NLT STUDY BIBLE

NLT STUDY BIBLE

LARGE PRINT

New Living Translation®

Tyndale House Publishers, Inc.
Carol Stream, Illinois

Library of Congress Cataloging-in-Publication Data

Bible. English. New Living Translation. 2008.
NLT study Bible.
p. cm.
Includes bibliographical references and index.
ISBN 978-0-8423-5570-4 (hc : alk. paper)
ISBN 978-1-4143-2448-7 (bndd blk : alk. paper)
[etc.]
I. Title.
BS195.N394 2008
220.'20834—dc22 2008017304

ISBN 978-1-4143-9175-5 Hardcover

Printed in China

19 18 17 16 15 14
6 5 4 3 2 1

Tyndale House Publishers and Wycliffe Bible Translators share the vision for an understandable, accurate translation of the Bible for every person in the world. Each sale of the *Holy Bible,* New Living Translation, benefits Wycliffe Bible Translators. Wycliffe is working with partners around the world to accomplish Vision 2025—an initiative to start a Bible translation program in every language group that needs it by the year 2025.

CONTENTS

OLD TESTAMENT

NEW TESTAMENT

REFERENCE HELPS

NLT STUDY BIBLE

INTRODUCTION

All of us at Tyndale House Publishers are pleased to present the *NLT Study Bible.* It brings together the best of scholarship in both the Bible translation and the study notes and features. We think you will find that the biblical text comes to life in a fresh, new way as a result of this Bible.

The creation of a study Bible represents a huge effort by many people. In this instance, a team of sixty scholars, writers, reviewers, editors, and designers worked together to bring you the study notes, introductions, maps, timelines, profiles, and theme notes in this Bible.

The Bible text used in the *NLT Study Bible* is the New Living Translation, second edition. The NLT was first published in 1996, and it quickly became one of the most popular English translations. Readers have especially appreciated the clarity of the language. The second edition text was first published in 2004. The NLT combines the best features of its predecessor, *The Living Bible,* with the world-class scholarship of the ninety scholars who worked on the translation.

The study notes and other features in the *NLT Study Bible* are designed to help today's readers understand the meaning and significance of the Bible in light of the world in which the text was first written. Our approach as writers and editors has been to help people understand the Bible clearly and accurately. We trust the Holy Spirit to be at work, bringing to people's minds and hearts the applications that he has for them. He does this in millions of different ways every day. As the editors of this study Bible, we hope to provide a context within which the Holy Spirit can work.

The rain and snow come down from the heavens
and stay on the ground to water the earth.
They cause the grain to grow,
producing seed for the farmer
and bread for the hungry.
It is the same with my word.
I send it out, and it always produces fruit.
It will accomplish all I want it to,
and it will prosper everywhere I send it. Isaiah 55:10-11

In the pages that follow, we describe the features of the *NLT Study Bible* and how to make the most use of them. We challenge you to try it. Come, walk through God's word, understand it for yourself, and let it change your life.

Study this Book of Instruction continually. Meditate on it day and night so you will be sure to obey everything written in it. Only then will you prosper and succeed in all you do.
Joshua 1:8

I will study your commandments and reflect on your ways. Psalm 119:15

THE EDITORS

NLT STUDY BIBLE

BOOK INTRODUCTIONS

Each book introduction helps readers understand that book as its original readers first understood it in their world. The book introduction discusses the book's setting, gives a summary of its literary structure, discusses historical issues such as authorship and date of writing, and explains the meaning and message of the book for its readers.

OVERVIEW

The Overview helps readers to find out quickly what this book of the Bible is about and why it is important. It gives a thumbnail sketch of the book and its contents and purpose.

SETTING

What is the story behind each book of the Bible? What was the need for each book in its setting? Every book of the Bible was written by flesh-and-blood people living in a particular time and place in history. They faced real challenges and difficulties. They wrote to other real flesh-and-blood people living at their own time in history. They wrote to address specific problems in their world, to help their readers understand God's mind regarding the issues and problems that they faced.

The world of the Bible is very different from our world today, but people are the same everywhere. If we understand the setting in which each book of the Bible was written, we will be in a much better position to understand what problems it addressed, what actions it was prompting, and what message it communicates.

THE BOOK OF

GENESIS

Genesis is the book of beginnings—of the universe and of humanity, of sin and its catastrophic effects, and of God's plan to restore blessing to the world through his chosen people. God began his plan when he called Abraham and made a covenant with him. Genesis traces God's promised blessings from generation to generation, to the time of bondage and the need for redemption from Egypt. It lays the foundation for God's subsequent revelation, and most other books of the Bible draw on its contents. Genesis is a source of instruction, comfort, and edification.

SETTING

When Genesis was written, the children of Israel had been slaves in Egypt for 400 years. They had recently been released from bondage and guided through the desert to meet the Lord at Mount Sinai, where he had established his covenant relationship with them and had given them his law through Moses. Israel was now poised to enter the Promised Land and receive the inheritance that God had promised Abraham.

While enslaved in Egypt, the Israelites had adopted many pagan ideas and customs from their Egyptian masters (e.g., Exod 32:1-4). They were influenced by false concepts of God, the world, and human nature (e.g., Exod 32), and were reduced to being slaves rather than owners and managers of the land. Perhaps they had forgotten the great promises that God had made to Abraham, Isaac, and Jacob, or perhaps they had concluded that the promises would never be fulfilled.

Before entering the Promised Land, the Israelites needed to understand the nature of God, his world, and their place in it more clearly. They needed to embrace their identity as descendants of Abraham, Isaac, and Jacob. Genesis provided the needed understanding.

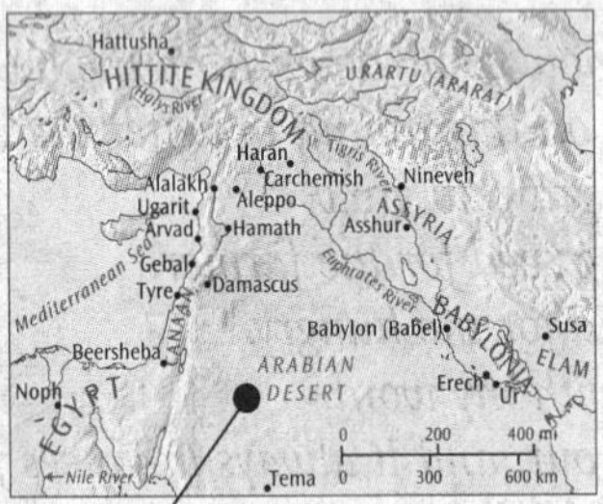

The Ancient Near East, about 2100 BC. Humanity spread out from the mountains of URARTU (ARARAT) and populated the early centers of civilization. By the time of the patriarchs (Abraham, Isaac, and Jacob), many of the cities were ancient.

ASSHUR 2:14; 10:22; 25:3; 25:18
ASSYRIA 10:11
BABYLON (BABEL), BABYLONIA 10:9-10; 11:1-9; 14:1, 9
CANAAN 9:18-27; 10:18-19; 12:5-10
DAMASCUS 14:15; 15:2
EGYPT 12:10–13:1; 15:18; 37:28-36; 39:1–50:26
ELAM 10:22; 14:1, 9
ERECH 10:10; Ezra 4:9
HAMATH 10:18; 2 Sam 8:9-10; 2 Kgs 14:28; 23:33
HARAN 11:26-32; 12:4-5; 27:43; 28:10; 29:4; Acts 7:2-4
SUSA Ezra 4:9; Neh 1:1; Esth 1:2; Dan 8:2
UR 11:28, 31; 15:7; Neh 9:7
URARTU (ARARAT) 8:4

MAP

The book introductions include maps of the setting to show where the events in each book of the Bible took place and how the places mentioned in that book fit into the world. Each map includes a caption that describes the map and how it relates to the book's setting. Along with a caption, most of these maps include a short index of places mentioned in the book.

FEATURES GUIDE

SUMMARY

What is the structure and flow of ideas in each book of the Bible? The Summary provides just that—a brief summary of the contents of the book. If the book is narrative, the Summary tells its story. If the book is a letter, the Summary explains its contents and the flow of its reasoning. If the book is an anthology, the Summary describes the structure and contents of the collection. If we have in mind the flow of the book, we can better understand each individual passage.

SUMMARY

Genesis traces God's work to overcome with blessing the curse that came on humankind because of sin. The book arranges family traditions, genealogies, historical events, and editorial comments into a single, sustained argument.

Every section but the first has the heading, "This is the account" (or *These are the generations;* Hebrew *toledoth*); each of the *toledoth* sections explains the history of a line of descent. In each case, a deterioration of well-being is followed by an increasing focus on God's plan to bless the world. This plan is the basis for God's covenant with his people; as the blessing develops, the covenant is clarified. By the end of the book, the reader is ready for the fulfillment of the promises in Israel's redemption from bondage (see Exodus).

The first section (1:1–2:3) does not have the *toledoth* heading, and logically so—it is the account of creation "in the beginning" (1:1). The work of creation is wrapped in God's approval and blessing as he fulfills his plan.

The next section (2:4–4:26) focuses on the creation of human life (2:4-25) and traces what became of God's creation because of Adam's and Eve's sin (3:1-13), the curse on their sin (3:14-24), and the extension of sin to their descendants (4:1-24). Humanity no longer enjoyed God's rest; instead, they experienced guilt and fear. So they fled from God and developed a proud civilization.

Independence from God resulted in the downward drift of human life (5:1–6:8). The genealogy of 5:1-32 begins by recalling that human beings were made in God's image and were blessed by him (5:1-2). As the genealogy is traced, the death of each generation reminds the reader of the curse, with Enoch providing a ray of hope that the curse is not final. In 6:1-8, we learn that God regretted having made humans and decided to judge the earth. Noah, however, received God's favor and provided a source of hope (5:29; 6:8).

The next section (6:9–9:29) brings the curse of judgment through the flood followed by blessing in a new beginning. A renewed creation began, purged of the abominable evil that had invaded and ruined the human race.

The world's population expanded into various nations (10:1–11:9) whose people were bent on disobedience. The population of the earth by Shem,

OUTLINE

1:1–2:3
Creation

2:4–4:26
What Happened to the Creation

5:1–6:8
The Account of Adam's Descendants

6:9–9:29
The Account of Noah's Family

10:1–11:9
The Account of Noah's Sons

11:10-26
The Account of Shem's Descendants

11:27–25:11
The Account of Terah's Descendants

25:12-18
The Account of Ishmael's Descendants

25:19–35:29
The Account of Isaac's Descendants

36:1–37:1
The Account of Esau's Descendants

37:2–50:26
The Account of Jacob's Descendants

TIMELINE

2166 / 1990 BC*
Abraham is born

2091 / 1915 BC
Abraham moves to Canaan

2080 / 1904 BC
Ishmael is born

2066 / 1890 BC
Sodom and Gomorrah are destroyed, Isaac is born

2006 / 1830 BC
Jacob and Esau are born

1898 / 1722 BC
Joseph is sold into slavery

1885 / 1709 BC
Joseph begins governing Egypt

1876 / 1661 BC
Jacob moves to Egypt

1446 / 1270 BC
Israel leaves Egypt (the Exodus), moves to Mount Sinai

1406 / 1230 BC
Israel enters Canaan

* *The two dates harmonize with the traditional "early" chronology and a more recent "late" chronology of the Exodus. All dates are approximate. Please see "Chronology: Abraham to Joshua," p. 118.*

TIMELINE

A timeline can be found in the margin of nearly all book introductions. The timelines show when the events in each book of the Bible took place and what was going on at the time. We can refer to the timeline while reading the setting and summary for the book, and again while reading the book, to help clarify and reinforce how the events fit into the flow of history.

OUTLINE

Each book includes an outline with up to three levels of headings. In the introduction, we provide the first level of the outline to give the reader an overview. The full outline is embedded in the NLT text as running headings. These book outlines follow the literary structure of the book—how the authors themselves thought about the organization and flow of ideas.

AUTHOR, DATE, AND OTHER HISTORICAL ISSUES

What do we know about who wrote this book and when it was written? What are the difficulties in determining the historical facts? Even though these issues might not be familiar ground, they are important. Understanding these things can help us appreciate the complexity of the Bible. Far from undermining confidence in Scripture, the issues discussed here give us a greater appreciation of how magnificent Scripture truly is. At the same time, we learn to be humble in how we interpret God's word.

Ham, and Japheth seemed fruitful (10:1-32), but the nations were divided by languages and boundaries (10:5, 20, 31). Because of their rebellion, God dispersed them to prevent greater wickedness (11:1-9).

After the chaos of the scattered nations, 11:10-26 brings the focus to Abram, through whom God chose to bring blessing to all. The rest of the book (11:27–50:26) tells of God's blessing Abram and his descendants. God first made a covenant with Abram (11:27–25:11), promising him a great nation, land, and name. As time went on, God made the specific terms of the covenant clearer, and Abram's faith grew deeper.

In each generation, Genesis gives a brief account of the families that are not Israel's ancestors before turning to the line of Israel. After briefly reporting what became of Ishmael (25:12-18), Genesis traces in detail what happened to Isaac and his family (25:19–35:29).

True to the pattern of the book, Esau's line (Edom) is dealt with briefly (36:1–37:1) before the chosen line of Jacob the heir. The final section (37:2–50:26) concerns Jacob's family, centering on the life of Joseph. In the land of Canaan, the family became corrupt under Canaanite influence to the point of beginning to merge with them (ch 38). To preserve the line of blessing, God sent the family into Egypt where they could flourish, remain separate (43:32; 46:34), and become a great nation. The book closes with the promise of the Lord's coming to rescue his people from Egypt (50:24-26).

> *"God rested on the seventh day from all his work that he had done. And he blessed the seventh day. . . ." And we ourselves will be a "seventh day" when we shall be filled with his blessing and remade by his sanctification. . . . Only when we are remade by God and perfected by a greater grace shall we have the eternal stillness of that rest in which we shall see that he is God.*
>
> ST. AUGUSTINE
> *City of God, sec. 22.30*

AUTHORSHIP

Both Scripture and tradition attribute the Pentateuch (Genesis—Deuteronomy) to Moses. No one was better qualified than Moses to have written this book. Since he was educated in all the wisdom of the Egyptians (Acts 7:22), he had the literary skills to collect and edit Israel's traditions and records and to compose this theological treatise. His unique communion with God gave him the spiritual illumination, understanding, and inspiration needed to guide him. He had good reason to write this work—to provide Israel with the theological and historical foundation for the Exodus and the covenant at Sinai, and to establish the new nation in accord with the promises made to their ancestors.

Most scholars, however, do not accept that Moses wrote Genesis. The prevailing critical view, called the *Documentary Hypothesis,* is that Genesis was compiled from various sources by different groups of people. In such approaches, there is seldom a word about divine revelation or inspiration. For those who understand the Bible as God's inspired word, such theories often seem unnecessarily complicated and conjectural. Genesis can be understood much more straightforwardly as the product of Moses' genius under God's inspiration with later editorial adjustments. (See further "Introduction to the Pentateuch: Authorship," p. 12).

COMPOSITION

Biblical scholars of all stripes have always acknowledged that various sources were used in writing Genesis and other historical texts in the Bible (such as Kings and Luke). Moses used collections of family records, oral traditions, ancient accounts of primeval events, and genealogies to write Genesis. Those sources could have been incorporated as received, or the author may have changed their style and wording, stitching them together with additional material for the particular purpose of tracing the foundations of Israelite faith.

Genesis is therefore a unique work. Theology, history, and tradition come together to instruct God's people and prepare them for blessing.

MEANING AND MESSAGE

Israel's most important questions were answered by the Genesis narratives. Life and death, the possession of the land of Canaan, and how Israel ended up in Egypt are explained as God's providential working in history. Israel was part of God's plan in this world. His plan had

MEANING AND MESSAGE

What is the message of each book of the Bible? What is its significance now? Here's where the rubber meets the road. Everything in a book's introduction—setting, summary, author, date, genre—is intended to prepare us to understand what that book of the Bible has to say, its message and significance. Reading these paragraphs carefully and reflectively will give us the keys to understanding that book of the Bible.

Genesis also includes passages and expressions that are obviously later editorial glosses. Some sections (such as the list of Edomite kings, 36:31-43) could have been added during the early days of the monarchy. There is no conflict in saying that Genesis was authored by Moses and augmented by subsequent editors whose work was guided by the Holy Spirit. Given these considerations, conservative scholars find it plausible that the biblical material accurately records actual events.

LITERARY CHARACTER

Genesis includes various types of literature. Several suggestions have been made as to the nature of the materials.

Myth. Mythological literature explains the origins of things symbolically through the deeds of gods and supernatural creatures. For ancient peoples, myths were beliefs that explained life and reality. Whole systems of ritual activities were developed to ensure that the forces of fertility, life, and death would continue year by year. Some of these rituals gave rise to cult prostitution (see 38:15, 21-22).

It would be very difficult to classify the material in Genesis as myth. Israel had one God, not a multitude. The nation of Israel had a beginning, a history, and a future hope. They saw God, rather than gods and other supernatural creatures, as the primary actor in the world. Their worship was not cosmic, magical, or superstitious, but a reenactment of their own rescue from Egypt and a celebration of God's factual intervention in history and their hope in his promises.

If Genesis uses elements of mythological language, it is to display a deliberate contrast with pagan concepts and to show that the Lord God is sovereign over such ideas. For example, the ancients worshiped the sun as a god, but in Genesis the sun serves the Creator's wishes (1:14-18). The book of Genesis is a cemetery for lifeless myths and dead gods. Genesis is not myth.

Etiology. A number of scholars describe the Genesis narratives as *etiologies*, stories that explain the causes of factual reality or traditional beliefs. The implication is that such stories were made up for explanatory purposes and do not describe historical events. For example, if one says that the story of Cain and Abel was made up to explain why shepherds and farmers do not get along, the account loses its integrity as factual history.

Etiological elements certainly occur in Genesis, because the book gives the foundation and rationale for almost everything that Israel would later do. For example, the creation account of Gen 2 ends with the explanation, "This explains why a man leaves his father and mother. . . ." The event as it happened explains why marriage was conducted the way it was, but to say that a story explains something is quite different from saying that the story was fabricated to explain it. The stories of Genesis are not fictional tales invented to explain later customs and beliefs.

History. Many scholars object to regarding Genesis as history, for two basic reasons: (1) Genesis explains events as caused by God, and the inclusion of the supernatural is regarded as proof that the material is theological reflection and thus not historically reliable; and (2) the events in Genesis cannot be validated from outside sources; no other records have demonstrated that Abraham existed or that any of his family history occurred.

Genesis is not interested in parading Abraham, Isaac, and Jacob as examples of morality. Therefore, it does not moralize on them. [Genesis] is bringing together the promises of God to the patriarchs and the faithfulness of God in keeping those promises.

VICTOR P. HAMILTON
The Book of Genesis: Chapters 1–17, p. 46

EPIGRAPHS
Sometimes other authors say insightful things about a book of the Bible, or they make a poignant observation about something that a given book discusses. The editors have gathered some of the best quotations they could find about each book and put them in the margins of the book introductions, to stimulate thinking and to promote meaningful interaction with each book of the Bible.

a starting point
when the prom

Israel, the Chose
made a covenan
make them his
to the world. G
its existence as
Israel could t
tiny to God's pr
of a great natio
cerns of the pat
birthrights and
protected the c
they had becon
was certainly n
would live as a
where they cou

Blessing and Cu
of blessing and
archs innumera
promise; the bl
them to flourisl
covenant blessi
disinherit peop
the whole race
These motifs
spoke of even g
for those who r
reminds God's
has the power t

Good and Evil.
produces, enha
evil is cursed: I
or destroys life.
and evil that ch
the greater goo
over all evil (cp

God's Plan. Genesis begins with the presupposition that God exists and that he has revealed himself in word and deed to Israel's ancestors. It does not argue for the existence of God; it simply begins with God and shows how everything falls into place when the sovereign God works out his plan to establish Israel as the means of restoring blessing to the whole world.

God's Rule. Genesis is the fitting introduction to the founding of theocracy, the rule of God over all creation that was to be established through his chosen people. Genesis lays down the initial revelation of God's sovereignty. He is the Lord of the universe who will move heaven and earth to bring about his plan. He desires to bless people, but he will not tolerate rebellion and unbelief. His promises are great, and he is fully able to bring them to fruition. To participate in his plan has always required faith, for without faith it is impossible to please him (Heb 11:6).

FURTHER READING

VICTOR P. HAMILTON
The Book of Genesis (199

DEREK KIDNER
Genesis (1967)

KENNETH A. MATHEWS
Genesis (1996)

ALLEN P. ROSS
Creation and Blessing (1988)
Genesis in *Cornerstone Biblical Commentary*, vol. 1 (2008)

GORDON WENHAM
Genesis 1–15 (1987)
Genesis 16–50 (1994)

FURTHER READING
Where can we learn more about each book of the Bible? The *NLT Study Bible* has plenty of resources for a lifetime journey of reading, studying, and discovering the riches of Scripture. Some readers, however, will want to go even further. At the end of each book introduction, the editors have recommended some of the resources that have helped them the most in studying and understanding that particular book of the Bible. They've chosen materials that are available in the general market—no seminary required! Nearly all of these books are as close as a visit to a local or online Christian retailer.

SECTION INTRODUCTIONS
For each major section of the Bible, the section introduction gives an overview of the books in that section and discusses issues that affect the interpretation of those books. (Not shown)

CHRONOLOGY ARTICLES
For each major period of biblical history, the chronology article provides a historical overview and discusses key issues regarding historical context. Each article includes a timeline of events during that period of history. (Not shown)

son of Ner, commander of the army of
Israel, and of Amasa son of Jether, commander of the army of Judah. 33May their
blood be on Joab and his descendants forever, and may the LORD grant peace forever
to David, his descendants, his dynasty, and
his throne."
34So Benaiah son of Jehoiada returned
to the sacred tent and killed Joab, and he
was buried at his home in the wilderness.
35Then the king appointed Benaiah to command the army in place of Joab, and he
installed Zadok the priest to take the place
of Abiathar.
36The king then sent for Shimei and told
him, "Build a house here in Jerusalem and
live there. But don't step outside the city
to go anywhere else. 37On the day you so
much as cross the Kidron Valley, you will
surely die; and your blood will be on your
own head."
38Shimei replied, "Your sentence is fair;
I will do whatever my lord the king commands." So Shimei lived in Jerusalem for a
long time.

would surely die? And you replied, 'The sentence is fair; I will do as you say.' 43Then why
haven't you kept your oath to the LORD and
obeyed my command?"
44The king also said to Shimei, "You certainly remember all the wicked things you
did to my father, David. May the LORD now
bring that evil on your own head. 45But may
I, King Solomon, receive the LORD's blessings, and may one of David's descendants
always sit on this throne in the presence of
the LORD." 46Then, at the king's command,
Benaiah son of Jehoiada took Shimei outside and killed him.
So the kingdom was now firmly in Solomon's grip.

Solomon's Great Wisdom (3:1–4:34)
Solomon Asks for Wisdom
1 Kgs 3:1-15 // 2 Chr 1:1-13

3 Solomon made an alliance with Pharaoh, the king of Egypt, and married
one of his daughters. He brought her to live
in the City of David until he could finish
building his palace and the Temple of the
LORD and the wall around the city. 2At that

2:33 2 Sam 3:29
2:35 1 Chr 29:22
2:36 2 Sam 16:5; 1 Kgs 2:8
2:37 2 Sam 15:23
2:39 1 Sam 27:2
2:44 1 Sam 25:39; 2 Sam 16:5-13
2:45 2 Sam 7:13
2:46 1 Kgs 2:12; 2 Chr 1:1
3:1 1 Kgs 7:8; 9:24
3:2 Lev 17:3-5; Deut 12:13-14
3:3 Deut 6:5; 1 Kgs 9:4; 11:4, 6, 38; Ps 31:23
3:4-15 //2 Chr 1:2-13
3:4 1 Chr 16:39; 21:29; 2 Chr 1:2-3
3:5 1 Kgs 9:2-3; Matt 1:20

1. CREATION (1:1–2:3)
In the Beginning (1:1-2)
1 In the beginning God [a]created the
[b]heavens and the [c]earth. 2The earth was
formless and empty, and darkness covered
the deep waters. And the [d]Spirit of God was
hovering over the surface of the waters.

Six Days of Creation (1:3-31)
Day One: Light, Darkness
3Then God said, "Let there be light," and
there was light. 4And God saw that the
light was good. Then he separated the
light from the darkness. 5God called
the light "day" and the darkness "night."
And evening passed and morning
came, marking the first day.

Day Two: Sky, Waters
6Then God said, "Let there be a space
between the waters, to separate the
waters of the heavens from the waters of
the earth." 7And that is what happened.
God made this space to separate the
waters of the earth from the waters of
the heavens. 8God called the space "sky."
And evening passed and morning
came, marking the second day.

Day Three: Land, Sea, Vegetation
9Then God said, "Let the waters beneath
the sky flow together into one place, so
dry ground may appear." And that is
what happened. 10God called the dry
ground "land" and the waters "seas."

1:1 Ps 89:11; 102:25; Isa 42:5; 48:13; John 1:1-2; [a]*bara'* (1254) ›Gen 1:27; [b]*shamayim* (8064) ›Exod 16:4; [c]*'erets* (0776) ›Gen 9:11
1:2 Isa 45:18; [d]*ruakh* (7307) ›Gen 45:27
1:3 Isa 45:7; 2 Cor 4:6
1:6 Job 26:10; Ps 136:5-6
1:9 Ps 95:5; Prov 8:29; Jer 5:22; 2 Pet 3:5

The Creation (1:1–2:3)

Ps 33:6-9; Prov 3:19; 8:22-31; Isa 40:26-28; 45:11-12, 18-19; Jer 10:11-16; John 1:1-4; Rom 8:18-25; 2 Cor 5:17; Col 1:15-20; Rev 4:11; 21:1-5

The creation account in Genesis is foundational to the message of the entire Bible, not just of Genesis or the Pentateuch. Understanding the early chapters of Genesis is thus crucial to forming a biblical worldview.

This part of Genesis deals with fundamental questions: Who created the world, and for what purpose? Why is the world in its present condition? Genesis answers these questions, dispelling the idolatry that Israel had acquired from their pagan masters in Egypt. In the Promised Land, they would also be surrounded by people who believed in many false gods and worshiped created things rather than the Creator. Genesis taught Israel that the one true God created and has absolute authority over all things; he alone is worthy of worship.

Every worldview attempts to explain where the world came from, what is wrong with the world, and how it can be set right again. The creation account in Genesis teaches that as God made the world, it was "very good" (1:31). Through creation, God turned disorder into restful order and emptiness into the fullness of abundant life. In this environment, humans enjoyed unbroken fellowship with their Creator until their rebellion severed that fellowship and implanted evil in human hearts (ch 3; see chs 4–6). The world's evil does not come from some defect in creation; God put the world under a curse because of human rebellion.

Since that first rebellion, humans have been alienated from the Creator and no longer recognize his presence and authority. This alienation results in shame, fractured relationships with God and other humans, estrangement from the rest of creation, and death (3:7-19). Since that time, God has been working purposefully in history to restore humans to fellowship with him, which he is doing through Jesus Christ. Restored humans are a new creation (Gal 6:15); through Jesus, eternal life is open to all and God will one day renew all things (see Isa 65:17-25; Rom 8:19-22). The whole cosmos will be made new (Rev 21:1).

1:1–2:3 These verses introduce the Pentateuch (Genesis—Deuteronomy) and teach Israel that the world was created, ordered, and populated by the one true God and not by the gods of surrounding nations. • God blessed three specific things: animal life (1:22-25), human life (1:27), and the Sabbath day (2:3). This trilogy of blessings highlights the Creator's plan: Humankind was made in God's image to enjoy sovereign dominion over the creatures of the earth and to participate in God's Sabbath rest.

1:1 ***In the beginning God created the heavens and the earth*** (or *In the beginning when God created the heavens and the earth, . . .* or *When God began to create the heavens and the earth, . . .*): This statement summarizes the entire creation account (1:3–2:3). Already a key question—Who created the world?—is answered (see also Prov 8:22-31; John 1:1-3). Although the modern naturalistic mindset rejects this question and that of creation's purpose, Genesis affirms God's role and purpose in creation. • The common name for ***God*** (Hebrew *'elohim*) emphasizes his grand supremacy. The word *'elohim* is plural, but the verbs used with it are usually singular, reflecting the consistent scriptural proclamation of a single, all-powerful God. • ***created*** (Hebrew *bara'*): In the OT, God is always the agent of creation expressed by this verb. It describes the making of something fresh and new—notably the cosmos (1:1, 21; 2:3), humankind (1:27), the Israelite nation (Isa 43:1), and the future new creation (Isa 65:17). • ***The heavens and the earth*** are the entire ordered cosmos.

1:2 This verse gives the background for the summary in 1:1 and the detailed description in 1:3–2:3. God's creative utterances bring order to the chaotic state of the universe. • ***formless . . . empty*** (Hebrew *tohu . . . bohu*): This terse idiom means something like "wild and waste." It sets a stark contrast to the final ordered state of the heavens and the earth (1:1). • ***deep waters***

PARALLEL PASSAGES

The NLT text indicates parallels with passages in other books. For example, the Gospel of Matthew has many parallels in Mark, Luke, and John. Similarly, the books of 2 Samuel through 2 Kings have many parallels to the books of 1–2 Chronicles. The parallel references are useful for making comparisons between different versions of the same events and gaining a deeper, fuller understanding of what was happening.

RUNNING OUTLINES

The NLT text of each book includes a running outline to show how the sections of that book fit together. The numbered top level of the outline matches the short outline in the book introduction. The second- and third-level headings describe the book's structure in greater detail, down to the level of individual passages. These outlines follow the literary structure of the book, so they show what the author of the book thought about how the book was put together.

THEME NOTES

How does the NLT Study Bible *explain the themes of the Bible?* Theme notes develop the main themes and topics that arise in each book. They are placed alongside particularly relevant passages but go beyond the passage at hand and extend to other books of the Bible. References for further study are included in the margin.

The topics in the theme notes have been chosen based on the major themes that occur in Scripture. They provide the first steps in developing a biblical theology without attempting to formulate a specific doctrinal system (such as reformed, charismatic, or Baptist). Because of this, the theme notes are designed to make us think and will stretch us to consider the teaching of Scripture more fully, whatever our doctrinal background.

wickedness on the earth, and he saw that
everything they thought or imagined was
consistently and totally evil. 6So the LORD
was sorry he had ever made them and put
them on the earth. It broke his heart. 7And
the LORD said, "I will wipe this human race I
have [c]created from the face of the earth. Yes,

Noah was a righteous man, the only [d]blame-
less person living on earth at the time, and
he walked in close fellowship with God.
10Noah was the father of three sons: Shem,
Ham, and Japheth.
11Now God saw that the earth had become corrupt and was filled with violence.

Exod 33:17
6:9
Job 1:1
Ezek 14:14
[d]*tamim* (8549)
›Gen 17:1
6:11
Deut 31:29
Judg 2:19
Ezek 8:17

NOAH (6:8-22)

Gen 5:28–10:1
1 Chr 1:4
Isa 54:9
Ezek 14:12-20
Matt 24:37-38
Luke 3:36; 17:26-27
Heb 11:7
1 Pet 3:20-21
2 Pet 2:5

Noah was the son of Lamech, a descendant of Seth (5:3-29). Lamech might have hoped that Noah (whose name means "rest" or "relief") would ease the curse of hardship in working the ground (see note on 5:29). God used Noah to help relieve the world of evil.

God intended to destroy creation because of pervasive human wickedness (6:1-7; see Matt 24:37-39; Luke 17:26-27), but he decided to preserve Noah (6:8). God gave Noah, a righteous and blameless man (6:9), precise instructions for building the ark in which only the eight people of his family would be saved, along with every kind of creature (6:14–8:19). When Noah and his family finally emerged from the ark after the flood, Noah pleased God by building an altar and sacrificing burnt offerings. God promised that he would never again flood the whole earth or disrupt the sequence of the seasons, despite human sin (8:20–9:17).

Noah's sons were Shem, Ham, and Japheth. All the nations of the earth descended from them (9:18-19). When Noah became drunk on wine from his vineyard, his sons and their descendants were cursed or blessed in accord with how they responded to him (9:22-27). Noah lived for 950 years, including 350 years after the flood (9:28-29); he is an example of righteousness, obedience, courage, and faith (see Ezek 14:12-20; Heb 11:7; 2 Pet 2:5).

society and allow human wickedness to run its full course. Others think it means that God would withdraw his life-giving breath from humans at an earlier age (*ruakh*, the Hebrew term for "spirit," can also mean "breath"; see 6:17; 7:22; see also Ps 104:29-30). • ***normal lifespan will be no more than 120 years*** (literally *his days will be 120 years*): It is possible that this was a new restriction on the number of years individuals would generally be allowed to live (so the NLT). However, for generations after the flood, humans lived well beyond 120 years (see, e.g., 11:10-26). An alternative interpretation sees this as a 120-year grace period before the arrival of the flood (see Jon 3:4; Matt 24:37-38; 1 Pet 3:20; 2 Pet 2:5).

6:4 ***giant Nephilites*** (Hebrew *nephilim*): The term may mean "fallen ones." The context implies that they were the offspring of the "sons of God" and would be destroyed in the flood. Num 13:31-33 uses the same term to describe other giants who were hostile toward God's people and would also be destroyed (see also Deut 2:11, which connects the Anakite *nephilim* with another group called the *rephaim*).

6:5 ***everything they thought or imagined*** (literally *every intention of the thoughts of their hearts*): In the OT, the heart is the core of volition, thought, and morality (see Prov 4:23). Wicked actions stem from a corrupt inner life. • ***consistently and totally evil:*** Strong language captures the pervasiveness, depth, and persistence of human wickedness. Human nature continued to be corrupt even after the flood (see 8:21).

6:6 ***the LORD was sorry:*** The extent of human wickedness made the Lord regret having created them (see also 6:7; cp. 1 Sam 15:11, 35). • ***It broke his heart:*** The evil in humanity's heart (6:5) pained God greatly. Sending the flood was a heart-wrenching act on God's part.

6:7 ***wipe . . . from the . . . earth:*** As Adam and Eve were banished from the garden sanctuary (3:23), all of humankind would be expunged from God's good creation. • ***every living thing:*** Human sin had so corrupted the earth that judgment fell on the animals and birds over which they had dominion (see 1:28 and note). The special role of humans in the created order (1:28-30) means that nature is affected by human moral choices (see 8:1; Job 38:41; Hos 4:3; Rom 8:19-22).

6:8 ***Noah*** and his godly life stand in stark contrast to the sinfulness of the rest of the people.

6:9 ***the account:*** See note on 2:4 • ***a righteous man, the only blameless person:*** The text does not claim that Noah was without sin (see Rom 5:12-14). Noah's righteousness and blamelessness came about because ***he walked in close fellowship with God.*** See also 7:1; 17:1; Heb 11:7.

6:11-13 See 6:5-7. • ***violence*** (Hebrew *khamas*): Murder had especially corrupted the line of Cain (4:8, 23-24).

PERSON PROFILES

The *NLT Study Bible* includes person profiles that describe the lives of the individuals who inhabit the pages of Scripture. Each of these people contributes significantly to the story and message of the Bible. Their lives instruct us with examples and counter-examples, and their stories help us better understand the Bible, its world, and its message. Their relationship with God, or lack of it, helps us to understand how we can have a relationship with God.

STUDY NOTES

Sometimes readers look at a note in a study Bible to understand the meaning of a verse and find themselves asking, "So what?" about a seemingly unrelated fact. The notes in the *NLT Study Bible* have been developed with the "So what?" test in mind—the editors' goal is that the study notes will clearly help us as readers to understand the verse or passage better.

The notes focus on the meaning and message of Scripture, not just facts. This means that there are notes on words, phrases, sentences, verses, paragraphs, and whole sections. The editors have included historical and literary notes to help draw us into the world of the Bible and the context in which it was originally read and heard.

Also included in the study notes is the full NLT textual footnote apparatus, which identifies variations in the Hebrew and Greek text as well as providing alternate translation possibilities.

Every excerpt from the NLT text is easily identified in bold italic type.

CROSS-REFERENCE SYSTEM

Some cross-reference systems are based on connections between individual words, without regard to whether there is any connection in meaning between the two verses or passages. With the *NLT Study Bible,* the cross-references relate to the meaning of the whole verse or passage, so the cross-references are always directly applicable.

To compare specific ideas within a verse, the study notes at the bottom of the page often include cross-references for individual words and phrases, along with a brief explanation of the nature of the connection.

In the cross-reference system, parallel lines (//) show that a particular cross-reference is a parallel passage that describes the same events or says much the same thing.

An asterisk (*) is used to indicate where the NT quotes the OT.

WORD STUDY SYSTEM

The *NLT Study Bible* includes a word study system in the cross-reference column. Because the NLT is a dynamic translation, a particular word in Greek or Hebrew is not always translated the same way, but is translated in a manner that is appropriate for the context. This makes word studies richer and more productive, because the range of meaning for a particular Greek or Hebrew word becomes very clear, and it is easier to avoid common misunderstandings about what the word means.

There are word studies for 100 Hebrew words and 100 Greek words. For each word, the editors have included enough occurrences to illustrate the range of meanings for that word. Each occurrence is indicated in the NLT text with a superscript letter (a, b, c, etc.). The same superscript letter occurs in the cross-reference column under that verse. After the superscript letter the Hebrew or Greek word is given, followed by a reference number that matches the glossary at the back and many widely available study tools, such as *Strong's Concordance.* On the next line is a chain-reference link to the next highlighted occurrence of the word. The word study system thus opens up a whole world of Greek and Hebrew word study.

VISUAL AIDS

If a picture is worth a thousand words, the *NLT Study Bible* has tens of thousands of words' worth of visual information. These visual aids include maps, timelines, illustrations, charts, and diagrams.

1:10 Ps 33:7; 95:5
1:11 Gen 2:9; Ps 104:14; Matt 6:30
1:14 Ps 74:16; 104:19
1:15 Gen 1:1
1:16 Ps 8:3; 19:1-6; 136:8-9; 1 Cor 15:41
1:18 Jer 33:20, 25
1:20 Gen 2:19; Ps 146:6; ᵉ*nepesh* (5315) ›Gen 2:7
1:21 Ps 104:25-28

And God saw that it was good. 11Then
God said, "Let the land sprout with
vegetation—every sort of seed-bearing
plant, and trees that grow seed-bearing
fruit. These seeds will then produce the
kinds of plants and trees from which
they came." And that is what happened.
12The land produced vegetation—all
sorts of seed-bearing plants, and trees
with seed-bearing fruit. Their seeds
produced plants and trees of the same
kind. And God saw that it was good.
13And evening passed and morning
came, marking the third day.

Day Four: Sun, Moon, Stars

14Then God said, "Let lights appear in the
sky to separate the day from the night.
Let them be signs to mark the seasons,
days, and years. 15Let these lights in
the sky shine down on the earth." And
that is what happened. 16God made two
great lights—the larger one to govern
the day, and the smaller one to govern
the night. He also made the stars. 17God
set these lights in the sky to light the
earth, 18to govern the day and night, and
to separate the light from the darkness.
And God saw that it was good.
19And evening passed and morning
came, marking the fourth day.

Day Five: Birds, Fish

20Then God said, "Let the waters swarm
with fish and other ᵉlife. Let the skies
be filled with birds of every kind." 21So
God created great sea creatures and
every living thing that scurries and

Formless	CHAOS	Empty
DAY 1 (1:3-5) Light, Dark	HEAVENS	DAY 4 (1:14-19) Sun, Moon, Stars
DAY 2 (1:6-8) Water, Sky	WATER & SKY	DAY 5 (1:20-23) Birds, Fish
DAY 3 (1:9-13) Sea, Land	EARTH	DAY 6 (1:24-31) Animals, Humans
Formed	COSMOS	Filled
	DAY 7 (2:2-3) Rest	

◂ **The Structure of the Creation Account** (1:1–2:3). God transformed chaos into the present cosmos. In the first three days, he transformed the formless void into the structured universe—the HEAVENS (outer space), the WATER and SKY, and the EARTH (cp. Exod 20:11; Ps 135:6). In the second three days, he populated each empty realm. The seventh day (2:1-3) stands apart: As God's day of rest, it provides the weekly pattern for human activity (Exod 20:8-11; 31:12-17) and speaks of the rest that God promised to those who live by faith in him (see Heb 3:7–4:11).

(Hebrew *tehom*): Some scholars say this alludes to the Mesopotamian goddess Tiamat (representing chaos), but Genesis views *tehom* as inhospitable chaos, not as a deity or goddess that God engaged in cosmic battle. • *the Spirit of God:* God directly superintended the creation process.

1:3-13 In the first three days, God formed the chaos into a habitable world.

1:3 *Then God said:* Nothing in Gen 1 is created apart from God's powerful word (cp. Ps 33:6, 9). • *"Let there be . . . ," and there was:* God's command enacted his will to create the world. God is not a part of creation or limited by it; he is the supreme ruler over everything (cp. Neh 9:6).

1:4 *Light* is antithetical to chaotic *darkness* (1:2); the light is declared *good* but the darkness is not (cp. John 1:5). God is the source of this light (cp. 1:14-19). God *separated* the light, as he did water (cp. 1:6-8), by his creative word. Light is associated with life and blessing (Job 38:19-20; Ps 19:1-6; 97:11; 104:19-20; Isa 60:19-20) and sets a boundary on the darkness that would destroy cosmic order. Darkness often typifies terror, death, and evil (see 15:12; Job 18:6, 18; Ps 88:12; Eph 5:11-12; 1 Jn 1:5).

1:5 *God called* (or *named*): To name something is to exercise authority over it (see also 2:19-20). • *day:* The Hebrew *yom* can refer to daylight (1:5a), to a 24-hour period (1:5b), or to an unspecified time period (2:4b, "When," literally *in the day*; cp. Exod 20:8-11). • *evening . . . morning:* The Hebrew day began at sundown, just as the first day began with darkness and brought the first morning light.

1:6-8 The creation account describes the appearance of things from a human perspective. The *sky* is viewed as a shiny dome that is a buffer between two collections of water (cp. Job 37:18; Ezek 1:22). In the ancient Near East, the cosmos was understood as a three-tier system, with rain originating from the outermost tier (see 7:11-12 and note).

1:9-10 *Let the waters . . . flow together:* Other ancient cultures viewed the sea as a hostile force. Genesis shows God as further restraining chaos (see note on 1:2) by prescribing specific boundaries for the sea. The flood—an act of God's judgment (6:7)—undid these boundaries and returned the earth to chaos (7:1-24).

1:14-31 On days 4–6, God filled the domains that had been formed during days 1–3 (1:3-13).

1:14 *Let them . . . mark the seasons, days, and years:* The movement of the heavenly bodies defined Israel's liturgical calendar, whose roots in creation gave a sacred timing to Israel's festivals and celebrations (see Exod 23:15; Lev 23:4).

1:16 In the surrounding pagan cultures, the *two great lights* were worshiped as deities, but in Genesis they serve God and humanity (see Ps 136:7-9; Jer 31:35). The sun and moon are not named; they are simply called *the larger one* and *the smaller one*. Not including their names may have reminded Israel that they were not gods. • *govern:* Cp. 1:26, 28; Ps 136:9. • *the stars:* The starry heavens testify to God's creative power as they proclaim his glory (Ps 19:1; 148:3). They do not predict the future, as Israel's neighbors believed (see Jer 10:2).

1:21 Contrary to the pagan idea that the *great sea creatures* were co-eternal with God, Genesis states that *God created* them and is sovereign over them. The Hebrew word *tanninim* ("*creatures*") elsewhere refers to crocodiles (Ezek 29:3), powerful monsters (Jer 51:34), or the sea creature, Leviathan (Isa 27:1; cp. Job 41:1-34).

19:13 Gen 18:20; 1 Chr 21:15; Jude 1:7
19:14 Exod 9:21; Jer 5:12; 43:1-2
19:17 Gen 13:10; 19:26; Jer 48:6
19:22 Gen 13:10
19:24 Luke 17:29; Jude 1:7
19:25 Deut 29:23; Isa 13:19; Lam 4:6; 2 Pet 2:6
19:26 Gen 19:17; Luke 17:32
19:27 Gen 18:22
19:28 Rev 9:2
19:29 Deut 7:8; 9:5; 2 Pet 2:7-8
19:30 Gen 13:10

the city?" they asked. "Get them out
place—your sons-in-law, sons, daught
anyone else. 13For we are about to d
this city completely. The outcry again
place is so great it has reached the
and he has sent us to destroy it."
14So Lot rushed out to tell his dau
fiancés, "Quick, get out of the city
LORD is about to destroy it." But the
men thought he was only joking.
15At dawn the next morning the
became insistent. "Hurry," they said
"Take your wife and your two dau
who are here. Get out right now, or yo
be swept away in the destruction
city!"
16When Lot still hesitated, the
seized his hand and the hands of hi
and two daughters and rushed th
safety outside the city, for the LOR
merciful. 17When they were safely
the city, one of the angels ordered,
for your lives! And don't look back o
anywhere in the valley! Escape to the
tains, or you will be swept away!"
18"Oh no, my lord!" Lot begged.
have been so gracious to me and sav
life, and you have shown such great
ness. But I cannot go to the mou
Disaster would catch up to me there, and
I would soon die. 20See, there is a small village nearby. Please let me go there instead;

Lot and His Daughters

30Afterward Lot left Zoar because he was
afraid of the people there, and he went to

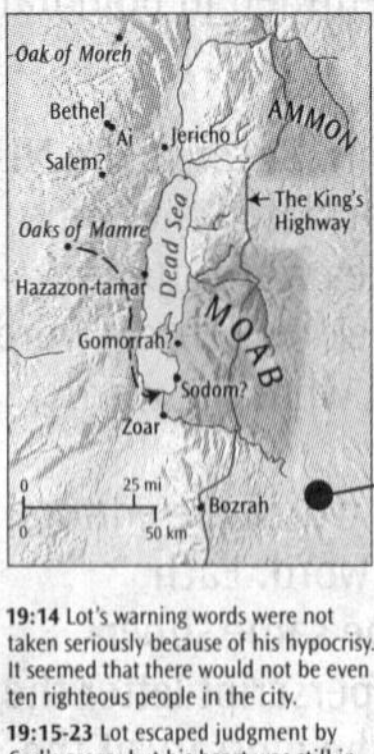

◂ **The Destruction of Sodom and Gomorrah** (18:16–19:38). The two angels apparently traveled, as shown, from Abraham's camp at the OAKS OF MAMRE to destroy SODOM and GOMORRAH. Lot and his daughters took refuge at ZOAR, then moved eastward into the mountains of MOAB. Lot fathered two sons by his daughters; the two sons became the nations of MOAB (see Num 21:10-20; 22:1–25:3; Deut 23:3, 6; Judg 3:12-30; Ruth 1:1-6) and AMMON (see Num 21:24; Deut 2:19-37; 23:3; Judg 10:6–12:3; 1 Sam 10:27–11:11).

19:14 Lot's warning words were not taken seriously because of his hypocrisy. It seemed that there would not be even ten righteous people in the city.

19:15-23 Lot escaped judgment by God's grace, but his heart was still in Sodom. Israel would forever remember Lot as lingering, halting, and being dragged to safety by angels. The Lord mercifully spared Lot for Abraham's sake (18:23; 19:29). Lot deserved judgment for his way of life, but he was a believer at heart and the Lord rescued him (2 Pet 2:7-8). • Lot is not alone in his conflicted lifestyle. Countless believers fall in with a corrupt world rather than flee a doomed society. God's people, living in a pagan world, must remain separate (1 Jn 2:15-17). The corrupt world system awaits God's coming judgment, which will be far greater than the destruction of Sodom and Gomorrah (Matt 11:23-24).

19:18-22 Lot demanded a concession from the angels even after he was delivered. He wanted to live in the small town of Zoar (*little place*).

19:23-25 Cp. Luke 17:29. The eruption of Vesuvius and the destruction of Pompeii in 79 AD, as well as recent natural disasters, show how quickly a thorough catastrophe like this could happen.

19:26 *looked back:* The verb indicates prolonged, intense gazing toward the world she loved, not a curious glance (15:5; Exod 33:8; Num 21:9; 1 Sam 2:32; cp. Exod 3:6). *Lot's wife* was too attached to Sodom to follow God's call of grace, so she was included in the judgment as she lingered on the valley slopes. Christ's return to judge the world will be as sudden and devastating as the destruction of Sodom (Luke 17:32-37). Those who crave the life of this wicked world will lose this world and the next.

19:29 God honored Abraham's intercession (cf. 18:23-32), but Lot's entire world was gone because he lived by instinct and desire, not by faith in God. He could no longer live in the good land he selfishly chose for himself (13:10-13; cp. Matt 16:26; 2 Cor 5:7).

19:30-38 The poverty of the cave contrasts with the wealth Lot shared with Abram and the good life he lived

CHARTS

Charts organize textual information into a form that is easy to understand quickly.

MAPS

Maps throughout the study materials visualize the events and places mentioned in the text of Scripture.

7:4
Gen 6:7, 13
7:6
Gen 5:32
7:7
Gen 6:18

female—into the boat with you to keep them alive during the flood. 20Pairs of every kind of bird, and every kind of animal, and every kind of small animal that scurries along the ground, will come to you to be kept alive.
5So Noah did everything as the LORD commanded him.
6Noah was 600 years old when the flood covered the earth. 7He went on board the boat to escape the flood—he and his wife

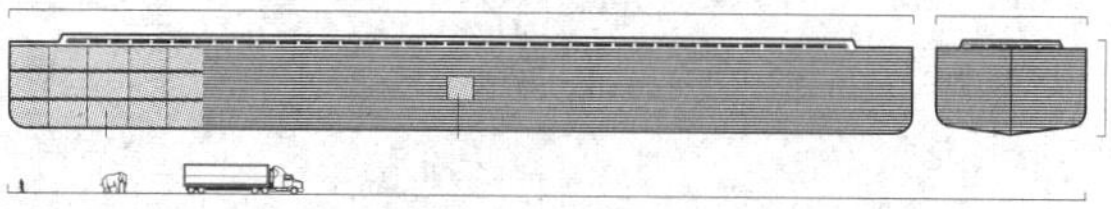

▲Noah's Ark (6:14-16). An ark built to the dimensions specified in Genesis would have been immense. Its ratio of length to width (6 to 1) is the most stable known and is used for the design of modern tankers and freight-hauling ships. The ark was able to carry 20,000 tons of cargo; the required number of young adult land animals would have occupied less than half of the available space. The design given was perfect for the ark's function.

6:14 *a large boat:* Traditionally rendered *an ark,* this was a long rectangular barge designed for survival, not for navigation. The Hebrew word *tebah* is used again only of the basket in which the baby Moses was floated on the Nile (Exod 2:3, 5). • *cypress wood:* Or *gopher wood.* It is not clear what kind of wood this was. It was possibly from a conifer, such as cypress.

6:15 The ark's dimensions: Hebrew *300 cubits* ... *bits* [23 m ... [13.8 met ... displaced

6:16 *An 1 ... opening o ... low the ro* ... ing light a ... *door* and ... was the c

with no sail or rudder. God also brought the animals to Noah (6:20).

6:17 *cover the earth with a flood:* Some propose that the flood might only have covered the ancient Near East as it was known to Noah or Moses. However, the flood's stated purpose—to *destroy every living thing that breathes* (see also 6:7, 11-13; 7:1, 4, 18-23; 8:21)—and its effect of undoing creation (see notes on 1:9-10; 7:11-12) suggest that the flood

These animals would procreate and repopulate the earth after the flood.

7:2 *of each animal I have approved for eating and for sacrifice* (literally *of each clean animal;* similarly in 7:8): In addition to the animals that were to repopulate the earth, these "clean" animals were for food and for Noah's sacrifice after the flood (8:20-21). This passage does not use the precise technical language that is found in the regulations

ILLUSTRATIONS
Illustrations help visualize objects that might be difficult to imagine without a picture. For example, the illustration of Noah's Ark on p. 33 shows just how big that floating storage box was and how much it was able to hold.

11:38
2 Sam 7:11, 27
11:40
1 Kgs 14:25
2 Chr 12:2
11:41-43
//2 Chr 9:29-31
12:1-24
//2 Chr 10:1–11:4
12:1
Judg 9:1, 6
2 Chr 10:1

the throne of Israel, and you will rule over all that your heart desires. 38If you listen to what I tell you and follow my ways and do whatever I consider to be right, and if you obey my decrees and commands, as my servant David did, then I will always be with you. I will establish an enduring dynasty for you as I did for David, and I will give Israel to you. 39Because of Solomon's sin I will punish the descendants of David—though not forever.' "
40Solomon tried to kill Jeroboam, but he fled to King Shishak of Egypt and stayed there until Solomon died.

Summary of Solomon's Reign
1 Kgs 11:41-43 // 2 Chr 9:29-31
41The rest of the events in Solomon's reign, including all his deeds and his wisdom, are recorded in *The Book of the Acts of Solomon.* 42Solomon ruled in Jerusalem over all Israel for forty years. 43When he died, he was buried in the City of David, named for his father. Then his son Rehoboam became the next king.

2. THE EARLY DIVIDED KINGDOM (12:1–16:14)
The Division of the Nation (12:1-24)
The Northern Tribes Revolt
1 Kgs 12:1-20 // 2 Chr 10:1-19
12 Rehoboam went to Shechem, where all Israel had gathered to make him king. 2When Jeroboam son of Nebat heard of this, he returned from Egypt, for he had fled to Egypt to escape from King Solomon. 3The leaders of Israel summoned him, and Jeroboam and the whole assembly of Israel

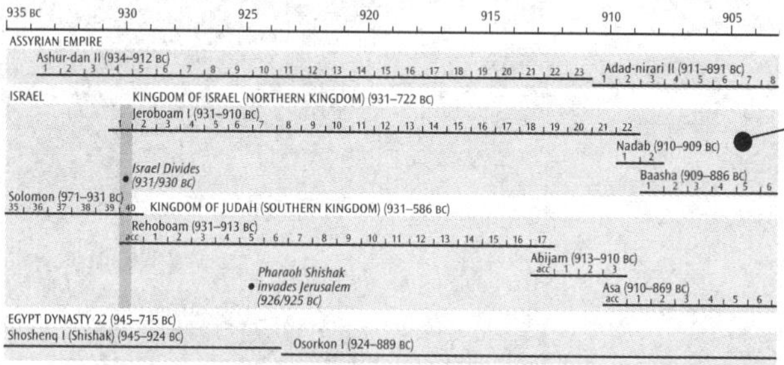

▲**Israel and Judah, 935–903 BC (11:41–15:34).** Each king's regnal years are numbered according to his own system of accounting (see "Chronology: Israel's Monarchy," p. 562). Each king's line on the chart runs from the beginning of the year in which his accession occurred to the end of the year in which he died. • SOLOMON's fortieth and final regnal year began in the fall (the month of Tishri) of 931 BC; his death and the division of the kingdom occurred sometime prior to the spring (the month of Nisan) of 930 BC. • The reign of JEROBOAM I started after that of REHOBOAM, but Jeroboam's first regnal was counted from the previous spring. • Pharaoh SHISHAK of Egypt invaded JERUSALEM during Rehoboam's fifth regnal year (see 14:25-28).

11:38 *an enduring dynasty:* Jeroboam had a great opportunity. God promised that if he was faithful and obedient to the Lord, his kingdom would be strong

pending difficulty, *tried to kill Jeroboam.* • *King Shishak of Egypt* later invaded Judah during the reign of Solomon's son Rehoboam (14:25-26).

tribes, had been a strategic site and religious center since the pre-Israelite occupation of Canaan (Gen 12:6-7; 33:18-20), and it became important in ... of ref- ... *boam* ... g over ... d the ... tically ... ibes. ... sional ... (12:25). ... 913 BC ... n Greek ... o 2 Chr ... *ypt.*

TIMELINES
Timelines show when in history various events took place and how they relate to other events in the Bible and in the surrounding world. The Bible is a record of history, and it is fascinating and stimulating to see just how the events of the Bible fit into recorded history as known from the surrounding cultures.

12:1
Gen 15:7
*Acts 7:3
Heb 11:8
'erets (0776)
›Gen 13:17
12:2
Gen 13:16; 15:5; 17:4; 18:18; 22:17
Zech 8:13
barak (1288)
›Gen 49:28
12:3
Gen 22:18; 26:4
Exod 23:22
Acts 3:25
*Gal 3:8
12:4
Gen 11:26, 31

still living. 29Meanwhile, Abram and Nahor both married. The name of Abram's wife was Sarai, and the name of Nahor's wife was Milcah. (Milcah and her sister Iscah were daughters of Nahor's brother Haran.) 30But Sarai was unable to become pregnant and had no children.
31One day Terah took his son Abram, his daughter-in-law Sarai (his son Abram's wife), and his grandson Lot (his son Haran's child) and moved away from Ur of the Chaldeans. He was headed for the land of Canaan, but they stopped at Haran and settled there. 32Terah lived for 205 years and died while still in Haran.

The Call of Abram (12:1-9)
12 The LORD had said to Abram, "Leave your native country, your relatives, and your father's family, and go to the land that I will show you. 2I will make you into a great nation. I will bless you and make you famous, and you will be a blessing to others. 3I will bless those who bless you and curse those who treat you with contempt. All the families on earth will be blessed through you."
4So Abram departed as the LORD had instructed, and Lot went with him. Abram was seventy-five years old when he left Haran. 5He took his wife, Sarai, his nephew Lot,

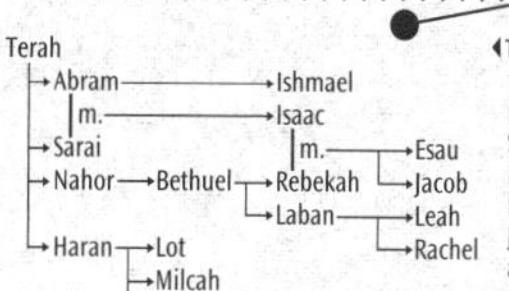

◄**Terah's Family (11:27-30),** to four generations. See profiles for ABRAHAM (p. 46), SARAH (p. 55), LOT (p. 58), ISHMAEL (p. 53), ISAAC (p. 63), REBEKAH (p. 69), ESAU (p. 71), JACOB (p. 76), LEAH (p. 79), and RACHEL (p. 78).

main city of Sumer in Mesopotamia near the mouth of the Persian Gulf. The family had moved there perhaps generations before the call. Their ances-

sovereignty of God, who miraculously gives children to barren women (see also 1 Sam 1:2; 2:5; Ps 113:9; Isa 54:1).

11:31 *Terah took:* The text is clear

and *be a blessing* (see note on 12:2). Each directive is followed by three promises conditioned upon obedience.

12:1 *Abram* knew that he should leave, but he did not know where he was going. Obedience required faith.

12:2 *and you will be a blessing* (or so *that you will be a blessing*): This clause is a command in Hebrew, but it is also a promise conditioned upon Abram's obedience to God's command (12:1): "Go . . . so that you will be a blessing. Be a blessing, so that I can bless and curse others." • *make you famous* (literally *make your name great*): Abram received

DIAGRAMS
Diagrams organize information visually in order to show relationships. For example, the genealogy of Terah, Abraham's father, on p. 43 helps sort out the relationships among many of the people who play a role in the book of Genesis.

HOW TO STUDY THE BIBLE WITH THE *NLT STUDY BIBLE*

Devoting yourself to understanding the text of the Bible is one of the greatest things that you can do. In the Bible, you can read about the things that God has done and said in the past. You can hear the stories of people who lived in a very different world from our own, yet whose lives were in so many ways just like ours. Most importantly, through the Bible you can hear God speak, and you can walk in fellowship with him.

The Bible, though, is a complex and very foreign book. It is true that some parts of it are not hard to understand. But other parts are, frankly, almost inscrutable, even when read in a clear, contemporary English translation like the NLT. Many people have set out to read and understand the Bible, only to put it aside in confusion and frustration. How can we "hear God speak" when his words seem so hard to understand?

The *NLT Study Bible* has been created to address this difficulty. The Bible *is* complex and foreign, but it is not an unscalable mountain or an impassable desert. It is, in fact, a well-traveled road. Having a guide can make the journey an interesting, enjoyable, and deeply rewarding experience. The *NLT Study Bible* has been designed to be your guide on the journey.

MAKING USE OF THE *NLT STUDY BIBLE*

Read the Bible Text. No feature of the *NLT Study Bible* is more important than Scripture, the text of the Bible itself. Read the Bible text as the record of God's dealings with specific people in the past. The Bible is not simply a set of theological propositions or moral instructions, although it does include them. Instead, it is primarily the record of God revealing himself and his purposes to people, and forming loving and faithful relationships with them. As you read, seek to understand the significance of what he was doing for them and saying to them. God does not change (1 Sam 15:29; Jas 1:17), so who he was in relation to the people of the past is who he is to you and me today, and he will be the same God in the future and for all eternity (Heb 13:8). Read the Bible text with the purpose of knowing God himself.

Read Each Book of the Bible as a Whole. It is best to study a book in its entirety, rather than picking and choosing individual verses. Each book is a unified whole, and each verse is a part of that whole. On your first reading, try to read the entire book in one sitting; for larger books, break it into chunks; you can use the outline in each book's introduction as a guide in dividing up your reading. During this reading, try to focus exclusively on the Bible text. We recommend that you leave the notes and other features for later. As you read, write down questions and thoughts that come to mind, and then keep going.

Read the Book Introductions, Section Introductions, and Chronology Articles. Each book of Scripture is situated in both literary and historical contexts that have important implications for understanding the book and individual passages. The *NLT Study Bible*

provides articles that will help you understand these contexts, and reading them will prepare you to engage the text with understanding. Our recommendation is that you begin by reading the Introductions to the Old and New Testaments (beginning on pp. 3 and 1557). Then read the introduction for the section of the Bible that you are studying and the book introduction for the book you are studying. Take time to understand what these introductions say—they were written by people who have devoted many years to understanding Scripture and helping others on the journey. Then refer back to these articles from time to time while you read the Bible text.

Read Slowly. After reading through the text of a Bible book quickly and reading the introductions that impact that book, you are ready to begin reading the Bible text and study materials together. We recommend that you take this part of your journey slowly. Give yourself time to read, understand, and ponder the words in the Bible text and the study materials—the notes, articles, and visual aids—that appear alongside it. Our recommendation is that you read and meditate on perhaps one chapter per day, or about one and one-half pages of Bible text and study materials. If you do so five days per week for fifty-two weeks each year, you will finish going through the *NLT Study Bible* one time in five years (the "Reading Plan" on p. 2209 will guide you at this pace). It sounds like a long time, but it will go quickly, and you will have the pleasure of many enjoyable discoveries along the way. Most importantly, you will be giving yourself time to breathe in God's words and breathe out your response to him in prayer.

Follow the Outline. Notice the outline headings in the text. Consider how each passage fits in the overall structure of the book.

Make Use of the Study Helps. The many study helps (see the "Features Guide," pp. A8–A15) are designed to help explain what the Bible *meant* to its first readers, and what it therefore *means* to us who read it today. Make use of the study helps to grasp the meaning and significance of what the Bible text says. When you read the Bible in this way, you can begin to hear God's voice speaking to you, just as he spoke to the people who first heard and read these words.

Keep a Journal. As you travel through the pages of Scripture, keep a journal of your discoveries, insights, epiphanies, questions, prayers, and perplexities. In past centuries, readers often kept a journal called a *commonplace book* containing their notes about the things they had read and discovered. More recently, many people have found it useful to keep a daily journal of their Bible reading, reflections, and prayers. You can use your Bible study journal to write questions as they come to mind, interesting things that you learn, your own thoughts about the passage, what you think God might be saying to you, and your prayers to God about what you have studied.

Mark the Bible Text and Study Materials. It can be helpful to highlight or mark the parts of the Bible text and study materials that answer your questions or speak to you in some way. Some ways of marking the text include underlining, circling, or highlighting words or phrases; putting brackets in the margins or around pieces of text; writing one to three words in the margin to prompt memory about a topic; and writing cross-references to other places in the *NLT Study Bible* or to your Bible journal (perhaps by date).

Develop a Sense of History. As you read the Bible, seek to develop a historical understanding of how the Bible fits together in time and space. We as people are designed to

enjoy and remember good stories. The Bible tells a great story, but sometimes we don't see how the parts of the story fit together. The *NLT Study Bible* includes a large number of timelines, maps, and explanations to help you do so. When we understand how it all fits together in one great story, it is possible to see connections and developments that could not be seen before.

Use the Reference Helps in the Back. The reference helps in the back of the *NLT Study Bible* will enable you to quickly find the key places where a particular person, place, or topic is covered. As you carefully read the notes and features that the index points to, also read the Bible text itself.

Go Further. Please do not treat the *NLT Study Bible* study notes and other features as the full and final word on any topic or passage. The Bible text itself is complete—you are holding a full and complete copy of God's revealed word. But the notes and other features are limited and incomplete. We who have prepared this Bible have packed in as much as we could in the 2200 pages from the beginning of the Old Testament to the end of the New Testament. But it is only a very small fraction of what could be said. Therefore, treat the *NLT Study Bible* notes and features as a very helpful but incomplete guide on your journey. For those who wish to go further with some aspect of study, there are many other resources available. To help point you in the right direction, each book and section introduction includes a list of "Further Reading" materials.

Go Ahead. Finally, don't hold back; jump in! Begin using the *NLT Study Bible* for your daily study, and don't worry about trying to do everything that we have suggested here. You can take small, manageable steps. The most important thing is that you begin your journey on the road of reading, studying, and understanding the Bible. After a while, come back and read this guide again; you might find something else here that will help you along the way.

As you use the *NLT Study Bible,* you will discover even more ways to grow in your understanding of God's word. We invite you to visit us and tell us about your experiences at www.NLTStudyBible.com, or send us an e-mail at NLTStudyBible@tyndale.com.

Come, . . . let us walk in the light of the LORD! Isaiah 2:5
Your word is a lamp to guide my feet and a light for my path. Psalm 119:105

THE EDITORS

NLT STUDY BIBLE
MASTER TIMELINE

How do the stories of Abraham, Isaac, and Jacob relate to history? What was going on in the world at the time of David and Solomon? How do the reigns of the kings of Israel and Judah fit together? What was happening during the time between the OT and the NT? How do the events in the life of Jesus and the early church correlate with other things that were happening in the Roman world?

CREATION TO ABRAHAM

Many of the events of Genesis 1–11 predate writing, so it is difficult to assign precise dates to these early events. We can, however, observe a close correlation between the biblical account and what is known from other historical sources. After the Flood, which Noah and his family survived, humanity spread out across the known world, and the ancient civilizations began. By the time of Abraham,

4500~950 BC
(300 years/inch)

See "Chronology of Abraham to Joshua," pp. 118–121

4000 BC | 3500 | 3000

EVENTS IN OT BOOKS: *GENESIS 1–11*

CREATION
(undated)

GREAT FLOOD?

MESOPOTAMIA
EARLY BRONZE AGE (3300–2000 BC)

Settlement of Asshur
(around 2800 BC)

SUMERIAN CIVILIZATION
(about 3000~1950 BC)

CANAAN

EGYPT
PREDYNASTIC PERIOD (4000–3000 BC)

ARCHAIC PERIOD /
DYNASTIES 1–2
(3000–2700 BC)

Egypt was well established, while Sumerian civilization in Mesopotamia was coming to a close.

ABRAHAM TO JOSHUA

We know that Abraham lived around 2000 BC, but we are not completely certain about the dates for his life. This uncertainty results from our uncertainty about the date of Israel's exodus from Egypt. Two dates for the Exodus are accepted as possibilities by biblical scholars, 1446 or 1270 BC. The dates for Abraham, Isaac, and Jacob are simply calculated from the date for the Exodus on the basis of information given in the biblical text. Although there is uncertainty, it is also quite clear that the things Scripture says about these people and their lives fit well with what we know about conditions in Canaan and Egypt during this period of history. For more information, see "Chronology of Abraham to Joshua," pp. 118–121.

THE TIME OF THE JUDGES

After Joshua led Israel's conquest of Canaan and the people of Israel began to settle in the land, a period of growing anarchy ensued. Periodic chaos and oppression were punctuated by rescue through the inspired leadership of the judges. For more information, see "Chronology of the Time of the Judges," pp. 414–415.

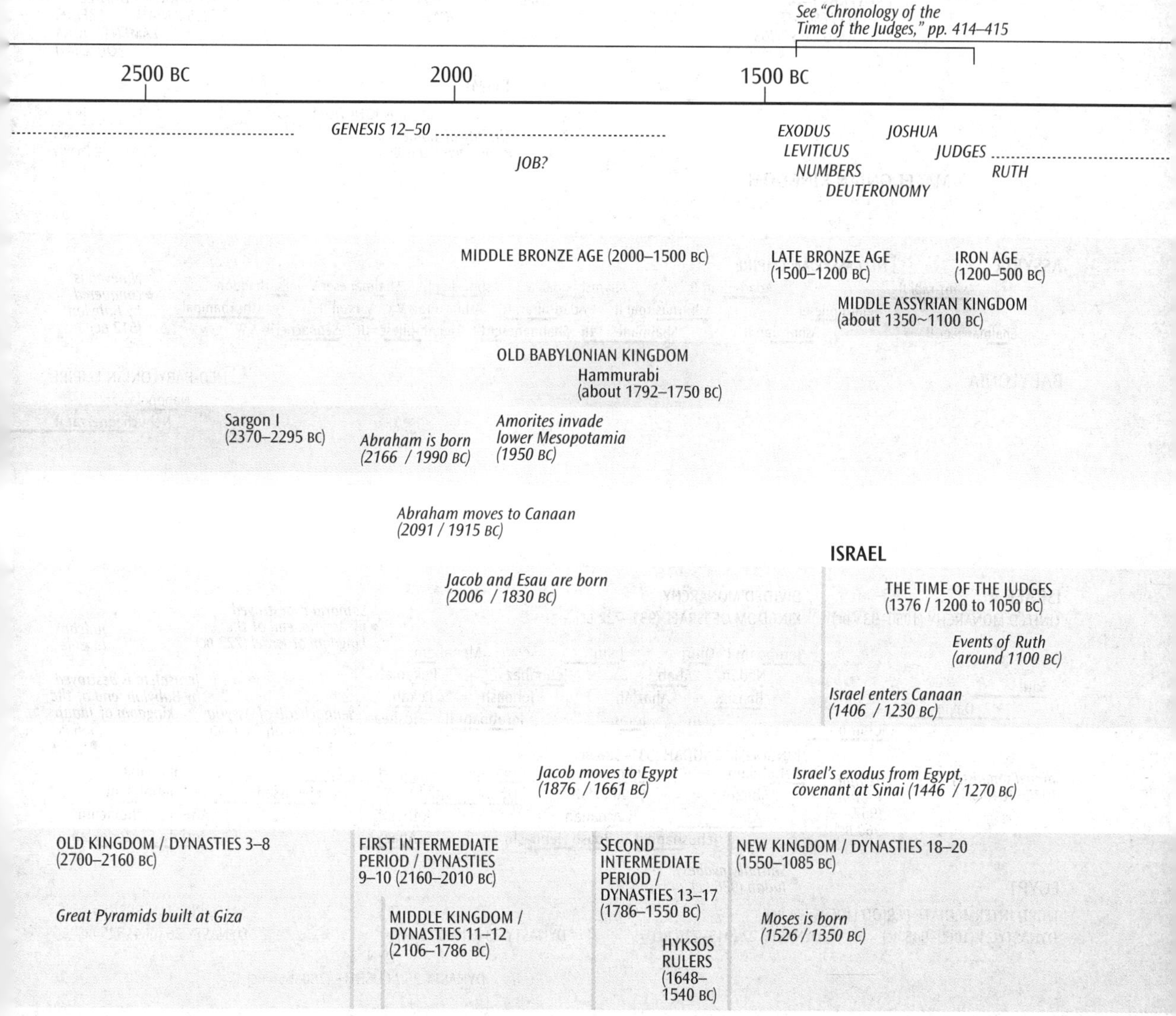

ISRAEL'S MONARCHY

The time of the judges came to a decisive end with the ministry of Samuel and the reigns of King Saul (about 1050~1011 BC) and King David (1011–971 BC). The dates for events from this time forward are much more precise, because we can correlate biblical information with the records of other ancient nations like the Assyrians and Babylonians, and with known astronomical phenomena such as solar eclipses. After the division of Israel into the northern kingdom (Israel) and the southern kingdom (Judah), the chronology becomes very complex, and good timelines are essential for understanding how the reigns of the kings fit together. For more information, see "Chronology of Israel's Monarchy," pp. 562–565. Detailed timelines are also included throughout the books of 1 & 2 Kings.

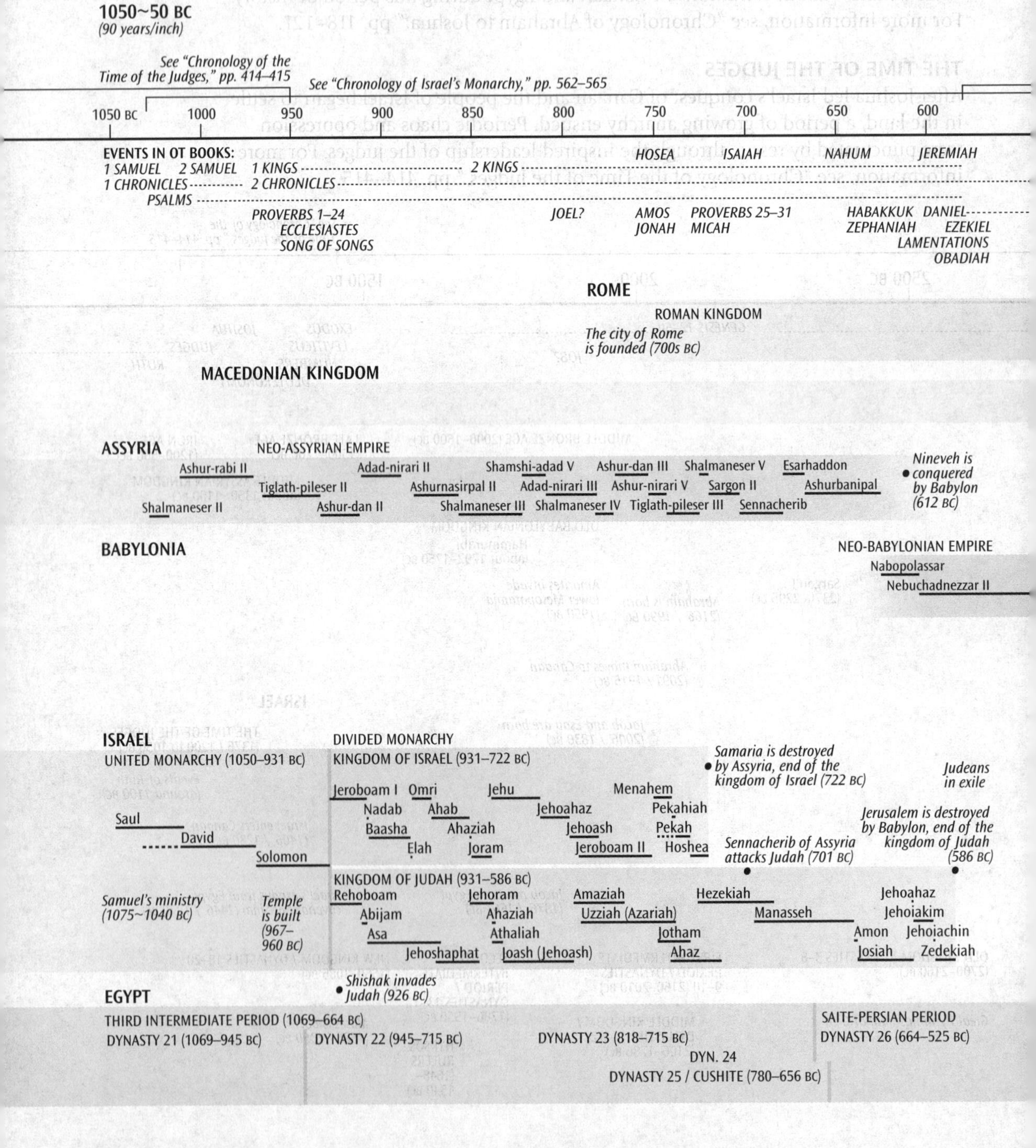

ISRAEL'S EXILE AND RETURN

The records of Israel's history are much more sparse during the period of the Exile than beforehand. Instead of a comprehensive, orderly account, as with Israel's monarchy, we have scattered accounts in books such as 2 Chronicles, Jeremiah, Ezekiel, Daniel, and Esther.

Nebuchadnezzar was the king in Babylon for much of the time of Israel's exile. After his death (562 BC), it was less than twenty-five years until Babylon was conquered by Cyrus the Great (539 BC). Cyrus issued a decree allowing Jewish people to return to Judea, and many did. The books of Ezra and Nehemiah narrate some of the events of the postexilic period in Judea, including the rebuilding of the Temple and the wall of Jerusalem. For more information about this period, see "Historical Background of Israel's Exile and Return," pp. 782–785.

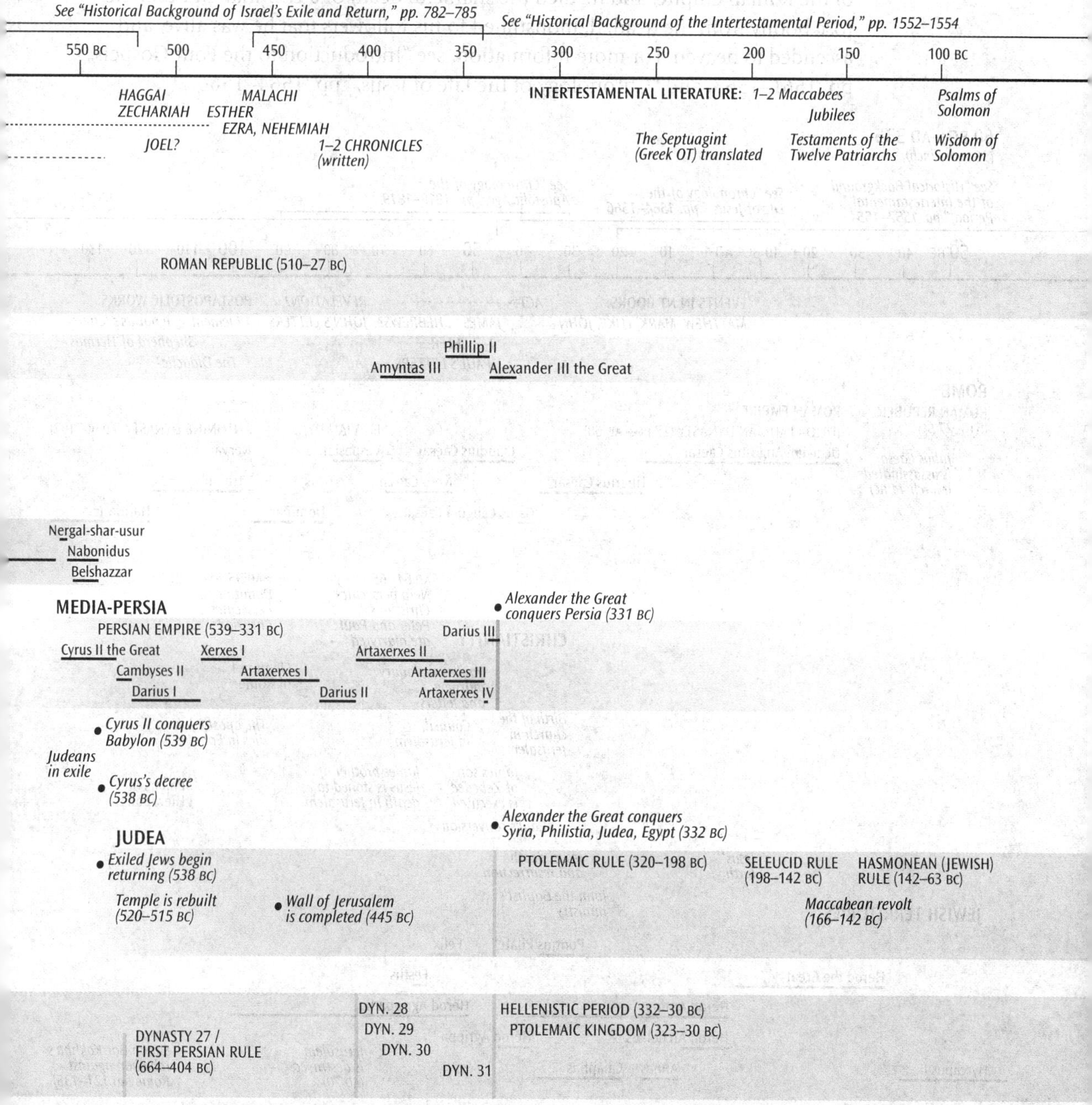

THE INTERTESTAMENTAL PERIOD

From the end of the OT to the beginning of the NT there was a period of about 400 years. It was not, however, an empty period or a lull in history. To the contrary, great changes took place. The Persian empire was replaced by Greek dominance, beginning with the conquests of Alexander the Great (332–323 BC). Greek culture began spreading inexorably throughout the Mediterranean world. Rome, too, grew in power and influence, until the Romans became the dominant power in the Mediterranean world in the first century BC. For more information, see "Historical Background of the Intertestamental Period," pp. 1552–1554.

THE LIFE OF JESUS

Jesus of Nazareth was born in Judea during the height of Greco-Roman culture and Roman power. Jesus lived a relatively short life in a tumultuous backwater of the Roman empire, and he died the shameful death of a criminal. But then he rose bodily from the dead, demonstrated to his followers that he was alive, and ascended to heaven. For more information, see "Introduction to the Four Gospels," pp. 1561–1563, and "Chronology of the Life of Jesus," pp. 1564–1566.

60 BC—AD 335
(36 years/inch)

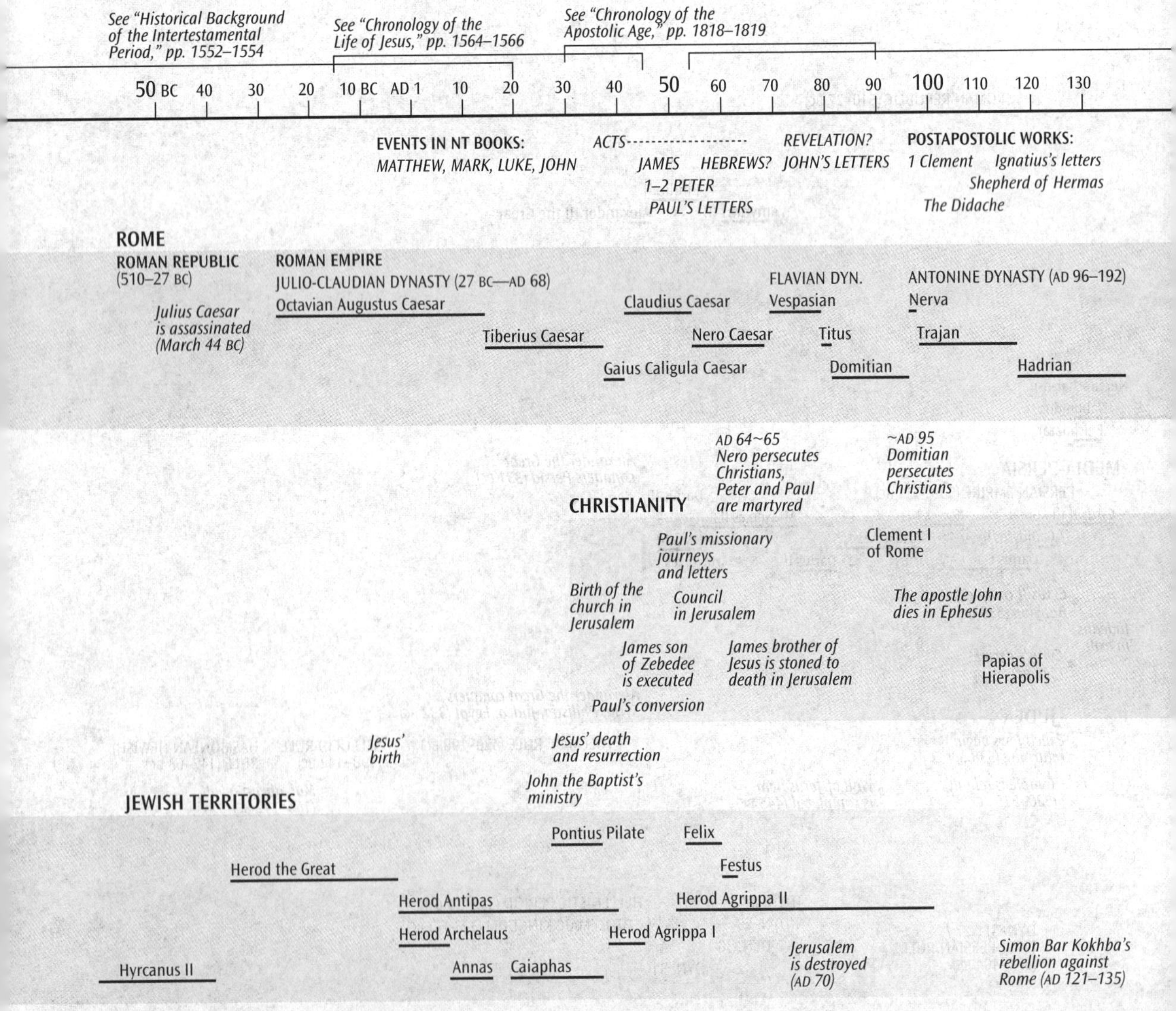

THE APOSTOLIC AGE

After Jesus rose from the dead, his followers quickly began proclaiming the news, and the movement of those who believed the message spread around the Roman world during the first century AD. The book of Acts and the letters of Paul and the other apostles record events in the Christian community during this period. For more information about the chronology of this time, see "Chronology of the Apostolic Age," pp. 1818–1819.

THE TIME AFTER THE APOSTLES

By the end of the first century, all of the apostles of Jesus had died, but the church continued growing. Those early, postapostolic Christians saw themselves and their communities as being in continuity with the apostles. They maintained the faith that the apostles had given them while experiencing periodic, harsh persecution from their neighbors and from the Roman government. For more information, see "Introduction to the Time after the Apostles," pp. 2201–2205.

See "Introduction to the Time after the Apostles," pp. 2201–2205

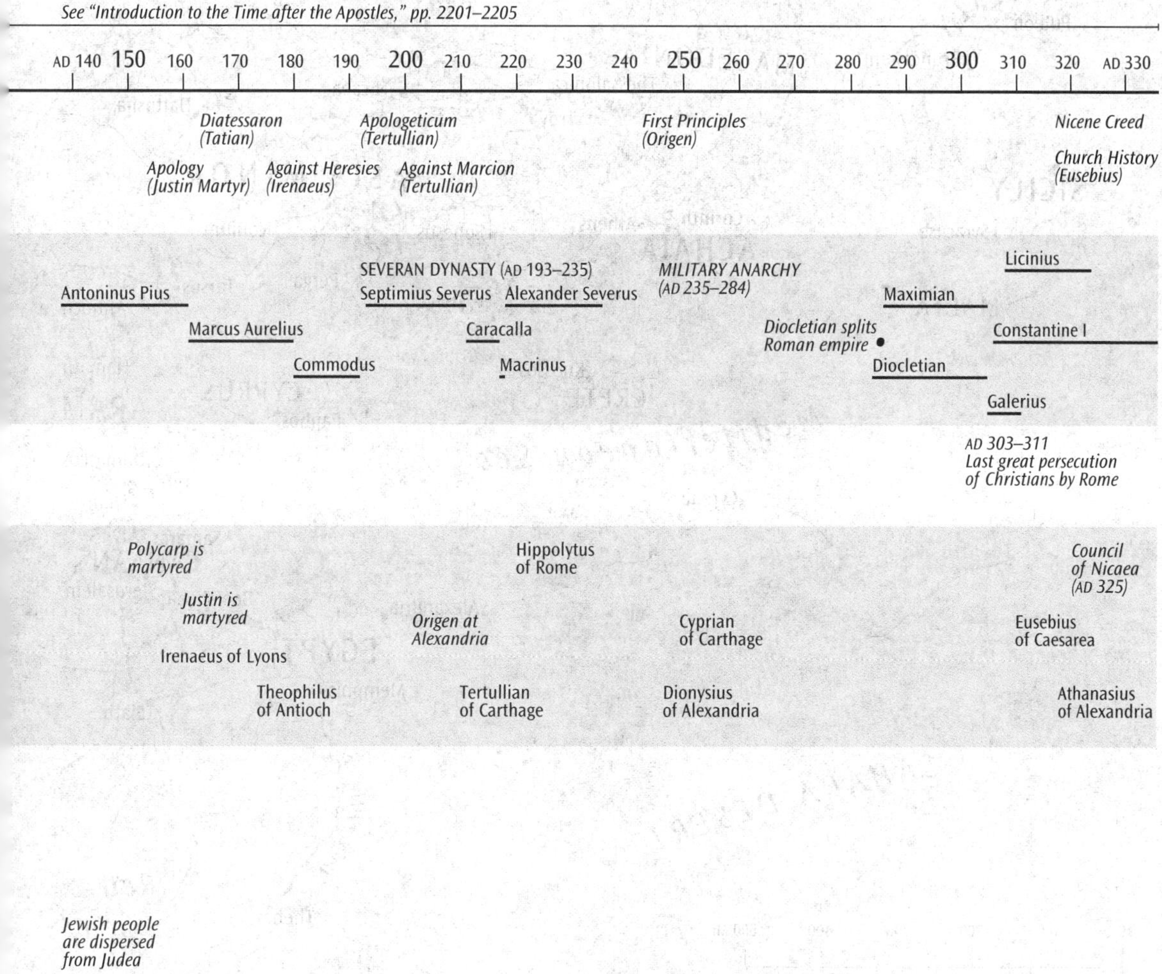

NLT STUDY BIBLE OVERVIEW MAPS

Where did Abraham live, travel, and obey God's instruction to sacrifice his son (Gen 12–22)? Why did Josiah confront Pharaoh Neco and lose his life (2 Kgs 23:29-30; 2 Chr 35:20-27; Jer 46)? When Jesus was making his final trip to Jerusalem, why did he go through Samaria (John 4:4)? How did Paul follow up with the churches he established during his first missionary

journey (Acts 13–14, 16)? The answers to questions such as these can be understood more readily through the study of the geography of the Bible.

THE EASTERN MEDITERRANEAN AND THE NEAR EAST

The events in the Bible took place in the lands around the eastern MEDITERRANEAN SEA and in the Near East—the area from EGYPT through CANAAN and ARAM, to MESOPOTAMIA and PERSIA. The ancient Near East is the setting for the earliest events of recorded history, and it is the world in which the nation of Israel was formed and grew. Abraham journeyed from HARAN in upper Mesopotamia to Canaan (Gen 12). His descendants then moved to Egypt (Gen 46) and spent hundreds of years there before returning to Canaan and establishing the nation of Israel (Exod—Josh).

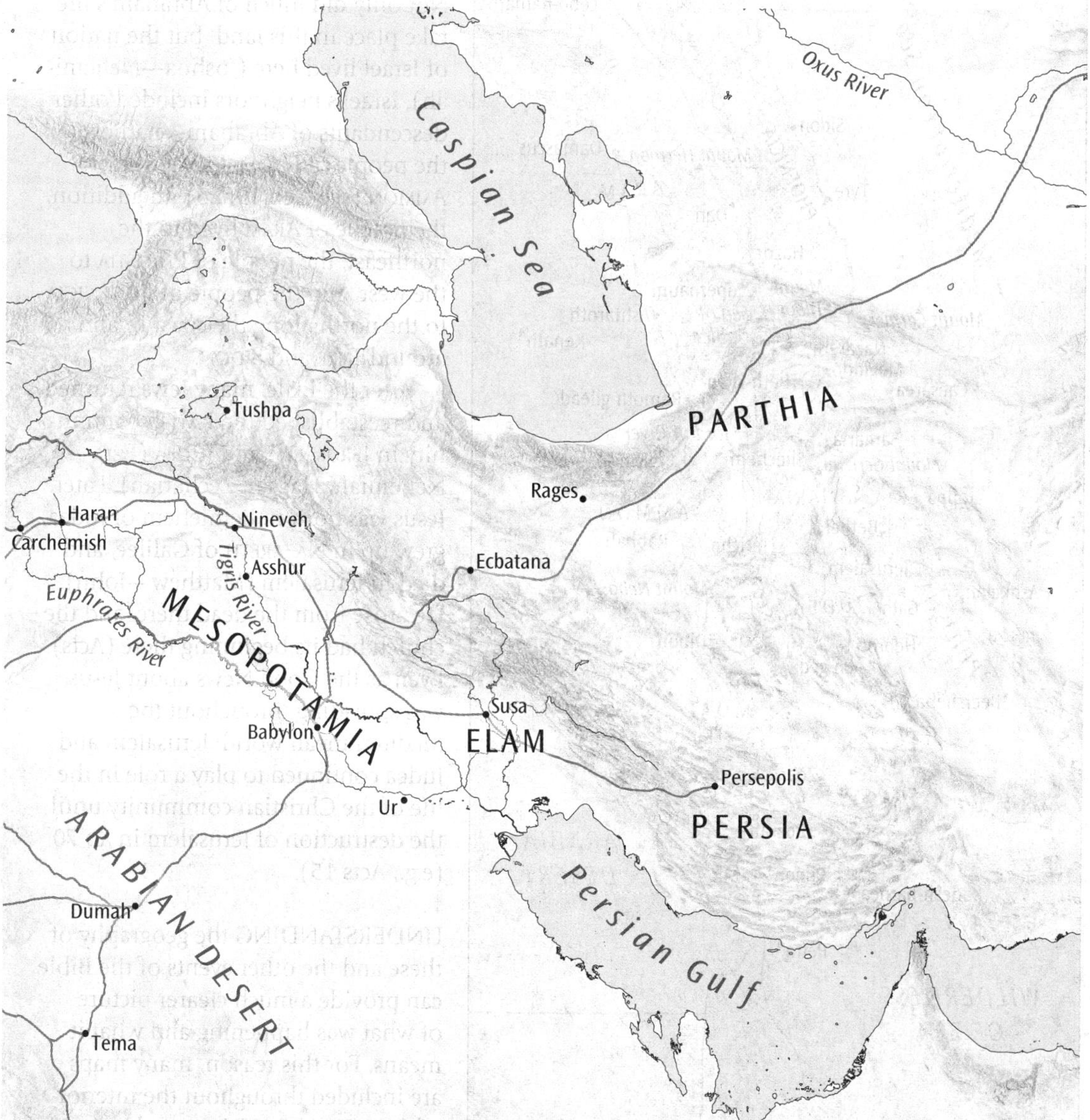

Almost 1,000 years later, after living in the land of Israel (see below), the descendants of Abraham returned to Mesopotamia as exiles (2 Kgs 17, 24–25). The Jewish people later returned to Jerusalem and Judea and reestablished their community (Ezra—Nehemiah). After Jesus' death and resurrection, the Christian community that began in Jerusalem spread as Paul and the other apostles took the Good News throughout the known world (Acts 2–28).

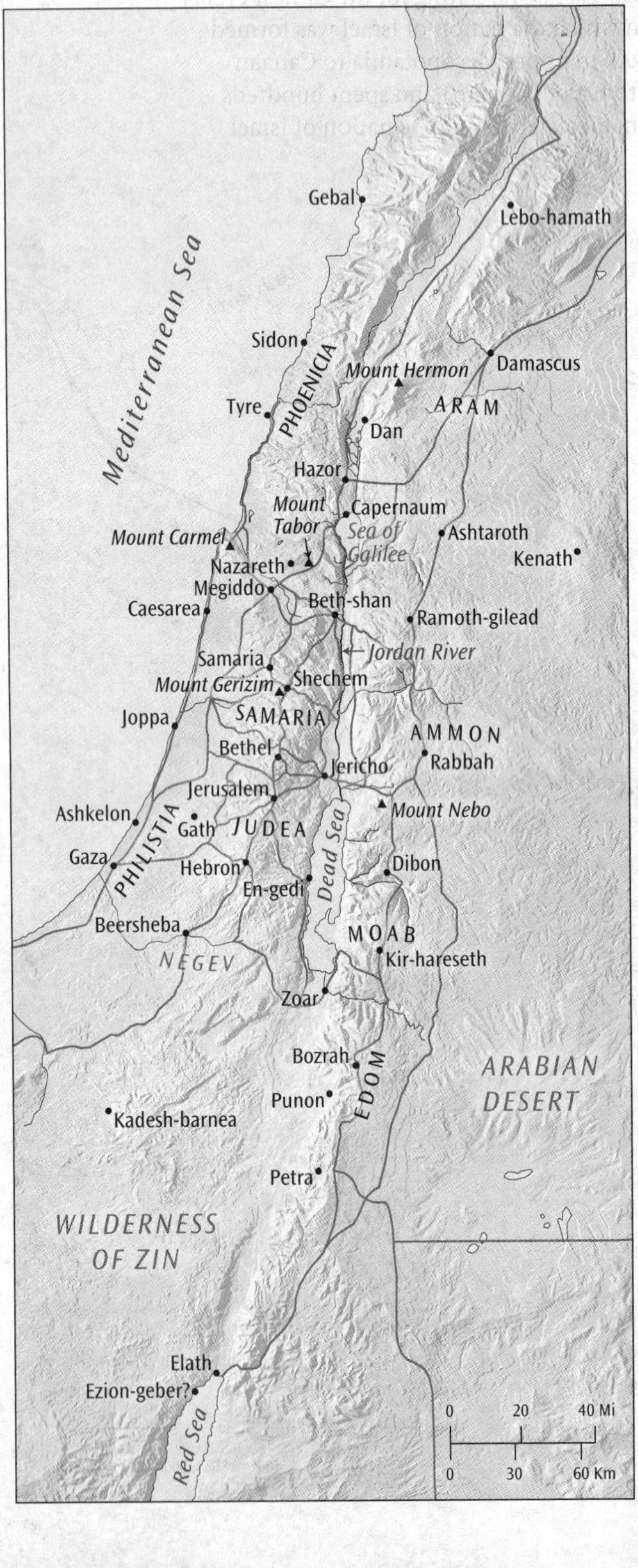

ISRAEL AND ITS NEIGHBORS

Many of the key events in the history of God's people took place in and around Canaan, which came to be called the land of Israel (from Dan in the north to Beersheba in the south). Not only did much of Abraham's life take place in this land, but the nation of Israel lived here (Joshua—Nehemiah). Israel's neighbors included other descendants of Abraham—namely, the people of Edom, Moab, and Ammon (see Gen 19, 25). In addition, the people of Aram lived to the northeast, the people of Philistia to the west, and the people of Phoenicia to the north along the coast in and around Tyre and Sidon.

After the Exile, many Jews returned and reestablished the Jewish community in Jerusalem and Judea (Ezra—Nehemiah, Haggai, Zechariah). Later, Jesus was born in Bethlehem of Judea, grew up in Nazareth of Galilee, and died in Jerusalem (Matthew—John). He arose from the dead there, and the church had its beginning there (Acts). Even as the Good News about Jesus was spreading throughout the Mediterranean world, Jerusalem and Judea continued to play a role in the life of the Christian community until the destruction of Jerusalem in AD 70 (e.g., Acts 15).

UNDERSTANDING the geography of these and the other events of the Bible can provide a much clearer picture of what was happening and what it means. For this reason, many maps are included throughout the interior of the *NLT Study Bible.* Most books of the Bible include a map in the book's introduction. All of the maps and many of the places on them are listed in the Subject Index, pp. 2227–2368.

NLT STUDY BIBLE
CONTRIBUTORS

EDITORS

GENERAL EDITOR
Sean A. Harrison

EXECUTIVE EDITOR
Mark D. Taylor

CONTENT EDITORS
David P. Barrett
G. Patrick LaCosse
Bradley J. Lewis
Henry M. Whitney III
Keith Williams

STYLISTIC EDITOR
Linda Schlafer

COPY EDITORS
Keith Williams, Coordinator
Leanne Roberts, Proofreading Coordinator
Paul Adams
Jason Driesbach
Adam Graber
Annette Hayward
Judy Modica
Jonathan Schindler
Caleb Sjogren
Cindy Szponder
Lisa Voth
Matthew Wolf

GENERAL REVIEWERS

GENESIS—DEUTERONOMY
Daniel I. Block

JOSHUA—ESTHER, MAPS
Barry J. Beitzel

JOB—SONG OF SONGS
Tremper Longman III

ISAIAH—MALACHI
John N. Oswalt

MATTHEW—ACTS
Grant R. Osborne

ROMANS—REVELATION
Norman R. Ericson

CONTRIBUTING SCHOLARS

GENESIS
Andrew Schmutzer
Allen P. Ross

EXODUS
John N. Oswalt

LEVITICUS
William C. Williams

NUMBERS
Gerald L. Mattingly

DEUTERONOMY
Eugene H. Merrill

JOSHUA
Joseph Coleson

JUDGES
Carl E. Armerding

RUTH
Joseph Coleson
Sean A. Harrison

1 & 2 SAMUEL
Victor P. Hamilton

1 & 2 KINGS
Richard D. Patterson

1 & 2 CHRONICLES
August Konkel

EZRA, NEHEMIAH, ESTHER
Gary V. Smith

JOB
Dale A. Brueggemann

PSALMS
Willem VanGemeren

PROVERBS
Tremper Longman III

ECCLESIASTES
Sean A. Harrison
Daniel C. Fredericks

SONG OF SONGS
Daniel C. Fredericks
Tremper Longman III

ISAIAH
Willem VanGemeren

JEREMIAH, LAMENTATIONS
G. Herbert Livingston

EZEKIEL
Iain Duguid

DANIEL
Gene Carpenter

HOSEA, JOEL
Owen Dickens

AMOS
William C. Williams

OBADIAH
Carl E. Armerding

JONAH
G. Patrick LaCosse

MICAH
Eugene Carpenter

NAHUM, HABAKKUK, ZEPHANIAH
Richard D. Patterson

HAGGAI, ZECHARIAH, MALACHI
Andrew Hill

MATTHEW
Scot McKnight

MARK
Robert Stein

LUKE
Mark Strauss

JOHN
Gary M. Burge

ACTS
Allison Trites

ROMANS
Douglas J. Moo

1 CORINTHIANS
Roger Mohrlang

2 CORINTHIANS
Ralph P. Martin

GALATIANS
Sean A. Harrison

EPHESIANS, PHILIPPIANS, PHILEMON
Roger Mohrlang

COLOSSIANS
Douglas J. Moo

1 & 2 THESSALONIANS
Gene L. Green

1 & 2 TIMOTHY, TITUS
Jon Laansma

HEBREWS
George Guthrie

JAMES
Norman R. Ericson

1 & 2 PETER, JUDE
Douglas J. Moo

1–3 JOHN
Philip W. Comfort

REVELATION
Gerald Borchert

OLD TESTAMENT PROFILES
Tremper Longman III

NEW TESTAMENT PROFILES
Roger Mohrlang

ARTICLES
Daniel I. Block
Eugene Carpenter
Philip W. Comfort
Iain Duguid
Sean A. Harrison
Tremper Longman III
Douglas J. Moo
Grant R. Osborne
Richard D. Patterson
Daniel H. Williams
William C. Williams

WORD STUDY SYSTEM
James A. Swanson
Keith Williams

SPECIAL REVIEWER
Kenneth N. Taylor (deceased)

BIBLE PUBLISHING TEAM

PUBLISHER
Douglas R. Knox

ASSOCIATE PUBLISHER
Blaine A. Smith

ACQUISITIONS DIRECTOR
Kevin O'Brien

ACQUISITIONS EDITOR
Kim Johnson

OTHER SERVICES

GRAPHIC DESIGNERS
Timothy R. Botts (Interior)
Dean Renninger (Cover)

CARTOGRAPHY
David P. Barrett

ILLUSTRATORS
Hugh Claycombe
Luke Daab
Sean A. Harrison

TYPESETTING
Joel Bartlett (The Livingstone Corporation)
Gwen Elliott

PROOFREADING
Peachtree Editorial Services

INDEXING
Karen Schmitt (Schmitt Indexing)

Many thanks to all who have had a hand in the creation of this study Bible, and most of all to the Lord of heaven and earth, who gave us his word and spirit so generously.

A NOTE TO READERS

THE *HOLY BIBLE*, NEW LIVING TRANSLATION, was first published in 1996. It quickly became one of the most popular Bible translations in the English-speaking world. While the NLT's influence was rapidly growing, the Bible Translation Committee determined that an additional investment in scholarly review and text refinement could make it even better. So shortly after its initial publication, the committee began an eight-year process with the purpose of increasing the level of the NLT's precision without sacrificing its easy-to-understand quality. This second-generation text was completed in 2004, with minor changes subsequently introduced in 2007.

The goal of any Bible translation is to convey the meaning and content of the ancient Hebrew, Aramaic, and Greek texts as accurately as possible to contemporary readers. The challenge for our translators was to create a text that would communicate as clearly and powerfully to today's readers as the original texts did to readers and listeners in the ancient biblical world. The resulting translation is easy to read and understand, while also accurately communicating the meaning and content of the original biblical texts. The NLT is a general-purpose text especially good for study, devotional reading, and reading aloud in worship services.

We believe that the New Living Translation—which combines the latest biblical scholarship with a clear, dynamic writing style—will communicate God's word powerfully to all who read it. We publish it with the prayer that God will use it to speak his timeless truth to the church and the world in a fresh, new way.

THE PUBLISHERS, *October 2007*

INTRODUCTION TO THE NEW LIVING TRANSLATION

Translation Philosophy and Methodology
English Bible translations tend to be governed by one of two general translation theories. The first theory has been called "formal-equivalence," "literal," or "word-for-word" translation. According to this theory, the translator attempts to render each word of the original language into English and seeks to preserve the original syntax and sentence structure as much as possible in translation. The second theory has been called "dynamic-equivalence," "functional-equivalence," or "thought-for-thought" translation. The goal of this translation theory is to produce in English the closest natural equivalent of the message expressed by the original-language text, both in meaning and in style.

Both of these translation theories have their strengths. A formal-equivalence translation preserves aspects of the original text—including ancient idioms, term consistency, and original-language syntax—that are valuable for scholars and professional study. It allows a reader to trace formal elements of the original-language text through the English translation. A dynamic-equivalence translation, on the other hand, focuses on translating the message of the original-language text. It ensures that the meaning of the text is readily apparent to the contemporary reader. This allows the message to come through with immediacy, without requiring the reader to struggle with foreign idioms and awkward syntax. It also facilitates serious study of the text's message and clarity in both devotional and public reading.

The pure application of either of these translation philosophies would create translations at opposite ends of the translation spectrum. But in reality, all translations contain a mixture of these two philosophies. A purely formal-equivalence translation would be unintelligible in English, and a purely dynamic-equivalence translation would risk being unfaithful to the original. That is why translations shaped by dynamic-equivalence theory are usually quite literal when the original text is relatively clear, and the translations shaped by formal-equivalence theory are sometimes quite dynamic when the original text is obscure.

The translators of the New Living Translation set out to render the message of the original texts of Scripture into clear, contemporary English. As they did so, they kept the concerns of both formal-equivalence and dynamic-equivalence in mind. On the one hand, they translated as simply and literally as possible when that approach yielded an accurate, clear, and natural English text. Many words and phrases were rendered literally and consistently into English, preserving essential literary and rhetorical devices, ancient metaphors, and word choices that give structure to the text and provide echoes of meaning from one passage to the next.

On the other hand, the translators rendered the message more dynamically when the literal rendering was hard to understand, was misleading, or yielded archaic or foreign wording. They clarified difficult metaphors and terms to aid in the reader's understanding. The translators first struggled with the meaning of the words and phrases in the ancient context; then they rendered the message into clear, natural English. Their goal was to be both faithful to the ancient texts and eminently readable. The result is a translation that is both exegetically accurate and idiomatically powerful.

Translation Process and Team
To produce an accurate translation of the Bible into contemporary English, the translation team needed the skills necessary to enter into the thought patterns of the ancient authors and then to render their ideas, connotations, and effects into clear, contemporary English. To begin this process, qualified biblical scholars were needed to interpret the meaning of the original text and to check it against our base English translation. In order to guard against personal and theological biases, the scholars needed to represent a diverse group of evangelicals who would employ the best exegetical tools. Then to work alongside the scholars, skilled English stylists were needed to shape the text into clear, contemporary English.

With these concerns in mind, the Bible Translation Committee recruited teams of scholars that represented a broad spectrum of denominations, theological perspectives, and backgrounds within the worldwide evangelical community. (These scholars are listed at the end of this introduction.) Each book of the Bible was assigned to three different scholars with proven expertise in the book or group of books to be reviewed. Each of these scholars made a thorough review of a base translation and submitted suggested revisions to the appropriate Senior Translator. The Senior Translator then reviewed and summarized these suggestions and proposed a first-draft revision of the base text. This draft served as the basis for several additional phases of exegetical and

stylistic committee review. Then the Bible Translation Committee jointly reviewed and approved every verse of the final translation.

Throughout the translation and editing process, the Senior Translators and their scholar teams were given a chance to review the editing done by the team of stylists. This ensured that exegetical errors would not be introduced late in the process and that the entire Bible Translation Committee was happy with the final result. By choosing a team of qualified scholars and skilled stylists and by setting up a process that allowed their interaction throughout the process, the New Living Translation has been refined to preserve the essential formal elements of the original biblical texts, while also creating a clear, understandable English text.

The New Living Translation was first published in 1996. Shortly after its initial publication, the Bible Translation Committee began a process of further committee review and translation refinement. The purpose of this continued revision was to increase the level of precision without sacrificing the text's easy-to-understand quality. This second-edition text was completed in 2004, and an additional update with minor changes was subsequently introduced in 2007. This printing of the New Living Translation reflects the updated 2007 text.

Written to Be Read Aloud

It is evident in Scripture that the biblical documents were written to be read aloud, often in public worship (see Nehemiah 8; Luke 4:16-20; 1 Timothy 4:13; Revelation 1:3). It is still the case today that more people will hear the Bible read aloud in church than are likely to read it for themselves. Therefore, a new translation must communicate with clarity and power when it is read publicly. Clarity was a primary goal for the NLT translators, not only to facilitate private reading and understanding, but also to ensure that it would be excellent for public reading and make an immediate and powerful impact on any listener.

The Texts behind the New Living Translation

The Old Testament translators used the Masoretic Text of the Hebrew Bible as represented in *Biblia Hebraica Stuttgartensia* (1977), with its extensive system of textual notes; this is an update of Rudolf Kittel's *Biblia Hebraica* (Stuttgart, 1937). The translators also further compared the Dead Sea Scrolls, the Septuagint and other Greek manuscripts, the Samaritan Pentateuch, the Syriac Peshitta, the Latin Vulgate, and any other versions or manuscripts that shed light on the meaning of difficult passages.

The New Testament translators used the two standard editions of the Greek New Testament: the *Greek New Testament*, published by the United Bible Societies (UBS, fourth revised edition, 1993), and *Novum Testamentum Graece*, edited by Nestle and Aland (NA, twenty-seventh edition, 1993). These two editions, which have the same text but differ in punctuation and textual notes, represent, for the most part, the best in modern textual scholarship. However, in cases where strong textual or other scholarly evidence supported the decision, the translators sometimes chose to differ from the UBS and NA Greek texts and followed variant readings found in other ancient witnesses. Significant textual variants of this sort are always noted in the textual notes of the New Living Translation.

Translation Issues

The translators have made a conscious effort to provide a text that can be easily understood by the typical reader of modern English. To this end, we sought to use only vocabulary and language structures in common use today. We avoided using language likely to become quickly dated or that reflects only a narrow subdialect of English, with the goal of making the New Living Translation as broadly useful and timeless as possible.

But our concern for readability goes beyond the concerns of vocabulary and sentence structure. We are also concerned about historical and cultural barriers to understanding the Bible, and we have sought to translate terms shrouded in history and culture in ways that can be immediately understood. To this end:

- We have converted ancient weights and measures (for example, "ephah" [a unit of dry volume] or "cubit" [a unit of length]) to modern English (American) equivalents, since the ancient measures are not generally meaningful to today's readers. Then in the textual footnotes we offer the literal Hebrew, Aramaic, or Greek measures, along with modern metric equivalents.
- Instead of translating ancient currency values literally, we have expressed them in common terms that communicate the message. For example, in the Old Testament, "ten shekels of silver" becomes "ten pieces of silver" to convey the intended message. In the New Testament, we have often translated the "denarius" as "the normal daily wage" to facilitate understanding. Then a footnote offers: "Greek *a denarius*, the payment for a full day's labor." In general, we give a clear English rendering and then state the literal Hebrew, Aramaic, or Greek in a textual footnote.
- Since the names of Hebrew months are unknown to most contemporary readers, and since the Hebrew lunar calendar fluctuates from year to year in relation to the solar calendar used today, we have looked for clear ways to communicate the time of year the Hebrew months (such as Abib) refer to. When an expanded or interpretive rendering is given in the text, a textual note gives the literal rendering. Where it is possible to define a specific ancient date in terms of our modern calendar, we use modern dates in the text. A textual footnote then gives the literal Hebrew date and states the rationale for our rendering. For example, Ezra 6:15 pinpoints the date when the postexilic Temple was completed in Jerusalem: "the third day of the month Adar." This was during the sixth year of King Darius's reign (that is, 515 B.C.). We have translated that date as March 12, with a footnote giving the Hebrew and identifying the year as 515 B.C.
- Since ancient references to the time of day differ from our modern methods of denoting time, we have used renderings that are instantly understandable to the

modern reader. Accordingly, we have rendered specific times of day by using approximate equivalents in terms of our common "o'clock" system. On occasion, translations such as "at dawn the next morning" or "as the sun was setting" have been used when the biblical reference is more general.

- When the meaning of a proper name (or a wordplay inherent in a proper name) is relevant to the message of the text, its meaning is often illuminated with a textual footnote. For example, in Exodus 2:10 the text reads: "The princess named him Moses, for she explained, 'I lifted him out of the water.' " The accompanying footnote reads: "*Moses* sounds like a Hebrew term that means 'to lift out.' "

  Sometimes, when the actual meaning of a name is clear, that meaning is included in parentheses within the text itself. For example, the text at Genesis 16:11 reads: "You are to name him Ishmael *(which means 'God hears')*, for the LORD has heard your cry of distress." Since the original hearers and readers would have instantly understood the meaning of the name "Ishmael," we have provided modern readers with the same information so they can experience the text in a similar way.
- Many words and phrases carry a great deal of cultural meaning that was obvious to the original readers but needs explanation in our own culture. For example, the phrase "they beat their breasts" (Luke 23:48) in ancient times meant that people were very upset, often in mourning. In our translation we chose to translate this phrase dynamically for clarity: "They went home *in deep sorrow.*" Then we included a footnote with the literal Greek, which reads: "Greek *went home beating their breasts.*" In other similar cases, however, we have sometimes chosen to illuminate the existing literal expression to make it immediately understandable. For example, here we might have expanded the literal Greek phrase to read: "They went home beating their breasts *in sorrow.*" If we had done this, we would not have included a textual footnote, since the literal Greek clearly appears in translation.
- Metaphorical language is sometimes difficult for contemporary readers to understand, so at times we have chosen to translate or illuminate the meaning of a metaphor. For example, the ancient poet writes, "Your neck is *like* the tower of David" (Song of Songs 4:4). We have rendered it "Your neck is *as beautiful as* the tower of David" to clarify the intended positive meaning of the simile. Another example comes in Ecclesiastes 12:3, which can be literally rendered: "Remember him . . . when the grinding women cease because they are few, and the women who look through the windows see dimly." We have rendered it: "Remember him before your teeth—your few remaining servants—stop grinding; and before your eyes—the women looking through the windows—see dimly." We clarified such metaphors only when we believed a typical reader might be confused by the literal text.
- When the content of the original language text is poetic in character, we have rendered it in English poetic form. We sought to break lines in ways that clarify and highlight the relationships between phrases of the text. Hebrew poetry often uses parallelism, a literary form where a second phrase (or in some instances a third or fourth) echoes the initial phrase in some way. In Hebrew parallelism, the subsequent parallel phrases continue, while also furthering and sharpening, the thought expressed in the initial line or phrase. Whenever possible, we sought to represent these parallel phrases in natural poetic English.
- The Greek term *hoi Ioudaioi* is literally translated "the Jews" in many English translations. In the Gospel of John, however, this term doesn't always refer to the Jewish people generally. In some contexts, it refers more particularly to the Jewish religious leaders. We have attempted to capture the meaning in these different contexts by using terms such as "the people" (with a footnote: Greek *the Jewish people*) or "the religious leaders," where appropriate.
- One challenge we faced was how to translate accurately the ancient biblical text that was originally written in a context where male-oriented terms were used to refer to humanity generally. We needed to respect the nature of the ancient context while also trying to make the translation clear to a modern audience that tends to read male-oriented language as applying only to males. Often the original text, though using masculine nouns and pronouns, clearly intends that the message be applied to both men and women. A typical example is found in the New Testament letters, where the believers are called "brothers" (*adelphoi*). Yet it is clear from the content of these letters that they were addressed to all the believers—male and female. Thus, we have usually translated this Greek word as "brothers and sisters" in order to represent the historical situation more accurately.

  We have also been sensitive to passages where the text applies generally to human beings or to the human condition. In some instances we have used plural pronouns (they, them) in place of the masculine singular (he, him). For example, a traditional rendering of Proverbs 22:6 is: "Train up a child in the way he should go, and when he is old he will not turn from it." We have rendered it: "Direct your children onto the right path, and when they are older, they will not leave it." At times, we have also replaced third person pronouns with the second person to ensure clarity. A traditional rendering of Proverbs 26:27 is: "He who digs a pit will fall into it, and he who rolls a stone, it will come back on him." We have rendered it: "If you set a trap for others, you will get caught in it yourself. If you roll a boulder down on others, it will crush you instead."

  We should emphasize, however, that all masculine nouns and pronouns used to represent God (for example, "Father") have been maintained without

exception. All decisions of this kind have been driven by the concern to reflect accurately the intended meaning of the original texts of Scripture.

Lexical Consistency in Terminology
For the sake of clarity, we have translated certain original-language terms consistently, especially within synoptic passages and for commonly repeated rhetorical phrases, and within certain word categories such as divine names and nontheological technical terminology (e.g., liturgical, legal, cultural, zoological, and botanical terms). For theological terms, we have allowed a greater semantic range of acceptable English words or phrases for a single Hebrew or Greek word. We have avoided some theological terms that are not readily understood by many modern readers. For example, we avoided using words such as "justification" and "sanctification," which are carryovers from Latin translations. In place of these words, we have provided renderings such as "made right with God" and "made holy."

The Spelling of Proper Names
Many individuals in the Bible, especially the Old Testament, are known by more than one name (e.g., Uzziah/Azariah). For the sake of clarity, we have tried to use a single spelling for any one individual, footnoting the literal spelling whenever we differ from it. This is especially helpful in delineating the kings of Israel and Judah. King Joash/Jehoash of Israel has been consistently called Jehoash, while King Joash/Jehoash of Judah is called Joash. A similar distinction has been used to distinguish between Joram/Jehoram of Israel and Joram/Jehoram of Judah. All such decisions were made with the goal of clarifying the text for the reader. When the ancient biblical writers clearly had a theological purpose in their choice of a variant name (e.g., Esh-baal/Ishbosheth), the different names have been maintained with an explanatory footnote.

For the names Jacob and Israel, which are used interchangeably for both the individual patriarch and the nation, we generally render it "Israel" when it refers to the nation and "Jacob" when it refers to the individual. When our rendering of the name differs from the underlying Hebrew text, we provide a textual footnote, which includes this explanation: "The names 'Jacob' and 'Israel' are often interchanged throughout the Old Testament, referring sometimes to the individual patriarch and sometimes to the nation."

The Rendering of Divine Names
All appearances of *'el, 'elohim,* or *'eloah* have been translated "God," except where the context demands the translation "god(s)." We have generally rendered the tetragrammaton (*YHWH*) consistently as "the LORD," utilizing a form with small capitals that is common among English translations. This will distinguish it from the name *'adonai,* which we render "Lord." When *'adonai* and *YHWH* appear together, we have rendered it "Sovereign LORD." This also distinguishes *'adonai YHWH* from cases where *YHWH* appears with *'elohim,* which is rendered "LORD God." When *YH* (the short form of *YHWH*) and *YHWH* appear together, we have rendered it "LORD GOD." When *YHWH* appears with the term *tseba'oth,* we have rendered it "LORD of Heaven's Armies" to translate the meaning of the name. In a few cases, we have utilized the transliteration, *Yahweh,* when the personal character of the name is being invoked in contrast to another divine name or the name of some other god (for example, see Exodus 3:15; 6:2-3).

In the New Testament, the Greek word *christos* has been translated as "Messiah" when the context assumes a Jewish audience. When a Gentile audience can be assumed, *christos* has been translated as "Christ." The Greek word *kurios* is consistently translated "Lord," except that it is translated "LORD" wherever the New Testament text explicitly quotes from the Old Testament, and the text there has it in small capitals.

Textual Footnotes
The New Living Translation provides several kinds of textual footnotes, all included within the study notes in this edition:

- When for the sake of clarity the NLT renders a difficult or potentially confusing phrase dynamically, we generally give the literal rendering in a textual footnote. This allows the reader to see the literal source of our dynamic rendering and how our translation relates to other more literal translations. These notes are prefaced with "literally." For example, in Acts 2:42 we translated the literal "breaking of bread" (from the Greek) as "the Lord's Supper" to clarify that this verse refers to the ceremonial practice of the church rather than just an ordinary meal. Then we attached a footnote to "the Lord's Supper," which reads: "Literally *the breaking of bread.*"
- Textual footnotes are also used to show alternative renderings, prefaced with the word "Or." These normally occur for passages where an aspect of the meaning is debated. On occasion, we also provide notes on words or phrases that represent a departure from long-standing tradition. These notes are prefaced with "Traditionally rendered." For example, the footnote to the translation "serious skin disease" at Leviticus 13:2 says: "Traditionally rendered *leprosy.* The Hebrew word used throughout this passage is used to describe various skin diseases."
- When our translators follow a textual variant that differs significantly from our standard Hebrew or Greek texts (listed earlier), we document that difference with a footnote. We also footnote cases when the NLT excludes a passage that is included in the Greek text known as the *Textus Receptus* (and familiar to readers through its translation in the King James Version). In such cases, we offer a translation of the excluded text in a footnote, even though it is generally recognized as a later addition to the Greek text and not part of the original Greek New Testament.
- All Old Testament passages that are quoted in the New Testament are identified by a textual footnote at the New Testament location. When the New Testament clearly quotes from the Greek

translation of the Old Testament, and when it differs significantly in wording from the Hebrew text, we also place a textual footnote at the Old Testament location. This note includes a rendering of the Greek version, along with a cross-reference to the New Testament passage(s) where it is cited (for example, see notes on Psalms 8:2; 53:3; Proverbs 3:12).

- Some textual footnotes provide cultural and historical information on places, things, and people in the Bible that are probably obscure to modern readers. Such notes should aid the reader in understanding the message of the text. For example, in Acts 12:1, "King Herod" is named in this translation as "King Herod Agrippa" and is identified in a footnote as being "the nephew of Herod Antipas and a grandson of Herod the Great."
- When the meaning of a proper name (or a wordplay inherent in a proper name) is relevant to the meaning of the text, it is either illuminated with a textual footnote or included within parentheses in the text itself. For example, the footnote concerning the name "Eve" at Genesis 3:20 reads: "*Eve* sounds like a Hebrew term that means 'to give life.' " This wordplay in the Hebrew illuminates the meaning of the text, which goes on to say that Eve "would be the mother of all who live."

Cross-References

There are a number of different cross-referencing tools that appear in New Living Translation Bibles, and they offer different levels of help in this regard. All straight-text Bibles include the standard set of textual footnotes that include cross-references connecting New Testament texts to their related Old Testament sources. (See more on this above.)

Many NLT Bibles include an additional short cross-reference system that sets key cross-references at the end of paragraphs and then marks the associated verses with a cross symbol. This space-efficient system, while not being obtrusive, offers many important key connections between passages. Larger study editions include a full-column cross-reference system. This system allows space for a more comprehensive listing of cross-references.

AS WE SUBMIT this translation for publication, we recognize that any translation of the Scriptures is subject to limitations and imperfections. Anyone who has attempted to communicate the richness of God's Word into another language will realize it is impossible to make a perfect translation. Recognizing these limitations, we sought God's guidance and wisdom throughout this project. Now we pray that he will accept our efforts and use this translation for the benefit of the church and of all people.

We pray that the New Living Translation will overcome some of the barriers of history, culture, and language that have kept people from reading and understanding God's Word. We hope that readers unfamiliar with the Bible will find the words clear and easy to understand and that readers well versed in the Scriptures will gain a fresh perspective. We pray that readers will gain insight and wisdom for living, but most of all that they will meet the God of the Bible and be forever changed by knowing him.

THE BIBLE TRANSLATION COMMITTEE, *October 2007*

BIBLE TRANSLATION TEAM
Holy Bible, New Living Translation

PENTATEUCH
Daniel I. Block, Senior Translator
Wheaton College

GENESIS
Allen Ross, *Beeson Divinity School, Samford University*
Gordon Wenham, *Trinity College, Bristol*

EXODUS
Robert Bergen, *Hannibal-LaGrange College*
Daniel I. Block, *Wheaton College*
Eugene Carpenter, *Bethel College, Mishawaka, Indiana*

LEVITICUS
David Baker, *Ashland Theological Seminary*
Victor Hamilton, *Asbury College*
Kenneth Mathews, *Beeson Divinity School, Samford University*

NUMBERS
Dale A. Brueggemann, *Assemblies of God Division of Foreign Missions*
R. K. Harrison, *Wycliffe College*
Paul R. House, *Beeson Divinity School, Samford University*
Gerald L. Mattingly, *Johnson Bible College*

DEUTERONOMY
J. Gordon McConville, *University of Gloucester*
Eugene H. Merrill, *Dallas Theological Seminary*
John A. Thompson, *University of Melbourne*

HISTORICAL BOOKS
Barry J. Beitzel, Senior Translator
Trinity Evangelical Divinity School

JOSHUA, JUDGES
Carl E. Armerding, *Schloss Mittersill Study Centre*
Barry J. Beitzel, *Trinity Evangelical Divinity School*
Lawson Stone, *Asbury Theological Seminary*

1 & 2 SAMUEL
Robert Gordon, *Cambridge University*
V. Philips Long, *Regent College*
J. Robert Vannoy, *Biblical Theological Seminary*

1 & 2 KINGS
Bill T. Arnold, *Asbury Theological Seminary*
William H. Barnes, *North Central University*
Frederic W. Bush, *Fuller Theological Seminary*

1 & 2 CHRONICLES
Raymond B. Dillard, *Westminster Theological Seminary*
David A. Dorsey, *Evangelical School of Theology*
Terry Eves, *Erskine College*

RUTH, EZRA—ESTHER
William C. Williams, *Vanguard University*
H. G. M. Williamson, *Oxford University*

WISDOM BOOKS
Tremper Longman III, Senior Translator
Westmont College

JOB
August Konkel, *Providence Theological Seminary*
Tremper Longman III, *Westmont College*
Al Wolters, *Redeemer College*

PSALMS 1–75
Mark D. Futato, *Reformed Theological Seminary*
Douglas Green, *Westminster Theological Seminary*
Richard Pratt, *Reformed Theological Seminary*

PSALMS 76–150
David M. Howard Jr., *Bethel Theological Seminary*
Raymond C. Ortlund Jr., *Immanuel Church, Nashville, Tennessee*
Willem VanGemeren, *Trinity Evangelical Divinity School*

PROVERBS
Ted Hildebrandt, *Gordon College*
Richard Schultz, *Wheaton College*
Raymond C. Van Leeuwen, *Eastern College*

ECCLESIASTES, SONG OF SONGS
Daniel C. Fredericks, *Belhaven College*
David Hubbard, *Fuller Theological Seminary*
Tremper Longman III, *Westmont College*

PROPHETS
John N. Oswalt, Senior Translator
Asbury Theological Seminary

ISAIAH
John N. Oswalt, *Asbury Theological Seminary*
Gary Smith, *Union University*
John Walton, *Wheaton College*

JEREMIAH, LAMENTATIONS
G. Herbert Livingston, *Asbury Theological Seminary*
Elmer A. Martens, *Mennonite Brethren Biblical Seminary*

EZEKIEL
Daniel I. Block, *Wheaton College*
David H. Engelhard, *Calvin Theological Seminary*
David Thompson, *Asbury Theological Seminary*

DANIEL, HAGGAI—MALACHI
Joyce Baldwin Caine, *Trinity College, Bristol*
Douglas Gropp, *Catholic University of America*
Roy Hayden, *Oral Roberts School of Theology*
Andrew Hill, *Wheaton College*
Tremper Longman III, *Westmont College*

HOSEA—ZEPHANIAH
Joseph Coleson, *Nazarene Theological Seminary*
Roy Hayden, *Oral Roberts School of Theology*

Andrew Hill, *Wheaton College*
Richard Patterson, *Liberty University*

GOSPELS AND ACTS
Grant R. Osborne, Senior Translator
Trinity Evangelical Divinity School

MATTHEW
Craig Blomberg, *Denver Seminary*
Donald A. Hagner, *Fuller Theological Seminary*
David Turner, *Grand Rapids Baptist Seminary*

MARK
Robert Guelich, *Fuller Theological Seminary*
George Guthrie, *Union University*
Grant R. Osborne, *Trinity Evangelical Divinity School*

LUKE
Darrell Bock, *Dallas Theological Seminary*
Scot McKnight, *North Park University*
Robert Stein, *The Southern Baptist Theological Seminary*

JOHN
Gary M. Burge, *Wheaton College*
Philip W. Comfort, *Coastal Carolina University*
Marianne Meye Thompson, *Fuller Theological Seminary*

ACTS
D. A. Carson, *Trinity Evangelical Divinity School*
William J. Larkin, *Columbia International University*
Roger Mohrlang, *Whitworth University*

LETTERS AND REVELATION
Norman R. Ericson, Senior Translator
Wheaton College

ROMANS, GALATIANS
Gerald Borchert, *Northern Baptist Theological Seminary*
Douglas J. Moo, *Wheaton College*
Thomas R. Schreiner, *The Southern Baptist Theological Seminary*

1 & 2 CORINTHIANS
Joseph Alexanian, *Trinity International University*
Linda Belleville, *Bethel College, Mishawaka, Indiana*
Douglas A. Oss, *Central Bible College*
Robert Sloan, *Houston Baptist University*

EPHESIANS—PHILEMON
Harold W. Hoehner, *Dallas Theological Seminary*
Moises Silva, *Gordon-Conwell Theological Seminary*
Klyne Snodgrass, *North Park Theological Seminary*

HEBREWS, JAMES, 1 & 2 PETER, JUDE
Peter Davids, *St. Stephen's University*
Norman R. Ericson, *Wheaton College*
William Lane, *Seattle Pacific University*
J. Ramsey Michaels, *S. W. Missouri State University*

1–3 JOHN, REVELATION
Greg Beale, *Westminster Theological Seminary*
Robert Mounce, *Whitworth University*
M. Robert Mulholland Jr., *Asbury Theological Seminary*

SPECIAL REVIEWERS
F. F. Bruce, *University of Manchester*
Kenneth N. Taylor, *Translator,* The Living Bible

COORDINATING TEAM
Mark D. Taylor, *Director and Chief Stylist*
Ronald A. Beers, *Executive Director and Stylist*
Mark R. Norton, *Managing Editor and O.T. Coordinating Editor*
Philip W. Comfort, *N.T. Coordinating Editor*
Daniel W. Taylor, *Bethel University, Senior Stylist*

TABLE OF ANCIENT WEIGHTS, MEASURES, AND COINS

WEIGHTS	talent (60 minas)	75 pounds	34 kilograms
	mina (50 shekels)	1.25 pounds	600 grams
	shekel	0.4 ounces	11.4 grams
	pim (2/3 shekel)	0.25 ounces	8 grams
	beka (1/2 shekel)	0.2 ounces	5.7 grams
	gerah (1/20 shekel)	0.02 ounces	0.6 grams
	litra	12 ounces	327 grams
LENGTHS	long cubit	21 inches	53 centimeters
	cubit	18 inches	45 centimeters
	span	9 inches	23 centimeters
	handbreadth	3 inches	8 centimeters
	fathom	6 feet	1.8 meters
	rod	10.5 feet	3.2 meters
	stadion	205 yards	187 meters
CAPACITIES	*Dry Measures*		
	cor/homer (10 ephahs)	5 bushels	182 liters
	lethek (5 ephahs)	2.5 bushels	91 liters
	ephah	0.5 bushels	18 liters
	seah (1/3 ephah)	6 quarts	6.6 liters
	omer (1/10 ephah)	2 quarts	2.2 liters
	cab (1/2 omer)	1 quart	1.1 liters
	Liquid Measures		
	bath	5.5 gallons	21 liters
	hin (1/6 bath)	1 gallon	3.8 liters
	log (1/72 bath)	0.3 quarts	0.3 liters
COINS	*Roman*		
	denarius	1 day's wages (for a laborer)	
	as	1/16 denarius	
	quadrans	1/64 denarius	
	Greek		
	drachma	~1 denarius	
	didrachma	2 drachmas	
	stater	4 drachmas	
	Jewish		
	lepton	1/2 quadrans	

OLD
TESTAMENT

INTRODUCTION TO THE OLD TESTAMENT

The Old Testament is God's word to his people through the ages. It describes the creation of the world and humanity, the origin of sin, and the beginning of God's plan of redemption. Through it we gain a much clearer understanding of who God is, what he is doing, and how we should live.

The Old Testament stimulates our imaginations and arouses our emotions. It is made up of gripping stories of real events, stirring poems, and bracing exhortations. It teaches us God's plan, reveals God's will, and helps us make decisions. Reading the Old Testament is like looking into a mirror, for it reveals our soul. It plants a seed that grows, ultimately transforming our character.

Jesus emphasized the importance of understanding the Old Testament (Luke 24:25-27), and Paul was speaking primarily of the Old Testament when he wrote, "All Scripture is inspired by God and is useful to teach us what is true and to make us realize what is wrong in our lives" (2 Tim 3:16). The Old Testament provides us with a profound knowledge of God, ourselves, and the world.

SETTING

Israel's geography encompasses rugged *wadis* (seasonally dry river beds), agriculturally rich valleys, rolling hills, arid wilderness, and sandy coasts. The Bible describes Israel as a fertile land, one "flowing with milk and honey" (Exod 3:8, 17; Num 13:27). But a lack of rainfall can trigger devastating famines.

The land of Israel was previously called Canaan. Before the people of Israel occupied the land, Canaan was composed of a number of loosely allied city-states, each with its own king. The Canaanite people remained a political threat until the time of King David, who decisively defeated both the Canaanites and the Philistines. The Canaanite worship of Baal and Ashtoreth, however, continued to plague Israel.

Compared to the superpowers of the day (Assyria, Babylon, the Hittites, Egypt, and Persia), Israel was a small but strategically significant nation, located along the main route between Mesopotamia and Egypt.

Various nations controlled Mesopotamia throughout the OT: Assyria to the north, Babylon to the south, and Persia to the east. All three of these powers constantly tried to expand their borders.

Egypt was also a superpower during much of the OT period. The Nile River defined ancient Egypt and was the source of its wealth. During the time between Joseph and the Exodus, Egypt oppressed and enslaved the people of Israel as they grew from a family of seventy individuals to a great nation. Egypt continued to play a role in the story of Israel. Toward the end of Israel's kingdom period, the last desperate kings hoped that Egypt would save Judah from the Babylonians. Egypt turned out to be "a reed that splinters beneath your weight and pierces your hand" (2 Kgs 18:21).

Directly north of Israel was Aram (Syria), with Damascus as its chief city. Israel experienced frequent conflicts with Aram, beginning during the time of David.

Toward the end of the OT period, the Persian empire gained power. Persia occupied the region just east of Mesopotamia. Persia's rise to power began in the mid-500s BC and included the defeat of Babylon in 539 BC. Judea became a province in the Persian empire and remained so until Alexander the Great defeated Persia in 331 BC.

THE OLD TESTAMENT STORY

The Bible begins with the account of creation (Gen 1–2). God created the heavens, the earth, and the first humans, and he pronounced it all "very good." God provided Eden, a wonderful place for human beings to live. Adam and Eve enjoyed a harmonious and fulfilling relationship with God and with each other.

All this changed quickly. Genesis 3 introduces the serpent, who injected discord into this harmonious world. The serpent taught Eve and Adam to distrust God, and they chose to rebel against God in the belief that they knew better than God. This sin placed a barrier between God and humans and brought death to all humanity. God's holy presence became deadly to Adam and Eve, and God ejected them from Eden. Even in the midst of judgment for their sin, however, God remained involved, working for their redemption.

After Eden, the OT describes a split between those who chose to follow God and those who rejected him: for example, Abel and Seth versus Cain, righteous Noah versus his wicked generation, Isaac versus Ishmael, and Jacob versus Esau and Laban.

A crucial transitional point came when God offered great promises to Abraham. He called Abraham to leave Ur (around 2100/1900 BC) and "go to the land that I will show you" (Gen 12:1). Unlike Adam and Eve, Abraham trusted God and responded obediently to him. As a result, God began carrying out his redemptive plan for humanity through Abraham and his descendants. Thus, Abraham became the father of a great nation, with many descendants and much land. Genesis 12—Joshua 24 describes how God multiplied the descendants of Abraham and ultimately brought them into possession of the Promised Land of Canaan.

God desired that Abraham's descendants, the nation of Israel, would obey God and prosper in the land he gave them and that the surrounding nations would turn to the true God. However, like Adam and Eve in Eden before them, the

Israelites were not satisfied with all that God gave them, instead turning to false gods to find happiness. The rest of the OT continues the story of Israel's persistent sin and God's unwavering commitment to them. Although God consistently judged their sin, he also remained patiently involved with his people.

Following Israel's settlement in Canaan, the period of the judges was marked by political fragmentation and spiritual confusion. God then allowed the people to choose a king to rule them. The monarchy began with the anointing of Saul (around 1050 BC), and it reached a high point with David (1011–971 BC) and the early part of Solomon's reign (971–931 BC). Due to Solomon's sin, however, God divided Israel into two parts, the northern and southern kingdoms, after Solomon's death in 931 BC.

From the beginning of the divided monarchy (931 BC) to the end of the OT period (about 400 BC), the prophets called the people of Israel and Judah to return to God, but most trusted the surrounding nations and their false gods. The northern kingdom of Israel, with its capital Samaria, lasted until 722 BC, when Assyria conquered it and deported its people. The southern kingdom of Judah, with its capital Jerusalem, lasted until the Babylonians defeated it in 586 BC, destroying the Temple and taking many of the people of Judah into exile.

The destruction of Jerusalem and the Exile of the Israelites did not end Israel's story. Even as the prophets had proclaimed devastating judgment on God's people, they also announced a future hope for the remnant. The Exile lasted until 539 BC, when Persia defeated Babylon and allowed the Jews to return to Judah to rebuild Jerusalem and the Temple. By 515 BC, the Jews had rebuilt a smaller, second Temple (see Ezra 6:15). Ezra arrived in 458 BC and reestablished God's law in Judah. In 445 BC, Nehemiah became governor of Judah and rebuilt the walls of Jerusalem. During the period after the Exile, many people of Judea finally worshiped the Lord, the God of Israel, exclusively. They also came to recognize the true significance of the OT records: God had been giving them a written revelation of his will, his purposes, and his acts in Israel's history.

The prophecy of Malachi, written a little before 400 BC, closes the OT story. The OT does not end with a strong sense of closure, but with anticipation of even greater things to come. The return to Jerusalem and the rebuilding of the Temple was a "down payment" of God's redemption for his people. However, the prophets understood that these events were not the ultimate realization of hope.

THE CANON OF THE OLD TESTAMENT

The text of the OT was written over a period of approximately 1,000 years, beginning with Moses and extending to the Persian period following the Jews' return to Judah from exile. God used Moses and many others—judges like Samuel, kings like David and Solomon, prophets like Isaiah and Jeremiah, priests like Ezra, and other people whose names we don't even know—to write parts of Israel's history and literature.

The Order of the Hebrew Bible

The order of books in the Hebrew Bible differs from the order of the books in English Bibles (see charts, below and at right). The Hebrew Bible is divided into three parts: Instruction (*Torah*), Prophets (*Nebi'im*) and Writings (*Ketubim*). Jesus referred to these divisions as "the law of Moses," "the prophets," and "the Psalms" (Luke 24:44). Jewish readers of the Hebrew Bible sometimes refer to their Scripture by taking the first letters of these three parts and forming the word "Tanak."

The Hebrew Bible combines into twenty-four books the same material that is presented as thirty-nine books in the English OT. In the Hebrew Bible, the first five books constitute the *Torah*. This section, also called the Pentateuch, is unchanged in English Bibles. The second section, the Prophets (*Nebi'im*), has two parts. The Former Prophets, called the historical books in English Bibles, are followed in the Hebrew Bible by the Latter Prophets. The third section, the Writings (*Ketubim*), contains miscellaneous books, including the books of poetry and wisdom.

In later Judaism, the "Five Scrolls" (*Megilloth*) were read at the important feasts and arranged in order of their observance in the holiday calendar (see chart, "Israel's Festivals," p. 235): Ruth was read at the Festival of Pentecost, Song of Songs at Passover, Ecclesiastes at the Festival of Shelters, Lamentations at the anniversary of the destruction of Jerusalem (the 9th of Ab), and Esther at Purim.

The Order of the English OT

English Bibles follow the order of the Greek translation of the OT (the

1. Instruction (*Torah*)	2. Prophets (*Nebi'im*)	3. Writings (*Ketubim*)
Genesis Exodus Leviticus Numbers Deuteronomy	*Former Prophets* Joshua Judges Samuel (1 & 2) Kings (1 & 2) *Latter Prophets* Isaiah Jeremiah Ezekiel The Twelve: Hosea Joel Amos Obadiah Jonah Micah Nahum Habakkuk Zephaniah Haggai Zechariah Malachi	Psalms Job Proverbs Five Scrolls (*Megilloth*): Ruth Song of Songs Ecclesiastes Lamentations Esther Daniel Ezra–Nehemiah Chronicles (1 & 2)

The Hebrew OT

Septuagint), which groups books according to genre and places the books within each genre in chronological order. The Greek and English OT begins with the Pentateuch. Next come the historical narratives; then the poetical books, arranged in chronological order according to their setting or traditional date of composition; and finally the prophets, in two parts. The major (largest) prophets appear in chronological order. They are followed by the twelve minor (shorter) prophets, which also follow a general chronological arrangement.

INTERPRETING THE OLD TESTAMENT

Christians sometimes find the OT difficult to read and understand, with content that seems strange and distant. What is the connection between Christianity and animal sacrifices, religious circumcision, strange dietary laws, the curses of the Psalms, and the history of ancient Israel? To understand the OT better, we must realize that it is an ancient book, with the oldest parts written some 3,500 years ago. It also comes from a culture, the ancient Near East, vastly different from ours. Most importantly, the books were written before the coming of Christ.

The following principles can help readers as they study the OT.

Read Each Passage in Context

With the Bible, as with all good literature, gaining a grasp of the whole helps us appreciate and understand the parts. We should not treat a biblical book as a collection of isolated sayings. Rather, the books contain connected stories, instructions, and poems. The meaning of the individual verses can be discovered only in the flow of the whole literary piece, which occurs by reading large blocks at a time. While this principle does not stop us from turning to the middle of a biblical book to read a few verses, we should also seek to develop an understanding of the message of the whole book. In other words, we should exercise great caution not to distort God's message when we read small pieces of Scripture. The book introductions in the *NLT Study Bible* help with this process by providing an overview of each book's contents and message.

Identify the Genre of the Book and Passage

Contemporary readers are familiar with a variety of genres such as biographies, textbooks, and newspaper editorials. The content of the OT can also be grouped into genres. The genres in the OT include history (e.g., Samuel), treaty/covenant (e.g., Exod 19–24), sermon (e.g., Deuteronomy), poetry and prayers (e.g., Psalms), wisdom (e.g., Proverbs), prophecy (e.g., Jeremiah), and apocalyptic (e.g., Dan 7–12). Different genres should trigger different reading strategies. Just as we approach a biography differently than we approach a novel, we should try to understand how to approach the different genres of the OT. The book and section introductions in the *NLT Study Bible* offer help in understanding OT genres.

Pentateuch	Historical Books	Poetry and Wisdom	Prophets
Genesis Exodus Leviticus Numbers Deuteronomy	Joshua Judges Ruth 1 Samuel 2 Samuel 1 Kings 2 Kings 1 Chronicles 2 Chronicles Ezra Nehemiah Esther	Job Psalms Proverbs Ecclesiastes Song of Songs	Isaiah Jeremiah Lamentations Ezekiel Daniel Minor Prophets: Hosea Joel Amos Obadiah Jonah Micah Nahum Habakkuk Zephaniah Haggai Zechariah Malachi

◀ **The English OT**

Consider the Historical and Cultural Background of the Book

The inspired authors of the OT lived and wrote in a time and culture very distant from ours. We should seek to understand what was taking place during the time period the author describes as well as the (often different) time period when the author was writing. For example, the book of Chronicles describes events that took place from the time of David to the Exile (about 1000–600 BC), but it was probably written in Judea following the return from exile (around 400 BC). Knowing the details and setting—both of the events that are described and of the time in which the book was written—will help us understand Chronicles and its message more clearly. The same holds true for other books of the OT.

Read the Old Testament in the Light of Christ's Coming

Jesus said that the whole OT anticipated his coming, suffering, and glory (Luke 24:25-27). Jesus is the center of biblical revelation. The OT anticipates him, and the NT describes him.

NT authors recognized this, so they frequently cited the OT to explain that the glorious events happening in their day were foreshadowed and foretold by the OT. Christians, too, should read the OT from the perspective of the death and resurrection of Christ. While it is crucial first to interpret each OT passage or book in the context of its original audience, we understand the OT better when we read it in light of its fulfillment in Jesus Christ.

MEANING AND MESSAGE

Scripture describes God's nature and explains his acts in history. By reading the OT, God's people learn about who God is by observing and participating in what he does.

God's Nature, Character, and Acts

God's special name in the OT is *Yahweh*. The name comes from the Hebrew word meaning "to be." God told Moses that his name means, "I AM WHO I AM" (Exod 3:14). In other words, God defines

himself. Nothing else defines him, but he defines everything. In most English translations, including the NLT, this name for God is usually translated "the LORD" (capitalized).

Most often, the OT describes God by picturing him in relationship. God relates to people as savior, king, shepherd, warrior, husband, and in many other roles. God also reveals who he is by what he does: for example, dividing the Red Sea, causing the walls of Jericho to fall, establishing David as king, allowing the Babylonian army to defeat Jerusalem, and restoring his people to the land after the Exile.

The primary message of the OT is that God saves his people and judges those who resist him. He passionately pursues his sinful people in order to establish a community that is in harmony with him, a kingdom that recognizes and serves its divine King.

There Is One God

The OT launches a sustained attack on the prevailing worldview of the ancient Near East, which was that the heavens and the earth, infused with deities, constitute the sum total of reality. The implications of this false worldview, which continues in much of the world today, are many and far-reaching:

- Because the heavens and the earth contain many diverse parts, many gods exist.
- Because the gods are the cosmos, we can manipulate the gods by manipulating the cosmos.
- Because humans are obsessed with sex, the gods are also.
- Because the universe exists without purpose, the gods have no purpose except survival through the acquisition of power—and so humans must pursue power as well.
- Because the gods are selfish and unmerciful, humans must seek their favor by appeasing their appetites.
- Because there are many gods, humans must seek the protection of their own gods against other people's gods.

The OT asserts the very opposite of these beliefs and all others that grow out of a pagan worldview:

- The universe is unified as the creation of the one true God.
- He alone is God, in no way comparable to other so-called gods, and he has a completely separate existence from the cosmos.
- God cannot be manipulated through the cosmos because he is not the cosmos.
- God created the world as a universe with his own unified purposes. Human beings have meaning by fulfilling God's purposes for them.
- Human beings are designed not to appease capricious and power-hungry gods but to worship and obey a loving Creator.
- Ultimate security and peace come from trusting and worshiping the Creator.

From beginning to end, the OT makes these and many related points in order to correct the seductive but incorrect and deadly pagan worldview.

God's Covenants with His People

The concept of *covenant* is central to the message of the OT. From Genesis onward, the covenant becomes the most persistent metaphor for God's relationship with his people (see "God's Covenant Relationships" at Gen 12:1-9, p. 44). A covenant is a relationship that gives promises and imposes obligations. OT covenants were similar to treaties between two nations, where a Great King would enter into a relationship with a vassal nation (see Deuteronomy Introduction, "Literary Form," p. 314). The term *covenant* describes the relationships God established with humanity and all creation through Noah (Gen 9:1-17), with Abraham and his descendants (Gen 15:1-21), with Israel through Moses (Exod 19:3–24:11), and with David and his offspring (2 Sam 7:8-16). God's relationship with Adam also had the character of a covenant, complete with commands, promises, and warnings. Each of God's covenants builds on the previous ones; new covenants do not replace the old.

Through his covenants, God established special relationships between himself and his people. In the covenants, God made promises, stated obligations, and threatened judgment if his people did not obey him. When they disobeyed, God sent his prophets to warn his disobedient people, urging them to turn from breaking his law and return to faithful obedience. The curses stipulated in the covenant provide the basis for God's judgment (see Deut 28), which he ultimately brought: Jerusalem was destroyed and most of the Israelites were sent into exile.

Yet God was not finished with his people: He brought some of them back from exile. They had been humbled and were more obedient—they finally stopped worshiping other gods and worshiped the Lord alone. God also promised to make a new covenant with them (Jer 31:31-34). In the context of this new covenant, God would "forgive their wickedness" and "never again remember their sins" (Jer 31:34), causing all Israel finally to know and obey him.

The establishment of the new covenant came with the Messiah. Jesus Christ, God's promised Savior and King, fulfilled the old covenant (Matt 5:17-20) and initiated the new covenant, a relationship with all who trust in him (John 3:16; Acts 2:38-39) based on his own sacrifice (Luke 22:20). Those who participate in this relationship inherit eternal fellowship with God and all his people (John 3:36; 5:24; Rom 5:21; 1 Jn 2:24-25).

FURTHER READING

BILL T. ARNOLD AND BRYAN E. BEYER
Encountering the Old Testament: A Christian Survey (1999)

CRAIG BARTHOLOMEW AND MICHAEL GOHEEN
The Drama of Scripture: Finding Our Place in the Biblical Story (2004)

RAYMOND B. DILLARD AND TREMPER LONGMAN III
An Introduction to the Old Testament, 2nd edition (2006)

ARCHAEOLOGY AND SOURCES FOR
OLD TESTAMENT BACKGROUND

In the past two hundred years, archaeology has experienced a huge information explosion in terms of both artifacts and texts from the ancient Near East. Every item must be placed into a large historical context, and, where relevant, must cautiously be placed in a proper relationship to biblical materials. Properly identified and interpreted, archaeological materials may illustrate, illuminate, demonstrate, confirm, or challenge the biblical text. These same artifacts and texts cannot be used at a theological level to "prove" the spiritual, religious, or theological claims of the biblical text. It is obviously impossible for a spade or a trowel to prove or disprove the spiritual revelations and assertions of Scripture. But these materials may confirm and make plausible certain historical perspectives and claims of those texts. It is fair to say that archaeology validates Hebrew history and explains many formerly obscure terms and traditions in both the OT and NT. It thus provides an authentic background for the prophecies culminating in Jesus Christ.

THE DEVELOPMENT OF BIBLICAL ARCHAEOLOGY

Modern archaeology in the Middle East began when Napoleon took with him into Egypt (1798) a team of specialists to record the ancient wonders of Egypt. They happened to find the Rosetta Stone (1799), which provided the unexpected key to the decipherment of Egyptian hieroglyphics (1819, 1822). The floodgates opened to a heightened interest in the wonders of the ancient Near East and to the light they might shed on the Bible—the ancient Near East's greatest religious, literary, and historical artifact. In 1845, Akkadian (the language of old Babylon) was deciphered using the Behistun Inscription (518 BC), which, like the Rosetta Stone, was inscribed in three languages. The deciphering of several other languages soon followed.

After that, the archaeology of the ancient Near East prospered and drew worldwide attention. Archaeologists, scholars, and treasure hunters were amazed at the creation and flood stories, legal documents, ancient civilizations and languages, religious and theological systems, sacrificial rituals, tabernacles, temples, palaces, wisdom literature, covenants and covenantal forms and rituals, war stories, birth stories, king lists, pagan prophetic parallels, and much more.

In the beginning, it was treasure hunters who made many of the significant finds, and their methods were often haphazard and caused destruction of important archaeological sites. The scientific study of ancient tells (strata of dirt and cultural debris compacted together into mounds over the millennia) began in Palestine in 1890, when Flinders Petrie adopted methods used to excavate Troy, systematically unearthing and studying the various strata (layers of occupation) of a city. This approach to archaeology in Palestine flourished as appropriate techniques, tools, and record-keeping developed. Today, a combination of methods is employed, including "surface surveys" and aerial photography used to get information about whole regions.

THE CONTRIBUTION OF BIBLICAL ARCHAEOLOGY

Various ancient Near Eastern texts and artifacts have helped scholars paint—both with a broad brush and in some cases with detail—a cultural and historical backdrop of OT eras across the centuries. Ancient texts and artifacts help us see the OT in its larger context and better understand its history, its literary qualities, and even its theological perspectives.

In principle, archaeologists have no particular interest in "proving the truth" of the Scriptures. And in fact, it is sometimes difficult to reconcile interpretations of archaeological data and the evidence of Scripture. Such conflicts are few in number, however, and tend to diminish noticeably as new information is forthcoming. The huge cache of ancient Near Eastern material makes the historical reliability of the OT arguably firm.

These archaeological source materials show the people of Israel as fellow participants in the ancient Near East of their day. It is possible to see the men and women of Scripture as real persons, as true children of their age, grappling with life's problems. And from time to time they catch a vision of God as all powerful and all holy, as guiding the destinies of individuals and nations, and as bringing about his purposes in history. Ancient texts and artifacts show that Israel shared in the social structures and worldviews of the surrounding cultures. But these texts and artifacts also show striking contrasts between the people of Israel and the world in which they lived—for Israel claimed a relationship with the Lord, the one true God, and did not worship many gods as neighboring nations did. The people of Israel's faith in and experience of the Lord make them unique in the ancient world, a uniqueness that comes into vibrant, colorful relief through the texts and artifacts of the ancient Near East.

PRIMARY SOURCES

[RANE] Bill T. Arnold and Bryan E. Beyer, *Readings from the Ancient Near East* (2002)

[COS] William W. Hallo, ed., *The Context of Scripture* (2003)

[AEL] Miriam Lichtheim, *Ancient Egyptian Literature* (1971–1980)

[OTP] Victor H. Matthews & Don C. Benjamin, eds., *Old Testament Parallels: Laws and Stories from the Ancient Near East* (2006)

[ANET] James B. Pritchard, ed., *Ancient Near Eastern Texts Relating to the Old Testament* (1969)

[ATSHB] Kenton L. Sparks, *Ancient Texts for the Study of the Hebrew Bible* (2005)

FURTHER READING

Susan Wise Bauer, *The History of the Ancient World* (2007)

Richard S. Hess, *Israelite Religions: An Archaeological and Biblical Survey* (2007)

Alfred J. Hoerth, *Archaeology and the Old Testament* (1998)

K. A. Kitchen, *On the Reliability of the Old Testament* (2006)

John H. Walton, *Ancient Near Eastern Thought and the Old Testament* (2006)

Michael O. Wise, et al., *The Dead Sea Scrolls* (2005)

Ancient Texts and Artifacts Relating to the Old Testament. The Old Testament was written in a complex era of history, and many parallels to the OT have been found in ancient artifacts and documents. This chart lists many of these items with their original date and a description. The "Sources" column lists English translations of the texts of these artifacts; the abbreviations are listed under "Primary Sources," above. The final column lists OT passages that parallel these sources in some manner: In some cases, the ancient source is similar to its OT parallels or provides cultural background; in other cases, the ancient source corroborates specific OT details.

Title	Date	Description	Sources	OT Parallels
Memphite Creation	2700 BC	Egyptian creation account	RANE 63–65; OTP 3–6	Gen 1–2
Famine Stela	2700 BC	Egyptian monumental texts with seven years of famine as a motif	COS 1.53	Gen 12, 41
Sumerian Proverbs	2600~2000 BC	Examples of Sumerian proverbs	COS 1.174–175	Proverbs, Ecclesiastes
Ebla Archives	2500 BC (about)	A huge cache of Sumerian texts that depict the pre-patriarchal world	OTP 240–243	Background of Genesis
Instructions of Ptah Hotep	2500 BC (about)	One of Egypt's great wise men teaches his son how to succeed in life and vocation	OTP 283–288; RANE 182–184	Prov 2, 6, 23, 25–26; Ecclesiastes
Ra and the Serpent	2400 BC	Egyptian story that pictures the sun and a serpent in opposition	OTP 28–31	Gen 3
Gudea Cylinders	2000s BC	Sumerian instructions to build a temple	ANET 268–269	Exod 25–40; 2 Sam 7–8; 1 Kgs 6
Sargon Legend	2000s BC	An Akkadian legend: Sargon I rescued from a river in a basket	RANE 75–76; OTP 55–58	Exod 2
Dream Interpretation	2000 or 1300 BC	An Egyptian list of how to interpret a dream	COS 1.33	Gen 40–41
Lament over Ur	2000 BC (about)	A Sumerian laments the fall of the city of Ur and abandonment by the gods	RANE 222–225	Lamentations
Prophecies of Neferti	1990 BC (about)	Egyptian prophecies: Neferti "predicts" Pharaoh Amenemhet I (1991–1960 BC)	RANE 210–212; OTP 235–240	1 Kgs 13; Dan 2–6
Epic of Gilgamesh	1900 BC	Sumerian and Akkadian epic: the great flood, death, a "Noah" figure, and the search for eternal life	RANE 66–70; COS 1.132; OTP 11–20	Gen 6–9
Lipit-Ishtar Laws	1800s BC	Collection of Sumerian laws	RANE 106–109	Exod 19–24; Deut 12–26
Travels of Sinuhe	1800–1000 BC	An Egyptian narrative that includes descriptions of Canaan and Syria	RANE 76–82; COS 1.38	Gen 37–50
Code of Hammurabi	1750 BC (about)	Akkadian laws that parallel the laws of Moses	RANE 111–114	Exod 20–24; Lev 16–26; Deut 12–26
Sumerian King Lists	1700s BC	Lists of Sumerian kings, including long life spans before the flood	RANE 150–151; OTP 21–32	Gen 5; Deut 17:14-20; 1 Sam 8; 12
Mari Tablets	1700s BC	Akkadian correspondence between famous kings reflecting conditions during the patriarchal era; mention of "Habiru"	OTP 318–322	Genesis—Numbers
Atrahasis Epic	1700s BC	Sumerian creation and flood stories; "Noah" figure	RANE 21–31; COS 1.130	Gen 1–11
Hittite Laws	1650–1200 BC	Hittite legal texts arranged by topics; scapegoat laws and levirate laws	RANE 115–116; OTP 70–72	Exod 19–24; Deut 12–26; Lev 17–26
Emar Tablets	1550–1200 BC	Akkadian tablets containing important legal, ritual, and religious texts	RANE 127; COS 1.123–126; 2.137	Lev 8:30; 23:1-44; Num 28–29; Deut 16, 31–32

Title	Date	Description	Sources	OT Parallels
Amarna Letters and Tell el-Amarna Tablets	1550~1150 BC	Akkadian letters written by Canaanite kings seeking Egypt's help against invading enemies, including "Habiru"	RANE 166–168; OTP 77–80	Joshua (Israel's invasion might be reflected)
Egyptian Love Songs	1400~1000 BC	Egyptian dialogues and monologues using sensual language	RANE 192–193; OTP 297–301	Song of Songs
Nuzi Tablets	1400s BC	Hurrian texts describing various social, religious, legal, and political customs	RANE 72–74; COS 3.121	General OT background; references to Baal cult
Ras Shamra Tablets	1400s BC	Hundreds of tablets that illuminate pagan religion in Ugarit and perhaps in Canaan	COS 1.88, 104; OTP 263–274	Understanding of pagan religious practices; references to Baal cult
Hittite Treaties	1400–1200 BC	Hittite documents that illustrate covenantal forms	RANE 97–100	Exod 19–24; Deuteronomy; Josh 24
Rituals against Reptiles	1350 BC	Ugaritic prayers to render a serpent's venom powerless	COS 1.94	Num 21:4-9; Deut 32:33
Hymn to Aten	1300s BC	An Egyptian poem praising the sun	RANE 196–197	cp. Ps 104
Urim and Thummin	1300, 800s, 600s BC	Hittite, Akkadian, and Egyptian texts related to discovering the gods' will	COS 1.78, 127	Exod 28:30; Lev 8:8; Deut 33:8; Ezra 2:63; Neh 7:65
Tale of Two Brothers	1225 BC	An Egyptian tale: A man rejects his sister-in-law's advances	COS 1.40	Gen 39
Merneptah Stela	1209 BC	Pharaoh Merneptah's monument recording his campaigns; first mention of Israel outside of OT	RANE 160; OTP 81–84; COS 2.6	Joshua
Hittite Proverbs	1200s BC?	Various Hittite proverbs	COS 1.81–82	Proverbs; Jer 31:29
Kherem: A Thing Devoted	1200s BC	A Hittite text that records things "devoted" to a god for destruction	COS 1.72	Lev 27:28-29; Josh 6:17-19, 24; 1 Sam 15:2-3
Annals of Rameses III	1200 BC (about)	Egyptian annals describing battle(s) of Rameses III with the Sea Peoples, including the future Philistines	ANET 262–263; OTP 151–154	Judg 13:1–16:31; 1 Samuel
Neo-Assyrian Laws	1100s BC	Laws of the Neo-Assyrian Empire	RANE 114–115	Exod 19–24; Deut 12–26
Travels of Wenamun	1090 BC	An Egyptian semi-fictional travelogue that includes descriptions of Canaan	RANE 212–215; COS 1.41	Gen 34
Ludlul Bel Nemeqi	1000s BC	The sufferings of a noble Babylonian, somewhat reminiscent of Job	RANE 177–179; COS 1.153	Job
Enuma Elish	1000 BC (about)	Akkadian cosmology and creation	RANE 31–50	Gen 1–2
Babylonian Theodicy	1000~500 BC	A sufferer and a companion dialogue about life and suffering	RANE 179–182	Job, Ecclesiastes
Dialogue of Pessimism	1000~500 BC	A slave and his master discuss the lack of real value in anything	COS 1.155	Job, Ecclesiastes
Inscription of Shoshenq I	920 BC	An inscription by Egyptian pharaoh Shoshenq I (Shishak)	ANET 242–243	1 Kgs 11:40; 14:25-28
Assyrian Eponym Canon	910–612 BC	A list of selected officials for each year along with natural events that facilitate dating with the modern calendar	COS 2.1131	1–2 Kings; see "The Chronology of Israel's Monarchy," p. 562
Gezer Calendar	900 BC	Oldest example of Canaanite (old Hebrew); describes agricultural cycles	RANE 171	
Annals of Shalmaneser III	850~824 BC	Royal annals describing Shalmaneser III's incursion into Syria–Palestine and mentioning Ahab and Hadadezer	OTP 176–181	1 Kgs 16–22; 2 Kgs 9:1–10:33
Tell Dan Inscription	850 BC (about)	An Aramaic inscription containing the first reference outside the OT to the "house of David"	RANE 165; COS 2.39; OTP 160–161	1 Samuel—2 Kings
Mesha Stela, Moabite Stone	850 BC	Moabite monuments that list Omri, Ahab, King Mesha, and possibly the house of David; concept of *kherem*	RANE 160–162; OTP 157–159	Deut 7:26; Josh 6:17, 40; 1 Kgs 11:44; 16:21-28; 2 Kgs 3:4; 25:30
Black Obelisk	827 BC	Akkadian monument that describes the successor of Shalmaneser III and mentions Jehu and Ahab	RANE 144–145; OTP 122–124	1 Kgs 19:16; 2 Kgs 8:7-15; 9:1-13; 10:31-36

Title	Date	Description	Sources	OT Parallels
Zakkur Inscription	800 BC	Zakkur, king of Hamath, honors his god, mentions Ben-hadad	RANE 163–165	1 Kgs 15; 19–20; 2 Kgs 6; 8; 13
Babylonian Chronicles	745–120 BC	Yearly records covering a period that included many biblical events, including 722, 605, 597, and 539 BC	RANE 155–159; COS 1.137	1 Kgs 2:10; 11:43; 2 Kgs 17–24; Jer 37:1; Dan 5:30; 6:28
Annals of Tiglath-Pileser IV (Pul)	744–727 BC	Annals of the king who founded the Neo-Assyrian empire; encounters with Israel	RANE 145; OTP 125–126	2 Kgs 15–16; 2 Chr 28:16-21; Isa 7:1–8:10
Annals of Sargon II	722–706 BC	Akkadian king Sargon II describes his conquest of Samaria and destruction of the northern kingdom of Israel	RANE 145–146; COS 2.118A; OTP 127–129	cp. 2 Kgs 17–18; Isa 10:27-32; 14:1-32; 20:1
Siloam Inscription	701 BC	Hebrew inscription describing the completion of Hezekiah's tunnel	RANE 171–172	2 Kgs 20:20; 2 Chr 32:30
Sennacherib Prism	701 BC	Akkadian inscription describing Sennacherib's invasion of Judah and siege of Jerusalem	RANE 146–147; OTP 139–140	2 Kgs 18–20; Isa 36:1–39:8
Balaam Inscription	700 BC	Inscription in Aramaic recording the name of Balaam, a "good prophet" who died as a result of his actions	RANE 225–226; COS 2.27; OTP 124–126	Num 22–24, 26
Wisdom of Ahiqar	700–650 BC	An Assyrian court tale and the instructions of a wise court official	RANE 189–191; OTP 283–288	Gen 37–50; Proverbs, Daniel, Esther
Yavneh Yam Ostracon	600s BC	A short inscription in Hebrew: A fieldworker pleads for his cloak, which his supervisor had unjustly confiscated	RANE 170; COS 3.41; OTP 331–332	Exod 22:25-27; Deut 24:12-17; Prov 14:9; 25:20
Seal of Baruch	600 BC (about)	A clay impression found in Jerusalem with Baruch's name		Jer 36; see "Baruch the Scribe," p. 1283
Instructions for Amenemope	600s–500s BC	Egyptian wisdom teaching: self-control, kindness, altruism, and the ideal man	RANE 187–189; COS 1.47	Prov 22–24
Babylonian Administrative Document	595–568 BC	Documents describe the good fortune of Judah's king Jehoiachin at the court of Babylonian king Evil-merodach	ANET 308	2 Kgs 25:27-30
Lachish Ostraca	589–586 BC	Clay tablets in Hebrew describing royal military administration and the plight of those under siege	RANE 168–169; OTP 134–136	1 Kgs 17:19; 19:7; Jer 26:20-22; 34:6-7
Nabonidus Chronicle	556–539 BC	Nabonidus's chronicle of his stay in Tema and the fall of Babylon	ANET 305–307; COS 1.89	Dan 5 (Belshazzar)
Seal of Temah	538~445 BC	A stone seal used by one of the Levitical families who went into exile	*The Jerusalem Post*, Jan 17, 2008	Neh 7:55
Cyrus Cylinder	518 BC	Cyrus recorded his conquest of Babylon in 539 BC and gave his theological explanation of the events	RANE 147–149; OTP 193–195	2 Chr 36:22-23; Ezra 1:1-4; 6:1-15; Isa 44:26-28; Dan 5:30; 6:28
Elephantine Papyri	400s BC	These Aramaic papyri describe life among Jews who fled to Egypt after the fall of Jerusalem	ANET 222, 491, 548–549	Jer 42–44
Murashu Tablets	400s BC	Akkadian tablets describing economic transactions between Babylonians and Jews who remained in Babylon	ATSHB 41	Ezra—Esther
Dead Sea Scrolls	300 BC (about)—AD 100	Some of the oldest copies of OT manuscripts and many extracanonical documents	Wise et al., *The Dead Sea Scrolls*	

INTRODUCTION TO THE PENTATEUCH

Yahweh! The LORD! The God of compassion and mercy!
I am slow to anger and filled with unfailing love and faithfulness.
I lavish unfailing love to a thousand generations. I forgive iniquity, rebellion, and sin.
But I do not excuse the guilty.
EXODUS 34:6b-7a

The Pentateuch, the first five books of the Bible, tells the story of how sin entered God's perfect world and how God responded. It introduces Abraham and his descendants as agents of blessing in a world under the curse of sin and death. This collection, Israel's foundational documents, thus offers a sobering yet inspiring picture of God's relationship with humankind.

SETTING

To help them remain true to God, the Israelites who had left Egypt needed a written record of their own history and mission. The Pentateuch recounts the story of God's grace to Israel. God rescued the people of Israel from slavery in Egypt, called them to a special covenant relationship with himself, revealed his will to them, and took care of them as they traveled through the wilderness. Finally, they stood on the verge of entering the land of Canaan, which God had promised to their ancestors.

SUMMARY

The Pentateuch begins with the book of Genesis, which recounts God's grace in the beginnings of human history and in the lives of Israel's ancestors. God created humankind in his image and authorized humans to govern the world in his place (cp. Ps 8). When Adam and Eve rebelled against God, he did not destroy them immediately, but their sin put them and their descendants under the curse of death. Eventually God judged humanity, but mercifully spared righteous Noah and his family. While the curse of sin and death continued to hang over the human race, God called Abraham and his family and established an eternal covenant with them that included a series of generous promises: innumerable descendants, permanent title to the land of Canaan, rule over the land, and blessing to all the nations of the earth. Often, Abraham's descendants proved themselves faithless and unworthy of the privilege. But God kept his commitment to save and bless the human race.

As the book of Exodus opens, the favored family had been enslaved by the Egyptians, and seventy individuals had grown into the nation of Israel. Then God rescued the Israelites from Egypt (Exod 1–18) so that he could establish them as his covenant people, a holy nation (Exod 19:4-6). God's revelation of himself at Sinai (Exod 19–40) is the pivotal event in the Pentateuch.

In the book of Leviticus, God revealed to his people how to maintain a relationship with him, the means of forgiveness for their sin, and how they should live.

Numbers describes Israel's journey from Sinai to the plains of Moab. God accompanied and provided for his people on their journey, despite their repeated rebellion.

Finally, Deuteronomy records Moses' final pastoral addresses to the community of Israel. Moses detailed the significance of God's covenant and urged the Israelites to stay true to their Redeemer. If the people were to enjoy the blessings of the covenant, they needed to be faithful to God. So Moses challenged them to devote themselves anew to God and God alone as they prepared to cross the Jordan River to enter the Promised Land.

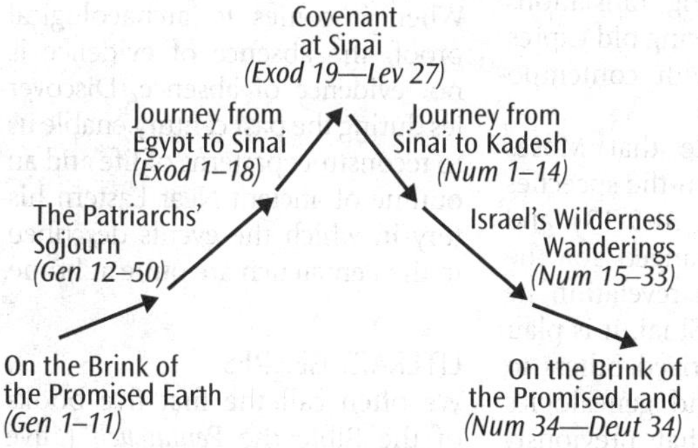

◀ **Outline of the Pentateuch**

AUTHORSHIP

Jewish and Christian tradition recognize Moses as the author of the Pentateuch, and many scholars continue to believe that Moses wrote much of the Pentateuch and that the entire document bears his stamp and authority.

Yet this view is not universal. Critical scholars since the mid-1800s have argued that the Pentateuch was written no earlier than the 600s BC and is the product of a complex literary evolution. The prevailing critical view, the *Documentary Hypothesis,* is that Genesis—Deuteronomy were

compiled from various sources by different groups of people. This hypothesis uses the different names for God, repeated stories, and theological emphases to propose that the Pentateuch comes from four sources: J ("Jahwist," from "Yahweh"), E ("Elohist," from "Elohim"), D ("Deuteronomic," from Deuteronomy), and P ("Priestly"). It is thought that these sources were written and collected between 850 BC and 445 BC, gradually being combined and edited until around Ezra's time (400s BC). This theory has prevailed in the scholarly world since Julius Wellhausen (1844–1918) made it popular.

However, advances in literary studies are again pointing back to Moses as the primary author of the Pentateuch. Critical scholars do not agree on the underlying sources for many passages, and additional sources have been invented to cover passages that do not fit the theory. The theory also fails to satisfactorily explain the emergence of Israel's monotheism in a totally polytheistic world. It assumes that the biblical writers borrowed most of their religious ideas from pagan predecessors. According to the biblical records, however, everything the Israelites borrowed from their neighbors was polytheistic and idolatrous. Israel's monotheism could not have been borrowed.

Archaeological discoveries have also called into question many of the criteria used in the Documentary Hypothesis. For instance, other writings from the ancient world confirm the use of different names for God, repeated stories, and ideas that were supposedly too advanced for ancient Israel, and the stories about the patriarchs fit their surrounding culture. These discoveries give background to the texts and contradict the assumptions of the Documentary Hypothesis. Archaeological finds continue to erode the rationale for dating the writing or editing of these books to later eras.

In recent years, with increased awareness of archaeology, critical scholars have begun to study the literary forms in the ancient Near East and in the Bible. *Form criticism* proposed that there was an oral tradition that lay behind the later written texts; by comparing these proposed oral forms, we could understand both the meaning and the function of the text. Other approaches have focused on tracing how the traditions developed, how the traditions were used in religious settings, or how the literary genres functioned.

Such theories often seem unnecessarily complicated and conjectural. Evidence in the Pentateuch itself suggests that Moses did keep records of some of Israel's experiences during the wilderness wanderings (Exod 17:14; 24:4, 7; 34:27; Num 33:1-2; Deut 31:9, 11). Many features in specific accounts point to a date of composition in the late Bronze Age (1500s–1200s BC, the era of the Exodus). The OT frequently credits Moses with writing the Pentateuch or portions of it (e.g., Josh 1:8; 8:31-32; 1 Kgs 2:3; 2 Kgs 14:6; Ezra 6:18; Neh 13:1; Dan 9:11-13; Mal 4:4), and the New Testament strongly connects the Torah with Moses (Matt 19:8; John 5:46-47; 7:19; Acts 3:22; Rom 10:5).

Do these facts confirm that Moses wrote the Pentateuch as we have it? Not necessarily. Several difficult factors remain. First, following the custom of literary works in the ancient Near East, the Pentateuch nowhere names its author. Second, Moses could not have recorded the account of his own death (Deut 34). Further, he would not have known of a place in northern Israel called Dan (Gen 14:14; cp. Josh 19:47; Judg 18:28-29), and he would not have referred to the conquest of Canaan as a past event (Deut 2:12). Thus, the text itself shows signs that it was updated for completeness (e.g., the death of Moses) or clarification for a later audience (e.g., Gen 14:14; 36:1; Deut 2:10-12). Some suggest that the reason the grammar and syntax of Deuteronomy resemble that of Jeremiah, who lived more than 500 years after Moses, is that later scribes updated the language. Such changes would be similar to updating translations of the Bible by replacing old expressions ("Behold") with contemporary ones ("Look").

We can conclude that Moses probably wrote down the speeches he delivered (Deut 31:9-13) and either wrote or arranged for the transcription of the revelation he received on Mount Sinai. It is plausible that he authorized others to write the stories and genealogies of the patriarchs that previously had been passed on orally. Just as the pieces of the Tabernacle were constructed and woven by skilled craftsmen and then finally assembled by Moses (Exod 35–40), so literary craftsmen might have composed bits and pieces that make up the Pentateuch and submitted them to Moses, who ultimately approved them. We can only speculate when these pieces were finally edited in their present form, although the narrative frame of Deuteronomy suggests it occurred sometime after the death of Moses. But by the time David organized Temple worship, the content of the Pentateuch as we know it was apparently fixed.

Genesis and the other books of the Pentateuch can thus be understood as the product of Moses' genius under God's inspiration, with later editorial adjustments. Later writers—including the New Testament authors—spoke of "The Torah of Moses," or "The Book of the Torah of Moses," or, as Jesus himself said, "Moses . . . wrote about me" (John 5:45-46). Moses might not have been the only author or editor of the Pentateuch, but the Pentateuch fundamentally and substantially comes from Moses, and the Israelites accepted it as bearing the full force of his authority.

HISTORICAL RELIABILITY

A number of critical scholars view the early chapters of Genesis as mythological *representations* of cosmic and human origins, like similar Babylonian accounts, rather than historical *presentations* of what actually happened. Recently, this same kind of skepticism has characterized views toward the patriarchs, as well as toward Moses and the Exodus. These scholars note that archaeological discoveries do not specifically identify any of the characters or the events in the Pentateuch. However, the issue is not quite so simple. When it comes to archaeological proof, the absence of evidence is not evidence of absence. Discoveries during the past century enable us to reconstruct patterns of life and an outline of ancient Near Eastern history in which the events described in the Pentateuch are quite at home.

LITERARY GENRES

We often call the first five books of the Bible the *Pentateuch* ("five

containers"). The New Testament refers to these books as "the law of Moses" (Luke 24:44). This designation comes from the early Greek translators of the Old Testament, who almost always rendered the Hebrew term *torah* as *nomos* ("law"), even though the Hebrew word *torah* actually means "instruction."

It is misleading to refer to the Pentateuch as "the law," because large portions are not law at all. It is, however, fitting to call the whole collection *torah* ("instruction"). The Torah includes inspired narrative (Genesis; Exod 1–20; 32–40; Lev 8–10; Numbers); poems and hymns (Gen 49; Exod 15; Deut 32; 33); genealogies (Gen 5, 10, 11, 36); covenant documents (Exod 19–24; Deuteronomy); civil, ceremonial, and moral laws (Exod 21–23); sermons (Deuteronomy); and prayers (Exod 32; Num 14).

INTERPRETATION

Several principles guide us as we read and interpret the Pentateuch:

1. These texts were originally read aloud, and the reading involved large sections at a time. Chapter and verse divisions were not part of the original and can detract from our understanding. Each verse and paragraph should be read within its larger context.

2. The Pentateuch was written more than 3,000 years ago. It used ancient literary standards and addressed ancient issues. For example, although Genesis 1–2 affects how Christians today respond to theories of evolution, the passage was written to address ancient rather than modern concerns.

3. The differences among genres of text require that we interpret them differently. Therefore, as we read the narratives and delight in the human interest elements, we should recognize that God is the ultimate hero in all the stories. Similarly, as we read the laws of Exodus and Leviticus, we should try to establish the theological significance that these regulations had for OT Israel and reflect on how their message applies to us today.

4. The Pentateuch records only the beginning and the early chapters of the larger story of divine revelation that ultimately culminates in Jesus Christ. The seeds of promise for a Messiah are found in God's promise to crush the head of the serpent through the offspring of the woman (Gen 3:15); in the offspring of Abraham (Gen 22:17); in the descendants of Judah (Gen 49:10), who received eternal title to the scepter of Israel; and in the star that the pagan prophet Balaam saw on the distant horizon (Num 24:17). These seeds bore fruit later in the biblical record.

MEANING AND MESSAGE

The Pentateuch provided ancient Israel with an awesome picture of God, an image that separated him from the false gods of other nations. Yahweh, the God of Israel, is the only God—no other god exists (Deut 4:32-40). Yahweh, the God of Israel, is the Creator of the heavens and the earth. Yahweh, the God of Israel, is a God of grace; he deals patiently with sinners, saving them and calling them to covenant relationship with himself, revealing his name and his will to them, providing for their needs, and walking with them in fellowship and love.

In the account of creation, the Pentateuch reveals important lessons about the universe. God created the world by speaking it into being. He created a perfect world, characterized by light and life and order. But the devastating effects of sin replaced light with darkness, life with death, and peace and order with confusion and pain. Yet God promised ultimate victory, guaranteeing that the head of the serpent who introduced sin to humankind would be crushed.

The Pentateuch introduces us to God's covenant relationships with human beings. All of God's covenants are gracious. He invites his human partners into a special relationship and calls on them to respond with holy living because of the special role they play in his plan of redemption. By grace, God drew Noah into covenant relationship by saving him from the Flood. By grace, God called Abraham out of the pagan city of Ur in Babylonia to establish a covenant relationship. By grace, God called Israel to be his people, and at Mount Sinai God confirmed for the nation his covenant with Abraham.

Although the covenants all originated in God's gracious heart, they still called for an obedient response from the human partners. However, God never wanted this obedience to be driven by a mere sense of duty or quid pro quo. Instead, the text of the Pentateuch reveals a consistent pattern of conduct for the Lord's people to follow in loving obedience and grateful response to God's saving work. Because God chose Israel to be his people and bound himself to them in covenant relationship, he desired that they express their faithfulness to him.

Despite the unified message of Scripture that people have never been saved by keeping the law (see Gen 15:6; Deut 7:7-8; Pss 40; 51; Isa 1:10-20; Rom 4:1-17; Gal 3:6-7), many people erroneously think that people in the Old Testament were saved by keeping the law. However, grace has always preceded law. God rescued Israel from their slavery in Egypt *before* he gave them the law. While God required the Israelites to obey the law in order to receive blessing and to fulfill the plan God had for them, the motivation for their obedience should have been gratitude that God had saved Israel and revealed his will to them.

In short, the Pentateuch contains the Torah—the instruction—that God gave Israel at its founding. Priests were to teach it and model it (Deut 33:10; 2 Chr 15:3; 19:8; Mal 2:6, 9; cp. Ezra 7:10; Jer 18:18; Ezek 7:26). Psalmists praised it (e.g., Ps 19:7-14; 119), prophets appealed to it (Isa 1:10; 5:24; 8:20; 30:9; 51:7), faithful kings ruled by it (1 Kgs 2:2-4; 2 Kgs 14:6; 22:11; 23:25), righteous citizens lived by it (Ps 1), and unfaithful Israel was judged by it (Deut 28:15-68; 2 Chr 36:11-21). Only Jesus Christ kept it and completely fulfilled it (Matt 3:15).

FURTHER READING

VICTOR HAMILTON
Handbook on the Pentateuch (2005)

G. HERBERT LIVINGSTON
The Pentateuch in Its Cultural Environment (1974)

THE BOOK OF GENESIS

Genesis is the book of beginnings—of the universe and of humanity, of sin and its catastrophic effects, and of God's plan to restore blessing to the world through his chosen people. God began his plan when he called Abraham and made a covenant with him. Genesis traces God's promised blessings from generation to generation, to the time of bondage and the need for redemption from Egypt. It lays the foundation for God's subsequent revelation, and most other books of the Bible draw on its contents. Genesis is a source of instruction, comfort, and edification.

SETTING

When Genesis was written, the children of Israel had been slaves in Egypt for 400 years. They had recently been released from bondage and guided through the desert to meet the Lord at Mount Sinai, where he had established his covenant relationship with them and had given them his law through Moses. Israel was now poised to enter the Promised Land and receive the inheritance that God had promised Abraham.

While enslaved in Egypt, the Israelites had adopted many pagan ideas and customs from their Egyptian masters (e.g., Exod 32:1-4). They were influenced by false concepts of God, the world, and human nature (e.g., Exod 32), and were reduced to being slaves rather than owners and managers of the land. Perhaps they had forgotten the great promises that God had made to Abraham, Isaac, and Jacob, or perhaps they had concluded that the promises would never be fulfilled.

Before entering the Promised Land, the Israelites needed to understand the nature of God, his world, and their place in it more clearly. They needed to embrace their identity as descendants of Abraham, Isaac, and Jacob. Genesis provided the needed understanding.

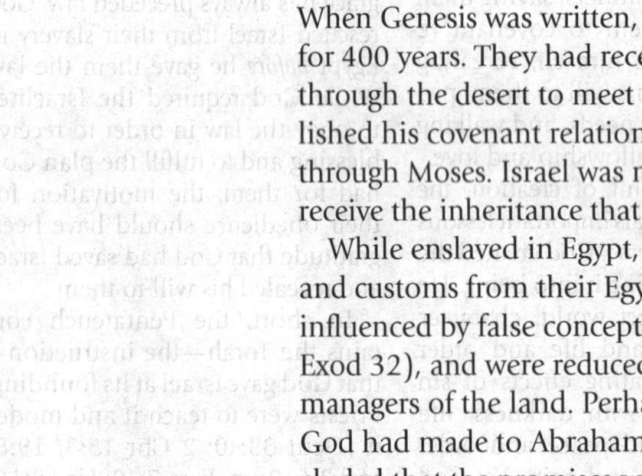

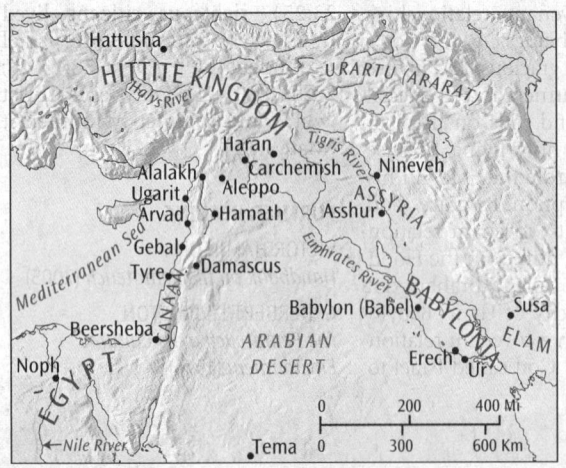

◂ **The Ancient Near East, about 2100 BC.** Humanity spread out from the mountains of URARTU (ARARAT) and populated the early centers of civilization. By the time of the patriarchs (Abraham, Isaac, and Jacob), many of the cities were ancient.

ASSHUR 2:14; 10:22; 25:3; 25:18
ASSYRIA 10:11
BABYLON (BABEL), BABYLONIA 10:9-10; 11:1-9; 14:1, 9
CANAAN 9:18-27; 10:18-19; 12:5-10
DAMASCUS 14:15; 15:2
EGYPT 12:10–13:1; 15:18; 37:28-36; 39:1–50:26
ELAM 10:22; 14:1, 9
ERECH 10:10; Ezra 4:9
HAMATH 10:18; 2 Sam 8:9-10; 2 Kgs 14:28; 23:33
HARAN 11:26-32; 12:4-5; 27:43; 28:10; 29:4; Acts 7:2-4
SUSA Ezra 4:9; Neh 1:1; Esth 1:2; Dan 8:2
UR 11:28, 31; 15:7; Neh 9:7
URARTU (ARARAT) 8:4

SUMMARY

Genesis traces God's work to overcome with blessing the curse that came on humankind because of sin. The book arranges family traditions, genealogies, historical events, and editorial comments into a single, sustained argument.

Every section but the first has the heading, "This is the account" (or *These are the generations*; Hebrew *toledoth*); each of the *toledoth* sections explains the history of a line of descent. In each case, a deterioration of well-being is followed by an increasing focus on God's plan to bless the world. This plan is the basis for God's covenant with his people; as the blessing develops, the covenant is clarified. By the end of the book, the reader is ready for the fulfillment of the promises in Israel's redemption from bondage (see Exodus).

The first section (1:1–2:3) does not have the *toledoth* heading, and logically so—it is the account of creation "in the beginning" (1:1). The work of creation is wrapped in God's approval and blessing as he fulfills his plan.

The next section (2:4–4:26) focuses on the creation of human life (2:4-25) and traces what became of God's creation because of Adam's and Eve's sin (3:1-13), the curse on their sin (3:14-24), and the extension of sin to their descendants (4:1-24). Humanity no longer enjoyed God's rest; instead, they experienced guilt and fear. So they fled from God and developed a proud civilization.

Independence from God resulted in the downward drift of human life (5:1–6:8). The genealogy of 5:1-32 begins by recalling that human beings were made in God's image and were blessed by him (5:1-2). As the genealogy is traced, the death of each generation reminds the reader of the curse, with Enoch providing a ray of hope that the curse is not final. In 6:1-8, we learn that God regretted having made humans and decided to judge the earth. Noah, however, received God's favor and provided a source of hope (5:29; 6:8).

The next section (6:9–9:29) brings the curse of judgment through the flood followed by blessing in a new beginning. A renewed creation began, purged of the abominable evil that had invaded and ruined the human race.

The world's population expanded into various nations (10:1–11:9) whose people were bent on disobedience. The population of the earth by Shem,

OUTLINE

1:1–2:3
Creation

2:4–4:26
What Happened to the Creation

5:1–6:8
The Account of Adam's Descendants

6:9–9:29
The Account of Noah's Family

10:1–11:9
The Account of Noah's Sons

11:10-26
The Account of Shem's Descendants

11:27–25:11
The Account of Terah's Descendants

25:12-18
The Account of Ishmael's Descendants

25:19–35:29
The Account of Isaac's Descendants

36:1–37:1
The Account of Esau's Descendants

37:2–50:26
The Account of Jacob's Descendants

TIMELINE

2166 / 1990 BC*
Abraham is born

2091 / 1915 BC
Abraham moves to Canaan

2080 / 1904 BC
Ishmael is born

2066 / 1890 BC
Sodom and Gomorrah are destroyed, Isaac is born

2006 / 1830 BC
Jacob and Esau are born

1898 / 1722 BC
Joseph is sold into slavery

1885 / 1709 BC
Joseph begins governing Egypt

1876 / 1661 BC
Jacob moves to Egypt

1446 / 1270 BC
Israel leaves Egypt (the Exodus), moves to Mount Sinai

1406 / 1230 BC
Israel enters Canaan

* *The two dates harmonize with the traditional "early" chronology and a more recent "late" chronology of the Exodus. All dates are approximate. Please see* *"Chronology: Abraham to Joshua," p. 118.*

Ham, and Japheth seemed fruitful (10:1-32), but the nations were divided by languages and boundaries (10:5, 20, 31). Because of their rebellion, God dispersed them to prevent greater wickedness (11:1-9).

After the chaos of the scattered nations, 11:10-26 brings the focus to Abram, through whom God chose to bring blessing to all. The rest of the book (11:27–50:26) tells of God's blessing Abram and his descendants. God first made a covenant with Abram (11:27–25:11), promising him a great nation, land, and name. As time went on, God made the specific terms of the covenant clearer, and Abram's faith grew deeper.

In each generation, Genesis gives a brief account of the families that are not Israel's ancestors before turning to the line of Israel. After briefly reporting what became of Ishmael (25:12-18), Genesis traces in detail what happened to Isaac and his family (25:19–35:29).

True to the pattern of the book, Esau's line (Edom) is dealt with briefly (36:1–37:1) before the chosen line of Jacob the heir. The final section (37:2–50:26) concerns Jacob's family, centering on the life of Joseph. In the land of Canaan, the family became corrupt under Canaanite influence to the point of beginning to merge with them (ch 38). To preserve the line of blessing, God sent the family into Egypt where they could flourish, remain separate (43:32; 46:34), and become a great nation. The book closes with the promise of the Lord's coming to rescue his people from Egypt (50:24-26).

"God rested on the seventh day from all his work that he had done. And he blessed the seventh day. . . ." And we ourselves will be a "seventh day" when we shall be filled with his blessing and remade by his sanctification. . . . Only when we are remade by God and perfected by a greater grace shall we have the eternal stillness of that rest in which we shall see that he is God.

ST. AUGUSTINE
City of God, sec. 22.30

AUTHORSHIP

Both Scripture and tradition attribute the Pentateuch (Genesis—Deuteronomy) to Moses. No one was better qualified than Moses to have written this book. Since he was educated in all the wisdom of the Egyptians (Acts 7:22), he had the literary skills to collect and edit Israel's traditions and records and to compose this theological treatise. His unique communion with God gave him the spiritual illumination, understanding, and inspiration needed to guide him. He had good reason to write this work—to provide Israel with the theological and historical foundation for the Exodus and the covenant at Sinai, and to establish the new nation in accord with the promises made to their ancestors.

Most scholars, however, do not accept that Moses wrote Genesis. The prevailing critical view, called the *Documentary Hypothesis,* is that Genesis was compiled from various sources by different groups of people. In such approaches, there is seldom a word about divine revelation or inspiration. For those who understand the Bible as God's inspired word, such theories often seem unnecessarily complicated and conjectural. Genesis can be understood much more straightforwardly as the product of Moses' genius under God's inspiration with later editorial adjustments. (See further "Introduction to the Pentateuch: Authorship," p. 12).

COMPOSITION

Biblical scholars of all stripes have always acknowledged that various sources were used in writing Genesis and other historical texts in the Bible (such as Kings and Luke). Moses used collections of family records, oral traditions, ancient accounts of primeval events, and genealogies to write Genesis. Those sources could have been incorporated as received, or the author may have changed their style and wording, stitching them together with additional material for the particular purpose of tracing the foundations of Israelite faith.

Genesis also includes passages and expressions that are obviously later editorial glosses. Some sections (such as the list of Edomite kings, 36:31-43) could have been added during the early days of the monarchy. There is no conflict in saying that Genesis was authored by Moses and augmented by subsequent editors whose work was guided by the Holy Spirit. Given these considerations, conservative scholars find it plausible that the biblical material accurately records actual events.

LITERARY CHARACTER

Genesis includes various types of literature. Several suggestions have been made as to the nature of the materials.

Myth. Mythological literature explains the origins of things symbolically through the deeds of gods and supernatural creatures. For ancient peoples, myths were beliefs that explained life and reality. Whole systems of ritual activities were developed to ensure that the forces of fertility, life, and death would continue year by year. Some of these rituals gave rise to cult prostitution (see 38:15, 21-22).

It would be very difficult to classify the material in Genesis as myth. Israel had one God, not a multitude. The nation of Israel had a beginning, a history, and a future hope. They saw God, rather than gods and other supernatural creatures, as the primary actor in the world. Their worship was not cosmic, magical, or superstitious, but a reenactment of their own rescue from Egypt and a celebration of God's factual intervention in history and their hope in his promises.

If Genesis uses elements of mythological language, it is to display a deliberate contrast with pagan concepts and to show that the Lord God is sovereign over such ideas. For example, the ancients worshiped the sun as a god, but in Genesis the sun serves the Creator's wishes (1:14-18). The book of Genesis is a cemetery for lifeless myths and dead gods. Genesis is not myth.

Etiology. A number of scholars describe the Genesis narratives as *etiologies,* stories that explain the causes of factual reality or traditional beliefs. The implication is that such stories were made up for explanatory purposes and do not describe historical events. For example, if one says that the story of Cain and Abel was made up to explain why shepherds and farmers do not get along, the account loses its integrity as factual history.

Etiological elements certainly occur in Genesis, because the book gives the foundation and rationale for almost everything that Israel would later do. For example, the creation account of Gen 2 ends with the explanation, "This explains why a man leaves his father and mother. . . ." The event as it happened explains why marriage was conducted the way it was, but to say that a story explains something is quite different from saying that the story was fabricated to explain it. The stories of Genesis are not fictional tales invented to explain later customs and beliefs.

History. Many scholars object to regarding Genesis as history, for two basic reasons: (1) Genesis explains events as caused by God, and the inclusion of the supernatural is regarded as proof that the material is theological reflection and thus not historically reliable; and (2) the events in Genesis cannot be validated from outside sources; no other records have demonstrated that Abraham existed or that any of his family history occurred.

Genesis is not interested in parading Abraham, Isaac, and Jacob as examples of morality. Therefore, it does not moralize on them. [Genesis] is bringing together the promises of God to the patriarchs and the faithfulness of God in keeping those promises.

VICTOR P. HAMILTON
The Book of Genesis: Chapters 1–17, p. 46

Modern philosophies of history exclude the supernatural as an explanation of historical events, but there is no reason to do so arbitrarily. If God exists and is able to act, then he might very well be the ultimate cause of all historical events and the immediate cause of specific historical events. The Israelites were not as distrustful of supernatural events as are modern critics; they experienced such events frequently as God acted among them to fulfill the promises recorded in Genesis.

It is true that no direct evidence of the patriarchs or the events in Genesis has been found, but archaeology confirms the plausibility of Genesis by showing that the historical situation in that era (Middle Bronze I, 2000–1800 BC) corresponds closely to what Genesis portrays. It is unlikely that this would be so if Genesis were not an accurate record of the facts. When all the archaeological and historical data are assembled around the events, they fit perfectly within the setting, and the details of the narratives make perfectly good sense.

Theological Interpretation. Genesis was not intended as a chronicle of the lives of the patriarchs, a history for history's sake, or a complete biography. It is clearly a theological interpretation of selected records of the nation's ancestors, but this does not destroy its historicity. Interpretations of an event can differ, but the offering of interpretations is a good witness to the actuality of the events. The author retold the events in his own way, but he did not invent them.

Tradition. What was thus committed to writing is tradition in the reverent care of literary genius. Scholars prefer words such as "traditions" or even "sagas" to describe these narratives. Doing so only makes the claim that the stories preserve the memory of the people of Israel; it makes no claim that the events themselves are historical. The biblical understanding, however, is that these stories were recorded under divine inspiration and are therefore historically true and reliable.

In all probability, Abram brought the primeval accounts and the family genealogies from Mesopotamia, and stories about the family were added to these collections. Joseph could easily have preserved all the traditions, both written and oral, in Egypt with his own records. Moses could then have compiled the works substantially in their present form while adding his editorial comments. Since he worked under God's inspiration and guidance, the narratives record exactly what God wanted written and correspond precisely to reality.

Instructional Literature. Since Genesis is the first book of the Pentateuch (the "Torah" or Law), it may be best to classify it as "Torah Literature" (Hebrew *torah*, "instruction, law"). Genesis is instructional literature that lays the foundation for the Law. It is theological interpretation of the historical traditions standing behind the covenant at Sinai. In the way it is written, one may discern that Moses was preparing his readers to receive God's law and the fulfillment of the promises made to their forefathers. Genesis is therefore a unique work. Theology, history, and tradition come together to instruct God's people and prepare them for blessing.

MEANING AND MESSAGE

Israel's most important questions were answered by the Genesis narratives. Life and death, the possession of the land of Canaan, and how Israel ended up in Egypt are explained as God's providential working in history. Israel was part of God's plan in this world. His plan had

a starting point at creation and will have an end point in the future when the promises are completely fulfilled.

Israel, the Chosen People. The central theme of Genesis is that God made a covenant with Abraham and his descendants. He promised to make them his own people, heirs of the land of Canaan, and a blessing to the world. Genesis gave Israel the theological and historical basis for its existence as God's chosen people.

Israel could trace its ancestry to the patriarch Abraham and its destiny to God's promises (12:1-3; 15:1-21; 17:1-8). Because the promise of a great nation was crucial, much of Genesis is devoted to family concerns of the patriarchs and their wives, their sons and heirs, and their birthrights and blessings. The record shows how God preserved and protected the chosen line through the patriarchs. Israel thus knew that they had become the great nation promised to Abraham. Their future was certainly not in slavery to the Egyptians, but in Canaan, where they would live as a free nation and as the people of the living God, and where they could mediate God's blessings to the people of the world.

Blessing and Curse. The entire message of Genesis turns on the motifs of blessing and cursing. The promised blessing would give the patriarchs innumerable descendants and give the descendants the land of promise; the blessing would make them famous in the earth, enable them to flourish and prosper, and appoint them to bring others into the covenant blessings. The curse, meanwhile, would alienate, deprive, and disinherit people from the blessings. The effects of the curse are felt by the whole race as death and pain and as God's judgment on the world.

These motifs continue throughout the Bible. Prophets and priests spoke of even greater blessings in the future and an even greater curse for those who refuse God's gift of salvation and its blessings. The Bible reminds God's people not to fear human beings, but to fear God, who has the power to bless and to curse.

Good and Evil. In Genesis, that which is good is blessed by God: It produces, enhances, preserves, and harmonizes with life. That which is evil is cursed: It causes pain, diverts from what is good, and impedes or destroys life. Genesis traces the perpetual struggle between good and evil that characterizes our fallen human race. God will bring about the greater good, build the faith of his people, and ultimately triumph over all evil (cp. Rom 8:28).

God's Plan. Genesis begins with the presupposition that God exists and that he has revealed himself in word and deed to Israel's ancestors. It does not argue for the existence of God; it simply begins with God and shows how everything falls into place when the sovereign God works out his plan to establish Israel as the means of restoring blessing to the whole world.

God's Rule. Genesis is the fitting introduction to the founding of theocracy, the rule of God over all creation that was to be established through his chosen people. Genesis lays down the initial revelation of God's sovereignty. He is the Lord of the universe who will move heaven and earth to bring about his plan. He desires to bless people, but he will not tolerate rebellion and unbelief. His promises are great, and he is fully able to bring them to fruition. To participate in his plan has always required faith, for without faith it is impossible to please him (Heb 11:6).

FURTHER READING

VICTOR P. HAMILTON
The Book of Genesis (1990)

DEREK KIDNER
Genesis (1967)

KENNETH A. MATHEWS
Genesis (1996)

ALLEN P. ROSS
Creation and Blessing (1988)
Genesis in *Cornerstone Biblical Commentary*, vol. 1 (2008)

GORDON WENHAM
Genesis 1–15 (1987)
Genesis 16–50 (1994)

1. CREATION (1:1–2:3)

In the Beginning (1:1-2)

1 In the beginning God [a]created the
[b]heavens and the [c]earth. 2The earth was
formless and empty, and darkness covered
the deep waters. And the [d]Spirit of God was
hovering over the surface of the waters.

Six Days of Creation (1:3-31)

Day One: Light, Darkness

3Then God said, "Let there be light," and
there was light. 4And God saw that the
light was good. Then he separated the
light from the darkness. 5God called
the light "day" and the darkness "night."
And evening passed and morning
came, marking the first day.

Day Two: Sky, Waters

6Then God said, "Let there be a space
between the waters, to separate the
waters of the heavens from the waters of
the earth." 7And that is what happened.
God made this space to separate the
waters of the earth from the waters of
the heavens. 8God called the space "sky."
And evening passed and morning
came, marking the second day.

Day Three: Land, Sea, Vegetation

9Then God said, "Let the waters beneath
the sky flow together into one place, so
dry ground may appear." And that is
what happened. 10God called the dry
ground "land" and the waters "seas."

1:1
Ps 89:11; 102:25
Isa 42:5; 48:13
John 1:1-2
[a]*bara'* (1254)
‣Gen 1:27
[b]*shamayim* (8064)
‣Exod 16:4
[c]*'erets* (0776)
‣Gen 9:11

1:2
Isa 45:18
[d]*ruakh* (7307)
‣Gen 45:27

1:3
Isa 45:7
2 Cor 4:6

1:6
Job 26:10
Ps 136:5-6

1:9
Ps 95:5
Prov 8:29
Jer 5:22
2 Pet 3:5

The Creation (1:1–2:3)

Ps 33:6-9
Prov 3:19; 8:22-31
Isa 40:26-28; 45:11-12, 18-19
Jer 10:11-16
John 1:1-4
Rom 8:18-25
2 Cor 5:17
Col 1:15-20
Rev 4:11; 21:1-5

The creation account in Genesis is foundational to the message of the entire Bible, not just of Genesis or the Pentateuch. Understanding the early chapters of Genesis is thus crucial to forming a biblical worldview.

This part of Genesis deals with fundamental questions: Who created the world, and for what purpose? Why is the world in its present condition? Genesis answers these questions, dispelling the idolatry that Israel had acquired from their pagan masters in Egypt. In the Promised Land, they would also be surrounded by people who believed in many false gods and worshiped created things rather than the Creator. Genesis taught Israel that the one true God created and has absolute authority over all things; he alone is worthy of worship.

Every worldview attempts to explain where the world came from, what is wrong with the world, and how it can be set right again. The creation account in Genesis teaches that as God made the world, it was "very good" (1:31). Through creation, God turned disorder into restful order and emptiness into the fullness of abundant life. In this environment, humans enjoyed unbroken fellowship with their Creator until their rebellion severed that fellowship and implanted evil in human hearts (ch 3; see chs 4–6). The world's evil does not come from some defect in creation; God put the world under a curse because of human rebellion.

Since that first rebellion, humans have been alienated from the Creator and no longer recognize his presence and authority. This alienation results in shame, fractured relationships with God and other humans, estrangement from the rest of creation, and death (3:7-19). Since that time, God has been working purposefully in history to restore humans to fellowship with him, which he is doing through Jesus Christ. Restored humans are a new creation (Gal 6:15); through Jesus, eternal life is open to all and God will one day renew all things (see Isa 65:17-25; Rom 8:19-22). The whole cosmos will be made new (Rev 21:1).

1:1–2:3 These verses introduce the Pentateuch (Genesis—Deuteronomy) and teach Israel that the world was created, ordered, and populated by the one true God and not by the gods of surrounding nations. • God blessed three specific things: animal life (1:22-25), human life (1:27), and the Sabbath day (2:3). This trilogy of blessings highlights the Creator's plan: Humankind was made in God's image to enjoy sovereign dominion over the creatures of the earth and to participate in God's Sabbath rest.

1:1 ***In the beginning God created the heavens and the earth*** (or *In the beginning when God created the heavens and the earth, . . .* or *When God began to create the heavens and the earth, . . .*): This statement summarizes the entire creation account (1:3–2:3). Already a key question—Who created the world?—is answered (see also Prov 8:22-31; John 1:1-3). Although the modern naturalistic mindset rejects this question and that of creation's purpose, Genesis affirms God's role and purpose in creation. • The common name for *God* (Hebrew *'elohim*) emphasizes his grand supremacy. The word *'elohim* is plural, but the verbs used with it are usually singular, reflecting the consistent scriptural proclamation of a single, all-powerful God. • ***created*** (Hebrew *bara'*): In the OT, God is always the agent of creation expressed by this verb. It describes the making of something fresh and new—notably the cosmos (1:1, 21; 2:3), humankind (1:27), the Israelite nation (Isa 43:1), and the future new creation (Isa 65:17). • ***The heavens and the earth*** are the entire ordered cosmos.

1:2 This verse gives the background for the summary in 1:1 and the detailed description in 1:3–2:3. God's creative utterances bring order to the chaotic state of the universe. • ***formless . . . empty*** (Hebrew *tohu . . . bohu*): This terse idiom means something like "wild and waste." It sets a stark contrast to the final ordered state of the heavens and the earth (1:1). • ***deep waters***

1:10
Ps 33:7; 95:5
1:11
Gen 2:9
Ps 104:14
Matt 6:30
1:14
Ps 74:16; 104:19
1:15
Gen 1:5
1:16
Ps 8:3; 19:1-6;
136:8-9
1 Cor 15:41
1:18
Jer 33:20, 25
1:20
Gen 2:19
Ps 146:6
[e]*nepesh* (5315)
›Gen 2:7
1:21
Ps 104:25-28

And God saw that it was good. 11 Then
God said, "Let the land sprout with
vegetation—every sort of seed-bearing
plant, and trees that grow seed-bearing
fruit. These seeds will then produce the
kinds of plants and trees from which
they came." And that is what happened.
12 The land produced vegetation—all
sorts of seed-bearing plants, and trees
with seed-bearing fruit. Their seeds
produced plants and trees of the same
kind. And God saw that it was good.
13 And evening passed and morning
came, marking the third day.

Day Four: Sun, Moon, Stars

14 Then God said, "Let lights appear in the
sky to separate the day from the night.
Let them be signs to mark the seasons,
days, and years. 15 Let these lights in
the sky shine down on the earth." And
that is what happened. 16 God made two
great lights—the larger one to govern
the day, and the smaller one to govern
the night. He also made the stars. 17 God
set these lights in the sky to light the
earth, 18 to govern the day and night, and
to separate the light from the darkness.
And God saw that it was good.
19 And evening passed and morning
came, marking the fourth day.

Day Five: Birds, Fish

20 Then God said, "Let the waters swarm
with fish and other [e]life. Let the skies
be filled with birds of every kind." 21 So
God created great sea creatures and
every living thing that scurries and

Formless	CHAOS	Empty
DAY 1 (1:3-5) Light, Dark	HEAVENS	DAY 4 (1:14-19) Sun, Moon, Stars
DAY 2 (1:6-8) Water, Sky	WATER & SKY	DAY 5 (1:20-23) Birds, Fish
DAY 3 (1:9-13) Sea, Land	EARTH	DAY 6 (1:24-31) Animals, Humans
Formed	COSMOS	Filled
	DAY 7 (2:2-3) Rest	

◂ **The Structure of the Creation Account** (1:1–2:3). God transformed chaos into the present cosmos. In the first three days, he transformed the formless void into the structured universe—the HEAVENS (outer space), the WATER and SKY, and the EARTH (cp. Exod 20:11; Ps 135:6). In the second three days, he populated each empty realm. The seventh day (2:1-3) stands apart: As God's day of rest, it provides the weekly pattern for human activity (Exod 20:8-11; 31:12-17) and speaks of the rest that God promised to those who live by faith in him (see Heb 3:7–4:11).

(Hebrew *tehom*): Some scholars say this alludes to the Mesopotamian goddess Tiamat (representing chaos), but Genesis views *tehom* as inhospitable chaos, not as a deity or goddess that God engaged in cosmic battle. • ***the Spirit of God:*** God directly superintended the creation process.

1:3-13 In the first three days, God formed the chaos into a habitable world.

1:3 ***Then God said:*** Nothing in Gen 1 is created apart from God's powerful word (cp. Ps 33:6, 9). • ***"Let there be . . . ," and there was:*** God's command enacted his will to create the world. God is not a part of creation or limited by it; he is the supreme ruler over everything (cp. Neh 9:6).

1:4 ***Light*** is antithetical to chaotic ***darkness*** (1:2); the light is declared ***good*** but the darkness is not (cp. John 1:5). God is the source of this light (cp. 1:14-19). God ***separated*** the light, as he did water (cp. 1:6-8), by his creative word. Light is associated with life and blessing (Job 38:19-20; Ps 19:1-6; 97:11; 104:19-20; Isa 60:19-20) and sets a boundary on the darkness that would destroy cosmic order. Darkness often typifies terror, death, and evil (see 15:12; Job 18:6, 18; Ps 88:12; Eph 5:11-12; 1 Jn 1:5).

1:5 ***God called*** (or *named*): To name something is to exercise authority over it (see also 2:19-20). • ***day:*** The Hebrew *yom* can refer to daylight (1:5a), to a 24-hour period (1:5b), or to an unspecified time period (2:4b, "When," literally *in the day;* cp. Exod 20:8-11). • ***evening . . . morning:*** The Hebrew day began at sundown, just as the first day began with darkness and brought the first morning light.

1:6-8 The creation account describes the appearance of things from a human perspective. The ***sky*** is viewed as a shiny dome that is a buffer between two collections of water (cp. Job 37:18; Ezek 1:22). In the ancient Near East, the cosmos was understood as a three-tier system, with rain originating from the outermost tier (see 7:11-12 and note).

1:9-10 ***Let the waters . . . flow together:*** Other ancient cultures viewed the sea as a hostile force. Genesis shows God as further restraining chaos (see note on 1:2) by prescribing specific boundaries for the sea. The flood—an act of God's judgment (6:7)—undid these boundaries and returned the earth to chaos (7:1-24).

1:14-31 On days 4–6, God filled the domains that had been formed during days 1–3 (1:3-13).

1:14 ***Let them . . . mark the seasons, days, and years:*** The movement of the heavenly bodies defined Israel's liturgical calendar, whose roots in creation gave a sacred timing to Israel's festivals and celebrations (see Exod 23:15; Lev 23:4).

1:16 In the surrounding pagan cultures, the ***two great lights*** were worshiped as deities, but in Genesis they serve God and humanity (see Ps 136:7-9; Jer 31:35). The sun and moon are not named; they are simply called ***the larger one*** and ***the smaller one.*** Not including their names may have reminded Israel that they were not gods. • ***govern:*** Cp. 1:26, 28; Ps 136:9. • ***the stars:*** The starry heavens testify to God's creative power as they proclaim his glory (Ps 19:1; 148:3). They do not predict the future, as Israel's neighbors believed (see Jer 10:2).

1:21 Contrary to the pagan idea that the ***great sea creatures*** were co-eternal with God, Genesis states that ***God created*** them and is sovereign over them. The Hebrew word *tanninim* ("***creatures***") elsewhere refers to crocodiles (Ezek 29:3), powerful monsters (Jer 51:34), or the sea creature, Leviathan (Isa 27:1; cp. Job 41:1-34).

swarms in the water, and every sort of
bird—each producing offspring of the
same kind. And God saw that it was
good. 22 Then God blessed them, saying,
"Be fruitful and multiply. Let the fish fill
the seas, and let the birds multiply on
the earth."
23 And evening passed and morning
came, marking the fifth day.

Day Six: Animals, Humankind

24 Then God said, "Let the earth produce
every sort of animal, each producing
offspring of the same kind—livestock,
small animals that scurry along the
ground, and wild animals." And that is
what happened. 25 God made all sorts
of wild animals, livestock, and small
animals, each able to produce offspring
of the same kind. And God saw that it
was good.
26 Then God said, "Let us make
human beings in our image, to be like
us. They will reign over the fish in the
sea, the birds in the sky, the livestock,
all the wild animals on the earth, and
the small animals that scurry along the
ground."

27 So God [f]created human beings in his
own image.
In the image of God he [f]created
them;
male and female he [f]created them.

28 Then God blessed them and said,
"Be fruitful and multiply. Fill the earth
and govern it. Reign over the fish in
the sea, the birds in the sky, and all the
animals that scurry along the ground."
29 Then God said, "Look! I have given
you every seed-bearing plant throughout
the earth and all the fruit trees for your
food. 30 And I have given every green
plant as food for all the wild animals, the
birds in the sky, and the small animals
that scurry along the ground—everything
that has life." And that is what happened.
31 Then God looked over all he had
made, and he saw that it was very good!
And evening passed and morning
came, marking the sixth day.

Sabbath Rest (2:1-3)

2 So the creation of the heavens and the
earth and everything in them was completed. 2 On the seventh day God had
finished his work of creation, so he rested
from all his work. 3 And God [g]blessed the
seventh day and declared it holy, because
it was the day when he rested from all his
work of [h]creation.

1:24 Gen 2:19
1:26 Gen 5:1; 9:6; Ps 8:6-8; Acts 17:28-29
1:27 *Matt 19:4; *Mark 10:6; [f]*bara'* (1254) ‣Gen 2:3
1:29 Gen 9:3; Ps 104:13; 136:25
1:30 Ps 104:14; 145:15
1:31 Ps 104:24
2:1 Deut 4:19; 17:3; Ps 104:2; Isa 45:12
2:2 Exod 20:11; 31:17; *Heb 4:4
2:3 Isa 58:13; [g]*barak* (1288) ‣Gen 12:2; [h]*bara'* (1254) ‣Gen 6:7
2:4 Gen 1:3-31; Job 38:4-11

1:22 ***God blessed them:*** God's blessing commissions and enables the fulfillment of what God has spoken (see "Blessing" at 48:8-20, p. 113). • ***Let the fish . . . let the birds:*** These directives define the blessing. The fish and birds are fertile by God's command, not by pagan ritual, as some of Israel's neighbors thought.

1:26 ***Let us make*** is more personal than the remote "Let there be" (e.g., 1:3, 6). • The plural ***us*** has inspired several explanations: (1) the Trinity; (2) the plural to denote majesty; (3) a plural to show deliberation with the self; and (4) God speaking with his heavenly court of angels. The concept of the Trinity—one true God who exists eternally in three distinct persons—was revealed at a later stage in redemptive history, making it unlikely that the human author intended that here. Hebrew scholars generally dismiss the plural of majesty view because the grammar does not clearly support it (the plural of majesty has not been demonstrated to be communicated purely through a plural verb). The plural of self-deliberation also lacks evidence; the only clear examples refer to Israel as a corporate unity (e.g., 2 Sam 24:14). God's speaking to the heavenly court, however, is well-attested in the OT (see 3:22; 11:7; 1 Kgs 22:19-22; Job 1:6-12; 2:1-6; 38:7; Ps 89:5-6; Isa 6:1-8; Dan 10:12-13). • ***human beings:*** Or *man;* Hebrew reads *'adam.* • The descriptors ***in our image*** and ***like us*** are virtually synonymous in Hebrew. Humans enjoy a unique relationship with God. • ***They will reign:*** Humans represent the Creator as his ambassadors, vice-regents, and administrators on earth.

1:27 The first poetry of Genesis reflectively celebrates God's climactic feat in creating humankind. • ***human beings*** (Or *the man;* Hebrew reads *ha-'adam*): This term is often used to denote humanity collectively (see 6:1, 5-7; 9:5-6). Though traditionally translated "man," gender is not at issue here; both ***male and female*** are included.

1:28 ***God blessed them:*** See note on 1:22; see also 17:16; 48:16; Deut 7:13. • ***said:*** God's message to humankind is direct and intimate; we are stewards of his delegated authority. • ***govern. . . . Reign:*** As God's vice-regents, humans are entrusted with the care and management of the world God created (see also 9:2; Ps 8:5-8).

1:29-30 These verses highlight the extent (***throughout the earth***) and variety (***every seed-bearing plant . . . all the fruit trees***) of God's provision for humans, ***animals***, and ***birds***.

1:31 The Creator declares his work ***good*** seven times in ch 1; following the creation of human beings, God declares it all ***very good***.

2:1-3 Humankind is the high point of God's creative acts (1:26-31), while day 7 is the climax of the creation week. When God ***rested*** (or *ceased*), he endorsed all of creation—there was nothing more to do! This seven-day framework structured Israel's week, with the ***seventh day*** as the precedent for their weekly Sabbath. The Sabbath was intended to celebrate God's finished work; the seventh day would be set apart as ***holy*** and dedicated to the Creator, who also rested (see Exod 20:8-11; 31:12-17; cp. Matt 12:1-8; Rom 14:5-6; Col 2:16-17; Heb 4:1-11).

2:3 The first six days of creation involved separation (light from darkness, day from night, water from dry land). The last act of creation separated what is ordinary from what is ***holy***, thus laying the foundation for Israel's worship. It also anticipated a coming age of rest (Heb 4:1-11; 12:2; 13:14). • The absence of the usual "morning and evening" reflects the Creator's willingness to enter into unending fellowship with humankind.

2:5
Gen 1:11
2:7
Gen 3:19
Job 33:4
Ps 103:14
Ezek 37:5
Zech 12:1
John 20:22
*1 Cor 15:45
[i]*nepesh* (5315)
‣Deut 12:23

2. WHAT HAPPENED TO THE CREATION (2:4–4:26)

Superscription (2:4a)

[4]This is the account of the creation of the
heavens and the earth.

Creation of Man and Woman (2:4b-25)

Creation of the Man

When the LORD God made the earth and
the heavens, [5]neither wild plants nor grains
were growing on the earth. For the LORD
God had not yet sent rain to water the earth,
and there were no people to cultivate the soil.
[6]Instead, springs came up from the ground
and watered all the land. [7]Then the LORD
God formed the man from the dust of the
ground. He breathed the breath of life into
the man's nostrils, and the man became a living [i]person.

Human Sexuality (1:27-28)

Gen 2:18-25
Lev 18:1-30
Deut 22:13-29
Ruth 4:11-13
2 Sam 11:2-27
Ps 127:3-5
Eccl 2:8-11
Song 1–8
Mal 2:15-16
Matt 19:3-12
1 Cor 6:12–7:40
Eph 5:31-33
1 Thes 4:3-8

When God created the first human beings in his own image, he created them as sexual beings, male and female (1:27). Through their sexuality, they were to fill and govern the world (1:28) and provide intimate companionship for one another in marriage (2:18-25). Male and female sexuality is central to what it means to be human.

Sexual intimacy united the first man and woman as one being, an effect that sexual intimacy continues to have. Since biblical sexuality is not just physical but has the total person in view, it validates sexual relations only as part of the partners' mutual commitment to each other's ultimate good. The Bible speaks of engaging in sexual intercourse as literally "knowing" another person intimately (see note on 4:1). Since creation, the purpose of sexuality has been to join people in an intimate union of marriage—a permanent and loving heterosexual commitment—that God blesses and calls "very good" (1:27-28, 31). The sexual relationship cements the marriage bond in an intimacy that continues even when reproduction is no longer possible.

Although sexuality was created before sin, it did not emerge unscathed from human rebellion. Sexuality is a powerful force that is easily corrupted if not carefully channeled (see Lev 18; 1 Thes 4:3-8). Sexual intimacy apart from marital commitment perverts the order that God intended for creation. Incest, for example, violates sexual boundaries (see Lev 18:7-14), collapses family structures (see 19:30-38), and fragments the community. Whereas perverted sexuality tears the community down (see 38:1-30; 39:7-9; Judg 19:1–20:48) and exalts the individual (see 2 Sam 13:11-14), biblical sexuality builds up the sexual partners and the community.

Our sexual identity has been damaged through our fall into sin (ch 3), but God has redeemed it through the death and resurrection of Jesus Christ (see 1 Cor 6:12-20; Eph 5:31-33). He restores sexual wholeness in those who trust his work in their lives by the Holy Spirit (1 Cor 6:9-11, 15-20; 1 Thes 4:1-5). Those who commit their sexuality to Christ can testify to God's love for his people (Eph 5:25-33).

2:4–4:26 This account (see note on 2:4) of the heavens and the earth is not a second creation account; rather, it is a theological and historical expansion on 1:1–2:3. The focus is now on what the cosmos produced rather than on its creation. Special attention is given to the first man and woman. As the story progresses, it is colored by contrasts of good and evil, knowledge and ignorance, life and death, harmony and discord.

2:4 ***This is the account*** (literally *These are the generations*): This or a similar phrase is repeated throughout Genesis, creating an internal outline for the book. In other occurrences, it introduces the genealogy or story of a key personality (5:1; 6:9; 10:1; 11:10; 11:27; 25:12; 25:19; 36:1; 37:2). • Some have argued that the first half of 2:4 belongs with 1:1–2:3, but it is more likely the introduction to the account that follows. • ***LORD God*** (Hebrew *Yahweh Elohim*) is the second name used for God in the early chapters of Genesis. *Elohim* (1:1–2:3) describes the all-powerful creator God. *Yahweh Elohim* speaks of the eternal God who formed a lasting covenant with Israel (Exod 3:6, 13-15). Accordingly, 2:4-25 focuses on God as provider more than as creator. The three themes of sexuality, dominion, and food in ch 1 are now addressed in reverse order (food, 2:8-17; dominion, 2:18-20; sexuality, 2:21-25).

2:5 ***cultivate:*** Work does not result from sin; it was part of the original structure of creation and is directly tied to human identity and purpose (1:28; 2:15).

2:6 ***springs*** (Or *mist,* as traditionally rendered): The word refers to subterranean springs that rose to the surface of the ground.

2:7 In 1:1–2:3, creation happens at a distance, by divine command ("Let there be . . . and that is what happened"). In this account, the creative act is much more intimate (see also 2:8-9, 21-22). • ***from the dust of the ground:*** In Hebrew, *'adamah* ("ground") forms a wordplay with *'adam* ("man"). The earth remains the definitive reference point for humans, who in death return to dust (3:17-19; 4:11; Job 4:19; 10:8-9; Isa 29:16). • ***breathed . . . into the man's nostrils:*** God's *breath* is not imparted to other animals; only humans are formed in God's image (1:27) and enjoy dialogue with their Creator (2:16-17; 3:8-13). They alone have spiritual awareness and moral conscience (see Job 32:8).

Creation of the Garden
8 Then the LORD God planted a garden in
Eden in the east, and there he placed the
man he had made. 9 The LORD God made
all sorts of trees grow up from the ground—
trees that were beautiful and that produced
delicious fruit. In the middle of the garden
he placed the tree of life and the tree of the
knowledge of good and evil.
10 A river flowed from the land of Eden,
watering the garden and then dividing into
four branches. 11 The first branch, called the
Pishon, flowed around the entire land of Havilah, where gold is found. 12 The gold of that
land is exceptionally pure; aromatic resin
and onyx stone are also found there. 13 The
second branch, called the Gihon, flowed
around the entire land of Cush. 14 The third
branch, called the Tigris, flowed east of the
land of Asshur. The fourth branch is called
the Euphrates.

The First Command
15 The LORD God placed the man in the
Garden of Eden to tend and watch over it.

2:8 Gen 3:23; 13:10; Isa 51:3; Joel 2:3
2:9 Gen 3:22; Prov 3:18; 11:30; Rev 2:7; 22:2, 14
2:10 Rev 22:1, 17
2:14 Gen 15:18; Deut 1:7; Dan 10:4
2:15 Gen 2:8

Biblical Marriage (2:18-25)

Gen 24:65-67; Ps 45:8-15; Is 54:5; Hos 2:19-20; Mal 2:10-16; 1 Cor 7:1-40; 2 Cor 6:14-16; Eph 5:21-33; Heb 13:4; 1 Pet 3:1-7

At the first wedding, God the Father gave the bride away to the groom and witnessed the couple's interaction in his sanctuary-garden (2:18-25). Married love is thus a binding covenant commitment before God. Breaching that covenant (e.g., through adultery) is a crime against persons and against God, who is a divine witness to and guarantor of the marriage covenant (see Mal 2:10-16; cp. Gen 39:6-9; Jer 3:1; 1 Cor 6:9-10; Heb 13:4). Although marriage is exclusive, it is not private. It is legally declared in public, with community recognition, witnesses, and accountability (see Lev 20:10-12; Deut 22:22; Jer 29:20-23).

Marriage is also a metaphor of the Lord's relationship with his people, first with Israel (see Exod 19:3-6; 20:2-6; 34:14; Isa 54:5; Ezek 16:1-63; Hos 2:19-20), and then with the church (see 2 Cor 11:2; Eph 5:21-33). A marriage points to something greater than itself—God's people (Christ's "bride") await the return of Christ (the "groom"). Married Christians are called to live in unity and dignity as they anticipate the wedding feast of the Lamb (Rev 19:6-9). Christ will live forever with his faithful people in glory (Rev 19:7; 21:2, 9).

2:8-14 Analogous to the sacred time marked out on the seventh day of creation (2:2-3), the sacred space of the ***garden in Eden*** was separate from the surrounding world. It functioned as a garden-temple or sanctuary because the Lord manifested his presence there in a special way.

2:8 ***Eden*** was the general location in which the ***garden*** was placed, not the garden itself. The term could mean "plain," "delight," or "fertility." The description that follows favors the idea of fertility. • ***in the east:*** The exact location of Eden is left to speculation, but it was east of Canaan, Israel's later home. • God ***placed the man*** in the garden for divine fellowship and physical blessing (see also 2:15 and note).

2:9 Beauty and bounty characterized humanity's original environment (cp. 13:10). • The ***tree of life*** represented God's presence and provision. The one who ate of it would have everlasting life (3:22), which made it a rich image for later Israelite and Christian reflection (Prov 3:18; 11:30; 13:12; Rev 2:7; 22:2, 14, 19). The candlestick in Israel's Tabernacle may have been a stylized representation of it (Exod 25:31-35). • Eating the fruit of the ***tree of the knowledge of good and evil*** enabled humanity's capacity for wisdom (3:6) and moral discernment (3:5, 22; cp. Deut 1:39, "innocent"). Eating from it represented a human grasp for autonomy and wisdom that were God's alone (cp. Prov 30:1-4). Humans sidestepped God's revelation as the means of moral discernment, flaunting their independence rather than submitting to God's will (cp. Prov 1:7). Choosing human wisdom over God's instruction brings death and destruction (see Ps 19:7-9; Ezek 28:6, 15-17).

2:10-14 This detailed description portrays the eastern region around Eden as a mountain with rivers flowing out to the world. Eden's beauty and fertility enriched the whole earth.

2:10 The ***river*** that was ***watering the garden*** was a material blessing (bringing agricultural fertility) and a symbol of God's presence (cp. Ps 46:4; Ezek 47:1-12; Zech 14:8; Rev 22:1-2). • ***dividing into four branches*** (literally *heads*): The common understanding is that one river had its source in Eden, flowed down through the garden, and then split into the four rivers named.

2:11 ***The Pishon*** and the Gihon (2:13) cannot be identified with certainty. If ***the land of Havilah*** was in southeast Arabia or on the African coast, as some biblical data suggest (see 10:7; 25:18; 1 Sam 15:7), then the Pishon was possibly the Nile River. Josephus thought that Havilah and the Pishon were in India (*Antiquities* 1.1.3). Two other proposals suggest: (1) rivers in the mountains of eastern Turkey where the Tigris and Euphrates (2:14) also flow, and (2) the marshy delta near the Persian Gulf. Current geographical conditions make any theory impossible to prove conclusively.

2:12 The magnificence and fertility of the garden are pictured as spreading to the surrounding regions through the rivers flowing out from it. The four rivers possibly imply that the garden's bounty flowed out to the four corners of the earth. • ***Gold*** and ***onyx*** were later used for decorating the Tabernacle, the Temple (Exod 25:3-9; 1 Chr 29:2), and the priests' clothing (Exod 28:9-14, 20). • ***Resin*** was used in sacred incense (Exod 30:34).

2:13 ***Gihon:*** Though unknown, proposals have included the Nile (as in the Greek version of Jer 2:18; Josephus, *Antiquities* 1.1.3), the Jordan, or, according to Jewish tradition, a river that formerly ran through the Kidron Valley (1 Kgs 1:33; 2 Chr 33:14). • Although ***Cush*** is the name of ancient Ethiopia, Mesopotamian regions associated with Babylon seem to be the immediate setting (see 10:8); Cush is possibly the land of the Kassites, a dynasty ruling in Babylonia.

2:14 ***Tigris . . . Euphrates:*** These well-known rivers flow from the mountains of eastern Turkey.

2:16 Gen 3:1-3
2:17 Gen 3:1, 16-17; Deut 30:15, 19-20; Rom 6:23; Jas 1:15
2:18 Gen 3:12; Prov 18:22
2:19 Gen 1:20-25
2:22 1 Cor 11:8-9; 1 Tim 2:13
2:23 Gen 29:14; Eph 5:28-30
2:24 *Matt 19:5; *1 Cor 6:16; Eph 5:31
2:25 Gen 3:7, 10-11

16 But the LORD God warned him, "You may
freely eat the fruit of every tree in the garden—17 except the tree of the knowledge
of good and evil. If you eat its fruit, you are
sure to die."

Creation of the Woman

18 Then the LORD God said, "It is not good
for the man to be alone. I will make a helper
who is just right for him." 19 So the LORD God
formed from the ground all the wild animals and all the birds of the sky. He brought
them to the man to see what he would call
them, and the man chose a name for each
one. 20 He gave names to all the livestock, all
the birds of the sky, and all the wild animals.
But still there was no helper just right for
him.

21 So the LORD God caused the man to
fall into a deep sleep. While the man slept,
the LORD God took out one of the man's
ribs and closed up the opening. 22 Then the
LORD God made a woman from the rib, and
he brought her to the man.

23 "At last!" the man exclaimed.

"This one is bone from my bone,
and flesh from my flesh!
She will be called 'woman,'
because she was taken from 'man.'"

24 This explains why a man leaves his father and mother and is joined to his wife,
and the two are united into one.
25 Now the man and his wife were both naked, but they felt no shame.

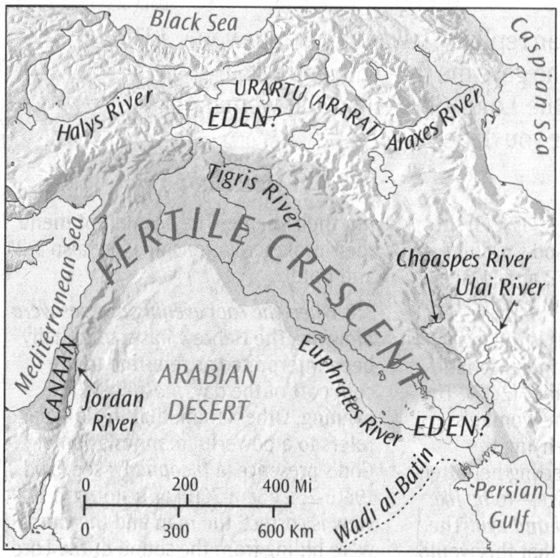

◂ **The Location of Eden (2:8-14).** Eden might have been located in the mountains of Ararat or near the Persian Gulf (see notes on 2:8-14). Possibilities for the four rivers (2:10-14) exist in either location (see note on 2:11). Eden represented God's presence on earth that was withdrawn at the Fall and reinaugurated at Sinai (see Exod 3:1-6; 24:9-18; 40:34-38).

2:15 ***to tend and watch over:*** The garden required maintenance and oversight. Tending the ***Garden*** was humanity's dignifying work. These roles in God's garden-sanctuary were later applied to God's Tabernacle (see Lev 8:35; Num 3:5-10; 4:46-49).

2:17 ***except*** (literally *but you must not eat*): This prohibition is given in the same legal format as Israel's Ten Commandments (see Exod 20:1-17; Deut 5:6-21). The Lord built law and obedience into the fabric of his covenant relationship with humanity. • ***the knowledge of good and evil:*** See note on 2:9. • ***you are sure to die:*** The consequences of disobedience would be immediate spiritual death (loss of relationship with God) and eventual physical death (see 3:22-23; Eccl 12:6-7).

2:18-23 As human creation was the climax of ch 1, so human intimacy is the high point of ch 2. God's concern for mutual human support and companionship finds no parallel in ancient Near Eastern literature.

2:18 ***It is not good:*** This is God's first negative assessment of an otherwise excellent creation (1:31). ***The LORD God*** is portrayed as a father who obtains a bride for his son (cp. 24:1-67). • The answer to the man's need is ***a helper who is just right for him***; she is his perfect complement, made in the same image of God (1:26-27), given the same commission (1:28; 2:15), and obligated by the same prohibition (2:17). The man cannot fulfill his created purpose alone.

2:19-20 ***to see what he would call them:*** Following God's example (1:5, 8, 10), the man ***chose a name for each*** of the creatures. In so doing, he was exercising his reign over creation (1:26, 28).

2:19 ***the man:*** Or *Adam,* and so throughout the chapter.

2:21 ***took out one of the man's ribs*** (or *took a part of the man's side*): Cp. 2:23; Eph 5:28.

2:23 Adam recognized the woman as a "helper just right for him" (2:20). His celebration of her in poetry and song observed his unity with her, not their distinctions (cp. 29:14). • Adam declares that "***She will be called 'woman'*** (Hebrew *'ishah*) ***because she was taken from 'man'*** (Hebrew *'ish*)." He understood the nature of their connection (see Eph 5:28-29). Adam had earlier assessed the animals without finding the characteristics he needed in a partner. How different this evaluation is!

2:24 Marriage between a man and a woman is not just a human social construct but is rooted in the created order. • ***a man leaves . . . and is joined:*** Marriage entails a shift of loyalty from parents to spouse. • ***the two are united into one:*** Marriage and its commitments make it the most fundamental covenant relationship observed among humans. Marriage is a powerful image of Israel's covenant with God (Hos 2:14-23) and of Christ's relationship to the church (Eph 5:22-32). Marriage is designed as an inseparable, exclusive relationship between a man and a woman. The family unit it creates is the basic building block of human society.

2:25 ***both naked:*** Prior to the Fall (ch 3), nakedness reflected innocence and trust. After the Fall, it denoted vulnerability and ***shame*** (see 9:22-23; Lev 18:1-23; Isa 47:3). Shame is more than embarrassment; it connotes exploitation and humiliation (see Deut 28:48; Isa 58:7; Jas 2:15-16).

The Ruin of God's Creation (3:1-24)

Temptation to Sin

3 The serpent was the shrewdest of all
the wild animals the LORD God had
made. One day he asked the woman, "Did
God really say you must not eat the fruit
from any of the trees in the garden?"
2"Of course we may eat fruit from the
trees in the garden," the woman replied.
3"It's only the fruit from the tree in the middle of the garden that we are not allowed to
eat. God said, 'You must not eat it or even
touch it; if you do, you will die.' "
4"You won't die!" the serpent replied to
the woman. 5"God knows that your eyes will
be opened as soon as you eat it, and you will
be like God, knowing both good and evil."

Man and Woman Rebel against the Creator

6The woman was convinced. She saw that
the tree was beautiful and its fruit looked
delicious, and she wanted the wisdom it
would give her. So she took some of the fruit
and ate it. Then she gave some to her husband, who was with her, and he ate it, too.
7At that moment their eyes were opened,
and they suddenly felt shame at their nakedness. So they sewed fig leaves together to
cover themselves.

God Interrogates the Man and Woman

8When the cool evening breezes were blowing, the man and his wife heard the LORD
God walking about in the garden. So they
hid from the LORD God among the trees.
9Then the LORD God called to the man,
"Where are you?"
10He replied, "I heard you walking in the
garden, so I hid. I was afraid because I was
naked."
11"Who told you that you were naked?"
the LORD God asked. "Have you eaten from
the tree whose fruit I commanded you not
to eat?"
12The man replied, "It was the woman you
gave me who gave me the fruit, and I ate it."
13Then the LORD God asked the woman,
"What have you done?"

3:1 2 Cor 11:3; Rev 12:9; 20:2
3:2 Gen 2:16
3:3 Gen 2:17; Exod 19:12
3:4 John 8:44; 2 Cor 11:3
3:5 Gen 2:17; 3:22; Isa 14:14; Ezek 28:2
3:6 2 Cor 11:3; 1 Tim 2:14; Jas 1:14-15; 1 Jn 2:16
3:8 Lev 26:12; Deut 23:14; Job 31:33
3:9 Gen 4:9; 18:9
3:10 Deut 5:5
3:12 Prov 28:13
3:13 2 Cor 11:3; 1 Tim 2:14

3:1-24 The rebellion of the man and the woman shattered their unity and harmony with earth, animals, each other, and God.

3:1 Genesis describes the deceiver as a *serpent*, one of the animals God created (see also 3:14 and note). He is later identified as Satan, the great enemy of God's people (Rev 12:9; 20:2). His manipulative language and his disguise as a serpent, ***the shrewdest of all*** creatures, show him as a master deceiver. Satan has various methods for opposing God's people (see 1 Chr 21:1; Zech 3:1-2); deception remains among his key strategies (cp. 2 Cor 11:3, 14). The Hebrew term for shrewd (*'arum*) can be positive ("prudent," Prov 14:8) or negative ("cunning," as here; Job 5:12). It forms a wordplay with "naked" (*'arummim*) in 2:25. Adam and Eve were naked and vulnerable; the serpent was shrewd and cunning. • Probably the serpent *asked the woman* because the prohibition was given to Adam prior to Eve's creation (see 2:16-17). Adam was probably aware of the serpent's cunning, having assessed and named all the animals before Eve was created (2:19-20, 23). • ***Did God really say?*** The deceiver began by twisting God's language to cast doubt on God's goodness. God's original prohibition applied to only one tree (2:16-17), not to all (*any*) of them.

3:2-3 The woman attempted to set the record straight; in the process, she belittled the privileges God had given her and her husband in several ways: (1) She reduced God's "freely eat" (2:16) to *may eat*; (2) she downplayed God's emphasis on the availability of fruit from every tree but one (2:17); (3) she added not touching to God's prohibition against eating (2:17); and (4) she softened the certainty of death (2:17).

3:4-5 *You won't die!* This is the exact negation of God's clear and emphatic words: "you are sure to die" (2:17). The serpent capitalizes on the woman's uncertainty by baldly denying the penalty and quickly diverting her attention to the supposed prize—to ***be like God, knowing both good and evil.*** The deceiver falsely implies that this would be an unqualified good for them. The term rendered God is *Elohim*; it can also mean "divine beings" (i.e., God and the angels; e.g., Ps 29:1; 89:7).

3:6 *She saw . . . she wanted:* The woman made two grave errors. (1) She assumed the right to decide what was and was not good, though God alone has this right; and (2) she coveted God's wisdom (see Deut 5:21). • ***her husband . . . with her:*** Although Scripture is clear about the woman's central role in the Fall (cp. 1 Tim 2:14), the man was clearly present and culpable as well. He comes to center stage in the verses that follow and in biblical theology. The consequence of his sin for the entire human race was immense. The Good News is that in Jesus Christ, the "second Adam," God has made salvation universally available (Rom 5:12-21).

3:7 *Shame* is opposite to the naked innocence Adam and Eve enjoyed prior to their rebellion (2:25). Their relationship with one another and with God was fractured. • ***sewed fig leaves together:*** These covered their physical bodies, but not their shame. They could not mend their broken relationships (see also 3:21 and note).

3:8 *When the cool evening breezes were blowing:* The Hebrew has traditionally been interpreted as referring to the cool part of the day, most likely the evening. Others think that the language refers to a powerful manifestation of God's presence (a *theophany;* see Exod 19:16-25; 1 Sam 7:10) as a storm. If this view is correct, the man and the woman were hiding from the sound of the Lord appearing in judgment (see 2 Sam 5:24; Ps 29). • ***the man:*** Or *Adam*, and so throughout the chapter. • God put ***trees*** in the garden as an environment for humanity to enjoy fellowship with God. Now the man and woman used them to evade the divine presence.

3:9-10 *Where are you?* The true intent of this rhetorical question is revealed in the man's answer (3:10). The real question was, why are you hiding? (cp. 4:9-10). • ***I was afraid because I was naked:*** Modesty was not the issue. The shame brought on by rebellion drove Adam and his wife to hide. Possibly they also feared punishment (see note on 3:8).

3:12 *It was the woman you gave me:* Rather than confessing, the man became evasive. He blamed the woman for giving him the fruit and God for giving him the woman.

3:13 *What have you done?* is another rhetorical question that is really an exclamation of horror (cp. 4:10). • ***The serpent deceived me:*** As the man implicated the woman (3:12), the woman accused the serpent. The serpent did play

3:14
Deut 28:15
Isa 65:25

3:15
John 8:44
Rom 16:20
Heb 2:14
[j]*zera'* (2233)
›Gen 12:7

3:16
1 Cor 11:3
Eph 5:22
1 Tim 2:15

3:17
Job 5:7
Eccl 1:3
Rom 8:20-22

"The serpent deceived me," she replied. "That's why I ate it."

God Indicts and Convicts

14Then the LORD God said to the serpent,

"Because you have done this, you are
cursed
more than all animals, domestic and
wild.
You will crawl on your belly,
groveling in the dust as long as you live.
15 And I will cause hostility between you
and the woman,
and between your [j]offspring and her
[j]offspring.
He will strike your head,
and you will strike his heel."

16Then he said to the woman,

"I will sharpen the pain of your
pregnancy,
and in pain you will give birth.
And you will desire to control your
husband,
but he will rule over you."

17And to the man he said,

ADAM (2:4–3:24)

Gen 1:26-31; 4:25–5:5
Hos 6:6-7
Luke 3:38
Rom 5:12-21
1 Cor 15:22, 45-49
1 Tim 2:13-14

Adam was the first man, the father of the human race. God created the first couple in his image to populate the earth and rule the created order (1:26-31). God made Adam from earth and breathed life into him (2:7); he was to cultivate the garden (2:15), name the animals (2:19-20), and follow God's instructions (1:28; 2:16-17). God created the woman as a companion and helper for Adam (2:18-22). Eve's creation from Adam's rib portrays the unity that God intended for man and woman in marriage (2:23-25).

After the serpent deceived Eve into rejecting God's rule, Adam also rebelled (3:1-6). Their willful disobedience disrupted their relationship (3:7) and separated them from God. God looked for Adam after his rebellion; he was hiding among the trees, already aware of his alienation (3:8). When God questioned him, Adam blamed Eve and, by implication, God (3:12). Adam's rebellion brought hardship in governing the earth as well as physical and spiritual death (3:17-19, 22). God provided animal skins to cover Adam and Eve (3:21), and promised that Eve's offspring would defeat Satan (3:15; see Rom 16:20; Rev 12:1-9; 20:1-10).

Adam was a historical individual (4:25; 5:1-5; 1 Chr 1:1; Hos 6:7; Luke 3:38; Rom 5:14; 1 Cor 15:22, 45; 1 Tim 2:13-14; Jude 1:14) who represents humanity as a whole. God's mandates (1:26-30) and curses (3:16-19) affected not only Adam and Eve, but the entire human race. Adam represents the separation from God that all humanity experiences.

The apostle Paul contrasted those represented by Adam, the first man, with those who follow Christ, the "last Adam" (1 Cor 15:45-50; see Rom 5:12-21; 8:5-11, 20-22). Those represented by Adam live only in him; they partake of his sin, his alienation from God and creation, and his spiritual death. Those who follow Christ live by faith in him. They are recreated in Christ's image and become "new people" who partake of a new creation (see Rom 8:29; 1 Cor 15:49; 2 Cor 5:17). The barriers Adam raised are removed by Christ (Rom 5:1; 2 Cor 5:19; Gal 3:27-28; 6:15; Eph 2:14-16); Christ restores what Adam lost.

a role and would be punished (3:14), but that did not release the woman or the man from their guilt.

3:14-19 The parties were judged in the order of their transgression—serpent, woman, man. Each received a punishment unique to his or her situation, and each had a key relationship altered. God is principled in judgment, not fickle; each punishment is proportionate to the offense.

3:14 ***to the serpent:*** Though later revelation identifies the deceiver as Satan, it is the created animal who was cursed, like the ground (3:17). • ***Groveling in the dust*** is a posture of humiliation and defeat (Ps 72:9; Mic 7:17).

3:15 ***hostility:*** The prophet Isaiah envisions the day when the Messiah's kingdom will restore all of creation to a harmonious state like the Garden of Eden before humans sinned (see Isa 11:8). • ***her offspring*** (literally *her seed*): This collective noun can refer to a single descendant or many. The ancient Near Eastern concept of corporate solidarity (e.g., "you and your descendants," 28:14) is also behind this description of the ongoing hostility that would exist between humans and snakes. The pattern is set using singular terms (***He . . . you***). Christian interpreters have traditionally understood this verse as a prophecy of Christ, the seed of Abraham and the culmination of the woman's seed (Gal 3:16; 4:4). • ***strike*** (Or *bruise*, in both occurrences): The striking of ***his heel*** is a reference to the suffering of God's servant (see Isa 53), while striking the serpent's ***head***—a more definitive blow—is ultimately fulfilled in Christ's death, resurrection, and final victory over Satan (1 Cor 15:55-57; Rev 12:7-9; 20:7-10).

3:16 Judgment falls on the woman's unique role of childbearing and on her relationship with her husband. • ***And you will desire to control your husband, but he will rule over you*** (Or *And though you will have desire for your husband, / he will rule over you*): The marriage relationship now included an element of antagonism rather than just security and fulfillment. New life in Christ allows for the restoration of a man and a woman's marriage relationship (Eph 5:18-32; cp. Matt 20:25-28).

3:17-19 God highlighted his original

"Since you listened to your wife and ate
from the tree
whose fruit I commanded you not to
eat,
the ground is cursed because of you.
All your life you will struggle to
scratch a living from it.
18 It will grow thorns and thistles for you,
though you will eat of its grains.
19 By the sweat of your brow
will you have food to eat
until you return to the ground
from which you were made.
For you were made from dust,
and to dust you will return."

Expulsion and Hope

20 Then the man—Adam—named his wife
Eve, because she would be the mother of all
who live. 21 And the LORD God made clothing from animal skins for Adam and his
wife.
22 Then the LORD God said, "Look, the
human beings have become like us, knowing both good and evil. What if they reach
out, take fruit from the tree of life, and eat
it? Then they will live [k]forever!" 23 So the
LORD God banished them from the Garden
of Eden, and he sent Adam out to cultivate
the ground from which he had been made.
24 After sending them out, the LORD God stationed mighty [a]cherubim to the east of the
Garden of Eden. And he placed a flaming
sword that flashed back and forth to guard
the way to the tree of life.

Results of Rebellion (4:1-24)

Cain and Abel

4 Now Adam had sexual relations with
his wife, Eve, and she became pregnant. When she gave birth to Cain, she said,
"With the LORD's help, I have produced a
man!" 2 Later she gave birth to his brother
and named him Abel.
When they grew up, Abel became a shepherd, while Cain cultivated the ground.
3 When it was time for the harvest, Cain
presented some of his crops as a gift to the
LORD. 4 Abel also brought a gift—the best
of the firstborn lambs from his flock. The
LORD accepted Abel and his gift, 5 but he did
not accept Cain and his gift. This made Cain
very angry, and he looked dejected.
6 "Why are you so angry?" the LORD asked
Cain. "Why do you look so dejected? 7 You
will be accepted if you do what is right. But
if you refuse to do what is right, then watch
out! Sin is crouching at the door, eager to

3:18 Job 31:40; Heb 6:8
3:19 Gen 2:7; Ps 90:3; 104:29; Eccl 12:7; 1 Cor 15:47
3:20 2 Cor 11:3; 1 Tim 2:13
3:21 2 Cor 5:2-3
3:22 Gen 1:26; [k]*olam* (5769) ‣Gen 9:16
3:24 Ezek 10:1; Rev 2:7; 22:2, 14; [a]*kerub* (3742) ‣Exod 25:18
4:2 Luke 11:50-51
4:3 Lev 2:1-2; Num 18:12
4:4 Exod 13:12; Heb 11:4
4:6 Jon 4:4
4:7 Rom 6:12, 16; Jas 1:15

command ***not to eat*** the fruit by speaking of eating several times in 3:17-19. The judgment affected humanity's ability to get food, and it was proportionate to their offense of eating what had been prohibited. • ***the ground is cursed:*** The relationship of the man to the ground (see note on 2:7) was now antagonistic as judgment fell on his primary role (2:5, 15). He must labor and toil to work the ground, but with diminished productivity. Human sin has broad effects on creation (see 4:12; 6:7; Lev 26; Deut 11:13-17, 28; Rom 8:22).

3:20-24 Soon after they were judged for their sin, Adam and Eve were banished from the garden.

3:20 *Eve* (Hebrew *khawah*) sounds like a Hebrew term (*khayah*) that means "to give life." Following God's pronouncement of Adam's impending death (3:19), Adam expressed hope by giving Eve a name associated with life. Adam's naming of Eve in such close proximity to 3:16 may suggest that the narrator views it as Adam's first act of ruling over the woman after the Fall (see note on 2:19-20).

3:21 God mercifully provided more substantial clothing for Adam and Eve (cp. 3:7) before expelling them into the harsh environment outside the garden.

3:22 ***human beings:*** Or *the man;* Hebrew reads *ha-'adam.* • ***like us:*** The plural probably reflects God's conversation with his angelic court (see note on 1:26). • ***the tree of life . . . live forever!*** Mercifully, God prevented humankind from eating of the tree of life and having to live forever in a fallen state. Through Jesus Christ, however, eternal life is once again made available (see Rev 2:7; 22:2, 14, 19).

3:23 ***So the LORD God banished them from the Garden of Eden:*** Before the Fall, the garden was a sanctuary in which humans could move freely in God's holy presence. Now their sin required expulsion from that environment. This same principle was behind the laws that restricted an Israelite's access to God's presence in the Tabernacle or Temple (e.g., Lev 16:1-2; Num 5:3).

3:24 *Cherubim* are a class of angelic beings that guard access to God's presence (Exod 26:31; Ezek 28:14). • ***east . . . of Eden:*** In Genesis, movement eastward often implies leaving the presence or blessing of God, whether in judgment (see also 4:16), self-aggrandizement (11:2; 13:11), or estrangement (25:6).

4:1 ***Adam:*** Or *the man;* also in 4:25. • ***had sexual relations*** (literally *knew*): In certain contexts, the Hebrew term meaning "to know" is an idiom for sexual knowledge of another person (4:17; 19:33, 35). It is never used of animals, which mate by instinct. • ***With the LORD's help:*** Eve fulfilled her God-given role of procreation despite the negative effects of the Fall (see 3:16, 20). • ***I have produced:*** Or *I have acquired. Cain* (Hebrew *qayin*) sounds like a Hebrew term (*qanah*) that can mean "produce" or "acquire."

4:2 ***his brother . . . Abel:*** The name (Hebrew *habel*) means "breath," "vapor," or "meaningless," anticipating his tragically brief life (cp. Eccl 1:2).

4:3 There was nothing wrong with offering grain to the Lord (Lev 2:14; Deut 26:2-4), but Cain brought only a token gift (*some of his crops*), whereas God requires the first and best (Exod 23:16, 19; 34:22, 26). Cain's heart attitude made his offering inferior to Abel's (cp. Heb 11:4).

4:4-5 ***the best of the firstborn lambs:*** Or *the firstborn of his flock and their fat portions.* Abel was giving God the best animals and the richest parts. Abel's offering, in contrast to Cain's, was the best he had to offer. True worship is a costly privilege.

4:7 ***Sin is crouching at the door . . . you must subdue it:*** Sin is pictured as a vicious animal lying in wait to pounce on Cain (cp. note on 3:16). Either sin will dominate Cain, or Cain will resist the temptation to sin. There is no neutral ground in that conflict.

4:8 Matt 23:35; 1 Jn 3:12
4:9 Gen 3:9
4:10 Num 35:33; Deut 21:1; Heb 12:24
4:11 Deut 27:15-26
4:12 Deut 28:15-24
4:14 Gen 9:6; Job 15:22
4:17 Ps 49:11

control you. But you must subdue it and be
its master."
[8]One day Cain suggested to his brother,
"Let's go out into the fields." And while they
were in the field, Cain attacked his brother,
Abel, and killed him.
[9]Afterward the LORD asked Cain, "Where
is your brother? Where is Abel?"
"I don't know," Cain responded. "Am I my
brother's guardian?"
[10]But the LORD said, "What have you
done? Listen! Your brother's blood cries
out to me from the ground! [11]Now you
are cursed and banished from the ground,
which has swallowed your brother's blood.
[12]No longer will the ground yield good
crops for you, no matter how hard you
work! From now on you will be a homeless
wanderer on the earth."
[13]Cain replied to the LORD, "My punishment is too great for me to bear! [14]You have
banished me from the land and from your
presence; you have made me a homeless wanderer. Anyone who finds me will kill me!"
[15]The LORD replied, "No, for I will give a
sevenfold punishment to anyone who kills
you." Then the LORD put a mark on Cain
to warn anyone who might try to kill him.
[16]So Cain left the LORD's presence and settled in the land of Nod, east of Eden.

The Descendants of Cain

[17]Cain had sexual relations with his wife,
and she became pregnant and gave birth to

Original Sin (3:1-19)

Gen 8:21; Exod 34:7; Job 4:17-21; Ps 51:5; Prov 22:15; Ezek 36:16-36; John 8:1-11; Rom 1:18–3:20; 5:12-21; 1 Cor 15:21-22; Gal 3:22; 5:17-24; Eph 2:1-10; 1 Jn 3:14

Genesis 3 describes how human moral innocence collapsed through rebellion (3:11, 17). What God declared as "very good" (1:31) was no longer completely so. Man and woman ate the fruit that promised knowledge of good and evil and thus broke God's command (2:17). Worse, they tried to become like God (3:5) and thus fell from their sinless state. Alienated from God, one another, and creation, they also became subject to death.

The term "original sin" denotes sin's complete, universal infiltration into individual lives and human society as a result of human rebellion. When the first man and woman ate the fruit in disobedience to God, they forfeited their own innocence and that of their children, the entire human race (Rom 5:12-14; 1 Cor 15:21-22, 45-49). All humans are "fallen," born in sin, predisposed to sin (8:21; Job 4:17-21; Ps 51:5; 103:10; 143:2; Prov 20:9), and awaiting death. As people yield to their inherited predisposition to sin, they become responsible for their own wrongdoing (Eccl 7:20; Rom 3:23).

The first man, Adam, introduced sin, but the "second Adam," Jesus Christ, is sin's antidote (1 Cor 15:3; 2 Cor 5:21). When Christ died as Redeemer, he made God's salvation from sin available to all (John 3:16; Rom 1:16).

4:8 The effects of the Fall on human relationships are tragically expressed in the first murder. • The word ***brother*** is used seven times in 4:2-11, highlighting Cain's fratricide in the face of familial responsibility. • ***Let's go out into the fields:*** As in Samaritan Pentateuch, Greek and Syriac versions, and Latin Vulgate; Masoretic Text lacks this phrase.

4:9 ***Where is your brother?*** The questions God asked Cain (4:6, 9, 10) recall those that God asked Cain's parents (3:9-13). In both cases, humans put up evasive answers (cp. 3:12-13). Cain's answer is shockingly defiant—another clue that the problem with his token offering was the attitude that lay behind it.

4:10 ***What have you done?*** is more an expression of horror and rebuke than a fact-finding question (cp. 3:13). • Abel's ***blood*** is personified as a legal witness that ***cries out*** against Cain. • ***from the ground:*** See note on 4:11-12.

4:11-12 As with his father (cp. 3:9-12, 17-19), Cain's interrogation (4:9-10) was followed by God's verdict. Adam's sin had already caused ***the ground*** to be cursed. Now Cain was ***cursed*** and ***banished*** from the land he farmed because he had contaminated it with innocent blood. • ***homeless wanderer:*** Cain was condemned to ceaseless roving in a land that would provide neither sustenance nor security. The effects of sin were escalating.

4:13-14 For Cain, eviction ***from the land***—the domain of his vocation as a farmer (see 4:2; cp. 3:23)—amounted to exile from God's ***presence.*** The Israelites were warned that unfaithfulness to the Sinai covenant would similarly result in eviction from the Promised Land and from God's presence in the Temple (see, e.g., Lev 26:27-32).

4:13 ***My punishment:*** Or *My sin.*

4:15 ***Sevenfold punishment*** was the full weight of justice. Cain complained that his punishment was too great, but the full sentence that would fall on anyone who committed Cain's crime against him shows how gracious the Lord was to Cain. Cain deserved death (see 9:5-6). • The ***mark*** graciously provided protection following Cain's judgment (cp. 3:21).

4:16 ***Nod*** means "wandering." The name speaks more of Cain's fate (see 4:12, 14) than of a specific geographical area (the location is unknown). Cain's sin denied him rest and a sense of belonging. • Cain's exile ***east of Eden*** is another point of connection with Adam's story (cp. 3:24). Cain did not learn from his father's mistake, so he also suffered estrangement from the ground and exile to the east (see note on 3:24).

4:17–5:32 These back-to-back genealogies do more than list names for the record. They contrast the ways that human culture spread, some in rebellion against God (Cain, 4:17-24) and some in obedience to God (Seth, 4:25–5:32). In Genesis, the history of the rejected branch is generally explained before carrying forward the line that led to Israel. Two points of contrast are especially worth noting: (1) Lamech, the seventh from Adam through the lineage

Enoch. Then Cain founded a city, which he
named Enoch, after his son. [18]Enoch had a
son named Irad. Irad became the father of
Mehujael. Mehujael became the father of
Methushael. Methushael became the father
of Lamech.

[19]Lamech married two women. The
first was named Adah, and the second was
Zillah. [20]Adah gave birth to Jabal, who was
the first of those who raise livestock and
live in tents. [21]His brother's name was Jubal, the first of all who play the harp and
flute. [22]Lamech's other wife, Zillah, gave
birth to a son named Tubal-cain. He became an expert in forging tools of bronze
and iron. Tubal-cain had a sister named
Naamah. [23]One day Lamech said to his
wives,

"Adah and Zillah, hear my voice;
listen to me, you wives of Lamech.
I have killed a man who attacked me,
a young man who wounded me.
[24]If someone who kills Cain is punished
seven times,
then the one who kills me will be
punished seventy-seven times!"

Epilogue: The Birth of Seth (4:25-26)

[25]Adam had sexual relations with his wife
again, and she gave birth to another son.
She named him Seth, for she said, "God has
granted me another son in place of Abel,
whom Cain killed." [26]When Seth grew up,
he had a son and named him Enosh. At that
time people first began to worship the LORD
by name.

3. THE ACCOUNT OF ADAM'S DESCENDANTS (5:1–6:8)

Human Identity Restated

5 This is the written account of the descendants of Adam. When God created
human beings, he made them to be like himself. [2]He created them male and female, and
he blessed them and called them "human."

Genealogy: Adam to Noah

[3]When Adam was 130 years old, he
became the father of a son who was just

4:23 Lev 19:18; Deut 32:35
4:25 Gen 4:8; 5:3; 1 Chr 1:1; Luke 3:38
4:26 Gen 12:8; 1 Kgs 18:24; Joel 2:32; Zeph 3:9; Acts 2:21
5:1 Gen 1:26; 6:9; 1 Chr 1:1
5:2 Gen 1:27; *Matt 19:4; *Mark 10:6
5:3-32 1 Chr 1:1-3; Luke 3:36-38
5:3 Gen 1:26; 4:25; 1 Cor 15:49

of Cain, is the main focus of the first genealogy. Like his ancestor, Lamech took human life and had to live in constant fear of death as a consequence (4:23-24). By contrast, Enoch, the seventh from Adam through the lineage of Seth (see 4:25–5:32), lived in a way that pleased God and avoided death altogether (5:24). (2) Advances in human culture and technology came through Cain's line (the first city, livestock, shelter, metallurgy, music), but the effects of sin still dominated. No technological advances are mentioned in Seth's line; instead, people began "to worship the LORD" (4:26) and to find "favor with the LORD" (see 6:8).

4:17 Cain's *wife* was probably one of his sisters (5:4). Cain's marriage to his sister would not have caused genetic problems so early in the development of the human gene pool. • Cain was condemned to be a wanderer. Perhaps he *founded a city* in rebellion against that verdict, seeking to defend himself by enclosing it in walls. Naming it *after his son* reflects a tendency among those who rebel against God to idolize humanity and its achievements.

4:18 *the father of:* Or *the ancestor of,* and so throughout the verse. Hebrew genealogies do not necessarily list every single generation.

4:19 Marrying *two women* was contrary to God's ideal pattern for marriage (2:24), and might be another manifestation of the arrogance and rebellion of Cain's descendants.

4:20-22 Technological advancement masks increasing self-assertion and distance from God (see note on 4:14–5:32).

4:23-24 Lamech's chilling taunt shows the further escalation of sin's effects on humanity. Cain's line had reached a crescendo of violence with Lamech's contempt for life. In his arrogance, he put his deed into poetic verse. • ***punished seventy-seven times!*** God warned that anyone who tried to kill Cain would experience the full weight of justice (4:15). Lamech's declaration that anyone who harmed him would receive an even more severe penalty is a claim to be accountable to no one, including God.

4:25–5:32 The story returns to Adam and follows the line of Seth, whose lineage led to Abraham and the Israelite nation.

4:25 ***another son . . . in place of Abel:*** Cain (4:8-16) and Lamech (4:19-24) illustrate sin's consequences; the birth of Seth brought renewed hope. See also note on 5:1-2. • ***Seth*** probably means "granted"; the name may also mean "appointed."

4:26 ***Enosh*** means "humankind." In the OT, the term is often used in poetic texts that emphasize human mortality, frailty, and weakness (e.g., Ps 144:3, "mere mortals"). Enosh was born at the time when people began to *worship the LORD by name* (literally *call on the name of the LORD*). In Genesis, that meant calling on the name of the Lord through sacrifice and prayer (similar Hebrew terminology is found in 12:8; 13:4; 21:33; 26:25).

5:1-32 The genealogies of Genesis go beyond simply recording history. By selective information and by structure, they communicate spiritual truth. The genealogies highlight God's blessing, authenticate the family heritage of important individuals, and hold the Genesis narrative together by showing familial continuity. Adam's genealogy through Seth traces ten generations to Noah (see 1 Chr 1:1-4; Luke 3:36-38), with the flood intervening before another ten generations from Noah to Abram. The number ten indicates completeness (ten plagues, Exod 7:8–11:10; Ten Commandments, Exod 20:2-17). Noah closed history before the flood, and Abram inaugurated a new era.

5:1-2 This is the prologue to the second *account* in Genesis (5:1–6:8; see note on 2:4); it connects God's purpose in creation with Seth's line rather than Cain's (4:17-24).

5:1 ***written account:*** Although the previous account (2:4–4:26) focused on Adam, Eve, and their first children, it was technically "the account of the heavens and the earth." Genesis 5:1-32 is a more typical genealogy. • ***human beings:*** Or *man;* Hebrew reads *'adam;* similarly in 5:2. • ***like himself:*** See 1:26 and note.

5:2 ***male and female . . . "human"*** (Hebrew *'adam*): See 1:27 and note. • ***blessed them:*** See 1:28 and note.

5:3 ***just like him—in his very image:*** The image and likeness of God (see note on 1:26) is preserved in human beings despite sin. Adam's sinful nature was also carried forward (Rom 5:12-14).

5:5
Gen 2:17
Heb 9:27

5:18
Jude 1:14

5:22
Gen 6:9; 48:15

5:24
2 Kgs 2:1, 11
Ps 73:24
Heb 11:5

5:29
Gen 3:17
Rom 8:20

5:32
Gen 7:6; 9:18

6:1
Gen 1:28

6:2
[b]*ben 'elohim* (1121, 0430)
‣Job 1:6

6:3
Ps 78:39
1 Pet 3:20

like him—in his very image. He named
his son Seth. 4After the birth of Seth,
Adam lived another 800 years, and he
had other sons and daughters. 5Adam
lived 930 years, and then he died.
6When Seth was 105 years old, he became
the father of Enosh. 7After the birth of
Enosh, Seth lived another 807 years, and
he had other sons and daughters. 8Seth
lived 912 years, and then he died.
9When Enosh was 90 years old, he became
the father of Kenan. 10After the birth of
Kenan, Enosh lived another 815 years,
and he had other sons and daughters.
11Enosh lived 905 years, and then he died.
12When Kenan was 70 years old, he
became the father of Mahalalel. 13After
the birth of Mahalalel, Kenan lived
another 840 years, and he had other
sons and daughters. 14Kenan lived
910 years, and then he died.
15When Mahalalel was 65 years old, he
became the father of Jared. 16After the
birth of Jared, Mahalalel lived another
830 years, and he had other sons and
daughters. 17Mahalalel lived 895 years,
and then he died.
18When Jared was 162 years old, he became
the father of Enoch. 19After the birth of
Enoch, Jared lived another 800 years, and
he had other sons and daughters. 20Jared
lived 962 years, and then he died.
21When Enoch was 65 years old, he became
the father of Methuselah. 22After the
birth of Methuselah, Enoch lived in
close fellowship with God for another
300 years, and he had other sons and
daughters. 23Enoch lived 365 years,
24walking in close fellowship with God.
Then one day he disappeared, because
God took him.
25When Methuselah was 187 years old, he
became the father of Lamech. 26After
the birth of Lamech, Methuselah lived
another 782 years, and he had other
sons and daughters. 27Methuselah lived
969 years, and then he died.
28When Lamech was 182 years old, he
became the father of a son. 29Lamech
named his son Noah, for he said, "May
he bring us relief from our work and the
painful labor of farming this ground
that the LORD has cursed." 30After the
birth of Noah, Lamech lived another
595 years, and he had other sons and
daughters. 31Lamech lived 777 years,
and then he died.
32By the time Noah was 500 years old,
he was the father of Shem, Ham, and
Japheth.

Corruption of the Human Race

6 Then the people began to multiply on
the earth, and daughters were born to
them. 2The [b]sons of God saw the beautiful
women and took any they wanted as their
wives. 3Then the LORD said, "My Spirit will
not put up with humans for such a long time,

5:5 ***he died:*** Death indeed came to Adam (see 2:17; 3:18-19) and his descendants (see Rom 5:12-14). Cain's violence is omitted (see 4:8, 15, 23-24) and key figures in Seth's line live in hope (5:29).

5:6 ***the father of:*** Or *the ancestor of;* also in 5:9, 12, 15, 18, 21, 25. Hebrew genealogies do not necessarily list every single generation.

5:7 ***After the birth of:*** Or *After the birth of this ancestor of;* also in 5:10, 13, 16, 19, 22, 26 (see note on 5:6).

5:22 ***Enoch lived in close fellowship with God*** (literally *Enoch walked with God*; also in 5:24): Enoch's position as seventh from Adam in the genealogy strikes a contrast with Lamech, the seventh from Adam in the line of Cain (see note on 4:17–5:32).

5:24 Unlike all other sons of Adam, Enoch did not succumb to death; rather, ***he disappeared, because God took him*** (cp. 2 Kgs 2:9-12; see also Heb 11:5).

5:27 ***969 years:*** This statement and the numbers given in 5:25, 28 and 7:6 mean that Methuselah died in the year of the flood.

5:28-29 As with Enoch (5:21-24), the normal genealogical formula is interrupted to highlight important theological information about Noah. ***Noah*** sounds like a Hebrew term (*nakham*) that can mean "relief" or "comfort," and another term (*nuakh*) that means "rest." As the first person born after Adam's death (see note on 5:5), Noah prompted his father ***Lamech*** to hope that the curse brought on by Adam's sin (3:17) might be lifted. See 8:21; 2 Cor 1:3-7; 2 Thes 2:16-17.

6:1-8 Human wickedness reached a climax, prompting God to send the flood to destroy all living things. A glimmer of hope appears in God's favor toward Noah (6:8).

6:1-2 The ***sons of God*** have generally been understood as fallen angels (cp. the same Hebrew phrase in Job 1:6; 2:1; 38:7; Ps 29:1; 89:7). This interpretation is prominent in ancient Jewish and Christian literature (e.g., *1 Enoch* 6:1–7:6; Justin Martyr, *Apology* 2.5) and is apparently supported by the NT (see 1 Pet 3:18-20; 2 Pet 2:4; Jude 1:6-7). Some interpreters do not believe that God would permit angels to procreate with humans and doubt that the above NT texts should be read in this way. Another possibility is that *sons of God* refers to the righteous descendants of Seth, while the ***beautiful women*** (6:2, literally *daughters of men;* also in 6:4) were female descendants of Cain's wicked line. This interpretation is in harmony with 4:17–5:32, but is weakened by the language of 6:1-2, which seems to refer to the daughters of humanity in general, not the daughters of Cain specifically. Others believe that *sons of God* refers to tyrannical human kings (possibly demon-possessed) who took Lamech's polygamy (4:19) to a new height of wickedness by seizing the daughters of the righteous. Language reminiscent of 3:6 (***saw . . . took***) shows the rebellious nature of this act.

6:3 ***will not put up with*** (Greek version reads *will not remain in*): Many think that this is an announcement of God's decision to withdraw the restraining influence of his ***Spirit*** from human

for they are only mortal flesh. In the future,
their normal lifespan will be no more than
120 years."
4In those days, and for some time after,
giant Nephilites lived on the earth, for whenever the sons of God had intercourse with
women, they gave birth to children who
became the heroes and famous warriors of
ancient times.
5The LORD observed the extent of human
wickedness on the earth, and he saw that
everything they thought or imagined was
consistently and totally evil. 6So the LORD
was sorry he had ever made them and put
them on the earth. It broke his heart. 7And
the LORD said, "I will wipe this human race I
have [c]created from the face of the earth. Yes,
and I will destroy every living thing—all the
people, the large animals, the small animals
that scurry along the ground, and even the
birds of the sky. I am sorry I ever made them."
8But Noah found favor with the LORD.

4. THE ACCOUNT OF NOAH'S FAMILY (6:9–9:29)

The Story of Noah

9This is the account of Noah and his family.
Noah was a righteous man, the only [d]blame-
less person living on earth at the time, and
he walked in close fellowship with God.
10Noah was the father of three sons: Shem,
Ham, and Japheth.
11Now God saw that the earth had become corrupt and was filled with violence.

6:4 Num 13:33; Jude 1:6-7
6:5 Ps 14:1-3
6:6 Exod 32:14; Num 23:19; 1 Sam 15:11, 35; 2 Sam 24:16
6:7 Deut 29:20; [c]*bara'* (1254) ‣Ps 51:10
6:8 Exod 33:17
6:9 Job 1:1; Ezek 14:14; [d]*tamim* (8549) ‣Gen 17:1
6:11 Deut 31:29; Judg 2:19; Ezek 8:17

NOAH (6:8-22)

Gen 5:28–10:1; 1 Chr 1:4; Isa 54:9; Ezek 14:12-20; Matt 24:37-38; Luke 3:36; 17:26-27; Heb 11:7; 1 Pet 3:20-21; 2 Pet 2:5

Noah was the son of Lamech, a descendant of Seth (5:3-29). Lamech might have hoped that Noah (whose name means "rest" or "relief") would ease the curse of hardship in working the ground (see note on 5:29). God used Noah to help relieve the world of evil.

God intended to destroy creation because of pervasive human wickedness (6:1-7; see Matt 24:37-39; Luke 17:26-27), but he decided to preserve Noah (6:8). God gave Noah, a righteous and blameless man (6:9), precise instructions for building the ark in which only the eight people of his family would be saved, along with every kind of creature (6:14–8:19). When Noah and his family finally emerged from the ark after the flood, Noah pleased God by building an altar and sacrificing burnt offerings. God promised that he would never again flood the whole earth or disrupt the sequence of the seasons, despite human sin (8:20–9:17).

Noah's sons were Shem, Ham, and Japheth. All the nations of the earth descended from them (9:18-19). When Noah became drunk on wine from his vineyard, his sons and their descendants were cursed or blessed in accord with how they responded to him (9:22-27). Noah lived for 950 years, including 350 years after the flood (9:28-29); he is an example of righteousness, obedience, courage, and faith (see Ezek 14:12-20; Heb 11:7; 2 Pet 2:5).

society and allow human wickedness to run its full course. Others think it means that God would withdraw his life-giving breath from humans at an earlier age (*ruakh*, the Hebrew term for "spirit," can also mean "breath"; see 6:17; 7:22; see also Ps 104:29-30). • ***normal lifespan will be no more than 120 years*** (literally *his days will be 120 years*): It is possible that this was a new restriction on the number of years individuals would generally be allowed to live (so the NLT). However, for generations after the flood, humans lived well beyond 120 years (see, e.g., 11:10-26). An alternative interpretation sees this as a 120-year grace period before the arrival of the flood (see Jon 3:4; Matt 24:37-38; 1 Pet 3:20; 2 Pet 2:5).

6:4 ***giant Nephilites*** (Hebrew *nepilim*): The term may mean "fallen ones." The context implies that they were the offspring of the "sons of God" and would be destroyed in the flood. Numbers 13:31-33 uses the same term to describe other giants who were hostile toward God's people and would also be destroyed (see also Deut 2:11, which connects the Anakite *nepilim* with another group called the *repa'im*).

6:5 ***everything they thought or imagined*** (literally *every intention of the thoughts of their hearts*): In the OT, the heart is the core of volition, thought, and morality (see Prov 4:23). Wicked actions stem from a corrupt inner life. • ***consistently and totally evil:*** Strong language captures the pervasiveness, depth, and persistence of human wickedness. Human nature continued to be corrupt even after the flood (see 8:21).

6:6 ***the LORD was sorry:*** The extent of human wickedness made the Lord regret having created them (see also 6:7; cp. 1 Sam 15:11, 35). • ***It broke his heart:*** The evil in humanity's heart (6:5) pained God greatly. Sending the flood was a heart-wrenching act on God's part.

6:7 ***wipe . . . from the . . . earth:*** As Adam and Eve were banished from the garden-sanctuary (3:23), all of humankind would be expunged from God's good creation. • ***every living thing:*** Human sin had so corrupted the earth that judgment fell on the animals and birds over which they had dominion (see 1:28 and note). The special role of humans in the created order (1:28-30) means that nature is affected by human moral choices (see 8:1; Job 38:41; Hos 4:3; Rom 8:19-22).

6:8 ***Noah*** and his godly life stand in stark contrast to the sinfulness of the rest of the people.

6:9 ***the account:*** See note on 2:4 • ***a righteous man, the only blameless person:*** The text does not claim that Noah was without sin (see Rom 5:12-14). Noah's righteousness and blamelessness came about because ***he walked in close fellowship with God.*** See also 7:1; 17:1; Heb 11:7.

6:11-13 See 6:5-7. • ***violence*** (Hebrew *khamas*): Murder had especially corrupted the line of Cain (4:8, 23-24).

6:12 Ps 14:1-3
6:13 Isa 34:1-4; Ezek 7:2-3
6:14 Exod 2:3; 1 Pet 3:20
6:17 Ps 29:10; 2 Pet 2:5
6:18 Gen 9:9-16; 17:7; 19:12
6:20 Gen 7:3
6:21 Gen 1:29
6:22 Gen 7:5; Exod 40:16
7:1 Gen 6:18; Matt 24:38; Luke 17:26-27; Heb 11:7; 1 Pet 3:20
7:2 Lev 11:1-47; Deut 14:3-20; Ezek 44:23
7:4 Gen 6:7, 13
7:6 Gen 5:32
7:7 Gen 6:18

12God observed all this corruption in the
world, for everyone on earth was corrupt.
13So God said to Noah, "I have decided to
destroy all living creatures, for they have
filled the earth with violence. Yes, I will
wipe them all out along with the earth!
14"Build a large boat from cypress wood
and waterproof it with tar, inside and out.
Then construct decks and stalls throughout
its interior. 15Make the boat 450 feet long,
75 feet wide, and 45 feet high. 16Leave an
18-inch opening below the roof all the way
around the boat. Put the door on the side,
and build three decks inside the boat—
lower, middle, and upper.
17"Look! I am about to cover the earth
with a flood that will destroy every living
thing that breathes. Everything on earth
will die. 18But I will confirm my covenant
with you. So enter the boat—you and your
wife and your sons and their wives. 19Bring
a pair of every kind of animal—a male and a
female—into the boat with you to keep them
alive during the flood. 20Pairs of every kind
of bird, and every kind of animal, and every
kind of small animal that scurries along the
ground, will come to you to be kept alive.
21And be sure to take on board enough food
for your family and for all the animals."
22So Noah did everything exactly as God
had commanded him.

The Universal Flood

7 When everything was ready, the LORD
said to Noah, "Go into the boat with all
your family, for among all the people of the
earth, I can see that you alone are righteous.
2Take with you seven pairs—male and female—of each animal I have approved for
eating and for sacrifice, and take one pair
of each of the others. 3Also take seven pairs
of every kind of bird. There must be a male
and a female in each pair to ensure that all
life will survive on the earth after the flood.
4Seven days from now I will make the rains
pour down on the earth. And it will rain
for forty days and forty nights, until I have
wiped from the earth all the living things I
have created."
5So Noah did everything as the LORD commanded him.
6Noah was 600 years old when the flood
covered the earth. 7He went on board the
boat to escape the flood—he and his wife

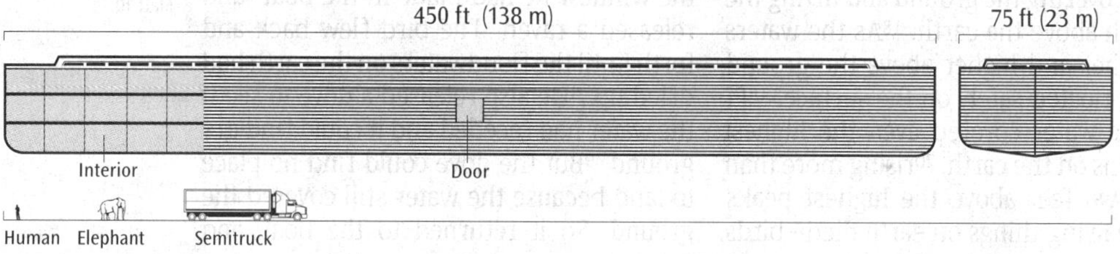

▲ **Noah's Ark (6:14-16).** An ark built to the dimensions specified in Genesis would have been immense. Its ratio of length to width (6 to 1) is the most stable known and is used for the design of modern tankers and freight-hauling ships. The ark was able to carry 20,000 tons of cargo; the required number of young adult land animals would have occupied less than half of the available space. The design given was perfect for the ark's function.

6:14 ***a large boat:*** Traditionally rendered *an ark*, this was a long rectangular barge designed for survival, not for navigation. The Hebrew word *tebah* is used again only of the basket in which the baby Moses was floated on the Nile (Exod 2:3, 5). • ***cypress wood:*** Or *gopher wood.* It is not clear what kind of wood this was. It was possibly from a conifer, such as cypress.

6:15 The ark's dimensions: Hebrew *300 cubits* [138 meters] *long, 50 cubits* [23 meters] *wide, and 30 cubits* [13.8 meters] *high.* This floating barge displaced around 43,300 tons of water.

6:16 ***An 18-inch opening*** (Hebrew *an opening of 1 cubit* [46 centimeters]) ***below the roof*** encircled ***the boat***, providing light and air. • Noah was to build a ***door*** and God would close it (7:16). God was the captain of this peculiar boat with no sail or rudder. God also brought the animals to Noah (6:20).

6:17 ***cover the earth with a flood:*** Some propose that the flood might only have covered the ancient Near East as it was known to Noah or Moses. However, the flood's stated purpose—to ***destroy every living thing that breathes*** (see also 6:7, 11-13; 7:1, 4, 18-23; 8:21)—and its effect of undoing creation (see notes on 1:9-10; 7:11-12) suggest that the flood covered the entire planet (see also 1 Pet 3:20; 2 Pet 2:5; 3:6).

6:18 This first explicit mention of a ***covenant*** in the Bible refers to the unilateral pact that God made with humankind and the world after the flood (see 9:9, 11, 14-17).

6:19-20 God's instructions to Noah repeat the language of creation (***every kind***, cp. 1:24). • ***a male and a female:*** These animals would procreate and repopulate the earth after the flood.

7:2 ***of each animal I have approved for eating and for sacrifice*** (literally *of each clean animal;* similarly in 7:8): In addition to the animals that were to repopulate the earth, these "clean" animals were for food and for Noah's sacrifice after the flood (8:20-21). This passage does not use the precise technical language that is found in the regulations concerning "clean" and "unclean" given to Israel at Sinai (see Lev 11:1-47; Deut 14:3-12), but the underlying concept is the same (perhaps God revealed it directly to Noah).

7:4 The number *forty* is often associated with affliction, trial, or punishment (see Exod 16:35; Judg 13:1; 1 Kgs 19:8; Ezek 4:6; Jon 3:4; Matt 4:2; Acts 1:3).

7:6 ***covered the earth:*** See note on 6:17.

and his sons and their wives. 8With them
were all the various kinds of animals—
those approved for eating and for sacrifice
and those that were not—along with all the
birds and the small animals that scurry
along the ground. 9They entered the boat
in pairs, male and female, just as God had
commanded Noah. 10After seven days, the
waters of the flood came and covered the
earth.

11When Noah was 600 years old, on the
seventeenth day of the second month, all
the underground waters erupted from the
earth, and the rain fell in mighty torrents
from the sky. 12The rain continued to fall
for forty days and forty nights.

13That very day Noah had gone into the
boat with his wife and his sons—Shem,
Ham, and Japheth—and their wives. 14With
them in the boat were pairs of every kind
of animal—domestic and wild, large and
small—along with birds of every kind. 15Two
by two they came into the boat, representing
every living thing that breathes. 16A male
and female of each kind entered, just as
God had commanded Noah. Then the LORD
closed the door behind them.

17For forty days the floodwaters grew
deeper, covering the ground and lifting the
boat high above the earth. 18As the waters
rose higher and higher above the ground,
the boat floated safely on the surface. 19Fi-
nally, the water covered even the highest
mountains on the earth, 20rising more than
twenty-two feet above the highest peaks.
21All the living things on earth died—birds,
domestic animals, wild animals, small animals that scurry along the ground, and all
the people. 22Everything that breathed and
lived on dry land died. 23God wiped out
every living thing on the earth—people, livestock, small animals that scurry along the
ground, and the birds of the sky. All were
destroyed. The only people who survived
were Noah and those with him in the boat.
24And the floodwaters covered the earth for
150 days.

The Floodwaters Recede

8 But God eremembered Noah and all
the wild animals and livestock with
him in the boat. He sent a wind to blow
across the earth, and the floodwaters began to recede. 2The underground waters
stopped flowing, and the torrential rains
from the sky were stopped. 3So the floodwaters gradually receded from the earth.
After 150 days, 4exactly five months from
the time the flood began, the boat came to
rest on the mountains of Ararat. 5Two and
a half months later, as the waters continued
to go down, other mountain peaks became
visible.

6After another forty days, Noah opened
the window he had made in the boat 7and
released a raven. The bird flew back and
forth until the floodwaters on the earth had
dried up. 8He also released a dove to see if
the water had receded and it could find dry
ground. 9But the dove could find no place
to land because the water still covered the
ground. So it returned to the boat, and

7:9 Gen 6:22
7:11 Ps 78:23; Ezek 26:19; Mal 3:10
7:13 1 Pet 3:20; 2 Pet 2:5
7:15 Gen 6:19; 7:9
7:19 Ps 104:6
7:20 2 Pet 3:6
7:23 Matt 24:38-39; Luke 17:26-27; 1 Pet 3:20; 2 Pet 2:5
7:24 Gen 8:3
8:1 Gen 19:29; 30:22; Exod 2:24; 14:21; Job 12:15; Isa 44:27; e*zakar* (2142) ▸Exod 2:24
8:2 Gen 7:4, 12
8:4 Gen 7:20
8:7 Lev 11:15; Deut 14:14; 1 Kgs 17:4; Luke 12:24
8:8 Isa 60:8; Hos 11:11; Matt 10:16

7:8 See note on 7:2.

7:11-12 ***on the seventeenth day of the second month:*** Such information gives the flood account a certain solemnity; it reminds readers that this was a true historical event. • ***underground waters:*** See 2:6. • ***rain fell:*** The flood undid the boundaries established on the second and third days of creation (1:6-13). Elsewhere, the Bible describes God's judgment as an undoing of creation (see Jer 4:23-26; Amos 7:4). • ***forty days and forty nights:*** See note on 7:4.

7:16 ***the LORD closed the door:*** The sovereign Judge took responsibility for the annihilation of all outside the boat and the protection of those within (see also 6:16 and note).

7:17 ***floodwaters grew deeper*** (literally *waters multiplied*): The same word used for the proliferation of humans and animals during creation (see 1:22, 28) is now used ironically of the water that would annihilate them. • ***covering the ground:*** The Hebrew word translated "ground" or "earth" is mentioned eight times in eight verses (7:17-24). The earth is the domain that humankind had polluted and that was now the object of a cleansing deluge.

7:20 ***more than twenty-two feet:*** Hebrew *15 cubits* [6.9 meters].

7:22 ***Everything that . . . lived:*** See note on 6:17.

8:1 ***But God remembered:*** This structural and theological center of the flood story does not mean that God had at any point forgotten Noah. This is covenant language reflecting God's faithfulness to his promise to ensure the safety of his covenant partner (cp. 6:18; 9:15-16; Exod 2:24; Lev 26:42, 45). • ***wind:*** The same word is translated "Spirit" in 1:2. This and other parallels (see 9:1-2) suggest that the restoration of the earth after the flood was effectively a new creation.

8:2 ***underground waters . . . torrential rains:*** See note on 7:11-12.

8:4 ***exactly five months from the time the flood began:*** Literally *on the seventeenth day of the seventh month;* see 7:11. • ***mountains of Ararat:*** These mountains might be in the region of Ararat (Urartu) southeast of the Black Sea near Lake Van, which touches parts of eastern Turkey, Armenia, and Iran. There is a Mount Ararat (*Agri Dag*) in Turkey, but this verse only identifies the region, not a specific mountain.

8:5 ***Two and a half months later:*** Literally *On the first day of the tenth month;* see 7:11 and note on 8:4. • ***the waters continued to go down:*** Another parallel with the creation week (see 1:9) suggests that the earth's restoration was effectively a new creation (see note on 8:1).

8:7 The ***raven*** is the largest member of the crow family, and was among Noah's unclean animals (Lev 11:15; Deut 14:14). As a scavenger and carrion eater, it was able to sustain itself without returning to the boat.

8:13
Gen 5:32
8:16
Gen 7:13
8:17
Gen 1:22
8:20
Gen 4:4; 12:7; 13:18; 22:2
8:21
Gen 3:17
Exod 29:18, 25
Lev 1:9, 13
Isa 54:9

Noah held out his hand and drew the dove
back inside. [10]After waiting another seven
days, Noah released the dove again. [11]This
time the dove returned to him in the evening with a fresh olive leaf in its beak. Then
Noah knew that the floodwaters were almost gone. [12]He waited another seven days
and then released the dove again. This time
it did not come back.

[13]Noah was now 601 years old. On the
first day of the new year, ten and a half months after the flood began, the floodwaters had almost dried up from the earth.
Noah lifted back the covering of the boat
and saw that the surface of the ground was
drying. [14]Two more months went by, and at
last the earth was dry!

Noah's Worship and God's Promise

[15]Then God said to Noah, [16]"Leave the boat,
all of you—you and your wife, and your
sons and their wives. [17]Release all the animals—the birds, the livestock, and the small
animals that scurry along the ground—so
they can be fruitful and multiply throughout the earth."

[18]So Noah, his wife, and his sons and their
wives left the boat. [19]And all of the large
and small animals and birds came out of
the boat, pair by pair.

[20]Then Noah built an altar to the LORD,
and there he sacrificed as burnt offerings
the animals and birds that had been approved for that purpose. [21]And the LORD
was pleased with the aroma of the sacrifice

Retribution (6:1–7:24)

Lev 26:14-39
Ps 7:6-17; 57:6; 95:8-11
Prov 6:27-35; 26:27
Mic 2:1-3
Rom 2:5-16
Gal 6:7-8
Heb 10:26-31
12:5-11, 25-29

God gave humans the commission of procreating and caring for the world (1:28). Instead, murder and violence multiplied with humanity's spiritual wickedness (4:8, 23; 6:11-13), resulting in a corrupt world that required cleansing.

The purpose of the flood was to enact God's global cleansing and retribution against evildoers. *Retribution* means "giving what is due" and usually refers to recompense for wrongdoing. Retribution is motivated by the conviction that moral order is woven into the fabric of the world and must be maintained or restored (see Ps 7:14-16; Prov 11:18; 26:27).

God maintains moral order by meting out justice, punishing wickedness, and rewarding right behavior (Gal 6:7). Since God oversees the world, it is never entirely overwhelmed by moral chaos; God holds people accountable for what they do. The judgment and exile of Adam and Eve (3:8-24), Cain's sentence and blood-revenge (4:10-15), and the worldwide flood and annihilation (chs 6–9) are OT examples of God's retribution. They reveal a sovereign God who exacts just punishment in the context of his good intentions for the world (see also Num 16; Deut 30:15-20; Josh 7; Mic 2:1-3).

Retribution is an application of God's righteousness; it purifies the world for his kingdom of peace. Through retribution, the divine King proclaims his universal rule and exercises his justice on all who reject his rule or defy his commands (Deut 7:10; 1 Sam 24:19; Ps 149; Prov 15:25; Mic 5:15; 1 Cor 16:22; Gal 1:8-9; 2 Thes 1:5-10).

For God's people, retribution is his discipline. It is intended to restore covenant fellowship with him (see Isa 44:22; Jer 3:12-14; Lam 3:19-33; Hos 14:1-2; Joel 2:12-13). When God's people experience his chastening, they can respond in hope because God's truth and righteousness will triumph (Ps 58:10-11) and God will redeem and restore his people who trust in him (Lev 26:40-45; Hos 2:2-23).

8:11 Unlike the raven (8:7), the *dove* feeds on vegetation. Since olive trees are not tall, Noah could tell that the water was *almost gone.*

8:13 ***On the first day of the new year, ten and a half months after the flood began*** (literally *On the first day of the first month;* see 7:11): This was two months after the peaks of the mountains first became visible (8:5).

8:14 ***Two more months went by:*** Literally *The twenty-seventh day of the second month arrived;* see note on 8:13. • ***the earth was dry!*** This special word for dry land is uniquely used in connection with the sea to portray God's sovereignty over both domains (see 1:9-10; Exod 14:22, 29; Ps 95:5; Jon 1:9).

8:17 ***be fruitful and multiply:*** See 9:1.

8:20 This first mention of an *altar* in the Bible (see "Altars" at 35:1-15, p. 91) shows Noah's gratitude for having passed through the judgment. • ***sacrificed as burnt offerings:*** The same term is used of the whole burnt offering in Leviticus (Lev 1:3-9); however, it can refer to any offering that is burned. Noah gave this offering to thank and worship God, who had delivered him and his family from the flood. • ***the animals and birds that had been approved for that purpose:*** Literally *every clean animal and every clean bird.*

8:21 ***pleased with the aroma of the sacrifice*** (literally *smelled the sweet aroma*): The narrator uses anthropomorphic language (i.e., he describes God's activity in human terms) to show God's acceptance of Noah's offering (see also Exod 29:18; Lev 1:9; Num 15:3). The common ancient Near Eastern notion that the gods ate the sacrifices offered to them is notably absent. • ***to himself*** (literally *in his heart*): The phrase echoes "broke his heart" (6:6), just as ***think or imagine*** echoes "everything they thought or imagined" (6:5). God's commitment to a new order replaced

and said to himself, "I will never again
curse the ground because of the human
race, even though everything they think or
imagine is bent toward evil from childhood.
I will never again destroy all living things.
22As long as the earth remains, there will
be planting and harvest, cold and heat, summer and winter, day and night."

God's Covenant with All Living Creatures

9 Then God blessed Noah and his sons
and told them, "Be fruitful and multiply. Fill the earth. 2All the animals of the
earth, all the birds of the sky, all the small
animals that scurry along the ground, and
all the fish in the sea will look on you with
fear and terror. I have placed them in your
power. 3I have given them to you for food,
just as I have given you grain and vegetables. 4But you must never eat any meat that
still has the [f]lifeblood in it.

5"And I will require the blood of anyone
who takes another person's life. If a wild
animal kills a person, it must die. And anyone who murders a fellow human must die.
6If anyone takes a human life, that person's
life will also be taken by human hands. For
God made human beings in his own image.
7Now be fruitful and multiply, and repopulate the earth."

8Then God told Noah and his sons, 9"I
hereby confirm my [g]covenant with you and
your descendants, 10and with all the animals
that were on the boat with you—the birds,
the livestock, and all the wild animals—every
living creature on earth. 11Yes, I am confirming my covenant with you. Never again will
floodwaters kill all living creatures; never
again will a flood destroy the [h]earth."

12Then God said, "I am giving you a sign
of my covenant with you and with all living creatures, for all generations to come.
13I have placed my rainbow in the clouds.
It is the sign of my covenant with you and
with all the earth. 14When I send clouds
over the earth, the rainbow will appear in
the clouds, 15and I will remember my covenant with you and with all living creatures.
Never again will the floodwaters destroy all
life. 16When I see the rainbow in the clouds,
I will remember the [i]eternal covenant between God and every living creature on
earth." 17Then God said to Noah, "Yes, this
rainbow is the sign of the covenant I am confirming with all the creatures on earth."

8:22 Ps 74:17
9:1 Gen 1:22
9:2 Gen 1:26-29; Ps 8:6-8
9:3 Ps 104:14
9:4 Lev 3:17; 7:26; 17:10; Deut 12:16; Acts 15:20, 29; [f]*dam* (1818) ▸Gen 49:11
9:5 Exod 21:28-32
9:6 Exod 20:13; 21:12; Num 35:33
9:9 [g]*berith* (1285) ▸Gen 15:18
9:11 Isa 24:5; [h]*'erets* (0776) ▸Gen 12:1
9:12 Gen 17:11
9:13 Ezek 1:28
9:15 Deut 7:9
9:16 [i]*'olam* (5769) ▸Gen 21:33

his grief over the old. • ***I will never again curse . . . destroy:*** The old curse was not lifted (5:29), but God promised not to add to it, thus establishing new limits for life in a disordered world (cp. Isa 54:9). The flood was to stop violence, not to reform the human heart (6:5). Humankind's ***bent toward evil*** would be contained to some degree through accountability to a new law (9:5-6).

8:22 God's promise to sustain the rhythm of the seasons reaffirmed the created order (1:14; see also Jer 33:20; Zech 14:7).

9:1-7 God's first post-flood speech opens and closes with blessing (9:1, 7). In it, human and animal relationships are again defined, with some modification of the original created order. The sanctity of life is given special focus.

9:1 ***Be fruitful and multiply:*** The blessing and mandate first given to Adam (1:28) are now reissued to Noah, the "Adam" of the newly cleansed world in need of repopulation.

9:2-3 There are two modifications to the original created order. (1) Previously, humans reigned over ***the animals*** (1:28), but now animals would live in ***terror*** of humans (similar military language is found in Exod 23:27-31; Deut 11:25; 31:8). (2) The animals' terror was related to a change in human diet. Humans were now permitted to eat the meat of animals to supplement their subsistence on grains, fruits, and vegetables (1:29).

9:4 A key restriction is imposed. Since blood was identified with life, it had to be drained from a slain animal before its ***meat*** could be eaten (see Lev 3:17; 7:26-27; 17:10-14; Deut 12:16, 23). The law of Moses prohibited eating animals that died naturally, since their blood had not been drained (Deut 14:21). God provided animal blood to atone for human sin (Lev 17:11; Heb 9:22).

9:5-6 Violence, including murder, was a major factor in bringing about God's judgment of the flood (4:8; 6:11, 13). At this new beginning for humans, God affirmed the sanctity of human life and established a system of retributive justice for the taking of human life (see also Ps 9:12; "Retribution" at 6:1–7:24, p. 35). The function of law is to restrain human wickedness and preserve moral order. This law was further developed in the law of Moses (Exod 21:12-14; Lev 24:17-22; Num 35:16-34; Deut 17:6-7; 19:15).

9:6 ***For God made human beings in his own image:*** The death penalty has a theological basis. God's image gives humans a unique status and authority within creation (1:26-28). Since murder destroys a person made in God's image, the ultimate penalty must be imposed on a murderer. See also Exod 21:23-25. We are not to pursue personal revenge (Rom 12:17-19), but are to uphold the justice of the "governing authorities" that God has established (Rom 13:1-7). • ***human beings:*** Or *man;* Hebrew reads *ha-'adam.*

9:7 ***Now be fruitful and multiply, and repopulate*** (literally *swarm and fill*): In contrast to those who would destroy human life (9:5-6), God's desire is that human life should abound and flourish.

9:8-17 God's second post-flood speech conveys his promise and plan for preserving creation.

9:9-10 God had promised this ***covenant*** before the flood (6:18). Its scope extends beyond humanity to include the earth and all animals.

9:11 This promise does not prohibit worldwide judgment, but it restricts the means by which God will do it (see 2 Pet 3:4-13).

9:12 In the Bible, covenants are frequently confirmed by some sort of ***sign*** (e.g., 17:11; Exod 31:13, 17; Luke 22:20).

9:13-16 God brought cataclysmic judgment through the rainstorm; now, the ***rainbow,*** a meteorological phenomenon associated with the rainstorm, would be an image of peace for ***all the earth*** (see 9:17). • "Rainbow" and "bow" are the same term in Hebrew. Since God is sometimes pictured as a warrior who shoots arrows of judgment (see Deut 32:42; Ps 7:12; 18:13-14; Hab 3:9-11),

9:21 Gen 19:35
9:22 Hab 2:15
9:25 Deut 27:16

Noah's Sons; Curse and Blessings
18 The sons of Noah who came out of the
boat with their father were Shem, Ham,
and Japheth. (Ham is the father of Canaan.)
19 From these three sons of Noah came all
the people who now populate the earth.
20 After the flood, Noah began to cultivate
the ground, and he planted a vineyard. 21 One
day he drank some wine he had made, and
he became drunk and lay naked inside his
tent. 22 Ham, the father of Canaan, saw that
his father was naked and went outside and
told his brothers. 23 Then Shem and Japheth
took a robe, held it over their shoulders, and
backed into the tent to cover their father. As
they did this, they looked the other way so
they would not see him naked.
24 When Noah woke up from his stupor,
he learned what Ham, his youngest son, had
done. 25 Then he cursed Canaan, the son of
Ham:

"May Canaan be cursed!
May he be the lowest of servants to
his relatives."

God's Covenant with Noah (9:1-17)

Ezek 14:12-23
Matt 24:37-39
Heb 11:7

The first explicit reference to a covenant in Scripture occurs after the flood (9:1-17). *Covenant* (Hebrew *berith*) means "bond": A covenant is a binding relationship rooted in a commitment that includes promises and obligations. Whether between individuals (e.g., 21:27), whole nations (e.g., Josh 9:15-18), or God and humans, the covenant relationship calls for faithfulness and makes peace and harmony possible.

Here God took the initiative to bind himself again to human beings and to the whole creation despite human faithlessness (see 6:1-7). When God charged Noah to build an ark to escape the impending deluge (6:13-17), he also promised to establish a covenant with him (6:18). The corruption and violence of the human race had provoked God's anger (6:11, 13), but his gracious favor remained with Noah (6:8). Through this covenant, God guaranteed that he would maintain a relationship with one family even as other divine-human relationships were being severed. God's covenant promise to Noah came with his command to build an ark (6:14); Noah's receipt of the covenant blessing depended on his obedience to this divine command (6:22; 7:5).

When Noah made an offering to God after the flood (8:20-22), God elaborated on his covenant with Noah as a universal covenant with humans and with all living creatures (9:8-10). God promised never to send such a flood again as judgment on the world.

This covenant helps us understand God as a covenant-maker. Although human beings deserve punishment because of their wickedness, God withholds ultimate destruction. God's covenant with Noah did not establish an intimate relationship between God and each living being, but it recalibrated moral and ecological life to be as God intended it (9:1-7), leaving open the possibility of a more intimate covenant to come (see 17:1-21). Despite their evil, human beings are allowed to live in God's world and seek a deeper relationship with the world's Creator during their time on earth. God's later covenants with his people made intimacy with him freely available to all (see Acts 2:22-40; 3:17-26).

some think that the imagery in 9:13-17 is of the Divine Warrior hanging up his bow of judgment.

9:18 ***Ham is the father of Canaan:*** See also 9:20-27; 10:6-20. The text emphasizes Canaan's ancestral connection to Ham to show that the Canaanite identity was inseparably linked to Ham's shameful behavior (9:20-27). The citizens of both Egypt (from which Israel escaped slavery) and Canaan (to which Israel was headed) were Ham's descendants (10:6; see Lev 18:3, 24-26; Ps 105:23, 27; 106:22). Later stories in Genesis emphasize the immoral climate of both Egypt (12:10-20) and Canaan (chs 34, 38). See 9:20-27 and 10:6-20.

9:20-27 The story of Noah begins with him walking in righteousness and obeying the Lord (6:9), but it ends with him lying drunk and naked in his tent and then delivering a curse on Canaan. Even after the great flood, the human race exhibited some of the same sinful characteristics that warranted the judgment in the first place. Special attention is given to the cursed origin of the Canaanites, the corrupt and idolatrous nation Israel would later displace from the Promised Land (see also 15:16 and note; Lev 18:3; 20:23).

9:21 ***wine . . . became drunk:*** Wine is a gift from God (Deut 14:26; Ps 104:15; Isa 55:1; see Luke 22:14-20; John 2:1-11). Scripture is clear, however, that excessive consumption of alcohol is a perilous sin (Prov 23:20-21, 29-35; 1 Cor 6:10).

9:22 ***the father of Canaan:*** See note on 9:18. • Ham's behavior was shameful. He gazed upon his naked father and, rather than covering him and keeping the matter secret, robbed him of his dignity by announcing it to his brothers (see Exod 21:15, 17; Lam 4:21; Hab 2:15). An ancient Near Eastern tale says that a son is expected to come to his father's aid when he is drunk (*Tale of Aqhat*; cp. Isa 51:17-18). Ham's neglect of familial duty explains why Noah praised Shem and Japheth but cursed Ham (9:24-27).

9:25 Noah's curse foresaw Ham's actions as morally representative of Ham's descendants through Canaan (see 10:6). • ***lowest of servants:*** Canaan was condemned to base servitude.

26Then Noah said,

"May the LORD, the God of Shem, be blessed,
and may Canaan be his servant!
27 May God expand the territory of Japheth!
May Japheth share the prosperity of Shem,
and may Canaan be his servant."

28Noah lived another 350 years after the great flood. 29He lived 950 years, and then he died.

5. THE ACCOUNT OF NOAH'S SONS (10:1–11:9)

Nations of the Ancient World (10:1-32)

Superscription

10 This is the account of the families of Shem, Ham, and Japheth, the three sons of Noah. Many children were born to them after the great flood.

Descendants of Japheth

2The descendants of Japheth were Gomer, Magog, Madai, Javan, Tubal, Meshech, and Tiras.
3The descendants of Gomer were Ashkenaz, Riphath, and Togarmah.
4The descendants of Javan were Elishah, Tarshish, Kittim, and Rodanim. 5Their
descendants became the seafaring peoples that spread out to various lands, each identified by its own language, clan, and national identity.

Descendants of Ham

6The descendants of Ham were Cush, Mizraim, Put, and Canaan.
7The descendants of Cush were Seba, Havilah, Sabtah, Raamah, and Sabteca. The descendants of Raamah were Sheba and Dedan.
8Cush was also the ancestor of Nimrod, who was the first heroic warrior on earth.

9:26 Gen 14:20
9:27 Gen 10:2-5; Isa 66:19
9:29 Gen 2:17
10:1 Gen 9:18; 1 Chr 1:4
10:2 1 Chr 1:5-7; Isa 66:19; Ezek 27:13; 38:2-3, 6
10:3 Jer 51:27; Ezek 27:14
10:4 1 Chr 1:6-7
10:6 1 Chr 1:8-10
10:7 Isa 43:3; Ezek 27:15, 20, 22

9:26 Noah refers to God as *the LORD*, who formed the covenant with Israel. *Shem* was the privileged forefather of the Israelites (see 10:21-32).

9:27 *May Japheth share the prosperity of Shem* (literally *May he live in the tents of Shem*): Japheth's descendants would live among Shem's descendants and share Shem's prosperity (cp. Rom 11:17-18).

10:1–11:9 The fifth *account* (10:1) in Genesis (see note on 2:4) unites the Table of Nations (10:2-32) and the Babel story (11:1-9) around the theme of scattering the nations (10:5, 18; 11:4, 8-9). The Table of Nations precedes the Babel story even though the Babel incident caused the geopolitical situation reflected in the Table of Nations. By reversing the order, Genesis links the repopulation of the earth with the blessing conferred upon Noah and his sons (see 9:1 and note) and shows that Abram's call (12:1-3) was God's solution to the problem of human estrangement from God as reflected in the Babel story (11:1-9).

10:1 *Many children were born . . . after the great flood:* This fulfilled the renewed creation mandate (9:1, 9; cp. 1:28).

10:2-32 This section describes the ancestral origin of the nations of the ancient Near East. Ham was at the center (10:6-20), while the descendants of Japheth and Shem spread out to the surrounding regions of Greece, Crete, Asia Minor, Mesopotamia, Madai, the Arabian peninsula, and northeast Africa. The list selectively highlights nations relevant to Israel. The total of seventy (seven times ten) names indicates completeness (see 46:27; Deut 32:8) and symbolizes the totality of the world, which would later be blessed by the descendants of Abraham (18:18). • Although Shem is mentioned first in 10:1, he is addressed last in the Table because of his connection to Abram (10:21-31; 11:10-32; 12:1). Although God established the boundaries of all nations (see Deut 32:8; Amos 9:7; Acts 17:26), Israel was his special creation—a microcosm of seventy people (46:27) called to be a blessing to a world of seventy nations (see 12:3).

10:2 The seven sons of *Japheth* settled in the region of Anatolia (the western plateau lands of Turkey) and spoke Indo-European languages. • *Gomer* was the ancestor of the later Cimmerians who lived north of the Black Sea. • *Magog* was probably the ancestor of those who settled in the region of Lydia (see Ezek 38:2). • The descendants of *Madai* were the later Medes of northwest Iran (see 2 Kgs 17:6; Jer 51:11; Dan 5:28). • The descendants of *Javan* were the later Ionian Greeks. • The descendants of *Tubal* and *Meshech* were sometimes allies in battle (Ezek 38:2). Both were possibly from the coastal regions of Anatolia (see Ezek 27:13). • The descendants of *Tiras* possibly became the Thracians that lived near the Aegean Sea.

10:3 The *descendants of Gomer* came from near the Upper Euphrates region north of the Black Sea (cp. Ezek 38:1-9). • The descendants of *Ashkenaz* were the later Scythians who inhabited the region between the Black and Caspian Seas. • *Riphath* is near Carchemish. • The descendants of *Togarmah* are associated with Til-garimmu, the capital of Kammanu in modern Armenia (see Ezek 38:6).

10:4 *Elishah* is probably Cyprus. • *Tarshish* is possibly southwest Spain (see note on Jon 1:3). • The *Kittim* were inhabitants of southern Cyprus. • The *Rodanim* (as in some Hebrew manuscripts and Greek version [see also 1 Chr 1:7]; most Hebrew manuscripts read *Dodanim*) were inhabitants of the island of Rhodes, later a territory of Greece.

10:5 *seafaring peoples . . . various lands:* They settled around the Mediterranean and on various islands. • *language:* This occurred after the Tower of Babel episode (11:1-9; see note on 10:1–11:9).

10:6 The peoples descended from Ham's four sons (Egyptians, Babylonians, Assyrians, Canaanites) were Israel's most hostile neighbors. • *Cush* was possibly in Ethiopia or ancient Nubia (northern Sudan). • *Mizraim* was the ancient name for Egypt (50:11). • *Put* was in Libya. • *Canaan* encompassed southern Syria, Phoenicia, and Palestine west of the Jordan River. In Moses' time, Egypt and Canaan were provinces of the same empire. Ham's descendants were excluded from the blessing of Shem's line (9:20-28).

10:7 The sons of *Cush* and *Raamah* together total seven. • *Seba* was in northern Africa (see Isa 43:3; 45:14). • *Havilah* was in southwest Arabia. • *Sabtah* was in southern Arabia, in ancient Hadramaut, near the Persian Gulf. • *Raamah* was in southwest Arabia near Najran. • *Sabteca* was in ancient Samudake near the Persian Gulf. • *Sheba* was a kingdom in southwest Arabia with commercial colonies (see 1 Kgs 10). • *Dedan* was in northern Arabia.

10:8-12 Special attention is given to the early history of *Babylonia* and *Assyria*, the Mesopotamian empires that would conquer and exile Israel and Judah.

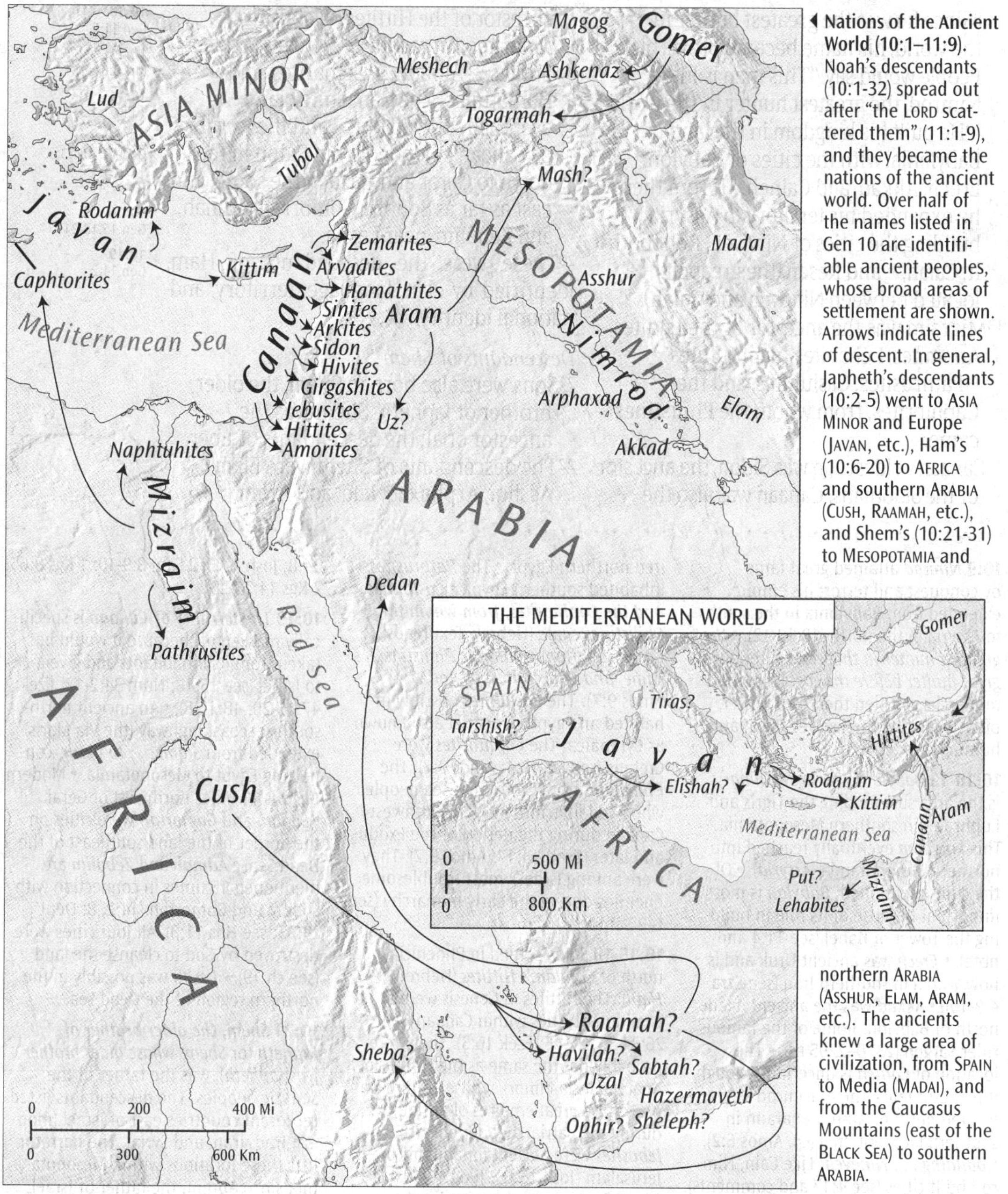

◀ **Nations of the Ancient World (10:1–11:9).** Noah's descendants (10:1-32) spread out after "the LORD scattered them" (11:1-9), and they became the nations of the ancient world. Over half of the names listed in Gen 10 are identifiable ancient peoples, whose broad areas of settlement are shown. Arrows indicate lines of descent. In general, Japheth's descendants (10:2-5) went to ASIA MINOR and Europe (JAVAN, etc.), Ham's (10:6-20) to AFRICA and southern ARABIA (CUSH, RAAMAH, etc.), and Shem's (10:21-31) to MESOPOTAMIA and northern ARABIA (ASSHUR, ELAM, ARAM, etc.). The ancients knew a large area of civilization, from SPAIN to Media (MADAI), and from the Caucasus Mountains (east of the BLACK SEA) to southern ARABIA.

Japheth *9:27*
Gomer *Ezek 38:6*
Ashkenaz *Jer 51:27*
Togarmah *Ezek 27:14; 38:6*
Magog *Ezek 38:2; 39:6; Rev 20:8*
Madai [Medes] *2 Kgs 17:6; Esth 1:19; Acts 2:9*
Javan
Elishah *Ezek 27:7*
Tarshish *Ps 72:10; Isa 23:1; 60:9; 66:19; Jer 10:9; Jon 1:3*
Tubal *Isa 66:19; Ezek 27:13; 38:2*
Meshech *Ps 120:5; Ezek 32:26; 39:1*

Ham *14:5; 1 Chr 4:38-41; Ps 105:27*
Cush *2:13; Num 12:1; 1 Chr 1:10*
Havilah *25:18; 1 Sam 15:7*
Raamah *Ezek 27:22*
Sheba *1 Kgs 10:1-13; Isa 60:6; Ezek 27:22-23; Matt 12:42*
Dedan *25:3; Jer 25:23; Ezek 25:13; 27:15*
Nimrod *1 Chr 1:10; Mic 5:6*
Mizraim *50:11*
Caphtorites *Deut 2:23*
Put *Nah 3:9*
Canaan *11:31; 12:5-10*
Sidon *Josh 13:4-6; 1 Kgs 5:6; 11:33; 16:31; Ezek 28:21-24; Matt 11:21-22; Luke 6:17; Acts 27:3*
Hittites *23:1-20; Num 13:29; Josh 1:4*
Jebusites *Josh 15:63; Judg 19:10-11; 2 Sam 5:6-8; Zech 9:7*
Amorites *14:7, 13; Num 21:21-35; Josh 5:1; 10:1-13*
Girgashites *15:21; Deut 7:1; Josh 3:10; 24:11; 1 Chr 1:14; Neh 9:8*
Hivites *34:1-2; 36:2; Deut 20:17; Josh 9:3-7; 11:3*
Arkites *Josh 16:2; 2 Sam 15:32*
Arvadites *Ezek 27:8, 11*
Zemarites *2 Chr 13:4*
Hamathites *2 Sam 8:9-10; 2 Kgs 14:28; 23:33*

Shem
Elam *14:1-9; Ezra 4:9; Isa 22:6; Jer 49:34-39; Ezek 32:24; Dan 8:2; Acts 2:9*
Asshur *2:14; 25:3; 25:18; Ezek 27:23*
Aram *24:10; 25:20; 28:5–31:21; Num 23:7; Judg 3:8; 2 Sam 8:5-6*

9 Since he was the greatest hunter in
the world, his name became proverbial.
People would say, "This man is like
Nimrod, the greatest hunter in the world."
10 He built his kingdom in the land of
Babylonia, with the cities of Babylon,
Erech, Akkad, and Calneh. 11 From there
he expanded his territory to Assyria,
building the cities of Nineveh, Rehoboth-
ir, Calah, 12 and Resen (the great city
located between Nineveh and Calah).
13 Mizraim was the ancestor of the Ludites,
Anamites, Lehabites, Naphtuhites,
14 Pathrusites, Casluhites, and the
Caphtorites, from whom the Philistines
came.
15 Canaan's oldest son was Sidon, the ancestor
of the Sidonians. Canaan was also the
ancestor of the Hittites, 16 Jebusites,
Amorites, Girgashites, 17 Hivites, Arkites,
Sinites, 18 Arvadites, Zemarites, and
Hamathites. The Canaanite clans
eventually spread out, 19 and the territory
of Canaan extended from Sidon in the
north to Gerar and Gaza in the south, and
east as far as Sodom, Gomorrah, Admah,
and Zeboiim, near Lasha.
20 These were the descendants of Ham,
identified by clan, language, territory, and
national identity.

Descendants of Shem

21 Sons were also born to Shem, the older
brother of Japheth. Shem was the
ancestor of all the descendants of Eber.
22 The descendants of Shem were Elam,
Asshur, Arphaxad, Lud, and Aram.

10:10 Gen 11:9
10:11 Mic 5:6
10:14 1 Chr 1:12
10:15 Gen 15:20; 23:3; 1 Chr 1:13; Jer 47:4
10:16 Gen 15:18-21
10:19 Gen 14:2

10:9 *Nimrod* attained great fame by conquest and terror; his empire extended from Babylonia in the south to Assyria in the north (10:10-12). • ***the greatest hunter in the world*** (literally *a great hunter before the* LORD): Assyrian monarchs glorified their own power, often depicting themselves as valiant hunter-conquerors.

10:10-12 ***Babylonia*** (Hebrew *Shinar*) is the area surrounding the Tigris and Euphrates in southern Mesopotamia. This ***kingdom*** eventually reached into northern Mesopotamia (*Assyria*). • Of the cities mentioned, ***Babylon*** is most important because of its role in building the Tower of Babel (see 11:4 and note). • ***Erech*** was ancient Uruk and is now Warka in southern Iraq (see Ezra 4:9-10). • ***Akkad*** was the ancient Agade north of Babylon, home of the famous ruler Sargon (2370–2295 BC). • The location of ***Calneh*** is uncertain, though it is presumably one of Nimrod's cities located north of Aram-naharaim in southern Mesopotamia (cp. Amos 6:2). • ***building . . . Nineveh:*** Like Cain, Nimrod built cities (see 4:17 and comments). Nineveh was an ancient Assyrian city on the east bank of the Tigris River in northern Iraq. • ***Rehoboth-ir*** was a daughter-city of Nineveh or was located nearby. • ***Calah*** is modern Tell Nimrud, south of Nineveh. • ***Resen*** is possibly modern Selamiyeh, northwest of Tell Nimrud.

10:11 ***From there he expanded his territory to Assyria:*** The Hebrew text can also be translated *From that land Assyria went out.*

10:13-14 The ***Ludites*** were Lydian tribes west of the Nile delta. • The identity of the ***Anamites*** is uncertain. They were possibly Egyptians near Cyrene, west of Egypt. • The ***Lehabites*** were possibly a Libyan tribe. • The ***Naphtuhites*** inhabited northern Egypt. • The ***Pathrusites*** inhabited southern Egypt. • ***Casluhites, and the Caphtorites, from whom the Philistines came*** (Hebrew text reads *Casluhites, from whom the Philistines came, and Caphtorites;* cp. Jer 47:4; Amos 9:7): The ***Casluhites*** possibly inhabited an Egyptian district also known as Cyrenaica. The ***Caphtorites*** were Cretans (see Jer 47:4; Amos 9:7). The ***Philistines*** from Crete were sea people who lived intermittently in southwest Canaan during the period of the Exodus and later (Exod 13:17; Amos 9:7). They were among Israel's most troublesome enemies during the early monarchy (see 1–2 Samuel).

10:15-18 ***Sidon*** settled in Phoenicia, north of ***Canaan.*** • ***Hittites*** (Hebrew *Heth*): The Hittites in Genesis were a coalition of cities within Canaan (see 26:34-35; 27:46; Ezek 16:3). They were probably not the same as the Hittites of Anatolia (Asia Minor), whose empire was one of the great empires of antiquity during the patriarchal period. • The ***Jebusites*** were ancient inhabitants of Jerusalem (Josh 15:63; Judg 19:10-11; 2 Sam 5:6-9). • The ***Amorites*** lived throughout the mountains of Palestine in Canaan (see 15:16; 48:22; Num 13:29; Deut 3:8; Josh 10:5; Judg 1:35; 10:8; Ezek 16:3). • Little is known of the ***Girgashites,*** a Canaanite tribe (15:21; Deut 7:1; Josh 3:10). • The ***Hivites*** were an uncircumcised Canaanite tribe (34:2, 13-24; Josh 9:1, 7; 11:3; Judg 3:3; 2 Sam 24:7). • The ***Arkites*** resided in Tell 'Arqa in Lebanon. • The ***Sinites*** formed a city-state and inhabited Phoenicia. • The ***Arvadites*** inhabited Ruad in northern Phoenicia, near the El Kebir River. They were known for shipping (cp. Ezek 27:8). • The ***Zemarites*** inhabited Sumur (modern Sumra), north of Arka on the Phoenician coast. • The ***Hamathites*** founded what is now Hama on the Orontes River, the northern boundary of Canaan (see Num 34:8; Josh 13:5; 2 Sam 8:9-10; 1 Kgs 8:65; 2 Kgs 14:25-28).

10:19 ***The territory of Canaan*** is specifically marked off because it would be taken from its inhabitants and given to Israel (see 15:18; Num 34:2-12; Ezek 47:15-20; 48:1-28). • An ancient north-south seacoast highway (the Via Maris) extended from ***Sidon . . . to Gerar,*** connecting Egypt to Mesopotamia. • Modern ***Gaza*** is 11 miles northwest of Gerar. • ***Sodom*** and ***Gomorrah*** were cities on the border of the land southeast of the Dead Sea. • ***Admah*** and ***Zeboiim*** are mentioned 15 times in connection with Sodom and Gomorrah (14:2, 8; Deut 29:23; see Hos 11:8). All four cities were destroyed by God to cleanse the land (see ch 19). • ***Lasha*** was possibly in the northern region of the Dead Sea.

10:21 ***Shem, the older brother of Japheth*** (or *Shem, whose older brother was Japheth*), was the father of the Semitic peoples. The descendants listed represent countries east of Israel (modern Iraq, Iran, and Syria). The narrator lists these locations within Mesopotamia since Abram, the father of Israel, originated from this area (see 11:27-32). • ***Eber*** receives special attention because of his connection with Abram (see note on 10:24).

10:22 The descendants of ***Elam*** lived in the region of modern southwestern Iran (see 14:1, 9; Ezra 4:9; Isa 11:11). • The descendants of ***Asshur*** were later Assyrians who lived under Nimrod's jurisdiction (see 10:11). Sumerians descended from Ham were ousted by Mesopotamian Semites. • ***Arphaxad*** possibly settled northeast of Nineveh; his descendants are further described in 11:12-26. • ***Lud*** was near the Tigris River; its people were related to the Lydians (see 10:13). • ***Aram*** was a kingdom of tribes that lived in the Mesopotamian plains.

10:23
Job 1:1
10:24
Luke 3:35
10:32
Gen 9:19; 10:1
11:2
Gen 10:10; 14:1
Isa 11:11
11:3
Gen 14:10
11:4
2 Sam 8:13
11:5
Gen 18:21
Exod 19:11
11:6
Gen 9:19; 11:1

23The descendants of Aram were Uz, Hul,
Gether, and Mash.
24Arphaxad was the father of Shelah, and
Shelah was the father of Eber.
25Eber had two sons. The first was named
Peleg (which means "division"), for during
his lifetime the people of the world were
divided into different language groups.
His brother's name was Joktan.
26Joktan was the ancestor of Almodad,
Sheleph, Hazarmaveth, Jerah,
27Hadoram, Uzal, Diklah, 28Obal,
Abimael, Sheba, 29Ophir, Havilah, and
Jobab. All these were descendants of
Joktan. 30The territory they occupied
extended from Mesha all the way to
Sephar in the eastern mountains.
31These were the descendants of Shem,
identified by clan, language, territory, and
national identity.

Conclusion

32These are the clans that descended from
Noah's sons, arranged by nation according
to their lines of descent. All the nations of
the earth descended from these clans after
the great flood.

The Dispersion at Babel (11:1-9)

The Tower of Babel

11 At one time all the people of the world
spoke the same language and used
the same words. 2As the people migrated
to the east, they found a plain in the land of
Babylonia and settled there.
3They began saying to each other, "Let's
make bricks and harden them with fire."
(In this region bricks were used instead of
stone, and tar was used for mortar.) 4Then
they said, "Come, let's build a great city for
ourselves with a tower that reaches into the
sky. This will make us famous and keep us
from being scattered all over the world."

The Lord Disperses the Nations

5But the Lord came down to look at the
city and the tower the people were building.
6"Look!" he said. "The people are united,

10:23 The patriarchs later interacted with ***the descendants of Aram*** (see 25:20; 31:20; Deut 26:5). • ***Uz*** was the chief Aramean tribe, possibly located northeast of the Jordan; it was Job's home (see Job 1:1; see also Lam 4:21). • ***Hul*** is unknown. He possibly founded Armenia. • ***Gether*** is unknown; he was possibly the founder of the Syrians. • ***Mash*** might be associated with Mount Masus in northern Mesopotamia or with a part of the Lebanon Mountains.

10:24 ***Arphaxad was the father of Shelah:*** Greek version reads *Arphaxad was the father of Cainan, Cainan was the father of Shelah.* Cp. Luke 3:36. • ***Shelah*** is unknown, but may be short for Methushelah (cp. 38:5, 11). • ***Eber*** was the ancestor of Abram the Hebrew (11:10-26); his name is at the root of the term "Hebrew" (see 14:13; 39:14; 40:15; 41:12; Exod 2:11; 3:18).

10:25 ***Peleg*** means ***division,*** anticipating the separation of people into ***language groups*** after Babel (11:1-9). Peleg's line led to Abram (see 11:16-26). • ***Joktan*** was the ancestor of the southern Arabian tribes. The Ishmaelite tribes were in northern Arabia (see 25:13-16).

10:26-32 There were fourteen sons of Shem by Eber through ***Joktan.*** The placement of the Babel story between the lines of Joktan and Peleg ties Joktan to the judgment of the Babel story (11:1-9) and ties Peleg to Abram (11:27–12:1).

10:26-29 ***Almodad*** was an ancestor, region, or tribe in modern Yemen. • ***Sheleph*** was a tribe of Yemen. • ***Hazarmaveth*** was related to Hadramaut in southern Arabia. • ***Jerah*** is unknown, but was possibly associated with Mount Barach. • ***Hadoram*** was an Arabian tribe. • ***Uzal*** was Sana'a, an old capital of Yemen in pre-Islamic times. • ***Diklah*** was a southern Arabian oasis in Mina. • ***Obal*** was between Hodeida and Sana'a in southwest Arabia. • ***Abimael*** was a Sabaean. • ***Sheba*** was in southern Arabia (see 10:7). • ***Ophir*** was a region of southern Arabia between Sheba and Havilah; it was a source of gold (Isa 13:12). • ***Havilah:*** See 10:7. • ***Jobab*** was possibly Jobebitai in southern Arabia.

10:30 ***Mesha*** was a region in northern Arabia, south of Hadramaut. • ***Sephar*** is identified with Isfar, south of Hadramaut in Yemen.

11:1-9 The story of the unfinished tower carries forward themes of language and solidarity from the Table of Nations (ch 10). The builders' desire for autonomy recalls the rebellion in Eden (ch 3) and establishes the need for Abram's redemptive faith in the midst of international disorder (ch 12). The scattering of the nations anticipates the warning to Israel that idolatry would result in their being scattered and their cities devastated (see Num 10:35; Lev 26:33; Deut 4:27; 28:64; 30:3). Chronologically, the story is a flashback that explains the rise of the nations during Peleg's time (see 10:25).

11:1 ***At one time:*** The events described in 11:1-9 led to the scattering of nations that is reflected in the genealogies of 10:2-30. The reversal of order has a theological purpose (see note on 10:1–11:9).

11:2 ***migrated to the east:*** See note on 3:24. • ***Babylonia*** (Hebrew *Shinar*) was located in southern Mesopotamia, the region of Nimrod's later empire and city-building campaign (see 10:10; Isa 11:11; Dan 1:2; Zech 5:11).

11:3 ***Stone*** was plentiful in Canaan; in Mesopotamia, stone was scarce and brick technology was developed. • ***Tar*** was made from bitumen, a natural, cement-like, waterproof asphalt (see 6:14; Exod 2:3).

11:4 Far from the original garden (2:15), the first cities of Genesis represent arrogance (4:17), tyranny (10:8-12), and wickedness (18:20-21). The city on the Babylonian plain was a magnet for human pride and idolatry. • ***a tower that reaches into the sky:*** This was probably a temple-tower (a ziggurat). Common in ancient Babylonian urban culture, ziggurats were regarded as sacred mountains by which deities descended to earth (Jacob's dream in 28:12 possibly reflects this idea). • ***This will make us famous*** (literally *let us make a name for ourselves*): The tower builders sought fame through idolatrous ambition. God promised to give Abram a famous name because of his humble obedience (12:2).

11:5 ***came down:*** The tower was a human attempt to ascend to God's realm (see Deut 26:15; Ps 2:4; 103:19; 115:16). The folly of that attempt was exposed by God's "coming down" to see their feeble efforts.

11:6 If left unchecked, the tower builders' solidarity and ambition would allow human wickedness to flourish in unimaginable ways.

and they all speak the same language. After this, nothing they set out to do will be
impossible for them! 7 Come, let's go down
and confuse the people with different
languages. Then they won't be able to understand each other."
8 In that way, the LORD scattered them all
over the world, and they stopped building
the city. 9 That is why the city was called Babel, because that is where the LORD confused
the people with different languages. In this
way he scattered them all over the world.

6. THE ACCOUNT OF SHEM'S DESCENDANTS (11:10-26)

10 This is the account of Shem's family.

Two years after the great flood, when
Shem was 100 years old, he became the
father of Arphaxad. 11 After the birth of
Arphaxad, Shem lived another 500 years
and had other sons and daughters.
12 When Arphaxad was 35 years old, he
became the father of Shelah. 13 After the
birth of Shelah, Arphaxad lived another
403 years and had other sons and
daughters.
14 When Shelah was 30 years old, he
became the father of Eber. 15 After the
birth of Eber, Shelah lived another
403 years and had other sons and
daughters.
16 When Eber was 34 years old, he became
the father of Peleg. 17 After the birth of
Peleg, Eber lived another 430 years and
had other sons and daughters.
18 When Peleg was 30 years old, he became
the father of Reu. 19 After the birth of
Reu, Peleg lived another 209 years and
had other sons and daughters.
20 When Reu was 32 years old, he became
the father of Serug. 21 After the birth of
Serug, Reu lived another 207 years and
had other sons and daughters.
22 When Serug was 30 years old, he
became the father of Nahor. 23 After
the birth of Nahor, Serug lived another
200 years and had other sons and
daughters.
24 When Nahor was 29 years old, he became
the father of Terah. 25 After the birth of
Terah, Nahor lived another 119 years and
had other sons and daughters.
26 After Terah was 70 years old, he became
the father of Abram, Nahor, and Haran.

7. THE ACCOUNT OF TERAH'S DESCENDANTS (11:27–25:11)

The Family of Terah (11:27-32)

27 This is the account of Terah's family. Terah was the father of Abram, Nahor, and
Haran; and Haran was the father of Lot.
28 But Haran died in Ur of the Chaldeans, the
land of his birth, while his father, Terah, was

11:7 Gen 1:26
11:8 Gen 9:19
11:9 Gen 10:10
11:10 Gen 10:22-25; Luke 3:36
11:12 Luke 3:36
11:13 1 Chr 1:17
11:14 Luke 3:35
11:16 Luke 3:35
11:18 Luke 3:35
11:20 Luke 3:35
11:22 Luke 3:34
11:24 Josh 24:2; Luke 3:34
11:26 Gen 22:20; 1 Chr 1:26-27; Luke 3:34
11:29 Gen 17:15; 20:11-12; 22:20
11:30 Gen 16:1; 18:11; 25:21; 1 Sam 1:5; Luke 1:7
11:31 Gen 27:43; Josh 24:2; Acts 7:4

11:7 ***Come, let's go down:*** God addresses his angelic court (see 1:26; 3:22; and notes). • ***won't be able to understand each other:*** Their inability to communicate would curtail their unified sinful ambition. The God-honoring unity of language on the day of Pentecost was a symbolic reversal of the Babel dispersion (Acts 2:5-13; see Zeph 3:9).

11:8 ***the LORD scattered them:*** Similarly, Adam and Eve's punishment for grasping at autonomy and Cain's punishment for murder involved banishment and dispersion (3:23; 4:12, 14; 9:19; 10:5, 25, 32).

11:9 ***Babel:*** Or *Babylon. Babel* sounds like a Hebrew term that means "confusion." The Babylonians viewed their city as the residence or gateway of the gods. The pun that concludes this account accurately reveals Babylon's spiritual confusion. Babylon achieved prominence under Nimrod (10:10) and in later biblical history (see 2 Kgs 25). Its role as an epicenter of arrogance and idolatry make it a fitting image for the anti-God forces associated with the end of time (e.g., Rev 14:8; 16:19; 18:2). • The tower builders had centralized to ascend into God's realm (11:3-4). God descended and ***scattered them all over the world*** to frustrate their idolatrous ambition.

11:10 This ***account of Shem's family*** resumes the line of Shem from 10:21-32, now with special focus on the line leading to Abram. Only Abram and Israel are heirs to Shem's God (see 9:26-27; Deut 32:8-9). The Babel story vividly depicts the culture that Abram was called to abandon (12:1; 24:6-7). Together with the account of Terah's descendants (11:27-32), this second account of Shem's line forms a bridge from the universal history of chs 1–11 to the national history of Israel that begins in ch 12. Abram is the remnant from Babel's confused world. God called him as an act of grace whereby the fractured world of Babel would be blessed (12:3). • ***the father of:*** Or *the ancestor of;* also in 11:12, 14, 16, 18, 20, 22, 24. Hebrew genealogies do not necessarily list every single generation.

11:11 ***After the birth of:*** Or *After the birth of this ancestor of;* also in 11:13, 15, 17, 19, 21, 23, 25 (see note on 11:10).

11:12-13 Greek version reads 12 *When Arphaxad was 135 years old, he became the father of Cainan.* 13 *After the birth of Cainan, Arphaxad lived another 430 years and had other sons and daughters, and then he died. When Cainan was 130 years old, he became the father of Shelah. After the birth of Shelah, Cainan lived another 330 years and had other sons and daughters, and then he died.* Cp. Luke 3:35-36.

11:18 ***Peleg:*** See note on 10:25.

11:27–25:11 ***This is the account*** (Hebrew *toledoth;* see note on 2:4) ***of Terah's family:*** What follows are the particulars about the family descended from Terah, notably about Abraham and God's covenant with him, and about Isaac, the child of promise, who carried forward the line and the blessing to the next generation.

11:27-32 This brief section provides a complete summary of Terah's life and accounts for his other sons and their marriages; it also introduces Lot, Abram's nephew, who later played a prominent role. The ancestors, including Terah and his family, were idolatrous, worshiping other gods in Mesopotamia (Josh 24:2).

11:27 ***Nahor*** was the father of Laban, whose daughters later became Jacob's wives (chs 29–31). • ***Lot:*** See "Lot," 19:1-38, p. 58.

11:28 The call of Abram occurred in ***Ur of the Chaldeans*** (15:7; Acts 7:2-4), the

12:1
Gen 15:7
*Acts 7:3
Heb 11:8
[i]*'erets* (0776)
‣Gen 13:17

12:2
Gen 13:16; 15:5; 17:4;
18:18; 22:17
Zech 8:13
[k]*barak* (1288)
‣Gen 49:28

12:3
Gen 22:18; 26:4
Exod 23:22
Acts 3:25
*Gal 3:8

12:4
Gen 11:26, 31

still living. [29]Meanwhile, Abram and Nahor
both married. The name of Abram's wife
was Sarai, and the name of Nahor's wife
was Milcah. (Milcah and her sister Iscah
were daughters of Nahor's brother Haran.)
[30]But Sarai was unable to become pregnant
and had no children.

[31]One day Terah took his son Abram, his
daughter-in-law Sarai (his son Abram's wife),
and his grandson Lot (his son Haran's child)
and moved away from Ur of the Chaldeans.
He was headed for the land of Canaan, but
they stopped at Haran and settled there.
[32]Terah lived for 205 years and died while
still in Haran.

The Call of Abram (12:1-9)

12 The LORD had said to Abram, "Leave
your native [j]country, your relatives,
and your father's family, and go to the [i]land
that I will show you. [2]I will make you into a
great nation. I will [k]bless you and make you
famous, and you will be a blessing to others.
[3]I will bless those who bless you and curse
those who treat you with contempt. All the
families on earth will be blessed through
you."

[4]So Abram departed as the LORD had instructed, and Lot went with him. Abram
was seventy-five years old when he left Haran. [5]He took his wife, Sarai, his nephew Lot,

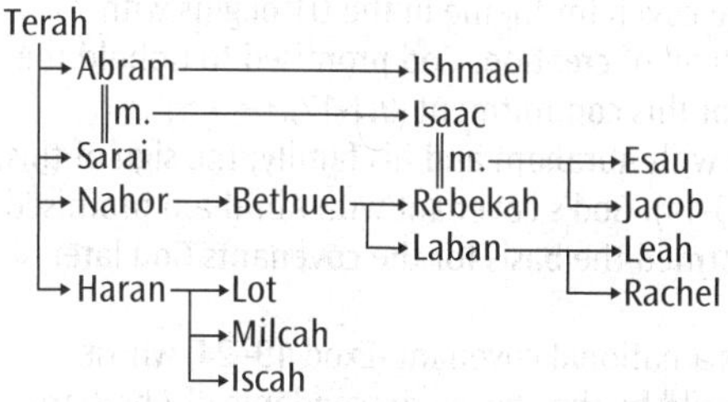

◂**Terah's Family (11:27-30),** to four generations. See profiles for ABRAHAM (p. 46), SARAH (p. 55), LOT (p. 58), ISHMAEL (p. 53), ISAAC (p. 63), REBEKAH (p. 69), ESAU (p. 71), JACOB (p. 76), LEAH (p. 79), and RACHEL (p. 78).

main city of Sumer in Mesopotamia near the mouth of the Persian Gulf. The family had moved there perhaps generations before the call. Their ancestral home ("native country," 12:1) was apparently near Haran, in the region of the descendants of Shem (11:10-26); thus they settled there when they left Ur (11:31) and were later described as "Aramaeans" (Deut 26:5). • ***land of his birth:*** The same Hebrew phrase is repeated in 12:1 ("native country"), making Ur, not Haran, the location of Abram's call (see 15:7; Neh 9:7; Acts 7:2).

11:29 ***Sarai*** means "princess" in Hebrew. No mention is made of Sarai's parentage, perhaps to add suspense to the Abimelech story, which reveals that she was Abram's half sister (20:9-12). Later, the law prohibited such a marriage (Lev 18:9; 20:17; Deut 27:22). • ***Nahor's wife was Milcah:*** Milcah was Haran's daughter and Nahor's niece (see 11:29). Her son Bethuel was the father of Rebekah, the wife of Abram's son Isaac (24:10, 15, 24). The name Milcah is related to the Hebrew word meaning "queen." In Akkadian, it is a title of the goddess Ishtar, the moon-god's daughter. Terah's name is related to the word for "moon" in Hebrew; his whole family appears to have worshiped Sin, the moon-god (see Josh 24:14).

11:30 ***Sarai,*** Rebekah (25:21), and Rachel (29:31) all suffered infertility. Sarai's situation in particular highlights the paradox between the apparent reality and God's promise to give many descendants (12:2). The Israelite nation's origin from barren women fixes its identity in the sovereignty of God, who miraculously gives children to barren women (see also 1 Sam 1:2; 2:5; Ps 113:9; Isa 54:1).

11:31 ***Terah took:*** The text is clear that Abram's departure from Ur was prompted by God's calling (see note on 11:28), but the event is described from Terah's perspective, in keeping with the patriarchy of ancient Near Eastern culture. This cultural deference to the oldest male is evidently why Abram did not continue on to Canaan by himself at this time (see Acts 7:2-4). • ***Haran*** was 550 miles northwest of Ur, near the Syrian-Turkish border. Despite the similar name, there is no connection with Terah's son Haran, who had died in Ur (11:28). • *Haran* means "caravan." Ancient commercial routes converged there, making it a key site for trade. • *Haran* was also well-known for the moon worship to which Terah's family was apparently devoted (see note on 11:29).

11:32 ***205 years:*** Some ancient versions read *145 years;* cp. 11:26 and 12:4.

12:1-9 Through Abram's faith and family, God began restoring the blessing. God called Abram from a pagan world to begin a new nation; his promises to Abram later became a covenant (ch 15). • God's call to Abram later helped convince the Israelites to leave Egypt and go to the land God promised to Abram. It also reminded the Babylonian exiles of their need to return to their own land (e.g., Isa 51).

12:1-3 These verses are structured around two commands to Abram: ***Leave*** and ***be a blessing*** (see note on 12:2). Each directive is followed by three promises conditioned upon obedience.

12:1 ***Abram*** knew that he should leave, but he did not know where he was going. Obedience required faith.

12:2 ***and you will be a blessing*** (or *so that you will be a blessing*): This clause is a command in Hebrew, but it is also a promise conditioned upon Abram's obedience to God's command (12:1): "Go . . . so that you will be a blessing. Be a blessing, so that I can bless and curse others." • ***make you famous*** (literally *make your name great*): Abram received the fame sought by the builders of Babel (see 11:4 and note).

12:3 Based on Abram's obedience to the command to be a blessing (12:2), God gave him three more promises. • ***those who treat you with contempt:*** People who disregarded Abram and his covenant were rejecting God's choice and plan. • ***All the families on earth will be blessed:*** By faith, they could participate in the covenant God was making with Abram. The blessing spread to the whole world through Abraham, Israel, the covenants, the prophets, Scripture, and the Messiah (Gal 3:8, 16; cp. Rom 9:4-5).

12:4-9 Abram's obedience to God's call corresponded to God's commands (see note on 12:1-3). He journeyed to Canaan (12:4-6) and became a blessing (12:5-9).

12:4 ***Abram*** was middle-aged, settled, prosperous, aristocratic, and polytheistic (see note on 11:27-32). When ***the LORD*** spoke to him (12:1-3), he obediently left his old ways in Ur to follow God's plan. Since Abram responded in faith, God's promises (12:2-3) could be confirmed in a binding covenant (15:8-21).

12:5 ***The people*** (Hebrew *hannepesh*, "the lives") ***he had taken into his household*** were probably converts; Abram first became a blessing by influencing people in his household to join him in following the Lord.

and all his wealth—his livestock and all the
people he had taken into his household at
Haran—and headed for the land of Canaan.
When they arrived in Canaan, 6Abram traveled through the land as far as Shechem.
There he set up camp beside the oak of Moreh. At that time, the area was inhabited by
Canaanites.
7Then the LORD appeared to Abram and
said, "I will give this land to your [a]descen-
dants." And Abram built an altar there and
dedicated it to the LORD, who had appeared
to him. 8After that, Abram traveled south
and set up camp in the hill country, with
Bethel to the west and Ai to the east. There
he built another altar and dedicated it to the
LORD, and he worshiped the LORD. 9Then
Abram continued traveling south by stages
toward the Negev.

Abram and Sarai in Egypt (12:10-20)

10At that time a severe famine struck the
land of Canaan, forcing Abram to go down

12:6 Gen 33:18; 35:4; Deut 11:30
12:7 Gen 13:15; *Gal 3:16; [a]*zera'* (2233); • Gen 26:3
12:8 Gen 4:26; 8:20; 22:9
12:9 Gen 13:1; 20:1
12:10 Gen 26:1; 42:5

God's Covenant Relationships (12:1-9)

Gen 9:1-17; 15:1-21; 17:9-14; Exod 6:2-5; 19:1–24:18; Lev 26:1-46; Deut 7:7-15; 29:2-29; Josh 8:30-35; 24:1-8; 2 Sam 7:5-16; Ezra 10:1-17; Isa 59:20-21; Jer 31:31-34; 33:19-26; 34:12-20; Ezek 16:1-63; Luke 22:20; Gal 4:21-31; Eph 2:11-13; Heb 8:6-13; 10:11-18; 12:24

The covenant relationships that God established and developed with his people may be the most important theological theme of the OT. The covenant theme in the OT begins with Noah, through whom God made a covenant with all of creation. God promised to uphold the created order and gave the rainbow as the sign of this commitment (9:1-17).

God later established a covenant relationship with Abraham and his family; the sign of this covenant was circumcision (12:1-9; 15:1-21; 17:9-14). God's covenant with Abraham promised descendants, land, and rulers; these promises formed the basis for the covenants God later made with his people.

God's covenant with Israel at Mount Sinai was a national covenant (Exod 19–24) whose sign was the Sabbath; it addressed how Israel would be the chosen descendants of Abraham. This covenant took the form of a suzerain-vassal treaty, an ancient relationship established between a great king and loyal subjects (see note on Exod 20:1–23:33).

The Sinai covenant was renewed in Deuteronomy and Josh 24:1-28. The renewal focused on God's promise of land and how Israel would conduct itself while inhabiting the land. Through his covenant with Israel, God affirmed that he was their God and they were his people, a relationship that required their complete loyalty (Jer 11:4; 24:7; Ezek 11:20; 14:11). God, the great king, would bless and protect the nation Israel. Israel's obligation was to keep God's commands, decrees, and regulations (Exod 19:5, 8; 24:3, 7; Deut 30:15-20).

God later formed a covenant with King David (2 Sam 7:5-16), which provided the line of kings promised to Abraham and Jacob (Gen 17:6, 16; 35:11).

Years later, at a low point in Israel's history, the prophet Jeremiah foretold a "new covenant" in Israel's future (Jer 31:31-33), in which the ideals of the covenants with Abraham and Israel would finally be realized. Jeremiah's prophecy found fulfillment in the person and work of Jesus Christ (see Luke 22:20; Heb 8:6-13; 12:24). This new covenant provides the ultimate fulfillment of the previous promises that were made to God's people.

God's covenants were motivated by God's faithful love (Hebrew *khesed*), which enabled a relationship to continue between God and his people. God initiated this relationship, announced its conditions, and rewarded his people accordingly. These covenants were not rewards but divine gifts. God may exclude people from the covenant relationship (Hos 1:9), but he will not break, revoke, or withdraw his covenants. If broken or annulled by the human parties, the covenant could be renewed only through a reapplication of God's faithful love (Exod 34:6-9; Jer 31:31-33). God's love has preserved the relationship, but his grace must not be mocked (Isa 54:7-10; 55:3; 61:8; 1 Cor 6:9-10; Gal 6:7).

12:6-7 ***The oak of Moreh*** was apparently a Canaanite shrine; fertile groves of trees were sacred to the Canaanites (cp. Isa 1:29), and *Moreh* means "teacher." Abram proclaimed (Luther: "preached") the Lord's name beside a pagan place of worship and instruction (12:8). • ***Abram*** continued to be a blessing when he ***built an altar*** to worship God at ***Shechem*** and east of Bethel (12:8).

12:7 ***The LORD appeared to Abram*** at Shechem (12:6) to confirm that ***this land*** was the Promised Land. Israel was to occupy this land, but sharing in God's promises required their faith (cp. Num 14; Josh 1:6-9). • ***to your descendants*** (literally *seed*): Abram did not yet possess the land; he lived as a temporary settler.

12:8-9 ***Abram*** had to keep moving ***camp*** because the Canaanites had the fertile land.

12:8 ***he worshiped the LORD*** (literally *he made proclamation of the LORD by name*): Proclaiming the name (identity and character) of the Lord is central to worship and witness (cp. 4:26; see Exod 34:5-7). Abram had to distinguish his sacrificial worship from that of the pagan Canaanites.

12:11 Gen 29:17
12:12 Gen 20:11
12:16 Gen 20:14; 24:35
12:17 1 Chr 16:21; Ps 105:14
12:18 Gen 20:9-10
12:19 Gen 20:5; 26:9
13:1 Gen 12:9
13:2 Gen 12:5

to Egypt, where he lived as a foreigner. 11As
he was approaching the border of Egypt,
Abram said to his wife, Sarai, "Look, you are
a very beautiful woman. 12When the Egyptians see you, they will say, 'This is his wife.
Let's kill him; then we can have her!' 13So
please tell them you are my sister. Then they
will spare my life and treat me well because
of their interest in you."
14And sure enough, when Abram arrived
in Egypt, everyone noticed Sarai's beauty.
15When the palace officials saw her, they
sang her praises to Pharaoh, their king,
and Sarai was taken into his palace. 16Then
Pharaoh gave Abram many gifts because of
her—sheep, goats, cattle, male and female
donkeys, male and female servants, and
camels.
17But the LORD sent terrible plagues upon
Pharaoh and his household because of Sarai, Abram's wife. 18So Pharaoh summoned
Abram and accused him sharply. "What
have you done to me?" he demanded. "Why
didn't you tell me she was your wife? 19Why
did you say, 'She is my sister,' and allow me to
take her as my wife? Now then, here is your
wife. Take her and get out of here!" 20Pha-
raoh ordered some of his men to escort
them, and he sent Abram out of the country,
along with his wife and all his possessions.

Abram and Lot Separate (13:1-18)

13 So Abram left Egypt and traveled
north into the Negev, along with
his wife and Lot and all that they owned.
2(Abram was very rich in livestock, silver,

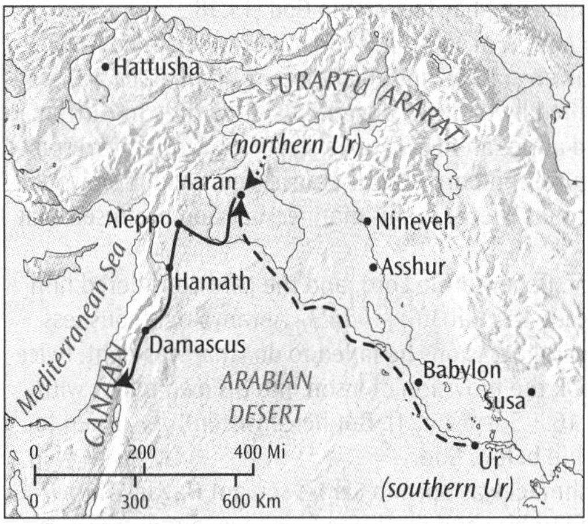

◀ **Abram's Journey to Canaan (12:1-9).** Traditionally, "Ur of the Chaldeans" (11:28, 31; 15:7) has been identified with UR in Mesopotamia (SOUTHERN UR), a chief city of ancient Sumer. Some scholars have proposed a NORTHERN UR to the north of HARAN, where Abram's extended family settled (see 27:43; 28:10; 29:4; Acts 7:2-4).

12:10-20 This episode shows that God would not allow Abram to jeopardize his promises. Just after Abram's obedience to the call, a famine tested his weak faith. God delivered him and his family, even though Abram foolishly used deception rather than trusting in God to preserve him in Egypt. • This story deliberately parallels Israel's later bondage in Egypt. Because of a famine (12:10 // 47:13), Abram/Israel went to Egypt (12:10 // 47:27); there was an attempt to kill the males and save the females (12:12 // Exod 1:22); God plagued Egypt (12:17 // Exod 7:14–11:10); Abram/Israel plundered Egypt (12:16 // Exod 12:35-36); they were expelled (Hebrew *shalakh*, "send"; 12:19-20 // Exod 12:31-33) and ascended to the Negev (13:1 // Num 13:17, 22). Israel was to believe that God would deliver them from bondage in Egypt through the plagues because their ancestor had already been rescued from bondage in Egypt.

12:10-13 Abram's scheme was rooted in fear that jeopardized his family and God's promises. Abram was not walking by faith when he went to Egypt. He stopped building altars and his deceptiveness took center stage. Deception would plague his family throughout Genesis (26:1-11; 27:1-29; 29:15-30; 30:34-36; 31:6-11; 37:18-35; 39:7-20). • Abram's plan was probably based on a social custom whereby a brother arranged the marriage of his sister (cp. 24:29-61). Abram may have thought that any potential suitor would have to deal with him, giving him time to leave with Sarai. He did not count on Pharaoh's acting without negotiation (12:14-16).

12:10 The Nile River provided ample irrigation, so ***Egypt*** was often the last region to suffer from ***famine***.

12:13 ***tell them you are my sister:*** This request occurs three times in Genesis (see also 20:2; 26:7). The text explains that this was Abram's usual strategy (20:13), and his son did likewise. This first occasion was outside the land, the second (ch 20) within, showing that God protected his promise in both regions.

12:14-16 Abram was bound by the king's gift to an unwanted agreement about Sarai that he could not prevent. His scheme had resulted in a terrible bind that endangered him, Sarai, and the promise. • Abram appeared to prosper from his deception, but the new possessions also caused crises. Abram and Lot had to separate (ch 13), and Hagar, an Egyptian maiden, became the mother of the Ishmaelites, perennial enemies of Israel (ch 16).

12:14-15 ***Sarai*** was 65 years old, but she lived to be 127; she was like a modern childless woman of about 35. She and Abram came from a noble family (see note on 11:29), so she was regal in her person and dress. Pharaoh was attracted by her physical appearance and her political assets.

12:15 ***Pharaoh*** was a title, not a personal name (37:36; Exod 1:15).

12:17-19 God's intervention rescued Sarai and preserved the marriage to fulfill the covenant promise. Sarai's restoration to Abram came with a rebuke from Pharaoh on God's behalf (12:18-19).

12:20 No answer to Pharaoh's questions (12:18-19) was needed, because the rebuke was followed by expulsion. Pharaoh's command paralleled God's command to Abram (12:1), but Pharaoh's demand brought shame and disgrace. God was faithful in preserving his promise.

13:1-7 This story is set in conflict amidst God's blessings. In the opening verses, Abram returns to a place where he had built an altar. Previous events are emphasized as Abram's return to the land is described (13:3-4); Abram renewed his worship and again proclaimed the Lord's name (cp. 12:8).

13:2 ***Abram*** already had powerful resources (12:5); his Egyptian sojourn augmented his wealth and power (12:16).

ABRAHAM (11:26–25:11)

Gen 26:2-5
Exod 3:15-16; 6:3; 32:13
Josh 24:2-3
1 Chr 1:27-34
2 Chr 20:7
Isa 29:22; 41:8; 51:1-2
Ezek 33:24
Matt 1:1-2; 3:9; 8:11; 22:31-32
Luke 16:19-31
John 8:31-58
Acts 7:2-8
Rom 4:1-23; 9:5-9; 11:16-17
Gal 3:6-29
Heb 6:13-15; 11:8-12; 11:17-19
Jas 2:21-23

"By faith . . . Abraham obeyed when God called him to leave home and go to another land. . . . He went without knowing where he was going. . . . By faith . . . Abraham offered Isaac as a sacrifice when God was testing him" (Heb 11:8, 17). These key events in Abraham's life illustrate the faithful obedience for which he is best known.

God called Abram from the city of Ur to become the patriarch of God's people. Abram's family relationships are recorded in Gen 11:26-32. Terah had three sons: Abram, Nahor, and Haran. Terah left Ur with Abram, Abram's wife Sarai, and Lot, whose father, Haran, had died. On his way to Canaan, Terah settled in the city of Haran (11:31). God had called Abram to a new land while he was still in Ur (Acts 7:2-4); God told Abram, "Leave your native country, your relatives, and your father's family, and go to the land that I will show you" (12:1). God blessed Abram by making a covenant with him that included promises of great blessing, numerous descendants, and a new land (12:1-3). These promises later saved Israel from destruction when they repeatedly failed to keep their covenant with God (see Lev 26:40-45).

Abram left Haran at age seventy-five. Entering Canaan, he went first to Shechem, a Canaanite city between Mount Gerizim and Mount Ebal. God appeared to Abram near the oak of Moreh, a Canaanite shrine (see note on 12:6-7). Abram built altars there and near Bethel (12:8), proclaiming the one true God at these centers of false worship. Abram later moved to Hebron by the oaks of Mamre, again building an altar to worship God (13:18).

When God again promised blessings to Abram in a vision (15:1), Abram exclaimed that he was still childless because Sarai was barren (11:30), and that Eliezer of Damascus was his heir (15:2). This obscure statement is clarified by the Nuzi documents. According to Hurrian custom, a childless couple of means could adopt an heir, often a slave who would be responsible for their burial and mourning. A natural son born after the slave-heir's adoption would supplant him. Apparently Abram had adopted Eliezer in this manner, but God promised that Abram's own son would be his heir (15:4).

The hallmark of Abram's life was that he believed the Lord, and the Lord considered him righteous because of his faith (15:6; see Rom 4:3; Gal 3:6; Jas 2:23). Abram's righteousness was not because he never sinned—on several occasions he failed to do what was right, twice he lied about Sarah out of fear, and he took the provision of a son into his own hands with Hagar rather than praying for God to act (16:1-5; cp. 25:21). But he consistently returned to faith as the fundamental principle of his life before God.

Abram was eighty-six years old when Ishmael was born to Sarai's servant Hagar. When Abram was ninety-nine, the Lord appeared to him and reaffirmed his covenant promise of a son and of blessing (ch 17), adding circumcision as the mark of the covenant relationship (17:9-14). God also changed Abram's and Sarai's names to Abraham and Sarah (17:5, 15). Abraham laughed at the promise of another son (17:17). Shortly afterward, the Lord appeared again to Abraham (ch 18) and again announced the promised son. This time, Sarah was caught laughing in disbelief (18:12-15). Abraham was 100 years old and his wife 90 when the Lord did "exactly what he had promised" (21:1). The long-promised son was born and was fittingly named Isaac ("he laughs!").

The supreme test of Abraham's faith came when God commanded him to sacrifice Isaac (ch 22). Abraham obeyed faithfully, trusting that God would not thwart his own purposes (see Heb 11:17-19). Just as the knife was about to fall, the angel of God stopped Abraham and provided a ram for him to sacrifice in Isaac's place (22:13). Abraham's faith was complete (22:12).

Christians understand the sacrifice of Isaac as prefiguring God's provision of his only Son, Jesus Christ, as a sacrifice for the sins of the world. God has fulfilled his covenant with Abraham through Jesus Christ, through whom the blessing of salvation is extended to all who have faith (Rom 4:16-17), and believers become Abraham's spiritual descendants (Gal 3:29). Abraham's life shows that God is faithful and worthy of belief and obedience. The full import of God's promise was realized when the gospel was preached to all nations and people from all families of the earth responded in faith (see Gal 3:6-9).

Abraham was God's friend (2 Chr 20:7; Jas 2:23). All who live by faith are challenged to live as he did, daily venturing into the unknown with trust in God's guidance and sustenance. Abraham is one of many great "witnesses" to a life of faith (Heb 12:1; see Heb 11), inspiring believers to persevere in faith because we know God is faithful.

13:3 Gen 12:8-9
13:5 Gen 12:5
13:6 Gen 12:5; 36:7
13:7 Gen 12:6; 26:20
13:8 Prov 15:18; 20:3
13:9 Gen 20:15
13:10 Gen 2:8-10
13:13 Gen 18:20; Num 32:23; Isa 1:10; 3:9; 2 Pet 2:8
13:14 Gen 28:14; Deut 3:27; 34:1-4
13:15 *Gal 3:16; Gen 12:2, 7; 15:18; 17:7-8
13:16 Num 23:10
13:17 Num 13:17-25
[b]*'erets* (0776) ▸Gen 15:18
13:18 Gen 14:13; 18:1

and gold.) [3]From the Negev, they continued traveling by stages toward Bethel, and they pitched their tents between Bethel and Ai, where they had camped before. [4]This was the same place where Abram had built the altar, and there he worshiped the LORD again.

[5]Lot, who was traveling with Abram, had also become very wealthy with flocks of sheep and goats, herds of cattle, and many tents. [6]But the land could not support both Abram and Lot with all their flocks and herds living so close together. [7]So disputes broke out between the herdsmen of Abram and Lot. (At that time Canaanites and Perizzites were also living in the land.)

[8]Finally Abram said to Lot, "Let's not allow this conflict to come between us or our herdsmen. After all, we are close relatives! [9]The whole countryside is open to you. Take your choice of any section of the land you want, and we will separate. If you want the land to the left, then I'll take the land on the right. If you prefer the land on the right, then I'll go to the left."

[10]Lot took a long look at the fertile plains of the Jordan Valley in the direction of Zoar. The whole area was well watered everywhere, like the garden of the LORD or the beautiful land of Egypt. (This was before the LORD destroyed Sodom and Gomorrah.) [11]Lot chose for himself the whole Jordan Valley to the east of them. He went there with his flocks and servants and parted company with his uncle Abram. [12]So Abram settled in the land of Canaan, and Lot moved his tents to a place near Sodom and settled among the cities of the plain. [13]But the people of this area were extremely wicked and constantly sinned against the LORD.

[14]After Lot had gone, the LORD said to Abram, "Look as far as you can see in every direction—north and south, east and west. [15]I am giving all this land, as far as you can see, to you and your descendants as a permanent possession. [16]And I will give you so many descendants that, like the dust of the earth, they cannot be counted! [17]Go and walk through the [b]land in every direction, for I am giving it to you."

[18]So Abram moved his camp to Hebron and settled near the oak grove belonging to Mamre. There he built another altar to the LORD.

Age	Event	Reference
10	Sarai is born	17:17; 20:12
75	Abram leaves Haran, moves to Canaan	12:4-6
85	Abram takes Hagar as a secondary wife	16:1-3
86	Ishmael is born	16:15-16
99	Abram is renamed Abraham, is promised a son through Sarah, is given circumcision	17:1–18:15
100	Isaac is born	21:1-7
~103	Isaac is weaned, Ishmael is sent away	21:8-14
137	Sarah dies	23:1
140	Abraham sends his servant to find a wife for Isaac	24:1-9; 25:20
160	Jacob and Esau are born	25:20, 26
175	Abraham dies	25:7-9

▲ **Abraham's Life (11:26–25:11).**

13:5-7 *Lot* was also *wealthy*, with ***flocks and herds. Tents*** figure prominently in Lot's story (13:12). • The ***Canaanites and Perizzites*** (see 34:30; Deut 7:1; Judg 1:4; 3:5) held the well-watered land; the quarrel between Abram's and Lot's herdsmen left Abram more vulnerable to attack.

13:8-13 Abram, to whom the land was promised, might have told Lot to find his own place. Abram's generosity was an act of faith; he knew that even if he gave the whole land away, God would still give it to him and his descendants. Abram did not have to cling to things, whereas Lot's choices were self-seeking.

13:8 ***Abram*** was concerned that there be no ***conflict*** (Hebrew *meribah*) between them, as they were ***close relatives*** (literally *brothers*). Moses later reproved Israel over the incident in the wilderness at Meribah (Exod 17:1-7; Num 20:1-13) and instructed them on exercising faith in such situations. Meribah thereafter became a watchword for testing and striving with the Lord in unbelief (see Ps 95).

13:10 What appealed to Lot would be short-lived. In the ***garden of the LORD***, Adam and Eve succumbed to their craving for what they saw; Israel was later enslaved in ***Egypt. Sodom and Gomorrah*** are reminders of putting intense desires ahead of obedience to God (3:5-6; see 1 Jn 2:16). • ***Zoar*** was a small town in the plain to which Lot and his daughters later fled (19:18-22); it was previously called Bela (14:2).

13:11-18 The narrator makes numerous contrasts between Lot and Abram.

13:11 Lot's choice was totally selfish, without concern for Abram or faith in the Lord. • The region called ***the whole Jordan Valley*** (literally *the circle of the Jordan*) is believed to have been near the south end of the Dead Sea, based on descriptions in ancient records that locate cities of the Plain. This area is now very desolate.

13:13 The implication is that Lot would not resist Sodom's influence because he, too, was living for himself.

13:14-17 Abram could give Lot the choice land because he believed in God's promise. Abram waited for God to give him the land; Lot just took what he wanted.

13:15 ***descendants:*** Literally *seed;* also in 13:16.

13:18 ***Hebron*** was an Anakite city (Num 13:22) originally called Kiriath-arba ("city of Arba"), located in forested highlands just north of the Negev (12:9; Josh 17:15). Abraham, Isaac, and Jacob all settled there (18:1; 35:27; 37:14), and Sarah, Abraham, Isaac, Rebekah, Jacob, and Leah were buried there (23:19; 35:27-29; 49:29-32; 50:13). • ***Mamre*** was an Amorite (14:13; 15:16).

Abram's Encounter with Kings (14:1-24)
Abram Rescues Lot

14 About this time war broke out in the
region. King Amraphel of Babylonia,
King Arioch of Ellasar, King Kedorlaomer
of Elam, and King Tidal of Goiim 2fought
against King Bera of Sodom, King Birsha
of Gomorrah, King Shinab of Admah, King
Shemeber of Zeboiim, and the king of Bela
(also called Zoar).
3This second group of kings joined forces
in Siddim Valley (that is, the valley of the
Dead Sea). 4For twelve years they had been
subject to King Kedorlaomer, but in the thirteenth year they rebelled against him.
5One year later Kedorlaomer and his allies arrived and defeated the Rephaites at
Ashteroth-karnaim, the Zuzites at Ham, the
Emites at Shaveh-kiriathaim, 6and the Horites at Mount Seir, as far as El-paran at the
edge of the wilderness. 7Then they turned
back and came to En-mishpat (now called
Kadesh) and conquered all the territory of
the Amalekites, and also the Amorites living
in Hazazon-tamar.
8Then the rebel kings of Sodom, Gomorrah, Admah, Zeboiim, and Bela (also called
Zoar) prepared for battle in the valley of the
Dead Sea. 9They fought against King Kedorlaomer of Elam, King Tidal of Goiim, King
Amraphel of Babylonia, and King Arioch of
Ellasar—four kings against five. 10As it happened, the valley of the Dead Sea was filled
with tar pits. And as the army of the kings
of Sodom and Gomorrah fled, some fell
into the tar pits, while the rest escaped into
the mountains. 11The victorious invaders
then plundered Sodom and Gomorrah and
headed for home, taking with them all the
spoils of war and the food supplies. 12They
also captured Lot—Abram's nephew who
lived in Sodom—and carried off everything
he owned.
13But one of Lot's men escaped and reported everything to Abram the Hebrew,
who was living near the oak grove belonging
to Mamre the Amorite. Mamre and his relatives, Eshcol and Aner, were Abram's allies.
14When Abram heard that his nephew

14:1 Gen 10:10; 11:2
14:2 Gen 10:19; 13:10; Deut 29:23
14:3 Num 34:3, 12; Deut 3:17; Josh 3:16
14:5 Gen 15:20; Deut 2:10, 20; 3:11; Josh 13:19
14:7 Gen 16:14; 20:1; Num 13:26; Deut 1:4; 2 Chr 20:2
14:12 Gen 11:27
14:13 Gen 10:16; 13:18; 39:14
14:14 Gen 12:5; Deut 34:1

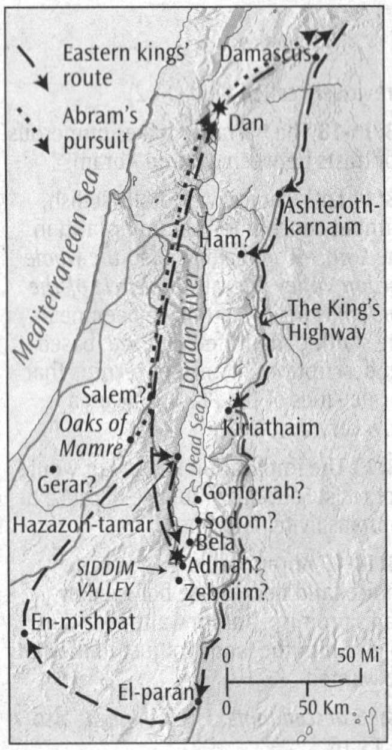

The Battle at Siddim Valley (14:1-24). When the kings in the Siddim Valley (the valley of the DEAD SEA) rebelled against King Kedorlaomer of Elam (14:4), Kedorlaomer and his Mesopotamian allies followed the King's Highway (see Num 20:17; 21:22) through Transjordan (the region east of the Jordan), then circled around from EL-PARAN through EN-MISHPAT (=Kadesh, 14:7; Num 13:26) to HAZAZON-TAMAR (=En-gedi, 2 Chr 20:2), conquering as they went. They then attacked the five Canaanite kings near BELA. When Abram heard that Lot had been taken captive, he chased after Kedorlaomer, attacked at DAN (=Laish, Josh 19:47), and pursued the fleeing armies north of DAMASCUS to Hobah, and he recovered the captives and their goods. On his return, Abram stopped by the Valley of Shaveh near SALEM (=Jerusalem) and was blessed by Melchizedek. • The location of the Siddim Valley is uncertain—it was probably at the south end of the Dead Sea.

14:1-16 In this skirmish typical of ancient politics, powerful kings formed a coalition to subjugate smaller vassal states.

14:1-2 Archaeology has not identified these kings, but similar names from antiquity corroborate the report's accuracy. The Mesopotamian kings were confederates under a suzerain, apparently *Amraphel*, who is mentioned first.

14:1 *Babylonia:* Hebrew *Shinar;* also in 14:9. • *Tidal* apparently ruled a number of city-states (*Goiim*, literally *nations*).

14:3 *Dead Sea:* Literally *Salt Sea.*

14:4-5 This was Kedorlaomer's war. Under the feudal system of tribal affiliations, those in covenant with him had to fight. It was also Abram's battle to rescue Lot, and those under treaty with him had to accompany him.

14:4 *King Kedorlaomer* apparently defeated the Siddim Valley kings at an earlier time and put them under tribute for asphalt, olive oil, and copper. *In the thirteenth year* they refused to send it; in the fourteenth year (14:5), the invaders returned to subjugate them again.

14:5-8 The invaders came down the King's Highway on the east side of the Jordan Valley to the Gulf of Aqaba, then circled back to *the valley of the Dead Sea* (Hebrew *Siddim Valley* [see 14:3]; also in 14:10).

14:8-12 The five cities of the plain were close together at the south end of the Dead Sea. The Mesopotamian kings defeated the frail uprising, looted the cities of Sodom and Gomorrah, and carried off Lot with the other captives.

14:13 The word *Hebrew* first occurs here in the Bible. It is not equivalent to the later term *Habiru* from Egyptian texts; the *Habiru* were mercenaries that roamed the land in the era of the judges. • *Mamre:* See note on 13:18. • *relatives:* Or *allies;* literally *brothers.*

14:14-16 God could give his people victory over any forces invading the Promised Land. Faithfulness to God was the prerequisite for victory. God promises to bless his people and give them victory over the world. He uses those who respond to his call and can skillfully use weapons of war (cp. Eph 4:8; 6:10-19).

14:14 *Abram . . . mobilized the 318 trained men who had been born into his household:* Abram was a formidable force, an outworking of God's promise to make him great (12:2-3). • *Dan* was a city

Lot had been captured, he mobilized the
318 trained men who had been born into his
household. Then he pursued Kedorlaomer's
army until he caught up with them at Dan.
15There he divided his men and attacked during the night. Kedorlaomer's army fled, but
Abram chased them as far as Hobah, north
of Damascus. 16Abram recovered all the
goods that had been taken, and he brought
back his nephew Lot with his possessions
and all the women and other captives.

Melchizedek Blesses Abram

17After Abram returned from his victory
over Kedorlaomer and all his allies, the king
of Sodom went out to meet him in the valley
of Shaveh (that is, the King's Valley).

18And Melchizedek, the king of Salem
and a [c]priest of God Most High, brought
Abram some bread and wine. 19Melchize-
dek blessed Abram with this blessing:

"Blessed be Abram by God Most High,
Creator of heaven and earth.
20 And blessed be God [d]Most High,
who has defeated your enemies for you."

Then Abram gave Melchizedek a [e]tenth of
all the goods he had recovered.

Abram Rejects Sodom's Goods (14:21-24)

21The king of Sodom said to Abram, "Give
back my people who were captured. But
you may keep for yourself all the goods you
have recovered."

14:15 Gen 15:2
14:17 2 Sam 18:18
14:18 Ps 76:2; 110:4; Heb 5:6, 10; 7:1; [c]*kohen* (3548) ‣Exod 18:1
14:19 Gen 27:25; 48:9; Mark 10:16
14:20 Gen 9:26; 24:27; *Heb 7:1-2; [d]*'elyon* (5945) ‣Num 24:16; [e]*ma'aser* (4643) ‣Lev 27:30

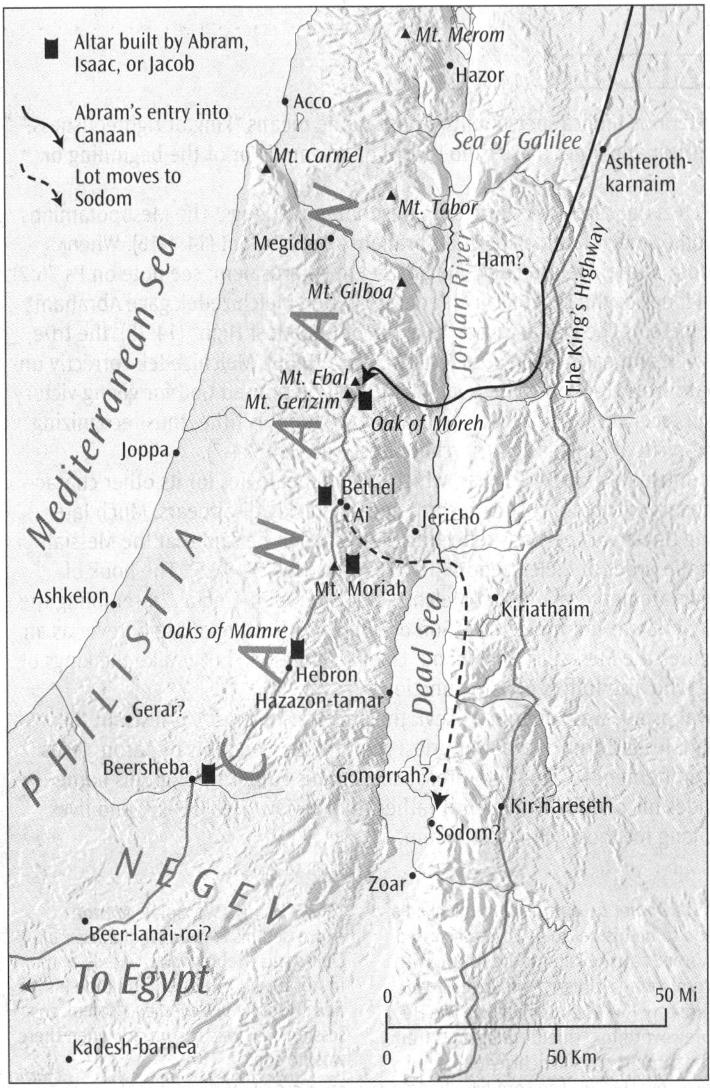

◀ **Abram in Canaan (12:1–25:11).** Abram probably entered CANAAN by following the King's Highway—an ancient and well-traveled route that ran just east of Canaan. Philistines had already begun settling along the coast (PHILISTIA; see 10:14; 21:32-34; 26:1-18). Some Canaanite settlements (JERICHO, MEGIDDO, HAZAZON-TAMAR=En-gedi) were very old by this time. Within Canaan, Abram traveled southward along the central ridge of the hill country, building altars at OAK OF MOREH (= Shechem, 12:6-7; see 33:18-19), BETHEL (12:8; 13:3; see 28:10-22; 35:1-15), MOUNT MORIAH (22:1-19), OAKS OF MAMRE (= HEBRON, 13:18; see 23:2), and BEERSHEBA (21:22-34; see 26:23-25; 46:1-7). Lot unwisely chose his portion in SODOM (13:10-13; see 18:16–19:29).

about 150 miles north of Abram's home in Hebron, then named Laish or Leshem (see Josh 19:47 and note; Judg 18:29). Dan, whose descendants migrated north in the days of the judges (Judg 18:1-29), had not yet been born (30:6). An editor apparently updated the text so that later readers could identify this city.

14:15 ***Damascus*** was 40 miles north of Dan. ***Hobah*** was about 60 miles ***north of Damascus.***

14:17 The ***valley of Shaveh*** or ***King's Valley*** was probably the Kidron Valley (see 2 Sam 18:18).

14:18 ***Melchizedek*** means "king of righteousness," suggesting that he was a righteous servant of God. He was probably a Jebusite priest and king; later authors regarded him as a type of Christ (Ps 110:4; Heb 7:1-19). • ***Salem*** is Jerusalem (cp. Ps 76:2). • ***God Most High:*** Hebrew *El-Elyon;* also in 14:19, 20, 22.

14:19-20 By paying a tithe (***a tenth***) to Melchizedek, Abram acknowledged Melchizedek as a spiritual superior (see Heb 7:4) and affirmed that God had given him victory.

14:21-24 Abram knew that accepting the offer of the ***king of Sodom*** (see note on 14:1-2) could make him his ally or subject, as Lot had been. This would jeopardize the fulfillment of God's promises. Faith looks beyond the riches of the world to the greater blessings that God has in store.

22Abram replied to the king of Sodom,
"I solemnly swear to the LORD, God Most
High, Creator of heaven and earth, 23that
I will not take so much as a single thread
or sandal thong from what belongs to you.
Otherwise you might say, 'I am the one
who made Abram rich.' 24I will accept only
what my young warriors have already eaten,
and I request that you give a fair share of
the goods to my allies—Aner, Eshcol, and
Mamre."

The LORD's Covenant Promise to Abram (15:1-21)

15 Some time later, the LORD spoke to
Abram in a vision and said to him,
"Do not be afraid, Abram, for I will [f]protect
you, and your reward will be great."
2But Abram replied, "O [g]Sovereign LORD,
what good are all your blessings when I
don't even have a son? Since you've given
me no children, Eliezer of Damascus, a servant in my household, will inherit all my
wealth. 3You have given me no descendants
of my own, so one of my servants will be my
heir."
4Then the LORD said to him, "No, your
servant will not be your heir, for you will
have a son of your own who will be your
heir." 5Then the LORD took Abram outside
and said to him, "Look up into the sky and
count the stars if you can. That's how many
descendants you will have!"
6And Abram [h]believed the LORD, and the
LORD counted him as righteous because of
his faith.

14:22 Gen 1:1
14:23 2 Kgs 5:16
15:1 Gen 21:17-18; 26:24; Ps 3:3; [f]*magen* (4043) ‣Deut 33:29
15:2 [g]*'adonay Yahweh* (0136, 3068) ‣Deut 3:24
15:4 *Gal 4:28
15:5 Gen 12:2; 22:17; 32:12; *Rom 4:18
15:6 Ps 106:31; *Rom 4:3, 9, 22; *Gal 3:6; [h]*'aman* (0539) ‣Gen 45:26

MELCHIZEDEK (14:17-24)

Ps 110:4; Heb 5:6-10; 6:20–7:28

Melchizedek is a mysterious biblical personality whose name means "king of righteousness." He was a Canaanite priest and king; there is no record of his family or of the beginning or end of his life.

Abraham met Melchizedek after defeating four Mesopotamian kings. The Mesopotamians had raided Sodom and Gomorrah and captured Abraham's nephew Lot (14:1-16). When Abraham returned from battle, Melchizedek, king of Salem (=Jerusalem; see note on Ps 76:2), was with the grateful kings of the Dead Sea confederacy. When Melchizedek gave Abraham bread, wine, and his blessing, he was acting as "a priest of God Most High" (14:18), the true God who created heaven and earth (see Ps 7:17; 47:2; 57:2; 78:56). Melchizedek correctly understood that Abraham worshiped the true God (14:22), and he praised God for giving victory to Abraham. Abraham received Melchizedek's gifts and gave him his tithe, thus recognizing Melchizedek's higher spiritual rank as a patriarchal priest (see Heb 7:4-7).

Melchizedek is an unusual figure in Genesis, which gives genealogies for its other characters. Melchizedek appears without any such record, and as quickly disappears. Much later in Israel's history, King David was perhaps reflecting on this when he said that the Messiah is "a priest forever in the order of Melchizedek" (Ps 110:4; cp. Heb 7:15-25). The book of Hebrews explains this statement, saying that Melchizedek is remembered as "resembling the Son of God" (Heb 7:3), but was not himself the Son of God. His priesthood lasts forever as an archetype that prefigures the Messiah's priesthood. Like Melchizedek (but unlike the kings of Israel), Jesus is a king who also fulfills priestly functions.

Melchizedek, a royal priest, was superior to Levi, the ancestor of Israel's priests. In the same way, the Messiah, Jesus Christ, is a better priest than the descendants of Aaron. Jesus provides permanent atonement for sins and direct access to his Father through his name (Heb 7:24-28). He guides his people by the Spirit rather than by law (Heb 8:7-13) and lives forever as priest and king for those who trust in him.

14:22 In the words of this oath, Abram may have been clarifying that his God, ***the LORD*** (*Yahweh*), was the ***God Most High*** that Melchizedek invoked. Perhaps Melchizedek had never heard the name *Yahweh*.

15:1-21 The Lord made a formal covenant with Abram, solemnly confirming the promises made at his call (12:1-3). There would be a long period of slavery for Abram's descendants before these promises would be completely fulfilled.

15:1 ***Do not be afraid:*** Abram lacked a son to be his heir. The Lord addressed Abram's anxiety about the future with comforting words. • ***I will protect you*** (literally *I will be your shield*): The Hebrew word for "shield" (*magen*) is from the same root as Melchizedek's word *defeated* (14:20). The Lord who had defeated Abram's enemies would continue to protect him. • ***your reward will be great:*** The promise of offspring (12:2-3; cp. Ps 127:3) was still unfulfilled.

15:2-3 Using a wordplay, ***Abram*** expressed his concern that ***Eliezer of Damascus*** (Hebrew *dammeseq*), a man in Abram's household, would be his ***heir*** (Hebrew *ben-mesheq*, "son of possession"), as was customary when there was no son.

15:4-6 God affirmed that the promise was for Abram's own offspring and showed him the stars as a promise of the vast number of descendants that he would have (22:17; 26:4). Paul quotes

15:7 Gen 12:1; 13:17 Acts 7:2-4
15:8 Luke 1:18
15:10 Lev 1:17
15:12 Gen 2:21; 28:11
15:13 Exod 12:40 *Acts 7:6 Gal 3:17
15:14 Exod 6:5
15:15 Gen 25:8
15:16 Exod 12:40

7Then the LORD told him, "I am the LORD
who brought you out of Ur of the Chaldeans
to give you this land as your possession."
8But Abram replied, "O Sovereign LORD,
how can I be sure that I will actually possess it?"
9The LORD told him, "Bring me a three-
year-old heifer, a three-year-old female
goat, a three-year-old ram, a turtledove, and
a young pigeon." 10So Abram presented all
these to him and killed them. Then he cut
each animal down the middle and laid the
halves side by side; he did not, however, cut
the birds in half. 11Some vultures swooped
down to eat the carcasses, but Abram
chased them away.
12As the sun was going down, Abram fell
into a deep sleep, and a terrifying darkness
came down over him. 13Then the LORD
said to Abram, "You can be sure that your
descendants will be strangers in a foreign
land, where they will be oppressed as slaves
for 400 years. 14But I will punish the nation
that enslaves them, and in the end they will
come away with great wealth. 15(As for you,
you will die in peace and be buried at a ripe
old age.) 16After four generations your descendants will return here to this land, for

God's Covenant with Abraham (15:1-21)

Gen 12:1-3; 17:1-14; 21:1-2; 22:15-18
Exod 2:24
Deut 1:8
Neh 9:7-8
Ps 105:7-45
Luke 3:7-9
Acts 3:24-26; 7:2-8
Rom 4:11-25; 9:7-8; 11:16-17
Gal 3:6-9; 3:29
Heb 6:13-15

The Lord had already established a relationship with Abraham (12:1-9) before he made a formal covenant with him (ch 15). God took all the initiative: He approached Abraham and spoke to him in a vision. God presented the impossible promise that the old man would have a son through whom his descendants would eventually be as numerous as the stars of heaven. Abraham believed God (15:6), and his faith proved to be an act of righteousness—faith is righteousness, and faith produces righteousness in covenant relationship with God (see Hab 2:4; Rom 1:17; 4:3, 17; Gal 3:6, 11; Heb 10:37-38). The covenant of ch 15 includes a royal grant (15:18-21) in which God, the king, gave land to Abraham, his subject, as a possession and an inheritance. (In the ancient Near East, kings sometimes granted land or other gifts to loyal subjects.) At the end of that day, Abraham knew that his own and his descendants' future was firmly in the hands of the covenant God. Later, the grant would be transferred to his descendants.

God later ratified his covenant with Abraham (17:1-22), giving him circumcision as its sign (17:10) and condition (17:4, 9). The almighty God once again took the initiative (17:1) in granting Abraham an extraordinary privilege. The covenant was not a relationship between equals, yet both partners in the covenant assumed responsibilities. God committed himself voluntarily to Abraham and his descendants, while requiring faithfulness from Abraham (17:1, 9-14). The blessing Abraham received as God's covenant partner was embodied in the new name that God gave him (17:5-6).

God's family covenant with Abraham also applied to his descendants (13:15-16; 15:3-5; 17:6-10). It pointed to blessing in the relatively near future when his descendants would possess the land (15:12-16). Much later, Abraham's faith became a blessing to all through his descendant, Jesus Christ, through whom all the families of the earth can share in God's blessing on Abraham (12:3; see Rom 4:11-25; Gal 3:8-9, 16).

this promise in Rom 4:18 to underscore the strength of Abram's faith.

15:6 ***And Abram believed:*** God made his covenant with a believer; the statement does not indicate when Abram came to faith. The Hebrew text does not link Abram's belief with the promise of the stars; it just says parenthetically that Abram believed God. Abram already had faith; his departure from Ur was his first great act that demonstrated it (see Heb 11:8-10). • God ***counted him as righteous because of his faith:*** This central statement about Abram's saving faith is quoted three times in the NT (Rom 4:3, 22-23; Gal 3:6; Jas 2:23) to support the doctrine of righteousness before God by faith.

15:7-21 With a solemn ceremony, God made a binding covenant with Abram that guaranteed the fulfillment of God's promises to him.

15:10 Obeying God's instructions, ***Abram*** gathered three herd animals for the ceremony and ***cut*** them ***in half.*** Cutting the animals symbolized the oath, indicating that the covenant maker staked his own life on his word (Jer 34:18).

15:11 ***Vultures*** are unclean birds of prey that symbolize those who unjustly attack Abraham's heirs (15:13-14).

15:13-16 Not even ***400 years*** of bondage could interfere with God's plan to fulfill the covenant.

15:13 ***oppressed:*** The same word is used in Exod 1:11-12. Egypt, like predatory birds (15:11), would try to destroy Israel and hinder the covenant's fulfillment. • Apparently ***400 years*** is a round number (also Acts 7:6; cp. Exod 12:40; Gal 3:17). Using the chronology in the Hebrew text, the family moved to Egypt around 1876 BC, and the Exodus occurred around 1446 BC (though many scholars date the Exodus later, around 1270 BC; see "Chronology: Abraham to Joshua," p. 118).

15:16 The reasons for Israel's bondage included God's justice. God would tolerate ***the sins of the Amorites*** until they fully deserved judgment. • ***do not yet warrant their destruction*** (literally *are not yet full*): To give the Promised Land to Israel, the Lord would dispossess the land's inhabitants in a way that satisfied

the sins of the Amorites do not yet warrant
their destruction."
17 After the sun went down and darkness
fell, Abram saw a smoking firepot and a
flaming torch pass between the halves of
the carcasses. 18 So the LORD made a [i]cov-
enant with Abram that day and said, "I have
given this [j]land to your descendants, all the
way from the border of Egypt to the great
Euphrates River—19 the land now occupied
by the Kenites, Kenizzites, Kadmonites,
20 Hittites, Perizzites, Rephaites, 21 Amorites,
Canaanites, Girgashites, and Jebusites."

God Provides the Promised Offspring (16:1–22:19)

Hagar and Ishmael

16 Now Sarai, Abram's wife, had not
been able to bear children for him.
But she had an Egyptian servant named
Hagar. 2 So Sarai said to Abram, "The LORD
has prevented me from having children. Go
and sleep with my servant. Perhaps I can
have children through her." And Abram
agreed with Sarai's proposal. 3 So Sarai,
Abram's wife, took Hagar the Egyptian servant and gave her to Abram as a wife. (This
happened ten years after Abram had settled
in the land of Canaan.)
4 So Abram had sexual relations with Hagar, and she became pregnant. But when
Hagar knew she was pregnant, she began
to treat her mistress, Sarai, with contempt.
5 Then Sarai said to Abram, "This is all your
fault! I put my servant into your arms, but
now that she's pregnant she treats me with
contempt. The LORD will show who's wrong—
you or me!"
6 Abram replied, "Look, she is your servant,

15:17 Jer 34:18-19
15:18 Num 34:1-15; Deut 1:7-8; [i]*berith* (1285) ‣Gen 17:2; [j]*'erets* (0776) ‣Gen 28:13
15:19 Num 24:21
15:21 Gen 10:15-16
16:1 Gen 11:30; Gal 4:24-25
16:2 Gen 30:3
16:3 Gen 12:4-5
16:4 Gen 16:15
16:5 Gen 31:53
16:7 Gen 21:17; 22:11, 15

HAGAR (16:1-16)

Gen 21:9-21; 25:12
Gal 4:22-31

Hagar was the Egyptian servant of Sarai, Abram's wife. When God commanded Abram to leave Mesopotamia, he promised him a multitude of descendants who would be given a new land (12:2, 7). After ten childless years in Canaan, Sarai followed the customary Mesopotamian strategy of giving Hagar to Abram as his concubine; any son born of the union of husband and concubine was considered the wife's child (cp. 30:1-6). Hagar bore a son, Ishmael (16:1-16; 21:9-21).

Hagar was so disrespectful to Sarai during her pregnancy (16:4-6) that Sarai dealt harshly with her and Hagar fled into the desert. The angel of the Lord appeared to her at a desert well, telling her to return to Abram's house and submit to Sarai.

Ishmael was born when Abram was eighty-six years old. Fourteen years later, God gave Abraham and Sarah their promised son, Isaac. When Isaac was weaned (at about three years), a traditional feast was held. At this event, Ishmael mocked Isaac (21:9), so Sarah insisted that Abraham send Hagar and Ishmael away. God confirmed this (21:12), so Hagar and Ishmael wandered in the wilderness of Beersheba. When their water was gone, God miraculously rescued them and assured Hagar that Ishmael would father a great nation (21:17-19).

Paul made an analogy (Gal 4:22-31) in which Hagar "represents Mount Sinai," where the old covenant was formed, while Sarah "represents the heavenly Jerusalem," the community of those who receive salvation by faith in Christ. As Isaac was Abraham's son by faith in the divine promise, Christians who are free of the law are spiritual children of Sarah.

his justice. The fulfillment of promises to Israel also brought retributive judgment on people of the land (though individuals were saved by faith; see Josh 2:1-15; 6:23-25; Heb 11:31; Jas 2:25). Until then, God would send the family to Egypt where Israel could become a great nation. Seeing all this in advance was terrifying (15:12), but it was comforting to know that nothing could interfere with God's plan.

15:17-18 *smoking firepot . . . flaming torch:* Fire represented the Lord's cleansing, consuming zeal and unapproachable holiness (cp. Isa 6:3-7). The holy God *made* (literally *cut*) a unilateral *covenant with Abram*; its promises were absolutely sure because they did not depend on what Abram or his descendants might do.

15:18-19 God specified the boundaries of the Promised Land. His clear message to Abram was that despite prospects of death and suffering (enslavement), he and his descendants would eventually receive the promises, for God had sworn an oath (see Heb 6:13-14). Nothing can separate God's people from his love or the fulfillment of his plans (see Rom 8:18-39; 2 Pet 1:3-4). • *the border of Egypt:* Literally *the river of Egypt*, referring either to an eastern branch of the Nile River or to the Brook of Egypt in the Sinai (see Num 34:5).

16:1-16 While waiting for their promised son to be born, Abram and Sarai attempted an alternate plan that was not in keeping with faith.

16:1-3 *Abram* and *Sarai* faced the tension of her being barren and beyond childbearing years. By custom, a barren woman could give her servant to her husband as a slave-wife; the child born to that union was considered the wife's child and could be adopted as the heir. Sarai's suggestion, unobjectionable by custom, set a problematic human plan in motion. God's promises would be fulfilled by faith.

16:4-6 Perhaps *Hagar* expected to become the favored wife instead of *Sarai* (cp. Prov 30:21-23).

[k]mal'ak (4397) ‣Gen 19:1
16:8 Gen 3:9; 4:9
16:9 Gen 21:12; Eph 6:5
16:10 Gen 17:20
16:11 Gen 16:15; Exod 3:7-8
16:12 Job 39:5-8
16:13 Gen 32:30
16:14 Gen 14:7
16:15 Gen 21:9; 25:12
16:16 Gen 12:4; 16:3

so deal with her as you see fit." Then Sarai
treated Hagar so harshly that she finally ran
away.
7The [k]angel of the LORD found Hagar
beside a spring of water in the wilderness,
along the road to Shur. 8The angel said to
her, "Hagar, Sarai's servant, where have you
come from, and where are you going?"
"I'm running away from my mistress, Sarai," she replied.
9The angel of the LORD said to her, "Return to your mistress, and submit to her
authority." 10Then he added, "I will give you
more descendants than you can count."
11And the angel also said, "You are now
pregnant and will give birth to a son. You
are to name him Ishmael (which means
'God hears'), for the LORD has heard your cry
of distress. 12This son of yours will be a wild
man, as untamed as a wild donkey! He will
raise his fist against everyone, and everyone
will be against him. Yes, he will live in open
hostility against all his relatives."
13Thereafter, Hagar used another name
to refer to the LORD, who had spoken to her.
She said, "You are the God who sees me."
She also said, "Have I truly seen the One
who sees me?" 14So that well was named
Beer-lahai-roi (which means "well of the Living One who sees me"). It can still be found
between Kadesh and Bered.
15So Hagar gave Abram a son, and Abram
named him Ishmael. 16Abram was eighty-
six years old when Ishmael was born.

ISHMAEL (16:11-16)

Gen 17:18-26; 21:8-21; 25:9-18; 28:9; Gal 4:21-31

Ishmael was Abraham's first son, born of Hagar, Sarah's Egyptian servant. The boy was born near Hebron when Abraham was 86 years old (13:18; 16:16). God had promised to make a great nation of the childless Abraham (12:2) and assured him that his son would be his heir (15:4). Ishmael was born in Abraham's attempt to fulfill God's promise by human means (see 16:1-16; Gal 4:23), but God would accomplish this through Sarah (see 17:15–18:15; 21:1-7).

When God announced that Sarah would have a son to fulfill the promise (17:15-16), Abraham asked God to accept Ishmael (17:17-18). Ishmael was not the promised son—the covenant would be established with Isaac (17:19)—but God did bless Ishmael and make him the father of a great nation (17:20-21).

At age thirteen, Ishmael was circumcised in witness to God's covenant with Abraham (17:9-14, 22-27). Then, at Isaac's weaning celebration (when Ishmael was about seventeen), Ishmael made fun of Isaac (21:9), and Abraham sent Ishmael and Hagar away with provisions. The angel of God helped Hagar survive in the wilderness, and Ishmael became a wild game hunter. He settled in the wilderness of Paran and married an Egyptian woman (21:20-21). He assisted in Abraham's burial (25:9-10), gave his daughter Mahalath in marriage to Esau (28:9), and died at age 137 (25:17). His twelve sons are named in 25:13-15.

Paul alluded to Ishmael when urging the Galatians to put their faith in God rather than in the law (see Gal 4:21-31). Those who trust the law will not inherit the kingdom, just as the slave woman's son did not inherit with the son of the free woman (Gal 4:30).

16:7 ***The angel of the LORD*** was the Lord himself (16:13; 21:17; 22:11-12; 31:11-13; 48:16; Exod 3:2; 32:34; Judg 6:11, 16, 22; 13:22-23; Zech 3:1-2), but was also distinct from the Lord (24:7; 2 Sam 24:16; Zech 1:12). The angel of the LORD was probably a *theophany* (a manifestation of God) or a *Christophany* (an appearance of the pre-incarnate Messiah; see 18:1-2; 19:1; Num 22:22; Judg 2:1-4; 5:23; Zech 12:8), speaking with the authority of the Lord himself.

16:8-12 The angel's rhetorical questions encouraged ***Hagar*** to pour out her heart to God. When she did, God commanded her to ***return*** and ***submit*** (16:9), promising that her son would have innumerable descendants. The angel of the Lord never referred to Hagar as Abram's wife, only as Sarai's servant. She would have Abram's child, but ***Ishmael*** was not central to God's covenant with Abram.

16:10-12 Hagar's son would become the father of a great but wild and hostile nation living in the Arabian Desert as perennial enemies of Israel (cp. 25:18). God blessed ***Ishmael*** as Abram's descendant, but not as the line chosen to carry on the covenant. That blessing was reserved for Abram's chosen heir.

16:11 Names in Genesis often capture the message of a passage and aid the remembrance of the events and their significance in the history of the faith. The name ***Ishmael,*** which means "***God hears***," commemorates that ***the LORD . . . heard*** Hagar's ***cry of distress*** (see also note on 16:14-15). This name would have greatly comforted Hagar; God listened to her prayers and acknowledged her complaint.

16:13 Hagar responded to God's messages by faith, in her words and in her obedience. • ***the God who sees me*** (Hebrew *El-roi*): God knew Hagar's plight and watched over her.

16:14-15 The names ***Beer-lahai-roi,*** which means ***"well of the Living One who sees me,"*** and ***Ishmael*** (see 16:11) were a message and a rebuke for Abram and Sarai. God sees affliction and hears the cries of those in need. Sarai and Abram should have prayed rather than taking the fulfillment of the promise into their own hands by following social custom (cp. 25:21). Giving children to the barren woman is God's work (Ps 113:9; cp. 1 Sam 1:1-28; Luke 1:1-25); impossible difficulties cannot be resolved by human intervention. The Lord hears the afflicted, sees them in their need, and will miraculously provide for them.

The Covenant Confirmed:
Abram Is Named Abraham

17 When Abram was ninety-nine years
old, the LORD appeared to him and
said, "I am El-Shaddai—'God [a]Almighty.'
Serve me faithfully and live a [b]blameless
life. [2]I will make a [c]covenant with you, by
which I will guarantee to give you countless
descendants."
[3]At this, Abram fell face down on the
ground. Then God said to him, [4]"This is
my covenant with you: I will make you the
father of a multitude of nations! [5]What's
more, I am changing your name. It will no
longer be Abram. Instead, you will be called
Abraham, for you will be the father of many
nations. [6]I will make you extremely fruitful. Your descendants will become many
nations, and kings will be among them!
[7]"I will confirm my covenant with you
and your descendants after you, from generation to generation. This is the everlasting

17:1
Gen 12:7; 28:3; 35:11; 48:3
Deut 18:13
Matt 5:48
[a]*shadday* (7706)
‣ Gen 28:3
[b]*tamim* (8549)
‣ Exod 12:5

17:2
Gen 12:2; 15:18
[c]*berith* (1285)
‣ Exod 19:5

17:3
Gen 17:17; 18:2

Circumcision (17:9-14)

Gen 17:23-27; 21:4; 34:1-26
Exod 4:24-26; 12:48
Lev 12:3
Josh 5:2-8
Jer 9:25-26
Ezek 44:7-9
Luke 1:59; 2:21
Acts 15:1-31; 16:1-5
Rom 2:25-29
1 Cor 7:17-19
Gal 5:1-6; 5:11-12; 6:12-16
Eph 2:11-18
Phil 3:2-7
Col 2:11; 3:11

Circumcision is the removal of the male foreskin. It was practiced by some cultures in the ancient world (see Jer 9:25-26); the Bible uses it to symbolize the removal of sin and an old identity, accompanied by inclusion in the covenant community.

God chose circumcision as the sign of a covenant that focuses on descendants. God had promised to make Abraham and his descendants into a great nation (17:7, 13, 19) and to use them to redeem the Gentile nations (12:3; 17:4-6; see Gal 3:8-9). Circumcision was God's signature in flesh; it would identify Abraham and his descendants as God's own people (17:9-14) and remind them to live in faithfulness to the covenant.

Although circumcision was applied to adult males when they joined the covenant community (17:23-27; Exod 12:48; Josh 5:3-7), it was usually performed on infants (21:4; Lev 12:3), who received God's promises and membership in the covenant community through their parents. Faith was required in order to receive God's blessings, however, as can be seen in the differentiation between Ishmael and Isaac, Esau and Jacob, and Joseph and his brothers. Non-Israelites could also obligate themselves to Israel's covenant (Exod 12:48; cp. Gen 34:15-24); circumcision marked their inclusion into the worshiping community (e.g., Exod 12:44).

Circumcision would help Israel recognize and remember that they must lay aside natural impurity. God's people had to be loyal to the covenant, to the family, and to their own marriages. Intermarriage with uncircumcised people who were not of the covenant was a violation of the covenant. Any man who refused to be circumcised (cut physically in this symbolic way) would be cut off from the covenant people because of his disobedience to God's command (17:14).

Circumcision is a symbol of separation from the world, of purity, and of loyalty to the covenant. It provides the powerful metaphor of "circumcision of the heart," which designates a heart that is committed to God and is inwardly set apart to God, rather than being stubbornly resistant (Jer 9:26; Lev 26:41; Deut 30:6; Jer 4:4; Eph 2:11). Circumcision of the heart evidences salvation and fellowship with God (see Ezek 18:31-32; 36:25-27; Rom 2:28-29; 4:11).

When Jesus Christ established God's new covenant, he fulfilled the requirements of the old covenant, so a new sign was given to identify members of the covenant community. Thus baptism replaces circumcision, and it too must be accompanied by faith. It is not necessary for Gentile believers to be circumcised, since they are incorporated into the people of God through faith in Christ (Acts 15:1-29; Rom 2:25-29; Gal 2:1-10; 6:15; Col 2:11-12). One must turn in confidence to God and his promises, lay aside natural strength and the customs of the world, and live a new life by faith (see Jer 31:33-34; Rom 8:1-17; Gal 5:16–6:10).

17:1-27 God now gave the family signs that the promises would be fulfilled. He changed Abram's name to Abraham (17:1-8), instituted the rite of circumcision as the sign of the covenant (17:9-14, 23-27), and changed Sarai's name to Sarah (17:15-22).

17:1 *El-Shaddai:* This name for God emphasizes his power (see also 28:3; 35:11; 43:14; 48:3; 49:25). • ***Serve me faithfully and live a blameless life:*** Being a blessing to the nations required obedience from Abram; his conduct would be guided by Almighty God.

17:4-5 God guaranteed his promise by changing Abram's name. ***Abram*** means "exalted father"; ***Abraham*** sounds like a Hebrew term that means "father of many" (*'ab hamon*). "Abram" referred to his noble lineage, as Terah was the "exalted father" (11:27). His new name was a wordplay on the promise of his own progeny (see also John 8:31-59; Rom 4:16-17; Gal 3:7, 15-19, 29). Whenever the new name was used, he and his household would remember that a multitude of nations would issue from him.

17:6 ***kings will be among them!*** This is the first indication that Israel would become a monarchy (see also 35:11; 36:31; Num 24:7; Deut 17:14-18; 28:36).

17:7-8 The land of Canaan was to be an

17:5 Neh 9:7 *Rom 4:17
17:6 Gen 35:11
17:7 Gen 15:18 Lev 11:45; 26:12 Ps 105:8-11 *Gal 3:16
17:9 Exod 19:5
17:10 John 7:22 Acts 7:8
17:11 Exod 12:48 Josh 5:2
17:12 Gen 21:4 Lev 12:3 Luke 1:59; 2:21
17:14 Exod 30:33 Lev 7:20
17:15 Gen 17:5
17:16 Gen 18:10
17:17 Gen 17:3; 18:11-13

covenant: I will always be your God and the
God of your descendants after you. 8And I
will give the entire land of Canaan, where
you now live as a foreigner, to you and your
descendants. It will be their possession forever, and I will be their God."

The Mark of the Covenant

9Then God said to Abraham, "Your responsibility is to obey the terms of the covenant.
You and all your descendants have this
continual responsibility. 10This is the
covenant that you and your descendants
must keep: Each male among you must be
circumcised. 11You must cut off the flesh
of your foreskin as a sign of the covenant
between me and you. 12From generation
to generation, every male child must be circumcised on the eighth day after his birth.
This applies not only to members of your
family but also to the servants born in your
household and the foreign-born servants
whom you have purchased. 13All must be
circumcised. Your bodies will bear the
mark of my everlasting covenant. 14Any
male who fails to be circumcised will be
cut off from the covenant family for breaking the covenant."

The Promise Affirmed: Sarai Is Named Sarah

15Then God said to Abraham, "Regarding
Sarai, your wife—her name will no longer
be Sarai. From now on her name will be
Sarah. 16And I will bless her and give you
a son from her! Yes, I will bless her richly,
and she will become the mother of many
nations. Kings of nations will be among her
descendants."

17Then Abraham bowed down to the
ground, but he laughed to himself in disbelief. "How could I become a father at the age
of 100?" he thought. "And how can Sarah
have a baby when she is ninety years old?"
18So Abraham said to God, "May Ishmael
live under your special blessing!"

SARAH (17:15-22)

Gen 11:29-31; 12:10-20; 16:1-6; 18:10-15; 21:1-10; 23:1-2
Isa 51:2
Rom 4:19; 9:9
Gal 4:21-31
Heb 11:11-12
1 Pet 3:6

Sarah is among the women in Scripture who were barren but miraculously bore a son (see also 30:22-24; 1 Sam 1:11, 19-20; 2 Kgs 4:14-17; Luke 1:5-25). Because Sarah was ninety years old when this happened (cp. 17:17; 21:1-5), she testifies to God's ability to do what is humanly impossible. She was Abraham's wife and the mother of Isaac, through whom God promised to multiply the Israelite nation (12:2; 17:19). Jesus was born from her descendants. Her name Sarai was changed to Sarah when Isaac's birth was promised (see note on 17:15-16). Sarah is honored for her faithfulness, even though she laughed at the prediction of Isaac's birth (18:10-15), twenty-five years after God's original promise to Abraham.

Sarah was also Abraham's half sister (11:29; 20:12). Sarah accompanied Abraham from Ur to Haran to Canaan (11:31; 12:5). On two occasions, in Egypt (12:10-20) and Gerar (20:1-18), Abraham asked Sarah to say that she was his sister rather than his wife because he was afraid that he would be killed as her husband. In both cases, despite Abraham's lack of faith, God protected Sarah, preserving her as Isaac's mother and preventing any doubt as to who Isaac's father was when he was born (21:1-5) about a year after his birth was promised (17:21; 18:10-14). God thus preserved his chosen line.

Sarah died at age 127 and was buried in the cave that Abraham purchased (ch 23) at Machpelah. She is known as the mother of the nation of Israel (Isa 51:2), just as Abraham is its father. She is a key player in accounts of Abraham's faith (Rom 4:19). She represents the freedom that Christians have, as children of Sarah the free woman, through faith in Christ (see Gal 4:21-31). Peter cites her as an example of holy submission (1 Pet 3:6). Sarah believed in God's ability to keep his promises, and her life shows that he does (Rom 9:6-9; Heb 11:11-12).

everlasting possession for the descendants of Abraham; the Lord would be their *God* forever (see Jer 31:31-40; Zech 8:8; Luke 1:68-79; Rev 21:1-4).

17:7 ***descendants:*** Literally *seed;* also in 17:8, 9, 10, 19.

17:9-14 God gave circumcision as a confirming sign that reminded all households of loyalty to ***the covenant.***

17:14 ***will be cut off:*** This punishment seems to have several applications. A person could be exiled from society or put to death by the community; most often it warned that a person might die prematurely as God cut him off from the land of the living (see Exod 31:14; Lev 7:20-27; 17:3-4; 20:17-18; 23:28-29; Num 15:30-31; see also Ps 31:22; Ezek 21:4; Rom 9:3; 11:22). Failure to be circumcised was a serious violation (see Exod 4:24-26; cp. Gal 5:2-4).

17:15-16 ***Sarai*** and ***Sarah*** both mean "princess"; the change in spelling may reflect the difference in dialect between Ur and Canaan. The new name, fitting for one who would be the mother of kings, was a milestone in Sarah's calling and brought attention to the promise.

17:17-18 Abraham ***laughed*** (Hebrew *yitskhaq*) because the promise seemed unbelievable; he had begun to believe that his line would come through ***Ishmael.*** But Abraham and Sarah would have a son of their own.

19But God replied, "No—Sarah, your wife,
will give birth to a son for you. You will
name him Isaac, and I will confirm my covenant with him and his descendants as an
everlasting covenant. 20As for Ishmael, I
will bless him also, just as you have asked.
I will make him extremely fruitful and multiply his descendants. He will become the
father of twelve princes, and I will make
him a great nation. 21But my covenant will
be confirmed with Isaac, who will be born
to you and Sarah about this time next year."
22When God had finished speaking, he left
Abraham.

Abraham Accepts the Covenant

23On that very day Abraham took his son,
Ishmael, and every male in his household, including those born there and those he had
bought. Then he circumcised them, cutting
off their foreskins, just as God had told him.
24Abraham was ninety-nine years old when
he was circumcised, 25and Ishmael, his son,
was thirteen. 26Both Abraham and his son,
Ishmael, were circumcised on that same
day, 27along with all the other men and
boys of the household, whether they were
born there or bought as servants. All were
circumcised with him.

A Son Is Promised to Sarah

18 The LORD appeared again to Abraham near the oak grove belonging to
Mamre. One day Abraham was sitting at the
entrance to his tent during the hottest part
of the day. 2He looked up and noticed three
men standing nearby. When he saw them,
he ran to meet them and welcomed them,
bowing low to the ground.

3"My lord," he said, "if it pleases you, stop
here for a while. 4Rest in the shade of this
tree while water is brought to wash your
feet. 5And since you've honored your servant with this visit, let me prepare some
food to refresh you before you continue on
your journey."

"All right," they said. "Do as you have
said."

6So Abraham ran back to the tent and
said to Sarah, "Hurry! Get three large measures of your best flour, knead it into dough,
and bake some bread." 7Then Abraham ran
out to the herd and chose a tender calf and
gave it to his servant, who quickly prepared
it. 8When the food was ready, Abraham
took some yogurt and milk and the roasted
meat, and he served it to the men. As they
ate, Abraham waited on them in the shade
of the trees.

9"Where is Sarah, your wife?" the visitors
asked.

"She's inside the tent," Abraham replied.

10Then one of them said, "I will return to
you about this time next year, and your wife,
Sarah, will have a son!"

Sarah was listening to this conversation
from the tent. 11Abraham and Sarah were
both very old by this time, and Sarah was
long past the age of having children. 12So
she laughed silently to herself and said,
"How could a worn-out woman like me
enjoy such pleasure, especially when my
master—my husband—is also so old?"

13Then the LORD said to Abraham, "Why
did Sarah laugh? Why did she say, 'Can an
old woman like me have a baby?' 14Is anything too hard for the LORD? I will return

17:19 Gen 21:2; 26:2-5
17:20 Gen 25:12-16
17:21 Gen 18:10, 14
17:22 Gen 18:33; 35:13
17:23 Gen 14:14
17:24 Rom 4:11
17:25 Gen 16:16
18:1 Gen 12:7; 13:18
18:2 Gen 32:24; Josh 5:13; Judg 13:6-11
18:4 Gen 19:2; 24:32
18:5 Judg 6:18-19; 13:15-16
18:10 *Rom 9:9
18:11 Gen 17:17
18:12 1 Pet 3:6
18:14 Gen 18:10; Jer 32:17, 27; *Rom 9:9

17:19 The name *Isaac* means "he laughs" (Hebrew *yitskhaq*); it would constantly recall Abraham's disbelieving laughter when he heard the promise. It was also a reminder of God's favor and his pleasure in the birth (cp. 21:6).

17:20-21 *Ishmael* would not be abandoned; his family would prosper (see 25:13-16), but the *covenant* promises were for *Isaac*.

17:23-27 Having received God's word about Isaac, Abraham immediately complied with God's instructions. He implemented the rite of circumcision as an act of faith; it signified their participation in the covenant (cp. Rom 4:11-12; Gal 5:2-6, 11; 6:15; Phil 3:2-3; Col 2:11-12; 1 Pet 3:21).

18:1-15 The Lord's visit to Abraham set the time for Isaac's birth. The three visitors were probably the Lord and two angels (see note on 16:7). Abraham's peaceful and generous reception of the visitors contrasts sharply with the chaos and corruption of Sodom (ch 19). Eating together was important in making or confirming covenants; when God was ready to fulfill the covenant promise, he came in person to share a meal with Abraham. Fellowship with God has always been signified by a communal meal (see Exod 24:9-11; Matt 26:17-30 // Luke 22:7-38; Acts 2:42; 1 Cor 11:20-34).

18:2-8 Abraham received his visitors as very important guests, perhaps realizing that they were messengers from God.

18:3 *My lord:* The Hebrew text uses *'adonay* ("Lord"), the word that is usually reserved for God. In Hebrew tradition, it was spoken in places where the holy name Yahweh (the LORD) was in the text. Perhaps the text uses *'adonay* rather than the more common *'adoni* to show that this was the angel of the Lord—i.e., the Lord himself (see note on 16:7). We don't know whether Abraham knew his visitors' identity at the outset, but by the story's end Abraham certainly knew he had been talking with God.

18:6 *three large measures:* Hebrew *3 seahs,* about half a bushel or 22 liters.

18:9 The visitors' rhetorical question focuses attention on *Sarah*, whom the visitors knew by name.

18:10 *I will return:* The Hebrew verb means "to intervene in someone's life to change their destiny." The statement announced a coming dramatic change.

18:13-15 Sarah thought her disbelieving laughter was hidden, but God knows human hearts (see Ps 69:5; Prov 20:27; Mark 4:22; Luke 8:43-48; Heb 4:13), whether they stagger at the promises or step out in faith (see Heb 11:11-12).

18:14 *Is anything too hard for the LORD?* The question is rhetorical. God is able to do marvelous things. Nothing is incredible to those in covenant fellowship

18:16 Gen 18:22; 19:1
18:17 Gen 19:24
18:18 Gen 12:2-3; *Gal 3:18
18:19 Neh 9:7
18:20 Gen 19:13
18:21 Gen 11:5; Exod 3:8
18:22 Gen 18:16; 19:1
18:23 Exod 23:7
18:25 Deut 1:16-17; 32:4; Ps 58:11; [d]*shapat* (8199) ‣Exod 2:14; [e]*mishpat* (4941) ‣Ps 9:16
18:27 Gen 2:7; Job 30:19; 42:6
18:30 Exod 32:32
18:33 Gen 17:22; 35:13
19:1 Gen 18:2; [f]*mal'ak* (4397) ‣Gen 28:12

about this time next year, and Sarah will have a son."

[15]Sarah was afraid, so she denied it, saying, "I didn't laugh."

But the LORD said, "No, you did laugh."

Abraham Intercedes for Sodom

[16]Then the men got up from their meal and looked out toward Sodom. As they left, Abraham went with them to send them on their way.

[17]"Should I hide my plan from Abraham?" the LORD asked. [18]"For Abraham will certainly become a great and mighty nation, and all the nations of the earth will be blessed through him. [19]I have singled him out so that he will direct his sons and their families to keep the way of the LORD by doing what is right and just. Then I will do for Abraham all that I have promised."

[20]So the LORD told Abraham, "I have heard a great outcry from Sodom and Gomorrah, because their sin is so flagrant. [21]I am going down to see if their actions are as wicked as I have heard. If not, I want to know."

[22]The other men turned and headed toward Sodom, but the LORD remained with Abraham. [23]Abraham approached him and said, "Will you sweep away both the righteous and the wicked? [24]Suppose you find fifty righteous people living there in the city—will you still sweep it away and not spare it for their sakes? [25]Surely you wouldn't do such a thing, destroying the righteous along with the wicked. Why, you would be treating the righteous and the wicked exactly the same! Surely you wouldn't do that! Should not the [d]Judge of all the earth do what is [e]right?"

[26]And the LORD replied, "If I find fifty righteous people in Sodom, I will spare the entire city for their sake."

[27]Then Abraham spoke again. "Since I have begun, let me speak further to my Lord, even though I am but dust and ashes. [28]Suppose there are only forty-five righteous people rather than fifty? Will you destroy the whole city for lack of five?"

And the LORD said, "I will not destroy it if I find forty-five righteous people there."

[29]Then Abraham pressed his request further. "Suppose there are only forty?"

And the LORD replied, "I will not destroy it for the sake of the forty."

[30]"Please don't be angry, my Lord," Abraham pleaded. "Let me speak—suppose only thirty righteous people are found?"

And the LORD replied, "I will not destroy it if I find thirty."

[31]Then Abraham said, "Since I have dared to speak to the Lord, let me continue—suppose there are only twenty?"

And the LORD replied, "Then I will not destroy it for the sake of the twenty."

[32]Finally, Abraham said, "Lord, please don't be angry with me if I speak one more time. Suppose only ten are found there?"

And the LORD replied, "Then I will not destroy it for the sake of the ten."

[33]When the LORD had finished his conversation with Abraham, he went on his way, and Abraham returned to his tent.

Sodom and Gomorrah Destroyed

19 That evening the two [f]angels came to the entrance of the city of Sodom. Lot was sitting there, and when he saw them,

with the Lord, because nothing is too difficult for him.

18:16-33 God took Abraham into his confidence as his prophet (18:16-21; see 20:7); Abraham, in turn, interceded for Sodom (18:23-32; see Heb 7:23-26). God is able to do whatever he chooses to do; this passage affirms that it will be just and right.

18:17-19 Abraham was responsible for teaching his descendants righteousness and justice so that they might enjoy God's blessings. It was important for Abraham to know how God's righteousness was at work in judgment.

18:20-21 The omniscient God was cautious in his judgment: He knew the sins of Sodom and Gomorrah, but this close scrutiny communicated God's justice in human terms—he would not destroy the people of the plain unless he was absolutely sure they were wicked.

18:20 ***a great outcry:*** See Ezek 16:49-50.

18:22-33 Abraham probably thought there were more righteous people in Sodom and Gomorrah than there were (see note on 19:14). In his concern for them, he ***approached*** the Lord with a legal appeal based on God's justice. His prayer seems too bold at times, as though he were bargaining with God, but he approached God with genuine humility and reverence. He did not try to talk God into doing something against his will, but prayed for the well-being of others (contrast Lot's prayer, 19:18-23). God is a righteous judge; righteousness exalts a nation (Prov 14:34), and righteous people help to preserve society (cp. Matt 5:13).

19:1-38 The Canaanites were an evil, corrupting people. God judged their morally bankrupt civilization and warned others against becoming like them. It was difficult to get Lot and his family out of Sodom; it was more difficult to get Sodom out of Lot and his family. This chapter helped later Israelites to understand the moral and spiritual threat of the peoples living in and around the Promised Land, such as the Canaanites and Lot's descendants, the Moabites and the Ammonites (see Num 22–25; Deut 23:3-6; Josh 24:9; Judg 10:7-9; 11:4-5; 1 Sam 10:27; 1 Kgs 11:1-3; 2 Kgs 24:2).

19:1-14 ***The two angels*** who were with the Lord at Mamre (cp. 18:2, 22) visited ***Sodom*** reluctantly, knowing what kind of people lived there. Despite Lot's hospitality, they preferred lodging in the square to entering Lot's house.

19:1 No longer living in tents next to Sodom (13:12), Lot had become a citizen and leader in Sodom, ***sitting there*** at the entrance of the city. Community leaders (elders) usually congregated in the gates, where legal and business

he stood up to meet them. Then he welcomed them and bowed with his face to the ground. 2“My lords,” he said, “come to my home to wash your feet, and be my guests for the night. You may then get up early in the morning and be on your way again.”

“Oh no,” they replied. “We’ll just spend the night out here in the city square.”

3But Lot insisted, so at last they went home with him. Lot prepared a feast for them, complete with fresh bread made without yeast, and they ate. 4But before they retired for the night, all the men of Sodom, young and old, came from all over the city and surrounded the house. 5They shouted to Lot, “Where are the men who came to spend the night with you? Bring them out to us so we can have sex with them!”

6So Lot stepped outside to talk to them, shutting the door behind him. 7“Please, my brothers,” he begged, “don’t do such a wicked thing. 8Look, I have two virgin daughters. Let me bring them out to you, and you can do with them as you wish. But please, leave these men alone, for they are my guests and are under my protection.”

9“Stand back!” they shouted. “This fellow came to town as an outsider, and now he’s acting like our judge! We’ll treat you far worse than those other men!” And they lunged toward Lot to break down the door.

10But the two angels reached out, pulled Lot into the house, and bolted the door. 11Then they blinded all the men, young and old, who were at the door of the house, so they gave up trying to get inside.

12Meanwhile, the angels questioned Lot. “Do you have any other relatives here in

19:2 Gen 18:4
19:3 Gen 18:6-8
19:4 Gen 13:13; 18:20
19:5 Lev 18:22; Judg 19:22
19:8 Deut 23:17
19:9 Exod 2:14
19:10 Gen 19:1
19:11 Deut 28:28-29; 2 Kgs 6:18; Acts 13:11

LOT (19:1-38)

Gen 11:27, 31; 12:4-5; 13:1-14; 14:12-16
Deut 2:9, 17-19
Ps 83:4-8
Luke 17:28-33
2 Pet 2:6-9

Lot was Abraham’s nephew and the ancestor of the Moabites and Ammonites. Like Abraham, Lot was born in Ur and accompanied Terah to Haran (11:27-32). After Terah’s death, he joined Abraham in journeying to Canaan and Egypt.

When Lot and Abraham returned from Egypt to Canaan, their flocks and herds grew too numerous for them to live together. Abraham gave Lot his choice of land on which to settle. Lot chose the fertile plain of the Jordan that was like “the garden of the Lord” (13:10), and eventually he took up residence in Sodom. His increasing involvement with the completely corrupt cities of the plain contaminated Lot and resulted in the loss of all his wealth.

While Lot lived in Sodom, four Mesopotamian kings defeated the kings of five towns in the area; in the subsequent plundering, they carried off Lot, his family, and his possessions (14:1-12). When word of this reached Abraham, he launched a rearguard action against the invaders and recovered the prisoners and property (14:13-16). Later, two angelic visitors called on Lot in Sodom to hasten his departure from the doomed city (ch 19). The homosexual attack on the visitors illustrates the city’s depravity, and Lot’s willingness to sacrifice his daughters shows how corrupt and compromised he had become. Lot was reluctant to leave Sodom. No one but his immediate family accompanied him, and his wife was destroyed when she turned back. His daughters, despairing of finding husbands, got Lot drunk enough to have sexual relations with them. Their two sons, Moab and Ben-ammi, were ancestors of the Moabites and Ammonites (19:30-38), two nations that became inveterate enemies of Israel (see Deut 23:3-6).

Lot was a fool and a hypocrite to the people of the town, and on his journey out of Sodom he was still bargaining with God. His drunkenness and incest with his two daughters also reveals his character. Despite his waywardness, Peter declares that Lot was a “righteous man who was tormented in his soul by the wickedness he saw and heard day after day” (see 2 Pet 2:6-9).

transactions were publicly finalized (cp. 23:18; Job 29:7, 12-17). As a righteous man (2 Pet 2:7-8), Lot tried to modify the townspeople’s wickedness by giving advice on good living (cp. 19:9). Although he denounced gross evil, Lot preferred Sodom’s sumptuous lifestyle to life in the hills (cp. 13:10-11), where there was clean living but no “good life.” As long as the Lord left Lot and his family alone in Sodom, he lived comfortably there and kept his personal belief in God; but finally, he could not hold to both. Sodom would have destroyed Lot if the Lord had not destroyed Sodom. • This account showed Israel that God is the righteous judge of the whole earth (18:25) who will judge evildoers with justice and equity. In wicked societies, moral and ethical failures lead to social injustice.

19:4-5 The townsmen’s vileness was matched by Lot’s hypocrisy (19:6-9).

19:6-9 Lot opposed homosexuality and rape and rebuked their wicked plans, but he was hypocritically willing to sacrifice his daughters to fend off the townsmen’s vice. Lot had originally pitched his tent next to Sodom; now Sodom controlled his life.

19:9 The men of the city were enraged by Lot’s attempts to curtail their wickedness. Lot had apparently not condemned them before, since they were amazed that he now judged them.

19:10 *angels:* Literally *men;* also in 19:12, 16. They first appeared to Abraham as men (18:2); the text identifies two of them as angels (19:1).

19:13 Gen 18:20; 1 Chr 21:15; Jude 1:7
19:14 Exod 9:21; Jer 5:12; 43:1-2
19:17 Gen 13:10; 19:26; Jer 48:6
19:22 Gen 13:10
19:24 Luke 17:29; Jude 1:7
19:25 Deut 29:23; Isa 13:19; Lam 4:6; 2 Pet 2:6
19:26 Gen 19:17; Luke 17:32
19:27 Gen 18:22
19:28 Rev 9:2
19:29 Deut 7:8; 9:5; 2 Pet 2:7-8
19:30 Gen 13:10

the city?" they asked. "Get them out of this place—your sons-in-law, sons, daughters, or anyone else. 13For we are about to destroy this city completely. The outcry against this place is so great it has reached the LORD, and he has sent us to destroy it."

14So Lot rushed out to tell his daughters' fiancés, "Quick, get out of the city! The LORD is about to destroy it." But the young men thought he was only joking.

15At dawn the next morning the angels became insistent. "Hurry," they said to Lot. "Take your wife and your two daughters who are here. Get out right now, or you will be swept away in the destruction of the city!"

16When Lot still hesitated, the angels seized his hand and the hands of his wife and two daughters and rushed them to safety outside the city, for the LORD was merciful. 17When they were safely out of the city, one of the angels ordered, "Run for your lives! And don't look back or stop anywhere in the valley! Escape to the mountains, or you will be swept away!"

18"Oh no, my lord!" Lot begged. 19"You have been so gracious to me and saved my life, and you have shown such great kindness. But I cannot go to the mountains. Disaster would catch up to me there, and I would soon die. 20See, there is a small village nearby. Please let me go there instead; don't you see how small it is? Then my life will be saved."

21"All right," the angel said, "I will grant your request. I will not destroy the little village. 22But hurry! Escape to it, for I can do nothing until you arrive there." (This explains why that village was known as Zoar, which means "little place.")

23Lot reached the village just as the sun was rising over the horizon. 24Then the LORD rained down fire and burning sulfur from the sky on Sodom and Gomorrah. 25He utterly destroyed them, along with the other cities and villages of the plain, wiping out all the people and every bit of vegetation. 26But Lot's wife looked back as she was following behind him, and she turned into a pillar of salt.

27Abraham got up early that morning and hurried out to the place where he had stood in the LORD's presence. 28He looked out across the plain toward Sodom and Gomorrah and watched as columns of smoke rose from the cities like smoke from a furnace.

29But God had listened to Abraham's request and kept Lot safe, removing him from the disaster that engulfed the cities on the plain.

Lot and His Daughters

30Afterward Lot left Zoar because he was afraid of the people there, and he went to

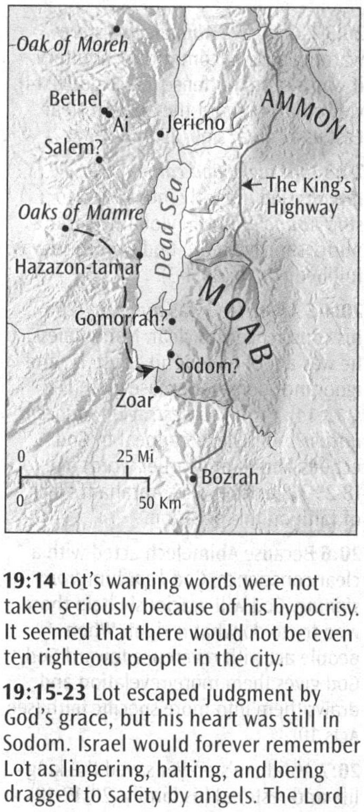

◀ **The Destruction of Sodom and Gomorrah (18:16–19:38).** The two angels apparently traveled, as shown, from Abraham's camp at the OAKS OF MAMRE to destroy SODOM and GOMORRAH. Lot and his daughters took refuge at ZOAR, then moved eastward into the mountains of MOAB. Lot fathered two sons by his daughters; the two sons became the nations of MOAB (see Num 21:10-20; 22:1–25:3; Deut 23:3, 6; Judg 3:12-30; Ruth 1:1-6) and AMMON (see Num 21:24; Deut 2:19-37; 23:3; Judg 10:6–12:3; 1 Sam 10:27–11:11).

19:14 Lot's warning words were not taken seriously because of his hypocrisy. It seemed that there would not be even ten righteous people in the city.

19:15-23 Lot escaped judgment by God's grace, but his heart was still in Sodom. Israel would forever remember Lot as lingering, halting, and being dragged to safety by angels. The Lord mercifully spared Lot for Abraham's sake (18:23; 19:29). Lot deserved judgment for his way of life, but he was a believer at heart and the Lord rescued him (2 Pet 2:7-8). • Lot is not alone in his conflicted lifestyle. Countless believers fall in with a corrupt world rather than flee a doomed society. God's people, living in a pagan world, must remain separate (1 Jn 2:15-17). The corrupt world system awaits God's coming judgment, which will be far greater than the destruction of Sodom and Gomorrah (Matt 11:23-24).

19:18-22 Lot demanded a concession from the angels even after he was delivered. He wanted to live in the small town of Zoar (***little place***).

19:23-25 Cp. Luke 17:29. The eruption of Vesuvius and the destruction of Pompeii in 79 AD, as well as recent natural disasters, show how quickly a thorough catastrophe like this could happen.

19:26 ***looked back:*** The verb indicates prolonged, intense gazing toward the world she loved, not a curious glance (15:5; Exod 33:8; Num 21:9; 1 Sam 2:32; cp. Exod 3:6). ***Lot's wife*** was too attached to Sodom to follow God's call of grace, so she was included in the judgment as she lingered on the valley slopes. Christ's return to judge the world will be as sudden and devastating as the destruction of Sodom (Luke 17:32-37). Those who crave the life of this wicked world will lose this world and the next.

19:29 God honored Abraham's intercession (cp. 18:23-32), but Lot's entire world was gone because he lived by instinct and desire, not by faith in God. He could no longer live in the good land he selfishly chose for himself (13:10-13; cp. Matt 16:26; 2 Cor 5:7).

19:30-38 The poverty of the cave contrasts with the wealth Lot shared with Abram and the good life he lived

live in a cave in the mountains with his two
daughters. 31One day the older daughter
said to her sister, "There are no men left
anywhere in this entire area, so we can't
get married like everyone else. And our father will soon be too old to have children.
32Come, let's get him drunk with wine, and
then we will have sex with him. That way
we will preserve our family line through our
father."
33So that night they got him drunk with
wine, and the older daughter went in and
had intercourse with her father. He was
unaware of her lying down or getting up
again.
34The next morning the older daughter
said to her younger sister, "I had sex with
our father last night. Let's get him drunk
with wine again tonight, and you go in and
have sex with him. That way we will preserve our family line through our father."
35So that night they got him drunk with
wine again, and the younger daughter went
in and had intercourse with him. As before,
he was unaware of her lying down or getting up again.
36As a result, both of Lot's daughters became pregnant by their own father. 37When
the older daughter gave birth to a son, she
named him Moab. He became the ancestor
of the nation now known as the Moabites.
38When the younger daughter gave birth
to a son, she named him Ben-ammi. He became the ancestor of the nation now known
as the Ammonites.

Abraham Deceives Abimelech

20 Abraham moved south to the Negev and lived for a while between
Kadesh and Shur, and then he moved on
to Gerar. While living there as a foreigner,
2Abraham introduced his wife, Sarah, by saying, "She is my sister." So King Abimelech of
Gerar sent for Sarah and had her brought to
him at his palace.
3But that night God came to Abimelech in
a dream and told him, "You are a dead man,
for that woman you have taken is already
married!"
4But Abimelech had not slept with her yet,
so he said, "Lord, will you destroy an innocent nation? 5Didn't Abraham tell me, 'She
is my sister'? And she herself said, 'Yes, he is
my brother.' I acted in complete innocence!
My hands are clean."
6In the dream God responded, "Yes, I
know you are innocent. That's why I kept
you from sinning against me, and why I
did not let you touch her. 7Now return the
woman to her husband, and he will pray
for you, for he is a [g]prophet. Then you will
live. But if you don't return her to him, you
can be sure that you and all your people will
die."

19:33 Gen 9:21
19:37 Gen 36:35; Exod 15:15; Num 21:29; Deut 2:9; Ruth 1:1
19:38 Num 21:24; Deut 2:19
20:1 Gen 14:7; 26:1
20:2 Gen 12:13
20:3 Gen 28:12; 31:24; 37:5
20:4 Gen 18:23-25
20:5 Gen 12:19; 1 Kgs 9:4; Ps 7:8; 26:6
20:7 1 Sam 7:5; Job 42:8
[g]*nabi'* (5030) ‣ Exod 7:1

---

in Sodom. Abraham would father a righteous nation (17:1), but Lot and his daughters gave birth to a new Sodom.

19:30-35 The character of Lot's *daughters* was formed by Sodom's culture more than by their father's heritage, so they had no qualms about having children by their drunk father (cp. 9:21-22). They saw no other way to carry on their line.

19:36-38 The daughters' plan worked, and they each ***became pregnant by their own father***. From these two incest-born sons came two perennial enemies of Israel, the nations of Moab and Ammon. Their grotesque wickedness was due in part to their origin. • Both daughters chose ambiguous names that hinted at their actions without raising the suspicions of those who did not know the stories. ***Moab*** sounds like a Hebrew term that means "from father." ***Ben-ammi*** means "son of my kinsman."

20:1-18 This second "sister story" in Genesis (cp. 12:10-20) occurred shortly before Sarah became pregnant with Isaac (ch 21). On both occasions, God protected Abraham and Sarah's marriage in purity for the sake of the covenant promises. Participation in God's plan requires separation from worldly corruption. • This story took place in the Promised Land; it showed Israel how God intervened in people's lives to fulfill his plan, how God continued to protect them against threats from other tribes, and how God used his chosen people to mediate his relationship with the nations. • God's preventing the destruction of Abraham's marriage by adultery reminded the Israelites to keep their marriages morally and racially pure (Ezra 9:1-4; Neh 13:23-27; Mal 2:10-17); they should not allow any opportunity for temptation (Exod 20:14, 17; Lev 20:10; 21:13-15). Adultery would eventually destroy the covenant and the covenant people.

20:1 ***Gerar*** was near the coast in Philistine land, about twelve miles south of Gaza and fifty miles southwest of Hebron.

20:2 ***Abraham*** told the same lie to Abimelech that he had told to Pharaoh (12:13); Isaac would later do the same (26:1-11), probably having learned this tactic from his father. • ***Abimelech*** (literally *my father the king*) was probably a title like "Pharaoh" (37:36; Exod 1:15), not a proper name (see note on 26:1).

20:3-7 ***God*** gave ***Abimelech*** a stern warning against committing adultery; it was a capital offense (cp. Exod 20:14), viewed throughout the ancient Near East as a "great sin" (20:9).

20:3 ***that night God came . . . in a dream:*** God urgently intervened to stop ***Abimelech*** from violating Sarah's purity shortly before God's promise was fulfilled (18:10; 21:1-3).

20:4-5 ***Abimelech*** was ***innocent*** (20:6); his conscience was clear. Nonetheless, he was about to commit adultery, and ignorance does not excuse guilt (Lev 4:13-14). • ***will you destroy an innocent nation?*** Abimelech's appeal to God echoes Abraham's earlier words (cp. 18:23-32) and rebukes Abraham's lack of faith on this occasion.

20:6 Because Abimelech acted with a clear conscience, God ***kept*** him ***from sinning***. God will graciously help those who try to do what is right. When people act with reverence toward God, God gives them more revelation and draws them into more specific faith (see Acts 10).

20:7 Abraham's prayer saved the king's life and restored his family (20:17-18).

20:9 Gen 12:18
20:11 Gen 12:12; 42:18
20:13 Gen 12:1
20:14 Gen 12:16
20:16 Gen 23:15
20:17 Num 12:13; 21:7 [h]*palal* (6419) ‣Deut 9:26
20:18 Gen 12:17
21:1 Gen 17:16, 21
21:2 Gen 18:10 Gal 4:22 Heb 11:11
21:3 Gen 17:19
21:4 Gen 17:10, 12
21:5 Gen 12:4 Heb 6:15
21:6 Isa 54:1
21:7 Gen 18:13
21:8 1 Sam 1:23
21:9 Gal 4:29
21:10 *Gal 4:30

8Abimelech got up early the next morning and quickly called all his servants
together. When he told them what had
happened, his men were terrified. 9Then
Abimelech called for Abraham. "What
have you done to us?" he demanded.
"What crime have I committed that deserves treatment like this, making me and
my kingdom guilty of this great sin? No
one should ever do what you have done!
10Whatever possessed you to do such a
thing?"
11Abraham replied, "I thought, 'This is a
godless place. They will want my wife and
will kill me to get her.' 12And she really
is my sister, for we both have the same
father, but different mothers. And I married her. 13When God called me to leave
my father's home and to travel from place
to place, I told her, 'Do me a favor. Wherever we go, tell the people that I am your
brother.' "
14Then Abimelech took some of his sheep
and goats, cattle, and male and female servants, and he presented them to Abraham.
He also returned his wife, Sarah, to him.
15Then Abimelech said, "Look over my land
and choose any place where you would like
to live." 16And he said to Sarah, "Look, I am
giving your 'brother' 1,000 pieces of silver
in the presence of all these witnesses. This
is to compensate you for any wrong I may
have done to you. This will settle any claim
against me, and your reputation is cleared."
17Then Abraham [h]prayed to God, and
God healed Abimelech, his wife, and his female servants, so they could have children.
18For the LORD had caused all the women to
be infertile because of what happened with
Abraham's wife, Sarah.

The Birth of Isaac

21 The LORD kept his word and did for
Sarah exactly what he had promised. 2She became pregnant, and she gave
birth to a son for Abraham in his old age.
This happened at just the time God had
said it would. 3And Abraham named their
son Isaac. 4Eight days after Isaac was born,
Abraham circumcised him as God had commanded. 5Abraham was 100 years old when
Isaac was born.
6And Sarah declared, "God has brought
me laughter. All who hear about this will
laugh with me. 7Who would have said to
Abraham that Sarah would nurse a baby? Yet
I have given Abraham a son in his old age!"

Hagar and Ishmael Are Sent Away

8When Isaac grew up and was about to be
weaned, Abraham prepared a huge feast
to celebrate the occasion. 9But Sarah saw
Ishmael—the son of Abraham and her Egyptian servant Hagar—making fun of her son,
Isaac. 10So she turned to Abraham and demanded, "Get rid of that slave woman and
her son. He is not going to share the inheritance with my son, Isaac. I won't have it!"
11This upset Abraham very much because Ishmael was his son. 12But God told

---

Abimelech learned that Abraham's God was sovereign, and that Abraham, God's ***prophet***, had received God's revelation and would intercede for others (see Num 12:13; Deut 9:20), even if he did not always live up to the office.

20:8-10 Abraham had earned rebukes from Abimelech and from God (cp. 12:17-19). Abimelech was angry that Abraham's deception had made him guilty ***of this great sin*** (see note on 20:3-7). He knew that taking a married woman into his harem was wrong.

20:11-13 Abraham's duplicity was not a momentary loss of faith. Despite the rebuke he received in Egypt, he practiced this strategy ***wherever*** he went (cp. 12:12-13). Living by faith requires perseverance.

20:14-16 ***Abimelech*** secured his ***reputation*** as a good man (see note on 20:4-5) and demonstrated his integrity. He made amends by allowing Abraham to live in the region, and by giving him slaves, livestock (cp. 21:27), and ***1,000 pieces of silver*** (Hebrew *1,000 [shekels] of silver*, about 25 pounds or 11.4 kilograms in weight) to ***compensate . . . for any wrong*** done to Sarah.

20:17-18 The infertility suggests that some time had passed. God controls births; he opens and closes wombs (25:21; 29:31; 30:2, 17, 22-23; 1 Sam 1:19-20; Ps 113:9; 127:3; Luke 1:13).

21:1-2 See 18:10.

21:3-4 ***Abraham*** responded in faith by naming his ***son Isaac*** and circumcising him according to the terms of the covenant (see 17:9-14).

21:5 Isaac was born twenty-five years after the promise was first given (cp. 12:4).

21:6-7 ***Sarah*** was filled with joy and praise for this amazing event—only ***God*** could enable her to have a child.

21:6 The name *Isaac* (Hebrew *yitskhaq*) means "he laughs." Sarah's wordplay shows that the laughter of unbelief when the promise was given (18:12) had changed to the laughter of joy at its fulfillment. Isaac's name could refer to the pleasure of God and of his parents at his birth. Sarah knew that everyone who heard about this would ***laugh with*** her and rejoice at the news.

21:8-21 God used the incident of Ishmael's mocking Isaac to separate Ishmael and Hagar from the family and the child of promise. They would constantly threaten the promised descendant if they remained with the family.

21:8-9 The ***feast*** for Isaac's weaning probably occurred when he was three and ***Ishmael*** about seventeen years old (16:16). Sarah saw Ishmael ***making fun of her son, Isaac*** (as in Greek version and Latin Vulgate; Hebrew lacks *of her son, Isaac*). The verb *metsakheq* ("making fun of") is related to the word for "laughter"; this theme (21:6) is given a sour twist by Ishmael's mockery.

21:10 Earlier, Sarah mistreated Hagar and pressured her to flee (16:6); when Hagar's son mistreated Isaac, Sarah demanded that ***that slave woman and her son*** leave.

21:11-13 Abraham was ***upset*** by Sarah's demand to oust Hagar and ***Ishmael***.

Abraham, "Do not be upset over the boy and
your servant. Do whatever Sarah tells you,
for Isaac is the son through whom your descendants will be counted. 13But I will also
make a nation of the descendants of Hagar's son because he is your son, too."
14So Abraham got up early the next morning, prepared food and a container of water,
and strapped them on Hagar's shoulders.
Then he sent her away with their son, and
she wandered aimlessly in the wilderness
of Beersheba.
15When the water was gone, she put the
boy in the shade of a bush. 16Then she went
and sat down by herself about a hundred
yards away. "I don't want to watch the boy
die," she said, as she burst into tears.
17But God heard the boy crying, and the
angel of God called to Hagar from heaven,
"Hagar, what's wrong? Do not be afraid! God
has heard the boy crying as he lies there.
18Go to him and comfort him, for I will
make a great nation from his descendants."
19Then God opened Hagar's eyes, and she
saw a well full of water. She quickly filled
her water container and gave the boy a
drink.
20And God was with the boy as he grew
up in the wilderness. He became a skillful
archer, 21and he settled in the wilderness
of Paran. His mother arranged for him to
marry a woman from the land of Egypt.

Abraham's Covenant with Abimelech

22About this time, Abimelech came with
Phicol, his army commander, to visit Abraham. "God is obviously with you, helping
you in everything you do," Abimelech said.
23"Swear to me in God's name that you will
never deceive me, my children, or any of my
descendants. I have been loyal to you, so
now swear that you will be loyal to me and
to this country where you are living as a foreigner."
24Abraham replied, "Yes, I swear to it!"
25Then Abraham complained to Abimelech
about a well that Abimelech's servants had
taken by force from Abraham's servants.
26"This is the first I've heard of it," Abimelech answered. "I have no idea who is
responsible. You have never complained
about this before."
27Abraham then gave some of his sheep,
goats, and cattle to Abimelech, and they
made a treaty. 28But Abraham also took
seven additional female lambs and set
them off by themselves. 29Abimelech asked,
"Why have you set these seven apart from
the others?"
30Abraham replied, "Please accept these
seven lambs to show your agreement that I
dug this well." 31Then he named the place
Beersheba (which means "well of the oath"),
because that was where they had sworn the
oath.

21:12 *Rom 9:7 *Heb 11:18
21:13 Gen 16:10; 21:18; 25:12-18
21:14 Gen 16:1
21:16 Jer 6:26
21:17 Exod 3:7 Deut 26:7 Ps 6:8
21:18 Gen 26:24
21:20 Gen 28:15
21:21 Gen 25:18
21:22 Gen 26:26
21:23 Gen 24:3
21:25 Gen 26:15
21:27 Gen 26:31
21:30 Gen 31:44
21:31 Gen 21:14; 26:33

God told him to comply, assuring Abraham that Ishmael would also have a future as Abraham's offspring.

21:14-21 God again rescued Hagar ***in the wilderness*** and guaranteed her future (cp. 16:7-14). This passage is similar to ch 16, but the differences are great. Here, Hagar and Ishmael are rescued, but there is no commemorative naming. God's earlier promise to Hagar is reiterated, but this time Hagar is not told to return to Sarah. The repeated motifs on the two occasions confirm God's sovereign plan for Hagar and Ishmael. As Joseph told Pharaoh, the twofold event showed that God confirmed it (41:32). God did not abandon Hagar and Ishmael but met them in their despair (cp. 16:7), provided sustenance for them, and promised again that Ishmael would found a great nation (21:13; cp. 16:11-12). Paul uses this event in his letter to the Galatians to illustrate how God's people must relinquish all that threatens the fulfillment of God's promise (Gal 4:21-31).

21:16 ***a hundred yards*** (literally *a bowshot*): This description connects with Ishmael's vocation (21:20).

21:22-34 This passage, at its climax, explains the name of ***Beersheba***, Abraham's home (21:31-34). Beersheba reflected the covenant Abraham made with the residents of the land, which enabled him to dwell there in peace and prosperity. God's promise was coming to fruition (12:7; 13:14-17; 15:7, 18-21; 17:8).

21:22-23 ***Abimelech*** pressed for the treaty so that ***Abraham*** would not cheat or ***deceive*** him. Abimelech knew that God was blessing Abraham even though Abraham was not entirely trustworthy (20:9-10). This sad contradiction made the treaty necessary. By contrast, God's faithful people are exhorted to speak the truth (Eph 4:15, 25), and Jesus warned against manipulating truth by the clever use of oaths (Matt 5:37; Jas 5:12).

21:25 The motif of the ***well*** appears again (cp. 16:14; 21:19). God provided water (a symbol of blessing) in the barren wilderness, and later even brought water out of a rock for Israel (Exod 15:22-27; 17:1-7; Num 20:1-13).

21:27-31 Abraham's gifts to Abimelech (cp. 20:14) secured his legal right to dwell peaceably in the land and to claim ownership of the well. ***Beersheba*** marked one more step toward the fulfillment of God's promise.

21:32 ***The Philistines*** in Genesis are different from the Philistines of Judges through Kings. The earlier Philistines had Semitic names (e.g., Abimelech) and Canaanite culture. The later Philistines were apparently of Greek origin, with Greek customs and culture. They seem to have arrived in Canaan by sea from the Aegean area around 1200 BC, during the time of the judges. Probably the name of the later Philistines was used here simply to describe the region's earlier inhabitants.

21:33-34 ***A tamarisk tree*** requires a lot of water; this act indicated Abraham's security in his land rights and his faith that God would provide water in this desert area. He settled ***as a foreigner*** in the land, but dwelling under his tree was a sign of peaceful security (cp. Zech 3:10). • ***there he worshiped the LORD:*** See note on 12:8. • ***the Eternal God:*** Hebrew *El-Olam*.

22:1-2 The greatest test in Abraham's life came after he had received the promised child following a long wait. He had grown to love Isaac and had enjoyed his presence for a number of years.

21:33
1 Sam 22:6; 31:13
Ps 90:2
Isa 9:6; 40:28
[i]*olam* (5769)
‣Deut 33:15

22:1
Exod 15:25; 16:4
Deut 8:2, 16

22:2
2 Chr 3:1
John 3:16

22:5
[j]*khawah* (7812)
‣Gen 42:6

32After making their covenant at Beersheba, Abimelech left with Phicol, the
commander of his army, and they returned
home to the land of the Philistines. 33Then
Abraham planted a tamarisk tree at Beersheba, and there he worshiped the LORD, the
[i]Eternal God. 34And Abraham lived as a foreigner in Philistine country for a long time.

Abraham's Faith Tested

22 Some time later, God tested Abraham's faith. "Abraham!" God called.
"Yes," he replied. "Here I am."
2"Take your son, your only son—yes, Isaac,
whom you love so much—and go to the land
of Moriah. Go and sacrifice him as a burnt
offering on one of the mountains, which I
will show you."
3The next morning Abraham got up
early. He saddled his donkey and took
two of his servants with him, along with
his son, Isaac. Then he chopped wood for
a fire for a burnt offering and set out for
the place God had told him about. 4On the
third day of their journey, Abraham looked
up and saw the place in the distance. 5"Stay
here with the donkey," Abraham told the
servants. "The boy and I will travel a little
farther. We will [j]worship there, and then
we will come right back."

ISAAC (21:1-12)

Gen 17:19-21; 22:1-19; 24:1-8, 14, 62-67; 25:5-11, 19-28; 26:1–28:9; 31:42; 35:12, 27-28; 48:15-16; 49:31
Exod 3:6
Josh 24:3-4
Rom 9:6-10
Gal 4:21-31
Heb 11:8-9, 17-20

At Isaac's birth, his parents, Abraham and Sarah, were beyond childbearing age. God had promised Abraham a son (15:4-6), but no son had come. Ishmael had been born through Hagar (16:1-16), but he was not the promised son.

Isaac means "he laughs," reflecting the circumstances of his birth. When God promised that Isaac would be born, both Abraham and Sarah first laughed in disbelief (17:15-19; 18:9-15). When he was born, they laughed for joy (21:6-7).

During Isaac's adolescence, God tested Abraham by telling him to sacrifice Isaac (22:1-19). Abraham's faith remained firm; he obeyed, and Isaac submitted to his father. God then intervened to provide a sacrificial ram in Isaac's place. Abraham's faith in God was rewarded with the promise of great blessings (22:15-18).

Isaac married Rebekah and was ready to carry on the chosen line, but Rebekah was unable to bear children (25:21). Rather than take matters into his own hands as his father had done (see 16:1-16), Isaac "pleaded with the LORD" and Rebekah bore twin sons. Isaac favored Esau, the older son, while Rebekah preferred Jacob. Favoritism remained a problem among Isaac's descendants (see notes on 29:30; 33:1-2; 37:4) and led to Isaac's being deceived by his son Jacob when he was old and blind (ch 27).

Isaac followed his father Abraham's example in relating to surrounding nations. When visiting another kingdom during a famine, he fearfully claimed that his wife was his sister (26:1-11; cp. 12:10-20; 20:1-18). Like his father, Isaac became prosperous in that land and was asked to leave (26:12-16; cp. 12:16-20); he experienced conflict over water and land with other herdsmen (26:17-22; cp. 21:25-31); and he made a treaty with the king of the Philistines (26:26-31; cp. 21:22-31). When Isaac worshiped the Lord at Beersheba, he was given the same promise that his father had received (26:2-5, 23-25; cp. 21:32-33; 22:16-18).

Isaac continued God's covenant with Abraham and linked Abraham with Jacob (see Acts 7:8; Heb 11:9-20). As the child of promise, Isaac represents all who are children of Abraham by faith in Christ and are thereby free to live as God's children rather than as slaves (see Gal 4:21–5:1).

22:1 *Some time later:* Abraham had sent Ishmael away and settled in the land. Now ***God tested Abraham's faith*** by telling him to give up Isaac. This pushed the limits of logic and of Abraham's knowledge of God. Would he still obey when God seemed to be working against him and against the covenant? Would he cling to the boy or surrender him to God (see Exod 13:11-13)? Did he believe that God would still keep his word and bless the world through Abraham's offspring?

22:2 Obedience to God's earlier call (12:1-3) was rewarded with great blessing; now Abraham had the opportunity to show even greater obedience. • ***Take your son . . . Isaac, whom you love so much:*** By this detailed description of Isaac, God reminded Abraham that the young man was his beloved son, and intensified his awareness of the cost of the sacrifice. • The name ***Moriah*** is explained by the Chronicler (2 Chr 3:1) as the place of the later Temple Mount in Jerusalem. • ***Go:*** By wording the command in this way, God helped Abraham to obey by recalling his former call (cp. 12:1-3).

22:3 Abraham's immediate, unquestioning obedience is almost as astounding as the test.

22:5 ***We will worship there, and then we will come*** (or *We will worship there so that we may come back*): Abraham's amazing statement makes us wonder what he was thinking. Abraham knew that God had planned the future of the covenant around Isaac, and that God wanted him to sacrifice Isaac. He could not reconcile these things in his mind; he could only do what God commanded him to do, and leave the future to God (cp. Heb 11:17-19).

6So Abraham placed the wood for the burnt offering on Isaac's shoulders, while he himself carried the fire and the knife. As the two of them walked on together, 7Isaac turned to Abraham and said, "Father?"

"Yes, my son?" Abraham replied.

"We have the fire and the wood," the boy said, "but where is the sheep for the burnt offering?"

8"God will provide a sheep for the burnt offering, my son," Abraham answered. And they both walked on together.

9When they arrived at the place where God had told him to go, Abraham built an altar and arranged the wood on it. Then he tied his son, Isaac, and laid him on the altar on top of the wood. 10And Abraham picked up the knife to kill his son as a sacrifice. 11At that moment the angel of the LORD called to him from heaven, "Abraham! Abraham!"

"Yes," Abraham replied. "Here I am!"

12"Don't lay a hand on the boy!" the angel said. "Do not hurt him in any way, for now I know that you truly fear God. You have not withheld from me even your son, your only son."

13Then Abraham looked up and saw a ram caught by its horns in a thicket. So he took the ram and sacrificed it as a burnt offering in place of his son. 14Abraham named the place Yahweh-Yireh (which means "the LORD will provide"). To this day, people still use that name as a proverb: "On the mountain of the LORD it will be provided."

15Then the angel of the LORD called again to Abraham from heaven. 16"This is what the LORD says: Because you have obeyed me and have not withheld even your son, your only son, I swear by my own name that 17I will certainly bless you. I will multiply your descendants beyond number, like the stars in the sky and the sand on the seashore. Your descendants will conquer the cities of their enemies. 18And through your descendants all the nations of the earth will be blessed—all because you have obeyed me."

19Then they returned to the servants and traveled back to Beersheba, where Abraham continued to live.

Nahor's Family (22:20-24)

20Soon after this, Abraham heard that Milcah, his brother Nahor's wife, had borne Nahor eight sons. 21The oldest was named Uz, the next oldest was Buz, followed by

22:6 John 19:17
22:7 Gen 8:20; Exod 29:38-42; John 1:29, 36; Rev 13:8
22:9 Heb 11:17-19; Jas 2:21
22:11 Gen 16:7; 21:17
22:12 Heb 11:17
22:13 Gen 8:20
22:14 Gen 22:7-8
22:16 *Heb 6:13-14
22:17 Gen 12:2; 15:5; 26:4; *Heb 6:14
22:18 *Acts 3:25; *Gal 3:8, 16
22:19 Gen 21:14
22:20 Gen 11:29

22:7-8 In response to Isaac's question, *Abraham* again showed his faith in the Lord, saying *God will provide,* although he was not sure how. This theme is central to the entire narrative.

22:9-19 God's intervention was dramatic and instructive, confirming that he never intended for Isaac to be sacrificed. God later made it clear that child sacrifice was an abomination to him (see Lev 18:21; 20:1-5; Deut 18:10; 2 Kgs 16:2-3; Isa 57:5; Jer 32:35). God wanted Abraham to sacrifice his own will and surrender it to God, and when he did, God intervened. This passage sets a pattern for all sacrificial worshipers. Like Abraham, true worshipers of God know that everything belongs to God—it all came from God and must therefore be acknowledged as God's possession. A true worshiper holds nothing back but obediently gives God what he asks, trusting that God will provide for all his needs, and then discovering through experience that God always does so.

22:11 *The angel of the LORD* stopped Abraham just as he was ready to plunge the knife into his son.

22:12 Now God knew that Abraham would hold nothing back from him, that he did *truly fear God.* To fear the Lord means to reverence him as sovereign, trust him implicitly, and obey him without protest. The sacrifice that pleases God is a heart broken of self-will, surrendered to God (Ps 40:6-8; 51:17) and offering its best to God. • *You have not withheld:* Cp. Rom 8:32, which uses the same verb ("spare") as the Greek OT uses here. If God gave us his dearest possession, he will surely provide all things for us.

22:13 God provided *a ram caught by its horns in a thicket* for the sacrifice. God graciously allowed Abraham to substitute an animal sacrifice *in place of* Isaac. Later, all Israel would offer animals to the Lord, knowing that God's grace had provided this substitution (Exod 29:10; Lev 4:15; 16:20-22). In the NT, God substituted his only son for all humanity; the perfect sacrifice was made once and for all (Isa 53:6, 10; John 1:29; Heb 7:27; 10:1-14; 1 Pet 3:18).

22:14 As with many patriarchal narratives, the heart of the matter is retained through commemorative naming. *Yahweh-Yireh . . . means "the LORD will provide"* (see 22:8). That Abraham used the holy name in this act shows that the patriarchs knew the name *Yahweh* (cp. Exod 6:2-3), but not its full meaning (see note on Exod 6:2-3). • *To this day:* Later Israelites understood this passage as a lesson about their own worship in Jerusalem. Abraham's sacrifice took place *on the mountain of the LORD*, later the location of the Temple in Jerusalem (see note on 22:2). Three times a year, the people of Israel brought their best to God as a sacrifice, trusting that he would continue to provide for their needs.

22:15-19 After the event, God again confirmed his covenant with Abraham (cp. 15:5, 18-21; 17:3-8). His descendants would be numerous *like the stars in the sky* (cp. 26:4), like *the sand on the seashore* (cp. 32:12), and like the dust of the earth (cp. 13:16; 28:14).

22:16 *by my own name:* There is no higher name by which God can *swear* (Heb 6:13-17).

22:17 *descendants:* Literally *seed;* also in 22:18. • Joshua and OT Israel partially fulfilled the promise that Abraham's descendants would *conquer the cities* (literally *take possession of the gates*) of God's *enemies*; this will be fulfilled fully by the church (cp. Matt 16:18 and note).

22:18–25:11 Abraham passed the test of faith; from this point, his task was to pass the covenant blessings to Isaac. He purchased a burial plot (ch 23), acquired a wife for Isaac (ch 24), and distributed his property (25:1-11).

22:20-24 A report came from the east that Abraham's brother Nahor (see 11:27-29) was flourishing. The actors in the following narrative are introduced here.

22:20 *Milcah*, Nahor's wife, was also his niece (see 11:29).

22:21 *Uz* might have been Job's forefather (Job 1:1).

22:23 Gen 24:15
23:2 Josh 14:15
23:3 Gen 10:15
23:4 Lev 25:23; 1 Chr 29:15; Ps 39:12; Heb 11:9
23:6 Gen 14:14-16
23:8-9 Gen 25:9
23:10 Ruth 4:1, 11
23:15 Exod 30:13
23:16 Jer 32:9
23:17-18 Gen 25:9; 49:29-30; 50:13

Kemuel (the ancestor of the Arameans),
22Kesed, Hazo, Pildash, Jidlaph, and Bethuel.
23(Bethuel became the father of Rebekah.)
In addition to these eight sons from Milcah,
24Nahor had four other children from his
concubine Reumah. Their names were Tebah, Gaham, Tahash, and Maacah.

The Burial of Sarah: Abraham's Land Purchase (23:1-20)

23 When Sarah was 127 years old, 2she
died at Kiriath-arba (now called
Hebron) in the land of Canaan. There Abraham mourned and wept for her.
3Then, leaving her body, he said to the
Hittite elders, 4"Here I am, a stranger and a
foreigner among you. Please sell me a piece
of land so I can give my wife a proper burial."
5The Hittites replied to Abraham, 6"Listen, my lord, you are an honored prince
among us. Choose the finest of our tombs
and bury her there. No one here will refuse
to help you in this way."
7Then Abraham bowed low before the
Hittites 8and said, "Since you are willing
to help me in this way, be so kind as to ask
Ephron son of Zohar 9to let me buy his cave
at Machpelah, down at the end of his field.
I will pay the full price in the presence of
witnesses, so I will have a permanent burial
place for my family."
10Ephron was sitting there among the
others, and he answered Abraham as the
others listened, speaking publicly before
all the Hittite elders of the town. 11"No, my
lord," he said to Abraham, "please listen to
me. I will give you the field and the cave.
Here in the presence of my people, I give it
to you. Go and bury your dead."
12Abraham again bowed low before the
citizens of the land, 13and he replied to Ephron as everyone listened. "No, listen to me. I
will buy it from you. Let me pay the full price
for the field so I can bury my dead there."
14Ephron answered Abraham, 15"My
lord, please listen to me. The land is worth
400 pieces of silver, but what is that between
friends? Go ahead and bury your dead."
16So Abraham agreed to Ephron's price
and paid the amount he had suggested—
400 pieces of silver, weighed according to
the market standard. The Hittite elders witnessed the transaction.
17So Abraham bought the plot of land
belonging to Ephron at Machpelah, near
Mamre. This included the field itself, the
cave that was in it, and all the surrounding
trees. 18It was transferred to Abraham as
his permanent possession in the presence
of the Hittite elders at the city gate. 19Then
Abraham buried his wife, Sarah, there in
Canaan, in the cave of Machpelah, near
Mamre (also called Hebron). 20So the field
and the cave were transferred from the
Hittites to Abraham for use as a permanent
burial place.

22:22-23 *Bethuel* was the youngest of Nahor's eight sons by Milcah; he was ***the father of Rebekah***, Isaac's future wife (see 24:15, 67). Rebekah would follow Sarah as matriarch of the clan (23:1-2).

23:1-20 When *Sarah . . . died*, Abraham acquired a parcel of land for a burial place. This transaction was the first sign that a permanent transition had taken place, as people were normally buried in their ancestral homeland (cp. 49:29–50:13). In burying Sarah, Abraham detached from his just-mentioned ancestral home (where his relatives still lived, 22:20-24); his future would be in Canaan, where his descendants would realize the promise.

23:1 *Sarah was 127 years old:* Isaac was 37 at this time (cp. 17:17). • ***Hebron:*** See note on 13:18.

23:3-4 Abraham bargained with local ***Hittite elders*** for a ***piece of land*** for a burial site. These Hittites had apparently migrated south to Canaan from the great Hittite empire in eastern Asia Minor (modern Turkey; cp. 10:15). • Abraham was ***a stranger and a foreigner*** among these people; his hope was in God's promise that he would eventually possess the land.

23:5-6 ***my lord, you are an honored prince:*** Either Abraham was highly regarded by these people, or they were politely appealing to his generosity. • ***Choose the finest. . . . No one here will refuse:*** They were willing to accommodate his request, especially if they could legally obligate him to themselves (23:11).

23:7-16 Abraham wanted to ***buy*** Ephron's ***cave at Machpelah***, but ***Ephron*** wanted him to buy the entire field.

23:9 This would be a ***permanent burial place*** for Abraham's ***family***. The site was near Mamre (23:19), where Abraham lived (see 13:18; 14:13; 18:1). Abraham and Sarah, Isaac and Rebekah, and Jacob and Leah would all be buried in this cave (23:19; 25:9; 35:27-29; 49:29-31; 50:13), their permanent place in the Promised Land.

23:11 Ephron did not intend to ***give*** the cave to Abraham; Abraham was expected to "give" the full price in return. Ephron wanted to sell as much as he could to avoid responsibility for caring for the cave and to receive as high a price as possible.

23:12-13 Abraham didn't want the whole field, but he was willing to take it to get the cave.

23:15 ***400 pieces*** (Hebrew *400 shekels*, about 10 pounds or 4.6 kilograms in weight; also in 23:16) ***of silver*** was a very high price. Ephron's politeness was typical of the bargaining process.

23:16-20 Abraham ***paid the amount*** and finalized the transaction, avoiding indebtedness by accepting no gifts from the people (cp. 14:21-24). The ***Hittite elders witnessed the transaction***, ensuring that no one could challenge Abraham's full ownership of the land. The transaction took place ***at the city gate***, where public legal and business dealings were conducted (cp. 19:1). The land became Abraham's ***permanent possession***, a down payment on God's promise to give him the land. Abraham knew that God's promise was not fulfilled (12:7) by this acquisition, so he planned for the future. By buying land for his dead, he declared that God's promises do not end with this life. This is the hope of all who die in faith.

A Wife for Isaac from Nahor's Family (24:1-67)
Commission to Find a Wife

24 Abraham was now a very old man,
and the LORD had blessed him in
every way. 2One day Abraham said to his
oldest servant, the man in charge of his
household, "Take an oath by putting your
hand under my thigh. 3Swear by the LORD,
the God of heaven and earth, that you will
not allow my son to marry one of these local
Canaanite women. 4Go instead to my homeland, to my relatives, and find a wife there
for my son Isaac."
5The servant asked, "But what if I can't
find a young woman who is willing to travel
so far from home? Should I then take Isaac
there to live among your relatives in the
land you came from?"
6"No!" Abraham responded. "Be careful
never to take my son there. 7For the LORD,
the God of heaven, who took me from
my father's house and my native land, solemnly promised to give this land to my
descendants. He will send his angel ahead
of you, and he will see to it that you find a
wife there for my son. 8If she is unwilling to
come back with you, then you are free from
this oath of mine. But under no circumstances are you to take my son there."

Dependence on God's Leading

9So the servant took an oath by putting
his hand under the thigh of his master,
Abraham. He swore to follow Abraham's
instructions. 10Then he loaded ten of Abraham's camels with all kinds of expensive
gifts from his master, and he traveled to
distant Aram-naharaim. There he went to
the town where Abraham's brother Nahor
had settled. 11He made the camels kneel
beside a well just outside the town. It was
evening, and the women were coming out
to draw water.
12"O LORD, God of my master, Abraham,"
he prayed. "Please give me success today,
and show unfailing love to my master, Abraham. 13See, I am standing here beside this
spring, and the young women of the town
are coming out to draw water. 14This is my
request. I will ask one of them, 'Please give
me a drink from your jug.' If she says, 'Yes,
have a drink, and I will water your camels,
too!'—let her be the one you have selected as
Isaac's wife. This is how I will know that you
have shown unfailing love to my master."
15Before he had finished praying, he saw
a young woman named Rebekah coming out
with her water jug on her shoulder. She was
the daughter of Bethuel, who was the son of
Abraham's brother Nahor and his wife, Milcah. 16Rebekah was very beautiful and old
enough to be married, but she was still a virgin. She went down to the spring, filled her
jug, and came up again. 17Running over to
her, the servant said, "Please give me a little
drink of water from your jug."
18"Yes, my lord," she answered, "have a
drink." And she quickly lowered her jug
from her shoulder and gave him a drink.
19When she had given him a drink, she said,
"I'll draw water for your camels, too, until
they have had enough to drink." 20So she
quickly emptied her jug into the watering
trough and ran back to the well to draw water for all his camels.
21The servant watched her in silence, wondering whether or not the LORD had given
him success in his mission. 22Then at last,
when the camels had finished drinking, he

24:1 Gen 12:2; 24:35
24:2 Gen 47:29
24:3 Gen 14:19
24:4 Gen 12:1
24:5 Gen 24:39
24:7 Gen 12:1, 7; 16:7; 22:11; Rom 4:13; *Gal 3:16
24:10 Gen 11:29; Deut 23:4
24:11 Gen 24:42
24:12 Gen 24:27, 48
24:14 Judg 6:17; 1 Sam 14:10
24:15 Gen 22:20-24
24:16 Gen 12:11; 29:17
24:17 1 Kgs 17:10; John 4:7
24:19 Gen 24:14
24:22 Gen 24:47

24:1-67 Isaac's marriage to Rebekah ensured that God's plan would continue into the next generation. God showed covenant faithfulness by working through his faithful people (24:12, 27, 49).

24:1-9 Confident in the Lord's promise, Abraham had his chief servant (probably Eliezer, 15:2) ***swear*** to ***find a wife*** among Abraham's ***relatives*** in his ***homeland***, some 450 miles away. Abraham was faithful to the covenant by preparing for Isaac's future.

24:2 Putting his ***hand under*** Abraham's ***thigh*** (cp. 47:29), the servant took a very solemn oath, assuming the burden of completing this mission.

24:3 Isaac knew how wicked and threatening the ***local Canaanite*** people were, so he maintained separation from them (cp. 26:34-35; 27:46; 28:8-9).

24:6-8 ***Under no circumstances*** was the servant to take Isaac from the Promised Land to seek a wife. Abraham ensured Isaac's safety and secured God's promises in the land of blessing.

24:7 ***descendants:*** Literally *seed;* also in 24:60.

24:10-60 The servant faithfully carried out the mission, and he glorified God for displaying faithful covenant love for Abraham's family by bringing all the details together. God sovereignly worked behind the scenes to accomplish his will through the circumstances of those acting responsibly in faith.

24:10-27 The servant obeyed his master's instructions and trusted God to lead him to the right woman.

24:10 ***Aram-naharaim*** ("Aram of the two rivers") was also called ***Paddan-aram*** ("the field of Aram," cp. 25:20). It was a two-week journey in each direction, so the servant had ***ten . . . camels*** for provisions and ***gifts*** (24:22, 53).

24:14 Abraham's future daughter-in-law manifested hospitality and industry like Abraham's (see 18:1-8). Ten thirsty camels could drink 250 gallons of water, so a woman who would work that hard for a stranger was certainly not lazy, but generous and hospitable.

24:15-22 The servant received a precise, immediate answer to his prayer for guidance.

24:22 The servant showed his gratitude by giving the girl expensive jewelry. • ***a gold ring for her nose and two large gold bracelets:*** Hebrew ***a gold nose-ring weighing a half shekel*** [0.2 ounces or 6 grams] ***and two gold bracelets weighing 10 shekels*** [4 ounces or 114 grams].

24:24 Gen 24:15
24:26 Exod 4:31
24:27 Gen 14:20; 24:12, 48
24:28 Gen 29:12
24:29 Gen 25:20; 29:5
24:30 Gen 24:10
24:31 Gen 26:29
24:34 Gen 15:2; 24:2
24:35 Gen 12:2
24:36 Gen 21:1-7; 25:5
24:37 Gen 24:2-4
24:40 Gen 24:7

took out a gold ring for her nose and two large gold bracelets for her wrists.

23"Whose daughter are you?" he asked. "And please tell me, would your father have any room to put us up for the night?"

24"I am the daughter of Bethuel," she replied. "My grandparents are Nahor and Milcah. 25Yes, we have plenty of straw and feed for the camels, and we have room for guests."

26The man bowed low and worshiped the LORD. 27"Praise the LORD, the God of my master, Abraham," he said. "The LORD has shown unfailing love and faithfulness to my master, for he has led me straight to my master's relatives."

The Success of the Mission

28The young woman ran home to tell her family everything that had happened. 29Now Rebekah had a brother named Laban, who ran out to meet the man at the spring. 30He had seen the nose-ring and the bracelets on his sister's wrists, and had heard Rebekah tell what the man had said. So he rushed out to the spring, where the man was still standing beside his camels. 31Laban said to him, "Come and stay with us, you who are blessed by the LORD! Why are you standing here outside the town when I have a room all ready for you and a place prepared for the camels?"

32So the man went home with Laban, and Laban unloaded the camels, gave him straw for their bedding, fed them, and provided water for the man and the camel drivers to wash their feet. 33Then food was served. But Abraham's servant said, "I don't want to eat until I have told you why I have come."

"All right," Laban said, "tell us."

34"I am Abraham's servant," he explained. 35"And the LORD has greatly blessed my master; he has become a wealthy man. The LORD has given him flocks of sheep and goats, herds of cattle, a fortune in silver and gold, and many male and female servants and camels and donkeys.

36"When Sarah, my master's wife, was very old, she gave birth to my master's son, and my master has given him everything he owns. 37And my master made me take an oath. He said, 'Do not allow my son to marry one of these local Canaanite women. 38Go instead to my father's house, to my relatives, and find a wife there for my son.'

39"But I said to my master, 'What if I can't find a young woman who is willing to go back with me?' 40He responded, 'The LORD, in whose presence I have lived, will send his angel with you and will make your mission successful. Yes, you must find a wife for my son from among my relatives, from my father's family. 41Then you will have fulfilled your obligation. But if you go to my relatives and they refuse to let her go with you, you will be free from my oath.'

42"So today when I came to the spring, I prayed this prayer: 'O LORD, God of my master, Abraham, please give me success on this mission. 43See, I am standing here beside this spring. This is my request. When a young woman comes to draw water, I will say to her, "Please give me a little drink of water from your jug." 44If she says, "Yes, have a drink, and I will draw water for your camels, too," let her be the one you have selected to be the wife of my master's son.'

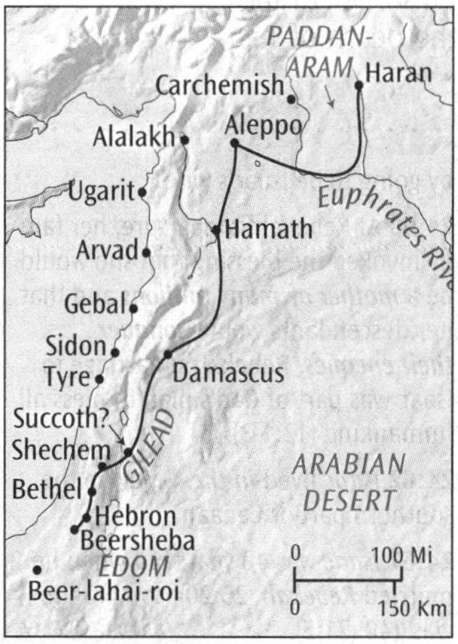

◀ **Journeys to Paddan-aram** (24:1-67; 28:1–29:14; 31:1–33:20). When Abraham's servant traveled to PADDAN-ARAM (=Aram-naharaim? cp. 24:10; 25:20) to find a wife for Isaac, he probably followed the same route that he had previously traveled from Haran (11:28–12:9). Jacob later made the same trip to and from Haran (28:1–29:14; 31:1–33:20; see "Jacob's Family in Canaan" at 32:1–38:30, p. 87).

24:23-24 God led the servant to Abraham's family.

24:25 Rebekah again showed kindness by offering lodging for the servant and food for his camels.

24:26 The servant ***bowed*** to the ground and ***worshiped the LORD*** for his loyal love and faithfulness in guiding him to the exact family he sought.

24:27 *The LORD has shown unfailing love and faithfulness to my master:* These words express this chapter's message (cp. 24:48). Believers can trust the Lord's leading because he is sovereign in all things. He never leaves his people to their own resources in carrying out his covenant work.

24:29-31 *Laban . . . ran:* He was not going to miss the chance to marry his sister off and receive more gifts. Laban's response to the servant's wealth foreshadows his avaricious character (see 24:54-56 and note; 29:21-27; 30:27-36; 31:1-13).

24:33-48 The ***servant*** was not diverted from his mission; he insisted on telling his story before he would eat. He recounted his mission and acknowledged God's providence in directing him to Rebekah before attending to his personal needs. The servant wanted everyone to know that this was God's work, not a chance or humanly arranged meeting.

45“Before I had finished praying in my
heart, I saw Rebekah coming out with her
water jug on her shoulder. She went down
to the spring and drew water. So I said to
her, ‘Please give me a drink.’ 46She quickly
lowered her jug from her shoulder and said,
‘Yes, have a drink, and I will water your camels, too!’ So I drank, and then she watered
the camels.
47“Then I asked, ‘Whose daughter are
you?’ She replied, ‘I am the daughter of Bethuel, and my grandparents are Nahor and
Milcah.’ So I put the ring on her nose, and
the bracelets on her wrists.
48“Then I bowed low and worshiped the
LORD. I praised the LORD, the God of my
master, Abraham, because he had led me
straight to my master’s niece to be his son’s
wife. 49So tell me—will you or won’t you
show unfailing love and faithfulness to my
master? Please tell me yes or no, and then
I’ll know what to do next.”
50Then Laban and Bethuel replied, “The
LORD has obviously brought you here, so
there is nothing we can say. 51Here is Rebekah; take her and go. Yes, let her be the
wife of your master’s son, as the LORD has
directed.”
52When Abraham’s servant heard their
answer, he bowed down to the ground and
worshiped the LORD. 53Then he brought
out silver and gold jewelry and clothing
and presented them to Rebekah. He also
gave expensive presents to her brother and
mother. 54Then they ate their meal, and the
servant and the men with him stayed there
overnight.
But early the next morning, Abraham’s
servant said, “Send me back to my master.”
55“But we want Rebekah to stay with us at
least ten days,” her brother and mother said.
“Then she can go.”
56But he said, “Don’t delay me. The LORD
has made my mission successful; now send
me back so I can return to my master.”
57“Well,” they said, “we’ll call Rebekah
and ask her what she thinks.” 58So they
called Rebekah. “Are you willing to go with
this man?” they asked her.
And she replied, “Yes, I will go.”
59So they said good-bye to Rebekah and
sent her away with Abraham’s servant and
his men. The woman who had been Rebekah’s childhood nurse went along with her.
60They gave her this blessing as she parted:

“Our sister, may you become
the mother of many millions!
May your descendants be strong
and conquer the cities of their
enemies.”

61Then Rebekah and her servant girls
mounted the camels and followed the man.
So Abraham’s servant took Rebekah and
went on his way.

The Marriage of Isaac and Rebekah

62Meanwhile, Isaac, whose home was in the
Negev, had returned from Beer-lahai-roi.
63One evening as he was walking and meditating in the fields, he looked up and saw
the camels coming. 64When Rebekah looked
up and saw Isaac, she quickly dismounted
from her camel. 65“Who is that man walking through the fields to meet us?” she
asked the servant.
And he replied, “It is my master.” So
Rebekah covered her face with her veil.
66Then the servant told Isaac everything he
had done.
67And Isaac brought Rebekah into his
mother Sarah’s tent, and she became his
wife. He loved her deeply, and she was a special comfort to him after the death of his
mother.

24:45 1 Sam 1:12
24:47 Gen 24:23-24
24:49 Gen 47:29
24:50 Ps 118:23
24:52 Gen 24:26
24:54 Gen 30:25
24:55 Judg 19:4
24:59 Gen 35:8
24:60 Gen 17:16; 22:17
24:62 Gen 16:14
24:63 Ps 119:15, 27, 48
24:67 Gen 23:1-2; 25:20; 29:18

24:48 The way that God directed this event from behind the scenes is different than in most of Genesis, but it is true to how the life of faith normally works. Faith, expressed in personal prayer and obedience, looks for evidence of God’s working. Believers usually have to make wise choices and remain faithful to the covenant, trusting that God will guide them through the circumstances of life to accomplish his will.

24:50-51 Following his testimony about God’s guidance, the servant secured the family’s blessing and permission to take *Rebekah* to his master’s son, Isaac.

24:53 The servant gave expensive gifts to *Rebekah*, her *mother*, and *her brother* to conclude the arrangements.

24:54-56 It was hard for Rebekah’s family to let her go so suddenly, and Laban may have hoped to gain more wealth. However, the servant had sworn an oath and would not rest until it was completed. There was no reason for him to stay.

24:57-58 Rebekah’s decision to leave immediately to be with her new husband settled the impasse. *Rebekah* submitted to the Lord’s obvious leading. Young women were normally eager to marry (not to marry was a catastrophe), and later accounts of Laban suggest why Rebekah preferred to leave (cp. 31:14-15). Rebekah displayed faithful love to the servant, Abraham’s family, and Isaac by going to be Isaac’s wife.

24:60 At Rebekah’s departure, her family invoked the blessing that she would be a ***mother of many millions*** and that her descendants would ***conquer . . . their enemies.*** Rebekah’s marriage to Isaac was part of God’s plan to bless all humankind (12:1-3).

24:62 ***Isaac*** lived ***in the Negev,*** in the southern part of Canaan.

24:67 ***Isaac*** was 40 years old when he married ***Rebekah*** (25:20), so Abraham was 140 (21:5).

25:1-11 Though Abraham had sons by another wife, he safeguarded Isaac’s inheritance and blessing.

25:1-4
//1 Chr 1:32-33
25:5
Gen 24:35-36
25:7
Gen 12:4
25:8
Gen 15:15; 25:17; 35:29; 49:29, 33
25:9-10
Gen 23:17-18; 49:29; 50:13
25:11
Gen 12:2; 24:62
25:12-16
//1 Chr 1:29-31

Abraham's Final Days (25:1-11)

Abraham's Family with Keturah

25 Abraham married another wife,
whose name was Keturah. 2She gave
birth to Zimran, Jokshan, Medan, Midian,
Ishbak, and Shuah. 3Jokshan was the father
of Sheba and Dedan. Dedan's descendants
were the Asshurites, Letushites, and Leum-
mites. 4Midian's sons were Ephah, Epher,
Hanoch, Abida, and Eldaah. These were all
descendants of Abraham through Keturah.

Isaac Receives the Inheritance

5Abraham gave everything he owned to his
son Isaac. 6But before he died, he gave gifts
to the sons of his concubines and sent them
off to a land in the east, away from Isaac.

The Death of Abraham

7Abraham lived for 175 years, 8and he died at
a ripe old age, having lived a long and satisfying life. He breathed his last and joined his
ancestors in death. 9His sons Isaac and Ishmael buried him in the cave of Machpelah,
near Mamre, in the field of Ephron son of Zohar the Hittite. 10This was the field Abraham
had purchased from the Hittites and where
he had buried his wife Sarah. 11After Abraham's death, God blessed his son Isaac, who
settled near Beer-lahai-roi in the Negev.

8. THE ACCOUNT OF ISHMAEL'S DESCENDANTS (25:12-18)

12This is the account of the family of Ishmael, the son of Abraham through Hagar,
Sarah's Egyptian servant. 13Here is a list, by
their names and clans, of Ishmael's descendants: The oldest was Nebaioth, followed
by Kedar, Adbeel, Mibsam, 14Mishma, Dumah, Massa, 15Hadad, Tema, Jetur, Naphish,
and Kedemah. 16These twelve sons of Ishmael became the founders of twelve tribes

REBEKAH (24:12-67)

Gen 22:23; 25:20-28; 26:7-8, 35; 27:5-17, 42-46; 29:12; 35:8; 49:31
Rom 9:10-13

Genesis 24 describes the mission of Abraham's servant to find a wife for Isaac. At Abraham's command, he went to Haran in Aram-naharaim (northwest Mesopotamia), to Abraham's relatives, because Abraham did not want Isaac to marry a local Canaanite. The servant prayed that the young woman God had selected to be Isaac's wife would answer his request for a drink by immediately giving it and watering his camels as well (24:12-14). Such a young woman would readily exercise hospitality and be willing to work hard (see note on 24:14). God abundantly answered his prayer with Rebekah, the daughter of Bethuel (22:23; 25:20), the son of Abraham's brother Nahor (11:27-32).

When Abraham's servant described how God had led him (24:34-49), Rebekah's father and brother recognized it as God's hand, but they were reluctant to let her go immediately (24:50-56). Rebekah, however, demonstrated faith in God's plan; she was willing to leave her family without delay to marry Isaac (24:57-58). Rebekah's faith was richly rewarded; the blessing her womenfolk gave her in parting (24:59-60) came true when she bore to Isaac the next generation of God's chosen line.

Rebekah bore twins, Esau and Jacob (25:20-26). She preferred Jacob, the younger, whom God had told her would be the stronger and the leader of the two (25:23). Rebekah helped Jacob seize the blessing of the firstborn by deceiving Isaac (27:1-40). Afterward, she arranged for Jacob to be sent to Haran to get away from his brother's anger over the stolen blessing (27:41–28:5). Rebekah's deceptive scheme created a lasting schism in the family, and she apparently never saw her favorite son again. She was, however, buried beside her husband in the family burial site (49:31), and she fulfilled God's plan as the mother of Jacob, the founding father of Israel.

25:1 Exactly when ***Abraham married . . . Keturah*** is unknown. It was probably, but not necessarily, after Sarah's death.

25:2-4 The birth of these nations from Abraham partially fulfilled God's promise to him (12:2; 17:4).

25:3 ***Sheba and Dedan:*** Cp. 10:7. Abraham's descendants probably settled in these regions and became identified by their names, along with people of other lineage.

25:5-6 ***Abraham*** loved all his sons, so ***before he died***, he ***gave*** them ***gifts*** and ***sent them*** away as he had sent Ishmael (21:8-14). In this way, he preserved Isaac's position as his heir.

25:7-8 Abraham's death is recorded before the births of Jacob and Esau, but he lived until they were fifteen years old (25:19-26; cp. 21:5; 25:26). This literary arrangement closes Abraham's story before focusing on Isaac's family.

25:11 God's blessing transferred to Isaac; Abraham's other sons had been sent away. Isaac lived ***near Beer-lahai-roi***—a special place where God had answered prayer (16:14) and where Isaac waited on the Lord (24:62).

25:12-18 This record lists Ishmael's descendants before tracing Isaac's (25:19–35:29), which is in keeping with the literary arrangement of Genesis (see Introduction to Genesis: "Summary," p. 15).

25:16 Ishmael's ***twelve sons*** fulfilled God's promise of blessing (17:20).

named after them, listed according to the
places they settled and camped. 17Ishmael
lived for 137 years. Then he breathed his
last and joined his ancestors in death. 18Ish-
mael's descendants occupied the region
from Havilah to Shur, which is east of Egypt
in the direction of Asshur. There they lived
in open hostility toward all their relatives.

9. THE ACCOUNT OF ISAAC'S DESCENDANTS (25:19–35:29)

The Births of Esau and Jacob (25:19-26)

19This is the account of the family of Isaac,
the son of Abraham. 20When Isaac was forty
years old, he married Rebekah, the daughter
of Bethuel the Aramean from Paddan-aram
and the sister of Laban the Aramean.
21Isaac pleaded with the LORD on behalf
of his wife, because she was unable to have
children. The LORD answered Isaac's prayer,
and Rebekah became pregnant with twins.
22But the two children struggled with each
other in her womb. So she went to ask the
LORD about it. "Why is this happening to
me?" she asked.
23And the LORD told her, "The sons in
your womb will become two nations. From
the very beginning, the two nations will be
rivals. One nation will be stronger than the
other; and your older son will serve your
younger son."
24And when the time came to give birth,
Rebekah discovered that she did indeed
have twins! 25The first one was very red at

25:17 Gen 25:8
25:18 Gen 16:12; 20:1
25:21 Gen 21:2
25:23 Gen 17:2-4; 27:29; 48:19; Num 20:14; Deut 2:4, 8; *Rom 9:11-12
25:25 Gen 27:11

Infertility (25:21)

Gen 16:1-6; 17:15-21; 20:17-18; 29:31; 30:1-2; 30:22-24
Exod 23:25-26
Deut 7:12-15
Judg 13:2-5
1 Sam 1:2-28; 2:5-7
Ps 113:5-9
Isa 54:1-3
Luke 1:5-25
Rom 4:19-22
Gal 4:24-28
Heb 11:11-12

With the possible exception of Leah, each of the patriarchs' wives suffered infertility for a time before having children (11:30; 25:21; 29:31; see also 1 Sam 1:1-18). Children continued the family line, helped protect the tribe, and provided labor. They ensured that hereditary property would stay within the family, guaranteed assistance in old age, and enacted the proper funeral rites. Infertility was therefore a crushing stigma for a woman (Ps 113:9; Prov 30:15-16; Isa 54:1), who understood herself to be created as a vessel of life (1:28; 3:20). It was considered a denial of blessing, design, and desire (1:28), and it brought shame (1 Sam 1:7), ridicule (16:4), and vicious jealousy (30:1).

In the OT, childlessness is a theological issue. Fertility is controlled by the Creator (20:17-18; 30:2, 23; 1 Sam 1:6, 27), who causes fertility and infertility according to his purpose and his promises (17:19; 30:2; Ps 113:9; Luke 1:11-20; Rom 4:19). God often chose infertility as a precursor to the birth of a promised or unique child, marking the birth as God's own work. Childlessness is thus a trial of patience that prompts prayer and faith (25:21; 1 Sam 1:11). Abraham learned to nurture faith in God's promise long before his child arrived (15:4-6; 17:15-21; Rom 4:20-22). When a couple has been infertile, a child's arrival is marked as a special display of God's faithfulness and creative authority.

God's delays are not necessarily denials, but they remind longing parents to use trials for growth and to see children as a gift that cannot be taken for granted. A childless home can be filled with devotion as human expectations submit to future glory (see, e.g., Luke 2:36-37).

25:18 ***Havilah*** was a region in north-central Arabia. • ***Shur*** was a region between Beersheba and Egypt. • ***in open hostility toward all their relatives:*** The meaning of the Hebrew is uncertain, but the wording is close to that of 16:12.

25:19–35:29 This *account of the family of Isaac*, the chosen *son of Abraham*, mostly recounts Jacob's struggle for the blessing (25:27-34; chs 27–33).

25:19-26 Jacob's struggle for supremacy began before the twins were born (see Hos 12:3).

25:19-20 ***Isaac . . . married Rebekah:*** Isaac's marriage tied him and his family even more closely to Abraham's ancestors. Had he married a Canaanite, the covenant faith would have been imperiled by this corrupt, syncretistic people.

25:21 For twenty years, Rebekah was barren (cp. 25:20, 26), like Sarah (see 16:1). This condition tested their faith (see note on 16:1-3). How could they be childless when God promised that nations would issue from them? • ***Isaac pleaded with the LORD*** and ***the LORD answered Isaac's prayer.*** Isaac apparently learned from his father's mistake and responded in faith.

25:22 When the pregnancy was difficult, Rebekah ***went to ask the LORD about it***, probably by visiting a prophet—perhaps Abraham (20:7; see note on 25:7-8).

25:23 ***rivals:*** Jacob and Esau fought in the womb, and their descendants (Israel and Edom) fought continuously throughout their history. In their many conflicts, Israel achieved supremacy over Edom. • ***your older son will serve your younger son:*** God's choice of the younger son over the elder ran against natural order (cp. 48:12-14; see Mal 1:1-3; Rom 9:11-16).

25:24-26 When the twins were born, the unusual circumstances inspired each boy's name and hinted at what would happen to him in the future.

25:25 Two wordplays anticipate Esau's later life. ***Esau*** sounds like a Hebrew term that means "hair" (Hebrew *se'ar*); Esau's later homeland, Edom, was known as *Seir* ("hairy") because it was wooded (as though covered with hair). • ***red*** (Hebrew *'admoni*) sounds like Esau's other name, Edom (25:27-34); Edom had red soil. • Esau's ***hair*** was ***like*** the ***fur coat*** of an animal, foreshadowing his unspiritual character (25:34; Heb 12:16; cp. Lev 26:22; Deut 7:22; 1 Cor 15:32). The description of the child uses words that highlight the Edomites' nature.

25:26
Hos 12:3
25:30
Gen 36:1, 8
25:31
Deut 21:16-17
1 Chr 5:1-2
25:33
Gen 27:36
Heb 12:16

birth and covered with thick hair like a fur
coat. So they named him Esau. 26 Then the
other twin was born with his hand grasping
Esau's heel. So they named him Jacob. Isaac
was sixty years old when the twins were
born.

Esau Sells His Birthright (25:27-34)

27 As the boys grew up, Esau became a skillful
hunter. He was an outdoorsman, but Jacob
had a quiet temperament, preferring to stay
at home. 28 Isaac loved Esau because he enjoyed eating the wild game Esau brought
home, but Rebekah loved Jacob.

29 One day when Jacob was cooking some
stew, Esau arrived home from the wilderness exhausted and hungry. 30 Esau said to
Jacob, "I'm starved! Give me some of that
red stew!" (This is how Esau got his other
name, Edom, which means "red.")

31 "All right," Jacob replied, "but trade me
your rights as the firstborn son."

32 "Look, I'm dying of starvation!" said
Esau. "What good is my birthright to me
now?"

33 But Jacob said, "First you must swear
that your birthright is mine." So Esau swore

ESAU (25:21-34)

Gen 26:34-35; 27:1-42; 28:6-9; 32:3-20; 33:1-16; 35:28-29; 36:1-43
Deut 2:1-8, 12, 22, 29
Josh 24:4
Mal 1:2-5
Rom 9:6-13
Heb 11:20; 12:16-17

Esau, the son of Isaac and Rebekah, was Jacob's older twin brother (25:24-26), so named because his body was hairy at birth. His descendants were called Edom ("red") on account of his reddish color at birth, the red lentil soup he received from Jacob (25:30), and the reddish color of the land in which he settled (see note on 25:25).

Esau was a proficient hunter who brought tasty wild meat to his father. Isaac enjoyed its strong flavor more than the mild meat Jacob provided from the family flocks. One day Esau returned home very hungry from an unsuccessful hunt, and Jacob persuaded Esau to surrender his birthright in exchange for food (25:29-34). Esau had little regard for his birthright and was controlled by his carnal desires (see Heb 12:16). He also married two local women who were not Abraham's descendants (26:34-35), which may be why Rebekah coached Jacob in obtaining the patriarchal blessing that would normally have belonged to the elder brother (ch 27). Esau's anger on discovering his brother's deception prompted Jacob to flee for Haran. The brothers were reunited 20 years later because of Esau's gracious forgiveness (33:1-16).

Jacob was born grasping Esau's heel; this omen was interpreted to mean that Esau's Edomite descendants would be subject to Jacob's offspring. The subservient relationship between the Edomites and the Israelites in David's time (2 Sam 8:11-15; 1 Chr 18:13) continued until the reign of Jehoram (2 Kgs 8:20-22; 2 Chr 21:8-10). Following a rebellion in 845 BC, the Edomites briefly gained their independence but were conquered again by Amaziah (796–767 BC). They regained their freedom in 735 BC and then remained independent of Judah.

In the NT, Esau represents the line of Abraham's descendants who lacked the gift of faith and were rejected by God as recipients of his promised blessings (see Rom 9:6-24).

25:26 The name *Jacob* (Hebrew *ya'aqob*) sounds like the Hebrew words for "heel" and "deceiver" (from Hebrew *'aqeb*). The name was originally positive, meaning "protect" (like a rear guard), but it took on the negative meaning of "heel grabber" or "deceiver" in the context of Jacob's deceptive, grasping, usurping character (see 27:36).

25:27-34 Jacob and Esau each developed in accord with his initial characteristics (25:24-26). Esau, the reddish, hairy man, cared about physical things rather than spiritual things (see Heb 12:16); he was finally overcome by physical appetites and sold his birthright. Jacob, the heel grabber, knew the birthright's value and drove a ruthless bargain to gain it presumptuously from his brother.

25:27 *Esau* was a ***skillful hunter*** and ***an outdoorsman***—a wild man who loved wild country. Jacob had a ***quiet*** (or *even*) ***temperament*** and preferred ***to stay at home*** (literally *dwelling in tents*)—i.e., he was civilized.

25:28 The parents each practiced favoritism. • ***because:*** Isaac's love for Esau was conditioned upon his son's performance. Rebekah's love for Jacob was constant and unconditional.

25:29 Ironically, ***Jacob*** proved the more cunning hunter. The word ***cooking*** (Hebrew *wayyazed*, "boiling") sounds like the word for "hunter" (Hebrew *tsayid*). While boiling stew, Jacob was laying a trap for the hairy red animal. He may have waited a long time for this opportunity. This word for "boil" was also used for presumptuous action (like water boiling over the rim of the pot). Jacob overstepped his boundaries when he seized the promise for himself. By contrast, Abraham knew the promise was his and was secure in giving the land away (see note on 13:8-13). • ***Esau*** was ***exhausted and hungry***, but his life was not in danger (25:32; see note on 25:33-34).

25:30 *Esau* was preoccupied with his appetite. Being driven by one's appetites leaves no place for spiritual values. The text emphasizes this by using a Hebrew word (translated ***give***) that was normally used for feeding animals. • ***Edom, which means "red":*** See note on 25:25.

25:31-33 ***Jacob*** was the better hunter on this occasion, but great danger lay in exercising such strong ambition. God's people should desire the things of God, but they must not seek them "in the flesh" (see Zech 4:6; Gal 5:16-17; Eph 6:10-12). The Lord dealt severely with Jacob to purge him of carnal methods. He later received the promise not as crafty Jacob the usurper, but as Israel (meaning, "God fights"), with God fighting on his behalf (32:28).

an oath, thereby selling all his rights as the
firstborn to his brother, Jacob.
34Then Jacob gave Esau some bread and
lentil stew. Esau ate the meal, then got up
and left. He showed contempt for his rights
as the firstborn.

Isaac and Abimelech (26:1-35)
Isaac Deceives Abimelech

26 A severe famine now struck the land,
as had happened before in Abra-
ham's time. So Isaac moved to Gerar, where
Abimelech, king of the Philistines, lived.
2The LORD appeared to Isaac and said,
"Do not go down to Egypt, but do as I tell you.
3Live here as a foreigner in this land, and I
will be with you and bless you. I hereby confirm that I will give all these lands to you and
your [k]descendants, just as I solemnly promised Abraham, your father. 4I will cause your
descendants to become as numerous as the
stars of the sky, and I will give them all
these lands. And through your descendants
all the nations of the earth will be blessed.
5I will do this because Abraham listened to
me and obeyed all my requirements, commands, decrees, and instructions." 6So Isaac
stayed in Gerar.
7When the men who lived there asked
Isaac about his wife, Rebekah, he said, "She
is my sister." He was afraid to say, "She is my
wife." He thought, "They will kill me to get
her, because she is so beautiful." 8But some
time later, Abimelech, king of the Philistines, looked out his window and saw Isaac
caressing Rebekah.
9Immediately, Abimelech called for Isaac
and exclaimed, "She is obviously your wife!
Why did you say, 'She is my sister'?"
"Because I was afraid someone would kill
me to get her from me," Isaac replied.
10"How could you do this to us?" Abimelech exclaimed. "One of my people might
easily have taken your wife and slept with
her, and you would have made us guilty of
great sin."
11Then Abimelech issued a public proclamation: "Anyone who touches this man or
his wife will be put to death!"

Conflict over Water Rights
12When Isaac planted his crops that year, he
harvested a hundred times more grain than
he planted, for the LORD blessed him. 13He
became a very rich man, and his wealth
continued to grow. 14He acquired so many
flocks of sheep and goats, herds of cattle,
and servants that the Philistines became
jealous of him. 15So the Philistines filled up
all of Isaac's wells with dirt. These were the
wells that had been dug by the servants of
his father, Abraham.
16Finally, Abimelech ordered Isaac to
leave the country. "Go somewhere else," he

26:1 Gen 12:10; 20:1-2
26:2 Gen 12:1, 7
26:3 Gen 12:7
[k]*zera'* (2233)
‣Gen 35:12
26:4 Gen 15:5; 22:17
Exod 32:13
*Acts 3:25
*Gal 3:8
26:7 Gen 12:11-13; 20:2, 12
26:10 Gen 20:7-10
26:12 Gen 26:3
26:13 Gen 24:35; 25:5
26:15 Gen 21:25
26:16 Exod 1:9

25:33-34 *Esau* eagerly took Jacob's bait and fell into the trap. He ate and left too quickly to have been near death (25:32). The final comment on the passage explains that Esau ***showed contempt for*** his birthright, considering it worthless (Heb 12:16). It is foolish to sacrifice spiritual blessings to satisfy physical appetites (cp. 3:6).

26:1-35 In this digression from Jacob's story, Isaac's prosperity (ch 26) shows that the blessing had passed to him (cp. 25:11) despite his failures of faith.

26:1 This *Abimelech* is probably not the man in ch 20, for these events could have been 90 years apart. Possibly Abimelech was a dynastic name or title (a later King Achish, 1 Sam 21:10, was also called Abimelech, Ps 34:TITLE).

26:2-5 The Lord assured Isaac that the covenant promises (cp. 12:2-3; 15:5-8; 17:3-8; 22:15-18; 28:13-14) would pass to him because Abraham faithfully ***listened*** to God and ***obeyed all*** his ***requirements, commands, decrees, and instructions.*** These terms were later used in Deuteronomy to describe God's full legal covenant with Israel. An Israelite reader would immediately think of the complete Torah when hearing these words and be prompted to obey God's law as Abraham did, though Abraham had only a few commands from the Lord. Through these words, the text emphasizes that Abraham would have obeyed the later commands if he had had them, because he was an obedient servant of the Lord.

26:3 *descendants:* Literally *seed;* also in 26:4, 24.

26:6-11 While staying in Gerar, Isaac, like his father, deceived people into believing that his wife was his sister. Some suppose that this story duplicates the stories of Abraham's deception (12:10-20; 20:1-18), but the differences are greater than the similarities, and the son's repetition of his father's lie is natural. Through numerous parallels with Abraham, ch 26 shows how God's plan continued with Isaac. Even when Isaac jeopardized the covenant as his father had, God prevented disaster and preserved the marriage. Abraham's descendants would be blessed because of Abraham, but they had to exercise their own faith to enjoy the blessings. Genuine faith in God's promises engenders a fearless walk with him; cowering in fear endangers the blessing and mocks the faith.

26:8 ***Abimelech . . . saw Isaac caressing Rebekah:*** The word for "caressing" (Hebrew *metsakheq*) is the same as the word used for Ishmael's "making fun of" Isaac (21:9); the word is related to the name "Isaac" (Hebrew *yitskhaq*). It is as though Isaac's lapse of faith made fun of Abimelech and made a mockery of Rebekah and the great promise embodied in Isaac's name.

26:10-11 Isaac, like his father, was rebuked by ***Abimelech*** (see note on 20:1-18). This legal wording would remind Israel of how important it was to preserve marital purity. Abimelech recognized the danger to his own people. Though his decree preserved his own society, it was also a word from God that preserved the sanctity of Isaac's and Israel's marriages. If Isaac's marriage had ended here, there would have been no Israelite society.

26:12-13 *Isaac* lived in the land as a temporary settler, enjoying abundant prosperity because of God's blessing; ***his crops*** flourished and he became ***very rich.***

26:14-16 ***The Philistines*** envied Isaac's prosperity and ***filled*** his ***wells with dirt.*** The king then ***ordered Isaac to leave*** that region because he was ***too powerful*** for them (cp. 21:22-23).

26:19 John 4:10-11
26:22 Ps 4:1; 18:19 Isa 54:2
26:23 Gen 22:19
26:24 Gen 17:7; 22:17 Exod 3:6
26:25 Gen 12:7-8; 13:4
26:26 Gen 21:22
26:27 Gen 26:16
26:28 Gen 21:22-23
26:30 Gen 31:54
26:31 Gen 21:31
26:33 Gen 21:31
26:34 Gen 28:8
26:35 Gen 27:46
27:1 Gen 25:25; 48:10
27:2 Gen 47:29
27:3 Gen 25:27
27:4 Gen 24:60; 27:19; 48:9

said, "for you have become too powerful
for us."
17So Isaac moved away to the Gerar Valley, where he set up their tents and settled
down. 18He reopened the wells his father
had dug, which the Philistines had filled in
after Abraham's death. Isaac also restored
the names Abraham had given them.
19Isaac's servants also dug in the Gerar
Valley and discovered a well of fresh water.
20But then the shepherds from Gerar came
and claimed the spring. "This is our water,"
they said, and they argued over it with Isaac's
herdsmen. So Isaac named the well Esek
(which means "argument"). 21Isaac's men
then dug another well, but again there was
a dispute over it. So Isaac named it Sitnah
(which means "hostility"). 22Abandoning
that one, Isaac moved on and dug another
well. This time there was no dispute over it,
so Isaac named the place Rehoboth (which
means "open space"), for he said, "At last the
LORD has created enough space for us to
prosper in this land."
23From there Isaac moved to Beersheba,
24where the LORD appeared to him on the
night of his arrival. "I am the God of your
father, Abraham," he said. "Do not be afraid,
for I am with you and will bless you. I will
multiply your descendants, and they will become a great nation. I will do this because
of my promise to Abraham, my servant."
25Then Isaac built an altar there and worshiped the LORD. He set up his camp at that
place, and his servants dug another well.

Isaac's Covenant with Abimelech

26One day King Abimelech came from Gerar
with his adviser, Ahuzzath, and also Phicol,
his army commander. 27"Why have you
come here?" Isaac asked. "You obviously
hate me, since you kicked me off your land."
28They replied, "We can plainly see that
the LORD is with you. So we want to enter
into a sworn treaty with you. Let's make a
covenant. 29Swear that you will not harm us,
just as we have never troubled you. We have
always treated you well, and we sent you
away from us in peace. And now look how
the LORD has blessed you!"
30So Isaac prepared a covenant feast to
celebrate the treaty, and they ate and drank
together. 31Early the next morning, they
each took a solemn oath not to interfere
with each other. Then Isaac sent them home
again, and they left him in peace.
32That very day Isaac's servants came
and told him about a new well they had dug.
"We've found water!" they exclaimed. 33So
Isaac named the well Shibah (which means
"oath"). And to this day the town that grew
up there is called Beersheba (which means
"well of the oath").

Esau's Hittite Wives (26:34-35)

34At the age of forty, Esau married two
Hittite wives: Judith, the daughter of Beeri,
and Basemath, the daughter of Elon. 35But
Esau's wives made life miserable for Isaac
and Rebekah.

Jacob Steals Esau's Blessing (27:1-40)

27 One day when Isaac was old and
turning blind, he called for Esau, his
older son, and said, "My son."
"Yes, Father?" Esau replied.
2"I am an old man now," Isaac said, "and I
don't know when I may die. 3Take your bow
and a quiver full of arrows, and go out into
the open country to hunt some wild game
for me. 4Prepare my favorite dish, and
bring it here for me to eat. Then I will pronounce the blessing that belongs to you, my
firstborn son, before I die."

26:17-22 ***Isaac moved . . . to the Gerar Valley*** (away from the city of Gerar itself, 26:6, but probably still within ten miles) and ***reopened*** his father's ***wells***. Isaac was also opposed there, but chose not to fight back; he relinquished one well after another until God's blessing outdid the opposition. Whenever Isaac reopened a well, and regardless of how often enemies caused them to cave in, he found water. God was blessing Isaac and that blessing could not be hindered. Finally, the Philistines left Isaac alone.

26:23-25 At ***Beersheba, . . . the LORD appeared to*** Isaac to confirm his covenant (cp. 21:31-33). ***Isaac*** responded in faith as his father had done by building ***an altar*** to the Lord and proclaiming the Lord's identity and nature (see note on 12:8; 21:33).

26:26-33 This ***treaty*** is similar to the one an earlier king had made with Abraham (cp. 21:22-31). This king acknowledged that God was blessing Isaac and realized that a treaty with Isaac would benefit him. No opposition can hinder God's blessing—it will flourish, and other nations will see it and seek peace with God's people to share in the blessing.

26:33 Since the earlier treaty was renewed with Isaac, the name of the well was also renewed by the oath.

26:34-35 Esau's marriages illustrate how unfit he was to lead the covenant people into God's blessings, and how foolish was Isaac's later attempt to bless Esau (27:1-40). Esau later married a third wife in a vain attempt to do the right thing (28:6-9).

27:1-40 Jacob got his father Isaac's blessing through deception. In this story, an entire family tries to carry out their responsibilities by physical means rather than by faith. Faith would have provided Rebekah and Jacob a more honorable solution to the crisis.

27:1-4 The first scene sets up the chapter's crisis. Isaac knew of God's oracle (25:22-23), yet he thwarted or ignored it by trying to bless Esau. • ***Isaac was old and turning blind:*** He was losing his senses, both physically and spiritually.

27:3-4 Like Esau, Isaac allowed his palate to govern his heart (cp. 25:28-34).

5But Rebekah overheard what Isaac had said to his son Esau. So when Esau left to hunt for the wild game, 6she said to her son Jacob, "Listen. I overheard your father say to Esau, 7'Bring me some wild game and prepare me a delicious meal. Then I will bless you in the LORD's presence before I die.' 8Now, my son, listen to me. Do exactly as I tell you. 9Go out to the flocks, and bring me two fine young goats. I'll use them to prepare your father's favorite dish. 10Then take the food to your father so he can eat it and bless you before he dies."

11"But look," Jacob replied to Rebekah, "my brother, Esau, is a hairy man, and my skin is smooth. 12What if my father touches me? He'll see that I'm trying to trick him, and then he'll curse me instead of blessing me."

13But his mother replied, "Then let the curse fall on me, my son! Just do what I tell you. Go out and get the goats for me!"

14So Jacob went out and got the young goats for his mother. Rebekah took them and prepared a delicious meal, just the way Isaac liked it. 15Then she took Esau's favorite clothes, which were there in the house, and gave them to her younger son, Jacob. 16She covered his arms and the smooth part of his neck with the skin of the young goats. 17Then she gave Jacob the delicious meal, including freshly baked bread.

18So Jacob took the food to his father. "My father?" he said.

"Yes, my son," Isaac answered. "Who are you—Esau or Jacob?"

19Jacob replied, "It's Esau, your firstborn son. I've done as you told me. Here is the wild game. Now sit up and eat it so you can give me your blessing."

20Isaac asked, "How did you find it so quickly, my son?"

"The LORD your God put it in my path!" Jacob replied.

21Then Isaac said to Jacob, "Come closer so I can touch you and make sure that you really are Esau." 22So Jacob went closer to his father, and Isaac touched him. "The voice is Jacob's, but the hands are Esau's," Isaac said. 23But he did not recognize Jacob, because Jacob's hands felt hairy just like Esau's. So Isaac prepared to bless Jacob. 24"But are you really my son Esau?" he asked.

"Yes, I am," Jacob replied.

25Then Isaac said, "Now, my son, bring me the wild game. Let me eat it, and then I will give you my blessing." So Jacob took the food to his father, and Isaac ate it. He also drank the wine that Jacob served him. 26Then Isaac said to Jacob, "Please come a little closer and kiss me, my son."

27So Jacob went over and kissed him. And when Isaac caught the smell of his clothes, he was finally convinced, and he blessed his son. He said, "Ah! The smell of my son is like the smell of the outdoors, which the LORD has blessed!

28 "From the dew of heaven
and the richness of the earth,
may God always give you abundant
harvests of grain
and bountiful new wine.
29 May many nations become your
servants,
and may they bow down to you.
May you be the master over your
brothers,
and may your mother's sons bow
down to you.
All who curse you will be cursed,
and all who bless you will be blessed."

30As soon as Isaac had finished blessing Jacob, and almost before Jacob had left his father, Esau returned from his hunt. 31Esau prepared a delicious meal and brought it to his father. Then he said, "Sit up, my father, and eat my wild game so you can give me your blessing."

32But Isaac asked him, "Who are you?"

Esau replied, "It's your son, your firstborn son, Esau."

33Isaac began to tremble uncontrollably and said, "Then who just served me wild game? I have already eaten it, and I blessed him just before you came. And yes, that blessing must stand!"

27:5-6 Gen 25:27-28
27:8 Gen 27:13, 43
27:11 Gen 25:25
27:12 Gen 9:25; 27:21-22
27:13 Gen 27:8
27:15 Gen 27:27
27:19 Gen 27:31
27:21 Gen 27:12
27:23 Gen 27:16
27:25 Gen 27:4
27:27 Ps 65:10; Heb 11:20
27:28 Deut 7:13; 33:13, 28; Zech 8:12
27:29 Gen 9:25-27; 12:3; Isa 45:14
27:31 Gen 27:4
27:32 Gen 27:18
27:33 Gen 27:35

27:5-17 The blessing seemed to be in jeopardy. In scene two, Rebekah and Jacob sought to achieve God's blessing by deception, without faith or love. Rebekah planned to deceive the old man into thinking that he was blessing Esau when he was actually blessing Jacob.

27:5 *Esau* agreed to Isaac's plan, thus breaking the oath he had sworn to Jacob (25:33).

27:11-12 *Jacob* had no qualms about this deception; he only feared that it might not work and that he would be cursed for trying.

27:18-29 In scene three, Jacob deceives his father and receives the blessing.

27:18-20 *Jacob* lied about his identity, and then came close to blasphemy by lying about *God*.

27:20-27 *Isaac* voiced his suspicion three times, but was finally deceived by his senses, which were not functioning well (see note on 27:1-4).

27:30-40 In scene four, everything is discovered and the family becomes even more divided.

27:33 When he realized what had happened, ***Isaac began to tremble uncontrollably***; he had been tampering with God's plan, and God had overruled him.

27:34 Heb 12:17
27:35 Gen 27:19
27:36 Gen 25:26
27:37 Gen 27:28-29
27:38 Heb 12:17
27:39 Heb 11:20
27:40 2 Kgs 8:20-22
27:41 Gen 32:3-11; 37:4
27:43 Gen 27:8
27:44 Gen 31:41
27:46 Gen 26:34-35
28:1 Gen 24:3
28:2 Gen 25:20
28:3 Gen 17:16; 35:11
[a]*shadday* (7706) ‣Gen 35:11
[b]*qahal* (6951) ‣Gen 35:11
28:4 Gen 12:1-3; 15:7; 35:11

34 When Esau heard his father's words, he let out a loud and bitter cry. "Oh my father, what about me? Bless me, too!" he begged.

35 But Isaac said, "Your brother was here, and he tricked me. He has taken away your blessing."

36 Esau exclaimed, "No wonder his name is Jacob, for now he has cheated me twice. First he took my rights as the firstborn, and now he has stolen my blessing. Oh, haven't you saved even one blessing for me?"

37 Isaac said to Esau, "I have made Jacob your master and have declared that all his brothers will be his servants. I have guaranteed him an abundance of grain and wine—what is left for me to give you, my son?"

38 Esau pleaded, "But do you have only one blessing? Oh my father, bless me, too!" Then Esau broke down and wept.

39 Finally, his father, Isaac, said to him,

"You will live away from the richness of
the earth,
and away from the dew of the heaven
above.
40 You will live by your sword,
and you will serve your brother.
But when you decide to break free,
you will shake his yoke from your
neck."

Jacob Flees to Paddan-Aram (27:41–28:5)

41 From that time on, Esau hated Jacob because their father had given Jacob the blessing. And Esau began to scheme: "I will soon be mourning my father's death. Then I will kill my brother, Jacob."

42 But Rebekah heard about Esau's plans. So she sent for Jacob and told him, "Listen, Esau is consoling himself by plotting to kill you. 43 So listen carefully, my son. Get ready and flee to my brother, Laban, in Haran. 44 Stay there with him until your brother cools off. 45 When he calms down and forgets what you have done to him, I will send for you to come back. Why should I lose both of you in one day?"

46 Then Rebekah said to Isaac, "I'm sick and tired of these local Hittite women! I would rather die than see Jacob marry one of them."

28 So Isaac called for Jacob, blessed him, and said, "You must not marry any of these Canaanite women. 2 Instead, go at once to Paddan-aram, to the house of your grandfather Bethuel, and marry one of your uncle Laban's daughters. 3 May God [a]Almighty bless you and give you many children. And may your descendants multiply and become [b]many nations! 4 May God pass on to you and your descendants the blessings he promised to Abraham. May you own this land where you are now living as a foreigner, for God gave this land to Abraham."

5 So Isaac sent Jacob away, and he went to Paddan-aram to stay with his uncle Laban, his mother's brother, the son of Bethuel the Aramean.

27:34-35 ***Esau*** was very ***bitter,*** and angry enough to kill (27:41).

27:36 ***Esau*** began to realize Jacob's true nature, saying ***he has cheated me*** (or *tripped me up,* or *deceived me)* ***twice,*** by taking the birthright (the right of inheritance, Hebrew *bekorah;* 25:27-34) and by deceiving their father to receive the ***blessing*** (the spoken pronouncement of the inheritance, Hebrew *berakah*). • ***Jacob*** sounds like the Hebrew words for "heel" and "deceiver." Esau's assessment of Jacob was correct, but he failed to see his own ungodliness in these transactions (see note on 27:5; Heb 12:16).

27:37 There was no going back. ***Isaac*** had declared an oracle from God, who had ***made Jacob*** to be Esau's ***master*** (see Rom 9:11-13).

27:39-40 All that remained for Esau was a promise of hardship and struggle (cp. 3:17-19; 16:11-12).

27:41-45 Rebekah and Jacob got the blessing but reaped hatred from Esau and separation from one another; there is no indication that Rebekah and Jacob ever saw each other again. They gained nothing that God was not already going to give them, and their methods were costly. Jacob fled from home to escape Esau's vengeance.

27:42–33:17 Jacob met the Lord on a route that Abraham had taken 125 years earlier. The story follows a chiastic structure that centers on Jacob's exile:

A: Jacob flees Esau (27:42–28:9)
  B: Angels of God meet Jacob at Bethel (28:10-22)
    C: Jacob is exiled in Paddan-aram (29:1–31:55)
  B': Angels of God meet Jacob at Mahanaim (32:1-2)
A': Jacob is reconciled to Esau (32:3–33:17)

27:46 ***Rebekah*** manipulated ***Isaac*** into sending ***Jacob*** away. Like Isaac, Jacob took a wife from among his relatives in the east.

28:1-2 ***Isaac*** remained in the land, but ***Jacob*** had to leave it. God would deal with Jacob under the hand of ***Laban,*** his ***uncle*** (see note on 29:1–31:55). • Believers in any age must remain spiritually pure by marrying other believers (2 Cor 6:14-18). The Canaanite people incorporated dozens of groups and clans into their society and religion by wars, treaties, and marriages (see 34:20-23). Abraham's family was to resist such mixing (cp. 24:3; ch 34); they were to marry within their clan to maintain the purity of the line and of the faith that identified them as the chosen seed. The surest way to lose their distinctiveness was to intermarry with people of other tribal backgrounds and beliefs (see Ezra 9–10; Neh 13:23-29).

28:3-5 Before Jacob departed, Isaac gave him a pure, legitimate blessing. He did not hold back, because he now knew what God wanted him to do. Isaac clearly passed on the blessing ***God Almighty*** (Hebrew *El-Shaddai*; see 17:1) had given to Abraham and to him regarding prosperity and the land (cp. 15:5, 18-20).

28:4 ***descendants:*** Literally *seed;* also in 28:13, 14.

JACOB (27:1–35:29)

Gen 25:19-34; 37:1-35; 42:1-4, 29-38; 43:1-13; 45:25–50:14
Exod 1:1-5
Num 23:7-10, 20-23; 24:5-9, 17-19
Deut 26:5
Josh 24:4, 32
Hos 12:2-14
Mal 1:2
John 4:5-6, 12
Acts 7:8-16
Rom 9:10-13
Heb 11:8-9, 20-21

Jacob, younger twin son of Isaac and Rebekah, struggled with his twin brother Esau in the womb and was born grasping his heel (25:24-26). God told Rebekah that the boys represented two nations and that the older son would serve the younger (25:23).

Isaac favored Esau, an outdoorsman; Rebekah preferred Jacob, who was happier at home. Once, Esau returned famished from hunting and Jacob bought his birthright with some red stew he had cooked (25:27-34; see Heb 12:16). Later, Isaac asked Esau to prepare wild game so he could eat and bless him (27:1-4; cp. 25:28). Rebekah sent Jacob to deceive Isaac into blessing him instead, and her ploy was successful (27:5-29). Jacob's ruse was soon discovered (27:30-35), but legally valid blessings were irrevocable promises (27:33). So Isaac gave Esau a lesser blessing (27:36-40), and Esau plotted to kill Jacob (27:41). Rebekah convinced Isaac to send Jacob away to her brother Laban so that Jacob would marry among relatives (27:46).

So Isaac transferred the covenant promises to Jacob and sent him to Haran (28:1-5). Along the way, God appeared to Jacob in a dream and affirmed the promises of land and descendants that he had given to Abraham and Isaac (28:10-15). Jacob worshiped the Lord and named the place Bethel ("house of God").

At Haran, Jacob began to serve his uncle Laban (chs 29–31). Jacob loved Laban's daughter Rachel and worked seven years to marry her, but Laban deceived him by substituting his older daughter Leah on Jacob's wedding night. Jacob worked seven more years for Rachel and an additional six years to acquire flocks for himself (30:25-43; see also 31:38-42). Despite many hardships, he had thirteen children and became very prosperous.

After twenty years, God told Jacob to return to Canaan (31:3). Fearing reprisals from Laban and his sons (31:1-2), Jacob organized his caravan and left while Laban was away (31:4-21). Laban gave chase, but God prevented him from harming Jacob (31:22-24, 29). Laban instead upbraided Jacob for leaving stealthily and for stealing his idols (31:25-30; see also 31:19). Jacob let Laban search his tents, but the idols were not found (31:33-35), and Jacob became angry (31:36-42). Though their conflict remained unresolved (31:43), the two men made a peace covenant (31:44-54); the location formed the lasting boundary between Israel and Aram.

Jacob now faced Esau and God. When Esau came to meet him with 400 men, Jacob sought God's protection and sent gifts to pacify his estranged brother (32:3-21). During a night that symbolized his whole life, Jacob wrestled alone with a man who dislocated his hip and gave him the blessing he sought (32:22-32). God changed his name to Israel ("God fights").

Jacob met Esau and the two were reconciled (33:1-11); Esau was gracious and forgiving, and Jacob shared some of his blessing. Esau then returned to Seir while Jacob continued to Canaan. In Shechem, Jacob bought land and built an altar (33:16-20), then moved to Bethel and expelled all foreign idols from his household (35:1-8). God reaffirmed Jacob's new name, Israel, and renewed his promises of land and descendants (35:9-15).

Jacob's favoritism for Rachel extended to her son Joseph, whom Jacob intended to anoint as the firstborn and heir (37:1-4), a plan that God confirmed through dreams (37:5-11). But then Joseph's brothers sold him as a slave (Gen 37:9-28) and for over twenty years Jacob believed he was dead. Only after letting Benjamin go to Egypt in Judah's care did Jacob learn that Joseph was alive and would be the source of famine relief for his family (43:1-14; 45:24-28). Jacob's spirits revived. He moved to Egypt and joyously reunited with his favorite son at Goshen (Gen 46:28-30), where he prospered for seventeen more years.

When Jacob approached death at age 147, he arranged for the future of his family. He made Joseph swear to bury him in Canaan (47:29-31; 49:29-32). He gave Joseph's sons his prime blessing (48:1-20) and put Ephraim, the younger son, first. He gave assurance that the family would return to Canaan (48:21-22), then blessed each of his sons and prophesied the future of their descendants (49:1-28). He died (49:33) and was buried at the cave of Machpelah, accompanied by his sons and a large Egyptian procession. His death marked the end of the patriarchal age and the beginning of Israel's growth as a nation in Egypt until they returned to live again in the Promised Land (see Exodus—Joshua).

The name "Jacob" became synonymous with the nation of Israel (see Num 23:7, 21; 24:5; Hos 12:2). God called the nation to serve him as their forefathers had done (Hos 12:3-13). He promised Israel the same love that he had shown toward Jacob (Mal 1:2). And he promised that a conquering ruler would come from Jacob's descendants (Gen 49:8-12; Num 24:17-19).

28:6
Gen 28:1
28:8
Gen 26:35
28:9
Gen 36:2
28:10
Gen 26:23
28:12
Gen 20:3
Num 12:6
*John 1:51
[c]*mal'ak* (4397)
‣Gen 48:16
28:13
[d]*'erets* (0776)
‣Num 13:27
28:14
Gen 12:2; 13:14; 22:17
28:15
Gen 48:21
Deut 7:9; 31:6, 8
28:17
Exod 3:5
Ps 68:35
28:18
Gen 35:14
28:19
Gen 12:8; 35:6; 48:3
28:21
Exod 15:2

Esau's Ishmaelite Wives (28:6-9)

6Esau knew that his father, Isaac, had blessed
Jacob and sent him to Paddan-aram to find
a wife, and that he had warned Jacob, "You
must not marry a Canaanite woman." 7He
also knew that Jacob had obeyed his parents
and gone to Paddan-aram. 8It was now very
clear to Esau that his father did not like the
local Canaanite women. 9So Esau visited his
uncle Ishmael's family and married one of
Ishmael's daughters, in addition to the wives
he already had. His new wife's name was Mahalath. She was the sister of Nebaioth and
the daughter of Ishmael, Abraham's son.

Jacob's Dream at Bethel: The Blessing Confirmed (28:10-22)

10Meanwhile, Jacob left Beersheba and traveled toward Haran. 11At sundown he arrived
at a good place to set up camp and stopped
there for the night. Jacob found a stone to
rest his head against and lay down to sleep.
12As he slept, he dreamed of a stairway that
reached from the earth up to heaven. And
he saw the [c]angels of God going up and
down the stairway.

13At the top of the stairway stood the
LORD, and he said, "I am the LORD, the God
of your grandfather Abraham, and the God
of your father, Isaac. The [d]ground you are
lying on belongs to you. I am giving it to you
and your descendants. 14Your descendants
will be as numerous as the dust of the earth!
They will spread out in all directions—to
the west and the east, to the north and the
south. And all the families of the earth will
be blessed through you and your descendants. 15What's more, I am with you, and I
will protect you wherever you go. One day
I will bring you back to this land. I will not
leave you until I have finished giving you
everything I have promised you."

16Then Jacob awoke from his sleep and
said, "Surely the LORD is in this place, and
I wasn't even aware of it!" 17But he was also
afraid and said, "What an awesome place
this is! It is none other than the house of
God, the very gateway to heaven!"

18The next morning Jacob got up very
early. He took the stone he had rested his
head against, and he set it upright as a memorial pillar. Then he poured olive oil over
it. 19He named that place Bethel (which
means "house of God"), although it was previously called Luz.

20Then Jacob made this vow: "If God will
indeed be with me and protect me on this
journey, and if he will provide me with food
and clothing, 21and if I return safely to my

Age	Event	Reference
15	Abraham dies	21:5; 25:7, 26
91	Joseph is born	See "Joseph's Life," p. 99
108	Joseph is sold into slavery	37:2
120	Isaac dies	25:26; 35:28
130	Jacob moves to Egypt	47:7-9
147	Jacob dies, is buried in Canaan	47:28

▲Jacob's Life (27:1–35:29).

28:6-9 *Esau*, the unchosen son still trying to please ***his father***, married a woman from the unchosen line of ***Ishmael***, which he thought would be more acceptable. He did not understand the uniqueness of the covenant family.

28:10-22 Despite Jacob's previous means of securing the blessing, God assured him of protection and provision. The God of Abraham and Isaac was also the God of Jacob. The revelation dramatically changed Jacob's outlook and brought faith into clearer focus.

28:11 The ***good place*** where Jacob ***set up camp*** was apparently a protected area at the foot of a hill. The ***stone to rest his head against*** was probably large, more for protection than for a pillow.

28:12-15 The point of the vision was that God and his angels were with Jacob on his journey. God reiterated to Jacob the covenant promises made to Abraham and Isaac, promising him land, descendants numerous as the dust (cp. 13:16; 22:17), and universal blessing through him (cp. 12:2-3; 15:5, 18; 17:3-8; 22:15-18; 35:11-12). God also promised to be with Jacob and watch over him until he returned.

28:12-13 *stairway* (traditionally *ladder*): This word occurs nowhere else in Scripture. The imagery probably reminded readers of a staircase or ramp up the front of a ziggurat that signified communication between heaven and earth (see note on 11:4). God initiated a divine communication between heaven and earth to guide and protect Jacob, the steward of his covenant (28:13-15; see Ps 91:11-15). • Jesus said that he himself is the stairway between heaven and earth (John 1:51).

28:14 Jacob inherited Abraham's entire covenant (see 22:17), which confirmed Isaac's blessing (28:3-4) and stipulated a temporary exile (28:15; see 15:12-16).

28:15 ***I am with you:*** The promise of God's presence meant that God would ***protect*** and provide for Jacob in a special way. God's promise to be with his people is repeated throughout Scripture (see also 26:24), prompting a response of worship and confidence in those who have faith (28:16-22).

28:16-22 The second half of the passage gives Jacob's response to the revelation. He felt reverential fear and awe in the Lord's presence, and his acts of devotion became archetypes of Israel's worship. When God graciously visits his people and promises to be with them and make them a blessing to the world, his people respond in faith with reverential fear, worship, offerings, and vows. They preserve their faith in memory for future worshipers.

28:18 Anointing with ***oil*** became a way of setting something apart for divine use in Israel's worship (Exod 29:1-7; 40:9; Lev 2:1; 1 Sam 10:1).

28:19 ***Bethel*** later became a holy site for Israel (see Judg 20:18-27; 1 Sam 7:16; 10:3; 1 Kgs 12:26–13:10; 2 Kgs 2:2-3).

28:20-22 In view of what God would do for him, Jacob vowed to do certain things for God. He believed the Lord's words and responded in gratitude. Jacob's ***vow*** influenced Israel's way of making commitments to God in worship.

father's home, then the LORD will certainly
be my God. 22And this memorial pillar I
have set up will become a place for worshiping God, and I will present to God a tenth of
everything he gives me."

Jacob in Paddan-Aram (29:1–31:55)
Jacob Meets Rachel and Laban

29 Then Jacob hurried on, finally arriving in the land of the east. 2He saw a
well in the distance. Three flocks of sheep
and goats lay in an open field beside it, waiting to be watered. But a heavy stone covered
the mouth of the well.
3It was the custom there to wait for all the
flocks to arrive before removing the stone
and watering the animals. Afterward the
stone would be placed back over the mouth
of the well. 4Jacob went over to the shepherds and asked, "Where are you from, my
friends?"
"We are from Haran," they answered.
5"Do you know a man there named Laban,
the grandson of Nahor?" he asked.
"Yes, we do," they replied.
6"Is he doing well?" Jacob asked.
"Yes, he's well," they answered. "Look,
here comes his daughter Rachel with the
flock now."
7Jacob said, "Look, it's still broad daylight—too early to round up the animals.
Why don't you water the sheep and goats so
they can get back out to pasture?"
8"We can't water the animals until all the
flocks have arrived," they replied. "Then the
shepherds move the stone from the mouth
of the well, and we water all the sheep and
goats."
9Jacob was still talking with them when
Rachel arrived with her father's flock, for
she was a [e]shepherd. 10And because Rachel
was his cousin—the daughter of Laban, his
mother's brother—and because the sheep
and goats belonged to his uncle Laban, Jacob
went over to the well and moved the stone
from its mouth and watered his uncle's
flock. 11Then Jacob kissed Rachel, and he
wept aloud. 12He explained to Rachel that

28:22 Gen 14:20; 35:7; Deut 14:22
29:1 Judg 6:3, 33
29:2 Gen 24:10-11
29:4 Gen 28:10
29:5 Gen 11:29
29:6 Exod 2:16
29:9 [e]*ro'ah* (7462) ›Gen 48:15
29:10 Exod 2:17
29:11 Gen 33:4
29:12 Gen 28:5

RACHEL (29:6–30:24)

Gen 31:4-19, 31-35; 33:1-7; 35:16-20; 46:19-22; 48:7
Ruth 4:11
1 Sam 10:2
Jer 31:15
Matt 2:18

Rachel, Laban's beautiful younger daughter, was Jacob's favorite wife. He first met her as he arrived at Paddan-aram in Haran, when he helped Rachel remove the stone from the well and watered her father's sheep (29:10). Jacob agreed to work seven years for Laban in order to have Rachel as his wife, and the time seemed like only a few days because of his great love for her.

Laban deceptively required Jacob to marry Leah, his older, less attractive daughter, before finally giving him Rachel. Unlike Leah, Rachel was barren in the early years of her marriage to Jacob (30:1). She gave her servant Bilhah to Jacob in order to have children, and Dan and Naphtali were born (30:3-8). In time, Rachel conceived and bore Joseph (30:22-25), and Jacob took his wives, children, and possessions away from Haran.

Somewhere between Bethel and Bethlehem, Rachel died while giving birth to Benjamin (35:16-20). Jacob set up a pillar over her tomb that was a landmark even in Saul's time (1 Sam 10:2). Rachel and Leah are highly regarded for having built up the house of Israel (Ruth 4:11). In Jer 31:15, Rachel is pictured as crying for her children being carried off into captivity, and Matthew recalls Jeremiah's words at Herod's slaughter of the male infants (Matt 2:18).

28:22 ***I will present to God a tenth:*** By paying a tithe (*a tenth*) as an act of worship, a person acknowledges that everything is a gift from God and belongs to God (see 14:19-20; Num 18:21-32; Deut 14:22-29; 2 Chr 31:5-6; Mal 3:7-12; Matt 23:23).

29:1–31:55 These chapters tell how God kept his promise by abundantly blessing Jacob with family and possessions. God also disciplined Jacob, leaving him to struggle with Laban for many years. Laban was Jacob's match in deception, and thus a means of correction. • The story of Jacob and Laban parallels Israel's later sojourn in Egypt. Jacob struggled while serving his uncle, but finally emerged with a large family (the founders of the twelve tribes) and great wealth. In Egypt, the Israelites suffered under their oppressors, but they also flourished, becoming a great nation of twelve large tribes and escaping with great riches.

29:1 ***Jacob hurried on:*** The Hebrew text says that he "picked up his feet" as if he felt the wind at his back; he continued his journey with fresh enthusiasm. His changed outlook was the direct result of the vision he received at Bethel, a marvelous revelation that God was going to protect and bless him. He now sought the fulfillment of God's promises to him, not just an escape from Esau. Jacob's attitude had become positive and magnanimous to the point of being naive and vulnerable.

29:2-12 Jacob's meeting Rachel at the well was providentially timed by the sovereign God who was leading Jacob to fulfillment of the promises (cp. 24:12-20). The well was a reminder of God's blessing (cp. 16:13-14; 21:19; 26:19-25, 33).

29:10 In contrast to the lazy, unhelpful shepherds (29:7-8), Jacob is portrayed as generous, industrious, and energetic. • ***Jacob . . . watered his uncle's flock:*** Laban's flocks would flourish under Jacob's care.

29:11 ***Jacob kissed Rachel:*** Kissing relatives was a proper greeting (29:13; cp. Song 8:1).

29:14 Judg 9:2; 2 Sam 5:1
29:15 Gen 30:28; 31:7, 41
29:16 Gen 29:25-26
29:17 Gen 12:11
29:18 Gen 24:67; Hos 12:12
29:20 Song 8:7
29:22 Judg 14:10
29:23 Gen 24:65; 38:14
29:24 Gen 30:9
29:25 Gen 12:18

he was her cousin on her father's side—the
son of her aunt Rebekah. So Rachel quickly
ran and told her father, Laban.
13As soon as Laban heard that his nephew
Jacob had arrived, he ran out to meet him.
He embraced and kissed him and brought
him home. When Jacob had told him his
story, 14Laban exclaimed, "You really are
my own flesh and blood!"

Jacob Marries Leah and Rachel

After Jacob had stayed with Laban for
about a month, 15Laban said to him, "You
shouldn't work for me without pay just because we are relatives. Tell me how much
your wages should be."
16Now Laban had two daughters. The
older daughter was named Leah, and the
younger one was Rachel. 17There was no
sparkle in Leah's eyes, but Rachel had a
beautiful figure and a lovely face. 18Since
Jacob was in love with Rachel, he told her
father, "I'll work for you for seven years if
you'll give me Rachel, your younger daughter, as my wife."
19"Agreed!" Laban replied. "I'd rather give
her to you than to anyone else. Stay and work
with me." 20So Jacob worked seven years to
pay for Rachel. But his love for her was so
strong that it seemed to him but a few days.
21Finally, the time came for him to marry
her. "I have fulfilled my agreement," Jacob
said to Laban. "Now give me my wife so I
can sleep with her."
22So Laban invited everyone in the neighborhood and prepared a wedding feast.
23But that night, when it was dark, Laban
took Leah to Jacob, and he slept with her.
24(Laban had given Leah a servant, Zilpah,
to be her maid.)
25But when Jacob woke up in the morning—
it was Leah! "What have you done to me?"

LEAH (29:14-35)

Gen 30:9-21; 31:4-16; 33:1-7; 34:1; 46:8-15; 49:31; Ruth 4:11

Leah was Laban's first daughter, Jacob's unloved first wife, and Rachel's older sister.

After Jacob deceived his father Isaac into giving him the blessing intended for Esau (27:1-40), Jacob went to his uncle Laban in Mesopotamia to find a wife (27:46–28:2) and escape Esau's revenge (27:41-42). He fell in love with his cousin Rachel and arranged with her father to marry her after seven years of work (29:17-18). At the wedding feast, Laban deceived Jacob by giving him Leah instead of Rachel (29:21-25), claiming that custom required the older daughter to marry first (29:26). Leah's eyes were not beautiful, but Rachel "had a beautiful figure and a lovely face" (29:17).

Jacob's love for Rachel (29:20) induced him to work another seven years to marry her. In the intense rivalry between the two sisters, Jacob favored Rachel, so the Lord blessed Leah with six sons and a daughter (Reuben, Simeon, Levi, Judah, Issachar, Zebulun, and Dinah) before Rachel was given any children (29:31–30:22). This barrenness became a great burden for Rachel. At one point she bargained with Leah for mandrakes, a plant believed to ensure conception, in exchange for conjugal rights. This increased her sister's advantage, because Leah conceived and bore her fifth son (30:14-17).

Leah was the mother of two tribes that played significant roles in Israelite history. The tribe of Levi was the tribe of the priesthood, and the tribe of Judah became the tribe of royalty through which the promised seed (3:15; 12:2-3; 2 Sam 7:16; Matt 1:1) came in the person of Jesus Christ.

29:14a ***You really are my own flesh and blood!*** Laban welcomed Jacob into his house and treated him much like a son.

29:14b-30 Jacob's joyful prospect of marriage to the lovely Rachel became an occasion for Laban's shrewdness and Jacob's discipline. Jacob and his mother had deceived his father and brother to gain the blessing; now his mother's brother deceived him. Jacob received a dose of his own duplicity through twenty years of labor, affliction, and deception in Laban's service (31:38). In God's justice, people harvest what they plant (Gal 6:7). Laban's deception was perfectly designed to make Jacob aware of his own craftiness. God often brings people into the lives of believers to discipline them. But Jacob was tenacious, and God blessed him abundantly with a large family and many possessions (30:25-43) during this time of service.

29:17 *There was no sparkle in Leah's eyes:* Or *Leah had dull eyes,* or *Leah had soft eyes.* The meaning of the Hebrew is uncertain.

29:18 *Seven years* of service was a high bride-price in the ancient world, but Rachel was beautiful (like Sarah and Rebekah), and ***Jacob was in love*** with her.

29:23-26 Like Isaac, Jacob was plied with food and wine (cp. 27:25), deprived of sight in the darkness (cp. 27:1), baffled by clothing (cp. 27:15), and misled by touch (cp. 27:23). The marriage had been consummated (29:23; see 2:24), so Jacob was bound to Leah, but Jacob only acknowledged Rachel as his wife (44:27) and her children as his own (42:38). • ***It's not our custom here to marry off a younger daughter ahead of the firstborn:*** Laban's words are a reminder of what Jacob did when he, the younger son, pretended to be his older brother to gain the blessing (ch 27). Now Leah, the older sister, pretended to be the younger sister to get a husband. God gave the deceiver a dose of his own deception as a discipline in his life.

Jacob raged at Laban. "I worked seven years for Rachel! Why have you tricked me?"

26"It's not our custom here to marry off a younger daughter ahead of the firstborn," Laban replied. 27"But wait until the bridal week is over, then we'll give you Rachel, too—provided you promise to work another seven years for me."

28So Jacob agreed to work seven more years. A week after Jacob had married Leah, Laban gave him Rachel, too. 29(Laban gave Rachel a servant, Bilhah, to be her maid.) 30So Jacob slept with Rachel, too, and he loved her much more than Leah. He then stayed and worked for Laban the additional seven years.

Children Born to Leah and Rachel

31When the LORD saw that Leah was unloved, he enabled her to have children, but Rachel could not conceive. 32So Leah became pregnant and gave birth to a son. She named him Reuben, for she said, "The LORD has noticed my misery, and now my husband will love me."

33She soon became pregnant again and gave birth to another son. She named him Simeon, for she said, "The LORD heard that I was unloved and has given me another son."

34Then she became pregnant a third time and gave birth to another son. She named him Levi, for she said, "Surely this time my husband will feel affection for me, since I have given him three sons!"

35Once again Leah became pregnant and gave birth to another son. She named him Judah, for she said, "Now I will praise the LORD!" And then she stopped having children.

30 When Rachel saw that she wasn't having any children for Jacob, she became jealous of her sister. She pleaded with Jacob, "Give me children, or I'll die!"

2Then Jacob became furious with Rachel. "Am I God?" he asked. "He's the one who has kept you from having children!"

3Then Rachel told him, "Take my maid, Bilhah, and sleep with her. She will bear children for me, and through her I can have a family, too." 4So Rachel gave her servant, Bilhah, to Jacob as a wife, and he slept with her. 5Bilhah became pregnant and presented him with a son. 6Rachel named him Dan, for she said, "God has vindicated me! He has heard my request and given me a son." 7Then Bilhah became pregnant again and gave Jacob a second son. 8Rachel named him Naphtali, for she said, "I have struggled hard with my sister, and I'm winning!"

9Meanwhile, Leah realized that she wasn't getting pregnant anymore, so she took her

29:27 Judg 14:12
29:29 Gen 30:3
29:30 Gen 29:16
29:31 Deut 21:15-17
29:32 Gen 30:23; 37:21; 46:8
29:33 Deut 21:15
29:34 Gen 49:5
29:35 Gen 49:8; Matt 1:2-3
30:1 1 Sam 1:5-6
30:2 Gen 20:18; 29:31
30:3-4 Gen 16:2-4
30:6 Gen 30:23
30:8 Gen 32:28

29:28-30 After the bridal week ended (29:27), Jacob also received Rachel as his wife, though he then would have to work an ***additional seven years*** (cp. 31:41). Laban seemed to have gained the upper hand.

29:30 Jacob ***loved*** Rachel ***much more than Leah:*** Favoritism was an ongoing cause of dysfunction in Jacob's family (cp. 25:28; 37:3). Jacob's favoritism had lasting effects: his family was never together, and their descendants, the tribes of Israel, were rarely unified.

29:31–30:24 The rivalry between these sisters explains much of the later rivalry among their sons, and then among the tribes, just as the rivalry between Jacob and Laban foreshadowed conflict between Israel and the Arameans of Damascus (2 Sam 8:5-6; 10:8-19; 1 Kgs 20:1-34; 2 Kgs 5–8; 13; Isa 7:1-9). • God champions the cause of the poor and oppressed; he exalted Leah, the despised first wife, as the first to become a mother. Judah's kingly tribe and Levi's priestly line came through her despite Jacob's favoritism for Rachel and her children. Despite the tension and jealousy resulting from Laban's treachery and Jacob's favoritism, God still built Jacob's family and brought about the births of the tribal ancestors.

29:31-35 Leah's first four sons were born in rapid succession, but ***Rachel could not conceive***. She was barren, like Sarah and Rebekah (cp. 16:1; 25:21; see also 1 Sam 1:1-28; Luke 1:5-25). • Each name is a memorable wordplay on Leah's experience and hopes.

29:32 ***Reuben*** (Hebrew *re'uben*) means "Look, a son!" It also sounds like the Hebrew for "He has seen my misery" (*ra'ah be'onyi*). His birth gave Leah consolation from God and hope for Jacob's love. Jacob seems not to have seen her misery, but God did (cp. 16:14; 24:62; 25:11). The name was a reminder of God's intervention.

29:33 Leah named her second son ***Simeon***. *Simeon* probably means "one who hears." ***The LORD heard that*** Leah ***was unloved***. The name suggests that she had cried out to the Lord (cp. 16:11).

29:34 ***Levi*** sounds like a Hebrew term that means "being attached" or "feeling affection for." Leah named her third son Levi, hoping that her ***husband*** would become attached to her since she had ***given him three sons***. This hope was not fulfilled.

29:35 Leah reconciled herself to the reality that nothing would turn Jacob's affections toward her. She named her fourth son ***Judah*** with the sentiment, ***"I will praise the LORD"*** (*Judah* is related to the Hebrew term for "praise"). She seems to have given up on Jacob, taking her consolation from the Lord.

30:1-8 Rachel's naming of sons through Bilhah does not reflect faith as Leah's namings had. Rachel felt wronged over the marriage and her barrenness. The names of Bilhah's sons reflect Rachel's bitter struggle with her sister and her feeling of some victory.

30:1-2 In that culture, it was like death for a woman not to have children (cp. 1 Sam 1); only God could open Rachel's womb.

30:3-4 Rachel's decision to have children through her servant, and Jacob's compliance, recall Sarai's use of Hagar (16:1-4). • ***bear children for me:*** Literally *bear children on my knees.*

30:5-6 ***Dan*** means "he judged" or "he vindicated." Rachel felt ***vindicated*** (Hebrew *dananni*) by Dan's birth.

30:7-8 ***Naphtali*** means "my struggle"; it is related to the clause ***I have struggled hard*** (Hebrew *naptule 'elohim niptalti*, "I have struggled the struggles of God"). This word for God expresses the superlative.

30:9 When Leah saw that she had stopped bearing children, she coun-

30:11 Gen 35:26; 46:16; 49:19
30:14 Song 7:13
30:17 Gen 25:21
30:18 Gen 49:14
30:22 1 Sam 1:19-20
30:23 Luke 1:25
30:24 Gen 35:17
30:26 Gen 29:18 Hos 12:12
30:27 Gen 39:2-5
30:28 Gen 29:15; 31:7
30:32 Gen 31:8, 12

servant, Zilpah, and gave her to Jacob as a
wife. 10 Soon Zilpah presented him with a
son. 11 Leah named him Gad, for she said,
"How fortunate I am!" 12 Then Zilpah gave
Jacob a second son. 13 And Leah named him
Asher, for she said, "What joy is mine! Now
the other women will celebrate with me."
14 One day during the wheat harvest, Reuben found some mandrakes growing in a field and brought them to his mother, Leah. Rachel begged Leah, "Please give me some of your son's mandrakes."
15 But Leah angrily replied, "Wasn't it enough that you stole my husband? Now will you steal my son's mandrakes, too?"

Rachel answered, "I will let Jacob sleep with you tonight if you give me some of the mandrakes."

16 So that evening, as Jacob was coming home from the fields, Leah went out to meet him. "You must come and sleep with me tonight!" she said. "I have paid for you with some mandrakes that my son found."
So that night he slept with Leah. 17 And God
answered Leah's prayers. She became pregnant again and gave birth to a fifth son for
Jacob. 18 She named him Issachar, for she
said, "God has rewarded me for giving my
servant to my husband as a wife." 19 Then
Leah became pregnant again and gave birth
to a sixth son for Jacob. 20 She named him
Zebulun, for she said, "God has given me a good reward. Now my husband will treat me with respect, for I have given him six
sons." 21 Later she gave birth to a daughter
and named her Dinah.
22 Then God remembered Rachel's plight and answered her prayers by enabling her
to have children. 23 She became pregnant
and gave birth to a son. "God has removed
my disgrace," she said. 24 And she named
him Joseph, for she said, "May the LORD add yet another son to my family."

Jacob's Wealth Increases

25 Soon after Rachel had given birth to Joseph, Jacob said to Laban, "Please release me so I can go home to my own country.
26 Let me take my wives and children, for I have earned them by serving you, and let me be on my way. You certainly know how hard I have worked for you."
27 "Please listen to me," Laban replied. "I have become wealthy, for the LORD has
blessed me because of you. 28 Tell me how
much I owe you. Whatever it is, I'll pay it."
29 Jacob replied, "You know how hard I've worked for you, and how your flocks and
herds have grown under my care. 30 You had
little indeed before I came, but your wealth has increased enormously. The LORD has blessed you through everything I've done. But now, what about me? When can I start providing for my own family?"
31 "What wages do you want?" Laban asked again.

Jacob replied, "Don't give me anything. Just do this one thing, and I'll continue to
tend and watch over your flocks. 32 Let me
inspect your flocks today and remove all the sheep and goats that are speckled or spotted, along with all the black sheep.
Give these to me as my wages. 33 In the fu-
ture, when you check on the animals you have given me as my wages, you'll see that I have been honest. If you find in my flock

tered Rachel's effort by giving ***her servant . . . to Jacob as a wife*** even though she already had four sons.

30:10-13 ***Gad*** means "good fortune" and was the name of a god of fortune. ***Asher*** means "happy" and was the name of a god of luck. These names reflect Leah's pagan background, but there is no indication that she believed in these gods.

30:14-17 ***Mandrakes*** were considered an aphrodisiac and aid to procreation (see Song 7:13). Rachel thought they would help her get pregnant and so traded Jacob for a night to get them. In the process, Leah got pregnant, not Rachel.

30:18 ***Issachar*** sounds like a Hebrew term that means "reward." The name captures the sense of Jacob's being hired (30:16) and of the Lord's rewarding Leah (Hebrew *sekari*, "my hire").

30:19-20 ***Zebulun*** probably means "honor"; it also means "gift," as in a dowry or tribute. Leah thought that God gave her Zebulun so that her husband would honor her. This hope never fully left her.

30:21 ***Dinah*** was Jacob's only daughter. See ch 34.

30:22-24 Rachel finally ***gave birth to*** her own ***son***, Joseph. His birth was brought about by God's intervention, not by superstitious practices (30:14-16) or the social custom of giving servants as wives. • ***Removed*** (Hebrew *'asap*, "take away") sounds similar to *Joseph* (Hebrew *yosep*). ***Joseph*** means "may he add." Rachel rejoiced over Joseph's birth, yet she prayed that the Lord would ***add yet another son to*** her ***family***.

30:25-34 After his fourteen years of service, Jacob asked Laban for permission to go home. The two bedouin leaders negotiated politely but remained cautiously on guard. Laban wanted to get more out of Jacob. Jacob wanted to gain his wages by selective breeding.

30:27 ***I have become wealthy, for*** (or *I have learned by divination that*): God had prospered Laban through Jacob's presence (see 22:18). Laban may have looked for omens, or simply have perceived what was happening. Since dark-colored sheep (30:32) were rare, a large number of them was considered an omen of God's blessing.

30:30-33 Jacob agreed that God had blessed Laban through him, so he made a plan to gain something for himself. He proposed for his wages the rare black and multicolored goats and the speckled and spotted sheep that were born.

30:32 As Abraham had done with Lot (13:9), Jacob gave Laban what he valued most. White sheep were more common and more valuable than dark or multicolored sheep; as a man of faith, Jacob was willing to take the rejects (cp. 1 Cor 1:26).

any goats without speckles or spots, or any
sheep that are not black, you will know that
I have stolen them from you."
34"All right," Laban replied. "It will be as
you say." 35But that very day Laban went
out and removed the male goats that were
streaked and spotted, all the female goats
that were speckled and spotted or had
white patches, and all the black sheep. He
placed them in the care of his own sons,
36who took them a three-days' journey from
where Jacob was. Meanwhile, Jacob stayed
and cared for the rest of Laban's flock.
37Then Jacob took some fresh branches
from poplar, almond, and plane trees and
peeled off strips of bark, making white
streaks on them. 38Then he placed these
peeled branches in the watering troughs
where the flocks came to drink, for that was
where they mated. 39And when they mated
in front of the white-streaked branches,
they gave birth to young that were streaked,
speckled, and spotted. 40Jacob separated
those lambs from Laban's flock. And at mating time he turned the flock to face Laban's
animals that were streaked or black. This
is how he built his own flock instead of increasing Laban's.
41Whenever the stronger females were
ready to mate, Jacob would place the peeled
branches in the watering troughs in front
of them. Then they would mate in front of
the branches. 42But he didn't do this with
the weaker ones, so the weaker lambs belonged to Laban, and the stronger ones
were Jacob's. 43As a result, Jacob became
very wealthy, with large flocks of sheep and
goats, female and male servants, and many
camels and donkeys.

Jacob Flees from Laban

31 But Jacob soon learned that Laban's
sons were grumbling about him. "Jacob has robbed our father of everything!"
they said. "He has gained all his [f]wealth at
our father's expense." 2And Jacob began to
notice a change in Laban's attitude toward
him.
3Then the LORD said to Jacob, "Return to
the land of your father and grandfather and
to your relatives there, and I will be with
you."
4So Jacob called Rachel and Leah out to
the field where he was watching his flock.
5He said to them, "I have noticed that your
father's attitude toward me has changed.
But the God of my father has been with
me. 6You know how hard I have worked
for your father, 7but he has cheated me,
changing my wages ten times. But God has
not allowed him to do me any harm. 8For if
he said, 'The speckled animals will be your
wages,' the whole flock began to produce
speckled young. And when he changed his
mind and said, 'The striped animals will be
your wages,' then the whole flock produced
striped young. 9In this way, God has taken
your father's animals and given them to me.
10"One time during the mating season, I
had a dream and saw that the male goats
mating with the females were streaked,
speckled, and spotted. 11Then in my dream,

30:43 Gen 13:2; 24:35; 26:13
31:1 [f]*kabod* (3519) ‣ Exod 16:10
31:3 Gen 28:15; 32:9
31:6 Gen 30:29
31:7 Gen 29:25; 31:41
31:8 Gen 30:32
31:11 Gen 16:7-11; 22:11, 15

30:34-36 ***Laban*** verbally agreed with Jacob's plan, but he tried to prevent Jacob from accruing wealth by removing animals from the flock that would fulfill the agreement. • Laban's deception with his ***goats*** reminds us of Jacob's deception of Esau (cp. 27:9; see note on 29:14b-30).

30:37-43 God blessed Jacob despite Laban's duplicity. Not to be outwitted, Jacob used selective breeding to acquire a flock, following the traditional belief that peeled sticks influenced the kind of animal that would be born. The peeled branches seemingly made his animals produce streaked and spotted young; Jacob later acknowledged that God had prospered him (31:7-12). Jacob gained ***stronger*** animals for himself and ***weaker ones*** for Laban (30:41-42).

30:37 ***making white streaks:*** A clever wordplay captures the meaning of this whole section. When Jacob exposed the white (Hebrew *laban*) streaks of wood underneath, he played the "white" game (the *Laban* game) and won. As he outwitted Laban ("Whitey"), Jacob's flocks flourished and Jacob prospered.

30:42 Laban now received due recompense for his treatment of Jacob. Laban's attempt to defraud Jacob resulted in Jacob's coming out ahead, because God was at work in his life.

30:43 ***Jacob became very wealthy***, in fulfillment of God's promises to him (27:28; 28:13-15).

31:1-21 Jacob's return journey precipitated a confrontation with Laban that set a permanent boundary between Israel (Jacob) and Aram (Laban). God kept his word to Jacob by prospering him in Paddan-aram and protecting him on his journey home.

31:1-2 The animosity of ***Laban's sons*** against ***Jacob*** grew because his flocks were multiplying faster than Laban's. They were jealous of God's blessing on Jacob and afraid that he would completely overrun them.

31:3 ***The land of your father and grandfather*** was the land of Canaan, to which Abraham had previously been called (12:1-7; 17:8). • ***Return . . . I will be with you:*** See notes on 26:2-5; 28:12-15. God protected Jacob ("Israel," 32:28) as he brought his family back to the land that was promised to them. God later brought Israel back to Canaan after long years of service in Egypt. That great return had many elements similar to this passage: God defeated foreign gods and beliefs, used dreams for rescue and protection, gave victory over those who threatened them, and established boundaries between nations and tribes (see Deut 32:8).

31:4-13 Jacob explained to his wives how God had blessed him despite Laban's opposition. He was not sure they would want to leave Laban and go to Canaan. He wanted to take a willing family, so he had to make an effective appeal. He rehearsed God's leading and provision over the years, and then told them that he had to keep the vow he had made at Bethel (28:20-22).

31:12 Gen 30:32 Exod 3:7
31:13 Gen 28:10-22
31:15 Gen 29:20, 27
31:18 Gen 25:20
31:19 Judg 17:5
31:20 Gen 31:27
31:21 Gen 37:25 Num 32:1
31:22 Gen 30:36
31:24 Gen 25:20
31:28 Gen 31:55
31:31 Gen 20:11
31:32 Gen 44:9

the angel of God said to me, 'Jacob!' And I
replied, 'Yes, here I am.'
12"The angel said, 'Look up, and you will
see that only the streaked, speckled, and
spotted males are mating with the females
of your flock. For I have seen how Laban has
treated you. 13I am the God who appeared to
you at Bethel, the place where you anointed
the pillar of stone and made your vow to me.
Now get ready and leave this country and return to the land of your birth.' "
14Rachel and Leah responded, "That's
fine with us! We won't inherit any of our father's wealth anyway. 15He has reduced our
rights to those of foreign women. And after
he sold us, he wasted the money you paid
him for us. 16All the wealth God has given
you from our father legally belongs to us
and our children. So go ahead and do whatever God has told you."
17So Jacob put his wives and children
on camels, 18and he drove all his livestock
in front of him. He packed all the belongings he had acquired in Paddan-aram and
set out for the land of Canaan, where his
father, Isaac, lived. 19At the time they left,
Laban was some distance away, shearing
his sheep. Rachel stole her father's household idols and took them with her. 20Jacob
outwitted Laban the Aramean, for they set
out secretly and never told Laban they were
leaving. 21So Jacob took all his possessions
with him and crossed the Euphrates River,
heading for the hill country of Gilead.

Dispute between Laban and Jacob

22Three days later, Laban was told that Jacob had fled. 23So he gathered a group of
his relatives and set out in hot pursuit. He
caught up with Jacob seven days later in the
hill country of Gilead. 24But the previous
night God had appeared to Laban the Aramean in a dream and told him, "I'm warning
you—leave Jacob alone!"
25Laban caught up with Jacob as he was
camped in the hill country of Gilead, and
he set up his camp not far from Jacob's.
26"What do you mean by deceiving me
like this?" Laban demanded. "How dare
you drag my daughters away like prisoners
of war? 27Why did you slip away secretly?
Why did you deceive me? And why didn't
you say you wanted to leave? I would have
given you a farewell feast, with singing and
music, accompanied by tambourines and
harps. 28Why didn't you let me kiss my
daughters and grandchildren and tell them
good-bye? You have acted very foolishly! 29I
could destroy you, but the God of your father appeared to me last night and warned
me, 'Leave Jacob alone!' 30I can understand
your feeling that you must go, and your intense longing for your father's home. But
why have you stolen my gods?"
31"I rushed away because I was afraid,"
Jacob answered. "I thought you would take
your daughters from me by force. 32But as
for your gods, see if you can find them, and
let the person who has taken them die! And
if you find anything else that belongs to
you, identify it before all these relatives of
ours, and I will give it back!" But Jacob did
not know that Rachel had stolen the household idols.
33Laban went first into Jacob's tent to
search there, then into Leah's, and then

31:13 ***the God who appeared to you at Bethel:*** As in Greek version and an Aramaic Targum; Hebrew reads *the God of Bethel.*

31:14-16 The women responded immediately that they would go with Jacob because God had blessed him. They were very willing to leave Laban, who had squandered their wealth (the property that would have provided for them). They knew that what God had given to Jacob would also be theirs.

31:17-21 Jacob left Laban secretly out of fear of reprisal (31:31).

31:19-20 ***Rachel stole her father's household idols:*** Rachel probably wanted to regain some of the assets Laban had squandered; possibly she also worshiped idols (cp. 35:2-4). To have the idols may have signified claiming the family inheritance, as customs in subsequent periods indicate. Laban apparently felt vulnerable without them. Whatever her reasons, Rachel's theft almost brought disaster on the fleeing family when Laban caught up with them. • A wordplay shows that Rachel and Jacob were very much alike—Rachel ***stole*** (Hebrew *wattignob*) Laban's household gods, and Jacob ***outwitted*** (Hebrew *wayyignob,* "stole the heart of, deceived") ***Laban.***

31:21 The journey took the family from Haran southwest to the land of ***Gilead,*** just east of the Jordan River in the north of today's kingdom of Jordan. • ***the Euphrates River:*** Literally *the river.*

31:22-23 The theft of the idols (31:19) was probably the main reason that Laban and his men chased Jacob. It was one thing for Jacob to take his family and flocks—Laban probably still believed they were all his—but another matter entirely to take his household gods. Laban may have feared that Jacob would return someday to claim all of Laban's estate. When he failed to find the gods, he asked for a treaty to keep Jacob away (31:43-53). • It took Laban ***seven days*** to catch up with Jacob.

31:24 ***leave Jacob alone!*** (literally *Do not speak to Jacob either good or evil*): God commanded Laban not to take justice into his own hands. When we try to enact our own sense of good and evil apart from God's command, we always do evil (see note on 2:9).

31:25-30 The dispute between the two men used the language of legal controversies and lawsuits (see also 31:36). In his first argument, Laban presented himself as a wounded party that Jacob had robbed.

31:32 Jacob, so convinced that he didn't have the gods, used an oath that unwittingly put Rachel under a death sentence.

31:33-35 ***Laban*** searched for the idols but ***found nothing***. Laban never

the tents of the two servant wives—but he
found nothing. Finally, he went into Rachel's
tent. 34But Rachel had taken the household
idols and hidden them in her camel saddle,
and now she was sitting on them. When
Laban had thoroughly searched her tent
without finding them, 35she said to her father, "Please, sir, forgive me if I don't get up
for you. I'm having my monthly period." So
Laban continued his search, but he could
not find the household idols.

36Then Jacob became very angry, and he
challenged Laban. "What's my crime?" he
demanded. "What have I done wrong to
make you chase after me as though I were
a criminal? 37You have rummaged through
everything I own. Now show me what you
found that belongs to you! Set it out here
in front of us, before our relatives, for all to
see. Let them judge between us!

38"For twenty years I have been with
you, caring for your flocks. In all that time
your sheep and goats never miscarried. In
all those years I never used a single ram
of yours for food. 39If any were attacked
and killed by wild animals, I never showed
you the carcass and asked you to reduce
the count of your flock. No, I took the loss
myself! You made me pay for every stolen
animal, whether it was taken in broad daylight or in the dark of night.

40"I worked for you through the scorching
heat of the day and through cold and sleepless nights. 41Yes, for twenty years I slaved
in your house! I worked for fourteen years
earning your two daughters, and then six
more years for your flock. And you changed
my wages ten times! 42In fact, if the God of
my father had not been on my side—the
God of Abraham and the fearsome God of
Isaac—you would have sent me away empty-
handed. But God has seen your abuse and
my hard work. That is why he appeared to
you last night and rebuked you!"

Jacob's Treaty with Laban

43Then Laban replied to Jacob, "These
women are my daughters, these children are
my grandchildren, and these flocks are my
flocks—in fact, everything you see is mine.
But what can I do now about my daughters
and their children? 44So come, let's make a
covenant, you and I, and it will be a witness
to our commitment."

45So Jacob took a stone and set it up as a
monument. 46Then he told his family members, "Gather some stones." So they gathered
stones and piled them in a heap. Then Jacob
and Laban sat down beside the pile of stones
to eat a covenant meal. 47To commemorate
the event, Laban called the place Jegar-
sahadutha (which means "witness pile" in
Aramaic), and Jacob called it Galeed (which
means "witness pile" in Hebrew).

48Then Laban declared, "This pile of
stones will stand as a witness to remind us
of the covenant we have made today." This
explains why it was called Galeed—"Witness Pile." 49But it was also called Mizpah
(which means "watchtower"), for Laban
said, "May the LORD keep watch between
us to make sure that we keep this covenant
when we are out of each other's sight. 50If
you mistreat my daughters or if you marry
other wives, God will see it even if no one
else does. He is a witness to this covenant
between us.

51"See this pile of stones," Laban continued, "and see this monument I have set
between us. 52They stand between us as witnesses of our vows. I will never pass this pile
of stones to harm you, and you must never
pass these stones or this monument to harm
me. 53I call on the God of our ancestors—the
God of your grandfather Abraham and the

31:37 Gen 31:33
31:38 Gen 27:44
31:39 Exod 22:10-13
31:41 Gen 29:30
31:42 Gen 29:32
31:44 Gen 21:27, 30
31:45 Gen 28:18; Josh 24:26-27
31:48 Gen 21:30
31:49 Judg 10:17; 11:29
31:50 Judg 11:10; 1 Sam 12:5; Jer 29:23; 42:5
31:52 Gen 31:29, 42
31:53 Gen 24:12

dreamed that a woman having her *monthly period* would desecrate the idols by *sitting on them* (cp. Lev 15:19-24).

31:36-42 Jacob retaliated by accusing Laban of false charges and humiliation. Laban now became the defendant, for his charges were demeaning and apparently groundless.

31:40 Jacob, who preferred domestic life (25:27), had for twenty years endured the rigors of the outdoors that Esau had loved.

31:42 ***on my side . . . and the fearsome God of Isaac*** (or *and the Fear of Isaac*): The God that Isaac feared was with Jacob (31:3), had seen his ***hard work*** and faithfulness despite Laban's ***abuse***, and had rewarded Jacob. Laban's dream only proved to Jacob that he was in the right.

31:43-44 ***Laban*** pushed for a treaty to settle the dispute—he felt vulnerable, so he wanted to secure the borders. Jacob did not need a treaty, since God had provided for him and protected him.

31:45-48 The ***stone*** and the ***heap*** of stones were a ***monument*** to the border treaty between the two men, as a witness to future generations. Each man named the monument ***witness pile*** in his native language. It remained the perpetual border between Israel and the kingdom of Aram (Syria), two nations often at war.

31:49 The witness pile was also called ***watchtower.*** God would watch over Jacob and Laban and keep them apart, for they could not trust each other.

31:50-53 Laban added some face-saving stipulations to the treaty, using many words to cover up his own untrustworthiness and portray Jacob as the unethical party. He even took credit for the monument Jacob had erected (***this monument I have set***, 31:51). The women and children would be much safer and better cared for with Jacob than they ever were with Laban.

31:53 ***the fearsome God of his father, Isaac:*** Or *the Fear of his father, Isaac.* See note on 31:42.

31:54 Exod 18:12
31:55 Gen 31:28
32:1 Gen 16:11; 2 Kgs 6:16-17
32:2 Josh 13:26; 21:38; 2 Sam 2:8
32:3 Gen 27:41-42
32:4 Gen 31:41
32:7 Gen 33:1
32:9 Gen 28:13-15; 31:13
32:10 Gen 24:27
32:11 Gen 27:41
32:12 Gen 28:14
32:18 Gen 32:13
32:20 1 Sam 25:19

God of my grandfather Nahor—to serve as a
judge between us."
So Jacob took an oath before the fearsome God of his father, Isaac, to respect
the boundary line. 54Then Jacob offered a
sacrifice to God there on the mountain and
invited everyone to a covenant feast. After
they had eaten, they spent the night on the
mountain.
55Laban got up early the next morning,
and he kissed his grandchildren and his
daughters and blessed them. Then he left
and returned home.

Jacob Returns Home (32:1–33:20)

Angels Meet Jacob

32 As Jacob started on his way again,
angels of God came to meet him.
2When Jacob saw them, he exclaimed, "This
is God's camp!" So he named the place Mahanaim.

Jacob Sends Gifts to Esau

3Then Jacob sent messengers ahead to his
brother, Esau, who was living in the region
of Seir in the land of Edom. 4He told them,
"Give this message to my master Esau: 'Humble greetings from your servant Jacob. Until
now I have been living with Uncle Laban,
5and now I own cattle, donkeys, flocks of
sheep and goats, and many servants, both
men and women. I have sent these messengers to inform my lord of my coming,
hoping that you will be friendly to me.' "

Jacob Prepares to Meet Esau

6After delivering the message, the messengers returned to Jacob and reported, "We
met your brother, Esau, and he is already
on his way to meet you—with an army
of 400 men!" 7Jacob was terrified at the
news. He divided his household, along
with the flocks and herds and camels, into
two groups. 8He thought, "If Esau meets
one group and attacks it, perhaps the other
group can escape."
9Then Jacob prayed, "O God of my grandfather Abraham, and God of my father,
Isaac—O LORD, you told me, 'Return to
your own land and to your relatives.' And
you promised me, 'I will treat you kindly.' 10I
am not worthy of all the unfailing love and
faithfulness you have shown to me, your
servant. When I left home and crossed
the Jordan River, I owned nothing except a
walking stick. Now my household fills two
large camps! 11O LORD, please rescue me
from the hand of my brother, Esau. I am
afraid that he is coming to attack me, along
with my wives and children. 12But you
promised me, 'I will surely treat you kindly,
and I will multiply your descendants until
they become as numerous as the sands
along the seashore—too many to count.' "
13Jacob stayed where he was for the
night. Then he selected these gifts from
his possessions to present to his brother,
Esau: 14200 female goats, 20 male goats,
200 ewes, 20 rams, 1530 female camels with
their young, 40 cows, 10 bulls, 20 female
donkeys, and 10 male donkeys. 16He divided these animals into herds and assigned
each to different servants. Then he told his
servants, "Go ahead of me with the animals,
but keep some distance between the herds."
17He gave these instructions to the men
leading the first group: "When my brother,
Esau, meets you, he will ask, 'Whose servants are you? Where are you going? Who
owns these animals?' 18You must reply,
'They belong to your servant Jacob, but they
are a gift for his master Esau. Look, he is
coming right behind us.' "
19Jacob gave the same instructions to the
second and third herdsmen and to all who
followed behind the herds: "You must say
the same thing to Esau when you meet him.
20And be sure to say, 'Look, your servant Jacob is right behind us.' "
Jacob thought, "I will try to appease him
by sending gifts ahead of me. When I see

31:55 Verse 31:55 is numbered 32:1 in Hebrew text.

32:1-32 Verses 32:1-32 are numbered 32:2-33 in Hebrew text.

32:1 God assured ***Jacob*** of his protection at a time when Jacob most needed such consolation. His journey was both a physical return to his homeland and a spiritual return to the land of God's promised blessing. God protects his people and fulfills his plan.

32:2 ***This is God's camp!*** Jacob must have seen the ***angels*** that revealed God's presence as a sign of protection, as with the earlier vision when he was departing the land (28:10-22). • ***Mahanaim*** means "two camps." Jacob's company and the company of angels were together in one place.

32:3-5 Apparently inspired by the vision of angels (32:1, Hebrew *mal'akim*), ***Jacob sent messengers*** (*mal'akim*) into Edom to meet Esau.

32:7-8 Jacob ***divided*** his company ***into two groups*** or camps (Hebrew *makhanoth*, related to "Mahanaim" in 32:2) because he was afraid, remembering Esau's character and his threat to kill Jacob (see 25:25; 27:41).

32:9-12 Jacob's prayer is a wonderful example of how to address God. He based his appeal on God's will, reminding God of his relationship with him, his command for him to return to the land, and his promise (32:9). He had a correct attitude of genuine humility and total dependence on God (32:10). Finally, he asked that God ***rescue*** him from his brother, and he repeated God's promises (see 22:17).

32:13-21 Taking a large portion of the wealth God had blessed him with (some 550 animals), Jacob prepared a gift to appease Esau's anger and gain his favor.

him in person, perhaps he will be friendly
to me." 21So the gifts were sent on ahead,
while Jacob himself spent that night in the
camp.

Jacob Wrestles with God and Becomes Israel

22During the night Jacob got up and took
his two wives, his two servant wives, and his
eleven sons and crossed the Jabbok River
with them. 23After taking them to the other
side, he sent over all his possessions.

24This left Jacob all alone in the camp,
and a man came and wrestled with him until the dawn began to break. 25When the
man saw that he would not win the match,
he touched Jacob's hip and wrenched it out
of its socket. 26Then the man said, "Let me
go, for the dawn is breaking!"

But Jacob said, "I will not let you go unless
you bless me."

27"What is your name?" the man asked.

He replied, "Jacob."

28"Your name will no longer be Jacob,"
the man told him. "From now on you will be
called Israel, because you have fought with
God and with men and have won."

29"Please tell me your name," Jacob said.

"Why do you want to know my name?" the
man replied. Then he blessed Jacob there.

30Jacob named the place Peniel (which
means "face of God"), for he said, "I have
seen God face to face, yet my life has been
spared." 31The sun was rising as Jacob left
Peniel, and he was limping because of the
injury to his hip. 32(Even today the people
of Israel don't eat the tendon near the hip
socket because of what happened that
night when the man strained the tendon of
Jacob's hip.)

Jacob and Esau Make Peace

33 Then Jacob looked up and saw Esau
coming with his 400 men. So he divided the children among Leah, Rachel, and

32:22 Deut 3:16; Josh 12:2
32:24 Gen 18:2
32:26 Hos 12:3-4
32:28 Gen 35:10; 1 Kgs 18:31
32:29 Exod 3:13; Judg 13:17
32:30 Gen 16:13; Exod 24:10; 33:20; Num 12:8; Deut 5:24; 34:10; Judg 6:22; John 1:18
32:31 Judg 8:8-9
33:1 Gen 32:6-7

32:22-32 Before Jacob returned to the land God had promised him, God met him, crippled him, and blessed him, changing his name to Israel. This episode was a significant turning point for him.

32:22-24 ***The Jabbok River*** flows westward to the Jordan Valley, dividing the region of Bashan on the north from Gilead on the south. Wordplays on Jacob's name and character preserve the memory of this encounter. ***Jacob*** (Hebrew *ya'aqob*), while at ***Jabbok*** (Hebrew *yabboq*), ***wrestled*** (Hebrew *wayye'abeq*). Through his fight with an adversary to receive the blessing, Jacob's name would be changed, and his deceptive striving would partially give way to faith as his way of life.

32:24 ***a man came:*** The narrative unfolds as the event did for Jacob. No details are given about the assailant, who later refused to identify himself (32:29). • ***until the dawn:*** The darkness fit Jacob's situation and increased the fear and uncertainty that seized him. In the darkness he had no idea who it was—it might have been one of Esau's men, or Laban's.

32:25 ***he touched Jacob's hip and wrenched it out of its socket:*** Jacob, the deceitful fighter, could fight no more. When his assailant fought him as man to man, Jacob could hold his own. But like so many of his own rivals, he had now more than met his match.

32:26 At daybreak, the significance of this fight began to dawn on Jacob. He realized who his assailant was, and since it was futile to fight, he held on to obtain God's blessing.

32:27 ***What is your name?*** The Lord's question was really about Jacob's character, not his identity (cp. 3:9; 4:9). By giving his name, ***Jacob*** confessed his nature, his way of doing things as "Heel-grabber, Deceiver, Usurper." Before God would bless him, he had to acknowledge who he was, and then God would change his identity.

32:28 ***Jacob*** sounds like the Hebrew words for "heel" and "deceiver." ***Israel*** means "God fights." God first had to fight with him, but now God would fight for him. Jacob's name was thus full of promise for Jacob and his descendants. • ***you have fought with God and with men:*** Through his entire life, Jacob had been seizing God's blessing by his own abilities and by any means possible. Jacob knew the importance of the blessing, but he was too self-sufficient and proud to let the blessing be given to him. He had been fighting God long before this encounter. • ***and have won:*** He had prevailed in his struggles with Esau and with Laban; now he prevailed in obtaining God's blessing.

32:29 ***Jacob*** knew who was with him (32:30); the request was his attempt to regain some control. God would not reveal his ***name***, which cannot be had on demand.

32:30 ***Peniel (which means "face of God"):*** The name shows that Jacob recognized the man as a manifestation of God (a *theophany*). • ***yet my life has been spared*** (or *and I have been rescued*): The saying probably meant that Jacob realized that his prayer to be rescued from Esau (32:11) had been answered, for if he could meet God like this and walk away, he had nothing to fear from Esau. The saying may also reflect an ancient understanding that no one could see God and live (see Exod 33:20).

32:31 ***Peniel:*** Hebrew *Penuel*, a variant spelling of Peniel. • ***he was limping:*** God injured Jacob's hip, thus curtailing his proud self-sufficiency. Since the Lord had restricted his natural strength, Jacob would have to rely on the Lord with greater faith. He had thought that returning to his land would be a matter of outwitting his brother once again (32:3-21), but here at the land's threshold he met its true proprietor. He would get the land, but only if God fought for him. Self-sufficiency—trying to achieve the blessing by our own strength or by the ways of the world—will not suffice. If we persist, God may have to cripple our self-sufficiency to make us trust him more.

32:32 The story includes a dietary restriction for Israel that became a custom but was not put into law. This custom helped preserve the memory of the story. Observant Jews still refuse to eat the tendons of an animal's hindquarters.

33:1-17 Jacob's long-anticipated meeting with his brother Esau turned out far better than he had feared. Esau's changed heart is an example of how "God fights" (32:28). Earlier, he had cared little about the birthright (25:32-34); now he cared little for old grudges. Jacob recognized that God had intervened.

33:1-2 Jacob's identity had been changed (32:27-28), but he had not yet learned to live up to the new name; he still showed the favoritism that divides families. He lined up his family and his possessions in the order of their

33:3
Gen 18:2; 42:6
33:4
Gen 45:14-15
33:5
Gen 48:9
33:8
Gen 32:14-16

his two servant wives. 2He put the servant
wives and their children at the front, Leah
and her children next, and Rachel and Joseph last. 3Then Jacob went on ahead. As
he approached his brother, he bowed to the
ground seven times before him. 4Then Esau
ran to meet him and embraced him, threw
his arms around his neck, and kissed him.
And they both wept.
5Then Esau looked at the women and
children and asked, "Who are these people
with you?"
"These are the children God has graciously given to me, your servant," Jacob
replied. 6Then the servant wives came forward with their children and bowed before
him. 7Next came Leah with her children,
and they bowed before him. Finally, Joseph
and Rachel came forward and bowed before him.
8"And what were all the flocks and herds
I met as I came?" Esau asked.
Jacob replied, "They are a gift, my lord, to
ensure your friendship."
9"My brother, I have plenty," Esau answered. "Keep what you have for yourself."
10But Jacob insisted, "No, if I have found
favor with you, please accept this gift from
me. And what a relief to see your friendly
smile. It is like seeing the face of God!
11Please take this gift I have brought you,
for God has been very gracious to me. I have
more than enough." And because Jacob insisted, Esau finally accepted the gift.

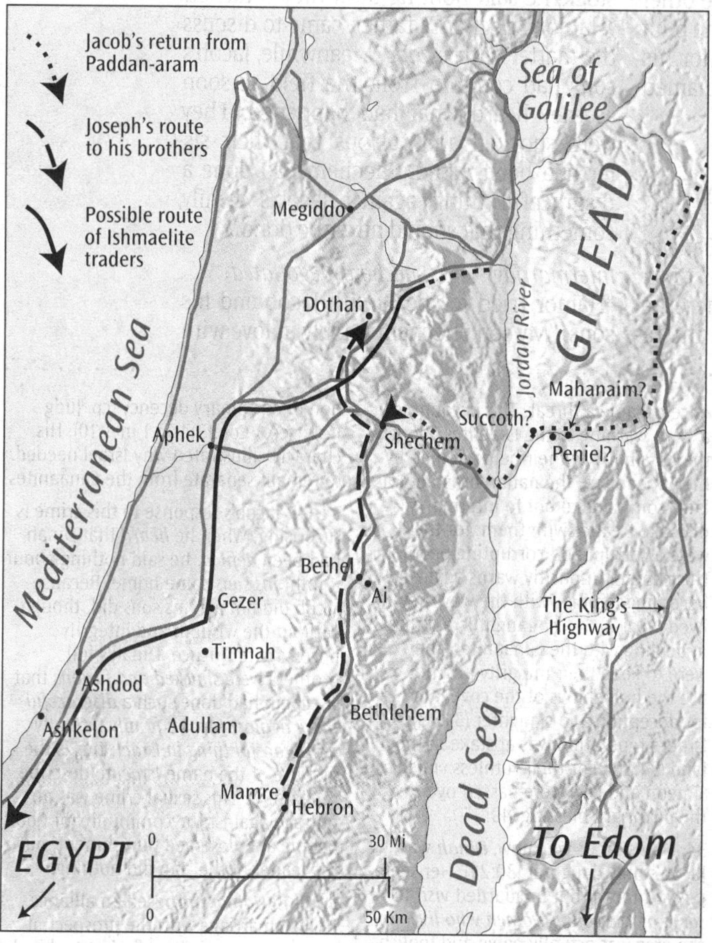

◀ **Jacob's Family in Canaan (32:1–38:30).** When Jacob returned to Canaan from Haran, after making a treaty with Laban at Mizpah (31:48-49), he met angels at MAHANAIM (32:1-2) and wrestled with God at PENIEL (32:22-32). After making peace with Esau (33:1-16), Jacob traveled to SUCCOTH (33:17) and then SHECHEM (33:18-20; cp. 12:6-7). After the conflict with the people of Shechem (ch 34), at God's instruction Jacob moved to BETHEL (35:1-15; cp. 12:8; 13:1-4; 28:10-22). After Jacob left Bethel, Rachel died in childbirth on the way to Ephrath (=BETHLEHEM, 35:16-20; cp. 1 Sam 10:2; Jer 31:15). Jacob continued to HEBRON (35:27), where he was reunited with his father. There he settled, and from there Joseph later went to find his brothers (37:14). Joseph's route to SHECHEM and then DOTHAN is shown (37:14-17), as is the possible route of the Ishmaelite traders from GILEAD to EGYPT (37:25-36). ADULLAM, where Judah moved (38:1), is also shown.

importance to him, with the slave wives and their children in front (to face danger first), Leah's group behind them, and Rachel and Joseph in the back, where it was safest.

33:3-13 Even though Jacob had nothing to fear, he was afraid and tried to appease his brother. He assumed the role of a servant before royalty by bowing (33:3), using an honorific title (33:8, 13), making introductions (33:6-7), and presenting gifts (33:8).

33:4 Esau's friendly greeting was an answer to prayer (32:11). God had rescued Jacob from Esau's revenge.

33:5 ***your servant:*** In talking with his brother, Jacob continued to refer to himself as Esau's servant (also 33:14) and to Esau as his lord (33:8, 13-15); Esau called Jacob "my brother" (33:9). Jacob was cautiously warding off any possible retaliation by reversing the words of the oracle (25:23).

33:7 Among Jacob's sons, only *Joseph* is named; he was Jacob's favorite son and the recipient of the blessing.

33:10 Jacob knew that Esau's friendly greeting was God's work, secured at Peniel when he saw God face to face.

33:11 ***this gift I have brought you*** (literally *my blessing*): Jacob perceived Esau as a threat and tried to appease him with a gift (cp. 2 Kgs 17:3-4; 18:7, 14; 2 Chr 28:21), perhaps in a guilty attempt to undo the past. Jacob would not take no for an answer.

12“Well,” Esau said, “let’s be going. I will
lead the way.”
13But Jacob replied, “You can see, my lord,
that some of the children are very young,
and the flocks and herds have their young,
too. If they are driven too hard, even for one
day, all the animals could die. 14Please, my
lord, go ahead of your servant. We will follow slowly, at a pace that is comfortable for
the livestock and the children. I will meet
you at Seir.”
15“All right,” Esau said, “but at least let me
assign some of my men to guide and protect
you.”
Jacob responded, “That’s not necessary.
It’s enough that you’ve received me warmly,
my lord!”
16So Esau turned around and started back
to Seir that same day. 17Jacob, on the other
hand, traveled on to Succoth. There he built
himself a house and made shelters for his
livestock. That is why the place was named
Succoth (which means “shelters”).

Jacob Moves to Shechem

18Later, having traveled all the way from
Paddan-aram, Jacob arrived safely at the
town of Shechem, in the land of Canaan.
There he set up camp outside the town.
19Jacob bought the plot of land where he
camped from the family of Hamor, the father of Shechem, for 100 pieces of silver.
20And there he built an altar and named it
El-Elohe-Israel.

The Danger of Intermarriage (34:1-31)

Dinah Is Defiled

34 One day Dinah, the daughter of Jacob and Leah, went to visit some
of the young women who lived in the area.
2But when the local prince, Shechem son of
Hamor the Hivite, saw Dinah, he seized her
and raped her. 3But then he fell in love with
her, and he tried to win her affection with
tender words. 4He said to his father, Hamor,
“Get me this young girl. I want to marry her.”
5Soon Jacob heard that Shechem had
defiled his daughter, Dinah. But since his
sons were out in the fields herding his livestock, he said nothing until they returned.
6Hamor, Shechem’s father, came to discuss
the matter with Jacob. 7Meanwhile, Jacob’s
sons had come in from the field as soon
as they heard what had happened. They
were shocked and furious that their sister had been raped. Shechem had done a
disgraceful thing against Jacob’s family,
something that should never be done.

Intermarriage with Shechem Negotiated

8Hamor tried to speak with Jacob and his
sons. “My son Shechem is truly in love with

33:14 Gen 32:3
33:17 Judg 8:5, 14; Ps 60:6
33:18 Gen 12:6; 25:20
33:19 Josh 24:32; John 4:5
34:1 Gen 30:21
34:2 Deut 21:14; 2 Sam 13:14
34:4 Gen 21:21
34:7 2 Sam 13:12

33:12-15 Despite Esau’s apparent magnanimity, Jacob was wary and cleverly avoided traveling with his brother. • ***I will meet you at Seir:*** Jacob’s lie manifests his old character, living by deception rather than by faith.

33:16-17 Instead of following ***Esau*** south ***to Seir*** as promised, ***Jacob*** again deceived his brother, then headed in the opposite direction ***to Succoth***, east of the Jordan River and north of the Jabbok.

33:18-20 These verses form an epilogue to Jacob’s adventures outside the land. He returned in peace with a large family and many possessions. • ***Jacob***, like Abraham, ***built an altar*** at ***Shechem*** (see 12:6-8) and purchased land ***from the family of Hamor***.

33:19 *100 pieces of silver:* Hebrew *100 kesitahs;* the value or weight of the kesitah is no longer known.

33:20 *El-Elohe-Israel* means “God, the God of Israel.” The name of the altar commemorated Jacob’s relationship with God. Jacob publicly proclaimed that God was his God, and that God had led him back to the land he would inherit.

34:1-31 Once Jacob and his family settled in the land, the Canaanite presence became a threat. This account is a stern warning to the Israelites about the possibility of their being defiled by the Canaanites. The nation of Israel was later commanded not to intermarry or make treaties with them, for they were a corrupt and corrupting people. This chapter implicitly warns against becoming familiar with the way they lived (34:1-2). It also taught Israel that in dealing with the Canaanites, they were to keep their integrity and not use the holy things of the covenant for deception and slaughter (34:13); Israel’s reputation was at stake in the land (34:30). For their ruthless violence, Simeon and Levi were passed over in the birthright blessing (49:5-7).

34:1-2 As far as we know, ***Dinah*** was Jacob’s only daughter (30:21). Her seemingly innocent but unguarded ***visit*** to ***some of the young women who lived in the area*** was actually naive and foolish, because the local Hivites were very corrupt, not safe or trustworthy. • ***Shechem . . . seized her and raped her:*** Shechem violated and debased Dinah, so she had no chance for a proper marriage.

34:3-4 While Shechem’s intense feelings for Dinah made him willing to undergo significant hardship (34:11-12, 17-18, 24), the way he showed his “love” for her was selfish, impetuous, and in violation of customary decency (cp. Judg 14:2; see 1 Cor 13:4-7; 1 Jn 4:10). His character illustrated why Israel needed to remain separate from the Canaanites.

34:5-7 Jacob’s response to this crime is surprising. When he ***heard*** that Dinah had been ***defiled***, he said nothing about it until ***his sons*** came home. Because Jacob did not act, his sons did, though without the wisdom and integrity necessary for justice. Dinah’s full brothers ***were shocked and furious*** that Shechem had done such a ***disgraceful thing against Jacob’s family*** (literally *a disgraceful thing in Israel*; this is the first use of the name *Israel* to describe the family). This sexual crime was an outrage against the community of God’s people and deserved punishment, but the leader of the clan did nothing.

34:8-10 ***Hamor*** proposed an alliance of intermarriage with the prospect of mutual economic benefit, but God had already promised Jacob everything, including the land (34:10; see 14:21-24). Hamor wanted to gain control of Israel’s wealth (34:23); no good could come of trusting the defiling Canaanites. For some of these reasons, intermarriage with Canaanites was not allowed under the law (see Exod 23:27-33; Deut 7:1-5)—unless, of course, they came to faith (see Josh 2:1-15; 6:23-25; Matt 1:5).

34:10
Gen 33:19
34:12
Exod 22:16
34:13
Gen 27:36
34:14
Gen 17:14
34:19
Gen 29:20
34:22
Gen 34:15
34:25
Gen 49:5-7
Josh 5:8
34:28
Gen 43:18
34:30
Gen 13:7; 49:5-7
Exod 5:21
2 Sam 10:6
1 Chr 16:19
35:1
Gen 12:8; 28:19

your daughter," he said. "Please let him
marry her. 9In fact, let's arrange other marriages, too. You give us your daughters for
our sons, and we will give you our daughters
for your sons. 10And you may live among
us; the land is open to you! Settle here and
trade with us. And feel free to buy property
in the area."

11Then Shechem himself spoke to Dinah's father and brothers. "Please be kind
to me, and let me marry her," he begged. "I
will give you whatever you ask. 12No matter
what dowry or gift you demand, I will gladly
pay it—just give me the girl as my wife."

13But since Shechem had defiled their
sister, Dinah, Jacob's sons responded deceitfully to Shechem and his father, Hamor.
14They said to them, "We couldn't possibly
allow this, because you're not circumcised.
It would be a disgrace for our sister to marry
a man like you! 15But here is a solution. If
every man among you will be circumcised
like we are, 16then we will give you our
daughters, and we'll take your daughters
for ourselves. We will live among you and
become one people. 17But if you don't agree
to be circumcised, we will take her and be
on our way."

18Hamor and his son Shechem agreed to
their proposal. 19Shechem wasted no time
in acting on this request, for he wanted Jacob's daughter desperately. Shechem was
a highly respected member of his family,
20and he went with his father, Hamor, to
present this proposal to the leaders at the
town gate.

21"These men are our friends," they said.
"Let's invite them to live here among us and
trade freely. Look, the land is large enough
to hold them. We can take their daughters
as wives and let them marry ours. 22But they
will consider staying here and becoming
one people with us only if all of our men are
circumcised, just as they are. 23But if we do
this, all their livestock and possessions will
eventually be ours. Come, let's agree to their
terms and let them settle here among us."

Jacob's Sons Destroy Shechem

24So all the men in the town council agreed
with Hamor and Shechem, and every male
in the town was circumcised. 25But three
days later, when their wounds were still
sore, two of Jacob's sons, Simeon and Levi,
who were Dinah's full brothers, took their
swords and entered the town without opposition. Then they slaughtered every male
there, 26including Hamor and his son Shechem. They killed them with their swords,
then took Dinah from Shechem's house and
returned to their camp.

27Meanwhile, the rest of Jacob's sons arrived. Finding the men slaughtered, they
plundered the town because their sister
had been defiled there. 28They seized all
the flocks and herds and donkeys—everything they could lay their hands on, both
inside the town and outside in the fields.
29They looted all their wealth and plundered their houses. They also took all their
little children and wives and led them away
as captives.

30Afterward Jacob said to Simeon and
Levi, "You have ruined me! You've made
me stink among all the people of this land—
among all the Canaanites and Perizzites.
We are so few that they will join forces and
crush us. I will be ruined, and my entire
household will be wiped out!"

31"But why should we let him treat our
sister like a prostitute?" they retorted angrily.

Jacob's Return to Bethel (35:1-15)

35 Then God said to Jacob, "Get ready
and move to Bethel and settle
there. Build an altar there to the God who
appeared to you when you fled from your
brother, Esau."

34:13-17 Dinah's brothers ***responded*** to the proposal without waiting for Jacob to respond, and they acted ***deceitfully***. They may not have thought that ***Shechem*** and his people would ever agree to the rite of circumcision, but they knew what they would do if the Canaanites accepted (34:25).

34:18-24 The Canaanites accepted the stipulation and ***every male in the town was circumcised***. This was not just to allow Shechem to marry Dinah, but to give them the opportunity to acquire everything that Jacob possessed (34:23).

34:25-29 When ***Simeon and Levi*** used circumcision to deceive and slaughter the Canaanites, they showed disdain for the sign of the covenant. Their slaughter of all the males and their plunder of the city was not justice, but brutal and excessive revenge. In their moral outrage and desire to right the wrong, they should have demanded compensation (see Exod 22:16-17; Deut 22:28-29). Instead, their passionate act of rage cost them their birthright blessing (49:5-7).

34:30 ***Jacob*** responded again out of fear of what would happen to him, but God caused ***the people of this land*** to fear him instead (35:5).

35:1-29 This chapter highlights God's promises, Jacob's vow, and the transition to Jacob's sons' carrying on the covenant. Deborah, Rachel, and Isaac all died, marking the end of an era and of the account of Isaac's family (25:19–35:29). • Idols were removed (35:1-4) and pure worship was established (35:6-7). During this transition, the faith had to be revitalized so that the covenant could be carried forward by Jacob's sons.

35:1-7 ***Jacob*** returned ***to Bethel***, about fifteen miles south of Shechem, to complete the vows he had made at Bethel (28:20-22).

[2]So Jacob told everyone in his household,
"Get rid of all your pagan idols, purify yourselves, and put on clean clothing. [3]We are
now going to Bethel, where I will build an
altar to the God who answered my prayers
when I was in distress. He has been with me
wherever I have gone."
[4]So they gave Jacob all their pagan idols
and earrings, and he buried them under the
great tree near Shechem. [5]As they set out,
a terror from God spread over the people
in all the towns of that area, so no one attacked Jacob's family.
[6]Eventually, Jacob and his household arrived at Luz (also called Bethel) in Canaan.
[7]Jacob built an altar there and named the
place El-bethel (which means "God of Bethel"),
because God had appeared to him there
when he was fleeing from his brother, Esau.
[8]Soon after this, Rebekah's old nurse,
Deborah, died. She was buried beneath the
oak tree in the valley below Bethel. Ever
since, the tree has been called Allon-bacuth
(which means "oak of weeping").
[9]Now that Jacob had returned from
Paddan-aram, God appeared to him again
at Bethel. God blessed him, [10]saying, "Your
name is Jacob, but you will not be called
Jacob any longer. From now on your name
will be Israel." So God renamed him Israel.
[11]Then God said, "I am El-Shaddai—'God
[g]Almighty.' Be fruitful and multiply. You
will become a great nation, even [h]many
nations. Kings will be among your descendants! [12]And I will give you the land I once
gave to Abraham and Isaac. Yes, I will give
it to you and your [i]descendants after you."
[13]Then God went up from the place where
he had spoken to Jacob.
[14]Jacob set up a stone pillar to mark the
place where God had spoken to him. Then
he poured wine over it as an offering to God
and anointed the pillar with olive oil. [15]And
Jacob named the place Bethel (which means
"house of God"), because God had spoken to
him there.

Jacob Moves to Mamre (35:16-29)

Rachel Dies in Childbirth

[16]Leaving Bethel, Jacob and his clan moved
on toward Ephrath. But Rachel went into
labor while they were still some distance
away. Her labor pains were intense. [17]After
a very hard delivery, the midwife finally exclaimed, "Don't be afraid—you have another
son!" [18]Rachel was about to die, but with
her last breath she named the baby Ben-
oni (which means "son of my sorrow"). The
baby's father, however, called him Benjamin
(which means "son of my right hand"). [19]So
Rachel died and was buried on the way to
Ephrath (that is, Bethlehem). [20]Jacob set up
a stone monument over Rachel's grave, and
it can be seen there to this day.

Reuben's Transgression

[21]Then Jacob traveled on and camped beyond Migdal-eder. [22]While he was living
there, Reuben had intercourse with Bilhah,
his father's concubine, and Jacob soon
heard about it.

35:2 Gen 31:19
35:3 Gen 28:15-22
35:4 Exod 32:3; Judg 8:24; Hos 2:13
35:5 Exod 15:16
35:6 Gen 28:19
35:7 Gen 28:19
35:8 Gen 24:59
35:9 Gen 28:13
35:10 Gen 32:28
35:11 Gen 12:2; 17:1, 6; [g]*shadday* (7706) ‣Gen 48:3; [h]*qahal* (6951) ‣Deut 23:2
35:12 Gen 13:15; 28:13; [i]*zera'* (2233) ‣Gen 48:4
35:13 Judg 6:21; 13:20
35:14 Gen 28:18-19
35:16 Ruth 4:11
35:17 Gen 30:22-24
35:18 Gen 49:27
35:19 Gen 48:7
35:22 Gen 49:4; Lev 18:8; 1 Chr 5:1

35:2-4 Jacob had vowed wholehearted devotion to the Lord (28:20-22); establishing this required that his family remove all ***pagan idols*** and cease their devotion to other gods. God permits no rivals; only the Lord was to be their God (cp. Josh 5:1-9).

35:3 ***He has been with me wherever I have gone:*** God had fulfilled his promises (28:15; 31:3), so Jacob must fulfill his vow.

35:5 ***a terror from God:*** People had heard about the massacre of Shechem (34:25-30).

35:6-7 Jacob ***built an altar*** at ***Bethel*** as God had instructed (35:1; cp. 12:8).

35:9-15 ***At Bethel,*** God confirmed the promise he had made there earlier; he reiterated Jacob's change of ***name*** from ***Jacob*** to ***Israel*** as proof that the blessing had been given.

35:10 Jacob's name change is reiterated and confirmed (cp. 41:32). • ***Jacob*** sounds like the Hebrew words for "heel" and "deceiver." ***Israel*** means "God fights."

35:11-12 God's reference to himself as ***God Almighty*** assured Jacob that his promise could and would be fulfilled. At Bethel, God had promised that Jacob would have descendants in the land (cp. 28:13-14); here he added that his descendants would include ***kings*** (see 17:6).

35:14-15 In fulfilling his vow (28:20-22), Jacob's actions were almost identical to his actions in the earlier experience at Bethel (cp. 28:16-19).

35:16-20 Benjamin's birth completed the family, but it was a sorrowful event because ***Rachel died*** in childbirth (see note on 31:32).

35:18 ***Rachel*** found the name ***son of my sorrow*** appropriate to the situation, but Jacob did not want such a sad name for his son, so he changed it to ***son of my right hand***. Jacob thus turned the day of sorrow into a day of hope that gave his son the prospect of success.

35:19 Jacob did not carry Rachel's body to the family tomb at Machpelah (23:1-20; 25:9; 49:30; 50:13), but buried her in the territory that would be Benjamin's (see Josh 18:21-28; 1 Sam 10:2).

35:20 ***it can be seen there to this day:*** This seems to be a later editorial comment by someone who was living in the land after the conquest and giving directions to the tomb (see Introduction to Genesis: "Composition," p. 16).

35:21 ***Jacob:*** Hebrew *Israel;* also in 35:22a. The names "Jacob" and "Israel" are often interchanged throughout the Old Testament, referring sometimes to the individual patriarch and sometimes to the nation.

35:22 ***Reuben had intercourse with Bilhah,*** thus defiling his father's marriage bed. Perhaps Reuben, as the oldest son, was trying to replace his father as head of the clan by a pagan procedure (cp. 2 Sam 16:15-22), but by this action he lost his birthright (see 49:3-4). • ***Jacob soon heard about it,*** but he again delayed his response (see 49:3-4; cp. 34:5).

35:23-26
//1 Chr 2:1-2
35:23
Gen 29:31-35; 30:18-20
35:24
Gen 30:24
35:25
Gen 30:5-8
35:26
Gen 30:10-13
35:27
Gen 13:18; 23:2
35:28
Gen 25:7-8, 20
36:1
Gen 25:30
36:2
Gen 26:34
1 Chr 1:40
36:3
Gen 25:13

The Twelve Sons of Jacob

These are the names of the twelve sons of
Jacob:

23 The sons of Leah were Reuben (Jacob's
oldest son), Simeon, Levi, Judah, Issachar,
and Zebulun.
24 The sons of Rachel were Joseph and Benjamin.
25 The sons of Bilhah, Rachel's servant, were
Dan and Naphtali.
26 The sons of Zilpah, Leah's servant, were
Gad and Asher.

These are the names of the sons who were born to Jacob at Paddan-aram.

Jacob Returns to Isaac; Isaac's Death

27 So Jacob returned to his father, Isaac, in
Mamre, which is near Kiriath-arba (now
called Hebron), where Abraham and Isaac
had both lived as foreigners. 28 Isaac lived
for 180 years. 29 Then he breathed his last
and died at a ripe old age, joining his ancestors in death. And his sons, Esau and Jacob,
buried him.

10. THE ACCOUNT OF ESAU'S DESCENDANTS (36:1–37:1)

Esau's Life

36 This is the account of the descendants of Esau (also known as Edom).
2 Esau married two young women from
Canaan: Adah, the daughter of Elon the
Hittite; and Oholibamah, the daughter of
Anah and granddaughter of Zibeon the Hivite. 3 He also married his cousin Basemath,
who was the daughter of Ishmael and the

Altars (35:1-15)

Gen 8:20-21; 12:7-8; 22:9-14; 26:25; 33:20
Exod 20:24-26; 24:4-5; 27:1-8
Josh 22:10-34
1 Kgs 18:20-40
2 Kgs 23:10-20
Hos 8:11
Matt 5:23-24
Heb 13:10-14
Rev 6:9; 8:3-5

The first recorded altar was built by Noah (8:20-21), though Cain and Abel gave the first offerings (4:3-4). The patriarchs built numerous altars (see 8:20-21; 12:7-8; 13:4, 18; 22:9; 26:25; 33:20; 35:1, 14-15). These altars designated sacred sites of divine revelation and personal land claims in the Promised Land, both north (in Shechem) and south (in Beersheba). Altars were made of stone, earth, brick, or metal and wood. Their table-like form allowed smoke to rise unhindered. Intended as memorials or places for sacrifice, an altar was the most common image of worship in the OT and in the wider ancient world. The typical altar was on a raised platform accessed by a ramp or stairway; this elevated the sacrificial worship toward heaven. The four horns on the corners of the altar marked off the sacred space of meeting between divine and human realms. Through sacrifice and burning, the offering was transferred from the visible to the invisible world. Altars were both religious monuments and places of refuge where fugitives could find asylum (see Exod 21:14).

Jesus unites the various aspects of the altar imagery in himself as high priest, sacrificial lamb, and altar (see Heb 4:14-15; 7:24, 27; 9:14, 26; 10:10; 13:10, 12). Jesus anticipated his own sacrifice in his reference to the blood of martyrs (see Matt 23:35; Luke 11:51). The enthroned Lamb in Revelation removes the need for temple and altar (Rev 21:22). The cross is the final altar; Jesus' death is the new covenant memorial and his body is the place of sanctuary (Heb 13:10).

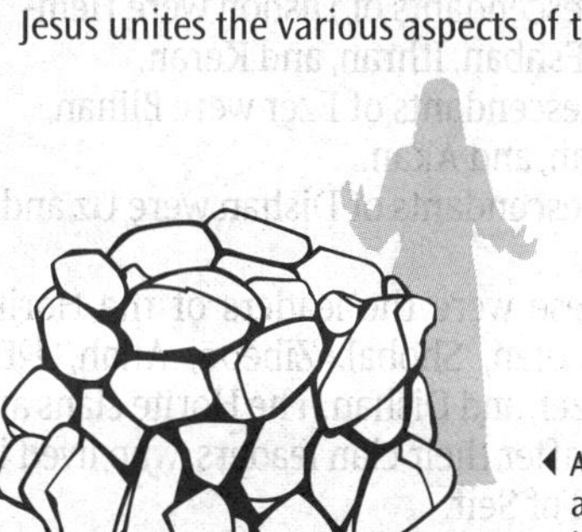

◀ **Altars of the Patriarchs** (35:1-15). Several of the patriarchs built altars, including Noah (8:20), Abraham (12:7, 8; 13:18; 22:9), Isaac (26:25), and Jacob (33:20; 35:7). These altars were probably made of piles of uncut stone, as God later instructed Israel (Exod 20:25; Deut 27:5-6; cp. Josh 8:30-31).

35:23-26 The twelve sons became leaders of the twelve tribes of Israel. Their names are the firstfruits of the nation.

35:27-29 ***Esau and Jacob*** (listed here in ordinary birth order) came together—probably for the first time since they had reconciled (33:16-17)—to bury ***Isaac*** in ***Hebron*** (see 13:18; 23:1-2, 17-19).

36:1-43 The book turns to the accounts of Isaac's sons, concluding the unchosen line of Esau (ch 36) before proceeding with the chosen line of Jacob (ch 37).

36:1-8 The ***account*** of ***Esau*** stresses two points. First, Esau's sons were ***born . . . in the land of Canaan*** (36:5) before he moved to ***Seir*** (36:8). Jacob's children, by contrast, were almost all born outside the land but then moved into it. God was giving the land to Jacob and his descendants and so made room for them by providing for Esau in a different place. Second, Esau's other name was ***Edom***. Israel often struggled with the Edomites (see 1 Sam 21:7; 22:9-22; Obad 1:1-21; see also "Herod the Great" at Matt 2:1-20, p. 1578).

36:2-3 Esau's three wives—***Adah***, ***Oholibamah***, and ***Basemath***—are listed. Two of these wives' names are different from those listed earlier (26:34; 28:9). Perhaps the others died, or Esau favored these three among a total of six, or these were just different names for the same three. There is not enough information to decide.

36:2 ***Oholibamah*** was a great-granddaughter of Seir the Horite, whose descendants lived in Edom when Esau went to live there (36:20, 25).

sister of Nebaioth. 4Adah gave birth to a
son named Eliphaz for Esau. Basemath gave
birth to a son named Reuel. 5Oholibamah
gave birth to sons named Jeush, Jalam, and
Korah. All these sons were born to Esau in
the land of Canaan.

6Esau took his wives, his children, and his
entire household, along with his livestock
and cattle—all the wealth he had acquired
in the land of Canaan—and moved away
from his brother, Jacob. 7There was not
enough land to support them both because
of all the livestock and possessions they had
acquired. 8So Esau (also known as Edom)
settled in the hill country of Seir.

Esau's Descendants

9This is the account of Esau's descendants,
the Edomites, who lived in the hill country
of Seir.

10These are the names of Esau's sons: Eliphaz, the son of Esau's wife Adah; and Reuel, the son of Esau's wife Basemath.
11The descendants of Eliphaz were Teman, Omar, Zepho, Gatam, and Kenaz.
12Timna, the concubine of Esau's son Eliphaz, gave birth to a son named Amalek. These are the descendants of Esau's wife Adah.
13The descendants of Reuel were Nahath, Zerah, Shammah, and Mizzah. These are the descendants of Esau's wife Basemath.
14Esau also had sons through Oholibamah, the daughter of Anah and granddaughter of Zibeon. Their names were Jeush, Jalam, and Korah.
15These are the descendants of Esau who became the leaders of various clans:

The descendants of Esau's oldest son, Eliphaz, became the leaders of the clans of Teman, Omar, Zepho, Kenaz,
16Korah, Gatam, and Amalek. These are the clan leaders in the land of Edom who descended from Eliphaz. All these were descendants of Esau's wife Adah.
17The descendants of Esau's son Reuel became the leaders of the clans of Nahath, Zerah, Shammah, and Mizzah. These are the clan leaders in the land of Edom who descended from Reuel. All these were descendants of Esau's wife Basemath.
18The descendants of Esau and his wife Oholibamah became the leaders of the clans of Jeush, Jalam, and Korah. These are the clan leaders who descended from Esau's wife Oholibamah, the daughter of Anah.
19These are the clans descended from Esau (also known as Edom), identified by their clan leaders.

Original Peoples of Edom

20These are the names of the tribes that
descended from Seir the Horite. They
lived in the land of Edom: Lotan, Shobal,
Zibeon, Anah,
21Dishon, Ezer, and Dishan.
These were the Horite clan leaders, the descendants of Seir, who lived in the land of Edom.

22The descendants of Lotan were Hori and Hemam. Lotan's sister was named Timna.
23The descendants of Shobal were Alvan, Manahath, Ebal, Shepho, and Onam.
24The descendants of Zibeon were Aiah and Anah. (This is the Anah who discovered the hot springs in the wilderness while he was grazing his father's donkeys.)
25The descendants of Anah were his son, Dishon, and his daughter, Oholibamah.
26The descendants of Dishon were Hemdan, Eshban, Ithran, and Keran.
27The descendants of Ezer were Bilhan, Zaavan, and Akan.
28The descendants of Dishan were Uz and Aran.
29So these were the leaders of the Horite
clans: Lotan, Shobal, Zibeon, Anah,
30Dishon, Ezer, and Dishan. The Horite clans are
named after their clan leaders, who lived in
the land of Seir.

Rulers of Edom

31These are the kings who ruled in the land
of Edom before any king ruled over the Israelites:

36:4 1 Chr 1:35
36:5 Gen 36:18
36:7 Gen 13:6
36:8 Gen 14:6; 25:30
36:9 Gen 36:43
36:10-14 //1 Chr 1:35-37
36:19 1 Chr 1:35
36:20-28 //1 Chr 1:38-42
36:20 Gen 14:6; Deut 2:12, 22
36:25 Gen 36:2, 5, 14, 18; 1 Chr 1:41
36:27 1 Chr 1:38, 42
36:29-30 Gen 36:20
36:31-43 //1 Chr 1:43-54

36:7-8 ***Esau***, like Lot, left for the eastern land (cp. 13:5-6).

36:9-43 This passage begins a second ***account of Esau's descendants*** (36:1); it traces the family to subsequent generations and alliances.

36:9-14 The ***descendants*** of Esau's five sons are named.

36:15-19 Thirteen of Esau's descendants had positions as ***leaders of various clans***. A picture begins to emerge of Esau as a grand overlord of tribes (cp. 36:40-43).

36:20-30 ***Seir the Horite*** was an early inhabitant of the land; his descendants populated the region until Esau moved in and displaced them (Deut 2:12).

36:26 Hebrew *Dishan*, a variant spelling of Dishon; cp. 36:21, 28.

36:31-39 It is not clear how these ***kings of Edom*** were related to Esau. The clans in Edom followed the same pattern of organization as the later tribes of Israel. They eventually chose a king from one of their tribes and carried on a line of succession from him.

36:31 ***before any king ruled over the Israelites*** (Or ***before an Israelite king ruled over them***): This editorial note was

37:1 Gen 17:8; 28:4
37:2 Gen 35:22-26; 41:46
37:3 Gen 37:23, 32; 44:20
37:4 Gen 27:41
37:5 Gen 28:12; Num 12:6; Dan 2:1

32Bela son of Beor, who ruled in Edom
from his city of Dinhabah.
33When Bela died, Jobab son of Zerah from
Bozrah became king in his place.
34When Jobab died, Husham from the land
of the Temanites became king in his
place.
35When Husham died, Hadad son of Bedad
became king in his place and ruled from
the city of Avith. He was the one who
defeated the Midianites in the land of
Moab.
36When Hadad died, Samlah from the city
of Masrekah became king in his place.
37When Samlah died, Shaul from the city
of Rehoboth-on-the-River became king
in his place.
38When Shaul died, Baal-hanan son of Acbor became king in his place.
39When Baal-hanan son of Acbor died,
Hadad became king in his place and
ruled from the city of Pau. His wife was
Mehetabel, the daughter of Matred and
granddaughter of Me-zahab.

40These are the names of the leaders of
the clans descended from Esau, who lived
in the places named for them: Timna, Alvah,
Jetheth, 41Oholibamah, Elah, Pinon, 42Ke-
naz, Teman, Mibzar, 43Magdiel, and Iram.
These are the leaders of the clans of Edom,
listed according to their settlements in the land they occupied. They all descended from Esau, the ancestor of the Edomites.

Recapitulation and Contrast with Jacob

37 So Jacob settled again in the land of Canaan, where his father had lived as a foreigner.

11. THE ACCOUNT OF JACOB'S DESCENDANTS (37:2–50:26)

Joseph's Dreams of Prominence (37:2-11)

2This is the account of Jacob and his family.
When Joseph was seventeen years old, he
often tended his father's flocks. He worked
for his half brothers, the sons of his father's
wives Bilhah and Zilpah. But Joseph reported to his father some of the bad things
his brothers were doing.
3Jacob loved Joseph more than any of his
other children because Joseph had been
born to him in his old age. So one day Jacob
had a special gift made for Joseph—a beautiful robe. 4But his brothers hated Joseph
because their father loved him more than
the rest of them. They couldn't say a kind
word to him.
5One night Joseph had a dream, and when
he told his brothers about it, they hated him
more than ever. 6"Listen to this dream," he

probably inserted into the text during Israel's monarchy (see note on 35:20).

36:39 *Hadad:* As in some Hebrew manuscripts, Samaritan Pentateuch, and Syriac version (see also 1 Chr 1:50); most Hebrew manuscripts read *Hadar.*

36:40-43 These chiefs descended from Esau, who was a great and powerful overlord. As father of the Edomites, he ruled over clans and regions, with eleven chiefs descended from him. By separating from Jacob, Esau was beginning to shake Jacob's yoke from his neck (27:39-40).

37:1 In ch 36, Esau was well on his way to power and prosperity; by contrast, ***Jacob***, still waiting for the promise, ***settled*** in the land ***as a foreigner,*** like ***his father.*** He was still a temporary resident with a single family. Worldly greatness often comes more swiftly than spiritual greatness. Waiting for the promised spiritual blessing while others prosper is a test of patience, faith, and perseverance.

37:2–50:26 The story of Joseph and his brothers comprises a separate unit in Genesis, distinct in tone and emphasis from the preceding material. It traces one continuous series of episodes with Joseph at their center. • Cycles of repeated motifs structure the entire Joseph account. The themes are closely related to those found in wisdom books such as Proverbs, Ecclesiastes, and Daniel. Wisdom literature assures the faithful that God brings good out of evil and joy out of pain—if not in this life, then certainly in the life to come. Though the wicked may prosper for a time, the righteous should hold fast to their integrity because a higher, more enduring principle of life is realized through obedience to God. Everyone who aspires to leadership in God's plan should observe how wisdom led to Joseph's success. Christ Jesus embodied the life of wisdom portrayed here as no one else could, for he is the wisdom of God. • Judah is also an important character in the story. He began as irresponsible and mean-spirited as his brothers; but he truly repented, put his life on the line to ransom a child for his father, and received a very important inheritance.

37:2 ***The account of Jacob and his family*** tells of ***Joseph*** and his brothers. Jacob is still prominent, but the focus is on Joseph, who is introduced as an obedient seventeen-year-old son. • ***Joseph reported . . . the bad things his brothers were doing:*** Bringing a bad report has never been popular, but it was the right thing to do and shows that Joseph was faithful from the beginning. As the story progresses, we see more of his brothers' wickedness displayed until, like Cain, they tried to eliminate the brother who pleased God.

37:3 ***Jacob:*** Hebrew *Israel;* also in 37:13. See note on 35:21. • Jacob ***loved Joseph more*** because ***Joseph had been born to him in his old age*** and because he was the first son of his favorite wife, Rachel. • ***A beautiful robe*** (traditionally rendered *a coat of many colors;* the exact meaning of the Hebrew is uncertain): Jacob gave Joseph this robe to demonstrate that he intended to grant him the largest portion of the inheritance.

37:4 Jacob's favoritism toward Joseph inflamed his other sons' hatred of their brother. Just as Isaac's and Rebekah's favoritism had separated their family, Jacob's favoritism would separate him from his son Joseph.

37:5-11 God confirmed his choice of this faithful son as the eventual leader of the whole family through two symbolic dreams. This is the first of three ***dream*** sequences in chs 37–50 (see 40:1–41:36; cp. 15:13; 20:3; 28:12-15; 31:24). Dreams carried weight as a form of divine communication, especially if the dream revelation was given twice. Everyone would have taken Joseph's dreams seriously.

said. 7“We were out in the field, tying up bundles of grain. Suddenly my bundle stood up,
and your bundles all gathered around and
bowed low before mine!”
8His brothers responded, “So you think
you will be our king, do you? Do you actually think you will reign over us?” And
they hated him all the more because of
his dreams and the way he talked about
them.
9Soon Joseph had another dream, and
again he told his brothers about it. “Listen,
I have had another dream,” he said. “The
sun, moon, and eleven stars bowed low before me!”
10This time he told the dream to his
father as well as to his brothers, but his father scolded him. “What kind of dream is
that?” he asked. “Will your mother and I
and your brothers actually come and bow
to the ground before you?” 11But while his
brothers were [j]jealous of Joseph, his father
wondered what the dreams meant.

Joseph Sold into Slavery in Egypt (37:12-36)

12Soon after this, Joseph’s brothers went to
pasture their father’s flocks at Shechem.
13When they had been gone for some time,
Jacob said to Joseph, “Your brothers are pasturing the sheep at Shechem. Get ready, and
I will send you to them.”
“I’m ready to go,” Joseph replied.
14“Go and see how your brothers and the
flocks are getting along,” Jacob said. “Then
come back and bring me a report.” So Jacob
sent him on his way, and Joseph traveled to
Shechem from their home in the valley of
Hebron.
15When he arrived there, a man from the
area noticed him wandering around the
countryside. “What are you looking for?”
he asked.
16“I’m looking for my brothers,” Joseph
replied. “Do you know where they are pasturing their sheep?”
17“Yes,” the man told him. “They have
moved on from here, but I heard them say,
‘Let’s go on to Dothan.’ ” So Joseph followed
his brothers to Dothan and found them
there.
18When Joseph’s brothers saw him coming, they recognized him in the distance.
As he approached, they made plans to kill
him. 19“Here comes the dreamer!” they said.
20“Come on, let’s kill him and throw him
into one of these cisterns. We can tell our
father, ‘A wild animal has eaten him.’ Then
we’ll see what becomes of his dreams!”
21But when Reuben heard of their scheme,
he came to Joseph’s rescue. “Let’s not kill
him,” he said. 22“Why should we shed any
blood? Let’s just throw him into this empty
cistern here in the wilderness. Then he’ll
die without our laying a hand on him.” Reuben was secretly planning to rescue Joseph
and return him to his father.
23So when Joseph arrived, his brothers
ripped off the beautiful robe he was wearing. 24Then they grabbed him and threw
him into the cistern. Now the cistern was
empty; there was no water in it. 25Then,

37:7 Gen 42:6, 9; 43:26
37:8 Deut 33:16
37:10 Gen 27:29
37:11 Luke 2:19, 51; Acts 7:9; [j]qana’ (7065) ‣ Exod 20:5
37:13 Gen 33:19
37:14 Gen 35:27
37:17 2 Kgs 6:13
37:20 Gen 37:33
37:21 Gen 42:22
37:22 Gen 37:29
37:23 Gen 37:3
37:24 Jer 38:6; 41:7
37:25 Gen 31:21; 37:28; Jer 8:22; 46:11

37:7 The ***bundles of grain*** hint at how Joseph’s authority over his family would be achieved (see 42:1-3).

37:8 The brothers’ angry response to the revelation, in contrast to Joseph’s honesty and faithfulness, clearly demonstrates why they were not chosen for leadership: Leaders in God’s plan cannot be consumed with jealousy and hatred. In their anger, they missed an important part of the revelation—they too would be rulers (stars, 37:9) who would productively bind their sheaves (37:7).

37:9 ***The sun, moon, and eleven stars:*** Astrological symbols often represent rulers. The dream predicted Joseph’s elevation to a position of authority over the whole clan of Israel.

37:10 *your mother and I:* Joseph’s birth mother, Rachel, was dead (35:19). Leah was now the matriarch of the clan.

37:11 ***His brothers*** hated Joseph because they ***were jealous*** of him. Rather than recognize the hand of God, the brothers tried to prevent the dream from being fulfilled (37:18-36). These actions show that they were not fit to lead the household of faith. God’s sovereign choice of a leader, especially if the one chosen is young or appears unqualified, often brings out the true colors of those who have to submit to that leader’s authority. The brothers represent people throughout history who have been driven by envy and malice because they were not committed to doing the Lord’s will. • Jacob ***wondered what the dreams meant*** because he knew that God would choose the next leader, that God could choose the younger son to rule over the older sons, and that God could reveal all this in dreams.

37:12-13 It was foolish for ***Jacob*** to ***send*** Joseph on such a mission, knowing how the brothers felt about him. ***Joseph*** obeyed his father by going to find his brothers despite their hatred for him.

37:14-17 The ***brothers*** ranged far and wide. ***Shechem*** was about fifty miles from ***Hebron***, and ***Dothan*** another fifteen miles beyond Shechem.

37:18-20 ***When Joseph’s brothers saw him coming***, they devised a plot ***to kill . . . the dreamer*** and end ***his dreams***. Earlier, they had unjustly killed the men of Shechem to avenge their sister (ch 34); in the region of Shechem, they now plotted unjustly to kill their own brother out of envy.

37:21-24 ***Reuben*** was perhaps trying to get back into his father’s good graces (35:22) by exercising the leadership of the firstborn (cp. 42:22). Reuben succeeded in saving Joseph’s life, but he failed to earn his father’s favor (37:29-30).

37:23 The recurring motif of changed clothes signifies changes in status, position, and authority (see 37:3, 23; 38:14, 19; 39:15-18; 41:14, 42).

37:25-28 The ***Ishmaelite traders*** were descendants of the slave child who was cast out for mocking Isaac. Now they would enslave Joseph. When he was sold for ***twenty pieces of silver*** and carried ***to Egypt***, he was at least preserved alive.

just as they were sitting down to eat, they looked up and saw a caravan of camels in the distance coming toward them. It was a group of Ishmaelite traders taking a load of gum, balm, and aromatic resin from Gilead down to Egypt.

26Judah said to his brothers, "What will we gain by killing our brother? We'd have to cover up the crime. 27Instead of hurting him, let's sell him to those Ishmaelite traders. After all, he is our brother—our own flesh and blood!" And his brothers agreed. 28So when the Ishmaelites, who were Midianite traders, came by, Joseph's brothers pulled him out of the cistern and sold him to them for twenty pieces of silver. And the traders took him to Egypt.

29Some time later, Reuben returned to get Joseph out of the cistern. When he discovered that Joseph was missing, he tore his clothes in grief. 30Then he went back to his brothers and lamented, "The boy is gone! What will I do now?"

31Then the brothers killed a young goat and dipped Joseph's robe in its blood. 32They sent the beautiful robe to their father with this message: "Look at what we found. Doesn't this robe belong to your son?"

33Their father recognized it immediately. "Yes," he said, "it is my son's robe. A wild animal must have eaten him. Joseph has clearly been torn to pieces!" 34Then Jacob tore his clothes and dressed himself in burlap. He [k]mourned deeply for his son for a long time. 35His family all tried to comfort him, but he refused to be comforted. "I will go to my [a]grave mourning for my son," he would say, and then he would weep.

36Meanwhile, the Midianite traders arrived in Egypt, where they sold Joseph to Potiphar, an officer of Pharaoh, the king of Egypt. Potiphar was captain of the palace guard.

Judah, Tamar, and the Birth of Judah's Offspring (38:1-30)

38 About this time, Judah left home and moved to Adullam, where he stayed with a man named Hirah. 2There he saw a Canaanite woman, the daughter of Shua, and he married her. When he slept with her, 3she became pregnant and gave birth to a son, and he named the boy Er. 4Then she became pregnant again and gave birth to another son, and she named him Onan. 5And when she gave birth to a third son, she named him Shelah. At the time of Shelah's birth, they were living at Kezib.

6In the course of time, Judah arranged for his firstborn son, Er, to marry a young woman named Tamar. 7But Er was a wicked man in the LORD's sight, so the LORD took his life. 8Then Judah said to Er's brother Onan, "Go and marry Tamar, as our law requires of the brother of a man who has died. You must produce an heir for your brother."

37:28 Gen 39:1; 45:4-5; Lev 27:5; Judg 8:22-24; Acts 7:9
37:29 Gen 37:34; 44:13; Num 14:6
37:30 Gen 42:13, 36
37:32 Luke 15:22
37:33 Gen 37:20; 44:28
37:34 Gen 37:29; [k]*'abal* (0056) ‣Exod 33:4
37:35 Gen 44:29; 2 Sam 12:17; Ps 77:2; [a]*she'ol* (7585) ‣Num 16:30
37:36 Gen 39:1; 40:3
38:1 Josh 15:35; 1 Sam 22:1
38:2 Gen 24:3; 34:2; 38:12
38:3 Gen 46:12; Num 26:19
38:6 Matt 1:3
38:7 Gen 6:5; 13:13; 19:13; 38:10; 1 Chr 2:3
38:8 Num 36:8; Deut 25:5-10; *Matt 22:24; *Mark 12:19

37:26 ***Judah*** began to exercise leadership that he would continue to develop as events unfolded (see 43:8-10). • ***cover up the crime:*** Literally *cover his blood.*

37:28 ***the Ishmaelites, who were Midianite traders*** (literally *the Midianite traders*): Ishmaelites were descendants of Abraham through Hagar (16:5), while Midianites were descendants of Abraham through Keturah (25:1-2). The term *Ishmaelite* may have described bedouin tribes generally. The Midianites might also have been traveling with a separate caravan of *Ishmaelite traders* (37:27). • ***Twenty pieces:*** Hebrew *20 shekels,* about 8 ounces or 228 grams in weight. • Kidnapping (see 40:15) was a capital offense (see Exod 21:16).

37:29-30 When ***Reuben returned,*** he ***tore his clothes in grief.*** His attempt to restore his relationship with his father by saving Joseph had gone awry.

37:31-35 The old family propensity for deception seized the brothers' imagination. Jacob had ***killed a young goat*** to deceive Isaac (27:5-17); now Jacob's sons deceived him with a goat (see note on 30:34-36).

37:32 ***your son:*** In their cold hatred, the brothers did not refer to Joseph by name or acknowledge him as their brother (see 21:10).

37:33 ***recognized:*** Cp. 27:23.

37:34-35 ***Jacob tore his clothes and dressed himself in burlap:*** These were signs of great distress and mourning (see 44:13; Job 1:20; 16:15). Jacob was devastated and ***refused to be comforted.*** The treachery thus affected everyone in his family. • ***go to my grave:*** Hebrew *go down to Sheol.*

37:36 ***the Midianite traders:*** As in the Greek version; Hebrew reads *the Medanites.* The relationship between the Midianites and Medanites is unclear; cp. 37:28. See also 25:2. • ***sold Joseph to Potiphar:*** Joseph found himself in a place of service that seemed congruent with his rise to authority, yet he still faced more testing.

38:1-30 The story of ***Judah*** and ***Tamar*** is a carefully placed interlude; it reports what was happening in the family of Judah, who would later rise to prominence, and it shows the beginnings of assimilation with the people of the land to help explain why God sent the family to Egypt (chs 39–47). The Egyptians were strict separatists (43:32); the Israelites would retain their unique identity better in Egypt than in Canaan.

38:7-10 In this story, ***the LORD*** is mentioned as the sovereign judge who took the lives of Judah's ***evil*** sons.

38:7 That ***Er was a wicked man*** is not surprising, since his mother was a Canaanite and his father a wayward Israelite.

38:8 ***as our law requires. . . . You must produce an heir for your brother:*** The custom that informs this episode is the law for levirate marriage (Latin *levir,* "husband's brother"). By this custom, which was later incorporated into God's law for Israel (Deut 25:5-10), if a man died childless, his brother or nearest relative would marry his widow to produce a child who would carry on the family name of the deceased and inherit his property. Apparently, the near kinsman had a right to refuse, but he would be disgraced in the family for refusing to perpetuate his brother's name.

9But Onan was not willing to have a child who would not be his own heir. So whenever he had intercourse with his brother's wife, he spilled the semen on the ground. This prevented her from having a child who would belong to his brother. 10But the LORD considered it evil for Onan to deny a child to his dead brother. So the LORD took Onan's life, too.

11Then Judah said to Tamar, his daughter-in-law, "Go back to your parents' home and remain a widow until my son Shelah is old enough to marry you." (But Judah didn't really intend to do this because he was afraid Shelah would also die, like his two brothers.) So Tamar went back to live in her father's home.

12Some years later Judah's wife died. After the time of mourning was over, Judah and his friend Hirah the Adullamite went up to Timnah to supervise the shearing of his sheep. 13Someone told Tamar, "Look, your father-in-law is going up to Timnah to shear his sheep."

14Tamar was aware that Shelah had grown up, but no arrangements had been made for her to come and marry him. So she changed out of her widow's clothing and covered herself with a veil to disguise herself. Then she sat beside the road at the entrance to the village of Enaim, which is on the road to Timnah. 15Judah noticed her and thought she was a prostitute, since she had covered her face. 16So he stopped and propositioned her. "Let me have sex with you," he said, not realizing that she was his own daughter-in-law.

"How much will you pay to have sex with me?" Tamar asked.

17"I'll send you a young goat from my flock," Judah promised.

"But what will you give me to guarantee that you will send the goat?" she asked.

18"What kind of guarantee do you want?" he replied.

She answered, "Leave me your identification seal and its cord and the walking stick you are carrying." So Judah gave them to her. Then he had intercourse with her, and she became pregnant. 19Afterward she went back home, took off her veil, and put on her widow's clothing as usual.

20Later Judah asked his friend Hirah the Adullamite to take the young goat to the woman and to pick up the things he had given her as his guarantee. But Hirah couldn't find her. 21So he asked the men who lived there, "Where can I find the shrine prostitute who was sitting beside the road at the entrance to Enaim?"

"We've never had a shrine prostitute here," they replied.

22So Hirah returned to Judah and told him, "I couldn't find her anywhere, and the men of the village claim they've never had a shrine prostitute there."

23"Then let her keep the things I gave her," Judah said. "I sent the young goat as we agreed, but you couldn't find her. We'd be the laughingstock of the village if we went back again to look for her."

24About three months later, Judah was told, "Tamar, your daughter-in-law, has acted like a prostitute. And now, because of this, she's pregnant."

"Bring her out, and let her be burned!" Judah demanded.

25But as they were taking her out to kill her, she sent this message to her father-in-law: "The man who owns these things made me pregnant. Look closely. Whose seal and cord and walking stick are these?"

26Judah recognized them immediately and said, "She is more righteous than I am, because I didn't arrange for her to marry

38:11 Ruth 1:13
38:12 Gen 31:19; Josh 15:10, 57
38:16 Lev 18:15; 2 Sam 13:11
38:17 Gen 38:20
38:18 Gen 41:42
38:24 Lev 20:10; 21:9
38:26 1 Sam 24:17

38:9-10 ***Onan*** married Tamar, but ***was not willing*** to provide an ***heir*** for his brother. He would have sex with Tamar but not fulfill his responsibility to his dead brother (38:8).

38:11 ***Judah*** is now presented as the model for his sons' behavior—he, too, was unfaithful to his levirate responsibility to Tamar as next kinsman (see note on 38:8). Judah and his sons were far too Canaanite in their ways (see note on 38:27-30; contrast Boaz, Ruth 3–4).

38:12-13 Without a marriage, the family's future was in jeopardy.
• ***Judah's wife died:*** This made Judah available to fulfill the responsibility of providing an heir.

38:14-19 ***Tamar*** realized that she would have to take matters into her own hands if the family were to have a future. Tamar acted in keeping with the levirate custom (see note on 38:8) out of loyalty to her deceased husband. She had a legal right to an heir by Judah's son or by Judah, so she lured her father-in-law into having sex with her. Jacob's family was deceived again, this time by a Canaanite daughter-in-law.

38:17 It would be normal for Tamar to ask for a pledge if the man did not have the money to pay. A woman in such a position would not trust anyone to send the money.

38:18 ***identification seal:*** A stone or metal cylinder was engraved with distinctive designs and was usually worn around the neck on a ***cord***; when rolled onto clay or wax, it left a distinct impression.

38:20-23 ***Judah*** had gone in to Tamar as a regular prostitute (Hebrew *zonah*, 38:15), whereas ***Hirah*** was mistakenly looking for a ***shrine prostitute*** (Hebrew *qedeshah*), of which there were none.

38:24-26 ***Judah*** played the hypocrite when he condemned ***Tamar*** to death for adultery. When she produced the ***seal and cord and walking stick*** that identified him as the father, he withdrew the condemnation.

38:26 ***She is more righteous than I am:*** Judah acknowledged that he had shirked his responsibility to provide an

38:27
Gen 25:24
38:29
Gen 46:12
Num 26:20-21
Ruth 4:12
1 Chr 2:4
Matt 1:3
Luke 3:33
39:1
Gen 37:25
39:2
Acts 7:9
39:4
Gen 40:4
Prov 22:29
39:5
Deut 28:3-4, 11
39:6
1 Sam 16:12, 18
Acts 7:20
39:7
Prov 7:15-20
39:8
Gen 39:4-5
Prov 6:23-24
39:9
[b]*khata'* (2398)
‣Exod 10:16
39:10
1 Thes 5:22
39:12
Prov 7:13
2 Tim 2:22
39:17
Exod 20:16; 23:1
Ps 55:3

my son Shelah." And Judah never slept with
Tamar again.
27When the time came for Tamar to give
birth, it was discovered that she was carrying
twins. 28While she was in labor, one of the
babies reached out his hand. The midwife
grabbed it and tied a scarlet string around
the child's wrist, announcing, "This one
came out first." 29But then he pulled back
his hand, and out came his brother! "What!"
the midwife exclaimed. "How did you break
out first?" So he was named Perez. 30Then
the baby with the scarlet string on his wrist
was born, and he was named Zerah.

Joseph's Rise to Power in Egypt (39:1–41:57)
Joseph's Rise in Potiphar's House

39 When Joseph was taken to Egypt
by the Ishmaelite traders, he was
purchased by Potiphar, an Egyptian officer.
Potiphar was captain of the guard for Pharaoh, the king of Egypt.
2The LORD was with Joseph, so he succeeded in everything he did as he served
in the home of his Egyptian master. 3Pot-
iphar noticed this and realized that the
LORD was with Joseph, giving him success
in everything he did. 4This pleased Potiphar, so he soon made Joseph his personal
attendant. He put him in charge of his entire household and everything he owned.
5From the day Joseph was put in charge of
his master's household and property, the
LORD began to bless Potiphar's household
for Joseph's sake. All his household affairs
ran smoothly, and his crops and livestock
flourished. 6So Potiphar gave Joseph complete administrative responsibility over
everything he owned. With Joseph there,
he didn't worry about a thing—except what
kind of food to eat!

Potiphar's Wife

Joseph was a very handsome and well-built
young man, 7and Potiphar's wife soon began to look at him lustfully. "Come and
sleep with me," she demanded.
8But Joseph refused. "Look," he told her,
"my master trusts me with everything in his
entire household. 9No one here has more
authority than I do. He has held back nothing from me except you, because you are his
wife. How could I do such a wicked thing? It
would be a great [b]sin against God."
10She kept putting pressure on Joseph
day after day, but he refused to sleep with
her, and he kept out of her way as much as
possible. 11One day, however, no one else
was around when he went in to do his work.
12She came and grabbed him by his cloak,
demanding, "Come on, sleep with me!" Joseph tore himself away, but he left his cloak
in her hand as he ran from the house.
13When she saw that she was holding
his cloak and he had fled, 14she called out
to her servants. Soon all the men came running. "Look!" she said. "My husband has
brought this Hebrew slave here to make
fools of us! He came into my room to rape
me, but I screamed. 15When he heard me
scream, he ran outside and got away, but he
left his cloak behind with me."
16She kept the cloak with her until her husband came home. 17Then she told him her
story. "That Hebrew slave you've brought into
our house tried to come in and fool around
with me," she said. 18"But when I screamed,
he ran outside, leaving his cloak with me!"

---

heir. It was sinful for Judah to go to a prostitute, but Tamar had a legal right to be the mother of Judah's child and had acted on that right. In the book of Ruth, the elders analogously blessed the marriage of Boaz and Ruth, praying that God would make Ruth like Tamar (Ruth 4:12; cp. Matt 1:3, 5).

38:27-30 Judah's line continued because of Tamar. The *twins* replaced Judah's two slain sons (38:7, 10); their birth was similar to the birth of Jacob and Esau (25:21-26) in that the "red" one was born first, but the other son pushed past him in later life. Jacob's gaining the right to rule over his older brother (27:29) seemed to be relived in Judah's line. The line was carried on through Perez and not through the elder son Shelah, whom he had gone to such lengths to protect (38:11; see 1 Chr 4:21), nor through the elder twin Zerah (see Ruth 4:13-22; Matt 1:3).

38:29-30 *Perez* means "breaking out." He pushed past his brother, just as Joseph would soon do in relation to his brothers (chs 39–47). • *Zerah* means "scarlet" or "brightness."

39:1–47:31 Joseph began as a slave, alienated from his brothers and separated from his father; he ended as Pharaoh's viceroy. Through the trips to Egypt, the covenant family went from the brink of apostasy, divided by jealousy and deception, to being reconciled and united by Judah's intercession and Joseph's forgiveness. • God is mentioned for the first time (apart from 38:7-10) since Jacob built his altar in Bethel (35:1-15); his covenant name, "the LORD," is used for the first time since Jacob left Laban (31:49).

39:1-23 Joseph's integrity in Potiphar's service contrasts with Judah's moral failure (ch 38). God was with Joseph (39:2-3, 21, 23) and enabled him to prosper and be a blessing (see notes on 12:1-9; 28:16-22) despite his slavery and imprisonment.

39:5 God *began to bless* Egypt through Joseph (see 22:18).

39:6-10 One of the major motifs of wisdom literature (see note on 37:2–50:26) is to warn young people that immorality will lead them to disaster (cp. Prov 5–7). Joseph was able to resist temptation because he had godly wisdom—he was guided by the fear of the Lord (Prov 1:7; 9:10).

39:14 Though Potiphar's wife was addressing slaves, she appealed to them as fellow Egyptians (*us*) to enlist them as witnesses against the despised *Hebrew* (see 43:32) who had won Potiphar's trust.

Joseph Put in Prison

19Potiphar was furious when he heard his
wife's story about how Joseph had treated
her. 20So he took Joseph and threw him into
the prison where the king's prisoners were
held, and there he remained. 21But the LORD
was with Joseph in the prison and showed
him his faithful love. And the LORD made
Joseph a favorite with the prison warden.
22Before long, the warden put Joseph in
charge of all the other prisoners and over
everything that happened in the prison.
23The warden had no more worries, because
Joseph took care of everything. The LORD
was with him and caused everything he did
to succeed.

Joseph Interprets Two Prisoners' Dreams

40 Some time later, Pharaoh's chief cup-
bearer and chief baker offended
their royal master. 2Pharaoh became angry
with these two officials, 3and he put them in
the prison where Joseph was, in the palace of
the captain of the guard. 4They remained in
prison for quite some time, and the captain
of the guard assigned them to Joseph, who
looked after them.

5While they were in prison, Pharaoh's
cup-bearer and baker each had a dream
one night, and each dream had its own
meaning. 6When Joseph saw them the next
morning, he noticed that they both looked
upset. 7"Why do you look so worried today?" he asked them.

8And they replied, "We both had dreams
last night, but no one can tell us what they
mean."

"Interpreting dreams is God's business,"
Joseph replied. "Go ahead and tell me your
dreams."

9So the chief cup-bearer told Joseph his
dream first. "In my dream," he said, "I saw
a grapevine in front of me. 10The vine had
three branches that began to bud and blossom, and soon it produced clusters of ripe
grapes. 11I was holding Pharaoh's wine cup
in my hand, so I took a cluster of grapes
and squeezed the juice into the cup. Then I
placed the cup in Pharaoh's hand."

12"This is what the dream means," Joseph
said. "The three branches represent three
days. 13Within three days Pharaoh will lift
you up and restore you to your position as
his chief cup-bearer. 14And please remember me and do me a favor when things go
well for you. Mention me to Pharaoh, so he
might let me out of this place. 15For I was
kidnapped from my homeland, the land of
the Hebrews, and now I'm here in prison,
but I did nothing to deserve it."

16When the chief baker saw that Joseph
had given the first dream such a positive
interpretation, he said to Joseph, "I had a
dream, too. In my dream there were three
baskets of white pastries stacked on my
head. 17The top basket contained all kinds
of pastries for Pharaoh, but the birds
came and ate them from the basket on my
head."

18"This is what the dream means," Joseph
told him. "The three baskets also represent
three days. 19Three days from now Pharaoh
will lift you up and impale your body on a
pole. Then birds will come and peck away
at your flesh."

20Pharaoh's birthday came three days
later, and he prepared a banquet for all his
officials and staff. He summoned his chief
cup-bearer and chief baker to join the other
officials. 21He then restored the chief cup-
bearer to his former position, so he could
again hand Pharaoh his cup. 22But Pharaoh
impaled the chief baker, just as Joseph had
predicted when he interpreted his dream.

39:20 Gen 40:1-3, 15; 41:10; Ps 105:18
39:21 Ps 105:19; Acts 7:9
39:22 Gen 39:4
39:23 Gen 39:3
40:1 Neh 1:11
40:4 Gen 37:36; 39:4
40:5 Gen 20:3; 41:11
40:8 Gen 41:15-16; Dan 2:27-28
40:12 Gen 41:12
40:13 Gen 40:19-20
40:14 1 Sam 20:14
40:15 Gen 37:26-28; 39:20
40:18 Gen 40:12
40:19 Deut 21:22-23
40:22 Gen 40:19

39:19-20 This was the second time that ***Joseph***, while faithfully doing the right thing, was thrown into bondage with his clothing used deceptively as evidence (cp. 37:23-24, 31-33).

39:21-23 ***Joseph*** thrived in ***prison*** because God was with him. Each time Joseph prospered, he was put ***in charge*** of something.

40:1-23 Joseph did not lose faith in God's promises, as evidenced by his readiness to interpret the dreams of two prisoners. He was still convinced that God's revelation in his own two dreams (37:5-11) was true, and he had not abandoned hope that they would be fulfilled. When the fellow prisoners' dreams were fulfilled exactly as Joseph said, this confirmed that his previous dreams were from God.

40:1-4 ***Joseph*** was so faithful and trustworthy that ***the captain of the guard*** trusted him with the care of two of Pharaoh's ***chief . . . officials***.

40:5-8 ***Pharaoh's cup-bearer and baker*** looked ***worried*** because they knew that their futures were somehow bound up in these ominous and disturbing dreams that they could not understand. • Joseph still had faith that ***interpreting dreams is God's business***, and that he would understand them with God's help. He knew he had not misinterpreted his own dreams.

40:9-19 Joseph listened to the dreams and offered their interpretations. These dreams were not trivial; they were ominous warnings from God about what everyone was going to face. These two dreams prepared for Pharaoh's two dreams, which revealed the periods of life and death that the nation would soon experience.

40:14-15 Because he knew that the chief cup-bearer was going back into Pharaoh's personal service, Joseph saw an opportunity to seek his own release from prison.

40:20-22 The interpretations Joseph gave the prisoners proved true. The death of the ***chief baker*** speaks of the harsh realities of life in ancient Egypt, with a king whose word was his land's highest law. • ***He summoned:*** Literally *He lifted up the head of.*

40:23 Gen 40:14
41:5 2 Kgs 4:42
41:6 Ezek 19:12

[23]Pharaoh's chief cup-bearer, however,
forgot all about Joseph, never giving him another thought.

Pharaoh's Dreams

41 Two full years later, Pharaoh
dreamed that he was standing on
the bank of the Nile River. [2]In his dream
he saw seven fat, healthy cows come up out
of the river and begin grazing in the marsh
grass. [3]Then he saw seven more cows come
up behind them from the Nile, but these
were scrawny and thin. These cows stood
beside the fat cows on the riverbank. [4]Then
the scrawny, thin cows ate the seven healthy,
fat cows! At this point in the dream, Pharaoh woke up.
[5]But he fell asleep again and had a second dream. This time he saw seven heads
of grain, plump and beautiful, growing on
a single stalk. [6]Then seven more heads of
grain appeared, but these were shriveled

JOSEPH (39:1–45:28)

Gen 30:22-24; 37:2-36; 48:1-22; 49:22-26; 50:1-26
Exod 13:19
Deut 33:13-17
Josh 24:32
Ps 105:16-22
Acts 7:9-14

Joseph is known for his dreams and for the beautiful coat his father Jacob gave him. He is an example of faith, prudence, and administrative ability. Despite overwhelming difficulties, Joseph saved Canaan, Egypt, and his own family from starvation during seven years of drought.

Joseph was Jacob's eleventh son, the first child of Jacob's favorite wife, Rachel. Joseph's name means "may he add," expressing Rachel's desire that God give her another son (30:24). Rachel later died at the birth of Benjamin, Joseph's only full brother.

Joseph's brothers resented him because of his dreams. They sold him to a passing caravan and led Jacob to believe an animal had killed him. In Egypt, Joseph quickly became prominent until he was jailed when his master's wife falsely accused him. Having correctly interpreted dreams for fellow inmates, he was summoned when Pharaoh couldn't understand his dreams. Joseph said they predicted seven good years followed by seven lean years, and Pharaoh directed him to prepare for famine. When Joseph's family had to buy grain in Egypt, Joseph eventually disclosed his identity. The family was reconciled and reunited when Jacob came to live in Egypt.

Because Jacob blessed Joseph's sons, Ephraim and Manasseh, and took them as his own (48:5-20), each was considered a separate tribe later in Israel. Ephraim, whom Jacob put first and to whom he gave the birthright (48:17-20), became one of the strongest tribes of Israel and the leading tribe in the northern kingdom after the division during Rehoboam's reign (see 1 Kgs 11:26–12:33). Several of the prophets refer to the northern kingdom under the names Ephraim (e.g., Ezek 37:15-19; Hos 5:3-5) and Joseph (e.g., Obad 1:18).

Age	Event	Reference
17	Joseph is sold into slavery	37:2, 18-36
30	Joseph begins serving Pharaoh	41:46
39	Joseph is reunited with his brothers, Jacob moves to Egypt	45:3-6
56	Jacob dies, is buried in Canaan	47:28
110	Joseph dies in Egypt	50:26

▲Joseph's Life (39:1–45:28).

Joseph's dying wish (which Moses later honored) was that his bones be buried in Canaan (Exod 13:19; Josh 24:32). Joseph's story dramatizes the life of a man of faith and godly character who fulfilled God's plan. His name is mentioned frequently in Scripture, showing that he was highly regarded by later Israelites. His story is summarized in the Psalms (Ps 105:16-22) and in Stephen's speech just prior to his martyrdom (Acts 7:9-14).

Joseph's life confirms God's control of the long course of history even when bad things happen (50:20). God expresses his sovereign power through his provident, faithful love for his people. Joseph also models for us a firm faith in the sovereign God and personal integrity in the face of adversity.

40:23 The *cup-bearer . . . forgot all about Joseph,* but God did not forget him. Joseph's faith was about to be rewarded (ch 41).

41:1-46 God had used two dreams to identify Joseph as a leader among his brothers (37:5-11). He used two dreams to test Joseph's faith in prison (40:5-14). Now he would use two dreams to elevate Joseph from prison to preeminence. Joseph had repeatedly proven faithful in small matters; now he would be put in charge of great things.

41:1-4 Pharaoh's first dream was about *cows.* Cows liked to stand half-submerged among the reeds in the Nile River to take refuge from the heat and flies. They would come out of the water to find pasture. The second cows disturbed Pharaoh because they were scrawny yet able to swallow the *fat cows.*

41:5-7 Pharaoh's *second dream* carried a similar message. Seven *plump heads of grain* on *a single stalk* were *swallowed up* by seven *shriveled and withered* heads that sprouted after them.

and withered by the east wind. 7And these
thin heads swallowed up the seven plump,
well-formed heads! Then Pharaoh woke up
again and realized it was a dream.
8The next morning Pharaoh was very disturbed by the dreams. So he called for all
the magicians and wise men of Egypt. When
Pharaoh told them his dreams, not one of
them could tell him what they meant.
9Finally, the king's chief cup-bearer
spoke up. "Today I have been reminded of
my failure," he told Pharaoh. 10"Some time
ago, you were angry with the chief baker
and me, and you imprisoned us in the palace of the captain of the guard. 11One night
the chief baker and I each had a dream, and
each dream had its own meaning. 12There
was a young Hebrew man with us in the
prison who was a slave of the captain of
the guard. We told him our dreams, and
he told us what each of our dreams meant.
13And everything happened just as he had
predicted. I was restored to my position as
cup-bearer, and the chief baker was executed and impaled on a pole."

Joseph's Interpretation and Counsel

14Pharaoh sent for Joseph at once, and he
was quickly brought from the prison. After he shaved and changed his clothes, he
went in and stood before Pharaoh. 15Then
Pharaoh said to Joseph, "I had a dream last
night, and no one here can tell me what it
means. But I have heard that when you hear
about a dream you can interpret it."
16"It is beyond my power to do this," Joseph replied. "But God can tell you what it
means and set you at ease."
17So Pharaoh told Joseph his dream. "In
my dream," he said, "I was standing on the
bank of the Nile River, 18and I saw seven fat,
healthy cows come up out of the river and
begin grazing in the marsh grass. 19But then
I saw seven sick-looking cows, scrawny and
thin, come up after them. I've never seen
such sorry-looking animals in all the land
of Egypt. 20These thin, scrawny cows ate the
seven fat cows. 21But afterward you wouldn't
have known it, for they were still as thin and
scrawny as before! Then I woke up.
22"Then I fell asleep again, and I had another dream. This time I saw seven heads
of grain, full and beautiful, growing on a
single stalk. 23Then seven more heads of
grain appeared, but these were blighted,
shriveled, and withered by the east wind.
24And the shriveled heads swallowed the
seven healthy heads. I told these dreams
to the magicians, but no one could tell me
what they mean."
25Joseph responded, "Both of Pharaoh's
dreams mean the same thing. God is telling Pharaoh in advance what he is about
to do. 26The seven healthy cows and the
seven healthy heads of grain both represent seven years of prosperity. 27The seven
thin, scrawny cows that came up later and
the seven thin heads of grain, withered
by the east wind, represent seven years of
famine.
28"This will happen just as I have described it, for God has revealed to Pharaoh
in advance what he is about to do. 29The
next seven years will be a period of great
prosperity throughout the land of Egypt.
30But afterward there will be seven years
of famine so great that all the prosperity
will be forgotten in Egypt. Famine will
destroy the land. 31This famine will be so
severe that even the memory of the good
years will be erased. 32As for having two
similar dreams, it means that these events
have been decreed by God, and he will soon
make them happen.
33"Therefore, Pharaoh should find an
intelligent and wise man and put him in
charge of the entire land of Egypt. 34Then

41:8 Exod 7:11-12; Dan 2:1-3; 4:5-7
41:9 Gen 40:14
41:10 Gen 40:2
41:11 Gen 40:5
41:12 Gen 40:12
41:13 Gen 40:22
41:14 Ps 105:20
41:15 Dan 2:25
41:16 Gen 40:8
41:17 Gen 41:1
41:27 2 Kgs 8:1
41:29 Gen 41:47
41:30 Gen 47:13
41:33 Gen 41:39

41:8 The ***magicians and wise men*** belonged to a guild of supposed experts in spiritual matters, including dreams and visions (cp. Exod 8:18-19; Dan 2:10-11), but they could not interpret these dreams. God used an Israelite slave to confound the wisdom of the world (cp. Dan 2). However powerful a nation becomes, it is still under God's sovereign control (Dan 2:20-23).

41:9-13 The ***chief cup-bearer*** finally remembered Joseph and testified that his interpretations were true.

41:14-15 ***Pharaoh*** immediately summoned ***Joseph*** from prison to interpret his dreams. • ***he shaved:*** As was the Egyptian custom.

41:16 ***Joseph*** knew that only ***God*** could tell what Pharaoh's dreams meant (cp. 40:8), and he was confident that God would do so, because he had given the dreams for a purpose (41:25, 28).

41:17-24 ***Pharaoh*** recounted his dreams and testified that no human wisdom could interpret them.

41:25-32 Both dreams predicted that ***seven years*** of abundant crops would be followed by ***seven years*** of severe ***famine***.

41:32 The ***two similar dreams*** confirmed that the message was ***decreed by God*** and would ***soon . . . happen***, just as the dreams of the two prisoners were quickly fulfilled (40:5-23). Joseph's own two dreams (37:5-11) were about to come true as well (41:37-46; 42:6-9).

41:33-36 God's revelation demanded a response—it was not given just to satisfy curiosity about the future. Joseph's advice about planning and preparing showed that he was the kind of ***intelligent and wise man*** that Pharaoh needed (41:37-40). • Joseph instituted central planning and control with a supervisor, local managers, a 20 percent tax on grain, and a rationing system. Later wisdom literature (see note on 37:2–50:26) teaches the principle of planning ahead rather than living just for the moment (see Prov 6:6-8; 27:12).

41:36
Gen 47:14
41:38
Dan 4:8, 18; 5:11, 14
41:39
Gen 41:33
41:40
Gen 39:9
Ps 105:21
Acts 7:10
41:41
Esth 8:2
Dan 6:3
41:42
Esth 3:10; 6:8
41:44
Gen 45:8
Ps 105:22
41:45
Ezek 30:17
41:46
Gen 37:2
41:51
Gen 48:1
Deut 33:17
41:52
Gen 17:6
41:54
Gen 41:30
Ps 105:16
Acts 7:11
41:55
Gen 41:41

Pharaoh should appoint supervisors over
the land and let them collect one-fifth of
all the crops during the seven good years.
[35]Have them gather all the food produced
in the good years that are just ahead and
bring it to Pharaoh's storehouses. Store it
away, and guard it so there will be food in
the cities. [36]That way there will be enough
to eat when the seven years of famine come
to the land of Egypt. Otherwise this famine
will destroy the land."

Pharaoh Promotes Joseph to Power

[37]Joseph's suggestions were well received
by Pharaoh and his officials. [38]So Pharaoh
asked his officials, "Can we find anyone else
like this man so obviously filled with the
spirit of God?" [39]Then Pharaoh said to Joseph, "Since God has revealed the meaning
of the dreams to you, clearly no one else is
as intelligent or wise as you are. [40]You will
be in charge of my court, and all my people
will take orders from you. Only I, sitting
on my throne, will have a rank higher than
yours."

[41]Pharaoh said to Joseph, "I hereby put
you in charge of the entire land of Egypt."
[42]Then Pharaoh removed his signet ring
from his hand and placed it on Joseph's
finger. He dressed him in fine linen clothing and hung a gold chain around his neck.
[43]Then he had Joseph ride in the chariot
reserved for his second-in-command. And
wherever Joseph went, the command was
shouted, "Kneel down!" So Pharaoh put Joseph in charge of all Egypt. [44]And Pharaoh
said to him, "I am Pharaoh, but no one will
lift a hand or foot in the entire land of Egypt
without your approval."

[45]Then Pharaoh gave Joseph a new Egyptian name, Zaphenath-paneah. He also gave
him a wife, whose name was Asenath. She
was the daughter of Potiphera, the priest of
On. So Joseph took charge of the entire land
of Egypt. [46]He was thirty years old when he
began serving in the court of Pharaoh, the
king of Egypt. And when Joseph left Pharaoh's presence, he inspected the entire
land of Egypt.

God Provides through Joseph and for Joseph

[47]As predicted, for seven years the land
produced bumper crops. [48]During those
years, Joseph gathered all the crops grown
in Egypt and stored the grain from the surrounding fields in the cities. [49]He piled up
huge amounts of grain like sand on the seashore. Finally, he stopped keeping records
because there was too much to measure.

[50]During this time, before the first of the
famine years, two sons were born to Joseph
and his wife, Asenath, the daughter of Potiphera, the priest of On. [51]Joseph named his
older son Manasseh, for he said, "God has
made me forget all my troubles and everyone
in my father's family." [52]Joseph named his
second son Ephraim, for he said, "God has
made me fruitful in this land of my grief."

The Beginning of the Famine

[53]At last the seven years of bumper crops
throughout the land of Egypt came to an
end. [54]Then the seven years of famine
began, just as Joseph had predicted. The
famine also struck all the surrounding countries, but throughout Egypt there was plenty
of food. [55]Eventually, however, the famine
spread throughout the land of Egypt as well.
And when the people cried out to Pharaoh
for food, he told them, "Go to Joseph, and
do whatever he tells you." [56]So with severe
famine everywhere, Joseph opened up

41:37-40 Pharaoh recognized that Joseph was the man for the job; he had ***the spirit of God*** and was ***intelligent*** and ***wise***. God showed his sovereign rule in Egypt; Israelites who later read the account could be confident that God would save them as he had promised.

41:41-46 Joseph was made the acting ruler or manager of Egypt.

41:42 Pharaoh's ***signet ring*** had a seal used for signing documents. The seal was impressed in soft clay, which hardened and left a permanent impression of the ruler's signature, which carried his authority. Numerous seals of this type have been found in archaeological digs. • The ***linen clothing*** and ***gold chain*** signified Joseph's new status as ruler.

41:43-44 Pharaoh made Joseph ***second-in-command***; all the people had to submit to him. Cp. Ps 105:16-22.

41:45 As token of Joseph's new status, ***Pharaoh gave*** him an ***Egyptian name*** and ***a wife*** from a high-ranking family. • ***Zaphenath-paneah*** probably means "God speaks and lives." • ***On:*** Greek version reads *Heliopolis;* also in 41:50. On was a center for sun worship that came to be known as Heliopolis ("sun city").

41:46 ***He was thirty years old:*** It had been approximately thirteen years since his brothers had sold Joseph into slavery (37:2). • ***he inspected the entire land of Egypt:*** As a wise manager, his first priority was to learn the scope of his responsibilities.

41:47-57 Pharaoh's dreams were fulfilled in keeping with Joseph's interpretation.

41:50-52 In spite of his position and authority, ***Joseph*** never abandoned his heritage; he gave Hebrew names to his ***two sons***. • ***Manasseh*** sounds like a Hebrew term that means "causing to forget." Joseph's prosperity and success made him forget the misery of separation from his family. • ***Ephraim*** sounds like a Hebrew term that means "fruitful." In so naming him, Joseph proclaimed his gratitude to God for the fruitfulness he was experiencing in Egypt.

41:53-57 Joseph's wisdom paid off, for the seven years of plenty were followed by seven years of severe famine, ***but throughout Egypt there was plenty of food***. Joseph had grain to sell to the Egyptians and to people from other countries as well.

the storehouses and distributed grain to the Egyptians, for the famine was severe throughout the land of Egypt. 57And people from all around came to Egypt to buy grain from Joseph because the famine was severe throughout the world.

Israel Moves to Egypt (42:1–47:31)

Joseph's Brothers Go to Egypt

42 When Jacob heard that grain was available in Egypt, he said to his sons, "Why are you standing around looking at one another? 2I have heard there is grain in Egypt. Go down there, and buy enough grain to keep us alive. Otherwise we'll die."

3So Joseph's ten older brothers went down to Egypt to buy grain. 4But Jacob wouldn't let Joseph's younger brother, Benjamin, go with them, for fear some harm might come to him. 5So Jacob's sons arrived in Egypt along with others to buy food, for the famine was in Canaan as well.

6Since Joseph was governor of all Egypt and in charge of selling grain to all the people, it was to him that his brothers came. When they arrived, they ᶜbowed before him with their faces to the ground. 7Joseph recognized his brothers instantly, but he pretended to be a stranger and spoke harshly to them. "Where are you from?" he demanded.

"From the land of Canaan," they replied. "We have come to buy food."

Joseph Accuses His Brothers to Have Benjamin Brought

8Although Joseph recognized his brothers, they didn't recognize him. 9And he remembered the dreams he'd had about them many years before. He said to them, "You are spies! You have come to see how vulnerable our land has become."

10"No, my lord!" they exclaimed. "Your servants have simply come to buy food. 11We are all brothers—members of the same family. We are honest men, sir! We are not spies!"

12"Yes, you are!" Joseph insisted. "You have come to see how vulnerable our land has become."

13"Sir," they said, "there are actually twelve of us. We, your servants, are all brothers, sons of a man living in the land of Canaan. Our youngest brother is back there with our father right now, and one of our brothers is no longer with us."

14But Joseph insisted, "As I said, you are spies! 15This is how I will test your story. I swear by the life of Pharaoh that you will never leave Egypt unless your youngest brother comes here! 16One of you must go and get your brother. I'll keep the rest of you here in prison. Then we'll find out whether or not your story is true. By the life of Pharaoh, if it turns out that you don't have a younger brother, then I'll know you are spies."

17So Joseph put them all in prison for three days. 18On the third day Joseph said to them, "I am a God-fearing man. If you do as I say, you will live. 19If you really are honest men, choose one of your brothers to remain in prison. The rest of you may go home with grain for your starving families. 20But you must bring your youngest brother back to me. This will prove that you are telling the truth, and you will not die." To this they agreed.

21Speaking among themselves, they said, "Clearly we are being punished because of what we did to Joseph long ago. We saw his anguish when he pleaded for his life, but we wouldn't listen. That's why we're in this trouble."

22"Didn't I tell you not to sin against the boy?" Reuben asked. "But you wouldn't

41:57 Gen 42:5; 47:15; Ps 105:16
42:1 Acts 7:12
42:2 Gen 43:2, 4
42:3 Gen 43:20
42:4 Gen 35:24
42:5 Gen 41:57; Acts 7:11
42:6 Ps 105:16-21; ᶜ*khawah* (7812) ‣Exod 4:31
42:7 Gen 42:30
42:8 Gen 37:2
42:9 Gen 42:16, 30-34
42:10 Gen 37:6-9
42:11 Gen 42:19, 31-34
42:13 Gen 37:30-33; 44:20; 46:31
42:14 Gen 42:9
42:17 Gen 40:4
42:18 Gen 20:11; Lev 25:43
42:20 Gen 42:34; 43:15
42:21 Gen 37:23-28; 45:3-5
42:22 Gen 9:5-6; 37:21-22

42:1–47:31 God used the famine to bring Israel to Egypt under Joseph's rule, thus fulfilling two prophecies (15:13; 37:7-11).

42:1–44:34 Joseph did several unusual things to his brothers when they came looking for grain. The last time Joseph had been with them, they were filled with jealousy, hatred, and anger; they attempted to destroy their brother, and they deceived their father. Joseph put them through various tests, similar to the trying situations they had put him through, to see if they had changed.

42:4 ***Jacob*** may have believed that ***Benjamin*** would not be safe with his brothers.

42:5 ***Jacob's:*** Hebrew *Israel's.* See note on 35:21.

42:6-7 Joseph's first dream (37:5-11) was partially fulfilled when his brothers ***bowed*** down to him without recognizing him (see also 43:26; 44:14). It was totally fulfilled in 50:18. Joseph recognized his brothers immediately, but he could not reveal himself because he did not yet trust them to be the honest men they claimed to be (42:10).

42:8 ***they didn't recognize him:*** Joseph was a grown man, not a boy. He was not wearing a beard, was dressed in Egyptian clothes, and was in an unexpected position, speaking to them through an interpreter (42:23).

42:9 ***You are spies!*** The brothers had considered Joseph a spy for their father and had treated him roughly (37:2, 14, 18-28). Joseph was putting them in a similar situation to see how they would respond.

42:11 Joseph knew that they had not always been the ***honest men*** they claimed to be.

42:15-17 Joseph put the brothers in jail for three days to see if they had a conscience functioning about what they had done (42:21-23). The brothers had similarly thrown Joseph into a cistern-prison while they decided what to do with him (37:24).

42:18-20 Rather than keep all but one, Joseph would release all but one to take ***grain*** home to their ***starving families.***

42:21-23 ***Clearly we are being punished:*** The brothers sensed that having to bring Benjamin back to Egypt against their

42:24 Gen 43:14, 23
42:25 Gen 44:1
42:28 Gen 43:23
[d]*leb* (3820)
‣Exod 15:8
42:30 Gen 42:7
42:31 Gen 42:11
42:32 Gen 42:13

listen. And now we have to answer for his
blood!"
23 Of course, they didn't know that Joseph
understood them, for he had been speaking
to them through an interpreter. 24 Now he
turned away from them and began to weep.
When he regained his composure, he spoke
to them again. Then he chose Simeon from
among them and had him tied up right before their eyes.
25 Joseph then ordered his servants to fill
the men's sacks with grain, but he also gave
secret instructions to return each brother's
payment at the top of his sack. He also gave
them supplies for their journey home. 26 So
the brothers loaded their donkeys with the
grain and headed for home.
27 But when they stopped for the night and
one of them opened his sack to get grain for
his donkey, he found his money in the top
of his sack. 28 "Look!" he exclaimed to his
brothers. "My money has been returned; it's
here in my sack!" Then their [d]hearts sank.
Trembling, they said to each other, "What
has God done to us?"

The Brothers Report to Jacob

29 When the brothers came to their father,
Jacob, in the land of Canaan, they told him
everything that had happened to them.
30 "The man who is governor of the land
spoke very harshly to us," they told him.
"He accused us of being spies scouting the
land. 31 But we said, 'We are honest men,
not spies. 32 We are twelve brothers, sons of

Famine (41:56-57)

Gen 12:10; 26:1; 41:33-36; 45:6-7
Lev 26:19-20
Deut 8:3; 11:16-17
Ruth 1:1
2 Sam 21:1
1 Kgs 18:1-2
2 Kgs 8:1-2
Jer 14:11-16
Ezek 34:29-31; 36:28-32
Joel 1:1-20
Amos 8:11-14
Hag 1:1-11
Luke 6:21
John 6:32-35
Acts 11:28-30
Rev 7:16

Famine occurred early in the lives of Abraham (12:10) and Isaac (26:1). When famine afflicted Jacob's family (41:56-57), God had already placed Joseph in Egypt to provide for his people through the disaster (45:5, 7). This famine was particularly severe, but famines were not uncommon in the ancient world (see 12:10; 26:1; see also Ruth 1:1; 2 Sam 21:1; 1 Kgs 18:1-2; Hag 1:1-11; Acts 11:28). Dependence on rainfall caused some people to stockpile food against possible famine. In Egypt, Joseph implemented a grain ration that saved the people, supplied seed, and filled Pharaoh's royal storehouses (41:33-36; 47:23-24). Israel's temple also contained storerooms (1 Chr 26:15; 2 Chr 31:11; Neh 10:37-39).

Famine was a devastating catastrophe in an agrarian society. Caused by drought, crop failure, or siege (Ruth 1:1-2; 2 Kgs 25), it was often accompanied by disease or war that brought adversity at many levels of society (Jer 14:12), even for animals (Job 38:41; Joel 1:20). Famines had far-reaching results in price inflation, robbery, social exploitation, agricultural collapse, migration, and even cannibalism (12:10; 26:1; 2 Kgs 6:24-29; Neh 5:1-3; Jer 19:9; Lam 2:20-21; 4:8-10). Therefore, faithfulness to God was a particularly vivid need (Ps 33:18-19; 37:19), and God's blessings on the nation included protection from famine (Ezek 34:29; 36:29-30). God sometimes used famine as divine judgment on the Israelites (Lev 26:14-20; Deut 11:16-17; 28:33; Jer 29:17-18).

Jesus relived Israel's experience in his own wilderness testing and refused to make bread just for himself (Matt 4:3-4; cp. Deut 8:3). His success showed that scarcity and hunger can develop humility and trust in divine providence (Matt 4:2), something that Israel did not learn very well. Jesus fed 5,000 to draw them to himself as the bread of life, God's true manna (John 6:32-35), but the crowds followed Jesus more for the food than for himself (John 6:26-27). Without ignoring physical food, Jesus highlighted spiritual hunger and thirst (Luke 6:21; John 4:34). Eating provides both a context and a metaphor for fellowship (43:34; Luke 22:15-16; Rev 19:9). Heaven will remove the desperation of hunger altogether (Rev 7:16).

father's wishes was God's punishment for their having sold Joseph to the traders. The sense of divine retribution began to awaken feelings of remorse that Joseph's cries for mercy and their father's tears (37:34-35) had failed to arouse.

42:22 ***you wouldn't listen:*** Reuben had lost the reins of leadership (see notes on 42:37; 49:3-4).

42:24 Joseph ***turned away from them and began to weep*** (cp. 43:30; 45:2, 14; 50:1, 17); perhaps he was hearing part of the story that he had never known (Reuben's attempt to save him, 37:21-22, 29), or his brothers' remorse moved him to forgiveness.

42:25-28 Joseph cared for his brothers' needs; he had forgiven them (see note on 42:24) and was fulfilling his role to provide for them. God used Joseph's care to convict the brothers even more fully of their sin.

42:25 ***return each brother's payment:*** He was now testing them to awaken their conscience and make them face their past guilt; once again, they were going home with silver instead of a brother (37:28-35).

42:28 ***What has God done to us?*** They knew that God was behind everything that had been happening, so they faced a day of reckoning for their sins.

42:29-34 The brothers' account focused on the accusation that they were spies and on the need to take Benjamin back to Egypt with them. They omitted their growing realization of divine retribution for their crime against Joseph.

one father. One brother is no longer with us, and the youngest is at home with our father in the land of Canaan.'

33"Then the man who is governor of the land told us, 'This is how I will find out if you are honest men. Leave one of your brothers here with me, and take grain for your starving families and go on home. 34But you must bring your youngest brother back to me. Then I will know you are honest men and not spies. Then I will give you back your brother, and you may trade freely in the land.' "

35As they emptied out their sacks, there in each man's sack was the bag of money he had paid for the grain! The brothers and their father were terrified when they saw the bags of money. 36Jacob exclaimed, "You are robbing me of my children! Joseph is gone! Simeon is gone! And now you want to take Benjamin, too. Everything is going against me!"

37Then Reuben said to his father, "You may kill my two sons if I don't bring Benjamin back to you. I'll be responsible for him, and I promise to bring him back."

38But Jacob replied, "My son will not go down with you. His brother Joseph is dead, and he is all I have left. If anything should happen to him on your journey, you would send this grieving, white-haired man to his grave."

The Brothers Return to Egypt with Benjamin

43 But the famine continued to ravage the land of Canaan. 2When the grain they had brought from Egypt was almost gone, Jacob said to his sons, "Go back and buy us a little more food."

3But Judah said, "The man was serious when he warned us, 'You won't see my face again unless your brother is with you.' 4If you send Benjamin with us, we will go down and buy more food. 5But if you don't let Benjamin go, we won't go either. Remember, the man said, 'You won't see my face again unless your brother is with you.' "

6"Why were you so cruel to me?" Jacob moaned. "Why did you tell him you had another brother?"

7"The man kept asking us questions about our family," they replied. "He asked, 'Is your father still alive? Do you have another brother?' So we answered his questions. How could we know he would say, 'Bring your brother down here'?"

8Judah said to his father, "Send the boy with me, and we will be on our way. Otherwise we will all die of starvation—and not only we, but you and our little ones. 9I personally guarantee his safety. You may hold me responsible if I don't bring him back to you. Then let me bear the blame forever. 10If we hadn't wasted all this time, we could have gone and returned twice by now."

11So their father, Jacob, finally said to them, "If it can't be avoided, then at least do this. Pack your bags with the best products of this land. Take them down to the man as gifts—balm, honey, gum, aromatic resin, pistachio nuts, and almonds. 12Also take double the money that was put back in your sacks, as it was probably someone's mistake. 13Then take your brother, and go back to the man. 14May God Almighty give you mercy as you go before the man, so that he will release Simeon and let Benjamin return. But if I must lose my children, so be it."

15So the men packed Jacob's gifts and double the money and headed off with Benjamin. They finally arrived in Egypt and presented themselves to Joseph. 16When Joseph saw Benjamin with them, he said to the manager of his household, "These

42:34 Gen 34:10
42:35 Gen 43:12, 15, 18
42:36 Gen 43:14; 44:20-22
42:37 Gen 43:9; 44:32
42:38 Gen 37:35; 44:29, 34
43:1 Gen 41:56-57
43:2 Gen 42:25
43:3 Gen 42:15; 44:23
43:7 Gen 42:13; 43:27
43:8 Gen 42:2
43:9 Gen 42:37; Phlm 1:18-19
43:11 Gen 32:13; 37:25
43:12 Gen 42:25, 35
43:13 Gen 43:3
43:14 Gen 42:24; Ps 106:46
43:16 Gen 44:1

42:36 Filled with grief over two sons lost already, Jacob feared that he would also lose Benjamin if he went to Egypt. • ***You are robbing me of my children!*** He did not realize the full truth of his words, but they must have stung his sons' guilty consciences.

42:37 ***Reuben*** tried to take the lead; perhaps he thought he could get back into his father's good favor (see 35:22), first by rescuing Joseph from certain death (37:21-22, 29-30) and now by keeping ***Benjamin*** safe.

42:38 ***Jacob*** was resolute in his favoritism toward Rachel's remaining son. Benjamin would not go to Egypt even if it meant that Leah's son Simeon never returned. Jacob's grief apparently weighed heavily on the brothers' conscience (44:18-34). • ***to his grave:*** Hebrew *to Sheol.*

43:1-7 As ***the famine continued***, Jacob's family needed more grain, but they could not return to Egypt without Benjamin (42:16, 20). Jacob realized that he was in a bind; he needed ***more food***, but was loath to lose ***Benjamin***.

43:6 ***Jacob:*** Hebrew *Israel;* also in 43:11. See note on 35:21.

43:8-10 ***Judah*** broke the deadlock by taking responsibility for Benjamin's well-being, thus succeeding where Reuben failed. His action was fitting, since it had been his idea to sell Joseph to the Ishmaelites (37:26-27) instead of killing him. Now he would secure Benjamin's safety with his own life (see 44:18-34).

43:11-13 ***Jacob*** provided everything he could to ensure a favorable reception from the Egyptian governor (***the man;*** cp. 32:13-21).

43:13-14 Jacob finally entrusted his family's future to ***God Almighty*** (Hebrew *El-Shaddai*), the divine title that stresses God's power (see also 17:1; 28:3; 35:11; 48:3; 1 Kgs 19:10, 14; Rev 21:22).

43:16 ***When Joseph saw Benjamin with them:*** Joseph now knew that Benjamin was well (see note on 42:1–44:34). The feast was both a celebration and a test.

43:18 Gen 42:28, 35
43:21 Gen 42:25, 35; 43:12
43:22 Gen 42:28
43:23 Gen 42:24
43:24 Gen 18:4; 24:32
43:27 Gen 43:7; 45:3
43:28 Exod 18:7
43:29 Num 6:25; Ps 67:1
43:30 Gen 42:24; 45:2, 14-15; 46:29
43:31 Gen 45:1
43:32 Gen 46:34; Exod 8:26
43:33 Gen 44:12
44:1 Gen 42:25; 43:16
44:4 Prov 17:13

men will eat with me this noon. Take them inside the palace. Then go slaughter an animal, and prepare a big feast." 17So the man did as Joseph told him and took them into Joseph's palace.

18The brothers were terrified when they saw that they were being taken into Joseph's house. "It's because of the money someone put in our sacks last time we were here," they said. "He plans to pretend that we stole it. Then he will seize us, make us slaves, and take our donkeys."

A Feast at Joseph's Palace

19The brothers approached the manager of Joseph's household and spoke to him at the entrance to the palace. 20"Sir," they said, "we came to Egypt once before to buy food. 21But as we were returning home, we stopped for the night and opened our sacks. Then we discovered that each man's money—the exact amount paid—was in the top of his sack! Here it is; we have brought it back with us. 22We also have additional money to buy more food. We have no idea who put our money in our sacks."

23"Relax. Don't be afraid," the household manager told them. "Your God, the God of your father, must have put this treasure into your sacks. I know I received your payment." Then he released Simeon and brought him out to them.

24The manager then led the men into Joseph's palace. He gave them water to wash their feet and provided food for their donkeys. 25They were told they would be eating there, so they prepared their gifts for Joseph's arrival at noon.

26When Joseph came home, they gave him the gifts they had brought him, then bowed low to the ground before him. 27After greeting them, he asked, "How is your father, the old man you spoke about? Is he still alive?"

28"Yes," they replied. "Our father, your servant, is alive and well." And they bowed low again.

29Then Joseph looked at his brother Benjamin, the son of his own mother. "Is this your youngest brother, the one you told me about?" Joseph asked. "May God be gracious to you, my son." 30Then Joseph hurried from the room because he was overcome with emotion for his brother. He went into his private room, where he broke down and wept. 31After washing his face, he came back out, keeping himself under control. Then he ordered, "Bring out the food!"

32The waiters served Joseph at his own table, and his brothers were served at a separate table. The Egyptians who ate with Joseph sat at their own table, because Egyptians despise Hebrews and refuse to eat with them. 33Joseph told each of his brothers where to sit, and to their amazement, he seated them according to age, from oldest to youngest. 34And Joseph filled their plates with food from his own table, giving Benjamin five times as much as he gave the others. So they feasted and drank freely with him.

Joseph's Silver Cup in Benjamin's Sack

44 When his brothers were ready to leave, Joseph gave these instructions to his palace manager: "Fill each of their sacks with as much grain as they can carry, and put each man's money back into his sack. 2Then put my personal silver cup at the top of the youngest brother's sack, along with the money for his grain." So the manager did as Joseph instructed him.

3The brothers were up at dawn and were sent on their journey with their loaded donkeys. 4But when they had gone only a short distance and were barely out of the city, Joseph said to his palace manager, "Chase after them and stop them. When you catch up

43:18 *The brothers were terrified:* Cp. 32:6-12. Their guilt would not let them see that something good might happen.

43:19-22 *The brothers,* completely vulnerable and feeling the weight of God's judgment on their consciences, ***approached the manager*** in desperation.

43:24 Joseph no longer treated his brothers harshly, but provided kind hospitality.

43:26 For the second time, the brothers ***bowed . . . before*** Joseph in fulfillment of his first dream (37:7; see 42:6-7; cp. 33:3).

43:29 ***May God be gracious to you, my son:*** Joseph's blessing to his full brother fulfilled Jacob's prayer (43:14).

43:30 ***he was overcome with emotion for his brother:*** Cp. 42:24. Joseph's tears were of painful memories and years of lost fellowship, as well as of joy and thanksgiving to see his brother again. • ***He went into his private room:*** He did not yet plan to reveal his identity.

43:33 ***to their amazement:*** This ruler knew more about the brothers than seemed possible (cp. 44:15).

43:34 The brothers were confronted with generous and gracious dealings from God through Joseph, who tested their tolerance by reenacting the favoritism toward Rachel's son that had galvanized their earlier hostility.

44:1-34 The brothers appeared to have changed; they had shown remorse over what they had done to Joseph, and they showed integrity in returning the money and in bringing Benjamin. Given a chance to get rid of Rachel's other son, Benjamin, would they do it?

44:2 Joseph was giving his brothers the chance to abandon Benjamin if they wanted to. Joseph was testing them to see if they were loyal to the family and faithful to their father.

with them, ask them, 'Why have you repaid
my kindness with such evil? [5]Why have you
stolen my master's silver cup, which he uses
to predict the future? What a wicked thing
you have done!' "
[6]When the palace manager caught up
with the men, he spoke to them as he had
been instructed.
[7]"What are you talking about?" the brothers responded. "We are your servants and
would never do such a thing! [8]Didn't we return the money we found in our sacks? We
brought it back all the way from the land of
Canaan. Why would we steal silver or gold
from your master's house? [9]If you find his
cup with any one of us, let that man die.
And all the rest of us, my lord, will be your
slaves."
[10]"That's fair," the man replied. "But only
the one who stole the cup will be my slave.
The rest of you may go free."
[11]They all quickly took their sacks from
the backs of their donkeys and opened
them. [12]The palace manager searched the
brothers' sacks, from the oldest to the youngest. And the cup was found in Benjamin's
sack! [13]When the brothers saw this, they
tore their clothing in despair. Then they
loaded their donkeys again and returned to
the city.
[14]Joseph was still in his palace when Judah and his brothers arrived, and they fell
to the ground before him. [15]"What have you
done?" Joseph demanded. "Don't you know
that a man like me can predict the future?"
[16]Judah answered, "Oh, my lord, what can
we say to you? How can we explain this? How
can we prove our innocence? God is punishing us for our sins. My lord, we have all
returned to be your slaves—all of us, not just
our brother who had your cup in his sack."
[17]"No," Joseph said. "I would never do
such a thing! Only the man who stole the
cup will be my slave. The rest of you may go
back to your father in peace."

Judah Intercedes for Benjamin

[18]Then Judah stepped forward and said,
"Please, my lord, let your servant say just one
word to you. Please, do not be angry with
me, even though you are as powerful as
Pharaoh himself.
[19]"My lord, previously you asked us, your
servants, 'Do you have a father or a brother?'
[20]And we responded, 'Yes, my lord, we have
a father who is an old man, and his youngest
son is a child of his old age. His full brother is
dead, and he alone is left of his mother's children, and his father loves him very much.'
[21]"And you said to us, 'Bring him here so
I can see him with my own eyes.' [22]But we
said to you, 'My lord, the boy cannot leave
his father, for his father would die.' [23]But
you told us, 'Unless your youngest brother
comes with you, you will never see my face
again.'
[24]"So we returned to your servant, our father, and told him what you had said. [25]Later,
when he said, 'Go back again and buy us
more food,' [26]we replied, 'We can't go unless you let our youngest brother go with us.
We'll never get to see the man's face unless
our youngest brother is with us.'
[27]"Then my father said to us, 'As you
know, my wife had two sons, [28]and one
of them went away and never returned.
Doubtless he was torn to pieces by some
wild animal. I have never seen him since.
[29]Now if you take his brother away from

44:5 Gen 30:27; Deut 18:10-14
44:8 Gen 43:21
44:9 Gen 31:32
44:12 Gen 44:2
44:13 Gen 37:29, 34
44:15 Gen 44:5
44:16 Gen 42:11; 43:18
44:18 Gen 37:7-8; 41:40-44
44:19 Gen 42:11; 43:7
44:21 Gen 42:11, 15
44:23 Gen 43:3
44:24 Gen 42:29-34
44:25 Gen 42:2
44:26 Gen 43:5
44:27 Gen 46:19
44:28 Gen 37:33
44:29 Gen 42:38

44:5 This description would make the brothers understand that the ruler knew things that others could not. • ***silver cup:*** As in Greek version; Hebrew lacks this phrase. *Hydromancy* (pouring water into oil) and *oenomancy* (pouring wine into other liquids) were methods of divination used in the ancient Near East that would have required such a cup. Joseph was continuing his ruse (see 42:7; cp. 30:27; see also Lev 19:26; Num 23:23; Deut 18:10-11)—he knew that only God grants revelation (see 37:5-9; 40:8; 41:16).

44:9-10 The punishment that the brothers proposed was harsher than necessary; it was normal in antiquity to stake your life on what you said. The palace manager was agreeable but enforced a punishment that matched Joseph's intentions (44:17).

44:11-12 The ***palace manager*** knew where the cup was, but he created more anxiety by beginning with the oldest.

44:13 *they tore their clothing in despair:* They knew what it would do to Jacob to lose Benjamin (42:38).

44:14 This time, the brothers did not bow politely (see 42:6-7; 43:26); they ***fell to the ground*** in desperation, fulfilling Joseph's first dream for the third time (see 37:10).

44:16 *Judah* again spoke for the group. • ***God is punishing us for our sins:*** God was completing the work of repentance in their hearts. Judah again proposed that they all be punished. Benjamin was seemingly guilty of this theft, but all of the others were guilty of sin against Joseph. They preferred not returning to Jacob at all versus seeing his grief at the loss of Benjamin (44:34).

44:18-34 *Judah* made good on his promise to pay for Benjamin's safety (43:8-10). His lengthy plea to be imprisoned in place of the lad (44:33) is one of the most moving acts of intercession in Scripture. It demonstrated Judah's concern for their father and his willingness to give up everything for the sake of his brother. With this kind of integrity (see John 15:13), Judah showed himself to be a true leader, qualified to receive the blessing of the firstborn, through whom the kings of Israel would come (see 49:10). • The brothers had fully repented, as expressed by Judah's intercession. Because of their change, Joseph could make himself known to them (45:1-15) and arrange for the family to join him in Egypt where there was food (45:16; 47:12).

44:29 *to his grave:* Hebrew *to Sheol;* also in 44:31.

44:30 1 Sam 18:1
44:32 Gen 43:9
45:1 Gen 43:31
45:3 Gen 43:7
45:4 Gen 37:28
45:5 Gen 50:20
45:6 Gen 41:30
45:8 Gen 41:41; Judg 17:10
45:9 Acts 7:14

me, and any harm comes to him, you will
send this grieving, white-haired man to his
grave.'
30"And now, my lord, I cannot go back to
my father without the boy. Our father's life
is bound up in the boy's life. 31If he sees that
the boy is not with us, our father will die.
We, your servants, will indeed be responsible for sending that grieving, white-haired
man to his grave. 32My lord, I guaranteed to
my father that I would take care of the boy. I
told him, 'If I don't bring him back to you, I
will bear the blame forever.'
33"So please, my lord, let me stay here as
a slave instead of the boy, and let the boy
return with his brothers. 34For how can I return to my father if the boy is not with me? I
couldn't bear to see the anguish this would
cause my father!"

Joseph Reveals His Identity and God's Plan

45 Joseph could stand it no longer.
There were many people in the
room, and he said to his attendants, "Out,
all of you!" So he was alone with his brothers when he told them who he was. 2Then
he broke down and wept. He wept so loudly
the Egyptians could hear him, and word of
it quickly carried to Pharaoh's palace.
3"I am Joseph!" he said to his brothers.
"Is my father still alive?" But his brothers
were speechless! They were stunned to realize that Joseph was standing there in front
of them. 4"Please, come closer," he said to
them. So they came closer. And he said
again, "I am Joseph, your brother, whom you
sold into slavery in Egypt. 5But don't be upset, and don't be angry with yourselves for
selling me to this place. It was God who sent
me here ahead of you to preserve your lives.
6This famine that has ravaged the land
for two years will last five more years, and
there will be neither plowing nor harvesting. 7God has sent me ahead of you to keep
you and your families alive and to preserve
many survivors. 8So it was God who sent me
here, not you! And he is the one who made
me an adviser to Pharaoh—the manager of
his entire palace and the governor of all
Egypt.
9"Now hurry back to my father and tell
him, 'This is what your son Joseph says:
God has made me master over all the land
of Egypt. So come down to me immediately!

JUDAH (44:14-34)

Gen 29:35; 37:26-27; 38:1-30; 43:1-10; 46:28; 49:8-12
Ruth 4:12
1 Chr 2:3-4; 5:2
Ps 108:8

Judah is remembered most often as the ancestor of King David and of Jesus Christ. Despite his indiscretions and his birth as a middle child, God chose Judah to carry the line of King David (1 Chr 2:1-16; 3:1-24) and of the Messiah (49:8-12; Matt 1:2-3; Luke 3:33).

Judah was the fourth of Jacob's twelve sons (35:23; 1 Chr 2:1). Leah, overjoyed to have borne her fourth son, named him Judah, meaning "praise" (29:35). Judah fathered five sons: Er, Onan, and Shelah by Bathshua, a woman from Canaan (38:3-5; 1 Chr 2:3); and the twins, Perez and Zerah, by his daughter-in-law Tamar (38:29-30; 1 Chr 2:4). God killed his first two sons, Er and Onan, in Canaan for disobedience (46:12). Judah eventually settled his family in Egypt with his father and brothers (Exod 1:2).

Though reckless in his behavior with Tamar (38:6-30), Judah took personal responsibility for Benjamin's safety in Egypt and interceded with Joseph for his brothers (44:14-18). When Jacob gave his dying blessing, he granted Judah the position of leadership; the future kings of Israel would come through Judah's offspring (see note on 49:10).

44:32-34 Judah was willing to give up his family, his future, and his freedom for others.

45:1-15 In one of the most dramatic scenes of the book, ***Joseph*** revealed his identity to his brothers, bringing the process of reconciling with them to a climax (see also 50:14-21).

45:2 This is the third of five times in the story that Joseph ***wept*** over his brothers (see also 42:24; 43:30; 45:14; 50:17; cp. 50:1).

45:3 The brothers were ***stunned*** at the news, unable to speak from amazement and fear (45:5; cp. 50:15).

45:5-8 ***God . . . sent me*** is the central message of the account of Jacob's family (37:2). As the Lord had told Abraham, he was leading the Israelites into Egypt (15:13). God had sent Joseph to Egypt to prepare for his family's rescue during the famine. In what has become a classic statement of God's sovereignty, Joseph explained that God had been working through all of the circumstances and human acts to bring about his plan. The certainty of God's will is the basis for forgiveness and reconciliation with those who do wrong, cause hurt, or bring harm. If people do not believe that God is sovereign, then they will blame others and retaliate. Those who are spiritual will trust that God is at work even through human wickedness (see also Rom 8:28-30).

45:7 ***to preserve many survivors:*** Or *and to save you with an extraordinary rescue.* The meaning of the Hebrew is uncertain.

45:8 ***an adviser:*** Literally *a father.*

45:9-13 Joseph instructed his brothers to inform Jacob. The whole family was to move to ***Egypt*** and live in ***Goshen***, a fertile region in the Nile delta (see 47:1-12). If they did not come to Egypt, they would not survive the ***five years of famine ahead.***

10You can live in the region of Goshen,
where you can be near me with all your
children and grandchildren, your flocks
and herds, and everything you own. 11I will
take care of you there, for there are still five
years of famine ahead of us. Otherwise you,
your household, and all your animals will
starve.' "
12Then Joseph added, "Look! You can
see for yourselves, and so can my brother
Benjamin, that I really am Joseph! 13Go tell
my father of my honored position here in
Egypt. Describe for him everything you
have seen, and then bring my father here
quickly." 14Weeping with joy, he embraced
Benjamin, and Benjamin did the same.
15Then Joseph kissed each of his brothers
and wept over them, and after that they began talking freely with him.

Pharaoh Invites Jacob to Egypt

16The news soon reached Pharaoh's palace:
"Joseph's brothers have arrived!" Pharaoh
and his officials were all delighted to hear
this.
17Pharaoh said to Joseph, "Tell your brothers, 'This is what you must do: Load your pack
animals, and hurry back to the land of Canaan. 18Then get your father and all of your
families, and return here to me. I will give
you the very best land in Egypt, and you will
eat from the best that the land produces.' "
19Then Pharaoh said to Joseph, "Tell your
brothers, 'Take wagons from the land of
Egypt to carry your little children and your
wives, and bring your father here. 20Don't
worry about your personal belongings, for
the best of all the land of Egypt is yours.' "
21So the sons of Jacob did as they were
told. Joseph provided them with wagons, as
Pharaoh had commanded, and he gave them
supplies for the journey. 22And he gave each
of them new clothes—but to Benjamin he
gave five changes of clothes and 300 pieces
of silver. 23He also sent his father ten male
donkeys loaded with the finest products
of Egypt, and ten female donkeys loaded
with grain and bread and other supplies he
would need on his journey.
24So Joseph sent his brothers off, and as
they left, he called after them, "Don't quarrel about all this along the way!" 25And they
left Egypt and returned to their father, Jacob, in the land of Canaan.
26"Joseph is still alive!" they told him.
"And he is governor of all the land of Egypt!"
Jacob was stunned at the news—he couldn't
[e]believe it. 27But when they repeated to Jacob everything Joseph had told them, and
when he saw the wagons Joseph had sent to
carry him, their father's [f]spirits revived.
28Then Jacob exclaimed, "It must be true!
My son Joseph is alive! I must go and see
him before I die."

Jacob and His Family Move to Egypt

46 So Jacob set out for Egypt with all
his possessions. And when he came
to Beersheba, he [g]offered sacrifices to the

45:10 Gen 46:28, 34
45:11 Gen 47:12
45:13 Acts 7:14
45:14 Gen 45:2
45:16 Acts 7:13
45:17 Gen 42:26
45:18 Gen 27:28
45:19 Gen 45:27; 46:5
45:20 Gen 46:6
45:22 Gen 24:53; 2 Kgs 5:5
45:23 Gen 43:11
45:24 Gen 42:21-22
45:26 Gen 37:31-35; [e]*'aman* (0539) ‣Exod 14:31
45:27 Gen 45:19; [f]*ruakh* (7307) ‣Exod 31:3
45:28 Gen 44:28
46:1 Gen 21:14; 26:24; 28:13; 31:42; [g]*zabakh* (2076) ‣Exod 22:20

45:10 *The region of Goshen* was in the northeast corner of Egypt, only a few days' walk from Canaan. Jacob's family stayed there because there was food and water for themselves and their flocks; later, they were kept there by Egyptians who put them to slave labor.

45:14-15 Joseph was reunited with his brothers—first with ***Benjamin*** and then with the rest. Their previous hatred and jealousy of Joseph (37:4-11) had come to an end. The brothers experienced forgiveness from God and from Joseph. Far from commanding ***his brothers*** to bow down to him (see 42:6-7), Joseph welcomed them. Joseph held no grudge because he accepted what had happened as God's work and saw the good that had resulted (see 50:14-21). This is how wisdom rules: The wise leader will forgive and restore (see note on 37:2–50:26).

45:16–47:12 This section is transitional, as the family moved from Canaan to Goshen, where they would live for the next four centuries.

45:16-25 Joseph sent his brothers with instructions to bring Jacob and the entire family to Egypt. Out of gratitude for Joseph's having saved all of Egypt (45:18; see 47:20), Pharaoh promised the ***best of all the land of Egypt,*** and Joseph gave them ***the finest products of Egypt.***

45:21 ***Jacob:*** Hebrew *Israel;* also in 45:28. See note on 35:21.

45:22 ***300 pieces:*** Hebrew *300 shekels,* about 7.5 pounds or 3.4 kilograms in weight.

45:24 ***Don't quarrel about all this along the way!*** When they were away from Joseph, they might begin to accuse one another about the past or argue about how to explain what had happened to Jacob. It was now time to put the past behind them and enjoy the reunion.

45:26-28 As might be expected, ***Jacob was stunned*** when he heard that his son ***Joseph*** was ***still alive*** and ruling ***all the land of Egypt.*** As he heard the details of their story and saw all that ***Joseph had sent*** him, he was convinced that it was ***true.*** He immediately prepared to move to Egypt and reunite with his son Joseph, whom he had not seen for twenty-two years.

45:27 ***their father's spirits revived:*** This royal invitation to Jacob, an old man near the end of hope, and to the ten brothers burdened with guilty fears, was a turning point in their lives. It was also a fulfillment of God's prediction (15:13-16) that they would go into seclusion in a foreign country and there become a great nation without losing their identity. The joyful news about Joseph changed the lives of everyone in this family for the good.

46:1-4 God reassured Jacob about his move to Egypt.

46:1 ***Jacob*** (Hebrew *Israel;* also in 46:29, 30; see note on 35:21) ***set out for Egypt:*** A little over 200 years earlier, Abraham had similarly gone down into Egypt during a famine in Canaan (12:10), and God had protected him there. • Jacob's first stop was at ***Beersheba,*** where Abraham had sacrificed to the Lord and worshiped him after settling his land and water rights with the Philistines (21:31-33). This was where Isaac had

46:2
Gen 22:11; 31:11
Num 12:6
46:3
Gen 17:1; 26:2
46:4
Gen 28:13
Exod 3:8
46:5
Gen 45:19
46:6
Num 20:15
Deut 26:5
Acts 7:15
46:8
Gen 29:32; 35:23
46:9
1 Chr 5:3
46:10
1 Chr 4:24
46:11
1 Chr 6:16
46:12
1 Chr 2:3
46:13
1 Chr 7:1
46:14
Gen 30:20
46:15
Gen 30:21
46:16
Gen 30:11
Num 26:15
46:17
Gen 30:13

God of his father, Isaac.
2During the night
God spoke to him in a vision. "Jacob! Jacob!"
he called.

"Here I am," Jacob replied.

3"I am God, the God of your father," the
voice said. "Do not be afraid to go down to
Egypt, for there I will make your family into
a great nation.
4I will go with you down to
Egypt, and I will bring you back again. You
will die in Egypt, but Joseph will be with you
to close your eyes."

5So Jacob left Beersheba, and his sons took
him to Egypt. They carried him and their
little ones and their wives in the wagons
Pharaoh had provided for them.
6They also
took all their livestock and all the personal
belongings they had acquired in the land of
Canaan. So Jacob and his entire family went
to Egypt—
7sons and grandsons, daughters
and granddaughters—all his descendants.

8These are the names of the descendants
of Israel—the sons of Jacob—who went to
Egypt:

Reuben was Jacob's oldest son.
9The sons
of Reuben were Hanoch, Pallu, Hezron,
and Carmi.

10The sons of Simeon were Jemuel, Jamin,
Ohad, Jakin, Zohar, and Shaul. (Shaul's
mother was a Canaanite woman.)

11The sons of Levi were Gershon, Kohath,
and Merari.

12The sons of Judah were Er, Onan,
Shelah, Perez, and Zerah (though
Er and Onan had died in the land
of Canaan). The sons of Perez were
Hezron and Hamul.

13The sons of Issachar were Tola, Puah,
Jashub, and Shimron.

14The sons of Zebulun were Sered, Elon,
and Jahleel.

15These were the sons of Leah and Jacob
who were born in Paddan-aram, in addition to their daughter, Dinah. The number
of Jacob's descendants (male and female)
through Leah was thirty-three.

16The sons of Gad were Zephon, Haggi,
Shuni, Ezbon, Eri, Arodi, and Areli.

17The sons of Asher were Imnah, Ishvah,
Ishvi, and Beriah. Their sister was
Serah. Beriah's sons were Heber and
Malkiel.

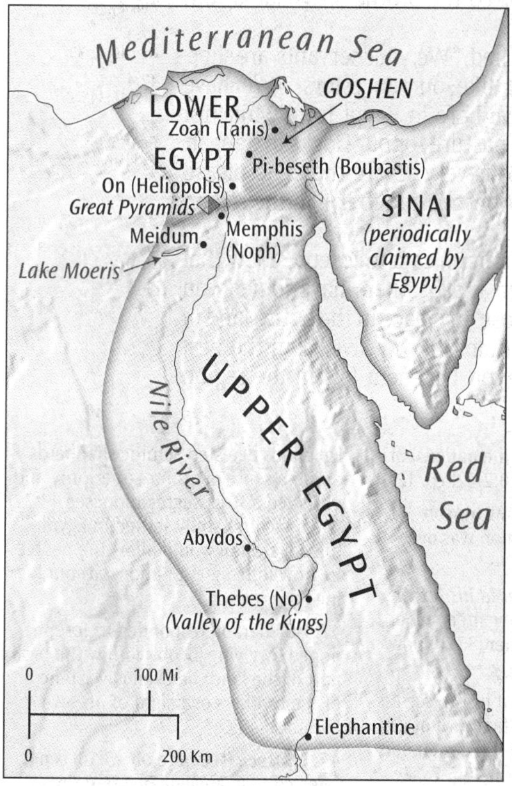

◂ **Egypt, about 1700 BC (39:1–50:26).** Egypt was already a great and ancient civilization when Joseph rose to power (chs 39–41) and Jacob's family traveled there for food (chs 42–46; cp. 12:10-20). As the breadbasket of the region, Egypt was synonymous with abundance. It was protected from enemies by natural barriers: the harborless MEDITERRANEAN SEA to the north, the rugged SINAI peninsula to the east, and a great desert to the west. ON (HELIOPOLIS) was the religious center (see 41:45, 50). Egypt was divided into two regions—LOWER EGYPT (the NILE delta region) and UPPER EGYPT (from the delta to the first cataract of the NILE at ELEPHANTINE). ZOAN and MEMPHIS were administrative centers (see Num 13:22; Ps 78:12, 43; Isa 19:11-13; 30:4; Ezek 30:14). THEBES, the chief city of Upper Egypt, was later conquered by the Assyrians (Nah 3:8-10; cp. Ezek 30:14-16). GOSHEN is also shown, the region where the Israelites settled (45:10; 46:28–47:6, 28-29; see Exod 8:22; 9:26).

lived, and where Jacob had lived before he fled from Esau's anger (28:10). • *all his possessions:* See 46:5-7.

46:2-4 In a night vision, the LORD repeated his promise to go with Jacob and make his family into a great nation in Egypt. The same God who led the family into Egypt promised to bring them out of Egypt to live once again in the land of Canaan.

46:3 *I am God:* Hebrew *I am El.*

46:4 *you will die:* He would have a peaceful death, surrounded by his family and many blessings from God (49:33).

46:8-27 This genealogy of *the sons of Jacob* shows that all the tribes *of Israel* went together to the land of Egypt; they would all leave together as well (see the book of Exodus).

46:13 *Puah:* As in Syriac version and Samaritan Pentateuch (see also 1 Chr 7:1); Hebrew reads *Puvah.* • *Jashub:* As in some Greek manuscripts and Samaritan Pentateuch (see also Num 26:24; 1 Chr 7:1); Hebrew reads *Iob.*

46:16 *Zephon:* As in Greek version and Samaritan Pentateuch (see also Num 26:15); Hebrew reads *Ziphion.*

18 These were the sons of Zilpah, the servant
given to Leah by her father, Laban. The number of Jacob's descendants through Zilpah
was sixteen.

19 The sons of Jacob's wife Rachel were
Joseph and Benjamin.
20 Joseph's sons, born in the land of Egypt,
were Manasseh and Ephraim. Their
mother was Asenath, daughter of
Potiphera, the priest of On.
21 Benjamin's sons were Bela, Beker, Ashbel,
Gera, Naaman, Ehi, Rosh, Muppim,
Huppim, and Ard.
22 These were the sons of Rachel and Jacob.
The number of Jacob's descendants through
Rachel was fourteen.

23 The son of Dan was Hushim.
24 The sons of Naphtali were Jahzeel, Guni,
Jezer, and Shillem.
25 These were the sons of Bilhah, the servant
given to Rachel by her father, Laban. The
number of Jacob's descendants through Bilhah was seven.

26 The total number of Jacob's direct descendants who went with him to Egypt, not
counting his sons' wives, was sixty-six. 27 In
addition, Joseph had two sons who were
born in Egypt. So altogether, there were seventy members of Jacob's family in the land
of Egypt.

Jacob's Family Arrives in Goshen

28 As they neared their destination, Jacob
sent Judah ahead to meet Joseph and get directions to the region of Goshen. And when
they finally arrived there, 29 Joseph prepared
his chariot and traveled to Goshen to meet
his father, Jacob. When Joseph arrived, he
embraced his father and wept, holding him
for a long time. 30 Finally, Jacob said to Joseph,
"Now I am ready to die, since I have seen your
face again and know you are still alive."

31 And Joseph said to his brothers and
to his father's entire family, "I will go to
Pharaoh and tell him, 'My brothers and my
father's entire family have come to me from
the land of Canaan. 32 These men are shepherds, and they raise livestock. They have
brought with them their flocks and herds
and everything they own.' "

33 Then he said, "When Pharaoh calls for
you and asks you about your occupation,
34 you must tell him, 'We, your servants, have
raised livestock all our lives, as our ancestors
have always done.' When you tell him this,
he will let you live here in the region of Goshen, for the Egyptians despise shepherds."

Jacob Blesses Pharaoh and Settles in Goshen

47 Then Joseph went to see Pharaoh
and told him, "My father and my
brothers have arrived from the land of Canaan. They have come with all their flocks
and herds and possessions, and they are
now in the region of Goshen."

2 Joseph took five of his brothers with
him and presented them to Pharaoh. 3 And
Pharaoh asked the brothers, "What is your
occupation?"

They replied, "We, your servants, are shepherds, just like our ancestors. 4 We have
come to live here in Egypt for a while, for
there is no pasture for our flocks in Canaan.
The famine is very severe there. So please,
we request permission to live in the region
of Goshen."

5 Then Pharaoh said to Joseph, "Now that
your father and brothers have joined you
here, 6 choose any place in the entire land of
Egypt for them to live. Give them the best
land of Egypt. Let them live in the region

46:19 Gen 44:27
46:20 Gen 41:45, 50-52
46:21 Num 26:38-41; 1 Chr 7:6-12
46:22 Gen 35:24
46:23 Gen 30:6; Num 26:42
46:24 Gen 30:8
46:25 Gen 35:25
46:27 Exod 1:5; Deut 10:22; Acts 7:14
46:28 Gen 43:3; 45:10
46:29 Gen 45:14-15
46:30 Gen 44:28
46:31 Gen 47:1
46:32 Gen 37:2; 47:3
46:33 Gen 47:3
46:34 Gen 13:7; 26:20; 37:2
47:1 Gen 46:31
47:2 Gen 43:15
47:3 Gen 46:32-33
47:4 Gen 46:34
47:6 Gen 45:18; Exod 18:21, 25

46:20 ***On:*** Greek version reads *of Heliopolis* (see note on 41:45).

46:26 ***The total number . . . was sixty-six:*** This is the number of those who traveled with Jacob to Egypt, excluding ***his sons' wives,*** the servants, and others attached to the household. It also omits Joseph, Ephraim, Manasseh, and Jacob.

46:27 ***two sons:*** Greek version reads *nine sons,* probably including Joseph's grandsons through Ephraim and Manasseh (see 1 Chr 7:14-20). • ***seventy*** (Greek version reads *seventy-five;* see note on Exod 1:5): This number includes Joseph, Ephraim, Manasseh, and Jacob. Seventy is also a symbolic number for perfection or completion (see "Symbolic Numbers" at Rev 4:4, p. 2173). From these seventy (i.e., all Israel) would grow the nation of Israel that would bless the seventy nations (i.e., all the nations) of the world (see note on 10:2-32; cp. 12:3).

46:28-34 Jacob finally saw his son Joseph again; their reunion was overwhelmingly joyful.

46:29 ***Joseph . . . embraced his father and wept:*** Joseph was seventeen when he had last seen his father (37:2); now he was thirty-nine.

46:30 ***Jacob*** was satisfied just to see his beloved son ***alive***—the firstborn of his chosen wife Rachel and the designated family leader (see note on 48:5-7; see also 1 Chr 5:1-2). More than just a family reunion, this was confirmation that God's plan was intact.

46:34 In contrast to the syncretistic Canaanites, who would have absorbed the Israelites had they stayed in Canaan, Egyptians detested Semitic shepherds out of a sense of ethnic superiority and observed a strict segregation (see 43:32). When Jacob's family settled in Egypt, this separation would allow the people to grow into a great nation without losing their identity.

47:1-6 Pharaoh responded as Joseph hoped by giving Jacob's family the best part of the land; he even gave some of the brothers oversight of his own livestock (47:6).

47:1 ***Goshen*** (see note on 45:10) is not referred to in ancient Egyptian texts; the name it bore in later Egyptian writings was "the region of Rameses" (47:11; see Exod 1:11). It was fertile and near to Joseph at court, which suggests that it was on the eastern side of the Nile delta.

47:7
Gen 47:10
2 Sam 14:22
1 Kgs 8:66
47:10
Gen 14:19
47:11
Exod 1:11; 12:37
47:12
Gen 45:11; 47:24
47:13
Gen 41:30
Acts 7:11
47:14
Gen 41:56
47:15
Gen 47:18-19
47:17
Exod 14:9
47:19
Neh 5:2
Job 2:4
Lam 1:11
47:22
Deut 14:28-29
47:24
Gen 41:34
47:25
Gen 32:5
47:26
Gen 47:22
47:27
Exod 1:7
47:29
Gen 24:2; 50:24-25

of Goshen. And if any of them have special
skills, put them in charge of my livestock,
too."
[7]Then Joseph brought in his father, Jacob,
and presented him to Pharaoh. And Jacob
blessed Pharaoh.
[8]"How old are you?" Pharaoh asked him.
[9]Jacob replied, "I have traveled this earth
for 130 hard years. But my life has been
short compared to the lives of my ancestors." [10]Then Jacob blessed Pharaoh again
before leaving his court.
[11]So Joseph assigned the best land of
Egypt—the region of Rameses—to his father and his brothers, and he settled them
there, just as Pharaoh had commanded.
[12]And Joseph provided food for his father
and his brothers in amounts appropriate to
the number of their dependents, including
the smallest children.

Joseph's Leadership in the Famine

[13]Meanwhile, the famine became so severe
that all the food was used up, and people
were starving throughout the lands of Egypt
and Canaan. [14]By selling grain to the people,
Joseph eventually collected all the money in
Egypt and Canaan, and he put the money in
Pharaoh's treasury. [15]When the people of
Egypt and Canaan ran out of money, all the
Egyptians came to Joseph. "Our money is
gone!" they cried. "But please give us food,
or we will die before your very eyes!"
[16]Joseph replied, "Since your money is
gone, bring me your livestock. I will give
you food in exchange for your livestock."
[17]So they brought their livestock to Joseph
in exchange for food. In exchange for their
horses, flocks of sheep and goats, herds of
cattle, and donkeys, Joseph provided them
with food for another year.
[18]But that year ended, and the next year
they came again and said, "We cannot hide
the truth from you, my lord. Our money is
gone, and all our livestock and cattle are
yours. We have nothing left to give but our
bodies and our land. [19]Why should we die
before your very eyes? Buy us and our land
in exchange for food; we offer our land and
ourselves as slaves for Pharaoh. Just give us
grain so we may live and not die, and so the
land does not become empty and desolate."
[20]So Joseph bought all the land of Egypt
for Pharaoh. All the Egyptians sold him
their fields because the famine was so
severe, and soon all the land belonged to
Pharaoh. [21]As for the people, he made them
all slaves, from one end of Egypt to the other.
[22]The only land he did not buy was the land
belonging to the priests. They received an
allotment of food directly from Pharaoh, so
they didn't need to sell their land.
[23]Then Joseph said to the people, "Look,
today I have bought you and your land for
Pharaoh. I will provide you with seed so you
can plant the fields. [24]Then when you harvest it, one-fifth of your crop will belong to
Pharaoh. You may keep the remaining four-
fifths as seed for your fields and as food for
you, your households, and your little ones."
[25]"You have saved our lives!" they exclaimed. "May it please you, my lord, to let
us be Pharaoh's servants." [26]Joseph then
issued a decree still in effect in the land
of Egypt, that Pharaoh should receive one-
fifth of all the crops grown on his land.
Only the land belonging to the priests was
not given to Pharaoh.
[27]Meanwhile, the people of Israel settled
in the region of Goshen in Egypt. There they
acquired property, and they were fruitful,
and their population grew rapidly. [28]Jacob
lived for seventeen years after his arrival in
Egypt, so he lived 147 years in all.

Joseph Promises to Bury Jacob in Canaan

[29]As the time of his death drew near, Jacob
called for his son Joseph and said to him,

47:7-10 When ***Jacob*** entered Pharaoh's court and when he left, he ***blessed Pharaoh***, an indication of Jacob's position as God's representative (see Heb 7:7). God had promised that he would bless those who blessed Abraham's family (12:2-3), so he now blessed Pharaoh and Egypt.

47:13-26 The Lord blessed Pharaoh because Pharaoh was blessing Abraham's descendants (12:3). Through Joseph's wise administration in Egypt, the Lord saved the people from starvation and prospered Pharaoh. In selling food to the Egyptians during the years of famine, Joseph accepted money, livestock, and finally land as payment, until almost all of Egypt belonged to Pharaoh. Meanwhile, God provided Israel with some of the best land in Egypt where they could live, work, and multiply.

47:21 ***he made them all slaves:*** As in Greek version and Samaritan Pentateuch; Hebrew reads *he moved them all into the towns,* where the food was. In Hebrew script, the difference is very slight between *slaves* (Hebrew *'abadim*) and *towns* (Hebrew *'arim*). Moving the people into the towns doesn't fit the context very well, so most translations select *slaves* as the reading that makes the most sense (cp. 47:20).

47:27 God blessed his people according to his promise to Abraham that his descendants would be innumerable (15:5; 22:17). They had to wait for the fulfillment of the second promise, that they would own the land of Canaan (17:8).

47:29-31 ***bury me with my ancestors:*** Cp. 49:29-33. Jacob wanted to be buried with Abraham and Isaac in the cave of Machpelah (see note on 49:29-33; see 23:1-20; 25:7-10; 35:27-29). • ***Put your hand under my thigh:*** This custom (cp. 24:1-9 and note on 24:2) was a serious oath to carry on the covenant, which had as its main promise innumerable descendants in the Promised Land.
• ***Jacob:*** Hebrew *Israel;* also in 47:31b. See note on 35:21.

"Please do me this favor. Put your hand under my thigh and swear that you will treat me with unfailing love by honoring this last request: Do not bury me in Egypt. 30When I die, please take my body out of Egypt and bury me with my ancestors."

So Joseph promised, "I will do as you ask."
31"Swear that you will do it," Jacob insisted. So Joseph gave his oath, and Jacob bowed humbly at the head of his bed.

Jacob Blesses His Children (48:1–50:26)

Jacob Blesses Manasseh and Ephraim

48 One day not long after this, word came to Joseph, "Your father is failing rapidly." So Joseph went to visit his father, and he took with him his two sons, Manasseh and Ephraim.

2When Joseph arrived, Jacob was told, "Your son Joseph has come to see you." So Jacob gathered his strength and sat up in his bed.

3Jacob said to Joseph, "God [h]Almighty appeared to me at Luz in the land of Canaan and blessed me. 4He said to me, 'I will make you fruitful, and I will multiply your descendants. I will make you a multitude of nations. And I will give this land of Canaan to your [i]descendants after you as an everlasting possession.'

5"Now I am claiming as my own sons these two boys of yours, Ephraim and Manasseh, who were born here in the land of Egypt before I arrived. They will be my sons, just as Reuben and Simeon are. 6But any children born to you in the future will be your own, and they will inherit land within the territories of their brothers Ephraim and Manasseh.

7"Long ago, as I was returning from Paddan-aram, Rachel died in the land of Canaan. We were still on the way, some distance from Ephrath (that is, Bethlehem). So with great sorrow I buried her there beside the road to Ephrath."

8Then Jacob looked over at the two boys.
"Are these your sons?" he asked.
9"Yes," Joseph told him, "these are the sons God has given me here in Egypt."

And Jacob said, "Bring them closer to me, so I can bless them."

10Jacob was half blind because of his age and could hardly see. So Joseph brought the boys close to him, and Jacob kissed and embraced them.
11Then Jacob said to Joseph, "I never thought I would see your face again, but now God has let me see your children, too!"

12Joseph moved the boys, who were at their grandfather's knees, and he bowed with his face to the ground.
13Then he positioned the boys in front of Jacob. With his right hand he directed Ephraim toward Jacob's left hand, and with his left hand he put Manasseh at Jacob's right hand.
14But Jacob crossed his arms as he reached out to lay his hands on the boys' heads. He put his right hand on the head of Ephraim, though he was the younger boy, and his left hand on the head of Manasseh, though he was the firstborn.
15Then he blessed Joseph and said,

"May the God before whom my
grandfather Abraham
and my father, Isaac, walked—
the God who has been my [j]shepherd
all my life, to this very day,

47:30 Gen 23:17-20; 25:9; 49:29; Acts 7:15-16
47:31 Heb 11:21
48:1 Gen 41:51-52; Heb 11:21
48:3 Gen 28:13-19; 35:9-12; [h]*shadday* (7706) ‣Gen 49:25
48:4 [i]*zera'* (2233) ‣Exod 32:13
48:5 Gen 29:32-33
48:7 Gen 35:19
48:9 Gen 33:5
48:10 Gen 27:1
48:11 Gen 44:28
48:12 Gen 33:3; 42:6
48:14 Gen 41:51-52
48:15 Gen 17:1; 49:24; [j]*ro'eh* (7462) ‣Gen 49:24

47:31 When the oath was taken, Jacob ***bowed humbly*** in worship ***at the head of his bed:*** Greek version reads *and Israel bowed in worship as he leaned on his staff;* cp. Heb 11:21. Jacob thanked the Lord for ensuring that he would be buried with his ancestors in the land of promise (cp. 1 Kgs 1:47).

48:1-22 In blessing Ephraim and Manasseh, Jacob reached out by faith for the promise to be continued, having learned that God's ways are not always the ways of men. Out of Jacob's long life, the writer to the Hebrews selected the blessing of Joseph's sons as his great act of faith (Heb 11:21). As Jacob acted in light of God's will, the primary blessing was again given to the younger instead of the older son, but without scheming and its bitter results.

48:2 ***Jacob:*** Hebrew *Israel;* also in 48:8, 10, 11, 13, 14, 21. See note on 35:21.

48:3-4 ***Jacob*** rehearsed how ***God Almighty*** (Hebrew *El-Shaddai*) had ***appeared*** to him and had promised him Abraham's blessing—innumerable ***descendants*** dwelling in the ***land . . . as an everlasting possession*** (cp. 28:10-22). • ***descendants:*** Literally *seed;* also in 48:19.

48:5-7 Jacob, prompted by his memory of Rachel (see 35:16-20), blessed Joseph by elevating his two sons as coheirs with his other sons—the tribes of Ephraim and Manasseh would have shares along with the other tribes that came from Jacob (see Josh 16–17). Jacob also gave Ephraim, Joseph's younger son, the birthright (see 1 Chr 5:1-2). As a result of this blessing, Ephraim and Manasseh became large and powerful tribes (see Josh 17:14-18).

48:10 As Isaac his father had done, Jacob now gave the blessing when his eyesight was failing (cp. 27:1).

48:14 The ***right hand*** was for the head of the firstborn, and Jacob was deliberately giving that position to the younger son. That pattern was followed for four consecutive generations: Isaac over Ishmael, Jacob over Esau, Joseph over Reuben, and Ephraim over Manasseh. Many years later, Ephraim became the leading tribe in the northern kingdom, superior to the tribe of Manasseh. The entire northern kingdom of Israel was occasionally called Ephraim (see notes on 2 Chr 28:12; Isa 11:13; Ezek 37:16-19; Hos 6:4; Zech 9:10).

48:15-16 In his blessing on Joseph, Jacob used a threefold invocation to describe the God in whom he trusted: (1) ***the God*** who was in covenant with his fathers ***Abraham*** and ***Isaac*** (28:13; 31:5, 42; 32:9; 46:3); (2) ***the God*** who had been his ***shepherd*** (cp. 49:24;

48:16
Gen 22:11; 28:13-15; 31:11
*Heb 11:21
[k]*mal'ak* (4397)
‣Exod 3:2

48:19
Gen 28:14; 46:3

48:20
Ruth 4:11

48:21
Gen 28:15; 46:4; 50:24

48:22
Josh 24:32
John 4:5

49:1
Num 24:14

16 the [k]Angel who has redeemed me from
all harm—
may he bless these boys.
May they preserve my name
and the names of Abraham and Isaac.
And may their descendants multiply
greatly
throughout the earth."

17 But Joseph was upset when he saw that
his father placed his right hand on Ephraim's head. So Joseph lifted it to move it from
Ephraim's head to Manasseh's head. 18 "No,
my father," he said. "This one is the firstborn. Put your right hand on his head."
19 But his father refused. "I know, my son;
I know," he replied. "Manasseh will also become a great people, but his younger brother
will become even greater. And his descendants will become a multitude of nations."
20 So Jacob blessed the boys that day with
this blessing: "The people of Israel will use
your names when they give a blessing. They
will say, 'May God make you as prosperous
as Ephraim and Manasseh.' " In this way, Jacob put Ephraim ahead of Manasseh.
21 Then Jacob said to Joseph, "Look, I am
about to die, but God will be with you and
will take you back to Canaan, the land of
your ancestors. 22 And beyond what I have
given your brothers, I am giving you an extra portion of the land that I took from the
Amorites with my sword and bow."

Jacob Blesses His Sons

49 Then Jacob called together all his
sons and said, "Gather around me,
and I will tell you what will happen to each
of you in the days to come.

Blessing (48:8-20)

Gen 1:22, 28; 9:26-27; 12:2-3; 14:19-20; 24:59-60; 27:1-41; 28:1-4; 32:24-30; 49:1-28
Lev 26:3-13
Num 6:22-27
Deut 7:12-15; 10:8; 28:1-14; 33:1-29
1 Sam 2:20-21
Ps 128:1-6
Matt 5:3-12
Luke 6:27-28
Rom 12:14
Gal 3:13-14
Eph 1:3
Heb 7:6-7
1 Pet 3:9

Jacob adopted Joseph's sons and blessed them (48:3-7), just as his father Isaac had blessed him (27:27-29). Blessing enables, enhances, and enriches life, whereas a curse diminishes it (Lev 26:14-39). Blessing is issued publicly by a benefactor and provides power for prosperity and success. Blessing is essential to covenant relationships in that it guides and motivates the parties to obey the covenant's stipulations (Lev 26:3-13; Deut 28:1-14). Obedience leads to blessing, whereas rebellion brings a curse.

The initial realm of blessing is creation, in which God as Creator is the ultimate granter of blessing for animals (1:22) and humans (1:28; see Ps 104; 128:3-4). Humans also serve as channels of divine blessing. Abraham was called to be a blessing to the nations (12:2-3). The institutions of family (27:27-29), government (1 Kgs 8:14, 44, 52, 66), and religion (14:19; Lev 9:22) are nurtured, commissioned, and purified through blessing. Israel's priests mediated God's blessing to Israel (Num 6:24-26; Deut 10:8).

Three basic characteristics can be observed in OT blessings: (1) They are conveyed from a greater party to a lesser one (32:26; Heb 7:6-7); (2) They are signs of favor that result in well-being and productivity (Deut 28:3-7); and (3) They acknowledge that all power and blessing stems from the Creator. All blessings have their source in God's love (Deut 7:7-8, 12-15).

God's blessings in Genesis are in striking contrast with the pagan religions of antiquity. For pagan religions, fortunes and fertility of flock, family, and fields came about through sympathetic magic in cultic observances at their shrines—profane customs that were designed to induce the deities to act on their behalf so that the cycle of life could be maintained. In Genesis, all of life, fertility, and blessing came by God's decree, for he is the only true and living God.

In the NT, the emphasis of blessing shifts from the material to the spiritual, from the nation to the church, and from the temporal to the eternal (Matt 6:25; Eph 1:3; 1 Pet 3:9). In his death, Jesus bore the consequences of sin's curse (Gal 3:13), established God's kingdom (Matt 3:2; 5:3-20; John 3:3-5), and blessed its citizens with forgiveness of sin (Rom 4:6-25). Now believers are called to bless the world (Luke 6:27-28; Rom 12:14; see also Isa 19:24; Zech 8:13).

Exod 6:6; Ps 23:1; Isa 59:20); and (3) *the Angel* who rescued him *from all harm.* He prayed the same blessings for Joseph's sons.

48:17-19 ***Joseph was upset:*** He expected God to act according to convention, but faith recognizes that God's ways are not man's ways, and God's thoughts are not man's thoughts. It took Jacob a lifetime to learn this lesson, but he did learn it, and here he acted on it.

48:22 ***an extra portion of the land:*** Or *an extra ridge of land.* The meaning of the Hebrew is uncertain. Joseph was later buried at Shechem (Josh 24:32) as a sign that he possessed this bequeathed portion (Hebrew *shekem*) of land. Jacob had apparently conquered this area though the occasion is not mentioned elsewhere.

49:1-28 Jacob, by faith and as God's spokesman, looked forward to Israel's settlement in the land, and beyond that to the glorious future. Here at the end of the patriarchal age, he foretold what would happen to each tribe as he evaluated his sons one by one, just as Noah had done at the end of the primeval era

2 "Come and listen, you sons of Jacob;
listen to Israel, your father.
3 "Reuben, you are my firstborn, my strength,
the child of my vigorous youth.
You are first in rank and first in power.
4 But you are as unruly as a flood,
and you will be first no longer.
For you went to bed with my wife;
you defiled my marriage couch.
5 "Simeon and Levi are two of a kind;
their weapons are instruments of
violence.
6 May I never join in their meetings;
may I never be a party to their plans.
For in their anger they murdered men,
and they crippled oxen just for sport.
7 A curse on their anger, for it is fierce;
a curse on their wrath, for it is cruel.
I will scatter them among the descendants of Jacob;
I will disperse them throughout Israel.

8 "Judah, your brothers will praise you.
You will grasp your enemies by the
neck.
All your relatives will bow before you.
9 Judah, my son, is a young lion
that has finished eating its prey.
Like a lion he crouches and lies down;
like a lioness—who dares to rouse
him?
10 The scepter will not depart from Judah,
nor the ruler's staff from his
descendants,
until the coming of the one to whom it
belongs,
the one whom all nations will honor.
11 He ties his foal to a grapevine,
the colt of his donkey to a choice vine.
He washes his clothes in wine,
his robes in the [a]blood of grapes.
12 His eyes are darker than wine,
and his teeth are whiter than milk.

13 "Zebulun will settle by the seashore
and will be a harbor for ships;
his borders will extend to Sidon.

14 "Issachar is a sturdy donkey,
resting between two saddlepacks.
15 When he sees how good the
countryside is
and how pleasant the land,
he will bend his shoulder to the load
and submit himself to hard labor.

16 "Dan will govern his people,
like any other tribe in Israel.
17 Dan will be a snake beside the road,
a poisonous viper along the path

49:3 Num 26:5; Deut 21:17; Ps 78:51; 105:36
49:4 Gen 35:22; Deut 27:20
49:5 Gen 29:33-34; 34:25-30
49:6 Gen 34:26
49:7 Josh 19:1, 9; 21:1-42
49:8 1 Chr 5:2; Heb 7:14
49:9 Num 24:9; Mic 5:8
49:10 Num 24:17; Ps 2:6-9; 60:7
49:11 Deut 8:7-8; 2 Kgs 18:32; [a]*dam* (1818) ‣Lev 3:17
49:13 Deut 33:18-19
49:15 Josh 19:17-23
49:16 Deut 33:22; Judg 18:26-27
49:19 Deut 33:20
49:20 Deut 33:24-25

(cp. 9:25-27). The character and acts of each ancestor affected the lives of his descendants (Exod 20:5-6; 34:6-7; Num 14:18; Jer 32:18).

49:1-2 Jacob's words were deliberately chosen prophetic oracles. The ***days to come*** refer to the conquest and settlement of the Promised Land, and beyond that to the messianic age. They would all share in the blessing; all the tribes would enter the land with Joshua, but they would not all participate equally.

49:3-4 As firstborn, ***Reuben*** was entitled to be head of the family, but because he had the ungoverned impulses of boiling or turbulent waters (35:22), Jacob prophesied that Reuben would fail in leadership (see 37:21-22, 29; 42:22, 37-38; cp. Judg 5:15-16; 1 Chr 5:1-2).

49:5-7 ***Simeon and Levi*** were violent and lawless; instead of serving justice, they indulged their uncontrolled anger and disregarded life (34:24-29). • ***I will scatter them:*** Simeon's land was largely absorbed into Judah's (Josh 19:1, 9); Levi was given a more honorable future because the Levites became the priestly tribe (see Exod 32:25-29), but they had no region of their own (Josh 21).

49:8-12 The blessing on ***Judah*** commands the most attention. In this oracle, Jacob predicted the fierce, ***lion***-like dominance of Judah over his enemies and over his brothers, who would ***praise*** him (cp. 29:35; see, e.g., Ruth 4:11-12; 1 Sam 18:6-7; Pss 2, 45, 72; Isa 11:1-13).

49:10 This verse anticipates the kingship in ***Judah*** (cp. 17:6, 16; 35:11). Although the birthright blessing went to Joseph, Judah would provide Israel's rulers (see 1 Chr 5:1-2). A long line of kings from Judah would retain ***the scepter***, the symbol of rule; the last king would be ***the one to whom it belongs***, the promised Messiah (see 2 Sam 7:4-16; Pss 2, 45, 60; Isa 11; Ezek 21:26-27; Zech 9:9; Rev 5:5). • ***from his descendants:*** Literally *from between his feet,* taking *between his feet* as a poetic euphemism for reproductive organs. • ***until the coming of the one to whom it belongs*** (Or *until tribute is brought to him and the peoples obey;* traditionally rendered *until Shiloh comes*): These differences arise from ambiguities in the Hebrew text. Rule of Israel *belongs* to Judah's descendant through David's line (2 Sam 7:8-16), and he will eventually rule all nations, as signified by the bringing of *tribute* (see Ps 68:29; 72:8-11; Isa 2:2-4; Eph 4:8-10).

49:11-12 These descriptions envision the abundance of the Messiah's kingdom (see Isa 61:6-7; 65:21-25; Zech 3:10). When the Messiah comes, there will be paradise-like splendor and abundance on the earth. • ***He ties his foal to a grapevine:*** Grapevines will be so abundant that they will be used for hitching posts, and ***wine*** will be as abundant as fresh water (see Amos 9:13-14; Zech 3:10). • The coming one will have ***eyes . . . darker than wine*** and ***teeth . . . whiter than milk:*** He will be vigorous and healthy, as will be the era of his rule. Jesus' miracle of changing water into wine (John 2:1-12), his first sign, was an announcement that the Messiah had come; it was a foretaste of even better things to come.

49:13 The oracle said ***Zebulun*** would dwell by the sea and be a safe harbor, but in the actual settlement they spread inland (see Josh 19:10-16). The oracle did not give specific borders for the tribes.

49:14-15 Like ***a sturdy donkey***, the tribe of ***Issachar*** would be forced to work for others. Issachar was often subjugated by invading armies. • ***saddlepacks:*** Or *sheepfolds,* or *hearths.* The meaning of the Hebrew is uncertain.

49:16-17 ***Dan*** was called to provide justice (*Dan* means "judge"), but the tribe would choose treachery, like ***a snake beside the road*** (see Judg 18).

49:21 Deut 33:23
49:22 Deut 33:13-17
49:23 Gen 37:24
49:24 Ps 132:2, 5; Isa 41:10; 49:26; [b]*ro'eh* (7462) ›Exod 3:1
49:25 Gen 28:13; [c]*shadday* (7706) ›Exod 6:3

that bites the horse's hooves
so its rider is thrown off.
18 I trust in you for salvation, O LORD!
19 "Gad will be attacked by marauding bands,
but he will attack them when they
retreat.
20 "Asher will dine on rich foods
and produce food fit for kings.
21 "Naphtali is a doe set free
that bears beautiful fawns.
22 "Joseph is the foal of a wild donkey,
the foal of a wild donkey at a spring—
one of the wild donkeys on the ridge.
23 Archers attacked him savagely;
they shot at him and harassed him.
24 But his bow remained taut,
and his arms were strengthened
by the hands of the Mighty One of
Jacob,
by the [b]Shepherd, the Rock of Israel.
25 May the God of your father help you;
may the [c]Almighty bless you

Death (49:29-33)

Gen 2:15-17; 3:19; 6:17; 9:5-6; Exod 21:12-17, 28-29; 23:7; 31:14-15; Lev 24:16; Deut 32:39; Job 10:18-22; 19:25-27; Ps 90:1-12; 94:17; Prov 14:32; Eccl 12:1-7; Isa 25:6-9; 26:19; 40:6-8; Dan 12:2-3; Mark 12:26-27; Rom 5:12-17; 1 Cor 15:20-26, 51-58; Rev 20:4-6, 11-15; 21:3-8

As Jacob lay dying in Egypt, he considered two promises regarding his death: that he would die peacefully (46:4) and that he would join his ancestors (49:29, 33). Humans are mortal, and death is the natural end of earthly life (Ps 90:1-6). Human identity began with the earth's dust being animated by the breath of God (2:7). This passive state returns at death as God withdraws his breath and the human body collapses again into dust (3:19; Job 4:19-21; Isa 40:6-8). Human life depends entirely and continuously on the Creator of life—his breath is a gift that sustains us in life for as long as he grants it (Ps 104:29).

Death entered the human race by sin and brought ruin to it; death comes suddenly, bringing mourning and an apparent end to hopes and dreams. Death is the severest penalty in human justice. In the OT, the death penalty was a punishment for murder (9:6; Exod 21:12) or blasphemy (Lev 24:16; John 10:30-31)—violations that threatened the living community.

In the OT, the opposite of "the land of the living" (Ps 27:13) was *Sheol,* the realm of the dead that was shrouded in darkness and silence (Job 10:21-22; Ps 94:17; Jon 2:6). Yet even in death, believers cannot be separated from God's presence (Ps 17:15; 49:15; Prov 14:32). God is sovereign and rules over death (Deut 32:39).

The OT mentions the fact of resurrection (see Job 19:25-27; Isa 25:6-9; 26:19; Dan 12:2). Eventually, God's redeemed people will triumph over death (1 Cor 15:54-55), the last enemy to be destroyed (1 Cor 15:26). Death results from sin (Rom 5:12), and sinners will be punished in the lake of fire, called the second death (Rev 21:8). Christ's death defeated death, making his resurrection the paradigm for all believers (Col 1:18). He is the Lord of the living and of the dead (Rom 14:9).

In Gen 49:29-33, death is joined with hope by faith. In life, the patriarchs were sojourners; in death, they were heirs of the promise and the occupied land. The patriarchs died without having received the promises (Heb 11:39-40), but that was not the end of the story. God's promises to people are not exhausted in this life, for God makes promises that necessitate a resurrection (see Matt 22:21-32 // Mark 12:26-27). The time of death—when the natural inclination is to mourn—should also be the time of the greatest demonstration of faith, for the recipient of God's promises has a hope beyond the grave.

49:18 At this point, Jacob interjected an expression of hope. He may have been indirectly reminding his sons of their need for dependence on the Lord or expressing his hope in the Messiah's reign, when he and his descendants would be rescued from all trouble, grief, and human treachery.

49:19 Three of the six Hebrew words in this verse are wordplays on the name *Gad* ("attack"). Gad will be ***attacked*** by ***marauding bands*** (attackers), but he will ***attack.*** The tribes that settled east of the Jordan River frequently experienced border raids (see Josh 13; 2 Kgs 10:32-33; 1 Chr 5:18-19).

49:20 ***Asher*** would be fertile and productive, providing ***rich foods.*** That tribe settled along the rich northern coast of Canaan.

49:21 ***Naphtali,*** like ***a doe,*** would be a ***free*** mountain people (cp. Judg 5:18). The tribe settled in the hilly region northwest of the Sea of Galilee.

49:22-26 This oracle treats ***Joseph*** more expansively than any of the others, for here the main blessing lay (see 1 Chr 5:1-2). Jacob lavished promises of victory and prosperity on Joseph's two tribes. Ephraimites recorded as victorious in battle include Joshua (Josh 6, 8, 10, 12) and Deborah (Judg 4). Victorious descendants of Manasseh include Gideon (Judg 6–8) and Jephthah (Judg 11:1–12:7).

49:22 Or *Joseph is a fruitful tree, / a fruitful tree beside a spring. / His branches reach over the wall.* The meaning of the Hebrew is uncertain.

49:24-26 Five names for God introduce five blessings; God is the giver of all good things.

49:25 The ***blessings of the heavens above*** meant rain for crops. • The ***blessings of the watery depths*** were streams and wells of water. • The ***blessings of the breasts and womb*** were abundant offspring.

with the blessings of the heavens above,
and blessings of the watery depths
below,
and blessings of the breasts and
womb.
26 May the blessings of your father
surpass the blessings of the ancient
mountains,
reaching to the heights of the eternal
hills.
May these blessings rest on the head of
Joseph,
who is a prince among his brothers.

27 "Benjamin is a ravenous wolf,
devouring his enemies in the morning
and dividing his plunder in the evening."

28 These are the twelve tribes of Israel,
and this is what their father said as he told
his sons good-bye. He [d]blessed each one
with an appropriate message.

Jacob's Death and Burial

29 Then Jacob instructed them, "Soon I will
die and join my ancestors. Bury me with my
father and grandfather in the cave in the
field of Ephron the Hittite. 30 This is the cave
in the field of Machpelah, near Mamre in
Canaan, that Abraham bought from Ephron
the Hittite as a permanent burial site.
31 There Abraham and his wife Sarah are
buried. There Isaac and his wife, Rebekah,
are buried. And there I buried Leah. 32 It is
the plot of land and the cave that my grandfather Abraham bought from the Hittites."

33 When Jacob had finished this charge
to his sons, he drew his feet into the bed,
breathed his last, and joined his ancestors
in death.

50 Joseph threw himself on his father and wept over him and kissed
him. 2 Then Joseph told the physicians who
served him to embalm his father's body;
so Jacob was embalmed. 3 The embalming
process took the usual forty days. And the
Egyptians mourned his death for seventy
days.

4 When the period of mourning was over,
Joseph approached Pharaoh's advisers and
said, "Please do me this favor and speak to
Pharaoh on my behalf. 5 Tell him that my
father made me swear an oath. He said to
me, 'Listen, I am about to die. Take my body
back to the land of Canaan, and bury me in
the tomb I prepared for myself.' So please
allow me to go and bury my father. After his
burial, I will return without delay."

6 Pharaoh agreed to Joseph's request. "Go
and bury your father, as he made you promise," he said. 7 So Joseph went up to bury his
father. He was accompanied by all of Pharaoh's officials, all the senior members of
Pharaoh's household, and all the senior officers of Egypt. 8 Joseph also took his entire
household and his brothers and their households. But they left their little children and
flocks and herds in the land of Goshen. 9 A
great number of chariots and charioteers
accompanied Joseph.

10 When they arrived at the threshing
floor of Atad, near the Jordan River, they
held a very great and solemn memorial service, with a seven-day period of mourning
for Joseph's father. 11 The local residents,
the Canaanites, watched them mourning at
the threshing floor of Atad. Then they renamed that place (which is near the Jordan)
Abel-mizraim, for they said, "This is a place
of deep mourning for these Egyptians."

49:26 Deut 33:15-16
49:27 Deut 33:12
49:28 [d]*barak* (1288) ‣Num 6:23
49:29 Gen 23:16-20; 25:8-9
49:31 Gen 23:19; 25:9; 35:29
49:33 Gen 25:8 Acts 7:15
50:1 Gen 46:4
50:2 Gen 50:26
50:3 Num 20:29 Deut 34:8
50:5 Gen 47:29-31
50:8 Gen 45:10
50:9 Gen 41:43

49:26 *of the ancient mountains:* Or *of my ancestors.* • ***Joseph . . . is a prince among his brothers:*** A reflection of both his character and his position.

49:27 The oracle about *Benjamin* describes a violent tribe (see Judg 20; 1 Sam 9:1-2; 19:10; 22:17).

49:28 These prophecies are broad in scope, foretelling the future of the different tribes in general terms. Individuals, by faith and obedience, could find great blessing from God regardless of what happened to their clan.

49:29-33 ***Bury me with my father:*** This grave in the land of Canaan represented hope for the future (cp. 47:29-30). Others buried at the cave of Machpelah near Hebron were Sarah (23:19), Abraham (25:7-9), Isaac (35:27-29), Rebekah, and Leah.

49:33 Jacob died at the age of 147 (47:28), bringing his life of struggle and sorrow to an end. Jacob had always had an unquenchable desire for God's blessing. He had a deep piety that habitually relied on God despite all else. In the end, he died a man of genuine faith. He learned where real blessings come from, and through his faith would be able to hand these on to his sons (Heb 11:21).

50:1-6 As with his father and grandfather, Jacob's death brought the end of an era.

50:2 *Jacob:* Hebrew *Israel;* see note on 35:21. His body was *embalmed* for burial in typical Egyptian fashion.

50:3 *The Egyptians mourned* for Jacob *for seventy days*, just two days short of the mourning period for a pharaoh. This showed the great respect that the Egyptians had for Joseph.

50:4-6 *Joseph* needed Pharaoh's permission to leave his post temporarily to *bury* his *father* in *Canaan*. Pharaoh readily granted this freedom to the former slave.

50:7-9 This was Joseph's first return to his homeland in thirty-nine years. The trip was temporary. Centuries later, the family of Israel would permanently leave Egypt, taking Joseph's bones with them for burial in the land of promise (see 50:25).

50:10-13 This journey into Canaan was made in sorrow to bury a man; the next journey into the land would be to live there. • *Abel-mizraim* means "mourning of the Egyptians."

50:12
Gen 49:29
50:13
Gen 23:16-18
50:15
Gen 42:21-22
50:16
Gen 49:29
50:17
Gen 45:5, 7
Matt 6:14
Luke 6:27
Rom 12:19
[e]*nasa'* (5375)
‣ Exod 10:17
[f]*pesha'* (6588)
‣ Exod 34:7
50:18
Gen 37:7-10
50:19
Gen 30:2
50:20
Gen 37:26-27
50:21
Gen 45:11
50:24
Gen 13:15; 28:13
50:25
Exod 13:19
Josh 24:32
Heb 11:22
50:26
Exod 1:6
[g]*'aron* (0727)
‣ Exod 25:22

12So Jacob's sons did as he had commanded them. 13They carried his body to
the land of Canaan and buried him in the
cave in the field of Machpelah, near Mamre.
This is the cave that Abraham had bought
as a permanent burial site from Ephron the
Hittite.

Joseph Reassures His Brothers

14After burying Jacob, Joseph returned to
Egypt with his brothers and all who had accompanied him to his father's burial. 15But
now that their father was dead, Joseph's
brothers became fearful. "Now Joseph will
show his anger and pay us back for all the
wrong we did to him," they said.

16So they sent this message to Joseph: "Before your father died, he instructed us 17to
say to you: 'Please [e]forgive your brothers for
the great wrong they did to you—for their
[f]sin in treating you so cruelly.' So we, the servants of the God of your father, beg you to
[e]forgive our [f]sin." When Joseph received the
message, he broke down and wept. 18Then
his brothers came and threw themselves
down before Joseph. "Look, we are your
slaves!" they said.

19But Joseph replied, "Don't be afraid of
me. Am I God, that I can punish you? 20You
intended to harm me, but God intended it all
for good. He brought me to this position so
I could save the lives of many people. 21No,
don't be afraid. I will continue to take care
of you and your children." So he reassured
them by speaking kindly to them.

The Death of Joseph

22So Joseph and his brothers and their families continued to live in Egypt. Joseph lived
to the age of 110. 23He lived to see three generations of descendants of his son Ephraim,
and he lived to see the birth of the children
of Manasseh's son Makir, whom he claimed
as his own.

24"Soon I will die," Joseph told his brothers, "but God will surely come to help you
and lead you out of this land of Egypt. He
will bring you back to the land he solemnly
promised to give to Abraham, to Isaac, and
to Jacob."

25Then Joseph made the sons of Israel
swear an oath, and he said, "When God
comes to help you and lead you back, you
must take my bones with you." 26So Joseph
died at the age of 110. The Egyptians embalmed him, and his body was placed in a
[g]coffin in Egypt.

50:15-18 The *brothers* pleaded for Joseph's forgiveness, referring to themselves as Joseph's *slaves* (cp. 37:7; 44:16, 33). The brothers were afraid that Joseph's earlier reconciliation with them had been motivated only by his desire to see his father again. With neither Jacob nor Pharaoh to restrain him, they feared that he might now take revenge on them. But *Joseph . . . wept* because they still feared reprisal.

50:19-21 Joseph reassured his brothers that God planned to fulfill the promised blessing (cp. 45:5, 7-9), and he promised kindness and provision (cp. 45:11).

50:22-23 Joseph lived to see his great-great-grandchildren by Ephraim, and his great-grandchildren by Manasseh—a sign of God's blessing (see Ps 128:6; Prov 17:6; Isa 53:10).

50:23 *whom he claimed as his own* (literally *who were born on Joseph's knees*): Placing them on his knees at their birth was a symbolic act signifying that they came from him and belonged to him (cp. Job 3:12).

50:24-25 *God will surely come to help you* (literally *visit you*): These words of Joseph, given twice, summarize the hope expressed throughout both the OT and NT. God's visitation in the person of the Messiah, the offspring of Abraham, would bring the curse to an end and establish the long-awaited blessing of God in a new creation. The company of the faithful would wait in expectation for that to happen. • Like his father before him, Joseph made his brothers promise that his bones would be taken out of Egypt when God would come to take them (*to help you and lead you . . . back*) to Canaan (see Exod 13:19; Josh 24:32; Heb 11:22).

50:26 Joseph's death signified the end of his generation (see notes on 25:7-8; 35:1-29; 35:27-29) and of the patriarchal age. From this point forward, God dealt with Israel as a nation. • Joseph's body was kept in Egypt as a pledge of hope for slaves awaiting the Promised Land (see Exod 13:19; Heb 11:39-40). He was eventually buried in Shechem (see Josh 24:32), where Jacob had originally sent him (37:13).

THE CHRONOLOGY OF
Abraham to Joshua

Serious study of the chronology of Israel's early history is rewarding, in spite of serious challenges. The Bible provides some information about the chronology of events and the ages of people. However, not enough information is available for us to be certain about the dates for various events and people's lives. Instead, we can discern a coherent general picture of how Israel's early history fits into the history of surrounding nations.

DATE OF THE EXODUS (1446 OR 1270 BC) The date of Israel's exodus from Egypt is the key question in determining Israel's early chronology. The Bible's focus on sequence of events and their meanings rather than a strict chronology makes it difficult, however, to assign exact dates for the Exodus. A number of chronological indicators help point the way.

First, according to 1 Kgs 14:25-26, Pharaoh Shishak raided Judah in the fifth year of King Rehoboam's reign. From sources outside the Bible, this date is known to be 926 BC. Earlier dates in Israel's history, such as the year Solomon began building the Temple (967 BC) and the date of the Exodus, are calculated by working backward from this fixed point and attempting to harmonize as much data as possible.

A second chronological indicator for the date of the Exodus is the "new king" who "knew nothing about Joseph" (Exod 1:8). This comment most likely signals the arrival of a new dynasty. In the 1700s BC, foreigners from Asia began migrating to Egypt. In 1648 BC, one group of such foreigners, the Hyksos, invaded Lower Egypt and gained control of the region. Joseph and Jacob very likely entered Egypt (Gen 39, 46) shortly before or during the Hyksos period. The Hyksos ruled until 1540 BC, when Pharaoh Ahmose (1550–1525 BC) expelled them. Ahmose and the pharaohs who followed him were probably the dynasty described by Exodus 1:8.

A third chronological indicator is the Merneptah Stela, an Egyptian monument dated to roughly 1209 BC, which mentions a clash with the Israelites in the southern part of Palestine. This is the first clear mention of Israel outside the Bible.

Based on the available data, two dates for Israel's exodus from Egypt appear to be possible: an earlier date around 1446 BC and a later date around 1270 BC.

3300 BC | 3200 | 3100 | 3000 | 2900

MESOPOTAMIA

EARLY BRONZE AGE (3300–2000 BC)

EGYPT

PREDYNASTIC PERIOD (4000–3000 BC)

ARCHAIC PERIOD / DYNASTIES 1–2 (3000–2700 BC)

Scenario 1: Early Exodus (about 1446 BC) The traditional scenario places the date of the Exodus around 1446 BC. According to 1 Kgs 6:1, Solomon began construction of the Temple in the fourth year of his reign (967 BC), 480 years after the Exodus from Egypt. If the number 480 refers to calendar years, then the date of the Exodus was about 1446 BC, and Israel's entry to Canaan was around 1406 BC. Archaeologists have discovered the Amarna letters, a cache of letters from Canaanite city chieftains asking Pharaoh Akhenaten (about 1352–1336 BC) to help them fight against certain rabble who were attacking them. This is a possible reference to the Israelites and would support the early dates for the Exodus and conquest. Additionally, in about 1100 BC Jephthah described Israel as having inhabited the Promised Land for 300 years (see Judg 11:26; cp. Num 21:21-35). The early date seems to fit best with the Bible's own chronological information. A date near 1446 BC, therefore, has long been accepted.

Scenario 2: Late Exodus (about 1270 BC) The late Exodus scenario places the Exodus from Egypt approximately 300 years before the dedication of Solomon's temple in 967 BC, early in the reign of Pharaoh Rameses II (1279–1213 BC). The city of Rameses, which the Israelites helped build (Exod 1:11), was named after this Pharaoh, and there is evidence of significant construction activity dating to the early 1200s BC at the site. Additionally, archaeologists working in Palestine between World Wars I and II reported that they were unable to find any evidence of the conquest taking place in the early 1300s BC, as required by the early

	Scenario 1: Early Exodus (1446 BC)		Scenario 2: Late Exodus (about 1270 BC)	
Description	**Hebrew (MT)**	**Greek (LXX)**	**Hebrew (MT)**	**Greek (LXX)**
Abraham is born	2166 BC	1951 BC	1990 BC	1775 BC
Abraham travels to Canaan	2091 BC	1876 BC	1915 BC	1700 BC
Jacob travels to Egypt	1876 BC	1661 BC	1700 BC	1485 BC
Hyksos (foreigners) rule Egypt	**1648–1540 BC**	**1648–1540 BC**	**1648–1540 BC**	**1648–1540 BC**
Moses is born (80 years before the Exodus, Exod 7:7)	1526 BC	1526 BC	1350 BC	1350 BC
The Exodus	1446 BC	1446 BC	1270 BC	1270 BC
Israel begins the conquest of Canaan (40 years after the Exodus, Num 14:33-34; 32:13)	1406 BC	1406 BC	1230 BC	1230 BC
Solomon begins building the Temple (1 Kgs 6:1)	**967 BC**	**967 BC**	**967 BC**	**967 BC**

▲ **Scenarios: Dates for the Patriarchs.** The dates of various key events from Abraham to Solomon depend on the date of the Exodus and the text of Exod 12:40. Each of the two scenarios for the date of the Exodus is shown with two columns of dates: one following the Hebrew text of Exod 12:40, the other following the Greek text. Fixed points of reference are shown in bold type; all other dates are relative to these events and the date of the Exodus.

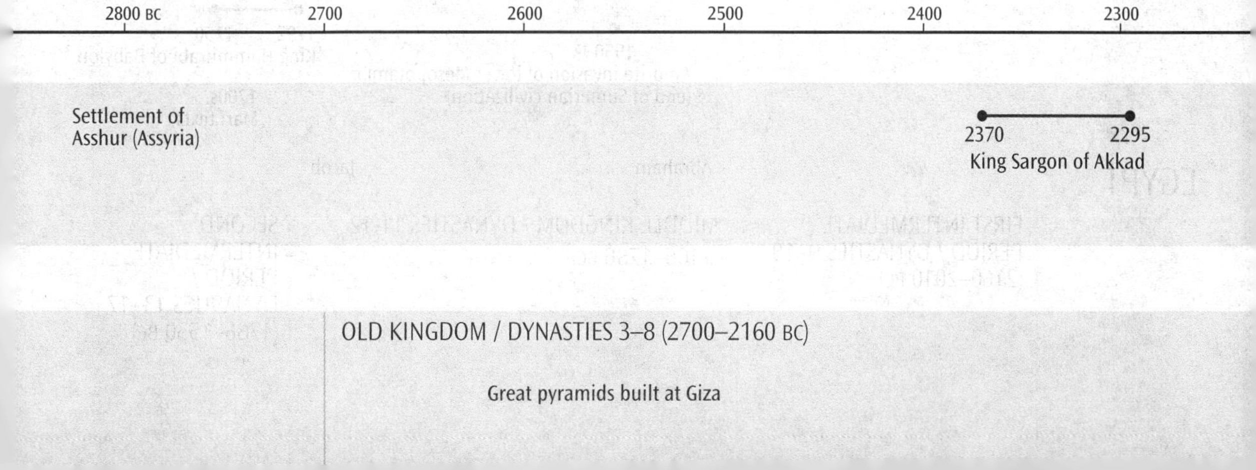

date. They did, however, claim to have found evidence of conquest and increased settlement activity in the late 1200s BC. If these findings are accurate and reflect Israelite activity in the Promised Land, they would support the idea that the Exodus occurred around 1270 BC. Those who opt for this later date contend that the number 480 in 1 Kgs 6:1 is a symbolic number (12 generations x 40 years to symbolize a generation); in that case, the actual length of time would have been closer to 300 years (12 generations x 25 years, the approximate length of an actual generation).

Egyptian Rulers, Dynasties 18–19

Dates BC*	Ruler
	Dynasty 18
1550–1525	Ahmose
1525–1504	Amenhotep I
1504–1492	Thutmose I
1492–1479	Thutmose II
1479–1457	Hatshepsut
1479–1425	Thutmose III
1427–1400	Amenhotep II
1400–1390	Thutmose IV
1390–1352	Amenhotep III
1352–1336	Amenhotep IV (Akhenaten)
1336–1327	Tutankhamen
1327–1323	Ay
1323–1295	Horemheb
	Dynasty 19
1295–1294	Rameses I
1294–1279	Seti I
1279–1213	Rameses II
1213–1203	Merneptah

* All Egyptian dates according to K. A. Kitchen, "Egypt, History of (Chronology)" in *Anchor Bible Dictionary*, vol. II, p. 329.

DATES FOR THE PATRIARCHS

Genesis provides the relative ages of Israel's patriarchs, Abraham to Joseph, but it does not fix absolute dates for their lives (see "Abraham" at Gen 11:26–25:11, p. 46; and "Jacob" at Gen 27:1–35:29, p. 76). Israel's patriarchs (Abraham, Isaac, and Jacob) were powerful family chiefs who moved from place to place. Unlike the leaders of empires who created permanent records, the patriarchs did not have palaces or libraries in which to deposit records. Also, the climate of Palestine is not favorable to the preservation of documents.

The date of the Exodus is therefore a key for calculating dates for the patriarchs. Calculations also take into account the lifespan of each patriarch; the chronological notations in Gen 12:4; 21:5; 25:26; 47:9 suggest that the patriarchs spent 215 years in Canaan.

The length of Israel's stay in Egypt is an additional factor, and here there is a difference in texts. The Hebrew Masoretic Text (MT) for Exod 12:40 says that Israel spent 430 years in Egypt, from the year that Jacob entered Egypt to the year of Israel's Exodus. However, the early Greek OT translation (the Septuagint, or LXX) and the Samaritan Pentateuch (another significant manuscript) both say that the

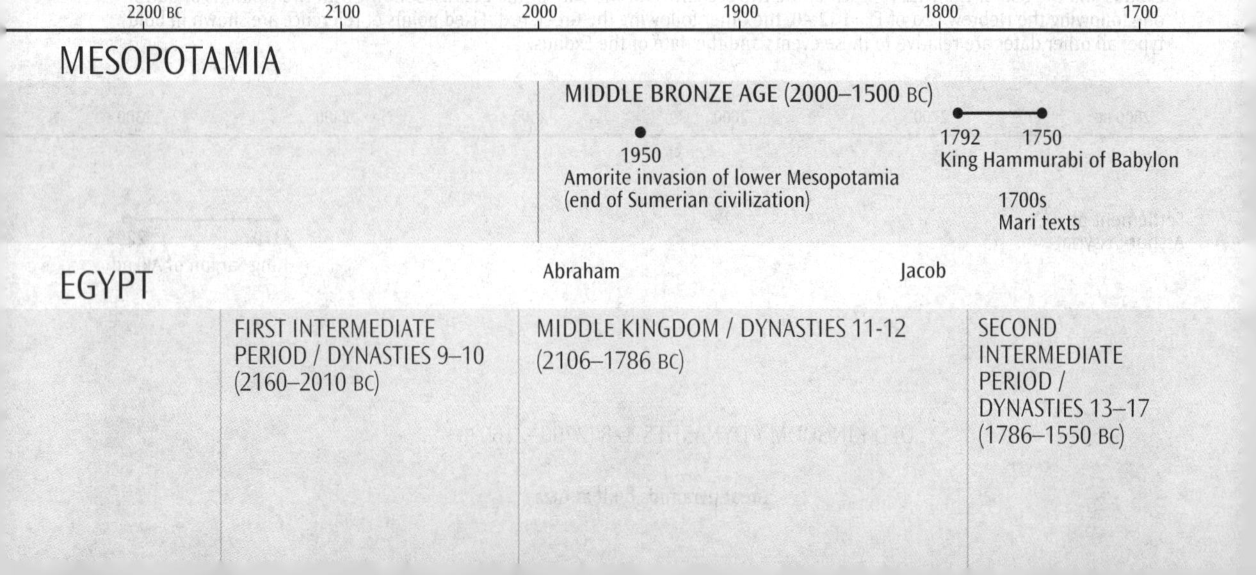

430-year period mentioned in Exodus 12:40 includes the time the Israelites spent in both Canaan and Egypt (a chronology that Paul apparently followed; see Gal 3:17). This chronology would reduce the time spent in Egypt to 215 years. Various biblical statements that Israel was in Egypt for 400 years or four generations (Gen 15:13-16; cp. Exod 6:16-20; Num 3:17-19; 26:58-59; 1 Chr 6:1-3; Acts 7:6) could support the reading of either the Hebrew or the Greek text. The chart on p. 119 provides a sense of how these variants play out.

CONCLUSION

Fitting all the data together is challenging. Still, although the two scenarios for dating the Exodus result in a 176-year difference, the middle two scenarios in the chart on p. 119 (Scenario 1 with the Greek text of Exod 12:40 and Scenario 2 with the Hebrew text) yield dates for Abraham and Jacob that are remarkably similar. Both of these scenarios also provide dates for the patriarchs that correlate well with information known from sources outside the Bible.

While the dates of the Exodus or the patriarchs cannot be determined with absolute certainty, perhaps they were never intended to be. The biblical authors did not set out to provide a complete chronological record. What we do have is an excellent correlation between Israel's historical records and those of the surrounding cultures.

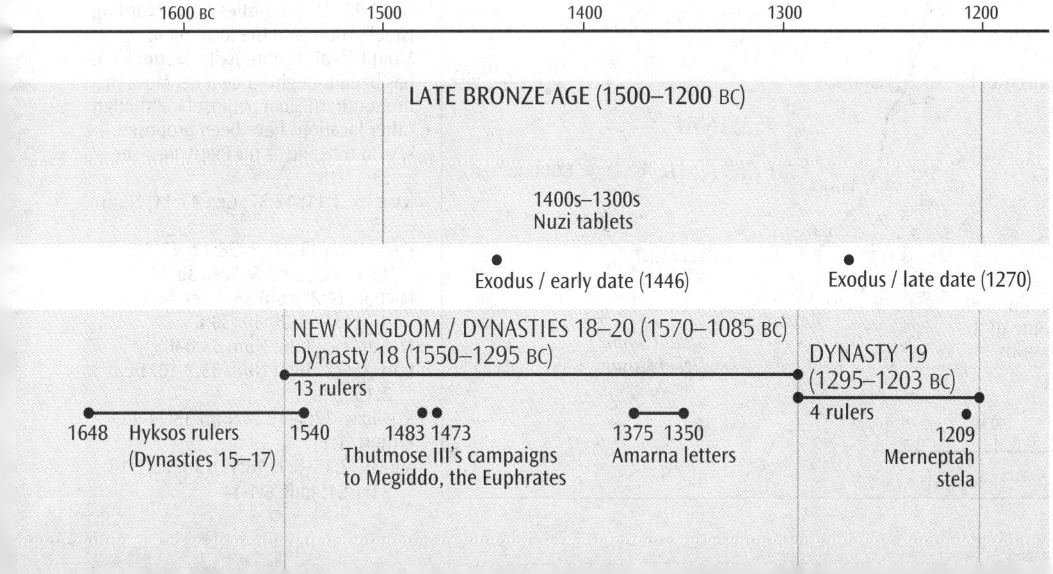

THE BOOK OF EXODUS

What does it mean to be in a relationship with God, the ultimate being in the universe? How does one establish that relationship? What is that relationship like, and what does it take to stay in it? These are questions that people around the world have been asking since the beginning of time. The book of Exodus provided the ancient Israelites with answers to such questions, revealing not only what was required of them in a relationship with God, but also what God had graciously done to make that relationship possible.

SETTING

The Exodus occurred sometime between 1450 and 1250 BC, when Egypt was arguably the greatest military and cultural power in the world. During Egypt's 18th dynasty (1550–1295 BC) the pharaohs built an empire beyond Egypt's borders, extending its control far into the north, up the Canaanite coast, and far to the south along the Nile. This imperial thrust seems to have fueled a megalomaniacal building program. As the house of the pharaoh grew in power, so the god of the royal house, Amon-Re, gained dominance. The land remained staunchly polytheistic, but worship of Amon-Re seems to have surpassed devotion to all other gods.

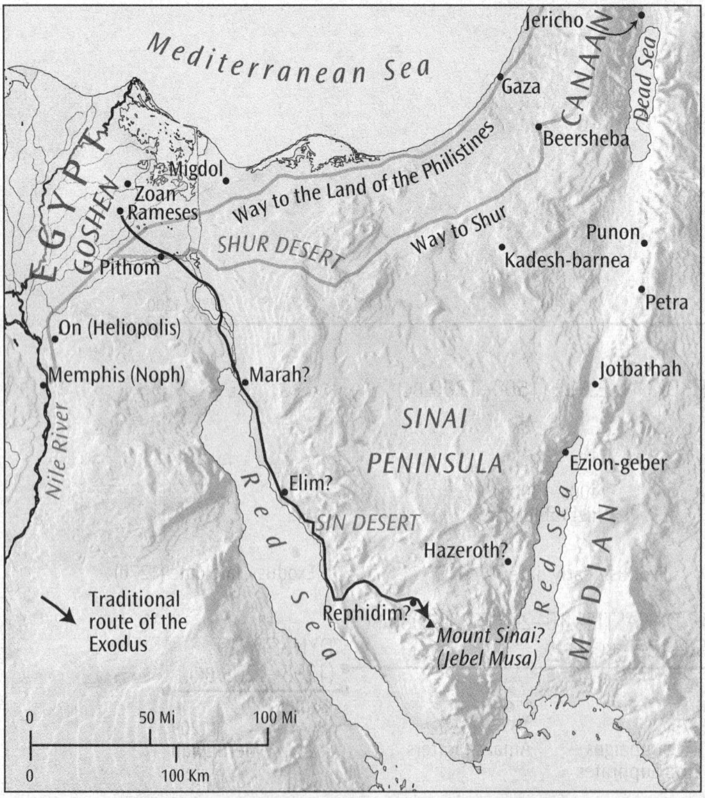

The Exodus: Egypt to Sinai. When the Israelites left Egypt following the first Passover, they traveled through the RED SEA and the SINAI PENINSULA to MOUNT SINAI. There they stayed for a full year (19:1; Num 10:11-12). Uncertainties exist regarding Israel's route and the location of Mount Sinai. Traditionally, Mount Sinai has been thought to be Jebel Musa in the southern Sinai peninsula, although other locations have been proposed.

WAY TO THE LAND OF THE PHILISTINES see 13:17-18

RAMESES 1:11; 12:37; Gen 47:11; Num 33:3

ZOAN Num 13:22; Ps 78:12, 43; Isa 19:11, 13; 30:3-5; Ezek 30:14

MIGDOL 14:2; Num 33:7; Jer 44:1; 46:14; Ezek 29:10; 30:6

MARAH 15:23-26; Num 33:8-9

ELIM 15:27; 16:1; Num 33:9-10; Deut 2:15

REPHIDIM 17:1–19:2; Num 33:14-15

PITHOM 1:11

MIDIAN 2:15–3:1; 18:1; Num 25:1-18; 31:1-54; Judg 6:1-14

It was during this period that the Israelites departed from Egypt. God did not sneak his people out during a time of Egyptian weakness; he led them forth when Egyptian strength was at its height.

SUMMARY

The term *Exodus* derives from the Greek word *exodos*, which means "the way out." Chapters 1–15 are about the Hebrews' "way out" of Egypt. The additional matters covered in the book (chs 16–40) reveal that the Hebrew people needed more than rescue from bondage in Egypt. They needed a way out of their sin and a way into fellowship with God. Exodus addresses Israel's great needs: to be set free from bondage (chs 1–15), to know who God is and what he is like through the covenant at Sinai (chs 16–24), and to experience fellowship with God through the Tabernacle (chs 25–40). All of us have the same need to be set free, to know God, and to experience fellowship with him.

OUTLINE

1:1–18:27
The Exodus Rescue: God's Power and Provision

19:1–24:18
The Sinai Covenant: God's Principles

25:1–40:38
The Tabernacle: God's Presence

AUTHORSHIP

Moses is traditionally considered the author of the Pentateuch (Genesis—Deuteronomy), though many scholars believe he was not. See "Introduction to the Pentateuch: Authorship," p. 11.

THE DATE OF THE EXODUS

Considerable debate revolves around the date of the Exodus. The evidence points to two main possibilities—an early date of about 1446 BC and a later date of about 1270 BC. See "Chronology: Abraham to Joshua," p. 118.

MEANING AND MESSAGE

The opening chapters of Genesis depict a serious problem: God made the world and human beings for blessing (Gen 1:27-28), but the world fell under a curse. Humanity had become deeply corrupted (Gen 6:5), alienated from their Creator (Gen 3:23-24) and from one another (Gen 4:14). Death, violence, and confusion were rampant (Gen 4:8, 23-24; 11:9). Was there a way back to the blessing that God originally intended?

In Gen 12–50, God's plan to restore the world begins to unfold. God chose Abraham and his descendants to be in a special covenant relationship with him, promising to make them into a prosperous nation through which the entire world would be blessed (Gen 12:1-3). Abraham believed God despite the fact that his wife seemed hopelessly barren (Gen 15:6), and God soon began to fulfill his promises (Gen 21:1-7).

As the book of Exodus begins, however, the validity of God's promises to Abraham is in question. Yes, Abraham's descendants had grown to a great number, but they were now slaves in Egypt, and pharaoh, the mightiest

TIMELINE

2166 / 1990 BC*
Abraham is born

2091 / 1915 BC
Abraham moves to Canaan

1876 / 1661 BC
Jacob moves to Egypt

1526 / 1350 BC
Moses is born

1446 / 1270 BC
Israel leaves Egypt (the Exodus), moves to Mount Sinai

1406 / 1230 BC
Moses dies, Israel enters Canaan

** The two dates harmonize with the traditional "early" chronology and a more recent "late" chronology of the Exodus. All dates are approximate. Please see "Chronology: Abraham to Joshua," p. 118.*

king in the world, was committed to keeping them subjugated. As for the Promised Land, Abraham and his descendants had never actually owned any of it except for a burial plot (Gen 23). How would a group of slaves, slated to be absorbed into the Egyptian underclass, ever inherit the Promised Land and become a blessing to the world? Could God keep his promises? Did he even want to keep them? Did he really care for the Israelites, and did he even know what they were going through? If not, then the promises of Genesis were of no real value.

In answering those questions, Exodus moves us far down the road to understanding who God is. God really does know our situation, and he values us. The Lord is in an altogether different category from "all other gods" (18:11). He is revealed in Exodus as the greatest being in existence (3:5-6, 14-15; 6:3), superior to human kings who think of themselves as gods and to all the forces of nature. He is the one true God.

The people of Israel had spent some 400 years absorbing Egypt's mistaken pagan beliefs. Now they would have to unlearn them: There are not many gods, only one. God is not the same as the natural world around them; he stands apart from the world, which he created. God cannot be manipulated by magic. Existence is not defined by an eternal struggle between positive and negative forces. God is holy, absolutely other, profoundly ethical in all of his relationships, passionately loyal to his creatures, and desiring to do good for them (34:5-6).

God used a covenant (chs 19–23) to teach his people who he is and what their relationship with him should be like (see "The Purpose of God's Covenant" at 19:3-6, p. 157). The covenant teaches us God's ethical nature. In the ancient world, ethics and religion were largely unrelated (see "Ancient Law Codes" at 20:1–23:33, p. 163). By contrast, most of the requirements of God's covenant have to do with how people treat one another (see 20:3-17). Those who are in a covenant relationship with God must treat one another ethically.

God rescues his people and calls us into a life of holiness in order that we may have a living, personal relationship with him. The Tabernacle chapters (chs 25–40) are not an add-on; they are what the Exodus was all about. Yes, God would keep his promise of taking the people to the Promised Land, but his goal was for them to live in his presence without being destroyed by his holiness, and that is what happened (40:34-38). Salvation is not merely the forgiveness of sins. God's goal for us is that, having been rescued from the bondage of sin, we might live daily in the glory of his presence and manifest his holy character.

Few events in history have had such far-reaching effects as Israel's Exodus out of Egypt. The Exodus event lies at the very heart of the Old Testament. The Exodus is to the Old Covenant what the resurrection is to the New.

PAGE H. KELLEY
Exodus: Called for Redemptive Mission

FURTHER READING

R. ALAN COLE
Exodus (1973)

JOHN I. DURHAM
Exodus (1987)

PETER ENNS
Exodus (2001)

ALEC MOTYER
The Message of Exodus (2004)

JOHN OSWALT
Exodus in *Cornerstone Biblical Commentary*, vol. 1 (2008)

1:1
Gen 46:8-27
1:5
Gen 46:26-27
1:7
Gen 35:11-12; 47:27
*Acts 7:17
1:8
Acts 7:18-19
[a]*melek* (4428)
‣1 Sam 18:6
1:9-10
Ps 105:24-25
Acts 7:18-19

1. THE EXODUS RESCUE: GOD'S POWER AND PROVISION (1:1–18:27)

The Need for Rescue (1:1-22)

1 These are the names of the sons of Israel
(that is, Jacob) who moved to Egypt with
their father, each with his family: 2 Reuben,
Simeon, Levi, Judah, 3 Issachar, Zebulun, Benjamin, 4 Dan, Naphtali, Gad, and Asher. 5 In
all, Jacob had seventy descendants in Egypt,
including Joseph, who was already there.
6 In time, Joseph and all of his brothers
died, ending that entire generation. 7 But
their descendants, the Israelites, had many
children and grandchildren. In fact, they
multiplied so greatly that they became extremely powerful and filled the land.
8 Eventually, a new [a]king came to power
in Egypt who knew nothing about Joseph
or what he had done. 9 He said to his people,
"Look, the people of Israel now outnumber
us and are stronger than we are. 10 We must
make a plan to keep them from growing
even more. If we don't, and if war breaks
out, they will join our enemies and fight

PHARAOH (1:8-22)

Exod 2:14-15, 23; 5:1–15:21

"Pharaoh" is an Egyptian word meaning "great house." It refers to the royal palace and is also used as a title for the king of Egypt. Two Pharaohs appear in the book of Exodus. The first was king when Moses was born. Out of fear, he ordered the murder of all Hebrew baby boys. Moses not only escaped death, but was raised by Pharaoh's daughter in the king's palace! This Pharaoh died after Moses had fled from Egypt (2:23).

Moses and Aaron later confronted the new Pharaoh who came to power. This Pharaoh was determined to prevent the Israelites from leaving Egypt; he remained stubborn even when confronted with God's power. The Bible describes his hardhearted unwillingness to change (8:32; 9:12, 34; see "A Hardened Heart" at 14:4, 8, p. 149; cp. Rom 1:18-32).

As king, the Pharaoh personified the rule of the gods over Egypt, which gave him absolute authority. The plagues were God's attacks on the false gods of Egypt (12:12). The final plague—the death of the firstborn—was an attack on Pharaoh's household. This climactic plague convinced Pharaoh to let Israel go, but after the Israelites left, Pharaoh again changed his mind. He chased them until he had cornered them at the Red Sea. This event—the rescue of the defenseless Israelites and the destruction of the powerful Egyptians—is among the most dramatic rescues recorded in the OT. The Lord revealed himself at the Red Sea as a warrior who fought for his people (15:3).

Neither of the Pharaohs in Exodus is mentioned by name, probably in keeping with Egyptian practice. However, speculation abounds regarding the identity of the Pharaoh of the Exodus. If the Exodus took place in the 1400s BC, the Pharaoh might have been Thutmose III (about 1479–1425 BC). If the Exodus occurred in the 1200s BC, the Pharaoh of the Exodus might have been Rameses II (about 1279–1213 BC). See further "Old Testament Chronology: Abraham to Joshua," p. 118.

1:1-22 The need for deliverance was obviously related to the Israelites' condition (***the Egyptians worked the people of Israel without mercy***, 1:13); it also was related to promises God had made to the patriarchs years earlier. The Lord had promised Abraham that his descendants would be a great nation, living in freedom in the land of Canaan. At this point, Abraham's descendants were slaves in Egypt under a pharaoh determined to decimate them as a people. God would have to rescue the people if his promises were to be kept.

1:1 *Israel* is the name God had given to ***Jacob***, son of Isaac and grandson of Abraham (Gen 32:28). • Many years earlier, Jacob and his family had ***moved to Egypt***, seeking refuge from severe drought (see Gen 46:1-7). Thanks to Joseph's wisdom and leadership (see Gen 41:25-49), a steady grain supply had been stored (see Gen 42:1-2; 45:5-7).

1:2-4 For the births of Jacob's sons, see Gen 29:31–30:24; 35:16-18.

1:5 ***seventy descendants:*** The Dead Sea Scrolls and the Greek version read *seventy-five;* see notes on Gen 46:27. The larger number might include the five sons of Ephraim and Manasseh (Num 26:29, 35). • Jacob's eleventh son, ***Joseph***, had been sold into Egyptian slavery by his jealous brothers (Gen 37:18-28). God accomplished good for his people in spite of the brothers' sin. With Joseph present in Egypt, God could use him to save the lives of the chosen people from the famine that would have destroyed them (Gen 42:1-2; 50:19-20).

1:6-7 The long sojourn of Jacob's family in Egypt was part of a divine design. God had told Abraham that his descendants could not receive the land of Canaan for 400 years—until the sin of the Canaanites had come to its full fruition (Gen 15:13-16). Even in Egypt, God's promises were at work, and the ***descendants*** of aged Abraham and barren Sarah ***multiplied . . . greatly*** as God had said (Gen 15:5), because God blessed them (Ps 105:24).

1:8-10 From about 1650 until about 1550 BC, the northern part of Egypt, where the Israelites lived, was ruled by Semitic invaders that the Egyptians called "shepherd kings," or *Hyksos.* Many scholars believe that these kings were sympathetic to the Israelites and that the Israelites may even have been allied with them. When these invaders were finally expelled about 1540 BC, it is easy to imagine that the new rulers (Egypt's 18th Dynasty) were very suspicious of any Semites, including the Israelites, who remained in the country.

1:10 The people whom Pharaoh referred to as ***our enemies*** would almost

against us. Then they will escape from the country."

11So the Egyptians made the Israelites their slaves. They appointed brutal slave drivers over them, hoping to wear them down with crushing labor. They forced them to build the cities of Pithom and Rameses as supply centers for the king. 12But the more the Egyptians oppressed them, the more the Israelites multiplied and spread, and the more alarmed the Egyptians became. 13So the Egyptians worked the people of Israel without mercy. 14They made their lives bitter, forcing them to mix mortar and make bricks and do all the work in the fields. They were ruthless in all their demands.

15Then Pharaoh, the king of Egypt, gave this order to the Hebrew midwives, Shiphrah and Puah: 16"When you help the Hebrew women as they give birth, watch as they deliver. If the baby is a boy, kill him; if it is a girl, let her live." 17But because the midwives [b]feared God, they refused to obey the king's orders. They allowed the boys to live, too.

18So the king of Egypt called for the midwives. "Why have you done this?" he demanded. "Why have you allowed the boys to live?"

19"The Hebrew women are not like the Egyptian women," the midwives replied. "They are more vigorous and have their babies so quickly that we cannot get there in time."

20So God was good to the midwives, and the Israelites continued to multiply, growing more and more powerful. 21And because the midwives feared God, he gave them families of their own.

22Then Pharaoh gave this order to all his people: "Throw every newborn Hebrew boy into the Nile River. But you may let the girls live."

Preparation of a Rescuer (2:1-25)

The Birth of Moses

2 About this time, a man and woman from the tribe of Levi got married. 2The woman became pregnant and gave birth to a son. She saw that he was a special baby and kept him hidden for three months. 3But when she could no longer hide him, she got a basket made of papyrus reeds and waterproofed it with tar and pitch. She put the baby in the basket and laid it among the

1:11 Exod 2:11; 3:7
1:14 Exod 2:23
1:16 Acts 7:19
1:17 [b]*yare'* (3372) ›Lev 19:14
1:19 Josh 2:4-6; 2 Sam 17:20
1:20 Exod 1:12
1:22 Acts 7:19
2:1 Exod 6:20; Num 26:59
2:2 Acts 7:20; Heb 11:23
2:3 Gen 6:14; Isa 18:2

certainly have been the remnants of the Hyksos (see note on 1:8-10). • *will escape from the country:* Or *will take the country.*

1:11 *Pithom and Rameses* have been identified with the modern cities of Tel el-Mashkutah and Qantir, which archaeology shows to have been built during the Late Bronze period (1550–1250 BC), the same period in which the Israelites were present.

1:12 In spite of the concerted Egyptian oppression, *the Israelites multiplied and spread;* God was keeping his promise about giving Abraham many descendants (Gen 15:5).

1:14 The only stone that the Egyptians could obtain for building purposes came from the far south of the country. Therefore, in the north where the Hebrews were settled, only the most important state and religious buildings were made of stone. The rest were constructed with *mortar* and *bricks* made of durable clay with a binder such as seashells or straw mixed in. After being sun dried in a form, they were surprisingly durable—especially in a land such as Egypt, where there was little rainfall or humidity.

1:15 *Pharaoh* is a title for the Egyptian ruler, not a personal name. • The origins of the word *Hebrew* are unclear. As used by the Egyptians and Philistines in reference to the Israelites, it was apparently a derogatory term for a despised underclass. • Whatever the number of Hebrew people (see note on 12:37), there were clearly more than two *midwives* for the whole nation. Probably the two named here, *Shiphrah and Puah,* are representatives of the whole group. The differences between Pharaoh and the midwives are dramatic. He had great political and military power; they had none. He had great official prestige; they had very little. He was a man; they were women. He was of the ruling people; they were slaves. He was rich; they were poor. They could easily have been cowed into obedience, but they were not.

1:16 *watch as they deliver* (literally *look upon the two stones*): The meaning of the Hebrew is uncertain, but perhaps the reference is to a birthstool. It might also refer to the genitalia. • *If the baby is a boy, kill him; if it is a girl, let her live:* Such selective genocide would not completely deprive the Egyptians of a free labor source. When grown, the girls would be married to slaves from other people groups, effectively destroying Hebrew cohesion while keeping the supply of slaves as high as possible.

1:17 The *midwives . . . refused to obey* the mighty Egyptian king because they feared God more than they feared Pharaoh (1:21). Fear of the Lord (reverent awe of him as the almighty Creator and Judge) is the foundation of true knowledge and of wisdom (Prov 1:7; 9:10). The Lord is a friend to those who fear him (Ps 25:14). The midwives understood that the Lord has more power than any human being.

1:19 It might trouble us that the *midwives* were not candid in giving their main reason for keeping the boy babies alive. Comprehensive honesty is less important to God than absolute faithfulness to him and to his believing community.

1:20-21 *he gave them families:* For most of history, children have had the worthy goal of growing up to raise a family. God graciously granted the universal wish of these women who served him courageously and faithfully.

2:1-25 Chapter 1 established the need for rescue; ch 2 describes the preparation of Moses, the rescuer. God used the destruction of the Hebrew boy babies to ensure that the rescuer would be trained (see note on 2:10) for his task.

2:1 The *man and woman* were named Amram and Jochebed (6:20). • *Levi* was Jacob's third son by his wife Leah (Gen 29:34).

2:2 *a special baby* (literally *he was good*): This is probably a reference to his appearance: He was a "perfect" baby.

2:3 *Papyrus reeds* grew plentifully along the many streams into which the *Nile River* divided in the delta region of northern Egypt. They were light and

2:4
Exod 15:20
Num 26:59

2:5
Exod 7:15; 8:20
Acts 7:21

2:10
1 Sam 1:20
2 Sam 22:17

2:11
Acts 7:23-24
Heb 11:24-26

2:12
Acts 7:24

2:13
Acts 7:26-28

2:14
*Acts 7:27, 35
[c]*shapat* (8199)
‣ Exod 18:26

2:15
Acts 7:29

reeds along the bank of the Nile River. 4The
baby's sister then stood at a distance, watching to see what would happen to him.
5Soon Pharaoh's daughter came down
to bathe in the river, and her attendants
walked along the riverbank. When the princess saw the basket among the reeds, she
sent her maid to get it for her. 6When the
princess opened it, she saw the baby. The
little boy was crying, and she felt sorry for
him. "This must be one of the Hebrew children," she said.
7Then the baby's sister approached the
princess. "Should I go and find one of the
Hebrew women to nurse the baby for you?"
she asked.
8"Yes, do!" the princess replied. So the
girl went and called the baby's mother.
9"Take this baby and nurse him for me,"
the princess told the baby's mother. "I will
pay you for your help." So the woman took
her baby home and nursed him.
10Later, when the boy was older, his
mother brought him back to Pharaoh's
daughter, who adopted him as her own son.
The princess named him Moses, for he explained, "I lifted him out of the water."

Moses Escapes to Midian
11Many years later, when Moses had grown
up, he went out to visit his own people, the
Hebrews, and he saw how hard they were
forced to work. During his visit, he saw
an Egyptian beating one of his fellow Hebrews. 12After looking in all directions to
make sure no one was watching, Moses
killed the Egyptian and hid the body in the
sand.
13The next day, when Moses went out to
visit his people again, he saw two Hebrew
men fighting. "Why are you beating up your
friend?" Moses said to the one who had
started the fight.
14The man replied, "Who appointed you
to be our prince and [c]judge? Are you going
to kill me as you killed that Egyptian yesterday?"
Then Moses was afraid, thinking, "Everyone knows what I did." 15And sure enough,
Pharaoh heard what had happened, and he
tried to kill Moses. But Moses fled from
Pharaoh and went to live in the land of
Midian.
When Moses arrived in Midian, he sat
down beside a well. 16Now the priest of

flexible, well-suited for ***basket*** weaving. It is possible that Moses' mother placed the basket in the water exactly where it was most likely to be found by the Egyptian princess.

2:5-6 Much like the Ganges River in modern India, the Nile was understood by the Egyptians to be a goddess who had life-giving and healing properties. When ***Pharaoh's daughter came down to bathe in the river,*** she was not merely washing but completing her morning devotions. The discovery of the baby floating on the river, in the embrace of the Nile goddess (as she saw it), would be very significant to her. It is also natural for a young woman to feel ***sorry*** for a ***crying*** baby. The combination of factors may account for her rescuing the child, though she recognized that he was ***Hebrew*** (Hebrews and Egyptians practiced circumcision differently).

2:7-9 It is ironic evidence of God's grace and sovereignty that Pharaoh's daughter paid Moses' ***mother*** to nurse her own ***baby*** rather than having him killed according to Pharaoh's command. The narrator seems to imply that the princess realized who the baby's mother was (since she didn't ask any embarrassing questions). Two women chose to understand each other while maintaining a legal fiction. Moses was saved because God was at work, not because anyone was fooled.

2:10 God not only saved Moses' life for his future calling, he also arranged for him to receive administrative, military, and leadership training from the oppressors of his people. A pharaoh was expected to sire as many children as was physically possible to prove his power. Male offspring were placed in civil and military positions. It is very likely that the ***adopted*** son of a princess would have had such experiences (see Acts 7:22). • ***Moses:*** The ***princess*** gave the child an Egyptian name that is found in the full names of many prominent Egyptians, including the 18th Dynasty pharaohs named *Ahmose* (1550~1525 BC) and *Thutmose* (1504~1390 BC). By naming the child Moses (meaning "to give birth"), the princess was perhaps saying that the Nile, revered as a source of life, had given birth to the baby. The Israelites drew a connection between the name *Moses* and the similar sounding Hebrew term *mashah,* which means "to lift out."

2:11-15 This section addresses Moses' first abortive attempt to rescue Israel in his own strength. This incident shows Moses' courage and decisiveness, but it also shows his tendency to assume the responsibility himself, which would later have tragic effects in his life (Num 20:1-13). Moses' concern for his people's welfare was good; his timing and manner did not accord with God's plan.

2:11-12 ***Moses*** had a privileged upbringing as compared with the toil and hardship of ***his own people, the Hebrews,*** but he was willing to identify with them and help them to the point of jeopardizing his own privileges.

2:13 ***Moses,*** who had put himself at risk to prevent an Egyptian from beating a Hebrew, must have been especially angered to see a Hebrew ***beating up*** a fellow Hebrew.

2:14 The arrogant response of the Hebrew man, ***"Who appointed you to be our prince and judge?"*** foreshadows how the rest of the Hebrews would respond to Moses in later years—they would not thank him for his efforts on their behalf. If Moses were to succeed, he would have to depend solely on a sense of his divine calling.

2:15 ***Moses fled:*** By trying to rescue Israel himself rather than through God's help, Moses made himself a fugitive rather than a leader in Egypt, forestalling God's purposes for him. Moses' life was drastically changed as a consequence of his actions (cp. Num 20:9-13; Deut 3:23-29). • ***Midian*** was located on both sides of the Gulf of Aqaba—in the southern Sinai Peninsula and on the western edge of the Arabian Peninsula. A major trade route from southern Arabia passed through this dry and barren area. Its people seem to have been nomadic shepherds and traders (see Gen 37:28). It was a good place for a fugitive to disappear.

2:16-25 This passage further reveals Moses' concern for the oppressed and

MOSES (2:1-22)

Exod 3:1–19:25; 20:19-21; 24:1-18; 31:18; 32:1–34:35; 39:42-43; 40:16
Lev 8:1-36; 10:1-20; 24:10-23
Num 7:1-11, 89; 9:1-14; 10:29–14:45; 15:32-36; 16:1–17:13; 20:1-29; 21:4-9; 25:1-5; 27:1-23; 31:1–32:33; 33:1-2
Deut 1:1-5; 31:1–34:12
1 Chr 23:13-17
Ps 77:20; 90; 103:7; 105:26-27; 106:32-33
Mark 9:2-13
Acts 7:17-44
1 Cor 10:1-14
2 Cor 3:7-18
Gal 3:19
Heb 3:1-19; 8:5; 9:19-22; 11:23-28; 12:18-29

Moses was the founding leader of Israel as a nation. God used Moses at a critical juncture in the history of his people. He was the prophet who received the law and mediated God's covenant with Israel at Mount Sinai (19:3-6). He was also the first known writer of Scripture.

Moses, the younger brother of Miriam and Aaron, was born in Egypt under dangerous circumstances (1:15–2:2; 6:20). The Egyptian pharaoh, fearing a rebellion, had decreed that all Hebrew boys be killed at birth. Moses' mother, Jochebed, entrusted her infant son to God and set him afloat in the Nile in a reed basket (2:3-10). Pharaoh's daughter found him and took him into the palace to raise as her own child.

Little is known about Moses' upbringing. Jewish tradition holds that he received both administrative and military training in Pharaoh's household. When he was about forty years old, he killed an Egyptian to rescue a Hebrew slave, and then he fled to Midian (2:11-15; cp. Acts 7:23-29). There he rescued some young women who were being harassed as they watered their flocks. Their father, Jethro, invited him home. Moses married one of the women, Zipporah, and began a family as he cared for his father-in-law's flocks.

About forty years later (Acts 7:30), God revealed himself to Moses in a burning bush and commissioned Moses to return to Egypt to rescue his people from slavery (3:1–4:17). Moses hesitated, fearful that the Israelites would not accept him as their leader. God revealed his covenant name, Yahweh, and assigned Aaron as Moses' spokesman.

Moses and Aaron went to Egypt and confronted Pharaoh, who stubbornly resisted Moses' demand that he free the Israelite slaves. Moses then announced a series of plagues, which eventually convinced Pharaoh to let the Israelites leave. After they had left Egypt, Pharaoh changed his mind and pursued them to the edge of the Red Sea. God enabled the Israelites to cross safely to the other side by dividing the waters; the pursuing Egyptian army was destroyed when the waters closed over them.

Moses led Israel to Mount Sinai, where he had encountered God at the burning bush. God again revealed himself to Moses on that mountain, giving him the law (including the Ten Commandments; 20:1–23:19) and directions for building the Tabernacle. But when Moses came down from the mountain, he found that the people had already deserted the true God by worshiping a gold calf. Moses threw down and broke the two tablets of the law and rallied the Levites to execute some of the offenders. After praying for the people, he received a new copy of the law and led the people in building the Tabernacle.

Moses led a grumbling, rebellious, and distrustful people through the wilderness. Even his own brother and sister challenged his leadership (Num 12), using his marriage to a Cushite woman as an excuse. Moses responded with great humility (Num 12:3), while God made it clear that Moses was his spokesman and confidant.

Moses was a great man, but not a perfect one. When the people stretched his patience by complaining about water, Moses failed to follow God's guidance and struck a certain rock rather than speaking to it (Num 20:1-13). His actions failed to demonstrate God's holiness, and by what he said, Moses implied that he had brought the water by his own power (Num 20:10; cp. Ps 106:32-33). As a result, God did not allow him to enter the Promised Land.

Before his death, Moses delivered his final sermon, known to us as the book of Deuteronomy. The first generation had died in the wilderness, so Moses was addressing a new generation. Deuteronomy renewed the covenant with this generation, reminded them of its terms, and encouraged them to obey it and serve the Lord alone.

After giving this sermon and before Israel entered Canaan, Moses climbed Pisgah Peak on Mount Nebo, where he died. "There has never been another prophet in Israel like Moses, whom the LORD knew face to face" (Deut 34:10). Only Jesus surpassed Moses as a mediator between God and human beings (Acts 3:17-26; Heb 3).

Moses is mentioned in the NT more than any other OT figure, and he appeared at Jesus' transfiguration. The NT emphasizes his role as lawgiver and draws from Moses' experiences to show patterns of life under the new covenant. Like Moses, Jesus was rescued as an infant from the evil designs of a human despot (Matt 2:13-18). Jesus' proclamation of a new law in his Sermon on the Mount (Matt 5–7) parallels the giving of the law at Sinai and presents Jesus as the authoritative interpreter of God's will. The letter to the Hebrews compares Christ with Moses, while Paul's letter to the Galatians and the Gospel of John contrast the law of Moses with a believer's new relationship with God (see John 1:17; Heb 3:5-6; 9:11-22).

2:16
Gen 24:11
Exod 3:1; 18:1
2:17
Gen 29:10
2:18
Num 10:29
2:20
Gen 18:5
2:21
Exod 4:25; 18:2
Acts 7:29
2:22
Gen 23:4
Heb 11:13
2:23
Exod 6:5, 9
Acts 7:34
2:24
Gen 22:16-18; 26:2-3; 28:13
Ps 105:10, 42
[d]*zakar* (2142)
‣Lev 26:45
3:2
*Acts 7:30
[e]*mal'ak* (4397)
‣Num 22:22
3:3
*Acts 7:31

Midian had seven daughters who came
as usual to draw water and fill the water
troughs for their father's flocks. 17But some
other shepherds came and chased them
away. So Moses jumped up and rescued the
girls from the shepherds. Then he drew water for their flocks.
18When the girls returned to Reuel, their
father, he asked, "Why are you back so soon
today?"
19"An Egyptian rescued us from the shepherds," they answered. "And then he drew
water for us and watered our flocks."
20"Then where is he?" their father asked.
"Why did you leave him there? Invite him to
come and eat with us."
21Moses accepted the invitation, and he
settled there with him. In time, Reuel gave
Moses his daughter Zipporah to be his wife.
22Later she gave birth to a son, and Moses
named him Gershom, for he explained, "I
have been a foreigner in a foreign land."
23Years passed, and the king of Egypt died.
But the Israelites continued to groan under
their burden of slavery. They cried out for
help, and their cry rose up to God. 24God
heard their groaning, and he [d]remembered
his covenant promise to Abraham, Isaac,
and Jacob. 25He looked down on the people
of Israel and knew it was time to act.

The Call of the Rescuer (3:1–4:28)
Moses and the Burning Bush

3 One day Moses was tending the flock
of his father-in-law, Jethro, the priest of
Midian. He led the flock far into the wilderness and came to Sinai, the mountain of God.
2There the [e]angel of the LORD appeared to
him in a blazing fire from the middle of a
bush. Moses stared in amazement. Though
the bush was engulfed in flames, it didn't
burn up. 3"This is amazing," Moses said to
himself. "Why isn't that bush burning up? I
must go see it."
4When the LORD saw Moses coming to
take a closer look, God called to him from
the middle of the bush, "Moses! Moses!"
"Here I am!" Moses replied.

Age	Event	References
birth	Moses is rescued by midwives	1:15-22
3 months	Moses is adopted by Pharaoh's daughter	2:1-10
40 years	Moses kills an Egyptian and flees to Midian	2:11-22; Acts 7:23
80	God commissions Moses; Israel is rescued from Egypt	7:7; Acts 7:30
120	Moses dies on Mount Nebo in Moab	Deut 34:1-8

▲Moses' Life (2:1-22)

tells of his transition to a new land (2:18-22). He married, had a child, and lived there for forty years (Acts 7:30). From a human perspective, there was no way for the Israelites to be rescued through Moses, but it is the divine perspective that matters. The end of this section (2:23-25) tells us that God had not forgotten his people; he was only waiting for the *time to act* (2:25).

2:16 The *priest of Midian* was named Reuel (2:18), but later he is called Jethro (18:1). It was common for a person to have both an official name and a personal name, though in this case it is not clear which is which. Perhaps, like Melchizedek (Gen 14:18), he represented an indigenous religious class that had not fallen prey to a pagan religion. Reuel's actions in bringing an offering and sacrifices to God (18:12) suggest that this was so.

2:17 ***rescued:*** Now a stranger in a strange land, Moses still could not stand by and allow oppression to continue—he was, by nature, a rescuer. The NLT has captured the correct sense of the Hebrew word, sometimes translated *deliver* or *save.*

2:18-20 The father of seven daughters was not about to leave a generous and courageous male—excellent husband material—unaccounted for! We see here the well-known hospitality (see also Gen 18:1-8) that characterizes the residents of this region to this day.

2:22 ***Gershom*** sounds like a Hebrew term that means "a foreigner there."

2:23 ***The king of Egypt*** who ***died*** was possibly Thutmose III (1504~1450 BC; see "Old Testament Chronology: Abraham to Joshua," p. 118). The new pharaoh did not change his predecessor's oppressive policies.

2:24-25 The verbs here speak of a ***God*** who is sensitive to his people's needs (***heard . . . looked down***), who is faithful and reliable (***remembered his covenant promise***), and who accepts his obligations in a relationship (***knew it was time to act***). The last phrase could also be translated *and acknowledged his obligation to help them.*

3:1–4:28 This section presents Moses' call to rescue the Israelites from Egyptian bondage. It is divided into two subsections, 3:1–4:17 and 4:18-28. The first deals with the call itself, while the second addresses the full implications of accepting that call. Moses was not presented with a mere vocational change; he faced an entire reorientation of his life.

3:1-10 In these verses, the stage is set for the reorientation of Moses' life.

3:1 ***Jethro:*** Moses' father-in-law went by two names, Jethro and Reuel. See note on 2:16. • ***Sinai:*** Hebrew *Horeb,* another name for Sinai. *Sinai* is the name usually used for the mountain where God later revealed himself in the covenant (for example, see 16:1; 19:1-2). Here and in 17:6 and 33:6 the Hebrew text uses the proper name *Horeb.* Both names presumably refer to the same mountain, so the NLT consistently uses Sinai.

3:2 Technically, ***the angel of the LORD*** is the Lord's officially authorized envoy, but the expression may be used more broadly of other visible manifestations of the Lord (see Gen 16:9-13; Judg 13:3, 6, 21-22). • In the Bible, ***blazing fire*** often represents God's transcendent holiness (see 19:18; Gen 15:17; 1 Kgs 18:38-39; Isa 33:14). • ***didn't burn up:*** This may show that God does not wish to consume the vehicle that he sets ablaze for his purposes.

3:4 ***Moses! Moses!*** God knows his people by name, and individuals are important to him.

5“Do not come any closer,” the LORD
warned. “Take off your sandals, for you are
standing on holy ground. 6I am the [f]God
of your father—the [f]God of Abraham, the
[f]God of Isaac, and the [f]God of Jacob.” When
Moses heard this, he covered his face because he was afraid to look at [f]God.

7Then the LORD told him, “I have certainly
seen the oppression of my people in Egypt.
I have heard their cries of distress because
of their harsh slave drivers. Yes, I am aware
of their suffering. 8So I have come down to
rescue them from the power of the Egyptians and lead them out of Egypt into their
own fertile and spacious land. It is a land
flowing with milk and honey—the land
where the Canaanites, Hittites, Amorites,
Perizzites, Hivites, and Jebusites now live.
9Look! The cry of the people of Israel has
reached me, and I have [g]seen how harshly
the Egyptians abuse them. 10Now go, for I
am sending you to Pharaoh. You must lead
my people Israel out of Egypt.”

11But Moses protested to God, “Who am I
to appear before Pharaoh? Who am I to lead
the people of Israel out of Egypt?”

12God answered, “I will be with you. And
this is your sign that I am the one who has
sent you: When you have brought the people out of Egypt, you will worship God at
this very mountain.”

13But Moses protested, “If I go to the people of Israel and tell them, ‘The God of your
ancestors has sent me to you,’ they will ask
me, ‘What is his name?’ Then what should
I tell them?”

14God replied to Moses, “I AM WHO I AM.
Say this to the people of Israel: I AM has sent
me to you.” 15God also said to Moses, “Say
this to the people of Israel: Yahweh, the God

3:5 Gen 28:17; Josh 5:15; *Acts 7:33
3:6 *Matt 22:32; *Mark 12:26; *Luke 20:37; *Acts 3:13; 7:32; [f]*'elohim* (0430) ‣ Num 23:21
3:7 *Acts 7:34
3:8 Gen 15:18-19; 46:4; 50:24; Exod 3:17; Deut 6:3; 8:7-9; 11:9; 26:9
3:9 [g]*ra'ah* (7462) ‣ 1 Sam 16:11
3:10 *Acts 7:34
3:11 Exod 4:10; 6:12
3:12 Exod 4:12; 19:2; *Acts 7:7

3:5 The soil around the bush was ***holy ground,*** while the soil on the bottom of Moses' sandals was common. The common cannot touch the holy without being transformed or destroyed (see “Clean and Unclean” at Lev 11:1–15:33, p. 213). At the outset of the Exodus, God was making it plain that he is absolutely “other” than his creation, a reality that cannot be overlooked in a proper divine-human relationship. The word ***holy*** occurs only a few times in the Bible prior to 3:5. It now becomes the central descriptor of God in the OT. In other Semitic languages, the same root occurs infrequently. It does not describe a moral quality in these other languages but simply what is “other than” human. The pagan gods, for instance, were “holy” only in the sense of being “other”—they did everything humans do, good and evil, but on a larger scale. In the Bible, by contrast, moral perfection is a central idea of the term *holy.* The one true God is the only being in the universe who truly stands apart from this world and is worthy of being called “holy” in this general sense. The true God is perfectly consistent and moral in his character. Here, at the burning bush, God revealed his otherness (see also “God's Absolute Holiness” at Lev 10:3, p. 210). Later at Sinai, he revealed his moral character in his requirements for those who would be his covenant partners (see 19:6; 20:1–23:33; see also Lev 11:45; 1 Pet 1:13-16).

3:6 This transcendent God had committed himself to Moses' ancestors in a faithful promise maintained for hundreds of years. Moses was in awe of the one, holy, and transcendent ***God of Abraham.*** • ***your father:*** The Greek version reads *your fathers.* • Jesus quoted this verse when he was sparring with the Sadducees about the concept of resurrection (Matt 22:32; Mark 12:26; Luke 20:37).

3:7 The continued slavery and ***distress*** of Israel touched God's heart.

3:8 God would not only ***rescue them*** but would take them to ***their own . . . land*** that he had promised to Abraham (Gen 13:14-18). • ***flowing with milk and honey:*** The land was agriculturally rich, with pasturage for cattle and crops with blooms from which bees could make honey. • ***Canaanites . . . Jebusites:*** The list of peoples who lived in Canaan indicates the importance of this strip of land between the Mediterranean Sea and the Arabian Desert. As a vital crossroads for trade and communication between Egypt and the rest of the ancient Near East, it was a hotly contested prize. That Israel could end up in sole possession of it seemed an impossibility.

3:10 God would act compassionately to save his suffering people, but it would be through a human agency. Often God is known among us because of the way his people carry out his will.

3:11–4:17 Moses, in his response to God, presented four reasons why he was not the one to fulfill God's call. Although each reason supposedly relates to Moses and his ability, God's answers show that they were really questions about God.

3:11-12 ***Moses*** first protested that he was unworthy of such a great task, but ***God*** responded that this was not the issue. Human worthiness is of no significance if God's presence is ***with*** that person.

3:12 In the Bible, a ***sign*** often occurred after a person or a nation had already had to decide whether to act in faith or not (see Isa 7:14). A sign cannot create faith where there is none (see Matt 12:39; 16:4). Rather, it encourages the one who has exercised the faith he or she already has.

3:13-22 Moses' second protest was that he had inadequate knowledge. He did not know God's name. This might mean that God's personal name had not yet been revealed (see notes on 6:2-3). It is also possible that Moses meant he did not know the secret, magic formula that a man of power might have been expected to make use of. Interest in such things was common in the ancient Near East. God's direct response is almost a riddle, but the majority of his answer is a statement of his faithfulness in the past and a demonstration of his knowledge of the future. There is nothing magical about the name *Yahweh.* Knowledge of secret formulas and magic powers is not the issue; the issue is the character of God and his lordship of history. The reason there is “something about that name” is because of the incomparable character and nature of the one who bears it.

3:14 ***I AM WHO I AM:*** This name could also be translated *I WILL BE WHAT I WILL BE.* It speaks of a God who is self-sufficient, self-existent, all encompassing, and without limitations, the one being in the universe who is not dependent on something else for his existence.

3:15 ***Yahweh*** is a transliteration of the proper name *YHWH.* This name is probably a form of the Hebrew verb “to be,” so it could mean “he causes to be,” or “he who is,” or “I am.” Later Jews were not permitted to speak God's name aloud, so the Hebrew text supplies the vowels from the word *'adonay* (which means “lord” or “master”) whenever God's proper name, YHWH, appears. In oral reading, the Hebrew reader would pronounce *'adonay,* even though the written text is *YHWH.* We do not know

3:13 Exod 15:3
3:14 Exod 6:3; John 8:58; Rev 1:8; 4:8
3:15 Ps 72:17; 102:12; 135:13; *Acts 3:13
3:16 Exod 4:29
3:17 Exod 3:8; Josh 24:11
3:18 Exod 4:23; 5:1, 3; Num 23:4, 16
3:19 Exod 5:2; 6:1; 7:4
3:20 Exod 11:1; 12:31-33; Neh 9:10; Acts 7:36
3:21 Exod 11:2-3
3:22 Exod 11:2; 12:35
4:1 Exod 3:15-16, 18
4:3 Exod 7:8-12, 15
4:5 Exod 4:31; 19:9
4:6 Num 12:10; 2 Kgs 5:27
4:7 2 Kgs 5:14; Matt 8:3; Luke 17:12-14
4:9 Exod 7:17-21

of your ancestors—the God of Abraham,
the God of Isaac, and the God of Jacob—has
sent me to you.

This is my eternal name,
my name to remember for all
generations.

16“Now go and call together all the elders
of Israel. Tell them, ‘The LORD, the God of
your ancestors—the God of Abraham, Isaac,
and Jacob—has appeared to me. He told
me, “I have been watching closely, and I
see how the Egyptians are treating you. 17I
have promised to rescue you from your oppression in Egypt. I will lead you to a land
flowing with milk and honey—the land
where the Canaanites, Hittites, Amorites,
Perizzites, Hivites, and Jebusites now live.”’
18“The elders of Israel will accept your
message. Then you and the elders must go
to the king of Egypt and tell him, ‘The LORD,
the God of the Hebrews, has met with us. So
please let us take a three-day journey into
the wilderness to offer sacrifices to the
LORD, our God.’
19“But I know that the king of Egypt will
not let you go unless a mighty hand forces
him. 20So I will raise my hand and strike the
Egyptians, performing all kinds of miracles
among them. Then at last he will let you
go. 21And I will cause the Egyptians to look
favorably on you. They will give you gifts
when you go so you will not leave empty-
handed. 22Every Israelite woman will ask
for articles of silver and gold and fine clothing from her Egyptian neighbors and from
the foreign women in their houses. You will
dress your sons and daughters with these,
stripping the Egyptians of their wealth.”

Signs of the LORD’s Power

4 But Moses protested again, “What if
they won’t believe me or listen to me?
What if they say, ‘The LORD never appeared
to you’?”
2Then the LORD asked him, “What is that
in your hand?”
“A shepherd’s staff,” Moses replied.
3“Throw it down on the ground,” the
LORD told him. So Moses threw down the
staff, and it turned into a snake! Moses
jumped back.
4Then the LORD told him, “Reach out and
grab its tail.” So Moses reached out and
grabbed it, and it turned back into a shepherd’s staff in his hand.
5“Perform this sign,” the LORD told him.
“Then they will believe that the LORD, the
God of their ancestors—the God of Abraham, the God of Isaac, and the God of
Jacob—really has appeared to you.”
6Then the LORD said to Moses, “Now put
your hand inside your cloak.” So Moses put
his hand inside his cloak, and when he took
it out again, his hand was white as snow
with a severe skin disease. 7“Now put your
hand back into your cloak,” the LORD said.
So Moses put his hand back in, and when
he took it out again, it was as healthy as the
rest of his body.
8The LORD said to Moses, “If they do
not believe you and are not convinced by
the first miraculous sign, they will be convinced by the second sign. 9And if they
don’t believe you or listen to you even after
these two signs, then take some water from
the Nile River and pour it out on the dry
ground. When you do, the water from the
Nile will turn to blood on the ground.”

the pronunciation of the divine name. The widely used *Yahweh* is an informed guess. The English word “Jehovah” is an artificial term made by combining the vowels of *’adonay* with the consonants Y-H-W-H. In the NLT, this name is usually translated “LORD” (with small capitals), but it is transliterated “Yahweh” in the few instances, like this verse, where a point is made about the name itself. Also in 6:2-3; 15:3; 33:19; 34:5-6.

3:16-17 Moses was to tell the people of Israel that the God who now spoke to them was the same God their ancestors knew and worshiped, and he would lead them into a fruitful ***land*** wrested from the hands of many others. Moses’ message was not a magical formula, but the word of a God who, standing outside of history, can yet enter and direct it. • ***flowing with milk and honey:*** See note on 3:8.

3:18 ***Hebrews:*** See note on 1:15. • ***a three-day journey . . . to offer sacrifices:*** If we think of the primary purpose of the Exodus as rescuing the Israelites from bondage, this seems like a disingenuous request. But God’s primary purpose was to create a people for himself, and he was taking them into the wilderness to teach them to worship him.

3:19 ***I know:*** See “A Hardened Heart” at 14:4, 8, p. 149. • ***will not let you go unless a mighty hand forces him:*** As translated from the Greek and Latin versions; Hebrew reads *will not let you go, not by a mighty hand.*

3:20-21 God’s power would be obvious, and the Egyptians would not only allow the Hebrews to leave, they would pay them to do so.

4:1-9 Moses’ third protest was that he lacked power. God answered in a very convincing demonstration of divine power by instantaneous creation of a ***snake*** and of a ***severe skin disease.***

4:3 Across the ancient Near East, the ***snake*** was a symbol of both death and healing. The person who demonstrated power in these areas was powerful indeed.

4:6 ***severe skin disease:*** The Hebrew word underlying this phrase has traditionally been translated “leprosy.” However, the symptoms of this condition as described in the Bible are not those of the disease we know as leprosy (Hansen’s disease). The biblical term seems to describe several kinds of highly contagious inflammations and skin lesions.

4:9 As with the previous two signs, the fact that ***the water from the Nile will turn to blood*** also demonstrated God’s power over life and death (see “The Plagues” at 7:14–11:10, p. 141).

10But Moses pleaded with the LORD,
"O Lord, I'm not very good with words. I
never have been, and I'm not now, even
though you have spoken to me. I get tongue-
tied, and my words get tangled."
11Then the LORD asked Moses, "Who
makes a person's mouth? Who decides
whether people speak or do not speak, hear
or do not hear, see or do not see? Is it not I,
the LORD? 12Now go! I will be with you as you
speak, and I will instruct you in what to say."
13But Moses again pleaded, "Lord, please!
Send anyone else."
14Then the LORD became angry with
Moses. "All right," he said. "What about your
brother, Aaron the Levite? I know he speaks
well. And look! He is on his way to meet you
now. He will be delighted to see you. 15Talk
to him, and put the words in his mouth.
I will be with both of you as you speak, and
I will instruct you both in what to do.
16Aaron will be your spokesman to the people. He will be your mouthpiece, and you
will stand in the place of God for him, telling
him what to say. 17And take your shepherd's
staff with you, and use it to perform the miraculous signs I have shown you."

Moses Returns to Egypt

18So Moses went back home to Jethro, his
father-in-law. "Please let me return to my
relatives in Egypt," Moses said. "I don't even
know if they are still alive."
"Go in peace," Jethro replied.
19Before Moses left Midian, the LORD
said to him, "Return to Egypt, for all those
who wanted to kill you have died."
20So Moses took his wife and sons, put
them on a donkey, and headed back to the
land of Egypt. In his hand he carried the
staff of God.
21And the LORD told Moses, "When you
arrive back in Egypt, go to Pharaoh and perform all the miracles I have empowered you
to do. But I will harden his heart so he will
refuse to let the people go. 22Then you will
tell him, 'This is what the LORD says: Israel is
my firstborn son. 23I commanded you, "Let
my son go, so he can worship me." But since
you have refused, I will now kill your firstborn son!' "
24On the way to Egypt, at a place where
Moses and his family had stopped for the
night, the LORD confronted him and was
about to kill him. 25But Moses' wife, Zipporah, took a flint knife and circumcised her
son. She touched his feet with the foreskin
and said, "Now you are a bridegroom of
blood to me." 26(When she said "a bridegroom of blood," she was referring to the
circumcision.) After that, the LORD left him
alone.
27Now the LORD had said to Aaron, "Go
out into the wilderness to meet Moses." So
Aaron went and met Moses at the mountain
of God, and he embraced him. 28Moses
then told Aaron everything the LORD had
commanded him to say. And he told him
about the miraculous signs the LORD had
commanded him to perform.

4:10 Exod 3:11; Jer 1:6
4:11 Ps 94:9; Matt 11:5
4:12 Deut 18:15, 18; Matt 10:19-20; Mark 13:11
4:14 Exod 4:27
4:15 Isa 51:16; Jer 1:9
4:16 Exod 7:1; 18:19-20
4:17 Exod 14:16; 17:9
4:19 Exod 2:15, 23
4:20 Exod 18:3; Acts 7:29
4:21 Exod 7:3, 13; 9:12; Deut 2:30; John 12:40
4:22 Isa 63:16; 64:8; Jer 31:9; Hos 11:1; Rom 9:4
4:23 Exod 5:1; 6:11; 7:16
4:24 Num 22:22; 1 Chr 21:16
4:25-26 Josh 5:2-3
4:27 Exod 4:14
4:28 Exod 4:16

4:10-17 Moses' fourth and final protest was that he could not speak effectively. Moses was apparently grasping at straws in trying to escape this dangerous and unpleasant assignment, and God was becoming angry at Moses' refusal to grasp the truth. The outcome did not depend on Moses' ability, but upon his willingness to let God's power operate through him.

4:11 God created the organs of speech and has ordained every person's particular abilities in this area. He is able to use what he has made and ordained.

4:13 Having run out of protests, Moses simply asked to be excused.

4:14-17 God would not let Moses evade responsibility, but he would accommodate Moses' concern by allowing Moses' brother ***Aaron*** to become Moses' ***mouthpiece*** (14:16). As the narrative unfolds, the text records fewer and fewer occasions of Aaron serving in this capacity. Moses' speaking problem was perhaps not as serious as he made it out to be, or the problem began to dissipate as his experience increased.

4:18 Moses was now eighty years old (see 7:7), but he was still formally subject to his father-in-law.

4:20 ***he carried the staff of God:*** Whatever he may have said to Jethro, Moses was going to Egypt in obedience to God and in the expectation of being used by God (see 4:17).

4:21-23 These verses summarize the events of the next several chapters, beginning with the request to let the people go so that they could worship God (5:3) and concluding with the final plague, the death of the firstborn (11:4-6). God was preparing the rescuer for the difficult task ahead (see 11:9).

4:24-26 This incident is shrouded in mystery. That ***Zipporah*** responded immediately and ***circumcised her son*** suggests that she and Moses had discussed the possibility of doing so previously and had decided it was not necessary. Why would having an uncircumcised son lead to God's intent to kill the rescuer he had carefully prepared and called? Perhaps if Moses had arrived in Egypt claiming to represent the God of the Israelites' ancestors and yet had not done the one thing God had commanded of his followers to this point (Gen 17:10), then the people would have been less inclined to follow God in a radically exclusive way.

4:25 The Hebrew word for ***feet*** may refer here to the male sex organ. See also note on Gen 49:10. • ***a bridegroom of blood:*** The context suggests that this statement was part of the circumcision ritual of that time. Perhaps it reflects a practice among some Semites (as among certain African groups today) of performing circumcision when the child had attained puberty.

4:27 Aaron's coming ***to meet Moses*** is the first recorded confirmation of God's promises (see 4:14). • ***mountain of God:*** A reference to Mount Sinai.

4:29–7:7 In this section, the Lord offered to rescue the Israelites. The people initially gave a favorable response but ultimately faced a crisis of faith.

4:29 Exod 3:16
4:30 Exod 4:15
4:31 Exod 3:18; 12:27
[h]*khawah* (7812)
‣ Num 25:2
5:1 Exod 3:18; 4:23
5:2 Exod 3:19
Job 21:15
5:3 Exod 3:18
Deut 28:21
5:4-5 Exod 1:11

The Offer of Rescue (4:29–7:7)

Moses and Aaron Speak to the People

29Then Moses and Aaron returned to Egypt
and called all the elders of Israel together.
30Aaron told them everything the LORD
had told Moses, and Moses performed the
miraculous signs as they watched. 31Then
the people of Israel were convinced that
the LORD had sent Moses and Aaron. When
they heard that the LORD was concerned
about them and had seen their misery, they
bowed down and [h]worshiped.

Moses and Aaron Speak to Pharaoh

5 After this presentation to Israel's leaders, Moses and Aaron went and spoke
to Pharaoh. They told him, "This is what the
LORD, the God of Israel, says: Let my people
go so they may hold a festival in my honor
in the wilderness."
2"Is that so?" retorted Pharaoh. "And who
is the LORD? Why should I listen to him and
let Israel go? I don't know the LORD, and I
will not let Israel go."
3But Aaron and Moses persisted. "The
God of the Hebrews has met with us," they
declared. "So let us take a three-day journey
into the wilderness so we can offer sacrifices to the LORD our God. If we don't, he
will kill us with a plague or with the sword."
4Pharaoh replied, "Moses and Aaron, why
are you distracting the people from their
tasks? Get back to work! 5Look, there are
many of your people in the land, and you
are stopping them from their work."

AARON (4:14-17, 27-31)

Exod 6:20-27; 7:1-2; 28:1-5; 32:1-25
Num 12:1-12; 20:1-13, 22-29
Acts 7:39-41

Moses' older brother, Aaron (6:20; 7:7), played a crucial role in founding Israel and its institutions, particularly the priesthood. He first appears after Moses' calling at the burning bush (3:1–4:17). Moses was reluctant to accept the divine commission, claiming that he was unfit to lead the Israelites out of Egypt because his words tended to "get tangled" (4:10). Despite God's assurances, Moses continued to object until God appointed Aaron as Moses' mouthpiece. Thereafter, Aaron was often at Moses' side, speaking to the Israelite leaders and demanding that Pharaoh let the Israelites leave Egypt (5:1-5).

During the Israelites' wilderness wanderings, Aaron became Israel's first high priest. God appointed Aaron and his sons to be set apart and dedicated as priests (28:1-5; 29:1-46; Lev 8:1-36). Aaron's role as high priest was especially prominent on the annual Day of Atonement, the only day on which the high priest entered the Most Holy Place to purify it from the effects of Israel's sins (Lev 16). Before he could do so, however, the high priest had to offer a sacrifice to atone for his own sins.

Aaron was an imperfect leader. While Moses was on Mount Sinai receiving the law from God, Aaron helped the people make an idol (ch 32). When Moses returned, Aaron gave poor excuses and blamed the people. Surprisingly, the Levite tribe, of whom Aaron and Moses were members, then supported Moses by executing many of the idol worshipers.

Aaron and his sister, Miriam, once wrongly challenged Moses' authority (Num 12). When other Levites later challenged Aaron's authority, God affirmed Aaron's role by making his staff bud with almond blossoms (Num 17). However, because Moses and Aaron challenged God's authority (Num 20:1-13), they both died in the wilderness without entering the Promised Land (Num 20:22-27).

Jesus has become the great high priest. Jesus far surpasses Aaron's priestly authority and effectiveness (see Heb 7–10).

Amram m. Jochebed
→ Miriam
→ Aaron → Nadab
→ Abihu
→ Eleazar → Phinehas
→ Ithamar
→ Moses

◂ **Aaron's Family (6:20-25).** Profiles are given for MOSES (p. 128) and ELEAZAR (p. 284).

4:31 ***the people of Israel were convinced:*** The initial response to the good news was one of faith and worship. Contrast the response of panic in 14:10-12, when they saw Pharaoh chasing them.

5:1-14 ***Pharaoh*** not only rejected Moses' request to release the Hebrew slaves, he also retaliated by making their work harder. The arrival of the rescuer had actually made the situation worse.

5:1 ***so they may hold a festival:*** See note on 3:18.

5:2 ***Pharaoh*** immediately moved to the heart of the issue. What god could possibly be superior to Pharaoh? What god could compel him to do what he did not want to do? This is a central issue for the whole human race. Is there someone or something greater than my self-interest?

5:3 ***he will kill us:*** God had not said this. Perhaps Moses and Aaron were trying to strengthen their case by saying that they had to obey God or die.

5:4-5 Evidently the people were anticipating their promised freedom and had stopped ***their work.***

Pharaoh Increases Israel's Oppression

6That same day Pharaoh sent this order to the Egyptian slave drivers and the Israelite foremen: 7"Do not supply any more straw for making bricks. Make the people get it themselves! 8But still require them to make the same number of bricks as before. Don't reduce the quota. They are lazy. That's why they are crying out, 'Let us go and offer sacrifices to our God.' 9Load them down with more work. Make them sweat! That will teach them to listen to lies!"

10So the slave drivers and foremen went out and told the people: "This is what Pharaoh says: I will not provide any more straw for you. 11Go and get it yourselves. Find it wherever you can. But you must produce just as many bricks as before!" 12So the people scattered throughout the land of Egypt in search of stubble to use as straw.

13Meanwhile, the Egyptian slave drivers continued to push hard. "Meet your daily quota of bricks, just as you did when we provided you with straw!" they demanded. 14Then they whipped the Israelite foremen they had put in charge of the work crews. "Why haven't you met your quotas either yesterday or today?" they demanded.

15So the Israelite foremen went to Pharaoh and pleaded with him. "Please don't treat your servants like this," they begged. 16"We are given no straw, but the slave drivers still demand, 'Make bricks!' We are being beaten, but it isn't our fault! Your own people are to blame!"

17But Pharaoh shouted, "You're just lazy! Lazy! That's why you're saying, 'Let us go and offer sacrifices to the LORD.' 18Now get back to work! No straw will be given to you, but you must still produce the full quota of bricks."

19The Israelite foremen could see that they were in serious trouble when they were told, "You must not reduce the number of bricks you make each day." 20As they left Pharaoh's court, they confronted Moses and Aaron, who were waiting outside for them. 21The foremen said to them, "May the LORD judge and punish you for making us stink before Pharaoh and his officials. You have put a sword into their hands, an excuse to kill us!"

22Then Moses went back to the LORD and protested, "Why have you brought all this trouble on your own people, Lord? Why did you send me? 23Ever since I came to Pharaoh as your spokesman, he has been even more brutal to your people. And you have done nothing to rescue them!"

Promises of Rescue

6 Then the LORD told Moses, "Now you will see what I will do to Pharaoh. When he feels the force of my strong hand, he will let the people go. In fact, he will force them to leave his land!"

2And God said to Moses, "I am Yahweh—'the LORD.' 3I appeared to Abraham, to Isaac, and to Jacob as El-Shaddai—'God [i]Almighty'—but I did not reveal my name, Yahweh, to them. 4And I reaffirmed my covenant with them. Under its terms, I promised to give them the land of Canaan,

5:6 Exod 3:7; 5:10, 14
5:7 Gen 11:3
5:14 Isa 10:24
5:17 Exod 5:8
5:21 Gen 16:5; 34:30
5:22 Num 11:11; Jer 4:10
5:23 Exod 3:8
6:1 Exod 3:19-20; 11:1; 12:31
6:2 Exod 3:14-15
6:3 Gen 17:1; Ps 83:18; Isa 52:6
[i]*shadday* (7706) ›Job 22:25

5:6-14 Pharaoh made the work harder in retaliation for their insubordination; he also believed they had too much time on their hands (5:8). He could not conceive of a god who would reveal himself outside of the established royal system of worship, so the only explanation he could imagine for their strange religious ideas was that they had dreamed them up themselves—when they should have been working (see also 5:17).

5:7 ***Straw*** is a binder to help clay and mud ***bricks*** retain their form while drying in the sun.

5:22-23 This was the crisis point. After the initial burst of enthusiasm (4:29-31), the offer of rescue produced nothing but skepticism, hostility, and worse oppression than before. Moses, the rescuer, was himself reduced to doubt.

5:22 The phrase ***brought all this trouble*** could be translated even more strongly as *done all this evil.* Is God really good or not? Instead of rescuing the people out of their evil circumstances as he had promised, it seems that God had only made the situation worse. Is he faithful or not? Is he powerful or not? (cp. Ps 105:25-27).

6:1-13 God renewed his promises. The offer of rescue brought the true question to the fore, the question articulated by Pharaoh: Who is the Lord (5:2)? As much as the Israelites needed rescue from bondage, their greater need was to know the Lord. The climax of God's renewed promises was ***"you will know that I am the LORD your God"*** (6:7).

6:1 ***Now you will see:*** Far from being daunted by the questions being raised about his integrity, his ability, and his very character, God looked forward to the clash of worldviews that lay ahead. ***Pharaoh***, thinking himself divine, would just be a pawn in the hand of the one true God.

6:2-8 Once again, God forcefully linked his promises to the patriarchs (Abraham's family) with what he was about to do. God's work in history shows his faithfulness. He has made promises, and he will keep them. God also wished to reveal more of himself than he had been able to do with the patriarchs. This generation would know more of God and his intentions than Abraham had, particularly regarding the implications of the ***covenant*** (6:4-5). Why does God ***redeem*** (6:6)? Why did he reveal himself to Abraham in the first place? God wanted the Israelites to be his ***own people*** and he wanted to be their God (6:7). God's goal is for humanity to be in a lovingly submissive covenant relationship with God, where we can be what he made us to be.

6:2-3 ***I am Yahweh . . . El-Shaddai:*** Here the NLT transliterates the divine names *Yahweh* and *El-Shaddai* because God was emphasizing that he was now using a different name than the name by which he was known to Abraham,

6:4 Gen 15:18
6:5 Exod 2:23-24
6:6 Exod 3:17; 13:3, 14 Deut 6:12; 26:8
6:7 Exod 16:12 Deut 4:20 Isa 60:16
6:8 Num 14:30 Josh 24:13
6:11 Exod 5:1; 7:2
6:12 Exod 4:10; 6:30

where they were living as foreigners. 5You
can be sure that I have heard the groans of
the people of Israel, who are now slaves to
the Egyptians. And I am well aware of my
covenant with them.
6"Therefore, say to the people of Israel:
'I am the LORD. I will free you from your
oppression and will rescue you from your
slavery in Egypt. I will redeem you with a
powerful arm and great acts of judgment.
7I will claim you as my own people, and I
will be your God. Then you will know that
I am the LORD your God who has freed you
from your oppression in Egypt. 8I will bring
you into the land I swore to give to Abraham,
Isaac, and Jacob. I will give it to you as your
very own possession. I am the LORD!' "
9So Moses told the people of Israel what
the LORD had said, but they refused to listen
anymore. They had become too discouraged by the brutality of their slavery.
10Then the LORD said to Moses, 11"Go
back to Pharaoh, the king of Egypt, and tell
him to let the people of Israel leave his country."
12"But LORD!" Moses objected. "My own
people won't listen to me anymore. How
can I expect Pharaoh to listen? I'm such a
clumsy speaker!"
13But the LORD spoke to Moses and Aaron
and gave them orders for the Israelites and
for Pharaoh, the king of Egypt. The LORD
commanded Moses and Aaron to lead the
people of Israel out of Egypt.

Hardship in Following God (5:1-23)

Exod 18:8; Gen 39:6-20; 1 Kgs 18:3-4; 19:1-10; Ps 6:6-7; 22:11-18; Matt 5:11-12; Mark 8:34; John 15:20; 16:33; Rom 16:20; 2 Cor 11:23-29; Eph 6:10-18; 2 Tim 3:12; Heb 10:32-36; 1 Pet 1:6-7; 3:9-17; 4:12-19

Sometimes people are urged to accept Christ because "he will solve your problems." But Christ did not promise to solve all of people's problems. In fact, he repeatedly warned people to consider what it would cost them to follow him (see, e.g., Luke 14:28), and he pointed out the hardships that would come into their lives as a result of choosing to follow him (see, e.g., Mark 8:34).

Exodus 5 gives us a case study: Pharaoh's earlier enslavement and persecution of the Hebrews was purely strategic. He worried that this growing sector of the population would cause trouble for him (1:8-22). In ch 5, the situation is different. Moses and Aaron had rallied the people's hopes that their God would soon rescue them (4:29-31). During their initial encounter with Pharaoh, Moses and Aaron confronted him with the reality of God's sovereign rule (5:2-3). Not surprisingly, Pharaoh considered this an affront to his own sovereignty and reacted strongly against the Israelites (5:6-21). When God's Kingdom clashes with God's enemies, there is often conflict and hardship for God's people.

We should not be surprised, therefore, when hardships come our way. Believers have changed allegiance from the realm of darkness to the realm of light (Col 1:12-13), and those who rule in the realm of darkness will certainly not let us leave their power without a fight. We, like the ancient Hebrews, must stand firm in our faith, knowing that God will secure the final victory on our behalf (6:1-8; see also Matt 5:11-12; John 16:33; Rom 16:20; Eph 6:10-18).

Isaac, and Jacob. To assist the English reader, the translators have also supplied the English terms usually used for these Hebrew terms: "the LORD" and "God Almighty." • Regarding the name *Yahweh*, see the note on 3:15. • *El-Shaddai*, which means "God Almighty," is the name for God used in Gen 17:1; 28:3; 35:11; 43:14; 48:3. • ***I did not reveal my name, Yahweh, to them:*** The name Yahweh in fact appears frequently in Genesis (translated "the LORD"). Two solutions are possible: (1) The name Yahweh was not known to the patriarchs, but Moses, the author of Genesis, was inspired to insert that name in those places in Genesis where God's grace and his nature as covenant-keeper were apparent. (2) While the patriarchs might have known the name Yahweh, it is possible that they had never seen God's nature displayed as it was in the Exodus and the Sinai Covenant. In Hebrew, a person's name has a broader significance than it does in English. People's names were intended to reflect their character and nature, not just serve as a label (see, e.g., Ps 8:1, 9; 148:13). Here *reveal* is a Hebrew word often translated "to know," which implies intimate knowledge and experience. In this case, the patriarchs knew God's name, but they did not know and experience his nature fully as he revealed himself in the Exodus.

6:7 ***Then you will know that I am the LORD:*** The Hebrew word translated *know* is always based on experience and relationship. The same word is used to describe human sexual relations. To *know* God as Yahweh is not just to know abstract facts about him, but to be in a relationship with him in which we are always learning who he is and what he wants us to do. This is the only true rescue from the human predicament of sin described in Gen 3–11. The importance of "knowing the Lord" in the book of Exodus is seen in its recurrence, especially in chs 5–18 (5:2; 7:5, 17; 8:10, 22; 9:29; 10:2; 11:7; 14:4, 18; 16:6, 12; 18:11).

6:9 The crisis deepened as the people ***refused to listen*** to the reaffirmation of the promises. They had not anticipated that their initial faith would produce greater problems for them.

6:10-13 The crisis hit bottom. Even Moses was back to the situation on Sinai, where he had first responded to God's call with protests of inadequacy (3:1–4:13): ***I'm such a clumsy speaker*** (literally *I have uncircumcised lips;* also in 6:30). But God renewed his ***orders.***

The Ancestors of Moses and Aaron
14These are the ancestors of some of the
clans of Israel:

The sons of Reuben, Israel's oldest son, were
Hanoch, Pallu, Hezron, and Carmi. Their
descendants became the clans of Reuben.
15The sons of Simeon were Jemuel, Jamin,
Ohad, Jakin, Zohar, and Shaul. (Shaul's
mother was a Canaanite woman.) Their
descendants became the clans of Simeon.
16These are the descendants of Levi, as
listed in their family records: The sons of
Levi were Gershon, Kohath, and Merari.
(Levi lived to be 137 years old.)
17The descendants of Gershon included Libni and Shimei, each of whom
became the ancestor of a clan.
18The descendants of Kohath included
Amram, Izhar, Hebron, and Uzziel. (Kohath lived to be 133 years old.)
19The descendants of Merari included
Mahli and Mushi.

These are the clans of the Levites, as listed
in their family records.

20Amram married his father's sister Jochebed, and she gave birth to his sons,
Aaron and Moses. (Amram lived to be
137 years old.)
21The sons of Izhar were Korah, Nepheg,
and Zicri.
22The sons of Uzziel were Mishael, Elzaphan, and Sithri.
23Aaron married Elisheba, the daughter of
Amminadab and sister of Nahshon, and
she gave birth to his sons, Nadab, Abihu,
Eleazar, and Ithamar.
24The sons of Korah were Assir, Elkanah,
and Abiasaph. Their descendants became the clans of Korah.
25Eleazar son of Aaron married one of the
daughters of Putiel, and she gave birth to
his son, Phinehas.
These are the ancestors of the Levite families, listed according to their clans.

26The Aaron and Moses named in this
list are the same ones to whom the LORD
said, "Lead the people of Israel out of the
land of Egypt like an army." 27It was Moses
and Aaron who spoke to Pharaoh, the king
of Egypt, about leading the people of Israel
out of Egypt.
28When the LORD spoke to Moses in the
land of Egypt, 29he said to him, "I am the
LORD! Tell Pharaoh, the king of Egypt, everything I am telling you." 30But Moses argued
with the LORD, saying, "I can't do it! I'm such
a clumsy speaker! Why should Pharaoh listen to me?"

The LORD's Command Renewed
7 Then the LORD said to Moses, "Pay
close attention to this. I will make you
seem like God to Pharaoh, and your brother,
Aaron, will be your [j]prophet. 2Tell Aaron
everything I command you, and Aaron must
command Pharaoh to let the people of Israel
leave his country. 3But I will make Pharaoh's

6:14 Gen 46:9; Num 26:5-11
6:15 Gen 46:10
6:16 Gen 46:11; Num 3:17; 1 Chr 6:1, 16-19
6:17 Num 3:18-20; 1 Chr 6:17
6:18 Num 3:25-30; 1 Chr 6:2, 18
6:19 1 Chr 6:19
6:20 Exod 2:1-2; Num 26:59
6:21 Num 16:1
6:22 Lev 10:4
6:23 Ruth 4:19-20
6:24 1 Chr 6:22-23, 37
6:25 Num 25:7, 11; Josh 24:33
6:26 Exod 6:13
6:29 Exod 6:2, 6, 8; 7:2
6:30 Exod 4:10; 6:12
7:1 Exod 4:16; *ʲnabi'* (5030) ‣Exod 15:20

6:14-30 This genealogical interlude places Moses and Aaron among the families of Israel. That it is an interlude is clear because 6:30 is a repetition of 6:12. There is a recurring emphasis in Exodus on Yahweh as the God of the ancestors, both explicitly (from 3:6 on) and implicitly (from 1:1 on). What was about to happen was not an unrelated action by some new god who was devaluing impotent older gods (a typical theme in ancient pagan literature). Unlike pagan gods, whose only purpose is personal power, and who are in constant conflict among themselves, the true God has a single, overarching purpose: He wants his creation to find its fulfillment in proper relation to him. Although he enacts that purpose in ever-expanding displays of creativity, the new activities are always consistent with what he has already revealed of himself. Moses and Aaron did not suddenly appear out of the unknown, but were an integral part of that same people to whom God first revealed himself and through whom he was about to give an even grander revelation. The genealogies of Jesus have a similar purpose (Matt 1:1-16; Luke 3:23-38).

6:14-16 The genealogy works its way through Jacob's first and second sons to the third, Levi, the ancestor of Moses and Aaron. Having reached Levi, it dispenses with the other nine sons.

6:16-20 This genealogy of Levi's descendants focuses on ***Aaron*** and ***Moses;*** four generations are given in the genealogy from Levi to Aaron and Moses (cp. Gen 15:16). Since the people of Israel had lived in Egypt for 430 years (see 12:40-41; Gen 15:13), this genealogy skips numerous generations. In Gen 46:11, ***Gershon, Kohath, and Merari*** are listed as the actual ***sons of Levi*** who moved down to Egypt with their father and the rest of Jacob's family. ***Amram's*** wife, Jochebed, ***gave birth to his sons*** (6:20). This is very concrete language, so there is no reason to believe that there were unnamed generations between Amram and ***Aaron and Moses.*** This suggests that the unnamed generations were between Kohath (son of Levi) and Amram (father of Aaron and Moses).

6:18 *The descendants* (literally *sons*) ***of Kohath included Amram, Izhar, Hebron, and Uzziel:*** The Hebrew word for "sons" can also mean "descendants," which accommodates the possibility of unnamed generations.

6:20-25 The descendants of Kohath's sons now become the focus of the genealogy. The families of ***Aaron*** son of Amram and ***Korah*** son of Izhar are given a more detailed listing (6:23-24), followed by one of Aaron's sons, ***Eleazar*** (6:25). The focus is clearly on Aaron's line through Eleazar, who received the high priesthood (see "Eleazar" at Num 20:22-29, p. 284). The fact that Aaron and Korah were cousins makes it easier to see why Aaron's elevation to high priesthood was so galling to Korah (see Num 16:1-3); family rivalry is nothing new. The later rebellion might explain why Korah and his sons are given particular mention in this genealogy.

7:1-7 In this final scene in the offer of rescue, the Lord once again answered Moses' fears of not being able to speak eloquently. He would allow Moses to

7:3 Exod 4:21
7:4 Exod 11:9
7:5 Exod 8:19
7:7 Deut 34:7; Acts 7:23, 30
7:9 Exod 4:3; Isa 7:11
7:11 Gen 41:8; Exod 8:7, 18; 2 Tim 3:8-9
7:13 Exod 4:21
7:14 Exod 8:15
7:15 Exod 2:5; 8:20
7:16 Exod 4:23
7:17 Rev 11:6; 16:4
7:19 Exod 14:21
7:20 Ps 78:44; 105:29
7:22 Exod 8:7

heart stubborn so I can multiply my miraculous signs and wonders in the land of Egypt.
4Even then Pharaoh will refuse to listen to
you. So I will bring down my fist on Egypt.
Then I will rescue my forces—my people,
the Israelites—from the land of Egypt with
great acts of judgment. 5When I raise my
powerful hand and bring out the Israelites,
the Egyptians will know that I am the LORD."
6So Moses and Aaron did just as the LORD
had commanded them. 7Moses was eighty
years old, and Aaron was eighty-three when
they made their demands to Pharaoh.

Opposition to Rescue and the Plagues (7:8–11:10)

Aaron's Staff Becomes a Serpent

8Then the LORD said to Moses and Aaron,
9"Pharaoh will demand, 'Show me a miracle.' When he does this, say to Aaron, 'Take
your staff and throw it down in front of Pharaoh, and it will become a serpent.' "
10So Moses and Aaron went to Pharaoh
and did what the LORD had commanded
them. Aaron threw down his staff before
Pharaoh and his officials, and it became a serpent! 11Then Pharaoh called in his own wise
men and sorcerers, and these Egyptian magicians did the same thing with their magic.
12They threw down their staffs, which also
became serpents! But then Aaron's staff
swallowed up their staffs. 13Pharaoh's heart,
however, remained hard. He still refused to
listen, just as the LORD had predicted.

A Plague of Blood

14Then the LORD said to Moses, "Pharaoh's
heart is stubborn, and he still refuses to
let the people go. 15So go to Pharaoh in the
morning as he goes down to the river. Stand
on the bank of the Nile and meet him there.
Be sure to take along the staff that turned
into a snake. 16Then announce to him, 'The
LORD, the God of the Hebrews, has sent me
to tell you, "Let my people go, so they can
worship me in the wilderness." Until now,
you have refused to listen to him. 17So this
is what the LORD says: "I will show you that
I am the LORD." Look! I will strike the water
of the Nile with this staff in my hand, and
the river will turn to blood. 18The fish in it
will die, and the river will stink. The Egyptians will not be able to drink any water
from the Nile.' "
19Then the LORD said to Moses: "Tell
Aaron, 'Take your staff and raise your hand
over the waters of Egypt—all its rivers, canals, ponds, and all the reservoirs. Turn all
the water to blood. Everywhere in Egypt
the water will turn to blood, even the water
stored in wooden bowls and stone pots.' "
20So Moses and Aaron did just as the
LORD commanded them. As Pharaoh and
all of his officials watched, Aaron raised
his staff and struck the water of the Nile.
Suddenly, the whole river turned to blood!
21The fish in the river died, and the water
became so foul that the Egyptians couldn't
drink it. There was blood everywhere
throughout the land of Egypt. 22But again
the magicians of Egypt used their magic,
and they, too, turned water into blood. So
Pharaoh's heart remained hard. He refused
to listen to Moses and Aaron, just as the
LORD had predicted. 23Pharaoh returned to

---

speak through Aaron (see 4:16), but ***Pharaoh will refuse to listen*** regardless. God's power, not Moses' eloquence, was the important factor. ***Moses and Aaron*** then took the step of faith and did what God ***had commanded.*** The first crisis (see note on 5:22-23) had passed.

7:3 The Lord would use ***miraculous signs and wonders*** to convince Pharaoh, just as he had promised to use signs to convince the Israelites that they should follow Moses (3:12; 4:5, 8, 9).

7:5 ***my powerful hand:*** A further revelation of God would take place in the Exodus of the Israelites from Egypt, revealing God's incomparable power.

7:7 Although ***eighty*** seems old to us, the typical age of Moses and Aaron's ancestors at death had been between 130 and 140 years (see 6:16, 18, 20).

7:8–12:30 This section divides the events of rescue into two parts: the plagues (7:8–11:10) and the Passover (12:1-30). God demonstrated that he is the Lord of life and death and nothing has any power against him (see Isa 43:13). The God of the patriarchs is also the God of the universe.

7:8–11:10 God showed that all the Egyptians' so-called gods, supposed to be sources of life, were really sources of death apart from the life-giving power of the Lord (see 12:12; 18:11).

7:9 ***Serpent*** (Hebrew *tannin*) is a different word than the word translated "snake" in 4:3. *Tannin* is often used to refer to a sea monster (the Greek version translates it "dragon"). In various places, Egypt is referred to as an ultimately impotent sea monster (Isa 30:7; Ezek 29:3). The image of a cobra's head was on the pharaoh's headdress.

7:11 ***these Egyptian magicians did the same thing*** (see also 7:22; 8:7): While demonic power might have been involved, it is also possible that some sleight of hand was being practiced. When they could not reproduce the plague of gnats, they declared that it was "the finger of God" (8:19), indicating that their own actions were not a manifestation of divine power. While the Egyptian magicians are not identified by name, tradition gives their names as Jannes and Jambres (see 2 Tim 3:8).

7:14-25 The first plague was the plague on the Nile, when ***the whole river turned to blood*** (7:20). The Egyptians correctly understood that without the Nile there would be no life in Egypt. They worshiped the Nile as the Mother of Egypt, but God showed that life is his to give or withhold.

7:14 ***stubborn*** (literally *heavy*): See "A Hardened Heart" at 14:4, 8, p. 149.

7:22 The Egyptian priests did not do anything as extensive as Moses and Aaron had done, but Pharaoh did not want to believe, so it took only the smallest thing to justify his unbelief.

his palace and put the whole thing out of his mind. 24Then all the Egyptians dug along the riverbank to find drinking water, for they couldn't drink the water from the Nile.

25Seven days passed from the time the LORD struck the Nile.

A Plague of Frogs

8 Then the LORD said to Moses, "Go back to Pharaoh and announce to him, 'This is what the LORD says: Let my people go, so they can worship me. 2If you refuse to let them go, I will send a plague of frogs across your entire land. 3The Nile River will swarm with frogs. They will come up out of the river and into your palace, even into your bedroom and onto your bed! They will enter the houses of your officials and your people. They will even jump into your ovens and your kneading bowls. 4Frogs will jump on you, your people, and all your officials.' "

5Then the LORD said to Moses, "Tell Aaron, 'Raise the staff in your hand over all the rivers, canals, and ponds of Egypt, and bring up frogs over all the land.' " 6So Aaron raised his hand over the waters of Egypt, and frogs came up and covered the whole land! 7But the magicians were able to do the same thing with their magic. They, too, caused frogs to come up on the land of Egypt.

8Then Pharaoh summoned Moses and Aaron and begged, "Plead with the LORD to take the frogs away from me and my people. I will let your people go, so they can offer sacrifices to the LORD."

9"You set the time!" Moses replied. "Tell me when you want me to pray for you, your officials, and your people. Then you and your houses will be rid of the frogs. They will remain only in the Nile River."

10"Do it tomorrow," Pharaoh said.

"All right," Moses replied, "it will be as you have said. Then you will know that there is no one like the LORD our God. 11The frogs will leave you and your houses, your officials, and your people. They will remain only in the Nile River."

12So Moses and Aaron left Pharaoh's palace, and Moses cried out to the LORD about the frogs he had inflicted on Pharaoh. 13And the LORD did just what Moses had predicted. The frogs in the houses, the courtyards, and the fields all died. 14The Egyptians piled them into great heaps, and a terrible stench filled the land. 15But when Pharaoh saw that relief had come, he became stubborn. He refused to listen to Moses and Aaron, just as the LORD had predicted.

A Plague of Gnats

16So the LORD said to Moses, "Tell Aaron, 'Raise your staff and strike the ground. The dust will turn into swarms of gnats throughout the land of Egypt.' " 17So Moses and Aaron did just as the LORD had commanded them. When Aaron raised his hand and struck the ground with his staff, gnats infested the entire land, covering the Egyptians and their animals. All the dust in the land of Egypt turned into gnats. 18Pharaoh's magicians tried to do the same thing with their secret arts, but this time they failed. And the gnats covered everyone, people and animals alike.

19"This is the finger of God!" the magicians exclaimed to Pharaoh. But Pharaoh's heart remained hard. He wouldn't listen to them, just as the LORD had predicted.

A Plague of Flies

20Then the LORD told Moses, "Get up early in the morning and stand in Pharaoh's way as he goes down to the river. Say to him, 'This

8:1 Exod 5:1
8:2 Ps 105:30
8:5 Exod 7:9-20
8:6 Ps 78:45; 105:30
8:7 Exod 7:11
8:10 Exod 9:14; 15:11; Deut 4:35; Isa 46:9
8:12 Exod 8:30; 9:33; 10:18
8:15 Exod 7:14; Eccl 8:11
8:16 Exod 4:2
8:17 Ps 105:31
8:18 Exod 7:11; 9:11
8:19 Exod 7:5; 1 Sam 6:9
8:20 Exod 7:15

8:1-32 Verses 8:1-4 are numbered 7:26-29 in the Hebrew text, and verses 8:5-32 are numbered 8:1-28 in the Hebrew text.

8:1-15 The second plague was the *plague of frogs* (8:2). The Egyptians gave special reverence to amphibians because of their ability to live in two different worlds; Egyptians were deeply concerned with survival in the next world, after death. God showed that frogs have no special hold on life. This plague is sometimes said to have been a natural result of whatever happened to make the Nile River uninhabitable. However, the extent of the plague was more than a natural result.

8:7-8 The *magicians* were able to duplicate the plague in some sense, but *Pharaoh* did not ask them to rid the land of the frogs. Instead, he *begged* Moses *to take* them *away*. He already knew where the real power was.

8:9 In this instance, the evidence of God's power was not in the event per se but in the timing. God could keep the frogs alive or he could end their lives. Pharaoh needed only to say when.

8:10 *you will know that there is no one like the LORD our God:* Once more the issue is highlighted (see 7:17). These events were not primarily about rescue, but about the nature of reality. Who was rescuing these people—one of the gods, or the one true God, the Lord?

8:13 *had predicted:* Moses predicted that the plague would stop the next day; God predicted that Pharaoh would refuse to listen (see 8:15). The element of prediction is central to God's lordship. God sees and controls the future; he is the Lord.

8:15 *became stubborn* (literally *made his heart heavy;* also in 8:32): See "A Hardened Heart" at 14:4, 8, p. 149.

8:16-19 The third plague was the plague of *gnats*. The word translated "gnats" is very general. Technical OT dictionaries often translate it as "vermin." The English term "bugs" would come close. The whole land was infested with insects of one sort or another.

8:19 *This is the finger of God!* See note on 7:11.

8:20-32 The fourth plague was the plague of *flies*. The Egyptians worshiped

8:22
Exod 9:4; 10:23
8:24
Ps 78:45; 105:31
8:25
Exod 8:8; 10:8
8:27
Exod 3:18
8:28
Exod 8:8
8:30
Exod 8:12
8:32
Exod 8:8, 15
9:1
Exod 8:1; 10:3
9:3
Exod 7:4
9:4
Exod 8:23; 9:26
9:7
Exod 7:14; 8:32

is what the LORD says: Let my people go, so
they can worship me. 21If you refuse, then
I will send swarms of flies on you, your officials, your people, and all the houses. The
Egyptian homes will be filled with flies, and
the ground will be covered with them. 22But
this time I will spare the region of Goshen,
where my people live. No flies will be found
there. Then you will know that I am the
LORD and that I am present even in the heart
of your land. 23I will make a clear distinction
between my people and your people. This
miraculous sign will happen tomorrow.' "
24And the LORD did just as he had said. A
thick swarm of flies filled Pharaoh's palace
and the houses of his officials. The whole
land of Egypt was thrown into chaos by the
flies.
25Pharaoh called for Moses and Aaron.
"All right! Go ahead and offer sacrifices to
your God," he said. "But do it here in this
land."
26But Moses replied, "That wouldn't be
right. The Egyptians detest the sacrifices
that we offer to the LORD our God. Look, if
we offer our sacrifices here where the Egyptians can see us, they will stone us. 27We
must take a three-day trip into the wilderness to offer sacrifices to the LORD our God,
just as he has commanded us."
28"All right, go ahead," Pharaoh replied. "I
will let you go into the wilderness to offer
sacrifices to the LORD your God. But don't go
too far away. Now hurry and pray for me."
29Moses answered, "As soon as I leave
you, I will pray to the LORD, and tomorrow
the swarms of flies will disappear from you
and your officials and all your people. But
I am warning you, Pharaoh, don't lie to us
again and refuse to let the people go to sacrifice to the LORD."
30So Moses left Pharaoh's palace and
pleaded with the LORD to remove all the
flies. 31And the LORD did as Moses asked
and caused the swarms of flies to disappear
from Pharaoh, his officials, and his people.
Not a single fly remained. 32But Pharaoh
again became stubborn and refused to let
the people go.

A Plague against Livestock

9 "Go back to Pharaoh," the LORD commanded Moses. "Tell him, 'This is what
the LORD, the God of the Hebrews, says:
Let my people go, so they can worship me.
2If you continue to hold them and refuse
to let them go, 3the hand of the LORD will
strike all your livestock—your horses, donkeys, camels, cattle, sheep, and goats—with
a deadly plague. 4But the LORD will again
make a distinction between the livestock of
the Israelites and that of the Egyptians. Not
a single one of Israel's animals will die! 5The
LORD has already set the time for the plague
to begin. He has declared that he will strike
the land tomorrow.' "
6And the LORD did just as he had said.
The next morning all the livestock of the
Egyptians died, but the Israelites didn't lose
a single animal. 7Pharaoh sent his officials
to investigate, and they discovered that the
Israelites had not lost a single animal! But
even so, Pharaoh's heart remained stubborn,
and he still refused to let the people go.

---

insects such as flies that seemed to be able to turn death into life, as their young seemed to emerge from decaying matter. If the Egyptians thought that insects had the secret of life, God would let them have all the insects they wanted. Some say that this infestation was the natural result of all the dead frogs, but there were ***no flies*** in ***Goshen*** (8:22), the northeastern delta area where the Hebrews lived. God's miraculous power was clearly seen in his ability to infest one area while sparing another at will.

8:23 ***I will make a clear distinction between:*** As translated from the Greek and Latin versions; Hebrew reads *I will set redemption between.*

8:25 ***Pharaoh*** attempted to bargain with God. He wanted to obey partially while still retaining control. James says of such people, "Their loyalty is divided between God and the world" (Jas 1:8), and such a person cannot receive anything from the Lord.

8:26-27 ***Moses*** pointed out the impossibility of what Pharaoh was asking on the grounds of the Egyptians' own prejudice: They considered all Semites to be uncultured and uncouth (see Gen 43:32). • The Hebrews were leaving Egypt in order to worship God (see, e.g., 5:1; 7:16; 8:1, 20). God's purpose for the Exodus was to lead his people into a proper relationship with him.

8:29-30 ***I will pray:*** Moses was learning the role of intercessor that would be so much a part of his life in future years (see, e.g., 32:11-13, 30-32; Num 14:13-19). It must have been increasingly tempting to let the Egyptians continue to experience the results of their king's stubbornness, but Moses was willing to ***plead with*** God not to leave them in a permanent state of grief and distress.

9:1-7 The fifth plague was against the ***livestock.*** As with the withholding of flies from the area where the Hebrews lived (8:22-23), the ***distinction between the livestock of the Israelites and that of the Egyptians*** (9:4) shows that a natural explanation of this event is insufficient, even if the previous plagues contributed. The Egyptians, like many in the ancient Near East, worshiped the ram, the goat, and the bull as representing power and fertility. These animals had no power before the Lord, in whom true power resides.

9:3 ***Your livestock*** refers specifically to field animals. Other animals would have boils inflicted upon them in the next plague. • The term ***all*** (also in 9:6) is not absolute; it does not mean that every single livestock animal was killed. There were still some left to be protected from or struck down by the hail of the seventh plague (9:20, 25).

9:5-6 Prediction again played an important role. These events were being directed by the One who is sovereign over all that happens.

9:7 ***stubborn*** (literally *heavy*): See "A Hardened Heart" at 14:4, 8, p. 149.

A Plague of Festering Boils
8 Then the LORD said to Moses and Aaron,
"Take handfuls of soot from a brick kiln,
and have Moses toss it into the air while Pharaoh watches. 9 The ashes will spread like
fine dust over the whole land of Egypt, causing festering boils to break out on people
and animals throughout the land."
10 So they took soot from a brick kiln and
went and stood before Pharaoh. As Pharaoh
watched, Moses threw the soot into the air,
and boils broke out on people and animals
alike. 11 Even the magicians were unable to
stand before Moses, because the boils had
broken out on them and all the Egyptians.
12 But the LORD hardened Pharaoh's heart,
and just as the LORD had predicted to Moses,
Pharaoh refused to listen.

A Plague of Hail
13 Then the LORD said to Moses, "Get up early
in the morning and stand before Pharaoh.
Tell him, 'This is what the LORD, the God of
the Hebrews, says: Let my people go, so they
can worship me. 14 If you don't, I will send
more plagues on you and your officials and
your people. Then you will know that there
is no one like me in all the earth. 15 By now
I could have lifted my hand and struck you
and your people with a plague to wipe you
off the face of the earth. 16 But I have spared
you for a purpose—to show you my power
and to spread my fame throughout the
earth. 17 But you still lord it over my people
and refuse to let them go. 18 So tomorrow at
this time I will send a hailstorm more devastating than any in all the history of Egypt.
19 Quick! Order your livestock and servants
to come in from the fields to find shelter.
Any person or animal left outside will die
when the hail falls.' "
20 Some of Pharaoh's officials were afraid
because of what the LORD had said. They
quickly brought their servants and livestock
in from the fields. 21 But those who paid no
attention to the word of the LORD left theirs
out in the open.
22 Then the LORD said to Moses, "Lift your
hand toward the sky so hail may fall on
the people, the livestock, and all the plants
throughout the land of Egypt."
23 So Moses lifted his staff toward the sky,
and the LORD sent thunder and hail, and
lightning flashed toward the earth. The
LORD sent a tremendous hailstorm against
all the land of Egypt. 24 Never in all the history of Egypt had there been a storm like
that, with such devastating hail and continuous lightning. 25 It left all of Egypt in
ruins. The hail struck down everything in
the open field—people, animals, and plants
alike. Even the trees were destroyed. 26 The
only place without hail was the region of Goshen, where the people of Israel lived.
27 Then Pharaoh quickly summoned
Moses and Aaron. "This time I have sinned,"
he confessed. "The LORD is the righteous
one, and my people and I are wrong. 28 Please
beg the LORD to end this terrifying thunder
and hail. We've had enough. I will let you go;
you don't need to stay any longer."
29 "All right," Moses replied. "As soon as I
leave the city, I will lift my hands and pray
to the LORD. Then the thunder and hail will
stop, and you will know that the earth belongs to the LORD. 30 But I know that you and
your officials still do not fear the LORD God."
31 (All the flax and barley were ruined
by the hail, because the barley had formed
heads and the flax was budding. 32 But the
wheat and the emmer wheat were spared,
because they had not yet sprouted from the
ground.)

9:9 Lev 13:18; Rev 16:2
9:11 Exod 8:18
9:12 Exod 4:21
9:13 Exod 8:20
9:14 Exod 8:10; 15:11
9:16 Exod 14:4, 17; *Rom 9:17
9:18 Exod 9:23-24
9:20 Prov 13:13
9:22 Rev 16:21
9:23 Gen 19:24; Josh 10:11; Ps 78:47; Rev 8:7; 16:21
9:25 Ps 105:32
9:26 Exod 8:22; 10:23
9:27 2 Chr 12:6; Ps 129:4
9:28 Exod 8:8; 10:16-17
9:29 Ps 24:1; 1 Cor 10:26
9:30 Exod 8:29

9:8-12 The sixth plague brought *festering boils* on humans and animals. At this point the magicians, far from being able to duplicate the sign, were unable to spare themselves from it. Their defeat was complete.

9:12 Plagues five and six apparently dissipated on their own, since there was no plea by Pharaoh to bring them to an end.

9:13-33 The seventh plague was a *hailstorm* (9:18). It rains in Egypt only a few days each year, and hail and thunderstorms are largely unknown, so this storm would have been terrifying. That may be why there is more theological reflection associated with it. The *devastating* effect of the plague was to destroy the *flax and barley* crops (9:31).

9:13 *so they can worship me:* See note on 8:26-27.

9:14-17 God explained the purpose of the plagues to Pharaoh: They were revelatory, designed to demonstrate (especially to Pharaoh) that *there is no one like me in all the earth* (9:14; see also Isa 46:9; Jer 10:6-7). God had not destroyed Pharaoh and Egypt in a single blow, as he *could have* done. Rather he had *spared* them (9:16), giving them an opportunity to submit to his power. But Pharaoh refused to humble himself and stop lording it *over* the Lord's *people* (9:17).

9:14 *on you:* Literally *on your heart.*

9:16 *to show you my power:* Greek version reads *to display my power in you;* cp. Rom 9:17, where Paul quotes from the Greek version of this verse as he describes the sovereignty of God.

9:20-21 *Some of Pharaoh's officials* were beginning to make appropriate deductions from their experiences thus far and to take precautions, while others imitated their master's refusal to submit. Pride often dominates reason.

9:26 The hail was not a natural event, either in extent or in selectivity (see note on 9:1-7).

9:27 *Pharaoh* was driven to a logical conclusion. In the face of such clear evidence to the contrary, pride was not merely a failure; it was a sin.

9:29 There is no one like the Lord in all the earth (9:14), and all *the earth belongs to the LORD.* This was the inescapable message of the plagues, though

9:35 Exod 4:21
10:1 Exod 4:21; 7:14
10:2 Exod 13:8, 14; Deut 4:9; Ps 44:1
10:3 Exod 4:23
10:4 Rev 9:3; ᵏ'*arbeh* (0697) ‣Exod 10:12
10:5 Exod 9:32; Joel 1:4; 2:25
10:7 Exod 7:5

33So Moses left Pharaoh's court and went out of the city. When he lifted his hands to the LORD, the thunder and hail stopped, and the downpour ceased. 34But when Pharaoh saw that the rain, hail, and thunder had stopped, he and his officials sinned again, and Pharaoh again became stubborn. 35Because his heart was hard, Pharaoh refused to let the people leave, just as the LORD had predicted through Moses.

A Plague of Locusts

10 Then the LORD said to Moses, "Return to Pharaoh and make your demands again. I have made him and his officials stubborn so I can display my miraculous signs among them. 2I've also done it so you can tell your children and grandchildren about how I made a mockery of the Egyptians and about the signs I displayed among them—and so you will know that I am the LORD."

3So Moses and Aaron went to Pharaoh and said, "This is what the LORD, the God of the Hebrews, says: How long will you refuse to submit to me? Let my people go, so they can worship me. 4If you refuse, watch out! For tomorrow I will bring a swarm of [k]locusts on your country. 5They will cover the land so that you won't be able to see the ground. They will devour what little is left of your crops after the hailstorm, including all the trees growing in the fields. 6They will overrun your palaces and the homes of your officials and all the houses in Egypt. Never in the history of Egypt have your ancestors seen a plague like this one!" And with that, Moses turned and left Pharaoh.

7Pharaoh's officials now came to Pharaoh and appealed to him. "How long will you let this man hold us hostage? Let the men go to worship the LORD their God! Don't you realize that Egypt lies in ruins?"

The Plagues (7:14–11:10)

Exod 7:3-5; 12:28-33; 32:35; Gen 12:15-20; 20:1-18; Num 11:33; 12:1-15; 16:43-50; 1 Kgs 13:4; 2 Kgs 2:24; 2 Chr 26:16-21; Acts 5:1-11

Rescuing the Hebrew people from oppression by the Egyptians was not the main purpose of the plagues. If that had been the case, one climactic miracle would have been sufficient. The real purpose of the plagues was to communicate who God is—to Israel, to Egypt, and to the surrounding nations.

The Israelites did not know who the Lord was. They had lived for hundreds of years in Egypt, one of the most polytheistic religious environments the world has ever known. Whatever they may have believed about God when they arrived in Egypt, it is certain that they were infected with the prevailing pagan views during their sojourn there (see ch 32).

The plagues revealed the Lord's absolute superiority over everything in creation. These cataclysmic events were specifically aimed at elements the Egyptians particularly revered and worshiped, such as the Nile River (plague one, 7:14-25), amphibians (plague two, 8:1-15), insects (plagues three and four, 8:16-32), animals (plagues five and six, 9:1-12), plants (plagues seven and eight, 9:13–10:20), the sun (plague nine, 10:21-29), and life itself (plague ten, 11:1-10; 12:29-32). Thus Yahweh demonstrated to both the Egyptians and the Israelites that he alone is God.

The plagues are often referred to as "signs," just as Jesus' miracles were (e.g., 7:3; 10:1-2; John 2:23; 4:48; 12:37). The plagues show that worship of the created order brings God's judgment. Jesus' miracles, on the other hand, show that with the Lord, all that is deadly in creation—illness, the demonic, nature run amok, and even death itself—can be overcome by life.

the Egyptians had difficulty accepting it.

9:34 ***became stubborn*** (literally *made his heart heavy*): See "A Hardened Heart" at 14:4, 8, p. 149.

10:1-20 The eighth plague was the plague of ***locusts*** (10:4). Evidently enough time had elapsed between this plague and the previous one that the wheat and emmer wheat had sprouted (see 9:32). The Egyptian god Osiris was especially revered as the god who descended into the underworld and brought plant life back in the spring. This second, climactic attack on the plant life demonstrated that even Osiris was helpless before the Lord. There is no eternal life in sprouting plants.

10:1 ***have made him and his officials stubborn*** (literally *have made his heart and his officials' hearts heavy*): See "A Hardened Heart" at 14:4, 8, p. 149.

10:2 The plagues were sent so that Israel ***will know that I am the LORD*** (similarly, with respect to Egypt, see 9:14-16).

10:4 These ***locusts*** were not the insects called locusts in North America, but a form of migratory grasshopper. Swarming out of desert regions, they could devastate large areas of land, devouring all the plant life before them.

10:7-11 The ***officials,*** with no royal prestige on the line, were willing to learn the lessons of God's sovereignty and ***let the men go. Pharaoh*** again resisted, in an effort to save face somehow. He would let them go only if they left their families behind and were thus bound to return, but Moses had never said they would return. While the purpose for going into the wilderness was to worship God, it was unthinkable that oppressed slaves would willingly return to their oppressors once they were free, and Pharaoh knew it.

8So Moses and Aaron were brought back
to Pharaoh. "All right," he told them, "go and
worship the LORD your God. But who exactly will be going with you?"
9Moses replied, "We will all go—young
and old, our sons and daughters, and our
flocks and herds. We must all join together
in celebrating a festival to the LORD."
10Pharaoh retorted, "The LORD will certainly need to be with you if I let you take
your little ones! I can see through your evil
plan. 11Never! Only the men may go and
worship the LORD, since that is what you requested." And Pharaoh threw them out of
the palace.
12Then the LORD said to Moses, "Raise
your hand over the land of Egypt to bring
on the [a]locusts. Let them cover the land and
devour every plant that survived the hailstorm."
13So Moses raised his staff over Egypt,
and the LORD caused an east wind to blow
over the land all that day and through the
night. When morning arrived, the east wind
had brought the locusts. 14And the locusts
swarmed over the whole land of Egypt, settling in dense swarms from one end of the
country to the other. It was the worst locust
plague in Egyptian history, and there has
never been another one like it. 15For the
locusts covered the whole country and darkened the land. They devoured every plant in
the fields and all the fruit on the trees that
had survived the hailstorm. Not a single leaf
was left on the trees and plants throughout
the land of Egypt.
16Pharaoh quickly summoned Moses and
Aaron. "I have [b]sinned against the LORD your
God and against you," he confessed. 17"[c]For-
give my sin, just this once, and plead with
the LORD your God to take away this death
from me."
18So Moses left Pharaoh's court and
pleaded with the LORD. 19The LORD responded by shifting the wind, and the
strong west wind blew the locusts into the
Red Sea. Not a single locust remained in all
the land of Egypt. 20But the LORD hardened
Pharaoh's heart again, so he refused to let
the people go.

A Plague of Darkness

21Then the LORD said to Moses, "Lift your
hand toward heaven, and the land of Egypt
will be covered with a darkness so thick you
can feel it." 22So Moses lifted his hand to
the sky, and a deep darkness covered the entire land of Egypt for three days. 23During
all that time the people could not see each
other, and no one moved. But there was light
as usual where the people of Israel lived.
24Finally, Pharaoh called for Moses. "Go
and worship the LORD," he said. "But leave
your flocks and herds here. You may even
take your little ones with you."
25"No," Moses said, "you must provide us
with animals for sacrifices and burnt offerings to the LORD our God. 26All our livestock
must go with us, too; not a hoof can be left
behind. We must choose our sacrifices for
the LORD our God from among these animals. And we won't know how we are to
worship the LORD until we get there."
27But the LORD hardened Pharaoh's heart
once more, and he would not let them go.
28"Get out of here!" Pharaoh shouted at
Moses. "I'm warning you. Never come back
to see me again! The day you see my face,
you will die!"
29"Very well," Moses replied. "I will never
see your face again."

10:8 Exod 8:8, 25
10:9 Exod 12:37
10:10 Gen 50:8; Exod 12:31
10:11 Exod 10:28
10:12 Exod 7:19; [a]*'arbeh* (0697) ‣Lev 11:22
10:13 Ps 78:46; 105:34
10:14 Joel 1:4, 7; 2:1-11
10:15 Exod 10:5; Ps 105:35
10:16 Exod 8:8; 9:27; [b]*khata'* (2398) ‣Deut 20:18
10:17 Exod 8:8, 29; 1 Sam 15:25; [c]*nasa'* (5375) ‣Exod 32:32
10:18 Exod 8:30
10:20 Exod 4:21; 11:10
10:21 Deut 28:29
10:22 Ps 105:28
10:23 Exod 8:22
10:24 Exod 8:8, 10
10:26 Exod 10:9
10:27 Exod 4:21; 14:4
10:28 Exod 10:11
10:29 Heb 11:27

10:13-15 The miraculous nature of the locust plague was indicated by its timing (when ***Moses raised his staff***) and by its extent and intensity (***from one end of the country to the other***, and ***there has never been another one like it***).

10:13 ***an east wind:*** The grasshopper swarms came from the Arabian Desert, across the Red Sea to the east.

10:17 ***Forgive my sin:*** Pharaoh's recognition grew deeper; he admitted that his pride and refusal to keep his word were sins, and he recognized that sin cannot be ignored but must be forgiven. Unfortunately, his correct theological understanding did not in itself change his heart.

10:19 ***Red Sea:*** Literally *sea of reeds*. See note on 13:18.

10:21-29 The ninth plague was the plague of ***darkness*** (10:21). The chief god of Egypt through the centuries, who appeared under several different names, was the sun. At this time he was known as Amon-Re. He was supreme over all the other gods and was considered to be the ultimate source of life. The Lord showed that the sun's light is completely under his control; he could shut it off from Egypt proper, while leaving it to shine in Goshen in the northeast part of the country (10:23; see note on 9:1-7).

10:24 ***leave your flocks and herds:*** Pharaoh again attempted to save some scrap of his prestige and authority from the debacle.

10:25-26 Moses was unrelenting. He knew that the Israelites, far from leaving any of their possessions behind, would be receiving gifts from the Egyptians in order to hurry them away (3:21-22). He also kept the focus on the worship of God. This continual refrain about the purpose for leaving Egypt (see note on 8:26-27) reflects the key purpose of their Exodus, to become the people of God.

10:27-29 Pharaoh seemed to realize that he had reached a point of no return. If he would not submit—the only action appropriate to what he had learned from the plagues—then he must kill the messenger. This reasoning is similar to that of the religious leaders later during the life of Christ. They refused to draw the appropriate conclusions from Jesus' life and ministry, so they decided to kill him (see John 11:45-53).

11:1 Exod 12:31, 33, 39
11:2 Exod 3:22; 12:35-36
11:3 Exod 3:21; 12:36; Deut 34:10-12
11:4 Exod 12:29
11:5 Exod 12:12, 29; Ps 78:51; 105:36; 135:8; 136:10
11:6 Exod 12:30; Amos 5:17
11:7 Exod 8:22
11:8 Exod 12:31-33; Heb 11:27
11:9 Exod 7:3-4
11:10 Exod 4:21; Rom 2:5; 9:17
12:2 Exod 13:4; 23:15; 34:18; Deut 16:1
12:3 Mark 14:12; 1 Cor 5:7
12:5 Lev 22:18-20; Heb 9:14; [d]*tamim* (8549) ‣Deut 32:4
12:6 Lev 23:5; Num 9:3; Deut 16:4, 6
12:7 Exod 12:22
12:8 Exod 34:25; Num 9:11-12; Deut 16:7
12:10 Exod 23:18; 34:25

Death for Egypt's Firstborn

11 Then the LORD said to Moses, "I will strike Pharaoh and the land of Egypt with one more blow. After that, Pharaoh will let you leave this country. In fact, he will be so eager to get rid of you that he will force you all to leave. [2]Tell all the Israelite men and women to ask their Egyptian neighbors for articles of silver and gold." [3](Now the LORD had caused the Egyptians to look favorably on the people of Israel. And Moses was considered a very great man in the land of Egypt, respected by Pharaoh's officials and the Egyptian people alike.)

[4]Moses had announced to Pharaoh, "This is what the LORD says: At midnight tonight I will pass through the heart of Egypt. [5]All the firstborn sons will die in every family in Egypt, from the oldest son of Pharaoh, who sits on his throne, to the oldest son of his lowliest servant girl who grinds the flour. Even the firstborn of all the livestock will die. [6]Then a loud wail will rise throughout the land of Egypt, a wail like no one has heard before or will ever hear again. [7]But among the Israelites it will be so peaceful that not even a dog will bark. Then you will know that the LORD makes a distinction between the Egyptians and the Israelites. [8]All the officials of Egypt will run to me and fall to the ground before me. 'Please leave!' they will beg. 'Hurry! And take all your followers with you.' Only then will I go!" Then, burning with anger, Moses left Pharaoh.

[9]Now the LORD had told Moses earlier, "Pharaoh will not listen to you, but then I will do even more mighty miracles in the land of Egypt." [10]Moses and Aaron performed these miracles in Pharaoh's presence, but the LORD hardened Pharaoh's heart, and he wouldn't let the Israelites leave the country.

Prelude to Rescue: The Passover (12:1-30)

12 While the Israelites were still in the land of Egypt, the LORD gave the following instructions to Moses and Aaron: [2]"From now on, this month will be the first month of the year for you. [3]Announce to the whole community of Israel that on the tenth day of this month each family must choose a lamb or a young goat for a sacrifice, one animal for each household. [4]If a family is too small to eat a whole animal, let them share with another family in the neighborhood. Divide the animal according to the size of each family and how much they can eat. [5]The animal you select must be a one-year-old male, either a sheep or a goat, with [d]no defects.

[6]"Take special care of this chosen animal until the evening of the fourteenth day of this first month. Then the whole assembly of the community of Israel must slaughter their lamb or young goat at twilight. [7]They are to take some of the blood and smear it on the sides and top of the doorframes of the houses where they eat the animal. [8]That same night they must roast the meat over a fire and eat it along with bitter salad greens and bread made without yeast. [9]Do not eat any of the meat raw or boiled in water. The whole animal—including the head, legs, and internal organs—must be roasted over a fire. [10]Do not leave any of it until the next

. . . .

11:1-9 The final plague was the death of the ***firstborn sons.*** The Egyptians worshiped life. They gave so much attention to preparations for life after death because they wanted to ensure that it would be at least as good as their lives in Egypt. Death itself is in God's hand. There is no underworld god who can ultimately defeat the God of life. Both life and death belong to the Lord.

11:3 Pharaoh refused to recognize the truth, but the Lord ensured that the rest of Egypt would recognize it.

11:5 In much of the world, the issue of survival is addressed through children, and it is through the ***firstborn sons*** that the family line is carried on. If we have a child, there is a sense of satisfaction that even when we are dead, we will live on through our children. In the death of the Egyptian firstborn, God was showing that humans can do nothing by themselves to guarantee survival. Life is a gift, and that gift is in the hand of the one Lord, the "I AM."

11:7 As stated explicitly in the fourth, fifth, seventh, and ninth plagues (8:23; 9:6; 9:26; 10:23), the Lord distinguished between his people and the Egyptians. These events clearly resulted from the express activity of God and were not just a chance collection of natural tragedies.

11:8 Pharaoh had lost control. Moses was no longer asking; he was now in a position to dictate the terms of the Israelites' departure from the country.

12:1-30 The Lord gave Moses instructions for the Passover meal and the Festival of Unleavened Bread (12:14-20), and Moses and the people observed the first Passover (12:21-30).

12:2 ***This month*** was the month Abib (13:4; 23:15; 34:18; Deut 16:1; later called by the Babylonian name, Nisan, Neh 2:1; Esth 3:7), which falls within the months of March and April. See chart, "Israel's Annual Calendar," p. 145. Many cultures held festivals about this time of the year, celebrating the renewal of plant life. Israel's festival celebrated the historic event in which God defeated death and rescued his people from bondage in Egypt.

12:5 ***with no defects:*** We must give God our best, just as he gave us his best: "the sinless, spotless Lamb of God" (1 Pet 1:19).

12:6 ***the whole assembly of the community:*** Both the benefits and the responsibility of a relationship with God are realized in community.

12:7 ***blood:*** God could not simply exempt his people from this plague as he had preserved them from the other plagues. Death reigns in the world because of sin, and in light of God's justice, sin cannot be ignored; it must be either punished or atoned for. Since the blood represents life (Lev 17:11), it alone is acceptable for the forgiveness of sins (Heb 9:22). As Deut 6:9 suggests, ***doorframes*** represent the totality of life as the place of going in and coming out.

12:10 Since this was not a regular meal, none of the meat was to be saved for another day.

morning. Burn whatever is not eaten before
morning.
11"These are your instructions for eating
this meal: Be fully dressed, wear your sandals, and carry your walking stick in your
hand. Eat the meal with urgency, for this is
the LORD's [e]Passover. 12On that night I will
pass through the land of Egypt and strike
down every firstborn son and firstborn
male animal in the land of Egypt. I will execute judgment against all the gods of Egypt,
for I am the LORD! 13But the blood on your
doorposts will serve as a sign, marking the
houses where you are staying. When I see
the blood, I will pass over you. This plague
of death will not touch you when I strike the
land of Egypt.
14"This is a day to remember. Each year,
from generation to generation, you must
celebrate it as a special festival to the LORD.
This is a law for all time. 15For seven days
the bread you eat must be made without
yeast. On the first day of the festival, remove every trace of yeast from your homes.
Anyone who eats bread made with yeast
during the seven days of the festival will be
cut off from the community of Israel. 16On
the first day of the festival and again on the
seventh day, all the people must observe an
official day for holy assembly. No work of
any kind may be done on these days except
in the preparation of food.
17"Celebrate this Festival of Unleavened
Bread, for it will remind you that I brought
your forces out of the land of Egypt on this
very day. This festival will be a permanent
law for you; celebrate this day from generation to generation. 18The bread you eat must
be made without yeast from the evening of
the fourteenth day of the first month until
the evening of the twenty-first day of that
month. 19During those seven days, there
must be no trace of yeast in your homes.
Anyone who eats anything made with yeast
during this week will be cut off from the
community of Israel. These regulations apply both to the foreigners living among you
and to the native-born Israelites. 20During
those days you must not eat anything made
with yeast. Wherever you live, eat only
bread made without yeast."
21Then Moses called all the [f]elders of Israel together and said to them, "Go, pick out
a lamb or young goat for each of your families, and slaughter the [g]Passover animal.
22Drain the blood into a basin. Then take a
bundle of hyssop branches and dip it into
the blood. Brush the hyssop across the top
and sides of the doorframes of your houses.
And no one may go out through the door
until morning. 23For the LORD will pass

12:11 Num 28:16
[e]*pesakh* (6453) ‣ Exod 12:21
12:12 Exod 11:4-5; Num 33:4
12:13 Heb 11:28
12:14-20 //Lev 23:4-8; //Num 28:16-25; //Deut 16:1-8
12:15 Exod 23:15; 34:18; Lev 23:5-6; Deut 16:3
12:16 Lev 23:7-8
12:17 Exod 13:3
12:18 Lev 23:5-8; Num 28:16-25
12:19 Exod 12:15
12:21 Mark 14:12-16; Heb 11:28
[f]*zaqen* (2205) ‣ Lev 4:15
[g]*pesakh* (6453) ‣ Exod 12:27
12:22 Lev 14:4, 6; Num 19:18; Ps 51:7; Heb 11:28
12:23 Exod 12:12; Isa 37:36

The Passover (12:1-51)

Lev 23:4-8; Num 9:1-14; 28:16-25; Deut 16:1-7; Matt 26:17-30; Luke 22:15-20; 1 Cor 5:6-8

The major festival associated with the Exodus does not celebrate political independence, but deliverance from death. Israel's main enemy was not bondage to Egypt but bondage to death, as it is for all people. The most fundamental problem facing humans is not political, but spiritual. Of course, only the death of the firstborn was prevented in Egypt. So was death really conquered? Furthermore, why did the Passover require that the Israelites apply blood to their doorposts? They were not required to perform such a ritual to escape harm in any of the other plagues.

These questions highlight the significance of Jesus' death and resurrection as associated with the Passover season. Death is the effect of sin (1 Cor 15:56). Passover shows that we can be delivered from death only by means of a sacrifice that takes our place. The Passover lamb took the place of the firstborn son of every family of Israel (12:12-13, 23; 13:2, 11-16). The Passover symbolizes the reality that would come later in Jesus Christ, who gave his life as "a ransom for many" (Matt 20:28; Mark 10:45) and became "the Lamb of God that takes away the sin of the world" (John 1:29). Jesus says to his disciples, "this is my blood, which confirms the covenant. . . . It is poured out as a sacrifice to forgive the sins of many" (Matt 26:28). He brings to reality the truths that were first symbolized in the Passover celebration: Through his sacrifice, sin and death were fully and finally defeated (see also Isa 25:7-8).

12:11 ***Be fully dressed*** (literally *Bind up your loins*): The Israelites were to be ready to depart at a moment's notice.

12:12 The plagues were primarily the Lord's ***judgment against all the gods of Egypt*** (see also Num 33:4).

12:14 The Jewish people still commemorate Passover, since it was instituted as ***a law for all time.***

12:15 ***without yeast:*** Israel needed unleavened bread for traveling (see 12:34, 39), which the festival commemorated. Later, yeast was seen as an image of sin, probably because it is an agent of fermentation ("Beware of the yeast of the Pharisees," Matt 16:6). • ***cut off from the community:*** This means either death or expulsion from the community.

12:22 ***Hyssop*** is a small bush with stiff, compact branches that can serve as a brush (see also Ps 51:7 and note).

12:24 Exod 13:4-5, 10
12:25 Exod 3:17
12:26 Exod 10:2; 13:14-15
12:27 Exod 4:31
[h]*pesakh* (6453) ‣Exod 12:43
12:29 Exod 4:23; 11:4 Ps 78:51; 105:36
12:30 Exod 11:6
12:31 Exod 8:8, 25
12:33 Exod 10:7; 11:1
12:35 Exod 3:22

through the land to strike down the Egyptians. But when he sees the blood on the top
and sides of the doorframe, the LORD will
pass over your home. He will not permit his
death angel to enter your house and strike
you down.
24"Remember, these instructions are a
permanent law that you and your descendants must observe forever. 25When you
enter the land the LORD has promised to
give you, you will continue to observe this
ceremony. 26Then your children will ask,
'What does this ceremony mean?' 27And you
will reply, 'It is the [h]Passover sacrifice to the
LORD, for he passed over the houses of the Israelites in Egypt. And though he struck the
Egyptians, he spared our families.' " When
Moses had finished speaking, all the people
bowed down to the ground and worshiped.
28So the people of Israel did just as the
LORD had commanded through Moses and
Aaron. 29And that night at midnight, the
LORD struck down all the firstborn sons in
the land of Egypt, from the firstborn son of
Pharaoh, who sat on his throne, to the firstborn son of the prisoner in the dungeon.
Even the firstborn of their livestock were
killed. 30Pharaoh and all his officials and
all the people of Egypt woke up during the
night, and loud wailing was heard throughout the land of Egypt. There was not a single
house where someone had not died.

The Rescue Realized (12:31–14:31)
Israel's Exodus from Egypt

31Pharaoh sent for Moses and Aaron during the night. "Get out!" he ordered. "Leave
my people—and take the rest of the Israelites with you! Go and worship the LORD as
you have requested. 32Take your flocks and
herds, as you said, and be gone. Go, but bless
me as you leave." 33All the Egyptians urged
the people of Israel to get out of the land as
quickly as possible, for they thought, "We
will all die!"
34The Israelites took their bread dough
before yeast was added. They wrapped their
kneading boards in their cloaks and carried
them on their shoulders. 35And the people

Hebrew (Babylonian) Month	References	Gregorian Month	Annual Festivals*
1 Abib (Nisan)	Exod 12:2; 13:4; 23:15; 34:18; Deut 16:1	Mar~Apr	Passover, Unleavened Bread, First Harvest
2 Ziv (Iyyar)	1 Kgs 6:1, 37	Apr~May	
3 (Sivan)	Esth 8:9	May~June	Harvest/Pentecost
4 (Tammuz)		June~July	
5 (Ab)		July~Aug	
6 (Elul)	Neh 6:15	Aug~Sept	
7 Ethanim (Tishri)	1 Kgs 8:2	Sept~Oct	Trumpets, Day of Atonement, Final Harvest, Shelters
8 Bul (Marheshvan)	1 Kgs 6:38	Oct~Nov	
9 (Kislev)	Neh 1:1	Nov~Dec	Dedication
10 (Tebeth)	Esth 2:16	Dec~Jan	
11 Shebat (Sebat)	Zech 1:7	Jan~Feb	
12 (Adar)	Esth 3:7	Feb~Mar	Purim
13 Second Adar			[see caption at right]

* See also chart, "Israel's Festivals," p. 235.

◀ **Israel's Annual Calendar (12:2).** The Exodus marked the first month of ancient Israel's annual calendar (12:2). Preexilic month names are shown, with postexilic (Babylonian) names in parentheses. Ancient Israel marked the beginning of each month at the new moon, which occurs every 29.5 days, resulting in a 354-day annual calendar, 11 days shorter than the solar year; thus the months in Israel's calendar do not align with modern (Gregorian) months. In later Judaism, an extra month, called "Second Adar," was an *intercalary* "leap month," inserted seven times every nineteen years to realign the calendar with the solar year. Such *intercalation* of a month occurs in many lunar calendars. In our modern solar calendar, intercalation is unnecessary because the months are not tied to the lunar cycle.

12:25 ***The land the LORD has promised to give you*** refers to the land of Canaan, which God had promised to Abraham (Gen 12:7; 13:14-17).

12:26-27 In the future, the ***Passover*** celebration would be a memorial reminding future generations of Israelites of God's grace in providing them a way of escape from death. For more than 3,000 years the Jewish people have celebrated this great formative event in their history.

12:28-30 The predicted plague was fulfilled. Just as death exempts no one, so no one in Egypt, from ***Pharaoh*** to the lowest ***prisoner***, escaped the effects of Pharaoh's pride.

12:31–14:31 The Lord delivered on his promises and rescued Israel, bringing them out of Egypt.

12:31-33 The same Pharaoh who had said that Moses would never again see his face and live (see 10:28) now asked for Moses to come and see him. Just as God had predicted, Pharaoh then ordered the Israelites to leave his land. He implicitly recognized the Lord's power as he asked Moses to ***bless*** him. He never formally admitted that the Lord is God and that he, Pharaoh, was not.

12:35 ***they asked the Egyptians:*** See 3:22; 11:2.

of Israel did as Moses had instructed; they asked the Egyptians for clothing and articles of silver and gold. [36]The LORD caused the Egyptians to look favorably on the Israelites, and they gave the Israelites whatever they asked for. So they stripped the Egyptians of their wealth!

[37]That night the people of Israel left Rameses and started for Succoth. There were about 600,000 men, plus all the women and children. [38]A rabble of non-Israelites went with them, along with great flocks and herds of livestock. [39]For bread they baked flat cakes from the dough without yeast they had brought from Egypt. It was made without yeast because the people were driven out of Egypt in such a hurry that they had no time to prepare the bread or other food.

[40]The people of Israel had lived in Egypt for 430 years. [41]In fact, it was on the last day of the 430th year that all the LORD's forces left the land. [42]On this night the LORD kept his promise to bring his people out of the land of Egypt. So this night belongs to him, and it must be commemorated every year by all the Israelites, from generation to generation.

Further Instructions for Passover

[43]Then the LORD said to Moses and Aaron, "These are the instructions for the festival of [i]Passover. No outsiders are allowed to eat the Passover meal. [44]But any slave who has been purchased may eat it if he has been circumcised. [45]Temporary residents and hired servants may not eat it. [46]Each Passover lamb must be eaten in one house. Do not carry any of its meat outside, and do not break any of its bones. [47]The whole community of Israel must celebrate this Passover festival.

[48]"If there are foreigners living among you who want to celebrate the LORD's [j]Passover, let all their males be circumcised. Only then may they celebrate the Passover with you like any native-born Israelite. But no uncircumcised male may ever eat the Passover meal. [49]This instruction applies to everyone, whether a native-born Israelite or a foreigner living among you."

[50]So all the people of Israel followed all the LORD's commands to Moses and Aaron. [51]On that very day the LORD brought the people of Israel out of the land of Egypt like an army.

Dedication of the Firstborn

13 Then the LORD said to Moses, [2]"Dedicate to me every firstborn among the Israelites. The first offspring to be born, of both humans and animals, belongs to me."

[3]So Moses said to the people, "This is a day to remember forever—the day you left Egypt, the place of your slavery. Today the LORD has brought you out by the power of his mighty hand. (Remember, eat no food containing yeast.) [4]On this day in early

12:36 Exod 3:22
12:37 Exod 38:26; Num 1:46
12:38 Num 11:4
12:39 Exod 11:1
12:40-41 Gen 15:13, 16; Acts 7:6; Gal 3:17
12:42 Exod 3:10; Deut 16:1
12:43 Num 9:14; [i]*pesakh* (6453) ‣Exod 12:48
12:44 Gen 17:12-13; Lev 22:11
12:46 Num 9:12; John 19:33, 36
12:48 Num 9:13-14; Gal 3:28; [j]*pesakh* (6453) ‣Deut 16:1
12:49 Lev 24:22; Num 15:15-16
12:50 Exod 12:28
13:2 Exod 13:12-13; 22:29; 34:20; Lev 27:26; Num 3:13; Deut 15:19; *Luke 2:23
13:3 Exod 3:20; 6:1
13:4 Exod 12:2

12:37 *Succoth* is usually identified with Tell el-Maskhutah. • ***600,000 men*** (or *fighting men;* literally *men on foot*): See also Num 1:46. This large number implies about 2.5 million people in the community as a whole, which raises logistical problems: (1) The area of encampment would be 400 sq. mi.; (2) A column of people 1,000 across would be nearly a mile wide and would take 20 hours to pass a single point; (3) As best we know, there were no other armies nearly so large in the ancient Near East at that time. As a result, scholars have proposed two viable alternatives: (1) The number might be symbolic, communicating not an actual number but the fact that God had greatly blessed Israel. While this use of a number seems strange to us, it would be acceptable in the ancient world. (2) The Hebrew word for "thousand" (*'elep*) might have been confused with the word for "troop" (*'allup*). If so, the original would have read "600 *troops* of fighting men." With a troop size of approximately 100 men, the total population would be significantly reduced. But despite the logistical difficulties, it is possible that there were in fact 2.5 million Israelites.

12:38 ***A rabble of non-Israelites:*** Some of these people later became disaffected and led the Israelites into complaining about their difficulties (see Num 11:4). We are never told their motivation for joining with the Israelites. Perhaps some had come to faith in the Lord as a result of the plagues. Others probably saw it as an opportunity for a better life elsewhere.

12:40 ***had lived in Egypt for 430 years:*** The Greek translation of the OT (the Septuagint) says that Israel had lived *in Egypt and Canaan* for 430 years. The Samaritan Pentateuch reads *in Canaan and Egypt.* According to these versions, 430 years would cover the full period from the promise to Abraham (Gen 12; 15) until the Exodus. Cp. Gal 3:17; see further "Old Testament Chronology: Abraham to Joshua," p. 118.

12:43-50 These additional instructions for the observance of Passover relate primarily to *outsiders* (12:43) and *foreigners* (12:48). Perhaps the presence of the non-Israelite rabble (12:38) in the community prompted these instructions. The key factor was whether or not the person was willing to become fully identified with Israel and with the Lord by submitting to circumcision.

12:46 ***do not break any of its bones:*** The apostle John makes reference to this instruction regarding the Passover lambs when reporting that Jesus' legs were not broken on the cross (John 19:36).

12:51 The Israelites left Egypt *like an army,* with the Lord as their commander-in-chief.

13:1-16 Like the Passover celebration, the practice of dedicating the firstborn memorialized what God did in the Passover event. Because he spared the firstborn, they now belonged to him and must be redeemed. The annual sacrifice and eating of the lamb symbolized what God would do in providing a substitute in his Son, Jesus Christ; we who deserve death must be redeemed with a price, the life of the Son.

13:1-10 This rehearsal of the customs surrounding Passover and the Festival of Unleavened Bread sets the stage for discussing the dedication of the firstborn (13:11-16).

13:5 Exod 3:8, 17; 12:25-26
13:6 Exod 12:15-20
13:9 Exod 12:14; Deut 6:8; [k]*torah* (8451) ‣Exod 18:20
13:10 Exod 12:24-25
13:12 Exod 13:2; 22:29; Num 3:13; *Luke 2:23
13:13 Exod 34:20; Num 18:15-16
13:14 Exod 12:26-27; Deut 6:20-23
13:15 Exod 12:29
13:16 Exod 13:9; Deut 6:8
13:17 Exod 14:11; Num 14:1-4; Deut 17:16
13:18 Josh 1:14; 4:13
13:19 Gen 50:24-25; Josh 24:32; Acts 7:16
13:20 Exod 12:37; Num 33:6-8
13:21 Exod 14:19, 24; 33:9-10; Ps 105:39; 1 Cor 10:1

spring, in the month of Abib, you have been set free. [5]You must celebrate this event in this month each year after the LORD brings you into the land of the Canaanites, Hittites, Amorites, Hivites, and Jebusites. (He swore to your ancestors that he would give you this land—a land flowing with milk and honey.) [6]For seven days the bread you eat must be made without yeast. Then on the seventh day, celebrate a feast to the LORD. [7]Eat bread without yeast during those seven days. In fact, there must be no yeast bread or any yeast at all found within the borders of your land during this time.

[8]"On the seventh day you must explain to your children, 'I am celebrating what the LORD did for me when I left Egypt.' [9]This annual festival will be a visible sign to you, like a mark branded on your hand or your forehead. Let it remind you always to recite this [k]teaching of the LORD: 'With a strong hand, the LORD rescued you from Egypt.' [10]So observe the decree of this festival at the appointed time each year.

[11]"This is what you must do when the LORD fulfills the promise he swore to you and to your ancestors. When he gives you the land where the Canaanites now live, [12]you must present all firstborn sons and firstborn male animals to the LORD, for they belong to him. [13]A firstborn donkey may be bought back from the LORD by presenting a lamb or young goat in its place. But if you do not buy it back, you must break its neck. However, you must buy back every firstborn son.

[14]"And in the future, your children will ask you, 'What does all this mean?' Then you will tell them, 'With the power of his mighty hand, the LORD brought us out of Egypt, the place of our slavery. [15]Pharaoh stubbornly refused to let us go, so the LORD killed all the firstborn males throughout the land of Egypt, both people and animals. That is why I now sacrifice all the firstborn males to the LORD—except that the firstborn sons are always bought back.' [16]This ceremony will be like a mark branded on your hand or your forehead. It is a reminder that the power of the LORD's mighty hand brought us out of Egypt."

Israel's Wilderness Detour

[17]When Pharaoh finally let the people go, God did not lead them along the main road that runs through Philistine territory, even though that was the shortest route to the Promised Land. God said, "If the people are faced with a battle, they might change their minds and return to Egypt." [18]So God led them in a roundabout way through the wilderness toward the Red Sea. Thus the Israelites left Egypt like an army ready for battle.

[19]Moses took the bones of Joseph with him, for Joseph had made the sons of Israel swear to do this. He said, "God will certainly come to help you. When he does, you must take my bones with you from this place."

[20]The Israelites left Succoth and camped at Etham on the edge of the wilderness. [21]The LORD went ahead of them. He guided them during the day with a pillar of cloud,

---

13:4 ***On this day in early spring, in the month of Abib*** (literally *On this day in the month of Abib*): See note on 12:2.

13:5 ***A land flowing with milk and honey*** refers to a land that was agriculturally rich, where there was pasturage for cattle and crops with blooms from which bees could make honey.

13:9 The annual celebration of the Passover was ***a visible sign*** to identify oneself as the Lord's possession. It was ***a mark*** of his ownership, the physical reinforcement of a spiritual reality. • ***Let it remind you always to recite this teaching of the LORD:*** The second part of the verse may be interpreted either as a statement to be recited (as in the NLT text) or simply as a description of the Lord's work (*Let it remind you always to keep the instructions of the LORD on the tip of your tongue, because with a strong hand, the LORD rescued you from Egypt*).

13:13 A ***firstborn son*** had to be ***bought back,*** or redeemed. He could not be sacrificed to the Lord, as child sacrifice is condemned throughout Scripture (see Lev 18:21; 20:2; Ezek 23:37-39).

13:16 Like the annual Passover celebration (13:9), dedicating the firstborn to the Lord was ***like a mark,*** a visible way to identify oneself as the Lord's possession.

13:17–14:4 The Lord's redemptive power was demonstrated as he brought Israel into a place where they were completely helpless and had to either rely on him for rescue or die. Although at the time it must have seemed completely foolish, Israel would thank God for the rest of its history for maneuvering them into such a spot (see Ps 106:7-12; cp. Isa 12:2-6).

13:17-18 ***faced with a battle:*** The Israelites had not yet seen God fight on their behalf. Even though they ***left Egypt like an army ready for battle*** (13:18; see also 12:51), it was only an appearance. Until they experienced the Lord as fighting for them (14:14) in the crossing of the sea, they were not ready to face enemies in the Promised Land.

13:18 ***roundabout way:*** There is disagreement among scholars about the identification of some of the sites mentioned (13:20; 14:2), so there is little consensus about the precise route the Israelites took. • ***Red Sea:*** Literally *sea of reeds.* The Red Sea proper is too far south. The Sea of Reeds was part of the Red Sea, probably located at the northern end of the Gulf of Suez. • ***left Egypt like an army ready for battle:*** Greek version reads *left Egypt in the fifth generation.*

13:19 ***Joseph*** had recognized that God would not leave his people in Egypt indefinitely because he had promised Canaan to them (see Gen 50:24-25).

13:20 The locations of ***Succoth*** and ***Etham*** are uncertain, although the reference to ***the edge of the wilderness*** suggests that they were in the region southeast of the Nile delta toward the Gulf of Suez.

13:21 The ***pillar of cloud*** and the ***pillar of fire*** were to be the Israelites' constant companions for the next forty years.

and he provided light at night with a pillar
of fire. This allowed them to travel by day
or by night. 22 And the LORD did not remove
the pillar of cloud or pillar of fire from its
place in front of the people.

14 Then the LORD gave these instructions to Moses: 2 "Order the Israelites
to turn back and camp by Pi-hahiroth between Migdol and the sea. Camp there
along the shore, across from Baal-zephon.
3 Then Pharaoh will think, 'The Israelites
are confused. They are trapped in the wilderness!' 4 And once again I will harden
Pharaoh's heart, and he will chase after you.
I have planned this in order to display my
glory through Pharaoh and his whole army.
After this the Egyptians will know that I am
the LORD!" So the Israelites camped there
as they were told.

The Egyptians Pursue Israel

5 When word reached the king of Egypt that
the Israelites had fled, Pharaoh and his officials changed their minds. "What have we
done, letting all those Israelite slaves get
away?" they asked. 6 So Pharaoh harnessed
his chariot and called up his troops. 7 He
took with him 600 of Egypt's best chariots,
along with the rest of the chariots of Egypt,
each with its commander. 8 The LORD hardened the heart of Pharaoh, the king of Egypt,
so he chased after the people of Israel, who
had left with fists raised in defiance. 9 The
Egyptians chased after them with all the
forces in Pharaoh's army—all his horses and
chariots, his charioteers, and his troops.
The Egyptians caught up with the people of
Israel as they were camped beside the shore
near Pi-hahiroth, across from Baal-zephon.
10 As Pharaoh approached, the people of Israel looked up and panicked when they saw
the Egyptians overtaking them. They cried
out to the LORD, 11 and they said to Moses,
"Why did you bring us out here to die in the
wilderness? Weren't there enough graves
for us in Egypt? What have you done to us?
Why did you make us leave Egypt? 12 Didn't
we tell you this would happen while we
were still in Egypt? We said, 'Leave us alone!
Let us be slaves to the Egyptians. It's better
to be a slave in Egypt than a corpse in the
wilderness!'"
13 But Moses told the people, "Don't be
afraid. Just stand still and watch the LORD
[a]rescue you today. The Egyptians you see
today will never be seen again. 14 The LORD
himself will fight for you. Just stay calm."

Escape through the Red Sea

15 Then the LORD said to Moses, "Why are
you crying out to me? Tell the people to get
moving! 16 Pick up your staff and raise your
hand over the sea. Divide the water so the
Israelites can walk through the middle of
the sea on dry ground. 17 And I will harden
the hearts of the Egyptians, and they will
charge in after the Israelites. My great glory
will be displayed through Pharaoh and his
troops, his chariots, and his charioteers.
18 When my glory is displayed through them,
all Egypt will see my glory and know that I
am the LORD!"
19 Then the angel of God, who had been
leading the people of Israel, moved to the

14:2 Num 33:7-8; Jer 44:1
14:4 Exod 4:21; 7:5; Rom 9:17, 22-23
14:5 Ps 105:25
14:7 Exod 15:4
14:8 Num 33:3; Acts 13:17
14:9 Exod 14:2; 15:9; Josh 24:6
14:10 Josh 24:7; Neh 9:9
14:11 Exod 5:21; 15:24; Ps 106:7-8
14:13 Gen 15:1; Exod 14:30; 15:2; [a]*yeshu'ah* (3444) ▸Exod 15:2
14:14 Exod 15:3; Deut 1:30; 3:22; Isa 30:15
14:15 Josh 7:10
14:16 Exod 4:17, 20; Num 20:8-9, 11
14:18 Exod 14:25
14:19 Exod 13:21-22

14:2 The precise locations of ***Pi-hahiroth, Migdol,*** and ***Baal-zephon*** are unknown. • ***the sea:*** See note on 13:18.

14:4 ***after you:*** Literally *after them.* • ***to display my glory through Pharaoh:*** See note on 9:16. • ***know that I am the LORD:*** This event was the climactic demonstration of the Lord's character and power in the Exodus. Rescue for humans is by means of God's self-revelation as he incarnates himself in our life and experience. • ***as they were told:*** In this part of the book, the Israelites were obedient to God's commands (12:35, 50). Unfortunately, this was not their continued pattern after the crossing.

14:5-14 Because there was no real repentance on the part of ***Pharaoh and his officials,*** once the immediate terror of their experience had worn off, their self-interest reasserted itself and they determined to recapture their slave labor.

14:6-7 ***chariot:*** At this point in history, the Egyptian light chariot was the ultimate weapon. Pulled by three horses, it was swift and highly maneuverable. Sometimes it was manned by only one person, but some ancient illustrations show a driver with a warrior. The reference to a ***commander*** may indicate such two-man teams. The greatest military power in the world of that day was being marshaled against the Hebrews.

14:9 Even though today we don't know exactly where these events took place (see note on 14:2), there is no question that the narrator and his readers did. This account is history and not literary fantasy.

14:10-12 This complaint is the first occurrence of what was to become a sad refrain over the next forty years. Instead of believing that the God who had demonstrated his power so overwhelmingly could now save them, the Israelites turned on their rescuer. The cry of the unsurrendered heart is always, "Give me the security of slavery rather than the risk of faith."

14:13-14 One person, at least, had learned the lessons of the plagues and applied it to this crisis of faith. ***Moses*** did not know what God would do, but in one of the great statements of faith in the Bible, Moses declared his confidence in God. It was not ***the LORD*** who would fail, but the ***Egyptians.***

14:15-31 The escape through the Red Sea was the climactic moment of rescue.

14:17 ***My great glory:*** The Hebrew word translated "glory" (*kabod*) connotes weightiness, significance, and reality (see "The Glory of God" at 24:15-17, p. 167). God demonstrated his authenticity while showing that all the political, military, and material glory of one of the greatest human cultures was only the thinnest of veils.

14:19-25 Whereas the Hebrews had been in a panic the night before, now the highly disciplined Egyptian army was thrown into disarray. They knew they were dealing with something far beyond their ability to comprehend or control.

14:21
Exod 7:19
Ps 106:9; 114:3, 5
Isa 63:12-13

14:22
Exod 15:19
Neh 9:11
Ps 66:6; 78:13
Heb 11:29

14:24
Exod 13:21

14:26
Exod 14:16

14:27
Exod 15:1, 7
Deut 11:4
Heb 11:29

14:28
Exod 15:19
Neh 9:11
Ps 78:53; 106:11

14:29
Ps 66:6
Isa 11:15

14:30
Ps 106:8
Isa 63:8, 11

14:31
Exod 4:31; 19:9
Ps 106:12

rear of the camp. The pillar of cloud also moved from the front and stood behind them. 20The cloud settled between the Egyptian and Israelite camps. As darkness fell, the cloud turned to fire, lighting up the night. But the Egyptians and Israelites did not approach each other all night.

21Then Moses raised his hand over the sea, and the LORD opened up a path through the water with a strong east wind. The wind blew all that night, turning the seabed into dry land. 22So the people of Israel walked through the middle of the sea on dry ground, with walls of water on each side!

23Then the Egyptians—all of Pharaoh's horses, chariots, and charioteers—chased them into the middle of the sea. 24But just before dawn the LORD looked down on the Egyptian army from the pillar of fire and cloud, and he threw their forces into total confusion. 25He twisted their chariot wheels, making their chariots difficult to drive. "Let's get out of here—away from these Israelites!" the Egyptians shouted. "The LORD is fighting for them against Egypt!"

26When all the Israelites had reached the other side, the LORD said to Moses, "Raise your hand over the sea again. Then the waters will rush back and cover the Egyptians and their chariots and charioteers." 27So as the sun began to rise, Moses raised his hand over the sea, and the water rushed back into its usual place. The Egyptians tried to escape, but the LORD swept them into the sea. 28Then the waters returned and covered all the chariots and charioteers—the entire army of Pharaoh. Of all the Egyptians who had chased the Israelites into the sea, not a single one survived.

29But the people of Israel had walked through the middle of the sea on dry ground, as the water stood up like a wall on both sides. 30That is how the LORD rescued Israel from the hand of the Egyptians that day. And the Israelites saw the bodies of the Egyptians washed up on the seashore. 31When the people of Israel saw the mighty

A Hardened Heart (14:4, 8)

Exod 3:19; 4:21; 8:15, 19, 32; 9:12; 10:1, 20; 11:10
Gen 8:21
Josh 11:19-20
2 Chr 36:11-13
Ps 95:8-11
Isa 6:9-10
Ezek 11:18-21; 36:22-27
Matt 12:34-35; 13:10-17
Luke 8:4-15
John 12:37-40
Acts 28:23-28
Rom 2:14-16; 11:7-12
2 Cor 3:13-18
Eph 4:17-24
Heb 3:6-19; 6:4-8

Exodus repeatedly states that the Lord hardened Pharaoh's heart (4:21; 9:12; 10:1, 20; 11:10; 14:4, 8). These statements are troubling to some. Was Pharaoh forced to sin against God?

Other facts from Exodus need to be taken into account: (1) The Lord knew ahead of time that Pharaoh would harden his heart (3:19); (2) Pharaoh himself became stubborn (8:15, 32); and (3) Pharaoh remained stubborn despite clear warnings (8:19). Pharaoh was not a well-meaning, misguided individual who was not allowed to repent. Although God was ultimately in control of Pharaoh, Pharaoh himself was accountable for his actions.

This interplay between human choice and divine sovereignty is found in other places in Scripture. (See Josh 11:20; Isa 6:9-10; Matt 13:15; John 12:40; Acts 28:27; Rom 11:7; 2 Cor 3:14; Eph 4:18; Heb 3:13.) The Israelites hardened their hearts and refused to believe God in the wilderness. God is said to have hardened the hearts of the Canaanites so that they did not seek to make peace with the Hebrews. The message God gave to Isaiah hardened the hearts of his hearers, and that Isaiah passage is referred to several times in the New Testament to explain the people's negative response to the message of the gospel. People are responsible for their choices, but no one makes choices in a vacuum. Rather, they make them in the context of the way God has made his world and providentially directs it.

The emphasis in Exodus on God's control of Pharaoh puts the conflict between the two belief systems into stark contrast. Pharaoh believed that he was sovereign and divine, able to do whatever he pleased. God showed that this was not the case; Pharaoh was dependent, as much the prisoner of his choices as any other creature on the planet. There is only one absolutely independent "I AM," and that is Yahweh (see 3:6-14; 6:2-8; 20:2; 34:6-7; Isa 45:3-7; 48:17; Mark 14:62; John 8:23-28).

14:22 As with the plagues, naturalistic explanations for this event are beside the point. A strong, steady wind blowing across a relatively shallow, contained body of water can change its depth dramatically, but that does not produce *dry ground, with walls of water on each side.* The Lord can intervene in nature and do with it as he wishes.

14:25 ***He twisted their chariot wheels:*** As translated from the Greek and Syriac versions and the Samaritan Pentateuch. Hebrew reads *He removed their chariot wheels.* The ancient versions differ among themselves on the translation of this phrase. Perhaps there was deep sand where the water had been, and this broke the light wheels of the chariots. At any rate, the Egyptian charge through the sea failed, and they became terrified. • ***The LORD is fighting for them:*** Certainly by this time everyone in Egypt was aware of the special relationship between the Lord and his people.

14:31 Finally, the ***people of Israel*** were moved to ***put their faith in the LORD:*** Sadly, it was very short-lived (see 15:24; 16:3). • To be the Lord's ***servant*** is a position of high honor (see Isa 42:1-4; Matt 12:18).

power that the LORD had unleashed against the Egyptians, they were filled with awe before him. They [b]put their faith in the LORD and in his servant Moses.

A Song of Rescue (15:1-21)

15 Then Moses and the people of Israel sang this song to the LORD:

"I will sing to the LORD,
for he has triumphed gloriously;
he has hurled both horse and rider
into the sea.
2 The LORD is my strength and my song;
he has given me [c]victory.
This is my God, and I will praise him—
my father's God, and I will [d]exalt him!
3 The LORD is a warrior;
Yahweh is his name!
4 Pharaoh's chariots and army
he has hurled into the sea.
The finest of Pharaoh's officers
are drowned in the Red Sea.
5 The deep waters gushed over them;
they sank to the bottom like a stone.

6 "Your right hand, O LORD,
is glorious in power.
Your right hand, O LORD,
smashes the enemy.
7 In the greatness of your majesty,
you overthrow those who rise against
you.
You unleash your blazing fury;
it consumes them like straw.
8 At the blast of your breath,
the waters piled up!
The surging waters stood straight like
a wall;
in the [e]heart of the sea the deep
waters became hard.
9 "The enemy boasted, 'I will chase them
and catch up with them.
I will plunder them
and consume them.
I will flash my sword;
my powerful hand will destroy them.'
10 But you blew with your breath,
and the sea covered them.
They sank like lead
in the mighty waters.
11 "Who is like you among the gods,
O LORD—
glorious in holiness,
awesome in splendor,
performing great wonders?
12 You raised your right hand,
and the earth swallowed our
enemies.

[b]*'aman* (0539) ▸Num 14:11
15:1 Ps 106:12; Jer 51:21; Rev 15:3
15:2 Exod 3:15-16; Deut 10:21; Isa 12:2
[c]*yeshu'ah* (3444) ▸Ps 6:4
[d]*rum* (7311) ▸1 Sam 2:7
15:3 Exod 14:14; Ps 24:8; 83:18
15:4 Exod 14:6-7, 17, 28
15:5 Exod 14:28; Neh 9:11
15:6 Exod 3:20; Ps 118:15-16
15:7 Exod 9:16; 14:24; Ps 78:49-50
15:8 Exod 14:22, 29; Ps 78:13
[e]*leb* (3820) ▸Deut 6:5
15:9 Exod 14:5-9
15:10 Exod 14:27-28
15:11 Exod 8:10; Deut 3:24; 1 Sam 2:2; 2 Sam 7:22; Isa 6:3

15:1-18 Scholars believe this *song* of rescue to be one of the oldest preserved examples of the Hebrew language, attesting to its importance in Israel's thought and faith. It is divided into three stanzas: 15:1-5, 6-12, 13-18. The first stanza rejoices in the Lord's personal rescue of Moses and his people (note the recurrence of the first-person pronouns). The second exults in the great contrast between the Lord and the Egyptians. The third stanza reflects on what these events would mean for the future.

15:1-5 God's salvation and rescue had implications for personal faith.

15:1 *Moses and the people:* In this triumphant moment there was no division between them; they sang as one. • *I will sing:* The highly personal declarations of the first two verses emphasize the personal nature of God's relation to humans. He is not an impersonal force, but relates to us as one person relates to another. The songs of thanks and hymns of praise in the Bible characteristically give the reason for the thanks or praise early in the piece (see Ps 95:1-3; 96:1-4). The reason for the song is that *the LORD . . . has triumphed gloriously.* The community's faith in God through the dark night had been dramatically vindicated.

15:2 This statement is quoted in two other places, Ps 118:14 and Isa 12:2, which shows its importance. The "God of your father" (3:6) had become *my God.* The Israelites now knew God for themselves and not just as a historical memory.

15:3 *The LORD is a warrior:* He will aggressively defend his own. He is not an oppressor, nor does he fight for the love of violence. But when his people are helpless before the enemy, whether external or internal, they can know that *Yahweh,* "He Who Is," is their defender (Isa 59:15-19; 63:1-6; Rev 11:17-18). Regarding the name *Yahweh,* see the note on 3:15. The NLT usually translates this name "the LORD" (with small capitals). Here the translators chose to transliterate the name because Moses was emphasizing the personal name of God.

15:4 *Red Sea:* Literally *sea of reeds;* also in 15:22. See note on 13:18.

15:6-12 The personal tone continues as the Lord is referred to as *you* and is contrasted dramatically with *them* (15:7). All that the enemy intended (15:9) was brought to nothing (15:10) before the mighty power of God.

15:6 *Your right hand:* This was typically a warrior's sword arm.

15:8 *blast* (literally *nostrils*): In other contexts, the same word may be translated "anger." The hot breath from God's nose is an image of God's anger. • *your breath:* The Hebrew word translated as "breath" (*ruakh*) is the same one translated as "wind" in 14:21 and as "Spirit" in Gen 1:2. Nature is not God, but God is everywhere at work in nature.

15:9-10 Compared to the Creator, all the plans of even the most powerful humans are nothing (see Ps 2:2-5). They are like dust that can be blown away with one puff of his *breath* (see Isa 40:15-17).

15:11 The *gods* of the pagan nations are not in the same category as the *LORD.* They do not deserve to be called holy (see note on 3:5).

15:13-18 *The people* God has *redeemed* have confidence for the future. In light of what the Lord had done in rescuing Israel from his enemies, there was no question that he would be able to carry through on his promise to take them safely into the Promised Land.

15:13 When God's *unfailing love* and his *might* are combined, there is no reason to doubt that he will be able to keep his promises. "Unfailing love" is a translation of the Hebrew word *khesed,* which

15:13
Neh 9:12
Ps 77:15, 20

15:14
Deut 2:25
Hab 3:7

15:15
Num 22:3
Deut 2:4
Josh 2:11; 5:1

15:17
Exod 23:20; 32:34
Ps 2:6; 78:54, 68

15:18
Ps 10:16; 29:10
Isa 57:15

15:19
Exod 14:22, 28

15:20
1 Sam 18:6
Ps 30:11; 150:4
ᶠ*nebi'ah* (5031)
‣ Deut 13:1

13 "With your unfailing love you lead
the people you have redeemed.
In your might, you guide them
to your sacred home.
14 The peoples hear and tremble;
anguish grips those who live in
Philistia.
15 The leaders of Edom are terrified;
the nobles of Moab tremble.
All who live in Canaan melt away;
16 terror and dread fall upon them.
The power of your arm
makes them lifeless as stone
until your people pass by, O LORD,
until the people you purchased
pass by.
17 You will bring them in and plant them
on your own mountain—
the place, O LORD, reserved for your
own dwelling,
the sanctuary, O Lord, that your hands
have established.
18 The LORD will reign forever and ever!"

19 When Pharaoh's horses, chariots, and
charioteers rushed into the sea, the LORD
brought the water crashing down on them.
But the people of Israel had walked through
the middle of the sea on dry ground!
20 Then Miriam the ᶠprophet, Aaron's sister,
took a tambourine and led all the women as
they played their tambourines and danced.
21 And Miriam sang this song:

The Exodus as History (14:15–15:21)

Exod 18:8-12
Judg 11:12-27
Acts 7:1-56

Israel's understanding of reality was radically different from that of all other ancient cultures. All of the other brilliant cultures surrounding Israel—from Sumer in southern Mesopotamia in 2000 BC to Rome in 200 AD—reached their views of reality by observing the world of nature. They concluded that there were many gods and that all events go in unending cycles. Ancient Israel believed that there is one God who is distinct from the world, who made the world with purpose, and who is guiding its events to realize his purposes. How did the Israelites come to their unique concept of reality? Was it not through encounters with the true God in actual events of history? The most reasonable explanation for the distinctiveness of Israel's understanding is that, as the Bible describes, God broke into their experience and showed himself to them in events that have been recorded as history.

There is nothing else like Israel's account of its past in the literature of the entire ancient world. There is no report in Egyptian texts of the kinds of events the Bible describes—but no ancient people except Israel ever reported the disasters they themselves experienced. Other ancient peoples only reported good things, with the belief that the reporting itself would determine the final outcome. The Bible's historical reporting is unlike anything else found in the ancient Near East.

Archaeology cannot prove that certain events happened, but it can demonstrate that conditions would have permitted the events to occur. That is true of the book of Exodus and of the Bible in general. Egyptian records and archaeology neither confirm nor contradict the Bible's record. However, the text of Exodus shows an intimate familiarity with Egyptian thought and culture.

The writers of the Bible believed they were reporting actual events, and they expected their readers to take them as such. If the Bible is in fact God's inspired word (2 Tim 3:16; 2 Pet 1:20-21), then these events cannot be fiction. Exodus 18:8-12 gives the first example of someone who put his faith in God because of a testimony to what had actually happened. Faith in God and in the Bible has a strong historical basis. God really has entered into history to act for the salvation of humanity. His acts include Israel's exodus from Egypt and climax in the life, death, and resurrection of Jesus Christ.

speaks of the undeserved kindness and loyalty of a superior to an inferior. It is the most frequent descriptor of God's character in the OT (see Ps 136). If God had such a character but did not have the *might* to carry out his good intentions toward his people, his character would be of little value to us. The good news is that he has both a loving character and all power. • *sacred home:* God has chosen his people and gathered them to himself in order to dwell in their midst (see also 15:17).

15:14-15 *Philistia, Edom, Moab,* and *Canaan* are the four peoples that would most feel the hand of God's judgment as he dispossessed them to give the land to the people of Israel. What God had done to Egypt would have been common news throughout that part of the world (see Rahab's report in Josh 2:9-11, where the same imagery as in 15:15, to *melt away,* is used).

15:17 *your own mountain:* Deities were believed to have their residence on mountains. Thus Canaan is figuratively portrayed as God's residence.

15:19-21 *Miriam* led the women in praise. In many ancient societies, men and women performed ceremonies separately. Women had special roles in ritual praise and lamentation.

"Sing to the LORD,
for he has triumphed gloriously;
he has hurled both horse and rider
into the sea."

En Route to Sinai (15:22–18:27)

Bitter Water at Marah

22Then Moses led the people of Israel away
from the Red Sea, and they moved out into
the desert of Shur. They traveled in this desert for three days without finding any water.
23When they came to the oasis of Marah, the
water was too bitter to drink. So they called
the place Marah (which means "bitter").
24Then the people complained and turned
against Moses. "What are we going to drink?"
they demanded. 25So Moses cried out to the
LORD for help, and the LORD showed him a
piece of wood. Moses threw it into the water,
and this made the water good to drink.
It was there at Marah that the LORD set
before them the following decree as a standard to test their faithfulness to him. 26He
said, "If you will listen carefully to the voice
of the LORD your God and do what is right in
his sight, obeying his commands and keeping all his decrees, then I will not make you
suffer any of the diseases I sent on the Egyptians; for I am the LORD who heals you."
27After leaving Marah, the Israelites traveled on to the oasis of Elim, where they
found twelve springs and seventy palm
trees. They camped there beside the water.

Manna and Quail from Heaven

16 Then the whole community of Israel
set out from Elim and journeyed into
the wilderness of Sin, between Elim and
Mount Sinai. They arrived there on the fifteenth day of the second month, one month
after leaving the land of Egypt. 2There, too,
the whole community of Israel complained
about Moses and Aaron.
3"If only the LORD had killed us back in
Egypt," they moaned. "There we sat around
pots filled with meat and ate all the bread we
wanted. But now you have brought us into
this wilderness to starve us all to death."
4Then the LORD said to Moses, "Look, I'm
going to rain down food from [g]heaven for
you. Each day the people can go out and
pick up as much food as they need for that
day. I will test them in this to see whether
or not they will follow my instructions. 5On
the sixth day they will gather food, and
when they prepare it, there will be twice as
much as usual."
6So Moses and Aaron said to all the people
of Israel, "By evening you will realize it was
the LORD who brought you out of the land of
Egypt. 7In the morning you will see the glory
of the LORD, because he has heard your complaints, which are against him, not against
us. What have we done that you should complain about us?" 8Then Moses added, "The
LORD will give you meat to eat in the evening
and bread to satisfy you in the morning, for
he has heard all your complaints against him.
What have we done? Yes, your complaints
are against the LORD, not against us."
9Then Moses said to Aaron, "Announce
this to the entire community of Israel: 'Present yourselves before the LORD, for he has
heard your complaining.' " 10And as Aaron
spoke to the whole community of Israel,

15:21 Exod 15:1
15:22 Num 33:8; Ps 77:20; 78:52
15:23 Num 33:8; Ruth 1:20
15:24 Exod 14:11; Ps 106:13
15:25 Exod 14:10; 16:4
15:26 Exod 19:5-6; Deut 7:15; Ps 103:3
15:27 Num 33:9
16:1 Exod 17:1; Num 33:11-12
16:2 Exod 14:11; 1 Cor 10:10
16:4 Deut 8:2-3, 16; Ps 78:24; 105:40; John 6:31; 1 Cor 10:3
[g]*shamayim* (8064) ›2 Kgs 1:10
16:5 Exod 16:22
16:6 Exod 6:6
16:7 Exod 16:12; Num 14:27; 16:11

15:22–18:27 On the journey from the sea to Sinai, God continued his providential care for the people's needs. In the events of rescue, he primarily revealed his power. Here he revealed that he cares about his people's basic needs.

15:22-27 First at *Marah* and then at *Elim*, God provided water for the people. • The precise location of the *desert of Shur* (15:22) is unknown.

15:23 The *water* was probably heavily alkaline, as is typical in the Sinai Desert.

15:24 Instead of reflecting on the lessons of faith so recently experienced, the people lost heart and began to complain, as we often do under adverse circumstances. If this complaining becomes a pattern, disaster can befall us in the ultimate test, as it did the Israelites (see Num 14; Ps 95:7-11; Heb 3:7-11).

15:25 See 2 Kgs 2:19-22 for a similar incident.

15:26 The connection between obedience to God's *commands* and health is not arbitrary. God made the body, and our bodies will last longer if we follow the Creator's guidelines. Since this statement was made in the context of a need for water, it might indicate that the Egyptians had been drinking polluted water.

16:1-36 God demonstrated care for his people by providing manna and quail as food for them.

16:1 The geographical name *Sin* is related to *Sinai* and should not be confused with the English word *sin*. • ***one month after leaving the land of Egypt:*** The Exodus had occurred on the fifteenth day of the first month (see Num 33:3).

16:2 ***complained:*** The people were developing a pattern of faithlessness manifested in complaining.

16:3 ***all the bread we wanted:*** The Israelites had been oppressed slaves in Egypt! One of the great dangers of complaining is that it blinds us to reality. Faith is grateful for what is, and believes the best is yet to come. Complaint focuses on what is wrong with the present and glorifies an unreal past.

16:4-5 These are the Lord's instructions for gathering the ***food*** that he would provide in the wilderness. Enough was provided for each day, with a double amount provided on ***the sixth day*** so that the people would not have to gather any on the Sabbath (see 16:21-30). The Israelites thus observed the Sabbath even before it was codified in the Decalogue. We instinctively resist a style of life in which it is necessary to depend on God each day to supply our needs. We wish to have supplies in advance so that we can feel independent. God was training the people for a life of faith (cp. Matt 6:11).

16:7 The Hebrew word translated ***glory*** connotes weightiness, substance, and reality. It is not the flimsy, ephemeral quality we often associate with the English term *glory.* It is more the idea of royal grandeur. See also "The Glory of God" at 24:15-17, p. 167.

16:10
Num 16:19
[h]*kabod* (3519)
‣ Num 14:10
16:12
Exod 16:7
16:13
Num 11:31
Ps 78:27-28; 105:40
16:14
Num 11:7-9
Deut 8:3
16:15
Exod 16:31
Neh 9:15
John 6:31
1 Cor 10:3
[i]*man* (4478)
‣ Exod 16:31
16:16
Exod 16:33, 36
16:18
*2 Cor 8:15
16:19
Exod 12:10; 23:18
16:22
Exod 16:5; 34:31
16:23
Gen 2:3
Exod 20:8; 23:12
Neh 9:14
[j]*shabbath* (7676)
‣ Exod 20:11
16:24
Exod 16:20
16:28
Ps 78:10
16:31
Num 11:7-9
Deut 8:3, 16
[k]*man* (4478)
‣ Exod 16:33
16:33
Heb 9:4
Rev 2:17
[a]*man* (4478)
‣ Exod 16:35
16:34
Exod 25:16, 21
Num 1:50
16:35
Josh 5:12
Neh 9:20-21
[b]*man* (4478)
‣ Num 11:6

they looked out toward the wilderness. There they could see the awesome [h]glory of the LORD in the cloud.

11 Then the LORD said to Moses, 12 "I have heard the Israelites' complaints. Now tell them, 'In the evening you will have meat to eat, and in the morning you will have all the bread you want. Then you will know that I am the LORD your God.' "

13 That evening vast numbers of quail flew in and covered the camp. And the next morning the area around the camp was wet with dew. 14 When the dew evaporated, a flaky substance as fine as frost blanketed the ground. 15 The Israelites were puzzled when they saw it. [i]"What is it?" they asked each other. They had no idea what it was.

And Moses told them, "It is the food the LORD has given you to eat. 16 These are the LORD's instructions: Each household should gather as much as it needs. Pick up two quarts for each person in your tent."

17 So the people of Israel did as they were told. Some gathered a lot, some only a little. 18 But when they measured it out, everyone had just enough. Those who gathered a lot had nothing left over, and those who gathered only a little had enough. Each family had just what it needed.

19 Then Moses told them, "Do not keep any of it until morning." 20 But some of them didn't listen and kept some of it until morning. But by then it was full of maggots and had a terrible smell. Moses was very angry with them.

21 After this the people gathered the food morning by morning, each family according to its need. And as the sun became hot, the flakes they had not picked up melted and disappeared. 22 On the sixth day, they gathered twice as much as usual—four quarts for each person instead of two. Then all the leaders of the community came and asked Moses for an explanation. 23 He told them, "This is what the LORD commanded: Tomorrow will be a day of complete rest, a holy [j]Sabbath day set apart for the LORD. So bake or boil as much as you want today, and set aside what is left for tomorrow."

24 So they put some aside until morning, just as Moses had commanded. And in the morning the leftover food was wholesome and good, without maggots or odor. 25 Moses said, "Eat this food today, for today is a Sabbath day dedicated to the LORD. There will be no food on the ground today. 26 You may gather the food for six days, but the seventh day is the Sabbath. There will be no food on the ground that day."

27 Some of the people went out anyway on the seventh day, but they found no food. 28 The LORD asked Moses, "How long will these people refuse to obey my commands and instructions? 29 They must realize that the Sabbath is the LORD's gift to you. That is why he gives you a two-day supply on the sixth day, so there will be enough for two days. On the Sabbath day you must each stay in your place. Do not go out to pick up food on the seventh day." 30 So the people did not gather any food on the seventh day.

31 The Israelites called the food [k]manna. It was white like coriander seed, and it tasted like honey wafers.

32 Then Moses said, "This is what the LORD has commanded: Fill a two-quart container with manna to preserve it for your descendants. Then later generations will be able to see the food I gave you in the wilderness when I set you free from Egypt."

33 Moses said to Aaron, "Get a jar and fill it with two quarts of [a]manna. Then put it in a sacred place before the LORD to preserve it for all future generations." 34 Aaron did just as the LORD had commanded Moses. He eventually placed it in the Ark of the Covenant—in front of the stone tablets inscribed with the terms of the covenant. 35 So the people of Israel ate [b]manna for forty years until they arrived at the land

16:15 The Hebrew *man hu'* (***What is it?***) came to be the name of the miraculous food ("manna," see 16:31). For forty years, the people ate *what is it?* Jesus referred to himself as the fulfillment of the meaning of this miracle. He was the "true bread from heaven" that gives life (John 6:32-35, 48, 51, 63).

16:16 ***two quarts:*** Hebrew *1 omer* (2 liters); also in 16:32, 33.

16:18 ***measured it out:*** Hebrew *measured it with an omer*; see note on 16:16.

16:19-20 Regarding these instructions, see note on 16:4-5.

16:21-30 Although ***the Sabbath*** was a ***day set apart for the LORD*** (16:23), it was also ***the LORD's gift*** to his people (16:29). Rest and worship are not meant to be an obligation, but a privilege. However, given the human determination to meet our needs in our own way, rest and worship are given as ***commands*** (16:28).

16:22 ***four quarts:*** Hebrew *2 omers* (4 liters).

16:31 ***Manna*** means "What is it?" See 16:15.

16:32-36 The ***container*** of ***manna*** was to be preserved as a reminder of God's providential care for his people. He is powerful and deeply caring. Not only can he supply our needs, he wants to do so.

16:34 Aaron was to place a jar of the manna ***in the Ark of the Covenant*** (literally *in front of the Testimony;* see note on 25:16), along with ***the stone tablets inscribed with the terms of the covenant.***

16:35 ***until they arrived at the land:*** God's care for us is normally demonstrated in ordinary ways, as it would usually be for Israel after they arrived in Canaan (see Josh 5:10-12). That care is just as real as when it comes in extraordinary ways, as it did while Israel was in the wilderness.

where they would settle. They ate [b]manna
until they came to the border of the land of
Canaan.
36The container used to measure the
manna was an omer, which was one-tenth
of an ephah; it held about two quarts.

Water from the Rock

17 At the LORD's command, the whole
community of Israel left the wilderness of Sin and moved from place to place.
Eventually they camped at Rephidim, but
there was no water there for the people
to drink. 2So once more the people complained against Moses. "Give us water to
drink!" they demanded.
"Quiet!" Moses replied. "Why are you
complaining against me? And why are you
testing the LORD?"
3But tormented by thirst, they continued
to argue with Moses. "Why did you bring us
out of Egypt? Are you trying to kill us, our
children, and our livestock with thirst?"
4Then Moses cried out to the LORD,
"What should I do with these people? They
are ready to stone me!"
5The LORD said to Moses, "Walk out in
front of the people. Take your staff, the one
you used when you struck the water of the
Nile, and call some of the elders of Israel to
join you. 6I will stand before you on the rock
at Mount Sinai. Strike the rock, and water
will come gushing out. Then the people will
be able to drink." So Moses struck the rock
as he was told, and water gushed out as the
elders looked on.
7Moses named the place Massah (which
means "test") and Meribah (which means
"arguing") because the people of Israel argued with Moses and tested the LORD by
saying, "Is the LORD here with us or not?"

Israel Enabled to Defeat the Amalekites

8While the people of Israel were still at
Rephidim, the warriors of Amalek attacked
them. 9Moses commanded Joshua, "Choose
some men to go out and fight the army of
Amalek for us. Tomorrow, I will stand at the
top of the hill, holding the staff of God in
my hand."
10So Joshua did what Moses had
commanded and fought the army of Amalek. Meanwhile, Moses, Aaron, and Hur
climbed to the top of a nearby hill. 11As
long as Moses held up the staff in his hand,
the Israelites had the advantage. But whenever he dropped his hand, the Amalekites
gained the advantage. 12Moses' arms soon
became so tired he could no longer hold
them up. So Aaron and Hur found a stone
for him to sit on. Then they stood on each
side of Moses, holding up his hands. So
his hands held steady until sunset. 13As a
result, Joshua overwhelmed the army of
Amalek in battle.
14After the victory, the LORD instructed
Moses, "Write this down on a scroll as a
permanent reminder, and read it aloud to
Joshua: I will erase the memory of Amalek
from under heaven." 15Moses built an altar
there and named it Yahweh-Nissi (which
means "the LORD is my banner"). 16He said,

[b]*man* (4478)
‣ Num 11:6

17:1
Exod 16:1; 19:2
Num 33:15

17:2
Exod 14:11-12
Num 20:3
Deut 6:16
1 Cor 10:10

17:3
Exod 16:2-3

17:4
Num 14:10; 16:19

17:5
Exod 7:20; 14:16

17:6
Num 20:8-10
Ps 78:15-16; 105:41
1 Cor 10:4

17:7
Deut 6:16; 9:22
Ps 81:7; 95:8

17:8
Gen 36:12, 16
Num 24:20
Deut 25:17-19

17:9
Exod 24:13
Num 11:28

17:10
Exod 24:14; 31:2

17:12
Isa 35:3

17:14
Exod 24:4; 34:27
Num 33:2

17:15
Gen 22:14

16:36 The Hebrew text of this verse reads *An omer is one-tenth of an ephah.*

17:1 *Sin:* See note on 16:1. • *from place to place:* With a large and diverse group, travel was undoubtedly slow and arduous. It is also possible that God was using this time to demonstrate his care by miraculously providing for their needs before bringing them to Mount Sinai and offering his covenant to them.

17:2 *testing the LORD* is explained in 17:7. They doubted that God was really with them or cared for them, and they demanded that he prove his presence and care. God invites a test based on faith ("I do believe, but help me overcome my unbelief," Mark 9:24), but he abhors a test based on doubt (i.e., *I don't believe, and I think God should prove himself to me,* as in John 6:30). The test based on doubt makes us the judge and God the defendant.

17:3 Regarding a similar complaint, see note on 16:3.

17:6 *Mount Sinai:* Hebrew *Horeb.* See note on 3:1. • *water gushed out:* Note the similar provision in Num 20:11 (see also Ps 78:15-16; 105:41; 114:8; Isa 48:21).

17:8-16 Israel was enabled to defeat the Amalekites only by God's blessing and providential care.

17:8 *Amalek* was Esau's grandson (Gen 36:11-12). His descendants were nomadic, though loosely based in the land of Edom. They seem to have supported themselves by raiding more settled peoples.

17:9-13 This victory was a gift from God, as the description here makes clear. The determining factor was God's blessing, as indicated by Moses' upraised *hands.* This principle was illustrated again and again in the conquest of the land of Canaan. Without God's blessing, Israel could do nothing (see Num 14:42-45; Josh 7:10-12).

17:9 *Joshua* was Moses' trusted assistant (33:11) who would eventually become his successor (Deut 31:7-8). This early experience was important training for leading the people later in the conquest of the land. The Hebrew name *Joshua,* which means "savior," is equivalent to the Greek name *Jesus* (see also note on Heb 4:8).

17:14-16 By their unprovoked attack on the people through whom God was extending his blessing, the Amalekites incurred the unending wrath of God. God's hand can be extended in blessing, or it can be extended in curse. Those who reject the hand of blessing experience the curse (see 1 Sam 15).

17:15 This *banner* was a battle flag. In Isa 5:26, God lifted up a banner to call the nations to war against Israel. In Isa 11:10, 12, the Messiah would be the banner calling the nations to bring his people home.

17:16 ***They have raised their fist against the LORD's throne, so now*** (or *Hands have been lifted up to the LORD's throne, and now*): The NLT sees the fist raised against the Lord's throne as Amalek's aggression against the Lord and his

18:1 Exod 2:16, 18; 3:1
ᶜ*kohen* (3548)
›Exod 19:6
18:2 Exod 2:21; 4:25
18:3 Exod 2:22
Acts 7:29
18:4 Gen 49:25
18:5 Exod 3:1
18:7 Gen 43:28
18:8 Exod 15:6, 16
Num 20:14
18:9 Isa 63:7-14
18:10 1 Kgs 8:56
Ps 68:19-20
18:11 Exod 12:12; 15:11
18:12 Gen 31:54
Exod 24:5

"They have raised their fist against the LORD's
throne, so now the LORD will be at war with
Amalek generation after generation."

Jethro's Visit to Moses

18 Moses' father-in-law, Jethro, the
ᶜpriest of Midian, heard about everything God had done for Moses and his
people, the Israelites. He heard especially
about how the LORD had rescued them from
Egypt.

[2]Earlier, Moses had sent his wife, Zipporah, and his two sons back to Jethro, who
had taken them in. [3](Moses' first son was
named Gershom, for Moses had said when
the boy was born, "I have been a foreigner
in a foreign land." [4]His second son was
named Eliezer, for Moses had said, "The
God of my ancestors was my helper; he
rescued me from the sword of Pharaoh.")
[5]Jethro, Moses' father-in-law, now came to
visit Moses in the wilderness. He brought
Moses' wife and two sons with him, and
they arrived while Moses and the people
were camped near the mountain of God.
[6]Jethro had sent a message to Moses,
saying, "I, Jethro, your father-in-law, am
coming to see you with your wife and your
two sons."
[7]So Moses went out to meet his father-in-
law. He bowed low and kissed him. They
asked about each other's welfare and then
went into Moses' tent. [8]Moses told his father-
in-law everything the LORD had done to
Pharaoh and Egypt on behalf of Israel. He
also told about all the hardships they had experienced along the way and how the LORD
had rescued his people from all their troubles. [9]Jethro was delighted when he heard
about all the good things the LORD had
done for Israel as he rescued them from the
hand of the Egyptians.

[10]"Praise the LORD," Jethro said, "for he
has rescued you from the Egyptians and
from Pharaoh. Yes, he has rescued Israel
from the powerful hand of Egypt! [11]I know
now that the LORD is greater than all other
gods, because he rescued his people from
the oppression of the proud Egyptians."

[12]Then Jethro, Moses' father-in-law,
brought a burnt offering and sacrifices to
God. Aaron and all the elders of Israel came
out and joined him in a sacrificial meal in
God's presence.

JETHRO/REUEL (18:1-27)

Exod 2:16-25; 3:1
Num 10:29
Judg 1:16; 4:11

Jethro, also called Reuel (2:16-18; Num 10:29), was "the priest of Midian" (2:16). We first encounter Jethro when Moses rescued his seven daughters from the rough treatment of other shepherds at a well and helped them water their flocks. At home they told their father of their surprising encounter with "an Egyptian." Jethro responded gratefully by inviting Moses for a meal. Moses married Jethro's daughter Zipporah, with whom he had two sons.

While Moses was living in Midian near his father-in-law (3:1), he encountered God at the burning bush. Before leaving for Egypt, Moses asked Jethro's permission to go; he later sent his family to stay with Jethro during the Exodus.

When Moses and the Israelites were in the wilderness, Jethro returned with Moses' family. Jethro, having heard of Yahweh's deliverance of his people from Egypt, acknowledged him as the God of all gods. He worshiped Yahweh with a burnt offering and sacrifices, thereby identifying himself with Israel (18:11). In response, Israel's leaders joined him for "a sacrificial meal in God's presence" (18:12).

Moses was overwhelmed with caring for the vast numbers of Israelites. Jethro gave Moses good administrative advice about organizing the people more efficiently and about judging disputes among the people (18:13-23). Moses listened to this counsel and appointed able men to assist him as leaders and judges over the people (18:24-27). Jethro returned to Midian and seems not to have interacted further with Israel, but his son (Num 10:29-33) and other descendants later became Israelites (Judg 1:16; 4:11).

people. The alternate interpretation sees a reference to Moses' own hands that were lifted to the Lord in prayer (17:15).

18:1-12 Moses had apparently *sent his wife* and children back from Egypt at some point to stay with his *father-in-law.* In the intense confrontation with Pharaoh, Moses might have been afraid for their lives. *Jethro* now came to meet Moses and the Israelites, bringing Moses' family with him (18:2-6). In the context of the visit, Moses gave him a report, and Jethro was brought to faith through the testimony of the Lord's work.

18:1 *Jethro:* See note on 2:16.

18:3-4 *Gershom* sounds like a Hebrew term that means "a foreigner there." *Eliezer* means "God is my helper." Hebrew parents often used names related to the circumstances of a child's birth.

18:7 ***bowed low and kissed him. They asked about each other's welfare:*** These were all typical customs of greeting in that society.

Jethro's Wise Advice

13 The next day, Moses took his seat to hear the people's disputes against each other. They waited before him from morning till evening.

14 When Moses' father-in-law saw all that Moses was doing for the people, he asked, "What are you really accomplishing here? Why are you trying to do all this alone while everyone stands around you from morning till evening?"

15 Moses replied, "Because the people come to me to get a ruling from God. 16 When a dispute arises, they come to me, and I am the one who settles the case between the quarreling parties. I inform the people of God's decrees and give them his instructions."

17 "This is not good!" Moses' father-in-law exclaimed. 18 "You're going to wear yourself out—and the people, too. This job is too heavy a burden for you to handle all by yourself. 19 Now listen to me, and let me give you a word of advice, and may God be with you. You should continue to be the people's representative before God, bringing their disputes to him. 20 Teach them God's decrees, and give them his [d]instructions. Show them how to conduct their lives. 21 But select from all the people some capable, honest men who fear God and hate bribes. Appoint them as leaders over groups of one thousand, one hundred, fifty, and ten. 22 They should always be available to solve the people's common disputes, but have them bring the major cases to you. Let the leaders decide the smaller matters themselves. They will help you carry the load, making the task easier for you. 23 If you follow this advice, and if God commands you to do so, then you will be able to endure the pressures, and all these people will go home in peace."

24 Moses listened to his father-in-law's advice and followed his suggestions. 25 He [e]chose capable men from all over Israel and appointed them as leaders over the people. He put them in charge of groups of one thousand, one hundred, fifty, and ten. 26 These men were always available to [f]solve the people's common disputes. They brought the major cases to Moses, but they [f]took care of the smaller matters themselves.

27 Soon after this, Moses said good-bye to his father-in-law, who returned to his own land.

THE SINAI COVENANT: GOD'S PRINCIPLES (19:1–24:18)

Preparation to Receive the Covenant (19:1-25)

19 Exactly two months after the Israelites left Egypt, they arrived in the wilderness of Sinai. 2 After breaking camp at Rephidim, they came to the wilderness of Sinai and set up camp there at the base of Mount Sinai.

3 Then Moses climbed the mountain to appear before God. The LORD called to him from the mountain and said, "Give these instructions to the family of Jacob; announce it to the descendants of Israel: 4 'You have seen what I did to the Egyptians. You know how I carried you on eagles' wings and brought you to myself. 5 Now if you will obey me and keep my [g]covenant, you will be my own special treasure from among all the peoples on earth; for all the earth belongs to me. 6 And you will be my kingdom of [h]priests, my holy nation.' This is the message you must give to the people of Israel."

18:15 Num 9:8; Deut 17:8-13
18:16 Exod 24:14
18:18 Num 11:14, 17; Deut 1:9
18:19-20 Deut 1:18
18:20 [d]*torah* (8451) ‣Deut 30:10
18:21 Deut 1:13, 15; Ps 15:1-5
18:22 Num 11:17; Deut 1:17-18
18:25 Deut 1:15; 16:18; [e]*bakhar* (0977) ‣Deut 7:6
18:26 Deut 16:18; [f]*shapat* (8199) ‣Lev 19:15
18:27 Num 10:29-30
19:1 Exod 12:51; 16:1
19:2 Exod 17:1; 18:5
19:3 Exod 20:21; Acts 7:38
19:4 Deut 29:2; Isa 40:31; 63:9; Rev 12:14
19:5 Exod 15:26; Deut 10:14; [g]*berith* (1285) ‣Num 25:12
19:6 Lev 11:44-45; Deut 33:3; *1 Pet 2:5, 9; Rev 1:6; 5:10; [h]*kohen* (3548) ‣Lev 1:5

18:13-27 Jethro's wise advice is a further example of God's providence, although it was not given in a miraculous way. Jethro introduced Moses to a style of leadership that involved delegation of authority. It appears that Moses had been following an Egyptian style of leadership that was heavily hierarchical and based on circumstances. No Egyptian law code has yet been discovered. It appears that all authority flowed downward from the Pharaoh, who ruled by fiat. Jethro proposed a structure of delegation that would make Moses' life easier.

18:13-16 Moses had set himself up in place of Pharaoh, making himself indispensable to the people.

18:17-18 Such a leader-centered approach is not good for either the leader or the people (see also 18:23).

18:19-22 Moses needed to distinguish between his teaching function, in which he received and declared God's *decrees* and *instructions* (18:19-20), and an administrative function, in which he applied all of those decrees and instructions (18:21-22).

19:1-9 God prepared his people to receive the covenant by first reminding them of the past and of what they had learned about him (19:4). He then made promises concerning the future, which were contingent upon obedience (19:5-6). The final result was their promise to obey what *the LORD has commanded* (19:8).

19:1 ***Exactly two months after the Israelites left Egypt:*** Literally *In the third month after the Israelites left Egypt, on the very day,* i.e., two lunar months to the day after leaving Egypt. Cp. Num 33:3. See also chart, "Israel's Annual Calendar," p. 145. It was now the fifteenth day of the third month.

19:2 The arrival at Sinai was a fulfillment of the promise made earlier to Moses at this same spot (3:12).

19:3 ***the family of Jacob . . . the descendants of Israel:*** The link between Jacob and the present generation reflected continuity with the past. God had kept all his promises thus far, and the promises he was yet to make would be equally trustworthy.

19:5-6 God, to whom ***all the earth belongs,*** promised to make Israel his ***own special treasure.*** This promise was contingent upon their accepting a ***covenant*** with God and keeping it faithfully. • ***my kingdom of priests, my holy nation:*** The nation was to become intermediaries between a holy God and a lost world. Through them God would reveal himself (see 1 Pet 2:9-10).

19:7
Exod 4:29-30; 24:9
19:8
Exod 24:3, 7
Deut 5:27; 26:17
19:9
Exod 19:16; 24:15
Deut 4:11
Ps 99:7
19:10
Gen 35:2
Lev 11:44-45
Num 8:7; 19:19
Heb 10:22
Rev 22:14
19:11
Exod 19:16
19:13
*Heb 12:20
19:15
1 Sam 21:4
1 Cor 7:5

7So Moses returned from the mountain
and called together the elders of the people
and told them everything the LORD had commanded him. 8And all the people responded
together, "We will do everything the LORD
has commanded." So Moses brought the
people's answer back to the LORD.
9Then the LORD said to Moses, "I will come
to you in a thick cloud, Moses, so the people
themselves can hear me when I speak with
you. Then they will always trust you."
Moses told the LORD what the people
had said. 10Then the LORD told Moses, "Go
down and prepare the people for my arrival.
Consecrate them today and tomorrow, and
have them wash their clothing. 11Be sure
they are ready on the third day, for on that
day the LORD will come down on Mount
Sinai as all the people watch. 12Mark off a
boundary all around the mountain. Warn
the people, 'Be careful! Do not go up on
the mountain or even touch its boundaries.
Anyone who touches the mountain will certainly be put to death. 13No hand may touch
the person or animal that crosses the boundary; instead, stone them or shoot them with
arrows. They must be put to death.' However, when the ram's horn sounds a long
blast, then the people may go up on the
mountain."
14So Moses went down to the people. He
consecrated them for worship, and they
washed their clothes. 15He told them, "Get
ready for the third day, and until then abstain from having sexual intercourse."

The Purpose of God's Covenant (19:3-6)

Exod 9:1
Lev 11:44-45
Jer 31:33-34; 32:40
John 16:5-11

Nearly everything the Israelites had learned about ultimate reality from the Egyptians was wrong (see "The Plagues" at 7:14–11:10, p. 141). There are not many gods; there is only one God. The Creator is perfectly good, and evil is the result of rebellion against him. God's blessings cannot be obtained through magic and manipulation; instead, they are free to those who lovingly submit to him.

The Israelites' real problem was not primarily their being slaves in Egypt; it was that they did not yet know God in the way that he intended. They left Egypt to worship the Lord (4:23; 5:3; 7:16; 8:1, 20, 26; 9:1, 13; 10:7, 24; 12:31). In the plagues and the Red Sea crossing, they learned of God's unique power. In the wilderness, they learned about God's providential care, but they still did not know God's character. The covenant at Sinai was designed to teach the Israelites about God's nature and character as they lived out his *Torah,* his instructions.

The covenant used a familiar political form, the *suzerain-vassal treaty,* in which a "great king" (the suzerain) made a treaty with a nation he had subjected as a vassal people. In such a treaty, the conquered people would declare their absolute loyalty to the king and obedience to his demands. The king, for his part, would promise to care for the conquered people and protect them from any enemies who might attack them (see also note on 20:1–23:33). In the covenant at Sinai, God called the people to absolute loyalty to himself as the only God and to a lifestyle that reflected his will and nature as their sovereign Creator.

Ever since the Fall (Gen 3), there has been something fundamentally wrong with the human spirit. Humans by nature oppose surrendering control to someone else. God wanted a very simple and straightforward response from the Israelites that was impossible for the unchanged human spirit. The covenant was a good thing, but it was weak in that it was incapable of making the Israelites able to follow it (Rom 7:12; 8:3). Unless God graciously bestows his Spirit upon us, we will never be able to do the things we must do; we will never share the character of the Creator. Through the cross of Christ, God has made it possible for us to be empowered by the Spirit and thus to fulfill his covenant purpose by sharing his holy character (see Jer 31:33-34; 32:40; John 16:8; Rom 8:5-14; 10:8-17; Gal 5:1-26).

19:7-8 The first phase of preparation was successful. The people agreed to ***do everything the LORD has commanded.***

19:9 See also Deut 4:12, 33.

19:10-15 In the second phase of preparation, the people received commands that would prepare them to receive God's covenant. They were to ***wash their clothing*** (19:10, 14) because God is pure. They were to prepare ***a boundary all around the mountain*** (19:12-13) and be careful not to cross it because God is holy. They were to ***abstain from having sexual intercourse*** (19:15) because God is not a sexual being, and his blessings are not produced through sexual activity. Things that are natural and right under ordinary circumstances were to be set aside for the extraordinary purpose of concentrating on the Lord, the King who was about to appear before the people. Only their compliance with the second of these commands is specifically reported (19:23), but it is safe to assume that they obeyed the other two as well since no negative response from the Lord is recorded. • Hebrews 12:18-22 contrasts this experience at Mount Sinai with the believer's experience at Mount Zion, "the heavenly Jerusalem."

19:13 ***up on the mountain:*** Or *up to the mountain.*

16 On the morning of the third day, thunder roared and lightning flashed, and a dense cloud came down on the mountain. There was a long, loud blast from a ram's horn, and all the people trembled. 17 Moses led them out from the camp to meet with God, and they stood at the foot of the mountain. 18 All of Mount Sinai was covered with smoke because the LORD had descended on it in the form of fire. The smoke billowed into the sky like smoke from a brick kiln, and the whole mountain shook violently. 19 As the blast of the ram's horn grew louder and louder, Moses spoke, and God thundered his reply. 20 The LORD came down on the top of Mount Sinai and called Moses to the top of the mountain. So Moses climbed the mountain.

21 Then the LORD told Moses, "Go back down and warn the people not to break through the boundaries to see the LORD, or they will die. 22 Even the priests who regularly come near to the LORD must purify themselves so that the LORD does not break out and destroy them."

23 "But LORD," Moses protested, "the people cannot come up to Mount Sinai. You already warned us. You told me, 'Mark off a boundary all around the mountain to set it apart as holy.' "

24 But the LORD said, "Go down and bring Aaron back up with you. In the meantime, do not let the priests or the people break through to approach the LORD, or he will break out and destroy them."

25 So Moses went down to the people and told them what the LORD had said.

Ten Commandments (20:1-21)

EXOD 20:2-17 // DEUT 5:6-21

20 Then God gave the people all these instructions:

2 "I am the LORD your God, who rescued you from the land of Egypt, the place of your slavery.

3 "You must not have any other god but me.

19:16-19 Deut 4:11; 5:4 Ps 68:7-8; 81:7; 104:32 Heb 12:18-19
19:20 Neh 9:13
19:21 Exod 3:5
19:22 Lev 10:3; 21:6-8
19:24 Exod 24:1, 9
20:1-17 //Deut 5:6-21
20:3 Deut 5:7; 6:14
20:4 Exod 23:13, 24; 34:14 Lev 26:1 Deut 4:15-19
20:5 Exod 34:6-7 Num 14:18 Deut 7:9-10

19:16-25 The final phase of preparation involved phenomena that moved the people toward acceptance of the covenant. Some of the experiences were visual: ***lightning*** and a ***cloud*** (19:16), ***smoke*** and ***fire*** (19:18). The people also heard ***thunder, a ram's horn,*** and the voice of ***God*** (19:16, 19), and ***the whole mountain shook violently*** (19:18). In the Bible, such phenomena are often associated with a *theophany,* which is a visible manifestation of God's holy presence.

19:21-25 The repeated warnings that no one should ***break through to approach the LORD*** reinforced the impact of the phenomena the people had just witnessed. God is utterly transcendent, and he must be approached in the way he ordains or not at all.

20:1–23:33 The Sinai Covenant follows very closely the form of the covenants, or *suzerain-vassal* treaties, that great kings (the *suzerains*) in the ancient Near East offered to subject peoples (the *vassals*) as follows: (1) An introduction named the Great King who was offering the covenant (20:1). (2) A historical preamble set out the circumstances that had led to the offer of a treaty (20:2). (3) Stipulations, the terms upon which the two parties were to agree, typically included the king's offer of protection from enemies and care during emergency, while the people would agree to behave in conformance to the preferences of that king. Exodus includes a brief setting forth of the terms of the covenant (20:3-17) followed by expanded terms (21:1–23:33). (4) Another statement indicated where a written copy of the covenant should be kept and when it should be read (24:7; 25:16). (5) The gods were called upon to witness the agreement (in Exodus, historical markers are substituted for the gods, 24:4). (6) The blessings and curses were stated that would follow upon obedience or disobedience to the covenant (23:20-33). Utilizing the political form of the covenant, God invited his people into a formal relationship with himself as king while avoiding the pagan overtones that contaminated religious forms of the time. Jesus' Sermon on the Mount (Matt 5:1–7:28) is a NT parallel to this section of Exodus, with the Beatitudes (Matt 5:3-12) paralleling the Ten Commandments.

20:1-17 The brief statement of the terms of the covenant (see also Deut 5:6-21).

20:1 This corresponds to the introductory statement in the ancient covenant format. • ***all these instructions*** (literally *all these words*): When these statements are referred to elsewhere (34:28; Deut 4:13; 10:4), the Hebrew text refers to them as the "Ten Words." These are not arbitrary commandments, but an explanation of God's basic instructions for human living given by the Creator of human life.

20:2 This sentence corresponds to the preamble in the ancient covenant format. It gives the historical setting that makes such an agreement between two parties both possible and reasonable. We are told that ***the LORD your God*** was offering the covenant. It was not some unknown deity that offered this special relationship, but the God of Israel's ancestors who had revealed his power and his care directly to them. Furthermore, that revelation was an act of gracious rescue on their behalf, demonstrating that he is the only God.

20:3-17 The terms of the covenant specify the behavior the people were expected to manifest if they were to be in a covenant with God. Only the first four instructions (20:2-11) relate directly to God, while the remaining six (20:12-17) have to do with human-to-human relationships. A covenant with God stipulates how we are to treat each other because God is profoundly ethical, and he expects us to manifest his character in all our relationships. Other law codes in the ancient Near East did not incorporate such absolute prohibitions, probably because polytheism mitigated against absolute principles. In contrast, covenants with a king did include absolute prohibitions because a single king could demand whatever he wished of his subjects. Here the single king is the sole Creator of the universe, who truly has authority to state absolute principles, demands, and prohibitions.

20:3-11 The first four commandments relate to one's relationship with God. Observing them would foster a correct understanding of God in contrast to the idolatrous notions of deity that the Israelites had encountered in Egypt and would yet encounter in Canaan.

20:3 Not recognizing ***any other god*** is the first step toward learning the truth that there are no other gods besides the Lord (see Deut 4:35; 6:4; Isa 43:10-11; 45:21-22).

[i]*qanna'* (7067)
‣ Exod 34:14

20:6
[j]*khesed* (2617)
‣ Josh 2:12

20:10
[k]*'ebed* (5650)
‣ Exod 21:2

20:11
*Acts 4:24
[a]*shabbath* (7676)
‣ Exod 31:15

20:12
*Matt 15:4
*Mark 7:10
*Luke 18:20
*Eph 6:2

20:13
Gen 9:5
*Matt 5:21; 19:18
*Rom 13:9
*Jas 2:11

20:14
*Matt 5:27

20:15
*Matt 19:18
*Mark 10:19
*Luke 18:20
*Rom 13:9

20:17
*Rom 7:7

4 “You must not make for yourself an idol
of any kind or an image of anything in
the heavens or on the earth or in the sea.
5 You must not bow down to them or worship them, for I, the LORD your God, am a
[i]jealous God who will not tolerate your affection for any other gods. I lay the sins
of the parents upon their children; the entire family is affected—even children in
the third and fourth generations of those
who reject me. 6 But I lavish unfailing
[j]love for a thousand generations on those
who love me and obey my commands.
7 “You must not misuse the name of the
LORD your God. The LORD will not let you
go unpunished if you misuse his name.
8 “Remember to observe the Sabbath day by
keeping it holy. 9 You have six days each
week for your ordinary work, 10 but the
seventh day is a Sabbath day of rest dedicated to the LORD your God. On that day
no one in your household may do any
work. This includes you, your sons and
daughters, your male and female [k]ser-
vants, your livestock, and any foreigners
living among you. 11 For in six days the
LORD made the heavens, the earth, the
sea, and everything in them; but on the
seventh day he rested. That is why the
LORD blessed the [a]Sabbath day and set it
apart as holy.
12 “Honor your father and mother. Then
you will live a long, full life in the land
the LORD your God is giving you.
13 “You must not murder.
14 “You must not commit adultery.
15 “You must not steal.
16 “You must not testify falsely against your
neighbor.
17 “You must not covet your neighbor's
house. You must not covet your neighbor's wife, male or female servant, ox or
donkey, or anything else that belongs to
your neighbor.”

20:4 Not making ***an image*** of God is the first step toward recognizing that he is transcendent—that he is the Creator of the universe and distinct from it. To represent God as something in creation was inevitably to end up worshiping the creation rather than the Creator, and this had deadly moral consequences (Rom 1:18-25).

20:5-6 ***jealous God:*** God is passionately opposed to our prostituting ourselves with false gods (see Josh 24:19-20). • ***in the third and fourth generations . . . for a thousand generations:*** It is important to keep both sides of this equation together. God does not punish children for their parents' sins. Rather, he is saying that our sins affect future generations of descendants. But he is also restricting the natural effects of those sins to three or four generations, while graciously extending the effects of obedience to ***a thousand generations*** (literally *for thousands;* see also Exod 34:6-7; Deut 7:9). • ***reject*** (literally *hate*): The Hebrew words commonly translated “love” (20:6) and “hate” are difficult to translate into English because they include an act of the will as well as the emotional element we are familiar with. In biblical thinking, to “love” is to choose something and to act consistently in accord with that choice. To “hate” is to reject something and to act in ways consistent with that choice. The choice is connected to emotion: Feeling expresses itself in choices, and our choices show how we really feel.

20:7 In Hebrew, one's ***name*** connotes nature and character (see note on 3:13-22). To make the name of God empty (NLT, ***misuse***) is to do anything that makes him appear insignificant or worthless. One way to do this is to invoke his name in an oath we do not mean to keep. But there are other, even more significant ways to bring shame on God's name (see Num 20:12; Amos 2:7; cp. Matt 6:9).

20:8-11 The ***Sabbath day*** is kept ***holy*** when it is ***dedicated to the LORD*** (20:10). Whatever belongs exclusively to God shares his character. This is not to say that the other six days are unholy, but simply that they are for ***ordinary work*** (20:9). On this day set apart, we are reminded that it is not our work that supplies our needs. Our needs are supplied by God as an act of his grace (see 20:6, ***unfailing love***).

20:11 To be in covenant with God is to do what God does; since he ***rested*** from his work (Gen 2:1-3), how can we think that we need no rest?

20:12-17 The remaining six instructions all have to do with human relationships. Many of the stipulations of the covenant with God relate to how people treat each other. This connection of ethical behavior with religious duty is unique in the OT world. There are several ethical law codes known in the ancient Near East, and several of these predate Moses, but all of them are imposed by a human king and have little to do with religion. The pagan gods, meanwhile, were all patently unethical and untrustworthy, unlike the God of Israel, whose people worship him by treating others as he does. See also Matt 19:17-19.

20:12 To ***honor your father and mother*** is to recognize that you are not self-sufficient and self-existent. This is one important step on the road to humility. Arrogance may produce notoriety, but humility and gratitude are the foundations of a ***long, full life.*** Both Jesus and Paul refer to this command (see Matt 15:4; Mark 7:10; Eph 6:1-3).

20:13 ***murder:*** This is the correct rendering of the Hebrew word. There is another word that connotes mere killing. Taking human life is not prohibited, per se, but the intentional killing of another for personal reasons is prohibited. This principle tells us that God values our individual, physical lives. Jesus expanded on this command in Matt 5:21-26.

20:14 ***adultery:*** Here this term represents all sexual sins, among which adultery most clearly indicates breaking faith. Adulterers satisfy their sexual desires as they please, and they break faith with their spouse in so doing. Jesus expanded on this command in Matt 5:27-30.

20:15 Stealing is another way of saying that I have an absolute right to my own way, whether I have earned it or not. From the divine side, the prohibition says that God values us even down to our possessions.

20:16 Not telling a lie can be a very individual act, and even a prideful one. But refusing to ***testify falsely against your neighbor*** is an unselfish act, in which your neighbor's reputation and well-being is more important to you than your own.

20:17 This final principle circles back to the first, for “a greedy person is an idolater” (Col 3:5). Covetousness is the worship of this world, the belief that possessions, especially those my ***neighbor*** possesses, will give me lasting happiness. To believe this is to break one's covenant of absolute loyalty to God, who alone supplies our needs. See also Rom 7:7.

18When the people heard the thunder and the loud blast of the ram's horn, and when they saw the flashes of lightning and the smoke billowing from the mountain, they stood at a distance, trembling with fear.

19And they said to Moses, "You speak to us, and we will listen. But don't let God speak directly to us, or we will die!"

20"Don't be afraid," Moses answered them, "for God has come in this way to test you, and so that your fear of him will keep you from sinning!"

21As the people stood in the distance, Moses approached the dark cloud where God was.

Covenant Requirements for the People (20:22–23:19)

Proper Use of Altars

22And the LORD said to Moses, "Say this to the people of Israel: You saw for yourselves that I spoke to you from heaven. 23Remember, you must not make any idols of silver or gold to rival me.

24"Build for me an altar made of earth, and offer your sacrifices to me—your burnt offerings and peace offerings, your sheep and goats, and your cattle. Build my altar wherever I cause my name to be remembered, and I will come to you and bless you. 25If you use stones to build my altar, use only natural, uncut stones. Do not shape the stones with a tool, for that would make the altar unfit for holy use. 26And do not approach my altar by going up steps. If you do, someone might look up under your clothing and see your nakedness.

Fair Treatment of Slaves

21 "These are the regulations you must present to Israel.

2"If you buy a Hebrew [b]slave, he may serve for no more than six years. Set him free in the seventh year, and he will owe you nothing for his freedom. 3If he was single when he became your slave, he shall leave single. But if he was married before he became a slave, then his wife must be freed with him.

4"If his master gave him a wife while he was a slave and they had sons or daughters, then only the man will be free in the seventh year, but his wife and children will still belong to his master. 5But the [c]slave may declare, 'I love my master, my wife, and my children. I don't want to go free.' 6If he does this, his master must present him before God. Then his master must take him to the door or doorpost and publicly pierce his ear with an awl. After that, the slave will serve his master for life.

7"When a man sells his daughter as a slave, she will not be freed at the end of six years

20:18 Exod 19:18; Heb 12:18
20:19 Deut 5:23-27
20:21 Deut 5:22; Ps 97:2
20:23 Exod 32:4; Deut 29:17-18
20:24 Exod 10:25; 18:12; 24:5; Lev 1:2; Deut 12:5
20:25 Deut 27:5-6; Josh 8:31
20:26 Exod 28:42
21:1 Deut 4:14
21:2-6 Lev 25:39-41; //Deut 15:12-18
21:2 Jer 34:14
[b]*'ebed* (5650) ›Exod 21:5
21:5 Deut 15:16
[c]*'ebed* (5650) ›Exod 21:20
21:6 Exod 22:8-9; Deut 15:17
21:7 Neh 5:5

20:18-26 This interlude is about access to God. The first part (20:18-21) deals with the need for a mediator between the people and God. In 20:22-26, we find the appropriate form for an altar in the interval before God revealed his plans for a more permanent sanctuary (see 25:1–30:28).

20:18-21 The *people* were very conscious of their sinfulness before a holy *God* and begged Moses to stand between them and God. Moses pointed out that God's goal was neither to overawe them nor to destroy them. Rather, he wanted their awe of him to ***keep*** them ***from sinning*** (20:20). Jesus is the ultimate mediator between God and people (1 Tim 2:5).

20:22-26 *The LORD* is transcendent, as shown by his speaking to the people in a disembodied voice ***from heaven*** (20:22). This would have two effects upon their practice: They were not to use ***silver or gold*** to make gods in human form (***idols***, 20:23), and they were not to carve ***stones*** for an ***altar*** (20:25). Perhaps this is because they would be tempted to carve stone gods in the process. The altar was to be made of ***earth*** (20:24) and ***uncut stones*** (20:25). • The prohibition against revealing one's ***nakedness*** (20:26) might have been to separate Israelite religious practice from the nature worship around them. Sexual activity was an integral part of many Canaanite rituals.

21:1–23:33 The terms of the covenant are now expanded. The beginning section (21:1–23:19) gives specific examples of the general principles stated in 20:3-17. The commitments to which God bound himself if the Israelites kept their side of the covenant are stated in 23:20-33, as are the blessings of obedience.

21:1–23:19 The statements found here are in the typical case-law format of ancient Near Eastern law codes (see "Ancient Law Codes" at 20:1–23:33, p. 163). This format begins with a hypothetical situation introduced by the word "if." The following statement of what is to be done in such a case is introduced by "then." While some cases are grouped into categories in these chapters, there is little attempt to separate personal, civil, or ceremonial laws from one another. For God, life is not compartmentalized. All of life is lived in relationship to God, so all kinds of behavior signify whether we are in loving submission to him or in defiance of him.

21:1-11 Slavery was a fact of life in the ancient world. In some cases, it was the only resort for those who were destitute. In much of the ancient world, people who were slaves felt that the gods had abandoned them. But the Lord cares about those who are in this helpless condition, so his covenant people must care also. Ultimately, the revelation that Jesus Christ had died for all people everywhere would make the practice of slavery untenable (Gal 3:28).

21:2 A man might sell himself into slavery in order to get money to pay his debts. This law states that the man was never to become the permanent property of the master.

21:3 If a man and a wife went into slavery together, they were also to go free together.

21:4-6 The master was not required to provide a slave with a wife who would then be freed with him. The slave in such a situation had to either abandon the family he began while he was a slave or become a permanent slave.

21:6 ***before God:*** Or *before the judges.*

21:7-9 A female slave was treated differently from a male, possibly because it was understood that she was sold to become a concubine. For such a woman to be released after seven years would not be just. She would either have to return to her father

21:10 1 Cor 7:3, 5
21:12 Gen 9:6; Lev 24:21
21:13 Num 35:22; Deut 19:4-5; Josh 20:9
21:14 Num 35:30-31; 1 Kgs 2:28-34
21:16 Deut 24:7
21:17 Lev 20:9; Deut 5:16; *Matt 15:4; *Mark 7:10
21:20 [d]*'ebed* (5650) ‣ Exod 21:26
21:21 Lev 25:44-46
21:23 Lev 24:19
21:24 Lev 24:20; *Matt 5:38
21:26 Job 31:13; [e]*'ebed* (5650) ‣ Exod 21:32
21:28 Gen 9:5
21:32 Gen 37:28; Zech 11:12-13; Matt 26:15; 27:3, 9; [f]*'ebed* (5650) ‣ Lev 25:6

as the men are. [8]If she does not satisfy her owner, he must allow her to be bought back again. But he is not allowed to sell her to foreigners, since he is the one who broke the contract with her. [9]But if the slave's owner arranges for her to marry his son, he may no longer treat her as a slave but as a daughter.

[10]"If a man who has married a slave wife takes another wife for himself, he must not neglect the rights of the first wife to food, clothing, and sexual intimacy. [11]If he fails in any of these three obligations, she may leave as a free woman without making any payment.

Cases of Personal Injury

[12]"Anyone who assaults and kills another person must be put to death. [13]But if it was simply an accident permitted by God, I will appoint a place of refuge where the slayer can run for safety. [14]However, if someone deliberately kills another person, then the slayer must be dragged even from my altar and be put to death.

[15]"Anyone who strikes father or mother must be put to death.

[16]"Kidnappers must be put to death, whether they are caught in possession of their victims or have already sold them as slaves.

[17]"Anyone who dishonors father or mother must be put to death.

[18]"Now suppose two men quarrel, and one hits the other with a stone or fist, and the injured person does not die but is confined to bed. [19]If he is later able to walk outside again, even with a crutch, the assailant will not be punished but must compensate his victim for lost wages and provide for his full recovery.

[20]"If a man beats his male or female [d]slave with a club and the slave dies as a result, the owner must be punished. [21]But if the slave recovers within a day or two, then the owner shall not be punished, since the slave is his property.

[22]"Now suppose two men are fighting, and in the process they accidentally strike a pregnant woman so she gives birth prematurely. If no further injury results, the man who struck the woman must pay the amount of compensation the woman's husband demands and the judges approve. [23]But if there is further injury, the punishment must match the injury: a life for a life, [24]an eye for an eye, a tooth for a tooth, a hand for a hand, a foot for a foot, [25]a burn for a burn, a wound for a wound, a bruise for a bruise.

[26]"If a man hits his male or female [e]slave in the eye and the eye is blinded, he must let the slave go free to compensate for the eye. [27]And if a man knocks out the tooth of his male or female slave, he must let the slave go free to compensate for the tooth.

[28]"If an ox gores a man or woman to death, the ox must be stoned, and its flesh may not be eaten. In such a case, however, the owner will not be held liable. [29]But suppose the ox had a reputation for goring, and the owner had been informed but failed to keep it under control. If the ox then kills someone, it must be stoned, and the owner must also be put to death. [30]However, the dead person's relatives may accept payment to compensate for the loss of life. The owner of the ox may redeem his life by paying whatever is demanded.

[31]"The same regulation applies if the ox gores a boy or a girl. [32]But if the ox gores a [f]slave, either male or female, the animal's

(who clearly did not want her, having previously sold her), marry (an unlikely prospect for a former concubine), or become a prostitute. Thus, it was best for her to remain in the home of her master. Presumably, if a man bought a girl to be his son's wife (21:9), it was understood that the purchase price was not actually buying her, but was the equivalent of a bride-price. Typically, a young man wishing to marry a girl had to give her father a gift of some sort, either money or a gift in kind (see 22:16; Gen 24:53). A woman for whom a bride-price had been paid was not a slave.

21:12-17 The crimes of murder, kidnapping, and dishonoring one's parents warranted the death penalty. A murderer forfeits his own life, and human life is so precious that even an accidental death cannot be overlooked. The *place of refuge* (see Num 35:6-28) was a place where an accidental killer could go so that the family of the deceased could not take vengeance on him (see notes on Num 35:6-34).

21:14 ***dragged . . . from my altar:*** See 1 Kgs 2:28-33.

21:17 ***Anyone who dishonors:*** Greek version reads *Anyone who speaks disrespectfully of.* Cp. Matt 15:4; Mark 7:10. See note on Lev 20:9; see also Exod 20:12; Deut 5:16; 21:18-21; Eph 6:1-4.

21:18-27 These laws governed compensation for injuries that did not lead to death.

21:22-25 ***so she gives birth prematurely:*** Or *so she has a miscarriage;* literally *so her children come out.* • It appears that if a child's birth was caused prematurely and the child died (i.e., there was *further injury*), the penalty for murder was to be enacted. The law of retaliation (the *lex talionis*) called for a penalty that matched the injury inflicted on a victim. But this law also served to limit the punishment so it was not more severe than the original injury. Cp. Matt 5:38-39.

21:28-32 If an animal caused a person's death and ***the owner*** was judged to be negligent, the relatives of the deceased could demand the death penalty for both the animal and its owner. However, that penalty was not mandatory, and the relatives could elect to accept compensation (21:30).

21:28 ***ox:*** Or *bull,* or *cow;* also in 21:29-36.

21:32 ***thirty silver coins:*** Literally *30 shekels of silver,* about 12 ounces or 342 grams in weight.

owner must pay the slave's owner thirty silver coins, and the ox must be stoned.
33“Suppose someone digs or uncovers a
pit and fails to cover it, and then an ox or a
donkey falls into it. 34The owner of the pit
must pay full compensation to the owner
of the animal, but then he gets to keep the
dead animal.
35“If someone's ox injures a neighbor's ox
and the injured ox dies, then the two owners must sell the live ox and divide the price
equally between them. They must also divide the dead animal. 36But if the ox had a
reputation for goring, yet its owner failed to
keep it under control, he must pay full compensation—a live ox for the dead one—but
he may keep the dead ox.

Protection of Property

22 “If someone steals an ox or sheep
and then kills or sells it, the thief
must pay back five oxen for each ox stolen,
and four sheep for each sheep stolen.
2“If a thief is caught in the act of breaking into a house and is struck and killed in
the process, the person who killed the thief
is not guilty of murder. 3But if it happens
in daylight, the one who killed the thief is
guilty of murder.
“A thief who is caught must pay in full
for everything he stole. If he cannot pay, he
must be sold as a slave to pay for his theft.
4If someone steals an ox or a donkey or a
sheep and it is found in the thief's possession, then the thief must pay double the
value of the stolen animal.
5“If an animal is grazing in a field or
vineyard and the owner lets it stray into
someone else's field to graze, then the animal's owner must pay compensation from
the best of his own grain or grapes.
6“If you are burning thornbushes and the
fire gets out of control and spreads into another person's field, destroying the sheaves
or the uncut grain or the whole crop, the
one who started the fire must pay for the
lost crop.
7“Suppose someone leaves money or
goods with a neighbor for safekeeping, and
they are stolen from the neighbor's house.
If the thief is caught, the compensation is
double the value of what was stolen. 8But if
the thief is not caught, the neighbor must
appear before God, who will determine if
he stole the property.
9“Suppose there is a dispute between two
people who both claim to own a particular
ox, donkey, sheep, article of clothing, or
any lost property. Both parties must come
before God, and the person whom God
declares guilty must pay double compensation to the other.
10“Now suppose someone leaves a donkey,
ox, sheep, or any other animal with a neighbor for safekeeping, but it dies or is injured
or gets away, and no one sees what happened.
11The neighbor must then take an oath in the
presence of the LORD. If the LORD confirms
that the neighbor did not steal the property,
the owner must accept the verdict, and no
payment will be required. 12But if the animal
was indeed stolen, the guilty person must pay
compensation to the owner. 13If it was torn
to pieces by a wild animal, the remains of the
carcass must be shown as evidence, and no
compensation will be required.
14“If someone borrows an animal from a
neighbor and it is injured or dies when the
owner is absent, the person who borrowed
it must pay full compensation. 15But if the
owner was present, no compensation is required. And no compensation is required
if the animal was rented, for this loss is covered by the rental fee.

Social Responsibility

16“If a man seduces a virgin who is not engaged to anyone and has sex with her, he
must pay the customary bride price and
marry her. 17But if her father refuses to
let him marry her, the man must still pay
him an amount equal to the bride price of
a virgin.
18“You must not allow a sorceress to live.
19“Anyone who has sexual relations with
an animal must certainly be put to death.
20“Anyone who [g]sacrifices to any god
other than the LORD must be [h]destroyed.

21:33
Luke 14:5

22:1
Lev 6:1-7
2 Sam 12:6
Prov 6:31
Luke 19:8

22:2
Num 35:26-27

22:3
Exod 21:2

22:4
Prov 6:31
Jer 2:26
John 12:6

22:5
Exod 21:34

22:7
Lev 6:1-7

22:8
Exod 21:6
Deut 17:8-9; 19:17

22:9
Deut 25:1

22:13
Gen 31:39

22:16-17
Deut 22:28-29

22:18
Lev 20:27
Deut 18:10

22:19
Lev 18:23; 20:15

22:20
Exod 32:8; 34:15
[g]*zabakh* (2076)
‣ Exod 23:18
[h]*kharam* (2763)
‣ Lev 27:28

21:33–22:15 In cases involving loss of property, the responsible person had to pay compensation equal to the value of what was lost. If the person had actually stolen the property, the compensation was multiplied (22:1, 4, 7). Where there was a question of responsibility, the parties were to ***appear before God*** for adjudication (22:8). The means by which the judgment was reached is not reported.

22:1 Verse 22:1 is numbered 21:37 in the Hebrew text. • *ox:* Or *bull,* or *cow;* also in 22:4, 9, 10.

22:2-31 Verses 22:2-31 are numbered 22:1-30 in the Hebrew text.

22:8 *before God:* Or *before the judges.*

22:9 *before God, and the person whom God declares guilty:* Or *before the judges, and the person whom the judges declare guilty.*

22:16-31 These miscellaneous cases involving social responsibility are not categorized. All parts of life are an expression of one's obedience to God (see note on 21:1–23:19).

22:16-17 ***bride price:*** See note on 21:7-9.

22:18 The practices of ***a sorceress*** represented the pagan worldview from which God was delivering his people. That worldview was utterly incompatible with the biblical one (see 20:3; 23:13).

22:20 ***must be destroyed:*** The Hebrew term used here refers to the complete

22:21 Lev 19:33
22:22 Deut 24:17-18
22:25 Lev 25:35-37; Deut 23:19-20
22:26 Deut 24:6, 10-13
22:28 Lev 24:15-16; Acts 23:5
22:29 Exod 13:2; 23:16, 19; 34:20; Deut 26:2
22:30 Gen 17:12; Lev 12:3; 22:27
22:31 Exod 19:6; Lev 7:24; 17:15; 22:8

21 “You must not mistreat or oppress
foreigners in any way. Remember, you yourselves were once foreigners in the land of
Egypt.
22 “You must not exploit a widow or an orphan. 23 If you exploit them in any way and
they cry out to me, then I will certainly hear
their cry. 24 My anger will blaze against you,
and I will kill you with the sword. Then your
wives will be widows and your children fatherless.
25 “If you lend money to any of my people
who are in need, do not charge interest as
a money lender would. 26 If you take your
neighbor’s cloak as security for a loan, you
must return it before sunset. 27 This coat may
be the only blanket your neighbor has. How
can a person sleep without it? If you do not
return it and your neighbor cries out to me
for help, then I will hear, for I am merciful.
28 “You must not dishonor God or curse
any of your rulers.
29 “You must not hold anything back when
you give me offerings from your crops and
your wine.
“You must give me your firstborn sons.
30 “You must also give me the firstborn of
your cattle, sheep, and goats. But leave the
newborn animal with its mother for seven
days; then give it to me on the eighth day.
31 “You must be my holy people. Therefore, do not eat any animal that has been
torn up and killed by wild animals. Throw
it to the dogs.

Ancient Law Codes (20:1–23:33)

Exod 34:1–35:3; Lev 1:1–27:34; Deut 4:1–33:29; Ezra 1:1-4; Esth 1:13-19; 8:9-14; Dan 6:6-9; Luke 2:1-3

Until the late 1800s, the law of Moses was believed to be a unique code of law, existing nearly a thousand years before anything comparable in the Greek and Roman laws. Excavations in Persia in the late 1800s, however, uncovered laws set forth by the Babylonian king Hammurabi (the 1700s BC) some 300 years prior to Moses. Surprisingly, a number of the laws in that list are almost identical to those in the Bible. Though this seemed to imply that the biblical laws had been taken from Hammurabi, subsequent discoveries produced law codes preceding Hammurabi’s by at least 500 years, and several laws are common to all of them, so Hammurabi did not originate them either.

What does this mean for the Bible? First, it is not surprising that we find similar laws from cultures neighboring Israel; similar societies require similar codes of conduct in order to ensure justice. Second, it is unique that the biblical laws are incorporated in a covenant with God. Elsewhere in the ancient Near East, religious laws (about sacrifice, prayers, offerings, etc.) and civil laws (covering theft, lying, sexual conduct, murder, etc.) were completely unrelated because ethics and religion were considered separate domains. Religion was a matter of prayer, devotion, offerings, and ritual behavior—the territory of priests. Ethics concerned social and civil behavior—the business of the king. The biblical view of things is different. A person who is in a relationship with the true God must not only participate in proper worship (religion), but also treat other people rightly (ethics).

Israel’s covenant with God made use of existing forms but invested them with new meaning. For example, the basic layout of Israel’s Tabernacle (chs 26–27) and Temple (see 1 Kgs 6–7) were the same as elsewhere in the ancient world, and the basic forms of the Hebrew sacrifices (see Lev 1–7) were largely identical to the forms of pagan sacrifices. But the meaning and purpose of the Temple and the sacrifices were significantly different from the meaning and purpose of such things in paganism (see notes on 20:3-17; 25:1–40:38; Lev 1–7).

While many of the laws of Moses were not new to the world at that time, the idea that the behavior they called for is written into the very fabric of the universe by its Creator was radically new.

consecration of things or people to the LORD, either by destroying them or by giving them as an offering. See also Lev 27:28-29.

22:21 The Hebrews were to treat ***foreigners*** kindly because they, too, had once been foreigners (see also 23:9; Deut 10:18-19). For further development of the principle, see Luke 6:31.

22:22-23 The ***widow***, the ***orphan***, and the foreigner were in a helpless and economically disadvantaged position. God, by his protective stance toward these persons, demonstrated that he does not value people on the basis of their power or wealth, the standards accepted by most humans. Instead, God values people because they share his image (Gen 1:27).

22:25-27 Although ***interest*** could not be charged on a loan to another Israelite, collateral, or ***security***, could be required. However, even the security had to be handled in a humane way. The requirements of the covenant mirrored the character of God.

22:30 God is considerate even of animals (see Jon 4:11).

22:31 Because of the symbolic significance of blood as life itself, God forbade eating meat with the blood still in it (see Lev 17:10-16).

A Call for Justice

23 "You must not pass along false rumors. You must not cooperate with
evil people by lying on the witness stand.
2"You must not follow the crowd in doing
wrong. When you are called to testify in a
dispute, do not be swayed by the crowd to
twist justice. 3And do not slant your testimony in favor of a person just because that
person is poor.
4"If you come upon your enemy's ox or
donkey that has strayed away, take it back
to its owner. 5If you see that the donkey of
someone who hates you has collapsed under its load, do not walk by. Instead, stop
and help.
6"In a lawsuit, you must not deny justice
to the poor.
7"Be sure never to charge anyone falsely
with evil. Never sentence an innocent or
blameless person to death, for I never declare a guilty person to be innocent.
8"Take no bribes, for a bribe makes you
ignore something that you clearly see. A
bribe makes even a righteous person twist
the truth.
9"You must not oppress foreigners. You
know what it's like to be a foreigner, for you
yourselves were once foreigners in the land
of Egypt.

Ceremonial Requirements

10"Plant and harvest your crops for six years,
11but let the land be renewed and lie uncultivated during the seventh year. Then let the
poor among you harvest whatever grows on
its own. Leave the rest for wild animals to
eat. The same applies to your vineyards and
olive groves.
12"You have six days each week for your
ordinary work, but on the seventh day you
must stop working. This gives your ox and
your donkey a chance to rest. It also allows
your slaves and the foreigners living among
you to be refreshed.
13"Pay close attention to all my instructions. You must not call on the name of any
other gods. Do not even speak their names.
14"Each year you must celebrate three
festivals in my honor. 15First, celebrate the
[i]Festival of Unleavened Bread. For seven
days the bread you eat must be made
without yeast, just as I commanded you.
Celebrate this festival annually at the appointed time in early spring, in the month
of Abib, for that is the anniversary of your
departure from Egypt. No one may appear
before me without an offering.
16"Second, celebrate the [j]Festival of Harvest, when you bring me the first crops of
your harvest.
"Finally, celebrate the [j]Festival of the Final Harvest at the end of the harvest season,
when you have harvested all the crops from
your fields. 17At these three times each year,
every man in Israel must appear before the
Sovereign, the LORD.
18"You must not [k]offer the blood of my
sacrificial offerings together with any
baked goods containing yeast. And do not
leave the fat from the festival offerings until the next morning.

23:1 Exod 20:16; Ps 35:11
23:2 Deut 1:17; 16:19
23:4-5 Deut 22:1-4
23:6 Exod 23:2-3
23:7 Exod 20:13, 16; Deut 27:25
23:8 Deut 16:19
23:9 Exod 22:21; Lev 19:33-34
23:10 Lev 25:3
23:11 Lev 25:1-7
23:12 Exod 20:8-11
23:13 Deut 4:9, 23
23:14 Exod 34:23-24; Deut 16:16
23:15 Exod 12:15; 13:4; Lev 23:5; [i]*khag* (2282) ‣Exod 23:16
23:16 Exod 34:22; Lev 23:34; Deut 16:13; [j]*khag* (2282) ‣Deut 16:10
23:17 Deut 16:16
23:18 Exod 12:8; 34:25; Lev 2:11; [k]*zabakh* (2076) ‣Num 15:8

23:1-9 This call for justice includes a miscellaneous list of covenant requirements, most of which have to do with fairness and integrity.

23:1-3 It is necessary to give true witness, even under the pressure of ***evil people*** (23:1), ***the crowd*** (23:2), or misguided motives (23:3, 7-8).

23:7 God's character is the motive for righteous behavior (see 22:22-24, 27).

23:9 See note on 22:21.

23:10-12 Renewal, *rest* (23:12), and refreshment are important. Just as humans and animals are to enjoy these in the weekly Sabbath, so ***the land*** is to be given rest every seven years (23:10-11; see note on 20:8-11).

23:13 See 20:3; 22:18 and notes.

23:14-17 God's command was that ***every man in Israel must appear before . . . the LORD*** (23:17), that is, at the Tabernacle, ***three times each year.*** While all the people were camped around the Tabernacle in the wilderness, this requirement did not create any problems. Later, when the people were dispersed throughout the land at a distance from the Tabernacle (later the Temple), it was more difficult. The stipulation seems to have been intended to keep the people from building local worship centers, which would splinter them as a people and allow for pagan influences on the worship of Yahweh. Sadly, these stipulations were not carefully carried out (see, e.g., 2 Kgs 23:21-23).

23:15 ***appointed time in early spring, in the month of Abib:*** Literally *appointed time in the month of Abib.* This first month of the ancient Hebrew lunar calendar usually occurs within the months of March and April. See also 13:4-5; Lev 23:5-8; Deut 16:1-8.

23:16 ***Festival of Harvest:*** Or *Festival of Weeks.* This festival was later called the Festival of Pentecost (see Acts 2:1). It is celebrated today as Shavuot (or Shabuoth). The Festival of Harvest was celebrated seven weeks after Passover, around the end of the barley harvest and the beginning of the wheat harvest (mid-May to mid-June). In postbiblical Judaism, this festival commemorated the giving of the Sinai Covenant, which was calculated to have occurred fifty days after the first Passover in Egypt (see Lev 23:15-21; Deut 16:9-12). • ***Festival of the Final Harvest:*** Or *Festival of Ingathering.* This festival was later called the Festival of Shelters or Festival of Tabernacles (see Lev 23:33-36). It is celebrated today as Sukkot (or Succoth). The Festival of Final Harvest was celebrated on the fifteenth day of the seventh month of the Hebrew calendar (mid-September to mid-October), after the final harvest of grapes was complete. This festival commemorated the wilderness wanderings when God provided for his people.

23:18 ***Blood*** symbolized life (Lev 17:11-14; Deut 12:23), so blood must not be mixed with ***yeast,*** which was not normally included in offerings (see note on Lev 2:11). • The ***fat,*** considered the best part of the offering, was to be burned at once (see Lev 3:3-5).

23:19 Exod 22:29; Deut 14:21
23:20 Exod 32:34
23:21 Exod 3:14; 34:5; Num 14:10-11
23:22 Num 24:9; Deut 30:7
23:23 Josh 24:8, 11
23:24 Exod 20:5; 34:13
23:25 Exod 15:26; Lev 26:3-13; Deut 7:12-15; 28:1-14
23:27 Gen 35:5; Exod 15:14; Deut 7:23
23:28 Deut 7:20
23:29-30 Deut 7:22
23:31 Gen 15:18; Josh 21:44; 24:12, 18
23:32 Deut 7:2
23:33 Deut 7:1-5, 16
24:1 Exod 6:23; 19:24
24:2 Num 12:6-8
24:3 Exod 19:8; 24:7; Deut 5:27; 11:1

19“As you harvest your crops, bring the
very best of the first harvest to the house of
the LORD your God.
“You must not cook a young goat in its
mother’s milk.

The LORD’s Covenant Promises (23:20-33)

20“See, I am sending an angel before you to
protect you on your journey and lead you
safely to the place I have prepared for you.
21Pay close attention to him, and obey his
instructions. Do not rebel against him, for
he is my representative, and he will not forgive your rebellion. 22But if you are careful
to obey him, following all my instructions,
then I will be an enemy to your enemies, and
I will oppose those who oppose you. 23For
my angel will go before you and bring you
into the land of the Amorites, Hittites, Perizzites, Canaanites, Hivites, and Jebusites, so
you may live there. And I will destroy them
completely. 24You must not worship the
gods of these nations or serve them in any
way or imitate their evil practices. Instead,
you must utterly destroy them and smash
their sacred pillars.
25“You must serve only the LORD your God.
If you do, I will bless you with food and water,
and I will protect you from illness. 26There
will be no miscarriages or infertility in your
land, and I will give you long, full lives.
27“I will send my terror ahead of you and
create panic among all the people whose
lands you invade. I will make all your enemies
turn and run. 28I will send terror ahead of
you to drive out the Hivites, Canaanites, and
Hittites. 29But I will not drive them out in a
single year, because the land would become
desolate and the wild animals would multiply and threaten you. 30I will drive them out
a little at a time until your population has
increased enough to take possession of the
land. 31And I will fix your boundaries from
the Red Sea to the Mediterranean Sea, and
from the eastern wilderness to the Euphrates River. I will hand over to you the people
now living in the land, and you will drive
them out ahead of you.
32“Make no treaties with them or their
gods. 33They must not live in your land, or
they will cause you to sin against me. If you
serve their gods, you will be caught in the
trap of idolatry.”

Israel Accepts the LORD’s Covenant (24:1-18)

24 Then the LORD instructed Moses:
“Come up here to me, and bring
along Aaron, Nadab, Abihu, and seventy of
Israel’s elders. All of you must worship from
a distance. 2Only Moses is allowed to come
near to the LORD. The others must not come
near, and none of the other people are allowed to climb up the mountain with him.”
3Then Moses went down to the people and repeated all the instructions and

23:19 The significance of the command not to ***cook a young goat in its mother’s milk*** is unknown. Its inclusion at this point suggests that it may have been a pagan religious practice.

23:20-33 If the people kept the covenant stipulations just listed, the Covenant Lord agreed to protect them from enemies (23:22-23) and from illness (23:25-26) and give them a land to possess (23:27-31). These covenant promises were contingent upon absolute loyalty to the Covenant Lord. In particular, it would be an act of ***rebellion*** (23:21) to ***worship the gods*** (23:24, 32-33) of the dispossessed peoples.

23:20-23 ***an angel:*** Probably the “Angel of the Lord,” who was often a manifestation of the Lord himself (see 3:2).

23:23 See note on 3:8.

23:24 In Canaanite worship, ***sacred pillars*** were erected to represent the deities. Sometimes they would have a human likeness carved on them.

23:25 ***I will bless:*** As translated from the Greek and Latin versions; Hebrew reads *he will bless.*

23:26 Pagan rites were carried out in an attempt to manipulate the forces of fertility and reproduction. God promised to give these gifts freely if the people would faithfully carry out the terms of their covenant with him.

23:28 ***terror:*** Often rendered *the hornet.* The meaning of the Hebrew is uncertain, but it probably does not refer to stinging insects.

23:29-31 ***I will:*** God, not Israel, would take the land. The land would be a gift from their Covenant Lord. Israel was being granted possession of it as long as they faithfully fulfilled the covenant.

23:31 ***from the Red Sea to the Mediterranean Sea*** (literally *from the sea of reeds to the sea of the Philistines*) . . . ***from the eastern wilderness to the Euphrates River*** (literally *from the wilderness to the river*): See Gen 15:18; Num 34:2-12; Deut 11:24; 2 Chr 9:26. • ***I will hand over to you the people:*** God had promised the land to Abraham (Gen 15:16). At that time, “the sin of the Amorites” had not yet run its course. Now it had. God was not arbitrarily dispossessing the Amorites (i.e., the Canaanites), but was using his people, the Israelites, to judge their wickedness.

23:33 ***they will cause you to sin against me:*** The Canaanites were to be destroyed because there could be no truce between a holy God and sin. Furthermore, the continuance of God’s revelation, which was to culminate in the incarnation of Jesus Christ, depended on the survival of that revelation through the people of Israel. If they fell back into paganism, that could not happen.

24:1-18 Israel agreed to the terms of the covenant (24:3), which was then ratified in several ceremonial activities. This included the formal writing and reading of the covenant (24:4, 7), the splattering of ***blood*** (24:6), a ***covenant meal*** (24:11), and the appearing of the ***glory of the LORD*** on the ***mountain*** (24:15-18).

24:1-2 Some commentators suggest that ***Moses, Aaron, Nadab, Abihu,*** and the ***elders*** made two trips up the mountain, here and in 24:9-11. However, this command was probably given in advance and obeyed at the proper time in 24:9.

24:3 ***went down:*** At this critical moment, would the people accept this relationship with God in which they would swear absolute loyalty to him and agree to live in ways that are in keeping with his character? Fortunately, they answered unanimously, ***with one voice,*** that they would abide by the covenant.

regulations the LORD had given him. All the people answered with one voice, "We will do everything the LORD has commanded."

4Then Moses carefully wrote down all the LORD's instructions. Early the next morning Moses got up and built an altar at the foot of the mountain. He also set up twelve pillars, one for each of the twelve tribes of Israel. 5Then he sent some of the young Israelite men to present burnt offerings and to sacrifice bulls as peace offerings to the LORD. 6Moses drained half the blood from these animals into basins. The other half he splattered against the altar.

7Then he took the Book of the Covenant and read it aloud to the people. Again they all responded, "We will do everything the LORD has commanded. We will obey."

8Then Moses took the blood from the basins and splattered it over the people, declaring, "Look, this blood confirms the covenant the LORD has made with you in giving you these instructions."

9Then Moses, Aaron, Nadab, Abihu, and the seventy elders of Israel climbed up the mountain. 10There they saw the God of Israel. Under his feet there seemed to be a surface of brilliant blue lapis lazuli, as clear as the sky itself. 11And though these nobles of Israel gazed upon God, he did not destroy them. In fact, they ate a covenant meal, eating and drinking in his presence!

12Then the LORD said to Moses, "Come up to me on the mountain. Stay there, and I will give you the tablets of stone on which I have inscribed the instructions and commands so you can teach the people." 13So Moses and his [a]assistant Joshua set out, and Moses climbed up the mountain of God.

14Moses told the elders, "Stay here and wait for us until we come back. Aaron and Hur are here with you. If anyone has a dispute while I am gone, consult with them."

15Then Moses climbed up the mountain, and the cloud covered it. 16And the glory of the LORD settled down on Mount Sinai, and the cloud covered it for six days. On the seventh day the LORD called to Moses from inside the cloud. 17To the Israelites at the foot of the mountain, the glory of the LORD appeared at the summit like a consuming fire. 18Then Moses disappeared into the cloud as he climbed higher up the mountain. He remained on the mountain forty days and forty nights.

THE TABERNACLE: GOD'S PRESENCE (25:1–40:38)

Instructions for the Primary Structure (25:1–27:19)

Offerings for the Tabernacle

25 The LORD said to Moses, 2"Tell the people of Israel to bring me their sacred offerings. Accept the contributions

24:4 Deut 31:9
24:5 Exod 18:12
24:6 Heb 9:18
24:7 Exod 19:8; 24:3 Heb 9:19
24:8 Zech 9:11 Matt 26:28 1 Cor 11:25 *Heb 9:20 1 Pet 1:2
24:10 Exod 33:20 Num 12:8 Isa 6:5 Ezek 1:26
24:12 Exod 31:18; 32:15-16 Jer 31:33 2 Cor 3:3
24:13 Exod 17:9-14; 33:11 [a]*sharath* (8334) ‣Num 1:50
24:15 Exod 19:9
24:16 Exod 16:10 Num 14:10
24:17 Exod 3:2 Deut 4:24, 36 Heb 12:18, 29
24:18 Exod 34:28 Deut 9:9; 10:10 1 Kgs 19:8
25:1-7 //Exod 35:4-9
25:2 1 Chr 29:2-5 Ezra 2:68 Neh 7:70-72 2 Cor 8:11-12; 9:7

24:4 ***Pillars*** were erected as historical markers, witnessing in history that something momentous had occurred at a certain time at this place. In Hittite treaties, pagan gods were called upon to witness the agreement. In this case, the Hebrews were forbidden to recognize other gods, so pillars served the purpose.

24:6 When Moses ***splattered*** half of the blood of the sacrificial animals ***against the altar,*** he symbolized God's formal oath to keep the covenant (see Gen 15:9-18; Heb 6:13).

24:7 Treaties were required to be written down and publicly ***read . . . aloud.*** Very likely Moses began at this time to write down, under God's inspiration, all the things that he believed were authoritative documents for his people.

24:8 ***Look, this blood confirms the covenant*** (literally *behold the blood of the covenant*): Jesus repeated this sentence almost verbatim at the Last Supper (Matt 26:28), when he said, "This is my blood, which confirms the covenant" (literally *"This is my blood of the covenant"*). See also Heb 9:20.

24:10 ***There they saw . . . God:*** This statement must be interpreted in the light of 33:20. They saw some representation of God, the description of which is limited to the surface under his feet. When Isaiah saw God, the only description given was of the hem of his robe (Isa 6:1).

24:11 Around the world, then and now, the act of eating a ***meal*** together is often a sign of peace and good relations.

24:12 The ***instructions and commands*** to be ***inscribed*** on ***the tablets of stone*** were the ten basic principles of 20:3-17 (see 34:28) on which the specific stipulations of 21:1–23:33 depended.

24:14 See 18:13-27 and notes.

24:16 ***the glory of the LORD:*** See 16:7.

24:17 ***consuming fire:*** See 3:2 and note.

25:1–40:38 Unlike our churches, the Tabernacle functioned primarily as a residence or palace of God, the divine king, rather than as a place for people to congregate. In this respect, churches are more like the later Jewish synagogues (see also note on 40:2). This last section of Exodus completes the revelation of God necessary for the people of Israel to come out of the theological darkness that had held them in bondage. This final section includes instructions for building the Tabernacle (25:1–31:18), the story of the gold calf (a wrong attempt to secure God's presence, 32:1–34:35), and the report of building the Tabernacle (the proper way to secure God's presence, 35:1–40:38). God's ultimate goal in delivering the people from bondage was to share his presence with them. Because of his holiness, that presence could only be experienced in his way, not through the pagan way of human manipulation. The construction of the Tabernacle is reported here, even though some of the instructions in Leviticus were actually given before this event (see 40:1-2; Lev 25:1; 27:34; Num 7:1). This event expresses the goal of the entire Exodus sequence, which is God taking up residence among his people.

25:1–27:19 These instructions first indicate the materials the Israelites could contribute for the construction of the Tabernacle (25:3-7). The instructions then move from the center outward, beginning with the Ark of the Covenant (25:10-22) and concluding with the courtyard (27:9-19). Two items, the altar of incense in the sanctuary and the washbasin in the courtyard, are included later (30:1-10, 17-21), in the section relating to the priesthood, perhaps

25:6 Exod 27:20; 30:23, 34
25:8 Exod 29:45; 36:1-5 Deut 12:11 Rev 21:3
25:9 Acts 7:44 Heb 8:5 [b]*mishkan* (4908) ‣Exod 35:11
25:10-20 //Exod 37:1-9
25:12 Exod 26:29; 27:7; 37:5; 38:7
25:13 Exod 30:5; 37:4; 40:20
25:15 1 Kgs 8:8
25:16 Exod 16:34 Heb 9:4

from all whose hearts are moved to offer
them. 3Here is a list of sacred offerings you
may accept from them:

gold, silver, and bronze;
4 blue, purple, and scarlet thread;
fine linen and goat hair for cloth;
5 tanned ram skins and fine goatskin leather;
acacia wood;
6 olive oil for the lamps;
spices for the anointing oil and the fragrant incense;
7 onyx stones, and other gemstones to be set in the ephod and the priest's chestpiece.

8"Have the people of Israel build me a
holy sanctuary so I can live among them.
9You must build this [b]Tabernacle and its furnishings exactly according to the pattern I will show you.

Plans for the Ark of the Covenant

10"Have the people make an Ark of acacia wood—a sacred chest 45 inches long,
27 inches wide, and 27 inches high. 11Overlay it inside and outside with pure gold, and
run a molding of gold all around it. 12Cast
four gold rings and attach them to its four
feet, two rings on each side. 13Make poles
from acacia wood, and overlay them with
gold. 14Insert the poles into the rings at the
sides of the Ark to carry it. 15These carrying poles must stay inside the rings; never
remove them. 16When the Ark is finished,

The Glory of God (24:15-17)

Exod 14:17-18; 16:6-12; 33:17-23
Lev 9:23-24; 10:1-3
Num 14:21-22
Deut 5:24
Josh 7:19
1 Kgs 8:11
2 Chr 7:1-3
Job 37:2-5
Ps 3:3; 8:4-6; 19:1; 29:3, 7-9; 48:8
Isa 6:3-5; 42:8; 43:7; 66:18-19
Jer 13:16
Ezek 1:28; 10:4
Hos 4:7
John 17:1-5
Rom 5:2
2 Cor 4:4
Col 1:27
Rev 21:10-11, 23-25

Glory has a rather different connotation in the OT than it does in English usage. The English word suggests something thin and passing—the glory of a sunset, the glory of last year's winning team. The root idea of the Hebrew word for *glory* is "heaviness" or "solidity." It connotes "significance" or "worth," the absolute opposite of "vanity" or "nothingness." When God's glory appears, it is not merely a bright light or a glittering cloud, but a visible expression of his absolute reality.

God's glory is the manifestation of his person, his power, and his majesty (see Ezek 1:28; 10:4). God's glory may be revealed in nature, such as in a thunderstorm (Job 37:2-5; Ps 29:3, 7) or in the plagues sent on the Egyptians (Num 14:21-22). God's glory can also be a unique manifestation, such as the revelation on Mount Sinai (Deut 5:24). At the dedication of the Tabernacle (40:34-35) and Solomon's Temple (1 Kgs 8:11), God's glory filled those structures, indicating his approval of them and that his presence would now reside there. Similarly, the glory of the Lord sent the fire that kindled the first sacrifices of the sanctuary (Lev 9:22-24).

When God reveals his glory to his creation (see, e.g., 24:16-18), it is often called a *theophany*. God gives limited (or veiled) glimpses of his glory because no one can see God and live (33:18-23; see also Isa 6:5). To "give glory" to God (Josh 7:19; Isa 24:15; Jer 13:16) means to speak or act in a manner that acknowledges who God is.

Christ is the glory and image of God (2 Cor 4:4), and he was glorified in his death and resurrection (John 17:1-5). When Christ appears again at last, he will further manifest God's glory in his restored Kingdom (Rev 21:11, 23). Paul declares that the presence of Christ in the lives of believers provides assurance that we will share in that glory (Rom 5:2; Col 1:27).

because their use was especially related to functions of the priests.

25:2 ***all whose hearts are moved:*** There is a marked difference in motivation between meeting needs in God's way and attempting to meet them in our own way, as when Aaron used coercion in creating the gold calf (see 32:1-4).

25:7 ***ephod:*** See 28:6-14 and notes. • ***chestpiece:*** See 28:15-30 and notes.

25:8 ***a holy sanctuary:*** If the people were to have a life-giving relationship with God, it was absolutely vital that they learn how utterly different God was from them (see note on 3:5). • The purpose of this activity was so God could ***live among them.***

25:9 ***exactly according to the pattern:*** We do not determine for ourselves how we want to come into the presence of a holy God. If we come into his presence at all, it will be on his terms and in accord with his desires and character.

25:10-22 ***an Ark of acacia wood:*** In translating the plans for the Ark of the Covenant, the NLT continues to use the word *Ark* because of its traditional associations. However, *ark* is simply an archaic English word meaning "box." The Ark was Israel's "covenant box." It was the most significant item in the whole complex, because it was there that God made his presence available (25:22). The presence of the stone tablets of the covenant in the box (25:16, 21) underlined the truth that God reveals himself in the context of a mutually binding commitment between himself and his people. See illustration, p. 170.

25:10 ***45 inches long, 27 inches wide, and 27 inches high:*** Hebrew *2.5 cubits* [115 centimeters] *long, 1.5 cubits* [69 centimeters] *wide, and 1.5 cubits* [69 centimeters] *high.*

25:12-15 The ***carrying poles*** were there so that no one would touch this representation of God's devastating holiness. Later, a death occurred when someone instinctively reached out to steady the Ark as it was being moved from one place to another (see 2 Sam 6:6-7).

25:16 ***When the Ark is finished, place inside it the stone tablets inscribed with***

place inside it the stone tablets inscribed
with the terms of the covenant, which I will
give to you.
17“Then make the Ark’s cover—the place
of atonement—from pure gold. It must be
45 inches long and 27 inches wide. 18Then
make two [c]cherubim from hammered gold,
and place them on the two ends of the
atonement cover. 19Mold the cherubim on
each end of the atonement cover, making
it all of one piece of gold. 20The [d]cherubim
will face each other and look down on the
atonement cover. With their wings spread
above it, they will protect it. 21Place inside
the Ark the stone tablets inscribed with the
terms of the covenant, which I will give to
you. Then put the atonement cover on top
of the Ark. 22I will meet with you there
and talk to you from above the atonement
cover between the gold cherubim that
hover over the [e]Ark of the Covenant. From
there I will give you my commands for the
people of Israel.

Plans for the Table

23“Then make a table of acacia wood, 36
inches long, 18 inches wide, and 27 inches
high. 24Overlay it with pure gold and run a
gold molding around the edge. 25Decorate it
with a 3-inch border all around, and run a
gold molding along the border. 26Make four
gold rings for the table and attach them at
the four corners next to the four legs. 27At-
tach the rings near the border to hold the
poles that are used to carry the table. 28Make
these poles from acacia wood, and overlay

25:17 Exod 37:6; Lev 16:13; Rom 3:25; Heb 9:5

25:18 [c]*kerub* (3742) ‣ Exod 25:20

25:20 1 Kgs 8:7; Heb 9:5; [d]*kerub* (3742) ‣ Num 7:89

25:21 Exod 26:34

25:22 Exod 30:6, 36; Lev 1:1; [e]*'aron* (0727) ‣ Exod 40:20

25:23-29 //Exod 37:10-16

The Tabernacle (25:1-9)

Exod 26:1-37; 35:4–36:38; 38:21-31; 39:32–40:35; 2 Chr 3:1–7:22; Heb 9:1-28

From the very beginning of creation, God’s plan was to share his life with humanity and allow people the joy of fellowship with him. However, the entrance of sin into the world (Gen 3) created a serious obstacle to realizing that goal, for if sinful people were to come into the presence of God, his holiness would destroy them. The Tabernacle provided a temporary means by which the Israelites could enjoy God’s presence without being destroyed by it (25:8).

The Tabernacle shows us in tangible ways what is required to enter God’s presence. The altar shows us that sin must be removed through a sacrificial death. The washbasin shows that fellowship with God demands removing uncleanness, that is, anything that conflicts with God’s ethical perfection. In the Holy Place, the lampstand and the table show that we must walk in God’s light and rely on him to provide for our needs. The incense altar represents prayer, and the constantly rising incense reminds those who are forgiven and washed, who are walking in his light and relying constantly on him, that they have unlimited access to him. The curtain between the Holy Place and the Most Holy Place reminds us that the Almighty, the most holy God who invites us into fellowship, cannot be approached casually. Behind the curtain, there is no idol, but the glorious Ark of the Covenant, over which God’s glory appeared, symbolizing his enthronement as Israel’s king. The centrality of the Ark reflects God’s central purpose for his people—a covenant relationship with the living God.

Our new covenant relationship with God is made possible by Jesus’ perfect sacrifice for sin and his ministry as our high priest before God (see especially Heb 9–10). He has fulfilled the requirements that are illustrated by the ancient Tabernacle.

the terms of the covenant (literally *Place inside the Ark the Testimony;* similarly in 25:21): The Hebrew word for “testimony” refers to the terms of the Lord’s covenant with Israel as written on the stone tablets, and also to the covenant itself.

25:17 The word translated ***atonement*** means “to cover over.” The ***cover*** of the covenant box was the place of “covering over” sin (see Lev 16:14-16). • ***45 inches long and 27 inches wide:*** Hebrew *2.5 cubits* [115 centimeters] *long and 1.5 cubits* [69 centimeters] *wide.*

25:18 The appearance of the ***cherubim*** is not described except to say that they had wings (25:20; see 2 Chr 3:10-13).

25:22 ***I will meet with you there:*** The *Ark* was located in the innermost part of the sanctuary (26:33), which was in effect God’s throne room (see note on Lev 16:2). In a comparable pagan sanctuary, one would find an idol in this location. The Tabernacle had no idol, only a box that physically represented the covenant faithfulness and grace of God. God meets his people in that context, not in the context of idolatry. An idol reflects the belief that a deity is continuous with the created order and that it can be manipulated with the right ritual. It assumes that we can secure blessings from the deity without regard to our own character or commitment. But God is completely distinct from this world, and he cannot be manipulated in any way. He wants to bless us, but those blessings can only be given to those who receive his grace as a gift and surrender to him in trust. • ***Ark of the Covenant:*** Or *Ark of the Testimony;* see note on 25:16.

25:23-30 The ***table of acacia wood*** stood on the north side of the main room of the sanctuary, the Holy Place (26:35). It reminded the people that God would provide sustenance for them. Above all, that sustenance was his presence (25:30). See illustration, p. 171.

25:23 ***36 inches long, 18 inches wide, and 27 inches high:*** Hebrew *2 cubits* [92 centimeters] *long, 1 cubit* [46 centimeters] *wide, and 1.5 cubits* [69 centimeters] *high.*

25:25 ***a 3-inch border:*** Literally *a border of a handbreadth* [8 centimeters].

25:29 Exod 37:16; Num 4:7
25:30 Exod 39:36; 40:23; Lev 24:5-9; Num 4:7
25:31-39 //Exod 37:17-24
25:31 Exod 37:17; 1 Kgs 7:49; Heb 9:2; Rev 1:12
25:37 Exod 27:21; Zech 4:2; Rev 1:4, 12, 20; 4:5
25:40 Acts 7:44; *Heb 8:5
26:1-37 //Exod 36:8-38
26:3 Exod 36:10
26:5 Exod 36:12
26:7 Exod 36:14

them with gold. [29]Make special containers of pure gold for the table—bowls, pans, pitchers, and jars—to be used in pouring out liquid offerings. [30]Place the Bread of the Presence on the table to remain before me at all times.

Plans for the Lampstand

[31]"Make a lampstand of pure, hammered gold. Make the entire lampstand and its decorations of one piece—the base, center stem, lamp cups, buds, and petals. [32]Make it with six branches going out from the center stem, three on each side. [33]Each of the six branches will have three lamp cups shaped like almond blossoms, complete with buds and petals. [34]Craft the center stem of the lampstand with four lamp cups shaped like almond blossoms, complete with buds and petals. [35]There will also be an almond bud beneath each pair of branches where the six branches extend from the center stem. [36]The almond buds and branches must all be of one piece with the center stem, and they must be hammered from pure gold. [37]Then make the seven lamps for the lampstand, and set them so they reflect their light forward. [38]The lamp snuffers and trays must also be made of pure gold. [39]You will need seventy-five pounds of pure gold for the lampstand and its accessories.

[40]"Be sure that you make everything according to the pattern I have shown you here on the mountain.

Plans for the Tabernacle

26 "Make the Tabernacle from ten curtains of finely woven linen. Decorate the curtains with blue, purple, and scarlet thread and with skillfully embroidered cherubim. [2]These ten curtains must all be exactly the same size—42 feet long and 6 feet wide. [3]Join five of these curtains together to make one long curtain, then join the other five into a second long curtain. [4]Put loops of blue yarn along the edge of the last curtain in each set. [5]The fifty loops along the edge of one curtain are to match the fifty loops along the edge of the other curtain. [6]Then make fifty gold clasps and fasten the long curtains together with the clasps. In this way, the Tabernacle will be made of one continuous piece.

[7]"Make eleven curtains of goat-hair cloth to serve as a tent covering for the Tabernacle. [8]These eleven curtains must all be

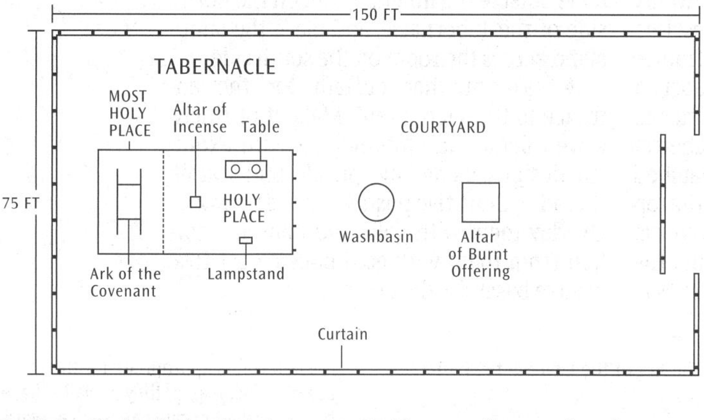

◀ **The Tabernacle (26:1-37).** The construction of the Tabernacle and its accessories is described in chs 36–40.

25:29 The *liquid offerings* included olive oil and wine (see 29:40).

25:31-39 The *lampstand of pure, hammered gold* stood on the south side of the Holy Place (26:35). It showed the light of God's presence to his people. The *lamps* (25:37) were flat dishes containing olive oil. A wick extended into the oil and hung down from a lip on one side of the dish. The dishes, resting on the upturned *almond blossoms* (25:33), were to be turned so that all their wicks faced the center of the room (25:37). The total number of lamps is not clear. Although *seven lamps* are mentioned in 25:37, there seem to be 22 *lamp cups* in 25:33-34. See illustration, p. 172.

25:39 *seventy-five pounds:* Hebrew *1 talent* [34 kilograms].

26:1-37 The *Tabernacle* proper (as distinct from the surrounding courtyard) was not very large. It was approximately 15 feet wide and 45 feet long. The supporting *framework* consisted of 48 vertical frames, *15 feet high and 27 inches wide* (26:16). They were made of *acacia wood* overlaid with *gold* (26:15, 29). The frames were locked together with horizontal *crossbars* to form a three-sided rectangle with an open end (26:26-28). Two large linen *curtains* (each composed of five smaller ones) were then linked together into one and draped across the top of this *framework*. The combined total was long enough to hang down on the sides and rear (26:1-6), forming coverings for the walls as well as the roof. Over the linen curtain was draped a curtain of *goat-hair cloth* constructed in the same way. It was three feet wider and six feet longer than the linen curtain (26:7-13), so that it hung down further than the linen curtain on all sides. Over these two curtains were two *protective* coverings, one of *tanned ram skins* and one of *fine goatskin leather* (26:14). The space so enclosed was divided in two with another beautifully *embroidered* curtain hanging crosswise on *four posts of acacia wood.* The resulting two spaces were *the Holy Place* and *the Most Holy Place* (26:31-33).

26:2-6 *42 feet long and 6 feet wide:* Hebrew *28 cubits* [12.9 meters] *long and 4 cubits* [1.8 meters] *wide.* A width of *6 feet* may have been dictated by the size of the largest loom available. Five of the six-foot strips were joined, probably by being sewn together, making one continuous piece of cloth 42 feet long and 30 feet wide. When joined to each other with the *loops* and *clasps* (26:5-6), the two cloths formed a single unit 42 feet by 60 feet.

26:8 *45 feet long and 6 feet wide:* Hebrew *30 cubits* [13.8 meters] *long and 4 cubits* [1.8 meters] *wide.*

exactly the same size—45 feet long and
6 feet wide. 9Join five of these curtains together to make one long curtain, and join
the other six into a second long curtain. Allow 3 feet of material from the second set
of curtains to hang over the front of the sacred tent. 10Make fifty loops for one edge
of each large curtain. 11Then make fifty
bronze clasps, and fasten the loops of the
long curtains with the clasps. In this way,
the tent covering will be made of one continuous piece. 12The remaining 3 feet of this
tent covering will be left to hang over the
back of the Tabernacle. 13Allow 18 inches
of remaining material to hang down over
each side, so the Tabernacle is completely
covered. 14Complete the tent covering with
a protective layer of tanned ram skins and a
layer of fine goatskin leather.

15"For the framework of the Tabernacle,
construct frames of acacia wood. 16Each
frame must be 15 feet high and 27 inches
wide, 17with two pegs under each frame.
Make all the frames identical. 18Make
twenty of these frames to support the curtains on the south side of the Tabernacle.
19Also make forty silver bases—two bases
under each frame, with the pegs fitting securely into the bases. 20For the north side
of the Tabernacle, make another twenty
frames, 21with their forty silver bases, two
bases under each frame. 22Make six frames
for the rear—the west side of the Tabernacle—23along with two additional frames to
reinforce the rear corners of the Tabernacle. 24These corner frames will be matched
at the bottom and firmly attached at the top
with a single ring, forming a single corner
unit. Make both of these corner units the
same way. 25So there will be eight frames at
the rear of the Tabernacle, set in sixteen silver bases—two bases under each frame.

26"Make crossbars of acacia wood to link
the frames, five crossbars for the north side
of the Tabernacle 27and five for the south
side. Also make five crossbars for the rear of
the Tabernacle, which will face west. 28The
middle crossbar, attached halfway up the
frames, will run all the way from one end
of the Tabernacle to the other. 29Overlay
the frames with gold, and make gold rings
to hold the crossbars. Overlay the crossbars
with gold as well.

30"Set up this Tabernacle according to the
pattern you were shown on the mountain.

31"For the inside of the Tabernacle, make
a special curtain of finely woven linen. Decorate it with blue, purple, and scarlet thread
and with skillfully embroidered cherubim.
32Hang this curtain on gold hooks attached
to four posts of acacia wood. Overlay the
posts with gold, and set them in four silver
bases. 33Hang the inner curtain from clasps,
and put the Ark of the Covenant in the
room behind it. This curtain will separate
the Holy Place from the Most Holy Place.

34"Then put the Ark's cover—the place
of atonement—on top of the Ark of the Covenant inside the Most Holy Place. 35Place the
table outside the inner curtain on the north
side of the Tabernacle, and place the lampstand across the room on the south side.

36"Make another curtain for the entrance to the sacred tent. Make it of finely
woven linen and embroider it with exquisite designs, using blue, purple, and scarlet
thread. 37Craft five posts from acacia wood.
Overlay them with gold, and hang the curtain from them with gold hooks. Cast five
bronze bases for the posts.

26:11 Exod 36:18
26:14 Exod 36:19
26:15 Exod 36:20-34
26:20 Exod 36:23
26:25 Exod 36:30
26:30 Exod 25:9, 40; Acts 7:44; *Heb 8:5
26:31 Exod 36:35; 2 Chr 3:14; Matt 27:51; Heb 9:3
26:33 Exod 25:16; 40:21; Heb 9:2-3
26:34 Exod 25:21; 37:6; Heb 9:5
26:36 Exod 40:28
26:37 Exod 36:38

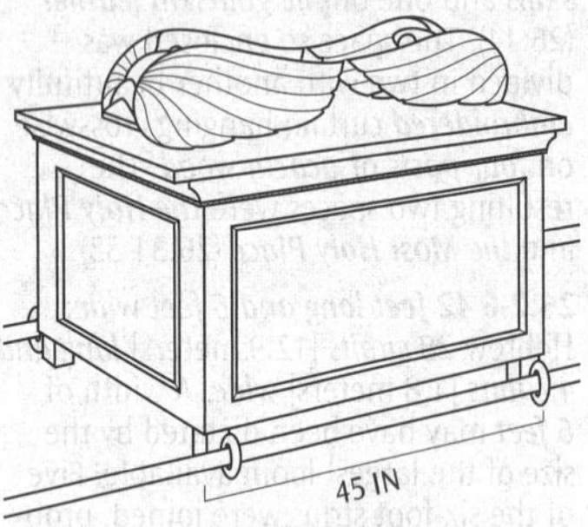

◀ **The Ark of the Covenant (25:10-22).**

26:9 The two goat-hair curtains (26:7) totaled 45 feet by 66 feet. The extra 6 feet were equally distributed to hang down over the front and back of the framework. • ***Allow 3 feet of material . . . to hang over the front:*** Literally *Double over the sixth sheet at the front.*

26:12 ***The remaining 3 feet:*** Literally *The half sheet that is left over.*

26:13 ***18 inches:*** Hebrew *1 cubit* [46 centimeters].

26:15 ***acacia wood:*** A hard wood found in the region of Sinai.

26:16 ***15 feet high and 27 inches wide:*** Hebrew *10 cubits* [4.6 meters] *high and 1.5 cubits* [69 centimeters] *wide.*

26:19 Apparently each of the ***bases*** stood beneath the junction where the frames met. The right peg of one frame and the left peg of the next frame went into one base. Along with the crossbars (26:27-28), this arrangement would contribute to the stability of the whole.

26:31 While ***blue, purple, and scarlet*** are rich colors appropriate for the palace of a divine king, they may also have been specified because these dyes were easiest to procure in the desert.

26:33 ***Ark of the Covenant:*** Or *Ark of the Testimony;* also in 26:34; see note on 25:16. • The ***Most Holy Place*** was the earthly dwelling of the Lord. It contained the Ark of the Covenant, from which the Lord would give his commands for the people of Israel (25:22). The Most Holy Place was approximately 15 feet wide, 15 feet deep, and 15 feet high.

26:34 ***atonement:*** See note on 25:17.

26:36-37 The ***curtain*** that covered the opening at the eastern end of the structure was similar to the one separating the Holy Place and the Most Holy Place. The ***bases*** of these supporting ***posts*** were of ***bronze*** instead of silver.

27:1-8 //Exod 38:1-7
27:1 Ezek 43:13
27:2 Exod 29:12; Lev 4:7
27:3 Num 4:14
27:6 Exod 25:13
27:8 Exod 25:40; 26:30
27:9-19 //Exod 38:9-20
27:10 Exod 38:17
27:14 Exod 38:15
27:16 Exod 36:37
27:20-21 //Lev 24:1-3; Zech 4:11-12

Plans for the Altar of Burnt Offering

27 "Using acacia wood, construct a square altar 7½ feet wide, 7½ feet long, and 4½ feet high. 2Make horns for each of its four corners so that the horns and altar are all one piece. Overlay the altar with bronze. 3Make ash buckets, shovels, basins, meat forks, and firepans, all of bronze. 4Make a bronze grating for it, and attach four bronze rings at its four corners. 5Install the grating halfway down the side of the altar, under the ledge. 6For carrying the altar, make poles from acacia wood, and overlay them with bronze. 7Insert the poles through the rings on the two sides of the altar. 8The altar must be hollow, made from planks. Build it just as you were shown on the mountain.

Plans for the Courtyard

9"Then make the courtyard for the Tabernacle, enclosed with curtains made of finely woven linen. On the south side, make the curtains 150 feet long. 10They will be held up by twenty posts set securely in twenty bronze bases. Hang the curtains with silver hooks and rings. 11Make the curtains the same on the north side—150 feet of curtains held up by twenty posts set securely in bronze bases. Hang the curtains with silver hooks and rings. 12The curtains on the west end of the courtyard will be 75 feet long, supported by ten posts set into ten bases. 13The east end of the courtyard, the front, will also be 75 feet long. 14The courtyard entrance will be on the east end, flanked by two curtains. The curtain on the right side will be 22½ feet long, supported by three posts set into three bases. 15The curtain on the left side will also be 22½ feet long, supported by three posts set into three bases.

16"For the entrance to the courtyard, make a curtain that is 30 feet long. Make it from finely woven linen, and decorate it with beautiful embroidery in blue, purple, and scarlet thread. Support it with four posts, each securely set in its own base. 17All the posts around the courtyard must have silver rings and hooks and bronze bases. 18So the entire courtyard will be 150 feet long and 75 feet wide, with curtain walls 7½ feet high, made from finely woven linen. The bases for the posts will be made of bronze.

19"All the articles used in the rituals of the Tabernacle, including all the tent pegs used to support the Tabernacle and the courtyard curtains, must be made of bronze.

Instructions Relating to the Priesthood (27:20–28:43)

Light for the Tabernacle

20"Command the people of Israel to bring you pure oil of pressed olives for the light, to

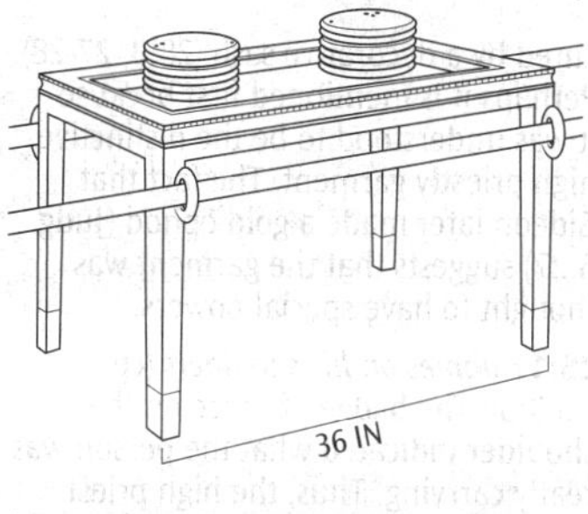

◀ **Table for the Bread of the Presence (25:23-30).**

27:1-19 These plans for the altar of burnt offering and the courtyard continue the movement outward from the center. As with the sanctuary, the plans for the furniture of the courtyard are given (27:1-8) before the plans for the courtyard itself (27:9-19).

27:1-8 Like the frames of the Tabernacle, the ***square altar*** of burnt offerings was made of ***acacia wood*** overlaid with metal. However, in keeping with the other features outside the sanctuary, it was overlaid with ***bronze*** (27:2-3; see 27:10, 17, 19). See illustration, p. 173.

27:1 ***7½ feet wide, 7½ feet long, and 4½ feet high:*** Hebrew *5 cubits* [2.3 meters] *wide, 5 cubits* [2.3 meters] *long, a square, and 3 cubits* [1.4 meters] *high.*

27:2 Archaeology has shown that the ***horns*** of the ***altar*** were protrusions sticking up from the corners of the structure. Perhaps they kept wood and offerings from falling off (see Ps 118:27). They also seem to have had a theological significance, representing God's gracious care. A person who held onto the horns of the altar was requesting leniency in judgment (see 1 Kgs 1:50-51; 2:28). The horns were anointed with blood in atonement and purification ceremonies (29:12; Lev 4:7).

27:5 The ***altar*** was evidently a hollow square (27:1, 8), with the ***grating*** placed inside it to allow ashes to fall to the ground underneath.

27:9-19 The plans for the ***courtyard*** called for walls of ***curtains made of finely woven linen*** hanging on ***posts*** with ***bronze bases.*** The posts seem to have been 7½ feet apart and 7½ feet high. The curtains formed a rectangle 150 feet long and 75 feet wide, with a 30-foot opening centered in the east end.

27:9 ***150 feet long:*** Hebrew *100 cubits* [46 meters]; also in 27:11.

27:12 ***75 feet long:*** Hebrew *50 cubits* [23 meters]; also in 27:13.

27:14 ***22½ feet long:*** Hebrew *15 cubits* [6.9 meters]; also in 27:15.

27:16 The ***curtain*** shielding the entry to the courtyard was similar in color and workmanship to the entry curtain and the dividing curtain of the Tabernacle (26:31, 36). • ***30 feet long:*** Hebrew *20 cubits* [9.2 meters].

27:18 ***150 feet long and 75 feet wide, with curtain walls 7½ feet high:*** Hebrew *100 cubits* [46 meters] *long and 50 by 50* [23 meters] *wide and 5 cubits* [2.3 meters] *high.*

27:19 The use of ***tent pegs*** suggests that the courtyard posts were not freestanding but were stabilized with guy wires.

27:20–30:38 Following the instructions for Tabernacle structure, instructions are now given for those who would serve in the Tabernacle and for the elements involved in that service. Included are priestly functions (27:20-21; 29:38-46), clothing (28:1-43), dedication ceremonies (29:1-37), furnishings (30:1-10, 17-21), and supplies (30:11-16, 22-38).

27:20-21 The first thing said about the function of the priests, ***Aaron and his sons,*** is that they were to ***keep the lamps burning continually*** through the night

keep the lamps burning continually. [21]The lampstand will stand in the Tabernacle, in front of the inner curtain that shields the Ark of the Covenant. Aaron and his sons must keep the lamps burning in the LORD's presence all night. This is a permanent law for the people of Israel, and it must be observed from generation to generation.

Clothing for the Priests

28 "Call for your brother, Aaron, and his sons, Nadab, Abihu, Eleazar, and Ithamar. Set them apart from the rest of the people of Israel so they may minister to me and be my priests. [2]Make sacred garments for Aaron that are glorious and beautiful. [3]Instruct all the skilled craftsmen whom I have filled with the spirit of wisdom. Have them make garments for Aaron that will distinguish him as a priest set apart for my service. [4]These are the garments they are to make: a chestpiece, an ephod, a robe, a patterned tunic, a turban, and a sash. They are to make these sacred garments for your brother, Aaron, and his sons to wear when they serve me as priests. [5]So give them fine linen cloth, gold thread, and blue, purple, and scarlet thread.

Design of the Ephod

[6]"The craftsmen must make the ephod of finely woven linen and skillfully embroider it with gold and with blue, purple, and scarlet thread. [7]It will consist of two pieces, front and back, joined at the shoulders with two shoulder-pieces. [8]The decorative sash will be made of the same materials: finely woven linen embroidered with gold and with blue, purple, and scarlet thread.

[9]"Take two onyx stones, and engrave on them the names of the tribes of Israel. [10]Six names will be on each stone, arranged in the order of the births of the original sons of Israel. [11]Engrave these names on the two stones in the same way a jeweler engraves a seal. Then mount the stones in settings of gold filigree. [12]Fasten the two stones on the shoulder-pieces of the ephod as a reminder that Aaron represents the people of Israel. Aaron will carry these names on his shoulders as a constant reminder whenever he goes before the LORD. [13]Make the settings of gold filigree, [14]then braid two cords of pure gold and attach them to the filigree settings on the shoulders of the ephod.

Design of the Chestpiece

[15]"Then, with great skill and care, make a chestpiece to be worn for seeking a decision from God. Make it to match the ephod, using finely woven linen embroidered with gold and with blue, purple, and scarlet thread. [16]Make the chestpiece of a single piece of cloth folded to form a pouch nine inches

27:21 Exod 25:22; Lev 3:17; 16:34
28:1 Exod 24:1, 9; Num 18:7; Ps 99:6; Heb 5:1, 4
28:2 Exod 29:5, 9; 31:10; Lev 8:7, 30; Num 20:26
28:5 Exod 25:3-4
28:6-14 //Exod 39:2-7
28:12 Exod 39:7
28:15-28 //Exod 39:8-21

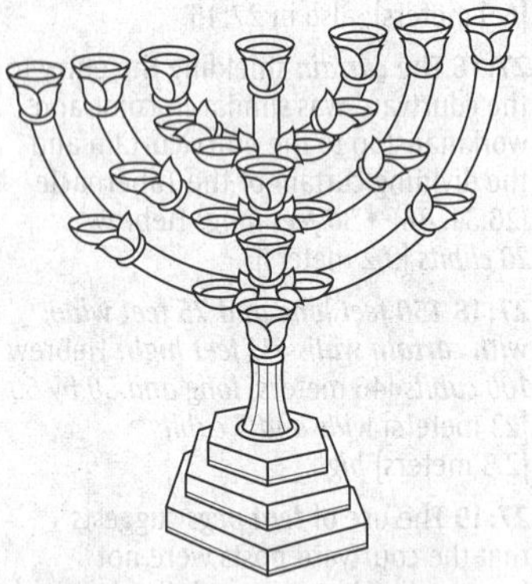

◀ **The Golden Lampstand (25:31-39).**

(see 30:8). As the lamps burned *in the LORD's presence*, they would indicate the continuity of his presence.

27:21 ***the Tabernacle*** (literally *the Tent of Meeting*): The term *Tent of Meeting* sometimes refers to the Tabernacle tent; in these cases the term is essentially synonymous with *Tabernacle*, and the NLT consistently renders it *Tabernacle*. In addition, a temporary tent also called the "Tent of Meeting" is mentioned in 33:7-11. See note on 40:2. • ***in front of the inner curtain that shields the Ark of the Covenant:*** Literally *outside the inner curtain that is in front of the Testimony*. See note on 25:16.

28:1-43 These ***glorious and beautiful*** (28:2) garments for Aaron were to ***distinguish him as a priest set apart*** (Hebrew *qadash*, "consecrated") ***for [the LORD's] service*** (28:3). See illustration, p. 174. The magnificence of these garments is in keeping with the grandeur of the Tabernacle, which functioned as a portable earthly palace for God. There would come a day when Jesus Christ, the true High Priest, would enter the Most Holy Place once for all, and the distinction between priests and people would fade away (Heb 10:11-22). Until that time, human mediators were needed to symbolize the wonderful thing that God was planning to do in the hearts, lives, and behavior of those with whom he shared his presence.

28:1-2 The garments described in this chapter are primarily those for Aaron, the first high priest. The clothing for Aaron's sons, who functioned as his assistants, is described in 28:40-43.

28:6-14 The ***ephod*** was a kind of apron consisting of front and back pieces joined by shoulder straps (28:7) and secured by a decorative sash (28:8, 27-28). Perhaps it is mentioned first because it was understood to be the distinctive high priestly garment. The fact that Gideon later made a gold ephod (Judg 8:27) suggests that the garment was thought to have special powers.

28:12 ***names on his shoulders*** (cp. Isa 9:6): The badge of office on the shoulder indicated what the person was really carrying. Thus, the high priest represented the people before God, and with his royal garments he represented the glory of God before the people.

28:15-30 More attention is given to the ***chestpiece*** than to any other item, suggesting the importance attached to it. It apparently symbolized the priest's representation of ***Israel*** (28:17-21, 29) and was a container for the ***Urim and Thummim***, by which God made his will known (28:30). The chestpiece represented the totality of the high priest's tasks of bringing the people to God and bringing God's word to the people.

28:15 ***a chestpiece to be worn for seeking a decision from God:*** Literally *a chestpiece for decision*.

28:16 ***nine inches:*** Hebrew *1 span* [23 centimeters].

28:17
Exod 39:10
28:21
Exod 39:14
28:24
Exod 39:17
28:26
Exod 39:17
28:29
Exod 28:12
28:30
Lev 8:8
Num 27:21
28:31-43
//Exod 39:22-31
28:36
Exod 39:30-31
Lev 8:9
28:38
Lev 10:17; 22:16
Num 18:1
Heb 9:28
1 Pet 2:24

square. 17Mount four rows of gemstones on
it. The first row will contain a red carnelian,
a pale-green peridot, and an emerald. 18The
second row will contain a turquoise, a blue
lapis lazuli, and a white moonstone. 19The
third row will contain an orange jacinth, an
agate, and a purple amethyst. 20The fourth
row will contain a blue-green beryl, an
onyx, and a green jasper. All these stones
will be set in gold filigree. 21Each stone will
represent one of the twelve sons of Israel,
and the name of that tribe will be engraved
on it like a seal.
22"To attach the chestpiece to the ephod,
make braided cords of pure gold thread.
23Then make two gold rings and attach
them to the top corners of the chestpiece.
24Tie the two gold cords to the two rings on
the chestpiece. 25Tie the other ends of the
cords to the gold settings on the shoulder-
pieces of the ephod. 26Then make two more
gold rings and attach them to the inside
edges of the chestpiece next to the ephod.
27And make two more gold rings and attach
them to the front of the ephod, below the
shoulder-pieces, just above the knot where
the decorative sash is fastened to the ephod.
28Then attach the bottom rings of the chestpiece to the rings on the ephod with blue
cords. This will hold the chestpiece securely
to the ephod above the decorative sash.
29"In this way, Aaron will carry the names
of the tribes of Israel on the sacred chestpiece over his heart when he goes into the
Holy Place. This will be a continual reminder
that he represents the people when he
comes before the LORD. 30Insert the Urim
and Thummim into the sacred chestpiece
so they will be carried over Aaron's heart
when he goes into the LORD's presence. In
this way, Aaron will always carry over his
heart the objects used to determine the
LORD's will for his people whenever he goes
in before the LORD.

Additional Clothing for the Priests

31"Make the robe that is worn with the
ephod from a single piece of blue cloth,
32with an opening for Aaron's head in the
middle of it. Reinforce the opening with
a woven collar so it will not tear. 33Make
pomegranates out of blue, purple, and scarlet yarn, and attach them to the hem of the
robe, with gold bells between them. 34The
gold bells and pomegranates are to alternate all around the hem. 35Aaron will wear
this robe whenever he ministers before the
LORD, and the bells will tinkle as he goes in
and out of the LORD's presence in the Holy
Place. If he wears it, he will not die.
36"Next make a medallion of pure gold,
and engrave it like a seal with these words:
HOLY TO THE LORD. 37Attach the medallion
with a blue cord to the front of Aaron's turban, where it must remain. 38Aaron must

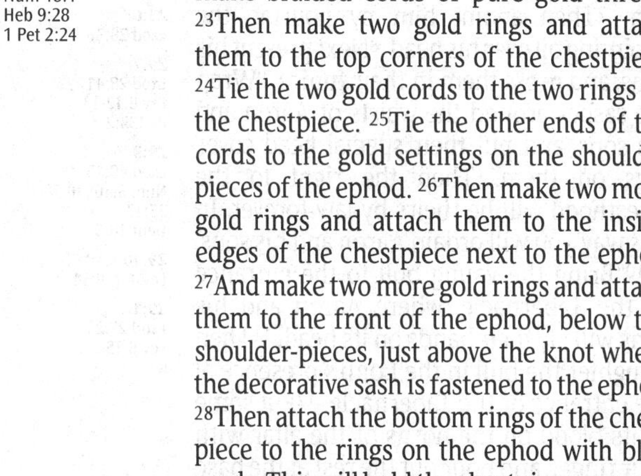

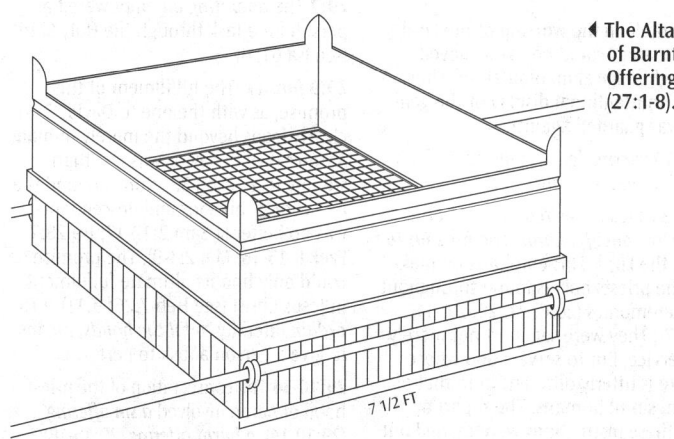

The Altar of Burnt Offering (27:1-8).

28:17-20 The identification of some of these ***gemstones*** is uncertain. Cp. Rev 21:19-20.

28:29 *the sacred chestpiece:* Literally *the chestpiece for decision;* also in 28:30. See 28:15. • The high priest would go into ***the Holy Place*** (the outer room of the sanctuary) to trim the lamp, replace the bread on the table, and replenish the incense on the altar that stood outside the Most Holy Place.

28:30 The ***Urim and Thummim*** (Hebrew terms that might translate as *lights* [or *curses*] *and perfections*) were apparently a pair of stones that were thrown down to get a yes or no answer from God. No physical description of these objects exists; their use is further explained in Num 27:21; Deut 33:8; 1 Sam 28:6; Ezra 2:63; and Neh 7:65.

28:31-35 The ***robe*** worn under the ephod is described. The ***bells*** signaled that the priest was still moving and had not been struck dead by God's presence (see Lev 10:1-2). Jewish tradition tells us that the priest had a cord tied to his ankle so that if he died in ***the Holy Place*** (28:35), his body could be dragged out.

28:32 *a woven collar:* The meaning of the Hebrew is uncertain.

28:36-38 Like all the other elements of the high priest's clothing and activities, the ***medallion*** worn on the front of the turban was to remind the people that God is holy, and his holiness had implications for their entering his presence. God wished to dwell with his people, but his holiness would destroy them unless he took preventative steps. God determines the way into his presence; we do not. The central question of the Bible is how a sinful people can live in the presence of a holy God so that God can share his holy character with them. Ultimately, the answer is provided in Jesus Christ, the Holy One of God who is the perfect mediator (Luke 4:34; Heb 9:11-15). He did not die only to rescue us from the consequences of our sin, but so that God can live in us, reproducing his holy character in us (Eph 2:10; 4:22; Phil 1:27; 1 Pet 1:13-16).

wear it on his forehead so he may take on
himself any guilt of the people of Israel
when they consecrate their sacred offerings. He must always wear it on his forehead
so the LORD will accept the people.
39“Weave Aaron’s patterned tunic from
fine linen cloth. Fashion the turban from
this linen as well. Also make a sash, and decorate it with colorful embroidery.
40“For Aaron’s sons, make tunics, sashes,
and special head coverings that are glorious and beautiful. 41Clothe your brother,
Aaron, and his sons with these garments,
and then anoint and ordain them. Consecrate them so they can serve as my priests.
42Also make linen undergarments for them,
to be worn next to their bodies, reaching
from their hips to their thighs. 43These
must be worn whenever Aaron and his sons
enter the Tabernacle or approach the altar
in the Holy Place to perform their priestly
duties. Then they will not incur guilt and
die. This is a permanent law for Aaron and
all his descendants after him.

Instructions for Ordination of the Priests (29:1-37)

29 “This is the ceremony you must follow when you consecrate Aaron and
his sons to serve me as priests: Take a young
bull and two rams with no defects. 2Then,
using choice wheat flour and no yeast, make
loaves of bread, thin cakes mixed with olive
oil, and wafers spread with oil. 3Place them
all in a single basket, and present them at
the entrance of the Tabernacle, along with
the young bull and the two rams.
4“Present Aaron and his sons at the entrance of the Tabernacle, and wash them
with water. 5Dress Aaron in his priestly garments—the tunic, the robe worn with the
ephod, the ephod itself, and the chestpiece.
Then wrap the decorative sash of the ephod
around him. 6Place the turban on his head,
and fasten the sacred medallion to the turban. 7Then anoint him by pouring the
anointing oil over his head. 8Next present his
sons, and dress them in their tunics. 9Wrap
the sashes around the waists of Aaron and
his sons, and put their special head coverings on them. Then the right to the
priesthood will be theirs by law forever. In
this way, you will ordain Aaron and his sons.
10“Bring the young bull to the entrance
of the Tabernacle, where Aaron and his
sons will lay their hands on its head. 11Then
slaughter the bull in the LORD’s presence at
the entrance of the Tabernacle. 12Put some
of its blood on the horns of the altar with
your finger, and pour out the rest at the base

28:40 Exod 39:27-29; Lev 8:13
28:41 Exod 29:7-9; Lev 8:1-36; Heb 7:28
28:42 Lev 6:10; 16:4; Ezek 44:18
28:43 Exod 20:26; 27:21
29:1-37 //Lev 8:1-36
29:2 Lev 6:19-23
29:4 Exod 40:12; Heb 10:22
29:5 Exod 28:2, 5
29:6 Exod 28:36
29:7 Exod 28:41; Lev 8:12-13; Ps 133:2
29:9 Exod 40:15; Num 3:10; 18:7; 25:13; Deut 18:5
29:10 Lev 1:4; 8:14
29:12 Exod 27:2; Lev 8:15

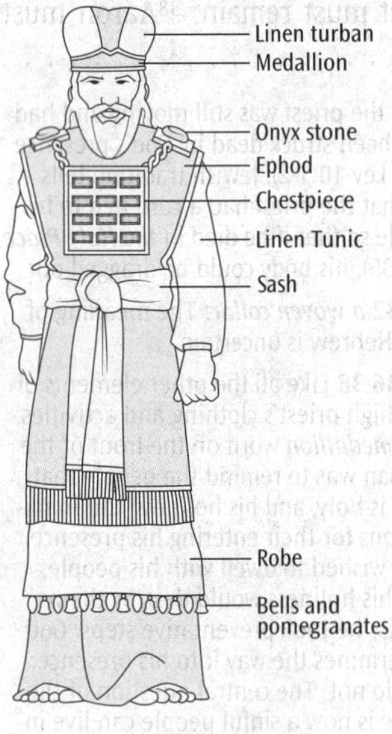

◀ **The High Priest’s Clothing (28:1-43).**

28:39 Apparently the *tunic* was a shirt worn under the robe (see 29:5).

28:42-43 Expressions of sexuality were a frequent part of pagan religion, as worshipers attempted to control the powers of fertility. In some cases, priests served their deities in the nude. Not even a hint of sexual manipulation was acceptable in the worship of the Lord. His blessings could not be achieved through magical manipulation. Thus, even unintentional display of the genitals was guarded against.

28:43 ***Tabernacle:*** Literally *Tent of Meeting.* See note on 27:21.

29:1-37 Moses was required to ***consecrate*** (or ***sanctify***) ***Aaron and his sons to serve*** the Lord. This emphasis on making the priests holy is found throughout the ceremonies (29:6, 21, 28, 29, 34, 36, 37). They were set apart not merely for service, but to serve a God whose nature is utterly different from that of fallen, sinful humans. The report of how these instructions were carried out is found in Lev 8.

29:1 ***with no defects:*** The same word is translated “blameless” and “perfect” in reference to human and divine behavior (e.g., Gen 17:1; Ps 18:30, 32). The sacrifice is representative of God’s own character and the character he seeks in humans.

29:4 ***Tabernacle:*** Literally *Tent of Meeting;* also in 29:10, 11, 30, 32, 42, 44. See note on 27:21. • ***wash them with water:*** This act dramatized the truth that no one can live in God’s presence with the filth of sin in their lives (29:21).

29:7 The ***anointing oil*** empowered a person for a task through the Holy Spirit (see Isa 61:1).

29:9 ***forever:*** The fulfillment of this promise, as with the one to David, clearly leads beyond the merely human. Aaron’s own behavior was less than sterling (e.g., Exod 32; Num 11), and the behavior of his sons and descendants was no better (1 Sam 2:12-17; Isa 28:7; Ezek 8:15-16; Mal 2:1-9). The promise could only find its ultimate fulfillment in Jesus Christ (see Heb 7:26; 9:11). • To ***ordain*** (literally *to fill the hands*) means to give a person a task to perform.

29:10-34 The consecration of the priesthood of Aaron involved ***a sin offering*** (29:10-14), ***a burnt offering*** (29:15-18), and an ***ordination*** offering (29:19-28). The same patterns established here are expanded to the regular offerings of the people (see 29:38-46; Lev 1–5). In all three cases, ***Aaron and his sons lay their hands on [the] head*** of the sacrificial animals (29:10, 15, 19), indicating that sin is a matter of life and death, and that it can only be removed by a death. Because it represents life, ***blood*** is prominent in these ceremonies (29:12, 16, 20, 21).

29:12 ***horns:*** See note on 27:2.

of the altar. 13Take all the fat around the internal organs, the long lobe of the liver, and
the two kidneys and the fat around them,
and burn it all on the altar. 14Then take the
rest of the bull, including its hide, meat, and
dung, and burn it outside the camp as a sin
offering.
15"Next Aaron and his sons must lay
their hands on the head of one of the rams.
16Then slaughter the ram, and splatter its
blood against all sides of the altar. 17Cut the
ram into pieces, and wash off the internal
organs and the legs. Set them alongside the
head and the other pieces of the body, 18then
burn the entire animal on the altar. This is a
burnt offering to the LORD; it is a pleasing
aroma, a special gift presented to the LORD.
19"Now take the other ram, and have
Aaron and his sons lay their hands on its
head. 20Then slaughter it, and apply some of
its blood to the right earlobes of Aaron and
his sons. Also put it on the thumbs of their
right hands and the big toes of their right
feet. Splatter the rest of the blood against all
sides of the altar. 21Then take some of the
blood from the altar and some of the anointing oil, and sprinkle it on Aaron and his sons
and on their garments. In this way, they and
their garments will be set apart as holy.
22"Since this is the ram for the ordination
of Aaron and his sons, take the fat of the
ram, including the fat of the broad tail, the
fat around the internal organs, the long lobe
of the liver, and the two kidneys and the fat
around them, along with the right thigh.
23Then take one round loaf of bread, one
thin cake mixed with olive oil, and one wafer from the basket of bread without yeast
that was placed in the LORD's presence.
24Put all these in the hands of Aaron and
his sons to be lifted up as a special offering
to the LORD. 25Afterward take the various
breads from their hands, and burn them on
the altar along with the burnt offering. It is
a pleasing aroma to the LORD, a special gift
for him. 26Then take the breast of Aaron's
ordination ram, and lift it up in the LORD's
presence as a special offering to him. Then
keep it as your own portion.
27"Set aside the portions of the ordination
ram that belong to Aaron and his sons. This
includes the breast and the thigh that were
lifted up before the LORD as a special offering. 28In the future, whenever the people of
Israel lift up a peace offering, a portion of it
must be set aside for Aaron and his descendants. This is their permanent right, and it
is a sacred offering from the Israelites to
the LORD.
29"Aaron's sacred garments must be preserved for his descendants who succeed
him, and they will wear them when they are
anointed and ordained. 30The descendant
who succeeds him as high priest will wear
these clothes for seven days as he ministers
in the Tabernacle and the Holy Place.
31"Take the ram used in the ordination
ceremony, and boil its meat in a sacred
place. 32Then Aaron and his sons will eat
this meat, along with the bread in the basket, at the Tabernacle entrance. 33They
alone may eat the meat and bread used for
their purification in the ordination ceremony. No one else may eat them, for these
things are set apart and holy. 34If any of the
ordination meat or bread remains until the
morning, it must be burned. It may not be
eaten, for it is holy.
35"This is how you will ordain Aaron and
his sons to their offices, just as I have commanded you. The ordination ceremony will
go on for seven days. 36Each day you must
sacrifice a young bull as a sin offering to purify them, making them right with the LORD.

29:13 Lev 3:3-5
29:14 Lev 4:11-12, 21; Heb 13:11
29:15 Exod 29:10
29:18 Gen 8:21
29:21 Exod 30:25, 31; Heb 9:22
29:23 Lev 8:26
29:24 Lev 7:30
29:26 Lev 7:31, 34; 8:29
29:27 Lev 7:31, 34; Num 18:11-12; Deut 18:3
29:29 Num 20:26, 28
29:28 Lev 10:15
29:30 Lev 8:35
29:33 Lev 22:10, 13
29:34-35 Lev 8:32-33
29:36 Exod 40:10; Heb 10:11

29:13 The *fat* was considered the best part and so was given to God.

29:14 The remains represented what was unclean in human behavior. • *sin offering:* See Lev 4:1-35 and notes.

29:15-18 The next offering was a gift of thanks to God; it also represented the complete giving of oneself to God.

29:18 *pleasing aroma:* Such language is *anthropomorphism,* describing God with human terms and experiences. God's delight in an appropriately offered sacrifice is like a human's enjoyment of a pleasing smell.

29:19-28 This ordination offering is very similar to the peace (or fellowship) offering later described in Lev 3. The *fat* was burned as a gift to the Lord, but the *breast* and the *thigh,* after having been dedicated to the Lord by lifting them up before him (29:24-26), became the portion for the priests to eat (29:26-28). In the regular peace offering, the remainder of the meat was to be eaten by the person making the offering in a fellowship meal (Lev 7:11-18), as the priests did here (29:31-34).

29:20-21 The placing of the *blood* on the *earlobes, thumbs,* and *big toes* represented dedication of the entire person to God. Sprinkling it on their clothes indicated that the clothing, too, could be used only for *holy* purposes.

29:30 *The descendant who succeeds him:* Each succeeding high priest was to be ordained in the same way.

29:31 This *sacred place* was probably in the courtyard of the Tabernacle.

29:32-34 Eating in the presence of the Lord signified an intimate relationship with him (as in 24:9-11).

29:33 *their purification:* Or *their atonement.* Traditionally, atonement has been described as a "covering over." Some more recent commentators seek to derive the term from another Semitic root (which does not occur elsewhere in the Hebrew Bible) and thus arrive at "blot out, erase, or cleanse." In either case, the effect is the same: Persons and objects are made capable of surviving in God's presence because of a negation of the effects of their sin.

29:36 *to purify them, making them*

Afterward, cleanse the altar by purifying it;
make it holy by anointing it with oil. [37]Pu-
rify the altar, and consecrate it every day
for seven days. After that, the altar will be
absolutely holy, and whatever touches it will
become holy.

Instructions for Priestly Activities (29:38–30:38)

The Daily Offerings

[38]"These are the sacrifices you are to offer regularly on the altar. Each day, offer two lambs
that are a year old, [39]one in the morning and
the other in the evening. [40]With one of them,
offer two quarts of choice flour mixed with
one quart of pure oil of pressed olives; also,
offer one quart of wine as a liquid offering.
[41]Offer the other lamb in the evening, along
with the same offerings of flour and wine as
in the morning. It will be a pleasing aroma, a
special gift presented to the LORD.
[42]"These burnt offerings are to be made
each day from generation to generation.
Offer them in the LORD's presence at the
Tabernacle entrance; there I will meet with
you and speak with you. [43]I will meet the
people of Israel there, in the place made
holy by my glorious presence. [44]Yes, I will
consecrate the Tabernacle and the altar,
and I will consecrate Aaron and his sons to
serve me as priests. [45]Then I will live among
the people of Israel and be their God, [46]and
they will know that I am the LORD their God.
I am the one who brought them out of the
land of Egypt so that I could live among
them. I am the LORD their God.

Plans for the Incense Altar

30 "Then make another altar of acacia
wood for burning incense. [2]Make it
18 inches square and 36 inches high, with
horns at the corners carved from the same
piece of wood as the altar itself. [3]Overlay the
top, sides, and horns of the altar with pure
gold, and run a gold molding around the entire altar. [4]Make two gold rings, and attach
them on opposite sides of the altar below
the gold molding to hold the carrying poles.
[5]Make the poles of acacia wood and overlay
them with gold. [6]Place the incense altar just
outside the inner curtain that shields the
Ark of the Covenant, in front of the Ark's
cover—the place of atonement—that covers
the tablets inscribed with the terms of the
covenant. I will meet with you there.
[7]"Every morning when Aaron maintains
the lamps, he must burn fragrant incense on
the altar. [8]And each evening when he lights
the lamps, he must again burn incense in the
LORD's presence. This must be done from
generation to generation. [9]Do not offer any
unholy incense on this altar, or any burnt offerings, grain offerings, or liquid offerings.
[10]"Once a year Aaron must purify the altar by smearing its horns with blood from
the offering made to purify the people
from their sin. This will be a regular, annual
event from generation to generation, for
this is the LORD's most holy altar."

Money for the Tabernacle

[11]Then the LORD said to Moses, [12]"Whenever
you take a census of the people of Israel,

29:37 Exod 40:10; Matt 23:19
29:38 Num 28:3-31; 29:6-38; 1 Chr 16:40; Dan 12:11
29:41 2 Kgs 16:15; Ezra 9:4-5; Ps 141:2
29:42 Exod 30:8
29:43 1 Kgs 8:11
29:45 Exod 25:8; Lev 26:12; Num 5:3; Deut 12:11; Ps 68:18; Zech 2:10; 2 Cor 6:16; Rev 21:3
29:46 Exod 20:2
30:1-5 //Exod 37:25-28; 1 Kgs 6:20; Rev 8:3
30:6 Exod 25:21-22
30:7 Exod 27:21; 30:34-35; 1 Sam 2:28; Luke 1:9
30:10 Lev 16:8
30:12 Exod 38:25-26; Num 1:2; 26:2; 2 Sam 24:1; Matt 20:28

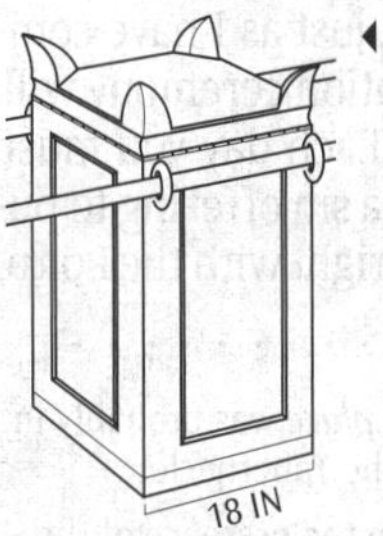

◀ **The Incense Altar (30:1-10).**

right with the LORD: Or *to make atonement.* See note on 29:33. • ***by purifying it:*** Or *by making atonement for it;* similarly in 29:37.

29:37 As with the priests, the *altar* was to be made ***holy*** so it could be used in service of the holy God.

29:38-41 Offering the daily sacrifices was one of the priest's chief functions.

29:40 *two quarts of choice flour . . . one quart of pure oil . . . one quart of wine:* Hebrew *1⁄10 of an ephah* [2.2 liters] *of choice flour . . . 1⁄4 of a hin* [1 liter] *of pure oil . . . 1⁄4 of a hin* [1 liter] *of wine.*

29:42-46 The purpose of the Tabernacle, the priesthood, and the sacrificial system was to facilitate human fellowship with God. The Lord would ***meet with*** his people there (29:42, 43) and ***speak with*** them (29:42). He would ***live among*** them as ***their God*** (29:45, 46).

29:46 The purpose of the Exodus was to reveal the grace, power, and holiness of God and to enable humans to experience God's presence in their lives.

30:1-10 Plans for the ***altar of acacia wood*** are included here rather than with the plans for the other items in the sanctuary (25:23-40), perhaps because of the reference to the priest's use of it in 30:7-10. See illustration at left.

30:2 *18 inches square and 36 inches high:* Hebrew *1 cubit* [46 centimeters] *long and 1 cubit wide, a square, and 2 cubits* [92 centimeters] *high.* • ***horns:*** See note on 27:2.

30:6 ***outside the inner curtain:*** That is, in the Holy Place, just outside the Most Holy Place where the ark was located. • The rising smoke of the ***incense*** symbolized prayer. Believers now have constant access to God in prayer through the continuous atonement provided through Christ (see Ps 141:2; Luke 1:10; Rev 5:8; 8:3-4). • ***Ark of the Covenant:*** Or *Ark of the Testimony;* also in 30:26. • ***that covers the tablets inscribed with the terms of the covenant:*** Literally *that covers the Testimony.* See note on 25:16.

30:10 ***purify:*** Or *make atonement for;* also in 30:10b. See note on 29:33.

30:12 ***no plague:*** Cp. 2 Sam 24, when a plague followed upon David's unauthorized census. Perhaps a census was often taken for reasons of pride and domination. Here the people are giving God a ***ransom*** for themselves. This standard payment would go into the Tabernacle treasury and initially be used in the construction of the Tabernacle (see 38:25-26).

30:13 Matt 17:24
30:15 Prov 22:2
30:18 Exod 38:8; 40:7, 30
30:19 Exod 40:31-32
30:21 Exod 28:43
30:25 Exod 37:29; 40:9
30:26 Lev 8:10; Num 7:1
30:29 Exod 29:37
30:30 Lev 8:2, 12, 30
30:33 Gen 17:14; Exod 12:15; Lev 7:20-21
30:36 Lev 2:3

each man who is counted must pay a ransom for himself to the LORD. Then no plague will strike the people as you count them. [13]Each person who is counted must give a small piece of silver as a sacred offering to the LORD. (This payment is half a shekel, based on the sanctuary shekel, which equals twenty gerahs.) [14]All who have reached their twentieth birthday must give this sacred offering to the LORD. [15]When this offering is given to the LORD to purify your lives, making you right with him, the rich must not give more than the specified amount, and the poor must not give less. [16]Receive this ransom money from the Israelites, and use it for the care of the Tabernacle. It will bring the Israelites to the LORD's attention, and it will purify your lives."

Plans for the Washbasin

[17]Then the LORD said to Moses, [18]"Make a bronze washbasin with a bronze stand. Place it between the Tabernacle and the altar, and fill it with water. [19]Aaron and his sons will wash their hands and feet there. [20]They must wash with water whenever they go into the Tabernacle to appear before the LORD and when they approach the altar to burn up their special gifts to the LORD—or they will die! [21]They must always wash their hands and feet, or they will die. This is a permanent law for Aaron and his descendants, to be observed from generation to generation."

The Anointing Oil

[22]Then the LORD said to Moses, [23]"Collect choice spices—12½ pounds of pure myrrh, 6¼ pounds of fragrant cinnamon, 6¼ pounds of fragrant calamus, [24]and 12½ pounds of cassia—as measured by the weight of the sanctuary shekel. Also get one gallon of olive oil. [25]Like a skilled incense maker, blend these ingredients to make a holy anointing oil. [26]Use this sacred oil to anoint the Tabernacle, the Ark of the Covenant, [27]the table and all its utensils, the lampstand and all its accessories, the incense altar, [28]the altar of burnt offering and all its utensils, and the washbasin with its stand. [29]Consecrate them to make them absolutely holy. After this, whatever touches them will also become holy.

[30]"Anoint Aaron and his sons also, consecrating them to serve me as priests. [31]And say to the people of Israel, 'This holy anointing oil is reserved for me from generation to generation. [32]It must never be used to anoint anyone else, and you must never make any blend like it for yourselves. It is holy, and you must treat it as holy. [33]Anyone who makes a blend like it or anoints someone other than a priest will be cut off from the community.' "

The Incense

[34]Then the LORD said to Moses, "Gather fragrant spices—resin droplets, mollusk shell, and galbanum—and mix these fragrant spices with pure frankincense, weighed out in equal amounts. [35]Using the usual techniques of the incense maker, blend the spices together and sprinkle them with salt to produce a pure and holy incense. [36]Grind some of the mixture into a very fine powder and put it in front of the Ark of the Covenant, where I will meet with you in the Tabernacle. You must treat this incense as most holy. [37]Never use this formula to make this incense for yourselves. It is reserved for the LORD, and you must treat it as holy. [38]Anyone who makes incense like this for personal use will be cut off from the community."

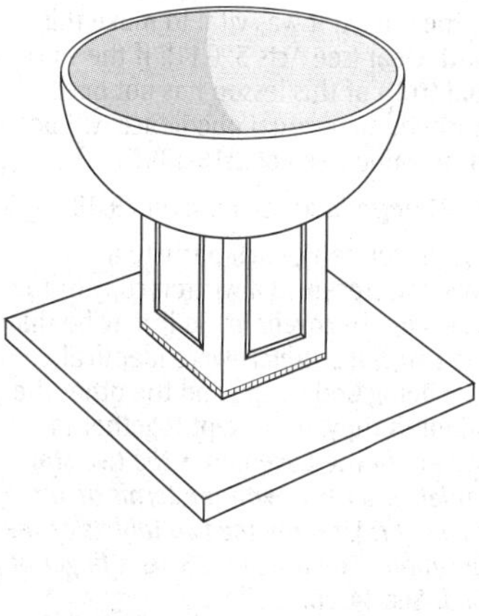

◀ The Bronze Washbasin (30:17-21).

30:13 ***half a shekel:*** Or *0.2 ounces,* or *6 grams.*

30:15 ***to purify your lives, making you right with him:*** Or *to make atonement for your lives;* similarly in 30:16. See note on 29:33.

30:16 ***Tabernacle:*** Literally *Tent of Meeting;* also in 30:18, 20, 26, 36. See note on 27:21.

30:17-21 On why the plans for the ***bronze washbasin*** are included here, see note on 30:1-10. See illustration at left.

30:20 ***wash with water:*** See note on 29:4.

30:22-38 Because God is absolutely unique (***holy***), what is used for his service cannot be used for any other purpose. This was the point made to Moses at the burning bush (see note on 3:5). It was so vital for the people to understand this point that disobedience in this matter involved a severe punishment (30:33).

30:23 ***12½ pounds of pure myrrh, 6¼ pounds of fragrant cinnamon, 6¼ pounds of fragrant calamus:*** Hebrew *500 shekels* [5.7 kilograms] *of pure myrrh, 250 shekels* [2.9 kilograms] *of fragrant cinnamon, 250 shekels of fragrant calamus.*

30:24 ***12½ pounds of cassia:*** Hebrew *500 shekels* [5.7 kilograms] *of cassia.* • ***one gallon of olive oil:*** Hebrew *1 hin* [3.8 liters] *of olive oil.*

30:33 ***cut off from the community:*** Either by death or by expulsion.

30:36 ***in front of the Ark of the Covenant:*** Literally *in front of the Testimony.* See note on 25:16.

Craftsmen: Bezalel and Oholiab (31:1-11)

31 Then the LORD said to Moses, 2“Look,
I have specifically chosen Bezalel
son of Uri, grandson of Hur, of the tribe of
Judah. 3I have filled him with the [f]Spirit of
God, giving him great wisdom, ability, and
expertise in all kinds of crafts. 4He is a master craftsman, expert in working with gold,
silver, and bronze. 5He is skilled in engraving and mounting gemstones and in carving
wood. He is a master at every craft!

6“And I have personally appointed Oholiab son of Ahisamach, of the tribe of Dan,
to be his assistant. Moreover, I have given
special skill to all the gifted craftsmen so
they can make all the things I have commanded you to make:

7 the Tabernacle;
the Ark of the Covenant;
the Ark’s cover—the place of atonement;
all the furnishings of the Tabernacle;
8 the table and its utensils;
the pure gold lampstand with all its accessories;
the incense altar;
9 the altar of burnt offering with all its utensils;
the washbasin with its stand;
10 the beautifully stitched garments—the sacred garments for Aaron the priest, and the garments for his sons to wear as they minister as priests;
11 the anointing oil;
the fragrant incense for the Holy Place.

The craftsmen must make everything as
I have commanded you.”

Instructions for the Sabbath (31:12-18)

12The LORD then gave these instructions
to Moses: 13“Tell the people of Israel: ‘Be
careful to keep my Sabbath day, for the Sabbath is a sign of the covenant between me
and you from generation to generation. It is
given so you may know that I am the LORD,
who makes you holy. 14You must keep the
Sabbath day, for it is a holy day for you. Anyone who desecrates it must be put to death;
anyone who works on that day will be cut
off from the community. 15You have six
days each week for your ordinary work, but
the seventh day must be a [g]Sabbath day of
complete rest, a holy day dedicated to the
LORD. Anyone who works on the [g]Sabbath
must be put to death. 16The people of Israel
must keep the [h]Sabbath day by observing
it from generation to generation. This is a
covenant obligation for all time. 17It is a permanent sign of my covenant with the people
of Israel. For in six days the LORD made
heaven and earth, but on the seventh day he
stopped working and was refreshed.’ ”

18When the LORD finished speaking
with Moses on Mount Sinai, he gave him
the two stone tablets inscribed with the
terms of the covenant, written by the finger of God.

The Gold Calf: A Wrong Attempt to Secure God’s Presence (32:1–34:35)

Making the Gold Calf

32 When the people saw how long
it was taking Moses to come back
down the mountain, they gathered around
Aaron. “Come on,” they said, “make us some

31:2-6 //Exod 35:30–36:1; 1 Chr 2:20
31:3 1 Kgs 7:14; [f]*ruakh* (7307) ‣ Num 11:25
31:6 Exod 35:31-34; 36:1
31:7 Exod 37:1-9
31:8 Exod 37:10-16; Lev 24:4
31:11 Exod 30:23-32
31:13 Lev 19:3, 30; Ezek 20:12-13
31:14 Exod 16:23; 35:2; John 7:23
31:15 [g]*shabbath* (7676) ‣ Exod 31:16
31:16 Exod 20:8; [h]*shabbath* (7676) ‣ Lev 23:32
31:17 Gen 2:2-3; Exod 20:11
31:18 Exod 24:12; 32:15-16; 34:1, 28
32:1 Exod 24:18; Deut 9:9-12; *Acts 7:40

31:1-11 God gave instructions for the Tabernacle complex and for those who would serve in it. He also chose and empowered those who would do the work.

31:3 ***I have filled him with the Spirit of God:*** This is one of the earliest references to being filled with the Spirit as an expression of divine empowerment for activities that are clearly beyond normal human abilities (see also Gen 41:38; Num 11:17; Judg 6:34; 14:19; 1 Sam 10:6; 16:13; Joel 2:28-29; Mic 3:8).

31:6 God ***commanded*** remarkable things, but he also provided ***gifted craftsmen*** who would be able to carry out all those instructions—much as Augustine prayed, “Give what you command, and command what you will” (Augustine, *Confessions* 10.29).

31:7 ***Tabernacle:*** Literally *Tent of Meeting.* See note on 27:21. • ***Ark of the Covenant:*** Literally *Ark of the Testimony.* See note on 25:16.

31:11 The point throughout this entire section (25:1–40:38) is that God intends to meet his people’s need for some tangible representation of his presence, but it must be done in the way he has ***commanded.*** He, not we, determines the terms by which we come to him.

31:12-18 The Sabbath was understood to be the unique ***sign of the covenant*** (31:13, 16, 17; see also 20:8-11; Isa 58:13-14; Jer 17:21-27; Neh 13:15-22). The Sabbath is also said to figure significantly in the achievement of God’s underlying purpose of making his people ***holy,*** that is, set apart for his exclusive use and sharing his character (31:13, 14, 15). Resting from their own work (31:15, 17) was also a practical way of demonstrating genuine dependence on God to meet their needs (see 20:8-11 and notes).

31:14-15 It is absolutely important to learn that we can find life in God only by coming to him in his way. This is underlined by the death sentence for disobedience (see also Num 15:32-36). This is not to say that followers of God must always punish those who commit these offenses in this way; but here at the outset, it was vital to make this truth clear (see Acts 5:1-11). If the spiritual truth of this lesson has not been learned, mere ritual obedience will be of no value (see Col 2:16-19).

31:17 ***refreshed:*** See note on 29:18.

31:18 Normally, each party to a covenant received a written copy of ***the terms of the covenant.*** So it may be that the ***two stone tablets*** were identical, one being God’s copy and the other the people’s copy, to be kept together in the Ark of the Covenant. • ***the two stone tablets inscribed with the terms of the covenant:*** Literally *the two tablets of the Testimony.* See note on 25:16. • ***finger of God:*** See 34:28.

32:1-35 At the foot of Mount Sinai, after Moses had been absent for many days, the people felt the need for protection, guidance, and a tangible way to express

32:2
Exod 35:22
32:4
Exod 20:23
Deut 9:16
Ps 106:19
Acts 7:41
32:6
Num 25:2
Acts 7:41
*1 Cor 10:7
32:7
Exod 19:24; 33:1
Deut 9:12
32:8
Exod 22:20; 34:15
Deut 32:17
32:9
Exod 33:5
Num 14:11
Acts 7:51
32:10
Num 14:12
Deut 9:14
32:11
Deut 9:18, 26
Ps 106:23
32:12
Num 14:13-16
Deut 9:28

gods who can lead us. We don't know what
happened to this fellow Moses, who brought
us here from the land of Egypt."
2So Aaron said, "Take the gold rings from
the ears of your wives and sons and daughters, and bring them to me."
3All the people took the gold rings from
their ears and brought them to Aaron.
4Then Aaron took the gold, melted it down,
and molded it into the shape of a calf. When
the people saw it, they exclaimed, "O Israel,
these are the gods who brought you out of
the land of Egypt!"
5Aaron saw how excited the people were,
so he built an altar in front of the calf. Then
he announced, "Tomorrow will be a festival
to the LORD!"
6The people got up early the next morning to sacrifice burnt offerings and peace
offerings. After this, they celebrated with
feasting and drinking, and they indulged in
pagan revelry.

The LORD's Response and Moses' Intercession

7The LORD told Moses, "Quick! Go down the
mountain! Your people whom you brought
from the land of Egypt have corrupted
themselves. 8How quickly they have turned
away from the way I commanded them to
live! They have melted down gold and made
a calf, and they have bowed down and sacrificed to it. They are saying, 'These are your
gods, O Israel, who brought you out of the
land of Egypt.' "
9Then the LORD said, "I have seen how
stubborn and rebellious these people are.
10Now leave me alone so my fierce anger
can blaze against them, and I will destroy
them. Then I will make you, Moses, into a
great nation."
11But Moses tried to pacify the LORD
his God. "O LORD!" he said. "Why are you
so angry with your own people whom you
brought from the land of Egypt with such
great power and such a strong hand? 12Why
let the Egyptians say, 'Their God rescued
them with the evil intention of slaughtering
them in the mountains and wiping them
from the face of the earth'? Turn away from
your fierce anger. Change your mind about
this terrible disaster you have threatened

their worship. God knew this and was eager to meet these needs (chs 25–31). The Israelites, however, tried to meet their needs for themselves. Fellowship with God requires depending on him (see John 15:5; 2 Cor 3:5).

32:1-6 The people were not willing to wait and see what God had been saying to Moses on the mountain for the forty days while he was there (see 24:18).

32:1 The Israelites' actions were motivated by fear, disrespect for ***this fellow Moses,*** disbelief in God's leadership, and denial of responsibility. They were unwilling to wait for God to reveal his plans of care for them. Refusal to wait on God is often a cause of sin (see 1 Sam 13:7-13; Isa 30:15-18).

32:2-4 The religious professional, ***Aaron,*** demanded a specific contribution of ***gold rings*** and then excluded ***the people*** from any further involvement in the process. This is very different from what God had commanded regarding the construction of the Tabernacle, where the people were invited to bring many different kinds of things as they felt led (25:1-9; 35:4–36:7) and to share in the work under the guidance of a Spirit-filled layperson (31:1-6; 36:1-2).

32:4 ***the shape of a calf:*** The idol might actually have been an image of a bull, like the images of the Egyptian god Amon-Re that the people had known in Egypt. The bull represented power, domination, and fertility. The writer would then be using the term *calf* as a way of expressing contempt for the idol. Alternatively, Aaron might have made a calf, feeling that this sin was not as serious as if the idol were a full-sized bull. • ***these are the gods who brought you out:*** The people attributed to the idol what they had just said that Moses had done (32:1). Idolatry expresses the belief that the divine realm and the visible world are continuous with one another. This worldview sees it as possible to lay hold of divine power through ritual manipulation of the god by means of the idol. God had been insisting that the very opposite is true: God is *not* contained in or restrained by his creation, and his blessings cannot be procured by manipulating creation, either ritually or otherwise. The blessings of God are for those who surrender their own efforts to make themselves secure and come to him using the ways and means that he has decreed.

32:5 Aaron attempted to control the process, but he was actually abdicating leadership by simply doing what he thought ***the people*** wanted. • Although the idol was referred to as "the gods" (32:4), Aaron also implied that it was a physical manifestation of ***the LORD.***

32:6 The Hebrew term translated ***pagan revelry*** is traditionally rendered ***they got up to play.*** As in English, the Hebrew word for *play* can have sexual overtones (see Gen 26:8, "caressing"), which is likely the case here. Worship of a fertility symbol such as a bull was often accompanied by sexual activities on the part of the worshipers (see 1 Cor 10:7-8).

32:7 ***Your people whom you brought from the land of Egypt:*** God here attributes his own work to Moses, which suggests that he was testing Moses, giving him an opportunity to make the same mistake the people had made (32:1). God was not "tempting" Moses in the sense of "seducing him to do evil" (see Jas 1:13-14), but he was putting Moses into a situation where he was faced with a clear choice that could take him in opposing directions (cp. 1 Kgs 22:19-23).

32:9-10 God was apparently prepared to disown his people, since they had broken their covenant with him.

32:10 ***Now leave me alone:*** This apparent command was in fact an invitation to Moses to intercede for his people. Although the people deserved destruction, God was willing not to destroy them if Moses continued to stand before him as an intercessor. • ***I will make you, Moses, into a great nation:*** If Moses were willing, God would start over again, abandoning the rest of the children of Abraham and beginning now with the children of Moses. This was apparently a test of Moses' understanding of God.

32:11-13 If a test was involved, Moses passed it. He refused to put himself in God's place (32:11). He knew that God is just and faithful and that he would not deliver people only to destroy them (32:12). He refused to accept the invitation to become the father of a great nation, since that would involve God's breaking his promises to ***Abraham, Isaac, and Jacob*** (32:13). Moses had learned who God really is.

against your people! 13Remember your servants Abraham, Isaac, and Jacob. You bound
yourself with an oath to them, saying, 'I will
make your ⁱdescendants as numerous as
the stars of heaven. And I will give them
all of this land that I have promised to your
ⁱdescendants, and they will possess it forever.' "
14So the LORD changed his mind about
the terrible disaster he had threatened to
bring on his people.

Moses' Response

15Then Moses turned and went down the
mountain. He held in his hands the two
stone tablets inscribed with the terms of
the covenant. They were inscribed on both
sides, front and back. 16These tablets were
God's work; the words on them were written by God himself.
17When Joshua heard the boisterous
noise of the people shouting below them,
he exclaimed to Moses, "It sounds like war
in the camp!"
18But Moses replied, "No, it's not a shout
of victory nor the wailing of defeat. I hear
the sound of a celebration."
19When they came near the camp, Moses
saw the calf and the dancing, and he burned
with anger. He threw the stone tablets to
the ground, smashing them at the foot of
the mountain. 20He took the calf they had
made and burned it. Then he ground it into
powder, threw it into the water, and forced
the people to drink it.
21Finally, he turned to Aaron and demanded, "What did these people do to you
to make you bring such terrible sin upon
them?"
22"Don't get so upset, my lord," Aaron replied. "You yourself know how evil these
people are. 23They said to me, 'Make us
gods who will lead us. We don't know
what happened to this fellow Moses, who
brought us here from the land of Egypt.'
24So I told them, 'Whoever has gold jewelry,
take it off.' When they brought it to me, I
simply threw it into the fire—and out came
this calf!"
25Moses saw that Aaron had let the people get completely out of control, much
to the amusement of their enemies. 26So
he stood at the entrance to the camp and
shouted, "All of you who are on the LORD's
side, come here and join me." And all the Levites gathered around him.
27Moses told them, "This is what the
LORD, the God of Israel, says: Each of you,
take your swords and go back and forth
from one end of the camp to the other. Kill
everyone—even your brothers, friends, and
neighbors." 28The Levites obeyed Moses'
command, and about 3,000 people died
that day.
29Then Moses told the Levites, "Today you
have ordained yourselves for the service of
the LORD, for you obeyed him even though
it meant killing your own sons and brothers.
Today you have earned a blessing."

32:13
Gen 15:5; 22:16-18
Heb 6:13
zera' (2233)
‣Deut 34:4

32:14
2 Sam 24:16
Ps 106:45

32:15
Exod 24:18
Deut 9:15

32:16
Exod 31:18

32:19
Exod 32:6
Deut 9:16-17

32:20
Deut 9:21

32:22
Deut 9:24

32:23
Exod 32:1

32:25
1 Kgs 12:28-30

32:26
2 Sam 20:11

32:27
Num 25:5
Deut 33:9

32:28
Num 16:32; 25:9

32:29
Deut 13:6; 33:9

32:13 ***Jacob:*** Literally *Israel.* The names "Jacob" and "Israel" are often interchanged throughout the OT, referring sometimes to the individual patriarch and sometimes to the nation; see Gen 32:28.

32:14 In response to Moses' argument, ***the LORD changed his mind.*** This is not the picture of a raging tyrant who is, with great difficulty, finally persuaded to back down. The Lord is much more inclined to be merciful than to insist on vengeance, and he invites those who are near him, like Moses, to give him an occasion for his mercy through faithful intercession.

32:15-29 When ***Moses*** actually saw what was going on, he was much less calm than he had been on the mountain. He smashed the tablets (32:15-19), destroyed the calf (32:20), confronted Aaron (32:21-25), and had the ringleaders killed (32:26-29).

32:15 ***the two stone tablets inscribed with the terms of the covenant:*** Literally *the two tablets of the Testimony.* See note on 25:16.

32:16 ***These tablets were God's work:*** The covenant was not merely a human agreement.

32:19 While the act of ***smashing*** the tablets might simply have been a reaction of fury, it might also have been Moses' way of saying that the covenant with God was now irrevocably broken. God later reminded Moses rather pointedly that Moses was the one who had smashed the tablets (see 34:1).

32:20 Passing the gold ***powder*** of the image through the bodies of the people effectively rendered it unclean.

32:21-25 ***Aaron*** denied responsibility even though he himself had made the molds and poured the gold (32:4). Aaron wanted Moses to believe that it all "just happened" (32:24) and that he had no choice because the ***people*** were so ***evil*** (32:22). Moses was not misled. He knew ***that Aaron*** could have led the people but had let them ***get completely out of control*** (32:25).

32:25 ***much to the amusement of their enemies:*** Or *and they mocked anyone who opposed them;* the meaning of the Hebrew is unclear. After the Israelites' great show of worshiping the Lord as a different kind of God, their actions proclaimed that he was merely another of the idols that their enemies had been worshiping all along (see Ezek 36:19-20).

32:26-29 ***Moses*** had asked God to spare the people, but now he called on those who followed the Lord to kill those who had sinned. The ***Levites*** (32:26) were willing to confront the sin that Aaron had let loose. Although Moses commanded them to ***kill everyone*** (32:27), the number ***3,000*** (32:28) makes it clear that the word *everyone* had a restricted meaning. The reference to ***your own sons and brothers*** suggests that as Aaron had led in the idolatry, many of the Levites had led in the worship of the idol, and they were the ones that the rest of the Levites killed. Aaron may have escaped because God had already designated him as high priest (28:1). • ***Today you have ordained yourselves:*** As in Greek and Latin versions; Hebrew reads *Today ordain yourselves.*

32:30
[j]*kapar* (3722)
‣ Lev 4:26

32:31
Exod 20:23

32:32
Ps 69:28
Isa 4:3
Dan 12:1
Mal 3:16-17
Phil 4:3
Rev 3:5; 21:27
[k]*nasa'* (5375)
‣ Exod 34:7

32:33
Deut 29:20
Ps 9:5
Rev 3:5

32:34
Exod 3:17; 23:20
Ps 99:8

33:1
Gen 12:7
Exod 32:7, 13

33:2
Exod 23:27-31

33:3
Exod 3:8, 17; 32:9-10

33:4
Num 14:1, 39
[a]*'abal* (0056)
‣ 1 Sam 6:19

33:5
Exod 33:3

33:7
Exod 29:42-43

33:8
Num 16:27

33:9
Exod 13:21; 19:9; 25:22
Ps 99:7

33:11
Num 12:8
Deut 34:10

Moses Intercedes for Israel

30The next day Moses said to the people,
"You have committed a terrible sin, but I will
go back up to the LORD on the mountain.
Perhaps I will be able to [j]obtain forgiveness
for your sin."
31So Moses returned to the LORD and
said, "Oh, what a terrible sin these people
have committed. They have made gods of
gold for themselves. 32But now, if you will
only [k]forgive their sin—but if not, erase my
name from the record you have written!"
33But the LORD replied to Moses, "No,
I will erase the name of everyone who has
sinned against me. 34Now go, lead the people to the place I told you about. Look! My
angel will lead the way before you. And
when I come to call the people to account,
I will certainly hold them responsible for
their sins."
35Then the LORD sent a great plague upon
the people because they had worshiped the
calf Aaron had made.

The LORD Will Go with Them

33 The LORD said to Moses, "Get going,
you and the people you brought up
from the land of Egypt. Go up to the land I
swore to give to Abraham, Isaac, and Jacob.
I told them, 'I will give this land to your descendants.' 2And I will send an angel before
you to drive out the Canaanites, Amorites,
Hittites, Perizzites, Hivites, and Jebusites.
3Go up to this land that flows with milk and
honey. But I will not travel among you, for
you are a stubborn and rebellious people. If
I did, I would surely destroy you along the
way."
4When the people heard these stern
words, they [a]went into mourning and
stopped wearing their jewelry and fine
clothes. 5For the LORD had told Moses to tell
them, "You are a stubborn and rebellious
people. If I were to travel with you for even
a moment, I would destroy you. Remove
your jewelry and fine clothes while I decide
what to do with you." 6So from the time
they left Mount Sinai, the Israelites wore no
more jewelry or fine clothes.
7It was Moses' practice to take the Tent of
Meeting and set it up some distance from
the camp. Everyone who wanted to make a
request of the LORD would go to the Tent of
Meeting outside the camp.
8Whenever Moses went out to the Tent
of Meeting, all the people would get up and
stand in the entrances of their own tents.
They would all watch Moses until he disappeared inside. 9As he went into the tent, the
pillar of cloud would come down and hover
at its entrance while the LORD spoke with
Moses. 10When the people saw the cloud
standing at the entrance of the tent, they
would stand and bow down in front of their
own tents. 11Inside the Tent of Meeting, the
LORD would speak to Moses face to face, as

32:30-35 This further intercession for the people may have been needed because of Moses' new recognition of how serious the sin really was.

32:30 ***to obtain forgiveness:*** Or *to make atonement.* See note on 29:33.

32:32 As if underlining his earlier refusal of God's invitation to become a great nation at the people's expense, Moses here rather piously asked God to destroy him, too, if he chose not to forgive the people.

32:33 God dismissed Moses' request. He would bring judgment only on those who had sinned in the incident.

32:34 ***the place I told you about:*** Canaan, which God had promised to give to Abraham's descendants (see 3:17; 32:13; 33:1). • ***when I come to call the people to account:*** Because of God's mercy, judgment may not always come immediately (though in this instance God soon sent a plague, 32:35), but it will come for those who persist in sin (see Matt 13:24-30).

33:1-6 God would not lead the people up to Canaan as he had previously led them (see 33:3; but see also 33:14-17). Instead, he would send an angel (33:2).

33:2-3 ***an angel. . . . But I will not travel:*** This angel was possibly not the "Angel of the Lord," since in Exodus and other parts of the OT, the Angel of the Lord is closely associated with the presence of the Lord himself (see 3:2; 23:20-23). Or, God might have been saying that while he would go ***before*** them in the person of the Angel (33:2), he would not dwell ***among*** them (33:3) in the Tabernacle, as he had planned. • ***Canaanites . . . Jebusites:*** See note on 3:8.

33:3 ***land that flows with milk and honey:*** Although Canaan was not as fertile as the Nile Valley in Egypt, it was a great deal more productive agriculturally than the Sinai Desert where they were. • ***stubborn and rebellious:*** They were covenant-breakers. • ***I would surely destroy you:*** As the Covenant Lord (see note on 23:20-33), he would enforce the terms of the covenant that called for the destruction of covenant-breakers (see 24:7-8 and notes).

33:4-6 The ***jewelry and fine clothes*** might have been worn while worshiping the gold calf. Here their removal signifies ***mourning*** (33:4) and repentance.

33:6 ***Sinai:*** Hebrew *Horeb,* another name for Sinai. See note on 3:1.

33:7-11 The means of communication between God and his people before the completion of the Tabernacle are probably recorded here to explain the communications in 33:1-6 and 33:12-23.

33:7 This ***Tent of Meeting*** is different from the Tabernacle described in chs 26 and 36. Although the Tabernacle is often referred to as the Tent of Meeting (see note on 27:21), the "Tent of Meeting" referred to here was another, temporary tent. When the Tabernacle was completed, it was located in the center of the camp (see Num 2:1-31).

33:8-11 ***get up and stand . . . stand and bow down:*** The people were awed by the thought that Moses was talking directly to God, ***face to face*** (33:11).

33:11 Just as ***Joshua*** had previously gained experience as a military leader (see 17:9-13), he was now gaining experience as a spiritual leader (see also 24:13). Here he may have remained ***behind*** to guard the tent, a function the Levites would later fulfill with the Tabernacle (1 Chr 26).

one speaks to a friend. Afterward Moses
would return to the camp, but the young man
who assisted him, Joshua son of Nun, would
remain behind in the Tent of Meeting.

12One day Moses said to the LORD, "You
have been telling me, 'Take these people up
to the Promised Land.' But you haven't told
me whom you will send with me. You have
told me, 'I know you by name, and I look
favorably on you.' 13If it is true that you look
favorably on me, let me know your ways so
I may understand you more fully and continue to enjoy your favor. And remember
that this nation is your very own people."

14The LORD replied, "I will personally go
with you, Moses, and I will give you rest—
everything will be fine for you."

15Then Moses said, "If you don't personally go with us, don't make us leave this
place. 16How will anyone know that you
look favorably on me—on me and on your
people—if you don't go with us? For your
presence among us sets your people and me
apart from all other people on the earth."

17The LORD replied to Moses, "I will indeed do what you have asked, for I look
favorably on you, and I know you by name."

18Moses responded, "Then show me your
glorious presence."

19The LORD replied, "I will make all my
goodness pass before you, and I will call
out my name, Yahweh, before you. For I
will show mercy to anyone I choose, and I
will [b]show compassion to anyone I choose.
20But you may not look directly at my face,
for no one may see me and live." 21The LORD
continued, "Look, stand near me on this
rock. 22As my glorious presence passes by, I
will hide you in the crevice of the [c]rock and
cover you with my hand until I have passed
by. 23Then I will remove my hand and let
you see me from behind. But my face will
not be seen."

Moses Sees the Goodness of the LORD

34 Then the LORD told Moses, "Chisel
out two stone tablets like the first
ones. I will write on them the same words
that were on the tablets you smashed. 2Be
ready in the morning to climb up Mount Sinai and present yourself to me on the top of
the mountain. 3No one else may come with
you. In fact, no one is to appear anywhere
on the mountain. Do not even let the flocks
or herds graze near the mountain."

4So Moses chiseled out two tablets of
stone like the first ones. Early in the morning he climbed Mount Sinai as the LORD had
commanded him, and he carried the two
stone tablets in his hands.

5Then the LORD came down in a cloud
and stood there with him; and he called out
his own name, Yahweh. 6The LORD passed
in front of Moses, calling out,

33:12 Exod 3:10; 32:34; John 10:14-15; 2 Tim 2:19
33:13 Exod 34:9; Ps 25:4; 27:11
33:14 Exod 13:21; Josh 22:4; Isa 63:9
33:15 Ps 80:3, 7, 19
33:16 Exod 34:10; Lev 20:24, 26; Num 14:14
33:17 Exod 33:12
33:18 Exod 33:20, 23
33:19 *Rom 9:15; [b]*rakham* (7355) ▸2 Kgs 13:23
33:20 Isa 6:5; John 1:18; 1 Tim 6:16
33:22 Ps 91:1, 4; Isa 49:2; 51:16; [c]*tsur* (6697) ▸Deut 32:4
33:23 John 1:18
34:1 Exod 24:12; 32:19; Deut 10:2, 4
34:3 Exod 19:12-13
34:5 Exod 33:19
34:6 Num 14:18; Neh 9:17

33:12-23 *Moses* begged for God to go with him and the people to the Promised Land. In these verses the word ***personally*** (33:14-15) usually reflects a Hebrew term literally rendered *face.* Moses wanted to continue experiencing the "face to face" relationship he had begun to have (33:11). He also wanted the people to have that experience in some sense.

33:12 ***I know you by name:*** Moses had been appointed by God himself.

33:13 ***let me know your ways:*** Moses did not merely want God's blessings; he wanted to know God's nature and character, as well as the manner of and reasons for his actions. God's goal of revealing himself was beginning to be realized, at least in one person. • Moses wanted God himself to accompany them, because they were the Lord's ***own people.***

33:14 ***I will give you rest:*** Literally *a place to roost,* as in a place where a bird can land and be at peace. Ever since Abraham left Ur, he and his descendants had had no such place.

33:15-16 ***Moses*** made his request even more direct. Again he showed his understanding of what God was doing. The Exodus was not merely about getting the Israelites out of Egypt so they could go to Canaan. It was about a personal experience of God that would change how they lived. If that was not possible, then they might just as well have stayed at Sinai. Going on to Canaan would be disastrous without the Lord.

33:17 ***The LORD*** reaffirmed his agreement to go with them and his personal appointment of Moses.

33:18 ***Moses*** asked for confirmation of God's promises. He asked to see God's ***glorious presence*** (literally *glory*). He was asking for an experience of seeing the very essence of God (see note on 16:7).

33:19 In his positive reply, God subtly changed the terms. He would grant Moses a glorious experience, but he would not show Moses his face. Rather, he would show him his ***goodness*** and express his character (***my name***), marked above all by ***mercy*** and ***compassion*** (see Rom 9:14-16). • ***Yahweh:*** See note on 3:15. Here God is emphasizing his own personal name.

33:20-23 God longs to show us his character, but to see his *face* (his essence) and his ***glorious presence*** (33:22) would be to die. Moses was permitted a glimpse of that, but nothing more.

34:1-35 God granted Moses' request (33:18), showed Moses his goodness (34:1-9), and renewed the covenant (34:10-35). This renewal was a unilateral statement by God. God would indeed go with his people, maintaining his covenant promises even though they had broken the covenant (32:1-6) and deserved nothing better than death and abandonment.

34:1-3 God called Moses to come back ***up Mount Sinai*** with ***two*** new ***stone tablets.*** The restrictions for the rest of the people are like those made at first (see 19:12-13, 21-25).

34:5-9 Moses experienced God's presence in a revelation of the ***name,*** or character, of God. As God had promised (33:19), he showed Moses the glory of his goodness.

34:5-6 ***Yahweh:*** See note on 3:15. Here God is emphasizing his personal name.

34:6 ***compassion and mercy*** (see 20:5-6; 33:19 and notes): The Creator who was revealing himself to the Israelites, and through them to the world, is a God of grace. Neither his justice nor his sovereignty are underlined here, as true as those attributes are. If God were merely just, the OT would have ended at this

"Yahweh! The LORD!
The God of compassion and mercy!
I am [d]slow to anger
and filled with unfailing love and
[e]faithfulness.
7 I lavish unfailing love to a thousand
generations.
I [f]forgive iniquity, [g]rebellion, and sin.
But I do not excuse the guilty.
I lay the sins of the parents upon their
children and grandchildren;
the entire family is affected—
even children in the third and fourth
generations."

8 Moses immediately threw himself to
the ground and worshiped. 9 And he said,
"O Lord, if it is true that I have found favor
with you, then please travel with us. Yes,
this is a stubborn and rebellious people,
but please forgive our iniquity and our sins.
Claim us as your own special possession."

The LORD Renews the Covenant

10 The LORD replied, "Listen, I am making
a covenant with you in the presence of all
your people. I will perform miracles that
have never been performed anywhere in
all the earth or in any nation. And all the
people around you will see the power of the
LORD—the awesome power I will display for
you. 11 But listen carefully to everything I
command you today. Then I will go ahead of
you and drive out the Amorites, Canaanites,
Hittites, Perizzites, Hivites, and Jebusites.

12 "Be very careful never to make a treaty
with the people who live in the land where
you are going. If you do, you will follow
their evil ways and be trapped. 13 Instead,
you must break down their pagan altars,
smash their sacred pillars, and cut down
their Asherah poles. 14 You must worship no
other gods, for the LORD, whose very name
is [h]Jealous, is a God who is [h]jealous about his
relationship with you.

15 "You must not make a treaty of any kind
with the people living in the land. They lust
after their gods, offering sacrifices to them.
They will invite you to join them in their
sacrificial meals, and you will go with them.
16 Then you will accept their daughters, who
sacrifice to other gods, as wives for your
sons. And they will seduce your sons to
commit adultery against me by worshiping
other gods. 17 You must not make any gods
of molten metal for yourselves.

18 "You must celebrate the Festival of Unleavened Bread. For seven days the bread
you eat must be made without yeast, just as
I commanded you. Celebrate this festival annually at the appointed time in early spring,
in the month of Abib, for that is the anniversary of your departure from Egypt.

19 "The firstborn of every animal belongs
to me, including the firstborn males from
your herds of cattle and your flocks of
sheep and goats. 20 A firstborn donkey may
be bought back from the LORD by presenting a lamb or young goat in its place. But if

Ps 86:15; 103:8
[d]*'arek 'appayim* (0750, 0639)
› Num 14:18
[e]*'emeth* (0571)
› Ps 25:5

34:7
Exod 20:6-7
Deut 5:10
Nah 1:3
[f]*nasa'* (5375)
› Josh 24:19
[g]*pesha'* (6588)
› Ps 32:1

34:9
Num 14:19
Deut 4:20; 32:9
Ps 25:11

34:10
Deut 5:2-3
Ps 72:18; 136:4

34:11
Exod 33:2
Deut 6:3

34:12
Exod 23:32-33

34:13
Exod 23:24
Deut 7:5; 12:3; 16:21
2 Chr 34:3-4

34:14
Exod 20:3
Deut 4:24
[h]*qanna'* (7067)
› Deut 4:24

34:15
Num 25:2
Judg 2:17

34:16
Deut 7:3
Josh 23:12

34:17
Exod 20:4, 23

34:18
Exod 12:2, 15-17

34:19
Exod 13:2; 22:29

34:20
Exod 13:13, 15
Num 3:45

point, or it would have picked up and started again with an entirely new family. This did not happen because God, in his unique character, is *slow to anger* and full of ***unfailing love and faithfulness***. These qualities were the basis for his renewal of the covenant.

34:7 God's ***unfailing love*** and his generous desire to *forgive* are not weakness or indecisiveness, nor are they reason to sin. Sin will have its effects, because God created a world of cause and effect. The murderer may repent, be forgiven, and lead a new life, but the effects of his previous choices will continue to play out. We should not sin just because we know that God will forgive (see note on 20:5-6). • ***a thousand generations:*** Literally *for thousands*. See Deut 7:9-11. • ***I lay the sins of the parents:*** Our sins affect future generations of descendants, but God restricts the natural effect of those sins to three or four generations. See also 20:5-6.

34:8-9 Since the Lord had already twice promised to go with them (33:14, 17), this renewed request seems to show a lack of faith. It may also be that God's presence had driven home to Moses how absolutely holy God is and how very different he is from this ***stubborn and rebellious people***. Here Moses took his request a step further and asked God to ***travel*** with the people and make them his ***own special possession*** (see 19:6). Moses asked for the complete restoration of the relationship.

34:10-26 Some of the terms of the covenant are restated, particularly those that prohibit the worship of other gods and that describe the proper worship of the Lord.

34:10-11 God committed himself again to the miraculous care of his people in bringing them into the land of Canaan. That care was contingent on obedience. In Hebrew, the word translated *listen* (34:11) also means *obey*. There is no distinction as there is in English, in which a disobedient person can hear a command but not obey.

34:12-17 Worship of idols was prohibited, particularly the idols of the peoples into whose lands the Israelites were going. Central to this restriction was the prohibition of treaties, or covenants, with these idol-worshiping peoples. Not only would the making of a ***treaty*** involve recognizing those peoples' gods (because ancient treaties would call upon the gods as witnesses; see note on 20:1–23:33), but the very existence of the treaties would predispose the Israelites to accept the ways of their treaty partners (34:12, 15-16).

34:13 *Asherah* was a Canaanite fertility goddess who would continue to be a temptation throughout Israel's history (see, e.g., Judg 6:25; 1 Kgs 14:15; 2 Kgs 23:15). • The ***poles*** seem to have been fertility symbols.

34:14 ***whose very name is Jealous:*** See note on 20:5-6.

34:16 Intermarriage with pagans was a problem throughout the OT (see Gen 24:3; Ezra 9:1-2; cp. 2 Cor 6:14-18).

34:18 ***appointed time in early spring, in the month of Abib:*** Literally *appointed time in the month of Abib*. See note on 23:15. See also chart, "Israel's Annual Calendar," p. 145.

you do not buy it back, you must break its neck. However, you must buy back every firstborn son.

"No one may appear before me without an offering.

21"You have six days each week for your ordinary work, but on the seventh day you must stop working, even during the seasons of plowing and harvest.

22"You must celebrate the Festival of Harvest with the first crop of the wheat harvest, and celebrate the Festival of the Final Harvest at the end of the harvest season. 23Three times each year every man in Israel must appear before the Sovereign, the LORD, the God of Israel. 24I will drive out the other nations ahead of you and expand your territory, so no one will covet and conquer your land while you appear before the LORD your God three times each year.

25"You must not offer the blood of my sacrificial offerings together with any baked goods containing yeast. And none of the meat of the Passover sacrifice may be kept over until the next morning.

26"As you harvest your crops, bring the very best of the first harvest to the house of the LORD your God.

"You must not cook a young goat in its mother's milk."

27Then the LORD said to Moses, "Write down all these instructions, for they represent the terms of the covenant I am making with you and with Israel."

28Moses remained there on the mountain with the LORD forty days and forty nights. In all that time he ate no bread and drank no water. And the LORD wrote the terms of the covenant—the Ten Commandments—on the stone tablets.

29When Moses came down Mount Sinai carrying the two stone tablets inscribed with the terms of the covenant, he wasn't aware that his face had become radiant because he had spoken to the LORD. 30So when Aaron and the people of Israel saw the radiance of Moses' face, they were afraid to come near him.

31But Moses called out to them and asked Aaron and all the leaders of the community to come over, and he talked with them. 32Then all the people of Israel approached him, and Moses gave them all the instructions the LORD had given him on Mount Sinai. 33When Moses finished speaking with them, he covered his face with a veil. 34But whenever he went into the Tent of Meeting to speak with the LORD, he would remove the veil until he came out again. Then he would give the people whatever instructions the LORD had given him, 35and the people of Israel would see the radiant glow of his face. So he would put the veil over his face until he returned to speak with the LORD.

Constructing the Tabernacle: Securing God's Presence in God's Way (35:1–40:38)

Instructions for the Sabbath

35 Then Moses called together the whole community of Israel and told them, "These are the instructions the LORD has commanded you to follow. 2You have six days each week for your ordinary work, but the seventh day must be a Sabbath day of complete rest, a holy day dedicated to the LORD. Anyone who works on that day must be put to death. 3You must not even light a fire in any of your homes on the Sabbath."

Offerings for the Tabernacle

4Then Moses said to the whole community of Israel, "This is what the LORD has commanded: 5Take a sacred offering for the LORD. Let those with generous hearts present the following gifts to the LORD:

34:21 Exod 31:15; 35:2
34:22 Exod 23:16
34:23 Exod 23:14-17; Deut 16:16
34:24 Exod 33:2; Josh 11:23
34:25 Exod 12:10; 23:18
34:26 Exod 23:19; Deut 26:2
34:27 Exod 17:14; 24:4
34:28 Exod 24:18; Deut 4:13; 10:4
34:29 Exod 32:15; Matt 17:2; 2 Cor 3:7, 13
34:33 2 Cor 3:13
34:34 2 Cor 3:16
34:35 2 Cor 3:13
35:1 Exod 34:32
35:2 Exod 20:9-10; 23:12; 31:15; 34:21; Num 15:32-36; Deut 5:13-14
35:3 Exod 16:23
35:4-9 //Exod 25:1-9

34:22 *Festival of Harvest:* Literally *Festival of Weeks.* • ***Festival of the Final Harvest:*** Or *Festival of Ingathering.* See notes on 23:16; Lev 23:15-19, 33-36, 39-43.

34:23 *Three times:* See 23:14-17.

34:24 *No one will . . . conquer your land:* If Israel would trust God and obey him, he would protect them.

34:27-28 *Moses* wrote down this reiteration of the general ***terms of the covenant*** (34:27), while ***the LORD*** (literally *he*) miraculously ***wrote . . . the Ten Commandments*** (literally *the ten words*), the summary of the terms, on the new ***tablets*** (34:28).

34:29-35 *Moses,* who had asked to see the glory of God, ***wasn't aware*** that his own face reflected that glory.

34:29 *the two stone tablets inscribed with the terms of the covenant:* Literally *the two tablets of the Testimony.* See note on 25:16.

34:33 *covered his face with a veil:* While Moses was reporting what God had said to him, he left his face unveiled. Then he covered it, perhaps because of the fright (34:30) its radiance caused during ordinary discourse (see 2 Cor 3:7-18 for Paul's reflection on this incident).

35:1–40:38 Much of the report of the building of the Tabernacle reiterates what was said in 25:1–31:18. There is a change from the imperative mood to the indicative, and there are certain changes in the order. This repetition underlines the point that the work was done exactly as God had commanded (see 40:16). The people had tried to secure God's presence in their own way with the gold calf, and the result was disaster. Now they were doing it in God's way, resulting in blessing (40:34-38).

35:4–36:7 Unlike the creation of the gold calf, where Aaron demanded that one type of material (earrings) be given (see note on 32:2-4), the people were again invited to bring a variety of gifts (35:4-9) as their ***hearts were stirred*** and

35:10-19
//Exod 39:32-41
35:11
[i]*mishkan* (4908)
‣Lev 8:10
35:21
Exod 25:2; 35:5
35:23
Exod 39:1
35:25
Exod 28:3
35:27
1 Chr 29:6
Ezra 2:68
35:29
1 Chr 29:9
35:30-35
//Exod 31:2-6
35:34
Exod 31:6
35:35
Exod 31:3, 6; 35:31
1 Kgs 7:14
36:1
Exod 25:8
[j]*khokmah* (2451)
‣1 Kgs 4:29

gold, silver, and bronze;
6 blue, purple, and scarlet thread;
fine linen and goat hair for cloth;
7 tanned ram skins and fine goatskin
leather;
acacia wood;
8 olive oil for the lamps;
spices for the anointing oil and the fragrant incense;
9 onyx stones, and other gemstones to be
set in the ephod and the priest's chestpiece.

10"Come, all of you who are gifted craftsmen. Construct everything that the LORD
has commanded:

11 the [i]Tabernacle and its sacred tent, its
covering, clasps, frames, crossbars,
posts, and bases;
12 the Ark and its carrying poles;
the Ark's cover—the place of atonement;
the inner curtain to shield the Ark;
13 the table, its carrying poles, and all its
utensils;
the Bread of the Presence;
14 for light, the lampstand, its accessories,
the lamp cups, and the olive oil for
lighting;
15 the incense altar and its carrying poles;
the anointing oil and fragrant incense;
the curtain for the entrance of the Tabernacle;
16 the altar of burnt offering;
the bronze grating of the altar and its
carrying poles and utensils;
the washbasin with its stand;
17 the curtains for the walls of the courtyard;
the posts and their bases;
the curtain for the entrance to the courtyard;
18 the tent pegs of the Tabernacle and
courtyard and their ropes;
19 the beautifully stitched garments for the
priests to wear while ministering in
the Holy Place—the sacred garments
for Aaron the priest, and the garments
for his sons to wear as they minister
as priests."

20So the whole community of Israel left
Moses and returned to their tents. 21All
whose hearts were stirred and whose spirits were moved came and brought their
sacred offerings to the LORD. They brought
all the materials needed for the Tabernacle, for the performance of its rituals, and
for the sacred garments. 22Both men and
women came, all whose hearts were willing.
They brought to the LORD their offerings of
gold—brooches, earrings, rings from their
fingers, and necklaces. They presented gold
objects of every kind as a special offering
to the LORD. 23All those who owned the following items willingly brought them: blue,
purple, and scarlet thread; fine linen and
goat hair for cloth; and tanned ram skins
and fine goatskin leather. 24And all who
had silver and bronze objects gave them
as a sacred offering to the LORD. And those
who had acacia wood brought it for use in
the project.

25All the women who were skilled in
sewing and spinning prepared blue, purple, and scarlet thread, and fine linen cloth.
26All the women who were willing used
their skills to spin the goat hair into yarn.
27The leaders brought onyx stones and the
special gemstones to be set in the ephod
and the priest's chestpiece. 28They also
brought spices and olive oil for the light,
the anointing oil, and the fragrant incense.
29So the people of Israel—every man and
woman who was eager to help in the work
the LORD had given them through Moses—
brought their gifts and gave them freely to
the LORD.

Craftsmen: Bezalel and Oholiab

30Then Moses told the people of Israel, "The
LORD has specifically chosen Bezalel son of
Uri, grandson of Hur, of the tribe of Judah.
31The LORD has filled Bezalel with the Spirit
of God, giving him great wisdom, ability,
and expertise in all kinds of crafts. 32He
is a master craftsman, expert in working
with gold, silver, and bronze. 33He is skilled
in engraving and mounting gemstones and
in carving wood. He is a master at every
craft. 34And the LORD has given both him
and Oholiab son of Ahisamach, of the tribe
of Dan, the ability to teach their skills to
others. 35The LORD has given them special
skills as engravers, designers, embroiderers in blue, purple, and scarlet thread on
fine linen cloth, and weavers. They excel as
craftsmen and as designers.

36 "The LORD has gifted Bezalel, Oholiab, and the other skilled craftsmen with [j]wisdom and ability to perform
any task involved in building the sanctuary.

their *spirits were moved* (35:21). Perhaps because the variety of gifts meant that everyone could bring something and because the giving was voluntary, the people gave too much and had to be commanded to stop (36:4-7).

35:21 *Tabernacle:* Literally *Tent of Meeting.* See note on 27:21.

Let them construct and furnish the Tabernacle, just as the LORD has commanded."
2So Moses summoned Bezalel and Oholiab and all the others who were specially
gifted by the LORD and were eager to get
to work. 3Moses gave them the materials
donated by the people of Israel as sacred
offerings for the completion of the sanctuary. But the people continued to bring
additional gifts each morning. 4Finally the
craftsmen who were working on the sanctuary left their work. 5They went to Moses
and reported, "The people have given more
than enough materials to complete the job
the LORD has commanded us to do!"
6So Moses gave the command, and this
message was sent throughout the camp:
"Men and women, don't prepare any more
gifts for the sanctuary. We have enough!"
So the people stopped bringing their sacred
offerings. 7Their contributions were more
than enough to complete the whole project.

Building the Tabernacle

8The skilled craftsmen made ten curtains of
finely woven linen for the Tabernacle. Then
Bezalel decorated the curtains with blue,
purple, and scarlet thread and with skillfully
embroidered cherubim. 9All ten curtains
were exactly the same size—42 feet long
and 6 feet wide. 10Five of these curtains
were joined together to make one long curtain, and the other five were joined to make
a second long curtain. 11He made fifty loops
of blue yarn and put them along the edge of
the last curtain in each set. 12The fifty loops
along the edge of one curtain matched the
fifty loops along the edge of the other curtain. 13Then he made fifty gold clasps and
fastened the long curtains together with
the clasps. In this way, the Tabernacle was
made of one continuous piece.
14He made eleven curtains of goat-hair
cloth to serve as a tent covering for the
Tabernacle. 15These eleven curtains were
all exactly the same size—45 feet long and
6 feet wide. 16Bezalel joined five of these
curtains together to make one long curtain,
and the other six were joined to make a second long curtain. 17He made fifty loops for
the edge of each large curtain. 18He also
made fifty bronze clasps to fasten the long
curtains together. In this way, the tent covering was made of one continuous piece. 19He
completed the tent covering with a layer of
tanned ram skins and a layer of fine goatskin leather.
20For the framework of the Tabernacle,
Bezalel constructed frames of acacia wood.
21Each frame was 15 feet high and 27 inches
wide, 22with two pegs under each frame. All
the frames were identical. 23He made twenty
of these frames to support the curtains on
the south side of the Tabernacle. 24He also
made forty silver bases—two bases under
each frame, with the pegs fitting securely
into the bases. 25For the north side of the
Tabernacle, he made another twenty frames,
26with their forty silver bases, two bases
under each frame. 27He made six frames
for the rear—the west side of the Tabernacle—28along with two additional frames to
reinforce the rear corners of the Tabernacle.
29These corner frames were matched at the
bottom and firmly attached at the top with
a single ring, forming a single corner unit.
Both of these corner units were made the
same way. 30So there were eight frames at
the rear of the Tabernacle, set in sixteen silver bases—two bases under each frame.
31Then he made crossbars of acacia
wood to link the frames, five crossbars for
the north side of the Tabernacle 32and five
for the south side. He also made five crossbars for the rear of the Tabernacle, which
faced west. 33He made the middle crossbar
to attach halfway up the frames; it ran all
the way from one end of the Tabernacle
to the other. 34He overlaid the frames with
gold and made gold rings to hold the crossbars. Then he overlaid the crossbars with
gold as well.
35For the inside of the Tabernacle, Bezalel made a special curtain of finely woven
linen. He decorated it with blue, purple, and
scarlet thread and with skillfully embroidered cherubim. 36For the curtain, he made
four posts of acacia wood and four gold
hooks. He overlaid the posts with gold and
set them in four silver bases.
37Then he made another curtain for the
entrance to the sacred tent. He made it of
finely woven linen and embroidered it with
exquisite designs using blue, purple, and
scarlet thread. 38This curtain was hung on
gold hooks attached to five posts. The posts
with their decorated tops and hooks were
overlaid with gold, and the five bases were
cast from bronze.

36:2 Exod 35:21, 26; 1 Chr 29:5
36:5 2 Chr 24:14; 31:6-10; 2 Cor 8:2-3
36:7 1 Kgs 8:64
36:8-38 //Exod 26:1-37
36:14 Exod 26:7
36:20-34 Exod 26:15-29; 40:18-19
36:35-38 Exod 26:31-37

36:8 *Bezalel:* Literally *he;* also in 36:16, 20, 35. See 37:1.
36:9 ***42 feet long and 6 feet wide:*** Hebrew *28 cubits* [12.9 meters] *long and 4 cubits* [1.8 meters] *wide.*
36:15 ***45 feet long and 6 feet wide:*** Hebrew *30 cubits* [13.8 meters] *long and 4 cubits* [1.8 meters] *wide.*
36:21 ***15 feet high and 27 inches wide:*** Hebrew *10 cubits* [4.6 meters] *high and 1.5 cubits* [69 centimeters] *wide.*

37:1-9
//Exod 25:10-20
37:1
Deut 10:3
37:10-16
//Exod 25:23-29; 40:22
37:17-24
//Exod 25:31-39; 40:24
37:17
Heb 9:2
Rev 1:12
37:25-28
//Exod 30:1-5
37:25
Heb 9:4
Rev 8:3
37:29
Exod 30:22-23; 40:9
Lev 8:10
38:1-7
//Exod 27:1-8; 40:10, 29

Building the Ark of the Covenant

37 Next Bezalel made the Ark of acacia wood—a sacred chest 45 inches long, 27 inches wide, and 27 inches high. 2He overlaid it inside and outside with pure gold, and he ran a molding of gold all around it. 3He cast four gold rings and attached them to its four feet, two rings on each side. 4Then he made poles from acacia wood and overlaid them with gold. 5He inserted the poles into the rings at the sides of the Ark to carry it.

6Then he made the Ark's cover—the place of atonement—from pure gold. It was 45 inches long and 27 inches wide. 7He made two cherubim from hammered gold and placed them on the two ends of the atonement cover. 8He molded the cherubim on each end of the atonement cover, making it all of one piece of gold. 9The cherubim faced each other and looked down on the atonement cover. With their wings spread above it, they protected it.

Building the Table

10Then Bezalel made the table of acacia wood, 36 inches long, 18 inches wide, and 27 inches high. 11He overlaid it with pure gold and ran a gold molding around the edge. 12He decorated it with a 3-inch border all around, and he ran a gold molding along the border. 13Then he cast four gold rings for the table and attached them at the four corners next to the four legs. 14The rings were attached near the border to hold the poles that were used to carry the table. 15He made these poles from acacia wood and overlaid them with gold. 16Then he made special containers of pure gold for the table—bowls, pans, jars, and pitchers—to be used in pouring out liquid offerings.

Building the Lampstand

17Then Bezalel made the lampstand of pure, hammered gold. He made the entire lampstand and its decorations of one piece—the base, center stem, lamp cups, buds, and petals. 18The lampstand had six branches going out from the center stem, three on each side. 19Each of the six branches had three lamp cups shaped like almond blossoms, complete with buds and petals. 20The center stem of the lampstand was crafted with four lamp cups shaped like almond blossoms, complete with buds and petals. 21There was an almond bud beneath each pair of branches where the six branches extended from the center stem, all made of one piece. 22The almond buds and branches were all of one piece with the center stem, and they were hammered from pure gold.

23He also made seven lamps for the lampstand, lamp snuffers, and trays, all of pure gold. 24The entire lampstand, along with its accessories, was made from seventy-five pounds of pure gold.

Building the Incense Altar

25Then Bezalel made the incense altar of acacia wood. It was 18 inches square and 36 inches high, with horns at the corners carved from the same piece of wood as the altar itself. 26He overlaid the top, sides, and horns of the altar with pure gold, and he ran a gold molding around the entire altar. 27He made two gold rings and attached them on opposite sides of the altar below the gold molding to hold the carrying poles. 28He made the poles of acacia wood and overlaid them with gold.

29Then he made the sacred anointing oil and the fragrant incense, using the techniques of a skilled incense maker.

Building the Altar of Burnt Offering

38 Next Bezalel used acacia wood to construct the square altar of burnt offering. It was 7½ feet wide, 7½ feet long, and 4½ feet high. 2He made horns for each of its four corners so that the horns and altar were all one piece. He overlaid the altar with bronze. 3Then he made all the altar utensils of bronze—the ash buckets, shovels, basins, meat forks, and firepans. 4Next he made a bronze grating and installed it halfway down the side of the altar, under

37:1-29 While it is said that *Bezalel made the Ark* and all the rest of the furnishings (37:1, 10, 17, 25) as well as the courtyard and its furnishings (38:1, 8, 9, 18), this is probably only a way of saying that he was responsible and directed the other craftsmen and seamstresses.

37:1 ***45 inches long, 27 inches wide, and 27 inches high:*** Hebrew *2.5 cubits* [115 centimeters] *long, 1.5 cubits* [69 centimeters] *wide, and 1.5 cubits high.*

37:6 ***45 inches long and 27 inches wide:*** Hebrew *2.5 cubits* [115 centimeters] *long and 1.5 cubits* [69 centimeters] *wide.*

37:10 ***Bezalel:*** Literally *he;* also in 37:17, 25. See 37:1. • ***36 inches long, 18 inches wide, and 27 inches high:*** Hebrew *2 cubits* [92 centimeters] *long, 1 cubit* [46 centimeters] *wide, and 1.5 cubits* [69 centimeters] *high.*

37:12 ***a 3-inch border:*** Hebrew *a border of a handbreadth* [8 centimeters].

37:24 ***seventy-five pounds:*** Hebrew *1 talent* [34 kilograms].

37:25 ***18 inches square and 36 inches high:*** Hebrew *1 cubit* [46 centimeters] *long and 1 cubit wide, a square, and 2 cubits* [92 centimeters] *high.*

38:1-20 This section reports on building the courtyard (38:9-20) and its equipment, including the altar of burnt offering (38:1-7) and the washbasin (38:8).

38:1 ***Bezalel:*** Literally *he;* also in 38:8, 9. See 37:1. • ***7½ feet wide, 7½ feet long, and 4½ feet high:*** Hebrew *5 cubits* [2.3 meters] *wide, 5 cubits long, a square, and 3 cubits* [1.4 meters] *high.*

the ledge. 5 He cast four rings and attached
them to the corners of the bronze grating to
hold the carrying poles. 6 He made the poles
from acacia wood and overlaid them with
bronze. 7 He inserted the poles through the
rings on the sides of the altar. The altar was
hollow and was made from planks.

Building the Washbasin

8 Bezalel made the bronze washbasin and its
bronze stand from bronze mirrors donated
by the women who served at the entrance of
the Tabernacle.

Building the Courtyard

9 Then Bezalel made the courtyard, which
was enclosed with curtains made of finely
woven linen. On the south side the curtains
were 150 feet long. 10 They were held up by
twenty posts set securely in twenty bronze
bases. He hung the curtains with silver
hooks and rings. 11 He made a similar set of
curtains for the north side—150 feet of curtains held up by twenty posts set securely in
bronze bases. He hung the curtains with silver hooks and rings. 12 The curtains on the
west end of the courtyard were 75 feet long,
hung with silver hooks and rings and supported by ten posts set into ten bases. 13 The
east end, the front, was also 75 feet long.

14 The courtyard entrance was on the east
end, flanked by two curtains. The curtain
on the right side was 22½ feet long and
was supported by three posts set into three
bases. 15 The curtain on the left side was also
22½ feet long and was supported by three
posts set into three bases. 16 All the curtains
used in the courtyard were made of finely
woven linen. 17 Each post had a bronze base,
and all the hooks and rings were silver. The
tops of the posts of the courtyard were overlaid with silver, and the rings to hold up the
curtains were made of silver.

18 He made the curtain for the entrance
to the courtyard of finely woven linen, and
he decorated it with beautiful embroidery
in blue, purple, and scarlet thread. It was
30 feet long, and its height was 7½ feet, just
like the curtains of the courtyard walls. 19 It
was supported by four posts, each set securely in its own bronze base. The tops of
the posts were overlaid with silver, and the
hooks and rings were also made of silver.

20 All the tent pegs used in the Tabernacle
and courtyard were made of bronze.

Inventory of Materials

21 This is an inventory of the materials
used in building the Tabernacle of the Covenant. The Levites compiled the figures, as
Moses directed, and Ithamar son of Aaron
the priest served as recorder. 22 Bezalel son
of Uri, grandson of Hur, of the tribe of Judah, made everything just as the LORD had
commanded Moses. 23 He was assisted by
Oholiab son of Ahisamach, of the tribe
of Dan, a craftsman expert at engraving,
designing, and embroidering with blue, purple, and scarlet thread on fine linen cloth.

24 The people brought special offerings
of gold totaling 2,193 pounds, as measured
by the weight of the sanctuary shekel. This
gold was used throughout the Tabernacle.

25 The whole community of Israel gave
7,545 pounds of silver, as measured by the
weight of the sanctuary shekel. 26 This silver came from the tax collected from each
man registered in the census. (The tax is
one beka, which is half a shekel, based on
the sanctuary shekel.) The tax was collected
from 603,550 men who had reached their
twentieth birthday. 27 The hundred bases for
the frames of the sanctuary walls and for the
posts supporting the inner curtain required
7,500 pounds of silver, about 75 pounds for
each base. 28 The remaining 45 pounds of

38:8
Exod 30:18

38:9-20
//Exod 27:9-19; 40:8

38:25-26
Exod 12:37; 30:11-16
Num 1:46; 26:51

38:8 While the plans for the ***washbasin*** (30:17-21) were included in the instructions to the priests (29:38–30:38), here its construction is reported in logical sequence. • This ***bronze,*** which could be polished to a mirror-like finish, was probably of especially high quality, as was fitting for use in God's Tabernacle. • ***Tabernacle:*** Literally *Tent of Meeting;* also in 38:30. See note on 27:21.

38:9 ***150 feet long:*** Hebrew *100 cubits* [46 meters]; also in 38:11.

38:12 ***75 feet long:*** Hebrew *50 cubits* [23 meters]; also in 38:13.

38:14 ***22½ feet long:*** Hebrew *15 cubits* [6.9 meters]; also in 38:15.

38:18 ***30 feet long, and its height was 7½ feet:*** Hebrew *20 cubits* [9.2 meters] *long and 5 cubits* [2.3 meters] *high.*

38:21-29 The immense amount of metal reported in this inventory of materials (more than a ton of ***gold,*** almost four tons of ***silver,*** and two and a half tons of ***bronze***) reflects the Egyptians' eagerness to get the Israelites out of Egypt, giving the Israelites anything they asked for in order to hurry them on their way (see 12:35-36).

38:21 Since the Tabernacle contained the Ark of the Covenant, it is called the ***Tabernacle of the Covenant*** (literally *the Tabernacle, the Tabernacle of the Testimony*; see note on 25:16).

38:24 ***2,193 pounds:*** Hebrew *29 talents and 730 shekels* [994 kilograms]. Each shekel weighed about 0.4 ounces.

38:25 ***7,545 pounds:*** Hebrew *100 talents and 1,775 shekels* [3,420 kilograms].

38:26 For the earlier discussion of this ***tax,*** see 30:11-16. • ***one beka, which is half a shekel:*** Or *0.2 ounces, or 6 grams.* The ***sanctuary shekel*** was evidently the standard against which other weights were measured for accuracy. • ***603,550:*** See note on 12:37.

38:27 ***7,500 pounds of silver, about 75 pounds for each base:*** Hebrew *100 talents* [3,400 kilograms] *of silver, 1 talent* [34 kilograms] *for each base.*

38:28 ***45 pounds:*** Hebrew *1,775 shekels* [20.2 kilograms].

39:1 Exod 35:23
39:2-7 //Exod 28:6-14
39:8-21 //Exod 28:15-28
39:14 Rev 21:12
39:22-31 //Exod 28:31-43
39:27 Exod 28:39-40, 42

silver was used to make the hooks and rings
and to overlay the tops of the posts.
29The people also brought as special offerings 5,310 pounds of bronze, 30which
was used for casting the bases for the posts
at the entrance to the Tabernacle, and for
the bronze altar with its bronze grating and
all the altar utensils. 31Bronze was also used
to make the bases for the posts that supported the curtains around the courtyard,
the bases for the curtain at the entrance of
the courtyard, and all the tent pegs for the
Tabernacle and the courtyard.

Clothing for the Priests

39 The craftsmen made beautiful sacred garments of blue, purple, and
scarlet cloth—clothing for Aaron to wear
while ministering in the Holy Place, just as
the LORD had commanded Moses.

Making the Ephod

2Bezalel made the ephod of finely woven
linen and embroidered it with gold and with
blue, purple, and scarlet thread. 3He made
gold thread by hammering out thin sheets
of gold and cutting it into fine strands.
With great skill and care, he worked it into
the fine linen with the blue, purple, and scarlet thread.
4The ephod consisted of two pieces, front
and back, joined at the shoulders with two
shoulder-pieces. 5The decorative sash was
made of the same materials: finely woven
linen embroidered with gold and with blue,
purple, and scarlet thread, just as the LORD
had commanded Moses. 6They mounted
the two onyx stones in settings of gold filigree. The stones were engraved with the
names of the tribes of Israel, just as a seal is
engraved. 7He fastened these stones on the
shoulder-pieces of the ephod as a reminder
that the priest represents the people of Israel. All this was done just as the LORD had
commanded Moses.

Making the Chestpiece

8Bezalel made the chestpiece with great
skill and care. He made it to match the
ephod, using finely woven linen embroidered with gold and with blue, purple, and
scarlet thread. 9He made the chestpiece
of a single piece of cloth folded to form a
pouch nine inches square. 10They mounted
four rows of gemstones on it. The first row
contained a red carnelian, a pale-green
peridot, and an emerald. 11The second row
contained a turquoise, a blue lapis lazuli,
and a white moonstone. 12The third row
contained an orange jacinth, an agate, and
a purple amethyst. 13The fourth row contained a blue-green beryl, an onyx, and a
green jasper. All these stones were set in
gold filigree. 14Each stone represented one
of the twelve sons of Israel, and the name of
that tribe was engraved on it like a seal.
15To attach the chestpiece to the ephod,
they made braided cords of pure gold thread.
16They also made two settings of gold filigree and two gold rings and attached them
to the top corners of the chestpiece. 17They
tied the two gold cords to the rings on the
chestpiece. 18They tied the other ends of
the cords to the gold settings on the shoulder-pieces of the ephod. 19Then they made
two more gold rings and attached them to
the inside edges of the chestpiece next to
the ephod. 20Then they made two more
gold rings and attached them to the front of
the ephod, below the shoulder-pieces, just
above the knot where the decorative sash
was fastened to the ephod. 21They attached
the bottom rings of the chestpiece to the
rings on the ephod with blue cords. In this
way, the chestpiece was held securely to the
ephod above the decorative sash. All this
was done just as the LORD had commanded
Moses.

Additional Clothing for the Priests

22Bezalel made the robe that is worn with
the ephod from a single piece of blue woven cloth, 23with an opening for Aaron's
head in the middle of it. The opening was
reinforced with a woven collar so it would
not tear. 24They made pomegranates of
blue, purple, and scarlet yarn, and attached
them to the hem of the robe. 25They also
made bells of pure gold and placed them
between the pomegranates along the hem
of the robe, 26with bells and pomegranates
alternating all around the hem. This robe
was to be worn whenever the priest ministered before the LORD, just as the LORD had
commanded Moses.
27They made tunics for Aaron and his
sons from fine linen cloth. 28The turban
and the special head coverings were made
of fine linen, and the undergarments were

38:29 ***5,310 pounds:*** Hebrew *70 talents and 2,400 shekels* [2,407 kilograms].

39:1-31 See 28:1-43 and notes.

39:2 *Bezalel:* Literally *He;* also in 39:8, 22. See 36:1-3.

39:9 *nine inches:* Hebrew *1 span* [23 centimeters].

39:10 The identification of some of these *gemstones* is uncertain.

39:23 ***The opening was reinforced with a woven collar:*** The meaning of the Hebrew is uncertain.

also made of finely woven linen. 29 The sashes were made of finely woven linen and embroidered with blue, purple, and scarlet thread, just as the LORD had commanded Moses.

30 Finally, they made the sacred medallion—the badge of holiness—of pure gold. They engraved it like a seal with these words: HOLY TO THE LORD. 31 They attached the medallion with a blue cord to Aaron's turban, just as the LORD had commanded Moses.

Moses Inspects the Work

32 And so at last the Tabernacle was finished. The Israelites had done everything just as the LORD had commanded Moses. 33 And they brought the entire Tabernacle to Moses:

the sacred tent with all its furnishings,
clasps, frames, crossbars, posts, and bases;
34 the tent coverings of tanned ram skins and fine goatskin leather;
the inner curtain to shield the Ark;
35 the Ark of the Covenant and its carrying poles;
the Ark's cover—the place of atonement;
36 the table and all its utensils;
the Bread of the Presence;
37 the pure gold lampstand with its symmetrical lamp cups, all its accessories, and the olive oil for lighting;
38 the gold altar;
the anointing oil and fragrant incense;
the curtain for the entrance of the sacred tent;
39 the bronze altar;
the bronze grating and its carrying poles and utensils;
the washbasin with its stand;
40 the curtains for the walls of the courtyard;
the posts and their bases;
the curtain for the entrance to the courtyard;
the ropes and tent pegs;
all the furnishings to be used in worship at the Tabernacle;
41 the beautifully stitched garments for the priests to wear while ministering in the Holy Place—the sacred garments for Aaron the priest, and the garments for his sons to wear as they minister as priests.

42 So the people of Israel followed all of the LORD's instructions to Moses. 43 Then Moses inspected all their work. When he found it had been done just as the LORD had commanded him, he blessed them.

Setting Up the Tabernacle

40 Then the LORD said to Moses, 2 "Set up the Tabernacle on the first day of the new year. 3 Place the Ark of the Covenant inside, and install the inner curtain to enclose the Ark within the Most Holy Place. 4 Then bring in the table, and arrange the utensils on it. And bring in the lampstand, and set up the lamps.

5 "Place the gold incense altar in front of the Ark of the Covenant. Then hang the curtain at the entrance of the Tabernacle. 6 Place the altar of burnt offering in front of the Tabernacle entrance. 7 Set the washbasin between the Tabernacle and the altar, and fill it with water. 8 Then set up the courtyard around the outside of the tent, and hang the curtain for the courtyard entrance.

9 "Take the anointing oil and [k]anoint the Tabernacle and all its furnishings to consecrate them and make them holy. 10 Anoint

39:30 Exod 28:36-37
39:32-41 //Exod 35:10-19
39:43 Lev 9:22-23; Num 6:23-26; 1 Kgs 8:14; 2 Chr 30:27
40:2 Exod 12:2; 40:17; Num 1:1
40:3 Exod 26:33; 40:21-30; Num 4:5
40:4 Exod 25:30
40:7 Exod 30:18
40:9 Exod 30:26
[k]*mashakh* (4886) ‣ Lev 8:11

39:30 The designation *badge of holiness* is perhaps a formal title; it does not appear in the first description of the *sacred medallion* in 28:36.

39:32-43 *Moses* inspected the finished work and confirmed that everything *had been done just as the LORD had commanded* (39:43). As a result, Moses *blessed them* instead of pronouncing judgment upon them, as when they had tried to meet their need for God's presence in their own ways (32:27).

39:32 *the Tabernacle:* Literally *the Tabernacle, the Tent of Meeting;* also in 39:40. See note on 27:21.

39:35 *Ark of the Covenant:* Literally *Ark of the Testimony.* See note on 25:16.

40:1-33 The report on setting up the Tabernacle begins with the Lord's commands to do so (40:1-15) and continues with the report on how Moses obeyed those commands (40:16-33). • The repeated statement that Moses did everything *just as the LORD had commanded him* (40:16, 19, 21, 23, 25, 27, 29, 32) is in radical contrast to Aaron's self-serving statement in 32:22-24. God wishes to share his presence with us, but his holiness is such that this can occur only if we renounce our own efforts to secure his presence and gifts.

40:2 *the Tabernacle:* Literally *the Tabernacle, the Tent of Meeting;* also in 40:6, 29. See note on 27:21. In the Tabernacle, the Tent of Meeting, the divine King met with Israel to communicate his will to them (see also notes on 25:1–40:38; 25:22). • *the first day of the new year* (literally *the first day of the first month*): This day of the ancient Hebrew lunar calendar occurred in March or April. The Tabernacle was set up one year after God announced the Passover and the start of Israel's calendar (see chart, "Israel's Annual Calendar," p. 145).

40:3 *Ark of the Covenant:* Or *Ark of the Testimony;* also in 40:5, 21. The Hebrew word translated *Covenant* is *'eduth* ("testimony"), which refers particularly to the covenant stipulations; see note on 25:16. The written copy of these stipulations contained in the Ark would serve as a testimony to the covenant Israel had entered into with God.

40:7 *Tabernacle:* Literally *Tent of Meeting;* also in 40:12, 22, 24, 26, 30, 32, 34, 35. See note on 27:21.

40:12 Lev 8:1-13
40:15 Exod 29:9; Num 25:13
40:17 Exod 40:2; Num 7:1
40:20 Exod 25:16; Deut 10:5; 1 Kgs 8:9; 2 Chr 5:10; Heb 9:4; *ᵃ'aron* (0727) ‣Num 10:33
40:23 Exod 25:30; Lev 24:5-8
40:31 Exod 30:19-21
40:34 Num 9:15-23; 1 Kgs 8:11
40:35 1 Kgs 8:10-11
40:36 Num 9:17; 10:11
40:37 Num 9:19-22
40:38 1 Cor 10:1

the altar of burnt offering and its utensils
to consecrate them. Then the altar will become absolutely holy. 11Next anoint the
washbasin and its stand to consecrate
them.

12"Present Aaron and his sons at the entrance of the Tabernacle, and wash them
with water. 13Dress Aaron with the sacred
garments and anoint him, consecrating
him to serve me as a priest. 14Then present
his sons and dress them in their tunics.
15Anoint them as you did their father, so
they may also serve me as priests. With
their anointing, Aaron's descendants are set
apart for the priesthood forever, from generation to generation."

16Moses proceeded to do everything just
as the LORD had commanded him. 17So the
Tabernacle was set up on the first day of
the first month of the second year. 18Moses
erected the Tabernacle by setting down its
bases, inserting the frames, attaching the
crossbars, and setting up the posts. 19Then
he spread the coverings over the Tabernacle
framework and put on the protective layers,
just as the LORD had commanded him.

20He took the stone tablets inscribed
with the terms of the covenant and placed
them inside the ᵃArk. Then he attached the
carrying poles to the ᵃArk, and he set the
Ark's cover—the place of atonement—on
top of it. 21Then he brought the Ark of the
Covenant into the Tabernacle and hung the
inner curtain to shield it from view, just as
the LORD had commanded him.

22Next Moses placed the table in the Tabernacle, along the north side of the Holy
Place, just outside the inner curtain. 23And
he arranged the Bread of the Presence on
the table before the LORD, just as the LORD
had commanded him.

24He set the lampstand in the Tabernacle
across from the table on the south side of
the Holy Place. 25Then he lit the lamps in
the LORD's presence, just as the LORD had
commanded him. 26He also placed the gold
incense altar in the Tabernacle, in the Holy
Place in front of the inner curtain. 27On it
he burned the fragrant incense, just as the
LORD had commanded him.

28He hung the curtain at the entrance
of the Tabernacle, 29and he placed the altar of burnt offering near the Tabernacle
entrance. On it he offered a burnt offering
and a grain offering, just as the LORD had
commanded him.

30Next Moses placed the washbasin between the Tabernacle and the altar. He
filled it with water so the priests could wash
themselves. 31Moses and Aaron and Aaron's
sons used water from it to wash their hands
and feet. 32Whenever they approached
the altar and entered the Tabernacle, they
washed themselves, just as the LORD had
commanded Moses.

33Then he hung the curtains forming
the courtyard around the Tabernacle and
the altar. And he set up the curtain at the
entrance of the courtyard. So at last Moses
finished the work.

The LORD's Glory Fills the Tabernacle

34Then the cloud covered the Tabernacle,
and the glory of the LORD filled the Tabernacle. 35Moses could no longer enter the
Tabernacle because the cloud had settled
down over it, and the glory of the LORD
filled the Tabernacle.

36Now whenever the cloud lifted from
the Tabernacle, the people of Israel would
set out on their journey, following it. 37But if
the cloud did not rise, they remained where
they were until it lifted. 38The cloud of the
LORD hovered over the Tabernacle during
the day, and at night fire glowed inside the
cloud so the whole family of Israel could
see it. This continued throughout all their
journeys.

40:20 ***He took the stone tablets inscribed with the terms of the covenant:*** Literally *He placed the Testimony.* See note on 25:16.

40:33 ***So at last Moses finished the work:*** See note on 37:1-29.

40:34-38 The climax of the Exodus occurred when the ***glory of the LORD filled the Tabernacle.*** God's goal from the outset was not merely to deliver his people from their bondage, but to bring them into a relationship with himself. Their real need was to know God personally in their lives. Without that, the Promised Land would not be a land of promise. Now it would be, because the glory that had been on Mount Sinai was in Israel's midst; it would not be left behind, but would travel with them wherever they might go.

40:38 ***the whole family of Israel:*** This description is reminiscent of the way the book began (see 1:1-7). Jacob's family had become slaves in Egypt. What a dramatic change had occurred! They were no longer slaves. They were now in a position to be a blessing to the earth, as God had promised to Abraham generations earlier (Gen 12:3).

THE BOOK OF

LEVITICUS

Leviticus enabled ancient Israel to live in relationship with a holy God. But what do laws governing ancient Israel's system of worship, with its priests and animal sacrifices, have to do with us? Jesus Christ became our High Priest and ultimate sacrifice, thereby fulfilling many of these requirements. Yet Leviticus is important to us today because it increases our understanding of God's holiness. God's demand for those who know him remains the same: "I am the LORD your God. . . . You must be holy because I am holy" (11:44-45; 1 Pet 1:15-16).

SETTING

Leviticus continues the great redemptive story that began with the promises made to Abraham (Gen 12, 15, 17) and the liberation of the Israelites from bondage in Egypt. The Israelites had not yet wandered in the wilderness or entered the Promised Land of Canaan. At the writing of this book, Israel was camped at the foot of Mount Sinai. With Moses as his mediator, God had already established his covenant with Israel, declaring the Israelites as his special treasure, royal priesthood, and chosen people (Exod 19:5-6). The people had received the Ten Commandments (Exod 20:1-17), the plans for the Tabernacle (Exod 25–27, 30), and the institution of the priesthood (Exod 28–29). The Tabernacle had been completed and dedicated (Exod 35–40). Here, in Leviticus, God spoke to Moses about his nature, providing instructions about worship and conduct appropriate for Israel as his covenant people.

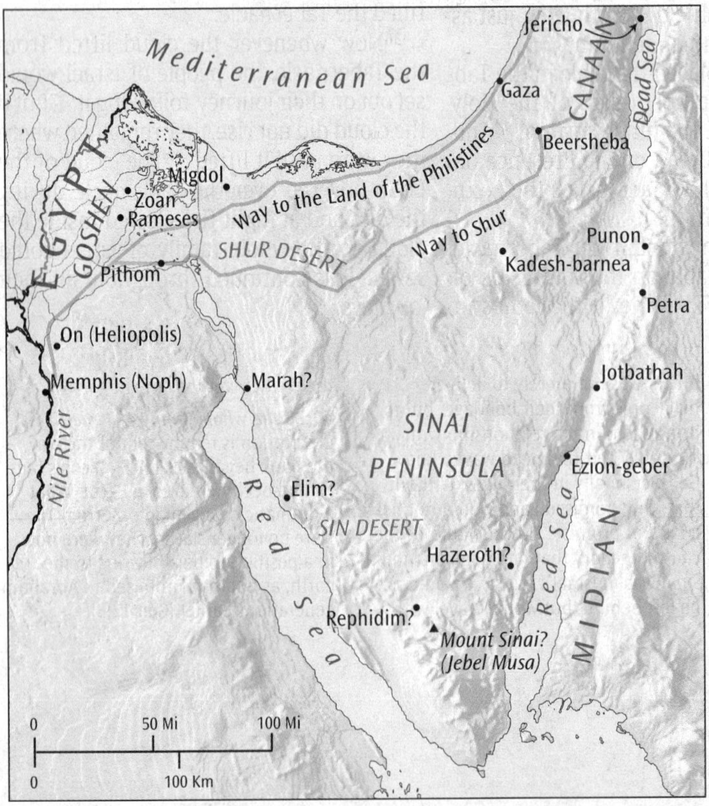

◂ **Israel at Sinai.** After leaving slavery in EGYPT, Israel camped at MOUNT SINAI for about a year (Exod 19:1; Num 10:11-12). The Lord gave many of his instructions to Israel during this time, including those recorded in the book of Leviticus. For information about Israel's route to and from Sinai, see map on p. 122 and map on p. 246.

SUMMARY

The regulations in Leviticus deal primarily with the activities and responsibilities of the priestly tribe of Levi, especially the high priest (Exod 28:1-43; Num 3:44–4:49). Moses recorded God's instructions about the Tabernacle, the priesthood, sacrifices, holy days, and ceremonial purity. Three main concerns are evident throughout Leviticus: the holiness of God, what is appropriate in worshiping a holy God, and how Israel was to be holy in relation to God.

A proper relationship with God begins with knowing who God is and understanding his nature. Yet finite human minds cannot fully comprehend God, the Eternal One. Worse, if left to our own intuition, we inevitably begin to worship idols rather than the true God. In Leviticus, God graciously reveals his holiness in tangible ways and instructs the people how to worship him acceptably. Each sacrifice and holy day teaches the Israelites something about God and what he requires of them.

God calls Israel to know him and to lovingly serve him (Deut 6:5; 11:1). As a result, they will also love and serve one another (Lev 19:18, 33-34). The rituals and regulations revealed in Leviticus teach the Israelites how to integrate love and service into their lives, both as individuals and as a nation.

OUTLINE

1:1–7:38
The Offering System

8:1–10:20
The Institution of the Priesthood

11:1–15:33
Regulations Pertaining to Purity

16:1-34
The Day of Atonement

17:1–26:46
Expressions of Holiness in the Community

27:1-34
Regulations Pertaining to Vows and Tithes

AUTHORSHIP

Some modern scholars believe that Leviticus was written during Israel's exile in Babylon (about 586–539 BC), long after the time of Moses. This view, however, does not explain why Judaism during the Exile, which was increasingly oriented around the rabbi and the synagogue, would be concerned with the priesthood and the Tabernacle. Nor does it explain the rituals followed in Israelite worship prior to the Exile, aside from the liturgy contained or implied in the Psalms.

It is most likely that Moses wrote Leviticus during Israel's time in the wilderness after the Exodus. Both Jewish tradition and the early Christian church identified Moses as the author of Leviticus. Moses, raised in the court of Egypt's king, would have been skilled in reading, writing, and mathematics (see Acts 7:20-22) and quite capable of writing Leviticus. The book begins (1:1) and ends (27:34) with statements affirming that the contents of Leviticus were given to Israel by God through Moses. Leviticus repeatedly describes how Moses received the Lord's instructions (e.g., 4:1; 5:14; 6:1, 8, 19, 24; 7:22, 28; 8:1) and carried them out (8:1–10:20). The OT often refers to Moses as the author of the Pentateuch (Genesis—Deuteronomy; see Josh 8:31-32; 23:6; 1 Kgs 2:3; 2 Kgs 14:6; 23:25; 2 Chr

TIMELINE

1500–1200 BC
Late Bronze Age

1446 / 1270 BC*
Israel leaves Egypt (the Exodus), moves to Mount Sinai
The covenant at Sinai

1406 / 1230 BC
Genesis—Deuteronomy are drafted
Moses dies
Israel enters Canaan

* *The two dates harmonize with the traditional "early" chronology and a more recent "late" chronology of the Exodus. All dates are approximate. Please see "Chronology: Abraham to Joshua," p. 118.*

God ordained diverse kinds of oblations and sacrifices. . . . He declared by these sacrifices and ceremonies that the reward of sin is death and that without the blood of Christ, the innocent Lamb of God, there can be no forgiveness of sins.

MATTHEW HENRY
Commentary on the Bible

No person can be his own saviour or mediator. An individual must come before God in penitence, confess his sin and obtain pardon from a merciful God who repudiates sin but shows covenant love to the sinner.

R. K. HARRISON
Leviticus, p. 32

23:18; 30:16; Ezra 3:2; 7:6; Neh 8:1; Dan 9:11-13). The NT does the same (Matt 19:7-8; Luke 2:22; 24:44; John 7:19, 23; 28:23; Rom 10:5; 1 Cor 9:9; Heb 10:28). See further "Introduction to the Pentateuch: Authorship," p. 11.

MEANING AND MESSAGE

"You must be holy because I, the L*ORD your God, am holy."*— Lev 19:2

Although it is set in an ancient time and culture, Leviticus communicates a timeless and vibrant message: God is holy, and he expects his people to be like him. God's holiness and his gracious redemption provide both the grounds and the motivation for his people's own holiness (11:44-45).

The priests, as mediators of the covenant, stood between God and the people. The priests interpreted what was holy and how holiness should be expressed in the community. The atoning sacrifices provided the way for the people to have their sins forgiven and to be made right with God (atonement). The non-atoning sacrifices celebrated the people's relationship with God through gifts and shared meals. While surrounding nations offered sacrifices to their gods to appease them and gain their favor, Israel's worship was not designed to manipulate God. Rather, the worship prepared and purified the people so they could approach their holy God. Each of the laws, ceremonies, and holy days teaches that God is holy and that he expects his people to be holy, a motif that embraces both Old and New Covenants (see 1 Cor 3:17; 1 Pet 1:15).

Forgiveness of sin and reconciliation to God directly relate to how people treat one another. Concern for social justice pervades Leviticus, which sets forth obligations to one's neighbor, to the poor, and to foreigners. God loves people (Exod 34:6-7), especially the people he calls his own. He expects those in covenant with him to love each other as an expression of his love (cp. Matt 22:39; Mark 12:31; Luke 10:27; Rom 13:9; Gal 5:14; Jas 2:8). Atonement and social justice are closely connected with the holiness that God requires of his people.

FURTHER READING

R. K. HARRISON
Leviticus (1980)

G. J. WENHAM
The Book of Leviticus (1979)

A. NOORDTZIJ
Leviticus (1982)

DAVID BAKER
Leviticus in *Cornerstone Biblical Commentary*, vol. 2 (2008)

1. THE OFFERING SYSTEM (1:1–7:38)

The Whole Burnt Offering (1:1-17)

1 The LORD called to Moses from the
Tabernacle and said to him, 2"Give the
following instructions to the people of Israel. When you present an animal as an
offering to the LORD, you may take it from
your herd of cattle or your flock of sheep
and goats.
3"If the animal you present as a burnt offering is from the herd, it must be a male
with no defects. Bring it to the entrance of

1:1
Exod 25:22
Num 7:89

1:2
Lev 6:9-13; 17:1-8; 22:19-25

1:3
Heb 9:14

1:1–7:38 The first major section of Leviticus deals with the institution of the sacrificial system and the priesthood. The sacrifices were either for atonement (the whole burnt offering, sin offering, and guilt offering) or for worship (grain offering and peace offering). Each one taught theology through a hands-on approach. Priests were required to officiate in the sacrificial worship at the Tabernacle, to instruct God's people in the revelation given to Moses at Sinai, and to represent the people before God, such as on the Day of Atonement (ch 16). Priests were provided for by receiving a portion of the offerings.

1:1 ***The LORD called to Moses from the Tabernacle:*** Leviticus is part of the ongoing narrative of the Pentateuch (Gen—Deut). It is part of the history of God's saving acts: God chose Israel to be his people, delivered them from slavery in Egypt, entered into a covenant relationship with them, and guided them through the desert to the Promised Land. Specifically, Leviticus picks up with events recorded in Exod 40:34-38, when construction of the Tabernacle is completed. It has been dedicated, and the Lord has filled it with his glory. Now the Lord gives Moses instructions for conducting worship at the Tabernacle. • The ***Tabernacle*** (literally *Tent of Meeting;* also in 1:3, 5) was an earthly representation of God's palace. Inside the Most Holy Place, the Ark of the Covenant represented God's throne (Exod 40:1-33). The Lord's glory resided between the outstretched wings of the cherubim. There he would meet with Israel to communicate his will to them (see Exod 25:22). The term "Tent of Meeting" sometimes refers to the actual tent of the Tabernacle and sometimes to the entire complex, including

1:4
Exod 29:10, 15, 19
Lev 4:13-35
Num 8:10-12; 15:25
2 Chr 29:23-24

1:5
Lev 1:11; 3:8
Heb 12:24
[a]*kohen* (3548)
‣ Num 3:6

1:6
Lev 7:8

1:8
Exod 29:13

1:9
Gen 8:21
Exod 29:17
Eph 5:2

the Tabernacle so you may be accepted by
the LORD. 4Lay your hand on the animal's
head, and the LORD will accept its death in
your place to purify you, making you right
with him. 5Then slaughter the young bull in
the LORD's presence, and Aaron's sons, the
[a]priests, will present the animal's blood by
splattering it against all sides of the altar
that stands at the entrance to the Tabernacle. 6Then skin the animal and cut it into
pieces. 7The sons of Aaron the priest will
build a wood fire on the altar. 8They will arrange the pieces of the offering, including
the head and fat, on the wood burning on
the altar. 9But the internal organs and the
legs must first be washed with water. Then
the priest will burn the entire sacrifice on
the altar as a burnt offering. It is a special
gift, a pleasing aroma to the LORD.

10"If the animal you present as a burnt offering is from the flock, it may be either a
sheep or a goat, but it must be a male with
no defects. 11Slaughter the animal on the
north side of the altar in the LORD's presence,
and Aaron's sons, the priests, will splatter its
blood against all sides of the altar. 12Then
cut the animal in pieces, and the priests will
arrange the pieces of the offering, including
the head and fat, on the wood burning on
the altar. 13But the internal organs and the
legs must first be washed with water. Then
the priest will burn the entire sacrifice on
the altar as a burnt offering. It is a special
gift, a pleasing aroma to the LORD.

. . . .

the courtyard. The term is essentially synonymous with "Tabernacle," so the NLT consistently renders it "Tabernacle."

1:2-3 *When:* This word introduces a major category (the process of presenting an offering), followed by a series of conditions introduced by *if* (1:3, 10, 14). This *when/if* pattern is generally followed through all the major offerings described in 1:2–6:7. • ***offering*** (Hebrew *qorban;* see note on Mark 7:11) is a general term referring to all kinds of offerings and gifts, including the various offerings described in Lev 1–7.

1:3-17 ***burnt offering*** (Hebrew *'olah,* "what goes up"): The Hebrew word implies the ascent of ***the animal*** in flame and smoke. Except for its hide, given in payment to the officiating priest (7:8), this offering was burned completely on the altar (1:9). Its purpose was to satisfy God's wrath against sin, ceremonially cleansing the worshiper and restoring him or her to fellowship with God (cp. Rom 3:25; 8:3; 2 Cor 5:18-21). The whole burnt offering occurs first in this list of offerings (1:1–7:38), providing a pattern for offerings that follow. It is the most common and most general atoning offering.

1:3 ***male with no defects:*** God allowed female and slightly deformed animals for certain types of non-atoning offerings (see 3:1; 4:27-31; 22:23), but not for the whole burnt offering. In the dry, brush-encrusted hills of southern Palestine, cattle were much more difficult to raise than sheep or goats. This meant a bull without defect was an animal of great value. Centuries later, the prophet Malachi confronted the people for offering sick and lame animals instead of those without defect (Mal 1:6-14). • ***so you may be accepted:*** Or *so it may be accepted.*

1:4 ***Lay your hand on the animal's head:*** The sacrificial animal represented the worshiper in the ceremony (4:4, 15, 24, 29, 33; 16:21). This act signified that the animal's death represented the death of its owner. In the ritual for the Day of Atonement, it signified that the sins of the owner were transferred to the animal (16:20-22). With the peace offering (3:2, 8, 13), the act seems to have indicated ownership of the animal being sacrificed. • The phrase ***in your place*** may mean "in payment for sin" (sometimes called *expiation*) or "as a substitute for the sinner's death" (sometimes called *propitiation*). • ***to purify you, making you right with him*** (or *to make atonement for you*): Although older commentaries describe this process as "covering over" sin, recent scholarship defines it as "blotting out, erasing, or cleansing from" sin. The concept involves satisfying God's wrath against sin, ceremonially cleansing the worshiper, and restoring fellowship with God in the community of God's people.

1:5 ***Aaron's sons:*** The descendants of Levi, Moses' own tribe, were divided into two categories: (1) priests, who were descendants of Aaron, the first high priest; and (2) Levites, who served in subordinate roles (Exod 28:1-4; Num 18:1-7). The instructions given here applied to later generations as well. • The ***blood*** was a symbol of life, not of death. The Israelite system of sacrifice was based on the principle of substitution, and the shedding of sacrificial blood was essential for atonement. It represented sacrificing the life of the animal as a substitute for the life of the worshiper (17:10-14; Heb 9:22). The blood of Jesus Christ was shed as the ultimate sacrifice for sin (Heb 9:11-14). • The ***altar*** of burnt offering was located in the east end of the courtyard, outside the Tabernacle but inside the entrance to the courtyard (Exod 40:6, 29).

1:6 The entire animal was to be burned, except for the ***skin,*** which was the priest's share of the offering (7:8).

1:8 The Hebrew word translated ***fat*** describes the suet, or hard fat, from around the kidneys and loins. This specific term occurs only here and in 1:12 and 8:20. All fat—not just this special fat—was considered God's portion (3:14-17; 7:23-25; see 1 Sam 2:15-17). Only the whole burnt offering was entirely consumed on the altar. With other offerings, the fatty portions and certain internal organs were burned; the rest belonged to the officiating priests and sometimes to the worshiper (7:11-18).

1:9 The offering was ***washed with water*** to remove dirt or debris that might contaminate the offering. Washing was also part of purification from ritual uncleanness, a prerequisite for Tabernacle service (6:27; 11:28). • ***special gift:*** The Hebrew term (*'isheh*) has traditionally been rendered "offering made by fire." Although the offering was to be burned (1:13, 17), recent scholarship suggests that the word had the more generic meaning of "gift." • ***pleasing aroma to the LORD*** (literally *a restful odor;* also in 1:13, 17): Pagan people of the ancient Near East believed that their gods smelled the offerings because they needed to eat them to sustain their lives. Although God's response is sometimes represented in language that reflects the cultural setting (e.g., 21:6; Num 28:2), the Bible is clear that God did not need offerings as food (Ps 50:9-13). Instead, they pleased him as sincere offerings for the purpose of atonement.

1:10-13 Permission to offer lesser animals was to make the animal, and therefore atonement, more affordable to common Israelites. The method of offering these animals closely parallels the offering of bulls outlined in 1:3-9.

14“If you present a bird as a burnt offering
to the LORD, choose either a turtledove or a
young pigeon. 15The priest will take the bird
to the altar, wring off its head, and burn it
on the altar. But first he must drain its blood
against the side of the altar. 16The priest
must also remove the crop and the feathers
and throw them in the ashes on the east side
of the altar. 17Then, grasping the bird by its
wings, the priest will tear the bird open, but
without tearing it apart. Then he will burn it
as a burnt offering on the wood burning on
the altar. It is a special gift, a pleasing aroma
to the LORD.

The Grain Offering (2:1-16)

2 “When you present grain as an offering
to the LORD, the offering must consist of
choice flour. You are to pour olive oil on it,
sprinkle it with frankincense, 2and bring it
to Aaron’s sons, the priests. The priest will
scoop out a handful of the flour moistened
with oil, together with all the frankincense,
and burn this representative portion on the
altar. It is a special gift, a pleasing aroma to
the LORD. 3The rest of the grain offering
will then be given to Aaron and his sons.
This offering will be considered a most
holy part of the special gifts presented to
the LORD.

4“If your offering is a grain offering baked
in an oven, it must be made of choice flour,
but without any yeast. It may be presented
in the form of thin cakes mixed with olive
oil or wafers spread with olive oil. 5If your
grain offering is cooked on a griddle, it must
be made of choice flour mixed with olive oil
but without any yeast. 6Break it in pieces and
pour olive oil on it; it is a grain offering. 7If
your grain offering is prepared in a pan, it
must be made of choice flour and olive oil.

8“No matter how a grain offering for the
LORD has been prepared, bring it to the
priest, who will present it at the altar. 9The
priest will take a representative portion of
the grain offering and burn it on the altar.
It is a special gift, a pleasing aroma to the
LORD. 10The rest of the grain offering will
then be given to Aaron and his sons as their
food. This offering will be considered a
most holy part of the special gifts presented
to the LORD.

11“Do not use yeast in preparing any of
the grain offerings you present to the LORD,
because no yeast or honey may be burned
as a special gift presented to the LORD.

1:14 Gen 15:9; Lev 12:8
1:15 Lev 5:8-9
2:1 Exod 29:2; Lev 6:14-18; 24:7; Num 15:4-21
2:2 Lev 5:12-13; 6:15-18
2:3 Lev 10:12-13
2:4 Exod 29:2; Lev 7:12
2:9 Gen 8:21; Lev 2:2; 6:15
2:10 Lev 2:3
2:11 Lev 6:16-17

1:14-17 Birds were plentiful, cheap, and easy to catch. This meant that atonement and worship through sacrifices were not only for the rich and privileged; the poor were also included (see also 5:7; 12:8; see Luke 2:24).

1:16 ***the crop and the feathers:*** Or *the crop and its contents.* The meaning of the Hebrew is uncertain.

1:17 ***tear . . . without tearing it apart:*** Cutting larger animals into pieces (1:6, 12) probably reflects the ancient rite of covenant-making, in which the participant passed between the two halves of a sacrificed animal (see Gen 15:10). Because of their small size, birds were not cut in half. If it was necessary to pass between them, they were arranged in pairs.

2:1-16 The *grain offering* (Hebrew *minkhah,* “gift, present”) was a way to express worship to the Lord through a gift, recognizing him as Lord over the life of the worshiper. The grain offering was to accompany each whole burnt offering (Num 28:3-6, 12-13), sin offering (Num 6:14-15), and peace offering (9:4; Num 6:17). The grain offering supplied the priest with bread for his daily sustenance, because no farmland was allocated to priests.

2:1 ***Choice flour*** was fine wheat flour (in contrast with common barley flour). See also 1 Kgs 4:22; Ezek 16:13, 19. • Israelites used ***olive oil*** as shortening in their cooking, as lamp fuel, and for medicinal and cosmetic purposes. Accordingly, it was associated with the rich produce of the land and with God’s provision (Deut 8:8). • Like choice flour, ***frankincense*** was frequently connected with the Tabernacle (Exod 30:34; Lev 24:7) or the Temple (1 Chr 9:29). This fragrant tree resin was also used by individuals on special occasions (Song 3:6; Matt 2:11). It was a primary ingredient of the holy incense burned in the Holy Place as a tangible expression of worship (Exod 30:34-38).

2:2 The ***representative portion*** of the grain offering was burned on the altar to remind the worshiper that the whole offering belonged to God.

2:3 ***rest of the grain offering:*** A portion of the fire offerings was generally reserved for the priest as food (see 6:16-17). Exceptions included the whole burnt offering (the priest received only the hide; see 7:8), offerings given by the priest for himself (4:3-12; 6:19-23), or offerings made for the entire community (4:13-21). In these cases, the offering was to be entirely burned. The grain offering provided the priests with bread for their diet. • ***most holy*** (Hebrew *qodesh qodashim,* “holy of holies”): Both God and what belongs to him are holy. “Most holy” designates the priestly share as taken from the holy offering and reserved for a special function. This description is used for the priest’s share of any gifts dedicated to the Lord (Num 18:8-10).

2:4 A large ceramic ***oven*** was placed in a hole, and around it a fire was kindled. Once the oven was hot, the flat bread baked against the inside of its wall. • ***without any yeast:*** See note on 2:11; see also Exod 12:8.

2:5 A ***griddle*** was a flat stone or clay surface propped above a fire and heated. Later griddles were made of metal (Ezek 4:3).

2:7 Dough ***prepared in a pan*** was fried with ***oil*** until crisp.

2:11 ***yeast:*** The bread commonly eaten in biblical times was comparable to modern sourdough. The substance that is often called “leaven” consisted of wild yeast spores mixed into moist dough or a flour mixture. The yeast would grow and cause the dough to ferment, souring and raising it. A reserved portion of the sour dough would be kneaded into subsequent batches (Matt 13:33). Unleavened bread was required for the Passover (Exod 12:8), in remembrance of Israel’s bondage in Egypt (Deut 16:3) and their speedy departure from that land (Exod 12:34; 13:3). Following the Exodus, unleavened bread acquired the status of altar bread. Leavened bread was not to be burned on the altar. • ***honey:*** The Hebrew word (*debash*) can also refer to fruit nectar. The reason for its exclusion is not stated, but perhaps the frequent

2:12
Lev 7:13; 23:9-14
2:13
Num 18:19
2 Chr 13:5
Ezek 43:24
Mark 9:50
2:14
Lev 23:9-14
2 Kgs 4:42
3:1
Lev 1:3; 7:11-21
3:2
Exod 29:11
Lev 1:4; 7:14

12You may add yeast and honey to an offering of the first crops of your harvest, but
these must never be offered on the altar as
a pleasing aroma to the LORD. 13Season all
your grain offerings with salt to remind you
of God's eternal covenant. Never forget to
add salt to your grain offerings.
14"If you present a grain offering to the
LORD from the first portion of your harvest,
bring fresh grain that is coarsely ground
and roasted on a fire. 15Put olive oil on this
grain offering, and sprinkle it with frankincense. 16The priest will take a representative
portion of the grain moistened with oil, together with all the frankincense, and burn it
as a special gift presented to the LORD.

The Peace Offering (3:1-17)

3 "If you present an animal from the herd
as a peace offering to the LORD, it may
be a male or a female, but it must have no
defects. 2Lay your hand on the animal's

Sacrifice	References	Description	Purpose	See Also
Burnt Offering	**1:2-17;** 6:8-13	*Atoning sacrifice* of a bull, ram, or male bird with no physical defect	To make atonement for sin; to cleanse and restore the worshiper to fellowship with God	Gen 8:20-22; Exod 29:42-46; Num 28–29; 1 Sam 7:9-10; 1 Chr 21:18–22:1; Ezra 3:1-6; Job 1:5; 42:8; Isa 1:11-20; Mark 12:33; Rom 3:25; 8:3; Heb 10:1-18
Grain Offering	**2:1-16;** 6:14-23; 7:9-10	*Non-atoning sacrifice* of grain, choice flour, or baked breads with olive oil, frankincense, and salt	To honor God with a worshipful gift	Exod 30:9; 40:29; Num 16:15; 28–29; Neh 10:33, 37; cp. 2 Cor 9:1-15; 1 Tim 5:17-18
Peace Offering	**3:1-17;** 7:11-36; 22:21	*Non-atoning sacrifice* of any animal from the flock or herd, along with baked breads	To express thanks and gratitude to God through worship and by a meal shared with family and friends	Exod 18:12; 24:9-11; 1 Sam 9:15-25; Acts 2:42; 10:36; Rom 5:1; 1 Cor 10:16; 11:17-34; 2 Cor 5:18-21
Sin Offering	**4:1–5:13;** 6:24-30; 16:3-22	*Atoning sacrifice* of animals with no physical defects. The required offering varied with the situation and station of the person receiving its benefits.	To make atonement for unintentional sins of ritual impurity, neglect, or thoughtlessness	Num 15:22-31; Gal 6:1; Heb 10:26-31; 1 Jn 1:8-9
Guilt Offering	**5:14–6:7;** 7:1-7	*Atoning sacrifice* of a ram or lamb with no physical defects	To pay for sins against God and against people in the community	Matt 5:23-24; Rom 6:12-23; 7:21–8:4

▲ **Israel's Sacrifices (1:1–7:38)** For each sacrifice, the primary references that define the sacrifice are given, followed by a description of the sacrifice and its spiritual purpose. The "See Also" column provides other references to the sacrifice and to passages that address the same spiritual purpose as the sacrifice.

use of honey in pagan offerings, particularly to gods of the underworld, was a contributing reason. If the word refers to fruit nectar, its association with wine and fermentation may have linked it with yeast, making it ineligible to be burned on the altar. However, both honey and yeast were allowed as part of an offering of first crops (2:12). Loaves of bread made with yeast were to be presented with thank offerings (7:13) and as a gift to the priest in the Festival of Harvest (23:17). In the NT, yeast becomes a spiritual metaphor, playing on its sour taste and on its tendency to spread (Matt 16:6, 11, 12; 1 Cor 5:6-8; cp. Matt 13:33).

2:12 ***offering of the first crops:*** This offering (called "firstfruits" in many translations) was brought from the first part of the harvest (23:15-21; Num 28:26-31). Like the representative portion of the grain offering, this offering acknowledged that the entire harvest belonged to God (23:10-11; Exod 22:29; 23:19; 34:26; Num 15:18-20; Deut 18:4-5; 26:1-2). It further recognized that the land itself, not just its products, belonged to God; Israel was merely the tenant (see Lev 25:23).

2:13 In ancient times, ***salt*** represented permanence, because it preserved food. A covenant of salt (see notes on Num 18:19; 2 Chr 13:5) denoted an enduring covenant that was renewed with successive generations.

3:1-17 The ***peace offering*** (Hebrew *shelem*) expressed worship through fellowship with the Lord and with others. The Hebrew word is from the same root as *shalom,* which speaks of wholeness, well-being, harmony, and peace. *Shalom* means more than a cessation of hostilities between God and the worshiper; it implies a bond of harmonious fellowship. The peace offering was therefore a shared meal celebrating fellowship with God and others (cp. Exod 18:12; 24:9-11; 1 Sam 9:15-24). It could be presented as an expression of thanks (7:12-15), as a voluntary offering, or in fulfillment of a vow (7:16-18; 22:21). Peace offerings often followed whole burnt offerings (e.g., 1 Kgs 9:25), showing that fellowship with God follows atonement. When we have experienced atonement through Christ, we are able to be at peace with God and with each other (see Acts 2:42; 10:36; Rom 5:1; 1 Cor 10:16; 11:17-34; 2 Cor 5:18-21).

3:1 ***a male or a female:*** The whole burnt offering allowed only the use of male animals because it made atonement (1:3, 10). The less formal peace offering permitted both male and female animals (see also 4:28, 32). • ***no defects:*** The sacrificial animals had to be healthy. The only exception was the voluntary offering, for which a slight blemish was permissible (22:23).

3:2 ***Tabernacle:*** Literally *Tent of Meeting;* also in 3:8, 13; see note on 1:1.

head, and slaughter it at the entrance of the
Tabernacle. Then Aaron's sons, the priests,
will splatter its blood against all sides of the
altar. 3The priest must present part of this
peace offering as a special gift to the LORD.
This includes all the fat around the internal
organs, 4the two kidneys and the fat around
them near the loins, and the long lobe of the
liver. These must be removed with the kidneys, 5and Aaron's sons will burn them on
top of the burnt offering on the wood burning on the altar. It is a special gift, a pleasing
aroma to the LORD.

6"If you present an animal from the flock
as a peace offering to the LORD, it may be
a male or a female, but it must have no
defects. 7If you present a sheep as your offering, bring it to the LORD, 8lay your hand
on its head, and slaughter it in front of the
Tabernacle. Aaron's sons will then splatter
the sheep's blood against all sides of the altar. 9The priest must present the fat of this
peace offering as a special gift to the LORD.
This includes the fat of the broad tail cut off
near the backbone, all the fat around the
internal organs, 10the two kidneys and the
fat around them near the loins, and the long
lobe of the liver. These must be removed
with the kidneys, 11and the priest will burn
them on the altar. It is a special gift of food
presented to the LORD.

12"If you present a goat as your offering,
bring it to the LORD, 13lay your hand on
its head, and slaughter it in front of the
Tabernacle. Aaron's sons will then splatter the goat's blood against all sides of the
altar. 14The priest must present part of this
offering as a special gift to the LORD. This includes all the fat around the internal organs,
15the two kidneys and the fat around them
near the loins, and the long lobe of the liver.
These must be removed with the kidneys,
16and the priest will burn them on the altar.
It is a special gift of food, a pleasing aroma
to the LORD. All the fat belongs to the LORD.

17"You must never eat any fat or [b]blood.
This is a permanent law for you, and it must
be observed from generation to generation,
wherever you live."

The Sin Offering (4:1–5:13)
Procedures for the Sin Offering

4 Then the LORD said to Moses, 2"Give the
following instructions to the people of
Israel. This is how you are to deal with those
who sin unintentionally by doing anything
that violates one of the LORD's commands.

3"If the high priest sins, bringing guilt
upon the entire community, he must give a

3:3 Exod 29:13, 22; Lev 3:9-11
3:5 Num 15:8-10
3:6 Lev 3:1
3:13 Lev 1:5
3:15-16 Lev 4:26; 7:23-25
3:17 Lev 7:25-26; 17:10; Deut 12:16; Acts 15:20
[b]*dam* (1818) ‣ Lev 17:11
4:2 Lev 4:22; 22:14; Num 15:22-29
4:3 Lev 4:14; 9:2; Ezek 43:19

3:3 *all the fat:* See 1:8 and note.

3:4 *kidneys . . . lobe of the liver:* The Israelites saw the kidneys as organs of understanding, much like how we think of the brain ("I am overwhelmed [literally *my kidneys are consumed*]," Job 19:27; "heart," Ps 7:9; 16:7; Prov 23:16; Jer 12:2; Lam 3:13; "motives," Ps 26:2; Jer 17:10; "thoughts," Jer 11:20; 20:12). The liver represented life and vitality, similar to how we think of the heart (Prov 7:23; "spirit," Lam 2:11).

3:5 The *burnt offering* is described in 1:3-17 and is best referred to as the "whole burnt offering." Because it was offered twice daily (see Num 28:4), and because the need for atonement preceded fellowship, the text assumes that the burnt offering would be on the altar already. The priest was to lay the fatty portions and certain internal organs (3:3-4) of the peace offering on top of it.

3:6-11 *Sheep* were smaller, easier to raise, and less expensive than cattle. Apart from the exceptions mentioned in these verses, offerings of sheep followed the same pattern as those of cattle.

3:9 *broad tail:* Sheep in this part of the ancient Near East had broad, fatty tails that were burned on the altar with the rest of the fat.

3:11 *special gift:* See note on 1:9.

• Offerings of *food* were called "God's food" (21:6, 8, 17, 21, 22; Num 28:2). However, Scripture is clear that the Lord did not eat the offerings, as pagans believed their deities did (Ps 50:9-13). Instead, these offerings belonged to God, and the priest ate a portion of this food as God's representative (Lev 21:21-22). These offerings sustained the priest and his family.

3:12-16 The offering of goats followed a similar pattern as for cattle and sheep. Both goats and sheep were considered offerings from the flock (see 3:6).

3:17 Human beings were not permitted to eat the *fat or blood* (see 1:5, 8 and notes).

4:1–5:13 The *sin offering* (Hebrew *khatta't*, from the root *khata'*, meaning "to lack, fall short, miss, fail") was for specific unintentional violations of God's commands (see also Num 15:22-29), intended to repair a loss or remedy a failure (e.g., 5:1-4). Although we all sin, God will forgive us if we confess it (Gal 6:1; 1 Jn 1:8-9). But we are warned against sinning "brazenly" or "deliberately" (Num 15:30-31; Heb 6:4-6; 10:26-29).

4:3-21 These verses distinguish two types of sin offerings: (1) the offering given for the sin of the ***high priest*** (4:3, 20) and ***the entire Israelite community*** (4:13), and (2) the offering given for ***one of Israel's leaders*** (4:22) and ***any of the common people*** (4:27). The former case required offering a bull, a large, expensive animal. It was not to be eaten (6:30), but was completely burned (4:12, 21), and some of its blood was presented in the Holy Place (4:6-7, 17-18). The latter case required a lesser animal—a male goat for a lay leader or a female sheep or goat for a common person. The priest ate a portion of the layperson's offering (6:24-29), and the blood was presented at the bronze altar in the courtyard (4:25, 30). The distinction stresses the responsibilities of leaders. The offering was the same for the priest as for the entire people, and the lay leader's offering was more than that of a common person. The NT also emphasizes the responsibility of religious leaders; those who teach (Jas 3:1) and those who serve as religious leaders (Matt 23:1-33; Luke 20:47) are judged more severely than those who follow them.

4:3 The ***high priest*** (literally *the anointed priest;* also in 4:5, 16) was designated by God and "anointed" (Hebrew *mashiakh*, "set apart by the ritual of anointing") for a particular service. In 1 Sam—2 Kgs, anointing most often refers to Israel's king (see 1 Sam 24:6; 2 Sam 1:14; 19:21). While

4:5 Lev 4:16; 16:14
4:7 Lev 8:15
4:8 Lev 3:3
4:11 Num 19:5
4:12 Heb 13:11
4:13 Num 15:23-26
4:14 Lev 4:3

sin offering for the sin he has committed.
He must present to the LORD a young bull
with no defects. 4He must bring the bull to
the LORD at the entrance of the Tabernacle,
lay his hand on the bull's head, and slaughter it before the LORD. 5The high priest will
then take some of the bull's blood into the
Tabernacle, 6dip his finger in the blood, and
sprinkle it seven times before the LORD
in front of the inner curtain of the sanctuary. 7The priest will then put some of the
blood on the horns of the altar for fragrant
incense that stands in the LORD's presence
inside the Tabernacle. He will pour out the
rest of the bull's blood at the base of the
altar for burnt offerings at the entrance
of the Tabernacle. 8Then the priest must
remove all the fat of the bull to be offered
as a sin offering. This includes all the fat
around the internal organs, 9the two kidneys and the fat around them near the loins,
and the long lobe of the liver. He must remove these along with the kidneys, 10just
as he does with cattle offered as a peace offering, and burn them on the altar of burnt
offerings. 11But he must take whatever is
left of the bull—its hide, meat, head, legs,
internal organs, and dung—12and carry it
away to a place outside the camp that is ceremonially clean, the place where the ashes
are dumped. There, on the ash heap, he will
burn it on a wood fire.

13"If the entire Israelite community sins
by violating one of the LORD's commands,
but the people don't realize it, they are still
guilty. 14When they become aware of their
sin, the people must bring a young bull as an
offering for their sin and present it before

Community Identity (4:3, 13-21)

Lev 20:1-5
Exod 20:5-6, 8-10
Josh 7:1-26
Neh 1:6-7
1 Cor 12:12-27
Gal 6:2
Eph 4:11-13

In Israel, an individual's identity and significance were determined by his or her membership in the community. This contrasts with Western society, where the individual is considered to be the primary social entity. All Israelites were expected to partake of the common identity of the community as the "children of Israel" and to embody the characteristics that marked the whole.

In the OT, the people are often referred to or addressed in the singular, emphasizing their oneness. The Decalogue (Exod 20:2-17) and the blessing of Aaron (Num 6:24-26), for example, are given in the singular. The individual could often represent the group, and the group could be referred to as an individual. Nehemiah, for example, asks forgiveness for the sins that caused the exile to Babylon as though he had been one of those transgressors ("we have sinned," Neh 1:6-7). Nehemiah was governor of Judea from 445 to 433 BC, about 140 years after the destruction of Jerusalem (586 BC), so he did not participate in the sins leading to the exile of Judeans to Babylon. Yet in his prayer, he identifies with his people in their sinfulness. In this same way, the high priest could represent the entire people on the Day of Atonement (see Lev 16). Because the individual Israelite was so strongly identified with the community, the sin of the individual would become the sin of the community if not addressed (see Lev 4:3, 13-21; 20:1-5).

In like manner, the Christian community is described as the "body of Christ" (1 Cor 12:27; Eph 4:12). The members partake of Christ's identity through the Holy Spirit. That is, as the body of Christ they manifest Christ's life in their lives, and as a unified whole they reveal him to the world. Paul exhorts the Galatians to share the burdens of others (Gal 6:2) and so to model Christ's example (Matt 11:29-30).

all priests were anointed (Exod 40:13-15), here the term probably refers to the high priest because he was specially anointed for service in the Tabernacle (6:20; 8:12). Since the high priest was mediator for all of Israel, including lesser priests, his sin would bring guilt on the entire assembly (see "Community Identity" above). • ***Guilt*** results from violating God's will; it is not just perceived or psychological guilt (see note on 5:17-19).

4:4 ***Tabernacle:*** Literally *Tent of Meeting;* also in 4:5, 7, 14, 16, 18; see note on 1:1.

4:5-6 The ***Tabernacle*** complex had a tent (sometimes called the "tent of meeting"; see note on 1:1) at the west end of the courtyard. Inside the tent, the ***inner curtain*** divided the first room, the Holy Place, from the second, the Most Holy Place. The Most Holy Place contained the Ark of the Covenant (Exod 26:31-33) and was God's throne room (see note on 1:1). Sprinkling the animal's ***blood*** before the curtain (4:6, 17) and applying it to the horns of the incense altar (4:7, 18) was done to atone for the anointed priest or for the entire congregation. This action demonstrated the gravity of the offenses being atoned for (cp. 4:25, 30-35).

4:7 The ***altar for fragrant incense*** stood in front of the inner curtain, just outside the Most Holy Place (4:6). It had four protrusions resembling ***horns,*** as did the altar for burnt offerings (see note on Exod 27:2). The priests burned incense on this altar to the Lord each morning and evening (Exod 30:1-10).

4:11-12 Only the offerings for the priest or the entire community were burned ***outside the camp.*** Perhaps this was commanded because the offering had figuratively absorbed the contamination of the high priest or the community and therefore had to be disposed of outside the camp. Those guilty should not partake of or reap any benefit from their own sin offerings, even if they were priests (6:19-23).

the Tabernacle. [15]The [c]elders of the community must then lay their hands on the bull's
head and slaughter it before the LORD. [16]The
high priest will then take some of the bull's
blood into the Tabernacle, [17]dip his finger in
the blood, and sprinkle it seven times before
the LORD in front of the inner curtain. [18]He
will then put some of the blood on the horns
of the altar for fragrant incense that stands
in the LORD's presence inside the Tabernacle. He will pour out the rest of the blood at
the base of the altar for burnt offerings at
the entrance of the Tabernacle. [19]Then the
priest must remove all the animal's fat and
burn it on the altar, [20]just as he does with
the bull offered as a sin offering for the high
priest. Through this process, the priest will
purify the people, making them right with
the LORD, and they will be forgiven. [21]Then
the priest must take what is left of the bull
and carry it outside the camp and burn it
there, just as is done with the sin offering
for the high priest. This offering is for the
sin of the entire congregation of Israel.

[22]"If one of Israel's leaders sins by violating one of the commands of the LORD his
God but doesn't realize it, he is still guilty.
[23]When he becomes aware of his sin, he
must bring as his offering a male goat with
no defects. [24]He must lay his hand on the
goat's head and slaughter it at the place
where burnt offerings are slaughtered before the LORD. This is an offering for his
sin. [25]Then the priest will dip his finger in
the blood of the sin offering and put it on
the horns of the altar for burnt offerings.
He will pour out the rest of the blood at
the base of the altar. [26]Then he must burn
all the goat's fat on the altar, just as he does
with the peace offering. Through this process, the priest will [d]purify the leader from
his sin, making him right with the LORD,
and he will be forgiven.

[27]"If any of the common people sin by
violating one of the LORD's commands, but
they don't realize it, they are still guilty.
[28]When they become aware of their sin,
they must bring as an offering for their sin
a female goat with no defects. [29]They must
lay a hand on the head of the sin offering
and slaughter it at the place where burnt offerings are slaughtered. [30]Then the priest
will dip his finger in the blood and put it on
the horns of the altar for burnt offerings.
He will pour out the rest of the blood at the
base of the altar. [31]Then he must remove all
the goat's fat, just as he does with the fat
of the peace offering. He will burn the fat
on the altar, and it will be a pleasing aroma
to the LORD. Through this process, the priest
will purify the people, making them right
with the LORD, and they will be forgiven.

[32]"If the people bring a sheep as their
sin offering, it must be a female with no defects. [33]They must lay a hand on the head of
the sin offering and slaughter it at the place
where burnt offerings are slaughtered.
[34]Then the priest will dip his finger in the
blood of the sin offering and put it on the
horns of the altar for burnt offerings. He
will pour out the rest of the blood at the base
of the altar. [35]Then he must remove all the

4:15 Lev 8:14; Num 8:10-12; [c]*zaqen* (2205) ‣Num 11:25
4:17 Lev 4:6
4:19 Lev 4:8
4:20 Num 15:25
4:21 Lev 4:12
4:22 Lev 4:2, 13
4:24 Lev 6:25
4:25 Lev 4:7
4:26 Lev 4:19-20; [d]*kapar* (3722) ‣Lev 9:7
4:27 Lev 4:2
4:28 Lev 4:23
4:30 Lev 4:7
4:31 Gen 8:21; Exod 29:18; Lev 2:2; 4:8; 6:15
4:32 Lev 4:28
4:35 Lev 3:5

4:15 The Hebrew term for *elders* is related to the word for beard. It implies mature but not necessarily elderly individuals. They were leaders of the community—typically, heads of families and tribes (cp. Exod 18:21-26; Deut 22:15-19). For this offering, the elders represented the entire people, as they would later in anointing David as king (2 Sam 5:3).

4:20 ***will purify the people, making them right with the LORD:*** Or *will make atonement for the people;* similarly in 4:26, 31, 35. See note on 1:4. • A similar form of the phrase ***they will be forgiven*** appears frequently in passages dealing with atonement (4:26, 31, 35; 5:10, 13, 16, 18; 6:7; 19:22; Num 15:25, 26, 28). God is willing to forgive a repentant person's sin and restore him or her to the community of faith.

4:22-35 The sin offerings described in this passage atoned for laypersons, whether leaders or other Israelite citizens. These offerings could be eaten (contrast 4:3-21), and they involved lesser animals. The blood of the offering was disposed of in the courtyard of the Tabernacle and not carried to the Holy Place. As with the peace offering (ch 3), the fat and certain internal organs were burned on the altar. However, the rest of the meat from these offerings was given to the priest as food for himself and the males in his family (6:29) and it was to be eaten in a holy place (6:26; cp. 10:16-20). A lay leader was to offer a male goat (4:23), while a common layperson could offer a female goat or lamb. The animal's lesser size and cost reflected the lesser influence of the common Israelite and, probably, his financial situation. Economic considerations allowed those who were poor to bring a pair of doves or young pigeons (5:7-8; 12:6, 8; cp. Luke 2:24). The desperately poor could offer two quarts of flour (5:11).

4:22 ***Israel's leaders*** included the elders (see 4:15), tribal heads, and family heads (see Num 1:16, 44; 1 Kgs 8:1).

4:23 The ***male goat*** offered by a lay leader was a lesser offering than was required for the priest (a bull) but more than was required for a common person (4:28, 32). However, like all offerings used for securing atonement, the animal could have no ***defects*** (see 1:3).

4:24 ***at the place where burnt offerings are slaughtered:*** See 1:3-5.

4:25 ***blood . . . horns of the altar:*** Unlike the blood of the bull for the priest, the blood of the offering of a leader (4:25) or a common Israelite (4:30, 34) was not to be carried into the Holy Place. Also, a portion of the meat was to be eaten by the priest who offered it (6:24-29).

4:27-35 The ***common people,*** who had less responsibility than a priest or leader, were permitted the lesser offering of a ***female*** sheep or goat. A greater position brings greater responsibility (cp. Amos 3:2; Matt 25:14-30; Jas 3:1).

5:1 Prov 29:24
5:2 Lev 11:4-11, 24-39; Num 19:11-16; Deut 14:3-21
5:4 Num 30:6-8
5:5 Lev 16:21; Num 5:7; Josh 7:19
5:6 Lev 4:28, 32
5:7 Lev 12:8; Luke 2:24
5:8 Lev 1:15, 17
5:9 Lev 4:7; 7:2
5:10 Lev 1:14-17
5:11 Lev 14:21; *Luke 2:24

sheep's fat, just as he does with the fat of a
sheep presented as a peace offering. He will
burn the fat on the altar on top of the special gifts presented to the LORD. Through
this process, the priest will purify the people from their sin, making them right with
the LORD, and they will be forgiven.

Sins Requiring a Sin Offering

5 "If you are called to testify about something you have seen or that you know
about, it is sinful to refuse to testify, and you
will be punished for your sin.
2"Or suppose you unknowingly touch
something that is ceremonially unclean,
such as the carcass of an unclean animal.
When you realize what you have done, you
must admit your defilement and your guilt.
This is true whether it is a wild animal, a
domestic animal, or an animal that scurries
along the ground.
3"Or suppose you unknowingly touch
something that makes a person unclean.
When you realize what you have done, you
must admit your guilt.
4"Or suppose you make a foolish vow of
any kind, whether its purpose is for good or
for bad. When you realize its foolishness,
you must admit your guilt.
5"When you become aware of your guilt
in any of these ways, you must confess your
sin. 6Then you must bring to the LORD as the
penalty for your sin a female from the flock,
either a sheep or a goat. This is a sin offering
with which the priest will purify you from
your sin, making you right with the LORD.
7"But if you cannot afford to bring a sheep,
you may bring to the LORD two turtledoves
or two young pigeons as the penalty for
your sin. One of the birds will be for a sin
offering, and the other for a burnt offering.
8You must bring them to the priest, who will
present the first bird as the sin offering. He
will wring its neck but without severing its
head from the body. 9Then he will sprinkle some of the blood of the sin offering
against the sides of the altar, and the rest of
the blood will be drained out at the base of
the altar. This is an offering for sin. 10The
priest will then prepare the second bird as a
burnt offering, following all the procedures
that have been prescribed. Through this
process the priest will purify you from your
sin, making you right with the LORD, and
you will be forgiven.
11"If you cannot afford to bring two
turtledoves or two young pigeons, you may

5:1-6 These verses list examples of sins covered by the sin offering (4:2). When a person realized he or she had committed an offense, the next step was to make it right by admitting guilt and bringing a sin offering.

5:1 The first infraction was the failure ***to testify*** when called as a witness before a court. Failure to testify was not a passive act because it actively aided the criminal. • ***you will be punished*** (literally *you become guilty* or *you realize your guilt*): Anticipating God's punishment for the sin, the guilty party offered the sacrifice to remove the guilt and escape the punishment.

5:2 ***ceremonially unclean:*** "Clean" and "unclean" did not pertain to hygiene (see 11:1–15:33) but to suitability for participating in worship or, in the case of animals, suitability for sacrifice or human consumption. A list of clean and unclean animals is found in 11:1-47. The requirement for becoming clean after touching an unclean animal was merely to wash one's clothes and remain apart from the community until evening (11:27-28). Most likely, therefore, the requirement of this sin offering indicates that the person had failed to follow the prescription for cleansing (11:27-28).

5:3 Any bodily discharge, even blood, would render a person temporarily ***unclean*** (chs 11–15). The uncleanness itself was not sin, but it was a sin to neglect the uncleanness, allowing it to spread. Once people became aware of their unclean state, they were guilty if they neglected it.

5:4 Oaths could be taken in the name of the Lord. However, a ***foolish vow,*** one thoughtlessly made, was a blasphemous misuse of the Lord's name (Exod 20:7). Accordingly, vows must be fulfilled (see Num 30:2; Deut 23:21-23; Eccl 5:4-6).

5:5 ***When you become aware of your guilt:*** All the situations that required a sin offering assumed guilt by accident or ignorance. As soon as a person became aware of having done something improper, he or she became guilty and was required to attend to it. Known sins were to be dealt with; it was a sin in itself to know what was right and not do it (see 5:17; Jas 4:17). • ***confess:*** Sacrifice for sin without admission of guilt would be a meaningless ritual. When the sacrificial animal was presented to the priest, the worshiper likely told the priest why it was being offered.

5:6 This ***penalty*** was apparently fulfilled by the required sacrifice (see note on 4:1–5:13). • The actions described in 5:1-5 best fit those of a layperson, so a ***female*** offering was permitted, in keeping with the principle demonstrated in 4:28, 32. • ***will purify you from your sin, making you right with the LORD:*** Or *will make atonement for you for your sin;* similarly in 5:10, 13, 16, 18. See note on 1:4.

5:7-13 The poor also needed to secure atonement and reconciliation. Birds (5:7) were permitted for those too poor to afford a lamb (cp. 1:14-17). Although an animal offering was typically required for atonement (17:11), God in his grace allowed the bloodless offering of flour if the worshiper could not afford two birds (5:11).

5:7 The sin offerings included both a portion as a burnt offering and a portion that was first offered, then given to the priests (cp. 4:22-35; 6:24-30). Because of their small size, two birds were required—one for each type of offering.

5:10 ***making you right:*** See notes on 1:4; 4:20.

5:11 ***two quarts:*** Hebrew *1/10 of an ephah* [2.2 liters]. • ***choice flour:*** See note on 2:1. • The sin offering was not to be adorned with ***olive oil or . . . frankincense.*** These were required for the grain offering, which was the individual's gift to the Lord (see 2:1), given to express worship. The sin offering made atonement; its purpose was to obtain forgiveness, requiring that the offering be completely unadorned.

bring two quarts of choice flour for your sin
offering. Since it is an offering for sin, you
must not moisten it with olive oil or put any
frankincense on it. [12]Take the flour to the
priest, who will scoop out a handful as a representative portion. He will burn it on the
altar on top of the special gifts presented to
the LORD. It is an offering for sin. [13]Through
this process, the priest will purify those
who are guilty of any of these sins, making
them right with the LORD, and they will be
forgiven. The rest of the flour will belong to
the priest, just as with the grain offering."

The Guilt Offering (5:14–6:7)

Procedures for the Guilt Offering

[14]Then the LORD said to Moses, [15]"If one of
you commits a sin by unintentionally defiling the LORD's sacred property, you must
bring a guilt offering to the LORD. The offering must be your own ram with no defects,
or you may buy one of equal value with silver,
as measured by the weight of the sanctuary
shekel. [16]You must make restitution for the
sacred property you have harmed by paying
for the loss, plus an additional 20 percent.
When you give the payment to the priest, he
will purify you with the ram sacrificed as
a guilt offering, making you right with the
LORD, and you will be forgiven.

[17]"Suppose you sin by violating one of the
LORD's commands. Even if you are unaware
of what you have done, you are guilty and
will be punished for your sin. [18]For a guilt
offering, you must bring to the priest your
own ram with no defects, or you may buy
one of equal value. Through this process
the priest will purify you from your unintentional sin, making you right with the LORD,
and you will be forgiven. [19]This is a guilt
offering, for you have been guilty of an offense against the LORD."

Sins Requiring a Guilt Offering

6 Then the LORD said to Moses, [2]"Suppose
one of you sins against your associate
and is unfaithful to the LORD. Suppose you
cheat in a deal involving a security deposit,
or you steal or commit fraud, [3]or you find
lost property and lie about it, or you lie while
swearing to tell the truth, or you commit
any other such sin. [4]If you have sinned in
any of these ways, you are guilty. You must
give back whatever you stole, or the money
you took by extortion, or the security deposit, or the lost property you found, [5]or
anything obtained by swearing falsely. You
must make restitution by paying the full
price plus an additional 20 percent to the
person you have harmed. On the same day
you must present a guilt offering. [6]As a guilt
offering to the LORD, you must bring to the
priest your own ram with no defects, or you
may buy one of equal value. [7]Through this
process, the priest will purify you before

5:15 Exod 30:13; Lev 6:6; 7:1-10
5:16 Lev 6:5; 22:14
5:17 Lev 5:15
6:2 Exod 22:7-15; Num 5:6; Col 3:9
6:3 Deut 22:1-3
6:5-6 Lev 5:15-16; Num 5:8

5:12 ***representative portion:*** See note on 2:2.

5:13 ***making them right:*** See notes on 1:4; 4:20. • ***rest of the flour:*** See note on 2:3.

5:14–6:7 The ***guilt offering*** (Hebrew *'asham,* "guilt") dealt with property loss and damages, whether sacred (5:14-16) or secular (6:1-7). It involved restitution as well as compensation for the loss (5:16; 6:5). It could be called a "penalty offering," because the ram was a penalty, or perhaps a "restitution offering," because of the need to make restitution for the loss before the ram was offered. In the guilt offering (5:14–6:7), the loss involved was not only a failure in God's sight, as with the sin offering, but also a loss of property to another person or to the sanctuary. Cp. Matt 5:23-24.

5:15 ***unintentionally defiling:*** Damage to sacred property was distinguished from damage to secular property. The sacrifice was effective only if the damage to sacred property had been committed accidentally. Deliberate damage, such as vandalism, to something sacred was blasphemous. As with other deliberate sins (Num 15:30-31), no means was specified for its atonement. No devout believer would defiantly continue in sin (see 1 Jn 3:9). • The ***sanctuary shekel*** was not a coin but a standardized unit for measuring weight; each ***shekel*** was about 0.4 ounces or 11 grams in weight. It was used to evaluate the ram being offered. Some scholars suggest that this text permits the substitution of the appropriate amount of silver for the ram.

5:16 The surcharge of ***an additional 20 percent*** provided compensation to the owner for loss or damage to property. The surcharge for sacred property was paid directly to the priests. Accidental damage to sacred property occurred when a person unintentionally ate the sacred offerings (22:14) or omitted the tithe (27:31). A similar surcharge was involved in redeeming an animal (27:13, 27).

5:17-19 This paragraph provides general principles for the guilt offering. Even if ***unaware*** of the infraction, an individual was ***guilty*** and had to provide the appropriate ***guilt offering.*** This applied to both sacred and secular property (5:14-16; 6:1-7).

6:1-7 Verses 6:1-7 are numbered 5:20-26 in the Hebrew text.

6:2 ***sins against your associate . . . unfaithful to the LORD:*** For believers, there really is no such thing as a "secular" sin. All sin involves God, even sin directed against another person or group. In the sins requiring a guilt offering, God's forgiveness was needed, but restitution to the injured individual had to be made first (6:5-7; cp. Matt 5:23-24). Unlike offenses against sacred property (5:14-16), both accidental and intentional offenses against secular property could be forgiven.

6:4 ***you are guilty:*** See note on 5:5.

6:5 The instructions for the guilt offering assumed that a person's conscience would induce voluntary reparation; when restitution was voluntary, the surcharge for loss of use to the owner was always ***20 percent.*** Penalties were more severe in other cases (cp. Exod 22:1-15). There is a clear difference between voluntary confession and simply admitting sin after being caught.

6:7 ***will purify you before the LORD, making you right with him*** (or ***will make atonement for you before the LORD***): God

6:9
Exod 29:38-42
Lev 6:12-13
Num 28:1-25
6:10
Exod 28:39-43
6:12
Lev 3:5
6:14
Lev 2:1
6:15
Lev 2:1-2, 9
6:16
Lev 10:12-15
Num 18:10

the LORD, making you right with him, and
you will be forgiven for any of these sins
you have committed."

Priestly Regulations Pertaining to the Offerings (6:8–7:38)

Further Instructions for the Burnt Offering

[8]Then the LORD said to Moses, [9]"Give Aaron
and his sons the following instructions
regarding the burnt offering. The burnt offering must be left on top of the altar until
the next morning, and the fire on the altar
must be kept burning all night. [10]In the
morning, after the priest on duty has put on
his official linen clothing and linen undergarments, he must clean out the ashes of the
burnt offering and put them beside the altar. [11]Then he must take off these garments,
change back into his regular clothes, and
carry the ashes outside the camp to a place
that is ceremonially clean. [12]Meanwhile, the
fire on the altar must be kept burning; it
must never go out. Each morning the priest
will add fresh wood to the fire and arrange
the burnt offering on it. He will then burn
the fat of the peace offerings on it. [13]Re-
member, the fire must be kept burning on
the altar at all times. It must never go out.

Further Instructions for the Grain Offering

[14]"These are the instructions regarding the
grain offering. Aaron's sons must present
this offering to the LORD in front of the altar. [15]The priest on duty will take from the
grain offering a handful of the choice flour
moistened with olive oil, together with all
the frankincense. He will burn this representative portion on the altar as a pleasing
aroma to the LORD. [16]Aaron and his sons
may eat the rest of the flour, but it must be

God's Instructions (6:9, 14)

Gen 26:5
Exod 16:4
Deut 17:8-13, 18-20
2 Kgs 10:30-31; 22:8-20
Job 22:21-23
Ps 40:8; 78:9-12
Prov 6:20-23; 13:14; 28:9
Isa 8:20
Col 3:16
2 Tim 3:14-17

The common Hebrew word *torah* is translated "law" in most English versions. This translation comes from the use of the Greek word *nomos* (which means "law") to translate *torah* in the Septuagint (the Greek OT). However, *torah* doesn't mean "law," but rather "teaching," "instruction," or "doctrine." This meaning is respected in the NLT by its translation as "instructions" (e.g., 6:9, 14).

The term *law* often brings to mind an authority imposed by an external force (such as a government) and is often perceived as harsh and unbending. The *torah* of Moses, however, is instructional. It might embody law, but it also included stories (10:1-3), poetry (Deut 32:1-43), genealogies (Exod 6:14-25), and a number of other literary forms.

There are other words properly translated "law." The first is *khoq,* or "statute," rendered "right" in 6:18 and "law" in 6:22. A statute is a law as it was given by the lawgiver—in this case, by God himself. It states a general principle, leaving its application open to interpretation by context or the courts. In 18:4-5 and 19:37, *khuqqah* ("decrees") is paired with *mishpatim* ("regulations"), a term indicating case laws. It would be impossible to write laws that cover every situation. A case law, therefore, refers to a court's previous interpretation of a statute in certain cases; the court's decisions in the past give guidance for deciding on similar cases in the present.

Law is necessary, for there will always be people who need its restraint. Instruction in doctrine and godly living are an integral part of the church and its life-giving message to the world (Col 3:16).

graciously gave his people a way to atone for their sins. See also notes on 1:4; 4:20.

6:8–7:38 The regulations in 1:2–6:7 include instructions for both priest and layperson. This section adds detail regarding the rights and obligations of the officiating priest. Because the tribe of Levi had been allotted no land for farming (Deut 18:1; Josh 13:14, 33), priests depended on the offering system for their income. The concern was that priests be adequately provided for. Like many human institutions, this system was eventually abused (1 Sam 2:12-25; Hos 4:8).

6:8-30 Verses 6:8-30 are numbered 6:1-23 in Hebrew text.

6:9 ***burnt offering:*** See note on 1:3-17.

6:10 The priest was required to wear ***official linen clothing,*** the attire of his office, when officiating at the Tabernacle. This allowed everyone to know that he was there to carry out his official duties (Exod 28:40-43). The priest was to dress appropriately for service to the divine King. He was not to wear his official garb outside the Tabernacle (6:11; Ezek 44:19). • ***undergarments:*** See Exod 20:26.

6:11 Most natural environments qualified as a ***place that is ceremonially clean.***

6:12-13 This passage cautions that ***the fire on the*** bronze ***altar*** must be constantly tended and ***never*** allowed to ***go out,*** perhaps anticipating the tragedy of the "wrong kind of fire" offered by Nadab and Abihu (10:1-2).

6:14 ***grain offering:*** See note on 2:1-16.

6:15 ***frankincense:*** See note on 2:1.

6:16 In this context ***sacred place*** does not refer to the Holy Place at the heart of the Tabernacle but to any location within the Tabernacle complex, all of which were ceremonially clean and holy. • ***Tabernacle:*** Literally *Tent of Meeting;* also in 6:26, 30; see note on 1:1.

baked without yeast and eaten in a sacred
place within the courtyard of the Tabernacle. 17Remember, it must never be prepared
with yeast. I have given it to the priests as
their share of the special gifts presented to
me. Like the sin offering and the guilt offering, it is most holy. 18Any of Aaron's male
descendants may eat from the special gifts
presented to the LORD. This is their permanent right from generation to generation.
Anyone or anything that touches these offerings will become holy."

Procedures for the Ordination Offering

19Then the LORD said to Moses, 20"On the
day Aaron and his sons are anointed, they
must present to the LORD a grain offering
of two quarts of choice flour, half to be offered in the morning and half to be offered
in the evening. 21It must be carefully mixed
with olive oil and cooked on a griddle. Then
slice this grain offering and present it as a
pleasing aroma to the LORD. 22In each generation, the high priest who succeeds Aaron
must prepare this same offering. It belongs
to the LORD and must be burned up completely. This is a permanent law. 23All such
grain offerings of a priest must be burned
up entirely. None of it may be eaten."

Further Instructions for the Sin Offering

24Then the LORD said to Moses, 25"Give
Aaron and his sons the following instructions regarding the sin offering. The animal
given as an offering for sin is a most holy
offering, and it must be slaughtered in the
LORD's presence at the place where the burnt
offerings are slaughtered. 26The priest who
offers the sacrifice as a sin offering must
eat his portion in a sacred place within the
courtyard of the Tabernacle. 27Anyone or
anything that touches the sacrificial meat
will become holy. If any of the sacrificial
blood spatters on a person's clothing, the
soiled garment must be washed in a sacred
place. 28If a clay pot is used to boil the sacrificial meat, it must then be broken. If a
bronze pot is used, it must be scoured and
thoroughly rinsed with water. 29Any male
from a priest's family may eat from this
offering; it is most holy. 30But the offering
for sin may not be eaten if its blood was
brought into the Tabernacle as an offering
for purification in the Holy Place. It must be
completely burned with fire.

Further Instructions for the Guilt Offering

7 "These are the instructions for the
guilt offering. It is most holy. 2The animal sacrificed as a guilt offering must be
slaughtered at the place where the burnt
offerings are slaughtered, and its blood
must be splattered against all sides of the
altar. 3The priest will then offer all its fat on
the altar, including the fat of the broad tail,
the fat around the internal organs, 4the two
kidneys and the fat around them near the
loins, and the long lobe of the liver. These
are to be removed with the kidneys, 5and
the priests will burn them on the altar as a
special gift presented to the LORD. This is

6:17 Lev 2:11; 6:29; 10:17
6:18 Lev 6:29; Num 18:10; 1 Cor 9:13
6:21 Lev 2:5, 8; 7:9
6:22-23 Exod 29:30
6:25 Lev 4:24, 29
6:27 Exod 29:37
6:28 Lev 11:33; 15:12
6:29 Lev 6:18
6:30 Lev 4:18
7:1 Lev 5:14–6:7
7:2 Lev 1:11
7:3 Lev 3:3, 9

6:17 *yeast:* See note on 2:11. • The priests' *share* of the grain offering had the practical value of providing their staple food—bread (7:9)—in addition to its theological significance as being *most holy.* See note on 2:3.

6:18 The priestly share did not belong exclusively to the priest conducting the sacrifice; it was to be shared with all ***of Aaron's male descendants.*** The text does not indicate why these offerings could be eaten only by the males while other offerings were available to all members of the priests' families (see note on 10:13-15; see also Num 18:20-24). • ***will become holy:*** Or *must be holy;* also in 6:27. Though uncleanness could be spread by touch (ch 15), Haggai implied that holiness could not (Hag 2:12). If an unclean person encountered that which was holy, disaster could result (10:1-3; 1 Sam 6:19-20; 2 Sam 6:6-8).

6:19-23 These instructions applied only to the grain portion of the ordination offering (see 2:1-16; for the rest of the ordination offering, see 8:22-32).

6:20 *two quarts:* Hebrew *1/10 of an ephah* [2.2 liters].

6:21 *slice:* The meaning of this Hebrew term is uncertain.

6:22 Only the *high priest* (literally *the anointed priest*) could represent the priesthood as an institution, with all its constituent priests.

6:23 Normally, the bulk of a grain offering would go to the officiating priest (2:9-10). However, the grain offering described in 6:19-23 was for a special occasion—the ordination of the priests—and therefore was to be *burned up entirely* and not *eaten.*

6:25 *sin offering:* See 4:2–5:10 and notes.

6:26 *sacred place:* See note on 6:16.

6:28 A *clay pot* was porous and could not be cleansed as thoroughly as a metal one—some of the holy food might stick to it or soak in. Reuse would cause an act of sacrilege. However, a ***bronze pot*** could be thoroughly ***scoured*** to prevent this problem (see also 11:33; 15:12).

6:29 ***Any male from a priest's family:*** See note on 6:18.

6:30 Some sin offerings for the anointed priest and for the entire congregation were not to be eaten. The blood of these offerings was carried into the Holy Place and sprinkled before the curtain (see 4:1-21). The sacrifices that could be eaten were those for the lay leader and for the common people. The blood of these animals was poured on and around the base of the altar in the courtyard of the Tabernacle (see 4:22-35). • ***an offering for purification:*** Or *an offering to make atonement.* See note on 1:4.

7:1 *guilt offering:* See notes on 5:14–6:7.

7:2 ***where the burnt offerings are slaughtered:*** See 1:3-5.

7:3-4 The guilt offering required the sacrifice of a ram (5:18). • ***fat . . . tail . . . organs:*** The parts of the guilt offering to be burned were the same as those for the peace offering (3:3-4, 9-10, 14-15) and the sin offering (4:8-9, 26, 31, 35).

7:6 Lev 6:18, 29; Num 18:10
7:7 Lev 14:13
7:9 Lev 2:5, 8
7:11 Lev 3:1-17
7:12 Lev 2:4; Num 6:15
7:13 Lev 2:12; 23:17
7:15 Lev 22:29-30; [e]*todah* (8426) ‣Lev 22:29
7:16 Lev 19:6-8
7:17 Exod 12:10
7:19 Lev 11:47
7:20 Gen 17:14; Lev 22:3-7; Num 19:13
7:21 Lev 5:2-3
7:23 Lev 3:17
7:24 Exod 22:31; Lev 17:15

the guilt offering. 6Any male from a priest's family may eat the meat. It must be eaten in a sacred place, for it is most holy.

7"The same instructions apply to both the guilt offering and the sin offering. Both belong to the priest who uses them to purify someone, making that person right with the LORD. 8In the case of the burnt offering, the priest may keep the hide of the sacrificed animal. 9Any grain offering that has been baked in an oven, prepared in a pan, or cooked on a griddle belongs to the priest who presents it. 10All other grain offerings, whether made of dry flour or flour moistened with olive oil, are to be shared equally among all the priests, the descendants of Aaron.

Further Instructions for the Peace Offering

11"These are the instructions regarding the different kinds of peace offerings that may be presented to the LORD. 12If you present your peace offering as an expression of thanksgiving, the usual animal sacrifice must be accompanied by various kinds of bread made without yeast—thin cakes mixed with olive oil, wafers spread with oil, and cakes made of choice flour mixed with olive oil. 13This peace offering of thanksgiving must also be accompanied by loaves of bread made with yeast. 14One of each kind of bread must be presented as a gift to the LORD. It will then belong to the priest who splatters the blood of the peace offering against the altar. 15The meat of the peace offering of [e]thanksgiving must be eaten on the same day it is offered. None of it may be saved for the next morning.

16"If you bring an offering to fulfill a vow or as a voluntary offering, the meat must be eaten on the same day the sacrifice is offered, but whatever is left over may be eaten on the second day. 17Any meat left over until the third day must be completely burned up. 18If any of the meat from the peace offering is eaten on the third day, the person who presented it will not be accepted by the LORD. You will receive no credit for offering it. By then the meat will be contaminated; if you eat it, you will be punished for your sin.

19"Meat that touches anything ceremonially unclean may not be eaten; it must be completely burned up. The rest of the meat may be eaten, but only by people who are ceremonially clean. 20If you are ceremonially unclean and you eat meat from a peace offering that was presented to the LORD, you will be cut off from the community. 21If you touch anything that is unclean (whether it is human defilement or an unclean animal or any other unclean, detestable thing) and then eat meat from a peace offering presented to the LORD, you will be cut off from the community."

The Forbidden Blood and Fat

22Then the LORD said to Moses, 23"Give the following instructions to the people of Israel. You must never eat fat, whether from cattle, sheep, or goats. 24The fat of an animal found dead or torn to pieces by wild

---

7:6 *Any male from a priest's family:* See note on 6:18. • *a sacred place:* See note on 6:16.

7:7 *to purify someone, making that person right with the LORD:* Or *to make atonement*; see note on 1:4; 4:20.

7:12-15 The *peace offering* could be presented as an expression of thanks (as here), as payment of a vow (7:16), or as a voluntary offering (see 3:1-7). A worshiper made it an *expression of thanksgiving* by presenting a grain offering along with his peace offering (2:1-16). A grain offering consisted of unleavened cakes, wafers, or cakes of fine flour, all mixed or spread with olive oil. A representative portion was set aside to be burned (2:9). The grain offering was to be accompanied by loaves of yeast bread (7:13).

7:15 The *thanksgiving* offering was given when the worshiper was thankful (Jer 17:26; 33:11). The sacrifice was to be *eaten on the same day* it was offered so that the event would not fade from the worshiper's memory.

7:16-18 In contrast to the "peace offering of thanksgiving," which was presented as an expression of thanks to the Lord (7:12-15), the *offering to fulfill a vow* related to a vow made by a worshiper. The festive meal that followed was more relaxed and could extend into the next day. However, because the vow offering involved a vow made to God, it was still more restrictive than the voluntary offering, which could even use a deformed animal (22:23).

7:18 The Hebrew term for *contaminated* (*piggul*) occurs only in three other places (19:7; Isa 65:4; Ezek 4:14). It is always used in reference to meat that is unacceptable for sacrifice or human consumption.

7:19-21 Anything that was *ceremonially unclean* could not come into contact with what was holy (7:20). Although uncleanness was not sinful in itself, it symbolized what was unholy (see Exod 19:10).

7:20-21 *cut off:* Three interpretations are possible for this expression, all of them very grave: (1) The person was subject to God's judgment and faced an early death by natural causes (17:10-14). (2) The person was to be executed by the community (cp. Exod 31:14). (3) The person lost communal membership in Israel, either by banishment (such as by excommunication) or by shunning the person and treating him or her as unclean (18:24-30; cp. 23:29-30, where "cut off" seems distinct from "destroy").

7:22-27 In the sacrificial system, the *fat* and *blood* of all altar offerings belonged to God. They were offered before any of the sacrifice could be eaten. Consuming blood was specifically forbidden because it represented the very life of the animal (17:10-16). The injunction against eating fat might have been because fat, considered to be the best part of the offering, belonged to God.

7:24 Animals *found dead* had not been drained of their blood and were therefore unclean. Their fat was unfit to offer to the Lord and could not be eaten. However, it could be *used for any other purpose*, such as greasing cart axles, waterproofing animal hides, and other household uses.

animals must never be eaten, though it may
be used for any other purpose. 25Anyone
who eats fat from an animal presented as a
special gift to the LORD will be cut off from
the community. 26No matter where you live,
you must never consume the blood of any
bird or animal. 27Anyone who consumes
blood will be cut off from the community."

A Portion for the Priests

28Then the LORD said to Moses, 29"Give the
following instructions to the people of Israel. When you present a peace offering
to the LORD, bring part of it as a gift to the
LORD. 30Present it to the LORD with your own
hands as a special gift to the LORD. Bring the
fat of the animal, together with the breast,
and lift up the breast as a special offering
to the LORD. 31Then the priest will burn the
fat on the altar, but the breast will belong to
Aaron and his descendants. 32Give the right
thigh of your peace offering to the priest
as a gift. 33The right thigh must always be
given to the priest who offers the blood and
the fat of the peace offering. 34For I have
reserved the breast of the special offering
and the right thigh of the sacred offering
for the priests. It is the permanent right of
Aaron and his descendants to share in the
peace offerings brought by the people of
Israel. 35This is their rightful share. The special gifts presented to the LORD have been
reserved for Aaron and his descendants
from the time they were set apart to serve
the LORD as priests. 36On the day they were
anointed, the LORD commanded the Israelites to give these portions to the priests as
their permanent share from generation to
generation."

37These are the instructions for the burnt
offering, the grain offering, the sin offering,
and the guilt offering, as well as the ordination offering and the peace offering. 38The
LORD gave these instructions to Moses on
Mount Sinai when he commanded the Israelites to present their offerings to the LORD
in the wilderness of Sinai.

2. THE INSTITUTION OF THE PRIESTHOOD (8:1–10:20)

The Priests Are Ordained and Begin Their Ministry (8:1–9:24)

Ordination of the Priests

8 Then the LORD said to Moses, 2"Bring
Aaron and his sons, along with their sacred garments, the anointing oil, the bull for
the sin offering, the two rams, and the basket of bread made without yeast, 3and call
the entire community of Israel together at
the entrance of the Tabernacle."

4So Moses followed the LORD's instructions, and the whole community assembled
at the Tabernacle entrance. 5Moses announced to them, "This is what the LORD
has commanded us to do!" 6Then he presented Aaron and his sons and washed
them with water. 7He put the official tunic on Aaron and tied the sash around his

7:26 Gen 9:4; Lev 17:10-14; Acts 15:20, 29
7:29 Lev 3:1
7:30 Exod 29:26-27; Lev 8:29; Num 6:20
7:31 Lev 7:34; Num 18:11
7:32 Num 18:18
7:34 Exod 29:22; Lev 10:15
7:36 Exod 29:22-34; 40:13-15
7:38 Lev 26:46
8:2 Exod 28:1
8:6 Exod 29:4

7:26-27 The prohibition against consuming blood was so important that the Council at Jerusalem included it in the instructions for Gentile believers (Acts 15:29).

7:29 ***peace offering:*** See 3:1-17.

7:34 ***breast of the special offering . . . right thigh of the sacred offering:*** The peace offering was a shared meal between God, the priest, the worshiper, and his guests. The breast (in some older translations called a "wave offering") and thigh (sometimes called the "contribution" or "heave offering") were specifically designated as the priest's portion (see 10:13-15). After these offerings were taken into the Tabernacle and presented before the Lord, they could then be eaten (see Exod 29:24, 26).

7:36 ***anointed:*** See 8:12, 30; also Exod 40:13-15.

7:37 ***ordination offering:*** See notes on 6:19-23; 8:22-32.

8:1-36 In Exod 28–29, the Lord gave Moses specific instructions for clothing and for ordaining Aaron and his sons as priests. In Exod 39:1-31; 40:12-16; and Lev 8:1-36, the commands were carried out. Moses didn't just pass along the instructions verbally; he enacted the rituals to provide an example for the priests down to the last detail, ***just as the LORD had commanded him*** (8:9, 13, 17, 21, 29). Because the penalty for disobedience was death, God made sure the priests knew exactly what to do.

8:2 These items are also mentioned in Exod 29:1-3, 7. • ***sacred garments:*** See Exod 28:1-43. • The ***anointing oil*** consisted of special ingredients to give it a unique scent. These included myrrh, cinnamon, cane, and cassia (dried flowers from the cinnamon tree) mixed into olive oil (see Exod 30:22-33). • ***bull for the sin offering:*** See 4:3-12. • The first of the ***two rams*** was to be a whole burnt offering (8:18), while the second was a special ordination sacrifice (8:22). • ***basket of bread made without yeast:*** See 6:19-23.

8:3 ***Tabernacle:*** Literally *Tent of Meeting;* also in 8:4, 31, 33, 35; see note on 1:1.

8:4 The text repeatedly emphasizes that ***Moses followed the LORD's instructions,*** obeying the commands given in Exod 29 (see also Lev 8:9, 13, 17, 21, 29, 36).

8:6 Being ***washed . . . with water*** was the first step for cleansing from impurity. The priests had to be ceremonially clean before they could serve the Lord in holiness (Exod 29:4; see Ps 24:4).

8:7-9 See the illustration of the high priest's clothing at Exod 28:1-43, p. 174.

8:7 The ***tunic*** (see Exod 28:39) was woven of patterned linen cloth. • The same type of material used for the Tabernacle curtains was used for the embroidered ***ephod*** (see Exod 28:4, 6-14). This garment's precise shape and size are unclear, but it seems to have been a long, sleeveless vest, fitted close to the body and tied about the waist. It was joined at the shoulders by gold settings; each setting bore an onyx stone engraved with the names of six of the tribes of Israel (Exod 28:9). Later, an ephod also referred to a venerated image (Judg 8:27; 18:17). • The ***decorative sash*** was embroidered and was made of the same materials as the ephod (see Exod 28:8).

8:8 Exod 28:30; Ezra 2:63
8:9 Exod 28:4, 36-38
8:10 Exod 30:26-33; [f]*mishkan* (4908) ‣ Lev 17:4
8:11 Exod 29:37; Lev 16:14; [g]*mashakh* (4886) ‣ Lev 8:12
8:12 Exod 28:41; 30:30; Lev 21:10-12; [h]*mashakh* (4886) ‣ 1 Sam 10:1
8:13 Exod 28:4, 39
8:14 Exod 29:10-14; Lev 4:4
8:15 Lev 4:7
8:17 Lev 4:11-12
8:18 Exod 29:15-19
8:22 Exod 29:31
8:23 Exod 29:20-21
8:25 Exod 29:22

waist. He dressed him in the robe, placed
the ephod on him, and attached the ephod
securely with its decorative sash. 8Then
Moses placed the chestpiece on Aaron and
put the Urim and the Thummim inside it.
9He placed the turban on Aaron's head and
attached the gold medallion—the badge of
holiness—to the front of the turban, just as
the LORD had commanded him.
10Then Moses took the anointing oil and
anointed the [f]Tabernacle and everything in
it, making them holy. 11He sprinkled the oil
on the altar seven times, [g]anointing it and all
its utensils, as well as the washbasin and its
stand, making them holy. 12Then he poured
some of the anointing oil on Aaron's head,
[h]anointing him and making him holy for his
work. 13Next Moses presented Aaron's sons.
He clothed them in their tunics, tied their
sashes around them, and put their special
head coverings on them, just as the LORD
had commanded him.
14Then Moses presented the bull for the
sin offering. Aaron and his sons laid their
hands on the bull's head, 15and Moses slaughtered it. Moses took some of the blood, and
with his finger he put it on the four horns
of the altar to purify it. He poured out the
rest of the blood at the base of the altar.
Through this process, he made the altar holy
by purifying it. 16Then Moses took all the
fat around the internal organs, the long lobe
of the liver, and the two kidneys and the fat
around them, and he burned it all on the altar. 17He took the rest of the bull, including
its hide, meat, and dung, and burned it on a
fire outside the camp, just as the LORD had
commanded him.
18Then Moses presented the ram for the
burnt offering. Aaron and his sons laid
their hands on the ram's head, 19and Moses
slaughtered it. Then Moses took the ram's
blood and splattered it against all sides of
the altar. 20Then he cut the ram into pieces,
and he burned the head, some of its pieces,
and the fat on the altar. 21After washing
the internal organs and the legs with water,
Moses burned the entire ram on the altar as
a burnt offering. It was a pleasing aroma, a
special gift presented to the LORD, just as
the LORD had commanded him.
22Then Moses presented the other ram,
which was the ram of ordination. Aaron
and his sons laid their hands on the ram's
head, 23and Moses slaughtered it. Then
Moses took some of its blood and applied
it to the lobe of Aaron's right ear, the thumb
of his right hand, and the big toe of his right
foot. 24Next Moses presented Aaron's sons
and applied some of the blood to the lobes
of their right ears, the thumbs of their right
hands, and the big toes of their right feet.
He then splattered the rest of the blood
against all sides of the altar.
25Next Moses took the fat, including the
fat of the broad tail, the fat around the internal organs, the long lobe of the liver, and the
two kidneys and the fat around them, along

8:8 The *chestpiece* (see Exod 28:15-30) was made of embroidered linen folded double. It bore twelve stones, each engraved with the name of a tribe of Israel. It was suspended over the heart by a gold chain from the gold shoulder-pieces of the ephod. • The *Urim and the Thummim* were placed in the pocket of the chestpiece (Exod 28:30; 1 Sam 23:9-12; 30:7-8); the precise function of these items is uncertain. They are generally thought of as two stones, perhaps each different in color, that were cast as lots. They apparently could give a positive, neutral, or negative answer to questions that could not otherwise be resolved (Exod 28:30; Num 27:21; 1 Sam 28:6). Their mention in OT prophetic literature written centuries later (Ezra 2:63; Neh 7:65) demonstrates how important these items were to the office of priest.

8:9 The *turban* worn by the high priest was made of linen and was distinct from the headdresses of the common priests (Exod 28:40). The *gold medallion* was suspended from the turban and bore an inscription that read, "HOLY TO THE LORD" (Exod 28:36). With the names of the tribes on his shoulders and over his heart and the dedication to the Lord on his forehead, the high priest was clearly marked as the people's representative to God and God's representative to the people. In this mediating role, the high priest modeled the standard for all priests.

8:10 *making them holy:* God is the Holy One (Ps 22:3; 78:41). In the strictest sense, only God can make a person or thing holy (Exod 31:13; Lev 20:8; 21:15, 23; 22:9, 16; 22:32; see Heb 2:11); the actions of Moses simply recognized and declared what God had done (also in 8:11, 12, 15).

8:13 For the attire of the common priests, see Exod 28:40-41.

8:14 *sin offering* (see 4:3-12): Two atoning offerings were made—the sin offering (8:14-17) and the whole burnt offering (8:18-21). • By placing *their hands on the bull's head* (see 1:4), Aaron and his sons were identifying themselves with the sacrifice (also in 8:18, 22).

8:15 Normally, the high priest performed these priestly duties. However, it would not be proper for the priests to ordain themselves, so *Moses*, acting as God's representative, instituted the priesthood. • *by purifying it:* Or *by making atonement for it;* or *that offerings for purification might be made on it*; see note on 1:4.

8:18 *ram for the burnt offering:* See note on 1:10-13.

8:22 *ram of ordination:* See Exod 29:19-34.

8:23 Aaron's *[ear]lobe, thumb,* and *big toe* represented his total person. This act emphasized the role of the priestly office, with the blood stressing the ties to the sacrificial system. The priest's basic function was mediation between God and his people. To do this effectively, he needed ears that could hear the words of God and the needs of his people, hands ready to do God's bidding, and feet ready to take him where he was needed.

with the right thigh. 26On top of these he
placed a thin cake of bread made without
yeast, a cake of bread mixed with olive oil,
and a wafer spread with olive oil. All these
were taken from the basket of bread made
without yeast that was placed in the LORD's
presence. 27He put all these in the hands of
Aaron and his sons, and he lifted them up
as a special offering to the LORD. 28Moses
then took all the offerings back from them
and burned them on the altar on top of the
burnt offering. This was the ordination offering. It was a pleasing aroma, a special gift
presented to the LORD. 29Then Moses took
the breast and lifted it up as a special offering to the LORD. This was Moses' portion of
the ram of ordination, just as the LORD had
commanded him.

30Next Moses took some of the anointing
oil and some of the blood that was on the
altar, and he sprinkled them on Aaron and
his garments and on his sons and their garments. In this way, he made Aaron and his
sons and their garments holy.

31Then Moses said to Aaron and his sons,
"Boil the remaining meat of the offerings
at the Tabernacle entrance, and eat it there,
along with the bread that is in the basket of
offerings for the ordination, just as I commanded when I said, 'Aaron and his sons
will eat it.' 32Any meat or bread that is left
over must then be burned up. 33You must
not leave the Tabernacle entrance for seven
days, for that is when the ordination ceremony will be completed. 34Everything we
have done today was commanded by the
LORD in order to purify you, making you
right with him. 35Now stay at the entrance
of the Tabernacle day and night for seven
days, and do everything the LORD requires.
If you fail to do this, you will die, for this
is what the LORD has commanded." 36So
Aaron and his sons did everything the LORD
had commanded through Moses.

The Priests Begin Their Work

9 After the ordination ceremony, on
the eighth day, Moses called together
Aaron and his sons and the elders of Israel.
2He said to Aaron, "Take a young bull for a
sin offering and a ram for a burnt offering,
both without defects, and present them to
the LORD. 3Then tell the Israelites, 'Take
a male goat for a sin offering, and take a
calf and a lamb, both a year old and without defects, for a burnt offering. 4Also take
a bull and a ram for a peace offering and
flour moistened with olive oil for a grain
offering. Present all these offerings to the
LORD because the LORD will appear to you
today.' "

5So the people presented all these things
at the entrance of the Tabernacle, just as
Moses had commanded. Then the whole
community came forward and stood before
the LORD. 6And Moses said, "This is what
the LORD has commanded you to do so that
the glory of the LORD may appear to you."

7Then Moses said to Aaron, "Come to the
altar and sacrifice your sin offering and your
burnt offering to [i]purify yourself and the
people. Then present the offerings of the
people to [i]purify them, making them right
with the LORD, just as he has commanded."

8So Aaron went to the altar and slaughtered the calf as a sin offering for himself.

8:26 Exod 29:23
8:27 Exod 29:24
8:28 Exod 29:25
8:29 Exod 29:26; Lev 7:31-34
8:30 Exod 29:21
8:31 Exod 29:31-32
8:32 Exod 29:34
8:33 Exod 29:35
8:34 Heb 7:16
8:35 Num 3:7; 9:19; Deut 11:1; 1 Kgs 2:3; Ezek 48:11
9:3 Lev 4:3
9:4 Exod 29:43
9:6 Lev 9:23
9:7 Heb 5:1-3; 7:27; [i]*kapar* (3722) ‣Num 15:25

8:29 Moses functioned as a priest in the ordination ceremony and so received the priest's ***portion*** of the offering (see 8:15).

8:30 ***anointing oil:*** See note on 8:2; see also Ps 133:2.

8:31 The ordination offering was a variation of the peace offering (Exod 29:28). It was a meal (7:11-18, 28-34) shared between God (the parts burned on the altar) and the priests. The command to ***boil . . . and eat*** the ordination offering first appears in Exod 29:32.

8:34 ***commanded by the LORD:*** The details of the sacrifice rituals were symbolic and important in their own right. Yet most important, the priests were to obey God's commands. Complete obedience to God is a major theme in both the OT and the NT: "Obedience is better than sacrifice" (1 Sam 15:22). • ***to purify you, making you right with him:*** Or *to make atonement for you.* See note on 1:4.

8:35 ***seven days:*** This command emphasized God's absolute holiness and mandated strict compliance with his commands. The priests, now anointed as God's holy servants, were to remain in the Tabernacle court for ***seven days*** before venturing out into everyday life.

9:1 ***eighth day:*** The priests had finished the seven-day period of probation commanded in 8:35. • ***elders:*** See note on 4:15.

9:2-4 These sacrifices—the sin and whole burnt offerings for the priests and the sin, burnt, peace, and grain offerings for the people—were offered at the beginning of the priests' ministry to make certain that all sin was atoned for and the covenant with God affirmed. Only the guilt offering was omitted.

9:4 ***bull:*** Or *cow;* also in 9:18, 19.

9:5 ***Tabernacle:*** Literally *Tent of Meeting;* also in 9:23; see note on 1:1.

9:6 Just as holiness describes God's person and nature, the ***glory of the LORD*** tangibly expresses his power and majesty (see Ezek 1:28; 10:4). His glory was revealed on Mount Sinai (Exod 24:16), at the dedication of the Tabernacle (Exod 40:34-35), and in Solomon's Temple (1 Kgs 8:11; 2 Chr 7:1). Yet it remained as vast as the heavens (Ps 19:1). The NT speaks of Christ's glory as the image of God (2 Cor 4:4), who manifested God's glory to the world (John 1:14). He was glorified in his death and resurrection (John 17:1-5). See also Exod 24:15-17.

9:7 ***your sin offering . . . burnt offering:*** Before the high priest could make atonement for the people, he had to be right with God himself. • ***to purify them, making them right with the LORD:*** Or *to make atonement for them*; see notes on 1:4; 4:20.

9:9 Lev 4:6-7
9:15 Lev 4:27-31; 9:3
9:16 Lev 1:3, 10
9:17 Lev 2:1-3; 3:5
9:18 Lev 3:1-11
9:19 Lev 3:9
9:21 Lev 7:30, 32
9:22 Num 6:24-26
9:23 Num 16:19, 42
9:24 1 Kgs 18:38
10:1 Exod 6:23; Num 3:2
10:2 Num 26:61
10:3 Exod 19:22; Ezek 38:16
10:4 Exod 6:18

[9]His sons brought him the blood, and he dipped his finger in it and put it on the horns of the altar. He poured out the rest of the blood at the base of the altar. [10]Then he burned on the altar the fat, the kidneys, and the long lobe of the liver from the sin offering, just as the LORD had commanded Moses. [11]The meat and the hide, however, he burned outside the camp.

[12]Next Aaron slaughtered the animal for the burnt offering. His sons brought him the blood, and he splattered it against all sides of the altar. [13]Then they handed him each piece of the burnt offering, including the head, and he burned them on the altar. [14]Then he washed the internal organs and the legs and burned them on the altar along with the rest of the burnt offering.

[15]Next Aaron presented the offerings of the people. He slaughtered the people's goat and presented it as an offering for their sin, just as he had first done with the offering for his own sin. [16]Then he presented the burnt offering and sacrificed it in the prescribed way. [17]He also presented the grain offering, burning a handful of the flour mixture on the altar, in addition to the regular burnt offering for the morning.

[18]Then Aaron slaughtered the bull and the ram for the people's peace offering. His sons brought him the blood, and he splattered it against all sides of the altar. [19]Then he took the fat of the bull and the ram—the fat of the broad tail and from around the internal organs—along with the kidneys and the long lobes of the livers. [20]He placed these fat portions on top of the breasts of these animals and burned them on the altar. [21]Aaron then lifted up the breasts and right thighs as a special offering to the LORD, just as Moses had commanded.

[22]After that, Aaron raised his hands toward the people and blessed them. Then, after presenting the sin offering, the burnt offering, and the peace offering, he stepped down from the altar. [23]Then Moses and Aaron went into the Tabernacle, and when they came back out, they blessed the people again, and the glory of the LORD appeared to the whole community. [24]Fire blazed forth from the LORD's presence and consumed the burnt offering and the fat on the altar. When the people saw this, they shouted with joy and fell face down on the ground.

The Priests Nadab and Abihu Disobey and Die (10:1-20)

10 Aaron's sons Nadab and Abihu put coals of fire in their incense burners and sprinkled incense over them. In this way, they disobeyed the LORD by burning before him the wrong kind of fire, different than he had commanded. [2]So fire blazed forth from the LORD's presence and burned them up, and they died there before the LORD.

[3]Then Moses said to Aaron, "This is what the LORD meant when he said,

'I will display my holiness
  through those who come near me.
I will display my glory
  before all the people.' "

And Aaron was silent.

[4]Then Moses called for Mishael and Elzaphan, Aaron's cousins, the sons of Aaron's

9:9 Both Aaron, the high priest (9:8, 12), and *his sons,* the common priests (9:9, 12, 13), participated in the sin offering (9:8-11) and the burnt offering (9:12-14). This made the atonement effective for the entire priesthood. • *horns of the altar:* See note on 4:25; see also Exod 27:1-8.

9:11 *burned outside the camp:* See note on 4:11-12.

9:17 *regular burnt offering for the morning:* A lamb was offered as a whole burnt offering each morning and evening (6:9; Num 28:2-4).

9:21 *breasts . . . thighs:* See note on 7:34.

9:22 *blessed them:* See Num 6:22-27.

9:24 *Fire blazed forth from the LORD's presence,* indicating that God had accepted the offerings, the atonement, and the priesthood (9:7; cp. 1 Kgs 18:36-38).

10:1-20 A fire was to burn constantly on the bronze altar (6:9) to supply coals for burning incense (16:12). Perhaps careless from drinking wine (10:8-11), Nadab and Abihu took coals from another source. This violation of God's instruction resulted in their deaths.

10:1 Aaron's two older sons, *Nadab and Abihu* (Exod 6:23), had accompanied Moses and the seventy elders on Mount Sinai (Exod 24:1, 9) and had witnessed the great theophany (appearance of God) there. They died without male heirs (see also Exod 28:1; Num 3:2-4; 26:60-61; 1 Chr 6:3; 24:1-2). • The *incense burners* were fire pans or trays that held hot coals. Incense was sprinkled on them (Exod 30:34-38; see also Lev 16:12-13; 2 Chr 26:19; Rev 8:3-4). • The *wrong kind of fire* (Hebrew *'esh zarah,* "strange fire") could mean "foreign," and thus "unauthorized" (see Exod 30:9) or even "pagan" (as in Ps 44:20; 81:9). Apparently, Nadab and Abihu used fire from a source not approved by God (Num 3:4; 26:61), possibly even a pagan source. It is also possible that they offered incense not prepared according to God's specifications (Exod 30:34-38), although the text does not mention that. They did not enter God's presence on his terms but on their own.

10:2 In 9:24, the *fire blazed forth* to show God's acceptance. It now indicates his disapproval by bringing death to Nadab and Abihu, who had demonstrated a careless approach toward the worship of God (cp. Acts 5:1-11).

10:3 God's *holiness* is his very essence, substance, and character, and it stands in contrast to the creaturely world. By performing this rash act, Nadab and Abihu failed to consider God's holiness and failed to honor him.

10:4 *Mishael and Elzaphan . . . uncle Uzziel:* See Exod 6:18, 22. • *carry away the bodies of your relatives:* Aaron, the high priest, and the priests Eleazar and Ithamar (10:6) could not defile themselves by making contact with a dead person (21:10-12).

uncle Uzziel. He said to them, “Come forward and carry away the bodies of your
relatives from in front of the sanctuary to a
place outside the camp.” 5So they came forward and picked them up by their garments
and carried them out of the camp, just as
Moses had commanded.
6Then Moses said to Aaron and his sons
Eleazar and Ithamar, “Do not show grief by
leaving your hair uncombed or by tearing
your clothes. If you do, you will die, and
the LORD’s anger will strike the whole community of Israel. However, the rest of the
Israelites, your relatives, may mourn because
of the LORD’s fiery destruction of Nadab and
Abihu. 7But you must not leave the entrance
of the Tabernacle or you will die, for you
have been anointed with the LORD’s anointing oil.” So they did as Moses commanded.
8Then the LORD said to Aaron, 9“You and
your descendants must never drink wine or
any other alcoholic drink before going into
the Tabernacle. If you do, you will die. This
is a permanent law for you, and it must be
observed from generation to generation.
10You must distinguish between what is sacred and what is common, between what
is ceremonially unclean and what is clean.
11And you must teach the Israelites all
the decrees that the LORD has given them
through Moses.”
12Then Moses said to Aaron and his remaining sons, Eleazar and Ithamar, “Take
what is left of the grain offering after a portion has been presented as a special gift to
the LORD, and eat it beside the altar. Make
sure it contains no yeast, for it is most holy.
13You must eat it in a sacred place, for it has

10:6 Lev 21:1-15; Num 1:53; 16:22; Josh 7:1
10:7 Lev 21:12
10:9 Ezek 44:21
10:10 Lev 11:47; Ezek 22:26
10:11 Deut 33:10
10:12 Lev 21:22; Num 3:2

God’s Absolute Holiness (10:3)

Lev 11:44-45; Exod 3:14; 34:6-7; 1 Sam 2:1-2; Isa 6:3-5; 52:10; Hos 11:9

Holiness is the fundamental descriptor of who God is. It is not merely one of his many attributes; it is the key to his very being. Calling God “the Holy One” speaks to the transcendence of his nature, in sharp contrast to the finite creation, whose creatures are bound by time and space. God speaks of himself as “I AM WHO I AM” (Exod 3:14), defining himself by himself. God is the Wholly Other, the One who is completely self-sufficient and distinct from the created order.

God’s holiness also speaks of his character. It is common to describe God’s holiness in terms of his separation from sin and his wrath against it, but holiness embraces all of God’s character, including his mercy. God revealed himself to Moses as the “God of compassion and mercy.” He said, “I am slow to anger and filled with unfailing love and faithfulness.” In his holiness, God shows this “unfailing love to a thousand generations. I forgive iniquity, rebellion, and sin. But I do not excuse the guilty” (Exod 34:6-7).

God’s holiness can be deadly to uninvited intruders (Isa 6:3, 5; see Exod 28:35) or to those who treat it with contempt. His infinite holiness is too much for finite, fallen mortals and would utterly destroy them apart from God’s sustaining grace. Understanding God’s holiness should thus trigger a response of awe and reverence. Anything less would be profane. Perhaps this was the error that cost Nadab and Abihu their lives (10:1-3). Only in recognizing the awesomeness of God can we appreciate his great love for us and worship him appropriately and authentically.

10:5 Carrying the bodies *by their garments* avoided defilement.

10:6 *Eleazar and Ithamar* were Aaron’s two remaining sons (Exod 6:23). • *by leaving your hair uncombed:* Or *by uncovering your heads.* This practice and others like it were ways to *show grief* in biblical times (cp. Gen 37:29; 44:13; Deut 14:1; 2 Sam 1:11; Job 1:20; Jer 16:6; 47:5). As high priest, Aaron was prohibited from participating in these rituals or in any way displaying his grief (21:10). The injunction extended to *Eleazar and Ithamar;* if God’s representatives had shown grief on this occasion, it might have been interpreted by observers as disagreeing with God’s justice. However, the laypeople were allowed to mourn.

10:7 *must not leave:* Eleazar and Ithamar were not to attend the funeral. • *Tabernacle:* Literally *Tent of Meeting;* also in 10:9; see note on 1:1. • *the LORD’s anointing oil:* Because they had recently been *anointed* as priests (see 7:36), they were to avoid any association with the dead.

10:8-10 The placement of this instruction suggests that Nadab and Abihu were under the influence of alcohol when they offered “the wrong kind of fire” (10:1). Priests were not to drink anything that could impair their judgment before serving in the Tabernacle. • *the LORD said to Aaron:* God had been communicating only to Moses, but he now accepted Aaron as the people’s representative, and he communicated directly with Aaron as well. • The word *common* means “secular” or “ordinary.” • *ceremonially unclean . . . clean:* See Lev 7:19-21; 11:1–15:33.

10:11 The *decrees that the LORD has given* were laws that came directly from God, rather than from a court decision (cp. “regulations” in 18:4).

10:12 The *grain offering* was part of the ordination ceremony (see Lev 8:26; Exod 29:2, 23). • *no yeast, for it is most holy:* Realizing that some time had passed, Moses wanted to be certain that no fermentation had occurred in the priest’s portion of the grain offering (6:14-18).

10:13-15 The priest’s share of the grain offering, the sin offering, and

10:14 Lev 7:28-36
10:15 Lev 7:30-34
10:16 Lev 9:3
10:17 Lev 6:24-30
10:18 Lev 6:26, 30
10:19 Lev 9:8, 12
11:1-23 //Deut 14:3-20

been given to you and your descendants as your portion of the special gifts presented to the LORD. These are the commands I have been given. 14But the breast and thigh that were lifted up as a special offering may be eaten in any place that is ceremonially clean. These parts have been given to you and your descendants as your portion of the peace offerings presented by the people of Israel. 15You must lift up the thigh and breast as a special offering to the LORD, along with the fat of the special gifts. These parts will belong to you and your descendants as your permanent right, just as the LORD has commanded."

16Moses then asked them what had happened to the goat of the sin offering. When he discovered it had been burned up, he became very angry with Eleazar and Ithamar, Aaron's remaining sons. 17"Why didn't you eat the sin offering in the sacred area?" he demanded. "It is a holy offering! The LORD has given it to you to remove the guilt of the community and to purify the people, making them right with the LORD. 18Since the animal's blood was not brought into the Holy Place, you should have eaten the meat in the sacred area as I ordered you."

19Then Aaron answered Moses, "Today my sons presented both their sin offering and their burnt offering to the LORD. And yet this tragedy has happened to me. If I had eaten the people's sin offering on such a tragic day as this, would the LORD have been pleased?" 20And when Moses heard this, he was satisfied.

3. REGULATIONS PERTAINING TO PURITY (11:1–15:33)

Clean (Permitted) and Unclean (Not Permitted) Animals (11:1-47)

11 Then the LORD said to Moses and Aaron, 2"Give the following instructions to the people of Israel.

Holiness by Relationship (11:44-45)

Lev 19:1-3; 20:3-8; 22:32
Exod 3:5; 20:8-11; 28:29-35; 29:44-46; 31:13
Ps 24:3-6
Isa 35:8-10
Dan 4:8-9
Rom 8:5-14
Gal 3:2-3; 5:16-26
1 Pet 1:13-16
1 Jn 3:2-3

Holiness refers to God's transcendent character (10:3). How can we, finite creatures who have fallen into sin, be holy as God is holy? We can never become transcendent like God. We will always be finite creatures. Our holiness is not absolute the way God's holiness is; it does not refer to our own nature and character. Instead, it refers to our relationship with God.

When God declares a place to be holy, it is because he manifests himself there (see Exod 3:5); if his presence is withdrawn, the place reverts to being ordinary. When God declares an object to be holy, such as an altar (Exod 29:44-46), it is because it was built in the manner prescribed by God and has been accepted by God for his service. Its relationship to God makes it holy as nothing else could.

It is the same for people. We are told to be holy because God is holy (see also 19:2; 1 Pet 1:16). Such holiness can only be imputed to humans. Without a relationship with God, true holiness remains elusive, no matter how good, pious, or disciplined a person's life might be. Only God can make people holy (20:8; 22:32; Exod 31:13). God promises to be with his people (Hos 11:9) and make their holiness possible (see Isa 35:8-10).

The church, like Israel of the OT, shares a relationship with God. Our adoption as God's children allows us to become godly people (see Exod 4:22; Rom 8:14; Gal 3:26; 1 Jn 3:2). The atoning death of Jesus, the Holy One, makes possible the perfection of holiness in all who claim its benefits by faith (Rom 5:12-21). We can be holy in our standing with God as well as in our conduct toward other people.

the guilt offering was "most holy" (see 2:3; 6:29; 7:6). Only the males in the priest's family could eat it, and it had to be consumed in a holy place (that is, the Tabernacle court). The priest's portion of the peace offering, though, was considered simply "holy." It could be eaten by any family member in any clean place (22:10-13).

10:16-17 ***The goat of the sin offering*** was the offering for the people (9:3, 15-17; cp. 9:2, 8-11). On this special occasion, its blood was not carried into the Holy Place as required. The remaining portion, after the portions allocated to God had been offered, should have been eaten by the priests (see 6:29). But the goat was entirely burned, even though its blood had not been taken into the sanctuary (10:18; see 6:30).

10:17 ***to purify the people, making them right with the LORD:*** Or *to make atonement for the people before the LORD*; see notes on 1:4; 4:20.

10:19 ***yet this tragedy has happened to me:*** Aaron was saying either that eating the goat of the sin offering would not have prevented the deaths of Nadab and Abihu or that it would not have been appropriate for him to eat it on the heels of such a grievous event.

11:1–15:33 These chapters detail the regulations pertaining to purity. The mixing of types of animals was forbidden (see Deut 22:9-11) because it represented a violation of the normal created order. "Abnormal" creatures—such as fish without fins and scales, carnivores, crawling insects, and animals without split hooves—cross boundaries between "normal" types and were unfit for food or offerings (see also Deut 14:1-21). The dietary laws were meant to distinguish Israel as a holy people from the surrounding nations (11:44-45).

"Of all the land animals, these are the
ones you may use for food. 3You may eat
any animal that has completely split hooves
and chews the cud. 4You may not, however,
eat the following animals that have split
hooves or that chew the cud, but not both.
The camel chews the cud but does not have
split hooves, so it is ceremonially unclean
for you. 5The hyrax chews the cud but does
not have split hooves, so it is unclean. 6The
hare chews the cud but does not have split
hooves, so it is unclean. 7The pig has evenly
split hooves but does not chew the cud, so
it is unclean. 8You may not eat the meat of
these animals or even touch their carcasses.
They are ceremonially unclean for you.

9"Of all the marine animals, these are
ones you may use for food. You may eat
anything from the water if it has both fins
and scales, whether taken from salt water
or from streams. 10But you must never eat
animals from the sea or from rivers that
do not have both fins and scales. They are
detestable to you. This applies both to little
creatures that live in shallow water and to
all creatures that live in deep water. 11They
will always be detestable to you. You must
never eat their meat or even touch their
dead bodies. 12Any marine animal that
does not have both fins and scales is detestable to you.

13"These are the birds that are detestable
to you. You must never eat them: the griffon
vulture, the bearded vulture, the black vulture, 14the kite, falcons of all kinds, 15ravens
of all kinds, 16the eagle owl, the short-eared
owl, the seagull, hawks of all kinds, 17the little owl, the cormorant, the great owl, 18the
barn owl, the desert owl, the Egyptian vulture, 19the stork, herons of all kinds, the
hoopoe, and the bat.

20"You must not eat winged insects that
walk along the ground; they are detestable
to you. 21You may, however, eat winged insects that walk along the ground and have
jointed legs so they can jump. 22The insects
you are permitted to eat include all kinds of
[i]locusts, bald locusts, crickets, and grasshoppers. 23All other winged insects that walk
along the ground are detestable to you.

24"The following creatures will make you
ceremonially unclean. If any of you touch
their carcasses, you will be defiled until
evening. 25If you pick up their carcasses,
you must wash your clothes, and you will remain defiled until evening.

26"Any animal that has split hooves that
are not evenly divided or that does not chew
the cud is unclean for you. If you touch
the carcass of such an animal, you will be
defiled. 27Of the animals that walk on all
fours, those that have paws are unclean. If
you touch the carcass of such an animal, you
will be defiled until evening. 28If you pick
up its carcass, you must wash your clothes,
and you will remain defiled until evening.
These animals are unclean for you.

29"Of the small animals that scurry along
the ground, these are unclean for you: the
mole rat, the rat, large lizards of all kinds,
30the gecko, the monitor lizard, the common
lizard, the sand lizard, and the chameleon.
31All these small animals are unclean for
you. If any of you touch the dead body of
such an animal, you will be defiled until evening. 32If such an animal dies and falls on

11:4
Acts 10:14

11:7
Isa 65:4; 66:3, 17

11:8
Heb 9:10

11:9-10
Deut 14:9-10

11:13
Deut 14:12-19

11:22
Matt 3:4
Mark 1:6
[i]*'arbeh* (0697)
‣ Deut 28:38

11:25
Lev 11:28, 40
Num 19:11-13

11:32
Lev 15:12

11:2-8 Some scholars have suggested that unclean animals were to be avoided for reasons of public health, but the evidence does not support this. Horse meat, for example, is no less healthy than beef, yet it was considered unclean because the horse does not have a split hoof (see 11:2-3). The regulations existed because an unclean animal was unacceptable as an offering to God and, therefore, it was also unacceptable as food for God's people. Jesus proclaimed all foods clean for Christians (Mark 7:14-19; Acts 10:9-16).

11:2-3 ***these . . . you may use for food:*** Animals that have ***split hooves*** and chew the ***cud*** were considered "normal" and ceremonially clean (see also Deut 14:3-21).

11:4-23 The identification of some of the animals, birds, and insects in this chapter is uncertain.

11:5-6 Neither the ***hyrax*** (or *coney*, or *rock badger*, or *Syrian hyrax*) nor the ***hare*** truly chews the cud, though both appear to. They are considered unclean because they do not have split hooves.

11:9 ***marine animals:*** Fish considered clean for the Israelites had both fins and scales (11:12).

11:10 The prohibition included fish such as eels and sharks that have ***fins*** but not ***scales,*** as well as crustaceans and mollusks, which have neither fins nor scales.

11:13-19 The list of unclean ***birds*** includes birds of prey and scavengers, both of which come in contact with dead animals and blood. This renders them unclean and unfit. Bats (11:19) fly, but are not birds; they are therefore "abnormal" and ceremonially unclean.

11:21-22 ***insects that walk along the ground and have jointed legs:*** This phrase eliminates creatures that creep or crawl low to the ground (11:27). Leviticus 11:42 indicates that multi-legged creatures, such as centipedes, are unclean. ***Locusts*** and ***grasshoppers*** are examples of clean insects (see Matt 3:4).

11:24-25 ***defiled until evening:*** Anyone who touched a carcass of an unclean animal would be unclean until evening, which marked the beginning of the next day in Israel.

11:29-31 This list of unclean creatures that crawl contains both warm-blooded and cold-blooded animals that scurry along the ground. Snakes are also included in this category (11:42).

11:32-40 Dead animals could make things and people unclean. Even a clean animal that died without having its blood drained was considered unclean (11:39-40). When a person became unclean from contact with an

11:33 Lev 6:28
11:40 Lev 11:25; 17:15 Deut 14:21 Ezek 4:14; 44:31
11:41 Lev 11:29

something, that object will be unclean. This
is true whether the object is made of wood,
cloth, leather, or burlap. Whatever its use,
you must dip it in water, and it will remain
defiled until evening. After that, it will be
ceremonially clean and may be used again.
33 "If such an animal falls into a clay pot,
everything in the pot will be defiled, and
the pot must be smashed. 34 If the water
from such a container spills on any food,
the food will be defiled. And any beverage
in such a container will be defiled. 35 Any
object on which the carcass of such an animal falls will be defiled. If it is an oven or
hearth, it must be destroyed, for it is defiled,
and you must treat it accordingly.
36 "However, if the carcass of such an animal falls into a spring or a cistern, the water
will still be clean. But anyone who touches
the carcass will be defiled. 37 If the carcass
falls on seed grain to be planted in the field,
the seed will still be considered clean. 38 But
if the seed is wet when the carcass falls on
it, the seed will be defiled.
39 "If an animal you are permitted to eat
dies and you touch its carcass, you will be
defiled until evening. 40 If you eat any of its
meat or carry away its carcass, you must
wash your clothes, and you will remain defiled until evening.
41 "All small animals that scurry along the
ground are detestable, and you must never
eat them. 42 This includes all animals that
slither along on their bellies, as well as those
with four legs and those with many feet. All
such animals that scurry along the ground

Clean and Unclean (11:1–15:33)

Lev 21:1-23; 22:3-8
Gen 7:2
Num 19:1-22
Deut 14:1-21; 21:1-9
Ps 19:9; 24:3-4; 51:7-10
Isa 52:11
Matt 8:2-4
John 13:10-11
Acts 10:9-28
Heb 9:13-15, 23

The rites and regulations establishing cleanness and uncleanness were to distinguish Israel from the surrounding nations. To understand a rationale behind these regulations, one suggestion has been that unclean things are associated with death or the ground (see, e.g., 21:1, 11; 22:8). Recent studies, however, suggest the principle of "normalcy." God is a God of order. Things that are normal in God's order are called "clean" and are "permitted." Abnormal things would be unfit for food or offerings and would be "unclean." A normal land animal would be a vegetarian (see Gen 1:30). A normal human body would have no infections or discharges. A normal piece of cloth would have no mildew on it. If abnormalities occurred, the animal, person, or cloth was unclean.

What is unclean is not sinful but represents a state of spiritual unworthiness that cannot come in contact with the holy (e.g., 11:44-45). If it is cleansed, it acquires the potential for holiness; it may be dedicated to God and become holy. If what is holy (such as the Sabbath) is treated like something common, God is blasphemed and the thing is profaned. If what is clean becomes unclean, it is defiled and requires cleansing. Some things, such as unclean animals, fish, or birds, remain unclean by definition and can never be cleansed, and, thus, can never become holy.

In the New Covenant, things that were previously unclean have been declared clean (Acts 10:15, 28, 45). Yet God is still a God of order (1 Cor 14:33) and wants worship to be conducted in an orderly way (1 Cor 14:40). While God's grace is abundant to repentant sinners, some things are still repulsive to his holiness and should never be brought into his presence (e.g., Ananias and Sapphira's offering; see Acts 5:1-11).

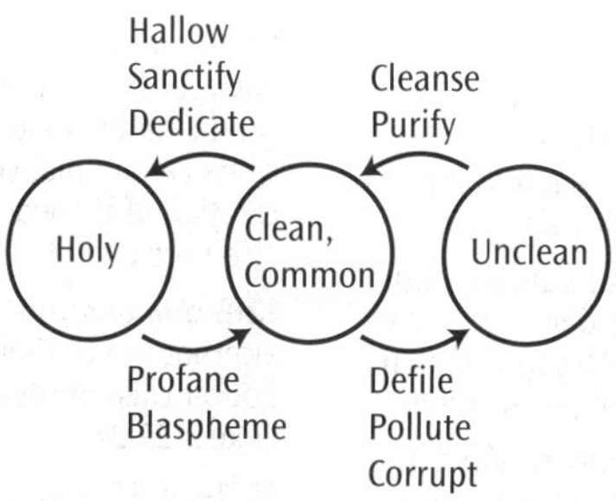

◀ **Holy, Clean, and Unclean** (11:1–15:33) This diagram depicts the states of being "holy," "clean," and "unclean" and the transitions between those states.

animal's carcass, it lasted only until evening. Household articles that came into contact with a carcass had to be purified (11:25, 28, 32, 40) or destroyed (11:33, 35).

11:33 ***pot must be smashed:*** See note on 6:28.

11:36 A *cistern* was a hole dug into the ground or rock, often lined with plaster, that retained rain and surface water.

11:37-38 ***Grain*** moistened with water was probably intended to be cooked for food; eating contaminated grain would be like eating a carcass. However, if the grain was sown, the new plant and the grain it bore were undefiled.

11:39-40 Israelites were not to consume blood (7:26). They could eat an animal only after the blood had been drained and properly disposed of (17:13). The undrained blood of an otherwise clean animal that died of natural causes rendered it unclean. An Israelite was permitted to give or sell such an animal to foreigners (Deut 14:21) but not to eat it.

are detestable, and you must never eat them.
43 Do not defile yourselves by touching them.
You must not make yourselves ceremonially
unclean because of them. 44 For I am the
LORD your God. You must consecrate yourselves and be holy, because I am holy. So
do not defile yourselves with any of these
small animals that scurry along the ground.
45 For I, the LORD, am the one who brought
you up from the land of Egypt, that I might
be your God. Therefore, you must be holy
because I am holy.
46 "These are the instructions regarding
land animals, birds, marine creatures, and
animals that scurry along the ground. 47 By
these instructions you will know what is unclean and clean, and which animals may be
eaten and which may not be eaten."

Purification after Childbirth (12:1-8)

12 The LORD said to Moses, 2 "Give the
following instructions to the people
of Israel. If a woman becomes pregnant
and gives birth to a son, she will be ceremonially unclean for seven days, just as she is
unclean during her menstrual period. 3 On
the eighth day the boy's foreskin must be
circumcised. 4 After waiting thirty-three
days, she will be purified from the bleeding
of childbirth. During this time of purification, she must not touch anything that is set
apart as holy. And she must not enter the
sanctuary until her time of purification is
over. 5 If a woman gives birth to a daughter,
she will be ceremonially unclean for two
weeks, just as she is unclean during her
menstrual period. After waiting sixty-six
days, she will be purified from the bleeding
of childbirth.
6 "When the time of purification is completed for either a son or a daughter, the
woman must bring a one-year-old lamb
for a burnt offering and a young pigeon or
turtledove for a purification offering. She
must bring her offerings to the priest at the
entrance of the Tabernacle. 7 The priest will
then present them to the LORD to purify her.
Then she will be ceremonially clean again after her bleeding at childbirth. These are the
instructions for a woman after the birth of
a son or a daughter.
8 "If a woman cannot afford to bring
a lamb, she must bring two turtledoves
or two young pigeons. One will be for the
burnt offering and the other for the purification offering. The priest will sacrifice
them to purify her, and she will be ceremonially clean."

Infections in People, Clothing, and Buildings (13:1–14:57)

Serious Skin Diseases

13 The LORD said to Moses and Aaron,
2 "If anyone has a swelling or a rash
or discolored skin that might develop into

11:44-45 Exod 6:7; 19:6; Lev 19:2; 1 Thes 4:7; *1 Pet 1:16
11:47 Lev 10:10; Ezek 22:26; 44:23
12:2 Lev 15:19; 18:19
12:3 Gen 17:12-14
12:6 Luke 2:22
12:8 Lev 5:7; Luke 2:24
13:2-3 Lev 14:56; Deut 24:8

11:44-45 ***I am the LORD your God:*** See note on 18:2. • ***be holy, because I am holy:*** These words express the dominant theme of Leviticus: God is holy. He must be regarded and treated as holy, and he expects holiness from his people (10:3; 19:2). The profound teaching of this verse is that God's own nature permeates those who covenant with him (see also 11:45; 20:7, 26; 21:8, 15; 22:9, 16, 32), and they become his holy people (Exod 22:31; Deut 28:9; cp. 1 Pet 1:16).

11:45 ***brought you up from the land of Egypt:*** This or a similar phrase is found often throughout the Pentateuch (see Exod 13:9; 20:2; Lev 19:36; 22:33; 25:38; 26:13; Num 15:41; Deut 4:37). Each time, it reminds the Israelites, God's covenant people, of God's great act in liberating them from Egypt. The Exodus event is frequently commemorated elsewhere in the OT (Ps 80:8; 106:21; Isa 11:16; Jer 34:13; Hos 12:9; 13:4; Amos 2:10).

12:1-8 These verses detail the regulations pertaining to childbirth. Any bodily discharge, even blood, was considered "abnormal" because it reduced the vitality of the individual and rendered the person ceremonially unclean (see notes on 5:3; 11:1–15:33). Accordingly, not childbirth but the discharge accompanying it is addressed in these verses (12:2, 5, 7). The uncleanness was not sinful in itself, but only if it was neglected and allowed to come into contact with what is holy (see 5:2-3).

12:2 ***menstrual period:*** See 15:19-24.

12:3 By the ***eighth day,*** a baby's system has developed to a point where the blood can clot properly, rendering circumcision relatively safe.

12:4 These ***thirty-three days*** are added to the seven previous days (12:2, 3) to yield a total of forty days to complete the mother's period of purification.

12:5 ***two weeks . . . sixty-six days:*** The total is eighty days, double the time required for the birth of a son (see also 27:2-7).

12:6 ***purification offering:*** The Hebrew word is the same as that for the sin offering (*khatta't,* see note on 4:1–5:13). This leads some scholars to think that this offering dealt only with purification or decontamination, including those cases mentioned in 5:1-6. The offering here was certainly part of a purification ritual, but it seems more likely that the sin offering repaired a lack or failure. In this context, the issue is purity rather than sin, and the focus is on restoring the woman to community fellowship, not forgiving a sinner. • ***Tabernacle:*** Literally *Tent of Meeting*; see note on 1:1.

12:7 ***to purify her:*** Or *to make atonement for her;* also in 12:8. "Atonement" can be understood in this context to stress ceremonial cleansing and reconciliation of the worshiper (see 4:20; see also note on 1:4).

12:8 ***cannot afford to bring a lamb:*** The alternative offering provided for the poorer class of society (see 5:7-13; cp. Luke 2:22-24).

13:1–14:57 Concerning the regulations pertaining to infections, the principle of normal and abnormal comes into play (see "Clean and Unclean" at 11:1–15:33, p. 213). Whether in a person, clothing, or a building, infections are not normal: They indicate disease and death, the antitheses of wholeness, and were therefore declared unclean.

13:1-46 ***a serious skin disease*** (Hebrew *tsara'at*): Traditionally rendered *leprosy.* The Hebrew word throughout this

13:6
Lev 11:25
13:10
Num 12:10
2 Kgs 5:27
13:16
Luke 5:12-14
13:18
Exod 9:9

a serious skin disease, that person must be
brought to Aaron the priest or to one of his
sons. [3]The priest will examine the affected
area of the skin. If the hair in the affected
area has turned white and the problem
appears to be more than skin-deep, it is a
serious skin disease, and the priest who
examines it must pronounce the person ceremonially unclean.

[4]"But if the affected area of the skin is
only a white discoloration and does not appear to be more than skin-deep, and if the
hair on the spot has not turned white, the
priest will quarantine the person for seven
days. [5]On the seventh day the priest will
make another examination. If he finds
the affected area has not changed and the
problem has not spread on the skin, the
priest will quarantine the person for seven
more days. [6]On the seventh day the priest
will make another examination. If he finds
the affected area has faded and has not
spread, the priest will pronounce the person ceremonially clean. It was only a rash.
The person's clothing must be washed, and
the person will be ceremonially clean. [7]But
if the rash continues to spread after the person has been examined by the priest and
has been pronounced clean, the infected
person must return to be examined again.
[8]If the priest finds that the rash has spread,
he must pronounce the person ceremonially unclean, for it is indeed a skin disease.

[9]"Anyone who develops a serious skin
disease must go to the priest for an examination. [10]If the priest finds a white swelling
on the skin, and some hair on the spot has
turned white, and there is an open sore in
the affected area, [11]it is a chronic skin disease, and the priest must pronounce the
person ceremonially unclean. In such cases
the person need not be quarantined, for it
is obvious that the skin is defiled by the disease.

[12]"Now suppose the disease has spread
all over the person's skin, covering the
body from head to foot. [13]When the priest
examines the infected person and finds
that the disease covers the entire body, he
will pronounce the person ceremonially
clean. Since the skin has turned completely
white, the person is clean. [14]But if any open
sores appear, the infected person will be
pronounced ceremonially unclean. [15]The
priest must make this pronouncement as
soon as he sees an open sore, since open
sores indicate the presence of a skin disease. [16]However, if the open sores heal and
turn white like the rest of the skin, the person must return to the priest [17]for another
examination. If the affected areas have
indeed turned white, the priest will then
pronounce the person ceremonially clean
by declaring, 'You are clean!'

[18]"If anyone has a boil on the skin that
has started to heal, [19]but a white swelling
or a reddish white spot develops in its place,
that person must go to the priest to be examined. [20]If the priest examines it and finds
it to be more than skin-deep, and if the
hair in the affected area has turned white,
the priest must pronounce the person ceremonially unclean. The boil has become
a serious skin disease. [21]But if the priest
finds no white hair on the affected area and
the problem appears to be no more than
skin-deep and has faded, the priest must
quarantine the person for seven days. [22]If
during that time the affected area spreads
on the skin, the priest must pronounce the
person ceremonially unclean, because it is
a serious disease. [23]But if the area grows no

passage is used to describe various skin diseases; it is much broader than the severely disfiguring Hansen's disease (see note on 13:2). This larger range included symptoms such as an open sore (13:10), a boil (13:18), a burn (13:24), a sore on the head or chin (13:29), shiny white patches (13:38), or abnormal baldness (13:40). A general test was whether or not the abnormality was spreading (13:5-8). If so, a quarantine was ordered for as long as the disorder persisted (13:46). Not just people, but clothing (13:47-59) and even buildings (14:33-53) could contract such infections.

13:2 Skin disorders that were potentially contagious, such as ***swelling or a rash or discolored skin,*** required precautions to arrest their spread. Until a disorder was healed, the person was deemed unclean. The diseases described in this section may range from something as simple as an allergic rash, ringworm, or eczema to something as serious as gangrene. In OT times, skin conditions were diagnosed by observation. The priests not only had a religious function, but they also served as physicians. • ***one of his sons:*** Or *one of his descendants.* These priestly functions were to apply to future generations of priests as well.

13:3 ***more than skin-deep:*** This indicates that either the infection had eaten away the skin or the infection was visible beneath the skin. The white hair, together with the depression in the skin, indicated a skin disease that could spread (13:21-23). This made the person unclean (13:8).

13:4-5 The purpose of a ***quarantine*** was primarily diagnostic. It gave the priest an opportunity to examine the patient's symptoms over a period of time.

13:8 If ***the rash*** had ***spread,*** then the priest declared the person unclean and the isolation became long-term.

13:10 The presence of an ***open sore*** was the crucial factor, because it indicated infection.

13:12-13 The ***completely white*** skin might refer simply to a loss of pigment (see also 13:3), whereas raw flesh (13:10, 14) indicated infection and ceremonial uncleanness.

13:20 ***skin-deep:*** See note on 13:3.

larger and does not spread, it is merely the scar from the boil, and the priest will pronounce the person ceremonially clean.

24“If anyone has suffered a burn on the skin and the burned area changes color, becoming either reddish white or shiny white, 25the priest must examine it. If he finds that the hair in the affected area has turned white and the problem appears to be more than skin-deep, a skin disease has broken out in the burn. The priest must then pronounce the person ceremonially unclean, for it is clearly a serious skin disease. 26But if the priest finds no white hair on the affected area and the problem appears to be no more than skin-deep and has faded, the priest must quarantine the infected person for seven days. 27On the seventh day the priest must examine the person again. If the affected area has spread on the skin, the priest must pronounce that person ceremonially unclean, for it is clearly a serious skin disease. 28But if the affected area has not changed or spread on the skin and has faded, it is simply a swelling from the burn. The priest will then pronounce the person ceremonially clean, for it is only the scar from the burn.

29“If anyone, either a man or woman, has a sore on the head or chin, 30the priest must examine it. If he finds it is more than skin-deep and has fine yellow hair on it, the priest must pronounce the person ceremonially unclean. It is a scabby sore of the head or chin. 31If the priest examines the scabby sore and finds that it is only skin-deep but there is no black hair on it, he must quarantine the person for seven days. 32On the seventh day the priest must examine the sore again. If he finds that the scabby sore has not spread, and there is no yellow hair on it, and it appears to be only skin-deep, 33the person must shave off all hair except the hair on the affected area. Then the priest must quarantine the person for another seven days. 34On the seventh day he will examine the sore again. If it has not spread and appears to be no more than skin-deep, the priest will pronounce the person ceremonially clean. The person’s clothing must be washed, and the person will be ceremonially clean. 35But if the scabby sore begins to spread after the person is pronounced clean, 36the priest must do another examination. If he finds that the sore has spread, the priest does not need to look for yellow hair. The infected person is ceremonially unclean. 37But if the color of the scabby sore does not change and black hair has grown on it, it has healed. The priest will then pronounce the person ceremonially clean.

38“If anyone, either a man or woman, has shiny white patches on the skin, 39the priest must examine the affected area. If he finds that the shiny patches are only pale white, this is a harmless skin rash, and the person is ceremonially clean.

40“If a man loses his hair and his head becomes bald, he is still ceremonially clean. 41And if he loses hair on his forehead, he simply has a bald forehead; he is still clean. 42However, if a reddish white sore appears on the bald area at the top or back of his head, this is a skin disease. 43The priest must examine him, and if he finds swelling around the reddish white sore anywhere on the man’s head and it looks like a skin disease, 44the man is indeed infected with a skin disease and is unclean. The priest must pronounce him ceremonially unclean because of the sore on his head.

45“Those who suffer from a serious skin disease must tear their clothing and leave their hair uncombed. They must cover their mouth and call out, ‘Unclean! Unclean!’ 46As long as the serious disease lasts, they will be ceremonially unclean. They must live in isolation in their place outside the camp.

13:27 Lev 13:5
13:33 Lev 14:8
13:34 Lev 14:8
13:40 2 Kgs 2:23; Isa 15:2; Ezek 29:18; Amos 8:10
13:45 Lam 4:15
13:46 Num 5:1-4; 12:14; 2 Kgs 7:3; 15:5; Luke 17:12

13:24-25 The priest was to inspect the ***burned area*** to see if the wound had become infected (see 13:9-17). • ***hair . . . turned white:*** See 13:18-23.

13:30 The ***scabby sore*** suggested a fungal infection in the scalp or beard, hidden by hair. The symptoms included loss of hair and crusty skin.

13:38-39 If a ***skin rash*** showed pus or inflammation (13:42), it was probably an infection. If it only showed as a whitened area, it was probably vitiligo (leucoderma). With this harmless disorder, patches of skin lose their pigmentation.

13:42 A ***reddish white sore*** perhaps indicated pus and inflammation.

13:45 ***and leave their hair uncombed:*** Or *and uncover their heads.* Tearing one’s ***clothing,*** letting one’s hair go ***uncombed,*** and covering the ***mouth*** were common ways of expressing mourning (10:6). • The cry of ***Unclean! Unclean!*** denoted social unacceptability as much as a health threat. It warned others that the individual’s skin disorder could be contagious and that holy things should not touch the unclean person.

13:46 The Tabernacle containing the Ark was in the center of the camp, so that God could be considered as being in the camp (Deut 23:14). As long as an individual’s skin disorder persisted, he was to stay ***in isolation . . . outside the camp.*** This ensured that the infection would not spread to others and that the uncleanness would not come in contact with holy things. Even Miriam, sister of Moses and Aaron, had to spend seven days outside the camp (Num 12:15). This area was not exclusive to those suffering from skin disorders. The uneaten sin offering was taken there and burned (4:21). Criminals were executed there (24:14, 23), and corpses were carried there to avoid contaminating the area where the people lived (10:4-5). Even bodily functions were attended to outside the camp (Deut 23:12-14).

13:51 Lev 14:44
14:2 Matt 8:4 Mark 1:40-45 Luke 5:12-14; 17:12-14
14:3 Lev 13:46
14:4 Lev 14:6, 49-52 Num 19:6
14:6 Ps 51:7
14:8 Lev 14:9 Num 8:7
14:9 Lev 13:33; 14:8 Num 6:9

Treatment of Contaminated Clothing

47“Now suppose mildew contaminates some woolen or linen clothing, 48woolen or linen fabric, the hide of an animal, or anything made of leather. 49If the contaminated area in the clothing, the animal hide, the fabric, or the leather article has turned greenish or reddish, it is contaminated with mildew and must be shown to the priest. 50After examining the affected spot, the priest will put the article in quarantine for seven days. 51On the seventh day the priest must inspect it again. If the contaminated area has spread, the clothing or fabric or leather is clearly contaminated by a serious mildew and is ceremonially unclean. 52The priest must burn the item—the clothing, the woolen or linen fabric, or piece of leather—for it has been contaminated by a serious mildew. It must be completely destroyed by fire.

53“But if the priest examines it and finds that the contaminated area has not spread in the clothing, the fabric, or the leather, 54the priest will order the object to be washed and then quarantined for seven more days. 55Then the priest must examine the object again. If he finds that the contaminated area has not changed color after being washed, even if it did not spread, the object is defiled. It must be completely burned up, whether the contaminated spot is on the inside or outside. 56But if the priest examines it and finds that the contaminated area has faded after being washed, he must cut the spot from the clothing, the fabric, or the leather. 57If the spot later reappears on the clothing, the fabric, or the leather article, the mildew is clearly spreading, and the contaminated object must be burned up. 58But if the spot disappears from the clothing, the fabric, or the leather article after it has been washed, it must be washed again; then it will be ceremonially clean.

59“These are the instructions for dealing with mildew that contaminates woolen or linen clothing or fabric or anything made of leather. This is how the priest will determine whether these items are ceremonially clean or unclean.”

Cleansing from Skin Diseases

14 And the LORD said to Moses, 2“The following instructions are for those seeking ceremonial purification from a skin disease. Those who have been healed must be brought to the priest, 3who will examine them at a place outside the camp. If the priest finds that someone has been healed of a serious skin disease, 4he will perform a purification ceremony, using two live birds that are ceremonially clean, a stick of cedar, some scarlet yarn, and a hyssop branch. 5The priest will order that one bird be slaughtered over a clay pot filled with fresh water. 6He will take the live bird, the cedar stick, the scarlet yarn, and the hyssop branch, and dip them into the blood of the bird that was slaughtered over the fresh water. 7The priest will then sprinkle the blood of the dead bird seven times on the person being purified of the skin disease. When the priest has purified the person, he will release the live bird in the open field to fly away.

8“The persons being purified must then wash their clothes, shave off all their hair, and bathe themselves in water. Then they will be ceremonially clean and may return to the camp. However, they must remain outside their tents for seven days. 9On the seventh day they must again shave all the hair from their heads, including the hair of the beard and eyebrows. They must also

---

13:47-59 The rainy season in Israel, when the weather is humid and cool, extends from mid-October through March. Mildew flourishes during this time, and the spores can trigger serious allergic reactions, posing a health problem. The regulations for mildew in clothing were similar to those for infections in people. If the mildew showed signs of spreading, it was serious. If it could be stopped or washed or cut out, a garment could be saved. This process was similar to the treatment of rot and mold in buildings (14:33-53).

13:47 ***mildew:*** Traditionally rendered *leprosy.* The Hebrew term used throughout this passage is the same term used for the various skin diseases described in 13:1-46. The word refers here to a variety of molds or mildews that infected cloth or leather.

13:55 ***the contaminated spot:*** The meaning of the Hebrew is uncertain.

14:1-32 These verses, dealing with the purification of infected individuals, are best understood when read in conjunction with 13:1-46.

14:2 ***skin disease:*** Traditionally rendered *leprosy;* see note on 13:2.

14:4 The items listed here were part of the cleansing ritual involving the ashes of the red heifer (Num 19:6), but their exact significance is unknown. See also Heb 9:18-22. ***Hyssop*** (or *juniper;* also in 14:6, 49, 51) was a small plant used for sprinkling blood (Exod 12:22) and in purification rites (Num 19:18).

14:5-7 Killing the bird and sprinkling its blood (14:7) reflects Exod 24:6-8, where all of Israel was sprinkled with blood to establish the people as God’s covenant community. Here the individual was cleansed by being sprinkled with blood and allowed to return to community membership. Fresh water was also used in cleansing ceremonies (Num 8:7) and in sacrifice preparation (1:9, 13).

14:7 Just as the goat released to Azazel symbolized the removal of sin from the community on the Day of Atonement (16:10, 20-22), the ***release*** of ***the live bird*** symbolized the removal of the individual’s uncleanness.

wash their clothes and bathe themselves in water. Then they will be ceremonially clean.
10"On the eighth day each person be-
ing purified must bring two male lambs and a one-year-old female lamb, all with no defects, along with a grain offering of six quarts of choice flour moistened with
olive oil, and a cup of olive oil. 11Then the
officiating priest will present that person for purification, along with the offerings, before the LORD at the entrance of the Tabernacle. 12The priest will take one of the male
lambs and the olive oil and present them as a guilt offering, lifting them up as a special
offering before the LORD. 13He will then
slaughter the male lamb in the sacred area where sin offerings and burnt offerings are slaughtered. As with the sin offering, the guilt offering belongs to the priest. It is a
most holy offering. 14The priest will then
take some of the blood of the guilt offering and apply it to the lobe of the right ear, the thumb of the right hand, and the big toe of the right foot of the person being purified.
15"Then the priest will pour some of the
olive oil into the palm of his own left hand.
16He will dip his right finger into the oil in
his palm and sprinkle some of it with his
finger seven times before the LORD. 17The
priest will then apply some of the oil in his palm over the blood from the guilt offering that is on the lobe of the right ear, the thumb of the right hand, and the big toe of the right foot of the person being purified.
18The priest will apply the oil remaining in
his hand to the head of the person being purified. Through this process, the priest will purify the person before the LORD.
19"Then the priest must present the sin of-
fering to purify the person who was cured of the skin disease. After that, the priest
will slaughter the burnt offering 20and offer
it on the altar along with the grain offering. Through this process, the priest will purify the person who was healed, and the person will be ceremonially clean.
21"But anyone who is too poor and cannot
afford these offerings may bring one male lamb for a guilt offering, to be lifted up as a special offering for purification. The person must also bring two quarts of choice flour moistened with olive oil for the grain
offering and a cup of olive oil. 22The offer-
ing must also include two turtledoves or two young pigeons, whichever the person can afford. One of the pair must be used for the sin offering and the other for a burnt
offering. 23On the eighth day of the purifi-
cation ceremony, the person being purified must bring the offerings to the priest in the LORD's presence at the entrance of the
Tabernacle. 24The priest will take the lamb
for the guilt offering, along with the olive oil, and lift them up as a special offering to
the LORD. 25Then the priest will slaughter
the lamb for the guilt offering. He will take some of its blood and apply it to the lobe of the right ear, the thumb of the right hand, and the big toe of the right foot of the person being purified.
26"The priest will also pour some of the
olive oil into the palm of his own left hand.
27He will dip his right finger into the oil
in his palm and sprinkle some of it seven
times before the LORD. 28The priest will
then apply some of the oil in his palm over the blood from the guilt offering that is on the lobe of the right ear, the thumb of the right hand, and the big toe of the right foot
of the person being purified. 29The priest
will apply the oil remaining in his hand to the head of the person being purified. Through this process, the priest will purify the person before the LORD.
30"Then the priest will offer the two
turtledoves or the two young pigeons,
whichever the person can afford. 31One of
them is for a sin offering and the other for a burnt offering, to be presented along with

14:10 Lev 23:12-13; Num 6:10; Matt 8:4; Mark 1:44; Luke 5:14
14:12 Exod 29:24
14:13 Lev 1:11-13; 6:24–7:10
14:14 Exod 29:20; Lev 8:23-24
14:20 Lev 14:8
14:21 Lev 5:7, 11; 12:8
14:22 Lev 5:7
14:23 Lev 14:11
14:25 Lev 14:14

14:10 ***grain offering:*** See note on 2:1-16. • ***six quarts:*** Hebrew *3⁄10 of an ephah* [6.6 liters]. • ***a cup:*** Hebrew *1 log* [0.3 liters]; also in 14:21.

14:11 ***Tabernacle:*** Literally *Tent of Meeting;* also in 14:23; see note on 1:1.

14:12 This ***guilt offering*** (sometimes called the "penalty offering" or "reparation offering") was offered because the unclean person living outside the camp could not bring sacrifices, tithes, and offerings during the period of uncleanness (see 5:14-16).

14:14 The ***lobe, thumb,*** and ***big toe*** represent what the whole person hears and does, and where he or she goes (also 14:17, 28; see note on 8:23).

14:15-17 In the ancient world, ***olive oil*** was commonly used to aid healing (see Isa 1:6; Luke 10:34). Its use here might symbolize the healing and cleansing of the infection, which allowed the person to return to the community. Perhaps it also represented restored union between God, the priest, and the worshiper.

14:18 ***will purify:*** Or *will make atonement for;* similarly in 14:19, 20, 21, 29, 31, 53; see note on 1:4.

14:19 This ***sin offering*** was the offering of purification mentioned in 12:6 (see 4:2-3). • The ***burnt offering*** provided atonement for sins committed during the period of uncleanness when the person was unable to bring offerings (see 1:4).

14:20 ***grain offering:*** See note on 2:1-16.

14:21-32 The ritual for the ***poor*** was very similar to the conventional purification offering, but it allowed for the use of less expensive birds in place of a lamb (see 5:7-13).

14:21 ***two quarts:*** Hebrew *1⁄10 of an ephah* [2.2 liters].

14:34 Gen 17:8; Num 32:22; Deut 7:1
14:35 Ps 91:10
14:39 Lev 13:5
14:49 Lev 14:4; Num 19:6
14:56 Lev 13:2
15:2 Lev 22:4; Num 5:2

the grain offering. Through this process, the priest will purify the person before the LORD. 32These are the instructions for purification for those who have recovered from a serious skin disease but who cannot afford to bring the offerings normally required for the ceremony of purification."

Treatment of Contaminated Houses

33Then the LORD said to Moses and Aaron, 34"When you arrive in Canaan, the land I am giving you as your own possession, I may contaminate some of the houses in your land with mildew. 35The owner of such a house must then go to the priest and say, 'It appears that my house has some kind of mildew.' 36Before the priest goes in to inspect the house, he must have the house emptied so nothing inside will be pronounced ceremonially unclean. 37Then the priest will go in and examine the mildew on the walls. If he finds greenish or reddish streaks and the contamination appears to go deeper than the wall's surface, 38the priest will step outside the door and put the house in quarantine for seven days. 39On the seventh day the priest must return for another inspection. If he finds that the mildew on the walls of the house has spread, 40the priest must order that the stones from those areas be removed. The contaminated material will then be taken outside the town to an area designated as ceremonially unclean. 41Next the inside walls of the entire house must be scraped thoroughly and the scrapings dumped in the unclean place outside the town. 42Other stones will be brought in to replace the ones that were removed, and the walls will be replastered.

43"But if the mildew reappears after all the stones have been replaced and the house has been scraped and replastered, 44the priest must return and inspect the house again. If he finds that the mildew has spread, the walls are clearly contaminated with a serious mildew, and the house is defiled. 45It must be torn down, and all its stones, timbers, and plaster must be carried out of town to the place designated as ceremonially unclean. 46Those who enter the house during the period of quarantine will be ceremonially unclean until evening, 47and all who sleep or eat in the house must wash their clothing.

48"But if the priest returns for his inspection and finds that the mildew has not reappeared in the house after the fresh plastering, he will pronounce it clean because the mildew is clearly gone. 49To purify the house the priest must take two birds, a stick of cedar, some scarlet yarn, and a hyssop branch. 50He will slaughter one of the birds over a clay pot filled with fresh water. 51He will take the cedar stick, the hyssop branch, the scarlet yarn, and the live bird, and dip them into the blood of the slaughtered bird and into the fresh water. Then he will sprinkle the house seven times. 52When the priest has purified the house in exactly this way, 53he will release the live bird in the open fields outside the town. Through this process, the priest will purify the house, and it will be ceremonially clean.

54"These are the instructions for dealing with serious skin diseases, including scabby sores; 55and mildew, whether on clothing or in a house; 56and a swelling on the skin, a rash, or discolored skin. 57This procedure will determine whether a person or object is ceremonially clean or unclean.

"These are the instructions regarding skin diseases and mildew."

Bodily Discharges (15:1-33)

15 The LORD said to Moses and Aaron, 2"Give the following instructions to the people of Israel.

14:33-53 The contamination of buildings by rot or mildew made them unhealthy or even unsafe. These buildings were considered diseased and therefore not whole or clean (see note on 11:1–15:33). The inspection and treatment process was similar to the one for mildew in clothing (13:47-59).

14:34 ***I may contaminate:*** In the absolute monotheism of biblical language, God causes or allows everything. For example, Exod 21:13 describes an accidental death as something that God allowed to happen (see also Deut 19:4-5). • ***mildew:*** Traditionally rendered *leprosy;* see note on 13:47.

14:36 Having ***the house emptied*** indicated that it was not actually unclean until the priest pronounced it so. The owner would remove furnishings so that they would not be included in the quarantine.

14:37 If the mildew extended ***deeper than the wall's surface*** it was more serious than if it were just on the surface. The same idea was expressed by "skin-deep" in the examination of infected individuals (see note on 13:3).

14:54-57 A summary statement about infections of all sorts (cp. 11:46-47).

14:54-55 ***serious skin diseases . . . mildew:*** This Hebrew word is traditionally rendered *leprosy;* see notes on 13:2, 47.

15:1-33 The principle of normal and abnormal and the created order again aids the interpretation of these regulations (see "Clean and Unclean" at 11:1–15:33, p. 213). Bodily discharges, such as infections (see note on 13:1-46), were not "normal" because they weakened the vitality of the person, so the person was not seen as whole. Whether male (15:1-18) or female (15:19-33), such a person became unclean.

"Any man who has a bodily discharge is
ceremonially unclean. 3This defilement is
caused by his discharge, whether the discharge continues or stops. In either case
the man is unclean. 4Any bed on which the
man with the discharge lies and anything
on which he sits will be ceremonially unclean. 5So if you touch the man's bed, you
must wash your clothes and bathe yourself
in water, and you will remain unclean until evening. 6If you sit where the man with
the discharge has sat, you must wash your
clothes and bathe yourself in water, and
you will remain unclean until evening. 7If
you touch the man with the discharge, you
must wash your clothes and bathe yourself
in water, and you will remain unclean until
evening. 8If the man spits on you, you must
wash your clothes and bathe yourself in
water, and you will remain unclean until
evening. 9Any saddle blanket on which the
man rides will be ceremonially unclean.
10If you touch anything that was under the
man, you will be unclean until evening. You
must wash your clothes and bathe yourself
in water, and you will remain unclean until
evening. 11If the man touches you without
first rinsing his hands, you must wash your
clothes and bathe yourself in water, and you
will remain unclean until evening. 12Any
clay pot the man touches must be broken,
and any wooden utensil he touches must be
rinsed with water.

13"When the man with the discharge is
healed, he must count off seven days for the
period of purification. Then he must wash
his clothes and bathe himself in fresh water, and he will be ceremonially clean. 14On
the eighth day he must get two turtledoves
or two young pigeons and come before the
LORD at the entrance of the Tabernacle and
give his offerings to the priest. 15The priest
will offer one bird for a sin offering and the
other for a burnt offering. Through this
process, the priest will purify the man before the LORD for his discharge.

16"Whenever a man has an emission of
semen, he must bathe his entire body in
water, and he will remain ceremonially unclean until the next evening. 17Any clothing
or leather with semen on it must be washed
in water, and it will remain unclean until
evening. 18After a man and a woman have
sexual intercourse, they must each bathe
in water, and they will remain unclean until
the next evening.

19"Whenever a woman has her menstrual
period, she will be ceremonially unclean
for seven days. Anyone who touches her
during that time will be unclean until evening. 20Anything on which the woman lies
or sits during the time of her period will
be unclean. 21If any of you touch her bed,
you must wash your clothes and bathe yourself in water, and you will remain unclean
until evening. 22If you touch any object she
has sat on, you must wash your clothes and
bathe yourself in water, and you will remain
unclean until evening. 23This includes her
bed or any other object she has sat on, you
will be unclean until evening if you touch it.
24If a man has sexual intercourse with her
and her blood touches him, her menstrual
impurity will be transmitted to him. He will

15:12 Lev 6:28; 11:32-33
15:13 Lev 15:28
15:15 Lev 14:30-31
15:16 Lev 22:4; Deut 23:10-11
15:18 1 Sam 21:4
15:19 Lev 12:2
15:24 Lev 18:19; 20:18; Ezek 18:6

15:2 ***bodily discharge*** (literally *a flowing from his flesh*): Most scholars interpret the word *flesh* as a euphemism for sexual organs and the symptoms described here as indicating an infection of gonorrhea. Others suggest that it refers to a discharge of semen or even diarrhea. A discharge of semen is unlikely, however, because that is singled out in 15:16-17 and required only washing with water. It is clear that this bodily discharge proceeded from "under the man" (15:10) and contaminated anything he sat on or lay upon (15:4, 6, 9).

15:7-12 ***touch . . . wash:*** See note on 11:24-25.

15:12 ***wooden utensil . . . rinsed:*** See note on 6:28.

15:13-15 In contrast to the man with a skin disease (see 13:46), a man with a bodily discharge was apparently allowed to live at home. He did not have to undergo the more elaborate cleansing ritual described in ch 14. He simply had to wait seven days after the discharge ceased, wash (15:13), and present the least expensive animal sacrifice of two birds—one as a ***sin offering*** and the other as a whole ***burnt offering.***

15:14 ***Tabernacle:*** Literally *Tent of Meeting;* also in 15:29; see note on 1:1.

15:15 ***will purify:*** Or *will make atonement for;* also in 15:30; see note on 1:4.

15:16-17 ***until the next evening:*** Literally *until evening;* also in 15:18. In the case of an ***emission of semen,*** the discharge was not a sign of illness (see note on 15:1-33). Still, the same rule applied; the man must wash and be considered unclean until the next evening.

15:18 If the seminal emission involved ***sexual intercourse,*** both the man and the woman became unclean and had to wash and remain unclean until the next evening. Although it involved a bodily emission, sexual intercourse was not an infection or abnormality, and it required no sacrifices.

15:19-23 There is nothing wrong or diseased about a woman's ***menstrual period.*** However, because it is accompanied by a bloody discharge, the woman was considered ceremonially unclean (see 15:32-33). The restrictions were similar to the restrictions on the man with the bodily discharge (15:2-12): She was allowed to live at home, but whatever she sat on became unclean. Anyone who touched her had to wash, and presumably she also did so at the end of the seven-day quarantine. However, no animal sacrifice was required.

15:24 ***Sexual intercourse*** with a woman during her menstrual period will later be forbidden and given a harsh penalty (18:19). This verse probably describes a case in which the woman's menstrual flow went unnoticed when the sexual activity began or in which the woman's period began during intercourse. The

15:25 Matt 9:20; Mark 5:25; Luke 8:43-44
15:30 Lev 5:7; 14:22
15:31 Num 5:3; 19:13, 20
16:1 Lev 10:1-2
16:2 Exod 25:21-22; 30:10; Heb 9:25
16:3 Lev 16:6-7
16:4 Exod 28:39-43; 39:27-29; Ezek 44:17-18
16:6 Lev 9:7; Heb 5:1-3; 7:27-28; 9:7

remain unclean for seven days, and any bed on which he lies will be unclean.

25"If a woman has a flow of blood for many days that is unrelated to her menstrual period, or if the blood continues beyond the normal period, she is ceremonially unclean. As during her menstrual period, the woman will be unclean as long as the discharge continues. 26Any bed she lies on and any object she sits on during that time will be unclean, just as during her normal menstrual period. 27If any of you touch these things, you will be ceremonially unclean. You must wash your clothes and bathe yourself in water, and you will remain unclean until evening.

28"When the woman's bleeding stops, she must count off seven days. Then she will be ceremonially clean. 29On the eighth day she must bring two turtledoves or two young pigeons and present them to the priest at the entrance of the Tabernacle. 30The priest will offer one for a sin offering and the other for a burnt offering. Through this process, the priest will purify her before the LORD for the ceremonial impurity caused by her bleeding.

31"This is how you will guard the people of Israel from ceremonial uncleanness. Otherwise they would die, for their impurity would defile my Tabernacle that stands among them. 32These are the instructions for dealing with anyone who has a bodily discharge—a man who is unclean because of an emission of semen 33or a woman during her menstrual period. It applies to any man or woman who has a bodily discharge, and to a man who has sexual intercourse with a woman who is ceremonially unclean."

4. THE DAY OF ATONEMENT (16:1-34)

16 The LORD spoke to Moses after the death of Aaron's two sons, who died after they entered the LORD's presence and burned the wrong kind of fire before him. 2The LORD said to Moses, "Warn your brother, Aaron, not to enter the Most Holy Place behind the inner curtain whenever he chooses; if he does, he will die. For the Ark's cover—the place of atonement—is there, and I myself am present in the cloud above the atonement cover.

3"When Aaron enters the sanctuary area, he must follow these instructions fully. He must bring a young bull for a sin offering and a ram for a burnt offering. 4He must put on his linen tunic and the linen undergarments worn next to his body. He must tie the linen sash around his waist and put the linen turban on his head. These are sacred garments, so he must bathe himself in water before he puts them on. 5Aaron must take from the community of Israel two male goats for a sin offering and a ram for a burnt offering.

6"Aaron will present his own bull as a sin offering to purify himself and his family, making them right with the LORD. 7Then he must take the two male goats and present

---

regulations required the man who came into contact with her blood to share the woman's seven-day quarantine.

15:25-29 Normal menstruation required no offering from the woman (15:19-24). A discharge of blood that exceeded seven days required a cleansing ceremony similar to that for the man cleansed of a bodily discharge (15:13-15; see also Matt 9:20-22).

15:32-33 A summary of the principles stated in 15:1-31. Bodily discharges—whether pus, semen, menstrual fluid, or blood—made an individual ceremonially unclean.

16:1-34 The Day of Atonement, the tenth day of the seventh month (see 16:29; 23:27; Num 29:7), was the most solemn day of the year for Israelites. It was the only required fast, and it was a Sabbath of rest for all the people (23:32). Introduced by the Festival of Trumpets (Num 29:1, 7-11), it was the day when the corporate sins of the community were atoned for. Only the high priest (Aaron) could officiate, because only he could represent all the people, including other priests (Aaron's sons). The Day of Atonement is celebrated today as Yom Kippur.

16:2 An *inner curtain* separated the Holy Place from the *Most Holy Place.* Conceptually, the sanctuary was God's palace, the Most Holy Place was his throne room, and the Ark was his throne (see 1:1). In the ancient Near East, entering the presence of a king without invitation meant risking death (Esth 4:11). The Most Holy Place, therefore, was not a place that Aaron could enter casually. It was off-limits even to the high priest, except when his presence was required by God as part of the ritual of the Day of Atonement.

16:4 For most of the ritual of the Day of Atonement, the high priest wore plain *linen* clothing rather than his normal robes. This seems to symbolize the humility that should characterize all the people on this solemn occasion. When the high priest stood before God on behalf of his people, he had nothing to commend himself or the people. But when he stood before the people on God's behalf, his official robes reflected the glory and splendor of God (16:23).

16:6 ***to purify himself and his family, making them right with the LORD:*** Or *to make atonement for himself and his family;* similarly in 16:11, 17, 24, 34; see notes on 1:4; 4:20. • The writer of the Epistle to the Hebrews makes a clear analogy between Aaron's work for Israel and Christ's work for the believer. Both brought atonement to their people. Before Aaron could offer a sin offering for the people, he had to offer a sacrifice for himself to make certain his own sins were forgiven (Heb 5:1-3). However, although Christ was tempted, he did not sin (Heb 4:15). Therefore, in his role as high priest for all Christians, he had no need to make a similar sacrifice (Heb 7:26-28).

16:7 ***Tabernacle:*** Literally *Tent of Meeting;* also in 16:16, 17, 20, 23, 33; see note on 1:1.

them to the LORD at the entrance of the
Tabernacle. 8He is to cast sacred lots to determine which goat will be reserved as an
offering to the LORD and which will carry
the sins of the people to the wilderness of
Azazel. 9Aaron will then present as a sin offering the goat chosen by lot for the LORD.
10The other goat, the scapegoat chosen by
lot to be sent away, will be kept alive, standing before the LORD. When it is sent away to
Azazel in the wilderness, the people will be
purified and made right with the LORD.
11"Aaron will present his own bull as a
sin offering to purify himself and his family, making them right with the LORD. After
he has slaughtered the bull as a sin offering,
12he will fill an incense burner with burning coals from the altar that stands before
the LORD. Then he will take two handfuls of
fragrant powdered incense and will carry
the burner and the incense behind the inner curtain. 13There in the LORD's presence
he will put the incense on the burning coals
so that a cloud of incense will rise over the
Ark's cover—the place of atonement—that
rests on the Ark of the Covenant. If he follows these instructions, he will not die.
14Then he must take some of the blood of
the bull, dip his finger in it, and sprinkle it
on the east side of the atonement cover. He
must sprinkle blood seven times with his
finger in front of the atonement cover.
15"Then Aaron must slaughter the first
goat as a sin offering for the people and
carry its blood behind the inner curtain.
There he will sprinkle the goat's blood over
the atonement cover and in front of it, just
as he did with the bull's blood. 16Through
this process, he will purify the Most Holy
Place, and he will do the same for the entire
Tabernacle, because of the defiling sin and
rebellion of the Israelites. 17No one else is
allowed inside the Tabernacle when Aaron
enters it for the purification ceremony in
the Most Holy Place. No one may enter until
he comes out again after purifying himself,
his family, and all the congregation of Israel,
making them right with the LORD.
18"Then Aaron will come out to purify the
altar that stands before the LORD. He will do
this by taking some of the blood from the
bull and the goat and putting it on each of
the horns of the altar. 19Then he must sprinkle the blood with his finger seven times
over the altar. In this way, he will cleanse it
from Israel's defilement and make it holy.
20"When Aaron has finished purifying
the Most Holy Place and the Tabernacle and
the altar, he must present the live goat. 21He
will lay both of his hands on the goat's head
and [k]confess over it all the wickedness, rebellion, and sins of the people of Israel. In
this way, he will transfer the people's sins to
the head of the goat. Then a man specially
chosen for the task will drive the goat into
the wilderness. 22As the goat goes into the
wilderness, it will carry all the people's sins
upon itself into a desolate land.
23"When Aaron goes back into the Tabernacle, he must take off the linen garments
he was wearing when he entered the Most
Holy Place, and he must leave the garments
there. 24Then he must bathe himself with
water in a sacred place, put on his regular
garments, and go out to sacrifice a burnt offering for himself and a burnt offering for
the people. Through this process, he will purify himself and the people, making them
right with the LORD. 25He must then burn
all the fat of the sin offering on the altar.
26"The man chosen to drive the scapegoat
into the wilderness of Azazel must wash his
clothes and bathe himself in water. Then he
may return to the camp.
27"The bull and the goat presented as sin
offerings, whose blood Aaron takes into the

16:10 Isa 53:4-10
16:11 Heb 9:7
16:12 Exod 30:34-38; Num 16:18, 46
16:13 Exod 25:22; Lev 22:9
16:14 Lev 4:17
16:15 Heb 6:19; 9:3, 7, 12
16:16 Exod 29:36; 30:10; Heb 2:17
16:18 Lev 4:7, 25; Ezek 43:20
16:19 Lev 4:6; 16:14
16:21 Lev 5:5; [k]*yadah* (3034) ‣2 Chr 5:13
16:22 Isa 53:12
16:23 Exod 28:42; Lev 16:4
16:24 Exod 29:4-9
16:27 Lev 4:11-12; 6:30

16:8 The term *Azazel* is found only in 16:8, 10, 26. This word has generally been interpreted in four different ways: (1) as a word meaning "the goat of going away"; (2) as a demon that lived in the wilderness; (3) as a strengthened form of the Hebrew word for "go, leave," meaning "utter loss"; and (4) as a rocky cliff over which the goat was pushed. Since this goat represented the removal of the sins of Israel from the camp (16:22), the first interpretation is probably the simplest solution.

16:10 ***wilderness, the people will be purified and made right with the LORD:*** Or *wilderness, it will make atonement for the people.*

16:12 ***inner curtain:*** See note on 16:2.

16:13 ***that rests on the Ark of the Covenant:*** Literally *that is above the Testimony.* The Hebrew word for "testimony" refers to the terms of the LORD's covenant with Israel as written on stone tablets, which were kept in the Ark.

16:16 The high priest needed to ***purify*** (or *make atonement for;* similarly in 16:17a, 18, 20, 27, 33) the ***Most Holy Place*** and the rest of the ***Tabernacle*** because, over the course of the year, the sins the Israelites had committed had brought uncleanness on the whole sanctuary. If the Tabernacle was to remain the place for meeting God in the coming year, it had to be purified. The same applied to the altar (16:18).

16:23-24 For this ceremony, the high priest had to put on special clothing (16:4), which he used for no other purpose. When the ceremony concluded, he was to ***leave the garments*** in ***the Most Holy Place.*** Many scholars believe that the bathing and changes of clothing were necessary because handling the sin offering brought defilement.

16:27 For the Day of Atonement, the high priest took the ***blood*** of the ***sin offerings . . . into the Most Holy Place.*** As a result, the offerings were ***burned*** and not eaten (4:3-12, 13-21).

16:28 Num 19:8, 10
16:29 Lev 23:26-32; Num 29:7
16:31 Lev 23:32; Ezra 8:21
16:34 Lev 23:14, 21, 30-31; Heb 9:7

Most Holy Place for the purification ceremony, will be carried outside the camp. The
animals' hides, internal organs, and dung
are all to be burned. 28The man who burns
them must wash his clothes and bathe himself in water before returning to the camp.
29"On the tenth day of the appointed
month in early autumn, you must deny yourselves. Neither native-born Israelites nor
foreigners living among you may do any
kind of work. This is a permanent law for
you. 30On that day offerings of purification
will be made for you, and you will be purified in the LORD's presence from all your
sins. 31It will be a Sabbath day of complete
rest for you, and you must deny yourselves.
This is a permanent law for you. 32In future
generations, the purification ceremony will
be performed by the priest who has been
anointed and ordained to serve as high
priest in place of his ancestor Aaron. He
will put on the holy linen garments 33and
purify the Most Holy Place, the Tabernacle,
the altar, the priests, and the entire congregation. 34This is a permanent law for you, to
purify the people of Israel from their sins,
making them right with the LORD once
each year."

Moses followed all these instructions exactly as the LORD had commanded him.

5. EXPRESSIONS OF HOLINESS IN THE COMMUNITY (17:1–26:46)

Inappropriate Worship of God (17:1-9)

17 Then the LORD said to Moses, 2"Give
the following instructions to Aaron
and his sons and all the people of Israel.
This is what the LORD has commanded.

Atonement (16:1-34)

Lev 1:1-17; 4:1–6:7; 17:10-14; 23:26-32; Exod 25:17-22; 30:10-16; Num 15:22-29; 29:7-11; Ps 51:7; Prov 16:6; Ezek 43:18-27; Dan 9:24; John 1:29; Eph 1:7; Col 1:20; Heb 2:16-17; 9:12-14

To worship a holy God, one must remove any obstacle that stands in the way. Atonement removes any sin or uncleanness that inhibits proper worship. In the atoning offerings (see chart, "Israel's Sacrifices," p. 197), the sacrifice represented the life of the worshiper, given in his place so that he might live. Blood was the symbol of life given by God and was reserved as God's portion of each animal offering. Blood represents life, and the blood of the offering represented the life of the worshiper. God had designated the victim's blood, representing the life of the victim, as the means of atonement (17:11). God's grace permitted the death of an animal to be accepted in exchange for the sinner's life.

Leviticus 16 describes the Day of Atonement. On this day, the sins of the community were presented to the Lord by the high priest. Atonement provides both *propitiation* and *expiation*. Expiation is the payment of what is owed. For example, the guilt offering (5:14–6:7) involves damages or loss to property, and the loss must be repaid with a 20 percent surcharge. Propitiation, on the other hand, involves appeasing or pacifying an offended party. The whole burnt offering (1:1-17) and the sin offering (4:1–5:13) require no discernable payment. Instead, the act of laying hands on the victim (4:4-33; 16:21) indicates identification of the worshiper with the animal being sacrificed. The blood, representing the life of the animal (17:14), is presented as a substitute for the life of the worshiper (17:11). The animal is slain, and its blood and certain parts are ceremonially presented to God, thus propitiating (appeasing) him and averting his wrath from the worshiper.

The blood of Jesus brings atonement (Eph 1:7; Col 1:20) and obtains eternal redemption for believers (Heb 9:12). Christ, God's lamb, reconciles us to God (John 1:29; Heb 9:14). He paid our debt of sin (expiation) and satisfied God's judgment against us (propitiation).

16:29 ***tenth day of the appointed month in early autumn:*** Literally *On the tenth day of the seventh month.* This day in the ancient Hebrew lunar calendar occurred in September or October; see note on 16:1-34. • ***must deny yourselves:*** Or *must fast;* also in 16:31. The Hebrew term (*'anah,* "humble, afflict yourselves") is closely connected with fasting (Isa 58:3, 5). • ***foreigners*** (Hebrew *ger*): The Hebrew term denotes those who were not Israelites yet lived among the Israelites. Foreigners participated to some extent in Israelite worship (see Num 9:14) and represented potential converts. They probably did not own land, but were day laborers, sharecroppers, or tenant farmers. However, if they lived among the Israelites, they were expected to abide by Israelite law and customs (see, e.g., 24:16).

16:30 ***offerings of purification will be made for you:*** Or *atonement will be made for you, to purify you.* See note on 1:4.

16:31 The Day of Atonement was regarded as a ***Sabbath day.*** No one in the camp, Israelite or foreigner, was permitted to work (see 19:30).

16:32 ***purification:*** Or *atonement.* See note on 1:4.

17:1–26:46 This section deals with how the community of Israel was to observe holiness. Holiness does not describe one attribute of God among many. Rather, it is the sum of all attributes of his person, nature, and character (see note on Exod 3:5). His "glory" is the manifestation of his perfect person, nature, and character (see 9:6). God's covenant with Israel meant that the people and the nation participated in God's holiness. This holiness depended on Israel's relationship with God. This relationship brought certain ethical and ritual expectations for Israel to uphold.

3“If any native Israelite sacrifices a bull
or a lamb or a goat anywhere inside or outside the camp 4instead of bringing it to the
entrance of the [a]Tabernacle to present it as
an offering to the LORD, that person will
be as guilty as a murderer. Such a person
has shed blood and will be cut off from
the community. 5The purpose of this rule
is to stop the Israelites from sacrificing
animals in the open fields. It will ensure
that they bring their sacrifices to the priest
at the entrance of the Tabernacle, so he
can present them to the LORD as peace
offerings. 6Then the priest will be able to
splatter the blood against the LORD’s altar
at the entrance of the Tabernacle, and he
will burn the fat as a pleasing aroma to the
LORD. 7The people must no longer be unfaithful to the LORD by offering sacrifices
to the goat idols. This is a permanent law
for them, to be observed from generation
to generation.

8“Give them this command as well. If any
native Israelite or foreigner living among
you offers a burnt offering or a sacrifice
9but does not bring it to the entrance of the
Tabernacle to offer it to the LORD, that person will be cut off from the community.

Regulations about Handling Blood (17:10-16)

10“And if any native Israelite or foreigner living among you eats or drinks blood in any
form, I will turn against that person and cut
him off from the community of your people, 11for the life of the body is in its [b]blood.
I have given you the blood on the altar to
purify you, making you right with the LORD.
It is the [b]blood, given in exchange for a life,
that makes purification possible. 12That is
why I have said to the people of Israel, ‘You
must never eat or drink blood—neither you
nor the foreigners living among you.’

13“And if any native Israelite or foreigner
living among you goes hunting and kills an
animal or bird that is approved for eating,
he must drain its blood and cover it with
earth. 14The life of every creature is in its
blood. That is why I have said to the people
of Israel, ‘You must never eat or drink blood,
for the life of any creature is in its blood.’ So
whoever consumes blood will be cut off
from the community.

15“And if any native-born Israelites or foreigners eat the meat of an animal that died
naturally or was torn up by wild animals,
they must wash their clothes and bathe

17:4 Deut 12:5-21
[a]*mishkan* (4908) ‣2 Sam 7:6
17:5 Lev 3:1-2; Deut 12:4-7
17:6 Exod 29:18; Num 18:17
17:7 Exod 22:20; 32:8; Deut 32:17; 2 Chr 11:15; 1 Cor 10:20
17:9 Lev 17:4
17:10 Lev 3:17; Deut 12:16, 23-25
17:11 Gen 9:4; Lev 17:14; Heb 9:22
[b]*dam* (1818) ‣Deut 12:23
17:13 Deut 12:16; Ezek 24:7
17:14 Gen 9:4; Lev 17:11
17:15 Exod 22:31; Lev 7:24; Deut 14:21

17:3-9 These regulations (see also Deut 12:15-21) indicate that unsupervised sacrifice could easily lead to the integration of pagan elements into the true worship of the Lord (17:7). Israel was camped around the Tabernacle (Num 2:2-34), so it was not inconvenient to bring an animal to the sanctuary for slaughter. Deut 12:20-24 anticipates Israel’s settlement in the land and the hardship imposed by this regulation. It permitted slaughtering and eating meat without bringing it to the sanctuary, as long as the blood was not consumed.

17:3 ***bull:*** Or *cow.*

17:4 ***Tabernacle:*** Literally *Tent of Meeting;* also in 17:5, 6, 9; see note on 1:1. • ***will be as guilty as a murderer:*** Literally *will be guilty of blood.* The person had shed an animal’s blood in an unlawful manner. The life of the animal had been given by God; it had to be returned to him in the blood of the sacrificed animal. • ***cut off:*** See note on 7:20-21.

17:5 ***peace offerings:*** See note on 3:1.

17:6 ***fat:*** See note on 1:8; 3:3.

17:7 ***be unfaithful*** (Hebrew *zanah,* “commit fornication”): Israel was not to worship any god but the Lord (Exod 20:3). Israel’s covenant relationship to the Lord was even compared to a marriage (see Hos 1:2), and worshiping other gods could be described as spiritual adultery. In addition, many of the Canaanite religions were fertility cults. This verb reflects the prostitution conducted at Canaanite shrines to induce fertility in the land through rites of magic involving sexual intercourse. • The Hebrew word translated *goat idols* (or *goat demons*) is the plural for a male goat. In the ancient world, the male goat was often a symbol of fertility or of a god of the underworld. During the reign of Jeroboam I, many Levites from the northern kingdom moved south to Jerusalem; they had been appalled by the use of goats and bulls in the northern kingdom’s worship (2 Chr 11:15-16).

17:8 ***foreigner:*** See note on 16:29.

17:10 ***drinks blood:*** See note on 17:4. • ***cut him off:*** See note on 7:20-21.

17:11 ***the life of the body is in its blood:*** Israel was forbidden to consume blood (17:10) because it was symbolic of the life given by God and was reserved as God’s portion of each animal offering. God had also designated the sacrificial blood as the means of atonement. In other words, God’s grace permitted the life of the animal to be accepted in exchange for the life of the sinner. In the NT, the blood of Christ—representing his life freely given—has provided eternal redemption for believers (Heb 9:12). • ***to purify you, making you right with the LORD:*** Or *to make atonement for you*; see notes on 1:4; 4:20.

17:13 ***cover it with earth:*** This restriction kept the hunter from using an animal’s blood for food. Just like the blood of animals presented in altar offerings, the blood of wild game also represented life. Uncovered blood was also the sign of violent crime; innocent blood defiled the land (Num 35:33) and cried out to God for justice (Gen 4:10; see Job 16:18). Covering the blood of a slain animal gave it a symbolic burial. This demonstrated reverence both for the animal’s life and for God, the life-giver. The burial signified the return of that life to God, just like the disposal of the blood by the priest in the altar offerings.

17:14 See 17:10; note on 17:4.

17:15-16 An animal killed by a predator or which died of natural causes still had undrained blood in its tissues. This rendered it ceremonially unclean and a potential source of defilement (22:8). Israelites were to throw such an animal to the dogs (Exod 22:31) or give or sell it to a non-Israelite (Deut 14:21). If an Israelite happened to eat an animal with undrained blood, he or she became ceremonially unclean and had to wash in water. The uncleanness itself was not a sin, but neglect of the unclean state brought punishment.

18:2 Exod 6:7; Lev 11:44
18:3 Exod 23:24; Lev 20:23; Rom 12:2
18:4 Deut 4:1
18:5 Ezek 20:11; Luke 10:28; *Rom 10:5; *Gal 3:12
18:7 Lev 20:11
18:8 Gen 35:22; Lev 20:11; Deut 27:20
18:9 Lev 20:17
18:12 Lev 20:19
18:14 Lev 20:20
18:15 Lev 20:12; Ezek 22:11
18:16 Lev 20:21

themselves in water. They will remain ceremonially unclean until evening, but then
they will be clean. 16But if they do not wash
their clothes and bathe themselves, they
will be punished for their sin."

Sexual Morality and Other Practical Matters (18:1–20:27)

Forbidden Sexual Practices

18 Then the LORD said to Moses, 2"Give
the following instructions to the people of Israel. I am the LORD your God. 3So do
not act like the people in Egypt, where you
used to live, or like the people of Canaan,
where I am taking you. You must not imitate
their way of life. 4You must obey all my regulations and be careful to obey my decrees,
for I am the LORD your God. 5If you obey my
decrees and my regulations, you will find
life through them. I am the LORD.

6"You must never have sexual relations
with a close relative, for I am the LORD.

7"Do not violate your father by having sexual relations with your mother. She is your
mother; you must not have sexual relations
with her.

8"Do not have sexual relations with any
of your father's wives, for this would violate
your father.

9"Do not have sexual relations with your
sister or half sister, whether she is your father's daughter or your mother's daughter,
whether she was born into your household
or someone else's.

10"Do not have sexual relations with your
granddaughter, whether she is your son's
daughter or your daughter's daughter, for
this would violate yourself.

11"Do not have sexual relations with your
stepsister, the daughter of any of your father's wives, for she is your sister.

12"Do not have sexual relations with your
father's sister, for she is your father's close
relative.

13"Do not have sexual relations with your
mother's sister, for she is your mother's
close relative.

14"Do not violate your uncle, your father's
brother, by having sexual relations with his
wife, for she is your aunt.

15"Do not have sexual relations with your
daughter-in-law; she is your son's wife, so
you must not have sexual relations with
her.

16"Do not have sexual relations with your
brother's wife, for this would violate your
brother.

18:1–20:27 Chapters 18 and 20 primarily discuss sexual matters, warning against engaging in pagan practices both religious and secular. These chapters bracket exhortations to pursue holiness in everyday life (ch 19).

18:2 Many Near Eastern treaties began with the name and titles of the ruler who was drawing up the treaty. The phrase ***I am the LORD your God*** gives the name of the Great King, Yahweh (English ***the LORD***), followed by his title, ***your God*** (see also Exod 20:2; Deut 5:6). These words were an abbreviated way to invoke Israel's covenant with God and all that it implied. By reminding the people that they were the Lord's, these words carried an authority that required a response (11:44; 18:4-5). Chapter 18 begins and ends (18:30) with these words, and they appear frequently throughout chs 19–26.

18:4-5 ***regulations . . . decrees:*** The Bible anticipated that the courts would need to interpret the laws that God had provided to apply them to different circumstances. Such interpretations became case laws; the body of these court decisions was called *mishpatim* in Hebrew (cp. "decrees" in 10:11). • Paul alludes to these verses in Rom 10:5 and Gal 3:12, where he contrasts the "way of faith" with the "way of law."

18:6-7 ***have sexual relations with:*** Literally *to uncover the nakedness of.* Similar regulations in Lev 20 use the Hebrew word *shakab* ("lie with"), a word frequently used to indicate an improper sexual relationship.

18:7-8 ***violate your father:*** The Hebrew text here equates having sexual relations with your mother or any of your father's wives with having sexual relations with him (cp. Gen 35:22; 49:4; see also 1 Cor 5:1). The husband and his wife were "two united into one" (Gen 2:24; cp. Eph 5:29). Always in the background of these commands are the commands to honor your parents (Exod 20:12; Lev 20:9) and, by extension, other members of the family (see also note on 20:17).

18:7 ***She is your mother:*** Incest was prohibited because of the disruption it created in families, so the commands concerning this sin included close relatives not necessarily related by blood. Incest was a serious crime because it brought competition and chaos into the family structure. It threatened the safety of the home by violating a family's appropriate intimacy and the sense of belonging shared by its members. • The commands were directly addressed to the male, even though the female could be older (such as one's mother). The male, especially if he was the head of the household or the firstborn, wielded more power than the female; with this position came the responsibility to use that power lawfully. In addition, the male was more likely to be the sexual aggressor in an illicit sexual union, although this was not always the case (e.g., Gen 39:6-18).

18:9 Sexual relations with a full ***sister*** dishonored both parents, and relations with a ***half sister*** dishonored one parent.

18:12-13 ***your father's sister . . . mother's sister:*** These actions would dishonor your father or mother.

18:14 Having sexual relations with ***your aunt*** would dishonor your uncle. In turn, this would also dishonor your father (see 20:20).

18:15 Just as having sexual relations with your father's wife would dishonor your father, having sexual relations with ***your daughter-in-law*** would dishonor your son. The law called for daughters-in-law to be treated like natural daughters (Exod 21:9; cp. Gen 38:1-30).

18:16 Sexual relations with your sister-in-law would be adulterous and disgrace your brother. The exception was the law of levirate marriage (see Deut 25:5-10), which called for a man to marry his brother's widow in order to produce an heir who was considered the dead brother's son.

17 "Do not have sexual relations with both a woman and her daughter. And do not take her granddaughter, whether her son's daughter or her daughter's daughter, and have sexual relations with her. They are close relatives, and this would be a wicked act.

18 "While your wife is living, do not marry her sister and have sexual relations with her, for they would be rivals.

19 "Do not have sexual relations with a woman during her period of menstrual impurity.

20 "Do not defile yourself by having sexual intercourse with your neighbor's wife.

21 "Do not permit any of your children to be offered as a sacrifice to Molech, for you must not bring shame on the name of your God. I am the LORD.

22 "Do not practice homosexuality, having sex with another man as with a woman. It is a detestable sin.

23 "A man must not defile himself by having sex with an animal. And a woman must not offer herself to a male animal to have intercourse with it. This is a perverse act.

24 "Do not defile yourselves in any of these ways, for the people I am driving out before you have defiled themselves in all these ways. 25 Because the entire land has become defiled, I am punishing the people who live there. I will cause the land to vomit them out. 26 You must obey all my decrees and regulations. You must not commit any of these detestable sins. This applies both to native-born Israelites and to the foreigners living among you.

27 "All these detestable activities are practiced by the people of the land where I am taking you, and this is how the land has become defiled. 28 So do not defile the land and give it a reason to vomit you out, as it will vomit out the people who live there now. 29 Whoever commits any of these detestable sins will be cut off from the community of Israel. 30 So obey my instructions, and do not defile yourselves by committing any of these detestable practices that were committed by the people who lived in the land before you. I am the LORD your God."

Holiness in Personal Conduct

19 The LORD also said to Moses, 2 "Give the following instructions to the entire community of Israel. You must be holy because I, the LORD your God, am holy.

3 "Each of you must show great respect for your mother and father, and you must always observe my Sabbath days of rest. I am the LORD your God.

4 "Do not put your trust in idols or make

18:17 Lev 20:14
18:19 Lev 15:24; 20:18
18:20 Exod 20:14; Lev 20:10; Matt 5:27-28; 1 Cor 6:9
18:21 Lev 19:12; 20:1-5; 21:6; Deut 12:31; 2 Kgs 23:10; Mal 1:12
18:22 Gen 19:5; Lev 20:13; Rom 1:27
18:23 Exod 22:19; Lev 20:15-16; Deut 27:21
18:24 Lev 18:3
18:25 Lev 20:22-23; Deut 9:5
18:26 Lev 18:2-3
19:2 Exod 19:6; Lev 11:44; *1 Pet 1:16
19:3 Exod 20:8, 12; Lev 11:44
19:4 Exod 20:23; Lev 26:1

18:17 As with all examples listed in ch 18, marrying a ***woman*** together with ***her daughter*** or ***granddaughter*** was prohibited because of the disruption it would cause in the family order. It would violate the intimacy of the family group by forcing a wife to compete for her husband's affections against a much younger woman. The penalty for this act was death by burning (20:14). • ***do not take:*** Or *do not marry.*

18:18 The word ***rival*** (Hebrew *tsarah*) vividly describes the relationship between Leah and Rachel (Gen 29:16–30:24) and Hannah and Peninnah (1 Sam 1:6); in both cases, the fellow wives were driven to bitter rivalry for their husband's affections.

18:19 See note on 15:24.

18:20 The Hebrew word translated ***defile yourself*** could be more literally translated *to become ceremonially unclean.* • Sexual intercourse with a ***neighbor's wife*** or any married woman defined adultery in the OT. Breaking this law was punishable by death (Deut 22:22). Like incest, adultery threatened the integrity and security of the home and family. In this case, it violated the covenant of marriage and divided the adulterer's affection between his spouse and his mistress.

18:21 ***Molech*** was the national god of the Ammonites (1 Kgs 11:7). This god was later worshiped by Israel during times of apostasy (2 Kgs 23:10; Jer 32:35). Molech probably appears in this list because Molech worship was associated with sexual sins; it seems to have included child sacrifice as well. • To ***bring shame on*** (literally *blaspheme, profane*) ***the name of your God*** meant using the name of the Lord as though it were not holy, such as in a false oath (19:12) or in the worship of a false god (Ezek 20:39).

18:22 In Gen 1:31, God pronounced all things good. This yielded a theology of the created order where good is defined by what God created and by the way he intended it to function. Part of this "good" was the creation of woman as man's companion (Gen 2:22-24). Marriage forms a microcosm of the human race, which stands as the corporate bearer of God's image. Sin, introduced by the Fall (Gen 3), disrupted the created order. ***Homosexuality*** is but one example of sinful violation of God's order; it is tied to the rejection of God by fallen humanity (Rom 1:25-32). • The Hebrew word translated ***detestable*** (*to'ebah*) indicates strong disapproval and disgust (20:13; see also 18:26-30).

18:23 Like homosexuality, bestiality is a violation of the natural order (see note on 18:22). • The phrase ***perverse act*** referred not only to a violation, but to a confusion of the order God created because it broke down clear boundaries that he had established.

18:24-25 ***any of these ways:*** Pagan worship (18:21), homosexuality (18:22), and bestiality (18:23). • ***The land*** was so nauseated by Canaanite practices that it would dramatically ***vomit them out*** (see 18:28).

18:26 ***foreigners:*** See note on 16:29.

18:28 Just as ***the land*** would ***vomit*** out the Canaanites, it would also ***vomit out*** the Israelites if they acted like the Canaanites (see note on 18:24-25; 20:22). This came to pass with the destruction and exile of the northern kingdom by the Assyrians in 722 BC (2 Kgs 17:6) and when the Babylonians destroyed and exiled Judah in 586 BC (2 Kgs 25:8-21).

18:29 ***cut off:*** See note on 7:20-21.

18:30 ***I am the LORD your God:*** See note on 18:2.

19:2 ***be holy:*** See note on 11:44-45.

19:3 ***I am the LORD*** (see 18:2): These words break ch 19 into terse, staccato sections (19:3, 4, 10, 12, 14, 16, 18, 25, 28, 30, 31, 34, 36, 37). Each use served to remind Israel why they were to obey God's regulations.

19:6-7
Lev 7:16-18
19:9
Lev 23:22
Deut 24:19-22
19:11
Exod 20:15-16
19:13
Exod 22:7-15, 21-27; 23:4-9
Deut 24:14-15
Mal 3:5
Jas 5:4
19:14
Deut 27:18
[c]*yare'* (3372)
‣ Lev 25:17
19:15
Exod 23:2-3, 6
Deut 1:17
Prov 24:23
Jas 2:1-4
[d]*shapat* (8199)
‣ Deut 25:1
[e]*tsedeq* (6664)
‣ Lev 19:36
19:16
Exod 23:1, 7
Ezek 22:9

metal images of gods for yourselves. I am
the LORD your God.
5"When you sacrifice a peace offering to
the LORD, offer it properly so you will be accepted by God. 6The sacrifice must be eaten
on the same day you offer it or on the next
day. Whatever is left over until the third
day must be completely burned up. 7If any
of the sacrifice is eaten on the third day, it
will be contaminated, and I will not accept
it. 8Anyone who eats it on the third day will
be punished for defiling what is holy to the
LORD and will be cut off from the community.
9"When you harvest the crops of your
land, do not harvest the grain along the
edges of your fields, and do not pick up
what the harvesters drop. 10It is the same
with your grape crop—do not strip every
last bunch of grapes from the vines, and
do not pick up the grapes that fall to the
ground. Leave them for the poor and the
foreigners living among you. I am the LORD
your God.
11"Do not steal.
"Do not deceive or cheat one another.
12"Do not bring shame on the name of
your God by using it to swear falsely. I am
the LORD.
13"Do not defraud or rob your neighbor.
"Do not make your hired workers wait until the next day to receive their pay.
14"Do not insult the deaf or cause the
blind to stumble. You must [c]fear your God;
I am the LORD.
15"Do not twist justice in legal matters by
favoring the poor or being partial to the rich
and powerful. Always [d]judge people [e]fairly.
16"Do not spread slanderous gossip
among your people.
"Do not stand idly by when your neighbor's life is threatened. I am the LORD.

Family and Community (18:6-30)

Lev 20:14, 21
Gen 19:30-38; 49:3-4
2 Sam 13:1-39
Matt 14:3-5
1 Cor 5:1-2; 6:13-20; 7:2
Gal 5:19-21
Eph 5:3
Jude 1:7
Rev 2:14-16, 20

In Israel, the family was the basic building block for the solidarity of the entire people. Each of the twelve tribes was a conglomeration of families and clans. The twelve tribes together comprised the people of Israel as a whole. Although the level of solidarity might decrease at a distance from one's immediate family, this familial notion permeated all of Israelite society. A kinsman was often called a brother, not just a relative, to express the closest intimacy. By extension of the family model, the term often translated "brother" could also be used of a fellow Israelite (see Deut 1:16, "fellow Israelites"; 3:18, "Israelite relatives").

Since Israel was seen as an extended family, its existence depended on the integrity of the home. Crimes such as incest and adultery were regarded very severely because they weakened the foundation of the family. Incest introduced competition, threatening the safety of the home by violating the trust, intimacy, and sense of belonging shared by its members. Adultery fragmented the home by allowing intimacy with someone outside it to divide the loyalties of its participants. These powerful enemies of family solidarity weakened the clan and tribe (see 18:6-23) and, by extension, the solidarity of the nation itself. Sexual sins are not "victimless crimes" but sins that eventually threaten the community itself. The importance given here to such crimes is echoed in NT warnings against sexual immorality (see especially 1 Cor 5:1-2; 6:13-20; 7:2; Gal 5:19-21; Eph 5:3; Jude 1:7; Rev 2:14-16, 20).

19:5 ***peace offering:*** See 3:1-17. • ***so you will be accepted:*** Or *so it will be accepted.*

19:8 ***cut off:*** See note on 7:20-21.

19:9-10 ***do not harvest. . . . Leave them for the poor:*** Israel's covenant with God included a social structure that created a leveling effect and resisted social divisions. Families were required to provide for family members who faced difficulties. Widows and orphans (Exod 22:22), the poor, and foreigners (19:10) were considered members of Israel's extended family. The poor were not only given special consideration in the offering system (5:7-13), but positive steps were taken to make sure they had food to eat.

19:11 A society that did not respect the property of others would quickly fall apart internally. To ***steal*** was prohibited (Exod 20:15), and those who would ***deceive or cheat*** were required to present a guilt offering (see 6:2-7).

19:12 To ***bring shame on the name*** means to blaspheme (see note on 18:21).

19:13 Day laborers had no land and were a part of Israel's lowest economic ranks. These ***hired workers*** depended on landowners for their livelihood. A hired man needed to receive his wages promptly so that he could feed his family (Deut 24:15); to withhold the wages of such a worker was to cheat him.

19:14 The ***deaf*** and ***blind*** were helpless people, easy to belittle and exploit. The Israelites were not to take advantage of them.

19:15 Neither the ***poor*** nor the ***rich*** were to be favored in a legal case. Justice was the priority at all times (see Exod 23:3, 6).

19:16 ***Do not spread slanderous gossip*** (literally *Do not act as a merchant toward your own people*): The image here is of a merchant who trades and sells harmful rumors and accusations. This practice would quickly erode and undermine the sense of community so valued in Israel (cp. Prov 11:13; 16:28; 20:19; 26:20; 2 Cor 12:20).

17"Do not nurse hatred in your heart for
any of your relatives. Confront people directly so you will not be held guilty for their
sin.
18"Do not seek revenge or bear a grudge
against a fellow Israelite, but love your neighbor as yourself. I am the LORD.
19"You must obey all my decrees.
"Do not mate two different kinds of
animals. Do not plant your field with two different kinds of seed. Do not wear clothing
woven from two different kinds of thread.
20"If a man has sex with a slave girl whose
freedom has never been purchased but
who is committed to become another man's
wife, he must pay full compensation to her
master. But since she is not a free woman,
neither the man nor the woman will be put
to death. 21The man, however, must bring
a ram as a guilt offering and present it to
the LORD at the entrance of the Tabernacle.
22The priest will then purify him before the
LORD with the ram of the guilt offering, and
the man's sin will be forgiven.
23"When you enter the land and plant
fruit trees, leave the fruit unharvested for
the first three years and consider it forbidden. Do not eat it. 24In the fourth year the
entire crop must be consecrated to the
LORD as a celebration of praise. 25Finally, in
the fifth year you may eat the fruit. If you follow this pattern, your harvest will increase.
I am the LORD your God.
26"Do not eat meat that has not been
drained of its blood.
"Do not practice fortune-telling or witchcraft.
27"Do not trim off the hair on your temples or trim your beards.
28"Do not cut your bodies for the dead,
and do not mark your skin with tattoos. I
am the LORD.
29"Do not defile your daughter by making
her a prostitute, or the land will be filled
with prostitution and wickedness.
30"Keep my Sabbath days of rest, and
show reverence toward my sanctuary. I am
the LORD.
31"Do not defile yourselves by turning to
mediums or to [f]those who consult the spirits of the dead. I am the LORD your God.
32"Stand up in the presence of the elderly,
and show respect for the aged. Fear your
God. I am the LORD.

19:17 Matt 18:15-17; 1 Jn 2:9, 11; 3:15
19:18 Ps 103:9; *Matt 19:19; 22:39; *Mark 12:31; *Luke 10:27; *Rom 13:9; *Gal 5:14; *Jas 2:8
19:19 Deut 22:9-11
19:20 Deut 22:23-27
19:21 Lev 5:15
19:26 Deut 18:10-12
19:27 Lev 21:5
19:28 Lev 21:5; Deut 14:1; Jer 16:6; 41:5
19:29 Lev 21:9; Deut 23:17-18
19:30 Exod 20:8-11; Lev 26:2
19:31 Lev 20:6; [f]*yidde'oni* (3049) ‣ Lev 20:6
19:32 1 Tim 5:1-2

19:17 *for any of your relatives:* Literally *for your brother.* The Hebrew term can refer to any fellow Israelite; all Israel was considered one family (cp. 1 Jn 3:15). • ***Confront people directly:*** Love does not mean closing one's eyes to wrong; reproof can help a person change.

19:18 *love your neighbor as yourself:* This is the cornerstone for biblical ethics in both the OT and the NT (see Matt 22:39; Mark 12:31; Luke 10:27; Rom 13:8-9; Gal 5:14; Jas 2:8). It includes foreigners (19:34; cp. Luke 10:30-37). Conversely, hate leads to a ***grudge*** that can bear violent fruit (see 1 Jn 2:10-11; 4:20).

19:19 *two different kinds:* God created a natural order (Gen 1:31; see Lev 18:22), and it is violated when God's boundaries are crossed. The prohibitions against intermixing were also object lessons for the Israelites, who were not to intermarry with the Canaanites.

19:20-22 Betrothal in the biblical world was considered equivalent to marriage. Sexual relations with a betrothed or engaged woman who was not a slave merited death, the same punishment as for adultery (Deut 22:22; see Lev 18:20). However, the situation was less clear when the woman was a slave who might be unable to refuse. While slaves in Israel had considerably more rights than those in Mesopotamia or Egypt, they were still not free. Because a ***slave girl*** could not be punished, ***the man*** was also left unpunished. Still, he was guilty in God's sight and had to sacrifice a ram for his sin.

19:21 *Tabernacle:* Literally *Tent of Meeting*; see note on 1:1.

19:22 *purify him:* Or *make atonement for him*; see notes on 1:4; 4:20.

19:23-25 For the ***first three years,*** a newly planted fruit tree was only to be pruned and cultivated. This allowed all the strength to go back into the tree. In the ***fourth year,*** all of the fruit was considered the "first crop" and was given to God (see Exod 23:16). Only in the ***fifth year*** could the fruit be eaten.

19:23 ***consider it forbidden:*** Literally *consider it uncircumcised.*

19:26 ***blood:*** See note on 7:22-27. • Priests were permitted to consult the Urim and Thummim (Exod 28:30) or to cast lots (16:8) to help decide cases not covered by Mosaic regulations. However, those who practiced ***fortune-telling or witchcraft*** were actually consulting a power apart from the Lord, which was forbidden under the first commandment (Exod 20:3).

19:27 *Do not trim:* As discovered in Egyptian wall paintings, Canaanites carefully trimmed their hair and beards. The Israelites were not to imitate this practice so that they would not be influenced by Canaanite religion and ethics.

19:28 *cut your bodies:* Cutting oneself was associated with Canaanite mourning practices (21:5; Deut 14:1). The word translated ***tattoo*** might refer to painting the body, a practice also associated with paganism.

19:29 Cp. 21:9; Deut 23:17.

19:30 ***Sabbath days:*** The Hebrew word translated "Sabbath" (*shabbath*) is related to a verb which means simply "to cease," implying rest from one's labor. The Sabbath commemorated God's resting on the seventh day after he had completed his work of creation (Gen 1:31; 2:1-3). It began at sundown on the sixth day. With the Exodus from Egypt, the Sabbath gained covenantal significance (Exod 16:23-25; 31:13). Because only free people, not slaves, had a regular day of rest, the Sabbath became symbolic of Israel's liberation from bondage in Egypt (see Deut 5:13-15). • The people were to ***show reverence*** (literally *fear*) because the ***sanctuary,*** like the Sabbath, was holy. They were not to enter it when they were unclean or bring anything unclean into it.

19:31 ***mediums:*** Cp. 1 Sam 28:7-25. • The Hebrew term for ***consult the spirits*** (*yidde'oni*) is derived from a root meaning "to know." It describes those who claim to have special occult knowledge and use it to communicate with the dead.

19:32 In the ancient world, ***the elderly*** and ***the aged*** were respected for their wisdom (Job 32:7). Honoring the elderly also honors God.

19:34 Lev 19:18
19:35 Deut 25:13-16
19:36 Deut 25:13-15; Prov 20:10; [g]*tsedeq* (6664) ‣Deut 16:20
20:2 Lev 18:21; 24:14-23
20:3 Lev 18:21; Num 19:20; Ezek 5:11
20:6 Lev 19:26, 31; [h]*yidde'oni* (3049) ‣Lev 20:27
20:7 Lev 11:44-45; *1 Pet 1:16
20:9 Exod 21:17; Deut 27:16; *Matt 15:4
20:10 Exod 20:14; Deut 22:22
20:11 Lev 18:7-8; Deut 27:20
20:12 Lev 18:15
20:13 Lev 18:22
20:14 Lev 18:17; Deut 27:23
20:15 Lev 18:23; Deut 27:21

[33]"Do not take advantage of foreigners who live among you in your land. [34]Treat them like native-born Israelites, and love them as you love yourself. Remember that you were once foreigners living in the land of Egypt. I am the LORD your God.

[35]"Do not use dishonest standards when measuring length, weight, or volume. [36]Your scales and weights must be [g]accurate. Your containers for measuring dry materials or liquids must be [g]accurate. I am the LORD your God who brought you out of the land of Egypt.

[37]"You must be careful to keep all of my decrees and regulations by putting them into practice. I am the LORD."

Punishments for Disobedience

20 The LORD said to Moses, [2]"Give the people of Israel these instructions, which apply both to native Israelites and to the foreigners living in Israel.

"If any of them offer their children as a sacrifice to Molech, they must be put to death. The people of the community must stone them to death. [3]I myself will turn against them and cut them off from the community, because they have defiled my sanctuary and brought shame on my holy name by offering their children to Molech. [4]And if the people of the community ignore those who offer their children to Molech and refuse to execute them, [5]I myself will turn against them and their families and will cut them off from the community. This will happen to all who commit spiritual prostitution by worshiping Molech.

[6]"I will also turn against those who commit spiritual prostitution by putting their trust in mediums or in [h]those who consult the spirits of the dead. I will cut them off from the community. [7]So set yourselves apart to be holy, for I am the LORD your God. [8]Keep all my decrees by putting them into practice, for I am the LORD who makes you holy.

[9]"Anyone who dishonors father or mother must be put to death. Such a person is guilty of a capital offense.

[10]"If a man commits adultery with his neighbor's wife, both the man and the woman who have committed adultery must be put to death.

[11]"If a man violates his father by having sex with one of his father's wives, both the man and the woman must be put to death, for they are guilty of a capital offense.

[12]"If a man has sex with his daughter-in-law, both must be put to death. They have committed a perverse act and are guilty of a capital offense.

[13]"If a man practices homosexuality, having sex with another man as with a woman, both men have committed a detestable act. They must both be put to death, for they are guilty of a capital offense.

[14]"If a man marries both a woman and her mother, he has committed a wicked act. The man and both women must be burned to death to wipe out such wickedness from among you.

[15]"If a man has sex with an animal, he must be put to death, and the animal must be killed.

[16]"If a woman presents herself to a male animal to have intercourse with it, she and the animal must both be put to death. You must kill both, for they are guilty of a capital offense.

19:33-34 The Israelites, ***once foreigners living in . . . Egypt,*** were to remember their own mistreatment and avoid inflicting similar abuse on others (see Deut 10:19).

19:35-36 ***dishonest standards:*** Merchants would sometimes use two different sets of weights, one heavy and one light (Deut 25:13-15), in order to cheat customers. The Bible makes it clear that this practice was abhorrent to God (Prov 11:1; 16:11; 20:10, 23; Mic 6:11).

19:36 ***Your containers for measuring dry materials or liquids must be accurate:*** Literally *Use an honest ephah* [a dry measure] *and an honest hin* [a liquid measure].

19:37 ***decrees and regulations:*** Together, these terms designated the entire body of law, both the law as first enacted ("decrees," see 10:11) and its interpretation by the courts ("regulations," see 18:4).

20:2 Stoning was the conventional means of enforcing capital punishment (see also 20:27; 24:14, 16, 23; Exod 19:13; Num 15:35-36; Deut 17:2-7; Josh 7:25-26; John 8:1-11).

20:9-27 Because pagan worship affected ethics, the regulations for families follow immediately after those dealing with pagan religious practices. To some extent, the laws of this section replicate those of 18:6-30, which precede the section dealing with proper expressions of holiness (19:1-37). These were all related issues, as the proper worship of God led to proper conduct toward other people, while improper worship of God led to moral violations.

20:9 ***Anyone who dishonors:*** Greek version reads *Anyone who speaks disrespectfully of;* cp. Matt 15:4; Mark 7:10; Eph 6:1-4. The Hebrew word for ***dishonors*** means "to make light of, treat with contempt," and is traditionally translated "curse," in the sense of calling someone a vulgar or profane name. Parental authority was given by God, not chosen by the child (see Exod 20:12; Deut 21:18-21).

20:10 See note on 18:20; see also Exod 20:14.

20:11 See note on 18:7-8. This injunction made it clear that the crime was seen as both incest and adultery.

20:12 See note on 18:15.

20:13 See note on 18:22.

20:14 See note on 18:17.

20:15-16 See note on 18:23.

17"If a man marries his sister, the daughter of either his father or his mother, and
they have sexual relations, it is a shameful
disgrace. They must be publicly cut off
from the community. Since the man has
violated his sister, he will be punished for
his sin.
18"If a man has sexual relations with a
woman during her menstrual period, both
of them must be cut off from the community, for together they have exposed the
source of her blood flow.
19"Do not have sexual relations with your
aunt, whether your mother's sister or your
father's sister. This would dishonor a close
relative. Both parties are guilty and will be
punished for their sin.
20"If a man has sex with his uncle's wife,
he has violated his uncle. Both the man and
woman will be punished for their sin, and
they will die childless.
21"If a man marries his brother's wife,
it is an act of impurity. He has violated his
brother, and the guilty couple will remain
childless.
22"You must keep all my decrees and
regulations by putting them into practice;
otherwise the land to which I am bringing
you as your new home will vomit you out.
23Do not live according to the customs of
the people I am driving out before you. It
is because they do these shameful things
that I detest them. 24But I have promised
you, 'You will possess their land because
I will give it to you as your possession—a
land flowing with milk and honey.' I am the
LORD your God, who has set you apart from
all other people.
25"You must therefore make a distinction
between ceremonially clean and unclean
animals, and between clean and unclean
birds. You must not defile yourselves by eating any unclean animal or bird or creature
that scurries along the ground. I have identified them as being unclean for you. 26You
must be holy because I, the LORD, am holy. I
have set you apart from all other people to
be my very own.
27"Men and women among you who act
as mediums or 'who consult the spirits of
the dead must be put to death by stoning.
They are guilty of a capital offense."

Priestly Regulations (21:1–22:33)

Instructions for the Priests

21 The LORD said to Moses, "Give the
following instructions to the priests,
the descendants of Aaron.
"A priest must not make himself ceremonially unclean by touching the dead body
of a relative. 2The only exceptions are his
closest relatives—his mother or father, son
or daughter, brother, 3or his virgin sister
who depends on him because she has no
husband. 4But a priest must not defile himself and make himself unclean for someone
who is related to him only by marriage.
5"The priests must not shave their heads
or trim their beards or cut their bodies.

20:17 Lev 18:9
20:18 Lev 15:24; 18:19
20:19 Lev 18:12-13
20:20 Lev 18:14
20:21 Lev 18:16
20:22 Lev 18:28
20:23 Lev 18:1-3, 24-30
20:24 Exod 13:5; 33:1-3, 16
20:25 Lev 11:1-47; Deut 14:3-5
20:26 Lev 20:24
20:27 Lev 19:31; *'yidde'oni* (3049) ›Deut 18:11
21:1 Lev 19:28; Ezek 44:25
21:2 Lev 21:11
21:5 Lev 19:27-28; Deut 14:1; Jer 16:6

20:17 See note on 18:9. • ***a shameful disgrace:*** Proper conduct brings honor both to individuals and their households; improper conduct brings shame. • Both parties are ***cut off*** (see 7:20-21), but the man ***will be punished*** (see 5:1; 18:6).

20:18 See note on 15:24.

20:19 See note on 18:12-13.

20:20-21 Being left ***childless*** carried a social stigma and was considered a judgment from God (see Gen 30:1-2; Deut 7:14). What situation is envisioned in these verses? Sexual relations with a sister-in-law (18:16) or an ***uncle's wife*** (18:14) have already been discussed. Adultery is dealt with elsewhere and would bring death to both parties (Deut 22:22). If the woman involved was a widow without a male heir, the law of levirate marriage could be invoked (Deut 25:5-6; see note on 18:16). Since those situations don't seem to apply, it would appear that this law refers to marrying an aunt or a sister-in-law after she has been divorced from her husband. John the Baptist apparently applied this law to condemn Herod Antipas's marriage to Herodias (see Mark 6:17-29).

20:22 ***vomit you out:*** See note on 18:28.

20:24 The expression ***flowing with milk and honey*** is common in Exodus—Deuteronomy. It conveys the idea of food being abundant and easy to get. This contrasts with Egypt, where everything depended on the flooding of the Nile and irrigation (Deut 11:9-12).

20:25 ***clean . . . unclean:*** See note on 11:1–15:33.

20:26 ***be holy:*** See note on 11:44-45.

20:27 ***mediums:*** See note on 19:31.

21:1–22:33 This section, which covers priestly regulations, is punctuated six times with the phrase ***I am the LORD who makes . . . holy*** (21:15, 23; 22:9, 16, 32; cp. 21:8). The words reaffirm the necessary connection between the holiness of God and the holiness expected of the priesthood, and by extension, of all Israel (see 8:10; 11:44-45; 19:2). Priests are specifically addressed in 21:1–22:16, while both clergy and laity are included in 22:17-33.

21:1-4 Touching a ***dead body*** rendered a person unclean for seven days. Because a priest had to be prepared to deal with holy things at all times, he was not allowed to handle a dead body, even of a relative, or else he could be unfit to minister when needed. The only exceptions were his ***closest relatives*** because there might not be anyone else who could bury the bodies.

21:5 ***shave . . . trim:*** See notes on 10:6; 19:27. • ***cut their bodies:*** See note on 19:28. Self-mutilation was a pagan custom. Just as defects of any kind precluded most animals as offerings (22:19-25), a defect similarly precluded a priest from officiating (see 21:17-23). For example, a eunuch could not serve as a priest (Deut 23:1) because he was not an adequate representative of the people. However, his priestly lineage was recognized as qualifying him to eat his priestly share (see 21:22). On the other hand, uncleanness disqualified any priest from ministry and from eating the priest's share as long as the condition persisted (22:2-8).

21:6 Lev 10:3
21:7 Lev 21:14; Ezek 44:22; [j]*garash* (1644) ‣Lev 21:14
21:8 Lev 11:44
21:9 Lev 19:29
21:10 Lev 10:6-7
21:11 Num 19:14
21:12 Lev 10:7; Num 19:11-13
21:13 Ezek 44:22
21:14 Lev 21:7, 13; [k]*garash* (1644) ‣Lev 22:13
21:17 Lev 21:6
21:21 Lev 21:17-21
21:22 1 Cor 9:13
21:23 Lev 21:12
22:3 Lev 7:20-21; Num 19:13
22:4 Lev 11:24, 28, 31, 39-40; 14:1-32
22:5 Lev 11:24-25, 41-44

6They must be set apart as holy to their God and must never bring shame on the name of God. They must be holy, for they are the ones who present the special gifts to the LORD, gifts of food for their God.

7"Priests may not marry a woman defiled by prostitution, and they may not marry a woman who is [j]divorced from her husband, for the priests are set apart as holy to their God. 8You must treat them as holy because they offer up food to your God. You must consider them holy because I, the LORD, am holy, and I make you holy.

9"If a priest's daughter defiles herself by becoming a prostitute, she also defiles her father's holiness, and she must be burned to death.

10"The high priest has the highest rank of all the priests. The anointing oil has been poured on his head, and he has been ordained to wear the priestly garments. He must never leave his hair uncombed or tear his clothing. 11He must not defile himself by going near a dead body. He may not make himself ceremonially unclean even for his father or mother. 12He must not defile the sanctuary of his God by leaving it to attend to a dead person, for he has been made holy by the anointing oil of his God. I am the LORD.

13"The high priest may marry only a virgin. 14He may not marry a widow, a woman who is [k]divorced, or a woman who has defiled herself by prostitution. She must be a virgin from his own clan, 15so that he will not dishonor his descendants among his clan, for I am the LORD who makes him holy."

16Then the LORD said to Moses, 17"Give the following instructions to Aaron: In all future generations, none of your descendants who has any defect will qualify to offer food to his God. 18No one who has a defect qualifies, whether he is blind, lame, disfigured, deformed, 19or has a broken foot or arm, 20or is hunchbacked or dwarfed, or has a defective eye, or skin sores or scabs, or damaged testicles. 21No descendant of Aaron who has a defect may approach the altar to present special gifts to the LORD. Since he has a defect, he may not approach the altar to offer food to his God. 22However, he may eat from the food offered to God, including the holy offerings and the most holy offerings. 23Yet because of his physical defect, he may not enter the room behind the inner curtain or approach the altar, for this would defile my holy places. I am the LORD who makes them holy."

24So Moses gave these instructions to Aaron and his sons and to all the Israelites.

22 The LORD said to Moses, 2"Tell Aaron and his sons to be very careful with the sacred gifts that the Israelites set apart for me, so they do not bring shame on my holy name. I am the LORD. 3Give them the following instructions.

"In all future generations, if any of your descendants is ceremonially unclean when he approaches the sacred offerings that the people of Israel consecrate to the LORD, he must be cut off from my presence. I am the LORD.

4"If any of Aaron's descendants has a skin disease or any kind of discharge that makes him ceremonially unclean, he may not eat from the sacred offerings until he has been pronounced clean. He also becomes unclean by touching a corpse, or by having an emission of semen, 5or by touching a small animal that is unclean, or by touching someone who is ceremonially unclean for any reason. 6The man who is defiled in

21:6 A priest should ***never bring shame*** by profaning God's name. • ***food:*** See note on 3:11.

21:7 The priest, to lead Israel in worship, had to model the highest standard of conduct for the people both in his personal life and in leadership of his family. He could have no ties to pagan culture (prostitution, 21:9), nor could the legitimacy of his family be questioned (divorce). Similar stringent standards applied to leaders of the early church (1 Tim 3:1-13).

21:8 ***food:*** See note on 3:11. • ***I make you holy:*** See note on 21:1–22:33.

21:10-15 The restrictions made on the common priests (21:1-4) applied even more stringently to the ***high priest*** because he had to represent all Israel, including the other priests. • The priest must ***never leave his hair uncombed*** (or *never uncover his head*) or ***tear his clothing*** in mourning, so that he would always be fit to minister. Although the common priest was permitted to marry a widow, the high priest was allowed to marry only a virgin. This made certain that the future high priest and the common priests descended from that union would have an unquestioned lineage (21:15).

21:17-23 See note on 21:5.

21:17, 21 ***food:*** See note on 3:11.

21:22 ***he may eat:*** Although a mutilation or defect (see 21:18-20) disqualified a descendant of Aaron from representing the people, it did not compromise his priestly lineage. He was eligible to eat the priest's share of the offerings (see 2:3, 10; 6:17-18).

22:2-6 The priest's portions of ***the sacred offerings*** were regarded as "most holy" (see 2:3) and were not to come into contact with anything unclean (11:1–15:33). Accordingly, any descendant of Aaron who was unclean was forbidden to eat this food.

22:4 ***skin disease:*** Traditionally rendered *leprosy;* see note on 13:2.

22:5 In Leviticus, the Hebrew word *sherets* always denotes an unclean ***small animal*** that swarms on land or in water (5:2; 11:10, 20-21, 23, 29, 31, 41-44).

any of these ways will remain unclean until
evening. He may not eat from the sacred offerings until he has bathed himself in water.
7When the sun goes down, he will be ceremonially clean again and may eat from the
sacred offerings, for this is his food. 8He
may not eat an animal that has died a natural death or has been torn apart by wild
animals, for this would defile him. I am the
LORD.
9"The priests must follow my instructions carefully. Otherwise they will be
punished for their sin and will die for violating my instructions. I am the LORD who
makes them holy.
10"No one outside a priest's family may
eat the sacred offerings. Even guests and
hired workers in a priest's home are not allowed to eat them. 11However, if the priest
buys a slave for himself, the slave may eat
from the sacred offerings. And if his slaves
have children, they also may share his food.
12If a priest's daughter marries someone
outside the priestly family, she may no longer eat the sacred offerings. 13But if she
becomes a widow or is [a]divorced and has no
children to support her, and she returns to
live in her father's home as in her youth, she
may eat her father's food again. Otherwise,
no one outside a priest's family may eat the
sacred offerings.
14"Any such person who eats the sacred
offerings without realizing it must pay the
priest for the amount eaten, plus an additional 20 percent. 15The priests must not
let the Israelites defile the sacred offerings
brought to the LORD 16by allowing unauthorized people to eat them. This would bring
guilt upon them and require them to pay
compensation. I am the LORD who makes
them holy."

Worthy and Unworthy Offerings

17And the LORD said to Moses, 18"Give
Aaron and his sons and all the Israelites
these instructions, which apply both to native Israelites and to the foreigners living
among you.
"If you present a gift as a burnt offering to
the LORD, whether it is to fulfill a vow or is
a voluntary offering, 19you will be accepted
only if your offering is a male animal with
no defects. It may be a bull, a ram, or a male
goat. 20Do not present an animal with defects, because the LORD will not accept it on
your behalf.
21"If you present a peace offering to the
LORD from the herd or the flock, whether
it is to fulfill a vow or is a voluntary offering, you must offer a perfect animal. It may
have no defect of any kind. 22You must not
offer an animal that is blind, crippled, or
injured, or that has a wart, a skin sore, or
scabs. Such animals must never be offered
on the altar as special gifts to the LORD. 23If
a bull or lamb has a leg that is too long or
too short, it may be offered as a voluntary
offering, but it may not be offered to fulfill
a vow. 24If an animal has damaged testicles
or is castrated, you may not offer it to the
LORD. You must never do this in your own
land, 25and you must not accept such an animal from foreigners and then offer it as a
sacrifice to your God. Such animals will not
be accepted on your behalf, for they are mutilated or defective."
26And the LORD said to Moses, 27"When
a calf or lamb or goat is born, it must be
left with its mother for seven days. From
the eighth day on, it will be acceptable as
a special gift to the LORD. 28But you must
not slaughter a mother animal and her
offspring on the same day, whether from
the herd or the flock. 29When you bring a

22:8 Exod 22:31; Lev 17:15
22:9 Exod 28:43; Lev 18:30; Num 18:1-7
22:10 Exod 29:31-34; Lev 22:13
22:11 Gen 17:13; Exod 12:44
22:13 Lev 22:10; [a]*garash* (1644) ‣ Deut 22:19
22:14 Lev 5:15-16
22:15 Lev 19:8
22:16 Lev 22:9
22:19 Lev 1:3
22:20 Lev 1:3; Deut 15:21; Heb 9:14; 1 Pet 1:19
22:25 Lev 21:6, 17
22:28 Deut 22:6

22:8 ***died a natural death:*** See note on 17:15-16.

22:9 ***will die for violating my instructions:*** As in 10:1-3. The temptation to offer improper offerings persisted throughout Israel's history until after the Exile (Mal 1:6-9).

22:11 The only male outside the priest's family who could eat the priest's share was the priest's *slave.* He would have no other food if this provision were denied him.

22:14-16 Similar to provisions for the guilt offering, a common person who accidentally ate the priestly portion had to repay 120 percent (see 5:14-16). However, the offering of a ram was not required in this case.

22:15 An Israelite who ate the "most holy" priestly portion as if it were common food would *defile* it.

22:18 Apparently individuals could present a whole *burnt offering* instead of a peace offering if they desired (see 1:3).

22:19 ***you will be accepted:*** Or *it will be accepted.*

22:21 A *peace offering* could function in several ways: as a thanksgiving offering, an offering to fulfill a vow, or a voluntary offering (see 3:1-17).

22:23 The requirements for the *voluntary offering* were more lenient, allowing the use of a deformed animal. Fulfilling a *vow,* however, still required an animal that was not maimed or diseased. In no case would God accept a sacrifice that could not be eaten by a person or that was not a whole animal. • ***bull:*** Or *cow.*

22:27 Leaving a newborn animal ***with its mother for seven days*** allowed time to determine the animal's health (see Exod 22:30).

22:28 ***on the same day:*** There are several possible explanations for this command, although none is certain: (1) Senseless slaughtering would leave nothing of the herd; (2) it would be inhumane to slaughter the young and the mother at the same time; or (3) it would be too similar to pagan worship rites, where the newborn animal was cooked in the milk of its slain mother (see Exod 23:19).

22:29 Lev 7:12
[b]*todah* (8426) ‣Josh 7:19
22:30 Lev 7:15
22:31 Lev 19:37
22:33 Lev 11:45
23:2 Lev 23:21; Num 29:39
23:3 Exod 20:8-11; 23:12; 31:15; Deut 5:13-14
23:5 Exod 12:3-20; Deut 16:1-8
23:6 Exod 12:14-20
23:10 Exod 23:19; 34:26
23:13 Lev 6:20
23:15 Num 28:26-31; Deut 16:9-12

[b]thanksgiving offering to the LORD, sacrifice it properly so you will be accepted. 30 Eat the entire sacrificial animal on the day it is presented. Do not leave any of it until the next morning. I am the LORD.

31 "You must faithfully keep all my commands by putting them into practice, for I am the LORD. 32 Do not bring shame on my holy name, for I will display my holiness among the people of Israel. I am the LORD who makes you holy. 33 It was I who rescued you from the land of Egypt, that I might be your God. I am the LORD."

The Religious Festivals (23:1-44)

The Appointed Festivals

23 The LORD said to Moses, 2 "Give the following instructions to the people of Israel. These are the LORD's appointed festivals, which you are to proclaim as official days for holy assembly.

3 "You have six days each week for your ordinary work, but the seventh day is a Sabbath day of complete rest, an official day for holy assembly. It is the LORD's Sabbath day, and it must be observed wherever you live.

4 "In addition to the Sabbath, these are the LORD's appointed festivals, the official days for holy assembly that are to be celebrated at their proper times each year.

Passover and the Festival of Unleavened Bread

5 "The LORD's Passover begins at sundown on the fourteenth day of the first month. 6 On the next day, the fifteenth day of the month, you must begin celebrating the Festival of Unleavened Bread. This festival to the LORD continues for seven days, and during that time the bread you eat must be made without yeast. 7 On the first day of the festival, all the people must stop their ordinary work and observe an official day for holy assembly. 8 For seven days you must present special gifts to the LORD. On the seventh day the people must again stop all their ordinary work to observe an official day for holy assembly."

Celebration of First Harvest

9 Then the LORD said to Moses, 10 "Give the following instructions to the people of Israel. When you enter the land I am giving you and you harvest its first crops, bring the priest a bundle of grain from the first cutting of your grain harvest. 11 On the day after the Sabbath, the priest will lift it up before the LORD so it may be accepted on your behalf. 12 On that same day you must sacrifice a one-year-old male lamb with no defects as a burnt offering to the LORD. 13 With it you must present a grain offering consisting of four quarts of choice flour moistened with olive oil. It will be a special gift, a pleasing aroma to the LORD. You must also offer one quart of wine as a liquid offering. 14 Do not eat any bread or roasted grain or fresh kernels on that day until you bring this offering to your God. This is a permanent law for you, and it must be observed from generation to generation wherever you live.

The Festival of Harvest

15 "From the day after the Sabbath—the day you bring the bundle of grain to be lifted

---

23:2 These ***appointed festivals*** included occasions for eating, resting, and even fasting. For additional details, see Num 28–29.

23:3 ***Sabbath:*** See note on 19:30.

23:5-8 ***Passover . . . Unleavened Bread:*** These feasts were instituted on the eve of the Exodus from Egypt (see Exod 12:1-28). Passover was the first of three great festivals (Deut 16:16), followed by the Festival of Harvest (23:15-21) and the Festival of Shelters (23:34-43).

23:5 ***Passover*** began ***at sundown of the fourteenth day of the first month,*** as the new day was beginning (see note on 11:24-25). This day in the ancient Hebrew lunar calendar occurred in late March, April, or early May. The Passover feast included a roast lamb, bitter salad greens, and bread made without yeast (Exod 12:8), all representing Israel's liberation from Egyptian bondage. • The ***first month*** marked the beginning of the Jewish calendar as late as Ezra 6:19. The month's earliest name, Abib ("spring, fresh grain"; Exod 13:4; 23:15; 34:18; Deut 16:1), was partially replaced by the name Nisan after the Babylonian exile (Neh 2:1; Esth 3:7).

23:6 Following Passover was the ***Festival of Unleavened Bread,*** during which Israel ate bread made without yeast (see note on 2:11) to remember the Egyptian slavery that it represented (Deut 16:3).

23:10-14 Just as the burned portion of each sacrifice represented the whole offering and the tithe symbolized that all of a person's money belonged to God, so also the first portions of each harvest, or ***first crops,*** symbolized the entire harvest, and even the land itself (25:23), as belonging to the Lord. In the barley harvest, the first portions were offered as part of the Festival of Unleavened Bread (23:6, 10-12). The first portions of the wheat harvest were offered during the Festival of Harvest (23:15-21; Exod 34:22). These gifts to God recognized God's prior gifts to Israel (see 2:1). The entire offering of first crops became the property and food of God's representatives, the priests (see 2:14-16).

23:11 The phrase ***lift it up*** symbolizes presenting the grain to the Lord (see note on 7:34).

23:13 ***four quarts:*** Hebrew *2/10 of an ephah* [4.4 liters]; also in 23:17. • ***one quart:*** Hebrew *1/4 of a hin* [1 liter].

23:14 Israelites could not eat food from the harvest ***on that day*** until they acknowledged God's provision by presenting him with the appropriate offering.

23:15-21 This celebration, called the Festival of Harvest (Exod 34:22; Num 28:26) or the Festival of Weeks, was later called the Festival of Pentecost (see Acts 2:1; 20:16; 1 Cor 16:8). It is celebrated today as Shavuot. Israel was to start the count of ***seven full weeks*** on the first day of the Festival of Unleavened Bread. The fiftieth day marked the beginning of the Festival of Harvest (the NT name of "Pentecost" is

up as a special offering—count off seven full weeks. [16]Keep counting until the day after the seventh Sabbath, fifty days later. Then present an offering of new grain to the LORD. [17]From wherever you live, bring two loaves of bread to be lifted up before the LORD as a special offering. Make these loaves from four quarts of choice flour, and bake them with yeast. They will be an offering to the LORD from the first of your crops. [18]Along with the bread, present seven one-year-old male lambs with no defects, one young bull, and two rams as burnt offerings to the LORD. These burnt offerings, together with the grain offerings and liquid offerings, will be a special gift, a pleasing aroma to the LORD. [19]Then you must offer one male goat as a sin offering and two one-year-old male lambs as a peace offering.

[20]"The priest will lift up the two lambs as a special offering to the LORD, together with the loaves representing the first of your crops. These offerings, which are holy to the LORD, belong to the priests. [21]That same day will be proclaimed an official day for holy assembly, a day on which you do no ordinary work. This is a permanent law for you, and it must be observed from generation to generation wherever you live.

[22]"When you harvest the crops of your land, do not harvest the grain along the edges of your fields, and do not pick up what the harvesters drop. Leave it for the poor and the foreigners living among you. I am the LORD your God."

The Festival of Trumpets

[23]The LORD said to Moses, [24]"Give the following instructions to the people of Israel.

23:19 Lev 3:1; Num 28:30
23:20 Exod 29:24
23:22 Lev 19:9-10; Deut 24:19-21
23:24 Num 10:9-10; 29:1

Concern for the Poor (23:22)

Lev 5:7, 11; 14:21-22; 19:9-10; Exod 22:22-27; 23:6-11; Deut 10:17-19; 15:4-11; 16:9-12; 24:6-22; 26:12-13; 27:17-19; 1 Sam 2:8; Ps 10:13-18; 35:10; 68:5; Prov 14:31; Isa 1:15-17; Amos 2:6; 4:1; 8:4-7; Mic 6:6-8, 12; Mark 12:41-44; Luke 6:20; 14:12-14; Jas 2:1-17

God commanded Israel to show concern for its people's well-being. Israel's covenant with God, together with its self-concept as an extended family, exerted a leveling effect that resisted pretensions to privilege. A family should provide for members who are facing difficulty. These members of the Israelite people included widows and orphans (Exod 22:22), the poor, and foreigners (19:10). In 19:9-10, the edges of the fields and the gleanings of field and vineyard were to be left for the needy (see 23:22). The crops that grew spontaneously each Sabbath year and Jubilee year were allocated to the poor and the foreigner (25:1-55). Those who were destitute were not to be victimized. Instead, loans were to be made at no charge, or the debtor was to be allowed to work off his debt with dignity as a bondservant (25:35-42). These positive steps ensured that the poor had food to eat.

The Bible first mentions concern for the poor in the radical accommodations of the offering system to those unable to afford more costly offerings. Birds could substitute for lambs in the whole burnt offering (1:14-17) and the sin offering (5:7-10), and there were other such concessions in the cleansing rituals (14:21-22). Perhaps the most striking is in the substitution of flour for the sin offering (5:11-13). The life-for-a-life symbolism is forfeited for economic reasons, showing clearly God's desire that the poor who cannot afford a lamb should nonetheless experience forgiveness of sins.

This theme is continued in the prophets' concern for the poor and helpless (e.g., Isa 1:17) and their pleas for social justice and compassion (e.g., Amos 2:6; 4:1; 8:4). Their concern was for a worship that was not geared to formalities, but to a proper attitude toward God and one's fellow human beings (e.g., Isa 1:15-20; Mic 6:6-8). The prophets regarded the wealthy and powerful with suspicion, often questioning their morality (e.g., Mic 6:12). Likewise in the Gospels, greater respect is paid to the widow's offering, not because of its monetary value, but because of the devotion it represented (Mark 12:41-44).

derived from the Greek word for "fifty"). For this festival the people were to offer the first portions of the wheat harvest. Each person was also required to take three quarts of fine flour and bake two loaves of yeast bread. These offerings were then presented to the priest officiating at the sanctuary. See also note on Exod 23:16.

23:18 *burnt offerings:* See note on 1:3-17. • *grain offerings:* See note on 2:1-16. • The *liquid offerings* probably consisted of two quarts of wine (see Exod 29:40; Num 15:5, 10). • *pleasing aroma to the LORD:* See note on 1:9.

23:19 *sin offering:* See note on 4:3-21. • *peace offering:* See note on 3:1-17.

23:20 *lift up:* See notes on 7:34; 23:11.

23:22 *along the edges . . . what the harvesters drop:* See note on 19:9-10. • *foreigners:* See note on 16:29.

23:24 *On the first day of the appointed month in early autumn:* Literally *On the first day of the seventh month.* This day in the ancient Hebrew lunar calendar occurred in September or October. This festival is celebrated today as Rosh Hashanah, the Jewish new year. The Israelite calendar was divided into two half-years. The first half-year began with the first month, Nisan (Babylonian name) or Abib (the more ancient agriculture name). The second half-year began with the seventh month (Tishri in the modern Jewish calendar). The celebration of this holiday marked the beginning of the second half-year (see chart, "Israel's Annual Calendar," at p. 145).

Festival	References	When	Description	See also
Sabbath	23:3	Every 7th day	A weekly day of rest from all work, commemorating God's rest from the work of creation and his rescue of Israel from slavery; its observance brought blessing to the individual and the community	Gen 2:1-3; Exod 16:29; 20:8-11; 31:13-17; 35:2-3; Num 15:32-36; 28:9-10; Deut 5:12-15; Neh 13:15-22; Ps 92:TITLE; Isa 56:2-6; 58:13-14; Jer 17:21-27; Ezek 20:12-26; 44:24; Matt 12:1-13; Luke 13:10-17; John 5:10-18; 7:21-24; 9:13-16; Acts 17:2; 18:4; Col 2:16-17; Heb 4:1-11; Rev 14:13
New Moon	Num 28:11-15	1st day of every month	Special sacrifices and a feast to remind Israel of God's faithful provision for his people	1 Sam 20:5-34; 1 Chr 23:28-31; Neh 10:32-33; Ps 81:3; Isa 1:13-14; Col 2:16-17
Sabbath Year	25:1-7	Every 7th year	A Sabbath rest for the land by not cultivating or harvesting	Exod 21:2-9; 23:10-11; Deut 15:1-6, 12-18; Neh 10:31; Jer 34:8-22
Jubilee Year	25:8-17	Every 50th year, counted from the Day of Atonement	An additional SABBATH YEAR; land reverted to its ancestral owners, debts were forgiven, and slaves were freed	25:27-28; 25:39-55; 27:16-25; Ezek 46:16-17
Annual Festivals				
Passover	23:5	14th day of 1st month (Mar~Apr)	Commemoration of God's sparing the Israelites when he killed the firstborn of Egypt; marked by a special meal and sacrificial blood on the doorposts	Exod 12:1-14; Num 9:1-14; Deut 16:1-8; 2 Chr 35:1-19; Luke 22:1, 7-13; John 1:29; 1 Cor 11:23-26
Unleavened Bread*	23:6-8	15th–21st days of 1st month (Mar~Apr)	A *pilgrimage festival** commemorating Israel's departure from Egypt. Bread without yeast was eaten for seven days, with a holy assembly on the first and last days.	Exod 12:15-20; 23:14-15; Num 28:16-25; Deut 16:1-8; Acts 12:3; 1 Cor 5:7-8
First Harvest (Firstfruits)	23:9-14	The day following the Sabbath during the FESTIVAL OF UNLEAVENED BREAD	Offering of new grain to celebrate the beginning of the grain harvest; commemoration of Israel's entry into the Promised Land	Exod 23:19; Deut 26:1-11; 1 Cor 15:20-23
Harvest* (Weeks, Pentecost)	23:15-22	50th day after FIRST HARVEST, at the end of the grain harvest	A *pilgrimage festival** of thanksgiving and covenant renewal with a celebratory offering of new grain.	Exod 23:16; 34:22; Num 28:26; Deut 16:9-12; Acts 2:1-47
Trumpets (Rosh Hashanah)	23:23-25	1st day (NEW MOON) of 7th month (Sep~Oct)	A special Sabbath observed with a holy assembly and loud trumpet blasts	Num 29:1-6
Day of Atonement (*Yom Kippur*)	16:1-34; 23:26-32	10th day of 7th month (Sep~Oct)	The year's most solemn day; a special Sabbath and fast when the high priest made atonement for all Israel's sins	25:8-10; Num 29:7-11; note on Acts 27:9; Heb 9:6–10:22; cp. Ezek 36:25-27; Zech 13:1; Eph 1:7; Col 1:20
Shelters* (Final Harvest, Tabernacles, Booths, Ingathering, Succoth)	23:33-43	15th–21st days of 7th month (Sep~Oct)	Celebration of the last harvest of the year. A *pilgrimage festival** to commemorate Israel's living in temporary shelters in the wilderness	Exod 23:16; Deut 16:13-17; Neh 8:13-18; Zech 14:16-19; John 7:2-39
added later:				
Purim (Lots)	Esth 9:1-32	14th or 15th day of 12th month (Feb~Mar)	Feasting, celebration, and gift-giving to commemorate God's rescue of the Jews from their enemies through Esther	The Book of Esther
Dedication (Hanukkah, Lights)	John 10:22	25th–31st days of 9th month (Nov~Dec)	Commemoration of the Temple's rededication in 164 BC after being defiled by Antiochus IV Epiphanes	*1 Maccabees* 4:36-59; *2 Maccabees* 10:1-8

▲ **Israel's Festivals (23:1-44).**

* *Pilgrimage festivals* were national gatherings in Jerusalem (Deut 16:16-17). See also chart, "Israel's Annual Calendar," p. 145.

On the first day of the appointed month in
early autumn, you are to observe a day of
complete rest. It will be an official day for
holy assembly, a day commemorated with
loud blasts of a trumpet. 25 You must do no
ordinary work on that day. Instead, you are
to present special gifts to the LORD."

The Day of Atonement

26 Then the LORD said to Moses, 27 "Be careful to celebrate the Day of Atonement on the
tenth day of that same month—nine days
after the Festival of Trumpets. You must observe it as an official day for holy assembly,
a day to deny yourselves and present special
gifts to the LORD. 28 Do no work during that
entire day because it is the Day of Atonement,
when offerings of purification are made for
you, making you right with the LORD your
God. 29 All who do not deny themselves that
day will be cut off from God's people. 30 And
I will destroy anyone among you who does
any work on that day. 31 You must not do any
work at all! This is a permanent law for you,
and it must be observed from generation
to generation wherever you live. 32 This will
be a Sabbath day of complete rest for you,
and on that day you must deny yourselves.
This day of [c]rest will begin at sundown on
the ninth day of the month and extend until
sundown on the tenth day."

The Festival of Shelters

33 And the LORD said to Moses, 34 "Give the
following instructions to the people of
Israel. Begin celebrating the Festival of Shelters on the fifteenth day of the appointed
month—five days after the Day of Atonement. This festival to the LORD will last for
seven days. 35 On the first day of the festival
you must proclaim an official day for holy
assembly, when you do no ordinary work.
36 For seven days you must present special
gifts to the LORD. The eighth day is another
holy day on which you present your special
gifts to the LORD. This will be a solemn occasion, and no ordinary work may be done
that day.

37 ("These are the LORD's appointed festivals. Celebrate them each year as official
days for holy assembly by presenting special gifts to the LORD—burnt offerings, grain
offerings, sacrifices, and liquid offerings—
each on its proper day. 38 These festivals
must be observed in addition to the LORD's
regular Sabbath days, and the offerings
are in addition to your personal gifts, the
offerings you give to fulfill your vows, and
the voluntary offerings you present to the
LORD.)

39 "Remember that this seven-day festival
to the LORD—the Festival of Shelters—begins on the fifteenth day of the appointed
month, after you have harvested all the
produce of the land. The first day and the
eighth day of the festival will be days of
complete rest. 40 On the first day gather
branches from magnificent trees—palm
fronds, boughs from leafy trees, and
willows that grow by the streams. Then celebrate with joy before the LORD your God
for seven days. 41 You must observe this festival to the LORD for seven days every year.
This is a permanent law for you, and it must
be observed in the appointed month from
generation to generation. 42 For seven days
you must live outside in little shelters. All
native-born Israelites must live in shelters.
43 This will remind each new generation of
Israelites that I made their ancestors live in

23:25 Lev 23:7
23:27 Lev 16:29-30
23:28 Lev 23:7
23:29 Gen 17:14
23:32 Lev 16:31
[c]*shabbath* (7676) ‣Lev 25:2
23:33-34 Num 29:12-39; Deut 16:13-16; Ezra 3:4; Neh 8:14; Zech 14:16; John 7:2
23:35 Lev 23:7
23:36 Num 29:12-38
23:37 Lev 23:2
23:38 Num 29:39
23:40 Neh 8:15
23:43 Deut 16:13-15; Ps 78:1-8

23:27-29 *deny yourselves . . . deny themselves:* See note on 16:29.

23:27 The *Day of Atonement* was the most solemn day in the Israelite calendar and the only day of fasting (Lev 16). The high priest made atonement for the corporate sin of the people, laying the theological foundation for the atonement made by Jesus Christ (Heb 9:11-12). • ***on the tenth day of that same month—nine days after the Festival of Trumpets:*** Literally *on the tenth day of the seventh month;* see 23:24 and the note there. This day in the ancient Hebrew lunar calendar occurred in September or October. It is celebrated today as Yom Kippur. • ***to deny yourselves:*** Or *to fast;* similarly in 23:29, 32.

23:28 ***when offerings of purification are made for you, making you right with:*** Or *when atonement is made for you before;* see notes on 1:4; 4:20.

23:29-30 ***cut off . . . destroy:*** See note on 7:20-21; cp. Exod 31:14, 15; 35:2.

23:34-43 During the Festival of Shelters, the Israelites lived in temporary shelters for seven days. This commemorated the time they had spent in tents and other temporary shelters during the wilderness wanderings and also recalled God's faithfulness to them during those times. For a list of sacrifices to be offered each day, see Num 29:12-34.

23:34 ***Festival of Shelters*** (Hebrew *sukkoth*): Or *Festival of Booths,* or *Festival of Tabernacles.* This was earlier called the Festival of the Final Harvest or Festival of Ingathering (see Exod 23:16b). It is celebrated today as Sukkot (or Succoth). • ***on the fifteenth day of the appointed month—five days after the Day of Atonement:*** Literally *on the fifteenth day of the seventh month;* see 23:27 and note.

23:38 ***offerings:*** See note on 7:16-18.

23:39 ***the appointed month:*** Literally *the seventh month.* • ***after you have harvested all the produce:*** The ***Festival of Shelters*** was also called the Festival of Final Harvest (Exod 34:22) because all of the unharvested fruit and vegetables were gathered.

23:40 ***gather branches from magnificent trees:*** Or *gather fruit from majestic trees.*

23:41 ***the appointed month:*** Literally *the seventh month.*

23:43 The Israelites were never to forget God's great acts of redemption on their behalf, but were to *remind each new generation* of what God had done (Deut 4:9; 11:19). Their understanding of who they were and of who God was

23:44 Lev 23:37
24:2 Exod 27:20-21
24:4 Exod 25:31
24:5-6 Exod 25:30; 40:23; Lev 23:13; Heb 9:2
24:9 Lev 6:16-17; Matt 12:4
24:11 Exod 22:28; Job 1:11; 2:5; Isa 8:21
24:14 Lev 20:2, 27; Deut 13:9; 17:7; 21:21
24:15 Exod 22:28
24:17 Gen 9:5-6; Exod 21:12, 14; Num 35:30-31; Deut 19:11-12
24:18 Lev 24:21

shelters when I rescued them from the land of Egypt. I am the LORD your God."

44So Moses gave the Israelites these instructions regarding the annual festivals of the LORD.

Provision for the Tabernacle (24:1-9)

24 The LORD said to Moses, 2"Command the people of Israel to bring you pure oil of pressed olives for the light, to keep the lamps burning continually. 3This is the lampstand that stands in the Tabernacle, in front of the inner curtain that shields the Ark of the Covenant. Aaron must keep the lamps burning in the LORD's presence all night. This is a permanent law for you, and it must be observed from generation to generation. 4Aaron and the priests must tend the lamps on the pure gold lampstand continually in the LORD's presence.

5"You must bake twelve loaves of bread from choice flour, using four quarts of flour for each loaf. 6Place the bread before the LORD on the pure gold table, and arrange the loaves in two rows, with six loaves in each row. 7Put some pure frankincense near each row to serve as a representative offering, a special gift presented to the LORD. 8Every Sabbath day this bread must be laid out before the LORD. The bread is to be received from the people of Israel as a requirement of the eternal covenant. 9The loaves of bread will belong to Aaron and his descendants, who must eat them in a sacred place, for they are most holy. It is the permanent right of the priests to claim this portion of the special gifts presented to the LORD."

The Penalty for Blasphemy (24:10-23)

10One day a man who had an Israelite mother and an Egyptian father came out of his tent and got into a fight with one of the Israelite men. 11During the fight, this son of an Israelite woman blasphemed the Name of the LORD with a curse. So the man was brought to Moses for judgment. His mother was Shelomith, the daughter of Dibri of the tribe of Dan. 12They kept the man in custody until the LORD's will in the matter should become clear to them.

13Then the LORD said to Moses, 14"Take the blasphemer outside the camp, and tell all those who heard the curse to lay their hands on his head. Then let the entire community stone him to death. 15Say to the people of Israel: Those who curse their God will be punished for their sin. 16Anyone who blasphemes the Name of the LORD must be stoned to death by the whole community of Israel. Any native-born Israelite or foreigner among you who blasphemes the Name of the LORD must be put to death.

17"Anyone who takes another person's life must be put to death.

18"Anyone who kills another person's animal must pay for it in full—a live animal for the animal that was killed.

19"Anyone who injures another person must be dealt with according to the injury

revolved around their knowledge of those things. See Deut 6:20-24; 26:5-9; Josh 24:2-13; Ps 136.

24:3 ***in the Tabernacle, in front of the inner curtain that shields the Ark of the Covenant:*** Literally *in the Tent of Meeting, outside the inner curtain of the Testimony;* see Exod 26:31-33; also see notes on 1:1; 4:6; 16:13.

24:5 Traditionally called the "shewbread" (KJV), ***twelve loaves*** (see Exod 25:30) of this flat bread, the "Bread of the Presence," were to be placed on the table in the Holy Place each Sabbath (Exod 25:23-30). This bread was considered part of the priest's portion of the offerings. David and his men ate this bread while fleeing from Saul (1 Sam 21:1-6; see Matt 12:1-8). • ***four quarts:*** Hebrew *2/10 of an ephah* [4.4 liters].

24:7 Since a portion of this bread was to be burned as ***a representative offering*** (see 2:2), it would have been made without yeast (that is, unleavened; see 2:11).

24:10-23 A large body of non-Israelites, including other Semitic people as well as Egyptians, came out of Egypt with Israel (Exod 12:38). Among them was a man of mixed parentage, whose mother was an Israelite and whose father was an Egyptian. A quarrel broke out between the man and a full-blooded Israelite. In the altercation, the man who was half-Egyptian verbally cursed the Israelite, using the name of God in an irreverent manner.

24:11 ***blasphemed . . . with a curse:*** In biblical times, a name was more than a means of identification; it represented a person's character, reputation, and origin. God is holy, and he was to be regarded as holy in all of Israel's life (see 10:3). The Israelites had been instructed to treat God's name with reverence (Exod 20:7). Using his name in a curse reflected a sinful attitude toward God himself (24:15), and it deserved death (24:13-16). The wording in the Hebrew text is very strong: Two verbs meaning "curse" are used, one that indicated a more formal type of curse, the other a blasphemous or irreverent expression. The two terms are synonymous in 24:15-16. • ***the Name of the LORD*** (literally *the Name;* also in 24:16): The Hebrew text refers simply to "the Name" to reflect care and reverence for God's name.

24:14 Those who heard a ***blasphemer*** curse were to ***lay their hands on his head.*** This indicated their own innocence by symbolically transferring the guilt (see 16:21), as well as their willingness to accept responsibility for the blasphemer's death. A single witness was not enough to cause a man to die (see Num 35:30; Deut 17:2-7; Matt 18:16; 2 Cor 13:1; 1 Tim 5:19; Heb 10:28).

24:17 Because human life was patterned after the life of God himself (Gen 1:26, 27), murder was a blasphemous act. It required the same penalty as oral blasphemy (Gen 9:6). For a similar law and its qualifiers, see Exod 21:12-14.

inflicted—20a fracture for a fracture, an eye
for an eye, a tooth for a tooth. Whatever anyone does to injure another person must be
paid back in kind.
21"Whoever kills an animal must pay for
it in full, but whoever kills another person
must be put to death.
22"This same standard applies both to
native-born Israelites and to the foreigners
living among you. I am the LORD your God."
23After Moses gave all these instructions
to the Israelites, they took the blasphemer
outside the camp and stoned him to death.
The Israelites did just as the LORD had commanded Moses.

The Sabbath Year and the Year of Jubilee (25:1-55)

The Sabbath Year

25 While Moses was on Mount Sinai,
the LORD said to him, 2"Give the
following instructions to the people of Israel. When you have entered the land I am
giving you, the land itself must observe a
[d]Sabbath rest before the LORD every seventh year. 3For six years you may plant your
fields and prune your vineyards and harvest
your crops, 4but during the seventh year the
land must have a Sabbath year of complete
rest. It is the LORD's Sabbath. Do not plant
your fields or prune your vineyards during
that year. 5And don't store away the crops
that grow on their own or gather the grapes
from your unpruned vines. The land must
have a year of complete rest. 6But you may
eat whatever the land produces on its own
during its Sabbath. This applies to you, your
male and female [e]servants, your hired workers, and the temporary residents who live
with you. 7Your livestock and the wild animals in your land will also be allowed to eat
what the land produces.

The Year of Jubilee

8"In addition, you must count off seven Sabbath years, seven sets of seven years, adding
up to forty-nine years in all. 9Then on the
Day of Atonement in the fiftieth year, blow
the ram's horn loud and long throughout
the land. 10Set this year apart as holy, a time
to proclaim freedom throughout the land
for all who live there. It will be a jubilee year
for you, when each of you may return to the
land that belonged to your ancestors and return to your own clan. 11This fiftieth year
will be a jubilee for you. During that year
you must not plant your fields or store away
any of the crops that grow on their own, and
don't gather the grapes from your unpruned
vines. 12It will be a jubilee year for you, and
you must keep it holy. But you may eat whatever the land produces on its own. 13In the
Year of Jubilee each of you may return to the
land that belonged to your ancestors.

24:20 Exod 21:24-25; Deut 19:21; Matt 5:38
24:21 Lev 24:17-18
24:22 Exod 12:49; Num 15:15-16, 29
25:2 Exod 23:11; [d]*shabbath* (7676) ‣Num 15:32
25:3 Exod 23:10
25:4 Lev 25:20-23
25:5 2 Kgs 19:29
25:6 Lev 25:20-21; [e]*'ebed* (5650) ‣Lev 25:39
25:9 Num 10:10
25:10 Lev 25:8-16, 28-54; Isa 61:1; Jer 34:8, 15, 17; Luke 4:18-19
25:13 Lev 25:10, 24-31

24:20 *eye for an eye:* The legal principle involved is often called *lex talionis* ("law of retaliation"), which is that the penalty must fit the crime. When an injured party sought revenge on behalf of his kinsman (see Num 35:19-21), excessive revenge naturally ensued instead of appropriate justice. This provoked even greater retaliation, resulting in a cycle of increasing violence. *Lex talionis* served to regulate the prosecution of crimes (see also 6:2-7; cp. Exod 21:24; Lev 24:20; Deut 19:21; Matt 5:28-39).

24:22 Although *foreigners* were not citizens, they were human beings entitled to equal justice under the law (see 16:29, 31).

25:1-55 Just as seven days equaled a week ending in a Sabbath day, each seven years ended with ***a Sabbath year***. Likewise, after ***seven Sabbath years*** (i.e., 49 years total) came a special year, the ***Year of Jubilee***. Like so many holidays, these occasions were times of reflection on Israel's corporate identity and how they were shaped by their relationship with God. Because every Israelite, bond or free, had a part in God's kingdom, those bound in servitude were freed in the Year of Jubilee (25:39-43). In order to curb economic hardship and foster well-being, land sales were limited to a maximum term of fifty years. The land was then to be returned to the original owner's family or clan. The land belonged to the Lord; the Israelites were merely tenants (25:23). It is unlikely, however, that these laws saw much use; the best land fell into the hands of rich landowners (Isa 5:8-10; cp. Amos 5:11).

25:2-7 During the ***year*** of ***Sabbath rest***, there was to be no formal cultivation or harvesting of the land; from what grew on its own the landowner could gather what he needed for his household day by day. Whatever remained uneaten was left for the poor and for foreigners (Exod 23:10-11), and what they left provided food for both wild and domestic animals. See also Exod 21:2; Deut 15:1-11.

25:4 ***land must have a Sabbath year:*** The principle behind the Sabbath (see note on 19:30) was that God rested and therefore man rests. Here the principle was extended to the land.

25:8-17 The ***Year of Jubilee*** took place every ***fiftieth year*** as a release from obligations and servitude. The same year was also treated as a Sabbath year with no farming. Some scholars argue that the forty-ninth year served as both Sabbath (seventh) and jubilee (fiftieth) years. A simple count of fifty years would place the Year of Jubilee immediately after the seventh Sabbath year, which would mean two consecutive years without harvests. • Each Year of Jubilee the land was to revert to the clan or tribe that had originally received it under Joshua (Josh 13–21). Land had two functions: (1) It provided an economic basis for existence; and (2) it tied the landowner to his ancestors and, through them, to the land allocation under Joshua and even to the covenant with Moses. The return of the land was to prevent powerful land monopolies that would close out the poor.

25:9 ***on the Day of Atonement in the fiftieth year:*** Literally *on the tenth day of the seventh month, on the Day of Atonement;* see 23:27 and note. See also 16:1-34.

25:10 ***proclaim freedom throughout the land for all who live there:*** See 25:39-43, 47-55. • ***return to the land that belonged to your ancestors:*** If the individual who originally owned the land had died, the land was returned to his heirs.

25:11-12 All the regulations of the Sabbath year also applied to the Year of Jubilee.

25:14
Lev 25:17
25:17
[f]*yare'* (3372)
‣Deut 5:5
25:23
Exod 19:5
1 Chr 29:15
25:25
Ruth 2:20; 4:4, 6
Jer 32:7
[g]*ga'al* (1350)
‣Lev 27:13
25:27
Lev 25:50-52
25:28
Lev 25:10, 13
25:34
Num 35:2-5

14"When you make an agreement with
your neighbor to buy or sell property, you
must not take advantage of each other.
15When you buy land from your neighbor,
the price you pay must be based on the number of years since the last jubilee. The seller
must set the price by taking into account the
number of years remaining until the next
Year of Jubilee. 16The more years until the
next jubilee, the higher the price; the fewer
years, the lower the price. After all, the person selling the land is actually selling you
a certain number of harvests. 17Show your
[f]fear of God by not taking advantage of each
other. I am the LORD your God.

18"If you want to live securely in the land,
follow my decrees and obey my regulations.
19Then the land will yield large crops, and
you will eat your fill and live securely in
it. 20But you might ask, 'What will we eat
during the seventh year, since we are not allowed to plant or harvest crops that year?'
21Be assured that I will send my blessing
for you in the sixth year, so the land will produce a crop large enough for three years.
22When you plant your fields in the eighth
year, you will still be eating from the large
crop of the sixth year. In fact, you will still
be eating from that large crop when the
new crop is harvested in the ninth year.

Redemption of Property

23"The land must never be sold on a permanent basis, for the land belongs to me. You
are only foreigners and tenant farmers
working for me.

24"With every purchase of land you must
grant the seller the right to buy it back. 25If
one of your fellow Israelites falls into poverty and is forced to sell some family land,
then a close relative should [g]buy it back for
him. 26If there is no close relative to buy the
land, but the person who sold it gets enough
money to buy it back, 27he then has the
right to redeem it from the one who bought
it. The price of the land will be discounted
according to the number of years until the
next Year of Jubilee. In this way the original
owner can then return to the land. 28But
if the original owner cannot afford to buy
back the land, it will remain with the new
owner until the next Year of Jubilee. In the
jubilee year, the land must be returned to
the original owners so they can return to
their family land.

29"Anyone who sells a house inside a
walled town has the right to buy it back for
a full year after its sale. During that year, the
seller retains the right to buy it back. 30But
if it is not bought back within a year, the
sale of the house within the walled town
cannot be reversed. It will become the permanent property of the buyer. It will not be
returned to the original owner in the Year
of Jubilee. 31But a house in a village—a settlement without fortified walls—will be
treated like property in the countryside.
Such a house may be bought back at any
time, and it must be returned to the original
owner in the Year of Jubilee.

32"The Levites always have the right to
buy back a house they have sold within
the towns allotted to them. 33And any property that is sold by the Levites—all houses
within the Levitical towns—must be returned in the Year of Jubilee. After all, the
houses in the towns reserved for the Levites are the only property they own in all
Israel. 34The open pastureland around the

25:15-16 ***the number of years:*** The law did not allow the land to be sold in perpetuity. It was God's, and Israel was simply permitted to use it (25:23). However, if the owner was forced to give it up due to financial distress, it could be leased for up to forty-nine years (until the next jubilee). The price was adjusted according to the length of the lease. At the end of that time, the land was to revert to the family of the original owner.

25:18-22 See note on 25:4.

25:23 ***the land belongs to me:*** Israel's ownership of the land was derivative, not absolute—ownership depended on the covenant, in which God himself allotted them the land (Deut 1:8, 39). The ideas of land stewardship and of sharing material resources stem naturally from this concept of God's ownership.

25:25 The Hebrew word translated ***buy it back*** (*ga'al*) is often translated "redeem." It means "to restore something to its original or proper state of existence." The noun derived from this root (*go'el*) indicates the ***close relative*** who will restore what is out of order. The relative's duties were to redeem the property of his kinsman and keep it in the family (see Ruth 4:1-4; Jer 32:6-15); to seek out the murderer of his kinsman and bring him to justice (Num 35:19); and to marry his brother's widow and father a male heir to inherit the estate of his dead kinsman (Deut 25:5-10; see Gen 38:6-30; Ruth 4:9-10).

25:29-31 A house in an unwalled ***village*** was apparently considered the same as land. It could be bought back, and if not, ownership reverted in the Year of Jubilee to the family of the individual who sold it. No farm or grazing acreage was involved in the sale of a ***house inside a walled town.*** Because such a house could be built on the town wall without having to rest on the earth (Josh 2:15), there was no land to redeem. Therefore, it could not be bought back unless the new owner desired to sell it, nor did it revert ***to the original owner in the Year of Jubilee.***

25:32-34 The tribe of Levi could not inherit tribal territory because, as the priestly tribe, they were scattered throughout the land (Deut 18:1; see Gen 49:5-7; Num 35:1-8; Josh 21:1-42). The Levites could inherit only certain cities and the pasturelands surrounding them (Num 35:2). Therefore, they were an exception to the rules regarding land ownership, and their meager holdings were carefully protected. Their houses could be redeemed even in walled cities, and the pasturelands outside their towns could not be sold.

Levitical towns may never be sold. It is their
permanent possession.

Redemption of the Poor and Enslaved

35“If one of your fellow Israelites falls into
poverty and cannot support himself, support him as you would a foreigner or a
temporary resident and allow him to live
with you. 36Do not charge interest or make
a profit at his expense. Instead, show your
fear of God by letting him live with you as
your relative. 37Remember, do not charge
interest on money you lend him or make a
profit on food you sell him. 38I am the LORD
your God, who brought you out of the land
of Egypt to give you the land of Canaan and
to be your God.

39“If one of your fellow Israelites falls
into poverty and is forced to sell himself
to you, do not treat him as a [h]slave. 40Treat
him instead as a hired worker or as a temporary resident who lives with you, and he will
serve you only until the Year of Jubilee. 41At
that time he and his children will no longer
be obligated to you, and they will return to
their clans and go back to the land originally
allotted to their ancestors. 42The people of
Israel are my servants, whom I brought out
of the land of Egypt, so they must never be
sold as slaves. 43Show your fear of God by
not treating them harshly.

44“However, you may purchase male and
female [i]slaves from among the nations
around you. 45You may also purchase the
children of temporary residents who live
among you, including those who have been
born in your land. You may treat them as
your property, 46passing them on to your
children as a permanent inheritance. You
may treat them as slaves, but you must never
treat your fellow Israelites this way.

47“Suppose a foreigner or temporary
resident becomes rich while living among
you. If any of your fellow Israelites fall into
poverty and are forced to sell themselves to
such a foreigner or to a member of his family, 48they still retain the right to be bought
back, even after they have been purchased.
They may be bought back by a brother, 49an
uncle, or a cousin. In fact, anyone from the
extended family may buy them back. They
may also redeem themselves if they have
prospered. 50They will negotiate the price
of their freedom with the person who
bought them. The price will be based on the
number of years from the time they were
sold until the next Year of Jubilee—whatever it would cost to hire a worker for that
period of time. 51If many years still remain
until the jubilee, they will repay the proper
proportion of what they received when
they sold themselves. 52If only a few years
remain until the Year of Jubilee, they will
repay a small amount for their redemption.
53The foreigner must treat them as workers
hired on a yearly basis. You must not allow
a foreigner to treat any of your fellow Israelites harshly. 54If any Israelites have not been
bought back by the time the Year of Jubilee
arrives, they and their children must be set
free at that time. 55For the people of Israel
belong to me. They are my servants, whom
I brought out of the land of Egypt. I am the
LORD your God.

25:35 Deut 15:7-11; Prov 21:26
25:36 Exod 22:25; Deut 23:19-20
25:38 Lev 11:45
25:39 Exod 21:2-11; Deut 15:12-18; [h]*'ebed* (5650) ‣Lev 25:44
25:40 Lev 25:53
25:43 Col 4:1
25:44 [i]*'ebed* (5650) ‣Deut 23:15
25:46 Lev 25:40, 53
25:48 Neh 5:5
25:49 Lev 25:26
25:50 Job 7:1
25:53 Lev 25:40, 46
25:54 Lev 25:10, 13, 28

25:35 An impoverished Israelite first looked to his family for help (see note on 25:25). Second, he relied on the community, which was commanded to help him rather than exploit his vulnerability.

25:36-37 The purpose of a loan was to help a poor man get back on his feet, not to make money from his vulnerability. ***Interest*** was forbidden on loans to Israelites, but permitted on loans to foreigners (Deut 23:19-20).

25:38 The mention of ***the land of Egypt*** reminded the Israelites that they had been slaves at one time. They were to help the poor among them because of God's covenant relationship with them (cp. Exod 20:2 and Deut 5:6, where God's covenant with them is initiated).

25:40 The terms ***hired worker . . . temporary resident*** appear in parallel, suggesting they were similar in Israel's socioeconomic system. Both terms describe day laborers who had no land and depended on landowners to hire them (see Matt 20:1-16; also see note on 19:13). • ***Jubilee:*** See note on 25:8-17.

25:42 The same Hebrew word is translated as both ***servants*** and ***slaves.*** Because the Israelites were God's slaves/servants, they could not be slaves/servants to other human beings, except temporarily to work off a debt.

25:43 As human beings created in God's image (Gen 1:26, 27; Prov 14:31; 17:5) and as fellow Israelites in covenant with God, even bondservants were to be treated with respect. God's law includes numerous provisions for their protection (see Exod 21:20, 26-27). All human beings must be treated in a way that reflects reverence for God (see Prov 14:31; 17:5; Jas 2:14-16; 3:9-10).

25:44-46 ***Slaves*** in Mesopotamia and Egypt were little more than chattel, with no protection or rights. Israelites were allowed to purchase non-Israelites as slaves, but they were to be treated well and not abused. Occasionally some slaves were even adopted into childless families (Gen 15:2-4). Slavery continued into NT times, but the foundations had been laid for its dissolution in the OT doctrine of the common origins of all mankind through God. Slavery stemmed from the Fall, when relationships based on power replaced those of fellowship and communication (see Gen 3:16). In the NT, believers uphold the ideas of fellowship and communication by accepting the title "Christ's slave" or "servant" (Rom 1:1; Col 4:12; 2 Pet 1:1). In Paul's doctrine of the body of Christ (1 Cor 12:27; Eph 4:12), all believers acquired a common identity (Gal 3:28; Col 3:11; Phlm 1:16).

25:47-55 An Israelite who sold himself or a family member to a foreigner in Israel retained the right to buy himself or the family member back. If he could not find the resources to do that, he was not released during the seventh year (cp. Exod 21:2), but had to await

26:1 Exod 20:4; 34:17 Lev 19:4 Num 33:52
26:2 Exod 20:8-11
26:4 Lev 25:19 Deut 11:14-15
26:6 Ps 29:11
26:8 Deut 28:7; 32:30
26:9 Gen 17:6-7
26:10 Lev 25:22
26:11 Exod 29:45-46
26:12 Exod 6:7 *2 Cor 6:16
26:13 Exod 20:2
26:16 Deut 28:22, 33, 65-67; 32:23-25
26:17 Lev 26:36-37 Deut 28:25 Ps 106:41 Prov 28:1
26:18 Lev 26:21, 24, 28
26:19 Deut 28:23 Isa 25:11; 26:5
26:20 Ps 127:1

Blessings for Obedience and Curses for Disobedience (26:1-46)

26 "Do not make idols or set up
carved images, or sacred pillars, or
sculptured stones in your land so you may
worship them. I am the LORD your God.
2You must keep my Sabbath days of rest
and show reverence for my sanctuary. I am
the LORD.
3"If you follow my decrees and are careful to obey my commands, 4I will send you
the seasonal rains. The land will then yield
its crops, and the trees of the field will produce their fruit. 5Your threshing season will
overlap with the grape harvest, and your
grape harvest will overlap with the season
of planting grain. You will eat your fill and
live securely in your own land.
6"I will give you peace in the land, and
you will be able to sleep with no cause for
fear. I will rid the land of wild animals and
keep your enemies out of your land. 7In
fact, you will chase down your enemies and
slaughter them with your swords. 8Five of
you will chase a hundred, and a hundred of
you will chase ten thousand! All your enemies will fall beneath your sword.
9"I will look favorably upon you, making
you fertile and multiplying your people. And
I will fulfill my covenant with you. 10You
will have such a surplus of crops that you
will need to clear out the old grain to make
room for the new harvest! 11I will live among
you, and I will not despise you. 12I will walk
among you; I will be your God, and you will
be my people. 13I am the LORD your God,
who brought you out of the land of Egypt so
you would no longer be their slaves. I broke
the yoke of slavery from your neck so you
can walk with your heads held high.
14"However, if you do not listen to me
or obey all these commands, 15and if you
break my covenant by rejecting my decrees,
treating my regulations with contempt, and
refusing to obey my commands, 16I will punish you. I will bring sudden terrors upon
you—wasting diseases and burning fevers
that will cause your eyes to fail and your
life to ebb away. You will plant your crops
in vain because your enemies will eat them.
17I will turn against you, and you will be defeated by your enemies. Those who hate
you will rule over you, and you will run even
when no one is chasing you!
18"And if, in spite of all this, you still disobey me, I will punish you seven times over
for your sins. 19I will break your proud spirit
by making the skies as unyielding as iron
and the earth as hard as bronze. 20All your
work will be for nothing, for your land will

---

the Year of Jubilee. During his service to the foreigner, the Israelite slave was to enjoy the status of a hired servant and not be treated like a slave (25:53). The people of Israel belonged to God; they were not to be sold as permanent slaves to anyone else.

26:1 Israel was to make no *idols* or *carved images* to worship (see Exod 20:4-6). Creating an image to worship would blaspheme God by confining him to time and space and by manufacturing a lifeless image to take the place of the living God. • Early in Israel's history, stones were set on end as memorials to various events (Gen 28:18; Exod 24:4). However, ***pillars*** and ***sculptured stones*** were associated with pagan worship (2 Kgs 3:2; 10:26, 27), especially when the carved image of a god rested on them. Some sculpture was clearly allowed (e.g., 1 Kgs 7:25); the focus here is on objects that might be worshiped and thereby become idolatrous.

26:3-39 These blessings and curses resemble a key element of ancient Near Eastern suzerain-vassal treaties. In such treaties, the suzerain king promised to defend the vassal king and his state, while the vassal took an oath of loyalty to his lord. Blessings and curses followed, with the curses generally being more lengthy (contrast 26:3-13 with 26:14-39; cp. Deut 27:15–28:68). Such treaties would call upon the gods as witnesses and enforcers. In God's covenant with Israel, however, the Lord was one of the parties to the treaty (Israel being the other); since the Lord could swear by no one greater, he swore by himself (see Gen 22:16; Heb 6:13).

26:3 Treaties and covenants had conditions attached to them. Israel's blessings were conditioned on the people's obedience to the terms revealed by God, to whom they had sworn obedience (Exod 24:7; Josh 24:21-22). The covenant itself, however, was irrevocable (26:44-45; see Rom 11:29); Israel could not cancel it. The people had only two choices: obedience, which brought blessing, or rebellion, which brought curse.

26:5 Israel's restoration following captivity also promised a harvest so plentiful that it would run over into the time of planting (see Amos 9:13; Joel 3:18).

26:7 Success in warfare would result from obedience to God (cp. 26:17, 36-37; Deut 28:6, 19).

26:9 ***fulfill my covenant:*** The fulfillment is seen in the "rest" spoken of in Hebrews (Heb 3:11–4:11). The Promised Land should have brought a state of security and prosperity, a state of "rest" to the Israelites (Exod 33:14; Deut 12:10; 25:19; Josh 1:13, 15). Israel succeeded in entering the Promised Land, but their rebellion kept them from seeing the covenant fulfilled.

26:12 ***your God . . . my people:*** The covenant bound the parties to one another, making each belong to the other.

26:13 ***yoke of slavery:*** A yoke would fit over a slave's shoulders and behind the base of the neck for carrying pairs of heavy items, such as pails of water. Cp. Rom 6:16-22.

26:14-39 The objective of God's punishment of his people is to change behavior and restore relationship. God responds to his disobedient people as a perfectly righteous and loving parent would to a child. The punishments designed to curb rebellious behavior gradually increase, giving Israel the opportunity to repent at any time (26:18-28). Even when Israel was punished with exile from the land in 722 and 586 BC, God was working to restore his people (see, e.g., Isa 40–66; Jer 29:10; Amos 9:11-15).

26:18 ***seven times over:*** I.e., many times (see also 26:21, 24, 28; Gen 4:15).

26:19-20 If God withholds rain, the ground will be hard and unproductive.

yield no crops, and your trees will bear no
fruit.
21"If even then you remain hostile toward
me and refuse to obey me, I will inflict disaster on you seven times over for your sins.
22I will send wild animals that will rob you
of your children and destroy your livestock.
Your numbers will dwindle, and your roads
will be deserted.
23"And if you fail to learn the lesson and
continue your hostility toward me, 24then
I myself will be hostile toward you. I will
personally strike you with calamity seven
times over for your sins. 25I will send armies
against you to carry out the curse of the covenant you have broken. When you run to
your towns for safety, I will send a plague to
destroy you there, and you will be handed
over to your enemies. 26I will destroy your
food supply, so that ten women will need
only one oven to bake bread for their families. They will ration your food by weight,
and though you have food to eat, you will
not be satisfied.
27"If in spite of all this you still refuse to
listen and still remain hostile toward me,
28then I will give full vent to my hostility. I
myself will punish you seven times over
for your sins. 29Then you will eat the flesh
of your own sons and daughters. 30I will destroy your pagan shrines and knock down
your places of worship. I will leave your
lifeless corpses piled on top of your lifeless
idols, and I will despise you. 31I will make
your cities desolate and destroy your places
of pagan worship. I will take no pleasure
in your offerings that should be a pleasing
aroma to me. 32Yes, I myself will devastate
your land, and your enemies who come to
occupy it will be appalled at what they see.
33I will scatter you among the nations and
bring out my sword against you. Your land
will become desolate, and your cities will lie
in ruins. 34Then at last the land will enjoy
its neglected Sabbath years as it lies desolate while you are in exile in the land of your
enemies. Then the land will finally rest and
enjoy the Sabbaths it missed. 35As long as
the land lies in ruins, it will enjoy the rest
you never allowed it to take every seventh
year while you lived in it.
36"And for those of you who survive, I will
demoralize you in the land of your enemies.
You will live in such fear that the sound of a
leaf driven by the wind will send you fleeing.
You will run as though fleeing from a sword,
and you will fall even when no one pursues
you. 37Though no one is chasing you, you
will stumble over each other as though fleeing from a sword. You will have no power
to stand up against your enemies. 38You will
die among the foreign nations and be devoured in the land of your enemies. 39Those
of you who survive will waste away in your
enemies' lands because of their sins and
the sins of their ancestors.
40"But at last my people will confess their
sins and the sins of their ancestors for betraying me and being hostile toward me.
41When I have turned their hostility back
on them and brought them to the land of
their enemies, then at last their stubborn
hearts will be humbled, and they will pay
for their sins. 42Then I will remember my
covenant with Jacob and my covenant with
Isaac and my covenant with Abraham, and I
will remember the land. 43For the land must
be abandoned to enjoy its years of Sabbath
rest as it lies deserted. At last the people will
pay for their sins, for they have continually
rejected my regulations and despised my
decrees.

26:21 Lev 26:18
26:22 Deut 32:24
26:23 Jer 2:30; 5:3
26:25 Deut 28:21-22, 27-29; 32:35
26:26 Isa 3:1; 9:19-20 Ezek 4:16
26:29 Deut 28:53-57 2 Kgs 6:26-30
26:30 1 Kgs 13:2 Isa 27:9
26:31 Ps 74:3 Isa 63:18
26:32 Jer 12:11; 18:16
26:33 Deut 28:64-68
26:34 Lev 26:43 2 Chr 36:21
26:36 Ezek 21:7
26:38 Deut 4:25-27
26:39 Ezek 33:10
26:40 Jer 3:12-15 Luke 15:18 1 Jn 1:9
26:42 Gen 12:1-3; 15:1-4, 13-16; 26:2-5; 28:13-15
26:43 Lev 26:34

26:29 Starvation would so pervade the land that when a child died of hunger, he or she would be eaten, in pagan fashion, by the others in the family (Deut 28:53-57; see 2 Kgs 6:24-31; Lam 2:20; cp. 2 Kgs 3:27).

26:30 The ***pagan shrines*** mentioned here were the infamous "high places" built on hilltops (see 2 Kgs 18:4). These shrines incorporated elements from pre-Israelite religions into Israel's worship and challenged the Temple for religious authority. • ***places of worship*** (Hebrew *khamman*): Perhaps "incense altars." Some of these altars were used in Baal worship (2 Chr 34:4). • ***idols:*** The Hebrew term (literally *round things*) probably alludes to dung.

26:34 With the people gone into captivity in a foreign land, there would be no one to work ***the land.*** It would ***at last*** have the "rest" of lying fallow that the people had denied it (see 25:1-7).

26:36-39 Disastrous defeat and captivity would later be the fate of both Israel and Judah (see notes on 18:28; 26:14-39).

26:40-45 The chapter ends with a message of hope: Even after Israel violated the covenant and experienced judgment, reconciliation and restoration remained possible if the people confessed and repented (see note on 4:20). God's grace had not been taken away. God did not want to destroy his people; he would restore them if they would only humble themselves and repent (see also 2 Chr 7:14).

26:41 Physical circumcision of males was the mark of God's covenant with Israel (Gen 17:9-14; Exod 4:25-26). ***Stubborn hearts*** (literally *uncircumcised hearts*) do not love God and demonstrate it by persistent disobedience. God promised to "circumcise" Israel's uncircumcised hearts so that the people could love him (see also Deut 10:16; 30:6; Jer 4:4; Ezek 36:25-27).

26:42 God had begun his ***covenant with Abraham*** (then called Abram, Gen 15:18) and continued it with ***Isaac*** (Gen 17:19) and ***Jacob*** (Exod 2:24). Jacob's twelve sons were the ancestors of Israel's twelve tribes. Israel's liberation from Egypt and settlement in Canaan were based on God's promises to their ancestors, not on the Israelites' own virtues (Deut 9:4-5).

26:44
Deut 4:29-31
Rom 11:2

26:45
Gen 17:7
Exod 6:6-8
[i]*zakar* (2142)
‣Num 10:9

26:46
Lev 27:34

27:3
Exod 30:13
Lev 5:15; 27:25

27:6
Num 3:46-48;
18:14-16

27:8
Lev 14:21-22

27:10
Lev 27:14-33

27:13
[k]*ga'al* (1350)
‣Num 35:12

44"But despite all this, I will not utterly reject or despise them while they are in exile
in the land of their enemies. I will not cancel
my covenant with them by wiping them out,
for I am the LORD their God. 45For their sakes
I will [i]remember my ancient covenant with
their ancestors, whom I brought out of the
land of Egypt in the sight of all the nations,
that I might be their God. I am the LORD."

46These are the decrees, regulations, and
instructions that the LORD gave through
Moses on Mount Sinai as evidence of the
relationship between himself and the Israelites.

6. REGULATIONS PERTAINING TO VOWS AND TITHES (27:1-34)

27 The LORD said to Moses, 2"Give the
following instructions to the people
of Israel. If anyone makes a special vow to
dedicate someone to the LORD by paying
the value of that person, 3here is the scale of
values to be used. A man between the ages
of twenty and sixty is valued at fifty shekels of silver, as measured by the sanctuary
shekel. 4A woman of that age is valued at
thirty shekels of silver. 5A boy between the
ages of five and twenty is valued at twenty
shekels of silver; a girl of that age is valued
at ten shekels of silver. 6A boy between the
ages of one month and five years is valued at
five shekels of silver; a girl of that age is valued at three shekels of silver. 7A man older
than sixty is valued at fifteen shekels of
silver; a woman of that age is valued at ten
shekels of silver. 8If you desire to make such
a vow but cannot afford to pay the required
amount, take the person to the priest. He
will determine the amount for you to pay
based on what you can afford.

9"If your vow involves giving an animal
that is acceptable as an offering to the LORD,
any gift to the LORD will be considered holy.
10You may not exchange or substitute it for
another animal—neither a good animal for
a bad one nor a bad animal for a good one.
But if you do exchange one animal for another, then both the original animal and its
substitute will be considered holy. 11If your
vow involves an unclean animal—one that is
not acceptable as an offering to the LORD—
then you must bring the animal to the priest.
12He will assess its value, and his assessment
will be final, whether high or low. 13If you
want to [k]buy back the animal, you must pay
the value set by the priest, plus 20 percent.

14"If someone dedicates a house to the
LORD, the priest will come to assess its

26:44-45 ***I am the LORD:*** See note on 19:3.

27:1-34 As a conclusion to the book, this chapter discusses various types of vows and ends with a provision for redeeming one's tithes (see also ch 25). Under certain circumstances, such as an emergency, an individual might make a vow promising something to God, usually in exchange for God's answering his or her prayer (see Jon 2:9). Once the prayer is answered, the individual might be tempted to discount the vow. Scripture requires that vows be made carefully (see 5:4; Eccl 5:4-6) and then carried out. Jesus taught that oaths should not be commonly or carelessly made (Matt 5:33-37; 23:16-22).

27:2 The vow taken to become a Nazirite is also called a ***special vow*** (Num 6:2), but the vow mentioned here was probably a promise made to God when seeking a desired answer to prayer (see Gen 28:20-22). Pagan religions of the time sacrificed infants to their gods, but God outlawed such a practice (18:21; 20:2-5; cp. Gen 22:12-13). Consequently, the concept of being vowed to the Lord was measured in terms of service given, not in the sacrifice of a life. Whether the vow was made by the person or by another acting for him or her, payment was to be made to the sanctuary, apparently for the person's expenses during the term of service. See also Num 6:1-21; Judg 13:5, 7; 1 Sam 1:11; Amos 2:11-12; Acts 18:18.

27:3-7 This section reflects social rank in ancient Near Eastern cultures. An adult ***man*** of working age had the highest rank, followed by an adult ***woman*** of working age. A ***boy*** ranked higher than a ***girl,*** and both ranked higher than toddlers. Senior citizens, who were past prime working age, ranked comparably to boys and girls. • The amount of ***fifty shekels*** (see note on 5:15) would have represented about 20 ounces (570 grams) of silver, a significant amount. Comparisons with other literature of the time indicates that the biblical valuation is quite high and would have been out of reach for most people.

27:3 *fifty shekels:* Or *20 ounces* [570 grams].

27:4 *thirty shekels:* Or *12 ounces* [342 grams].

27:5 Or *A boy . . . 8 ounces* [228 grams] *of silver; a girl . . . 4 ounces* [114 grams] *of silver.*

27:6 Or *A boy . . . 2 ounces* [57 grams] *of silver; a girl . . . 1.2 ounces* [34 grams] *of silver.*

27:7 Or *A man . . . 6 ounces* [171 grams] *of silver; a woman . . . 4 ounces* [114 grams] *of silver.*

27:8 As in the offering system (see 5:7-13), special consideration was given to the poor person who wanted to contribute to the sanctuary. In such cases, the amount of silver to accompany the pledge was left to the priest's discretion.

27:9-10 Once an acceptable ***animal*** had been vowed and the priest at the sanctuary had accepted it on God's behalf, the animal became ***holy*** and belonged to God.

27:11-13 An ***unclean animal,*** one unfit either for food or sacrifice, could be bought back by the worshiper for its assessed value ***plus 20 percent.*** No doubt the reasoning behind this rule was to preserve the sanctity of vows and to minimize thoughtless dedications. For the 20 percent surcharge on property, see 27:15, 19, 31.

27:14-15 The Hebrew term translated as ***dedicates*** is quite strong and means "declares holy." • This ruling would apply only to ***a house*** in a walled town. Other houses, whether in unwalled villages or on open land, reverted to the owner in the Year of Jubilee (25:29-31). If the owner decided to redeem it, he had to pay a surcharge of ***20 percent.*** If the house was not redeemed in the first year, it became the property of the sanctuary and priests, and it could be used however they wished.

value. The priest's assessment will be final,
whether high or low. 15If the person who
dedicated the house wants to buy it back,
he must pay the value set by the priest, plus
20 percent. Then the house will again be
his.
16"If someone dedicates to the LORD a
piece of his family property, its value will
be assessed according to the amount of
seed required to plant it—fifty shekels of
silver for a field planted with five bushels
of barley seed. 17If the field is dedicated
to the LORD in the Year of Jubilee, then the
entire assessment will apply. 18But if the
field is dedicated after the Year of Jubilee,
the priest will assess the land's value in proportion to the number of years left until
the next Year of Jubilee. Its assessed value
is reduced each year. 19If the person who
dedicated the field wants to buy it back,
he must pay the value set by the priest,
plus 20 percent. Then the field will again
be legally his. 20But if he does not want to
buy it back, and it is sold to someone else,
the field can no longer be bought back.
21When the field is released in the Year of
Jubilee, it will be holy, a field specially set
apart for the LORD. It will become the property of the priests.
22"If someone dedicates to the LORD a
field he has purchased but which is not part
of his family property, 23the priest will assess its value based on the number of years
left until the next Year of Jubilee. On that
day he must give the assessed value of
the land as a sacred donation to the LORD.
24In the Year of Jubilee the field must be
returned to the person from whom he purchased it, the one who inherited it as family
property. 25(All the payments must be measured by the weight of the sanctuary shekel,
which equals twenty gerahs.)
26"You may not dedicate a firstborn animal to the LORD, for the firstborn of your
cattle, sheep, and goats already belong to
him. 27However, you may buy back the firstborn of a ceremonially unclean animal by
paying the priest's assessment of its worth,

27:18 Lev 25:14-16
27:21 Lev 25:8-54; Num 18:14; Ezek 44:29
27:24 Lev 25:28
27:25 Exod 30:13; Num 3:47; 18:16; Ezek 45:12
27:26 Exod 13:2, 12

Complete Dedication (27:28-29)

Exod 22:20; Num 18:8-14; 21:2-3; Deut 7:1-6, 26; 13:12-18; Josh 6:17-19, 24; 7:11-15; 1 Sam 15:2-3; 1 Kgs 20:42; Isa 43:26-28; Mal 4:5-6; Rom 9:3; 1 Cor 16:22; Gal 1:8-9

The Hebrew word *kherem* ("specially set apart") is difficult to translate because it represents a concept for which there is no exact parallel in modern English. In the conquest of Canaan under Joshua, *kherem* designated something deemed holy to a pagan god and therefore hostile to the LORD. Such things were to be destroyed (27:29). In the case of valuable metal items, they were brought to the sanctuary, where they became holy to the LORD (27:28; see also Josh 6:19, 24). The concept of being "specially set apart" was also applied to Israel's enemies when they and their property were destroyed (Josh 6:17-19; 1 Sam 15:2-3).

In 27:21, 28, *kherem* indicates an acceptable vow devoting something to the Lord for use in the sanctuary (see Num 18:14). This made the item, land, or person holy. The thing or person could not be bought back and remained in the Lord's service permanently.

The concept of complete dedication through total destruction underlies several passages in the apostle Paul's writings, especially Romans 9:3 and Galatians 1:8-9 (see also 1 Cor 16:22). In Romans 9:3, Paul was even willing to be declared *anathema* (the Greek equivalent of *kherem*) if it would bring about the salvation of his fellow Jews. In Galatians 1:8-9, the same Greek word indicates an appropriate end for those who preach a false gospel. In 1 Corinthians 12:3, Paul warns that no one speaking in the Spirit can call Jesus *anathema*, that is, no one who has God's Spirit will interpret Jesus' crucifixion as a sign of God's rejection of him, as the Jews of Paul's day did. Instead, they will recognize it as an act of atonement for sinful humanity.

27:16-21 ***fifty shekels of silver for a field planted with five bushels of barley seed:*** Hebrew *50 shekels* [20 ounces, or 570 grams] *of silver for a homer* [182 liters] *of barley seed.* The price for dedicating a ***field*** was determined by ***the number of years*** remaining ***until the next Year of Jubilee*** (see 25:24-28). If this property was not redeemed, it became the property of the priests to do with as they wished. The price of redeeming a field was 120 percent of the valuation (see 27:11-13). If a landowner dedicated his field without redeeming it, it did not revert to his family in the Year of Jubilee.

27:21 ***Year of Jubilee:*** See 25:8-55. • ***specially set apart*** (Hebrew *kherem*): The Hebrew term refers to the complete consecration of things or people to the LORD, either by destroying them or by giving them as an offering; also in 27:28, 29. Here, an acceptable vow devoting something to the Lord made it holy; it could not be redeemed.

27:25 ***sanctuary shekel:*** Each shekel was about 0.4 ounces [11 grams] in weight. See note on 5:15. • Each of the ***gerahs*** weighed about 0.02 ounces or 0.6 grams.

27:26 ***You may not dedicate:*** Every ***firstborn*** male, be it man or animal, already belonged to God (Exod 13:2; 34:19-20). Therefore, dedicating a firstborn was a useless exercise. The priest clearly had a use for the firstborn of animals fit for food or sacrifice (clean animals). The ***firstborn of a ceremonially unclean animal*** such as a donkey could be redeemed for 20 percent more than its value. Human firstborns had to be redeemed (Exod 13:11-13).

27:28
Josh 6:17-19
[a]*kharam* (2763)
‣Num 21:2
27:30
Gen 28:22
Num 18:26
2 Chr 31:5-6
Neh 13:12
Mal 3:8
[b]*ma'aser* (4643)
‣Lev 27:31
27:31
[c]*ma'aser* (4643)
‣Num 18:21
27:33
Lev 27:10
27:34
Lev 26:46

plus 20 percent. If you do not buy it back,
the priest will sell it at its assessed value.
28"However, anything specially [a]set apart
for the LORD—whether a person, an animal,
or family property—must never be sold or
bought back. Anything devoted in this way
has been set apart as holy, and it belongs to
the LORD. 29No person specially set apart
for destruction may be bought back. Such
a person must be put to death.
30"One-[b]tenth of the produce of the land,
whether grain from the fields or fruit from
the trees, belongs to the LORD and must be
set apart to him as holy. 31If you want to
buy back the LORD's [c]tenth of the grain or
fruit, you must pay its value, plus 20 percent. 32Count off every tenth animal from
your herds and flocks and set them apart
for the LORD as holy. 33You may not pick and
choose between good and bad animals, and
you may not substitute one for another. But
if you do exchange one animal for another,
then both the original animal and its substitute will be considered holy and cannot be
bought back."
34These are the commands that the LORD
gave through Moses on Mount Sinai for the
Israelites.

27:28 ***specially set apart*** (Hebrew *kherem*): Such an act of devotion was irrevocable. The person, animal, or property devoted this way was dedicated to the service of the sanctuary in a manner defined by the priest.

27:29 ***set apart for destruction*** (Hebrew *kherem*): The context here is the war for the conquest of Canaan, when cities, animals, and people deemed holy to some other god were set apart to be destroyed.

27:30 ***One-tenth*** (the "tithe") of the harvest belonged ***to the LORD*** (Deut 14:22-26; cp. Lev 23:10-14). Members of the tribe of Levi, the priests and Levites, received no tribal lands. Accordingly, they were allotted one-tenth of all produce from those who did own land (Num 18:21-29). This tithe was set aside every year (Deut 14:22) and was taken to the sanctuary; part of it was eaten there in a ritual meal (Deut 14:23-26). A second tithe was paid locally every third year to the local Levites and the poor (Deut 14:27-29; 26:12; contrast Amos 4:4). The Levites then paid a tithe of what they received to the Tabernacle priests (Num 18:26), who used it to support themselves and maintain the sanctuary. Some interpreters think there were three tithes, the first paid to the Levites, the second consumed at the sanctuary, and the third paid every third year for the poor. Others suggest that there was just one tithe, paid at the sanctuary for two years, then paid locally every third year.

27:31 The penalty to ***buy back*** the tithed harvest was the same amount assessed for an individual who had accidentally withheld his tithe (see 5:16).

27:32 Just like the produce of the fields (27:29-34), the flocks and herds were also tithed to the Lord.

27:34 The book closes as it opened (see 1:1), clearly noting the divine origin of its contents as mediated through Moses.

THE BOOK OF NUMBERS

The book of Numbers tells the story of Israel in the wilderness, journeying toward the Promised Land from Mount Sinai. As Moses led Israel from Egypt to Canaan, God tested his people in the crucible of the wilderness to see if they would be faithful to him as a unified nation. Numbers documents their successes and failures. Israel's disobedience resulted in the Lord's judgment, always counterbalanced by his patient persistence in raising a new generation to fulfill his plan. With its many stories and the detailed exposition of God's laws, Numbers gives us a dramatic account of the Lord's nature, his covenant, and his plan for his people.

SETTING

After leaving Egypt, the Israelites journeyed to Mount Sinai, where God gave them the law (see Exodus). They remained at Sinai for a year before traveling through the wilderness into Transjordan (the region east of the Jordan River) to camp on the plains of Moab. God tested Israel in the wilderness as the generation that made the Exodus from Egypt passed away and a new generation prepared to enter the Promised Land. The book of Numbers instructed the new generation camped on the plains of Moab to obey the Lord.

Israel was shaped and purified during this wilderness sojourn. Through Moses' literary efforts (and those of later scribes and editors), Numbers enabled successive generations to hear that story. It thus became a vital component of Hebrew memory. Numbers was written so that those who learned from history need not repeat mistakes from the past.

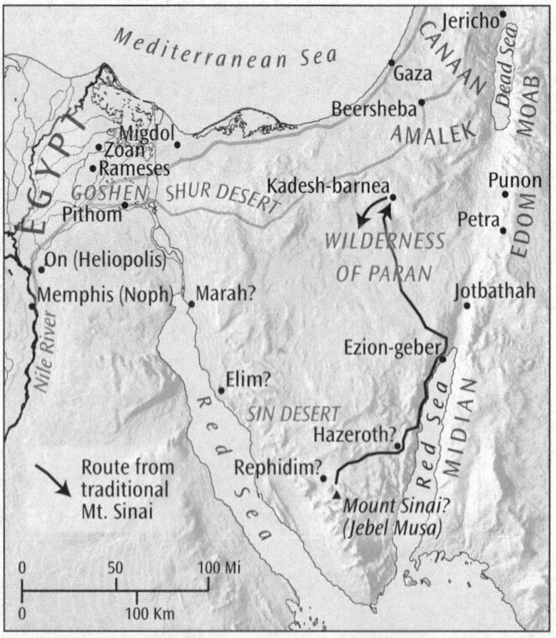

◀ **Israel in the Wilderness.** Israel's approximate route is shown from MOUNT SINAI into the WILDERNESS OF PARAN near KADESH-BARNEA (chs 1–13). After their rebellion against the Lord (ch 14), Israel wandered in the wilderness for nearly forty years (14:26–22:1) before beginning to move toward the Promised Land (see map, p. 285). Many of the places shown are listed in ch 33.

ZOAN 13:22
RAMESES 33:3, 5; Exod 12:37
MOUNT SINAI 1:1, 19; 9:1; 10:12; 33:15-16
HAZEROTH 12:1-16; 33:17-18
MIDIAN 10:29; 22:4, 7; 25:6, 14-18; 31:2-10
KADESH-BARNEA 13:26; 20:1, 14-16, 22; 32:8; 33:36-37; 34:4
EDOM 20:14-21; 21:4; 24:18; 33:37; 34:3
MOAB chs 21–26; Deut 1:5
JERICHO 22:1; 26:63; 33:48; 36:13

SUMMARY

Three stages of Israel's journey through the wilderness give the book of Numbers its structure: (1) the nineteen days in which Israel prepared for departure from their camp at Sinai (1:1–10:10), (2) the approximately thirty-nine-year journey from Sinai to the plains of Moab (10:11–22:1), and (3) the final months of Israel's encampment on the plains of Moab shortly before they entered Canaan (21:1–36:13).

The registrations of Israel's men of military age (chs 1–4, 26) also shape Numbers. The two registrations primarily measured the strength of Israel's fighting force and the number of Levites, with the totals at the beginning of the book and toward the end of the book representing two completely different generations. The first census tallied the rebellious generation that left Egypt, received the law at Sinai, and died in the wilderness. The second registration numbered the new generation of Israelites that entered the Promised Land. The two counts are very close, showing that the second generation completely replaced the first.

Along the way, the Hebrews that left Egypt committed serious acts of disobedience (chs 11, 12, 14, 16–17, 20, 25); they all died in the wilderness except for Joshua and Caleb, whose faith was exemplary (13:30; 14:6-9). Israel's army was tested on several occasions before they entered Canaan (chs 14, 21, 31), and the famous story of Balaam is recounted in great detail in chs 22–24. Arrangements were made for settling Transjordan (ch 32), the wilderness journey was reviewed (ch 33), and Moses anticipated the occupation of Canaan (chs 34–36) prior to his sermons in the book of Deuteronomy.

Numbers focuses on the role of the Levites, including their duties when the Hebrews were on the march. Numbers is a case study in how Israel maintained—and failed to maintain—covenant regulations in their day-to-day experiences.

OUTLINE

1:1–10:10
The Israelites Camp in the Wilderness of Sinai

10:11–22:1
The Israelites Move from Sinai to the Plains of Moab

22:2–36:13
The Israelites Camp in the Plains of Moab and Prepare to Invade Canaan

AUTHORSHIP

As with the other books of the Pentateuch, Moses has traditionally been recognized as the author of Numbers. Until the advent of modern scholarship, both Jewish and Christian scholars held to Moses' authorship; the OT, the NT, and much ancient Jewish literature also made this assumption. References to Moses' role as author occur throughout the Pentateuch (e.g., 33:1-2). On the basis of content or the level of literacy feasible at the time of the Exodus and conquest, there is no need to exclude Moses out of hand as the primary author, except in passages such as the account of Moses' death (Deut 34). It is also possible that Moses supervised the compilation of books credited to him or, like the apostle Paul, dictated parts of his writings. Numbers refers to representatives and elders who helped Moses in various ways (chs 1, 11).

TIMELINE

1500–1200 BC
Late Bronze Age

1446 / 1270 BC*
Israel leaves Egypt (the Exodus), moves to Mount Sinai
The covenant at Sinai

1445 / 1269 BC
Israel enters the wilderness

1445–1406 / 1269–1230 BC
Events recorded in Numbers occur

1406 / 1230 BC
Genesis—Deuteronomy are drafted
Moses dies
Israel enters Canaan

* *The two dates harmonize with the traditional "early" chronology and a more recent "late" chronology of the Exodus. All dates are approximate. Please see "Chronology: Abraham to Joshua," p. 118.*

History repeats itself . . . because it is based on two factors which do not change: God's character and man's sinfulness.

GORDON J. WENHAM
Numbers, p. 15

Many scholars postulate various sources from which later editors created the books of the Pentateuch, but this "Documentary Hypothesis" remains speculative (see "Introduction to the Pentateuch: Authorship," p. 11). Even allowing for later modifications by scribes and editors, Numbers substantially represents itself as Moses' work.

DATE & GEOGRAPHY

The geographical, cultural, and linguistic data related to Numbers fit either an early or a late date (1400s or 1200s BC) for the Exodus and conquest (see "Chronology: Abraham to Joshua," p. 118).

The archaeological evidence from Sinai, the Negev, and Transjordan (Edom, Moab, and Ammon) also contributes significantly to discussion about the historical background of the conquest. Scholars are unable to identify exact locations for many place-names mentioned in the wilderness itinerary, and there are problems with various other sites named in Numbers (e.g., see notes on 20:1; 21:1–22:1).

LITERARY ISSUES

Title of the Book. The name "Numbers" derives from this book's interest in statistics (as in chs 1–4, 26). It is the English translation of Latin *Numeri* and Greek *Arithmoi,* the name given to this book by the Latin Vulgate and Greek Septuagint translations of the OT. The registration accounts show with mathematical precision that the Israelites that left Egypt were not the same people that crossed the Jordan into Canaan. In the Hebrew Bible, the book of Numbers is called *bemidbar* ("in the wilderness"), the fourth word of 1:1 in Hebrew. This title is certainly appropriate, since it reflects the book's geographical setting and chronological framework.

Just as the Israelites were not intended to pass thirty-eight years in journeying from one place to another in the wilderness, so the Christian is not expected to have prolonged wilderness experiences through disobedience. . . . The book of Numbers is . . . a warning against indulging in the kind of sin that brought death to a whole generation of Israelites so long ago.

R. K. HARRISON
Numbers, p. 28

Literary Genres. The book of Numbers includes a variety of common literary genres, such as narrative (e.g., 10:11–14:45), poetry (e.g., chs 23–24), and law (e.g., chs 4–6). It also contains detailed lists of facts and figures, such as registration tallies (e.g., chs 1–4), offerings (e.g., ch 7), and travel itineraries (e.g., ch 33). The NLT compiles various prose lists into concise tables of names and numbers (chs 1–2, 13, 34).

Literary Sources. The Hebrew Bible identifies ancient sources that Moses (and perhaps later editors) consulted, such as the *Book of the Wars of the LORD* (21:14-15); the "Song of the Well" (21:17-18); and the "Song of Heshbon" (21:27-30). Chapters 23–24 contain many poetic lines from the non-Israelite prophet Balaam; 31:32-47 seems to be based on an actual booty record; and ch 33 appears to derive from a written diary.

Text. The Hebrew text of Numbers is very well preserved, except for a few sections of poetry in chs 21–24 that are difficult to interpret. The generally good condition of the Hebrew text is evident when comparing the Hebrew Masoretic Text (AD 900s) with much earlier fragments of Numbers found in the Dead Sea Scrolls (150 BC—AD 125); there are only a few insignificant variations between the two. Greater differences exist between the Masoretic Text, equivalent sections in the Greek OT (the Septuagint), and the Samaritan Pentateuch, but they represent deliberate differences of interpretation, not just variant readings of the manuscripts.

MEANING AND MESSAGE

Numbers explains how God provided for his people's needs, and it documents the repeated disobedience that marred this period as they rebelled against the Lord's commands. The Israelites did not wander in the wilderness for forty years because they were lost, but because of their faithlessness and rebellion.

Numbers highlights Israel's struggle with God. As often as God called the Israelites to strictly adhere to the law, they disobeyed him. The Israelites could count on God's provision for their physical necessities and for guidance and instruction through their chosen leaders. Yet God's constant purpose was often met with lack of faith. Numbers illustrates the swift judgment of a holy God while teaching that the Lord is faithful, patient, holy, and just. These characteristics were held in tension, but there was no doubt about the outcome when Israel was disobedient.

As in ancient Israel, all communities of believers still need unwavering leadership, and Numbers still warns those who too easily forget God's holy nature. In Rom 15:4, Paul says that the OT narratives were written for our benefit. Specific episodes from Numbers are used in the NT as powerful object lessons:

- In 1 Cor 10:1-11, the apostle Paul warns his readers to avoid idolatry, immorality, and grumbling so that they will not perish like the Israelites in the wilderness. God is not pleased with such behavior, and Christians must not put God to the test (10:9).
- The author of Hebrews identifies repeated instances of Israel's hardhearted and disobedient spirit and says that God responded to this waywardness with swift and certain wrath (Heb 3:7–4:11). These verses, which draw heavily on the language of Ps 95, are saturated with terms that reflect God's judgment of Israel's sin.
- Jude 1:5 summarizes Numbers to educate Christians based on the past.

The same God who liberated his people from Egypt destroyed that rebellious generation because they did not believe. Like ancient Israel, Christians should learn from the mistakes of the past and live in faith and obedience to their Lord.

FURTHER READING

RONALD B. ALLEN
Numbers (1990)

TIMOTHY R. ASHLEY
The Book of Numbers (1993)

DALE A. BRUEGGEMANN
Numbers in *Cornerstone Biblical Commentary,* vol. 2 (2008)

ERYL W. DAVIES
Numbers (1995)

R. K. HARRISON
Numbers (1990)

GORDON J. WENHAM
Numbers (1981)

1:1 Exod 40:2, 17
1:2 Exod 38:25-26; Num 26:2
1:4 Exod 18:21; Num 34:18

1. THE ISRAELITES CAMP IN THE WILDERNESS OF SINAI (1:1–10:10)

The First Registration and Organization of the Camp (1:1–3:51)

The First Census of Israel's Troops

1 A year after Israel's departure from
Egypt, the LORD spoke to Moses in the
Tabernacle in the wilderness of Sinai. On
the first day of the second month of that
year he said, 2"From the whole community
of Israel, record the names of all the warriors by their clans and families. List all the
men 3twenty years old or older who are able
to go to war. You and Aaron must register
the troops, 4and you will be assisted by one
family leader from each tribe.

1:1–10:10 The Israelites prepared to leave for the Promised Land by registering all the troops eligible to participate in the conquest. The nation was transitioning from slavery to nationhood.

1:1-16 One family leader from each tribe (except Levi) was appointed to count Israel's men of fighting age.

1:1 In the *year after Israel's departure from Egypt, the LORD* frequently communicated his will to the people through *Moses* and gave them every opportunity to conform to his divine plan. • God's self-disclosure often took place at the *Tabernacle* (literally *the Tent of Meeting*; see notes on Exod 27:21; 40:2). • *The wilderness of Sinai* was a great, terrifying, and inhospitable desert (Deut 1:19). This relatively unpopulated region was the anvil on which God forged Israel as the environmental challenges of Sinai tested Israel's dependence upon the Lord throughout the book of Numbers. Sinai reminded later biblical authors of the law and of Israel's rebellious spirit (Ps 106:19; Heb 12:25-26). • *the first day of the second month:* This day in the ancient Hebrew lunar calendar occurred in April or May.

1:2-16 *men twenty years old or older who are able to go to war:* In this effort

5"These are the tribes and the names of
the leaders who will assist you:

Tribe	*Leader*
Reuben	Elizur son of Shedeur
6 Simeon	Shelumiel son of Zurishaddai
7 Judah	Nahshon son of Amminadab
8 Issachar	Nethanel son of Zuar
9 Zebulun	Eliab son of Helon
10 Ephraim son of Joseph	Elishama son of Ammihud
Manasseh son of Joseph	Gamaliel son of Pedahzur
11 Benjamin	Abidan son of Gideoni
12 Dan	Ahiezer son of Ammishaddai
13 Asher	Pagiel son of Ocran
14 Gad	Eliasaph son of Deuel
15 Naphtali	Ahira son of Enan

16These are the chosen leaders of the community, the leaders of their ancestral tribes,
the heads of the clans of Israel."
17So Moses and Aaron called together
these chosen leaders, 18and they assembled the whole community of Israel on that
very day. All the people were registered
according to their ancestry by their clans
and families. The men of Israel who were
twenty years old or older were listed one
by one, 19just as the LORD had commanded
Moses. So Moses recorded their names in
the wilderness of Sinai.
20-21This is the number of men twenty
years old or older who were able to go to war,
as their names were listed in the records of
their clans and families:

Tribe	*Number*
Reuben (Jacob's oldest son)	46,500
22-23 Simeon	59,300
24-25 Gad	45,650
26-27 Judah	74,600
28-29 Issachar	54,400
30-31 Zebulun	57,400
32-33 Ephraim son of Joseph	40,500
34-35 Manasseh son of Joseph	32,200
36-37 Benjamin	35,400
38-39 Dan	62,700
40-41 Asher	41,500
42-43 Naphtali	53,400

44These were the men registered by Moses
and Aaron and the twelve leaders of Israel, all listed according to their ancestral
descent. 45They were registered by families—all the men of Israel who were twenty
years old or older and able to go to war.
46The total number was 603,550.

Special Status of the Levites

47But this total did not include the Levites.
48For the LORD had said to Moses, 49"Do not
include the tribe of Levi in the registration;
do not count them with the rest of the Israelites. 50Put the Levites in charge of the
Tabernacle of the Covenant, along with all
its furnishings and equipment. They must
carry the Tabernacle and all its furnishings
as you travel, and they must [a]take care of it
and camp around it. 51Whenever it is time
for the Tabernacle to move, the Levites will
take it down. And when it is time to stop, they
will set it up again. But any unauthorized
person who goes too near the Tabernacle
must be put to death. 52Each tribe of Israel
will camp in a designated area with its own
family banner. 53But the Levites will camp
around the Tabernacle of the Covenant to
protect the community of Israel from the
LORD's anger. The Levites are responsible to
stand guard around the Tabernacle."
54So the Israelites did everything just as
the LORD had commanded Moses.

1:5 Gen 29:32; Rev 7:5
1:7 Ruth 4:20; 1 Chr 2:10
1:14 Num 2:14
1:16 Num 7:2; 16:2; 26:9
1:18 Num 1:2-3; Ezra 2:59
1:20 Num 26:5-11
1:22 Num 26:12-14
1:24 Num 26:15-18
1:26 Num 26:19-22
1:28 Num 26:23-25
1:30 Num 26:26-27
1:32 Num 26:35-37
1:34 Num 26:28-34
1:36 Num 26:38-41
1:38 Num 26:42-43
1:40 Num 26:44-47
1:42 Num 26:48-50
1:44 Num 26:64
1:46 Exod 38:26; Num 2:32; 26:51
1:47 Num 2:33; 26:57
1:50 Num 3:25-37; [a]*sharath* (8334) ‣ Deut 10:8
1:51 Num 4:1-33
1:52 Num 2:2
1:53 Num 1:50

to register Israel's men of military age, more information was gathered than in the previous registration (cp. Exod 38:26). • *the tribes and the names of the leaders:* Hebrew culture was tribal, built around clans and families. The tribal leaders were readily identified and appear again as a group in ch 7. • Moses and Aaron did not include Levi's tribe in this registration, since it had a special status in Israelite society (cp. 1:47-53; 26:51-62; Deut 18:5; 33:8-11).

1:16 These tribal *leaders* had apparently shown themselves responsible and trustworthy by fulfilling other important duties.

1:17-46 The tabulation yields the same number of qualified men (*603,550*) as mentioned in Exod 38:26. Exodus 12:37 and Num 11:21 give an approximate number of 600,000. These numbers have been interpreted in different ways. They might reflect the literal size of this army (cp. Exod 1:9-10); alternatively, the figures might be symbolic, projected backward from a later period, or simply misunderstood in translation. See also note on Exod 12:37.

1:18 *on that very day:* Literally *on the first day of the second month;* see 1:1.

1:20-43 In this second list of the tribes, *Gad* is placed alongside *Reuben* and *Simeon,* the tribes with whom Gad would camp while Israel was on the march.

1:20-21 *This is the number of men . . . clans and families:* In the Hebrew text, this sentence is repeated in 1:22, 24, 26, 28, 30, 32, 34, 36, 38, 40, 42. • *Jacob's* (literally *Israel's*): The names "Jacob" and "Israel" are often interchanged throughout the Old Testament, referring sometimes to the individual patriarch and sometimes to the nation.

1:47-54 The tribe of Levi did not serve in Israel's army with the other tribes. This section of Numbers describes the organization of *Levites* for service in the Tabernacle, which was their primary responsibility.

1:50-53 *The Levites* inherited the task of erecting, dismantling, transporting, and guarding *the Tabernacle.* By keeping unauthorized persons from getting too close or desecrating it, they protected the Hebrews *from the LORD's anger.*

1:50 *Tabernacle of the Covenant:* Or *Tabernacle of the Testimony;* also in 1:53. This portable sanctuary symbolized the presence of the Lord and represented Israel's covenant relationship with him.

2:2 Num 1:52
2:3 Num 10:14
2:5 Num 1:8
2:9 Num 10:14
2:10 Num 1:5
2:12 Num 1:6
2:14 Num 1:14
2:17 Num 1:53
2:20 Num 1:10
2:24 Num 10:22
2:25 Num 1:12
2:27 Num 1:13
2:31 Num 10:25
2:32 Exod 38:26; Num 1:45-46
2:33 Num 1:47

Organization for Israel in Camp and on the March

2 Then the LORD gave these instructions to Moses and Aaron: 2“When the Israelites set up camp, each tribe will be assigned its own area. The tribal divisions will camp beneath their family banners on all four sides of the Tabernacle, but at some distance from it.

3-4“The divisions of Judah, Issachar, and Zebulun are to camp toward the sunrise on the east side of the Tabernacle, beneath their family banners. These are the names of the tribes, their leaders, and the numbers of their registered troops:

	Tribe	*Leader*	*Number*
	Judah	Nahshon son of Amminadab	74,600
5-6	Issachar	Nethanel son of Zuar	54,400
7-8	Zebulun	Eliab son of Helon	57,400

9So the total of all the troops on Judah’s side of the camp is 186,400. These three tribes are to lead the way whenever the Israelites travel to a new campsite.

10-11“The divisions of Reuben, Simeon, and Gad are to camp on the south side of the Tabernacle, beneath their family banners. These are the names of the tribes, their leaders, and the numbers of their registered troops:

	Tribe	*Leader*	*Number*
	Reuben	Elizur son of Shedeur	46,500
12-13	Simeon	Shelumiel son of Zurishaddai	59,300
14-15	Gad	Eliasaph son of Deuel	45,650

16So the total of all the troops on Reuben’s side of the camp is 151,450. These three tribes will be second in line whenever the Israelites travel.

17“Then the Tabernacle, carried by the Levites, will set out from the middle of the camp. All the tribes are to travel in the same order that they camp, each in position under the appropriate family banner.

18-19“The divisions of Ephraim, Manasseh, and Benjamin are to camp on the west side of the Tabernacle, beneath their family banners. These are the names of the tribes, their leaders, and the numbers of their registered troops:

	Tribe	*Leader*	*Number*
	Ephraim	Elishama son of Ammihud	40,500
20-21	Manasseh	Gamaliel son of Pedahzur	32,200
22-23	Benjamin	Abidan son of Gideoni	35,400

24So the total of all the troops on Ephraim’s side of the camp is 108,100. These three tribes will be third in line whenever the Israelites travel.

25-26“The divisions of Dan, Asher, and Naphtali are to camp on the north side of the Tabernacle, beneath their family banners. These are the names of the tribes, their leaders, and the numbers of their registered troops:

	Tribe	*Leader*	*Number*
	Dan	Ahiezer son of Ammishaddai	62,700
27-28	Asher	Pagiel son of Ocran	41,500
29-30	Naphtali	Ahira son of Enan	53,400

31So the total of all the troops on Dan’s side of the camp is 157,600. These three tribes will be last, marching under their banners whenever the Israelites travel.”

32In summary, the troops of Israel listed by their families totaled 603,550. 33But as the LORD had commanded, the Levites were

2:1-34 Israel’s camps were to be organized by tribal groupings. This arrangement may have reflected concerns for social status, access to water, and security for the Tabernacle, which represented the Lord’s presence. The Egyptian army from approximately this same era camped in a similar defensive formation to protect the sacred objects that accompanied their field campaigns.

2:2 Each area of the Hebrew *camp* was identified by *family banners,* which were probably flags or streamers (1:52). The use of such tribal symbols or battle flags finds an analogy in modern bedouin life, where the divisions of tribe, clan, and family have long held great importance. • The tribes camped around the sanctuary at a safe distance (cp. Josh 3:4) that respected the gap between God’s holiness and the non-Levitical tribes.

2:2 *Tabernacle:* Literally *the Tent of Meeting;* also in 2:17. See notes on Exod 27:21; 40:2.

2:3-9 The tribes of ***Judah, Issachar, and Zebulun*** camped in the most prestigious place ***on the east side of the Tabernacle*** and led the way when Israel was on the move. This largest of the tribal groups (***186,400***) could provide adequate protection for the sacred tent and its attendants.

2:10-16 The tribes of ***Reuben, Simeon, and Gad*** camped ***on the south.*** With their ***151,450*** warriors, they took second place in the line of march.

2:14-15 *son of Deuel:* As in many Hebrew manuscripts, Samaritan Pentateuch, and Latin Vulgate (see also 1:14); most Hebrew manuscripts read *son of Reuel.*

2:18-24 The tribes of ***Ephraim, Manasseh, and Benjamin*** marched behind the Tabernacle and the Levites.

2:25-31 The tribes of ***Dan, Asher, and Naphtali*** brought up the rear.

not included in this registration. 34 So the people of Israel did everything as the LORD had commanded Moses. Each clan and family set up camp and marched under their banners exactly as the LORD had instructed them.

Family of Aaron

3 This is the family line of Aaron and Moses as it was recorded when the LORD spoke to Moses on Mount Sinai: 2 The names of Aaron's sons were Nadab (the oldest), Abihu, Eleazar, and Ithamar. 3 These sons of Aaron were anointed and ordained to minister as priests. 4 But Nadab and Abihu died in the LORD's presence in the wilderness of Sinai when they burned before the LORD the wrong kind of fire, different than he had commanded. Since they had no sons, this left only Eleazar and Ithamar to serve as priests with their father, Aaron.

Levites Appointed for Service

5 Then the LORD said to Moses, 6 "Call forward the tribe of Levi, and present them to Aaron the [b]priest to serve as his assistants. 7 They will serve Aaron and the whole community, performing their sacred duties in and around the Tabernacle. 8 They will also maintain all the furnishings of the sacred tent, serving in the Tabernacle on behalf of all the Israelites. 9 Assign the Levites to Aaron and his sons. They have been given from among all the people of Israel to serve as their assistants. 10 Appoint Aaron and his sons to carry out the duties of the priesthood. But any unauthorized person who goes too near the sanctuary must be put to death."

11 And the LORD said to Moses, 12 "Look, I have chosen the Levites from among the Israelites to serve as substitutes for all the firstborn sons of the people of Israel. The Levites belong to me, 13 for all the firstborn males are mine. On the day I struck down all the firstborn sons of the Egyptians, I set apart for myself all the firstborn in Israel, both of people and of animals. They are mine; I am the LORD."

Registration of the Levites

14 The LORD spoke again to Moses in the wilderness of Sinai. He said, 15 "Record the names of the members of the tribe of Levi by their families and clans. List every male who is one month old or older." 16 So Moses listed them, just as the LORD had commanded.

17 Levi had three sons, whose names were
Gershon, Kohath, and Merari.
18 The clans descended from Gershon were
named after two of his descendants,
Libni and Shimei.
19 The clans descended from Kohath were
named after four of his descendants,
Amram, Izhar, Hebron, and Uzziel.
20 The clans descended from Merari were
named after two of his descendants,
Mahli and Mushi.

These were the Levite clans, listed according to their family groups.

21 The descendants of Gershon were composed of the clans descended from Libni and Shimei. 22 There were 7,500 males one month old or older among these Gershonite clans. 23 They were assigned the area to the west of the Tabernacle for their camp.

3:2 Num 26:60
3:3 Exod 28:41
3:4 Lev 10:1-2; Num 26:61
3:6 Num 8:6-22; 18:2-6; [b]*kohen* (3548) ‣ Num 5:16
3:7 Num 3:41; 8:16-18
3:10 Num 1:51
3:12 Num 3:41
3:13 Exod 13:2, 12, 15; Num 8:17
3:15 Num 1:47

2:34 The Hebrews initially obeyed God by camping and marching in the manner Moses had specified, but this obedient spirit did not last for long.

3:1–4:49 The organization and duties of Israel's priests and Levites included the transportation, assembly, safety, and upkeep of the Tabernacle. The physical arrangement of Israel's tribes reflected concern for these activities.

3:1-4 ***The family line of Aaron*** provided the professional priests who led Israel's worship. Aaron's four sons were the foundation of Israel's priesthood; they stood in God's presence and served him on behalf of the people. They were appointed to lead the people and serve the Lord as ministers in the Tabernacle and as guardians of God's covenant with his people.

3:4 The deaths of ***Nadab and Abihu*** (see Lev 10:1-2) highlighted the importance of guarding the holiness of the sanctuary and of strict obedience to God's instructions (26:61; Lev 16:1; 1 Chr 24:2; cp. Acts 5:1-11; 1 Cor 10:6-11; 11:29-30). • ***Eleazar and Ithamar:*** See "Eleazar" at 20:22-29, p. 284.

3:5-13 The Levites were appointed as ***assistants*** to the priests, who were represented by ***Aaron.*** Their ministry included ***sacred duties*** (3:7) in maintaining ***the Tabernacle*** and its ***furnishings*** (3:8; described in greater detail in 4:1-33).

3:7 ***around the Tabernacle:*** Literally *around the Tent of Meeting, doing service at the Tabernacle.*

3:8 ***sacred tent:*** Literally *the Tent of Meeting;* also in 3:25. See note on Exod 27:21.

3:10 The ***sanctuary*** was sacred (1:51; 3:38; 18:7); it was not to be approached by the unqualified (cp. 3:4).

3:11-13 ***The firstborn sons . . . of Israel*** belonged to God, having been spared when the Egyptian firstborn sons died (3:13; see Exod 11–12). ***The Levites*** were ***chosen . . . to serve as substitutes*** in their place.

3:14-39 This first phase of a two-stage registration ***of the tribe of Levi*** (see 4:34-49 for stage two) summarized each family group's special responsibilities (described in greater detail in 4:1-33). This numbering was not linked with military duties, so it enrolled male Levites from the age of one month (3:40-41). • Three family groups are descended from ***Gershon, Kohath, and Merari,*** the three sons of Levi. These clans (often called the Gershonites, Kohathites, and Merarites) later inherited the "cities of refuge" (Josh 21) and filled various important posts in the Jerusalem Temple (2 Chr 29:3-17).

3:25 Num 4:24-26
3:27 Exod 6:18; 1 Chr 26:23
3:33 Exod 6:19
3:38 Num 1:51; 3:10
3:39 Num 26:62
3:41 Num 3:12, 45
3:43 Num 3:39
3:45 Lev 11:44
3:46 Exod 13:13, 15; Num 18:14-16
3:47 Exod 30:13; Lev 27:1-8
3:50 Num 3:46-48

24The leader of the Gershonite clans was Eliasaph son of Lael. 25These two clans were responsible to care for the Tabernacle, including the sacred tent with its layers of coverings, the curtain at its entrance, 26the curtains of the courtyard that surrounded the Tabernacle and altar, the curtain at the courtyard entrance, the ropes, and all the equipment related to their use.

27The descendants of Kohath were composed of the clans descended from Amram, Izhar, Hebron, and Uzziel. 28There were 8,600 males one month old or older among these Kohathite clans. They were responsible for the care of the sanctuary, 29and they were assigned the area south of the Tabernacle for their camp. 30The leader of the Kohathite clans was Elizaphan son of Uzziel. 31These four clans were responsible for the care of the Ark, the table, the lampstand, the altars, the various articles used in the sanctuary, the inner curtain, and all the equipment related to their use. 32Eleazar, son of Aaron the priest, was the chief administrator over all the Levites, with special responsibility for the oversight of the sanctuary.

33The descendants of Merari were composed of the clans descended from Mahli and Mushi. 34There were 6,200 males one month old or older among these Merarite clans. 35They were assigned the area north of the Tabernacle for their camp. The leader of the Merarite clans was Zuriel son of Abihail. 36These two clans were responsible for the care of the frames supporting the Tabernacle, the crossbars, the pillars, the bases, and all the equipment related to their use. 37They were also responsible for the posts of the courtyard and all their bases, pegs, and ropes.

38The area in front of the Tabernacle, in the east toward the sunrise, was reserved for the tents of Moses and of Aaron and his sons, who had the final responsibility for the sanctuary on behalf of the people of Israel. Anyone other than a priest or Levite who went too near the sanctuary was to be put to death.

39When Moses and Aaron counted the Levite clans at the LORD's command, the total number was 22,000 males one month old or older.

Redeeming the Firstborn Sons

40Then the LORD said to Moses, "Now count all the firstborn sons in Israel who are one month old or older, and make a list of their names. 41The Levites must be reserved for me as substitutes for the firstborn sons of Israel; I am the LORD. And the Levites' livestock must be reserved for me as substitutes for the firstborn livestock of the whole nation of Israel."

42So Moses counted the firstborn sons of the people of Israel, just as the LORD had commanded. 43The number of firstborn sons who were one month old or older was 22,273.

44Then the LORD said to Moses, 45"Take the Levites as substitutes for the firstborn sons of the people of Israel. And take the livestock of the Levites as substitutes for the firstborn livestock of the people of Israel. The Levites belong to me; I am the LORD. 46There are 273 more firstborn sons of Israel than there are Levites. To redeem these extra firstborn sons, 47collect five pieces of silver for each of them (each piece weighing the same as the sanctuary shekel, which equals twenty gerahs). 48Give the silver to Aaron and his sons as the redemption price for the extra firstborn sons."

49So Moses collected the silver for redeeming the firstborn sons of Israel who exceeded the number of Levites. 50He collected 1,365 pieces of silver on behalf of

3:27-32 Aaron and Moses, sons of Amram, were ***descendants of Kohath*** (see Exod 6:18, 20, 26). Because they were caretakers of the *sanctuary* (the Most Holy Place) and its very sacred furnishings (described in chs 3–4), the Kohathites were the most highly regarded of the three clans.

3:28 *8,600:* Some Greek manuscripts read *8,300;* see total in 3:39. The "six" (Hebrew *shsh*) in 8,600 could result from misreading a "three" (Hebrew *shlsh*).

3:32 *Eleazar,* Aaron's third son, presided over the Levites as ***administrator*** (perhaps as an executive secretary) while his father dealt with other matters; he had ***special . . . oversight*** of the Tabernacle (4:16-20). He played an important role in Israel's wilderness period and later succeeded his father as high priest (see 16:37-39; 19:3-6; 20:25-28; 26:1-3).

3:38 The preeminent campsite east of the Tabernacle ***was reserved for . . . Moses,*** Aaron, and his priestly sons. • ***toward the sunrise:*** Literally *toward the sunrise, in front of the Tent of Meeting.*

3:39 *22,000:* The numbers listed for each clan (3:22, 28, 34) add up to 22,300. See note on 3:28.

3:40-51 There were 273 more ***firstborn sons in Israel*** (in the non-Levite tribes) than there were Levite males (cp. 3:39). Because the Levites served ***as substitutes*** for the firstborn of Israel (3:41; see note on 3:11-13), a ***redemption price*** (3:48) of ***five pieces of silver*** (3:47) had to be paid for each of the ***extra firstborn sons*** (3:46; cp. Lev 27:6). It is not clear who covered this cost. This provision for a special class of substitutes points to Christ's role as a substitute; through his death, Christ paid the ***redemption price*** for all humanity (see Mark 10:45; Gal 3:13; Eph 1:7; Heb 9:15).

3:47 ***five pieces of silver:*** Hebrew *5 shekels* [2 ounces or 57 grams].

3:50 ***1,365 pieces of silver:*** Hebrew *1,365 shekels* [34 pounds or 15.5 kilograms].

these firstborn sons of Israel (each piece weighing the same as the sanctuary shekel). [51]And Moses gave the silver for the redemption to Aaron and his sons, just as the LORD had commanded.

Duties of the Levites (4:1-49)

Duties of the Kohathite Clan

4 Then the LORD said to Moses and Aaron, [2]"Record the names of the members of the clans and families of the Kohathite division of the tribe of Levi. [3]List all the men between the ages of thirty and fifty who are eligible to serve in the Tabernacle.

[4]"The duties of the Kohathites at the Tabernacle will relate to the most sacred objects. [5]When the camp moves, Aaron and his sons must enter the Tabernacle first to take down the inner curtain and cover the Ark of the Covenant with it. [6]Then they must cover the inner curtain with fine goatskin leather and spread over that a single piece of blue cloth. Finally, they must put the carrying poles of the Ark in place.

[7]"Next they must spread a blue cloth over the table where the Bread of the Presence is displayed, and on the cloth they will place the bowls, pans, jars, pitchers, and the special bread. [8]They must spread a scarlet cloth over all of this, and finally a covering of fine goatskin leather on top of the scarlet cloth. Then they must insert the carrying poles into the table.

[9]"Next they must cover the lampstand with a blue cloth, along with its lamps, lamp snuffers, trays, and special jars of olive oil. [10]Then they must cover the lampstand and its accessories with fine goatskin leather and place the bundle on a carrying frame.

[11]"Next they must spread a blue cloth over the gold incense altar and cover this cloth with fine goatskin leather. Then they must attach the carrying poles to the altar. [12]They must take all the remaining furnishings of the sanctuary and wrap them in a blue cloth, cover them with fine goatskin leather, and place them on the carrying frame.

[13]"They must remove the ashes from the altar for sacrifices and cover the altar with a purple cloth. [14]All the altar utensils—the firepans, meat forks, shovels, basins, and all the containers—must be placed on the cloth, and a covering of fine goatskin leather must be spread over them. Finally, they must put the carrying poles in place. [15]The camp will be ready to move when Aaron and his sons have finished covering the sanctuary and all the sacred articles. The Kohathites will come and carry these things to the next destination. But they must not touch the sacred objects, or they will die. So these are the things from the Tabernacle that the Kohathites must carry.

[16]"Eleazar son of Aaron the priest will be responsible for the oil of the lampstand, the fragrant incense, the daily grain offering, and the anointing oil. In fact, Eleazar will be responsible for the entire Tabernacle and everything in it, including the sanctuary and its furnishings."

4:3 Num 4:23; 8:24-25
4:6 Num 4:25
4:7 Exod 37:10-16; Lev 24:5-8
4:9 Exod 25:37-38
4:15 Num 4:19-20
4:16 Exod 25:1-7; 30:22-34

4:1-49 This section expands the discussion begun in 3:21-37 on the duties of the three clans of Levites. The Levites—on the march and encamped—carried and cared for the Tabernacle and were always surrounded by the other tribes so that they and their precious cargo would be safe (2:17). The sacred things associated with God were placed in the middle of the tribes, and the role of the priests and their Levitical assistants was to keep them holy by keeping them separate. • God, in his holiness, is worthy of attention to the details of his will. His Tabernacle and its furnishings were sacred, and the tribe of Levi was responsible to maintain the distinction between holy and common, between clean and unclean. This explains why so much information is provided about the duties of the three clans of Levites.

4:1 *Moses and Aaron* were mediators of God's will regarding the care and transport of the Tabernacle, the primary charge of the three Levitical families.

4:3 Of the 22,000 Levites (3:39), only *men between the ages of thirty and fifty,* those in the prime of their life, were allowed to serve in the sanctuary. The summary of this registration (another "numbering") found in 4:34-49 gives the total number of qualified males as 8,580. • *the Tabernacle:* Literally *the Tent of Meeting;* also in 4:4, 15, 23, 25, 28, 30, 31, 33, 35, 37, 39, 41, 43, 47. See note on Exod 27:21.

4:4-20 *The duties of the Kohathites* (see 3:27-32) are listed first because they performed a special service related to *the most sacred objects* (perhaps because Aaron and the priests came from this clan; 1 Chr 6:2-3). The tasks of carrying, setting up, and disassembling these sacred coverings and furnishings were extremely important. All the things entrusted to Kohath's descendants—*the Ark of the Covenant,* the table of *the Bread of the Presence, the lampstand* (Hebrew *menorah*), *the gold incense altar,* and *the altar for sacrifices*—held tremendous value. These objects are first described in Exod 25–30, but Numbers shows how they were integrated into Hebrew life. The Kohathites carried these items on poles or in frames, and they were not to *touch* them or *enter the sanctuary to look at* them on penalty of death.

4:5 *Ark of the Covenant:* Or *Ark of the Testimony.*

4:15 Aaron and his surviving sons Eleazar and Ithamar had to cover *the sanctuary and all the sacred articles* completely before the camp was *ready to move,* with the groups of non-Levitical tribes marching before and behind the Levites who carried the Tabernacle. The royalty of these objects is seen in the symbolic colors of the coverings, and their sacredness underlies the stern warning that even though the Kohathites were the designated handlers, *they must not touch the sacred objects, or they* would *die.* Such respect marked the holiness of Israel's Lord. The dangers of disregarding these instructions are apparent in 1 Sam 6:19-20 and 2 Sam 6:6-7.

4:16-20 *Eleazar:* See note on 3:32.

4:23 Num 4:3
4:25 Num 3:25-26
4:30 Num 4:3
4:46 Num 1:19
4:49 Num 1:47-49

17Then the LORD said to Moses and Aaron, 18"Do not let the Kohathite clans be destroyed from among the Levites! 19This is what you must do so they will live and not die when they approach the most sacred objects. Aaron and his sons must always go in with them and assign a specific duty or load to each person. 20The Kohathites must never enter the sanctuary to look at the sacred objects for even a moment, or they will die."

Duties of the Gershonite Clan

21And the LORD said to Moses, 22"Record the names of the members of the clans and families of the Gershonite division of the tribe of Levi. 23List all the men between the ages of thirty and fifty who are eligible to serve in the Tabernacle.

24"These Gershonite clans will be responsible for general service and carrying loads. 25They must carry the curtains of the Tabernacle, the Tabernacle itself with its coverings, the outer covering of fine goatskin leather, and the curtain for the Tabernacle entrance. 26They are also to carry the curtains for the courtyard walls that surround the Tabernacle and altar, the curtain across the courtyard entrance, the ropes, and all the equipment related to their use. The Gershonites are responsible for all these items. 27Aaron and his sons will direct the Gershonites regarding all their duties, whether it involves moving the equipment or doing other work. They must assign the Gershonites responsibility for the loads they are to carry. 28So these are the duties assigned to the Gershonite clans at the Tabernacle. They will be directly responsible to Ithamar son of Aaron the priest.

Duties of the Merarite Clan

29"Now record the names of the members of the clans and families of the Merarite division of the tribe of Levi. 30List all the men between the ages of thirty and fifty who are eligible to serve in the Tabernacle.

31"Their only duty at the Tabernacle will be to carry loads. They will carry the frames of the Tabernacle, the crossbars, the posts, and the bases; 32also the posts for the courtyard walls with their bases, pegs, and ropes; and all the accessories and everything else related to their use. Assign the various loads to each man by name. 33So these are the duties of the Merarite clans at the Tabernacle. They are directly responsible to Ithamar son of Aaron the priest."

Summary of the Registration

34So Moses, Aaron, and the other leaders of the community listed the members of the Kohathite division by their clans and families. 35The list included all the men between thirty and fifty years of age who were eligible for service in the Tabernacle, 36and the total number came to 2,750. 37So this was the total of all those from the Kohathite clans who were eligible to serve at the Tabernacle. Moses and Aaron listed them, just as the LORD had commanded through Moses.

38The Gershonite division was also listed by its clans and families. 39The list included all the men between thirty and fifty years of age who were eligible for service in the Tabernacle, 40and the total number came to 2,630. 41So this was the total of all those from the Gershonite clans who were eligible to serve at the Tabernacle. Moses and Aaron listed them, just as the LORD had commanded.

42The Merarite division was also listed by its clans and families. 43The list included all the men between thirty and fifty years of age who were eligible for service in the Tabernacle, 44and the total number came to 3,200. 45So this was the total of all those from the Merarite clans who were eligible for service. Moses and Aaron listed them, just as the LORD had commanded through Moses.

46So Moses, Aaron, and the leaders of Israel listed all the Levites by their clans and families. 47All the men between thirty and fifty years of age who were eligible for service in the Tabernacle and for its transportation 48numbered 8,580. 49When their names were recorded, as the LORD had commanded through Moses, each man was assigned his task and told what to carry.

And so the registration was completed, just as the LORD had commanded Moses.

4:21-28 The men of the ***Gershonite*** clan (see 3:21-26) were ***responsible for general service and carrying loads*** (4:24). This involved handling the curtains and coverings, ropes, and related equipment that was less central to Israel's worship. Their duties focused on the Tabernacle in general instead of on the sacred objects of the inner sanctuary that were the responsibility of Kohath's clan.

4:29-33 Even this assignment to the ***Merarite*** clan, which focused on items of lesser priority than those handled by the Kohathites and Gershonites, had to be done in a specific way, and ***the various loads*** were assigned ***to each man by name*** (4:32; cp. 1 Cor 14:40). While the Gershonites and Merarites lacked the status of Kohath's family, each group contributed to the process of moving and erecting the Tabernacle.

4:34-49 The process of numbering and recording the Levites' names and making sure that each man understood his assignment was an important step in organizing Israel to travel and camp in the correct manner and in safeguarding the Tabernacle.

Laws Regarding Ritual and Moral Purity (5:1–6:27)

Purity in Israel's Camp

5 The LORD gave these instructions to Moses: 2"Command the people of Israel to remove from the camp anyone who has a skin disease or a discharge, or who has become ceremonially unclean by touching a dead person. 3This command applies to men and women alike. Remove them so they will not defile the camp in which I live among them." 4So the Israelites did as the LORD had commanded Moses and removed such people from the camp.

5Then the LORD said to Moses, 6"Give the following instructions to the people of Israel: If any of the people—men or women—betray the LORD by doing wrong to another person, they are guilty. 7They must confess their sin and make full restitution for what they have done, adding an additional 20 percent and returning it to the person who was wronged. 8But if the person who was wronged is dead, and there are no near relatives to whom restitution can be made, the payment belongs to the LORD and must be given to the priest. Those who are guilty must also bring a ram as a sacrifice, and they will be purified and made right with the LORD. 9All the sacred offerings that the Israelites bring to a priest will belong to him. 10Each priest may keep all the sacred donations that he receives."

A Test for Adultery

11And the LORD said to Moses, 12"Give the following instructions to the people of Israel.

"Suppose a man's wife goes astray, and she is unfaithful to her husband 13and has sex with another man, but neither her husband nor anyone else knows about it. She has defiled herself, even though there was no witness and she was not caught in the act. 14If her husband becomes jealous and is suspicious of his wife and needs to know whether or not she has defiled herself, 15the husband must bring his wife to the priest. He must also bring an offering of two quarts of barley flour to be presented on her behalf. Do not mix it with olive oil or frankincense, for it is a jealousy offering—an offering to prove whether or not she is guilty.

16"The ᶜpriest will then present her to stand trial before the LORD. 17He must take some holy water in a clay jar and pour into

5:2 Lev 13:3, 46; 15:2
5:3 Lev 26:12; 2 Cor 6:16
5:7 Lev 5:5, 16; 6:4-5
5:9 Lev 6:17
5:12 Num 5:19-21, 29
5:15 Ezek 29:16
5:16 ᶜ*kohen* (3548) ‣Deut 17:9

5:1–10:10 These legal matters were to ensure the purity of the Israelites, their priesthood, and the Tabernacle. Such regulations drew constant attention to ancient Israel's identity as a theocracy of which Moses was the primary spokesman.

5:1-31 These laws concern purity, restitution, and marital faithfulness.

5:1-4 Modern Westerners find the need for ceremonial or ritual purity difficult to understand. Westerners view skin diseases, bodily discharge, and contact with corpses as concerns of health and hygiene, but the primary issue in the OT is guarding God's holiness against ceremonial uncleanness (see Lev 11–15). The community had to safeguard the holiness of the camp so that unclean things or people did not ceremonially defile things associated with the Lord (5:2-3). The community had to choose between having God in the camp or letting a defiled person remain in the camp, because both could not remain (5:3). • The importance of purity extends from Leviticus and Numbers to the book of Revelation: All that is ceremonially unclean will be forbidden to enter the New Jerusalem where God resides (see note on Rev 21:27). In the NT, however, impurity is limited to what is morally impure (Acts 10:28; Eph 5:5; 1 Thes 2:3; 4:7).

5:2 *skin disease:* Traditionally rendered *leprosy.* The Hebrew word used here describes various skin diseases that were regarded as contagious (cp. Lev 13–14). • ***Discharge*** refers to fluids associated with sexual organs (Lev 15; cp. Luke 8:43-48). • ***touching a dead person:*** See 6:6-11; 19:11.

5:5-10 Guidelines regarding confession and ***restitution*** for wrongdoing emphasize the strong Hebrew concern for morality (Lev 6:1-7).

5:6 Doing something wrong to another human being is the same as betraying—literally *breaking faith with*—the Lord (cp. 5:8). A right relationship with God produces right relationships with people; a wrong relationship with others shows a wrong relationship with the Lord.

5:7 This ***restitution*** and the guilt offering (see Lev 6–7) associated with the sin was intended to inculcate a heightened sense of individual responsibility to God's holiness.

5:8 Because sin is ultimately against God (5:6; Ps 51:4), the perpetrator had a moral obligation to make restitution ***to the LORD,*** who authorized the human victims of the sin to receive that payment; if none were living, the Lord received payment through the priest. Perpetrators also had to offer a valuable sacrifice that restored their ritual purity (5:1-4) and their relationship with God. • ***bring a ram as a sacrifice, and they will be purified and made right with the LORD:*** Or *bring a ram for atonement, which will make atonement for them.* See note on Lev 1:4.

5:9-10 Priests supported their families partly by receiving a share of the sacrifices. In some instances, surplus sacrifices could be sold to provide funds for the priesthood, for maintaining the sanctuary, and for other religious needs (cp. 1 Cor 8:4-13).

5:11-31 This detailed test for adultery, a "trial by ordeal," is the only such case found in the OT, though trial by ordeal was a common procedure in the ancient Near East. God had a special interest in safeguarding marriage as the foundation of Hebrew society, and the purpose of this ordeal was to promote marital faithfulness. We cannot determine how commonly such ordeals actually occurred. This procedure appealed to God's own intervention to ensure justice in cases lacking evidence (cp. 1 Cor 5:5).

5:14-15 ***The husband*** presented his case before ***the priest,*** and the "ritual law for dealing with suspicion" (5:29) took the husband's jealousy and suspicion to a higher court.

5:15 ***two quarts:*** Hebrew ***¹⁄₁₀ of an ephah*** [2.2 liters].

5:17 The ***holy water*** and the ***dust*** were sacred because of their association with the sanctuary.

5:21 Josh 6:26; 1 Sam 14:24; Neh 10:29
5:22 [d]*'amen* (0543) ‣Deut 27:15
5:26 Lev 2:2
5:27 Jer 29:18; 42:18
5:29 Num 5:12
6:2 Judg 13:4-5; 16:17; Amos 2:11-12
6:3 Luke 1:15
6:5 1 Sam 1:11

it dust he has taken from the Tabernacle floor. 18When the priest has presented the woman before the LORD, he must unbind her hair and place in her hands the offering of proof—the jealousy offering to determine whether her husband's suspicions are justified. The priest will stand before her, holding the jar of bitter water that brings a curse to those who are guilty. 19The priest will then put the woman under oath and say to her, 'If no other man has had sex with you, and you have not gone astray and defiled yourself while under your husband's authority, may you be immune from the effects of this bitter water that brings on the curse. 20But if you have gone astray by being unfaithful to your husband, and have defiled yourself by having sex with another man—'

21"At this point the priest must put the woman under oath by saying, 'May the people know that the LORD's curse is upon you when he makes you infertile, causing your womb to shrivel and your abdomen to swell. 22Now may this water that brings the curse enter your body and cause your abdomen to swell and your womb to shrivel.' And the woman will be required to say, [d]'Yes, let it be so.' 23And the priest will write these curses on a piece of leather and wash them off into the bitter water. 24He will make the woman drink the bitter water that brings on the curse. When the water enters her body, it will cause bitter suffering if she is guilty.

25"The priest will take the jealousy offering from the woman's hand, lift it up before the LORD, and carry it to the altar. 26He will take a handful of the flour as a token portion and burn it on the altar, and he will require the woman to drink the water. 27If she has defiled herself by being unfaithful to her husband, the water that brings on the curse will cause bitter suffering. Her abdomen will swell and her womb will shrink, and her name will become a curse among her people. 28But if she has not defiled herself and is pure, then she will be unharmed and will still be able to have children.

29"This is the ritual law for dealing with suspicion. If a woman goes astray and defiles herself while under her husband's authority, 30or if a man becomes jealous and is suspicious that his wife has been unfaithful, the husband must present his wife before the LORD, and the priest will apply this entire ritual law to her. 31The husband will be innocent of any guilt in this matter, but his wife will be held accountable for her sin."

Nazirite Laws

6 Then the LORD said to Moses, 2"Give the following instructions to the people of Israel.

"If any of the people, either men or women, take the special vow of a Nazirite, setting themselves apart to the LORD in a special way, 3they must give up wine and other alcoholic drinks. They must not use vinegar made from wine or from other alcoholic drinks, they must not drink fresh grape juice, and they must not eat grapes or raisins. 4As long as they are bound by their Nazirite vow, they are not allowed to eat or drink anything that comes from a grapevine—not even the grape seeds or skins.

5"They must never cut their hair throughout the time of their vow, for they are holy and set apart to the LORD. Until the time of

---

5:21 ***when he makes you infertile, causing your womb to shrivel:*** Literally *when he causes your thigh to waste away.* "Thigh" is a euphemism for the reproductive organs (cp. Gen 24:2; 47:29); something would go wrong with her reproductive abilities. The punishment suited the crime as sexual immorality resulted in the inability to have children.

5:22 ***cause . . . your womb to shrivel:*** Literally *cause . . . your thigh to waste away.*

5:23-24 The symbolism of drinking disturbing words is repeated in Ezek 2:8–3:3 and Rev 10:8-11.

5:27 ***and her womb will shrink:*** Literally *and her thigh will waste away.*

5:29-31 As the trial by ordeal is summarized and justified, it is clear that a husband's questions about his wife's guilt or innocence did not burden him with any guilt. We might raise the question of a double standard, but it was very common for ancient laws to draw attention to the woman's failure in the matter of adultery. However, Israel's legal system provided for the punishment of both parties to an affair (as in Lev 20:10; Deut 22:21-22).

6:1-21 The voluntary Nazirite vow allowed men or women to set themselves apart for the Lord. There was considerable variation in how the Nazirite lifestyle was practiced in various periods of Hebrew history. Vows were taken very seriously in ancient times as a well-established means of expressing devotion or gratitude to God. This vow could be temporary or permanent; it involved refraining from alcoholic drinks, hair cutting, and contact with corpses. Nazirite restrictions gave members of non-Levitical tribes a way to enter into a more demanding and highly respected relationship with God. The Nazirite vow is probably best known because of Samson (Judg 13–16). See also 1 Sam 1:11; Jer 35; Acts 18:8; 21:23-26; cp. Luke 1:15.

6:2 ***Nazirite:*** The Hebrew term *nazir* is derived from a verb that means "to separate."

6:3-4 The law required priests to avoid drinking ***wine*** before they served in the Tabernacle (Lev 10:9); the Nazirite vow allowed non-Levites to broaden that law to include all places, all times, and ***anything that comes from a grapevine.***

6:5 Hair had special symbolic significance (cp. Lev 19:27); religious persons often left their hair uncut or shaved it off entirely (8:5-7). The Israelites were not expected to leave their hair entirely uncut, but the Nazirites were.

their vow has been fulfilled, they must let
their hair grow long. 6And they must not
go near a dead body during the entire period of their vow to the LORD. 7Even if the
dead person is their own father, mother,
brother, or sister, they must not defile themselves, for the hair on their head is the
symbol of their separation to God. 8This requirement applies as long as they are set
apart to the LORD.
9"If someone falls dead beside them, the
hair they have dedicated will be defiled.
They must wait for seven days and then shave
their heads. Then they will be cleansed from
their defilement. 10On the eighth day they
must bring two turtledoves or two young
pigeons to the priest at the entrance of the
Tabernacle. 11The priest will offer one of the
birds for a sin offering and the other for a
burnt offering. In this way, he will purify
them from the guilt they incurred through
contact with the dead body. Then they must
reaffirm their commitment and let their
hair begin to grow again. 12The days of their
vow that were completed before their defilement no longer count. They must rededicate
themselves to the LORD as a Nazirite for the
full term of their vow, and each must bring a
one-year-old male lamb for a guilt offering.
13"This is the ritual law for Nazirites. At the
conclusion of their time of separation as Nazirites, they must each go to the entrance of
the Tabernacle 14and offer their sacrifices to
the LORD: a one-year-old male lamb without
defect for a burnt offering, a one-year-old female lamb without defect for a sin offering, a
ram without defect for a peace offering, 15a
basket of bread made without yeast—cakes of
choice flour mixed with olive oil and wafers
spread with olive oil—along with their prescribed grain offerings and liquid offerings.
16The priest will present these offerings before the LORD: first the sin offering and the
burnt offering; 17then the ram for a peace offering, along with the basket of bread made
without yeast. The priest must also present
the prescribed grain offering and liquid offering to the LORD.
18"Then the Nazirites will shave their
heads at the entrance of the Tabernacle.
They will take the hair that had been dedicated and place it on the fire beneath the
peace-offering sacrifice. 19After the Nazirite's head has been shaved, the priest will
take for each of them the boiled shoulder of
the ram, and he will take from the basket a
cake and a wafer made without yeast. He
will put them all into the Nazirite's hands.
20Then the priest will lift them up as a special offering before the LORD. These are
holy portions for the priest, along with the
breast of the special offering and the thigh
of the sacred offering that are lifted up
before the LORD. After this ceremony the
Nazirites may again drink wine.
21"This is the ritual law of the Nazirites,
who vow to bring these offerings to the
LORD. They may also bring additional offerings if they can afford it. And they must be
careful to do whatever they vowed when
they set themselves apart as Nazirites."

The Priestly Blessing

22Then the LORD said to Moses, 23"Tell
Aaron and his sons to ᵉbless the people of
Israel with this special blessing:

24 'May the LORD bless you
and protect you.
25 May the LORD smile on you
and be gracious to you.

6:6 Lev 21:1-3 Num 19:11-22
6:9 Num 6:18
6:11 Lev 5:7; 12:6-8
6:12 Lev 5:6
6:14 Lev 14:10
6:15 Num 15:1-7
6:18 Num 6:9
6:20 Lev 7:28-34
6:23 Deut 21:5 1 Chr 23:13 ᵉ*barak* (1288) ‣Num 22:6
6:24 Deut 28:3-6
6:25 Ps 80:3, 7, 19

6:6-8 Dead bodies defiled whoever touched them (9:6-10). Priests were only allowed to touch the dead bodies of close relatives (Lev 21:1-4), but even that was forbidden to Nazirites.

6:9-21 Provisions were made for restoring purity in cases of unavoidable contact with a corpse. Special procedures and offerings brought the period of the Nazirite vow to a conclusion. A stern warning is added about actually fulfilling the vow (6:21).

6:10 ***the Tabernacle:*** Literally *the Tent of Meeting;* also in 6:13, 18. See note on Exod 27:21.

6:11 ***purify them:*** Or *make atonement for them.*

6:22-27 The priestly benediction is related to the overall theme of worship and purity in chs 5–6. This is a prayer on behalf of the people as the priests sought God's blessings for Israel. Since the priest represented God, such prayer was part of the priestly duty (cp. Lev 9:23; Deut 10:8). This prayer is not unlike Jesus' high priestly prayer in John 17.

6:24-26 Psalm 67:1 contains an abbreviated version of this benediction, much like one inscribed on a silver amulet excavated at Ketef Hinnom, southwest of Jerusalem's Old City (see "The Priest's Blessing," facing page). On a second, larger silver amulet from the same tomb, the complete benediction was inscribed in words almost identical to those here. In the days of the Second Temple (from Ezra to the time of Jesus), priests pronounced a blessing at each day's sacrifice or at the end of services. This blessing is still used in Jewish and Christian liturgy as a way of seeking divine blessing (as in 6:27).

6:24 The blessings sought in the first half of this verse include health, wealth, and fertility, while the protection mentioned in the second half was needed for all manner of dangers. This supplication is echoed in the language of Ps 121:3-8; 140:4; and 141:9. These heartfelt appeals are still good models for prayer and for the blessings that God's people can seek for all humanity. The entire poem draws attention to the Lord as the source of all good things.

6:25 The desire for God's *smile* is often translated more literally *may he make his face shine upon you.* • ***be gracious to you:*** God's people need his grace and mercy in a dangerous world (cp. Ps 31:16; 67:1; 80:3, 7, 19).

6:26 Ps 4:6; 29:11; 44:3
7:1 Exod 40:9-11
7:2 Num 1:2-16

26 May the LORD show you his favor
and give you his peace.'
27 Whenever Aaron and his sons bless the people of Israel in my name, I myself will bless them."

Israel's Final Preparations to Leave Sinai (7:1–10:10)

Offerings for the Dedication of the Tabernacle

7 On the day Moses set up the Tabernacle, he anointed it and set it apart as
holy. He also anointed and set apart all its
furnishings and the altar with its utensils.
2 Then the leaders of Israel—the tribal leaders who had registered the troops—came
and brought their offerings. 3 Together they
brought six large wagons and twelve oxen.
There was a wagon for every two leaders and
an ox for each leader. They presented these
to the LORD in front of the Tabernacle.
4 Then the LORD said to Moses, 5 "Receive
their gifts, and use these oxen and wagons
for transporting the Tabernacle. Distribute
them among the Levites according to the

The Priest's Blessing (6:22-27)

Num 24:1-9
Gen 1:28; 9:1, 26-27; 12:1-3; 14:19-20; 28:1-4; 48:15-20; 49:25-26
Lev 9:22
Deut 10:8; 33:11-29
1 Sam 2:20
1 Kgs 8:55-65
2 Chr 30:27
Ps 115:12-15; 128:1-6
Matt 5:3-11
Luke 11:27-28
2 Cor 13:14
Eph 6:23
1 Thes 5:23-24

The priest's blessing (6:22-27) is one of the most familiar and best-loved passages in the Hebrew Bible. Through the centuries, worshipers have found comfort in its brief but profound lines. This famous text is simple and elegant.

The priest's blessing invokes the Lord's blessing by repeating his name in each appeal ("the LORD" = *Yahweh;* see note on Exod 3:15). The repetition of God's name reminds God's people of his interest and involvement in their lives. This benediction emphasizes the relationship between God and his people and helps them to remember the source of their blessings.

Many OT passages refer to blessings pronounced by God and by people (e.g., Gen 12:1-3; 27:1-40; Deut 7:14-16; 28:1-14). The Israelites needed God's blessings—his help and favor—as they prepared to leave Sinai. Although the modern reader tends to think of a blessing in general terms, the Israelites in the wilderness must have understood it in terms of food, water, health, children, protection from enemies, and settlement in the Promised Land. Throughout the book of Numbers, God dealt with Israel through these down-to-earth concerns.

The Lord blessed Israel through the good words of Aaron and his sons, the priests (6:22-23). In addition to their work in the Tabernacle (and later the Temple), the priests played an important role in Israelite life. For example, the priests helped administer justice in the land (Deut 17:8-12) and assisted the king in his duties, according to a principle established in Deut 17:18-20. Eli the priest comforted Hannah and took an active role in the spiritual formation of young Samuel (1 Sam 1–3). The priests and Levites were active in Israel's spiritual instruction (see, e.g., Deut 33:9-10; Neh 8:9-12; Mal 2:6-9).

An important archaeological discovery draws attention to the significance of this ancient priestly blessing. In 1979, excavators recovered two small silver scrolls from a rock-cut tomb at Ketef Hinnom, southwest of the Old City of Jerusalem. Scholars date these small amulets to the late 600s or early 500s BC. When these delicate scrolls were unrolled through a lengthy and tedious process, they were found to contain the blessing from 6:24-26 in words that are very close to the text in the Hebrew Bible. In ancient times, such scrolls were sometimes worn as charms, similar in function to the *tefillin,* or "phylacteries" or "prayer boxes" (see Deut 6:8; Matt 23:5). These small scrolls are the earliest manuscripts (written documents) of the biblical text and contain the earliest reference to *Yahweh,* the OT name of God, found in Jerusalem. These artifacts point to the timeless appeal of this brief text.

6:26 God's ***favor***—the display of his face, or countenance—refers to his approval and special attention (cp. Ps 30:7). Divine ***peace*** (Hebrew *shalom*) is not just the absence of conflict or violence; God's peace brings complete well-being, health, and wholeness.

6:27 The priests were the mediators of God's covenant with Israel, so their duty was to pray for God's people and invoke his blessing on them. Jesus has the same role in relation to the church (see Rom 8:34; Heb 2:17-18; 4:14-16).

7:1-89 This detailed description of offerings presented by Israel's twelve tribes at the dedication of the Tabernacle includes the dedicatory gifts brought on twelve successive days.

7:1 ***The day Moses set up the Tabernacle*** was the first day of the second year after the Exodus (Exod 40:1-2). • Once Moses finished setting up the Tabernacle, he ***anointed and set apart*** (or *consecrated*) its furnishings, the altar, and its utensils (cp. Exod 40:9-10; Lev 8:10-11). As the locus of sacrifice, the altar held special importance among the sacred furniture.

7:2-9 The same tribal leaders that assisted in the registration of ch 1 are found in 7:2-3. The non-Levitical tribes supplied the Gershonites and Merarites with the wagons and oxen needed to transport the heavy structural components of the Tabernacle and other items (cp. Num 4). • These vehicles and draft animals were the first offerings from the Hebrew tribes (7:2); these practical gifts were accompanied by more elaborate dedicatory offerings that were also presented by the tribal leaders (7:10, 12-83).

7:5 ***the Tabernacle:*** Literally *the Tent*

work they have to do." 6So Moses took the wagons and oxen and presented them to the Levites. 7He gave two wagons and four oxen to the Gershonite division for their work, 8and he gave four wagons and eight oxen to the Merarite division for their work. All their work was done under the leadership of Ithamar son of Aaron the priest. 9But he gave none of the wagons or oxen to the Kohathite division, since they were required to carry the sacred objects of the Tabernacle on their shoulders.

10The leaders also presented dedication gifts for the altar at the time it was anointed. They each placed their gifts before the altar. 11The LORD said to Moses, "Let one leader bring his gift each day for the dedication of the altar."

12On the first day Nahshon son of Amminadab, leader of the tribe of Judah, presented his offering.

13His offering consisted of a silver platter weighing 3¼ pounds and a silver basin weighing 1¾ pounds (as measured by the weight of the sanctuary shekel). These were both filled with grain offerings of choice flour moistened with olive oil. 14He also brought a gold container weighing four ounces, which was filled with incense. 15He brought a young bull, a ram, and a one-year-old male lamb for a burnt offering, 16and a male goat for a sin offering. 17For a peace offering he brought two bulls, five rams, five male goats, and five one-year-old male lambs. This was the offering brought by Nahshon son of Amminadab.

18On the second day Nethanel son of Zuar, leader of the tribe of Issachar, presented his offering.

19His offering consisted of a silver platter weighing 3¼ pounds and a silver basin weighing 1¾ pounds (as measured by the weight of the sanctuary shekel). These were both filled with grain offerings of choice flour moistened with olive oil. 20He also brought a gold container weighing four ounces, which was filled with incense. 21He brought a young bull, a ram, and a one-year-old male lamb for a burnt offering, 22and a male goat for a sin offering. 23For a peace offering he brought two bulls, five rams, five male goats, and five one-year-old male lambs. This was the offering brought by Nethanel son of Zuar.

24On the third day Eliab son of Helon, leader of the tribe of Zebulun, presented his offering.

25His offering consisted of a silver platter weighing 3¼ pounds and a silver basin weighing 1¾ pounds (as measured by the weight of the sanctuary shekel). These were both filled with grain offerings of choice flour moistened with olive oil. 26He also brought a gold container weighing four ounces, which was filled with incense. 27He brought a young bull, a ram, and a one-year-old male lamb for a burnt offering, 28and a male goat for a sin offering. 29For a peace offering he brought two bulls, five rams, five male goats, and five one-year-old male lambs. This was the offering brought by Eliab son of Helon.

30On the fourth day Elizur son of Shedeur, leader of the tribe of Reuben, presented his offering.

31His offering consisted of a silver platter weighing 3¼ pounds and a silver basin weighing 1¾ pounds (as measured by the weight of the sanctuary shekel). These were both filled with grain offerings of choice flour moistened with olive oil. 32He also brought a gold container weighing four ounces, which was filled with incense. 33He brought a young bull, a ram, and a one-year-old

7:7 Num 4:26
7:8 Num 4:33
7:9 Num 4:5-15
7:14 Exod 30:34
7:16 Lev 4:3
7:17 Lev 3:1
7:18 Num 1:8
7:29 Lev 7:32
7:30 Num 1:5

of Meeting; also in 7:89. See note on Exod 27:21.

7:9 A later Israelite attempt to transport the Ark by cart ended in tragedy (1 Sam 6:8, 11; 2 Sam 6:3, 6-7).

7:10-11 In addition to the wagons and oxen, the tribal leaders also presented gifts of silver and gold vessels and other religious offerings ***for the altar at the time it was anointed.*** Beginning with the tribe of Judah, the tribal leaders brought these gifts to the Tabernacle on twelve consecutive days. The gifts came from items collected from the Egyptians when Israel departed from Egypt (cp. Exod 12:35-36; 25:3).

7:12-83 One by one, the tribal leaders brought their dedicatory gifts and offerings until the entire Hebrew confederation had participated. The repetitious pattern of describing each tribal gift emphasizes the communal nature of this ceremony; all tribes played a role in consecrating their place of worship. The detailed listing might reflect the meticulous record keeping of an archive or ledger. As noted in the record for each tribe, the ***silver*** vessels contained ***grain offerings,*** and the ***gold*** vessels held *incense.* Every tribe also brought animals as ***a burnt offering, a sin offering,*** and ***a peace offering,*** as specified in Leviticus.

7:13 ***silver platter weighing 3¼ pounds and a silver basin weighing 1¾ pounds:*** Hebrew *silver platter weighing 130 shekels* [1.5 kilograms] *and a silver basin weighing 70 shekels* [800 grams]; also in 7:19, 25, 31, 37, 43, 49, 55, 61, 67, 73, 79, 85.

7:14 ***four ounces:*** Hebrew *10 shekels* [114 grams]; also in 7:20, 26, 32, 38, 44, 50, 56, 62, 68, 74, 80, 86.

7:34 Heb 10:4
7:36 Num 1:6
7:42 Num 1:14
7:48 Num 1:10
7:52 Heb 10:4
7:60 Num 1:11
7:66 Num 1:12
7:70 Heb 10:4

male lamb for a burnt offering, 34 and
a male goat for a sin offering. 35 For a
peace offering he brought two bulls, five rams, five male goats, and five one-year-old male lambs. This was the offering brought by Elizur son of Shedeur.

36 On the fifth day Shelumiel son of Zurishaddai, leader of the tribe of Simeon, presented his offering.

37 His offering consisted of a silver platter weighing 3¼ pounds and a silver basin weighing 1¾ pounds (as measured by the weight of the sanctuary shekel). These were both filled with grain offerings of choice flour moistened
with olive oil. 38 He also brought a gold container weighing four ounces, which
was filled with incense. 39 He brought
a young bull, a ram, and a one-year-old
male lamb for a burnt offering, 40 and
a male goat for a sin offering. 41 For a
peace offering he brought two bulls, five rams, five male goats, and five one-year-old male lambs. This was the offering brought by Shelumiel son of Zurishaddai.

42 On the sixth day Eliasaph son of Deuel, leader of the tribe of Gad, presented his offering.

43 His offering consisted of a silver platter weighing 3¼ pounds and a silver basin weighing 1¾ pounds (as measured by the weight of the sanctuary shekel). These were both filled with grain offerings of choice flour moistened
with olive oil. 44 He also brought a gold container weighing four ounces, which
was filled with incense. 45 He brought
a young bull, a ram, and a one-year-old
male lamb for a burnt offering, 46 and
a male goat for a sin offering. 47 For a
peace offering he brought two bulls, five rams, five male goats, and five one-year-old male lambs. This was the offering brought by Eliasaph son of Deuel.

48 On the seventh day Elishama son of Ammihud, leader of the tribe of Ephraim, presented his offering.

49 His offering consisted of a silver platter weighing 3¼ pounds and a silver basin weighing 1¾ pounds (as measured by the weight of the sanctuary shekel). These were both filled with grain offerings of choice flour moistened
with olive oil. 50 He also brought a gold container weighing four ounces, which
was filled with incense. 51 He brought
a young bull, a ram, and a one-year-old
male lamb for a burnt offering, 52 and
a male goat for a sin offering. 53 For a
peace offering he brought two bulls, five rams, five male goats, and five one-year-old male lambs. This was the offering brought by Elishama son of Ammihud.

54 On the eighth day Gamaliel son of Pedahzur, leader of the tribe of Manasseh, presented his offering.

55 His offering consisted of a silver platter weighing 3¼ pounds and a silver basin weighing 1¾ pounds (as measured by the weight of the sanctuary shekel). These were both filled with grain offerings of choice flour moistened
with olive oil. 56 He also brought a gold container weighing four ounces, which
was filled with incense. 57 He brought
a young bull, a ram, and a one-year-old
male lamb for a burnt offering, 58 and
a male goat for a sin offering. 59 For a
peace offering he brought two bulls, five rams, five male goats, and five one-year-old male lambs. This was the offering brought by Gamaliel son of Pedahzur.

60 On the ninth day Abidan son of Gideoni, leader of the tribe of Benjamin, presented his offering.

61 His offering consisted of a silver platter weighing 3¼ pounds and a silver basin weighing 1¾ pounds (as measured by the weight of the sanctuary shekel). These were both filled with grain offerings of choice flour moistened
with olive oil. 62 He also brought a gold container weighing four ounces, which
was filled with incense. 63 He brought
a young bull, a ram, and a one-year-old
male lamb for a burnt offering, 64 and
a male goat for a sin offering. 65 For a
peace offering he brought two bulls, five rams, five male goats, and five one-year-old male lambs. This was the offering brought by Abidan son of Gideoni.

66 On the tenth day Ahiezer son of Ammishaddai, leader of the tribe of Dan, presented his offering.

67 His offering consisted of a silver platter weighing 3¼ pounds and a silver basin weighing 1¾ pounds (as measured by the weight of the sanctuary shekel). These were both filled with grain offerings of choice flour moistened
with olive oil. 68 He also brought a gold container weighing four ounces, which
was filled with incense. 69 He brought
a young bull, a ram, and a one-year-old
male lamb for a burnt offering, 70 and
a male goat for a sin offering. 71 For a

peace offering he brought two bulls, five
rams, five male goats, and five one-year-
old male lambs. This was the offering
brought by Ahiezer son of Ammishaddai.

72On the eleventh day Pagiel son of Ocran,
leader of the tribe of Asher, presented his
offering.

73His offering consisted of a silver
platter weighing 3¼ pounds and a silver
basin weighing 1¾ pounds (as measured
by the weight of the sanctuary shekel).
These were both filled with grain
offerings of choice flour moistened
with olive oil. 74He also brought a gold
container weighing four ounces, which
was filled with incense. 75He brought
a young bull, a ram, and a one-year-old
male lamb for a burnt offering, 76and
a male goat for a sin offering. 77For a
peace offering he brought two bulls, five
rams, five male goats, and five one-year-
old male lambs. This was the offering
brought by Pagiel son of Ocran.

78On the twelfth day Ahira son of Enan,
leader of the tribe of Naphtali, presented
his offering.

79His offering consisted of a silver
platter weighing 3¼ pounds and a silver
basin weighing 1¾ pounds (as measured
by the weight of the sanctuary shekel).
These were both filled with grain
offerings of choice flour moistened
with olive oil. 80He also brought a gold
container weighing four ounces, which
was filled with incense. 81He brought
a young bull, a ram, and a one-year-old
male lamb for a burnt offering, 82and
a male goat for a sin offering. 83For a
peace offering he brought two bulls, five
rams, five male goats, and five one-year-
old male lambs. This was the offering
brought by Ahira son of Enan.

84So this was the dedication offering
brought by the leaders of Israel at the time
the altar was anointed: twelve silver platters,
twelve silver basins, and twelve gold incense
containers. 85Each silver platter weighed
3¼ pounds, and each silver basin weighed
1¾ pounds. The total weight of the silver
was 60 pounds (as measured by the weight
of the sanctuary shekel). 86Each of the
twelve gold containers that was filled with
incense weighed four ounces (as measured
by the weight of the sanctuary shekel). The
total weight of the gold was three pounds.
87Twelve young bulls, twelve rams, and
twelve one-year-old male lambs were donated for the burnt offerings, along with
their prescribed grain offerings. Twelve
male goats were brought for the sin offerings. 88Twenty-four bulls, sixty rams, sixty
male goats, and sixty one-year-old male
lambs were donated for the peace offerings.
This was the dedication offering for the altar after it was anointed.

89Whenever Moses went into the Tabernacle to speak with the LORD, he heard the
voice speaking to him from between
the two ᶠcherubim above the Ark's cover—
the place of atonement—that rests on the
Ark of the Covenant. The LORD spoke to
him from there.

Preparing the Lamps

8 The LORD said to Moses, 2"Give Aaron
the following instructions: When you
set up the seven lamps in the lampstand,
place them so their light shines forward in
front of the lampstand." 3So Aaron did this.
He set up the seven lamps so they reflected
their light forward, just as the LORD had
commanded Moses. 4The entire lampstand,
from its base to its decorative blossoms,
was made of beaten gold. It was built according to the exact design the LORD had shown
Moses.

The Levites Dedicated

5Then the LORD said to Moses, 6"Now set the
Levites apart from the rest of the people of

7:78 Num 1:15
7:84 Num 7:10
7:88 Num 7:1, 10
7:89 Exod 25:21-22; 33:9-11; Ps 80:1; 99:1; ᶠ*kerub* (3742) ‣ 1 Sam 4:4
8:2 Exod 25:37
8:4 Exod 25:18, 31-36, 40

7:84-88 The gifts and offerings of each tribe having been described, this paragraph tabulates these expensive containers, their offerings and incense, and the sacrificial animals. These large and costly gifts and sacrifices drew attention to the importance of the altar, the Tabernacle, and the God who was served there. The sacrifices were required by law; the Hebrews presented the special gifts with a generous spirit.

7:85 ***60 pounds:*** Hebrew *2,400 shekels* [27.6 kilograms].

7:86 ***three pounds:*** Hebrew *120 shekels* [1.4 kilograms].

7:89 Once ***the Tabernacle*** had been dedicated and set apart as holy, it was the center of divine revelation. There ***Moses*** spoke with God, God's will was disclosed, and his presence came to rest (Lev 16:2, 13-17). Such communication emanated from the Ark of the Covenant ***between the two cherubim above the Ark's cover,*** also known as the "mercy seat" (cp. Exod 25:17-22). • For the Israelites, this was the special place associated with atonement, even as the Cross has assumed that significance in Christian faith (see Heb 9–10, especially 9:5). God's voice, as heard by Moses the mediator, fulfilled the expectation established by Exod 25:22 and 30:6. The Lord's presence guaranteed the holiness of Israel's wilderness sanctuary. • ***Ark of the Covenant:*** Or *Ark of the Testimony.*

8:1-4 Here are specific guidelines for the placement of the elaborate ***lampstand*** (Hebrew *menorah;* see Exod 25:31-40) in the Tabernacle. Since the inside of the Tabernacle was dark, the illumination provided by this stylized tree of lamps aided Israel's worship.

8:5-22 The Lord prescribed the dedication and cleansing of the Levites.

8:7 Lev 14:8-9; Num 19:9, 17-18
8:8 Num 15:3-12
8:10 Lev 3:2
8:12 Exod 29:10-14
8:14 Num 3:12
8:16 Num 3:13
8:17 Exod 13:12-13
8:19 Num 1:53
8:24 Num 4:3

Israel and make them ceremonially clean.
7Do this by sprinkling them with the water
of purification, and have them shave their
entire body and wash their clothing. Then
they will be ceremonially clean. 8Have them
bring a young bull and a grain offering of
choice flour moistened with olive oil, along
with a second young bull for a sin offering.
9Then assemble the whole community of Israel, and present the Levites at the entrance
of the Tabernacle. 10When you present the
Levites before the LORD, the people of Israel
must lay their hands on them. 11Raising his
hands, Aaron must then present the Levites
to the LORD as a special offering from the
people of Israel, thus dedicating them to
the LORD's service.
12"Next the Levites will lay their hands on
the heads of the young bulls. Present one
as a sin offering and the other as a burnt
offering to the LORD, to purify the Levites
and make them right with the LORD. 13Then
have the Levites stand in front of Aaron and
his sons, and raise your hands and present
them as a special offering to the LORD. 14In
this way, you will set the Levites apart from
the rest of the people of Israel, and the Levites will belong to me. 15After this, they
may go into the Tabernacle to do their work,
because you have purified them and presented them as a special offering.
16"Of all the people of Israel, the Levites
are reserved for me. I have claimed them for
myself in place of all the firstborn sons of
the Israelites; I have taken the Levites as their
substitutes. 17For all the firstborn males
among the people of Israel are mine, both
of people and of animals. I set them apart
for myself on the day I struck down all the
firstborn sons of the Egyptians. 18Yes, I have
claimed the Levites in place of all the firstborn sons of Israel. 19And of all the Israelites,
I have assigned the Levites to Aaron and his
sons. They will serve in the Tabernacle on
behalf of the Israelites and make sacrifices
to purify the people so no plague will strike
them when they approach the sanctuary."
20So Moses, Aaron, and the whole community of Israel dedicated the Levites, carefully
following all the LORD's instructions to
Moses. 21The Levites purified themselves
from sin and washed their clothes, and
Aaron lifted them up and presented them
to the LORD as a special offering. He then
offered a sacrifice to purify them and make
them right with the LORD. 22After that the
Levites went into the Tabernacle to perform
their duties, assisting Aaron and his sons. So
they carried out all the commands that the
LORD gave Moses concerning the Levites.
23The LORD also instructed Moses,
24"This is the rule the Levites must follow:
They must begin serving in the Tabernacle
at the age of twenty-five, 25and they must
retire at the age of fifty. 26After retirement
they may assist their fellow Levites by serving as guards at the Tabernacle, but they
may not officiate in the service. This is how
you must assign duties to the Levites."

The Second Passover

9 A year after Israel's departure from
Egypt, the LORD spoke to Moses in the
wilderness of Sinai. In the first month of

8:7 The ceremony to make the Levites ***ceremonially clean*** consisted of sprinkling with water, shaving all hair, and donning clean clothes; this resembled the ceremonies of cleansing from ritual defilement. • ***water of purification:*** This term appears only here. This sprinkling symbolized the washing of sin from their lives and thus contained some of the symbolic significance of later Jewish washings and even of Christian baptism. Perhaps this water was the same as the sin-removing mixture that included ashes from the red heifer mentioned in 19:9 (see Heb 9:13). • The requirement to ***shave their entire body*** was also part of the process of being declared clean from the ritual impurity of defiling diseases (Lev 14:8). • The washing of clothing accompanied all instances of cleansing from ritual defilement (e.g., Lev 15:5-27).

8:9 *the Tabernacle:* Literally *the Tent of Meeting;* also in 8:15, 19, 22, 24, 26. See note on Exod 27:21.

8:10-11 By the laying on of hands, Israel recognized the Levites' special status and offered them as their representatives before the Lord (8:16).

8:11 The reference to Aaron's raised hands suggests that Israel offered the Levites to the Lord as a "wave offering"—the type of offering lifted up to the Lord (cp. Lev 7:30). The Levites were dedicated to duties that made them "living and holy sacrifices" (cp. Rom 12:1).

8:12-22 The Levites had to offer appropriate sacrifices before they performed their duties in the Tabernacle (8:15).

8:12 *to purify the Levites and make them right with the LORD:* Or *to make atonement for the Levites.* See note on Lev 1:4.

8:19 *purify:* Or *make atonement for.* • A ***plague*** was an appropriate punishment for unlawful actions (11:33; 14:37).

8:21 *then offered a sacrifice to purify them and make them right with the LORD:* Or *then made atonement for them to purify them.*

8:23-26 Guidelines regarding the Levites' length of service. • Whereas 4:3 states that their Tabernacle service began at age 30, 8:24 gives the age as 25. The discrepancy might reflect age requirements followed in different periods when the number of Levite men available for service varied, or those aged 25–29 may have been considered unofficial workers or apprentices. • Both passages establish the retirement age at 50; retired Levites could serve the Tabernacle as guards (cp. Ps 84:10).

9:1-14 *A year after Israel's* exodus ***from Egypt,*** the time came for Israel to celebrate their second Passover ***in the wilderness of Sinai.*** Those unable to celebrate it on time were given permission to do so a month later.

9:1 The ***first month*** of the ancient Hebrew lunar calendar usually occurs within the months of March and April.

that year he said, 2"Tell the Israelites to celebrate the Passover at the prescribed time, 3at twilight on the fourteenth day of the first month. Be sure to follow all my decrees and regulations concerning this celebration."

4So Moses told the people to celebrate the Passover 5in the wilderness of Sinai as twilight fell on the fourteenth day of the month. And they celebrated the festival there, just as the LORD had commanded Moses. 6But some of the men had been ceremonially defiled by touching a dead body, so they could not celebrate the Passover that day. They came to Moses and Aaron that day 7and said, "We have become ceremonially unclean by touching a dead body. But why should we be prevented from presenting the LORD's offering at the proper time with the rest of the Israelites?"

8Moses answered, "Wait here until I have received instructions for you from the LORD."

9This was the LORD's reply to Moses. 10"Give the following instructions to the people of Israel: If any of the people now or in future generations are ceremonially unclean at Passover time because of touching a dead body, or if they are on a journey and cannot be present at the ceremony, they may still celebrate the LORD's Passover. 11They must offer the Passover sacrifice one month later, at twilight on the fourteenth day of the second month. They must eat the Passover lamb at that time with bitter salad greens and bread made without yeast. 12They must not leave any of the lamb until the next morning, and they must not break any of its bones. They must follow all the normal regulations concerning the Passover.

13"But those who neglect to celebrate the Passover at the regular time, even though they are ceremonially clean and not away on a trip, will be cut off from the community of Israel. If they fail to present the LORD's offering at the proper time, they will suffer the consequences of their guilt. 14And if foreigners living among you want to celebrate the Passover to the LORD, they must follow these same decrees and regulations. The same laws apply both to native-born Israelites and to the foreigners living among you."

The Guidance of the Fiery Cloud

15On the day the Tabernacle was set up, the cloud covered it. But from evening until morning the cloud over the Tabernacle looked like a pillar of fire. 16This was the regular pattern—at night the cloud that covered the Tabernacle had the appearance of fire. 17Whenever the cloud lifted from over the sacred tent, the people of Israel would break camp and follow it. And wherever the cloud settled, the people of Israel would set up camp. 18In this way, they traveled and camped at the LORD's command wherever he told them to go. Then they remained in their camp as long as the cloud stayed over the Tabernacle. 19If the cloud remained over the Tabernacle for a long time, the Israelites stayed and performed their duty to the LORD. 20Sometimes the cloud would stay over the Tabernacle for only a few days, so the people would stay for only a few days, as the LORD commanded. Then at the LORD's command they would break camp and move on. 21Sometimes the cloud stayed only overnight and lifted the next morning. But day or night, when the cloud lifted, the people broke camp and moved on. 22Whether the

9:2 Exod 12:1-6
9:5 Josh 5:10
9:6 Num 19:11-22
9:8 Exod 18:15
9:11 Exod 12:8
9:12 Exod 12:10, 43, 46 *John 19:36
9:13 Exod 12:15 Num 15:30-31
9:14 Exod 12:48-49
9:15 Exod 13:21-22; 40:2, 17, 34 Neh 9:12, 19 Ps 78:14
9:17 Exod 40:36-38 Num 10:11, 33-34
9:18 1 Cor 10:1
9:22 Exod 40:36-37

See chart, "Israel's Annual Calendar," p. 145.

9:2-3 The Hebrews were told to celebrate ***the Passover at the prescribed time*** (see Exod 12:6), ***on the fourteenth day of the first month.*** This day in the ancient Hebrew lunar calendar occurred in late March, April, or early May. • ***at twilight:*** The Hebrew day begins at sundown.

9:4-7 When it was time to celebrate the Passover, some men were prevented by the restrictions of Lev 7:20-21. Their objection arose from a desire to keep the regulation in a case where there seemed to be no good way for them to do so.

9:8 Moses agreed to inquire of the Lord regarding this difficult case (cp. 7:89).

9:9-14 God's response to the quandary was to allow a makeup ceremony one month later for two special cases (see also 2 Chr 30), but with this provision he warned that the Israelites must not neglect the Passover and must celebrate it according to the regulations.

9:11 ***the fourteenth day of the second month:*** This day in the ancient Hebrew lunar calendar occurred in late April, May, or early June. See chart, "Israel's Annual Calendar," p. 145.

9:12 The bones of the Passover lamb were not to be broken (see Exod 12:46; Ps 34:20; John 19:32-36; cp. John 1:29; 1 Cor 5:7). The apostle John made reference to this instruction when reporting that Jesus' legs were not broken on the cross (John 19:36).

9:13 If they ignored the required ***Passover***, they must ***be cut off from the community.*** It is not clear whether this refers to the death penalty or banishment (see note on Lev 7:20-21).

9:14 ***Foreigners*** who lived among the Hebrews and wanted ***to celebrate the Passover*** could do so by following ***the same laws,*** but circumcision was required for males who desired to eat the Passover meal (see also Exod 12:48-49).

9:15-23 This passage parallels Exod 40:17, 34-38 and provides additional details about God's use of the pillar of cloud and fire to lead his people (see also Exod 13:21-22). The Lord faithfully and unmistakably guided his people in the wilderness.

9:15 ***covered it:*** Literally *covered the Tabernacle, the Tent of the Testimony.*

9:19-23 The fiery cloud, witnessed even by Israel's enemies (14:14), was a clear symbol of God's glorious presence and

10:5 Num 10:14
10:7 Joel 2:1
10:8 Num 31:6; Josh 6:3-9; 2 Chr 5:11-12

cloud stayed above the Tabernacle for two days, a month, or a year, the people of Israel stayed in camp and did not move on. But as soon as it lifted, they broke camp and moved on. 23So they camped or traveled at the LORD's command, and they did whatever the LORD told them through Moses.

The Silver Trumpets

10 Now the LORD said to Moses, 2"Make two trumpets of hammered silver for calling the community to assemble and for signaling the breaking of camp. 3When both trumpets are blown, everyone must gather before you at the entrance of the Tabernacle. 4But if only one trumpet is blown, then only the leaders—the heads of the clans of Israel—must present themselves to you.

5"When you sound the signal to move on, the tribes camped on the east side of the Tabernacle must break camp and move forward. 6When you sound the signal a second time, the tribes camped on the south will follow. You must sound short blasts as the signal for moving on. 7But when you call the people to an assembly, blow the trumpets with a different signal. 8Only the priests, Aaron's descendants, are allowed to blow the trumpets. This is a permanent law for you, to be observed from generation to generation.

The Cloud and Fire (9:15-23)

Num 10:11-12, 34; 11:25; 12:5, 10; 14:14; 16:42; Exod 13:20-22; 14:19-24; 16:10; 19:16-18; 24:15-18; 33:7-11; 40:34-38; Lev 16:2; Deut 31:15; 1 Kgs 8:11; 2 Chr 5:14; Neh 9:19-21; Ps 78:14; 99:7; 104:3; Ezek 1:4-5; 10:3; Matt 17:5; 24:30; 26:64; Luke 9:34-35; Acts 1:9; 1 Cor 10:2; 1 Thes 4:17; Rev 1:7; 14:14-16

When Israel was in the wilderness, God led the nation with a pillar of cloud and fire. The pillar joined the Israelites when they "left Succoth and camped at Etham on the edge of the wilderness" (Exod 13:20-22; cp. Num 33:8). This happened right after the first Passover, immediately after Israel left Egypt.

The pillar served a variety of functions. When the Egyptians pursued the Israelites, the cloud moved behind the people of Israel and prevented an Egyptian advance (Exod 14:19-20). Through the rest of Israel's travels, it was a visible indication that "the LORD went ahead of them" (Exod 13:21). When the pillar settled over the Tabernacle and the camp of Israel, it represented the Lord's presence and protection. The cloud and fire also provided divine guidance by indicating when the Israelites should move (9:17-23; Exod 40:36-38). When the pillar was stationary, Israel stayed where they were. When it lifted and moved on, the Israelites broke camp and followed. They camped in different places for varying amounts of time, sometimes briefly and sometimes for a longer period. Israel thus "camped or traveled at the Lord's command" (9:23). The pillar of cloud and fire was like a divine banner flying over the tribes on the march (cp. 10:14, 18, 22, 25).

The pillar regularly appeared as a cloud by day and a pillar of fire by night (9:15-16; Exod 13:21). In the Bible, both fire and clouds often indicate the presence and glory of God (e.g., Exod 19:16-18; 24:15-18; Matt 17:5; 24:30; Acts 1:9; cp. Ps 18:8-13). The cloud and fire imagery indicated that God's presence and glory moved with Israel through the wilderness. Exodus 14:19 refers to the pillar as "the angel of God" (i.e., a representative or representation of God). This special manifestation of God (a *theophany*) stayed with them "throughout all their journeys" while they were in the wilderness (Exod 40:38; see also Exod 13:22). Sometimes, "the cloud covered the Tabernacle, and the glory of the LORD filled the Tabernacle," so that "Moses could no longer enter the Tabernacle" (Exod 40:34-35). On other occasions, the cloud descended and hovered near the entrance to the Tent of Meeting, indicating that the Lord was speaking with Moses "face to face" (Exod 33:7-11; cp. Num 11:25; 12:5; Deut 31:15). The pillar of cloud and fire was a constant, reassuring reminder of the Lord's presence. We are not given any specific description of the fire and the cloud other than that it was shaped like a pillar, but it was a powerful symbol of God's special care for Israel (see Neh 9:19-21; cp. Ps 46:1; 139; John 1:14; Rom 8:31-39).

the means by which he directed their movement.

10:1-10 Israel needed signals that were loud and clear so that the tribes could receive instructions. Two silver trumpets provided a simple, effective means to signal all the tribes to move. • These trumpets were not the ram's horns (Hebrew *shopar*) mentioned frequently in the OT (e.g., Josh 6:4-6); they were fashioned by Israelite craftsmen from ***hammered silver*** brought out of Egypt.

10:2-4 The ***two trumpets*** were used to get people's attention for important pronouncements (cp. Rev 8–11).

10:3 ***Tabernacle:*** Literally *Tent of Meeting*. See note on Exod 27:21.

10:5-8 When it was time to ***break camp***, the sound of the trumpets supplemented the movement of the pillar of cloud (cp. 9:15-22) by signaling when to camp and when to move on (see ch 2).

10:8 ***Only the priests . . . are allowed to blow the trumpets:*** All uses of these trumpets were related to God and his government of Israel, both of which the priests served.

9“When you arrive in your own land and
go to war against your enemies who attack
you, sound the alarm with the trumpets.
Then the LORD your God will [g]remember
you and rescue you from your enemies.
10Blow the trumpets in times of gladness,
too, sounding them at your annual festivals
and at the beginning of each month. And
blow the trumpets over your burnt offerings and peace offerings. The trumpets will
remind the LORD your God of his covenant
with you. I am the LORD your God.”

2. THE ISRAELITES MOVE FROM SINAI TO THE PLAINS OF MOAB (10:11–22:1)

The Israelites Move from Sinai to Kadesh (10:11–12:16)

The Israelites Leave Sinai

11In the second year after Israel’s departure
from Egypt—on the twentieth day of the
second month—the cloud lifted from the
Tabernacle of the Covenant. 12So the Israelites set out from the wilderness of Sinai and
traveled on from place to place until the
cloud stopped in the wilderness of Paran.
13When the people set out for the first
time, following the instructions the LORD
had given through Moses, 14Judah’s troops
led the way. They marched behind their
banner, and their leader was Nahshon son
of Amminadab. 15They were joined by the
troops of the tribe of Issachar, led by Nethanel son of Zuar, 16and the troops of the
tribe of Zebulun, led by Eliab son of Helon.
17Then the Tabernacle was taken down,
and the Gershonite and Merarite divisions
of the Levites were next in the line of march,
carrying the Tabernacle with them. 18Reu-
ben’s troops went next, marching behind
their banner. Their leader was Elizur son of
Shedeur. 19They were joined by the troops of
the tribe of Simeon, led by Shelumiel son of
Zurishaddai, 20and the troops of the tribe
of Gad, led by Eliasaph son of Deuel.
21Next came the Kohathite division of the
Levites, carrying the sacred objects from the
Tabernacle. Before they arrived at the next
camp, the Tabernacle would already be set
up at its new location. 22Ephraim’s troops
went next, marching behind their banner.
Their leader was Elishama son of Ammihud.
23They were joined by the troops of the tribe
of Manasseh, led by Gamaliel son of Pedahzur, 24and the troops of the tribe of Benjamin,
led by Abidan son of Gideoni.
25Dan’s troops went last, marching behind
their banner and serving as the rear guard for
all the tribal camps. Their leader was Ahiezer
son of Ammishaddai. 26They were joined by
the troops of the tribe of Asher, led by Pagiel
son of Ocran, 27and the troops of the tribe of
Naphtali, led by Ahira son of Enan.
28This was the order in which the Israelites marched, division by division.

Hobab the Guide

29One day Moses said to his brother-in-law,
Hobab son of Reuel the Midianite, “We are
on our way to the place the LORD promised
us, for he said, ‘I will give it to you.’ Come
with us and we will treat you well, for the
LORD has promised wonderful blessings for
Israel!”
30But Hobab replied, “No, I will not go. I
must return to my own land and family.”
31“Please don’t leave us,” Moses pleaded.
“You know the places in the wilderness
where we should camp. Come, be our guide.
32If you do, we’ll share with you all the blessings the LORD gives us.”

10:9 Judg 2:18; Ps 106:4; [g]*zakar* (2142) ‣Num 15:39
10:10 Lev 23:24; Num 29:1; Ps 81:3-5
10:11 Exod 40:17
10:12 Gen 21:20-21; Num 12:16
10:13 Deut 1:6
10:14 Num 2:3-31
10:17 Num 4:21-23
10:18 Num 2:10-16
10:21 Num 4:1-20
10:22 Num 2:3-31
10:29 Exod 2:18-21; 3:1; Judg 4:11
10:32 Ps 22:27-31

10:9-10 ***The trumpets*** marked holy events that might not readily be recognized as such. Trumpets that sounded a call to arms (Hos 5:8; Joel 2:1) would ***remind the LORD*** to rescue the Hebrews from their enemies.

10:11-36 Leaving Sinai was a pivotal moment in Israel’s history. Now the Israelites had the law and would be tested as to how they would keep it. The departure from Sinai was the beginning of the march toward Canaan, though it turned into a long journey (cp. Deut 1:6-8, 19). This passage summarizes the daily procedures on the journey.

10:11 ***the twentieth day of the second month:*** This day in the ancient Hebrew lunar calendar occurred in late April, May, or early June. • ***Tabernacle of the Covenant:*** Or *Tabernacle of the Testimony.*

10:12 ***The Israelites*** marched to ***the wilderness of Paran,*** an arid or semi-arid region in the northeastern part of the Sinai Peninsula, south of the Negev and west of the Dead Sea/Arabah Rift (cp. Gen 21:21).

10:13-28 The order of march is different here than in 2:3-34, which specifies that all three clans of Levites were to carry the Tabernacle and its furnishings in the middle of the troop, between the groups headed by Judah and Reuben and the groups headed by Ephraim and Dan. Here, the Gershonites and Merarites carried the components of the Tabernacle structure between Judah and Reuben, and the Kohathites carried the most sacred furniture between Reuben and Ephraim. This useful arrangement allowed time for the Gershonites and Merarites to set up the Tabernacle before the Kohathites arrived with the sacred objects. It also provided security for their special cargo, and it spread the Levites out among the tribes, perhaps enhancing the leavening effect of their influence (cp. Matt 13:33; 16:6, 11-12; 1 Cor 5:6-7).

10:29-32 After the trek toward Paran had begun, Moses took the practical step of asking ***his brother-in-law Hobab*** (cp. Judg 4:11) to join the Israelites as their ***guide*** (literally *to serve as Israel’s eyes*) and so to share in their promised blessings. As a Midianite shepherd, Hobab knew the routes and possible sources of food and water in this region of the Sinai Peninsula. • ***Reuel the Midianite:*** See “Jethro/Reuel” at Exod 18:1-27, p. 155. • ***my own land and family:*** Midian was probably in northwestern Arabia. Judges 1:16 suggests that Hobab accepted the appeal.

10:33
Deut 1:33
[h]*'aron* (0727)
‣1 Sam 3:3
10:34
Num 9:15-23
10:35
Ps 68:1-2
10:36
Deut 1:10-11
11:1
Lev 10:1-2
Num 14:2; 16:35; 17:5
11:3
Deut 9:22
11:4
Exod 12:38
Lev 24:10-11
Ps 78:18
1 Cor 10:6
11:6
Num 21:5
[i]*man* (4478)
‣Num 11:7
11:7
Exod 16:14, 31
[j]*man* (4478)
‣Num 11:9

The Ark Leads the Way

33They marched for three days after leaving the mountain of the LORD, with the [h]Ark
of the LORD's Covenant moving ahead of
them to show them where to stop and rest.
34As they moved on each day, the cloud of
the LORD hovered over them. 35And whenever the Ark set out, Moses would shout,
"Arise, O LORD, and let your enemies be scattered! Let them flee before you!" 36And
when the Ark was set down, he would say,
"Return, O LORD, to the countless thousands of Israel!"

The People Complain to Moses

11 Soon the people began to complain
about their hardship, and the LORD
heard everything they said. Then the LORD's
anger blazed against them, and he sent a
fire to rage among them, and he destroyed
some of the people in the outskirts of the
camp. 2Then the people screamed to Moses
for help, and when he prayed to the LORD,
the fire stopped. 3After that, the area was
known as Taberah (which means "the place
of burning"), because fire from the LORD
had burned among them there.

4Then the foreign rabble who were traveling with the Israelites began to crave the
good things of Egypt. And the people of Israel also began to complain. "Oh, for some
meat!" they exclaimed. 5"We remember the
fish we used to eat for free in Egypt. And we
had all the cucumbers, melons, leeks, onions,
and garlic we wanted. 6But now our appetites
are gone. All we ever see is this [i]manna!"

7The [j]manna looked like small coriander
seeds, and it was pale yellow like gum resin.
8The people would go out and gather it from
the ground. They made flour by grinding it

Bread from Heaven (11:1-15)

Exod 16:1-36
Deut 8:3, 16
Josh 5:10-12
Neh 9:20-21
Ps 78:24; 105:40
John 6:1-15, 22-64
1 Cor 10:3-5
Rev 2:17

As the Israelites left Egypt behind and entered the wilderness, God sent manna to sustain them and to show them his "awesome glory" (Exod 16:1-36). The Lord gave them food adequate for their daily needs (see Neh 9:20-21). This "bread from heaven" (Ps 78:24; 105:40) showed God's people his love and mercy.

Manna illustrates God's special provision for Israel in the wilderness (see Deut 8:3, 16; Ps 78:24; 105:40; cp. Rev 2:17). Although manna was actual food, some passages use the term in a spiritual sense to symbolize a spiritual relationship with the Lord and as a sign of God's miraculous provision for his people (see 1 Cor 10:3-4). At the same time, manna was associated with Israel's complaining against God and with their lack of trust in his provision (11:1-15; see 1 Cor 10:5).

Shortly after Jesus had miraculously fed the 5,000 near the Sea of Galilee, he taught about the "bread of life" in the synagogue at Capernaum (John 6:22-59). He identified himself as the "true bread of God" and "the bread of life" (John 6:32-35); he even linked eternal life with the need to eat his flesh and drink his blood (John 6:50-58). Just as the manna provided food in the wilderness, Jesus—the true bread from God—offers spiritual sustenance. Israel was humbled by their need for food in the wilderness (Deut 8:3). Now followers of Jesus must humble themselves and receive the fullness of his life by faith (John 6:35-40, 47-51, 63-64).

10:33 ***The mountain of the LORD*** refers here to Mount Sinai; elsewhere the expression refers to Mount Moriah or Zion in Jerusalem (Gen 22:14; Ps 24:3; Isa 2:3; Zech 8:3).

10:35 Moses' invocation, spoken when ***the Ark set out***, acknowledged the Lord as a warrior who would give Israel the Promised Land and called him to fight Israel's battles (cp. Ps 68:1).

10:36 This invocation called the Lord to join his people and protect Israel while they camped.

11:1-35 This is the first of many occasions in the wilderness when Israel was disobedient to the Lord.

11:1 ***Soon the people began to complain. . . . Then the LORD's anger blazed:*** The link between Israel's complaints and God's anger is a major theme of Numbers and throughout the OT (e.g., Deut 9:22; Ps 78). God is holy and just, and he demands obedience from his people. Complaints are equivalent to rejecting him (cp. 11:20). • ***their hardship:*** Mount Sinai had provided a stable residence for a year; the road to Paran provided heat, thirst, and fatigue. • ***fire . . . destroyed some:*** Cp. Lev 10:2.

11:2-3 The people sought Moses' intercession again (cp. Exod 15:25; 32:11-14), which brought an end to the fire of God's judgment. • ***Taberah:*** Cp. 11:34-35; see Deut 9:22.

11:4-15 Israel had not relinquished the attitude that brought about the judgment at Taberah (11:1-3), so they readily joined the ***foreign rabble*** in craving the delicacies of Egypt, forgetting the misery of slavery there.

11:4-6 ***Oh, for some meat!*** The Israelites had flocks and herds (e.g., Exod 12:32, 38; 17:3; 34:3; Num 32:1), but the animals were more valuable for their dairy products and other benefits produced while alive and were only butchered for meat on a selective basis. The Hebrews would not have had enough meat to feed such a large population regularly (cp. 11:21-22).

11:6 The Lord had earlier provided ***manna*** and quail (Exod 16).

11:7-9 ***The manna*** has often been explained as one of various edible substances that occur naturally (but see Deut 8:3); even so, its quantity and duration were miraculous.

with hand mills or pounding it in mortars.
Then they boiled it in a pot and made it into
flat cakes. These cakes tasted like pastries
baked with olive oil. 9The [k]manna came
down on the camp with the dew during the
night.
10Moses heard all the families standing
in the doorways of their tents whining, and
the LORD became extremely angry. Moses
was also very aggravated. 11And Moses said
to the LORD, "Why are you treating me, your
servant, so harshly? Have mercy on me!
What did I do to deserve the burden of all
these people? 12Did I give birth to them?
Did I bring them into the world? Why did
you tell me to carry them in my arms like
a mother carries a nursing baby? How can
I carry them to the land you swore to give
their ancestors? 13Where am I supposed
to get meat for all these people? They keep
whining to me, saying, 'Give us meat to eat!'
14I can't carry all these people by myself!
The load is far too heavy! 15If this is how you
intend to treat me, just go ahead and kill me.
Do me a favor and spare me this misery!"

Moses Chooses Seventy Leaders

16Then the LORD said to Moses, "Gather before me seventy men who are recognized as
elders and leaders of Israel. Bring them to
the Tabernacle to stand there with you. 17I
will come down and talk to you there. I will
take some of the Spirit that is upon you, and
I will put the Spirit upon them also. They
will bear the burden of the people along
with you, so you will not have to carry it
alone.
18"And say to the people, 'Purify yourselves, for tomorrow you will have meat to
eat. You were whining, and the LORD heard
you when you cried, "Oh, for some meat!
We were better off in Egypt!" Now the
LORD will give you meat, and you will have
to eat it. 19And it won't be for just a day or
two, or for five or ten or even twenty. 20You
will eat it for a whole month until you gag
and are sick of it. For you have rejected the
LORD, who is here among you, and you have
whined to him, saying, "Why did we ever
leave Egypt?"'"
21But Moses responded to the LORD,
"There are 600,000 foot soldiers here with
me, and yet you say, 'I will give them meat
for a whole month!' 22Even if we butchered
all our flocks and herds, would that satisfy
them? Even if we caught all the fish in the
sea, would that be enough?"
23Then the LORD said to Moses, "Has
my arm lost its power? Now you will see
whether or not my word comes true!"
24So Moses went out and reported the
LORD's words to the people. He gathered the
seventy elders and stationed them around
the Tabernacle. 25And the LORD came down
in the cloud and spoke to Moses. Then he
gave the seventy [a]elders the same [b]Spirit
that was upon Moses. And when the [b]Spirit
rested upon them, they prophesied. But this
never happened again.
26Two men, Eldad and Medad, had stayed
behind in the camp. They were listed among
the elders, but they had not gone out to the
Tabernacle. Yet the Spirit rested upon them
as well, so they prophesied there in the
camp. 27A young man ran and reported to
Moses, "Eldad and Medad are prophesying
in the camp!"
28Joshua son of Nun, who had been Moses'
assistant since his youth, protested, "Moses,
my master, make them stop!"
29But Moses replied, "Are you jealous for
my sake? I wish that all the LORD's people
were prophets and that the LORD would put
his Spirit upon them all!" 30Then Moses returned to the camp with the elders of Israel.

11:9 Exod 16:13; [k]*man* (4478) ›Deut 8:3
11:10 Ps 78:21
11:11 Exod 5:22
11:12 Gen 26:3; Exod 13:4-5; Isa 49:23
11:14 Exod 18:18; Deut 1:12
11:15 Exod 32:32
11:16 Exod 24:1, 9
11:17 Exod 34:5-6; Num 11:25; 12:5
11:18 Exod 19:10, 14-15
11:21 Exod 12:37
11:23 Isa 50:2
11:25 Num 11:16-17; [a]*zaqen* (2205) ›Deut 19:12; [b]*ruakh* (7307) ›Deut 34:9
11:28 Josh 1:1; Mark 9:38-40

11:10-15 The Israelites' persistent ***whining*** led a frustrated Moses to register his own complaints with God. With biting sarcasm, Moses reminded God that he had not wanted this job in the first place (cp. Exod 4:10). Israel became such a burden that Moses wished that God would do him the favor of killing him (cp. Job 6:9). • Moses' complaint was acceptable, unlike the complaints of the people, because he was seeking the Lord rather than pining for the delights of Egypt.

11:16-30 When Jethro proposed a judicial hierarchy (Exod 18:13-26), he was concerned with practical matters, as were the tribal leaders who helped Moses with the registration (1:5-15). By contrast, this group of ***seventy . . . elders*** would provide Israel with spiritual guidance. They needed a share of God's ***Spirit*** that already rested upon Moses and made him the Lord's special spokesman. Their capacity as leaders depended on the presence of God's Spirit (cp. 1 Sam 10:6; 19:20; Joel 2:28; Acts 2:16-18; 1 Cor 12:10; 2 Pet 1:20-21).

11:16 ***the Tabernacle:*** Literally *the Tent of Meeting*. See note on Exod 27:21.

11:24 ***the Tabernacle:*** Literally *the tent;* also in 11:26.

11:25 We are not told what happened when ***the Spirit rested upon them*** and ***they prophesied.*** Whatever happened (possibly ecstatic utterances; cp. Acts 2:4; 1 Cor 14:2), it was a unique occurrence.

11:28-29 ***Joshua son of Nun:*** See "Joshua" at Josh 1:1-18, p. 377. • Joshua's zealous protest was prompted by his jealousy in a worthy but immature desire to safeguard his master's status. Moses was humble (12:3) and was not threatened by Eldad and Medad's prophecy. Instead, he was magnanimous about sharing the spotlight and happy to learn that God was working through others in such special ways. Moses had leadership qualities that the younger Joshua had not yet acquired (cp. Mark 9:38-40).

11:31
Exod 16:13
Ps 78:26-33; 105:40
11:33
Num 11:10
11:34
Deut 9:22
11:35
Num 33:17
12:1
Exod 2:21; 15:20
12:2
Num 16:3

The Lord Sends Quail and a Plague
31Now the Lord sent a wind that brought quail from the sea and let them fall all around the camp. For miles in every direction there were quail flying about three feet above the ground.
32So the people went out and caught quail all that day and throughout the night and all the next day, too. No one gathered less than fifty bushels! They spread the quail all around the camp to dry.
33But while they were gorging themselves on the meat—while it was still in their mouths—the anger of the Lord blazed against the people, and he struck them with a severe plague.
34So that place was called Kibroth-hattaavah (which means "graves of gluttony") because there they buried the people who had craved meat from Egypt.
35From Kibroth-hattaavah the Israelites traveled to Hazeroth, where they stayed for some time.

The Complaints of Miriam and Aaron
12 While they were at Hazeroth, Miriam and Aaron criticized Moses because he had married a Cushite woman.
2They said, "Has the Lord spoken only through Moses? Hasn't he spoken through us, too?"

Spirit Empowerment (11:16-17, 24-30)

Num 24:1-9; 27:18-23
Deut 34:10-12
Judg 3:9-10; 6:34; 11:29; 14:5-6, 19; 15:14
1 Sam 16:13
Isa 61:1
Ezek 11:5
Joel 2:28-29
Zech 4:6
Matt 12:18
Luke 4:1, 14, 18
John 3:34
Acts 1:8; 2:4, 16-18; 4:31; 10:38; 19:6; 20:28
1 Cor 12:1-31
Gal 3:2-5

The account of Moses, the seventy elders, and the Spirit of the Lord (11:16-30) reminds us that God has moved and worked among his people in special ways throughout the ages. When Moses reached the end of his patience and his ability to manage rebellious Israel (11:1-15), God told him to select seventy men to help him (11:16-17; cp. Exod 18:14-26). Then the Lord redistributed the Spirit that Moses already possessed and empowered these men for service (11:24-25).

The presence, indwelling, and special awareness of God's Spirit have made a great difference in the lives of God's people. God empowers those who are committed to his service in special ways when the need arises (see Ps 23:1-6; 46:1; 94:16-19; 116:1-9; 121:1-8; 143:10-12), and the Spirit moves as circumstances require to provide spiritual renewal and strength to God's people.

Joshua was empowered by the Lord's Spirit (27:18; cp. Deut 34:9), though not to the same degree as Moses (Deut 34:10-12; cp. Num 12:6-8). In the period of the Judges, the Spirit of the Lord came to the aid of Israel's leaders as, for example, in the work of Othniel (Judg 3:10), Gideon (Judg 6:34), Jephthah (Judg 11:29), and Samson (Judg 13:25; 14:6, 19; 15:14). David had access to the strength of God's presence, and his awareness of God's actions—in history and in his own experience—made him a great leader (e.g., 1 Sam 16:13; 17:45; 18:12, 28). The prophets knew that their special ministry was possible because of the Spirit's presence and power (e.g., Isa 61:1; Ezek 11:5; Zech 4:6).

Jesus was filled with God's Spirit and empowered for a unique ministry (see Matt 12:18; Luke 4:1, 14, 18; Acts 10:38), and he spoke about the Spirit's special role in the church (John 3:34; Acts 1:8). The arrival of the Spirit enabled the assembled believers to speak powerfully on the Day of Pentecost (Acts 2:4-5, 16-18; cp. Joel 2:28-29). The Spirit emboldened and empowered the church after Pentecost (Acts 4:31; 19:6; 20:28; 1 Cor 12:1-31; Gal 3:2-5) and remains with God's people today.

11:31-35 God responded to the people's complaints by sending a storm of quail and a plague. God had provided ***quail*** along with manna in Exod 16:13, but here they expressed God's judgment in their sickeningly overabundant supply.

11:31 ***there were quail flying about three feet above the ground:*** Or *there were quail about 3 feet* [2 cubits or 92 centimeters] *deep on the ground.*

11:32 ***fifty bushels:*** Hebrew *10 homers* [1.8 kiloliters].

11:34-35 The precise locations of ***Kibroth-hattaavah*** and ***Hazeroth*** are unknown.

12:1-16 Rebellion was not restricted to the "foreign rabble" or to the Israelites who were bored with manna (11:4). Moses' own brother and sister, Aaron the high priest (Exod 29:30) and Miriam the prophet (Exod 15:20), rebelled against him. Israel was near the nadir of its rebellion against God (13:25–14:12).

12:1-2 ***Miriam and Aaron*** might have perceived Moses' marriage as a threat to their status and ambitions. Miriam is named first, which suggests that she instigated this family feud and could explain why God punished her and not Aaron (12:9-10).

12:1 Most interpreters understand the ***Cushite woman*** to be Moses' wife Zipporah from Midian (Exod 2:16-22), understanding *Cush* as referring here to Cushan, a region and people near Midian (Hab 3:7). Other interpreters, taking *Cushite* in its usual sense as referring to Kusi (in northern Arabia), Ethiopia, or Sudan, think that she was a different wife. In either case, it is possible that Miriam and Aaron disapproved of his having married a non-Israelite or that they were jealous of her influence over Moses.

12:2 The challenge to Moses' authority was, by implication, a rejection of the Lord's choice of Moses as Israel's leader. • ***the Lord heard:*** The same phrase in 11:1 foreshadows the Lord's response.

But the LORD heard them. 3(Now Moses was
very [c]humble—more humble than any other
person on earth.)
4So immediately the LORD called to
Moses, Aaron, and Miriam and said, "Go
out to the Tabernacle, all three of you!" So
the three of them went to the Tabernacle.
5Then the LORD descended in the pillar of
cloud and stood at the entrance of the Tabernacle. "Aaron and Miriam!" he called, and
they stepped forward. 6And the LORD said
to them, "Now listen to what I say:

"If there were prophets among you,
I, the LORD, would reveal myself in
visions.
I would speak to them in dreams.
7 But not with my servant Moses.
Of all my house, he is the one I trust.
8 I speak to him face to face,
clearly, and not in riddles!
He sees the LORD as he is.
So why were you not afraid
to criticize my servant Moses?"

9The LORD was very angry with them, and
he departed. 10As the cloud moved from
above the Tabernacle, there stood Miriam,
her skin as white as snow from leprosy.
When Aaron saw what had happened to her,
11he cried out to Moses, "Oh, my master!
Please don't punish us for this sin we have so
foolishly committed. 12Don't let her be like a
stillborn baby, already decayed at birth."
13So Moses cried out to the LORD, "O God,
I beg you, please heal her!"
14But the LORD said to Moses, "If her father had done nothing more than spit in her
face, wouldn't she be defiled for seven days?
So keep her outside the camp for seven days,
and after that she may be accepted back."
15So Miriam was kept outside the camp
for seven days, and the people waited until
she was brought back before they traveled
again. 16Then they left Hazeroth and
camped in the wilderness of Paran.

Israel Camps in the Region of Kadesh (13:1–20:13)

Twelve Scouts Explore Canaan

13 The LORD now said to Moses, 2"Send
out men to explore the land of Canaan, the land I am giving to the Israelites.
Send one leader from each of the twelve ancestral tribes." 3So Moses did as the LORD
commanded him. He sent out twelve men,
all tribal leaders of Israel, from their camp
in the wilderness of Paran. 4These were the
tribes and the names of their leaders:

Tribe	*Leader*
Reuben	Shammua son of Zaccur
5 Simeon	Shaphat son of Hori
6 Judah	Caleb son of Jephunneh
7 Issachar	Igal son of Joseph
8 Ephraim	Hoshea son of Nun
9 Benjamin	Palti son of Raphu
10 Zebulun	Gaddiel son of Sodi
11 Manasseh son of Joseph	Gaddi son of Susi
12 Dan	Ammiel son of Gemalli
13 Asher	Sethur son of Michael
14 Naphtali	Nahbi son of Vophsi
15 Gad	Geuel son of Maki

16These are the names of the men Moses
sent out to explore the land. (Moses called
Hoshea son of Nun by the name Joshua.)
17Moses gave the men these instructions
as he sent them out to explore the land:
"Go north through the Negev into the hill
country. 18See what the land is like, and

12:3 Matt 11:29
[c]*anaw* (6035)
‣Ps 25:9
12:5 Num 11:25
12:6 Gen 15:1; 31:10-11; 46:2
1 Kgs 3:5
12:7 Ps 105:26
Heb 3:2, 5
12:8 Exod 33:11, 19
Deut 34:10
12:10 Deut 24:9
12:11 2 Sam 19:19
12:14 Lev 13:46
Num 5:1-3
Deut 25:9
13:2 Deut 1:22-25
Josh 1:3
13:8 Num 13:16
13:16 Num 13:8
13:17 Gen 12:9; 13:1
Num 13:21

12:3 Moses' incomparable humility contrasts his godly character (see also Prov 3:34; Matt 5:5) with Miriam and Aaron's jealousy. • This parenthetical comment, a simple statement of the truth from God's perspective, could be the words of Moses or of a later editor.

12:4-8 In response, the Lord reconfirmed Moses' special status and authority.

12:4 *the Tabernacle:* Literally *the Tent of Meeting.* See note on Exod 27:21.

12:5 *the Tabernacle:* Literally *the tent;* also in 12:10.

12:6-8 The Lord's *trust* in Moses resulted in an intimate relationship. God spoke to prophets in visions and dreams, but he spoke to Moses *face to face* (literally *mouth to mouth;* see Exod 33:8-11, 18-24; Deut 34:10).

12:9-16 *Miriam* bore the brunt of God's wrath (see note on 12:1-2). Once *Aaron saw what had happened to her,* he admitted his error and sought Moses' intercession (cp. 11:2). Both *Moses* and *the LORD* accepted Aaron's confession.

12:10 *from leprosy:* Or *with a skin disease.* The Hebrew word used here can describe various skin diseases. See note on 5:2.

12:14 Miriam was required to follow the normal procedure for achieving ritual purity after a skin disease (5:2-4; Lev 13–14).

12:16 The camp in *the wilderness of Paran* was at Kadesh-barnea (13:26; Deut 1:19-22).

13:1–14:45 Twelve spies investigated the rich land of Canaan and found it defended by formidable foes. Israel's disobedience in earlier chapters foreshadows more of the same. The Israelites lacked the obedience, courage, and faith to take the land, so the Lord destined them to spend forty years in the Sinai wilderness; that generation failed to receive their inheritance in the Promised Land.

13:1-16 Moses selected a leader from each tribe to explore the territory that God had promised to give the Hebrews. The tribes listed are those of ch 1, though the order is different. Caleb and Joshua are later shown to be men of faith (14:30).

13:17-20 The military purpose of the scouting mission is evident; the spies were also to gather information about natural resources and food, which had been on the Israelites' minds since they left Egypt (ch 11; Exod 16).

13:20 Deut 1:25
13:21 Num 20:1; 27:14; Josh 19:28; Judg 1:31; Amos 6:14
13:22 Num 13:33; Josh 11:21; 15:14; Judg 1:20
13:23 Num 13:24; 32:9; Deut 1:24-25

find out whether the people living there
are strong or weak, few or many. 19See what
kind of land they live in. Is it good or bad?
Do their towns have walls, or are they unprotected like open camps? 20Is the soil fertile
or poor? Are there many trees? Do your best
to bring back samples of the crops you see."
(It happened to be the season for harvesting
the first ripe grapes.)
21So they went up and explored the land
from the wilderness of Zin as far as Rehob,
near Lebo-hamath. 22Going north, they
passed through the Negev and arrived at
Hebron, where Ahiman, Sheshai, and Talmai—all descendants of Anak—lived. (The
ancient town of Hebron was founded seven
years before the Egyptian city of Zoan.)
23When they came to the valley of Eshcol,
they cut down a branch with a single cluster
of grapes so large that it took two of them to
carry it on a pole between them! They also
brought back samples of the pomegranates
and figs. 24That place was called the valley
of Eshcol (which means "cluster"), because
of the cluster of grapes the Israelite men
cut there.

The Servant-Leader (12:7-8)

Num 12:3; Gen 13:8-12; 14:11-24; 30:31-32; Exod 14:31; Deut 34:10-12; 2 Sam 15:1-6; 1 Kgs 12:1-7; Isa 52:13–53:12; Matt 18:4; 20:24-28; 23:11-12; Mark 10:35-45; John 10:11; 12:27-28; Acts 3:1-11; 4:13-22; 5:12-16; 9:32-42; Rom 8:17; 2 Cor 11:23-27; Gal 5:13; Phil 2:25-30; Col 4:7; 2 Tim 1:8; 2:3; 1 Pet 4:10-11; 5:1-5

The servant-leader is characterized by an overwhelming desire to accomplish a purpose through service. The leader's heart compels this person to assume a servant role. Jesus of Nazareth and the apostle Paul fit this definition of servant-leaders, along with Moses, Joshua, and Caleb.

The OT describes Moses as the Lord's servant (12:7-8; Exod 14:31). Moses did not seek power, prestige, or material gain, but assumed his leadership role reluctantly. He used his prophetic authority with humility (12:3), knowing that he was subject to God (Deut 34:10-12; Hos 12:13). Every event in Moses' story indicates that he understood his leadership as derived from his service to God. He was submissive, selfless, and faithful. His interactions with his fellow Israelites were characterized by empathy, persuasiveness, and vision. Moses stood in the gap at a critical moment in Israelite history and fulfilled a role comparable to that of the apostle Paul during early Christianity. Like Paul, Moses' outstanding attribute was his humble submission to God; his humility was the basis for his role as a dedicated servant who became a great leader.

Jesus of Nazareth is the ideal servant-leader. The Gospels portray Jesus as the Lord's "Suffering Servant" (see Isa 52:13–53:12), especially in his sacrificial death, which was his ultimate act of service (Mark 10:45). Jesus spoke with great authority (e.g., John 13:12-16), but humbly, understanding his role as a shepherd who sacrifices his life for his sheep (John 10:11). He spent time with children and used them as models for those who desire to follow God wholeheartedly (Matt 18:4). When James and John asked him to give them an elevated rank in his Kingdom, Jesus criticized their worldly ambition (Mark 10:35-45). He set their priorities straight by instructing them to follow his example (Matt 20:24-28; 23:11-12; Mark 10:43-45). As a model for all who want to lead others through a life of service, Jesus understood that his purpose was to bring glory to God's name (John 12:27-28).

The apostles Paul and Peter followed Christ's example and fulfilled his ideal of servant-leadership. Paul's life of service demonstrates humility and tireless efforts on behalf of others (see 2 Cor 11:23-27). He taught Christians to do the same (Rom 8:17; Gal 5:13; 2 Tim 1:8; 2:3) and praised those who did so (e.g., Phil 2:25-30; Col 4:7). Peter also exemplified self-sacrificing service to Christ (e.g., Acts 3:1-11; 4:13-22; 5:12-16; 9:32-42); his instructions define the character of a servant-leader clearly and concisely (see 1 Pet 4:10-11; 5:1-5).

13:20 ***The season for harvesting the first ripe grapes*** came in late July or August.

13:21-24 The spies explored the land, which was unusually fertile in contrast with the Sinai wilderness.

13:21 It was about 275 miles ***from the wilderness of Zin,*** located roughly between the wilderness of Paran and the southern frontier of Canaan (see 34:3-5; Josh 15:1-4), to ***Lebo-hamath*** ("entrance of Hamath," either a notable mountain pass or another city near Hamath) in Syria. • The exact location of ***Rehob*** is uncertain, but it was probably the same as OT Beth-rehob, situated near a major route to Hamath. The text thus already identifies the approximate borders of the Promised Land (see 1 Kgs 8:65). The phrase "from Dan to Beersheba" (Judg 20:1; 2 Sam 3:10), frequently used to demarcate Israel's traditional boundaries, referred to a considerably smaller area than the territory visited by Israel's spies.

13:22 Israel's spies made their way into Canaan's hill country via the ***Negev,*** the dry southland next to the wilderness of Zin. In the southern part of Canaan's central hill country, they came to ***Hebron,*** where Israel's ancestors had lived (Gen 13:18; 23:19; 35:27; 37:14). • The ***descendants of Anak*** were famous for their size and strength (e.g., Deut 9:2). • ***Zoan*** (later called Tanis by the Greeks) was a famous city in Egypt's eastern delta (see also Ps 78:12, 43; Isa 19:11-13; 30:3-5).

The Scouting Report
25After exploring the land for forty days,
the men returned 26to Moses, Aaron, and
the whole community of Israel at Kadesh
in the wilderness of Paran. They reported
to the whole community what they had
seen and showed them the fruit they had
taken from the land. 27This was their report to Moses: "We entered the [d]land you
sent us to explore, and it is indeed a bountiful country—a land flowing with milk and
honey. Here is the kind of fruit it produces.
28But the people living there are powerful,
and their towns are large and fortified. We
even saw giants there, the descendants of
Anak! 29The Amalekites live in the Negev,
and the Hittites, Jebusites, and Amorites
live in the hill country. The Canaanites live
along the coast of the Mediterranean Sea
and along the Jordan Valley."
30But Caleb tried to quiet the people as
they stood before Moses. "Let's go at once
to take the land," he said. "We can certainly
conquer it!"
31But the other men who had explored
the land with him disagreed. "We can't go
up against them! They are stronger than we
are!" 32So they spread this bad report about
the land among the Israelites: "The land we
traveled through and explored will devour
anyone who goes to live there. All the people we saw were huge. 33We even saw giants
there, the descendants of Anak. Next to
them we felt like grasshoppers, and that's
what they thought, too!"

The People Rebel
14 Then the whole community began
weeping aloud, and they cried all
night. 2Their voices rose in a great chorus of
protest against Moses and Aaron. "If only we
had died in Egypt, or even here in the wilderness!" they complained. 3"Why is the LORD
taking us to this country only to have us die
in battle? Our wives and our little ones will
be carried off as plunder! Wouldn't it be better for us to return to Egypt?" 4Then they
plotted among themselves, "Let's choose a
new leader and go back to Egypt!"
5Then Moses and Aaron fell face down on
the ground before the whole community of
Israel. 6Two of the men who had explored
the land, Joshua son of Nun and Caleb son of
Jephunneh, tore their clothing. 7They said
to all the people of Israel, "The land we traveled through and explored is a wonderful
land! 8And if the LORD is pleased with us, he
will bring us safely into that land and give
it to us. It is a rich land flowing with milk
and honey. 9Do not rebel against the LORD,
and don't be afraid of the people of the land.
They are only helpless prey to us! They have
no protection, but the LORD is with us! Don't
be afraid of them!"
10But the whole community began to talk
about stoning Joshua and Caleb. Then the

13:26 Num 12:16; 13:3; 20:1; 32:8
13:27 Exod 13:5; Deut 1:25; [d]*'erets* (0776) ‣Deut 4:39
13:28 Num 13:22-23
13:29 Num 14:43
13:30 Num 14:6, 24
13:31 Deut 1:28
13:32 Num 14:36
13:33 Deut 1:28
14:2 Exod 15:24; 16:3; Num 11:1; 16:13; 20:4; 21:5
14:3 Exod 5:21; 16:3; Num 14:31; Deut 1:39
14:5 Num 16:22, 45
14:7 Num 13:27; Deut 1:25
14:8 Exod 3:8; Num 13:27
14:9 Deut 1:21, 29; 7:18; 9:7, 23-24
14:10 Exod 16:7, 10; 17:4; 24:16-17; 32:9-13; Lev 9:23

13:25-29 The spies agreed that the land was good, but most doubted that Israel could conquer it. The strong, well-fed Canaanites had built fortified towns to protect themselves.

13:26 ***Kadesh*** is often identified with 'Ain el-Qudeirat, a spring at the northern border of Sinai and the southern edge of Canaan. There is no evidence of a Hebrew camp at this site during the period of the Exodus or the wilderness wanderings, so some scholars have suggested that ancient Kadesh was located elsewhere.

13:27 The Promised Land is often described as ***a land flowing with milk and honey.*** Milk and dairy products constituted a major part of the diet in biblical times, and "milk" is used in figurative language for abundance (see Deut 32:14; Isa 55:1; Joel 3:18). Honey provided sweetness (see Ps 19:10; 119:103; Ezek 3:3; Rev 10:9-10). The phrase thus refers to a highly desirable destination, a land with an abundance of food and resources (cp. 16:13-14; see also Exod 3:8; Deut 6:3; 26:15; Jer 11:4-5; Ezek 20:6). The NT emphasizes the spiritual nature of God's promises, pointing to a promised inheritance in heaven (see Rom 9:6-8; Gal 6:14-16; Rev 21:1-2).

13:29 The spies answer the question of 13:18. Many ethnic groups occupied ancient Canaan. • ***the Mediterranean Sea:*** Literally *the sea.*

13:30 ***Caleb*** and Joshua (see 14:6, 10, 30) were more optimistic in their assessment of the land than the other spies were (cp. 14:31-33).

13:33 ***giants:*** Hebrew *nephilim;* see note on Gen 6:4.

14:1-45 The testimony of the faithful spies Joshua and Caleb was rejected, and rebellion spread through the entire community. Only Moses' intervention saved Israel from complete destruction. Those who failed to obey God died during a forty-year wilderness sojourn.

14:3-4 The threats about which they complained were real, but the Israelites should have trusted the Lord. In the ancient Near East, women and children were often taken as ***plunder*** in the aftermath of battle. • ***return to Egypt:*** How quickly the Israelites forgot their bondage (Exod 2:23-24) and the hardship of the wilderness (11:1)!

14:5 ***Moses and Aaron*** prostrated themselves out of humility, fear, grief, and anguish.

14:6 ***Joshua*** and ***Caleb*** joined in the effort to reverse the rebellion and avert God's wrath; they ***tore their clothing*** in a gesture of grief.

14:7-9 Joshua and Caleb understood that Israel's lack of courage and their criticism of Moses and Aaron were rebellion against the Lord, and they knew what results this would produce. • ***the LORD is with us:*** This was the source of their confidence (cp. Rom 8:31).

14:10 ***Joshua and Caleb,*** with their encouragement and expression of trust in God, brought even more opposition; the protests against the leaders were converted into threats of violence against the faithful spies. All of the Israelites' objections came to a sudden stop when the Lord's ***glorious presence*** (Hebrew *kabod;* see Exod 24:15-18; Ezek 1) appeared ***at the Tabernacle,*** the site of divine communication. • ***the Tabernacle:*** Literally *the Tent of Meeting.* See note on Exod 27:21.

[e]*kabod* (3519)
‣1 Sam 4:21

14:11
[f]*'aman* (0539)
‣Ps 106:12

14:12
Exod 32:10
Lev 26:25
Deut 28:21

14:13
Exod 9:28; 32:12

14:14
Exod 13:21; 33:11
Deut 5:4

14:16
Exod 32:12
Deut 9:28
Josh 7:7

14:18
[g]*'arek 'appayim* (0750, 0639)
‣Neh 9:17

14:19
Exod 34:9
Ps 106:45

14:20
Ps 106:23
Mic 7:18-20

14:23
Num 26:65; 32:11

14:24
Num 32:12
Josh 14:6-15

14:25
Num 13:29

14:28
Num 14:2, 21

14:29
Num 1:17-19; 26:2
Heb 3:17

14:30
Num 14:24, 38

14:31
Num 14:3

14:32
Num 26:64-65; 32:13
1 Cor 10:5

14:33
Deut 2:7; 8:2

[e]glorious presence of the LORD appeared
to all the Israelites at the Tabernacle. [11]And
the LORD said to Moses, "How long will
these people treat me with contempt? Will
they never [f]believe me, even after all the miraculous signs I have done among them? [12]I
will disown them and destroy them with a
plague. Then I will make you into a nation
greater and mightier than they are!"

Moses Intercedes for the People

[13]But Moses objected. "What will the Egyptians think when they hear about it?" he
asked the LORD. "They know full well the
power you displayed in rescuing your people from Egypt. [14]Now if you destroy them,
the Egyptians will send a report to the inhabitants of this land, who have already
heard that you live among your people.
They know, LORD, that you have appeared to
your people face to face and that your pillar
of cloud hovers over them. They know that
you go before them in the pillar of cloud by
day and the pillar of fire by night. [15]Now if
you slaughter all these people with a single
blow, the nations that have heard of your
fame will say, [16]'The LORD was not able to
bring them into the land he swore to give
them, so he killed them in the wilderness.'

[17]"Please, Lord, prove that your power is
as great as you have claimed. For you said,
[18]'The LORD is [g]slow to anger and filled
with unfailing love, forgiving every kind of
sin and rebellion. But he does not excuse
the guilty. He lays the sins of the parents
upon their children; the entire family is
affected—even children in the third and
fourth generations.' [19]In keeping with your
magnificent, unfailing love, please pardon
the sins of this people, just as you have forgiven them ever since they left Egypt."

[20]Then the LORD said, "I will pardon them
as you have requested. [21]But as surely as I
live, and as surely as the earth is filled with
the LORD's glory, [22]not one of these people
will ever enter that land. They have all seen
my glorious presence and the miraculous
signs I performed both in Egypt and in the
wilderness, but again and again they have
tested me by refusing to listen to my voice.
[23]They will never even see the land I swore
to give their ancestors. None of those who
have treated me with contempt will ever see
it. [24]But my servant Caleb has a different
attitude than the others have. He has remained loyal to me, so I will bring him into
the land he explored. His descendants will
possess their full share of that land. [25]Now
turn around, and don't go on toward the
land where the Amalekites and Canaanites
live. Tomorrow you must set out for the wilderness in the direction of the Red Sea."

The LORD Punishes the Israelites

[26]Then the LORD said to Moses and Aaron,
[27]"How long must I put up with this wicked
community and its complaints about me?
Yes, I have heard the complaints the Israelites are making against me. [28]Now tell them
this: 'As surely as I live, declares the LORD,
I will do to you the very things I heard you
say. [29]You will all drop dead in this wilderness! Because you complained against me,
every one of you who is twenty years old or
older and was included in the registration
will die. [30]You will not enter and occupy the
land I swore to give you. The only exceptions will be Caleb son of Jephunneh and
Joshua son of Nun.

[31]" 'You said your children would be carried off as plunder. Well, I will bring them
safely into the land, and they will enjoy what
you have despised. [32]But as for you, you will
drop dead in this wilderness. [33]And your
children will be like shepherds, wandering
in the wilderness for forty years. In this way,

14:11 God marveled that Israel had not yet learned to trust him, even after he had miraculously rescued them from slavery and provided for their needs as they traveled in the wilderness (cp. Deut 4:32-40; Matt 11:21; Luke 10:13).

14:12 God is patient, but he will not tolerate outright rebellion from his people (cp. Exod 32:7-10). The writer of Hebrews refers to this episode in his effort to strengthen the faith of Christians whose trust in the Good News was wavering (Heb 3:7-19; 12:3, 25; cp. Ps 95:8-11).

14:13-25 Moses interceded on behalf of his people, reminding God that his reputation was bound up with that of Israel and appealing to his faithfulness.

14:17-18 Moses had used this same argument earlier when he sought pardon for Israel's rebellion (Exod 32:10-14). Moses knew that God would not let the Israelites off without punishment (Deut 7:9-10).

14:19 Israel's history since leaving Egypt had been a series of transgressions forgiven by the Lord (Exod 15:22-27; 17:1-7; 32:1-14; Lev 10:1-20; Num 11:1–12:16).

14:20-25 As a result of Moses' argument, the Lord pardoned Israel's rebellion and did not obliterate them, but the obstinate adult generation would never see the Promised Land.

14:22 The people's lack of obedience and faith was a refusal to listen to God's voice, since they were eyewitnesses of the Lord's ***glorious presence*** (see note on 14:10) and ***miraculous signs*** (Exod 4:29-31; 7:1–11:10; 14:15-31; 16:1–17:13).

14:23-25 Having turned their backs on the Promised Land, the Israelites were now ordered to march the other way.
• ***The Red Sea*** (literally *sea of reeds*) could refer to bodies of water on either side of the Sinai Peninsula (the Gulf of Aqaba or the Gulf of Suez).

14:27 ***I have heard:*** See 11:1; 12:2.

14:28 Israel's disobedience brought on the consequences they feared would come from obeying.

14:29 ***registration:*** See 1:3; note on 1:2-16.

they will pay for your faithlessness, until the
last of you lies dead in the wilderness.
34" 'Because your men explored the land
for forty days, you must wander in the wilderness for forty years—a year for each day,
suffering the consequences of your sins.
Then you will discover what it is like to have
me for an enemy.' 35I, the LORD, have spoken!
I will certainly do these things to every member of the community who has conspired
against me. They will be destroyed here in
this wilderness, and here they will die!"
36The ten men Moses had sent to explore
the land—the ones who incited rebellion
against the LORD with their bad report—
37were struck dead with a plague before the
LORD. 38Of the twelve who had explored the
land, only Joshua and Caleb remained alive.

Israelite Defeat at Hormah

39When Moses reported the LORD's words
to all the Israelites, the people were filled
with grief. 40Then they got up early the next
morning and went to the top of the range of
hills. "Let's go," they said. "We realize that
we have sinned, but now we are ready to enter the land the LORD has promised us."
41But Moses said, "Why are you now disobeying the LORD's orders to return to the
wilderness? It won't work. 42Do not go up
into the land now. You will only be crushed
by your enemies because the LORD is not
with you. 43When you face the Amalekites
and Canaanites in battle, you will be slaughtered. The LORD will abandon you because
you have abandoned the LORD."
44But the people defiantly pushed ahead
toward the hill country, even though neither
Moses nor the Ark of the LORD's Covenant
left the camp. 45Then the Amalekites and
the Canaanites who lived in those hills came
down and attacked them and chased them
back as far as Hormah.

Laws concerning Offerings

15 Then the LORD told Moses, 2"Give the
following instructions to the people
of Israel.
"When you finally settle in the land I am
giving you, 3you will offer special gifts as
a pleasing aroma to the LORD. These gifts
may take the form of a burnt offering, a sacrifice to fulfill a vow, a voluntary offering, or
an offering at any of your annual festivals,
and they may be taken from your herds of
cattle or your flocks of sheep and goats.
4When you present these offerings, you
must also give the LORD a grain offering of
two quarts of choice flour mixed with one
quart of olive oil. 5For each lamb offered as
a burnt offering or a special sacrifice, you
must also present one quart of wine as a liquid offering.
6"If the sacrifice is a ram, give a grain offering of four quarts of choice flour mixed
with a third of a gallon of olive oil, 7and give
a third of a gallon of wine as a liquid offering. This will be a pleasing aroma to the
LORD.
8"When you present a young bull as a
burnt offering or as a [h]sacrifice to fulfill a
vow or as a peace offering to the LORD, 9you
must also give a grain offering of six quarts
of choice flour mixed with two quarts of
olive oil, 10and give two quarts of wine as a
liquid offering. This will be a special gift, a
pleasing aroma to the LORD.
11"Each sacrifice of a bull, ram, lamb, or
young goat should be prepared in this way.
12Follow these instructions with each offering you present. 13All of you native-born

14:36 Num 13:4-16
14:39 Exod 33:4
14:40 Deut 1:41-44
14:44 Num 10:33; 31:6
14:45 Num 21:3; Judg 1:17
15:3 Lev 1:2; 2:1-16; 22:21; 23:37-38; 27:2
15:5 Num 28:7
15:8 Lev 3:1; 7:11-18; [h]*zebakh* (2077) › Deut 15:21
15:10 Num 28:14

14:34 *each day:* Cp. 13:25. • *to have me for an enemy:* Cp. Ezek 5:8; 21:3.

14:39-45 The threat of divine punishment for their sins brought grief to the people of Israel, but their hearts were still rebellious and they again disobeyed the Lord's command (14:25). The promise of God's presence had been the basis for Caleb and Joshua's initial confidence (14:9), but God would not fight alongside the Israelites until all the rebels had died.

14:43 ***The LORD will abandon you because you have abandoned the LORD:*** Moses' prediction summarizes the whole chapter.

14:44 ***The Ark*** symbolized God's presence and blessings (cp. 1 Sam 4:1-11).

14:45 ***Hormah*** means "destruction" in Hebrew (see 21:1-3).

15:1-41 Chapters 1–14 took place in a relatively short period of time, but ch 15 describes the beginning of a long period—the bulk of the forty years in the wilderness—about which relatively little is known, though there are references to events that took place during the wilderness wanderings (e.g., Deut 8:2-6; 29:5-6; Josh 5:4-8; Ezek 20:10-26; Amos 5:25-26; Acts 7:42-43). During this period, Moses continued to deliver legislation to govern Israelite society, especially for that day when survivors of the wilderness would finally enter the Promised Land. This chapter deals with three categories of legal matters. Presented in the middle of stories about a stubborn and disobedient Israel, ch 15 raises hope that the Promised Land still awaited Israel's descendants.

15:1-3 The implication of these *instructions* is that the Israelites would someday settle in the Promised Land (14:31; 15:18).

15:3 ***special gifts . . . a pleasing aroma to the LORD:*** God is pleased by the honor and thanksgiving that sacrifices and offerings show him.

15:4 *two quarts:* Hebrew *1⁄10 of an ephah* [2.2 liters]. • *one quart:* Hebrew *¼ of a hin* [1 liter]; also in 15:5.

15:6 *four quarts:* Hebrew *2⁄10 of an ephah* [4.4 liters]. • *a third of a gallon:* Hebrew *⅓ of a hin* [1.3 liters]; also in 15:7.

15:9 *six quarts:* Hebrew *3⁄10 of an ephah* [6.6 liters]. • *two quarts:* Hebrew *½ of a hin* [2 liters]; also in 15:10.

15:12-16 All inhabitants of the land, Israelite and foreign-born, were to be

15:15 Num 9:14; 15:29
15:19 Josh 5:11-12
15:22 Lev 4:2
15:25 Lev 4:20
[i]*kapar* (3722) ‣Num 15:28
15:28 [i]*kapar* (3722) ‣Num 35:33
15:29 Num 15:15
15:30 Num 14:40-44; Deut 1:43; 17:13
15:32 Exod 31:14-15; 35:2-3
[k]*shabbath* (7676) ‣Deut 5:12
15:35 Lev 24:14, 23; Deut 21:21

Israelites must follow these instructions when you offer a special gift as a pleasing aroma to the LORD. 14 And if any foreigners visit you or live among you and want to present a special gift as a pleasing aroma to the LORD, they must follow these same procedures. 15 Native-born Israelites and foreigners are equal before the LORD and are subject to the same decrees. This is a permanent law for you, to be observed from generation to generation. 16 The same instructions and regulations will apply both to you and to the foreigners living among you."

17 Then the LORD said to Moses, 18 "Give the following instructions to the people of Israel.

"When you arrive in the land where I am taking you, 19 and you eat the crops that grow there, you must set some aside as a sacred offering to the LORD. 20 Present a cake from the first of the flour you grind, and set it aside as a sacred offering, as you do with the first grain from the threshing floor. 21 Throughout the generations to come, you are to present a sacred offering to the LORD each year from the first of your ground flour.

22 "But suppose you unintentionally fail to carry out all these commands that the LORD has given you through Moses. 23 And suppose your descendants in the future fail to do everything the LORD has commanded through Moses. 24 If the mistake was made unintentionally, and the community was unaware of it, the whole community must present a young bull for a burnt offering as a pleasing aroma to the LORD. It must be offered along with its prescribed grain offering and liquid offering and with one male goat for a sin offering. 25 With it the priest will [i]purify the whole community of Israel, making them right with the LORD, and they will be forgiven. For it was an unintentional sin, and they have corrected it with their offerings to the LORD—the special gift and the sin offering. 26 The whole community of Israel will be forgiven, including the foreigners living among you, for all the people were involved in the sin.

27 "If one individual commits an unintentional sin, the guilty person must bring a one-year-old female goat for a sin offering. 28 The priest will sacrifice it to [i]purify the guilty person before the LORD, and that person will be forgiven. 29 These same instructions apply both to native-born Israelites and to the foreigners living among you.

30 "But those who brazenly violate the LORD's will, whether native-born Israelites or foreigners, have blasphemed the LORD, and they must be cut off from the community. 31 Since they have treated the LORD's word with contempt and deliberately disobeyed his command, they must be completely cut off and suffer the punishment for their guilt."

Penalty for Breaking the Sabbath

32 One day while the people of Israel were in the wilderness, they discovered a man gathering wood on the [k]Sabbath day. 33 The people who found him doing this took him before Moses, Aaron, and the rest of the community. 34 They held him in custody because they did not know what to do with him. 35 Then the LORD said to Moses, "The

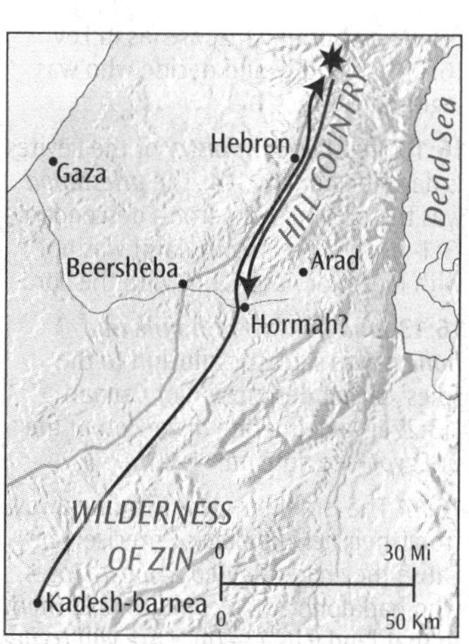

◂ **Defeat in the Hill Country of Canaan** (14:39-45). The approximate route of Israel's ill-fated attempt to conquer the HILL COUNTRY of Canaan. The location of HORMAH is not certain (see notes on 21:1-3).

equal before the LORD in all matters (see also Lev 24:22).

15:17-21 These gifts, signs of gratitude to God for agricultural bounty, were expected to begin after the Hebrews reached the Promised Land and had begun planting crops.

15:22-29 Unintentional sins were treated differently than intentional sins (15:30-31), and the actions of the community were distinguished from those of an individual (see also Lev 4–5).

15:25 ***will purify the whole community of Israel, making them right with the LORD:*** Or *will make atonement for the whole community of Israel.* See note on Lev 1:4.

15:28 ***to purify:*** Or *to make atonement for.*

15:30-31 While atonement could be made for unwitting or inadvertent sins (15:22-29), anyone who ***brazenly*** (literally *with a high hand;* cp. Exod 14:8) violated ***the LORD's will*** was guilty of blasphemy and suffered the consequences (cp. Lev 24:10-16; see also Deut 17:2-6; Heb 10:26-31). • ***cut off from the community:*** See notes on Exod 31:14; Lev 7:20-21.

15:32-36 This case illustrates 15:30-31. ***The Sabbath*** was the Lord's holy day, which was not to be disregarded (Exod 20:8-11; 31:14-15; 35:1-3).

15:34 Though there was no question about the man's guilt, it is possible that the community was uncertain how to punish him. The death sentence was an appropriate penalty, because disregard of the Sabbath signaled a rejection of God's gracious covenant with Israel (Exod 31:12-17) and was akin to blasphemy (15:30; Lev 24:10-16; cp. 1 Tim 1:20).

man must be put to death! The whole community must stone him outside the camp."
36So the whole community took the man
outside the camp and stoned him to death,
just as the LORD had commanded Moses.

Tassels on Clothing

37Then the LORD said to Moses, 38"Give
the following instructions to the people of
Israel: Throughout the generations to come
you must make tassels for the hems of your
clothing and attach them with a blue cord.
39When you see the tassels, you will [a]remem-
ber and obey all the commands of the LORD
instead of following your own desires and
defiling yourselves, as you are prone to do.
40The tassels will help you remember that
you must obey all my commands and be
holy to your God. 41I am the LORD your God
who brought you out of the land of Egypt
that I might be your God. I am the LORD
your God!"

Korah's Rebellion

16 One day Korah son of Izhar, a descendant of Kohath son of Levi, conspired
with Dathan and Abiram, the sons of Eliab,
and On son of Peleth, from the tribe of
Reuben. 2They incited a rebellion against
Moses, along with 250 other leaders of the
community, all prominent members of the
assembly. 3They united against Moses and
Aaron and said, "You have gone too far!
The whole community of Israel has been
set apart by the LORD, and he is with all of
us. What right do you have to act as though
you are greater than the rest of the LORD's
people?"

4When Moses heard what they were saying, he fell face down on the ground. 5Then
he said to Korah and his followers, "Tomorrow morning the LORD will show us who
belongs to him and who is holy. The LORD
will allow only those whom he selects to
enter his own presence. 6Korah, you and all
your followers must prepare your incense
burners. 7Light fires in them tomorrow, and
burn incense before the LORD. Then we will
see whom the LORD chooses as his holy one.
You Levites are the ones who have gone too
far!"

8Then Moses spoke again to Korah: "Now
listen, you Levites! 9Does it seem insignificant to you that the God of Israel has chosen
you from among all the community of Israel
to be near him so you can serve in the LORD's
Tabernacle and stand before the people to
minister to them? 10Korah, he has already
given this special ministry to you and your
fellow Levites. Are you now demanding the
priesthood as well? 11The LORD is the one
you and your followers are really revolting
against! For who is Aaron that you are complaining about him?"

12Then Moses summoned Dathan and
Abiram, the sons of Eliab, but they replied,
"We refuse to come before you! 13Isn't it
enough that you brought us out of Egypt, a
land flowing with milk and honey, to kill us
here in this wilderness, and that you now
treat us like your subjects? 14What's more,
you haven't brought us into another land
flowing with milk and honey. You haven't
given us a new homeland with fields and
vineyards. Are you trying to fool these men?
We will not come."

15:38 Lev 3:17; Num 10:8; Deut 22:12; Matt 23:5

15:39 Deut 4:23; 6:12; 8:11, 14; [a]*zakar* (2142) ‣ Deut 5:15

15:40 Lev 11:44; Rom 12:1; Col 1:22; 1 Pet 1:15-16

15:41 Exod 20:2

16:1 Exod 6:21; Num 26:9; Deut 11:6; Jude 1:11

16:2 Num 1:16

16:3 Exod 19:6; Num 16:7; 35:34

16:4 Num 14:5

16:5 Lev 10:3; Num 17:5, 8; Ps 65:4

16:7 Num 16:3

16:10 Num 3:6-10

16:11 Exod 16:7; 1 Cor 10:10

16:13 Num 11:5; 14:2-3; 20:3-4

16:14 Exod 22:5; Num 20:5

15:37-41 Had the Hebrews remembered their special relationship with the Lord, they might have avoided the problems reported in Numbers. ***The tassels*** reminded Israel of their special relationship with a holy God and his demands. He had redeemed his people from Egypt, and in keeping with his call to covenant relationship with himself he expected them to observe the law (cp. Deut 6:6-9; Matt 9:20; 14:36; 23:5). • The color ***blue*** signified royalty and reflected God's holiness.

16:1–17:13 Another rebellion called for a clear delineation of the duties of priests and Levites. This power struggle was a more serious challenge than any of the previous rebellions against God's authority (11:1-35; 12:1-15; 14:1-45). As in all of these historical episodes, the coconspirators protested relatively minor issues and questioned the actions of their leaders, but Moses reminded them that they were really rebelling against God. Once again, the Israelites suffered the deadly consequences of their rebellion.

16:3 The rebels were "jealous of Moses and envious of Aaron" (Ps 106:16). The rebels insisted that ***Moses and Aaron*** had ***gone too far*** because all Israelites were God's chosen people (Exod 19:6). Their egalitarian protest against Moses and Aaron's authority was probably intended to replace that authority with their own.

16:4-7 ***Moses . . . fell face down on the ground*** in intercession (cp. 14:5; 16:22), then challenged ***Korah and his followers*** to a test.

16:5 ***Tomorrow morning the LORD will show us who belongs to him:*** Greek version reads *God has visited and knows those who are his.* Cp. 2 Tim 2:19.

16:6 ***prepare your incense burners:*** Korah and his company were to act like priests by burning incense (as in Lev 16:11-13); God would decide who was legitimate.

16:10 The ***special ministry*** of the Levites is described in chs 3–4. The ***priesthood*** was the province of Aaron's descendants (3:1-4). The rebels' complaint was not with Moses or Aaron, but with the Lord.

16:13 ***land flowing with milk and honey:*** This sarcastic allusion to the spies' earlier description of Canaan (13:27) is a deliberate distortion of life in ***Egypt*** (see note on 11:4-15).

16:14 The Israelites were heading away from their ***new homeland*** precisely because they had rebelled against Moses, who had done all he could to take them to that land (chs 13–14). • ***Are you trying to fool these men?*** Literally *Are you trying to put out the eyes of these men?* They were accusing Moses and Aaron of trying to mislead the Israelites (to "pull the wool over their eyes").

16:15
Gen 4:5
1 Sam 12:3
16:19
Lev 9:6
Num 14:10; 16:42; 20:6
16:21
Exod 32:10
16:22
Gen 18:23-32
16:24
Num 16:45
16:26
Gen 19:12-17
16:28
Exod 3:12; 4:1-9; 7:9
16:30
[b]*she'ol* (7585)
‣1 Sam 2:6
16:32
Num 16:30; 26:10
16:35
Lev 10:2
Num 11:1-3; 26:10

15 Then Moses became very angry and
said to the LORD, "Do not accept their grain
offerings! I have not taken so much as a
donkey from them, and I have never hurt a
single one of them." 16 And Moses said to Korah, "You and all your followers must come
here tomorrow and present yourselves
before the LORD. Aaron will also be here.
17 You and each of your 250 followers must
prepare an incense burner and put incense
on it, so you can all present them before
the LORD. Aaron will also bring his incense
burner."

18 So each of these men prepared an
incense burner, lit the fire, and placed
incense on it. Then they all stood at the entrance of the Tabernacle with Moses and
Aaron. 19 Meanwhile, Korah had stirred up
the entire community against Moses and
Aaron, and they all gathered at the Tabernacle entrance. Then the glorious presence of
the LORD appeared to the whole community,
20 and the LORD said to Moses and Aaron,
21 "Get away from all these people so that I
may instantly destroy them!"

22 But Moses and Aaron fell face down on
the ground. "O God," they pleaded, "you are
the God who gives breath to all creatures.
Must you be angry with all the people when
only one man sins?"

23 And the LORD said to Moses, 24 "Then
tell all the people to get away from the tents
of Korah, Dathan, and Abiram."

25 So Moses got up and rushed over to the
tents of Dathan and Abiram, followed by
the elders of Israel. 26 "Quick!" he told the
people. "Get away from the tents of these
wicked men, and don't touch anything
that belongs to them. If you do, you will be
destroyed for their sins." 27 So all the people
stood back from the tents of Korah, Dathan,
and Abiram. Then Dathan and Abiram came
out and stood at the entrances of their tents,
together with their wives and children and
little ones.

28 And Moses said, "This is how you will
know that the LORD has sent me to do all
these things that I have done—for I have not
done them on my own. 29 If these men die
a natural death, or if nothing unusual happens, then the LORD has not sent me. 30 But if
the LORD does something entirely new and
the ground opens its mouth and swallows
them and all their belongings, and they go
down alive into the [b]grave, then you will
know that these men have shown contempt
for the LORD."

31 He had hardly finished speaking the
words when the ground suddenly split
open beneath them. 32 The earth opened its
mouth and swallowed the men, along with
their households and all their followers
who were standing with them, and everything they owned. 33 So they went down
alive into the grave, along with all their belongings. The earth closed over them, and
they all vanished from among the people
of Israel. 34 All the people around them fled
when they heard their screams. "The earth
will swallow us, too!" they cried. 35 Then fire
blazed forth from the LORD and burned up
the 250 men who were offering incense.

36 And the LORD said to Moses, 37 "Tell Eleazar son of Aaron the priest to pull all the
incense burners from the fire, for they are
holy. Also tell him to scatter the burning
coals. 38 Take the incense burners of these
men who have sinned at the cost of their

16:15 *Do not accept their grain offerings!* Cp. Ps 109:7; Prov 28:9.

16:16-17 *Moses* gave final instructions concerning the test to see if the Lord would accept what the rebels brought or what Aaron offered.

16:18-22 At the height of the insurrection, the Lord intervened to save *Moses and Aaron,* and they interceded for the people.

16:18 *the Tabernacle:* Literally *the Tent of Meeting;* also in 16:19, 42, 43, 50. See note on Exod 27:21.

16:19 The *community . . . gathered at the Tabernacle entrance,* either to see the test or to overthrow Moses and Aaron. • *the glorious presence of the LORD:* See note on 14:10.

16:21-26 The Lord threatened to *destroy* the entire community because of its pervasive sin (cp. Gen 18:16-33). *Moses and Aaron* interceded to narrow the Lord's judgment down to those who were guilty of this particular rebellion.

16:26 *don't touch anything that belongs to them:* These men and their belongings were now "set apart for destruction" (see Lev 27:28-29; cp. Deut 7:26; 13:17; Josh 6:18; 7:1-26).

16:28-30 Moses had faith that God would enact his own justice, and God did so (16:31-35; cp. 1 Kgs 18:18-40). • *into the grave:* (Hebrew *into Sheol;* also in 16:33): *Sheol* was the place of the dead (see 1 Sam 2:6; 2 Sam 22:5-6; Job 3:20-22; Ps 16:10; Acts 2:27-33; 1 Cor 15:15; Rev 20:13-14).

16:31-33 Korah's sons did not die at this time (26:10-11). In fact, his descendants eventually became gatekeepers and musicians in the Temple (1 Chr 9:19, 31; 26:19; 2 Chr 20:19; cp. the titles of Pss 42, 45–49, 84–85, 87–88).

16:34-35 The *250* Israelite leaders who attempted to offer *incense* shared the fate of Nadab and Abihu (Lev 10:1-2) and of those who complained about the hardships of the wilderness (11:1; cp. 2 Kgs 1:10).

16:36-50 Verses 16:36-50 are numbered 17:1-15 in Hebrew text.

16:37 Although the men who used the *incense burners* were wicked, the vessels themselves were *holy* and had to be treated with care and respect. The *burning coals* were also holy and had to be scattered so that they would not be used for any other purpose.

16:38-40 The bronze *sheet* made by Eleazar to cover the altar replaced or supplemented the one made previously (Exod 38:2). Like the simple blue tassels of 15:37-41, it reminded *the people of Israel* of their need to obey God.

lives, and hammer the metal into a thin
sheet to overlay the altar. Since these burners were used in the LORD's presence, they
have become holy. Let them serve as a warning to the people of Israel."
39So Eleazar the priest collected the
250 bronze incense burners that had been
used by the men who died in the fire, and he
hammered them into a thin sheet to overlay
the altar. 40This would warn the Israelites
that no unauthorized person—no one who
was not a descendant of Aaron—should
ever enter the LORD's presence to burn incense. If anyone did, the same thing would
happen to him as happened to Korah and
his followers. So the LORD's instructions to
Moses were carried out.
41But the very next morning the whole
community of Israel began muttering again
against Moses and Aaron, saying, "You have
killed the LORD's people!" 42As the community gathered to protest against Moses and
Aaron, they turned toward the Tabernacle
and saw that the cloud had covered it, and
the glorious presence of the LORD appeared.
43Moses and Aaron came and stood in
front of the Tabernacle, 44and the LORD
said to Moses, 45"Get away from all these
people so that I can instantly destroy them!"
But Moses and Aaron fell face down on the
ground.
46And Moses said to Aaron, "Quick, take
an incense burner and place burning coals
on it from the altar. Lay incense on it, and
carry it out among the people to purify
them and make them right with the LORD.
The LORD's anger is blazing against them—
the plague has already begun."
47Aaron did as Moses told him and ran out
among the people. The plague had already
begun to strike down the people, but Aaron
burned the incense and purified the people.
48He stood between the dead and the living,
and the plague stopped. 49But 14,700 people died in that plague, in addition to those
who had died in the affair involving Korah.
50Then because the plague had stopped,
Aaron returned to Moses at the entrance of
the Tabernacle.

The Budding of Aaron's Staff

17 Then the LORD said to Moses, 2"Tell
the people of Israel to bring you
twelve wooden staffs, one from each leader
of Israel's ancestral tribes, and inscribe each
leader's name on his staff. 3Inscribe Aaron's
name on the staff of the tribe of Levi, for
there must be one staff for the leader of each
ancestral tribe. 4Place these staffs in the Tabernacle in front of the Ark containing the
tablets of the Covenant, where I meet with
you. 5Buds will sprout on the staff belonging
to the man I choose. Then I will finally put
an end to the people's murmuring and complaining against you."
6So Moses gave the instructions to the
people of Israel, and each of the twelve
tribal leaders, including Aaron, brought
Moses a staff. 7Moses placed the staffs in
the LORD's presence in the Tabernacle of the
Covenant. 8When he went into the Tabernacle of the Covenant the next day, he found
that Aaron's staff, representing the tribe of
Levi, had sprouted, budded, blossomed, and
produced ripe almonds!
9When Moses brought all the staffs out

16:40 Num 1:51; 3:10, 38
16:41 Num 16:3
16:42 Exod 40:34; Num 14:10; 16:19
16:45 Num 16:21, 24
16:46 Lev 10:1, 6; Num 8:19; 18:5; 25:13; Deut 9:22
16:47 Num 25:7-8, 13
16:49 Num 16:32-35; 25:9
17:4 Exod 25:22; Num 17:10
17:5 Num 16:5; 17:8
17:7 Num 18:2
17:8 Num 17:5; Heb 9:4

16:41 The Israelites still exhibited the same self-destructive, defiant behavior that had caused all their troubles. Then they blamed *Moses and Aaron* for what happened.

16:42-48 In reply, the Lord's *glorious presence* reappeared and threatened to *destroy* the people of Israel (cp. 16:19-20). Once again, *Moses and Aaron* intervened by falling *face down on the ground.*

16:46-50 Moses and Aaron acted quickly to rescue the Israelites from God's wrath. In an unusual procedure, Aaron carried *an incense burner* with burning coals among the people and thus stopped the plague.

16:46 *to purify them and make them right with the LORD:* Or *to make atonement for them.*

16:47 *and purified:* Or *and made atonement for.*

17:1-13 The Lord prescribed another trial to reinforce the lessons taught by the incidents in ch 16 and to introduce the instructions of ch 18. • Verses 17:1-13 are numbered 17:16-28 in Hebrew text.

17:1-5 The shepherd's staff was a common possession (cp. Ps 23:4) and, like the scepter, was a symbol of authority (cp. Jer 48:17). This trial was especially appropriate because the Hebrew words translated *staffs* and *tribes* are homonyms; the Lord's choice of staff would indicate his choice of tribe.

17:4 Moses placed the staffs *in the Tabernacle in front of the Ark containing the tablets of the Covenant* (literally *in the Tent of Meeting before the Testimony*): The Hebrew word for "testimony" refers to the terms of the Lord's covenant with Israel as written on stone tablets, which were kept in the Ark, and also to the covenant itself. The staffs were in the Lord's presence (17:7), a safe spot where no one would tamper with them.

17:7 *Tabernacle of the Covenant:* Or *Tabernacle of the Testimony;* also in 17:8.

17:8 *Aaron's staff . . . produced ripe almonds!* This was more than enough proof that Aaron was God's chosen leader and that the Levites held a special position. The cups on the Tabernacle's lampstand were shaped like almond blossoms (Exod 25:33-36). Later, Jeremiah's vision of an almond branch represented the Lord's vigil and his intention to carry out his plans (see Jer 1:11-12). • There is no natural explanation for the budding of Aaron's staff. Almond wood is soft while alive and only becomes hard enough for use as a staff long after it has been cut off and allowed to dry.

17:9-11 After each tribal leader *claimed his own staff,* it was clear that *Aaron's* deserved special treatment. It was placed *permanently before the Ark*

17:10 Num 17:4; Deut 9:7, 24
17:12 Isa 6:5
17:13 Num 1:51-53
18:1 Exod 28:38
18:2 Num 3:5-10
18:5 Num 16:46
18:6 Num 3:9, 12
18:7 Exod 29:9; Num 1:51; 3:10
18:8 Lev 7:28-34; Deut 12:6
18:9 Lev 2:1-16; 6:25-30

from the LORD's presence, he showed them to the people. Each man claimed his own staff. [10]And the LORD said to Moses: "Place Aaron's staff permanently before the Ark of the Covenant to serve as a warning to rebels. This should put an end to their complaints against me and prevent any further deaths." [11]So Moses did as the LORD commanded him.

[12]Then the people of Israel said to Moses, "Look, we are doomed! We are dead! We are ruined! [13]Everyone who even comes close to the Tabernacle of the LORD dies. Are we all doomed to die?"

Duties of Priests and Levites

18 Then the LORD said to Aaron: "You, your sons, and your relatives from the tribe of Levi will be held responsible for any offenses related to the sanctuary. But you and your sons alone will be held responsible for violations connected with the priesthood.

[2]"Bring your relatives of the tribe of Levi—your ancestral tribe—to assist you and your sons as you perform the sacred duties in front of the Tabernacle of the Covenant. [3]But as the Levites go about all their assigned duties at the Tabernacle, they must be careful not to go near any of the sacred objects or the altar. If they do, both you and they will die. [4]The Levites must join you in fulfilling their responsibilities for the care and maintenance of the Tabernacle, but no unauthorized person may assist you.

[5]"You yourselves must perform the sacred duties inside the sanctuary and at the altar. If you follow these instructions, the LORD's anger will never again blaze against the people of Israel. [6]I myself have chosen your fellow Levites from among the Israelites to be your special assistants. They are a gift to you, dedicated to the LORD for service in the Tabernacle. [7]But you and your sons, the priests, must personally handle all the priestly rituals associated with the altar and with everything behind the inner curtain. I am giving you the priesthood as your special privilege of service. Any unauthorized person who comes too near the sanctuary will be put to death."

Support for the Priests and Levites

[8]The LORD gave these further instructions to Aaron: "I myself have put you in charge of all the holy offerings that are brought to me by the people of Israel. I have given all these consecrated offerings to you and your sons as your permanent share. [9]You are allotted the portion of the most holy offerings that is not burned on the fire. This portion of all the most holy offerings—including the grain offerings, sin offerings, and guilt

to warn potential ***rebels*** and to deter Israelites who complained about the Lord and his appointed leaders. The Ark eventually contained this staff, a jar of manna, and the stone tablets of the law (cp. Heb 9:4) to remind the Israelites of their wilderness wanderings.

17:10 *before the Ark of the Covenant:* Literally *before the Testimony;* see note on 17:4.

17:12-13 The Lord and his Tabernacle were holy, and because of God's holiness, his sanctuary could be a dangerous place for those who were not qualified to enter it. Moses' efforts to make the people understand and respect the God of Israel were bearing fruit.

18:1-32 The instructions given here arose from the need demonstrated in ch 17 for clear boundaries between the people and the priests and Levites. The distinctive privileges of the Levites were matched by significant responsibilities. One very important aspect of their work was to safeguard the Tabernacle from unauthorized entry (ch 16).

18:1-4 ***The LORD*** gave special authority to ***Aaron,*** his ***sons*** (the priests), and his ***relatives*** (the ***Levites***), all of whom were ***held responsible*** for offenses against ***the sanctuary.*** But the priests alone were held responsible for their own ***violations*** of God's instructions for their service.

18:2 ***the Tabernacle of the Covenant:*** Or *Tabernacle of the Testimony.*

18:3-4 ***all their assigned duties:*** See 1:47-53; 3:5-38; 4:1-33. • ***they must be careful:*** The Levites could ***go near*** only when ***the sacred objects*** were covered for transport.

18:4 ***the Tabernacle:*** Literally *the Tent of Meeting;* also in 18:6, 21, 22, 23, 31. See note on Exod 27:21.

18:5-7 Only the priests (Aaron and his descendants) could perform ***sacred duties inside the sanctuary*** proper or approach ***the altar,*** a sacred space that deserved special reverence. Only the high priest could serve in the Most Holy Place. The Levites were to serve only in the courtyard, away from the altar, except when it was time to assemble or disassemble the Tabernacle (ch 4).

18:5 Aaron and the priests were the people's representatives before the Lord, so their actions had consequences for all of Israel (cp. 16:18-21).

18:6-7 ***Levites . . . your special assistants:*** As explained in chs 3–4; see also 3:9; 8:16, 19.

18:7 ***Any unauthorized person . . . will be put to death:*** This verse warned Israelites at all levels in the sacred hierarchy to avoid areas where they were not allowed. Certain sacred places were off limits to those not qualified in a technical religious sense. Access to the most sacred areas was restricted, set apart for the holiest members of the religious community. Those who broke that taboo violated God's holiness at the cost of their lives (see also 1:51, 53; 3:10, 29-38; 4:1-20).

18:8-14 The priests and Levites were to be supported by the sacrificial system (see, e.g., Lev 7:28-36). God's appointed representatives deserve compensation for their efforts (cp. Matt 10:9-10; 1 Cor 9:3-10).

18:9-11 ***The most holy offerings*** were consumed only by Aaron and his sons, the priests set apart to serve in God's presence (Exod 28:1; 29:44-46). • ***This portion*** was a holy offering presented to God, and the priests had to respect it as such (18:10). Other categories of offerings provided food for the priests and their families (18:11-12), but only if they were ***ceremonially clean.***

offerings—will be most holy, and it belongs
to you and your sons. 10You must eat it as a
most holy offering. All the males may eat of
it, and you must treat it as most holy.
11"All the sacred offerings and special offerings presented to me when the Israelites
lift them up before the altar also belong to
you. I have given them to you and to your
sons and daughters as your permanent share.
Any member of your family who is ceremonially clean may eat of these offerings.
12"I also give you the harvest gifts brought
by the people as offerings to the LORD—the
best of the olive oil, new wine, and grain.
13All the first crops of their land that the
people present to the LORD belong to you.
Any member of your family who is ceremonially clean may eat this food.
14"Everything in Israel that is specially
set apart for the LORD also belongs to you.
15"The firstborn of every mother, whether
human or animal, that is offered to the
LORD will be yours. But you must always redeem your firstborn sons and the firstborn
of ceremonially unclean animals. 16Re-
deem them when they are one month old.
The redemption price is five pieces of silver
(as measured by the weight of the sanctuary
shekel, which equals twenty gerahs).
17"However, you may not redeem the firstborn of cattle, sheep, or goats. They are holy
and have been set apart for the LORD. Sprinkle their blood on the altar, and burn their
fat as a special gift, a pleasing aroma to the
LORD. 18The meat of these animals will be
yours, just like the breast and right thigh that
are presented by lifting them up as a special
offering before the altar. 19Yes, I am giving
you all these holy offerings that the people of
Israel bring to the LORD. They are for you and
your sons and daughters, to be eaten as your
permanent share. This is an eternal and unbreakable covenant between the LORD and
you, and it also applies to your descendants."
20And the LORD said to Aaron, "You
priests will receive no allotment of land
or share of property among the people of
Israel. I am your share and your allotment.
21As for the tribe of Levi, your relatives, I
will compensate them for their service in
the Tabernacle. Instead of an allotment of
land, I will give them the [c]tithes from the entire land of Israel.
22"From now on, no Israelites except
priests or Levites may approach the Tabernacle. If they come too near, they will be
judged guilty and will die. 23Only the Levites may serve at the Tabernacle, and they
will be held responsible for any offenses
against it. This is a permanent law for you,
to be observed from generation to generation. The Levites will receive no allotment
of land among the Israelites, 24because I
have given them the Israelites' tithes, which
have been presented as sacred offerings
to the LORD. This will be the Levites' share.
That is why I said they would receive no allotment of land among the Israelites."
25The LORD also told Moses, 26"Give these
instructions to the Levites: When you receive from the people of Israel the tithes
I have assigned as your allotment, give a
tenth of the tithes you receive—a tithe of
the tithe—to the LORD as a sacred offering.
27The LORD will consider this offering to be
your harvest offering, as though it were the
first grain from your own threshing floor or
wine from your own winepress. 28You must
present one-tenth of the tithe received
from the Israelites as a sacred offering to
the LORD. This is the LORD's sacred portion,
and you must present it to Aaron the priest.
29Be sure to give to the LORD the best portions of the gifts given to you.
30"Also, give these instructions to the
Levites: When you present the best part
as your offering, it will be considered as
though it came from your own threshing

18:11 Lev 22:2-3, 11-13
18:12 Exod 23:19; Deut 18:4
18:14 Lev 27:28
18:19 2 Chr 13:5
18:20 Deut 10:9; 18:2; Josh 13:33; Ezek 44:28
18:21 Lev 27:30-33; [c]*ma'aser* (4643) ‣Deut 12:6
18:23 Num 18:1, 20
18:26 Num 18:28; Neh 10:38
18:28 Num 18:21

18:14 Offerings ***specially set apart for the LORD*** were available to Aaron and his extended family. The Hebrew term used here refers to the complete consecration of things or people to the LORD, either by destroying them or by giving them as an offering (see Lev 27:28-29); the second sense is intended here.

18:15-16 The Lord provided for the Hebrew priests and their families out of what was set aside for the Lord. The priests had rights to firstborn animal offerings and to the redemption fee for Israel's firstborn sons. Both the firstborn sons and the offspring of unclean animals had to be redeemed by a fee paid in silver, since neither could be sacrificed (see 3:13, 40-51; Exod 13:2).

18:16 *five pieces of silver:* Hebrew *5 shekels* [2 ounces or 57 grams] *of silver.*

18:19 These arrangements were part of ***an eternal and unbreakable covenant*** (literally *a covenant of salt*; cp. 2 Chr 13:5). The covenant was apparently meant to be permanent, since salt (a preservative) was a symbol of permanence (Lev 2:13).

18:20-21 The priests and Levites did not have a tribal homeland but were scattered among Israel's other tribes (cp. 35:1-8; Deut 12:12; Josh 21:1-42). • ***I am your share and your allotment:*** Instead of their own territory, Israel's priests received the assurance that God himself would be their homeland, while ***the tribe of Levi*** received ***tithes*** in compensation for their sacred service.

18:22 See 18:7.

18:23-24 The ***Israelites' tithes*** were one tenth of the year's production of goods (see Deut 14:22-29; 26:12; Neh 10:35-39; Mal 3:8-12; Matt 23:23; cp. Gen 14:17-20; Heb 7:5-10).

18:25-32 Just as the Levites received a tithe of the Israelites' goods (18:24), they in turn were required to ***give . . . a tithe of the tithe*** to the priests as their own ***harvest offering*** (18:27).

18:31 Matt 10:10; Luke 10:7; 1 Cor 9:13; 1 Tim 5:18
18:32 Lev 22:2, 15-16
19:2 Lev 22:20-25; Deut 21:3
19:4 Lev 4:6, 17; 16:14
19:6 Lev 14:4, 6, 49
19:7 Lev 11:25; 16:26-28
19:9 Num 8:7; 19:13, 20-21
19:10 Num 19:7-8, 19
19:11 Lev 21:1
19:12 Num 19:17-19
19:13 Lev 7:20-21; 15:31; 20:3; 22:3

floor or winepress. 31 You Levites and your families may eat this food anywhere you wish, for it is your compensation for serving in the Tabernacle. 32 You will not be considered guilty for accepting the LORD's tithes if you give the best portion to the priests. But be careful not to treat the holy gifts of the people of Israel as though they were common. If you do, you will die."

The Red Heifer and the Water of Purification

19 The LORD said to Moses and Aaron, 2 "Here is another legal requirement commanded by the LORD: Tell the people of Israel to bring you a red heifer, a perfect animal that has no defects and has never been yoked to a plow. 3 Give it to Eleazar the priest, and it will be taken outside the camp and slaughtered in his presence. 4 Eleazar will take some of its blood on his finger and sprinkle it seven times toward the front of the Tabernacle. 5 As Eleazar watches, the heifer must be burned—its hide, meat, blood, and dung. 6 Eleazar the priest must then take a stick of cedar, a hyssop branch, and some scarlet yarn and throw them into the fire where the heifer is burning.

7 "Then the priest must wash his clothes and bathe himself in water. Afterward he may return to the camp, though he will remain ceremonially unclean until evening. 8 The man who burns the animal must also wash his clothes and bathe himself in water, and he, too, will remain unclean until evening. 9 Then someone who is ceremonially clean will gather up the ashes of the heifer and deposit them in a purified place outside the camp. They will be kept there for the community of Israel to use in the water for the purification ceremony. This ceremony is performed for the removal of sin. 10 The man who gathers up the ashes of the heifer must also wash his clothes, and he will remain ceremonially unclean until evening. This is a permanent law for the people of Israel and any foreigners who live among them.

11 "All those who touch a dead human body will be ceremonially unclean for seven days. 12 They must purify themselves on the third and seventh days with the water of purification; then they will be purified. But if they do not do this on the third and seventh days, they will continue to be unclean even after the seventh day. 13 All those who touch a dead body and do not purify themselves in the proper way defile the LORD's Tabernacle, and they will be cut off from the community of Israel. Since the water of purification was not sprinkled on them, their defilement continues.

14 "This is the ritual law that applies when someone dies inside a tent: All those who enter that tent and those who were inside when the death occurred will be ceremonially

---

18:31 Any food received in tithes could be consumed by Levites and their families. That food was ***compensation*** (i.e., a salary) for Tabernacle service.

18:32 The food tithes had a sacred origin as ***holy gifts of the people of Israel;*** they were not to turn these gifts into something ***common*** by neglecting to give a tithe to the priests.

19:1-22 This account considers the procedure by which ordinary Israelites defiled by contact with a corpse (see 9:4-12; Lev 17:15; 21:1-4, 11-12) could regain ceremonial purity and keep from defiling the Tabernacle. God's holiness requires that the place where his presence dwells be kept pure and set apart from pollution (cp. 1 Cor 6:9-11, 18-20).

19:1-10 The ***water for the purification ceremony*** (19:9), prepared with ashes of the red heifer, may have been the same as the water of purification in 8:7; see also 31:19-24. This ceremony required the ***ashes*** of a ***red heifer;*** the color probably represented blood (cp. Heb 9:13-14).

19:3-5 The need to safeguard Aaron's consecrated status (see Lev 21:10-12) required that ***Eleazar*** perform the offering of the red ***heifer,*** since it caused ritual impurity. The ceremony of the red heifer contrasted with the regular sacrifice (cp. Lev 4:3-12).

19:4 ***the Tabernacle:*** Literally *the Tent of Meeting.* See note on Exod 27:21.

19:6 The only other passage where ***a stick of cedar*** (or *juniper*), ***a hyssop branch, and some scarlet yarn*** occur together is Lev 14, which describes another ceremony (also "outside the camp") that brought about ceremonial purification. Some scholars suggest that Eleazar added cedarwood and hyssop to produce an aroma. Hyssop is associated with purification (Exod 12:22; Ps 51:7; cp. Heb 9:19), and the scarlet yarn, like the red heifer, probably symbolized blood. Taken together, the cedarwood, hyssop, and scarlet symbolize cleansing.

19:7-10 Three people were needed to produce and collect the heifer's ashes—Eleazar, the man who burned the animal, and the man who gathered its ashes. All three became ritually impure for a day because of this process. This was also true for the person who used the finished product, a potion made from the ash dust and water (cp. 19:21) that had the same defiling effect as blood associated with sacrifices (Lev 6:27-28).

19:9 The purpose of the ceremony of burning the red heifer was to produce ***ashes.*** These were collected and deposited ***in a purified place outside the camp*** until the Israelites needed them ***in the water for the purification ceremony*** to remove such defilement as coming into contact with a corpse (19:11-22).

19:11-19 Coming into contact with a human corpse produced ritual impurity for ***seven days*** (cp. Lev 21:1-3). The remedy was the ***water of purification,*** applied ***on the third and seventh days.***

19:13 The impurity caused by contact with a corpse was especially dangerous since a ceremonially defiled person would ***defile the LORD's Tabernacle*** (cp. Lev 15:31). This was grounds for being ***cut off from the community of Israel*** (cp. 9:13; Exod 12:15; Lev 7:20-21; 17:4-14; 20:17-18).

19:14-16 Death's contagion could be transmitted to an object or to a place where death had occurred (cp. Lev 15:1-12).

unclean for seven days. 15 Any open container in the tent that was not covered with
a lid is also defiled. 16 And if someone in an
open field touches the corpse of someone
who was killed with a sword or who died a
natural death, or if someone touches a human bone or a grave, that person will be
defiled for seven days.
17 "To remove the defilement, put some
of the ashes from the burnt purification
offering in a jar, and pour fresh water over
them. 18 Then someone who is ceremonially
clean must take a hyssop branch and dip it
into the water. That person must sprinkle
the water on the tent, on all the furnishings
in the tent, and on the people who were in
the tent; also on the person who touched
a human bone, or touched someone who
was killed or who died naturally, or touched
a grave. 19 On the third and seventh days
the person who is ceremonially clean must
sprinkle the water on those who are defiled.
Then on the seventh day the people being
cleansed must wash their clothes and bathe
themselves, and that evening they will be
cleansed of their defilement.
20 "But those who become defiled and do
not purify themselves will be cut off from
the community, for they have defiled the
sanctuary of the LORD. Since the water of purification has not been sprinkled on them,
they remain defiled. 21 This is a permanent
law for the people. Those who sprinkle the
water of purification must afterward wash
their clothes, and anyone who then touches
the water used for purification will remain
defiled until evening. 22 Anything and anyone that a defiled person touches will be
ceremonially unclean until evening."

Moses Strikes the Rock in Disobedience

20 In the first month of the year, the
whole community of Israel arrived
in the wilderness of Zin and camped at Kadesh. While they were there, Miriam died
and was buried.
2 There was no water for the people to
drink at that place, so they rebelled against
Moses and Aaron. 3 The people blamed
Moses and said, "If only we had died in the
LORD's presence with our brothers! 4 Why
have you brought the congregation of the
LORD's people into this wilderness to die,
along with all our livestock? 5 Why did you
make us leave Egypt and bring us here to
this terrible place? This land has no grain,
no figs, no grapes, no pomegranates, and no
water to drink!"
6 Moses and Aaron turned away from
the people and went to the entrance of the
Tabernacle, where they fell face down on
the ground. Then the glorious presence of
the LORD appeared to them, 7 and the LORD
said to Moses, 8 "You and Aaron must take
the staff and assemble the entire community. As the people watch, speak to the rock
over there, and it will pour out its water. You
will provide enough water from the rock to
satisfy the whole community and their livestock."
9 So Moses did as he was told. He took
the staff from the place where it was kept
before the LORD. 10 Then he and Aaron summoned the people to come and gather at the
rock. "Listen, you rebels!" he shouted. "Must
we bring you water from this rock?" 11 Then
Moses raised his hand and struck the rock
twice with the staff, and water gushed out.
So the entire community and their livestock
drank their fill.

19:16 Num 19:11; 31:19
19:17 Num 19:9
19:19 Ezek 36:25-27; Heb 10:22
19:20 Num 19:13
19:21 Lev 11:25, 40; 16:26-28; Num 19:7
19:22 Lev 5:2-3; 7:21
20:1 Num 13:21
20:2 Exod 17:1
20:3 Exod 17:2; Num 14:2-3; 16:31-35
20:5 Num 16:14
20:8 Exod 4:17, 20
20:11 Ps 78:16; Isa 48:21; 1 Cor 10:4

19:17-22 To cleanse with the heifer's ashes, a special purifying mixture was made by combining ***ashes from the burnt purification offering*** with ***fresh water*** (cp. 5:17).

19:20 See note on 19:13.

20:1 The ***first month*** of the ancient Hebrew lunar calendar usually occurs within the months of March and April. The number of years since leaving Egypt is not specified, but Aaron's death (20:22-29) took place in Israel's fortieth year in the wilderness (33:36-39).
• ***Miriam died:*** All in her generation shared this fate (14:26-30), including Moses and Aaron (20:2-13, 22-29).

20:2-13 In the face of yet another complaint by the people of Israel about a lack of water and food (cp. 11:4-35; 21:4-5; Exod 15:22-25), Moses and Aaron disobeyed the Lord and lost the privilege of entering the Promised Land.

20:2 ***There was no water:*** Throughout most of the year, Sinai and the Negev are very hot and dry.

20:3 ***our brothers!*** The Israelites identified themselves with Nadab and Abihu (Lev 10:1-5), the gluttons killed by the first plague (11:33), the skeptics who had already died in the wilderness (14:29), the ten unfaithful spies (14:36-37), Korah, Abiram, and Dathan, the 250 prominent men, and the 14,700 who died in the second plague (16:32, 35, 49).

20:6 ***the Tabernacle:*** Literally *the Tent of Meeting.* See note on Exod 27:21.
• ***they fell face down on the ground:*** As in previous conflicts (14:5, 10; 16:4, 19, 22), they prostrated themselves and awaited ***the glorious presence of the LORD*** to resolve the crisis.

20:7-9 God heard Israel's complaints, regarded them as legitimate, and commanded Moses to solve the problem.

20:8-9 The ***staff*** was kept before the Ark of the Covenant to prevent the Israelites from complaining (cp. 17:10); it represented God's authority in the hands of Moses and Aaron. The instructions that God gives his representatives are very precise and must be followed exactly (cp. Jas 3:1; see also 2 Tim 2:24-26).

20:10-12 Instead of reverently obeying God's instructions, Moses rebuked the people (***Must we bring you water from this rock?***) and angrily ***struck the rock twice with the staff*** (20:11). God regarded Moses' words and actions as a serious breach of faith; Moses "spoke foolishly" (Ps 106:32-33; cp. Jas 1:20) and ***did not trust*** God ***enough to demonstrate*** his ***holiness.*** By not doing exactly as he was

20:12 Lev 10:3; Num 20:24
20:13 Exod 17:7; Ps 95:8
20:14 Gen 36:31-39; Josh 2:10; 9:9
20:16 Exod 3:2-6; 14:19
20:21 Num 21:4; Deut 2:8; Judg 11:18
20:25 Num 3:4; 19:3-4
20:26 Num 20:24
20:28 Num 33:38

12But the LORD said to Moses and Aaron,
"Because you did not trust me enough to
demonstrate my holiness to the people of
Israel, you will not lead them into the land
I am giving them!" 13This place was known
as the waters of Meribah (which means "arguing") because there the people of Israel
argued with the LORD, and there he demonstrated his holiness among them.

The Israelites Move from Kadesh to the Plains of Moab (20:14–22:1)

Edom Refuses Israel Passage

14While Moses was at Kadesh, he sent ambassadors to the king of Edom with this
message:

"This is what your relatives, the people
of Israel, say: You know all the hardships
we have been through. 15Our ancestors
went down to Egypt, and we lived there
a long time, and we and our ancestors
were brutally mistreated by the Egyptians. 16But when we cried out to the
LORD, he heard us and sent an angel
who brought us out of Egypt. Now we
are camped at Kadesh, a town on the
border of your land. 17Please let us travel
through your land. We will be careful
not to go through your fields and vineyards. We won't even drink water from
your wells. We will stay on the king's
road and never leave it until we have
passed through your territory."

18But the king of Edom said, "Stay out of
my land, or I will meet you with an army!"
19The Israelites answered, "We will stay
on the main road. If our livestock drink
your water, we will pay for it. Just let us pass
through your country. That's all we ask."
20But the king of Edom replied, "Stay out!
You may not pass through our land." With
that he mobilized his army and marched
out against them with an imposing force.
21Because Edom refused to allow Israel
to pass through their country, Israel was
forced to turn around.

The Death of Aaron

22The whole community of Israel left Kadesh and arrived at Mount Hor. 23There, on
the border of the land of Edom, the LORD
said to Moses and Aaron, 24"The time has
come for Aaron to join his ancestors in
death. He will not enter the land I am giving
the people of Israel, because the two of you
rebelled against my instructions concerning the water at Meribah. 25Now take Aaron
and his son Eleazar up Mount Hor. 26There
you will remove Aaron's priestly garments
and put them on Eleazar, his son. Aaron will
die there and join his ancestors."
27So Moses did as the LORD commanded.
The three of them went up Mount Hor together as the whole community watched.
28At the summit, Moses removed the
priestly garments from Aaron and put them
on Eleazar, Aaron's son. Then Aaron died

---

told, Moses demonstrated a lack of faith in God to provide for his people. This lack of faith is also apparent in Moses' words to the people. The Lord requires obedience and faith; anything less is an affront to his holy character (20:24; 27:14). Such serious lack of obedience and faith had the same result as it had earlier (14:20-23; see also 1 Cor 10:4-12).

20:13 ***Meribah:*** As they had at Rephidim (Exod 17:1-7), the Israelites coined a name (***"arguing"***) that referred more to the incident than to a geographical location. • God ***demonstrated his holiness*** through his judgment on Aaron and Moses' sin.

20:14–21:35 Here the Israelites began their trek toward the Promised Land. Moving from Kadesh, they left the Sinai Peninsula behind and entered the area east of the Jordan (Transjordan), approaching the Promised Land from the east by a less direct point of entry (see 14:25; cp. Deut 2:2-6).

20:14-21 Israel tried unsuccessfully to establish peaceful relations with ***Edom,*** with which it had apparently had no dealings since Esau (Edom) and Jacob (Israel) buried their father, Isaac (Gen 35:29; 36:6-8; cp. Gen 32:28). Moses' appeal resembles the formal diplomatic correspondence of that era. While contacts with the Canaanites and other people groups were marked by hostility, communication with Edom was polite because of kinship ties (cp. Deut 2:4; 23:7). Those ties, however, were apparently not strong enough to overcome the ancient tension between Jacob and Esau (Gen 27:41).

20:17 ***We won't even drink water from your wells:*** Edom is very dry; food and water were too scarce to provide for this substantial number of Hebrew immigrants. • ***We will stay on the king's road:*** The "King's Highway" (also 21:22) is well known in the OT, though its exact route is not certain. As its name indicates, this route was maintained for official purposes, including the movement of troops and trade. Along this trail, travelers could find settlements, food, and water between the Red Sea and Damascus. The route remained important into Roman and even modern times. This royal road contrasted with a much less hospitable route farther to the east called the Desert Highway.

20:18-21 ***Stay out of my land:*** As their ancestor Esau had distrusted Jacob (Gen 27:36), the Edomites now distrusted Jacob's descendants. So ***Israel was forced to turn around*** and find another way to approach Canaan (cp. Deut 2:4-6).

20:22-23 Israel did not follow the more direct route through the southern region east of the Jordan, the Edomite heartland (20:21). • After leaving Kadesh, the Hebrews reached ***Mount Hor,*** located ***on the border of the land of Edom.*** The precise location of Mount Hor remains unknown, though Josephus (writing in AD 70–100) linked it with the Petra region (at Jebel Haroun, "mountain of Aaron").

20:24-26 Aaron's participation in the rebellion of his generation resulted in his death outside the Promised Land (20:10-12).

20:27-29 Priestly authority was transferred when Moses placed Aaron's ***priestly garments*** (cp. Lev 8:7-9) ***on Eleazar.*** Afterward, ***Aaron died*** at the age of 123, in the fortieth year after the Hebrews left Egypt (see 33:37-39). • ***all Israel mourned for him thirty days:*** This was an unusually high honor (see also

there on top of the mountain, and Moses and Eleazar went back down. [29]When the people realized that Aaron had died, all Israel mourned for him thirty days.

Victory over the Canaanites at Hormah

21 The Canaanite king of Arad, who lived in the Negev, heard that the Israelites were approaching on the road through Atharim. So he attacked the Israelites and took some of them as prisoners.
[2]Then the people of Israel made this vow to the LORD: "If you will hand these people over to us, we will [d]completely destroy all their towns." [3]The LORD heard the Israelites' request and gave them victory over the Canaanites. The Israelites completely destroyed them and their towns, and the place has been called Hormah ever since.

Fiery Serpents and the Bronze Snake

[4]Then the people of Israel set out from Mount Hor, taking the road to the Red Sea

21:1 Num 33:40; Josh 12:14; Judg 1:16
21:2 [d]*kharam* (2763) ‣Deut 7:2
21:3 Num 14:45
21:4 Deut 2:8

ELEAZAR (20:22-29)

Num 3:1-4; 16:36-40; Exod 6:23-25; Lev 10:6-7; Josh 14:1

Eleazar was the third son of Aaron, the first high priest (Exod 6:23; see "Aaron" at Exod 4:14-17, 27-31, p. 133). His two older brothers, Nadab and Abihu, offended God by offering incense in a different way than what God had commanded (Lev 10:1-7). God alone determines the right way for people to worship him; the brothers acted as though they knew better than God, so God sent fire to kill them. Since Eleazar was the next oldest son, he succeeded Aaron as high priest. During Aaron's lifetime, Eleazar performed priestly duties. He helped his father and Moses when some Levites rebelled because they wanted equal status with Aaron's priestly family (16:36-40).

Aaron died in the wilderness a short time before the Israelites entered the Promised Land. He was not allowed to enter because he and Moses had rebelled against God by striking the rock at Meribah (20:1-13). Before Aaron's death, he, Moses, and Eleazar went up on Mount Hor. Moses removed the priestly garments from Aaron and put them on his son (20:22-29). After this, Eleazar was high priest for the rest of his life, which included the time of Canaan's conquest.

When it was time to divide the land among the tribes, Eleazar and Joshua cast the sacred lots to determine where each tribe would settle (Josh 14:1-5). When Eleazar died, he was succeeded by his son Phinehas, who had distinguished himself by his covenant faithfulness at Baal-peor (ch 25). Eleazar's descendants included Zadok, the faithful priest who replaced Abiathar (1 Kgs 2:26-27, 35; see 1 Chr 6:3-8, 50-53; see also "Zadok" at 2 Sam 15:23-37, p. 545) and Ezra the priest, who was instrumental in reestablishing Judea after the Exile (see Ezra 7:1-5; see also "Ezra the Scribe" at Ezra 7:1–10:44, p. 800). In Ezekiel's ideal temple, only the descendants of Eleazar through Zadok would be permitted to serve (Ezek 44:15).

Deut 34:8), since the normal period of public mourning was seven days (Gen 50:10; 1 Sam 31:13).

21:1–22:1 In the march toward the Promised Land, Israel moved from Mount Hor to the plains of Moab (22:1). The account of Israel's march is punctuated by the book's emphasis on the Lord's patient plan to lead Israel into Canaan despite their frailties. • Although the general direction of travel is clear, the exact route taken by the Hebrews remains unknown. Many of the places are hard to identify, and the archaeological evidence from some sites does not fit the time frame usually associated with the wilderness period. An honest appraisal of the wilderness itinerary is still beset by significant geographical and historical uncertainties.

21:1 It is possible that ***the Canaanite king of Arad*** was provoked by many enemies to the south of his territory (cp. 14:44-45). • ***Arad*** and Hormah (21:3) were far to the north of Mount Hor (20:22-29; 21:4; see note on 20:22-23). Ancient *Arad* is usually identified with Tel Arad, located west of the modern Israeli town of Arad and about fifty miles north of Kadesh. While excavation at Tel Arad has revealed important ruins from the Early Bronze Age (about 3300–2000 BC) and the Iron Age (about 1200–500 BC), there is no evidence of occupation during Israel's exodus and wilderness period (the Late Bronze Age, 1500–1200 BC). Some solutions link ancient Arad with another archaeological site in the region. Others claim that all such stories come from a much later period and that there is no reason to expect a correlation between excavated data and literary traditions. Another set of solutions recognizes that the evidence is fragmentary, insufficient to settle scholarly debate or to reach a definitive conclusion. The same general kinds of problems with geographical and archaeological details are found in other parts of the OT, and the solutions are often uncertain. • ***Atharim*** is otherwise unknown.

21:2-3 ***completely destroy*** (Hebrew *kharam*): The Hebrew term used here refers to the complete consecration of things or people to the Lord, either by destroying them or by giving them as an offering. Israel was instructed to completely destroy their enemies and their enemies' property (see Lev 27:28-29; Deut 7:2; 20:17; Josh 6–7, 10–11). • This battle reflects a play on words between *kharam* and ***Hormah*** (Hebrew *khormah,* 21:3). It marks a turning point in Israel's interaction with the Canaanites, who remained a formidable enemy throughout the period of the conquest. • ***Hormah*** means "destruction" (see also Josh 12:14; Judg 1:16-17).

21:4-9 The ***vow to the LORD*** and consequent victory (21:2-3) did not eliminate Israel's criticisms ***against God and***

21:5
Num 11:5-6; 14:2-3
Ps 78:19
21:6
Deut 8:15
1 Cor 10:9
21:7
Ps 78:34
21:8
Isa 14:29
John 3:14-15
21:9
2 Kgs 18:4
John 3:14; 12:32
21:10
Num 33:43
21:15
Num 21:28
Deut 2:9
21:16
Judg 9:21

to go around the land of Edom. But the people grew impatient with the long journey,
[5]and they began to speak against God and
Moses. "Why have you brought us out of
Egypt to die here in the wilderness?" they
complained. "There is nothing to eat here
and nothing to drink. And we hate this horrible manna!"
[6]So the LORD sent poisonous snakes
among the people, and many were bitten
and died. [7]Then the people came to Moses
and cried out, "We have sinned by speaking against the LORD and against you. Pray
that the LORD will take away the snakes." So
Moses prayed for the people.
[8]Then the LORD told him, "Make a replica
of a poisonous snake and attach it to a pole.
All who are bitten will live if they simply
look at it!" [9]So Moses made a snake out of
bronze and attached it to a pole. Then anyone who was bitten by a snake could look at
the bronze snake and be healed!

Israel's Journey around Southern Moab
[10]The Israelites traveled next to Oboth and
camped there. [11]Then they went on to Iye-
abarim, in the wilderness on the eastern
border of Moab. [12]From there they traveled
to the valley of Zered Brook and set up camp.
[13]Then they moved out and camped on the
far side of the Arnon River, in the wilderness
adjacent to the territory of the Amorites.
The Arnon is the boundary line between
the Moabites and the Amorites. [14]For this
reason *The Book of the Wars of the LORD*
speaks of "the town of Waheb in the area of
Suphah, and the ravines of the Arnon River,
[15]and the ravines that extend as far as the
settlement of Ar on the border of Moab."
[16]From there the Israelites traveled to
Beer, which is the well where the LORD said

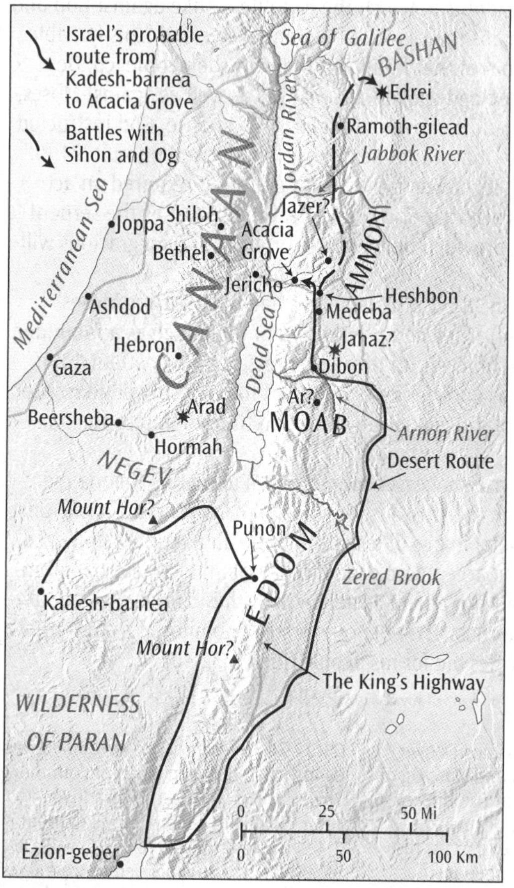

◀ **Journey toward the Promised Land** (20:22–22:1). This passage documents Israel's journey from KADESH-BARNEA to ACACIA GROVE (see also 33:37-49; Deut 2–3). The Israelites traveled from KADESH to MOUNT HOR, where Aaron died (20:22-29). Along the way they waged their first successful battle in CANAAN against the king of ARAD (21:1-3). From MOUNT HOR they were forced to travel the long way around EDOM (21:4) and pass to the east of EDOM and MOAB (21:10-20). They entered the area north of the ARNON RIVER and conquered the area of two Amorite kings, Sihon and Og (21:21-35). The map shows key battles against these kings at JAHAZ (21:23) and EDREI (21:33).

Moses, even though the ***long journey*** was punishment for the same kind of complaining (14:26-35).

21:4 *Red Sea:* Literally *sea of reeds.*

21:6 This whole region provided (and still provides) habitat for extremely ***poisonous snakes*** (cp. Isa 30:6).

21:7-9 Jesus alluded to this incident when discussing his identity and mission (John 3:14-15). • By Hezekiah's day (around 700 BC), this ***bronze snake*** had become an object of worship in Jerusalem (2 Kgs 18:4).

21:10 The location of ***Oboth*** is uncertain.

21:11-12 The Israelites made their way along the east side of Edom. • ***Iye-abarim*** ("ruins of Abarim" or "ruins of the region beyond") was probably near the northern bank of ***Zered Brook*** (cp. Deut 2:13-14) which separated ancient Edom from ***Moab*** (Deut 2:8-25).

21:13 The Israelites traveled to the east of the Moabite territory that lay between the Zered Brook on the south and the Arnon River on the north. ***The far side of the Arnon River*** was probably north and east of the main east–west canyon of the Arnon; this "Grand Canyon" was an effective natural ***boundary line*** between Moab and ***the territory of the Amorites*** north of the Arnon (see 21:26). • The ***Amorites*** were a group of nomadic peoples who had conquered areas from Mesopotamia to Canaan in the Middle Bronze Age (about 2000–1500 BC), including Babylon (around 1830 BC) and Assur (around 1750 BC). Amorites living in the hill country of Canaan had terrified Israel's spies (Deut 1:26-28) and had then repelled Israel's misguided attempt to enter Canaan (14:44-45; see Deut 1:42-44). At the time of Israel's arrival, Amorites had gained control of much of Transjordan (the area east of the Jordan); see note on 21:26.

21:14-15 ***The Book of the Wars of the LORD,*** analogous to *The Book of Jashar* (Josh 10:13; 2 Sam 1:18), is otherwise unknown. • ***Waheb*** (a town) and ***Suphah*** (a region) are otherwise unknown, but ***Ar*** was one of the major Moabite settlements of that day (cp. 21:28; Deut 2:18; Isa 15:1).

21:16-18a *Beer* means "well"; its location is unknown (cp. Isa 15:8). The poetic fragment describes the excavation of a new well and reflects the joy that this occasioned in a semiarid region. That the laborers were ***princes***

to Moses, "Assemble the people, and I will
give them water." 17 There the Israelites sang
this song:

"Spring up, O well!
Yes, sing its praises!
18 Sing of this well,
which princes dug,
which great leaders hollowed out
with their scepters and staffs."

Then the Israelites left the wilderness
and proceeded on through Mattanah, 19 Na-
haliel, and Bamoth. 20 After that they went
to the valley in Moab where Pisgah Peak
overlooks the wasteland.

Victory over Sihon and Og

21 The Israelites sent ambassadors to King Sihon of the Amorites with this message:
22 "Let us travel through your land. We
will be careful not to go through your
fields and vineyards. We won't even
drink water from your wells. We will
stay on the king's road until we have
passed through your territory."

23 But King Sihon refused to let them cross
his territory. Instead, he mobilized his entire
army and attacked Israel in the wilderness,
engaging them in battle at Jahaz. 24 But the Israelites slaughtered them with their swords
and occupied their land from the Arnon
River to the Jabbok River. They went only
as far as the Ammonite border because the
boundary of the Ammonites was fortified.

25 So Israel captured all the towns of the
Amorites and settled in them, including the

21:21 Deut 2:26-28; Judg 11:19-21
21:22 Num 20:17
21:23 Num 20:21; Deut 2:32; Judg 11:20
21:24 Deut 2:19, 31-37; Josh 12:1-2; 13:10
21:25 Amos 2:10

The Bronze Snake (21:4-9)

2 Kgs 18:1-4; John 3:14-15; 6:32-40; 8:28; 12:30-34

Numbers 21:4-9 contains one of many incidents in which the Israelites spoke against God and Moses. When the Israelites complained about their lack of food and water and "this horrible manna" (21:5), the Lord sent poisonous snakes that fatally bit many of the people (cp. Deut 8:15). When the Israelites realized that they had spoken against God as well as against Moses, they asked Moses to pray that the Lord would remove the snakes. In response, God instructed Moses to make a bronze replica of a snake that would heal those who looked upon it (21:8). What kind of medical treatment was this? Its power came from God, but it required an act of faith to look at the bronze image and trust that God would heal them. Just as the serpent bites resulted from God's wrath, the Lord provided deliverance through his own gracious will (see *Wisdom of Solomon* 16:5-7).

When Hezekiah became king of Judah in 715 BC, the Israelites had begun using Moses' bronze serpent as an idol (see 2 Kgs 18:1-4). They had probably kept the image as a reminder of God's power, even as they kept other artifacts from the wilderness period (cp. Deut 10:5; Heb 9:4-5), but they began worshiping it as another deity, so it had to be destroyed like other pagan shrines and sacred pillars. Such idolatry is a serious threat to the worship of the one true God (cp. Exod 32).

Jesus referred to the incident of the bronze snake (see John 3:14-15) to predict the manner of his execution: He would be "lifted up" on the cross just as Moses had lifted up the snake on a pole (see also John 8:28; 12:32-34). The metal image of a snake offered an antidote to injected venom, but those who look at the cross and accept God's sacrifice lay claim to an eternal promise (John 3:14-16). The Lord sent the serpents to punish Israel because they complained about the manna God had sent them in the wilderness (21:4-9). Jesus referred to himself as the "true bread from heaven," the manna that provides life for his people (John 6:32-40).

and *leaders* and the tools were *scepters and staffs* may indicate that digging the well included a festive ceremony.

21:18b-20 After moving north of the Arnon, the Hebrews *left the wilderness* on the eastern side of Moab and the recently conquered Amorite territory (see note on 21:21-35). They turned westward toward the ridgeline that rises up from the Jordan Rift Valley, then traveled north to *Pisgah Peak* (see also 23:14; Deut 3:17, 27; 34:1, 5). • *overlooks the wasteland:* Or *overlooks Jeshimon*, north of the Dead Sea (cp. 23:28; 1 Sam 23:19, 24; 26:1, 3).

21:21-35 The Israelite victories over King Sihon of Heshbon and King Og of Bashan were previews of the Hebrew conquest of Canaan and came to represent God's promise to assist his people in their time of need (cp. Deut 2:24–3:7; Josh 2:10; 9:10; 12:1-6; 13:10-12; Judg 11:19-22; Neh 9:22; Ps 135:10-12; 136:17-22; Jer 48:45-46). • Because Israel had left the wilderness (cp. 21:18, 23) before arriving at Pisgah (21:20), this account is probably a flashback of something that took place before the movement described in 21:18-20.

21:21-24 The territory of *King Sihon* was sandwiched between Moab and Ammon. The Israelites were not to invade Ammon (Deut 2:19), Edom, or Moab (Deut 2:4-9) because they were kin (Gen 19:30-38; 32:3), but Israel needed to cross Transjordan to enter Canaan. Sihon's territory was the natural route.

21:21-22 Cp. 20:14-17.

21:24 *because the boundary of the Ammonites was fortified:* Or *because the terrain of the Ammonite frontier was rugged;* Hebrew reads *because the boundary of the Ammonites was strong.*

21:26 Ps 135:11
21:28 Deut 2:9, 18; Jer 48:45-46
21:29 Judg 11:24; 1 Kgs 11:7, 33
21:32 Num 32:1, 35; Jer 48:32
21:33 Deut 3:3-4
22:1 Num 33:48-49
22:2 Exod 15:15; Deut 2:25
22:4 Num 22:7; 25:16-18

city of Heshbon and its surrounding villages.
26 Heshbon had been the capital of King
Sihon of the Amorites. He had defeated a
former Moabite king and seized all his land
as far as the Arnon River. 27 Therefore, the
ancient poets wrote this about him:

"Come to Heshbon and let it be rebuilt!
Let the city of Sihon be restored.
28 A fire flamed forth from Heshbon,
a blaze from the city of Sihon.
It burned the city of Ar in Moab;
it destroyed the rulers of the Arnon heights.
29 What sorrow awaits you, O people of Moab!
You are finished, O worshipers of Chemosh!
Chemosh has left his sons as refugees,
his daughters as captives of Sihon, the Amorite king.
30 We have utterly destroyed them,
from Heshbon to Dibon.
We have completely wiped them out
as far away as Nophah and Medeba."

31 So the people of Israel occupied the territory of the Amorites. 32 After Moses sent
men to explore the Jazer area, they captured
all the towns in the region and drove out
the Amorites who lived there. 33 Then they
turned and marched up the road to Bashan,
but King Og of Bashan and all his people
attacked them at Edrei. 34 The LORD said to
Moses, "Do not be afraid of him, for I have
handed him over to you, along with all his
people and his land. Do the same to him as
you did to King Sihon of the Amorites, who
ruled in Heshbon." 35 And Israel killed King
Og, his sons, and all his subjects; not a single
survivor remained. Then Israel occupied
their land.

Israel Reaches the Plains of Moab, Opposite Jericho

22 Then the people of Israel traveled to
the plains of Moab and camped east
of the Jordan River, across from Jericho.

3. THE ISRAELITES CAMP IN THE PLAINS OF MOAB AND PREPARE TO INVADE CANAAN (22:2–36:13)

Balak, Balaam, and the Israelites (22:2–24:25)

Balak Sends for Balaam

2 Balak son of Zippor, the Moabite king, had
seen everything the Israelites did to the
Amorites. 3 And when the people of Moab
saw how many Israelites there were, they
were terrified. 4 The king of Moab said to
the elders of Midian, "This mob will devour

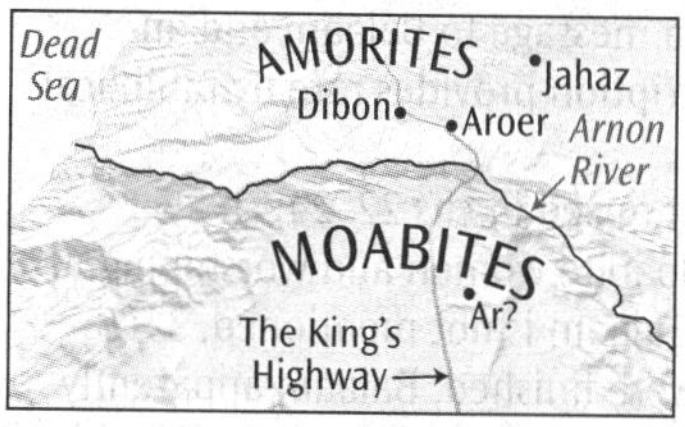

◄ **The Arnon Gorge (21:13-15).** The canyon of the ARNON RIVER (modern Wadi al-Mujib) is the natural northern barrier of MOABITE territory (cp. 2 Kgs 10:33). It marks the southern boundary of the AMORITES' territory, which was the first territory that Israel conquered (21:21-35; see also Deut 2:24, 36; 4:48).

21:25 The area conquered at this time became home to the tribes of Reuben, Gad, and Manasseh (cp. ch 32).

21:26 ***King Sihon of the Amorites*** had taken the area north of the Arnon from the Moabites, who earlier controlled it. After Israel occupied this region for several hundred years, it was reclaimed by King Mesha of Moab (see 2 Kgs 3:4-27) through a campaign described in detail around 830 BC on the Mesha Inscription (also known as the Moabite Stone). • ***Heshbon*** is usually identified with Tell Hesban, which has not yielded evidence of Late Bronze Age occupation; see note on 21:1.

21:27-30 This ancient ballad was apparently an old Amorite song focusing on the exploits of King Sihon. Other interpreters assume that Israelite balladeers created it as a taunt song to ridicule Sihon's defeat and celebrate Israel's victory. The logical flow of thought from 21:26 to 21:27 would favor the former interpretation, with Israel applying the song to their own victory: Sihon and the Amorites had defeated Moab; now Israel had defeated them! Cp. Judg 11:12-28.

21:28 King Sihon had destroyed Moab's towns from his center of operations at ***Heshbon***.

21:29 From the ancient point of view, even ***Moab***'s supreme god ***Chemosh*** suffered defeat at the hands of the Amorite conquerors, while the people of Moab became ***refugees*** and ***captives***.

21:30 The area described here is the one that Israel had just conquered (21:24), making the ballad celebrating Sihon a fitting tribute to Israel's victory. • ***as far away as Nophah and Medeba:*** Or *until fire spread to Medeba.* The meaning of the Hebrew is uncertain.

21:33-35 Ancient ***Bashan*** was located east of the Sea of Galilee. • ***King Og,*** like Sihon, was an Amorite (see note on 21:13). This brief account of Israel's defeat of Og is expanded in Deut 3:1-11.

21:35 ***Then Israel occupied their land:*** See ch 32.

22:1 Following their victories over the Amorite kingdoms (21:21-35 and note), Israel took up residence in ***the plains of Moab*** on the eastern side of the Jordan Valley, northeast of the Dead Sea and across the river from the oasis of ***Jericho***. The Hebrews camped there until they crossed the Jordan to enter Canaan (Josh 3:1).

22:2–24:25 The narrative of Balak and Balaam describes a pivotal moment in Israel's history and contains humor, drama, and profound theological insights. The Lord's will must be accomplished—nothing could thwart his plan for Israel.

22:2-3 ***Balak*** is unknown outside of this incident (Josh 24:9; Judg 11:25; Mic 6:5; Rev 2:14). His territory had been seized by Sihon, the Amorite king (21:26), whom Israel had just defeated (21:21-31). Balak may have imagined that his tiny kingdom was next.

22:4 ***Midian:*** This desert people was descended from Abraham (Gen 25:1-2; Exod 2:15-16). Their alliance with Moab was the beginning of their conflicts with

everything in sight, like an ox devours grass in the field!"

So Balak, king of Moab, 5sent messengers to call Balaam son of Beor, who was living in his native land of Pethor near the Euphrates River. His message said:

"Look, a vast horde of people has arrived from Egypt. They cover the face of the earth and are threatening me. 6Please come and curse these people for me because they are too powerful for me. Then perhaps I will be able to conquer them and drive them from the land. I know that [e]blessings fall on any people you [e]bless, and curses fall on people you curse."

7Balak's messengers, who were elders of Moab and Midian, set out with money to pay Balaam to place a curse upon Israel. They went to Balaam and delivered Balak's message to him. 8"Stay here overnight," Balaam said. "In the morning I will tell you whatever

22:5 Num 23:7 Deut 23:4
22:6 [e]*barak* (1288) ‣Deut 30:19
22:7 Num 23:23

BALAAM (22:1–25:18)

Num 31:8, 16
Josh 13:22
2 Pet 2:15-16
Jude 1:11
Rev 2:14

Balaam was a diviner—a person who read signs and omens to determine the future and performed rituals to change future events (see note on 22:5-6; cp. Josh 13:22). He was a diviner for hire, so when Balak, king of Moab, wanted to hire him to curse Israel, he was eager to get started. Even when God told him not to go, he hoped God would change his mind because he was very interested in the money (2 Pet 2:15).

Finally, God allowed Balaam to go, but only if Balaam agreed to say what God told him to say, and only to frustrate Balak's purposes (Deut 23:4-5). On the road, Balaam's donkey refused to move because the angel of the Lord blocked the way. The donkey could see, but Balaam was blind and foolish. Still, Balaam was smart enough not to curse the Israelites when God told him to bless them, and to Balak's great frustration, that was all Balaam could do.

Recently, an inscription was found that mentions Balaam son of Beor, a diviner who had visions at night (cp. Num 22:9-12, 20). The inscription was written on a plaster wall at Deir 'Alla, eight miles east of the Jordan River, and not far north of where the Hebrews were camped at the time of the Balaam incident. This nonbiblical text, dated 850–650 BC, identifies Balaam as a "seer of the gods" and reports that the gods, whose names in the inscription are similar to *Shaddai* ("Almighty"; cp. 24:3, 16), delivered a message to Balaam and announced judgment upon the world (cp. 24:15-25). The inscription provides rare extrabiblical evidence about a Bible character.

While Balaam's character and motives appear somewhat mixed in chs 22–24, ch 25 describes how the men of Israel sinned by sleeping with Moabite women and worshiping their gods, which made God angry with his people. While Balaam is not mentioned, 31:16 names him as the originator of this plot. After his visions were finished, Balaam apparently remained in Moab and kept working the angles until he found a way to damage Israel and get the money. The Israelites killed him a short time later (31:8). Balaam became known as a magician with bad motives (see Deut 23:4-5; Josh 13:22) and a false teacher who was only interested in pay (see Neh 13:2; 2 Pet 2:15; Jude 1:11), who led Israel into idolatry and immorality (31:16; see Rev 2:14).

Israel (22:7; see 25:6, 14-18; 31:2-10; Judg 6–8).

22:5-6 ***Balaam*** was a pagan religious specialist (a *diviner*) from northwest Mesopotamia (see "Balaam" at 22:1–25:18, above). Like other ancient peoples, Moab and Midian believed that the spoken word—in the form of a blessing or curse—was powerful when uttered by a skilled diviner. Members of this trained profession claimed to possess special powers to learn about and manipulate the future course of events (see Deut 18:14; 1 Sam 6:2; 2 Kgs 21:6; Isa 44:25; Dan 2:1-12; 2:27-28; Mic 5:12; Zech 10:2). Israel's enemies appealed to Balaam to pronounce curses upon the Hebrews, for they believed that such spoken words would be effective against them. Ancient armies pronounced such curses on their enemies before they entered battle. Belief in the power of the spoken word was common in ancient Israel even when not linked with divination (e.g., Gen 27:1-40; Deut 27:15-26; 1 Sam 14:24-28; cp. Matt 21:18-22). • ***Pethor*** (22:5) is probably ancient Pitru, located on the west side of the Euphrates River south of Carchemish, 400 miles from Moab (see map, p. 14, for the general area).

22:5 ***who was living in his native land of Pethor:*** Or *who was at Pethor in the land of the Amavites.* • ***the Euphrates River:*** Literally *the river.*

22:7 ***set out with money to pay Balaam to place a curse upon Israel*** (literally *set out with the money of divination in their hand*): As a professional diviner, Balaam could command considerable payment for his services (22:7, 17-18; cp. 1 Sam 9:7-8; 2 Kgs 8:7-9).

22:8 ***Stay here overnight:*** Balaam expected to receive a message from God at night (22:9, 19-20; cp. Job 4:12-16; Zech 1:8). • ***the LORD*** (Hebrew *Yahweh*): Balaam knew about Yahweh, the God of Israel, and expected a message from him as to what he could or could not do.

22:12 Num 23:11-12
22:17 Num 22:6
22:18 Num 23:26; 24:13
22:20 Num 22:35; 23:12, 26
22:21 2 Pet 2:15
22:22 [f]*mal'ak* (4397) ‣Josh 6:17
22:28 2 Pet 2:16

the LORD directs me to say." So the officials
from Moab stayed there with Balaam.
9That night God came to Balaam and asked
him, "Who are these men visiting you?"
10Balaam said to God, "Balak son of Zippor, king of Moab, has sent me this message:
11'Look, a vast horde of people has arrived
from Egypt, and they cover the face of the
earth. Come and curse these people for me.
Then perhaps I will be able to stand up to
them and drive them from the land.' "
12But God told Balaam, "Do not go with
them. You are not to curse these people, for
they have been blessed!"
13The next morning Balaam got up and
told Balak's officials, "Go on home! The
LORD will not let me go with you."
14So the Moabite officials returned to
King Balak and reported, "Balaam refused
to come with us." 15Then Balak tried again.
This time he sent a larger number of even
more distinguished officials than those he
had sent the first time. 16They went to Balaam and delivered this message to him:

"This is what Balak son of Zippor says:
Please don't let anything stop you from
coming to help me. 17I will pay you very
well and do whatever you tell me. Just
come and curse these people for me!"

18But Balaam responded to Balak's messengers, "Even if Balak were to give me his
palace filled with silver and gold, I would be
powerless to do anything against the will of
the LORD my God. 19But stay here one more
night, and I will see if the LORD has anything
else to say to me."
20That night God came to Balaam and
told him, "Since these men have come for
you, get up and go with them. But do only
what I tell you to do."

Balaam and His Donkey Travel to Moab

21So the next morning Balaam got up, saddled his donkey, and started off with the
Moabite officials. 22But God was angry that
Balaam was going, so he sent the [f]angel of
the LORD to stand in the road to block his
way. As Balaam and two servants were riding along, 23Balaam's donkey saw the angel
of the LORD standing in the road with a
drawn sword in his hand. The donkey bolted
off the road into a field, but Balaam beat it
and turned it back onto the road. 24Then
the angel of the LORD stood at a place where
the road narrowed between two vineyard
walls. 25When the donkey saw the angel of
the LORD, it tried to squeeze by and crushed
Balaam's foot against the wall. So Balaam
beat the donkey again. 26Then the angel of
the LORD moved farther down the road and
stood in a place too narrow for the donkey
to get by at all. 27This time when the donkey
saw the angel, it lay down under Balaam. In
a fit of rage Balaam beat the animal again
with his staff.
28Then the LORD gave the donkey the ability to speak. "What have I done to you that
deserves your beating me three times?" it
asked Balaam.

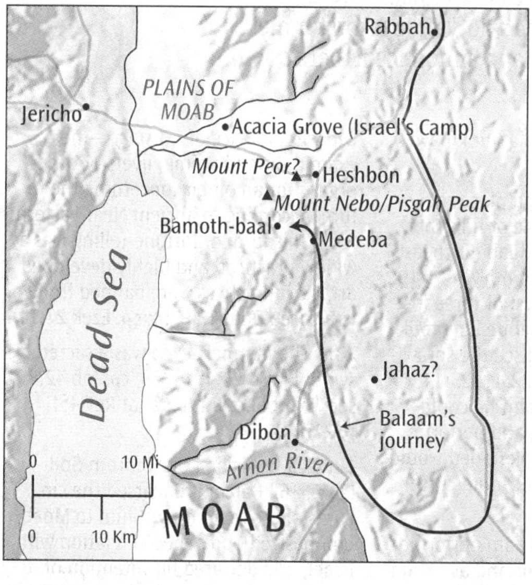

◂ **Balaam Blesses Israel (22:21-41).** Balaam probably traveled southward on the eastern desert route and avoided HESHBON, which had been occupied by Israel (21:25-30). After he met Balak near the ARNON RIVER (22:36), the two traveled north to the mountains overlooking the Israelite camp.

22:9-18 God prohibited Balaam from going with Balak's messengers.

22:18 Some have read Balaam's reply to this second delegation as his attempt to prompt a more lucrative offer, but his refusal (24:13) weighs against this view. Instead, Balaam seemed determined to obey the Lord and called him ***my God***.

22:19-20 Balaam agreed to inquire about the Lord's wishes one more time. God allowed him to accompany Balak's representatives, but admonished him to do exactly what God commanded (cp. 22:35).

22:21-41 The passage is clearly making fun of this professional seer, whose spiritual insights and obedience to God are not equal to those of his donkey.

22:22 God's anger is puzzling in light of the permission he granted to Balaam in 22:20. The Lord knew that the diviner's intentions and character were not as honorable as he claimed in conversation with Balak's messengers. Balaam's foolish beating of the donkey demonstrates his ungodly character (Prov 12:10; cp. 1 Sam 25).

22:28-31 The only scriptural parallel to this phenomenon of a talking animal is the serpent who spoke with Eve (Gen 3:1-5). God used the donkey to rebuke the foolish diviner (2 Pet 2:15-16).

29“You have made me look like a fool!” Balaam shouted. “If I had a sword with me, I
would kill you!”
30“But I am the same donkey you have
ridden all your life,” the donkey answered.
“Have I ever done anything like this before?”
“No,” Balaam admitted.
31Then the LORD opened Balaam’s eyes,
and he saw the angel of the LORD standing
in the roadway with a drawn sword in his
hand. Balaam bowed his head and fell face
down on the ground before him.
32“Why did you beat your donkey those
three times?” the angel of the LORD demanded. “Look, I have come to block your
way because you are stubbornly resisting
me. 33Three times the donkey saw me and
shied away; otherwise, I would certainly
have killed you by now and spared the donkey.”
34Then Balaam confessed to the angel of
the LORD, “I have sinned. I didn’t realize you
were standing in the road to block my way.
I will return home if you are against my going.”
35But the angel of the LORD told Balaam,
“Go with these men, but say only what I tell
you to say.” So Balaam went on with Balak’s
officials. 36When King Balak heard that Balaam was on the way, he went out to meet
him at a Moabite town on the Arnon River
at the farthest border of his land.
37“Didn’t I send you an urgent invitation?
Why didn’t you come right away?” Balak
asked Balaam. “Didn’t you believe me when
I said I would reward you richly?”
38Balaam replied, “Look, now I have come,
but I have no power to say whatever I want.
I will speak only the message that God puts
in my mouth.” 39Then Balaam accompanied
Balak to Kiriath-huzoth, 40where the king
sacrificed cattle and sheep. He sent portions of the meat to Balaam and the officials
who were with him. 41The next morning Balak took Balaam up to Bamoth-baal. From
there he could see some of the people of Israel spread out below him.

Balaam’s First Message

23 Then Balaam said to King Balak,
“Build me seven altars here, and
prepare seven young bulls and seven rams
for me to sacrifice.” 2Balak followed his instructions, and the two of them sacrificed a
young bull and a ram on each altar.
3Then Balaam said to Balak, “Stand here
by your burnt offerings, and I will go to see if
the LORD will respond to me. Then I will tell
you whatever he reveals to me.” So Balaam
went alone to the top of a bare hill, 4and God
met him there. Balaam said to him, “I have
prepared seven altars and have sacrificed a
young bull and a ram on each altar.”
5The LORD gave Balaam a message for
King Balak. Then he said, “Go back to Balak
and give him my message.”
6So Balaam returned and found the king
standing beside his burnt offerings with
all the officials of Moab. 7This was the message Balaam delivered:

“Balak summoned me to come from
Aram;
the king of Moab brought me from
the eastern hills.
‘Come,’ he said, ‘curse Jacob for me!
Come and announce Israel’s doom.’

22:31 Josh 5:13-15
22:34 1 Sam 15:24
22:35 Num 22:20
22:37-38 Num 22:18
22:41 Num 23:13
23:1 Num 22:40
23:5 Num 22:20, 35; 23:16
23:7 Num 22:6

22:34 *I have sinned:* Balaam admitted his mistake in not perceiving the angel of the Lord or his intention and offered to go back.

22:35 The Lord ensured that Balaam would say only what God commanded (cp. 22:20).

22:36 It is likely that this meeting place was in the northeastern corner of Balak’s small kingdom.

22:37 Balak thought Balaam did not understand how *urgent* the situation was nor how great the offered payment.

22:38 Balaam’s reply reflected the lesson he had learned in the donkey incident (cp. 22:20, 35).

22:39-41 Balak attempted to secure Balaam’s curse on Israel, first through a ritual offering and meal that would invoke the gods and Balaam, and second by taking Balaam to see the Israelite camp. • *Kiriath-huzoth* is an unknown location.

22:41 *Bamoth-baal* (“high places of Baal”) was along the ridge of hills that overlooks the plains of Moab northeast of the Dead Sea (cp. “Bamoth” in 21:19; Josh 13:17). It was the first of three locations to which the Moabite king took Balaam so that he could see the sprawling Israelite camp (also 22:41; 23:14, 28). From such a high point he could see the Israelites (22:11) and perform the ceremonies that Balak hoped would lead to a powerful imprecation (curse) against them.

23:1-30 As a diviner, Balaam performed rituals to interpret omens and ascertain Israel’s future (cp. 23:23; 24:1). Balak had summoned him to pronounce imprecations, but God repeatedly prohibited him from doing so. • It is possible that these sacrifices were connected with the practice of *extispicy*—the examination of animal livers or other organs for an omen concerning the future. According to ancient Near Eastern texts, this form of fortune-telling was a widely practiced and highly developed art. Such practices were banned from Israel (see Deut 18:9-14; cp. Ezek 21:21).

23:1 The number *seven* was a sacred symbol (also 23:4, 14, 29; cp. Job 42:8; see “Symbolic Numbers” at Rev 4:4, p. 2173).

23:7-10 In his first oracle from God (23:5, 16), Balaam rehearsed the circumstances that brought him to Moab, emphasized God’s special relation with Israel, and declared his intention of protecting them from harm. • These poetic oracles illustrate the parallelism of Hebrew poetry. Parallel lines reinforce the content by repeating important concepts in a highly structured pattern

23:8 Num 22:12
23:9 Num 22:41
23:10 Gen 13:16; Ps 37:37; Isa 57:1
23:12 Num 22:20, 38
23:16 Num 22:38
23:19 1 Sam 15:29; Isa 40:8; 55:11; [g]ben 'adam (1121, 0120) ›Job 25:6
23:20 Isa 43:13
23:21 Exod 3:12; Deut 31:23; [h]'elohim (0430) ›Josh 24:2
23:22 Num 24:8
23:23 Num 22:7
23:24 Gen 49:9
23:26 Num 22:38

8 But how can I curse those
whom God has not cursed?
How can I condemn those
whom the LORD has not condemned?
9 I see them from the cliff tops;
I watch them from the hills.
I see a people who live by themselves,
set apart from other nations.
10 Who can count Jacob's descendants, as
numerous as dust?
Who can count even a fourth of
Israel's people?
Let me die like the righteous;
let my life end like theirs."

11Then King Balak demanded of Balaam,
"What have you done to me? I brought you
to curse my enemies. Instead, you have
blessed them!"

12But Balaam replied, "I will speak only
the message that the LORD puts in my
mouth."

Balaam's Second Message

13Then King Balak told him, "Come with
me to another place. There you will see another part of the nation of Israel, but not
all of them. Curse at least that many!" 14So
Balak took Balaam to the plateau of Zophim
on Pisgah Peak. He built seven altars there
and offered a young bull and a ram on each
altar.

15Then Balaam said to the king, "Stand
here by your burnt offerings while I go over
there to meet the LORD."

16And the LORD met Balaam and gave him
a message. Then he said, "Go back to Balak
and give him my message."

17So Balaam returned and found the king
standing beside his burnt offerings with all
the officials of Moab. "What did the LORD
say?" Balak asked eagerly.

18This was the message Balaam delivered:
"Rise up, Balak, and listen!
Hear me, son of Zippor.
19 God is not a man, so he does not lie.
He is not [g]human, so he does not
change his mind.
Has he ever spoken and failed to act?
Has he ever promised and not carried
it through?
20 Listen, I received a command to bless;
God has blessed, and I cannot
reverse it!
21 No misfortune is in his plan for Jacob;
no trouble is in store for Israel.
For the LORD their [h]God is with them;
he has been proclaimed their king.
22 God brought them out of Egypt;
for them he is as strong as a wild ox.
23 No curse can touch Jacob;
no magic has any power against Israel.
For now it will be said of Jacob,
'What wonders God has done for
Israel!'
24 These people rise up like a lioness,
like a majestic lion rousing itself.
They refuse to rest
until they have feasted on prey,
drinking the blood of the slaughtered!"

25Then Balak said to Balaam, "Fine, but
if you won't curse them, at least don't bless
them!"

26But Balaam replied to Balak, "Didn't
I tell you that I can do only what the LORD
tells me?"

Balaam's Third Message

27Then King Balak said to Balaam, "Come, I
will take you to one more place. Perhaps it
will please God to let you curse them from
there."

(see "Introduction to the Books of Poetry and Wisdom," p. 849). • ***Aram:*** Aram-naharaim (Gen 24:10) is another name for North Mesopotamia, where Balaam's home of Pethor was located (22:5). • The ***eastern hills*** are a line of mountains in North Syria.

23:7-8 Instead of cursing Israel, the seer noted their special status (cp. Exod 19:5-6; Deut 7:6-9) and observed that God's blessing had turned a humble people into a great nation (cp. Gen 12:2-3; 13:16; 28:14). Balaam wished for similar good fortune to come his way (23:10).

23:13-26 ***Balak*** hoped that he would get different results if he changed the venue. The precise location of ***the plateau of Zophim on Pisgah Peak*** is unknown, though Pisgah is part of the ridgeline that overlooks the plains of Moab (Deut 34:1) in the vicinity of Bamoth-baal (22:41) and Mount Peor (23:28).

23:18-24 This oracle emphasizes God's faithfulness to his people—he would stay with them and keep all of his promises.

23:19 Because of God's reliable character, Balaam could do nothing but bless Israel.

23:20-21 Since the Lord would follow through on his promises to bless his people (bringing them no misfortune or trouble), Balaam was in no position to reverse God's intentions. Though God punished the Hebrews for acts of disobedience, his advocacy of Israel's cause was evident from the time he delivered them from Egypt.

23:23-24 No curse could succeed against Israel because they had been blessed (22:12; cp. Gen 12:2-3; 22:17-18). Israel was safe from the harm that Moab and Midian sought to inflict through divination (cp. 24:1); Israel would become famous because God protected them from harm (see Josh 2:9-11; cp. Num 14:13-19).

23:27–24:14 Disappointed with Balaam's blessing, Balak hoped that yet another change of location would produce different results. Though the location of ***Mount Peor*** is unknown, this place was probably near a worship site of Baal of Peor (cp. 25:3, 5) and the Beth-peor of Deut 3:29; 34:6, where Moses was buried.

28 So Balak took Balaam to the top of
Mount Peor, overlooking the wasteland.
29 Balaam again told Balak, "Build me seven
altars, and prepare seven young bulls and
seven rams for me to sacrifice." 30 So Balak
did as Balaam ordered and offered a young
bull and a ram on each altar.

24 By now Balaam realized that the
LORD was determined to bless Israel,
so he did not resort to divination as before.
Instead, he turned and looked out toward
the wilderness, 2 where he saw the people
of Israel camped, tribe by tribe. Then the
Spirit of God came upon him, 3 and this is
the message he delivered:

"This is the message of Balaam son of Beor,
the message of the man whose eyes
see clearly,
4 the message of one who hears the words
of God,
who sees a vision from the Almighty,
who bows down with eyes wide open:
5 How beautiful are your tents, O Jacob;
how lovely are your homes, O Israel!
6 They spread before me like palm groves,
like gardens by the riverside.
They are like tall trees planted by the
LORD,
like cedars beside the waters.
7 Water will flow from their buckets;
their offspring have all they need.
Their king will be greater than Agag;
their kingdom will be exalted.
8 God brought them out of Egypt;
for them he is as strong as a wild ox.
He devours all the nations that oppose
him,
breaking their bones in pieces,
shooting them with arrows.
9 Like a lion, Israel crouches and lies down;
like a lioness, who dares to arouse her?
Blessed is everyone who blesses you,
O Israel,
and cursed is everyone who curses you."

10 King Balak flew into a rage against Balaam. He angrily clapped his hands and
shouted, "I called you to curse my enemies!
Instead, you have blessed them three times.
11 Now get out of here! Go back home! I promised to reward you richly, but the LORD has
kept you from your reward."

12 Balaam told Balak, "Don't you remember what I told your messengers? I said,
13 'Even if Balak were to give me his palace
filled with silver and gold, I would be powerless to do anything against the will of the
LORD.' I told you that I could say only what
the LORD says! 14 Now I am returning to my
own people. But first let me tell you what
the Israelites will do to your people in the
future."

Balaam's Final Messages

15 This is the message Balaam delivered:

"This is the message of Balaam son of
Beor,
the message of the man whose eyes
see clearly,
16 the message of one who hears the words
of God,
who has knowledge from the [i]Most
High,
who sees a vision from the Almighty,
who bows down with eyes wide open:
17 I see him, but not here and now.
I perceive him, but far in the distant
future.
A star will rise from Jacob;
a scepter will emerge from Israel.

23:28 Num 31:16; Josh 22:17
24:2 Num 11:25-26; 1 Sam 10:10; 2 Chr 15:1
24:3 Num 23:7-10, 18-24
24:4 Num 12:6; 22:20
24:6 Ps 45:8
24:7 1 Sam 15:8-9; Ps 145:11-13
24:8 Ps 45:5
24:9 Gen 12:3; 27:29; 49:9; Num 23:24
24:11 Num 22:17, 37
24:13 Num 22:18, 20
24:15 Gen 49:1; Num 24:3-4
24:16 [i]*'elyon* (5945) ▸Deut 32:8
24:17 Gen 49:10; Isa 15:1–16:4; Matt 2:2

23:28 *overlooking the wasteland:* Or *overlooking Jeshimon.*

24:1-2 Unlike previously (23:3, 15), Balaam ***did not resort to divination*** this time. He already knew that auguries and omens could not harm Israel (23:23), so he quit looking for them. Instead, Balaam was directly inspired by ***the Spirit of God.***

24:3-9 The third oracle contains another description of God's plan to bless Israel.

24:5-6 God's love for his people was reflected in the blessings he showered upon them.

24:6-7a The Lord's favor is emphasized by the comparison of Israel's situation with groves and gardens that have access to abundant water. Their growing population already reflected God's blessing (24:7), as mentioned in 23:10. This would also become clear in the second registration (ch 26).

24:6 *like palm groves:* Or *like a majestic valley.*

24:7b-9 God's blessing would enable the Israelites to overcome their enemies (see 24:15-24). • ***Agag*** was an Amalekite king defeated by Saul (1 Sam 15:7-9, 32-33). The Amalekites, a desert people, were traditional enemies of the Hebrews (cp. Exod 17:8-16; Num 14:45), and it is likely that Agag was the traditional designation for their king. Since God brought Israel out of Egypt, he fought on their behalf, like a warrior and like a wild animal (ox and lion; 24:8-9). • ***Blessed . . . cursed:*** See Gen 12:3; 27:29.

24:10 Balak ***clapped his hands*** in reproach (cp. Job 27:23; Lam 2:15).

24:14 ***let me tell you what the Israelites will do to your people in the future:*** Since Balak sought to curse Israel, he and his people would be cursed (24:9). The damage that Balak hoped to inflict on Israel would fall on Moab.

24:15-25 This prophecy provides more specific details than the first three. Based on another ***vision from the Almighty*** (24:16), it lists some of the enemies that Israel would defeat in the future and predicts the emergence of an outstanding leader who would play a major role in these military victories (24:17).

24:17 ***A star*** was a symbol for a king (cp. Isa 14:12; Matt 2:1-10), and ***a scepter***

24:18 Amos 9:12
24:19 Gen 49:10
24:20 Exod 17:14
24:21 Gen 15:19
24:22 Gen 10:22
24:24 Gen 10:4, 21
25:1 Num 33:49; Josh 2:1
25:2 Exod 34:15-16; *ikhawah* (7812) ‣ Deut 5:9
25:3 Num 25:5; Deut 4:3
25:6 Num 22:4

It will crush the foreheads of Moab's
people,
cracking the skulls of the people of
Sheth.
18 Edom will be taken over,
and Seir, its enemy, will be
conquered,
while Israel marches on in triumph.
19 A ruler will rise in Jacob
who will destroy the survivors of Ir."

20Then Balaam looked over toward the people of Amalek and delivered this message:

"Amalek was the greatest of nations,
but its destiny is destruction!"

21Then he looked over toward the Kenites and delivered this message:

"Your home is secure;
your nest is set in the rocks.
22 But the Kenites will be destroyed
when Assyria takes you captive."

23Balaam concluded his messages by saying:

"Alas, who can survive
unless God has willed it?
24 Ships will come from the coasts of
Cyprus;
they will oppress Assyria and afflict
Eber,
but they, too, will be utterly destroyed."

25Then Balaam and Balak returned to their homes.

Moab Seduces Israel into Apostasy (25:1-18)

25 While the Israelites were camped at Acacia Grove, some of the men defiled themselves by having sexual relations with local Moabite women.
2These women invited them to attend sacrifices to their gods, so the Israelites feasted with them and iworshiped the gods of Moab.
3In this way, Israel joined in the worship of Baal of Peor, causing the LORD's anger to blaze against his people.

4The LORD issued the following command to Moses: "Seize all the ringleaders and execute them before the LORD in broad daylight, so his fierce anger will turn away from the people of Israel."

5So Moses ordered Israel's judges, "Each of you must put to death the men under your authority who have joined in worshiping Baal of Peor."

6Just then one of the Israelite men brought a Midianite woman into his tent, right

---

was an image of power and majesty (cp. Gen 49:10; Ps 45:6). King David fits the description historically. The Moabites, whose defeat is mentioned in 24:17, were among the many peoples conquered during his reign (2 Sam 8:2), though Moab remained a dangerous enemy of Israel after David's time (cp. 2 Kgs 3; Isa 15–16; Jer 48). Many interpreters have extended the image beyond David. Christians identify Jesus of Nazareth with a star (cp. Matt 2:2; 2 Pet 1:19; Rev 2:28; 22:16) and a scepter (cp. Heb 1:8). • ***The people of Sheth*** were probably the ancient Sutu, though it might refer to Edom/Seir (also conquered by David; 24:18), Ir (or Ar) of Moab (24:19; cp. 21:28), or Amalek, one of Israel's earliest and most persistent enemies (24:20).

24:21-22 The *Kenites,* a desert people who occupied some of the same regions as the Amalekites and Midianites, would be destroyed by ***Assyria*** (Hebrew *'Ashur;* also in 24:24). Moses married a Kenite (Judg 1:16; 4:11; cp. Num 10:29-32), and the Kenites remained mostly friendly with Israel thereafter (e.g., 1 Sam 15:6; 27:10; 30:27-30).

24:23-24 The oracle ends with a word about the rise and fall of invaders from ***Cyprus*** (Hebrew *Kittim*); this term probably referred to a number of Mediterranean people groups (cp. Gen 10:4; Jer 2:10; Dan 11:30).

24:23 This verse, like 22:12, sums up the lesson of the entire incident.

24:24 *Eber,* spelled the same as the ancestor of the Hebrews (cp. Gen 10:21-25; 11:10-16), possibly refers to a people beyond the Euphrates River, a region that fits the parallel reference to Assyria (Josh 24:3; Isa 7:20).

24:25 ***Balaam*** did not yet go back to Pethor (31:8).

25:1-18 Israel was camped across the Jordan from Jericho, almost on the eve of conquest, but they plunged to a new low in moral failure and spiritual bankruptcy. Balaam's advice led to the immorality and apostasy of Baal-peor (31:16); he found a way to damage Israel, if not through a curse, then through lust and idolatry. The same temptation to idolatry and immorality existed for the early church (1 Cor 10:6, 11).

25:1 *Acacia Grove* (Hebrew *Shittim*): This type of tree thrives in arid regions. From here, Joshua later sent spies across the Jordan, and the Hebrews launched their conquest (Josh 2:1; 3:1). • ***some of the men defiled themselves by having:*** As in Greek version; Hebrew reads *some of the men began having.* • ***Moabite women:*** The Moabites and Midianites shared culpability in the episode involving Balaam (22:2-4, 7; 31:8, 15-16).

25:2 The Israelites participated in worship feasts associated with the ***gods of Moab*** (see Ps 106:28).

25:3 ***Baal of Peor*** might refer to Chemosh (21:29) by a different name, but probably Baal ("lord"), the Canaanite god, was included on the list of deities honored by the Moabites. Numerous place-names were formed with this deity's name (e.g., Baal-gad, Baal-hermon, Baal-meon, Baal-peor), representing shrines for local manifestations of Baal. Peor was a mountain from which Balaam could see the Israelite camp in the plains of Moab; the mountain and the related shrine of Beth-peor (23:28; 25:3, 5, 18; 31:16; Deut 3:29; 4:3, 46; 34:6; Josh 13:20; 22:17) were somewhere in the vicinity of Mount Nebo. • Israel's idolatry caused ***the LORD's anger to blaze against his people;*** this included a plague (25:8-9; 26:1; cp. 11:1, 10; 12:9).

25:4 As he had at Sinai (Exod 32:27-28), the Lord required swift justice. • ***execute . . . in broad daylight:*** The guilty parties were perhaps impaled and left out in the sun (see 2 Sam 21:6, 9) so that everyone could see them and learn from their mistakes (cp. 2 Sam 12:12).

25:6 Here another ***Israelite*** defiled himself with a foreign woman; apparently both Moabite and ***Midianite*** women had been involved in the scandal (25:1-3, 16-18; 31:1-2). The man's sin was

before the eyes of Moses and all the people, as everyone was weeping at the entrance of the Tabernacle. 7When Phinehas son of Eleazar and grandson of Aaron the priest saw this, he jumped up and left the assembly. He took a spear 8and rushed after the man into his tent. Phinehas thrust the spear all the way through the man's body and into the woman's stomach. So the plague against the Israelites was stopped, 9but not before 24,000 people had died.

10Then the LORD said to Moses, 11"Phinehas son of Eleazar and grandson of Aaron the priest has turned my anger away from the Israelites by being as zealous among them as I was. So I stopped destroying all Israel as I had intended to do in my zealous anger. 12Now tell him that I am making my special [k]covenant of peace with him. 13In this covenant, I give him and his descendants a permanent right to the priesthood, for in his zeal for me, his God, he purified the people of Israel, making them right with me."

14The Israelite man killed with the Midianite woman was named Zimri son of Salu, the leader of a family from the tribe of Simeon. 15The woman's name was Cozbi; she was the daughter of Zur, the leader of a Midianite clan.

16Then the LORD said to Moses, 17"Attack the Midianites and destroy them, 18because they assaulted you with deceit and tricked you into worshiping Baal of Peor, and because of Cozbi, the daughter of a Midianite leader, who was killed at the time of the plague because of what happened at Peor."

The Second Registration (26:1-65)

The Second Registration of Israel's Troops

26 After the plague had ended, the LORD said to Moses and to Eleazar son of Aaron the priest, 2"From the whole community of Israel, record the names of all the warriors by their families. List all the men twenty years old or older who are able to go to war."

3So there on the plains of Moab beside the Jordan River, across from Jericho, Moses and Eleazar the priest issued these instructions to the leaders of Israel: 4"List all the men of Israel twenty years old and older, just as the LORD commanded Moses."

This is the record of all the descendants of Israel who came out of Egypt.

The Tribe of Reuben

5These were the clans descended from the sons of Reuben, Jacob's oldest son:

The Hanochite clan, named after their ancestor Hanoch.
The Palluite clan, named after their ancestor Pallu.
6The Hezronite clan, named after their ancestor Hezron.
The Carmite clan, named after their ancestor Carmi.

7These were the clans of Reuben. Their registered troops numbered 43,730.

8Pallu was the ancestor of Eliab, 9and Eliab was the father of Nemuel, Dathan, and Abiram. This Dathan and Abiram are the same community leaders who conspired with Korah against Moses and Aaron, rebelling against the LORD. 10But the earth opened up its mouth and swallowed them with Korah, and fire devoured 250 of their followers. This served as a warning to the entire nation of Israel. 11However, the sons of Korah did not die that day.

The Tribe of Simeon

12These were the clans descended from the sons of Simeon:

25:7-8 Ps 106:30
25:9 *1 Cor 10:8
25:12 Ps 106:30-31; Isa 54:10; [k]*berith* (1285) ‣Deut 29:1
25:15 Num 25:18; 31:8; Josh 13:21
25:17 Num 31:2
25:18 Num 23:28
26:1 Num 25:6-9
26:2 Num 1:2-15
26:5 Exod 6:14
26:9 Num 16:1
26:10 Num 16:32, 35, 38
26:12 1 Chr 4:24-43

particularly brazen, as he apparently disregarded the judgment and mourning around him. • Some suggest that *his tent* was an unauthorized shrine associated with the worship of Yahweh, and not just Zimri's dwelling. • ***the Tabernacle:*** Literally *the Tent of Meeting.* See note on Exod 27:21.

25:7-9 ***Phinehas,*** acting as a representative of the priestly family, killed Zimri and Cozbi with one *thrust* of a *spear* (25:7-8), which probably indicates that they were engaged in sexual intercourse. Phinehas's zeal *stopped* the plague (25:1-3).

25:10-13 Israel's identity as the Lord's people was severely threatened by their unfaithfulness on this occasion. Phinehas was *as zealous* as God in his pursuit of holiness and justice. As a result, Phinehas and his descendants were granted a special status; God made a ***special covenant of peace*** with Phinehas, and qualified men in his family inherited ***a permanent right to the priesthood*** (cp. Mal 2:5). This unconditional covenant was similar to that extended to David (see Jer 33:19-22).

25:13 ***he purified the people of Israel, making them right with me*** (or *he made atonement for the people of Israel*): The deaths of Zimri and Cozbi helped to purify Israel from its sin; Phinehas's act had atoning value (see note on Lev 1:4).

25:16-18 ***Attack the Midianites and destroy them:*** This war is recorded in ch 31.

26:1-65 After nearly forty years, Israel again registered their men of military age (cp. chs 1–4) as they camped ***in the plains of Moab . . . across from Jericho.*** The overall population had changed only slightly, with 603,550 in the first registration and ***601,730*** in the second. This nearly complete replacement of population (26:63-65) showed that the Lord was faithful to Israel in spite of their repeated acts of rebellion.

26:1-4 As in the first registration, Moses and Eleazar (who had replaced Aaron) instructed the tribal leaders in the tabulation process.

26:5 ***Jacob's:*** Literally *Israel's;* see note on 1:20-21.

26:8-11 ***the sons of Korah did not die that day:*** See note on 16:31-33.

26:23
1 Chr 7:1-5
26:28
Gen 46:19-21

The Jemuelite clan, named after their ancestor Jemuel.
The Jaminite clan, named after their ancestor Jamin.
The Jakinite clan, named after their ancestor Jakin.
13 The Zoharite clan, named after their ancestor Zohar.
The Shaulite clan, named after their ancestor Shaul.

14 These were the clans of Simeon. Their registered troops numbered 22,200.

The Tribe of Gad

15 These were the clans descended from the sons of Gad:
The Zephonite clan, named after their ancestor Zephon.
The Haggite clan, named after their ancestor Haggi.
The Shunite clan, named after their ancestor Shuni.
16 The Oznite clan, named after their ancestor Ozni.
The Erite clan, named after their ancestor Eri.
17 The Arodite clan, named after their ancestor Arodi.
The Arelite clan, named after their ancestor Areli.

18 These were the clans of Gad. Their registered troops numbered 40,500.

The Tribe of Judah

19 Judah had two sons, Er and Onan, who
had died in the land of Canaan. 20 These
were the clans descended from Judah's surviving sons:
The Shelanite clan, named after their ancestor Shelah.
The Perezite clan, named after their ancestor Perez.
The Zerahite clan, named after their ancestor Zerah.

21 These were the subclans descended from the Perezites:
The Hezronites, named after their ancestor Hezron.
The Hamulites, named after their ancestor Hamul.

22 These were the clans of Judah. Their registered troops numbered 76,500.

The Tribe of Issachar

23 These were the clans descended from the sons of Issachar:
The Tolaite clan, named after their ancestor Tola.
The Puite clan, named after their ancestor Puah.
24 The Jashubite clan, named after their ancestor Jashub.
The Shimronite clan, named after their ancestor Shimron.

25 These were the clans of Issachar. Their registered troops numbered 64,300.

The Tribe of Zebulun

26 These were the clans descended from the sons of Zebulun:
The Seredite clan, named after their ancestor Sered.
The Elonite clan, named after their ancestor Elon.
The Jahleelite clan, named after their ancestor Jahleel.

27 These were the clans of Zebulun. Their registered troops numbered 60,500.

The Tribe of Manasseh

28 Two clans were descended from Joseph through Manasseh and Ephraim.

29 These were the clans descended from Manasseh:
The Makirite clan, named after their ancestor Makir.
The Gileadite clan, named after their ancestor Gilead, Makir's son.

30 These were the subclans descended from the Gileadites:
The Iezerites, named after their ancestor Iezer.
The Helekites, named after their ancestor Helek.
31 The Asrielites, named after their ancestor Asriel.
The Shechemites, named after their ancestor Shechem.
32 The Shemidaites, named after their ancestor Shemida.
The Hepherites, named after their ancestor Hepher.
33 (One of Hepher's descendants, Zelophehad, had no sons, but his daughters' names were Mahlah, Noah, Hoglah, Milcah, and Tirzah.)

26:12 *Jemuelite . . . Jemuel:* As in Syriac version (see also Gen 46:10; Exod 6:15); Hebrew reads *Nemuelite . . . Nemuel.*

26:13 *Zoharite . . . Zohar:* As in parallel texts at Gen 46:10 and Exod 6:15; Hebrew reads *Zerahite . . . Zerah.*

26:17 *Arodi:* As in Samaritan Pentateuch and Greek and Syriac versions (see also Gen 46:16); Hebrew reads *Arod.*

26:23 *The Puite clan, named after their ancestor Puah:* As in Samaritan Pentateuch, Greek and Syriac versions, and Latin Vulgate (see also 1 Chr 7:1); Hebrew reads *The Punite clan, named after its ancestor Puvah.*

26:33 The daughters of *Zelophehad* initiated important legal reform (see 27:1-11; 36:1-12).

34 These were the clans of Manasseh. Their registered troops numbered 52,700.

The Tribe of Ephraim

35 These were the clans descended from the sons of Ephraim:

The Shuthelahite clan, named after their ancestor Shuthelah.
The Bekerite clan, named after their ancestor Beker.
The Tahanite clan, named after their ancestor Tahan.

36 This was the subclan descended from the Shuthelahites:

The Eranites, named after their ancestor Eran.

37 These were the clans of Ephraim. Their registered troops numbered 32,500.

These clans of Manasseh and Ephraim were all descendants of Joseph.

The Tribe of Benjamin

38 These were the clans descended from the sons of Benjamin:

The Belaite clan, named after their ancestor Bela.
The Ashbelite clan, named after their ancestor Ashbel.
The Ahiramite clan, named after their ancestor Ahiram.
39 The Shuphamite clan, named after their ancestor Shupham.
The Huphamite clan, named after their ancestor Hupham.

40 These were the subclans descended from the Belaites:

The Ardites, named after their ancestor Ard.
The Naamites, named after their ancestor Naaman.

41 These were the clans of Benjamin. Their registered troops numbered 45,600.

The Tribe of Dan

42 These were the clans descended from the sons of Dan:

The Shuhamite clan, named after their ancestor Shuham.

43 These were the Shuhamite clans of Dan. Their registered troops numbered 64,400.

The Tribe of Asher

44 These were the clans descended from the sons of Asher:

The Imnite clan, named after their ancestor Imnah.
The Ishvite clan, named after their ancestor Ishvi.
The Beriite clan, named after their ancestor Beriah.

45 These were the subclans descended from the Beriites:

The Heberites, named after their ancestor Heber.
The Malkielites, named after their ancestor Malkiel.

46 Asher also had a daughter named Serah.

47 These were the clans of Asher. Their registered troops numbered 53,400.

The Tribe of Naphtali

48 These were the clans descended from the sons of Naphtali:

The Jahzeelite clan, named after their ancestor Jahzeel.
The Gunite clan, named after their ancestor Guni.
49 The Jezerite clan, named after their ancestor Jezer.
The Shillemite clan, named after their ancestor Shillem.

50 These were the clans of Naphtali. Their registered troops numbered 45,400.

Results of the Registration

51 In summary, the registered troops of all
Israel numbered 601,730.
52 Then the LORD said to Moses, 53 "Divide the land among the tribes, and
distribute the grants of land in proportion
to the tribes' populations, as indicated by
the number of names on the list. 54 Give
the larger tribes more land and the smaller
tribes less land, each group receiving a
grant in proportion to the size of its population. 55 But you must assign the land by
lot, and give land to each ancestral tribe
according to the number of names on the
list. 56 Each grant of land must be assigned
by lot among the larger and smaller tribal
groups."

26:35 1 Chr 7:20-25
26:37 Num 1:32-35
26:38 Gen 46:21; 1 Chr 8:1
26:40 1 Chr 8:3
26:42 Gen 46:23-25
26:44 Gen 46:17
26:48 1 Chr 7:13
26:51 Num 1:43-46
26:54 Num 33:54
26:55 Num 33:54; 34:13

26:39 *Shupham:* As in some Hebrew manuscripts, Samaritan Pentateuch, Greek and Syriac versions, and Latin Vulgate; most Hebrew manuscripts read *Shephupham.*

26:40 ***The Ardites, named after their ancestor Ard:*** As in Samaritan Pentateuch, some Greek manuscripts, and Latin Vulgate; Hebrew lacks *named after their ancestor Ard.*

26:51 In spite of warfare, plagues, and punishments, God had been faithful to Israel. The number of male warriors had shrunk by 1,820 compared to the first registration (cp. 2:32), a difference of 0.3 percent.

26:52-56 The second registration, like the first, was a military one, but it also provided the basis for distributing land to Israel's tribes ***in proportion to the tribes' populations*** (cp. Josh 15–19). • ***assign the land by lot:*** Lots were used to seek divine guidance and avoid favoritism in important matters (e.g.,

26:57
Gen 46:11
1 Chr 6:1

26:58
Num 3:16-35

26:60
Num 3:2

26:61
Lev 10:1-2
Num 3:4

26:62
Num 3:39

26:64
Num 14:20-43
Deut 2:14-15

27:1
Num 26:28-37; 36:1-4

27:7
Num 36:1-4
Josh 17:4

27:11
Num 35:29

The Tribe of Levi

57 This is the record of the Levites who were counted according to their clans:

The Gershonite clan, named after their ancestor Gershon.
The Kohathite clan, named after their ancestor Kohath.
The Merarite clan, named after their ancestor Merari.

58 The Libnites, the Hebronites, the Mahlites, the Mushites, and the Korahites were all subclans of the Levites.

Now Kohath was the ancestor of Amram, 59 and Amram's wife was named Jochebed. She also was a descendant of Levi, born among the Levites in the land of Egypt. Amram and Jochebed became the parents of Aaron, Moses, and their sister, Miriam. 60 To Aaron were born Nadab, Abihu, Eleazar, and Ithamar. 61 But Nadab and Abihu died when they burned before the LORD the wrong kind of fire, different than he had commanded.

62 The men from the Levite clans who were one month old or older numbered 23,000. But the Levites were not included in the registration of the rest of the people of Israel because they were not given an allotment of land when it was divided among the Israelites.

Summary of the Registration

63 So these are the results of the registration of the people of Israel as conducted by Moses and Eleazar the priest on the plains of Moab beside the Jordan River, across from Jericho. 64 Not one person on this list had been among those listed in the previous registration taken by Moses and Aaron in the wilderness of Sinai. 65 For the LORD had said of them, "They will all die in the wilderness." Not one of them survived except Caleb son of Jephunneh and Joshua son of Nun.

Preparations for the Invasion (27:1–36:13)

The Daughters of Zelophehad

27 One day a petition was presented by the daughters of Zelophehad—Mahlah, Noah, Hoglah, Milcah, and Tirzah. Their father, Zelophehad, was a descendant of Hepher son of Gilead, son of Makir, son of Manasseh, son of Joseph. 2 These women stood before Moses, Eleazar the priest, the tribal leaders, and the entire community at the entrance of the Tabernacle. 3 "Our father died in the wilderness," they said. "He was not among Korah's followers, who rebelled against the LORD; he died because of his own sin. But he had no sons. 4 Why should the name of our father disappear from his clan just because he had no sons? Give us property along with the rest of our relatives."

5 So Moses brought their case before the LORD. 6 And the LORD replied to Moses, 7 "The claim of the daughters of Zelophehad is legitimate. You must give them a grant of land along with their father's relatives. Assign them the property that would have been given to their father.

8 "And give the following instructions to the people of Israel: If a man dies and has no son, then give his inheritance to his daughters. 9 And if he has no daughter either, transfer his inheritance to his brothers. 10 If he has no brothers, give his inheritance to his father's brothers. 11 But if his father has no brothers, give his inheritance to the nearest relative in his clan. This is a legal requirement for the people of Israel, just as the LORD commanded Moses."

27:21; 1 Sam 10:20; 14:41-42; Prov 18:18; Acts 1:26).

26:57-61 The family of ***Kohath*** received special attention as the clan of ***Aaron, Moses,*** and ***Miriam.***

26:62 The Levites were numbered separately (cp. 1:47-49; 3:14-39). • ***one month old or older:*** Cp. 3:15. • ***they were not given an allotment of land when it was divided among the Israelites:*** The Levites were given forty-eight towns for their use, but they received no large territory through the process described in 26:52-56 (35:1-8; cp. 18:23-24).

26:63-65 The registration figures represent an entirely new generation of Hebrews, for everyone who came out of Egypt died in the wilderness except Caleb and Joshua. ***Joshua*** inherited Moses' position as the leader of Israel (27:12-23; see "Joshua" at Josh 1:1-18, p. 377), and ***Caleb*** later played an important role (see "Caleb" at Josh 14:6-15, p. 399). Chapter 26 documents Israel's transition from a generation under God's condemnation (ch 14) to a people with a future, as predicted by Balaam's four prophecies (chs 23–24).

27:1-11 Zelophehad's lack of male heirs created an opportunity to refine the inheritance laws, which would later be refined even further (cp. 36:1-13).

27:2 ***The entrance of the Tabernacle*** (literally *the Tent of Meeting*) was the most important public place, where significant decisions were made. The reference to this event in Josh 17:4 specifically mentions Eleazar, Joshua, and the Hebrew leaders, but omits Moses' name. These women requested an exception to the law as it stood, and they brought their case to the highest tribal authorities.

27:3-4 Zelophehad had not been part of ***Korah's*** rebellion (16:1-50); if he had been, his property rights would apparently have been voided (see 15:30; cp. 1 Kgs 21:7-16). Israelite society was patriarchal and patrilineal, tracing ancestry and property through the male line. Zelophehad had no sons, but his daughters wanted his family ***property*** rights to continue. Zelophehad's daughters thus made a reasonable appeal for property rights equal to those of males.

27:5-11 Moses took their case ***before the LORD,*** who accepted the women's appeal and established their case as a principle in order to preserve property within families.

Joshua Chosen to Lead Israel
12One day the LORD said to Moses, "Climb
one of the mountains east of the river, and
look out over the land I have given the people of Israel. 13After you have seen it, you
will die like your brother, Aaron, 14for you
both rebelled against my instructions in
the wilderness of Zin. When the people of
Israel rebelled, you failed to demonstrate
my holiness to them at the waters." (These
are the waters of Meribah at Kadesh in the
wilderness of Zin.)
15Then Moses said to the LORD, 16"O LORD,
you are the God who gives breath to all creatures. Please appoint a new man as leader
for the community. 17Give them someone
who will guide them wherever they go and
will lead them into battle, so the community
of the LORD will not be like sheep without a
shepherd."
18The LORD replied, "Take Joshua son
of Nun, who has the Spirit in him, and lay
your hands on him. 19Present him to Eleazar the priest before the whole community,
and publicly commission him to lead the
people. 20Transfer some of your authority
to him so the whole community of Israel
will obey him. 21When direction from the
LORD is needed, Joshua will stand before Eleazar the priest, who will use the Urim—one
of the sacred lots cast before the LORD—to
determine his will. This is how Joshua and
the rest of the community of Israel will determine everything they should do."
22So Moses did as the LORD commanded.
He presented Joshua to Eleazar the priest
and the whole community. 23Moses laid his
hands on him and commissioned him to
lead the people, just as the LORD had commanded through Moses.

The Daily Offerings
28 The LORD said to Moses, 2"Give
these instructions to the people of
Israel: The offerings you present as special
gifts are a pleasing aroma to me; they are
my food. See to it that they are brought at
the appointed times and offered according
to my instructions.
3"Say to the people: This is the special
gift you must present to the LORD as your
daily burnt offering. You must offer two
one-year-old male lambs with no defects.
4Sacrifice one lamb in the morning and the
other in the evening. 5With each lamb you
must offer a grain offering of two quarts of
choice flour mixed with one quart of pure
oil of pressed olives. 6This is the regular
burnt offering instituted at Mount Sinai as
a special gift, a pleasing aroma to the LORD.
7Along with it you must present the proper
liquid offering of one quart of alcoholic

27:12 Num 33:47; Deut 32:49
27:13 Deut 32:50-51
27:14 Num 20:9-13; Deut 32:48-52
27:17 1 Kgs 22:17; Ezek 34:1-24; Zech 10:2; Matt 9:36; *Mark 6:34
27:18 Deut 34:9
27:20 Josh 1:16-17
27:21 Exod 28:30; 1 Sam 28:6
28:3 Exod 29:38-41
28:4 Lev 6:19-20
28:5 Num 15:3-12
28:7 Exod 29:42; Lev 23:13

27:12-23 Israel would need leadership when they entered the land of Canaan. Joshua was commissioned to succeed Moses.

27:12 ***The mountains east of the river*** (or *the mountains of Abarim*) probably included Mount Nebo (Deut 32:49), from which Moses viewed the Promised Land just before his death (Deut 34:1).

27:13-14 ***waters of Meribah at Kadesh:*** Literally *waters of Meribath-kadesh*; cp. 20:12-13.

27:15-17 Israel was on the threshold of a long battle for Canaan; Moses did not want them to flounder without a leader or lose their way ***like sheep without a shepherd*** (cp. 1 Kgs 22:17; Ezek 34:5; Matt 9:36).

27:18-19 ***Joshua*** had a solid background for the role (cp. Exod 17:8-16). He had been Moses' assistant for a long time (11:28; cp. Exod 33:11). He was also one of the faithful spies (chs 13–14) who knew the people of Israel well. Joshua possessed ***the Spirit*** and recognized the special presence of God in his life (cp. 11:25-29). His relationship with God also gave him wisdom for the tasks ahead (e.g., Deut 34:9). • ***lay your hands on him:*** This act symbolized the transfer of authority from an elder statesman to his assistant (cp. 8:10-14). Moses did this ***publicly*** so that Joshua's leadership would be incontestable.

27:20-21 Joshua assumed only ***some*** of Moses' ***authority***. Moses had face-to-face contact with God (12:6-8; Deut 34:10-12), but Joshua had only indirect access to revelation, since he had to consult with ***Eleazar the priest*** on important matters (27:21; cp. Exod 28:30; Lev 8:8). Israel would keep military and spiritual leadership separate hereafter.

28:1–29:40 These two chapters contain information about Israel's ritual calendar, including a list of required daily, weekly, and monthly offerings and a list of annual religious events. Thus Israel was instructed to worship God "properly and in order" (1 Cor 14:40). The annual cycle of sacrifices involved a tremendous investment of animals, grain, oil, and wine. Israel marked these special days by stopping their normal work, a kind of sacrifice that recognized the importance of these holy days. This annual cycle included eight different occasions for worship, all of which recalled Israel's relationship with the Lord. Each worship event included a different combination of burnt, grain, liquid, and/or sin offerings. • For details on the grain and liquid offerings, see 15:1-16. For explanations of the different types of offerings, see chart, "Israel's Sacrifices," p. 197. For a description of Israel's festivals, see chart, "Israel's Festivals," p. 235. For the details of Israel's annual calendar, see chart, "Israel's Annual Calendar" p. 145. For the NT perspective on the OT sacrificial system, see John 1:29; Rom 12:1; Heb 9:9-15; 10:1-2; 1 Pet 2:5.

28:1-2 The Lord accepted ***special gifts*** (cp. 15:3) as ***a pleasing aroma***, a figurative expression describing God's acceptance and enjoyment of these gifts (see also Gen 8:21; Lev 1:9; Eph 5:2; Phil 4:18). Offerings were made at ***appointed times*** according to specific ***instructions*** (see 28:3–29:39).

28:2 ***they are my food:*** See notes on Exod 29:18; Deut 8:2.

28:3-8 The daily offering was the foundation of the sacrificial system. Its practice was ***instituted at Mount Sinai*** (see Exod 29:38-46). • ***alcoholic drink:*** Cp. 6:3; Lev 10:9; Deut 14:26.

28:5 ***two quarts:*** Hebrew *1/10 of an ephah* [2.2 liters]; also in 28:13, 21, 29. • ***one quart:*** Hebrew *1/4 of a hin* [1 liter]; also in 28:7.

28:11 Num 10:10; 28:19 Ezek 46:6-7
28:12 Num 15:4-12
28:15 Num 28:3
28:16 Exod 12:6, 18 Lev 23:5-14 Deut 16:1-8
28:19 Num 28:11
28:26 Exod 23:16 Lev 23:9-22 Deut 16:9-12
28:31 Num 28:3

drink with each lamb, poured out in the Holy Place as an offering to the LORD. [8]Offer the second lamb in the evening with the same grain offering and liquid offering. It, too, is a special gift, a pleasing aroma to the LORD.

The Sabbath Offerings

[9]"On the Sabbath day, sacrifice two one-year-old male lambs with no defects. They must be accompanied by a grain offering of four quarts of choice flour moistened with olive oil, and a liquid offering. [10]This is the burnt offering to be presented each Sabbath day, in addition to the regular burnt offering and its accompanying liquid offering.

The Monthly Offerings

[11]"On the first day of each month, present an extra burnt offering to the LORD of two young bulls, one ram, and seven one-year-old male lambs, all with no defects. [12]These must be accompanied by grain offerings of choice flour moistened with olive oil—six quarts with each bull, four quarts with the ram, [13]and two quarts with each lamb. This burnt offering will be a special gift, a pleasing aroma to the LORD. [14]You must also present a liquid offering with each sacrifice: two quarts of wine for each bull, a third of a gallon for the ram, and one quart for each lamb. Present this monthly burnt offering on the first day of each month throughout the year.

[15]"On the first day of each month, you must also offer one male goat for a sin offering to the LORD. This is in addition to the regular burnt offering and its accompanying liquid offering.

Offerings for the Passover

[16]"On the fourteenth day of the first month, you must celebrate the LORD's Passover. [17]On the following day—the fifteenth day of the month—a joyous, seven-day festival will begin, but no bread made with yeast may be eaten. [18]The first day of the festival will be an official day for holy assembly, and no ordinary work may be done on that day. [19]As a special gift you must present a burnt offering to the LORD—two young bulls, one ram, and seven one-year-old male lambs, all with no defects. [20]These will be accompanied by grain offerings of choice flour moistened with olive oil—six quarts with each bull, four quarts with the ram, [21]and two quarts with each of the seven lambs. [22]You must also offer a male goat as a sin offering to purify yourselves and make yourselves right with the LORD. [23]Present these offerings in addition to your regular morning burnt offering. [24]On each of the seven days of the festival, this is how you must prepare the food offering that is presented as a special gift, a pleasing aroma to the LORD. These will be offered in addition to the regular burnt offerings and liquid offerings. [25]The seventh day of the festival will be another official day for holy assembly, and no ordinary work may be done on that day.

Offerings for the Festival of Harvest

[26]"At the Festival of Harvest, when you present the first of your new grain to the LORD, you must call an official day for holy assembly, and you may do no ordinary work on that day. [27]Present a special burnt offering on that day as a pleasing aroma to the LORD. It will consist of two young bulls, one ram, and seven one-year-old male lambs. [28]These will be accompanied by grain offerings of choice flour moistened with olive oil—six quarts with each bull, four quarts with the ram, [29]and two quarts with each of the seven lambs. [30]Also, offer one male goat to purify yourselves and make yourselves right with the LORD. [31]Prepare these

---

28:9-10 Special days called for additional offerings. The ***Sabbath day*** required a sacrifice over and above the ***regular burnt offering and its accompanying liquid offering.*** Other passages highlight the importance of the Sabbath (e.g., Exod 20:8-11; Lev 23:3; Deut 5:12-15).

28:9 ***four quarts:*** Hebrew $\frac{2}{10}$ *of an ephah* [4.4 liters]; also in 28:12, 20, 28.

28:11-15 The offering of the ***first day of each month***—the New Moon—called for the sacrifice of bulls, rams, and lambs as burnt offerings, along with a male goat as a sin offering (see also chart, "Israel's Festivals," p. 235).

28:12 ***six quarts:*** Hebrew $\frac{3}{10}$ *of an ephah* [6.6 liters]; also in 28:20, 28.

28:14 ***two quarts:*** Hebrew $\frac{1}{2}$ *of a hin* [2 liters]. • ***a third of a gallon:*** Hebrew $\frac{1}{3}$ *of a hin* [1.3 liters]. • ***one quart:*** Hebrew $\frac{1}{4}$ *of a hin* [1 liter].

28:16-25 The Passover, followed by the Festival of Unleavened Bread, was the first of five great annual festivals; it was held in early spring (March~April). The Passover required no public sacrifices—it was a family occasion celebrated at home (see also 9:1-4; Exod 12:1–13:10; Lev 23:5-8; Deut 16:1-8). This festival played a special role in the background of the Last Supper (see Matt 26:17-19, 26-27; Mark 14:12; John 11:55; 12:1; 13:1; 18:28, 39; 19:14, 31; cp. 1 Cor 5:7).

28:16 ***the fourteenth day of the first month:*** This day in the ancient Hebrew lunar calendar occurred in late March, April, or early May.

28:22 ***to purify yourselves and make yourselves right with the LORD:*** Or *to make atonement for yourselves;* also in 28:30.

28:26-31 The ***Festival of Harvest*** (literally *Festival of Weeks*) was later called the Festival of Pentecost (see Acts 2:1). It is celebrated today as Shavuot (or Shabuoth); see also Lev 23:15-22. It celebrated the end of the barley harvest and the beginning of the wheat harvest in early summer (May~June). The Greek name *Pentecost* means "fiftieth day" (i.e., after Passover; see Acts 20:16; 1 Cor 16:8).

special burnt offerings, along with their liquid offerings, in addition to the regular burnt offering and its accompanying grain offering. Be sure that all the animals you sacrifice have no defects.

Offerings for the Festival of Trumpets

29 "Celebrate the Festival of Trumpets each year on the first day of the appointed month in early autumn. You must call an official day for holy assembly, and you may do no ordinary work. 2On that day you must present a burnt offering as a pleasing aroma to the LORD. It will consist of one young bull, one ram, and seven one-year-old male lambs, all with no defects. 3These must be accompanied by grain offerings of choice flour moistened with olive oil—six quarts with the bull, four quarts with the ram, 4and two quarts with each of the seven lambs. 5In addition, you must sacrifice a male goat as a sin offering to purify yourselves and make yourselves right with the LORD. 6These special sacrifices are in addition to your regular monthly and daily burnt offerings, and they must be given with their prescribed grain offerings and liquid offerings. These offerings are given as a special gift to the LORD, a pleasing aroma to him.

Offerings for the Day of Atonement

7"Ten days later, on the tenth day of the same month, you must call another holy assembly. On that day, the Day of Atonement, the people must go without food and must do no ordinary work. 8You must present a burnt offering as a pleasing aroma to the LORD. It will consist of one young bull, one ram, and seven one-year-old male lambs, all with no defects. 9These offerings must be accompanied by the prescribed grain offerings of choice flour moistened with olive oil—six quarts of choice flour with the bull, four quarts of choice flour with the ram, 10and two quarts of choice flour with each of the seven lambs. 11You must also sacrifice one male goat for a sin offering. This is in addition to the sin offering of atonement and the regular daily burnt offering with its grain offering, and their accompanying liquid offerings.

Offerings for the Festival of Shelters

12"Five days later, on the fifteenth day of the same month, you must call another holy assembly of all the people, and you may do no ordinary work on that day. It is the beginning of the Festival of Shelters, a seven-day festival to the LORD. 13On the first day of the festival, you must present a burnt offering as a special gift, a pleasing aroma to the LORD. It will consist of thirteen young bulls, two rams, and fourteen one-year-old male lambs, all with no defects. 14Each of these offerings must be accompanied by a grain offering of choice flour moistened with olive oil—six quarts for each of the thirteen bulls, four quarts for each of the two rams, 15and two quarts for each of the fourteen lambs. 16You must also sacrifice a male goat as a sin offering, in addition to the regular burnt offering with its accompanying grain offering and liquid offering.

17"On the second day of this seven-day festival, sacrifice twelve young bulls, two rams, and fourteen one-year-old male lambs, all with no defects. 18Each of these offerings of bulls, rams, and lambs must be accompanied by its prescribed grain offering and liquid offering. 19You must also sacrifice a male goat as a sin offering, in addition to the regular burnt offering with its accompanying grain offering and liquid offering.

29:1 Lev 23:23-25; Num 28:26
29:6 Num 28:3
29:7 Lev 16:29-34; 23:26-32
29:11 Lev 16:1-34
29:12 Lev 23:33-43; Deut 16:13-14
29:19 Num 28:3, 11, 31

29:1-6 *the Festival of Trumpets:* See also Lev 23:23-25.

29:1 ***the first day of the appointed month in early autumn*** (literally *the first day of the seventh month*): This day in the ancient Hebrew lunar calendar occurred in September or October. This festival is celebrated today as Rosh Hashanah, the Jewish new year.

29:3 ***six quarts:*** Hebrew *3/10 of an ephah* [6.6 liters]; also in 29:9, 14. • ***four quarts:*** Hebrew *2/10 of an ephah* [4.4 liters]; also in 29:9, 14.

29:4 ***two quarts:*** Hebrew *1/10 of an ephah* [2.2 liters]; also in 29:10, 15.

29:5 ***to purify yourselves and make yourselves right with the LORD:*** Or *to make atonement for yourselves.*

29:7-11 ***The Day of Atonement*** was a solemn occasion, a day of fasting (see also Lev 16:1-34; 23:26-32; Rom 3:23-25; Heb 9:7-12, 23-28).

29:7 ***Ten days later, on the tenth day of the same month*** (literally *On the tenth day of the seventh month;* see 29:1 and note): This day in the ancient Hebrew lunar calendar occurred in September or October. It is celebrated today as Yom Kippur (from Hebrew *yom hakkippurim,* Lev 23:27).

29:12-38 ***The Festival of Shelters*** began on the fifteenth day of the seventh month. It was an eight-day harvest celebration (29:12, 35; Exod 34:22) that required an enormous number of offerings. This harvest festival was an especially joyous occasion and a time for thanksgiving (see Neh 8:13-18). The shelters also reminded the Israelites of dwelling in tents during their wilderness sojourn (see also Lev 23:33-43; 1 Kgs 8:1-2).

29:12 ***on the fifteenth day of the same month*** (literally *On the fifteenth day of the seventh month;* see 29:1, 7 and notes): This day in the ancient Hebrew lunar calendar occurred in late September, October, or early November. • The ***Festival of Shelters*** (or *Festival of Booths,* or *Festival of Tabernacles*) was earlier called the Festival of the Final Harvest or Festival of Ingathering (see Exod 23:16b). It is celebrated today as Sukkot (or Succoth).

29:22 Num 28:15
29:35 Lev 23:36
29:39 Lev 23:2; 2 Chr 31:3; Ezra 3:5
30:2 Deut 23:21-25

20“On the third day of the festival, sacrifice eleven young bulls, two rams, and
fourteen one-year-old male lambs, all with
no defects. 21Each of these offerings of
bulls, rams, and lambs must be accompanied by its prescribed grain offering and
liquid offering. 22You must also sacrifice a
male goat as a sin offering, in addition to
the regular burnt offering with its accompanying grain offering and liquid offering.

23“On the fourth day of the festival, sacrifice ten young bulls, two rams, and fourteen
one-year-old male lambs, all with no defects. 24Each of these offerings of bulls,
rams, and lambs must be accompanied by
its prescribed grain offering and liquid offering. 25You must also sacrifice a male goat
as a sin offering, in addition to the regular
burnt offering with its accompanying grain
offering and liquid offering.

26“On the fifth day of the festival, sacrifice nine young bulls, two rams, and
fourteen one-year-old male lambs, all with
no defects. 27Each of these offerings of
bulls, rams, and lambs must be accompanied by its prescribed grain offering and
liquid offering. 28You must also sacrifice a
male goat as a sin offering, in addition to
the regular burnt offering with its accompanying grain offering and liquid offering.

29“On the sixth day of the festival, sacrifice eight young bulls, two rams, and
fourteen one-year-old male lambs, all with
no defects. 30Each of these offerings of
bulls, rams, and lambs must be accompanied by its prescribed grain offering and
liquid offering. 31You must also sacrifice a
male goat as a sin offering, in addition to
the regular burnt offering with its accompanying grain offering and liquid offering.

32“On the seventh day of the festival,
sacrifice seven young bulls, two rams, and
fourteen one-year-old male lambs, all with
no defects. 33Each of these offerings of
bulls, rams, and lambs must be accompanied by its prescribed grain offering and
liquid offering. 34You must also sacrifice
one male goat as a sin offering, in addition
to the regular burnt offering with its accompanying grain offering and liquid offering.

35“On the eighth day of the festival, proclaim another holy day. You must do no
ordinary work on that day. 36You must
present a burnt offering as a special gift, a
pleasing aroma to the LORD. It will consist
of one young bull, one ram, and seven one-
year-old male lambs, all with no defects.
37Each of these offerings must be accompanied by its prescribed grain offering and
liquid offering. 38You must also sacrifice
one male goat as a sin offering, in addition to the regular burnt offering with its
accompanying grain offering and liquid
offering.

39“You must present these offerings to
the LORD at your annual festivals. These
are in addition to the sacrifices and offerings you present in connection with vows,
or as voluntary offerings, burnt offerings,
grain offerings, liquid offerings, or peace
offerings.”

40So Moses gave all of these instructions
to the people of Israel as the LORD had commanded him.

Laws concerning Vows

30 Then Moses summoned the leaders of the tribes of Israel and told
them, “This is what the LORD has commanded: 2A man who makes a vow to the
LORD or makes a pledge under oath must
never break it. He must do exactly what he
said he would do.

3“If a young woman makes a vow to the
LORD or a pledge under oath while she is
still living at her father’s home, 4and her father hears of the vow or pledge and does not
object to it, then all her vows and pledges
will stand. 5But if her father refuses to let
her fulfill the vow or pledge on the day he
hears of it, then all her vows and pledges
will become invalid. The LORD will forgive
her because her father would not let her fulfill them.

29:39 Public offerings were supplemented by a variety of ***voluntary*** individual gifts (cp. Lev 23:38).

29:40 Verse 29:40 is numbered 30:1 in Hebrew text.

30:1-16 Vows were an important way to express devotion or piety, but were sometimes made in haste and were often forgotten. Voluntary pledges were commonly made on special religious occasions or in times of war. Perhaps the reference to vows and voluntary offerings (29:39) prompted the further discussion here (cp. 15:3; see also Lev 5:4-5; 27:1-34; Num 6:1-21; Deut 23:21-23). These instructions were applied in the case of Hannah and Elkanah (1 Sam 1). Such practices, which included fasting, continued into the NT period (e.g., Matt 6:16; 15:3-9; Acts 18:18; 21:23). Vows of females—young and unmarried or adult and married—were subject to approval by the responsible male who would be a financial partner in the vow. Nobody, male or female, young or old, should make a vow to God and then neglect it. • Verses 30:1-16 are numbered 30:2-17 in Hebrew text.

30:1-2 Vows included promises of offerings (e.g., Hannah’s vow, 1 Sam 1) and pledges of abstinence (e.g., the Nazirite vow, Num 6). Jesus made reference to the instruction regarding vows in the Sermon on the Mount (Matt 5:33).

30:3-5 A ***young woman*** was under the authority of ***her father***, who was responsible for her actions and her financial obligations.

6“Now suppose a young woman makes
a vow or binds herself with an impulsive
pledge and later marries. 7If her husband
learns of her vow or pledge and does not object on the day he hears of it, her vows and
pledges will stand. 8But if her husband refuses to accept her vow or impulsive pledge
on the day he hears of it, he nullifies her
commitments, and the LORD will forgive
her. 9If, however, a woman is a widow or is
divorced, she must fulfill all her vows and
pledges.
10“But suppose a woman is married and
living in her husband’s home when she
makes a vow or binds herself with a pledge.
11If her husband hears of it and does not object to it, her vow or pledge will stand. 12But
if her husband refuses to accept it on the
day he hears of it, her vow or pledge will be
nullified, and the LORD will forgive her. 13So
her husband may either confirm or nullify
any vows or pledges she makes to deny herself. 14But if he does not object on the day
he hears of it, then he is agreeing to all her
vows and pledges. 15If he waits more than a
day and then tries to nullify a vow or pledge,
he will be punished for her guilt.”
16These are the regulations the LORD gave
Moses concerning relationships between a
man and his wife, and between a father and
a young daughter who still lives at home.

Conquest of the Midianites

31 Then the LORD said to Moses, 2“On
behalf of the people of Israel, take
revenge on the Midianites for leading them
into idolatry. After that, you will die and
join your ancestors.”
3So Moses said to the people, “Choose some
men, and arm them to fight the LORD’s war of
revenge against Midian. 4From each tribe of
Israel, send 1,000 men into battle.” 5So they
chose 1,000 men from each tribe of Israel, a
total of 12,000 men armed for battle. 6Then
Moses sent them out, 1,000 men from each
tribe, and Phinehas son of Eleazar the priest
led them into battle. They carried along the
holy objects of the sanctuary and the trumpets for sounding the charge. 7They attacked
Midian as the LORD had commanded Moses,
and they killed all the men. 8All five of the
Midianite kings—Evi, Rekem, Zur, Hur, and
Reba—died in the battle. They also killed Balaam son of Beor with the sword.
9Then the Israelite army captured the
Midianite women and children and seized
their cattle and flocks and all their wealth
as plunder. 10They burned all the towns

30:8 Gen 3:16
30:12 Eph 5:22; Col 3:18
31:2 Num 25:16-17
31:6 Num 10:8-9
31:8 Josh 13:21-22

30:6-8 When a *young* Hebrew *woman* married, she came under the authority of *her husband,* who could void the obligations of a *vow or pledge* made by his wife while she was under her father’s authority by nullifying it as soon as he heard about it.

30:9 A *widow* or a *divorced* woman usually returned to her father’s family (Lev 22:13), but a mature single woman who made a vow or pledge was required to *fulfill* her religious duties.

30:10-15 A *married* woman also needed the approval of *her husband* to make vows and pledges. Her husband could *nullify* her religious promise, but he had to make this decision on the day he heard about it. God did not hold the married woman guilty of breaking this promise if her husband cancelled it in the proper manner (cp. 30:5, 8, 12). The self-denial mentioned in 30:13 probably refers to fasting. If he raised no objection, the husband’s silence implied consent. He could not delay in his objection, or he would incur the guilt of a broken vow (cp. Lev 5:4-13).

31:1-2 The Lord ordered Moses to lead Israel in a war of retaliation against the Midianites, who had joined the Moabites in leading the Hebrews into idolatry (25:1-18). The *Midianites* were a tribal people who inhabited the arid and semiarid regions south and east of Palestine and east of the Jordan River; they were counted among the “people of the east” (Judg 6:3, 33; 7:12). They lived in camps or settlements and were famous for their knowledge of desert transportation (cp. Gen 37:28, 36; Isa 60:6). While they were descended from Abraham (Gen 25:1-2) and had been friendly toward Moses (Exod 2:15–3:1; cp. Num 10:29), the elders of Midian had joined Balak in hiring Balaam to curse Israel (22:4, 7), whose presence threatened the peoples of Transjordan (the region east of the Jordan).

31:3-5 *Each tribe* contributed ***1,000 men*** for the ***battle,*** which enabled all of them to gain experience in combat and share in the victory.

31:6 *Phinehas, son of Eleazar* (the high priest), led this force of 12,000 into battle. His leadership helped to define this engagement as “holy war,” an act of revenge for the spiritual harm that Midian had inflicted on Israel (cp. 25:6-18; 31:15-16; see “Holy War” at 2 Chr 20:20-24, p. 757). His zeal in this situation (25:11, 13) was equal to what he demonstrated in the case of Zimri and Cozbi (25:7-8). • Many believe that ***holy objects of the sanctuary*** meant the Ark, which the Hebrews sometimes carried into battle (e.g., 10:35-36; Josh 6:6; 1 Sam 4:3-11; cp. Num 14:44). Others suggest that they were a variety of sacred vessels associated with the Tabernacle rituals (3:31; 4:15; 18:3; cp. 1 Kgs 8:4; 1 Chr 9:29; 2 Chr 5:5). The Israelites probably took some or all of these holy objects as symbols of God’s participation in their holy war.

31:7 The Israelites ***killed all*** of the Midianite *men* in the particular groups they attacked from their camp in the plains of Moab (31:12), not all of the people who were part of the larger Midianite confederation (cp. Judg 6–8). The number of animals and virgins mentioned in 31:32-35 indicates that the 12,000 Hebrews fought a sizable enemy force.

31:8 *Balaam son of Beor* deserved to die because his counsel “caused the people of Israel to rebel against the LORD at Mount Peor” (31:16). Balaam was punished for his villainous deeds (cp. 2 Pet 2:15; Jude 1:11).

31:9-13 After the battle, the Hebrews began the practice that they sometimes followed throughout the period of conquest and beyond (e.g., Josh 6, 8, 10–11). They destroyed their enemies (sometimes the total population), burned towns, and set aside spoils for their own use or as dedicated to the Lord.

31:10 *towns and villages:* These were larger settlements and smaller unfortified encampments.

31:16 Num 25:1-18; 2 Pet 2:15-16
31:17 Deut 7:2; 20:16-18; Judg 21:10-12
31:24 Lev 11:25; 14:9
31:27 Josh 22:8
31:28 Num 18:21
31:29 Num 18:25-26
31:49 Num 1:19

and villages where the Midianites had lived. 11After they had gathered the plunder and captives, both people and animals, 12they brought them all to Moses and Eleazar the priest, and to the whole community of Israel, which was camped on the plains of Moab beside the Jordan River, across from Jericho. 13Moses, Eleazar the priest, and all the leaders of the community went to meet them outside the camp. 14But Moses was furious with all the generals and captains who had returned from the battle.

15"Why have you let all the women live?" he demanded. 16"These are the very ones who followed Balaam's advice and caused the people of Israel to rebel against the LORD at Mount Peor. They are the ones who caused the plague to strike the LORD's people. 17So kill all the boys and all the women who have had intercourse with a man. 18Only the young girls who are virgins may live; you may keep them for yourselves. 19And all of you who have killed anyone or touched a dead body must stay outside the camp for seven days. You must purify yourselves and your captives on the third and seventh days. 20Purify all your clothing, too, and everything made of leather, goat hair, or wood."

21Then Eleazar the priest said to the men who were in the battle, "The LORD has given Moses this legal requirement: 22Anything made of gold, silver, bronze, iron, tin, or lead—23that is, all metals that do not burn—must be passed through fire in order to be made ceremonially pure. These metal objects must then be further purified with the water of purification. But everything that burns must be purified by the water alone. 24On the seventh day you must wash your clothes and be purified. Then you may return to the camp."

Division of the Plunder

25And the LORD said to Moses, 26"You and Eleazar the priest and the family leaders of each tribe are to make a list of all the plunder taken in the battle, including the people and animals. 27Then divide the plunder into two parts, and give half to the men who fought the battle and half to the rest of the people. 28From the army's portion, first give the LORD his share of the plunder—one of every 500 of the prisoners and of the cattle, donkeys, sheep, and goats. 29Give this share of the army's half to Eleazar the priest as an offering to the LORD. 30From the half that belongs to the people of Israel, take one of every fifty of the prisoners and of the cattle, donkeys, sheep, goats, and other animals. Give this share to the Levites, who are in charge of maintaining the LORD's Tabernacle." 31So Moses and Eleazar the priest did as the LORD commanded Moses.

32The plunder remaining from everything the fighting men had taken totaled 675,000 sheep and goats, 3372,000 cattle, 3461,000 donkeys, 35and 32,000 virgin girls.

36Half of the plunder was given to the fighting men. It totaled 337,500 sheep and goats, 37of which 675 were the LORD's share; 3836,000 cattle, of which 72 were the LORD's share; 3930,500 donkeys, of which 61 were the LORD's share; 40and 16,000 virgin girls, of whom 32 were the LORD's share. 41Moses gave all the LORD's share to Eleazar the priest, just as the LORD had directed him.

42Half of the plunder belonged to the people of Israel, and Moses separated it from the half belonging to the fighting men. 43It totaled 337,500 sheep and goats, 4436,000 cattle, 4530,500 donkeys, 46and 16,000 virgin girls. 47From the half-share given to the people, Moses took one of every fifty prisoners and animals and gave them to the Levites, who maintained the LORD's Tabernacle. All this was done as the LORD had commanded Moses.

48Then all the generals and captains came to Moses 49and said, "We, your servants,

---

31:13 *outside the camp:* Probably to keep from contaminating the Tabernacle and all of the people, the returning troops were subjected to purification rituals because of their contact with corpses (31:19-24).

31:14-16 *Moses was furious:* God had commanded total destruction, but the Midianite ***women*** who had ***followed Balaam's advice*** and were largely responsible for the apostasy of Baal-peor had wrongly been given clemency.

31:14 *the generals and captains:* Literally *the commanders of thousands, and the commanders of hundreds;* also in 31:48, 52, 54.

31:17-18 Only young virgin women were to be spared, since they had not participated in the incident at Baal-peor.

31:19-24 Israelite warriors who had contact with corpses subjected themselves and their equipment to routine, but important, purification rituals (see 5:1-4; 19:1-22).

31:25-31 ***The plunder*** was divided ***into two*** equal ***parts,*** with half going to those who fought against the Midianites and half going to the Israelites who stayed behind (cp. 1 Sam 30:21-25). In this sense, everyone participated in the armed conflict, but the relatively small number of warriors each received a larger portion than the much larger number of those who stayed behind.

31:32-35 The total number of animals and young girls who were not killed was quite large, which indicates that Israel fought against many Midianites.

31:36-47 ***The plunder*** was distributed according to the principles established in 31:25-30.

31:48-49 Though it is unusual for no soldiers from an army to be killed in battle, it is not impossible. Classical authors also reported battles in which

have accounted for all the men who went
out to battle under our command; not one
of us is missing! [50]So we are presenting the
items of gold we captured as an offering to
the LORD from our share of the plunder—
armbands, bracelets, rings, earrings, and
necklaces. This will purify our lives before
the LORD and make us right with him."
[51]So Moses and Eleazar the priest
received the gold from all the military commanders—all kinds of jewelry and crafted
objects. [52]In all, the gold that the generals
and captains presented as a gift to the LORD
weighed about 420 pounds. [53]All the fighting men had taken some of the plunder for
themselves. [54]So Moses and Eleazar the
priest accepted the gifts from the generals
and captains and brought the gold to the
Tabernacle as a reminder to the LORD that
the people of Israel belong to him.

The Settlement of Israelite Tribes
East of the Jordan

32 The tribes of Reuben and Gad
owned vast numbers of livestock.
So when they saw that the lands of Jazer
and Gilead were ideally suited for their
flocks and herds, [2]they came to Moses, Eleazar the priest, and the other leaders of the
community. They said, [3]"Notice the towns
of Ataroth, Dibon, Jazer, Nimrah, Heshbon,
Elealeh, Sibmah, Nebo, and Beon. [4]The LORD
has conquered this whole area for the community of Israel, and it is ideally suited for
all our livestock. [5]If we have found favor
with you, please let us have this land as our
property instead of giving us land across the
Jordan River."
[6]"Do you intend to stay here while your
brothers go across and do all the fighting?"
Moses asked the men of Gad and Reuben.
[7]"Why do you want to discourage the rest
of the people of Israel from going across
to the land the LORD has given them? [8]Your
ancestors did the same thing when I sent
them from Kadesh-barnea to explore the
land. [9]After they went up to the valley of
Eshcol and explored the land, they discouraged the people of Israel from entering the
land the LORD was giving them. [10]Then the
LORD was very angry with them, and he
vowed, [11]'Of all those I rescued from Egypt,
no one who is twenty years old or older will
ever see the land I swore to give to Abraham,
Isaac, and Jacob, for they have not obeyed
me wholeheartedly. [12]The only exceptions
are Caleb son of Jephunneh the Kenizzite
and Joshua son of Nun, for they have wholeheartedly followed the LORD.'
[13]"The LORD was [a]angry with Israel and
made them wander in the wilderness for
forty years until the entire generation that
sinned in the LORD's sight had died. [14]But
here you are, a brood of sinners, doing exactly the same thing! You are making the
LORD even angrier with Israel. [15]If you
turn away from him like this and he abandons them again in the wilderness, you will
be responsible for destroying this entire
nation!"

31:53 Deut 20:14
32:1 Num 21:32
32:3 Num 32:33-42; Josh 13:17; Isa 15:4; 16:9
32:8 Num 13:2-26; Deut 1:19-21
32:9 Num 13:23-24
32:10 Num 14:28-30; Deut 1:34
32:12 Num 14:6, 24, 30; Deut 1:36; Josh 14:8-9
32:13 Num 14:31-39; [a]*'ap* (0639) ›Deut 7:4
32:15 Deut 30:17-18

few or no Roman soldiers were killed. If the Israelites had the advantages of preparation, surprise, and overwhelming force, they could have defeated the Midianites and lost no troops, especially in light of God's blessing.

31:50-54 The commanders gladly offered ***gold*** objects in gratitude for a great victory that resulted in no loss of life (cp. Exod 30:12). Ancient art and literature indicate that the Midianites and other desert peoples, both males and females, wore gold jewelry as adornment and as a form of portable wealth (e.g., Judg 8:24-26). ***Moses and Eleazar*** brought this large collection ***to the Tabernacle*** as a memorial of this special event (cp. 16:39-40; Zech 6:14).

31:50 ***will purify our lives before the LORD and make us right with him:*** Or *will make atonement for our lives before the LORD.*

31:52 ***420 pounds:*** Hebrew *16,750 shekels* [191 kilograms].

31:54 ***the Tabernacle:*** Literally *the Tent of Meeting.* See note on Exod 27:21.

32:1-5 From the time that Israel occupied the central part of the area east of the Jordan—during the military encounters described in ch 21—Israel had been preparing to invade Canaan. At a moment when the Hebrews needed to safeguard their unity, two tribes asked to settle east of the Jordan River.

32:1 ***vast numbers of livestock:*** The Israelites had flocks and herds when they left Egypt (cp. Exod 12:38); they acquired many more animals as loot in the war with Midian (cp. 31:32-33) and perhaps in their victories over Sihon and Og (21:21-35). • ***Gilead*** can refer either to the whole northern region of the plateau east of the Jordan (e.g., 32:29) or only to the part of that territory between the Jabbok and the Arnon.

32:3 Reuben, Gad, and half of Manasseh settled in the land that Israel had recently captured from Sihon the Amorite and Og of Bashan (cp. 21:21-35). • ***Ataroth, Dibon, Jazer, Nimrah, Heshbon,*** and ***Elealeh*** have been linked with archaeological sites. • ***Sibmah:*** As in Samaritan Pentateuch and Greek version (see also 32:38); Hebrew reads *Sebam;* its location is unknown. • Though the location of a town called ***Nebo*** is unknown, it was certainly near a mountain or ridge of that same name, which was located along the escarpment that rises above the northern end of the Dead Sea. • The site named ***Beon*** is almost certainly the place called "Baal-meon" in 32:38, which probably corresponds to the ruins at Ma'in.

32:6-15 Moses assumed that Reuben and Gad wanted to stay east of the Jordan River to avoid the dangers that awaited the other tribes in Canaan (cp. chs 13–14).

32:12 ***Caleb*** is identified as a ***Kenizzite,*** a descendant of Esau (cp. Gen 36:10-11). Apparently Caleb was not a native Israelite, but a convert who was so thoroughly integrated into the life and faith of Israel that he was called upon to represent the tribe of Judah when the 12 scouts were sent out to survey the Promised Land (Num 13:6).

32:17
Josh 4:12-13
32:18-19
Josh 13:8; 22:4
32:20
Deut 3:18
32:22
Deut 3:20
Josh 22:4
32:24
Num 30:2
32:33
Num 21:23-26; 34:14
Deut 3:8-17
Josh 12:1-6
32:41
Deut 3:14
Josh 13:30
1 Chr 2:23

[16]But they approached Moses and said,
"We simply want to build pens for our
livestock and fortified towns for our wives
and children. [17]Then we will arm ourselves
and lead our fellow Israelites into battle until we have brought them safely to their land.
Meanwhile, our families will stay in the fortified towns we build here, so they will be
safe from any attacks by the local people.
[18]We will not return to our homes until all
the people of Israel have received their portions of land. [19]But we do not claim any of
the land on the other side of the Jordan. We
would rather live here on the east side and
accept this as our grant of land."

[20]Then Moses said, "If you keep your
word and arm yourselves for the LORD's
battles, [21]and if your troops cross the Jordan and keep fighting until the LORD has
driven out his enemies, [22]then you may
return when the LORD has conquered the
land. You will have fulfilled your duty to the
LORD and to the rest of the people of Israel.
And the land on the east side of the Jordan
will be your property from the LORD. [23]But
if you fail to keep your word, then you will
have sinned against the LORD, and you may
be sure that your sin will find you out. [24]Go
ahead and build towns for your families
and pens for your flocks, but do everything
you have promised."

[25]Then the men of Gad and Reuben replied, "We, your servants, will follow your
instructions exactly. [26]Our children, wives,
flocks, and cattle will stay here in the towns
of Gilead. [27]But all who are able to bear
arms will cross over to fight for the LORD,
just as you have said."

[28]So Moses gave orders to Eleazar the
priest, Joshua son of Nun, and the leaders
of the clans of Israel. [29]He said, "The men
of Gad and Reuben who are armed for battle must cross the Jordan with you to fight
for the LORD. If they do, give them the land
of Gilead as their property when the land
is conquered. [30]But if they refuse to arm
themselves and cross over with you, then
they must accept land with the rest of you
in the land of Canaan."

[31]The tribes of Gad and Reuben said
again, "We are your servants, and we will
do as the LORD has commanded! [32]We will
cross the Jordan into Canaan fully armed to
fight for the LORD, but our property will be
here on this side of the Jordan."

[33]So Moses assigned land to the tribes of
Gad, Reuben, and half the tribe of Manasseh
son of Joseph. He gave them the territory of
King Sihon of the Amorites and the land of
King Og of Bashan—the whole land with its
cities and surrounding lands.

[34]The descendants of Gad built the towns
of Dibon, Ataroth, Aroer, [35]Atroth-shophan,
Jazer, Jogbehah, [36]Beth-nimrah, and Beth-
haran. These were all fortified towns with
pens for their flocks.

[37]The descendants of Reuben built the
towns of Heshbon, Elealeh, Kiriathaim,
[38]Nebo, Baal-meon, and Sibmah. They
changed the names of some of the towns
they conquered and rebuilt.

[39]Then the descendants of Makir of the
tribe of Manasseh went to Gilead and conquered it, and they drove out the Amorites
living there. [40]So Moses gave Gilead to
the Makirites, descendants of Manasseh,
and they settled there. [41]The people of
Jair, another clan of the tribe of Manasseh,
captured many of the towns in Gilead and
changed the name of that region to the
Towns of Jair. [42]Meanwhile, a man named
Nobah captured the town of Kenath and its
surrounding villages, and he renamed that
area Nobah after himself.

32:16-19 The Reubenites and Gadites assured Moses that they would not discourage their fellow Israelites and would support the war to its very end. There were still dangers east of the Jordan River, so they wanted to safeguard their livestock and families.

32:20-24 Moses accepted the terms offered by Reuben and Gad. If they joined their kindred in fighting the Canaanites, they would fulfill their end of the agreement and could then return to their settlements east of the Jordan (32:22). If they failed to keep their promise, it would be a serious sin against God (32:23).

32:25-27 Reuben and Gad did in fact fulfill the agreement (Josh 4:12-13; 22:1-9).

32:28-30 Israel's leaders—***Eleazar, Joshua***, and the heads of ***clans***—would help enforce Moses' terms (cp. Josh 22:1-2) since his death was imminent.

32:31-32 ***Gad and Reuben*** reaffirmed their pledge before all of Israel's leaders.

32:33-42 The tribes of ***Gad*** and ***Reuben***, along with ***half the tribe of Manasseh***, settled east of the Jordan (e.g., Deut 3:12-13; 4:43; 29:7-8). These tribes occupied territory and towns taken from ***King Sihon*** the Amorite and ***King Og of Bashan*** (32:33; see 21:21-35). • ***Half the tribe of Manasseh*** suddenly appears in the discussion of territorial distribution. Part of Manasseh settled east of the Jordan River, while another part of the tribe settled in Canaan, west of the Jordan (cp. Josh 17:1-12; 22:7).

32:35-36 The precise locations of ***Atroth-shophan, Jogbehah***, and ***Beth-haran*** are unknown. ***Aroer*** was located on the northern rim of the Arnon canyon.

32:37-38 If ***names of some of the towns*** were ***changed*** to avoid pagan associations (e.g., "Baal," the well-known Canaanite god, or "Nebo," a Babylonian deity; see Isa 46:1), the alternate designations are not provided here.

32:39-42 Three clans of Manasseh conquered part of Gilead and Bashan (cp. Deut 3:13-15; Josh 13:29-31). The location of ***Nobah*** remains uncertain (cp. Judg 8:11). • ***Towns of Jair:*** Hebrew *Havvoth-jair* (cp. Deut 3:14; Josh 13:30; Judg 10:4; 1 Kgs 4:13; 1 Chr 2:21-23).

Remembering Israel's Journey

33 This is the route the Israelites followed as they marched out of Egypt
under the leadership of Moses and Aaron.
2 At the LORD's direction, Moses kept a written record of their progress. These are the
stages of their march, identified by the different places where they stopped along the
way.
3 They set out from the city of Rameses
in early spring—on the fifteenth day of
the first month—on the morning after the
first Passover celebration. The people of
Israel left defiantly, in full view of all the
Egyptians. 4 Meanwhile, the Egyptians were
burying all their firstborn sons, whom the
LORD had killed the night before. The LORD
had defeated the gods of Egypt that night
with great acts of judgment!

5 After leaving Rameses, the Israelites set up camp at Succoth.
6 Then they left Succoth and camped at Etham on the edge of the wilderness.
7 They left Etham and turned back toward Pi-hahiroth, opposite Baal-zephon, and camped near Migdol.
8 They left Pi-hahiroth and crossed the Red Sea into the wilderness beyond. Then they traveled for three days into the Etham wilderness and camped at Marah.
9 They left Marah and camped at Elim, where there were twelve springs of water and seventy palm trees.
10 They left Elim and camped beside the Red Sea.
11 They left the Red Sea and camped in the wilderness of Sin.
12 They left the wilderness of Sin and camped at Dophkah.
13 They left Dophkah and camped at Alush.
14 They left Alush and camped at Rephidim, where there was no water for the people to drink.
15 They left Rephidim and camped in the wilderness of Sinai.
16 They left the wilderness of Sinai and camped at Kibroth-hattaavah.
17 They left Kibroth-hattaavah and camped at Hazeroth.
18 They left Hazeroth and camped at Rithmah.
19 They left Rithmah and camped at Rimmon-perez.
20 They left Rimmon-perez and camped at Libnah.
21 They left Libnah and camped at Rissah.
22 They left Rissah and camped at Kehelathah.
23 They left Kehelathah and camped at Mount Shepher.
24 They left Mount Shepher and camped at Haradah.
25 They left Haradah and camped at Makheloth.
26 They left Makheloth and camped at Tahath.
27 They left Tahath and camped at Terah.
28 They left Terah and camped at Mithcah.
29 They left Mithcah and camped at Hashmonah.

33:3 Exod 12:33-37
33:5 Exod 13:20
33:7 Exod 14:2, 9
33:8 Exod 14:21-22
33:9 Exod 15:27; 16:1
33:11 Exod 16:1; 17:1
33:14 Exod 17:1-8
33:15 Exod 19:1
33:16-17 Num 11:34-35

33:1-56 This review of the entire wilderness period contains the longest integrated list of place-names in the OT, from Israel's departure from Egypt (33:3; cp. Exod 12:37) until their arrival in the plains of Moab, opposite Jericho (33:49; cp. 22:1). The forty-two way stations on this itinerary represent far more than a geographical journey; they recall Israel's forty-year spiritual pilgrimage. In their travels between Rameses in Egypt (33:3) and Acacia on the plains of Moab (33:49), Israel finally became the people who could invade the land of Canaan and claim the promises God made to Abraham. • This itinerary does not provide enough data to plot an accurate, specific route. Most of the places cannot be identified with certainty; many of the sites appear nowhere else in the Hebrew Bible, and there are not enough clues to pinpoint their locations precisely. Furthermore, this list is partial or selective, omitting some of the place-names mentioned earlier in the journey. See maps "The Exodus: Egypt to Sinai," Exodus Introduction, p. 122; "Israel in the Wilderness," Numbers Introduction, p. 246; and "Balaam Blesses Israel," 22:21-41, p. 289.

33:1-2 The itinerary contains features that reflect detailed record keeping. This is the only place where Numbers says that Moses kept a record of Israel's history (cp. Exod 24:4).

33:3 ***the fifteenth day of the first month—on the morning after the first Passover celebration:*** This day in the ancient Hebrew lunar calendar occurred in late March, April, or early May. • ***left defiantly:*** See Exod 14:8.

33:4 ***defeated the gods of Egypt:*** See Exod 6:6; 12:12. This historical review draws attention to those special events that forced Pharaoh to allow the Israelite exodus from Egypt.

33:5-15 For Israel's wilderness itinerary between *Rameses* and the desert of *Sinai,* see Exod 13:17–19:1.

33:6 ***Etham:*** See Exod 13:20.

33:8 ***the Red Sea:*** Literally *the sea.*

33:9 ***Elim*** remains impossible to identify with certainty, but it may have been the oasis (with springs and palm trees) at Wadi Gharandel.

33:10 ***the Red Sea:*** Literally *the sea of reeds;* also in 33:11.

33:11 The geographical name *Sin* is related to *Sinai* and should not be confused with the English word *sin.*

33:14 The entry for ***Rephidim*** (see note on 20:13) adds a reminder of Israel's rebellion there (Exod 17:1-7).

33:15 Tradition associates the ***wilderness of Sinai*** with a mountainous region in the southern Sinai Peninsula near Jebel Musa (Arabic for "mountain of Moses"), though scholars have suggested other locations.

33:16-36 The journey between *Sinai* and *Kadesh.* Our ability to locate the named sites depends on the identification of Mount Sinai.

33:16-17 ***Kibroth-hattaavah . . . Hazeroth:*** See 11:34–12:16.

33:18-30 Most of the place-names in this section appear nowhere else in the OT.

33:30 Deut 10:6
33:33 Deut 10:7
33:36 Num 20:1
33:38 Num 20:25-28
33:40 Num 21:1
33:43 Num 21:10-11
33:47 Num 27:12
33:48 Num 22:1
33:49 Num 25:1
33:52 Exod 23:24; 34:13 Deut 7:2-5, 25-26
33:54 Num 26:53-56
33:55 Josh 23:13 Ps 106:34-36

30They left Hashmonah and camped at Moseroth.
31They left Moseroth and camped at Bene-jaakan.
32They left Bene-jaakan and camped at Hor-haggidgad.
33They left Hor-haggidgad and camped at Jotbathah.
34They left Jotbathah and camped at Abronah.
35They left Abronah and camped at Ezion-geber.
36They left Ezion-geber and camped at Kadesh in the wilderness of Zin.
37They left Kadesh and camped at Mount
Hor, at the border of Edom. 38While
they were at the foot of Mount Hor, Aaron the priest was directed by the LORD to go up the mountain, and there he died. This happened in midsummer, on the first day of the fifth month of the fortieth year after Israel's
departure from Egypt. 39Aaron was
123 years old when he died there on Mount Hor.
40At that time the Canaanite king of Arad, who lived in the Negev in the land of Canaan, heard that the people of Israel were approaching his land.
41Meanwhile, the Israelites left Mount Hor and camped at Zalmonah.
42Then they left Zalmonah and camped at Punon.
43They left Punon and camped at Oboth.
44They left Oboth and camped at Iye-abarim on the border of Moab.
45They left Iye-abarim and camped at Dibon-gad.
46They left Dibon-gad and camped at Almon-diblathaim.
47They left Almon-diblathaim and camped in the mountains east of the river, near Mount Nebo.
48They left the mountains east of the river and camped on the plains of Moab beside the Jordan River, across from Jericho.
49Along the Jordan River they camped from Beth-jeshimoth as far as the meadows of Acacia on the plains of Moab.

Commands for Israel after They Enter Canaan

50While they were camped near the Jordan River on the plains of Moab opposite Jericho, the LORD said to Moses,
51"Give the following instructions to the people of Israel: When you cross the Jordan River into the land of Canaan,
52you must drive out all the people living there. You must destroy all their carved and molten images and demolish all their pagan shrines.
53Take possession of the land and settle in it, because I have given it to you to occupy.
54You must distribute the land among the clans by sacred lot and in proportion to their size. A larger portion of land will be allotted to each of the larger clans, and a smaller portion will be allotted to each of the smaller clans. The decision of the sacred lot is final. In this way, the portions of land will be divided among your ancestral tribes.
55But if you fail to drive out the people who live in the land, those who remain will be like splinters in your eyes and thorns in your sides. They will harass you in the land where you live.
56And I will do to you what I had planned to do to them."

33:30-31 *Moseroth* was also called "Moserah" (Deut 10:6). This is where Aaron died and was buried (cp. Num 20:22-29; 33:37-39).

33:35 *Ezion-geber* (cp. Deut 2:8) was located near the northern end of the Gulf of Aqaba.

33:36 Israel was residing in *Kadesh* (13:26; 27:14; cp. "Kadesh-barnea," 32:8) when the spies reported on their trip through Canaan.

33:37-49 Israel traveled from *Kadesh* to *the plains of Moab.*

33:38-39 These details about Aaron's death (cp. 20:22-29) and his age show that he was about three years older than Moses (cp. Deut 31:1-2; 34:7).

33:38 *the first day of the fifth month:* This day in the ancient Hebrew lunar calendar occurred in July or August.

33:42-49 Good candidates for the locations of most of these sites are found east of the Jordan between the southern Arabah and the plains of Moab, opposite Jericho.

33:45 As in 33:44; Hebrew reads *Iyim,* another name for *Iye-abarim.*

33:47 *Almon-diblathaim* is probably the same place as "Beth-diblathaim" (Jer 48:22), also mentioned in the famous Mesha Inscription (see note on 21:26). • *the mountains east of the river:* Or *the mountains of Abarim;* also in 33:48.

33:49 *as far as the meadows of Acacia:* Hebrew *as far as Abel-shittim.*

33:50-56 After the Israelites reached *the plains of Moab opposite Jericho* (22:1), they camped there for the rest of the period covered in Numbers (see 36:13) and Deuteronomy (Deut 34:8). While they were camped there, God gave Israel specific *instructions* for dealing with the population of Canaan. The Lord commanded his people to destroy the people groups that occupied Canaan and to obliterate all vestiges of their religious practices (cp. Exod 23:23-33; 34:11-17; Deut 7:1-6; 12:2-4; Josh 23:4-8). Moses' commands included the destruction of ***their carved and molten images*** (cp. Lev 26:1) and the demolition of their ***pagan shrines*** (see Deut 12:2-3).

33:54 *distribute the land . . . by sacred lot:* See 26:53-56. Chapter 34 describes the boundaries of the land of Canaan, which they would soon conquer and divide.

33:55-56 Israel failed to carry out God's instructions (33:51-53) and suffered the consequences predicted here (see Judg 1:1–2:5; 2:11–3:6). Israel's enemies in the period of the Judges were like *splinters* and *thorns* (33:55), harassing them militarily and spiritually (cp. 2 Cor 12:7).

Boundaries of the Land

34 Then the LORD said to Moses, 2“Give
these instructions to the Israelites:
When you come into the land of Canaan,
which I am giving you as your special possession, these will be the boundaries. 3The
southern portion of your country will extend
from the wilderness of Zin, along the edge
of Edom. The southern boundary will begin
on the east at the Dead Sea. 4It will then run
south past Scorpion Pass in the direction of
Zin. Its southernmost point will be Kadesh-
barnea, from which it will go to Hazar-addar,
and on to Azmon. 5From Azmon the boundary will turn toward the Brook of Egypt and
end at the Mediterranean Sea.
6“Your western boundary will be the
coastline of the Mediterranean Sea.
7“Your northern boundary will begin
at the Mediterranean Sea and run east to
Mount Hor, 8then to Lebo-hamath, and on
through Zedad 9and Ziphron to Hazar-enan.
This will be your northern boundary.
10“The eastern boundary will start at
Hazar-enan and run south to Shepham,
11then down to Riblah on the east side of
Ain. From there the boundary will run down
along the eastern edge of the Sea of Galilee,
12and then along the Jordan River to the Dead
Sea. These are the boundaries of your land.”
13Then Moses told the Israelites, “This
territory is the homeland you are to divide
among yourselves by sacred lot. The LORD
has commanded that the land be divided
among the nine and a half remaining tribes.
14The families of the tribes of Reuben, Gad,
and half the tribe of Manasseh have already
received their grants of land 15on the east
side of the Jordan River, across from Jericho toward the sunrise.”

Leaders to Divide the Land

16And the LORD said to Moses, 17“Eleazar the
priest and Joshua son of Nun are the men designated to divide the grants of land among
the people. 18Enlist one leader from each
tribe to help them with the task. 19These are
the tribes and the names of the leaders:

Tribe	*Leader*
Judah	Caleb son of Jephunneh
20 Simeon	Shemuel son of Ammihud
21 Benjamin	Elidad son of Kislon
22 Dan	Bukki son of Jogli
23 Manasseh son of Joseph	Hanniel son of Ephod
24 Ephraim son of Joseph	Kemuel son of Shiphtan

34:2 Gen 17:8; Deut 1:7-8; Ezek 47:15
34:3 Josh 15:1-4
34:4 Num 32:8
34:6 Josh 15:4
34:7 Ezek 47:15-17
34:10 Josh 15:5
34:11 2 Kgs 23:33; 25:6; Jer 52:9
34:13 Josh 14:1-2
34:14 Num 32:33
34:18 Num 1:4, 16

34:1-29 Chapter 34 gives the borders of ***the land of Canaan***, which Israel was to settle according to the guidelines in 26:52-56. Ever since the call of Abraham (Gen 12:1-7), the Promised Land of Canaan had stood at the heart of the OT story. Though an entire generation of Hebrews died in the wilderness because they refused to believe the report of the faithful spies (ch 13), God had reaffirmed his promise of land (33:53). Here, God reviewed the plan and identified the boundaries of the Promised Land in an idealized form (cp. Josh 13–19; Ezek 47–48). OT Israel did not possess the exact extent of the territory described here (though it came close in the days of David and Solomon; e.g., 2 Sam 24:1-9), but these borders describe the province of Canaan as generally defined by Egyptian texts dating 1500–1200 BC (the period of the Hebrew invasion). The region actually occupied by Israel changed from time to time.

34:3-5 Portions of the southern boundary of Canaan were familiar to Israel from earlier experiences in ***the wilderness of Zin*** on the northwestern *edge of Edom* (see chs 13–14). This southern frontier ran east to west in an arc from the southern end of the ***Dead Sea*** (literally *Salt Sea;* also in 34:12) to ***the Mediterranean Sea*** (literally *the sea;* also in 34:6, 7).

34:4 From the southern end of the Dead Sea, the boundary ran through ***Scorpion Pass*** (or *the ascent of Akrabbim*) toward *Zin* (cp. 13:21). The ***southernmost point*** was ***Kadesh-barnea*** (cp. 13:26). ***Hazar-addar*** and ***Azmon*** are unknown.

34:5 ***The Brook of Egypt*** (not to be confused with the Nile) designates the wadi that separates the land of Canaan from Egypt; it drains toward ***the Mediterranean Sea*** (cp. 1 Kgs 8:65). In OT times, Israel exercised little control over this southern coastal region.

34:6-9 The natural ***western boundary*** of Canaan was the ***Mediterranean*** coast (34:6). The ***northern*** border began at the Mediterranean and ran eastward to ***Mount Hor*** somewhere in the Lebanon range (not the place of Aaron’s death, 20:22-29). • ***Lebo-hamath:*** Cp. 13:21; 1 Kgs 8:65; Amos 6:14.

34:11 ***Sea of Galilee:*** Hebrew *Sea of Kinnereth*. Its ***eastern edge*** (literally *shoulder*) is the ridge that rises rather abruptly from its eastern shoreline.

34:12 The natural eastern border of Canaan followed the ***Jordan River*** down to the ***Dead Sea***. As part of the Great Rift Valley, the Jordan and the Dead Sea were formidable, though not impassable, barriers. This boundary excluded the lands east of the Jordan that were occupied by Reuben, Gad, and the half-tribe of Manasseh. Those settlements were not part of Canaan per se and stood outside the Promised Land as originally defined.

34:13-15 ***you are to divide . . . by sacred lot:*** Cp. 26:55-56. Because of the settlement of two and a half tribes (***Reuben, Gad, and half the tribe of Manasseh***) in Transjordan (cp. 32:33), Canaan was to ***be divided among the nine and a half remaining tribes***.

34:16-29 Eleazar (the high priest) and Joshua (the political leader) were to divide the land among the remaining tribes. The ten tribal leaders who would help them are listed in 34:19-28.

34:19-28 ***Caleb son of Jephunneh*** is the only tribal leader who appears elsewhere in Numbers (13:6, 30; 14:6-38; see also “Caleb” at Josh 14:6-15, p. 399). Nearly all of the older generation had already died during the wilderness period (26:63-65), but the two faithful spies were still leading their people.

35:1-34 The tribe of Levi received no territory, so ch 35 describes their allotment of 48 towns dispersed among the territories of Israel’s other tribes (see Josh 21; see also Lev 25:32-34; 1 Chr 13:2; 2 Chr 11:14). Just as the Levites had lived in the center of the Israelite camp during the wilderness period (cp. 2:17), in the Promised Land they were to live among the other tribes and have a leavening influence among them (see Deut 33:9-10; 2 Chr 17:7-9; 19:8-11; 35:3). The cities and their surrounding pastureland were not a “homeland” (cp. 18:23; 26:62), but only a tiny fraction of the Canaanite territory dispersed among the other tribes.

35:2 Lev 25:32-34; Josh 14:3-4
35:6 Josh 20:2-9; 21:3, 13, 21-38
35:7 Josh 21:3-42
35:8 Num 26:54
35:11 Num 35:22-25
35:12 Josh 20:3; [b]*ga'al* (1350) ‣Ps 77:15

25Zebulun . . . . Elizaphan son of Parnach
26Issachar . . . . Paltiel son of Azzan
27Asher. . . . . Ahihud son of Shelomi
28Naphtali . . . . Pedahel son of Ammihud
29These are the men the LORD has appointed
to divide the grants of land in Canaan
among the Israelites."

Towns for the Levites

35 While Israel was camped beside
the Jordan on the plains of Moab
across from Jericho, the LORD said to Moses,
2"Command the people of Israel to give to
the Levites from their property certain
towns to live in, along with the surrounding
pasturelands. 3These towns will be for the
Levites to live in, and the surrounding lands
will provide pasture for their cattle, flocks,
and other livestock. 4The pastureland assigned to the Levites around these towns
will extend 1,500 feet from the town walls
in every direction. 5Measure off 3,000 feet
outside the town walls in every direction—
east, south, west, north—with the town at
the center. This area will serve as the larger
pastureland for the towns.
6"Six of the towns you give the Levites
will be cities of refuge, where a person who
has accidentally killed someone can flee
for safety. In addition, give them forty-two
other towns. 7In all, forty-eight towns with
the surrounding pastureland will be given
to the Levites. 8These towns will come from
the property of the people of Israel. The
larger tribes will give more towns to the
Levites, while the smaller tribes will give
fewer. Each tribe will give property in proportion to the size of its land."

Cities of Refuge

9The LORD said to Moses, 10"Give the following instructions to the people of Israel.
"When you cross the Jordan into the land
of Canaan, 11designate cities of refuge to
which people can flee if they have killed
someone accidentally. 12These cities will be
places of protection from a dead person's
relatives who want to [b]avenge the death.
The slayer must not be put to death before

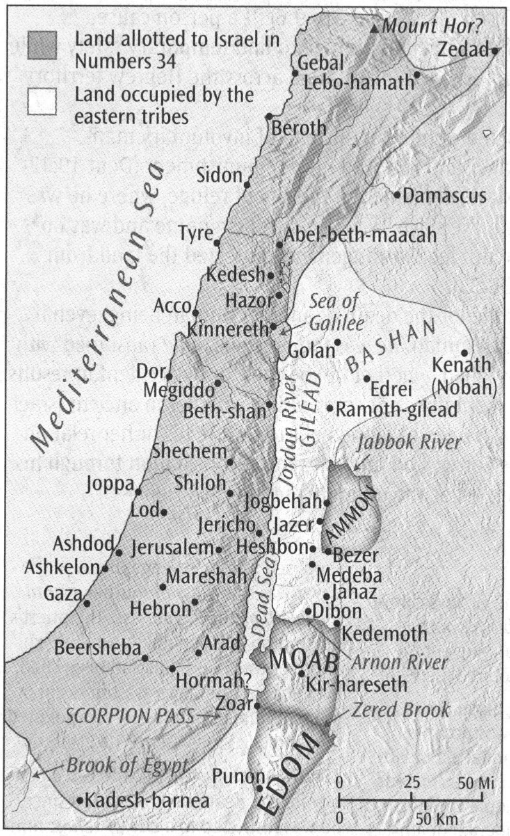

◂ **Boundaries of the Promised Land** (34:1-15). The boundaries of the land allotted to Israel in ch 34 are shown, along with the area east of the Jordan (Transjordan) occupied by Reuben, Gad, and Manasseh (see 32:1-5, 33-42). Cp. Josh 13:8–20:9.

35:4-5 Readers have long attempted to explain the alleged contradiction between the ***1,500 feet*** (Hebrew *1,000 cubits* [460 meters]) and the ***3,000 feet*** (Hebrew *2,000 cubits* [920 meters]). If the Hebrews conceived of a town as a fixed point, then the square of territory around each town would measure 3,000 feet on each side. Another solution is to see a distinction between ***pastureland*** (35:4) and ***larger pastureland*** (35:5) around the town. On the basis of this text, some Jewish interpreters restricted the distance that one could walk on the Sabbath to 3,000 feet (2,000 cubits) from home.

35:6-34 *Six* of the Levites' ***towns*** had a special purpose as ***cities of refuge***, places ***where a person who has accidentally killed someone can flee for safety***. This unusual institution illustrates the humanitarian aspect of Hebrew law (see also Deut 4:41-43; 19:1-13; Josh 20:1-9). These six Levitical towns provided a safe haven in cases of accidental or involuntary manslaughter (cp. Exod 21:12-14). Just as the forty-eight Levite towns were widely distributed across Israel's territories, the six cities of refuge were dispersed so they would be widely accessible (see Josh 20:7-8; see map, p. 397). These designated settlements supplemented the role of the altar as a temporary place of asylum (e.g., 1 Kgs 1:50-53; 2:28-34; cp. Exod 21:14). Other ancient peoples provided special places of asylum or refuge, often at the altar (see Exod 21:12-14; 1 Kgs 2:28-34), but only ancient Israel established whole settlements as places of sanctuary, reflecting a special interest in social justice.

35:12 ***protection from a dead person's relatives who want to avenge the death:*** Justice was enacted through vengeance at the hand of a designated avenger, usually a relative.

being tried by the community. [13]Designate
six cities of refuge for yourselves, [14]three on
the east side of the Jordan River and three
on the west in the land of Canaan. [15]These
cities are for the protection of Israelites,
foreigners living among you, and traveling
merchants. Anyone who accidentally kills
someone may flee there for safety.

[16]"But if someone strikes and kills another
person with a piece of iron, it is murder,
and the murderer must be executed. [17]Or
if someone with a stone in his hand strikes
and kills another person, it is murder, and the
murderer must be put to death. [18]Or if someone strikes and kills another person with a
wooden object, it is murder, and the murderer
must be put to death. [19]The victim's nearest
relative is responsible for putting the murderer to death. When they meet, the avenger
must put the murderer to death. [20]So if someone hates another person and pushes him or
throws a dangerous object at him and he dies,
it is murder. [21]Or if someone hates another
person and hits him with a fist and he dies,
it is murder. In such cases, the avenger must
put the murderer to death when they meet.

[22]"But suppose someone pushes another
person without having shown previous hostility, or throws something that unintentionally
hits another person, [23]or accidentally drops a
huge stone on someone, though they were not
enemies, and the person dies. [24]If this should
happen, the community must follow these
regulations in making a judgment between
the slayer and the avenger, the victim's nearest relative: [25]The community must protect
the slayer from the avenger and must escort
the slayer back to live in the city of refuge to
which he fled. There he must remain until the
death of the high priest, who was anointed
with the sacred oil.

[26]"But if the slayer ever leaves the limits
of the city of refuge, [27]and the avenger finds
him outside the city and kills him, it will not

35:16
Exod 21:12-14
Lev 24:17

The Cities of Refuge (35:6-34)

Deut 19:1-13
Josh 20:1-9; 21:13, 21, 27, 32, 38
1 Kgs 1:50-53; 2:28-34

The cities of refuge were built to protect innocent people from blood revenge. An avenger had the legal right to put a murderer to death (35:19; see Gen 9:6). If a person caused someone's death accidentally, the slayer fled to a city of refuge to find temporary safety while awaiting trial (35:22-28). The six cities of refuge were distributed across the Hebrew territory so that any Israelite could seek asylum.

If, after the trial, the fugitive was convicted of murder (instead of involuntary manslaughter), he was turned over to the avenger and received his due punishment (Deut 19:12). If he was found innocent of murder, the slayer remained in the city of refuge, where he was granted asylum. When the high priest died, the slayer was free to return home and was no longer subject to blood revenge. This merciful legal arrangement protected the land from further pollution by innocent blood (see 35:33).

It was not acceptable to pay a fine to atone for the death of another human being, even if that death was not premeditated (35:31-33). Human life was too precious to be ransomed with a simple payment. When a human being is killed, whether deliberately or by accident, it results in alienation or exile as all sin does. Atonement does not come easily, whether in ancient Israelite times or in our own day; each person is in need of atonement to restore his or her relationship with God (see Rom 3:23-26). Jesus, the Son of God, provides this reconciliation through his work as a great High Priest who offered himself as the ultimate sacrifice (see Heb 4–9).

35:15-24 The OT makes a clear distinction between deliberate murder and involuntary manslaughter (35:11, 22-23; Exod 21:12-14; cp. 15:22-31). Murder required a penalty of execution, but an accidental death did not. The cities of refuge provided protection only for those who killed another person by accident. • The use of a weapon was proof of malicious intent.

35:15 ***Israelites, foreigners living among you, and traveling merchants. Anyone:*** The same law applied impartially to everyone; Israel had one standard of justice, not two (one for citizens, another for noncitizens), as in many societies (see also Lev 19:15; Deut 1:16-17; 1 Tim 5:21; Jas 2:2-4).

35:19 The *avenger* was the victim's closest relative; he was ***responsible for putting the murderer to death***, carrying out the vengeance that justice required (Gen 9:6).

35:22-23 Here are some instances in which a victim died but was not murdered through an intentional act of violence. The cities of refuge were created as places of safety for people who were responsible for such accidental deaths.

35:24-25 If the *slayer* was cleared of the murder charge in his trial or hearing before the ***community*** (cp. Deut 19:11-12), he had to remain in ***the city of refuge to which he fled***, and the avenger was not supposed to seek revenge, because the slayer was not guilty of murder. • ***until the death of the high priest:*** The priest's death probably provided a kind of expiation for the blood that had been shed; even though the slayer was innocent of murder, human bloodshed had polluted the land (35:33; cp. Gen 4:10-11).

35:26-29 The *slayer* still suffered a penalty for the death he had caused since he was restricted to a *city of refuge* until he or the high priest died. ***But after the death of the high priest***, the ***slayer*** was free to return to his own home, and the avenger was not to seek revenge.

35:30 ***All murderers*** were condemned

35:30 Deut 17:6-7; 19:15
Matt 18:16
2 Cor 13:1
Heb 10:28

35:33 [c]*kapar* (3722)
▸1 Sam 3:14

35:34 Lev 18:25

36:1-2 Num 27:1-11

36:8 1 Chr 23:22

36:11 Num 26:33; 27:1

36:13 Lev 7:38; 27:34

be considered murder. 28The slayer should have stayed inside the city of refuge until the death of the high priest. But after the death of the high priest, the slayer may return to his own property. 29These are legal requirements for you to observe from generation to generation, wherever you may live.

30"All murderers must be put to death, but only if evidence is presented by more than one witness. No one may be put to death on the testimony of only one witness. 31Also, you must never accept a ransom payment for the life of someone judged guilty of murder and subject to execution; murderers must always be put to death. 32And never accept a ransom payment from someone who has fled to a city of refuge, allowing a slayer to return to his property before the death of the high priest. 33This will ensure that the land where you live will not be polluted, for murder pollutes the land. And no sacrifice except the execution of the murderer can [c]purify the land from murder. 34You must not defile the land where you live, for I live there myself. I am the LORD, who lives among the people of Israel."

Women Who Inherit Property

36 Then the heads of the clans of Gilead—descendants of Makir, son of Manasseh, son of Joseph—came to Moses and the family leaders of Israel with a petition. 2They said, "Sir, the LORD instructed you to divide the land by sacred lot among the people of Israel. You were told by the LORD to give the grant of land owned by our brother Zelophehad to his daughters. 3But if they marry men from another tribe, their grants of land will go with them to the tribe into which they marry. In this way, the total area of our tribal land will be reduced. 4Then when the Year of Jubilee comes, their portion of land will be added to that of the new tribe, causing it to be lost forever to our ancestral tribe."

5So Moses gave the Israelites this command from the LORD: "The claim of the men of the tribe of Joseph is legitimate. 6This is what the LORD commands concerning the daughters of Zelophehad: Let them marry anyone they like, as long as it is within their own ancestral tribe. 7None of the territorial land may pass from tribe to tribe, for all the land given to each tribe must remain within the tribe to which it was first allotted. 8The daughters throughout the tribes of Israel who are in line to inherit property must marry within their tribe, so that all the Israelites will keep their ancestral property. 9No grant of land may pass from one tribe to another; each tribe of Israel must keep its allotted portion of land."

10The daughters of Zelophehad did as the LORD commanded Moses. 11Mahlah, Tirzah, Hoglah, Milcah, and Noah all married cousins on their father's side. 12They married into the clans of Manasseh son of Joseph. Thus, their inheritance of land remained within their ancestral tribe.

13These are the commands and regulations that the LORD gave to the people of Israel through Moses while they were camped on the plains of Moab beside the Jordan River across from Jericho.

to *death*, but their conviction required a high standard of evidence—the testimony of two or more witnesses (cp. Deut 17:6; 19:15).

35:31-32 The payment of a *ransom* (monetary compensation) to free a convicted murderer from *execution* was prohibited, since the death penalty was required (cp. 2 Sam 21:2-9). Similarly, the *slayer* in an involuntary manslaughter could not pay a ransom to get around his confinement in a city of refuge.

35:33 ***for murder pollutes the land:*** If the slayer in either a homicide or involuntary manslaughter were not dealt with as commanded, God regarded the *land* as *polluted*, because human bloodshed required death (Gen 4:10-11; 9:6; contrast Exod 21:29-30; see also Lev 18:28; Ezek 36:17-18; Hos 4:2-3). In its stern warning about the evil of murder, this entire passage highlights the absolute value of human life (Exod 20:13). • ***can purify the land from murder:*** Or *can make atonement for murder.*

35:34 The Lord lived ***among the people of Israel*** even as the Tabernacle stood in the middle of the Hebrew camp (see chs 1–4). This meant that they must not ***defile*** their ***land*** by ignoring God's commands or by failing to uphold justice (cp. 5:1-4).

36:1-13 The five daughters of Zelophehad had petitioned for, and had been granted, equitable property rights (27:1-11). Here the ramifications of that decision are discussed.

36:1-4 Women who inherited land might ***marry men from another tribe;*** their land would then be lost by their ancestral tribe and transferred to their husband's tribe. The Year of Jubilee (Lev 25:8-55) normally provided the means for land to return to its original owner, but it pertained only to land that was sold, not to land acquired through marriage.

36:5 The Lord readily provided the justice that ***the men of the tribe of Joseph*** (i.e., of the tribe of Manasseh, the son of Joseph) sought in their petition.

36:6-9 These stipulations resolved the quandary, guaranteeing the stability and continuity of the tribal land allotments.

36:10-12 As they had been instructed, Zelophehad's five daughters ***all married cousins on their father's side,*** keeping their father's allotment within his clan. Marriage to a first cousin was acceptable in ancient Hebrew society (cp. Lev 18, 20; see also 1 Chr 23:22) as well as in other Near Eastern cultures.

36:13 ***Commands and regulations*** might refer to legal pronouncements from the whole book (cp. Lev 27:34) or only to those given ***on the plains of Moab*** (chs 26–36). • All that remained to make the Israelites ready to enter Canaan was for Moses to remind them of their history and covenant obligations—the subjects of the book of Deuteronomy.

THE BOOK OF DEUTERONOMY

God first revealed Israel's national "constitution" to Moses at Sinai (Exod 20–23). The great leader Moses was now about to die. God had appointed a younger man, Joshua, to replace Moses, but he was not yet fully tested. Israel had been rescued from slavery in Egypt and miraculously preserved through forty years of wandering in the wilderness. The Israelites now stood on the verge of the land promised to them, but it was inhabited by powerful and hostile enemies. Although God had been faithful in the past, the future seemed uncertain. Deuteronomy is the story of Israel's renewed covenant with God—a covenant that would guide Israel to God's blessings throughout the remainder of their history as a nation.

SETTING

Forty years after their exodus from Egypt, the Israelites arrived at the plains of Moab, just across the Jordan River from Jericho. After four decades of wandering, they were poised to cross the Jordan, conquer the Canaanite nations, and settle their land in fulfillment of God's promises to Abraham. First, however, God would renew his covenant with them.

Moses was aware that he would die before leading his people to their destination. However, prior to his death, he needed

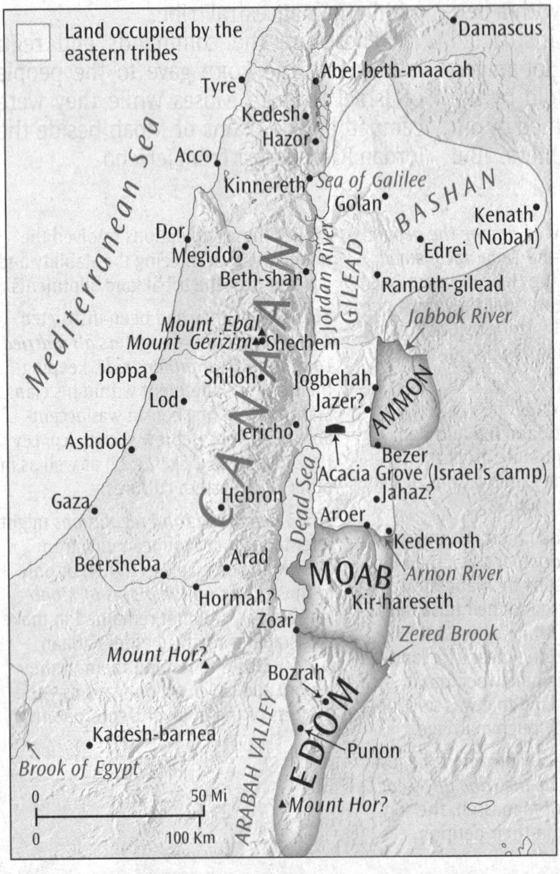

◀ **Key Places in Deuteronomy.** While Israel was camped at ACACIA GROVE on the plains of MOAB (34:1, 8; see Num 22:1; 33:49; Josh 13:32), Moses gave his people the messages now recorded in Deuteronomy. In these messages, Moses mentioned many of the places where Israel had traveled. For the details of Israel's route, see maps "The Exodus: Egypt to Sinai," p. 122; "Israel in the Wilderness," p. 246; and "Journey toward the Promised Land," p. 285.

AMMON: 2:19-21, 37; Num 21:24; Judg 11:4-36; 1 Sam 10:27–11:11
ARABAH VALLEY: 2:8
AROER: 2:36; 3:12; 4:48; Josh 12:2; Isa 17:2
BASHAN: 3:1-14; 29:7-8; Num 21:33-35; Mic 7:14
BEZER: 4:43
EDOM: 2:4; 23:7-8; Num 20:14-21; 24:18; Obadiah
EDREI: 1:4; 3:1; Num 21:33
GOLAN: 4:43
HORMAH: 1:44; Num 14:45; 21:3
JAHAZ: 2:32; Num 21:23
KADESH-BARNEA: 1:2, 19, 46; 2:14; 9:23; 32:51; 33:2
MOAB: 1:5; 2:8-9, 29; 23:3, 6; 34:1-8
MOUNT EBAL, MOUNT GERIZIM: 11:29; 27:4-26; Josh 8:30-35
RAMOTH-GILEAD: 4:43; 1 Kgs 22:3-29

to remind the people of the terms of the covenant that God had revealed to him. The initial covenant, suitable for Israel while en route to Canaan, had been made thirty-eight years earlier at Sinai (Exod 19–24). Now, in anticipation of Israel's establishment as a settled community, the original covenant must be restated and enlarged. The book of Deuteronomy is this restatement.

OUTLINE

1:1-5
Preamble: Narrative Setting

1:6–4:40
First Address: Historical Review

4:41-49
Narrative Interlude

5:1–26:19
Second Address: The Covenant Text

27:1–30:20
Third Address: Ratification of the Covenant

31:1–34:12
Moses' Farewell

SUMMARY

Deuteronomy is Moses' farewell address to the tribes he had served as prophetic leader. The book includes narratives, exhortations, warnings, instructions, and promises of blessing for Israel's faithfulness. Using elements common to covenants between nations, Deuteronomy is composed as a treaty text. It is similar to other treaties known from ancient Near Eastern sources, particularly from Hittite archives. Moses, clearly aware of the patterns used in typical covenants, communicates God's purposes to Israel in a familiar literary and legal form.

Paying careful attention to the formal structures of Deuteronomy yields a great deal of insight into the theological nature of the book. As a covenant text, it underscores the seriousness of God's promises and of Israel's need (as the covenant partner) to obey the terms of the treaty so that God can fulfill his promises. As a farewell speech, Deuteronomy is rooted in a historical and geographical setting.

The following outline reflects the analysis of Deuteronomy as a covenant document:

1:1-5 Preamble to the covenant
1:6–4:49 Historical prologue
5:1–26:15 Stipulations of the covenant
26:16–29:1 Blessings for obedience and curses for disobedience
29:2–30:20 Review of the covenant and choice between life and death
31:1-29 Deposit of the text of the covenant
31:30–32:43 Witnesses of the covenant

The outline embedded in the Bible text reflects Deuteronomy's structure both as a covenant text and as a farewell speech and series of sermons.

AUTHORSHIP

Long-standing Jewish and Christian tradition holds that Moses wrote Deuteronomy. Deuteronomy 1:1 also asserts that Moses is the book's author. Both the OT and NT acknowledge Moses' authorship of the book (see Josh 1:7-8; Judg 1:20; 3:4; 1 Kgs 2:3; 2 Kgs 14:6; 2 Chr 25:4; Ezra 3:2; Matt 19:7; Mark 12:19; Luke 20:28; Acts 3:22; Rom 10:19; 1 Cor 9:9).

TIMELINE

1526 / 1350 BC*
Moses is born

1446 / 1270 BC
Israel leaves Egypt (the Exodus), moves to Mount Sinai
The covenant at Sinai

1406 / 1230 BC
▸ **Deuteronomy is written**
Moses dies
Israel enters Canaan

1376 / 1200 BC
Joshua dies
Beginning of the Judges period

* *The two dates harmonize with the traditional "early" chronology and a more recent "late" chronology of the Exodus. All dates are approximate. Please see "Chronology: Abraham to Joshua," p. 118.*

Deuteronomy is one of the greatest books of the Old Testament. Its influence on the domestic and personal religion of all ages has not been surpassed by any other book of the Bible.

J. A. THOMPSON
Deuteronomy

However, during the past 200 years, critical scholars have denied that Moses wrote Deuteronomy. Some scholars identify Deuteronomy as the scroll found in the Temple in King Josiah's time (about 621 BC; see 2 Kgs 22:8-20); consequently, critical scholars date Deuteronomy to that time, and attribute editorial additions as late as the period following the Exile (538 BC and later).

Archaeologists have discovered Hittite treaty texts originating in the Late Bronze Age (1500–1200 BC), about the time of Moses. These texts provide support for an early authorship of Deuteronomy (see "Literary Form," below). Some scholars compare Deuteronomy to seventh-century Assyrian treaty texts that are closer to Josiah's time. However, the Hittite texts are more similar to Deuteronomy in structure and content than the Assyrian examples, making it less likely that Deuteronomy was written during the later period.

In short, there is no good reason to deny that Moses wrote the book shortly before his death. The account of his death (34:5-12) was added later. See further "Introduction to the Pentateuch: Authorship," p. 11.

Though the scene is set more than three thousand years in the past, Deuteronomy is still a book of considerable contemporary relevance. Then, as now, the surrounding world was experiencing a time of change, of political tension and military engagement. . . . The book provides a paradigm for the kingdom of God in the modern world; it is a time for renewing commitment within the New Covenant and turning to the future with a view to possessing the promise of God.

PETER C. CRAIGIE
The Book of Deuteronomy

LITERARY FORM

Deuteronomy's structure resembles other treaty texts drawn up between various nations in the period of the Exodus and the conquest. Some of these were treaties between equals, while others were suzerain-vassal treaties. In a suzerain-vassal treaty, the superior party (the suzerain, or "Great King") would make demands of and offer promises to subject peoples (the vassals) in return for their unqualified obedience.

Deuteronomy is a suzerain-vassal treaty between God and Israel. God called the Israelites out of bondage in Egypt to be his servant people. He took the lead in the relationship, determined the terms for maintaining the treaty, and offered promises of blessing if Israel obeyed and judgment if the nation disobeyed.

Moses' use of the suzerain-vassal treaty format makes it clear that Deuteronomy is a covenant text. God chose Israel to be his special people. It was not the covenant that made them so, for they were already identified as God's people before the Exodus (Exod 4:22-23). Rather, the text of the covenant regulated their behavior. By reviewing the covenant with this generation of Israelites, Moses ensured that they would enter the Promised Land as God's covenant people.

MEANING AND MESSAGE

The covenant is the leading theme of Deuteronomy—and perhaps of the entire OT. The covenant provided the means for the Lord to unite himself to Israel. The covenant stated that the Lord was ancient Israel's God, Israel was God's people, and the relationship between them would achieve God's redemptive purposes. This awesome privilege also included profound responsibility. Could Israel conduct itself in a manner that would guarantee the success of its mission? What standards of behavior would enable them to fulfill their heavenly calling?

Israel had the freedom to accept or reject God's covenant (Exod 19:7-8). Once accepted, the blessings and curses within the covenant depended on whether Israel obeyed or disobeyed (28:1-6, 15-19). God promised that even disobedience could be overcome if the nation would repent, return, and be restored to covenant fellowship (30:1-10; Lev 26:40-45).

This covenant did not make Israel God's people; God's promise of a national offspring to Abraham had already done that (Gen 17:1-8). This document reiterated the covenant made at Sinai, where Israel was given the privilege of serving the Lord as a kingdom of priests (Exod 19:4-6). If Israel could remain faithful to its role as a "kingdom of priests and my holy nation," it would direct God's blessings to the whole world.

The Israelites were the unique people of God. God made promises to the nation's forefathers that he fulfilled in the Exodus and in creating the nation. He was ready to solidify Israel in the conquest of the Promised Land and move the nation forward until his purposes were complete. The book of Deuteronomy established the principles of faithful life and ministry that would ensure Israel's ongoing relationship with God in achieving those objectives. Israel had the indescribable honor of partnering with Almighty God to bring about his plan for the ages.

FURTHER READING

P. C. CRAIGIE
The Book of Deuteronomy (1976)

J. G. MCCONVILLE
Deuteronomy (2002)

J. A. THOMPSON
Deuteronomy (1974)

E. MERRILL
Deuteronomy in *Cornerstone Biblical Commentary,* vol. 2 (2008)

1:1 Deut 2:8, 24; 3:3; 4:1, 44-46
1:4 Num 21:24, 33
1:6 Num 10:11-13

1. PREAMBLE: NARRATIVE SETTING (1:1-5)

1 These are the words that Moses spoke
to all the people of Israel while they
were in the wilderness east of the Jordan
River. They were camped in the Jordan Valley near Suph, between Paran on one side
and Tophel, Laban, Hazeroth, and Di-zahab
on the other.
2 Normally it takes only eleven days to
travel from Mount Sinai to Kadesh-barnea,
going by way of Mount Seir. 3 But forty years
after the Israelites left Egypt, on the first day
of the eleventh month, Moses addressed
the people of Israel, telling them everything
the LORD had commanded him to say. 4 This
took place after he had defeated King Sihon
of the Amorites, who had ruled in Heshbon,
and King Og of Bashan, who had ruled in
Ashtaroth and Edrei.
5 While the Israelites were in the land of
Moab east of the Jordan River, Moses carefully explained the LORD's instructions as
follows.

2. FIRST ADDRESS: HISTORICAL REVIEW (1:6–4:40)

God's Guidance of Israel (1:6–3:29)

The Command to Leave Sinai

6 "When we were at Mount Sinai, the LORD
our God said to us, 'You have stayed at this

1:1-5 Ancient Near Eastern treaty texts usually began with a brief section introducing the partners in the covenant, their relationship to each other, and their immediate ancestry. This introduction provides information primarily about the social and geographic setting.

1:1 ***These are the words that Moses spoke:*** Although Deuteronomy is modeled after a covenant or treaty document, it is essentially a series of addresses delivered by Moses to the assembly of Israel. • ***the Jordan Valley*** (Hebrew *the Arabah;* also in 1:7): *Arabah* is a common word usually translated "wilderness" or "desert." It generally refers to the Great Rift Valley that extends from the Sea of Galilee southward to the Red Sea (the Gulf of Aqaba). In this context, the Arabah is the wasteland of the lower Jordan River, just north of the Dead Sea.

1:2 The distance from *Mount Sinai* in the southern part of the Sinai Peninsula to ***Kadesh-barnea*** (see note on 1:19) in the north is only 150 miles. Even the massive Hebrew population could easily have covered this distance in *eleven days* had they proceeded without detour or interruption. Their rebellion against the Lord resulted in a 38-year delay and a circuitous route (2:14; Num 14:34). • ***Mount Sinai*** (Hebrew *Horeb,* another name for Sinai; also in 1:6, 19): Horeb is the name consistently used in Deuteronomy for the sacred mountain where the covenant was given. Its likely connection to a word meaning "drought" or "devastation" suggests the conditions the people of Israel had to face. • The ***way of Mount Seir*** was the route from Mount Sinai to Mount Seir. *Seir,* another name for Edom, was located east-southeast of the Dead Sea. The ordinary route took travelers through the Arabah north from the Gulf of Aqaba and then west to Kadesh-barnea, just south of the Dead Sea.

1:3 ***forty years after the Israelites left Egypt:*** Literally *In the fortieth year, on the first day of the eleventh month.* This day in the ancient Hebrew lunar calendar occurred in January or February (see chart, "Israel's Annual Calendar," p. 145).

1:4 The ***Amorites*** were a Semitic people, linguistically related to the Canaanites. They originally lived in what is now north-central Syria, but they had migrated into Canaan to settle on both sides of the Jordan River, primarily in the hill country. At the time of Israel's conquest, many Amorites lived in Transjordan (east of the Jordan), north of the Arnon River, with their capital at Heshbon (see also note on Num 21:13). The Israelites had already displaced many of them before this time (Num 22:21-35). • ***Bashan*** was also an Amorite area, located north of the Yarmuk River and east of the Sea of Galilee. It was known for its prized livestock (cp. Ps 22:12; Ezek 39:18; Amos 4:1 and note). Its capital was Ashtaroth. • The kings ***Sihon*** and ***Og*** are not known outside the Bible (see Num 21:21-35).

1:6–4:40 Secular treaties typically included a section detailing the past relations between the treaty partners. The purpose here was to point out Israel's successes and failures since the Exodus and to remind the people that God had been true to his word regardless of how they had acted toward him. In order to prepare the Israelites for life

mountain long enough. 7It is time to break
camp and move on. Go to the hill country
of the Amorites and to all the neighboring
regions—the Jordan Valley, the hill country,
the western foothills, the Negev, and the
coastal plain. Go to the land of the Canaanites and to Lebanon, and all the way to the
great Euphrates River. 8Look, I am giving all
this land to you! Go in and occupy it, for it
is the land the LORD swore to give to your
ancestors Abraham, Isaac, and Jacob, and to
all their descendants.' "

Moses Appoints Leaders from Each Tribe

9Moses continued, "At that time I told you,
'You are too great a burden for me to carry
all by myself. 10The LORD your God has
increased your population, making you
as numerous as the stars! 11And may the
LORD, the God of your ancestors, multiply
you a thousand times more and bless you
as he promised! 12But you are such a heavy
load to carry! How can I deal with all your
problems and bickering? 13Choose some
well-respected men from each tribe who
are known for their wisdom and understanding, and I will appoint them as your
leaders.'

14"Then you responded, 'Your plan is a
good one.' 15So I took the wise and respected
men you had selected from your tribes and
appointed them to serve as judges and officials over you. Some were responsible for a
thousand people, some for a hundred, some
for fifty, and some for ten.

16"At that time I instructed the judges,
'You must hear the cases of your fellow Israelites and the foreigners living among you.
Be perfectly fair in your decisions 17and impartial in your judgments. Hear the cases
of those who are poor as well as those who
are rich. Don't be afraid of anyone's anger,
for the decision you make is God's decision.
Bring me any cases that are too difficult for
you, and I will handle them.'

18"At that time I gave you instructions
about everything you were to do.

Scouts Explore the Land

19"Then, just as the LORD our God commanded us, we left Mount Sinai and traveled
through the great and terrifying wilderness, as you yourselves remember, and
headed toward the hill country of the Amorites. When we arrived at Kadesh-barnea,
20I said to you, 'You have now reached the
hill country of the Amorites that the LORD
our God is giving us. 21Look! He has placed
the land in front of you. Go and occupy it
as the LORD, the God of your ancestors, has
promised you. Don't be afraid! Don't be discouraged!'

22"But you all came to me and said, 'First,
let's send out scouts to explore the land for
us. They will advise us on the best route to
take and which towns we should enter.'

23"This seemed like a good idea to me,
so I chose twelve scouts, one from each
of your tribes. 24They headed for the hill
country and came to the valley of Eshcol
and explored it. 25They picked some of its
fruit and brought it back to us. And they
reported, 'The land the LORD our God has
given us is indeed a good land.'

1:7 Gen 15:18-21; Josh 10:5, 40
1:8 Gen 12:7; 26:3; Exod 33:1; Num 32:10-11
1:9 Exod 18:18, 24
1:10 Gen 15:5; 22:17; Deut 10:22; 26:5; 28:62
1:11 Deut 1:8, 10
1:12 Exod 18:13-14
1:13 Exod 18:21-22; Num 11:16-17
1:16 Deut 16:18
1:17 Exod 18:25-26; Deut 10:17; 16:19; 24:17; Prov 24:23; Jas 2:1, 9
1:19 Deut 1:2; 8:15; 32:10
1:22-23 Num 13:1-3
1:24 Num 13:21-25

in Canaan, Moses reminded them of life in Egypt, of the forty years of wandering in the wilderness, and of their past blunders. He warned them to obey God's covenant and assured them that God's grace would follow them as they learned to trust and obey the Lord.

1:6-8 See Num 10:11-13.

1:7 The ***hill country*** consisted of interior areas of Canaan that were also inhabited by the Amorites (see 1:4; Num 13:29; Josh 10:6). The Canaanites apparently once lived throughout Palestine, but with the incursion of the Amorites they were restricted to the valleys and lowlands. • ***the western foothills*** (Hebrew *the Shephelah*): This term is still used in modern Israel for the region between the hills of Judah and the coastal plain, an area that specializes in orchards and vineyards. • ***the Negev:*** This great desert area lies to the south of Canaan. The Hebrew word could also designate "the south."

1:8 ***occupy it*** (literally *acquire it as an inheritance*): The land was already Israel's because God had promised it to the nation's ancestors centuries earlier (Gen 15:18-21; 26:3; Exod 23:31). Israel was not seizing new territory from its rightful owners but was taking possession of land occupied by squatters.

1:9-18 See Exod 18:13-27.

1:10 ***as numerous as the stars:*** This figure of speech deliberately exaggerates for effect. Abraham's descendants had not approached the actual number of stars in the universe, though they exceeded the number of stars visible to the naked eye. Moses meant that God had begun fulfilling his promises to Abraham (see Gen 15:5; 22:17) by making Israel numerous, bringing them to the Promised Land, and preparing them to conquer it.

1:13 Those who were ***well-respected*** had lives and reputations that were above reproach, even on close scrutiny.

1:15 ***thousand . . . hundred . . . fifty . . . ten:*** This was standard military organization, so some of these officials were probably military officers (see 1 Sam 8:12; 22:7; 2 Sam 18:1).

1:16-17 ***Be . . . impartial*** (literally *do not notice faces*): People appearing before the court should be treated as though they were wearing a mask to conceal their identity. Judges were not to be influenced by rich and powerful persons in the community but were to judge on the basis of God's own impartiality (10:17) and treat all persons equally under the law.

1:19-25 See Num 13:1-33.

1:19 ***Kadesh-barnea***, a great oasis with abundant wells and springs, was about fifty miles south of Beersheba, the traditional southern point of Israel (see 2 Sam 3:10; 1 Chr 21:2).

1:24-25 ***Eshcol*** means "cluster"; the ***fruit*** grown there was grapes (see Num 13:23-27).

1:26 Num 14:1-3
1:27 Deut 9:28; Ps 106:25
1:28 Num 13:28, 33; Deut 9:1-2
1:29 Deut 3:22; 7:18
1:30 Exod 14:14; Deut 20:4
1:31 Deut 32:11; Acts 13:18
1:33 Exod 13:21; Num 9:15-23; 10:33-36
1:34-35 Num 14:23; 32:14
1:36 Num 14:24; Josh 14:6
1:37 Num 20:12
1:38 Num 27:18; 34:17; Deut 3:28; 31:7
1:39 Num 14:3, 31

Israel's Rebellion against the LORD

26"But you rebelled against the command
of the LORD your God and refused to go
in. 27You complained in your tents and
said, 'The LORD must hate us. That's why he
has brought us here from Egypt—to hand
us over to the Amorites to be slaughtered.
28Where can we go? Our brothers have demoralized us with their report. They tell us,
"The people of the land are taller and more
powerful than we are, and their towns are
large, with walls rising high into the sky! We
even saw giants there—the descendants of
Anak!" '

29"But I said to you, 'Don't be shocked or
afraid of them! 30The LORD your God is going ahead of you. He will fight for you, just
as you saw him do in Egypt. 31And you saw
how the LORD your God cared for you all
along the way as you traveled through the
wilderness, just as a father cares for his
child. Now he has brought you to this place.'

32"But even after all he did, you refused
to trust the LORD your God, 33who goes before you looking for the best places to camp,
guiding you with a pillar of fire by night and
a pillar of cloud by day.

34"When the LORD heard your complaining, he became very angry. So he solemnly
swore, 35'Not one of you from this wicked
generation will live to see the good land
I swore to give your ancestors, 36except
Caleb son of Jephunneh. He will see this
land because he has followed the LORD
completely. I will give to him and his descendants some of the very land he explored
during his scouting mission.'

37"And the LORD was also angry with me
because of you. He said to me, 'Moses, not
even you will enter the Promised Land! 38In-
stead, your assistant, Joshua son of Nun, will
lead the people into the land. Encourage him,
for he will lead Israel as they take possession of it. 39I will give the land to your little
ones—your innocent children. You were
afraid they would be captured, but they will

God's War (1:30)

Deut 2:9-12; 7:2; 20:1-4; 23:9-14; 32:8-9; Gen 12:1; 13:14-17; 15:18-21; Judg 3:27-30; 1 Sam 7:8-10; 2 Chr 13:12-16; Isa 13:3; Jer 6:1-9; 51:20-28; Joel 3:1-16; Matt 5:9; 26:52; Rev 19:11-21; 20:7-10

The Lord's command to Israel to annihilate its enemies poses a major ethical problem. How could the God of love mandate genocide? What justification could Israel have had for invading, conquering, and destroying the land of Canaan and its peoples? From a human perspective, it appears that Israel's aggressive campaigns to settle Canaan were illegal and immoral.

However, the war against the Canaanites was led by God, not by mere human whim (see Deut 7:2). The conquest was directed against wicked people who had rebelled against the Lord and his purposes. Their sin had reached its full measure and now warranted their destruction (cp. Gen 15:16). Israel became God's instrument to carry out his judgment.

The war that Israel was authorized to wage was limited historically and theologically to its OT setting. Medieval campaigns, such as the Crusades by European "Christians" against Middle Eastern "infidels," or the more recent *jihads* of Islamic terrorism cannot be justified based on OT practice. Jesus made it very clear that "God blesses those who work for peace" (Matt 5:9) and that "those who use the sword will die by the sword" (Matt 26:52). No justification for such action exists in the modern world. In the final judgment, God himself will pour out his holy wrath on human wickedness (see Rev 19:11-21; 20:7-10).

1:26-46 See Num 14:1-45.

1:28 ***Anak*** was a well-known man of gigantic physical stature (2:10, 21; 9:2; Num 13:33). Goliath (1 Sam 17:4) might have been one of the ***descendants of Anak*** who migrated to the Philistine coastal plain (2:23; Josh 11:21-23; 15:14; 1 Chr 20:4-8).

1:30 ***He will fight for you:*** This phrase refers to the defeat of the Canaanite nations. The Lord would initiate the battle, lead it, fight it, and bring it to a successful conclusion. The only other use of this phrase refers to God's activity in the Exodus (Exod 14:14).

1:31 God's tender care ***as a father*** reflected his covenant relationship with Israel (Exod 4:22; Hos 11:1-4; cp. Matt 6:26-33; John 14:21; Acts 13:18; Rom 8:15-17; 1 Pet 1:2-3; 1 Jn 3:1). Israel was God's ***child*** by descent from Abraham and because God had chosen and adopted Israel from among all the nations (14:2; Exod 19:4-6). The imagery is similar to that found in secular covenant texts in which a Great King regarded a vassal with whom he had made a treaty as his son (see Deuteronomy Introduction, "Literary Form," p. 314).

1:33 Physical manifestations of God (called *theophanies*), such as the ***pillar of fire*** and the ***pillar of cloud***, assured God's people of his presence and power. As he moved forward by these visible displays, they could also move, knowing that he would faithfully lead them to their final destination (Exod 13:21-22; 14:24; Ps 18:9-10).

1:36 ***Caleb*** was one of the twelve spies whom Moses sent to discern the political and military situation in Canaan. Caleb and Joshua alone brought back the report that God would give Israel success in conquering Canaan (Num 13:6, 8, 16, 30). Caleb later became the father-in-law of Othniel, Israel's first judge (Judg 1:13). For his faithfulness, Caleb was given the vicinity of Hebron as his inheritance, and he expelled the Anakites (see Josh 14:12-15; Judg 1:20).

1:37 God was ***angry with me because of you:*** In his frustration against rebellious Israel, Moses had disobeyed God by striking the rock rather than merely speaking to it (Num 20:10-13).

be the ones who occupy it. 40As for you, turn
around now and go on back through the wilderness toward the Red Sea.'

41"Then you confessed, 'We have sinned
against the LORD! We will go into the land
and fight for it, as the LORD our God has
commanded us.' So your men strapped on
their weapons, thinking it would be easy to
attack the hill country.

42"But the LORD told me to tell you, 'Do
not attack, for I am not with you. If you go
ahead on your own, you will be crushed by
your enemies.'

43"This is what I told you, but you would
not listen. Instead, you again rebelled
against the LORD's command and arrogantly
went into the hill country to fight. 44But the
Amorites who lived there came out against
you like a swarm of bees. They chased and
battered you all the way from Seir to Hormah. 45Then you returned and wept before
the LORD, but he refused to listen. 46So you
stayed there at Kadesh for a long time.

Remembering Israel's Wanderings

2"Then we turned around and headed
back across the wilderness toward the
Red Sea, just as the LORD had instructed me,
and we wandered around in the region of
Mount Seir for a long time.

2"Then at last the LORD said to me, 3'You
have been wandering around in this hill
country long enough; turn to the north.
4Give these orders to the people: "You will
pass through the country belonging to your
relatives the Edomites, the descendants of
Esau, who live in Seir. The Edomites will feel
threatened, so be careful. 5Do not bother
them, for I have given them all the hill country around Mount Seir as their property,
and I will not give you even one square foot
of their land. 6If you need food to eat or water to drink, pay them for it. 7For the LORD
your God has blessed you in everything you
have done. He has watched your every step
through this great wilderness. During these
forty years, the LORD your God has been
with you, and you have lacked nothing."'

8"So we bypassed the territory of our relatives, the descendants of Esau, who live in
Seir. We avoided the road through the Arabah Valley that comes up from Elath and
Ezion-geber.

"Then as we turned north along the desert route through Moab, 9the LORD warned
us, 'Do not bother the Moabites, the descendants of Lot, or start a war with them. I have
given them Ar as their property, and I will
not give you any of their land.'"

10(A race of giants called the Emites had
once lived in the area of Ar. They were as
strong and numerous and tall as the Anakites, another race of giants. 11Both the
Emites and the Anakites are also known
as the Rephaites, though the Moabites call
them Emites. 12In earlier times the Horites
had lived in Seir, but they were driven out
and displaced by the descendants of Esau,

1:40 Num 14:25
1:41 Num 14:40
1:42 Num 14:41-43
1:43 Num 14:44
1:44 Num 14:45
2:1 Num 21:4
2:4 Exod 15:15; Num 20:14
2:5 Deut 23:7; Josh 24:4
2:7 Deut 8:2; 29:5
2:8 Num 20:20
2:9 Gen 19:37; Deut 2:18, 29
2:10 Gen 14:5; Num 13:22, 33
2:12 Gen 14:6; Num 21:25, 35; Deut 2:22

1:40 *Red Sea:* Literally *sea of reeds.*

1:44 ***Hormah*** is perhaps modern Khirbet el-Meshash, a site seven miles southeast of Beersheba. The ancient name is derived from the verb *kharam,* which means to "devastate" or "annihilate." The Israelites indeed devastated Hormah (Num 14:45; 21:3).

2:1 *Red Sea:* Literally *sea of reeds.*
• ***Mount Seir*** was a mountainous territory north of the Gulf of Aqaba, east of the Arabah (see note on 1:1) and the Dead Sea. It was originally settled by the Horites (Gen 14:6), now identified by many scholars as the Hurrians. The Hurrians are described in many ancient texts as wandering tradesmen and adventurers who found a home in many parts of the ancient Near East. In time, the Horites of Mount Seir were supplanted by the descendants of Esau (2:22), and the region was called Edom ("red"), perhaps because of the rose-red stone typical of the area.

2:2-25 Num 21:10-20 covers the same time period.

2:5 *I have given them:* God's gift of a promised land was not limited to Israel. He also distributed lands to Edom, Moab (2:9), Ammon (2:19), and the Caphtorites (2:22-23). Although God had chosen Israel as a special nation (1:31; see also 7:6; 14:2; Exod 19:5), he is also the God of all nations and has a place and purpose for each (32:8; Acts 17:26)—even for those that do not recognize his sovereignty (Rom 1:16-23).

2:8 *our relatives:* Isaac had two sons, ***Esau,*** the firstborn, and Jacob, who obtained Esau's birthright and blessing as the firstborn (Gen 25:27-34; 27:1-36). The result was intense hostility between Esau and Jacob and between their descendants. Israel still recognized and honored the kinship, however; out of fraternal good faith, if not affection, Israel bypassed Edom and did not engage the Edomites in battle (see Num 20:14-21). • ***Arabah Valley:*** See note on 1:1. • ***Elath and Ezion-geber*** were twin port cities on the Red Sea. They later harbored the merchant ships of Solomon (1 Kgs 9:26), Jehoshaphat (1 Kgs 22:48), and Uzziah (2 Kgs 14:22).

2:9 Following the destruction of Sodom, Gomorrah, and the other cities of the plain, ***Lot*** (Abraham's nephew and Isaac's cousin) and his two unmarried daughters sheltered in a cave east of the Dead Sea (see Gen 19:30-38), where Lot's daughters plied their father with drink until he had sexual relations with them. Their descendants became the nations of Moab and Ammon. Because of their kinship with Israel, ***the Moabites*** were to be left undisturbed. David's great-grandmother Ruth descended from Moab (Ruth 1:4), and David sent his own family to the land of Moab for protection when he was pursued by Saul (1 Sam 22:3-5). • ***Ar*** was probably the capital of Moab.

2:10 The ***Emites*** were also located at Shaveh-kiriathaim (Gen 14:5), perhaps ten miles east of the Dead Sea's north end.

2:11 The ***Rephaites*** lived near Ashteroth-karnaim (Gen 14:5; perhaps modern Tel Ashtarah), due east of the Sea of Galilee (see 1:4).

2:12 ***just as Israel drove out:*** The Hebrew does not include the phrase ***the people of Canaan.*** This passage is often cited as a later addition to Deuteronomy because it seems to presuppose

2:14
Num 14:29-35; 26:64-65
Deut 2:7
1 Cor 10:5

2:15
Ps 106:26
Jude 1:5

2:18
Num 21:15
Deut 2:9

2:20
Deut 2:11

2:23
Gen 10:13-14
1 Chr 1:11-12
Jer 47:4
Amos 9:7

2:24
Num 21:13
Judg 11:18

2:25
Exod 15:14-16; 23:27
Deut 11:25
Josh 2:9

2:26
Num 21:21
Deut 20:10
Judg 11:19

2:29
Deut 2:8-9; 23:3

2:30
Exod 4:21
Num 21:23
Josh 11:20

just as Israel drove out the people of Canaan
when the LORD gave Israel their land.)
13Moses continued, "Then the LORD said
to us, 'Get moving. Cross the Zered Brook.'
So we crossed the brook.
14"Thirty-eight years passed from the
time we first left Kadesh-barnea until we
finally crossed the Zered Brook! By then,
all the men old enough to fight in battle
had died in the wilderness, as the LORD had
vowed would happen. 15The LORD struck
them down until they had all been eliminated from the community.
16"When all the men of fighting age had
died, 17the LORD said to me, 18'Today you
will cross the border of Moab at Ar 19and
enter the land of the Ammonites, the descendants of Lot. But do not bother them or
start a war with them. I have given the land
of Ammon to them as their property, and I
will not give you any of their land.' "
20(That area was once considered the
land of the Rephaites, who had lived there,
though the Ammonites call them Zamzummites. 21They were also as strong and
numerous and tall as the Anakites. But the
LORD destroyed them so the Ammonites
could occupy their land. 22He had done
the same for the descendants of Esau who
lived in Seir, for he destroyed the Horites so
they could settle there in their place. The descendants of Esau live there to this day. 23A
similar thing happened when the Caphtorites from Crete invaded and destroyed the
Avvites, who had lived in villages in the area
of Gaza.)
24Moses continued, "Then the LORD said,
'Now get moving! Cross the Arnon Gorge.
Look, I will hand over to you Sihon the Amorite, king of Heshbon, and I will give you
his land. Attack him and begin to occupy
the land. 25Beginning today I will make people throughout the earth terrified because
of you. When they hear reports about you,
they will tremble with dread and fear.' "

Victory over Sihon of Heshbon

26Moses continued, "From the wilderness of
Kedemoth I sent ambassadors to King Sihon
of Heshbon with this proposal of peace:

27'Let us travel through your land. We will
stay on the main road and won't turn off
into the fields on either side. 28Sell us food
to eat and water to drink, and we will pay
for it. All we want is permission to pass
through your land. 29The descendants
of Esau who live in Seir allowed us to
go through their country, and so did
the Moabites, who live in Ar. Let us pass
through until we cross the Jordan into the
land the LORD our God is giving us.'

30"But King Sihon of Heshbon refused to
allow us to pass through, because the LORD
your God made Sihon stubborn and defiant
so he could help you defeat him, as he has
now done.

---

the conquest under Joshua. However, it refers in part to the defeat of peoples east of the Jordan, such as the Amorites under King Sihon and King Og (3:12-17).

2:13 The ravine of ***Zered Brook*** marked the boundary between Moab and Edom. Rising in the highlands of Mount Seir, this waterway empties into the southeast bend of the Dead Sea.

2:19 Like the Moabites, the ***Ammonites*** were descendants of the incestuous relationship between Lot and his daughters (see note on 2:9). Throughout most of their history, the Ammonites lived south and east of the Jabbok River. The nation's capital was Rabbath Ammon (modern Amman, Jordan). David arranged for Uriah, Bathsheba's husband, to be slain in the siege of this city (2 Sam 11:1, 14-21).

2:20-21 The *Zamzummites* are probably the same as the Zuzites (Gen 14:5). The Lord had removed them from the land in the past so that the Ammonites could occupy their lands. The God of Israel is also the God of all the earth; he is mindful of all nations and has a place and purpose for each.

2:23 The *Caphtorites* were descendants of Ham and were originally ***from Crete*** (Hebrew *from Caphtor*), a large island south of the Greek peninsula. The Caphtorites are usually identified with the Philistines (see Gen 10:6-14; 1 Chr 1:8-12). The Philistine presence in Canaan resulted from two separate movements, one in the time of the Hebrew patriarchs (see note on Gen 21:32) and another that began about 1200 BC (see notes on Josh 13:2; Judg 3:3). This passage apparently refers to the earlier settlement. • The *Avvites* were indigenous inhabitants of the lower Mediterranean coastal plain; they were supplanted in Gaza by the early wave of Philistines (cp. Josh 13:2-4).

2:24 The ***Arnon Gorge*** is the deep canyon formed by the Arnon River; it sometimes marked the border between Moab and Edom (see Num 21:13). It rises deep in the Arabian Desert and empties into the Dead Sea midway along its eastern shore. • ***Sihon the Amorite*** controlled the area east of the Jordan, north of the Arnon, and south of the Ammonite territories (see Num 21:21-35). He is not known outside of the Bible. His capital, ***Heshbon***, was probably about fifteen miles southwest of Rabbath Ammon and is usually identified with the impressive ruins at Tell Hesban.

2:26-37 See Num 21:21-32.

2:26 The ***wilderness of Kedemoth*** might refer to the area north of the Arnon Gorge between Dibon and Mattanah (Josh 13:18; 21:37).

2:30 ***made Sihon stubborn and defiant*** (literally *had hardened his spirit and strengthened his heart*): Like Pharaoh (see Exod 7:13), Sihon was incorrigibly unrepentant and thus experienced God's wrath. God knew that any further extension of grace to these rulers would be useless. Mystery surrounds the relationship between statements that people harden their own hearts (e.g., Exod 7:13, 22; 8:15) and statements that God hardens people's hearts (e.g., Exod 4:21; 7:3; 9:12). What is clear is that God appeals for repentance and is ready to forgive, but when people continually ignore or reject his appeals, they can become incapable of hearing and obeying God (see "A Hardened Heart" at Exod 14:4, 8, p. 149; Rom 1:21-28; 9:17-24).

31“Then the LORD said to me, ‘Look, I have
begun to hand King Sihon and his land over
to you. Begin now to conquer and occupy
his land.’
32“Then King Sihon declared war on us
and mobilized his forces at Jahaz. 33But
the LORD our God handed him over to
us, and we crushed him, his sons, and all
his people. 34We conquered all his towns
and completely destroyed everyone—men,
women, and children. Not a single person
was spared. 35We took all the livestock as
plunder for ourselves, along with anything
of value from the towns we ransacked.
36“The LORD our God also helped us conquer Aroer on the edge of the Arnon Gorge,
and the town in the gorge, and the whole
area as far as Gilead. No town had walls too
strong for us. 37However, we avoided the
land of the Ammonites all along the Jabbok
River and the towns in the hill country—all
the places the LORD our God had commanded us to leave alone.

Victory over Og of Bashan

3 “Next we turned and headed for the
land of Bashan, where King Og and
his entire army attacked us at Edrei. 2But
the LORD told me, ‘Do not be afraid of him,
for I have given you victory over Og and his
entire army, and I will give you all his land.
Treat him just as you treated King Sihon of
the Amorites, who ruled in Heshbon.’
3“So the LORD our God handed King Og
and all his people over to us, and we killed
them all. Not a single person survived. 4We
conquered all sixty of his towns—the entire
Argob region in his kingdom of Bashan. Not
a single town escaped our conquest. 5These
towns were all fortified with high walls and
barred gates. We also took many unwalled
villages at the same time. 6We completely
destroyed the kingdom of Bashan, just as
we had destroyed King Sihon of Heshbon.
We destroyed all the people in every town
we conquered—men, women, and children
alike. 7But we kept all the livestock for ourselves and took plunder from all the towns.
8“So we took the land of the two Amorite
kings east of the Jordan River—all the way
from the Arnon Gorge to Mount Hermon.
9(Mount Hermon is called Sirion by the Sidonians, and the Amorites call it Senir.) 10We
had now conquered all the cities on the
plateau and all Gilead and Bashan, as far as
the towns of Salecah and Edrei, which were
part of Og’s kingdom in Bashan. 11(King Og
of Bashan was the last survivor of the giant
Rephaites. His bed was made of iron and
was more than thirteen feet long and six
feet wide. It can still be seen in the Ammonite city of Rabbah.)

Land Division East of the Jordan

12“When we took possession of this land, I
gave to the tribes of Reuben and Gad the territory beyond Aroer along the Arnon Gorge,
plus half of the hill country of Gilead with its
towns. 13Then I gave the rest of Gilead and
all of Bashan—Og’s former kingdom—to the
half-tribe of Manasseh. (This entire Argob
region of Bashan used to be known as the

2:33 Num 21:24-30; Deut 3:6; 29:7
2:35 Deut 3:7, 10
2:36 Ps 44:3
2:37 Deut 3:16
3:1 Num 21:33-35
3:2 Num 21:34
3:3 Josh 9:10
3:4 1 Kgs 4:13
3:6 Deut 2:33-34; 20:16
3:7 Deut 2:35
3:8 Num 32:33-42; Josh 12:1-6; 13:8-13
3:9 Deut 4:48; Josh 11:17; Ps 29:5-6
3:11 Deut 2:11, 20; 2 Sam 11:1; 12:26-27; Jer 49:2
3:12 Num 32:33-42; Deut 2:35-36; Josh 13:8-13

2:34 ***completely destroyed*** (Hebrew *kharam*): The Hebrew term used here refers to the complete consecration of things or people to the LORD, either by destroying them or by giving them as an offering. The underlying rationale was to maintain the Lord’s holiness in the face of pagan idolatry and moral corruption (see also Lev 27:28-29).

2:36 ***Aroer,*** on the north rim of the Arnon Gorge three miles from Dibon, marked the southernmost extent of the Amorite kingdom (3:12; 4:48; Josh 12:2; 13:9, 16, 25). • The identity of ***the town in the gorge*** is uncertain but was probably ***Aroer.*** • ***Gilead,*** famous for its balm and other aromatic spices (Jer 8:22; 46:11), lay north of the Jabbok River, the northernmost border of the Amorites under Sihon.

2:37 Like the Moabites, ***the Ammonites*** were related to Israel and were thus to be left undisturbed (cp. 2:9). • The ***Jabbok River,*** a great tributary of the Jordan River, marked the border between Gilead to the north and the Amorite kingdom of Sihon to the south. The Ammonites lived east and south of the Jabbok (2:19). It was somewhere at the Jabbok that Jacob wrestled with the stranger at night (Gen 32:22-32).

3:1-11 See Num 21:33-35.

3:1 ***Bashan:*** See note on 1:4.

3:4 ***Argob*** might be synonymous with Bashan or might refer to a heavily populated part of Bashan.

3:6 ***completely destroyed:*** See note on 2:34.

3:8 ***Mount Hermon*** is the southernmost peak in the Anti-Lebanon Mountains northeast of the Sea of Galilee; at 9,300 feet above sea level, it is also the highest. On a clear day, this impressive landmark is visible from many miles away.

3:9 The alternative names ***Sirion*** and ***Senir*** suggest that Hermon was perhaps a later name given by the Israelites. Hermon is apparently related to the verb *kharam,* which means “to destroy” (see note on 2:34) and perhaps describes the destruction summarized in 3:3-7.

3:11 ***His bed*** was probably wooden, inlaid with iron. Alternatively, the Hebrew word might suggest a sarcophagus or coffin. • ***thirteen feet long and six feet wide:*** Hebrew *9 cubits* [4.1 meters] *long and 4 cubits* [1.8 meters] *wide.* • ***Rabbah*** is the same city as Rabbath Ammon (2:19). Apparently there was some kind of museum at Rabbah when Deuteronomy was written, and this artifact could be seen there.

3:12-20 See Num 32.

3:12 The tribes of ***Reuben and Gad*** had asked Moses to let them settle east of the Jordan rather than in Canaan, and he allowed them to do so (Num 32:1-5). • ***Aroer:*** See note on 2:36.

3:13 ***The half-tribe of Manasseh*** made the same request as Reuben and Gad (3:12), and Moses accepted their request. Gad and Reuben settled between the Arnon (see 2:24) and the middle of ***Gilead*** (see 2:36), and Manasseh took everything north of that, including ***Bashan*** (see 3:1).

3:15 Num 32:40
3:17 Josh 13:27
3:18 Num 32:20; Josh 4:12-13
3:19 Num 32:16; Josh 1:14
3:22 Deut 1:29-30; 20:4
3:24 Ps 86:8; [a]*'adonay Yahweh* (0136, 3068) ›Josh 7:7
3:26 Deut 1:37; 31:2
3:27 Num 27:12; Deut 1:37
3:28 Num 27:18
4:1 Lev 19:37; Deut 5:32-33; 8:1; 16:20; 30:16; Ezek 20:11; Rom 10:5
4:2 Deut 12:32; Prov 30:6; Matt 5:18; Rev 22:18-19
4:3 Num 25:1-9

land of the Rephaites. [14]Jair, a leader from the tribe of Manasseh, conquered the whole Argob region in Bashan, all the way to the border of the Geshurites and Maacathites. Jair renamed this region after himself, calling it the Towns of Jair, as it is still known today.) [15]I gave Gilead to the clan of Makir. [16]But I also gave part of Gilead to the tribes of Reuben and Gad. The area I gave them extended from the middle of the Arnon Gorge in the south to the Jabbok River on the Ammonite frontier. [17]They also received the Jordan Valley, all the way from the Sea of Galilee down to the Dead Sea, with the Jordan River serving as the western boundary. To the east were the slopes of Pisgah.

[18]"At that time I gave this command to the tribes that would live east of the Jordan: 'Although the LORD your God has given you this land as your property, all your fighting men must cross the Jordan ahead of your Israelite relatives, armed and ready to assist them. [19]Your wives, children, and numerous livestock, however, may stay behind in the towns I have given you. [20]When the LORD has given security to the rest of the Israelites, as he has to you, and when they occupy the land the LORD your God is giving them across the Jordan River, then you may all return here to the land I have given you.'

Moses Forbidden to Enter the Land

[21]"At that time I gave Joshua this charge: 'You have seen for yourself everything the LORD your God has done to these two kings. He will do the same to all the kingdoms on the west side of the Jordan. [22]Do not be afraid of the nations there, for the LORD your God will fight for you.'

[23]"At that time I pleaded with the LORD and said, [24]'O [a]Sovereign LORD, you have only begun to show your greatness and the strength of your hand to me, your servant. Is there any god in heaven or on earth who can perform such great and mighty deeds as you do? [25]Please let me cross the Jordan to see the wonderful land on the other side, the beautiful hill country and the Lebanon mountains.'

[26]"But the LORD was angry with me because of you, and he would not listen to me. 'That's enough!' he declared. 'Speak of it no more. [27]But go up to Pisgah Peak, and look over the land in every direction. Take a good look, but you may not cross the Jordan River. [28]Instead, commission Joshua and encourage and strengthen him, for he will lead the people across the Jordan. He will give them all the land you now see before you as their possession.' [29]So we stayed in the valley near Beth-peor.

Exhortation to Covenant Faithfulness (4:1-40)

Moses Urges Israel to Obey

4 "And now, Israel, listen carefully to these decrees and regulations that I am about to teach you. Obey them so that you may live, so you may enter and occupy the land that the LORD, the God of your ancestors, is giving you. [2]Do not add to or subtract from these commands I am giving you. Just obey the commands of the LORD your God that I am giving you.

[3]"You saw for yourself what the LORD did to you at Baal-peor. There the LORD your God destroyed everyone who had worshiped Baal, the god of Peor. [4]But all of you who were faithful to the LORD your God are still alive today—every one of you.

• The ***Rephaites,*** a giant people related to the Anakites (see 2:11), are noted here as being indigenous to Bashan.

3:14 ***Jair*** was a descendant of Manasseh from Makir and Gilead (1 Chr 2:22). • ***Geshurites and Maacathites,*** kingdoms of Bashan, lay along the west side of the Golan Heights, east of the Sea of Galilee. • ***The Towns of Jair*** (Hebrew *Havvoth-jair*) was the name given Argob (see 3:4) after Jair brought it under Israelite control.

3:15 ***Makir*** was a clan in the tribe of Manasseh (Num 26:29) to which Jair was related (1 Chr 2:21-23). The clan of Makir settled south of Bashan in the northern part of Gilead (see 3:13).

3:17 ***from the Sea of Galilee down to the Dead Sea*** (Hebrew *from Kinnereth to the Sea of the Arabah, the Salt Sea*): The Hebrew name for the beautiful ***Sea of Galilee*** is *kinnereth,* which might come from *kinnor* ("harp") because of its shape. • The ***Dead Sea*** (Hebrew *yam hammelakh,* "Salt Sea"), here also called the Sea of the Arabah (see note on 1:1), has a very high mineral content (about 30 percent). • ***Pisgah*** is a section of the Abarim mountain range; its most prominent peak is Mount Nebo, where Moses died (see Deut 34:1).

3:21-29 See Num 20:2-13; Ps 106:32-33.

3:21 ***He will do the same:*** Israel's military success under Moses' leadership could be expected to continue under Joshua because the Lord promised to remain with them.

3:24 ***Is there any god?*** Moses did not believe that other gods existed; he was simply affirming that only the Lord is God. Nothing and no one else, real or imaginary, can rival the one true God.

3:29 ***Beth-peor,*** otherwise known as Baal Peor (see 4:3) or simply Peor (Num 23:28; Josh 22:17), became Moses' burial place (34:6). At that place the false prophet Balaam had earlier attempted to curse Israel on behalf of Balak, king of Moab (Num 23:27–24:25).

4:1-40 Moses' lengthy exhortation to the Israelite community was based on the people's recent failures and his anticipation of what lay ahead in Canaan.

4:1 The pairing of the terms ***decrees and regulations*** in Deuteronomy (e.g., 4:5, 8, 14, 45; 5:1, 31) is a way of referring to the covenant stipulations and the detailed application of the great principles of the Law (see note on 4:44).

4:3 ***Baal*** was the Canaanite god associated with the fertility of the soil and of human and animal life. Major pagan worship centers linked Baal with their own shrines and cultic rituals, as with ***the god of Peor*** (see 3:29).

5“Look, I now teach you these decrees and regulations just as the LORD my God commanded me, so that you may obey them in the land you are about to enter and occupy. 6Obey them completely, and you will display your wisdom and intelligence among the surrounding nations. When they hear all these decrees, they will exclaim, ‘How wise and prudent are the people of this great nation!’ 7For what great nation has a god as near to them as the LORD our God is near to us whenever we call on him? 8And what great nation has decrees and regulations as righteous and fair as this body of instructions that I am giving you today?

9“But watch out! Be careful never to forget what you yourself have seen. Do not let these memories escape from your mind as long as you live! And be sure to pass them on to your children and grandchildren. 10Never forget the day when you stood before the LORD your God at Mount Sinai, where he told me, ‘Summon the people before me, and I will personally instruct them. Then they will learn to fear me as long as they live, and they will teach their children to fear me also.’

11“You came near and stood at the foot of the mountain, while flames from the mountain shot into the sky. The mountain was shrouded in black clouds and deep darkness. 12And the LORD spoke to you from the heart of the fire. You heard the sound of his words but didn’t see his form; there was only a voice. 13He proclaimed his covenant—the Ten Commandments—which he commanded you to keep, and which he wrote on two stone tablets. 14It was at that time that the LORD commanded me to teach you his decrees and regulations so you would obey them in the land you are about to enter and occupy.

A Warning against Idolatry

15“But be very careful! You did not see the LORD’s form on the day he spoke to you from the heart of the fire at Mount Sinai. 16So do not corrupt yourselves by making an idol in any form—whether of a man or a woman, 17an animal on the ground, a bird in the sky, 18a small animal that scurries along the ground, or a fish in the deepest sea. 19And when you look up into the sky and see the sun, moon, and stars—all the [b]forces of heaven—don’t be seduced into worshiping them. The LORD your God gave them to all the peoples of the earth. 20Remember that the LORD rescued you from the iron-smelting furnace of Egypt in order to make you his very own people and his special possession, which is what you are today.

21“But the LORD was angry with me because of you. He vowed that I would not cross the Jordan River into the good land the LORD your God is giving you as your special possession. 22You will cross the Jordan to occupy the land, but I will not. Instead, I will die here on the east side of the river. 23So be

4:5 Lev 26:46; 27:34
4:6 Ps 19:7-8; Prov 1:7-9
4:7 Ps 148:14
4:8 Ps 89:14-15
4:10 Exod 19:9, 16
4:11 Exod 19:18; Heb 12:18
4:13 Exod 31:18; 34:28; Deut 10:4
4:15 Exod 19:9, 18, 21
4:16 Exod 20:4-5; 32:8; Deut 9:12; 31:29
4:19 2 Kgs 17:16; Acts 7:43; [b]*tsaba’* (6635) ‣ Deut 17:3
4:20 1 Kgs 8:51; Jer 11:4
4:21 Num 20:12; Deut 1:37
4:23 Exod 20:4-5

4:6 ***Obey . . . wisdom and intelligence:*** Wisdom is linked to obedience—obeying the Lord is the essence of wisdom (see 10:12-13; Prov 1:7; 9:10; 15:33). If God’s people were ***wise and prudent*** enough to keep the Lord’s perfect covenant, all the world would marvel.

4:8 Israel’s laws were ***righteous and fair*** because they originated with God.

4:10 ***Mount Sinai:*** Hebrew *Horeb,* another name for Sinai; also in 4:15. See note on 1:2. • ***fear me:*** See notes on 7:21; 10:12-13.

4:11 ***flames . . . clouds:*** In these contrasting displays of God’s presence (*theophanies;* see note on 1:33), he revealed himself while also remaining hidden (see Exod 19:16-19).

4:13 The ***covenant*** is the key theological idea of Deuteronomy and perhaps of the entire OT. A covenant was a legal arrangement involving two or more parties who entered into agreements with mutually binding obligations. The covenant at Sinai (Exod 20:1–23:33) codified this relationship between the Lord and Israel; in Deuteronomy, Moses interpreted and expanded the covenant for the new generation that was about to conquer and occupy the Promised Land. • The ***Ten Commandments*** (literally *the ten words,* “decalogue”) are so much at the heart of the covenant text and its requirements as to be equated with the covenant. The first four *words* regulate relationship with God, while the last six regulate human relationships. • ***two stone tablets:*** All legal documents, including covenant texts, were copied for the benefit of all involved parties. God had his copy (the stone tablets) laid inside the ark of the covenant in the sanctuary (see Exod 25:16, 21; 31:18; 40:20; cp. Deut 31:26); Israel’s copy was written in the books of Exodus (Exod 20:1-17) and Deuteronomy (5:6-21).

4:15 ***form:*** No image could capture the transcendent glory and power of the invisible God (Neh 9:20; Isa 63:10-14; Zech 4:6; John 4:24). Any *form* of the Lord could become an object of worship in lieu of worshiping God himself.

4:16 ***idol:*** Idolatry inherently confined the Lord to the artist’s imagination. Israel was not to make idols in the form of any of his creatures (4:17-18). Idols and images could lead to worship of the creature rather than the Creator (5:8-9; Rom 1:23-25).

4:19 ***forces of heaven:*** This phrase refers to the stars and other heavenly bodies, which, like earthly creations, were thought to embody or represent deities. Instead, they are servants of God, named by him to carry out their duties of marking the times and seasons (Gen 1:14-19; Isa 40:26). • ***The LORD your God gave them:*** Rather than worshiping these heavenly bodies, the people of Israel were to recognize that God’s creation was made, among other reasons, to serve mankind (Gen 1:28).

4:20 An ***iron-smelting furnace*** was used to refine metal ores and separate the pure metal from the dross. Israel’s trials in Egypt made the Israelites more spiritually and morally pure. • ***special possession*** (literally *people of inheritance*): Israel itself was God’s inheritance. This concept is confirmed by the parallel phrase describing Israel as ***his very own people.*** As such, the Israelites were now fit to enter, conquer, and occupy the land (cp. 1 Pet 2:9-12).

4:24
Exod 24:17; 34:14
Heb 12:29
[c]*qanna'* (7067)
‣Job 5:2

4:25
Deut 4:16; 31:29

4:26
Deut 7:4; 8:19; 31:29

4:27
Deut 28:64

4:28
Deut 28:36, 64; 29:17
Ps 115:4-8

4:29
Deut 6:5; 10:12; 30:1-3
2 Chr 15:4

4:30
[d]*shama'* (8085)
‣Deut 11:27

4:31
Deut 31:6, 8
Josh 1:5
Heb 13:5

4:33
Exod 20:22
Deut 5:24, 26

careful not to break the covenant the LORD
your God has made with you. Do not make
idols of any shape or form, for the LORD your
God has forbidden this. 24The LORD your
God is a devouring fire; he is a [c]jealous God.
25"In the future, when you have children
and grandchildren and have lived in the
land a long time, do not corrupt yourselves
by making idols of any kind. This is evil
in the sight of the LORD your God and will
arouse his anger.
26"Today I call on heaven and earth as
witnesses against you. If you break my covenant, you will quickly disappear from the
land you are crossing the Jordan to occupy.
You will live there only a short time; then
you will be utterly destroyed. 27For the LORD
will scatter you among the nations, where
only a few of you will survive. 28There, in
a foreign land, you will worship idols made
from wood and stone—gods that neither see
nor hear nor eat nor smell. 29But from there
you will search again for the LORD your God.
And if you search for him with all your heart
and soul, you will find him.
30"In the distant future, when you are
suffering all these things, you will finally
return to the LORD your God and [d]listen to
what he tells you. 31For the LORD your God
is a merciful God; he will not abandon you
or destroy you or forget the solemn covenant he made with your ancestors.

There Is Only One God

32"Now search all of history, from the time
God created people on the earth until now,
and search from one end of the heavens
to the other. Has anything as great as this
ever been seen or heard before? 33Has any
nation ever heard the voice of God speaking from fire—as you did—and survived?

Biblical Law (4:1-2)

Deut 5:6-21, 32-33; 6:1-9; 8:1; 30:1-20
Exod 19:4-6
Lev 18:5
Matt 5:17-48; 22:36-40
John 14:15-21
Rom 3:19-24; 7:1-12
1 Cor 9:20-21
Gal 3:1-22; 5:14
Heb 7:18-19; 10:1

Biblical law is more than lists of dos and don'ts. It is a system of divine expectations regarding belief and behavior which, if faithfully carried out, will bring God's richest blessing. Life itself depends on keeping the law (4:1; see also 5:32-33; 8:1; 16:20).

The exodus from Egypt freed the nation of Israel to become God's servant. When God delivered Israel from bondage by "a strong hand, a powerful arm, and terrifying acts" (4:34), it was not because Israel had earned this right through its own righteousness but because God is gracious and faithful to his promises to Abraham. The purpose of the rescue from Egypt was not just to relieve the Israelites of their onerous burdens (Exod 1:11-22; 5:4-23), but to make a covenant with them. The covenant relationship did not make the Israelites God's people; they already were his people (see Exod 4:22-23). Obedience was not a precondition to the covenant but the proper response to it. It placed on them the responsibility of serving God as a priestly kingdom and a holy nation (Exod 19:4-6).

The covenant guaranteed the people of Israel abundant and meaningful life if they kept the law. The covenant document consists of broad principles, patterns, and standards. God's instructions are embodied most famously in the Ten Commandments (5:6-21) and most succinctly in the *Shema* (6:4-5). All other laws of God are interpretations and applications of these primary principles. The law was given to regulate Israel's affairs as a nation so that God's people would be a beacon of his grace to the whole world.

The life that resulted from obedience to the law was not eternal life in the NT sense. It was God's promise that if the Israelites were faithful to the covenant, the nation could expect long and prosperous days in the land (4:1; 5:16, 33; 10:8-9). Jesus also exhorted his disciples to keep the Ten Commandments and the demands of the *Shema* (Matt 22:37-40)—not to have eternal life but as an expression of commitment to him (cp. Matt 5:17-19; John 14:15-21).

4:24 God does not have the petty human emotion of jealousy. Rather, the phrase ***jealous God*** shows that God was asserting his uniqueness and claiming exclusive worship (6:15; Lev 10:2; Num 16:35). The Hebrew word can be rendered as "jealous" or "zealous." God zealously protects his own reputation as the universal sovereign.

4:26 ***Heaven and earth*** would be ***witnesses*** against Israel if the people were disloyal to the Lord. In a covenant partnership, the parties to the agreement were held accountable to the oaths of loyalty and commitment they made to each other in the presence of witnesses (Isa 1:2-7; Mic 6:1-8). In Deuteronomy, the natural creation plays that role of witness (see also 30:19).

4:27 ***scatter you:*** One of the curses directed against Israel if it violated the terms of the covenant was the dispersion of the people to the ends of the earth (28:64). This judgment later came to pass repeatedly, especially when the Assyrians occupied the northern kingdom in 722 BC, when the Babylonians conquered Judah in 605–586 BC, and when Jerusalem was destroyed in AD 70.

4:30 ***distant future*** (literally *last* [or *latter*] *days*): Israel would eventually return from the Exile and worldwide dispersion (see 30:1-10; Lev 26:40-45; Jer 31:27-34; Ezek 36:22-31).

4:33 ***the voice of God:*** Or *the voice of a god.*

34Has any other god dared to take a nation
for himself out of another nation by means
of trials, miraculous signs, wonders, war, a
strong hand, a powerful arm, and terrifying
acts? Yet that is what the LORD your God did
for you in Egypt, right before your eyes.
35"He showed you these things so you
would know that the LORD is God and there
is no other. 36He let you hear his voice from
heaven so he could instruct you. He let you
see his great fire here on earth so he could
speak to you from it. 37Because he loved your
ancestors, he chose to bless their descendants, and he personally brought you out
of Egypt with a great display of power. 38He
drove out nations far greater than you, so he
could bring you in and give you their land as
your special possession, as it is today.
39"So remember this and keep it firmly
in mind: The LORD is God both in heaven
and on [e]earth, and there is no other. 40If you
obey all the decrees and commands I am
giving you today, all will be well with you
and your children. I am giving you these
instructions so you will enjoy a long life
in the land the LORD your God is giving you
for all time."

3. NARRATIVE INTERLUDE (4:41-49)

Eastern Cities of Refuge

41Then Moses set apart three cities of refuge east of the Jordan River. 42Anyone who
killed another person unintentionally, without previous hostility, could flee there to live
in safety. 43These were the cities: Bezer on
the wilderness plateau for the tribe of Reuben; Ramoth in Gilead for the tribe of Gad;
Golan in Bashan for the tribe of Manasseh.

Introduction to Moses' Second Address

44This is the body of instruction that Moses
presented to the Israelites. 45These are the
laws, decrees, and regulations that Moses
gave to the people of Israel when they left
Egypt, 46and as they camped in the valley
near Beth-peor east of the Jordan River.
(This land was formerly occupied by the
Amorites under King Sihon, who ruled from
Heshbon. But Moses and the Israelites destroyed him and his people when they came
up from Egypt. 47Israel took possession of
his land and that of King Og of Bashan—the
two Amorite kings east of the Jordan. 48So
Israel conquered the entire area from Aroer
at the edge of the Arnon Gorge all the way
to Mount Sirion, also called Mount Hermon.
49And they conquered the eastern bank of
the Jordan River as far south as the Dead
Sea, below the slopes of Pisgah.)

4. SECOND ADDRESS: THE COVENANT TEXT (5:1–26:19)

The Principles of the Covenant (5:1–11:32)

Ten Commandments for the Covenant Community

5 Moses called all the people of Israel
together and said, "Listen carefully, Israel. Hear the decrees and regulations I am

4:34 Exod 14:30; Deut 5:15; 6:21; 7:19; 33:29; Ps 136:12
4:35 Exod 8:10; 9:14; Deut 4:39; 1 Sam 2:2; Mark 12:29; *Mark 12:32
4:36 Exod 19:9, 19; Neh 9:13
4:37 Deut 7:8
4:38 Num 32:4
4:39 *'erets* (0776) ›Josh 1:15
4:40 Exod 23:26; Deut 4:2; 5:16, 29, 33; 32:47
4:41 Num 35:6; Deut 19:1-13
4:48 Deut 2:35-36
5:2 Exod 19:5; Mal 4:4
5:4 Num 14:14

4:34 ***strong hand, a powerful arm:*** Describing divine qualities in human terms is called *anthropomorphism* (see note on 8:2). Here it represents God's sovereign power in delivering Israel from bondage in Egypt.

4:36 ***great fire:*** God revealed the covenant law at Mount Sinai with a magnificent and terrifying display of power and glory comparable to the eruption of a great volcano (see note on 1:33; see Exod 3:1-4; 24:16-18).

4:39 The Lord is unique, ***and there is no other*** besides him. This instruction reaffirms the first two commandments (5:6-8; Exod 20:2-4) and foreshadows the *Shema* (6:4-5). God's uniqueness had to be underscored because Israel's neighbors worshiped many gods.

4:40 More than a promise of individual longevity, ***long life*** described Israel's tenure in the land of promise.

4:41-49 Moses was ready to set forth the covenant in all its magisterial authority. This section bridges the review of the past (1:6–4:40) and the presentation of the covenant text proper (5:1–26:19).

4:41-43 When Israel settled in Canaan and adopted an urban lifestyle, crimes such as homicide would inevitably need judicial resolution. In order to protect alleged perpetrators from premature vengeance and to guarantee them a fair trial, they needed safe haven in accessible ***cities of refuge.*** These towns were first assigned east of the Jordan and later in Canaan (see Num 35:9-28). The laws governing these matters occur again in Deut 19:1-13, but they appear here because of the just-mentioned promise of a long and safe life in the land (4:40). Establishing places of refuge to protect the innocent from false accusations would help secure that promise.

4:43 ***Bezer*** (probably modern Umm al-'Amad) lay some six miles east of Heshbon. • ***Ramoth in Gilead*** was thirty-five miles east-southeast of the Sea of Galilee. • The town of ***Golan*** was about forty miles north of *Ramoth in Gilead.*

4:44 ***body of instruction*** (Hebrew *torah*): The Hebrew noun is derived from the verb *yarah,* "to teach"; its basic meaning is ***instruction.*** The Greek OT understands the term to mean "law." In this context, the term introduces the *body of instruction* in the remainder of Deuteronomy (see note on 5:1–26:19).

4:48 ***Mount Sirion:*** As in Syriac version (see also 3:9); Hebrew reads *Mount Sion.* The Sidonians used the name *Sirion* for Mount Hermon.

4:49 ***conquered the eastern bank of the Jordan River as far south as the Dead Sea*** (Hebrew *took the Arabah on the east side of the Jordan as far as the sea of the Arabah*): The Arabah ("wilderness" or "wasteland") usually refers to the Great Rift Valley south of the Dead Sea; in Deuteronomy, it also pertains to the lower Jordan Valley (see 1:1; 3:17).

5:1–26:19 This section contains the heart of the covenant document, the stipulations. The first subdivision (5:1–11:32) sets forth the major stipulations relating especially to the first two commandments (5:7-10). The more specific minor stipulations make up the rest of the section.

5:1-32 The rest of the covenant laws expand and comment upon the Ten Commandments (5:6-21), on which they are based. Moses had first given the Ten

5:5
Exod 19:16, 25
[f]*yare'* (3372)
‣Deut 10:20

5:6-21
//Exod 20:2-17

5:7
Exod 20:3

5:8
Exod 20:4
Lev 26:1
Deut 4:16-17

5:9
Exod 34:7, 14
[g]*khawah* (7812)
‣Deut 29:26

5:12
Exod 20:8-11
[h]*shabbath* (7676)
‣2 Chr 36:21

5:15
Exod 20:11
Deut 15:15; 16:12
[i]*zakar* (2142)
‣Judg 16:28

5:16
Exod 20:12; 21:17
*Matt 15:4; 19:19
*Mark 7:10; 10:9
*Luke 18:20
*Eph 6:2-3

5:17
Exod 20:13
*Matt 5:21

5:18
Exod 20:14
*Mark 10:19
*Luke 18:20
*Rom 13:9
*Jas 2:11

5:19
Exod 20:15
*Matt 19:18
*Mark 10:19
*Luke 18:20
*Rom 13:9

5:20
*Matt 19:18
*Mark 10:19
*Luke 18:20

5:21
*Rom 7:7; 13:9

5:22
Exod 19:16-19

giving you today, so you may learn them and
obey them!
2"The LORD our God made a covenant with
us at Mount Sinai. 3The LORD did not make
this covenant with our ancestors, but with all
of us who are alive today. 4At the mountain the
LORD spoke to you face to face from the heart
of the fire. 5I stood as an intermediary between you and the LORD, for you were [f]afraid
of the fire and did not want to approach the
mountain. He spoke to me, and I passed his
words on to you. This is what he said:

6"I am the LORD your God, who rescued
you from the land of Egypt, the place of
your slavery.
7"You must not have any other god but me.
8"You must not make for yourself an idol
of any kind, or an image of anything
in the heavens or on the earth or in
the sea. 9You must not [g]bow down to
them or worship them, for I, the LORD
your God, am a jealous God who will
not tolerate your affection for any
other gods. I lay the sins of the parents
upon their children; the entire family is
affected—even children in the third and
fourth generations of those who reject
me. 10But I lavish unfailing love for a
thousand generations on those who love
me and obey my commands.
11"You must not misuse the name of the
LORD your God. The LORD will not let you
go unpunished if you misuse his name.
12"Observe the [h]Sabbath day by keeping
it holy, as the LORD your God has
commanded you. 13You have six days
each week for your ordinary work, 14but
the seventh day is a Sabbath day of rest
dedicated to the LORD your God. On that
day no one in your household may do any
work. This includes you, your sons and
daughters, your male and female servants,
your oxen and donkeys and other
livestock, and any foreigners living among
you. All your male and female servants
must rest as you do. 15[i]Remember that
you were once slaves in Egypt, but the
LORD your God brought you out with his
strong hand and powerful arm. That is
why the LORD your God has commanded
you to rest on the Sabbath day.
16"Honor your father and mother, as the
LORD your God commanded you. Then
you will live a long, full life in the land
the LORD your God is giving you.
17"You must not murder.
18"You must not commit adultery.
19"You must not steal.
20"You must not testify falsely against your
neighbor.
21"You must not covet your neighbor's
wife. You must not covet your neighbor's
house or land, male or female servant, ox
or donkey, or anything else that belongs
to your neighbor.

22"The LORD spoke these words to all of
you assembled there at the foot of the mountain. He spoke with a loud voice from the
heart of the fire, surrounded by clouds and
deep darkness. This was all he said at that
time, and he wrote his words on two stone
tablets and gave them to me.
23"But when you heard the voice from the
heart of the darkness, while the mountain

Commandments to the people of Israel nearly forty years earlier (Exod 20:2-17).

5:1 ***decrees and regulations:*** These technical terms describe the stipulations that Israel must obey as the junior partner in the covenant.

5:2 ***Mount Sinai:*** Hebrew *Horeb,* another name for Sinai (see note on 1:2).

5:9 ***jealous God:*** See note on 4:24. • The children of sinful *parents* are not punished for the wrongdoings of their mothers and fathers, but the sins of any generation have consequences that last for generations (see 2 Sam 12:10). • The term ***reject*** (literally *hate*) does not relate to having bitter and hostile feelings but to forsaking a relationship.

5:10 ***for a thousand generations on those:*** Literally *for thousands of those.* • ***who love me:*** Those who choose to accept the Lord do not hate or reject him.

5:11 ***misuse the name*** (literally *take up the name in vain*): Someone who "takes the name of the Lord in vain" uses it manipulatively to achieve a desired end, uses it thoughtlessly, or takes an oath by God's name that a falsehood is true.

5:12 ***keeping it holy:*** Certain holy days were set apart from others and were given extraordinary significance (see chart, "Israel's Festivals," p. 235). On the ***Sabbath day,*** the community stopped working and worshiped the Lord (cp. 1 Cor 16:2; Heb 10:25).

5:15 ***That is why:*** God commanded Israel to observe a day of rest to remember that God ceased his work of creation on the seventh day (Exod 20:11). In Deuteronomy, the Sabbath also celebrated Israel's release from Egyptian bondage. In the Christian tradition, the first day rather than the seventh is generally set apart to observe the most significant event in Christian history, the resurrection of Jesus Christ (see note on Rev 1:10).

5:16-20 Jesus quoted these five commands in response to the question, "What must I do to inherit eternal life?" (Matt 19:17-19; Mark 10:19; Luke 18:20).

5:16 ***Honor:*** Since parents are representatives of divine authority, children are to recognize them as worthy of obedience and great respect (cp. Eph 6:1-3).

5:17 ***murder:*** The Hebrew word can mean either "kill" or "murder." Killing was permitted in war and as punishment in capital cases, so here it must refer to premeditated homicide. See Jesus' comments in Matt 5:21-22.

5:18 ***adultery:*** See Jesus' comments about adultery in Matt 5:27-28.

5:21 ***covet:*** This commandment differs from the others because it pertains to a desire rather than to an act. An evil desire is no less offensive to God than an evil deed (see Matt 5:27-28).

5:22 ***fire . . . clouds:*** See note on 4:11. • ***two stone tablets:*** See note on 4:13.

was blazing with fire, all your tribal leaders
and elders came to me. 24They said, 'Look,
the LORD our God has shown us his glory and
greatness, and we have heard his voice from
the heart of the fire. Today we have seen that
God can speak to us humans, and yet we live!
25But now, why should we risk death again?
If the LORD our God speaks to us again, we
will certainly die and be consumed by this
awesome fire. 26Can any living thing hear
the voice of the living God from the heart
of the fire as we did and yet survive? 27Go
yourself and listen to what the LORD our God
says. Then come and tell us everything he
tells you, and we will listen and obey.'
28"The LORD heard the request you made
to me. And he said, 'I have heard what the
people said to you, and they are right. 29Oh,
that they would always have hearts like this,
that they might fear me and obey all my
commands! If they did, they and their descendants would prosper forever. 30Go and
tell them, "Return to your tents." 31But you
stand here with me so I can give you all my
commands, decrees, and regulations. You
must teach them to the people so they can
obey them in the land I am giving them as
their possession.' "
32So Moses told the people, "You must be
careful to obey all the commands of the LORD
your God, following his instructions in every
detail. 33Stay on the path that the LORD your
God has commanded you to follow. Then you
will live long and prosperous lives in the land
you are about to enter and occupy.

A Call for Wholehearted Commitment

6 "These are the commands, decrees,
and regulations that the LORD your
God commanded me to teach you. You must
obey them in the land you are about to enter and occupy, 2and you and your children
and grandchildren must fear the LORD your
God as long as you live. If you obey all his decrees and commands, you will enjoy a long
life. 3Listen closely, Israel, and be careful to
obey. Then all will go well with you, and you
will have many children in the land flowing
with milk and honey, just as the LORD, the
God of your ancestors, promised you.
4"Listen, O Israel! The LORD is our God,
the LORD alone. 5And you must love the
LORD your God with all your heart, all your
soul, and all your strength. 6And you must
commit yourselves[j] wholeheartedly to these
commands that I am giving you today. 7Re-
peat them again and again to your children.
Talk about them when you are at home and
when you are on the road, when you are going to bed and when you are getting up. 8Tie
them to your hands and wear them on your
forehead as reminders. 9Write them on the
doorposts of your house and on your gates.
10"The LORD your God will soon bring
you into the land he swore to give you when
he made a vow to your ancestors Abraham,
Isaac, and Jacob. It is a land with large, prosperous cities that you did not build. 11The
houses will be richly stocked with goods
you did not produce. You will draw water
from cisterns you did not dig, and you will

5:25 Exod 20:18-19; Deut 18:16; Heb 12:19
5:26 Exod 24:2
5:28 Deut 18:17
5:29 Deut 5:16, 33; Ps 81:13; Isa 48:18
5:31 Exod 24:12
5:32 Deut 17:20; Josh 1:7; 23:6
5:33 Exod 20:12; Deut 4:1, 40
6:2 Deut 4:9; 10:12
6:3 Exod 3:8, 17; Deut 5:33
6:4-5 Deut 4:35, 39; *Matt 22:37; *Mark 12:29-30; Luke 10:27; 1 Cor 8:4, 6
6:6 Deut 11:18; [j]*lebab* (3824) ‣Deut 8:2
6:7 Deut 4:9; Eph 6:4
6:8 Exod 13:9
6:9 Deut 11:20
6:10 Deut 9:1; Josh 24:13

5:33 *Stay on the path:* This figure of speech compares the course of life to making a journey. Israel was called to live in such a way that the nation would not be sidetracked from the purposes for which it had been chosen and equipped.

6:1-25 Moses here explains how the stipulations in the following sections should be applied and handed on to future generations.

6:1 Moses added ***commands*** to ***decrees and regulations,*** the usual formula for covenant stipulations (see 4:1; 5:1); ***commands*** is a general term for the whole body of instruction.

6:2 God's awesome power and glory (see 4:10) require that God's people ***fear*** him, treating him with respect and reverence (see notes on 7:21; 10:12-13).

6:3 The ***milk and honey*** abundant in Canaan represented both agriculture and forage. Compared to the desert fare, Canaan's food was sumptuous indeed (see Exod 3:8, 17).

6:4-5 *Listen* (Hebrew *shema'*): The *Shema* is the fundamental statement of Israel's faith. Jesus described these verses as the greatest of the commandments (Matt 22:34-39; Mark 12:28-31; Luke 10:25-28), a sentiment shared by ancient and modern Judaism. The rabbi Hillel (first century BC) spoke of the *Shema* as the central theological idea of the Hebrew Bible (the OT), calling the rest mere commentary.

6:4 *The LORD is our God, the LORD alone* (or *The LORD our God is one LORD;* or *The LORD our God, the LORD is one;* or *The LORD is our God, the LORD is one*): Only God is worthy of worship (5:7).

6:5 *love the LORD:* See note on Josh 23:11. • The words ***heart, . . . soul, and . . . strength*** represent the intellect, the will, the emotions, the spirituality, and the physical being—all that a person is and can do for God. This commandment is the core of God's covenant with Israel (see Jesus' comments in Matt 22:37; Mark 12:30; Luke 10:27).

6:7 *Repeat them:* The Hebrew verb (*shanan*) might suggest "engraving" a text into a medium that cannot be obliterated, or it might simply mean "repeat." Either way, the teaching of the *Shema* was to be indelibly imparted to children by constant repetition so that it would never be forgotten.

6:8 *Tie them:* The Lord's commandments (6:6) were to be as interwoven into the hearts and minds of children as though they were tied to them. Eventually, this figurative phrase in Judaism was practiced literally by wrapping the forearm with cords representing the Torah (see note on 4:44). • *wear them:* This figure of speech was represented literally in later Judaism by a small box containing a few brief Torah texts. The box and its contents (Hebrew *tefillin;* Greek *phylactery*) were reminders of the need to teach and obey the covenant (cp. 11:18; Matt 23:5).

6:9 *Write them on the doorposts:* In later Judaism, people placed portions of Deuteronomy in a small metal case (a *mezuzah*) attached to the doorframes of houses or other buildings. It was customary to touch the mezuzah when passing through the doorway to show respect for and dependence upon the Scripture.

6:13
*Matt 4:10
*Luke 4:8

6:15
Deut 4:24; 5:9

6:16
Exod 17:7
*Matt 4:7
*Luke 4:12

6:17
Deut 11:22

6:18
Deut 4:40

6:20
Exod 13:8, 14

6:24
Deut 6:17; 10:12

7:1
Deut 20:17
Acts 13:19

7:2
Exod 23:32
[k]*kharam* (2763)
‣Deut 7:26

7:3
Josh 23:12

7:4
[a]*'ap* (0639)
‣Judg 6:39

7:5
Exod 23:24

7:6
Exod 19:5-6
Deut 14:2; 26:18
1 Pet 2:9
[b]*bakhar* (0977)
‣Deut 14:2

eat from vineyards and olive trees you did not plant. When you have eaten your fill in this land, 12be careful not to forget the LORD, who rescued you from slavery in the land of Egypt. 13You must fear the LORD your God and serve him. When you take an oath, you must use only his name.

14"You must not worship any of the gods of neighboring nations, 15for the LORD your God, who lives among you, is a jealous God. His anger will flare up against you, and he will wipe you from the face of the earth. 16You must not test the LORD your God as you did when you complained at Massah. 17You must diligently obey the commands of the LORD your God—all the laws and decrees he has given you. 18Do what is right and good in the LORD's sight, so all will go well with you. Then you will enter and occupy the good land that the LORD swore to give your ancestors. 19You will drive out all the enemies living in the land, just as the LORD said you would.

20"In the future your children will ask you, 'What is the meaning of these laws, decrees, and regulations that the LORD our God has commanded us to obey?'

21"Then you must tell them, 'We were Pharaoh's slaves in Egypt, but the LORD brought us out of Egypt with his strong hand. 22The LORD did miraculous signs and wonders before our eyes, dealing terrifying blows against Egypt and Pharaoh and all his people. 23He brought us out of Egypt so he could give us this land he had sworn to give our ancestors. 24And the LORD our God commanded us to obey all these decrees and to fear him so he can continue to bless us and preserve our lives, as he has done to this day. 25For we will be counted as righteous when we obey all the commands the LORD our God has given us.'

The Privilege of Holiness

7 "When the LORD your God brings you into the land you are about to enter and occupy, he will clear away many nations ahead of you: the Hittites, Girgashites, Amorites, Canaanites, Perizzites, Hivites, and Jebusites. These seven nations are greater and more numerous than you. 2When the LORD your God hands these nations over to you and you conquer them, you must [k]completely destroy them. Make no treaties with them and show them no mercy. 3You must not intermarry with them. Do not let your daughters and sons marry their sons and daughters, 4for they will lead your children away from me to worship other gods. Then the [a]anger of the LORD will burn against you, and he will quickly destroy you. 5This is what you must do. You must break down their pagan altars and shatter their sacred pillars. Cut down their Asherah poles and burn their idols. 6For you are a holy people, who belong to the LORD your God. Of all the people on earth, the LORD your God has [b]chosen you to be his own special treasure.

6:13 Jesus quoted this verse when tempted by Satan (Matt 4:10; Luke 4:8).

6:15 ***jealous God:*** See note on 4:24.

6:16 When Israel journeyed through the Sinai desert after the Exodus, they came to Rephidim, where they found no water (Exod 17:1-7). Moses saw the people's demand for water as testing the Lord; hence the name ***Massah*** ("testing") for this place. Jesus quoted this verse to rebut Satan (Matt 4:7; Luke 4:12).

6:21 The phrase ***his strong hand*** is an anthropomorphism (see note on 8:2).

6:22 The ***signs and wonders*** were the ten plagues God sent to impress Israel and Egypt with his power when he brought about the Exodus (Exod 7–12; see also Exod 3:20; 4:5; Josh 4:23-24).

6:25 ***righteous when we obey:*** Obedience shows that one is already in a state of righteousness, a standing before God obtained by faith (see 24:13; Hab 2:4; Rom 1:17; 4:1-5; Gal 3:6-7; see also Gen 15:6; Eph 2:8-9). When other nations observed Israel's commitment to the covenant, they could rightly conclude that Israel was righteous.

7:1-26 Before Israel could occupy the land of promise (cp. Gen 13:14-17; 15:18-21), the nations already living there had to be removed. The land was the Lord's, and only he could determine who the inhabitants should be.

7:1 The ***Hittites*** were native to Anatolia (now north-central Turkey). They established colonies in far-flung areas such as Syria and were also linked to Canaan in the list of ancient nations (see Gen 10:15; 23:3-20). The Hittite empire came to a sudden end around 1200 BC, but people known as Hittites continued to live in Israel (e.g., Uriah the Hittite, 2 Sam 11:3; 23:39). It is impossible to prove that the Hittites of Anatolia were the same as those mentioned in the OT, but some commonality is probable. • ***Girgashites*** were an otherwise unknown Canaanite people (Gen 10:16-17). • ***Amorites:*** See note on 1:4. • The ***Canaanites*** were the native people of Canaan; their habitation there can be traced back to 3000 BC. They descended from Noah's son Ham (see Gen 9:18-27). • The ***Perizzites*** are not listed in the Table of Nations (Gen 10:16-17), so they might not have been related to the Canaanites. • Many scholars identify the ***Hivites*** as the Horites (or Hurrians; see note on 2:1), a non-Semitic people found throughout the ancient Near East. • The ***Jebusites*** were associated with Jerusalem (Judg 1:21; 2 Sam 5:6-8). David bought a piece of land from Araunah the Jebusite to build an altar (2 Sam 24:15-25); this property later became the site of the Temple (2 Chr 3:1).

7:2 ***completely destroy:*** See note on 2:34.

7:5 Engraved stone pillars called *stelae* usually represented pagan male deities. These ***sacred pillars*** were commonly found at shrines dedicated to Baal. • ***Asherah poles,*** usually made of wood, represented Canaanite fertility goddesses, particularly Asherah, the mother of the gods. These shrines might have developed as stylized sacred trees associated with fertility (see note on 12:2).

7:6 Of all peoples on earth, God chose Israel as his ***special treasure.*** Israel had not done anything commendable; rather, God acted out of grace that was undeserved and freely given.

7“The LORD did not set his heart on you
and choose you because you were more numerous than other nations, for you were the
smallest of all nations! 8Rather, it was simply
that the LORD loves you, and he was keeping
the oath he had sworn to your ancestors.
That is why the LORD rescued you with such a
strong hand from your slavery and from the
oppressive hand of Pharaoh, king of Egypt.
9Understand, therefore, that the LORD your
God is indeed God. He is the faithful God
who keeps his covenant for a thousand generations and lavishes his unfailing love on
those who love him and obey his commands.
10But he does not hesitate to punish and destroy those who reject him. 11Therefore, you
must obey all these commands, decrees, and
regulations I am giving you today.
12“If you listen to these regulations and
faithfully obey them, the LORD your God
will keep his covenant of unfailing love with
you, as he promised with an oath to your ancestors. 13He will love you and bless you,
and he will give you many children. He will
give fertility to your land and your animals.
When you arrive in the land he swore to give
your ancestors, you will have large harvests
of grain, new wine, and olive oil, and great
herds of cattle, sheep, and goats. 14You will
be blessed above all the nations of the earth.
None of your men or women will be childless, and all your livestock will bear young.
15And the LORD will protect you from all
sickness. He will not let you suffer from the
terrible diseases you knew in Egypt, but he
will inflict them on all your enemies!
16“You must destroy all the nations the
LORD your God hands over to you. Show
them no mercy, and do not worship their
gods, or they will trap you. 17Perhaps you
will think to yourselves, ‘How can we ever
conquer these nations that are so much
more powerful than we are?’ 18But don’t
be afraid of them! Just remember what the
LORD your God did to Pharaoh and to all the
land of Egypt. 19Remember the great terrors the LORD your God sent against them.
You saw it all with your own eyes! And remember the miraculous signs and wonders,
and the strong hand and powerful arm with
which he brought you out of Egypt. The
LORD your God will use this same power
against all the people you fear. 20And then
the LORD your God will send terror to drive
out the few survivors still hiding from you!
21“No, do not be afraid of those nations,
for the LORD your God is among you, and
he is a great and awesome God. 22The LORD
your God will drive those nations out ahead
of you little by little. You will not clear them
away all at once, otherwise the wild animals
would multiply too quickly for you. 23But
the LORD your God will hand them over
to you. He will throw them into complete
confusion until they are destroyed. 24He
will put their kings in your power, and you
will erase their names from the face of the
earth. No one will be able to stand against
you, and you will destroy them all.
25“You must burn their idols in fire, and
you must not covet the silver or gold that
covers them. You must not take it or it will
become a trap to you, for it is detestable
to the LORD your God. 26Do not bring any
detestable objects into your home, for then
you will be [c]destroyed, just like them. You

7:7 Deut 4:37
7:9 Exod 20:6; Deut 4:39; 5:9-10; 1 Cor 1:9; 1 Thes 5:24; 2 Tim 2:13
7:12 Lev 26:3; Deut 28:1
7:13 Lev 26:9; Deut 28:4; 30:5-6
7:14 Exod 23:26
7:15 Exod 15:26
7:16 Exod 23:32; Deut 7:2
7:17 Num 33:53
7:18 Num 14:9; Deut 1:21, 29
7:19 Deut 4:34
7:20 Exod 23:28; Josh 24:12
7:21 Exod 29:45
7:22 Exod 23:28-30
7:24 Deut 11:25; Josh 1:5; 10:8; 23:9
7:25 Deut 7:2; 12:3; Josh 7:1, 21
7:26 Lev 27:28-29; [c]*kherem* (2764) ›Josh 6:21

7:9 A *faithful God* is absolutely dependable and can be leaned upon. Abraham was commended as being righteous because he believed God; he was wholly dependent upon God’s faithfulness (Gen 15:6). • Contrasted with human agents, who often break their pledges, the Lord faithfully *keeps his covenant.*

7:10 *those who reject him:* See note on 5:9.

7:12 *promised with an oath* (literally *swore*): In a covenant or treaty, the parties to the covenant had to swear to keep its terms in order for it to be valid. God’s promises are always guaranteed by his character (7:9; 32:4; Heb 6:18; Jas 1:17). He fulfilled the requirements of the covenant with Israel by swearing to keep its terms (see Gen 22:16).

7:15 The *terrible diseases . . . in Egypt* were perhaps illnesses related to the plagues (e.g., Exod 9:9) or other serious diseases that regularly afflicted the Egyptians.

7:19 The familiar word pair *signs and wonders* signifies the miraculous deeds God performed to induce fear in his enemies and to inspire awe and praise in his people (see 6:22). • *strong hand and powerful arm:* See notes on 4:34 and 8:2.

7:20 *terror:* Often rendered *the hornet.* The meaning of the Hebrew is uncertain. Whether God sent stinging insects or some other source of terror, he would expel surviving Canaanites from the land (Exod 23:28; Josh 24:12).

7:21 *awesome* (literally *one to be feared*): This fear is not the terror induced by a bully who strikes without reason or plan, but the reverential fear of a loving God whose nature is so majestic that it inspires a kind of dread (see “Fear of the LORD” at Prov 1:7, p. 1030).

7:24 *erase their names:* An individual’s name represented that person’s existence as it would be carried into the future through generations of descendants. By destroying an entire nation, God cut off its line of descent and thus also its future. The Canaanites who suffered God’s war against them lost all their descendants and thus their existence and identity.

7:25-26 Worship of false gods is *detestable to the LORD:* It denies that God is unique and rejects his demand for exclusive worship (5:7-9). The horrific and disgusting rituals typically associated with pagan worship were antithetical to God’s holy nature, but Israel was in danger of being led into similar beliefs and practices (12:31; 13:12-17). An Israelite who acknowledged false gods committed an act of treason. The only remedy was complete and total destruction of these *detestable objects.*

7:26 *set apart for destruction* (Hebrew *kherem*): See note on 2:34.

8:1 Lev 26:3; Deut 4:1; 7:11
8:2 Exod 15:25; 2 Chr 32:31; [d]*lebab* (3824) ‣Deut 29:19
8:3 Ps 78:24; *Matt 4:4; *Luke 4:4; [e]*man* (4478) ‣Deut 8:16
8:4 Deut 29:5; Neh 9:21
8:5 Prov 3:11-12; Heb 12:6
8:7 Deut 11:10-12; Jer 2:7
8:8 Deut 32:13
8:10 Deut 6:11-12
8:11 Deut 4:9
8:12 Prov 30:9; Hos 13:6
8:15 Exod 17:6; Num 20:11; 21:6; Deut 1:19-21; 32:13; Ps 78:15; 114:8
8:16 Exod 16:15; Deut 8:2; John 6:30-31; [f]*man* (4478) ‣Josh 5:12
8:18 Prov 10:22; Hos 2:8
8:19 Deut 4:26; 30:18
8:20 Ezek 5:15-17
9:1 Deut 11:23

must utterly detest such things, for they are
[c]set apart for destruction.

A Call to Remember and Obey

8 "Be careful to obey all the commands
I am giving you today. Then you will
live and multiply, and you will enter and
occupy the land the LORD swore to give
your ancestors. 2Remember how the LORD
your God led you through the wilderness
for these forty years, humbling you and
testing you to prove your [d]character, and to
find out whether or not you would obey his
commands. 3Yes, he humbled you by letting
you go hungry and then feeding you with
[e]manna, a food previously unknown to you
and your ancestors. He did it to teach you
that people do not live by bread alone; rather,
we live by every word that comes from the
mouth of the LORD. 4For all these forty years
your clothes didn't wear out, and your feet
didn't blister or swell. 5Think about it: Just
as a parent disciplines a child, the LORD your
God disciplines you for your own good.
6"So obey the commands of the LORD your
God by walking in his ways and fearing him.
7For the LORD your God is bringing you into
a good land of flowing streams and pools of
water, with fountains and springs that gush
out in the valleys and hills. 8It is a land of
wheat and barley; of grapevines, fig trees,
and pomegranates; of olive oil and honey.
9It is a land where food is plentiful and nothing is lacking. It is a land where iron is as
common as stone, and copper is abundant
in the hills. 10When you have eaten your fill,
be sure to praise the LORD your God for the
good land he has given you.
11"But that is the time to be careful! Beware that in your plenty you do not forget the
LORD your God and disobey his commands,
regulations, and decrees that I am giving you
today. 12For when you have become full and
prosperous and have built fine homes to live
in, 13and when your flocks and herds have
become very large and your silver and gold
have multiplied along with everything else,
be careful! 14Do not become proud at that
time and forget the LORD your God, who rescued you from slavery in the land of Egypt.
15Do not forget that he led you through the
great and terrifying wilderness with its poisonous snakes and scorpions, where it was
so hot and dry. He gave you water from the
rock! 16He fed you with [f]manna in the wilderness, a food unknown to your ancestors. He
did this to humble you and test you for your
own good. 17He did all this so you would
never say to yourself, 'I have achieved this
wealth with my own strength and energy.'
18Remember the LORD your God. He is the
one who gives you power to be successful, in
order to fulfill the covenant he confirmed
to your ancestors with an oath.
19"But I assure you of this: If you ever
forget the LORD your God and follow other
gods, worshiping and bowing down to
them, you will certainly be destroyed. 20Just
as the LORD has destroyed other nations in
your path, you also will be destroyed if you
refuse to obey the LORD your God.

Victory by God's Grace

9 "Listen, O Israel! Today you are about to
cross the Jordan River to take over the
land belonging to nations much greater and

8:1-20 Once Israel inhabited the land, they might have the human tendency to take credit for the blessings that followed. Moses warned the people to guard against a self-congratulatory attitude. God alone is the source of all prosperity and achievement.

8:2 ***to prove your character*** (literally *to know what is in your heart*): God already knew the Israelites' innermost thoughts (Ps 51:6; 139:1, 4, 23); he wanted their character to come out in their actions. • ***to find out whether:*** The OT often describes God in human terms, even in ways that appear to limit God. *Anthropomorphism* (assigning human characteristics to God) and *anthropopathism* (assigning human feelings or emotions to God) are ways of representing God on a human level so the human mind can better grasp his ways, but God is not limited in his knowledge, power, or transcendence. Here, God is figuratively described as having only a human knowledge of the future, but other passages make it clear that God knows everything—past, present, and future (Ps 139:1-18; Heb 4:13).

8:3 The word ***manna*** is derived from the Hebrew words *man hu* (meaning "what is it?"). God miraculously provided this food to teach his people total dependence on him (Exod 16:1-30; Num 11:4-9). Manna represented the word of God, which is even more essential to life and well-being than food is. • ***people do not live by bread alone:*** Jesus quoted this phrase to rebut Satan (Matt 4:4; Luke 4:4).

8:6 ***fearing him:*** See note on 7:21.

8:9 ***Iron*** was not widely used in this period of the Bronze Age because the process of smelting and working it was known to only a few cultures (see 1 Sam 13:19-21). The time would come when Israel would exploit this vastly superior metal (see Josh 17:16-18; 1 Kgs 6:7; 2 Kgs 6:5; 1 Chr 22:3).

8:15 ***water from the rock!*** See Exod 17:6; Num 20:2-13; see also Deut 1:37.

8:18 This was not ***the covenant*** that God made with the previous generation of Israelites at Sinai but the one he first made with Abraham (Gen 15:1-21; 17:1-21), then Isaac (Gen 26:1-5) and Jacob (Gen 28:1-4, 13-15; 46:1-4). • In order to be legal and proper, a covenant had to be sworn to with ***an oath*** that all parties to the agreement uttered. Although by his very nature God could never rescind a promise, he honored the protocol (see 7:12).

9:1 ***walls that reach to the sky:*** This figurative language emphasizes the impossibility of breaching these walls by human effort alone (Num 13:28). If Israel were to enjoy success, God must lead the way and fight the battle (9:5).

more powerful than you. They live in cities
with walls that reach to the sky! 2The people are strong and tall—descendants of the
famous Anakite giants. You've heard the
saying, 'Who can stand up to the Anakites?'
3But recognize today that the LORD your
God is the one who will cross over ahead
of you like a devouring fire to destroy them.
He will subdue them so that you will quickly
conquer them and drive them out, just as
the LORD has promised.
4"After the LORD your God has done this
for you, don't say in your hearts, 'The LORD
has given us this land because we are such
good people!' No, it is because of the wickedness of the other nations that he is pushing
them out of your way. 5It is not because you
are so good or have such integrity that you
are about to occupy their land. The LORD
your God will drive these nations out ahead
of you only because of their wickedness,
and to fulfill the oath he swore to your ancestors Abraham, Isaac, and Jacob. 6You
must recognize that the LORD your God is
not giving you this good land because you
are good, for you are not—you are a stubborn people.

Remembering the Gold Calf

7"Remember and never forget how angry
you made the LORD your God out in the
wilderness. From the day you left Egypt
until now, you have been constantly rebelling against him. 8Even at Mount Sinai you
made the LORD so angry he was ready to
destroy you. 9This happened when I was on
the mountain receiving the tablets of stone
inscribed with the words of the covenant
that the LORD had made with you. I was
there for forty days and forty nights, and
all that time I ate no food and drank no water. 10The LORD gave me the two tablets on
which God had written with his own finger
all the words he had spoken to you from the
heart of the fire when you were assembled
at the mountain.
11"At the end of the forty days and nights,
the LORD handed me the two stone tablets
inscribed with the words of the covenant.
12Then the LORD said to me, 'Get up! Go down
immediately, for the people you brought out
of Egypt have corrupted themselves. How
quickly they have turned away from the way
I commanded them to live! They have melted
gold and made an idol for themselves!'
13"The LORD also said to me, 'I have seen
how stubborn and rebellious these people
are. 14Leave me alone so I may destroy them
and erase their name from under heaven.
Then I will make a mighty nation of your
descendants, a nation larger and more powerful than they are.'
15"So while the mountain was blazing
with fire I turned and came down, holding
in my hands the two stone tablets inscribed
with the terms of the covenant. 16There
below me I could see that you had sinned
against the LORD your God. You had melted
gold and made a calf idol for yourselves.
How quickly you had turned away from the
path the LORD had commanded you to follow! 17So I took the stone tablets and threw
them to the ground, smashing them before
your eyes.
18"Then, as before, I threw myself down
before the LORD for forty days and nights.
I ate no bread and drank no water because
of the great sin you had committed by doing what the LORD hated, provoking him
to anger. 19I feared that the furious anger
of the LORD, which turned him against you,

9:3 Deut 4:24; Heb 12:29
9:4 Lev 18:23-30; Deut 7:24; 12:31; 18:9-14
9:6 Deut 9:13-14; 10:16; 31:27
9:7 Exod 14:11; Num 14:20-22
9:8 Exod 32:7; Ps 106:19-20
9:9 Exod 24:18; Deut 9:18
9:12 Exod 32:7-8
9:13 Exod 32:9
9:15 Exod 32:15
9:16 Exod 32:19
9:18 Exod 34:8-9, 28; Deut 9:9; 10:10
9:19 Exod 32:10-11; *Heb 12:21

9:3 The graphic metaphor ***like a devouring fire*** depicts God's war against his enemies (see 1:30). God will not just use fire but will himself be a raging inferno, consuming everything in his path. In the end, Israel would simply have to step in and occupy the subdued land.

9:5 *to fulfill the oath:* In the covenant promises made to the patriarchs, God swore that their descendants would inherit the land of Canaan (Gen 13:14-17; 15:18-21; see Deut 1:8; 8:18).

9:6 *Stubborn* (literally *stiff-necked*) describes a draft animal that is unwilling to bend its neck to the yoke (Exod 32:9; 33:3, 5; Isa 48:4). Sadly, Israel was not just occasionally stubborn; stubbornness was the nation's characteristic behavior and attitude.

9:8 *Mount Sinai:* Hebrew *Horeb*, another name for Sinai; see note on 1:2.

9:9 *tablets of stone:* See note on 4:13. • ***Covenant*** here refers to the promises God made with Israel nearly forty years earlier at Sinai (see 4:13). • The common biblical expression ***forty days and forty nights*** represents trial or testing (Exod 34:28). Moses' fast was like Jesus' fast (Matt 4:2). It is physically possible to go without food for forty days, but a person cannot ordinarily survive without water for more than a few days. Moses was directly sustained by God (cp. Matt 4:11).

9:10 Speaking of God's ***own finger*** (see notes on 4:34 and 8:2) emphasizes God's personal interest and involvement in communicating the text of the covenant (Exod 31:18; 32:15-16; 34:1, 28).

9:12 The type of ***idol*** (from a Hebrew word meaning *cast* or *pour*) mentioned here was formed by pouring liquid metal into a mold (Exod 32:1-4). Other idols were made of carved wood, stone, clay, or precious metals hammered in thin sheets over wooden cores.

9:14 *erase their name:* The Lord threatened to destroy Israel's identity and existence (see note on 7:24).

9:16 The gold ***calf idol*** Israel made at Sinai (Exod 32) was probably modeled after bovine deities of Egypt, such as the bull god Apis and the cow goddess Hathor, both associated with fertility. When the Israelites entered Canaan, they would be confronted with the fertility gods of the Canaanite cults. They would be tempted to rely upon these false gods, rather than the one true God, as the source of their blessings (cp. 8:18-20).

9:21 Exod 32:20
9:22 Exod 17:7; Num 11:3, 34
9:24 Exod 32:9; Deut 9:7; 31:27
9:25 Deut 9:18
9:26 Exod 32:11-13
[g]*palal* (6419) ‣1 Sam 1:10
9:27 Exod 32:9
9:29 Deut 4:34
10:1 Exod 25:10; 34:1
10:2 Exod 25:16; Deut 4:13
10:3 Exod 34:4; 37:1
10:4 Exod 34:28; Deut 4:13
10:5 Exod 40:20
10:6 Num 20:25-26
10:8 Num 3:6; 18:1; Deut 18:5; 21:5; 31:9
[h]*sharath* (8334) ‣1 Sam 2:11
10:9 Num 18:20, 24; Deut 18:2; Ezek 44:28

would drive him to destroy you. But again
he listened to me. 20The LORD was so angry
with Aaron that he wanted to destroy him,
too. But I prayed for Aaron, and the LORD
spared him. 21I took your sin—the calf you
had made—and I melted it down in the fire
and ground it into fine dust. Then I threw
the dust into the stream that flows down the
mountain.
22"You also made the LORD angry at Taberah, Massah, and Kibroth-hattaavah. 23And
at Kadesh-barnea the LORD sent you out
with this command: 'Go up and take over
the land I have given you.' But you rebelled
against the command of the LORD your God
and refused to put your trust in him or obey
him. 24Yes, you have been rebelling against
the LORD as long as I have known you.
25"That is why I threw myself down before
the LORD for forty days and nights—for the
LORD said he would destroy you. 26I [g]prayed
to the LORD and said, 'O Sovereign LORD, do
not destroy them. They are your own people. They are your special possession, whom
you redeemed from Egypt by your mighty
power and your strong hand. 27Please overlook the stubbornness and the awful sin of
these people, and remember instead your
servants Abraham, Isaac, and Jacob. 28If you
destroy these people, the Egyptians will say,
"The Israelites died because the LORD wasn't
able to bring them to the land he had promised to give them." Or they might say, "He
destroyed them because he hated them; he
deliberately took them into the wilderness
to slaughter them." 29But they are your people and your special possession, whom you
brought out of Egypt by your great strength
and powerful arm.'

A New Copy of the Covenant

10 "At that time the LORD said to me,
'Chisel out two stone tablets like the
first ones. Also make a wooden Ark—a sacred chest to store them in. Come up to me
on the mountain, 2and I will write on the tablets the same words that were on the ones
you smashed. Then place the tablets in the
Ark.'
3"So I made an Ark of acacia wood and
cut two stone tablets like the first two. Then
I went up the mountain with the tablets in
my hand. 4Once again the LORD wrote the
Ten Commandments on the tablets and gave
them to me. They were the same words the
LORD had spoken to you from the heart of
the fire on the day you were assembled at
the foot of the mountain. 5Then I turned and
came down the mountain and placed the
tablets in the Ark of the Covenant, which I
had made, just as the LORD commanded me.
And the tablets are still there in the Ark."
6(The people of Israel set out from the
wells of the people of Jaakan and traveled
to Moserah, where Aaron died and was
buried. His son Eleazar ministered as high
priest in his place. 7Then they journeyed
to Gudgodah, and from there to Jotbathah,
a land with many brooks and streams.
8At that time the LORD set apart the tribe
of Levi to carry the Ark of the LORD's Covenant, and to stand before the LORD as his
[h]ministers, and to pronounce blessings in
his name. These are their duties to this day.
9That is why the Levites have no share of
property or possession of land among the
other Israelite tribes. The LORD himself is
their special possession, as the LORD your
God told them.)

9:22 Shortly after Israel left Sinai, the people began to murmur against the Lord so incessantly and bitterly that he sent a fiery judgment to slay some of them at ***Taberah*** (Taberah means "place of burning." See Num 11:1-3). • Even earlier, the people came to ***Massah***, a place where they tested the Lord to see whether he could supply their need for water (*Massah* means "place of testing." See Exod 17:1-7). • At ***Kibroth-hattaavah***, the Israelites demanded food other than manna. The Lord miraculously provided quail, with which they gorged themselves. Many of them paid for this sin of gluttony with their lives. *Kibroth-hattaavah* means "graves of gluttony." See Num 11:31-34.

9:23 Israel made ***Kadesh-barnea*** its major headquarters for the thirty-eight years of wandering in the wilderness (see also note on 1:19).

9:26 ***special possession:*** See note on 4:20. • The Lord ***redeemed*** Israel from their bondage in Egypt by his own gracious efforts on their behalf.

9:27 In Hebrew, the term translated ***remember*** does not always mean to recall something that has been forgotten, especially when God is the subject (see notes on 8:2 and 32:36). Here the meaning is that God would honor the promises he made to the patriarchs by doing what he said he would do. Appealing to God to remember goes beyond urging him to be aware of a need; it is a petition for him to act in the face of that need (cp. Luke 23:42-43).

10:1 ***two stone tablets:*** See note on 4:13. • The ***Ark*** was a gold-plated wooden chest that contained the stone tablets; it was kept in the Most Holy Place in the Tabernacle or Temple (Exod 25:10). Later, a pot of manna and Aaron's flowering rod were also placed in the Ark (Heb 9:4). The Ark was the throne upon which the invisible Lord sat on earth among his people (see notes on Exod 25:22 and Lev 16:2).

10:3 ***acacia wood:*** This durable desert tree is probably the species *Acacia raddiana;* it is the only variety that grows large enough in the Negev to produce timber for building.

10:4 ***the Ten Commandments:*** Literally *the ten words.* See note on 4:13.

10:5 ***still there:*** Occasionally, phrases such as this one appear in Deuteronomy, indicating that the book received final touches sometime after Moses originally composed it. At the time the book was finally edited, the stone tablets were ***still*** in the Ark.

10:6 ***set out from the wells of the people of Jaakan:*** Or *set out from Beeroth of Bene-jaakan.*

10“As for me, I stayed on the mountain
in the LORD’s presence for forty days and
nights, as I had done the first time. And
once again the LORD listened to my pleas
and agreed not to destroy you. 11Then the
LORD said to me, ‘Get up and resume the
journey, and lead the people to the land I
swore to give to their ancestors, so they may
take possession of it.’

A Call to Love and Obedience

12“And now, Israel, what does the LORD your
God require of you? He requires only that
you fear the LORD your God, and live in a way
that pleases him, and love him and serve
him with all your heart and soul. 13And you
must always obey the LORD’s commands
and decrees that I am giving you today for
your own good.

14“Look, the highest heavens and the
earth and everything in it all belong to the
LORD your God. 15Yet the LORD chose your
ancestors as the objects of his love. And
he chose you, their descendants, above all
other nations, as is evident today. 16There-
fore, change your hearts and stop being
stubborn.

17“For the LORD your God is the God of
gods and Lord of lords. He is the great God,
the mighty and awesome God, who shows
no partiality and cannot be bribed. 18He
ensures that orphans and widows receive
justice. He shows love to the foreigners
living among you and gives them food and
clothing. 19So you, too, must show love to
foreigners, for you yourselves were once
foreigners in the land of Egypt. 20You must
[i]fear the LORD your God and worship him
and cling to him. Your oaths must be in his
name alone. 21He alone is your God, the only
one who is worthy of your praise, the one
who has done these mighty miracles that
you have seen with your own eyes. 22When
your ancestors went down into Egypt, there
were only seventy of them. But now the
LORD your God has made you as numerous
as the stars in the sky!

11 “You must love the LORD your God
and obey all his requirements, decrees, regulations, and commands. 2Keep
in mind that I am not talking now to your
children, who have never experienced the
discipline of the LORD your God or seen his
greatness and his strong hand and powerful
arm. 3They didn’t see the miraculous signs
and wonders he performed in Egypt against
Pharaoh and all his land. 4They didn’t see
what the LORD did to the armies of Egypt
and to their horses and chariots—how he
drowned them in the Red Sea as they were
chasing you. He destroyed them, and they
have not recovered to this very day!

5“Your children didn’t see how the LORD
cared for you in the wilderness until you
arrived here. 6They didn’t see what he did
to Dathan and Abiram (the sons of Eliab, a
descendant of Reuben) when the earth
opened its mouth in the Israelite camp and
swallowed them, along with their households and tents and every living thing that
belonged to them. 7But you have seen the
LORD perform all these mighty deeds with
your own eyes!

The Blessings of Obedience

8“Therefore, be careful to obey every command I am giving you today, so you may
have strength to go in and take over the land
you are about to enter. 9If you obey, you will
enjoy a long life in the land the LORD swore
to give to your ancestors and to you, their

10:10 Deut 9:18
10:12 Deut 6:5; Mic 6:8
10:14 1 Kgs 8:27; Ps 68:33; 115:16
10:16 Lev 26:41-42; Deut 9:6; Jer 4:4
10:17 Deut 1:17; 16:19; Ps 136:2
10:18 Exod 22:22-24; Ps 68:5; 103:6
10:19 Exod 22:21; Lev 19:34
10:20 Deut 5:11; 6:13; *‘yare’* (3372) ‣ Deut 17:19
10:21 Exod 15:2; Ps 109:1
10:22 Gen 46:27; Deut 1:10
11:1 Lev 18:29-30; Deut 6:5-6; 10:12-13
11:2 Deut 5:24
11:4 Exod 14:28; 15:4
11:6 Num 16:31; 26:10-11
11:8 Deut 31:6-7, 23; Josh 1:6-7
11:9 Deut 4:40; 5:33; 9:5; Prov 10:27

10:12–11:32 Moses here appends to the covenant stipulations (chs 5–11) a list of curses and blessings similar to those that follow the whole covenant text in chs 27–28.

10:12-13 *fear the LORD your God:* The fear of God is not terror from dread of his wrath. Rather, God wanted his people to recognize their finiteness and unworthiness in his divine presence (see notes on 7:21 and Prov 1:7).

10:16 *change your hearts* (literally *circumcise the foreskin of your hearts*): This figure of speech encompasses both inward and outward conformity to the covenant (Gen 17:9-14; Rom 2:28-29).

10:17 The phrase *God of gods* does not affirm the existence of other gods; rather, it affirms God’s absolute sovereignty over all powers in heaven and earth. The Hebrew *’elohim,* translated *gods,* can also refer to angels or other powerful beings (see Ps 82:1). • *shows no partiality:* God is not impressed with people who hold power and influence, and therefore he offers them no privileged consideration (see 1:17).

10:18 *foreigners* (literally *sojourners*): “A rabble of non-Israelites” (Exod 12:38) came out of Egypt with the Israelites, and others later took up residence in Israel for various reasons. Some of these non-Israelites had no intention of becoming part of the covenant nation, but other foreigners, while not citizens of Israel, were God-fearers or potential proselytes. They lacked full equality with the Israelites and thus were often victims of neglect and discrimination.

10:22 *numerous as the stars:* See note on 1:10.

11:3 *signs and wonders:* See notes on 6:22 and 7:19.

11:4 The common translation *Red Sea* (literally *sea of reeds*) comes from the Greek OT. It was called the “Sea of Reeds” because of the marshy plants that grew along its shores.

11:6 *Dathan and Abiram:* See Num 16:1-40. In the Lord’s administration of his kingdom, he established levels of authority and command that were not to be transgressed. Because the Lord had appointed Moses and Aaron as leaders, the rebellion of Dathan and Abiram against Moses was the same as rebellion against God’s sovereign rule.

11:9 *milk and honey:* See note on 6:3.

11:11 Deut 8:7-9
11:13 Deut 4:29; 6:17; 10:12
11:14 Lev 26:4-5; Deut 28:12
11:15 Deut 6:10-12
11:16 Deut 8:19; 29:18
11:17 Deut 4:26; 28:24
11:18 Exod 13:9, 16
11:19 Deut 4:9; 6:7
11:22 Deut 6:17; 10:20
11:23 Deut 4:38; 7:1
11:24 Gen 15:18; Exod 23:31; Deut 1:7-8; Josh 1:3
11:25 Exod 23:27; Deut 7:24
11:26 Deut 30:1, 15-20
11:27 [j]*shama'* (8085) ‣Deut 13:4
11:29 Deut 27:12-26; Josh 8:30-35
11:30 Gen 12:6; Josh 4:19
11:31 Josh 1:11
12:1 Deut 4:9-10; 6:15
12:2 2 Kgs 17:10

descendants—a land flowing with milk and
honey! 10For the land you are about to enter
and take over is not like the land of Egypt
from which you came, where you planted
your seed and made irrigation ditches with
your foot as in a vegetable garden. 11Rather,
the land you will soon take over is a land
of hills and valleys with plenty of rain—12a
land that the LORD your God cares for. He
watches over it through each season of the
year!

13"If you carefully obey all the commands
I am giving you today, and if you love the
LORD your God and serve him with all your
heart and soul, 14then he will send the rains
in their proper seasons—the early and late
rains—so you can bring in your harvests of
grain, new wine, and olive oil. 15He will give
you lush pastureland for your livestock, and
you yourselves will have all you want to eat.

16"But be careful. Don't let your heart be
deceived so that you turn away from the
LORD and serve and worship other gods. 17If
you do, the LORD's anger will burn against
you. He will shut up the sky and hold back
the rain, and the ground will fail to produce
its harvests. Then you will quickly die in
that good land the LORD is giving you.

18"So commit yourselves wholeheartedly
to these words of mine. Tie them to your
hands and wear them on your forehead as
reminders. 19Teach them to your children.
Talk about them when you are at home
and when you are on the road, when you
are going to bed and when you are getting
up. 20Write them on the doorposts of your
house and on your gates, 21so that as long
as the sky remains above the earth, you and
your children may flourish in the land the
LORD swore to give your ancestors.

22"Be careful to obey all these commands
I am giving you. Show love to the LORD your
God by walking in his ways and holding
tightly to him. 23Then the LORD will drive
out all the nations ahead of you, though they
are much greater and stronger than you,
and you will take over their land. 24Wher-
ever you set foot, that land will be yours.
Your frontiers will stretch from the wilderness in the south to Lebanon in the north,
and from the Euphrates River in the east
to the Mediterranean Sea in the west. 25No
one will be able to stand against you, for the
LORD your God will cause the people to fear
and dread you, as he promised, wherever
you go in the whole land.

26"Look, today I am giving you the choice
between a blessing and a curse! 27You will
be blessed if you [j]obey the commands of
the LORD your God that I am giving you today. 28But you will be cursed if you reject
the commands of the LORD your God and
turn away from him and worship gods you
have not known before.

29"When the LORD your God brings you
into the land and helps you take possession of it, you must pronounce the blessing
at Mount Gerizim and the curse at Mount
Ebal. 30(These two mountains are west of
the Jordan River in the land of the Canaanites who live in the Jordan Valley, near the
town of Gilgal, not far from the oaks of Moreh.) 31For you are about to cross the Jordan
River to take over the land the LORD your
God is giving you. When you take that land
and are living in it, 32you must be careful to
obey all the decrees and regulations I am
giving you today.

The Specific Stipulations of the Covenant (12:1–26:15)

The LORD's Chosen Place for Worship

12 "These are the decrees and regulations you must be careful to obey
when you live in the land that the LORD, the
God of your ancestors, is giving you. You
must obey them as long as you live.

2"When you drive out the nations that
live there, you must destroy all the places
where they worship their gods—high on the

11:12 ***a land . . . your God cares for:*** God's care included blessing the land with all the resources his people would need to survive and prosper there.

11:24 ***you set foot*** (literally *you tread the sole of your foot*): This idea suggests claiming a territory by placing a foot on it or walking through it (see Gen 13:17; Josh 1:3; 14:9). • ***to the Mediterranean Sea in the west:*** Literally *to the western sea.*

11:26 In covenant contexts, ***a blessing*** is the outcome of obedience, while ***a curse*** is the result of disobedience (see chs 27–28).

11:29 ***Mount Gerizim*** is a prominent hill lying just west of Shechem. In later times, the Samaritans built a temple there (cp. John 4:20). • ***Mount Ebal*** is across the valley from Mount Gerizim, to the east of Shechem.

11:30 ***the Jordan Valley*** (Hebrew *the Arabah*): See notes on 1:1 and 4:49. • ***Gilgal*** was the site of the first camp the Israelites would make in Canaan after crossing the Jordan (Josh 4:19). It was about two miles northeast of Jericho, although its exact location is no longer certain. A line from Jericho to Shechem would pass near Gilgal. • The ***oaks of Moreh*** were near Shechem; they were where Abram had set up his first camp in Canaan (Gen 12:6) and where Jacob had later buried Laban's idols (Gen 35:4).

12:1–26:15 After Moses laid out the principles of the covenant (5:1–11:32), he moved to the application of these principles in everyday life. Passages in this section expand on the Ten Commandments and cover some of the contingencies that inevitably arise in the complexity of human relationships.

12:2 ***green tree:*** The Canaanites selected groves of trees for worship sites because

mountains, up on the hills, and under every
green tree. 3Break down their altars and
smash their sacred pillars. Burn their Asherah poles and cut down their carved idols.
Completely erase the names of their gods!
4"Do not worship the LORD your God in
the way these pagan peoples worship their
gods. 5Rather, you must seek the LORD your
God at the place of worship he himself will
choose from among all the tribes—the place
where his name will be honored. 6There you
will bring your burnt offerings, your sacrifices, your ktithes, your sacred offerings,
your offerings to fulfill a vow, your voluntary offerings, and your offerings of the
firstborn animals of your herds and flocks.
7There you and your families will feast in
the presence of the LORD your God, and you
will rejoice in all you have accomplished because the LORD your God has blessed you.
8"Your pattern of worship will change.
Today all of you are doing as you please, 9be-
cause you have not yet arrived at the place
of rest, the land the LORD your God is giving you as your special possession. 10But
you will soon cross the Jordan River and
live in the land the LORD your God is giving
you. When he gives you rest from all your
enemies and you're living safely in the land,
11you must bring everything I command
you—your burnt offerings, your sacrifices,
your tithes, your sacred offerings, and your
offerings to fulfill a vow—to the designated
place of worship, the place the LORD your
God chooses for his name to be honored.
12"You must celebrate there in the presence of the LORD your God with your sons
and daughters and all your servants. And
remember to include the Levites who live
in your towns, for they will receive no allotment of land among you. 13Be careful
not to sacrifice your burnt offerings just
anywhere you like. 14You may do so only at
the place the LORD will choose within one
of your tribal territories. There you must offer your burnt offerings and do everything
I command you.
15"But you may butcher your animals and
eat their meat in any town whenever you
want. You may freely eat the animals with
which the LORD your God blesses you. All
of you, whether ceremonially clean or unclean, may eat that meat, just as you now eat
gazelle and deer. 16But you must not consume the blood. You must pour it out on the
ground like water.
17"But you may not eat your offerings in
your hometown—neither the atithe of your
grain and new wine and olive oil, nor the
firstborn of your flocks and herds, nor any
offering to fulfill a vow, nor your voluntary offerings, nor your sacred offerings.
18You must eat these in the presence of the
LORD your God at the place he will choose.
Eat them there with your children, your
servants, and the Levites who live in your
towns, celebrating in the presence of the
LORD your God in all you do. 19And be very
careful never to neglect the Levites as long
as you live in your land.
20"When the LORD your God expands
your territory as he has promised, and you
have the urge to eat meat, you may freely eat
meat whenever you want. 21It might happen

12:5 Exod 20:24; Deut 26:2
12:6 Deut 14:22; kma'aser (4643) ›Deut 12:17
12:7 Deut 12:12, 18; 14:26; 15:20
12:8 Judg 17:6
12:10 Josh 3:17; 11:23
12:12 Deut 10:9; 12:7, 18-19; 26:11
12:13 Deut 12:5
12:15 Deut 12:20-23; 14:3-5
12:16 Lev 17:10-12; Deut 15:23
12:17 Deut 12:26; 14:22-23; ama'aser (4643) ›Deut 14:23
12:18 Deut 12:4-5, 26
12:20 Deut 11:24

their lush foliage demonstrated fertility. Sometimes trees were stylized in the form of wooden poles driven into the ground and dedicated to the worship of the mother goddess, Asherah (see 7:5).

12:3 *sacred pillars:* See note on 7:5. • *Asherah poles:* The feminine counterpart to the sacred pillar was a wooden pole dedicated to the mother goddess, Asherah. • *erase the names:* With the destruction of all idols and every vestige of pagan worship, the names of these deities would be forgotten. Future generations would know nothing of them (see also note on 7:24).

12:5 *his name will be honored:* The name of the Lord represents the Lord himself. God lived among his people in a designated location by placing *his name* there (see Exod 3:13-14).

12:6 All of the *offerings* listed here are expressions of thanksgiving, fellowship, and loyalty to the Lord. In covenant relationships, the vassal offered tribute to the Great King as a sign of submission and a promise of dependability (see note on 1:31).

12:8 *doing as you please:* Until the Exodus, the Israelites probably worshiped at multiple shrines in Egypt. With the construction of the Tabernacle, worship was centralized and remained so with the later building of the Temple. In the future, the community would be required to assemble on stated occasions to worship the Lord collectively at the central sanctuary, although local worship by individuals, families, and even villages would continue (see Exod 20:24-26; 1 Sam 9:11-14).

12:12 *The Levites,* descendants of Jacob's son Levi, were set apart to serve the Lord full time in Israel's religious life (Num 18:1-7). The primary task of the Levites was to assist the priests in their various responsibilities. Because the priests and the Levites could not engage in secular pursuits, they depended on the generosity of Israel's other tribes for their livelihood (Num 18:21-24).

12:15 *butcher your animals . . . whenever you want:* This instruction refers to animals for eating, not for a ritual sacrifice. • *ceremonially clean or unclean:* The slaughter of animals for food could take place without the slayer undergoing the purification rituals necessary when sacrificial animals were slain.

12:16 The prohibition against consuming *blood* pertained both to sacrificial animals and to those slain for meat. Because it represented life, blood was sacred and was to be rendered only to God. This principle is inherent in creation and preceded the law (Gen 4:10-11; 9:4-6; Lev 17:11). See also note on Lev 7:26-27.

12:18 The *place he will choose* was the central sanctuary—first the Tabernacle and then the Temple.

12:23
[b]*dam* (1818)
‣2 Kgs 21:16
[c]*nepesh* (5315)
‣Job 7:11

12:25
Deut 4:40

12:26
Num 5:9-10
Deut 12:17

12:28
Deut 4:40

12:31
Lev 18:21
Deut 9:5; 18:10
Ps 106:37-38

12:32
Deut 4:2

13:1
Matt 24:24
Mark 13:22
2 Thes 2:9
[d]*nabi'* (5030)
‣Deut 18:15

that the designated place of worship—the place the LORD your God chooses for his name to be honored—is a long way from your home. If so, you may butcher any of the cattle, sheep, or goats the LORD has given you, and you may freely eat the meat in your hometown, as I have commanded you. [22]Anyone, whether ceremonially clean or unclean, may eat that meat, just as you do now with gazelle and deer. [23]But never consume the [b]blood, for the [b]blood is the [c]life, and you must not consume the [c]lifeblood with the meat. [24]Instead, pour out the blood on the ground like water. [25]Do not consume the blood, so that all may go well with you and your children after you, because you will be doing what pleases the LORD.

[26]"Take your sacred gifts and your offerings given to fulfill a vow to the place the LORD chooses. [27]You must offer the meat and blood of your burnt offerings on the altar of the LORD your God. The blood of your other sacrifices must be poured out on the altar of the LORD your God, but you may eat the meat. [28]Be careful to obey all my commands, so that all will go well with you and your children after you, because you will be doing what is good and pleasing to the LORD your God.

[29]"When the LORD your God goes ahead of you and destroys the nations and you drive them out and live in their land, [30]do not fall into the trap of following their customs and worshiping their gods. Do not inquire about their gods, saying, 'How do these nations worship their gods? I want to follow their example.' [31]You must not worship the LORD your God the way the other nations worship their gods, for they perform for their gods every detestable act that the LORD hates. They even burn their sons and daughters as sacrifices to their gods.

[32]"So be careful to obey all the commands I give you. You must not add anything to them or subtract anything from them.

A Warning against Idolatry

13 "Suppose there are [d]prophets among you or those who dream dreams about the future, and they promise you signs or miracles, [2]and the predicted signs or miracles occur. If they then say, 'Come,

The Central Sanctuary (12:4-7)

Deut 31:14-15
Exod 25:8-9, 22, 40; 26:30; 33:7-11; 40:34-35
Num 7:1; 11:16
1 Kgs 8:10-11, 27
John 1:14; 2:19-21
Acts 7:44
1 Cor 3:16-17; 6:19-20
2 Cor 6:16
Eph 2:21
Heb 8:2, 5
Rev 21:22

God wanted worship to be carried out only in the place where he had established his name. For Israel, this place was the Tabernacle and later the Temple in Jerusalem.

God is *transcendent* (above all things) and *omnipresent* (present everywhere), yet he chose one place for Israel to worship him. Solomon later asked how the God of heaven could be housed in a human structure (1 Kgs 8:27). The answer is that God's name stands in his place. The Tabernacle and then the Temple belonged to him and bore his name, so they were, in a sense, his dwelling places. In the ancient Near East, names were more than labels: They represented the character and nature of the named individuals (e.g., Jacob, Gen 27:36; Jesus, Matt 1:21; Barnabas, Acts 4:36; Peter, John 1:42; 1 Cor 1:12; 9:5). Thus the ancient Hebrew sage could advise, "Choose a good reputation [literally *name*] over great riches" (Prov 22:1).

God made his home in a sanctuary that bore his name. His glorious presence manifested in fire and cloud during the wilderness wanderings served as a constant reminder that his name was there (Exod 40:34-35; see also 1 Kgs 8:10-11) and that he was at home among his people (cp. John 1:14; 2:19-21; 1 Cor 3:16-17; 6:19-20; 2 Cor 6:16; Eph 2:21; Rev 21:22).

12:21 ***you may butcher:*** Because an animal's blood was considered sacred (see Gen 9:4-6), even meat intended for human consumption was to be slaughtered at the central ***designated place of worship*** if that was at all practical (cp. Lev 17:8-9); if not, the animal could be sacrificed locally, but the blood still had to be disposed of in a ritually appropriate manner (12:23-25; cp. Lev 17:10-12).

12:23 ***the blood is the life:*** In this figure of speech, the means (***blood***) is equated with the effect (***life***). Since ***life*** is sacred, its vehicle, ***the blood,*** is also sacred (see also Lev 17:11).

12:27 ***you may eat the meat:*** The exception was meat sacrificed in burnt offerings, which was to be given to the Lord and wholly consumed in the fire (see Lev 1:3-17 and note).

12:31 ***burn their sons and daughters:*** Human sacrifice was one of the most abhorrent practices of ancient pagan religions. The Ammonites believed that their god Molech required such sacrifice from his worshipers (Lev 18:21; 20:2; 2 Kgs 23:10; Jer 32:35).

12:32 Verse 12:32 is numbered 13:1 in the Hebrew text.

13:1-18 Prophets who tried to lead Israel away from the one true God were guilty of treason, which carried the death penalty. No other religion insisted on exclusive worship of their national gods; consequently, such harsh penalties for the worship of competing deities were unknown elsewhere in the ancient Near East.
• Verses 13:1-18 are numbered 13:2-19 in Hebrew text.

13:1 God performed ***signs*** and ***miracles*** to induce amazement and faith in those who witnessed them (see 6:22). False prophets and magicians were able to replicate these feats to a degree and thus sometimes led God's people astray (see Exod 7:11, 22; 8:7).

let us worship other gods'—gods you have
not known before—3do not listen to them.
The LORD your God is testing you to see if
you truly love him with all your heart and
soul. 4Serve only the LORD your God and
fear him alone. Obey his commands, [e]listen
to his voice, and cling to him. 5The false
prophets or visionaries who try to lead
you astray must be put to death, for they
encourage rebellion against the LORD your
God, who redeemed you from slavery and
brought you out of the land of Egypt. Since
they try to lead you astray from the way the
LORD your God commanded you to live, you
must put them to death. In this way you will
purge the evil from among you.

6"Suppose someone secretly entices
you—even your brother, your son or daughter, your beloved wife, or your closest
friend—and says, 'Let us go worship other
gods'—gods that neither you nor your ancestors have known. 7They might suggest that
you worship the gods of peoples who live
nearby or who come from the ends of the
earth. 8But do not give in or listen. Have no
pity, and do not spare or protect them. 9You
must put them to death! Strike the first blow
yourself, and then all the people must join
in. 10Stone the guilty ones to death because
they have tried to draw you away from the
LORD your God, who rescued you from the
land of Egypt, the place of slavery. 11Then
all Israel will hear about it and be afraid,
and no one will act so wickedly again.

12"When you begin living in the towns
the LORD your God is giving you, you may
hear 13that [f]scoundrels among you are leading their fellow citizens astray by saying,
'Let us go worship other gods'—gods you
have not known before. 14In such cases,
you must examine the facts carefully. If
you find that the report is true and such a
detestable act has been committed among
you, 15you must attack that town and completely destroy all its inhabitants, as well
as all the livestock. 16Then you must pile
all the plunder in the middle of the open
square and burn it. Burn the entire town as
a burnt offering to the LORD your God. That
town must remain a ruin forever; it may
never be rebuilt. 17Keep none of the plunder that has been set apart for destruction.
Then the LORD will turn from his fierce
anger and be merciful to you. He will have
compassion on you and make you a large
nation, just as he swore to your ancestors.

18"The LORD your God will be merciful
only if you listen to his voice and keep all
his commands that I am giving you today,
doing what pleases him.

Ceremonially Clean and Unclean Animals

14 "Since you are the people of the
LORD your God, never cut yourselves
or shave the hair above your foreheads in
mourning for the dead. 2You have been set
apart as holy to the LORD your God, and he
has [g]chosen you from all the nations of the
earth to be his own special treasure.

3"You must not eat any detestable animals that are ceremonially unclean. 4These
are the animals you may eat: the ox, the
sheep, the goat, 5the deer, the gazelle, the
roe deer, the wild goat, the addax, the ante-
lope, and the mountain sheep.

6"You may eat any animal that has completely split hooves and chews the cud, 7but
if the animal doesn't have both, it may not

13:3
Deut 6:5; 8:2, 16
13:4
Deut 10:20
[e]*shama'* (8085)
▸Deut 28:1
13:5
Deut 13:9; 17:5; 22:21
13:6
Deut 17:2-7; 29:18
13:8
Deut 7:2
13:9
Lev 24:13-14
Deut 13:5; 17:7
13:11
Deut 19:20
13:13
Deut 13:2
[f]*beliya'al* (1100)
▸Judg 19:22
13:16
Deut 7:25-26
Josh 6:24
13:17
Exod 32:12
Num 25:4
Deut 7:13; 30:3
13:18
Deut 12:28
14:1
Lev 19:27-28
Jer 16:6
14:2
Exod 19:5
[g]*bakhar* (0977)
▸Deut 21:5
14:3-20
//Lev 11:1-43
14:3
Ezek 4:14
14:4
Acts 10:14

13:3 ***testing you to see if:*** See note on 8:2.

13:5 ***visionaries:*** Literally *dreamer of dreams.* • ***purge*** (literally *burn*): God wanted false prophets to be completely eliminated, leaving no residue of their evil ways. See also 17:12; 19:13.

13:6 ***neither you nor your ancestors have known:*** The Israelites had heard of these false gods before, but they had never worshiped them. Doing so would violate the first two commandments, the essence of the covenant.

13:9 ***Strike the first blow yourself:*** Because the guilty parties would be members of one's own family (13:6), this difficult demand would test the depth of a person's commitment to worship the Lord exclusively. Love for God must take priority over love for family members and friends (Matt 10:34-39).

13:13 ***scoundrels*** (literally *sons of Belial*): In Hebrew, "son(s) of" often expresses group affiliation or shared characteristics. *Scoundrels* typically deceived others and led them astray (Prov 6:12; 16:27; 19:28; Nah 1:11).

13:14 A ***detestable act*** is any deed or even thought that is offensive to God (see notes on 7:25-26; 12:31).

13:15 ***completely destroy:*** See note on 2:34; similarly in 13:17.

13:16 The spoils of war, or ***plunder,*** were not to be kept. God had designated them for complete destruction (see 2:34; Lev 27:28-29).

14:1-21 See "Clean and Unclean" at Lev 11:1–15:33, p. 213.

14:1 ***cut yourselves:*** This pagan custom was usually associated with mourning rites, perhaps to induce the dead to come back to life (see 1 Kgs 18:28; Zech 13:4-6). • ***shave the hair:*** This practice also pertained to lament for the dead (see Lev 19:27-28; 21:5-6), but the exact meaning of this rite is unknown.

14:2 The fundamental Hebrew meaning of ***holy*** focuses on separation of a person or thing for a particular function or use. A derivative meaning is "pure" or "morally and spiritually upright." • ***special treasure:*** See note on 7:6.

14:4 ***These are the animals:*** The identification of some of the animals and birds listed in this chapter is uncertain.

14:6 ***split hooves and chews the cud:*** These criteria distinguished edible animals listed in 14:4-5 from those listed in 14:7-8. Although the people experienced health benefits from observing these restrictions, a thing was actually clean or unclean only because God declared it to be such.

14:7 The ***hyrax*** (or *coney,* or *rock badger*) was a rabbit-sized, hoofed mammal.

be eaten. So you may not eat the camel, the
hare, or the hyrax. They chew the cud but
do not have split hooves, so they are ceremonially unclean for you. 8And you may not
eat the pig. It has split hooves but does not
chew the cud, so it is ceremonially unclean
for you. You may not eat the meat of these
animals or even touch their carcasses.

9"Of all the marine animals, you may eat
whatever has both fins and scales. 10You
may not, however, eat marine animals that
do not have both fins and scales. They are
ceremonially unclean for you.

11"You may eat any bird that is ceremonially clean. 12These are the birds you may not
eat: the griffon vulture, the bearded vulture,
the black vulture, 13the kite, the falcon, buzzards of all kinds, 14ravens of all kinds, 15the
eagle owl, the short-eared owl, the seagull,
hawks of all kinds, 16the little owl, the great
owl, the barn owl, 17the desert owl, the Egyptian vulture, the cormorant, 18the stork,
herons of all kinds, the hoopoe, and the bat.

19"All winged insects that walk along the
ground are ceremonially unclean for you
and may not be eaten. 20But you may eat any
winged bird or insect that is ceremonially
clean.

21"You must not eat anything that has
died a natural death. You may give it to a
foreigner living in your town, or you may
sell it to a stranger. But do not eat it yourselves, for you are set apart as holy to the
Lord your God.

"You must not cook a young goat in its
mother's milk.

The Giving of Tithes

22"You must set aside a tithe of your crops—
one-tenth of all the crops you harvest each
year. 23Bring this tithe to the designated
place of worship—the place the Lord your
God chooses for his name to be honored—
and eat it there in his presence. This applies
to your [h]tithes of grain, new wine, olive oil,
and the firstborn males of your flocks and
herds. Doing this will teach you always to
fear the Lord your God.

24"Now when the Lord your God blesses
you with a good harvest, the place of worship he chooses for his name to be honored
might be too far for you to bring the tithe.
25If so, you may sell the tithe portion of your
crops and herds, put the money in a pouch,
and go to the place the Lord your God has
chosen. 26When you arrive, you may use the
money to buy any kind of food you want—
cattle, sheep, goats, wine, or other alcoholic
drink. Then feast there in the presence of
the Lord your God and celebrate with your
household. 27And do not neglect the Levites
in your town, for they will receive no allotment of land among you.

28"At the end of every third year, bring
the entire tithe of that year's harvest and
store it in the nearest town. 29Give it to the
Levites, who will receive no allotment of
land among you, as well as to the foreigners living among you, the orphans, and the
widows in your towns, so they can eat and
be satisfied. Then the Lord your God will
bless you in all your work.

Release for Debtors

15 "At the end of every seventh year you
must cancel the debts of everyone
who owes you money. 2This is how it must
be done. Everyone must cancel the loans
they have made to their fellow Israelites.

14:12 Lev 11:13
14:19 Lev 11:20
14:21 Exod 23:19; 34:26; Lev 17:15; 22:8; Deut 14:2; Ezek 4:14
14:22 Deut 12:6, 17
14:23 Deut 4:10; 12:4; [h]*ma'aser* (4643) ›2 Chr 31:5
14:24 Deut 12:5, 21
14:26 Deut 12:7
14:27 Num 18:20; Deut 12:12
14:28 Deut 26:12
14:29 Deut 16:11; 24:19
15:1 Deut 31:10-11

14:8 The instruction not to *touch their carcasses* was primarily to maintain ritual purity.

14:11-18 These animals are grouped as flying animals that eat rotting flesh.

14:19-20 *winged insects:* Cp. Lev 11:20-23.

14:21 Animals that had *died a natural death* were considered unclean (even if considered clean while living) because they had not been slaughtered according to ritual protocol and their blood had not been properly drained and disposed of (see 12:23-25). • *You must not cook a young goat in its mother's milk:* A common explanation for why this pagan practice was improper is that it displayed insensitivity to the natural feelings of affection and trust between mothers and their offspring (see 28:56-57).

14:22-27 *set aside a tithe:* The ancient practice of giving a tenth preceded the law of Moses (Gen 14:20; 28:22) and existed in other ancient cultures. Here it is viewed as a tax or tribute collected by the sovereign Lord from his vassals (see notes on 1:31 and 12:6).

14:23 *The place the Lord your God chooses for his name to be honored* (literally *the place he will cause his name to dwell*) was the central sanctuary, the Lord's dwelling on the earth among his people (see 12:5, 18).

14:26 Both *wine* and *other alcoholic drink* were used in worship ceremonies (Gen 14:18; 35:14; Exod 29:40-41; Matt 26:27) and in celebrations; they signified God's blessing (Gen 27:25, 28; 49:11; 1 Chr 12:40; Ps 104:15; Song 4:10; 5:1; Isa 25:6; Matt 26:29).

14:27 Because *the Levites* had no geographic inheritance of their own and were forbidden to engage in secular work, they depended on the support of other tribes (see 12:12).

14:28 An annual *tithe* was required of all adult Israelite males as part of their festival observances (15:20; 16:16-17). The tithe *every third year* met the needs of the Levites and other dependent classes in Israelite society (14:29). See note on Lev 27:30.

15:1-23 The Law included the regulation of borrowing and lending so that the poor could survive deprivation. It provided restrictions to allow the rich to minister to the needs of the poor without exploiting them.

15:1 *cancel the debts:* This technical term refers to releasing people in financial bondage from their creditors and from any penalty for their default.

15:2 The *time of release* was to occur every seventh year across the nation

They must not demand payment from their
neighbors or relatives, for the LORD's time of
release has arrived. 3This release from debt,
however, applies only to your fellow Israelites—not to the foreigners living among you.
4"There should be no poor among you, for
the LORD your God will greatly bless you in
the land he is giving you as a special possession. 5You will receive this blessing if you
are careful to obey all the commands of the
LORD your God that I am giving you today.
6The LORD your God will bless you as he
has promised. You will lend money to many
nations but will never need to borrow. You
will rule many nations, but they will not rule
over you.
7"But if there are any poor Israelites in
your towns when you arrive in the land
the LORD your God is giving you, do not be
hard-hearted or tightfisted toward them.
8Instead, be generous and lend them whatever they need. 9Do not be mean-spirited
and refuse someone a loan because the year
for canceling debts is close at hand. If you refuse to make the loan and the needy person
cries out to the LORD, you will be considered
guilty of sin. 10Give generously to the poor,
not grudgingly, for the LORD your God will
bless you in everything you do. 11There will
always be some in the land who are poor.
That is why I am commanding you to share
freely with the poor and with other Israelites in need.

Release for Hebrew Slaves

12"If a fellow Hebrew sells himself or herself to be your servant and serves you for
six years, in the seventh year you must set
that servant free.
13"When you release a male servant, do
not send him away empty-handed. 14Give
him a generous farewell gift from your
flock, your threshing floor, and your winepress. Share with him some of the bounty
with which the LORD your God has blessed
you. 15Remember that you were once slaves
in the land of Egypt and the LORD your God
redeemed you! That is why I am giving you
this command.
16"But suppose your servant says, 'I will
not leave you,' because he loves you and your
family, and he has done well with you. 17In
that case, take an awl and push it through
his earlobe into the door. After that, he will
be your servant for life. And do the same for
your female servants.
18"You must not consider it a hardship
when you release your servants. Remember that for six years they have given you
services worth double the wages of hired
workers, and the LORD your God will bless
you in all you do.

Sacrificing Firstborn Male Animals

19"You must set aside for the LORD your God
all the firstborn males from your flocks
and herds. Do not use the firstborn of your
herds to work your fields, and do not shear
the firstborn of your flocks. 20Instead, you
and your family must eat these animals in
the presence of the LORD your God each
year at the place he chooses. 21But if this
firstborn animal has any defect, such as
lameness or blindness, or if anything else
is wrong with it, you must not ˈsacrifice it
to the LORD your God. 22Instead, use it for
food for your family in your hometown.
Anyone, whether ceremonially clean or
unclean, may eat it, just as anyone may eat
a gazelle or deer. 23But you must not consume the blood. You must pour it out on the
ground like water.

15:3 Deut 23:20
15:4 Deut 28:8
15:6 Deut 28:12-13
15:7 Deut 15:11
15:9 Exod 22:22-23; Deut 15:1; 24:14-15; Job 34:28
15:10 2 Cor 9:5, 7
15:11 John 12:8
15:12-18 //Exod 21:2-6
15:12 Lev 25:39; Jer 34:14
15:15 Deut 5:15; 16:12
15:16 Exod 21:5-6
15:19 Exod 13:2, 12; 34:19
15:20 Deut 12:7
15:21 Lev 22:19; Mal 1:8; ˈ*zabakh* (2076) ▸Josh 22:27
15:22 Deut 12:15
15:23 Deut 12:16, 23-24

(the Sabbath year, Lev 25:1-7). The time frame followed the calendar rather than the length of the loan arrangement. This meant that the year of release could fall as soon as a year after a loan was made.

15:4 If Israel lived in perfect obedience to the covenant, there would ***be no poor*** in the nation. However, this ideal was never realized in ancient Israel, and poverty was very much an issue.

15:6 ***You will lend money to many nations:*** An obedient Israel would become an affluent nation able to provide international aid. This bounty would bear testimony to God's promise to Abraham that his seed would be a blessing to all nations (Gen 12:2-3; 17:4-6; 26:3-4).

15:11 The reality that there ***will always be some . . . who are poor*** in a fallen world is no excuse for indifference to their plight. Instead, it should emphasize the need for the rich to contribute to the well-being of the poor (Matt 26:6-13).

15:12 ***If a fellow Hebrew sells himself or herself to be your servant*** (or ***If a Hebrew man or woman is sold to you***): This arrangement allowed a debtor to work off financial obligations to a creditor. The limit of this arrangement was seven years (but see 15:16-17).

15:16 ***he loves you:*** In the context of a covenant, this phrase speaks of a binding relationship with both legal and emotional overtones.

15:17 ***push it through his earlobe:*** This disfigurement publicly indicated that a bondservant had voluntarily indentured himself to his master for life. This might be what Paul meant when he said "I bear on my body the scars that show I belong to Jesus" (Gal 6:17).

15:18 ***worth double the wages:*** Because a bondservant worked all day, every day, his output was more than that of a day laborer, who merely put in his shift.

15:19 The ***firstborn males*** of livestock represented the firstborn sons of Israel who had been spared from death in the tenth plague (Exod 12:12, 29; 13:2, 12; 22:29).

15:21 A ***defect*** was any imperfection that devalued an animal; it was no sacrifice to give up something that was of little or no worth to begin with (2 Sam 24:24).

15:23 The ***blood*** of an animal was seen as synonymous with its life, the most sacred of God's creations, so it was sacrilegious to ***consume*** it (see 12:16).

16:1-8
//Exod 12:14-20
//Lev 23:4-8
//Num 28:16-25
16:1
Exod 12:2
Num 28:16
[j]*pesakh* (6453)
‣ Josh 5:10
16:2
Exod 12:5
16:3
Exod 12:8, 15; 34:18
16:4
Exod 13:7; 34:25
16:6
Deut 12:5
16:7
2 Chr 35:13
16:9-12
//Lev 23:15-22
//Num 28:26-31
16:9
Exod 23:16; 34:22
Lev 23:15
Num 28:26
16:10
[k]*khag* (2282)
‣ Deut 16:14
16:11
Deut 12:7, 12; 14:29; 24:19
16:12
Deut 15:15
16:13-17
//Lev 23:33-43
//Num 29:12-39
16:13
Lev 23:16, 40
16:14
[a]*khag* (2282)
‣ Deut 16:16
16:16
Exod 23:14-17; 34:20, 22-24
[b]*khag* (2282)
‣ 2 Chr 30:21

Passover and the Festival
of Unleavened Bread

16 "In honor of the LORD your God, celebrate the [j]Passover each year in the
early spring, in the month of Abib, for that
was the month in which the LORD your God
brought you out of Egypt by night. 2Your
Passover sacrifice may be from either the
flock or the herd, and it must be sacrificed
to the LORD your God at the designated
place of worship—the place he chooses
for his name to be honored. 3Eat it with
bread made without yeast. For seven days
the bread you eat must be made without
yeast, as when you escaped from Egypt in
such a hurry. Eat this bread—the bread of
suffering—so that as long as you live you
will remember the day you departed from
Egypt. 4Let no yeast be found in any house
throughout your land for those seven days.
And when you sacrifice the Passover lamb
on the evening of the first day, do not let
any of the meat remain until the next
morning.

5"You may not sacrifice the Passover in
just any of the towns that the LORD your
God is giving you. 6You must offer it only
at the designated place of worship—the
place the LORD your God chooses for his
name to be honored. Sacrifice it there in
the evening as the sun goes down on the
anniversary of your exodus from Egypt.
7Roast the lamb and eat it in the place the
LORD your God chooses. Then you may go
back to your tents the next morning. 8For
the next six days you may not eat any bread
made with yeast. On the seventh day proclaim another holy day in honor of the
LORD your God, and no work may be done
on that day.

The Festival of Harvest

9"Count off seven weeks from when you
first begin to cut the grain at the time of
harvest. 10Then celebrate the [k]Festival of
Harvest to honor the LORD your God. Bring
him a voluntary offering in proportion
to the blessings you have received from
him. 11This is a time to celebrate before
the LORD your God at the designated place
of worship he will choose for his name to
be honored. Celebrate with your sons and
daughters, your male and female servants,
the Levites from your towns, and the foreigners, orphans, and widows who live
among you. 12Remember that you were
once slaves in Egypt, so be careful to obey
all these decrees.

The Festival of Shelters

13"You must observe the Festival of Shelters for seven days at the end of the harvest
season, after the grain has been threshed
and the grapes have been pressed. 14This
[a]festival will be a happy time of celebrating
with your sons and daughters, your male
and female servants, and the Levites, foreigners, orphans, and widows from your
towns. 15For seven days you must celebrate
this festival to honor the LORD your God at
the place he chooses, for it is he who blesses
you with bountiful harvests and gives you
success in all your work. This festival will
be a time of great joy for all.

16"Each year every man in Israel must
celebrate these three festivals: the [b]Festival
of Unleavened Bread, the [b]Festival of Harvest, and the [b]Festival of Shelters. On each
of these occasions, all men must appear
before the LORD your God at the place he
chooses, but they must not appear before

16:1-17 See chart, "Israel's Festivals," p. 235.

16:1-8 The *Passover* (Hebrew *pesakh*) was the festival marking Israel's deliverance from the tenth plague and from bondage in Egypt (see Exod 11–12; Lev 23:5-8). • The Exodus was such a significant event in Israel's history that *the month of Abib,* when the Exodus took place, became the beginning of Israel's annual calendar (see Exod 12:2).

16:1 ***In honor of the LORD your God, celebrate the Passover each year in the early spring, in the month of Abib:*** Literally *Observe the month of Abib, and keep the Passover unto the LORD your God.* Abib, the first month of the ancient Hebrew lunar calendar, usually occurs within the months of March and April.

16:2 ***the place . . . for his name to be honored:*** The Lord's name represented the Lord himself. When he placed *his name* in the Tabernacle or Temple, he was effectively taking up residence there (see 12:5, 18).

16:3 Although *yeast* frequently symbolizes corruption (Lev 6:14-17; Matt 16:11-12), it was avoided at the original Passover because the Israelites had no time to wait for yeast bread to rise (see Exod 12:10-14). The elements of the yearly Passover celebration reminded the Israelites of what God had done for them.

16:10 ***Festival of Harvest:*** Literally *Festival of Weeks;* also in 16:16. This was later called the Festival of Pentecost (see Acts 2:1). It is celebrated today as Shavuot (or Shabuoth). The Festival of Harvest took place seven weeks after Passover to celebrate the wheat harvest (Exod 34:22; Lev 23:15-22).

16:11 ***the . . . place . . . for his name to be honored:*** See 12:5, 18.

16:13-17 ***Festival of Shelters:*** Or *Festival of Booths,* or *Festival of Tabernacles;* also in 16:16. This was earlier called the Festival of the Final Harvest or Festival of Ingathering (see Exod 23:16). It is celebrated today as Sukkot (or Succoth). It is called the Festival of Shelters because the people of Israel were instructed to camp out for a week in crude huts made of tree limbs as a memorial to their years of wilderness wandering (Lev 23:33-43). It was also a celebration of the fall harvests.

16:16 Participation in the festival was required of *every man,* but women and children could participate as well (16:11, 14; cp. Luke 2:41).

the LORD without a gift for him. 17All must give as they are able, according to the blessings given to them by the LORD your God.

Justice for the People

18"Appoint judges and officials for yourselves from each of your tribes in all the towns the LORD your God is giving you. They must judge the people fairly. 19You must never twist justice or show partiality. Never accept a bribe, for bribes blind the eyes of the wise and corrupt the decisions of the godly. 20Let true [c]justice prevail, so you may live and occupy the land that the LORD your God is giving you.

21"You must never set up a wooden Asherah pole beside the altar you build for the LORD your God. 22And never set up sacred pillars for worship, for the LORD your God hates them.

17 "Never sacrifice sick or defective cattle, sheep, or goats to the LORD your God, for he detests such gifts.

2"When you begin living in the towns the LORD your God is giving you, a man or woman among you might do evil in the sight of the LORD your God and violate the covenant. 3For instance, they might serve other gods or worship the sun, the moon, or any of the stars—the [d]forces of heaven—which I have strictly forbidden. 4When you hear about it, investigate the matter thoroughly. If it is true that this detestable thing has been done in Israel, 5then the man or woman who has committed such an evil act must be taken to the gates of the town and stoned to death. 6But never put a person to death on the testimony of only one witness. There must always be two or three witnesses. 7The witnesses must throw the first stones, and then all the people may join in. In this way, you will purge the evil from among you.

8"Suppose a case arises in a local court that is too hard for you to decide—for instance, whether someone is guilty of murder or only of manslaughter, or a difficult lawsuit, or a case involving different kinds of assault. Take such legal cases to the place the LORD your God will choose, 9and present them to the Levitical [e]priests or the judge on duty at that time. They will hear the case and declare the verdict. 10You must carry out the verdict they announce and the sentence they prescribe at the place the LORD chooses. You must do exactly what they say. 11After they have interpreted the law and declared their verdict, the sentence they impose must be fully executed; do not modify it in any way. 12Anyone [f]arrogant enough to reject the verdict of the judge or of the priest who represents the LORD your God must die. In this way you will purge the evil from Israel. 13Then everyone else will hear about it and be afraid to act so arrogantly.

16:18 Exod 18:21, 26; Deut 1:16
16:19 Exod 23:2-3; Lev 19:15
16:20 [c]*tsedeq* (6664) ‣Ps 9:8
16:21 Exod 34:13; Deut 7:5
16:22 Lev 26:1
17:1 Deut 15:21
17:2 Deut 13:6-11
17:3 [d]*tsaba'* (6635) ‣Josh 5:14
17:4 Deut 13:12-14
17:5 Lev 24:14
17:6 Num 35:30; Deut 19:15
17:7 Lev 24:13-14; Deut 13:9; *1 Cor 5:13
17:8 Deut 12:5
17:9 [e]*kohen* (3548) ‣Deut 18:3
17:11 Deut 25:1
17:12 [f]*zadon* (2087) ‣1 Sam 17:28

16:18–17:13 The community of Israel, like any political entity, needed leaders of different kinds to provide cohesion and guidance. The Lord directed Moses to establish an appropriate leadership structure. He also laid out the criteria for selecting the leaders and the responsibilities of each office.

16:18 The combination of the words ***judges and officials*** might suggest that here the two terms are functionally synonymous. Usually ***officials*** is a generic title applied to any public leader, but here it seems to refer to an administrator of law and justice or something like police officers, as in modern Hebrew. • ***fairly:*** The idea was to measure up to an objective standard of equity that neither public nor private pressure could alter.

16:19 ***show partiality:*** See note on 1:17; also see 10:17.

16:21-22 ***Asherah pole . . . sacred pillars:*** See note on 7:5; also see 12:3; Isa 27:8-9; Mic 5:13-15.

17:1 A ***sick or defective*** animal had little monetary value, so it was no sacrifice to surrender it to the Lord (cp. 15:21).

17:3 The ***forces of heaven*** are visible objects such as the ***sun, moon,*** and ***stars,*** as well as invisible beings such as angels. Worship of anyone or anything created by God is a clear violation of the second commandment (see 5:9).

17:4 Anything offensive to the Lord could be called a ***detestable thing*** (see 7:25; 12:31; 13:14).

17:5 ***the gates:*** A typical town in ancient Israel was small (about 10 acres or less) and crowded. It had few open areas except for a plaza just inside or outside the main gate where public meetings were held, including trials and other judicial proceedings. The place here is clearly outside of the town because stoning to death would not occur inside the walls (22:24; 1 Kgs 21:10) except under unusual circumstances (22:21).

17:7 The instruction for ***witnesses*** to ***throw the first stones*** guarded against unfounded allegations. False testimony carried serious consequences. Requiring a witness to take the leading role in an execution helped guarantee the reliability of his testimony; he would personally bear the guilt if he took the life of an innocent person (see John 8:1-11). • ***The people*** would ***purge the evil from among you*** by executing those whose sin brought the stain of guilt upon the community of Israel (see "Purge the Evil," facing page; cp. 1 Cor 5:13 and note).

17:8 ***whether someone is guilty of murder or only of manslaughter:*** In OT law, as in modern jurisprudence, murder was intentional; manslaughter was accidental (cp. 19:1-13).

17:9 ***priests or the judge:*** Both types of officials could decide matters of either a religious or a secular nature.

17:11 ***do not modify it:*** This Hebrew term envisions keeping on a straight path (cp. Prov 4:25-27; Heb 12:13). Once a verdict has been rendered, the sentence must be applied according to the law and the rules of evidence. Justice must be carried out on an unswerving path of fairness and righteousness.

17:12 ***purge the evil:*** The effects of evil should not be allowed to fester in the community. Like a cancer, they must be completely eradicated.

17:14 Deut 11:31; Josh 21:43
17:16 1 Kgs 4:26; Ezek 17:15
17:17 2 Sam 5:13; 1 Kgs 11:3-4
17:18 Deut 31:9, 24
17:19 Deut 4:9-10; Josh 1:8; [g]*yir'ah* (3374) ›1 Sam 7:7
17:20 Deut 5:32
18:1 Deut 10:9; 1 Cor 9:13
18:2 Num 18:20
18:3 Lev 7:32; Num 18:11; [h]*kohen* (3548) ›1 Sam 2:35

Guidelines for a King

14"You are about to enter the land the LORD your God is giving you. When you take it over and settle there, you may think, 'We should select a king to rule over us like the other nations around us.' 15If this happens, be sure to select as king the man the LORD your God chooses. You must appoint a fellow Israelite; he may not be a foreigner.

16"The king must not build up a large stable of horses for himself or send his people to Egypt to buy horses, for the LORD has told you, 'You must never return to Egypt.' 17The king must not take many wives for himself, because they will turn his heart away from the LORD. And he must not accumulate large amounts of wealth in silver and gold for himself.

18"When he sits on the throne as king, he must copy for himself this body of instruction on a scroll in the presence of the Levitical priests. 19He must always keep that copy with him and read it daily as long as he lives. That way he will learn to [g]fear the LORD his God by obeying all the terms of these instructions and decrees. 20This regular reading will prevent him from becoming proud and acting as if he is above his fellow citizens. It will also prevent him from turning away from these commands in the smallest way. And it will ensure that he and his descendants will reign for many generations in Israel.

Gifts for the Priests and Levites

18 "Remember that the Levitical priests—that is, the whole of the tribe of Levi—will receive no allotment of land among the other tribes in Israel. Instead, the priests and Levites will eat from the special gifts given to the LORD, for that is their share. 2They will have no land of their own among the Israelites. The LORD himself is their special possession, just as he promised them.

3"These are the parts the [h]priests may claim as their share from the cattle, sheep, and goats that the people bring as offerings: the shoulder, the cheeks, and the stomach.

Purge the Evil (17:2-13)

Deut 9:3-6; 13:5; Lev 19:1-2; Josh 7:1-26; 2 Chr 34:3-8; Isa 1:24-26; 4:2-6; 33:14; Ezek 20:32-38; Matt 18:8-9; Acts 5:1-11; Rom 14:10; 1 Cor 11:27-30; 2 Cor 5:10; Heb 9:27-28; 10:31; 12:28-29; Jas 5:19-20; 1 Pet 4:5

Sin is so abhorrent to God that it cannot coexist with him. The same should be true for his people. God is holy, and he expects his people to reflect his holiness (Lev 11:45; 19:2).

God required severe measures to remove sins and sinners from the covenant community. God offered forgiveness, but only for the truly repentant; those who hardened their hearts could expect God's judgment—a devouring fire, a purging process that devours sinners and their sins and leaves nothing behind (see 9:3; 13:5; Isa 33:14; Heb 12:28-29). Such cleansing is meant to heal the community of believers and deter others from rebelling against the Lord (17:13).

Early in the OT, God's judgment among his people was often immediate (see, e.g., Num 11:1-3; 16:1-50; Josh 7:1-26; cp. Acts 5:1-11). God made his people aware of his demand for obedience and of the penalty for those who did not comply.

God's retribution is now reserved for the future day of judgment, when the sins of the unrighteous and the saints will be exposed and judged (Rom 14:10; 2 Cor 5:10; Heb 9:27; 1 Pet 4:5). However, some instances of calamity can be understood as God's judgment on his disobedient children (see 1 Cor 11:27-30; Jas 5:19-20). It is still a "terrible thing to fall into the hands of the living God" (Heb 10:31).

17:15 ***the man the LORD your God chooses:*** Human monarchy was not contrary to God's will for Israel (cp. 1 Sam 8:6-7). God promised Abraham and Sarah that their descendants would include kings (Gen 17:6, 16; see also Gen 35:11), but the abuses of kingship were condemned. The theology that views the Messiah in a kingly role (2 Sam 7:11-15; Pss 2; 110; Isa 9:6-7) provides for both human and divine royalty.

17:16 ***never return to Egypt:*** Going there would show a king's lack of dependence on God, who had redeemed Israel from bondage to Egypt. The best horses were found in Egypt (see 1 Kgs 10:28-29).

17:17 ***many wives:*** Polygamy is neither prohibited nor sanctioned here. This guideline was meant to moderate and regulate the practice. In the ancient world, kings married many wives to cement political alliances with other kingdoms, showing trust in human power rather than God's provision. David (2 Sam 5:13; 12:11) and Solomon (1 Kgs 11:3-4) both ignored this warning to their own great harm and that of the nation. • ***must not accumulate:*** The amassing of wealth was another sign of dependence on human resources.

17:18 ***This body of instruction*** (literally *this torah*) refers to the book of Deuteronomy or perhaps only to this passage concerning the Israelite monarchy. For *torah,* see note on 4:44.

18:1 The term ***Levitical priests*** described the entire ***tribe of Levi.*** Technically, however, only Aaron's descendants were priests. The non-priestly Levites were their assistants (see 12:12).

18:2 ***The LORD himself is their special possession:*** The allotment of the Levites was spiritual, not territorial or material. They possessed the Lord by giving their whole lives to his service. This idea is a remarkable inverse of the idea that Israel was the Lord's possession (see 7:6).

18:3 In the dietary fare of ancient Israel, ***the shoulder, the cheeks, and the stomach*** of oxen and sheep were the choice cuts. God's priestly servants were to be honored by receiving the very best (see Lev 7:28-34).

4You must also give to the priests the first
share of the grain, the new wine, the olive
oil, and the wool at shearing time. 5For the
LORD your God chose the tribe of Levi out
of all your tribes to minister in the LORD's
name forever.
6"Suppose a Levite chooses to move from
his town in Israel, wherever he is living, to
the place the LORD chooses for worship. 7He
may minister there in the name of the LORD
his God, just like all his fellow Levites who
are serving the LORD there. 8He may eat his
share of the sacrifices and offerings, even if
he also receives support from his family.

A Call to Holy Living

9"When you enter the land the LORD your
God is giving you, be very careful not to imitate the detestable customs of the nations
living there. 10For example, never sacrifice
your son or daughter as a burnt offering.
And do not let your people practice fortune-
telling, or use sorcery, or interpret omens,
or engage in witchcraft, 11or cast spells, or
function as mediums or [i]psychics, or call
forth the spirits of the dead. 12Anyone who
does these things is detestable to the LORD.
It is because the other nations have done
these detestable things that the LORD your
God will drive them out ahead of you. 13But
you must be blameless before the LORD your
God. 14The nations you are about to displace consult sorcerers and fortune-tellers,
but the LORD your God forbids you to do
such things."

True and False Prophets

15Moses continued, "The LORD your God
will raise up for you a [j]prophet like me from
among your fellow Israelites. You must listen to him. 16For this is what you yourselves
requested of the LORD your God when you
were assembled at Mount Sinai. You said,
'Don't let us hear the voice of the LORD our
God anymore or see this blazing fire, for we
will die.'
17"Then the LORD said to me, 'What they
have said is right. 18I will raise up a [k]prophet
like you from among their fellow Israelites. I
will put my words in his mouth, and he will
tell the people everything I command him.
19I will personally deal with anyone who will
not listen to the messages the prophet proclaims on my behalf. 20But any [a]prophet who
falsely claims to speak in my name or who
speaks in the name of another god must die.'
21"But you may wonder, 'How will we
know whether or not a prophecy is from the
LORD?' 22If the [b]prophet speaks in the LORD's
name but his prediction does not happen or
come true, you will know that the LORD did
not give that message. That [b]prophet has
spoken without my authority and need not
be feared.

Cities of Refuge

19 "When the LORD your God destroys
the nations whose land he is giving
you, you will take over their land and settle
in their towns and homes. 2Then you must
set apart three cities of refuge in the land

18:4 Exod 22:29
18:5 Exod 28:1; Deut 10:8
18:6 Num 35:2-3
18:8 Lev 27:30; Num 18:21
18:9 Deut 9:5; 12:29-30
18:10 Exod 22:18; Lev 19:26, 31; 20:6; Deut 12:31; Jer 27:9-10
18:11 [i]*yidde'oni* (3049) ›1 Sam 28:3
18:13 Gen 6:7-10; Matt 5:48
18:15 Luke 24:19; John 1:21, 24-25; *Acts 3:22; 7:37; [j]*nabi'* (5030) ›Deut 18:18
18:16 Deut 5:23-27
18:18 *Acts 3:22; [k]*nabi'* (5030) ›Deut 18:20
18:19 Deut 17:12; *Acts 3:22; Heb 12:25
18:20 Deut 13:1-4; [a]*nabi'* (5030) ›Deut 18:22
18:22 Jer 28:9; [b]*nabi'* (5030) ›Judg 4:4
19:1 Deut 6:10-12

18:8 *support from his family:* Although Levites were in full-time ministry at the Tabernacle and (later) the Temple, they could still hold material assets of their own (see Num 35:1-8). The Levites were to be supported by the regular offerings designated for that purpose without having to forfeit any of their own assets.

18:10 *never sacrifice your son or daughter as a burnt offering* (or *never make your son or daughter pass through the fire*): Some Canaanite religions included child sacrifice to appease their gods. Israel was strictly warned never to engage in this practice (Exod 34:15-16; Lev 18:21; 20:2-5). When they did, it aroused God's judgment (2 Kgs 17:16-17; 21:6; Ezek 23:37). • ***fortune-telling:*** Throughout the ancient Near East, diviners were considered experts at reading and interpreting omens. Divination was commonly done through *extispicy*, the examination of livers, kidneys, and other internal organs of various animals. • ***sorcery:*** Sorcerers conjured up the spirits of the dead. • Divining cups were often used to ***interpret omens*** (see Gen 44:5). Drops of oil would be placed in containers of water, and the spread of the oil communicated some message to the expert. A parallel would be reading tea leaves. • The practice of ***witchcraft*** included performing unusual acts or signs (Exod 7:11) to mislead people (Mal 3:5).

18:11 *cast spells:* These incantations were to destroy or injure others by invoking curses on them. The false prophet Balaam was hired for this purpose against Israel (Num 22:2-6). • ***Mediums*** and ***psychics*** were especially adept at conjuring up and communicating with the spirits of the dead (see 1 Sam 28:3-25).

18:15 *A prophet like me* would be beyond the ordinary because Moses was without peer among the prophets (see 34:10-11). This prophet would be ***from among your fellow Israelites*** (literally *from among your brothers*), and Israel was required to listen to him (18:19). The prophets of OT Israel would partially fulfill the function of God's spokesman to whom Israel ***must listen.*** Later, Judaism looked for this prophet as a major messianic figure (see John 1:21; 6:14; 7:40); the NT identifies Jesus as this prophet (Acts 3:18-26).

18:16 *Mount Sinai:* Hebrew *Horeb*, another name for Sinai; see note on 1:2.

18:18 The ***prophet*** (18:15) would be the Lord's spokesman, as Moses was (see 4:10-17; Exod 7:1).

18:19 Not to listen to the Lord's spokesman is not to listen to the Lord.

18:22 Any prophet whose ***prediction*** fails must be branded as false, even if he claims to speak for God. The mere claim is insufficient if it goes unfulfilled.

19:1-13 *Cities of refuge* (19:2) were strategically located throughout the land so those accused of homicide could find protective sanctuary until their cases came to trial (see 4:41; Num 35:6-29).

19:2 The ***three cities*** were those in Canaan, west of the Jordan; there were three more in Transjordan (see Num 35:13-14; Josh 20:7).

19:2 Deut 4:41-42; Josh 20:2
19:4 Num 35:9-34
19:8 Deut 11:24
19:9 Deut 6:5; 11:22
19:10 Num 35:33; Deut 21:1-9
19:12 [c]*zaqen* (2205) ‣Deut 21:3
19:13 Deut 7:2
19:14 Deut 27:17; Prov 23:10-11
19:15 Num 35:30; Deut 17:6; *Matt 18:16; *2 Cor 13:1
19:16 Exod 23:1
19:17 Deut 17:9; 21:5
19:19 *1 Cor 5:13; Prov 19:5
19:21 Exod 21:24; Lev 20:20; *Matt 5:38
20:1 Deut 3:22; 31:6-8
20:2 Num 10:8; 31:6
20:3 Josh 23:10

the LORD your God is giving you. 3Survey the
territory, and divide the land the LORD your
God is giving you into three districts, with
one of these cities in each district. Then anyone who has killed someone can flee to one
of the cities of refuge for safety.
4"If someone kills another person unintentionally, without previous hostility, the
slayer may flee to any of these cities to live
in safety. 5For example, suppose someone
goes into the forest with a neighbor to cut
wood. And suppose one of them swings
an ax to chop down a tree, and the ax head
flies off the handle, killing the other person.
In such cases, the slayer may flee to one of
the cities of refuge to live in safety.
6"If the distance to the nearest city of refuge is too far, an enraged avenger might be
able to chase down and kill the person who
caused the death. Then the slayer would die
unfairly, since he had never shown hostility
toward the person who died. 7That is why I
am commanding you to set aside three cities of refuge.
8"And if the LORD your God enlarges your
territory, as he swore to your ancestors, and
gives you all the land he promised them,
9you must designate three additional cities
of refuge. (He will give you this land if you
are careful to obey all the commands I have
given you—if you always love the LORD your
God and walk in his ways.) 10That way you
will prevent the death of innocent people in
the land the LORD your God is giving you as
your special possession. You will not be held
responsible for the death of innocent people.
11"But suppose someone is hostile toward
a neighbor and deliberately ambushes and
murders him and then flees to one of the
cities of refuge. 12In that case, the [c]elders of
the murderer's hometown must send agents
to the city of refuge to bring him back and
hand him over to the dead person's avenger
to be put to death. 13Do not feel sorry for
that murderer! Purge from Israel the guilt
of murdering innocent people; then all will
go well with you.

Concern for Justice

14"When you arrive in the land the LORD
your God is giving you as your special possession, you must never steal anyone's land
by moving the boundary markers your ancestors set up to mark their property.
15"You must not convict anyone of a
crime on the testimony of only one witness.
The facts of the case must be established by
the testimony of two or three witnesses.
16"If a malicious witness comes forward
and accuses someone of a crime, 17then
both the accuser and accused must appear
before the LORD by coming to the priests and
judges in office at that time. 18The judges
must investigate the case thoroughly. If the
accuser has brought false charges against
his fellow Israelite, 19you must impose on
the accuser the sentence he intended for
the other person. In this way, you will purge
such evil from among you. 20Then the rest
of the people will hear about it and be
afraid to do such an evil thing. 21You must
show no pity for the guilty! Your rule should
be life for life, eye for eye, tooth for tooth,
hand for hand, foot for foot.

Regulations concerning War

20 "When you go out to fight your
enemies and you face horses and
chariots and an army greater than your
own, do not be afraid. The LORD your God,
who brought you out of the land of Egypt, is
with you! 2When you prepare for battle, the
priest must come forward to speak to the
troops. 3He will say to them, 'Listen to me,
all you men of Israel! Do not be afraid as you

19:3 *Survey the territory:* Or *Keep the roads in good repair.*

19:4 A *slayer* who *kills . . . unintentionally* does not plan ahead of time to commit the act (see 17:8).

19:6 *avenger* (literally *the redeemer of blood*): The law allowed murder to be avenged by members of the victim's family. When they found the killer, they could put him to death (Num 35:16-21). The idea was that blood shed by the victim must be paid for by the blood of the person responsible for the act (see Gen 4:15; 9:6). In this way, the land polluted by the shed blood could be purified (Num 35:33-34).

19:9 If Israel proved faithful to the covenant (19:8), God would grant the nation even more territory, so much so that *three additional cities of refuge* would be needed. Sadly, this need never arose because of Israel's disobedience to the Lord.

19:11 The Hebrew term rendered *is hostile* (literally *is a hater*) indicates a constant and long-standing hateful attitude, which constituted evidence that the killer was predisposed to commit a crime and therefore probably did it.

19:13 *Purge* (literally *burn*): The only way for the land to be free of culpability in matters of homicide was for blood vengeance to be enacted, which would burn out the impurity. See also 13:5; 17:12.

19:15 The word of one witness alone would count no more than the word of the accused. However, *two or three witnesses* would confirm or discount each other's testimony. For NT references to this law, see Matt 18:15-20; John 8:17-18; 2 Cor 13:1 and note.

19:21 The legal principle described as *life for life* is known as *lex talionis* ("law of retaliation"), according to which the punishment must fit the crime (see Exod 21:23; Lev 24:20); it should be neither too lenient nor too severe. Appropriate punishment is a necessary function of government (cp. Rom 13:1-7), and it served to maintain Israel's spiritual integrity as God's people (see note on 17:7). But vengeance belongs to God, not individuals (see 1 Sam 25:26, 33; Matt 5:38-39; 1 Cor 6:1-8).

go out to fight your enemies today! Do not
lose heart or panic or tremble before them.
4For the LORD your God is going with you!
He will fight for you against your enemies,
and he will give you victory!'
5"Then the officers of the army must address the troops and say, 'Has anyone here
just built a new house but not yet dedicated
it? If so, you may go home! You might be
killed in the battle, and someone else would
dedicate your house. 6Has anyone here just
planted a vineyard but not yet eaten any of
its fruit? If so, you may go home! You might
die in battle, and someone else would eat the
first fruit. 7Has anyone here just become engaged to a woman but not yet married her?
Well, you may go home and get married!
You might die in the battle, and someone
else would marry her.'
8"Then the officers will also say, 'Is anyone here afraid or worried? If you are, you
may go home before you frighten anyone
else.' 9When the officers have finished
speaking to their troops, they will appoint
the unit commanders.
10"As you approach a town to attack it, you
must first offer its people terms for peace.
11If they accept your terms and open the
gates to you, then all the people inside will
serve you in forced labor. 12But if they refuse to make peace and prepare to fight, you
must attack the town. 13When the LORD your
God hands the town over to you, use your
swords to kill every man in the town. 14But
you may keep for yourselves all the women,
children, livestock, and other plunder. You
may enjoy the plunder from your enemies
that the LORD your God has given you.
15"But these instructions apply only to distant towns, not to the towns of the nations
in the land you will enter. 16In those towns
that the LORD your God is giving you as a special possession, destroy every living thing.
17You must completely destroy the Hittites,
Amorites, Canaanites, Perizzites, Hivites,
and Jebusites, just as the LORD your God has
commanded you. 18This will prevent the
people of the land from teaching you to imitate their detestable customs in the worship
of their gods, which would cause you to [d]sin
deeply against the LORD your God.
19"When you are attacking a town and
the war drags on, you must not cut down
the trees with your axes. You may eat the
fruit, but do not cut down the trees. Are the
trees your enemies, that you should attack
them? 20You may only cut down trees that
you know are not valuable for food. Use
them to make the equipment you need to
attack the enemy town until it falls.

Cleansing for Unsolved Murder

21 "When you are in the land the LORD
your God is giving you, someone
may be found murdered in a field, and you
don't know who committed the murder. 2In
such a case, your elders and judges must
measure the distance from the site of the
crime to the nearby towns. 3When the nearest town has been determined, that town's
[e]elders must select from the herd a young
cow that has never been trained or yoked to
a plow. 4They must lead it down to a valley
that has not been plowed or planted and that
has a stream running through it. There in
the valley they must break the young cow's
neck. 5Then the Levitical priests must step
forward, for the LORD your God has [f]chosen
them to minister before him and to pronounce blessings in the LORD's name. They
are to decide all legal and criminal cases.
6"The elders of the town must wash their

20:5 Neh 12:27
20:6 Lev 19:23
20:7 Deut 24:5
20:8 Judg 7:3
20:10 Luke 14:31-32
20:13 Num 31:7
20:14 Josh 8:2
20:16 Exod 23:31; Deut 7:1-2
20:18 Deut 7:4; 9:5; 12:30
[d]*khata'* (2398) ▸1 Sam 12:23
21:3 [e]*zaqen* (2205) ▸Deut 21:20
21:5 Deut 10:8; 17:9; 19:17
[f]*bakhar* (0977) ▸1 Sam 2:28
21:6 Matt 27:24

20:4 *He will fight for you:* This promise affirms that God initiates wars, carries them out, and brings them to successful conclusion against his enemies. The purpose of war initiated by God was to eradicate hopelessly unrepentant enemies and prevent them from contaminating his people (see 1:30).

20:7 *someone else would marry her:* In this situation, a man who died would be deprived of offspring to carry on his name, which was a great tragedy in ancient Israel.

20:10-15 The people in the land had already been placed under the ban (7:1-6), so this instruction refers to those whom Israel would engage outside the land (20:15).

20:11 *forced labor:* Involuntary service was pressed upon prisoners of war and sometimes on Israelites (1 Kgs 5:13-18; 9:15, 21; 12:18).

20:15 Places described as *distant towns* were outside the boundaries of the Promised Land.

20:17 *completely destroy:* See note on 2:34.

20:19 *do not cut down the trees:* Ordinarily, trees might be cut down during a war so the enemy could not benefit from them. However, since the Israelites were occupying the enemy's former land, the trees could be of use to them.

20:20 This *equipment* consisted of the materials built up against a city wall as part of the effort to bring it under siege.

21:1-9 The guilt of murder was usually removed through the death of the murderer (19:11-13; Num 35:30-34). However, if the murderer was unknown, the guilt could still be removed by using this ritual.

21:1 In contrast to the the word translated *murder* in the Ten Commandments (see note on 5:17), the Hebrew verb here translated *murdered* (literally *pierced through*) indicates clear evidence that the death was not by natural causes.

21:3-8 An avenger from the victim's family (19:6-7; Num 35:16-29) could not hold the whole community responsible.

21:4 The *stream* would be an ever-flowing (perennial) brook located in an isolated area, free of contaminants.

21:6 *wash their hands:* This ancient practice asserted innocence (cp. Matt

21:8 Num 35:33-34; Jon 1:14
21:9 Deut 19:13
21:10 Josh 21:44
21:12 Lev 14:8-9; Num 6:9
21:13 Ps 45:10
21:14 Gen 34:2
21:17 Gen 49:3
21:18 Prov 1:8
21:20 [g]*zaqen* (2205) ‣ Deut 22:15
21:21 Lev 20:2, 27; Num 15:35
21:22 Matt 26:65-66; Mark 14:63-64
21:23 Josh 8:29; John 19:31; *Gal 3:13
22:1 Exod 23:4

hands over the young cow whose neck was broken. 7Then they must say, 'Our hands did not shed this person's blood, nor did we see it happen. 8O LORD, forgive your people Israel whom you have redeemed. Do not charge your people with the guilt of murdering an innocent person.' Then they will be absolved of the guilt of this person's blood. 9By following these instructions, you will do what is right in the LORD's sight and will cleanse the guilt of murder from your community.

Marriage to a Captive Woman

10"Suppose you go out to war against your enemies and the LORD your God hands them over to you, and you take some of them as captives. 11And suppose you see among the captives a beautiful woman, and you are attracted to her and want to marry her. 12If this happens, you may take her to your home, where she must shave her head, cut her nails, 13and change the clothes she was wearing when she was captured. She will stay in your home, but let her mourn for her father and mother for a full month. Then you may marry her, and you will be her husband and she will be your wife. 14But if you marry her and she does not please you, you must let her go free. You may not sell her or treat her as a slave, for you have humiliated her.

Rights of the Firstborn

15"Suppose a man has two wives, but he loves one and not the other, and both have given him sons. And suppose the firstborn son is the son of the wife he does not love. 16When the man divides his inheritance, he may not give the larger inheritance to his younger son, the son of the wife he loves, as if he were the firstborn son. 17He must recognize the rights of his oldest son, the son of the wife he does not love, by giving him a double portion. He is the first son of his father's virility, and the rights of the firstborn belong to him.

Dealing with a Rebellious Son

18"Suppose a man has a stubborn and rebellious son who will not obey his father or mother, even though they discipline him. 19In such a case, the father and mother must take the son to the elders as they hold court at the town gate. 20The parents must say to the [g]elders, 'This son of ours is stubborn and rebellious and refuses to obey. He is a glutton and a drunkard.' 21Then all the men of his town must stone him to death. In this way, you will purge this evil from among you, and all Israel will hear about it and be afraid.

Various Regulations

22"If someone has committed a crime worthy of death and is executed and hung on a tree, 23the body must not remain hanging from the tree overnight. You must bury the body that same day, for anyone who is hung is cursed in the sight of God. In this way, you will prevent the defilement of the land the LORD your God is giving you as your special possession.

22 "If you see your neighbor's ox or sheep or goat wandering away, don't ignore your responsibility. Take it back to its owner. 2If its owner does not live

---

27:24); by it the community would declare that it was not responsible for a crime committed in its vicinity.

21:12 To *shave her head* and *cut her nails* demonstrated a captive woman's separation from her home and family. She was cutting off the past to join a new family and community.

21:13 To *change the clothes she was wearing* symbolically communicated taking on a new life and identifying with a new family.

21:14 *humiliated her:* By first taking her prisoner and then divorcing her, a captive woman's husband devalued her. To protect her from further disgrace, the law prohibited him from selling her as a slave or from using her as one. Instead, she must be allowed to *go free.*

21:15-17 The law required that a *firstborn son* receive the greater share of his father's inheritance (see 21:15-16; 2 Kgs 2:9). The custom of giving the firstborn son a *double portion* is first recorded here but was implied in earlier practice (see Gen 25:31-34; 27:1-4; 48:8-22). • *son of his father's virility:* The eldest male child carried this distinction because he proved that the man was capable of siring children, and a boy in particular.

21:20 Calling someone *a glutton and a drunkard* was probably a proverbial cliché suggesting self-indulgence and laziness. Such a son was a good-for-nothing who rebelled against his parents and thus also against the community and divine authority (see Prov 23:20-21).

21:21 *purge* (literally *burn*): See note on 13:5; also 17:12; 19:13.

21:22 *hung on a tree* (or *impaled on a pole;* similarly in 21:23): This was not the method of execution, at least in this text. It was a shameful display of those put to death for capital offenses, probably to show the Lord's hatred of sin and to deter others who might commit such acts (see also Gen 40:19, 22; Josh 10:26; 2 Sam 4:12; 21:12; Esth 2:23; 7:10).

21:23 *for anyone who is hung:* Greek version reads *for everyone who is hung on a tree.* Cp. Gal 3:13, which explains how this proverb applies to Jesus. • *cursed in the sight of God:* Unrepentant sinners do fall under God's judgment. However, the idea of this proverb is probably that whoever saw a person in this condition would naturally conclude that God had cursed that person, when in fact the person could have been misjudged or even lynched.

22:1 *don't ignore your responsibility* (literally *don't hide yourself;* similarly in 22:3): An individual was not to avoid a troubled scene by pretending not to see what was going on. To do so would be a failure of the individual's responsibility to the covenant community.

nearby or you don't know who the owner is, take it to your place and keep it until the owner comes looking for it. Then you must return it. 3Do the same if you find your neighbor's donkey, clothing, or anything else your neighbor loses. Don't ignore your responsibility.

4"If you see that your neighbor's donkey or ox has collapsed on the road, do not look the other way. Go and help your neighbor get it back on its feet!

5"A woman must not put on men's clothing, and a man must not wear women's clothing. Anyone who does this is detestable in the sight of the LORD your God.

6"If you happen to find a bird's nest in a tree or on the ground, and there are young ones or eggs in it with the mother sitting in the nest, do not take the mother with the young. 7You may take the young, but let the mother go, so that you may prosper and enjoy a long life.

8"When you build a new house, you must build a railing around the edge of its flat roof. That way you will not be considered guilty of murder if someone falls from the roof.

9"You must not plant any other crop between the rows of your vineyard. If you do, you are forbidden to use either the grapes from the vineyard or the other crop.

10"You must not plow with an ox and a donkey harnessed together.

11"You must not wear clothing made of wool and linen woven together.

12"You must put four tassels on the hem of the cloak with which you cover yourself—on the front, back, and sides.

Regulations for Sexual Purity

13"Suppose a man marries a woman, but after sleeping with her, he turns against her 14and publicly accuses her of shameful conduct, saying, 'When I married this woman, I discovered she was not a virgin.' 15Then the woman's father and mother must bring the proof of her virginity to the [h]elders as they hold court at the town gate. 16Her father must say to them, 'I gave my daughter to this man to be his wife, and now he has turned against her. 17He has accused her of shameful conduct, saying, "I discovered that your daughter was not a virgin." But here is the proof of my daughter's virginity.' Then they must spread her bed sheet before the elders. 18The elders must then take the man and punish him. 19They must also fine him 100 pieces of silver, which he must pay to the woman's father because he publicly accused a virgin of Israel of shameful conduct. The woman will then remain the man's wife, and he may never [i]divorce her.

20"But suppose the man's accusations are true, and he can show that she was not a virgin. 21The woman must be taken to the door of her father's home, and there the men of the town must stone her to death, for she has committed a disgraceful crime in Israel by being promiscuous while living in her parents' home. In this way, you will purge this evil from among you.

22"If a man is discovered committing adultery, both he and the woman must die. In this way, you will purge Israel of such evil.

23"Suppose a man meets a young woman, a virgin who is engaged to be married, and he has sexual intercourse with her. If this happens within a town, 24you must take both of them to the gates of that town and stone them to death. The woman is guilty because she did not scream for help. The man must die because he violated another man's wife. In this way, you will purge this evil from among you.

22:6 Lev 22:28
22:9 Lev 19:19
22:10 2 Cor 6:14
22:12 Num 15:37-39; Matt 23:5
22:13 Deut 24:1
22:15 [h]*zaqen* (2205) ‣Deut 25:8
22:19 [i]*shalakh* (7971) ‣Deut 22:29
22:21 Deut 23:17-18
22:22 Lev 20:10; Ezek 16:38; John 8:5
22:23 Lev 19:20-22

22:5 Adopting the dress and behavior of the opposite gender unnaturally blurs the lines between things that should be kept separate and distinct (also 22:9-11).

22:9 ***any other crop between the rows:*** This would bring about a mingling of things that should be kept separate.

22:10 Plowing ***with an ox and a donkey*** would be inefficient; this example illustrates the principle of separation and order (see also 2 Cor 6:14-18).

22:11 Keeping ***wool and linen*** separate illustrated Israel's separation as God's holy people (see also Lev 19:19).

22:12 Placing ***four tassels on the hem*** of a garment probably reminded the wearer to be loyal to the covenant, similar to tying a string around one's finger (see Num 15:37-41).

22:14 A husband who discovered evidence that his wife had lost her virginity prior to marriage (see 22:15) would accuse her of ***shameful conduct.***

22:15 ***proof of her virginity:*** A blood-stained cloth would indicate that the woman's hymen was ruptured by her first act of intercourse with her husband. • ***town gate:*** See note on 17:5.

22:17 The ***bed sheet*** (literally *covering*) might also have been a garment of some kind, such as a nightgown.

22:19 ***100 pieces of silver*** (Hebrew *100 shekels of silver,* about 2.5 pounds or 1.1 kilograms in weight): The husband, who had already paid the woman's father the normal bride price, must now pay additional compensation for defaming her character.

22:21 ***by being promiscuous*** (literally *acting as a prostitute*): A single act of sexual intercourse by an unmarried woman was enough to earn this ***disgraceful*** label and the death penalty. • ***purge*** (literally *burn):* See note on 13:5; see also 17:12; 19:13.

22:24 ***the gates of that town:*** See note on 17:5. • Because betrothal was tantamount to marriage in the OT, ***another man's wife*** in this passage technically refers to a fiancée.

22:28
Exod 22:16
22:29
[j]*shalakh* (7971)
‣Deut 24:1
22:30
Lev 18:8; 20:11
Deut 27:20
23:1
Lev 21:20; 22:24
23:2
[k]*qahal* (6951)
‣1 Kgs 8:55
23:3
Neh 13:1-2
23:4
Num 23:4, 7-10
2 Pet 2:15
Jude 1:11
23:7
Lev 19:34
Deut 10:19
23:11
Lev 15:16
23:14
Lev 26:12
23:15
1 Sam 30:15
[a]*'ebed* (5650)
‣2 Kgs 10:23

25“But if the man meets the engaged
woman out in the country, and he rapes her,
then only the man must die. 26Do nothing
to the young woman; she has committed no
crime worthy of death. She is as innocent
as a murder victim. 27Since the man raped
her out in the country, it must be assumed
that she screamed, but there was no one to
rescue her.

28“Suppose a man has intercourse with a
young woman who is a virgin but is not engaged to be married. If they are discovered,
29he must pay her father fifty pieces of silver. Then he must marry the young woman
because he violated her, and he may never
[j]divorce her as long as he lives.

30“A man must not marry his father’s former wife, for this would violate his father.

Regulations concerning Worship

23 “If a man’s testicles are crushed or
his penis is cut off, he may not be
admitted to the assembly of the LORD.

2“If a person is illegitimate by birth,
neither he nor his descendants for ten generations may be admitted to the [k]assembly
of the LORD.

3“No Ammonite or Moabite or any of their
descendants for ten generations may be admitted to the assembly of the LORD. 4These
nations did not welcome you with food and
water when you came out of Egypt. Instead,
they hired Balaam son of Beor from Pethor
in distant Aram-naharaim to curse you.
5But the LORD your God refused to listen to
Balaam. He turned the intended curse into
a blessing because the LORD your God loves
you. 6As long as you live, you must never
promote the welfare and prosperity of the
Ammonites or Moabites.

7“Do not detest the Edomites or the
Egyptians, because the Edomites are your
relatives and you lived as foreigners among
the Egyptians. 8The third generation of
Edomites and Egyptians may enter the assembly of the LORD.

Miscellaneous Regulations

9“When you go to war against your enemies,
be sure to stay away from anything that is
impure.

10“Any man who becomes ceremonially
defiled because of a nocturnal emission
must leave the camp and stay away all day.
11Toward evening he must bathe himself,
and at sunset he may return to the camp.

12“You must have a designated area outside the camp where you can go to relieve
yourself. 13Each of you must have a spade as
part of your equipment. Whenever you relieve yourself, dig a hole with the spade and
cover the excrement. 14The camp must be
holy, for the LORD your God moves around
in your camp to protect you and to defeat
your enemies. He must not see any shameful thing among you, or he will turn away
from you.

15“If [a]slaves should escape from their
masters and take refuge with you, you
must not hand them over to their masters.
16Let them live among you in any town they
choose, and do not oppress them.

17“No Israelite, whether man or woman,
may become a temple prostitute. 18When
you are bringing an offering to fulfill a
vow, you must not bring to the house of the
LORD your God any offering from the earnings of a prostitute, whether a man or a
woman, for both are detestable to the LORD
your God.

22:29 *fifty pieces of silver* (Hebrew *50 shekels of silver,* about 1.25 pounds or 570 grams in weight): The father could still expect a dowry for his unmarried daughter (see Gen 34:12; Exod 22:16). • *he must marry:* The assumption is that the girl and her father were willing to undertake the arrangement (see Exod 22:17).

22:30 Verse 22:30 is numbered 23:1 in the Hebrew text. • The phrase *his father’s former wife* does not refer to a man’s own mother because incest was a more serious crime (see Lev 18:7-8, 29).

23:1-25 Verses 23:1-25 are numbered 23:2-26 in Hebrew text.

23:1 Emasculation, associated with certain pagan rituals and customs, was abhorrent to the Lord (cp. Isa 56:3-4).

23:3 *No Ammonite or Moabite:* These nations were Lot’s descendants by his incestuous daughters (see notes on 2:9, 19). In addition, they had forbidden Israel access to their lands during their desert wanderings (23:4). • Exclusion for *ten generations* means an indefinitely long period of time.

23:4 *Pethor* is now identified with Pitru in Mesopotamia (see note on Num 22:5-6). • *Aram-naharaim* (“Aram of the two rivers”) lies between the Euphrates and the Balih Rivers in upper Mesopotamia.

23:7 The *Edomites* were descendants of Jacob’s brother, Esau (see 2:8).

23:8 *third generation:* Following a long period of probation, Edomites and Egyptians who lived in Israel could worship the Lord as converts to the faith.

23:10 *nocturnal emission:* Although they might have been unintentional or involuntary, these discharges rendered a man ceremonially unclean (see Lev 15:16-18).

23:12 *outside the camp:* Defecation is a normal bodily function, but it brought ritual impurity and therefore violated God’s holiness.

23:13 It would be disgusting and shameful to have an open latrine outside the camp, let alone within it.

23:14 *shameful thing* (literally *nakedness of a thing*): Because the camp of God’s army was holy, it was necessary that nakedness, especially of the genitalia, not be exposed within the camp (cp. Gen 2:25; 3:7-11; 9:21-23; Exod 20:26; Isa 47:3; Rev 3:18).

23:17 *A temple prostitute* was commonly a part of Canaanite religious rituals, so they were forbidden in Israel.

23:18 *a man:* The Hebrew word (literally *a dog*) was a derogatory term for homosexual men, who often took part in Canaanite religious ceremonies.

19"Do not charge interest on the loans you make to a fellow Israelite, whether you loan money, or food, or anything else. 20You may charge interest to foreigners, but you may not charge interest to Israelites, so that the LORD your God may bless you in everything you do in the land you are about to enter and occupy.

21"When you make a vow to the LORD your God, be prompt in fulfilling whatever you promised him. For the LORD your God demands that you promptly fulfill all your vows, or you will be guilty of sin. 22However, it is not a sin to refrain from making a vow. 23But once you have voluntarily made a vow, be careful to fulfill your promise to the LORD your God.

24"When you enter your neighbor's vineyard, you may eat your fill of grapes, but you must not carry any away in a basket. 25And when you enter your neighbor's field of grain, you may pluck the heads of grain with your hand, but you must not harvest it with a sickle.

24 "Suppose a man marries a woman but she does not please him. Having discovered something wrong with her, he writes her a letter of [b]divorce, hands it to her, and sends her away from his house. 2When she leaves his house, she is free to marry another man. 3But if the second husband also turns against her and [c]divorces her, or if he dies, 4the first husband may not marry her again, for she has been defiled. That would be detestable to the LORD. You must not bring guilt upon the land the LORD your God is giving you as a special possession.

5"A newly married man must not be drafted into the army or be given any other official responsibilities. He must be free to spend one year at home, bringing happiness to the wife he has married.

6"It is wrong to take a set of millstones, or even just the upper millstone, as security for a loan, for the owner uses it to make a living.

7"If anyone kidnaps a fellow Israelite and treats him as a slave or sells him, the kidnapper must die. In this way, you will purge the evil from among you.

8"In all cases involving serious skin diseases, be careful to follow the instructions of the Levitical priests; obey all the commands I have given them. 9Remember what the LORD your God did to Miriam as you were coming from Egypt.

10"If you lend anything to your neighbor, do not enter his house to pick up the item he is giving as security. 11You must wait outside while he goes in and brings it out to you. 12If your neighbor is poor and gives you his cloak as security for a loan, do not keep the cloak overnight. 13Return the cloak to its owner by sunset so he can stay warm through the night and bless you, and the LORD your God will count you as righteous.

14"Never take advantage of poor and destitute laborers, whether they are fellow Israelites or foreigners living in your towns. 15You must pay them their wages each day before sunset because they are poor and are counting on it. If you don't, they might cry out to the LORD against you, and it would be counted against you as sin.

16"Parents must not be put to death for the sins of their children, nor children for the sins of their parents. Those deserving to die must be put to death for their own crimes.

17"True justice must be given to foreigners living among you and to orphans, and you

23:19 Exod 22:25; Lev 25:36
23:20 Deut 28:12
23:21 Num 30:1-2; Eccl 5:4; Matt 5:33
23:25 Matt 12:1-2; Mark 2:23; Luke 6:1
24:1 Num 5:12-28; Deut 22:13-21; *Matt 5:31; 19:7; Mark 10:4-5; [b]*kerituth* (3748) ‣Deut 24:3
24:3 [c]*kerituth* (3748) ‣2 Sam 13:16
24:5 Deut 20:7
24:8 Lev 13:2
24:9 Num 12:10
24:10 Exod 22:24-26
24:14 Lev 19:13; 1 Tim 5:18
24:16 //2 Kgs 14:6; 2 Chr 25:4; Ezek 18:20
24:17 Exod 22:21-22; 23:2-3; Deut 1:17; 10:17

23:19-20 The word translated *interest* is related to a noun meaning "bite." Charging interest was to "put the bite" on the debtor. See also Exod 22:25; Lev 25:36-37; Neh 5:1-13; Ps 15:5.

23:24 ***your neighbor's vineyard:*** In a certain sense, God owned all the land and provided it to its human occupants. Therefore, no one had the right to make an exclusive claim to it. On the other hand, renters had rights to privacy and to a measure of control over what had been allotted to them. Trespassing was permitted within this context but not with the intention of theft. One could, however, pluck a few grapes or kernels of grain to eat along the way (see Matt 12:1-8; Mark 2:23-28; Luke 6:1-5).

24:1 ***something wrong:*** This phrase indicates sexual impurity or some other impropriety. It does not pertain to adultery, which would have required the death penalty (22:22). • ***a letter of divorce:*** This procedure was a concession; initiating a divorce in such cases was optional and not necessarily desirable (see Mal 2:16; Matt 5:31-32; Mark 10:2-12).

24:4 Perhaps the woman is described as *defiled* because she had two husbands; returning to the first husband would be considered adultery. • ***guilt upon the land:*** The concept of community was so strong in ancient Israel that the individual's identity almost merged with that of the community. The sin of one individual had collective, corporate consequences.

24:6 ***the owner uses it to make a living*** (literally *it is his life*): Without his tool, the owner of the millstone might perish. The law imposed a limit on what could secure a loan. The millstone probably represents any means by which an individual made his living.

24:7 ***purge*** (literally *burn*): See note on 13:5; see also 17:12; 19:13.

24:8 ***serious skin diseases:*** Traditionally rendered *leprosy.* The Hebrew word used here can describe various skin diseases. Medical science has determined that it does not refer to leprosy per se (i.e., Hansen's disease).

24:11 ***wait outside:*** Even debtors were to be allowed their dignity and spared unnecessary embarrassment. A creditor was not to invade the debtor's privacy when collecting from him.

24:13 ***Return the cloak . . . by sunset:*** The law was merciful.

24:17 ***True justice must be given*** (literally *do not deprive of justice*): The

24:18 Deut 5:15
24:19 Lev 19:9-10; Deut 14:28-29
24:20 Lev 19:10
25:1 Deut 17:11; [d]*shapat* (8199) ‣Judg 2:16
25:3 2 Cor 11:24
25:4 *1 Cor 9:9; *1 Tim 5:18
25:5 *Matt 22:24; Mark 12:19; *Luke 20:28
25:6 Ruth 4:5
25:8 [e]*zaqen* (2205) ‣Deut 32:7

must never accept a widow's garment as security for her debt. [18]Always remember that
you were slaves in Egypt and that the LORD
your God redeemed you from your slavery.
That is why I have given you this command.
[19]"When you are harvesting your crops
and forget to bring in a bundle of grain from
your field, don't go back to get it. Leave it for
the foreigners, orphans, and widows. Then
the LORD your God will bless you in all you
do. [20]When you beat the olives from your
olive trees, don't go over the boughs twice.
Leave the remaining olives for the foreigners, orphans, and widows. [21]When you
gather the grapes in your vineyard, don't
glean the vines after they are picked. Leave
the remaining grapes for the foreigners, orphans, and widows. [22]Remember that you
were slaves in the land of Egypt. That is why
I am giving you this command.

25 "Suppose two people take a dispute
to court, and the judges [d]declare
that one is right and the other is wrong. [2]If
the person in the wrong is sentenced to
be flogged, the judge must command him
to lie down and be beaten in his presence
with the number of lashes appropriate to
the crime. [3]But never give more than forty
lashes; more than forty lashes would publicly humiliate your neighbor.
[4]"You must not muzzle an ox to keep it
from eating as it treads out the grain.
[5]"If two brothers are living together
on the same property and one of them
dies without a son, his widow may not be
married to anyone from outside the family. Instead, her husband's brother should
marry her and have intercourse with her to
fulfill the duties of a brother-in-law. [6]The
first son she bears to him will be considered the son of the dead brother, so that his
name will not be forgotten in Israel.
[7]"But if the man refuses to marry his
brother's widow, she must go to the town
gate and say to the elders assembled there,
'My husband's brother refuses to preserve
his brother's name in Israel—he refuses
to fulfill the duties of a brother-in-law by
marrying me.' [8]The [e]elders of the town will

True Justice (24:17)

Deut 10:17-19; 16:19; 24:12-22; 25:13-16; 27:19
Exod 23:3
Lev 19:15
Ps 82:1-5
Prov 11:1
Isa 1:17; 10:1-4; 11:3-4; 59:14-19
Jer 22:13-17
Ezek 22:23-29; 45:9-10
Amos 2:6-8; 8:5-6
Hab 1:4
Matt 23:23
Luke 18:6-8
Jas 2:1-7

The community of God's people in OT Israel was to be responsible for the well-being of widows, orphans, and foreigners (27:19). The Israelites were to represent the just God whom they served (see 10:17-19) and always remember that they had been an enslaved and defenseless people in Egypt (see 10:19; 24:18-22). How could they, the beneficiaries of God's grace, ignore the rights and needs of the most vulnerable who lived among them?

Every society has social structures that separate the powerful from the weak and the privileged from the ill-favored. This was true of OT Israel despite its unique constitution and commission as a "holy nation" (Exod 19:6). Judges and other officials charged with upholding the law might tend to favor individuals with financial means, high social standing, or community influence, especially when these individuals offer bribes (16:19). However, God cannot be bribed, nor does he show partiality (10:17). The rich and the poor, the powerful and the weak, the exalted and the downtrodden are all alike to him.

Those charged with applying the law in God's name must be scrupulously honest and upright in carrying out their duties. Justice that falls short of God's standard is not true justice, and those responsible for its corruption can expect full retribution from the Judge of all the earth (16:18-20; 25:13-16). The prophets of Israel understood the need for equity and justice and often called for the application of these principles to community and national life (Isa 1:17; 10:1-4; 59:14-19; Ezek 22:23-29; Amos 2:6-8; Hab 1:4). The NT also appeals for proper treatment of the poor and disadvantaged and speaks of God's displeasure when they are neglected (Matt 23:23; 2 Cor 9:6-10; Jas 2:1-7).

people of Israel were to vigorously resist discrimination against the weakest and most vulnerable people in society. Israel had been redeemed from such a status in Egypt, and their experience should help them realize how to treat others in similar circumstances (24:18).

25:3 At a flogging, the maximum number of strikes allowed was ***forty lashes.*** Fewer could be applied depending on the case (25:2). As people created in the image of God, even wrongdoers were entitled to mercy and respect. In later Judaism, thirty-nine lashes were given (see 2 Cor 11:24 and note).

25:4 ***You must not muzzle an ox:*** The animal had to be able to eat the grain as it worked (cp. 1 Cor 9:9-14; 1 Tim 5:17-18).

25:5 The term ***duties of a brother-in-law*** refers to the *levirate* (Latin for *brother-in-law*) marriage custom. The brother of a deceased man was encouraged to marry his brother's widow and father her children so that the name of the dead brother would not be forgotten. For examples of this custom, see Gen 38:6-11; Ruth 3:12-13; 4:1-12; Luke 20:27-33.

then summon him and talk with him. If he
still refuses and says, 'I don't want to marry
her,' 9the widow must walk over to him in
the presence of the elders, pull his sandal
from his foot, and spit in his face. Then
she must declare, 'This is what happens to
a man who refuses to provide his brother
with children.' 10Ever afterward in Israel
his family will be referred to as 'the family
of the man whose sandal was pulled off'!

11"If two Israelite men get into a fight
and the wife of one tries to rescue her husband by grabbing the testicles of the other
man, 12you must cut off her hand. Show her
no pity.

13"You must use accurate scales when you
weigh out merchandise, 14and you must use
full and honest measures. 15Yes, always use
honest weights and measures, so that you
may enjoy a long life in the land the LORD
your God is giving you. 16All who cheat with
dishonest weights and measures are detestable to the LORD your God.

17"Never forget what the Amalekites did
to you as you came from Egypt. 18They attacked you when you were exhausted and
weary, and they struck down those who
were straggling behind. They had no fear of
God. 19Therefore, when the LORD your God
has given you rest from all your enemies in
the land he is giving you as a special possession, you must destroy the Amalekites and
erase their memory from under heaven.
Never forget this!

Harvest Offerings and Tithes

26 "When you enter the land the LORD
your God is giving you as a special possession and you have conquered
it and settled there, 2put some of the first
produce from each crop you harvest into a
basket and bring it to the designated place
of worship—the place the LORD your God
chooses for his name to be honored. 3Go
to the priest in charge at that time and say
to him, 'With this gift I acknowledge to the
LORD your God that I have entered the land
he swore to our ancestors he would give us.'
4The priest will then take the basket from
your hand and set it before the altar of the
LORD your God.

5"You must then say in the presence of
the LORD your God, 'My ancestor Jacob was
a wandering Aramean who went to live as a
foreigner in Egypt. His family arrived few
in number, but in Egypt they became a large
and mighty nation. 6When the Egyptians
oppressed and humiliated us by making us
their slaves, 7we cried out to the LORD, the
God of our ancestors. He heard our cries
and saw our hardship, toil, and oppression.
8So the LORD brought us out of Egypt with
a strong hand and powerful arm, with
overwhelming terror, and with miraculous
signs and wonders. 9He brought us to this
place and gave us this land flowing with
milk and honey! 10And now, O LORD, I have
brought you the first portion of the harvest
you have given me from the ground.' Then
place the produce before the LORD your
God, and bow to the ground in worship
before him. 11Afterward you may go and
celebrate because of all the good things the
LORD your God has given to you and your
household. Remember to include the Levites and the foreigners living among you
in the celebration.

25:9-10 Ruth 4:7-8
25:12 Deut 7:2
25:13 Lev 19:35; Prov 11:1; 16:11; Ezek 45:10-11
25:16 Prov 11:1
25:17 Exod 17:8-16
26:2 Exod 22:29; 23:16, 19
26:5 Gen 46:27; Deut 1:10; 10:22
26:6 Exod 1:11-12
26:8 Deut 4:34
26:9 Exod 3:8, 17
26:11 Deut 12:7, 12

25:9 ***pull his sandal from his foot:*** Using footwear, which touched the ground, the brother-in-law showed that he relinquished any claim to his dead brother's estate (Ruth 4:7). • ***spit in his face:*** This is an almost universal gesture of utter contempt (see Num 12:14).

25:10 ***his family will be referred to:*** If a man refused to perpetuate his brother's name, he would be spoken of in a derogatory way.

25:11-12 ***cut off her hand:*** The woman's act would emasculate the man, depriving him of (or *cutting off* from him) any offspring. As with the previous law (25:9), the punishment fits the crime (*lex talionis;* see note on 19:21).

25:13-14 ***You must use accurate scales . . . full and honest measures*** (Hebrew *you must not have stone and stone, large and small, . . . ephah and ephah, large and small*): Merchants were not to use two sets of weights and measures for cheating customers—a heavier weight or measure when purchasing goods (thus reducing their own cost) and a lighter one when selling them (thus increasing their own profit).

25:17 The ***Amalekites*** were tribal peoples who attacked Israel's rear flanks during the Sinai wilderness wandering (Exod 17:8-16). They were apparently related to the Edomites (Gen 36:12).

25:19 ***destroy:*** God authorized war against his enemies. Later, Samuel commanded Saul to completely destroy ***the Amalekites,*** something he only partially accomplished (1 Sam 15). As a result, God rejected Saul as king. • ***from under heaven:*** The Amalekites were to be obliterated completely (see note on 2:34).

26:1-15 Under the terms of the covenant, the Great King required that his subjects render him tribute annually or even more frequently. Since Israel was an agrarian society, God required offerings of animal, vegetable, or grain products. This tribute specifically celebrated the mighty Exodus redemption.

26:2 ***the place . . . for his name to be honored:*** See notes on 12:5; 14:23; 16:2.

26:5 ***Jacob's*** mother (Rebekah) was an ***Aramean*** (Gen 24:10; 25:20, 26), and Jacob also lived in Aram for many years (Gen 31:41-42). His lifestyle was seminomadic (***wandering***). • ***few in number:*** Jacob and his family totaled only seventy when they went to Egypt (see Gen 46:27; Exod 1:5).

26:8 ***strong hand and powerful arm:*** See notes on 4:34 and 8:2. • ***signs and wonders:*** See notes on 6:22 and 7:19.

26:9 ***milk and honey:*** See note on 6:3.

26:11 ***Levites:*** See note on 12:12. • In Israelite society, ***foreigners*** (literally *sojourners*) were resident aliens; see also note on 10:18.

26:12 Deut 14:28-29 Heb 7:5, 9-10
26:15 Zech 2:13
26:16 Deut 4:29
26:17 Ps 48:14
26:18 Deut 7:6
26:19 Deut 28:1
27:2 Josh 8:30-32
27:9 Deut 26:17

12"Every third year you must offer a special tithe of your crops. In this year of the special tithe you must give your tithes to the Levites, foreigners, orphans, and widows, so that they will have enough to eat in your towns. 13Then you must declare in the presence of the LORD your God, 'I have taken the sacred gift from my house and have given it to the Levites, foreigners, orphans, and widows, just as you commanded me. I have not violated or forgotten any of your commands. 14I have not eaten any of it while in mourning; I have not handled it while I was ceremonially unclean; and I have not offered any of it to the dead. I have obeyed the LORD my God and have done everything you commanded me. 15Now look down from your holy dwelling place in heaven and bless your people Israel and the land you swore to our ancestors to give us—a land flowing with milk and honey.'

Exhortation to Obey (26:16-19)

16"Today the LORD your God has commanded you to obey all these decrees and regulations. So be careful to obey them wholeheartedly. 17You have declared today that the LORD is your God. And you have promised to walk in his ways, and to obey his decrees, commands, and regulations, and to do everything he tells you. 18The LORD has declared today that you are his people, his own special treasure, just as he promised, and that you must obey all his commands. 19And if you do, he will set you high above all the other nations he has made. Then you will receive praise, honor, and renown. You will be a nation that is holy to the LORD your God, just as he promised."

5. THIRD ADDRESS: RATIFICATION OF THE COVENANT (27:1–30:20)

Covenant Curses and Blessings (27:1–29:1)

The Altar on Mount Ebal

27 Then Moses and the leaders of Israel gave this charge to the people: "Obey all these commands that I am giving you today. 2When you cross the Jordan River and enter the land the LORD your God is giving you, set up some large stones and coat them with plaster. 3Write this whole body of instruction on them when you cross the river to enter the land the LORD your God is giving you—a land flowing with milk and honey, just as the LORD, the God of your ancestors, promised you. 4When you cross the Jordan, set up these stones at Mount Ebal and coat them with plaster, as I am commanding you today.

5"Then build an altar there to the LORD your God, using natural, uncut stones. You must not shape the stones with an iron tool. 6Build the altar of uncut stones, and use it to offer burnt offerings to the LORD your God. 7Also sacrifice peace offerings on it, and celebrate by feasting there before the LORD your God. 8You must clearly write all these instructions on the stones coated with plaster."

9Then Moses and the Levitical priests addressed all Israel as follows: "O Israel, be quiet and listen! Today you have become the people of the LORD your God. 10So you must obey the LORD your God by keeping all these commands and decrees that I am giving you today."

26:12 ***Every third year*** the tithe was gathered for the Levites and other dependents; see also note on 14:28.

26:13 ***I have taken*** (literally *burned*) ***the sacred gift:*** This phrase means that the donor had given his own property to the Levites and to others in need.

26:14 ***offered any of it to the dead:*** These pagan rituals were intended to sustain the dead through food offerings. Such food would be unacceptable as a part of the tithe given to the Levites.

26:15 ***flowing with milk and honey:*** See note on 6:3.

26:16-19 Having laid out the great covenant principles (chs 5–11) and clarified their application (chs 12–26), Moses urged the people to obey the covenant with all their hearts. The Lord had called them into a special relationship with himself, a privilege that required obedience to the covenant prescriptions. The result of this submission was holiness, a state that reflected God's character and that would flow naturally from unbroken fellowship with him.

26:16 ***wholeheartedly*** (literally *with all your heart and with all your soul*): This Hebrew phrase is a clear reference to the *Shema,* the foundational statement of Israel's faith and covenant commitment (see 6:4-5 and notes). There could be no halfhearted compliance with God's high and holy expectations; it must be all or nothing.

26:18 ***special treasure:*** See note on 7:6.

27:3 ***this whole body of instruction*** (literally *all the words of this torah*): This phrase could refer to the entire book of Deuteronomy, but considering the small surface (27:2) on which the text was to be inscribed, it probably just refers to the Ten Commandments. • ***flowing with milk and honey:*** See note on 6:3.

27:4 The covenant ceremony was to take place at ***Mount Ebal,*** a mountain east of Shechem (see Josh 8:30-35). The Samaritan Pentateuch reads "Mount Gerizim" here, an obvious attempt to justify the existence of the Samaritan temple on that mountain (see 11:29).

27:5 ***natural, uncut stones:*** Archaeological research has uncovered a number of Canaanite altars, all built of hewn blocks. In contrast to this practice, the Israelites were to build their altars only of rough field stones (Exod 20:22-26; see "Altars" at Gen 35:1-15, p. 91).

27:7 Some offerings atoned for sins and trespasses; others affirmed that all was well between the Lord and the donor. For example, ***peace offerings*** (sometimes called *fellowship offerings*) testified to wholeness in the divine–human relationship (see Lev 3:1-16).

27:9 ***Today:*** The Israelites were already the Lord's people prior to this moment, but each time Israel affirmed itself to be God's people and renewed the covenant (as here), they became God's people in a fresh, new way. Recommitment to the Lord is like beginning a new relationship with him.

Curses from Mount Ebal

11 That same day Moses also gave this charge
to the people: 12 "When you cross the Jordan
River, the tribes of Simeon, Levi, Judah, Issachar, Joseph, and Benjamin must stand on
Mount Gerizim to proclaim a blessing over
the people. 13 And the tribes of Reuben, Gad,
Asher, Zebulun, Dan, and Naphtali must
stand on Mount Ebal to proclaim a curse.

14 "Then the Levites will shout to all the
people of Israel:

15 'Cursed is anyone who carves or casts an
idol and secretly sets it up. These idols,
the work of craftsmen, are detestable to
the LORD.'
And all the people will reply, [f]'Amen.'

16 'Cursed is anyone who dishonors father
or mother.'
And all the people will reply, 'Amen.'

17 'Cursed is anyone who steals property
from a neighbor by moving a boundary
marker.'
And all the people will reply, 'Amen.'

18 'Cursed is anyone who leads a blind
person astray on the road.'
And all the people will reply, 'Amen.'

19 'Cursed is anyone who denies justice to
foreigners, orphans, or widows.'
And all the people will reply, 'Amen.'

20 'Cursed is anyone who has sexual
intercourse with one of his father's
wives, for he has violated his father.'
And all the people will reply, 'Amen.'

21 'Cursed is anyone who has sexual
intercourse with an animal.'
And all the people will reply, 'Amen.'

22 'Cursed is anyone who has sexual
intercourse with his sister, whether
she is the daughter of his father or his
mother.'
And all the people will reply, 'Amen.'

23 'Cursed is anyone who has sexual
intercourse with his mother-in-law.'
And all the people will reply, 'Amen.'

24 'Cursed is anyone who attacks a neighbor
in secret.'
And all the people will reply, 'Amen.'

25 'Cursed is anyone who accepts payment
to kill an innocent person.'
And all the people will reply, 'Amen.'

26 'Cursed is anyone who does not
affirm and obey the terms of these
instructions.'
And all the people will reply, 'Amen.'

Blessings for Obedience

28 "If you fully [g]obey the LORD your
God and carefully keep all his commands that I am giving you today, the LORD
your God will set you high above all the nations of the world. 2 You will experience all
these blessings if you obey the LORD your
God:

3 Your towns and your fields
will be blessed.
4 Your children and your crops
will be blessed.
The offspring of your herds and flocks
will be blessed.
5 Your fruit baskets and breadboards
will be blessed.
6 Wherever you go and whatever you do,
you will be blessed.

27:12 Deut 11:26; Josh 8:33-35
27:15 Exod 20:4, 23; Lev 19:4; Deut 4:16; 5:8; [f]*'amen* (0543) › 1 Kgs 1:36
27:16 Exod 21:17; Lev 20:9; Ezek 22:7
27:17 Deut 19:14
27:18 Lev 19:14
27:19 Exod 22:21; Lev 19:33; Deut 10:18
27:20 Lev 18:8; 20:11; Deut 22:30
27:21 Exod 22:19; Lev 18:23; 20:15
27:22 Lev 18:9; 20:17
27:23 Lev 18:17; 20:14
27:24 Exod 21:12; Lev 24:17; Num 35:30
27:25 Exod 23:8; Deut 10:17
27:26 Deut 28:15; Gal 3:10
28:1 Exod 15:26; 23:22; Lev 26:3; Deut 7:12; 11:13; [g]*shama'* (8085) › Deut 30:10
28:2 Deut 30:20
28:3 Ps 144:15
28:4 Gen 49:25
28:6 Ps 121:8

27:12-26 ***Mount Gerizim*** lies just south of Mount Ebal (27:4), and Shechem lies in the valley between (see 11:29; Josh 8:30-35). • ***proclaim a blessing:*** The tribes or their representatives were carefully placed so that as the Levites (27:14) read the covenant from the valley below, the other tribes antiphonally proclaimed their adherence to its terms by shouting *Amen,* a Hebrew term that means "May it be so."

27:13 ***proclaim a curse:*** By invoking curses on themselves if they disobeyed the terms of the covenant, these tribes served as witnesses and judges of their own future disobedience.

27:14 ***The Levites*** as a group were stationed on Mount Gerizim (27:12). The Ark of the Covenant accompanied them, and they offered sacrifices (Josh 8:30-35). It was part of the Levites' role to teach and proclaim the Torah (33:10; see note on 6:8; see also Lev 10:11).

27:15 ***carves or casts an idol:*** Such behavior would strike at the very heart of the covenant ideal by violating the second commandment (see 5:7-10).

27:16 ***dishonors father or mother:*** In the various spheres of human relationships, duty to parents ranked just below duty to God (see 5:16). To disrespect and disobey parents was just short of disrespecting God.

27:17 ***Moving a boundary marker*** to one's own advantage is tantamount to theft and clearly violates the eighth commandment (see 5:19; 19:14).

27:18 ***blind person:*** This curse would apply to treatment of physically disabled or disadvantaged people in general. Such a mean and callous act was not worthy of a member of the covenant community, in which all were to be treated alike.

27:19 It would be easy to put ***foreigners, orphans,*** and ***widows*** at a legal disadvantage or to deny them justice altogether (see 10:18; 24:17).

27:20 ***violated his father:*** See 22:30.

27:22 ***whether . . . the daughter of his father or his mother:*** Though this instruction concerns a relationship with a half sister or foster sibling, it precludes a sexual relationship with one's full sibling as well (see Lev 18:9; 20:17).

28:1-68 This section presents the conditions for receiving the covenant blessing, the nature of the blessings (28:1-14), and the curses that will come if these mandates are ignored or disobeyed (28:15-68).

28:5 The ***breadboards*** were blessed because the harvest was blessed.

28:7
Lev 26:8, 17
28:8
Deut 15:4
28:9
Exod 19:5
28:11
Deut 28:2-6, 8
28:12
Lev 26:4
Deut 11:14; 23:20
28:13
Deut 28:1, 44
28:14
Deut 5:32-33
28:15
Lev 26:14
Josh 23:15-16
28:20
Deut 8:11; 28:25
28:21
Lev 26:25
Num 14:12
Amos 4:10

7"The LORD will conquer your enemies
when they attack you. They will attack you
from one direction, but they will scatter
from you in seven!
8"The LORD will guarantee a blessing on
everything you do and will fill your storehouses with grain. The LORD your God will
bless you in the land he is giving you.
9"If you obey the commands of the LORD
your God and walk in his ways, the LORD
will establish you as his holy people as he
swore he would do. 10Then all the nations
of the world will see that you are a people
claimed by the LORD, and they will stand in
awe of you.
11"The LORD will give you prosperity
in the land he swore to your ancestors to
give you, blessing you with many children,
numerous livestock, and abundant crops.
12The LORD will send rain at the proper
time from his rich treasury in the heavens
and will bless all the work you do. You will
lend to many nations, but you will never
need to borrow from them. 13If you listen
to these commands of the LORD your God
that I am giving you today, and if you carefully obey them, the LORD will make you the
head and not the tail, and you will always be
on top and never at the bottom. 14You must
not turn away from any of the commands I
am giving you today, nor follow after other
gods and worship them.

Curses for Disobedience

15"But if you refuse to listen to the LORD
your God and do not obey all the commands
and decrees I am giving you today, all these
curses will come and overwhelm you:

16 Your towns and your fields
  will be cursed.
17 Your fruit baskets and breadboards
  will be cursed.
18 Your children and your crops
  will be cursed.
The offspring of your herds and flocks
  will be cursed.
19 Wherever you go and whatever you do,
  you will be cursed.

20"The LORD himself will send on you
curses, confusion, and frustration in everything you do, until at last you are completely
destroyed for doing evil and abandoning
me. 21The LORD will afflict you with diseases until none of you are left in the land

Curses and Blessings (27:1–29:1)

Deut 8:7-20; 11:29
Gen 9:24-27
Lev 26:3-45
Josh 8:33-35
2 Kgs 17:7-20
2 Chr 36:17-21

Nearly all treaty or covenant texts from the ancient Near East contained curses and blessings. The curses were leveled against those who violated the terms of the agreement, while blessings were promised to the faithful. This was particularly true of suzerain-vassal covenants like Deuteronomy (see Deuteronomy Introduction, "Literary Form," p. 314).

Deuteronomy presented to the assembly of Israel what God expected of the nation. The covenant required the nation of Israel to obey the Lord, and the Israelites had pledged themselves to obey (Exod 19:8). The curses and blessings section (27:1–29:1) spells out how God would reward their obedience and judge their disobedience. The curses receive more emphasis than the blessings, perhaps because people naturally pay more attention to promises than to warnings. Promised blessings in the future can easily be understood as providing well-being. However, judgment is more abstract and needs detailed, graphic description. God emphasizes the curses to drive home the consequences of wrongdoing. These warnings were very much in line with Jesus' warnings about things to come (Matt 24:1–25:46).

Israel's subsequent history bears witness to God's promise of both the blessings and the curses. When Israel was faithful to the covenant God, he blessed the people. When they rebelled, he brought judgment upon them. Israel's whole history is summarized in 2 Kgs 17:7-20. When the Israelites broke the first two commandments (5:7-10), they proceeded to violate the whole covenant. Their rebellion brought upon them the curses of ch 28.

28:7 In the Bible, the number *seven* generally conveys fullness or completion (see "Symbolic Numbers" at Rev 4:4, p. 2173). Here, the number indicates that Israel's enemies would be completely removed from the land (see note on 2:34).

28:10 When the *nations* saw the blessings of Israel, they would know that it had happened because ***you are a people claimed by the LORD*** (literally *the name of the LORD is called over you*). When the nations saw Israel, they would think of the Lord and his faithfulness.

28:12 ***his rich treasury in the heavens:*** This metaphor describes the clouds that provide life-giving rain to the earth.

28:13 ***the head and not the tail:*** If Israel obeyed the terms of the covenant, it would lead the nations and not be subject to them.

28:17 If they disobeyed the commands of the covenant, Israel could expect God to judge them with the curse of agricultural barrenness (cp. 28:5).

28:21 The diseases that ***afflict*** (or *cling to*) Israel would be chronic, not releasing their hold until the nation had succumbed.

you are about to enter and occupy. 22The LORD will strike you with wasting diseases, fever, and inflammation, with scorching heat and drought, and with blight and mildew. These disasters will pursue you until you die. 23The skies above will be as unyielding as bronze, and the earth beneath will be as hard as iron. 24The LORD will change the rain that falls on your land into powder, and dust will pour down from the sky until you are destroyed.

25"The LORD will cause you to be defeated by your enemies. You will attack your enemies from one direction, but you will scatter from them in seven! You will be an object of horror to all the kingdoms of the earth. 26Your corpses will be food for all the scavenging birds and wild animals, and no one will be there to chase them away.

27"The LORD will afflict you with the boils of Egypt and with tumors, scurvy, and the itch, from which you cannot be cured. 28The LORD will strike you with madness, blindness, and panic. 29You will grope around in broad daylight like a blind person groping in the darkness, but you will not find your way. You will be oppressed and robbed continually, and no one will come to save you.

30"You will be engaged to a woman, but another man will sleep with her. You will build a house, but someone else will live in it. You will plant a vineyard, but you will never enjoy its fruit. 31Your ox will be butchered before your eyes, but you will not eat a single bite of the meat. Your donkey will be taken from you, never to be returned. Your sheep and goats will be given to your enemies, and no one will be there to help you. 32You will watch as your sons and daughters are taken away as slaves. Your heart will break for them, but you won't be able to help them. 33A foreign nation you have never heard about will eat the crops you worked so hard to grow. You will suffer under constant oppression and harsh treatment. 34You will go mad because of all the tragedy you see around you. 35The LORD will cover your knees and legs with incurable boils. In fact, you will be covered from head to foot.

36"The LORD will exile you and your king to a nation unknown to you and your ancestors. There in exile you will worship gods of wood and stone! 37You will become an object of horror, ridicule, and mockery among all the nations to which the LORD sends you.

38"You will plant much but harvest little, for [h]locusts will eat your crops. 39You will plant vineyards and care for them, but you will not drink the wine or eat the grapes, for worms will destroy the vines. 40You will grow olive trees throughout your land, but you will never use the olive oil, for the fruit will drop before it ripens. 41You will have sons and daughters, but you will lose them, for they will be led away into captivity. 42Swarms of insects will destroy your trees and crops.

43"The foreigners living among you will become stronger and stronger, while you become weaker and weaker. 44They will lend money to you, but you will not lend to them. They will be the head, and you will be the tail!

45"If you refuse to listen to the LORD your God and to obey the commands and decrees he has given you, all these curses will pursue and overtake you until you are destroyed. 46These horrors will serve as a sign and warning among you and your descendants forever. 47If you do not serve the LORD your God with joy and enthusiasm for the abundant benefits you have received, 48you will serve your enemies whom the LORD will send against you. You will be left hungry, thirsty, naked, and lacking in everything. The LORD will put an iron yoke on your neck, oppressing you harshly until he has destroyed you.

28:23
Lev 26:19

28:24
Deut 11:17
1 Kgs 17:1
Jer 14:1

28:25
2 Chr 29:8
Isa 30:17
Jer 15:4

28:26
Ps 79:2
Jer 7:33; 16:4; 19:7; 34:20

28:27
Exod 9:9; 15:26
Deut 7:15
1 Sam 5:6, 9, 12

28:29
Exod 10:21
Job 5:14
Isa 59:10

28:30
Deut 20:6-7
Job 31:10
Isa 65:22
Amos 5:11

28:35
Job 2:7

28:36
2 Kgs 17:4, 6; 24:12, 14; 25:7, 11

28:38
Lev 26:20
Isa 5:10
Mic 6:15
[h]*'arbeh* (0697)
›Judg 6:5

28:41
Deut 28:32

28:42
Deut 28:38

28:44
Deut 28:12-13

28:45
Deut 4:25-26

28:47
Deut 32:15

28:22 Some scholars identify these symptoms with tuberculosis.

28:23 In this graphic picture of drought and famine, the sky dams up the rain, making the earth hard and unfruitful.

28:24 The only thing even resembling rain would be the swirling *dust* that coats everything to suffocation.

28:25 This verse reverses the blessing of 28:7; Israel would be forced to *scatter from* their enemies in *seven* directions—i.e., completely and totally.

28:27 *the boils of Egypt:* See Exod 9:8-12. • *tumors:* Cp. 1 Sam 5:6, 9, 12. • *scurvy:* Perhaps dermatitis. • *The itch* is also symptomatic of dermatitis.

28:36 *exile you:* This prediction had two major fulfillments in OT times—the Assyrian exile of Samaria in 722 BC and the Babylonian conquest and exile of Jerusalem in 586 BC.

28:43 *foreigners* (literally *sojourners*): In God's day of judgment, those regarded as the weakest and most vulnerable elements of Israelite society (see 29:11) would dominate.

28:44 *the head . . . the tail:* Rather than Israel's leading the nations, the reverse would be true when God punishes his people (see 28:13).

28:46 *sign and warning* (literally *sign and wonder*): This expression indicates God's miraculous acts that arrest the attention of those who witness them and attest to his power and sovereignty (see 6:22). They are intended to produce intense fear among his own people.

28:48 An *iron yoke* is portrayed in various inscriptions and artistic representations. The use of this hard, unyielding metal emphasizes the cruelty and severity of the bondage Israel would experience if it remained unrepentant.

28:49
Isa 5:26; 7:18
Jer 5:15
28:52
Jer 10:17-18
Zeph 1:14-15
28:53
Lev 26:29
Jer 19:9
Lam 2:20; 4:10
28:60
Deut 28:21, 27
28:62
Deut 1:10
28:63
Jer 45:4
28:64
Lev 26:33
Deut 4:27; 32:17
Neh 1:8
28:65
Lam 1:3
28:66
Heb 10:27

49"The LORD will bring a distant nation
against you from the end of the earth, and
it will swoop down on you like a vulture.
It is a nation whose language you do not
understand, 50a fierce and heartless nation that shows no respect for the old and
no pity for the young. 51Its armies will
devour your livestock and crops, and you
will be destroyed. They will leave you no
grain, new wine, olive oil, calves, or lambs,
and you will starve to death. 52They will
attack your cities until all the fortified
walls in your land—the walls you trusted
to protect you—are knocked down. They
will attack all the towns in the land the
LORD your God has given you.

53"The siege and terrible distress of the
enemy's attack will be so severe that you
will eat the flesh of your own sons and
daughters, whom the LORD your God has
given you. 54The most tenderhearted man
among you will have no compassion for his
own brother, his beloved wife, and his surviving children. 55He will refuse to share
with them the flesh he is devouring—the
flesh of one of his own children—because
he has nothing else to eat during the siege
and terrible distress that your enemy will
inflict on all your towns. 56The most tender
and delicate woman among you—so delicate
she would not so much as touch the ground
with her foot—will be selfish toward the
husband she loves and toward her own son
or daughter. 57She will hide from them the
afterbirth and the new baby she has borne,
so that she herself can secretly eat them.
She will have nothing else to eat during the
siege and terrible distress that your enemy
will inflict on all your towns.

58"If you refuse to obey all the words
of instruction that are written in this
book, and if you do not fear the glorious
and awesome name of the LORD your God,
59then the LORD will overwhelm you and
your children with indescribable plagues.
These plagues will be intense and without
relief, making you miserable and unbearably sick. 60He will afflict you with all the
diseases of Egypt that you feared so much,
and you will have no relief. 61The LORD
will afflict you with every sickness and
plague there is, even those not mentioned
in this Book of Instruction, until you are
destroyed. 62Though you become as numerous as the stars in the sky, few of you
will be left because you would not listen to
the LORD your God.

63"Just as the LORD has found great pleasure in causing you to prosper and multiply,
the LORD will find pleasure in destroying
you. You will be torn from the land you are
about to enter and occupy. 64For the LORD
will scatter you among all the nations from
one end of the earth to the other. There you
will worship foreign gods that neither you
nor your ancestors have known, gods made
of wood and stone! 65There among those
nations you will find no peace or place to
rest. And the LORD will cause your heart
to tremble, your eyesight to fail, and your
soul to despair. 66Your life will constantly
hang in the balance. You will live night and
day in fear, unsure if you will survive. 67In
the morning you will say, 'If only it were
night!' And in the evening you will say, 'If
only it were morning!' For you will be terrified by the awful horrors you see around
you. 68Then the LORD will send you back to
Egypt in ships, to a destination I promised
you would never see again. There you will
offer to sell yourselves to your enemies as
slaves, but no one will buy you."

28:49 ***like a vulture*** (or ***eagle***): This simile indicates how rapidly the enemy would come. • ***whose language you do not understand:*** Both Assyrian and Babylonian were dialects of Akkadian, a language that was related to Hebrew but vastly different in grammar, syntax, and vocabulary (see Isa 36:11-13).

28:50 The Assyrians were ***fierce and heartless*** toward their defeated enemies. A favorite instrument of torture was a stake on which they impaled their victims alive (see Isa 33:19; Nah 2:1-7).

28:54 A ***tenderhearted man*** was sheltered from the dark and disgusting side of life. He had never experienced the horrors that would befall him.

28:56 ***not . . . touch the ground:*** This woman was so fastidious that she avoided walking barefoot on the soil.

28:57 ***afterbirth:*** This horrific scenario depicts a mother so hungry as to eat a human placenta and ***the new baby she has borne.***

28:58 The context suggests that ***all the words of instruction*** (literally ***all the words of this torah***) refers to the entire book of Deuteronomy, in which lists of blessings and curses were a major part (see 27:3). • ***If you do not fear the . . . name***—i.e., do not fear God himself (see note on 7:21).

28:60 The ***diseases of Egypt*** were not just general plagues but those associated with physical illness (see Exod 9:8-12).

28:64 ***foreign gods:*** This phrase does not suggest the actual existence of other deities. The OT is clear that there is only one God, the Lord. However, the pagans among whom Israel would live did worship other gods; the danger was that Israel would adopt the same practices.

28:68 The threat of being sent ***back to Egypt*** referred to any future exile of God's people, a reversal of the exodus from freedom to bondage. • ***no one will buy you:*** The disobedient and cursed Israelites would be so little esteemed that they would be unable to command any price as slaves. By contrast, the Lord had redeemed Israel from enslavement at great cost (see 9:26).

29 These are the terms of the [i]cov-
enant the LORD commanded Moses
to make with the Israelites while they were
in the land of Moab, in addition to the [i]cov-
enant he had made with them at Mount
Sinai.

Covenant Epilogue (29:2–30:20)
Moses Reviews the Covenant
2Moses summoned all the Israelites and
said to them, "You have seen with your own
eyes everything the LORD did in the land of
Egypt to Pharaoh and to all his servants and
to his whole country—3all the great tests
of strength, the miraculous signs, and the
amazing wonders. 4But to this day the LORD
has not given you minds that understand,
nor eyes that see, nor ears that hear! 5For
forty years I led you through the wilderness, yet your clothes and sandals did not
wear out. 6You ate no bread and drank no
wine or other alcoholic drink, but he gave
you food so you would know that he is the
LORD your God.

7"When we came here, King Sihon of
Heshbon and King Og of Bashan came out
to fight against us, but we defeated them.
8We took their land and gave it to the tribes
of Reuben and Gad and to the half-tribe of
Manasseh as their grant of land.

9"Therefore, obey the terms of this covenant so that you will prosper in everything
you do. 10All of you—tribal leaders, elders,
officers, all the men of Israel—are standing today in the presence of the LORD your
God. 11Your little ones and your wives are
with you, as well as the foreigners living
among you who chop your wood and carry
your water. 12You are standing here today
to enter into the covenant of the LORD your
God. The LORD is making this covenant, including the curses. 13By entering into the
covenant today, he will establish you as his
people and confirm that he is your God, just
as he promised you and as he swore to your
ancestors Abraham, Isaac, and Jacob.

14"But you are not the only ones with
whom I am making this covenant with its
curses. 15I am making this covenant both
with you who stand here today in the presence of the LORD our God, and also with the
future generations who are not standing
here today.

16"You remember how we lived in the
land of Egypt and how we traveled through
the lands of enemy nations as we left. 17You
have seen their detestable practices and
their idols made of wood, stone, silver, and
gold. 18I am making this covenant with you
so that no one among you—no man, woman,
clan, or tribe—will turn away from the LORD
our God to worship these gods of other nations, and so that no root among you bears
bitter and poisonous fruit.

19"Those who hear the warnings of this
curse should not congratulate themselves,
thinking, 'I am safe, even though I am following the desires of my own stubborn [i]heart.'
This would lead to utter ruin! 20The LORD
will never pardon such people. Instead his
anger and jealousy will burn against them.
All the curses written in this book will come
down on them, and the LORD will erase their
names from under heaven. 21The LORD will
separate them from all the tribes of Israel,

29:1 Lev 27:34; Deut 1:1-5; 5:1; [i]*berith* (1285) ›Deut 33:9
29:2 Exod 19:4
29:4 Isa 6:9-10; Acts 28:26; *Rom 11:8
29:5 Deut 8:2, 4
29:7 Num 21:21; Deut 1:2-5; 2:26
29:8 Num 32:31; Deut 3:12
29:9 Exod 19:5; Deut 4:6; Josh 1:7
29:11 Josh 9:21, 23, 27
29:13 Gen 17:7; Exod 6:7
29:14 Jer 31:31; Heb 8:7
29:17 Exod 20:23; Deut 4:28; 28:36
29:18 Deut 13:6; 32:32; Heb 12:15
29:19 [i]*leb* (3820) ›2 Sam 17:10
29:20 Deut 9:14; 2 Kgs 14:27; Ps 74:1; 80:4

29:1 Verse 29:1 is numbered 28:69 in the Hebrew text. • The ***land of Moab*** was the region east of the Jordan where Deuteronomy was composed and delivered to Israel. • ***Mount Sinai:*** Hebrew *Horeb*, another name for Sinai; see note on 1:2.

29:2–30:20 Anticipating his death, Moses composed a farewell address, briefly reviewing Israel's history since the Exodus. He charged the nation to pledge their fidelity to the Lord. This section of Deuteronomy makes it clear that grace is not just a NT doctrine: It undergirds every aspect of Israel's relationship with the Lord.

29:2-29 Verses 29:2-29 are numbered 29:1-28 in the Hebrew text.

29:3 ***signs . . . wonders:*** See notes on 6:22; 7:19.

29:6 ***but he gave you food:*** This clause does not appear in the Hebrew but is implied by its context.

29:7 ***King Sihon of Heshbon,*** ruler of the Amorites, had controlled an area from the Arnon River to the Ammonite border. See Num 21:31-35. • ***Heshbon:*** See 1:4; 2:24. • ***King Og of Bashan*** had ruled an Amorite kingdom east of the Sea of Galilee (see 3:1).

29:8 ***Reuben and Gad and . . . the half-tribe of Manasseh*** were granted their request to settle in the area east of the Jordan (see 3:12-13).

29:11 ***foreigners*** (literally *sojourners*): See note on 10:18. • The saying ***chop your wood and carry your water*** was a cliché for any servile work (see Josh 9:22-27).

29:12 The technical phrase ***to enter into the covenant*** meant subscribing to the terms of the agreement.

29:15 ***future generations:*** The covenant made with Moses' generation was also for generations yet to be born. Abraham's descendants of the future would have the privileges of the covenant, but they would also need to obey it personally to enjoy its blessings (see 4:9).

29:17 The ***detestable practices*** were abominable manifestations of paganism, especially regarding worship (see 7:25-26; 12:31; 13:14). • ***idols:*** The Hebrew term, meaning *round things*, probably alludes to dung. These objects were so reprehensible that they were compared to excrement.

29:18 This metaphor describes idolatry (the ***root***), which, if cultivated, would result in idol worship (the ***fruit***).

29:19 An attitude of nonchalance or smugness regarding God's judgment would ***lead to utter ruin.***

29:20 ***jealousy:*** See note on 4:24. • ***erase their names:*** To forget the name of a people resulted in eventually forgetting their very existence. The most unspeakable tragedy would be for God to treat the people of Israel as though they had never existed (see 7:24; Exod 32:32-33; 2 Kgs 14:27).

29:22 Jer 19:8
29:23 Gen 19:24; Isa 1:7; 34:9; 64:11
29:24 1 Kgs 9:8; Jer 22:8-9
29:25 2 Kgs 17:9; 2 Chr 36:13
29:26 [k]*khawah* (7812) ‣Neh 8:6
29:27 Deut 29:20
29:28 1 Kgs 14:15; Ezek 19:12
29:29 John 5:39; Acts 1:7; 17:11
30:1 Lev 26:40-41; Deut 4:30; 11:26
30:2 Deut 4:29-30; Neh 1:9
30:3 Gen 28:15; Matt 23:37; John 11:51-52
30:4 Isa 43:6
30:5 Deut 13:17; Jer 29:14; 30:3
30:7 Deut 7:15
30:9 Deut 15:10; 29:9
30:10 Deut 4:29; [a]*shama'* (8085) ‣Josh 1:18; [b]*torah* (8451) ‣Deut 31:9; [c]*shub* (7725) ‣2 Kgs 23:25
30:11 Isa 45:19

to pour out on them all the curses of the covenant recorded in this Book of Instruction.
22“Then the generations to come, both
your own descendants and the foreigners
who come from distant lands, will see the
devastation of the land and the diseases
the LORD inflicts on it. 23They will exclaim,
‘The whole land is devastated by sulfur and
salt. It is a wasteland with nothing planted
and nothing growing, not even a blade of
grass. It is like the cities of Sodom and Gomorrah, Admah and Zeboiim, which the
LORD destroyed in his intense anger.’
24“And all the surrounding nations will
ask, ‘Why has the LORD done this to this
land? Why was he so angry?’
25“And the answer will be, ‘This happened
because the people of the land abandoned
the covenant that the LORD, the God of their
ancestors, made with them when he brought
them out of the land of Egypt. 26Instead,
they turned away to serve and [k]worship
gods they had not known before, gods that
were not from the LORD. 27That is why the
LORD’s anger has burned against this land,
bringing down on it every curse recorded
in this book. 28In great anger and fury the
LORD uprooted his people from their land
and banished them to another land, where
they still live today!’
29“The LORD our God has secrets known
to no one. We are not accountable for them,
but we and our children are accountable
forever for all that he has revealed to us, so
that we may obey all the terms of these instructions.

A Call to Return to the LORD

30 “In the future, when you experience all these blessings and curses I
have listed for you, and when you are living
among the nations to which the LORD your
God has exiled you, take to heart all these
instructions. 2If at that time you and your children return to the LORD your God, and if you
obey with all your heart and all your soul all
the commands I have given you today, 3then
the LORD your God will restore your fortunes.
He will have mercy on you and gather you
back from all the nations where he has scattered you. 4Even though you are banished to
the ends of the earth, the LORD your God will
gather you from there and bring you back
again. 5The LORD your God will return you
to the land that belonged to your ancestors,
and you will possess that land again. Then
he will make you even more prosperous and
numerous than your ancestors!
6“The LORD your God will change your
heart and the hearts of all your descendants,
so that you will love him with all your heart
and soul and so you may live! 7The LORD
your God will inflict all these curses on your
enemies and on those who hate and persecute you. 8Then you will again obey the
LORD and keep all his commands that I am
giving you today.
9“The LORD your God will then make you
successful in everything you do. He will give
you many children and numerous livestock,
and he will cause your fields to produce
abundant harvests, for the LORD will again
delight in being good to you as he was to
your ancestors. 10The LORD your God will delight in you if you [a]obey his voice and keep
the commands and decrees written in this
Book of [b]Instruction, and if you [c]turn to the
LORD your God with all your heart and soul.

The Choice of Life or Death

11“This command I am giving you today is
not too difficult for you to understand, and

29:21 ***Book of Instruction*** (literally *book of the torah*): Here, this phrase refers to all of Deuteronomy, of which the list of curses (ch 28) is a part (see 27:3).

29:23 ***like . . . Sodom and Gomorrah, Admah and Zeboiim:*** In the days of Abraham and Lot, these cities were destroyed because of their gross immorality; their destruction was associated with ***sulfur and salt*** (Gen 19:23-28).

29:25-28 This explanation anticipates a future when people would look back at Israel’s history of rebellion and easily understand why they were in exile.

29:27 The phrase *this book* refers at least to Deuteronomy and perhaps to the first five books of the OT (the Pentateuch).

29:29 ***secrets known to no one:*** There is an apparent contradiction between God’s covenant promises to Israel on the one hand and Israel’s being sent into exile on the other. What purpose could there be in such a mysterious turn of events? Only God knows. • ***the terms of these instructions*** (literally *the words of this torah*): See 4:44; 27:3.

30:1-10 Repentance was the only solution to the threat of judgment. The possibility of blessing and the prevention of judgment both depended on a proper relationship with the Lord.

30:1 ***These blessings and curses:*** See 27:1–28:68.

30:2-3 ***with all your heart and all your soul:*** The expectation of these verses was clearly articulated in the *Shema*, Israel’s great statement of covenant faith and commitment (cp. 6:4). Obedience to the covenant was a prerequisite necessary for Israel to receive God’s forgiveness and return to its land.

30:6 ***change your heart*** (literally *circumcise your heart*): This work of God, initiated by his grace, would result in Israel’s regeneration and identify the nation as the Lord’s true people (see 10:16; Jer 4:4; Rom 4:1-12).

30:11-20 Adherence to the covenant terms that Moses had outlined would give life; disobedience would surely bring death. Life and death refer to physical, mortal life in the land—of individuals and of the community of Israel.

30:11 ***This command*** refers to the whole covenant text, all of Deuteronomy (see 4:2; 5:29; 7:9).

it is not beyond your reach. 12It is not kept in
heaven, so distant that you must ask, 'Who
will go up to heaven and bring it down so
we can hear it and obey?' 13It is not kept beyond the sea, so far away that you must ask,
'Who will cross the sea to bring it to us so
we can hear it and obey?' 14No, the message
is very close at hand; it is on your lips and in
your heart so that you can obey it.
15"Now listen! Today I am giving you a
choice between life and death, between
prosperity and disaster. 16For I command
you this day to love the LORD your God and
to keep his commands, decrees, and regulations by walking in his ways. If you do this,
you will live and multiply, and the LORD
your God will bless you and the land you are
about to enter and occupy.
17"But if your heart turns away and you
refuse to listen, and if you are drawn away
to serve and worship other gods, 18then I
warn you now that you will certainly be destroyed. You will not live a long, good life
in the land you are crossing the Jordan to
occupy.
19"Today I have given you the choice between life and death, between [d]blessings
and curses. Now I call on heaven and earth
to witness the choice you make. Oh, that you
would choose life, so that you and your descendants might live! 20You can make this
choice by loving the LORD your God, obeying him, and committing yourself firmly to
him. This is the key to your life. And if you
love and obey the LORD, you will live long in
the land the LORD swore to give your ancestors Abraham, Isaac, and Jacob."

6. MOSES' FAREWELL (31:1–34:12)

Deposit of the Text and Provision for Implementation (31:1-29)

Joshua Becomes Israel's Leader

31
When Moses had finished giving
these instructions to all the people
of Israel, 2he said, "I am now 120 years old,
and I am no longer able to lead you. The
LORD has told me, 'You will not cross the
Jordan River.' 3But the LORD your God himself will cross over ahead of you. He will
destroy the nations living there, and you
will take possession of their land. Joshua
will lead you across the river, just as the
LORD promised.
4"The LORD will destroy the nations living in the land, just as he destroyed Sihon
and Og, the kings of the Amorites. 5The
LORD will hand over to you the people who
live there, and you must deal with them as
I have commanded you. 6So be strong and
courageous! Do not be afraid and do not
panic before them. For the LORD your God
will personally go ahead of you. He will neither fail you nor abandon you."
7Then Moses called for Joshua, and as all
Israel watched, he said to him, "Be strong
and courageous! For you will lead these
people into the land that the LORD swore
to their ancestors he would give them. You
are the one who will divide it among them
as their grants of land. 8Do not be afraid or
discouraged, for the LORD will personally
go ahead of you. He will be with you; he will
neither fail you nor abandon you."

Public Reading of the Book of Instruction

9So Moses wrote this entire body of [e]instruc-
tion in a book and gave it to the priests, who

30:12-14
*Rom 10:6-8
30:15
Deut 11:26
Jer 21:8
Matt 7:13-14
30:16
Deut 4:1; 6:5
30:18
Deut 4:26
30:19
Deut 4:26; 30:1
[d]*berakah* (1293)
▸Deut 33:1
30:20
Deut 10:20; 13:4
31:2
Deut 34:7
31:3
Num 27:18
31:6
Deut 20:1
*Heb 13:5
31:7
Deut 1:38; 3:28
31:9
Num 4:5-6
Deut 10:8
[e]*torah* (8451)
▸Deut 32:46

30:12 ***not kept in heaven:*** The revelation of God is not known only to him but is accessible to human beings (see Rom 10:6-8).

30:13 ***not kept beyond the sea:*** God's purposes are not in the custody of faraway nations but are available to his people (see Rom 10:6-8).

30:14 The message of salvation is objectively close (***on your lips***) and subjectively near (***in your heart***). It is capable of being taught and learned (see 6:6-7).

30:16 ***love the LORD your God:*** This paraphrases the *Shema*, Israel's central covenant affirmation (see 6:5). To love God means to obey him in every respect, which results in divine blessing.

30:19 ***life and death . . . blessings and curses:*** This grammatical structure suggests an equivalence between *life* and *blessing* and between *death* and *curses.* The essence of a blessing is life, and the essence of a curse is death. • ***I call on heaven and earth to witness:*** See note on 4:26.

30:20 ***This is the key:*** Or *He is the key.* • ***the key to your life:*** In its most meaningful sense, life consists of absolute commitment to the Lord.

31:1-29 For covenant documents to have abiding authority and relevance, they must be kept perpetually in a place where both parties could have easy access to them. The book of Deuteronomy had to be preserved for future reference so that Israel would always be reminded to submit to the Lord's sovereignty.

31:1-8 Moses' impending death meant that his role as covenant administrator would soon be over. Joshua had to be properly and publicly introduced as his successor with the same authority.

31:1 ***Moses had finished giving these instructions:*** As in Dead Sea Scrolls and Greek version; Masoretic Text reads *Moses went and spoke.* Based on the context, ***these instructions*** refers to all of Deuteronomy (see 1:1).

31:3 ***The LORD . . . will cross over ahead of you:*** The conquest would be God's war. The conflict would be commanded, initiated, and led by the Divine Warrior, the Lord God of Israel (see 1:30). • From the earliest days of the Sinai wandering (Exod 17:8) to the present, ***Joshua*** had served as Moses' attendant; now he was divinely appointed as Moses' successor (see 1:38; 3:23-29; Num 27:15-23).

31:4 ***Sihon and Og:*** See note on 2:24; Num 21:21-35.

31:6 ***He will neither fail you nor abandon you:*** This encouragement for Israel on the verge of taking possession of the Promised Land also states a general principle of God's care for his people (see also Heb 13:5).

31:9-13 So that future generations in Israel could be reminded of their

31:10 Deut 15:1
31:12 Deut 4:10
31:14 Num 27:13; Deut 34:5
31:15 Exod 33:9
31:16 Deut 4:25; 32:50; Judg 2:11; 10:6
31:17 Judg 2:12-14
31:20 Deut 6:10-12; 8:19; 11:16-17
31:21 Lev 26:41

carried the Ark of the LORD's Covenant, and
to the elders of Israel. [10]Then Moses gave
them this command: "At the end of every
seventh year, the Year of Release, during
the Festival of Shelters, [11]you must read
this Book of Instruction to all the people of
Israel when they assemble before the LORD
your God at the place he chooses. [12]Call
them all together—men, women, children,
and the foreigners living in your towns—so
they may hear this Book of Instruction
and learn to fear the LORD your God and
carefully obey all the terms of these instructions. [13]Do this so that your children who
have not known these instructions will hear
them and will learn to fear the LORD your
God. Do this as long as you live in the land
you are crossing the Jordan to occupy."

Israel's Disobedience Predicted

[14]Then the LORD said to Moses, "The time
has come for you to die. Call Joshua and
present yourselves at the Tabernacle, so that
I may commission him there." So Moses and
Joshua went and presented themselves at
the Tabernacle. [15]And the LORD appeared
to them in a pillar of cloud that stood at the
entrance to the sacred tent.

[16]The LORD said to Moses, "You are about
to die and join your ancestors. After you are
gone, these people will begin to worship foreign gods, the gods of the land where they
are going. They will abandon me and break
my covenant that I have made with them.
[17]Then my anger will blaze forth against
them. I will abandon them, hiding my face
from them, and they will be devoured. Terrible trouble will come down on them, and on
that day they will say, 'These disasters have
come down on us because God is no longer
among us!' [18]At that time I will hide my face
from them on account of all the evil they
commit by worshiping other gods.

[19]"So write down the words of this song,
and teach it to the people of Israel. Help
them learn it, so it may serve as a witness
for me against them. [20]For I will bring them
into the land I swore to give their ancestors—
a land flowing with milk and honey. There
they will become prosperous, eat all the
food they want, and become fat. But they
will begin to worship other gods; they will
despise me and break my covenant. [21]And
when great disasters come down on them,
this song will stand as evidence against
them, for it will never be forgotten by their
descendants. I know the intentions of these
people, even now before they have entered
the land I swore to give them."

[22]So that very day Moses wrote down the
words of the song and taught it to the Israelites.

[23]Then the LORD commissioned Joshua
son of Nun with these words: "Be strong

---

covenant obligations, the covenant text was to be read publicly. Doing so was a practical necessity in an era when personal copies of documents were not generally available.

31:9 ***Ark of the LORD's Covenant:*** This gold-plated wooden chest contained the two stone tablets bearing the text of the Ten Commandments. It was also the Lord's throne, as he sat there invisibly among his people (see note on 10:1).

31:10 The ***Year of Release*** was the ***seventh year*** of the calendar, not the seventh year of a given transaction between individuals. All debts were to be cancelled and Hebrew bond servants released from obligation to their creditors (see 15:1-3). • ***Festival of Shelters*** (also known as the Feast of Tabernacles): The people observed this celebration in the seventh month (*Tishri,* September/October) of every year to commemorate God's miraculous preservation of Israel in the wilderness. It also celebrated the fall harvest (see 16:13-15).

31:11 ***the place he chooses:*** See note on 12:18.

31:12 Even ***foreigners*** living among the Israelites were to submit to the requirements of the covenant law. Despite their disadvantaged status, the Lord would provide for them (see 10:18).

31:14 ***Tabernacle*** (literally *Tent of Meeting*): At first, the Tent of Meeting was a provisional place of encounter between God and his people (especially Moses). Later, the term became synonymous with the Tabernacle (see Exod 28:43; 33:7-11; 40:2; Num 11:16, 24, 26; 12:4). See note on Lev 1:1.

31:15 Since God is spirit, he cannot be seen unless he chooses to manifest his glory physically. The ***pillar of cloud*** was such a manifestation, sometimes called a *theophany* (see note on 1:33). When the pillar appeared, those who saw it recognized in it the presence of God (see Exod 33:9; Num 12:5).

31:18 ***I will hide my face:*** The invisible God used this figure of speech (see note on 8:2) to communicate the breaking of fellowship between himself and his people. He turned away to indicate his rejection and repudiation.

31:19-22 When sung by the collective community in days to come, ***this song*** (32:1-43) would remind the people of God's faithfulness in the past and of their too-frequent disloyalty. The major blessings for obedience and curses for disobedience were implicit in the song. The people of Israel would sing it as a sign that they had placed themselves under these promises and threats. Through music, they would be reminded of God's blessings for obedience and would invoke God's judgment should they prove unfaithful.

31:19 ***a witness:*** See note on 4:26.

31:20 ***land flowing with milk and honey:*** See note on 6:3. • ***become fat:*** Fatness did not imply obesity or self-indulgence but blessing and prosperity. • ***despise me:*** Israel would disregard the Lord and treat him lightly by falsely assuming that their prosperity had come through their own efforts or through the false gods of the land.

31:22 ***Moses wrote down the words:*** This statement is good evidence for the traditional view that Moses wrote Deuteronomy (see Deuteronomy Introduction, "Authorship," p. 313).

31:23 ***I will be with you:*** These words given to Joshua were the same words God spoke to Moses at the burning bush, when he called him to lead Israel out of Egypt (Exod 3:12). The same God, with the same assurance, was able to guarantee the same results.

and courageous, for you must bring the
people of Israel into the land I swore to give
them. I will be with you."
24 When Moses had finished writing this
entire body of instruction in a book, 25 he
gave this command to the Levites who
carried the Ark of the LORD's Covenant:
26 "Take this Book of Instruction and place
it beside the Ark of the Covenant of the
LORD your God, so it may remain there as
a witness against the people of Israel. 27 For
I know how rebellious and stubborn you
are. Even now, while I am still alive and am
here with you, you have rebelled against the
LORD. How much more rebellious will you
be after my death!
28 "Now summon all the elders and officials of your tribes, so that I can speak to
them directly and call heaven and earth to
witness against them. 29 I know that after my
death you will become utterly corrupt and
will turn from the way I have commanded
you to follow. In the days to come, disaster
will come down on you, for you will do what
is evil in the LORD's sight, making him very
angry with your actions."

The Song of Moses (31:30–32:47)

30 So Moses recited this entire song publicly
to the assembly of Israel:

32 1 "Listen, O heavens, and I will speak!
Hear, O earth, the words that I say!
2 Let my teaching fall on you like rain;
let my speech settle like dew.
Let my words fall like rain on tender grass,
like gentle showers on young plants.
3 I will proclaim the name of the LORD;
how glorious is our God!
4 He is the [f]Rock; his deeds are [g]perfect.
Everything he does is just and fair.
He is a faithful God who does no wrong;
how just and upright he is!

5 "But they have acted corruptly toward him;
when they act so perversely,
are they really his children?
They are a deceitful and twisted generation.
6 Is this the way you repay the LORD,
you foolish and senseless people?
Isn't he your Father who created you?
Has he not made you and established you?
7 Remember the days of long ago;
think about the generations past.
Ask your father, and he will inform you.
Inquire of your [h]elders, and they will tell you.
8 When the [i]Most High assigned lands to the nations,
when he divided up the human race,
he established the boundaries of the peoples
according to the number in his heavenly court.

9 "For the people of Israel belong to the LORD;
Jacob is his special possession.

31:25 Deut 31:9
31:27 Deut 9:7, 24
31:28 Deut 30:19; 32:1
31:29 Deut 32:5
32:1 Deut 4:26; Isa 1:2
32:2 Ps 72:6; Isa 55:10
32:3 Gen 18:25; Exod 34:5-6; Deut 3:24
32:4 Gen 49:24; Deut 32:18; 2 Sam 22:2
[f]*tsur* (6697) ▸Deut 32:13
[g]*tamim* (8549) ▸2 Sam 22:24
32:5 Deut 4:25; 31:27; Matt 17:17
32:6 Deut 1:31; 32:28
32:7 Deut 7:18-19
[h]*zaqen* (2205) ▸Josh 20:4
32:8 [i]*'elyon* (5945) ▸Ps 7:17
32:9 1 Kgs 8:51; Jer 10:16

31:25 ***Ark of the LORD's Covenant:*** See note on 31:9.

31:26 ***beside the Ark:*** Unlike the stone tablets, the scroll of Deuteronomy was not to be placed in the Ark but near it, in the inner sanctuary of the Tabernacle and, later, of the Temple (see 31:9; Exod 25:16; 26:33). • ***a witness:*** Like the song that the Israelites were to sing (see 31:19), the presence of the scroll of Deuteronomy would be a perpetual reminder of Israel's covenant obligations and privileges (see 31:10, 19).

31:28 ***call heaven and earth to witness:*** See note on 4:26; see also 30:19.

31:30–32:47 In ancient times, the validity of a treaty arrangement between individuals or nations was secured by both parties' vows. Israel's promise was in the song of witness that Moses composed under divine inspiration (31:19-22). When Israel sang the song (presumably as part of a regular covenant-renewal ceremony; 31:21), they invoked upon themselves the covenant's judgments and reminded themselves of its promises.

32:1 ***Listen, O heavens. . . . Hear, O earth:*** Moses appealed to the witnesses of the covenant to note Israel's confession and commitment as well as its anticipated disobedience and disloyalty (see 30:19).

32:2 ***like rain . . . like dew:*** This simile shows the refreshing gentleness of Moses' teaching. It should produce the fruit of obedience in the hearts of God's people.

32:4 ***the Rock:*** This metaphor represents the Lord as strong, stable, and reliable; he is more than capable of providing righteousness and justice (see 32:15, 18, 30; Hab 1:12).

32:5 ***are they really his children?*** The meaning of the Hebrew is uncertain.

32:7 ***Ask your father:*** History instructs those who are willing to learn from it. In the wisdom tradition of the OT, the father was given the task of teaching his children the lessons that had previously been transmitted to him (see, e.g., Prov 1:8; 2:1; 3:1).

32:8 ***the Most High*** (Hebrew *'Elyon*): Abraham learned this name for God when he encountered Melchizedek (Gen 14:19). This ancient name describes God's universal sovereignty. • ***assigned lands:*** One evidence of God's sovereignty was his distribution of lands to the nations (see Gen 10). • ***the number in his heavenly court:*** As in Dead Sea Scrolls, which read *the number of the sons of God,* and Greek version, which reads *the number of the angels of God;* Masoretic Text reads *the number of the sons of Israel.* These different translations reflect different textual traditions. The point is clear: God is sovereign over and concerned with all nations and has allotted their land in accord with his own purposes (see Ps 74:17; Acts 17:26).

32:9 ***his special possession*** (literally *his inheritance*): God declared Israel to be his son, whom he redeemed from bondage in Egypt (see Exod 4:22-23; 13:15; Deut 7:6).

32:10 Ps 17:8
32:11 Exod 19:4; Ps 17:8; 18:10-18
32:12 Deut 4:35; Isa 43:12
32:13 Job 29:6; Ps 81:16; [j]*tsur* (6697) ‣Deut 32:18
32:14 Ps 147:14
32:15 Judg 10:6
32:16 Ps 78:58; 106:29
32:17 Lev 17:7; 1 Cor 10:20
32:18 Deut 8:11; 32:4; Ps 106:21; [k]*tsur* (6697) ‣Deut 32:31
32:19 Lev 26:30; Ps 106:40
32:20 Deut 32:5
32:21 1 Kgs 16:13, 26; *Rom 10:19
32:22 Lev 26:20; Ps 18:7-8
32:23 Deut 28:15-19; Ps 85:5
32:24 Deut 28:53; Ps 91:6
32:25 2 Chr 36:17; Lam 1:20; 2:21; Ezek 7:15

10 He found them in a desert land,
in an empty, howling wasteland.
He surrounded them and watched over them;
he guarded them as he would guard his own eyes.
11 Like an eagle that rouses her chicks
and hovers over her young,
so he spread his wings to take them up
and carried them safely on his pinions.
12 The LORD alone guided them;
they followed no foreign gods.
13 He let them ride over the highlands
and feast on the crops of the fields.
He nourished them with honey from the rock
and olive oil from the [j]stony ground.
14 He fed them yogurt from the herd
and milk from the flock,
together with the fat of lambs.
He gave them choice rams from Bashan, and goats,
together with the choicest wheat.
You drank the finest wine,
made from the juice of grapes.

15 "But Israel soon became fat and unruly;
the people grew heavy, plump, and stuffed!
Then they abandoned the God who had made them;
they made light of the Rock of their salvation.
16 They stirred up his jealousy by worshiping foreign gods;
they provoked his fury with detestable deeds.
17 They offered sacrifices to demons, which are not God,
to gods they had not known before,
to new gods only recently arrived,
to gods their ancestors had never feared.
18 You neglected the [k]Rock who had fathered you;
you forgot the God who had given you birth.

19 "The LORD saw this and drew back,
provoked to anger by his own sons and daughters.
20 He said, 'I will abandon them;
then see what becomes of them.
For they are a twisted generation,
children without integrity.
21 They have roused my jealousy by worshiping things that are not God;
they have provoked my anger with their useless idols.
Now I will rouse their jealousy through people who are not even a people;
I will provoke their anger through the foolish Gentiles.
22 For my anger blazes forth like fire
and burns to the depths of the grave.
It devours the earth and all its crops
and ignites the foundations of the mountains.
23 I will heap disasters upon them
and shoot them down with my arrows.
24 I will weaken them with famine,
burning fever, and deadly disease.
I will send the fangs of wild beasts
and poisonous snakes that glide in the dust.
25 Outside, the sword will bring death,
and inside, terror will strike
both young men and young women,
both infants and the aged.

32:10 ***as he would guard his own eyes:*** Literally *as the pupil of his eye.*

32:14 ***rams from Bashan, and goats:*** This high plateau east of the Sea of Galilee was famous for such livestock (see note on 1:4; see also Ps 22:12; Ezek 39:18; Amos 4:1).

32:15 ***Israel:*** Hebrew *Jeshurun,* a term of endearment for Israel that demonstrates the Lord's strong affection for his people. The name appears to be derived from a verb meaning "to be upright" (see 33:5, 26; Isa 44:2). • ***the Rock:*** This metaphor describes God's strength and reliability, especially regarding salvation (see 32:4).

32:16 ***his jealousy:*** See note on 4:24. Just as a husband is properly jealous when another man tries to draw his wife away (Prov 6:34), God was jealous when Israel worshiped other gods.

32:17 ***demons:*** In the ancient Near East, the gods were thought to protect individuals and places from harm, but worshiping these pagan deities actually amounted to worshiping evil spirits (cp. 1 Cor 10:20-21; Rev 9:20). • ***New gods*** were false deities that Israel had never before encountered.

32:18 ***the Rock:*** This expression draws attention to God's reliability as Father (see 32:4, 9).

32:20 The phrase ***without integrity*** indicates disloyalty to the covenant. Israel had promised to be true to the Lord but had consistently been unfaithful (see Exod 19:8).

32:21 ***roused my jealousy:*** The Lord was not petulant because of attention paid to false gods. Rather, Israel had broken their covenant with him by worshiping other gods, demonstrating their disdain for him and his sovereignty (see 32:16). • ***people who are not even a people:*** God's purpose for Israel was not just to redeem them, but through them to redeem all nations of the earth. In Israel's eyes, other peoples were worthless, but through God's attention to other nations, Israel would be drawn back to obedience (see Hos 1:9; 2:23; Rom 9:25; 10:19).

32:22 ***of the grave*** (Hebrew *of Sheol*): The realm of the dead was thought to be in ***the depths*** beneath the earth, and the entrance to that world was the grave. God is omnipresent, and his judgment reaches the most inaccessible places (see Ps 139:7-12).

26 I would have annihilated them,
wiping out even the memory of them.
27 But I feared the taunt of Israel's enemy,
who might misunderstand and say,
"Our own power has triumphed!
The LORD had nothing to do with this!"'
28 "But Israel is a senseless nation;
the people are foolish, without understanding.
29 Oh, that they were wise and could understand this!
Oh, that they might know their fate!
30 How could one person chase a thousand of them,
and two people put ten thousand to flight,
unless their Rock had sold them,
unless the LORD had given them up?
31 But the [a]rock of our enemies is not like our [a]Rock,
as even they recognize.
32 Their vine grows from the vine of Sodom,
from the vineyards of Gomorrah.
Their grapes are poison,
and their clusters are bitter.
33 Their wine is the venom of serpents,
the deadly poison of cobras.

34 "The LORD says, 'Am I not storing up these things,
sealing them away in my treasury?
35 I will take revenge; I will pay them back.
In due time their feet will slip.
Their day of disaster will arrive,
and their destiny will overtake them.'
36 "Indeed, the LORD will give justice to his people,
and he will change his mind about his servants,
when he sees their strength is gone
and no one is left, slave or free.
37 Then he will ask, 'Where are their gods,
the rocks they fled to for refuge?
38 Where now are those gods,
who ate the fat of their sacrifices
and drank the wine of their offerings?
Let those gods arise and help you!
Let them provide you with shelter!
39 Look now; I myself am he!
There is no other god but me!
I am the one who kills and gives life;
I am the one who wounds and heals;
no one can be rescued from my powerful hand!
40 Now I raise my hand to heaven
and declare, "As surely as I live,
41 when I sharpen my flashing sword
and begin to carry out justice,
I will take revenge on my enemies
and repay those who reject me.
42 I will make my arrows drunk with blood,
and my sword will devour flesh—
the blood of the slaughtered and the captives,
and the heads of the enemy leaders."'

32:26 Deut 4:27; 28:64
32:29 Deut 5:29
32:30 Lev 26:7-8; Deut 32:4, 18
32:31 [a]*tsur* (6697) ‣1 Sam 2:2
32:32 Deut 29:18
32:35 Jer 23:12; Ezek 7:5; *Rom 12:19
32:36 Lev 26:44-45; Deut 30:2-3; *Heb 10:30
32:37 Jer 2:28
32:38 Num 25:1-2; Jer 11:12
32:39 1 Sam 2:6; Ps 50:22; Isa 41:4; 43:10
32:41 Isa 34:6-8; Jer 12:12; 46:10; 50:28-32

32:27 ***I feared:*** God is never terrified or intimidated. This fear is concern that Israel's enemies would attribute their success to their own efforts rather than to God's sovereign judgment of his people (see Exod 32:11-14).

32:29 ***their fate*** (literally *their latter end*): Israel's future had not been predetermined; this statement expresses how things would turn out if Israel continued on its rebellious course.

32:30 ***How could one person chase a thousand:*** When God gives his people over to destruction, they are vulnerable against all odds. • ***their Rock:*** Here the metaphor is used ironically. The very one upon whom Israel should stand as the source of their strength will desert them because of their own wickedness and unfaithfulness (see 32:4).

32:31 ***the rock of our enemies:*** In this sarcastic comparison between the pagan gods and the Lord God of Israel, the false deities come up woefully short. • ***as even they recognize:*** The meaning of the Hebrew is uncertain. Greek version reads *our enemies are fools.* Either way, those gods are inadequate.

32:32 ***Sodom . . . Gomorrah:*** These cities were the epitome of evil (see Gen 18:16–19:38). Pagan perversity and godlessness found their inspiration and source in these cities, and because they were unrepentant, they were utterly destroyed (see 29:23).

32:34 Metaphorically, ***my treasury*** is the place where God, as Divine Warrior, lays up his implements of war and judgment until the time comes for them to be put to use (see 1:30).

32:36 ***will change his mind about*** (or ***will take revenge for,*** or ***will be sorry for***): When speaking of God, the OT frequently uses figurative language (see note on 8:2). Human beings cannot understand God's mind (Isa 55:8), so God uses human language and gives himself human physical characteristics and feelings. Although the Bible frequently speaks of God's eyes, arms, hands, and feet, he is invisible and has no body; these metaphors describe his activity. Similarly, when the Bible says that God fears (32:27) or changes his mind, it expresses how God's actions appear to humans. See also "God's Change of Mind" at 1 Sam 15:11, 29, 35, p. 493.

32:37 ***the rocks:*** This sarcastic metaphor concerns the impotence of pagan gods (see 32:31).

32:38 ***ate the fat . . . drank the wine:*** Most polytheistic religious systems that practice sacrifice include the notion that the gods find nourishment in the sacrifices made to them. Israel fell victim to this superstitious belief for a time before the Lord graciously taught them otherwise and restored them to himself (32:36).

32:40 ***I raise my hand to heaven:*** This anthropomorphism (see notes on 4:34 and 8:2) asserts God's solemn intention to keep his covenant promises to deliver his people from their enemies. When God makes an oath, he is not bound to some course of action in the event that he proves undependable. Rather, the statement emphasizes the reliability of God's promises above and beyond his character alone (see Num 14:21, 28; Isa 49:18; Ezek 20:5-6).

32:42 The phrase ***arrows drunk with blood*** combines personification and hyperbole to show the extent of the carnage that will result from God's judgment of the nations.

32:43
*Rom 15:10

32:46
Deut 4:9
Ezek 40:4; 44:5
[b]*torah* (8451)
‣Josh 1:8

32:47
Deut 4:40; 8:3; 30:20

32:49
Num 27:12
Deut 3:27

32:50
Gen 25:8
Num 27:13

32:51
Num 20:12

32:52
Deut 1:37; 3:27

33:1
Josh 14:6
[c]*berakah* (1293)
‣1 Kgs 8:14

33:2
Exod 19:18, 20
Judg 5:4
Ps 68:8, 17
Dan 7:10
Hab 3:3
Gal 3:19

33:3
Deut 4:37; 6:1-9; 7:6; 14:2

33:4
Deut 4:2
Ps 119:111

33:5
Num 23:18-24
Ps 10:16

43 “Rejoice with him, you heavens,
and let all of God’s angels worship him.
Rejoice with his people, you nations,
and let all the angels be strengthened
in him.
For he will avenge the blood of his
servants;
he will take revenge against his
enemies.
He will repay those who hate him
and cleanse the land for his people.”

44 So Moses came with Joshua son of Nun
and recited all the words of this song to the
people.
45 When Moses had finished reciting all
these words to the people of Israel, 46 he
added: “Take to heart all the words of warning I have given you today. Pass them on as a
command to your children so they will obey
every word of these [b]instructions. 47 These
instructions are not empty words—they are
your life! By obeying them you will enjoy a
long life in the land you will occupy when
you cross the Jordan River.”

Moses’ Impending Death (32:48-52)

48 That same day the LORD said to Moses,
49 “Go to Moab, to the mountains east of the
river, and climb Mount Nebo, which is across
from Jericho. Look out across the land of
Canaan, the land I am giving to the people
of Israel as their own special possession.
50 Then you will die there on the mountain.
You will join your ancestors, just as Aaron,
your brother, died on Mount Hor and joined
his ancestors. 51 For both of you betrayed
me with the Israelites at the waters of Meribah at Kadesh in the wilderness of Zin. You
failed to demonstrate my holiness to the people of Israel there. 52 So you will see the land
from a distance, but you may not enter the
land I am giving to the people of Israel.”

Moses Blesses the People (33:1-29)

33 This is the [c]blessing that Moses, the
man of God, gave to the people of Israel before his death:

2 “The LORD came from Mount Sinai
and dawned upon us from Mount Seir;
he shone forth from Mount Paran
and came from Meribah-kadesh
with flaming fire at his right hand.
3 Indeed, he loves his people;
all his holy ones are in his hands.
They follow in his steps
and accept his teaching.
4 Moses gave us the LORD’s instruction,
the special possession of the people
of Israel.
5 The LORD became king in Israel—
when the leaders of the people
assembled,
when the tribes of Israel gathered as
one.”

32:43 *Rejoice with him, you heavens . . . angels worship him:* As in Dead Sea Scrolls and Greek version; Masoretic Text lacks the first two lines (cp. Heb 1:6). • *and let all the angels be strengthened in him:* As in Greek version; Hebrew text lacks this line. • *He will repay those who hate him:* As in Dead Sea Scrolls and Greek version; Masoretic Text lacks this line.

32:44 *Joshua:* Hebrew *Hoshea,* a variant name for Joshua.

32:47 *they are your life:* Obeying the Lord’s words brings life (see 8:3; 30:20). • *long life:* This promise does not guarantee individual longevity and certainly not immortality; it is about Israel’s long tenure in the Land of Promise.

32:49 The *mountains east of the river* (Hebrew *the mountains of Abarim*) are a range of mountains overlooking the Jordan Valley. *Mount Nebo,* a prominent peak in this range, was the point from which Moses could view Canaan to the east and also where he died (32:50; see 3:17).

32:50 The location of *Mount Hor* is uncertain, but the traditional location (Jebel Haroun) is some ten miles northeast of Kadesh-barnea, within sight of the Nabatean city of Petra (see 1:19; Num 20:22-29). • The phrase *joined his ancestors* is a euphemism for burial.

32:51 *you betrayed me:* During the wilderness sojourn, Moses dishonored the Lord by striking a water-producing rock. This fit of impatient anger disqualified Moses from entering the Promised Land (Num 20:1-13; see Deut 1:37; 3:26-27). • *waters of Meribah at Kadesh:* Hebrew *waters of Meribath-kadesh.*

33:1-29 On the eve of his death, Jacob blessed his twelve sons (Gen 49:1-28). As the founding father of his country, Moses blessed these same sons, now grown into mighty tribes.

33:2 *upon us:* As in Greek and Syriac versions; Hebrew reads *upon them.* • *Mount Seir:* See notes on 1:2 and 2:1; also see Judg 5:4. • *Mount Paran* is the highlands of Paran in the northeast region of the Sinai Peninsula (see 1:1). • *came from Meribah-kadesh with flaming fire at his right hand* (Or *came from myriads of holy ones, from the south, from his mountain slopes.* The meaning of the Hebrew is uncertain): This poetic account does not establish an itinerary that God followed. Instead, it portrays God in his splendor as he came at certain times and places to lead his people against their foes in God’s war.

33:3 *Indeed, he loves his people:* As in Greek version; Hebrew reads *Indeed, lover of the peoples.* In covenant contexts, *to love* is frequently synonymous with *to choose.* The Lord does indeed love his people, but here it means that he chooses them as his special possession (4:20). • *his hands:* This phrase figuratively conveys the security that Israel (*his holy ones*) had in the Lord. • *his steps:* Following the Lord requires adopting his lifestyle and going where he goes. • *His teaching* refers particularly and pertinently to the Torah in all its fullness.

33:4 *of Israel:* Literally *of Jacob.* The names “Jacob” and “Israel” are often interchanged throughout the Old Testament, referring sometimes to the individual patriarch and sometimes to the nation. Hebrew probably uses *Jacob* because the tribes descended from Jacob’s twelve sons are here listed by name as recipients of God’s blessing (33:6-25; cp. Gen 49:1-28).

33:5 *in Israel:* Hebrew *in Jeshurun,* a term of endearment for Israel showing God’s great love for his people. The noun is derived from a verb meaning “to be upright” (see 32:15).

6 Moses said this about the tribe of Reuben:

"Let the tribe of Reuben live and not die out,
though they are few in number."

7 Moses said this about the tribe of Judah:

"O LORD, hear the cry of Judah
and bring them together as a people.
Give them strength to defend their cause;
help them against their enemies!"

8 Moses said this about the tribe of Levi:

"O LORD, you have given your Thummim
and Urim—the sacred lots—
to your faithful servants the Levites.
You put them to the test at Massah
and struggled with them at the waters of Meribah.
9 The Levites obeyed your word
and guarded your [d]covenant.
They were more loyal to you
than to their own parents.
They ignored their relatives
and did not acknowledge their own children.
10 They teach your regulations to Jacob;
they give your instructions to Israel.
They present incense before you
and offer whole burnt offerings on the altar.
11 Bless the ministry of the Levites, O LORD,
and accept all the work of their hands.
Hit their enemies where it hurts the most;
strike down their foes so they never rise again."

12 Moses said this about the tribe of Benjamin:

"The people of Benjamin are loved by the LORD
and live in safety beside him.
He surrounds them continuously
and preserves them from every harm."

13 Moses said this about the tribes of Joseph:

"May their land be blessed by the LORD
with the precious gift of dew from the heavens
and water from beneath the earth;
14 with the rich fruit that grows in the sun,
and the rich harvest produced each month;
15 with the finest crops of the ancient mountains,
and the abundance from the [e]everlasting hills;
16 with the best gifts of the earth and its bounty,
and the favor of the one who appeared in the burning bush.
May these blessings rest on Joseph's head,
crowning the brow of the prince among his brothers.
17 Joseph has the majesty of a young bull;
he has the horns of a wild ox.

33:6 Gen 49:3
33:7 Gen 49:8-12
33:8 Exod 17:7; Lev 8:8; Num 20:13, 24; Deut 6:16
33:9 Exod 32:27; Mal 2:5; [d]*berith* (1285) ‣Josh 24:25
33:10 Lev 10:11; 16:12-13; Deut 17:9; 31:9
33:12 Deut 12:10; 32:8
33:13 Gen 27:27-29; 49:22
33:15 [e]*'olam* (5769) ‣2 Sam 7:13
33:16 Exod 3:2
33:17 Num 23:22; 24:8; 1 Kgs 22:11

33:6 Hebrew lacks *Moses said this about the tribe of Reuben.* The NLT adds this line for clarity (cp. 33:7, 8, 12, etc.). • *Reuben* was Jacob's eldest son by Leah (see Gen 29:32). His sin against his father (Gen 35:22) might explain his tribe's lack of prominence (Gen 49:3-4).

33:7 *Judah* was Jacob's fourth son by Leah (Gen 29:35). The anticipated messianic ruler would come through this tribe. This promise was fulfilled first in David (Ruth 4:18-22; 1 Chr 2:3-15) and then in Jesus Christ (Matt 1:1-6a; see Gen 49:10).

33:8 *Levi* was Jacob's third son by Leah (Gen 29:34). The Levites, particularly those descended from Aaron, were entrusted with the priesthood (see Exod 28:1; 32:29; Num 3:9). • *Thummim and Urim* were precious stones embedded in or suspended from the breastpiece of the ephod, a garment worn by the chief priest. These stones could be consulted to determine God's will. Their names may be translated "perfections" and "lights," respectively (see note on Exod 28:30). • *to your faithful servants the Levites:* As in Greek version; Hebrew lacks *the Levites.* • *Massah* means "[place of] testing," referring to an incident when the people ran out of water and tested the Lord (see note on 6:16; Exod 17:1-7). • *Meribah* means "[place of] contention," referring to another occasion when the people of Israel fought with the Lord until he brought them water from a rock (Num 20:13, 24).

33:9 *guarded your covenant:* The verse alludes to the incident of the gold calf at Mount Sinai (Exod 32:25-29) and to the affair at Baal-peor (Num 25:6-9). The Levites' love for the Lord and loyalty to his covenant eclipsed their devotion to their own families, averted God's judgment, and brought them the honor expressed here.

33:10 *They teach your regulations . . . instructions:* In addition to carrying out priestly duties such as sacrifices and otherwise assisting at the Tabernacle and the Temple, the Levites had the task of teaching the Torah (31:9-13). • *present incense:* This ministry was limited to Levitical priests (Num 16:39-40). Later, when King Uzziah entered the Temple to offer *incense,* he was roundly condemned for his arrogant breach of the priests' privilege and was afflicted by a skin disease for the rest of his life (2 Chr 26:16-21).

33:12 *Benjamin* was Jacob's youngest son (Gen 35:18; 49:27). Because Rachel was Jacob's favorite wife, Benjamin was also favored. His tribe was blessed by the Lord's special protection.

33:13-17 *Joseph* was Jacob's eleventh son (Gen 30:23-24) and his favorite child (Gen 37:3). Joseph and his two sons, Ephraim and Manasseh, received Jacob's special blessing (Gen 48:1-22; 49:22-26). As a result, *the tribes of Joseph* prospered and multiplied, becoming two separate tribes.

33:16 *the one who appeared in the burning bush:* See Exod 3:2-4. The same Lord who favored Israel by rescuing them from bondage blessed the tribes of Joseph. • *the prince among his brothers:* Joseph's dream that he would rule over his siblings was fulfilled when they submitted to him in Egypt (Gen 37:5-11; 42:6).

33:17 *Ephraim* is listed first because he received the blessing of the firstborn over *Manasseh* (Gen 48:8-22). Manasseh, the firstborn, would normally have received the double portion belonging to

33:18 Gen 49:13
33:19 Ps 4:5; 51:19
33:20 Gen 49:19
33:21 Num 32:1; 34:14 Josh 4:12; 22:1
33:22 Gen 49:16 Ezek 19:2-3
33:23 Gen 49:21

He will gore distant nations,
driving them to the ends of the earth.
This is my blessing for the multitudes of Ephraim
and the thousands of Manasseh."

18Moses said this about the tribes of Zebulun and Issachar:

"May the people of Zebulun prosper in their travels.
May the people of Issachar prosper at home in their tents.
19 They summon the people to the mountain
to offer proper sacrifices there.
They benefit from the riches of the sea
and the hidden treasures in the sand."

20Moses said this about the tribe of Gad:

"Blessed is the one who enlarges Gad's territory!
Gad is poised there like a lion
to tear off an arm or a head.
21 The people of Gad took the best land for themselves;
a leader's share was assigned to them.
When the leaders of the people were assembled,
they carried out the LORD's justice
and obeyed his regulations for Israel."

22Moses said this about the tribe of Dan:

"Dan is a lion's cub,
leaping out from Bashan."

23Moses said this about the tribe of Naphtali:

"O Naphtali, you are rich in favor
and full of the LORD's blessings;
may you possess the west and the south."

God's Covenant Love (33:3)

Deut 7:6-11
Isa 38:15-20; 49:14-18; 63:7-10
Hos 11:1-11
Mal 1:2-3
Matt 3:16-17
Luke 15:1-32
John 3:16; 16:25-27; 17:23-24
Rom 5:6-8; 8:37; 9:13-26
Gal 2:20
Eph 1:4; 2:4-7
Heb 12:6-11
1 Jn 3:1; 4:8-9, 16

Often in the Bible, God's love is understood in the ordinary sense that God has strongly affectionate feelings toward humankind. In certain contexts, such as the covenant document of Deuteronomy, love refers to God's commitment to his people.

In the ancient Near East, a conquering king would characteristically speak of his relationship to vassal peoples as a relationship of love, meaning that he had chosen those people to enjoy his favor and to benefit from his protection in exchange for their loyal service. Similarly, God chose Israel to be his servant nation not because the Israelites deserved it but because he loved them (7:6-11). Put another way, he loved them because he had chosen them.

The strongest affirmation of God's love-choice can be found in Mal 1:2-3. God chose Jacob but rejected Esau (Rom 9:13-26). God loves the entire world (John 3:16), but only those he chooses experience his saving grace (Eph 1:4; 2 Thes 2:13).

the firstborn (cp. 21:17), but Jacob gave it to Ephraim, Joseph's younger son. Moses' blessing reflects Jacob's blessing by listing the tribe of Ephraim as numbering in ***multitudes*** (literally *tens of thousands*) and Manasseh in ***thousands.*** After the conquest and establishment of the nation, Ephraim became the dominant tribe of the north; later, after the kingdom was divided following Solomon's death (1 Kgs 12), the name Ephraim was used interchangeably with Israel in speaking of the northern kingdom.

33:18 ***Zebulun and Issachar*** (Hebrew lacks *and Issachar*; the NLT adds it for clarity) were the sixth and fifth sons of Jacob by Leah (Gen 30:18, 20). • ***in their travels . . . in their tents:*** This figure of speech (a *merism*) encompasses life in all its fullness for both tribes, from activity (***travels***) to inactivity (***tents***).

33:19 ***to the mountain:*** Issachar was allotted much of the plains of Jezreel or Esdraelon. Mount Tabor, a prominent landmark of this region, was probably the mountain in view because later tradition knows this as a place of worship (Hos 5:1). The nature of that worship is unclear, but it was probably proper even though it was not carried out at the Temple (see 1 Kgs 18:30, 32). • The phrase ***riches of the sea*** might refer to the maritime industry of the people of Zebulun when their western border extended to the Mediterranean Sea (see Gen 49:13).

33:20 ***Gad*** was the elder of two sons of Jacob by Leah's servant Zilpah (Gen 30:10-11). His name means "good fortune," but the message is that the one who enables the tribe to enlarge its territory is the fortunate one. That territory was east of the Jordan and the Sea of Galilee.

33:21 ***the best land:*** Gad chose this territory prior to the conquest. It was the famously rich and productive land of Bashan (Num 32:1-5). The commendation of Gad for carrying out the Lord's justice and obeying his regulations probably refers to the tribe's faithfulness in assisting the western tribes in their conquest of Canaan (Josh 22:1-3).

33:22 ***Dan*** was the elder of two sons of Jacob by Rachel's servant Bilhah (Gen 30:5-6). The name means "he judged." The tribe of Dan was originally given territory between Judah and the Mediterranean. However, because of fierce hostility in that region, they were unable to settle there (Josh 19:40-48). The tribe then moved to the far north, destroyed the people who lived there, and settled in their place near Mount Hermon, north of the Sea of Galilee and adjacent to Bashan. The historical record doesn't mention Dan's staging area from which an attack was made against Laish, but the phrase ***leaping out from Bashan*** might suggest that Dan would attack from Bashan (Judg 18:27-28; see Gen 49:16-17).

33:23 ***Naphtali*** was the younger of two sons of Jacob by Rachel's servant Bilhah (Gen 30:7-8). The name means something like "my struggle." • ***the west and the south*** (or *southward to the sea*): The Hebrew word (*yam*) can mean either "west" or "sea." This phrase might refer to the region this tribe settled in near the Sea of Galilee (see Matt 4:12-17), known for its fishing and farming.

24 Moses said this about the tribe of Asher:

"May Asher be blessed above other
 sons;
may he be esteemed by his brothers;
may he bathe his feet in olive oil.
25 May the bolts of your gates be of iron
 and bronze;
may you be secure all your days."
26 "There is no one like the God of Israel.
He rides across the heavens to help
 you,
across the skies in majestic splendor.
27 The eternal God is your refuge,
and his everlasting arms are under
 you.
He drives out the enemy before you;
he cries out, 'Destroy them!'
28 So Israel will live in safety,
prosperous Jacob in security,
in a land of grain and new wine,
while the heavens drop down dew.
29 How blessed you are, O Israel!
Who else is like you, a people saved by
 the LORD?
He is your protecting [f]shield
 and your triumphant sword!
Your enemies will cringe before you,
 and you will stomp on their backs!"

Narrative Epilogue: Moses' Death (34:1-12)

34 Then Moses went up to Mount
Nebo from the plains of Moab and
climbed Pisgah Peak, which is across from
Jericho. And the LORD showed him the
whole land, from Gilead as far as Dan; 2 all
the land of Naphtali; the land of Ephraim
and Manasseh; all the land of Judah, extending to the Mediterranean Sea; 3 the Negev;
the Jordan Valley with Jericho—the city of
palms—as far as Zoar. 4 Then the LORD said
to Moses, "This is the land I promised on
oath to Abraham, Isaac, and Jacob when
I said, 'I will give it to your [g]descendants.'
I have now allowed you to see it with your
own eyes, but you will not enter the land."
5 So Moses, the servant of the LORD, died
there in the land of Moab, just as the LORD
had said. 6 The LORD buried him in a valley near Beth-peor in Moab, but to this

33:24 Gen 49:20; Job 29:6
33:25 Ps 147:13
33:26 Exod 15:11; Deut 4:35; Ps 68:33
33:27 Gen 49:24; Deut 7:2; Josh 24:18; Ps 90:1
33:28 Gen 27:27-29, 37; Deut 33:12-13
33:29 Gen 15:1; Deut 4:32; Ps 66:3; 115:11; [f]*magen* (4043) › 2 Sam 1:21
34:1 Num 21:20; Deut 32:49, 52
34:2 Exod 23:31; Deut 11:24
34:4 Gen 12:7; 26:3; [g]*zera'* (2233) › Josh 24:3
34:5 Num 12:7-8; Deut 32:50

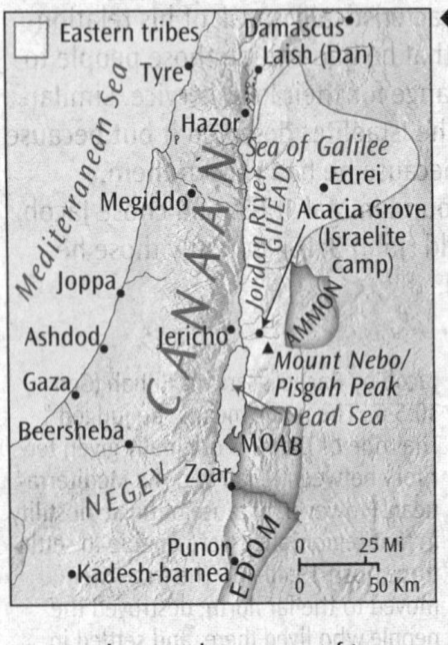

◀ **Moses' Death on Mount Nebo (34:1-8).** When Moses had finished teaching Israel to follow the Lord, he climbed PISGAH PEAK, saw the Promised Land, and then died. See also 3:26-28; 32:48-52.

33:24 ***Asher*** was the younger of two sons of Jacob by Leah's servant Zilpah (Gen 30:12-13). The name means "happy" or "blessed," evident in the abundance of ***olive oil*** from the orchards that cover the lower Galilean hills and Mount Carmel, as well as the security from danger that these hills and other natural formations provided (33:25).

33:26 ***of Israel:*** Hebrew *of Jeshurun;* see note on 32:15. • ***He rides across the heavens:*** Moses' blessing of the tribes climaxes with praise to the Lord. Like a mighty warrior, God rides triumphantly through the skies on chariots of cloud (see 1:30).

33:27 God's ***everlasting arms*** suggest his eternal nature (he has always existed and always will), omnipotence (power), and care. God's power would evict the Canaanites from the Promised Land so that Israel could enter and occupy it.

33:29 ***stomp on their backs:*** Treading on an enemy's back figuratively meant having complete victory over him. The word *backs* can also be translated "high places," meaning the heights of the land and the traditional places of pagan worship—a way of suggesting total physical and spiritual conquest. The Lord promised to lead the way and guarantee success in the forthcoming conquest (see 11:24-25; Josh 1:3; 14:9; cp. Amos 4:13; Mic 1:3; Hab 3:15).

34:1-12 Moses fell short of entry into the land of promise (see note on 32:51), but God did permit him to share a moment of glory in the land at Jesus' transfiguration (Luke 9:28-36).

34:1 ***Mount Nebo*** is a high elevation in the Abarim hills east of the Jordan River. Virtually the whole land west of the Jordan can be seen from this vantage point (32:49). • Nebo was part of ***Pisgah Peak*** (see note on 3:17). • ***Gilead as far as Dan*** was the northernmost part of the land. The Sea of Galilee and Mount Hermon lie straight north from Nebo. Gilead is just east of the Sea, and Dan (Laish; Judg 18:29) was south and west of Hermon.

34:2 The ***land of Naphtali*** was northwest of Nebo and west of the Sea of Galilee. • ***The land of Ephraim and Manasseh*** was a large area to the west-northwest of Nebo, the present West Bank area of Palestine. • The ***land of Judah*** lay to the immediate west-southwest of Nebo, from the Jordan River to ***the Mediterranean Sea*** (literally *the western sea*).

34:3 The desert region of ***the Negev*** (meaning "desert" or "south") extends south from Judah to the Gulf of Eilat (or Aqaba) and thus to the far southwest of Mount Nebo. • ***Jericho . . . as far as Zoar:*** These two sites marked the northern and southern ends of the ***Jordan Valley*** from the viewpoint of Mount Nebo. Zoar was a city of the plain that was not destroyed in the days of Abraham and Lot (see Gen 19:21-22, 30).

34:4 ***you will not enter:*** See note on 32:51.

34:6 ***The LORD buried him:*** Literally *He buried him;* Samaritan Pentateuch and some Greek manuscripts read *They buried him.* • ***Beth-peor*** was where Israel engaged in pagan ritual (see 3:29; 4:3; Num 25) and where Moses presented his farewell address (see 4:44-46). • The phrase ***to this day*** refers to the time of Deuteronomy's final composition (see Introduction to the Pentateuch, "Authorship," p. 11).

34:6
Deut 3:29; 4:46
Jude 1:9
34:7
Deut 31:2
34:9
Num 27:18
Isa 11:2
[h]*ruakh* (7307)
‣1 Sam 16:15
34:10
Num 12:8
34:11-12
Deut 4:34

day no one knows the exact place. 7Moses
was 120 years old when he died, yet his
eyesight was clear, and he was as strong
as ever. 8The people of Israel mourned
for Moses on the plains of Moab for thirty
days, until the customary period of mourning was over.
9Now Joshua son of Nun was full of the
[h]spirit of wisdom, for Moses had laid his
hands on him. So the people of Israel obeyed
him, doing just as the LORD had commanded
Moses.
10There has never been another prophet
in Israel like Moses, whom the LORD knew
face to face. 11The LORD sent him to perform all the miraculous signs and wonders
in the land of Egypt against Pharaoh, and
all his servants, and his entire land. 12With
mighty power, Moses performed terrifying
acts in the sight of all Israel.

34:7 At age 120, Moses was ***as strong as ever*** and in full possession of his faculties. He did not fail to enter Canaan because he died; he died because he failed to enter Canaan.

34:9 ***full of the spirit of wisdom:*** When Joshua was selected as Moses' successor, he had to be invested with the Spirit of God to fill the office (Num 27:15-23; cp. Num 11:16-30). Now that Moses had died, God showed that Joshua was Moses' divinely appointed successor by giving continuing evidence of the Spirit's power and blessing.

34:10 ***face to face:*** Moses and the Lord had an intimate relationship, and there was no need for an intercessor between them. Aaron and Miriam once challenged Moses' leadership and were severely rebuked by the Lord (Num 12:8), who reminded them that they were ordinary prophets that received revelation by dreams and visions. Moses was not such a prophet. God said, "I speak to him face to face, clearly, and not in riddles" (Num 12:8). No other prophet in OT times could rival Moses' relationship with God (see note on 18:15).

34:11 ***signs and wonders:*** See note on 6:22.

34:12 ***terrifying acts in the sight of all Israel:*** The people of Israel as well as the Egyptians were impressed by the power of God. They needed a constant reminder to submit to him in reverential fear (see 4:10; 5:29; 6:2; Prov 1:7).

INTRODUCTION TO THE OLD TESTAMENT
HISTORICAL BOOKS

"Believers will be persuaded that they hold in their hands an absolutely unique literary creation. . . . It must be addressed as the word of God with all that implies concerning its worth and authority as historical source."
Eugene H. Merrill, *Kingdom of Priests*, p. 16

The Old Testament books from Joshua to Esther tell the story of the ancient nation of Israel from its entrance into the Promised Land to its return from exile during the era of Zerubbabel, Ezra, and Nehemiah. We meet illustrious leaders of Israel such as Joshua, Gideon, Samuel, David, and Solomon. We meet notable prophets such as Elijah and Elisha, and godly women such as Ruth, Hannah, and Esther. We read of spectacular events such as the fall of the walls of Jericho, the day the sun stood still, David's slaying of the giant Goliath, and the building of Solomon's Temple.

These books illustrate that people who forsake God will experience his judgment and failure, whereas those who honor and serve God will receive his blessings, fulfillment, and satisfaction. In our own age, when the study of history is often seen as irrelevant compared to great technical advances, the OT historical books remind us that those who ignore the past are doomed to repeat its errors.

SETTING AND SUMMARY

The OT historical books (Joshua—Esther) tell Israel's story from the conquest of Canaan to the time of Israel's exile and return.

Conquest and Settlement

Israel's conquest and settling in Canaan are recorded in the book of Joshua. Joshua encountered only a group of disorganized Canaanite city-states. With God's help, Israel was able to take possession of the land they had been promised.

Tribal Fragmentation, Oppression, and Period of the Judges

Following Joshua's death, Israel's loss of vital worship led to growing political fragmentation, which allowed nearby nations to gain sufficient strength to harass God's people. The surrounding Arameans, Moabites, and Canaanites each launched a series of oppressions against the Israelite tribes, as recorded in the book of Judges. By the mid-1100s BC, other small nations became oppressive—the Midianites to the south, the Ammonites to the east, and the Philistines to the west. The Philistines remained a threat until David's time.

In addition to oppression, the people of Israel also experienced natural disasters such as famines. One such famine forms the background for events in the book of Ruth. By the end of the Judges era, Israel's degraded situation was characterized by chaos and brutality (Judg 21:25; see Judg 19–21; cp. 1 Sam 2:12-36).

United Kingdom (1050~931 BC)

During the time of Samuel, Israel's last judge (1 Sam 1–7), Israel made a decisive change: The people asked Samuel to give them a king. The Lord responded by appointing Saul as Israel's first king (1 Sam 8–10).

Saul's reign as king was characterized by disobedience to the Lord and ongoing conflict with the Philistines to the west. After Saul was killed by the Philistines (1 Sam 31; 2 Sam 1), David began reigning in Judah, while Saul's son Ishbosheth ruled Israel's northern tribes. After seven years of conflict, Ishbosheth was killed and David was crowned king of a united Israel (2 Sam 5, about 1004 BC). During his reign, David brought many of the surrounding peoples into subjection, including the Philistines (2 Sam 5:17-25; 8:1-14).

Israel became a recognized power in the ancient Near East during the reign of David, and especially during the reign of his son Solomon (971–931 BC, 1 Kgs 1–11). With the traditional superpowers in decline

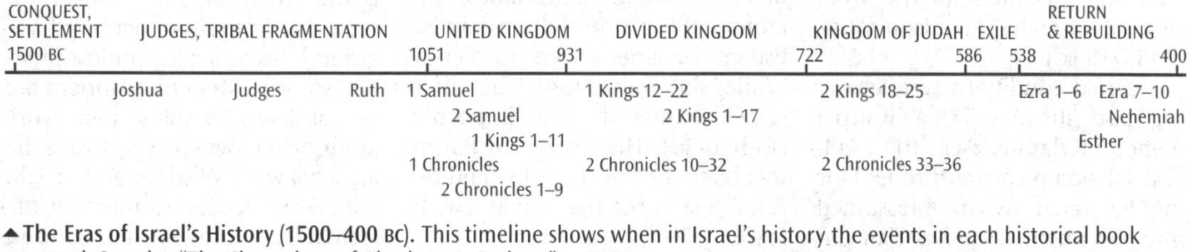

▲ **The Eras of Israel's History (1500–400 BC).** This timeline shows when in Israel's history the events in each historical book occurred. See also "The Chronology of Abraham to Joshua," p. 118.

and the lesser nearby states in subjection, Solomon's strong kingdom and commercial ventures brought prosperity at home and good relations abroad.

Divided Kingdom (971–722 BC)

After Solomon's death and as a result of his sins (1 Kgs 11:29-39), internal tensions between the north and south erupted, and the kingdom was divided (1 Kgs 12). In the north, Jeroboam son of Nebat founded the kingdom of Israel, while in the south, Solomon's son Rehoboam retained rule over the kingdom of Judah. The early part of this era was marked by skirmishes between the two kingdoms and an invasion by the Egyptian Pharaoh Shishak (Shoshenq I) in 926 BC.

Beginning with Israel's third dynasty (Omri–Joram, 885–841 BC), the two Israelite kingdoms were increasingly caught up in political turmoil that grew with the rising power and expansion of Assyria. By 841 BC, Assyrian king Shalmaneser III (858–824 BC) extended Assyria's dominance westward into Aram, bringing some stability to the area. When Shalmaneser was occupied elsewhere, however, Israel was plagued by renewed Aramean incursions under Hazael (2 Kgs 13:3). Relief came only with the intervention of an Assyrian king, probably Adad-nirari III (810–783 BC; see 2 Kgs 13:4-5). After Adad-nirari's death, weak kings ruled Assyria, so Assyrian domination declined, and the twin kingdoms of Israel and Judah were able to gather their strength and expand their influence. Israel under Jeroboam II (793–753 BC, 2 Kgs 14:23-25) and Judah under Uzziah (792–740 BC, 2 Chr 26:1-15) achieved their greatest power since Solomon.

After Jeroboam II died in 752 BC, kings of lesser ability often vied with one another for supremacy, and the northern kingdom fell into chaos. Judah's spiritual fiber also went into decline with the accession of Uzziah's grandson Ahaz (743–715 BC).

External conditions were changing also. In Assyria, a usurper named Tiglath-pileser III (744–727 BC) occupied the throne. During his reign Assyria blossomed into the mighty Neo-Assyrian empire. His successor, Shalmaneser V, destroyed the northern kingdom of Israel (722 BC) and took its people into exile.

Kingdom of Judah (722–586 BC)

Although Judah survived for over a century after the kingdom of Israel fell in 722 BC, only two good kings reigned during this period: Hezekiah (728–686 BC) and Josiah (640–609 BC). Judah was plagued by apostasy and caught in the web of international intrigue involving the declining Assyria, the growing Neo-Babylonian empire, and a strengthened Egypt. With Josiah's death, Judah's fate was already sealed. Judah and Jerusalem suffered a series of Babylonian invasions (605, 597, 588 BC) that brought the southern kingdom to an end in 586 BC. Jerusalem was sacked, the Temple was destroyed, and many of the people were taken to Babylon in exile.

Exile and Return (605–400 BC)

The period of exile is described by several Israelite prophets (Jer 39:11–44:30; Ezekiel; Daniel). Judah's exile lasted until Cyrus II of Persia conquered Babylon in October, 539 BC, and brought the Neo-Babylonian empire to an end.

After Cyrus defeated Babylon, Persia became the dominant power. Cyrus issued decrees that allowed exiled peoples to return to their native lands and rebuild them. This included a decree allowing the Jews to return to Jerusalem (538 BC, Ezra 1:1-4), which they did (Ezra 1:5–2:70). By early autumn of 537 BC, the altar in Jerusalem was rebuilt and the sacrificial service was reestablished (Ezra 3:1-6). With the prophetic encouragement of Haggai and Zechariah, the rebuilt Temple was completed in 515 BC despite opposition (Ezra 3–6).

Several decades later, the Jewish people were rescued from possible extermination. Many of the Jews had remained in foreign lands, and around 480 BC one of them, named Esther, became queen of Persia. While she was queen, she intervened to save the Jewish people (Esth 1–10). The Festival of Purim was celebrated at that time and became one of the traditional Jewish feasts.

A couple decades later, Ezra the priest returned to Jerusalem in 458 BC to stimulate civil and spiritual reform (Ezra 7–10). In 445 BC, Nehemiah returned from Persia to oversee rebuilding Jerusalem's walls and to effect further reforms. The last books of the OT were also written during this time: Malachi sometime in the 400s BC, 1–2 Chronicles around 400 BC, and Ezra—Esther around the same time. Judea remained under Persian control until Alexander the Great defeated the Persian empire in 331 BC.

HISTORICAL AND LITERARY ISSUES

The historical chronology of the OT is covered in separate articles (see "The Chronology of Israel's Monarchy," p. 562; "The Historical Background of Israel's Exile and Return," p. 782). Specific historical issues are also examined in the introductions to the various books.

Narrative as History

The OT historical books contain all the usual elements of narrative, such as plot, characterization, and point of view. In writing history, the authors portray people in ways that reveal their personal character and their roles in events.

Modern historians who take pride in their analytic, factual approach sometimes look askance at the biblical histories, which tell a compelling story rather than presenting a dispassionate record. This difference may be misleading, however. Modern historians are confronted with the distance between themselves and the time they study; they are dependent upon the accuracy of their sources, and they are often faced with gaps in the materials. They also sometimes select sources so as to harmonize with their particular view of historiography. Using an objective voice does not guarantee greater objectivity or truthfulness. "The modern writer's purpose in writing a history, then, is important, and it is usually inseparable from his or her own background, experience, philosophies, and so on."[1] Modern historians are just as likely to shape their work around their own perspective as the ancients were. Wisdom and insight are always needed to interpret the factual data of history and write an

[1] David M. Howard, Jr., *An Introduction to the Old Testament Historical Books* (Chicago: Moody, 1993), 40.

accurate and compelling account. The use of narrative techniques and the existence of perspective in the writing do not in themselves cast doubt on reliability. In fact, appreciating a biblical author's point of view helps us to understand his purpose in writing the account.

Date and Sources of Writing

Although the existing OT historical books were compiled and edited much later than the events they describe, they need not be assumed to be inaccurate, because they are based on earlier records. Both Kings and Chronicles, for example, cite many of their sources (see, e.g., "Sources Consulted by the Chronicler," p. 742). Their sources include such documents as the annals and court memoirs of various kings (e.g., 1 Kgs 11:41) and short historical abstracts (e.g., 2 Kgs 25:22-30).

Ideally, historical sources can be supported by other sources, which validate and authenticate them as reliable records. As it turns out, all of the historical books of the OT can be supported by a host of texts from the nations of the ancient Near East as well as by archaeological data.[2] These sources are of immense importance in helping to build a coherent picture of the history of Israel and the surrounding nations. With the help of these sources, it is reasonable to conclude that "we have a consistent level of good, fact-based correlations right through from circa 2000 BC . . . to 400 BC. In terms of general reliability . . . the Old Testament comes out remarkably well."[3] Moreover, a growing body of archaeological data, both textual and material, illumines and authenticates the historical, linguistic, literary, and cultural background of the Bible.

INTERPRETATION

All available evidence suggests that the OT historical books faithfully and accurately reflect the history of ancient Israel, so readers should approach them as history. Within that basic guideline, readers should follow several important steps:

- Examine any individual historical account by noting its literary boundaries as well as its function within the full historical presentation.
- Compare the data recorded with other scriptural passages covering the same event(s).
- Use relevant material from the records of other ancient Near Eastern peoples.
- Look for the author's purpose and goals in recording the event(s) he has selected.
- Apply the meaning of the text to contemporary issues and personal needs.

MEANING AND MESSAGE

Fidelity to God

The unifying theme of the OT historical books is fidelity to God. Individual and national success in Israel was directly attributable to the people's commitment to God. Times of obedience brought blessing; disobedience brought judgment and failure. Faithfulness and surrender to God enabled Israel to enter the Promised Land and divide it among its twelve tribes (Joshua). Deepening apostasy in the era of the judges brought moral failure, political and civil upheaval, and incursions from hostile nations. In those troubled times, Ruth shines as an example of how God blesses his people's faithfulness.

Israel's demand for a king did little to alleviate conditions, for Saul's establishment of a monarchy brought scant spiritual progress, and Saul failed to meet God's standards (1 Samuel). David stands in contrast to Saul. Despite his occasional moral lapses, David's heart for God earned God's approval, and political stability emerged (2 Sam 5–24; 1 Chr 1–21). God also made an unconditional covenant with David to bless Israel through his heirs (2 Sam 7; 1 Chr 17). David also prepared for the building of the Temple (1 Chr 22–29).

Faithfulness to God brought widespread success (1 Kgs 1–11), but spiritual decay occasioned the division of the kingdom (1 Kgs 12) and eventually brought the demise of both Israel and Judah and the deportation of many of God's people (1 Kgs 12—2 Kgs 25). When his people again became obedient and mindful of him, God directed international affairs so that his people could return to their land with a new potential for experiencing his blessings (Ezra, Nehemiah).

The Importance of Godly Leadership

A second theme of the OT historical books is the importance of godly leadership. Joshua guided the people in the conquest and division of the land. Judges such as Deborah, Gideon, and Samuel stemmed the advance of apostasy. When David and Solomon committed themselves to God, God blessed the people and had Solomon build the Lord's Temple in Jerusalem. Ungodly leaders led the people into moral and political failure, while godly kings such as Jehoshaphat, Hezekiah, and Josiah prolonged God's blessings. The people could also look to prophets such as Elijah, Elisha, and Isaiah during the divided monarchy, and to Haggai, Zechariah, and Malachi after Israel returned to the land.

God's Faithfulness to His Promises

A third theme is that God is faithful to his covenant promises. The conquest of the Promised Land bore testimony to God's covenant keeping (Josh 21:43-45). Israel's periods of success and judgment bore further witness to God's upholding of the covenant formed at Sinai. Additional blessings came through God's covenant with David, in which the earlier covenant with Abraham would be channeled through David's line. From that line an everlasting King would emerge—the Messiah who would establish God's Kingdom. In the Messiah the anticipated messianic kingship, redemption, righteousness, and blessing would be realized (Gen 49:10; Num 24:17-19; Deut 17:15; cp. 2 Chr 6:42).

FURTHER READING

DAVID M. HOWARD, JR.
An Introduction to the Old Testament Historical Books (1993)

K. A. KITCHEN
On the Reliability of the Old Testament (2006)

V. PHILIPS LONG
The Art of Biblical History (1994)

[2] See K. A. Kitchen, *On the Reliability of the Old Testament* (Grand Rapids: Eerdmans, 2006).
[3] Ibid., 500.

THE BOOK OF JOSHUA

The account of Israel's soldiers walking around Jericho until its walls came tumbling down is one of the most famous in the Bible. Joshua had served as Moses' apprentice, so when God appointed Joshua as Israel's leader, he was ready. He led the Israelites across the Jordan River and through two campaigns that enabled them to settle the hill country of Canaan. As they began to live there, Joshua divided the land among Israel's twelve tribes. The book of Joshua reveals much about God, who judges sin and faithfully keeps his promises.

SETTING

When Israel left Egypt, they left a nation that had been the most powerful, prosperous, and secure on earth. But God intervened on Israel's behalf, and Egypt was devastated. Then the Israelites spent forty years in the wilderness because they refused to believe that God could do for them in Canaan what he had already done in bringing them out of Egypt. The disbelieving generation died and a new generation came of age. The new generation believed God's promises and was ready to invade the land of Canaan.

Ancient Canaan was subdivided by geographical features into four narrow north–south strips. (1) The eastern border of Israel's settlement was on the plateau

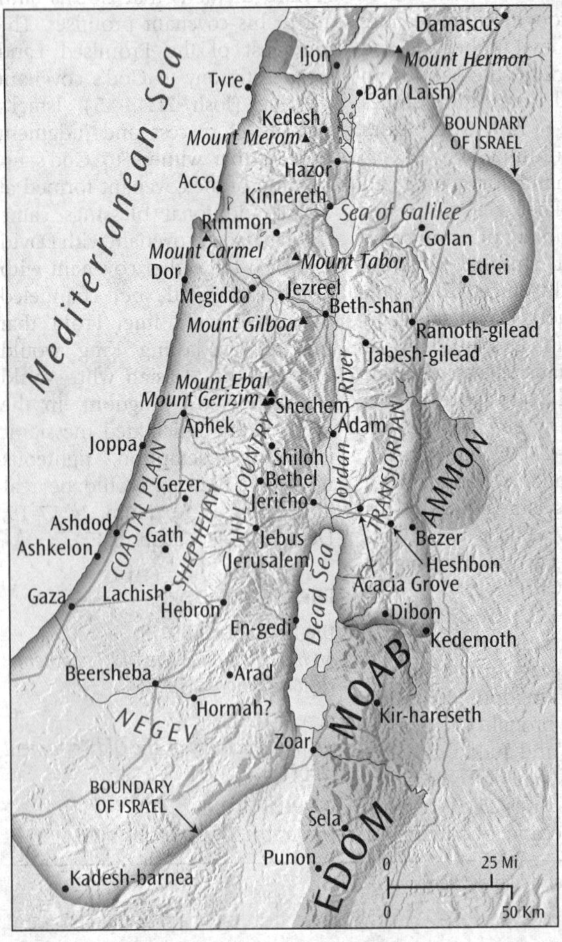

◂ **The Setting of Joshua.** The geography of the Promised Land is defined by several north–south regions: the plateau of Transjordan (the area "across the Jordan"); the deep Jordan River valley; the central Hill Country; the Shephelah ("western foothills"); and the Coastal Plain along the Mediterranean Sea. In the narrative of Joshua, Israel began at Acacia Grove in Transjordan, crossed the Jordan River, conquered Jericho and the central hill country, and took up settlements in the regions that had been cleared.

Acacia Grove 2:1; 3:1
Bethel 7:2; 8:9-17
Beth-shan 17:11, 16
Dan 19:47; Judg 18
Gezer 10:33; 16:10
Hazor 11:1-15
Hebron 10:36-37; 11:21; 14:13-15
Jericho 2:1-22; 6:1-26; 9:3-4; 24:11
Jezreel 17:16
Jordan River 1:2-15; 3:1–4:22; 22:10-34; 23:4
Lachish 10:31-33
Mount Ebal and Mount Gerizim 8:30-35
Shechem 24:1-28, 32
Shiloh 18:1-10; 21:1-3; 22:9-12

of Transjordan (the land "across the Jordan"). (2) Looking westward from Transjordan, the land drops steeply into the deep cut of the Great Rift Valley, where the Jordan River valley lies. The deepest dry point of this valley, the shores of the Dead Sea, marks the lowest dry land on the surface of the earth. (3) Continuing westward, the central hill country runs from the mountains and hills of Galilee in the north to the Negev in the south. (4) The Coastal Plain lies along the Mediterranean, interrupted near its northern end by the ridge of Mount Carmel that juts into the sea.

Much of Canaan was organized into small city-states, each with its own king. These city-states were grouped in ever-shifting coalitions. The assembling of a southern and then a northern coalition against the invading Israelites was as close to total unity as these city-states ever came. However, even these coalitions were not enough to save the Canaanites.

OUTLINE

1:1–6:27
God Brings Israel into the Land of Promise

7:1–12:24
God Gives Israel Victory

13:1–21:45
Joshua Distributes the Land

22:1–24:33
Joshua Bids Israel Farewell

SUMMARY

The story told in the first half of Joshua (chs 1–12) is among the most dramatic in the Bible. In preparing Israel to cross the Jordan, Joshua sent two young men to scout out Jericho, a town Israel would have to conquer in order to enter the hill country. The young scouts were aided by Rahab, and they promised to spare her and her family in return for her help (ch 2). As the priests stepped into the waters of the Jordan, the river's flow temporarily ceased so that the Israelites could cross (ch 3). Israel did not conquer Jericho; God gave them the city by causing its walls to fall (ch 6).

Possession of Jericho opened the routes that ascended westward into the hill country. Yet God was displeased when a man named Achan disobeyed his instructions, and Israel suffered a setback before Achan's sin was discovered and judged (ch 7). God then gave Joshua a resounding victory over the hastily gathered coalition of southern Canaanite city-states; God even granted Joshua's request for the sun and moon to stand still until the victory was complete (ch 10). Joshua then turned northward, where he gained a similarly decisive victory over a northern coalition of city-states (ch 11). The entire hill country, from the Negev in the south to Upper Galilee in the north, now lay open for Israelite settlement.

The second half of Joshua (chs 13–24) is not as heart-thumping as the first half, yet its account of the allotment of territory to Israel's twelve tribes is informative and inspiring. The narrator describes in detail the territories given to Judah, Benjamin, and Joseph (chs 15–19); these tribes became the central tribes of Israel throughout its history. Caleb's and Joshua's inheritances begin and end this section of territorial allotments (chs 15, 19). The designation of six cities of refuge (ch 20) and the assignment of towns to the Levites within each tribal territory (ch 21) complete the process of allotting the land to the tribes. The 2½ tribes given the land

TIMELINE

1446 / 1270 BC*
Israel leaves Egypt (the Exodus), moves to Mount Sinai
The covenant at Sinai

1445 / 1269 BC
Israel enters the wilderness

1406 / 1230 BC
Genesis—Deuteronomy are written
Moses dies
Israel enters Canaan

1376 / 1200 BC
Joshua dies
Beginning of the Judges period

about 1050 BC
Saul becomes king of Israel

about 1011 BC
David becomes king of Israel

* *The two dates harmonize with the traditional "early" chronology and a more recent "late" chronology of the Exodus. All dates are approximate. Please see "Chronology: Abraham to Joshua," p. 118.*

Scripture presents historical facts in order to show that history is en route to a goal: that there is dynamic movement, and that the earlier leads to a later and a last.

MARTEN WOUDSTRA
Joshua, p. 4

on the east side of the Jordan River were then free to return home, but they had to work with the western tribes to clear up a misunderstanding about the building of a memorial (ch 22). Joshua's farewell (ch 23), his convening of the people to renew their covenant with God, and three important funerals (ch 24) conclude the narrative of Joshua.

AUTHOR AND DATE

Nowhere does the book of Joshua claim that Joshua was its author. Both the frequent occurrence of the phrase "to this day" and the reference to *The Book of Jashar* as a source for Joshua indicate that the book was written after Joshua's death. Yet the occurrence of the pronoun "we" in portions of the narrative provides evidence that at least some of the book is based on personal recollections of Joshua and of those under his command. It is likely that the book of Joshua existed in more or less its present form no later than Israel's early monarchy (the time of David and Solomon). The human author or authors of Joshua remain anonymous.

JOSHUA AS HISTORY

In the last two centuries, some scholars have attempted to discredit the historical validity of Joshua by arguing that Transjordan (the area east of the Jordan River) and the cities of Jericho and Ai were not occupied when Israel entered Canaan, so Israel could not have conquered them. However, archaeological surveys show that Transjordan was occupied when Israel entered Canaan and that Jericho was indeed destroyed as Joshua describes.

Other scholars argue that accounts having an explanatory purpose (such as those explaining the origin of a name) cannot be historical. However, although some explanatory accounts found in ancient texts are mythical or false, many others are historically accurate. The book of Joshua was probably first written down near the time of the events it includes. It shows every indication of being historically accurate, even though it does not answer every historical question readers might bring to it.

For most of the time that it has been part of the Scriptures, the book of Joshua has been regarded as reliable history. Joshua records only the broad outlines of Israel's entry into Canaan. As the world's earliest history writings, the books of Joshua, Judges, Samuel, and Kings stand in contrast with the epic, mythical, and royal self-congratulatory literature produced by surrounding cultures. These biblical books provide a selective history of ancient Israel in the land where God placed them. They were written from a prophetic perspective—from the same point of view as Isaiah, Jeremiah, Ezekiel, and the twelve Minor Prophets—which regarded Israel as living in a covenant relationship with God.

An air of joyful optimism pervades the book of Joshua. Its keynote is the fulfillment of the promise made to the forefathers regarding the possession of the land of Canaan.

MARTEN WOUDSTRA
Joshua, p. 32

The book of Joshua neither states nor implies that Israel destroyed all of the Canaanites and their cities. Many Canaanites remained, as the following book of Judges also makes clear. The multi-generation history of Israel recorded in Judges shows that Israel gradually became stronger and absorbed the Canaanites. By the time of King David, most people of the land regarded themselves as Israelites, although some distinct groups still remained (e.g., 2 Sam 5:6-8; 24:16-18).

MEANING AND MESSAGE

The book of Joshua emphasizes the fulfillment of God's covenant promises to Abraham, Isaac, and Jacob. The patriarchs had traversed the land as resident aliens; now their descendants occupied it as the beneficiaries of God's faithfulness to his promise. Even the burials at the close of the book emphasize that point. Whereas Abraham had to buy a small parcel of land to bury Sarah, now Joseph, Joshua, and Eleazar were honored with burials in the territory God had given to their descendants.

God desires and pursues relationships with people. God began to bring the human race back to himself by calling out a man (Abraham), his family, and finally the nation descended from him (Israel), through whom he could bring redemption to the world. The book of Joshua demonstrates how God brought the Israelites into the land promised to their ancestors. The book proves that God speaks and acts with integrity, and it shows that God can be trusted to fulfill his promises.

The book of Joshua conveys this message in both subtle and obvious ways. The scouts' faithfulness to Rahab and her family reflects and affirms the faithfulness of the God who had brought them to her house. Caleb's inheritance at the beginning of the tribal allotments and Joshua's at the end bear testimony to God's recognition of those who remain faithful to him throughout their lifetime.

Joshua records that Israel constructed stone memorials throughout the country. These monuments served as visual aids for teaching generations of Israelite children about God's absolute faithfulness. These stone monuments crumbled or were carried away for use in construction, but the book of Joshua itself remains as an enduring memorial, still giving testimony of God's goodness and faithfulness.

The book of Joshua records disturbing events. Israel destroyed Jericho and Ai and all their people. Many Israelites, including Achan and his family, died because of Achan's sin. God fought the Canaanite coalitions that tried to prevent Israel from establishing themselves in the land. These and other episodes remind readers of the deadly seriousness of sin.

In a culture where women and their rights were held with little or no regard, Joshua records divine enlightenment. When the land was allocated among the clans of Manasseh, the daughters of Zelophehad received their father's inheritance, as God had instructed. Rahab's saving of the two young scouts in the dramatic opening episode of the book also provides a radically positive assessment of a woman's place in God's economy.

The book of Joshua has much for contemporary readers to ponder—about God himself, the consequences of human good and evil, and God's passionate commitment to human redemption and the restoration of the divine-human relationship.

FURTHER READING

JAMES MONTGOMERY BOYCE
Joshua (2005)

RICHARD HESS
Joshua (1996)

MARTEN WOUDSTRA
Joshua (1981)

GOD BRINGS ISRAEL INTO THE LAND OF PROMISE (1:1–6:27)

Joshua Assumes Command in Israel (1:1-18)

The LORD's Charge to Joshua

1 After the death of Moses the LORD's
servant, the LORD spoke to Joshua son
of Nun, Moses' assistant. He said, 2"Moses
my servant is dead. Therefore, the time has
come for you to lead these people, the Israelites, across the Jordan River into the land I
am giving them. 3I promise you what I promised Moses: 'Wherever you set foot, you will
be on land I have given you—4from the Negev wilderness in the south to the Lebanon
mountains in the north, from the Euphrates
River in the east to the Mediterranean Sea
in the west, including all the land of the Hittites.' 5No one will be able to stand against
you as long as you live. For I will be with you
as I was with Moses. I will not fail you or
[a]abandon you.
6"Be strong and courageous, for you are
the one who will lead these people to possess all the land I swore to their ancestors I
would give them. 7Be strong and very courageous. Be careful to obey all the instructions
Moses gave you. Do not deviate from them,
turning either to the right or to the left.
Then you will be successful in everything
you do. 8Study this Book of [b]Instruction continually. [c]Meditate on it day and night so you
will be sure to obey everything written in it.
Only then will you prosper and succeed in
all you do. 9This is my command—be strong
and courageous! Do not be afraid or discouraged. For the LORD your God is with you
wherever you go."

Joshua's Charge to Israel and Israel's Response

10Joshua then commanded the officers
of Israel, 11"Go through the camp and tell

1:2 Num 12:7; Deut 34:5
1:3 Deut 11:24
1:5 Deut 7:24; 31:6-8; Heb 13:5; [a]*'azab* (5800) ▸Josh 24:16
1:7 Deut 5:29, 32; 28:14; 29:9
1:8 Deut 29:9; Ps 1:1-3; [b]*torah* (8451) ▸Neh 9:13; [c]*hagah* (1897) ▸Ps 1:2
1:9 Deut 31:6-8
1:10-11 Deut 3:2-4, 15-17

Obedience and God's Blessing (1:1-9)

Gen 22:18; Exod 19:5; Deut 6:10-19; 7:9-12; 28:1-14; 30:16; 1 Kgs 8:23; Isa 1:19; 56:1-8; Zech 6:15; Matt 5:3-12; Rom 1:5; Phil 2:6-9; Heb 5:7-9; Jas 1:22-25

God made Abraham a specific promise to bring his descendants into possession of the land of Canaan (Gen 12:7; 15:7; 17:8). God repeated his promise to Moses (Exod 3:6-8; 13:3-5; Deut 1:6-8; 6:10-19). Now God was ready to fulfill his promise, using Moses' successor, Joshua, to begin the process.

God always keeps his unconditional promises. Joshua led Israel's first generation of settlers into the Promised Land, and his victories against two Canaanite coalitions—first in the south and then in the north—opened the hill country for settlement by the Israelites.

Whether or not an individual or a whole generation benefits from God's faithfulness depends on obedience. The history of God's people in the OT era alternates between their partnering with God—and enjoying the fulfillment of his generous promises—and their turning from God and reaping the harvests of defeat, dispersion, and death.

Just as God fulfilled through Joshua the promise of land to Abraham and Moses, he later fulfilled through Jesus the promise of an unfailing dynasty to David (2 Sam 7:11-16; see Matt 21:9; Rev 11:15). God's fulfillment of his promises will continue into eternity.

1:1-9 God confirmed *Joshua* as Israel's leader and Moses' successor.

1:1-2 *Moses* had died on Mount Nebo east of the Jordan (Deut 34:1-5).

1:3 Moses' death did not end God's presence with or guidance of Israel.

1:4 Ancient Israel's southernmost settlement was in *the Negev*, in the vicinity of Beersheba (15:28). Israel's northernmost tribes settled in portions of *the Lebanon mountains*, which made them neighbors of the Sidonians. • *the Mediterranean Sea:* Literally *the Great Sea.* • The *Hittites* were one of the subgroups that made up Canaan's population (see note on 3:10).

1:5 God promised never to *fail* or *abandon* Joshua, just as he had promised Moses (cp. Deut 31:6-8).

1:6-9 For emphasis, God told Joshua three times that he would need to *be strong and courageous* in order to *be successful* against the Canaanites, who outnumbered Israel. The people would also need to *be careful to obey all the instructions Moses* had given them if Israel were to settle the land, establish productive farms, and build homes, villages, and cities. The land is God's land, as is the whole earth (Ps 24:1); God brought Israel into Canaan as tenants, not as owners (Lev 25:23).

1:6 *you are the one:* God delegated Joshua as the primary agent to fulfill the promise he had given to *their ancestors* (see Exod 6:8).

1:8 *This Book of Instruction* (Hebrew *torah*) probably refers to the book of Deuteronomy (see Deut 4:44; 29:21; 30:10; 31:9-12). It includes Israel's foundational law codes as well as God's moral and spiritual instructions (see Introduction to the Pentateuch, "Literary Genres," p. 11). • God commanded Joshua to think and speak of God's instruction *day and night*—i.e., continually (cp. Deut 6:6-7; 17:18-20).

1:9 As the Israelites entered Canaan, they would fight the worshipers of the Canaanite gods, but they were *afraid* these gods would grant the Canaanites victory in battle. In reassuring Joshua, God used his personal name *the LORD* (Hebrew *Yahweh;* see note on Exod 3:15) to remind Joshua that the Lord was more powerful than any false gods the Canaanites might invoke. • *your God is with you:* God's continuous presence made it possible for Joshua to heed God's instruction.

1:10 *commanded:* Joshua now began leading God's people.

1:11 Because of fear and unbelief, the previous generation had refused to enter the Promised Land from the south forty years earlier (see Num

1:12 Num 32:20-22, 33
1:13 Deut 3:18-20
1:15 Josh 22:1-4
[d]*'erets* (0776) ‣Josh 23:14
1:16 Num 32:25
1:17 Josh 1:5, 9
1:18 [e]*shama'* (8085) ‣1 Sam 15:22

the people to get their provisions ready. In
three days you will cross the Jordan River
and take possession of the land the LORD
your God is giving you."
12 Then Joshua called together the tribes
of Reuben, Gad, and the half-tribe of Manasseh. He told them, 13 "Remember what
Moses, the servant of the LORD, commanded
you: 'The LORD your God is giving you a
place of rest. He has given you this land.'
14 Your wives, children, and livestock may
remain here in the land Moses assigned
to you on the east side of the Jordan River.
But your strong warriors, fully armed, must
lead the other tribes across the Jordan to
help them conquer their territory. Stay with
them 15 until the LORD gives them rest, as he
has given you rest, and until they, too, possess the [d]land the LORD your God is giving
them. Only then may you return and settle
here on the east side of the Jordan River
in the [d]land that Moses, the servant of the
LORD, assigned to you."
16 They answered Joshua, "We will do
whatever you command us, and we will go
wherever you send us. 17 We will obey you
just as we obeyed Moses. And may the LORD
your God be with you as he was with Moses.
18 Anyone who rebels against your orders
and does not [e]obey your words and everything you command will be put to death. So
be strong and courageous!"

JOSHUA (1:1-18)

Josh 4:1–24:33
Exod 17:8-15
Num 13:1–14:38; 27:15-23; 34:17
Deut 34:9
Judg 2:6-9
Heb 11:30

Joshua, son of Nun, was Moses' assistant and successor as Israel's leader. Joshua brought the young nation across the Jordan River into Canaan. He faithfully followed God's leadership.

Before Israel reached Mount Sinai, Joshua led Israel's warriors when Amalek attacked Israel (Exod 17:8-13). Shortly thereafter, he was among the twelve men Moses sent to scout the Promised Land (Num 13:8, 16). Joshua and Caleb urged Israel to occupy Canaan immediately (Num 14:6-9), and only they entered Canaan (Num 14:30, 38).

God directed Moses to designate Joshua as his successor (Num 27:15-23; Deut 34:9). After Moses died, Joshua led Israel across the Jordan River (1:1-18; 3:1–4:24) to the conquest of Jericho (6:1-27). When Israel suffered defeat at Ai, Joshua turned to the Lord and followed his instructions to purge Israel of sin (7:1-26); then Israel conquered Ai (8:1-29). Following God's instructions to Moses (Deut 11:29-32; 27:1–28:68), Joshua built an altar on Mount Ebal (8:30-32) and read the blessings and curses of the covenant (8:33-35). Joshua conducted campaigns against two coalitions of Canaanite kings, a southern and a northern coalition (10:1-43; 11:1-15). Joshua's victories in these campaigns opened the hill country to settlement by the Israelites.

After supervising the allotment of territories to the tribes of Israel, Joshua received his own portion in Ephraim (19:49-50). He established the cities of refuge (ch 20) and Levitical cities (ch 21) and released the 2½ tribes that had settled east of the Jordan River to return home (ch 22). As he grew old, Joshua charged Israel to remain faithful to God (chs 23–24). His farewell message at Shechem summarized God's dealings with Israel and concluded with the familiar challenge, "Choose today whom you will serve. . . . But as for me and my family, we will serve the LORD" (24:15). Joshua died at the age of 110 and was buried in Timnath-serah (24:29-30; see also Judg 2:8-9).

Joshua demonstrated exceptional faithfulness throughout his life, except in dealing with the Gibeonites (ch 9). Israel served God faithfully under Joshua and the elders Joshua trained (24:31; Judg 2:7). Stephen mentions Joshua in his martyr's sermon (Acts 7:45), and the writer of Hebrews uses Joshua's conquest of Jericho as an illustration of faith (Heb 11:30). It is fitting that Joshua and Jesus are the same name in Hebrew: Joshua led Israel into physical salvation in Canaan; Jesus leads all who believe him into eternal salvation.

13–14). The current generation would now enter from the east, across ***the Jordan River.***

1:12-15 ***Reuben, Gad, and the half-tribe of Manasseh*** had requested and received from *Moses* the conquered land east of the Jordan (Num 32:33).

1:13 God wanted the people of Israel to experience the spiritual, cultural, and emotional *rest* of a right relationship with him and each other, not just the physical rest of living in a secure and abundant land (see Heb 4:1-11).

1:14 The *warriors* of the 2½ tribes had promised to cross the Jordan with the rest of Israel ***to help them*** conquer their land (Num 32:16-19). Joshua reminded them of their obligation.

1:17 Israel often did not ***obey . . . Moses.*** However, the tribes living east of the Jordan did cross with the rest of Israel, and they did not return to their own land and homes until Joshua dismissed them (22:6).

1:18 Disobeying God's chosen ruler was treason against God himself.

Joshua Sends Spies into Jericho (2:1-24)
Rahab Hides Two Israelite Spies

2 Then Joshua secretly sent out two spies
from the Israelite camp at Acacia Grove.
He instructed them, "Scout out the land on
the other side of the Jordan River, especially
around Jericho." So the two men set out and
came to the house of a prostitute named Rahab and stayed there that night.
2But someone told the king of Jericho,
"Some Israelites have come here tonight to
spy out the land." 3So the king of Jericho
sent orders to Rahab: "Bring out the men
who have come into your house, for they
have come here to spy out the whole land."
4Rahab had hidden the two men, but she
replied, "Yes, the men were here earlier, but
I didn't know where they were from. 5They
left the town at dusk, as the gates were about
to close. I don't know where they went. If
you hurry, you can probably catch up with
them." 6(Actually, she had taken them up to
the roof and hidden them beneath bundles
of flax she had laid out.) 7So the king's men
went looking for the spies along the road
leading to the shallow crossings of the Jordan River. And as soon as the king's men
had left, the gate of Jericho was shut.

Rahab Asks That Her Family Be Spared
8Before the spies went to sleep that night,
Rahab went up on the roof to talk with
them. 9"I know the LORD has given you this
land," she told them. "We are all afraid of
you. Everyone in the land is living in terror.
10For we have heard how the LORD made a
dry path for you through the Red Sea when

2:1 Num 25:1; Heb 11:31; Jas 2:25
2:4 2 Sam 17:19
2:6 Jas 2:25
2:9 Exod 23:27; Deut 2:25; Josh 9:24
2:10 Exod 14:21; Num 21:21-35

RAHAB (2:1-21)

Josh 6:17, 22-25; Matt 1:5; Heb 11:31; Jas 2:25

Rahab, a prostitute and a woman of faith, remains enigmatic centuries after her brief appearance in Israel's history. Because she placed her faith in Israel's God and helped the two young Israelite scouts who came to her house, her life was spared when Israel captured Jericho. Because Rahab's house stood on the wall of the city, Joshua's scouts went there when they entered Jericho. Rahab might have been an innkeeper as well as a prostitute; other documents from the OT era record women innkeepers who were also prostitutes. If Rahab's house was in fact an inn, it would have been a reasonable destination; Joshua's scouts could hope they would not attract unwanted attention.

Rahab's arrangement with the scouts was a stirring declaration of faith in Yahweh, Israel's God (2:8-21). As a Canaanite woman, Rahab would have practiced the fertility cult of Baal, god of the storm and life-giving rain, and of his consort Asherah, the mother earth goddess. Yet based on reports of Israel's progress toward her land, Rahab recognized that Yahweh, the God of Israel, is "the supreme God of the heavens above and the earth below" (2:11).

After Joshua's conquest of Jericho, Rahab married Salmon of the tribe of Judah; she gave birth to a son, whom they named Boaz (Ruth 4:21; Matt 1:5). Thus, Rahab was the mother-in-law of Ruth, another foreign woman adopted into Israel. Rahab was King David's great-great-grandmother. She is listed with Moses, David, Samson, and Samuel as examples of faith demonstrated by good deeds (Heb 11:31; Jas 2:25). She is one of five women (including Mary) mentioned in Matthew's genealogy of Jesus, the human family tree of God's Son (Matt 1:5). Along with these outsiders and their stories, Rahab bears especially poignant witness to the breathtaking scope of God's grace.

2:1-24 Like any good military commander, Joshua sent out *spies* or scouts to get information about his objective. • Because Israel planned to approach Canaan from the east, they could not bypass *Jericho.*

2:1 *Acacia Grove* (Hebrew *Shittim*) was about eight miles east of the Jordan River on the plains of Moab, across from *Jericho* (see Num 25:1). • In *the house of a prostitute* strangers could avoid unwanted attention. According to tradition, Rahab was an innkeeper as well as a prostitute (Josephus, *Antiquities* 5.1.2). Other evidence from the ancient Near East suggests that women who owned and operated inns were often prostitutes.

2:2 The spies' speech probably gave them away. Hebrew and Canaanite were both dialects of the same language but with differences in vocabulary and grammar.

2:3 Jericho's *king* assumed *Rahab* was both loyal to the city and unaware of the men's mission.

2:4-5 It is not necessary either to condone or condemn Rahab's lying to the king's messengers. She might have had no concept of any ethical standards God had given Israel. Or the higher ethical value of saving lives might supersede the normal requirement to be truthful.

2:6 The inner fibers of *flax* were processed to make linen. The first step involved laying out the flax stems to dry on the flat rooftop.

2:7 Medium-sized towns such as *Jericho* had one main *gate* made of two very large wooden doors reinforced with bronze. The gate was barred for the night and opened again in the morning. By shutting the gate immediately after the pursuers departed, the authorities took a sensible precaution: If the spies had not left the town as Rahab implied, they might still be found in Jericho during the night.

2:9-10 Rahab began to declare her

2:11 Deut 4:39
2:12 Josh 2:17-18; [f]*khesed* (2617) ▸Ruth 1:8
2:15 Josh 2:18, 21
2:16 Jas 2:25
2:24 Josh 2:9; 6:2
3:1 Josh 2:1
3:2 Josh 1:11

you left Egypt. And we know what you did to Sihon and Og, the two Amorite kings east of the Jordan River, whose people you completely destroyed. 11No wonder our hearts have melted in fear! No one has the courage to fight after hearing such things. For the LORD your God is the supreme God of the heavens above and the earth below.

12"Now swear to me by the LORD that you will be [f]kind to me and my family since I have [f]helped you. Give me some guarantee that 13when Jericho is conquered, you will let me live, along with my father and mother, my brothers and sisters, and all their families."

The Scarlet Cord Becomes the Sign

14"We offer our own lives as a guarantee for your safety," the men agreed. "If you don't betray us, we will keep our promise and be kind to you when the LORD gives us the land."

15Then, since Rahab's house was built into the town wall, she let them down by a rope through the window. 16"Escape to the hill country," she told them. "Hide there for three days from the men searching for you. Then, when they have returned, you can go on your way."

17Before they left, the men told her, "We will be bound by the oath we have taken only if you follow these instructions. 18When we come into the land, you must leave this scarlet rope hanging from the window through which you let us down. And all your family members—your father, mother, brothers, and all your relatives—must be here inside the house. 19If they go out into the street and are killed, it will not be our fault. But if anyone lays a hand on people inside this house, we will accept the responsibility for their death. 20If you betray us, however, we are not bound by this oath in any way."

21"I accept your terms," she replied. And she sent them on their way, leaving the scarlet rope hanging from the window.

22The spies went up into the hill country and stayed there three days. The men who were chasing them searched everywhere along the road, but they finally returned without success.

23Then the two spies came down from the hill country, crossed the Jordan River, and reported to Joshua all that had happened to them. 24"The LORD has given us the whole land," they said, "for all the people in the land are terrified of us."

Israel Crosses the Jordan River (3:1–5:1)

Israel Prepares to Cross the Jordan

3 Early the next morning Joshua and all the Israelites left Acacia Grove and arrived at the banks of the Jordan River, where they camped before crossing. 2Three days later the Israelite officers went through the camp, 3giving these instructions to the people: "When you see the Levitical priests carrying the Ark of the Covenant of the LORD your God, move out from your positions and follow them. 4Since you have never traveled this way before, they will guide you. Stay about a half mile behind them, keeping a clear distance between you and the Ark. Make sure you don't come any closer."

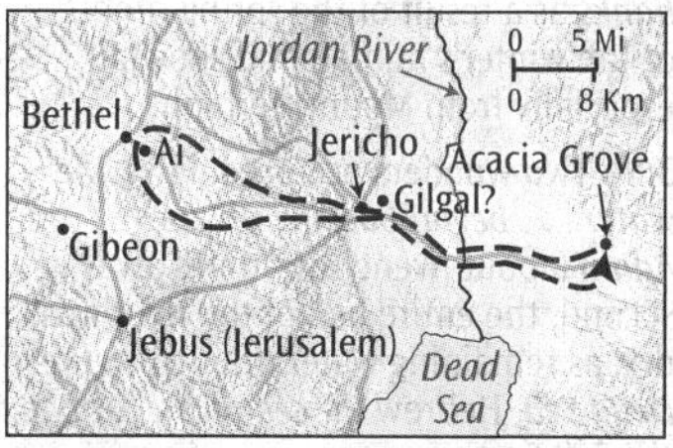

faith in ***the LORD***. • ***made a dry path:*** God had parted the waters of the *Red Sea* (literally *sea of reeds*) for Israel (Exod 14:21-28). • Israel had defeated ***Sihon and Og*** (Num 21:21-35). • ***completely destroyed:*** The Hebrew term used here refers to the complete consecration of things or people to the LORD, either by destroying them or by giving them as an offering. See Lev 27:28-29; 1 Sam 15:3.

2:11 Although the people of Canaan incurred God's judgment, Rahab's declaration of faith (proven genuine by her aid to the spies) brought her into the people of God (Heb 11:31).

◂ **Spies Sent to Jericho (2:1-24).** From Israel's camp at ACACIA GROVE, the two spies traveled to JERICHO, where they hid for the night, then went on into the hill country (probably near BETHEL and AI) before returning to Israel's camp.

2:12-13 Rahab's request demonstrated her faith in Israel and Israel's God.

2:14 When Israel attacked Jericho, Joshua and the two spies kept their ***promise*** to spare Rahab (6:22).

2:15 Because ***Rahab's house*** stood on the ***town wall***, she could hide the men on the flat roof of her house (2:6) and let them out ***through the window***, down the outer side of the wall.

2:16 The ***hill country*** of central Canaan began its steep rise just west of Jericho. Thinking that the two spies would head directly to Israel's camp across the Jordan, the pursuers from Jericho would naturally head eastward. When the pursuers gave up, the spies could slip across the Jordan unhindered.

2:19 ***it will not be our fault. But . . . we will accept the responsibility:*** The spies used a standard formula to accept responsibility for any of Rahab's family remaining with her in her house, but not for those who did not.

2:23-24 The spies' report surely raised the spirits and morale of the Israelites.

3:1 Israel had camped at *Acacia Grove* (Hebrew *Shittim*; see note on 2:1) since before Balaam's oracles (Num 22–24).

3:3 ***The Ark of the Covenant of the LORD*** was God's dwelling place among the Israelites and symbolized his throne. Whenever Israel moved, a contingent of priests carried the Ark before them (Exod 25:13-15; Num 10:33-36).

3:4 ***Stay about a half mile*** (Hebrew *about 2,000 cubits* [920 meters]) ***behind them:*** God did not want his people to take his presence for granted. They were to acknowledge his holiness with reverence, respect, and awe.

5Then Joshua told the people, "Purify
yourselves, for tomorrow the LORD will do
great wonders among you."
6In the morning Joshua said to the priests,
"Lift up the Ark of the Covenant and lead the
people across the river." And so they started
out and went ahead of the people.
7The LORD told Joshua, "Today I will begin to make you a great leader in the eyes
of all the Israelites. They will know that I
am with you, just as I was with Moses. 8Give
this command to the priests who carry the
Ark of the Covenant: 'When you reach the
banks of the Jordan River, take a few steps
into the river and stop there.' "

Joshua Promises a Miracle

9So Joshua told the Israelites, "Come and listen to what the LORD your God says. 10Today
you will know that the living God is among
you. He will surely drive out the Canaanites,
Hittites, Hivites, Perizzites, Girgashites, Amorites, and Jebusites ahead of you. 11Look,
the Ark of the Covenant, which belongs to
the Lord of the whole earth, will lead you
across the Jordan River! 12Now choose
twelve men from the tribes of Israel, one
from each tribe. 13The priests will carry the
Ark of the LORD, the Lord of all the earth. As
soon as their feet touch the water, the flow
of water will be cut off upstream, and the
river will stand up like a wall."

Israel Crosses on Dry Ground

14So the people left their camp to cross the
Jordan, and the priests who were carrying
the Ark of the Covenant went ahead of
them. 15It was the harvest season, and the
Jordan was overflowing its banks. But as
soon as the feet of the priests who were
carrying the Ark touched the water at the
river's edge, 16the water above that point began backing up a great distance away at a
town called Adam, which is near Zarethan.
And the water below that point flowed on
to the Dead Sea until the riverbed was dry.
Then all the people crossed over near the
town of Jericho.
17Meanwhile, the priests who were carrying the Ark of the LORD's Covenant stood on
dry ground in the middle of the riverbed
as the people passed by. They waited there
until the whole nation of Israel had crossed
the Jordan on dry ground.

Israel Erects Memorials of the Crossing

4 When all the people had crossed the
Jordan, the LORD said to Joshua, 2"Now
choose twelve men, one from each tribe.
3Tell them, 'Take twelve stones from the
very place where the priests are standing
in the middle of the Jordan. Carry them out
and pile them up at the place where you will
camp tonight.' "
4So Joshua called together the twelve
men he had chosen—one from each of the
tribes of Israel. 5He told them, "Go into the
middle of the Jordan, in front of the Ark
of the LORD your God. Each of you must
pick up one stone and carry it out on your
shoulder—twelve stones in all, one for each

3:5 Exod 19:10; Josh 7:13
3:7 Josh 4:14
3:8 Josh 3:17
3:10 Deut 7:1
3:12 Josh 4:2-4
3:13 Exod 15:8
3:15 1 Chr 12:15
3:16 Ps 66:6; 74:15; 114:3, 5
3:17 Exod 14:21-22, 29
4:1 Deut 27:2
4:2 Josh 3:12

3:5 ***Purify yourselves:*** They had to separate themselves from anything unclean that would bar an Israelite from coming into God's presence (cp. Exod 19:9-20; Lev 11:44).

3:7 To reassure the people that he had not brought them this far to abandon them, God made Joshua ***a great leader*** like ***Moses***.

3:8 As they crossed ***the Jordan River,*** the Ark led the way until the feet of the priests entered the water; the priests were to stand in the Jordan, not on the dry land. By carrying the Ark into the water first, the obedient priests would show their faith (cp. Jas 2:18).

3:10 ***Today you will know:*** The Israelites who were adults when Moses led Israel out of Egypt had died. The people now entering Canaan with Joshua had taken their place. The events about to unfold would signify God's presence with them and demonstrate his intention to fulfill his promises. • In Canaan, the Israelites would be living among pagan neighbors and might be tempted to join them in worshiping their gods and goddesses. None of these false gods were worthy of worship. By contrast, the Lord is ***the living God,*** and he was present among the Israelites. • The ***Canaanites*** and ***Amorites*** were distinct peoples, but their names sometimes indicated all the pre-Israelite peoples of Canaan. The ***Hittites*** were related to the earlier Hittite Empire of Asia Minor that controlled much of Canaan. The ***Jebusites*** were from the city-state of Jerusalem, which Israel did not conquer permanently until David's time. Little is known about the other three groups.

3:11 Because ***the Ark of the Covenant*** went ahead of the Israelites, they knew that ***the Lord of the whole earth*** was leading them into Canaan. Their God was not a limited local deity.

3:12 Joshua told the people to ***choose twelve men*** but did not reveal what this group of men would be doing (4:2-8).

3:13 Even though the Jordan was in its spring flood stage, ***the water*** stopped abruptly, an obvious miracle.

3:15 ***The Jordan was overflowing its banks*** as a result of the spring runoff of the winter's rainfall and snowfall, especially from Mount Hermon.

3:16 Two wonders occurred. First, ***the water . . . began backing up*** above ***Adam*** (about twenty-five miles away). Second, the entire bed of the river was dry, as remaining water drained to ***the Dead Sea*** (Hebrew *the sea of the Arabah, the Salt Sea*).

3:17 The repetition of the phrase ***on dry ground*** emphasizes that God performed a miracle.

4:2 The ***twelve men*** (see note on 3:12) represented Jacob's twelve sons. The tribe of Levi was not counted because the Levites settled in designated cities among the other tribes (Gen 49:5-7; Num 1:49-52; 18:20). However, the number of tribes remained at twelve because Joseph's two sons (Ephraim and Manasseh) were accounted as separate tribes (Gen 48:5).

4:5 Carrying the ***stone*** on a ***shoulder*** implies that the men each chose ***stones*** weighing some 100 pounds.

4:6 Exod 12:26; 13:14
4:8 Josh 4:20
4:9 Gen 28:18
4:12 Num 32:17
4:14 Josh 3:7
4:18 Josh 3:15
4:19 Josh 5:9
4:22 Josh 3:17
4:24 1 Kgs 8:42-43; Ps 89:13

of the twelve tribes of Israel. 6We will use
these stones to build a memorial. In the
future your children will ask you, 'What
do these stones mean?' 7Then you can
tell them, 'They remind us that the Jordan
River stopped flowing when the Ark of the
LORD's Covenant went across.' These stones
will stand as a memorial among the people
of Israel forever."

8So the men did as Joshua had commanded them. They took twelve stones
from the middle of the Jordan River, one for
each tribe, just as the LORD had told Joshua.
They carried them to the place where they
camped for the night and constructed the
memorial there.

9Joshua also set up another pile of twelve
stones in the middle of the Jordan, at the
place where the priests who carried the Ark
of the Covenant were standing. And they
are there to this day.

The Jordan Resumes Its Flow

10The priests who were carrying the Ark
stood in the middle of the river until all of
the LORD's commands that Moses had given
to Joshua were carried out. Meanwhile, the
people hurried across the riverbed. 11And
when everyone was safely on the other side,
the priests crossed over with the Ark of the
LORD as the people watched.

12The armed warriors from the tribes
of Reuben, Gad, and the half-tribe of Manasseh led the Israelites across the Jordan,
just as Moses had directed. 13These armed
men—about 40,000 strong—were ready for
battle, and the LORD was with them as they
crossed over to the plains of Jericho.

14That day the LORD made Joshua a great
leader in the eyes of all the Israelites, and
for the rest of his life they revered him as
much as they had revered Moses.

15The LORD had said to Joshua, 16"Command the priests carrying the Ark of the
Covenant to come up out of the riverbed."
17So Joshua gave the command. 18As soon
as the priests carrying the Ark of the LORD's
Covenant came up out of the riverbed and
their feet were on high ground, the water
of the Jordan returned and overflowed its
banks as before.

The Meaning of the Stone Memorials

19The people crossed the Jordan on the
tenth day of the first month. Then they
camped at Gilgal, just east of Jericho. 20It
was there at Gilgal that Joshua piled up the
twelve stones taken from the Jordan River.

21Then Joshua said to the Israelites, "In
the future your children will ask, 'What
do these stones mean?' 22Then you can tell
them, 'This is where the Israelites crossed
the Jordan on dry ground.' 23For the LORD
your God dried up the river right before
your eyes, and he kept it dry until you were
all across, just as he did at the Red Sea when
he dried it up until we had all crossed over.
24He did this so all the nations of the earth
might know that the LORD's hand is powerful, and so you might fear the LORD your
God forever."

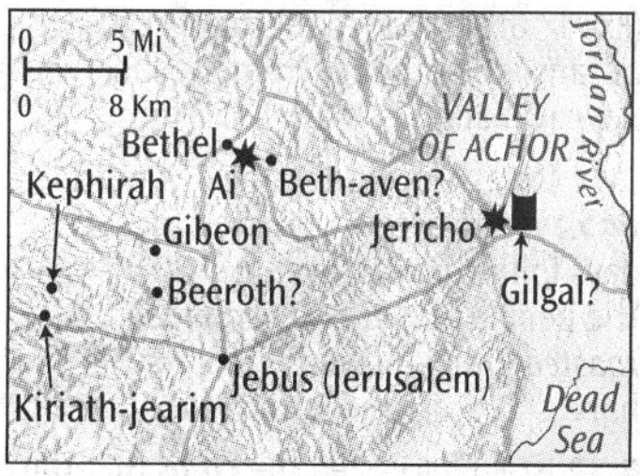

◀ **Israel's Entry into Canaan (3:1–9:27).** When Israel left ACACIA GROVE (see map on 2:1-24, p. 379), they crossed the JORDAN RIVER (chs 3–4) then camped at GILGAL (4:19-20), where the Lord renewed his covenant with them (5:2-15). Israel then fought against JERICHO (ch 6) and AI (chs 7–8). The ambassadors from GIBEON traveled only a few miles to GILGAL in their successful bid for peace (ch 9).

4:6 Joshua twice (see 4:21) told the Israelites to prepare to answer ***future*** generations. The stone ***memorial*** would serve as a teaching aid.

4:9 A second memorial ***of twelve stones in the middle of the Jordan*** was submerged as soon as the river resumed its flow. The monument's top would be visible in the dry summer seasons. • Their existence ***to this day*** indicates that the memorials stood for generations, until the final editing of the book (see Introduction to Joshua, "Author and Date," p. 374).

4:12 ***Reuben, Gad, and . . . Manasseh:*** See note on 1:12-15.

4:14 Now that God had brought the Israelites safely across the Jordan River, Israel recognized God's presence with Joshua as ***a great leader*** and ***revered him as much as they had revered Moses.*** Their confidence in Joshua would be crucial in the years ahead.

4:16 ***Ark of the Covenant:*** Literally *Ark of the Testimony.*

4:18 After Israel crossed the river, the Jordan ***overflowed its banks as before.*** These events could not occur without God's intervention.

4:19-20 ***the tenth day of the first month:*** This day in the ancient Hebrew lunar calendar occurred in late March, April, or early May, a few days before Passover (see chart, "Israel's Annual Calendar" at Exod 12:2, p. 145). • ***Gilgal*** became an important worship center for early Israel. Although its location is uncertain, it was somewhere just east or northeast of Jericho. Its name (which means "wheel of a cart," cp. Isa 28:28) implies that Joshua set the twelve stones in a circle (cp. note on 5:9).

4:23 ***Red Sea:*** Literally *sea of reeds.*

4:24 In addition to future generations of Israelites, ***all the nations of the earth*** were to understand God's power. At least some individuals in every group respond to the God who cares for them (Rev 7:9-10).

5 When all the Amorite kings west of the
Jordan and all the Canaanite kings who
lived along the Mediterranean coast heard
how the LORD had dried up the Jordan River
so the people of Israel could cross, they lost
heart and were paralyzed with fear because
of them.

Israel Reestablishes Covenant Ceremonies (5:2-12)

Joshua Circumcises Israel's Males

2At that time the LORD told Joshua, "Make
flint knives and circumcise this second generation of Israelites." 3So Joshua made flint
knives and circumcised the entire male population of Israel at Gibeath-haaraloth.

4Joshua had to circumcise them because
all the men who were old enough to fight in
battle when they left Egypt had died in the
wilderness. 5Those who left Egypt had all
been circumcised, but none of those born
after the Exodus, during the years in the
wilderness, had been circumcised. 6The
Israelites had traveled in the wilderness
for forty years until all the men who were
old enough to fight in battle when they left
Egypt had died. For they had disobeyed the
LORD, and the LORD vowed he would not let
them enter the land he had sworn to give
us—a land flowing with milk and honey.
7So Joshua circumcised their sons—those
who had grown up to take their fathers'
places—for they had not been circumcised
on the way to the Promised Land. 8After
all the males had been circumcised, they
rested in the camp until they were healed.

9Then the LORD said to Joshua, "Today I
have rolled away the shame of your slavery
in Egypt." So that place has been called Gilgal to this day.

Israel Celebrates the First Passover in the Land

10While the Israelites were camped at Gilgal on the plains of Jericho, they celebrated
[g]Passover on the evening of the fourteenth
day of the first month. 11The very next
day they began to eat unleavened bread
and roasted grain harvested from the land.
12No [h]manna appeared on the day they first
ate from the crops of the land, and it was
never seen again. So from that time on the
Israelites ate from the crops of Canaan.

The Fall of Jericho (5:13–6:27)

The LORD's Commander Confronts Joshua

13When Joshua was near the town of Jericho, he looked up and saw a man standing
in front of him with sword in hand. Joshua
went up to him and demanded, "Are you
friend or foe?"

5:1 Num 13:29; Josh 2:9-11
5:2-3 Gen 17:9-10, 23
5:4 Deut 2:14
5:6 Num 14:29-35; 26:63-65; Deut 2:7
5:10 Exod 12:18; Josh 4:19; [g]*pesakh* (6453) ‣2 Kgs 23:21
5:12 Exod 16:35; [h]*man* (4478) ‣Neh 9:20
5:13 Gen 18:1-2; 32:24; Exod 23:23; Num 22:31

5:1 After news of Israel's crossing of the Jordan River spread, all of southern Canaan was in a state of alert awaiting Israel's expected invasion. • ***Amorite kings . . . Canaanite kings:*** See note on 3:10. • ***along the Mediterranean coast:*** Literally *along the sea.* • With Israel's impossible crossing of the Jordan, the Canaanites ***lost heart and were paralyzed with fear***. They knew they faced the people of a God more powerful than any they worshiped.

5:2 Before the Israelites turned their attention to Jericho, God directed Joshua to perform the covenant renewal ceremony of circumcising all the males born in the forty years since the exodus from Egypt (see "Circumcision" at Gen 17:9-14, p. 54). Because the land was part of the covenant promise, Israel's men needed to demonstrate their personal participation in the covenant through circumcision in order to enter into the land. • Flint is found in a natural state, so ***flint knives*** were mandated for circumcision as a symbol of purity or holiness.• ***circumcise this second generation of Israelites:*** Or *circumcise the Israelites a second time.*

5:3 ***Gibeath-haaraloth*** means "hill of foreskins," suggesting that the circumcision ritual took place on a hill outside Israel's camp at Gilgal.

5:4-7 This unexpected detour in the narrative provides an important reminder of Israel's earlier refusal to believe that God would bring them safely into the land of Canaan (Num 14). This summary of God's judgment upon their fathers reminded the present generation that trusting in God was still necessary if they were to occupy the land their ancestors had forfeited. Further, it signaled the completion of God's judgment upon the earlier generation.

5:8 ***until they were healed:*** Recovery from circumcision, a relatively minor surgery, usually takes about three days if no complications occur.

5:9 ***Gilgal*** sounds like the Hebrew word *galal,* meaning "to roll," indicating that this place was where God ***rolled away*** the reproach of Egypt.

5:10 The Passover lamb was slain ***on the evening of the fourteenth day of the first month*** (see note on 4:19-20). Just as the Passover in Egypt marked the exodus from slavery, the celebration of this ***Passover*** in Canaan marked the attainment of the goal God had been leading the Israelites toward. This Passover also anticipated God's promised rest for his people in their new land. • This was apparently the first Passover Israel had celebrated since they had been encamped at Sinai (Num 9:1-5). For the younger Israelites, it was their first Passover ever; for the older ones, their first since childhood. Celebrating the Passover after such a long lapse, particularly on the eve of the campaign to take the Promised Land, heightened both the joy and the solemnity of the occasion.

5:11-12 God's daily provision of ***manna*** (Exod 16:31; Num 11:9) could cease because the produce from the land was now available.

5:11 Israel reinstituted the Festival of Unleavened Bread, observed for seven days following Passover (Lev 23:6). The people ate ***unleavened bread and roasted grain,*** a favorite food of the harvest season (see Ruth 2:14).

5:12 Israel harvested the ***crops*** that the people of Jericho did not have time to harvest before Israel crossed the Jordan.

5:13-15 ***The commander of the LORD's army*** gave Joshua instructions for conducting the siege of Jericho (6:2-5). Like God's earlier message to Joshua (1:1-9), this encounter was to encourage Joshua on the eve of action against the enemy.

5:13 ***Joshua*** was scouting the land and the city's defenses ***near the town of Jericho*** to follow up on the report of the two spies (2:23-24). Joshua demonstrated personal courage when he approached the unknown figure whose ***sword*** was already drawn.

5:14 Gen 17:3
'*tsaba'* (6635)
›1 Sam 17:45
6:2 Deut 7:24
6:4 Lev 25:9
6:7 Exod 14:15
6:9 Isa 52:12
6:13 Josh 6:4
6:17 Lev 27:28
Deut 20:17

14“Neither one,” he replied. “I am the commander of the LORD’s 'army.”
At this, Joshua fell with his face to the
ground in reverence. “I am at your command,” Joshua said. “What do you want your
servant to do?”
15The commander of the LORD’s army replied, “Take off your sandals, for the place
where you are standing is holy.” And Joshua
did as he was told.

God’s Strategy for Taking Jericho

6 Now the gates of Jericho were tightly
shut because the people were afraid of
the Israelites. No one was allowed to go out
or in. 2But the LORD said to Joshua, “I have
given you Jericho, its king, and all its strong
warriors. 3You and your fighting men should
march around the town once a day for six
days. 4Seven priests will walk ahead of the
Ark, each carrying a ram’s horn. On the seventh day you are to march around the town
seven times, with the priests blowing the
horns. 5When you hear the priests give one
long blast on the rams’ horns, have all the
people shout as loud as they can. Then the
walls of the town will collapse, and the people can charge straight into the town.”

The Israelites Circle Jericho

6So Joshua called together the priests and
said, “Take up the Ark of the LORD’s Covenant, and assign seven priests to walk
in front of it, each carrying a ram’s horn.”
7Then he gave orders to the people: “March
around the town, and the armed men will
lead the way in front of the Ark of the
LORD.”
8After Joshua spoke to the people, the
seven priests with the rams’ horns started
marching in the presence of the LORD, blowing the horns as they marched. And the Ark
of the LORD’s Covenant followed behind
them. 9Some of the armed men marched
in front of the priests with the horns and
some behind the Ark, with the priests continually blowing the horns. 10“Do not shout;
do not even talk,” Joshua commanded. “Not
a single word from any of you until I tell you
to shout. Then shout!” 11So the Ark of the
LORD was carried around the town once
that day, and then everyone returned to
spend the night in the camp.
12Joshua got up early the next morning,
and the priests again carried the Ark of the
LORD. 13The seven priests with the rams’
horns marched in front of the Ark of the
LORD, blowing their horns. Again the armed
men marched both in front of the priests
with the horns and behind the Ark of the
LORD. All this time the priests were blowing their horns. 14On the second day they
again marched around the town once and
returned to the camp. They followed this
pattern for six days.

Jericho Falls on the Seventh Day

15On the seventh day the Israelites got up at
dawn and marched around the town as they
had done before. But this time they went
around the town seven times. 16The seventh time around, as the priests sounded
the long blast on their horns, Joshua commanded the people, “Shout! For the LORD
has given you the town! 17Jericho and everything in it must be completely destroyed

5:14 ***Joshua fell with his face to the ground in reverence*** when he understood who stood before him. Joshua’s action demonstrated that he was available for God’s service, wholeheartedly and without reservation. • Scholars disagree whether the ***commander*** was an appearance of God, the pre-incarnate Christ, or an angel. His reference to himself as ***commander of the LORD’s army*** might imply that he was an angel. However, he did not prevent Joshua from worshiping him, as angels usually did (e.g., Rev 22:8-9; cp. Acts 10:25-26).

5:15 ***Take off your sandals, for the place . . . is holy:*** This was what God told Moses at the burning bush (Exod 3:5). Joshua certainly recognized the similarity. This encounter would have encouraged Joshua of God’s blessing on Israel’s first action against Canaan.

6:1 ***Jericho*** guarded two important entrances into the heart of the hill country. If the Israelites did not conquer the city first, they would leave a well-armed enemy at their back, standing between the Israelite forces and their families encamped at Gilgal. They had to conquer Jericho first.

6:2 God’s reassuring words, ***“I have given you Jericho,”*** must have lifted Joshua’s spirits. All Joshua had to do was obey God, and he had a lifetime of practice at that.

6:4 ***Seven*** is a biblical number of perfection. • The seven ***priests*** were to precede ***the Ark***, the emblem of God’s presence, at the head of Israel’s forces. This arrangement symbolized that God himself fought against the town. Israel had only to march and observe, then shout and observe, and finally mop up after God delivered the town into their hands. • The ***ram’s horn*** (Hebrew *shofar*) could sound several pitches to signal either battle or worship. In battle, the shofar alerted troops or townsfolk to an enemy’s approach or sounded the call to advance or retreat.

6:6-9 ***The Ark***, the priests ***blowing the horns***, and the military honor guard all symbolized God’s presence and his leadership of the siege.

6:10-11 Warriors would often ***shout*** in battle to lift their morale and intimidate the enemy. • ***Until I tell you:*** After thirteen circuits of Jericho by Israel’s army with only the sound of trumpets, the psychological shock when Jericho’s defenders heard shouting would be devastating.

6:15 Marching around Jericho ***seven times*** on ***the seventh day*** again symbolized that this was God’s battle.

6:16 Joshua’s command, ***“Shout! For the LORD has given you the town!”*** was not a device to cause Jericho’s walls to fall. Rather, Joshua exhorted the Israelites to celebrate God’s victory.

6:17 ***completely destroyed:*** See note on 2:9-10; similarly in 6:18, 21. Joshua reminded his troops that the town and

as an offering to the LORD. Only Rahab the
prostitute and the others in her house will
be spared, for she protected our [j]spies.
18"Do not take any of the things set apart
for destruction, or you yourselves will be
completely destroyed, and you will bring
trouble on the camp of Israel. 19Everything
made from silver, gold, bronze, or iron is sacred to the LORD and must be brought into
his treasury."
20When the people heard the sound of
the rams' horns, they shouted as loud as
they could. Suddenly, the walls of Jericho collapsed, and the Israelites charged straight
into the town and captured it. 21They completely [k]destroyed everything in it with
their swords—men and women, young and
old, cattle, sheep, goats, and donkeys.
22Meanwhile, Joshua said to the two spies,
"Keep your promise. Go to the prostitute's
house and bring her out, along with all her
family."
23The men who had been spies went in
and brought out Rahab, her father, mother,
brothers, and all the other relatives who
were with her. They moved her whole family to a safe place near the camp of Israel.

Joshua Burns and Curses Jericho

24Then the Israelites burned the town and
everything in it. Only the things made
from silver, gold, bronze, or iron were kept
for the treasury of the LORD's house. 25So
Joshua spared Rahab the prostitute and her
relatives who were with her in the house, because she had hidden the spies Joshua sent
to Jericho. And she lives among the Israelites to this day.
26At that time Joshua invoked this curse:

"May the curse of the LORD fall on
anyone
who tries to rebuild the town of
Jericho.
At the cost of his firstborn son,
he will lay its foundation.
At the cost of his youngest son,
he will set up its gates."

27So the LORD was with Joshua, and his
reputation spread throughout the land.

2. GOD GIVES ISRAEL VICTORY (7:1–12:24)

Achan's Sin, Israel's Judgment (7:1-26)

Achan's Sin

7 But Israel violated the instructions
about the things set apart for the LORD.
A man named Achan had stolen some of
these dedicated things, so the LORD was
very angry with the Israelites. Achan was
the son of Carmi, a descendant of Zimri son
of Zerah, of the tribe of Judah.

Ai Defeats the Israelites

2Joshua sent some of his men from Jericho
to spy out the town of Ai, east of Bethel,

6:17 [j]*mal'ak* (4397) ›Judg 13:3
6:18 Deut 20:17; Josh 7:1, 25
6:19 Num 31:21-23
6:20 Heb 11:30
6:21 Deut 20:16; [k]*kharam* (2763) ›Josh 7:12
6:22 Josh 2:14; Heb 11:31
6:25 Josh 2:6; Heb 11:31
6:26 1 Kgs 16:34
6:27 Josh 9:1
7:1 Josh 6:18-19; 1 Chr 2:7
7:2 Gen 28:19; Josh 16:2

---

everything in it belonged to God as the firstfruits of their inheritance in the land of Canaan. • ***Rahab:*** See 2:12-21.

6:19 See note on 6:24.

6:20 Following Joshua's last-minute commands, a final blast of the ***rams' horns*** signaled the climax.

6:22-23 The ***two spies*** fulfilled Joshua's command and their oath to Rahab. Through the actions of God's people, a pagan household saw that God is trustworthy. • ***the prostitute's house:*** See note on 2:1. • Moving Rahab and her family ***near the camp of Israel*** provided security.

6:24-27 Jericho's citizens had already been executed (6:21). Now Joshua destroyed the town and its contents. The firstfruits of the spoils of war, as with all else, belonged to God.

6:24 The fire melted and purified the ***silver, gold, bronze,*** and ***iron.*** These metals had probably been used for the figures of pagan gods. As these images melted, the metals were purified and made fit for dedication to God.

6:25 The statement that Rahab ***lives among the Israelites to this day*** affirms the breadth and depth of God's grace. Rahab was not only accepted into Israel; she ultimately was an ancestor of the Messiah (see Matt 1:5).

6:26 ***Joshua*** placed a ***curse*** upon the site because ***Jericho*** was the first Canaanite town to resist God's purposes in bringing Israel into the land. Jericho was also the first town to experience God's judgment upon Canaan's great wickedness. As the firstfruits of Israel's conquest of Canaan, it belonged to God (Exod 13:2; 23:19). God executed Joshua's curse on the first man to defy it (1 Kgs 16:34; cp. 7:1-26).

6:27 As the first chapter in Israel's conquest of Canaan closed, both the Israelites and the Canaanites could see that ***the LORD was with Joshua,*** as he had promised (1:5, 9; cp. 4:14). Crossing the Jordan and taking Jericho established Israel's presence in ***the land,*** causing the people of Canaan to fear Israel and Israel's God.

7:1–12:24 This second major section of the book records Joshua's southern and northern campaigns against two coalitions of Canaanite kings. Joshua's victories enabled Israel to settle the hill country from Galilee in the north to the Negev in the south.

7:1-26 Now that Jericho belonged to Israel, Joshua's first military problem involved securing a foothold in the hill country. The conquest of Jericho inspired Israel's confidence and consigned the people of Canaan to discouragement and despair. Yet everything hinged on Israel's obedience to God. One man's sin and its consequences demonstrate how serious was the command to destroy Jericho (see "Complete Dedication" at Lev 27:28-29, p. 244).

7:1 ***things set apart for the LORD:*** The Hebrew term used here refers to the complete consecration of things or people to the LORD, either by destroying them or by giving them as an offering; similarly in 7:11, 12, 13, 15. Also see note on 2:9-10. • ***Zimri*** (as in parallel text at 1 Chr 2:6; Hebrew reads *Zabdi;* also in 7:17, 18) ***son of Zerah:*** Achan belonged to a prominent family (Num 26:19-20) and was a leader or a potential leader, so his actions would be influential.

7:2 As he did before the battle for Jericho, ***Joshua sent some of his men*** to assess the situation at ***Ai.*** This town stood about ten miles west of Jericho at the entrance to a plateau north of Jerusalem called the Plateau of Benjamin;

7:5 Josh 2:11
7:6 Job 2:12; 42:6; Lam 2:10; Rev 18:19
7:7 Exod 5:22; [a]'adonay Yahweh (0136, 3068) ›Judg 6:22
7:9 Exod 32:12; Deut 9:28
7:10 Exod 14:15; 1 Sam 15:24

near Beth-aven. 3When they returned, they
told Joshua, "There's no need for all of us
to go up there; it won't take more than two
or three thousand men to attack Ai. Since
there are so few of them, don't make all our
people struggle to go up there."
4So approximately 3,000 warriors were
sent, but they were soundly defeated. The
men of Ai 5chased the Israelites from the
town gate as far as the quarries, and they
killed about thirty-six who were retreating
down the slope. The Israelites were paralyzed with fear at this turn of events, and
their courage melted away.

Joshua Prays, God Responds

6Joshua and the elders of Israel tore their
clothing in dismay, threw dust on their
heads, and bowed face down to the ground
before the Ark of the LORD until evening.
7Then Joshua cried out, "Oh, [a]Sovereign
LORD, why did you bring us across the
Jordan River if you are going to let the Amorites kill us? If only we had been content to
stay on the other side! 8Lord, what can I say
now that Israel has fled from its enemies?
9For when the Canaanites and all the other
people living in the land hear about it, they
will surround us and wipe our name off the
face of the earth. And then what will happen to the honor of your great name?"
10But the LORD said to Joshua, "Get up!
Why are you lying on your face like this? 11Is-
rael has sinned and broken my covenant!
They have stolen some of the things that I
commanded must be set apart for me. And
they have not only stolen them but have lied

Communal Responsibility (7:1-26)

Gen 9:24-27; Exod 20:5; 2 Kgs 14:6; 21:10-15; Ezra 9:6-15; Neh 9:16-37; Jer 31:29-30; Ezek 18:20; Dan 9:4-19; Matt 23:29-36; John 9:1-3; Rom 5:12-21; 1 Cor 15:21

Why did so many of Israel's soldiers die at Ai because of Achan's sin? Why did the Israelites stone Achan's family along with him? A significant part of the answer to these questions comes by understanding the concept of communal responsibility.

If Achan's family knew of his theft, they were accomplices and shared Achan's guilt. A community becomes responsible for sin when people either actively participate in an act of sin or silently condone sinful actions or attitudes.

But what about Achan's children who were too young to understand or those who had no knowledge of his theft? What about Israel's soldiers who died at Ai because Achan stole what belonged to God?

To understand, we have to go back to the beginning. The sin of our first parents, Adam and Eve (Gen 3), was at least twofold. First, they chose not to trust God, even though he was their true and intimate friend. Instead, they listened to the voice of a stranger. Second, though they were unsuccessful, they declared their independence from God by trying to become gods themselves. Because we all make that same choice for ourselves, no one is truly innocent.

Thus, we are all subject to the consequences of sin in the world. We may die as the result of another's sin, carelessness, or ignorance, or as a result of our own. Because one person drives under the influence of alcohol, someone else might die on the highway. Because one person wants to maximize profits, others can suffer in wretched conditions. And because Achan sinned, others in Israel died at Ai. None of this is "fair." However, God promises to bring perfect justice in his own time. God's justice will be mediated through his grace and mercy, brought to us through Jesus' death in our place.

conquering Ai would open the way for Israel to control the hill country. • ***Beth-aven,*** "house of iniquity," was probably an intentionally derogatory wordplay on the name ***Bethel,*** the "house of God." A pagan shrine stood on this site later in Israel's history (1 Kgs 12:28-33).

7:3-4 God's provision of victory at Jericho apparently bred complacency and overconfidence; Joshua did not even consult with God before sending a small contingent of troops to Ai.

7:5 Ai's defenders left through ***the town gate*** and attacked Israel's troops directly (see 8:5). • ***as far as the quarries:*** Or *as far as Shebarim*, an otherwise unknown place.

7:6 Israel's leaders ***tore their clothing*** and ***threw dust on their heads,*** common public gestures of grief or despair in the ancient Near East. By falling face down ***before the Ark of the LORD,*** Joshua belatedly acknowledged that Israel needed God's direction in the battle against Ai.

7:7 ***Joshua*** expressed his anger toward God; this explains the sharp tone of God's reply (7:10-15). Though the battle had been lost because of Achan's sin, Joshua and Israel's elders had neglected to seek God's guidance (7:3). • Joshua did not really believe that Israel should have stayed ***on the other side*** of the Jordan. Rather, he used hyperbole to show that he was at a loss over what to do next.

7:8-9 Joshua's fears were realistic. All Canaan had thought that Israel was invincible. However, because tiny Ai had defeated Israel, the Canaanites might think it could happen again. • If God allowed the wicked to ***wipe*** his people ***off the face of the earth,*** the nations would not have a witness that God continues to be involved with his world. • ***your great name:*** Cp. Exod 32:11-12; Num 14:13-19.

7:10-11 ***Get up!*** God's command was abrupt, stern, and outwardly unsympathetic. For Israel to regain God's favor, Joshua needed to act swiftly and decisively.

about it and hidden the things among their
own belongings. 12That is why the Israelites
are running from their enemies in defeat.
For now Israel itself has been set apart for
[b]destruction. I will not remain with you any
longer unless you destroy the things among
you that were set apart for [b]destruction.
13"Get up! Command the people to purify
themselves in preparation for tomorrow.
For this is what the LORD, the God of Israel,
says: Hidden among you, O Israel, are things
set apart for the LORD. You will never defeat
your enemies until you remove these things
from among you.
14"In the morning you must present yourselves by tribes, and the LORD will point out
the tribe to which the guilty man belongs.
That tribe must come forward with its clans,
and the LORD will point out the guilty clan.
That clan will then come forward, and the
LORD will point out the guilty family. Finally,
each member of the guilty family must
come forward one by one. 15The one who
has stolen what was set apart for destruction will himself be burned with fire, along
with everything he has, for he has broken
the covenant of the LORD and has done a
horrible thing in Israel."

Achan's Judgment

16Early the next morning Joshua brought
the tribes of Israel before the LORD, and the
tribe of Judah was singled out. 17Then the
clans of Judah came forward, and the clan
of Zerah was singled out. Then the families
of Zerah came forward, and the family of
Zimri was singled out. 18Every member of
Zimri's family was brought forward person
by person, and Achan was singled out.
19Then Joshua said to Achan, "My son,
give glory to the LORD, the God of Israel, by
[c]telling the truth. Make your confession
and tell me what you have done. Don't hide
it from me."
20Achan replied, "It is true! I have
sinned against the LORD, the God of Israel.
21Among the plunder I saw a beautiful robe
from Babylon, 200 silver coins, and a bar of
gold weighing more than a pound. I wanted
them so much that I took them. They are
hidden in the ground beneath my tent, with
the silver buried deeper than the rest."
22So Joshua sent some men to make a
search. They ran to the tent and found the
stolen goods hidden there, just as Achan
had said, with the silver buried beneath the
rest. 23They took the things from the tent
and brought them to Joshua and all the Israelites. Then they laid them on the ground in
the presence of the LORD.
24Then Joshua and all the Israelites took
Achan, the silver, the robe, the bar of gold,
his sons, daughters, cattle, donkeys, sheep,
goats, tent, and everything he had, and
they brought them to the valley of Achor.
25Then Joshua said to Achan, "Why have
you brought trouble on us? The LORD will
now bring trouble on you." And all the Israelites stoned Achan and his family and
burned their bodies. 26They piled a great
heap of stones over Achan, which remains
to this day. That is why the place has been
called the Valley of Trouble ever since. So
the LORD was no longer angry.

7:12 [b]*kherem* (2764) ‣1 Sam 15:3
7:17 Num 26:20
7:19 Jer 13:16; John 9:24; [c]*todah* (8426) ‣Neh 12:27
7:24 Josh 15:7
7:25 Josh 6:18
7:26 Isa 65:10; Hos 2:15

7:12 ***Israel itself has been set apart for destruction:*** With his individual sin, Achan made all Israel liable to destruction (see "Communal Responsibility" at 7:1-26, p. 385).

7:13 ***Command the people to purify themselves:*** See note on 3:5.

7:14 Israel's twelve ***tribes*** were descendants of Jacob's sons. A ***clan*** represented a smaller unit within the tribes; later, as Israel's allotments in the land were distributed, a clan usually received possession of a town and its surrounding fields, forest, and pastureland. A man's ***family*** included his sons and their dependents.

7:15 God had commanded that all the stolen goods were to be destroyed by fire. Now they would be, because Achan and ***everything*** he had would ***be burned with fire.*** Breaking ***the covenant of the LORD*** was treason, a capital offense (e.g., Exod 22:20; Deut 4:25-27).

7:16-18 Achan might have been ***singled out*** by use of the Urim and Thummim, a God-given system of sacred lots. These items remained in the care of the high priest, probably in a bag or a pouch (see Exod 28:30; Num 27:21). They might have been two different-colored objects, perhaps stones or gems. Inquiries were phrased as "yes" or "no" questions.

7:19-20 ***My son:*** This gentle, compassionate form of address reveals Joshua as a caring leader, sorry for this young man trapped by impulsive greed. Although Joshua and Achan both knew that Achan would die for his crime, Joshua entreated him to repent. Achan responded with a full confession.

7:21 The ***robe*** should have been burned with the rest of Jericho's goods. It was ***from Babylon*** (Hebrew *Shinar*), evidence that long-distance trade was a significant part of life in the ancient Near East. • ***200 silver coins*** (Hebrew *200 shekels of silver,* about 5 pounds or 2.3 kilograms in weight): Achan took pieces or lumps of silver that functioned as money; coinage was not invented until the 600s BC. • ***more than a pound:*** Hebrew *50 shekels,* about 20 ounces or 570 grams in weight. • ***I wanted them so much*** is translated "covet" in the tenth commandment (Exod 20:17). Achan's coveting had prompted his theft.

7:22 Because the matter was urgent, Joshua's messengers ***ran to the tent*** to confirm Achan's confession.

7:24 This careful listing of Achan's relatives and possessions, including the stolen items, has the tone of a legal statement. Achan compromised all that pertained to him through his contact with the stolen items; thus, all had to be included in his judgment.

7:25 Stoning was one prescribed means of execution (see, e.g., Exod 19:13).

7:26 ***the Valley of Trouble:*** Literally *valley of Achor* (Hebrew *'akor,* "trouble"). • God had not been ***angry*** without basis. God's people must be holy. To trifle with things belonging to God signifies

8:1
Deut 1:19-21
Josh 1:9; 6:2; 10:8

8:2
Deut 20:14
Josh 8:27

8:8
Judg 20:29-38

8:14
Deut 1:1
Judg 20:34

8:18
Exod 14:16; 17:9-13
Josh 8:26

The Israelites Defeat Ai (8:1-35)

Joshua Lays an Ambush against Ai

8 Then the LORD said to Joshua, "Do
not be afraid or discouraged. Take
all your fighting men and attack Ai, for I
have given you the king of Ai, his people,
his town, and his land. 2You will destroy
them as you destroyed Jericho and its king.
But this time you may keep the plunder
and the livestock for yourselves. Set an ambush behind the town."
3So Joshua and all the fighting men set
out to attack Ai. Joshua chose 30,000 of
his best warriors and sent them out at night
4with these orders: "Hide in ambush close
behind the town and be ready for action.
5When our main army attacks, the men of
Ai will come out to fight as they did before,
and we will run away from them. 6We will
let them chase us until we have drawn them
away from the town. For they will say, 'The
Israelites are running away from us as they
did before.' Then, while we are running
from them, 7you will jump up from your
ambush and take possession of the town,
for the LORD your God will give it to you.
8Set the town on fire, as the LORD has commanded. You have your orders."
9So they left and went to the place of
ambush between Bethel and the west side
of Ai. But Joshua remained among the people in the camp that night. 10Early the next
morning Joshua roused his men and started
toward Ai, accompanied by the elders of Israel. 11All the fighting men who were with
Joshua marched in front of the town and
camped on the north side of Ai, with a valley
between them and the town. 12That night
Joshua sent 5,000 men to lie in ambush between Bethel and Ai, on the west side of the
town. 13So they stationed the main army
north of the town and the ambush west of
the town. Joshua himself spent that night in
the valley.

Joshua Captures and Destroys Ai

14When the king of Ai saw the Israelites
across the valley, he and all his army hurried
out early in the morning and attacked the
Israelites at a place overlooking the Jordan
Valley. But he didn't realize there was an
ambush behind the town. 15Joshua and the
Israelite army fled toward the wilderness as
though they were badly beaten. 16Then all
the men in the town were called out to chase
after them. In this way, they were lured away
from the town. 17There was not a man left in
Ai or Bethel who did not chase after the Israelites, and the town was left wide open.
18Then the LORD said to Joshua, "Point
the spear in your hand toward Ai, for I will
hand the town over to you." Joshua did as
he was commanded. 19As soon as Joshua
gave this signal, all the men in ambush
jumped up from their position and poured
into the town. They quickly captured it and
set it on fire.
20When the men of Ai looked behind
them, smoke from the town was filling the
sky, and they had nowhere to go. For the Israelites who had fled in the direction of the
wilderness now turned on their pursuers.
21When Joshua and all the other Israelites

---

rebellion against God, and such sin always brings trouble (*'akor*) upon God's people. Achan's sin brought disaster on Israel, so the severe punishment he received was just.

8:1-13 The first attempt to conquer Ai had been done without consulting God; the second attempt would be made at God's command and direction. Before the second attempt, God spoke to Joshua again and gave him a strategy. More importantly, in light of Israel's recent disaster, God gave him encouragement and a promise.

8:1 ***Do not be afraid or discouraged:*** God gave Joshua similar encouragement before sending him against Jericho (6:2).

8:2 Unlike other ancient nations, who went to war to gain wealth, Israel served as God's agent of judgment upon the Canaanites; the ***plunder and the livestock*** were incidental. • The strategy for capturing Ai was to plan ***an ambush.*** Joshua executed God's simple instructions well. • ***behind the town:*** On its west side (see 8:12).

8:3 ***set out to attack Ai:*** This first sentence provides a summary; details are filled in over the next several paragraphs. • The Hebrew words translated *30,000* might mean *30 units* (see note on Exod 12:37) or *30 chieftains.* As the battle developed, this group would wait in ambush until Joshua called them out (8:18-19).

8:4-9 Joshua told the select squad what to expect from Israel's main army. Because this special unit would be separated from Joshua's command for nearly forty-eight hours, they needed to understand exactly what to do. Israel's success in this second attempt on Ai depended on the precise timing of their rush into the town.

8:11-13 That the main army ***marched in front of the town*** indicates that ***Joshua*** did not try to hide them from the defenders of Ai. The main army came from the east and ended the day ***camped on the north side of Ai.*** The men in ***ambush*** were ***west*** of Ai, between Ai and Bethel. • ***5,000 men:*** See note on 8:3.

8:14 The ***king of Ai . . . and all his army*** were recklessly eager to repeat their heroics of the previous battle. As Joshua and Israel had learned, such overconfidence is dangerous. • ***the Jordan Valley:*** Hebrew *the Arabah,* the desert plain north of the Dead Sea.

8:15 ***Joshua and the Israelite army fled*** as in the first attack (7:4-5).

8:17 ***not a man left in Ai or Bethel:*** Much of an individual soldier's gain from warfare was his share of the spoils taken from the defeated enemy or a reward given by his king for each enemy he killed. • The warriors of ***Bethel*** likely joined those of Ai because they also feared Israel's advance. • Some manuscripts lack ***or Bethel.***

8:18-19 Israel succeeded in this second attack on Ai because this time God directed the battle.

saw that the ambush had succeeded and that smoke was rising from the town, they turned and attacked the men of Ai. 22Meanwhile, the Israelites who were inside the town came out and attacked the enemy from the rear. So the men of Ai were caught in the middle, with Israelite fighters on both sides. Israel attacked them, and not a single person survived or escaped. 23Only the king of Ai was taken alive and brought to Joshua.

24When the Israelite army finished chasing and killing all the men of Ai in the open fields, they went back and finished off everyone inside. 25So the entire population of Ai, including men and women, was wiped out that day—12,000 in all. 26For Joshua kept holding out his spear until everyone who had lived in Ai was completely destroyed. 27Only the livestock and the treasures of the town were not destroyed, for the Israelites kept these as plunder for themselves, as the LORD had commanded Joshua. 28So Joshua burned the town of Ai, and it became a permanent mound of ruins, desolate to this very day.

29Joshua impaled the king of Ai on a sharpened pole and left him there until evening. At sunset the Israelites took down the body, as Joshua commanded, and threw it in front of the town gate. They piled a great heap of stones over him that can still be seen today.

Joshua Leads Israel in Renewing God's Covenant

30Then Joshua built an altar to the LORD, the God of Israel, on Mount Ebal. 31He followed the commands that Moses the LORD's servant had written in the Book of Instruction: "Make me an altar from stones that are uncut and have not been shaped with iron tools." Then on the altar they presented burnt offerings and peace offerings to the LORD. 32And as the Israelites watched, Joshua copied onto the stones of the altar the instructions Moses had given them.

33Then all the Israelites—foreigners and native-born alike—along with the elders, officers, and judges, were divided into two groups. One group stood in front of Mount Gerizim, the other in front of Mount Ebal. Each group faced the other, and between them stood the Levitical priests carrying the Ark of the LORD's Covenant. This was all done according to the commands that Moses, the servant of the LORD, had previously given for blessing the people of Israel.

34Joshua then read to them all the blessings and curses Moses had written in the Book of Instruction. 35Every word of every command that Moses had ever given was read to the entire assembly of Israel, including the women and children and the foreigners who lived among them.

The Gibeonites Deceive Israel (9:1-27)

Joshua Meets the Gibeonite Envoys

9 Now all the kings west of the Jordan River heard about what had happened. These were the kings of the Hittites, Amorites, Canaanites, Perizzites, Hivites, and Jebusites, who lived in the hill country, in

8:22 Deut 7:2
8:25 Deut 20:16-18
8:26 Exod 17:11-12
8:27 Josh 8:2
8:28 Deut 13:16
8:29 Deut 21:22-23
8:30 Deut 27:2-8
8:31 Exod 20:24-25; Deut 27:5-6
8:33 Deut 27:12-13
8:34 Deut 28:61; 31:11
8:35 Deut 31:12
9:1 Num 13:17, 29; Josh 3:10; 11:19

8:24-26 ***completely destroyed:*** See note on 2:9-10.

8:27 ***the livestock and the treasures of the town were not destroyed:*** See note on 8:2.

8:28 ***a permanent mound of ruins: Ai*** means "ruin." Prior to its destruction, the town was called by an unknown name. For clarity, the writer of Joshua always referred to the town as Ai, the name it was given after its destruction.

8:29 The public executions of the kings (see also 10:26; 11:10, 12) emphasized that Israel was God's agent in the judgment of the leaders and people of Canaan for their wickedness. • ***at sunset:*** See Deut 21:22-23. • ***that can still be seen today:*** See Introduction to Joshua, "Author and Date," p. 374.

8:30-31 Archaeologists have recently discovered ***an altar . . . on Mount Ebal*** built of ***uncut*** stones and not ***shaped with iron tools*** (see Exod 20:25; Deut 27:5-6). However, no inscription was found with it (8:32). • ***Burnt offerings and peace offerings*** were prescribed in the laws of sacrifice that God gave Moses while Israel was still at Mount Sinai (Lev 1; 3). ***Moses*** gave specific ***commands*** for this ceremony (see Deut 11:26-32; 27:1–28:68).

8:32 ***onto the stones of the altar*** (literally *onto the stones*): Joshua fulfilled Moses' command to set up stones and coat them with plaster (Deut 27:2-8). After the plaster hardened, ***the instructions*** (Hebrew *torah*) would permanently be on public display at the first location where Israel formally worshiped the Lord after entering the land. The public display of laws occurred in other places; the best-known example is the famous Code of Hammurabi, which that king set up in Babylon.

8:33-35 This ceremony marked the formal possession of the land, even though major campaigns against the Canaanites were still to come. The ritual of sacrifice and reading of the law highlighted the promises and obligations of God's covenant with them and anticipated the eventual possession of all of Canaan.

8:33 The town of Shechem, located between ***Mount Gerizim*** to the south and ***Mount Ebal*** to the north, guarded the pass between the two mountains. Although the covenant renewal ceremony took place at Shechem, neither Joshua nor Judges records that Israel conquered the town. • With every Israelite involved and ***the Ark*** positioned in the valley between the two groups, this ceremony was a promise to keep the covenant God had made with Israel at Sinai.

8:34 ***blessings . . . curses:*** See Deut 27:1–28:68.

8:35 OT religion was not just for the men of Israel; ***the entire assembly*** included ***the women and children.*** • The ***foreigners who lived among*** the Israelites included people who came out of Egypt with Israel in the Exodus (Exod 12:38, 48-49). These converts had accepted the Lord as their God and joined Israel when they saw the great things God had done for Israel.

9:1-27 Joshua once again failed to consult God (9:14; cp. 7:2-4), this time over an unexpected request. Other

9:3
Josh 10:2; 11:19
9:7
Exod 23:32
Josh 11:19
9:9
Josh 9:16-17
9:10
Num 21:24, 33
9:14
Num 27:21
9:15
[d]*shalom* (7965)
‣Judg 6:24

the western foothills, and along the coast of the Mediterranean Sea as far north as the Lebanon mountains. 2These kings combined their armies to fight as one against Joshua and the Israelites.

3But when the people of Gibeon heard what Joshua had done to Jericho and Ai, 4they resorted to deception to save themselves. They sent ambassadors to Joshua, loading their donkeys with weathered saddlebags and old, patched wineskins. 5They put on worn-out, patched sandals and ragged clothes. And the bread they took with them was dry and moldy. 6When they arrived at the camp of Israel at Gilgal, they told Joshua and the men of Israel, "We have come from a distant land to ask you to make a peace treaty with us."

7The Israelites replied to these Hivites, "How do we know you don't live nearby? For if you do, we cannot make a treaty with you."

8They replied, "We are your servants."

"But who are you?" Joshua demanded. "Where do you come from?"

9They answered, "Your servants have come from a very distant country. We have heard of the might of the LORD your God and of all he did in Egypt. 10We have also heard what he did to the two Amorite kings east of the Jordan River—King Sihon of Heshbon and King Og of Bashan (who lived in Ashtaroth). 11So our elders and all our people instructed us, 'Take supplies for a long journey. Go meet with the people of Israel and tell them, "We are your servants; please make a treaty with us." '

12"This bread was hot from the ovens when we left our homes. But now, as you can see, it is dry and moldy. 13These wineskins were new when we filled them, but now they are old and split open. And our clothing and sandals are worn out from our very long journey."

14So the Israelites examined their food, but they did not consult the LORD. 15Then Joshua made a [d]peace treaty with them and guaranteed their safety, and the leaders of

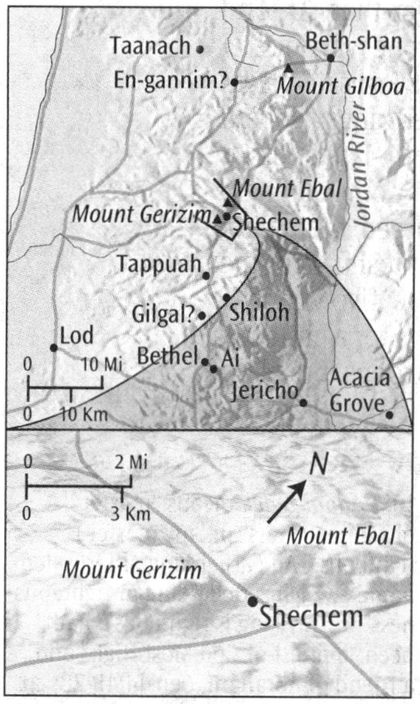

◂ **Mount Ebal and Mount Gerizim** (8:30-35). After Israel's victories over JERICHO and AI, the Israelites traveled north to SHECHEM, and Joshua followed the instructions given in the law for renewing the covenant at MOUNT EBAL and MOUNT GERIZIM (see also 24:1-28; see Deut 11:26-32).

ancient Near Eastern accounts tell only of a leader's triumphs; this author also recorded the shortcomings of Joshua and Israel's elders. The real hero of the story is God, whose accomplishments the author wished to tell.

9:1 ***Hittites . . . Jebusites:*** See note on 3:10. • The fertile region of lower hills between the highlands of Judah and the southern coastal plain was known as ***the western foothills*** (Hebrew *the Shephelah*). • Although not all of the coastal plain of ***the Mediterranean Sea*** (literally *the Great Sea*) was occupied during this period, several important cities did exist. The kings of those small city-states, ***as far north*** as Mount Carmel, joined the southern coalition to resist Israel's advances.

9:2 Chapter 10 provides a more complete description of ***these kings*** and their reasons for forming a coalition to ***fight . . . the Israelites.***

9:3 The ***people of Gibeon*** deceitfully attempted to make a covenant with Israel. The town of ***Gibeon*** was on the plateau just north of Jerusalem (see note on 7:2), not more than fifteen miles from Israel's camp at Gilgal.

9:4-6 Long-distance travel was difficult, dirty, and dangerous in those days. If they were to carry off their deception, the Gibeonite supplies, ***clothes,*** and even food had to look the part.

9:7-8 The name ***Hivites*** is known only from the Bible and refers to a non-Semitic ethnic group that lived in various parts of Canaan (see Gen 34:2; 36:2; Exod 23:23, 28). • ***How do we know you don't live nearby?*** Israel's leaders raised the possibility of deception. Joshua followed the Gibeonites' evasive reply by asking two direct questions. However, Joshua could have received a direct answer by consulting the Lord (9:14).

9:9-10 ***in Egypt:*** See Exod 7–14. • ***kings . . . Sihon . . . Og:*** See Num 21.

9:11-13 Distracted by the flattering words about God and the notion that a foreign people wanted to make a treaty with them, none of Israel's leaders noticed that the Gibeonites had failed to answer Joshua's questions. • If the Israelites spared their lives, the Gibeonites were willing to be Israel's ***servants*** and swear to a ***treaty*** with Israel. This request should have raised suspicions among Israel's leaders: Why would people from a distant land be concerned about a treaty of protection?

9:14 Israel's leaders ***examined*** the bread to verify the Gibeonites' story, but Joshua neglected to ***consult the LORD.*** This same oversight had cost lives at Ai, whereas the victories at Jericho and Ai had both been won when Israel followed God's instructions precisely.

9:15 Israel entered into a ***peace treaty*** with the Gibeonites. The Israelites were God's vassals, having entered into a suzerain-vassal treaty with God at Sinai (see note on Exod 20:1–23:33). Israel did not have authority to enter into treaties without the approval of their own suzerain. • ***guaranteed their safety*** (literally *cut with them a covenant for their lives*): Nations ratified covenants by a ceremony that involved cutting sacrificial animals in half. The parties to the covenant walked between the two animal halves (cp. Gen 15:9-18) to symbolize their commitment to be cut in two like the sacrifice if one violated the terms of the covenant. Covenants also were written documents, sometimes chiseled in stone and set up in a public area for all to see and remember (see note on 8:32). • In Israel, ***a binding oath*** was sworn in the name of the Lord. Violating the oath invited the Lord's judgment for swearing falsely (Exod 20:7).

the community ratified their agreement with a binding oath.

Israel Sets the Gibeonites to Menial Labor

16Three days after making the treaty, they learned that these people actually lived nearby! 17The Israelites set out at once to investigate and reached their towns in three days. The names of these towns were Gibeon, Kephirah, Beeroth, and Kiriath-jearim. 18But the Israelites did not attack the towns, for the Israelite leaders had made a vow to them in the name of the LORD, the God of Israel.

The people of Israel grumbled against their leaders because of the treaty. 19But the leaders replied, "Since we have sworn an oath in the presence of the LORD, the God of Israel, we cannot touch them. 20This is what we must do. We must let them live, for divine anger would come upon us if we broke our oath. 21Let them live." So they made them woodcutters and water carriers for the entire community, as the Israelite leaders directed.

22Joshua called together the Gibeonites and said, "Why did you lie to us? Why did you say that you live in a distant land when you live right here among us? 23May you be cursed! From now on you will always be servants who cut wood and carry water for the house of my God."

24They replied, "We did it because we—your servants—were clearly told that the LORD your God commanded his servant Moses to give you this entire land and to destroy all the people living in it. So we feared greatly for our lives because of you. That is why we have done this. 25Now we are at your mercy—do to us whatever you think is right."

26So Joshua did not allow the people of Israel to kill them. 27But that day he made the Gibeonites the woodcutters and water carriers for the community of Israel and for the altar of the LORD—wherever the LORD would choose to build it. And that is what they do to this day.

Joshua Defeats the Southern Canaanite Coalition (10:1-43)

Gibeon Calls on Joshua for Help

10 Adoni-zedek, king of Jerusalem, heard that Joshua had captured and completely destroyed Ai and killed its king, just as he had destroyed the town of Jericho and killed its king. He also learned that the Gibeonites had made peace with Israel and were now their allies. 2He and his people became very afraid when they heard all this because Gibeon was a large town—as large as the royal cities and larger than Ai. And the Gibeonite men were strong warriors.

3So King Adoni-zedek of Jerusalem sent messengers to several other kings: Hoham of Hebron, Piram of Jarmuth, Japhia of Lachish, and Debir of Eglon. 4"Come and help me destroy Gibeon," he urged them, "for they have made peace with Joshua and the people of Israel." 5So these five Amorite kings combined their armies for a united attack. They moved all their troops into place and attacked Gibeon.

9:17 Josh 15:9, 60; 18:25-28
9:21 Deut 29:11
9:24 Deut 7:1-2
9:27 Deut 12:5
10:1 Josh 8:22-28; 9:15
10:3 2 Chr 11:9
10:5 Num 13:29; Josh 9:2

9:16 ***lived nearby!*** In reporting Israel's discovery, the author repeated the word the Israelites had used to voice their suspicion of the Gibeonites (9:7).

9:17 ***Gibeon, Kephirah, Beeroth, and Kiriath-jearim*** were on the plateau northwest of Jerusalem and southwest of Bethel and Ai (see note on 7:2).

9:18-21 Israel was not entitled to break this *treaty* even though the Gibeonites deceived the Israelites into making it. Breaking a covenant sworn by ***an oath in the presence of the LORD*** would have made light of God's name and honor (cp. Gen 27:30-38).

9:22 As the leader of Israel, ***Joshua*** was within his rights when he ***called together the Gibeonites*** to question them. • ***you live right here among us?*** See notes on 9:7-8 and 9:16. Joshua's use of this phrase tacitly acknowledged that he should not have accepted the word of the Gibeonites without consulting the Lord.

9:23 The Gibeonites were ***cursed***, meaning they were diminished to the status of ***servants***. • At that time, ***the house of . . . God*** was the Tabernacle; later, it was the Temple at Jerusalem.

9:24-25 The response of the Gibeonites amounted to a statement of faith in the Lord: They acted deceptively because they believed that God would enable Israel to conquer Canaan.

9:26-27 This summary closes the account of Joshua's second and last major mistake in leadership. • ***to this day:*** See note on 4:9.

10:1-43 Gibeon and its neighboring cities occupied a plateau north of Jerusalem (see note on 7:2). With Gibeon now allied to Israel, control of the plateau and of the central hill country in the vicinity of Gibeon belonged to Israel. Throughout history, whoever has controlled the plateau has, in general, also controlled the hill country. The Canaanite kings had to conquer Gibeon or their cause was lost.

10:1 ***Adoni-zedek*** means "master of righteousness" or "my master is righteous." An earlier king of Jerusalem named Melchizedek ("king of righteousness" or "my king is righteous") had been "a priest of God Most High" and a friend of Abraham (Gen 14:18-20; cp. note on Ps 76:2). However, Adoni-zedek was not a friend to Joshua or a believer in the Lord. • ***completely destroyed:*** See note on 2:9-10; also in 10:28, 35, 37, 39, 40.

10:2 ***Gibeon*** was apparently not one of ***the royal cities.*** Gibeon might have been subservient to Canaan-controlled Jerusalem before making the covenant with Joshua, or it might have been an independent town controlled by a few leading families.

10:5 When the OT makes a distinction between Amorites and Canaanites (see note on 3:10), the ***Amorite kings*** controlled the hill country, while the Canaanites occupied the valleys and the coastal plain.

10:8
Josh 1:5, 9
10:10
Deut 7:23
10:13
2 Sam 1:18
Isa 38:8
10:14
Exod 14:14
Deut 1:30
10:15
Josh 10:6, 43
10:16
Josh 10:5
10:20
Deut 20:16
10:21
Josh 10:16
10:22
Deut 7:24

[6]The men of Gibeon quickly sent messengers to Joshua at his camp in Gilgal. "Don't
abandon your servants now!" they pleaded.
"Come at once! Save us! Help us! For all the
Amorite kings who live in the hill country
have joined forces to attack us."
[7]So Joshua and his entire army, including
his best warriors, left Gilgal and set out for
Gibeon. [8]"Do not be afraid of them," the
LORD said to Joshua, "for I have given you
victory over them. Not a single one of them
will be able to stand up to you."

The Sun and Moon Stand Still

[9]Joshua traveled all night from Gilgal and
took the Amorite armies by surprise. [10]The
LORD threw them into a panic, and the Israelites slaughtered great numbers of them
at Gibeon. Then the Israelites chased the
enemy along the road to Beth-horon, killing
them all along the way to Azekah and Makkedah. [11]As the Amorites retreated down the
road from Beth-horon, the LORD destroyed
them with a terrible hailstorm from heaven
that continued until they reached Azekah.
The hail killed more of the enemy than the
Israelites killed with the sword.
[12]On the day the LORD gave the Israelites
victory over the Amorites, Joshua prayed to
the LORD in front of all the people of Israel.
He said,

"Let the sun stand still over Gibeon,
and the moon over the valley of Aijalon."

[13]So the sun stood still and the moon stayed
in place until the nation of Israel had defeated its enemies.
Is this event not recorded in *The Book of
Jashar*? The sun stayed in the middle of the
sky, and it did not set as on a normal day.
[14]There has never been a day like this one
before or since, when the LORD answered
such a prayer. Surely the LORD fought for
Israel that day!
[15]Then Joshua and the Israelite army returned to their camp at Gilgal.

Joshua Executes the Five Southern Kings

[16]During the battle the five kings escaped
and hid in a cave at Makkedah. [17]When
Joshua heard that they had been found,
[18]he issued this command: "Cover the opening of the cave with large rocks, and place
guards at the entrance to keep the kings inside. [19]The rest of you continue chasing the
enemy and cut them down from the rear.
Don't give them a chance to get back to their
towns, for the LORD your God has given you
victory over them."
[20]So Joshua and the Israelite army continued the slaughter and completely crushed
the enemy. They totally wiped out the five
armies except for a tiny remnant that managed to reach their fortified towns. [21]Then
the Israelites returned safely to Joshua in
the camp at Makkedah. After that, no one
dared to speak even a word against Israel.
[22]Then Joshua said, "Remove the rocks
covering the opening of the cave, and bring
the five kings to me." [23]So they brought the
five kings out of the cave—the kings of Jerusalem, Hebron, Jarmuth, Lachish, and Eglon.
[24]When they brought them out, Joshua told
the commanders of his army, "Come and

10:7 ***Joshua*** had sworn to rescue ***Gibeon***, so now he ***set out*** to do it.

10:8 God once again urged Joshua ***not*** to ***be afraid***, assuring him of victory over Israel's enemies (see also 1:9; 8:1).

10:9 Joshua's army walked ***all night*** to travel the fifteen miles up the rugged passes and steep slopes and across the plateau. By attacking ***the Amorite armies*** from the east at sunrise, Joshua's army came out of the sun, blinding the Amorites as they faced eastward to fight. • Israel's covenant required the nation to respond to Gibeon's plea for help, but Joshua responded more promptly than any treaty required. Defeating the Canaanite force with a swift strike gave Israel a tremendous advantage.

10:10-13 Three miracles—supernatural panic, a terrible hailstorm, and a lengthened day—demonstrated that the destruction of the Canaanites was entirely God's doing.

10:10 It was about forty miles from ***Gibeon***, down the ***Beth-horon*** road, then south through the western foothills to ***Azekah and Makkedah***.

10:12 ***Joshua prayed*** to have the day lengthened so the Israelites could finish the task without allowing the Amorite forces time to organize a new defense against Israel. • The ***sun*** and ***moon***, two of Canaan's most powerful gods, proved powerless against the Lord. • ***Aijalon*** was a city near the western end of the Beth-horon road.

10:13 God caused the ***sun*** to stay ***in the middle of the sky*** and it ***did not set as on a normal day*** (or ***did not set for about a whole day***). Not all miracles can be understood, whether in purpose, in scope, or in mechanism. • ***The Book of Jashar*** (or ***The Book of the Upright***) served as one of the ancient sources for Israel's historians. While well known in ancient Israel, it did not survive as a separate document.

10:16 ***The five kings*** (see 10:3) had led the southern coalition against God's people. • Although the location of ***Makkedah*** is uncertain, it was in the same district as Lachish (15:39-41) in the southern part of the western foothills, about twenty-five miles southwest of Jerusalem. Limestone caves are numerous in that region.

10:18-19 By blocking ***the opening of the cave***, Joshua reduced the number of guards needed to keep the kings from escaping. This also eliminated danger to the guards and freed more men to pursue the fleeing people.

10:21 The armies ***returned safely***, indicating that Israel suffered few or no casualties in this battle, a sign of God's presence in the battle. • ***no one dared:*** The Canaanites in the south now had firsthand experience that Israel's powerful God was fighting them.

10:24 Victorious commanders in the ancient Near East would commonly ***put*** their ***feet on*** defeated ***kings' necks*** to symbolize their subjugation.

put your feet on the kings' necks." And they
did as they were told.
25"Don't ever be afraid or discouraged,"
Joshua told his men. "Be strong and courageous, for the LORD is going to do this to all
of your enemies." 26Then Joshua killed each
of the five kings and impaled them on five
sharpened poles, where they hung until
evening.
27As the sun was going down, Joshua gave
instructions for the bodies of the kings to
be taken down from the poles and thrown
into the cave where they had been hiding.
Then they covered the opening of the cave
with a pile of large rocks, which remains to
this very day.

Joshua Destroys the Southern Towns

28That same day Joshua captured and destroyed the town of Makkedah. He killed
everyone in it, including the king, leaving
no survivors. He destroyed them all, and he
killed the king of Makkedah as he had killed
the king of Jericho. 29Then Joshua and the
Israelites went to Libnah and attacked it.
30There, too, the LORD gave them the town
and its king. He killed everyone in it, leaving
no survivors. Then Joshua killed the king of
Libnah as he had killed the king of Jericho.
31From Libnah, Joshua and the Israelites
went to Lachish and attacked it. 32Here
again, the LORD gave them Lachish. Joshua
took it on the second day and killed everyone in it, just as he had done at Libnah.
33During the attack on Lachish, King Ho-
ram of Gezer arrived with his army to help
defend the town. But Joshua's men killed
him and his army, leaving no survivors.
34Then Joshua and the Israelite army went
on to Eglon and attacked it. 35They captured
it that day and killed everyone in it. He completely destroyed everyone, just as he had
done at Lachish. 36From Eglon, Joshua and
the Israelite army went up to Hebron and
attacked it. 37They captured the town and
killed everyone in it, including its king, leaving no survivors. They did the same thing to
all of its surrounding villages. And just as he
had done at Eglon, he completely destroyed
the entire population.
38Then Joshua and the Israelites turned
back and attacked Debir. 39He captured the
town, its king, and all of its surrounding villages. He completely destroyed everyone in
it, leaving no survivors. He did to Debir and
its king just what he had done to Hebron
and to Libnah and its king.

Summary of the Southern Campaign

40So Joshua conquered the whole region—
the kings and people of the hill country,
the Negev, the western foothills, and the
mountain slopes. He completely destroyed
everyone in the land, leaving no survivors,
just as the LORD, the God of Israel, had commanded. 41Joshua slaughtered them from
Kadesh-barnea to Gaza and from the region
around the town of Goshen up to Gibeon.
42Joshua conquered all these kings and their
land in a single campaign, for the LORD, the
God of Israel, was fighting for his people.
43Then Joshua and the Israelite army returned to their camp at Gilgal.

Joshua Defeats the Northern Canaanite Coalition (11:1-15)

11 When King Jabin of Hazor heard
what had happened, he sent messages to the following kings: King Jobab of
Madon; the king of Shimron; the king of

10:25 Josh 10:8
10:26 Josh 8:29
10:27 Deut 21:22-23
10:29 Num 33:20-21; Josh 15:42
10:36 Josh 14:13; 15:13
10:40 Deut 1:7; 7:24; 20:16
10:41 Josh 11:16; 15:51
10:42 Josh 10:14
11:1 Josh 11:10

10:25 Joshua encouraged his men at Makkedah, using the same words God had used to encourage him before Israel crossed the Jordan and again before the battle of Ai (1:9; 8:1).

10:26-27 Joshua's execution of the *five kings* followed the pattern established with the king of Ai (see note on 8:29).

10:28-39 Joshua led the Israelites throughout southern Canaan, where they captured but did not burn a number of important cities. God had promised that Israel would dwell in cities they had not built (Deut 6:10).

10:28 ***He destroyed them all:*** See note on 2:9-10.

10:29-30 ***Libnah*** was probably about six miles north of Lachish. Because the location of Makkedah is uncertain, how far it was from Libnah is also unknown.

10:31-33 ***Lachish,*** by far the most important of the six cities taken at this time, was defended so well that it took Joshua until ***the second day*** to capture it. • ***Gezer*** was about twenty-five miles north of Lachish. Lachish and Gezer might have had a mutual aid treaty.

10:38-39 Because settlement in the hill country was sparse, the ***surrounding villages***—walled towns that could not maintain their independence—depended on the kingdoms of the dominant cities for protection.

10:40 Joshua's southern campaign cleared the way for the southern tribes to occupy this ***whole region*** when the settlement process began. • ***the western foothills:*** Hebrew *the Shephelah*; see map, facing page; note on Deut 1:7.

10:41 This ***Goshen*** was not the region in Egypt's Nile delta (Gen 47:27) but a town in the hill country (15:51) south of Jerusalem. From ***Goshen up to Gibeon*** describes the eastern reach of Joshua's southern campaign.

10:43 ***Joshua*** and his ***army*** were free to return ***to their camp at Gilgal*** in the Jordan Valley and turn their thoughts to the northern region of Canaan.

11:1-16 Through the more detailed accounts of Joshua's campaign in southern Canaan (chs 6-10), the narrator established firmly that the Israelites needed God's help to succeed. Because what had been true in the southern campaign would also be true in the northern (ch 11), those details were unnecessary here.

11:1-3 ***Hazor*** lay along the international trade route and was by far the largest and most important inland city of Canaan (see 11:10). • Virtually all of

11:2 Josh 12:3
11:4 Judg 7:12
11:6 Josh 10:8; 2 Sam 8:4
11:10 Judg 4:2; 1 Sam 12:9; 1 Kgs 9:15; 2 Kgs 15:29
11:11 Deut 20:16-17

Acshaph; [2]all the kings of the northern hill
country; the kings in the Jordan Valley south
of Galilee; the kings in the Galilean foothills;
the kings of Naphoth-dor on the west; [3]the
kings of Canaan, both east and west; the
kings of the Amorites, the Hittites, the Perizzites, the Jebusites in the hill country, and
the Hivites in the towns on the slopes of
Mount Hermon in the land of Mizpah.
[4]All these kings came out to fight. Their
combined armies formed a vast horde. And
with all their horses and chariots, they covered the landscape like the sand on the
seashore. [5]The kings joined forces and established their camp around the water near
Merom to fight against Israel.
[6]Then the LORD said to Joshua, "Do not
be afraid of them. By this time tomorrow I
will hand all of them over to Israel as dead
men. Then you must cripple their horses
and burn their chariots."
[7]So Joshua and all his fighting men traveled to the water near Merom and attacked
suddenly. [8]And the LORD gave them victory over their enemies. The Israelites
chased them as far as Greater Sidon and
Misrephoth-maim, and eastward into the
valley of Mizpah, until not one enemy warrior was left alive. [9]Then Joshua crippled
the horses and burned all the chariots, as
the LORD had instructed.
[10]Joshua then turned back and captured
Hazor and killed its king. (Hazor had at one
time been the capital of all these kingdoms.)
[11]The Israelites completely destroyed every
living thing in the city, leaving no survivors.
Not a single person was spared. And then
Joshua burned the city.

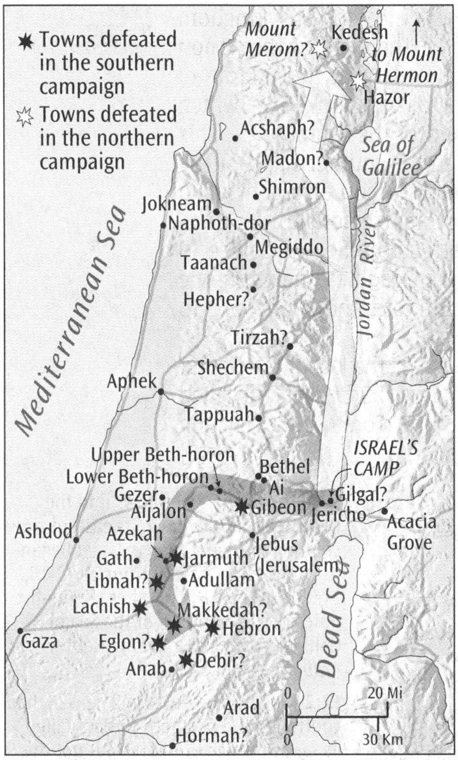

◀ **Israel's Conquest of Canaan (10:1–12:24).** Israel's initial conquest took place in two major campaigns, a southern campaign and a northern one. The southern campaign began when a coalition of armies, led by the king of JERUSALEM, attacked GIBEON and were defeated by Israelite forces in a surprise attack (10:1-15). Then, after killing the kings of the defeated armies (10:16-27), the Israelites swept through and destroyed a number of southern towns (10:28-42), effectively clearing the hill country of Judea for settlement before returning to camp at GILGAL. The northern campaign, too, was instigated by Canaanites, with the king of HAZOR in the lead (11:1-5). Joshua defeated the northern coalition, also in a surprise attack, then destroyed the great city of Hazor (11:6-15). This victory cleared the way for Israel to conquer the rest of the hill country and Jordan Valley (11:16-22). Chapter 12 summarizes all the kings Israel defeated, both east of the Jordan and within Canaan.

northern Canaan joined the coalition of ***King Jabin*** against Israel. This region stretched from the Mediterranean Sea in the west to the desert in the east and from the borders of Phoenicia in the north to the hill country and the Jordan Valley in the south. • The term ***Jebusites*** typically refers to the people of Jerusalem and surrounding towns under its control. Perhaps men from Jebus were mercenaries to ***Jabin.*** • ***Mizpah*** means "watchtower" or "lookout." Several places had this name; this one was the extensive region of the lower ***slopes of Mount Hermon,*** the highest peak of the Promised Land.

11:2 ***in the Jordan Valley south of Galilee:*** Hebrew *in the Arabah south of Kinnereth.* • ***the Galilean foothills:*** Hebrew *the Shephelah*; also in 11:16.

11:4 In the ancient Near East at this time, ***horses*** only pulled chariots; cavalry and mounted bowmen did not appear until centuries later. • Israel probably faced ***chariots*** for the first time in this battle against the northern coalition, where the land was flatter than in southern Canaan. As the heavy weapons of the battlefield, chariots easily overpowered foot soldiers. Scythes were often attached to the axles, and charioteers drove at opposing infantry to mow them down.

11:5 The location of ***Merom*** is unclear. The most likely site was in Upper Galilee a few miles west of Hazor.

11:6 God again urged Joshua ***not*** to ***be afraid,*** promising Israel the victory, even against horses and chariots. • ***cripple their horses and burn their chariots:*** God wanted Israel to rely on him rather than weaponry and equipment (cp. Deut 17:16; Isa 31:1).

11:7 ***Joshua . . . traveled:*** Jabin might have planned to move from Merom out of Upper Galilee to meet Israel on a more advantageous battlefield when all his forces were assembled. However, Joshua attacked suddenly, before Jabin could choose the battleground.

11:8 The Canaanites scattered widely, fleeing north and west into the territory of ***Greater Sidon*** on the Mediterranean coast and ***eastward into the valley of Mizpah.***

11:11 ***completely destroyed:*** See note on 2:9-10; also in 11:12, 20, 21. • Archaeological excavation confirms that ***the city*** of Hazor was destroyed by fire during this period.

12Joshua slaughtered all the other kings
and their people, completely destroying
them, just as Moses, the servant of the LORD,
had commanded. 13But the Israelites did
not burn any of the towns built on mounds
except Hazor, which Joshua burned. 14And
the Israelites took all the plunder and livestock of the ravaged towns for themselves.
But they killed all the people, leaving no
survivors. 15As the LORD had commanded
his servant Moses, so Moses commanded
Joshua. And Joshua did as he was told, carefully obeying all the commands that the
LORD had given to Moses.

Summary of Joshua's Campaigns (11:16-23)

16So Joshua conquered the entire region—
the hill country, the entire Negev, the whole
area around the town of Goshen, the western
foothills, the Jordan Valley, the mountains
of Israel, and the Galilean foothills. 17The
Israelite territory now extended all the way
from Mount Halak, which leads up to Seir
in the south, as far north as Baal-gad at the
foot of Mount Hermon in the valley of Lebanon. Joshua killed all the kings of those
territories, 18waging war for a long time
to accomplish this. 19No one in this region
made peace with the Israelites except the Hivites of Gibeon. All the others were defeated.
20For the LORD hardened their hearts and
caused them to fight the Israelites. So they
were completely destroyed without mercy,
as the LORD had commanded Moses.
21During this period Joshua destroyed all
the descendants of Anak, who lived in the hill
country of Hebron, Debir, Anab, and the entire hill country of Judah and Israel. He killed
them all and completely destroyed their
towns. 22None of the descendants of Anak
were left in all the land of Israel, though some
still remained in Gaza, Gath, and Ashdod.
23So Joshua took control of the entire
land, just as the LORD had instructed Moses.
He gave it to the people of Israel as their special possession, dividing the land among the
tribes. So the land finally had rest from war.

List of Defeated Canaanite Kings (12:1-24)

Kings Defeated East of the Jordan

12 These are the kings east of the Jordan River who had been killed by the
Israelites and whose land was taken. Their
territory extended from the Arnon Gorge
to Mount Hermon and included all the land
east of the Jordan Valley.
2King Sihon of the Amorites, who lived
in Heshbon, was defeated. His kingdom
included Aroer, on the edge of the Arnon
Gorge, and extended from the middle of
the Arnon Gorge to the Jabbok River, which
serves as a border for the Ammonites. This
territory included the southern half of the
territory of Gilead. 3Sihon also controlled
the Jordan Valley and regions to the east—
from as far north as the Sea of Galilee to
as far south as the Dead Sea, including the
road to Beth-jeshimoth and southward to
the slopes of Pisgah.
4King Og of Bashan, the last of the Rephaites, lived at Ashtaroth and Edrei. 5He ruled
a territory stretching from Mount Hermon

11:14 Num 31:11-12
11:15 Exod 34:11-12
11:16 Josh 10:40
11:17 Deut 7:24; Josh 12:7
11:19 Josh 9:3-15
11:20 Exod 14:17; Deut 7:16
11:21 Num 13:33; Deut 9:1-2; Josh 14:12; 15:13
11:23 Deut 1:38; 12:9-10; 25:19; Heb 4:8
12:1 Num 32:33; Deut 3:8; Josh 11:1-3
12:2 Num 21:23; Deut 2:36
12:4 Num 21:33; Josh 13:12

11:13 ***the towns built on mounds:*** In the ancient Near East it was common practice to rebuild cities on the same sites after they had been destroyed. All the elements that made a city site advantageous remained after a city's destruction. Many cities were rebuilt numerous times, slowly rising in height as more debris accumulated after each destruction. • Joshua burned only ***Hazor*** in the north, just as he had destroyed Jericho (6:24) and Ai (8:28) in the center of the land.

11:15 God commanded Joshua to exercise faithfulness to Moses' *torah*, or "Book of Instruction" (1:7-10). At the conclusion of the two major campaigns to occupy Canaan, the narrator reported that Joshua had obeyed ***all the commands*** faithfully.

11:16 ***the western foothills, the Jordan Valley:*** Hebrew *the Shephelah, the Arabah.*

11:18 Although the initial victories in both the southern and the northern campaigns were quick and decisive, it took ***a long time*** to take fortified cities. After Israel crossed the Jordan River, the total campaign for Canaan lasted perhaps five years (see 14:10).

11:19-20 The judgment on Canaan was God's, not Israel's. God had extended mercy to the Canaanites for several generations. Now, however, God determined that "the sin of the Amorites" had "reached its full measure" (Gen 15:16), and he ***hardened their hearts.*** God used Israel as the instrument and agent of his judgment, just as in later centuries God used other nations to execute judgment upon Israel and Judah for their sins.

11:21-22 ***the descendants of Anak:*** See Num 13:28, 33.

11:23 The major theme of the second half of Joshua is ***dividing the land.*** • ***rest:*** See note on 1:13.

12:1-24 This chapter summarizes Israel's conquests on both sides of the Jordan and transitions to Joshua's distribution of the land of Canaan among the tribes of Israel (ch 13).

12:1 The Arnon River flows into the Dead Sea midway down its eastern side, creating ***the Arnon Gorge.*** Israel began its conquests here (see Num 21:13-15, 21-35). • ***Mount Hermon*** lies twenty-five miles north-northeast of the Sea of Galilee. • ***the Jordan Valley:*** Hebrew *the Arabah;* also in 12:3, 8.

12:2 ***King Sihon*** (see Num 21:24-25) had controlled the northern Jordan Valley as far as the Sea of Galilee but not the northern part of Gilead (12:5).

12:3 ***from . . . Galilee . . . Dead Sea:*** Hebrew *from the Sea of Kinnereth to the Sea of the Arabah, which is the Salt Sea.* • ***Beth-jeshimoth*** was Israel's camp in the plains of Moab (Num 33:49). • Moses had viewed the Promised Land from ***Pisgah*** (Deut 34:1).

12:4 ***King Og of Bashan:*** See Num 21:33-35. • The ***Rephaites*** were an indigenous people who lived on both sides of the Jordan. Many scholars have concluded that the Rephaites were unusually tall (see Deut 3:11). • ***Ashtaroth and Edrei:*** Many rulers of large kingdoms had

12:5 Deut 3:10
12:7 Josh 11:17
12:8 Josh 11:16
12:9 Josh 6:2; 8:29
12:12 Josh 10:33
12:13 Josh 10:3
12:24 Deut 7:24
13:1 Josh 14:10
13:2 Judg 3:3

to Salecah in the north and to all of Bashan
in the east, and westward to the borders of
the kingdoms of Geshur and Maacah. This
territory included the northern half of Gilead, as far as the boundary of King Sihon of
Heshbon.
6 Moses, the servant of the LORD, and the
Israelites had destroyed the people of King
Sihon and King Og. And Moses gave their
land as a possession to the tribes of Reuben,
Gad, and the half-tribe of Manasseh.

Kings Defeated West of the Jordan

7 The following is a list of the kings that
Joshua and the Israelite armies defeated on
the west side of the Jordan, from Baal-gad in
the valley of Lebanon to Mount Halak, which
leads up to Seir. (Joshua gave this land to the
tribes of Israel as their possession, 8 including the hill country, the western foothills,
the Jordan Valley, the mountain slopes, the
Judean wilderness, and the Negev. The people who lived in this region were the Hittites,
the Amorites, the Canaanites, the Perizzites,
the Hivites, and the Jebusites.) These are the
kings Israel defeated:

9 The king of Jericho
The king of Ai, near Bethel
10 The king of Jerusalem
The king of Hebron
11 The king of Jarmuth
The king of Lachish
12 The king of Eglon
The king of Gezer
13 The king of Debir
The king of Geder
14 The king of Hormah
The king of Arad
15 The king of Libnah
The king of Adullam
16 The king of Makkedah
The king of Bethel
17 The king of Tappuah
The king of Hepher
18 The king of Aphek
The king of Lasharon
19 The king of Madon
The king of Hazor
20 The king of Shimron-meron
The king of Acshaph
21 The king of Taanach
The king of Megiddo
22 The king of Kedesh
The king of Jokneam in Carmel
23 The king of Dor in the town of
Naphoth-dor
The king of Goyim in Gilgal
24 The king of Tirzah.

In all, thirty-one kings were defeated.

3. JOSHUA DISTRIBUTES THE LAND (13:1–21:45)

The Land Yet to Be Conquered (13:1-7)

13 When Joshua was an old man, the
LORD said to him, "You are growing
old, and much land remains to be conquered.
2 This is the territory that remains: all the regions of the Philistines and the Geshurites,
3 and the larger territory of the Canaanites,
extending from the stream of Shihor on the
border of Egypt, northward to the boundary

palaces in more than one of their cities. The fact that Joshua credits only Og with more than one capital indicates that his kingdom was much larger than others Israel encountered, except for Sihon's.

12:6 ***Reuben, Gad, and the half-tribe of Manasseh:*** See Num 32. The author of Joshua reminded the Israelites that their kin who lived east of the Jordan also belonged to Israel.

12:7-24 ***Joshua and the Israelite armies*** faithfully carried out the tasks God gave them. This summary showcases their successes, providing proper recognition for their faithfulness. God gave the Israelites their promised inheritance while bringing about the long-delayed judgment of the Canaanites. This roster of defeated kings, identified by their city-states, provides evidence of God's accomplished purposes. A solemn yet joyful recital for Israel, the list symbolizes God's mighty acts for his people and exalts his own great name.

12:7 ***Baal-gad*** was at the western foot of Mount Hermon, the northern limit of Joshua's conquests west of the Jordan. • ***The valley of Lebanon*** divided the coastal Lebanon range and the inland Anti-Lebanon range. • ***Mount Halak, which leads up to Seir*** (i.e., Edom), marked the southern limit of Joshua's conquests.

12:8 ***the western foothills:*** Hebrew *the Shephelah.* • ***Hittites . . . Jebusites:*** See note on 3:10.

12:23 ***Naphoth-dor:*** Hebrew *Naphath-dor,* a variant spelling of *Naphoth-dor.* • ***Goyim in Gilgal:*** Greek version reads *Goyim in Galilee.*

13:1–21:45 As he had promised, God brought Israel into the land. Joshua next turned his attention to the allotment of the land to Israel's tribes. • The tribal allotments gave geographical reality to the Israelites' covenant with God and expressed the fulfillment of God's promise to Abraham, Isaac, and Jacob. Because God owned the land, the apportionment to the tribes was a gift. God gave them the land to dwell in and directed its distribution. • In these lists of tribal allotments, the author describes some borders in such detail that they can be plotted on a map while others were far less well defined.

13:1-7 Israel did not conquer the entire land of Canaan while Joshua was alive. The unconquered areas, lying mostly in the valleys and plains, were the most populous regions. Several generations passed before Israel became strong enough to absorb or subjugate these regions and their peoples.

13:2 ***The Philistines*** were one of several groups in the great migration of the Sea Peoples from the Aegean region within a few decades after Israel's entry into Canaan. They settled along the southwestern Mediterranean coast, west and southwest of Judah. They came from Caphtor or Crete (Deut 2:23; Amos 9:7). • These ***Geshurites*** were people from a southern territory, not the northern Geshurites (cp. 12:5).

13:3 ***The stream of Shihor*** probably marked the traditional boundary between Canaan and Egypt, bisecting

of Ekron. It includes the territory of the five Philistine rulers of Gaza, Ashdod, Ashkelon, Gath, and Ekron. The land of the Avvites 4 in the south also remains to be conquered. In the north, the following area has not yet been conquered: all the land of the Canaanites, including Mearah (which belongs to the Sidonians), stretching northward to Aphek on the border of the Amorites; 5 the land of the Gebalites and all of the Lebanon mountain area to the east, from Baal-gad below Mount Hermon to Lebo-hamath; 6 and all the hill country from Lebanon to Misrephoth-maim, including all the land of the Sidonians.

"I myself will drive these people out of the land ahead of the Israelites. So be sure to give this land to Israel as a special possession, just as I have commanded you. 7 Include all this territory as Israel's possession when you divide this land among the nine tribes and the half-tribe of Manasseh."

The Land East of the Jordan (13:8-33)

The Land Divided East of the Jordan

8 Half the tribe of Manasseh and the tribes of Reuben and Gad had already received their grants of land on the east side of the Jordan, for Moses, the servant of the LORD, had previously assigned this land to them.

9 Their territory extended from Aroer on
the edge of the Arnon Gorge (including
the town in the middle of the gorge)
to the plain beyond Medeba, as far as
Dibon. 10 It also included all the towns
of King Sihon of the Amorites, who had
reigned in Heshbon, and extended as far
as the borders of Ammon. 11 It included
Gilead, the territory of the kingdoms
of Geshur and Maacah, all of Mount
Hermon, all of Bashan as far as Salecah,
12 and all the territory of King Og of
Bashan, who had reigned in Ashtaroth
and Edrei. King Og was the last of the
Rephaites, for Moses had attacked them
and driven them out. 13 But the Israelites
failed to drive out the people of Geshur
and Maacah, so they continue to live
among the Israelites to this day.

An Allotment for the Tribe of Levi

14 Moses did not assign any allotment of land to the tribe of Levi. Instead, as the LORD had

13:6 Josh 11:8
13:8 Josh 12:1-6
13:9 Num 32:34
13:12 Num 21:33-35
13:14 Deut 18:1-2

Inheriting the Land (13:1–21:45)

Gen 1:31; 12:7; 13:14-17; 15:12-21; 17:7-8; 35:11-13; 50:24
Ps 37:9-34
Luke 12:22-34; 16:9-11

Is the material world evil? Are spirit, soul, and energy the pure good toward which we are striving on our earthly journey? Will we only be truly spiritual and truly happy when we are finally free from the prison of this earth-bound flesh?

The Bible answers these and similar questions with an emphatic "No!" The universe, including this earth and all its bodily creatures, came perfect and holy from the skilled and expert hand of the loving Creator (Gen 1:31). As a result of our sin, this material world needs redeeming, and by God's grace, it will have its share in God's redemption at the end of time.

One of the ways Scripture affirms this is by a prominent theology of land. All land belongs to God. God evicted the Canaanite peoples from the Promised Land because of their wickedness. He brought Israel into that land because of his promises to the patriarchs and because he wants the earth to be under human stewards who are attuned to its Maker.

In ancient Israel, this stewardship was provided through the allotment of a livable portion to each household. Strictly speaking, the allotment of the land, rather than the land itself, was the stewardship trust. The allotment passed down from fathers to sons as the main part of most family inheritances. Following these principles and God's specific instruction, Joshua divided the land among the tribes, and the tribes divided it among their clans, families, and individual households. God's gift of stewardship over a specific portion of land was the gift of life to each household (see also note on 17:3-6).

the northern Sinai peninsula. • The Philistine territory included *five* main cities: ***Gaza, Ashdod,*** and ***Ashkelon*** were on the Mediterranean coast, and ***Gath*** and ***Ekron*** were a few miles inland. • The Philistines displaced ***the Avvites*** (Deut 2:23).

13:4-6a The ***Sidonians*** (that is, Phoenicians; see Isa 23:11; Obad 1:20; Acts 11:19) lived ***in the north*** along the coast, from north of Mount Carmel to above Gebal (Byblos). They also apparently occupied the Lebanon and Anti-Lebanon mountain ranges. Sidon was the dominant Phoenician city when Israel entered Canaan. • ***Baal-gad:*** See note on 12:7.

13:6b-7 The lands just listed had not yet been conquered, but God directed Joshua to show his faith by allotting them to the tribes against the future, when they would be taken.

13:8-14 ***Half the tribe of Manasseh and the tribes of Reuben and Gad*** had asked Moses for their inheritance ***on the east side of the Jordan*** in the land that had been the kingdoms of Sihon and Og (Num 21:21-35; 32:1-42). In return, they had helped the rest of Israel take possession of their inheritance west of the Jordan (1:12-18; 4:12-13). Here, the author confirmed their possession of these lands.

13:16 Josh 12:2
13:21-22 Num 31:8

promised them, their allotment came from
the offerings burned on the altar to the
LORD, the God of Israel.

The Land Given to the Tribe of Reuben
15Moses had assigned the following area to
the clans of the tribe of Reuben.

16Their territory extended from Aroer on
the edge of the Arnon Gorge (including
the town in the middle of the gorge) to the
plain beyond Medeba. 17It included
Heshbon and the other towns on the
plain—Dibon, Bamoth-baal, Beth-baal-
meon, 18Jahaz, Kedemoth, Mephaath,
19Kiriathaim, Sibmah, Zereth-shahar on
the hill above the valley, 20Beth-peor, the
slopes of Pisgah, and Beth-jeshimoth.
21The land of Reuben also included
all the towns of the plain and the
entire kingdom of Sihon. Sihon was
the Amorite king who had reigned in
Heshbon and was killed by Moses along
with the leaders of Midian—Evi, Rekem,
Zur, Hur, and Reba—princes living in the
region who were allied with Sihon. 22The
Israelites had also killed Balaam son of
Beor, who used magic to tell the future.
23The Jordan River marked the western
boundary for the tribe of Reuben. The
towns and their surrounding villages in
this area were given as a homeland to
the clans of the tribe of Reuben.

The Land Given to the Tribe of Gad
24Moses had assigned the following area to
the clans of the tribe of Gad.

25Their territory included Jazer, all the
towns of Gilead, and half of the land
of Ammon, as far as the town of Aroer
just west of Rabbah. 26It extended

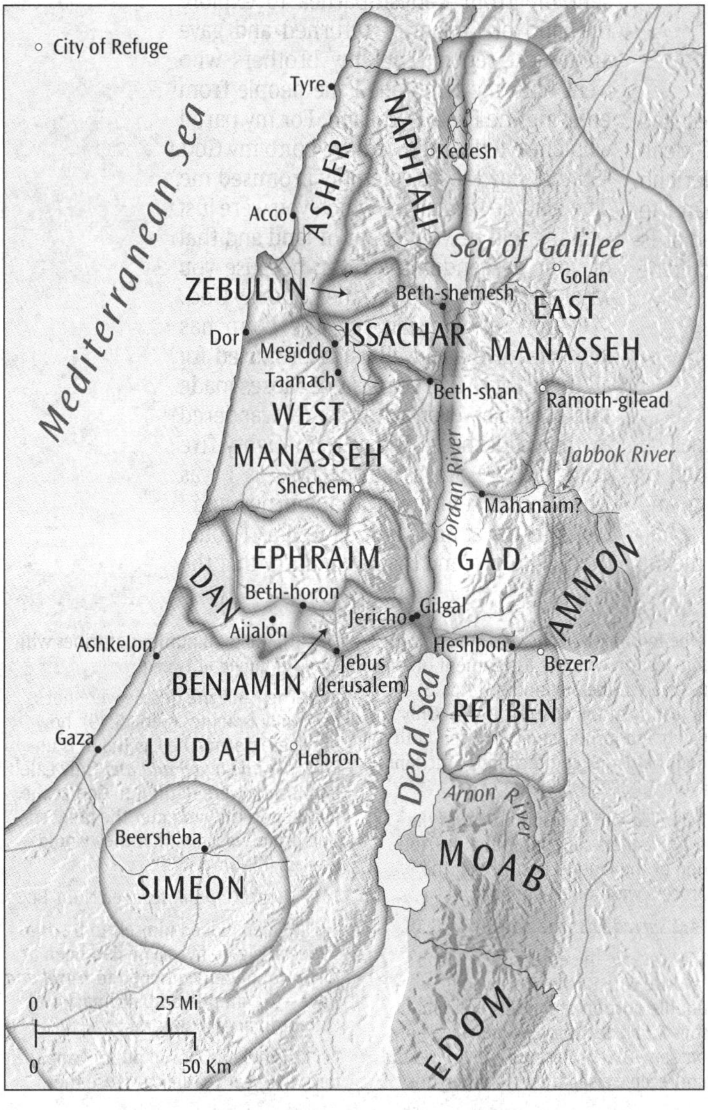

◂ **Allotment of the Land (13:1–21:45).** After Joshua and the Israelites had conquered the hill country, the land was divided among the twelve tribes, as shown. Much of this land remained unconquered, however (see map, p. 416), and the tribe of DAN later moved to a completely different area (19:47; Judg 18).

13:14 The *tribe of Levi* inherited no tribal land of its own (see Deut 18:1-8). Levitical cities were located in the territories of the other tribes (ch 21).

13:15-23 Because *Reuben,* Jacob's firstborn son by Leah (Gen 29:32), forfeited his birthright by sleeping with his father's concubine (Gen 35:22), the inheritance of his tribe was not of central importance. Although the tribe received a fertile portion of land, it was difficult to defend from neighboring nations. The tribe of Reuben eventually lost the southern portion to Moab.

13:21 The *leaders of Midian* were apparently kings (Num 31:8) or sheiks of small city-states south of Sihon's kingdom. The nomadic Midianites depended mostly on sheep and goats for their livelihood.

13:22 *Balaam son of Beor* had initiated a successful plan to seduce Israel into sexually expressed idolatry (Num 31:16), even though God had forbidden Balaam to curse Israel (Num 22–25).

13:24-28 *Gad* was Jacob's seventh son, born to Zilpah, Leah's servant. Just as Gad's position in his family was peripheral, the tribe of Gad was peripheral to Israel.

13:25 *just west of:* Literally *in front of.*

from Heshbon to Ramath-mizpeh and
Betonim, and from Mahanaim to the
territory of Lo-debar. [27]In the valley
were Beth-haram, Beth-nimrah, Succoth,
Zaphon, and the rest of the kingdom of
King Sihon of Heshbon. The western
boundary ran along the Jordan River,
extended as far north as the tip of the
Sea of Galilee, and then turned eastward.
[28]The towns and their surrounding
villages in this area were given as a
homeland to the clans of the tribe of Gad.

The Land Given to the Half-Tribe of Manasseh

[29]Moses had assigned the following area to
the clans of the half-tribe of Manasseh.

[30]Their territory extended from
Mahanaim, including all of Bashan, all the
former kingdom of King Og, and the sixty
towns of Jair in Bashan. [31]It also included
half of Gilead and King Og's royal cities
of Ashtaroth and Edrei. All this was
given to the clans of the descendants of
Makir, who was Manasseh's son.

[32]These are the allotments Moses had
made while he was on the plains of Moab,
across the Jordan River, east of Jericho.
[33]But Moses gave no allotment of land to
the tribe of Levi, for the LORD, the God of Israel, had promised that he himself would be
their allotment.

Caleb's Inheritance and the Allotment for Judah (14:1–15:63)

The Land Divided West of the Jordan

14 The remaining tribes of Israel received land in Canaan as allotted by
Eleazar the priest, Joshua son of Nun, and
the tribal leaders. [2]These nine and a half
tribes received their grants of land by means
of sacred lots, in accordance with the LORD's
command through Moses. [3]Moses had already given a grant of land to the two and
a half tribes on the east side of the Jordan
River, but he had given the Levites no such
allotment. [4]The descendants of Joseph had
become two separate tribes—Manasseh and
Ephraim. And the Levites were given no land
at all, only towns to live in with surrounding
pasturelands for their livestock and all their
possessions. [5]So the land was distributed
in strict accordance with the LORD's commands to Moses.

Caleb Requests His Land

[6]A delegation from the tribe of Judah, led by
Caleb son of Jephunneh the Kenizzite, came
to Joshua at Gilgal. Caleb said to Joshua, "Remember what the LORD said to Moses, the
man of God, about you and me when we
were at Kadesh-barnea. [7]I was forty years
old when Moses, the servant of the LORD,
sent me from Kadesh-barnea to explore
the land of Canaan. I returned and gave
an honest report, [8]but my brothers who
went with me frightened the people from
entering the Promised Land. For my part, I
wholeheartedly followed the LORD my God.
[9]So that day Moses solemnly promised me,
'The land of Canaan on which you were just
walking will be your grant of land and that
of your descendants forever, because you
wholeheartedly followed the LORD my God.'

[10]"Now, as you can see, the LORD has
kept me alive and well as he promised for
all these forty-five years since Moses made
this promise—even while Israel wandered
in the wilderness. Today I am eighty-five
years old. [11]I am as strong now as I was
when Moses sent me on that journey, and I
can still travel and fight as well as I could
then. [12]So give me the hill country that the

13:27 Num 34:11
13:30 Num 32:41
13:33 Num 18:20; Josh 13:14
14:1 Num 34:16-17
14:3 Num 32:33; Josh 13:14
14:6 Num 13:30; 14:6, 24, 30
14:9 Deut 1:36

13:26 *Lo-debar:* Hebrew *Li-debir*, apparently a variant spelling of *Lo-debar* (cp. 2 Sam 9:4; 17:27; Amos 6:13).

13:27 *Sea of Galilee:* Hebrew *Sea of Kinnereth.*

13:29-33 ***Manasseh*** was Joseph's elder son. Jacob gave Joseph's sons each a full inheritance, thus giving Joseph a double portion of the birthright (see 14:4).

13:30-31 ***Jair*** was a great-grandson of Manasseh (1 Chr 2:21-22). ***Makir*** was one of Manasseh's sons. It is unclear whether the land allotted to these tribes in north Gilead was distinguished from the land that the tribe of Gad received there.

14:1–19:51 The allotment of land to the tribes on the west side of the Jordan describes what God intended for each tribe to possess. • The narrator frames this section with the assignment of land to Caleb at the beginning (14:6-15) and to Joshua at the end (19:49-51). Only Caleb and Joshua had expressed faith in God that Israel could conquer the land (Num 13:30; 14:6-9).

14:1 ***Eleazar . . . Joshua . . . and the tribal leaders*** supervised the distribution of the land to ensure that the process was honest and just.

14:2 ***sacred lots:*** See note at 7:16-18.

14:4 ***Joseph***, the elder son of Jacob's favorite wife Rachel, received a double portion of land through his sons ***Manasseh and Ephraim*** (see note on Gen 48:5-7). Because ***the Levites*** did not receive a separate tribal territory (13:14), the total number of tribes with land remained at twelve.

14:6 The ***Kenizzite*** people were not originally Israelites (Gen 15:19); how they became attached to Judah is unknown. • ***about you and me:*** Only Caleb and Joshua were faithful to God at the first opportunity to enter the land, so God promised them that they would possess it (Num 14:24).

14:9 ***Moses . . . promised:*** See Num 14:24.

14:11 Caleb judged himself to be ***as strong*** at eighty-five as he had been at forty. He still felt equipped to ***travel and fight***—to continue both ordinary and extraordinary pursuits.

14:12 Israel had stayed out of Canaan forty-five years earlier because they

14:12 Num 13:33
14:15 Josh 11:23
15:1 Num 34:3-4 Deut 32:51
15:3-4 Num 34:4-5
15:5-6 Josh 18:15-19

LORD promised me. You will remember that
as scouts we found the descendants of Anak
living there in great, walled towns. But if the
LORD is with me, I will drive them out of the
land, just as the LORD said."
13So Joshua blessed Caleb son of Jephunneh and gave Hebron to him as his portion
of land. 14Hebron still belongs to the descendants of Caleb son of Jephunneh the
Kenizzite because he wholeheartedly followed the LORD, the God of Israel. 15(Previously Hebron had been called Kiriath-arba.
It had been named after Arba, a great hero
of the descendants of Anak.)

And the land had rest from war.

The Land Given to the Tribe of Judah

15 The allotment for the clans of the
tribe of Judah reached southward to
the border of Edom, as far south as the wilderness of Zin.
2The southern boundary began at the
south bay of the Dead Sea, 3ran south of
Scorpion Pass into the wilderness of Zin,
and then went south of Kadesh-barnea
to Hezron. Then it went up to Addar,
where it turned toward Karka. 4From
there it passed to Azmon until it finally
reached the Brook of Egypt, which it
followed to the Mediterranean Sea. This
was their southern boundary.
5The eastern boundary extended
along the Dead Sea to the mouth of the
Jordan River.

The northern boundary began at the
bay where the Jordan River empties
into the Dead Sea, 6went up from
there to Beth-hoglah, then proceeded
north of Beth-arabah to the Stone
of Bohan. (Bohan was Reuben's son.)
7From that point it went through the
valley of Achor to Debir, turning north

CALEB (14:6-15)

Josh 15:13-19
Num 13:1–14:38; 26:65; 32:12; 34:19
Deut 1:36
Judg 1:11-15, 20
1 Chr 4:15

Caleb stands as an inspiring example of faith in God. He was the son of Jephunneh the Kenizzite (14:6; Num 32:12). The Kenizzites lived in the Negev, the southern desert region of Canaan (see Gen 15:18-21). Jephunneh apparently married into the tribe of Judah a generation before Israel left Egypt.

Caleb first appears as one of twelve spies Moses sent to scout out the land of Canaan. Upon returning, all twelve confirmed the land's magnificence, but ten of the scouts focused on the land's fearsome inhabitants (Num 13:31-33). Only Joshua and Caleb believed that God would enable Israel to conquer the Canaanites (Num 14:6-9), advising that the Israelites immediately take the land (Num 13:30). Although the people wanted to stone both Caleb and Joshua (Num 14:1-4, 10), God protected them and punished the people (Num 14:11-38). God ultimately rewarded Caleb and Joshua for their faithfulness. Among all those who left Egypt, they were the only ones to enter the Promised Land.

After many years in the wilderness, Joshua and Caleb received their personal inheritance in the land. Caleb's faith did not diminish in the intervening forty-five years; his testimony reveals his character and rock-solid faith in God. Although Caleb was eighty-five years old, he was still strong and able to fight. Caleb drove out the Anakites to acquire Hebron. Caleb's city of Hebron, about twenty miles south of Jerusalem (not far from Kenizzite territory), was occupied by giant Anakites who had terrified the earlier scouts (14:6-15; Num 13:28, 33). Hebron later became a Levitical city of refuge (21:13; 1 Chr 6:55-57).

Caleb looked beyond serious obstacles to God's unbreakable promise that Israel would occupy Canaan. With unabated vigor, he stood ready to conquer the territory Joshua assigned him. Caleb's staunch confidence in God's reliable promises earned him an honored place among the faithful. Even when outnumbered by enemies, Caleb trusted God, and God richly rewarded him.

feared ***the descendants of Anak***, a tall, strong people who lived in ***the hill country*** of Judah (Num 13:32-33).

14:15 *rest from war:* See note on 1:13.

15:1-63 Judah's tribal allotment is described in greater detail than that of the other tribes. The failures of Judah's elder brothers (Gen 34:25-31; 35:22) put him in line to receive the mantle of leadership. Thus, ***the tribe of Judah*** received a central geographical position among the tribes, guaranteeing its leadership in the nation (Gen 49:8-12; Deut 33:7).

15:2-4 Judah's ***southern boundary*** extended well into the desert of the Negev, which had little if any settled population throughout the OT period.

15:2 *the Dead Sea:* Literally *the Salt Sea;* also in 15:5.

15:3 *Scorpion Pass:* Hebrew *Akrabbim.*

15:4 *the Mediterranean Sea:* Literally *the sea;* also in 15:11. • ***their:*** Literally *your.*

15:5-11 Although Judah's ***northern boundary*** is described in great detail, some sections of this border cannot be determined with certainty.

15:7 This ***Debir*** was not the same town as the Debir/Kiriath-sepher of 15:15.

toward Gilgal, which is across from the
slopes of Adummim on the south side
of the valley. From there the boundary
extended to the springs at En-shemesh
and on to En-rogel. 8 The boundary
then passed through the valley of Ben-
Hinnom, along the southern slopes of
the Jebusites, where the city of Jerusalem
is located. Then it went west to the top
of the mountain above the valley of
Hinnom, and on up to the northern end
of the valley of Rephaim. 9 From there
the boundary extended from the top of
the mountain to the spring at the waters
of Nephtoah, and from there to the
towns on Mount Ephron. Then it turned
toward Baalah (that is, Kiriath-jearim).
10 The boundary circled west of Baalah to
Mount Seir, passed along to the town of
Kesalon on the northern slope of Mount
Jearim, and went down to Beth-shemesh
and on to Timnah. 11 The boundary then
proceeded to the slope of the hill north of
Ekron, where it turned toward Shikkeron
and Mount Baalah. It passed Jabneel and
ended at the Mediterranean Sea.
12 The western boundary was the
shoreline of the Mediterranean Sea.

These are the boundaries for the clans of
the tribe of Judah.

The Land Given to Caleb

13 The LORD commanded Joshua to assign
some of Judah's territory to Caleb son of
Jephunneh. So Caleb was given the town
of Kiriath-arba (that is, Hebron), which had
been named after Anak's ancestor. 14 Caleb
drove out the three groups of Anakites—the
descendants of Sheshai, Ahiman, and Talmai, the sons of Anak.
15 From there he went to fight against
the people living in the town of Debir (formerly called Kiriath-sepher). 16 Caleb said, "I
will give my daughter Acsah in marriage to
the one who attacks and captures Kiriath-
sepher." 17 Othniel, the son of Caleb's brother
Kenaz, was the one who conquered it, so Acsah became Othniel's wife.
18 When Acsah married Othniel, she
urged him to ask her father for a field. As
she got down off her donkey, Caleb asked
her, "What's the matter?"
19 She said, "Give me another gift. You
have already given me land in the Negev;
now please give me springs of water, too." So
Caleb gave her the upper and lower springs.

The Towns Allotted to Judah

20 This was the homeland allocated to the
clans of the tribe of Judah.

21 The towns of Judah situated along
the borders of Edom in the extreme
south were Kabzeel, Eder, Jagur,
22 Kinah, Dimonah, Adadah, 23 Kedesh,
Hazor, Ithnan, 24 Ziph, Telem, Bealoth,
25 Hazor-hadattah, Kerioth-hezron (that
is, Hazor), 26 Amam, Shema, Moladah,
27 Hazar-gaddah, Heshmon, Beth-pelet,
28 Hazar-shual, Beersheba, Biziothiah,
29 Baalah, Iim, Ezem, 30 Eltolad, Kesil,
Hormah, 31 Ziklag, Madmannah,
Sansannah, 32 Lebaoth, Shilhim, Ain, and
Rimmon—twenty-nine towns with their
surrounding villages.
33 The following towns situated in
the western foothills were also given to

15:8 Josh 15:63
15:9 Josh 18:15
15:13 Josh 14:13-15
15:14 Num 13:33; Deut 9:2; Josh 11:21-22
15:17 Judg 1:12-13; 3:9
15:21 Gen 35:21
15:31 1 Sam 27:6
15:33 Judg 13:25; 16:31

• This *Gilgal* was not the same Gilgal where the Israelites earlier established their camp (4:19).

15:8 The ***valley of Ben-Hinnom*** marked Judah's northern border. ***Jerusalem*** occupied a ridge rising northward from the lower end of this valley within the tribe of Benjamin's territory. Neither tribe occupied Jerusalem, so when David captured it, it became the royal city of his dynasty rather than just another tribal city.

15:9 ***the spring at the waters of Nephtoah:*** Or *the spring at Me-nephtoah;* also in 18:15. It is possible that the place name is a reference to Egyptian Pharaoh Merneptah (late 1200s BC); an Egyptian papyrus refers to the "wells of Merneptah" on the mountain ridges of Canaan.

15:12 ***the Mediterranean Sea:*** Literally *the Great Sea;* also in 15:47. • ***These*** were ***the boundaries*** of ***Judah*** when the settlement process began. Later, the tribes of Simeon and Dan received their allotments from some of Judah's southern and western territories, and within a few decades the Philistines came from the Greek islands, settling all the southern coastal plain allotted to Judah (see note on 13:2).

15:16 Cp. 1 Sam 17:25; 18:27.

15:17 ***Othniel***, Caleb's nephew, became Israel's first judge (Judg 3:9-11).

15:18-19 ***she urged him:*** Some Greek manuscripts read *he urged her.* • ***What's the matter?*** No water source existed for the town Othniel conquered in ***the Negev*** ("dry land"), the southernmost of Judah's districts, which was semi-arid. • ***The upper and lower springs*** were close together but too far from Debir to belong to it naturally, so ***Acsah*** asked for the rights to the water.

15:20-63 Not all of these locations can be identified with certainty. Many are unknown except for their occurrence in this and other lists. Some receive passing reference in other texts.

15:21 ***in the extreme south:*** Or *in the Negev* (see note on 1:4). The Hebrew word *negeb* can refer either to the general direction ("south") or the desert region named "Negev." • The location of ***Eder*** is otherwise unknown. Some propose translating this word as "Arad" because Arad should be about here in the list and was too important to have been left out. This translation would simply reverse two Hebrew letters that are very similar in shape.

15:33 From the perspective of the highlanders of the Judean hill country, the lower hills between them and the coastal plain were ***the western foothills*** (Hebrew *the Shephelah*). These hills were separated geologically from the hill country by a series of north–south valleys. In this list, the western foothills are divided into four districts.

15:39 Josh 10:3; 2 Kgs 14:19
15:47 Num 34:6
15:63 Judg 1:21; 2 Sam 5:6
16:1 Josh 8:15; 18:12
16:2 Josh 18:13

Judah: Eshtaol, Zorah, Ashnah, 34Zanoah,
En-gannim, Tappuah, Enam, 35Jarmuth,
Adullam, Socoh, Azekah, 36Shaaraim,
Adithaim, Gederah, and Gederothaim—
fourteen towns with their surrounding
villages.
37Also included were Zenan, Hadashah,
Migdal-gad, 38Dilean, Mizpeh, Joktheel,
39Lachish, Bozkath, Eglon, 40Cabbon,
Lahmam, Kitlish, 41Gederoth, Beth-
dagon, Naamah, and Makkedah—sixteen
towns with their surrounding villages.
42Besides these, there were Libnah,
Ether, Ashan, 43Iphtah, Ashnah, Nezib,
44Keilah, Aczib, and Mareshah—nine
towns with their surrounding villages.
45The territory of the tribe of Judah
also included Ekron and its surrounding
settlements and villages. 46From Ekron
the boundary extended west and
included the towns near Ashdod with
their surrounding villages. 47It also
included Ashdod with its surrounding
settlements and villages and Gaza with
its settlements and villages, as far as the
Brook of Egypt and along the coast of
the Mediterranean Sea.
48Judah also received the following
towns in the hill country: Shamir, Jattir,
Socoh, 49Dannah, Kiriath-sannah (that
is, Debir), 50Anab, Eshtemoh, Anim,
51Goshen, Holon, and Giloh—eleven
towns with their surrounding villages.
52Also included were the towns of Arab,
Dumah, Eshan, 53Janim, Beth-tappuah,
Aphekah, 54Humtah, Kiriath-arba (that is,
Hebron), and Zior—nine towns with their
surrounding villages.
55Besides these, there were Maon,
Carmel, Ziph, Juttah, 56Jezreel, Jokdeam,
Zanoah, 57Kain, Gibeah, and Timnah—ten
towns with their surrounding villages.
58In addition, there were Halhul,
Beth-zur, Gedor, 59Maarath, Beth-anoth,
and Eltekon—six towns with their
surrounding villages.
60There were also Kiriath-baal (that is,
Kiriath-jearim) and Rabbah—two towns
with their surrounding villages.
61In the wilderness there were the
towns of Beth-arabah, Middin, Secacah,
62Nibshan, the City of Salt, and En-gedi—
six towns with their surrounding villages.

63But the tribe of Judah could not drive
out the Jebusites, who lived in the city of Jerusalem, so the Jebusites live there among
the people of Judah to this day.

The Western Allotments for Ephraim and Manasseh (16:1–17:18)

The Land Given to Ephraim and West Manasseh

16 The allotment for the descendants
of Joseph extended from the Jordan
River near Jericho, east of the springs
of Jericho, through the wilderness and
into the hill country of Bethel. 2From
Bethel (that is, Luz) it ran over to Ataroth
in the territory of the Arkites. 3Then it
descended westward to the territory
of the Japhletites as far as Lower Beth-
horon, then to Gezer and over to the
Mediterranean Sea.

4This was the homeland allocated to the
families of Joseph's sons, Manasseh and
Ephraim.

15:45-47 The fourth district of the western foothills included most of the territory soon to be occupied by the Philistines—*the tribe of Judah* held it only briefly.

15:48 The *hill country* was in the central highlands of Judah from Jerusalem in the north to just past Debir (15:15) in the south. It was divided into five districts.

15:56 This *Jezreel* in Judah was not the northern Jezreel. This city was the hometown of Ahinoam, David's wife and the mother of his eldest son, Amnon (2 Sam 3:2).

15:59 Following this verse, the Greek OT includes another district of 11 cities: Tekoa, Ephrathah (that is, Bethlehem), Phagor, Etam, Kulon, Tatam, Saris, Karem, Gallim, Bether, Manoch—eleven towns with their surrounding villages. The inclusion of this district accounts for Bethlehem; this town's omission would be surprising. Perhaps an early copyist of the Hebrew text accidentally omitted this twelfth district.

15:61 The *wilderness* of Judea included the eastern slopes of the central mountain highlands and extended to the western shore of the Dead Sea; three of its six towns were on or near that shoreline.

15:63 Even though *Jerusalem* was assigned to the tribe of Benjamin (18:28), it was not conquered in Joshua's day. • *to this day:* The Jebusites' continued presence later caused Judah trouble (Judg 1:21).

16:1–17:18 *Joseph* had two *sons, Manasseh and Ephraim* (Gen 41:50-52). Half of Manasseh's descendants had received their inheritance east of the Jordan River. The tribe of Ephraim and the rest of the tribe of Manasseh now received their allotments. This brought the total number of allotments to twelve and fulfilled the blessing Jacob had pronounced upon Joseph (Gen 49:22-26). Like Judah in the south, Joseph's tribes exercised leadership from their central position in the north.

16:1 *Jericho* was assigned to the tribe of Benjamin (18:21).

16:2 *From Bethel (that is, Luz):* As in Greek version (also see 18:13); Hebrew reads *From Bethel to Luz.*

16:3 Ephraim's border followed the ascent from lower to upper Beth-horon (see 16:5), giving this tribe control of one of the two main roads to Jerusalem from the west. • *Gezer,* a large and important Canaanite town at the juncture of the coastal plain and the hill country, apparently did not come into Israel's possession until the time of Solomon (see Judg 1:29; 1 Kgs 9:16). • *the Mediterranean Sea:* Literally *the sea;* also in 16:6, 8.

The Land Given to Ephraim

5The following territory was given to the clans of the tribe of Ephraim.

The boundary of their homeland began
at Ataroth-addar in the east. From
there it ran to Upper Beth-horon, 6then
on to the Mediterranean Sea. From
Micmethath on the north, the boundary
curved eastward past Taanath-shiloh
to the east of Janoah. 7From Janoah
it turned southward to Ataroth and
Naarah, touched Jericho, and ended at
the Jordan River. 8From Tappuah the
boundary extended westward, following
the Kanah Ravine to the Mediterranean
Sea. This is the homeland allocated to
the clans of the tribe of Ephraim.
9In addition, some towns with their
surrounding villages in the territory
allocated to the half-tribe of Manasseh
were set aside for the tribe of Ephraim.
10They did not drive the Canaanites
out of Gezer, however, so the people of
Gezer live as slaves among the people of
Ephraim to this day.

The Land Given to West Manasseh

17 The next allotment of land was given to the half-tribe of Manasseh, the descendants of Joseph's older son. Makir, the firstborn son of Manasseh, was the father of Gilead. Because his descendants were experienced soldiers, the regions of Gilead and Bashan on the east side of the Jordan had already been given to them. 2So the allotment on the west side of the Jordan was for the remaining families within the clans of the tribe of Manasseh: Abiezer, Helek, Asriel, Shechem, Hepher, and Shemida. These clans represent the male descendants of Manasseh son of Joseph.

3However, Zelophehad, a descendant of Hepher son of Gilead, son of Makir, son of Manasseh, had no sons. He had only daughters, whose names were Mahlah, Noah, Hoglah, Milcah, and Tirzah. 4These women came to Eleazar the priest, Joshua son of Nun, and the Israelite leaders and said, "The LORD commanded Moses to give us a grant of land along with the men of our tribe."

So Joshua gave them a grant of land along with their uncles, as the LORD had commanded. 5As a result, Manasseh's total allocation came to ten parcels of land, in addition to the land of Gilead and Bashan across the Jordan River, 6because the female descendants of Manasseh received a grant of land along with the male descendants. (The land of Gilead was given to the rest of the male descendants of Manasseh.)

7The boundary of the tribe of Manasseh
extended from the border of Asher to
Micmethath, near Shechem. Then the
boundary went south from Micmethath
to the settlement near the spring
of Tappuah. 8The land surrounding
Tappuah belonged to Manasseh, but the
town of Tappuah itself, on the border
of Manasseh's territory, belonged to
the tribe of Ephraim. 9From the spring
of Tappuah, the boundary of Manasseh
followed the Kanah Ravine to the
Mediterranean Sea. Several towns south
of the ravine were inside Manasseh's
territory, but they actually belonged
to the tribe of Ephraim. 10In general,
however, the land south of the ravine
belonged to Ephraim, and the land north
of the ravine belonged to Manasseh.
Manasseh's boundary ran along the
northern side of the ravine and ended
at the Mediterranean Sea. North of
Manasseh was the territory of Asher, and
to the east was the territory of Issachar.
11The following towns within the
territory of Issachar and Asher, however,
were given to Manasseh: Beth-shan,
Ibleam, Dor (that is, Naphoth-dor), Endor,

16:5 Josh 18:13
16:6 Josh 17:7
16:8 Josh 17:8-9
16:10 Josh 15:63; 17:12-13; Judg 1:29; 1 Kgs 9:16
17:1 Josh 13:8
17:3 Num 26:33; 27:1-7
17:6 Josh 13:30-31
17:11 1 Chr 7:29

16:5-8 This description of Ephraim's northern boundary with Manasseh is general and incomplete. Because Shechem belonged to Manasseh, the border between the two tribes ran south of that town.

16:9 See 17:7-10.

17:1 See 13:29-33 and notes.

17:3-6 In ancient Israel, inheritance usually passed from a father to his sons. Without ***sons***, a man's name could pass into oblivion. However, Zelophehad's ***daughters*** had petitioned Moses, Moses had inquired of God, and God had ruled that they should inherit their father's portion (see Num 27:1-11). God's ruling established a general principle, declaring that no family would be excluded from a portion of God's material blessings (see "Inheriting the Land" at 13:1–21:45, p. 396).

17:7-13 As with the tribe of Ephraim, Manasseh's territory was defined by a general description of its borders.

17:7 ***Asher*** was north-northwest of Manasseh, across the Jezreel Valley.

17:8-10 This general description of Manasseh's southern border with the land given to the tribe of Ephraim provides more detail than the description of Ephraim's northern border in 16:8.

17:9 ***the Mediterranean Sea:*** Literally *the sea;* also in 17:10.

17:11-13 All the towns mentioned here except ***Endor*** were important, but the military strength of the ***Canaanites*** prevented the tribe of Manasseh from inhabiting them for a time.

17:11 ***Beth-shan:*** Hebrew *Beth-shean,* a variant spelling of *Beth-shan;* also in 17:16. • ***Dor (that is, Naphoth-dor):*** The meaning of the Hebrew here is uncertain.

17:12 Judg 1:27-28
17:14 Num 26:28-37
17:16 Judg 1:19; 4:3, 13
18:1 Josh 19:51
Judg 21:19
Jer 7:12
18:3 Judg 18:9
18:5 Josh 15:1; 16:1-4
18:7 Num 18:7, 20
Josh 13:33

Taanach, and Megiddo, each with their
surrounding settlements.

12But the descendants of Manasseh were
unable to occupy these towns. They could
not drive out the Canaanites who continued
to live there. 13Later, however, when the Israelites became strong enough, they forced
the Canaanites to work as slaves. But they
did not drive them out of the land.

14The descendants of Joseph came to
Joshua and asked, "Why have you given us
only one portion of land as our homeland
when the LORD has blessed us with so many
people?"

15Joshua replied, "If there are so many of
you, and if the hill country of Ephraim is not
large enough for you, clear out land for yourselves in the forest where the Perizzites and
Rephaites live."

16The descendants of Joseph responded,
"It's true that the hill country is not large
enough for us. But all the Canaanites in the
lowlands have iron chariots, both those in
Beth-shan and its surrounding settlements
and those in the valley of Jezreel. They are
too strong for us."

17Then Joshua said to the tribes of
Ephraim and Manasseh, the descendants of
Joseph, "Since you are so large and strong,
you will be given more than one portion.
18The forests of the hill country will be
yours as well. Clear as much of the land as
you wish, and take possession of its farthest
corners. And you will drive out the Canaanites from the valleys, too, even though they
are strong and have iron chariots."

The Allotments for the Remaining Seven Tribes (18:1–19:51)

Survey of the Remaining Land

18 Now that the land was under Israelite control, the entire community of
Israel gathered at Shiloh and set up the Tabernacle. 2But there remained seven tribes
who had not yet been allotted their grants
of land.

3Then Joshua asked them, "How long are
you going to wait before taking possession
of the remaining land the LORD, the God
of your ancestors, has given to you? 4Select
three men from each tribe, and I will send
them out to explore the land and map it out.
They will then return to me with a written
report of their proposed divisions of their
new homeland. 5Let them divide the land
into seven sections, excluding Judah's territory in the south and Joseph's territory in
the north. 6And when you record the seven
divisions of the land and bring them to me,
I will cast sacred lots in the presence of the
LORD our God to assign land to each tribe.

7"The Levites, however, will not receive
any allotment of land. Their role as priests
of the LORD is their allotment. And the
tribes of Gad, Reuben, and the half-tribe of
Manasseh won't receive any more land, for
they have already received their grant of
land, which Moses, the servant of the LORD,

17:13 Throughout the period of the judges and beyond, the ***Israelites*** gradually grew stronger and the Canaanite people weaker. After the time of Joshua, the Israelites ***forced the Canaanites to work as slaves.*** They eventually absorbed these people and were influenced to worship the Canaanite gods. This idolatry ultimately cost them the land.

17:14 Joseph's ***one portion*** is described in 16:1-4. The descendants of Ephraim and Manasseh received portions that, when combined, were larger than the allotment of any other tribe.

17:15 The ***Perizzites*** lived in Canaan when Israel's conquest began. • ***Rephaites:*** See note on 12:4; see also Deut 2:10-11, 20-21; 3:11.

17:16 As a result of the Canaanites' ***iron chariots,*** Ephraim and Manasseh were restricted to ***the hill country*** in the early part of the settlement period (see note on 11:4). • The ***valley of Jezreel,*** a geological interruption of the hill country, separated Lower Galilee to the north from the hill country of Manasseh to the south. The Canaanites living in and near it and the valley of ***Beth-shan*** restricted Manasseh's expansion and apparently Ephraim's as well. Most of the towns named in 17:11-12 were on the edges of these valleys.

17:17-18 Rather than rebuke the people for their fear, Joshua repeated his instructions to clear forest land for settlement. His promise that ***the tribes of Ephraim and Manasseh*** would eventually ***drive out the Canaanites*** gave them a hope by which they could enlarge their faith and conquer their fear. • Much of the hill country was forested, and Canaanite settlement was sparse there. If Ephraim and Manasseh had contented themselves with land already cleared, they would have had little room for settlement. With the introduction of iron technology at about this time, including iron axe heads, the people of these tribes could clear the virgin forests and open up new land for settlement. Joshua might have set an example by being the first to clear his own homestead at Timnath-serah (19:50), a forested region in the Ephraimite hill country.

18:1 Israel had been encamped at Gilgal in the Jordan Valley (14:6). ***Shiloh*** was about twenty miles north of Jerusalem, in the hill country of Ephraim. By setting up ***the Tabernacle*** (literally *Tent of Meeting*) there, Joshua made Shiloh Israel's religious and political center. The Tabernacle remained at Shiloh until the Philistines captured the Ark (1 Sam 4:10-11).

18:4 The ***three*** selected representatives ***from each tribe*** came from the seven tribes that had not yet received their allotments. • ***a written report:*** Israel was not an entirely oral society. If an event or record was important enough to be remembered over time, leaders ordered that it be written down.

18:5 The remaining land was divided into ***seven sections,*** one for each tribe not yet assigned its territory.

18:6 Joshua publicly cast ***sacred lots*** to eliminate envy or suspicion (see also note on 7:16-18).

18:7 ***The Levites:*** See ch 21. • ***Gad . . . Manasseh:*** See 13:15-33.

gave them on the east side of the Jordan
River."
8As the men started on their way to map
out the land, Joshua commanded them, "Go
and explore the land and write a description
of it. Then return to me, and I will assign
the land to the tribes by casting sacred lots
here in the presence of the LORD at Shiloh."
9The men did as they were told and mapped
the entire territory into seven sections, listing the towns in each section. They made a
written record and then returned to Joshua
in the camp at Shiloh. 10And there at Shiloh,
Joshua cast sacred lots in the presence of
the LORD to determine which tribe should
have each section.

The Land Given to Benjamin

11The first allotment of land went to the
clans of the tribe of Benjamin. It lay between the territory assigned to the tribes of
Judah and Joseph.

12The northern boundary of Benjamin's
land began at the Jordan River, went
north of the slope of Jericho, then
west through the hill country and the
wilderness of Beth-aven. 13From there
the boundary went south to Luz (that is,
Bethel) and proceeded down to Ataroth-
addar on the hill that lies south of Lower
Beth-horon.
14The boundary then made a turn and
swung south along the western edge of
the hill facing Beth-horon, ending at the
village of Kiriath-baal (that is, Kiriath-
jearim), a town belonging to the tribe of
Judah. This was the western boundary.
15The southern boundary began at the
outskirts of Kiriath-jearim. From that
western point it ran to the spring at the
waters of Nephtoah, 16and down to the
base of the mountain beside the valley
of Ben-Hinnom, at the northern end of
the valley of Rephaim. From there it went
down the valley of Hinnom, crossing
south of the slope where the Jebusites
lived, and continued down to En-rogel.
17From En-rogel the boundary proceeded
in a northerly direction and came to
En-shemesh and on to Geliloth (which
is across from the slopes of Adummim).
Then it went down to the Stone of Bohan.
(Bohan was Reuben's son.) 18From there
it passed along the north side of the slope
overlooking the Jordan Valley. The border then went down into the valley, 19ran
past the north slope of Beth-hoglah, and
ended at the north bay of the Dead Sea,
which is the southern end of the Jordan
River. This was the southern boundary.
20The eastern boundary was the Jordan River.

These were the boundaries of the homeland
allocated to the clans of the tribe of Benjamin.

The Towns Given to Benjamin

21These were the towns given to the clans of
the tribe of Benjamin.

Jericho, Beth-hoglah, Emek-keziz, 22Beth-
arabah, Zemaraim, Bethel, 23Avvim,
Parah, Ophrah, 24Kephar-ammoni,
Ophni, and Geba—twelve towns with
their surrounding villages. 25Also Gibeon,
Ramah, Beeroth, 26Mizpah, Kephirah,
Mozah, 27Rekem, Irpeel, Taralah, 28Zela,
Haeleph, Jebus (that is, Jerusalem),
Gibeah, and Kiriath—fourteen towns
with their surrounding villages.

This was the homeland allocated to the
clans of the tribe of Benjamin.

The Land Given to Simeon

19 The second allotment of land went
to the clans of the tribe of Simeon.
Their homeland was surrounded by Judah's
territory.

18:8 Josh 18:1
18:10 Num 34:16-29; Josh 19:51
18:14-15 Josh 15:5-9
18:16 2 Kgs 23:10
18:17 Josh 15:7-8
18:24 Isa 10:29
18:28 Josh 15:8; 2 Sam 21:14

18:9 The Canaanites of the hill country now feared Israel and allowed twenty-one men (18:4) to walk through these territories and return unharmed. • The ***written record*** was probably a scroll, which might have provided the original source for the descriptions of the tribal allotments in chs 18–19.

18:11 ***Benjamin*** was Jacob's twelfth and last son, and the second son of Rachel, Jacob's favorite wife. The land received by his descendants reflected this favored position; they received a small but central portion ***between . . . Judah and Joseph.***

18:15 ***From that western point it ran:*** Or *From there it went to Mozah.* The meaning of the Hebrew is uncertain. • ***the spring at the waters of Nephtoah:*** Or *the spring at Me-nephtoah.* See note on 15:9.

18:18 ***overlooking the Jordan Valley:*** Hebrew *overlooking the Arabah*, or *overlooking Beth-arabah.*

18:19 ***Dead Sea:*** Literally *Salt Sea.*

18:21-28 While Judah's land included eleven or twelve districts (see note on 15:59), the tribe of Benjamin had two, totaling twenty-six towns. However, the location between the lands of Judah and Joseph gave Benjamin an economic and military importance significantly greater than its size.

18:28 ***Jerusalem:*** See note on 15:8. • ***Kiriath*** (some Greek manuscripts read *Kiriath-jearim*): The Kiriath-jearim of 18:14 belonged to Judah; another town with this name might have existed but is otherwise unknown. The word *Kiriath* here was probably originally followed by a word that has been lost in the process of copying.

19:1 ***Simeon***, Jacob and Leah's second son, was older than Judah. However, he had forfeited a leading role with his violent actions against Shechem (Gen 34:25-26). The tribal inheritance of his

19:5 1 Sam 30:1
19:11 Josh 21:34
19:15 Mic 5:2
19:18 1 Sam 28:4
19:28 Josh 11:8

2Simeon's homeland included Beersheba,
Sheba, Moladah, 3Hazar-shual, Balah,
Ezem, 4Eltolad, Bethul, Hormah, 5Ziklag,
Beth-marcaboth, Hazar-susah, 6Beth-
lebaoth, and Sharuhen—thirteen towns
with their surrounding villages. 7It
also included Ain, Rimmon, Ether, and
Ashan—four towns with their villages,
8including all the surrounding villages as
far south as Baalath-beer (also known as
Ramah of the Negev).

This was the homeland allocated to the
clans of the tribe of Simeon. 9Their allocation of land came from part of what had
been given to Judah because Judah's territory was too large for them. So the tribe of
Simeon received an allocation within the
territory of Judah.

The Land Given to Zebulun

10The third allotment of land went to the
clans of the tribe of Zebulun.

The boundary of Zebulun's homeland
started at Sarid. 11From there it went
west, going past Maralah, touching
Dabbesheth, and proceeding to the brook
east of Jokneam. 12In the other direction,
the boundary went east from Sarid to the
border of Kisloth-tabor, and from there
to Daberath and up to Japhia. 13Then it
continued east to Gath-hepher, Eth-kazin,
and Rimmon and turned toward Neah.
14The northern boundary of Zebulun
passed Hannathon and ended at the
valley of Iphtah-el. 15The towns in these
areas included Kattath, Nahalal, Shimron,
Idalah, and Bethlehem—twelve towns
with their surrounding villages.

16The homeland allocated to the clans of
the tribe of Zebulun included these towns
and their surrounding villages.

The Land Given to Issachar

17The fourth allotment of land went to the
clans of the tribe of Issachar.

18Its boundaries included the following towns: Jezreel, Kesulloth, Shunem,
19Hapharaim, Shion, Anaharath,
20Rabbith, Kishion, Ebez, 21Remeth, En-
gannim, En-haddah, and Beth-pazzez.
22The boundary also touched Tabor,
Shahazumah, and Beth-shemesh, ending
at the Jordan River—sixteen towns with
their surrounding villages.

23The homeland allocated to the clans of
the tribe of Issachar included these towns
and their surrounding villages.

The Land Given to Asher

24The fifth allotment of land went to the
clans of the tribe of Asher.

25Its boundaries included these
towns: Helkath, Hali, Beten, Acshaph,
26Allammelech, Amad, and Mishal. The
boundary on the west touched Carmel
and Shihor-libnath, 27then it turned
east toward Beth-dagon, and ran as far
as Zebulun in the valley of Iphtah-el,
going north to Beth-emek and Neiel. It
then continued north to Cabul, 28Abdon,
Rehob, Hammon, Kanah, and as far as
Greater Sidon. 29Then the boundary
turned toward Ramah and the fortress
of Tyre, where it turned toward Hosah
and came to the Mediterranean Sea. The
territory also included Mehebel, Aczib,

descendants reflected this; their land was carved out of ***Judah's territory*** on the southern periphery of the Negev. This arid land was far from any centers of influence and power (see also 19:9).

19:2-9 Some of the towns given to the tribe of Simeon were also part of Judah's allocation because ***Judah's territory was too large for them*** (cp. 17:14-18). Judah apparently absorbed most of Simeon's territory into its own before the end of the OT period.

19:10-48 The five small remaining tribes received land on the edges of the Israelite territory and had little national influence.

19:10-23 The lands given to the tribes of Zebulun and Issachar were strategically located; the major international trading route from Egypt to Mesopotamia ran through their territories. When Israel was strong, this position brought prosperity. However, when Israel was weak, these tribes were vulnerable both to the armies of Egypt and the successive Mesopotamian powers that fought for control of the ancient Near East.

19:10-16 ***The tribe of Zebulun*** received land partly in the valley of Jezreel and partly in the hills of Lower Galilee.

19:13 ***Gath-hepher*** was the hometown of the prophet Jonah (2 Kgs 14:25).

19:15 This ***Bethlehem*** was not the birthplace of David and Jesus in Judah. • More than ***twelve towns*** are named; some apparently did not belong to Zebulun but were on its borders.

19:16 Both by number of towns and by size of its territory, ***Zebulun*** was smallest of all the tribes. However, the NT village of Nazareth, where Jesus grew up, was in the tribal territory of Zebulun (Matt 2:19-23; 4:13-16).

19:17-23 The land given to ***the tribe of Issachar*** included much of the fertile ***Jezreel*** Valley. During OT times, this valley was largely a swamp surrounded by prosperous and important cities. This area was a center of Canaanite strength, so this small tribe had trouble gaining a foothold at first.

19:24-31 The land allocated to ***the tribe of Asher*** included the Plain of Acco on the Mediterranean coast and western Galilee. To the southwest, Asher ***touched Carmel,*** sharing at least a short common border with land allotted to the tribe of Manasseh. To the north, the Phoenician cities of ***Tyre*** and Sidon limited Asher's expansion.

19:28 ***Abdon:*** As in some Hebrew manuscripts (see also 21:30); most Hebrew manuscripts read *Ebron.*

19:29 ***the Mediterranean Sea:*** Literally *the sea.*

30 Ummah, Aphek, and Rehob—twenty-
two towns with their surrounding
villages.

31 The homeland allocated to the clans of
the tribe of Asher included these towns and
their surrounding villages.

The Land Given to Naphtali

32 The sixth allotment of land went to the
clans of the tribe of Naphtali.

33 Its boundary ran from Heleph, from
the oak at Zaanannim, and extended
across to Adami-nekeb, Jabneel, and
as far as Lakkum, ending at the Jordan
River. 34 The western boundary ran
past Aznoth-tabor, then to Hukkok, and
touched the border of Zebulun in the
south, the border of Asher on the west,
and the Jordan River on the east. 35 The
fortified towns included in this territory
were Ziddim, Zer, Hammath, Rakkath,
Kinnereth, 36 Adamah, Ramah, Hazor,
37 Kedesh, Edrei, En-hazor, 38 Yiron,
Migdal-el, Horem, Beth-anath, and Beth-
shemesh—nineteen towns with their
surrounding villages.

39 The homeland allocated to the clans of
the tribe of Naphtali included these towns
and their surrounding villages.

The Land Given to Dan

40 The seventh allotment of land went to the
clans of the tribe of Dan.

41 The land allocated as their homeland
included the following towns: Zorah,
Eshtaol, Ir-shemesh, 42 Shaalabbin,
Aijalon, Ithlah, 43 Elon, Timnah, Ekron,
44 Eltekeh, Gibbethon, Baalath, 45 Jehud,
Bene-berak, Gath-rimmon, 46 Me-jarkon,
Rakkon, and the territory across from
Joppa.

47 But the tribe of Dan had trouble
taking possession of their land, so
they attacked the town of Laish. They
captured it, slaughtered its people, and
settled there. They renamed the town
Dan after their ancestor.

48 The homeland allocated to the clans of
the tribe of Dan included these towns and
their surrounding villages.

The Land Given to Joshua

49 After all the land was divided among the
tribes, the Israelites gave a piece of land to
Joshua as his allocation. 50 For the LORD had
said he could have any town he wanted. He
chose Timnath-serah in the hill country of
Ephraim. He rebuilt the town and lived there.

51 These are the territories that Eleazar the
priest, Joshua son of Nun, and the tribal leaders allocated as grants of land to the tribes of
Israel by casting sacred lots in the presence
of the LORD at the entrance of the Tabernacle at Shiloh. So the division of the land was
completed.

Cities of Refuge and Levitical Cities (20:1–21:45)

The Cities of Refuge

20 The LORD said to Joshua, 2 "Now tell
the Israelites to designate the cities
of refuge, as I instructed Moses. 3 Anyone
who kills another person accidentally and
unintentionally can run to one of these
cities; they will be places of refuge from relatives seeking revenge for the person who
was killed.

19:30 Josh 21:31
19:34 Deut 33:23
19:42 Judg 1:35
19:47 Judg 18:27-31
19:50 Josh 24:30
19:51 Josh 14:1; 18:10
20:2 Num 35:6, 11; Deut 4:41; 19:2

19:30 The *twenty-two towns* did not include Tyre and Sidon, which the nation of Israel never controlled.

19:32-39 *The tribe of Naphtali* occupied eastern Galilee and overlooked the Sea of Galilee. Because a branch of an international trade route from Egypt to Mesopotamia ran through the territory of Naphtali, this tribe enjoyed periods of prosperity when Israel's kings were strong. The city of *Hazor* was within Naphtali's territory, guarding a section of that route. Naphtali is mentioned in Matt 4:13-16 in connection with Jesus' ministry in Galilee.

19:34 *and the Jordan River:* Hebrew reads *and Judah at the Jordan River.*

19:40-48 The original allotment given to *the tribe of Dan* lay west of Judah and southwest of Ephraim's main territory, between Judah and Philistia.

19:43 About fifty years after Israel came into Canaan under Joshua, the Philistines moved into the southern coastal plain and occupied the cities of *Timnah* and *Ekron* (Judg 14:1-2; 1 Sam 5:1-10). The Philistines were among the Sea Peoples who had perhaps been driven out of the Greek mainland and the Greek islands by an invasion from the north. The Sea Peoples also invaded and destroyed the Hittite Empire to the north of Israel. (Some scholars think that Homer's *Iliad* reflects this movement.)

19:47 ***The tribe of Dan had trouble taking possession of their land*** (or ***had trouble holding on to their land***) because of the Philistines, so a group of Danites moved northward (see Judg 18). • ***Laish*** (Hebrew *Leshem*, a variant spelling of *Laish*) was later renamed Dan, on the northern border of Israel's territory.

19:49-50 The ***piece of land*** given ***to Joshua*** closes the section on the allocation of land to the tribes of Israel (see note on 14:1–19:51).

19:51 ***the Tabernacle:*** Literally *Tent of Meeting.* • After Joshua received his inheritance, ***the division of the land was completed.*** Joshua served God and led Israel faithfully for many years, and God was gracious to Joshua.

20:1–21:45 Before the land was fully allotted, Joshua needed to establish six cities of refuge and assign cities for the Levites to live in.

20:1-6 These verses contain a review of the law concerning ***cities of refuge*** (see also Num 35:6-34).

20:3 The ***relatives*** of a murder or manslaughter victim had the responsibility of ***seeking revenge*** for the death. If the avenger (Hebrew *go'el*) found the killer outside a city ***of refuge***, he could kill him without punishment.

20:4
Ruth 4:1-2
ᵉ*zaqen* (2205)
‣Ruth 4:11

20:7
Josh 21:11, 32
1 Chr 6:76
Luke 1:39

20:8
Josh 21:27, 36, 38

21:1
Josh 14:1

21:2
Num 35:2

21:4-39
//1 Chr 6:54-80

21:11
Josh 15:13-14
1 Chr 6:57

21:13
Josh 15:42, 54; 20:7
1 Chr 6:55

21:15
Josh 15:49, 51
1 Chr 6:58

[4]"Upon reaching one of these cities, the one who caused the death will appear before the ᵉelders at the city gate and present his case. They must allow him to enter the city and give him a place to live among them. [5]If the relatives of the victim come to avenge the killing, the leaders must not release the slayer to them, for he killed the other person unintentionally and without previous hostility. [6]But the slayer must stay in that city and be tried by the local assembly, which will render a judgment. And he must continue to live in that city until the death of the high priest who was in office at the time of the accident. After that, he is free to return to his own home in the town from which he fled."

[7]The following cities were designated as cities of refuge: Kedesh of Galilee, in the hill country of Naphtali; Shechem, in the hill country of Ephraim; and Kiriath-arba (that is, Hebron), in the hill country of Judah. [8]On the east side of the Jordan River, across from Jericho, the following cities were designated: Bezer, in the wilderness plain of the tribe of Reuben; Ramoth in Gilead, in the territory of the tribe of Gad; and Golan in Bashan, in the land of the tribe of Manasseh. [9]These cities were set apart for all the Israelites as well as the foreigners living among them. Anyone who accidentally killed another person could take refuge in one of these cities. In this way, they could escape being killed in revenge prior to standing trial before the local assembly.

The Towns Given to the Levites

21 Then the leaders of the tribe of Levi came to consult with Eleazar the priest, Joshua son of Nun, and the leaders of the other tribes of Israel. [2]They came to them at Shiloh in the land of Canaan and said, "The LORD commanded Moses to give us towns to live in and pasturelands for our livestock." [3]So by the command of the LORD the people of Israel gave the Levites the following towns and pasturelands out of their own grants of land.

[4]The descendants of Aaron, who were members of the Kohathite clan within the tribe of Levi, were allotted thirteen towns that were originally assigned to the tribes of Judah, Simeon, and Benjamin. [5]The other families of the Kohathite clan were allotted ten towns from the tribes of Ephraim, Dan, and the half-tribe of Manasseh.

[6]The clan of Gershon was allotted thirteen towns from the tribes of Issachar, Asher, Naphtali, and the half-tribe of Manasseh in Bashan.

[7]The clan of Merari was allotted twelve towns from the tribes of Reuben, Gad, and Zebulun.

[8]So the Israelites obeyed the LORD's command to Moses and assigned these towns and pasturelands to the Levites by casting sacred lots.

[9]The Israelites gave the following towns from the tribes of Judah and Simeon [10]to the descendants of Aaron, who were members of the Kohathite clan within the tribe of Levi, since the sacred lot fell to them first: [11]Kiriath-arba (that is, Hebron), in the hill country of Judah, along with its surrounding pasturelands. (Arba was an ancestor of Anak.) [12]But the open fields beyond the town and the surrounding villages were given to Caleb son of Jephunneh as his possession.

[13]The following towns with their pasturelands were given to the descendants of Aaron the priest: Hebron (a city of refuge for those who accidentally killed someone), Libnah, [14]Jattir, Eshtemoa, [15]Holon, Debir,

20:7-9 Joshua ***designated*** six ***cities of refuge:*** three ***on the east side of the Jordan***, and three on the west. From anywhere in the land, one of these six well-known Levitical cities was no more than two days' travel away.

20:9 The treatment of ***foreigners*** in Israel was a great advance in human relations. Resident aliens were to receive every justice offered to native Israelites (see Exod 22:21; Lev 19:33-34; 24:22; Num 15:15-16).

21:1-8 The towns given to ***the tribe of Levi*** were determined by lot (see note at 7:16-18) by Israel's leaders.

21:2-3 ***The LORD commanded Moses:*** See Num 35:1-7. One of the priestly duties was to teach God's *torah* (see note at 1:8) to Israel. The Levites could accomplish this better by living throughout the tribal territories.

21:4 The ***descendants of Aaron*** served as Israel's priests. The cities they received ***were allotted*** by sacred lots. The priestly towns were in the tribal territories closest to Jerusalem, where the Temple was later built.

21:5 The remaining ***families of the Kohathite clan*** received cities in the central part of the hill country, north of Jerusalem.

21:6 The ***clan of Gershon*** received cities among the four northernmost tribes in Israel.

21:7 The ***clan of Merari*** did not stay together as other Levitical clans did.

21:8 The ***pasturelands*** were grazing ground surrounding the cities. The repetition of this word throughout the list (21:8-42) gave the allotment the character of a legal record, guaranteeing the Levites access to lands immediately surrounding each of the Levitical cities (Num 35:4-5).

21:9-42 ***The descendants of Aaron*** received thirteen cities, ***the rest of the Kohathite clan*** received ten, ***the descendants of Gershon*** received thirteen, and ***the Merari clan*** received twelve. There were a total of ***forty-eight*** Levitical cities. Each tribe had four Levitical cities, except Judah had eight, Simeon had one, and Naphtali had three. Six of the Levitical cities were also cities of refuge (20:7-8).

[16]Ain, Juttah, and Beth-shemesh—nine
towns from these two tribes.
[17]From the tribe of Benjamin the priests
were given the following towns with their
pasturelands: Gibeon, Geba, [18]Anathoth,
and Almon—four towns. [19]So in all, thirteen
towns with their pasturelands were given to
the priests, the descendants of Aaron.
[20]The rest of the Kohathite clan from
the tribe of Levi was allotted the following
towns and pasturelands from the tribe of
Ephraim: [21]Shechem in the hill country of
Ephraim (a city of refuge for those who accidentally killed someone), Gezer, [22]Kibzaim,
and Beth-horon—four towns.
[23]The following towns and pasturelands
were allotted to the priests from the tribe
of Dan: Eltekeh, Gibbethon, [24]Aijalon, and
Gath-rimmon—four towns.
[25]The half-tribe of Manasseh allotted the
following towns with their pasturelands
to the priests: Taanach and Gath-rimmon—
two towns. [26]So in all, ten towns with their
pasturelands were given to the rest of the
Kohathite clan.
[27]The descendants of Gershon, another
clan within the tribe of Levi, received the following towns with their pasturelands from
the half-tribe of Manasseh: Golan in Bashan
(a city of refuge for those who accidentally
killed someone) and Be-eshterah—two
towns.
[28]From the tribe of Issachar they received
the following towns with their pasturelands: Kishion, Daberath, [29]Jarmuth, and
En-gannim—four towns.
[30]From the tribe of Asher they received
the following towns with their pasturelands:
Mishal, Abdon, [31]Helkath, and Rehob—four
towns.
[32]From the tribe of Naphtali they received
the following towns with their pasturelands: Kedesh in Galilee (a city of refuge
for those who accidentally killed someone),
Hammoth-dor, and Kartan—three towns.
[33]So in all, thirteen towns with their pasturelands were allotted to the clan of Gershon.
[34]The rest of the Levites—the Merari
clan—were given the following towns
with their pasturelands from the tribe of
Zebulun: Jokneam, Kartah, [35]Dimnah, and
Nahalal—four towns.
[36]From the tribe of Reuben they received
the following towns with their pasturelands:
Bezer, Jahaz, [37]Kedemoth, and Mephaath—
four towns.
[38]From the tribe of Gad they received the
following towns with their pasturelands:
Ramoth in Gilead (a city of refuge for those
who accidentally killed someone), Mahanaim, [39]Heshbon, and Jazer—four towns.
[40]So in all, twelve towns were allotted to the
clan of Merari.
[41]The total number of towns and pasturelands within Israelite territory given to the
Levites came to forty-eight. [42]Every one of
these towns had pasturelands surrounding it.
[43]So the LORD gave to Israel all the land
he had sworn to give their ancestors, and
they took possession of it and settled there.
[44]And the LORD gave them rest on every side,
just as he had solemnly promised their ancestors. None of their enemies could stand
against them, for the LORD helped them conquer all their enemies. [45]Not a single one of
all the good promises the LORD had given
to the family of Israel was left unfulfilled;
everything he had spoken came true.

4. JOSHUA BIDS ISRAEL FAREWELL (22:1–24:33)

The Eastern Tribes Return to Their Homes (22:1-34)

The Eastern Tribes Return Home

22 Then Joshua called together the
tribes of Reuben, Gad, and the half-
tribe of Manasseh. [2]He told them, "You have
done as Moses, the servant of the LORD, commanded you, and you have obeyed every
order I have given you. [3]During all this time
you have not deserted the other tribes. You
have been careful to obey the commands of
the LORD your God right up to the present
day. [4]And now the LORD your God has given
the other tribes rest, as he promised them.
So go back home to the land that Moses, the
servant of the LORD, gave you as your pos-

21:16 Josh 15:10; 1 Chr 6:59
21:18 1 Chr 6:60
21:21 Josh 20:7
21:32 Josh 20:7
21:36 Josh 20:8
21:41 Num 35:7
21:43 Num 33:53; Deut 11:31; 17:14; 34:4
21:44 Exod 23:31; Deut 7:24
22:2 Num 32:20-22; Josh 1:12-18
22:4 Num 32:18; Deut 3:20

21:36 *Jahaz:* Hebrew *Jahzah,* a variant spelling of Jahaz.

21:45 God had made Israel many *good promises,* and not one had failed. He kept his promise to give Israel possession of the land and to save them from their surrounding enemies.

22:1–24:33 Israel completed the conquest and allotment of the land, but much of the hard work of actually settling it still lay ahead. However, all that remained for Joshua in his role as leader of Israel was to say farewell.

22:1-34 Joshua's first farewell was to the tribes east of the Jordan as he sent them home. Characteristically, he exhorted them to remain faithful.

22:2-3 Joshua commended the eastern tribes for their faithful obedience and the fulfillment of their promise to help the rest of Israel inhabit Canaan (see 1:12-18; Num 32:1-32).

22:4-6 Joshua's words recall God's words to Joshua at the beginning of the conquest (1:1-9). In order to live in *the land,* Israel needed to be faithful to God by being ***very careful to obey all the commands and the instructions*** given to Moses.

22:5 Deut 5:10; *Mark 12:32
22:7 Num 32:33; Josh 17:1-2
22:9 Num 32:1, 26, 29
22:11 Deut 12:5
22:13 Num 25:7, 11; 31:6
22:17 Num 25:1-9

session on the east side of the Jordan River.
5 But be very careful to obey all the commands and the instructions that Moses gave to you. Love the LORD your God, walk in all his ways, obey his commands, hold firmly to him, and serve him with all your heart and all your soul."
6 So Joshua blessed them and sent them away, and they went home.

7 Moses had given the land of Bashan, east of the Jordan River, to the half-tribe of Manasseh. (The other half of the tribe was given land west of the Jordan.) As Joshua sent them away and blessed them,
8 he said to them, "Go back to your homes with the great wealth you have taken from your enemies—the vast herds of livestock, the silver, gold, bronze, and iron, and the large supply of clothing. Share the plunder with your relatives."

9 So the men of Reuben, Gad, and the half-tribe of Manasseh left the rest of Israel at Shiloh in the land of Canaan. They started the journey back to their own land of Gilead, the territory that belonged to them according to the LORD's command through Moses.

The Eastern Tribes Build an Altar

10 But while they were still in Canaan, and when they came to a place called Geliloth near the Jordan River, the men of Reuben, Gad, and the half-tribe of Manasseh stopped to build a large and imposing altar.

11 The rest of Israel heard that the people of Reuben, Gad, and the half-tribe of Manasseh had built an altar at Geliloth at the edge of the land of Canaan, on the west side of the Jordan River.
12 So the whole community of Israel gathered at Shiloh and prepared to go to war against them.
13 First, however, they sent a delegation led by Phinehas son of Eleazar, the priest, to talk with the tribes of Reuben, Gad, and the half-tribe of Manasseh.
14 In this delegation were ten leaders of Israel, one from each of the ten tribes, and each the head of his family within the clans of Israel.

15 When they arrived in the land of Gilead, they said to the tribes of Reuben, Gad, and the half-tribe of Manasseh,
16 "The whole community of the LORD demands to know why you are betraying the God of Israel. How could you turn away from the LORD and build an altar for yourselves in rebellion against him?
17 Was our sin at Peor not enough? To this day we are not fully cleansed of it, even after the plague that struck the entire community of the LORD.
18 And yet today you are turning away from following the LORD. If you rebel against the LORD today, he will be angry with all of us tomorrow.

19 "If you need the altar because the land you possess is defiled, then join us in the LORD's land, where the Tabernacle of the LORD is situated, and share our land with us. But do not rebel against the LORD or against us by building an altar other than the one true altar of the LORD our God.
20 Didn't divine anger fall on the entire community of

22:5 ***all your heart and all your soul:*** See Deut 6:5.

22:7 ***Moses had given:*** The author takes great care to emphasize that the tribes east of the Jordan were part of Israel.

22:8 The ***great wealth*** represented these tribes' share of the spoils from the cities Israel had taken. • ***Share . . . with your relatives:*** While most of the fighting men assisted the rest of Israel, some men had remained to protect the women, children, and herds.

22:10-20 ***Reuben, Gad, and the half-tribe of Manasseh*** built their own altar, triggering a confrontation with ***the rest of Israel***.

22:10 ***to a place called Geliloth*** (or *to the circle of stones;* similarly in 22:11): It is reasonable to presume that Geliloth and the ***altar*** were on the west bank of the Jordan (see note on 22:19).

22:11 The tribes referred to here as ***the rest of Israel*** (literally *the sons of Israel*) consisted of the tribes given land west of the Jordan River, in ***Canaan*** proper. They already referred to themselves as Israel, excluding the tribes east of the Jordan (see 22:24-25).

22:12 The western tribes were ready ***to go to war*** because they saw the altar as violating Lev 17:8-9 and Deut 13:12-15.

22:13-14 ***delegation:*** See Deut 13:14. • The ***ten tribes*** west of the Jordan included Ephraim and the western half of Manasseh but not the tribe of Levi.

22:15-20 The direct and hard-hitting statements and questions of the delegation made sure that God's wrath would not come upon the nation because of rebellion like Achan's (7:1-15) or the episode at Peor (Num 25).

22:15 The delegation crossed the Jordan River to meet the leaders of the eastern tribes in ***the land of Gilead,*** probably in southern Gad.

22:16 The delegation brought the message the ten tribes had agreed upon when they met at Shiloh. • ***The whole community of the LORD demands to know*** (literally *Thus says the whole congregation of the LORD*): The formula using "thus says" was a typical introduction to a messenger's report (e.g., Ezra 1:2; Isa 28:16).

22:17 The ***sin at Peor*** was Israel's idolatrous rebellion in Moab, just at the point of entering the Promised Land (Num 25). Phinehas, now the leader of this delegation, had acted to save Israel from complete destruction at that time. He did not want to see any part of Israel turn away from God again.

22:19 Being ***defiled*** was not necessarily the result of rebellion or a moral lapse, but it did prevent persons or groups from participating in regular worship activities, including the offering of sacrifices. If the eastern tribes had defiled the land itself, the Israelites could not offer sacrifices to the Lord within it. This concern provides evidence that the eastern tribes had built their altar on the western bank of the Jordan. • The land west of the Jordan was considered ***the LORD's land***. The delegation from the western tribes made a very generous offer, inviting the eastern tribes to ***share*** their ***land.*** This demonstrated their commitment to national unity in faithfulness to God.

22:20 ***Achan:*** See ch 7. The delegation of western tribes feared that Achan's

Israel when Achan, a member of the clan of Zerah, sinned by stealing the things set apart for the LORD? He was not the only one who died because of his sin."

21Then the people of Reuben, Gad, and the half-tribe of Manasseh answered the heads of the clans of Israel: 22"The LORD, the Mighty One, is God! The LORD, the Mighty One, is God! He knows the truth, and may Israel know it, too! We have not built the altar in treacherous rebellion against the LORD. If we have done so, do not spare our lives this day. 23If we have built an altar for ourselves to turn away from the LORD or to offer burnt offerings or grain offerings or peace offerings, may the LORD himself punish us.

24"The truth is, we have built this altar because we fear that in the future your descendants will say to ours, 'What right do you have to worship the LORD, the God of Israel? 25The LORD has placed the Jordan River as a barrier between our people and you people of Reuben and Gad. You have no claim to the LORD.' So your descendants may prevent our descendants from worshiping the LORD.

26"So we decided to build the altar, not for burnt offerings or sacrifices, 27but as a memorial. It will remind our descendants and your descendants that we, too, have the right to worship the LORD at his sanctuary with our burnt offerings, [f]sacrifices, and peace offerings. Then your descendants will not be able to say to ours, 'You have no claim to the LORD.'

28"If they say this, our descendants can reply, 'Look at this copy of the LORD's altar that our ancestors made. It is not for burnt offerings or sacrifices; it is a reminder of the relationship both of us have with the LORD.' 29Far be it from us to rebel against the LORD or turn away from him by building our own altar for burnt offerings, grain offerings, or sacrifices. Only the altar of the LORD our God that stands in front of the Tabernacle may be used for that purpose."

30When Phinehas the priest and the leaders of the community—the heads of the clans of Israel—heard this from the tribes of Reuben, Gad, and the half-tribe of Manasseh, they were satisfied. 31Phinehas son of Eleazar, the priest, replied to them, "Today we know the LORD is among us because you have not committed this treachery against the LORD as we thought. Instead, you have rescued Israel from being destroyed by the hand of the LORD."

32Then Phinehas son of Eleazar, the priest, and the other leaders left the tribes of Reuben and Gad in Gilead and returned to the land of Canaan to tell the Israelites what had happened. 33And all the Israelites were satisfied and praised God and spoke no more of war against Reuben and Gad.

34The people of Reuben and Gad named the altar "Witness," for they said, "It is a witness between us and them that the LORD is our God, too."

Joshua's Farewell to Israel (23:1–24:33)

Joshua's Final Words to Israel

23 The years passed, and the LORD had given the people of Israel rest from all their enemies. Joshua, who was now very old, 2called together all the elders, leaders, judges, and officers of Israel. He said to them, "I am now a very old man. 3You have seen everything the LORD your God has done for you during my lifetime. The LORD your God has fought for you against your enemies. 4I have allotted to you as your homeland all

22:20 Josh 7:1-26
22:22 Deut 10:17
22:27 Josh 24:27
[f]*zebakh* (2077) ▸1 Kgs 8:5
22:29 Deut 12:13
22:31 Lev 26:11-12; 2 Chr 15:2
22:34 Gen 31:47-49
23:1 Josh 21:44
23:2 Josh 24:1
23:4 Exod 23:30

sin and its consequences would be repeated. • ***set apart for the LORD:*** The Hebrew term used here refers to the complete consecration of things or people to the LORD, either by destroying them or by giving them as an offering.

22:21-34 The eastern tribes defended their action.

22:22 ***The LORD . . . is God!*** The two-fold repetition of this dramatic affirmation indicated how shocked the eastern tribes were when accused of rebellion.

22:23 The eastern tribes swore by the name of ***the LORD*** that they were not guilty. • The instructions for sacrifices prescribed ***burnt offerings or grain offerings or peace offerings*** (Lev 1–3). At this time, Israel's worship was centered at the Tabernacle in Shiloh. To offer sacrifices anywhere but the central sanctuary was a violation of God's covenant (see note on 22:12).

22:24-29 The eastern tribes feared exclusion from Israel at a later time because the ***Jordan River*** divided them from the western tribes.

22:27 The altar near the bank of the Jordan would stand ***as a memorial*** (literally *witness*) through the generations that the eastern tribes were also part of Israel.

22:28 This altar was a ***copy***, intended to be seen, not used.

22:31 ***you have rescued:*** In his reply to the eastern tribes, Phinehas used very similar language to the words God had spoken when Phinehas turned God's anger from Israel at Peor (Num 25:11).

22:33 Both the eastern and western tribes were relieved that the crisis had been averted, and they joyfully ***praised God*** to renew their affirmation of national unity in faithfulness to God.

22:34 ***Witness:*** Some manuscripts lack this word. Hebrew texts that include it interpret the last statement as an explanation of the name. Texts that omit the word understand the last quotation to be the name of the altar.

23:1-11 ***Joshua*** urged Israel's leaders to be faithful.

23:2-3 The ***leaders . . . of Israel*** had experienced what God had done for them and to their enemies. Throughout the lifetimes of these leaders who outlived Joshua, Israel continued to be faithful to God (Judg 2:7).

23:4-5 Some of the land that Joshua had assigned to the various tribes

23:5 Num 33:53
23:6 Deut 5:32; Josh 1:7
23:7 Exod 20:5; 23:13; Ps 16:4
23:8 Deut 10:20
23:9 Deut 7:24
23:10 Lev 26:8; Deut 28:7
23:12 Deut 7:3-4; Ezra 9:2
23:13 Exod 23:33; 34:12; Deut 7:16
23:14 [g]*'erets* (0776) ‣Josh 23:16
23:15 Lev 26:14-33; Deut 28:15
23:16 Deut 4:25-26; [h]*'erets* (0776) ‣Ps 24:1
24:1 Josh 23:2
24:2 Gen 11:27-32; [i]*'elohim* (0430) ‣Ps 16:1

the land of the nations yet unconquered, as well as the land of those we have already conquered—from the Jordan River to the Mediterranean Sea in the west. 5This land will be yours, for the LORD your God will himself drive out all the people living there now. You will take possession of their land, just as the LORD your God promised you.

6"So be very careful to follow everything Moses wrote in the Book of Instruction. Do not deviate from it, turning either to the right or to the left. 7Make sure you do not associate with the other people still remaining in the land. Do not even mention the names of their gods, much less swear by them or serve them or worship them. 8Rather, cling tightly to the LORD your God as you have done until now.

9"For the LORD has driven out great and powerful nations for you, and no one has yet been able to defeat you. 10Each one of you will put to flight a thousand of the enemy, for the LORD your God fights for you, just as he has promised. 11So be very careful to love the LORD your God.

12"But if you turn away from him and cling to the customs of the survivors of these nations remaining among you, and if you intermarry with them, 13then know for certain that the LORD your God will no longer drive them out of your land. Instead, they will be a snare and a trap to you, a whip for your backs and thorny brambles in your eyes, and you will vanish from this good land the LORD your God has given you.

14"Soon I will die, going the way of everything on [g]earth. Deep in your hearts you know that every promise of the LORD your God has come true. Not a single one has failed! 15But as surely as the LORD your God has given you the good things he promised, he will also bring disaster on you if you disobey him. He will completely destroy you from this good land he has given you. 16If you break the covenant of the LORD your God by worshiping and serving other gods, his anger will burn against you, and you will quickly vanish from the good [h]land he has given you."

The LORD's Covenant Renewed

24 Then Joshua summoned all the tribes of Israel to Shechem, including their elders, leaders, judges, and officers. So they came and presented themselves to God.

2Joshua said to the people, "This is what the LORD, the [i]God of Israel, says: Long ago

remained *unconquered.* Israel's gradual occupation of the land had an ecological reason (see Exod 23:29-30), a military reason (see Judg 1:19), and a theological reason (see Judg 2:20–3:4). Israel's ensuing unfaithfulness delayed the settlement process by several centuries; instead of driving out the remaining Canaanites, Israel absorbed them, bringing God's people even greater temptations to unfaithfulness. Joshua knew this to be a real danger (23:15-16). • *the Mediterranean Sea:* Literally *the Great Sea.*

23:6 Since before crossing the Jordan River to take the land of Canaan, Joshua's guiding principle had been to ***be very careful to follow everything Moses wrote*** and ***not deviate.*** Now he passed on these instructions to the leaders who would succeed him in leading Israel.

23:7 ***Do not even mention . . . swear by . . . serve . . . or worship them:*** These four actions describe progressive involvement with idolatry.

23:8 To ***cling tightly*** or passionately to God would render impotent the temptation to stray off toward other gods. This same verb described a man clinging to his wife (Gen 2:24) and Ruth clinging to Naomi (Ruth 1:14).

23:9 Examples of ***great and powerful nations*** included the Anakim (11:21-22) and the city of Hazor (11:10).

23:10 ***God fights for you:*** Just as God had fought for the Israelites in the past (e.g., 10:11-14), he would continue to fight for them in the future.

23:11 ***be very careful to love:*** Love is a function of will and intention. Emotion and attraction are the results, not the essence, of love. Because love is (or is not) willed, love can be commanded but not coerced.

23:12-16 Apostasy—turning away from the true God—is fatal. • Because God is holy, Joshua could speak with optimism regarding God's promises and the good land into which God had brought them. God will not change his holy character even if his people change. The rebellion of God's people cannot damage his holiness, but rebellion will destroy those who rebel.

23:12 Joshua warned God's people not to ***intermarry with*** their polytheistic neighbors because such an intimate relationship would lead the Israelites astray (Deut 7:3-4). However, Canaanites who desired to worship the Lord and join God's people were welcomed (6:25; Ruth 4:10). Race, language, and ethnicity had no bearing on God's prohibition of intermarriage; it was a matter of faithfulness to the Lord (cp. 2 Cor 6:14-15).

23:13 ***will no longer drive them out:*** If Israel associated with the Canaanite remnant, God would oblige the Israelites by not driving out that remnant. God ultimately gives people what they seek.

23:15-16 God had blessed the Israelites, and he would also certainly judge them if they turned away from him. Joshua's warning against apostasy was prophetic; Israel did turn away, and God did not drive out the remaining Canaanites (Judg 2:20-23).

24:1-27 In both form and content, this statement of covenant resembled an ancient Near Eastern suzerain-vassal treaty. It begins with a preamble (24:2) and continues with a historical prologue relating the suzerain's (God's) gracious acts on behalf of the people (24:3-13), followed by a list of stipulations (24:14-15) and curses and blessings (24:19-20). It then notes where the text was to be deposited for periodic reading and renewal (implied, 24:26) and lists witnesses to the covenant (24:22, 27). See also note on Exod 20:1–23:33.

24:1-13 Joshua recounted God's grace toward Israel.

24:1 ***Shechem*** was the location of the first affirmation of the covenant shortly after Israel had entered the land of Canaan (see 8:30-35 and notes).

24:2 ***Terah:*** See Gen 11:27-32. • ***the Euphrates River:*** Literally *the river;* also in 24:3, 14, 15.

your ancestors, including Terah, the father
of Abraham and Nahor, lived beyond the
Euphrates River, and they worshiped other
[i]gods. 3But I took your ancestor Abraham
from the land beyond the Euphrates and
led him into the land of Canaan. I gave him
many [j]descendants through his son Isaac.
4To Isaac I gave Jacob and Esau. To Esau I
gave the mountains of Seir, while Jacob and
his children went down into Egypt.

5"Then I sent Moses and Aaron, and I
brought terrible plagues on Egypt; and afterward I brought you out as a free people.
6But when your ancestors arrived at the Red
Sea, the Egyptians chased after you with
chariots and charioteers. 7When your ancestors cried out to the LORD, I put darkness
between you and the Egyptians. I brought
the sea crashing down on the Egyptians,
drowning them. With your very own eyes
you saw what I did. Then you lived in the wilderness for many years.

8"Finally, I brought you into the land of
the Amorites on the east side of the Jordan.
They fought against you, but I destroyed
them before you. I gave you victory over
them, and you took possession of their land.
9Then Balak son of Zippor, king of Moab,
started a war against Israel. He summoned
Balaam son of Beor to curse you, 10but I
would not listen to him. Instead, I made Balaam bless you, and so I rescued you from
Balak.

11"When you crossed the Jordan River
and came to Jericho, the men of Jericho
fought against you, as did the Amorites, the
Perizzites, the Canaanites, the Hittites, the
Girgashites, the Hivites, and the Jebusites.
But I gave you victory over them. 12And
I sent terror ahead of you to drive out the
two kings of the Amorites. It was not your
swords or bows that brought you victory. 13I
gave you land you had not worked on, and
I gave you towns you did not build—the
towns where you are now living. I gave you
vineyards and olive groves for food, though
you did not plant them.

14"So fear the LORD and serve him wholeheartedly. Put away forever the idols your
ancestors worshiped when they lived beyond the Euphrates River and in Egypt.
Serve the LORD alone. 15But if you refuse
to serve the LORD, then choose today whom
you will serve. Would you prefer the gods
your ancestors served beyond the Euphrates? Or will it be the gods of the Amorites in
whose land you now live? But as for me and
my family, we will serve the LORD."

16The people replied, "We would never
[k]abandon the LORD and serve other gods.
17For the LORD our God is the one who rescued us and our ancestors from slavery in
the land of Egypt. He performed mighty
miracles before our very eyes. As we traveled through the wilderness among our
enemies, he preserved us. 18It was the LORD
who drove out the Amorites and the other
nations living here in the land. So we, too,
will serve the LORD, for he alone is our God."

19Then Joshua warned the people, "You
are not able to serve the LORD, for he is a
holy and jealous God. He will not [a]forgive
your rebellion and your sins. 20If you abandon the LORD and serve other gods, he will
turn against you and destroy you, even
though he has been so good to you."

[i]*elohim* (0430) ‣Ps 16:1

24:3 Gen 12:1; 15:5; 21:3; 24:7

[j]*zera'* (2233) ‣2 Sam 7:12

24:4 Gen 25:25-26; 46:5-7 Deut 2:5

24:5 Exod 3:10; 4:14-17

24:6 Exod 14:2-22

24:7 Exod 14:19-31 Deut 1:46; 2:14

24:8 Num 21:21-31

24:9 Num 22:2-6

24:11 Exod 23:23 Deut 7:1 Josh 3:14-17

24:12 Exod 23:28 Deut 7:20 Ps 44:3, 6

24:13 Deut 6:10-11

24:14 Deut 10:12; 18:13 1 Sam 12:24

24:15 Ruth 1:15 1 Kgs 18:21

24:16 [k]*azab* (5800) ‣Judg 2:12

24:19 Exod 20:5; 23:21; 34:14 Lev 19:2; 20:7, 26 [a]*nasa'* (5375) ‣1 Sam 15:25

24:20 Deut 4:25-26 Josh 23:15 1 Chr 28:9 Acts 7:42

24:3-13 Israel's faith was always the result of God's initiative. Joshua's repetition of God's words ***I took . . . I gave . . . I sent . . . I brought*** reminded the Israelites why they should continue to be loyal to God.

24:3 ***Abraham*** lived at Haran in Mesopotamia ***beyond the Euphrates*** until his father Terah died (Gen 11:31-32). • ***led him into . . . Canaan:*** See Gen 12:1-9.

24:4 ***Jacob and Esau:*** See Gen 25:19-26. • The ***mountains of Seir*** stood at the heart of Edom, the homeland of Esau's descendants (Gen 36:8-9).

24:5-7 The Exodus, which culminated with the crossing of ***the Red Sea***, was the climactic salvation event of ancient Israel's history. A number of psalms, several of the later prophets, and several NT writers all celebrated this defining event.

24:6 ***Red Sea:*** Literally *sea of reeds.* See note on Exod 13:18.

24:7 Even though the older Israelites present here had been children at the time of the Exodus, they had seen the events with their ***very own eyes.***

24:8 ***Amorites . . . their land:*** See Num 21:21-35.

24:9-10 See Num 22–25; 31.

24:11 See note on 3:10.

24:12 ***terror:*** Often rendered *the hornet.* The meaning of the Hebrew is uncertain. • Israel's successes were not because of their ***swords or bows*** or other military advantage; all were God's doing.

24:13 The Israelites received wealth, including ***land . . . towns*** and ***food,*** that they had not earned or created.

24:14 ***Put away forever the idols:*** Israel had not yet broken with the old polytheistic traditions of Mesopotamia ***beyond the Euphrates River,*** and some Israelites had added to their supply of gods while living ***in Egypt.***

24:15 Joshua threw the influence of his leadership and accomplishments behind his declaration to ***serve the LORD.***

24:16-18 ***The people*** recognized that it was ***God*** who ***rescued*** them, ***preserved*** them, and ***drove out the Amorites.***

24:16 ***The people*** responded emphatically, reflecting their determination to follow Joshua's lead in following ***the LORD.***

24:19-24 Joshua pressed the Israelites from a different perspective to underscore the seriousness of their commitment and to ensure that they were not merely responding to the enthusiasm of the moment.

24:19 God is ***holy:*** See "God's Absolute Holiness" at Lev 10:3, p. 210. • God is also ***jealous;*** he created every human being for relationship with himself.

24:24
Exod 19:8; 24:3, 7
Deut 5:27

24:25
Exod 24:8
[b]*berith* (1285)
‣2 Kgs 11:17

24:27
Josh 22:27

24:29
Judg 2:8

24:30
Josh 19:50

24:32
Gen 50:24-25
Exod 13:19
John 4:5
Acts 7:16

24:33
Josh 22:13

21 But the people answered Joshua, "No,
we will serve the LORD!"
22 "You are a witness to your own decision," Joshua said. "You have chosen to
serve the LORD."
"Yes," they replied, "we are witnesses to
what we have said."
23 "All right then," Joshua said, "destroy
the idols among you, and turn your hearts
to the LORD, the God of Israel."
24 The people said to Joshua, "We will
serve the LORD our God. We will obey him
alone."
25 So Joshua made a [b]covenant with the
people that day at Shechem, committing
them to follow the decrees and regulations
of the LORD. 26 Joshua recorded these things
in the Book of God's Instructions. As a reminder of their agreement, he took a huge
stone and rolled it beneath the terebinth
tree beside the Tabernacle of the LORD.
27 Joshua said to all the people, "This stone
has heard everything the LORD said to us. It
will be a witness to testify against you if you
go back on your word to God."
28 Then Joshua sent all the people away to
their own homelands.

Leaders Buried in the Promised Land

29 After this, Joshua son of Nun, the servant
of the LORD, died at the age of 110. 30 They
buried him in the land he had been allocated, at Timnath-serah in the hill country
of Ephraim, north of Mount Gaash.
31 The people of Israel served the LORD
throughout the lifetime of Joshua and of
the elders who outlived him—those who
had personally experienced all that the
LORD had done for Israel.
32 The bones of Joseph, which the Israelites had brought along with them when
they left Egypt, were buried at Shechem, in
the parcel of ground Jacob had bought from
the sons of Hamor for 100 pieces of silver.
This land was located in the territory allotted to the descendants of Joseph.
33 Eleazar son of Aaron also died. He was
buried in the hill country of Ephraim, in the
town of Gibeah, which had been given to
his son Phinehas.

24:22 ***a witness to your own decision:*** Joshua pressed the people to repeat their declaration as a legal affirmation and commitment.

24:23 Some Israelites had continued to worship ***idols*** since they left Egypt and after experiencing forty years of God's love and power. Joshua directed them to ***destroy the idols*** and ***turn*** their ***hearts to the LORD*** to serve him alone.

24:25 ***made a covenant:*** Literally *cut a covenant* (see note at 9:15).

24:26 ***The Book of God's Instructions*** was a scroll containing the writings of Moses (see note on 1:8). It was probably carried to Shiloh and stored with other documents of national importance. • The ***huge stone*** was probably a *stela,* a standing stone monument. Joshua might have had a memorial inscription chiseled into this stone monument.

24:27 ***This stone has heard:*** See note at 22:27.

24:29-33 The tombs of a venerated ancestor and two revered leaders provided the final notice that Canaan was indeed Israel's land. However, significant work, vigilance, and even fighting still lay ahead.

24:29 Joshua's ancestor Joseph had also attained ***the age of 110,*** which was considered the ideal lifespan by ancient Egyptians.

24:30 ***Timnath-serah:*** See 19:49-51.

24:31 Joshua's legacy was so strong that Israel remained faithful to God even ***throughout the lifetime . . . of the elders who outlived him.***

24:32 Israel had carried ***the bones of Joseph*** out of ***Egypt***, through the years of their journeys, and into Canaan to honor Joseph's last request to be buried in the land God had promised Israel (Gen 50:25; Exod 13:19). • ***Shechem*** was part of the inheritance of Joseph's descendants, at the border between Ephraim and Manasseh. Jacob had purchased it centuries before for ***100 pieces of silver*** (Hebrew *100 kesitahs;* the value or weight of the kesitah is no longer known).

24:33 ***Eleazar*** the high priest had stood beside Joshua during the process of allotting portions of the land to the tribes of Israel. • Joshua, Joseph, and Eleazar were all buried in ***Ephraim,*** in the central part of the newly conquered land. Their burial served as a final sign that God had fulfilled his promise to give Israel the land.

THE CHRONOLOGY OF

The Time of the Judges

The time of the judges marks the period after Joshua down through Samuel's ministry, to the beginning of Saul's reign as the first king of Israel (1 Sam 10). The judges were men and women whom God used during this period to rescue his people from their enemies. One long-standing question has been how to fit these stories into the chronology of this period.

The people of Israel entered the Promised Land of Canaan in either 1406 or 1230 BC, depending on the date of the Exodus (see "The Chronology of Abraham to Joshua," pp. 118–121). The people of Israel then lived in the land and experienced cycles of oppression by neighboring countries and rescue through various judges until the prophet Samuel anointed Saul as king of all Israel around 1050 BC.

The stories of the judges themselves are told as a sequence, giving the impression that one judge followed another. Most of the accounts of judges also provide chronological indications, specifying how long oppressors dominated God's people and the period of peace that followed their rescue by each judge (see chart, facing page). However, simply adding these numbers produces a sum of years that significantly exceeds the time available in this period of history.

A solution to this difficulty is to realize that the judges did not always work sequentially, but sometimes they overlapped with one another. For example, Judges 10:7 states, "So the LORD burned with anger against Israel, and he turned them over to the Philistines and the Ammonites." Jephthah freed his people from the Ammonite threat in the northeast while Samson began to rescue Israel from Philistia in the southwest.

In certain cases, the text does point to a sequence between judges. For instance, Shamgar judged "after Ehud" (Judg 3:31) and Deborah "after Ehud's death" (Judg 4:1, see also Judg 5:6). Nonetheless, Judges does not provide these types of connections between most of the judges. Indeed, in at least one case, it is explicit that two judges overlapped. Most of the judges held influence over only a limited part of the land of Israel. The period of the judges was characterized not only by moral depravity and spiritual darkness but also by political fragmentation. It is worth noting that none of the judges had a national following—each was followed only by a few tribes, usually those in the vicinity of the judge's hometown.

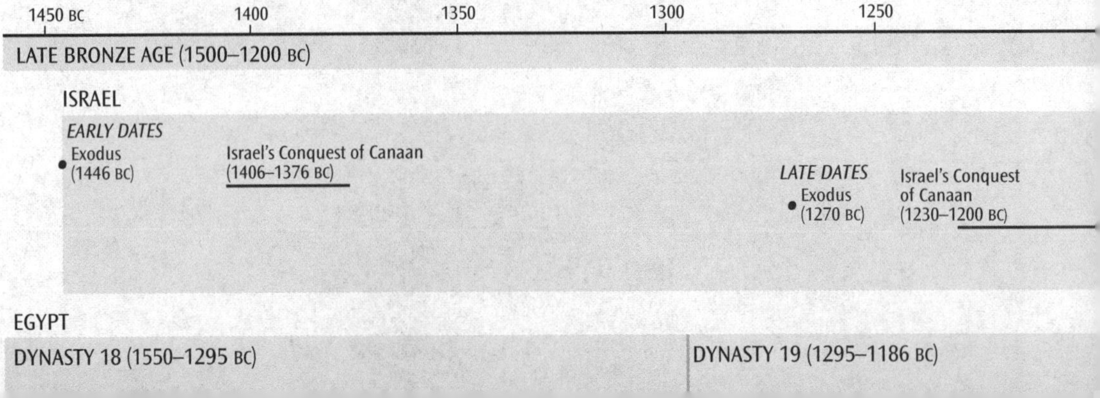

The period of the judges can thus be seen as fitting into history when we realize that the judges were local and often overlapped. Indeed, there is no reason to think that we have a full list of Israel's judges, only a representative number (cp. "Bedan" in 1 Sam 12:11; see Judges Introduction, "Summary," pp. 417–418).

Oppressor		Judge		Reference
Cushan-rishathaim (from Aram-naharaim)	8 yrs	Othniel	40 yrs	Judg 3:7-11
Eglon (from Moab)	18 yrs	Ehud	80 yrs	Judg 3:12-30
Philistines		Shamgar		Judg 3:31
Jabin & Sisera (from Hazor in Canaan)	20 yrs	Deborah/Barak	40 yrs	Judg 4:1–5:31
Midianites	7 yrs	Gideon	40 yrs	Judg 6:1–8:35
		Abimelech	3+ yrs	Judg 8:31; 9:1-57
		Tola	23 yrs	Judg 10:1-2
		Jair	22 yrs	Judg 10:3
Ammonites	18 yrs	Jephthah	6 yrs	Judg 10:6–12:7
		Ibzan	7 yrs	Judg 12:9
		Elon	10 yrs	Judg 12:11
		Abdon	8 yrs	Judg 12:14
Philistines	40 yrs	Samson	20 yrs	Judg 13:1–16:31
		Eli	40 yrs	1 Sam 1:9–4:22
TOTAL	*111 yrs*	*TOTAL*	*339 yrs*	

▲**Years of Oppression and Peace in Judges.** Simply adding up the years of oppression and peace recorded in Judges leads to a total of 450 years from the death of Joshua's generation (about 1350 or 1175 BC) to the beginning of Saul's reign (about 1050 BC). Clearly, there had to be overlap between the judges, whose leadership was local and tribal rather than nationwide.

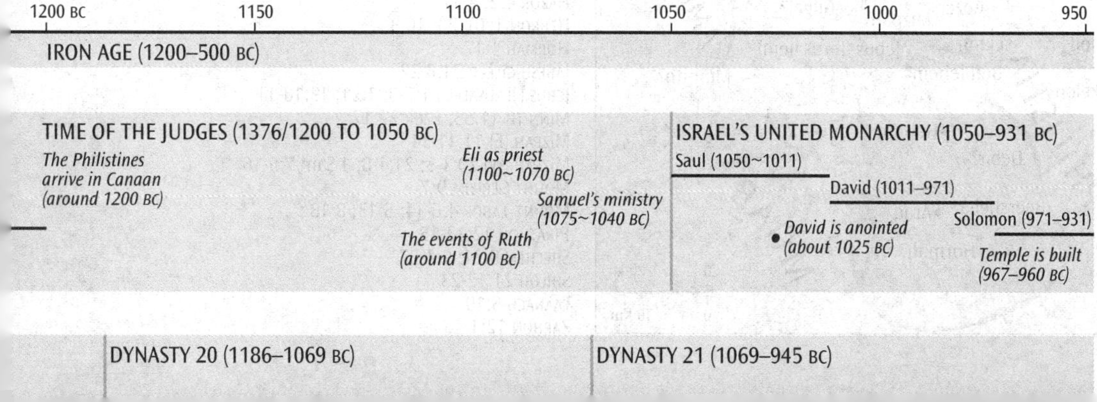

THE BOOK OF

JUDGES

The book of Judges tells the stories of the judges, the inspired leaders who rescued Israel time after time. During this period, the people were unfaithful to God's covenant, and God allowed their enemies to oppress them. Israel repeatedly turned to the Lord for help, and the Lord repeatedly sent charismatic judges to lead Israel. These powerful leaders did amazing things, but they were unable to transcend Israel's anarchy and lawlessness. Israel needed a leader whose authority could give them national coherence and unity.

SETTING

The period of the judges is best understood against the backdrop of its own age. Historians and sociologists have compared the book of Judges with the epics of Homer, the sagas of old Iceland, and the French *La Chanson de Roland,* each of which represents the "Heroic Age" in a civilization's adolescence. During these times, unorthodox men and women marched to a different drum, exhibiting behavior at odds with accepted norms.

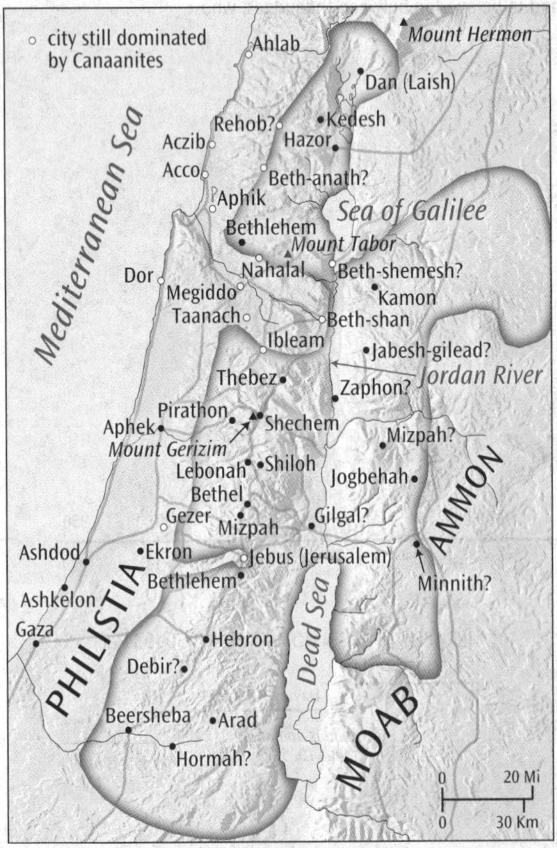

Setting of the Judges (about 1200 BC). Israel's approximate border during the time of the judges is shown. Israel had conquered Transjordan during the time of Moses, and the hill country of Canaan during the time of Joshua (see Josh 11:16–12:24), but the rest of the land remained largely unconquered (Josh 13:1-7). Open circles on this map designate the cities still dominated by Canaanites (see 1:19-36). In addition, the cities of PHILISTIA were under Philistine control. The people who were not driven out of the land became a source of both temptation and oppression to the Israelites (2:11–3:6).

ARAD 1:16
ASHKELON 1:18; 14:19; 1 Sam 6:17; 2 Sam 1:20
BETHEL 1:22-23; 4:5; 20:18, 23, 26-27; 21:2, 19
BETHLEHEM (N) see note on 12:8
BETHLEHEM (S) 17:7-9; 19:1-3, 18
BETH-SHEMESH 1:33
DAN (LAISH) 18:1-31
EKRON 1:18
GAZA 1:18; 6:4; 16:1-2; 16:21
GILGAL 2:1; 3:19
HAZOR 4:2; 4:17
HEBRON 1:10, 20; 16:3
HORMAH 1:17
JABESH-GILEAD 21:8-22
JEBUS (JERUSALEM) 1:7-8; 1:21; 19:10-11
MINNITH 11:33; Ezek 27:17
MIZPAH (E) 11:11-34
MIZPAH (W) 20:1-3; 21:1-8; 1 Sam 7:5-16
MOUNT GERIZIM 9:7
MOUNT TABOR 4:6-14; 5:13; 8:18
PIRATHON 12:13-15
SHECHEM 8:31; 9:1-57
SHILOH 21:12-23
TAANACH 5:19
ZAPHON 12:1

After Moses died, the Israelites' campaigns under Joshua provided the desert nomads with a settled land, but hardly a settled society. That would take hundreds of years and the emergence of a stable monarchy under King David. But Moses and Joshua did leave the Israelites with an organized society. According to the biblical text, the tribal structure was well-established and the lands were clearly apportioned. A few central shrines (Gilgal, Shiloh) had emerged, with leaders that included priests, Levites, and tribal elders who brought Israel a degree of order. The people continued to remember the old traditions—the covenant promise to Abraham, the sojourn in Egypt from which Israel had been rescued by divine strength, the desert wanderings, and the ratification of the covenant—but something was still lacking.

According to Judges, Israel's shortcomings had two sources. First, the prologues (1:1–2:5 and 2:6–3:6) explain that the tribes failed to possess their alloted territories because they capitulated to the norms of Canaan rather than adhering to the divine covenant given under Moses. The second issue looms large in the epilogues (17:1–21:25) and is summarized in the repeated sentence, "In those days Israel had no king; all the people did whatever seemed right in their own eyes" (17:6; 18:1; 19:1; 21:25). The prologues highlight Israel's unfaithfulness to God; the epilogues are concerned with a failed social structure. The age of heroes could not produce the stable political institutions required for implementing God's rule over the children of Israel.

OUTLINE

1:1–3:6
Prologues

3:7–16:31
Cycles of the Judges

17:1–21:25
Epilogues

The book of Judges does not, however, reject the principle of charismatic leadership embodied in the judges. The judges' inspiration came at God's initiative and fulfilled God's purpose in leading and saving Israel (see 2:16-19). The stories celebrate the principle of heroic leadership, making it clear that the Achilles' heel of the era was not in the divinely inspired leaders but in the sinfulness of the people's hearts, which had to be addressed by a different form of governance. "In those days" something was missing.

SUMMARY

Judges follows an A-B-A structure, beginning with two prologues. Each is introduced by the death of Joshua, thus picking up the narrative from Josh 24:28-31 by means of this pivotal event in Israel's national life. The first prologue (1:1–2:5) recalls the failures of individual tribes to follow through on God's covenant. By contenting themselves with partial occupation of the land, they demonstrated their disregard for the Lord's promise and provoked the withdrawal of his protection (2:1-3).

The second prologue (2:6–3:6) turns from the failures of the tribes to introduce the individuals whom the Lord used to keep the flame of conquest and settlement alive in a chaotic time. The story moves from Joshua to the elders who outlived him but had experienced God's power in the wilderness

TIMELINE

2091 / 1915 BC*
Abraham leaves Ur of the Chaldeans

1876 / 1661 BC
Jacob's family goes to Egypt

1446 / 1270 BC
Israel's exodus from Egypt

1406 / 1230 BC
Beginning of the conquest

about 1376 / 1200 BC
Beginning of the judges period

1075~1040 BC
Samuel as judge

1050~1011 BC
Saul's reign as king

1011–971 BC
David's reign as king

* *The two dates accord with the traditional "early" date and the more recent "late" date of the Exodus. All dates are approximate. Please see "Chronology: Abraham to Joshua," p. 118.*

and conquest, and finally to the third generation "who did not acknowledge the LORD or remember the mighty things he had done for Israel" (2:10). The account then introduces the central feature of the book, the judges (2:16) whom God raised up to rescue Israel and call them back to covenant obedience, the evidence of which would be faithful occupation of the Promised Land. Judges 3:1-6, like the close of the earlier prologue, informs readers in advance that the effort will end in failure.

The central section (3:7–16:31) contains "cycles"—longer accounts of the six major judges (Othniel, Ehud, Deborah, Gideon, Jephthah, and Samson), and shorter accounts of the six minor judges (Shamgar, Tola, Jair, Ibzan, Elon, and Abdon). The section is punctuated by the rise of an anti-charismatic leader, Abimelech (ch 9), whose rule was like that of a king. Following Abimelech, the spiral is clearly downward. The figures at the beginning of the story are more ideal (Othniel to Gideon), while the characters toward the end are more questionable (Jephthah, Samson). In all, there were twelve leaders, apparently representing each of the twelve tribes of Israel (see note on 12:8). The inexorable march toward chaos throughout the book points to their need for a more centralized society.

Judges culminates in two epilogues (chs 17–18; 19–21) that highlight the historical and theological failure of Israel under the judges, and the ensuing spiritual and social chaos. The epilogues are marked by the summary refrain, "In those days Israel had no king," to which is twice added, "all the people did whatever seemed right in their own eyes" (see 17:6; 18:1; 19:1; 21:25). This conclusion begs for a sequel in which a new tribal covenant reverses the declining effectiveness of individual charismatic leaders.

AUTHORS AND DATE OF COMPOSITION

Nothing is known about the author(s) or compiler(s) of Judges. The historical books (Joshua—2 Kings) are a connected narrative. Tradition tells us that various sources were combined into a theological narrative under the influence of Israel's prophetic schools.

Evidence from the last chapter of this history (2 Kgs 25:27-30) suggests the Exile to Babylon as a final date for the composition or collection of this material. Judges may have received its final form at the same time, although there is little in the book of Judges itself that points beyond the early monarchy. Judges knows nothing of a central shrine or national capital in Jerusalem; the social structures reflected in the book indicate a nation still struggling with issues of settlement and governance.

The church has her way of dealing with embarrassing Scripture: ignore it. Yet that is difficult to do with Judges. It's so interesting. Only people who take tranquilizers before sitting down can doze off while they read it.

DALE RALPH DAVIS
Such a Great Salvation, p. 7

CHRONOLOGY OF THE JUDGES

Dating and ordering the judges is notoriously difficult; the results depend to a great extent on whether one adopts the long or short chronology of the period, which in turn depends on whether the Exodus is seen as having occurred in the 1400s or in the 1200s BC (see "Chronology: Abraham to Joshua," p. 118). The long chronology harmonizes well with 1 Kgs 6:1 and Judg 11:26 and allows for the possibility that the cycles of judges occurred sequentially. The shorter chronology seems to fit better with external evidence (such as archaeological findings), but it forces the period of the judges into a short time frame and makes overlaps in the story inevitable. See further "Chronology: The Time of the Judges," p. 414.

MEANING AND MESSAGE

What kind of leadership does God's work require, and where can God's people find such leaders? Judges gives a partial answer to both questions but stops short of providing the final word.

Judges celebrates charismatic (gifted) leadership while recognizing its limitations. One enduring biblical principle of leadership is that God raises up heroes and fills them with his Spirit to rescue his people. Moses and Joshua had been such rescuer-leaders, and Saul and David would be. The heroes of Judges had flaws, but God used them. The true charismatic is a man or woman who is given a divine gift (Greek *charisma*) to lead. Following this kind of leader is part of the divine order.

A second kind of leadership, often called "official," has authority that does not come directly from God but flows from an office or appointment. Just as the Israelite judges were classic charismatic leaders, the kings represented official authority in the military and political sphere. Prophets and priests presented the same contrast in Israel's spiritual life—the prophets were inspired leaders while the priests were official leaders.

Which type of leader has God's approval? How do those who want to follow the Lord faithfully know which structures of leadership are worthy of obedience? The book of Judges demonstrates God's unmistakable commitment to raise up powerfully endowed, spirit-filled leaders appropriate for the occasion. The principle of charismatic leadership, despite its limitations, is never set aside in biblical narrative.

Even in the transition to kingship in 1 and 2 Samuel, there is ambivalence toward the new form of official leadership. Kingship began with Saul, a charismatic judge-king in whom the weaknesses of both systems combined to bring about his downfall. The charismatic principle is then affirmed and renewed in the life of David, a great hero-king. David was so distinctly a charismatic king that it is initially difficult to distinguish him from a successful judge. What answers the plaintive cry of Judges is not the rejection of charismatic leaders but the addition of God's covenant with his chosen king, David (2 Sam 7). God's ideal is in the combination of inspired and official leadership. Israel's judges and kings, with all their limitations, look forward to Jesus, the perfect charismatic king, who combines in his person all the perfections so lacking in each of his predecessors.

Old Israel's narrative art survives in its purest form in the Book of Judges.

ROBERT BOLING
Judges, p. 29

FURTHER READING

ROBERT G. BOLING
Judges (1975)

ARTHUR CUNDALL
Judges (1968)

DALE RALPH DAVIS
Such a Great Salvation: Expositions of the Book of Judges (1990)

MICHAEL WILCOCK
The Message of Judges (1992)

1:1 Num 27:21
1:2 Gen 49:8
1:3 Judg 1:17

1. PROLOGUES (1:1–3:6)

Partial Conquest and Tribal Unfaithfulness (1:1–2:5)

Judah and Simeon Conquer the Land

1 After the death of Joshua, the Israelites asked the LORD, "Which tribe should go first to attack the Canaanites?"
[2]The LORD answered, "Judah, for I have given them victory over the land."
[3]The men of Judah said to their relatives from the tribe of Simeon, "Join with us to fight against the Canaanites living in the territory allotted to us. Then we will help you

1:1–3:6 Two prologues (1:1–2:5 and 2:6–3:6) preface the body of the book. Both begin with ***the death of Joshua*** (1:1; cp. 2:8), thus connecting Judges with the preceding narrative (Josh 24:29-33; cp. Josh 1:1; 2 Sam 1:1).

1:1–2:5 The first prologue describes the unfaithfulness of the tribes in their failure to carry out Joshua's farewell charge (Josh 23).

1:1 The request for divine guidance (see Exod 28:30; Num 27:21; 1 Sam 14:41; 28:6; cp. Josh 7:14) is a reminder that the Lord's covenant with Israel included the taking of the land.

1:2 This verse, which is paralleled in the epilogues (20:18), shows the primacy of ***Judah***. This tribe did not figure in the downward cycles of the judges (cp. 15:9-13) after Othniel, the model judge who was linked to Judah through Caleb (Josh 14:6; 15:13, 17).

1:3 ***The tribe of Simeon*** virtually disappeared within the land assigned to Judah (Josh 19:1). • ***fight against the Canaanites . . . help you conquer:*** See Josh 16:10; 17:13; 23:4-13.

conquer your territory." So the men of Simeon went with Judah.
[4]When the men of Judah attacked, the
LORD gave them victory over the Canaanites
and Perizzites, and they killed 10,000 enemy warriors at the town of Bezek. [5]While at
Bezek they encountered King Adoni-bezek
and fought against him, and the Canaanites
and Perizzites were defeated. [6]Adoni-bezek
escaped, but the Israelites soon captured
him and cut off his thumbs and big toes.
[7]Adoni-bezek said, "I once had seventy
kings with their thumbs and big toes cut
off, eating scraps from under my table.
Now God has paid me back for what I did
to them." They took him to Jerusalem, and
he died there.
[8]The men of Judah attacked Jerusalem
and captured it, killing all its people and setting the city on fire. [9]Then they went down to
fight the Canaanites living in the hill country,
the Negev, and the western foothills. [10]Judah
marched against the Canaanites in Hebron
(formerly called Kiriath-arba), defeating the
forces of Sheshai, Ahiman, and Talmai.
[11]From there they went to fight against
the people living in the town of Debir (formerly called Kiriath-sepher). [12]Caleb said,
"I will give my daughter Acsah in marriage
to the one who attacks and captures Kiriath-
sepher." [13]Othniel, the son of Caleb's younger
brother, Kenaz, was the one who conquered
it, so Acsah became Othniel's wife.
[14]When Acsah married Othniel, she
urged him to ask her father for a field. As
she got down off her donkey, Caleb asked
her, "What's the matter?"
[15]She said, "Let me have another gift. You
have already given me land in the Negev;
now please give me springs of water, too." So
Caleb gave her the upper and lower springs.
[16]When the tribe of Judah left Jericho—
the city of palms—the Kenites, who were
descendants of Moses' father-in-law, traveled with them into the wilderness of Judah.
They settled among the people there, near
the town of Arad in the Negev.
[17]Then Judah joined with Simeon to fight
against the Canaanites living in Zephath,
and they completely destroyed the town.
So the town was named Hormah. [18]In addition, Judah captured the towns of Gaza,
Ashkelon, and Ekron, along with their surrounding territories.

Israel Fails to Conquer the Land

[19]The LORD was with the people of Judah,
and they took possession of the hill country. But they failed to drive out the people
living in the plains, who had iron chariots.
[20]The town of Hebron was given to Caleb as
Moses had promised. And Caleb drove out
the people living there, who were descendants of the three sons of Anak.
[21]The tribe of Benjamin, however, failed
to drive out the Jebusites, who were living in
Jerusalem. So to this day the Jebusites live in
Jerusalem among the people of Benjamin.
[22]The descendants of Joseph attacked
the town of Bethel, and the LORD was with
them. [23]They sent men to scout out Bethel

1:4 Gen 13:7; 1 Sam 11:8
1:8 Josh 15:63
1:10-15 //Josh 15:13-19
1:13 Judg 3:9
1:16 Deut 34:3; Judg 3:13; 4:11
1:17 Num 21:3
1:19 Josh 17:16; Judg 4:3
1:20 Josh 14:6-9; 15:14
1:21 Josh 15:63
1:22 Gen 28:19; Josh 14:3-4

1:9 ***the western foothills:*** Hebrew *the Shephelah.*

1:10 ***Hebron*** was the city nearest to Abraham's dwelling by the oaks of Mamre (Gen 13:18); the patriarchs later lived and were buried there (Gen 23:19; 35:27; 49:29-32). It was originally called ***Kiriath-arba*** ("City of Arba"), after the legendary Arba, who was "a great hero of the descendants of Anak" and "Anak's ancestor" (Josh 14:15; 15:13). The Anakites, in turn, are identified with the dreaded Nephilites (Num 13:33; see Gen 6:4).

1:11 ***Debir*** or ***Kiriath-sepher*** ("City of the Book"): This major Anakite town of the hill country (Josh 11:21) is not firmly identified, but was traditionally understood as being either southwest or east of Hebron.

1:14 ***she urged him:*** Greek version and Latin Vulgate read ***he urged her.*** See note on Josh 15:18-19.

1:16 The ***Kenites*** were a southern desert tribe associated with ***Moses'*** in-laws, who were also called Midianites (Exod 18:1; Num 10:29). Moses offered them a share in the covenant blessing (Num 10:29-32). At least one clan of Kenites accepted the offer and was adopted into Judah, though members of the clan later shifted allegiance to King Jabin of Hazor (4:11, 17).

1:17 ***completely destroyed:*** The Hebrew term used here refers to the complete consecration of things or people to the LORD, either by destroying them or by giving them as an offering. See Lev 27:28-29. • ***Hormah*** means "destruction." See note on Num 21:2-3.

1:18 ***Gaza, Ashkelon, and Ekron,*** with Gath and Ashdod, later made up the five main cities of the Philistines (3:3).

1:19-20 Despite the Lord's presence, the conquest was not completed because of ***iron chariots*** and lack of obedience (see Josh 23:12-13; 24:14).

1:21-36 The tribes of Israel failed to keep the covenant; their complacency was rebellion against the Lord, as the rest of the book of Judges shows.

1:21 Though ***the tribe of Benjamin*** produced more than its share of heroes (e.g., Ehud, Saul), it was also the nadir of covenant unfaithfulness, in contrast to Judah (see 20:18). Like Judah in its first battle (1:4-8), Benjamin faced challenges from a great people dwelling in a great city, but Benjamin settled for sharing the city with them. Reference to the Lord's personal presence is absent (cp. 1:19, 22). The Jebusite city remained in Canaanite hands until David's day. • The phrase ***to this day*** highlights either ongoing historical circumstances (here and 6:24) or the survival of certain customs to a later time (1:26; 10:4; 15:19; 18:12).

1:22-36 Two references to the descendants of Joseph (1:22, 35) frame this litany of the northern tribes' failures to drive out the enemy.

1:22 ***The LORD was with*** the descendants of Joseph (the tribes of Ephraim and Manasseh), but only in their united attack on Bethel, a place sacred to Israelite memories from the days of Jacob (Gen 28:19). They failed in attacks made separately (1:27-29). • ***Bethel*** is associated

1:24 Josh 2:12
1:25 Josh 6:25
1:27 Josh 17:11-13
1:29 Josh 16:10
1:34 Judg 18:1
1:36 Josh 15:3
2:1 Gen 17:7; Exod 20:2; Judg 6:11
2:2 Exod 23:32; 34:12-13
2:3 Num 33:55
2:5 Josh 7:26
2:6 Josh 24:28-31

(formerly known as Luz). 24They confronted
a man coming out of the town and said to
him, "Show us a way into the town, and we
will have mercy on you." 25So he showed
them a way in, and they killed everyone in
the town except that man and his family.
26Later the man moved to the land of the
Hittites, where he built a town. He named it
Luz, which is its name to this day.

27The tribe of Manasseh failed to drive
out the people living in Beth-shan, Taanach, Dor, Ibleam, Megiddo, and all their surrounding settlements, because the Canaanites were determined to stay in that
region. 28When the Israelites grew stronger,
they forced the Canaanites to work as slaves,
but they never did drive them completely
out of the land.

29The tribe of Ephraim failed to drive out
the Canaanites living in Gezer, so the Canaanites continued to live there among them.

30The tribe of Zebulun failed to drive out
the residents of Kitron and Nahalol, so the
Canaanites continued to live among them.
But the Canaanites were forced to work as
slaves for the people of Zebulun.

31The tribe of Asher failed to drive out
the residents of Acco, Sidon, Ahlab, Aczib,
Helbah, Aphik, and Rehob. 32Instead, the
people of Asher moved in among the Canaanites, who controlled the land, for they
failed to drive them out.

33Likewise, the tribe of Naphtali failed to
drive out the residents of Beth-shemesh and
Beth-anath. Instead, they moved in among
the Canaanites, who controlled the land.
Nevertheless, the people of Beth-shemesh
and Beth-anath were forced to work as
slaves for the people of Naphtali.

34As for the tribe of Dan, the Amorites
forced them back into the hill country and
would not let them come down into the
plains. 35The Amorites were determined
to stay in Mount Heres, Aijalon, and Shaalbim, but when the descendants of Joseph
became stronger, they forced the Amorites
to work as slaves. 36The boundary of the Amorites ran from Scorpion Pass to Sela and
continued upward from there.

The LORD's Messenger Comes to Bokim

2 The angel of the LORD went up from Gilgal to Bokim and said to the Israelites, "I
brought you out of Egypt into this land that
I swore to give your ancestors, and I said I
would never break my covenant with you.
2For your part, you were not to make any covenants with the people living in this land;
instead, you were to destroy their altars. But
you disobeyed my command. Why did you
do this? 3So now I declare that I will no longer drive out the people living in your land.
They will be thorns in your sides, and their
gods will be a constant temptation to you."

4When the angel of the LORD finished
speaking to all the Israelites, the people
wept loudly. 5So they called the place Bokim
(which means "weeping"), and they offered
sacrifices there to the LORD.

Leadership Failure and the Raising Up of Judges (2:6–3:6)

The Death of Joshua

6After Joshua sent the people away, each of
the tribes left to take possession of the land
allotted to them. 7And the Israelites served
the LORD throughout the lifetime of Joshua
and the leaders who outlived him—those
who had seen all the great things the LORD
had done for Israel.

8Joshua son of Nun, the servant of the
LORD, died at the age of 110. 9They buried
him in the land he had been allocated, at

---

with the battle against Ai (Josh 7:2) and is listed in the summary statement of kings that Israel had defeated (Josh 12:16).

1:24 To *have mercy* (Hebrew *khesed*) has the overtones of making a covenant (see also 8:35, "loyalty").

1:26 *The land of the Hittites* was probably a general name for North Syria, not the Hittite Kingdom of Anatolia (now Turkey). Nothing is known of the new *Luz.*

1:27 This chain of Canaanite cities stretched from *Dor* on the Mediterranean to *Beth-shan* (Hebrew *Beth-shean,* a variant spelling of *Beth-shan*) in the Jordan Valley and effectively cut off the northern tribes from those south of the Jezreel Valley. Likewise, a number of the cities listed in the south (1:35) probably cut Judah off from the northern tribes.

1:34 Dan's failure to take the land represents total infidelity and led to the complete abandonment of a portion of the Promised Land (chs 17–18).

1:36 *Scorpion Pass:* Hebrew *Akrabbim.*

2:1-5 The sanctuary had been set up at Gilgal (Josh 4:19-20; 5:10); ***Bokim*** is an unknown place, where ***the angel of the LORD*** gave an announcement that led to ***weeping*** and an attempt to reverse the judgment by offering sacrifice.

2:1 Even when Israel was unfaithful, God's ***covenant***, originally given to Abraham, remained unconditional (Gen 12:1-3; 17:1-22; cp. 2 Tim 2:13).

2:2 The gods of the nations were not a neutral force, so destroying the pagan ***altars*** was basic to covenant obedience. Not doing so would inevitably involve social and religious compromise, and the people of the land would oppress Israel (see Deut 20:17-18).

2:3 ***They will be thorns in your sides:*** Literally *They will be in your sides;* cp. Num 33:55.

2:6–3:6 The second prologue also follows from the events of Josh 23–24 (see note on 1:1–3:6), adding the element of a third generation (2:10) who had no personal experience of the Lord's mighty acts.

2:8 Cp. 1:1; Josh 24:29-31.

2:9 ***Timnath-serah:*** As in parallel text at Josh 24:30; Hebrew reads *Timnath-heres,* a variant spelling of *Timnath-serah.*

Timnath-serah in the hill country of Ephraim,
north of Mount Gaash.

Israel Disobeys the LORD

10After that generation died, another generation grew up who did not acknowledge the
LORD or remember the mighty things he
had done for Israel.

11The Israelites did evil in the LORD's
sight and served the images of Baal. 12They
[a]abandoned the LORD, the God of their ancestors, who had brought them out of Egypt.
They went after other gods, worshiping the
gods of the people around them. And they
angered the LORD. 13They abandoned the
LORD to serve Baal and the images of Ashtoreth. 14This made the LORD burn with anger
against Israel, so he handed them over to raiders who stole their possessions. He turned
them over to their enemies all around, and
they were no longer able to resist them. 15Ev-
ery time Israel went out to battle, the LORD
fought against them, causing them to be
defeated, just as he had warned. And the
people were in great distress.

The LORD Rescues His People

16Then the LORD raised up [b]judges to rescue
the Israelites from their attackers. 17Yet
Israel did not listen to the judges but prostituted themselves by worshiping other gods.
How quickly they turned away from the
path of their ancestors, who had walked in
obedience to the LORD's commands.

18Whenever the LORD raised up a judge
over Israel, he was with that judge and
rescued the people from their enemies
throughout the judge's lifetime. For the LORD
took pity on his people, who were burdened
by oppression and suffering. 19But when the
judge died, the people returned to their corrupt ways, behaving worse than those who
had lived before them. They went after other
gods, serving and worshiping them. And

2:10 Exod 5:2; 1 Sam 2:12
2:11 Judg 4:1; 6:1; 8:33; 10:6
2:12 Deut 31:16; 32:12; Judg 10:6; Ps 106:40
[a]*'azab* (5800) ‣1 Sam 12:10
2:13 Judg 10:6
2:16 Ps 106:43-45
[b]*shapat* (8199) ‣Ruth 1:1
2:17 Ps 81:11-12
2:19 Judg 4:1; 8:33

The Oppression of God's People (2:10-15)

Judg 2:2-3; 2:18; 3:1-8
Lev 26:14-39
Deut 8:19-20; 28:15-68
2 Kgs 17:5-23
Ezek 22:27-29
Amos 4:1
Jas 2:1-7

God does not want his people to be oppressed. From the Exodus under Moses to Joshua's conquest and David's battles, God's goal for Israel was complete victory over their enemies (Josh 1:1-9). The NT, too, consistently speaks of freedom from the oppression of sin (Rom 6:1-14; Gal 5:1-15) as an inalienable blessing of a relationship with Christ.

Why, then, does oppression exist? The book of Judges suggests that it is because of human disobedience to God's covenant. Israel was promised victory in the conquest if they would obey God, but the reality (1:19-36) was partial obedience, at best. With the rewards of victory in view, why did God's people of old—and why does the church today—fall short?

In Judges, the answer was that "another generation" arose that had not participated in the Exodus or the conquest under Joshua, so their faith was increasingly based on stories of divine intervention "in the olden days." They had not personally "seen all the great things the LORD had done for Israel" (2:7). This generation failed to "acknowledge the LORD or remember the mighty things he had done for Israel" (2:10). God had left enemies in the land to test the Israelites (3:1-4), but it was Israel who failed to drive out these enemies as God had commanded. The rest of the book of Judges illustrates the tragic results of that failure.

God only turns away from his people when they have turned away from him (2:12-14); he never abandons people who truly worship him (see "God's Grief over Apostasy" at 10:6-16, p. 439). Yet grace notes are sounded even in divine retribution: God turned his anger to a beneficial purpose: to teach his people obedience. The very foes who robbed Israel of its divine inheritance and blessing became part of God's gracious testing. We can learn from oppression, as both physical and spiritual warfare require discipline. The experience can produce a "peaceful harvest of right living" (see Heb 12:5-11).

2:10-19 Joshua was dead, the new generation had not experienced God's saving power, and the Canaanites continued to live in the land. What resulted was the cycle of rebellion and partial restoration. This section introduces that cycle, which the body of the book exemplifies.

2:11-13 Israel rebelled against the Lord and began serving the gods of their neighbors, especially the Canaanite deities of Baal and Asherah. • ***Baal*** means "lord"; ***Ashtoreth*** (most likely the plural form of *Asherah*) might be a Hebrew form of the Canaanite "Astarte," a goddess with various manifestations. See also 6:25-32 and notes.

2:14-15 As Israel served other gods, God withdrew his support. Their rebellion brought ***great distress*** from military defeat by their enemies.

2:15 God was not simply absent; he was actively involved in Israel's defeat, and the outcome of the battle belonged to the Lord (cp. 2 Chr 20:15).

2:16-19 ***The LORD raised up judges*** whose leadership brought partial, temporary restoration. They were later described as "judging" Israel (e.g., 3:10; 4:4; 10:2-3), but they were primarily known for their military victories.

2:20-23 The remaining Canaanites and their religion would become a source of temptation to the Israelites, offering an alternative to faithfully following

2:21 Josh 23:13
3:1 Judg 1:1; 2:21-22
3:3 Josh 13:3
3:4 Deut 8:2; Judg 2:22
3:5 Ps 106:35
3:6 Exod 34:16; Deut 7:3-4

they refused to give up their evil practices
and stubborn ways.
20 So the LORD burned with anger against
Israel. He said, "Because these people have
violated my covenant, which I made with
their ancestors, and have ignored my commands, 21 I will no longer drive out the
nations that Joshua left unconquered when
he died. 22 I did this to test Israel—to see
whether or not they would follow the ways
of the LORD as their ancestors did." 23 That
is why the LORD left those nations in place.
He did not quickly drive them out or allow
Joshua to conquer them all.

The Nations Left in Canaan

3 These are the nations that the LORD left
in the land to test those Israelites who
had not experienced the wars of Canaan.
2 He did this to teach warfare to generations
of Israelites who had no experience in battle. 3 These are the nations: the Philistines
(those living under the five Philistine rulers),
all the Canaanites, the Sidonians, and the
Hivites living in the mountains of Lebanon
from Mount Baal-hermon to Lebo-hamath.
4 These people were left to test the Israelites—to see whether they would obey the
commands the LORD had given to their ancestors through Moses.
5 So the people of Israel lived among the
Canaanites, Hittites, Amorites, Perizzites,
Hivites, and Jebusites, 6 and they intermarried with them. Israelite sons married their
daughters, and Israelite daughters were
given in marriage to their sons. And the Israelites served their gods.

2. CYCLES OF THE JUDGES (3:7–16:31)

The Period of Stability (3:7–8:35)

Othniel Becomes Israel's Judge

7 The Israelites did evil in the LORD's sight.
They forgot about the LORD their God, and

Charismatic, Inspired Leadership (2:16-19)

Judg 3:10, 27-28; 6:34-35; 11:29; 14:6, 19; 15:14
Exod 31:2-5
1 Sam 10:6; 16:13-18
2 Sam 23:2
Isa 61:1
Ezek 11:5
Mic 3:8
Matt 3:16–4:2
Acts 6:8; 8:4-40
Rom 1:11; 12:6-8
1 Cor 12:4-11
Eph 4:11-12

The judges are often described as *charismatic* (gifted) because their authority did not come from an office or a structure but from personal qualities. These qualities came from the inspiration of God's Spirit. Charismatic leaders arose in troubled and unsettled times and in response to a crisis. In Judges, the crisis was that "Again the people did evil in the LORD's sight" (10:6; 13:1; cp. 3:12; 4:1; 6:1), with enemy oppression as the inevitable result.

The inspired leadership of the judges fits a pattern. The judges were "raised up" by the Spirit and were sustained by prophetic affirmation. What might have led to prophetic utterance in other periods of Israel's history (e.g., 1 Sam 10:6; 2 Sam 23:2; Isa 61:1; Ezek 11:5; Mic 3:8), in the times of the judges led to physical prowess (e.g., Samson, 14:6, 19; 15:14), skill (1 Sam 16:13-18), or commanding authority (3:10; 6:34; 11:29).

In the NT, Jesus is clearly a Spirit-inspired leader, especially in the Gospel of Luke; and as the Jewish authorities were fond of pointing out, he had no "official" authority. Although the apostles were appointed to what we might consider to be an "office," there was virtually no structure to back up the office; when they exercised authority, it was purely charismatic leadership. Peter's healing of the beggar (Acts 3:6) provides the classic contrast between the accoutrements of office, such as "silver and gold," and true spiritual power.

Charisma has been a powerful tool for effective leadership from the heroes of Israel to the present time. Along with its successes, charismatic leadership is subject to tragic failure when the Spirit has departed (16:20; 1 Sam 16:14; Isa 63:10).

the Lord and his covenant ways. This result was known and even planned by God (cp. 3:4). God does not deliberately set his people up to sin (Jas 1:12-15). Temptations abound, but the choice to obey God or yield to temptation rests with those who claim to know him. Israel had a duty to possess the land fully, but God, not humankind, determines victory or failure.

3:1-4 The ongoing presence of ***the Philistines*** and ***Canaanites*** in the land had an instructional purpose. Skills in warfare were necessary for survival in the ancient world. God allowed a continuing presence of enemies, but they would become his provision for Israel's training and well-being.

3:3 ***The Philistines*** were never listed with the native Canaanite tribes; they were invaders from the sea who settled on the southwest coast of Israel in about 1200 BC. The Philistines were organized into five cities, each with its own ruler (cp. 1 Sam 6:16-17). They are included here with the ***Canaanites***, anticipating the prominent role they would have as Israel's major foe from Samson's time onward. • The text includes ***Sidonians*** and northern ***Hivites*** to show that Israel's ideal boundaries were well to the north and east of what they actually possessed. • The ***Hivites*** were Canaanite (Hamitic) peoples (Gen 10:17); little is known about them. The Gibeonites, who tricked Joshua (Josh 9:3-27) were Hivites. • ***Baal-hermon*** is possibly the largest of the three peaks that make up Mount Hermon in the northeast corner of Israel; ***Lebo-hamath***, in southern Lebanon, marks Israel's northernmost ideal boundary (1 Kgs 8:65).

3:5-6 Israel failed God's test (3:1-4). Intermarriage led Israel to worship in the fertility cult of the Canaanite ***gods***.

3:7-11 The account of Othniel is typical of the cycles in Judges. Evildoing led to apostasy, most frequently in the ***Baal*** and ***Asherah*** cults (see notes on 2:11-13; 6:25-32). Apostasy provoked the Lord

they served the images of Baal and the
Asherah poles. 8Then the LORD burned
with anger against Israel, and he turned
them over to King Cushan-rishathaim of
Aram-naharaim. And the Israelites served
Cushan-rishathaim for eight years.
9But when the people of Israel cried out
to the LORD for help, the LORD raised up a
rescuer to save them. His name was Othniel,
the son of Caleb's younger brother, Kenaz.
10The Spirit of the LORD came upon him,
and he became Israel's judge. He went to war
against King Cushan-rishathaim of Aram,
and the LORD gave Othniel victory over him.
11So there was peace in the land for forty
years. Then Othniel son of Kenaz died.

Ehud Becomes Israel's Judge

12Once again the Israelites did evil in the
LORD's sight, and the LORD gave King Eglon
of Moab control over Israel because of their
evil. 13Eglon enlisted the Ammonites and
Amalekites as allies, and then he went out
and defeated Israel, taking possession of Jericho, the city of palms. 14And the Israelites
served Eglon of Moab for eighteen years.
15But when the people of Israel cried out
to the LORD for help, the LORD again raised
up a rescuer to save them. His name was
Ehud son of Gera, a left-handed man of the
tribe of Benjamin. The Israelites sent Ehud
to deliver their tribute money to King Eglon
of Moab. 16So Ehud made a double-edged
dagger that was about a foot long, and he
strapped it to his right thigh, keeping it hidden under his clothing. 17He brought the
tribute money to Eglon, who was very fat.
18After delivering the payment, Ehud
started home with those who had helped
carry the tribute. 19But when Ehud reached
the stone idols near Gilgal, he turned back.
He came to Eglon and said, "I have a secret
message for you."

So the king commanded his servants, "Be
quiet!" and he sent them all out of the room.
20Ehud walked over to Eglon, who was
sitting alone in a cool upstairs room. And
Ehud said, "I have a message from God
for you!" As King Eglon rose from his seat,
21Ehud reached with his left hand, pulled
out the dagger strapped to his right thigh,
and plunged it into the king's belly. 22The
dagger went so deep that the handle disappeared beneath the king's fat. So Ehud
did not pull out the dagger, and the king's
bowels emptied. 23Then Ehud closed and
locked the doors of the room and escaped
down the latrine.
24After Ehud was gone, the king's servants returned and found the doors to
the upstairs room locked. They thought
he might be using the latrine in the room,

3:8 Judg 2:14
3:9 Judg 1:13
3:10 Num 11:25-29; 24:2 Judg 6:34; 11:29
3:11 Judg 5:31; 8:28
3:12 Judg 2:11
3:13 Judg 1:16
3:15 Judg 20:16 1 Chr 12:2
3:24 1 Sam 24:3
3:28 Judg 7:24; 12:5

and resulted in foreign oppression. Then the cry of the people evoked divine compassion and the raising up of a rescuer-judge as the agent of God's Spirit. The rescuer ended the oppression, and the land enjoyed a period of peace before the cycle started again. ***Othniel*** depicts an ideal judge.

3:8 ***Cushan-rishathaim*** means "Cushan of Double Wickedness." • ***Aram-naharaim*** means "Aram of the two rivers," thought to have been located between the Euphrates and Balih Rivers in northwestern Mesopotamia. Some scholars, however, think that Aram-naharaim is equivalent to all of Mesopotamia (a word that means "Midst of the Two Rivers," the region between the Tigris and the Euphrates).

3:12-30 In this epic account of intrigue and cunning, Ehud manifested heroic qualities when a coalition of nations from east of the Jordan penetrated the hill country of Ephraim and Benjamin. The cycle follows formulaic language, and highlights the repeated apostasy of the people ***once again.***

3:12-13 The people of ***Moab*** and the ***Ammonites*** were descendants of Lot's incestuous relationship with his daughters (Gen 19:30-38). Despite their kinship with Israel, both nations were Israel's enemies. • The ***Amalekites*** were nomads who had attacked Israel in the desert, and toward whom unbroken hostility had been commanded (Num 24:20; Deut 25:17-19). That the three nations joined in coalition probably reflected their growing fear of Israelite expansion.

3:15 ***left-handed*** (literally *restricted in the right hand*): This characteristic enabled ***Ehud*** to hide his weapon on the right hip. The Greek OT translates this phrase to mean "ambidextrous." The term used here is associated with the tribe of Benjamin ("son of my right hand," Gen 35:18; see Judg 20:16) and was connected with heroic military skills (cp. 1 Chr 12:1-2). • The ***tribute money*** was either pieces of metal or, more likely, agricultural goods requiring a team of bearers (3:18).

3:16 A knife for cutting would have a single blade. This ***doubled-edged dagger*** was fashioned to facilitate driving it into a victim. • ***foot:*** Hebrew *gomed,* the length of which is uncertain.

3:19-21 The ***message*** had to be ***secret*** to ensure that Ehud would be left alone with the king; it had to be ***from God*** to guarantee that the ploy would be effective. Eglon probably stood up because he expected some kind of message from the Lord, which is precisely what he received.

3:19 ***Gilgal*** became the Israelites' initial base of operations after they crossed the Jordan and was the site of important events associated with the conquest (Josh 4–6). The ***stone idols*** may have been a pagan shrine created from the twelve stones that Joshua set up (Josh 4:20). Later, Gilgal was still an important center for the faithful (1 Sam 7:16) and for idolators (Hos 4:15; 9:15; 12:11; Amos 4:4; 5:5).

3:20 The ***cool upstairs room*** was probably some kind of rooftop chamber, a common summer meeting place in hot countries.

3:22 ***and the king's bowels emptied:*** Or *and it came out behind,* which could refer to the dagger.

3:23 ***and escaped down the latrine:*** Or *and went out through the porch;* the meaning of the Hebrew is uncertain. The latrine might have been similar to those in medieval Europe, where it was not uncommon for a latrine to extend out from the wall of a building, with an external chute not unlike today's laundry or chimney ash chutes.

3:24-25 While the king's servants, perhaps reacting to familiar odors, dithered over protocol for a king with bowel problems, Ehud made his escape.

3:31
Judg 5:6
4:1
Judg 2:19
4:2
Josh 11:1
Ps 83:9
4:4
ᶜnebi'ah (5031)
‣1 Sam 10:10
4:6
1 Sam 12:11
Heb 11:32
4:7
Ps 83:9

25so they waited. But when the king didn't
come out after a long delay, they became
concerned and got a key. And when they
opened the doors, they found their master
dead on the floor.
26While the servants were waiting, Ehud
escaped, passing the stone idols on his way
to Seirah. 27When he arrived in the hill
country of Ephraim, Ehud sounded a call to
arms. Then he led a band of Israelites down
from the hills.
28"Follow me," he said, "for the LORD has
given you victory over Moab your enemy."
So they followed him. And the Israelites
took control of the shallow crossings of the
Jordan River across from Moab, preventing
anyone from crossing.
29They attacked the Moabites and killed
about 10,000 of their strongest and most
able-bodied warriors. Not one of them escaped. 30So Moab was conquered by Israel
that day, and there was peace in the land for
eighty years.

Shamgar Becomes Israel's Judge

31After Ehud, Shamgar son of Anath rescued Israel. He once killed 600 Philistines
with an ox goad.

Deborah Becomes Israel's Judge

4 After Ehud's death, the Israelites again
did evil in the LORD's sight. 2So the
LORD turned them over to King Jabin of Hazor, a Canaanite king. The commander of
his army was Sisera, who lived in Harosheth-
haggoyim. 3Sisera, who had 900 iron chariots, ruthlessly oppressed the Israelites for
twenty years. Then the people of Israel
cried out to the LORD for help.
4Deborah, the wife of Lappidoth, was a
ᶜprophet who was judging Israel at that time.
5She would sit under the Palm of Deborah,
between Ramah and Bethel in the hill country of Ephraim, and the Israelites would go
to her for judgment. 6One day she sent for
Barak son of Abinoam, who lived in Kedesh
in the land of Naphtali. She said to him,
"This is what the LORD, the God of Israel,
commands you: Call out 10,000 warriors
from the tribes of Naphtali and Zebulun
at Mount Tabor. 7And I will call out Sisera,
commander of Jabin's army, along with his
chariots and warriors, to the Kishon River.
There I will give you victory over him."
8Barak told her, "I will go, but only if you
go with me."

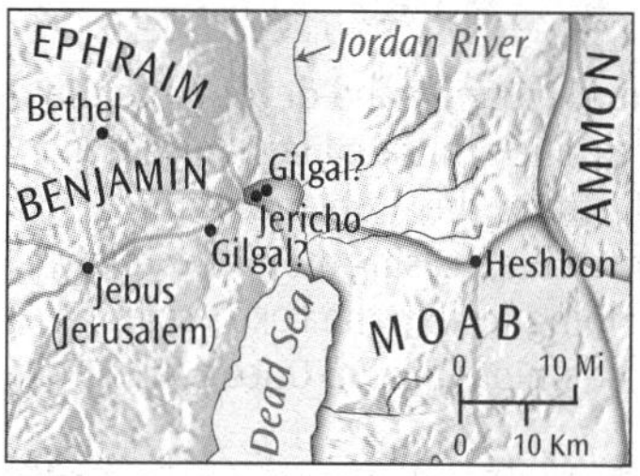

◂ **Ehud Defeats the Moabites (3:12-30).** MOAB was normally located further south than shown here (see map, p. 416; cp. Num 21:21-34; 32:33), but the Moabites had encroached on Israelite territory even to the point of capturing JERICHO. King Eglon's location when Ehud met him is uncertain.

3:26 *Seirah* is unknown, but it was accessible to the hill country, from which Ephraim and Benjamin could be rallied.

3:27-28 *sounded a call to arms* (literally *blew a trumpet*): The trumpet blast and the call *"Follow me"* were accompanied by the assurance of divine victory through the God-appointed rescuer.

3:31 *Shamgar* is nowhere specifically identified as an Israelite or as a judge (see 5:6-7). • *son of Anath:* Anath was perhaps a Canaanite goddess or shrine (cp. 1:33, "Beth-anath"); from similar references in ancient literature, some have seen him as part of a Canaanite warrior class.

4:1–5:31 The account of *Deborah* and *Barak*, given in both prose (ch 4) and poetry (ch 5), is the only large-scale military operation recorded against a major Canaanite foe after the initial conquest. Another king named *Jabin*, who also ruled in the city of *Hazor*, was defeated in an earlier battle against Joshua along with a vast northern coalition, and Hazor was burned (see Josh 11:1-15). Although Josh 11 and Judg 4–5 have often been compared, there are too many differing details to consider them to be parallel records of the same battle. Instead, Jabin is probably a dynastic name; the name occurs in the Mari texts for an even earlier king of Hazor, around 1800 BC.

4:1 The opening of ch 4 provides chronological continuity with *Ehud* and reinforces the cyclical nature of Israel's experience during this period.

4:2 *Hazor,* located north of the Sea of Galilee, dominated the intersection of major trade routes running north–south and east–west. References to Hazor appear frequently in ancient Near Eastern documents, and the site has been extensively excavated. Its position as a one-time "capital of all [those] kingdoms" (Josh 11:10) is confirmed by history and archaeology. • *Harosheth-haggoyim* ("Forest/Farmland of the Nations") was possibly a staging area for the battle; its location and history are debated.

4:3 Contemporary records confirm that armies like Sisera's had large numbers of *iron chariots.* Such a force would have expected overwhelming victory over the lightly-armed Israelite infantry.

4:4-7 Deborah was *a prophet* (Hebrew *'ishah nebi'ah,* "a woman, a female prophet") *who was judging* (*shoptah*, a feminine verb; see note on 2:16-19). She is the protagonist of this story, though much of the action surrounds her surrogate, Barak. Unlike most of the characters in the book of Judges, Deborah fulfilled both the judicial and the military functions implied by the label "judge." As a prophet, she foreshadowed Samuel's later work (1 Sam 7:15-17). Deborah called for a holy war in which the Lord would fight for his people (4:6-7; see notes on Deut 1:30; 2 Chr 20:21).

4:6 Though *Barak* appears in a list of Israelite heroes (Heb 11:32), Judges never gives him more than an equal place with Deborah. • *Mount Tabor* was in the territory of Issachar, just north of the Jezreel Valley.

4:7 The *Kishon River* formed the Jezreel Valley, which runs northwest into the Mediterranean just north of Mount Carmel.

4:8 The theme of the reluctant rescuer surfaces again with Gideon (6:15; cp. Exod 3:11).

9“Very well,” she replied, “I will go with
you. But you will receive no honor in this
venture, for the LORD’s victory over Sisera
will be at the hands of a woman.” So Deborah went with Barak to Kedesh. 10At Kedesh,
Barak called together the tribes of Zebulun
and Naphtali, and 10,000 warriors went up
with him. Deborah also went with him.
11Now Heber the Kenite, a descendant of
Moses’ brother-in-law Hobab, had moved
away from the other members of his tribe
and pitched his tent by the oak of Zaanannim near Kedesh.
12When Sisera was told that Barak son of
Abinoam had gone up to Mount Tabor, 13he
called for all 900 of his iron chariots and
all of his warriors, and they marched from
Harosheth-haggoyim to the Kishon River.
14Then Deborah said to Barak, “Get ready!
This is the day the LORD will give you victory
over Sisera, for the LORD is marching ahead
of you.” So Barak led his 10,000 warriors
down the slopes of Mount Tabor into battle.
15When Barak attacked, the LORD threw Sisera and all his chariots and warriors into a
panic. Sisera leaped down from his chariot
and escaped on foot. 16Then Barak chased
the chariots and the enemy army all the way
to Harosheth-haggoyim, killing all of Sisera’s
warriors. Not a single one was left alive.
17Meanwhile, Sisera ran to the tent of
Jael, the wife of Heber the Kenite, because
Heber’s family was on friendly terms with
King Jabin of Hazor. 18Jael went out to meet
Sisera and said to him, “Come into my tent,
sir. Come in. Don’t be afraid.” So he went
into her tent, and she covered him with a
blanket.
19“Please give me some water,” he said.
“I’m thirsty.” So she gave him some milk
from a leather bag and covered him again.
20“Stand at the door of the tent,” he told
her. “If anybody comes and asks you if there
is anyone here, say no.”
21But when Sisera fell asleep from exhaustion, Jael quietly crept up to him with a
hammer and tent peg in her hand. Then she
drove the tent peg through his temple and
into the ground, and so he died.
22When Barak came looking for Sisera,
Jael went out to meet him. She said, “Come,
and I will show you the man you are looking

4:10 Judg 5:18
4:11 Josh 19:33; Judg 1:16
4:15 Josh 10:10; Judg 7:21
4:16 Exod 14:28; Ps 83:9
4:19 Judg 5:25

DEBORAH (4:1–5:31)

Deborah the prophet was one of the early judges, a woman of integrity and devotion to the Lord. As a prophet, she received divine revelation; as a judge, she arbitrated legal disputes.

Deborah’s interaction with Barak, the military leader, illustrates the problems of this period of Israel’s history. The period of the judges was a time of increasing moral depravity, spiritual blindness, and political fragmentation. Israel was doing “evil in the LORD’s sight” (4:1), so God once again turned Israel over to an oppressor, Jabin of Canaan. Once again, Israel “cried out to the LORD for help” (4:3).

Through Deborah, God called Barak to fight against Sisera. But Barak did not receive God’s call with enthusiasm and courage. Instead, he set a condition: Deborah must go with him. Deborah agreed, but with a cost: The glory for the victory would not go to Barak but to a woman. And so it happened: Barak defeated Sisera and his army, but the glory went to Jael, the woman who killed Sisera and fulfilled Deborah’s prophecy. Barak’s lack of courage and leadership contrasts with the courage and leadership of these two women.

4:9 ***Honor*** for the ***victory*** would go to ***a woman***, which meant a loss of face for Barak. • This ***Kedesh*** appears to have been near Mount Tabor (cp. 4:6, 12), a different location than the Kedesh in Naphtali (4:6), which would have been too far north for the action described.

4:10 The warriors came from Barak’s tribe of ***Naphtali*** and its southern neighbor, ***Zebulun***.

4:11 Kenites related to Moses’ father-in-law had settled in Judah (1:16), in the southern desert (Exod 2:16-22) near the Amalekites in the mountainous country near Moab (Num 24:21-22). Part of the tribe had apparently migrated north and settled near the Sea of Galilee.

• ***brother-in-law:*** Or *father-in-law.*

4:12-13 Upon hearing of Barak’s muster of troops, ***Sisera*** fell into the trap set by the Lord. He headed for the Jezreel Valley with his ***chariots***, marching along the ***Kishon River*** where wheeled vehicles could operate freely.

4:14-16 ***Mount Tabor***, with its forest cover, was a strategic location, and the rush down the hill must have surprised the unsuspecting Canaanites. The battle was won, however, because it was the Lord’s war, not because of human strategy and tactics. • Nothing is said here about why the ***chariots*** were so ineffective; this awaits the poetic version of the account (5:21).

4:17-20 ***Sisera*** felt that he was back in ***friendly*** circles (cp. 4:11). A woman whose husband was absent would normally invite a man into her tent only for sex, but Sisera would have interpreted this invitation as an opportunity for safe haven. ***Jael*** did nothing to shake his confidence as she concealed and refreshed him.

4:19 The ***milk*** was probably the curds so favored by the Arabs (cp. “yogurt,” 5:25); many believe that it is soporific.

4:21-22 ***Jael*** completed what seems to have been her intention all along. There is a more graphic description of the event in 5:26-27.

5:1 Exod 15:1
5:2 Ps 110:3
5:4 Deut 33:2; Hab 3:6
5:5 Exod 19:18; Ps 97:5; 114:4; Isa 64:3
5:6 Judg 3:31; 4:17
5:8 Deut 32:17

for." So he followed her into the tent and found Sisera lying there dead, with the tent peg through his temple.

23So on that day Israel saw God defeat
Jabin, the Canaanite king. 24And from that
time on Israel became stronger and stronger against King Jabin until they finally destroyed him.

The Song of Deborah

5 On that day Deborah and Barak son of Abinoam sang this song:

2 "Israel's leaders took charge,
  and the people gladly followed.
Praise the LORD!

3 "Listen, you kings!
  Pay attention, you mighty rulers!
For I will sing to the LORD.
  I will make music to the LORD, the God of Israel.

4 "LORD, when you set out from Seir
  and marched across the fields of Edom,
the earth trembled,
  and the cloudy skies poured down rain.
5 The mountains quaked in the presence of the LORD,
  the God of Mount Sinai—
in the presence of the LORD,
  the God of Israel.

6 "In the days of Shamgar son of Anath,
  and in the days of Jael,
people avoided the main roads,
  and travelers stayed on winding pathways.
7 There were few people left in the villages of Israel—
  until Deborah arose as a mother for Israel.
8 When Israel chose new gods,
  war erupted at the city gates.
Yet not a shield or spear could be seen
  among forty thousand warriors in Israel!
9 My heart is with the commanders of Israel,
  with those who volunteered for war.
Praise the LORD!

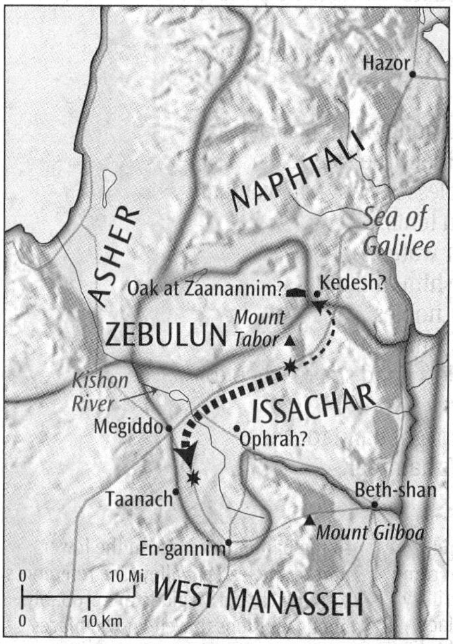

◀ **Barak Defeats Sisera at Mount Tabor (4:1–5:31).** One reconstruction of this battle is as shown: Deborah met Barak and the armies of NAPHTALI and ZEBULUN at KEDESH near MOUNT TABOR (see note on 4:9). Then Barak stationed himself on Mount Tabor. Sisera and his army marched down from near HAZOR and were passing Mount Tabor on their way to the KISHON RIVER when Barak attacked (4:12-16). Then Sisera fled north toward the OAK AT ZAANANNIM, where he met Jael. His forces fled south toward TAANACH, only to be intercepted and crushed by the armies of Ephraim, Benjamin, and Manasseh (4:16; 5:14-21).

4:23 ***God*** defeated ***Jabin*** by orchestrating people and events.

4:24 Sisera's army was gone, but ***Jabin*** and his kingdom were subdued more gradually.

5:1-31 ***This song,*** a victory hymn usually credited to ***Deborah,*** presents a second, more poetic account of the entire battle with various details that supplement the prose account. It is one of the most ancient Hebrew poems. It blesses the Lord, those tribes who responded to the muster, and Jael. It curses those who remained at home, Sisera, and his mother's entourage. It contrasts conditions before Barak's victory, when the Lord's curse was on the land, with the life of blessing in the wake of the warriors' righteous acts. It ends with a prayer that the Lord's enemies will perish like Sisera (5:31).

5:3 The victory song is primarily a hymn to ***the LORD, the God of Israel.*** It is also a wisdom song that gives instruction to ***kings*** and ***rulers,*** as other wisdom psalms do (see "Wisdom Psalms" at Ps 37, p. 937).

5:4-5 In the poem, the ***LORD*** is on the march from his home in the mountains of Edom (cp. Hab 3:3), or ***Mount Sinai*** (one tradition places Sinai east of the Jordan Valley, in the region of Edom; cp. Gal 4:25). The fire and earthquake that had so terrified Israel at the giving of the law (Exod 19:18) here symbolize God's power and fury on the battlefield against his enemies. • Torrential ***rain*** would have created a quagmire, making Sisera's chariots a liability rather than an asset (4:15-16).

5:6 During this period of chaos and uncertainty, there was little security for those living outside the main walled cities. Even ***Shamgar*** (see 3:31) did little to alleviate the misery of the common people, who suffered under the hand of the Canaanites and their cruel commander, Sisera.

5:7 ***There were few people left in the villages of Israel:*** The meaning of the Hebrew is uncertain. • ***Deborah*** was God's agent in bringing relief during this general social breakdown. Deborah did not muster or command the troops, but she was Israel's spiritual and emotional pillar; she is described as ***a mother*** in Israel.

5:8 ***Israel*** was in social chaos and also lacked defensive weapons. • ***Forty thousand warriors:*** The Hebrew word translated *thousand* could also be translated *clans* (see note on Exod 12:37).

10 "Consider this, you who ride on fine donkeys,
you who sit on fancy saddle blankets,
and you who walk along the road.
11 Listen to the village musicians
gathered at the watering holes.
They recount the righteous victories of the LORD
and the victories of his villagers in Israel.
Then the people of the LORD
marched down to the city gates.

12 "Wake up, Deborah, wake up!
Wake up, wake up, and sing a song!
Arise, Barak!
Lead your captives away, son of Abinoam!

13 "Down from Tabor marched the few
against the nobles.
The people of the LORD marched
down against mighty warriors.
14 They came down from Ephraim—
a land that once belonged to the Amalekites;
they followed you, Benjamin, with your troops.
From Makir the commanders marched down;
from Zebulun came those who carry a commander's staff.
15 The princes of Issachar were with Deborah and Barak.
They followed Barak, rushing into the valley.
But in the tribe of Reuben
there was great indecision.
16 Why did you sit at home among the sheepfolds—
to hear the shepherds whistle for their flocks?
Yes, in the tribe of Reuben
there was great indecision.
17 Gilead remained east of the Jordan.
And why did Dan stay home?
Asher sat unmoved at the seashore,
remaining in his harbors.
18 But Zebulun risked his life,
as did Naphtali, on the heights of the battlefield.

19 "The kings of Canaan came and fought,
at Taanach near Megiddo's springs,
but they carried off no silver treasures.
20 The stars fought from heaven.
The stars in their orbits fought against Sisera.
21 The Kishon River swept them away—
that ancient torrent, the Kishon.
March on with courage, my soul!
22 Then the horses' hooves hammered the ground,
the galloping, galloping of Sisera's mighty steeds.
23 'Let the people of Meroz be cursed,' said the angel of the LORD.
'Let them be utterly cursed,
because they did not come to help the LORD—
to help the LORD against the mighty warriors.'

24 "Most blessed among women is Jael,
the wife of Heber the Kenite.
May she be blessed above all women
who live in tents.
25 Sisera asked for water,
and she gave him milk.
In a bowl fit for nobles,
she brought him yogurt.
26 Then with her left hand she reached for a tent peg,
and with her right hand for the workman's hammer.

5:10 Judg 10:4; 12:14
5:11 Gen 24:11; 1 Sam 12:7
5:16 Num 32:1-2, 24
5:17 Josh 13:24-28
5:19 Josh 11:1-5; Judg 1:27
5:21 Judg 4:7
5:22 Job 39:19-25
5:24-25 Judg 4:17-19
5:26-27 Judg 4:21-22

5:10 Both the rich (those ***who ride***) and the poor (those ***who walk***) were to listen and spread the song, which would have both a spiritual and a social impact as it was disseminated.

5:11 ***Listen to the village musicians:*** The meaning of the Hebrew is uncertain, but the picture is of divine exploits being recited where people gathered. Much OT narrative and psalmody probably took shape in this way. "Remembering" in song and poetry is foundational to both Jewish and Christian worship.

5:13 ***The few*** were Barak's army, marching ***down*** against the ***mighty warriors*** of Sisera's army.

5:14-18 These verses honor those who volunteered and shame those who did not. • ***Ephraim, Benjamin***, and Manasseh (represented by ***Makir***) came from the south. ***Issachar***, the territory where the battle actually took place, was joined by ***Zebulun*** and ***Naphtali***, the two tribes closest to Barak's home base. • The tribes that were too irresolute and fainthearted to join the fight included ***Reuben***, Gad (represented by ***Gilead***), ***Dan***, and ***Asher***.

5:19-23 The battle is described. The brave warriors who followed Deborah and Barak faded into the background as the Lord mustered ***the stars*** of ***heaven*** and ***the Kishon River*** to obliterate Sisera's host.

5:19 ***Taanach*** was southeast of the great administrative center of Megiddo, so the battle took place in the lower part of the Jezreel Valley. The references to Taanach and Megiddo are probably poetic allusions to well-known places in the Jezreel Valley, rather than exact locations of any fighting, which appears to have taken place between Mount Tabor and the lowlands around the Kishon stream.

5:23 The location of ***Meroz*** is unknown, but it should not be confused with Merom (Josh 11:5), which was approximately twenty miles to the north in the hills of Galilee.

5:24-27 Sisera's end is described in a brief celebration of ***Jael***.

5:25 ***milk . . . yogurt:*** See note on 4:19.

5:30 Exod 15:9
5:31 Ps 68:1-2; 92:9
6:1 Num 25:15-18; 31:1-3; Judg 2:11
6:3 Isa 11:14
6:5 Num 22:4; Judg 7:12; [d]*'arbeh* (0697) ‣1 Kgs 8:37
6:6 Deut 28:43
6:8 Exod 18:9; Judg 2:1-2
6:10 Josh 24:15
6:11 Judg 13:3; Heb 11:32
6:13 Deut 31:17; Ps 44:1

She struck Sisera with the hammer,
crushing his head.
With a shattering blow, she pierced
his temples.
27 He sank, he fell,
he lay still at her feet.
And where he sank,
there he died.

28 "From the window Sisera's mother
looked out.
Through the window she watched for
his return, saying,
'Why is his chariot so long in coming?
Why don't we hear the sound of
chariot wheels?'
29 "Her wise women answer,
and she repeats these words to
herself:
30 'They must be dividing the captured
plunder—
with a woman or two for every man.
There will be colorful robes for Sisera,
and colorful, embroidered robes
for me.
Yes, the plunder will include
colorful robes embroidered on both
sides.'

31 "LORD, may all your enemies die like
Sisera!
But may those who love you rise like
the sun in all its power!"

Then there was peace in the land for forty years.

Gideon Becomes Israel's Judge

6 The Israelites did evil in the LORD's sight.
So the LORD handed them over to the
Midianites for seven years. 2 The Midianites
were so cruel that the Israelites made hiding places for themselves in the mountains,
caves, and strongholds. 3 Whenever the Israelites planted their crops, marauders from
Midian, Amalek, and the people of the east
would attack Israel, 4 camping in the land
and destroying crops as far away as Gaza.
They left the Israelites with nothing to eat,
taking all the sheep, goats, cattle, and donkeys. 5 These enemy hordes, coming with
their livestock and tents, were as thick as [d]lo-
custs; they arrived on droves of camels too
numerous to count. And they stayed until
the land was stripped bare. 6 So Israel was reduced to starvation by the Midianites. Then
the Israelites cried out to the LORD for help.
7 When they cried out to the LORD because
of Midian, 8 the LORD sent a prophet to the Israelites. He said, "This is what the LORD, the
God of Israel, says: I brought you up out of
slavery in Egypt. 9 I rescued you from the
Egyptians and from all who oppressed you.
I drove out your enemies and gave you their
land. 10 I told you, 'I am the LORD your God.
You must not worship the gods of the Amorites, in whose land you now live.' But you
have not listened to me."
11 Then the angel of the LORD came and
sat beneath the great tree at Ophrah, which
belonged to Joash of the clan of Abiezer.
Gideon son of Joash was threshing wheat
at the bottom of a winepress to hide the
grain from the Midianites. 12 The angel of
the LORD appeared to him and said, "Mighty
hero, the LORD is with you!"
13 "Sir," Gideon replied, "if the LORD is
with us, why has all this happened to us?
And where are all the miracles our ancestors told us about? Didn't they say, 'The
LORD brought us up out of Egypt'? But now

5:28 The natural confidence of *Sisera's mother* was beginning to crumble.

5:29-30 The *wise women* betrayed Sisera's evil intentions as they tried to encourage his mother. • The poet didn't need to tell how the story concluded.

5:31 *Sisera* typifies the Lord's *enemies;* Jael represents those who *love* the Lord. • *there was peace in the land:* Rest followed the Lord's rescue.

6:1–8:35 Gideon's judgeship brings to a close the first period of judges.

6:1-6 After forty years of peace, religious syncretism had brought about political instability, and marauding nomads had reduced *the Israelites* to living as fugitives. • *The Midianites* were once thought to be a purely nomadic tribe centered in northwest Arabia, but they are now understood to have built cities and for a time to have dominated much of the Arabian peninsula and southern Transjordan (the area east of the Jordan). They are joined here by Amalekites (who earlier were part of a Moabite coalition; see note on 3:12-13) and the mysterious *people of the east* (cp. 1 Kgs 4:30; Ezek 25:4, 10). The pattern of attack was seasonal but devastating.

6:5 *Camels*, known in some contexts from as early as 3000 BC, are frequently associated with eastern nomads and their raids. This may be one of the first recorded instances of camels being used in a large military force.

6:8-10 This unnamed *prophet* and Deborah are the only prophets to appear in Judges. This prophet rebuked Israel's apostasy in language familiar from Deuteronomy onward.

6:11-32 Gideon encountered *the angel of the LORD* and emerged as a hero. He overthrew the syncretistic Baal cult of his family and town and called his people to fight in the Lord's name.

6:12 *Mighty hero* translates a Hebrew term that is elsewhere translated as "strong warriors" (Josh 6:2), pointing to Gideon's potential military heroism, and as "the rich" (2 Kgs 15:20), pointing to his social standing as a member of a leading family. • *the LORD is with you:* A commission to fight God's war is usually accompanied by assurance of his presence (see Deut 1:30; Josh 1:1-9).

6:13-15 Like others called to be prophets or judges, *Gideon* was reluctant to obey. He questioned God's presence and his own adequacy (see note on 4:8; Exod 3:1–4:17; Jer 1:4-19).

the LORD has abandoned us and handed us over to the Midianites."

14Then the LORD turned to him and said, "Go with the strength you have, and rescue Israel from the Midianites. I am sending you!"

15"But Lord," Gideon replied, "how can I rescue Israel? My clan is the weakest in the whole tribe of Manasseh, and I am the least in my entire family!"

16The LORD said to him, "I will be with you. And you will destroy the Midianites as if you were fighting against one man."

17Gideon replied, "If you are truly going to help me, show me a sign to prove that it is really the LORD speaking to me. 18Don't go away until I come back and bring my offering to you."

He answered, "I will stay here until you return."

19Gideon hurried home. He cooked a young goat, and with a basket of flour he baked some bread without yeast. Then, carrying the meat in a basket and the broth in a pot, he brought them out and presented them to the angel, who was under the great tree.

20The angel of God said to him, "Place the meat and the unleavened bread on this rock, and pour the broth over it." And Gideon did as he was told. 21Then the angel of the LORD touched the meat and bread with the tip of the staff in his hand, and fire flamed up from the rock and consumed all he had brought. And the angel of the LORD disappeared.

22When Gideon realized that it was the angel of the LORD, he cried out, "Oh, [e]Sovereign LORD, I'm doomed! I have seen the angel of the LORD face to face!"

23"It is all right," the LORD replied. "Do not be afraid. You will not die." 24And Gideon built an altar to the LORD there and named it Yahweh-Shalom (which means "the LORD is [f]peace"). The altar remains in Ophrah in the land of the clan of Abiezer to this day.

25That night the LORD said to Gideon, "Take the second bull from your father's herd, the one that is seven years old. Pull down your father's altar to Baal, and cut down the Asherah pole standing beside it. 26Then build an altar to the LORD your God here on this hilltop sanctuary, laying the stones carefully. Sacrifice the bull as a burnt offering on the altar, using as fuel the wood of the Asherah pole you cut down."

27So Gideon took ten of his servants and did as the LORD had commanded. But he did it at night because he was afraid of the other members of his father's household and the people of the town.

28Early the next morning, as the people of the town began to stir, someone discovered that the altar of Baal had been broken down and that the Asherah pole beside it had been cut down. In their place a new altar had been built, and on it were the remains of the bull that had been sacrificed. 29The people said to each other, "Who did this?" And after asking around and making a careful search, they learned that it was Gideon, the son of Joash.

30"Bring out your son," the men of the town demanded of Joash. "He must die for destroying the altar of Baal and for cutting down the Asherah pole."

31But Joash shouted to the mob that confronted him, "Why are you defending Baal? Will you argue his case? Whoever pleads his case will be put to death by morning! If Baal truly is a god, let him defend himself and destroy the one who broke down his altar!" 32From then on Gideon was called Jerub-baal, which means "Let Baal defend himself," because he broke down Baal's altar.

Gideon Asks for a Sign

33Soon afterward the armies of Midian, Amalek, and the people of the east formed an alliance against Israel and crossed the Jordan, camping in the valley of Jezreel. 34Then the Spirit of the LORD took possession of Gideon. He blew a ram's horn as a call to arms, and the men of the clan of Abiezer came to him. 35He also sent messengers

6:15 Exod 3:11
6:17 Isa 38:7
6:19 Gen 18:6-8
6:21 Lev 9:24
6:22 Gen 32:30; Exod 33:20; Judg 13:21-22; [e]*'adonay Yahweh* (0136, 3068) ‣2 Sam 7:18
6:24 [f]*shalom* (7965) ‣1 Chr 22:9
6:25 Exod 34:13; Deut 7:5
6:33 Josh 17:16
6:34 Judg 3:10
6:35 Judg 7:23

6:15 Gideon's personal and clan status (see note on 6:12) was itself insufficient to muster troops.

6:19 ***a basket:*** Hebrew *an ephah* [20 quarts or 22 liters].

6:22 Encounters with divine holiness are inherently dangerous (cp. Gen 32:30; Deut 5:4-5).

6:24 The symbolically named ***altar*** commemorates the divine presence and favor. By the time the account was written down (***to this day***), the altar had probably become a pilgrimage site.

6:25-32 In a provocative act that was commanded by God, Gideon destroyed and desecrated a community altar to Baal and its Asherah pole.

6:25 In Canaanite worship, ***Baal*** was a storm and fertility god, while ***Asherah*** was often represented as a sacred tree.

6:31 The first person to follow Gideon's inspired act of leadership and abandon Baal for the Lord was Gideon's father ***Joash***, who was, ironically, the keeper of the Baal shrine.

6:33 The nomadic coalition (6:1-6) set up camp at the eastern end of the ***valley of Jezreel,*** which divided Israel's central tribes from the Galilean hills.

6:34 As is typical of the inspired leaders in Judges, the Spirit ***took possession of Gideon.*** This Hebrew expression points to an individual being "clothed" in or by the Spirit. A similar metaphor is frequent in Paul's letters (e.g., Rom 13:12; Gal 3:27; Eph 4:24; 6:11; Col 3:10, 12, 14).

6:36 Judg 6:14
6:39 Gen 18:32
^{g}'ap (0639) ›2 Sam 12:5
7:1 Gen 12:6 Deut 11:30 Judg 6:32
7:2 Deut 8:17-18 Isa 10:13 2 Cor 4:7
7:3 Deut 20:8
7:4 1 Sam 14:6
7:9 Josh 2:24; 10:8; 11:6

throughout Manasseh, Asher, Zebulun, and Naphtali, summoning their warriors, and all of them responded.

[36]Then Gideon said to God, "If you are truly going to use me to rescue Israel as you promised, [37]prove it to me in this way. I will put a wool fleece on the threshing floor tonight. If the fleece is wet with dew in the morning but the ground is dry, then I will know that you are going to help me rescue Israel as you promised." [38]And that is just what happened. When Gideon got up early the next morning, he squeezed the fleece and wrung out a whole bowlful of water.

[39]Then Gideon said to God, "Please don't be [g]angry with me, but let me make one more request. Let me use the fleece for one more test. This time let the fleece remain dry while the ground around it is wet with dew." [40]So that night God did as Gideon asked. The fleece was dry in the morning, but the ground was covered with dew.

Gideon Defeats the Midianites

7 So Jerub-baal (that is, Gideon) and his army got up early and went as far as the spring of Harod. The armies of Midian were camped north of them in the valley near the hill of Moreh. [2]The LORD said to Gideon, "You have too many warriors with you. If I let all of you fight the Midianites, the Israelites will boast to me that they saved themselves by their own strength. [3]Therefore, tell the people, 'Whoever is timid or afraid may leave this mountain and go home.' " So 22,000 of them went home, leaving only 10,000 who were willing to fight.

[4]But the LORD told Gideon, "There are still too many! Bring them down to the spring, and I will test them to determine who will go with you and who will not." [5]When Gideon took his warriors down to the water, the LORD told him, "Divide the men into two groups. In one group put all those who cup water in their hands and lap it up with their tongues like dogs. In the other group put all those who kneel down and drink with their mouths in the stream." [6]Only 300 of the men drank from their hands. All the others got down on their knees and drank with their mouths in the stream.

[7]The LORD told Gideon, "With these 300 men I will rescue you and give you victory over the Midianites. Send all the others home." [8]So Gideon collected the provisions and rams' horns of the other warriors and sent them home. But he kept the 300 men with him.

The Midianite camp was in the valley just below Gideon. [9]That night the LORD said, "Get up! Go down into the Midianite camp, for I have given you victory over them! [10]But if you are afraid to attack, go down to the camp with your servant Purah. [11]Listen to what the Midianites are saying, and you will be greatly encouraged. Then you will be eager to attack."

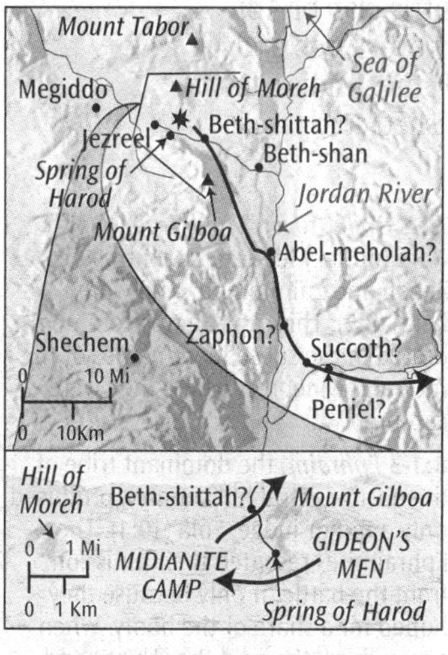

◀ **Gideon Defeats the Midianites** (7:1-25). After the Lord reduced Gideon's army to 300 men at the SPRING OF HAROD, they gathered on MOUNT GILBOA, overlooking the Midianites camped in the valley below (7:1-8). Gideon and his men went down to the MIDIANITE CAMP and attacked, then routed and chased the Midianites past SUCCOTH and PENIEL into Transjordan, where he killed the Midianite kings near Jogbehah (8:4-12; see map, p. 416). On his return, Gideon killed the men of Succoth and Peniel for their refusal to help his army (8:4-9, 13-17).

6:36-40 The *fleece* incident was not a confirmation of God's intention to use Gideon (which had already been established, 6:17-24), but God's indulgence in responding to the reluctant hero's uncertainty.

7:1 The *spring of Harod* and *the hill of Moreh* were just east of the town of Jezreel; they guarded the pass that connects the valley of Jezreel to the fords of the Jordan near Beth-shan. Gideon's army was located on the north slope of Mount Gilboa. The Midianite hosts were in the valley below, with the hill behind them.

7:2 *The LORD* does not require a large force to save his people (cp. 1 Sam 14:6). A large number might even have hindered success because the element of surprise was crucial to the Lord's battle plan. *Gideon* was to pare down the army to maintain godly humility, not for reasons of military strategy.

7:3 The first reduction sorted out those who initially responded with enthusiasm but then had second thoughts. • *may leave this mountain:* Literally *may leave Mount Gilead.* The identity of Mount Gilead is uncertain in this context. It is perhaps used here as another name for Mount Gilboa.

7:4-8 The choice of those who lapped from their hands over those who knelt was apparently arbitrary, but it enabled the Lord to reduce the size of the army.

7:8 The jars (in which the men carried *provisions*) and trumpets borrowed from the warriors who were sent home would be used in the coming battle.

7:10-15 The Lord *encouraged* Gideon with a third sign (see 6:17-21, 36-40).

7:11 With the *enemy camp* (next page) spread out across the valley (7:1, 12), it was easy for Gideon and his servant to sneak undetected into the camp.

So Gideon took Purah and went down to the edge of the enemy camp. 12The armies of Midian, Amalek, and the people of the east had settled in the valley like a swarm of locusts. Their camels were like grains of sand on the seashore—too many to count! 13Gideon crept up just as a man was telling his companion about a dream. The man said, "I had this dream, and in my dream a loaf of barley bread came tumbling down into the Midianite camp. It hit a tent, turned it over, and knocked it flat!"

14His companion answered, "Your dream can mean only one thing—God has given Gideon son of Joash, the Israelite, victory over Midian and all its allies!"

15When Gideon heard the dream and its interpretation, he bowed in worship before the LORD. Then he returned to the Israelite camp and shouted, "Get up! For the LORD has given you victory over the Midianite hordes!" 16He divided the 300 men into three groups and gave each man a ram's horn and a clay jar with a torch in it.

17Then he said to them, "Keep your eyes on me. When I come to the edge of the camp, do just as I do. 18As soon as I and those with me blow the rams' horns, blow your horns, too, all around the entire camp, and shout, 'For the LORD and for Gideon!' "

19It was just after midnight, after the changing of the guard, when Gideon and the 100 men with him reached the edge of the Midianite camp. Suddenly, they blew the rams' horns and broke their clay jars. 20Then all three groups blew their horns and broke their jars. They held the blazing torches in their left hands and the horns in their right hands, and they all shouted, "A sword for the LORD and for Gideon!"

21Each man stood at his position around the camp and watched as all the Midianites rushed around in a panic, shouting as they ran to escape. 22When the 300 Israelites blew their rams' horns, the LORD caused the warriors in the camp to fight against each other with their swords. Those who were not killed fled to places as far away as Beth-shittah near Zererah and to the border of Abel-meholah near Tabbath.

23Then Gideon sent for the warriors of Naphtali, Asher, and Manasseh, who joined in chasing the army of Midian. 24Gideon also sent messengers throughout the hill country of Ephraim, saying, "Come down to attack the Midianites. Cut them off at the shallow crossings of the Jordan River at Beth-barah."

So all the men of Ephraim did as they were told. 25They captured Oreb and Zeeb, the two Midianite commanders, killing Oreb at the rock of Oreb, and Zeeb at the winepress of Zeeb. And they continued to chase the Midianites. Afterward the Israelites brought the heads of Oreb and Zeeb to Gideon, who was by the Jordan River.

Gideon Kills Zebah and Zalmunna

8 Then the people of Ephraim asked Gideon, "Why have you treated us this way? Why didn't you send for us when you first went out to fight the Midianites?" And they argued heatedly with Gideon.

2But Gideon replied, "What have I accomplished compared to you? Aren't even the leftover grapes of Ephraim's harvest better than the entire crop of my little clan of Abiezer? 3God gave you victory over Oreb and Zeeb, the commanders of the Midianite army. What have I accomplished compared

7:12 Josh 11:4; Judg 6:5; 8:10
7:21 2 Kgs 7:7
7:24 Judg 3:27-28
7:25 Judg 8:4; Ps 83:11; Isa 10:26
8:1 Judg 12:1

7:13-14 Dreams and their interpretations were often discussed in Egypt and Babylonia. The OT teaches that dreams are inspired by God and are best interpreted by his revelation (see Gen 41:15-16, 25; Dan 2:28). The point of this dream is clear: Gideon's band, represented as a rounded *loaf of barley bread*, would come *tumbling down* and overturn *the Midianite camp*.

7:15 ***he bowed in worship before the LORD:*** As in Greek version. Hebrew reads *he bowed*.

7:16 Dividing the small band ***into three groups*** created the impression of a much larger force.

7:17-20 Surprise and deception took the place of a massive army. The war cry, the sudden blast of 300 trumpets, and the torches bursting into light created the impression of a large force.

7:19 ***just after midnight:*** Literally *at the beginning of the second watch.*

7:21 The warriors ***stood*** in place while God fought the battle (cp. Exod 14:13; 1 Sam 12:16; Rev 19:11-16). • The Midianites' camels (6:5) might have contributed to the ***panic***. Camels usually provided a military advantage, but in this situation they would have been a liability. They had probably been hobbled for the night, and camels themselves are subject to panic.

7:22 The fugitives fled in a southeasterly direction, past Beth-shan and toward the fords of the Jordan, trying to reach more friendly and favorable surroundings.

7:24 The ***shallow crossings of the Jordan*** were key to cutting off the escape of an army (cp. 3:28; 12:4-6).

7:25 ***Oreb*** ("raven") and ***Zeeb*** ("wolf") were military leaders, in contrast to Zebah and Zalmunnah, who were kings (8:5). This capture was commemorated in the subsequent names of the rock and winepress where they were captured.

8:1-3 ***Ephraim***, the dominant tribe of the north-central hill country, produced only a minor judge, Tola (10:1). The Ephraimites resented their omission from the battle, if only because they hoped for a share of the booty. When summoned, they did the job at hand. ***Gideon*** gave a gracious and humble answer, which turned away Ephraim's ***anger*** (see Prov 15:1; contrast Jephthah, 12:1-4). Gideon's and Ephraim's victories ***over Oreb and Zeeb*** and their armies became the stuff of legend (cp. Ps 83:11-12; Isa 10:26).

8:5 Gen 33:17
8:7 Judg 7:15
8:8 Gen 32:30; 1 Kgs 12:25
8:10 Isa 9:4
8:12 Ps 83:11

to that?" When the men of Ephraim heard
Gideon's answer, their anger subsided.
4 Gideon then crossed the Jordan River
with his 300 men, and though exhausted,
they continued to chase the enemy. 5 When
they reached Succoth, Gideon asked the
leaders of the town, "Please give my warriors some food. They are very tired. I am
chasing Zebah and Zalmunna, the kings of
Midian."
6 But the officials of Succoth replied,
"Catch Zebah and Zalmunna first, and then
we will feed your army."
7 So Gideon said, "After the LORD gives me
victory over Zebah and Zalmunna, I will return and tear your flesh with the thorns and
briers from the wilderness."
8 From there Gideon went up to Peniel
and again asked for food, but he got the
same answer. 9 So he said to the people of
Peniel, "After I return in victory, I will tear
down this tower."
10 By this time Zebah and Zalmunna were
in Karkor with 15,000 warriors—all that remained of the allied armies of the east, for
120,000 had already been killed. 11 Gideon
circled around by the caravan route east of
Nobah and Jogbehah, taking the Midianite
army by surprise. 12 Zebah and Zalmunna,
the two Midianite kings, fled, but Gideon
chased them down and captured all their
warriors.
13 After this, Gideon returned from the
battle by way of Heres Pass. 14 There he

GIDEON (6:1–8:35)

Judg 8:33–9:57; 1 Sam 12:11; Isa 10:26; Heb 11:32

Gideon, an Israelite judge, was son of Joash, from the tribe of Manasseh. Gideon described his clan as the least powerful in Manasseh and himself as the least important in the clan. His story tells how God can take a weak person and use him for great purposes.

At the time, Israel was being oppressed by Midian and cried to God for relief (6:6). In response, God sent a prophet to chastise them for neglecting the Lord and worshiping other gods. He also sent his angel to call Gideon to rescue Israel.

Gideon's first appearance is not promising. He was threshing wheat in the bottom of a winepress because he did not want the Midianites to know what he was doing. When the angel of the Lord appeared to Gideon in the winepress, Gideon questioned why God had not rescued his people as at the Exodus. God said that Gideon was chosen to be Israel's deliverer, and that God himself would be with him. Gideon was slow to believe, so he brought an offering; when the angel touched the sacrifice, fire came from the rock beneath it.

This sign gave Gideon enough faith to act locally. God told him to knock down his father's altar to Baal, cut down the Asherah pole, and build an altar to the Lord instead. Gideon did what God had commanded. Gideon became a warrior for God against false gods.

Then the Spirit of God came on Gideon, and he raised an army to fight the Midianites and their allies. Gideon was still cautious. He put out a fleece on two nights and asked God to confirm Gideon's calling. God did, and Gideon now knew God was calling him.

No army recruiter had greater success than Gideon as 32,000 men responded to his call. God, though, directed him to pare down the numbers to 300 men. Gideon led these 300 men against an overwhelming force and defeated them.

Gideon rightly resisted the people's call to be their ruler, but then he made an ephod from the earrings of the defeated soldiers, and the ephod became an idol (8:22-27). Gideon, weak in faith and dependent on visible signs, eventually turned away from worshiping the invisible God and worshiped idols. Israel enjoyed peace during his time, but his lack of faith bore bitter fruit after his death (8:33–9:57).

8:4-12 At this point, *Gideon* seemed as bent on revenge as on victory, and there is an abrupt cessation of his earlier dialogue with the Lord. The core of ***300 men*** made this final run against the Midianites. • Gideon pursued the fleeing ***kings of Midian*** through the Jabbok gorge, then southward toward Rabbah (see map, p. 441), following ***the caravan route*** onto the Transjordan plateau. • ***Succoth*** and ***Peniel*** were Israelite cities, but their loyalty to Gideon, an upstart general, was thin. The tribes east of the Jordan were continually exposed to the Midianites pressure and apparently feared the Midianites.

8:7 It was a common practice in the ancient Near East to ***tear*** the ***flesh*** of a defeated foe (cp. Amos 1:3; Mic 4:13).

8:8-9 ***Peniel:*** Hebrew *Penuel,* a variant spelling of Peniel; also in 8:9, 17. • ***this tower:*** Towers were common in the period and have been excavated at both Succoth and Shechem (see 9:46-49).

8:10-12 Apparently the ***Midianite*** remnant with its ***two kings*** felt reasonably secure, having reached the Transjordan plateau en route to their traditional desert haunts. This put them well beyond typically Israelite territory. As he had done before (7:19-22), ***Gideon*** took ***the Midianite army by surprise.*** He ***captured*** the two kings and routed the army, thus eliminating the threat of Midianite retribution feared by the leaders of Succoth and Peniel.

8:13-17 The return journey was probably a straight course (through the

captured a young man from Succoth and demanded that he write down the names of all the seventy-seven officials and elders in the town. 15 Gideon then returned to Succoth and said to the leaders, “Here are Zebah and Zalmunna. When we were here before, you taunted me, saying, ‘Catch Zebah and Zalmunna first, and then we will feed your exhausted army.’ ” 16 Then Gideon took the elders of the town and taught them a lesson, punishing them with thorns and briers from the wilderness. 17 He also tore down the tower of Peniel and killed all the men in the town.

18 Then Gideon asked Zebah and Zalmunna, “The men you killed at Tabor—what were they like?”

“Like you,” they replied. “They all had the look of a king’s son.”

19 “They were my brothers, the sons of my own mother!” Gideon exclaimed. “As surely as the LORD lives, I wouldn’t kill you if you hadn’t killed them.”

20 Turning to Jether, his oldest son, he said, “Kill them!” But Jether did not draw his sword, for he was only a boy and was afraid.

21 Then Zebah and Zalmunna said to Gideon, “Be a man! Kill us yourself!” So Gideon killed them both and took the royal ornaments from the necks of their camels.

Gideon’s Sacred Ephod

22 Then the Israelites said to Gideon, “Be our ruler! You and your son and your grandson will be our rulers, for you have rescued us from Midian.”

23 But Gideon replied, “I will not rule over you, nor will my son. The LORD will rule over you! 24 However, I do have one request—that each of you give me an earring from the plunder you collected from your fallen enemies.” (The enemies, being Ishmaelites, all wore gold earrings.)

25 “Gladly!” they replied. They spread out a cloak, and each one threw in a gold earring he had gathered from the plunder. 26 The weight of the gold earrings was forty-three pounds, not including the royal ornaments and pendants, the purple clothing worn by the kings of Midian, or the chains around the necks of their camels.

27 Gideon made a sacred ephod from the gold and put it in Ophrah, his hometown. But soon all the Israelites prostituted themselves by worshiping it, and it became a trap for Gideon and his family.

28 That is the story of how the people of Israel defeated Midian, which never recovered. Throughout the rest of Gideon’s lifetime—about forty years—there was peace in the land.

29 Then Gideon son of Joash returned home. 30 He had seventy sons born to him, for he had many wives. 31 He also had a concubine in Shechem, who gave birth to a son, whom he named Abimelech. 32 Gideon died when he was very old, and he was buried in the grave of his father, Joash, at Ophrah in the land of the clan of Abiezer.

33 As soon as Gideon died, the Israelites prostituted themselves by worshiping the images of Baal, making Baal-berith their god. 34 They forgot the LORD their God, who had rescued them from all their enemies surrounding them. 35 Nor did they show any loyalty to the family of Jerub-baal (that is, Gideon), despite all the good he had done for Israel.

8:15 Judg 8:6
8:17 Judg 8:8
8:23 1 Sam 12:12
8:27 Exod 28:6; Judg 17:5
8:30 Judg 9:2, 5
8:31 Judg 9:1
8:33 Judg 2:11
8:34 Deut 4:9; Judg 3:7

---

unknown ***Heres Pass)*** rather than the circular approach needed for the ambush. • That a typical ***young man from Succoth*** could ***write down the names*** is evidence that the newly developed alphabetic writing system had taken root in Israel. • Gideon’s practice of retribution and execution was the norm in his time, though Gideon’s reputation as the Lord’s servant was better served by his skillful diplomacy (8:1-3) than by vindictive punishment.

8:18-21 It is not clear just when the slaughter ***at Tabor*** took place; it may have occurred during the earlier battle.

8:20-21 Matters of honor dominated this interaction. Death at the hand of a woman or a child was considered dishonorable (5:24-27; 9:54).

8:21 ***royal ornaments*** (or “crescent necklaces,” Isa 3:18): Desert nomads tended to carry their wealth with them; jewelry maximized value for weight.

8:24 ***Ishmaelites*** and Midianites were both descendants of Abraham (Gen 16:15; 25:2).

8:26 ***forty-three pounds:*** Hebrew *1,700 shekels* [19.4 kilograms].

8:27 An ***ephod*** was normally considered part of the priestly garments (Exod 28:6-30); one was also worn by Samuel and David (1 Sam 2:18; 2 Sam 6:14; 1 Chr 15:27). But here, as in 17:5 and 18:14-18, the ***ephod*** appears to have been some kind of ***gold*** image, which in turn became an object of idolatrous worship.

8:28 When ***there was peace in the land*** (see note on 3:7-11) before Abimelech, it was for multiples of twenty years (3:11, 30; 5:31). After Gideon, the lengths were shorter. Israel’s ongoing apostasy led to increased social instability (cp. chs 17–21).

8:29-32 Advanced age is generally a sign of divine blessing, but Gideon was tarnished by a decline of spiritual blessing and leadership.

8:29 ***Gideon:*** Hebrew *Jerub-baal;* see 6:32.

8:31 ***concubine:*** See note on 19:1.

8:33-35 Gideon’s ephod (8:27) quickly became part of a pagan shrine honoring ***images of*** the ever-present Canaanite deity ***Baal***, here called ***Baal-berith*** (“Baal of the covenant”). Fundamental to this apostasy were the twin themes of forgetting the Lord and his works and disloyalty to godly leadership. Remembering is basic to biblical, covenantal worship, from the time of the Exodus (Exod 12:14, 24) to the ongoing Christian celebration of the Lord’s Supper (1 Cor 11:25). • ***loyalty:*** See note on 1:24.

9:1 Judg 8:31
9:4 Judg 8:33
9:5 Judg 6:11; 8:32
9:7 Deut 11:29; 27:12 John 4:20
9:8 2 Kgs 14:9 Ezek 17:3 Dan 4:10

Abimelech: the "Anti-Judge" (9:1-57)
Abimelech Rules over Shechem

9 One day Gideon's son Abimelech went
to Shechem to visit his uncles—his
mother's brothers. He said to them and to
the rest of his mother's family, 2"Ask the
leading citizens of Shechem whether they
want to be ruled by all seventy of Gideon's
sons or by one man. And remember that I
am your own flesh and blood!"
3So Abimelech's uncles gave his message to all the citizens of Shechem on his
behalf. And after listening to this proposal,
the people of Shechem decided in favor of
Abimelech because he was their relative.
4They gave him seventy silver coins from
the temple of Baal-berith, which he used
to hire some reckless troublemakers who
agreed to follow him. 5He went to his father's home at Ophrah, and there, on one
stone, they killed all seventy of his half
brothers, the sons of Gideon. But the youngest brother, Jotham, escaped and hid.
6Then all the leading citizens of Shechem
and Beth-millo called a meeting under the
oak beside the pillar at Shechem and made
Abimelech their king.

Jotham's Parable

7When Jotham heard about this, he climbed
to the top of Mount Gerizim and shouted,

"Listen to me, citizens of Shechem!
Listen to me if you want God to listen
to you!
8 Once upon a time the trees decided to
choose a king.
First they said to the olive tree,
'Be our king!'
9 But the olive tree refused, saying,
'Should I quit producing the olive oil
that blesses both God and people,
just to wave back and forth over the
trees?'
10 "Then they said to the fig tree,
'You be our king!'
11 But the fig tree also refused, saying,
'Should I quit producing my sweet fruit
just to wave back and forth over the
trees?'
12 "Then they said to the grapevine,
'You be our king!'
13 But the grapevine also refused, saying,
'Should I quit producing the wine
that cheers both God and people,
just to wave back and forth over the
trees?'
14 "Then all the trees finally turned to the
thornbush and said,
'Come, you be our king!'
15 And the thornbush replied to the trees,
'If you truly want to make me your king,
come and take shelter in my shade.
If not, let fire come out from me
and devour the cedars of Lebanon.' "

16Jotham continued, "Now make sure you
have acted honorably and in good faith by

9:1-57 The reign of Abimelech was the turning point between the comparative rest of the early period of judges (3:7–8:35) and the decline of the later years (10:1–16:31).

9:1-3 ***Abimelech***, son of a concubine (8:31; see note on 19:1), now argued that he could fulfill Israel's desire for the kind of royal dynasty rejected by his father. • The lack of any account of a conquest of Shechem, despite Israel's covenant activities in the city (Josh 24), suggests that Shechem's inhabitants were assimilated into Israel. Abimelech's ***uncles*** and his mother might thus have been of non-Israelite heritage (see also note on 9:28).

9:1 ***Gideon's:*** Hebrew *Jerub-baal's* (see 6:32); also in 9:2, 24.

9:3-5 Abimelech's appeal raised funding from the local ***temple of Baal-berith***, the worship center for a mixed Canaanite-Israelite religious cult.

9:4 True leaders do not buy loyalty and they appeal to the noble in society, not to ***reckless troublemakers*** like Abimelech's mercenary followers.

9:5 The murder of the ***seventy . . . sons of Gideon . . . on one stone*** was probably some kind of ritual slaying. • ***Gideon:*** Hebrew *Jerub-baal* (see 6:32); also in 9:16, 19, 28, 57. • ***youngest brother . . . escaped:*** Cp. 2 Kgs 11:1-3.

9:6 ***Beth-millo*** ("house of filling") was probably an elevated terrace on which an inner keep or tower was built (cp. 2 Sam 5:9; 1 Kgs 9:15, 24). The irony is thick: Abimelech—empty of divine appointment, priestly anointing, and popular acclaim—met at the "house of filling." His kingship was a sham. • ***under the oak beside the pillar:*** The meaning of the Hebrew is uncertain.

9:7-21 ***Jotham*** told a fable (a story in which plants and animals take on human attributes to make a moral point) to show what was happening (9:7-15). He then cursed ***Abimelech*** and ***the leading citizens of Shechem*** (9:16-21). If they had acted in bad faith, it would become evident (see 9:56-57).

9:7 ***Mount Gerizim*** was the mountain of blessing opposite Mount Ebal, the mountain of cursing (Deut 11:29). Gerizim, situated immediately south of Shechem, was a natural stage for Jotham's speech and also allowed him to escape when he was finished (see map, p. 389).

9:8-13 Olives, figs, and grapes were fundamental to the agriculture of Canaan, yielding important produce and adding to the beauty of the landscape. • To ***wave back and forth over the trees*** implied being visible and active while accomplishing nothing.

9:14-15 The trees, preferring an evil king to none at all (cp. 1 Sam 8:18-19), called on the ***thornbush***, who, though neither useful nor pleasing to the eye, accepted the job. The person who had agreed to be king did not have more profitable work to do. • ***Shade*** from the burning Middle Eastern sun was precisely what the thornbush could not produce. Accepting such an offer was both futile and foolish.

9:16-18 The people of Shechem had chosen to follow an unworthy man; they had also acted in bad faith by conspiring with Abimelech against Gideon's family.

making Abimelech your king, and that you have done right by Gideon and all of his descendants. Have you treated him with the honor he deserves for all he accomplished? 17For he fought for you and risked his life when he rescued you from the Midianites. 18But today you have revolted against my father and his descendants, killing his seventy sons on one stone. And you have chosen his slave woman's son, Abimelech, to be your king just because he is your relative.

19"If you have acted honorably and in good faith toward Gideon and his descendants today, then may you find joy in Abimelech, and may he find joy in you. 20But if you have not acted in good faith, then may fire come out from Abimelech and devour the leading citizens of Shechem and Beth-millo; and may fire come out from the citizens of Shechem and Beth-millo and devour Abimelech!"

21Then Jotham escaped and lived in Beer because he was afraid of his brother Abimelech.

Shechem Rebels against Abimelech

22After Abimelech had ruled over Israel for three years, 23God sent a spirit that stirred up trouble between Abimelech and the leading citizens of Shechem, and they revolted. 24God was punishing Abimelech for murdering Gideon's seventy sons, and the citizens of Shechem for supporting him in this treachery of murdering his brothers. 25The citizens of Shechem set an ambush for Abimelech on the hilltops and robbed everyone who passed that way. But someone warned Abimelech about their plot.

26One day Gaal son of Ebed moved to Shechem with his brothers and gained the confidence of the leading citizens of Shechem. 27During the annual harvest festival at Shechem, held in the temple of the local god, the wine flowed freely, and everyone began cursing Abimelech. 28"Who is Abimelech?" Gaal shouted. "He's not a true son of Shechem, so why should we be his servants? He's merely the son of Gideon, and this Zebul is merely his deputy. Serve the true sons of Hamor, the founder of Shechem. Why should we serve Abimelech? 29If I were in charge here, I would get rid of Abimelech. I would say to him, 'Get some soldiers, and come out and fight!' "

30But when Zebul, the leader of the city, heard what Gaal was saying, he was furious. 31He sent messengers to Abimelech in Arumah, telling him, "Gaal son of Ebed and his brothers have come to live in Shechem, and now they are inciting the city to rebel against you. 32Come by night with an army and hide out in the fields. 33In the morning, as soon as it is daylight, attack the city. When Gaal and those who are with him come out against you, you can do with them as you wish."

34So Abimelech and all his men went by night and split into four groups, stationing themselves around Shechem. 35Gaal was standing at the city gates when Abimelech and his army came out of hiding. 36When Gaal saw them, he said to Zebul, "Look, there are people coming down from the hilltops!"

Zebul replied, "It's just the shadows on the hills that look like men."

37But again Gaal said, "No, people are coming down from the hills. And another group is coming down the road past the Diviners' Oak."

9:18 Judg 8:31
9:23 1 Sam 16:14
9:24 Num 35:33; Deut 27:25
9:27 Judg 8:33
9:33 1 Sam 10:7

9:19-20 The Shechemites were invited to decide whether their actions merited blessing or cursing. The implication was that they had acted in bad faith, so they and Abimelech would destroy each other. The Lord is a devouring fire (Heb 12:29), and those who act unfaithfully prove his justice.

9:22-57 Theological statements in 9:23-24 and 9:56-57 frame the account of the civil strife that led to the destruction of Abimelech and Shechem, which was divine fulfillment of the curse set out by Jotham (9:19-20).

9:22-25 As prophesied in the fable (9:8-15), ***Abimelech*** was unable to live up to the Shechemites' expectations, so they conspired against him.

9:22-23 It took ***three years*** to bring about what God had decreed. The ***spirit that stirred up trouble*** found willing hearts. Those condemned for their folly participated fully in their own demise; they brought it on themselves.

9:25 An informer foiled the ***plot*** against Abimelech, but social conditions were deteriorating as God's curse played out.

9:26-41 ***Gaal son of Ebed*** ("vile son of a slave") led an unsuccessful rebellion against Abimelech in which many of Shechem's citizens were killed. This partially fulfilled Jotham's curse (9:20).

9:27-29 Disillusionment with Abimelech, social unrest, and lots of ***wine*** and loose talk made it easy for ***Gaal*** to gain initial acceptance.

9:28 ***Who is Abimelech? . . . He's not a true son of Shechem*** (literally *Who is Abimelech? And who is Shechem?*): Gaal focused on Abimelech's pedigree through his father, Gideon (a non-Shechemite) rather than through his mother (8:31; 9:2). • ***Serve the true sons of Hamor:*** Gaal's pedigree apparently went back to Hamor, ***the founder of Shechem*** (Gen 33:18–34:31).

9:29 ***I would say:*** As in Greek version; Hebrew reads *And he said.*

9:30-41 The second plot, like the first (9:22-25), was foiled by an informer, in this case probably an official appointed by the absent Abimelech. ***Zebul*** proposed a bold ***morning*** ambush, in which he would presumably help to draw ***Gaal*** and his followers out into the open country where they could be engaged. The plan worked. Perhaps because of his boasting and possibly in response to Zebul's mocking challenge, Gaal and his men ventured out only to be driven from town by the faithful Zebul, the agent for cleansing the city.

9:31 ***in Arumah:*** Or *in secret;* Hebrew reads *in Tormah;* cp. 9:41.

9:37 ***the hills:*** Or *the center of the land.* • ***the Diviners' Oak:*** Hebrew *Elon-meonenim.*

9:45 Deut 29:23
9:46 Judg 8:33
9:48 Ps 68:14
9:50 2 Sam 11:21
9:53 2 Sam 11:21

38Then Zebul turned on him and asked, "Now where is that big mouth of yours? Wasn't it you that said, 'Who is Abimelech, and why should we be his servants?' The men you mocked are right outside the city! Go out and fight them!"

39So Gaal led the leading citizens of Shechem into battle against Abimelech. 40But Abimelech chased him, and many of Shechem's men were wounded and fell along the road as they retreated to the city gate. 41Abimelech returned to Arumah, and Zebul drove Gaal and his brothers out of Shechem.

42The next day the people of Shechem went out into the fields to battle. When Abimelech heard about it, 43he divided his men into three groups and set an ambush in the fields. When Abimelech saw the people coming out of the city, he and his men jumped up from their hiding places and attacked them. 44Abimelech and his group stormed the city gate to keep the men of Shechem from getting back in, while Abimelech's other two groups cut them down in the fields. 45The battle went on all day before Abimelech finally captured the city. He killed the people, leveled the city, and scattered salt all over the ground.

46When the leading citizens who lived in the tower of Shechem heard what had happened, they ran and hid in the temple of Baal-berith. 47Someone reported to Abimelech that the citizens had gathered in the temple, 48so he led his forces to Mount Zalmon. He took an ax and chopped some branches from a tree, then put them on his shoulder. "Quick, do as I have done!" he told his men. 49So each of them cut down some branches, following Abimelech's example. They piled the branches against the walls of the temple and set them on fire. So all the people who had lived in the tower of Shechem died—about 1,000 men and women.

50Then Abimelech attacked the town of Thebez and captured it. 51But there was a strong tower inside the town, and all the men and women—the entire population—fled to it. They barricaded themselves in and climbed up to the roof of the tower. 52Abimelech followed them to attack the tower. But as he prepared to set fire to the entrance, 53a woman on the roof dropped a millstone that landed on Abimelech's head and crushed his skull.

54He quickly said to his young armor bearer, "Draw your sword and kill me! Don't let it be said that a woman killed Abimelech!" So the young man ran him through with his sword, and he died. 55When Abimelech's men saw that he was dead, they disbanded and returned to their homes.

56In this way, God punished Abimelech for the evil he had done against his father by murdering his seventy brothers. 57God also punished the men of Shechem for all their evil. So the curse of Jotham son of Gideon was fulfilled.

The Period of Decline (10:1–16:31)

Tola Becomes Israel's Judge

10 After Abimelech died, Tola son of Puah, son of Dodo, was the next person to rescue Israel. He was from the tribe

---

9:42 The NLT supplies the words ***to battle***, with the understanding that the Shechemites ***went out into the fields*** to keep Abimelech from reasserting power over them. Others think that the Shechemites returned to the fields to continue the harvest (9:27), believing that Abimelech would be satisfied now that Gaal had been driven out.

9:43-45 Abimelech forfeited any claim he might have had to being an inspired leader; he turned ***his men*** on ***the people*** of Shechem, slaughtered them all, and destroyed the city.

9:45 Scattering ***salt*** prevented anything from growing and ensured destruction.

9:46-49 The ***leading citizens*** (literally *lords*) of ***Shechem*** who had first plotted against Abimelech now crowded into ***the temple of Baal-berith*** (Hebrew *El-berith*, another name for Baal-berith; cp. 9:4) only to have it burn around them. This destruction has been confirmed by archaeologists at the site.

9:48 ***Mount Zalmon*** is probably another name for Mount Ebal, the mountain opposite Gerizim and next to Shechem (see note on 9:7).

9:50 ***Thebez*** was a stronghold a few miles northeast of Shechem. Abimelech was probably reclaiming Thebez, but he might have been attempting an initial takeover.

9:53 Women frequently ground grain on a stationary lower millstone, on which the lighter upper ***millstone*** was turned by hand. This incident is referenced in the story of David's murder of Uriah (2 Sam 11:21).

9:54-55 To die at the hands of ***a woman*** or a child was shameful (see note on 8:20-21). Abimelech was not given a peace formula or burial notice, because his reign was not legitimate.

9:56-57 The theological summary returns to the theme of Jotham's fable (9:24). Abimelech had no divine charisma, and his death as a result of divine vengeance meant that justice was finally served for Gideon's family. Israel's experiment with uninspired kingship was a stark example of leadership that was not from God.

10:1-5 Each of the five minor judges (see also 12:8-15) ***judged Israel*** for a specific number of years; in this period of decline after Gideon, the formula "there was peace in the land" (3:11, 30; 5:31; 8:28) never recurs. The details given for these enigmatic figures include their places of origin and burial, and perhaps a brief genealogy or something notable about their families. Four of the five names appear in other genealogical records: Tola and Puah as clans of Issachar (Gen 46:13; Num 26:23), Elon as a descendant of Zebulun (Gen 46:14; Num 26:26), and Jair at various points (see Num 32:41; Deut 3:14; Josh 13:30; 1 Kgs 4:13). The lack of specific military exploits and the common reference to "judging" suggests that they had some kind of administrative or judicial function.

of Issachar but lived in the town of Shamir
in the hill country of Ephraim. 2He judged
Israel for twenty-three years. When he died,
he was buried in Shamir.

Jair Becomes Israel's Judge

3After Tola died, Jair from Gilead judged
Israel for twenty-two years. 4His thirty
sons rode around on thirty donkeys, and
they owned thirty towns in the land of Gilead, which are still called the Towns of Jair.
5When Jair died, he was buried in Kamon.

The Ammonites Oppress Israel

6Again the Israelites did evil in the LORD's
sight. They served the images of Baal and
Ashtoreth, and the gods of Aram, Sidon,
Moab, Ammon, and Philistia. They abandoned the LORD and no longer served him at
all. 7So the LORD burned with anger against
Israel, and he turned them over to the Philistines and the Ammonites, 8who began to
oppress them that year. For eighteen years
they oppressed all the Israelites east of the
Jordan River in the land of the Amorites
(that is, in Gilead). 9The Ammonites also
crossed to the west side of the Jordan and
attacked Judah, Benjamin, and Ephraim.
The Israelites were in great distress. 10Fi-
nally, they cried out to the LORD for help,
saying, "We have sinned against you because we have abandoned you as our God
and have served the images of Baal."
11The LORD replied, "Did I not rescue you
from the Egyptians, the Amorites, the Ammonites, the Philistines, 12the Sidonians,
the Amalekites, and the Maonites? When
they oppressed you, you cried out to me for
help, and I rescued you. 13Yet you have abandoned me and served other gods. So I will
not rescue you anymore. 14Go and cry out to
the gods you have chosen! Let them rescue
you in your hour of distress!"
15But the Israelites pleaded with the LORD
and said, "We have sinned. Punish us as you
see fit, only rescue us today from our enemies." 16Then the Israelites put aside their
foreign gods and served the LORD. And he
was grieved by their misery.
17At that time the armies of Ammon had
gathered for war and were camped in Gilead, and the people of Israel assembled and
camped at Mizpah. 18The leaders of Gilead
said to each other, "Whoever attacks the
Ammonites first will become ruler over all
the people of Gilead."

Jephthah Becomes Israel's Judge

11 Now Jephthah of Gilead was a great
warrior. He was the son of Gilead, but
his mother was a prostitute. 2Gilead's wife
also had several sons, and when these half
brothers grew up, they chased Jephthah
off the land. "You will not get any of our father's inheritance," they said, "for you are
the son of a prostitute." 3So Jephthah fled
from his brothers and lived in the land of
Tob. Soon he had a band of worthless rebels
following him.
4At about this time, the Ammonites began
their war against Israel. 5When the Ammonites attacked, the elders of Gilead sent for
Jephthah in the land of Tob. The elders said,

10:4 Num 32:41
10:6 Judg 2:11-13
10:7 1 Sam 12:9
10:10 Judg 3:9
10:11 Exod 14:30; Judg 3:13
10:14 Deut 32:37
10:15 1 Sam 3:18
10:16 Deut 32:36; Josh 24:23; Jer 18:8
11:1 1 Sam 12:11; Heb 11:32
11:3 Judg 9:4; 2 Sam 10:6, 8
11:4 Judg 10:9

10:1 *Tola* was the first of five minor judges; little is known about him. Of the five, only Tola was said ***to rescue Israel***. He came ***after Abimelech died***, when Israel was in need of rescue, though not from a foreign enemy.

10:3-4 ***Jair*** was apparently a descendant of an earlier Jair of the tribe of Manasseh (see Num 32:41; Deut 3:14; cp. 1 Kgs 4:13). The ***Towns of Jair*** (Hebrew *Havvoth-jair*) that Jair and his sons controlled had been conquered by the earlier Jair.

10:6-16 The Lord responded to his people's total apostasy by allowing crushing oppression (10:8). As usual, Israel ***cried out to the LORD for help*** (10:10) only after experiencing ***great distress*** (10:9). Normally, Israel's cry led to divine intervention, but God's decision to leave them to their chosen gods marks a shift in the cycle described in 2:10-19. Only when ***the Israelites put aside their foreign gods and served the LORD*** did he again act to redeem them (10:17–11:33).

10:6 ***Again the Israelites did evil. . . . They abandoned the LORD:*** This period of apostasy was more complete than any described earlier—it included the worship of ***Baal and Ashtoreth*** along with other local ***gods***.

10:7-8 ***The Philistines:*** See notes on 3:3; 13:1. • ***The Ammonites*** lived east of the Jordan (see note on 3:12-13), and they began by oppressing the Israelite tribes of Transjordan (see map, p. 397); then they attacked the tribes west of the Jordan as well.

10:17-18 The narrative returns to the Ammonite oppression, which sets the stage for Jephthah's story.

10:18 ***The leaders of Gilead***, in their desperation for leadership, did not consult the Lord (cp. 1:1; 20:18) but said that ***whoever*** stepped up to lead would ***become ruler over*** Gilead.

11:1-3 In ***Jephthah***, inspired leadership took a new turn. He had humble origins, attracted followers, was eloquent in debate, and had Spirit-filled military prowess, but all of these were overshadowed by the fatal flaws of his untimely vow (11:30-31, 34-35) and his petulant civil war with Ephraim (12:1-6). Even his victory was short-lived (six years, 12:7). The period of decline was underway, which increased the demand for kingship.

11:1-2 ***great warrior:*** Jephthah had military prowess and possibly social prominence (see note on 6:12, where ***great warrior*** is translated "mighty hero"). ***Gilead*** was a descendant of Manasseh (Num 26:29-33; 32:39-40; 1 Chr 7:14-17). Jephthah's social standing raised his visibility despite the ignominy of his ***prostitute*** mother. His ***half brothers*** had no obligation to accept Jephthah's status or leadership.

11:3 Jephthah's ***worthless rebels*** are reminiscent of Abimelech's "reckless troublemakers" (see 9:4), but Jephthah had no need to buy their loyalty.

11:4 ***Ammonites . . . war:*** See 10:17.

11:5-6 These ***elders*** were apparently distinct from Jephthah's brothers,

11:10 Gen 31:50
11:11 Judg 10:17
11:13 Num 21:24-26
11:16 Num 20:1
11:17 Num 20:14-21; Josh 24:9

6“Come and be our commander! Help us
fight the Ammonites!”
7But Jephthah said to them, “Aren’t you
the ones who hated me and drove me from
my father’s house? Why do you come to me
now when you’re in trouble?”
8“Because we need you,” the elders replied. “If you lead us in battle against the
Ammonites, we will make you ruler over all
the people of Gilead.”
9Jephthah said to the elders, “Let me get
this straight. If I come with you and if the
LORD gives me victory over the Ammonites,
will you really make me ruler over all the
people?”
10“The LORD is our witness,” the elders replied. “We promise to do whatever you say.”
11So Jephthah went with the elders of
Gilead, and the people made him their
ruler and commander of the army. At Mizpah, in the presence of the LORD, Jephthah
repeated what he had said to the elders.
12Then Jephthah sent messengers to the
king of Ammon, asking, “Why have you
come out to fight against my land?”
13The king of Ammon answered Jephthah’s messengers, “When the Israelites
came out of Egypt, they stole my land from
the Arnon River to the Jabbok River and all
the way to the Jordan. Now then, give back
the land peaceably.”
14Jephthah sent this message back to the
Ammonite king:

15“This is what Jephthah says: Israel did
not steal any land from Moab or Ammon.
16When the people of Israel arrived at
Kadesh on their journey from Egypt
after crossing the Red Sea, 17they sent
messengers to the king of Edom asking
for permission to pass through his land.
But their request was denied. Then
they asked the king of Moab for similar
permission, but he wouldn’t let them
pass through either. So the people of
Israel stayed in Kadesh.

God’s Grief over Apostasy (10:6-16)

Gen 6:5-7; Isa 5:1-7; 53:3-12; 63:10; Hos 11:8-9; Eph 4:30

The entire era of the judges shows what happens in God’s heart when his people repeatedly spurn him. In the psalms, God asked, “How long will you people ruin my reputation? How long will you make groundless accusations? How long will you continue your lies?” (Ps 4:2). There will be a time, as in the time of Noah (Gen 6:5-7), when God’s patience runs out. For the Israelites who inhabited the land of the judges, that time had come. God’s verdict was, “Go and cry out to the gods you have chosen! Let them rescue you” (10:14). Israel repeated its plea for mercy (10:10, 15-16), but this time they rid themselves of the foreign gods who were powerless to help them and submitted to the Lord’s justice.

The God of the universe is grieved by his people’s misery (10:16; Hos 11:8-9). Even when repeatedly spurned, God’s love is more powerful than his wrath, and his compassion exceeds his indignation. God’s love does not negate his justice, however, “for he himself is fair and just, and he declares sinners to be right in his sight when they believe in Jesus” (Rom 3:26). He has taken upon himself the grievous weight of our sin (see Isa 53:3-12; 2 Cor 5:19-21).

although Jephthah’s initial response (11:7) appears to equate the two groups. They had promised (10:18) that whoever took the military initiative and attacked the Ammonites would become the ruler. Here, in typical Middle Eastern bargaining style, they only offered the status of ***commander***, trying to diminish their initial promise.

11:7-8 When Jephthah challenged the offer, the elders returned to the stronger word, ***ruler***.

11:9-10 Jephthah made sure that the elders really were offering him the position of ***ruler***, not just “commander.”

11:11 At the end of the negotiations, Jephthah was sworn in as both ***ruler and commander***. • This ***Mizpah*** (“watchtower”) was a shrine east of the Jordan in Gilead, which was Jephthah’s home (10:17; 11:29, 34); it should not be confused with Mizpah in Benjamin, the place near Bethel where the tribes later assembled and swore oaths for the final battle of Judges (20:1; 21:1). • The ceremony at Mizpah ***in the presence of the LORD*** appears to have been the making of a suzerain-vassal covenant, in which a ruler (the suzerain) promises to protect and defend a vassal people in exchange for authority over them (see note on Exod 20:1–23:33; see Deuteronomy Introduction, “Literary Form,” p. 314).

11:12-28 Jephthah initially tried to solve the problem by diplomatic rather than military means (cp. Deut 20:10-11). • Unlike the nomadic, marauding Midianites of Gideon’s day, the Ammonites were a settled tribe whose territory lay to the east of Israel’s holdings in Transjordan (east of the Jordan); Rabbah was the Ammonite capital. The Ammonites, like the Moabites (both descendants of Lot) and the Edomites (Esau’s descendants), were to be left alone, as their territories were assigned to them by the Lord (Deut 2:16-23). • Contrary to the Ammonite king’s contention, the Amorites, not Ammon or Moab, lived between the Arnon and Jabbok rivers at the time of the conquest. In response to Sihon’s refusal to let Israel pass, the Lord had given the land of the Amorite kings Sihon and Og to Israel. The Ammonite king had no legitimate quarrel with Israel.

11:16 ***Red Sea:*** Literally *sea of reeds*.

11:17 ***Kadesh*** had been Israel’s base for spying out the land (Num 32:8; Deut 1:19; 2:14). The name comes from the Hebrew root *qadesh* (“holy”) and presumably is named for a shrine.

18“Finally, they went around Edom
and Moab through the wilderness.
They traveled along Moab’s eastern
border and camped on the other side
of the Arnon River. But they never once
crossed the Arnon River into Moab, for
the Arnon was the border of Moab.
19“Then Israel sent messengers to
King Sihon of the Amorites, who ruled
from Heshbon, asking for permission
to cross through his land to get to their
destination. 20But King Sihon didn’t
trust Israel to pass through his land.
Instead, he mobilized his army at Jahaz
and attacked them. 21But the LORD, the
God of Israel, gave his people victory
over King Sihon. So Israel took control
of all the land of the Amorites, who lived
in that region, 22from the Arnon River to
the Jabbok River, and from the eastern
wilderness to the Jordan.
23“So you see, it was the LORD, the
God of Israel, who took away the land
from the Amorites and gave it to Israel.
Why, then, should we give it back to you?
24You keep whatever your god Chemosh
gives you, and we will keep whatever the
LORD our God gives us. 25Are you any
better than Balak son of Zippor, king of
Moab? Did he try to make a case against
Israel for disputed land? Did he go to
war against them?
26“Israel has been living here for
300 years, inhabiting Heshbon and its
surrounding settlements, all the way to
Aroer and its settlements, and in all the
towns along the Arnon River. Why have
you made no effort to recover it before
now? 27Therefore, I have not sinned
against you. Rather, you have wronged
me by attacking me. Let the LORD, who
is judge, decide today which of us is
right—Israel or Ammon.”
28But the king of Ammon paid no attention
to Jephthah’s message.

Jephthah’s Vow

29At that time the Spirit of the LORD came
upon Jephthah, and he went throughout
the land of Gilead and Manasseh, including
Mizpah in Gilead, and from there he led an
army against the Ammonites. 30And Jephthah made a vow to the LORD. He said, “If
you give me victory over the Ammonites, 31I
will give to the LORD whatever comes out of
my house to meet me when I return in triumph. I will sacrifice it as a burnt offering.”
32So Jephthah led his army against the
Ammonites, and the LORD gave him victory.
33He crushed the Ammonites, devastating about twenty towns from Aroer to an
area near Minnith and as far away as Abel-
keramim. In this way Israel defeated the
Ammonites.
34When Jephthah returned home to
Mizpah, his daughter came out to meet
him, playing on a tambourine and dancing
for joy. She was his one and only child; he
had no other sons or daughters. 35When
he saw her, he tore his clothes in anguish.
“Oh, my daughter!” he cried out. “You have
completely destroyed me! You’ve brought
disaster on me! For I have made a vow to the
LORD, and I cannot take it back.”
36And she said, “Father, if you have made
a vow to the LORD, you must do to me what

11:18 Num 21:4; Deut 2:1-9, 18-19
11:19 Num 21:21-22
11:21 Deut 2:32-34
11:24 Num 21:27-30; 1 Kgs 11:7
11:25 Num 22:2
11:26 Num 21:25
11:29 Judg 3:10
11:34 Exod 15:20; 1 Sam 18:6; Jer 31:4
11:35 Num 30:2; Eccl 5:2, 4-5
11:36 2 Sam 18:19; Luke 1:38

11:24 *Chemosh* was the god of the related tribe of Moabites. If the land occupied by Israel east of the Jordan originally belonged to Moab (see note on 11:25), the Ammonite king would still have regarded Chemosh as the god of that land. Whether Jephthah regarded Chemosh as a god or was accommodating himself to the king’s belief system is not clear.

11:25 *Moab* and Ammon were related (descendants of Lot). Moab, as opposed to Ammon, may have had a legitimate claim to the land that Israel occupied north of the Arnon, which was taken from them earlier by Sihon, king of the Amorites (Num 21:24). The Israelites had conquered Sihon and annexed the disputed territory, but Moab had not attempted to claim it. Neither should Ammon, because the land in question had never belonged to them.

11:26 Whether the conquest and settlement took place in the 1400s BC or the 1200s BC (see Chronology: The Time of the Judges, p. 414), Jephthah’s *300 years* is probably a round figure.

11:27 Jephthah appealed to *the LORD*, the great *judge*, to decide between *Israel* and *Ammon*. The Lord’s response (11:29-33) was his answer.

11:29-31 *The Spirit of the LORD*, a consistent sign of inspired authority, *came upon Jephthah*, and he journeyed through the tribal lands of *Gilead and Manasseh, including* his hometown of *Mizpah in Gilead*, gathering troops. During this time leading up to battle, he made his infamous *vow*.

11:31 Nowhere does the Lord demand such bargaining for his favor. Vows were made under a variety of circumstances and usually involved some gift (offering) dedicated to the Lord in response to his aid (cp. Gen 28:20-22). The more common preparation for battle was priestly sacrifice (1 Sam 13:8-12). Jephthah’s vow created the possibility that some person in his household would become a human sacrifice, an act strictly forbidden in Israelite law (Deut 18:10).

11:32 No connection is drawn between the *victory*, which was the Lord’s gift, and Jephthah’s vow.

11:35 Having made an impulsive *vow*, Jephthah now compounded his folly by blaming the result on his *daughter* and by failing to respond in light of Scripture. Vows taken were usually inviolable (Num 30:2), though the OT recognizes a few circumstances under which an unwise vow could be set aside (Num 30:6-8). Since human sacrifice was forbidden in the law, a substitute could have been made (see Lev 27:1-8). Jephthah was apparently unaware of these principles in God’s law, perhaps because of his upbringing in an area far from Israel’s major centers.

12:1
Judg 8:1
12:3
1 Sam 19:5
Job 13:14
12:5
Josh 2:7
Judg 3:28; 7:24
12:7
Heb 11:32

you have vowed, for the LORD has given you a great victory over your enemies, the Ammonites. 37But first let me do this one thing: Let me go up and roam in the hills and weep with my friends for two months, because I will die a virgin."

38"You may go," Jephthah said. And he sent her away for two months. She and her friends went into the hills and wept because she would never have children. 39When she returned home, her father kept the vow he had made, and she died a virgin.

So it has become a custom in Israel 40for young Israelite women to go away for four days each year to lament the fate of Jephthah's daughter.

Ephraim Fights with Jephthah

12 Then the people of Ephraim mobilized an army and crossed over the Jordan River to Zaphon. They sent this message to Jephthah: "Why didn't you call for us to help you fight against the Ammonites? We are going to burn down your house with you in it!"

2Jephthah replied, "I summoned you at the beginning of the dispute, but you refused to come! You failed to help us in our struggle against Ammon. 3So when I realized you weren't coming, I risked my life and went to battle without you, and the LORD gave me victory over the Ammonites. So why have you now come to fight me?"

4The people of Ephraim responded, "You men of Gilead are nothing more than fugitives from Ephraim and Manasseh." So Jephthah gathered all the men of Gilead and attacked the men of Ephraim and defeated them.

5Jephthah captured the shallow crossings of the Jordan River, and whenever a fugitive from Ephraim tried to go back across, the men of Gilead would challenge him. "Are you a member of the tribe of Ephraim?" they would ask. If the man said, "No, I'm not," 6they would tell him to say "Shibboleth." If he was from Ephraim, he would say "Sibboleth," because people from Ephraim cannot pronounce the word correctly. Then they would take him and kill him at the shallow crossings of the Jordan. In all, 42,000 Ephraimites were killed at that time.

7Jephthah judged Israel for six years. When he died, he was buried in one of the towns of Gilead.

Ibzan Becomes Israel's Judge

8After Jephthah died, Ibzan from Bethlehem judged Israel. 9He had thirty sons and thirty daughters. He sent his daughters to marry men outside his clan, and he brought

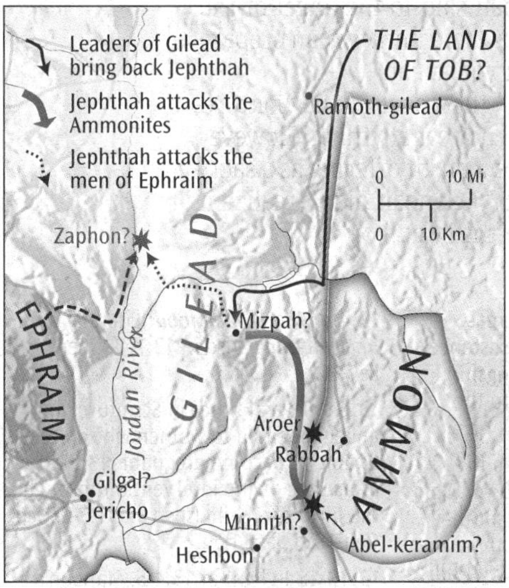

◂ **Jephthah Defeats the Ammonites and Ephraimites** (11:1–12:7). When the Ammonites attacked GILEAD, the elders of Gilead convinced Jephthah to come from the LAND OF TOB (location uncertain), where he had been living. At MIZPAH, the people of Gilead made him their ruler (11:1-11). Then Jephthah attacked and defeated the Ammonites from AROER to ABEL-KERAMIM (11:12-33). Afterward, Ephraim mobilized to ZAPHON to attack Gilead, so Jephthah met and defeated them there (12:1-7).

11:39 Jephthah *kept the vow* by sacrificing his daughter—there is no evidence that he merely kept her permanently celibate (cp. 11:37). Jephthah's folly demonstrates just how far Israel's society had descended into lawlessness and apostasy.

12:1-6 *Ephraim* once again felt neglected (cp. 8:1-3) and sought revenge. In contrast to Gideon's policy, Jephthah's response blamed Ephraim and resulted in civil war.

12:1 *Zaphon* was just east of the Jordan River, across from the tribal area of Ephraim (see map above).

12:2 There is no record of Jephthah's earlier appeal.

12:4 It is unclear why *the people of Ephraim* were taunting the *men of Gilead.* Perhaps they resented or looked down on the Israelites who lived east of the Jordan River.

12:5 The *Jordan River* could only be forded at *shallow crossings* where tributaries had deposited silt, as was probably the case where the Jabbok flowed into the Jordan.

12:6 The term *Shibboleth* has come to mean any password used to identify imposters. Such linguistic litmus tests have been used by armies throughout history. • *42,000 Ephraimites:* This number could possibly be translated as "42 troops" (see note on Exod 12:37).

12:7 *six years:* Like all the judges after Gideon, Jephthah's years as judge were specific and short (see note on 8:28). Jephthah was *buried* honorably, so despite his limitations he was an inspired and successful warrior (11:29; contrast Abimelech, note on 9:54-55).

12:8-15 The account continues with these minor judges (see note on 10:1-5).

12:8 If this was the northern *Bethlehem* located in Zebulun (see map, p. 397), it can be understood as part of the structure of Judges, in which each of the tribes supply one of the twelve judges (see Judges Introduction, "Summary," p. 417).

in thirty young women from outside his
clan to marry his sons. Ibzan judged Israel
for seven years. 10When he died, he was buried at Bethlehem.

Elon Becomes Israel's Judge

11After Ibzan died, Elon from the tribe
of Zebulun judged Israel for ten years.
12When he died, he was buried at Aijalon in
Zebulun.

Abdon Becomes Israel's Judge

13After Elon died, Abdon son of Hillel, from
Pirathon, judged Israel. 14He had forty sons
and thirty grandsons, who rode on seventy
donkeys. He judged Israel for eight years.
15When he died, he was buried at Pirathon
in Ephraim, in the hill country of the Amalekites.

The Birth of Samson

13 Again the Israelites did evil in the
LORD's sight, so the LORD handed
them over to the Philistines, who oppressed
them for forty years.
2In those days a man named Manoah from
the tribe of Dan lived in the town of Zorah.
His wife was unable to become pregnant,
and they had no children. 3The [h]angel of the
LORD appeared to Manoah's wife and said,
"Even though you have been unable to have
children, you will soon become pregnant
and give birth to a son. 4So be careful; you
must not drink wine or any other alcoholic
drink nor eat any forbidden food. 5You will
become pregnant and give birth to a son, and
his hair must never be cut. For he will be dedicated to God as a Nazirite from birth. He will
begin to rescue Israel from the Philistines."
6The woman ran and told her husband,
"A man of God appeared to me! He looked
like one of God's angels, terrifying to see. I
didn't ask where he was from, and he didn't
tell me his name. 7But he told me, 'You will
become pregnant and give birth to a son.
You must not drink wine or any other alcoholic drink nor eat any forbidden food. For
your son will be dedicated to God as a Nazirite from the moment of his birth until the
day of his death.'"
8Then Manoah prayed to the LORD, saying, "Lord, please let the man of God come
back to us again and give us more instructions about this son who is to be born."
9God answered Manoah's prayer, and the
angel of God appeared once again to his
wife as she was sitting in the field. But her
husband, Manoah, was not with her. 10So
she quickly ran and told her husband, "The
man who appeared to me the other day is
here again!"
11Manoah ran back with his wife and
asked, "Are you the man who spoke to my
wife the other day?"
"Yes," he replied, "I am."
12So Manoah asked him, "When your
words come true, what kind of rules should
govern the boy's life and work?"
13The angel of the LORD replied, "Be sure
your wife follows the instructions I gave her.
14She must not eat grapes or raisins, drink
wine or any other alcoholic drink, or eat any
forbidden food."
15Then Manoah said to the angel of the
LORD, "Please stay here until we can prepare
a young goat for you to eat."
16"I will stay," the angel of the LORD replied, "but I will not eat anything. However,
you may prepare a burnt offering as a sacrifice to the LORD." (Manoah didn't realize it
was the angel of the LORD.)

12:14 Judg 5:10
13:1 Judg 2:11
13:2 Josh 19:41
13:3 Gen 16:7; Judg 6:12; [h]*mal'ak* (4397) ‣2 Sam 14:17
13:4-5 Num 6:1-5; Judg 13:14; Luke 1:15
13:6 1 Sam 2:27
13:15 Judg 6:19

12:11 *Elon:* See note on 10:1-5.

12:15 The *Amalekites* had earlier occupied parts of *Ephraim* (5:14).

13:1–16:31 *Samson*, who receives more attention in the book of Judges than any other judge, is even more of an enigma than Jephthah. Samson reflects a high level of inspiration as a leader. He also personifies the inexorable march toward chaos that highlights the need for a more centralized society under a godly ruler.

13:1 Though mentioned earlier, ***the Philistines*** (3:3; 10:7) were a relatively new presence in the territory of Canaan, which would later be named for them (Palestine). This warlike race of sea people were of Greek rather than Canaanite ancestry and settled into the southwestern coastal areas about 1200 BC. From then on, Philistia was Israel's natural enemy and increasingly threatened its national existence. Israel's institutions, such as kingship, developed partly in response to the Philistine challenge.

13:2 Prior to their migration to the extreme north (ch 18), ***the tribe of Dan*** attempted to settle in Israel's southwest (Josh 19:40-48). This put them in direct conflict with the incoming Philistines. • ***Zorah*** was west of Judah, in the area newly occupied by the Philistines. Both Dan and neighboring Judah submitted to Philistine dominance (14:4; 15:11).

13:3-5 ***Manoah's wife*** was promised ***a son*** who was to be set aside from his birth as a ***Nazirite*** (see Num 6:1-21; cp. 1 Sam 1:11). The requirement that Samson's ***hair must never be cut*** would be central to his story.

13:4 ***any forbidden food:*** Literally *any unclean thing;* also in 13:7, 14. See Lev 11.

13:6-7 Several times in Scripture, an angel appeared to women who were unable to become pregnant (13:2) to announce divine intervention through the birth of a child (see Luke 1:5-25; cp. Gen 18; 1 Sam 1).

13:12-13 In light of 13:4-5, Manoah's question may seem redundant, but from 13:8 it is apparent that ***Manoah*** felt a keen personal responsibility for raising such a child. The angel responded graciously, but again stressed the wife's responsibility, which explains why it was she, not Manoah, who was first approached.

13:15-16 ***Manoah*** would only send a visitor on his way after providing a meal, in accord with eastern hospitality. ***The***

13:17 Gen 32:29
13:19 Judg 6:20-21
13:22 Gen 32:30; Judg 6:22
13:24 1 Sam 3:19; Luke 1:80; Heb 11:32
13:25 Judg 3:10; 18:11-12; 1 Sam 10:6, 10

17Then Manoah asked the angel of the
LORD, "What is your name? For when all
this comes true, we want to honor you."
18"Why do you ask my name?" the angel
of the LORD replied. "It is too wonderful for
you to understand."
19Then Manoah took a young goat and a
grain offering and offered it on a rock as a
sacrifice to the LORD. And as Manoah and his
wife watched, the LORD did an amazing thing.
20As the flames from the altar shot up toward
the sky, the angel of the LORD ascended in
the fire. When Manoah and his wife saw this,
they fell with their faces to the ground.
21The angel did not appear again to Manoah and his wife. Manoah finally realized
it was the angel of the LORD, 22and he said to
his wife, "We will certainly die, for we have
seen God!"
23But his wife said, "If the LORD were going to kill us, he wouldn't have accepted
our burnt offering and grain offering. He
wouldn't have appeared to us and told us this
wonderful thing and done these miracles."
24When her son was born, she named
him Samson. And the LORD blessed him as
he grew up. 25And the Spirit of the LORD
began to stir him while he lived in Mahaneh-
dan, which is located between the towns of
Zorah and Eshtaol.

Samson's Riddle

14 One day when Samson was in Timnah, one of the Philistine women
caught his eye. 2When he returned home,

SAMSON (13:1–16:31)

Heb 11:32

Samson, Israel's best-known judge, is a prime illustration of God's using a person for good in spite of that person's indifference and sin. Samson was a rescuer of Israel without even trying or caring. He did not care about his people, his family, or his God. All he cared about was himself. God, though, put him in situation after situation where he brought harm to the Philistines, whom God had allowed to oppress Israel because they had sinned against him.

The first example of how God used Samson occurred when he told his shocked parents that he wanted to marry a Philistine girl. Israelites were commanded not to intermarry with the people of the land (Deut 7:3; Josh 23:12-13; cp. 2 Cor 6:14-17), but Samson persisted over his parents' objections. As he was on his way to the wedding party, he scooped honey out of the dead lion he had earlier killed. He was born a Nazirite (Num 6:1-21), and Nazirites were absolutely forbidden from touching a dead body, but Samson didn't care. He then made up a riddle about the lion (14:14) and bet thirty young Philistine men that they could not solve his riddle. The men pestered his wife into telling them the answer. Samson became so angry that he killed thirty Philistine men and took their clothing to pay off the bet. God used the self-serving hero to "begin to rescue Israel from the Philistines" (13:5).

In the final, climactic story of Samson's life (16:4-31), Samson's lover, the infamous Delilah, nagged Samson until he revealed the secret of his strength and thus betrayed his Nazirite vow. She cut his hair, and the Philistines were finally able to overpower him. They blinded him, tied him up securely, and loaded him with menial work. While in captivity, Samson's hair began to grow again. One day, when the Philistines were celebrating and making fun of him, he asked to be led to the two central pillars of the pagan temple. He then prayed to God to give him the strength to kill the Philistines and take his own life. So he pulled the temple down on the heads of about 3,000 Philistines as well as himself. Even this act, however, was not done for his people or his God, but to "pay back the Philistines for the loss of [his] two eyes" (16:28). Even though it was all in God's plan, the story of Samson makes the reader long for a better savior.

angel insisted that any food be given *as a sacrifice to the LORD*. That and his reluctance to eat (cp. Gideon's visitor, 6:17-22) suggest that this was a *theophany* (an appearance of God). To that point, Manoah had failed to recognize his visitor's divinity.

13:17-18 The Lord's *name* is a divine secret (Gen 32:29; Exod 3:13-14). God knows our names, but in addressing him we are limited to terms of wonder and adoration, for the true essence of the infinite cannot be expressed or understood by the finite.

13:19-22 It is not possible for human beings to take in the full revelation of God's holy presence and still live (cp. 6:20-24; Exod 19:21; 33:20). The OT frequently reports divine visitations on earth in human form; these visitations foreshadow the full appearance of God on earth in the incarnation of Jesus.

13:25 Inspired leaders are filled with the divine *Spirit*. In spite of Samson's evident failures, the Spirit's presence was powerfully at work in him. • ***Mahaneh-dan*** (literally *camp of Dan*) is mentioned again in 18:12; the phrase could describe a temporary settlement rather than a fixed location. • ***Zorah*** (13:2) and ***Eshtaol*** were in the valley of Sorek, about fifteen miles west of Jerusalem at the pass that leads down to Philistine territory.

14:1–15:20 Samson's choice to marry a Philistine woman was the Lord's

he told his father and mother, "A young Philistine woman in Timnah caught my eye. I
want to marry her. Get her for me."
3His father and mother objected. "Isn't
there even one woman in our tribe or
among all the Israelites you could marry?"
they asked. "Why must you go to the pagan
Philistines to find a wife?"
But Samson told his father, "Get her for
me! She looks good to me." 4His father and
mother didn't realize the LORD was at work
in this, creating an opportunity to work
against the Philistines, who ruled over Israel at that time.
5As Samson and his parents were going
down to Timnah, a young lion suddenly
attacked Samson near the vineyards of
Timnah. 6At that moment the Spirit of the
LORD came powerfully upon him, and he
ripped the lion's jaws apart with his bare
hands. He did it as easily as if it were a
young goat. But he didn't tell his father or
mother about it. 7When Samson arrived in
Timnah, he talked with the woman and was
very pleased with her.
8Later, when he returned to Timnah for
the wedding, he turned off the path to look
at the carcass of the lion. And he found that a
swarm of bees had made some honey in the
carcass. 9He scooped some of the honey into
his hands and ate it along the way. He also
gave some to his father and mother, and they
ate it. But he didn't tell them he had taken
the honey from the carcass of the lion.
10As his father was making final arrangements for the marriage, Samson threw a
party at Timnah, as was the custom for elite
young men. 11When the bride's parents saw
him, they selected thirty young men from
the town to be his companions.
12Samson said to them, "Let me tell you a
riddle. If you solve my riddle during these
seven days of the celebration, I will give you
thirty fine linen robes and thirty sets of festive clothing. 13But if you can't solve it, then
you must give me thirty fine linen robes and
thirty sets of festive clothing."
"All right," they agreed, "let's hear your
riddle."
14So he said:

"Out of the one who eats came
something to eat;
out of the strong came something
sweet."

Three days later they were still trying to
figure it out. 15On the fourth day they said
to Samson's wife, "Entice your husband to explain the riddle for us, or we will burn down
your father's house with you in it. Did you
invite us to this party just to make us poor?"
16So Samson's wife came to him in tears
and said, "You don't love me; you hate me!
You have given my people a riddle, but you
haven't told me the answer."
"I haven't even given the answer to my father or mother," he replied. "Why should I
tell you?" 17So she cried whenever she was
with him and kept it up for the rest of the celebration. At last, on the seventh day he told
her the answer because she was tormenting
him with her nagging. Then she explained
the riddle to the young men.
18So before sunset of the seventh day, the
men of the town came to Samson with their
answer:

"What is sweeter than honey?
What is stronger than a lion?"

Samson replied, "If you hadn't plowed
with my heifer, you wouldn't have solved my
riddle!"
19Then the Spirit of the LORD came powerfully upon him. He went down to the town

14:2 Gen 21:21
14:3 Deut 7:3
14:4 Josh 11:20
14:6 Judg 13:25; 1 Sam 17:34-36
14:12 Gen 29:27; Ezek 17:2
14:15 Judg 15:6; 16:5
14:19 Judg 3:10

means (14:4) of beginning to confront the Philistine challenge (see 13:5). One thing led to another, punctuated by three occasions when the Spirit *came powerfully upon him* (14:6, 19; 15:14). Throughout these events, Samson was a powerful but flawed hero.

14:1 *Timnah* was probably about four miles down the valley of Sorek from Mahaneh-dan, at the intersection of the Israelite and Philistine territories.

14:2 Samson's choice of a bride was informed only by his pleasure in her appearance. Intermarriage was a significant mark of covenant infidelity (Josh 23:12-13), but God is able to work through human sinfulness.

14:3 The epithet *pagan* (literally *uncircumcised*) was regularly applied to Philistines, who, unlike many nations in the Middle East, did not practice any form of circumcision.

14:5-6 Samson was first explicitly empowered by *the Spirit* (cp. 13:25) when he was *attacked* by a *lion*.

14:11 *the bride's parents:* Literally *they.* • The reason for *thirty . . . companions* is not clear (cp. 2 Sam 23:13). *Companions,* a word that normally means "friends," may lend a touch of irony here (14:12-20).

14:12 Riddles were common tests of skill or a form of entertainment that usually employed double meanings. Despite some evidence for bees building hives in the bodies of dead animals, there was no apparent way to crack the mystery apart from knowing what Samson knew.

14:14-19 Israel's hero, like Sisera, was defeated by a woman (4:21; see note at 8:20-21).

14:15 *fourth:* As in Greek version; Hebrew reads *seventh.*

14:18 It was common to answer a riddle with another riddle. In this case, the Philistines used a similar poetic couplet, not to reveal all they knew, but simply to win the contest.

14:19 *Samson* kept his side of the deal (cp. 1 Sam 18:20-27). He apparently returned home without consummating his marriage, which traditionally would have happened at the end of the seven days of feasting.

14:20 John 3:29
15:2 Judg 14:20
15:6 Judg 14:15
15:11 Judg 13:1; 14:4; 15:20
15:14 Judg 14:19
15:15 Lev 26:8

of Ashkelon, killed thirty men, took their belongings, and gave their clothing to the men
who had solved his riddle. But Samson was
furious about what had happened, and he
went back home to live with his father and
mother. 20 So his wife was given in marriage
to the man who had been Samson's best
man at the wedding.

Samson's Vengeance on the Philistines

15 Later on, during the wheat harvest,
Samson took a young goat as a present to his wife. He said, "I'm going into my
wife's room to sleep with her," but her father wouldn't let him in.

2 "I truly thought you must hate her," her
father explained, "so I gave her in marriage
to your best man. But look, her younger sister is even more beautiful than she is. Marry
her instead."

3 Samson said, "This time I cannot be
blamed for everything I am going to do
to you Philistines." 4 Then he went out and
caught 300 foxes. He tied their tails together
in pairs, and he fastened a torch to each
pair of tails. 5 Then he lit the torches and let
the foxes run through the grain fields of the
Philistines. He burned all their grain to the
ground, including the sheaves and the uncut
grain. He also destroyed their vineyards and
olive groves.

6 "Who did this?" the Philistines demanded.

"Samson," was the reply, "because his
father-in-law from Timnah gave Samson's
wife to be married to his best man." So the
Philistines went and got the woman and her
father and burned them to death.

7 "Because you did this," Samson vowed,
"I won't rest until I take my revenge on you!"
8 So he attacked the Philistines with great
fury and killed many of them. Then he went
to live in a cave in the rock of Etam.

9 The Philistines retaliated by setting up
camp in Judah and spreading out near the
town of Lehi. 10 The men of Judah asked
the Philistines, "Why are you attacking
us?"

The Philistines replied, "We've come to
capture Samson. We've come to pay him
back for what he did to us."

11 So 3,000 men of Judah went down to
get Samson at the cave in the rock of Etam.
They said to Samson, "Don't you realize the
Philistines rule over us? What are you doing
to us?"

But Samson replied, "I only did to them
what they did to me."

12 But the men of Judah told him, "We
have come to tie you up and hand you over
to the Philistines."

"All right," Samson said. "But promise that
you won't kill me yourselves."

13 "We will only tie you up and hand you
over to the Philistines," they replied. "We
won't kill you." So they tied him up with two
new ropes and brought him up from the
rock.

14 As Samson arrived at Lehi, the Philistines
came shouting in triumph. But the Spirit of
the LORD came powerfully upon Samson,
and he snapped the ropes on his arms as
if they were burnt strands of flax, and they
fell from his wrists. 15 Then he found the jawbone of a recently killed donkey. He picked
it up and killed 1,000 Philistines with it.
16 Then Samson said,

"With the jawbone of a donkey,
I've piled them in heaps!

14:20 According to some ancient customs, giving the bride to the *best man*, even if the marriage was not consummated, was forbidden. The father's action appears to have been treacherous (cp. 15:2-3, 6).

15:1 *Wheat harvest* came at the end of May; how long this was after the wedding feast is not known. There was some precedent for a bride's remaining in her parents' home for a few months before moving to the groom's home, while allowing conjugal visits.

15:2 The *father* may have thought that his daughter had been abandoned (see note on 14:20). The father's offer of the *younger sister* might have been an attempt to remedy his own treachery

15:3-5 In revenge, Samson devastated the harvest of *grain*, wine (*vineyards*), and cooking oil (*olive groves*).

15:6-10 The chain of revenge was complicated (cp. 9:7-21). First, *Samson* took revenge on the community of Philistines, not on his in-laws. Next, *the Philistines* accepted that Samson was a victim of injustice (see note on 14:20) and took revenge on Samson's in-laws, which then led Samson to avenge his in-laws by attacking the Philistines. It all triggered a potential war with Israel. God was beginning to rescue Israel through Samson (13:5; cp. 1 Sam 7:3).

15:11 Completely missing what might have been a divine opportunity to throw off Philistine oppression, the tribe of *Judah* showed itself ready to continue living under foreign occupation. We can only wonder what might have happened if the Judeans had been fully committed to the Lord's covenant, which provided for them to take the land and drive out the inhabitants (see note on 1:1).

15:12 *promise that you won't kill me:* Samson's superhuman abilities might have been limited to use against the enemies of Israel; he broke these ropes only after the Spirit of the Lord came upon him (15:14).

15:13 *New ropes* were stronger, more pliable, and less brittle than older ones.

15:14-15 Both Samson and the Judeans seem to have been satisfied with this relatively small victory and did not follow up by overthrowing Philistine oppression. This failure reflects Israel's declining confidence in God's promises.

15:16 Like other warrior-heroes (e.g., Moses, Deborah, and David), Samson celebrated his victory in poetry, a

With the jawbone of a donkey,
I've killed a thousand men!"

17When he finished his boasting, he threw away the jawbone; and the place was named Jawbone Hill.

18Samson was now very thirsty, and he cried out to the LORD, "You have accomplished this great victory by the strength of your servant. Must I now die of thirst and fall into the hands of these pagans?" 19So God caused water to gush out of a hollow in the ground at Lehi, and Samson was revived as he drank. Then he named that place "The Spring of the One Who Cried Out," and it is still in Lehi to this day.

20Samson judged Israel for twenty years during the period when the Philistines dominated the land.

Samson Carries Away Gaza's Gates

16 One day Samson went to the Philistine town of Gaza and spent the night with a prostitute. 2Word soon spread that Samson was there, so the men of Gaza gathered together and waited all night at the town gates. They kept quiet during the night, saying to themselves, "When the light of morning comes, we will kill him."

3But Samson stayed in bed only until midnight. Then he got up, took hold of the doors of the town gate, including the two posts, and lifted them up, bar and all. He put them on his shoulders and carried them all the way to the top of the hill across from Hebron.

Samson and Delilah

4Some time later Samson fell in love with a woman named Delilah, who lived in the valley of Sorek. 5The rulers of the Philistines went to her and said, "Entice Samson to tell you what makes him so strong and how he can be overpowered and tied up securely. Then each of us will give you 1,100 pieces of silver."

6So Delilah said to Samson, "Please tell me what makes you so strong and what it would take to tie you up securely."

7Samson replied, "If I were tied up with seven new bowstrings that have not yet been dried, I would become as weak as anyone else."

8So the Philistine rulers brought Delilah seven new bowstrings, and she tied Samson up with them. 9She had hidden some men in one of the inner rooms of her house, and she cried out, "Samson! The Philistines have come to capture you!" But Samson snapped the bowstrings as a piece of string snaps when it is burned by a fire. So the secret of his strength was not discovered.

10Afterward Delilah said to him, "You've been making fun of me and telling me lies! Now please tell me how you can be tied up securely."

11Samson replied, "If I were tied up with brand-new ropes that had never been used, I would become as weak as anyone else."

12So Delilah took new ropes and tied him up with them. The men were hiding in the inner room as before, and again Delilah cried out, "Samson! The Philistines have

15:19 Gen 45:27; 1 Sam 30:12; Isa 40:29
15:20 Judg 13:1; 16:31; Heb 11:32
16:1 Josh 15:47
16:2 Ps 118:10-12
16:5 Judg 14:15
16:11 Judg 15:13

short couplet that combines colorful speech with word-play. "Lehi" (15:9) and ***jawbone*** are the same Hebrew word (*lekhi*), as are ***heaps*** and ***donkey*** (Hebrew *khamor*). • ***piled them in heaps!*** Or *made donkeys of them.*

15:17 ***Jawbone Hill:*** Hebrew *Ramath-lehi.*

15:18 Samson ***cried out to the LORD,*** as he feared dying of ***thirst*** and falling prey to the defeated ***pagans*** (literally *uncircumcised ones;* see note on 14:3). Samson twice prayed deep and passionate prayers, once when he feared being attacked, and once when he was attacking others (16:28-30).

15:19 ***The Spring of the One Who Cried Out:*** Hebrew *En-hakkore.*

15:20 Though this summary formula is repeated in 16:31, its occurrence here indicates that Samson's period as judge was effectively over (cp. 10:2, 3; 12:7). He had done little more than show Israel the potential of rescue; ***the Philistines*** still ***dominated the land.***

16:1-31 There is nothing of judgeship in this last chapter of Samson's checkered history. Samson effectively abandoned his calling and was eventually stripped of his gifting as well. Only in his final encounter, when he again turned to the Lord in prayer, did any of his heroic stature revive.

16:2-3 City ***gates*** of the period were locked ***during the night*** to prevent passage in or out, and the men of the city, having seen the gates locked, probably slept (***kept quiet***) in one of the gate houses, thinking that they could resume their vigil in the morning.

16:2 This verse is translated as in the Greek and Syriac versions and Latin Vulgate; Hebrew lacks ***word soon spread.***

16:3 Samson had to pick up the entire six- to twelve-foot-wide ***gate*** system and take it to the hills ***across from Hebron,*** a town about forty miles distant. Samson humiliated the Philistines but did nothing to defeat them.

16:4-22 Samson's dissipation and defeat by ***Delilah*** the temptress has the universal appeal of great tragedy.

16:5 The Philistine rulers knew that direct confrontation with Samson would not succeed, so they resorted to subterfuge. The generous offer by the ***rulers*** (literally ***lords***) of the five Philistine cities (3:3) shows how seriously the Philistines took this matter. • ***1,100 pieces:*** Hebrew *1,100 shekels,* about 28 pounds or 12.5 kilograms in weight.

16:6 The desire for silver rather than self-preservation (cp. 14:15) seems to have motivated Delilah; she apparently did not reciprocate Samson's love.

16:7 ***Bowstrings*** were commonly made of dried animal tendons or gut. ***Seven*** was a symbolic number, perhaps connected with the Philistines' sense of magical power. Samson seems more at home in a Philistine cultural setting than in keeping his Israelite vows that bound him as a Nazirite.

16:11 ***Brand-new ropes*** had already been tried (15:13-14).

16:15
Judg 14:16
16:17
Num 6:2, 5
Judg 13:5
16:20
1 Sam 16:14; 18:12
16:23
1 Sam 5:2
16:24
[i]*halal* (1984)
‣2 Chr 5:13
16:28
Judg 15:18
[j]*zakar* (2142)
‣1 Sam 1:19

come to capture you!" But again Samson
snapped the ropes from his arms as if they
were thread.
13 Then Delilah said, "You've been making
fun of me and telling me lies! Now tell me
how you can be tied up securely."
Samson replied, "If you were to weave the
seven braids of my hair into the fabric on
your loom and tighten it with the loom shuttle, I would become as weak as anyone else."
So while he slept, Delilah wove the seven
braids of his hair into the fabric.
14 Then she
tightened it with the loom shuttle. Again
she cried out, "Samson! The Philistines have
come to capture you!" But Samson woke up,
pulled back the loom shuttle, and yanked
his hair away from the loom and the fabric.
15 Then Delilah pouted, "How can you tell
me, 'I love you,' when you don't share your
secrets with me? You've made fun of me
three times now, and you still haven't told
me what makes you so strong!"
16 She tor-
mented him with her nagging day after day
until he was sick to death of it.
17 Finally, Samson shared his secret with
her. "My hair has never been cut," he confessed, "for I was dedicated to God as a
Nazirite from birth. If my head were shaved,
my strength would leave me, and I would become as weak as anyone else."
18 Delilah realized he had finally told her
the truth, so she sent for the Philistine rulers. "Come back one more time," she said,
"for he has finally told me his secret." So the
Philistine rulers returned with the money
in their hands.
19 Delilah lulled Samson to
sleep with his head in her lap, and then she
called in a man to shave off the seven locks
of his hair. In this way she began to bring
him down, and his strength left him.
20 Then she cried out, "Samson! The Philistines have come to capture you!"
When he woke up, he thought, "I will do
as before and shake myself free." But he
didn't realize the LORD had left him.
21 So the Philistines captured him and
gouged out his eyes. They took him to Gaza,
where he was bound with bronze chains
and forced to grind grain in the prison.
22 But before long, his hair began to grow
back.

Samson's Final Victory

23 The Philistine rulers held a great festival,
offering sacrifices and praising their god,
Dagon. They said, "Our god has given us victory over our enemy Samson!"
24 When the people saw him, they [i]praised
their god, saying, "Our god has delivered our
enemy to us! The one who killed so many of
us is now in our power!"
25 Half drunk by now, the people demanded, "Bring out Samson so he can amuse
us!" So he was brought from the prison to
amuse them, and they had him stand between the pillars supporting the roof.
26 Samson said to the young servant who
was leading him by the hand, "Place my
hands against the pillars that hold up the
temple. I want to rest against them."
27 Now
the temple was completely filled with people.
All the Philistine rulers were there, and there
were about 3,000 men and women on the
roof who were watching as Samson amused
them.
28 Then Samson prayed to the LORD, "Sovereign LORD, [j]remember me again. O God,
please strengthen me just one more time.
With one blow let me pay back the Philistines for the loss of my two eyes."
29 Then
Samson put his hands on the two center
pillars that held up the temple. Pushing
against them with both hands,
30 he prayed,
"Let me die with the Philistines." And the
temple crashed down on the Philistine rulers and all the people. So he killed more
people when he died than he had during
his entire lifetime.

16:13-14 These verses are translated as in the Greek version and Latin Vulgate; Hebrew lacks *I would become as weak as anyone else. / So while he slept, Delilah wove the seven braids of his hair into the fabric. 14Then she tightened it with the loom shuttle.* Possibly Samson's hair was actually woven into the fabric, perhaps as weft on the loom's warp, which was then tightened as in normal weaving.

16:16 Samson should have recognized his danger (cp. 14:17), but spiritual blindness had led to mental exhaustion.

16:17-19 Samson's ***hair*** was the sign of his vow to the Lord; when his hair was shorn, his vow would be broken. The ***seven*** braided ***locks*** were only a sign; the Lord's presence was the reality behind ***his strength***.

16:18 After being fooled three times, the ***rulers*** had given up and left. Now, however, they ***returned with the money in their hands***—they knew that this was the moment they had dreamed of.

16:19 ***she began to bring him down:*** Or *she began to torment him.* Greek version reads *He began to grow weak.*

16:20 Like the remorseful but presumptuous earlier Israelites (Num 14:40-45), Samson ***didn't realize*** that his hair was gone and that the divine presence had departed (cp. Hos 7:9).

16:22 There was no certainty that the Lord would revive Samson's strength when ***his hair began to grow back;*** there was only the hope that the Lord's earlier promise—that he would begin to rescue Israel through this strange and now broken hero—still stood.

16:23-24 In their boundless rejoicing, the Philistines gave all the credit to ***their god, Dagon***. In the pagan mind, the relative strength of nations reflected the power of their gods.

16:28-30 Though only for personal revenge, ***Samson*** furthered God's purpose of rescuing his people.

31Later his brothers and other relatives
went down to get his body. They took him
back home and buried him between Zorah and Eshtaol, where his father, Manoah,
was buried. Samson had judged Israel for
twenty years.

3. EPILOGUES (17:1–21:25)

Micah and the Tribe of Dan (17:1–18:31)

Micah's Idols

17 There was a man named Micah, who
lived in the hill country of Ephraim.
2One day he said to his mother, "I heard you
place a curse on the person who stole 1,100
pieces of silver from you. Well, I have the
money. I was the one who took it."

"The LORD bless you for admitting it," his
mother replied. 3He returned the money to
her, and she said, "I now dedicate these silver coins to the LORD. In honor of my son, I
will have an image carved and an idol cast."

4So when he returned the money to his
mother, she took 200 silver coins and gave
them to a silversmith, who made them into
an image and an idol. And these were placed
in Micah's house. 5Micah set up a shrine for
the idol, and he made a sacred ephod and
some household idols. Then he installed
one of his sons as his personal priest.

6In those days Israel had no king; all the
people did whatever seemed right in their
own eyes.

7One day a young Levite, who had been
living in Bethlehem in Judah, arrived in that
area. 8He had left Bethlehem in search of
another place to live, and as he traveled, he
came to the hill country of Ephraim. He happened to stop at Micah's house as he was
traveling through. 9"Where are you from?"
Micah asked him.

He replied, "I am a Levite from Bethlehem
in Judah, and I am looking for a place to live."

10"Stay here with me," Micah said, "and
you can be a father and priest to me. I will
give you ten pieces of silver a year, plus a
change of clothes and your food." 11The
Levite agreed to this, and the young man became like one of Micah's sons.

12So Micah installed the Levite as his personal priest, and he lived in Micah's house.
13"I know the LORD will bless me now," Micah said, "because I have a Levite serving as
my priest."

Idolatry in the Tribe of Dan

18 Now in those days Israel had no king.
And the tribe of Dan was trying to
find a place where they could settle, for they
had not yet moved into the land assigned to
them when the land was divided among the
tribes of Israel. 2So the men of Dan chose
from their clans five capable warriors from
the towns of Zorah and Eshtaol to scout out
a land for them to settle in.

16:31 Judg 15:20
17:3 Exod 20:4, 23; 34:17
17:5 Gen 31:19; Judg 8:27
17:6 Deut 12:8; Judg 18:1; 19:1; 21:25
17:7 Judg 19:1; Ruth 1:1-2; Mic 5:2; Matt 2:1
17:10 Judg 18:19
17:12 Num 16:10; Judg 18:1-7
18:1 Josh 19:40-48; Judg 17:6; 19:1
18:2 Judg 13:25

17:1–21:25 These two epilogues (17:1–18:31 and 19:1–21:25) attest that inspired but unstructured leadership cannot endure. During the relentless march toward social disintegration and civil war, the refrain, "In those days Israel had no king," occurs four times, and "all the people did whatever seemed right in their own eyes" is added twice (17:6; 18:1; 19:1; 21:25). The era of inspired leadership spiraled downward and culminated in chaos. Something was clearly missing.

17:1 *Micah* is the short form of a name that means "Who is like the LORD?" The name highlights the contrast between the Lord and a carved image or cast idol. • ***The hill country of Ephraim*** was a natural gathering place in central Israel (17:7-8; 18:2, 13; 19:1, 16).

17:2-3 Micah's ***mother*** was indulgent and idolatrous, yet she invoked the Lord's name in both cursing and blessing. • ***I heard you place a curse:*** The words uttered in curses and blessings were understood to have power, particularly if the speaker had the authority to utter such pronouncements (cp. Gen 27; Isa 55:11). • ***1,100 pieces:*** Hebrew *1,100 shekels,* about 28 pounds or 12.5 kilograms in weight. This same large number was given to Delilah (16:5). It was probably Micah's mother's life savings or dowry. • ***The LORD bless you:*** Micah's mother was hoping that the blessing would effectively neutralize her earlier curse.

17:4-5 We are not told what Micah's ***mother*** did with the other 900 shekels. Perhaps they went to pay for the ***shrine*** (literally *house of gods*).

17:5 ***ephod:*** See note on 8:27. • ***household idols:*** Cp. Gen 31:19-32; 2 Kgs 23:24; Zech 10:2. The Bible mocks the inabilities of these personal deities. Micah's installing ***one of his sons as his personal priest*** was triply irregular: The father was meant to be the religious head of the household (Deut 6:7; Job 1:5), only descendants of Aaron were to be priests (Exod 28:1–29:37; 30:30-33; 40:12-15), and priests were for the whole community of Israel, not for individuals or families.

17:7-8 Not much about this ***Levite*** fits into orthodox biblical categories. Some Levites were priests, while others were temple servants (cp. Num 3–4). Levites were scattered throughout Israel (Gen 49:5-7; Josh 21). This young man, apparently a descendant of Gershom (18:30; cp. Exod 2:21-22), was based in Judah, but not in a Levitical town, and was looking for ***another place to live.***

17:10 ***ten pieces:*** Hebrew *10 shekels,* about 4 ounces or 114 grams in weight.

17:13 The contract ***priest,*** in Micah's view, conferred some additional legitimacy on the shrine, though his expectation that ***the LORD*** would ***bless*** him was based on superstition rather than obedience to the Lord. Micah's abandonment of God's covenant would bring a curse on him that no unemployed ***Levite*** could ward off. Micah was not the last Israelite to seek out a priest or Levite in an attempt to legitimize irregular religious practices (cp. 1 Kgs 12:28-31; 2 Kgs 16:10-18).

18:1-31 The migration of the Danites (cp. Josh 19:40-48) is the story of that tribe's failure to obey God's covenant, and it is indicative of Israel's decline. What began as Micah's private heresy (17:4-5) would become the apostasy of an entire tribe (18:30-31). What began as covenant failure (1:19-36) turned into social breakdown in the days of Jephthah and Samson (chs 11–16). In the end, law and order were replaced by banditry and pillaging (18:27-28).

18:4
Judg 17:10-12
18:7
Josh 19:47
18:10
Deut 8:9

When these warriors arrived in the hill
country of Ephraim, they came to Micah's
house and spent the night there. [3]While at
Micah's house, they recognized the young
Levite's accent, so they went over and asked
him, "Who brought you here, and what are
you doing in this place? Why are you here?"
[4]He told them about his agreement with Micah and that he had been hired as Micah's
personal priest.
[5]Then they said, "Ask God whether or not
our journey will be successful."
[6]"Go in peace," the priest replied. "For the
LORD is watching over your journey."
[7]So the five men went on to the town of
Laish, where they noticed the people living
carefree lives, like the Sidonians; they were
peaceful and secure. The people were also
wealthy because their land was very fertile.
And they lived a great distance from Sidon
and had no allies nearby.
[8]When the men returned to Zorah and
Eshtaol, their relatives asked them, "What
did you find?"
[9]The men replied, "Come on, let's attack
them! We have seen the land, and it is very
good. What are you waiting for? Don't hesitate to go and take possession of it. [10]When

Social Chaos (17:1–21:25)

Judg 5:6-8; 6:25-27; 8:1-35; 12:1-15
Ps 11:2-7
Prov 28:2-3
Jer 5:7-9; 12:1-17
Mic 3:9-12; 7:2-7
Rom 1:21-32
Gal 5:19-23

The book of Judges celebrates divine rescue through heroes while chronicling the inadequacy of the status quo. A decline in individual piety throughout the period was accompanied by a rise in social dysfunction, powerfully expressed in ch 5 (e.g., 5:6-8). Three features of the times stand out: First, the tribes had little ability to function in unison, even when faced by a common enemy—as in the Gideon and Jephthah stories (chs 8, 12). The civil strife within and between tribes constantly recalls the results of covenant disobedience.

Jael's cunning assassination of Sisera, though it was part of God's plan to deliver Israel, illustrates the breakdown of civil society. The words of Sisera's mother and her circle (5:28-30) show that they expected a normal social order to be dominated by murder, rape, and plunder. Jephthah's apparent sacrifice of his daughter and Samson's revenge on his in-laws and their town similarly bespeak a world in which "might makes right."

Religious apostasy was widespread in those days. The altar to Baal and the Asherah pole in Gideon's town of Ophrah (6:23-27) indicate flagrant abandonment of the Lord. Gideon's ephod (8:22-27) was no innocent mistake in judgment; Gideon was hypocritical, rejecting human kingship while trying to establish it. Samson's intermarriage with the Philistines also directly contradicted the covenant commands (Deut 7:3).

Social chaos culminates in the closing chapters (chs 17–21). The incident of Micah, the Levite, and the Danites (chs 17–18) combines religious irregularities with lawless marauding, theft, and violence. The climactic final epilogue (chs 19–21) describes a tragic civil war and the abandonment of civility. Marital breakdown, inhospitality, rape, and murder (ch 19) led to the virtual elimination of the Benjamites (ch 20), who were spared only by the complete decimation of a historic city (Jabesh-gilead) and a sham ceremony in which maidens were seized as concubines (21:19-23). Little wonder that the book concludes, "In those days Israel had no king; all the people did whatever seemed right in their own eyes" (21:25).

18:2 ***Zorah and Eshtaol:*** Scouts were selected from the area where the Spirit of the Lord began to stir Samson (13:25). The mention of the two towns is a grim reminder that what began with Samson had not been completed, either by his own tribe (Dan) or by their powerful neighbor (Judah). These ***capable warriors***, rather than fighting the Lord's battles, bullied their fellow Israelites (18:24-25) and attacked a defenseless city (18:27; cp. Gen 49:17).

18:3-4 The Danites either ***recognized the young Levite's accent*** (literally *voice*) as belonging to the region of Judah (17:7) or recognized his voice because they had known him personally. Their line of questioning went beyond simply establishing his credentials to providing them with a bit of divine guidance (18:5). His reply (18:6) established his willingness to be a mercenary priest.

18:5-6 ***The LORD*** had already promised to give Dan an allotment in the southwest that they had failed to possess (see 1:34; Josh 19:40-48). Now they were asking God's blessing from a hired priest whose "blessing," like that of Micah's mother (17:2), sounded religious while having no basis in Israel's covenant with the Lord.

18:7 ***Laish*** has been extensively excavated and was an impressive city at this time. • ***they were peaceful and secure:*** The meaning of the Hebrew is uncertain. The description of Laish and its relationship to the port of ***Sidon*** is not entirely clear in the text or from recorded history. Perhaps the people of Laish expected, as a Phoenician outpost, to be exempt from Israel's attack on the Canaanites. This language is substantially repeated in 18:28.

18:9-10 The language resembles the report following the mission to spy out the land (Num 14:7-8; Deut 1:25), but the context is sharply different. Joshua and Caleb overcame their fear and acted in faith by remembering the Lord's promise (cp. Josh 2:9, 24; 6:2; 10:19, 30). The Danite warriors invoked God's blessing and recognized the value of the land, but their cocky self-assurance contrasts sharply with the godly faith of Joshua and Caleb.

you get there, you will find the people living
carefree lives. God has given us a spacious
and fertile land, lacking in nothing!"
11So 600 men from the tribe of Dan,
armed with weapons of war, set out from Zorah and Eshtaol. 12They camped at a place
west of Kiriath-jearim in Judah, which is
called Mahaneh-dan to this day. 13Then
they went on from there into the hill country of Ephraim and came to the house of
Micah.
14The five men who had scouted out the
land around Laish explained to the others,
"These buildings contain a sacred ephod, as
well as some household idols, a carved image, and a cast idol. What do you think you
should do?" 15Then the five men turned off
the road and went over to Micah's house,
where the young Levite lived, and greeted
him kindly. 16As the 600 armed warriors
from the tribe of Dan stood at the entrance
of the gate, 17the five scouts entered the
shrine and removed the carved image, the sacred ephod, the household idols, and the cast
idol. Meanwhile, the priest was standing at
the gate with the 600 armed warriors.
18When the priest saw the men carrying
all the sacred objects out of Micah's shrine,
he said, "What are you doing?"
19"Be quiet and come with us," they said.
"Be a father and priest to all of us. Isn't it better to be a priest for an entire tribe and clan
of Israel than for the household of just one
man?"
20The young priest was quite happy to
go with them, so he took along the sacred
ephod, the household idols, and the carved
image. 21They turned and started on their
way again, placing their children, livestock,
and possessions in front of them.
22When the people from the tribe of Dan
were quite a distance from Micah's house,
the people who lived near Micah came chasing after them. 23They were shouting as
they caught up with them. The men of Dan
turned around and said to Micah, "What's
the matter? Why have you called these men
together and chased after us like this?"
24"What do you mean, 'What's the matter?' " Micah replied. "You've taken away all
the gods I have made, and my priest, and I
have nothing left!"
25The men of Dan said, "Watch what you
say! There are some short-tempered men
around here who might get angry and kill
you and your family." 26So the men of Dan
continued on their way. When Micah saw
that there were too many of them for him
to attack, he turned around and went home.
27Then, with Micah's idols and his priest,
the men of Dan came to the town of Laish,
whose people were peaceful and secure.
They attacked with swords and burned the
town to the ground. 28There was no one
to rescue the people, for they lived a great
distance from Sidon and had no allies
nearby. This happened in the valley near
Beth-rehob.
Then the people of the tribe of Dan rebuilt
the town and lived there. 29They renamed
the town Dan after their ancestor, Israel's
son, but it had originally been called Laish.

18:14 Judg 17:5
18:19 Judg 17:10
18:27 Josh 19:47
18:28 2 Sam 10:6

18:12 ***Kiriath-jearim:*** In this town northwest of Jerusalem the Ark rested for twenty years (1 Sam 7:1-2) on its return from Philistine captivity. It lay on the border of Judah and Benjamin, and was given a memorial name associated with Dan's wanderings (cp. the different site of 13:25). The name ***Mahaneh-dan*** means "the camp of Dan."

18:14-26 The perfidy and insincerity of this exchange expose the ignoble values of all concerned.

18:14 ***sacred ephod . . . household idols . . . carved image . . . cast idol:*** See notes on 8:27 and 17:5.

18:15 Bypassing the host, the five unscrupulous scouts went straight to their target, the naive and unprincipled ***young Levite.***

18:16 The ***600 armed warriors*** were prepared to attack the single Levite. In contrast to Gideon's army of 300 arrayed against the Midianite hordes (7:2-11), the Danites were merely armed bullies.

18:18 The priest's rhetorical question was less an attempt to stop the theft than an expression of concern about his own future (cp. 18:20).

18:19 Using Micah's language (***be a father and priest***, 17:10), but without its generosity, the Danites' question was moot in light of the 600 men standing at the door.

18:20 ***The young priest*** was receptive to the offer; ignoring his generous benefactor, he joined in absconding with Micah's prized objects. The blessing of Micah's mother (17:3) was becoming ever more tarnished.

18:22 Some of Micah's neighbors had apparently become converts to the cult of his shrine.

18:23 The question was only intended to cow Micah into abandoning the fight.

18:24 Micah's last speech is pathetic and pitiful. He began by stealing from his own mother and ended by losing it all to worse thieves than himself. The narrative drips with irony, including Micah's loss of ***the gods I have made.*** His fate was that of all who forsake the Lord's covenant: ***I have nothing left!***

18:25 ***short-tempered*** (literally ***bitter of soul;*** "in deep anguish," 1 Sam 1:10; "discontented," 1 Sam 22:2; "enraged," 2 Sam 17:8): This term describes those whose bitter disappointment with life has made their actions unpredictable.

18:28 ***Beth-rehob*** was perhaps an Aramean kingdom to the north (2 Sam 10:6). Nothing heroic, and no holy war, accrued to these Danite warriors who captured this defenseless city. Dan fulfilled Jacob's mixed blessing by turning from the high calling of governing his people (Gen 49:16) to becoming "a snake beside the road, a poisonous viper along the path that bites the horse's hooves so its rider is thrown off" (Gen 49:17).

18:29-31 The city of ***Dan*** became the northernmost landmark of Israel's territory (e.g., 20:1; 2 Sam 3:10; 1 Kgs 4:25; 2 Chr 30:5). Its identity as a center of idolatry continued throughout its history (see 1 Kgs 12:28-30; Amos 8:14).

18:30 Exod 2:22; 18:3
18:31 Josh 18:1
19:1 Judg 18:1
19:3 Gen 34:3; 50:21
19:5 Gen 18:5
19:10 Josh 15:8; 1 Chr 11:4

30 Then they set up the carved image, and they appointed Jonathan son of Gershom, son of Moses, as their priest. This family continued as priests for the tribe of Dan until the Exile. 31 So Micah's carved image was worshiped by the tribe of Dan as long as the Tabernacle of God remained at Shiloh.

The Levite and the Tribe of Benjamin (19:1–21:25)

The Levite and His Concubine

19 Now in those days Israel had no king. There was a man from the tribe of Levi living in a remote area of the hill country of Ephraim. One day he brought home a woman from Bethlehem in Judah to be his concubine. 2 But she became angry with him and returned to her father's home in Bethlehem.

After about four months, 3 her husband set out for Bethlehem to speak personally to her and persuade her to come back. He took with him a servant and a pair of donkeys. When he arrived at her father's house, her father saw him and welcomed him. 4 Her father urged him to stay awhile, so he stayed three days, eating, drinking, and sleeping there.

5 On the fourth day the man was up early, ready to leave, but the woman's father said to his son-in-law, "Have something to eat before you go." 6 So the two men sat down together and had something to eat and drink. Then the woman's father said, "Please stay another night and enjoy yourself." 7 The man got up to leave, but his father-in-law kept urging him to stay, so he finally gave in and stayed the night.

8 On the morning of the fifth day he was up early again, ready to leave, and again the woman's father said, "Have something to eat; then you can leave later this afternoon." So they had another day of feasting. 9 Later, as the man and his concubine and servant were preparing to leave, his father-in-law said, "Look, it's almost evening. Stay the night and enjoy yourself. Tomorrow you can get up early and be on your way."

10 But this time the man was determined to leave. So he took his two saddled donkeys and his concubine and headed in the direction of Jebus (that is, Jerusalem). 11 It was late in the day when they neared Jebus, and the man's servant said to him, "Let's stop at this Jebusite town and spend the night there."

12 "No," his master said, "we can't stay in this foreign town where there are no Israelites. Instead, we will go on to Gibeah. 13 Come on, let's try to get as far as Gibeah or Ramah, and we'll spend the night in one of those towns."

18:30 The wandering Levite is now called *Jonathan*; he was a descendant of *Moses* through *Gershom* (Exod 2:21-22). • *son of Moses:* As in an ancient Hebrew tradition, some Greek manuscripts, and Latin Vulgate; Masoretic Text reads *son of Manasseh.* Later Hebrew scribes inserted a letter "n" into the Hebrew text, changing *Moses* to *Manasseh,* probably to preserve Moses' memory by distancing him from Jonathan's behavior. • *The Exile* is traditionally understood to have begun with the fall of the northern kingdom in 722 BC. In light of the reference to Shiloh (18:31), the exile of the Ark from Shiloh (1 Sam 4–6) might be in view.

18:31 The religious infidelity of *the tribe of Dan* continued at least through the period of the judges; whether it was corrected by Samuel, Saul, or David is nowhere stated. • Joshua took *Shiloh,* a town in the hill country of Ephraim, as his command post and central shrine (Josh 18:1) during the conquest and distribution of the land (Josh 18–22). The priest Eli and his sons ministered before the Lord at Shiloh (1 Sam 1:3). The town and sanctuary were probably destroyed by Philistines about 1050 BC (see 1 Sam 4:1-11). Shiloh was later remembered as an example of God's judgment on false worship conducted in his name (see Jer 7:12-14; 26:6; cp. Ps 78:60).

19:1–21:25 This second epilogue (see note on 17:1–21:25) shifts the focus from individuals to whole tribes. Beginning with the outrage in the Benjamite town of Gibeah (ch 19), which led to civil war (ch 20) and the decimation of Benjamin, and moving on to the attempt to rescue the tribe from oblivion (ch 21), the book concludes with the now-familiar refrain, ***in those days Israel had no king; all the people did whatever seemed right in their own eyes.*** This was perhaps the low point in Israel's own remembered history; these are the "days of Gibeah" that Hosea, 400 years later, would liken to the depths to which Ephraim had sunk (Hos 9:9; 10:9). • The way had been cleared for a transition from charismatic leadership to what might be called "covenant-charismatic kingship," i.e., kingship that combined living under the Lord's covenant (Deut 17:14-20) with the anointing of the Spirit for the task of ruling, as with Saul and David.

19:1 A ***concubine*** was a second-class wife. In a society where polygamy was common, a concubine could be purchased, acquired as repayment of debt, or taken in war. A concubine was sometimes added to make up for a deficiency in a legitimate wife (e.g., Gen 16:1-4; 30:3-13; 35:22), but in the case of the Levite there appears to have been no other wife.

19:2 ***she became angry with him:*** Or *she was unfaithful to him.*

19:3 ***When he arrived at:*** As in Greek version; Hebrew reads *When she brought him to.*

19:4 The woman's ***father*** demonstrated typical Near Eastern hospitality, in contrast to what would later transpire in Gibeah (19:14-28). The scene in Bethlehem offers reconciliation and the promise of a new beginning.

19:5-7 Although some have suggested that the delay in leaving was analogous to Samson's seven-day bridal feast (14:10-20), the picture may reflect nothing more than the father's reluctance to bid his daughter farewell.

19:10 ***Jebus:*** See note on 1:21. The city's old name and its foreign status in Israel persisted until its capture by David (2 Sam 5:6-10).

19:13 The two Benjamite towns of ***Gibeah*** and ***Ramah*** have a prominent place in Israelite history, connected as they are with judges (Deborah, 4:5), priests (Eleazar, Josh 24:33), prophets (Samuel, 1 Sam 8:4), and kings (Saul, 1 Sam 10:26). The account of Gibeah's noble history compounds the tragedy of the events that followed.

14So they went on. The sun was setting as
they came to Gibeah, a town in the land of
Benjamin, 15so they stopped there to spend
the night. They rested in the town square, but
no one took them in for the night.
16That evening an old man came home
from his work in the fields. He was from the
hill country of Ephraim, but he was living in
Gibeah, where the people were from the
tribe of Benjamin. 17When he saw the travelers sitting in the town square, he asked
them where they were from and where they
were going.
18"We have been in Bethlehem in Judah,"
the man replied. "We are on our way to a
remote area in the hill country of Ephraim,
which is my home. I traveled to Bethlehem,
and now I'm returning home. But no one
has taken us in for the night, 19even though
we have everything we need. We have straw
and feed for our donkeys and plenty of
bread and wine for ourselves."
20"You are welcome to stay with me," the
old man said. "I will give you anything you
might need. But whatever you do, don't
spend the night in the square." 21So he took
them home with him and fed the donkeys.
After they washed their feet, they ate and
drank together.
22While they were enjoying themselves,
a crowd of [k]troublemakers from the town
surrounded the house. They began beating
at the door and shouting to the old man,
"Bring out the man who is staying with you
so we can have sex with him."
23The old man stepped outside to talk
to them. "No, my brothers, don't do such
an evil thing. For this man is a guest in my
house, and such a thing would be shameful.
24Here, take my virgin daughter and this
man's concubine. I will bring them out to
you, and you can abuse them and do whatever you like. But don't do such a shameful
thing to this man."
25But they wouldn't listen to him. So
the Levite took hold of his concubine and
pushed her out the door. The men of the
town abused her all night, taking turns
raping her until morning. Finally, at dawn
they let her go. 26At daybreak the woman
returned to the house where her husband
was staying. She collapsed at the door of the
house and lay there until it was light.
27When her husband opened the door
to leave, there lay his concubine with her
hands on the threshold. 28He said, "Get up!
Let's go!" But there was no answer. So he put
her body on his donkey and took her home.
29When he got home, he took a knife
and cut his concubine's body into twelve
pieces. Then he sent one piece to each tribe
throughout all the territory of Israel.
30Everyone who saw it said, "Such a horrible crime has not been committed in all
the time since Israel left Egypt. Think about
it! What are we going to do? Who's going to
speak up?"

Israel's War with Benjamin

20 Then all the Israelites were united
as one man, from Dan in the north
to Beersheba in the south, including those
from across the Jordan in the land of Gilead.
The entire community assembled in the presence of the LORD at Mizpah. 2The leaders of
all the people and all the tribes of Israel—
400,000 warriors armed with swords—took
their positions in the assembly of the people
of God. 3(Word soon reached the land of
Benjamin that the other tribes had gone up
to Mizpah.) The Israelites then asked how
this terrible crime had happened.

19:16 Ps 104:23
19:18 Judg 18:31
19:21 Gen 24:32-33
19:22 Gen 19:4-5
[k]*beliya'al* (1100) ▸1 Sam 1:16
19:23 Gen 34:7; 2 Sam 13:12
19:24 Gen 19:8
19:28 Judg 20:5
19:29 1 Sam 11:7
19:30 Judg 20:7
20:1 1 Sam 7:5

19:15 The normal rules of hospitality in Israel and the rest of the Near East obligated a citizen of the town to take them in (cp. Isa 58:7; Luke 14:13-14; Rom 12:13; 1 Tim 3:2; 5:10; Heb 13:2; 1 Pet 4:9). The Levite had funds and provisions (19:19), so there was even less excuse. This erosion of common civility is yet another evidence of social dysfunction at the time of Judges.

19:16 The *old man* was *from the hill country of Ephraim* rather than the territory of Benjamin. The natives of Gibeah were all unwilling to help.

19:18 *now I'm returning home:* As in Greek version (see also 19:29); Hebrew reads *now I'm going to the Tabernacle of the LORD.* The Levite said nothing about his own status, or about why he was traveling.

19:20 The note of urgency in the old man's response foreshadowed the coming trouble (cp. Gen 19:2-3).

19:22 *troublemakers:* Hebrew *sons of Belial;* see notes on 1 Kgs 21:10; 1 Sam 1:16; 2 Cor 6:15. Their goal was homosexual rape. Cp. Gen 19:4-5.

19:23 *For this man is a guest in my house:* It was *shameful* to be inhospitable to a visitor, but the *evil* demands of the crowd went beyond lack of hospitality. They intended violence against the visitor (see 20:5).

19:24 The old man attempted to preserve the social obligation of hospitality at the cost of handing over the vulnerable to be harmed (cp. Jas 1:27). There is no way, for our age or theirs, to soften the horror of what followed. The period of the judges was coming to an end in deepest depravity. Something was fundamentally amiss.

19:25 Contrast the instruction to husbands in Eph 5:25-28.

19:28-29 The Levite's actions exemplify the horror of a corrupt culture.

19:28 Greek version adds *for she was dead.*

20:1 This was not the *Mizpah* east of the Jordan associated with Jephthah (10:17; 11:11, 29, 34), but a place in central Israel. This common name means "watchtower."

20:3 The tribe of *Benjamin* had probably received the summons (19:29), so they knew that trouble was brewing.

20:5 Judg 19:22, 25-26
20:6-7 Judg 19:29-30
20:12 Deut 13:14
20:13 1 Cor 5:13
20:16 Judg 3:15
20:18 Num 27:21; Judg 1:1
20:23 Josh 7:6-7

[4]The Levite, the husband of the woman
who had been murdered, said, "My concubine and I came to spend the night in Gibeah,
a town that belongs to the people of Benjamin. [5]That night some of the leading citizens
of Gibeah surrounded the house, planning
to kill me, and they raped my concubine
until she was dead. [6]So I cut her body into
twelve pieces and sent the pieces throughout the territory assigned to Israel, for these
men have committed a terrible and shameful crime. [7]Now then, all of you—the entire
community of Israel—must decide here and
now what should be done about this!"

[8]And all the people rose to their feet
in unison and declared, "None of us will
return home! No, not even one of us! [9]In-
stead, this is what we will do to Gibeah;
we will draw lots to decide who will attack
it. [10]One-tenth of the men from each tribe
will be chosen to supply the warriors with
food, and the rest of us will take revenge
on Gibeah of Benjamin for this shameful
thing they have done in Israel." [11]So all the
Israelites were completely united, and they
gathered together to attack the town.

[12]The Israelites sent messengers to the
tribe of Benjamin, saying, "What a terrible
thing has been done among you! [13]Give up
those evil men, those troublemakers from
Gibeah, so we can execute them and purge
Israel of this evil."

But the people of Benjamin would not
listen. [14]Instead, they came from their
towns and gathered at Gibeah to fight the
Israelites. [15]In all, 26,000 of their warriors
armed with swords arrived in Gibeah to
join the 700 elite troops who lived there.
[16]Among Benjamin's elite troops, 700 were
left-handed, and each of them could sling a
rock and hit a target within a hairsbreadth
without missing. [17]Israel had 400,000 experienced soldiers armed with swords, not
counting Benjamin's warriors.

[18]Before the battle the Israelites went to
Bethel and asked God, "Which tribe should
go first to attack the people of Benjamin?"

The LORD answered, "Judah is to go first."

[19]So the Israelites left early the next
morning and camped near Gibeah. [20]Then
they advanced toward Gibeah to attack the
men of Benjamin. [21]But Benjamin's warriors, who were defending the town, came
out and killed 22,000 Israelites on the battlefield that day.

[22]But the Israelites encouraged each other
and took their positions again at the same
place they had fought the previous day.
[23]For they had gone up to Bethel and wept
in the presence of the LORD until evening.
They had asked the LORD, "Should we fight
against our relatives from Benjamin again?"

And the LORD had said, "Go out and fight
against them."

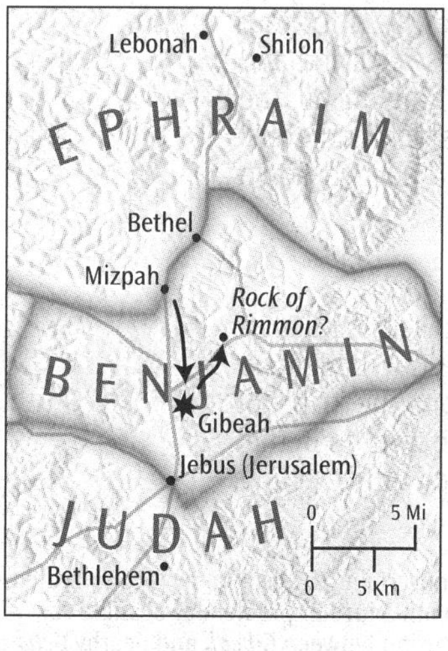

◀ **Israel's War with Benjamin (20:1-48).** In response to the episode of the Levite and his concubine (ch 19), the forces of Israel assembled at MIZPAH on the border of BENJAMIN. They then attacked and destroyed GIBEAH and most of the men of Benjamin. The remaining 600 Benjamites escaped to the ROCK OF RIMMON, where they were captured. The people of Israel then assembled at BETHEL (21:1-25).

20:5 The "troublemakers" (19:22) were *leading citizens* (literally *lords*). • ***planning to kill me:*** The death of his concubine convinced the Levite that the men of Gibeah intended his death.

20:9 The *lots* may have been the Urim and Thummim on the priest's breastplate (Exod 28:30; cp. Josh 14:2; 1 Sam 14:41; Ezra 2:63).

20:10 *One tenth of the men:* Literally *10 men from every hundred, 100 men from every thousand, and 1,000 men from every 10,000.* • ***Gibeah:*** Hebrew *Geba*, in this case a variant spelling of Gibeah; also in 20:33.

20:12-13 Israel recognized corporate responsibility. The leading citizens of *Gibeah* were guilty (20:5), and all of Gibeah became an accessory to their crimes by failing to discipline them. *The tribe of Benjamin*, in turn, had a responsibility to bring *Gibeah* to justice; failing that, they all shared the guilt. Had Israel not done something about Benjamin's sin, the guilt would then have extended to the entire nation.

20:13-17 Benjamin's response was consistent with its independent and warlike character (cp. Gen 49:27). The tribe had justifiable confidence in the warriors for which it was famous (3:12-30; 1 Chr 12:2). Though outnumbered almost three to one, they defeated the rest of Israel twice and inflicted heavy casualties (20:18-24).

20:16 *left-handed:* See note on 3:15. • The *sling* was of the same type as the one David used to kill Goliath (1 Sam 17:40-51). The slinger buried a stone in a small pouch attached to a leather thong, then swung it around his head to gain momentum before releasing one end of the thong to shoot the missile. A slinger had the advantage of distance over a swordsman.

20:18 To *go first* means to lead, not necessarily to precede (Gen 49:10).

20:19-21 The three battles took place around the guilty city. Despite superior numbers and having asked the Lord for guidance, the Israelite troops facing the defenders behind their walls were soundly beaten back the first day.

20:22-23 Following a time of weeping and probably confession (cp. Josh 7) the Israelite troops received divine guidance and regained confidence.

24 So the next day they went out again to fight against the men of Benjamin, 25 but the men of Benjamin killed another 18,000 Israelites, all of whom were experienced with the sword.

26 Then all the Israelites went up to Bethel and wept in the presence of the LORD and fasted until evening. They also brought burnt offerings and peace offerings to the LORD. 27 The Israelites went up seeking direction from the LORD. (In those days the Ark of the Covenant of God was in Bethel, 28 and Phinehas son of Eleazar and grandson of Aaron was the priest.) The Israelites asked the LORD, "Should we fight against our relatives from Benjamin again, or should we stop?"

The LORD said, "Go! Tomorrow I will hand them over to you."

29 So the Israelites set an ambush all around Gibeah. 30 They went out on the third day and took their positions at the same place as before. 31 When the men of Benjamin came out to attack, they were drawn away from the town. And as they had done before, they began to kill the Israelites. About thirty Israelites died in the open fields and along the roads, one leading to Bethel and the other leading back to Gibeah.

32 Then the warriors of Benjamin shouted, "We're defeating them as we did before!" But the Israelites had planned in advance to run away so that the men of Benjamin would chase them along the roads and be drawn away from the town.

33 When the main group of Israelite warriors reached Baal-tamar, they turned and took up their positions. Meanwhile, the Israelites hiding in ambush to the west of Gibeah jumped up to fight. 34 There were 10,000 elite Israelite troops who advanced against Gibeah. The fighting was so heavy that Benjamin didn't realize the impending disaster. 35 So the LORD helped Israel defeat Benjamin, and that day the Israelites killed 25,100 of Benjamin's warriors, all of whom were experienced swordsmen. 36 Then the men of Benjamin saw that they were beaten.

The Israelites had retreated from Benjamin's warriors in order to give those hiding in ambush more room to maneuver against Gibeah. 37 Then those who were hiding rushed in from all sides and killed everyone in the town. 38 They had arranged to send up a large cloud of smoke from the town as a signal. 39 When the Israelites saw the smoke, they turned and attacked Benjamin's warriors.

By that time Benjamin's warriors had killed about thirty Israelites, and they shouted, "We're defeating them as we did in the first battle!" 40 But when the warriors of Benjamin looked behind them and saw the smoke rising into the sky from every part of the town, 41 the men of Israel turned and attacked. At this point the men of Benjamin became terrified, because they realized disaster was close at hand. 42 So they turned around and fled before the Israelites toward the wilderness. But they couldn't escape the battle, and the people who came out of the nearby towns were also killed. 43 The Israelites surrounded the men of Benjamin and chased them relentlessly, finally overtaking them east of Gibeah. 44 That day 18,000 of Benjamin's strongest warriors died in battle. 45 The survivors fled into the wilderness toward the rock of Rimmon, but Israel killed 5,000 of them along the road. They continued the chase until they had killed another 2,000 near Gidom.

46 So that day the tribe of Benjamin lost 25,000 strong warriors armed with swords, 47 leaving only 600 men who escaped to the rock of Rimmon, where they lived for four months. 48 And the Israelites returned and slaughtered every living thing in all the towns—the people, the livestock, and everything they found. They also burned down all the towns they came to.

Israel Provides Wives for Benjamin

21 The Israelites had vowed at Mizpah, "We will never give our daughters in marriage to a man from the tribe of Benjamin." 2 Now the people went to Bethel and sat in the presence of God until evening,

20:26 Judg 21:2-4
20:27 Judg 20:18
20:31 Josh 8:16
20:33 Josh 8:19
20:34 Josh 8:14
20:36 Josh 8:15
20:37-38 Josh 8:19-20
20:40-41 Josh 8:20-21
20:42 Josh 8:15, 24
20:45 Judg 21:13

20:24-25 A second debacle shook the confidence of the Israelites (20:26-28).

20:26-28 The pressure was building to admit defeat and go home. The activities *in the presence of the LORD* increased in intensity as the Israelites sought the Lord's direction.

20:29-44 The third day's battle followed the same strategies of deception and ambush that were used to conquer Ai (Josh 8:1-29).

20:33 *Baal-tamar* is an unidentified town. • *hiding in ambush to the west:* As in Greek and Syriac versions and Latin Vulgate; Hebrew reads *hiding in the open space.*

20:36b-45 This section gives a second account of the battle.

20:42 *battle, and the people who came out of the nearby towns were also killed:* Or *battle, for the people from the nearby towns also came out and killed them.*

20:43 *finally overtaking them east of Gibeah:* The meaning of the Hebrew is uncertain. The geography is complicated, with a further problem of possible confusion between *Gibeah* and nearby *Geba* (1 Sam 13:3–14:5; see also 1 Kgs 15:22).

20:47 *the rock of Rimmon:* "Rimmon" was a Benjamite personal name (2 Sam 4:2) and the place was about four miles east of Bethel. It was a stronghold, probably a cliff dwelling that protected fugitives by its inaccessibility.

21:1 For the second time in Judges, an unwise vow put its makers in a difficult position (see note on 11:31).

21:1 Judg 21:7, 18
21:2 Judg 20:18, 26
21:4 Deut 12:5; 2 Sam 24:25
21:10 Num 31:17-18
21:13 Deut 20:10
21:19 Josh 18:1; Judg 18:31; 1 Sam 1:3
21:21 Exod 15:20; Judg 11:34
21:23 Judg 20:48

weeping loudly and bitterly. 3"O LORD, God of Israel," they cried out, "why has this happened in Israel? Now one of our tribes is missing from Israel!"

4Early the next morning the people built an altar and presented their burnt offerings and peace offerings on it. 5Then they said, "Who among the tribes of Israel did not join us at Mizpah when we held our assembly in the presence of the LORD?" At that time they had taken a solemn oath in the LORD's presence, vowing that anyone who refused to come would be put to death.

6The Israelites felt sorry for their brother Benjamin and said, "Today one of the tribes of Israel has been cut off. 7How can we find wives for the few who remain, since we have sworn by the LORD not to give them our daughters in marriage?"

8So they asked, "Who among the tribes of Israel did not join us at Mizpah when we assembled in the presence of the LORD?" And they discovered that no one from Jabesh-gilead had attended the assembly. 9For after they counted all the people, no one from Jabesh-gilead was present.

10So the assembly sent 12,000 of their best warriors to Jabesh-gilead with orders to kill everyone there, including women and children. 11"This is what you are to do," they said. "Completely destroy all the males and every woman who is not a virgin." 12Among the residents of Jabesh-gilead they found 400 young virgins who had never slept with a man, and they brought them to the camp at Shiloh in the land of Canaan.

13The Israelite assembly sent a peace delegation to the remaining people of Benjamin who were living at the rock of Rimmon. 14Then the men of Benjamin returned to their homes, and the 400 women of Jabesh-gilead who had been spared were given to them as wives. But there were not enough women for all of them.

15The people felt sorry for Benjamin because the LORD had made this gap among the tribes of Israel. 16So the elders of the assembly asked, "How can we find wives for the few who remain, since the women of the tribe of Benjamin are dead? 17There must be heirs for the survivors so that an entire tribe of Israel is not wiped out. 18But we cannot give them our own daughters in marriage because we have sworn with a solemn oath that anyone who does this will fall under God's curse."

19Then they thought of the annual festival of the LORD held in Shiloh, south of Lebonah and north of Bethel, along the east side of the road that goes from Bethel to Shechem. 20They told the men of Benjamin who still needed wives, "Go and hide in the vineyards. 21When you see the young women of Shiloh come out for their dances, rush out from the vineyards, and each of you can take one of them home to the land of Benjamin to be your wife! 22And when their fathers and brothers come to us in protest, we will tell them, 'Please be sympathetic. Let them have your daughters, for we didn't find wives for all of them when we destroyed Jabesh-gilead. And you are not guilty of breaking the vow since you did not actually give your daughters to them in marriage.' "

23So the men of Benjamin did as they were told. Each man caught one of the women as she danced in the celebration and carried her off to be his wife. They returned to their own land, and they rebuilt their towns and lived in them.

24Then the people of Israel departed by tribes and families, and they returned to their own homes.

25In those days Israel had no king; all the people did whatever seemed right in their own eyes.

21:3 The concept of a twelve-tribe league was deeply rooted in Israel, having survived the separation of Levi from the secular tribes, the virtual disappearance of Simeon and Asher, and the division of Joseph into two (Manasseh and Ephraim). The loss of one tribe would have suggested that God's covenant with Abraham, Isaac, and Jacob was coming unglued.

21:8-9 ***Jabesh-gilead*** was an important town east of the Jordan whose failure to participate in the war against Benjamin made a grievous break in solidarity (see 21:5).

21:11 ***Completely destroy:*** The Hebrew term used here refers to the complete consecration of things or people to the LORD, either by destroying them or by giving them as an offering. See Lev 27:28-29.

21:15-17 ***The people felt sorry for Benjamin:*** Israel was concerned about the brokenness of the nation. • The *gap* in Israel was an act of *the LORD*, because the war against Benjamin had been a response to the Lord's covenant.

21:19 The *annual* grape harvest *festival . . . in Shiloh* may originally have been a Canaanite feast.

21:23 ***Their own land*** was the land allotted to the tribe of Benjamin by the Lord's covenant (2:6).

21:24 ***The people of Israel*** pulled through despite the lack of inspired leadership (chs 17–18) and the failure of the tribal league (chs 19–21). ***Tribes and families*** were intact; Israel and all its tribes would survive.

21:25 The conclusion of chs 17–21 gives the reason for the social disorder of the time. Following the period of the judges, God would make a new covenant with Israel involving King David (2 Sam 7) and the promise of messianic rule. The fulfillment of that promise would go far beyond anything that could be imagined in the time when Israel had no king.

THE BOOK OF RUTH

Ruth was a dedicated daughter-in-law to Naomi, her bereaved mother-in-law. Boaz was the kindly owner of a busy farm and the second-nearest family redeemer. In their story, there is loss and loyalty, a homecoming, a secret midnight meeting, a public transfer of property, a marriage, and a child. The book of Ruth records no miracles, but it is full of God's love.

SETTING

The events in Ruth took place during Israel's period of the judges, about 1100 BC. The book of Judges records violent, momentous events, but Ruth shows a peaceful, ordinary side of life at the time.

During this period, Israel had few political structures. The average person focused more on tribal and clan ties than on national identity. Virtually every family in Israel depended on their own crops and animals for food and for most other necessities. Israel's hill country was fertile, but the water supply was variable. Two or three years of low rainfall could cause famine.

SUMMARY

When drought and famine came to Bethlehem, Elimelech moved to Moab with his wife, Naomi, and their two sons, who married Moabite women. Elimelech died in Moab, then the young men also died, leaving Naomi destitute. Hearing that the famine in Bethlehem had ended, Naomi decided to return home. Ruth, one of Naomi's Moabite daughters-in-law, declared her loyalty to Naomi, so the two of them set out together and arrived in Bethlehem at the beginning of the spring barley harvest. To obtain food for the coming year, Ruth went out to glean, beginning in Boaz's field. When he learned who she was, Boaz instructed his workers to be generous to Ruth.

Hearing of Boaz's kindness, Naomi sent Ruth to the threshing floor one night to meet him for a private conversation. Ruth asked Boaz to act as her family redeemer by marrying her. Boaz knew that a closer relative had the first right to act as family redeemer, but Boaz promised to do so if that man refused. He went to the town gate and arranged the matter so that the first man would decline. So, Boaz married Ruth, who bore a son named Obed.

Having a grandson guaranteed Naomi's security in old age and brought back what she thought she had

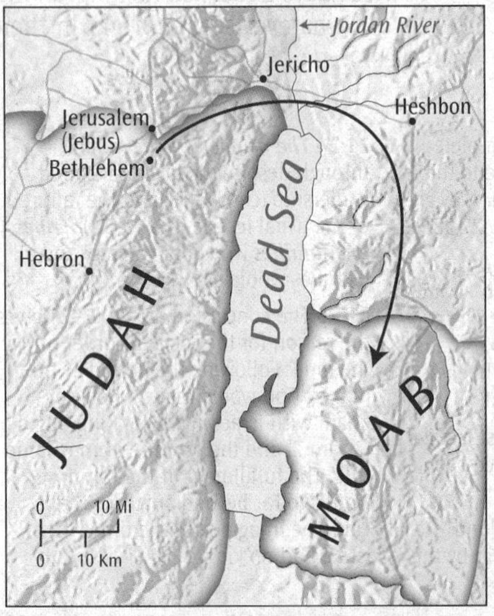

◂ **The Setting of Ruth.** Elimelech and his family moved from BETHLEHEM in JUDAH to MOAB during a famine (1:1-2). The traditional boundaries for Moab are shown, although its boundaries crept northward during the time of the judges (see map, p. 425) and later during the divided monarchy (see 2 Kgs 3:4-27).

lost forever. Eventually, Obed became the grandfather of David, Israel's first great king. The book of Ruth ends with a genealogy of ten generations, from Perez, the son of Judah, to David.

AUTHORSHIP AND DATE

In recent years, some biblical scholars have questioned the historicity of early Israelite stories, including Ruth, and proposed that they might be fictional. As biblical scholars discover more about ancient history, ancient writing conventions, and everyday life in the ancient Near East, however, we see more fully that Ruth and other stories from Israel's early periods are firmly grounded in history. We don't know who wrote Ruth, and archaeologists may never recover direct physical evidence of Ruth, Boaz, and Naomi, but the story rings true to its time and place and gives genealogical details for King David. We can be confident that this early account from the family of David is historical.

MEANING AND MESSAGE

God usually works in the ordinary events of everyday life. Miracles do happen, but God regularly accomplishes his purposes and blesses his people through routine occurrences. If we learn faithfulness in the everyday, we are equipped to be faithful when crises come.

Ruth contains at least nine spoken blessings. God's people have the privilege of blessing each other in God's name. We often help fulfill those blessings, as Naomi and Boaz fulfilled the blessings they gave to Ruth.

Naomi felt abandoned by God; but God had not abandoned Naomi, and by the end of the book Naomi knew that God had restored more to her than she could have dreamed. God is trustworthy in our darkest hours.

Faith in God involves willingness to take risks. The unnamed family redeemer who wanted to preserve his good name through his own heirs lost an opportunity to be generously faithful. Boaz, by contrast, took the risk of faithfulness and generosity, and he was richly rewarded.

The everyday and the ordinary can have breathtaking eternal results. Ruth's and Boaz's daily faithfulness in the unremarkable rhythms of farming, marriage, childbirth, and parenthood resulted in eternal blessings that still multiply through King David and his descendant Jesus Christ.

OUTLINE

1:1-5
Prologue: Elimelech Moves His Family to Moab

1:6-22
Naomi and Ruth Return to Bethlehem

2:1-23
Ruth Works in Boaz's Field

3:1-18
Meeting at the Threshing Floor

4:1-12
Transaction at the City Gate

4:13-17
Boaz Marries Ruth

4:18-22
Epilogue: Descendants of Perez

TIMELINE

about 1376–1050 BC
The era of the judges

late 1100s BC
Elimelech moves his family to Moab

about 1100 BC
Ruth gives birth to Obed

about 1075–1040 BC
The ministry of Samuel

1050–1011 BC
Saul's reign as king of Israel

1011–971 BC
David as king of Israel

Sure, I said,
heaven did
not mean,
Where I reap
thou shouldst
but glean;
Lay thy sheaf
a-down and
come,
Share my
harvest and
my home.

THOMAS HOOD
(1799–1845)
from "Ruth"

FURTHER READING

DANIEL I. BLOCK
Judges & Ruth (1998)

FREDERICK W. BUSH
Ruth/Esther (1996)

ROBERT L. HUBBARD, JR.
The Book of Ruth (1988)

LEON MORRIS
Judges & Ruth (1968)

1. PROLOGUE: ELIMELECH MOVES HIS FAMILY TO MOAB (1:1-5)

1 In the days when the [a]judges ruled in Israel, a severe famine came upon the land. So a man from Bethlehem in Judah left his home and went to live in the country of Moab, taking his wife and two sons with him. [2]The man's name was Elimelech, and his wife was Naomi. Their two sons were Mahlon and Kilion. They were Ephrathites from Bethlehem in the land of Judah. And when they reached Moab, they settled there.

[3]Then Elimelech died, and Naomi was left with her two sons. [4]The two sons married Moabite women. One married a woman named Orpah, and the other a woman named Ruth. But about ten years later, [5]both Mahlon and Kilion died. This left Naomi alone, without her two sons or her husband.

2. NAOMI AND RUTH RETURN TO BETHLEHEM (1:6-22)

[6]Then Naomi heard in Moab that the LORD had blessed his people in Judah by giving them good crops again. So Naomi and her daughters-in-law got ready to leave Moab to return to her homeland. [7]With her two daughters-in-law she set out from the place where she had been living, and they took the road that would lead them back to Judah.

[8]But on the way, Naomi said to her two daughters-in-law, "Go back to your mothers' homes. And may the LORD reward you for your [b]kindness to your husbands and to me. [9]May the LORD bless you with the security of another marriage." Then she kissed them good-bye, and they all broke down and wept.

[10]"No," they said. "We want to go with you to your people."

[11]But Naomi replied, "Why should you go on with me? Can I still give birth to other sons who could grow up to be your husbands? [12]No, my daughters, return to your parents' homes, for I am too old to marry again. And even if it were possible, and I were to get married tonight and bear sons, then what? [13]Would you wait for them to grow up and refuse to marry someone else? No, of course not, my daughters! Things are far more bitter for me than for you, because the LORD himself has raised his fist against me."

[14]And again they wept together, and Orpah kissed her mother-in-law good-bye. But Ruth clung tightly to Naomi. [15]"Look," Naomi said to her, "your sister-in-law has gone back to her people and to her gods. You should do the same."

[16]But Ruth replied, "Don't ask me to leave you and turn back. Wherever you go, I will go; wherever you live, I will live. Your people will be my people, and your God will be my God. [17]Wherever you die, I will die, and there I will be buried. May the LORD punish me severely if I allow anything but death to separate us!" [18]When Naomi saw that Ruth was determined to go with her, she said nothing more.

[19]So the two of them continued on their journey. When they came to Bethlehem, the entire town was excited by their arrival. "Is it really Naomi?" the women asked.

[20]"Don't call me Naomi," she responded. "Instead, call me Mara, for the Almighty has made life very bitter for me. [21]I went away full, but the LORD has brought me home empty. Why call me Naomi when the LORD has caused me to suffer and the Almighty has sent such tragedy upon me?"

1:1 Judg 2:16-18
[a]*shapat* (8199) ›1 Sam 8:1
1:2 Gen 35:19 Judg 3:30
1:6 Exod 4:31
1:8 2 Tim 1:16
[b]*khesed* (2617) ›2 Sam 9:1
1:9 Ruth 3:1
1:11 Deut 25:5
1:13 Judg 2:15
1:16 2 Kgs 2:2
1:18 Acts 21:14
1:20 Exod 6:3; 15:23 Ruth 1:13 Job 6:4
1:21 Job 1:21

1:1 ***The judges ruled*** from the death of Joshua (about 1376 or 1200 BC) to the beginning of Saul's reign as king (about 1050 BC). The events in Ruth occurred around 1100 BC. • ***Famine*** in Israel's hill country was usually caused by drought. • ***Bethlehem*** was a small town in the hill country of northern ***Judah***. • ***Moab***, the land southeast of Judah, sometimes received sufficient rain when Judah did not.

1:2 ***Ephrathites*** were from the clan of Ephrathah, centered in Bethlehem of Judah (see Gen 35:19; 1 Chr 4:4).

1:4 Kilion ***married . . . Orpah***; Mahlon married ***Ruth*** (see 4:10).

1:5 ***This left Naomi alone*** (literally *the woman was bereft*): Naomi suffered devastating emotional losses. She was also without economic support, and with the loss of heirs, she had no hope for the future of her family.

1:6 ***giving:*** This same Hebrew verb is used in 4:13 ("enabled"). These two notices of God's acts enclose the story between similar phrases (an *inclusio*, literary "bookends"). God gives good things, such as food and children, and he works providentially behind the scenes in the ordinary course of things.

1:8 ***But on the way:*** They had probably gone only a short distance when Naomi released Ruth and Orpah to return to their ***mothers' homes.***

1:9 Naomi here speaks the first of the book's several blessings.

1:14 ***Ruth clung tightly to Naomi:*** The Hebrew verb used here emphasizes the strength of Ruth's love for her mother-in-law; it is the same word used to describe a man being "joined to" his wife (Gen 2:24) and to describe a person staying faithful to the Lord (Deut 4:4; 10:20; Josh 22:5).

1:15 ***to her gods:*** Every nation believed in its own territorial god. Naomi assumed that Ruth would continue to worship Moabite gods.

1:16-17 ***Ruth*** swore an oath in the name of ***the LORD*** to seal her firm commitment to Israel's God (cp. 2:11-12) and to Naomi.

1:20 ***Naomi*** means "pleasant"; ***Mara*** means "bitter." • ***Almighty*** translates the Hebrew *shadday*, which pictures God's strength and provision. Naomi's complaint was real, but God provided exactly what she needed (see 4:14-17).

1:21 ***has caused me to suffer:*** Or *has testified against me.*

1:22 Exod 9:31
2:1 Ruth 1:2
2:2 Lev 19:9-10; 23:22
2:4 Ps 129:8 Luke 1:28
2:6 Ruth 1:22

22So Naomi returned from Moab, accompanied by her daughter-in-law Ruth, the young Moabite woman. They arrived in Bethlehem in late spring, at the beginning of the barley harvest.

3. RUTH WORKS IN BOAZ'S FIELD (2:1-23)

2 Now there was a wealthy and influential man in Bethlehem named Boaz, who was a relative of Naomi's husband, Elimelech.

2One day Ruth the Moabite said to Naomi, "Let me go out into the harvest fields to pick up the stalks of grain left behind by anyone who is kind enough to let me do it."

Naomi replied, "All right, my daughter, go ahead." 3So Ruth went out to gather grain behind the harvesters. And as it happened, she found herself working in a field that belonged to Boaz, the relative of her father-in-law, Elimelech.

4While she was there, Boaz arrived from Bethlehem and greeted the harvesters. "The LORD be with you!" he said.

"The LORD bless you!" the harvesters replied.

5Then Boaz asked his foreman, "Who is that young woman over there? Who does she belong to?"

6And the foreman replied, "She is the young woman from Moab who came back with Naomi. 7She asked me this morning if she could gather grain behind the harvesters. She has been hard at work ever since, except for a few minutes' rest in the shelter."

8Boaz went over and said to Ruth, "Listen, my daughter. Stay right here with us when you gather grain; don't go to any other

RUTH (1:4–4:13)

Matt 1:5

The story of Ruth tells of a kind and loyal woman and of the hidden providence of God, who makes all things work together for the good of those who love him (Rom 8:28). This story, part of the history that leads to the Messiah himself, starts with sadness but ends happily.

Ruth lived during the turbulent period of the judges. A foreigner from Moab, she married into an Israelite family from Bethlehem when that family was in Moab. All the men of this Israelite family died in Moab, leaving behind three widows—Ruth, her mother-in-law Naomi, and her sister-in-law Orpah. When Naomi decided to return to her hometown of Bethlehem, Ruth cast her lot with her mother-in-law. Ruth's declaration of love, loyalty, and faith in the LORD (Naomi's God) has few equals (1:16-17).

As Naomi had expected, the situation in Bethlehem was difficult for her and her daughter-in-law. Ruth, by her own initiative, undertook solving the problem of food for herself and Naomi through the hard and risky task of gleaning in the grain fields (2:2). She acted with modesty, grace, and courtesy, but also with determination, focus, and endurance.

On Naomi's encouragement, Ruth then took the initiative in asking Boaz, the wealthy landowner who was supporting Ruth's gleaning, to marry her and to act as the family redeemer (3:9). In doing this, Ruth was exercising great "family loyalty" (3:10); Ruth's generous and diligent care for Naomi and her family is a major theme throughout this little book. Boaz responded to Ruth's proposal by calling her a "virtuous woman" (3:11), and she certainly embodied the characteristics of a virtuous and capable wife (cp. Prov 31:10-31, which uses the same Hebrew phrase and is placed immediately before Ruth in the Hebrew Bible).

Boaz settled legal matters and then married Ruth. The book ends by announcing the birth of a baby boy, Obed. With this ending we see an important purpose of the book of Ruth. Obed became the grandfather of King David. The NT includes Ruth as one of only five women mentioned in the genealogy of Jesus Christ (Matt 1:5). The everyday faithfulness of Ruth and Boaz had eternal significance as God worked out his purposes through them.

1:22 ***The beginning of the barley harvest*** was between late March and mid-April by our calendar.

2:1 ***Boaz*** was ***a relative of . . . Elimelech*** and thus was qualified to be a family redeemer for the two widows, Ruth and Naomi (see note on 2:20).

2:2 ***to pick up the stalks of grain left behind:*** Harvesters were to leave some grain for the poor to glean (see Lev 19:9-10; 23:22; Deut 24:19-22). God provided the poor with food.

2:3 ***as it happened, she found herself:*** Ruth seemingly selected at random the field in which she would glean; God works through ordinary choices to provide for those who trust him.

2:5 ***Boaz*** recognized Ruth as a marriageable ***young woman*** (Hebrew *na'arah*).

2:7 ***in the shelter:*** Many farmers in Israel's hill country erected shelters beside their fields for use during the harvest. Workers used these shelters for shade during lunch or other break times during the long, hard workday. Such shelters can still be seen in parts of the hill country.

2:8-9 ***Boaz*** gave ***Ruth*** the special privilege of gleaning ***right behind the young women***. After the men cut the grain and tied it in small bundles, the women gathered the bundles into larger sheaves. The Torah did not

fields. Stay right behind the young women working in my field. 9See which part of the field they are harvesting, and then follow them. I have warned the young men not to treat you roughly. And when you are thirsty, help yourself to the water they have drawn from the well."

10Ruth fell at his feet and thanked him warmly. "What have I done to deserve such kindness?" she asked. "I am only a foreigner."

11"Yes, I know," Boaz replied. "But I also know about everything you have done for your mother-in-law since the death of your husband. I have heard how you left your father and mother and your own land to live here among complete strangers. 12May the LORD, the God of Israel, under whose wings you have come to take refuge, reward you fully for what you have done."

13"I hope I continue to please you, sir," she replied. "You have comforted me by speaking so kindly to me, even though I am not one of your workers."

14At mealtime Boaz called to her, "Come over here, and help yourself to some food. You can dip your bread in the sour wine." So she sat with his harvesters, and Boaz gave her some roasted grain to eat. She ate all she wanted and still had some left over.

15When Ruth went back to work again, Boaz ordered his young men, "Let her gather grain right among the sheaves without stopping her. 16And pull out some heads of barley from the bundles and drop them on purpose for her. Let her pick them up, and don't give her a hard time!"

17So Ruth gathered barley there all day, and when she beat out the grain that evening, it filled an entire basket. 18She carried it back into town and showed it to her mother-in-law. Ruth also gave her the roasted grain that was left over from her meal.

19"Where did you gather all this grain today?" Naomi asked. "Where did you work? May the LORD bless the one who helped you!"

So Ruth told her mother-in-law about the man in whose field she had worked. She said, "The man I worked with today is named Boaz."

20"May the LORD bless him!" Naomi told her daughter-in-law. "He is showing his kindness to us as well as to your dead husband. That man is one of our closest relatives, one of our [c]family redeemers."

21Then Ruth said, "What's more, Boaz even told me to come back and stay with his harvesters until the entire harvest is completed."

22"Good!" Naomi exclaimed. "Do as he said, my daughter. Stay with his young women right through the whole harvest. You might be harassed in other fields, but you'll be safe with him."

23So Ruth worked alongside the women in Boaz's fields and gathered grain with them until the end of the barley harvest. Then she continued working with them through the wheat harvest in early summer. And all the while she lived with her mother-in-law.

4. MEETING AT THE THRESHING FLOOR (3:1-18)

3 One day Naomi said to Ruth, "My daughter, it's time that I found a permanent home for you, so that you will be provided for. 2Boaz is a close relative of ours, and he's been very kind by letting you gather grain with his young women. Tonight he

2:10 1 Sam 25:23
2:12 Ruth 1:16
2:20 Ruth 3:9-10; 4:6
go'el (1350) ›Ruth 3:9
3:1 Ruth 1:9
3:2 Deut 25:5-10

require farmers to allow gleaners into the fields until the sheaves had been taken to the threshing floor. • ***I have warned the young men not to treat you roughly:*** Boaz assured Ruth that no one under his authority would taunt her or try to drive her away from his fields even though she was present before the proper time for gleaners to come in. • ***help yourself to the water:*** Boaz's generosity saved Ruth the trouble of drawing her own water.

2:13 ***your workers*** (literally *your maidservants*): By her use of this term, Ruth placed herself lower on the social scale than Boaz.

2:14 By sharing his meal with Ruth, ***Boaz*** extended hospitality far beyond the call of duty.

2:15-16 Boaz's instructions to his reapers as they returned to work after lunch made Ruth's gleaning a great deal more productive. Boaz provided for Ruth much more than the law of gleaning required of him.

2:17 ***it filled an entire basket:*** Hebrew *it was about an ephah* [20 quarts or 22 liters].

2:18 In giving Naomi ***the roasted grain that was left over***, Ruth was conscientious and generous.

2:19 ***all this grain:*** Ruth could not normally have gleaned nearly as much as an ephah of barley (about two-thirds of a bushel).

2:20 ***family redeemers*** (Hebrew *go'el*): The law specified that the *go'el*, the nearest male kinsman, was to help a relative who fell into economic difficulty (see "The Family Redeemer," facing page; see also note on Lev 25:25). • ***to us as well as to your dead husband:*** Literally *to the living and to the dead.*

2:21 ***Ruth:*** Literally *Ruth the Moabite.* The author refers to Ruth as "the Moabite" five times (1:22; 2:2, 21; 4:5, 10), reminding us repeatedly that Ruth was not an Israelite.

3:1 ***a permanent home*** (literally *a resting place*): Naomi used a related word in 1:9 when she prayed for Ruth and Orpah. Now she suggested a course of action that might encourage Boaz to act on Ruth's behalf.

3:2 As a *close relative*, Boaz might act as a redeemer for Ruth and Naomi (see notes on 2:20; 3:9). • The ***threshing floor*** was a flat surface of stone or hardened earth. The farmer spread sheaves of grain over its surface and beat them to separate the grain from the straw. Then the farmer would begin *winnowing* by

3:9
Ruth 2:20
[d]*go'el* (1350)
▸Ruth 4:6
3:11
Prov 12:4; 31:10
3:12
Ruth 4:1

will be winnowing barley at the threshing floor. 3Now do as I tell you—take a bath and put on perfume and dress in your nicest clothes. Then go to the threshing floor, but don't let Boaz see you until he has finished eating and drinking. 4Be sure to notice where he lies down; then go and uncover his feet and lie down there. He will tell you what to do."

5"I will do everything you say," Ruth replied. 6So she went down to the threshing floor that night and followed the instructions of her mother-in-law.

7After Boaz had finished eating and drinking and was in good spirits, he lay down at the far end of the pile of grain and went to sleep. Then Ruth came quietly, uncovered his feet, and lay down. 8Around midnight Boaz suddenly woke up and turned over. He was surprised to find a woman lying at his feet! 9"Who are you?" he asked.

"I am your servant Ruth," she replied. "Spread the corner of your covering over me, for you are my [d]family redeemer."

10"The LORD bless you, my daughter!" Boaz exclaimed. "You are showing even more family loyalty now than you did before, for you have not gone after a younger man, whether rich or poor. 11Now don't worry about a thing, my daughter. I will do what is necessary, for everyone in town knows you are a virtuous woman. 12But while it's true that I am one of your family redeemers, there is another man who is more closely

The Family Redeemer (2:20; 3:9, 12; 4:1-10)

Lev 25:23-55
Num 35:9-34
Isa 59:20
Jer 32:6-15
Matt 20:28
Rom 3:24-25
Eph 1:7
Titus 2:14
Rev 5:9

In the book of Ruth, the phrase "family redeemer" has a specific, technical meaning. Elsewhere, the underlying Hebrew term *go'el* is translated "nearest relative" (Num 27:11; 35:19, 24). According to the law, family redeemers had three main responsibilities in Israel:

1. Leviticus 25:23-34 stipulates that if an Israelite became so poor that he had to sell his land, a family member was to pay off the debt so the land would remain in the family. If no relative could purchase the land and the seller was unable to buy it back, the land still reverted to the seller or his heirs in the Jubilee (fiftieth) Year. Two examples of family redeemers buying land for their relatives are Boaz (4:1-12) and Jeremiah (Jer 32:6-15).

2. Similarly, if an Israelite became so poor he had to sell himself into debt-slavery, a family redeemer was to buy his relative from service to a non-relative (Lev 25:35-55). The poor Israelite would pay off his debt by working for his relative, who could be expected to treat him better than a stranger would.

3. The family redeemer was to pursue justice for an Israelite killed by another's hand, under conditions described in Numbers 35:9-34.

The concept of the family redeemer reminds us that God is the true owner of all things, and he commands us to love our neighbor as ourselves (Lev 19:18; Matt 22:39-40). The NT presents Jesus as the perfect family redeemer, buying us from the slavery to sin and death into which we had sold ourselves (Matt 20:28; Rom 3:24-25; Eph 1:7; Titus 2:14; Rev 5:9; cp. Exod 6:6; 15:13; Ps 130:8; Isa 44:22; 59:20; 63:9; Jer 31:11). In the spirit of the OT family redeemer (such as Boaz) and following the example of our great Redeemer, we, too, are commanded to act with love and compassion toward others (Lev 19:11-18; Matt 5:43-48; 19:19; 22:37-40; Rom 13:8-10; Gal 5:14; Jas 2:8-9).

throwing the mixed straw and grain into the air with a wooden fork or shovel. The breeze carried the lighter straw and chaff downwind, while the heavier grains fell to the threshing floor.

3:3 *take a bath* (literally *wash yourself*): Ruth probably bathed herself with a cloth dipped in water (only the wealthy had facilities for immersing themselves). Bathing was not an everyday expectation; this was a special occasion.

3:4 Ruth was to ***uncover*** Boaz's ***feet*** to ensure that he would waken.

3:7 ***he lay down:*** The owner slept at the threshing floor to deter petty theft.

3:8 ***He was surprised*** (literally *He was terrified*): Boaz knew that a female lay ***at his feet***, but he did not know who she was or why she was there.

3:9 ***your servant:*** Ruth deliberately identified herself with the female workers. • ***Spread . . . your covering over me:*** This was a way of asking Boaz to marry her (cp. Ezek 16:8). • Ruth appealed to Boaz's status as a ***family redeemer*** (Hebrew *go'el;* see "The Family Redeemer," above) to persuade him to marry her (see 4:5).

3:10 ***You are showing even more family loyalty:*** Ruth was not obligated to come to Bethlehem with Naomi, nor did she have to marry within Elimelech's family or provide them with an heir to the land (see 4:5).

3:11 ***what is necessary*** (literally *what you are asking*): Boaz agreed to act on Ruth's behalf. Some interpreters understand Boaz's statement as an unconditional agreement to marry Ruth (see also note on 4:5); most take it to mean that Boaz would act to provide for Ruth and Naomi by presenting to the nearer kinsman the opportunity to act as family redeemer before taking the opportunity himself (4:1-12). By voluntarily taking on the role of the family redeemer for Ruth and Naomi, Boaz became a forerunner of Jesus (see "The Family Redeemer," above).

3:12-13 ***Another man*** was ***more closely related*** to Elimelech than Boaz. He had the first right of refusal to act as

related to you than I am. 13Stay here tonight, and in the morning I will talk to him. If he is willing to redeem you, very well. Let him marry you. But if he is not willing, then as surely as the LORD lives, I will redeem you myself! Now lie down here until morning."

14So Ruth lay at Boaz's feet until the morning, but she got up before it was light enough for people to recognize each other. For Boaz had said, "No one must know that a woman was here at the threshing floor." 15Then Boaz said to her, "Bring your cloak and spread it out." He measured six scoops of barley into the cloak and placed it on her back. Then he returned to the town.

16When Ruth went back to her mother-in-law, Naomi asked, "What happened, my daughter?"

Ruth told Naomi everything Boaz had done for her, 17and she added, "He gave me these six scoops of barley and said, 'Don't go back to your mother-in-law empty-handed.' "

18Then Naomi said to her, "Just be patient, my daughter, until we hear what happens. The man won't rest until he has settled things today."

5. TRANSACTION AT THE CITY GATE (4:1-12)

4 Boaz went to the town gate and took a seat there. Just then the family redeemer he had mentioned came by, so Boaz called out to him, "Come over here and sit down, friend. I want to talk to you." So they sat down together. 2Then Boaz called ten leaders from the town and asked them to sit as witnesses. 3And Boaz said to the family redeemer, "You know Naomi, who came back from Moab. She is selling the land that belonged to our relative Elimelech. 4I thought I should speak to you about it so that you can redeem it if you wish. If you want the land, then buy it here in the presence of these witnesses. But if you don't want it, let me know right away, because I am next in line to redeem it after you."

The man replied, "All right, I'll redeem it."

5Then Boaz told him, "Of course, your purchase of the land from Naomi also requires that you marry Ruth, the Moabite widow. That way she can have children who will carry on her husband's name and keep the land in the family."

6"Then I can't redeem it," the [e]family

3:13 Ruth 4:5; Matt 22:24
3:18 Ps 37:3-5
4:1 Ruth 3:12
4:3 Lev 25:25
4:4 Lev 25:25; Jer 32:7-8
4:5 Deut 25:5-6
4:6 Lev 25:25; Ruth 3:12-13; [e]*go'el* (1350) ‣Job 19:25

---

family redeemer and (according to most interpreters) to marry Ruth.

3:15 *six scoops:* Literally *six measures,* an unknown quantity. There were two scoop sizes. The smaller measure (the *omer*) was $\frac{1}{10}$ of an ephah (about 2 quarts); the larger measure (the *seah*) was $\frac{1}{3}$ of an ephah (about 6 $\frac{2}{3}$ quarts). The latter quantity is more likely and indicates a very generous gift, twice the amount that Ruth gleaned on her first day (2:17); it was a significant token of good faith. • ***Then he:*** Most Hebrew manuscripts read *he*; many Hebrew manuscripts, Syriac version, and Latin Vulgate read *she.*

4:1 Most legal transactions, including property transfers, were carried out at ***the town gate.*** • ***friend:*** Boaz might or might not have used the man's name, but the author of Ruth avoided doing so (see note on 4:6).

4:3 ***Naomi . . . is selling the land:*** Naomi probably did not have control of Elimelech's ancestral land, though she did have legal title. She was selling the right to redeem it, or buy it back, from whoever was currently using it (see 4:4).

4:4 *redeem it:* The law called for a near relative, the family redeemer, to buy land when a landowner had to sell it (see Lev 25:23-34). This practice kept land in the family; the redeemer was a conservator for the land until the destitute landowner could recover economically and buy it back. • ***All right, I'll redeem it:*** The kinsman could see a great opportunity—there was no male heir and no apparent likelihood that there would be one, so he could add the land to his own estate while doing his social duty for the family.

4:5 ***your purchase . . . requires that you marry Ruth*** (literally *on the day you purchase . . . you acquire Ruth*): In the Hebrew manuscripts that we have, the body of this verse reads *I acquire,* but a scribal correction in the margin reads *you acquire,* a difference of one letter. (The scribe believed *you acquire* was the original reading and that the body of the text contained an error.) Some interpreters believe the body of the Hebrew text (*I acquire*) is the original reading of the text, indicating that the marriage between Boaz and Ruth was already set to occur (see note on 3:11). Most translators, however, believe that the marginal correction (*you acquire*) represents the original reading of the text because: (1) The scribe who made the marginal correction believed that *you acquire* was the original reading; (2) most ancient translations of Ruth, which predate our oldest copies of the Hebrew text, also read *you acquire*; and (3) it is easy to envision that an earlier Hebrew scribe (working before our earliest manuscript copies) substituted the word *I acquire*—as it appears in 4:10—in place of *you acquire.* • ***That way she can have children who will carry on her husband's name and keep the land in the family:*** This sentence draws heavily on Deut 25:7. Boaz connected the duties of a family redeemer (see notes on 2:20; Lev 25:25) with the duties of a brother-in-law (Latin *levir*) to provide an heir for a deceased brother (see Deut 25:5-10 for a description of *levirate marriage;* cp. Gen 38). There is no precise precedent for Boaz's legal maneuver. The duty of the *levir* as stated in Deut 25:5-10 was not binding in this situation (neither Boaz nor the other kinsman was Elimelech's brother, and Ruth was not Elimelech's widow). Boaz was apparently using the spirit of the law concerning the *go'el* (family redeemer) to establish a moral, if not a legal, obligation to serve as *levir* and provide the deceased with an heir to inherit the land (see note on Lev 25:25). The concepts of land ownership and provision for an heir were intimately connected in ancient Israel (cp. Num 27:1-11). Because Naomi was beyond childbearing age, Ruth, the widow of Elimelech's son, would be the mother for such an heir. This maneuver apparently surprised the other kinsman (4:6), but it is clear from what follows that Boaz's argument, while perhaps novel, was accepted as valid.

4:6 ***Then I can't redeem it:*** The addition of Ruth to the transaction completely changed the equation for the other kinsman. • ***this might endanger my own estate:*** If he bought the land, married Ruth, and raised an heir for Elimelech,

4:7
Deut 25:8-10

4:11
Gen 29:25-30
[f]*zaqen* (2205)
‣ Ps 105:22

4:12
Gen 38:29; 46:12

4:13
Gen 29:31; 33:5

4:14
Luke 1:58

4:15
Ruth 1:16-17; 2:11-12

4:18-22
//1 Chr 2:5-15
//Matt 1:3-6
//Luke 3:31-33

redeemer replied, "because this might endanger my own estate. You redeem the land; I cannot do it."

7Now in those days it was the custom in Israel for anyone transferring a right of purchase to remove his sandal and hand it to the other party. This publicly validated the transaction. 8So the other family redeemer drew off his sandal as he said to Boaz, "You buy the land."

9Then Boaz said to the elders and to the crowd standing around, "You are witnesses that today I have bought from Naomi all the property of Elimelech, Kilion, and Mahlon. 10And with the land I have acquired Ruth, the Moabite widow of Mahlon, to be my wife. This way she can have a son to carry on the family name of her dead husband and to inherit the family property here in his hometown. You are all witnesses today."

11Then the [f]elders and all the people standing in the gate replied, "We are witnesses! May the LORD make this woman who is coming into your home like Rachel and Leah, from whom all the nation of Israel descended! May you prosper in Ephrathah and be famous in Bethlehem. 12And may the LORD give you descendants by this young woman who will be like those of our ancestor Perez, the son of Tamar and Judah."

6. BOAZ MARRIES RUTH (4:13-17)

13So Boaz took Ruth into his home, and she became his wife. When he slept with her, the LORD enabled her to become pregnant, and she gave birth to a son. 14Then the women of the town said to Naomi, "Praise the LORD, who has now provided a redeemer for your family! May this child be famous in Israel. 15May he restore your youth and care for you in your old age. For he is the son of your daughter-in-law who loves you and has been better to you than seven sons!"

16Naomi took the baby and cuddled him to her breast. And she cared for him as if he were her own. 17The neighbor women said, "Now at last Naomi has a son again!" And they named him Obed. He became the father of Jesse and the grandfather of David.

7. EPILOGUE: DESCENDANTS OF PEREZ (4:18-22)

18This is the genealogical record of their ancestor Perez:

Perez was the father of Hezron.
19Hezron was the father of Ram.
Ram was the father of Amminadab.
20Amminadab was the father of Nahshon.
Nahshon was the father of Salmon.
21Salmon was the father of Boaz.
Boaz was the father of Obed.
22Obed was the father of Jesse.
Jesse was the father of David.

he might invest many resources only to lose control of the new land, and he might not have enough to maintain his own land. If he then failed to have a second son with Ruth as his own heir, his land would be inherited by Elimelech's heir, and his own name would die out. Even if this kinsman had acquired the land and not Ruth (see notes on 3:11; 4:5), he still might lose his investment in the land to the heir born to Ruth. By acting to preserve his own name, this man became the no-name who refused to help his close relative.

4:7 *in those days:* The book of Ruth was not written immediately after these events. By the time Ruth was written, most people had forgotten this custom of removing a *sandal* and what it meant. The transfer of a sandal symbolized ***transferring a right of purchase*** to redeem the land. See also Deut 25:9 for a similar (but not identical) custom in relation to levirate marriage; in both cases, the sandal apparently signified the right of redemption.

4:10 *And with the land* (literally *And besides*): Boaz intended to raise an heir for Mahlon, the first son, who would ***carry on the family name of her dead husband*** and inherit his land.

4:11 *Rachel and Leah*, Jacob's two wives, were the mothers of Israel. • *Ephrathah:* See note on 1:2.

4:12 Like Ruth, *Tamar* had been a foreigner; she became the mother of *Perez* and Zerah, through whom Judah's descendants came.

4:13 *the LORD enabled:* See note on 1:6.

4:14 This child replaced the family *Naomi* had lost when her own two sons died in Moab. ***The women of the town*** recognized that *this child* completed the circle of redemption for Naomi.

4:15 *care for you in your old age* (literally *cause your old age to be full*): With the birth of Obed, Naomi's life was full again (cp. 1:21).

4:18-22 The book of Ruth ends with a genealogy of ten generations, from Perez, the son of Judah (Jacob's son), to David, the grandson of Obed. Besides being one of the world's great stories, this tale concerns the family history of David, Israel's greatest king. That Ruth and Boaz were ancestors of Israel's greatest king is a major reason for the inclusion of this small book in the OT.

4:20 *Salmon:* As in some Greek manuscripts (see also 4:21); Hebrew reads *Salma.*

THE FIRST BOOK OF SAMUEL

When neighboring nations are hostile, the right leadership can give people a sense of safety. In Samuel's time, Israel faced external threats and internal discord, and the judges did not satisfy the people's desire for leadership and security. Israel wanted a king. The book of 1 Samuel records Israel's transition from a federation of tribes to a centralized kingdom. Israel's first king, Saul, was not faithful to God. However, God's plan to save Israel—and the world—began to unfold in the person of King David.

SETTING

As early as Moses' final address on the plains of Moab (Deut 17:14-20), God had said that the people of Israel would ask for a king to reign over them. God spelled out the requirements for a king (Deut 17:15) but also warned of the evils commonly associated with human kings. A king would want many horses, numerous wives, and large amounts of gold and silver (Deut 17:16-17). To correct these tendencies, God required that each king of Israel immerse himself in God's law (Deut 17:18-20).

Throughout the days of the judges, discontent grew over the lack of unity among Israel's tribes (see Judg 17–21). By Samuel's time, Israel was looking for a king to unite the nation and protect it from internal and external threats.

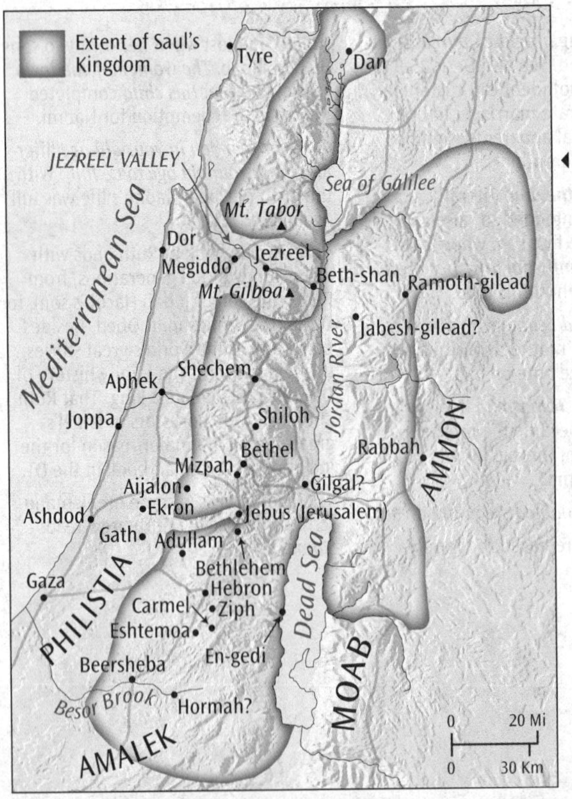

Israel at the Time of Samuel and Saul, 1075~1011 BC. Enemies surrounded Israel throughout this period. Samuel, Saul, and David were all instrumental in overcoming these enemies and establishing Israel in the region. The map shows the extent of Saul's kingdom along with many of the key places in the lives of Samuel, Saul, and David.

ADULLAM 22:1-2
AMALEK 14:48; 15:1-35; 27:8; 28:18; 30:1-20
AMMON 10:27–11:11; 12:12
ASHDOD 5:1-8
BEERSHEBA 3:20; 8:2
BESOR BROOK 30:9, 21
BETHEL 7:16; 10:3; 13:2; 30:27
BETHLEHEM 16:1-13, 18; 17:12, 15; 20:6, 28
BETH-SHAN 31:10-12
CARMEL 15:12; 25:2-40
EKRON 5:10-12; 6:16-17; 17:52
EN-GEDI 23:29; 24:1
GATH 5:8-9; 17:4, 52; 21:10–22:1; 27:2-12
GILGAL 7:16; 10:8; 11:14-15; 13:4-15; 15:12-33
JABESH-GILEAD 11:1-11; 31:11-13
JEZREEL 25:43; 29:1-11; 30:5; 31:7
MIZPAH 7:5-16; 10:17
MOAB 12:9; 14:47; 22:3-4
MOUNT GILBOA 28:4; 31:1-8
SHILOH 1:3-18, 24; 2:14; 3:19–4:12
ZIPH 23:14-24; 26:1-2

Gideon, who judged Israel about 100 years before the time of Samuel, had acted a lot like a monarch. Gideon rejected the invitation to inaugurate a hereditary dynasty (Judg 8:22-23), but he began to act like a king: He accumulated gold and used it to build a religious idol (Judg 8:24-27), he took many wives (Judg 8:30), and he even named one of his sons Abimelech, which means "my father is king" (Judg 8:31). Gideon acted like the kind of king God wanted Israel never to have. A monarchy would give an imperfect human even more control than the judges exercised. This book records the trouble that surrounded Israel's first king, Saul, as well as God's unfolding plan to establish an eternal kingship through the line of David.

TIMELINE

about 1376–1050 BC
The era of the judges

around 1200 BC
The Philistines arrive in Canaan

about 1100–950 BC
The period covered by the books of Samuel

about 1100–1070 BC
Eli as priest at Shiloh

about 1075–1040 BC
The ministry of Samuel

1050–1011 BC
The reign of Saul

about 1025 BC
David is anointed as king

about 1020 BC
David fights Goliath

about 1011 BC
The death of Saul and Jonathan

1011–971 BC
David as king of Israel

SUMMARY

In 1 Sam 1–7, Samuel emerges as one of God's key servants. Samuel was born to a devout woman who had been barren (1:1-23). He became an apprentice in the Tabernacle as a young child under the supervision of Eli the priest (1:24–3:18). It is possible that Samuel, a Levite (1 Chr 6:33-34), was originally being groomed to be a Tabernacle assistant. Instead, he became a prophet with a growing national reputation (3:19–4:1a). When the Philistines harassed the Israelites and captured the Ark of the Covenant (4:1b–7:2), Samuel is absent from the narrative—he was not yet prominent in Israel's national life. In ch 7, Samuel reappears strongly. He called Israel to repentance and, acting as a judge, drove out the Philistine oppressors, something Samson had failed to do.

OUTLINE

1:1–7:17
Establishment of Samuel's Leadership

8:1–12:25
Establishment of Saul's Kingship

13:1–16:13
Rejection of Saul's Kingship

16:14–31:13
Dissolution of Saul's Reign

Samuel's leadership as Levite, prophet, and judge spanned religious, spiritual, and political spheres. However, his sons did not prove worthy of carrying on in his place (8:1-3). Israel asked Samuel to appoint a king to lead them and make them like other nations. Samuel was outspoken in his opposition (8:10-21), yet the Lord instructed Samuel to anoint Saul as king (chs 9–10). In Samuel's farewell address (ch 12), he reminded the Israelites of God's power and care for them. He wanted them to realize their sin in asking for a king rather than trusting in the Lord.

Initially, Saul was a good king. He defeated the neighboring Ammonites and saved a city east of the Jordan from doom (ch 11). But by his disobedience to God, Saul soon proved that he was unworthy to be Israel's king (chs 13, 15). By contrast, Saul's noble son Jonathan (ch 14) seemed to be an ideal successor to his father. God, however, had different plans (chs 16–31). Jonathan would not succeed Saul. Instead, God instructed Samuel to anoint David secretly as Saul's successor while Saul was still king (16:1-13).

Saul's relationship with David was good at first, thanks in part to David's musical gifts (16:14-23). However, David's success with Goliath (ch 17) made Saul jealous (18:6-16), and their relationship turned sour, and Saul

Samuel and David . . . make a frame round the dark, problematical figure of King Saul. . . . All three . . . are forerunners and heralds of the real king.

HANS W. HERTZBERG
I & II Samuel

tried to eliminate the threat David posed to his kingship. He brought David into his family through marriage to have him nearby so it would be easier to kill him (18:17-29). He attacked David directly (19:1-10) and executed anybody who harbored David (chs 21–22). All of Saul's attempts to get rid of David proved unsuccessful.

Both Saul and Jonathan died in battle against the Philistines (31:1-6). This paved the way for David to begin his reign, though not without further difficulties (2 Sam 1:1–5:5).

AUTHOR

The title "Samuel" comes from the important role Samuel played in Israel's transition to a monarchy, not from the book's authorship. Samuel could have written parts of 1 Samuel, but he could not have written any part of 2 Samuel, as his death is recorded in 1 Sam 25:1. As with many OT books, the author of 1 Samuel is never identified.

COMPOSITION

1–2 Samuel were originally one book, the book of Samuel. The translators of the Septuagint (the Greek OT) divided it into two books, 1–2 Kingdoms. Later Hebrew tradition also divided the book but retained the name Samuel, as do most English versions.

Some scholars contend that 1–2 Samuel (along with 1–2 Kings, also one book originally) were created from a variety of sources during or after the Babylonian exile (586–538 BC). It is indeed possible that multiple sources were used in 1–2 Samuel. We know from 1 Chr 29:29, for example, that Samuel and the prophets Nathan and Gad chronicled events from the life of David. There is no reason to insist that the inspired author of 1–2 Samuel could not have made use of such information. However, the book could have been near its final form during or shortly after the reign of Solomon (971–931 BC).

Shortly after the exile to Babylon, the book of Samuel was incorporated into the larger body of material that includes Joshua, Judges, 1–2 Samuel, and 1–2 Kings. This section of Scripture has a clear purpose: It traces Israel's sacred history, beginning with blessing (conquering the land) and ending with judgment (losing the land). It explains to an audience in exile how their grave misfortune came about.

> *Simply as a source of stories to hold children spellbound [the books of Samuel] are incomparable, and moreover they provide an abundance of raw material from which to study the human condition, for they present real life with all its ambiguities. . . . The theology in these books is . . . an offer to those who will respond to the invitation to read and ponder the lives of those depicted here.*
>
> JOYCE G. BALDWIN
> *1 & 2 Samuel*

TEXT

The text of 1–2 Samuel that is found in the Greek OT (the Septuagint, 200s BC) is different in many places from the Hebrew (Masoretic) text (about AD 1000). The Hebrew texts of Samuel in the Dead Sea Scrolls (about 250–50 BC) found at Qumran agree in some places with the Septuagint, in other places with the Masoretic Text. In still other places they have their own readings. Readers will encounter notes such as "Hebrew lacks . . ." or "Greek reads . . ." more frequently in 1–2 Samuel than in other OT books. However, few of these textual variants significantly alter the book's meaning.

MEANING AND MESSAGE

The emphasis on kingship in 1 Samuel first appears in Hannah's Prayer of Praise (see 2:10). Hannah is the first person in Scripture to announce Israel's coming kingship. However, the idea that Israel would have a king was as old as God's promise to Abraham and Sarah (Gen 17:6, 16).

God neither mandated nor forbade a monarchy but only spelled out the excesses from which Israel's kings must abstain (see Deut 17:14-20).

During the period of the judges, Israel changed dramatically for the worse—both spiritually and nationally. This steady disintegration reaches a horrible climax in Judg 17–21. To help correct this decline, the book of Judges hints, Israel needed a king. Israel's greatest threat was not the Philistines or any other predatory neighbor but Israel itself and its breaking of the covenant. Israel needed a king to guard the covenant, which the pre-monarchical order had put at risk.

If the king's responsibility was to administer the covenant (Deut 17:18-20), the prophet's duty was to interpret its stipulations. For this reason, a prophet such as Samuel protected his divinely authorized claim over kings with a holy zeal. Not only did Samuel anoint Israel's first two kings (10:1; 16:13), but he was compelled to censure the king when he stepped outside of covenantal boundaries (13:8-15; 15:10-33).

Saul did not have the character or integrity needed to lead Israel into a successful, God-honoring monarchy. Saul was not fated to fall, as though he had no control over his decisions. In fact, God wanted him to be a good king and made every provision for that to happen (such as changing his heart and giving him his Spirit). But God does not force righteousness, holiness, or obedience. His grace is persuasive but not coercive.

Despite the deep disappointments of the era of the judges and the early monarchy, God's sovereign control over Israel's history is demonstrated in several ways: (1) A once-barren woman gave birth to Samuel, God's agent for the transition to monarchy (ch 1); (2) a devastating Philistine victory became a Philistine defeat without human help (chs 4–6); (3) the king whom the people demanded became God's anointed (chs 8–10); (4) this king was rejected for his unfaithfulness (chs 13, 15); and (5) the eighth son of an obscure family, a man after God's own heart, was chosen as the future king of Israel (ch 16).

Unlike Saul's rule, David's kingship over Israel lasted, and one of his descendants later became the sovereign and eternal King of the whole world. Jesus is the final heir to David's throne (John 7:42; Rev 5:5; 11:15). He perpetuates his ancestor's virtues but never exhibits his flaws. Jesus is the world's perfect and eternal Shepherd and King.

FURTHER READING

R. ALTER
The David Story: A Translation with Commentary of 1 and 2 Samuel (1999)

JOYCE G. BALDWIN
1 & 2 Samuel (1988)

R. D. BERGEN
1, 2 Samuel (1996)

WALTER BRUEGGEMANN
First and Second Samuel (1990)

T. W. CARTLEDGE
1 & 2 Samuel (2001)

A. R. MILLARD, J. K. HOFFMEIER, AND D. W. BAKER, EDS.
Faith, Tradition, and History: Old Testament Historiography in Its Near Eastern Context (1994)

J. ROBERT VANNOY
1 Samuel in *Cornerstone Biblical Commentary*, vol. 4a (2009)

1:1 1 Chr 6:22-28, 33-38
1:2 Deut 21:15-17
1:3 Exod 34:23; Deut 12:4-7; Josh 18:1; Luke 2:41-42

1. ESTABLISHMENT OF SAMUEL'S LEADERSHIP (1:1–7:17)

Samuel and the Word of the LORD (1:1–4:1a)

The Birth and Dedication of Samuel

1 There was a man named Elkanah who lived in Ramah in the region of Zuph in the hill country of Ephraim. He was the son of Jeroham, son of Elihu, son of Tohu, son of Zuph, of Ephraim. [2]Elkanah had two wives, Hannah and Peninnah. Peninnah had children, but Hannah did not.

[3]Each year Elkanah would travel to Shiloh to worship and sacrifice to the LORD of Heaven's Armies at the Tabernacle. The

---

1:1 *Elkanah* was a Levite (1 Chr 6:22-27). After the conquest of the Promised Land, the Levites were given towns in the territories of the other Israelite tribes, including *Ephraim* (Josh 21:20). • Elkanah's hometown was *Ramah* (as in Greek version; Hebrew reads *Ramathaim-zophim;* cp. 1:19; 2:11). This location should not be confused with the Ramah in the tribal area of Benjamin (see Josh 18:25; Judg 19:13; Matt 2:18). • The *region of Zuph* was named after one of Elkanah's ancestors, a Levite of the clan of Kohath (1 Chr 6:35). Saul first met Samuel in Zuph while searching for his father's donkeys (9:5). • Elkanah's lengthy genealogy suggests he was socially prominent.

1:2 Hardly an instance exists in Scripture where a man's simultaneous marriage to *two wives* did not produce serious friction (1:6-7; Gen 16; 21; 29).

1:3 Elkanah made this trip *each year;* the law required that people attend three annual festivals (Exod 23:14-17). • According to God's law, Israelites were to *sacrifice* at God's chosen sanctuary (Deut 12:1-28). From the days of Joshua (Josh 18:1) through Samuel's era, God's sanctuary—the Tabernacle—was at *Shiloh*, a town in Ephraim some 8.5 miles north of Bethel en route to Shechem. King David eventually moved it to Jerusalem (2 Sam 6). • *the LORD of Heaven's Armies:* Throughout the Hebrew OT, God

priests of the Lord at that time were the
two sons of Eli—Hophni and Phinehas. 4On
the days Elkanah presented his sacrifice, he
would give portions of the meat to Peninnah
and each of her children. 5And though he
loved Hannah, he would give her only one
choice portion because the Lord had given
her no children. 6So Peninnah would taunt
Hannah and make fun of her because the
Lord had kept her from having children.
7Year after year it was the same—Peninnah
would taunt Hannah as they went to the
Tabernacle. Each time, Hannah would be reduced to tears and would not even eat.
8"Why are you crying, Hannah?" Elkanah
would ask. "Why aren't you eating? Why be
downhearted just because you have no children? You have me—isn't that better than
having ten sons?"
9Once after a sacrificial meal at Shiloh,
Hannah got up and went to pray. Eli the priest
was sitting at his customary place beside
the entrance of the Tabernacle. 10Hannah
was in deep anguish, crying bitterly as she
[a]prayed to the Lord. 11And she made this
vow: "O Lord of Heaven's Armies, if you will
look upon my sorrow and answer my prayer
and give me a son, then I will give him back
to you. He will be yours for his entire lifetime,
and as a sign that he has been dedicated to
the Lord, his hair will never be cut."
12As she was praying to the Lord, Eli
watched her. 13Seeing her lips moving but
hearing no sound, he thought she had been
drinking. 14"Must you come here drunk?"
he demanded. "Throw away your wine!"
15"Oh no, sir!" she replied. "I haven't been
drinking wine or anything stronger. But I
am very discouraged, and I was pouring out
my heart to the Lord. 16Don't think I am a
[b]wicked woman! For I have been praying
out of great anguish and sorrow."
17"In that case," Eli said, "go in peace! May
the God of Israel grant the request you have
asked of him."
18"Oh, thank you, sir!" she exclaimed.

1:5 Gen 30:1-2
1:8 Ruth 4:15
1:9 1 Sam 3:3
1:10 [a]*palal* (6419) ‣1 Kgs 8:35
1:11 Gen 29:32; Num 6:1-6; 30:6-11; Judg 13:5; Luke 1:15
1:14 Acts 2:13
1:15 Ps 42:4; Lam 2:19
1:16 [b]*beliya'al* (1100) ‣1 Sam 2:12
1:17 Ps 20:3-5
1:18 Ruth 2:13

Vows to God (1:11, 24-28)

1 Sam 14:24-45; Gen 28:20-22; Lev 27:1-34; Num 21:2-3; 30:1-16; Deut 12:11; 23:18-23; Judg 11:30-40; Ps 76:11; Prov 20:25; Eccl 5:3-5; Mal 1:14; Matt 5:33-37; Acts 18:18; 21:23-24; Jas 5:12

The essence of a vow to God is, "If God will do X, then I will dedicate Y" to God or his sanctuary. Examples include Jacob's tithing (Gen 28:20-22), the Israelites' dealing with the Canaanite spoils of war (Num 21:2), Hannah's dedicating her son as a lifelong servant of the Lord (1:11), and Absalom's sacrificing to God at Hebron (2 Sam 15:8).

Guidelines for vows are frequently mentioned in the sacrificial laws. Israelites made vows conditional upon God's granting their requests. Then they would pay or fulfill their vows to God, often by giving offerings (e.g., Lev 7:16; 22:23; Deut 12:11).

However, vows could be abused. The law itself warns against this (Deut 23:21-23), as do the wisdom teachings (e.g., Prov 7:10-14; 20:25) and the books of the prophets (see, e.g., Jer 44:25). Saul was prone both to make foolish vows (14:24-28) and not to keep the vows he made (19:6). Impulsive vows might go unfulfilled and never paid, arousing God's anger. Not making a vow is better than backing out of one (Eccl 5:3-5). Jesus counsels us not to make vows, but simply to keep our word (Matt 5:33-37; cp. Jas 5:12).

is often referred to as *Yahweh Tseba'oth* or *'Elohim Tseba'oth.* Traditionally, these titles have been translated "Lord of hosts" and "God of hosts." The term "hosts" (Hebrew *tseba'oth,* traditionally "sabaoth") usually means "armies." It can refer to human armies, such as the armies of Israel (e.g., 17:45) or foreign armies sent to fulfill the Lord's purposes (e.g., Isa 9:11-13). However, most often it refers to God's angelic armies sent from heaven to do his bidding and wage war on earth (e.g., 2 Kgs 6:17). This designation anticipates God's role as a mighty warrior in the episode involving the Ark of the Covenant and the Philistines (chs 4–6).

1:4 ***sacrifice . . . portions of the meat:*** Certain sacrifices involved sharing part of the sacrificial animal in a communal meal (see Lev 7:11-34).

1:5 ***And though he loved Hannah, he would give her only one choice portion:*** Or *And because he loved Hannah, he would give her a choice portion.* The meaning of the Hebrew is uncertain.

1:7 ***the Tabernacle:*** Literally *the house of the Lord;* also in 1:24. Also called "the Temple of the Lord" in 1:9. These designations reflect that the Tabernacle, a portable structure, served as the central sanctuary at Shiloh.

1:9 ***the Tabernacle:*** Literally *the Temple of the Lord.* Solomon's Temple had not yet been constructed, so the word *Temple* here means the Lord's sanctuary.

1:11 Hannah's *vow* was a promise to give the child back to the Lord as a Nazirite (see Num 6:1-21). Hannah might have hoped that her child would be another Samson (cp. Judg 13), a deliverer of God's people. • Some manuscripts add *He will drink neither wine nor intoxicants* at the end of the verse.

1:13-14 Some people might have used the feast times at Shiloh as an occasion to get *drunk* rather than to worship. Eli mistakenly assumed Hannah was another drunken reveler (cp. Acts 2:13-15).

1:16 *wicked woman* (Hebrew *a daughter of Belial*): An expression used to describe a worthless person. Belial ("worthlessness") is later used as a name for Satan (2 Cor 6:15). In Hebrew, a *son of* or *daughter of* a quality is a person who exemplifies that quality.

1:17-18 A blessing was more than mere wishful thinking. It was often God's means of conferring a real benefit (see, e.g., Gen 27:1-40; 28:1-4; 32:22-32; 48:1–49:28). Because this blessing from God's high priest provided assurance

1:19
Gen 21:1-2; 30:22
ᶜ*zakar* (2142)
▸2 Kgs 20:3

1:21
Luke 2:22

1:24
Num 15:8-10

2:1
Luke 1:46-55

Then she went back and began to eat again, and she was no longer sad.

19The entire family got up early the next morning and went to worship the LORD once more. Then they returned home to Ramah. When Elkanah slept with Hannah, the LORD ᶜremembered her plea, 20and in due time she gave birth to a son. She named him Samuel, for she said, "I asked the LORD for him."

21The next year Elkanah and his family went on their annual trip to offer a sacrifice to the LORD. 22But Hannah did not go. She told her husband, "Wait until the boy is weaned. Then I will take him to the Tabernacle and leave him there with the LORD permanently."

23"Whatever you think is best," Elkanah agreed. "Stay here for now, and may the LORD help you keep your promise." So she stayed home and nursed the boy until he was weaned.

24When the child was weaned, Hannah took him to the Tabernacle in Shiloh. They brought along a three-year-old bull for the sacrifice and a basket of flour and some wine. 25After sacrificing the bull, they brought the boy to Eli. 26"Sir, do you remember me?" Hannah asked. "I am the woman who stood here several years ago praying to the LORD. 27I asked the LORD to give me this boy, and he has granted my request. 28Now I am giving him to the LORD, and he will belong to the LORD his whole life." And they worshiped the LORD there.

Hannah's Prayer of Praise

2 Then Hannah prayed:

"My heart rejoices in the LORD!
The LORD has made me strong.

SAMUEL (1:19–2:11)

1 Sam 3:1–4:1; 7:3–16:13; 19:18-24; 25:1; 28:1-25
Ps 99:6
Jer 15:1
Acts 3:24; 13:20
Heb 11:32

Samuel lived at the end of the period of the judges and ushered in the period of kingship. He was Israel's last judge (7:6, 15-17) and first prophet (3:20; Acts 3:24; 13:20). He functioned as a priest (2:18) and was a great man of faith (Heb 11:32).

Samuel was born in response to his mother Hannah's prayers. Samuel's parents traveled annually from Ramah to the Shiloh sanctuary (1:3). While at the sanctuary, Hannah, who was barren, prayed for a son and promised him to God for full-time service (1:9-11). God answered the prayer, and Samuel was born (1:19-20). When Samuel was weaned, Hannah took him to serve in the sanctuary with Eli, the high priest (1:24-28).

Eli's sons were wicked and pagan, but Samuel served the Lord. Soon it became clear that God spoke more intimately with Samuel than with Eli. God spoke to Samuel (3:1-18) to warn Eli of the coming disaster when the Philistines defeated Israel, killed Eli's sons, and took the Ark of the Covenant (chs 4–6). Later, under Samuel's leadership, the people repented of their sin of idolatry and succeeded in winning an important battle against the Philistines (7:3-17).

But as Samuel grew older, it became obvious that he suffered from the same weakness as Eli did before him. Samuel's sons were evil (8:1-3), and the people did not want them to assume leadership over the nation. So the people saw the need for a king who could lead them in battle against their enemies (8:4-5).

The transition from the era of the judges to kingship was turbulent. As priest, Samuel prayed for the people; as prophet, he reproved Saul for impatience and disobedience (13:5-14; 15:20-23). When God rejected Saul as king, Samuel anointed David as God's chosen one (16:1-13) and protected David from Saul (19:18-24).

Through prayer and perseverance, Samuel was a faithful leader (Jer 15:1; Acts 13:20; Heb 11:32) who cherished his people's well-being and courageously rebuked kings and elders. He led Israel from tribal disunity to national solidarity and established the monarchy. He wrote *The Record of Samuel the Seer* (1 Chr 29:29) and defined ideal kingship (10:25). When he died, he was mourned by all Israel. He was buried in Ramah, his hometown (25:1).

that Hannah's prayer would be answered, she was ***no longer sad.***

1:20 ***Samuel*** sounds like the Hebrew term for "asked of God" or "heard by God." We may ask God to fulfill the desires of our hearts.

1:22 ***until the boy is weaned:*** Hannah would have nursed Samuel two to four years. • Some manuscripts add *I will offer him as a Nazirite for all time* at the end of the verse.

1:23 Elkanah could have overridden Hannah's ***promise*** (Num 30:12-14), but instead he affirmed and supported it.

1:24 ***a three-year-old bull:*** As in Dead Sea Scrolls, Greek and Syriac versions; Masoretic Text reads *three bulls.* • ***and a basket:*** Hebrew *and an ephah* [20 quarts or 22 liters].

1:28 ***they:*** Literally *he.*

2:1-10 Hannah's prayer celebrates Samuel's dedication to the Lord's service by rejoicing in God's uniqueness (2:1-2), his ability to reverse fortunes

Now I have an answer for my enemies;
I rejoice because you rescued me.
2 No one is holy like the LORD!
There is no one besides you;
there is no [d]Rock like our God.

3 "Stop acting so proud and haughty!
Don't speak with such arrogance!
For the LORD is a God who knows what
you have done;
he will judge your actions.
4 The bow of the mighty is now broken,
and those who stumbled are now
strong.
5 Those who were well fed are now starving,
and those who were starving are now
full.
The childless woman now has seven
children,
and the woman with many children
wastes away.
6 The LORD gives both death and life;
he brings some down to the [e]grave but
raises others up.
7 The LORD makes some poor and others
rich;
he brings some down and [f]lifts
others up.
8 He lifts the poor from the dust
and the needy from the garbage dump.
He sets them among princes,
placing them in seats of honor.
For all the earth is the LORD's,
and he has set the world in order.

9 "He will protect his faithful ones,
but the wicked will disappear in
darkness.
No one will succeed by strength alone.
10 Those who fight against the LORD will
be shattered.
He thunders against them from heaven;
the LORD judges throughout the earth.
He gives power to his king;
he increases the strength of his
anointed one."

11 Then Elkanah returned home to Ramah without Samuel. And the boy [g]served the LORD by assisting Eli the priest.

Corruption in the Priestly House of Eli

12 Now the sons of Eli were [h]scoundrels who had no respect for the LORD 13 or for their

2:2
Deut 4:35; 32:30-31
[d]*tsur* (6697)
‣ 2 Sam 23:3

2:3
1 Sam 16:7
Prov 8:13; 16:2

2:4
Ps 37:15; 46:7-9

2:5
Ps 113:9
Jer 15:9

2:6
[e]*she'ol* (7585)
‣ Job 7:9

2:7
Deut 8:18
Job 1:21; 5:10-11
Ps 75:7
[f]*rum* (7311)
‣ 2 Sam 22:47

2:8
Job 38:4-7; 42:10
Jas 2:5

2:9
Ps 91:11-12

2:10
1 Sam 7:10
Ps 18:13; 21:1, 7

2:11
1 Sam 3:1
[g]*sharath* (8334)
‣ 1 Sam 2:18

2:12
Jer 2:8; 9:3, 6
[h]*beliya'al* (1100)
‣ 1 Sam 25:17

Hannah's Prayer of Praise (2:1-10)

Exod 15:21
Judg 5:1-31
Luke 1:46-55, 67-79

Hannah's Prayer of Praise (2:1-10) and Mary's Song of Praise (Luke 1:46-55) both emphasize God bringing down the rich and powerful and exalting the poor and the downtrodden (2:7-8; Luke 1:52-53). The rich, unrighteous rulers of the land (Eli, Saul, Herod) will be brought down, while the leaders who fulfill God's purposes (Samuel, David, Jesus) will be exalted.

Like Samuel, Jesus was dedicated at God's Temple (Luke 2:22-38). As Samuel had anointed David for service (16:13), John the Baptist and the Holy Spirit anointed Jesus (Matt 3:13-17; Mark 1:9-11; Luke 3:21-22). Samuel and David were the God-ordained means of fulfilling God's purposes for Israel. Hannah's song gives us a key to understanding God's purposes for Jesus; like Samuel and David, he would be a ruler and the Savior of God's people.

At the births of Samuel and Jesus, their mothers' songs represented the right response of all of God's people. God, who works decisively and redemptively, is worthy of praise.

(2:3-9), and his ability to strengthen his chosen king (2:10). David's prayer in 2 Sam 22 is another beautiful proclamation of God's saving power as it relates to his chosen king (2:10).

2:1 *made me strong* (literally *has exalted my horn*; cp. 2:10): The horn of a powerful animal, such as an ox or bull, was a symbol of strength that was held high in triumph after defeating an enemy (cp. 1 Kgs 22:11).

2:2 ***no one besides you:*** David responded similarly after receiving God's promises concerning his kingship (2 Sam 7:22). • ***Rock*** (cp. 2 Sam 22:2-3, 32): God provides stability and security for those who trust in him.

2:3 ***proud and haughty:*** Peninnah typified this attitude (see 1:6-7). Hannah, by contrast, was humbly dependent on God.

2:4-8 Hannah celebrated God's sovereign ability to radically reverse human circumstances.

2:5 *those who were starving are now full:* Cp. 1:7, 18. • The phrase *seven children* poetically means that the ***childless woman*** would be blessed with a house full of children (cp. 2:21).

2:6 *to the grave:* Hebrew *to Sheol.*

2:7-8 Cp. Ps 113:7-9.

2:8 *all the earth is the LORD's:* God, the creator and ruler of all things, is able to change circumstances (2:4-8), protect the faithful (2:9), judge the wicked, and empower his anointed king (2:10).

2:10 The king was to fulfill the descriptions of 2:4-9 by using his God-given ***power*** to care for the oppressed, the hungry, and the barren (see Ps 72:1-4, 12-14; Prov 31:8-9). • ***he increases the strength:*** Literally *he exalts the horn.* See note on 2:1. • ***anointed one*** (Hebrew *Messiah*): This climax to Hannah's prayer is prophetic both of Israel's anointed kings and of God's supreme Anointed King—the Messiah, Jesus Christ (see 12:3-5; 24:6, 10; Ps 132:17; Dan 9:25-26).

2:12 ***scoundrels*** (Hebrew *sons of Belial*): See note on 1:16. • ***had no respect for*** (literally *did not know*) ***the LORD:*** Although they were priests among God's people, they did not acknowledge God or seek to abide by his will (cp. Jer 2:8).

2:13-17 The priests were supposed to receive their portion of the meat only after it had been boiled (see Num 6:19). Eli's sons disregarded God's instructions (2:13-14, 17).

2:13 Lev 7:20, 28-36
2:15 Lev 3:2-5
2:17 Mal 2:7-9
2:18 1 Sam 2:11; [i]*sharath* (8334) ‣1 Kgs 19:21
2:19 1 Sam 1:3
2:21 Gen 21:1; 1 Sam 3:19-21; Luke 2:40
2:22 Exod 38:8
2:23 Num 15:30

duties as priests. Whenever anyone offered a sacrifice, Eli's sons would send over a servant with a three-pronged fork. While the meat of the sacrificed animal was still boiling, 14 the servant would stick the fork into the pot and demand that whatever it brought up be given to Eli's sons. All the Israelites who came to worship at Shiloh were treated this way. 15 Sometimes the servant would come even before the animal's fat had been burned on the altar. He would demand raw meat before it had been boiled so that it could be used for roasting.

16 The man offering the sacrifice might reply, "Take as much as you want, but the fat must be burned first." Then the servant would demand, "No, give it to me now, or I'll take it by force." 17 So the sin of these young men was very serious in the LORD's sight, for they treated the LORD's offerings with contempt.

18 But Samuel, though he was only a boy, [i]served the LORD. He wore a linen garment like that of a priest. 19 Each year his mother made a small coat for him and brought it to him when she came with her husband for the sacrifice. 20 Before they returned home, Eli would bless Elkanah and his wife and say, "May the LORD give you other children to take the place of this one she gave to the LORD." 21 And the LORD gave Hannah three sons and two daughters. Meanwhile, Samuel grew up in the presence of the LORD.

22 Now Eli was very old, but he was aware of what his sons were doing to the people of Israel. He knew, for instance, that his sons were seducing the young women who assisted at the entrance of the Tabernacle. 23 Eli said to them, "I have been hearing reports from all the people about the wicked things you are doing. Why do you keep sinning? 24 You must stop, my sons! The reports I hear among the LORD's people are

ELI (2:11–4:22)

1 Sam 1:9-18, 25-28
1 Kgs 2:27

Eli was Israel's chief priest at the Tabernacle at Shiloh, Israel's central shrine, during the period of the judges. Eli apparently descended from Ithamar, Aaron's youngest son (cp. 1 Kgs 2:27; 1 Chr 18:16; 24:3). Eli was sincere and devout, but he was weak and indulgent in parenting his wicked sons, Hophni and Phinehas.

When Eli encountered Hannah at the Tabernacle, he accused her of drunkenness as she fervently but silently asked God for a child. Upon realizing his mistake, Eli blessed Hannah, and God answered Hannah's prayer by giving her Samuel.

Samuel "grew in favor with the LORD and with the people" (2:26), but Eli's sons "were scoundrels who had no respect for the LORD" (2:12). They stole from the offerings and seduced women who served at the Tabernacle. When Eli reproached them, they disregarded him. God sent a prophet to denounce Eli's weakness and his sons' wickedness and to announce that God would withdraw the priesthood from Eli's family (2:27-36). This oracle was confirmed when God spoke to Samuel at night, telling him that he would soon punish Eli's family (3:1-14). Shortly thereafter, Israel's army was defeated in battle against the Philistines, the Ark of the Covenant was captured, and Eli's sons were killed (4:1-11). When Eli heard the news, he fell over backward and broke his neck (4:12-18). Eli was ninety-eight years old when he died. His daughter-in-law went into labor and died delivering Eli's grandson, named Ichabod ("where is the glory?" 4:19-22) because the glory had departed from Israel.

Eli's priestly line survived, however, until David's reign ended. Abiathar was Eli's last descendant to serve as chief priest. Since he supported Adonijah's attempt to usurp David's throne, Solomon removed Abiathar from office and replaced him with Zadok (1 Kgs 2:27).

2:15 God's law stipulated that the sacrificial ***animal's fat*** was the Lord's portion and had to be ***burned on the altar*** first (Lev 3:3-17).

2:18 The clause ***Samuel . . . served the LORD*** describes the ritual service of Levites and priests (see, e.g., Num 3:4; 8:19, 24; Deut 18:7). Like Eli's sons, Samuel was a Levite (see note on 1:1). But unlike Eli's sons, he lived up to his calling. • ***He wore a linen garment like that of a priest:*** Literally *He wore a linen ephod*, as did the priests who ministered in the sanctuary (see 22:18, "priestly garments").

2:20 ***Eli would bless:*** Blessing was one of the functions of a priest (Num 6:23-27; Deut 10:8; 1 Chr 23:13). See note on 1:17-18. • ***this one she gave to the LORD:*** As in Dead Sea Scrolls and Greek version; Masoretic Text reads *this one he requested of the LORD.*

2:21 ***Samuel grew up:*** See note on 2:26.

2:22-25 Eli's weak attempts to change his sons' behavior (cp. 2:29) indicate that he had raised them without discipline (3:13).

2:22 ***seducing . . . women:*** Eli's sons had probably been influenced by Canaanite religious practices, which included sex as part of the ritual. • ***who assisted at the entrance:*** See Exod 38:8. • ***Tabernacle:*** Literally *Tent of Meeting.* Some manuscripts lack this entire sentence.

not good. 25If someone sins against another
person, God can mediate for the guilty
party. But if someone sins against the LORD,
who can intercede?" But Eli's sons wouldn't
listen to their father, for the LORD was already planning to put them to death.
26Meanwhile, the boy Samuel grew taller
and grew in favor with the LORD and with
the people.
27One day a man of God came to Eli and
gave him this message from the LORD: "I revealed myself to your ancestors when the
people of Israel were slaves in Egypt. 28I
[j]chose your ancestor Aaron from among all
the tribes of Israel to be my priest, to offer
sacrifices on my altar, to burn incense, and
to wear the priestly vest as he served me.
And I assigned the sacrificial offerings to
you priests. 29So why do you scorn my sacrifices and offerings? Why do you give your
sons more honor than you give me—for you
and they have become fat from the best offerings of my people Israel!
30"Therefore, the LORD, the God of Israel,
says: I promised that your branch of the tribe
of Levi would always be my priests. But I will
honor those who honor me, and I will despise
those who think lightly of me. 31The time is
coming when I will put an end to your family,
so it will no longer serve as my priests. All the
members of your family will die before their
time. None will reach old age. 32You will
watch with envy as I pour out prosperity on
the people of Israel. But no members of your
family will ever live out their days. 33Those
who survive will live in sadness and grief,
and their children will die a violent death.
34And to prove that what I have said will
come true, I will cause your two sons, Hophni
and Phinehas, to die on the same day!
35"Then I will raise up a faithful [k]priest
who will serve me and do what I desire. I will
establish his family, and they will be priests
to my anointed kings forever. 36Then all of
your surviving family will bow before him,
begging for money and food. 'Please,' they
will say, 'give us jobs among the priests so
we will have enough to eat.' "

Samuel's Call to God's Service

3 Meanwhile, the boy Samuel served the
LORD by assisting Eli. Now in those days
messages from the LORD were very rare, and
[a]visions were quite uncommon.
2One night Eli, who was almost blind by
now, had gone to bed. 3The lamp of God
had not yet gone out, and Samuel was sleeping in the Tabernacle near the [b]Ark of God.
4Suddenly the LORD called out, "Samuel!"
"Yes?" Samuel replied. "What is it?" 5He
got up and ran to Eli. "Here I am. Did you
call me?"
"I didn't call you," Eli replied. "Go back to
bed." So he did.
6Then the LORD called out again, "Samuel!"
Again Samuel got up and went to Eli.
"Here I am. Did you call me?"
"I didn't call you, my son," Eli said. "Go
back to bed."

2:25 Josh 11:20
2:26 Luke 2:40, 52
2:27 Judg 13:6
2:28 Exod 28:1-4; 30:7-8
[j]*bakhar* (0977) ‣1 Sam 10:24
2:29 Deut 12:5; Matt 10:37
2:30 Num 25:12-13; Ps 50:23; Mal 2:7-9
2:31 1 Sam 4:11-18; 22:17-20
2:34 1 Sam 4:11, 17; 1 Kgs 13:3
2:35 [k]*kohen* (3548) ‣Jer 33:18
3:1 1 Sam 2:11; Ps 74:9; Amos 8:11
[a]*khazon* (2377) ‣2 Chr 32:32
3:3 [b]*'aron* (0727) ‣2 Sam 6:6

2:25 ***God*** (or ***the judges***; Hebrew *'elohim*): The Hebrew verb translated ***mediate*** is plural here, and when *'elohim* means "God," it often appears with a singular verb. In addition, some ancient translations render *'elohim* as "judges" here. If that is the correct translation, then the judges would ***mediate for the guilty party*** in a common human court. However, many Hebrew scholars believe that *'elohim* should never be translated "judges." If this is the case, in what sense could God *mediate for the guilty party*? Possibly Eli considered the court verdict to come directly from God. God might work through his revealed law or other circumstances to either acquit or convict an individual charged with wrongdoing. Or Eli might have been referring to the sacrificial system. • The sexual immorality (2:22) and gluttony (2:12-17) of Eli's sons were ***sins against the LORD*** because they were corrupting Israel's worship of him. No one can ***intercede*** for sinners who rebel so completely against God's will (cp. Matt 12:31). • Eli's sons did not ***listen to their father*** because the Lord had already begun to punish them by hardening their hearts (cp. Exod 4:21; 7:3; 8:15-32; 10:27; 11:10).

2:26 As children, both Samuel and Jesus possessed extraordinary qualities (2:21; see also Luke 2:40, 52). Samuel was one of Christ's forerunners.

2:27 ***Man of God*** is another name for a prophet (9:6; 1 Kgs 13:1; 2 Kgs 1:9). • ***I revealed myself:*** As in Greek and Syriac versions; Hebrew reads *Did I reveal myself.*

2:28 ***your ancestor Aaron:*** Literally *your father.* • ***the priestly vest:*** Literally *an ephod* (see note on 2:18).

2:29 By failing to stop his sons' wickedness, Eli showed contempt for God's ***sacrifices and offerings.*** Eli benefited from his sons' activities, and God held Eli responsible for letting them continue.

2:30 ***that your branch of the tribe of Levi*** (literally *that your house and your father's house*) ***would always be my priests:*** See Exod 29:9; Num 25:13. God would ***honor*** another of Aaron's descendants (see note on 2:35) and ***despise*** Eli's family, removing them from the priesthood (2:31-35).

2:32-33 ***live out their days . . . in sadness and grief:*** In the OT, a short life often expresses God's disfavor, while long life represents God's blessing (cp. Gen 15:15; 1 Kgs 3:14; Ps 91:16).

2:33 ***die a violent death:*** As in Dead Sea Scrolls, which read *die by the sword;* Masoretic Text reads *die like mortals.*

2:35 ***a faithful priest:*** Zadok and his descendants later replaced Eli's family in the priesthood (1 Kgs 2:26-27, 35).

3:1 ***messages . . . were very rare . . . visions were quite uncommon:*** God was not disclosing his will through prophets or priests, so the period was spiritually dark. However, that darkness was about to end when God communicated with Samuel (3:2–4:1a).

3:2 Eli was ***almost blind,*** both physically and spiritually (3:1).

3:3 The priests were responsible for keeping ***the lamp of God*** burning through the night (Exod 27:20-21; 30:7-8). • That Samuel ***was sleeping in the Tabernacle*** (literally *the Temple of the LORD;* see note on 1:7) ***near the Ark*** symbolizes his nearness to God's presence and purpose, in contrast to Eli and his sons.

3:7
Amos 3:7
3:11
2 Kgs 21:12
Jer 19:3
3:12
1 Sam 2:27-36
3:14
Lev 15:31
1 Sam 2:25
Isa 22:14
[c]*kapar* (3722)
› Ps 65:3
3:18
Job 2:10
Isa 39:8
3:19
Gen 21:22
Judg 13:24
3:20
Judg 20:1
4:1
1 Sam 7:12; 29:1
4:3
Num 10:35
Josh 7:7
4:4
2 Sam 6:2
Ps 80:1

[7]Samuel did not yet know the LORD because he had never had a message from the
LORD before. [8]So the LORD called a third
time, and once more Samuel got up and went
to Eli. "Here I am. Did you call me?"
Then Eli realized it was the LORD who was
calling the boy. [9]So he said to Samuel, "Go
and lie down again, and if someone calls
again, say, 'Speak, LORD, your servant is listening.'" So Samuel went back to bed.
[10]And the LORD came and called as before, "Samuel! Samuel!"
And Samuel replied, "Speak, your servant
is listening."
[11]Then the LORD said to Samuel, "I am
about to do a shocking thing in Israel. [12]I am
going to carry out all my threats against Eli
and his family, from beginning to end. [13]I
have warned him that judgment is coming
upon his family forever, because his sons
are blaspheming God and he hasn't disciplined them. [14]So I have vowed that the sins
of Eli and his sons will never be [c]forgiven by
sacrifices or offerings."

Samuel Speaks for the LORD

[15]Samuel stayed in bed until morning, then
got up and opened the doors of the Tabernacle as usual. He was afraid to tell Eli what
the LORD had said to him. [16]But Eli called
out to him, "Samuel, my son."
"Here I am," Samuel replied.
[17]"What did the LORD say to you? Tell me
everything. And may God strike you and
even kill you if you hide anything from me!"
[18]So Samuel told Eli everything; he didn't
hold anything back. "It is the LORD's will," Eli
replied. "Let him do what he thinks best."
[19]As Samuel grew up, the LORD was with
him, and everything Samuel said proved to
be reliable. [20]And all Israel, from Dan in the
north to Beersheba in the south, knew that
Samuel was confirmed as a prophet of the
LORD. [21]The LORD continued to appear at
Shiloh and gave messages to Samuel there
at the Tabernacle. [4:1]And Samuel's words
went out to all the people of Israel.

The Ark in Exile (4:1b–7:17)

The Philistines Capture the Ark

4 At that time Israel was at war with the
Philistines. The Israelite army was
camped near Ebenezer, and the Philistines
were at Aphek. [2]The Philistines attacked
and defeated the army of Israel, killing
4,000 men. [3]After the battle was over, the
troops retreated to their camp, and the
elders of Israel asked, "Why did the LORD
allow us to be defeated by the Philistines?"
Then they said, "Let's bring the Ark of the
Covenant of the LORD from Shiloh. If we
carry it into battle with us, it will save us
from our enemies."
[4]So they sent men to Shiloh to bring the
Ark of the Covenant of the LORD of Heaven's

3:7 ***Samuel did not yet know the LORD:*** He lacked direct experience of the Lord. In contrast, Eli's sons did not know the Lord (see note on 2:12) in that they were morally and spiritually deficient.

3:8 ***Eli realized:*** Despite his many shortcomings, Eli was not completely without spiritual insight.

3:10 The doubling of the name calls attention to the seriousness of the moment (cp. Gen 22:11; Exod 3:4; Matt 27:46; Luke 22:31; Acts 9:4). • Samuel omits "LORD" (see 3:9) from his response either out of reverence for the name or because of a lingering uncertainty about who was speaking.

3:11 The phrase ***a shocking thing*** conveys the magnitude and severity of God's judgment. God's actions would also be of national significance for Israel (cp. 2 Kgs 21:12; Jer 19:3).

3:12 ***my threats:*** See 2:27-36.

3:13 ***his sons are blaspheming God:*** As in Greek version; Hebrew reads *his sons have made themselves contemptible.* They were expressing contempt for God through their actions. • ***hasn't disciplined them:*** Eli rebuked his sons (2:23-25), but he did not restrain them.

3:14 Neither blood ***sacrifices*** nor ***offerings*** would be acceptable on behalf of Eli and his sons. The offerings of Lev 4–5 were for sins committed inadvertently or unintentionally, whereas ***the sins of Eli and his sons*** were deliberate and rebellious.

3:15 ***the Tabernacle:*** Literally *the house of the LORD.* See note on 1:7. • Samuel ***was afraid to tell Eli*** of God's plans for him and his family either because he respected Eli's position or he feared for his own safety.

3:19 ***proved to be reliable:*** Samuel was an authentic prophet (3:20; see Deut 18:21-22).

3:20 The whole nation, ***from Dan in the north to Beersheba in the south,*** acknowledged that Samuel was God's prophet. • ***confirmed as a prophet:*** The reliability of Samuel's message (3:19) made it evident that God was speaking through him.

3:21–4:1a ***The LORD continued to appear:*** God reopened the lines of communication with Israel through Samuel (cp. 3:1). • ***Shiloh:*** See note on 1:3.

4:1b–7:2 The crisis surrounding the Ark of the Covenant demonstrated Israel's need for Samuel's leadership and fulfilled prophecies about Eli and his sons (3:11-14).

4:1b ***the Philistines:*** See "The Philistines" at 5:1–6:18, p. 477. • The exact location of ***Ebenezer*** is unknown. It was probably just east of Aphek (see also 7:12 and note). • ***Aphek*** was west of Shiloh, well inland and well north of Philistine territory. By camping there, the Philistines might have been trying to seize more Israelite territory.

4:3 The Israelites were often ***defeated*** in war because of the sin of one individual or the entire nation (Josh 7). In this defeat, no one inquired whether sin was the cause; apparently no one had even asked the Lord whether they should engage the Philistines in the first place (cp. 1 Chr 14:13-16). Instead, the Israelites treated the ***Ark,*** the most sacred symbol of the Lord's presence, as a charm to ward off misfortune. Carrying the Ark ***into battle*** was not necessarily wrong (cp. Josh 6:2-21), but neither would this act ensure God's blessing and victory. • ***it will save us:*** Or *he will save us.*

4:4 ***LORD of Heaven's Armies:*** See note on 1:3. • ***enthroned between the cherubim:*** A representation of God's glorious

Armies, who is enthroned between the
[d]cherubim. Hophni and Phinehas, the sons
of Eli, were also there with the Ark of the
Covenant of God. 5When all the Israelites
saw the Ark of the Covenant of the LORD
coming into the camp, their shout of joy was
so loud it made the ground shake!
6"What's going on?" the Philistines asked.
"What's all the shouting about in the Hebrew
camp?" When they were told it was because
the Ark of the LORD had arrived, 7they panicked. "The gods have come into their camp!"
they cried. "This is a disaster! We have never
had to face anything like this before! 8Help!
Who can save us from these mighty gods of Israel? They are the same gods who destroyed
the Egyptians with plagues when Israel was
in the wilderness. 9Fight as never before,
Philistines! If you don't, we will become the
Hebrews' slaves just as they have been ours!
Stand up like men and fight!"
10So the Philistines fought desperately,
and Israel was defeated again. The slaughter was great; 30,000 Israelite soldiers died
that day. The survivors turned and fled to
their tents. 11The Ark of God was captured,
and Hophni and Phinehas, the two sons of
Eli, were killed.

The Death of Eli

12A man from the tribe of Benjamin ran
from the battlefield and arrived at Shiloh
later that same day. He had torn his clothes
and put dust on his head to show his grief.
13Eli was waiting beside the road to hear the
news of the battle, for his heart trembled for
the safety of the Ark of God. When the messenger arrived and told what had happened,
an outcry resounded throughout the town.
14"What is all the noise about?" Eli asked.
The messenger rushed over to Eli, 15who
was ninety-eight years old and blind. 16He
said to Eli, "I have just come from the battlefield—I was there this very day."
"What happened, my son?" Eli demanded.
17"Israel has been defeated by the Philistines," the messenger replied. "The people
have been slaughtered, and your two sons,
Hophni and Phinehas, were also killed. And
the Ark of God has been captured."
18When the messenger mentioned what
had happened to the Ark of God, Eli fell
backward from his seat beside the gate. He

[d]*kerub* (3742)
▸2 Sam 22:11

4:5 Josh 6:5
4:7 Exod 14:25; 15:14
4:9 Judg 13:1
4:10 Deut 28:15, 25
4:11 1 Sam 2:34; Ps 78:60-61
4:12 Josh 7:6; 2 Sam 1:2; Neh 9:1
4:15 Gen 27:1; 1 Sam 3:2
4:17 1 Sam 22:18; Ps 78:61, 64

The Ark of the Covenant (4:3, 6-11)

1 Sam 5:1–7:2
Exod 25:10-22; 40:20-21
Lev 16:2
Num 10:33-36
Deut 31:25-26
Josh 3:4-6; 6:6-13
Judg 20:26-28
2 Sam 6:1-17
Jer 3:16-18

The Ark was "The Ark of the LORD's Covenant" (Num 10:33; Deut 10:8; 31:9, 25-26). Its contents included the tablets of the covenant (the Ten Commandments). The Ark reminded Israel of God's covenant with them and was placed within the Most Holy Place in the sanctuary.

The Ark served as a sign of God's presence. It was carried around Jericho before that city was invaded (Josh 6:6-7). It also appeared when Israel headed out into the wilderness (Num 10:33-36) and crossed the Jordan River into the Promised Land (Josh 3:4-6), and in the siege of the Ammonite city of Rabbah during David's time (2 Sam 11:11).

The Philistines equated the Ark with Israel's God (4:6-8). This is understandable, because the Philistines brought images of their own gods into battle (2 Sam 5:21). The Israelites were not to use images of the divine, so they viewed the Ark as the Lord's footstool and temporary residence rather than his image. However, the Israelites developed an idolatrous, pagan point of view. They treated the sacred symbol as a fetish and tried to manipulate God's presence for their own benefit. They reasoned, "If the Ark is with us, then God's presence and favor in battle will also be with us." As their defeat that day showed, God cannot be manipulated—he is the ruler of his people, and he must be obeyed and trusted (cp. Josh 5:13-15).

presence hovered over the Ark in the Most Holy Place (God's "throne room"). • The involvement of Eli's sons, ***Hophni and Phinehas***, foreshadows the disaster that ensued (see 3:11-14).

4:6-7 Like the Israelites, ***the Philistines*** regarded the ***Ark*** as a powerful talisman (see 4:2-3) and believed that its presence in battle would mean sure ***disaster*** for them. • ***the gods have come:*** Or *A god has come.*

4:8 ***the same gods who destroyed the Egyptians:*** The Philistines, who worshiped many gods, knew of the Lord's power. Yet they knew nothing of his nature as the one true God. • ***destroyed . . . with plagues:*** The Lord later showed his power against the Philistines similarly (see 5:6–6:6).

4:10 ***30,000*** was more than seven times as many as had ***died*** previously without the Ark (4:2). The Israelites learned the hard way that the Ark was not a talisman to ward off misfortune.

4:11 That the ***Ark . . . was captured*** was devastating to the Israelites (4:12-22). • The deaths of ***Hophni and Phinehas*** fulfilled the Lord's word to Eli (2:34). Although they are the only casualties named, they were not the only Israelites who had sinned (see 7:3-6).

4:12 ***had torn his clothes and put dust on his head:*** This phrase indicates ***grief*** and loss (e.g., Josh 7:6; 2 Sam 1:2; 15:32; Job 2:12).

4:15 ***blind:*** See 3:2 and note.

4:18 ***Eli fell backward:*** Either he was startled or he had a heart attack when he heard the message. Eli's fatal fall symbolizes his family's fall from the priesthood and the end of the abomination that his sons began (2:12-17).

4:20
Gen 35:17-18
4:21
Ps 78:61; 106:20
[e]*kabod* (3519)
‣2 Chr 32:27
5:2
Judg 16:23
5:3
Isa 19:1; 46:7
5:4
Ezek 6:6
Mic 1:7
5:6
Exod 9:3
1 Sam 6:4-5
5:8
Judg 16:18

broke his neck and died, for he was old and overweight. He had been Israel's judge for forty years.

[19]Eli's daughter-in-law, the wife of Phinehas, was pregnant and near her time of delivery. When she heard that the Ark of God had been captured and that her father-in-law and husband were dead, she went into labor and gave birth. [20]She died in childbirth, but before she passed away the midwives tried to encourage her. "Don't be afraid," they said. "You have a baby boy!" But she did not answer or pay attention to them.

[21]She named the child Ichabod (which means "Where is the glory?"), for she said, "Israel's [e]glory is gone." She named him this because the Ark of God had been captured and because her father-in-law and husband were dead. [22]Then she said, "The glory has departed from Israel, for the Ark of God has been captured."

The Ark in Philistine Territory

5 After the Philistines captured the Ark of God, they took it from the battleground at Ebenezer to the town of Ashdod. [2]They carried the Ark of God into the temple of Dagon and placed it beside an idol of Dagon. [3]But when the citizens of Ashdod went to see it the next morning, Dagon had fallen with his face to the ground in front of the Ark of the LORD! So they took Dagon and put him in his place again. [4]But the next morning the same thing happened—Dagon had fallen face down before the Ark of the LORD again. This time his head and hands had broken off and were lying in the doorway. Only the trunk of his body was left intact. [5]That is why to this day neither the priests of Dagon nor anyone who enters the temple of Dagon in Ashdod will step on its threshold.

[6]Then the LORD's heavy hand struck the people of Ashdod and the nearby villages with a plague of tumors. [7]When the people realized what was happening, they cried out, "We can't keep the Ark of the God of Israel here any longer! He is against us! We will all be destroyed along with Dagon, our god." [8]So they called together the rulers of the Philistine towns and asked, "What should we do with the Ark of the God of Israel?"

The rulers discussed it and replied, "Move it to the town of Gath." So they moved the

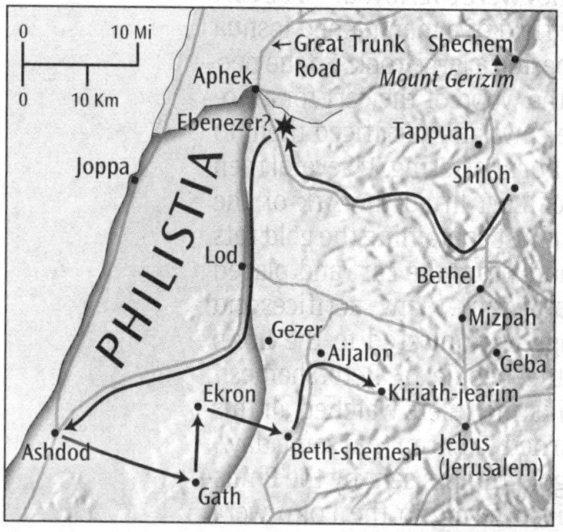

◀ **The Ark of the Covenant in Philistia (4:1-11; 5:1–7:2).** The arrows show the route that the Ark traveled. Israel carried the Ark into battle thinking it had magical powers to protect them (4:1-5). The Philistines, however, captured the Ark (4:6-11) and took it along the GREAT TRUNK ROAD to ASHDOD, then to GATH and EKRON (5:1-12). The Ark itself was no talisman, but it represented the Lord's holy presence. The Philistine idol fell before it, and in each city, the Lord's holiness brought a plague against the Philistines themselves. Finally, the Philistines sent the Ark back to the Israelites, who took it with joy to KIRIATH-JEARIM (6:1–7:2).

• ***Israel's judge:*** See Judges Introduction, p. 416. Priesthood and judgeship were not incompatible (cp. Exod 18:13-26; Deut 17:8-13). Samuel replaced Eli as Israel's judge and provided leadership that Eli had failed to provide (see 7:12-17). • The phrase ***for forty years*** incorporates Eli's career into the conceptual and temporal framework of the book of Judges (cp. Judg 3:11; 5:31; 8:28; 13:1).

4:20-21 The name *Ichabod* contains the Hebrew word *kabod* (*glory;* see Exod 24:15-17). A similar word is used to describe Eli in 4:18 (Hebrew *kabed,* "heavy"). The disappearance of the Ark parallels the demise of Eli's house. Although the Israelites experienced a stunning loss of divine glory and protection (cp. Ezek 8–10; Luke 19:41-44; 21:20-24), God's glorious presence would subsequently return to his people (ch 6; cp. Ezek 43:1-8).

5:1 ***Ebenezer:*** See note on 4:1b. • ***Ashdod,*** one of the five important Philistine cities (see 6:17), was located along the same major trade highway (the Great Trunk Road) as Aphek.

5:2 ***Dagon*** was one of the Philistines' gods (see Judg 16:23-24). The name could be related to the Hebrew *dag* ("fish"), an appropriate name for a god of seafaring people. More likely, it reflects the Hebrew *dagan* ("grain"), suggesting a fertility or agriculture god.

5:4 ***his head and hands had broken off:*** A symbol of God's supremacy over the idol (5:7; see also 17:51).

5:5 ***step on its threshold:*** While the Philistines might have believed that Dagon's amputations resulted from their failure to honor the god properly, the true failure was in worshiping an idol rather than honoring the one true God (Isa 44:6-20).

5:6 ***tumors:*** Greek version and Latin Vulgate read *tumors; and rats appeared in their land, and death and destruction were throughout the city* (cp. 6:4). The Hebrew term can mean simply "swellings." A possible alternative translation is "hemorrhoids." They were possibly the fatal *buboes* of bubonic plague, which attack the lower body, especially the rectal area. Rats are known carriers of the plague.

5:8 ***rulers*** (or *overlords*): Each of the five major Philistine cities had its own ruler (6:16-18). • ***Move it:*** Despite the obvious danger, the Philistines relished their captured trophy enough to relocate it rather than return it. • ***Gath,*** one of the five major Philistine cities, was nearby.

Ark of the God of Israel to Gath. 9But when the Ark arrived at Gath, the LORD's heavy hand fell on its men, young and old; he struck them with a plague of tumors, and there was a great panic.

10So they sent the Ark of God to the town of Ekron, but when the people of Ekron saw it coming they cried out, "They are bringing the Ark of the God of Israel here to kill us, too!" 11The people summoned the Philistine rulers again and begged them, "Please send the Ark of the God of Israel back to its own country, or it will kill us all." For the deadly plague from God had already begun, and great fear was sweeping across the town. 12Those who didn't die were afflicted with tumors; and the cry from the town rose to heaven.

The Return of the Ark to Israel

6 The Ark of the LORD remained in Philistine territory seven months in all. 2Then the Philistines called in their priests and diviners and asked them, "What should we do about the Ark of the LORD? Tell us how to return it to its own country."

3"Send the Ark of the God of Israel back with a gift," they were told. "Send a guilt offering so the plague will stop. Then, if you are healed, you will know it was his hand that caused the plague."

4"What sort of guilt offering should we send?" they asked.

And they were told, "Since the plague has struck both you and your five rulers, make five gold tumors and five gold rats, just like those that have ravaged your land. 5Make these things to show honor to the God of Israel. Perhaps then he will stop afflicting you, your gods, and your land. 6Don't be stubborn and rebellious as Pharaoh and the Egyptians were. By the time God was finished with them, they were eager to let Israel go.

7"Now build a new cart, and find two cows that have just given birth to calves. Make sure the cows have never been yoked to a cart. Hitch the cows to the cart, but shut their calves away from them in a pen. 8Put the Ark of the LORD on the cart, and beside it place a chest containing the gold rats and gold tumors you are sending as a guilt offering. Then let the cows go wherever they want. 9If they cross the border of our land and go to Beth-shemesh, we will know it was the LORD who brought this great disaster upon us. If they don't, we will know it was not his hand that caused the plague. It came simply by chance."

10So these instructions were carried out. Two cows were hitched to the cart, and their newborn calves were shut up in a pen. 11Then the Ark of the LORD and the chest containing the gold rats and gold tumors were placed on the cart. 12And sure enough, without veering off in other directions, the cows went straight along the road toward Beth-shemesh, lowing as they went. The Philistine rulers followed them as far as the border of Beth-shemesh.

13The people of Beth-shemesh were harvesting wheat in the valley, and when they saw the Ark, they were overjoyed! 14The cart came into the field of a man named Joshua and stopped beside a large rock. So the people broke up the wood of the cart for a fire and killed the cows and sacrificed them to the LORD as a burnt offering. 15Several men of the tribe of Levi lifted the Ark of the LORD and the chest containing the gold rats and gold tumors from the cart and placed them on the large rock. Many sacrifices and burnt offerings were offered to the LORD that day by the people of Beth-shemesh. 16The five Philistine rulers watched all this and then returned to Ekron that same day.

17The five gold tumors sent by the Philistines as a guilt offering to the LORD were

5:9 1 Sam 7:13; 12:15
5:10 Josh 13:3
6:2 Gen 41:8; Exod 7:11
6:3 Lev 5:15-16
6:4 Josh 13:3; 1 Sam 5:6, 11
6:6 Exod 8:15, 31-32; 12:31
6:7 Deut 21:3; 2 Sam 6:3
6:9 Josh 15:10; 1 Sam 6:3
6:14 2 Sam 24:22
6:15 Josh 3:2-4
6:17 1 Sam 6:4

5:9 God often used ***great panic*** to incapacitate and overwhelm Israel's enemies (14:15, 20; Deut 7:23; Ezek 22:5; Amos 3:9).

5:10 ***Ekron***, another of the five major Philistine cities (see 6:17), was just five miles north of Gath.

5:11 ***it will kill us:*** Or *he will kill us.*

6:2 ***priests and diviners:*** Divination was a part of Philistine religion (cp. 28:7; Deut 18:10-14).

6:3 It is unlikely the Philistines were aware of Israelite worship regulations. A Philistine *guilt offering* would have been a payment to the deity in an attempt to avert his wrath (contrast "Atonement" at Lev 16:1-34, p. 223).

6:4 ***rats:*** See note on 5:6.

6:6 The Philistines had thought they could overcome the Lord by fighting harder (4:9). They had defeated the Israelites, but they now realized that they could not defeat Israel's God.

6:7 ***shut their calves away:*** If the *cows* went against their maternal nature and left their calves to take the Ark to Israel, it would prove that the plague was from Israel's God (6:9).

6:9 ***Beth-shemesh*** was the closest Israelite town to Ekron (5:10).

6:13 ***Harvesting wheat*** was usually done in May or June.

6:14 This ***burnt offering*** could have been for forgiveness of sin (see 7:9-10; Lev 1:3-17), but it was more likely a freewill expression of love or thanksgiving (see Lev 22:18-22).

6:15 Providentially, ***the Ark*** had arrived in ***Beth-shemesh*** (6:13), which was a Levite city (Josh 21:13-16). The ***men of the tribe of Levi*** who lived there could safely move the Ark (see Num 4:15).

6:17 ***guilt offering:*** See note on 6:3. • ***Ashdod, Gaza, Ashkelon, Gath, and***

6:18
Deut 3:5
6:19
2 Sam 6:7
ʼ*abal* (0056)
‣2 Sam 13:37
6:20
Lev 11:44-45
2 Sam 6:9
Mal 3:2
6:21
Josh 15:9, 60
7:1
2 Sam 6:3-4
7:3
Deut 6:13; 13:4
Josh 24:14, 23
Judg 2:12-13; 10:16
Joel 2:12-14

gifts from the rulers of Ashdod, Gaza, Ashkelon, Gath, and Ekron. 18The five gold rats
represented the five Philistine towns and
their surrounding villages, which were controlled by the five rulers. The large rock at
Beth-shemesh, where they set the Ark of
the LORD, still stands in the field of Joshua
as a witness to what happened there.
19But the LORD killed seventy men from
Beth-shemesh because they looked into the
Ark of the LORD. And the people [f]mourned
greatly because of what the LORD had done.
20"Who is able to stand in the presence of
the LORD, this holy God?" they cried out.
"Where can we send the Ark from here?"
21So they sent messengers to the people
at Kiriath-jearim and told them, "The Philistines have returned the Ark of the LORD.
Come here and get it!"

7 So the men of Kiriath-jearim came to
get the Ark of the LORD. They took it
to the hillside home of Abinadab and ordained Eleazar, his son, to be in charge of it.
2The Ark remained in Kiriath-jearim for a
long time—twenty years in all. During that
time all Israel mourned because it seemed
the LORD had abandoned them.

Samuel, the Last of Israel's Judges

3Then Samuel said to all the people of Israel,
"If you are really serious about wanting to
return to the LORD, get rid of your foreign
gods and your images of Ashtoreth. Determine to obey only the LORD; then he will
rescue you from the Philistines." 4So the Israelites got rid of their images of Baal and
Ashtoreth and worshiped only the LORD.
5Then Samuel told them, "Gather all of

The Philistines (5:1–6:18)

1 Sam 13:16–14:23; 21:10-15; 23:1-5, 26-28; 31:1-10
Gen 10:13-14
Judg 3:1-3
2 Sam 5:17-25; 8:1; 21:15-22
2 Kgs 18:8
2 Chr 17:10-11; 21:16-17; 26:6-7; 28:18-19
Isa 2:6
Ezek 25:15-17
Amos 1:6-8; 9:7

The Philistines, situated on the southeast coastal plain of the Mediterranean, were part of a larger group of maritime immigrants from the Aegean area known by the Egyptians as the "Sea Peoples." They settled on Palestine's lower coastal plain around 1200 BC and established the five cities of Ashdod, Ashkelon, Ekron, Gaza, and Gath. Far from being unenlightened and unsophisticated, the Philistines were politically capable and technologically advanced.

The Philistines were fierce warriors. Their advances in iron technology made them an almost invincible foe (13:19-22). They were constant adversaries of the Israelites in the days of the judges (approximately 1350~1050 BC) and the early united monarchy (approximately 1050~970 BC). Saul eventually died at the hands of the Philistines (ch 31). David vanquished them before becoming king (18:20-30; 19:8; 23:1-5) and after (2 Sam 5:17-25; 8:1; 21:15, 18-22). While the Philistines never completely disappeared while Israel was a nation (2 Kgs 18:8; 2 Chr 17:11; 21:16-17; 26:6-7; 28:18), David effectively ended this menacing threat.

In 1 Samuel, God used the Philistines to eliminate the sinful family of Eli (4:10-22). The Philistines were also God's tool for building David's military and political career (17:32-58; 18:20-29). They distracted Saul when he was about to capture David (23:26-28), provided David with refuge from Saul (21:10-15; 27:1-12), prevented David from having to fight his own people (ch 29), and by killing Saul and his sons (ch 31), opened the way for David to become king. In the end, the Philistines experienced God's judgment (see Ezek 25:15-16; Amos 1:6-8).

Ekron: These five major Philistine cities were located on or near the Great Trunk Road. This major ancient trade route connected Egypt with Mesopotamia via the coastal plain of Canaan. Each city was governed by a kinglike ruler (6:16).

6:19 ***seventy men:*** As in a few Hebrew manuscripts; most Hebrew manuscripts read *70 men, 50,000 men.* Perhaps the text should be understood to read *the LORD killed 70 men and 50 oxen.* The smaller death toll is more likely than 50,070 because ***Beth-shemesh*** was a small village. • ***because they looked into the Ark:*** Physical contact with the Ark was prohibited (Num 4:15; 2 Sam 6:6-8), as was looking inside it (Num 4:20). Those who were killed lacked reverence for God's holiness.

6:20 ***Who is able to stand?*** Even God's people were not immune to his wrath when his holiness was violated. • ***Where can we send the Ark?*** When faced with God's holiness, the Israelites echoed the distress of the pagan Philistines (6:2).

6:21 ***Kiriath-jearim*** was nearby, about ten miles northeast of Beth-shemesh.

7:1 The ***men of Kiriath-jearim*** who transported ***the Ark*** and ***Eleazar*** were probably Levites (see 6:15; Num 1:47-51). • ***in charge of it:*** The same verb describes the Levites' duty of guarding the Tabernacle (Num 1:53; 3:7).

7:2 ***Twenty years*** covers the time until Samuel assembled the people at Mizpah (7:5-6). David later brought the Ark to Jerusalem (2 Sam 6:1-19).

7:3-10 The change in the people's standing with God, not the presence of the Ark (see 4:3-11), led Israel to victory against the Philistines.

7:3 People cannot expect God's blessing unless they ***get rid of*** what is contrary to his will (see Gen 35:2; Josh 24:14). • ***Ashtoreth*** (also called *Asherah*) was the Canaanite goddess of fertility associated with Baal (7:4). Worship of Asherah was an ongoing problem throughout Israel's history (e.g., Deut 12:3; 1 Kgs 16:33). The people started worshiping idols during the twenty-year period mentioned in 7:2, or perhaps they had done so ever since the days of the judges (8:8; Judg 6:25; cp. Amos 5:25-26). Israel's devastating defeat by the Philistines was due not only to the sins of Eli's two sons but to several generations of unfaithfulness to God.

Israel to Mizpah, and I will pray to the LORD
for you." 6So they gathered at Mizpah and,
in a great ceremony, drew water from a well
and poured it out before the LORD. They also
went without food all day and confessed
that they had sinned against the LORD. (It
was at Mizpah that Samuel became Israel's
judge.)

7When the Philistine rulers heard that
Israel had gathered at Mizpah, they mobilized their army and advanced. The
Israelites were badly [g]frightened when they
learned that the Philistines were approaching. 8"Don't stop pleading with the LORD our
God to save us from the Philistines!" they
begged Samuel. 9So Samuel took a young
lamb and offered it to the LORD as a whole
burnt offering. He pleaded with the LORD to
help Israel, and the LORD answered him.

10Just as Samuel was sacrificing the burnt
offering, the Philistines arrived to attack
Israel. But the LORD spoke with a mighty
voice of thunder from heaven that day, and
the Philistines were thrown into such confusion that the Israelites defeated them. 11The
men of Israel chased them from Mizpah to
a place below Beth-car, slaughtering them
all along the way.

12Samuel then took a large stone and
placed it between the towns of Mizpah and
Jeshanah. He named it Ebenezer (which
means "the stone of help"), for he said, "Up
to this point the LORD has helped us!"

13So the Philistines were subdued and
didn't invade Israel again for some time.
And throughout Samuel's lifetime, the
LORD's powerful hand was raised against
the Philistines. 14The Israelite villages near
Ekron and Gath that the Philistines had captured were restored to Israel, along with the
rest of the territory that the Philistines had
taken. And there was peace between Israel
and the Amorites in those days.

15Samuel continued as Israel's judge for
the rest of his life. 16Each year he traveled
around, setting up his court first at Bethel,
then at Gilgal, and then at Mizpah. He
judged the people of Israel at each of these
places. 17Then he would return to his home
at Ramah, and he would hear cases there,
too. And Samuel built an altar to the LORD
at Ramah.

2. ESTABLISHMENT OF SAUL'S KINGSHIP (8:1–12:25)

The People's Demand for a King (8:1-22)

8 As Samuel grew old, he appointed his
sons to be [h]judges over Israel. 2Joel and
Abijah, his oldest sons, held court in Beersheba. 3But they were not like their father,
for they were greedy for money. They accepted bribes and perverted justice.

4Finally, all the elders of Israel met at
Ramah to discuss the matter with Samuel.
5"Look," they told him, "you are now old,
and your sons are not like you. Give us a
king to judge us like all the other nations
have."

7:6 Judg 10:10; Neh 9:1; Lam 2:19
7:7 1 Sam 13:6; 17:11; [g]*yare'* (3372) ‣1 Sam 21:12
7:8 1 Sam 12:19; Isa 37:4
7:9 Lev 22:26-27; Ps 99:6; Jer 15:1
7:10 1 Sam 2:10; 2 Sam 22:14; Ps 18:14
7:12 Gen 35:13-15; Josh 4:9; 24:26
7:13 Judg 13:1; 1 Sam 13:5
7:15 1 Sam 7:6; 12:11
7:16 Gen 28:19; 1 Sam 7:5
7:17 1 Sam 1:1, 19; 2:11; 15:34
8:1 Deut 16:18-19; [h]*shapat* (8199) ‣Ps 7:11
8:2 1 Kgs 19:3; Amos 5:5
8:3 Exod 23:6, 8; Deut 16:19
8:4 1 Sam 7:17
8:5 Deut 17:14-15; 1 Sam 12:2

7:5 *Mizpah* was an administrative center and rallying point for the nation (see 7:16; 10:17; Judg 20:1). • *I will pray . . . for you:* Eli's question in 2:25 is answered here; Samuel was the intercessor Israel needed.

7:6 *drew water . . . poured it out:* This type of ceremony is not mentioned elsewhere in the OT. • At times Israelites *went without food* to express grief or to seek the Lord's favor (2 Sam 1:12; 12:22-23; 1 Kgs 21:27; Ezra 8:21-23; Neh 9:1; Esth 4:3, 16; Joel 2:12; cp. Luke 2:37; Acts 13:2-3; 14:23). • To have *Samuel* as *Israel's judge* was refreshing compared to Eli's failed leadership (see 4:18 and note) and the leadership of some other judges (e.g., Gideon, Judg 8:22-27; Jephthah, Judg 11:30–12:7; and Samson, Judg 13:1–16:21).

7:9 The *whole burnt offering* was probably for forgiveness of sin (see Lev 1:1-4). • *The LORD answered* with a forceful thunderclap (7:10).

7:10 *voice of thunder:* See 2:10. God often used similar tactics to throw Israel's enemies into *confusion* and defeat them (e.g., Exod 14:24; 23:27; Josh 10:10; Judg 4:15).

7:12 *Ebenezer:* The location of this *stone* memorial is unknown. The Philistines had defeated Israel and captured the Ark at a place with the same name (4:1; 5:1). Samuel erected this memorial to commemorate God's help in turning the tide against the Philistine attacks. • *Jeshanah:* As in Greek and Syriac versions; Hebrew reads *Shen.*

7:13 The Philistines were quiet *for some time*—until Saul became king (see 13:5). • God's *powerful hand,* not Samuel's giftedness, was the key factor in Israel's deliverance from the Philistines.

7:14 The *Amorites* had inhabited Canaan and the region east of the Jordan before Israel's conquest of the Promised Land (see Gen 15:16; Deut 3:8; Josh 2:10). Some Amorites remained in the area after the conquest (see 2 Sam 21:2).

7:15 *judge for the rest of his life:* Once Saul became king (ch 10), Samuel's role was more judicial than military.

7:16 *Bethel* and *Mizpah* were places of national assembly in the judges era (Judg 20:1, 18, 26; 21:1-2). Bethel's significance went back to the days of Abraham (Gen 12:8; 13:3-4; 28:10-22; 35:1-15). • *Gilgal,* located near Jericho, had been a sacred place since Joshua's day (Josh 4:19-24; 5:2-10). From this circuit, Samuel influenced "all the people of Israel" (10:17).

7:17 *Ramah* was Samuel's hometown (see 1:1).

8:1–12:25 During Israel's transition to a monarchy, neither God (8:7-9) nor Samuel (12:1-25) was pleased by the people's demand for a king. Saul, the first king (chs 9–11), failed in his role (chs 13–31) and fulfilled Samuel's warnings (see 8:10-18; cp. 16:1-13).

8:2 Samuel's two *oldest sons* functioned as judges *in Beersheba,* fifty miles south of their father's home.

8:3 *they were not like their father:* They were more like Eli's two sons (2:12-17). Their corruption was a primary reason the era of the judges ended.

8:5 *you are now old, and your sons are not like you:* Judges tended to be local leaders; kings, as national leaders, were more capable of uniting a whole nation

8:6 1 Sam 12:17; 15:11
8:7 Exod 16:8
8:9 1 Sam 8:11-18
8:11 Deut 17:16; 1 Sam 14:52; 2 Sam 15:1; 1 Kgs 1:5
8:12 1 Sam 22:7; 1 Kgs 4:7
8:14 1 Sam 22:7; 1 Kgs 21:7; Ezek 46:18
8:18 Job 27:9; Prov 1:25-28; Mic 3:4
8:19 Jer 44:16
8:22 1 Sam 8:7

6Samuel was displeased with their request and went to the LORD for guidance.
7"Do everything they say to you," the LORD
replied, "for it is me they are rejecting, not
you. They don't want me to be their king
any longer. 8Ever since I brought them from
Egypt they have continually abandoned me
and followed other gods. And now they are
giving you the same treatment. 9Do as they
ask, but solemnly warn them about the way
a king will reign over them."
10So Samuel passed on the LORD's warning to the people who were asking him for
a king. 11"This is how a king will reign over
you," Samuel said. "The king will draft your
sons and assign them to his chariots and
his charioteers, making them run before
his chariots. 12Some will be generals and
captains in his army, some will be forced to
plow in his fields and harvest his crops, and
some will make his weapons and chariot
equipment. 13The king will take your daughters from you and force them to cook and
bake and make perfumes for him. 14He will
take away the best of your fields and vineyards and olive groves and give them to his
own officials. 15He will take a tenth of your
grain and your grape harvest and distribute
it among his officers and attendants. 16He
will take your male and female slaves and demand the finest of your cattle and donkeys
for his own use. 17He will demand a tenth
of your flocks, and you will be his slaves.
18When that day comes, you will beg for relief from this king you are demanding, but
then the LORD will not help you."
19But the people refused to listen to Samuel's warning. "Even so, we still want a king,"
they said. 20"We want to be like the nations
around us. Our king will judge us and lead
us into battle."
21So Samuel repeated to the LORD what
the people had said, 22and the LORD replied,
"Do as they say, and give them a king." Then
Samuel agreed and sent the people home.

Monarchy (8:5-22)

1 Sam 10:1, 24-25; Deut 17:14-20; 33:5; Judg 17:6; 21:25; 2 Sam 7:8-16; Ps 89:35-37; Eccl 8:2-5; Isa 33:22; Matt 21:1-11; 22:42-46; 27:11; 1 Tim 1:17; 1 Pet 2:13-14; Rev 5:5; 11:15; 15:3

One reason the nation of Israel wanted a king was to be "like all the other nations." The institution of kingship in other ancient Near Eastern nations was almost 2,000 years old by the time of Saul and David, especially in the Egyptian and Babylonian empires. Other much smaller nations—such as Philistia, Moab, and Edom—also had kings with permanent bureaucracies and standing armies. Kings were believed to be the chosen instruments through which deities governed human affairs, so kings reigned either as gods or for the gods.

The Israelites envied other nations and were not interested in the long-term implications of monarchy, in spite of Samuel's warnings (8:10-18). Several hundred years of monarchy would prove that Samuel's apprehensions were justified: Wicked kings eventually led God's chosen nation into foreign domination and exile. Yet the monarchy would also provide the Messiah through David and his dynasty, and God established the Messiah's kingdom forever (see 2 Sam 7:8-16; Matt 21:1-11; Rev 5:5; 11:15). God used monarchy to fulfill his purposes.

in times of crisis (8:20). However, a spiritual problem underlay the request for a king (8:7-8). • *Other nations,* such as Egypt and Sumer, had monarchies for almost 2,000 years before Samuel's time.

8:6 *Samuel was displeased:* He probably felt personally rejected (8:7).

8:7 *Do everything they say:* God rarely instructed a prophet to heed the voice of the errant populace. The will of the people and the will of God would converge in King David (see 2 Sam 7:8-17). • *it is me they are rejecting:* Their rejection of judgeship was a deeper rejection of God's rule and sovereignty (see also 12:1-17).

8:8 *followed other gods:* The people's request for a king was tantamount to idolatry. Israel's monarchy was a divine concession rather than a divine gift. Kingship or any other human institution becomes idolatrous when it replaces trust in God.

8:10-18 These verses list the disadvantages of kingship. Each sentence begins with something the king would take. A king would be a confiscator, not just a protector.

8:11 While the people wanted a king to *judge* them, Samuel warned that the king would *reign over* them. They wanted a leader but received a ruler.

8:12-17 The king would take people as well as possessions.

8:12 *generals and captains in his army:* Literally *commanders of thousands and commanders of fifties.*

8:15 A *tenth* of the harvest was already required as a sacred donation to support God's Temple and servants (Deut 12:6, 17-18; 14:22-29; 26:12-15). The king would demand an additional tenth, a burdensome amount given the uncertainties of agriculture.

8:16 *cattle:* As in Greek version; Hebrew reads *young men.*

8:17 *you will be his slaves:* By demanding a king, the people whose ancestors had once been slaves in Egypt were risking a new enslavement (cp. 1 Kgs 12:1-20).

8:18 The people would *beg for relief* as their ancestors had done in Egypt under another punishing and exacting ruler (see Exod 3:7).

8:20 God had set Israel apart from the nations (Lev 20:26; Num 23:9). By insisting on a king and desiring *to be like the nations,* they were rejecting God's plan (see 8:5-7; cp. Deut 17:14). • *judge us and lead us into battle:* Kings performed three basic functions: (1) waging offensive and defensive war, (2) administering law, and (3) ensuring economic well-being.

8:21 *repeated to the LORD:* The role of a prophet included bringing the people's case before God (cp. Num 27:5).

8:22 *give them a king:* See note on 8:7; cp. Rom 1:24-26.

Saul Becomes an Effective King (9:1–12:25)

Samuel Anoints Saul

9 There was a wealthy, influential man
named Kish from the tribe of Benjamin. He was the son of Abiel, son of Zeror,
son of Becorath, son of Aphiah, of the tribe
of Benjamin. 2His son Saul was the most
handsome man in Israel—head and shoulders taller than anyone else in the land.
3One day Kish's donkeys strayed away,
and he told Saul, "Take a servant with you,
and go look for the donkeys." 4So Saul took
one of the servants and traveled through
the hill country of Ephraim, the land of Sha-
lishah, the Shaalim area, and the entire land
of Benjamin, but they couldn't find the donkeys anywhere.
5Finally, they entered the region of Zuph,
and Saul said to his servant, "Let's go home.
By now my father will be more worried
about us than about the donkeys!"
6But the servant said, "I've just thought of
something! There is a man of God who lives
here in this town. He is held in high honor
by all the people because everything he
says comes true. Let's go find him. Perhaps
he can tell us which way to go."
7"But we don't have anything to offer
him," Saul replied. "Even our food is gone,
and we don't have a thing to give him."
8"Well," the servant said, "I have one
small silver piece. We can at least offer it to
the man of God and see what happens!" 9(In
those days if people wanted a message from
God, they would say, "Let's go and ask the
seer," for prophets used to be called seers.)
10"All right," Saul agreed, "let's try it!" So
they started into the town where the man
of God lived.
11As they were climbing the hill to the
town, they met some young women coming
out to draw water. So Saul and his servant
asked, "Is the seer here today?"
12"Yes," they replied. "Stay right on this
road. He is at the town gates. He has just arrived to take part in a public sacrifice up at
the place of worship. 13Hurry and catch him
before he goes up there to eat. The guests
won't begin eating until he arrives to bless
the food."
14So they entered the town, and as they
passed through the gates, Samuel was coming out toward them to go up to the place
of worship.
15Now the LORD had told Samuel the previous day, 16"About this time tomorrow I will
send you a man from the land of Benjamin.
Anoint him to be the leader of my people,
Israel. He will rescue them from the Philistines, for I have looked down on my people
in mercy and have heard their cry."
17When Samuel saw Saul, the LORD said,
"That's the man I told you about! He will rule
my people."
18Just then Saul approached Samuel at
the gateway and asked, "Can you please tell
me where the seer's house is?"
19"I am the seer!" Samuel replied. "Go up
to the place of worship ahead of me. We
will eat there together, and in the morning
I'll tell you what you want to know and send
you on your way. 20And don't worry about
those donkeys that were lost three days ago,
for they have been found. And I am here to
tell you that you and your family are the focus of all Israel's hopes."
21Saul replied, "But I'm only from the tribe
of Benjamin, the smallest tribe in Israel, and

9:1 1 Chr 8:33; 9:36-39
9:2 1 Sam 10:23-24; 2 Sam 14:25
9:3 1 Sam 10:2, 14
9:5 1 Sam 1:1
9:6 Deut 33:1; 1 Sam 3:19-20; 2 Kgs 5:8
9:7 1 Kgs 14:3; 2 Kgs 5:15; 8:8-9; Ezek 13:19
9:9 2 Sam 24:11; 1 Chr 26:28
9:12 Luke 9:16; John 6:11
9:15 1 Sam 15:1
9:16 Exod 3:7, 9; Acts 13:21
9:17 1 Sam 16:12
9:20 1 Sam 12:13
9:21 Judg 20:46-48; 1 Sam 15:17

9:1–11:15 Saul's rise to power involved a threefold sequence: (1) his secret anointing by Samuel (9:1–10:16), (2) his selection by lot (10:17-27), and (3) his victory over the Ammonites (11:1-15). See also note on 13:1–16:13.

9:1 ***influential man named Kish:*** Saul came from a wealthy family.

9:2 Saul's mere appearance—***most handsome . . . taller than anyone else***—inspired loyalty among the people (see 10:23; cp. 16:12; 2 Sam 14:25-26).

9:5 ***Zuph,*** which was probably located in Ephraim, was Samuel's home region (1:1). God's providence led Saul there.

9:6 The phrase *man of God* was used to describe a prophet (2:27; also Deut 33:1; Josh 14:6; 1 Kgs 13:1-32).

9:7 ***anything to offer him:*** Evidently, it was customary to take a gift when one sought the help of a prophet (cp. 1 Kgs 14:2-3; 2 Kgs 5:5, 15; 8:8). Some false prophets demanded gifts in return for their services (Mic 3:11). Saul's concern might reflect the spiritual ignorance of thinking that advice from a prophet of God could be purchased (Acts 8:20).

9:8 ***one small silver piece:*** Hebrew *¼ shekel of silver,* about 0.1 ounces or 3 grams in weight.

9:12 Leaders of a community would normally convene for business at the ***town gates*** (cp. Ruth 4:1-2). • ***take part in a public sacrifice:*** Samuel is one of very few individuals in whom prophetic and priestly ministries unite (also Moses, Jeremiah, Ezekiel, and Jesus). • ***place of worship*** (literally *high place*): An open-air altar or platform on a hill near the city gate. High places easily became sites for pagan idolatry (see Num 33:52; 1 Kgs 15:14; 22:43; 2 Kgs 12:3; 14:4; 15:4, 35).

9:13 ***to eat:*** Part of a sacrifice made during worship was burned on the altar, while the remainder was eaten in a ceremonial feast by the ***guests*** (see also 1:4). • ***to bless the food:*** As a Levite, Samuel's priestly role included offering blessings (see Deut 10:8; 21:5).

9:16 God's directive to ***anoint him*** (by pouring olive oil on the head) marked Saul's elevation in status and consecration for a special purpose (see Exod 30:22-33; Lev 8:12; 1 Kgs 19:16; Isa 45:1). • ***He will rescue them:*** As they had requested (8:20; cp. Judg 13:5). David eventually subdued ***the Philistines*** (2 Sam 5:17-25; 8:1; 21:15, 18-22). • ***for I have . . . heard their cry*** (cp. Exod 3:7-9): The Philistines were again threatening to conquer Israel and demand homage from them as vassals.

9:21 ***the smallest tribe:*** Saul tried to downplay Benjamin's prominence, but they were powerful warriors (Judg 20:14-31; cp. note on 10:17). What better tribe to lead in battle? • ***least important of all the families:*** Cp. 9:1.

9:25
Deut 22:8
Acts 10:9-10

10:1
1 Sam 9:16; 16:13; 26:9
2 Sam 1:14
2 Kgs 9:3, 6
[i]*mashakh* (4886)
▸1 Sam 15:1

10:2
Gen 35:19; 48:7

10:3
Gen 35:1, 3, 7

10:5
1 Sam 19:20
2 Kgs 2:3, 5, 15
1 Chr 25:1

my family is the least important of all the
families of that tribe! Why are you talking
like this to me?"
[22]Then Samuel brought Saul and his servant into the hall and placed them at the
head of the table, honoring them above
the thirty special guests. [23]Samuel then instructed the cook to bring Saul the finest cut
of meat, the piece that had been set aside for
the guest of honor. [24]So the cook brought
in the meat and placed it before Saul. "Go
ahead and eat it," Samuel said. "I was saving
it for you even before I invited these others!"
So Saul ate with Samuel that day.
[25]When they came down from the place
of worship and returned to town, Samuel
took Saul up to the roof of the house and
prepared a bed for him there. [26]At daybreak the next morning, Samuel called to
Saul, "Get up! It's time you were on your
way." So Saul got ready, and he and Samuel left the house together. [27]When they
reached the edge of town, Samuel told Saul
to send his servant on ahead. After the servant was gone, Samuel said, "Stay here, for
I have received a special message for you
from God."

10 Then Samuel took a flask of olive
oil and poured it over Saul's head.
He kissed Saul and said, "I am doing this
because the LORD has [i]appointed you to be
the ruler over Israel, his special possession.
[2]When you leave me today, you will see two
men beside Rachel's tomb at Zelzah, on the
border of Benjamin. They will tell you that
the donkeys have been found and that your
father has stopped worrying about them
and is now worried about you. He is asking,
'Have you seen my son?'
[3]"When you get to the oak of Tabor, you
will see three men coming toward you who
are on their way to worship God at Bethel.
One will be bringing three young goats, another will have three loaves of bread, and
the third will be carrying a wineskin full
of wine. [4]They will greet you and offer you
two of the loaves, which you are to accept.
[5]"When you arrive at Gibeah of God,
where the garrison of the Philistines is

SAUL (9:1–11:15)

1 Sam 13:1–31:13
2 Sam 1:1-27
1 Chr 9:35–10:14

Saul was the first king of Israel. He was chosen by God and the people, but he failed tremendously because he lacked confidence in himself and in God. Saul was a very complex character who sometimes elicits our sympathy. He was also the source of his own problems, especially as he brought heartache and trouble into the lives of those close to him.

Saul, the son of a wealthy landowner, became king unexpectedly and reluctantly. The people had requested a king to help them fight their battles, so they were happy with Saul, who was a head taller than anyone else (10:23). Their military problems were overwhelming, however, and Saul was not a confident military leader. Had it not been for the prophet Samuel and Saul's son Jonathan, Saul's reign might have been marked by complete disaster.

Saul offended God by taking rash vows during wartime (14:16-46) and wrongly performing sacrifices before battle rather than waiting for Samuel (13:7b-14). He also failed to obey God's instruction to destroy all the people and plunder of the Amalekites (ch 15). So God determined to remove Saul from the kingship and sent Samuel to anoint David. Soon Saul was deeply suspicious of David, his son's best friend and his own most loyal servant. The reluctant king became a despot, clinging to power at all costs.

Saul was wounded in battle against the Philistines, then fell on his own sword. His death was a result of God's judgment. Although David had spent considerable time fleeing from Saul, he honored the first king and his son Jonathan with a moving eulogy (2 Sam 1:17-27).

9:25 A typical house had a flat *roof* that was used for a variety of purposes, such as sleeping in warm weather (see Deut 22:8; 2 Kgs 4:10). • ***and prepared a bed for him there:*** As in Greek version; Hebrew reads *and talked with him there.*

10:1 Samuel later repeated this process by anointing David with *olive oil* (16:13). • The people of Israel did not belong to the king but to the Lord. The king was to act as manager rather than owner (cp. 8:10-18). • ***over Israel, his special possession:*** Greek version reads *over Israel. And you will rule over the LORD's people and save them from their enemies around them. This will be the sign to you that the LORD has appointed you to be leader over his special possession.*

10:2-6 These three "signs" were to convince a reluctant Saul (9:21) that he had in fact been chosen to be king.

10:2 ***Rachel's tomb at Zelzah:*** See Gen 35:16-20; the precise location is unknown.

10:3 ***oak of Tabor:*** This location, somewhere in Benjamin, is not to be confused with the village of the same name in Zebulun (1 Chr 6:77). • ***Bethel:*** See note on 7:16.

10:5 *Gibeah of God* (Hebrew *Gibeath-elohim*), Saul's hometown (10:26), had been a lawless city (Judg 19–21). Nowhere else is it described as being "of God." This description might point to God's ownership of the town despite the occupation of the *Philistines.* • ***band:*** Prophets often lived in groups

located, you will meet a band of prophets coming down from the place of worship. They will be playing a harp, a tambourine, a flute, and a lyre, and they will be prophesying. 6At that time the Spirit of the LORD will come powerfully upon you, and you will prophesy with them. You will be changed into a different person. 7After these signs take place, do what must be done, for God is with you. 8Then go down to Gilgal ahead of me. I will join you there to sacrifice burnt offerings and peace offerings. You must wait for seven days until I arrive and give you further instructions."

9As Saul turned and started to leave, God gave him a new heart, and all Samuel's signs were fulfilled that day. 10When Saul and his servant arrived at Gibeah, they saw a group of [j]prophets coming toward them. Then the Spirit of God came powerfully upon Saul, and he, too, began to prophesy. 11When those who knew Saul heard about it, they exclaimed, "What? Is even Saul a prophet? How did the son of Kish become a prophet?"

12And one of those standing there said, "Can anyone become a prophet, no matter who his father is?" So that is the origin of the [k]saying "Is even Saul a prophet?"

13When Saul had finished prophesying, he went up to the place of worship. 14"Where have you been?" Saul's uncle asked him and his servant.

"We were looking for the donkeys," Saul replied, "but we couldn't find them. So we went to Samuel to ask him where they were."

15"Oh? And what did he say?" his uncle asked.

16"He told us that the donkeys had already been found," Saul replied. But Saul didn't tell his uncle what Samuel said about the kingdom.

Saul Publicly Proclaimed King

17Later Samuel called all the people of Israel to meet before the LORD at Mizpah. 18And he said, "This is what the LORD, the God of Israel, has declared: I brought you from Egypt and rescued you from the Egyptians and from all of the nations that were oppressing you. 19But though I have rescued you from your misery and distress, you have rejected your God today and have said, 'No, we want a king instead!' Now, therefore, present yourselves before the LORD by tribes and clans."

20So Samuel brought all the tribes of Israel before the LORD, and the tribe of Benjamin was chosen by lot. 21Then he brought each family of the tribe of Benjamin before the LORD, and the family of the Matrites was chosen. And finally Saul son of Kish was chosen from among them. But when they looked for him, he had disappeared! 22So they asked the LORD, "Where is he?"

And the LORD replied, "He is hiding among the baggage." 23So they found him and brought him out, and he stood head and shoulders above anyone else.

24Then Samuel said to all the people, "This is the man the LORD has [a]chosen as your king. No one in all Israel is like him!"

And all the people shouted, "Long live the king!"

25Then Samuel told the people what the rights and duties of a king were. He wrote them down on a scroll and placed it before the LORD. Then Samuel sent the people home again.

10:6 Num 11:25, 29; Judg 3:10; 14:6; 1 Sam 19:23-24
10:8 1 Sam 7:16; 11:14-15; 13:8
10:9 1 Sam 10:6
10:10 1 Sam 10:5; [j]*nabi'* (5030) ‣1 Kgs 18:19
10:11 1 Sam 19:24; Amos 7:14-15; Matt 13:54-57
10:12 [k]*mashal* (4912) ‣1 Sam 24:13
10:14 1 Sam 9:3
10:16 1 Sam 9:20
10:17 Judg 20:1; 1 Sam 7:5-6
10:18 Judg 6:8
10:19 1 Sam 8:5-7
10:23 1 Sam 9:2
10:24 1 Kgs 1:25, 34, 39; 2 Kgs 11:12; [a]*bakhar* (0977) ‣1 Sam 17:40
10:25 Deut 17:15; 1 Sam 8:11-18

(e.g., 2 Kgs 2:3). • ***harp . . . lyre:*** Ancient prophets sometimes used musical instruments to stimulate and accompany *prophesying* (e.g., 2 Kgs 3:15).

10:6 *prophesy:* Cp. 2 Sam 23:2; Acts 2:29-31. • ***different person:*** Saul would become a spiritual and charismatic national leader (cp. 16:14).

10:7 *for God is with you:* God's presence empowered Saul to carry out his responsibilities.

10:8 *Gilgal:* See note on 7:16. • ***wait for seven days:*** Saul apparently fulfilled this instruction in 11:14-15 (cp. 13:8).

10:9 *a new heart:* God gave Saul courage and strength, helping him overcome his hesitancy and enabling him to be king (10:6).

10:10 *the Spirit of God came powerfully upon Saul:* See "The Spirit's Presence" at 16:13-23, p. 494; see also 11:6; Judg 14:6, 19; 15:14; cp. Acts 2:17-18, 39). • When ***Saul . . . began to prophesy,*** it was a clear sign that he had been chosen to lead Israel (see also 19:18-23).

10:11 *Those who knew Saul* might have known him to be nonreligious and thus an unlikely candidate for prophet. Their surprise might indicate disappointment at receiving a prophet instead of a king (cp. John 6:14-15).

10:12 *"Can anyone become a prophet, no matter who his father is?"* (literally "*Who is their father?*"): Unlike priests and kings, prophets never inherited their office. Possibly the people were asking why Saul, whose well-to-do father was well known, would associate himself with a group of people who had no pedigree.

10:16 Perhaps ***Saul didn't tell his uncle*** because he had lingering uncertainty about what had transpired.

10:17 An earlier generation had gathered at ***Mizpah*** to decimate the tribe of Benjamin (Judg 20:1-4), making the city an ironic place to inaugurate a man of Benjamin as king.

10:18 *rescued you . . . from all of the nations:* Israel did not need a human king to rescue them; they needed God, but they had rejected him (10:19).

10:19 *rejected your God:* See also 8:7. Israel was rejecting God's ability to protect and save them. • ***Clans*** are subdivisions of ***tribes.***

10:20 *chosen by lot:* Cp. Lev 16:8; Josh 18:6; 1 Chr 26:12-16; Acts 1:26.

10:25 *rights and duties of a king:* See Deut 17:14-20. • ***He wrote them:*** Cp. Exod 24:4; Josh 24:26. • Samuel placed the document *before the LORD*—presumably in the Tabernacle. This position showed that God would honor those who lived by the covenant and punish those who violated it.

10:27
1 Kgs 10:24-25
11:1
Judg 11:4-6; 21:8
1 Sam 12:12; 31:11
11:2
1 Sam 17:26
11:4
1 Sam 10:26; 30:4
11:5
1 Kgs 19:19
11:6
Judg 3:10; 6:34
1 Sam 10:10
11:7
Judg 19:29; 20:1
11:8
Judg 1:4-6
11:10
1 Sam 11:3
11:11
Judg 7:16
11:12
1 Sam 10:27
Luke 19:27
11:13
Exod 14:13
1 Sam 19:5
2 Sam 19:22
11:14
1 Sam 10:1, 8

26 When Saul returned to his home at Gibeah, a group of men whose hearts God had
touched went with him. 27 But there were
some scoundrels who complained, "How
can this man save us?" And they scorned
him and refused to bring him gifts. But Saul
ignored them.

[Nahash, king of the Ammonites, had been grievously oppressing the people of Gad and Reuben who lived east of the Jordan River. He gouged out the right eye of each of the Israelites living there, and he didn't allow anyone to come and rescue them. In fact, of all the Israelites east of the Jordan, there wasn't a single one whose right eye Nahash had not gouged out. But there were 7,000 men who had escaped from the Ammonites, and they had settled in Jabesh-gilead.]

Saul Saves Jabesh-gilead from Destruction

11 About a month later, King Nahash
of Ammon led his army against the
Israelite town of Jabesh-gilead. But all the
citizens of Jabesh asked for peace. "Make a
treaty with us, and we will be your servants,"
they pleaded.
2 "All right," Nahash said, "but only on one
condition. I will gouge out the right eye of
every one of you as a disgrace to all Israel!"
3 "Give us seven days to send messengers
throughout Israel!" replied the elders of Jabesh. "If no one comes to save us, we will
agree to your terms."
4 When the messengers came to Gibeah
of Saul and told the people about their
plight, everyone broke into tears. 5 Saul
had been plowing a field with his oxen,
and when he returned to town, he asked,
"What's the matter? Why is everyone crying?" So they told him about the message
from Jabesh.
6 Then the Spirit of God came powerfully
upon Saul, and he became very angry. 7 He
took two oxen and cut them into pieces
and sent the messengers to carry them
throughout Israel with this message: "This
is what will happen to the oxen of anyone
who refuses to follow Saul and Samuel into
battle!" And the LORD made the people
afraid of Saul's anger, and all of them came
out together as one. 8 When Saul mobilized
them at Bezek, he found that there were
300,000 men from Israel and 30,000 men
from Judah.
9 So Saul sent the messengers back to
Jabesh-gilead to say, "We will rescue you by
noontime tomorrow!" There was great joy
throughout the town when that message
arrived!
10 The men of Jabesh then told their enemies, "Tomorrow we will come out to you,
and you can do to us whatever you wish."
11 But before dawn the next morning, Saul
arrived, having divided his army into three
detachments. He launched a surprise attack
against the Ammonites and slaughtered
them the whole morning. The remnant of
their army was so badly scattered that no
two of them were left together.
12 Then the people exclaimed to Samuel,
"Now where are those men who said, 'Why
should Saul rule over us?' Bring them here,
and we will kill them!"
13 But Saul replied, "No one will be executed today, for today the LORD has rescued
Israel!"
14 Then Samuel said to the people, "Come,

10:26–11:13 Saul proved his capacity for leadership by tolerating opposition and rescuing the town of Jabesh-gilead.

10:26 ***whose hearts God had touched:*** God gave people confidence in Saul's ability to lead (cp. 10:9).

10:27 These men were *scoundrels* (cp. 2:12) because they *scorned* God's chosen king. • ***Gifts*** were given to show homage (Gen 32:13, 18, 20), political friendship (2 Kings 20:12), or submission (Judg 3:15, 17). • ***ignored them:*** Saul's self-restraint while being insulted was a sign of maturity. In contrast, Prov 16:14 speaks of a king's potentially explosive rage when somebody crosses him. See also 11:12-13. • ***[Nahash . . . Jabesh-gilead]:*** This paragraph, which is not included in the Masoretic Text, is found in Dead Sea Scroll 4QSam[a]. Whether it was part of the original text is unknown, but it provides historical context for ch 11 (e.g., 11:2).

11:1-15 Saul's kingship was confirmed through a military victory, the very reason the people wanted a king (8:20).

11:1 This paragraph begins as in Greek version; Hebrew lacks ***About a month later.*** • ***Ammon*** (see Gen 19:38), located on the east side of the Jordan, represented a threat to Israel similar to the Philistines to the southwest (see also Judg 10:6–11:33). • ***Make a treaty with us:*** Cp. Josh 9; 2 Sam 10:19.

11:2 ***gouge out the right eye:*** Mutilation of captured soldiers was a common practice in the ancient Near East. These disfigured soldiers would have lost all depth perception, seriously curtailing their potential for fighting in a revolt.

11:3 Nahash agreed to grant a reprieve of *seven days,* reflecting his arrogant confidence of victory and his desire to humiliate Israel as much as possible.

11:6 ***Spirit of God:*** See note on 10:10.

11:7 Not to participate would indicate rejection of the leadership of both *Saul* as king and *Samuel* as prophet.

11:8 ***Bezek*** was about fourteen miles west of Jabesh-gilead. • The narrator's use of the terms ***Israel*** and ***Judah*** anticipates the later division of the kingdom (1 Kgs 12). • ***30,000:*** Dead Sea Scrolls and Greek version read *70,000.*

11:13 ***No one will be executed:*** This was a time for rejoicing, not revenge.

11:14 ***renew the kingdom:*** "Renew" indicates that someone or something had deteriorated or had been damaged (cp. Ps 51:10). Whatever effect the scoundrels (10:27; 11:12) might have had in undermining the people's confidence was now rectified by Saul's victory over the Ammonites.

let us all go to Gilgal to [b]renew the kingdom." 15So they all went to Gilgal, and in a solemn ceremony before the LORD they made Saul king. Then they offered peace offerings to the LORD, and Saul and all the Israelites were filled with joy.

Samuel's Farewell Address to Israel

12 Then Samuel addressed all Israel: "I have done as you asked and given you a king. 2Your king is now your leader. I stand here before you—an old, gray-haired man—and my sons serve you. I have served as your leader from the time I was a boy to this very day. 3Now testify against me in the presence of the LORD and before his anointed one. Whose ox or donkey have I stolen? Have I ever cheated any of you? Have I ever oppressed you? Have I ever taken a bribe and perverted justice? Tell me and I will make right whatever I have done wrong."

4"No," they replied, "you have never cheated or oppressed us, and you have never taken even a single bribe."

5"The LORD and his anointed one are my witnesses today," Samuel declared, "that my hands are clean."

"Yes, he is a witness," they replied.

6"It was the LORD who appointed Moses and Aaron," Samuel continued. "He brought your ancestors out of the land of Egypt. 7Now stand here quietly before the LORD as I remind you of all the great things the LORD has done for you and your ancestors.

8"When the Israelites were in Egypt and cried out to the LORD, he sent Moses and Aaron to rescue them from Egypt and to bring them into this land. 9But the people soon forgot about the LORD their God, so he handed them over to Sisera, the commander of Hazor's army, and also to the Philistines and to the king of Moab, who fought against them.

10"Then they cried to the LORD again and confessed, 'We have sinned by [c]turning away from the LORD and worshiping the images of Baal and Ashtoreth. But we will worship you and you alone if you will rescue us from our enemies.' 11Then the LORD sent Gideon, Bedan, Jephthah, and Samuel to save you, and you lived in safety.

12"But when you were afraid of Nahash, the king of Ammon, you came to me and said that you wanted a king to reign over you, even though the LORD your God was already your king. 13All right, here is the king you have chosen. You asked for him, and the LORD has granted your request.

14"Now if you fear and worship the LORD and listen to his voice, and if you do not rebel against the LORD's commands, then both you and your king will show that you recognize the LORD as your God. 15But if you rebel against the LORD's commands and refuse to listen to him, then his hand will be as heavy upon you as it was upon your ancestors.

16"Now stand here and see the great thing the LORD is about to do. 17You know

11:14 [b]*khadash* (2318) ›2 Chr 24:4
12:1 1 Sam 8:7, 9, 22
12:2 1 Sam 3:10, 19-20
12:3 Exod 23:8; Num 16:15; Deut 16:19
12:5 2 Sam 4:9; Rom 9:1; 2 Cor 1:23
12:6 Exod 6:26
12:7 Judg 5:11; Ps 78:4; Mic 6:4
12:8 Exod 2:23-25; 3:10; 4:14-16
12:9 Deut 32:18; Judg 3:7; 10:7; 13:1
12:10 Judg 10:10, 15-16; [c]*'azab* (5800) ›1 Kgs 11:33
12:11 Judg 4:6; 6:32; 11:1
12:12 Judg 8:22-23
12:13 1 Sam 8:5; 10:24; Hos 13:11
12:14 Josh 24:14, 20
12:15 Josh 24:20; Isa 1:2, 20
12:16 Exod 14:13, 21, 31
12:17 1 Sam 7:10; 8:6-7

11:15 The ***solemn ceremony before the LORD*** acknowledged Saul's sovereignty as king while affirming that the Lord was Israel's true King. • ***Peace offerings*** were common on historic occasions that inaugurated important institutions (see Exod 24:5; Lev 9:4, 18, 22; 1 Kgs 8:63-64).

12:1-25 The reaffirmation of Saul's kingship at Gilgal (11:12-15) was the final step in his installation as king. The event was a fitting occasion for Samuel's farewell address as leader of Israel.

12:3 God's ***anointed one*** was Saul (see 9:16). • ***Whose ox or donkey:*** Cp. Num 16:15. • ***have I stolen?*** In contrast to the behavior of kings (8:11-16). • ***Have I ever taken a bribe and perverted justice?*** No, but Samuel's sons did (8:3).

12:5 ***my hands are clean:*** Samuel's life and leadership before Israel had been above reproach (cp. 1 Cor 9:1-14; 2 Cor 7:2; 11:7-9; 1 Thes 2:1-12). Saul, David, and Solomon—kings rather than prophetic judges—would not be able to make this claim.

12:6-25 In 12:1-5, Samuel put himself on trial and was found innocent. In 12:6-25, he put the nation on trial and found it guilty.

12:6 ***Moses and Aaron*** were not self-made leaders but were ***appointed*** by God as leaders.

12:8 ***When the Israelites were:*** Literally *When Jacob was.* The names "Jacob" and "Israel" are often interchanged throughout the OT, referring sometimes to the individual patriarch and sometimes to the nation.

12:9 ***handed them over:*** See Judg 3:8; 4:1-3. • ***the king of Moab:*** See Judg 3:12. Not all of Israel's enemies in the era of the judges are listed (e.g., the Ammonites and Midianites). This list is representative to emphasize the highs and lows of that era.

12:10 ***Then they cried to the LORD:*** Sometimes only suffering turns people's hearts toward God. During the period of the judges, Israel repeatedly went through cycles of sin, oppression, repentance, and rescue. • ***Baal and Ashtoreth:*** When people turn *away from* God, they inevitably turn to idols (see 7:3; Judg 2:13; 10:6). • An attitude such as ***if you will rescue us*** turns ***worship*** into a debased bargain, in which God must perform some action to a person's liking. God deserves obedience and *worship* because he is God, not because of favors he can perform.

12:11 As in 12:9, this list of leaders is representative. • ***Gideon:*** Literally *Jerubbaal,* another name for Gideon (see Judg 6:32). • ***Bedan:*** Greek and Syriac versions read *Barak* (see Judg 4:6-24; 5:1, 12, 15). The identity of this judge remains unknown. • ***Samuel:*** Greek and Syriac versions read *Samson.*

12:12 ***you were afraid of Nahash:*** Israel's trouble with Nahash apparently preceded 11:1-11 (cp. 8:5, 20; 10:27).

12:13 Even though the Israelites' *request* amounted to a rejection of God as king, ***the LORD . . . granted*** it (see notes on 8:7-8).

12:14-15 To show that even under a monarchy Israel must still keep its covenant with the Lord—who was always to be their true king—Samuel echoed language from the Sinai covenant (e.g., Exod 19:5-6; Lev 26; Deut 30:11-20).

12:14 ***Worship*** is meaningless if it does not result in obedience.

12:20
Exod 32:30
Deut 11:16
12:21
Deut 11:16
Hab 2:18
12:22
Exod 32:12
Num 14:13
Deut 7:6; 31:6
Josh 7:9
1 Pet 2:9
12:23
1 Kgs 8:36
Prov 4:11
Rom 1:9
Col 1:9
1 Thes 3:10
[d]*khata'* (2398)
‣1 Sam 14:33
12:24
Deut 10:21
Eccl 12:13
12:25
Josh 24:20
1 Sam 31:1-5
Isa 1:20
13:2
1 Sam 10:26
13:3
Judg 3:27; 6:34
1 Sam 10:5
2 Sam 2:28; 20:1

that it does not rain at this time of the year
during the wheat harvest. I will ask the
LORD to send thunder and rain today. Then
you will realize how wicked you have been
in asking the LORD for a king!"
18 So Samuel called to the LORD, and the
LORD sent thunder and rain that day. And all
the people were terrified of the LORD and of
Samuel. 19 "Pray to the LORD your God for us,
or we will die!" they all said to Samuel. "For
now we have added to our sins by asking for
a king."
20 "Don't be afraid," Samuel reassured
them. "You have certainly done wrong, but
make sure now that you worship the LORD
with all your heart, and don't turn your
back on him. 21 Don't go back to worshiping
worthless idols that cannot help or rescue
you—they are totally useless! 22 The LORD
will not abandon his people, because that
would dishonor his great name. For it has
pleased the LORD to make you his very own
people.
23 "As for me, I will certainly not [d]sin
against the LORD by ending my prayers for
you. And I will continue to teach you what
is good and right. 24 But be sure to fear the
LORD and faithfully serve him. Think of all
the wonderful things he has done for you.
25 But if you continue to sin, you and your
king will be swept away."

3. REJECTION OF SAUL'S KINGSHIP (13:1–16:13)

Saul's Exploits and Rejection (13:1–15:35)

Samuel Rebukes Saul for His Disobedience

13 Saul was thirty years old when he
became king, and he reigned for
forty-two years.
2 Saul selected 3,000 special troops from
the army of Israel and sent the rest of the
men home. He took 2,000 of the chosen men
with him to Micmash and the hill country of
Bethel. The other 1,000 went with Saul's son
Jonathan to Gibeah in the land of Benjamin.
3 Soon after this, Jonathan attacked and
defeated the garrison of Philistines at
Geba. The news spread quickly among the
Philistines. So Saul blew the ram's horn
throughout the land, saying, "Hebrews, hear

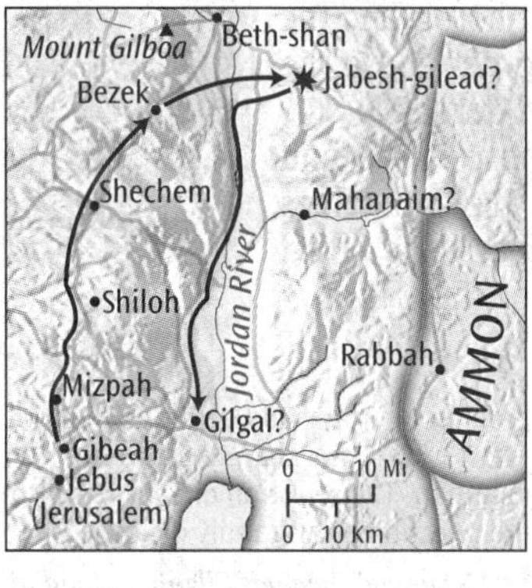

◀ **Saul's Victory at Jabesh-gilead (11:1-15).** Saul and his army traveled from GIBEAH and mobilized at BEZEK before attacking the Ammonites at JABESH-GILEAD. After defeating the Ammonites, they traveled at Samuel's instruction to GILGAL, where Saul's kingship was confirmed.

12:17 The *wheat harvest* occurred in late spring or early summer, when little or no rain fell in Israel. ***Thunder and rain*** would thus demonstrate God's power as a sign of the people's wickedness in asking for a king.

12:18 ***terrified:*** Cp. Exod 19:16.

12:19 The people asked Samuel to intercede for them (see also 7:8) rather than praying themselves probably because they were out of fellowship with God (note the use of ***your God*** rather than "our God"). • ***added to our sins:*** The sins included idol worship (12:21; see note on 8:8).

12:21 ***worthless . . . totally useless:*** Israel was slow to learn this lesson (e.g., Isa 40:18-26; 44:9-20).

12:22 ***because that would dishonor his great name:*** God will never contradict his own character and detract from his glory (see also Isa 37:35; 43:25; 48:9-11). Therefore, he always keeps his covenant promises, even if his people do not.

• ***his very own people:*** Israel is God's treasured possession (see Exod 19:5; Deut 9:25-29). He will never abandon them (see Rom 11:1-5, 25-32).

12:23 ***I will continue to teach you:*** Samuel was both intercessor and educator. • Although this address marked the end of Samuel's political leadership, he continued his spiritual ministry for some time (e.g., 19:24).

12:25 ***swept away:*** David later used this same Hebrew verb for Saul's death (26:10, "die . . . in battle") and for his own possible death at Saul's hands (27:1, "get me"). The warning would remain in force throughout Israel's history as a monarchy.

13:1–16:13 Saul's fall from power involved a threefold sequence, as had his rise to power (see note on 9:1–11:15): (1) He offered the sacrifices himself and did not wait for Samuel (13:1-14); (2) he made a rash oath that put Jonathan's life in danger (14:1-46); and (3) he failed to obey God by eliminating the Amalekites and their belongings (15:1-35).

13:1 For the kings of Israel and Judah, Scripture normally records the age of ascension and the length of reign (e.g., 2 Sam 5:4-5; 1 Kgs 14:21). • ***thirty years old:*** As in a few Greek manuscripts; the number is missing in the Hebrew. The number represents a plausible age for Saul's ascension. The Hebrew text and most Greek manuscripts omit the number, making it difficult to know the original wording. • ***reigned for forty-two years:*** Literally *reigned . . . and two;* the number is incomplete in the Hebrew. Cp. Acts 13:21. Most scholars agree that something has fallen out of the original manuscript, most likely due to a copyist's error. The majority of English translations have *forty-two* based on the approximate number in Acts 13:21.

13:2 Earlier, ***Saul*** had employed 330,000 troops to fight against a much less formidable foe (11:8). The selection here of ***3,000 special troops*** probably does not reflect overconfidence (cp. Josh 7:3-4). Rather, Saul likely recognized the need for a smaller, highly trained, elite militia to deal with the troublesome Philistines (see 14:52). • ***Micmash*** was located in Benjamin about two miles northwest of Saul's home in Gibeah.

13:3 ***Geba*** was located between Jonathan's forces at Gibeah and Saul's forces at Micmash. A deep gorge separated Geba and Micmash (see 13:23; 14:5). • ***The ram's horn*** (Hebrew *shofar*) was used to raise a signal—e.g., to muster an army (Judg 3:27). For other uses, see Lev 25:9; 2 Sam 6:15; 15:10; 18:16; 20:1; Hos 5:8; Joel 2:15. • Non-Israelites often used the term ***Hebrews*** disdainfully (see 14:11; 29:3; see also Gen 39:14; 43:32). Saul might have used it to strike a nerve and arouse the people's pride in their identity.

this! Rise up in revolt!" 4All Israel heard the news that Saul had destroyed the Philistine garrison at Geba and that the Philistines now hated the Israelites more than ever. So the entire Israelite army was summoned to join Saul at Gilgal.

5The Philistines mustered a mighty army of 3,000 chariots, 6,000 charioteers, and as many warriors as the grains of sand on the seashore! They camped at Micmash east of Beth-aven. 6The men of Israel saw what a tight spot they were in; and because they were hard pressed by the enemy, they tried to hide in caves, thickets, rocks, holes, and cisterns. 7Some of them crossed the Jordan River and escaped into the land of Gad and Gilead.

Meanwhile, Saul stayed at Gilgal, and his men were trembling with fear. 8Saul waited there seven days for Samuel, as Samuel had instructed him earlier, but Samuel still didn't come. Saul realized that his troops were rapidly slipping away. 9So he demanded, "Bring me the burnt offering and the peace offerings!" And Saul sacrificed the burnt offering himself.

10Just as Saul was finishing with the burnt offering, Samuel arrived. Saul went out to meet and welcome him, 11but Samuel said, "What is this you have done?"

Saul replied, "I saw my men scattering from me, and you didn't arrive when you said you would, and the Philistines are at Micmash ready for battle. 12So I said, 'The Philistines are ready to march against us at Gilgal, and I haven't even asked for the LORD's help!' So I felt compelled to offer the burnt offering myself before you came."

13"How foolish!" Samuel exclaimed. "You have not kept the command the LORD your God gave you. Had you kept it, the LORD would have established your kingdom over Israel forever. 14But now your kingdom must end, for the LORD has sought out a man after his own heart. The LORD has already appointed him to be the leader of his people, because you have not kept the LORD's command."

15Samuel then left Gilgal and went on his way, but the rest of the troops went with Saul to meet the army. They went up from Gilgal to Gibeah in the land of Benjamin. When Saul counted the men who were still with him, he found only 600 were left! 16Saul and Jonathan and the troops with them were staying at Geba in the land of Benjamin. The Philistines set up their camp at Micmash. 17Three raiding parties soon left the camp of the Philistines. One went north toward Ophrah in the land of Shual, 18another went west to Beth-horon, and the third moved toward the border above the valley of Zeboim near the wilderness.

19There were no blacksmiths in the land of Israel in those days. The Philistines wouldn't allow them for fear they would make swords and spears for the Hebrews.

13:5 Josh 11:4
13:6 Judg 6:2
13:8 1 Sam 10:8
13:9 2 Sam 24:25; 1 Kgs 3:4
13:10 1 Sam 15:13
13:13 1 Sam 15:23-24, 28; 2 Chr 16:9
13:14 *Acts 13:22
13:15 1 Sam 14:2
13:16 Josh 18:24
13:18 Neh 11:31-35
13:19 Judg 5:8; 1 Sam 17:47; 2 Kgs 24:14; Jer 24:1

13:4 ***Saul had destroyed:*** The commander in chief often got credit for what his soldiers accomplished. • Saul's kingship had been reaffirmed at ***Gilgal*** (11:15). Now the Lord would reject his kingship there because of his disobedience (13:7-14).

13:5 The Israelites were massively outnumbered, hence their fearful responses. • The Philistine army's ***3,000 chariots*** (as in Greek and Syriac versions; Hebrew reads *30,000 chariots*) and ***6,000 charioteers*** indicate Israel's underdog status. Nowhere in 1 Samuel is Israel said to have had any chariots (see note on 13:19-22; see also "The Philistines" at 5:1–6:18, p. 477).

13:7 The ***land of Gad and Gilead*** ran the length of Transjordan (the region just east of the Jordan River).

13:8 ***seven days . . . as Samuel had instructed:*** This instruction most likely was not the instruction in 10:8 but an unrecorded instruction on a separate occasion (see note on 10:8).

13:9 ***the burnt offering and the peace offerings:*** These general-purpose offerings (see Exod 24:5; 32:6; Num 10:10; 15:8; Deut 27:6-7) were always offered on a solemn occasion filled with either danger or joy. Typically, only priests were to offer these sacrifices (but see note on 13:13).

13:10 ***meet and welcome:*** Saul seemed unaware he had done anything wrong.

13:11 ***What is this you have done?*** Samuel's question was a rebuke, not a request for information (cp. Gen 3:13).

13:12 ***asked for the LORD's help:*** The purpose of the ***burnt offering*** was to entreat God to grant victory in battle. Samuel himself had offered a similar sacrifice, which did lead to victory in battle (see 7:7-11). But Samuel, unlike Saul, served in a priestly role.

13:13 ***the command the LORD . . . gave you:*** Other kings offered sacrifices without censure (David, 2 Sam 6:13, 17-18; Solomon, 1 Kgs 3:15; 8:64; Ahaz, 2 Kgs 16:12-13), as did judges (Gideon, Judg 6:26), illustrating that on occasion nonpriests could conduct sacrifices in a way that pleased the Lord. However, Samuel, God's prophet, had given Saul the order to wait (see note on 13:8).

13:14 ***a man after his own heart:*** This prophecy pertains to David (see also Acts 13:22) rather than to Saul's son Jonathan. The rejection of Saul was also the rejection of his family dynasty.

13:15 ***Samuel then left Gilgal . . . land of Benjamin:*** As in Greek version; Hebrew reads *Samuel then left Gilgal and went to Gibeah in the land of Benjamin.* • ***only 600 were left:*** Most of the 3,000 troops (13:2) had abandoned Saul (13:6-7).

13:17-18 Armies would send out ***raiding parties*** to plunder and sow panic among the enemy. These raiders embarked north (***Ophrah***), west (***Beth-horon***), and east (***Zeboim***), but not south, where Israelite strength was consolidated and where the terrain did not allow easy movement of forces (see note on 13:23).

13:19-22 ***no blacksmiths:*** The Philistines kept the Israelites unarmed by gaining a monopoly on the iron necessary to make weapons. Iron technology had not existed long in Canaan; it might have developed in the Aegean area, and metalworking skills were possibly introduced into Canaan through seafaring peoples, including the Philistines.

13:23
1 Sam 14:4
Isa 10:28

14:2
1 Sam 13:15

14:3
1 Sam 1:3; 22:11-12

14:6
Judg 7:4

20So whenever the Israelites needed to sharpen their plowshares, picks, axes, or sickles, they had to take them to a Philistine blacksmith. 21(The charges were as follows: a quarter of an ounce of silver for sharpening a plowshare or a pick, and an eighth of an ounce for sharpening an ax, a sickle, or an ox goad.) 22So on the day of the battle none of the people of Israel had a sword or spear, except for Saul and Jonathan.

23The pass at Micmash had meanwhile been secured by a contingent of the Philistine army.

Saul and Jonathan Fight the Philistines

14 One day Jonathan said to his armor bearer, "Come on, let's go over to where the Philistines have their outpost." But Jonathan did not tell his father what he was doing.

2Meanwhile, Saul and his 600 men were camped on the outskirts of Gibeah, around the pomegranate tree at Migron. 3Among Saul's men was Ahijah the priest, who was wearing the ephod, the priestly vest. Ahijah was the son of Ichabod's brother Ahitub, son of Phinehas, son of Eli, the priest of the LORD who had served at Shiloh.

No one realized that Jonathan had left the Israelite camp. 4To reach the Philistine outpost, Jonathan had to go down between two rocky cliffs that were called Bozez and Seneh. 5The cliff on the north was in front of Micmash, and the one on the south was in front of Geba. 6"Let's go across to the outpost of those pagans," Jonathan said to his armor bearer. "Perhaps the LORD will help us, for nothing can hinder the LORD. He can win a battle whether he has many warriors or only a few!"

JONATHAN (13:1–14:46)

1 Sam 18:1-4; 20:1-42; 23:16-18; 31:2
2 Sam 1:1-27; 4:4

Jonathan, the oldest son of King Saul, was in line to be the next king. Yet when God rejected Saul and chose David, Jonathan welcomed and supported his rise to power (18:1-5; 19:1-7).

Jonathan was a magnificent military leader. He led his father's army to victory over the Philistine garrison at Geba (13:3-4). In another daring move, Jonathan and his armor bearer attacked a Philistine outpost by themselves; the ensuing confusion threw the Philistine army into disarray, allowing the main Israelite army to attack and win the day (14:1-23; see also David's eulogy of Jonathan, 2 Sam 1:22). Saul had unwisely taken an oath that no one should eat until victory had been won. Jonathan did not know of the vow and ate some honey. When he learned of Saul's vow, Jonathan criticized it harshly, and Saul would have executed Jonathan after the battle he had helped to win if the people had not intervened.

When Jonathan and David met, they became fast friends (18:1-4). Jonathan expressed his deep love for David by giving him his robe, tunic, sword, bow, and belt, which may have represented Jonathan's belief that David should be the next ruler. When Saul tried to have David killed, Jonathan interceded for him and finally helped David slip away unharmed.

Jonathan remained with his father even after the Lord had made it clear that he had abandoned Saul. As a result, Jonathan died with Saul as they fought the Philistines (31:2; 1 Chr 10:2). Jonathan was a virtuous, daring, and selfless man who always spoke and acted with integrity. His love and courage helped David survive the demented attacks of King Saul.

13:20 *sickles:* As in Greek version; Hebrew reads *or plowshares.*

13:21 *a quarter of an ounce of silver:* Hebrew *1 pim* [8 grams]. • *an eighth of an ounce:* Hebrew *⅓ of a shekel* [4 grams].

13:23 *The pass at Micmash* was a strategic passage through the canyon that separated Micmash from Geba, Gibeah, and other towns to the south.

14:1-52 Saul's behavior in this chapter further justifies his dismissal as king (13:8-14; see also ch 15). Saul was alienated from both Samuel and his heroic son Jonathan. Chapter 14 anticipates the significant role that Jonathan played in the transition from Saul's kingship to David's.

14:1-15 Jonathan again fought in his father's battles (see also 13:2-4; ch 31).

14:1 *armor bearer:* See note on 16:21. • *Jonathan did not tell his father* because he knew that Saul would not grant permission for the dangerous plan. But he also knew that Saul wanted no one—not even his own son—to upstage him.

14:2 *camped:* Saul's inactivity contrasts with Jonathan's initiative (see also 22:6). • *around the pomegranate tree:* Or *around the rock of Rimmon;* cp. Judg 20:45, 47; 21:13.

14:3 *Ahijah the priest* was an adviser who could give Saul divine guidance through *the ephod* (14:18-19; see also 2:18 and note; 23:9-10). • *son of Eli:* Saul, the rejected king (13:13-14), kept in his company a priest from the rejected priesthood (2:27-36). • *Ichabod:* See 4:21.

14:4-5 The Philistines had already secured this area (13:23), so Jonathan and his armor bearer had to move carefully.

14:6 *pagans* (literally *uncircumcised*): A disdainful term for enemies of Israel (see also 17:36; 31:4). • *Perhaps:* Jonathan had no guarantee of survival, but he was certain that God could grant them victory despite the odds. Victory was in God's hands; Jonathan offered himself as an instrument God could use. • *many warriors or only a few:* Jonathan knew what Gideon had learned many years earlier (see Judg 7:2-8).

7 "Do what you think is best," the armor
bearer replied. "I'm with you completely,
whatever you decide."
8 "All right then," Jonathan told him. "We
will cross over and let them see us. 9 If they
say to us, 'Stay where you are or we'll kill
you,' then we will stop and not go up to them.
10 But if they say, 'Come on up and fight,'
then we will go up. That will be the LORD's
sign that he will help us defeat them."
11 When the Philistines saw them coming,
they shouted, "Look! The Hebrews are crawling out of their holes!" 12 Then the men from
the outpost shouted to Jonathan, "Come on
up here, and we'll teach you a lesson!"
"Come on, climb right behind me," Jonathan said to his armor bearer, "for the LORD
will help us defeat them!"
13 So they climbed up using both hands
and feet, and the Philistines fell before Jonathan, and his armor bearer killed those
who came behind them. 14 They killed some
twenty men in all, and their bodies were
scattered over about half an acre.
15 Suddenly, panic broke out in the Philistine army, both in the camp and in the field,
including even the outposts and raiding
parties. And just then an earthquake struck,
and everyone was terrified.
16 Saul's lookouts in Gibeah of Benjamin
saw a strange sight—the vast army of Philistines began to melt away in every direction.
17 "Call the roll and find out who's missing,"
Saul ordered. And when they checked, they
found that Jonathan and his armor bearer
were gone.
18 Then Saul shouted to Ahijah, "Bring the
ephod here!" For at that time Ahijah was
wearing the ephod in front of the Israelites.
19 But while Saul was talking to the priest,
the confusion in the Philistine camp grew
louder and louder. So Saul said to the priest,
"Never mind; let's get going!"
20 Then Saul and all his men rushed out to
the battle and found the Philistines killing
each other. There was terrible confusion
everywhere. 21 Even the Hebrews who had
previously gone over to the Philistine army
revolted and joined in with Saul, Jonathan,
and the rest of the Israelites. 22 Likewise,
the men of Israel who were hiding in the
hill country of Ephraim joined the chase
when they saw the Philistines running
away. 23 So the LORD saved Israel that day,
and the battle continued to rage even beyond Beth-aven.
24 Now the men of Israel were pressed
to exhaustion that day, because Saul had
placed them under an oath, saying, "Let a
curse fall on anyone who eats before evening—before I have full revenge on my
enemies." So no one ate anything all day,
25 even though they had all found honeycomb on the ground in the forest. 26 They
didn't dare touch the honey because they
all feared the oath they had taken.
27 But Jonathan had not heard his father's
command, and he dipped the end of his
stick into a piece of honeycomb and ate
the honey. After he had eaten it, he felt refreshed. 28 But one of the men saw him
and said, "Your father made the army take
a strict oath that anyone who eats food today will be cursed. That is why everyone is
weary and faint."
29 "My father has made trouble for us
all!" Jonathan exclaimed. "A command like
that only hurts us. See how refreshed I am
now that I have eaten this little bit of honey.
30 If the men had been allowed to eat freely
from the food they found among our enemies, think how many more Philistines we
could have killed!"

14:10 Gen 24:14; Judg 6:36
14:11 1 Sam 13:6
14:12 2 Sam 5:24
14:15 1 Sam 7:10; 2 Kgs 7:6
14:18 1 Sam 23:9; 30:7
14:19 Num 27:21
14:20 Judg 7:21-22; 2 Chr 20:23
14:21 1 Sam 29:4
14:22 1 Sam 13:6; 31:7
14:23 Exod 14:30; 2 Chr 32:22
14:24 Josh 6:26
14:29 1 Kgs 18:18

14:11 *Hebrews:* See note on 13:3. • *crawling out of their holes:* See 13:6.

14:14 *half an acre:* Literally *half a yoke;* a "yoke" was the amount of land plowed by a pair of yoked oxen in one day.

14:15 *panic broke out:* This parallel with the Gideon story depicts Jonathan as a judge-like figure (cp. Judg 7:19-22). God had not anointed or expressly gifted Jonathan to be leader, yet God used him to rescue his people. • *raiding parties:* See note on 13:17-18.

14:18 *Bring . . . Israelites:* As in some Greek manuscripts; Hebrew reads "*Bring the Ark of God." For at that time the Ark of God was with the Israelites.* The Greek text is likely original: The Ark remained at Kiriath-jearim for twenty years (7:2), and it was never used for getting information about the future, as the ephod was (see note on 2:18).

14:19 *Never mind; let's get going!* Literally *Withdraw your hand.*

14:21-22 *Previously,* a large group of Israelites had gone into *hiding* out of fear (13:6-7). Others might have joined *the Philistine army.* However, the statement that they *revolted* when the opportunity arose suggests they might have been taken as prisoners of war and forced into the Philistines' service.

14:23 It was God, not Saul, who *saved Israel;* Jonathan was just a willing instrument in the Lord's hands. • *Beth-aven* was due west of Micmash (see 13:5). The Israelites forced the Philistines to retreat all the way to Aijalon that day (see 14:31).

14:24 With his *oath,* Saul forced abstinence from food on men who were already hungry and exhausted from battle. This oath was probably a pagan-like attempt to manipulate God into giving them a favorable result (cp. notes on Exod 23:26; 25:22; 32:4). • That Saul said *my enemies* rather than "our enemies" reflects his self-centered pride.

14:27 *he felt refreshed:* Or *his eyes brightened;* similarly in 14:29.

14:29 *made trouble:* Joshua had used this verb in speaking with Achan (Josh 7:25), and Jephthah had used it with his innocent daughter (Judg 11:35). Saul's foolish oath limited Israel's victory (14:30) and put his son's life at risk (see also Josh 6:18; 1 Chr 2:7).

14:31 Josh 10:12
14:32 Gen 9:4; Lev 17:10; 1 Sam 15:19; Acts 15:20
14:33 ᵉ*khata'* (2398) ‣Neh 9:29
14:35 1 Sam 7:12, 17
14:37 1 Sam 28:5-6; 30:7-8
14:38 Josh 7:10-12
14:39 2 Sam 12:5
14:41 Acts 1:24
14:43 Josh 7:19; 1 Sam 14:27
14:44 Ruth 1:17; 1 Sam 3:17; 14:39; 25:22
14:45 2 Sam 14:11; Luke 21:18; Acts 27:34

31 They chased and killed the Philistines all day from Micmash to Aijalon, growing more and more faint. 32 That evening they rushed for the battle plunder and butchered the sheep, goats, cattle, and calves, but they ate them without draining the blood. 33 Someone reported to Saul, "Look, the men are ᵉsinning against the LORD by eating meat that still has blood in it."

"That is very wrong," Saul said. "Find a large stone and roll it over here. 34 Then go out among the troops and tell them, 'Bring the cattle, sheep, and goats here to me. Kill them here, and drain the blood before you eat them. Do not sin against the LORD by eating meat with the blood still in it.' "

So that night all the troops brought their animals and slaughtered them there. 35 Then Saul built an altar to the LORD; it was the first of the altars he built to the LORD.

36 Then Saul said, "Let's chase the Philistines all night and plunder them until sunrise. Let's destroy every last one of them."

His men replied, "We'll do whatever you think is best."

But the priest said, "Let's ask God first."

37 So Saul asked God, "Should we go after the Philistines? Will you help us defeat them?" But God made no reply that day.

38 Then Saul said to the leaders, "Something's wrong! I want all my army commanders to come here. We must find out what sin was committed today. 39 I vow by the name of the LORD who rescued Israel that the sinner will surely die, even if it is my own son Jonathan!" But no one would tell him what the trouble was.

40 Then Saul said, "Jonathan and I will stand over here, and all of you stand over there."

And the people responded to Saul, "Whatever you think is best."

41 Then Saul prayed, "O LORD, God of Israel, please show us who is guilty and who is innocent." Then they cast sacred lots, and Jonathan and Saul were chosen as the guilty ones, and the people were declared innocent.

42 Then Saul said, "Now cast lots again and choose between me and Jonathan." And Jonathan was shown to be the guilty one.

43 "Tell me what you have done," Saul demanded of Jonathan.

"I tasted a little honey," Jonathan admitted. "It was only a little bit on the end of my stick. Does that deserve death?"

44 "Yes, Jonathan," Saul said, "you must die! May God strike me and even kill me if you do not die for this."

45 But the people broke in and said to Saul, "Jonathan has won this great victory for Israel. Should he die? Far from it! As surely as the LORD lives, not one hair on his head will be touched, for God helped him do a great deed today." So the people rescued Jonathan, and he was not put to death.

46 Then Saul called back the army from chasing the Philistines, and the Philistines returned home.

47 Now when Saul had secured his grasp on Israel's throne, he fought against his enemies in every direction—against Moab,

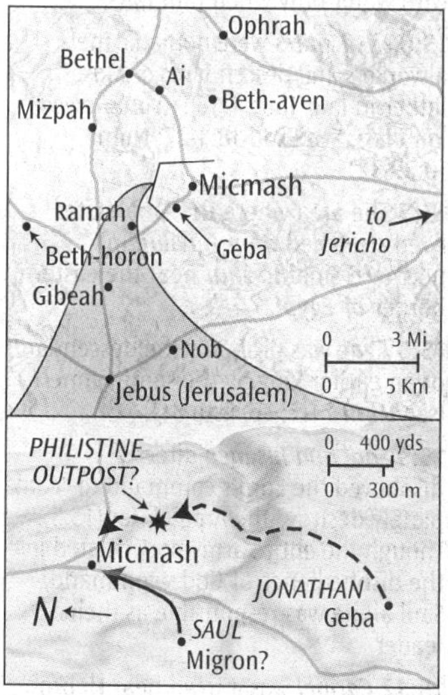

◂ **Saul & Jonathan's Victories at Micmash** (13:15–14:46). The top map shows the area around MICMASH; the bottom elevation looks eastward toward Micmash and GEBA and shows one possible reconstruction of the battle. Jonathan's surprise attack on the PHILISTINE OUTPOST threw the Philistines into panic. When Saul and his army saw what was happening, they joined the attack.

14:31 ***Aijalon:*** If the Philistines fled along the likely route through Beth-horon, then the Israelites kept up the pursuit for close to twenty miles.

14:32-34 The men were famished, so they ate meat ***without draining the blood.*** This act violated God's law (see Lev 17:10-14) and thus constituted ***sinning against the LORD.*** To prevent more sin, Saul used a large rock as a field altar so that the animals' blood could be properly drained. The incident would never have occurred had it not been for Saul's foolish oath.

14:35 ***first of the altars:*** This altar is the only one mentioned. David later built an altar that would become the site of God's Temple (2 Sam 24:18-25).

14:37-38 ***God made no reply:*** Neither the "no" lot nor the "yes" lot of the Urim and Thummim appeared.

14:41 Casting ***sacred lots*** involved the Urim and Thummim (Exod 28:30; Lev 8:8), which David also used when soliciting God's guidance (23:2; 30:8; 2 Sam 2:1). The Urim and Thummim were two small objects (perhaps flat stones, sticks, or arrows) that may have been cast like dice. They would provide a positive answer, a neutral response, or a negative answer. • Greek version adds *If the fault is with me or my son Jonathan, respond with Urim; but if the men of Israel are at fault, respond with Thummim.*

14:45 ***The people,*** aware of God's blessing on the real hero of the day, were wiser than their king.

14:47-52 In contrast to the folly described in 14:1-46, these verses summarize Saul's military successes. A similar summary of achievements ends the description of each king's reign in 1 Samuel—2 Kings.

14:47 ***secured his grasp:*** Samuel had used this verb repeatedly when

Ammon, Edom, the kings of Zobah, and the
Philistines. And wherever he turned, he was
victorious. 48He performed great deeds and
conquered the Amalekites, saving Israel
from all those who had plundered them.
49Saul's sons included Jonathan, Ishbosheth, and Malkishua. He also had two
daughters :Merab, who was older, and Michal.
50Saul's wife was Ahinoam, the daughter of
Ahimaaz. The commander of Saul's army was
Abner, the son of Saul's uncle Ner. 51Saul's father, Kish, and Abner's father, Ner, were both
sons of Abiel.
52The Israelites fought constantly with
the Philistines throughout Saul's lifetime.
So whenever Saul observed a young man
who was brave and strong, he drafted him
into his army.

The LORD Rejects Saul as King

15 One day Samuel said to Saul, "It was
the LORD who told me to [f]anoint you
as king of his people, Israel. Now listen to
this message from the LORD! 2This is what
the LORD of Heaven's Armies has declared:
I have decided to settle accounts with
the nation of Amalek for opposing Israel
when they came from Egypt. 3Now go and
completely [g]destroy the entire Amalekite nation—men, women, children, babies, cattle,
sheep, goats, camels, and donkeys."
4So Saul mobilized his army at Telaim.
There were 200,000 soldiers from Israel and
10,000 men from Judah. 5Then Saul and his
army went to a town of the Amalekites and
lay in wait in the valley. 6Saul sent this warning to the Kenites: "Move away from where
the Amalekites live, or you will die with them.
For you showed kindness to all the people of
Israel when they came up from Egypt." So
the Kenites packed up and left.
7Then Saul slaughtered the Amalekites
from Havilah all the way to Shur, east of
Egypt. 8He captured Agag, the Amalekite
king, but completely destroyed everyone else.
9Saul and his men spared Agag's life and kept
the best of the sheep and goats, the cattle, the
fat calves, and the lambs—everything, in fact,
that appealed to them. They destroyed only
what was worthless or of poor quality.
10Then the LORD said to Samuel, 11"I am
sorry that I ever made Saul king, for he has
not been loyal to me and has refused to
obey my command." Samuel was so deeply
moved when he heard this that he cried out
to the LORD all night.
12Early the next morning Samuel went to
find Saul. Someone told him, "Saul went to
the town of Carmel to set up a monument
to himself; then he went on to Gilgal."
13When Samuel finally found him, Saul
greeted him cheerfully. "May the LORD

14:48
1 Sam 15:3, 7

14:49
1 Sam 18:17, 20, 27; 19:11-12; 31:2
2 Sam 6:20
1 Chr 8:33; 10:2

14:50
2 Sam 2:8

14:51
1 Sam 9:1

14:52
1 Sam 8:11

15:1
1 Sam 9:16; 10:1
[f]*mashakh* (4886)
‣1 Sam 15:17

15:2
Exod 17:8-16
Num 24:20
Deut 25:17

15:3
Deut 20:16-18
Josh 6:17-18
[g]*kharam* (2763)
‣Isa 43:28

15:6
Num 24:21-22
Judg 1:16; 4:11

15:7
Gen 16:7; 25:18
Exod 15:22
1 Sam 27:8

15:8
Num 24:7

15:9
1 Sam 15:15, 21

15:11
Gen 6:6-7
Exod 32:9, 11, 14
2 Sam 24:16
Luke 6:12

15:12
Josh 15:55

---

speaking about what a king would do: "He will take . . . take . . . take" (8:10-18). • ***Moab, Ammon, Edom, . . . Zobah:*** David confronted these same foes during his reign and expanded Israel's territory in the process (see 2 Sam 8:1-14). • ***he was victorious:*** As in Greek version; Hebrew reads *he acted wickedly.*

14:48 ***conquered the Amalekites:*** See ch 15. The Amalekites, a nomadic group in the south, periodically raided and pillaged Israel (see Exod 17:8-16; Num 14:45; Judg 3:13; 6:3, 33; 7:12; 10:12).

14:49-51 This information about Saul's family, placed here rather than at the end of his reign, hints that his reign was essentially over and he would not be succeeded by one of his sons.

14:49 ***Saul's sons included:*** Another of Saul's sons was named Abinadab (31:2). • ***Ishbosheth:*** Hebrew *Ishvi,* a variant name for Ishbosheth; also known as Esh-baal. Esh-baal means "man of Baal." Ishbosheth means "man of shame" (see note on 2 Sam 2:8). He served briefly as a rival king over the northern tribes during David's early years (2 Sam 2:8-11).

14:50 ***Ahinoam*** is mentioned only here in Saul's story. In 25:43, David marries a woman also called Ahinoam (who might or might not have been the same person; cp. 2 Sam 12:8).

14:52 Saul had easily defeated the Ammonites (11:11) but was having much less success with ***the Philistines,*** given their well-organized fighting machine and their monopoly on iron and bronze (13:19-22). • ***he drafted him:*** Samuel had warned earlier that the king would take people as well as possessions (8:11).

15:1-35 After Saul failed to obey God and completely destroy the Amalekites, God rejected him in even stronger terms than before (cp. 13:8-14).

15:2 ***LORD of Heaven's Armies:*** See note on 1:3. • ***to settle accounts:*** In Moses' time, ***the nation of Amalek*** had inhabited southern Judah and the Negev area south of Judah. As Israel traveled to Canaan, the Amalekites preyed on the sick and the weak and those traveling at the rear. They were the first people to attack Israel after the exodus from Egypt, for which God had promised to judge them (Exod 17:8-16; Deut 25:17-19).

15:3 ***completely destroy:*** The Hebrew term used here refers to the complete consecration of things or people to the LORD, either by destroying them or by giving them as an offering; also in 15:8, 9, 15, 18, 20, 21.

15:4 ***Telaim:*** Possibly Telem (Josh 15:24).

15:5 The unnamed town ***in the valley*** was located somewhere near a Negev *wadi,* a streambed or riverbed that fills with water only when rain falls.

15:6 ***The Kenites*** were nomadic metalworkers and descendants of Moses' father-in-law (Judg 1:16). • ***you showed kindness:*** See Exod 18:1-27; Num 10:29-32.

15:7 The area where the Amalekites lived stretched ***from Havilah*** in northern Sinai ***to Shur*** near the eastern border ***of Egypt.***

15:8 ***Agag*** was probably the descendant of an earlier king by the same name (see Num 24:7; cp. Esth 3:1).

15:9 ***Saul and his men*** directly disobeyed the Lord's command to "completely destroy" the Amalekites (15:3). Though the entire army participated in the disobedience of God's command, Saul alone was responsible as their leader.

15:12 ***Carmel*** was a town near Hebron in southern Judah. • ***Saul*** commemorated his own accomplishments by erecting ***a monument to himself.*** In reality, he had earned shame (15:16-19). • ***Gilgal:*** See 13:4.

15:15 Gen 3:12-13; 1 Sam 15:9, 21
15:17 1 Sam 9:21; 10:22; [h]*mashakh* (4886) ›1 Sam 16:13
15:19 1 Sam 14:32
15:21 1 Sam 15:9, 15
15:22 Ps 40:6-8; 51:16-17; Isa 1:11-15; Jer 7:22-23; Hos 6:6; Mic 6:7-8; Mark 12:33; [i]*shama'* (8085) ›1 Kgs 12:24
15:23 Deut 18:10; 1 Sam 13:14
15:24 Num 22:34; 2 Sam 12:13; Ps 51:4; Isa 51:12-13
15:25 Exod 10:17; [j]*nasa'* (5375) ›Ps 32:1
15:27 1 Kgs 11:30-31
15:28 1 Sam 28:17-18

bless you," he said. "I have carried out the
LORD's command!"
14"Then what is all the bleating of sheep
and goats and the lowing of cattle I hear?"
Samuel demanded.
15"It's true that the army spared the best of
the sheep, goats, and cattle," Saul admitted.
"But they are going to sacrifice them to the
LORD your God. We have destroyed everything else."
16Then Samuel said to Saul, "Stop! Listen
to what the LORD told me last night!"
"What did he tell you?" Saul asked.
17And Samuel told him, "Although you may
think little of yourself, are you not the leader
of the tribes of Israel? The LORD has [h]anointed
you king of Israel. 18And the LORD sent you on
a mission and told you, 'Go and completely destroy the sinners, the Amalekites, until they
are all dead.' 19Why haven't you obeyed the
LORD? Why did you rush for the plunder and
do what was evil in the LORD's sight?"
20"But I did obey the LORD," Saul insisted. "I
carried out the mission he gave me. I brought
back King Agag, but I destroyed everyone
else. 21Then my troops brought in the best
of the sheep, goats, cattle, and plunder to
sacrifice to the LORD your God in Gilgal."
22But Samuel replied,

"What is more pleasing to the LORD:
your burnt offerings and sacrifices
or your [i]obedience to his voice?
Listen! [i]Obedience is better than sacrifice,
and submission is better than
offering the fat of rams.
23Rebellion is as sinful as witchcraft,
and stubbornness as bad as
worshiping idols.
So because you have rejected the
command of the LORD,
he has rejected you as king."

24Then Saul admitted to Samuel, "Yes,
I have sinned. I have disobeyed your instructions and the LORD's command, for I
was afraid of the people and did what they
demanded. 25But now, please [j]forgive my
sin and come back with me so that I may
worship the LORD."
26But Samuel replied, "I will not go back
with you! Since you have rejected the LORD's
command, he has rejected you as king of
Israel."
27As Samuel turned to go, Saul tried to
hold him back and tore the hem of his robe.
28And Samuel said to him, "The LORD has

Complete Destruction (15:3)

Exod 22:20; Lev 27:28-29; Num 21:2-3; Deut 7:1-6, 26; 13:12-18; Josh 6:17-19; 7:11-26; 1 Kgs 20:42; Isa 43:26-28

God instructed Saul to "completely destroy" the Amalekites, who had ambushed the Israelites after the Exodus (see Exod 17:8-16; Deut 25:17-19). The Hebrew word *kharam* ("completely destroy") often means dedicating something or someone completely to the Lord, either by destroying it (15:3; Josh 6:17-18) or by giving it as an offering (see Lev 27:28-29; Josh 6:19).

Complete destruction was called for in cases where those to be destroyed had committed a severe offense against God, such as worshiping false gods (Deut 7:1-6; 13:12-18). In 1 Sam 15:3, complete destruction is prescribed as God's judgment on a nation that mistreated his chosen people. Those who curse God's family are, in turn, cursed (Gen 12:3).

God still judges the godless and impenitent. But in the new covenant, Christians are not called to be agents of such judgment. God calls us to exercise his mercy toward those who wrong us (cp. Luke 9:51-56). We must completely destroy whatever within ourselves wars against Christ (Rom 8:13; Col 3:5). And we must overcome the enemies of Christ by our faith, by the Good News, and by our love (Eph 6:10-20; 1 Jn 2:9-17). God will mete out judgment according to his justice and in his time (Rom 12:19; 2 Thes 1:6-10).

15:13 ***I have carried out the LORD's command!*** Cp. 15:3. Saul apparently thought his actions were justified (15:15; cp. Lev 22:19). Samuel, however, cut through Saul's pretense (15:17-19) and carried out God's command himself (15:32-33).

15:15 Saul blamed *the army* even though he was the commander. Certainly, his real motivation was not spiritual (15:9).

15:17 As the ***anointed . . . king of Israel,*** Saul bore the responsibility for disobeying God, which neither false humility nor making excuses could diminish.

15:21 ***my troops:*** Saul persisted in blaming others (see 15:15). • ***Gilgal*** was a religious center. Saul tried to use religion to justify disobedience to God.

15:22 ***What is more pleasing:*** God values ***obedience*** much more than ritual (see also Ps 40:6; Hos 6:6; Matt 12:7). • ***the fat of rams:*** The choicest parts of the animal were offered to God.

15:23 ***Rebellion . . . and stubbornness,*** sins of the heart, are as bad as the sinful practices of idolatrous pagans. • Scripture condemns *witchcraft* (see note on Deut 18:10).

15:24-30 Saul finally confessed his sin. But it was too little, too late—and still accompanied by excuses.

15:24 ***I was afraid of the people:*** Saul continued to blame others (see 15:15, 21). • ***what they demanded:*** There is no hint of such pressure in the chapter. Saul's confession appears dishonest (cp. David, 2 Sam 12:13; Ps 51).

15:28 Samuel soon discovered who this *someone else* was (18:8-9; cp. ch 16).

torn the kingdom of Israel from you today and has given it to someone else—one who is better than you. 29And he who is the Glory of Israel will not lie, nor will he change his mind, for he is not human that he should change his mind!"

30Then Saul pleaded again, "I know I have sinned. But please, at least honor me before the elders of my people and before Israel by coming back with me so that I may worship the LORD your God." 31So Samuel finally agreed and went back with him, and Saul worshiped the LORD.

32Then Samuel said, "Bring King Agag to me." Agag arrived full of hope, for he thought, "Surely the worst is over, and I have been spared!" 33But Samuel said, "As your sword has killed the sons of many mothers, now your mother will be childless." And Samuel cut Agag to pieces before the LORD at Gilgal.

34Then Samuel went home to Ramah, and Saul returned to his house at Gibeah of Saul. 35Samuel never went to meet with Saul again, but he mourned constantly for him. And the LORD was sorry he had ever made Saul king of Israel.

David Anointed as King (16:1-13)

16 Now the LORD said to Samuel, "You have mourned long enough for Saul. I have rejected him as king of Israel, so fill your flask with olive oil and go to Bethlehem. Find a man named Jesse who lives there, for I have selected one of his sons to be my king."

2But Samuel asked, "How can I do that? If Saul hears about it, he will kill me."

"Take a heifer with you," the LORD replied, "and say that you have come to make a sacrifice to the LORD. 3Invite Jesse to the sacrifice, and I will show you which of his sons to anoint for me."

4So Samuel did as the LORD instructed. When he arrived at Bethlehem, the elders of the town came trembling to meet him. "What's wrong?" they asked. "Do you come in peace?"

5"Yes," Samuel replied. "I have come to sacrifice to the LORD. Purify yourselves and come with me to the sacrifice." Then Samuel performed the purification rite for Jesse and his sons and invited them to the sacrifice, too.

6When they arrived, Samuel took one look at Eliab and thought, "Surely this is the LORD's anointed!"

7But the LORD said to Samuel, "Don't judge by his appearance or height, for I have rejected him. The LORD doesn't see things the way you see them. People judge by outward appearance, but the LORD looks at the heart."

8Then Jesse told his son Abinadab to step forward and walk in front of Samuel. But Samuel said, "This is not the one the LORD has chosen." 9Next Jesse summoned Shimea,

15:29 Num 23:19; Ezek 24:14
15:30 Isa 29:13
15:33 Gen 9:5-6; Judg 1:7
15:34 1 Sam 7:17; 11:4
15:35 1 Sam 16:1; 19:24
16:1 1 Sam 9:16; 13:13-14; 2 Kgs 9:1-2
16:2 1 Sam 20:28-29
16:3 Deut 17:14-15
16:4 1 Kgs 2:13; Luke 2:4
16:5 Gen 35:2; Exod 19:10
16:6 1 Sam 17:13
16:7 1 Sam 9:2; 1 Kgs 8:39; 1 Chr 28:9; Luke 16:15
16:8 1 Sam 17:13

15:29 ***nor will he change his mind:*** Samuel spoke prophetically of God's commitment to make David king and to preserve his dynasty. God had rejected Saul, but he would never reject David (see 2 Sam 7:8-17).

15:30 ***honor me before the elders:*** To help Saul save face.

15:32 ***Agag arrived full of hope, for he thought, "Surely the worst is over, and I have been spared!"*** Dead Sea Scrolls and Greek version read *Agag arrived hesitantly, for he thought, "Surely this is the bitterness of death."*

15:35 The verb phrase ***mourned constantly*** is usually used for grieving over someone's death. Although Saul was still living, his royalty was coming to an end. Samuel might have been grieving out of personal attachment to Saul, a sense of failure, or concern that Israel's condition would be worse. • ***the LORD was sorry:*** See "God's Change of Mind," facing page.

16:1-23 David was Saul's replacement. There are striking similarities between the two: Samuel anointed both. Neither was pursuing the position. Both were unlikely candidates (Saul was from the smallest tribe; David was the youngest son). Both were impressive in appearance (9:2; 16:12). And the Spirit came mightily on each when he was anointed king (10:10; 11:6; 16:13). The key difference was that David was a man "after [God's] own heart" (13:14; cp. 16:7), while Saul was not.

16:1 ***mourned long enough:*** See note on 15:35. • ***Bethlehem*** was about five miles south of Jerusalem. It was later known as the City of David (Luke 2:11) and the birthplace of Jesus. • ***Jesse*** was the grandson of Boaz and Ruth (Ruth 4:22). • ***I have selected:*** This Hebrew verb implies that God had seen ***one of [Jesse's] sons*** and based his choice on what he saw. God, the eternal king, knows better than the people of Israel how to choose a good ***king*** to serve the nation, and he provided a replacement for Saul that would lead Israel well.

16:2 ***say that you have come to make a sacrifice:*** God sometimes leads his servants into dangerous situations. He protects his own—sometimes by miracle, sometimes by strategy (cp. Exod 3:18-22). In Samuel's role as a priestly judge, he would not have raised any suspicions by offering a sacrifice (see 10:8).

16:4 ***the elders . . . came trembling:*** News of Samuel's rebuke of Saul and execution of Agag had likely reached Bethlehem.

16:5 ***purify yourselves:*** Self-purification included bathing and abstaining from sexual intercourse (see Exod 19:10-15; cp. Gen 35:2-4). • ***The sacrifice*** likely took place the following morning (see Num 11:18; Josh 3:5; 7:13-14). • ***Samuel performed the purification rite for Jesse and his sons*** to make sure they were ready for the sacrifice and for the anointing of the new king (cp. Exod 19:10; Josh 3:5).

16:6-7 ***his appearance or height:*** Like Saul, ***Eliab***, Jesse's oldest son, had an impressive outward appearance (cp. 9:2). Also like Saul, he was ***rejected*** (cp. 15:23). God had another man in mind to anoint as king. • ***the LORD looks at the heart:*** God can give a new heart (10:9), touch hearts (10:26), and peer into the deep motivations of the heart (Ps 139:1). God sees what people cannot see—a person's true character. Eliab's character comes out in 17:28.

16:9 ***Shimea:*** Hebrew *Shammah*, a variant spelling of Shimea; cp. 1 Chr 2:13; 20:7.

16:11
2 Sam 7:8
[k]*ro'eh* (7462)
›1 Chr 11:2

16:12
Gen 39:6
Exod 2:1-2
1 Sam 9:17
Acts 7:20

16:13
[a]*mashakh* (4886)
›1 Kgs 1:34

16:14
Judg 16:20
1 Sam 11:6; 18:10-12; 19:9
1 Kgs 22:22

16:15
[b]*ruakh* (7307)
›2 Sam 23:2

16:18
1 Sam 3:19; 17:32-37

16:21
Gen 41:46

but Samuel said, "Neither is this the one the LORD has chosen." [10]In the same way all seven of Jesse's sons were presented to Samuel. But Samuel said to Jesse, "The LORD has not chosen any of these." [11]Then Samuel asked, "Are these all the sons you have?"

"There is still the youngest," Jesse replied. "But he's out in the fields [k]watching the sheep and goats."

"Send for him at once," Samuel said. "We will not sit down to eat until he arrives."

[12]So Jesse sent for him. He was dark and handsome, with beautiful eyes.

And the LORD said, "This is the one; anoint him."

[13]So as David stood there among his brothers, Samuel took the flask of olive oil he had brought and [a]anointed David with the oil. And the Spirit of the LORD came powerfully upon David from that day on. Then Samuel returned to Ramah.

4. DISSOLUTION OF SAUL'S REIGN (16:14–31:13)

David's and Saul's Lives Interact (16:14–18:30)

David Serves as Court Musician

[14]Now the Spirit of the LORD had left Saul, and the LORD sent a tormenting spirit that filled him with depression and fear.

[15]Some of Saul's servants said to him, "A tormenting [b]spirit from God is troubling you. [16]Let us find a good musician to play the harp whenever the tormenting spirit troubles you. He will play soothing music, and you will soon be well again."

[17]"All right," Saul said. "Find me someone who plays well, and bring him here."

[18]One of the servants said to Saul, "One of Jesse's sons from Bethlehem is a talented harp player. Not only that—he is a brave warrior, a man of war, and has good judgment. He is also a fine-looking young man, and the LORD is with him."

[19]So Saul sent messengers to Jesse to say, "Send me your son David, the shepherd." [20]Jesse responded by sending David to Saul, along with a young goat, a donkey loaded with bread, and a wineskin full of wine.

[21]So David went to Saul and began serving him. Saul loved David very much, and David became his armor bearer.

[22]Then Saul sent word to Jesse asking, "Please let David remain in my service, for I am very pleased with him."

[23]And whenever the tormenting spirit from God troubled Saul, David would play the harp. Then Saul would feel better, and the tormenting spirit would go away.

God's Change of Mind (15:10-11, 29, 35)

Gen 6:6-7
Exod 32:11-14
Num 23:19
Deut 32:36
2 Sam 24:15-16
Jer 4:28; 18:7-10; 26:2-19
Ezek 24:14
Joel 2:13-14
Amos 7:2-6
Jon 3:9–4:11

Thirty-four times in the OT, God is said to "change his mind" or "be sorry" (Hebrew *nakham*). What could this mean? Did he relent, or did he have pity? Was he sorry, or did he grieve?

One thing is clear: God never repents of sin or moral failure, because he is perfect (see 15:29; Num 23:19). He may "change his mind" regarding calamity or judgment that he initiated—that is, he may decide to stop it—in response to prayers of repentance (Jer 18:7-10; Joel 2:14; Jon 3:9-10), a human intercessor (Exod 32:11-14; Amos 7:2-6), or with no apparent human mediation (Judg 2:18; 2 Sam 24:16). On a few occasions, God is "sorry" about something he has already done, such as choosing Saul to be king (15:11, 35; cp. Gen 6:6). God is not admitting past mistakes; he is expressing anguish over lives gone awry.

Theologians debate the degree to which God, who is all-wise and all-powerful, can "change his mind." In the Bible, any language that refers to a change in God's mind reflects a human perspective on God's activity. Any change in God, therefore, is a change as humans experience him—a reflection of his unchanging love, mercy, faithfulness, and holy will. It does not suggest a change in God's power, omniscience, foreknowledge, wisdom, or holiness.

16:12 ***anoint him:*** See note on 9:16.

16:13 ***the Spirit of the LORD came . . . upon David:*** As was consistently evident (e.g., 16:23; 17:48-54; 18:5, 12-16). The Spirit of the Lord had also come upon Saul (10:10) but had left him because of disobedience (16:14). • ***Ramah:*** Samuel's hometown (1:1).

16:14–31:13 Saul's kingship continued its downward spiral after God's Spirit departed from him. His reign ended in shame and defeat (ch 31).

16:14 ***Spirit . . . left Saul:*** In contrast with David's receiving the Spirit (see "The Spirit's Presence" at 16:13-23, p. 494). • ***The LORD sent a tormenting spirit*** (or *an evil spirit;* also in 16:15, 16, 23) as a consequence of Saul's disobedience (see also 18:10; 19:9; cp. Judg 9:23; Rom 1:28-29).

16:18 ***harp:*** The instrument was probably a lyre (as in 10:5). • ***the LORD is with him:*** People recognized that God's Spirit was upon David (16:13).

16:21 Although at first ***Saul loved David very much,*** this love soon turned to intense jealousy and hatred (see 18:8-14). • An ***armor bearer*** in ancient Israel served as the personal attendant of a warrior chieftain (see 14:1-15; 31:4-6; Judg 9:54; 2 Sam 18:15).

16:22 David's father, ***Jesse*** (16:18), arranged for David to continue serving Saul while still fulfilling his shepherding duties at home (see 17:14-15).

16:23 ***Saul would feel better:*** David was more than a handsome lad gifted in music; he was the anointed king. Here

David Defeats Goliath

17 The Philistines now mustered their
army for battle and camped between
Socoh in Judah and Azekah at Ephes-
dammim. 2 Saul countered by gathering
his Israelite troops near the valley of Elah.
3 So the Philistines and Israelites faced each
other on opposite hills, with the valley between them.

4 Then Goliath, a Philistine champion
from Gath, came out of the Philistine ranks
to face the forces of Israel. He was over nine
feet tall! 5 He wore a bronze helmet, and his
bronze coat of mail weighed 125 pounds.
6 He also wore bronze leg armor, and he carried a bronze javelin on his shoulder. 7 The
shaft of his spear was as heavy and thick
as a weaver's beam, tipped with an iron
spearhead that weighed 15 pounds. His armor bearer walked ahead of him carrying
a shield.

8 Goliath stood and shouted a taunt across
to the Israelites. "Why are you all coming
out to fight?" he called. "I am the Philistine
champion, but you are only the servants of
Saul. Choose one man to come down here
and fight me! 9 If he kills me, then we will be
your slaves. But if I kill him, you will be our
slaves! 10 I defy the armies of Israel today!
Send me a man who will fight me!" 11 When
Saul and the Israelites heard this, they were
terrified and deeply shaken.

12 Now David was the son of a man named
Jesse, an Ephrathite from Bethlehem in the
land of Judah. Jesse was an old man at that
time, and he had eight sons. 13 Jesse's three
oldest sons—Eliab, Abinadab, and Shimea—
had already joined Saul's army to fight the
Philistines. 14 David was the youngest son.
David's three oldest brothers stayed with
Saul's army, 15 but David went back and
forth so he could help his father with the
sheep in Bethlehem.

16 For forty days, every morning and evening, the Philistine champion strutted in
front of the Israelite army.

17 One day Jesse said to David, "Take
this basket of roasted grain and these ten

17:1 1 Sam 13:5; 1 Chr 11:13
17:2 1 Sam 21:9
17:4 Josh 11:21-22; 2 Sam 21:19
17:9 2 Sam 2:12-16
17:10 1 Sam 17:26, 45
17:12 Gen 35:19; Ruth 4:18-22; 1 Chr 2:13
17:13 1 Sam 16:6-9
17:15 1 Sam 16:19
17:17 1 Sam 25:18

The Spirit's Presence (16:13-23)

1 Sam 10:1-10; 11:6-7; 19:19-23
Gen 41:37-40
Exod 31:1-6
Judg 3:9-11; 6:34; 11:29; 14:5-6; 16:20-21
2 Chr 20:13-19; 24:20-22
Ps 51:11-12
Isa 11:1-5
Jer 31:33-34
Joel 2:28-29
Mark 3:28-29
Acts 2:1-21; 4:31
Eph 1:13-14; 4:30
Heb 6:4-8

In the OT, the Spirit of the Lord came upon a person or group when they were called to do a task or ordained for an office. The Spirit "came upon" the judges Othniel, Gideon, and Jephthah (Judg 3:10; 6:34; 11:29), empowering them for service. Saul and David both received the Spirit of God when they were anointed king (10:1, 9-10; 16:13). The Spirit would depart when the task had been completed or when the officeholder was removed from office. When Samuel anointed David as the next king (16:13), the Spirit left Saul (16:14), who was disobedient and had been rejected by God as king (13:7b-14; 15:10-29; cp. 28:15; Judg 16:20). After David had sinned with Bathsheba, he prayed to be spared this same judgment (Ps 51:11).

In the NT, God's Holy Spirit is given to all who put their faith in Christ for salvation, not just to individuals in specific roles (see Acts 2:14-21; Eph 1:13-14; 1 Cor 12:1-11). Still, the Spirit performs a similar role in equipping God's servants to do the work that God has called them to do (see "The Holy Spirit's Presence" at Acts 5:32, p. 1834). The OT departure of the Spirit from Saul also has a NT parallel, found in warnings not to sin against the Spirit and not to bring sorrow to the Holy Spirit (see Mark 3:28-29; Eph 4:30; Heb 6:1-8).

David illustrated what a king should be: one who brings relief. Later, David composed dozens of psalms that have brought comfort and relief through the ages. • ***the tormenting spirit would go away:*** Even those who are disobedient and rejected can receive relief and comfort through the Lord's servant.

17:1 ***The Philistines*** presented an ongoing threat throughout Saul's reign (see 14:47-52). • ***Socoh in Judah*** was fourteen miles west of Bethlehem toward Philistine territory. • ***Azekah*** was a few miles northwest of Socoh (the precise location of *Ephes-dammim* is unknown). The Philistines were encroaching on Israelite territory.

17:2 The ***valley of Elah*** was a fertile area that ran east–west, fifteen miles southwest of Bethlehem.

17:4 ***champion:*** In ancient times, rival forces would sometimes agree to let selected individuals from each side decide a conflict. This reduced casualties and other costs. The same kind of combat is reflected in 2 Sam 2:12-17. • ***Gath*** was one of five Philistine cities with a reputation for having giants as citizens (2 Sam 21:15-22). • ***over nine feet:*** Hebrew *6 cubits and 1 span* [which totals about 9.75 feet or 3 meters]; Dead Sea Scrolls and Greek version read *4 cubits and 1 span* [which totals about 6.75 feet or 2 meters].

17:5-7 Although Goliath was a fully armored warrior of terrifying size, he did not have God—a far mightier warrior—on his side (17:45-47).

17:5 ***125 pounds:*** Hebrew *5,000 shekels* [57 kilograms].

17:7 ***15 pounds:*** Hebrew *600 shekels* [6.8 kilograms].

17:12 ***Ephrathite:*** Ephrath is a name for Bethlehem (Gen 35:19; 1 Chr 4:4).

17:13 ***Shimea:*** Hebrew *Shammah*, a variant spelling of Shimea; cp. 1 Chr 2:13; 20:7.

17:15 ***went back and forth:*** David apparently served as a musician and armor bearer in Saul's court (see 16:19-23) while maintaining his duties at home. The intermittent nature of David's service might explain why Saul was unfamiliar with David during the encounter with Goliath (see 17:55-58).

17:17 ***basket:*** Hebrew *ephah* [20 quarts or 22 liters].

DAVID (16:1–17:58)

1 Sam 18:1–27:12; 29:1–30:31
Ruth 4:13-22
2 Sam 1:1–24:25
1 Kgs 1:1–2:12
1 Chr 11:1–29:30
Psalms
Matt 1:1; 9:27; 22:41-46
Mark 12:35-37
Luke 20:41-44
John 7:40-44
Acts 2:22-37; 13:20-43
Rom 1:3
Rev 22:16

David is one of the monumental figures of biblical history. His reign was a high point in God's plan for Israel, and it had great and lasting significance.

David was born in Bethlehem as Jesse's youngest son; his lineage is traced back to Judah (Ruth 4:18-22; 1 Chr 2:3-15; Matt 1:3-6; Luke 3:31-33). At the time, Jerusalem was occupied by the Jebusites, and large parts of the Promised Land were still occupied by foreign people, most notably the Philistines. God would use David to complete the conquest of the land.

As a youth, David was a simple shepherd, watching his father's sheep (16:11; 17:15). His life took an unexpected turn when the prophet Samuel came to Jesse and anointed David as the next king of Israel. However, David's kingship was not initiated by a coup or an assassination. Indeed, David became a faithful servant to King Saul. David first entered Saul's service as a musician, playing songs that soothed Saul's tormented soul (16:14-23). This service anticipates David's role as the composer of many of the psalms. The youthful David also helped Saul by famously defeating the Philistine champion Goliath in individual combat (17:32-51). This victory anticipates David's role as a victorious military leader.

Although David was loyal, Saul grew deeply suspicious of him, and David had to flee. He was able to escape with help from Saul's own children, Jonathan and Michal. David led a virtual kingdom in exile. He had a standing army of 600 men. The prophet Gad and the priest Abiathar were also with him, providing direction and guidance from the Lord.

God's long-suffering patience finally ran out with Saul, and Saul was killed on the battlefield. Yet it was still not easy for David to establish his rule over all Israel. Judah immediately proclaimed him its king, but at first the northern tribes chose Ishbosheth, a son of Saul, to be their leader. Ishbosheth was not a powerful or good leader; he only stayed in power because of the protection of his father's military leader, Abner. However, Ishbosheth foolishly insulted Abner, so the general helped turn the kingdom over to David.

As king over a united Israel, David proceeded to solidify the kingdom. He and his men captured Jerusalem from the Jebusites and made this central city his capital. He also expelled the remaining Philistines from the land. He then brought the Ark of the Covenant into Jerusalem. David wanted to build a permanent temple to God in Jerusalem to replace the Tabernacle. God denied this wish, but he showed his love for David by entering into a covenant with him that established his descendants as a dynasty (2 Sam 7).

David's life soon took a turn for the worse, however (2 Sam 11–12). At a time when he probably should have been on the battlefield with his army, he was lounging around on the palace roof. He saw a beautiful woman named Bathsheba taking a bath. He wanted her, so, like a Near Eastern despot, he took her. She became pregnant, and his attempt to cover up his adultery failed. In a desperate attempt to keep things secret, he had her husband, Uriah, killed. But not even a great king like David can keep secrets from God, and God sent his prophet Nathan to confront David. David repented (see Pss 32, 51), but the consequences of his actions plagued his family and the rest of his reign.

From that point on, David's family fell apart. David's son Amnon raped his half sister Tamar (2 Sam 13:1-14). Her brother Absalom then murdered Amnon (2 Sam 13:20-22, 28-29). Absalom later created a civil war as he tried to steal the throne from his father (2 Sam 15–18). Another son, Adonijah, tried to take the throne from David by having himself proclaimed king while his father was still alive (1 Kgs 1:5-10). But David was able to muster enough strength to ensure that Solomon would succeed him (1 Kgs 1:28-40). David died, Solomon was proclaimed king, and David's long dynasty began (as promised in 2 Sam 7).

David's successors rarely measured up. Only rarely did his descendants lead the nation to worship God faithfully; the united monarchy did not even outlive Solomon. In the centuries that followed, the descendants of David ruled only Judah in the south. Finally, the kingdom of Judah was destroyed. Never again did a descendant of David reign as king in Israel.

What, then, of the promise to David that "your throne will be secure forever" (2 Sam 7:16)? The NT points to Jesus. He was the descendant of David, and God proclaimed him the Christ, or Messiah—the anointed king (see Matt 1:1; 9:27; 12:23; Mark 10:48; 11:10; 12:35; Luke 18:38-39; 20:41; John 7:42; Rev 5:5; 22:16). The life and rule of David foreshadows the messianic reign of Jesus Christ, which will last forever (see Luke 1:33; Rev 11:15).

loaves of bread, and carry them quickly to your brothers. [18]And give these ten cuts of cheese to their captain. See how your brothers are getting along, and bring back a report on how they are doing." [19]David's brothers were with Saul and the Israelite army at the valley of Elah, fighting against the Philistines.

[20]So David left the sheep with another shepherd and set out early the next morning with the gifts, as Jesse had directed him. He arrived at the camp just as the Israelite army was leaving for the battlefield with shouts and battle cries. [21]Soon the Israelite and Philistine forces stood facing each other, army against army. [22]David left his things with the keeper of supplies and hurried out to the ranks to greet his brothers. [23]As he was talking with them, Goliath, the Philistine champion from Gath, came out from the Philistine ranks. Then David heard him shout his usual taunt to the army of Israel.

[24]As soon as the Israelite army saw him, they began to run away in fright. [25]"Have you seen the giant?" the men asked. "He comes out each day to defy Israel. The king has offered a huge reward to anyone who kills him. He will give that man one of his daughters for a wife, and the man's entire family will be exempted from paying taxes!"

[26]David asked the soldiers standing nearby, "What will a man get for killing this Philistine and ending his defiance of Israel? Who is this pagan Philistine anyway, that he is allowed to defy the armies of the living God?"

[27]And these men gave David the same reply. They said, "Yes, that is the reward for killing him."

[28]But when David's oldest brother, Eliab, heard David talking to the men, he was angry. "What are you doing around here anyway?" he demanded. "What about those few sheep you're supposed to be taking care of? I know about your [c]pride and deceit. You just want to see the battle!"

[29]"What have I done now?" David replied. "I was only asking a question!" [30]He walked over to some others and asked them the same thing and received the same answer. [31]Then David's question was reported to King Saul, and the king sent for him.

[32]"Don't worry about this Philistine," David told Saul. "I'll go fight him!"

[33]"Don't be ridiculous!" Saul replied. "There's no way you can fight this Philistine and possibly win! You're only a boy, and he's been a man of war since his youth."

[34]But David persisted. "I have been taking care of my father's sheep and goats," he said. "When a lion or a bear comes to steal a lamb from the flock, [35]I go after it with a club and rescue the lamb from its mouth. If the animal turns on me, I catch it by the jaw and club it to death. [36]I have done this to both lions and bears, and I'll do it to this pagan Philistine, too, for he has defied the armies of the living God! [37]The LORD who rescued me from the claws of the lion and the bear will rescue me from this Philistine!"

Saul finally consented. "All right, go ahead," he said. "And may the LORD be with you!"

[38]Then Saul gave David his own armor—a bronze helmet and a coat of mail. [39]David put it on, strapped the sword over it, and took a step or two to see what it was like, for he had never worn such things before.

"I can't go in these," he protested to Saul. "I'm not used to them." So David took them off again. [40]He [d]picked up five smooth stones from a stream and put them into his shepherd's bag. Then, armed only with his shepherd's staff and sling, he started across the valley to fight the Philistine.

[41]Goliath walked out toward David with his shield bearer ahead of him, [42]sneering in contempt at this ruddy-faced boy. [43]"Am I a dog," he roared at David, "that you come at me with a stick?" And he cursed David by

17:18 Gen 37:13-14
17:23 1 Sam 17:8-10
17:25 Josh 15:16; 1 Sam 18:17
17:26 1 Sam 11:2; 14:6; 2 Kgs 19:4
17:28 Gen 37:4, 8; [c]*zadon* (2087) ‣ Prov 11:2
17:32 Deut 20:1
17:35 Amos 3:12
17:37 1 Sam 20:13; 2 Tim 4:17
17:40 [d]*bakhar* (0977) ‣ 1 Chr 28:5
17:42 1 Sam 16:12
17:43 1 Sam 24:14; 2 Sam 3:8; 9:8; 1 Kgs 20:10

17:18 ***bring back a report on how they are doing:*** Literally *take their pledge.*

17:26 ***What will a man get:*** Cp. 18:17-27. David's interest in a reward was overshadowed by his determination to silence Goliath's defiance of God (17:45-47). • ***pagan:*** Literally *uncircumcised.* See note on 14:6.

17:28 ***Eliab . . . was angry,*** perhaps resentful that David, rather than he, was anointed to be king (16:6-13).

17:32 ***I'll go fight him!*** David's courage stands in contrast to Saul's fear (17:11).

17:40 A ***stream*** flowed through the valley of Elah (17:2). • A ***sling*** was a leather pouch attached to two leather thongs. When the sling containing a stone was whirled rapidly, one of the thongs could be released, sending the stone toward its target. David probably became deadly accurate with a sling as a shepherd, but the sling was used by warriors as well (Judg 20:16).

17:42 ***ruddy-faced:*** The same Hebrew word is translated "dark" (16:12) and "very red" (Gen 25:25). Here, it emphasizes David's youthfulness and inexperience. • ***boy:*** Saul had expressed similar disbelief (17:33). As a champion, Goliath expected to be met by an Israelite warrior of similar rank.

17:43 ***a dog:*** A metaphor for a compliant, bowing servant (cp. 2 Sam 9:8). • ***a stick:*** David had concealed his sling, and Goliath could see only his staff. • ***by the names of his gods:*** Since Goliath appealed to his gods, David's victory over Goliath would also symbolize God's victory over Dagon, the chief god of the Philistines (5:2, 5).

17:45
2 Chr 32:8
Ps 124:8
Heb 11:32-34
[e]*tsaba'* (6635)
‣1 Kgs 22:19

17:46
Exod 7:5
Josh 4:24
1 Kgs 18:36
2 Kgs 19:19
Isa 37:20

17:47
1 Sam 14:6
2 Chr 14:11; 20:15
Ps 44:6
Hos 1:7

17:50
1 Sam 25:29

17:52
Josh 15:11, 36

18:1
Gen 44:30
2 Sam 1:26; 9:1

the names of his gods. [44]"Come over here,
and I'll give your flesh to the birds and wild
animals!" Goliath yelled.
[45]David replied to the Philistine, "You
come to me with sword, spear, and javelin,
but I come to you in the name of the LORD of
Heaven's [e]Armies—the God of the armies of
Israel, whom you have defied. [46]Today the
LORD will conquer you, and I will kill you
and cut off your head. And then I will give
the dead bodies of your men to the birds
and wild animals, and the whole world will
know that there is a God in Israel! [47]And
everyone assembled here will know that
the LORD rescues his people, but not with
sword and spear. This is the LORD's battle,
and he will give you to us!"
[48]As Goliath moved closer to attack, David quickly ran out to meet him. [49]Reaching
into his shepherd's bag and taking out a
stone, he hurled it with his sling and hit the
Philistine in the forehead. The stone sank
in, and Goliath stumbled and fell face down
on the ground.
[50]So David triumphed over the Philistine
with only a sling and a stone, for he had no
sword. [51]Then David ran over and pulled Goliath's sword from its sheath. David used it
to kill him and cut off his head.
When the Philistines saw that their champion was dead, they turned and ran. [52]Then
the men of Israel and Judah gave a great
shout of triumph and rushed after the Philistines, chasing them as far as Gath and the
gates of Ekron. The bodies of the dead and
wounded Philistines were strewn all along
the road from Shaaraim, as far as Gath and
Ekron. [53]Then the Israelite army returned
and plundered the deserted Philistine
camp. [54](David took the Philistine's head to
Jerusalem, but he stored the man's armor in
his own tent.)
[55]As Saul watched David go out to fight
the Philistine, he asked Abner, the commander of his army, "Abner, whose son is
this young man?"
"I really don't know," Abner declared.
[56]"Well, find out who he is!" the king told
him.
[57]As soon as David returned from killing
Goliath, Abner brought him to Saul with the
Philistine's head still in his hand. [58]"Tell me
about your father, young man," Saul said.
And David replied, "His name is Jesse,
and we live in Bethlehem."

Saul Is Jealous of David's Success

18 After David had finished talking
with Saul, he met Jonathan, the
king's son. There was an immediate bond
between them, for Jonathan loved David.
[2]From that day on Saul kept David with him

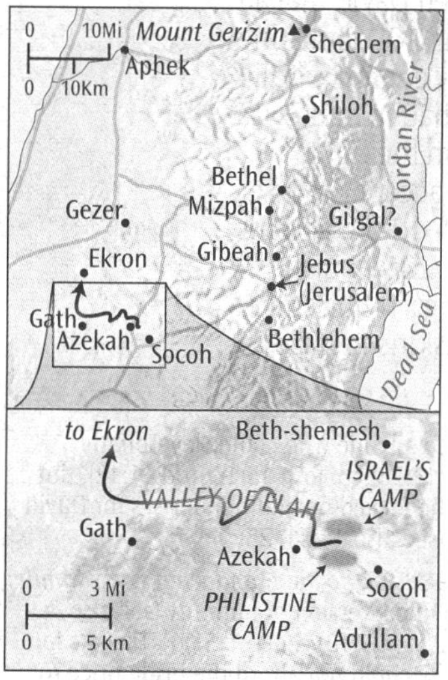

◀ **David vs. Goliath and the Battle of Elah (17:1-52).** The bottom map shows a close-up view of the PHILISTINE CAMP, ISRAEL'S CAMP, and the VALLEY OF ELAH between them; the top map shows the wider region. After David crossed the valley and killed Goliath, the Philistines fled toward their homeland, and the Israelites chased them "as far as GATH and the gates of EKRON" (17:52), westward along the valley floor.

17:44 A corpse left to scavengers such as ***birds and wild animals*** was grievously cursed (cp. Deut 21:23; 28:26).

17:45-47 ***the LORD of Heaven's Armies:*** See note on 1:3. Despite the Philistines' apparent military advantage, David knew that Israel had the supreme advantage in the one true God.

17:49 Goliath's ***forehead*** remained exposed beneath his enormous helmet. • ***stumbled and fell face down:*** The stone only incapacitated Goliath; David killed him by decapitating him (17:51).

17:52 The Israelites chased the Philistines to ***Gath*** (as in some Greek manuscripts; Hebrew reads *a valley*), some six miles to the west. • ***Ekron*** was a Philistine city five miles north of Gath. • ***Shaaraim*** was a city of Judah near Azekah (17:1).

17:53 Unless expressly prohibited (e.g., 15:3; Josh 6:18), victory in battle allowed for the taking of war spoils (Deut 2:35; Josh 8:2).

17:54 ***Jerusalem*** became an Israelite city later, when David captured it from the Jebusites (2 Sam 5:6-7). Jerusalem was probably the final destination of Goliath's head, after David had become king. But David might have taken it to Jerusalem earlier to intimidate the non-Israelite occupants.

17:55-58 In light of 16:14-23, it is surprising that neither Saul nor Abner knew who David was. It is possible that the events of ch 17 happened either before or long after David's tenure of intermittent service mentioned in ch 16 (Saul probably served as king for forty-two years, 13:1).

18:1 ***David*** and ***Jonathan*** had much in common: both were young and capable, were military heroes, had a robust faith in God, and had a claim to the throne of Israel. It is a testimony to Jonathan's true character that he recognized and supported God's choice of David to be the next king of Israel (see 18:3-4; 20:12-17). • ***Jonathan loved David:*** See 20:17; 2 Sam 1:26. Others in this chapter are also said to love David: all Israel and Judah (18:16), Saul's daughter Michal (18:20), and Saul's servants (18:22). Some modern interpreters see a homosexual relationship between David and Jonathan, but the text implies nothing other than a deep and loyal friendship.

18:2 David had previously served Saul part-time (see 17:15 and note); now ***Saul kept David with him*** full-time.

and wouldn't let him return home. 3And Jonathan made a solemn pact with David, because he loved him as he loved himself. 4Jonathan sealed the pact by taking off his robe and giving it to David, together with his tunic, sword, bow, and belt.

5Whatever Saul asked David to do, David did it successfully. So Saul made him a commander over the men of war, an appointment that was welcomed by the people and Saul's officers alike.

6When the victorious Israelite army was returning home after David had killed the Philistine, women from all the towns of Israel came out to meet [f]King Saul. They sang and danced for joy with tambourines and cymbals. 7This was their song:

"Saul has killed his thousands,
  and David his ten thousands!"

8This made Saul very angry. "What's this?" he said. "They credit David with ten thousands and me with only thousands. Next they'll be making him their king!" 9So from that time on Saul kept a jealous eye on David.

10The very next day a tormenting spirit from God overwhelmed Saul, and he began to rave in his house like a madman. David was playing the harp, as he did each day. But Saul had a spear in his hand, 11and he suddenly hurled it at David, intending to pin him to the wall. But David escaped him twice.

12Saul was then afraid of David, for the LORD was with David and had turned away from Saul. 13Finally, Saul sent him away and appointed him commander over 1,000 men, and David faithfully led his troops into battle.

14David continued to succeed in everything he did, for the LORD was with him. 15When Saul recognized this, he became even more afraid of him. 16But all Israel and Judah loved David because he was so successful at leading his troops into battle.

17One day Saul said to David, "I am ready to give you my older daughter, Merab, as your wife. But first you must prove yourself to be a real warrior by fighting the LORD's battles." For Saul thought, "I'll send him out against the Philistines and let them kill him rather than doing it myself."

18"Who am I, and what is my family in Israel that I should be the king's son-in-law?" David exclaimed. "My father's family is nothing!" 19So when the time came for Saul to give his daughter Merab in marriage to David, he gave her instead to Adriel, a man from Meholah.

20In the meantime, Saul's daughter Michal had fallen in love with David, and Saul was delighted when he heard about it. 21"Here's another chance to see him killed by the Philistines!" Saul said to himself. But to David he said, "Today you have a second chance to become my son-in-law!"

22Then Saul told his men to say to David, "The king really likes you, and so do we. Why don't you accept the king's offer and become his son-in-law?"

23When Saul's men said these things to David, he replied, "How can a poor man from a humble family afford the bride price for the daughter of a king?"

24When Saul's men reported this back to the king, 25he told them, "Tell David that all I want for the bride price is 100 Philistine foreskins! Vengeance on my enemies is all I really want." But what Saul had in mind was that David would be killed in the fight.

26David was delighted to accept the offer. Before the time limit expired, 27he and his men went out and killed 200 Philistines. Then David fulfilled the king's requirement by presenting all their foreskins to him. So

18:4 Gen 41:42; Esth 6:8
18:6 Exod 15:20; Judg 11:34; Ps 68:25; 149:3
[f] *melek* (4428) ▸ 2 Sam 5:3
18:7 1 Sam 21:11; 29:5
18:8 1 Sam 15:28-29
18:10 1 Sam 16:14
18:11 1 Sam 19:10
18:13 2 Sam 5:2
18:14 Gen 39:3-4
18:17 1 Sam 17:25; 25:28
18:18 1 Sam 9:21; 2 Sam 7:18
18:19 Judg 7:22; 2 Sam 21:8
18:20 1 Sam 18:28
18:23 Gen 29:20; 34:12
18:27 2 Sam 3:14

18:3-4 Out of his love for David and recognition that God had chosen David to be Israel's next king (see 20:13-17, 30-31; 23:17), ***Jonathan made a solemn pact*** of friendship with David. By giving David items that symbolized his official status as the king's son and crown prince, Jonathan symbolically gave David his right of succession to the throne.

18:6 The type of instrument represented by the word ***cymbals*** is uncertain.

18:7 ***thousands . . . ten thousands:*** This dramatic increase in number between two lines of Hebrew poetry was a way of intensifying the statement (cp. Deut 32:30; Ps 91:7). Because of his great military victories, David was beginning to eclipse Saul (18:16, 30; 21:11).

18:8-15 Saul came to view David as a threat rather than an ally and would do anything to get rid of him.

18:10 ***tormenting spirit*** (or *an evil spirit*): See note on 16:14.

18:11 In his jealousy and fear, Saul would have been happier with one dead David than with thousands of dead Philistines (18:7).

18:12 ***the LORD . . . had turned away from Saul*** as king as punishment for his disobedience. Saul's kingship would fail, and David's would succeed (18:14).

18:17-19 *Saul* offered his ***older daughter, Merab,*** to David. But it was an insincere gesture.

18:17 Saul had promised his ***daughter*** to anyone who could slay Goliath (17:25; cp. Josh 15:16; Judg 1:12), but he tacked on additional risks for David (see also 18:21, 25).

18:18 ***Who am I, and what is my family:*** An expression of humility (see also 2 Sam 7:18; cp. Exod 3:11). David's family could not afford the bride price to marry the king's daughter (18:23-25).

18:19 ***So:*** Or *But.* Either David declined the offer, or Saul reneged.

18:22 ***really likes you:*** The same Hebrew word describes Jonathan's love for David (18:3; 19:1-2, "strong affection"). Here, it was completely untrue.

18:23 The future son-in-law would give the ***bride price*** as a gift to his bride's father (see Gen 34:12; Exod 22:16-17).

19:1 1 Sam 18:1-3
19:3 1 Sam 20:9, 12
19:5 Deut 19:10-13; 1 Sam 11:13; 17:49-50; Ps 94:21
19:7 1 Sam 16:21
19:9 1 Sam 16:14; 18:10-12
19:11 Judg 16:2; Ps 59:TITLE, 3-4, 6
19:12 Josh 2:15; Acts 9:25

Saul gave his daughter Michal to David to be his wife.

28 When Saul realized that the LORD was with David and how much his daughter Michal loved him, 29 Saul became even more afraid of him, and he remained David's enemy for the rest of his life.

30 Every time the commanders of the Philistines attacked, David was more successful against them than all the rest of Saul's officers. So David's name became very famous.

Saul's Anger Makes David a Fugitive (19:1–23:29)

Jonathan and Michal Defend David

19 Saul now urged his servants and his son Jonathan to assassinate David. But Jonathan, because of his strong affection for David, 2 told him what his father was planning. "Tomorrow morning," he warned him, "you must find a hiding place out in the fields. 3 I'll ask my father to go out there with me, and I'll talk to him about you. Then I'll tell you everything I can find out."

4 The next morning Jonathan spoke with his father about David, saying many good things about him. "The king must not sin against his servant David," Jonathan said. "He's never done anything to harm you. He has always helped you in any way he could. 5 Have you forgotten about the time he risked his life to kill the Philistine giant and how the LORD brought a great victory to all Israel as a result? You were certainly happy about it then. Why should you murder an innocent man like David? There is no reason for it at all!"

6 So Saul listened to Jonathan and vowed, "As surely as the LORD lives, David will not be killed."

7 Afterward Jonathan called David and told him what had happened. Then he brought David to Saul, and David served in the court as before.

8 War broke out again after that, and David led his troops against the Philistines. He attacked them with such fury that they all ran away.

9 But one day when Saul was sitting at home, with spear in hand, the tormenting spirit from the LORD suddenly came upon him again. As David played his harp, 10 Saul hurled his spear at David. But David dodged out of the way, and leaving the spear stuck in the wall, he fled and escaped into the night.

11 Then Saul sent troops to watch David's house. They were told to kill David when he came out the next morning. But Michal, David's wife, warned him, "If you don't escape tonight, you will be dead by morning." 12 So she helped him climb out through a

MICHAL (18:17-30)

1 Sam 14:49; 19:11-17; 2 Sam 3:13-16; 6:16-23

Michal was King Saul's younger daughter (14:49) and David's first wife (18:17-27). She played a significant role in the transition from Saul's reign to David's.

In the ancient Near East, marriages of leading families were often politically motivated. Saul baited David into a dangerous situation by promising him his older daughter Merab if he would fight the Philistines. As a powerful warrior, David was an emerging leader in Saul's kingdom. The king should have been happy to have such an ally, but he soon grew jealous of David's accomplishments and suspicious of his ambition. Saul hoped that David would die in the attempt, but the deal fell through. Later, Saul learned that his younger daughter, Michal, loved David (18:20), which gave the king another opportunity to bait David into fighting the Philistines. This time David agreed. When David returned victorious, Saul could not avoid giving David his daughter in marriage. This marriage alliance helped David establish his credentials with the northern tribes when he became king (2 Sam 3:13-16).

Michal loved David early in their relationship and even deceived her father to help David escape from a plot to kill him (19:11-17). After David left the court, Saul arranged another marriage for her (25:44), but David broke up that marriage to bolster his claim to the throne (2 Sam 3:13-16). Michal came to despise David, and she expressed her contempt when he danced joyfully before the Ark of the Covenant as it was being brought into Jerusalem (2 Sam 6:16-23). Because of her contempt for the king (1 Chr 15:29), Michal did not bear children.

18:29 ***even more afraid:*** Saul's fear was unfounded. Although he made himself ***David's enemy***, David consistently honored Saul as king (see chs 24; 26).

19:4 ***Jonathan*** addressed his father as ***the king*** out of reverence.

19:6 ***vowed:*** Violating a vow is a serious offense against God (see Num 30:2; Deut 23:21-23; cp. Eccl 5:4-5). But Saul soon disregarded his promise and again sought to kill David (19:9-24).

19:9 ***tormenting spirit:*** Or *evil spirit.* See note on 16:14; see also 18:10.

19:10 ***hurled his spear:*** See also 18:11; 20:33.

19:11 See Ps 59:TITLE.

window, and he fled and escaped. [13]Then she took an idol and put it in his bed, covered it with blankets, and put a cushion of goat's hair at its head.

[14]When the troops came to arrest David, she told them he was sick and couldn't get out of bed.

[15]But Saul sent the troops back to get David. He ordered, "Bring him to me in his bed so I can kill him!" [16]But when they came to carry David out, they discovered that it was only an idol in the bed with a cushion of goat's hair at its head.

[17]"Why have you betrayed me like this and let my enemy escape?" Saul demanded of Michal.

"I had to," Michal replied. "He threatened to kill me if I didn't help him."

[18]So David escaped and went to Ramah to see Samuel, and he told him all that Saul had done to him. Then Samuel took David with him to live at Naioth. [19]When the report reached Saul that David was at Naioth in Ramah, [20]he sent troops to capture him. But when they arrived and saw Samuel leading a group of prophets who were prophesying, the Spirit of God came upon Saul's men, and they also began to prophesy. [21]When Saul heard what had happened, he sent other troops, but they, too, prophesied! The same thing happened a third time. [22]Finally, Saul himself went to Ramah and arrived at the great well in Secu. "Where are Samuel and David?" he demanded.

"They are at Naioth in Ramah," someone told him.

[23]But on the way to Naioth in Ramah the Spirit of God came even upon Saul, and he, too, began to prophesy all the way to Naioth! [24]He tore off his clothes and lay naked on the ground all day and all night, prophesying in the presence of Samuel. The people who were watching exclaimed, "What? Is even Saul a prophet?"

David and Jonathan Part as Allies and Friends

20 David now fled from Naioth in Ramah and found Jonathan. "What have I done?" he exclaimed. "What is my crime? How have I offended your father that he is so determined to kill me?"

[2]"That's not true!" Jonathan protested. "You're not going to die. He always tells me everything he's going to do, even the little things. I know my father wouldn't hide something like this from me. It just isn't so!"

[3]Then David took an oath before Jonathan and said, "Your father knows perfectly well about our friendship, so he has said to himself, 'I won't tell Jonathan—why should I hurt him?' But I swear to you that I am only a step away from death! I swear it by the LORD and by your own soul!"

[4]"Tell me what I can do to help you," Jonathan exclaimed.

[5]David replied, "Tomorrow we celebrate the new moon festival. I've always eaten with the king on this occasion, but tomorrow I'll hide in the field and stay there until the evening of the third day. [6]If your father asks where I am, tell him I asked permission to go home to Bethlehem for an annual family sacrifice. [7]If he says, 'Fine!' you will know all is well. But if he is angry and loses his temper, you will know he is determined to kill me. [8]Show me this loyalty as my sworn friend—for we made a solemn pact before the LORD—or kill me yourself if I have sinned against your father. But please don't betray me to him!"

[9]"Never!" Jonathan exclaimed. "You know that if I had the slightest notion my

19:13 Judg 18:14, 17
19:18 1 Sam 7:17; 19:22-23
19:20 Num 11:24-25; 1 Sam 10:5-6, 10; Joel 2:28
19:23 1 Sam 10:13
19:24 1 Sam 10:10-12; 2 Sam 6:20; Mic 1:8
20:1 1 Sam 24:9
20:3 Deut 6:13; 2 Kgs 2:6-7
20:5 Num 10:10; 28:11-17; 1 Sam 19:2
20:6 1 Sam 16:2; 17:58
20:7 1 Sam 25:17
20:8 1 Sam 18:1-3; 2 Sam 1:26; 14:32

19:13 ***an idol*** (Hebrew *teraphim;* also in 19:16): *Teraphim* were household idols (see Gen 31:30; Judg 17:5; 2 Kgs 23:24). The presence of an idol in the home of David and Michal might show the pervasive influence of pagan idol worship among the Israelites; perhaps the idol belonged to Michal. Apparently David did not object to its presence. (Cp. Rachel's theft of her father's household idols in Gen 31:19.) • Siblings Jonathan (19:1-7) and Michal (19:11-18) saved David from their father and undermined their father's plans to eliminate him. Members of Saul's royal family played a significant role in David's rise, though David did not usurp Saul's throne.

19:18 ***Ramah:*** Samuel's hometown (1:1). • ***Naioth*** was a tiny village not far from the other Ramah in Benjamin.

19:20 ***Prophets*** often assembled in groups under a single leader (see 2 Kgs 2:15; 4:38; 6:1-7). • The ***Spirit of God came upon Saul's men*** to allow David to escape (20:1).

19:21 ***other troops . . . a third time:*** Each time Saul sent troops, David's would-be captors were captured by the Spirit. Prophesying diverted them from pursuing David.

19:24 When Saul ***tore off his clothes and lay naked***, he unwittingly acted out his true spiritual condition of having been stripped of the kingship (13:14; 15:10-11, 23; see "Prophetic Sign Acts" at Ezek 4:1-17, p. 1319). • ***Is even Saul a prophet?*** In 10:9-13, Saul was rising as God's chosen king; here, he is descending under the weight of God's rejection.

20:2-3 ***Jonathan*** was naive about his father's intentions. David's willingness to ***swear . . . by the LORD*** showed how convinced he was about Saul's intentions.

20:5 ***new moon festival:*** The ancient Hebrews followed a lunar calendar, and the new moon marked the start of a new month (see "Israel's Annual Calendar" at Exod 12:2, p. 145). Every month was begun with a special sacrifice (Num 28:11-15), which became a monthly festival (see "Israel's Festivals" at Lev 23:1-44, p. 235).

20:6-7 Israelite families might designate one of the new moon festivals as an opportunity for ***an annual family sacrifice*** (see, e.g., 1:3).

20:8 ***Loyalty*** (Hebrew *khesed*) denotes faithfulness between covenant partners. • ***a solemn pact:*** See 18:3; 20:16.

20:13
Ruth 1:17
1 Sam 3:17; 14:44; 18:11-12
1 Chr 28:20

20:15
2 Sam 9:1

20:23
Gen 31:49-50, 53

father was planning to kill you, I would tell
you at once."
10Then David asked, "How will I know
whether or not your father is angry?"
11"Come out to the field with me," Jonathan replied. And they went out there
together. 12Then Jonathan told David, "I
promise by the LORD, the God of Israel, that
by this time tomorrow, or the next day at
the latest, I will talk to my father and let you
know at once how he feels about you. If he
speaks favorably about you, I will let you
know. 13But if he is angry and wants you
killed, may the LORD strike me and even kill
me if I don't warn you so you can escape and
live. May the LORD be with you as he used to
be with my father. 14And may you treat me
with the faithful love of the LORD as long as
I live. But if I die, 15treat my family with this
faithful love, even when the LORD destroys
all your enemies from the face of the earth."
16So Jonathan made a solemn pact with
David, saying, "May the LORD destroy all
your enemies!" 17And Jonathan made David
reaffirm his vow of friendship again, for
Jonathan loved David as he loved himself.
18Then Jonathan said, "Tomorrow we
celebrate the new moon festival. You will
be missed when your place at the table is
empty. 19The day after tomorrow, toward
evening, go to the place where you hid before, and wait there by the stone pile. 20I will
come out and shoot three arrows to the side
of the stone pile as though I were shooting
at a target. 21Then I will send a boy to bring
the arrows back. If you hear me tell him,
'They're on this side,' then you will know, as
surely as the LORD lives, that all is well, and
there is no trouble. 22But if I tell him, 'Go farther—the arrows are still ahead of you,' then
it will mean that you must leave immediately,
for the LORD is sending you away. 23And
may the LORD make us keep our promises
to each other, for he has witnessed them."

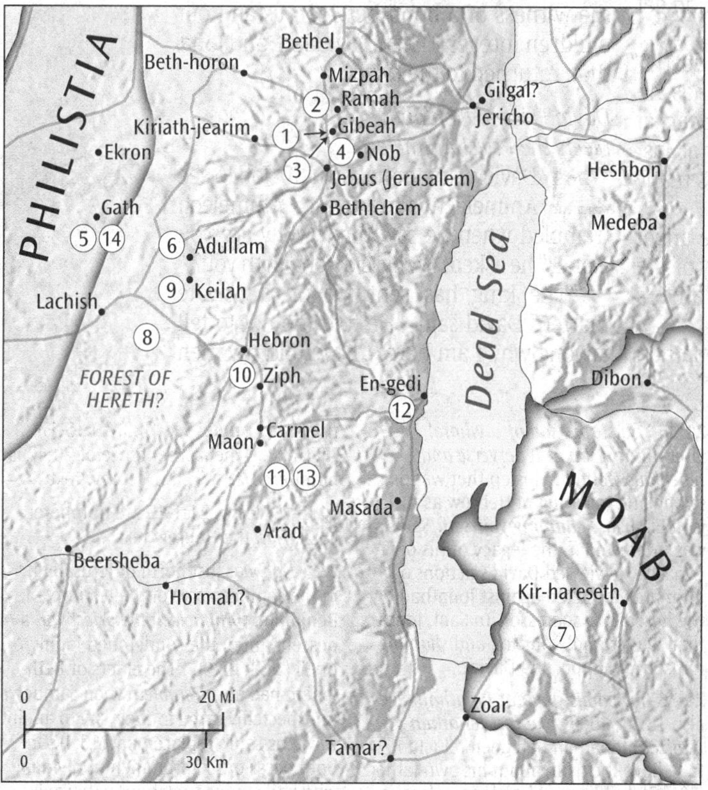

◀ **David's Escapes from Saul (19:11–27:12).** The map shows many of the places David went while avoiding being captured and killed by Saul: (1) GIBEAH (19:1-17); (2) RAMAH (19:18-24); (3) GIBEAH (20:1-42); (4) NOB (21:1-9); (5) GATH (21:10-15); (6) ADULLAM (22:1-5); (7) MOAB (22:3-4); (8) FOREST OF HERETH (22:5-6); (9) KEILAH (23:1-12); (10) the wilderness of ZIPH (23:13-18); (11) the wilderness of MAON (23:24-28); (12) EN-GEDI (23:29–24:22); (13) the wilderness of MAON (25:2–26:25); (14) GATH (27:1-12). In addition, MASADA (Hebrew *matsuda*) might have been the location of David's "stronghold" (Hebrew *metsuda*, 22:4; 24:22).

20:13 ***may the LORD strike me:*** Jonathan invoked a curse upon himself to reassure David that he would keep his promise. • ***as he used to be with my father:*** Jonathan recognized that David had received the blessing from God that his father had once had. The divine favor that had brought Saul into royal office (9:14–10:1) would bring David into royal office as Saul's replacement. Jonathan accepted this even though he was the natural successor to Saul.

20:14-16 ***faithful love:*** Hebrew *khesed* (see note on 20:8). Jonathan was reminding David to keep his commitment to him when he became king. It was reasonable for Jonathan to be concerned that David might kill any descendant of Saul who could make a rival claim to his throne. Saul later made a similar request of David (24:21).

20:15 ***treat my family:*** David later treated Jonathan's son, Mephibosheth, as one of his own sons (2 Sam 9:1-13).

20:16 ***with David:*** Literally *with the house of David.*

20:17 See 18:3; 23:16-18.

20:18-22 Jonathan's ruse would allow David to get the message even if there could be no face-to-face meeting; the boy's presence would allay suspicion and provide Jonathan an alibi for going to the field. As it happened, no one but the boy accompanied Jonathan to the field, so when the boy left, David was able to speak with Jonathan face to face (20:40-42).

20:19 ***the stone pile:*** Literally *the stone Ezel.* The meaning of the Hebrew is uncertain.

24 So David hid himself in the field, and when the new moon festival began, the king sat down to eat. 25 He sat at his usual place against the wall, with Jonathan sitting opposite him and Abner beside him. But David's place was empty. 26 Saul didn't say anything about it that day, for he said to himself, "Something must have made David ceremonially unclean." 27 But when David's place was empty again the next day, Saul asked Jonathan, "Why hasn't the son of Jesse been here for the meal either yesterday or today?"

28 Jonathan replied, "David earnestly asked me if he could go to Bethlehem. 29 He said, 'Please let me go, for we are having a family sacrifice. My brother demanded that I be there. So please let me get away to see my brothers.' That's why he isn't here at the king's table."

30 Saul boiled with rage at Jonathan. "You stupid son of a whore!" he swore at him. "Do you think I don't know that you want him to be king in your place, shaming yourself and your mother? 31 As long as that son of Jesse is alive, you'll never be king. Now go and get him so I can kill him!"

32 "But why should he be put to death?" Jonathan asked his father. "What has he done?" 33 Then Saul hurled his spear at Jonathan, intending to kill him. So at last Jonathan realized that his father was really determined to kill David.

34 Jonathan left the table in fierce anger and refused to eat on that second day of the festival, for he was crushed by his father's shameful behavior toward David.

35 The next morning, as agreed, Jonathan went out into the field and took a young boy with him to gather his arrows. 36 "Start running," he told the boy, "so you can find the arrows as I shoot them." So the boy ran, and Jonathan shot an arrow beyond him. 37 When the boy had almost reached the arrow, Jonathan shouted, "The arrow is still ahead of you. 38 Hurry, hurry, don't wait." So the boy quickly gathered up the arrows and ran back to his master. 39 He, of course, suspected nothing; only Jonathan and David understood the signal. 40 Then Jonathan gave his bow and arrows to the boy and told him to take them back to town.

41 As soon as the boy was gone, David came out from where he had been hiding near the stone pile. Then David bowed three times to Jonathan with his face to the ground. Both of them were in tears as they embraced each other and said good-bye, especially David.

42 At last Jonathan said to David, "Go in peace, for we have sworn loyalty to each other in the LORD's name. The LORD is the witness of a bond between us and our children forever." Then David left, and Jonathan returned to the town.

David Flees to Nob and Meets the Priest Ahimelech

21 David went to the town of Nob to see Ahimelech the priest. Ahimelech trembled when he saw him. "Why are you alone?" he asked. "Why is no one with you?"

2 "The king has sent me on a private matter," David said. "He told me not to tell anyone why I am here. I have told my men

20:26 Lev 7:20-21; 1 Sam 16:5
20:28 1 Sam 20:6
20:32 Matt 27:23
20:33 1 Sam 18:11; 19:10-11
20:36 1 Sam 20:20-21
20:42 1 Sam 20:14-15
21:1 1 Sam 16:4; 22:19; Neh 11:32

20:24 ***new moon festival:*** See note on 20:5.

20:25 ***Abner*** was Saul's cousin and served as commander of Saul's army (14:50; 17:55). His importance is indicated by his position *beside* the king at this festival. • ***with Jonathan sitting opposite him:*** As in Greek version; Hebrew reads *with Jonathan standing.*

20:26-27 A number of circumstances could render a person *ceremonially unclean* and thus unfit for attending a sacred festival (see Lev 7:20-21). Often, an unclean person was required to be excluded from such functions only until the evening of the same day (Lev 15:1-33). This explains why Saul became suspicious after David did not arrive *the next day.* • Saul referred to David as *the son of Jesse* (also in 20:31; 22:7), a description that functioned as David's surname.

20:29 ***get away:*** This verb also describes David's earlier escape from Saul (19:10, 11, 12, 17, 18).

20:30 ***You stupid son of a whore!*** Literally *You son of a perverse and rebellious woman.* This epithet was as strong and insulting in Hebrew as it is in English. • ***shaming yourself:*** Saul was interested in the legacy of his own dynasty. He viewed David's actions as ultimately directed against Jonathan, the hereditary successor. To Saul, Jonathan was stupidly hurting and *shaming* himself by supporting David.

20:33 ***hurled his spear at Jonathan:*** See also 18:11; 19:10. • ***at last Jonathan realized:*** Jonathan had been reluctant to believe the truth about his own father (20:2-3), but he could no longer deny it.

20:41 ***near the stone pile:*** As in Greek version; Hebrew reads *near the south edge.* • ***David bowed:*** Jonathan had the higher social rank, so David's homage was fitting. • ***Both of them were in tears:*** For the first time, the record of the emotion between these two men shows mutuality (see 18:1, 3-4; 20:17).

20:42 ***sworn loyalty to each other in the LORD's name:*** See 18:3; 20:15-17; 23:16-18. • The last sentence of 20:42 is numbered 21:1 in the Hebrew text.

21:1-15 Verses 21:1-15 are numbered 21:2-16 in the Hebrew text.

21:1 ***Nob*** was just north of Jerusalem, in the southern part of the territory of Benjamin. • ***Ahimelech the priest*** was a descendant of the condemned family of Eli (14:3; 22:9). • The elders of Bethlehem had also *trembled* when Samuel unexpectedly came to their city to anoint David as Saul's replacement (16:4). On both occasions, a prominent individual who had strained relations with Saul showed up unannounced. Both Ahimelech and the Bethlehem elders were concerned about being suspected of supporting an enemy of the king, which could result in death. In this case, what was feared came about (see 22:9-19).

21:2 ***The king has sent me:*** David lied to conceal his outlaw status and to dispel Ahimelech's worries.

21:4
Exod 19:14-15
Lev 24:5-9
Matt 12:4

21:6
Matt 12:3-4
Mark 2:25-28
Luke 6:3-4

21:7
1 Sam 22:9, 22
Ps 52:TITLE

21:9
1 Sam 17:2, 50-51

21:10
1 Sam 27:2

21:11
1 Sam 18:7; 29:5

21:12
yare' (3372)
›2 Kgs 17:35

21:13
Ps 34:TITLE

22:1-2
2 Sam 23:13

22:5
2 Sam 24:11
1 Chr 21:9; 29:29
2 Chr 29:25-26

where to meet me later. 3Now, what is there to eat? Give me five loaves of bread or anything else you have."

4"We don't have any regular bread," the priest replied. "But there is the holy bread, which you can have if your young men have not slept with any women recently."

5"Don't worry," David replied. "I never allow my men to be with women when they are on a campaign. And since they stay clean even on ordinary trips, how much more on this one!"

6Since there was no other food available, the priest gave him the holy bread—the Bread of the Presence that was placed before the LORD in the Tabernacle. It had just been replaced that day with fresh bread.

7Now Doeg the Edomite, Saul's chief herdsman, was there that day, having been detained before the LORD.

8David asked Ahimelech, "Do you have a spear or sword? The king's business was so urgent that I didn't even have time to grab a weapon!"

9"I only have the sword of Goliath the Philistine, whom you killed in the valley of Elah," the priest replied. "It is wrapped in a cloth behind the ephod. Take that if you want it, for there is nothing else here."

"There is nothing like it!" David replied. "Give it to me!"

David Flees to Gath and Meets King Achish

10So David escaped from Saul and went to King Achish of Gath. 11But the officers of Achish were unhappy about his being there. "Isn't this David, the king of the land?" they asked. "Isn't he the one the people honor with dances, singing,

'Saul has killed his thousands,
and David his ten thousands'?"

12David heard these comments and was very [g]afraid of what King Achish of Gath might do to him. 13So he pretended to be insane, scratching on doors and drooling down his beard.

14Finally, King Achish said to his men, "Must you bring me a madman? 15We already have enough of them around here! Why should I let someone like this be my guest?"

David Flees to a Cave in Adullam

22 So David left Gath and escaped to the cave of Adullam. Soon his brothers and all his other relatives joined him there. 2Then others began coming—men who were in trouble or in debt or who were just discontented—until David was the captain of about 400 men.

David Flees to Mizpeh in Moab

3Later David went to Mizpeh in Moab, where he asked the king, "Please allow my father and mother to live here with you until I know what God is going to do for me." 4So David's parents stayed in Moab with the king during the entire time David was living in his stronghold.

5One day the prophet Gad told David,

21:4 Only priests were permitted to partake of ***holy bread*** (see Exod 25:22-30; Lev 24:5-9), and only within the sacred precincts. • ***slept with any women:*** The consecrated bread was to be eaten only by the ritually pure, so the priest verified that David's men were free from ritual impurity caused by sexual activity (see Lev 15:16-18). Typically, such bread would not be available for consumption by laity. The priest made an exception in this case probably because he sensed the men's physical needs and he believed they were on a royal mission.

21:6 ***gave him the holy bread:*** Jesus referred to this incident to teach that meeting people's physical needs takes precedence over rigid adherence to sacred institutions (see Matt 12:1-8; Mark 2:23-28; Luke 6:1-5). • ***The Bread of the Presence*** consisted of twelve loaves (possibly one representing each tribe) that were laid out on a table in the Holy Place. They were ***replaced*** every Sabbath (see Exod 25:30; Lev 24:5-9).

21:7 ***having been detained before the LORD:*** The meaning of the Hebrew is uncertain. Ahimelech sought guidance from God on others' behalf (22:15), so it is possible that ***Doeg*** was awaiting a response to an inquiry.

21:9 ***The sword of Goliath,*** which David used to decapitate the giant (17:51), had been taken as war spoils, as had Goliath's head (17:54). • The ***ephod*** mentioned here might not have been the priestly garment of the same name; some passages give the impression that an ephod could also be a statue (Judg 8:27; 18:17).

21:10-15 ***Gath,*** a major Philistine city and the hometown of Goliath, was a clever but dangerous place for David to seek refuge from Saul.

21:11 ***the king of the land:*** David's reputation as a mighty warrior even greater than King Saul (see 18:7) had grown to the point where foreigners began referring to him as Israel's king.

21:12-13 The lengthy title of Ps 34 refers to this incident but names the Philistine king Abimelech rather than ***Achish.*** "Abimelech" might have been the common title for Philistine kings (in Hebrew it means "my father the king"). The name Abimelech also appears in Gen 20:2; 26:1.

22:1-23 Saul's character becomes evident here. Unable to exact revenge on David himself, Saul slaughtered those he believed to be guilty of giving aid and comfort to David.

22:1 ***Adullam*** was some sixteen miles southwest of Jerusalem, near Philistine territory. • Had David's ***brothers and all his other relatives*** stayed in Bethlehem, they would have been vulnerable to Saul's revenge.

22:2 ***in trouble . . . in debt . . . discontented:*** By attracting such down-and-out people to himself, David foreshadowed Jesus, who would attract to himself the hurting, the burdened, and the outcast (Matt 11:25-30).

22:3-4 ***Mizpeh in Moab*** lay east of the Dead Sea and the Jordan River—not an easy trip from Adullam, especially if the 400 men (22:2) accompanied David. • ***David's parents stayed in Moab:*** Jesse's grandmother was Ruth, a Moabite (Ruth 4:13-22).

22:5 The ***prophet Gad*** was David's special adviser (2 Sam 24:11). God was no longer communicating with Saul but was guiding David.

"Leave the stronghold and return to the land of Judah." So David went to the forest of Hereth.

Saul Massacres the Priests at Nob

6 The news of his arrival in Judah soon reached Saul. At the time, the king was sitting beneath the tamarisk tree on the hill at Gibeah, holding his spear and surrounded by his officers.

7 "Listen here, you men of Benjamin!" Saul shouted to his officers when he heard the news. "Has that son of Jesse promised every one of you fields and vineyards? Has he promised to make you all generals and captains in his army? 8 Is that why you have conspired against me? For not one of you told me when my own son made a solemn pact with the son of Jesse. You're not even sorry for me. Think of it! My own son—encouraging him to kill me, as he is trying to do this very day!"

9 Then Doeg the Edomite, who was standing there with Saul's men, spoke up. "When I was at Nob," he said, "I saw the son of Jesse talking to the priest, Ahimelech son of Ahitub. 10 Ahimelech consulted the LORD for him. Then he gave him food and the sword of Goliath the Philistine."

11 King Saul immediately sent for Ahimelech and all his family, who served as priests at Nob. 12 When they arrived, Saul shouted at him, "Listen to me, you son of Ahitub!"

"What is it, my king?" Ahimelech asked.

13 "Why have you and the son of Jesse conspired against me?" Saul demanded. "Why did you give him food and a sword? Why have you consulted God for him? Why have you encouraged him to kill me, as he is trying to do this very day?"

14 "But sir," Ahimelech replied, "is anyone among all your servants as faithful as David, your son-in-law? Why, he is the captain of your bodyguard and a highly honored member of your household! 15 This was certainly not the first time I had consulted God for him! May the king not accuse me and my family in this matter, for I knew nothing at all of any plot against you."

16 "You will surely die, Ahimelech, along with your entire family!" the king shouted. 17 And he ordered his bodyguards, "Kill these priests of the LORD, for they are allies and conspirators with David! They knew he was running away from me, but they didn't tell me!" But Saul's men refused to kill the LORD's priests.

18 Then the king said to Doeg, "You do it." So Doeg the Edomite turned on them and killed them that day, eighty-five priests in all, still wearing their priestly garments. 19 Then he went to Nob, the town of the priests, and killed the priests' families—men and women, children and babies—and all the cattle, donkeys, sheep, and goats.

20 Only Abiathar, one of the sons of Ahimelech, escaped and fled to David. 21 When he told David that Saul had killed the priests of the LORD, 22 David exclaimed, "I knew it! When I saw Doeg the Edomite there that day, I knew he was sure to tell Saul. Now I have caused the death of all your father's family. 23 Stay here with me, and don't be afraid. I will protect you with my own life, for the same person wants to kill us both."

David Fights the Philistines

23 One day news came to David that the Philistines were at Keilah stealing grain from the threshing floors. 2 David asked the LORD, "Should I go and attack them?"

"Yes, go and save Keilah," the LORD told him.

3 But David's men said, "We're afraid even here in Judah. We certainly don't want to go to Keilah to fight the whole Philistine army!"

22:6 Judg 4:5; 1 Sam 14:2
22:7 1 Sam 8:12, 14; 1 Chr 12:16-18
22:8 1 Sam 23:21
22:9 1 Sam 21:1, 7
22:10 1 Sam 21:6
22:14 1 Sam 19:4-5; 20:32
22:15 2 Sam 5:19, 23
22:17 1 Sam 14:45; 2 Kgs 10:25
22:18 1 Sam 2:18, 30-33
22:20 1 Sam 2:30-33; 23:6; 30:7; 1 Kgs 2:26-27
22:22 1 Sam 21:7
23:1 Josh 15:44; Neh 3:17
23:2 1 Sam 23:4, 12; 30:8; 2 Sam 5:19, 23

22:7-8 ***men of Benjamin:*** Saul was suspicious of his own tribesmen, believing that David had bought their loyalty. Worse, Saul did not even trust his ***own son***, convinced that he had joined the supposed conspiracy.

22:7 ***generals and captains in his army?*** Literally *commanders of thousands and commanders of hundreds?*

22:13 David had deceived Ahimelech into thinking he was on a mission for Saul (21:1-9), so Saul's accusations of conspiracy were baseless.

22:14 ***your son-in-law:*** David had married Saul's daughter (18:17-29).

22:18 ***Doeg the Edomite . . . killed them:*** As a non-Israelite, Doeg had no concern for the sanctity of God-anointed priests. He knew he was executing innocent men. This evil foreigner partially fulfilled the prophecy about the condemned priestly line of Eli (2:27-34; see 1 Kgs 2:27). • ***still wearing their priestly garments:*** This incident illustrates how mad Saul had become. Not even those holding a sacred office were safe.

22:19 Saul had been unwilling to carry out God's orders to destroy completely the Amalekites and their possessions (15:3, 9). Yet now, in his rage, he did not hesitate to decimate ***the priests' families*** and their possessions (see Prov 14:29; 16:14; 27:4).

22:20 ***Abiathar*** became an adviser to David, providing guidance from the Lord through the ephod (23:2-12; 2 Sam 15:24-36). Later, he conspired with Adonijah against David and Solomon (1 Kgs 1–2).

23:1-29 Thanks to informants (23:7, 13), Saul was able to stay on David's trail. David also had informants, allowing him to keep one step ahead of Saul (23:1, 9, 15, 25). David's chief advantage was access to divine guidance and resources (23:2, 4, 12), which Saul lacked.

23:1 ***Keilah*** was near Adullam (22:1) at the western edge of Judah, not far from the Philistine border (see Josh 15:44; Neh 3:17-18).

23:4
Josh 8:7
Judg 7:7

23:6
1 Sam 22:20

23:9
1 Sam 22:20; 30:7

23:13
1 Sam 22:2; 25:13
2 Sam 15:20

23:14
Josh 15:55
2 Chr 11:8

23:17
1 Sam 20:31; 24:20

23:18
1 Sam 18:3
2 Sam 9:1

23:19
1 Sam 26:1

23:21
1 Sam 22:8

23:24
Josh 15:55

[4]So David asked the LORD again, and again the LORD replied, "Go down to Keilah, for I will help you conquer the Philistines."

[5]So David and his men went to Keilah. They slaughtered the Philistines and took all their livestock and rescued the people of Keilah. [6]Now when Abiathar son of Ahimelech fled to David at Keilah, he brought the ephod with him.

David Narrowly Escapes Saul

[7]Saul soon learned that David was at Keilah. "Good!" he exclaimed. "We've got him now! God has handed him over to me, for he has trapped himself in a walled town!" [8]So Saul mobilized his entire army to march to Keilah and besiege David and his men.

[9]But David learned of Saul's plan and told Abiathar the priest to bring the ephod and ask the LORD what he should do. [10]Then David prayed, "O LORD, God of Israel, I have heard that Saul is planning to come and destroy Keilah because I am here. [11]Will the leaders of Keilah betray me to him? And will Saul actually come as I have heard? O LORD, God of Israel, please tell me."

And the LORD said, "He will come."

[12]Again David asked, "Will the leaders of Keilah betray me and my men to Saul?"

And the LORD replied, "Yes, they will betray you."

[13]So David and his men—about 600 of them now—left Keilah and began roaming the countryside. Word soon reached Saul that David had escaped, so he didn't go to Keilah after all. [14]David now stayed in the strongholds of the wilderness and in the hill country of Ziph. Saul hunted him day after day, but God didn't let Saul find him.

[15]One day near Horesh, David received the news that Saul was on the way to Ziph to search for him and kill him. [16]Jonathan went to find David and encouraged him to stay strong in his faith in God. [17]"Don't be afraid," Jonathan reassured him. "My father will never find you! You are going to be the king of Israel, and I will be next to you, as my father, Saul, is well aware." [18]So the two of them renewed their solemn pact before

ABIATHAR (22:20-23)

1 Sam 23:6, 9; 30:7
2 Sam 15:27-37; 17:15
1 Kgs 1:1–2:35
1 Chr 15:11

Abiathar was high priest during David's reign and into Solomon's reign. He first encountered David before David became king. When David fled from Saul, he stopped at the city of Nob. Pretending that he was acting on Saul's orders, David got food and supplies from the priests there. Saul discovered what had happened and was so angry that he killed all but one of the priests; only Abiathar escaped.

Abiathar was among the first people from Saul's administration to support David. His support was formidable; he represented the priesthood of Eli's line and brought with him the holy ephod containing the Urim and Thummim (Exod 28:29-30), which allowed him to seek God's will for David during crises (23:1-12; 30:7-8). After David became king, Abiathar served as priest along with Zadok, who was not a descendant of Eli (1 Chr 6:8; 18:16; 24:3; see "Zadok" at 2 Sam 15:23-37, p. 545). Both served David well; during Absalom's rebellion, for example, they reported to David what was happening in the capital (2 Sam 15:27-37; 17:15).

In David's old age, Abiathar wrongly supported Adonijah's attempt to become king in his father's place; Zadok remained loyal to David and supported Solomon (1 Kgs 1:5-8). As a result, once Solomon was on the throne, he removed Abiathar's priestly authority and banished him to his estate in Anathoth (1 Kgs 2:26-27), a village about four miles northeast of Jerusalem. Zadok became the high priest, and that role passed to Zadok's descendants rather than to Abiathar's. This removal fulfilled the "prophecy the LORD had given at Shiloh concerning the descendants of Eli" (1 Kgs 2:27; see 1 Sam 2:27-36).

23:4 ***David asked the LORD*** either directly in prayer or by using the ephod (see 23:6, 9; 2 Sam 2:1; 5:23-24). God's answers were a sign of his blessing and protection (cp. 28:6).

23:6 ***the ephod:*** Saul had slain eighty-five priests who were wearing their ephods (22:18; see note on 2:18), but the priest who escaped had the high priest's ephod, which contained the Urim and Thummim.

23:7 ***God has handed him over to me:*** To the contrary, see 23:14.

23:11 Some manuscripts lack the first sentence of 23:11.

23:14 The ***strongholds of the wilderness*** were not man-made structures but natural rock formations that provided refuge. • ***Ziph*** was approximately ten miles southeast of Keilah (23:1).

23:16 ***Jonathan . . . encouraged*** David because he knew that God had chosen David to be king.

23:17 ***You are going to be the king. . . . I will be next to you*** (literally *second to you*): Jonathan recognized God's selection of David and renounced any personal ambition to the throne. Jonathan never occupied an official position in David's court but was killed in battle along with his father (31:2).

23:18 ***their solemn pact:*** See 18:3-4; 20:12-17. • ***Jonathan returned home:*** This was probably the last time David and Jonathan saw each other.

the LORD. Then Jonathan returned home, while David stayed at Horesh.

[19]But now the men of Ziph went to Saul in Gibeah and betrayed David to him. "We know where David is hiding," they said. "He is in the strongholds of Horesh on the hill of Hakilah, which is in the southern part of Jeshimon. [20]Come down whenever you're ready, O king, and we will catch him and hand him over to you!"

[21]"The LORD bless you," Saul said. "At last someone is concerned about me! [22]Go and check again to be sure of where he is staying and who has seen him there, for I know that he is very crafty. [23]Discover his hiding places, and come back when you are sure. Then I'll go with you. And if he is in the area at all, I'll track him down, even if I have to search every hiding place in Judah!" [24]So the men of Ziph returned home ahead of Saul.

Meanwhile, David and his men had moved into the wilderness of Maon in the Arabah Valley south of Jeshimon. [25]When David heard that Saul and his men were searching for him, he went even farther into the wilderness to the great rock, and he remained there in the wilderness of Maon. But Saul kept after him in the wilderness.

[26]Saul and David were now on opposite sides of a mountain. Just as Saul and his men began to close in on David and his men, [27]an urgent message reached Saul that the Philistines were raiding Israel again. [28]So Saul quit chasing David and returned to fight the Philistines. Ever since that time, the place where David was camped has been called the Rock of Escape. [29]David then went to live in the strongholds of En-gedi.

David Shows Restraint (24:1–26:25)

David Spares Saul's Life at En-gedi

24 After Saul returned from fighting the Philistines, he was told that David had gone into the wilderness of En-gedi. [2]So Saul chose 3,000 elite troops from all Israel and went to search for David and his men near the rocks of the wild goats.

[3]At the place where the road passes some sheepfolds, Saul went into a cave to relieve himself. But as it happened, David and his men were hiding farther back in that very cave!

[4]"Now's your opportunity!" David's men whispered to him. "Today the LORD is telling you, 'I will certainly put your enemy into your power, to do with as you wish.' " So David crept forward and cut off a piece of the hem of Saul's robe.

[5]But then David's conscience began bothering him because he had cut Saul's robe. [6]"The LORD knows I shouldn't have done that to my lord the king," he said to his men. "The LORD forbid that I should do this to my lord the king and attack the LORD's anointed one, for the LORD himself has chosen him." [7]So David restrained his men and did not let them kill Saul.

After Saul had left the cave and gone on his way, [8]David came out and shouted after him, "My lord the king!" And when Saul looked around, David bowed low before him.

[9]Then he shouted to Saul, "Why do you listen to the people who say I am trying to harm you? [10]This very day you can see with your own eyes it isn't true. For the LORD placed you at my mercy back there in the cave. Some of my men told me to kill you, but I spared you. For I said, 'I will never harm the king—he is the LORD's anointed one.' [11]Look, my father, at what I have in my

23:26 Ps 17:9
23:29 Josh 15:62; 2 Chr 20:2
24:2 1 Sam 26:2
24:3 Judg 3:24
24:4 1 Sam 26:8, 11
24:5 2 Sam 24:10
24:6 1 Sam 26:11
24:7 1 Kgs 1:31
24:9 1 Sam 26:19
24:11 1 Sam 23:14, 23; 26:20

23:19 *Hakilah* was a hill in the wilderness region of Ziph (23:14). • The term *Jeshimon* is sometimes translated as "wasteland" rather than as a place name. It refers here to a specific wasteland located north of the Dead Sea, on both banks of the Jordan River (see Num 21:20).

23:20 Both Keilah (23:12) and Ziph (23:14; Ps 54:TITLE) were located in Judah, but neither one provided sanctuary for David, a native of Judah. David's ascension to power was not the result of his own tribe's loyalty but because of the will of God.

23:24 *Maon* was about three miles directly south of the wilderness of Ziph (23:14), approximately ten miles south of Hebron. • The *Arabah Valley* is a deep rift stretching from above the Sea of Galilee down both sides of the Jordan River to the Dead Sea.

23:28 *the Rock of Escape* (Hebrew *Sela-hammahlekoth.*): It is not uncommon for a place name to commemorate thankfulness to God (e.g., Gen 22:14; 28:19; 32:30). The exact rock formation that received this name is unknown.

23:29 Verse 23:29 is numbered 24:1 in the Hebrew text. • *David* traveled eastward from the area of Ziph (23:14) and took refuge in *the strongholds of En-gedi.* These rocky highlands were located on the western shore of the Dead Sea. There was an oasis in this region, making it an ideal place to find water and food.

24:1-22 Verses 24:1-22 are numbered 24:2-23 in the Hebrew text.

24:2 *3,000 elite troops:* David's force was outnumbered five to one (23:13).

24:4 David's men believed, as Saul did, that if the circumstances seem right, *the LORD is telling you* through those circumstances what to do (cp. 23:7). • Perhaps David was able to *cut off a piece of the hem of Saul's robe* without being apprehended because Saul had taken off the robe and laid it aside, or perhaps he fell asleep in the cave.

24:5 *David's conscience began bothering him* because he had dishonored God's anointed king.

24:6 *The LORD's anointed one* was not to be violated (26:9, 11, 16, 23; 2 Sam 1:14, 16; 19:21). David would not harm Saul even though God had anointed him to be the next king (16:13).

24:12 Gen 31:53; Judg 11:27
24:13 Matt 7:16-20; [h]*mashal* (4912) ‣1 Kgs 4:32
24:14 1 Sam 26:20
24:15 Ps 35:1
24:16 1 Sam 26:17
24:17 1 Sam 26:21; Matt 5:44
24:18 1 Sam 26:23
24:19 Ruth 2:12
24:20 1 Sam 13:14; 23:17
24:21 Gen 21:23; 1 Sam 20:14-17; 2 Sam 21:7
24:22 1 Sam 23:29
25:1 Deut 34:8; 1 Sam 7:17; 15:35; 28:3
25:2 Josh 15:55
25:3 Josh 15:13; 1 Sam 30:14
25:6 1 Chr 12:18
25:7 1 Sam 25:15
25:8 Neh 8:10
25:10 Judg 9:28
25:13 1 Sam 23:13

hand. It is a piece of the hem of your robe! I cut it off, but I didn't kill you. This proves that I am not trying to harm you and that I have not sinned against you, even though you have been hunting for me to kill me.

12"May the LORD judge between us. Perhaps the LORD will punish you for what you are trying to do to me, but I will never harm you. 13As that old [h]proverb says, 'From evil people come evil deeds.' So you can be sure I will never harm you. 14Who is the king of Israel trying to catch anyway? Should he spend his time chasing one who is as worthless as a dead dog or a single flea? 15May the LORD therefore judge which of us is right and punish the guilty one. He is my advocate, and he will rescue me from your power!"

16When David had finished speaking, Saul called back, "Is that really you, my son David?" Then he began to cry. 17And he said to David, "You are a better man than I am, for you have repaid me good for evil. 18Yes, you have been amazingly kind to me today, for when the LORD put me in a place where you could have killed me, you didn't do it. 19Who else would let his enemy get away when he had him in his power? May the LORD reward you well for the kindness you have shown me today. 20And now I realize that you are surely going to be king, and that the kingdom of Israel will flourish under your rule. 21Now swear to me by the LORD that when that happens you will not kill my family and destroy my line of descendants!"

22So David promised this to Saul with an oath. Then Saul went home, but David and his men went back to their stronghold.

Abigail Prevents David from Committing Murder

25 Now Samuel died, and all Israel gathered for his funeral. They buried him at his house in Ramah.

Then David moved down to the wilderness of Maon. 2There was a wealthy man from Maon who owned property near the town of Carmel. He had 3,000 sheep and 1,000 goats, and it was sheep-shearing time. 3This man's name was Nabal, and his wife, Abigail, was a sensible and beautiful woman. But Nabal, a descendant of Caleb, was crude and mean in all his dealings.

4When David heard that Nabal was shearing his sheep, 5he sent ten of his young men to Carmel with this message for Nabal: 6"Peace and prosperity to you, your family, and everything you own! 7I am told that it is sheep-shearing time. While your shepherds stayed among us near Carmel, we never harmed them, and nothing was ever stolen from them. 8Ask your own men, and they will tell you this is true. So would you be kind to us, since we have come at a time of celebration? Please share any provisions you might have on hand with us and with your friend David." 9David's young men gave this message to Nabal in David's name, and they waited for a reply.

10"Who is this fellow David?" Nabal sneered to the young men. "Who does this son of Jesse think he is? There are lots of servants these days who run away from their masters. 11Should I take my bread and my water and my meat that I've slaughtered for my shearers and give it to a band of outlaws who come from who knows where?"

12So David's young men returned and told him what Nabal had said. 13"Get your swords!" was David's reply as he strapped on his own. Then 400 men started off with David, and 200 remained behind to guard their equipment.

14Meanwhile, one of Nabal's servants went to Abigail and told her, "David sent messengers from the wilderness to greet our master, but he screamed insults at them.

24:11 *my father:* Saul was, in fact, David's father-in-law (18:27). David was demonstrating his respect for the king and recalling a day when their relationship had been much friendlier.

24:12 *May the LORD judge:* There was no human authority to adjudicate between Saul and David (cp. Gen 16:5; 31:53; Exod 5:21; Judg 11:27). • ***Perhaps the LORD will punish you:*** David rested in God's will rather than trying to force God's hand.

24:13 The ***proverb*** vindicates David and indicts Saul. David refrained from ***evil deeds,*** such as killing Saul. Saul, however, repeatedly tried to kill David.

24:20 ***I realize that you are surely going to be king:*** This was Saul's first open admission of the truth (cp. 23:17).

24:21-22 ***Now swear to me . . . you will not kill my family:*** Having descendants was a way that Saul's name would endure among the living. David had already sworn such an ***oath*** with Jonathan (20:14-17).

25:1-44 This episode about Nabal falls between two accounts in which Saul pursued David and David spared Saul's life. Nabal was similar to Saul.

25:1 *Maon:* as in Greek version (see also 25:2); Hebrew reads *Paran.* This town in southern Judah (see note on 23:24) was likely Nabal's home. The wilderness of Paran, located in the northern half of the Sinai peninsula, was too far south. The wilderness of Paran served as a place of refuge (Gen 21:21; 1 Kgs 11:18).

25:2 *Carmel* was a village near Maon, not to be confused with the famous mountain from the Elijah narrative in 1 Kgs 18. It was in this village that Saul had erected his monument to celebrate victory over the Amalekites (15:12).

25:3 *Nabal:* See 25:25 for insight into the irony of his name. • Unlike her husband, ***Abigail was a sensible*** and wise person, as the narrative shows.

25:8 Sheep-shearing time for herdsmen was like harvest time for farmers, ***a time of celebration*** and thankfulness for blessings.

25:10 *son of Jesse:* Like Saul (20:27, 31; 22:7), Nabal used this designation disrespectfully.

15These men have been very good to us, and
we never suffered any harm from them.
Nothing was stolen from us the whole time
they were with us. 16In fact, day and night
they were like a wall of protection to us and
the sheep. 17You need to know this and figure out what to do, for there is going to be
trouble for our master and his whole family.
He's so [i]ill-tempered that no one can even
talk to him!"
18Abigail wasted no time. She quickly
gathered 200 loaves of bread, two wineskins full of wine, five sheep that had been
slaughtered, nearly a bushel of roasted
grain, 100 clusters of raisins, and 200 fig
cakes. She packed them on donkeys 19and
said to her servants, "Go on ahead. I will
follow you shortly." But she didn't tell her
husband Nabal what she was doing.
20As she was riding her donkey into a
mountain ravine, she saw David and his
men coming toward her. 21David had just
been saying, "A lot of good it did to help
this fellow. We protected his flocks in the
wilderness, and nothing he owned was lost
or stolen. But he has repaid me evil for good.
22May God strike me and kill me if even one
man of his household is still alive tomorrow
morning!"
23When Abigail saw David, she quickly
got off her donkey and bowed low before
him. 24She fell at his feet and said, "I accept
all blame in this matter, my lord. Please listen to what I have to say. 25I know Nabal is a
[i]wicked and ill-tempered man; please don't
pay any attention to him. He is a fool, just as
his name suggests. But I never even saw the
young men you sent.
26"Now, my lord, as surely as the LORD
lives and you yourself live, since the LORD
has kept you from murdering and taking
vengeance into your own hands, let all your
enemies and those who try to harm you be
as cursed as Nabal is. 27And here is a present that I, your servant, have brought to you
and your young men. 28Please forgive me if
I have offended you in any way. The LORD
will surely reward you with a lasting dynasty,
for you are fighting the LORD's battles. And
you have not done wrong throughout your
entire life.
29"Even when you are chased by those
who seek to kill you, your life is safe in the
care of the LORD your God, secure in his treasure pouch! But the lives of your enemies
will disappear like stones shot from a sling!
30When the LORD has done all he promised
and has made you leader of Israel, 31don't
let this be a blemish on your record. Then
your conscience won't have to bear the staggering burden of needless bloodshed and
vengeance. And when the LORD has done
these great things for you, please remember
me, your servant!"
32David replied to Abigail, "Praise the
LORD, the God of Israel, who has sent you to
meet me today! 33Thank God for your good
sense! Bless you for keeping me from murder and from carrying out vengeance with
my own hands. 34For I swear by the LORD,
the God of Israel, who has kept me from
hurting you, that if you had not hurried out
to meet me, not one of Nabal's men would
still be alive tomorrow morning." 35Then
David accepted her present and told her,
"Return home in peace. I have heard what
you said. We will not kill your husband."
36When Abigail arrived home, she found
that Nabal was throwing a big party and was
celebrating like a king. He was very drunk,
so she didn't tell him anything about her
meeting with David until dawn the next day.
37In the morning when Nabal was sober, his
wife told him what had happened. As a result he had a stroke, and he lay paralyzed on
his bed like a stone. 38About ten days later,
the LORD struck him, and he died.
39When David heard that Nabal was dead,
he said, "Praise the LORD, who has avenged
the insult I received from Nabal and has
kept me from doing it myself. Nabal has
received the punishment for his sin." Then

25:15 1 Sam 25:7
25:16 Exod 14:22
25:17 [i]*beliya'al* (1100) ▸1 Sam 25:25
25:18 2 Sam 16:1; 1 Chr 12:40
25:19 Gen 32:16, 20
25:21 Ps 109:5
25:22 1 Sam 3:17; 1 Kgs 14:10
25:25 [i]*beliya'al* (1100) ▸2 Sam 22:5
25:26 2 Sam 18:32
25:27 Gen 33:11; 1 Sam 30:26
25:28 1 Sam 18:17; 2 Sam 7:11, 16
25:29 1 Sam 20:1; Jer 10:18
25:30 1 Sam 13:14
25:32 Exod 18:10
25:33 1 Sam 25:26
25:35 Gen 19:21

25:18 ***nearly a bushel:*** Hebrew 5 *seahs* [30 liters].

25:21 ***he has repaid me evil for good:*** Cp. 24:17.

25:22 ***May God strike me and kill me:*** As in Greek version; Hebrew reads *May God strike and kill the enemies of David.* Like Saul, David was capable of extreme speech against enemies.

25:25 The name *Nabal* means "fool."

25:26 Abigail began and ended (25:31) her plea by declaring that God had *kept you from murdering and taking vengeance:* David could have killed Nabal (and Saul), but he didn't.

25:28 ***a lasting dynasty:*** See 2 Sam 7. • ***fighting the LORD's battles:*** David was known and loved for his victories over Israel's enemies (18:7, 13, 16). • ***have not done wrong:*** This comment does not indicate that David was sinless, but rather that he was innocent in his quest for the throne (as 25:29-31 make clear).

25:29 The phrase *like stones shot from a sling* is a fitting metaphor for David, considering his defeat of Goliath with a sling (17:32-51).

25:36 ***like a king:*** Nabal was like Saul (see note on 25:1-44).

25:37 ***Nabal*** was so stunned by the revelation that ***he had a stroke*** or a heart attack (literally *his heart failed him*).

25:39 Nabal's death was God's ***punishment for his sin.*** David could not be accused of vengeful murder. • David lost no time in asking Abigail ***to become his wife.*** She had already shown herself to be a woman of good sense, and she was also beautiful (25:3).

25:42 Gen 24:61-67
25:43 1 Sam 27:2-3; 30:5
25:44 1 Sam 18:27; 2 Sam 3:14-15
26:1 1 Sam 23:19
26:2 1 Sam 13:2; 24:2
26:3 1 Sam 23:19
26:5 1 Sam 14:50-51
26:6 1 Chr 2:16
26:9 1 Sam 24:6; 2 Sam 1:14, 16
26:10 Deut 31:14; 1 Sam 25:38; 31:6
26:12 Gen 2:21; 15:12; Isa 29:10
26:17 1 Sam 24:16

David sent messengers to Abigail to ask her
to become his wife.
40When the messengers arrived at Carmel, they told Abigail, "David has sent us to
take you back to marry him."
41She bowed low to the ground and responded, "I, your servant, would be happy
to marry David. I would even be willing
to become a slave, washing the feet of his
servants!" 42Quickly getting ready, she took
along five of her servant girls as attendants,
mounted her donkey, and went with David's
messengers. And so she became his wife.
43David also married Ahinoam from Jezreel, making both of them his wives. 44Saul,
meanwhile, had given his daughter Michal,
David's wife, to a man from Gallim named
Palti son of Laish.

David Spares Saul's Life Again

26 Now some men from Ziph came to
Saul at Gibeah to tell him, "David
is hiding on the hill of Hakilah, which overlooks Jeshimon."
2So Saul took 3,000 of Israel's elite
troops and went to hunt him down in the
wilderness of Ziph. 3Saul camped along the
road beside the hill of Hakilah, near Jeshimon, where David was hiding. When David
learned that Saul had come after him into
the wilderness, 4he sent out spies to verify
the report of Saul's arrival.
5David slipped over to Saul's camp one
night to look around. Saul and Abner son
of Ner, the commander of his army, were
sleeping inside a ring formed by the slum-
bering warriors. 6"Who will volunteer to
go in there with me?" David asked Ahimelech the Hittite and Abishai son of Zeruiah,
Joab's brother.
"I'll go with you," Abishai replied. 7So David and Abishai went right into Saul's camp
and found him asleep, with his spear stuck
in the ground beside his head. Abner and
the soldiers were lying asleep around him.
8"God has surely handed your enemy over
to you this time!" Abishai whispered to David. "Let me pin him to the ground with one
thrust of the spear; I won't need to strike
twice!"
9"No!" David said. "Don't kill him. For
who can remain innocent after attacking
the LORD's anointed one? 10Surely the LORD
will strike Saul down someday, or he will die
of old age or in battle. 11The LORD forbid
that I should kill the one he has anointed!
But take his spear and that jug of water beside his head, and then let's get out of here!"
12So David took the spear and jug of water that were near Saul's head. Then he and
Abishai got away without anyone seeing
them or even waking up, because the LORD
had put Saul's men into a deep sleep.
13David climbed the hill opposite the
camp until he was at a safe distance. 14Then
he shouted down to the soldiers and to Abner son of Ner, "Wake up, Abner!"
"Who is it?" Abner demanded.
15"Well, Abner, you're a great man, aren't
you?" David taunted. "Where in all Israel is
there anyone as mighty? So why haven't you
guarded your master the king when someone came to kill him? 16This isn't good at all!
I swear by the LORD that you and your men
deserve to die, because you failed to protect your master, the LORD's anointed! Look
around! Where are the king's spear and the
jug of water that were beside his head?"
17Saul recognized David's voice and
called out, "Is that you, my son David?"

25:43 ***Ahinoam*** was also the name of Saul's wife (14:50). If she was the same woman, then David took Saul's widow after his death (ch 31), which would make another parallel between Nabal and Saul. However, see 27:3; 30:5. • This ***Jezreel*** was a village in the vicinity of Maon, Ziph, and Carmel in Judah (Josh 15:55-56) and not the better-known northern city of Jezreel.

25:44 Saul's motive for giving away ***Michal*** to another man was probably political, an attempt to remove any claim David might have on the throne by dissolving David's marriage with a member of the royal family.

26:1-25 This was the last time Saul and David were together. The Ziphites told Saul for the second time where David was hiding (see 23:19-20), and David spared Saul's life a second time as he did in the cave at En-gedi (see ch 24).

26:1 ***Men from Ziph*** had previously volunteered to capture David and hand him over to Saul (23:19-20). • ***Hakilah . . . Jeshimon*** is the same geographical location they had mentioned to Saul before (23:19). David had not moved far, probably because the hilly terrain was dotted with numerous caves, providing many good hiding places.

26:3 ***Saul had come after*** David again, despite his earlier remorse (24:17-21). Saul had become incapable of acting rationally or speaking truthfully.

26:5 ***Abner son of Ner:*** See note on 20:25.

26:6 This is the only reference to ***Ahimelech the Hittite.*** • ***Zeruiah*** was David's sister (1 Chr 2:16), so ***Abishai*** was David's nephew. The sons of Zeruiah (Abishai, Joab, and Asahel) were three of David's most faithful followers (e.g., 2 Sam 2:18), but they sometimes caused David difficulty (see 2 Sam 3:39; 16:10; 19:22).

26:8 ***God has surely handed your enemy over to you:*** Cp. 24:4.

26:9 ***the LORD's anointed:*** See note on 24:6.

26:10 David was confident that God would judge between him and Saul just as he had done between him and Nabal (see 25:38). Saul did ***die . . . in battle*** against the Philistines (31:6).

26:14 ***Abner:*** See note on 20:25.

26:16 ***deserve to die:*** Death was the punishment for dereliction of duty.

26:17 ***Is that you, my son David?*** Cp. 24:16.

And David replied, "Yes, my lord the king.
18Why are you chasing me? What have I
done? What is my crime? 19But now let my
lord the king listen to his servant. If the
LORD has stirred you up against me, then let
him accept my offering. But if this is simply a
human scheme, then may those involved be
cursed by the LORD. For they have driven me
from my home, so I can no longer live among
the LORD's people, and they have said, 'Go,
worship pagan gods.' 20Must I die on foreign
soil, far from the presence of the LORD? Why
has the king of Israel come out to search for
a single flea? Why does he hunt me down
like a partridge on the mountains?"

21Then Saul confessed, "I have sinned.
Come back home, my son, and I will no
longer try to harm you, for you valued my
life today. I have been a fool and very, very
wrong."

22"Here is your spear, O king," David replied. "Let one of your young men come over
and get it. 23The LORD gives his own reward
for doing good and for being loyal, and I refused to kill you even when the LORD placed
you in my power, for you are the LORD's
anointed one. 24Now may the LORD value
my life, even as I have valued yours today.
May he rescue me from all my troubles."

25And Saul said to David, "Blessings on
you, my son David. You will do many heroic
deeds, and you will surely succeed." Then
David went away, and Saul returned home.

Saul's Life and Reign End in Disaster (27:1–31:13)

David Serves with the Philistines

27 But David kept thinking to himself, "Someday Saul is going to get
me. The best thing I can do is escape to the
Philistines. Then Saul will stop hunting for
me in Israelite territory, and I will finally
be safe."

2So David took his 600 men and went
over and joined Achish son of Maoch, the
king of Gath. 3David and his men and their
families settled there with Achish at Gath.
David brought his two wives along with
him—Ahinoam from Jezreel and Abigail,
Nabal's widow from Carmel. 4Word soon
reached Saul that David had fled to Gath, so
he stopped hunting for him.

5One day David said to Achish, "If it is all
right with you, we would rather live in one
of the country towns instead of here in the
royal city."

6So Achish gave him the town of Ziklag
(which still belongs to the kings of Judah to
this day), 7and they lived there among the
Philistines for a year and four months.

8David and his men spent their time
raiding the Geshurites, the Girzites, and
the Amalekites—people who had lived
near Shur, toward the land of Egypt, since
ancient times. 9David did not leave one person alive in the villages he attacked. He took
the sheep, goats, cattle, donkeys, camels,
and clothing before returning home to see
King Achish.

10"Where did you make your raid today?"
Achish would ask.

And David would reply, "Against the south
of Judah, the Jerahmeelites, and the Kenites."

11No one was left alive to come to Gath and
tell where he had really been. This happened
again and again while he was living among
the Philistines. 12Achish believed David and
thought to himself, "By now the people of Israel must hate him bitterly. Now he will have
to stay here and serve me forever!"

26:19 1 Sam 24:9; 2 Sam 16:11
26:20 1 Sam 24:14
26:21 1 Sam 15:24, 30; 24:17
26:23 1 Sam 24:19
26:24 Ps 54:7
27:2 1 Sam 21:10; 1 Kgs 2:39
27:3 1 Sam 25:43; 2 Sam 2:2-3
27:6 Josh 15:31; 19:5; Neh 11:28
27:7 1 Sam 29:3
27:8 Exod 17:8; Josh 13:2-7, 13; 1 Sam 15:7-8
27:9 1 Sam 15:3
27:10 Judg 1:16; 4:11; 1 Sam 30:27-31; 1 Chr 2:9, 25

26:19 *If the LORD has stirred you up against me:* David was perplexed by Saul's behavior and concerned with the possibility of unintentional sin on his part. • *a human scheme:* Possibly a reference to Doeg (22:9-10). • *worship pagan gods:* The sentiment parallels Ps 137:4. Anyone who was exiled from the holy land was unable to worship the Lord by participating in sacrifice at the central sanctuary.

26:20 *a single flea:* Cp. 24:14.

26:21 *I have sinned:* Saul had seen the error of his ways once before (24:16-19). David had no good reason to trust him this time (see 27:1). • *I have been a fool:* This Hebrew term (*sakal*, "play the fool," see also 13:13) is different from the word meaning "fool" (*nabal*) used in ch 25. However, the two words have parallel meanings. Saul and Nabal are parallel figures.

26:23 David did not harm Saul (24:6; 26:9) because Saul was *the LORD's anointed one* (see note on 24:6).

26:24 *may the LORD value my life, even as I have valued yours:* David could not count on Saul to reciprocate. Thus, his fate was in God's hands.

26:25 *Saul returned home,* and this may have been David's last personal encounter with him.

27:1-12 David fled to the Philistines to get away from Saul for good. Rather than killing Saul, David chose the dangerous life of a fugitive.

27:2 This was David's second sojourn with *Achish*, the Philistine king (see 21:10-15). On both occasions, David lied to him (see 27:10).

27:6 *Ziklag* was about twenty-two miles southwest of Gath. • *still belongs to the kings of Judah:* This note was written between Solomon's death (931 BC) and the start of the Babylonian exile (586 BC).

27:8 *Geshurites . . . Girzites . . . Amalekites:* These groups, who lived on the edges of the southern desert, had been troublesome to both Philistines and Israelites. (On the Amalekites, see 14:48; 15; on the Geshurites, see Josh 13:2, 13; 2 Sam 3:3.) • *Shur* was somewhere east of Egypt (15:7; Gen 16:7; 20:1; 25:18).

27:9 *David did not leave one person alive:* At least some of these people were among those whom God had commanded Israel to destroy (see 15:3; 28:18; Deut 25:17-19; Josh 13:13).

27:10 David misled Achish by claiming his attacks were *against* his own people *of Judah* and two other related groups. The text does not commend David for lying to the foreign king, but neither does

28:1-2
1 Sam 29:1-2

28:3
Lev 19:31
Deut 18:10
1 Sam 15:23; 25:1
[k]*yidde'oni* (3049)
‣1 Sam 28:9

28:4
1 Sam 31:1, 3
2 Sam 1:6

28:6
Exod 28:30

28:7
Ps 83:10
Acts 16:16

28:8
Isa 8:19

28:9
1 Sam 28:3
[a]*yidde'oni* (3049)
‣2 Kgs 21:6

28:14
1 Sam 15:27

28:15
1 Sam 16:14

28:17
1 Sam 15:28

28:19
1 Sam 31:2, 6

28 About that time the Philistines mustered their armies for another war with Israel. King Achish told David, "You and your men will be expected to join me in battle."

2 "Very well!" David agreed. "Now you will see for yourself what we can do."

Then Achish told David, "I will make you my personal bodyguard for life."

A Medium Summons Samuel's Ghost

3 Meanwhile, Samuel had died, and all Israel had mourned for him. He was buried in Ramah, his hometown. And Saul had banned from the land of Israel all mediums and those who [k]consult the spirits of the dead.

4 The Philistines set up their camp at Shunem, and Saul gathered all the army of Israel and camped at Gilboa. 5 When Saul saw the vast Philistine army, he became frantic with fear. 6 He asked the LORD what he should do, but the LORD refused to answer him, either by dreams or by sacred lots or by the prophets. 7 Saul then said to his advisers, "Find a woman who is a medium, so I can go and ask her what to do."

His advisers replied, "There is a medium at Endor."

8 So Saul disguised himself by wearing ordinary clothing instead of his royal robes. Then he went to the woman's home at night, accompanied by two of his men.

"I have to talk to a man who has died," he said. "Will you call up his spirit for me?"

9 "Are you trying to get me killed?" the woman demanded. "You know that Saul has outlawed all the mediums and all who [a]consult the spirits of the dead. Why are you setting a trap for me?"

10 But Saul took an oath in the name of the LORD and promised, "As surely as the LORD lives, nothing bad will happen to you for doing this."

11 Finally, the woman said, "Well, whose spirit do you want me to call up?"

"Call up Samuel," Saul replied.

12 When the woman saw Samuel, she screamed, "You've deceived me! You are Saul!"

13 "Don't be afraid!" the king told her. "What do you see?"

"I see a god coming up out of the earth," she said.

14 "What does he look like?" Saul asked.

"He is an old man wrapped in a robe," she replied. Saul realized it was Samuel, and he fell to the ground before him.

15 "Why have you disturbed me by calling me back?" Samuel asked Saul.

"Because I am in deep trouble," Saul replied. "The Philistines are at war with me, and God has left me and won't reply by prophets or dreams. So I have called for you to tell me what to do."

16 But Samuel replied, "Why ask me, since the LORD has left you and has become your enemy? 17 The LORD has done just as he said he would. He has torn the kingdom from you and given it to your rival, David. 18 The LORD has done this to you today because you refused to carry out his fierce anger against the Amalekites. 19 What's more, the LORD will hand you and the army of Israel over to the Philistines tomorrow, and you and your sons will be here with me. The LORD will bring down the entire army of Israel in defeat."

it condemn him. • The ***Jerahmeelites*** were a Semitic tribe in southern Judah (1 Chr 2:9, 25-27, 33, 42). • ***Kenites:*** Moses' father-in-law was a Kenite (Judg 1:16; 4:11; see also note on 1 Sam 15:6).

28:1 ***another war:*** Hostilities between Israel and the Philistines were now routine. In exchange for providing refuge, Achish expected David's military involvement and cooperation.

28:3-14 Saul consulted the dead, a practice forbidden by God's law (see Lev 20:27; Deut 18:9-11).

28:3 ***banned from the land:*** Saul had either expelled or killed most mediums, or he had merely outlawed the practice of necromancy (see note on 28:9).

28:4 ***Shunem,*** a border town in the territory of Issachar (Josh 19:18), overlooked the valley of Jezreel. • Mount ***Gilboa*** is at the east end of the valley of Jezreel. The mountain took its name from a nearby village.

28:6 ***refused to answer:*** Earlier, Saul had consulted the Lord ***by sacred lots*** (literally *by Urim*) with mixed results (14:36-42). God's refusal to speak was a sign of his judgment (14:37; Lam 2:9; Ezek 7:26; Amos 8:11-12; Mic 3:6-7).

28:7 Excluded from God's counsel, Saul resorted to illegitimate methods for finding God's will. Saul had earlier prohibited the occult practice that he now engaged in himself (28:3). • ***Endor*** was on the boundary between Israel and Philistia; the area near Israel's border was probably a safer location for a banned practice.

28:9 ***outlawed:*** Literally *cut off,* suggesting that Saul might have had most of the mediums executed.

28:12 It is not clear why seeing Samuel caused ***the woman*** to recognize ***Saul.***

28:13 Saul asked the medium to describe what she saw that caused her to scream. She described a divine being, ***a god*** (or *gods;* Hebrew *'elohim*) ***coming up.*** Perhaps she observed a human figure with a godlike or angelic appearance, or her use of the term *god* might reflect a pagan belief that a person becomes *a god*—a spirit possessing supernatural abilities—after death.

28:15 ***God has left me:*** The same Hebrew term is used in 16:14 and Judg 16:20. • ***won't reply by prophets or dreams:*** Cp. 28:6.

28:16 Saul's *enemy* was not David but the Lord himself.

28:17 ***torn the kingdom from you:*** See 15:28.

28:18 ***you refused:*** Samuel's message to Saul had not changed (cp. 15:19).

28:19 ***here with me:*** In *Sheol,* the abode of the dead (cp. 2:6, "the grave"; see also Num 16:30-33; Job 17:1-16; Ps 49:11; Rev 1:18).

[20]Saul fell full length on the ground,
paralyzed with fright because of Samuel's
words. He was also faint with hunger, for he
had eaten nothing all day and all night.
[21]When the woman saw how distraught he
was, she said, "Sir, I obeyed your command at
the risk of my life. [22]Now do what I say, and
let me give you a little something to eat so you
can regain your strength for the trip back."
[23]But Saul refused to eat anything. Then
his advisers joined the woman in urging
him to eat, so he finally yielded and got up
from the ground and sat on the couch.
[24]The woman had been fattening a calf,
so she hurried out and killed it. She took
some flour, kneaded it into dough and
baked unleavened bread. [25]She brought the
meal to Saul and his advisers, and they ate it.
Then they went out into the night.

David Is Dismissed from the Philistine Army

29 The entire Philistine army now mobilized at Aphek, and the Israelites
camped at the spring in Jezreel. [2]As the Philistine rulers were leading out their troops
in groups of hundreds and thousands, David and his men marched at the rear with
King Achish. [3]But the Philistine commanders demanded, "What are these Hebrews
doing here?"
And Achish told them, "This is David, the
servant of King Saul of Israel. He's been
with me for years, and I've never found a
single fault in him from the day he arrived
until today."
[4]But the Philistine commanders were
angry. "Send him back to the town you've
given him!" they demanded. "He can't go
into the battle with us. What if he turns
against us in battle and becomes our adversary? Is there any better way for him to
reconcile himself with his master than by
handing our heads over to him? [5]Isn't this
the same David about whom the women of
Israel sing in their dances,

'Saul has killed his thousands,
and David his ten thousands'?"

[6]So Achish finally summoned David and
said to him, "I swear by the LORD that you
have been a trustworthy ally. I think you
should go with me into battle, for I've never
found a single flaw in you from the day you
arrived until today. But the other Philistine
rulers won't hear of it. [7]Please don't upset
them, but go back quietly."
[8]"What have I done to deserve this treatment?" David demanded. "What have you
ever found in your servant, that I can't go
and fight the enemies of my lord the king?"

28:21 Judg 12:3
28:23 2 Kgs 5:13
28:24 Gen 18:6-7
29:1 Josh 12:18; 1 Sam 4:1; 2 Kgs 9:30
29:2 1 Sam 28:2
29:3 1 Sam 27:1-7; 1 Chr 12:19-20
29:4 1 Sam 14:21
29:5 1 Sam 18:7; 21:11
29:6 1 Sam 27:12; 29:3

Calling up the Dead (28:1-25)

Lev 19:31; 20:6-8, 27
Deut 18:9-12
2 Kgs 21:6; 23:24
1 Chr 10:13-14
Job 14:10-12
Isa 3:1-3; 8:19-22

The OT forbids occult practices, such as spiritism, divination, and necromancy, in which someone attempts to contact the dead, usually to seek guidance about the future (see Deut 18:9-12). Practicing necromancy and consulting a necromancer were capital offenses (Lev 20:6, 27; cp. 1 Sam 28:9). God's people were instead to rely on God for divine guidance.

God buried Moses in an unmarked grave (Deut 34:6) because of Moses' stature and his role in mediating Israel's covenant with God. God did not want the Israelites to make Moses' grave a shrine, present offerings to his spirit, worship him, or attempt to consult his spirit.

The OT makes it plain that the dead cannot be contacted (cp. 2 Sam 12:23; Job 14:10-12; Ps 88:10; 115:17). Samuel is the only known exception; God apparently commanded him to return and speak (28:12-19). However, Saul's sin in consulting a medium was so severe that the Chronicler singles out this failure in commenting on Saul's downfall (see 1 Chr 10:13-14). There is never any justification for seeking advice from the dead when we have the living word of God to guide us (2 Tim 3:15-17; Heb 4:12-13).

28:24 ***fattening a calf . . . dough . . . bread:*** This meal was a major undertaking, a model of hospitality (cp. Gen 18:5-7). This meal the medium shared with Saul recalls the fine meal Samuel had shared with Saul (9:22-24) before he anointed Saul as king. That meal with God's prophet marked the beginning of Saul's kingship. This meal with a condemned spiritist came shortly before his death.

29:1-11 David was spared by divine providence from actually fighting against his own people.

29:1 *Aphek* was the site of an earlier confrontation between Israel and the Philistines (4:1). • *Jezreel* was about forty miles north of Aphek.

29:3 ***servant of King Saul:*** To Achish, David was a valued defector. The other Philistine rulers suspected that David was a plant, planning to mount an attack from within the Philistine defenses. • ***never found a single fault:*** This was the first of three times that Achish defended David (see also 29:6, 9). Yet David had been deceiving Achish the whole time (see 27:1-12).

29:4 ***handing our heads over:*** The commanders' fears were justified (cp. 17:51; 18:27).

29:5 This jingle referred to slain Philistines (18:7). It is remarkable that David could find refuge in their midst.

29:6 ***by the LORD:*** Achish used the unique name of Israel's God to prove his own sincerity. • ***a trustworthy ally:*** This assertion was not completely true, though Achish did not realize it (27:8-12).

29:9 2 Sam 14:17, 20; 19:27
30:1 1 Sam 15:7; 27:6, 8
30:5 1 Sam 25:39-43; 2 Sam 2:2
30:6 Exod 17:4; 1 Sam 23:16; Ps 18:2
30:7 1 Sam 23:9
30:8 1 Sam 23:2, 4
30:9 1 Sam 27:2
30:12 Judg 15:19
30:14 1 Sam 30:1; 2 Sam 1:1; 15:17-18; 1 Chr 18:17
30:15 Deut 23:15

9But Achish insisted, "As far as I'm concerned, you're as perfect as an angel of God. But the Philistine commanders are afraid to have you with them in the battle. 10Now get up early in the morning, and leave with your men as soon as it gets light."

11So David and his men headed back into the land of the Philistines, while the Philistine army went on to Jezreel.

David Conducts a Holy War against the Amalekites

30 Three days later, when David and his men arrived home at their town of Ziklag, they found that the Amalekites had made a raid into the Negev and Ziklag; they had crushed Ziklag and burned it to the ground. 2They had carried off the women and children and everyone else but without killing anyone.

3When David and his men saw the ruins and realized what had happened to their families, 4they wept until they could weep no more. 5David's two wives, Ahinoam from Jezreel and Abigail, the widow of Nabal from Carmel, were among those captured. 6David was now in great danger because all his men were very bitter about losing their sons and daughters, and they began to talk of stoning him. But David found strength in the LORD his God.

7Then he said to Abiathar the priest, "Bring me the ephod!" So Abiathar brought it. 8Then David asked the LORD, "Should I chase after this band of raiders? Will I catch them?"

And the LORD told him, "Yes, go after them. You will surely recover everything that was taken from you!"

9So David and his 600 men set out, and they came to the brook Besor. 10But 200 of the men were too exhausted to cross the brook, so David continued the pursuit with 400 men.

11Along the way they found an Egyptian man in a field and brought him to David. They gave him some bread to eat and water to drink. 12They also gave him part of a fig cake and two clusters of raisins, for he hadn't had anything to eat or drink for three days and nights. Before long his strength returned.

13"To whom do you belong, and where do you come from?" David asked him.

"I am an Egyptian—the slave of an Amalekite," he replied. "My master abandoned me three days ago because I was sick. 14We were on our way back from raiding the Kerethites in the Negev, the territory of Judah, and the land of Caleb, and we had just burned Ziklag."

15"Will you lead me to this band of raiders?" David asked.

The young man replied, "If you take an oath in God's name that you will not kill me or give me back to my master, then I will guide you to them."

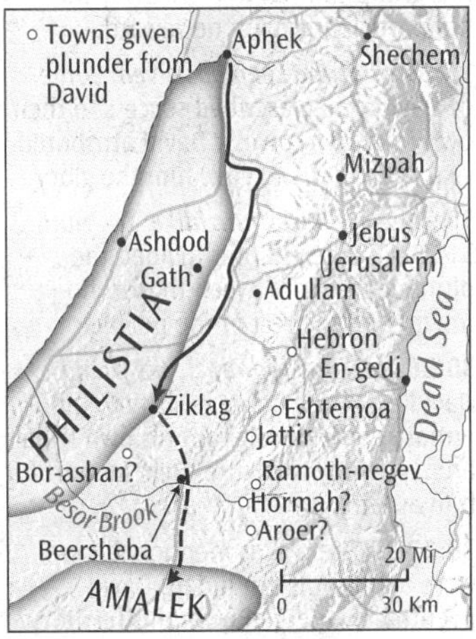

◂ **David's Destruction of the Amalekites (29:1–30:31).** When the Philistine army mobilized at APHEK to fight against Saul, David was sent back to ZIKLAG, his home in PHILISTIA. When he arrived, he found that the Amalekites had attacked and destroyed Ziklag, probably in retribution for David's earlier raids (27:8-9), and had carried everything and everyone away as plunder. David and his men chased the Amalekites into their territory and recovered everything. From Ziklag, David sent gifts from the plunder to many of the towns of Judah (shown as white circles; see note on 30:26; towns whose location is unknown are not shown).

30:1 ***Ziklag:*** See note on 27:6. • Perhaps the ***Amalekites*** were retaliating for David's raids against them (27:8).

30:2 There were no fighting men left in Ziklag to protect ***the women and children.*** The Amalekites had a reputation for preying on the weak and vulnerable (see Deut 25:17-18). • ***without killing anyone:*** The Amalekites were not being compassionate; women and children were more useful alive than dead.

30:5 ***Ahinoam:*** See note on 25:43. • ***Abigail:*** See 25:3-42.

30:6 ***in great danger:*** Saul had used the same expression about himself: When "in deep trouble" (28:15), Saul turned to necromancy, with disastrous results. David, by contrast, ***found strength*** and success ***in the LORD his God.***

30:7 ***the ephod:*** See notes on 2:18; 23:6.

30:8 Unlike Saul (28:6), David inquired of the Lord successfully (see 23:9-12; 2 Sam 2:1; 5:19, 23).

30:9 ***Besor*** was a large ***brook*** in Philistine territory that emptied into the Mediterranean southwest of Gaza.

30:10 ***too exhausted:*** David's men had traveled for three days (30:1) and were now in hot pursuit of the Amalekites without having rested. David did not upbraid them or drive them on mercilessly. See 30:23-25.

30:11-12 David had once received ***bread*** when he was famished (21:3-7). He and his men helped this ***Egyptian man*** before they even knew his identity or his ability to help their cause.

30:13 ***because I was sick:*** Only healthy and vigorous slaves were valuable to the Amalekites; the rest were expendable.

30:14 The ***land of Caleb*** was in the wilderness of Judah, south of Hebron (see Josh 14:6-15).

16So he led David to them, and they found the Amalekites spread out across the fields, eating and drinking and dancing with joy because of the vast amount of plunder they had taken from the Philistines and the land of Judah. 17David and his men rushed in among them and slaughtered them throughout that night and the entire next day until evening. None of the Amalekites escaped except 400 young men who fled on camels. 18David got back everything the Amalekites had taken, and he rescued his two wives. 19Nothing was missing: small or great, son or daughter, nor anything else that had been taken. David brought everything back. 20He also recovered all the flocks and herds, and his men drove them ahead of the other livestock. "This plunder belongs to David!" they said.

21Then David returned to the brook Besor and met up with the 200 men who had been left behind because they were too exhausted to go with him. They went out to meet David and his men, and David greeted them joyfully. 22But some evil troublemakers among David's men said, "They didn't go with us, so they can't have any of the plunder we recovered. Give them their wives and children, and tell them to be gone."

23But David said, "No, my brothers! Don't be selfish with what the LORD has given us. He has kept us safe and helped us defeat the band of raiders that attacked us. 24Who will listen when you talk like this? We share and share alike—those who go to battle and those who guard the equipment." 25From then on David made this a decree and regulation for Israel, and it is still followed today.

26When he arrived at Ziklag, David sent part of the plunder to the elders of Judah, who were his friends. "Here is a present for you, taken from the LORD's enemies," he said.

27The gifts were sent to the people of the following towns David had visited: Bethel, Ramoth-negev, Jattir, 28Aroer, Siphmoth, Eshtemoa, 29Racal, the towns of the Jerahmeelites, the towns of the Kenites, 30Hormah, Bor-ashan, Athach, 31Hebron, and all the other places David and his men had visited.

The Death of Saul
1 Sam 31:1-13 // 1 Chr 10:1-14

31 Now the Philistines attacked Israel, and the men of Israel fled before them. Many were slaughtered on the slopes

30:17 1 Sam 15:3
30:21 1 Sam 30:10
30:24 Num 31:27; Josh 22:7-8
30:26 Gen 33:11; 1 Sam 25:27
30:27 Josh 15:48
30:28 Josh 13:16
30:29 1 Sam 27:10
31:1-13 //2 Sam 1:4-12; //1 Chr 10:1-12
31:1 1 Sam 28:4

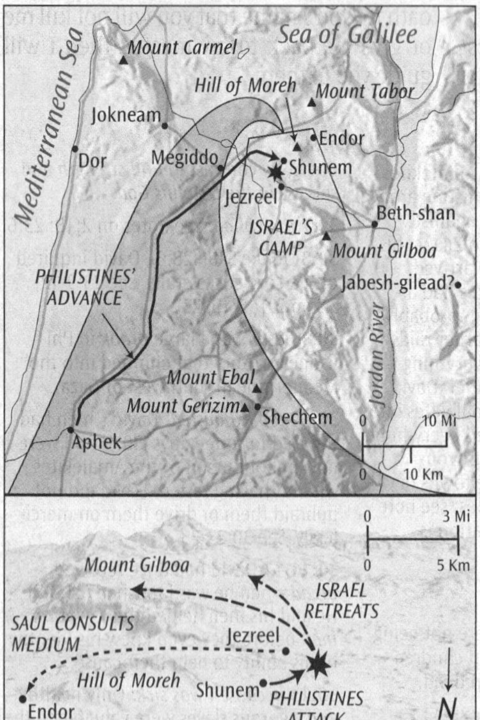

◂ **Saul's Death at Mount Gilboa (31:1-13).** The Philistine army marched from APHEK to JEZREEL (29:1, 11), where they attacked Saul's army. The bottom frame shows a southward elevation of the battle area, while the top frame shows the region. Before the battle, Saul sought counsel from Samuel through a medium at ENDOR (28:1-25). In the battle, Saul and his sons were killed on the slopes of MOUNT GILBOA as the Israelites fled from the Philistines (31:1-6).

30:17 The total number of Amalekite raiders must have been quite large if *400 young men* escaped.

30:21-31 David generously divided the spoils among those who participated in the battle and those who were too exhausted to take part.

30:21 ***greeted them joyfully:*** David did not reprimand them for not participating in the battle.

30:22 ***tell them to be gone:*** This heartless group wanted to drive away the nonparticipants with no reward.

30:23 ***what the LORD has given:*** Some of David's men ascribed success to their own military prowess; David attributed victory to God and gave him the glory.

30:24 ***share and share alike:*** Cp. Num 31:25-47, where Moses divided the plunder of war between those who fought and the rest of the people.

30:26 ***elders of Judah . . . his friends:*** David extended his generosity to influential people throughout his own tribal area, possibly to secure their support for him as king.

30:27-30 The places mentioned here were all in southern Judah. David eventually emerged from this territory as king (see 2 Sam 2:1-4).

30:29 ***Racal:*** Greek version reads *Carmel.*

30:31 From ***Hebron***, David reigned as king over Judah for 7½ years (2 Sam 2:1-7; 5:5).

31:1-13 While David was in the south successfully fighting the Amalekites (ch 30), Saul was in the north unsuccessfully fighting the Philistines.

31:3
2 Sam 1:6, 10

31:4
Judg 9:54

31:9
Judg 16:23-24
2 Sam 1:20

31:10
Josh 17:11
Judg 2:12-14
1 Sam 7:3

31:11-12
1 Sam 11:1-13
2 Sam 2:4-7; 21:12-14

of Mount Gilboa. 2The Philistines closed in
on Saul and his sons, and they killed three
of his sons—Jonathan, Abinadab, and Malkishua. 3The fighting grew very fierce around
Saul, and the Philistine archers caught up
with him and wounded him severely.

4Saul groaned to his armor bearer, "Take
your sword and kill me before these pagan
Philistines come to run me through and
taunt and torture me."

But his armor bearer was afraid and
would not do it. So Saul took his own sword
and fell on it. 5When his armor bearer realized that Saul was dead, he fell on his own
sword and died beside the king. 6So Saul,
his three sons, his armor bearer, and his
troops all died together that same day.

7When the Israelites on the other side
of the Jezreel Valley and beyond the Jordan saw that the Israelite army had fled
and that Saul and his sons were dead, they
abandoned their towns and fled. So the Philistines moved in and occupied their towns.

8The next day, when the Philistines went
out to strip the dead, they found the bodies
of Saul and his three sons on Mount Gilboa.
9So they cut off Saul's head and stripped off
his armor. Then they proclaimed the good
news of Saul's death in their pagan temple
and to the people throughout the land of
Philistia. 10They placed his armor in the temple of the Ashtoreths, and they fastened his
body to the wall of the city of Beth-shan.

11But when the people of Jabesh-gilead
heard what the Philistines had done to Saul,
12all their mighty warriors traveled through
the night to Beth-shan and took the bodies of
Saul and his sons down from the wall. They
brought them to Jabesh, where they burned
the bodies. 13Then they took their bones
and buried them beneath the tamarisk tree
at Jabesh, and they fasted for seven days.

31:1 The Israelites ***fled*** southeast from the Jezreel Valley (29:1) to higher and hillier ground. With their chariots, the Philistines had the advantage in the more level valley. • ***Mount Gilboa*** is southwest of the Sea of Galilee, far from the territory of the Philistines.

31:2 ***Jonathan . . . Malkishua:*** See 14:49. This is the first mention of Saul's son ***Abinadab*** (cp. 1 Chr 8:33; 9:39).

31:4 David had once held the position of ***armor bearer*** (16:21). • ***kill me:*** This is one of many parallels between the death of Abimelech in the time of the Judges (Judg 9) and Saul, Israel's first national king (cp. Judg 9:54).

31:8 The victorious army would ***strip the dead*** to search for anything valuable (such as clothing, weapons, or jewelry) on the corpses.

31:9 In the ancient world, the death of an enemy king was ***good news***, for it meant that the enemy's god had been defeated. However, little did the Philistines know that their victory would be short lived and hollow. David, the Lord's true anointed king, would soon come to power and pay back the Philistines mightily. Far from defeating Israel's God, the Philistines were simply fulfilling his purpose.

31:10 ***the Ashtoreths:*** See 7:3. • ***fastened his body:*** This practice further degraded the executed person by depriving him of proper burial. It also served as a deterrent to other potential enemies (see also Gen 40:19; Deut 21:21-22; Josh 10:26; Esth 9:6-14). • ***Beth-shan*** was a short distance east of Mount Gilboa.

31:11 The ***people of Jabesh-gilead*** were returning the favor Saul had done for them when he saved them from the Ammonites and their king Nahash (11:1-13). Jabesh-gilead was about twelve miles southeast of Beth-shan and across the Jordan River.

31:12 ***burned the bodies:*** Cremation was rare. It is possible the bodies were burned because decomposition had already set in.

31:13 ***bones . . . Jabesh:*** This was not the final resting place of Saul's remains (see 2 Sam 21:12-14). • The ending of 1 Samuel brings Israel's history back to the situation at the end of Judges, when "there was no king in Israel." Once again, the Philistines were in control. David had God's anointing but no crown. He had wives but no sons. His affiliation with the hated Philistines might jeopardize his standing among his own people. David's future path would be challenging, but God was clearly with him.

THE SECOND BOOK OF

SAMUEL

David's ascension to power over all the tribes of Israel was anything but smooth. Violence, politics, and intrigue lined the way. David was far from a perfect king—2 Samuel records his murder of the noble Uriah to cover up his adultery with Bathsheba and the political chaos that followed. Yet God was eternally committed to David and his dynasty. He protected David during the many challenges to his authority and mercifully forgave and restored him when he sinned.

SETTING

The book of 2 Samuel is a key part of the history of Israel's monarchy. It follows 1 Samuel as a unified composition that traces David's life and reign. While Saul was still reigning, Samuel anointed David as Israel's next king (1 Sam 16:1-13), but it was several years before David began to reign. Throughout most of this waiting period, David was the object of Saul's wrath and jealousy. Saul tried many times to kill David, but David never reciprocated. David trusted in the Lord's plan for him and in God's timing.

David's reign brought significant changes to Israel, both internally and externally. Internally, the nation began to develop a new awareness of itself as a unified nation. During Saul's reign and the early part of David's reign, the monarchy was not completely unified as it would be during Solomon's reign,

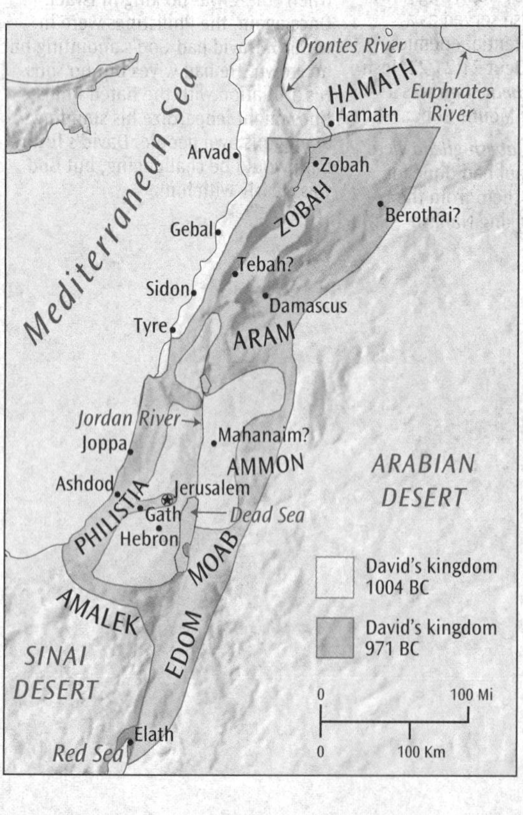

◀ **David's Kingdom** (1004–971 BC). After Saul's death, David began his reign over Judah from Hebron (1011–1004 BC), while Saul's son Ishbosheth reigned over the northern tribes from Mahanaim (see map, p. 521). After David gained the loyalty of the northern tribes in 1004 BC, he conquered Jerusalem from the Jebusites and made that city the administrative center of the kingdom (see 5:6-10). At that time, David's kingdom had roughly the same extent as Saul's, which was also the boundary of Israel's settlement from the time of the judges (cp. maps in the introductions to Judges, p. 416; and 1 Samuel, p. 464). Throughout his reign, David expanded his kingdom and created a small empire over surrounding nations.

Amalek 1:1; 8:12
Ammon 8:12; 10:1–11:1; 12:26-31
Aram 8:5-6; 10:6; 15:8
Berothai 8:7-8
Damascus 8:5-6
Edom 8:12-14
Gath 1:20; 6:10; 8:1; 15:18-19; 18:2; 21:19-22
Hamath 8:9
Hebron 2:1-11; 3:19-32; 4:1–5:5; 15:7-10
Jerusalem 5:5-13; 11:1; 15:13-14; 19:15–20:3; 24:16
Jordan River 2:29; 10:17; 16:14; 17:16-24; 19:15-39
Mahanaim 2:8-12, 29; 17:24-27; 18:23; 19:32
Moab 8:2
Tyre 5:11; 24:7
Zobah 8:3, 12; 10:6

and the twelve tribes still primarily found their identity at the tribal level rather than as a nation. By the end of David's reign, a sense of national unity was in place that set the stage for the glory days of King Solomon.

Externally, Israel's relationship with a number of its neighbors changed significantly during David's reign. Most notably, the constant threat posed by the Philistines, so obvious in the book of Judges and throughout Saul's reign, largely vanished as the result of David's skillful leadership (see, e.g., 5:17-25; 21:15-22; 23:9-17).

SUMMARY

For 7½ years after the deaths of Saul and Jonathan (ch 1), David reigned as king of Judah only. For two years of that time, Saul's only surviving son, Ishbosheth, was king of the northern tribes, and this led to a murderous civil war. David became progressively stronger while Ishbosheth became weaker. In the end, Ishbosheth and his top commander, Abner, were assassinated against David's wishes (3:22–4:12). Following Ishbosheth's death, the leaders of the northern tribes pledged their loyalty to David. David immediately relocated his capital from Hebron to the more centrally located Jerusalem, driving out its Jebusite inhabitants (5:6-16).

Jerusalem was more than David's political capital. By bringing the Ark of the Covenant to Jerusalem, David made it Israel's spiritual capital as well (6:1-15). Shortly thereafter, God made an eternal covenant with David and his house (7:1-29). In these early years, David enjoyed success on every side (chs 8, 10) and fulfilled his vow to treat the descendants of Saul and Jonathan kindly (ch 9).

Then David made the worst mistake of his life: When he saw the beautiful Bathsheba, he brought her to his house for sexual intimacy (11:1-5). She became pregnant, and David arranged for her husband's murder (11:6-27). God was displeased with David's actions and chastised him (12:1-12). Although David repented and experienced God's forgiveness, the child conceived in the affair died (12:13-23). Yet David remained God's chosen king (12:24-31).

From this point forward, problems escalated for David. Amnon, one of David's sons, raped his half sister, Tamar, and her brother Absalom avenged the act (ch 13). Absalom tried to overthrow and replace David, but he was killed in the coup (chs 14–19). Sheba, a Benjamite, also led a revolt against David but was defeated and executed (ch 20).

As king, David was responsible for the nation's well-being and twice acted to allay God's wrath against the nation (chs 21, 24). In the second instance, David built an altar in Jerusalem (24:18-25) that became the site of the future Temple (see 1 Chr 21:18–22:1). Sandwiched between these

OUTLINE

1:1-27
Introduction: The Close of Saul's Era

2:1–9:13
The Emergence of David's Monarchy

10:1–20:26
The Peak of David's Reign

21:1–24:25
The Celebration of David's Reign

TIMELINE

1050–1011 BC
Saul's reign as king of Israel

about 1025 BC
David is anointed as king

about 1020 BC
David fights Goliath

1011 BC
The death of Saul and Jonathan

1011–971 BC
David as king of Israel

1011–1004 BC
David's 7½-year reign at Hebron

1004–971 BC
David's 33-year reign at Jerusalem

about 980 BC
Absalom's revolt

971–931 BC
Solomon as king of Israel

two episodes are passages that celebrate God's power working through David and descriptions of the loyalty and heroism of David's special warriors (chs 22–23).

What a man! . . . I am more impressed than ever with [David's] life. Not perfect by any means, but authentic to the core.

CHARLES SWINDOLL
David: A Man of Passion and Destiny

AUTHOR

The same anonymous author who wrote 1 Samuel probably also wrote 2 Samuel (see "Author" in the Introduction to 1 Samuel).

HISTORICAL ISSUES

Evidence for David. For a long time, David's name had not been discovered in any document from antiquity outside of the Bible. This led some critical scholars to claim that David and his story were fictitious. However, in 1993, archaeologists working at Tell Dan in northern Israel found an inscription in Aramaic about Hazael, king of Syria (about 842–800 BC), who was celebrating a military victory over Israel and Judah. The inscription reads, "I put Jeho . . . , son of . . . ruler of Israel, and . . .iahu, son of . . .g of the house of David to death" (ellipses represent portions of the text illegible in the inscription). This inscription provides evidence of David's existence and acknowledgment that he founded a dynasty in Judah.

Violence. To a greater degree than any other biblical book, 2 Samuel tells of murders and executions. Most notable are those involving David's political rivals and their supporters (Saul and Jonathan, 1:1-15; Abner, 3:30; Ishbosheth, 4:6-8; Absalom, 18:14-15; other male descendants of Saul, 21:8-9; Amasa, 20:10; Sheba, 20:21-22). However, the narrator is careful to show that David was not responsible for these murders. Contrary to the claims of some (see 16:5-8), David could not be accused of murderous political ambition. David was guilty of murder only in the case of Uriah. Without question, this was a horrible sin, but it was devoid of political motive.

David had no involvement in the many murders surrounding his rise to power. He was not a usurper who violently eliminated the previous royal family. In fact, he genuinely lamented the deaths of Saul and Jonathan and ordered the executions of those who killed Saul and Ishbosheth (1:1-16; 4:12). David had deep respect for Saul as the Lord's anointed king. Although David was aware that God had anointed him to replace Saul, he refused to take the matter into his own hands.

[The book of] 1 and 2 Samuel . . . makes even the most sophisticated ancient biography seem like a cartoon in comparison. . . . [David] grows, he learns, he travails, he triumphs, and he suffers immeasurable tragedy and loss. He is the first human being in world literature.

BARUCH HALPERN
David's Secret Demons: Messiah, Murderer, Traitor, King

MEANING AND MESSAGE

The book of 2 Samuel reports how God brought the private anointing of David as king (1 Sam 16:1-13) to public fruition. Moreover, God solidified with a covenant his commitment to David's dynasty.

God's covenant with David bears significant similarities to the covenant with Abraham. Both include promises of great fame (Gen 12:2; 2 Sam 7:9) and of rest from their enemies (Gen 15:18-21; 2 Sam 7:10). Both are binding forever (Gen 13:15; 2 Sam 7:16), and the land God promised to Abraham and his descendants (Gen 15:18) was acquired through David's expansion of his empire (5:17-25; 8:1-14; 10:1-9).

God's commitment to David was crucial to David's successes despite civil war, revolts, the murderous ambition of some loyal to him, and

his personal failures. His shortcomings—particularly his adultery with Bathsheba and the murder of Uriah—lead readers to wonder if David would become like Saul, rejected by God and replaced by another. God certainly did punish David when he sinned (chs 12–20; 24). Yet God's commitment to David and to his dynasty remained (see especially 7:14-16). God's commitment rather than David's merit explains his success.

Kingship was central in God's plan for his people and his creation. God's commitment to David points beyond David and his immediate descendants to a distant son, Jesus Christ. The NT both begins (Matt 1:1) and ends (Rev 22:16) by focusing on Jesus, the Eternal King, as the descendant of David.

FURTHER READING

BILL T. ARNOLD
1 and 2 Samuel (2003)

JOYCE G. BALDWIN
1 & 2 Samuel (1988)

R. D. BERGEN
1, 2 Samuel (1996)

WALTER BRUEGGEMANN
First and Second Samuel (1990)

J. ROBERT VANNOY
2 Samuel in *Cornerstone Biblical Commentary*, vol. 4a (2009)

1:1 1 Sam 30:1, 17
1:2 1 Sam 4:12
1:4-12 //1 Sam 31:1-13 //1 Chr 10:1-12
1:4 1 Sam 4:16-17
1:6 1 Sam 28:4; 31:1-6
1:8 1 Sam 15:2-3; 30:1, 13, 17
1:11 Gen 37:29, 34
1:14 1 Sam 26:9-11
1:15 2 Sam 4:10, 12

1. INTRODUCTION: THE CLOSE OF SAUL'S ERA (1:1-27)

The Report of Saul's Death

1 After the death of Saul, David returned from his victory over the Amalekites and spent two days in Ziklag. 2On the third day a man arrived from Saul's army camp. He had torn his clothes and put dirt on his head to show that he was in mourning. He fell to the ground before David in deep respect.

3"Where have you come from?" David asked.

"I escaped from the Israelite camp," the man replied.

4"What happened?" David demanded. "Tell me how the battle went."

The man replied, "Our entire army fled from the battle. Many of the men are dead, and Saul and his son Jonathan are also dead."

5"How do you know Saul and Jonathan are dead?" David demanded of the young man.

6The man answered, "I happened to be on Mount Gilboa, and there was Saul leaning on his spear with the enemy chariots and charioteers closing in on him. 7When he turned and saw me, he cried out for me to come to him. 'How can I help?' I asked him.

8"He responded, 'Who are you?'

"'I am an Amalekite,' I told him.

9"Then he begged me, 'Come over here and put me out of my misery, for I am in terrible pain and want to die.'

10"So I killed him," the Amalekite told David, "for I knew he couldn't live. Then I took his crown and his armband, and I have brought them here to you, my lord."

11David and his men tore their clothes in sorrow when they heard the news. 12They mourned and wept and fasted all day for Saul and his son Jonathan, and for the LORD's army and the nation of Israel, because they had died by the sword that day.

13Then David said to the young man who had brought the news, "Where are you from?"

And he replied, "I am a foreigner, an Amalekite, who lives in your land."

14"Why were you not afraid to kill the LORD's anointed one?" David asked.

15Then David said to one of his men, "Kill him!" So the man thrust his sword

1:1-27 The forty years of Saul's reign came to a painful end. The Philistines inflicted a crushing blow on Saul's people, killing his sons and dismembering Saul's body after his suicide (1 Sam 31). On the heels of these tragedies, David's career as leader came into focus.

1:1-16 An unnamed Amalekite sought out David, claiming to have killed Saul. This was a lie, as Saul had committed suicide (1 Sam 31:4-6). The Amalekite might have hoped that David would reward him for making it possible for David to assume the throne. Instead, David ordered him killed for harming the Lord's anointed.

1:1 ***David returned from his victory:*** Just prior to this encounter, David and his men had killed many ***Amalekites*** because of what they had done to David's city and family (see 1 Sam 30).

1:4 ***What happened?*** David was not aware of what had happened to Saul—he had no part in Saul's death. • ***Saul and . . . Jonathan are also dead:*** Two other sons of Saul, Abinadab and Malkishua, were killed as well (1 Sam 31:2). The Amalekite was either unaware of their deaths or he mentioned only the son who would stand in the way of David's uncontested path to Israel's throne.

1:6 The Amalekite man's second lie is, ***I happened to be on Mount Gilboa***. Instead, he had probably scoured the area after the battle, looking for victims whose valuables he could take.

1:9 ***Then he begged me:*** This is the Amalekite's third lie; instead, Saul was probably already dead (cp. 1 Sam 31:4-6).

1:10 ***The Amalekite*** apparently got to Saul's corpse before the Philistines did, for they would not have left royal items such as ***his crown and his armband*** on his body. • Israel's king wore a ***crown*** (Hebrew *nezer*, "consecration") as a sign of his consecration to God and status as the Lord's anointed (1:14).

1:13 ***Where are you from?*** David's asking again (1:8) likely reflects the depth of his grief.

1:15-16 The Amalekite expected a reward for killing David's rival but was instead condemned for killing ***the LORD's anointed***. David himself had twice refused the opportunity to kill Saul (see 1 Sam 24:5-7; 26:9-11).

into the Amalekite and killed him. [16]"You have condemned yourself," David said, "for you yourself confessed that you killed the LORD's anointed one."

David's Lament for Saul and Jonathan

[17]Then David composed a funeral song for Saul and Jonathan, [18]and he commanded that it be taught to the people of Judah. It is known as the Song of the Bow, and it is recorded in *The Book of Jashar.*

[19] Your pride and joy, O Israel, lies dead on the hills!
Oh, how the mighty heroes have fallen!
[20] Don't announce the news in Gath,
don't proclaim it in the streets of Ashkelon,
or the daughters of the Philistines will rejoice
and the pagans will laugh in triumph.
[21] O mountains of Gilboa,
let there be no dew or rain upon you,
nor fruitful fields producing offerings of grain.
For there the [a]shield of the mighty heroes was defiled;
the [a]shield of Saul will no longer be anointed with oil.
[22] The bow of Jonathan was powerful,
and the sword of Saul did its mighty work.
They shed the blood of their enemies
and pierced the bodies of mighty heroes.
[23] How beloved and gracious were Saul and Jonathan!
They were together in life and in death.
They were swifter than eagles,
stronger than lions.
[24] O women of Israel, weep for Saul,
for he dressed you in luxurious scarlet clothing,
in garments decorated with gold.

[25] Oh, how the mighty heroes have fallen in battle!
Jonathan lies dead on the hills.
[26] How I weep for you, my brother Jonathan!
Oh, how much I loved you!
And your love for me was deep,
deeper than the love of women!
[27] Oh, how the mighty heroes have fallen!
Stripped of their weapons, they lie dead.

2. THE EMERGENCE OF DAVID'S MONARCHY (2:1–9:13)

David Becomes King of Judah

2 After this, David asked the LORD, "Should I move back to one of the towns of Judah?"

"Yes," the LORD replied.

Then David asked, "Which town should I go to?"

"To Hebron," the LORD answered.

[2]David's two wives were Ahinoam from Jezreel and Abigail, the widow of Nabal

1:16 1 Sam 26:9; 2 Sam 1:10
1:17 2 Chr 35:25
1:18 Josh 10:13
1:19 2 Sam 3:38
1:20 1 Sam 31:8; Mic 1:10
1:21 1 Sam 31:1; Ezek 31:15
[a]*magen* (4043) ‣2 Sam 22:31
1:23 Judg 14:18
1:25 2 Sam 1:19
1:26 1 Sam 18:1
2:1 Josh 14:13-14; 1 Sam 23:2, 4, 9-12
2:2 1 Sam 25:39, 42-43

1:18 The extrabiblical *Book of Jashar* (or *Book of the Upright*) is no longer available. It was probably an Israelite epic poem or an anthology of poetry that covered, at minimum, Joshua's conquest of Canaan (see Josh 10:13) and the ascension of David.

1:19 ***Your pride and joy:*** David's description focused more on Saul's royal position than on his personal characteristics.

1:20 ***Gath*** and ***Ashkelon*** were major Philistine cities. Announcing the ***news*** of Saul's death to the Philistines would give this hated foe the opportunity to gloat and glorify their false god, Dagon, while mocking Israel's God, Yahweh. • ***daughters of the Philistines:*** In ancient war culture, young women sometimes celebrated victories in song (cp. Exod 15:20-21; 1 Sam 18:7).

1:21 Saul and Jonathan died in the ***mountains of Gilboa*** (1 Sam 31:1). • ***let there be no dew or rain:*** David was invoking a curse on the place of their death. In a Canaanite text from the 1300s BC, a father invokes a very similar curse on the place of his son's death. • ***fruitful . . . grain:*** The meaning of the Hebrew is uncertain. • ***The shield of Saul*** symbolizes his military exploits as king. It would ***no longer be anointed with oil*** for the same reason that Saul was no longer the anointed king, because of his death.

1:22 ***the blood of their enemies:*** Saul and Jonathan were known as military heroes (see 1 Sam 11:1-11; 14:1-23, 47-48), though neither to the degree that David was (1 Sam 18:7; 21:11).

1:23 ***beloved and gracious . . . together in life and in death:*** Although the relationship between Saul and Jonathan was strained, especially due to Saul's treatment of David (see 1 Sam 20:30-33), Jonathan nevertheless fought and died alongside his father while defending Israel against the Philistine menace.

1:26 ***deeper than the love of women:*** Jonathan's loyalty and friendship to David involved personal risk and sacrifice. This commitment was unmatched in David's experience, including the love of his wives. The phrase in no way implies a homosexual relationship. Jonathan's love for David is highlighted three times in 1 Samuel (1 Sam 18:1, 3; 20:17).

2:1-32 After Saul died, those loyal to David (the tribe of Judah) clashed with those loyal to Saul's son Ishbosheth (the remaining tribes of Israel). The Philistines, who at this time were essentially overlords of all Palestine west of the Jordan River, likely favored and encouraged this division because it made it easier for them to divide and conquer.

2:1 ***David asked the LORD*** (cp. 5:23-24; Judg 1:1-2; 20:18; 1 Sam 10:22) by consulting the Urim and Thummim (see Exod 28:30; Lev 8:8; Deut 33:8; 1 Sam 14:41) administered by Abiathar, David's priest (1 Sam 23:1-12; 30:7-8). David acted when God directed, not before. • ***Hebron*** was nineteen miles southeast of Jerusalem. Abraham had lived in this area for a time and eventually purchased a nearby cave for a family burial plot (Gen 23). The people of the area were sympathetic toward David (see 1 Sam 30:26-31).

2:2 ***Ahinoam:*** See note on 1 Sam 25:43. David's other wife, Saul's daughter Michal, had been given to another man after David fled from Saul (1 Sam 25:44). • ***Abigail:*** See 1 Sam 25.

2:4
1 Sam 16:13; 31:11-13
2 Sam 5:3-5
2:5
1 Sam 23:21; 24:19
2:6
Exod 34:5-6
2:8
1 Sam 14:50
2 Sam 17:24
2:12
Josh 10:12
2:13
2 Sam 8:16
1 Chr 2:16; 11:5-6

from Carmel. So David and his wives
[3]and his men and their families all moved to Judah, and they settled in the villages near Hebron.
[4]Then the men of Judah came to David and anointed him king over the people of Judah.

When David heard that the men of Jabesh-gilead had buried Saul,
[5]he sent them this message: "May the LORD bless you for being so loyal to your master Saul and giving him a decent burial.
[6]May the LORD be loyal to you in return and reward you with his unfailing love! And I, too, will reward you for what you have done.
[7]Now that Saul is dead, I ask you to be my strong and loyal subjects like the people of Judah, who have anointed me as their new king."

[8]But Abner son of Ner, the commander of Saul's army, had already gone to Mahanaim with Saul's son Ishbosheth.
[9]There he proclaimed Ishbosheth king over Gilead, Jezreel, Ephraim, Benjamin, the land of the Ashurites, and all the rest of Israel.

[10]Ishbosheth, Saul's son, was forty years old when he became king, and he ruled from Mahanaim for two years. Meanwhile, the people of Judah remained loyal to David.
[11]David made Hebron his capital, and he ruled as king of Judah for seven and a half years.

Civil War between Israel and Judah

[12]One day Abner led Ishbosheth's troops from Mahanaim to Gibeon.
[13]About the same time, Joab son of Zeruiah led David's troops out and met them at the pool of Gibeon. The two groups sat down there, facing each other from opposite sides of the pool.

[14]Then Abner suggested to Joab, "Let's have a few of our warriors fight hand to hand here in front of us."

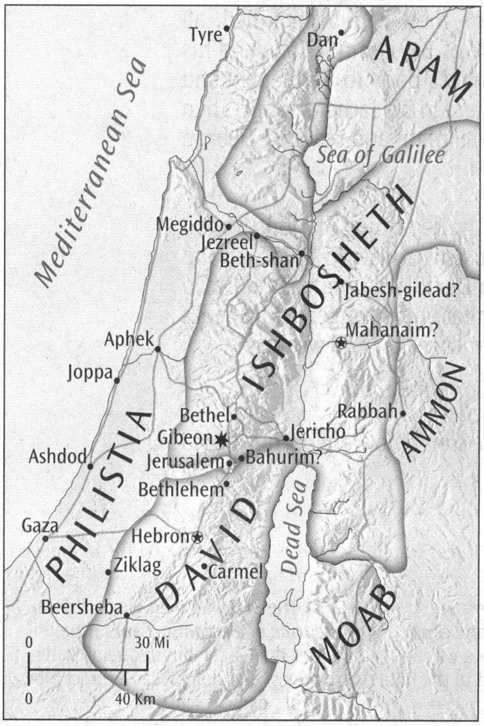

◀ **David vs. Ishbosheth** (2:1-32). After Saul's death, David ruled over Judah from HEBRON (2:1-4, 11), while Saul's son Ishbosheth ruled over the northern tribes from MAHANAIM (2:8-10). The result was "a long war" (3:1) between the north and the south; one of the key battles took place at GIBEON (2:12-17). Eventually, after both Ishbosheth and Abner his general were murdered (3:22-30; 4:1-12), all the tribes of Israel united under David's kingship (5:1-5).

2:4b-7 Once established in Hebron, ***David*** made good faith gestures to those still loyal to Saul, such as ***the men of Jabesh-gilead.*** However, because they were ***loyal to . . . Saul*** and his dynasty, they rejected David as king (2:8-11). David was also in league with Nahash, king of the Ammonites (see 10:2; 17:27-29), who had caused havoc in Jabesh-gilead (1 Sam 11).

2:7 David's anointing by ***the people of Judah*** provided the legal basis of his kingship, just as it had for Saul (1 Sam 11:15). He had been anointed by the prophet Samuel years earlier (1 Sam 16:13).

2:8 *Abner:* See note on 1 Sam 20:25. • ***Mahanaim*** was located east of the Jordan River, deep in the highlands of Gilead near a plentiful source of fresh water. Saul and his family had close ties to Gilead (1 Sam 11:1-11; 31:11-13). Locating east of the Jordan made Ishbosheth's regime less susceptible to attack by David's forces. This same area was later King David's temporary refuge after Absalom's coup (17:24, 27). • ***Ishbosheth*** is another name for Esh-baal (1 Chr 8:33; 9:39). *Ishbosheth* means "man of shame." *Esh-baal* means "man of Baal." The name *Baal* ("lord, master, possessor") was associated with a pagan Canaanite deity (e.g., see Num 25:3), so it is likely that Esh-baal, Ishbosheth's original name, was later changed because of that association.

2:9 ***Gilead*** was the easternmost district of the northern kingdom, ***Jezreel*** the northernmost, and ***Benjamin*** the southernmost, with ***Ephraim*** in the middle. It is unclear which area was the ***land of the Ashurites. All the rest of Israel*** refers to the tribes that Ishbosheth ruled over rather than to the geographical area of his kingdom.

2:10-11 ***Ishbosheth . . . ruled from Mahanaim for two years*** at some point during David's 7½-year reign from Hebron. Apparently a gap of five years occurred in which the northern tribes were without a king.

2:12-32 A protracted civil war ensued between Judah (led by David) and the northern tribes (led by Saul's dynasty). These events set the stage for Abner's murder (3:22-39).

2:12 ***Gibeon,*** about five miles northwest of Jerusalem, was a key city in Benjamin.

2:13 ***The pool of Gibeon*** extends down some 80 feet to the water table. Archaeologists estimate that the original diggers had to remove about 3,000 tons of limestone to create it.

2:14 ***a few of our warriors:*** In the ancient world, enemy armies would sometimes choose individuals or small groups to fight each other as representative gladiators—a custom often referred to as champion warfare (see also 1 Sam 17). • ***fight hand to hand:***

"All right," Joab agreed. 15So twelve men were chosen to fight from each side—twelve men of Benjamin representing Ishbosheth son of Saul, and twelve representing David. 16Each one grabbed his opponent by the hair and thrust his sword into the other's side so that all of them died. So this place at Gibeon has been known ever since as the Field of Swords.

17A fierce battle followed that day, and Abner and the men of Israel were defeated by the forces of David.

18Joab, Abishai, and Asahel—the three sons of Zeruiah—were among David's forces that day. Asahel could run like a gazelle, 19and he began chasing Abner. He pursued him relentlessly, not stopping for anything. 20When Abner looked back and saw him coming, he called out, "Is that you, Asahel?"

"Yes, it is," he replied.

21"Go fight someone else!" Abner warned. "Take on one of the younger men, and strip him of his weapons." But Asahel kept right on chasing Abner.

22Again Abner shouted to him, "Get away from here! I don't want to kill you. How could I ever face your brother Joab again?"

23But Asahel refused to turn back, so Abner thrust the butt end of his spear through Asahel's stomach, and the spear came out through his back. He stumbled to the ground and died there. And everyone who came by that spot stopped and stood still when they saw Asahel lying there.

24When Joab and Abishai found out what had happened, they set out after Abner. The sun was just going down as they arrived at the hill of Ammah near Giah, along the road to the wilderness of Gibeon. 25Abner's troops from the tribe of Benjamin regrouped there at the top of the hill to take a stand.

26Abner shouted down to Joab, "Must we always be killing each other? Don't you realize that bitterness is the only result? When will you call off your men from chasing their Israelite brothers?"

27Then Joab said, "God only knows what would have happened if you hadn't spoken, for we would have chased you all night if necessary." 28So Joab blew the ram's horn, and his men stopped chasing the troops of Israel.

29All that night Abner and his men retreated through the Jordan Valley. They crossed the Jordan River, traveling all through the morning, and didn't stop until they arrived at Mahanaim.

30Meanwhile, Joab and his men also returned home. When Joab counted his casualties, he discovered that only 19 men were missing in addition to Asahel. 31But 360 of Abner's men had been killed, all from the tribe of Benjamin. 32Joab and his men took Asahel's body to Bethlehem and buried him there in his father's tomb. Then they traveled all night and reached Hebron at daybreak.

3 That was the beginning of a long war between those who were loyal to Saul and those loyal to David. As time passed David became stronger and stronger, while Saul's dynasty became weaker and weaker.

David's Sons Born in Hebron
2 Sam 3:2-5 // 1 Chr 3:1-4

2These are the sons who were born to David in Hebron:

2:17 2 Sam 3:1
2:18 1 Chr 2:16; 11:26; 12:8
2:22 2 Sam 3:27
2:26 Deut 32:42
2:29 Deut 3:17
2:32 Gen 49:29
3:1 1 Kgs 14:30
3:2-5 //1 Chr 3:1-4
3:2 1 Sam 25:43; 2 Sam 13:1; 1 Chr 3:1

The Hebrew term usually includes a component of play. A contest of champions might have been seen as a type of high-stakes game. In this instance, it settled nothing; the fighting expanded into a much wider confrontation with heavier casualties (2:17-32).

2:16 ***the Field of Swords:*** Hebrew *Helkath-hazzurim.*

2:17 The casualty count of this ***fierce battle*** is noted in 2:30-31.

2:18 ***Zeruiah*** was David's sister (1 Chr 2:15-16), so ***Joab, Abishai, and Asahel*** were his nephews.

2:20-22 ***Go fight someone else! . . . Get away from here!*** Abner's words reflect respect between peers trained for the same career, as well as a sense of fair play. The youthful ***Asahel*** would have been no match for the more experienced Abner. Abner also knew that if he killed Asahel, the conflict with David would escalate and David's forces would seek revenge (see 3:22-39).

2:24 ***they set out after Abner:*** See 3:27. • ***Ammah*** ("conduit") and ***Giah*** ("gushing") suggest that there was an aqueduct system connected to the pool at Gibeon (2:12-13).

2:26 ***bitterness is the only result:*** Realizing that such wars go on generation after generation, Abner wisely negotiated a truce.

2:28 The ***ram's horn*** signaled the beginning and end of combat (see also 18:16; Josh 6:15-16). For other uses of the ram's horn, see note on 2 Sam 6:15.

2:29 ***Abner*** was wise to put as much distance as possible between his troops and Joab's forces, recognizing that their desire for blood vengeance could overpower the truce. • ***the Jordan Valley:*** Hebrew *the Arabah.* • ***through the morning:*** Or *continued on through the Bithron.* The meaning of the Hebrew is uncertain.

2:31 The ***360*** who died were ***all from the tribe of Benjamin***, Saul's tribe, under the leadership of one of Saul's relatives. This defeat was a direct blow to Saul's dynasty (cp. 3:1).

3:1-39 The house of David increased, while Saul's house dwindled. The crucial occasion came when Abner, the real political power in Saul's camp, switched allegiance to David, taking a considerable number of his northern kinsmen with him.

3:1 ***a long war:*** This civil war likely continued for most of the seven-plus years that David ruled from Hebron. The truce called by Joab and Abner (2:26-28) was short-lived.

3:2-5 One way ***David*** "became stronger and stronger" (3:1) was by taking more wives and having a son through each.

3:3 1 Sam 25:42; 1 Chr 3:1-2
3:4 1 Chr 3:2-3
3:5 1 Chr 3:3
3:7 2 Sam 21:8-11
3:8 1 Sam 24:14; 2 Sam 9:8; 16:9
3:9 1 Sam 15:28
3:13 1 Sam 18:20
3:14 1 Sam 18:25-27
3:15 1 Sam 25:44
3:16 2 Sam 16:5

The oldest was Amnon, whose mother
was Ahinoam from Jezreel.
[3] The second was Daniel, whose mother
was Abigail, the widow of Nabal from
Carmel.
The third was Absalom, whose mother
was Maacah, the daughter of Talmai,
king of Geshur.
[4] The fourth was Adonijah, whose mother
was Haggith.
The fifth was Shephatiah, whose mother
was Abital.
[5] The sixth was Ithream, whose mother
was Eglah, David's wife.

These sons were all born to David in Hebron.

Abner Joins Forces with David

[6]As the war between the house of Saul and the house of David went on, Abner became a powerful leader among those loyal to Saul. [7]One day Ishbosheth, Saul's son, accused Abner of sleeping with one of his father's concubines, a woman named Rizpah, daughter of Aiah.

[8]Abner was furious. "Am I some Judean dog to be kicked around like this?" he shouted. "After all I have done for your father, Saul, and his family and friends by not handing you over to David, is this my reward—that you find fault with me about this woman? [9]May God strike me and even kill me if I don't do everything I can to help David get what the LORD has promised him! [10]I'm going to take Saul's kingdom and give it to David. I will establish the throne of David over Israel as well as Judah, all the way from Dan in the north to Beersheba in the south." [11]Ishbosheth didn't dare say another word because he was afraid of what Abner might do.

[12]Then Abner sent messengers to David, saying, "Doesn't the entire land belong to you? Make a solemn pact with me, and I will help turn over all of Israel to you."

[13]"All right," David replied, "but I will not negotiate with you unless you bring back my wife Michal, Saul's daughter, when you come."

[14]David then sent this message to Ishbosheth, Saul's son: "Give me back my wife Michal, for I bought her with the lives of 100 Philistines."

[15]So Ishbosheth took Michal away from her husband, Palti son of Laish. [16]Palti followed along behind her as far as Bahurim, weeping as he went. Then Abner told him, "Go back home!" So Palti returned.

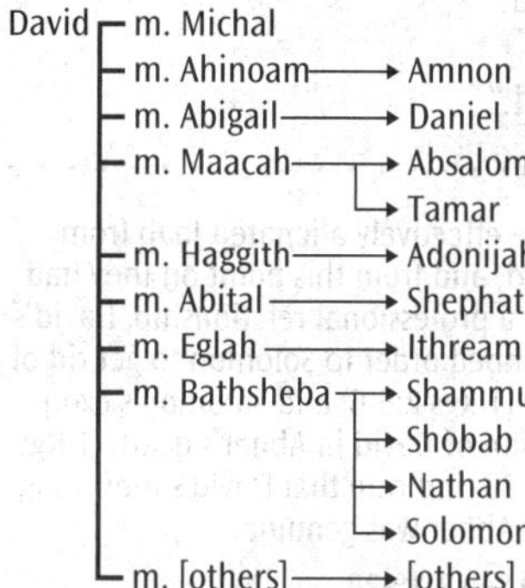

▲ **David's Wives and Children** (3:2-5; see also 5:14-16; 1 Chr 3:5-8).

Three of David's Hebron-born sons died violent deaths, two during David's reign (*Amnon, Absalom*), and one shortly after his death (*Adonijah*).

3:3 *Daniel:* As in parallel text at 1 Chr 3:1 (see also Greek version, which reads *Daluia*, and Dead Sea Scrolls, which read *Dan[iel]*); Hebrew reads *Kileab.* • *Geshur* was a small Canaanite kingdom in upper Transjordan (the area east of the Jordan) near the Sea of Galilee. Marrying into neighboring royal families created political alliances and secured David's position against the northern tribes. Solomon also followed this practice (1 Kgs 3:1; 11:1).

3:7 *Ishbosheth* is another name for Esh-baal (see note on 2:8). • *accused Abner of sleeping with one of [Saul's] concubines:* It is unclear whether Abner actually did so. Taking a king's wife or concubine was often part of a usurper's attempt to replace the king (see 12:8; 16:21; 1 Kgs 2:17-25). • *Rizpah:* See also 21:8-14.

3:8 *some Judean dog:* Cp. 1 Sam 17:43. • *by not handing you over to David:* Abner had control over the life and death of Saul's son.

3:9 *help David get what the LORD has promised him!* Abner was aware that God had chosen David to be king over all Israel (see also 3:18).

3:10 *and give it to David:* Cp. 1 Sam 28:17. • *I will establish the throne of David:* Whether an ally or enemy, Abner was a powerful man. Here he speaks like God (see 7:13).

3:11 *didn't dare say another word:* Ishbosheth's silence speaks loudly of his weakness as a ruler. Abner, who had installed him as king (2:8-9), was the real power behind Ishbosheth's reign.

3:12 In the proposed *solemn pact* (or *covenant*), Abner recognized that David would be king, while perhaps he hoped to be second-in-command.

3:13 Saul had given his daughter *Michal* to David as his wife (1 Sam 18:20-27). However, when Michal saved David's life from her father (1 Sam 19:11-17), Saul terminated the marriage and gave Michal to another man, Palti (1 Sam 25:44). For David to get her back now would further cement his claim to Saul's kingdom (cp. 1 Kgs 2:13-25).

3:14 *the lives* (literally *the foreskins*) *of 100 Philistines:* Saul had hoped that David would be killed in his attempt to secure the bride-price (see 1 Sam 18:17-27).

3:15 *Ishbosheth took:* Although Abner made the deal with David (3:12-13), it was Ishbosheth who gave Michal to David. This transaction illustrates Ishbosheth's weakness as a king and his fear of Abner (3:11). • *Palti:* As in 1 Sam 25:44; Hebrew reads *Paltiel,* a variant spelling of Palti.

3:16 In spite of Palti's anguished *weeping,* he was powerless to stop what was happening (cp. Judg 18:1-26). • *Bahurim* was probably a center of support for Saul's clan just east of Jerusalem (cp. 16:5).

17 Meanwhile, Abner had consulted with the elders of Israel. "For some time now," he told them, "you have wanted to make David your king. 18 Now is the time! For the LORD has said, 'I have chosen David to save my people Israel from the hands of the Philistines and from all their other enemies.' " 19 Abner also spoke with the men of Benjamin. Then he went to Hebron to tell David that all the people of Israel and Benjamin had agreed to support him.

20 When Abner and twenty of his men came to Hebron, David entertained them with a great feast. 21 Then Abner said to David, "Let me go and call an assembly of all Israel to support my lord the king. They will make a covenant with you to make you their king, and you will rule over everything your heart desires." So David sent Abner safely on his way.

The Murder of Abner

22 But just after David had sent Abner away in safety, Joab and some of David's troops returned from a raid, bringing much plunder with them. 23 When Joab arrived, he was told that Abner had just been there visiting the king and had been sent away in safety.

24 Joab rushed to the king and demanded, "What have you done? What do you mean by letting Abner get away? 25 You know perfectly well that he came to spy on you and find out everything you're doing!"

26 Joab then left David and sent messengers to catch up with Abner, asking him to return. They found him at the well of Sirah and brought him back, though David knew nothing about it. 27 When Abner arrived back at Hebron, Joab took him aside at the gateway as if to speak with him privately. But then he stabbed Abner in the stomach and killed him in revenge for killing his brother Asahel.

28 When David heard about it, he declared, "I vow by the LORD that I and my kingdom are forever innocent of this crime against Abner son of Ner. 29 Joab and his family are the guilty ones. May the family of Joab be cursed in every generation with a man who has open sores or leprosy or who walks on crutches or dies by the sword or begs for food!"

30 So Joab and his brother Abishai killed Abner because Abner had killed their brother Asahel at the battle of Gibeon.

31 Then David said to Joab and all those who were with him, "Tear your clothes and put on burlap. Mourn for Abner." And King David himself walked behind the procession to the grave. 32 They buried Abner in Hebron, and the king and all the people wept at his graveside. 33 Then the king sang this funeral song for Abner:

"Should Abner have died as fools die?
34 Your hands were not bound;
your feet were not chained.
No, you were murdered—
the victim of a wicked plot."

3:18 1 Sam 9:16; 15:28
3:19 1 Sam 10:20-21; 1 Chr 12:29
3:21 1 Kgs 11:37
3:22 1 Sam 27:8
3:27 2 Sam 2:22-23; 20:8-10; 1 Kgs 2:5
3:29 Lev 13:45-46; Deut 21:7-8; 1 Kgs 2:31-33
3:30 2 Sam 2:23
3:31 Gen 37:34; Judg 11:35
3:32 Prov 24:17

3:17 Apparently, there had been growing momentum among *the elders of Israel* in the north to accept *David* as *king*, though the text has made no mention of it to this point.

3:18 See also 3:9. By bringing relief from *the Philistines*, David would accomplish what Saul had failed to do (1 Sam 9:16).

3:19 Because Saul was from their tribe, *the men of Benjamin* no doubt viewed David, from Judah, as a usurper of Saul's throne. However, Abner was well-respected in Saul's regime and so was able to elicit support for David even among Saul's own tribe.

3:21 The narrator emphasized that *David sent Abner safely on his way* as a friend and an ally (restated in 3:22-23). David was at peace with Abner and was not involved in the renowned military leader's murder (cp. 3:28-29). • Despite the murder of Abner (3:27), the northern tribes eventually did *make a covenant* with David to make him their king, just as Abner had promised (5:1-3).

3:26 The precise location of the *well of Sirah* is unknown; presumably it was not far from Hebron. • *David knew nothing about it:* See note on 3:21.

3:27 *as if to speak with him privately:* Joab accused Abner of deception (3:25), but he used deception himself to lure Abner to his death. • *in revenge:* Joab was motivated by the practice of blood vengeance, avenging the death of a kinsman by killing the killer. See "Joab" at 18:2–19:13, p. 551.

3:28 *David* made it clear that he had nothing to do with Abner's death, labeling it as a *crime.* David knew that because his second-in-command had killed Abner, rumors would circulate among those loyal to Saul's dynasty that David had ordered the killing. • *I vow by the LORD:* David called on the Lord to hold him accountable if he were lying.

3:29 *leprosy:* Or *a contagious skin disease.* The Hebrew word used here can describe various skin diseases. While *leprosy* is a possible translation, the Hebrew here probably refers to a broader range of skin inflammations, not only Hansen's disease. • *who walks on crutches:* Or *who is effeminate;* Hebrew reads *who handles a spindle.* This curse effectively alienated Joab from David, and from this point on they had only a professional relationship. David's deathbed order to Solomon to get rid of Joab (1 Kgs 2:5-6) and Solomon's exoneration of David in Abner's death (1 Kgs 2:31-33) indicate that David's mourning over Abner was genuine.

3:30 See 2:18-28.

3:31 *David himself walked:* David's public presence in the mourning procession, his open weeping at the gravesite (3:32), and his dramatic fast (3:35) made evident to the public that he had not ordered Abner's killing (3:37).

3:32 Burying *Abner in Hebron*, David's capital city at the time, rather than at some northern site reinforced Abner's shift of support from Saul to David. Presumably it encouraged others from the northern tribes to follow Abner's example.

3:33 *as fools die:* Abner was deceived by Joab, an enemy who posed as a friend (see 3:27).

3:34 *a wicked plot:* Normal warfare could not defeat Abner, a seasoned warrior. Only treachery could.

3:35 2 Sam 1:12; 12:17
3:39 2 Sam 19:5-7
4:1 2 Sam 3:27
4:2 Josh 9:17; 18:25
4:3 Neh 11:33
4:4 1 Sam 31:1-4; 2 Sam 9:3, 5-6; 1 Chr 8:34; 9:40
4:5 2 Sam 2:8
4:6 2 Sam 2:23

All the people wept again for Abner. 35David had refused to eat anything on the day of the funeral, and now everyone begged him to eat. But David had made a vow, saying, "May God strike me and even kill me if I eat anything before sundown."

36This pleased the people very much. In fact, everything the king did pleased them! 37So everyone in Judah and all Israel understood that David was not responsible for Abner's murder.

38Then King David said to his officials, "Don't you realize that a great commander has fallen today in Israel? 39And even though I am the anointed king, these two sons of Zeruiah—Joab and Abishai—are too strong for me to control. So may the LORD repay these evil men for their evil deeds."

The Murder of Ishbosheth

4 When Ishbosheth, Saul's son, heard about Abner's death at Hebron, he lost all courage, and all Israel became paralyzed with fear. 2Now there were two brothers, Baanah and Recab, who were captains of Ishbosheth's raiding parties. They were sons of Rimmon, a member of the tribe of Benjamin who lived in Beeroth. The town of Beeroth is now part of Benjamin's territory 3because the original people of Beeroth fled to Gittaim, where they still live as foreigners.

4(Saul's son Jonathan had a son named Mephibosheth, who was crippled as a child. He was five years old when the report came from Jezreel that Saul and Jonathan had been killed in battle. When the child's nurse heard the news, she picked him up and fled. But as she hurried away, she dropped him, and he became crippled.)

5One day Recab and Baanah, the sons of Rimmon from Beeroth, went to Ishbosheth's house around noon as he was taking his midday rest. 6The doorkeeper, who had been sifting wheat, became drowsy and fell asleep. So Recab and Baanah slipped past

ABNER (3:6-39)

2 Sam 2:8-29; 1 Sam 14:49-52; 17:55-58; 26:5-16; 1 Kgs 2:5, 32

Abner son of Ner was King Saul's cousin as well as his general (1 Sam 14:49-52). Saul's armies won important battles against the Philistines under Abner's command (1 Sam 17:1-58), and Abner ate at the king's table with David and Jonathan (1 Sam 20:25). Yet Jonathan and David both outshone Abner in Saul's army.

David shamed Abner on one occasion (1 Sam 26:1-25). When Saul was trying to kill David, Saul and his troops camped in a circle with Saul sleeping at the center and Abner beside him. Abishai and David sneaked into the camp and could have killed Saul. They took some items from beside Saul's head; then, after retreating, they shouted to waken Saul and Abner and berate Abner for his carelessness.

After Saul and Jonathan died, Abner promoted the interests of Saul's son Ishbosheth (2:8-12) when Judah made David king. During this time, Abner was the real power in the north. When Ishbosheth accused Abner of sleeping with one of Saul's concubines, Abner turned the northern kingdom over to David. Ishbosheth was later murdered (4:1-12).

During the battle between Ishbosheth and David, Abner was forced in self-defense to kill Joab's brother Asahel, whom he did not want to kill and had warned to turn back (2:18-32). Abner was then murdered by Joab in calculated revenge (3:22-30), an evil act that David could not prevent (3:38-39). David honored Abner with a eulogy, public mourning, and a state funeral (3:31-37). Later, David remembered what had happened and made certain that the murder of Saul's general did not go unpunished (1 Kgs 2:5-6).

3:35 ***begged him to eat:*** See also 12:17.

3:37 See note on 3:31.

3:39 ***too strong for me to control:*** Just as Ishbosheth could not control Abner, David could not control Joab. However, David had faith that ***the LORD*** would ***repay*** Joab for murdering Abner.

4:1 ***Ishbosheth*** is another name for Esh-baal (see note on 2:8). • ***all Israel became paralyzed with fear:*** Abner's true power was evident in Ishbosheth's reaction to his death (cp. Josh 2:9-11; 5:1). Ishbosheth's timidity bred the same among his followers.

4:2-3 ***Beeroth*** was located in Benjamin near Gibeon. Probably because of Saul's persecution of the non-Israelite residents in that region (see 21:1-9), the citizens of *Beeroth* had ***fled to Gittaim,*** the location of which is unknown.

4:4 This parenthetical statement shows that, with the death of Ishbosheth (4:5-7), Saul's dynasty was unable to continue—the only other heir was a young child who was crippled (see also 9:1-13). • ***Mephibosheth*** is another name for Merib-baal (see 1 Chr 9:40). *Mephibosheth* is a nickname meaning "from the mouth of shame," possibly referring to his physical condition. No crippled animal could ever be offered to God, and no disabled priest was allowed to stand before God with the people's offerings (Lev 21:19). Likewise, Mephibosheth's condition probably disqualified him from the crown. His name change from Merib-baal also removed association with Baal (see note on 2:8).

4:6 ***The doorkeeper . . . past her:*** As in Greek version; Hebrew reads *So they went into the house pretending to fetch*

her. 7They went into the house and found
Ishbosheth sleeping on his bed. They struck
and killed him and cut off his head. Then,
taking his head with them, they fled across
the Jordan Valley through the night. 8When
they arrived at Hebron, they presented
Ishbosheth's head to David. "Look!" they
exclaimed to the king. "Here is the head of
Ishbosheth, the son of your enemy Saul who
tried to kill you. Today the LORD has given
my lord the king revenge on Saul and his entire family!"

9But David said to Recab and Baanah,
"The LORD, who saves me from all my enemies, is my witness. 10Someone once told
me, 'Saul is dead,' thinking he was bringing
me good news. But I seized him and killed
him at Ziklag. That's the reward I gave him
for his news! 11How much more should I reward evil men who have killed an innocent
man in his own house and on his own bed?
Shouldn't I hold you responsible for his
blood and rid the earth of you?"

12So David ordered his young men to kill
them, and they did. They cut off their hands
and feet and hung their bodies beside the pool
in Hebron. Then they took Ishbosheth's head
and buried it in Abner's tomb in Hebron.

David Becomes King of All Israel

2 Sam 5:1-5 // 1 Chr 11:1-3

5 Then all the tribes of Israel went to David at Hebron and told him, "We are your
own flesh and blood. 2In the past, when Saul

4:9 1 Kgs 1:29
4:10 2 Sam 1:1-2, 4, 15
4:11 Gen 9:5; Ps 9:12
4:12 2 Sam 1:15; 3:32
5:1-3 //1 Chr 11:1-3
5:2 1 Sam 18:5, 14; 25:30

Jerusalem (5:6-9)

Josh 15:63; Judg 1:8; 1:21; 1 Kgs 8:1; 2 Kgs 18:13-17; 25:1-10; 2 Chr 3:1; 12:1-12; 26:9, 15; 32:1-5, 27-30; Ezra 1:1-6; Neh 1:1–6:19; Ps 48:1-3; 125:2; Isa 14:32; 52:1-3; Gal 4:25-26; Heb 12:22-24

Jerusalem was a functioning city as early as 400 years before David. It was never fully captured during the conquest and the period of the judges (Josh 15:63; Judg 1:8, 21), and peaceful relations were evidently established between the autonomous Jebusite enclave and the surrounding Israelites (Judg 19:10-12). So impregnable was Jerusalem that the OT records only three successful invaders, David, Jehoash (2 Kgs 14:11-14), and Nebuchadnezzar of Babylon (2 Kgs 25:1-10). Even Sennacherib, one of Assyria's mightiest emperors, preferred accepting tribute money over attempting to seize the city (2 Kgs 18:14-16).

Whatever David's method of capturing Jerusalem (his use of a water tunnel is debatable—see note on 5:8), he secured Jerusalem as the political, and eventually spiritual, capital of Israel. Psalm 48 speaks beautifully and powerfully of Jerusalem as a fortress. Its towers, bulwarks, and easily defensible citadels with their rugged terrain could produce a false sense of security, if not idolatry (cp. Obad 1:3-4). Psalm 48:1-3 reminds the reader that God's living presence, not the topography of the city, made Jerusalem safe.

Both the Old Testament and the New Testament call Jerusalem a "holy city" (see Neh 11:1, 18; Isa 52:1; Dan 9:24; Matt 4:5; 27:53; Rev 21:2). It is the only city so described in the Bible. Wherein lies this city's holiness? It cannot be a reflection of the holiness of its occupants. In fact, so unholy was the populace that the city was decimated by the Babylonians in 586 BC. Nor was it a holy city because it was Israel's capital for several centuries. Jerusalem was a holy city, first of all, because God chose it (1 Kgs 8:44, 48; 11:13, 32, 36; 2 Chr 6:5, 34). Because he chose it, he put his glory and his name there (see 1 Kgs 14:21; 2 Chr 12:13; Ezek 8–10; 43). His presence and choice made Jerusalem holy.

In the Gospels and Acts, Jerusalem was still an earthly city of great importance. It was the location of the Temple and was the center of Israel's spiritual life (e.g., see Acts 2:46; 3:1-26; 5:12). But the NT also introduces the new Jerusalem, the heavenly city comprised of God's holy people (Heb 11:10; Rev 3:12; 21:2). As the earthly Jerusalem was the sphere in which the glorious presence and reign of God was partially actualized through King David and his successors, the new Jerusalem represents the government of Jesus Christ, the son of David, and his everlasting presence with his people (cp. John 1:14; Rev 21:3).

wheat, but they stabbed him in the stomach. Then Recab and Baanah escaped. ***Recab*** and ***Baanah*** believed they would gain David's favor by committing this treacherous act.

4:7 ***the Jordan Valley:*** Hebrew *the Arabah.*

4:8 ***your enemy Saul:*** As far as we know, David never referred to Saul as an enemy. • ***the LORD has given . . . revenge:*** Wrongdoers often presume upon God's favor to justify political ambition. However, David would not reward treachery.

4:9-11 ***Someone once told me:*** Cp. 1:1-16.

4:12 ***cut off their hands and feet:*** Displaying the dismembered bodies of Ishbosheth's killers shamed them by denying them proper burial (cp. 1 Sam 31:8-13); it was also a public testimony of David's innocence in Ishbosheth's death.

5:1-25 After the murder of Abner and Ishbosheth, the elders of the northern tribes accepted David as their king. David thus obtained an extended empire (5:1-5), a new capital city (5:6-10), a new palace (5:11), a new family (5:13-16), and renewed confidence (5:17-25).

5:1 ***your own flesh and blood:*** Years of civil war had set brother against

5:3
1 Sam 16:1, 13
2 Sam 2:4; 3:21
[b]*melek* (4428)
›1 Kgs 1:34
5:4
Gen 41:46
1 Kgs 2:11
Luke 3:23
5:6-10
//1 Chr 11:4-9
5:7
1 Kgs 2:10
5:9
1 Kgs 9:15, 24

was our king, you were the one who really
led the forces of Israel. And the LORD told
you, 'You will be the shepherd of my people
Israel. You will be Israel's leader.' "
3So there at Hebron, [b]King David made
a covenant before the LORD with all the elders of Israel. And they anointed him [b]king
of Israel.
4David was thirty years old when he began to reign, and he reigned forty years in
all. 5He had reigned over Judah from Hebron for seven years and six months, and
from Jerusalem he reigned over all Israel
and Judah for thirty-three years.

David Captures Jerusalem
2 Sam 5:6-10 // 1 Chr 11:4-9

6David then led his men to Jerusalem to
fight against the Jebusites, the original
inhabitants of the land who were living
there. The Jebusites taunted David, saying,
"You'll never get in here! Even the blind and
lame could keep you out!" For the Jebusites
thought they were safe. 7But David captured
the fortress of Zion, which is now called the
City of David.
8On the day of the attack, David said to
his troops, "I hate those 'lame' and 'blind'
Jebusites. Whoever attacks them should
strike by going into the city through the water tunnel." That is the origin of the saying,
"The blind and the lame may not enter the
house."
9So David made the fortress his home,
and he called it the City of David. He extended the city, starting at the supporting
terraces and working inward. 10And David
became more and more powerful, because

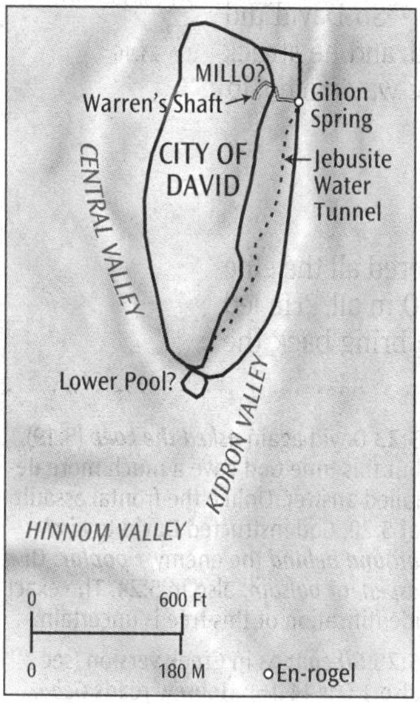

◂ **David's Capture of Jebus (Jerusalem) (5:6-12 // 1 Chr 11:4-8).** Jerusalem was a small walled city when David defeated its Jebusite inhabitants. The water tunnel that David might have used to enter the city (see note on 5:8) ran from GIHON SPRING outside the wall to the LOWER POOL at the lowest point inside the city wall. We don't know exactly where in the city David built his palace. The location of the MILLO ("supporting terraces," 5:9) is also uncertain. The original walled city continued to be called the CITY OF DAVID in later times (e.g., see 1 Kgs 3:1; 2 Kgs 15:7; 2 Chr 32:5; Neh 3:15).

brother, resulting in much bloodshed (see 3:1).

5:2 ***In the past:*** Or *For some time.* • ***you were the one:*** In the ancient world, a covenant relationship (a suzerain-vassal treaty) was sometimes formed between subjects (the vassals) and a ruler (the suzerain) because of past aid, often rescue from enemies (see Judg 8:22, Gideon; Judg 11:8-11, Jephthah; 1 Sam 11:1-15, Saul). This type of relationship is the background for the covenant concept in Scripture: God was Israel's covenant Lord because he had freed them from Egypt (cp. Exod 19:4; 20:1-2). • ***the LORD told you:*** Israel was already aware of God's selection of David (cp. 3:9). • ***shepherd for my people Israel:*** This phrase is quoted in Matt 2:6 when King Herod asks the leading priests about the prophecies concerning the Messiah.

5:3 ***King David made a covenant*** that demanded the people's loyalty, yet allowed them to maintain a sense of tribal privilege and individual dignity. It served as a constitution, containing stipulations obligating both the king and the people. • ***they anointed him king:*** While David had already been anointed by Samuel (1 Sam 16:13), this public ceremony demonstrated the people's acceptance of David as king.

5:4-5 ***Hebron:*** See note on 2:1.

5:6-10 ***David*** acquired a new capital city, ***Jerusalem,*** for the newly extended kingdom.

5:6 ***The Jebusites*** resided in Jerusalem prior to its conquest by David (see Exod 34:11; Deut 7:1-6; 20:17; Josh 15:63; Judg 1:21). Nothing is known of them outside the Bible. In archaeological discoveries from Mari in Syria, a similar name (*Yabasi*) appears as both a clan name and a geographic location. • ***Even the blind and lame:*** The Jebusites had a false notion of invincibility. Another possible translation is *you won't enter here unless you can get rid of the blind and lame,* implying that David's capture of Jerusalem was as likely as achieving a miraculous cure for blindness and lameness.

5:7 ***the fortress of Zion:*** At this time Jerusalem was probably a small site of nine to twelve square acres. The Jebusites' arrogance, and the fact that the city had not been conquered previously, suggests that it was well fortified.

5:8 ***I hate those 'lame' and 'blind' Jebusites:*** Or *Those 'lame' and 'blind' Jebusites hate me.* • ***through the water tunnel*** (or *with scaling hooks;* the meaning of the Hebrew is uncertain): How David conquered Jerusalem is debated. Possibly he used a water tunnel as a conduit for his troops to enter the city, but not all interpreters agree. Another possibility is that David and his men conquered Jerusalem with the more traditional siege works and by scaling the walls. The term translated *water tunnel* occurs only here and in Ps 42:7 ("raging seas"); the statement might be metaphorical, referring to the ferocity of the attack. • ***The blind and the lame may not enter the house:*** The meaning of this saying is uncertain. *House* could refer either to the Temple, which had not yet been built, or to David's palace. The proverb may explain why Mephibosheth, Saul's descendant, was barred from the throne (see note on 4:4). • David also promised that those who undertook the siege of Jerusalem would become the commanders of his army (see 1 Chr 11:6).

5:9 ***made the fortress his home:*** Jerusalem was a practical place from which David could effectively administer the extended kingdom. It was a centrally located neutral city on the border between Judah and the northern territories, and its natural fortifications and water tunnel were useful in case of siege. • ***the supporting terraces:*** Hebrew *the millo.* The meaning of the Hebrew is uncertain; see note on 1 Kgs 9:15.

the LORD God of Heaven's Armies was with
him.

The LORD Blesses David in Jerusalem
2 Sam 5:11-16 // 1 Chr 14:1-7

11Then King Hiram of Tyre sent messengers to David, along with cedar timber and
carpenters and stonemasons, and they built
David a palace. 12And David realized that
the LORD had confirmed him as king over
Israel and had blessed his kingdom for the
sake of his people Israel.

13After moving from Hebron to Jerusalem, David married more concubines and
wives, and they had more sons and daughters. 14These are the names of David's sons
who were born in Jerusalem: Shammua,
Shobab, Nathan, Solomon, 15Ibhar, Elishua,
Nepheg, Japhia, 16Elishama, Eliada, and
Eliphelet.

David Conquers the Philistines
2 Sam 5:17-25 // 1 Chr 14:8-17

17When the Philistines heard that David
had been anointed king of Israel, they mobilized all their forces to capture him. But
David was told they were coming, so he
went into the stronghold. 18The Philistines
arrived and spread out across the valley
of Rephaim. 19So David asked the LORD,
"Should I go out to fight the Philistines? Will
you hand them over to me?"

The LORD replied to David, "Yes, go ahead.
I will certainly hand them over to you."

20So David went to Baal-perazim and defeated the Philistines there. "The LORD did
it!" David exclaimed. "He burst through my
enemies like a raging flood!" So he named
that place Baal-perazim (which means "the
Lord who bursts through"). 21The Philistines had abandoned their idols there, so
David and his men confiscated them.

22But after a while the Philistines returned and again spread out across the
valley of Rephaim. 23And again David asked
the LORD what to do. "Do not attack them
straight on," the LORD replied. "Instead, circle around behind and attack them near the
poplar trees. 24When you hear a sound like
marching feet in the tops of the poplar trees,
be on the alert! That will be the signal that
the LORD is moving ahead of you to strike
down the Philistine army." 25So David did
what the LORD commanded, and he struck
down the Philistines all the way from Gibeon to Gezer.

The Death of Uzzah
2 Sam 6:1-11 // 1 Chr 13:1-14

6 Then David again gathered all the elite
troops in Israel, 30,000 in all. 2He led
them to Baalah of Judah to bring back the

5:10 2 Sam 3:1
5:11-16 //1 Chr 3:5-9; 14:1-7
5:11 1 Kgs 5:10, 18; 1 Chr 14:1
5:12 Num 24:7
5:13 Deut 17:17; 1 Chr 3:9
5:14 1 Chr 3:5
5:17-25 //1 Chr 14:8-17
5:18 Josh 15:8; 18:16
5:19 1 Sam 23:2
5:20 1 Chr 14:11
5:24 Judg 4:14
5:25 Josh 12:12; 21:20-22
6:1-11 //1 Chr 13:1-14
6:2 Lev 24:16

5:10 ***the LORD . . . was with him:*** While David was a skilled and charismatic leader, his growing success was ultimately due to God's blessing.

5:11 ***Hiram of Tyre:*** Although the meeting of these two neighboring kings is reported just after Jerusalem's conquest, it probably happened much later. Hiram remained on the throne in Tyre at least until Solomon's twenty-fourth year, and one ancient source notes that he had a reign of thirty-four years. Another tradition implies that Hiram became king of Tyre just eight years before Solomon became king of Israel. The same king performed a similar act for Solomon (1 Kgs 5:1-18). The report of Hiram's support is perhaps given here because it ties in with the theme of David's confirmation and establishment as Israel's king (5:12).

5:12 ***David realized*** that his reign ***as king over Israel*** was ***for the sake of*** God's ***people Israel,*** not just for his personal benefit or enrichment.

5:13-16 The expansion of David's family reflected his growing success and power as Israel's king. ***Solomon*** was David's most important Jerusalem-born son (see 12:24-25).

5:17-25 For the first time as king, ***David*** engaged ***the Philistines*** in battle. • David's life has been portrayed thus far in 2 Samuel with a repeated pattern: He was crowned king in Hebron (2:4), won a battle (2:12-17), became stronger (3:1), and started a large family (3:2-5). Now he was crowned in Jerusalem (5:3), became stronger (5:10), expanded his family (5:13-14), and won a battle (5:17-25). This parallel structure draws attention to both of David's coronations with signs of divine blessing and prosperity.

5:18 ***The valley of Rephaim*** is located between Bethlehem and Jerusalem (cp. 23:13-14).

5:20 ***Baal-perazim:*** David used the term *Baal* to honor the Lord for the victory he gave Israel. The title means "the lord of earthquakes/openings," and was evidently an acceptable title for Yahweh until the Canaanite worship of Baal became an overwhelming problem in Israel. Every time David engaged in combat with the Philistines in 2 Samuel (5:17-25; 8:1; 21:15-22; 23:13-17), he won without losing a single soldier. How different from Saul, for whom victory over the Philistines was impossible!

5:21 ***David . . . confiscated them:*** David's confiscation of the Philistines' ***idols*** was payback for their capture of the Ark during Eli's time (1 Sam 4:1b-11). David burned the idols rather than carrying them off as trophies (1 Chr 14:12).

5:23 David again ***asked the LORD*** (5:19), but this time God gave a much more detailed answer. Unlike the frontal assault of 5:20, God instructed David to ***circle around behind*** the enemy. • ***poplar:*** Or *aspen,* or *balsam;* also in 5:24. The exact identification of this tree is uncertain.

5:25 ***Gibeon:*** As in Greek version (see also 1 Chr 14:16); Hebrew reads *Geba.* David cleared the Philistines from the central hill country of Israel between *Gibeon* in the east (in Benjamin, north of Jerusalem) ***to Gezer*** in the west.

6:1-23 Except for the brief reference in 1 Sam 14:18 (see note), ***the Ark*** of the Covenant has not been mentioned since 1 Sam 7:1-2, when the Philistines returned the captured Ark to Beth-shemesh and then to Kiriath-jearim, where it was placed in Abinadab's home. The Ark's virtual absence during Saul's forty-year reign highlights that Saul, in his spiritual insensitivity, did not seek the Lord (see 1 Chr 10:13-14; 13:3). David brought the Ark into Jerusalem, effectively acknowledging and enthroning (see 6:2) Yahweh as the true king over Israel in the new capital.

6:2 ***Baalah of Judah*** is another name for Kiriath-jearim; cp. 1 Chr 13:6; see also Josh 15:9. • ***the Ark of God, which bears the name of the LORD of Heaven's***

6:3
Num 7:4-9
1 Sam 6:7
6:5
1 Chr 13:7-8; 16:5
6:6
Num 4:15
ʿaron (0727)
‣1 Kgs 8:1
6:7
1 Sam 6:19
6:10
1 Chr 26:4-5
6:12-19
1 Chr 15:25–16:3
6:12
1 Kgs 8:1
6:13
1 Kgs 8:5
6:14
Exod 15:20
1 Sam 2:18, 28

Ark of God, which bears the name of the LORD of Heaven's Armies, who is enthroned between the cherubim. 3They placed the Ark of God on a new cart and brought it from Abinadab's house, which was on a hill. Uzzah and Ahio, Abinadab's sons, were guiding the cart as it left the house, 4carrying the Ark of God. Ahio walked in front of the Ark. 5David and all the people of Israel were celebrating before the LORD, singing songs and playing all kinds of musical instruments—lyres, harps, tambourines, castanets, and cymbals.

6But when they arrived at the threshing floor of Nacon, the oxen stumbled, and Uzzah reached out his hand and steadied the [c]Ark of God. 7Then the LORD's anger was aroused against Uzzah, and God struck him dead because of this. So Uzzah died right there beside the Ark of God.

8David was angry because the LORD's anger had burst out against Uzzah. He named that place Perez-uzzah (which means "to burst out against Uzzah"), as it is still called today.

9David was now afraid of the LORD, and he asked, "How can I ever bring the Ark of the LORD back into my care?" 10So David decided not to move the Ark of the LORD into the City of David. Instead, he took it to the house of Obed-edom of Gath. 11The Ark of the LORD remained there in Obed-edom's house for three months, and the LORD blessed Obed-edom and his entire household.

Moving the Ark to Jerusalem
2 Sam 6:12-19 // 1 Chr 15:25–16:6

12Then King David was told, "The LORD has blessed Obed-edom's household and everything he has because of the Ark of God." So David went there and brought the Ark of God from the house of Obed-edom to the City of David with a great celebration. 13After the men who were carrying the Ark of the LORD had gone six steps, David sacrificed a bull and a fattened calf. 14And David danced before the LORD with all his might, wearing a priestly garment. 15So David and all the people of Israel brought up the Ark of the LORD with shouts of joy and the blowing of rams' horns.

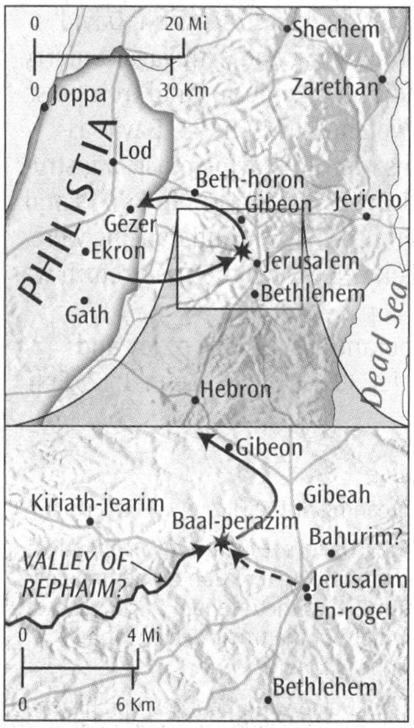

◂ **David's Defeat of the Philistines** (5:17-25). The first two battles between King David and the Philistines are shown. In the first, David engaged and defeated the Philistines at BAAL-PERAZIM (bottom inset). When the Philistines remustered their troops, David again came out from JERUSALEM, this time defeating them from GIBEON in Judah to GEZER in Philistine territory (5:25).

Armies: Or *the Ark of God where the Name is proclaimed—the name of the LORD of Heaven's Armies.* • ***is enthroned between the cherubim:*** See also 1 Sam 4:4; 2 Kgs 19:15; Ps 80:1; 99:1.

6:3-4 According to God's instructions (Exod 25:14; 37:5; Num 4:6), ***the Ark*** was to be carried by Levites of the clan of Kohath, holding two poles slipped through four rings at the corners of the Ark. God's instructions were ignored in this instance. • ***Uzzah and Ahio:*** In 1 Sam 7:1, Eleazar, another son of Abinadab, was put in charge of the Ark.

6:5 ***before the LORD, singing songs:*** As in Dead Sea Scrolls and Greek version (see also 1 Chr 13:8); Masoretic Text reads *before the LORD with all manner of cypress wood.* • The ***musical instruments*** were played by Levites (1 Chr 16:4-6).

6:6-7 ***steadied the Ark:*** Although Uzzah meant well and acted instinctively, he violated the Ark by touching it (cp. Exod 19:12-13; Num 4:15). He suffered the same penalty as the people from Beth-shemesh (1 Sam 6:19). David later had the Levites carry the Ark into Jerusalem in accordance with God's will (see 1 Chr 15:2, 13-15).

6:7 ***because of this:*** As in Dead Sea Scrolls; Masoretic Text reads *because of his irreverence.*

6:8 ***David was angry . . . the LORD's anger:*** Cp. Gen 4:5; 1 Sam 15:11; Jon 4:1; Luke 15:27-28. • ***Perez-uzzah:*** The first part of this name appears in 5:20 (*Baal-perazim*) as the place where God burst through the Philistine ranks.

6:9 ***David was . . . afraid:*** Similarly, Moses trembled at the display of divine wrath (Deut 9:19) and at the dramatic display of God's fiery presence (see Heb 12:21).

6:10 ***Obed-edom*** was a Levite (1 Chr 15:18, 21; 16:38; 26:4, 8, 15; 2 Chr 25:24) who lived either in the Philistine city of ***Gath*** or in an Israelite town of a similar name (e.g., Gath-rimmon, a city given to the Levites, Josh 21:25).

6:11 God ***blessed Obed-edom*** with health, prosperity, and family. God's presence, which is a curse to the ungodly (1 Sam 5), is a blessing to his people. Obed-edom must have taken care to preserve the Ark's sanctity.

6:12 David reasoned that if God ***blessed*** Obed-edom simply for storing ***the Ark***, God would surely bless David for placing the Ark in a dwelling specifically built for it in the capital city.

6:13 David offered this sacrifice of praise to God immediately, just ***six steps*** into the journey.

6:14 ***a priestly garment*** (literally *a linen ephod*): The *ephod* (Hebrew *'epod*) is associated with an Akkadian word, *epattu*, meaning "a costly garment." Richly ornamented with gold, this garment was used for robing statues of gods. Because priests and (sometimes) kings were considered sacred persons, they traditionally used garments of this type (see 1 Sam 2:18, 28; 14:3; 22:18; 23:6, 9).

6:15 In 15:10, ***rams' horns*** announce the crowning of a new king; in 20:1, they proclaim rebellion. Here they celebrate placing the Ark in its own tent (see note on 6:17), which in effect installed Yahweh's throne in Jerusalem.

Michal's Contempt for David
16But as the Ark of the LORD entered the
City of David, Michal, the daughter of Saul,
looked down from her window. When she
saw King David leaping and dancing before
the LORD, she was filled with contempt for
him.
17They brought the Ark of the LORD and
set it in its place inside the special tent
David had prepared for it. And David sacrificed burnt offerings and peace offerings to
the LORD. 18When he had finished his sacrifices, David blessed the people in the name
of the LORD of Heaven's Armies. 19Then he
gave to every Israelite man and woman in
the crowd a loaf of bread, a cake of dates,
and a cake of raisins. Then all the people returned to their homes.
20When David returned home to bless
his own family, Michal, the daughter of
Saul, came out to meet him. She said in disgust, "How distinguished the king of Israel
looked today, shamelessly exposing himself
to the servant girls like any vulgar person
might do!"
21David retorted to Michal, "I was dancing before the LORD, who chose me above
your father and all his family! He appointed
me as the leader of Israel, the people of the
LORD, so I celebrate before the LORD. 22Yes,
and I am willing to look even more foolish
than this, even to be humiliated in my own
eyes! But those servant girls you mentioned
will indeed think I am distinguished!" 23So
Michal, the daughter of Saul, remained
childless throughout her entire life.

6:16
1 Sam 18:27

6:17
1 Kgs 8:62-65
1 Chr 15:1
2 Chr 1:4

6:21
1 Sam 13:14

Celebration (6:1-15)

Exod 5:1; 12:17; 15:20-21
1 Sam 18:6
2 Chr 7:6-10
Ezra 3:10-11
Ps 30:11; 69:30; 98:4-6; 107:32; 149:1-9; 150:1-6
Isa 30:29; 54:1
Jer 30:18-19; 31:4, 13
Lam 5:14-15
Zeph 3:17
Luke 15:22-25
1 Cor 5:8
Eph 5:18-20
Col 3:16
Rev 18:20

It took two attempts for David to bring the Ark of the Covenant to Jerusalem (6:1-11, 12-23). In the second attempt, there was a notable change in David's mode of celebrating. Three Hebrew terms for "danced/dancing" are found in the account of the second procession of the ark (see also 1 Chr 15:25-29): *karar* (6:14, 16), *pazaz* (NLT, "leaping," 6:16), and *raqad* (1 Chr 15:29, "skipping about"). All three words refer to vigorous physical expression beyond the meaning of the Hebrew term for "celebrate" (6:5). Thus, in the first procession, David celebrated; in the second procession he engaged in exultant dancing and extravagant merry-making with intensified musical expression through the addition of shouting and trumpets.

Musical instruments played a significant role in Temple worship. In 1 Chr 25, David assigned various groups to the ministry of music. Many Psalms refer to playing musical instruments in praise and worship of God (see Ps 33:2-3; 57:8; 81:2; 92:1-3; 98:4-6). In Ps 149 and 150, dance and music are combined as a praise offering. Similarly, music and dancing were heard in the father's house in the parable of the lost son (Luke 15:25), as the son's return was truly a joyful occasion.

All these instances demonstrate that God welcomes exuberant expressions of joy and delight from those who worship and praise him (Isa 30:29; Jer 30:19; 31:13; Zeph 3:17; Eph 5:19; Col 3:16).

6:16 ***Michal*** is identified as ***the daughter of Saul*** three times (6:16, 20, 23). The use of her father's name underscores the ambiguity of David's relationship to her. Was she more David's wife or Saul's daughter? Had David reunited with her (3:13) because he loved her or because she was politically useful to him?
• Michal might have been ***filled with contempt*** for any of the following reasons: (1) She thought David's behavior was too sexually suggestive in front of a young female audience; (2) she was jealous over the glory David was receiving while she sat at home, a neglected wife; (3) she resented David's indifference to her for many years, his taking of other wives, and her being torn away from her second husband Palti (3:16-17); or (4) she felt sorrow for her late father and David's success at the expense of Saul's dynasty (see note on 6:21).

6:17 While ***the special tent*** for the Ark was not as opulent as the tent used during the wilderness wandering, this tent was a return to the wilderness tradition suspended two generations earlier at the destruction of Shiloh (Ps 78:60-61). David's special tent was the very last Tabernacle; Solomon, David's successor, built a permanent Temple for the Lord. Because this occasion was joyous, not penitential, the sacrifice included ***burnt offerings and peace offerings*** but not sin or guilt offerings (see "Israel's Sacrifices," Lev 1:1–7:38, p. 197).

6:18 ***blessed the people:*** Although blessing was typically the express function of priests, kings also offered blessings at significant national occasions (Solomon, 1 Kgs 8:14, 55; 2 Chr 6:3; Hezekiah, 2 Chr 31:8).

6:19 David's gifts of food to ***every Israelite*** anticipated other royal gifts they would receive under his reign. • ***a cake of dates:*** Or *a portion of meat.* The meaning of the Hebrew is uncertain.

6:21 David's response ***to Michal*** might hint at the real reason for her indignation—that she resented David's success in light of the tragic decline of her father's family.

6:22 David would not restrain his enthusiasm in celebrating before the Lord. In fact, he would exceed the enthusiasm he had shown thus far.

6:23 ***Michal*** was the only one of David's many wives who did not bear him at least one child. Either God was punishing her (cp. Gen 20:17-18) for her disdainful attitude toward David's exuberant praise, or David and Michal's relationship had become so strained that they never again shared the marriage bed. Because Michal ***remained childless,*** yet another aspect of Saul's dynasty was cut off. This occasion is Michal's last appearance in the text.

7:1-17
//1 Chr 17:1-15

7:2
2 Sam 5:11
1 Kgs 1:22
1 Chr 29:29

7:5
1 Kgs 5:3, 5; 8:17-19

7:6
Exod 40:18, 34
1 Kgs 8:16
[d]*mishkan* (4908)
‣1 Chr 21:29

7:7
Lev 26:11-12

The Lord's Covenant Promise to David
2 Sam 7:1-17 // 1 Chr 17:1-15

7When King David was settled in his
palace and the LORD had given him rest
from all the surrounding enemies, 2the king
summoned Nathan the prophet. "Look," David said, "I am living in a beautiful cedar
palace, but the Ark of God is out there in a
tent!"
3Nathan replied to the king, "Go ahead
and do whatever you have in mind, for the
LORD is with you."
4But that same night the LORD said to Nathan,
5"Go and tell my servant David, 'This is
what the LORD has declared: Are you the
one to build a house for me to live in?
6I have never lived in a house, from the
day I brought the Israelites out of Egypt
until this very day. I have always moved
from one place to another with a tent
and a [d]Tabernacle as my dwelling. 7Yet
no matter where I have gone with the
Israelites, I have never once complained
to Israel's tribal leaders, the shepherds
of my people Israel. I have never asked
them, "Why haven't you built me a
beautiful cedar house?"'

God's Covenant with David (7:5-16)

1 Kgs 8:20-24; 11:9-13; 15:1-5
2 Kgs 8:18-19
2 Chr 7:17-22
Ps 89:3-4, 18-51; 132:10-12
Isa 9:6-7; 11:1-10
Jer 33:20-26
Matt 1:1; 20:30-31; 21:1-9
Luke 1:30-33, 67-79
Acts 2:22-36
Rev 22:16

God made covenants with his people five times in the OT: (1) when he promised Noah that humanity would never again be destroyed by a flood (Gen 6:18; 9:1-17); (2) when he promised Abraham that he would inherit the land of Canaan and establish a great nation (Gen 15:1-21; 17:1-27); (3) when he formed a unique relationship with Israel at Mount Sinai through Moses (Exod 19–23); (4) when he promised a priestly dynasty to Phinehas (Num 25:10-13); and (5) when he promised a royal dynasty to David. In addition, God promised through Jeremiah to make a "new covenant" in the future (Jer 31:31-34).

God's promise to David is not explicitly identified as a covenant in 2 Sam 7. However, other passages do identify the event as a covenant (see 23:5; 2 Chr 7:18; 21:7; Ps 89:3-4, 28-29; 132:11-12; Isa 55:3; Jer 33:20-21). God's promise to David, that his "favor will not be taken from him" (7:15), speaks of a covenant relationship. Like God's promise to Abraham, his covenant with David is unconditional: It does not depend on human obedience or faithfulness but only on God's unchanging love.

At the heart of this covenant is God's promise to raise up David's successors forever and to be a father to them (cp. 1 Kgs 11:36; 15:4; 2 Kgs 8:19). God's blessing on Solomon's reign is a partial fulfillment of this promise (cp. 7:10-11 with 1 Kgs 8:56; see also 1 Kgs 8:20, 24). God's patience with the kings of Judah even when they turned away from him was the result of his covenant promise to David (see 1 Kgs 11:12-13; 15:3-5).

The complete and final fulfillment of God's covenant with David is found in the Messiah, Jesus Christ, the "son of David" (e.g., see Matt 9:27; 20:30-31; 21:9, 15). Isaiah foretold one who will rule "from the throne of his ancestor David for all eternity" (Isa 9:7) and called him the "shoot" growing "out of the stump of David's family" (Isa 11:1). Both of these references point to the coming Messiah. Four passages in the NT teach that Jesus is the ultimate fulfillment of the promises made to David by referring directly to 2 Sam 7 (Luke 1:32-33; Acts 2:29-31; 13:22-23; Heb 1:5). The NT opens (Matt 1:1) and closes (Rev 22:16) with reference to Jesus as the son of David, the successor to his throne.

7:1-29 *David* was not satisfied merely building *a tent* for the Ark (6:17). He wanted *to build a house* for God.

7:1-2 If God had only a tent while David had a palace, it might create the impression that David was the real king rather than God. Thus, David intended to build a temple for God.

7:1 ***from all . . . enemies:*** See Deut 12:9-10; 1 Kgs 5:4; 8:56. David's *rest* was temporary because shortly he was at war again (see ch 8).

7:2 ***Nathan*** is recorded in David's life on three occasions: (1) here with a promise for David; (2) in 12:1-15 with a parable of judgment against David; (3) in 1 Kgs 1:11-27 with a plan for installing Solomon as David's successor. • A *cedar palace* (literally *a house of cedar*) would have been made of stone with cedar paneling inside.

7:3 ***Go ahead and do whatever you have in mind:*** Nathan's counsel to David was Nathan's own idea. As it turned out, God disqualified David from building the Temple (see 1 Chr 22:8). Even true prophets are fallible when speaking on their own initiative rather than from God's revelation.

7:5 ***Are you the one?*** God wanted someone to build him a house, but David wasn't the right person.

7:6 ***never lived in a house:*** Prior to the building of the Temple in one fixed location, God's dwelling was the Tabernacle, a mobile, tentlike structure. The text here uses language of human experience to describe a truth about God (see notes on Exod 29:18; Deut 8:2). Although God is omnipresent, he chose the Tabernacle and Temple as his "dwelling place" in the OT (see note on 2 Chr 2:5-6; cp. Acts 17:24).

7:7 ***I have never once complained . . . never asked:*** While it was a less impressive structure than the Temple, the Tabernacle honored God because he had ordained its use for that period of Israel's history.

8“Now go and say to my servant David,
‘This is what the LORD of Heaven’s
Armies has declared: I took you from
tending sheep in the pasture and
selected you to be the leader of my
people Israel. 9I have been with you
wherever you have gone, and I have
destroyed all your enemies before your
eyes. Now I will make your name as
famous as anyone who has ever lived
on the earth! 10And I will provide a
homeland for my people Israel, planting
them in a secure place where they will
never be disturbed. Evil nations won’t
oppress them as they’ve done in the past,
11starting from the time I appointed
judges to rule my people Israel. And I
will give you rest from all your enemies.
“ ‘Furthermore, the LORD declares that
he will make a house for you—a dynasty
of kings! 12For when you die and are
buried with your ancestors, I will raise
up one of your [e]descendants, your own
offspring, and I will make his kingdom
strong. 13He is the one who will build a
house—a temple—for my name. And I will
secure his royal [f]throne [g]forever. 14I will
be his father, and he will be my son. If he
sins, I will correct and discipline him with
the rod, like any father would do. 15But my
favor will not be taken from him as I took
it from Saul, whom I removed from your
sight. 16Your house and your kingdom
will continue before me for all time, and
your throne will be secure forever.’ ”
17So Nathan went back to David and told him
everything the LORD had said in this vision.

David’s Prayer of Thanks

2 Sam 7:18-29 // 1 Chr 17:16-27

18Then King David went in and sat before
the LORD and prayed,

“Who am I, O [h]Sovereign LORD, and what
is my family, that you have brought me
this far? 19And now, Sovereign LORD, in
addition to everything else, you speak
of giving your servant a lasting dynasty!
Do you deal with everyone this way,
O Sovereign LORD?
20“What more can I say to you? You
know what your servant is really like,
Sovereign LORD. 21Because of your
promise and according to your will, you
have done all these great things and have
made them known to your servant.
22“How great you are, O Sovereign
LORD! There is no one like you. We have

7:8 1 Sam 16:10-11; Ps 78:70-71; *2 Cor 6:18
7:9 Ps 18:37-42
7:10 Ps 89:22; Isa 60:18
7:11 1 Sam 12:9-11; 25:28
7:12 1 Kgs 2:1; *Acts 2:30; [e]*zera‘* (2233) ‣Ps 89:4
7:13 1 Kgs 6:11-12; 8:19; Isa 9:7; [f]*kisse‘* (3678) ‣1 Kgs 10:18; [g]*‘olam* (5769) ‣Ps 10:16
7:14 Ps 89:26-27; Heb 1:5-6
7:15 1 Sam 15:23; 16:14; Ps 89:33
7:16 1 Sam 25:28; Ps 89:36-37
7:18-29 //1 Chr 17:16-27
7:18 Exod 3:11; 1 Sam 18:18; [h]*’adonay Yahweh* (0136, 3068) ‣Ps 73:28

7:8-17 Instead of David’s building God a house, God promised to build David a ***house***, a permanent ***dynasty of kings*** from David’s descendants.

7:8 ***tending sheep:*** Kings in the ancient Near East were often called shepherds (see 1 Kgs 22:17; Isa 44:28; Ezek 34:2; 37:24; Nah 3:18; Zech 10:3). David, who had been a shepherd, called the Lord his shepherd (Ps 23:1).

7:9 ***I have been with you:*** Through his guidance and protection, God was actively involved in shaping David’s entire life. • ***I will make your name . . . famous:*** God made this promise only to Abraham and David. (see Gen 12:2).

7:10-11a ***never be disturbed:*** Through David and his heirs, a lasting peace would engulf the land, in contrast with the intermittent and temporary periods of peace during the days of the ***judges***, when one predatory nation after another shattered Israel’s well-being. God’s promise of ***rest from all your enemies*** was first mentioned by Joshua (Josh 1:13, 15; 22:4), and later realized in the ministry of some of the judges (Judg 3:11, 30; 5:31; 8:28).

7:11b ***he will make a house for you:*** God wanted to do infinitely more for David than David could conceive of doing for God. While David was primarily interested in projects such as building a temple, God was interested in bringing blessing to his people through one righteous ***dynasty of kings.***

7:12-13 ***one of your descendants . . . will build a house . . . for my name:*** David’s son Solomon would build the Temple; David’s personal involvement in military conflict and bloodshed disqualified him from building God’s Temple (1 Chr 22:8-9).

7:14 ***I will be his father, and he will be my son:*** Kings in David’s line would enjoy a special covenant relationship with God, as the whole nation of Israel did (cp. Exod 6:7; Lev 26:12). Jesus later became the ultimate fulfillment of this prophecy (see Heb 1:5). Paul quotes this phrase in 2 Cor 6:18 and applies it to all believers. • ***If he sins, I will correct and discipline him:*** God would steer David’s offspring, the future kings of Israel, back onto the right track whenever they sinned. Cp. the experience of Jesus, who never sinned, yet endured God’s discipline (see Heb 4:15; 5:8; 12:1-11).

7:16 ***for all time . . . forever:*** God’s promises do not negate human responsibility and accountability (7:14). Wrongdoing requires a just response from God. However, no wayward son of David could move God to withdraw his promise to preserve David’s dynasty. Although the dynasty disappeared for hundreds of years, David’s ***house*** and ***kingdom*** were renewed in Jesus Christ, the sinless descendant of David who reigns forever. • ***before me:*** As in Greek version and some Hebrew manuscripts; Masoretic Text reads *before you.*

7:18-29 ***David*** responded prayerfully to God’s promise of a dynasty, repeatedly acknowledging God’s true kingship as ***Sovereign LORD.***

7:18 David’s question, ***“Who am I?”*** was an expression of genuine humility (cp. Exod 4:11).

7:19 God’s plan to give David ***a lasting dynasty*** stretched well beyond his lifetime. The promise is fulfilled forever in the eternal reign of Christ (Rev 11:15). • ***Do you deal with everyone this way, O Sovereign LORD?*** Or *This is your instruction for all humanity, O Sovereign LORD.*

7:20 ***You know what your servant is really like:*** God made his promises to David with full knowledge that David had both strengths and weaknesses.

7:21 God’s ***will,*** rather than David’s personal ambition, enabled David to accomplish ***great things.*** • ***you have done:*** David spoke of what God promised to do for his heirs over the generations as an already-accomplished fact, showing his unshakable belief in God’s faithfulness.

7:22 ***There is no one like you:*** David affirms God’s uniqueness (see also 22:32; Deut 4:39; 1 Sam 2:2).

7:19
1 Chr 17:17
Isa 55:8-9
7:20
1 Sam 16:7
John 21:17
7:22
Exod 10:2
Deut 3:24
1 Sam 2:2
Ps 44:1
7:23
Deut 4:32; 9:26; 10:21
7:24
Gen 17:7-8
Exod 6:7
Deut 32:6
Ps 48:14
7:28
Exod 34:5-6
John 17:17
7:29
Num 6:23-27
8:1-14
//1 Chr 18:1-13
8:2
2 Kgs 3:4; 17:3
8:3
1 Sam 14:47
2 Sam 10:16, 19
8:4
Josh 11:6, 9
8:5
1 Kgs 11:23-25
8:6
2 Sam 3:18
8:7
1 Kgs 10:16

never even heard of another God like you!
23What other nation on earth is like your
people Israel? What other nation, O God,
have you redeemed from slavery to be your
own people? You made a great name for
yourself when you redeemed your people
from Egypt. You performed awesome
miracles and drove out the nations and
gods that stood in their way. 24You made
Israel your very own people forever, and
you, O LORD, became their God.
25"And now, O LORD God, I am your
servant; do as you have promised
concerning me and my family. Confirm it
as a promise that will last forever. 26And
may your name be honored forever so
that everyone will say, 'The LORD of
Heaven's Armies is God over Israel!' And
may the house of your servant David
continue before you forever.
27"O LORD of Heaven's Armies, God
of Israel, I have been bold enough to
pray this prayer to you because you have
revealed all this to your servant, saying,
'I will build a house for you—a dynasty
of kings!' 28For you are God, O Sovereign
LORD. Your words are truth, and you
have promised these good things to your
servant. 29And now, may it please you to
bless the house of your servant, so that
it may continue forever before you. For
you have spoken, and when you grant
a blessing to your servant, O Sovereign
LORD, it is an eternal blessing!"

Expansion of the Kingdom
2 Sam 8:1-18 // 1 Chr 18:1-17

8 After this, David defeated and subdued
the Philistines by conquering Gath,
their largest town. 2David also conquered
the land of Moab. He made the people lie
down on the ground in a row, and he measured them off in groups with a length of
rope. He measured off two groups to be executed for every one group to be spared. The
Moabites who were spared became David's
subjects and paid him tribute money.
3David also destroyed the forces of Hadadezer son of Rehob, king of Zobah, when
Hadadezer marched out to strengthen his
control along the Euphrates River. 4David
captured 1,000 chariots, 7,000 charioteers, and 20,000 foot soldiers. He crippled
all the chariot horses except enough for
100 chariots.
5When Arameans from Damascus arrived
to help King Hadadezer, David killed 22,000
of them. 6Then he placed several army garrisons in Damascus, the Aramean capital, and
the Arameans became David's subjects and
paid him tribute money. So the LORD made
David victorious wherever he went.
7David brought the gold shields of Hadadezer's officers to Jerusalem, 8along with

7:23 *You made . . . in their way:* As in Greek version (see also 1 Chr 17:21); Hebrew reads *You made a great name for yourself and performed awesome miracles for your land. You did this in the sight of your people, whom you redeemed from Egypt, from nations and their gods.* Israel was set apart from every ***other nation*** by the uniqueness of its God and by the relationship the people had with him.

7:24 David praised God for his goodness in redeeming and establishing the nation of ***Israel*** (7:23-24), not just David and his royal line (7:18-21). His prayer is corporate rather than just personal.

7:25 *Confirm it:* David was not asking God for a sign (as Gideon had done, Judg 6:17). Rather, David was saying, "God, may it be so."

7:26 Although God had promised to make David's name great (7:9), David was concerned that God's ***name be honored.*** David knew that if God were not the focus of the people's praise, then David's dynasty would count for nothing.

8:1-18 The expansion of David's empire through military victories (8:1-14) and the establishment of his royal bureaucracy (8:15-18) fulfilled God's promise of a famous name (7:9; cp. 8:13).

8:1 ***by conquering Gath, their largest town:*** Literally *by conquering Metheg-ammah,* a name that means "the bridle," possibly referring to the size of the town or the tribute money taken from it. Cp. 1 Chr 18:1.

8:2 ***Moab*** was on the east side of the Dead Sea. Earlier, the people of Moab had provided David's parents with refuge during Saul's reign (1 Sam 22:3-4); David's great-grandmother, Ruth, was from Moab. For whatever reason, no such fraternal relationship existed any longer. • ***two groups to be executed for every one group to be spared:*** This is the only time in 2 Samuel that David executed captives taken in battle (see Num 21:29; 24:17; Deut 2:9).

8:3 ***Hadadezer*** reappears in 10:16 as David's foe. He was either the direct ***son of Rehob*** and his successor or the reigning king of a dynasty established by a king named Rehob, whose kingdom was near the northern city of Dan (see Judg 18:28; cp. Num 13:21). • ***Zobah*** was north and east of David's kingdom. • It is possible that David, not Hadadezer (literally *he*), ***marched out to strengthen his control.*** • ***the Euphrates River:*** Literally *the river;* 1 Chr 18:3 specifically identifies the Euphrates. Cp. 10:16.

8:4 ***1,000 chariots, 7,000 charioteers:*** As in Dead Sea Scrolls and Greek version (see also 1 Chr 18:4); Masoretic Text reads *captured 1,700 charioteers.* • David would have ***crippled . . . horses*** to prevent their reuse by the enemy and because kings in Israel were not to accumulate horses (Deut 17:16).

8:5 Hadadezer's neighbors, ***Arameans from Damascus,*** were of no help to him in repelling David. They would later be more successful against Solomon (1 Kgs 11:23-25) but less successful in their attack of Samaria during the days of King Ahab of Israel (1 Kgs 20).

8:6 David established ***army garrisons*** in Aram but not in Moab (8:2), which suggests that Aram was a more formidable force and that David needed a military presence there to maintain control. • ***the LORD made David victorious:*** Cp. 8:14. God was the real source of David's growth and power.

8:7 ***gold shields:*** See also 2 Kgs 11:10. • ***brought . . . to Jerusalem:*** In conformity with God's stipulations for a good king (Deut 17:17), David dedicated these valuable items to God (see 8:11)

a large amount of bronze from Hadadezer's
towns of Tebah and Berothai.
9When King Toi of Hamath heard that
David had destroyed the entire army of
Hadadezer, 10he sent his son Joram to congratulate King David for his successful
campaign. Hadadezer and Toi had been
enemies and were often at war. Joram presented David with many gifts of silver, gold,
and bronze.
11King David dedicated all these gifts to
the LORD, as he did with the silver and gold
from the other nations he had defeated—
12from Edom, Moab, Ammon, Philistia, and
Amalek—and from Hadadezer son of Rehob, king of Zobah.
13So David became even more famous
when he returned from destroying 18,000
Edomites in the Valley of Salt. 14He placed
army garrisons throughout Edom, and all
the Edomites became David's subjects. In
fact, the LORD made David victorious wherever he went.
15So David reigned over all Israel and
did what was just and right for all his people. 16Joab son of Zeruiah was commander
of the army. Jehoshaphat son of Ahilud was
the royal historian. 17Zadok son of Ahitub
and Ahimelech son of Abiathar were the
priests. Seraiah was the court secretary.
18Benaiah son of Jehoiada was captain of
the king's bodyguard. And David's sons
served as priestly leaders.

David's Kindness to Mephibosheth

9 One day David asked, "Is anyone in
Saul's family still alive—anyone to
whom I can show kindness for Jonathan's
sake?" 2He summoned a man named Ziba,
who had been one of Saul's servants. "Are
you Ziba?" the king asked.
"Yes sir, I am," Ziba replied.
3The king then asked him, "Is anyone
still alive from Saul's family? If so, I want to
show God's kindness to them."
Ziba replied, "Yes, one of Jonathan's sons
is still alive. He is crippled in both feet."
4"Where is he?" the king asked.
"In Lo-debar," Ziba told him, "at the home
of Makir son of Ammiel."
5So David sent for him and brought
him from Makir's home. 6His name was

8:8 Ezek 47:16
8:11 1 Kgs 7:51
8:13 2 Kgs 14:7; 1 Chr 18:12
8:14 Gen 27:30, 37-40
8:15-18 //1 Chr 18:14-17
8:16 2 Sam 2:13
8:18 2 Sam 20:7, 23; 1 Kgs 1:38, 44; 1 Chr 18:17
9:1 1 Sam 20:14-17, 42; *khesed* (2617) ‣1 Kgs 3:6
9:2 2 Sam 16:1-4; 19:17
9:3 1 Sam 20:14-15; 2 Sam 4:4
9:4 2 Sam 17:27-29

rather than hoarding them for his own wealth and splendor.

8:8 ***Tebah:*** As in some Greek manuscripts (see also 1 Chr 18:8); Hebrew reads *Betah.*

8:9 ***Hamath*** was northwest of Hadadezer's Zobah.

8:10 ***his son:*** King Toi dispatched the crown prince rather than another entourage on this mission because he considered it vital to stay properly connected with David. • ***Joram:*** The prefix *Jo-* is an abbreviated form of Yahweh; *Joram* means "Yahweh is exalted." In 1 Chr 18:10 the prince's name is Hadoram, which means "Hadad [a Canaanite god] is exalted." It is possible that Toi changed the prince's name for diplomatic reasons, to make it more agreeable to David.

8:11-12 Captured war booty and diplomatic exchanges went into God's treasury rather than the king's treasury. Voluntary gifts (8:11a) and plunder exacted from defeated foes (8:11b-12) also were ***dedicated . . . to the LORD.***

8:12 ***Edom:*** As in a few Hebrew manuscripts and in Greek and Syriac versions (see also 8:14; 1 Chr 18:11); most Hebrew manuscripts read *Aram.*

8:13-14 These two verses highlight three of David's war policies: (1) inflict heavy damage on the enemy (***18,000*** casualties); (2) reduce them to vassalage (they ***became David's subjects***); (3) place ***army garrisons*** in the conquered territory to maintain control over them. • ***Edomites:*** As in a few Hebrew manuscripts and in Greek and Syriac versions (see also 8:14; 1 Chr 18:12; Ps 60:TITLE); most Hebrew manuscripts read *Arameans.* The two names are very similar in old Hebrew script. *Edomites* is more likely, however, because ***the Valley of Salt*** (the Dead Sea area) was adjacent to Edomite, not Aramean, territory.

8:15-18 David's bureaucracy included (1) military officials (***Joab***); (2) a court historian (***Jehoshaphat***); (3) priests (***Zadok*** and ***Ahimelech***); (4) a scribe or court secretary (***Seraiah***); and (5) a security officer (***Benaiah,*** who became a commander under Solomon; see also 1 Kgs 2:25-46).

8:18 ***the king's bodyguard:*** Hebrew *the Kerethites and Pelethites.* Both peoples were probably foreigners, especially the Kerethites, who might have come from the island of Crete (see also 1 Sam 30:14; Ezek 25:16). These groups might have been Philistine mercenaries. • ***David's sons served as priestly leaders:*** Literally *David's sons were priests;* cp. parallel text at 1 Chr 18:17. David was from Judah and was not a Levite. Alongside the traditional priesthood, David might have inaugurated a religious class specifically tied to his dynasty, probably to serve the royal court (see also note on 20:26).

9:1-13 David showed mercy to Mephibosheth, Jonathan's crippled son. The incident is sandwiched between David's victories in battle (chs 8, 10), indicating that David also had concern for individuals and a compassionate heart.

9:1 ***show kindness:*** The Hebrew word (*khesed*) speaks of covenant loyalty and faithfulness. The word frequently describes God's commitment to his people, but it can also describe the devotion and loyalty between any two persons. David's use of the word here echoes the language of the covenant of friendship between himself and Jonathan (1 Sam 20:12-17). • ***for Jonathan's sake:*** Mephibosheth was Saul's only remaining descendant and the only son of Jonathan.

9:3 Mephibosheth was ***crippled in both feet*** from a childhood accident (see 4:4).

9:4 ***Lo-debar*** was a small town in northern Transjordan (the area east of the Jordan), close to Mahanaim, the capital city of Mephibosheth's late uncle, Ish-bosheth. The town was also near Jabesh-gilead, where Saul first made a name for himself (1 Sam 11:1-13). • ***Makir son of Ammiel,*** Mephibosheth's host, later supported David during Absalom's revolt (17:27).

9:5 As Saul had once sent for David (1 Sam 16:19), now ***David sent for*** Mephibosheth. However, Saul sent for someone to minister to him, whereas David sent for someone to whom he could minister.

9:6 ***Mephibosheth*** is another name for Merib-baal (see note on 4:4). • Given

9:7
2 Sam 19:28
2 Kgs 25:29

9:9
2 Sam 16:4; 19:29

9:10
2 Sam 19:28

10:1-19
//1 Chr 19:1-19

10:4
Isa 15:2; 20:4
Jer 41:5

10:6
Gen 34:30
2 Kgs 7:6

Mephibosheth; he was Jonathan's son and Saul's grandson. When he came to David, he bowed low to the ground in deep respect. David said, "Greetings, Mephibosheth."

Mephibosheth replied, "I am your servant."

7"Don't be afraid!" David said. "I intend to show kindness to you because of my promise to your father, Jonathan. I will give you all the property that once belonged to your grandfather Saul, and you will eat here with me at the king's table!"

8Mephibosheth bowed respectfully and exclaimed, "Who is your servant, that you should show such kindness to a dead dog like me?"

9Then the king summoned Saul's servant Ziba and said, "I have given your master's grandson everything that belonged to Saul and his family. 10You and your sons and servants are to farm the land for him to produce food for your master's household. But Mephibosheth, your master's grandson, will eat here at my table." (Ziba had fifteen sons and twenty servants.)

11Ziba replied, "Yes, my lord the king; I am your servant, and I will do all that you have commanded." And from that time on, Mephibosheth ate regularly at David's table, like one of the king's own sons.

12Mephibosheth had a young son named Mica. From then on, all the members of Ziba's household were Mephibosheth's servants. 13And Mephibosheth, who was crippled in both feet, lived in Jerusalem and ate regularly at the king's table.

3. THE PEAK OF DAVID'S REIGN (10:1–20:26)

David Defeats the Ammonites (10:1-19)

2 Sam 10:1-19 // 1 Chr 19:1-19

10 Some time after this, King Nahash of the Ammonites died, and his son Hanun became king. 2David said, "I am going to show loyalty to Hanun just as his father, Nahash, was always loyal to me." So David sent ambassadors to express sympathy to Hanun about his father's death.

But when David's ambassadors arrived in the land of Ammon, 3the Ammonite commanders said to Hanun, their master, "Do you really think these men are coming here to honor your father? No! David has sent them to spy out the city so they can come in and conquer it!" 4So Hanun seized David's ambassadors and shaved off half of each man's beard, cut off their robes at the buttocks, and sent them back to David in shame.

5When David heard what had happened, he sent messengers to tell the men, "Stay at Jericho until your beards grow out, and then come back." For they felt deep shame because of their appearance.

6When the people of Ammon realized how seriously they had angered David, they sent and hired 20,000 Aramean foot soldiers from the lands of Beth-rehob and Zobah, 1,000 from the king of Maacah, and 12,000 from the land of Tob. 7When David heard about this, he sent Joab and all his warriors to fight them. 8The Ammonite troops came out and drew up their battle lines at the entrance of the city gate, while the Arameans from Zobah and Rehob and

---

Mephibosheth's physical limitations, bowing *low to the ground* must have been very difficult.

9:7 David had confiscated *all the property* that had *belonged to . . . Saul.*

9:8 *a dead dog like me:* Mephibosheth knew that anyone with a possible claim to the throne might be killed as a threat.

9:10 *your master's household:* As in Greek version; Hebrew reads *your master's grandson.*

9:11 Both Ziba and Mephibosheth (9:6) used the phrase *"I am your servant"* when presenting themselves before King David. By referring to himself as David's servant, Ziba showed that he was no longer loyal to Saul's dynasty. The sincerity of both later came into question (16:1-4; 19:17-30). • *David's table:* As in Greek version; Hebrew reads *my table.*

9:13 *crippled in both feet:* See 4:4.

10:1-19 Following the interlude of ch 9, the narrative returns to David's military feats. The Ammonites were likely the dominant political power in Transjordan (the area east of the Jordan) during Saul's reign and the early years of David's reign.

10:1-5 The king of Ammon insulted David's ambassadors, which led to two battles between Israel and Ammon (10:6–12:31).

10:1 *Some time after this:* King Hadadezer appears in ch 10 as David's active and capable foe (10:16), yet in ch 8 David had defeated him (8:3) and plundered his city (8:7, 12). Either Hadadezer was still alive, had regrouped, and revolted in ch 10; or possibly ch 10 unpacks the events of ch 8 as a prelude to ch 11. • *King Nahash:* As in parallel text at 1 Chr 19:1; Hebrew reads *the king.*

10:2 In both chs 9 and 10, David wanted to *show loyalty* (*khesed;* also in 9:1, 3).

10:4 Shaving *half of each man's beard* was intended to maximize the humiliation and ridicule. • *cut off their robes:* The humiliating display of genitalia or *the buttocks* was associated with military defeat and exile (Isa 20:1-6).

10:5 The city of *Jericho* had not yet been formally reconstructed (see 1 Kgs 16:34), but the site was located adjacent to the largest and most plentiful spring in the land, so people continued to dwell in the area. Anyone traveling from Ammon to Jerusalem would pass right by it. It was a place of seclusion from the men's humiliation.

10:6 *Aramean foot soldiers:* See 8:5-6. • *Beth-rehob and Zobah:* See 8:3, 12. • *the land of Tob* (literally *the man of Tob*) possibly refers to a vassal king and region under Hadadezer's sovereignty.

10:8 The Israelites had a double battle: against the Ammonites in front of their fortifications *at the entrance of the city gate* and against the Aramean army *in the open fields.*

the men from Tob and Maacah positioned
themselves to fight in the open fields.
[9]When Joab saw that he would have
to fight on both the front and the rear, he
chose some of Israel's elite troops and
placed them under his personal command
to fight the Arameans in the fields. [10]He left
the rest of the army under the command
of his brother Abishai, who was to attack
the Ammonites. [11]"If the Arameans are
too strong for me, then come over and help
me," Joab told his brother. "And if the Ammonites are too strong for you, I will come
and help you. [12]Be courageous! Let us fight
bravely for our people and the cities of our
God. May the LORD's will be done."
[13]When Joab and his troops attacked, the
Arameans began to run away. [14]And when
the Ammonites saw the Arameans running,
they ran from Abishai and retreated into
the city. After the battle was over, Joab returned to Jerusalem.
[15]The Arameans now realized that they
were no match for Israel. So when they regrouped, [16]they were joined by additional
Aramean troops summoned by Hadadezer
from the other side of the Euphrates River.
These troops arrived at Helam under the
command of Shobach, the commander of
Hadadezer's forces.
[17]When David heard what was happening, he mobilized all Israel, crossed the
Jordan River, and led the army to Helam.
The Arameans positioned themselves in
battle formation and fought against David.
[18]But again the Arameans fled from the
Israelites. This time David's forces killed
700 charioteers and 40,000 foot soldiers,
including Shobach, the commander of their
army. [19]When all the kings allied with Hadadezer saw that they had been defeated
by Israel, they surrendered to Israel and
became their subjects. After that, the Arameans were afraid to help the Ammonites.

David's Sin with Bathshebsa and Uriah (11:1–12:31)

David and Bathsheba
2 Sam 11:1 // 1 Chr 20:1

11 In the spring of the year, when kings
normally go out to war, David sent
Joab and the Israelite army to fight the Ammonites. They destroyed the Ammonite
army and laid siege to the city of Rabbah.
However, David stayed behind in Jerusalem.
[2]Late one afternoon, after his midday rest,
David got out of bed and was walking on the
roof of the palace. As he looked out over the
city, he noticed a woman of unusual beauty
taking a bath. [3]He sent someone to find out
who she was, and he was told, "She is Bathsheba, the daughter of Eliam and the wife of
Uriah the Hittite." [4]Then David sent messengers to get her; and when she came to the
palace, he slept with her. She had just completed the purification rites after having
her menstrual period. Then she returned
home. [5]Later, when Bathsheba discovered
that she was pregnant, she sent David a message, saying, "I'm pregnant."

10:12 Deut 31:6; 1 Sam 3:18; 1 Cor 16:13
10:13 1 Kgs 20:13-21
10:18 1 Chr 19:17-18
10:19 2 Sam 8:6
11:1 2 Sam 12:26-29; 1 Chr 20:1; Amos 1:14
11:2 Deut 22:8; Matt 5:27-28
11:3 2 Sam 23:39; 1 Chr 3:5
11:4 Lev 15:19; 18:20-28; Ps 51:TITLE
11:5 Lev 20:10; Deut 22:22

10:12 ***Be courageous!*** Often the priest or another leader offered prebattle exhortations (cp. Num 31:6; Deut 20:2; Judg 4:14; 1 Sam 4:4; 14:3; 23:9).

10:16 ***Hadadezer:*** See note on 10:1. • ***Helam*** is unknown. • Apparently David had extended his empire as far north as ***the Euphrates River*** (literally *the river*; see also note on 8:3).

10:18 ***foot soldiers:*** As in some Greek manuscripts (see also 1 Chr 19:18); Hebrew reads *charioteers.*

11:1-27 David's affair with Bathsheba and the murder of her husband Uriah show that David was capable of great failure and cast a dark shadow over David's life and career. These failures came during a time of great military success against the Ammonites (10:1–11:1; 12:26-31).

11:1 ***In the spring of the year:*** Literally *At the turn of the year.* The first day of the year in the ancient Hebrew lunar calendar occurred in March or April, when the land began to dry out after the heavy winter rains. ***Kings*** avoided ***war*** during the rainy season. • ***David stayed behind*** either because he was irresponsible in carrying out his royal duties or because he trusted Joab to efficiently handle the Ammonite problem (cp. 10:7). This is the first mention of a leader of Israel staying off the battlefield in a time of war.

11:2 ***walking on the roof:*** The roofs of houses were flat and were regularly used for a variety of purposes, such as drying and storing produce (Josh 2:6), strolling and socializing, and sleeping in warm weather. • Bathsheba was ***taking a bath*** in plain view of the roof of the king's palace, but perhaps she assumed everyone would be inside, seeking refuge from the heat or having a ***midday rest.***

11:3 ***Bathsheba*** means "daughter of seven" or "daughter of oath." Her father ***Eliam*** was the son of Ahithophel (see 23:34), an adviser sought by David and then by Absalom (15:12; 16:23). Much to David's chagrin (15:31), Ahithophel later shifted his allegiance from David to Absalom (17:1-4, 14) and advised Absalom to sleep with David's concubines on a rooftop, in open view (16:20-22). • ***Uriah*** is a Hebrew name (meaning "Yahweh [is] my light"); either he was a foreign mercenary, a convert to Israelite religion, or an Israelite of ***Hittite*** heritage. Uriah might also have been a member of the non-Israelite aristocracy in Jerusalem that predated David's conquest of the city. He was one of the Thirty—David's mightiest warriors (23:39).

11:4 It is not clear whether Bathsheba ***came to*** David's ***palace*** voluntarily. That no protestations are recorded (cp. 13:12-13) and that she married David, bore him another child, and persuaded him to designate their child as heir (1 Kgs 1:11-21) suggest that she might have been a willing partner. However, Bathsheba mourned for her husband (11:26-27), and only David was condemned for this act (11:27), so she might have been violated against her will. • The phrase ***after having her menstrual period*** (see Lev 15:19-24) is included to show that the child Bathsheba conceived could not possibly have been Uriah's.

11:11
2 Sam 7:2
11:14
1 Kgs 21:8-10
11:15
2 Sam 12:9
11:21
Judg 9:50-54
11:26
Gen 50:10
Deut 34:8
1 Sam 31:13
11:27
2 Sam 12:9
Ps 51:4-5

6Then David sent word to Joab: "Send me Uriah the Hittite." So Joab sent him to David. 7When Uriah arrived, David asked him how Joab and the army were getting along and how the war was progressing. 8Then he told Uriah, "Go on home and relax." David even sent a gift to Uriah after he had left the palace. 9But Uriah didn't go home. He slept that night at the palace entrance with the king's palace guard.

10When David heard that Uriah had not gone home, he summoned him and asked, "What's the matter? Why didn't you go home last night after being away for so long?"

11Uriah replied, "The Ark and the armies of Israel and Judah are living in tents, and Joab and my master's men are camping in the open fields. How could I go home to wine and dine and sleep with my wife? I swear that I would never do such a thing."

12"Well, stay here today," David told him, "and tomorrow you may return to the army." So Uriah stayed in Jerusalem that day and the next. 13Then David invited him to dinner and got him drunk. But even then he couldn't get Uriah to go home to his wife. Again he slept at the palace entrance with the king's palace guard.

David Arranges for Uriah's Death

14So the next morning David wrote a letter to Joab and gave it to Uriah to deliver. 15The letter instructed Joab, "Station Uriah on the front lines where the battle is fiercest. Then pull back so that he will be killed." 16So Joab assigned Uriah to a spot close to the city wall where he knew the enemy's strongest men were fighting. 17And when the enemy soldiers came out of the city to fight, Uriah the Hittite was killed along with several other Israelite soldiers.

18Then Joab sent a battle report to David. 19He told his messenger, "Report all the news of the battle to the king. 20But he might get angry and ask, 'Why did the troops go so close to the city? Didn't they know there would be shooting from the walls? 21Wasn't Abimelech son of Gideon killed at Thebez by a woman who threw a millstone down on him from the wall? Why would you get so close to the wall?' Then tell him, 'Uriah the Hittite was killed, too.' "

22So the messenger went to Jerusalem and gave a complete report to David. 23"The enemy came out against us in the open fields," he said. "And as we chased them back to the city gate, 24the archers on the wall shot arrows at us. Some of the king's men were killed, including Uriah the Hittite."

25"Well, tell Joab not to be discouraged," David said. "The sword devours this one today and that one tomorrow! Fight harder next time, and conquer the city!"

26When Uriah's wife heard that her husband was dead, she mourned for him. 27When the period of mourning was over, David sent for her and brought her to the

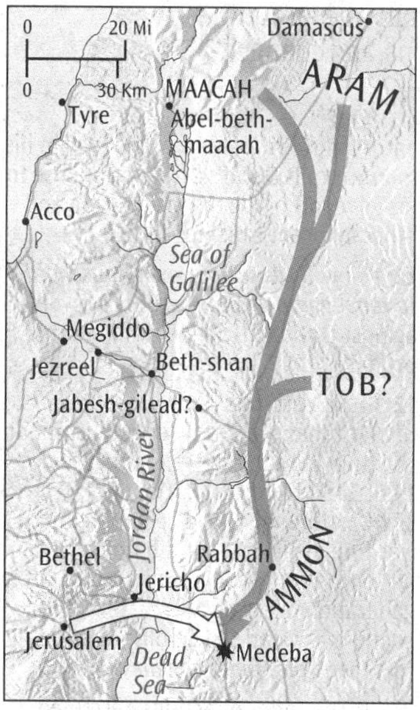

◀ **David's Defeat of the Ammonites (10:1-19).** When king Hanun of AMMON had humiliated David's ambassadors (10:1-5), Hanun hired mercenary soldiers (broad grey lines) to fight David's men (white line). David sent Joab in command of his army (10:7). The parallel passage (1 Chr 19:6-19) indicates that the Ammonites and Arameans were camped at MEDEBA (1 Chr 19:7), so the first battle likely took place nearby. Later battles took place at Helam (10:16) and at RABBAH, the capital of Ammon (12:26-31).

11:8 ***and relax:*** Literally *and wash your feet,* an expression that may also have a connotation of ritualistic washing. David assumed that Uriah would have sex with Bathsheba while on this weekend pass. Then everyone except Bathsheba would assume that the child was Uriah's, conceived on this night. • ***a gift:*** David might not have even cared whether the husband and wife were intimate. Uriah's return to his house would stifle any rumors as to how and when Bathsheba became pregnant.

11:11 ***in tents*** (or *at Succoth;* Hebrew, *sukkoth,* the name behind *Sukkot,* "the Festival of Shelters," Deut 16:13-17): These were temporary structures made of branches and foliage used by soldiers in the field, herdsmen protecting their cattle, or grape harvesters in the vineyard. • ***wine and dine and sleep with my wife?*** Uriah was willing to wine and dine with David (11:13), so it was not sharing the table with Bathsheba that Uriah wished to avoid but sharing the marriage bed. The Israelites considered the war camp a holy place because God was present to fight for his people. Thus, soldiers on duty avoided anything that caused impurity, such as sexual intercourse (Lev 15:18; see also 1 Sam 21:5-6).

11:16-17 ***Uriah*** was not the only casualty: David sacrificed ***several other Israelite soldiers*** while attempting to hide his sin.

11:21 ***Wasn't Abimelech . . . killed . . . by a woman:*** Cp. Judg 9:54. • ***son of Gideon:*** Literally *son of Jerub-besheth.* Jerub-besheth is a variation on the name Jerub-baal, which is another name for Gideon; see Judg 6:32; see also notes on 2:8; 4:4.

11:25 ***The sword devours this one today and that one tomorrow!*** David's callous attitude toward the unnecessary deaths he caused is chilling.

palace, and she became one of his wives. Then she gave birth to a son. But the LORD was displeased with what David had done.

Nathan Rebukes David

12 So the LORD sent Nathan the prophet to tell David this story: "There were two men in a certain town. One was rich, and one was poor. 2The rich man owned a great many sheep and cattle. 3The poor man owned nothing but one little lamb he had bought. He raised that little lamb, and it grew up with his children. It ate from the man's own plate and drank from his cup. He cuddled it in his arms like a baby daughter. 4One day a guest arrived at the home of the rich man. But instead of killing an animal from his own flock or herd, he took the poor man's lamb and killed it and prepared it for his guest."

5David was [j]furious. "As surely as the LORD lives," he vowed, "any man who would do such a thing deserves to die! 6He must repay four lambs to the poor man for the one he stole and for having no pity."

7Then Nathan said to David, "You are that man! The LORD, the God of Israel, says: I anointed you king of Israel and saved you from the power of Saul. 8I gave you your master's house and his wives and the kingdoms of Israel and Judah. And if that had not been enough, I would have given you much, much more. 9Why, then, have you despised the word of the LORD and done this horrible deed? For you have murdered Uriah the Hittite with the sword of the Ammonites and stolen his wife. 10From this time on, your family will live by the sword because you have despised me by taking Uriah's wife to be your own.

11"This is what the LORD says: Because of what you have done, I will cause your own household to rebel against you. I will give your wives to another man before your very eyes, and he will go to bed with them in public view. 12You did it secretly, but I will make this happen to you openly in the sight of all Israel."

David Confesses His Guilt

13Then David confessed to Nathan, "I have sinned against the LORD."

Nathan replied, "Yes, but the LORD has forgiven you, and you won't die for this sin. 14Nevertheless, because you have shown utter contempt for the LORD by doing this, your child will die."

15After Nathan returned to his home, the LORD sent a deadly illness to the child of David and Uriah's wife. 16David begged God to spare the child. He went without food and lay all night on the bare ground. 17The elders of his household pleaded with him to get up and eat with them, but he refused.

18Then on the seventh day the child died. David's advisers were afraid to tell him. "He wouldn't listen to reason while the child was ill," they said. "What drastic thing will he do when we tell him the child is dead?"

19When David saw them whispering, he realized what had happened. "Is the child dead?" he asked.

"Yes," they replied, "he is dead."

20Then David got up from the ground, washed himself, put on lotions, and changed

12:1 2 Sam 7:2, 17; Ps 51:TITLE
12:5 1 Kgs 20:40; [j]*'ap* (0639) › 2 Kgs 23:26
12:6 Exod 22:1
12:7 1 Sam 16:13; 1 Kgs 20:42
12:8 2 Sam 9:7
12:9 2 Sam 11:14-17, 27
12:10 2 Sam 13:28-29; 18:14; 1 Kgs 2:23
12:11 2 Sam 16:21-22
12:13 Lev 20:10; 24:17; Prov 28:13; Mic 7:18; Luke 18:13
12:14 Isa 52:5; Rom 2:23-24
12:17 2 Sam 3:35

12:1-31 Ch 12 expands on the last phrase of 11:27.

12:1 ***The LORD sent Nathan*** **to** ***David*** at least nine months after his adulterous sin. • *This story* is a rare OT instance of a parable (see also Judg 9:8-15). Such stories can be effective for communicating truth. • David *was rich* in the royal treasures he possessed, the number of wives he had, and all the promises of God for his future. Uriah by contrast *was poor*: he had one wife, one home, and no lineage.

12:3 *like a baby daughter:* Nathan's comparison of this lamb to a daughter (Hebrew *bath*) strikes a parallel with *Bath*sheba's name (see note on 11:3).

12:4 *he took the poor man's lamb:* Samuel had previously warned that a king would take what was not his (1 Sam 8:11-17).

12:5-6 The rich man of the parable did not deserve *to die* according to the law; instead, *he must repay four lambs* (cp. Exod 22:1). Intriguingly, David would later lose four of his sons (Bathsheba's first child, 12:18; Amnon, 13:29; Absalom, 18:14-15; Adonijah, 1 Kgs 2:25).

12:7-8 *You are that man!* David did deserve to die for his crime (Lev 20:10). • *I anointed . . . I gave . . . I would have given you:* David's sin not only violated God's commandments against murder, adultery, and coveting (Exod 20:1-17) but also amounted to a brazen disregard for all that the Lord had graciously given him.

12:8 *His wives* were probably the concubines of Saul's harem (cp. 3:7). The phrase could refer to Saul's wife Ahinoam, although David probably married a different woman with the same name (cp. 1 Sam 14:50; 25:43).

12:10 *from this time on* (literally *forever*): Contrast God's gracious "forever" promises of 7:13-29. • The reminder of what David had done with *the sword* (12:9) and what role *the sword* would play in his *family* recalls David's cavalier response to Joab's report of the deaths of Uriah and other innocent Israelites (11:25).

12:11 *I will cause your own household to rebel against you:* Absalom's revolt against David (chs 14–19) fulfilled this promise.

12:14 *Nevertheless . . . your child will die:* At times, God transfers punishment of fathers to their descendants (Exod 20:5; 34:7; Num 14:18; Deut 5:9; Jer 32:18). Although David repented and was forgiven (12:13), it did not cancel all retribution; it delayed it until a later generation (cp. 1 Kgs 21:27-29). • *the LORD:* As in Dead Sea Scrolls; Masoretic Text reads *the LORD's enemies.*

12:20 The series of actions described here show David resuming normal life activities. That he did so this soon after his son's death amazed his advisers (12:21). • *put on lotions:* Literally *anointed himself.*

12:22
Isa 38:1-5
Jon 3:9
12:23
Gen 37:35
Job 7:9-10
12:24
1 Chr 22:9
12:26
Deut 3:11
1 Chr 20:1-3
12:29-31
//1 Chr 20:1-3

his clothes. He went to the Tabernacle and
worshiped the LORD. After that, he returned
to the palace and was served food and ate.
21 His advisers were amazed. "We don't
understand you," they told him. "While the
child was still living, you wept and refused
to eat. But now that the child is dead, you
have stopped your mourning and are eating
again."
22 David replied, "I fasted and wept while
the child was alive, for I said, 'Perhaps the
LORD will be gracious to me and let the child
live.' 23 But why should I fast when he is dead?
Can I bring him back again? I will go to him
one day, but he cannot return to me."
24 Then David comforted Bathsheba, his
wife, and slept with her. She became pregnant and gave birth to a son, and David
named him Solomon. The LORD loved the
child 25 and sent word through Nathan the
prophet that they should name him Jedidiah (which means "beloved of the LORD"),
as the LORD had commanded.

David Captures Rabbah
2 Sam 12:29-31 // 1 Chr 20:2-3

26 Meanwhile, Joab was fighting against
Rabbah, the capital of Ammon, and he captured the royal fortifications. 27 Joab sent
messengers to tell David, "I have fought
against Rabbah and captured its water supply. 28 Now bring the rest of the army and
capture the city. Otherwise, I will capture it
and get credit for the victory."
29 So David gathered the rest of the army

BATHSHEBA (11:1–12:25)

1 Kgs 1:5–2:25
Ps 51

Bathsheba, wife of Uriah, was the daughter of Ammiel or Eliam (11:3; 1 Chr 3:5) and the granddaughter of Ahithophel, the king's adviser (15:12; 23:34). Her husband Uriah was a Hittite mercenary in King David's service and was one of David's mighty men (23:39).

One spring, David stayed home in Jerusalem while the army went to the battlefield (11:1). Resting at midday, David strolled on his roof overlooking the city and saw the beautiful Bathsheba taking a bath. He arranged for her to be brought to his private chambers. Then he had sexual relations with her, and she became pregnant (11:2-4).

Not wanting this scandal to become public, David arranged a cover-up: He told Joab, the general, to have Uriah bring back a report from the battle lines. David hoped that Uriah would return home and sleep with Bathsheba, thus legitimizing her pregnancy. But Uriah considered himself still on active duty, so he slept at the palace gate (11:5-13). When David asked him about this, he replied that he could not sleep with his wife while the Ark and the armies of Israel were on the battlefield. This answer put David in a very bad light: Uriah, who was not even an Israelite, was standing ready to return to battle by avoiding intercourse with his wife (see Lev 15:16-18), while David was staying at home and trying to cover up adultery! Then David sent Uriah back and ordered Joab to have him killed in battle (11:14-25). Uriah's death did not keep David's sin a secret, however. The Lord sent the prophet Nathan to confront David, and David confessed his sin and repented (12:1-14; see Ps 51).

Bathsheba's baby became sick and died, as Nathan had predicted. After Bathsheba's period of mourning, David installed her in the palace as his seventh wife. David and Bathsheba had other children (Shimea, Shobab, Nathan, and Solomon; 12:15-25; 1 Chr 3:5). The rest of 2 Samuel is filled with intrigue among the different factions of David's wives and children, culminating in David's old age when Bathsheba sought to ensure the kingship for her son Solomon (1 Kgs 1).

In Matthew's genealogy of Jesus the Messiah, both Solomon and Bathsheba appear (Matt 1:6); she is described there as "the widow of Uriah," a reminder of the sin that brought her into David's family and of God's gracious favor toward her descendants.

12:21-23 David grieved before his son's death, hoping to ward off punishment.

12:23 ***Can I bring him back again? I will go to him one day:*** The irreversibility of his son's death forced David to face his own mortality. But he also showed his confidence in the afterlife.

12:24 Even after Uriah's death, ***Bathsheba*** was still called Uriah's wife (12:9; see also Matt 1:6). Only here is she called David's ***wife.*** • ***David:*** literally *he;* an alternate Hebrew reading and some Hebrew manuscripts read *she.* • ***Solomon:*** Pronounced *Shelomoh* in Hebrew, it probably means "his peace," from the Hebrew *shalom.* It might mean "his replacement"; cp. *Shelemiah* (Jer 36:14, "Yahweh has provided compensation") and *Shelumiel* (Num 1:6, "God [is] my compensation"); both contain the root *shelem* ("replacement, compensation").

12:25 ***Jedidiah*** means "loved by Yahweh." This God-given second name for Solomon, mentioned only here, guaranteed his future, as it expressed God's special love for him. • ***as the LORD had commanded:*** As in Greek version; Hebrew reads *because of the LORD.*

12:26-31 David's battle with the Ammonites, begun in ch 10, ended in success.

12:26 ***the royal fortifications:*** Or *the royal city.*

12:27 ***captured its water supply:*** Or *captured the city of water.*

and went to Rabbah, and he fought against it and captured it. 30 David removed the crown from the king's head, and it was placed on his own head. The crown was made of gold and set with gems, and it weighed seventy-five pounds. David took a vast amount of plunder from the city. 31 He also made slaves of the people of Rabbah and forced them to labor with saws, iron picks, and iron axes, and to work in the brick kilns. That is how he dealt with the people of all the Ammonite towns. Then David and all the army returned to Jerusalem.

Amnon and Tamar (13:1-39)
Amnon Rapes Tamar

13 Now David's son Absalom had a beautiful sister named Tamar. And Amnon, her half brother, fell desperately in love with her. 2 Amnon became so obsessed with Tamar that he became ill. She was a virgin, and Amnon thought he could never have her.

3 But Amnon had a very crafty friend—his cousin Jonadab. He was the son of David's brother Shimea. 4 One day Jonadab said to Amnon, "What's the trouble? Why should the son of a king look so dejected morning after morning?"

So Amnon told him, "I am in love with Tamar, my brother Absalom's sister."

5 "Well," Jonadab said, "I'll tell you what to do. Go back to bed and pretend you are ill. When your father comes to see you, ask him to let Tamar come and prepare some food for you. Tell him you'll feel better if she prepares it as you watch and feeds you with her own hands."

6 So Amnon lay down and pretended to be sick. And when the king came to see him, Amnon asked him, "Please let my sister Tamar come and cook my favorite dish as I watch. Then I can eat it from her own hands." 7 So David agreed and sent Tamar to Amnon's house to prepare some food for him.

8 When Tamar arrived at Amnon's house, she went to the place where he was lying down so he could watch her mix some dough. Then she baked his favorite dish for him. 9 But when she set the serving tray before him, he refused to eat. "Everyone get out of here," Amnon told his servants. So they all left.

10 Then he said to Tamar, "Now bring the food into my bedroom and feed it to me here." So Tamar took his favorite dish to him. 11 But as she was feeding him, he grabbed her and demanded, "Come to bed with me, my darling sister."

12 "No, my brother!" she cried. "Don't be foolish! Don't do this to me! Such wicked things aren't done in Israel. 13 Where could I go in my shame? And you would be called one of the greatest fools in Israel. Please, just speak to the king about it, and he will let you marry me."

14 But Amnon wouldn't listen to her, and since he was stronger than she was, he raped her. 15 Then suddenly Amnon's love turned to hate, and he hated her even more

13:1 2 Sam 3:2-3; 1 Chr 3:1-2, 9
13:3 1 Sam 16:9
13:9 Gen 45:1
13:11 Gen 39:12
13:12 Lev 20:17

12:30 *David removed the crown:* David had, in effect, become the Ammonites' king. • *from the king's head:* Or *from the head of Milcom* (as in Greek version); the consonants of the Hebrew text can be read either way. Milcom, also called Molech, was the god of the Ammonites. • *seventy-five pounds:* Hebrew *1 talent* [34 kilograms]. • *a vast amount of plunder:* Instructions against taking such booty during a conquest (Deut 7:25-26) show how dangerous David's actions were. Such wealth might seduce the king's heart away from God.

12:31 *He also made slaves of the people of Rabbah and forced them to labor with:* Or *He also brought out the people of Rabbah and put them under.* Enslaving defeated peoples was in accord with Deut 20:11. Solomon later did the same with the Canaanites (1 Kgs 9:20-22; see also Judg 1:30, 33). The alternate reading might indicate torture inflicted on the defeated Ammonites (cp. note on 1 Chr 20:3). • *and to work in the brick kilns:* Or *and he made them pass through the brick kilns.*

13:1 *Absalom had a beautiful sister:* Tamar was Absalom's full sister but Amnon's half sister (see 3:2-3). Absalom would later avenge Tamar as her nearest relative (13:23-29; cp. Gen 34; Num 35:19).

13:2 *obsessed . . . ill:* As the story reveals, Amnon's "love" (13:4) for Tamar was a sickly erotic obsession. • *She was a virgin:* Amnon's fixation deepened because Tamar was sexually untouched. • *thought he could never have her:* The law prohibited marriage between brother and sister (Lev 18:9, 11; 20:17; Deut 27:22). But Amnon did not want to marry Tamar; he only wanted to have sex with her.

13:3 *crafty* (literally *wise*): Jonadab's "wisdom" was akin to the serpent's shrewdness (Gen 3:1). • In the context of a royal court, the Hebrew term for *friend* is closer to "counselor" or "adviser." • *Shimea:* Hebrew *Shimeah* (also in 13:32), a variant spelling of Shimea; compare 1 Chr 2:13.

13:4 *morning after morning:* Amnon's obsession was all-consuming and ongoing.

13:6 *my favorite dish:* Or *a couple of cakes;* also in 13:8, 10.

13:12 *wicked things:* The Hebrew word *nebalah* ("outrage," "deplorable act") often describes sexual crimes such as rape and adultery (Gen 34:7; Deut 22:21; Judg 20:6, 10; Jer 29:23) that the perpetrator must pay for with his life. • *in Israel:* The addition of this phrase either indicates indignation that the crime happened among Israelites or characterizes the act as a violation of Israelite standards of sexual morality.

13:13 *he will let you marry me:* Tamar said this to gain time; Amnon knew that the law prohibited marriage between half siblings (see note on 13:2), and he refused to back off.

13:14 *since he was stronger:* Tamar resisted as much as she could.

13:15 That Amnon's feelings for Tamar so quickly *turned to hate* shows that his so-called "love" for her (13:4) was really only selfish lust.

13:16
[k]*shalakh* (7971)
‣ Isa 50:1

13:18
Gen 37:23

13:19
Gen 37:29
2 Sam 1:11
Esth 4:1

13:22
Gen 31:24
Lev 19:17-18
1 Jn 2:9-11

13:29
2 Sam 18:9

13:31
2 Sam 12:16

13:32
2 Sam 13:3-5

13:34
2 Sam 18:24

13:37
2 Sam 3:3; 14:23, 32
[a]*'abal* (0056)
‣ 1 Chr 7:22

than he had loved her. "Get out of here!" he snarled at her.

16"No, no!" Tamar cried. "[k]Sending me away now is worse than what you've already done to me."

But Amnon wouldn't listen to her. 17He shouted for his servant and demanded, "Throw this woman out, and lock the door behind her!"

18So the servant put her out and locked the door behind her. She was wearing a long, beautiful robe, as was the custom in those days for the king's virgin daughters. 19But now Tamar tore her robe and put ashes on her head. And then, with her face in her hands, she went away crying.

20Her brother Absalom saw her and asked, "Is it true that Amnon has been with you? Well, my sister, keep quiet for now, since he's your brother. Don't you worry about it." So Tamar lived as a desolate woman in her brother Absalom's house.

21When King David heard what had happened, he was very angry. 22And though Absalom never spoke to Amnon about this, he hated Amnon deeply because of what he had done to his sister.

Absalom's Revenge on Amnon

23Two years later, when Absalom's sheep were being sheared at Baal-hazor near Ephraim, Absalom invited all the king's sons to come to a feast. 24He went to the king and said, "My sheep-shearers are now at work. Would the king and his servants please come to celebrate the occasion with me?"

25The king replied, "No, my son. If we all came, we would be too much of a burden on you." Absalom pressed him, but the king would not come, though he gave Absalom his blessing.

26"Well, then," Absalom said, "if you can't come, how about sending my brother Amnon with us?"

"Why Amnon?" the king asked. 27But Absalom kept on pressing the king until he finally agreed to let all his sons attend, including Amnon. So Absalom prepared a feast fit for a king.

28Absalom told his men, "Wait until Amnon gets drunk; then at my signal, kill him! Don't be afraid. I'm the one who has given the command. Take courage and do it!" 29So at Absalom's signal they murdered Amnon. Then the other sons of the king jumped on their mules and fled.

30As they were on the way back to Jerusalem, this report reached David: "Absalom has killed all the king's sons; not one is left alive!" 31The king got up, tore his robe, and threw himself on the ground. His advisers also tore their clothes in horror and sorrow.

32But just then Jonadab, the son of David's brother Shimea, arrived and said, "No, don't believe that all the king's sons have been killed! It was only Amnon! Absalom has been plotting this ever since Amnon raped his sister Tamar. 33No, my lord the king, your sons aren't all dead! It was only Amnon." 34Meanwhile Absalom escaped.

Then the watchman on the Jerusalem wall saw a great crowd coming down the hill on the road from the west. He ran to tell the king, "I see a crowd of people coming from the Horonaim road along the side of the hill."

35"Look!" Jonadab told the king. "There they are now! The king's sons are coming, just as I said."

36They soon arrived, weeping and sobbing, and the king and all his servants wept bitterly with them. 37And David [a]mourned many days for his son Amnon.

13:16 ***worse than what you've already done:*** A virgin who had been raped became unmarriageable (13:20; see Deut 22:28-29).

13:18 ***a long, beautiful robe:*** Or *a robe with sleeves,* or *an ornamented robe.* The meaning of the Hebrew is uncertain; the same phrase is used to describe Joseph's robe in Gen 37:3.

13:19 Tamar ***tore her robe*** to symbolize the violation of her virginity and honor and to mourn the death of her future (13:16). • ***Ashes*** represented death; sitting amidst ashes or putting ashes on one's head were signs of mourning (Esth 4:1-3; Job 42:6; Dan 9:3; Jon 3:6).

13:20 ***keep quiet for now . . . Don't you worry about it:*** Absalom's words of comfort seem hollow in light of her disgrace and mourning; this toned-down response hid Absalom's rage (13:22) from the already distraught Tamar. • ***as a desolate woman:*** See note on 13:16.

13:21 ***King David . . . was very angry:*** Dead Sea Scrolls and Greek version add *But he did not punish his son Amnon, because he loved him, for he was his firstborn.* Another possibility is that as an adulterer himself (see 11:1–12:24), David considered himself in no position to punish his son's sexual sin. A third possibility is that David thought this was God's "eye for an eye" punishment for his own sexual indiscretion.

13:23 ***Baal-hazor*** should not be confused with the famous fortified city of Hazor located north of the Sea of Galilee. The generally accepted location of Baal-hazor is Jebel el-Asur, some fifteen miles north of Jerusalem. • ***a feast:*** Sheep shearing was a time for sharing bounty and blessing with others (see 1 Sam 25:2-8).

13:27 ***So Absalom prepared a feast fit for a king:*** As in Greek and Latin versions (compare also Dead Sea Scrolls); the Hebrew text lacks this sentence.

13:31 David ***tore his robe,*** as Tamar had done after being violated (13:19)—a sign of great distress or remorse (see also Gen 37:34).

13:34-39 ***Absalom,*** now a fugitive, sought refuge among his mother's family.

13:34 ***He ran to tell . . . along the side of the hill:*** As in Greek version; Hebrew lacks this sentence.

13:37 ***fled to his grandfather:*** See 3:3. • ***Geshur*** was in Aram, northeast of Israel's territory (see 15:8; Josh 13:13).

Absalom fled to his grandfather, Talmai son of Ammihud, the king of Geshur. 38He stayed there in Geshur for three years. 39And King David, now reconciled to Amnon's death, longed to be reunited with his son Absalom.

Absalom and David (14:1–19:43)
David Meets with Absalom

14 Joab realized how much the king longed to see Absalom. 2So he sent for a woman from Tekoa who had a reputation for great wisdom. He said to her, "Pretend you are in mourning; wear mourning clothes and don't put on lotions. Act like a woman who has been mourning for the dead for a long time. 3Then go to the king and tell him the story I am about to tell you." Then Joab told her what to say.

4When the woman from Tekoa approached the king, she bowed with her face to the ground in deep respect and cried out, "O king! Help me!"

5"What's the trouble?" the king asked.

"Alas, I am a widow!" she replied. "My husband is dead. 6My two sons had a fight out in the field. And since no one was there to stop it, one of them was killed. 7Now the rest of the family is demanding, 'Let us have your son. We will execute him for murdering his brother. He doesn't deserve to inherit his family's property.' They want to extinguish the only coal I have left, and my husband's name and family will disappear from the face of the earth."

8"Leave it to me," the king told her. "Go home, and I'll see to it that no one touches him."

9"Oh, thank you, my lord the king," the woman from Tekoa replied. "If you are criticized for helping me, let the blame fall on me and on my father's house, and let the king and his throne be innocent."

10"If anyone objects," the king said, "bring him to me. I can assure you he will never complain again!"

11Then she said, "Please swear to me by the LORD your God that you won't let anyone take vengeance against my son. I want no more bloodshed."

"As surely as the LORD lives," he replied, "not a hair on your son's head will be disturbed!"

12"Please allow me to ask one more thing of my lord the king," she said.

"Go ahead and speak," he responded.

13She replied, "Why don't you do as much for the people of God as you have promised to do for me? You have convicted yourself in making this decision, because you have refused to bring home your own banished son. 14All of us must die eventually. Our lives are like water spilled out on the ground, which cannot be gathered up again. But God does not just sweep life away; instead, he devises ways to bring us back when we have been separated from him.

15"I have come to plead with my lord the king because people have threatened me. I said to myself, 'Perhaps the king will listen to me 16and rescue us from those who would cut us off from the inheritance God has given us. 17Yes, my lord the king will give us peace of mind again.' I know that you are like an [b]angel of God in discerning good from evil. May the LORD your God be with you."

18"I must know one thing," the king replied, "and tell me the truth."

"Yes, my lord the king," she responded.

19"Did Joab put you up to this?"

And the woman replied, "My lord the king, how can I deny it? Nobody can hide anything from you. Yes, Joab sent me and

13:39 2 Sam 12:19-23
14:2 2 Chr 11:5-10; Amos 1:1
14:3 2 Sam 14:19
14:7 Num 35:19; Deut 19:12-13
14:9 Gen 43:9; 1 Sam 25:24
14:11 Num 35:12, 19, 21; Deut 19:4-10; 1 Sam 14:45
14:13 2 Sam 13:37-39; 1 Kgs 20:40-42
14:14 Job 34:14-15; Heb 9:27
14:17 1 Sam 29:9; 2 Sam 19:27; [b]*mal'ak* (4397) ▸2 Kgs 19:35
14:19 2 Sam 14:3

13:39 *And King David:* Dead Sea Scrolls and Greek version read *And the spirit of the king.* • ***longed to be reunited with his son Absalom:*** Or *no longer felt a need to go out after Absalom.* David's grief over Amnon's death was evidently alleviated; any desire David might have had to execute Absalom had dissipated.

14:2 The woman with ***a reputation for great wisdom*** was summoned to carry out a delicate mission in the royal court (cp. 20:16). • ***don't put on lotions:*** Literally *don't anoint yourself with oil.*

14:9 *If you are criticized:* If David allowed a murder to go unavenged, he would be liable for not carrying out justice and would likely draw criticism.

14:11 *As surely as the LORD lives:* When the woman pressed David for a greater commitment of protection, David responded with this solemn oath (cp. 4:9; 12:5; 15:21; 1 Sam 20:3; 28:10; 29:6).

14:13 *for the people of God:* The woman argued that David was harming everyone in his kingdom by leaving Absalom in exile, perhaps because alienation in the royal family would be reproduced in the larger society or because David's obsession with Absalom would distract him from attending to more important matters (14:16).

14:14 *God . . . devises ways:* The woman encouraged David to be reconciled with Absalom as God does with his people. God did not remain estranged from David when he sinned; he forgave the repentant king.

14:16 The woman again addressed her specific situation. The king's concern for Absalom (see 13:39 and note) was keeping him from attending to matters of justice among his people. • ***cut us off:*** If her only remaining son were killed, the woman's family would lose ownership of its ancestral property (cp. Num 27:1-11).• ***the inheritance:*** Or *the property;* or *the people.*

14:17 *you are like an angel of God:* This flattering expression is not used for anyone else in the Bible but appears four times to describe David (see also 14:20; 19:27; 1 Sam 29:9). The woman was expressing confidence that David would act with God-given wisdom and justice.

14:23 2 Sam 13:37-39
14:27 2 Sam 13:1
14:28 2 Sam 14:24
14:32 1 Sam 20:8
14:33 Gen 33:4; Luke 15:20
15:1 1 Kgs 1:5
15:4 Judg 9:29

told me what to say. 20He did it to place the matter before you in a different light. But you are as wise as an angel of God, and you understand everything that happens among us!"

21So the king sent for Joab and told him, "All right, go and bring back the young man Absalom."

22Joab bowed with his face to the ground in deep respect and said, "At last I know that I have gained your approval, my lord the king, for you have granted me this request!"

23Then Joab went to Geshur and brought Absalom back to Jerusalem. 24But the king gave this order: "Absalom may go to his own house, but he must never come into my presence." So Absalom did not see the king.

Absalom Reconciled to David

25Now Absalom was praised as the most handsome man in all Israel. He was flawless from head to foot. 26He cut his hair only once a year, and then only because it was so heavy. When he weighed it out, it came to five pounds! 27He had three sons and one daughter. His daughter's name was Tamar, and she was very beautiful.

28Absalom lived in Jerusalem for two years, but he never got to see the king. 29Then Absalom sent for Joab to ask him to intercede for him, but Joab refused to come. Absalom sent for him a second time, but again Joab refused to come. 30So Absalom said to his servants, "Go and set fire to Joab's barley field, the field next to mine." So they set his field on fire, as Absalom had commanded.

31Then Joab came to Absalom at his house and demanded, "Why did your servants set my field on fire?"

32And Absalom replied, "Because I wanted you to ask the king why he brought me back from Geshur if he didn't intend to see me. I might as well have stayed there. Let me see the king; if he finds me guilty of anything, then let him kill me."

33So Joab told the king what Absalom had said. Then at last David summoned Absalom, who came and bowed low before the king, and the king kissed him.

Absalom's Rebellion

15 After this, Absalom bought a chariot and horses, and he hired fifty bodyguards to run ahead of him. 2He got up early every morning and went out to the gate of the city. When people brought a case to the king for judgment, Absalom would ask where in Israel they were from, and they would tell him their tribe. 3Then Absalom would say, "You've really got a strong case here! It's too bad the king doesn't have anyone to hear it. 4I wish I were the judge. Then everyone could bring their cases to me for judgment, and I would give them justice!"

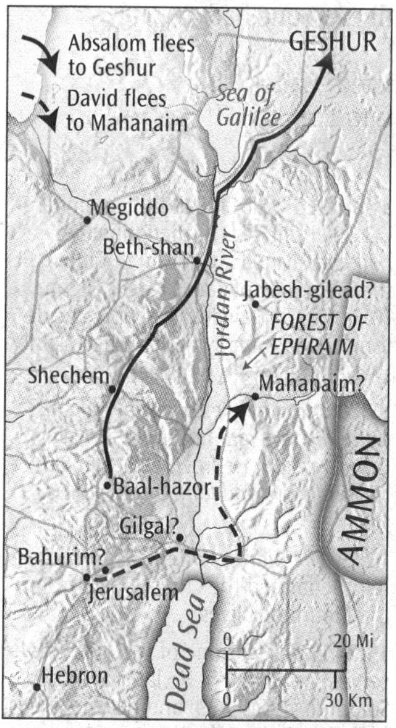

◀ **Absalom & David (13:23–18:18).** David's conflict with his son Absalom caused both to flee at different times. After Absalom killed his brother Amnon (13:23-37), he fled to GESHUR and stayed with his grandfather (see 3:3). Later, when Absalom had returned and staged a coup (15:1-12), David fled to MAHANAIM (15:13–17:29) until the coup was defeated (18:1-18) and he returned to JERUSALEM for the remainder of his reign (19:15-40).

14:20 ***as wise as an angel of God:*** This wise woman (14:2) knew it was good policy to flatter a king rather than risk insulting him.

14:21 ***bring back . . . Absalom:*** It seems that David was not yet interested in full reconciliation with his son (14:24).

14:23 ***Geshur:*** See 13:37-38.

14:26 ***cut his hair only once a year:*** Absalom's hair, an aspect of his attractiveness, ended up being a deadly snare for him (see 18:9-15). • ***five pounds:*** Hebrew *200 shekels* [2.3 kilograms] *by the royal standard.*

14:27 Absalom's ***three sons*** apparently died before he did (see 18:18). • Absalom named his daughter ***Tamar*** after his sister, and she too was ***very beautiful*** (13:1).

14:29 ***Joab*** persuaded David to welcome Absalom back (14:21-22) but then backed off from assisting Absalom further; perhaps Joab wanted to avoid aiding a would-be usurper (15:1-12).

14:33 Absalom ***bowed low***, assuming a posture of respect and deference to the king's majesty (see also 14:4, 22). • ***and the king kissed him:*** The lack of conversation, hugging (cp. Luke 15:20), or weeping (cp. Gen 33:4; 45:2, 14) suggests that this was a formal meeting rather than an affectionate reunion.

15:1-19 Absalom revolted against David eleven years after Amnon violated Tamar (cp. 13:23, 38; 14:28; 15:7), approximately the twenty-fifth year of David's thirty-three-year reign in Jerusalem.

15:1 ***a chariot and horses, and . . . fifty bodyguards:*** These three items, distinct signs of kingship, were also the first items that Samuel said the king would take from the people (1 Sam 8:11). Another of David's sons, Adonijah, collected the same items when he coveted the throne (1 Kgs 1:5).

5When people tried to bow before him, Absalom wouldn't let them. Instead, he took them by the hand and kissed them. 6Absalom did this with everyone who came to the king for judgment, and so he stole the hearts of all the people of Israel.

7After four years, Absalom said to the king, "Let me go to Hebron to offer a sacrifice to the LORD and fulfill a vow I made to him. 8For while your servant was at Geshur in Aram, I promised to sacrifice to the LORD in Hebron if he would bring me back to Jerusalem."

9"All right," the king told him. "Go and fulfill your vow."

So Absalom went to Hebron. 10But while he was there, he sent secret messengers to all the tribes of Israel to stir up a rebellion against the king. "As soon as you hear the ram's horn," his message read, "you are to say, 'Absalom has been crowned king in Hebron.' " 11He took 200 men from Jerusalem with him as guests, but they knew nothing of his intentions. 12While Absalom was offering the sacrifices, he sent for Ahithophel, one of David's counselors who lived in Giloh. Soon many others also joined Absalom, and the conspiracy gained momentum.

David Escapes from Jerusalem

13A messenger soon arrived in Jerusalem to tell David, "All Israel has joined Absalom in a conspiracy against you!"

14"Then we must flee at once, or it will be too late!" David urged his men. "Hurry! If we get out of the city before Absalom arrives, both we and the city of Jerusalem will be spared from disaster."

15"We are with you," his advisers replied. "Do what you think is best."

16So the king and all his household set out at once. He left no one behind except ten of his concubines to look after the palace. 17The king and all his people set out on foot, pausing at the last house 18to let all the king's men move past to lead the way. There were 600 men from Gath who had come with David, along with the king's bodyguard.

19Then the king turned and said to Ittai, a leader of the men from Gath, "Why are you coming with us? Go on back to King Absalom, for you are a guest in Israel, a foreigner in exile. 20You arrived only recently, and should I force you today to wander with us? I don't even know where we will go. Go on back and take your kinsmen with you, and may the LORD show you his unfailing love and faithfulness."

21But Ittai said to the king, "I vow by the LORD and by your own life that I will go wherever my lord the king goes, no matter what happens—whether it means life or death."

22David replied, "All right, come with us." So Ittai and all his men and their families went along.

23Everyone cried loudly as the king and his followers passed by. They crossed the Kidron Valley and then went out toward the wilderness.

24Zadok and all the Levites also came along, carrying the Ark of the Covenant of God. They set down the Ark of God, and Abiathar offered sacrifices until everyone had passed out of the city.

25Then the king instructed Zadok to take the Ark of God back into the city. "If

15:5 2 Sam 14:33
15:6 Rom 16:18
15:8 Gen 28:20; 2 Sam 13:37-39
15:10 1 Kgs 1:34; 2 Kgs 9:13
15:12 Josh 15:51; 2 Sam 17:14; Ps 3:1
15:13 Judg 9:3
15:14 2 Sam 12:11; Ps 3:TITLE
15:16 2 Sam 16:21-22
15:19 2 Sam 18:2
15:21 Ruth 1:16-17
15:24 Num 4:15; 1 Sam 4:4-5; 2 Sam 8:17; 20:25
15:25 1 Sam 3:18; Ps 43:3

15:5 To *bow before . . . Absalom* was, in effect, to honor him as king (see 14:33).

15:6 *stole the hearts:* Absalom's accessibility and false pretense of care for the people gained their loyalty.

15:7 *After four years:* As in Greek and Syriac versions; Hebrew reads *forty years.* The Hebrew text would put Absalom's uprising in David's last year as king and create many chronological difficulties with events that happened afterward (also see note on 15:1-19). The Greek and Syriac reading is much more likely. • *fulfill a vow:* Unlike the freewill offering of devotion and gratitude that a worshiper promised to God, this type of offering was to fulfill a promise to God (see Gen 28:20-22; Judg 11:30-31; 1 Sam 1:11). Absalom was probably lying (cp. 1 Sam 20:28-29).

15:8 *Geshur in Aram:* After killing Amnon, Absalom had sought refuge in the homeland of his mother (also see notes on 13:34-39; 13:37). • The perfect place for Absalom to turn his grassroots popularity into a full-fledged revolt against David was *in Hebron* (as in some Greek manuscripts; Hebrew lacks *in Hebron*), David's first capital.

15:12 *Ahithophel* was Bathsheba's grandfather (cp. 11:3; 23:34); years later, he might still have been angry over what David did to his granddaughter. • *Giloh* was located in the region of Hebron (Josh 15:51, 54).

15:15-16 Possibly David left *ten of his concubines* behind because he believed his exile would be short-lived. See 16:21-22.

15:18 *600 men from Gath:* This alliance went back to David's relationship with the Philistines in Saul's day (1 Sam 21:10-15; 27:1-12; 29:1-11). • *the king's bodyguard:* Hebrew *the Kerethites and Pelethites.* See note on 8:18.

15:19 *Ittai,* a Philistine from Gath, was associated with Gibeah in Benjamin (23:29; 1 Chr 11:31); the Philistines had established a garrison in Gibeah at the beginning of Saul's career (1 Sam 10:5; 13:3). • David was stepping aside for *King Absalom,* who had successfully swayed the loyalty of Israel.

15:20 *and may the LORD show you his unfailing love and faithfulness:* As in Greek version; Hebrew reads *and may unfailing love and faithfulness go with you.*

15:23 *The Kidron Valley,* east of Jerusalem, separated the City of David from the Mount of Olives.

15:24 *Zadok* was one of two priests who served David (8:17). He later anointed Solomon (1 Kgs 1:39) and became the high priest after Abiathar was deposed (1 Kgs 2:26-27). • *Abiathar offered sacrifices:* Or *Abiathar went up.*

15:25 *take the Ark of God back:* People fleeing invasion normally took their

15:27 2 Sam 17:17
15:28 2 Sam 17:16
15:30 Ezek 24:23
15:31 2 Sam 15:12; 16:23; 17:14, 23
15:32 Josh 16:2
15:34 2 Sam 16:19
15:35 2 Sam 17:15-16

the LORD sees fit," David said, "he will bring me back to see the Ark and the Tabernacle again. [26]But if he is through with me, then let him do what seems best to him."

[27]The king also told Zadok the priest, "Look, here is my plan. You and Abiathar should return quietly to the city with your son Ahimaaz and Abiathar's son Jonathan. [28]I will stop at the shallows of the Jordan River and wait there for a report from you." [29]So Zadok and Abiathar took the Ark of God back to the city and stayed there.

[30]David walked up the road to the Mount of Olives, weeping as he went. His head was covered and his feet were bare as a sign of mourning. And the people who were with him covered their heads and wept as they climbed the hill. [31]When someone told David that his adviser Ahithophel was now backing Absalom, David prayed, "O LORD, let Ahithophel give Absalom foolish advice!"

[32]When David reached the summit of the Mount of Olives where people worshiped God, Hushai the Arkite was waiting there for him. Hushai had torn his clothing and put dirt on his head as a sign of mourning. [33]But David told him, "If you go with me, you will only be a burden. [34]Return to Jerusalem and tell Absalom, 'I will now be your adviser, O king, just as I was your father's adviser in the past.' Then you can frustrate and counter Ahithophel's advice. [35]Zadok and Abiathar, the priests, will be there. Tell them about the plans being made in the

ZADOK (15:23-37)

2 Sam 8:17
1 Kgs 1:5-53; 2:35
1 Chr 6:1-15, 50-53
Ezra 7:2
Ezek 40:46; 43:19; 44:15; 48:11

Zadok was an important transitional figure in the history of Israel's priesthood. Since he seemingly appears out of nowhere in the narrative of 2 Samuel (8:17), some scholars suggest that he was not really born into a priestly family. However, there is no reason to doubt the biblical record that he was Aaron' descendant (1 Chr 6:1-15, 50-53). Zadok's descent is traced back to Eleazar, Aaron's eldest son (1 Chr 6:5-8; 18:16; 24:3; Ezr 7:2-5). Zadok served alongside Abiathar, a descendant of Eli. Zadok and Abiathar were priests of Israel under King David (8:17; 20:25).

When Absalom revolted against King David, both Zadok and Abiathar showed their loyalty to David by taking the Ark to him, fully prepared to share his exile (15:24-29). Instead, David sent them to Jerusalem as his spies.

Later, when David's son Adonijah tried to seize the aged David's throne with the support of Joab and Abiathar, Zadok wisely refrained from supporting him (1 Kgs 1:5-10). Abiathar, though, was banished (1 Kgs 2:26-27), fulfilling the prophecy that Eli's family would be removed from the priesthood (1 Sam 2:27-36) and replaced by "a faithful priest who will serve me and do what I desire. I will establish his family, and they will be priests to my anointed kings forever" (1 Sam 2:35).

The loyal Zadok fulfilled this prophecy and became the sole high priest under Solomon (1 Kgs 2:35). Zadok's descendants served as Israel's priests throughout the monarchy and beyond. Azariah, chief priest in Hezekiah's reign, was of Zadok's line (2 Chr 31:10). During the exile, Ezekiel's eschatological vision of the new Temple refers to Zadok's priestly line (Ezek 40:46; 43:19; 44:15; 48:11). When the Jews later came under Seleucid domination in the early 100s BC, the high priesthood, by then regarded as a political appointment, was taken away from Zadok's descendants. As a result of Ezekiel's prophecies, Jewish groups such as the Qumran community continued to await the restoration of Zadok to the high priesthood. The NT teaches that the office of the high priest now rests on Jesus Christ (Heb 9:11; 10:12-25).

idols to avoid having the items fall into an enemy's hands. The capture of a god could be interpreted by rebel elements to mean that the gods had abandoned the ruling dynasty. However, the Ark was not a mere idol or talisman (cp. 1 Sam 4:3-11; 5:6–6:9). It was the central object in the sanctuary and represented the presence of the Lord, the God of Israel (see Exod 40:34-35). David intentionally permitted the Ark to fall into Absalom's hands, trusting God's grace and promises (15:26; see 7:8-16) whether or not the Ark was with him. • ***and the Tabernacle:*** Literally *and his dwelling place.*

15:27 ***Look:*** As in Greek version; Hebrew reads *Are you a seer?* or *Do you see?* • Hebrew lacks ***and Abiathar;*** cp. 15:29. • ***Ahimaaz*** and ***Jonathan*** supported David during Absalom's coup d'etat by serving as his secret messengers (see 15:36; 17:17-22).

15:28 ***at the shallows of the Jordan River:*** Literally *at the crossing points of the wilderness.*

15:31 ***let Ahithophel give . . . foolish advice:*** David also sent a double-agent, Hushai, to confound Ahithophel's advice (15:32-37; 17:1-14).

15:32 At this point in Israel's history, ***people worshiped God*** at multiple altars across the land. The Tabernacle as it had existed from the time of Joshua and Samuel was gone and the Temple was yet to be built. • An ***Arkite*** was possibly a non-Israelite from the region south of Bethel (Josh 16:2).

15:34 While David was confident that God's providence was at work behind the scenes, he also took strategic action to further his own cause.

king's palace, [36]and they will send their
sons Ahimaaz and Jonathan to tell me what
is going on."
[37]So David's friend Hushai returned to
Jerusalem, getting there just as Absalom arrived.

David and Ziba

16 When David had gone a little beyond
the summit of the Mount of Olives,
Ziba, the servant of Mephibosheth, was
waiting there for him. He had two donkeys
loaded with 200 loaves of bread, 100 clusters of raisins, 100 bunches of summer
fruit, and a wineskin full of wine.
[2]"What are these for?" the king asked
Ziba.
Ziba replied, "The donkeys are for the
king's people to ride on, and the bread and
summer fruit are for the young men to
eat. The wine is for those who become exhausted in the wilderness."
[3]"And where is Mephibosheth, Saul's
grandson?" the king asked him.
"He stayed in Jerusalem," Ziba replied.
"He said, 'Today I will get back the kingdom
of my grandfather Saul.' "
[4]"In that case," the king told Ziba, "I give
you everything Mephibosheth owns."
"I bow before you," Ziba replied. "May I always be pleasing to you, my lord the king."

Shimei Curses David

[5]As King David came to Bahurim, a man
came out of the village cursing them. It was
Shimei son of Gera, from the same clan as
Saul's family. [6]He threw stones at the king
and the king's officers and all the mighty
warriors who surrounded him. [7]"Get out
of here, you murderer, you scoundrel!" he
shouted at David. [8]"The LORD is paying you
back for all the bloodshed in Saul's clan.
You stole his throne, and now the LORD has
given it to your son Absalom. At last you will
taste some of your own medicine, for you
are a murderer!"
[9]"Why should this dead dog curse my lord
the king?" Abishai son of Zeruiah demanded.
"Let me go over and cut off his head!"
[10]"No!" the king said. "Who asked your
opinion, you sons of Zeruiah! If the LORD
has told him to curse me, who are you to
stop him?"
[11]Then David said to Abishai and to all his
servants, "My own son is trying to kill me.
Doesn't this relative of Saul have even more
reason to do so? Leave him alone and let
him curse, for the LORD has told him to do
it. [12]And perhaps the LORD will see that I am
being wronged and will bless me because of
these curses today." [13]So David and his men
continued down the road, and Shimei kept
pace with them on a nearby hillside, cursing as he went and throwing stones at David
and tossing dust into the air.
[14]The king and all who were with him
grew weary along the way, so they rested
when they reached the Jordan River.

Ahithophel Advises Absalom

[15]Meanwhile, Absalom and all the army of
Israel arrived at Jerusalem, accompanied by
Ahithophel. [16]When David's friend Hushai
the Arkite arrived, he went immediately to
see Absalom. "Long live the king!" he exclaimed. "Long live the king!"
[17]"Is this the way you treat your friend David?" Absalom asked him. "Why aren't you
with him?"
[18]"I'm here because I belong to the man
who is chosen by the LORD and by all the men
of Israel," Hushai replied. [19]"And anyway,
why shouldn't I serve you? Just as I was your
father's adviser, now I will be your adviser!"

15:36 2 Sam 15:27
15:37 1 Chr 27:33
16:1 2 Sam 9:1-13
16:2 2 Sam 17:27-29
16:3 2 Sam 9:9-10; 19:26-27
16:5 Exod 22:28; 1 Sam 17:43; 2 Sam 19:16-23; 1 Kgs 2:8
16:7 2 Sam 12:9
16:9 Exod 22:28; 1 Sam 26:8; 2 Sam 19:21
16:10 2 Sam 3:39; 19:22; John 18:11; Rom 9:20
16:11 Gen 45:5; 1 Sam 26:19; 2 Sam 12:11
16:12 Deut 23:5; Rom 8:28
16:15 2 Sam 15:12, 37
16:16 1 Sam 10:24; 2 Sam 15:33-34; 2 Kgs 11:12
16:19 2 Sam 15:33-34

16:1 *Ziba:* See note on 9:11; see also 9:1-13; 19:24-30. • ***Mephibosheth*** is another name for Merib-baal (see notes on 4:4; 9:1-13). As Saul's grandson (16:3), he was a potential rival for the throne.

16:3-4 *Ziba* was lying to David for his own gain; ***Mephibosheth*** later set the record straight (19:24-30).

16:5 ***Bahurim*** was in the territory of Benjamin east of the Mount of Olives on the way to the Jordan River. It is likely that many people from Benjamin, Saul's tribe, harbored lingering resentment against David's rule. In the case of ***Shimei,*** his loyalty to Saul was even stronger because they were from the same clan in the tribe of Benjamin.

16:7-8 Shimei cursed *David,* holding him responsible for the violent death of Saul and his *clan.*

16:8 ***The LORD is paying you back:*** Shimei interpreted Absalom's rebellion as the Lord's retribution. However, David was innocent (see notes on 1:4, 15-16).

16:9 ***Abishai*** was David's nephew (1 Chr 2:13-16) and evidently a member of his personal guard. He believed that no one should talk this way to the king and live to tell about it (cp. 19:21). David was slower to judge (cp. 1 Kgs 2:8-9).

16:10 ***If the LORD has told him to curse me:*** David felt it might have been punishment for past sins. • David was—contrary to Shimei's charges—reducing the violence that surrounded him.

16:11-12 ***this relative of Saul:*** Literally *this Benjaminite.* • ***even more reason:*** David understood why a supporter of Saul might hate him.

16:14 ***when they reached the Jordan River:*** As in Greek version (see also 17:16); Hebrew reads *when they reached their destination.*

16:16 ***Long live the king!*** Hushai's words were deliberately ambiguous. He was in fact an agent of the true king—David was truly "the man . . . chosen by the LORD" (16:18). Hushai avoided using the king's name, leading Absalom to believe that Hushai was loyal to him rather than to David.

16:19 ***Why shouldn't I serve you?*** (literally *and second, to whom will I do service? Not before his son?*): The

16:21 2 Sam 15:16
16:22 2 Sam 12:11; 20:3
16:23 2 Sam 15:12; 17:14, 23
17:2 2 Sam 16:14; 1 Kgs 22:31
17:5 2 Sam 15:32-34
17:7 2 Sam 16:21
17:8 Hos 13:8

[20]Then Absalom turned to Ahithophel and asked him, "What should I do next?"

[21]Ahithophel told him, "Go and sleep with your father's concubines, for he has left them here to look after the palace. Then all Israel will know that you have insulted your father beyond hope of reconciliation, and they will throw their support to you." [22]So they set up a tent on the palace roof where everyone could see it, and Absalom went in and had sex with his father's concubines.

[23]Absalom followed Ahithophel's advice, just as David had done. For every word Ahithophel spoke seemed as wise as though it had come directly from the mouth of God.

17 Now Ahithophel urged Absalom, "Let me choose 12,000 men to start out after David tonight. [2]I will catch up with him while he is weary and discouraged. He and his troops will panic, and everyone will run away. Then I will kill only the king, [3]and I will bring all the people back to you as a bride returns to her husband. After all, it is only one man's life that you seek. Then you will be at peace with all the people." [4]This plan seemed good to Absalom and to all the elders of Israel.

Hushai Counters Ahithophel's Advice

[5]But then Absalom said, "Bring in Hushai the Arkite. Let's see what he thinks about this." [6]When Hushai arrived, Absalom told him what Ahithophel had said. Then he asked, "What is your opinion? Should we follow Ahithophel's advice? If not, what do you suggest?"

[7]"Well," Hushai replied to Absalom, "this time Ahithophel has made a mistake. [8]You know your father and his men; they are mighty warriors. Right now they are as

ABISHAI (16:9-12)

2 Sam 2:18; 3:30, 39; 10:10-14; 18:1-8; 19:21-23; 20:6-10; 21:17; 23:18-19
1 Sam 26:6-12
1 Chr 2:16; 11:20-21; 18:12-13; 19:11-15

Abishai was a powerful and successful warrior and a leader in David's army. He was David's nephew, a son of David's sister Zeruiah and the brother of Joab and Asahel (1 Chr 2:16).

Abishai was completely devoted to David and quick to suggest violence against David's enemies. When God allowed David and Abishai to penetrate Saul's war camp while the troops were sleeping (1 Sam 26:1-25), Abishai wanted to assassinate Saul, but David restrained him. Later, when the revolt of Absalom required that David leave Jerusalem, the king was cursed by Shimei, a member of Saul's family (16:5-14). Abishai wanted to execute Shimei (16:5-12; 19:18-23), but David twice rejected that proposal. The vengeful spirit of Abishai and his brothers also came out in the earlier conflict: Saul's general, Abner, was forced to kill Asahel, so Joab and Abishai took revenge by killing Abner (3:22-30).

Abishai was brave and very capable. He once killed 300 soldiers in a single battle. For this, he was made leader of the Thirty, a group of especially skillful warriors surpassed only by the Three (1 Chr 11:20-21). Abishai won a major victory over the Edomites (1 Chr 18:12-13). In a battle with the Philistines, Abishai saved David's life by killing the giant Ishbi-benob (21:15-17). Abishai also led the army, and when it divided for strategic purposes, Abishai led one group while his brother Joab led the other (10:1-19; 18:1-18; 1 Chr 19:1-19). Their military efforts were usually very successful.

Though Joab's actions eventually led to his death, we nowhere read about the death of Abishai, a violently impulsive military leader who was one of David's bravest warriors (23:18-19; 1 Chr 11:20-21).

ambiguous language continues. Hushai phrased his profession of loyalty as a question rather than as a commitment. His intent, lost on Absalom, was to serve David while fooling Absalom into thinking that he had changed sides. Similarly, ***just as I was your father's adviser, now I will be your adviser!*** is literally, *as I served before your father, so I will* [serve your father] *before you.*

16:21 ***Go and sleep with your father's concubines:*** A usurper took a predecessor's harem to assert or strengthen his claim to the throne (see 3:7). Absalom's action was in violation of Deut 22:30.

16:22 ***Absalom*** intended to show the people that he had assumed the throne with its royal prerogatives. His shameful act echoed David's adultery with Bathsheba, which also began on that *roof* (11:2-4); the episode fulfilled Nathan's prophecy (12:11-12).

16:23 ***from the mouth of God:*** Cp. 17:14.

17:1-14 ***Ahithophel*** proposed a quick surprise strike against David with a small force (***12,000 men***, 17:1), which would give David no time to organize and fight back. Then David's double-agent ***Hushai*** suggested taking more time to ***mobilize the entire army of Israel*** (17:11). This plan would supposedly give them an insurmountable numerical advantage and prevent David from engaging in guerilla tactics. Because the Lord was working against Absalom, he rejected Ahithophel's good strategy and accepted Hushai's bad advice (17:14; cp. 1 Kgs 12:1-15).

17:3 ***as a bride . . . you seek:*** As in Greek version; Hebrew reads *like the return of all is the man whom you seek.* The Hebrew text has the loyalty of all the people depend on the death of David. The Greek OT pictures a young wife who returns to her husband after a short quarrel.

enraged as a mother bear who has been robbed of her cubs. And remember that your father is an experienced man of war. He won't be spending the night among the troops. [9]He has probably already hidden in some pit or cave. And when he comes out and attacks and a few of your men fall, there will be panic among your troops, and the word will spread that Absalom's men are being slaughtered. [10]Then even the bravest soldiers, though they have the [c]heart of a lion, will be paralyzed with fear. For all Israel knows what a mighty warrior your father is and how courageous his men are.

[11]"I recommend that you mobilize the entire army of Israel, bringing them from as far away as Dan in the north and Beersheba in the south. That way you will have an army as numerous as the sand on the seashore. And I advise that you personally lead the troops. [12]When we find David, we'll fall on him like dew that falls on the ground. Then neither he nor any of his men will be left alive. [13]And if David were to escape into some town, you will have all Israel there at your command. Then we can take ropes and drag the walls of the town into the nearest valley until every stone is torn down."

[14]Then Absalom and all the men of Israel said, "Hushai's advice is better than Ahithophel's." For the LORD had determined to defeat the counsel of Ahithophel, which really was the better plan, so that he could bring disaster on Absalom!

[15]Hushai told Zadok and Abiathar, the priests, what Ahithophel had said to Absalom and the elders of Israel and what he himself had advised instead. [16]"Quick!" he told them. "Find David and urge him not to stay at the shallows of the Jordan River tonight. He must go across at once into the wilderness beyond. Otherwise he will die and his entire army with him."

[17]Jonathan and Ahimaaz had been staying at En-rogel so as not to be seen entering and leaving the city. Arrangements had been made for a servant girl to bring them the message they were to take to King David. [18]But a boy spotted them at En-rogel, and he told Absalom about it. So they quickly escaped to Bahurim, where a man hid them down inside a well in his courtyard. [19]The man's wife put a cloth over the top of the well and scattered grain on it to dry in the sun; so no one suspected they were there.

[20]When Absalom's men arrived, they asked her, "Have you seen Ahimaaz and Jonathan?"

The woman replied, "They were here, but they crossed over the brook." Absalom's men looked for them without success and returned to Jerusalem.

[21]Then the two men crawled out of the well and hurried on to King David. "Quick!" they told him, "cross the Jordan tonight!" And they told him how Ahithophel had advised that he be captured and killed. [22]So David and all the people with him went across the Jordan River during the night, and they were all on the other bank before dawn.

[23]When Ahithophel realized that his advice had not been followed, he saddled his donkey, went to his hometown, set his affairs in order, and hanged himself. He died there and was buried in the family tomb.

[24]David soon arrived at Mahanaim. By now, Absalom had mobilized the entire army of Israel and was leading his troops across the Jordan River. [25]Absalom had appointed Amasa as commander of his army, replacing Joab, who had been commander under David. (Amasa was Joab's cousin. His father was Jether, an Ishmaelite. His mother, Abigail daughter of Nahash, was the sister of Joab's mother, Zeruiah.) [26]Absalom and the Israelite army set up camp in the land of Gilead.

[27]When David arrived at Mahanaim, he was warmly greeted by Shobi son of Nahash,

17:10 Josh 2:9, 11
[c]*leb* (3820)
›1 Kgs 3:12

17:13 Mic 1:6

17:14 2 Sam 15:31-34

17:15 2 Sam 15:35-36

17:16 2 Sam 15:28

17:17 Josh 15:7
2 Sam 15:27, 35-36; 18:19

17:18 2 Sam 3:16; 16:5

17:19 Josh 2:4-6

17:20 Exod 1:19
Lev 19:11
1 Sam 19:12-17

17:23 2 Sam 16:23
2 Kgs 20:1
Matt 27:5

17:24 Gen 32:2
2 Sam 2:8

17:25 2 Sam 19:13; 20:12
1 Kgs 2:5
1 Chr 2:16-17

17:27 2 Sam 9:4; 10:1-2; 12:26, 29
1 Kgs 2:7

17:11 The nationwide military conscription *from . . . Dan* to *Beersheba* (the northern and southern limits of Israel) was intended to produce an overwhelmingly superior fighting force.

17:14 *Ahithophel's* strategy was actually *better.* However, Hushai had the psychological and rhetorical advantage as well as the Lord's purpose, so he won Absalom's favor. • *the LORD had determined to defeat:* Despite early advances, Absalom's power grab was doomed from the start.

17:16 *at the shallows of the Jordan River:* Literally *at the crossing points of the wilderness.*

17:17 *Jonathan and Ahimaaz:* See 15:27, 36. • The location of *En-rogel* is uncertain, but it cannot have been too far east of Jerusalem.

17:18-20 *Bahurim* was the home of Shimei, the pro-Saul Benjaminite (16:5; 19:16). Shimei's cursing of David at Bahurim reflected David's decline, while the escape of *Ahimaaz and Jonathan* pictured the hope of David's resurgence.

17:23 *hanged himself:* Ahithophel foresaw David's victory and Absalom's undoing, and he preferred to die by his own hand rather than by David's.

17:24 *Mahanaim,* once the capital city of Ishbosheth and Abner (2:8, 12, 29), became David's base of operations.

17:25 *Jether:* Hebrew *Ithra,* a variant spelling of Jether. • *an Ishmaelite:* As in some Greek manuscripts (see also 1 Chr 2:17); Hebrew reads *an Israelite.* • According to 1 Chr 2:15-16, *Abigail* and *Zeruiah* were David's sisters. But since Abigail is called the *daughter of Nahash,* she and *Zeruiah* were apparently David's half sisters (Nahash was probably their father; his widow would then have married Jesse and given birth to David and his brothers).

17:27 *Shobi* was probably the brother of Hanun, who had humiliated David's

17:29
2 Sam 16:2

18:1
Exod 18:25
1 Sam 22:7

18:2
1 Sam 11:11
2 Sam 15:19-22

18:3
2 Sam 21:17

18:4
2 Sam 18:24

18:6
Josh 17:15

18:9
2 Sam 14:26

18:13
2 Sam 14:19-20

18:16
2 Sam 2:28; 20:22

18:17
Josh 7:26; 8:29

who came from Rabbah of the Ammonites, and by Makir son of Ammiel from Lo-debar, and by Barzillai of Gilead from Rogelim. 28They brought sleeping mats, cooking pots, serving bowls, wheat and barley, flour and roasted grain, beans, lentils, 29honey, butter, sheep, goats, and cheese for David and those who were with him. For they said, "You must all be very hungry and tired and thirsty after your long march through the wilderness."

Absalom's Defeat and Death

18 David now mustered the men who were with him and appointed generals and captains to lead them. 2He sent the troops out in three groups, placing one group under Joab, one under Joab's brother Abishai son of Zeruiah, and one under Ittai, the man from Gath. The king told his troops, "I am going out with you."

3But his men objected strongly. "You must not go," they urged. "If we have to turn and run—and even if half of us die—it will make no difference to Absalom's troops; they will be looking only for you. You are worth 10,000 of us, and it is better that you stay here in the town and send help if we need it."

4"If you think that's the best plan, I'll do it," the king answered. So he stood alongside the gate of the town as all the troops marched out in groups of hundreds and of thousands.

5And the king gave this command to Joab, Abishai, and Ittai: "For my sake, deal gently with young Absalom." And all the troops heard the king give this order to his commanders.

6So the battle began in the forest of Ephraim, 7and the Israelite troops were beaten back by David's men. There was a great slaughter that day, and 20,000 men laid down their lives. 8The battle raged all across the countryside, and more men died because of the forest than were killed by the sword.

9During the battle, Absalom happened to come upon some of David's men. He tried to escape on his mule, but as he rode beneath the thick branches of a great tree, his hair got caught in the tree. His mule kept going and left him dangling in the air. 10One of David's men saw what had happened and told Joab, "I saw Absalom dangling from a great tree."

11"What?" Joab demanded. "You saw him there and didn't kill him? I would have rewarded you with ten pieces of silver and a hero's belt!"

12"I would not kill the king's son for even a thousand pieces of silver," the man replied to Joab. "We all heard the king say to you and Abishai and Ittai, 'For my sake, please spare young Absalom.' 13And if I had betrayed the king by killing his son—and the king would certainly find out who did it—you yourself would be the first to abandon me."

14"Enough of this nonsense," Joab said. Then he took three daggers and plunged them into Absalom's heart as he dangled, still alive, in the great tree. 15Ten of Joab's young armor bearers then surrounded Absalom and killed him.

16Then Joab blew the ram's horn, and his men returned from chasing the army of Israel. 17They threw Absalom's body into a deep pit in the forest and piled a great heap

---

messengers after the death of ***Nahash*** (ch 10; see note on 10:1-5). • ***Makir*** was Mephibosheth's host before David summoned him (9:4-5). • ***Barzillai of Gilead*** was probably not the same as Barzillai from Meholah (21:8).

18:1 ***appointed generals and captains:*** Literally *appointed commanders of thousands and commanders of hundreds.*

18:3 ***You are worth 10,000 of us:*** As in two Hebrew manuscripts and some Greek and Latin manuscripts; most Hebrew manuscripts read *Now there are 10,000 like us.* Although David's men flattered him, their insistence that he stay behind might actually suggest David's advancing frailty (see 21:15-17).

18:5 ***Joab*** violated David's order to ***deal gently with young Absalom*** (18:11-15). This was the second time Joab killed someone against David's wishes (see 3:22-37).

18:6 The ***forest of Ephraim*** was an area east of the Jordan settled by the tribe of Ephraim.

18:8 ***more men died because of the forest:*** The topographical conditions of the forest apparently took away the numerical advantage of Absalom's forces.

18:9 Absalom, who took such pride in ***his hair*** (literally *his head*; 14:25-26), died because of it. He who had built "a monument to himself" (18:18) was then thrown into a pit after his death (18:17) and denied the dignity of a proper burial. These ironies highlight the difference between Absalom's aspirations and his destiny.

18:11 ***ten pieces of silver:*** Hebrew *10 shekels of silver,* about 4 ounces or 114 grams in weight. • Perhaps ***a hero's belt*** was a sword belt that decorated a soldier for bravery and courage in battle (cp. 1 Sam 18:4).

18:12 ***a thousand pieces of silver:*** Hebrew *1,000 shekels,* about 25 pounds or 11.4 kilograms in weight.

18:14 ***plunged them into Absalom's heart:*** Earlier, Joab had played the role of reconciler between David and Absalom (ch 14). It is possible Joab believed that allowing Absalom to live would only invite ongoing trouble for David and for himself. (Absalom had appointed Amasa, Joab's first cousin, to fill Joab's position as commander of Israel's army; see 17:25.)

18:15 ***surrounded . . . and killed him:*** Perhaps Joab had his ***armor bearers*** finish the job so that he could make the case to David that he himself had not killed Absalom.

18:17 ***all Israel fled to their homes:*** Absalom's supporters (17:11) knew their lives were in danger (cp. 19:8). They had backed a usurper whose coup d'etat had been thwarted.

of stones over it. And all Israel fled to their homes.

18During his lifetime, Absalom had built a monument to himself in the King's Valley, for he said, "I have no son to carry on my name." He named the monument after himself, and it is known as Absalom's Monument to this day.

David Mourns Absalom's Death

19Then Zadok's son Ahimaaz said, "Let me run to the king with the good news that the LORD has rescued him from his enemies."

20"No," Joab told him, "it wouldn't be good news to the king that his son is dead. You can be my messenger another time, but not today."

21Then Joab said to a man from Ethiopia, "Go tell the king what you have seen." The man bowed and ran off.

22But Ahimaaz continued to plead with Joab, "Whatever happens, please let me go, too."

"Why should you go, my son?" Joab replied. "There will be no reward for your news."

23"Yes, but let me go anyway," he begged.

Joab finally said, "All right, go ahead." So Ahimaaz took the less demanding route by way of the plain and ran to Mahanaim ahead of the Ethiopian.

24While David was sitting between the inner and outer gates of the town, the watchman climbed to the roof of the gateway by the wall. As he looked, he saw a lone man running toward them. 25He shouted the news down to David, and the king replied, "If he is alone, he has news."

As the messenger came closer, 26the watchman saw another man running toward them. He shouted down, "Here comes another one!"

The king replied, "He also will have news."

27"The first man runs like Ahimaaz son of Zadok," the watchman said.

"He is a good man and comes with good news," the king replied.

28Then Ahimaaz cried out to the king, "Everything is all right!" He bowed before the king with his face to the ground and said, "Praise to the LORD your God, who has handed over the rebels who dared to stand against my lord the king."

29"What about young Absalom?" the king demanded. "Is he all right?"

Ahimaaz replied, "When Joab told me to come, there was a lot of commotion. But I didn't know what was happening."

30"Wait here," the king told him. So Ahimaaz stepped aside.

31Then the man from Ethiopia arrived and said, "I have good news for my lord the king. Today the LORD has rescued you from all those who rebelled against you."

32"What about young Absalom?" the king demanded. "Is he all right?"

And the Ethiopian replied, "May all of your enemies, my lord the king, both now and in the future, share the fate of that young man!"

33The king was overcome with emotion. He went up to the room over the gateway and burst into tears. And as he went, he cried, "O my son Absalom! My son, my son Absalom! If only I had died instead of you! O Absalom, my son, my son."

Joab Rebukes the King

19 Word soon reached Joab that the king was weeping and mourning for Absalom. 2As all the people heard of the king's deep grief for his son, the joy of that day's victory was turned into deep sadness. 3They crept back into the town that day as though they were ashamed and had deserted in battle. 4The king covered his face with his hands and kept on crying, "O my son Absalom! O Absalom, my son, my son!"

5Then Joab went to the king's room and said to him, "We saved your life today and the lives of your sons, your daughters, and your wives and concubines. Yet you act like this, making us feel ashamed of ourselves. 6You seem to love those who hate you and hate those who love you. You have made

18:18
Gen 14:17
1 Sam 15:12
2 Sam 14:27

18:19
2 Sam 15:36

18:24
2 Sam 13:34; 19:8-10
2 Kgs 9:17

18:27
1 Kgs 1:42

18:28
1 Sam 17:46; 25:23

18:32
1 Sam 25:26

18:33
Exod 32:32
2 Sam 19:4
Rom 9:1-3

19:1
2 Sam 18:5, 14

19:4
2 Sam 15:30; 18:33

18:18 ***I have no son:*** See note on 14:27. In the absence of a lineage, Absalom hoped a ***monument*** would preserve his name and memory. • ***to this day:*** The narrator was probably writing during Solomon's reign; the monument's location is now unknown.

18:19 ***Zadok:*** See note on 15:24.

18:21 ***a man from Ethiopia*** (Hebrew *from Cush;* similarly in 18:23, 31, 32): Joab thought it would be better to send a foreigner to tell the king of Absalom's death. If David overreacted, the loss of a foreigner was not as critical as the loss of a priest's son.

18:25 ***If he is alone, he has news:*** A solitary runner was usually a courier.

18:28-29 ***Everything is all right!*** (Hebrew *shalom*): David then asked, "Is it *shalom* with the young Ab-*shalom?*" (***What about young Absalom? . . . Is he all right?***). Even though Absalom was David's rival, he was also David's son. David was more concerned about his son's fate than the well-being of his fighting servants (19:5-6).

18:33 David was not afraid to show his emotions openly, whether engulfed by rapturous joy (6:14-19) or crushed by sadness. His feelings for Absalom were real, not theatrical. • Verse 18:33 is numbered 19:1 in the Hebrew text.

19:1-43 Verses 19:1-43 are numbered 19:2-44 in the Hebrew text.

19:5-7 These verses provide the only recorded instance of Joab openly rebuking the king (cp. 24:3).

19:8 2 Sam 8:1; 15:2; 18:24
19:9 2 Sam 8:1-14; 15:14
19:11 2 Sam 15:24
19:13 2 Sam 17:25
19:15 Josh 5:8-9; 1 Sam 11:14-15

it clear today that your commanders and
troops mean nothing to you. It seems that if
Absalom had lived and all of us had died,
you would be pleased. 7Now go out there
and congratulate your troops, for I swear by
the LORD that if you don't go out, not a single
one of them will remain here tonight. Then
you will be worse off than ever before."
8So the king went out and took his seat
at the town gate, and as the news spread
throughout the town that he was there,
everyone went to him.

David Returns to Jerusalem

Meanwhile, the Israelites who had supported Absalom fled to their homes. 9And
throughout all the tribes of Israel there was
much discussion and argument going on.
The people were saying, "The king rescued
us from our enemies and saved us from the
Philistines, but Absalom chased him out
of the country. 10Now Absalom, whom we
anointed to rule over us, is dead. Why not
ask David to come back and be our king
again?"
11Then King David sent Zadok and Abiathar, the priests, to say to the elders of Judah,
"Why are you the last ones to welcome back
the king into his palace? For I have heard
that all Israel is ready. 12You are my relatives,
my own tribe, my own flesh and blood! So
why are you the last ones to welcome back
the king?" 13And David told them to tell Amasa, "Since you are my own flesh and blood,
like Joab, may God strike me and even kill
me if I do not appoint you as commander of
my army in his place."
14Then Amasa convinced all the men of
Judah, and they responded unanimously.
They sent word to the king, "Return to us,
and bring back all who are with you."
15So the king started back to Jerusalem.
And when he arrived at the Jordan River, the
people of Judah came to Gilgal to meet him

JOAB (18:2–19:13)

2 Sam 2:13-32; 3:22-39; 8:16; 10:7-14; 11:1-25; 12:26-28; 14:1-33; 17:25; 20:7-23; 24:2-9
1 Kgs 1:7, 19; 2:28-35; 11:15-16
1 Chr 2:16; 11:6-8; 18:15; 19:8-15; 20:1; 21:2-6; 26:28; 27:24, 34
Ps 60:TITLE

Joab was David's nephew, son of David's sister Zeruiah (1 Chr 2:16); his brothers were Abishai and Asahel. Joab became commander of David's armies because of his bravery and military skill (2:18; 8:16; 11:1; 1 Chr 18:15). As the first to attack the Jebusite city of Jerusalem, he was awarded the commander's position (1 Chr 11:4-9). Joab also suppressed a rebellion among the Arameans and Ammonites (10:1-19; 1 Chr 19:8-15) and won many key battles for David against the northern army of Israel under Abner's impressive command (2:12-32).

Joab often acted to promote what he perceived were David's interests. For example, he colluded with David in the death of Uriah the Hittite to cover up the king's adultery with Bathsheba (11:1-27). He persuaded David to allow Absalom's return to court (14:1-33), and he tried to talk David out of taking a census that provoked God's anger (24:1-9; 1 Chr 21:1-6).

Though he was always loyal to David, Joab sometimes acted in his own interest, and sometimes he disregarded the king's orders. When Abner killed Joab's brother Asahel (2:23), Joab killed Abner in revenge (3:26-30), despite Abner's new loyalty to David (3:12-19). Joab probably saw him as a rival. Later, Joab killed his own cousin Amasa (20:8-10), who commanded Absalom's army (17:25), because David had appointed Amasa commander in Joab's place (19:13; 20:4). Joab also killed Absalom against David's direct order (18:5, 10-17). He then rebuked David for grieving Absalom's death rather than congratulating the army (19:5-7). Joab was ruthless, and he regained the most powerful position in David's army (20:23; 24:2; 1 Kgs 1:19).

Joab sealed his fate by supporting Adonijah's bid for David's throne (1 Kgs 1:5-7). David's deathbed instructions to Solomon included having Joab killed because of his murders of Abner (3:30) and Amasa (20:8-10). When Solomon became king, he sent Benaiah to kill Joab even as he clung to the horns of the altar (1 Kgs 2:28-34). Joab met the same fate that he dealt to others throughout his life, and his executioner replaced him as commander of Israel's armies (1 Kgs 2:35).

19:9-10 The ***argument*** among the ***tribes of Israel*** (possibly referring only to the northern tribes) resulted in the consensus that they should ***ask David to come back***, perhaps instead of going back to the semiautonomy of the era of the judges (cp. 20:1).

19:11-12 When David realized that the northern tribes would welcome him (19:9-10), he sent emissaries to goad Judah, his own tribesmen, into welcoming him as well. See also note on 19:41-43.

19:13 ***commander . . . in his place:*** Amasa's appointment would be short-lived (20:7-10).

19:14 *Amasa:* Or *David;* Hebrew reads *he.*

19:15-23 On his return to Jerusalem, David showed mercy to Shimei, the pro-Saul northerner who had cursed David when he fled from Jerusalem (see 16:5-14), but Shimei's action did not go unpunished (1 Kgs 2:8, 36-46).

19:15 *Gilgal* was an important city in the days of Samuel and Saul (see note on 19:40; 1 Sam 7:16; 11:15).

and escort him across the river. 16Shimei son of Gera, the man from Bahurim in Benjamin, hurried across with the men of Judah to welcome King David. 17A thousand other men from the tribe of Benjamin were with him, including Ziba, the chief servant of the house of Saul, and Ziba's fifteen sons and twenty servants. They rushed down to the Jordan to meet the king. 18They crossed the shallows of the Jordan to bring the king's household across the river, helping him in every way they could.

As the king was about to cross the river, Shimei fell down before him. 19"My lord the king, please forgive me," he pleaded. "Forget the terrible thing your servant did when you left Jerusalem. May the king put it out of his mind. 20I know how much I sinned. That is why I have come here today, the very first person in all Israel to greet my lord the king."

21Then Abishai son of Zeruiah said, "Shimei should die, for he cursed the LORD's anointed king!"

22"Who asked your opinion, you sons of Zeruiah!" David exclaimed. "Why have you become my adversary today? This is not a day for execution but for celebration! Today I am once again the king of Israel!" 23Then, turning to Shimei, David vowed, "Your life will be spared."

24Now Mephibosheth, Saul's grandson, came down from Jerusalem to meet the king. He had not cared for his feet, trimmed his beard, or washed his clothes since the day the king left Jerusalem. 25"Why didn't you come with me, Mephibosheth?" the king asked him.

26Mephibosheth replied, "My lord the king, my servant Ziba deceived me. I told him, 'Saddle my donkey so I can go with the king.' For as you know I am crippled. 27Ziba has slandered me by saying that I refused to come. But I know that my lord the king is like an angel of God, so do what you think is best. 28All my relatives and I could expect only death from you, my lord, but instead you have honored me by allowing me to eat at your own table! What more can I ask?"

29"You've said enough," David replied. "I've decided that you and Ziba will divide your land equally between you."

30"Give him all of it," Mephibosheth said. "I am content just to have you safely back again, my lord the king!"

31Barzillai of Gilead had come down from Rogelim to escort the king across the Jordan. 32He was very old, about eighty, and very wealthy. He was the one who had provided food for the king during his stay in Mahanaim. 33"Come across with me and live in Jerusalem," the king said to Barzillai. "I will take care of you there."

34"No," he replied, "I am far too old to go with the king to Jerusalem. 35I am eighty years old today, and I can no longer enjoy anything. Food and wine are no longer tasty, and I cannot hear the singers as they sing. I would only be a burden to my lord the king. 36Just to go across the Jordan River with the king is all the honor I need! 37Then let me return again to die in my own town, where my father and mother are buried. But here is your servant, my son Kimham. Let him go with my lord the king and receive whatever you want to give him."

38"Good," the king agreed. "Kimham will go with me, and I will help him in any way

19:16 2 Sam 16:5-13; 1 Kgs 2:8
19:17 2 Sam 9:2
19:19 2 Sam 16:6-9
19:21 Exod 22:28
19:22 1 Sam 11:13; 2 Sam 16:9-10
19:23 1 Kgs 2:8
19:24 2 Sam 9:5-10
19:25 2 Sam 16:17
19:26 2 Sam 9:2-3, 13
19:27 2 Sam 14:17, 20
19:28 2 Sam 9:7
19:31 2 Sam 17:27-29; 1 Kgs 2:7
19:35 Ps 90:10
19:37 1 Kgs 2:7; Jer 41:17

19:17 *Ziba:* See 16:1-4.

19:20 *I know how much I sinned:* Shimei's repentance might have been genuine, or he might simply have been backpedaling in a desperate attempt to save his life. David's concern for Absalom's safety had shown that David was not a self-promoting, bloodthirsty throne-stealer, as Shimei had thought; and Absalom had not replaced him (16:8), as Shimei had charged. • *in all Israel* (literally *in all the house of Joseph*): Just as Jacob's name could stand for all Israel (e.g., Num 24:19; Isa 10:20), Joseph's name could stand for all the northern tribes (e.g., notes on Amos 5:6; Zech 10:6).

19:21-22 Cp 16:9-12. • *Abishai:* See note on 16:9. • *you sons of Zeruiah:* See notes on 2:18; 17:25. While it was Abishai who consistently wanted to kill those hostile to David (cp. 16:9; 1 Sam 26:8), David also expressed his frustration with Joab, Abishai's brother (see 3:28-29, 39; 19:13; 1 Kgs 2:5-6). • *my adversary:* Or *my prosecutor.*

19:23 David's oath of protection was not binding on David's heir, Solomon, who later ordered Shimei's execution for far less serious crimes (1 Kgs 2:36-46).

19:24-30 See 16:1-4.

19:24 *Mephibosheth* is another name for Merib-baal (see note on 4:4). Mephibosheth's inattention to grooming throughout David's absence from Jerusalem was an act of mourning and that proved his loyalty to David. If Mephibosheth had designs on the throne (16:3), he would not have retained such an unkempt appearance.

19:26 *Saddle my donkey:* As in Greek, Syriac, and Latin versions; Hebrew reads *I will saddle a donkey for myself.*

19:27-28 *like an angel of God:* See note on 14:17. • *I could expect only death. . . . What more can I ask?* If Mephibosheth had wanted to betray David, it would have been a profound show of ingratitude for all that David had done for him.

19:30 Mephibosheth's disinterest in claiming even half of his property showed conclusively that his happiness over David's return was genuine.

19:31-40 Because *he was very old* and frail, *Barzillai* declined David's invitation to the royal court in Jerusalem as reward for his assistance. David took Barzillai's *son Kimham* instead (see also 1 Kgs 2:7).

19:31 *Gilead* was part of Manasseh's territory on the east side of the Jordan (Josh 17:5).

19:39 Gen 31:55; Ruth 1:14; 2 Sam 14:33
19:43 2 Sam 5:1
20:1 1 Sam 22:7-8; 1 Kgs 12:16; 2 Chr 10:16
20:3 2 Sam 15:16; 16:21-22
20:4 2 Sam 17:25; 19:13
20:6 2 Sam 21:17
20:7 2 Sam 8:18; 15:17-18; 1 Kgs 1:38
20:8 2 Sam 2:18
20:10 1 Kgs 2:5

you would like. And I will do for you anything you want." 39So all the people crossed
the Jordan with the king. After David had
blessed Barzillai and kissed him, Barzillai
returned to his own home.
40The king then crossed over to Gilgal,
taking Kimham with him. All the troops of
Judah and half the troops of Israel escorted
the king on his way.
41But all the men of Israel complained to
the king, "The men of Judah stole the king
and didn't give us the honor of helping
take you, your household, and all your men
across the Jordan."
42The men of Judah replied, "The king is
one of our own kinsmen. Why should this
make you angry? We haven't eaten any of
the king's food or received any special favors!"
43"But there are ten tribes in Israel," the
others replied. "So we have ten times as
much right to the king as you do. What right
do you have to treat us with such contempt?
Weren't we the first to speak of bringing
him back to be our king again?" The argument continued back and forth, and the
men of Judah spoke even more harshly than
the men of Israel.

Sheba's Rebellion (20:1-22)

20 There happened to be a trouble-
maker there named Sheba son of
Bicri, a man from the tribe of Benjamin.
Sheba blew a ram's horn and began to chant:

"Down with the dynasty of David!
We have no interest in the son of Jesse.
Come on, you men of Israel,
back to your homes!"

2So all the men of Israel deserted David
and followed Sheba son of Bicri. But the
men of Judah stayed with their king and
escorted him from the Jordan River to Jerusalem.
3When David came to his palace in Jerusalem, he took the ten concubines he had left
to look after the palace and placed them in
seclusion. Their needs were provided for,
but he no longer slept with them. So each of
them lived like a widow until she died.
4Then the king told Amasa, "Mobilize the
army of Judah within three days, and report
back at that time." 5So Amasa went out to
notify Judah, but it took him longer than
the time he had been given.
6Then David said to Abishai, "Sheba son
of Bicri is going to hurt us more than Absalom did. Quick, take my troops and chase
after him before he gets into a fortified
town where we can't reach him."
7So Abishai and Joab, together with the
king's bodyguard and all the mighty warriors, set out from Jerusalem to go after
Sheba. 8As they arrived at the great stone in
Gibeon, Amasa met them. Joab was wearing
his military tunic with a dagger strapped to
his belt. As he stepped forward to greet Amasa, he slipped the dagger from its sheath.
9"How are you, my cousin?" Joab said and
took him by the beard with his right hand
as though to kiss him. 10Amasa didn't notice the dagger in his left hand, and Joab
stabbed him in the stomach with it so that
his insides gushed out onto the ground.
Joab did not need to strike again, and Amasa soon died. Joab and his brother Abishai
left him lying there and continued after
Sheba.
11One of Joab's young men shouted to
Amasa's troops, "If you are for Joab and David, come and follow Joab." 12But Amasa lay
in his blood in the middle of the road, and
Joab's man saw that everyone was stopping
to stare at him. So he pulled him off the

19:39 *kissed him:* This was a genuine and affectionate kiss, in contrast with David's cold kiss for Absalom (14:33) and Absalom's calculating one for the people (15:5).

19:40 *Gilgal,* a natural stop along David's westward route, was also a politically significant location: It was where the people had proclaimed Saul king (1 Sam 11:15) and Samuel later announced the end of Saul's reign (1 Sam 13:13-15). David's kingship now had a new beginning at Gilgal.

19:41-43 This dispute, prompted by David's favoring his own tribe of Judah, reflects the roots of the division that eventually split Judah and Israel into separate nations (1 Kgs 11:31; 12:16, 20). • ***Weren't we the first:*** See 19:11-12.

20:1 *Down with the dynasty of David!* By the same rallying cry, the northern Israelites later dissociated themselves from Solomon (1 Kgs 12:16). Sheba's failed revolt foreshadowed the ultimate failure of the northern kingdom, which was founded on a similar revolt by Jeroboam (1 Kgs 12).

20:3 The fate of the *ten concubines* (15:16) whom Absalom had publicly violated (16:21-22) was like Michal's (see 6:23 and note).

20:4-5 *The king* had installed *Amasa* in Joab's place as commander of the armies (19:13-14). David apparently expected from Amasa the same efficiency and effectiveness as Joab had provided.

20:7 *So Abishai and Joab:* Literally *So Joab's men.* • ***the king's bodyguard:*** Hebrew *the Kerethites and Pelethites;* also in 20:23; see note on 8:18.

20:8 *As he stepped forward . . . sheath:* Literally *As he stepped forward, it fell out.*

20:9 *to kiss him:* This affectionate greeting was not always genuine (cp. 14:33).

20:10 *Amasa . . . died:* For the second time, Joab killed a commander of the opposing army by treachery (the first was Abner, 3:26-27). Twice, David tried to merge feuding parties by absorbing the military leader of the opposing side (see 3:6-13; 17:25; 19:13); twice Joab scuttled David's plans by treacherously murdering the rival commander (see also 3:22-30).

road into a field and threw a cloak over him.
13With Amasa's body out of the way, everyone went on with Joab to capture Sheba son
of Bicri.
14Meanwhile, Sheba traveled through all
the tribes of Israel and eventually came to
the town of Abel-beth-maacah. All the members of his own clan, the Bicrites, assembled
for battle and followed him into the town.
15When Joab's forces arrived, they attacked
Abel-beth-maacah. They built a siege ramp
against the town's fortifications and began battering down the wall. 16But a wise
woman in the town called out to Joab, "Listen to me, Joab. Come over here so I can talk
to you." 17As he approached, the woman
asked, "Are you Joab?"
"I am," he replied.
So she said, "Listen carefully to your servant."
"I'm listening," he said.
18Then she continued, "There used to be
a saying, 'If you want to settle an argument,
ask advice at the town of Abel.' 19I am one
who is peace loving and faithful in Israel.
But you are destroying an important town
in Israel. Why do you want to devour what
belongs to the LORD?"
20And Joab replied, "Believe me, I don't
want to devour or destroy your town!
21That's not my purpose. All I want is a man
named Sheba son of Bicri from the hill country of Ephraim, who has revolted against
King David. If you hand over this one man
to me, I will leave the town in peace."
"All right," the woman replied, "we will
throw his head over the wall to you." 22Then
the woman went to all the people with her
wise advice, and they cut off Sheba's head
and threw it out to Joab. So he blew the
ram's horn and called his troops back from
the attack. They all returned to their homes,
and Joab returned to the king at Jerusalem.

David's Officers (20:23-26)

23Now Joab was the commander of the
army of Israel. Benaiah son of Jehoiada
was captain of the king's bodyguard. 24Ad-
oniram was in charge of the labor force.
Jehoshaphat son of Ahilud was the royal
historian. 25Sheva was the court secretary.
Zadok and Abiathar were the priests. 26And
Ira, a descendant of Jair, was David's personal priest.

4. THE CELEBRATION OF DAVID'S REIGN (21:1–24:25)

David Avenges the Gibeonites

21 There was a famine during David's
reign that lasted for three years,
so David asked the LORD about it. And the
LORD said, "The famine has come because
Saul and his family are guilty of murdering
the Gibeonites."

20:15 Ezek 4:2
20:16 2 Sam 14:2
20:19 Deut 20:10; 2 Sam 14:15-16
20:21 Josh 24:33; 2 Sam 20:2
20:22 Eccl 9:14-15
20:23 2 Sam 8:16-18
20:24 1 Kgs 12:18
20:25 1 Sam 2:35
21:1 Gen 12:10; 26:1; 42:5

20:14 *Abel-beth-maacah* was in the northernmost region of Israelite territory, four miles west of the city of Dan. • *All . . . the Bicrites:* As in Greek and Latin versions; Hebrew reads *All the Berites.*

20:15 A *siege ramp* was often an earthen ramp built up against the wall, a well-known tactic for breaching a walled city's defenses (see also 2 Kgs 25:1; Jer 52:4).

20:16 *wise woman:* Cp. 14:2.

20:18-19 The woman told a *saying* to convince Joab not to slaughter an entire city, especially such a noble city as *Abel* (a shortened form of Abel-beth-maacah, 20:15), just to capture one criminal. • *an important town in Israel* (literally *a town that is a mother in Israel*): It was common to refer to outlying villages around a larger city as its "daughters."

20:23-26 This list of David's leaders and the similar list in 8:15-18 bracket chs 9–20 in David's life. Even after the major crises described in these 12 chapters, David's monarchy did not fall apart; he still had an intact administration.

20:23 In 8:16, *Joab* was called "commander of the army," but here he is *commander of the army of Israel.* David's wider control of Israel was established when the northern secessionist movements were defeated.

20:24 *Adoniram:* As in Greek version (see also 1 Kgs 4:6; 5:14); Hebrew reads *Adoram.* The addition of the officer *in charge of the labor force* (not mentioned in 8:15-18; see also 1 Kgs 4:6) shows that David had now gained sufficient control of Israel to require the payment of taxes and to conscript labor throughout the kingdom (cp. 1 Sam 8:11-17).

20:25 In contrast to David's personal priest (see 8:18; 20:26 and notes), *Zadok and Abiathar* presided over public worship.

20:26 David's personal *priest* was probably not a Levite but rather a special class of religious servant appointed for his royal court (see note on 8:18).

21:1–24:25 The final chapters of 2 Samuel are a *coda,* a concluding section that summarizes the important themes from the preceding material. These chapters are thematic, not chronological, and not all the events described here happened at the end of David's reign (e.g., 22:1). The materials are arranged according to a common Hebrew literary device, a *chiasm* (mirror-image):

- A: Saul's sin against the Gibeonites and its collective punishment (21:1-14)
  - B: David's heroes and their exploits (21:15-22)
    - C: David's Psalm (22:1-51)
    - C': David's Psalm (23:1-7)
  - B': David's heroes and their exploits (23:8-39)
- A': David's sin against the census taboo and its collective punishment (24:1-25).

A chiasm highlights the central section—here David's hymns, which focus not on David but on David's God.

21:1 *asked the LORD:* The Hebrew verb is the same as that used when David "begged" for the life of Bathsheba's child (12:16). On these two occasions, "seeking" was in the desperation of a moment of crisis. However, most often in the OT, "seeking God" refers not to a specific prayer of petition but to the dynamics of daily devotion and obedience to God (e.g., Ps 40:16; 105:4; Prov 28:5). • *Saul and his family are guilty:* The *famine* resulted from violating an oath taken before the Lord (Josh 9:19-20). • *murdering the Gibeonites:* This incident is not elsewhere recorded.

21:2 Josh 9:15-20
21:3 1 Sam 26:19
21:4 Num 35:33-34
21:5 2 Sam 21:1
21:6 Num 25:4; 1 Sam 10:24
21:7 1 Sam 18:1-3; 20:12-17; 23:18; 2 Sam 4:4
21:8 1 Sam 18:19; 2 Sam 3:7
21:10 Deut 21:23; 1 Sam 17:44
21:12 1 Sam 31:11-13
21:15-22 //1 Chr 20:4-8
21:16 Num 13:28
21:17 2 Sam 18:2-3; 20:6
21:18 1 Chr 11:29; 20:4-8; 27:11
21:19 1 Sam 17:4-7
21:22 1 Chr 20:8
22:1-51 //Ps 18:1-50
22:1 Exod 15:1; Deut 31:30; Judg 5:1; Ps 18:TITLE

2So the king summoned the Gibeonites.
They were not part of Israel but were all that
was left of the nation of the Amorites. The
people of Israel had sworn not to kill them,
but Saul, in his zeal for Israel and Judah, had
tried to wipe them out. 3David asked them,
"What can I do for you? How can I make
amends so that you will bless the LORD's
people again?"

4"Well, money can't settle this matter
between us and the family of Saul," the Gibeonites replied. "Neither can we demand the
life of anyone in Israel."

"What can I do then?" David asked. "Just
tell me and I will do it for you."

5Then they replied, "It was Saul who
planned to destroy us, to keep us from having any place at all in the territory of Israel.
6So let seven of Saul's sons be handed over to
us, and we will execute them before the LORD
at Gibeon, on the mountain of the LORD."

"All right," the king said, "I will do it." 7The
king spared Jonathan's son Mephibosheth,
who was Saul's grandson, because of the
oath David and Jonathan had sworn before
the LORD. 8But he gave them Saul's two sons
Armoni and Mephibosheth, whose mother
was Rizpah daughter of Aiah. He also gave
them the five sons of Saul's daughter Merab,
the wife of Adriel son of Barzillai from Meholah. 9The men of Gibeon executed them
on the mountain before the LORD. So all
seven of them died together at the beginning of the barley harvest.

10Then Rizpah daughter of Aiah, the
mother of two of the men, spread burlap on
a rock and stayed there the entire harvest
season. She prevented the scavenger birds
from tearing at their bodies during the day
and stopped wild animals from eating them
at night. 11When David learned what Rizpah,
Saul's concubine, had done, 12he went to the
people of Jabesh-gilead and retrieved the
bones of Saul and his son Jonathan. (When
the Philistines had killed Saul and Jonathan
on Mount Gilboa, the people of Jabesh-gilead
stole their bodies from the public square of
Beth-shan, where the Philistines had hung
them.) 13So David obtained the bones of
Saul and Jonathan, as well as the bones of the
men the Gibeonites had executed.

14Then the king ordered that they bury
the bones in the tomb of Kish, Saul's father,
at the town of Zela in the land of Benjamin.
After that, God ended the famine in the land.

Battles against Philistine Giants
2 Sam 21:18-22 // 1 Chr 20:4-8

15Once again the Philistines were at war with
Israel. And when David and his men were in
the thick of battle, David became weak and
exhausted. 16Ishbi-benob was a descendant
of the giants; his bronze spearhead weighed

Illicit bloodshed had polluted the land, making it sterile and unfruitful (cp. Gen 4:10-12; Num 35:30-34).

21:2 Though the *Amorites* were a specific people group (Gen 10:16), here it is a general term for the pre-Israelite inhabitants of Canaan. • When properly directed, *zeal* is commendable (e.g., Num 25:11; 1 Kgs 19:10). Saul's misdirected zeal, however, involved blatant disregard for Israel's covenant with the Gibeonites.

21:3 Saul's actions had caused the Gibeonites to curse Israel (cp. Rom 2:24); once David had made ***amends,*** the Gibeonites would ***bless the LORD's people again.***

21:6 ***seven of Saul's sons:*** Although the law codes of other ancient Near Eastern nations sometimes permitted members of a family to be punished for crimes a guilty individual had committed, Deut 24:16 prohibited such punishment among the Israelites. This penalty was God's prerogative alone (Deut 5:9). The few instances in the Bible when offspring were punished were not regular criminal cases. Rather, they involved offenses against God, such as violation of the *kherem* (the taboo on goods in wars of total destruction ordered by God; Josh 7:24-25) or of national oaths (as here). • ***at Gibeon, on the mountain of the LORD*** (as in Greek version (see also 21:9); Hebrew reads *at Gibeah of Saul, the chosen of the LORD*): This probably refers to the high place at Gibeon that Solomon later visited (1 Kgs 3:3-4; 2 Chr 1:3). If the Hebrew reading is correct, the Gibeonites were sarcastically referring to Saul as "the chosen of the LORD."

21:7 ***the oath:*** See 1 Sam 20:14-15. In contrast to Saul, David was honoring his oath while dealing with the deadly fallout of Saul's violation of an oath. • ***Mephibosheth*** is another name for Merib-baal. See note on 4:4.

21:8 ***Armoni and Mephibosheth*** were Saul's only two remaining sons. • ***Saul's daughter Merab*** (as in a few Hebrew and Greek manuscripts and Syriac version (see also 1 Sam 18:19); most Hebrew manuscripts read *Michal*): The NLT follows the Greek here because Michal remained childless (6:22-23). Also, Merab was married to *Adriel* (1 Sam 18:19), whereas Michal's other husband was Palti (3:15). • ***Barzillai from Meholah*** (cp. 1 Sam 18:19) should not be confused with Barzillai of Gilead (19:31).

21:9 ***The beginning of the barley harvest*** was in April. • ***Before the LORD*** means "before the Lord's altar" (see note on 21:6).

21:10 Because the Gibeonites were not Israelites (21:2), they had no law such as the Israelite one in Deut 21:22-23 requiring the quick and proper burial of a criminal. *Rizpah* was intent that her sons not be further shamed after their death.

21:11-13 Rizpah's action shamed *David* into likewise honoring the dead of Saul's family.

21:14 The precise location of *Zela* is unknown. • ***the famine:*** See 21:1-2.

21:15-22 The extended account of battles with ***the Philistines*** highlights some notable accomplishments of David's mighty warriors (see also 23:8-39).

21:15 The description of ***David*** as ***weak and exhausted*** helps shift the focus from his ability and accomplishments to God as the source of his success (ch 22).

21:16 ***a descendant of the giants*** (Or *a descendant of the Rapha;* also in 21:18, 20, 22): cp. Gen 14:5; Deut 2:10-11, 20-21; 3:11. • ***more than seven pounds:*** Hebrew *300 shekels* [3.4 kilograms].

more than seven pounds, and he was armed
with a new sword. He had cornered David
and was about to kill him. 17 But Abishai son
of Zeruiah came to David's rescue and killed
the Philistine. Then David's men declared,
"You are not going out to battle with us again!
Why risk snuffing out the light of Israel?"
18 After this, there was another battle
against the Philistines at Gob. As they
fought, Sibbecai from Hushah killed Saph,
another descendant of the giants.
19 During another battle at Gob, Elhanan son of Jair from Bethlehem killed the
brother of Goliath of Gath. The handle of
his spear was as thick as a weaver's beam!
20 In another battle with the Philistines at
Gath, they encountered a huge man with six
fingers on each hand and six toes on each
foot, twenty-four in all, who was also a descendant of the giants. 21 But when he defied
and taunted Israel, he was killed by Jonathan,
the son of David's brother Shimea.
22 These four Philistines were descendants of the giants of Gath, but David and
his warriors killed them.

David's Psalm of Thanksgiving

2 Sam 22:1-51 // Ps 18:1-50

22 David sang this song to the LORD on
the day the LORD rescued him from
all his enemies and from Saul. 2 He sang:

"The LORD is my rock, my fortress, and
my savior;
3 my God is my rock, in whom I find
protection.
He is my shield, the power that saves me,
and my place of safety.
He is my refuge, my savior,
the one who saves me from violence.
4 I called on the LORD, who is worthy of
praise,
and he saved me from my enemies.

5 "The waves of death overwhelmed me;
floods of [d]destruction swept over me.
6 The grave wrapped its ropes around me;
death laid a trap in my path.
7 But in my distress I cried out to the LORD;
yes, I cried to my God for help.
He heard me from his sanctuary;
my cry reached his ears.

8 "Then the earth quaked and trembled.
The foundations of the heavens shook;
they quaked because of his anger.
9 Smoke poured from his nostrils;
fierce flames leaped from his mouth.
Glowing coals blazed forth from him.
10 He opened the heavens and came down;
dark storm clouds were beneath his
feet.
11 Mounted on a mighty [e]angelic being, he
flew,
soaring on the wings of the wind.
12 He shrouded himself in darkness,
veiling his approach with dense rain
clouds.
13 A great brightness shone around him,
and burning coals blazed forth.
14 The LORD thundered from heaven;
the voice of the Most High resounded.

22:2 1 Sam 2:2; Ps 31:3; 71:3
22:3 Gen 15:1; Deut 33:29; Ps 3:3; Luke 1:69
22:4 Ps 48:1; 96:4
22:5 Ps 69:14; 93:4; Jon 2:3; [d]*beliya'al* (1100) ‣Ps 18:4
22:6 Ps 116:3-4
22:7 Ps 116:4; 120:1
22:8 Judg 5:4; Job 26:11; Ps 97:4
22:9 Deut 32:22; Heb 12:29
22:10 Exod 20:21; 1 Kgs 8:12-13; Ps 97:2; Nah 1:3
22:11 [e]*kerub* (3742) ‣1 Kgs 6:23
22:12 Ps 104:3
22:14 Job 37:2; Ps 29:3
22:15 Deut 32:23; Josh 10:10; 1 Sam 7:10
22:16 Exod 15:8; Nah 1:4
22:17 Ps 144:7

21:17 *Abishai* was an accomplished warrior and fiercely loyal to David, whom he heroically rescued (see "Abishai," 16:9-12, p. 547). • ***the light of Israel?*** Cp. 18:3. Both passages reflect the glowing adoration that David's men had for him.

21:18 The location of ***Gob*** is uncertain.

21:19 ***son of Jair:*** As in parallel text at 1 Chr 20:5; Hebrew reads *son of Jaare-oregim*. • ***killed the brother of Goliath of Gath:*** As in parallel text at 1 Chr 20:5; Hebrew reads *killed Goliath of Gath*. Some traditions identify ***Elhanan*** as David, principally because Elhanan was also from Bethlehem and because David killed Goliath (1 Sam 17:48-51). But it is more likely that the words *brother of* were omitted from the Masoretic Text by scribal error.

21:21 ***Shimea:*** As in parallel text at 1 Chr 20:7; Hebrew reads *Shimei*, a variant spelling of Shimea.

22:1-51 Although this prayer of thanksgiving (also recorded in Ps 18:1-50) is placed near the end of David's story, David probably offered it to God much earlier in his life. This prayer and Hannah's (1 Sam 2:1-10) together enclose the book of Samuel with an *inclusio* (literary bookends). Hannah was saved from barrenness; David was saved from his enemies. The placement of this hymn also provides a parallel to Moses. The stories of both Moses and David end with a song or hymn giving lavish praise to God (see also Deut 31:30–32:43). Both highlight God as a "Rock" (Deut 32:4, 15, 18, 30, 31; 2 Sam 22:2, 3, 32, 47). Both are followed by second and shorter poetic pieces—Moses' final blessing to the Israelite tribes (Deut 33:1-29), and David's last words (23:1-7).

22:2 Hannah had said, "there is no Rock like our God" (1 Sam 2:2), while David said, ***the LORD is my rock***, which recalls God's rescue of David from Saul at the Rock of Escape (1 Sam 23:28). The Hebrew word translated "rock" in 22:3 (different from 22:2) refers in 1 Sam 24:2 to "the rocks of the wild goats," where Saul suspected that David was hiding. • ***fortress:*** The same word referred to David's physical "stronghold" (1 Sam 22:4), where David and his men sought refuge from Saul.

22:3 The phrase ***the power that saves me*** (literally *the horn that has saved me*) is similar to Hannah's "Oh, how the LORD has blessed me!" (literally *my horn is raised high in the LORD*, 1 Sam 2:1).

22:6 ***The grave:*** Hebrew *Sheol*.

22:7 Although ***his sanctuary*** sometimes refers to the Tabernacle or Temple, here it refers to God's heavenly dwelling; neither the Tabernacle nor the Temple were in existence at this time.

22:8-20 David vividly expands on how God heard him (22:7). David describes God's rescue as a *theophany* (manifestation of God's presence; see notes on Exod 19:16-25; Deut 1:33) that recalls God's manifestation at Sinai (Exod 19:16-20; cp. Judg 5:4-5).

22:11 ***a mighty angelic being*** (Hebrew *a cherub*): see notes on Ezek 1:5-14; 10:1-2. • ***soaring:*** As in some Hebrew manuscripts (see also Ps 18:10); other Hebrew manuscripts read *appearing*.

22:13 ***burning coals:*** Or *and lightning bolts*.

22:14 ***the LORD thundered from heaven:*** Cp. 1 Sam 2:10.

22:18
Ps 23:4
22:19
Ps 23:4
22:20
Ps 31:8; 118:5
22:21
1 Sam 26:23
Ps 24:4-5; 128:1
22:22
Gen 18:19
Ps 128:1
22:23
Deut 6:6-9
22:24
Gen 6:9-10; 7:1
Eph 1:4
[f]*tamim* (8549)
‣Job 12:4
22:26
Matt 5:7
22:27
Lev 26:23-24
Matt 5:8
22:28
Exod 3:7-8
Ps 72:12-13
Isa 2:11-12, 17; 5:15
22:29
Ps 27:1
22:31
Deut 32:4
2 Sam 22:3
Ps 12:6; 119:140
Prov 30:5
Matt 5:48
[g]*magen* (4043)
‣1 Kgs 10:17
22:32
1 Sam 2:2
22:35
Ps 144:1
22:36
Eph 6:16-17
22:39
Mal 4:3
22:41
Exod 23:27
22:42
1 Sam 28:5-6
Isa 1:15
22:43
Isa 10:6
Mic 7:10
22:44
2 Sam 3:1; 8:1-14; 19:8-10
Isa 55:5
22:45
Ps 66:3
Isa 55:5; 60:12
22:46
Mic 7:17

15 He shot arrows and scattered his
enemies;
his lightning flashed, and they were
confused.
16 Then at the command of the LORD,
at the blast of his breath,
the bottom of the sea could be seen,
and the foundations of the earth were
laid bare.

17 "He reached down from heaven and
rescued me;
he drew me out of deep waters.
18 He rescued me from my powerful enemies,
from those who hated me and were
too strong for me.
19 They attacked me at a moment when I
was in distress,
but the LORD supported me.
20 He led me to a place of safety;
he rescued me because he delights
in me.
21 The LORD rewarded me for doing right;
he restored me because of my
innocence.
22 For I have kept the ways of the LORD;
I have not turned from my God to
follow evil.
23 I have followed all his regulations;
I have never abandoned his decrees.
24 I am [f]blameless before God;
I have kept myself from sin.
25 The LORD rewarded me for doing right.
He has seen my innocence.

26 "To the faithful you show yourself faithful;
to those with integrity you show
integrity.
27 To the pure you show yourself pure,
but to the wicked you show yourself
hostile.
28 You rescue the humble,
but your eyes watch the proud and
humiliate them.
29 O LORD, you are my lamp.
The LORD lights up my darkness.
30 In your strength I can crush an army;
with my God I can scale any wall.

31 "God's way is perfect.
All the LORD's promises prove true.
He is a [g]shield for all who look to him
for protection.
32 For who is God except the LORD?
Who but our God is a solid rock?
33 God is my strong fortress,
and he makes my way perfect.
34 He makes me as surefooted as a deer,
enabling me to stand on mountain
heights.
35 He trains my hands for battle;
he strengthens my arm to draw a
bronze bow.
36 You have given me your shield of victory;
your help has made me great.
37 You have made a wide path for my feet
to keep them from slipping.

38 "I chased my enemies and destroyed them;
I did not stop until they were conquered.
39 I consumed them;
I struck them down so they did not
get up;
they fell beneath my feet.
40 You have armed me with strength for
the battle;
you have subdued my enemies under
my feet.
41 You placed my foot on their necks.
I have destroyed all who hated me.
42 They looked for help, but no one came to
their rescue.
They even cried to the LORD, but he
refused to answer.
43 I ground them as fine as the dust of the
earth;
I trampled them in the gutter like dirt.

44 "You gave me victory over my accusers.
You preserved me as the ruler over
nations;
people I don't even know now serve me.
45 Foreign nations cringe before me;
as soon as they hear of me, they submit.
46 They all lose their courage
and come trembling from their
strongholds.

22:21-30 David's divine rescue and success were related to his own obedient walk with God. God honors those who order their lives in a way that pleases him (see also Lev 26:1-13; Deut 28:1-14; Ps 1).

22:22-24 David composed these words much earlier (22:1), before his sin with Bathsheba. Still, his claim to being blameless should not be construed as a claim to perfection. David was simply noting that he had kept the covenant and followed its law (see also "Job's Innocence" at Job 27:5-6, p. 883).

22:31-51 David glorifies God for rescue in the past and for his *promises* to David's house for coming generations (see 7:8-16).

22:32 See Isa 43:11; 44:6, 8; 45:5, 21.

22:34 David probably encountered *deer* during his many days of hiding out in hilly terrain and caves (1 Sam 19:11–27:12).

22:36 *your help:* As in Dead Sea Scrolls (see also Ps 18:35); Masoretic Text reads *your answering.*

22:38-40 David's military accomplishments before he became king were impressive (see 1 Sam 17:12-58; 18:17-30; 23:1-5; 30:1-31). Yet rather than exalting himself, David glorified God and gave him the credit.

22:43 *I trampled them:* As in Dead Sea Scrolls (see also Ps 18:42); Masoretic Text reads *I crushed and trampled them.*

22:46 *come trembling:* As in parallel text at Ps 18:45; Hebrew reads *come girding themselves.*

47 "The LORD lives! Praise to my Rock!
May God, the Rock of my salvation, be [h]exalted!
48 He is the God who pays back those who harm me;
he brings down the nations under me
49 and delivers me from my enemies.
You hold me safe beyond the reach of my enemies;
you save me from violent opponents.
50 For this, O LORD, I will praise you among the nations;
I will sing praises to your name.
51 You give great victories to your king;
you show unfailing love to your anointed,
to David and all his descendants forever."

David's Last Words

23 These are the last words of David:
"David, the son of Jesse, speaks—
David, the man who was raised up so high,
David, the man anointed by the God of Jacob,
David, the sweet psalmist of Israel.
2 "The [i]Spirit of the LORD speaks through me;
his words are upon my tongue.
3 The God of Israel spoke.
The [j]Rock of Israel said to me:
'The one who rules righteously,
who rules in the fear of God,
4 is like the light of morning at sunrise,
like a morning without clouds,
like the gleaming of the sun
on new grass after rain.'
5 "Is it not my family God has chosen?
Yes, he has made an everlasting covenant with me.
His agreement is arranged and guaranteed in every detail.
He will ensure my safety and success.
6 But the godless are like thorns to be thrown away,
for they tear the hand that touches them.
7 One must use iron tools to chop them down;
they will be totally consumed by fire."

The Three: David's Elite Commanders
2 Sam 23:8-17 // 1 Chr 11:10-19

8These are the names of David's mightiest
warriors. The first was Jashobeam the Hacmonite, who was leader of the Three—the
three mightiest warriors among David's
men. He once used his spear to kill 800 enemy warriors in a single battle.
9Next in rank among the Three was Eleazar son of Dodai, a descendant of Ahoah.
Once Eleazar and David stood together
against the Philistines when the entire Israelite army had fled. 10He killed Philistines
until his hand was too tired to lift his sword,
and the LORD gave him a great victory that
day. The rest of the army did not return until it was time to collect the plunder!
11Next in rank was Shammah son of Agee
from Harar. One time the Philistines gathered at Lehi and attacked the Israelites in a
field full of lentils. The Israelite army fled,
12but Shammah held his ground in the middle of the field and beat back the Philistines.
So the LORD brought about a great victory.
13Once during the harvest, when David
was at the cave of Adullam, the Philistine
army was camped in the valley of Rephaim.
The Three (who were among the Thirty—an

22:47 2 Sam 22:2, 32; Ps 89:26; [h]*rum* (7311) ▸Neh 9:5
22:48 1 Sam 24:12; 25:39; Ps 94:1; 144:2
22:49 Ps 44:5; 140:1, 4, 11
22:50 *Rom 15:9
22:51 2 Sam 7:12-16; Ps 89:20; 144:9-10
23:1 1 Sam 16:12-13; 2 Sam 7:8-9; Ps 78:70-72; 89:20
23:2 2 Pet 1:20-21; [i]*ruakh* (7307) ▸2 Kgs 2:15
23:3 2 Sam 22:2, 32; 2 Chr 19:7, 9; Ps 72:1-3; Isa 11:1-5; [j]*tsur* (6697) ▸Job 14:18
23:4 Judg 5:31; Ps 72:6; 110:3
23:5 2 Sam 7:12; Ps 89:29; Isa 55:3
23:6 Matt 13:41-42
23:8 1 Chr 11:11-47
23:9 1 Chr 27:4
23:13 1 Sam 22:1; 2 Sam 5:18

22:51 Cp. 7:5-29; 1 Sam 2:10.

23:1-7 This passage comes from the end of David's career and reflects on his experience as king, even as ch 22 reflects on his experience before becoming king.

23:1 David's ***last words*** were not necessarily the last words he actually spoke (see 1 Kgs 1:16, 29-30, 33-35; 2:1-9) but his final public expression of worship to God as king (cp. 1 Sam 12:1-25). • ***David . . . speaks:*** The language indicates that he was about to utter an oracle, a revelation from God (23:2). • ***the sweet psalmist of Israel*** (Or *the favorite subject of the songs of Israel;* or *the favorite of the Strong One of Israel.*): For other references to David as musician and poet, see 1 Chr 23:5; 2 Chr 29:26, 27; Neh 12:36; Amos 6:5.

23:2 ***the Spirit of the LORD speaks through me:*** David spoke of God, and in the process, God spoke through David.

23:5 ***my family . . . everlasting covenant:*** David is referring to the prophecy Nathan made about David and his descendants (7:12-16). Jesus is the everlasting king who is the "son of David" (Matt 1:1).

23:6 Cp. Ps 1:4-5.

23:8-39 This section is a listing of David's elite warriors by name, the most prominent of whom are listed with a notable accomplishment. These warriors were some of the "iron tools" that God used to "chop down" the godless (23:7). • The list divides into *the Three* and *the Thirty*. Some Hebrew scholars have suggested that *the Thirty* be translated as "Officers." If that is correct, then it is possible that *the Three* was originally a term for a specific military office.

23:8 ***Jashobeam the Hacmonite*** (as in parallel text at 1 Chr 11:11; Hebrew reads *Josheb-basshebeth the Tahkemonite*): One version of the Greek OT calls him Ishbaal ("man of Baal"). Most likely it is the same individual in both cases and scribal copying errors caused variations in the spelling of the name. • ***the Three:*** As in Greek and Latin versions (see also 1 Chr 11:11); the meaning of the Hebrew is uncertain. • ***the Three—the three mightiest warriors among David's men. . . . a single battle:*** As in some Greek manuscripts (see also 1 Chr 11:11); the meaning of the Hebrew is uncertain, though it might be rendered *the Three. It was Adino the Eznite who killed 800 men at one time.*

23:10 ***to collect the plunder:*** Cp. 1 Sam 30:9-10, 21-25.

23:12 ***Shammah:*** Literally *he.*

23:13 The ***cave of Adullam*** was a place of refuge for David from Saul (see

23:14 1 Sam 22:4-5
23:16 Gen 35:13-14
23:17 Lev 17:10
23:18 2 Sam 10:10, 14; 18:2; 1 Chr 11:20-21
23:20 Josh 15:21; 2 Sam 8:18; 20:23
23:24 2 Sam 2:18
23:25 Judg 7:1
23:27 Josh 21:18
23:28 2 Kgs 25:23
23:30 Josh 24:30
23:34 2 Sam 11:3; 15:12

elite group among David's fighting men)
went down to meet him there. 14David was
staying in the stronghold at the time, and
a Philistine detachment had occupied the
town of Bethlehem.
15David remarked longingly to his men,
"Oh, how I would love some of that good water from the well by the gate in Bethlehem."
16So the Three broke through the Philistine
lines, drew some water from the well by the
gate in Bethlehem, and brought it back to
David. But he refused to drink it. Instead,
he poured it out as an offering to the LORD.
17"The LORD forbid that I should drink this!"
he exclaimed. "This water is as precious as
the blood of these men who risked their
lives to bring it to me." So David did not
drink it. These are examples of the exploits
of the Three.

The Thirty: David's Mighty Men
2 Sam 23:18-39 // 1 Chr 11:20-47

18Abishai son of Zeruiah, the brother of
Joab, was the leader of the Thirty. He once
used his spear to kill 300 enemy warriors
in a single battle. It was by such feats that he
became as famous as the Three. 19Abishai
was the most famous of the Thirty and was
their commander, though he was not one of
the Three.
20There was also Benaiah son of Jehoiada, a valiant warrior from Kabzeel. He did
many heroic deeds, which included killing
two champions of Moab. Another time, on
a snowy day, he chased a lion down into a
pit and killed it. 21Once, armed only with a
club, he killed a great Egyptian warrior who
was armed with a spear. Benaiah wrenched
the spear from the Egyptian's hand and
killed him with it. 22Deeds like these made
Benaiah as famous as the Three mightiest
warriors. 23He was more honored than the
other members of the Thirty, though he
was not one of the Three. And David made
him captain of his bodyguard.
24Other members of the Thirty included:

Asahel, Joab's brother;
Elhanan son of Dodo from Bethlehem;
25 Shammah from Harod;
Elika from Harod;
26 Helez from Pelon;
Ira son of Ikkesh from Tekoa;
27 Abiezer from Anathoth;
Sibbecai from Hushah;
28 Zalmon from Ahoah;
Maharai from Netophah;
29 Heled son of Baanah from Netophah;
Ithai son of Ribai from Gibeah (in the
land of Benjamin);
30 Benaiah from Pirathon;
Hurai from Nahale-gaash;
31 Abi-albon from Arabah;
Azmaveth from Bahurim;
32 Eliahba from Shaalbon;
the sons of Jashen;
Jonathan 33son of Shagee from Harar;
Ahiam son of Sharar from Harar;
34 Eliphelet son of Ahasbai from Maacah;
Eliam son of Ahithophel from Giloh;
35 Hezro from Carmel;
Paarai from Arba;
36 Igal son of Nathan from Zobah;
Bani from Gad;

---

1 Sam 22:1). • The *valley of Rephaim* was located between Bethlehem and Jerusalem (see 5:17-25).

23:15-16 *remarked longingly:* This Hebrew verb elsewhere carries the idea of excessive desire (see Num 11:4, "began to crave"; Ps 106:14, "desires ran wild"). It is unclear whether David's craving for water was excessive, but it certainly led to dangerous exploits. • *well by the gate:* David had memories from his younger days of growing up *in Bethlehem.* The location of the well is unknown.

23:17 *This water . . . these men:* Literally *Shall I drink the blood of these men?* When David poured the hard-won water on the ground, it did not signal ingratitude. Rather, he regarded the water as equivalent to the warriors' *blood;* it represented life that only God was worthy to receive (Lev 17:10-13; Deut 12:23-24).

23:18-23 Here are examples of the prowess of *Abishai* and *Benaiah.* Elsewhere, *Abishai* was intensely combative toward David's enemies, especially Saul (1 Sam 26:6-9) and Saul's kinsman Shimei (16:9-11). Abishai had saved David's life during one of the Philistine wars (21:16-17). • *Benaiah* appeared first as the commander of the mercenaries who served as David's bodyguard, independent of the regular army (8:18; 20:23). He was also the leader of a 24,000-man division of the regular army that served the king in the third month of every year (1 Chr 27:5-6). He played a major role in Solomon's ascension to the throne (1 Kgs 1:32-49) and became the commander of Solomon's army, as Joab was for David.

23:18 *the Thirty:* As in a few Hebrew manuscripts and Syriac version; most Hebrew manuscripts read *the Three.*

23:19 *the Thirty:* As in Syriac version; Hebrew reads *the Three.*

23:20 *son of Jehoiada, a valiant warrior:* Or *son of Jehoiada, son of Ish-hai.* • *two champions:* Literally *two of Ariel.*

23:24 *Asahel,* David's nephew, was killed by Abner during the war between David and Ishbosheth (2:18-32). Asahel's inclusion here suggests that parts of these lists go back to the beginning of David's career. • *Elhanan son of Dodo* should not be confused with Elhanan son of Jair (21:19; 1 Chr 20:5).

23:26 *from Pelon:* As in parallel text at 1 Chr 11:27 (see also 1 Chr 27:10); Hebrew reads *from Palti.*

23:27 *Sibbecai:* As in some Greek manuscripts (see also 1 Chr 11:29); Hebrew reads *Mebunnai.*

23:29 *Heled:* As in some Hebrew manuscripts (see also 1 Chr 11:30); most Hebrew manuscripts read *Heleb.* • *Ithai:* As in parallel text at 1 Chr 11:31; Hebrew reads *Ittai.*

23:30 *Hurai:* As in some Greek manuscripts (see also 1 Chr 11:32); Hebrew reads *Hiddai.* • *from Nahale-gaash:* Or *from the ravines of Gaash.*

23:32-33 *Jonathan son of Shagee:* As in parallel text at 1 Chr 11:34; Hebrew reads *Jonathan, Shammah;* some Greek manuscripts read *Jonathan son of Shammah.*

23:34 *Eliam:* See note on 23:39.

37 Zelek from Ammon;
Naharai from Beeroth, Joab's armor bearer;
38 Ira from Jattir;
Gareb from Jattir;
39 Uriah the Hittite.

There were thirty-seven in all.

David Takes a Census
2 Sam 24:1-9 // 1 Chr 21:1-6

24 Once again the anger of the LORD
burned against Israel, and he caused
David to harm them by taking a census. "Go
and count the people of Israel and Judah,"
the LORD told him.
2So the king said to Joab and the commanders of the army, "Take a census of all
the tribes of Israel—from Dan in the north
to Beersheba in the south—so I may know
how many people there are."
3But Joab replied to the king, "May the LORD
your God let you live to see a hundred times
as many people as there are now! But why, my
lord the king, do you want to do this?"
4But the king insisted that they take the
census, so Joab and the commanders of the
army went out to count the people of Israel.
5First they crossed the Jordan and camped at
Aroer, south of the town in the valley, in the
direction of Gad. Then they went on to Jazer,
6then to Gilead in the land of Tahtim-hodshi
and to Dan-jaan and around to Sidon. 7Then
they came to the fortress of Tyre, and all the
towns of the Hivites and Canaanites. Finally,
they went south to Judah as far as Beersheba.
8Having gone through the entire land for
nine months and twenty days, they returned
to Jerusalem. 9Joab reported the number of
people to the king. There were 800,000 capable warriors in Israel who could handle a
sword, and 500,000 in Judah.

Judgment for David's Sin
2 Sam 24:10-17 // 1 Chr 21:7-17

10But after he had taken the census, David's
conscience began to bother him. And he
said to the LORD, "I have sinned greatly by
taking this census. Please forgive my guilt,
LORD, for doing this foolish thing."
11The next morning the word of the LORD
came to the prophet Gad, who was David's
seer. This was the message: 12"Go and say to
David, 'This is what the LORD says: I will give
you three choices. Choose one of these punishments, and I will inflict it on you.' "
13So Gad came to David and asked him,
"Will you choose three years of famine
throughout your land, three months of
fleeing from your enemies, or three days of
severe plague throughout your land? Think

23:39 2 Sam 11:3
24:1-17 1 Chr 21:1-17
24:1 1 Chr 27:23
24:2 Judg 20:1; 2 Sam 3:9-10
24:3 Deut 1:11
24:5 Num 21:32; 32:34-36; Josh 13:9, 16
24:6 Josh 19:28
24:9 Num 1:20-46; 1 Chr 21:5
24:10 1 Sam 24:5; 2 Sam 12:13
24:11 1 Sam 9:9; 22:5
24:13 1 Chr 21:12

23:39 The very last name mentioned is ***Uriah the Hittite***. There is an earlier reference to his father-in-law, Eliam, father of Bathsheba (23:34; see 11:3). By contrast, the Chronicler, who never mentioned David's sins against Bathsheba and Uriah, placed Uriah's name inconspicuously in the middle of the list of David's mighty men (1 Chr 11:10-47). This author not only described the sins (ch 11) but puts emphasis on Uriah's name by placing it at the end of this list. Uriah was no ordinary conscript but a loyal member of David's elite guard, which makes David's treachery against him all the worse. • ***There were thirty-seven in all:*** Only thirty-six names are mentioned, assuming that "Shammah . . . from Harar" (23:11) is different from "Shammah from Harod" (23:25), and that "Benaiah son of Jehoiada" (23:20) is different from "Benaiah from Pirathon" (23:30). Perhaps the thirty-seventh warrior was Joab, who is mentioned only peripherally (23:18, 37) and is absent from the list of names. Many commentators say that he is excluded because he was David's chief military leader and did not need to be included. The omission could also represent David's long and troubled association with Joab, who was eventually executed when Solomon carried out David's deathbed command (1 Kgs 2:5-6, 28-34).

24:1 The reason God's ***anger . . . burned against Israel*** is unknown (but see Deut 4:25; 6:14-15; 29:22-28; 31:16-18). • ***Caused . . . to harm*** reflects a Hebrew verb (*suth*) used elsewhere in the sense of enticing or inciting someone to do wrong (1 Sam 26:19, "stirred you up against me"). ***Census***-taking was usually unpopular with citizens, who resented it as an intrusion into their private affairs. They regarded it as a prelude to taxation or forced military service (see note on 24:9). If David was motivated by pride or was preparing for an illegitimate war (as 24:9 might suggest), this might explain why it was a sin for him (24:10).

24:2 ***Joab and the commanders:*** As in Greek version (see also 24:4 and 1 Chr 21:2); Hebrew reads *Joab the commander.* • ***Dan*** and ***Beersheba*** were the traditional northern and southern boundaries of Israel. This phrase meant the entire land of Israel.

24:3 ***why . . . do you want to do this?*** Joab either realized that such a move would be unpopular among the people, or he believed that it was wrong before God.

24:6 ***to Gilead in the land of Tahtim-hodshi:*** Greek version reads *to Gilead and to Kadesh in the land of the Hittites.*

24:7 ***they went south to Judah:*** Or *they went to the Negev of Judah.*

24:9 The phrase ***capable warriors*** shows that the census focused largely on those fit for military service. The total for Judah here might be rounded up from the total in 1 Chr 21:5; the different number for Israel in 1 Chr 21:5 (1,100,000) might come from combining a regular standing army of 300,000 (elsewhere unrecorded) with the 800,000 discovered through the census.

24:10 ***I have sinned:*** See note on 24:1. David believed his sin was the cause of the plague and that the removal of his sin would make things right (see also 24:17). It is clear, however, that Israel rather than David was the true object of God's wrath (24:1).

24:11 ***Gad . . . David's seer*** appears only here and in 1 Sam 22:5. *Seer* is an early name for a prophet (1 Sam 9:9, 19). Unlike pagan magicians or sorcerers, biblical seers had divinely inspired visions (see also 2 Kgs 17:13; Isa 29:10; 30:9-10; Amos 7:12; Mic 3:7) and functioned as God's messengers.

24:13 David had already experienced the first two options—fleeing from Saul and Absalom, and famine because Saul had murdered the Gibeonites (21:1). While ***three days of severe plague*** sounded less traumatic, 70,000 people perished (24:15). • ***three:*** As in Greek version (see also 1 Chr 21:12); Hebrew reads *seven.*

24:14 Ps 51:1; 130:3-4, 7-8
24:15 1 Chr 21:14; 27:24
24:16 Exod 12:23; 2 Kgs 19:35
24:17 Ps 74:1
24:18-25 //1 Chr 21:18-26
24:21 Num 16:44-50
24:22 1 Sam 6:14; 1 Kgs 19:21
24:24 Gen 23:16
24:25 2 Sam 21:14

this over and decide what answer I should
give the LORD who sent me."
14"I'm in a desperate situation!" David replied to God. "But let us fall into the hands
of the LORD, for his mercy is great. Do not
let me fall into human hands."
15So the LORD sent a plague upon Israel
that morning, and it lasted for three days. A
total of 70,000 people died throughout the
nation, from Dan in the north to Beersheba
in the south. 16But as the angel was preparing to destroy Jerusalem, the LORD relented
and said to the death angel, "Stop! That is
enough!" At that moment the angel of the
LORD was by the threshing floor of Araunah
the Jebusite.
17When David saw the angel, he said to
the LORD, "I am the one who has sinned and
done wrong! But these people are as innocent as sheep—what have they done? Let
your anger fall against me and my family."

David Builds an Altar
2 Sam 24:18-25 // 1 Chr 21:18-30
18That day Gad came to David and said to
him, "Go up and build an altar to the LORD on
the threshing floor of Araunah the Jebusite."
19So David went up to do what the LORD
had commanded him. 20When Araunah saw
the king and his men coming toward him,
he came and bowed before the king with
his face to the ground. 21"Why have you
come, my lord the king?" Araunah asked.
David replied, "I have come to buy your
threshing floor and to build an altar to the
LORD there, so that he will stop the plague."
22"Take it, my lord the king, and use it as
you wish," Araunah said to David. "Here are
oxen for the burnt offering, and you can use
the threshing boards and ox yokes for wood
to build a fire on the altar. 23I will give it all
to you, Your Majesty, and may the LORD your
God accept your sacrifice."
24But the king replied to Araunah, "No,
I insist on buying it, for I will not present
burnt offerings to the LORD my God that
have cost me nothing." So David paid him
fifty pieces of silver for the threshing floor
and the oxen.
25David built an altar there to the LORD
and sacrificed burnt offerings and peace offerings. And the LORD answered his prayer
for the land, and the plague on Israel was
stopped.

God or Satan? (24:1-25)

1 Chr 21:1-30; Job 1:8–2:10; Matt 4:1-11; 12:22-37; Mark 8:31-33; John 13:21-31; Rom 8:28; 1 Cor 5:1-5; 2 Cor 12:6-10; Eph 2:1-7; Rev 20:1-3, 7-10

There is a notable difference between the accounts of David's census in Samuel and in Chronicles. 2 Samuel 24:1 attributes the census taking to God ("the LORD . . . caused David to harm them by taking a census"), while 1 Chr 21:1 attributes the action to Satan ("Satan rose up against Israel and caused David to take a census of the people of Israel"). How can this be?

The difference is one of perspective. 2 Samuel 24 tells the census story from God's perspective as the primary agent; God permitted Satan's action in order to fulfill his own purpose.

This phenomenon is not uncommon in Scripture. Matthew 4:1 contains a similar instance of dual agency, where Jesus is led out into the wilderness by the Holy Spirit to be tempted by the devil. Perhaps the most notable similar experience is Job's trial: It was permitted by God and then brought on by Satan after the Lord spoke glowingly about Job (Job 1:8; 2:3). Through all the trials that followed, Job's heart was righteous despite Satan's attempts to elicit a curse against God. Similarly, 2 Cor 12:7 teaches that a God-sent affliction can be delivered by a messenger from Satan. When Paul wrote that he was given a "thorn," he used a passive verb, indicating that this affliction was given by God.

Satan works in many ways in an attempt to destroy or discourage God's people. Yet God is sovereign. God does not author evil, but sometimes God makes use of others' evil deeds to accomplish his good purposes (Gen 50:20).

24:15 *for three days:* Literally *for the designated time.*

24:16 *the LORD relented:* God might stop his judgment when a third party intercedes for the intended target (Exod 32:12-14), when the sinful person repents (Jer 18:8), or simply because he decides to do so. • *the death angel:* Cp. Exod 12:23. • A *threshing floor* was an unwalled space where harvested grain was threshed and winnowed to separate the kernels from the chaff. Gideon encountered God at a threshing floor (Judg 6:37). Araunah's threshing floor later became the site of the Temple (1 Chr 21:18–22:1; 2 Chr 3:1). • *Araunah the Jebusite:* Even though David had taken Jerusalem from the Jebusites (5:6-9), he had not eliminated them or driven them away.

24:17 *I am the one who has sinned:* David's earlier confession of sin was limited to his circumstances ("forgive my guilt"; 24:10); now he prayed for those he considered *innocent* (but see 24:1) and offered to die in their place. • *as sheep:* David was the shepherd of Israel (see note on 7:8).

24:21 *so that he will stop the plague:* David did not know that God had already announced the end of the plague to the angel (24:16).

24:24 *fifty pieces of silver:* Hebrew *50 shekels of silver,* about 20 ounces or 570 grams in weight.

24:25 David performed priestly functions when he ***built an altar,*** offered ***burnt offerings and peace offerings,*** and prayed for his people; in response, ***the LORD answered his prayer*** (cp. 21:14).

THE CHRONOLOGY OF
Israel's Monarchy

The time of Israel's kings is a fascinating period in history. The chronological data of Israel's monarchy, however, present a time-honored conundrum. Several factors contribute to the complexity, but what emerges is a coherent historical narrative, and events in the books of Samuel, Kings, and Chronicles fit the historical record.

REGNAL-YEAR DATING In the ancient Near East, events were dated with reference to the reign of an individual king rather than with reference to an absolute calendar. For instance, the people of Judah would have described an event in 701 BC as happening in the fourteenth year of King Hezekiah's reign in Judah (2 Kgs 18:13). This system can be called *regnal-year dating,* dating by reference to the years of a king's reign.

The books of Kings contain records of the regnal years for all of the kings of Israel and Judah from Solomon down to Judah's exile to Babylon. Archaeological records of Assyria and Babylon give us the regnal years for their kings. Some of these kings appear in the OT, which helps us see how the dates in Assyrian, Babylonian, and Israelite records are related to each other and to our own calendar.

ACCESSION-YEAR DATING Some nations, such as Babylon and Assyria, counted the year in which a new king took the throne (his *accession*) as belonging only to the previous king. A new king's accession year was not counted as one of his regnal years; his first regnal year was

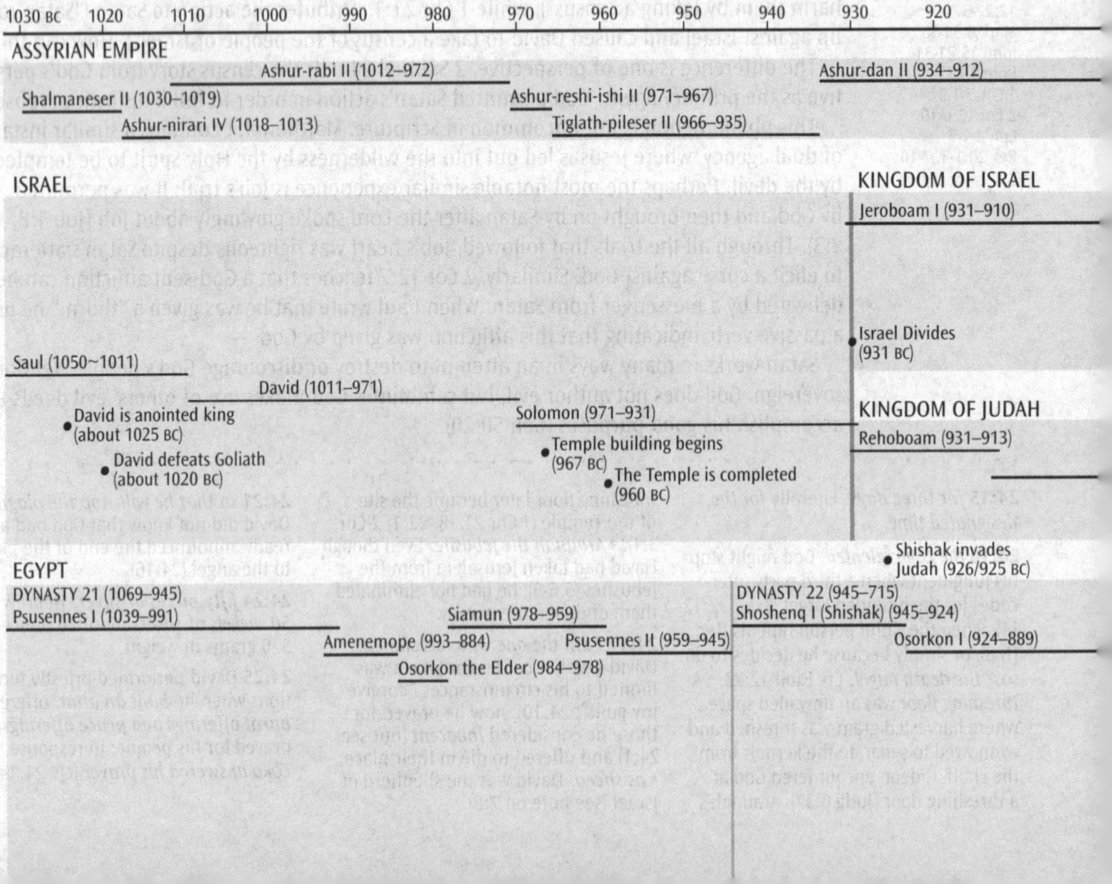

the following year. This system is called *accession-year dating* because it has separate accession years that are excluded from the count. Other nations, such as Egypt, counted the year of a king's accession while also counting that year as the last year of the old king's reign. As a result, a single calendar year would be counted twice—once for the previous king, once for the new king. This system is called *non-accession-year dating* because there are no distinct accession years in the system.

Edwin R. Thiele showed[1] that Israel's monarchy under David and Solomon probably used accession-year dating (i.e., accession years were not counted as regnal years). This practice was continued in the kingdom of Judah. The kingdom of Israel, by contrast, apparently followed Egypt's practice with non-accession-year dating. The kingdom of Israel was founded by Jeroboam I, who had spent several years in Egypt and was differentiating his kingdom from Judah (1 Kgs 12:26-33).

THE ANCIENT CALENDAR YEAR

The annual calendars of ancient Israel, Assyria, Babylon, and Egypt did not correlate with our modern calendar. Israel's united monarchy under David and Solomon evidently used a royal year beginning around September or October, and the kingdom of Judah continued to use this royal year[2] (see chart, "Israel's Annual Calendar," p. 145). For Babylon and the northern kingdom of Israel, the first month of the calendar year occurred around March or April.

Because the calendars of the ancient world do not correlate with our own, sometimes a variation of one year occurs in assigning a modern calendar date for an event. For instance, Solomon's last regnal year began in autumn 931 BC, and Jeroboam's first regnal year ended in spring 930 BC. We know therefore that between autumn 931 BC and spring 930 BC Solomon died, Rehoboam became king, and the kingdom split immediately thereafter. We do not know, however,

[1] Edwin R. Thiele, *The Mysterious Number of the Hebrew Kings*, 3rd ed. (Grand Rapids: Kregel, 1983), 47–51. With some modification, Thiele's influential solution is reflected in the *NLT Study Bible*.
[2] Ibid., 51–54.

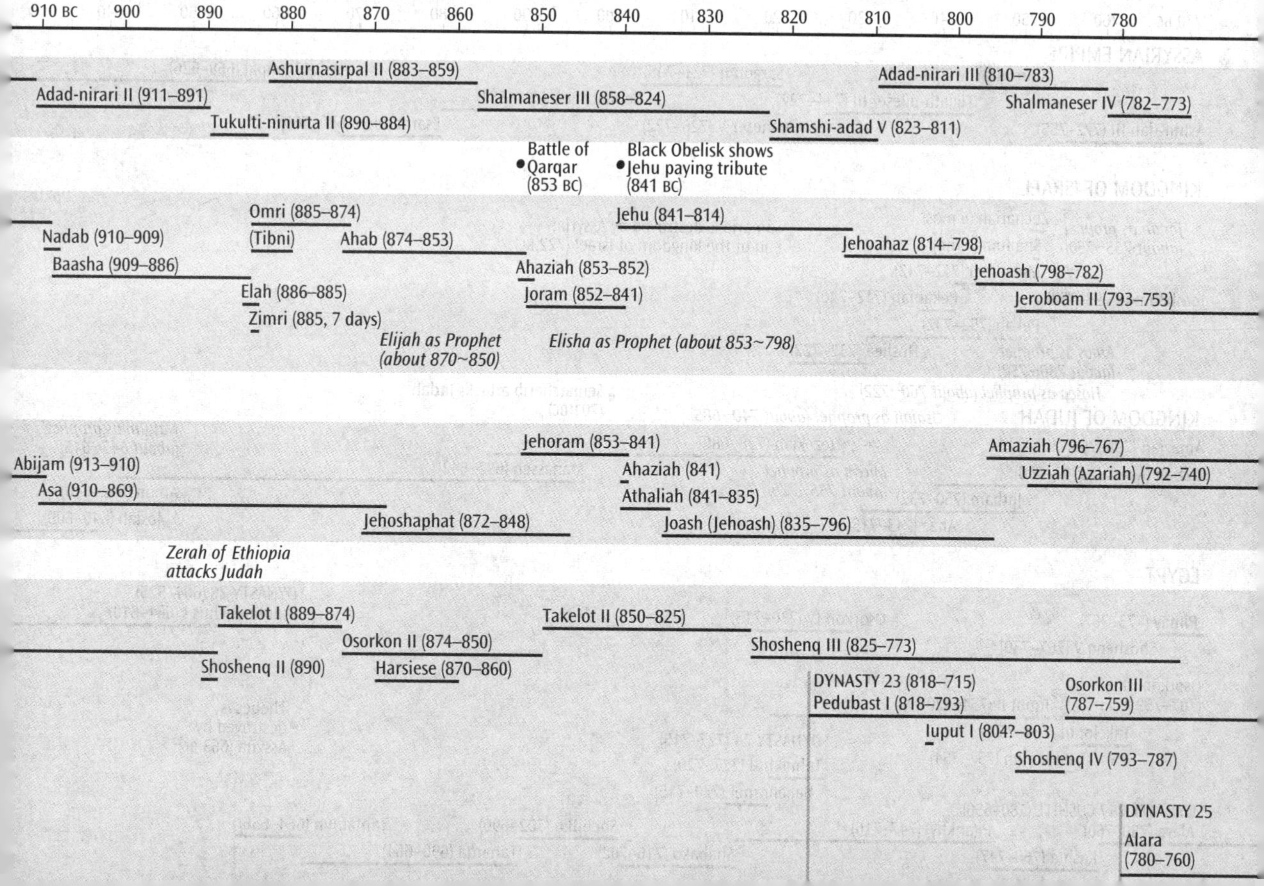

exactly when during that six-month period the division of the kingdom took place. Therefore some authors use 931 BC, while others use 930 BC. This variation simply reflects the "resolution" of the data in ancient records.

CO-REGENCIES Kings sometimes made their sons co-regents, perhaps to provide on-the-job training and to ensure an orderly transfer of power. The practice of co-regency became very common in Judah: Jehoshaphat, Jehoram, Uzziah, Jotham, Ahaz, Hezekiah, and Manasseh all began as co-regents. Co-regency also occurred in Babylon: Belshazzar (553–539 BC) served as co-regent (and acting ruler) for most of his father Nabonidus's reign (556–539 BC). The son's years are variously counted from when he became co-regent or from when he began his sole reign.

FIXING RELATIVE DATES IN HISTORY Can the relative dates of the Old Testament monarchs be converted to absolute dates in our calendar? The answer is usually yes, at least within a range of months.

A key document is the Assyrian Eponym Canon, which lists the names of Assyrian officials and kings between 910 and 612 BC. The Assyrians included in the list significant events that occurred during each year, including statements about war, flooding, and astronomical phenomena such as eclipses. Since eclipses occur at regular and predictable times, astronomers today can calculate when they occurred in ancient Assyria. The eclipses that the Assyrians observed and recorded give us a basis for fixing their records to our calendar.

Other Assyrian texts mention events in Israel. For example, the Assyrian king Shalmaneser III (858–824 BC) fought the Battle of Qarqar in 853 BC. The Kurkh Monolith, an Assyrian monument that describes that battle, says that King Ahab of Israel participated, so we know that Ahab's reign lasted until 853 BC. Later, the Black Obelisk, another Assyrian record, mentions Shalmaneser III making Jehu of

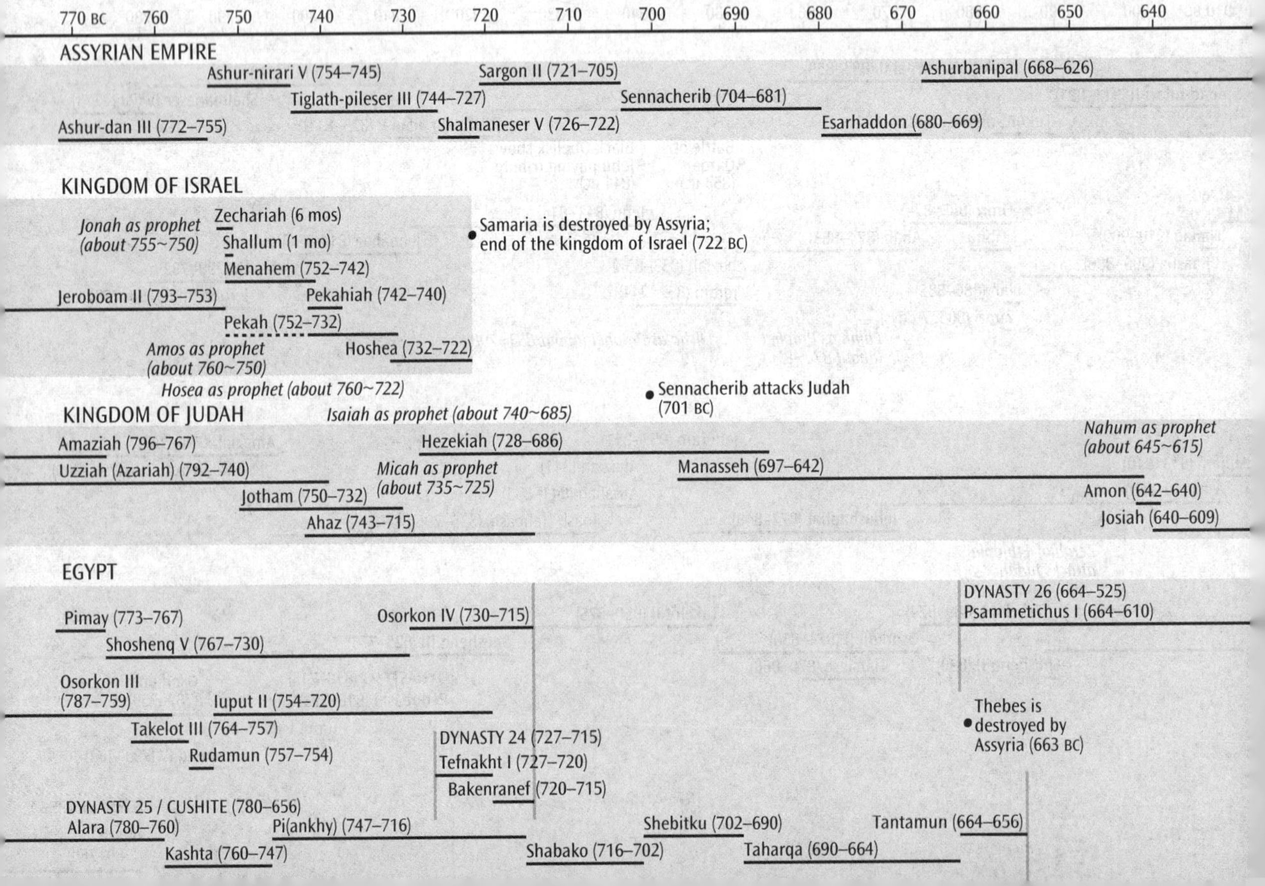

Israel pay tribute in 841 BC, so we know that Jehu was reigning by that date. In this way, the relative dates in the biblical text can be converted into absolute dates. Egyptian and Babylonian sources can also be correlated.[3] Assyrian and Aramean records explicitly and accurately refer to nearly half of the kings of the divided monarchy, beginning as early as Ahaziah (in Judah) and Omri (in Israel).

There is a remarkable harmony between the records of Assyria, Babylon, Aram, Egypt, and Israel. This harmony highlights the historical reliability of these records and gives confidence in the dating of biblical events during the divided monarchy.

FURTHER READING

K. A. KITCHEN
On the Reliability of the Old Testament (2006)

EDWIN R. THIELE
The Mysterious Numbers of the Hebrew Kings (1983)

[3] For Babylonian chronology, we rely on Richard A. Parker and Waldo H. Dubberstein, *Babylonian Chronology 626 B.C.—A.D. 75* (Providence, RI: Brown University Press, 1956). For Egyptian chronology, we use K. A. Kitchen, "Egypt, History of (Chronology)" in *Anchor Bible Dictionary*, David Noel Freedman, ed. (New York: Doubleday, 1992).

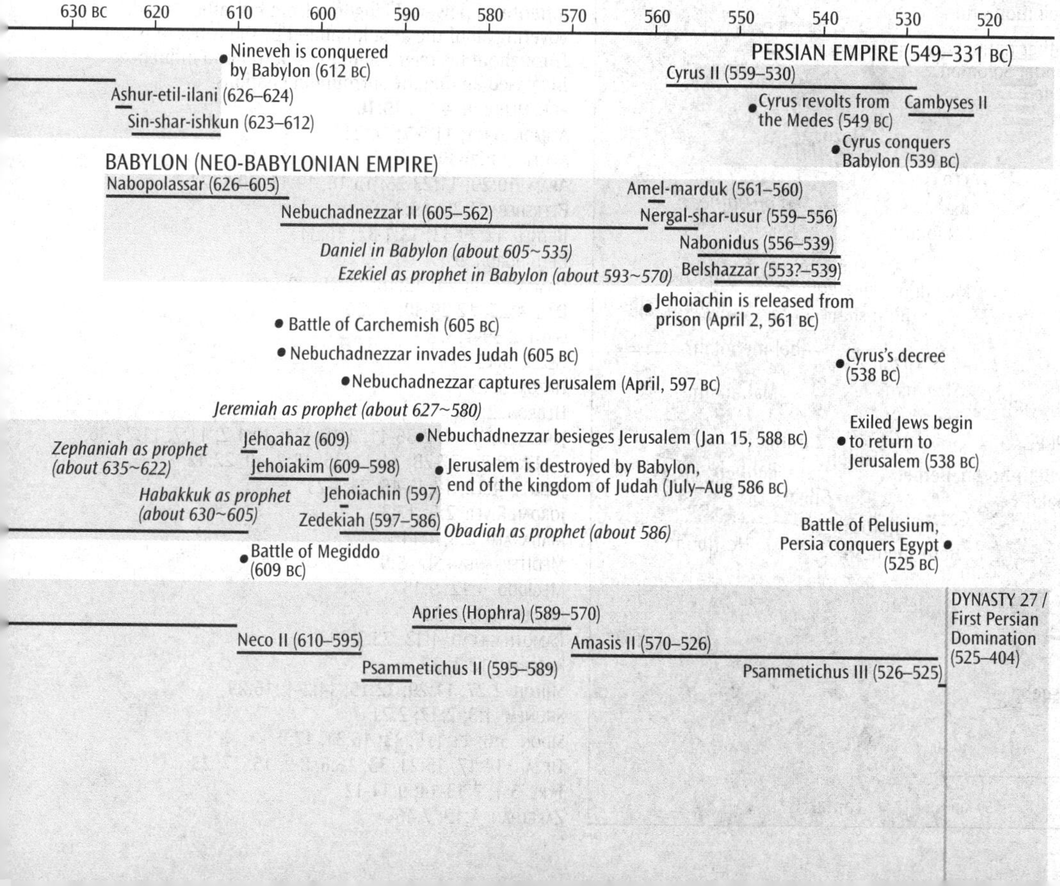

THE FIRST BOOK OF KINGS

Solomon's kingdom was the pinnacle of Israel's glory. "King Solomon became richer and wiser than any other king on earth" (10:23). The Queen of Sheba confirmed the glory of Solomon's kingdom, saying, "Everything I heard in my country about your achievements and wisdom is true! I didn't believe what was said until I arrived here and saw it with my own eyes" (10:6-7). First Kings celebrates the splendor of Solomon's kingdom. But Solomon's reign also illustrates the dangers of spiritual infidelity, and 1 Kings warns about the results of preoccupation with luxury, fame, self, and security. It is a timeless warning to us all.

SETTING

At the height of his power, Solomon administered a kingdom that stretched "from the Euphrates River in the north to the land of the Philistines and the border of Egypt in the south" (4:21).

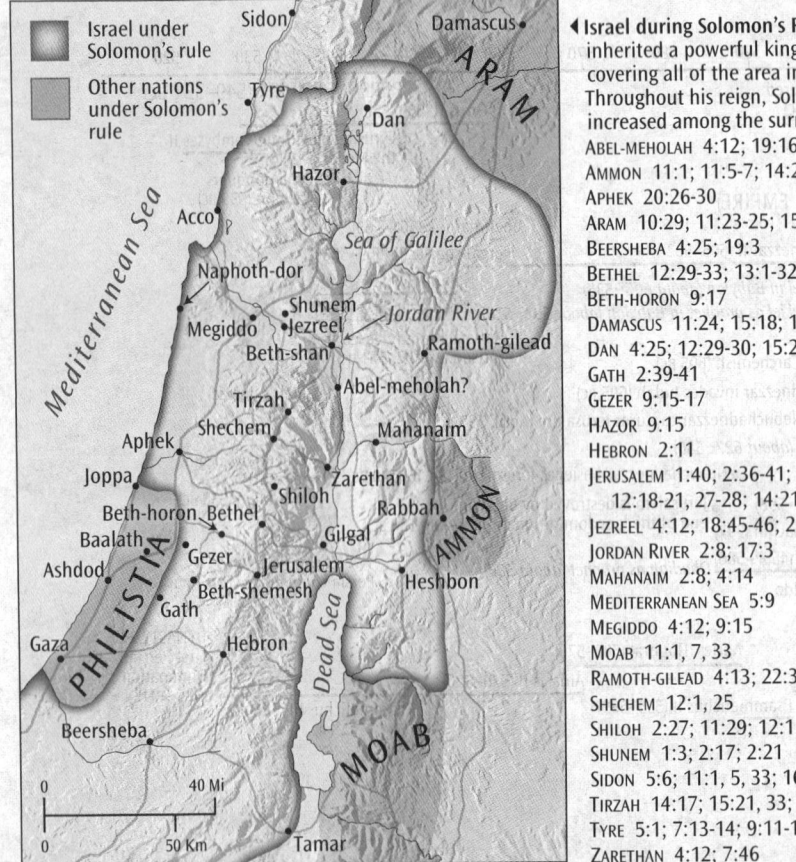

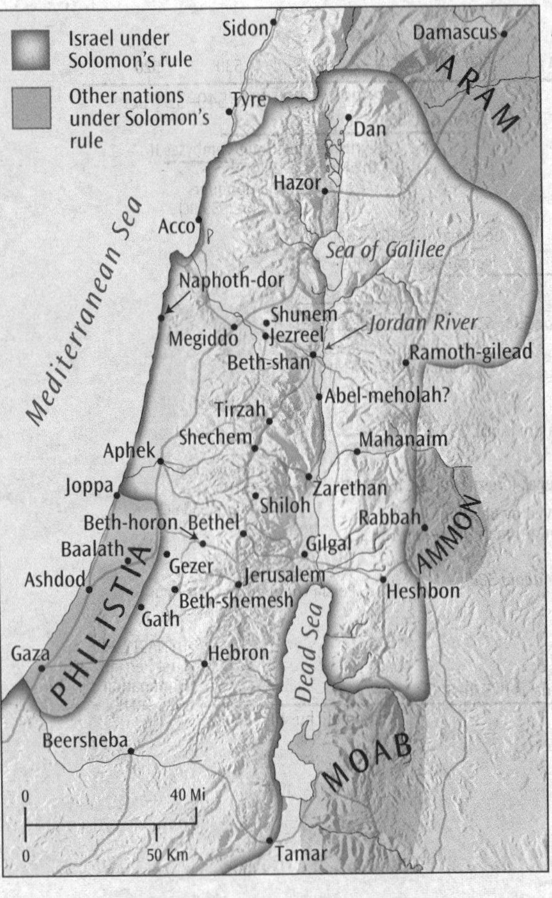

Israel during Solomon's Reign, 971–931 BC. Solomon inherited a powerful kingdom from his father David, covering all of the area inhabited by the tribes of Israel. Throughout his reign, Solomon's power and influence increased among the surrounding nations.

Abel-meholah 4:12; 19:16
Ammon 11:1; 11:5-7; 14:21
Aphek 20:26-30
Aram 10:29; 11:23-25; 15:18; 19:15; 20:1; 22:1
Beersheba 4:25; 19:3
Bethel 12:29-33; 13:1-32; 16:34
Beth-horon 9:17
Damascus 11:24; 15:18; 19:15; 20:34
Dan 4:25; 12:29-30; 15:20
Gath 2:39-41
Gezer 9:15-17
Hazor 9:15
Hebron 2:11
Jerusalem 1:40; 2:36-41; 3:15; 8:1; 10:1-2; 11:7; 11:29-36; 12:18-21, 27-28; 14:21, 25; 15:2, 10; 22:42
Jezreel 4:12; 18:45-46; 21:1-23
Jordan River 2:8; 17:3
Mahanaim 2:8; 4:14
Mediterranean Sea 5:9
Megiddo 4:12; 9:15
Moab 11:1, 7, 33
Ramoth-gilead 4:13; 22:3-29
Shechem 12:1, 25
Shiloh 2:27; 11:29; 12:15; 14:2-4; 15:29
Shunem 1:3; 2:17; 2:21
Sidon 5:6; 11:1, 5, 33; 16:31; 17:9
Tirzah 14:17; 15:21, 33; 16:6, 8-9, 15, 17, 23
Tyre 5:1; 7:13-14; 9:11-12
Zarethan 4:12; 7:46

Solomon's power and wealth brought him in contact with many surrounding nations—especially the important maritime city-state of Tyre and the age-old empire of Egypt.

It was an ideal time for Solomon's kingdom to expand, for the traditional political powers of the area were in decline (see map on p. 595). The strong Hittite kingdom to the north had broken up into a number of small states. In Mesopotamia, years of struggle with the Arameans and the Hittites had weakened Assyria, which remained weak until the accession of Ashur-dan II (934–912 BC). In the south, Egypt's presence in Canaan had weakened during the 21st dynasty (1069–945 BC). Egypt would not make an effective military effort until the rule of the 22nd dynasty pharaoh Shoshenq I (Shishak, 945–924 BC).

OUTLINE

1:1–11:43
The Reign of Solomon

12:1–16:14
The Early Divided Kingdom

16:15–22:53
The Era of Israel's Third Dynasty

Unfortunately, Solomon's foreign diplomacy involved marriages with the daughters of foreign kings. This was a common way to cement alliances in the ancient Near East, but it was spiritually disastrous, for "in Solomon's old age, they turned his heart to worship other gods instead of being completely faithful to the LORD his God" (11:4).

Tensions that had been smoldering between the northern and southern Hebrew tribes surfaced with Solomon's death in 931 BC. An outright schism eventually restructured the kingdom into Israel (the northern ten tribes) and Judah (the remaining two southern tribes). Israel and Judah skirmished repeatedly during the era of the first two northern dynasties and Judah's first three kings (931~874 BC). The hostility subsided when King Ahab of Israel and King Jehoshaphat of Judah found a common cause against the Arameans (chs 20, 22).

The Hebrew kingdoms were increasingly entangled by the expansionist ambitions of their neighbors. They were invaded by Shoshenq I of Egypt in 926 BC, and throughout the 800s BC they faced the constant menace of the Arameans and the rising power of Assyria. During the reigns of Assyrian kings Ashurnasirpal II (883–859 BC) and Shalmaneser III (858–824 BC), Assyrian troops moved steadily westward to the Mediterranean Sea. At the famous Battle of Qarqar (853 BC), a coalition of western allies, including Israel's King Ahab, withstood the Assyrian king Shalmaneser and temporarily sidetracked Assyria's advance.

During this time, the two Hebrew kingdoms struggled spiritually. Israel stopped worshiping the Lord at Solomon's Temple, and Jeroboam I, first king of the northern kingdom of Israel (931–910 BC), instituted apostate religious practices that led the northern kingdom astray (see 2 Kgs 17:21-23). Judah's first two kings, Rehoboam and Abijah, lapsed spiritually, while the subsequent two, Asa and Jehoshaphat, maintained greater, though not perfect, spiritual fidelity (15:11; 22:43).

TIMELINE

971–931 BC
Solomon as king of Israel

967–960 BC
The Temple is built

945–924 BC
Shoshenq I (Shishak) as pharaoh of Egypt

931 BC
The kingdom is divided

931–913 BC
Rehoboam as king of Judah

931–910 BC
Jeroboam I as king of Israel

926/925 BC
Shishak invades Judah

913–910 BC
Abijam as king of Judah

910–869 BC
Asa as king of Judah

910–909 BC
Nadab as king of Israel

909–886 BC
Baasha as king of Israel

890s BC
Zerah of Ethiopia attacks Judah

886–885 BC
Elah as king of Israel

885 BC
Zimri as king of Israel

885–874 BC
Omri as king of Israel

874–853 BC
Ahab as king of Israel

872–848 BC
Jehoshaphat as king of Judah

about 870~850 BC
Elijah as prophet

853–841 BC
Jehoram as king of Judah

853 BC
Battle of Qarqar

853–852 BC
Ahaziah as king of Israel

SUMMARY OF 1 KINGS

Beginning with King David's last days, 1 Kings describes the establishment of Solomon's glorious empire (971–931 BC) and the events that subsequently divided the kingdom into two parts, the kingdom of Israel in the north and the kingdom of Judah in the south. The book then traces the varying fortunes of the two kingdoms to about 853 BC, into the reign of Ahaziah in Israel (853–852 BC).

The first eleven chapters center on King Solomon, recounting both his fabulous reign and his later spiritual compromise. Solomon's story begins and ends in controversy. Solomon was David's chosen successor, but his older brother Adonijah attempted to seize the throne (chs 1–2). Having triumphed over Adonijah's rival claim, Solomon used his God-given wisdom to reorganize the government and make it more efficient. He facilitated the kingdom's commercial expansion on land and sea and undertook extensive building projects, including the marvelous Temple and palace complex. However, toward the end of his reign, Solomon's spiritual decline (11:1-13) and oppressive administrative measures (e.g., 5:13-18) incited political adversaries both in and out of the country (11:14-40).

Kings . . . records Israel's spiritual response to God who had taken her into covenant relationship with himself. . . . Within its pages is found a detailed summary of the spiritual experiences of her people—particularly her kings, prophets, and priests, whose activities largely point to the need for the advent of the one who would combine the intended ideal of these three offices in himself.

RICHARD D. PATTERSON AND HERMANN J. AUSTEL
1, 2 Kings, p. 4

God appeared three times to Solomon, giving us a glimpse of his personal spiritual journey. Early in Solomon's reign, God honored his request for wisdom to rule the kingdom (3:5-15), resulting in great prosperity and honor (3:16–8:66). After Solomon finished building the Temple and palace, God visited him again to remind him that, as heir of God's covenant with David, Solomon's continued success would depend on spiritual fidelity (9:1-9). However, his great fame (9:10–10:29) led him into foreign alliances, cemented by customary marriages with the daughters of foreign kings. This spiritual compromise eventually led Solomon so far as to sponsor the worship of pagan deities (11:1-8). God visited Solomon a third and final time, but this time he rebuked Solomon for his failure to honor the covenant. This unfaithfulness would be the ultimate cause of the kingdom's division after his death (11:9-13).

After Solomon died, God's judgment came quickly. King Rehoboam, Solomon's son, antagonized the northern tribes, who were seeking relief from forced labor and heavy taxation. Consequently, the kingdom was divided into Israel in the north, with Jeroboam I as king, and Judah in the south, where Rehoboam remained on the throne (12:1-24). Israel's first two dynasties (Jeroboam I to Tibni) spiritually degraded the northern kingdom, while the kings of Judah degraded the southern kingdom. Political instability continued in the northern kingdom, resulting in royal assassinations, contests for power, and the establishment of Israel's notorious third dynasty, founded by King Omri, who was one of the most powerful and evil kings of Israel (16:25-26).

The final section of 1 Kings is primarily devoted to the reign of Omri's son Ahab (16:29–22:40). Since Israel had begun worshiping the Canaanite storm-god Baal, the Lord commissioned Elijah to confront Ahab and to demonstrate the Lord's power, showing that he alone is God (17:1–18:46). After Elijah fled from the wrath of Queen Jezebel, God reclaimed and recommissioned him, with Elisha as his successor (19:1-21).

On the political front, King Ahab faced repeated challenges from the Aramean king Ben-hadad, against whom Ahab fought three

campaigns (20:1-25, 26-43; 22:1-40), the last of which cost Ahab his life. Between the second and third campaign, Ahab, aided by his ruthless wife Jezebel, murdered innocent Naboth and confiscated his property (ch 21).

God's prophets figured prominently in the events of Ahab's reign. In Ahab's first two campaigns against the Arameans, the king was first counseled (20:22) and then rebuked by an unnamed prophet (20:35-43). Elijah later censured Ahab's seizure of Naboth's vineyard (ch 21). Before Ahab's third battle against the Arameans, the prophet Micaiah warned of Ahab's impending death (22:5-28).

The book of 1 Kings closes with a brief word concerning the character and reign of Judah's King Jehoshaphat (22:41-50) and introduces Ahab's successor, Ahaziah (22:51-53), whose story begins 2 Kings.

COMPOSITION AND AUTHORSHIP

The books of 1 & 2 Kings reflect the coherent perspective of a single unknown author. Theories that suggest multiple authors are unconvincing. Jewish tradition identifies the author as the prophet Jeremiah (*Baba Batra* 15a). All that can be said with certainty, however, is that the author witnessed firsthand the fall of Jerusalem and was well acquainted with sources that enabled him to compose a rich history of the varying fortunes of the divided monarchy. Skillfully weaving many sources into a unified presentation, the author shows why God brought about the collapse of Solomon's empire and the subsequent twin kingdoms. His central concern is his people's repeated failure to honor their covenant relationship with God. (Whether the author was still alive and wrote the final appendix concerning Jehoiachin's release [2 Kgs 25:27-30; cp. Jer 52:31-34] is uncertain. If not, these verses were appended by someone well acquainted with 1 & 2 Kings and of a kindred spirit.)

The books of 1 & 2 Kings cover essentially the same time period as 2 Chronicles. Accordingly, there are numerous parallel passages with similar wording. But the authors had different purposes in writing, and these differences can be highlighted by comparing the similarities and the differences in the various parallel passages.

The account of the rise and fall of Solomon drives home in an impressive manner the lesson that so long as man walks in the path of righteousness all is well with him; but no sooner does he deviate [from it] than he becomes subject to Divine retribution. . . . As with the individual, a people's obedience to God is rewarded by national security and prosperity while disobedience is punished by national calamity.

I. W. SLOTKI
"Kings" in *Soncino Books of the Bible*, p. xi

DATE

Because 2 Kings records the fall of Jerusalem in 586 BC (2 Kgs 24:18–25:21), 1 & 2 Kings must have been written after this event. By that time, the author had a number of sources available, including official archives of the palace and Temple and records kept in various prophetic centers. The books of 1 & 2 Kings thus form a unified work that records a major period in Israel's redemptive history, centering on Israel's kings and prophets from the end of David's reign to the author's day.

The dating of the reigns of various kings and the chronological arrangement of 1 & 2 Kings remain somewhat problematic (see "Chronology," next page), but the general dating of the period seems clear. The basic period for 1 Kings stretches from approximately 973 BC (including approximately the last two years of David's reign in Jerusalem, 2 Sam 5:4-5) to about 853 BC, during the reigns of Jehoshaphat of Judah (872–848 BC) and Ahaziah of Israel (853–852 BC). The final appendix to 2 Kings (25:27-30) was written shortly after the death of Nebuchadnezzar II in 562 BC.

CHRONOLOGY

The dates for the reigns of the kings of Israel and Judah are determined by comparing biblical data with information from other sources from the period, including historical annals and records of astronomical phenomena. The data frequently highlight the practice of co-regency, whereby a reigning king designated his son as both heir apparent and co-ruler. This practice was common in both Israel and Judah. The resulting data are reflected in the study notes. See further "Chronology: Israel's Monarchy," p. 562.

MEANING AND MESSAGE

The primary concern of 1 Kings is Israel's spiritual condition: How well did Israel's rulers and people keep God's covenants? God enacted with David a special covenant that had conditions for blessing Israel's king and his kingdom (2 Sam 7:12-16; Ps 89:20-37). God's three appearances to Solomon highlight the potential for a successful and meaningful spiritual life, as well as the tragic consequences of spiritual infidelity and relying upon expediency. Each succeeding king is evaluated by his faithfulness to God—by his success or failure in keeping God's covenants.

The book of 1 Kings emphasizes the role of God's prophets in advising, admonishing, and warning the kings. While particular attention is devoted to Elijah's ministry (chs 17–19, 21), God also works through other prophets to claim his people's loyalty.

The spiritual odysseys of Israel's kings and prophets challenge all of God's people to faithful devotion and service. Israel's frequent preference for what is tangible and expedient reminds us to "keep away from anything that might take God's place in [our] hearts" (1 Jn 5:21). Like the prophets of old, God's servants today are to proclaim God's priority in the world.

FURTHER READING

PAUL HOUSE
1, 2 Kings (1998)

PETER LEITHART
1 & 2 Kings (2006)

RICHARD D. PATTERSON AND HERMANN J. AUSTEL
1, 2 Kings in *Expositor's Bible Commentary,* vol. 3 (2009)

JEROME T. WALSH
1 Kings (1996)

1. THE REIGN OF SOLOMON (1:1–11:43)

Solomon's Rise Amidst Adversaries (1:1–2:46)

David in His Old Age

1 King David was now very old, and no
matter how many blankets covered him,
he could not keep warm. 2So his advisers
told him, "Let us find a young virgin to wait
on you and look after you, my lord. She will
lie in your arms and keep you warm."
3So they searched throughout the land
of Israel for a beautiful girl, and they found
Abishag from Shunem and brought her to
the king. 4The girl was very beautiful, and
she looked after the king and took care of
him. But the king had no sexual relations
with her.

Adonijah Claims the Throne

5About that time David's son Adonijah,
whose mother was Haggith, began boasting,
"I will make myself king." So he provided
himself with chariots and charioteers and
recruited fifty men to run in front of him.
6Now his father, King David, had never disciplined him at any time, even by asking,
"Why are you doing that?" Adonijah had

1:3 Josh 19:18; 1 Sam 28:4

1:5 2 Sam 3:4

1:1–2:12 The book of 1 Kings opens by emphasizing the continuity of the Lord's covenant with David (see 2 Sam 7:11-16). Solomon was the legitimate and divinely chosen heir to what God had granted his father David. The challenges to Solomon's succession to the throne (1:1–2:46) foreshadowed challenges to his kingship at the end of his reign (11:1-43) and the continuing struggles between Israel and Judah thereafter.

1:1-3 At seventy years of age (2 Sam 5:4-5), David was feeble, perhaps because of years of warfare and stress. He needed a young person to impart warmth, a medical remedy also described in Josephus's *Antiquities* and by the Greek physician Galen. David's diminishing powers encouraged Adonijah's attempts to take the throne.

1:5-6 ***Adonijah*** was ***David's*** fourth ***son***. Because his older brothers, Amnon, Daniel, and Absalom, were all dead, Adonijah assumed he would succeed ***his father***. Yet, in keeping with ancient Near Eastern custom, Solomon—the son of David's favored wife, Bathsheba—was to succeed him as king. David had already communicated this fact to Solomon (1:13, 17; 1 Chr 22:6-10). Adonijah's self-seeking nature, likely encouraged by his father's lax discipline, surfaced in his declaration, ***"I will make myself king."***

1:7
1 Sam 22:20
2 Sam 20:25
1 Kgs 2:22, 28
1:8
2 Sam 8:18; 12:1; 20:25; 23:8-39
1:10
2 Sam 12:24
1:13
1 Chr 22:9-13

been born next after Absalom, and he was
very handsome.
7 Adonijah took Joab son of Zeruiah and
Abiathar the priest into his confidence,
and they agreed to help him become king.
8 But Zadok the priest, Benaiah son of Jehoiada, Nathan the prophet, Shimei, Rei, and
David's personal bodyguard refused to support Adonijah.
9 Adonijah went to the Stone of Zoheleth
near the spring of En-rogel, where he sacrificed sheep, cattle, and fattened calves. He
invited all his brothers—the other sons of
King David—and all the royal officials of
Judah. 10 But he did not invite Nathan the
prophet or Benaiah or the king's bodyguard
or his brother Solomon.
11 Then Nathan went to Bathsheba, Solomon's mother, and asked her, "Haven't
you heard that Haggith's son, Adonijah,
has made himself king, and our lord David
doesn't even know about it? 12 If you want
to save your own life and the life of your
son Solomon, follow my advice. 13 Go at
once to King David and say to him, 'My lord
the king, didn't you make a vow and say
to me, "Your son Solomon will surely be
the next king and will sit on my throne"?
Why then has Adonijah become king?'
14 And while you are still talking with him,
I will come and confirm everything you
have said."
15 So Bathsheba went into the king's bedroom. (He was very old now, and Abishag

SOLOMON (1:1–11:43)

2 Sam 12:24-25
2 Chr 1:1–9:31
Pss 72, 127
Prov 1:1
Matt 6:28-30; 12:42
Luke 11:31; 12:27

Solomon was the third king of Israel, the second son of David and Bathsheba (2 Sam 12:13-25); he reigned forty years (971–931 BC). Solomon began with promising confidence in God but ended his life as an idol-worshiper who destroyed his kingdom.

As King David neared death, his son Adonijah made an attempt on the throne, supported by the priest Abiathar and general Joab (ch 1). The kingdom had been promised to Solomon, however (1:17; see 2 Sam 12:24-25; 1 Chr 28:4-7), so Bathsheba and the prophet Nathan informed David of Adonijah's intentions. David immediately arranged Solomon's coronation. David advised Solomon to follow God faithfully (ch 2).

Solomon loved God and sought his help. God asked him to choose a gift, and since he chose wisdom rather than long life, riches, or fame, God gave him all of these. Solomon governed wisely (3:16-28), received worldwide respect (4:20-34; 10:1-29), and wrote parts of Proverbs, Ecclesiastes, and the Song of Songs. Rabbis said that these books came from three stages of his life: "When a man is young he composes songs; when he grows older he makes sententious remarks; and when he becomes an old man he speaks of the vanity of things" (*Midrash Rabbah*). He also built the Temple in Jerusalem and his own palace, developed trade, and increased the wealth and security of Israel. His reputation for wisdom and wealth was very great, and the queen of Sheba traveled to Jerusalem to see for herself (ch 10).

Unfortunately, Solomon made many foreign alliances and married many foreign women, beginning with the daughter of Egypt's pharaoh (3:1). His foreign wives turned Solomon's heart away from God and toward idols. Later in life, the wise Solomon became extremely foolish under his wives' influence; he worshiped false gods and oppressed his people. So God used Jeroboam to remove a large part of his kingdom.

Nonetheless, the NT remembers Solomon's wisdom and glory as the standard against which others are measured. Jesus is the incarnation of God's wisdom, which far surpassed that of Solomon (Matt 12:42; Luke 11:31).

1:7 ***Joab***, David's military commander, and ***Abiathar***, the high ***priest***, gave ***Adonijah*** powerful military and religious backing in his pursuit of the throne.

1:8 Solomon also had influential friends supporting his right to become king. ***Zadok*** was in the priestly line of Eleazar, ***Benaiah*** commanded David's ***bodyguard*** and his thirty mighty men (2 Sam 23:20-23), ***Shimei*** was one of Solomon's district governors (4:18), and ***Nathan*** was David's trusted ***prophet***. ***Rei*** is unknown beyond this verse.

1:9 ***En-rogel*** (modern Bir Ayyub, "Job's well") lay south of Jerusalem at the intersection of the Kidron and Hinnom valleys. Earlier, it harbored David's two informants, Jonathan and Ahimaaz, during Absalom's rebellion (see 2 Sam 17:17). • ***to the Stone of Zoheleth:*** Or *to the Serpent's Stone;* the Greek version supports reading *Zoheleth* as a proper name.

1:11-14 ***Bathsheba*** was Solomon's mother and David's favored wife. Their affair led to the death of Bathsheba's husband, Uriah the Hittite (see 2 Sam 11). • ***Nathan***, the prophet who revealed God's covenant with David (2 Sam 7:1-17) and announced God's love for Solomon at his birth (2 Sam 12:24-25), confirmed God's selection of ***Solomon*** to succeed David as king (see 1 Chr 28:4-7). Although Nathan had sharply rebuked David for his affair with Bathsheba and his murder of Uriah (2 Sam 12:1-15), the king respected the prophet. •***Adonijah*** certainly observed Nathan's close association with Bathsheba and Solomon. All three could expect to be killed if Adonijah's plot to seize the throne succeeded (see 15:29; 16:11).

was taking care of him.) 16Bathsheba bowed down before the king.

"What can I do for you?" he asked her.

17She replied, "My lord, you made a vow before the LORD your God when you said to me, 'Your son Solomon will surely be the next king and will sit on my throne.' 18But instead, Adonijah has made himself king, and my lord the king does not even know about it. 19He has sacrificed many cattle, fattened calves, and sheep, and he has invited all the king's sons to attend the celebration. He also invited Abiathar the priest and Joab, the commander of the army. But he did not invite your servant Solomon. 20And now, my lord the king, all Israel is waiting for you to announce who will become king after you. 21If you do not act, my son Solomon and I will be treated as criminals as soon as my lord the king has died."

22While she was still speaking with the king, Nathan the prophet arrived. 23The king's officials told him, "Nathan the prophet is here to see you."

Nathan went in and bowed before the king with his face to the ground. 24Nathan asked, "My lord the king, have you decided that Adonijah will be the next king and that he will sit on your throne? 25Today he has sacrificed many cattle, fattened calves, and sheep, and he has invited all the king's sons to attend the celebration. He also invited the commanders of the army and Abiathar the priest. They are feasting and drinking with him and shouting, 'Long live King Adonijah!' 26But he did not invite me or Zadok the priest or Benaiah or your servant Solomon. 27Has my lord the king really done this without letting any of his officials know who should be the next king?"

David Makes Solomon King

28King David responded, "Call Bathsheba!" So she came back in and stood before the king. 29And the king repeated his vow: "As surely as the LORD lives, who has rescued me from every danger, 30your son Solomon will be the next king and will sit on my throne this very day, just as I vowed to you before the LORD, the God of Israel."

31Then Bathsheba bowed down with her face to the ground before the king and exclaimed, "May my lord King David live forever!"

32Then King David ordered, "Call Zadok the priest, Nathan the prophet, and Benaiah son of Jehoiada." When they came into the king's presence, 33the king said to them, "Take Solomon and my officials down to Gihon Spring. Solomon is to ride on my own mule. 34There Zadok the priest and Nathan the prophet are to [a]anoint him [b]king over Israel. Blow the ram's horn and shout, 'Long live [b]King Solomon!' 35Then escort him back here, and he will sit on my throne. He will succeed me as king, for I have appointed him to be ruler over Israel and Judah."

36"[c]Amen!" Benaiah son of Jehoiada replied. "May the LORD, the God of my lord the king, decree that it happen. 37And may the LORD be with Solomon as he has been with you, my lord the king, and may he make Solomon's reign even greater than yours!"

38So Zadok the priest, Nathan the prophet, Benaiah son of Jehoiada, and the king's bodyguard took Solomon down to Gihon Spring, with Solomon riding on King David's own mule. 39There Zadok the priest took the flask of olive oil from the sacred tent and anointed Solomon with the oil. Then they sounded the ram's horn

1:19
1 Kgs 1:9

1:25
1 Sam 10:24
1 Kgs 1:9

1:28-53
//1 Chr 29:21-25

1:29
2 Sam 4:9

1:34
1 Sam 10:1; 16:3, 12
2 Sam 15:10
[a]*mashakh* (4886)
‣1 Kgs 19:16
[b]*melek* (4428)
‣1 Kgs 4:1

1:36
[c]*'amen* (0543)
‣1 Chr 16:36

1:37
Josh 1:5, 17
1 Sam 20:13
1 Kgs 1:47

1:39
1 Kgs 1:34
1 Chr 16:39; 29:22
Ps 89:20

1:28-30 *David* reassured *Bathsheba* that *Solomon* would ***be the next king*** by repeating his earlier *vow* in God's name (see 1:17).

1:31-32 *David* affirmed his pledge by ordering a public display of support by the priestly, prophetic, and military representatives, ***Zadok***, ***Nathan***, and ***Benaiah***.

1:33 Riding the king's ***own mule*** was a sign of prestige. In an ancient text from Mari, King Zimri-Lim was advised that royal protocol would be served by his riding in a donkey cart. David's sons rode mules (2 Sam 13:29; 18:9). Similarly Zechariah predicts that Israel's king will come "riding on a donkey's colt" (Zech 9:9), a prophecy fulfilled by Jesus (Matt 21:4-7; John 12:14-15). With Solomon mounted on David's royal mule, the people would know that Solomon's anointing as king had David's blessing. • The ***Gihon Spring***, just outside Jerusalem's eastern slopes, was the city's major water source. In this common gathering place, Solomon's anointing would be well known, yet not visible to Adonijah's supporters at En-rogel.

1:34 ***Solomon***'s anointing followed established protocol in being administered by a ***prophet*** (see 1 Sam 16:1-13). • ***Priests*** also played significant roles in royal matters, and the populace would welcome ***Zadok***'s blessing. David later confirmed Solomon's kingship in a public ceremony (1 Chr 29:22).

1:35 ***sit on my throne:*** Due to David's age and infirmities, Solomon officiated publicly for about two years before his father died. Co-regency provided for orderly royal succession and became commonplace during Israel's divided monarchy. It was also practiced in Egypt. • The Hebrew term for ***ruler***, used for various leadership positions, can have theological significance; the king was seen as both a spiritual and administrative leader of God's people (see Deut 31:10-11; 1 Chr 28:4-6; Ps 89:3-4; Isa 55:3-4).

1:38 ***The king's bodyguard*** (Hebrew *the Kerethites and Pelethites;* also in 1:44) were foreign mercenaries from Crete; they served David throughout his reign (2 Sam 8:18; 15:18; 20:7).

1:39 ***The priest . . . anointed Solomon*** with ***olive oil***. This act, a widely accepted Near Eastern practice, gave the ceremony divine sanction.

1:40
1 Sam 10:5
[d]*simkhah* (8057)
‣1 Chr 29:22
1:42
2 Sam 18:26-27
1:47
1 Kgs 1:37
1:48
2 Sam 7:12
1 Kgs 3:6
1:50
1 Kgs 2:28
2:2
Josh 23:14
2:3
Deut 18:18-19
Josh 1:6-7; 23:14
1 Chr 22:12
2:4
2 Sam 7:12-13, 25
1 Kgs 8:25; 9:5

and all the people shouted, "Long live King
Solomon!" 40 And all the people followed
Solomon into Jerusalem, playing flutes and
shouting for [d]joy. The celebration was so
joyous and noisy that the earth shook with
the sound.
41 Adonijah and his guests heard the celebrating and shouting just as they were
finishing their banquet. When Joab heard
the sound of the ram's horn, he asked,
"What's going on? Why is the city in such
an uproar?"
42 And while he was still speaking, Jonathan son of Abiathar the priest arrived.
"Come in," Adonijah said to him, "for you are
a good man. You must have good news."
43 "Not at all!" Jonathan replied. "Our
lord King David has just declared Solomon
king! 44 The king sent him down to Gihon
Spring with Zadok the priest, Nathan the
prophet, and Benaiah son of Jehoiada, protected by the king's bodyguard. They had
him ride on the king's own mule, 45 and
Zadok and Nathan have anointed him at Gihon Spring as the new king. They have just
returned, and the whole city is celebrating
and rejoicing. That's what all the noise is
about. 46 What's more, Solomon is now sitting on the royal throne as king. 47 And all
the royal officials have gone to King David
and congratulated him, saying, 'May your
God make Solomon's fame even greater
than your own, and may Solomon's reign
be even greater than yours!' Then the king
bowed his head in worship as he lay in his
bed, 48 and he said, 'Praise the LORD, the
God of Israel, who today has chosen a successor to sit on my throne while I am still
alive to see it.'"
49 Then all of Adonijah's guests jumped up
in panic from the banquet table and quickly
scattered. 50 Adonijah was afraid of Solomon,
so he rushed to the sacred tent and grabbed
on to the horns of the altar. 51 Word soon
reached Solomon that Adonijah had seized
the horns of the altar in fear, and that he was
pleading, "Let King Solomon swear today
that he will not kill me!"
52 Solomon replied, "If he proves himself
to be loyal, not a hair on his head will be
touched. But if he makes trouble, he will
die." 53 So King Solomon summoned Adonijah, and they brought him down from
the altar. He came and bowed respectfully
before King Solomon, who dismissed him,
saying, "Go on home."

David's Final Instructions to Solomon

2 As the time of King David's death approached, he gave this charge to his son
Solomon:
2 "I am going where everyone on earth
must someday go. Take courage and be a
man. 3 Observe the requirements of the
LORD your God, and follow all his ways.
Keep the decrees, commands, regulations,
and laws written in the Law of Moses so
that you will be successful in all you do
and wherever you go. 4 If you do this, then
the LORD will keep the promise he made to
me. He told me, 'If your descendants live as
they should and follow me faithfully with
all their heart and soul, one of them will always sit on the throne of Israel.'

1:40-41 Those attending Adonijah's banquet at En-rogel could not see the celebration, but it was so joyously ***noisy*** that they could hear it.

1:42-49 ***Solomon*** was proclaimed as ***king*** and warmly welcomed by the people. ***Adonijah*** and his followers panicked and fled, aborting the attempted coup.

1:50-53 Fearing for his life, ***Adonijah*** sought refuge at ***the horns*** (projections at the corners) ***of the altar*** (Exod 27:2), hoping for mercy according to biblical precedent (cp. Exod 21:12-14). However, such protection was provided only for unintentional homicide, so Adonijah's treason could only be forgiven by the king. ***Solomon*** treated him graciously on the condition that he remain loyal. Appearances aside, Adonijah was still looking for ways to usurp the kingship and was later killed as a troublemaker (2:13-25).

2:1-12 David gave his final charge to Solomon in two sections: personal advice for spiritual living (2:2-4) and instructions about people David had dealt with (2:5-9).

2:2-4 David's advice to Solomon combined the spiritual and ethical standards of Deuteronomy, the standards of the covenant through Moses (see Lev 18:4-5; Deut 5:33; 6:4-5; 8:6; 10:12), and the promises of the covenant with David (2 Sam 7:12-16, 25). If Solomon would keep God's standards of righteousness, the promises would be transmitted to his heir, who in turn could claim God's blessings and convey them to subsequent generations (Ps 89:3-4, 20, 24, 27-37). • The preeminent heir of David, the Messiah, would embody true righteousness (Isa 11:1-5), receive the full benefits of the covenant (Jer 33:14-16), and enact a new covenant with the people of Israel and Judah (Jer 31:31-34; Ezek 34:24-31; 37:24-28). The NT reveals Jesus as that son of David who has come (Matt 1:1; Rom 1:1-4); he will come again to fulfill OT prophecies and bless all people (Luke 1:67-79; Gal 3:26-29; Rev 3:21).

2:2 ***Take courage and be a man:*** God and Moses had given this same charge to Joshua at the time of the conquest (Deut 31:6-7; Josh 1:6-7, 9). Joshua and Hezekiah gave this admonition to Israelite forces when facing enemies (Josh 1:16-18; 10:24-28; 2 Chr 32:7). David had learned the value of godly courage (Ps 27:13-14; 31:23-24). When Paul urged Christians to be courageous (literally *be men*) and strong (1 Cor 16:13), he used the same words as the Greek OT uses for the charges by Moses, Joshua, Hezekiah, and the Lord. An interesting parallel is found in the account of Bishop Polycarp's martyrdom. As he was led into the stadium facing execution, Polycarp heard a voice from heaven saying, "Be strong, Polycarp, be a man!" (*Martyrdom of Polycarp* 9:1).

5"And there is something else. You know
what Joab son of Zeruiah did to me when
he murdered my two army commanders,
Abner son of Ner and Amasa son of Jether.
He pretended that it was an act of war, but
it was done in a time of peace, staining his
belt and sandals with innocent blood. 6Do
with him what you think best, but don't let
him grow old and go to his grave in peace.
7"Be kind to the sons of Barzillai of Gilead. Make them permanent guests at your
table, for they took care of me when I fled
from your brother Absalom.
8"And remember Shimei son of Gera, the
man from Bahurim in Benjamin. He cursed
me with a terrible curse as I was fleeing to
Mahanaim. When he came down to meet
me at the Jordan River, I swore by the LORD
that I would not kill him. 9But that oath does
not make him innocent. You are a wise man,
and you will know how to arrange a bloody
death for him."

Summary of David's Reign

1 Kgs 2:10-12 // 1 Chr 29:26-30

10Then David died and was buried with his
ancestors in the City of David. 11David had
reigned over Israel for forty years, seven of
them in Hebron and thirty-three in Jerusalem. 12Solomon became king and sat on the
throne of David his father, and his kingdom
was firmly established.

Solomon Establishes His Rule

13One day Adonijah, whose mother was
Haggith, came to see Bathsheba, Solomon's
mother. "Have you come with peaceful intentions?" she asked him.
"Yes," he said, "I come in peace. 14In fact, I
have a favor to ask of you."
"What is it?" she asked.
15He replied, "As you know, the kingdom
was rightfully mine; all Israel wanted me to
be the next king. But the tables were turned,
and the kingdom went to my brother instead; for that is the way the LORD wanted it.
16So now I have just one favor to ask of you.
Please don't turn me down."
"What is it?" she asked.
17He replied, "Speak to King Solomon on
my behalf, for I know he will do anything
you request. Ask him to let me marry Abishag, the girl from Shunem."
18"All right," Bathsheba replied. "I will
speak to the king for you."
19So Bathsheba went to King Solomon to
speak on Adonijah's behalf. The king rose
from his throne to meet her, and he bowed
down before her. When he sat down on his
throne again, the king ordered that a throne
be brought for his mother, and she sat at his
right hand.
20"I have one small request to make of
you," she said. "I hope you won't turn me
down."
"What is it, my mother?" he asked. "You
know I won't refuse you."
21"Then let your brother Adonijah marry
Abishag, the girl from Shunem," she replied.
22"How can you possibly ask me to give
Abishag to Adonijah?" King Solomon demanded. "You might as well ask me to give
him the kingdom! You know that he is my
older brother, and that he has Abiathar the
priest and Joab son of Zeruiah on his side."
23Then King Solomon made a vow before
the LORD: "May God strike me and even kill
me if Adonijah has not sealed his fate with

2:5 2 Sam 3:27; 20:10
2:7 2 Sam 17:27-29; 19:31-38
2:8 2 Sam 16:5-8; 19:18-23
2:10-12 //1 Chr 29:26-28
2:10 2 Sam 5:7; 1 Chr 29:28; Acts 2:29; 13:36
2:11 2 Sam 5:4-5
2:12 1 Chr 29:23; 2 Chr 1:1
2:17 1 Kgs 1:3
2:19 Ps 45:9
2:23 Ruth 1:17

2:5-6 ***Joab*** had supported David's bid for kingship but had become too ambitious. He had murdered former military rivals ***Abner*** (2 Sam 3:22-30) and ***Amasa*** (2 Sam 20:10), as well as David's son Absalom (2 Sam 18:1-18). A party to David's murder of Uriah the Hittite (2 Sam 11:14-27), Joab had grown very powerful (2 Sam 20:23), and his backing of Adonijah posed a serious threat to Solomon.

2:5 ***He pretended . . . time of peace:*** Or *He murdered them during a time of peace as revenge for deaths they had caused in time of war.* • ***with innocent blood:*** As in some Greek and Old Latin manuscripts; Hebrew reads *with the blood of war.*

2:6 ***don't let him grow old and go to his grave in peace:*** Literally *don't let his white head go down to Sheol in peace.*

2:7-9 ***Barzillai*** unwaveringly supported David during his trouble with ***Absalom***, while ***Shimei*** openly opposed David (2 Sam 16:5-13; 19:6-23).

2:7 ***at your table:*** As he had done for Mephibosheth (2 Sam 9:6-13), David provided for ***Barzillai*** and his family. This privilege assured their continued loyalty.

2:8 ***Mahanaim*** was David's refuge during Absalom's rebellion (2 Sam 17:24). The Egyptian pharaoh, Shishak, invaded it during Rehoboam's reign (see 14:25).

2:9 ***how to arrange a bloody death for him:*** Literally *how to bring his white head down to Sheol in blood.*

2:10-12 ***David died*** peacefully after a forty-year reign, knowing that the kingdom was ***firmly established*** in ***Solomon***, his designated heir. Various locations have been proposed for David's tomb, but none has been confirmed (cp. Acts 2:29). Royal tombs were used at least until Hezekiah's days (2 Kgs 20:21).

2:13-15 ***Adonijah*** contradicted his supposed ***peaceful intentions*** when he declared, ***the kingdom was rightfully mine.***

2:16-18 ***let me marry Abishag:*** Possessing the king's concubine was a mark of royal legitimacy. When David became king, he was given Saul's wives (2 Sam 12:7-8). The rebellious Absalom claimed David's concubines (2 Sam 16:20-22).

2:19-21 ***Solomon*** understood the intentions behind Adonijah's ***small request***. Adonijah's desire to ***marry Abishag*** could have launched a claim to the throne, whether or not she was officially in David's harem.

2:22-25 Because ***Adonijah*** violated his terms of submission to ***Solomon*** (1:52-53), the king ordered ***Benaiah*** (see 1:8, 26, 38) to execute him.

2:25 2 Sam 8:18
2:26 Josh 21:17-18; 1 Sam 22:20; 26:16; 2 Sam 15:24; Jer 1:1
2:27 1 Sam 2:27-36
2:28 2 Sam 17:25; 1 Kgs 1:49-50
2:31 Exod 21:14; Num 35:33; Deut 19:13
2:32 Gen 9:5-6; Judg 9:24, 56-57; 2 Sam 3:27; 20:8-10; 2 Chr 21:13

this request. 24 The LORD has confirmed me
and placed me on the throne of my father,
David; he has established my dynasty as he
promised. So as surely as the LORD lives,
Adonijah will die this very day!" 25 So
King Solomon ordered Benaiah son of Jehoiada to execute him, and Adonijah was
put to death.
26 Then the king said to Abiathar the
priest, "Go back to your home in Anathoth.
You deserve to die, but I will not kill you
now, because you carried the Ark of the Sovereign LORD for David my father and you
shared all his hardships." 27 So Solomon deposed Abiathar from his position as priest
of the LORD, thereby fulfilling the prophecy
the LORD had given at Shiloh concerning
the descendants of Eli.
28 Joab had not joined Absalom's earlier
rebellion, but he had joined Adonijah's
rebellion. So when Joab heard about Adonijah's death, he ran to the sacred tent of the
LORD and grabbed on to the horns of the
altar. 29 When this was reported to King Solomon, he sent Benaiah son of Jehoiada to
execute him.
30 Benaiah went to the sacred tent of the
LORD and said to Joab, "The king orders you
to come out!"
But Joab answered, "No, I will die here."
So Benaiah returned to the king and told
him what Joab had said.
31 "Do as he said," the king replied. "Kill
him there beside the altar and bury him.
This will remove the guilt of Joab's senseless murders from me and from my father's
family. 32 The LORD will repay him for the
murders of two men who were more righteous and better than he. For my father
knew nothing about the deaths of Abner

God's Covenant with Israel's Kings (2:2-4)

1 Kgs 3:3-15; 8:22-26; 9:1-9; 11:1-13, 29-39; 14:7-16; 15:1-5, 11; 2 Sam 7:5-17; 2 Kgs 17:13-23; 21:11-15; Acts 13:21-23

In David's charge to Solomon, the aged king admonished his son to keep all of God's requirements in the law of Moses in order to "be successful in all you do and wherever you go" (2:3). Solomon's faithfulness would allow the fulfillment of God's promises to David (2:4; see "God's Covenant with David" at 2 Sam 7:5-16, p. 531). Solomon understood his role as David's successor (2:33; 3:7). Early in his reign, he consciously emulated his father's love for and faithfulness to God (3:3). In his address dedicating the Temple, Solomon acknowledged God as keeping his promises to David (8:23-26), and God often reasserted the inviolability of that covenant (3:14; 9:4-5; 11:38; 15:4).

God ultimately judged Solomon and the subsequent kings of the southern kingdom against the standards of love and faithfulness to the covenant that David demonstrated (11:12-13; 14:8; 15:3-5, 11). God's covenant with Israel at Sinai forms the ethical and spiritual benchmark of the OT. His commendation and blessing or disapproval and judgment were conditioned upon whether people kept or violated his written word (see Deut 28). During the days of the kings, the people of Israel were condemned for willfully turning away from the clear precepts of the Lord contained in the law and spoken through God's prophets (2 Kgs 17:13-17). Their rejection of God resulted in judgment (2 Kgs 17:18-23; 21:11-15).

God's dealings with the kings of Israel still provide an example to those who are now in covenant with God through Christ (cp. Matt 25:21; Luke 16:10-12; John 14:21; 2 Tim 3:14; 4:7-8; Rev 2:10). God's people today are to love the Lord and keep his commandments (John 14:21) and be faithful to him in all things (Matt 25:21; Luke 16:10-12; 2 Tim 3:14; 4:7). Those who follow David's good example of faithfulness (see Acts 13:22) will similarly receive God's praise (cp. Matt 21:9; John 8:29; Heb 13:20-21). Those who confess the name of David's heir (Acts 13:32-37), who have a heart of devotion to God and his word (John 8:29), will seek to live lives that are pure and pleasing to God (Rom 15:16; Heb 13:20-21). They look forward to an abundant, eternal inheritance (2 Tim 4:8; Rev 2:10; cp. Gal 5:21).

2:26-35 Solomon presumed that Adonijah's chief supporters, ***Abiathar*** and ***Joab***, remained involved in ***Adonijah***'s schemes, so ***Solomon*** dealt with them as well.

2:26-27 ***Abiathar*** had treasonously supported Adonijah (1:7, 25). But he was ***deposed*** rather than killed because he had ***carried the Ark*** (2 Sam 15:24, 29, 35), had supported David, and had ***shared all his hardships***. Abiathar's removal from the priesthood fulfilled the Lord's word about the house of ***Eli*** in Ithamar's line (1 Sam 2:30-35). Zadok's appointment (4:2) returned the high priesthood to Eleazar's line as it had been before Eli (Num 20:22-28; 25:11-13; 2 Sam 8:17; 1 Chr 6:1-8, 50-53; Ezra 7:2-5) and as it continued throughout the divided monarchy (2 Chr 31:10; Ezek 43:19).

2:28-29 Following Adonijah's example (1:50), ***Joab*** hoped to find mercy by grasping ***the horns of the altar*** according to the provisions of the law of Moses (Exod 21:12-14; Num 35:22-25; Deut 19:4-5). But because *Joab* was a murderer, he could not claim clemency (see 2 Sam 3:27; 18:14; 20:10).

2:32 ***will repay him:*** Literally *will return his blood on his own head.*

son of Ner, commander of the army of
Israel, and of Amasa son of Jether, commander of the army of Judah. 33May their
blood be on Joab and his descendants forever, and may the LORD grant peace forever
to David, his descendants, his dynasty, and
his throne."
34So Benaiah son of Jehoiada returned
to the sacred tent and killed Joab, and he
was buried at his home in the wilderness.
35Then the king appointed Benaiah to command the army in place of Joab, and he
installed Zadok the priest to take the place
of Abiathar.
36The king then sent for Shimei and told
him, "Build a house here in Jerusalem and
live there. But don't step outside the city
to go anywhere else. 37On the day you so
much as cross the Kidron Valley, you will
surely die; and your blood will be on your
own head."
38Shimei replied, "Your sentence is fair;
I will do whatever my lord the king commands." So Shimei lived in Jerusalem for a
long time.
39But three years later two of Shimei's
slaves ran away to King Achish son of Maacah of Gath. When Shimei learned where
they were, 40he saddled his donkey and went
to Gath to search for them. When he found
them, he brought them back to Jerusalem.
41Solomon heard that Shimei had left Jerusalem and had gone to Gath and returned.
42So the king sent for Shimei and demanded,
"Didn't I make you swear by the LORD and
warn you not to go anywhere else or you
would surely die? And you replied, 'The sentence is fair; I will do as you say.' 43Then why
haven't you kept your oath to the LORD and
obeyed my command?"
44The king also said to Shimei, "You certainly remember all the wicked things you
did to my father, David. May the LORD now
bring that evil on your own head. 45But may
I, King Solomon, receive the LORD's blessings, and may one of David's descendants
always sit on this throne in the presence of
the LORD." 46Then, at the king's command,
Benaiah son of Jehoiada took Shimei outside and killed him.

So the kingdom was now firmly in Solomon's grip.

Solomon's Great Wisdom (3:1–4:34)

Solomon Asks for Wisdom

1 Kgs 3:1-15 // 2 Chr 1:1-13

3 Solomon made an alliance with Pharaoh, the king of Egypt, and married
one of his daughters. He brought her to live
in the City of David until he could finish
building his palace and the Temple of the
LORD and the wall around the city. 2At that
time the people of Israel sacrificed their
offerings at local places of worship, for a
temple honoring the name of the LORD had
not yet been built.
3Solomon loved the LORD and followed
all the decrees of his father, David, except
that Solomon, too, offered sacrifices and
burned incense at the local places of worship. 4The most important of these places
of worship was at Gibeon, so the king went
there and sacrificed 1,000 burnt offerings.

2:33 2 Sam 3:29
2:35 1 Chr 29:22
2:36 2 Sam 16:5; 1 Kgs 2:8
2:37 2 Sam 15:23
2:39 1 Sam 27:2
2:44 1 Sam 25:39; 2 Sam 16:5-13
2:45 2 Sam 7:13
2:46 1 Kgs 2:12; 2 Chr 1:1
3:1 1 Kgs 7:8; 9:24
3:2 Lev 17:3-5; Deut 12:13-14
3:3 Deut 6:5; 1 Kgs 9:4; 11:4, 6, 38; Ps 31:23
3:4-15 //2 Chr 1:2-13
3:4 1 Chr 16:39; 21:29; 2 Chr 1:2-3
3:5 1 Kgs 9:2-3; Matt 1:20

2:36-38 The confinement of ***Shimei*** prevented him from reaching his kinsmen in Benjamin to stir up trouble for the king.

2:39-46 ***Shimei's*** journey to ***Gath***, ostensibly to recover his runaway ***slaves***, violated his agreement. Technically, he did not cross the Kidron Valley in going to ***Gath***, but the penalty was understood by both parties to apply to Shimei's going ***anywhere else***. Because Shimei violated his ***oath to the LORD*** (2:42) and because of his past hostilities toward David (2 Sam 16:5-13; 19:16-23), Solomon instructed ***Benaiah*** to execute him.

3:1 As was common in the ancient Near East, Solomon sealed a political ***alliance*** with ***the king of Egypt*** by marrying ***one of his daughters***. The bestowal of an Egyptian princess and the city of Gezer to Solomon as a wedding present (9:16) demonstrated the Egyptians' high regard for him. The pharaoh was probably Siamun, of Egypt's weakened 21st dynasty. The alliance was mutually beneficial: ***Pharaoh*** gained access to trade routes through Israel, while ***Solomon*** increased security on his southern border. Apparently, Solomon had previously married the Ammonite Naamah (see 11:42-43 with 14:21). • ***City of David:*** This section of Jerusalem was the old Jebusite city in the southern portion of the eastern ridge. When Solomon extended his building activities northward, he built a special palace for Pharaoh's daughter (7:8; 9:24; 2 Chr 8:11).

3:2-3 The Ark of the Covenant sat in David's tent in Jerusalem before the Temple was built, and ***the people . . . sacrificed their offerings at local places of worship*** (see note on 8:1). However, this detracted from unified worship at a central sanctuary (12:1-24) and increased the danger of mixing with Canaanite religious practices. Israel's worship at such places was forbidden (Deut 12:1-14).

3:4-15 God's gift of wisdom to Solomon is narrated as a *chiasm* (a symmetrical arrangement in which sections A and B are mirrored by sections B' and A'), drawing the focus in on Solomon's transaction with the Lord:

A: While he sacrificed at ***Gibeon . . . the LORD appeared to Solomon in a dream*** (3:4-5).

B: Solomon prayed for wisdom to ***govern*** his ***people*** equitably and efficiently (3:6-9).

B': ***The Lord*** favorably answered his request and granted additional blessings (3:10-14).

A': Solomon awoke from the dream and offered additional sacrifices to the Lord (3:15).

3:4 The city of ***Gibeon*** lay six miles northwest of Jerusalem. Its altar, ***the most important of these*** [local] ***places of worship*** (literally *the great high place*), accommodated sacrifices of royal proportions. ***Gibeon*** was also the site of the Tabernacle (1 Chr 16:39-40; 21:29; 2 Chr 1:2-6).

3:6
2 Sam 7:8; 12:7
1 Kgs 1:48; 9:4
2 Chr 1:8
[e]*khesed* (2617)
‣Ps 25:6

3:7
1 Chr 22:9-13; 29:1
Jer 1:6-7

3:8
Gen 13:16; 15:5; 22:17
Exod 19:6
Deut 7:6

3:9
2 Sam 14:17
1 Kgs 3:12-13
2 Chr 1:10
Ps 72:1
Prov 2:3-5, 9
Jas 1:5

3:12
1 Kgs 4:29-31
1 Jn 5:14-15
[f]*leb* (3820)
‣1 Chr 29:17

3:13
1 Kgs 3:28; 4:20-24; 10:23

3:14
Ps 91:16
Prov 3:1-2, 16

3:15
1 Kgs 8:63, 65

5That night the LORD appeared to Solomon
in a dream, and God said, "What do you
want? Ask, and I will give it to you!"
6Solomon replied, "You showed faithful
[e]love to your servant my father, David, because he was honest and true and faithful to you. And you have continued your faithful [e]love to him today by giving him a son to sit on his throne.
7"Now, O LORD my God, you have made me king instead of my father, David, but I am like a little child who doesn't know his way around.
8And here I am in the midst of your own chosen people, a nation so great and numerous they cannot be counted!
9Give me an understanding heart so that I can govern your people well and know the difference between right and wrong. For who by himself is able to govern this great people of yours?"
10The Lord was pleased that Solomon
had asked for wisdom.
11So God replied, "Because you have asked for wisdom in governing my people with justice and have not asked for a long life or wealth or the death of your enemies—
12I will give you what you asked for! I will give you a wise and understanding [f]heart such as no one else has had or ever will have!
13And I will also give you what you did not ask for—riches and fame! No other king in all the world will be compared to you for the rest of your life!
14And if you follow me and obey my decrees and my commands as your father, David, did, I will give you a long life."
15Then Solomon woke up and realized it had been a dream. He returned to Jerusalem and stood before the Ark of the Lord's Covenant, where he sacrificed burnt offerings and peace offerings. Then he invited all his officials to a great banquet.

Solomon Judges Wisely

16Some time later two prostitutes came to the king to have an argument settled.

Solomon's Wisdom (3:5-14)

1 Kgs 3:16-28; 4:29-34; 5:2-7; 10:1-13
Exod 31:1-6
2 Chr 1:7-12
Ps 72:1-20; 111:10; 127:1-5
Eccl 12:9-14
Isa 11:1-5
Jer 9:23-24
Matt 12:42
Jas 1:5

When God gave Solomon the opportunity to ask for anything he wanted, Solomon chose wisdom, "so that I can govern your people well and know the difference between right and wrong" (3:9). In response to this selfless choice, God granted the wisdom he desired (3:12) and the rewards of its proper use (3:13-14).

Solomon's subsequent behavior provided immediate evidence of his wisdom. He resolved an argument over a child (3:16-27) with such insight that the people were "in awe of the king" (3:28). Later, the queen of Sheba came to test him with difficult questions and found his wisdom exceeding all that she had heard about it (10:1-9). His administration (4:1-28), his diplomacy (3:12; 5:1-9), his building projects (5:10–7:51), and his commerce (9:18, 26-28; 10:15-29) all demonstrated his wisdom. Solomon accumulated vast knowledge (4:29-33) and wrote proverbs (the book of Proverbs), songs (Ps 72, 127), love poetry (the Song of Songs), and philosophical literature (Ecclesiastes).

In Chronicles, the wisdom of Solomon (2 Chr 1:7-12) is principally directed toward the building of the Temple (2 Chr 2:12), even as Bezalel had previously been endowed with wisdom to build the Tabernacle (Exod 31:1-3). For the Chronicler, God's gift of wisdom is manifest in Solomon's wealth and honor (2 Chr 1:14-17).

Jesus noted Solomon's great wisdom and reminded his hearers that someone even greater than Solomon was among them (Matt 12:42). Jesus is the true wisdom of God (1 Cor 1:24) in whom one can find ultimate wisdom (Col 2:7). A life of wisdom is centered in Christ (1 Cor 1:18-25; 2 Pet 3:18) and in Scripture (Col 3:16; 2 Tim 3:14-16).

3:6 The Hebrew word translated ***faithful love*** (*khesed*) expresses God's gracious treatment and loving kindness toward humanity (Ps 118:1-2), especially to his covenant nation Israel (Deut 7:9, 12).

3:7-9 The Hebrew term translated ***little child*** was often used of someone who lacked experience in his profession ("assistant," 19:21). Solomon humbly recognized his inexperience and his need for an ***understanding heart.*** If he desired to govern the ***people well*** and render proper decisions, he knew that he needed God's help.

3:10-12 God ***was pleased*** with Solomon's unselfish request and granted him ***a wise and understanding heart.*** These incomparable qualities are demonstrated in the next section (3:16-28) and as Solomon sets up his administration (ch 4), business dealings, building activities, international relations, and worship practices (chs 5–10).

3:15 Solomon's sacrifice after the ***dream*** completes the narrative.

3:16-28 Solomon's judgment concerning the real mother of the living baby illustrates his wisdom in cases of civil jurisprudence. Chapters 4–10 illustrate his wisdom in all areas of his rule.

3:16 ***prostitutes:*** While the law condemned prostitution (Lev 19:29; Deut 23:18), it still existed in ancient Israel. Though these women were of the most despised class of women in Israelite society, Solomon demonstrated his kindness and availability to all people by dealing justice to them as mothers, not as prostitutes.

17“Please, my lord,” one of them began, “this woman and I live in the same house. I gave birth to a baby while she was with me in the house. 18Three days later this woman also had a baby. We were alone; there were only two of us in the house.

19“But her baby died during the night when she rolled over on it. 20Then she got up in the night and took my son from beside me while I was asleep. She laid her dead child in my arms and took mine to sleep beside her. 21And in the morning when I tried to nurse my son, he was dead! But when I looked more closely in the morning light, I saw that it wasn’t my son at all.”

22Then the other woman interrupted, “It certainly was your son, and the living child is mine.”

“No,” the first woman said, “the living child is mine, and the dead one is yours.” And so they argued back and forth before the king.

23Then the king said, “Let’s get the facts straight. Both of you claim the living child is yours, and each says that the dead one belongs to the other. 24All right, bring me a sword.” So a sword was brought to the king.

25Then he said, “Cut the living child in two, and give half to one woman and half to the other!”

26Then the woman who was the real mother of the living child, and who loved him very much, cried out, “Oh no, my lord! Give her the child—please do not kill him!”

But the other woman said, “All right, he will be neither yours nor mine; divide him between us!”

27Then the king said, “Do not kill the child, but give him to the woman who wants him to live, for she is his mother!”

28When all Israel heard the king’s decision, the people were in awe of the king, for they saw the wisdom God had given him for rendering justice.

Solomon’s Officials and Governors

4 1King Solomon now ruled over all Israel, 2and these were his high officials:

Azariah son of Zadok was the priest.
3 Elihoreph and Ahijah, the sons of Shisha, were court secretaries.
Jehoshaphat son of Ahilud was the royal historian.
4 Benaiah son of Jehoiada was commander of the army.
Zadok and Abiathar were priests.
5 Azariah son of Nathan was in charge of the district governors.
Zabud son of Nathan, a priest, was a trusted adviser to the king.
6 Ahishar was manager of the palace property.
Adoniram son of Abda was in charge of the labor force.

7Solomon also had twelve district governors who were over all Israel. They were responsible for providing food for the king’s household. Each of them arranged provisions for one month of the year. 8These are the names of the twelve governors:

Ben-hur, in the hill country of Ephraim.
9 Ben-deker, in Makaz, Shaalbim, Beth-shemesh, and Elon-bethhanan.
10 Ben-hesed, in Arubboth, including Socoh and all the land of Hepher.
11 Ben-abinadab, in all of Naphoth-dor. (He was married to Taphath, one of Solomon’s daughters.)
12 Baana son of Ahilud, in Taanach and Megiddo, all of Beth-shan near Zarethan below Jezreel, and all the territory from Beth-shan to Abel-meholah and over to Jokmeam.

3:26 Isa 49:15; Jer 31:20; Hos 11:8
3:28 1 Kgs 3:9-12; 4:29
4:1 *melek* (4428) ‣Ps 2:2
4:3 2 Sam 8:16
4:9 Judg 1:35
4:10 Josh 12:17
4:12 Josh 17:11

3:28 Kings often claimed special *wisdom* and the ability to make just *decisions*. As God promised, Solomon’s wisdom was greater than that of other wise men (4:29-34; 10:6-9, 23-24).

4:2 Because *Zadok* was now quite old, his grandson (see 1 Chr 6:8-9) *Azariah* succeeded him as high priest.

4:3 The *court secretaries* were state officials and Solomon’s private secretaries. *Shisha*, the father of *Elihoreph and Ahijah*, had served David in this capacity (2 Sam 8:17; 20:25; 1 Chr 18:16). • *The royal historian* functioned as chief of protocol for palace affairs and ceremonies. As elsewhere in ancient Egypt and Mesopotamia, such officials often represented the king in important negotiations (see 2 Kgs 18:18; 2 Chr 34:8).

4:4 *Benaiah . . . Zadok and Abiathar:* All three men had also held special posts in David’s administration. Though deposed as high priest (2:26-27), *Abiathar* still functioned as a *priest*.

4:5 Two sons of *Nathan* also served in Solomon’s inner circle. *Azariah* supervised the twelve *district governors*, while *Zabud . . . was a trusted adviser*, a post held by Hushai under David (2 Sam 15:37).

4:6 *Ahishar* functioned as *manager of the palace property*, an office that became powerful under Uzziah’s son Jotham (2 Kgs 15:5). Later, this position was held by Eliakim, one of Hezekiah’s representatives, who met with emissaries from King Sennacherib of Assyria during negotiations concerning the siege of Jerusalem (2 Kgs 18:18). • *Adoniram* was head of the corvée (the system of forced *labor*). Samuel had warned about this loathsome institution (1 Sam 8:12-17), and the leaders of Israel later complained about it to Solomon’s son Rehoboam (12:4).

4:7-19 The *twelve district governors* probably handled lesser administrative duties, such as securing revenue and *providing food for the king’s household*. Solomon’s twelve districts did not exactly coincide with the old tribal allotments.

4:11 *Naphoth-dor:* Hebrew *Naphath-dor*, a variant spelling of Naphoth-dor.

4:12 *Beth-shan:* Hebrew *Beth-shean*, a variant spelling of Beth-shan; also in 4:12b.

4:13 Num 32:41 Deut 3:4
4:19 Deut 3:8-10
4:20 Gen 32:12
4:21 2 Sam 8:2, 6 2 Chr 9:26 Ps 72:10-11

13 Ben-geber, in Ramoth-gilead,
including the Towns of Jair (named for Jair of the tribe of Manasseh) in Gilead, and in the Argob region of Bashan, including sixty large fortified towns with bronze bars on their gates.
14 Ahinadab son of Iddo, in Mahanaim.
15 Ahimaaz, in Naphtali. (He was married to Basemath, another of Solomon's daughters.)
16 Baana son of Hushai, in Asher and in Aloth.
17 Jehoshaphat son of Paruah, in Issachar.
18 Shimei son of Ela, in Benjamin.
19 Geber son of Uri, in the land of Gilead, including the territories of King Sihon of the Amorites and King Og of Bashan.

There was also one governor over the land of Judah.

Solomon's Prosperity and Wisdom
1 Kgs 4:21 // 2 Chr 9:26

20The people of Judah and Israel were as
numerous as the sand on the seashore.
They were very contented, with plenty to
eat and drink. 21Solomon ruled over all
the kingdoms from the Euphrates River
in the north to the land of the Philistines
and the border of Egypt in the south. The
conquered peoples of those lands sent tribute money to Solomon and continued to
serve him throughout his lifetime.
22The daily food requirements for Solomon's palace were 150 bushels of choice
flour and 300 bushels of meal; 23also 10
oxen from the fattening pens, 20 pasture-fed cattle, 100 sheep or goats, as well as deer, gazelles, roe deer, and choice poultry.

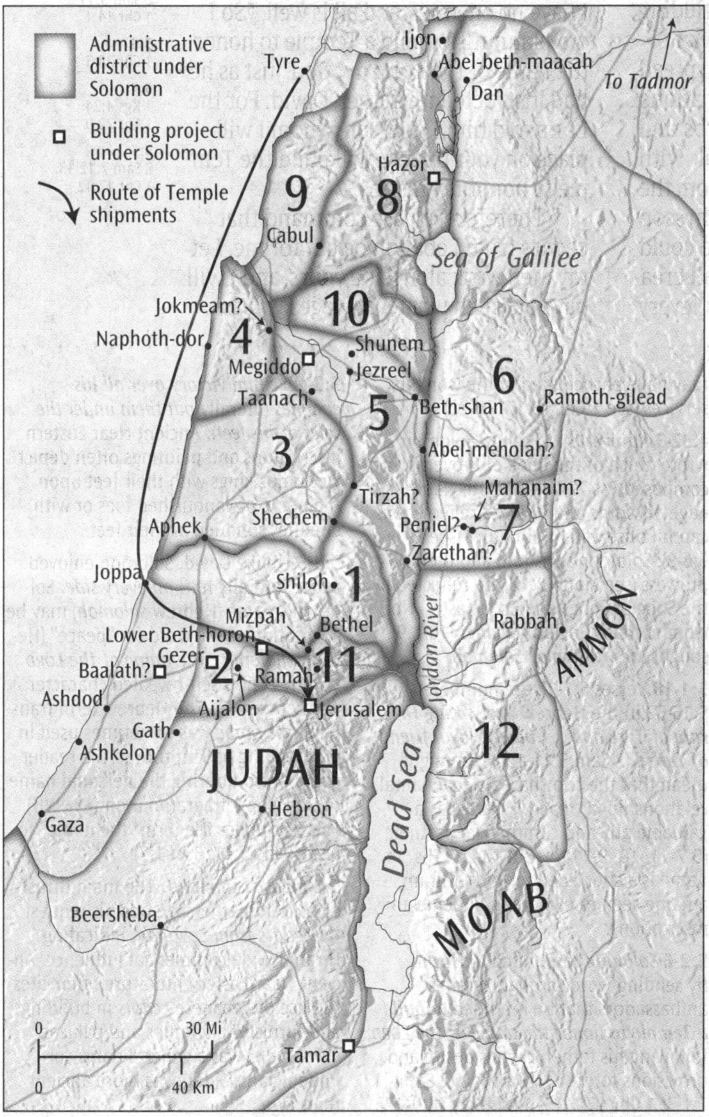

◀ **Solomon's Administrative Districts, 971–931 BC (4:7-19).** Solomon developed Israel's infrastructure and undertook many building projects throughout his vast kingdom. He maintained his lavish household by organizing his kingdom into twelve administrative districts and appointing a governor over each district. Each district was responsible for providing for the king's household for one month each year. • JOKMEAM (4:12) might be identified with Jokneam (as shown here); some scholars would place Jokmeam instead along the east side of the JORDAN RIVER near PENIEL.

4:13 ***Jair of the tribe of Manasseh:*** Literally *Jair son of Manasseh;* cp. 1 Chr 2:22.

4:19 ***of Gilead:*** Greek version reads *of Gad;* cp. 4:13. • The last sentence is as in some Greek manuscripts; Hebrew lacks *of Judah.* The meaning of the Hebrew is uncertain.

4:20-21 God's promise to Abraham (Gen 15:18-21; 17:8; 22:17) finds historical fulfillment in his blessing of ***Solomon.*** The surrounding lands conquered by David and ***Solomon*** (2 Chr 8:3) remained loyal to Solomon. They ***sent tribute money . . . and continued to serve him throughout*** his long reign.

4:21-34 Verses 4:21-34 are numbered 5:1-14 in the Hebrew text. • ***the Euphrates River:*** Literally *the river;* also in 4:24.

4:22-23 Solomon's court was enormous and splendid, as indicated by its ***daily food requirements.*** • ***150 bushels of choice flour and 300 bushels of meal:*** Hebrew *30 cors* [5.5 kiloliters] *of choice flour and 60 cors* [11 kiloliters] *of meal.* • ***and choice poultry:*** Or *and fattened geese.*

[24]Solomon's dominion extended over all
the kingdoms west of the Euphrates River,
from Tiphsah to Gaza. And there was peace
on all his borders. [25]During the lifetime
of Solomon, all of Judah and Israel lived
in peace and safety. And from Dan in the
north to Beersheba in the south, each family had its own home and garden.
[26]Solomon had 4,000 stalls for his chariot horses, and he had 12,000 horses.
[27]The district governors faithfully provided food for King Solomon and his court;
each made sure nothing was lacking during
the month assigned to him. [28]They also
brought the necessary barley and straw for
the royal horses in the stables.
[29]God gave Solomon very great [h]wisdom
and understanding, and knowledge as vast
as the sands of the seashore. [30]In fact, his
wisdom exceeded that of all the wise men
of the East and the wise men of Egypt.
[31]He was wiser than anyone else, including
Ethan the Ezrahite and the sons of Mahol—
Heman, Calcol, and Darda. His fame spread
throughout all the surrounding nations.
[32]He composed some 3,000 [i]proverbs and
wrote 1,005 songs. [33]He could speak with
authority about all kinds of plants, from the
great cedar of Lebanon to the tiny hyssop
that grows from cracks in a wall. He could
also speak about animals, birds, small creatures, and fish. [34]And kings from every
nation sent their ambassadors to listen to
the wisdom of Solomon.

Solomon's Building Activities (5:1–8:66)

Preparations for Building the Temple

1 Kgs 5:1-18 // 2 Chr 2:1-18

5 King Hiram of Tyre had always been
a loyal friend of David. When Hiram
learned that David's son Solomon was the
new king of Israel, he sent ambassadors to
congratulate him.
[2]Then Solomon sent this message back to
Hiram:

[3]"You know that my father, David, was
not able to build a Temple to honor the
name of the LORD his God because of
the many wars waged against him by
surrounding nations. He could not build
until the LORD gave him victory over
all his enemies. [4]But now the LORD my
God has given me peace on every side;
I have no enemies, and all is well. [5]So I
am planning to build a Temple to honor
the name of the LORD my God, just as he
had instructed my father, David. For the
LORD told him, 'Your son, whom I will
place on your throne, will build the Temple to honor my name.'
[6]"Therefore, please command that
cedars from Lebanon be cut for me. Let
my men work alongside yours, and I will
pay your men whatever wages you ask.

4:24 1 Chr 22:9
4:25 Jer 23:5-6; Mic 4:4; Zech 3:10
4:26 1 Kgs 10:26; 2 Chr 1:14
4:29 1 Kgs 3:12; [h]*khokmah* (2451) ‣Ps 111:10
4:30 Isa 19:11; Acts 7:22
4:31 1 Kgs 3:12
4:32 Prov 1:1; Eccl 12:9; Song 1:1; [i]*mashal* (4912) ‣Job 13:12
4:34 1 Kgs 10:1; 2 Chr 9:23
5:1-16 //2 Chr 2:1-18
5:1 2 Sam 5:11; 1 Chr 14:1
5:3 1 Chr 28:3
5:4 1 Kgs 4:24; 1 Chr 22:9
5:5 2 Sam 7:12-13; 1 Chr 17:12

4:24-25 ***each family had its own home and garden*** (literally *each family lived under its own grapevine and under its own fig tree*): Solomon's subjects lived under ideal conditions that foreshadowed the coming messianic era (Mic 4:4), enjoying widespread prosperity and tranquility.

4:26 ***4,000 stalls:*** As in some Greek manuscripts (see also 2 Chr 9:25); Hebrew reads *40,000 stalls.* The number *4,000* reflects the parallel text in 2 Chr 9:25, a suitable number for Solomon's 1,400 chariots (10:26; 2 Chr 1:14). • ***12,000 horses*** (or *12,000 charioteers*): The Hebrew can be translated as "horsemen" (Exod 15:19-21) or "horses" (Joel 2:4). To be prepared for battles, Solomon built towns to accommodate his forces (9:19).

4:29-30 ***wise men of the East:*** Babylon was well-known for wise men. Yet Solomon's God-given ***wisdom*** (3:9, 12, 28; Prov 1:7; Eccl 12:13) exceeded them all (4:34).

4:31 ***Ethan*** and ***Heman*** were among the musicians appointed by David (see 1 Chr 6:33-47; 15:16-19; Pss 88; 89). • ***The sons of Mahol*** were Temple singers, so ***Heman, Calcol, and Darda*** may have participated in the worship services (see 1 Chr 15:17, 19-22).

4:32-34 ***proverbs . . . songs:*** Solomon wrote much of the book of Proverbs and composed Pss 72 and 127. His knowledge of ***plants*** and ***animals*** reflected his careful observation of nature (see Prov 6:6-8). Solomon's wisdom and literary prowess (see Matt 12:42) are reflected in the Song of Songs and Ecclesiastes. No wonder many, including ***kings*** (10:1-9), sought ***the wisdom of Solomon.***

5:1-18 Verses 5:1-18 are numbered 5:15-32 in the Hebrew text. • ***King Hiram of Tyre had . . . been a loyal friend of David*** (2 Sam 5:11-12). This might mean that the two shared a covenantal relationship (a treaty). Hiram was a valuable ally and commercial partner (5:7-11, 18; 9:11, 26-28; 10:22). His name is a shortened form of Ahiram, a name seen elsewhere in Phoenician inscriptions.

5:2-6 ***Solomon*** responded to ***Hiram*** by sending word through Hiram's ambassadors that he intended to ***build a Temple to honor the name of the LORD,*** following his father David's desire and provisions for its construction (2 Sam 7:1-3; 1 Chr 17:1-15; 22:14-19; 28:9-12).

5:3 ***gave him victory over all his enemies*** (literally *put them under the soles of his feet*): Ancient Near Eastern inscriptions and paintings often depict victorious kings with their feet upon the necks of vanquished foes or with enemies subdued at their feet.

5:4-5 Unlike David, Solomon enjoyed ***peace*** [literally *rest*] ***on every side.*** Solomon's name (Hebrew *shlomoh*) may be a variation of the word for "peace" (Hebrew *shalom*). • ***The name of the LORD*** signifies God's self-revealed character and reputation. The Hebrew term translated *the name* was sometimes used in oral reading of Scripture so the reader could avoid uttering the personal name of God (the tetragrammaton—YHWH). The NT applies the term "the name" to Jesus (Acts 5:41; 3 Jn 1:7).

5:6 ***please command:*** The main thrust of Solomon's message was his request for ***cedars from Lebanon***, indicating Hiram's wide commercial influence. Ancient Near Eastern literature often cites the use of Lebanese *cedars* in building and furnishing temples and palaces. • ***Sidonians*** was a general name for Phoenicians; Sidon was more ancient than Tyre.

5:9
2 Chr 2:16
Ezra 3:7
Ezek 27:17

5:12
1 Kgs 3:12

5:14
1 Kgs 4:6

As you know, there is no one among us
who can cut timber like you Sidonians!"

7When Hiram received Solomon's message, he was very pleased and said, "Praise
the LORD today for giving David a wise son
to be king of the great nation of Israel."
8Then he sent this reply to Solomon:

"I have received your message, and I will
supply all the cedar and cypress timber
you need. 9My servants will bring the
logs from the Lebanon mountains to the
Mediterranean Sea and make them into
rafts and float them along the coast to
whatever place you choose. Then we will
break the rafts apart so you can carry
the logs away. You can pay me by supply-
ing me with food for my household."

10So Hiram supplied as much cedar and
cypress timber as Solomon desired. 11In return, Solomon sent him an annual payment
of 100,000 bushels of wheat for his household and 110,000 gallons of pure olive oil.
12So the LORD gave wisdom to Solomon, just
as he had promised. And Hiram and Solomon made a formal alliance of peace.

13Then King Solomon conscripted a labor
force of 30,000 men from all Israel. 14He
sent them to Lebanon in shifts, 10,000
every month, so that each man would be
one month in Lebanon and two months at
home. Adoniram was in charge of this labor

Pure Worship (5:3-5)

Gen 8:20; Exod 4:31; 25:10-22; Lev 1:1–8:36; Deut 5:7-9; 6:4-9; 10:12, 20; 16:13-17; 26:1-15; Ps 24:3-6; 51:1-19; Hos 6:6; 14:1-2; Mic 6:6-8; Matt 4:10; 5:16; 6:1-18; John 4:19-24; 5:23; 14:6; Acts 2:40-47; Rom 12:1-2; 1 Cor 3:16-17; 14:1-40; Phil 3:3; Heb 10:1-25; 1 Pet 3:15; 1 Jn 5:21; Rev 5:9-13; 15:3

One of the Lord's key purposes for his people is that they offer him pure worship. From the beginning of God's relationship with Israel, he made provision for their worship of him to be pleasing to him (Exod 20–40; Lev 1–8). When Solomon built the Temple as a permanent worship sanctuary, he took great care to erect "a Temple to honor the name of the LORD" (5:3-5). He built in accordance with the pattern he was given, placing the Ark in the inner sanctuary in the proper manner and dedicating the Temple to the Lord (8:1-11; see Deut 16:13-17). In all of this, Solomon kept the requirements laid down in the law (see, e.g., Exod 25:10-22), which were intended to keep Israel's worship purely focused on the Lord and his word.

Unfortunately, people tend to worship according to their own inclinations rather than according to God's instructions, and Israel was no different. In his later years, Solomon turned away from the Lord to other gods (11:7-8). After Solomon's death, Jeroboam in the north established a competing, idolatrous religion in clear violation of God's law (14:9-10, 15-16). False worship characterized the northern kingdom throughout the reigns of the kings that followed (e.g., 15:26; 16:13, 25-26, 30-34; 21:25-26). Meanwhile, in Judah, the southern kingdom, tolerance for local pagan altars became a persistent spiritual distraction (15:14; 22:43). Neither Judah nor Israel remained pure in their worship of the Lord.

There is but one God whom God's people must worship (8:23; see Deut 5:7, 9; 6:4; John 14:6; Acts 4:12). Our worship must come from a pure heart; we must remain completely faithful to the Lord in dedicated service to him (15:14; 17:1; see Deut 10:12, 20; Ps 24:3-4; Matt 4:10; John 4:24). Our daily and weekly worship of God should have a sense of God's presence, which will be a source of genuine joy (8:56; cp. Ps. 63:1-3; Phil. 4:4). Our whole life should include daily worship of Christ, acknowledging him as Lord (1 Pet 3:15). Just as Israel's Temple was a sanctuary intended to attract all people (8:41-43), believers are the temple of the living God (1 Cor 3:16-17). We are to live so as to attract and motivate others to desire to know the Lord and worship him (Matt 5:16; Acts 2:40-47; 2 Tim 4:5; 1 Pet 2:12). We must not let any idol take God's place in our hearts (1 Jn 5:21).

5:7-12 Hiram's ***reply to Solomon*** confirmed and perpetuated the cordial relations that he had with David. The venture was mutually beneficial. Solomon received needed construction materials for the Temple; in return, he supplied necessities for Hiram's ***household*** (5:9-10) and paid Hiram's workers (5:6). The passage illustrates the Phoenicians' skillful commercial enterprises and Solomon's immense wealth, and it again emphasizes Solomon's God-given ***wisdom.*** The largely commercial venture led to ***a formal alliance of peace*** (5:12).

5:7 ***Praise the LORD:*** Hiram did not acknowledge Israel's God as his own but, following ancient Near Eastern protocol, he politely recognized Solomon's God (see 10:9; 2 Kgs 18:22-25; Ezra 1:2-4; 6:12; Dan 2:47; 3:29; 6:26-27).

5:9 ***the Mediterranean Sea:*** Literally *the sea.*

5:11 ***100,000 bushels:*** Hebrew *20,000 cors* [3,640 kiloliters]. • ***110,000 gallons:*** As in Greek version, which reads *20,000 baths* [420 kiloliters] (see also 2 Chr 2:10); Hebrew reads *20 cors,* about 800 gallons or 3.6 kiloliters in volume.

5:13-18 This passage describes Solomon's work force and the division of ***labor.*** Forced labor was a common practice in the ancient Near East (see note on 4:6).

5:13 Aliens with permanent residency in ***Israel*** comprised the bulk of Solomon's ***labor force.*** Native Israelites were apparently temporary supervisors for Solomon's building projects (9:22-23; 11:28).

force. 15Solomon also had 70,000 common laborers, 80,000 quarry workers in the hill country, 16and 3,600 foremen to supervise the work. 17At the king's command, they quarried large blocks of high-quality stone and shaped them to make the foundation of the Temple. 18Men from the city of Gebal helped Solomon's and Hiram's builders prepare the timber and stone for the Temple.

Solomon Builds the Temple
1 Kgs 6:1-3 // 2 Chr 3:1-4

6 It was in midspring, in the month of Ziv, during the fourth year of Solomon's reign, that he began to construct the Temple of the LORD. This was 480 years after the people of Israel were rescued from their slavery in the land of Egypt.

2The Temple that King Solomon built for the LORD was 90 feet long, 30 feet wide, and 45 feet high. 3The entry room at the front of the Temple was 30 feet wide, running across the entire width of the Temple. It projected outward 15 feet from the front of the Temple. 4Solomon also made narrow recessed windows throughout the Temple.

5He built a complex of rooms against the outer walls of the Temple, all the way around the sides and rear of the building. 6The complex was three stories high, the bottom floor being 7½ feet wide, the second floor 9 feet wide, and the top floor 10½ feet wide. The rooms were connected to the walls of the Temple by beams resting on ledges built out from the wall. So the beams were not inserted into the walls themselves.

7The stones used in the construction of the Temple were finished at the quarry, so there was no sound of hammer, ax, or any other iron tool at the building site.

8The entrance to the bottom floor was on the south side of the Temple. There were winding stairs going up to the second floor, and another flight of stairs between the second and third floors. 9After completing the Temple structure, Solomon put in a ceiling made of cedar beams and planks. 10As already stated, he built a complex of rooms on three sides of the building, attached to the Temple walls by cedar timbers. Each story of the complex was 7½ feet high.

11Then the LORD gave this message to Solomon: 12"Concerning this Temple you are building, if you keep all my decrees and regulations and obey all my commands, I will fulfill through you the promise I made to your father, David. 13I will live among the Israelites and will never abandon my people Israel."

The Temple's Interior
1 Kgs 6:23-28 // 2 Chr 3:10-13

14So Solomon finished building the Temple.

5:17 1 Chr 22:2
6:1-29 //2 Chr 3:1-14
6:4 Ezek 41:16
6:5 Ezek 41:5-6
6:7 Exod 20:25; Deut 27:5-6
6:9 1 Kgs 6:14, 38
6:12 2 Sam 7:12-16; 1 Kgs 9:4-5
6:13 Exod 25:8; Deut 31:6; Josh 1:5

5:16 ***3,600 foremen:*** As in some Greek manuscripts (see also 2 Chr 2:2, 18); Hebrew reads *3,300.* In 2 Chronicles (2 Chr 2:2, 17-18; 8:10) the *foremen* total 3,600 non-Israelite and 250 Israelite chief supervisors. The numbers in the Hebrew text of 5:16 and 9:23 are 3,300 *foremen* and 550 chief supervisors. It is possible that 250 of the chief supervisors were Israelites, with 300 non-Israelites holding the same rank.

5:17-18 ***Large blocks of high-quality stone*** were probably cut to size (see 7:10) in a quarry near Jerusalem (6:7). The need to handle these massive stones is probably what led Solomon to institute forced labor. The craftsmen included ***men from . . . Gebal*** (Byblos), a port known for exporting timber, according to ancient Egyptian inscriptions.

6:1–8:66 The building of the Temple and palace complex and the celebration of the Temple dedication are central to the 1 Kings account of Solomon's era. The Temple, erected to glorify God, was Israel's most important building, so the writer of 1 Kings carefully recorded details of its construction.

6:1 Solomon's ***fourth year*** was about 967 BC. Treating the number *480* as representing calendar years yields a date of about 1446 BC for Israel's exodus from ***Egypt.*** Those who view the number as symbolic (12 generations times 40 years each) suggest that the Exodus occurred at a later date, around 1270 BC (see "Chronology: Abraham to Joshua," p. 118). • ***It was in midspring, in the month of Ziv:*** Literally *It was in the month of Ziv, which is the second month.* This month of the ancient Hebrew lunar calendar usually occurs within the months of April and May.

6:2 Like the Tabernacle before it, the ***Temple*** (literally *house*) was the place where God met with his people. David had stored up materials to be used in its construction (1 Chr 22:2-4, 14) and had drawn up plans for the Temple and given them to ***Solomon*** (1 Chr 28:11-12). The Temple's floor plan resembled that of the Tabernacle but doubled its length and width and increased its height (cp. Exod 26:3, 15-30; 36:26-34). • ***90 feet long, 30 feet wide, and 45 feet high:*** Hebrew *60 cubits* [27.6 meters] *long, 20 cubits* [9.2 meters] *wide, and 30 cubits* [13.8 meters] *high.*

6:3-4 Unlike the Tabernacle, the ***Temple*** had an east ***entry room*** (or porch) and two freestanding pillars before the entrance (7:15-22).

6:3 ***30 feet:*** Hebrew *20 cubits* [9.2 meters]; also in 6:16, 20. • ***15 feet:*** Hebrew *10 cubits* [4.6 meters].

6:6 ***the bottom floor . . . wide:*** Hebrew *the bottom floor being 5 cubits* [2.3 meters] *wide, the second floor 6 cubits* [2.8 meters] *wide, and the top floor 7 cubits* [3.2 meters] *wide.*

6:8 ***the bottom floor:*** As in Greek version; Hebrew reads *middle floor.*

6:10 ***7½ feet:*** Hebrew *5 cubits* [2.3 meters].

6:11-13 ***The LORD*** had an encouraging ***message*** for ***Solomon.*** Because God appeared to Solomon before (3:5) and after (9:2) this event, this *message* probably came to him by a prophet. The words reminded the king of God's prior ***promise*** (3:14): If Solomon remained faithful to God, the Temple that he was building would become an eternal dwelling place for God.

6:14-35 The focus shifts to the ***Temple*** interior. While the Temple site is not mentioned here, the Chronicler located it at the former threshing floor of Araunah (1 Chr 21:18-25; 2 Chr 3:1). This site is traditionally thought to be the location of Mount Moriah (Gen 22:2). Solomon's Temple was in

6:16
Exod 26:33
Lev 16:1-2
2 Chr 3:8

15 The entire inside, from floor to ceiling,
was paneled with wood. He paneled the
walls and ceilings with cedar, and he used
planks of cypress for the floors. 16 He par-
titioned off an inner sanctuary—the Most
Holy Place—at the far end of the Temple.
It was 30 feet deep and was paneled with
cedar from floor to ceiling. 17 The main
room of the Temple, outside the Most
Holy Place, was 60 feet long. 18 Cedar paneling completely covered the stone walls
throughout the Temple, and the paneling
was decorated with carvings of gourds and
open flowers.
19 He prepared the inner sanctuary at
the far end of the Temple, where the Ark

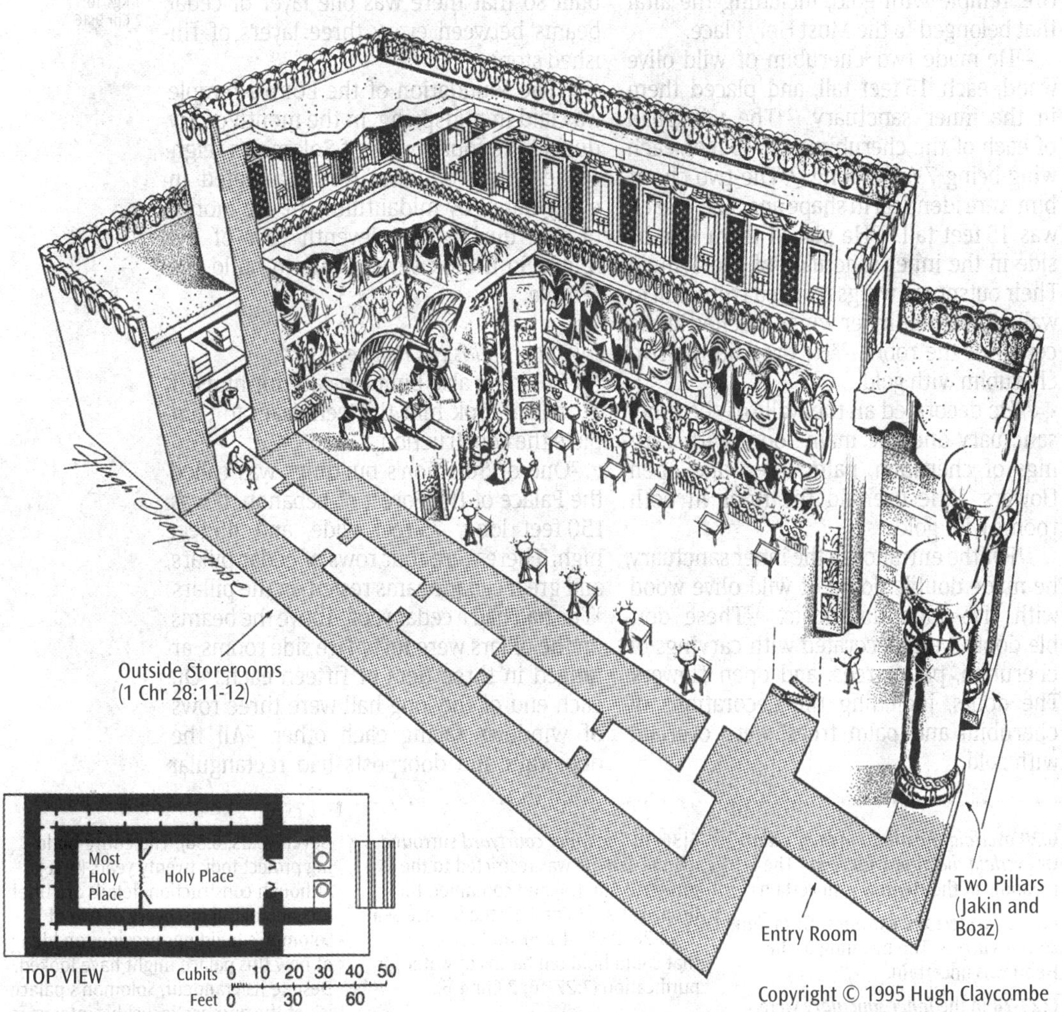

▲**Solomon's Temple, 967~586 BC (6:1–9:1 // 2 Chr 3:1–5:14).** It took Solomon seven years to build the Temple in Jerusalem, beginning in the fourth year of his reign (967 BC). The Temple, laid out like the Tabernacle before it, stood until Jerusalem was destroyed in 586 BC. This drawing is one rendition of how Solomon's Temple might have been designed.

the northeastern corner of Jerusalem (now called the "old city") in the area now associated with the Dome of the Rock.

6:15-18 *paneled with wood:* the interior walls were ***paneled with cedar from floor to ceiling*** so that no exterior stones could be seen. The effect was exquisitely beautiful, reflecting painstaking care and great expense.

6:17 *60 feet:* Hebrew *40 cubits* [18.4 meters].

6:19-22 Following the pattern of the Tabernacle, the *inner sanctuary*, which was *overlaid . . . inside with solid gold*, was separated from the main room *of the Temple* by a curtain (2 Chr 3:14) and *gold chains*. Like the Most Holy Place in the Tabernacle, the *inner sanctuary* was a perfect cube. It housed the ***Ark of the LORD's Covenant*** that symbolized God's presence. The place of atonement was atop the *Ark* (Exod 25:17); the high priest annually made propitiation for the Israelites by sprinkling the sacrificial blood of the atonement on it (Lev 16:1-19). • The ***altar that belonged to the Most Holy Place*** stood in the main room. The priests burned incense there daily (Exod 30:34-38; 37:25-29). The altar was made of ***cedar*** and covered with *gold*. • Like the *inner sanctuary*, the main room was also completely *overlaid with gold*, which reminded the priests that Almighty God was present. The main room also housed ten golden lampstands, ten tables (2 Chr 4:7-8), and other furnishings (7:48-50).

of the LORD's Covenant would be placed.
[20]This inner sanctuary was 30 feet long,
30 feet wide, and 30 feet high. He overlaid
the inside with solid gold. He also overlaid
the altar made of cedar. [21]Then Solomon
overlaid the rest of the Temple's interior
with solid gold, and he made gold chains
to protect the entrance to the Most Holy
Place. [22]So he finished overlaying the entire Temple with gold, including the altar
that belonged to the Most Holy Place.

[23]He made two [j]cherubim of wild olive
wood, each 15 feet tall, and placed them
in the inner sanctuary. [24]The wingspan
of each of the cherubim was 15 feet, each
wing being 7½ feet long. [25]The two cherubim were identical in shape and size; [26]each
was 15 feet tall. [27]He placed them side by
side in the inner sanctuary of the Temple.
Their outspread wings reached from wall to
wall, while their inner wings touched at the
center of the room. [28]He overlaid the two
cherubim with gold.

[29]He decorated all the walls of the inner
sanctuary and the main room with carvings of cherubim, palm trees, and open
flowers. [30]He overlaid the floor in both
rooms with gold.

[31]For the entrance to the inner sanctuary,
he made double doors of wild olive wood
with five-sided doorposts. [32]These double doors were decorated with carvings of
cherubim, palm trees, and open flowers.
The doors, including the decorations of
cherubim and palm trees, were overlaid
with gold.

[33]Then he made four-sided doorposts
of wild olive wood for the entrance to the
Temple. [34]There were two folding doors of
cypress wood, and each door was hinged to
fold back upon itself. [35]These doors were
decorated with carvings of cherubim, palm
trees, and open flowers—all overlaid evenly
with gold.

[36]The walls of the inner courtyard were
built so that there was one layer of cedar
beams between every three layers of finished stone.

[37]The foundation of the LORD's Temple
was laid in midspring, in the month of Ziv,
during the fourth year of Solomon's reign.
[38]The entire building was completed in
every detail by midautumn, in the month
of Bul, during the eleventh year of his
reign. So it took seven years to build the
Temple.

Solomon Builds His Palace

7 Solomon also built a palace for himself,
and it took him thirteen years to complete the construction.

[2]One of Solomon's buildings was called
the Palace of the Forest of Lebanon. It was
150 feet long, 75 feet wide, and 45 feet
high. There were four rows of cedar pillars,
and great cedar beams rested on the pillars.
[3]The hall had a cedar roof. Above the beams
on the pillars were forty-five side rooms, arranged in three tiers of fifteen each. [4]On
each end of the long hall were three rows
of windows facing each other. [5]All the
doorways and doorposts had rectangular

6:23 Exod 25:20; 37:1-9; 2 Chr 3:10-12
[j]*kerub* (3742) ‣ Isa 6:2
6:34 Ezek 41:23-25
6:36 1 Kgs 7:12
7:1 1 Kgs 3:1; 9:10; 2 Chr 8:1
7:2 1 Kgs 10:17; 2 Chr 9:16

6:20 ***overlaid the altar made of cedar:*** Or *overlaid the altar with cedar.* The meaning of the Hebrew is uncertain.

6:21 ***to protect the entrance:*** Or *to draw curtains across.* The meaning of the Hebrew is uncertain.

6:23-28 In the *inner sanctuary* were ***two cherubim*** (see note on 1 Chr 28:18) made of *olive wood* and ***overlaid . . . with gold.*** Standing like sentries facing the door (2 Chr 3:13), their combined wingspan reached from wall to wall. Along with the two smaller *cherubim* facing each other atop the Ark (Exod 25:17-21), they symbolized the awe-some presence of the Most Holy God.

6:23 ***wild olive:*** Or *pine;* Hebrew reads *oil tree;* also in 6:31, 33. • ***15 feet:*** Hebrew *10 cubits* [4.6 meters]; also in 6:24, 26.

6:24 ***7½ feet:*** Hebrew *5 cubits* [2.3 meters].

6:31 ***with five-sided doorposts:*** The meaning of the Hebrew is uncertain.

6:36-38 The *inner courtyard* surrounding the ***Temple*** was restricted to the priests (2 Chr 4:9) and contained the bronze altar (2 Chr 4:1), the bronze Sea (7:23-26; 2 Chr 4:2-5), and ten carts that could hold ten basins of water for purification (7:27-40; 2 Chr 4:6).

6:37 ***was laid in midspring, in the month of Ziv:*** Literally *was laid in the month of Ziv.* This month of the ancient Hebrew lunar calendar usually occurs within the months of April and May. See "Israel's Annual Calendar" at Exod 12:2, p. 145.

6:38 ***midautumn, in the month of Bul:*** Literally *by the month of Bul, which is the eighth month.* This month of the ancient Hebrew lunar calendar usually occurs within the months of October and November. The year was 960 BC.

7:1-12 Before describing the Temple's furnishings, the writer mentions the construction of Solomon's *palace* complex. The multiple buildings within this complex took nearly twice as long to build (***thirteen years***) as the Temple (seven years, 6:38). The entire building project took twenty years (9:16). Although construction details are brief, archaeological discovery of two of Solomon's buildings provides an idea of how this palace might have looked. Despite its grandeur, Solomon's palace is not the author's focus; his interest is in the Temple, God's dwelling place.

7:2-5 ***The Palace of the Forest of Lebanon*** was named for the abundant use of *cedar* in its construction. It would house 300 gold shields (10:16-17) and possibly served as both treasury and armory (see 12:25-28; Isa 22:8). The Egyptian Pharaoh Shishak later carried away the shields as booty (14:27).

7:2 ***150 feet long, 75 feet wide, and 45 feet high:*** Hebrew *100 cubits* [46 meters] *long, 50 cubits* [23 meters] *wide, and 30 cubits* [13.5 meters] *high.*

7:3 ***forty-five side rooms:*** Or *45 rafters,* or *45 beams,* or *45 pillars.* The architectural details in 7:2-6 can be interpreted in many different ways.

7:7
1 Kgs 6:9, 15-16
7:8
1 Kgs 3:1
2 Chr 8:11
7:12
1 Kgs 6:36
7:13
2 Chr 2:13-14
7:15
2 Kgs 25:17
2 Chr 3:15; 4:12
7:20
2 Chr 3:16; 4:13
7:21
2 Chr 3:17
7:23-26
//2 Chr 4:2-5
7:23
2 Kgs 25:13

frames and were arranged in sets of three, facing each other.

[6]Solomon also built the Hall of Pillars, which was 75 feet long and 45 feet wide. There was a porch in front, along with a canopy supported by pillars.

[7]Solomon also built the throne room, known as the Hall of Justice, where he sat to hear legal matters. It was paneled with cedar from floor to ceiling. [8]Solomon's living quarters surrounded a courtyard behind this hall, and they were constructed the same way. He also built similar living quarters for Pharaoh's daughter, whom he had married.

[9]From foundation to eaves, all these buildings were built from huge blocks of high-quality stone, cut with saws and trimmed to exact measure on all sides. [10]Some of the huge foundation stones were 15 feet long, and some were 12 feet long. [11]The blocks of high-quality stone used in the walls were also cut to measure, and cedar beams were also used. [12]The walls of the great courtyard were built so that there was one layer of cedar beams between every three layers of finished stone, just like the walls of the inner courtyard of the LORD's Temple with its entry room.

Furnishings for the Temple

[13]King Solomon then asked for a man named Huram to come from Tyre. [14]He was half Israelite, since his mother was a widow from the tribe of Naphtali, and his father had been a craftsman in bronze from Tyre. Huram was extremely skillful and talented in any work in bronze, and he came to do all the metal work for King Solomon.

Huram's Craftsmanship
1 Kgs 7:15-26// 2 Chr 3:15–4:5
1 Kgs 7:38-39 // 2 Chr 4:6, 10

[15]Huram cast two bronze pillars, each 27 feet tall and 18 feet in circumference. [16]For the tops of the pillars he cast bronze capitals, each 7½ feet tall. [17]Each capital was decorated with seven sets of latticework and interwoven chains. [18]He also encircled the latticework with two rows of pomegranates to decorate the capitals over the pillars. [19]The capitals on the columns inside the entry room were shaped like water lilies, and they were six feet tall. [20]The capitals on the two pillars had 200 pomegranates in two rows around them, beside the rounded surface next to the latticework. [21]Huram set the pillars at the entrance of the Temple, one toward the south and one toward the north. He named the one on the south Jakin, and the one on the north Boaz. [22]The capitals on the pillars were shaped like water lilies. And so the work on the pillars was finished.

[23]Then Huram cast a great round basin, 15 feet across from rim to rim, called the

---

7:5 ***the doorways and doorposts:*** Greek version reads *windows.*

7:6-8 ***The Hall of Pillars*** was apparently a colonnaded entry to the ***Hall of Justice***, where Solomon ***sat to hear legal matters*** (see also 10:18-20). Similar throne rooms have been found in Syria and Mesopotamia. • Solomon erected separate ***living quarters for Pharaoh's daughter*** (see 3:1; 9:24; 2 Chr 8:11).

7:6 ***75 feet long and 45 feet wide:*** Hebrew *50 cubits* [23 meters] *long and 30 cubits* [13.8 meters] *wide.*

7:7 ***from floor to ceiling:*** As in Syriac version and Latin Vulgate; Hebrew reads *from floor to floor.*

7:9-11 As with the Temple, the ***stones*** for Solomon's palace complex were ***high-quality stone, cut . . . and trimmed to exact*** specifications. Similar stonework has been found at Megiddo. ***Cedar beams*** between the courses of the wall provided better protection against earthquakes.

7:10 ***15 feet . . . 12 feet:*** Hebrew *10 cubits* [4.6 meters] . . . *8 cubits* [3.7 meters].

7:12 ***The great courtyard*** that encircled the Temple and palace complex provided a gathering place for the people (see Jer 7:1-2; 36:10).

7:13-14 ***Huram:*** Hebrew *Hiram* (also in 7:40, 45); cp. 2 Chr 2:13. This is not the same person mentioned in 5:1. Like his father, he was a master ***craftsman in bronze*** and other materials (2 Chr 2:12-14). His skillful ***metal work*** is detailed in the following verses (7:15-50). • ***skillful and talented*** (literally *filled with wisdom and understanding and knowledge*): The Israelites placed great emphasis on practical skills and considered them a form of wisdom (Prov 22:29).

7:15-22 The ***two bronze pillars*** were probably free-standing since the narrator describes them here rather than in the earlier discussion of the Temple structure (6:3-6).

7:15 ***27 feet tall and 18 feet in circumference:*** Hebrew *18 cubits* [8.3 meters] *tall and 12 cubits* [5.5 meters] *in circumference.* Cp. 2 Chr 3:15 and note; see also 2 Kgs 25:17; Jer 52:21.

7:16 ***7½ feet:*** Hebrew *5 cubits* [2.3 meters]. Cp. 2 Kgs 25:17 and note.

7:19 ***six feet:*** Hebrew *4 cubits* [1.8 meters]; also in 7:38.

7:21 ***Jakin*** probably means "he establishes"; ***Boaz*** probably means "in him is strength." The names of the pillars might represent Solomon's dedication to God in ruling his empire.

7:23-26 The giant bronze basin ***called the Sea*** replaced the smaller bronze washbasin used in the Tabernacle service (see Exod 30:17-21). The Sea was cast as one solid piece, excluding the ***twelve bronze oxen*** on which it sat. The oxen were placed so that ***three faced*** each direction, perhaps to remind priests that they served God on behalf of all twelve tribes of Israel. Ahaz later replaced the oxen with a stone base (2 Kgs 16:17). The priests used the Sea, like the bronze washbasin before it, for ceremonial washing (2 Chr 4:6) as they prepared to minister before God (see Exod 30:17-21). The apparent discrepancy in the volume of water it could hold (see 2 Chr 4:5) is probably due to standards of measurement that varied according to place and time.

7:23 ***15 feet across . . . 7½ feet deep and about 45 feet in circumference:*** Hebrew *10 cubits* [4.6 meters] *across. . . . 5 cubits* [2.3 meters] *deep and 30 cubits* [13.8 meters] *in circumference.*

Sea. It was 7½ feet deep and about 45 feet
in circumference. [24]It was encircled just
below its rim by two rows of decorative
gourds. There were about six gourds per
foot all the way around, and they were cast
as part of the basin.
[25]The Sea was placed on a base of twelve
bronze oxen, all facing outward. Three
faced north, three faced west, three faced
south, and three faced east, and the Sea
rested on them. [26]The walls of the Sea were
about three inches thick, and its rim flared
out like a cup and resembled a water lily
blossom. It could hold about 11,000 gallons
of water.
[27]Huram also made ten bronze water
carts, each 6 feet long, 6 feet wide, and
4½ feet tall. [28]They were constructed
with side panels braced with crossbars.
[29]Both the panels and the crossbars were
decorated with carved lions, oxen, and cherubim. Above and below the lions and oxen
were wreath decorations. [30]Each of these
carts had four bronze wheels and bronze
axles. There were supporting posts for the
bronze basins at the corners of the carts;
these supports were decorated on each side
with carvings of wreaths. [31]The top of each
cart had a rounded frame for the basin. It
projected 1½ feet above the cart's top like a
round pedestal, and its opening was 2¼ feet
across; it was decorated on the outside with
carvings of wreaths. The panels of the carts
were square, not round. [32]Under the panels
were four wheels that were connected to axles that had been cast as one unit with the
cart. The wheels were 2¼ feet in diameter
[33]and were similar to chariot wheels. The
axles, spokes, rims, and hubs were all cast
from molten bronze.
[34]There were handles at each of the four
corners of the carts, and these, too, were
cast as one unit with the cart. [35]Around the
top of each cart was a rim nine inches wide.
The corner supports and side panels were
cast as one unit with the cart. [36]Carvings of
cherubim, lions, and palm trees decorated
the panels and corner supports wherever
there was room, and there were wreaths all
around. [37]All ten water carts were the same
size and were made alike, for each was cast
from the same mold.
[38]Huram also made ten smaller bronze
basins, one for each cart. Each basin was six
feet across and could hold 220 gallons of
water. [39]He set five water carts on the south
side of the Temple and five on the north
side. The great bronze basin called the Sea
was placed near the southeast corner of
the Temple. [40]He also made the necessary
washbasins, shovels, and bowls.

The Completion of the Temple

1 Kgs 7:40-51 // 2 Chr 4:11–5:1

So at last Huram completed everything
King Solomon had assigned him to make
for the Temple of the LORD:

[41] the two pillars;
the two bowl-shaped capitals on top of the pillars;
the two networks of interwoven chains that decorated the capitals;
[42] the 400 pomegranates that hung from the chains on the capitals (two rows of pomegranates for each of the chain networks that decorated the capitals on top of the pillars);
[43] the ten water carts holding the ten basins;
[44] the Sea and the twelve oxen under it;
[45] the ash buckets, the shovels, and the bowls.

Huram made all these things of burnished
bronze for the Temple of the LORD, just as
King Solomon had directed. [46]The king had
them cast in clay molds in the Jordan Valley
between Succoth and Zarethan. [47]Solomon
did not weigh all these things because there
were so many; the weight of the bronze
could not be measured.
[48]Solomon also made all the furnishings
of the Temple of the LORD:

7:27 2 Kgs 16:17
7:38-51 //2 Chr 4:6, 10–5:1
7:47 1 Chr 22:3, 14
7:48 Exod 37:10-16

7:24 ***six gourds per foot:*** Or *20 gourds per meter;* Hebrew reads *10 per cubit.*

7:25 ***twelve bronze oxen:*** Hebrew *12 oxen;* cp. 2 Kgs 16:17, which specifies *bronze oxen.*

7:26 ***about three inches:*** Hebrew *a handbreadth* [8 centimeters]. • ***11,000 gallons:*** Hebrew *2,000 baths* [42 kiloliters].

7:27-39 The ***ten bronze water carts*** each held a basin for rinsing burnt offerings (2 Chr 4:6). ***Five*** stood on either side of the ***Temple.*** Because they had ***wheels,*** they could be moved as needed.

7:27 ***6 feet long, 6 feet wide, and 4½ feet tall:*** Hebrew *4 cubits* [1.8 meters] *long, 4 cubits wide, and 3 cubits* [1.4 meters] *high.*

7:31 ***1½ feet:*** Hebrew *a cubit* [46 centimeters]. • ***2¼ feet:*** Hebrew *1½ cubits* [69 centimeters]; also in 7:32.

7:35 ***nine inches wide:*** Hebrew *half a cubit wide* [23 centimeters].

7:38 ***220 gallons:*** Hebrew *40 baths* [840 liters].

7:40-45 ***Huram*** had great skill in casting items of varying size and complexity. He also made the bronze altar for the inner court that was used for burnt offerings (2 Chr 4:1).

7:46-47 ***between Succoth and Zarethan:*** This area east of the Jordan River (see Josh 3:16; Judg 8:4-5) was known for metallurgy. Abundant clay for molds, wood for fuel, and a prevailing north wind facilitated the casting process.

7:48-49 ***The gold altar*** replaced the altar for burning incense used in the Tabernacle (Exod 30:1-10). The one table and one lampstand used in the Tabernacle (Exod 25:23-40) were

7:49
Exod 25:31
7:50
2 Kgs 25:14-15
7:51
2 Sam 8:11
2 Chr 5:1
8:1-21
2 Chr 5:2–6:11
8:1
Num 7:2
2 Sam 5:7; 6:17
[k]*aron* (0727)
‣2 Kgs 12:9
8:2
Lev 23:33-34
2 Chr 5:3; 7:8-10
8:3
Num 7:9
8:5
2 Sam 6:13
2 Chr 1:5-6
[a]*zabakh* (2076)
‣Ps 4:5
8:8
Exod 25:13-15; 37:4-5
8:9
Exod 24:7; 25:16
Deut 4:13-14; 10:2
Heb 9:4
8:10
Exod 40:34-35
2 Chr 7:1-2

the gold altar;
the gold table for the Bread of the
Presence;
49 the lampstands of solid gold, five on the
south and five on the north, in front of
the Most Holy Place;
the flower decorations, lamps, and
tongs—all of gold;
50 the small bowls, lamp snuffers, bowls,
dishes, and incense burners—all of
solid gold;
the doors for the entrances to the Most
Holy Place and the main room of the
Temple, with their fronts overlaid with
gold.

51 So King Solomon finished all his
work on the Temple of the LORD. Then he
brought all the gifts his father, David, had
dedicated—the silver, the gold, and the various articles—and he stored them in the
treasuries of the LORD's Temple.

The Ark Brought to the Temple
1 Kgs 8:1-11 // 2 Chr 5:2-14

8 Solomon then summoned to Jerusalem
the elders of Israel and all the heads of
the tribes—the leaders of the ancestral families of the Israelites. They were to bring the
[k]Ark of the LORD's Covenant to the Temple
from its location in the City of David, also
known as Zion. 2 So all the men of Israel assembled before King Solomon at the annual
Festival of Shelters, which is held in early autumn in the month of Ethanim.
3 When all the elders of Israel arrived, the
priests picked up the Ark. 4 The priests and
Levites brought up the Ark of the LORD along
with the special tent and all the sacred items
that had been in it. 5 There, before the Ark,
King Solomon and the entire community of
Israel [a]sacrificed so many sheep, goats, and
cattle that no one could keep count!
6 Then the priests carried the Ark of the
LORD's Covenant into the inner sanctuary
of the Temple—the Most Holy Place—and
placed it beneath the wings of the cherubim. 7 The cherubim spread their wings
over the Ark, forming a canopy over the Ark
and its carrying poles. 8 These poles were so
long that their ends could be seen from the
Temple's main room—the Holy Place—but
not from the outside. They are still there
to this day. 9 Nothing was in the Ark except
the two stone tablets that Moses had placed
in it at Mount Sinai, where the LORD made
a covenant with the people of Israel when
they left the land of Egypt.
10 When the priests came out of the Holy
Place, a thick cloud filled the Temple of the

replaced by ten such sets in the Temple. Although the author lists a single ***gold table for the Bread of the Presence,*** the Chronicler reports ten tables, five on each side of the Temple's main room (cp. 2 Chr 4:8), along with ten ***lampstands of solid gold.*** The bread represented God's provision for his people, and the lampstand characterized God as the source of life and truth. Both symbols pointed to Christ, the bread of life (John 6:35) and the light of the world (John 8:12).

7:50-51 The writer emphasizes Solomon's abundant use of gold in furnishing the Temple. David and the people had collected an enormous amount of gold to be used for the Temple (1 Chr 29:1-9), and Solomon also amassed gold annually (10:14), so he had a ready supply (see 10:21).

8:1-66 Solomon's building activities climaxed with the Ark's move to the newly erected Temple. The king offered both prayer (8:22-53) and words of praise and blessing (8:56-61) to dedicate the Temple for the Lord's service. After the dedication, the assembled gathering enjoyed the great Festival of Shelters. The focus of the account is on Solomon praising God and blessing the people (8:12-61).

8:1 The ***Ark*** was being kept in a tent in the ***City of David*** (2 Sam 6:3-17; 1 Chr 13:7-14; 15:1–16:43). Solomon had gone there earlier to sacrifice after the Lord appeared to him in a dream in Gibeon (3:4-15).

8:2 Although the Temple was completed in the eighth month (6:38), Solomon apparently delayed the dedication until the following year so it could take place ***at the annual Festival of Shelters, which is held in early autumn in the month of Ethanim*** (literally *at the festival in the month Ethanim, which is the seventh month*). The Festival of Shelters began on the fifteenth day of the seventh month of the ancient Hebrew lunar calendar. This day occurred in late September, October, or early November (see "Israel's Festivals" at Lev 23:1-44, p. 235). This schedule allowed time to prepare for the spectacular celebration and gave the occasion double significance. As prescribed in the law, Solomon and the people expressed their gratitude to God for the completed harvest season. They also celebrated the fulfillment of Moses' song of deliverance, which promised that God would one day settle his people in the Promised Land and make his dwelling there (Exod 15:17; Deut 12:10-14). Solomon's dedicatory prayer and blessing may indicate that he was consciously leading his people in covenantal renewal, as prescribed in Deut 31:10-13, in the seventh month of the seventh year of his reign.

8:3-4 ***The priests and Levites brought up the Ark of the LORD*** as prescribed in the law (Exod 25:14-15; Num 4:5-8; cp. 2 Sam 6:1-15).

8:4 ***the special tent:*** Literally *the Tent of Meeting;* i.e., the tent mentioned in 2 Sam 6:17 and 1 Chr 16:1.

8:5 The incalculable sacrifices by the Israelites marked both the joy and the solemnity of this occasion.

8:8 In accordance with the law (Exod 25:15), the carrying ***poles*** were required to stay with the Ark.

8:9 The focus on the ***two stone tablets*** that Moses placed in the Ark (cp. 8:21; see Exod 25:21; Deut 31:26) suggests that Solomon had in mind both a renewal of the Mosaic covenant and the Temple dedication. • ***at Mount Sinai:*** Hebrew *at Horeb,* another name for Sinai (see note on Exod 3:1).

8:10-11 As ***the priests came out of the Holy Place,*** they were greeted with music praising the Lord (2 Chr 5:11-14). Previously, ***the glorious presence of the LORD*** had filled the Tabernacle (Exod 40:34-35). Now it filled the ***Temple*** to show that God was again dwelling among his people. Ezekiel recorded

LORD. 11The priests could not continue their service because of the cloud, for the glorious presence of the LORD filled the Temple.

Solomon Praises the LORD
1 Kgs 8:12-21 // 2 Chr 6:1-11

12Then Solomon prayed, "O LORD, you have said that you would live in a thick cloud of darkness. 13Now I have built a glorious Temple for you, a place where you can live forever!"

14Then the king turned around to the entire community of Israel standing before him and gave this [a]blessing: 15"Praise the LORD, the God of Israel, who has kept the promise he made to my father, David. For he told my father, 16'From the day I brought my people Israel out of Egypt, I have never chosen a city among any of the tribes of Israel as the place where a Temple should be built to honor my name. But I have chosen David to be king over my people Israel.'"

17Then Solomon said, "My father, David, wanted to build this Temple to honor the name of the LORD, the God of Israel. 18But the LORD told him, 'You wanted to build the Temple to honor my name. Your intention is good, 19but you are not the one to do it. One of your own sons will build the Temple to honor me.'

20"And now the LORD has fulfilled the promise he made, for I have become king in my father's place, and I now sit on the throne of Israel, just as the LORD promised. I have built this Temple to honor the name of the LORD, the God of Israel. 21And I have prepared a place there for the Ark, which contains the covenant that the LORD made with our ancestors when he brought them out of Egypt."

Solomon's Prayer of Dedication
1 Kgs 8:22-53 // 2 Chr 6:12-40

22Then Solomon stood before the altar of the LORD in front of the entire community of Israel. He lifted his hands toward heaven, 23and he prayed,

"O LORD, God of Israel, there is no God
like you in all of heaven above or on the
earth below. You keep your covenant
and show unfailing love to all who walk
before you in wholehearted devotion.
24You have kept your promise to your
servant David, my father. You made
that promise with your own mouth, and
with your own hands you have fulfilled
it today.

25"And now, O LORD, God of Israel,
carry out the additional promise
you made to your servant David, my
father. For you said to him, 'If your descendants guard their behavior and
faithfully follow me as you have done,
one of them will always sit on the
throne of Israel.' 26Now, O God of Israel, fulfill this promise to your servant
David, my father.

27"But will God really live on earth?
Why, even the highest heavens cannot
contain you. How much less this Temple
I have built! 28Nevertheless, listen to my
prayer and my [c]plea, O LORD my God.
Hear the cry and the prayer that your
servant is making to you today. 29May
you watch over this Temple night and
day, this place where you have said, 'My

8:12 2 Chr 6:1; Ps 97:2
8:14 [b]*barak* (1288) ‣2 Chr 6:3
8:15 2 Sam 7:12-13; 1 Chr 22:10
8:16 Deut 12:4-5, 11; 1 Sam 16:1
8:17 2 Sam 7:2-3; 1 Chr 17:1-2
8:19 2 Sam 7:12-13; 1 Chr 17:11-12; 22:8-10
8:20 1 Chr 28:6
8:23 Deut 7:9; Neh 1:5; 9:32
8:25 2 Sam 7:25; 1 Kgs 2:4; 1 Chr 17:23
8:27 2 Chr 2:6; Ps 139:7-16; Isa 66:1; Jer 23:24; Acts 7:48-49
8:28 [c]*tekhinnah* (8467) ‣1 Kgs 8:38
8:29 Deut 12:11; 2 Chr 7:12, 15-16

its later departure from the Temple (Ezek 10:18-19), to return at a blessed future time (Ezek 43:1-5). In the NT, John wrote that God dwells among his people through his son, Jesus Christ (John 1:14). Paul affirmed that Christ now dwells in each believer (Col 1:27) as a foretaste of a future when "God's home is . . . among his people" (Rev 21:3).

8:12-21 Solomon began with prayer (8:12-13), then blessed the people while praising God for fulfilling his promises (8:14-21). As in many praise psalms, Solomon elevated God, subordinated himself, and testified to God's great goodness.

8:12-13 ***thick cloud of darkness:*** Solomon recognized the cloud filling the inner sanctuary as a manifestation of God's presence, but he also understood that God could not be contained in a man-made ***Temple*** (see 8:27). Solomon fulfilled his commission to build the Temple (8:19; 1 Chr 28:10), believing the promises that God would dwell in the sanctuary (see Exod 15:17).

8:13 Some Greek texts add the line *Is this not written in the Book of Jashar?* See Josh 10:13 and 2 Sam 1:18 and notes.

8:14-16 Solomon's ***blessing*** was expressed as praise to God, who had kept his covenant promises and blessed his people (see 2 Sam 7:12-16; cp. 2 Chr 6:1-11).

8:22-61 Like Solomon's preceding prayer, his prayer of dedication for the Temple praised God and blessed the people. He emphasized God's covenant faithfulness and his own role in building the Temple and prayed for God's continued response to their prayers (8:22-30). Solomon then made seven distinct petitions to God (8:31-53) and concluded with a blessing (8:54-61).

8:22 As Solomon prayed, ***he lifted his hands toward heaven*** and knelt before the Lord on a platform erected in clear view of the congregation (8:54; 2 Chr 6:13). Jesus condemned hypocritical individuals that displayed religiosity without true, heartfelt belief (Matt 6:5-8). But Solomon's public piety was genuine, leading his people in worship and encouraging them to live in full dependence upon God. The nation that knows and obeys the Lord, and whose leaders rule in righteousness, is particularly blessed (2 Chr 7:14; Ps 33:12; 45:6-7; 144:15; Prov 29:2; Isa 11:1-5).

8:23-26 Solomon's prayer affirmed God's incomparable nature and the fulfillment of his promises to David. Solomon also prayed that God would keep his promise that David's ***descendants . . . will always sit on the throne.***

8:29-51 Solomon asked God to hear the prayers of his people from the Temple.

8:30
Neh 1:5-7
8:31
Exod 22:8-11
Lev 5:1
8:32
Deut 25:1
8:33
Lev 26:14-17, 40-42
Deut 28:25, 47-48
8:35
Lev 26:19
Deut 11:16-17
[d]*palal* (6419)
‣2 Kgs 6:18
8:36
1 Sam 12:23
Ps 27:11

name will be there.' May you always hear
the prayers I make toward this place.
30May you hear the humble and earnest
requests from me and your people Israel
when we pray toward this place. Yes,
hear us from heaven where you live, and
when you hear, forgive.
31"If someone wrongs another person and is required to take an oath of innocence in front of your altar in this
Temple, 32then hear from heaven and judge between your servants—the accuser and the accused. Punish the guilty as they deserve. Acquit the innocent because of their innocence.
33"If your people Israel are defeated
by their enemies because they have sinned against you, and if they turn to you and acknowledge your name and
pray to you here in this Temple, 34then
hear from heaven and forgive the sin of your people Israel and return them to this land you gave their ancestors.
35"If the skies are shut up and there is
no rain because your people have sinned against you, and if they [d]pray toward this Temple and acknowledge your name and turn from their sins because you have
punished them, 36then hear from heaven
and forgive the sins of your servants, your people Israel. Teach them to follow the right path, and send rain on your land that you have given to your people as their special possession.

The Land (8:29-51)

1 Kgs 9:3-9
Gen 12:1-3; 13:14-17
Lev 26:1-46
Deut 28:1-68
2 Kgs 17:18-23
Ps 24:1; 89:11
1 Pet 1:4
Rev 21:1-7

Land was extremely important to a largely agrarian society such as ancient Israel. As a key provision of God's covenant with them, Israel was given the privilege and responsibility of living in the land of Canaan, God's own land (8:33-40; see also Deut 28). The land was part of Israel's relationship with God: God had promised this land to Abraham and his descendants (Gen 12:1-3; 13:14-17). Throughout the period from Joshua through Chronicles, the nation of Israel lived in the land as its custodians and earthly possessors (4:17-19; 15:12; 22:46; see Ps 24:1; 89:11). The land was Israel's "special possession" (Deut 4:21), given by God, who required their fidelity (Deut 4:40). God expected the people to be proper stewards of the land and to serve him faithfully.

Solomon understood his people's propensity to sin and the judgment that would result (8:30-40, 46). Therefore, he asked that when the people prayed from a repentant heart, God would forgive them and restore the ancestral land that was their everlasting gift (8:46-51). Unfortunately, they turned to their own ways, serving pagan gods and self (2 Kgs 17:7-17). So God allowed foreign nations to gradually take away Israel's ownership of the land (e.g., 2 Kgs 8:20-22; 13:1-3; 17:3). Through these events God warned his people that if they failed to respond, they would forfeit the land (2 Kgs 21:8). Sadly, they refused to listen (2 Kgs 21:9). Their unfaithfulness eventually resulted in expulsion from the land (9:7; Lev 26:27-33; 2 Kgs 17:22-23; 25:1-7, 21).

Israel's failure to properly manage the land that God entrusted to them serves as a warning to us. God has redeemed us in Christ Jesus so that we may live faithful and productive lives (John 15:16; Eph 2:4-10; Col 1:11-14). Our infidelity and lack of productivity may cause us to lose our place of service for Christ (John 15:1-2, 6). It is by abiding in him that we "produce much fruit" and grow in our faith (John 15:5; 2 Pet 3:18).

God's people always have a propensity to sin (1 Jn 1:8, 10) and to exclude themselves from the place where God's grace operates freely (Gal 5:4). Nevertheless, God always stands ready to forgive and restore those who turn back to him (1 Jn 1:9) and to reinstate the blessings of his covenant. The one who mediates the new covenant between God and his people (Matt 26:27) is also their advocate in heaven (1 Jn 2:1), the place of permanent blessing with God (see Col 1:12-13; 1 Pet 1:4; Rev 21:1-7).

He then addressed specific instances in which they would need God's answers.

8:31-32 Solomon asked that God render the proper decision and carry out justice in court cases when the litigant's ***innocence*** could not be determined due to a lack of witnesses (cp. Exod 22:7-12). Perhaps Solomon realized that later officials would not have the special wisdom God had given him (3:12; e.g., 3:16-27).

8:33-34 Solomon asked concerning future situations when the people of Israel ***sinned*** and God allowed the enemy to defeat them (see Lev 26:14-17; Deut 28:15, 25-26, 45, 49; Josh 7) and then the people genuinely repented. Solomon asked that God honor his covenant and ***forgive*** them (Lev 26:39-42).

8:35-36 Solomon prayed about drought brought on by the people's sin (Lev 26:19; Deut 28:23-24). If the people confessed and truly repented, Solomon prayed that God would ***forgive*** them and restore fertility to the land so that the people would learn to live righteously before God.

37“If there is a famine in the land or a plague or crop disease or attacks of [e]locusts or caterpillars, or if your people’s enemies are in the land besieging their towns—whatever disaster or disease there is—38and if your people Israel [f]pray about their troubles, raising their hands toward this Temple, 39then hear from heaven where you live, and forgive. Give your people what their actions deserve, for you alone know each human heart. 40Then they will fear you as long as they live in the land you gave to our ancestors.

41“In the future, foreigners who do not belong to your people Israel will hear of you. They will come from distant lands because of your name, 42for they will hear of your great name and your strong hand and your powerful arm. And when they pray toward this Temple, 43then hear from heaven where you live, and grant what they ask of you. In this way, all the people of the earth will come to know and fear you, just as your own people Israel do. They, too, will know that this Temple I have built honors your name.

44“If your people go out where you send them to fight their enemies, and if they pray to the LORD by turning toward this city you have chosen and toward this Temple I have built to honor your name, 45then hear their [g]prayers from heaven and uphold their cause.

46“If they sin against you—and who has never sinned?—you might become angry with them and let their enemies conquer them and take them captive to their land far away or near. 47But in that land of exile, they might turn to you in repentance and pray, ‘We have sinned, done evil, and acted wickedly.’ 48If they turn to you with their whole heart and soul in the land of their enemies and pray toward the land you gave to their ancestors—toward this city you have chosen, and toward this Temple I have built to honor your name—49then hear their prayers and their petition from heaven where you live, and uphold their cause. 50Forgive your people who have sinned against you. Forgive all the offenses they have committed against you. Make their captors merciful to them, 51for they are your people—your special possession—whom you brought out of the iron-smelting furnace of Egypt.

52“May your eyes be open to my requests and to the requests of your people Israel. May you hear and answer them whenever they cry out to you. 53For when you brought our ancestors out of Egypt, O Sovereign LORD, you told your servant Moses that you had set Israel apart from all the nations of the earth to be your own special possession.”

The Dedication of the Temple

1 Kgs 8:62-66 // 2 Chr 7:4-10

54When Solomon finished making these prayers and [h]petitions to the LORD, he stood up in front of the altar of the LORD, where he had been kneeling with his hands raised toward heaven. 55He stood and in a loud voice blessed the entire [i]congregation of Israel:

56“Praise the LORD who has given rest to his people Israel, just as he promised. Not one word has failed of all the wonderful promises he gave through his servant Moses. 57May the LORD our God be with us as he was with our ancestors; may he never leave us or abandon us. 58May he give us the desire to do his will in everything and to obey

8:37 Lev 26:16, 25-26; Deut 28:21-23; [e]*'arbeh* (0697) ‣Ps 78:46
8:38 [f]*tekhinnah* (8467) ‣1 Kgs 8:45
8:39 1 Sam 2:3; 1 Chr 28:9; Jer 17:10; John 2:24-25
8:42 Deut 3:24
8:43 1 Sam 17:46
8:44 2 Chr 14:11
8:45 [g]*tekhinnah* (8467) ‣1 Kgs 8:54
8:46 2 Kgs 17:6, 18; 25:21; Prov 20:9; 1 Jn 1:8-10
8:47 Lev 26:40-42; Ezra 9:5-7; Neh 1:6-7; Ps 106:6-7; Dan 9:5
8:48 Deut 4:29; 1 Sam 7:3-4
8:50 2 Chr 30:9; Ps 106:46
8:51 Exod 32:11-12; Deut 4:20; 9:26-29; Jer 11:4
8:53 Exod 19:5-6
8:54 [h]*tekhinnah* (8467) ‣1 Kgs 9:3
8:55 [i]*qahal* (6951) ‣2 Chr 29:28
8:56 Josh 21:45; 23:14-15; 2 Kgs 10:9-10
8:57 Josh 1:5; 1 Sam 12:22; Heb 13:5
8:58 Ps 119:36; Jer 31:33

8:37-40 Solomon prayed concerning various disasters caused by individual or corporate sin (Lev 26:16, 19-26; Deut 28:21-22, 38-40, 42, 58-61). If his people confessed and truly repented, Solomon again asked that God deal justly so that all might live in reverence before him (Deut 8:6; 2 Chr 7:14; Prov 1:7; 9:10; 15:33).

8:41-43 Solomon asked that non-Israelites would learn to *fear* the Lord and live in relationship with him. Solomon realized that Israel must properly represent the Lord to those outside the covenant (see Gen 12:7; Ps 102:15; Hab 2:14; Matt 28:19).

8:44-45 On behalf of those without access to the *Temple*, particularly when far away fighting for God’s cause (Lev 26:7-8; Deut 20:1-4), Solomon asked that God hear their prayers directed toward the Lord and his *Temple* in Jerusalem (see Dan 6:10).

8:46-51 Solomon prayed concerning a time when Israel might be carried away ***captive*** (Lev 26:33). If the people genuinely repented and confessed their sin, Solomon prayed that God would listen, forgive them, and grant them favor with ***their captors*** (Lev 26:40-45; 2 Kgs 25:27-30; Dan 6:10; 9:3-19).

8:52-53 Solomon concluded his prayer of dedication with a general petition for God to be accessible to all of Israel and respond to their requests. Returning to the theme of the Exodus (8:16; see also “God’s Covenant with Israel’s Kings” at 2:2-4, p. 575), Solomon reminded God that he had selected Israel as his ***special possession*** (Exod 19:5; Deut 7:6; 14:1-2; 26:18; Ps 135:4; cp. Titus 2:11-14; 1 Pet 2:9-10).

8:54-56 Solomon praised God’s faithfulness and goodness to Israel in giving the people ***rest*** as ***promised*** (see Josh 21:43-45; 23:14; 2 Sam 7:1). Some Israelites failed to appropriate the rest that only God provides (Ps 95:10-11; Heb 3:7-19; 4:1-11).

8:57-61 Solomon asked that God continue to be with his people and mold them into an obedient and faithful nation. Through God’s grace and their faithfulness, Israel could experience God’s righteous justice and teach people ***all over the earth*** that ***the LORD alone is God***.

8:60
Deut 4:35
1 Sam 17:46
1 Kgs 18:39
Jer 10:10-12

8:61
Deut 18:13
1 Kgs 11:4
2 Kgs 20:3

8:62-66
2 Chr 7:1-10

8:64
2 Chr 4:1

8:65
Gen 15:18

9:1-9
//2 Chr 7:11-22

9:1
1 Kgs 7:1-2
2 Chr 8:6

9:2
1 Kgs 3:5; 11:9

9:3
2 Kgs 20:5
[i]*tekhinnah* (8467)
‣ Ps 6:9

all the commands, decrees, and regulations
that he gave our ancestors. 59And may these
words that I have prayed in the presence of
the LORD be before him constantly, day and
night, so that the LORD our God may give justice to me and to his people Israel, according
to each day's needs. 60Then people all over
the earth will know that the LORD alone is
God and there is no other. 61And may you
be completely faithful to the LORD our God.
May you always obey his decrees and commands, just as you are doing today."

62Then the king and all Israel with him
offered sacrifices to the LORD. 63Solomon
offered to the LORD a peace offering of
22,000 cattle and 120,000 sheep and goats.
And so the king and all the people of Israel
dedicated the Temple of the LORD.

64That same day the king consecrated
the central area of the courtyard in front of
the LORD's Temple. He offered burnt offerings, grain offerings, and the fat of peace
offerings there, because the bronze altar in
the LORD's presence was too small to hold
all the burnt offerings, grain offerings, and
the fat of the peace offerings.

65Then Solomon and all Israel celebrated
the Festival of Shelters in the presence of
the LORD our God. A large congregation had
gathered from as far away as Lebo-hamath
in the north and the Brook of Egypt in the
south. The celebration went on for fourteen
days in all—seven days for the dedication of
the altar and seven days for the Festival of
Shelters. 66After the festival was over, Solomon sent the people home. They blessed
the king and went to their homes joyful and
glad because the LORD had been good to his
servant David and to his people Israel.

Solomon's Post-Building Accomplishments (9:1-28)

The LORD's Response to Solomon
1 Kgs 9:1-9 // 2 Chr 7:11-22

9 So Solomon finished building the Temple of the LORD, as well as the royal
palace. He completed everything he had
planned to do. 2Then the LORD appeared to
Solomon a second time, as he had done before at Gibeon. 3The LORD said to him,

"I have heard your prayer and your
[j]petition. I have set this Temple apart

God's Faithfulness to His People (8:29-53)

1 Kgs 6:12-13; 9:3-9
Gen 32:10
Exod 3:13-17; 34:6
Deut 7:9; 31:6
Josh 1:5; 21:45
2 Sam 7:16
Ps 31:1-5; 91:4
Isa 40:1-11; 54:8
Lam 3:22-24
Mic 7:18-20
John 14:16
Rom 3:3-4; 11:25-29
1 Cor 10:13
2 Cor 1:20
2 Tim 2:13
Titus 1:2
Heb 10:23; 11:11
1 Pet 4:19
Rev 1:4-5; 19:11

After Solomon had finished dedicating the Temple, the Lord appeared to him and reminded him that if the people were unfaithful to his covenant, sure judgment would follow (9:6-9). Conversely, if they were faithful, God would dwell among them and never forsake them (6:12-13).

God had called the nation Israel to be his covenant people (8:51-53). Despite this unique identity as God's people, the people of Israel "sacrificed their offerings at local places of worship" (3:2), an expression of their ongoing commitment to pagan worship. Both the northern and southern kingdoms fell into this sin (12:31-32; 13:2, 32-33; 14:22-24; 15:14; 22:43), but the people of the northern kingdom received particular denunciation. Separated from Judah (12:1, 16, 20), they soon followed their corrupt leaders into idolatry and apostate religious practices (12:25-33; 16:2-4, 12-16, 19, 26, 33). They were unfaithful covenant breakers (19:10, 14), and God's judgment was certain to follow (14:15; 21:20-25). Still, God retained a faithful remnant among them (cp. 19:18) and had plans for their future well-being (e.g., Isa 40:1-11).

God still has a people who are his own (1 Cor 1:2; 1 Pet 1:1). God's own people now constitute the temple of God and are to live holy lives (1 Pet 2:9-10; 2 Cor 6:14–7:1), "totally committed to doing good deeds" (Titus 2:14; cp. Heb 12:28). Their assured hope is to live with the Lord forever (1 Thes 4:15-17; Rev 2:3). They have God's promise that he will never forsake them but will always be faithful to his promises to them (John 14:16; 2 Tim 2:13).

8:62-66 The closing *sacrifices* (see Deut 12:5-14) and the observance of ***the Festival of Shelters*** close the narrative frame that was opened with the sacrifices made when the Ark was installed in the Most Holy Place (8:1-11; cp. 2 Chr 7:1-6).

8:65 ***Lebo-hamath*** to the ***north*** in Aram and ***the Brook of Egypt*** (Wadi al Arish) to the south are the geographic boundaries that defined the Promised Land (Josh 13:5; 15:4). • ***seven days for the dedication of the altar and seven days for the Festival of Shelters:*** Literally *seven days and seven days, fourteen days;* cp. parallel text at 2 Chr 7:8-10. When the seven days for the dedication were completed, the *Festival of Shelters* (literally *the festival;* see note on 8:2) was observed for another seven days.

8:66 ***After the festival was over:*** Literally *On the eighth day,* probably referring to the day following the seven-day Festival of Shelters; cp. parallel text at 2 Chr 7:9-10.

9:2 ***The LORD*** had previously ***appeared to Solomon*** when granting his desire for wisdom (3:3-15). The Chronicler provides additional details of God's blessings or judgment, depending on the faithfulness of Solomon and Israel (2 Chr 7:11-22).

9:3-9 The Lord answered Solomon's ***prayer*** by reviewing the conditions of the covenant. Obedience would bring prosperity and the Lord's blessing; disobedience could mean utter disaster, including destruction of the city and

to be holy—this place you have built
where my name will be honored forever. I will always watch over it, for it
is dear to my heart.
4"As for you, if you will follow me with
integrity and godliness, as David your
father did, obeying all my commands,
decrees, and regulations, 5then I will establish the throne of your dynasty over Israel
forever. For I made this promise to your
father, David: 'One of your descendants
will always sit on the throne of Israel.'
6"But if you or your descendants abandon me and disobey the commands and
decrees I have given you, and if you serve
and worship other gods, 7then I will
uproot Israel from this land that I have
given them. I will reject this Temple that I
have made holy to honor my name. I will
make Israel an object of mockery and
ridicule among the nations. 8And though
this Temple is impressive now, all who
pass by will be appalled and will shake
their heads in amazement. They will
ask, 'Why did the LORD do such terrible
things to this land and to this Temple?'
9"And the answer will be, 'Because
his people abandoned the LORD their
God, who brought their ancestors out of
Egypt, and they worshiped other gods
instead and bowed down to them. That
is why the LORD has brought all these
disasters on them.' "

Solomon's Agreement with Hiram
1 Kgs 9:10-14 // 2 Chr 8:1-2

10It took Solomon twenty years to build the
LORD's Temple and his own royal palace.
At the end of that time, 11he gave twenty
towns in the land of Galilee to King Hiram
of Tyre. (Hiram had previously provided
all the cedar and cypress timber and gold
that Solomon had requested.) 12But when
Hiram came from Tyre to see the towns
Solomon had given him, he was not at all
pleased with them. 13"What kind of towns
are these, my brother?" he asked. So Hiram called that area Cabul (which means
"worthless"), as it is still known today.
14Nevertheless, Hiram paid Solomon 9,000
pounds of gold.

Solomon's Many Achievements
1 Kgs 9:17b-28 // 2 Chr 8:3-18

15This is the account of the forced labor
that King Solomon conscripted to build the
LORD's Temple, the royal palace, the supporting terraces, the wall of Jerusalem, and the
cities of Hazor, Megiddo, and Gezer. 16(Pharaoh, the king of Egypt, had attacked and
captured Gezer, killing the Canaanite population and burning it down. He gave the city
to his daughter as a wedding gift when she
married Solomon. 17So Solomon rebuilt the
city of Gezer.) He also built up the towns of
Lower Beth-horon, 18Baalath, and Tamar in
the wilderness within his land. 19He built
towns as supply centers and constructed
towns where his chariots and horses could
be stationed. He built everything he desired
in Jerusalem and Lebanon and throughout
his entire realm.
20There were still some people living in
the land who were not Israelites, including
Amorites, Hittites, Perizzites, Hivites, and
Jebusites. 21These were descendants of the

9:4 1 Kgs 3:14; 11:4
9:5 2 Sam 7:12
9:6 2 Sam 7:14-16; 1 Chr 28:9
9:7 Lev 18:24-29; Deut 4:26-27; 2 Kgs 17:23; Jer 7:4
9:8 Deut 29:24-26; 2 Chr 7:21; Jer 22:8-9, 28
9:9 Deut 29:25-28
9:10-28 2 Chr 8:1-18
9:10 1 Kgs 6:37-38
9:11 1 Kgs 5:1; 2 Chr 2:3
9:13 Josh 19:27
9:15 2 Sam 5:9
9:19 1 Kgs 4:26
9:21 Josh 15:63

Temple, and deportation of God's people (see Deut 28:36-37, 63-68). Although God's covenant was irrevocable, receiving its blessings depended upon faithfulness to its terms (Ps 89:24-37).

9:10-14 In Solomon's business agreement with ***King Hiram***, he exchanged wheat and olive oil for timber and ***gold*** (5:10-11). When ***Solomon*** became indebted to Hiram, he gave him ***twenty towns in . . . Galilee*** as compensation. However, Hiram was dissatisfied with the towns, so he returned them to Solomon's control (see 2 Chr 8:2). The two friends settled upon other means of compensation and remained active allies and trading partners (9:26-28; 10:22).

9:14 ***Nevertheless, Hiram paid:*** Or *For Hiram had paid.* • ***9,000 pounds:*** Hebrew *120 talents* [4,000 kilograms].

9:15-24 Solomon used ***forced labor*** to complete many building projects (4:6; 5:13-18; 9:20-23; 12:4, 18-19; cp. 1 Sam 8:10-18).

9:15 ***supporting terraces:*** Hebrew *the millo;* also in 9:24. The meaning of the Hebrew is uncertain, but the NLT rendering follows the strong consensus of current research. Solomon strengthened these *terraces,* which were on a slope of the southeastern ridge in the traditional City of David area of Jerusalem (see 2 Sam 5:9), and the ***wall of Jerusalem.*** He also fortified the key cities of ***Hazor, Megiddo, and Gezer.*** Archaeological research shows that the walls and gates of all three cities have distinctive traits attributable to Solomon's time. *Hazor,* in the north, was a first line of defense against invasion. *Megiddo,* in the Plain of Sharon, also had strategic military importance (2 Kgs 23:29-30; Rev 16:12-16).

9:16 ***Gezer,*** west of Jerusalem, was not previously occupied by Israelites. It was conquered by the Egyptian pharaoh and given to his daughter as a wedding gift when she married Solomon. An inscription in the Amon Temple in Tanis, apparently depicting a victory by the 21st dynasty Pharaoh Siamun (978–959 BC) against a Philistine campaign, suggests that Siamun was the pharaoh involved.

9:17-18 ***Lower Beth-horon*** was an important defensive site for western Judah. Several cities in Canaan were called ***Baalath***; the one here was probably also known as Kiriath-jearim (2 Sam 6:2; see Josh 15:9; 1 Chr 13:5, 6). ***Tamar*** (an alternate reading in the Masoretic Text reads *Tadmor;* see Ezek 47:19; 48:28) was probably located in the southeastern quarter of the Holy Land.

9:19 ***and horses:*** Or *and charioteers.*

9:20-23 Solomon's conscripted ***labor force*** was made up of early Canaanite settlers; 550 chief supervisors superintended the ***labor force,*** of which 250 were Israelites (2 Chr 8:9-10; see 5:15-16 with 2 Chr 2:17-18).

9:22 Lev 25:39
9:24 1 Kgs 3:1; 7:8; 11:1, 27; 2 Chr 32:5
9:25 Exod 23:14-17; Deut 16:16
9:26 Num 33:35; 1 Kgs 22:48
9:27 1 Kgs 10:11
10:1-13 //2 Chr 9:1-12
10:1 2 Chr 9:1; Ps 72:10, 15; Matt 12:42

nations whom the people of Israel had not
completely destroyed. So Solomon conscripted them for his labor force, and they
serve in the labor force to this day. 22But
Solomon did not conscript any of the Israelites for forced labor. Instead, he assigned
them to serve as fighting men, government
officials, officers and captains in his army,
commanders of his chariots, and charioteers. 23Solomon appointed 550 of them to
supervise the people working on his various projects.
24Solomon moved his wife, Pharaoh's
daughter, from the City of David to the new
palace he had built for her. Then he constructed the supporting terraces.
25Three times each year Solomon presented burnt offerings and peace offerings
on the altar he had built for the LORD. He
also burned incense to the LORD. And so he
finished the work of building the Temple.
26King Solomon also built a fleet of ships
at Ezion-geber, a port near Elath in the land
of Edom, along the shore of the Red Sea.
27Hiram sent experienced crews of sailors to sail the ships with Solomon's men.
28They sailed to Ophir and brought back to
Solomon some sixteen tons of gold.

Solomon's Wisdom Demonstrated (10:1-29)

Visit of the Queen of Sheba

1 Kgs 10:1-13 // 2 Chr 9:1-12

10 When the queen of Sheba heard
of Solomon's fame, which brought
honor to the name of the LORD, she came to

Successful Leadership (9:1-9)

1 Kgs 3:5-14; 4:1–8:66; 11:1-13; Deut 17:14-20; 2 Chr 32:20-23; Prov 11:14; 14:34; 15:22; 24:5-6; 29:2; Mark 10:42-45; Luke 22:24-27; John 10:11-15; Acts 6:3, 10; 1 Tim 3:1-12; Titus 1:6-9

The success of government depends on good leadership. Many of the kings whose reigns are narrated in 1 Kings left a record of good accomplishments that stemmed from a solid spiritual commitment. Where a high regard for the Lord's direction in their lives wavered, however, even these kings who received the narrator's commendation experienced failure.

Solomon serves as an example. When he initially encountered the Lord, he petitioned the Lord in humility for God's guidance and wisdom (3:5-9). Therefore, the Lord blessed him with wisdom, honor, and prosperity (3:10-14), which Solomon used to lead Israel well (chs 4–8). When the Lord appeared to him a second time, he commended Solomon (9:1-3) and challenged him to keep following the Lord "with integrity and godliness" (9:4) so that he would continue to experience blessing and success (9:5). God then solemnly warned Solomon what would happen if he abandoned God (9:6-9). The warning foreshadows Solomon's spiritual decline. By the time the Lord appeared to Solomon a third time, his quest for fame and power had led first to tolerance of, then to support for, the pagan practices of his foreign wives (11:1-8). Therefore, the Lord announced the division of the kingdom after Solomon's death (11:9-13).

Solomon's leadership in his early days demonstrates the wisdom of humble reliance on God for wisdom and guidance. Dedication to God made Solomon great, and Israel with him (Prov 14:34). Where leaders and their people humble themselves and pray, God's blessings follow (2 Chr 7:14; 32:20-23). Such leaders will be remembered long after their passing (2 Chr 34:25). God's people are always in need of spiritually dedicated and mature leaders (see 1 Tim 3:1-12; Titus 1:6-9) who rely on God for guidance and wisdom (see Luke 21:15; Acts 6:3, 10).

9:21 ***completely destroyed:*** The Hebrew term used here refers to the complete consecration of things or people to the Lord, either by destroying them or by giving them as an offering (see Lev 27:28-29; 1 Sam 15:3).

9:24 The ***new palace*** Solomon ***built for . . . Pharoah's daughter*** was separate from Solomon's own residence because his palace was deemed holy, "for the Ark of the LORD has been there" (2 Chr 8:11). The place where the Ark resided was considered sacred, since it embodied God's presence and sanctified its surroundings (Exod 25:22; see also 2 Sam 6:7; 1 Chr 15:11-13).

9:25 ***Three times each year Solomon*** provided exemplary leadership for Israel as he ***presented . . . offerings*** at the national festivals of Unleavened Bread, Harvest (or Pentecost, or Weeks), and Shelters (Deut 16:16).

9:26-28 The seaport of ***Ezion-geber*** was situated on the Gulf of Aqaba, which opens onto the ***Red Sea.*** The location of ***Ophir*** is uncertain but may have been located in southwestern Arabia, eastern Africa, or India; the mention of ***gold*** and other precious commodities (see 10:11-12) indicates its strategic importance for trade.

9:26 ***Elath:*** As in Greek version (see also 2 Kgs 14:22; 16:6); Hebrew reads *Eloth,* a variant spelling of *Elath.* • ***Red Sea:*** Literally *sea of reeds.*

9:28 ***sixteen tons:*** Hebrew *420 talents* [14 metric tons].

10:1-13 The queen of Sheba visited to test the accuracy of accounts concerning Solomon's wisdom (10:1, 3, 6-7). She may also have sought commercial partnership (10:2, 10, 13). All of Solomon's accomplishments resulted from his God-given wisdom, as the queen of Sheba testifies in the central speech of the narrative (10:6-9).

10:1 ***The queen*** likely ***heard*** tales of ***Solomon's*** wisdom and wealth because of his trading ventures to Ophir (10:11; see 9:26-28). ***Sheba,*** located in southwestern Arabia (modern Yemen), was a notably fertile commercial center. The trading enterprises of the ancient Sabeans encompassed great swaths of territory, including Syria, Africa, and India. • ***test . . . with hard questions***

test him with hard questions. 2She arrived in Jerusalem with a large group of attendants and a great caravan of camels loaded with spices, large quantities of gold, and precious jewels. When she met with Solomon, she talked with him about everything she had on her mind. 3Solomon had answers for all her questions; nothing was too hard for the king to explain to her. 4When the queen of Sheba realized how very wise Solomon was, and when she saw the palace he had built, 5she was overwhelmed. She was also amazed at the food on his tables, the organization of his officials and their splendid clothing, the cup-bearers, and the burnt offerings Solomon made at the Temple of the LORD.

6She exclaimed to the king, "Everything I heard in my country about your achievements and wisdom is true! 7I didn't believe what was said until I arrived here and saw it with my own eyes. In fact, I had not heard the half of it! Your wisdom and prosperity are far beyond what I was told. 8How happy your people must be! What a privilege for your officials to stand here day after day, listening to your wisdom! 9Praise the LORD your God, who delights in you and has placed you on the throne of Israel. Because of the LORD's eternal love for Israel, he has made you king so you can rule with justice and righteousness."

10Then she gave the king a gift of 9,000 pounds of gold, great quantities of spices, and precious jewels. Never again were so many spices brought in as those the queen of Sheba gave to King Solomon.

11(In addition, Hiram's ships brought gold from Ophir, and they also brought rich cargoes of red sandalwood and precious jewels. 12The king used the sandalwood to make railings for the Temple of the LORD and the royal palace, and to construct lyres and harps for the musicians. Never before or since has there been such a supply of sandalwood.)

13King Solomon gave the queen of Sheba whatever she asked for, besides all the customary gifts he had so generously given. Then she and all her attendants returned to their own land.

Solomon's Wealth and Splendor

1 Kgs 10:14-25 // 2 Chr 9:13-24
1 Kgs 10:26-29 // 2 Chr 1:14-17 // 2 Chr 9:25-28

14Each year Solomon received about 25 tons of gold. 15This did not include the additional revenue he received from merchants and traders, all the kings of Arabia, and the governors of the land.

16King Solomon made 200 large shields of hammered gold, each weighing more

10:8 Prov 8:34
10:9 2 Sam 8:15; 23:3; 1 Kgs 5:7; 2 Chr 2:11
10:11 1 Kgs 9:27
10:14-29 //2 Chr 1:14-17; 9:13-28
10:16 1 Kgs 14:26-28; 2 Chr 12:9-10

(literally *riddles*): Arabian literature is famous for its riddles and proverbs. The queen tested Solomon's wisdom and explored perplexities of her own. • ***which brought honor to the name of the LORD:*** Or *which was due to the name of the LORD.* The meaning of the Hebrew is uncertain.

10:2 The queen of Sheba arrived as royalty, with a large entourage and ***camels loaded*** with precious commodities. This was a high-level meeting, as demonstrated by Solomon's generous gifts to her (10:13).

10:3-5 The queen was satisfied with Solomon's wisdom. He answered all of her questions well, and she was ***overwhelmed*** by the applied wisdom in his building activities, well-organized administration and staff, and commitment to his God. Jesus commended the queen's search for truth while condemning the Pharisees and teachers of religious law who failed to recognize him—the one who was greater than Solomon (Matt 12:42).

10:6-9 The queen's testimony confirmed her amazement. Not only was everything she had heard true, but now that she had seen it with her *own eyes,* she realized that Solomon's accomplishments had been understated. She recognized that the Lord was Solomon's benefactor and that Solomon should steward his God-given wisdom ***with justice and righteousness.***

10:6 ***your achievements:*** Literally *your words.*

10:8 ***your people:*** Greek and Syriac versions and Latin Vulgate read *your wives.*

10:10-12 Solomon possessed and used abundant ***gold*** during his reign. What the ***queen*** provided supplemented what Solomon already possessed through his trading partnership with Hiram of Tyre. The precious metal was put to good use (see 6:20-22, 28, 30, 32, 35; 7:49-51; 10:18, 21). • Arabian traders dealt in ***spices*** such as frankincense and myrrh. Both were used for medicinal purposes; frankincense was also used in the sacred incense (Exod 30:34-38; Lev 2:2), and myrrh was used both for perfume and for embalming the dead. These spices and gold were presented to Jesus by wise men from eastern lands (Matt 2:1-11).

10:10 ***9,000 pounds:*** Hebrew *120 talents* [4,000 kilograms].

10:11 ***Sandalwood*** (literally *almug wood;* also in 10:12) is a reddish-brown wood native to India and valued for its aromatic essential oil. Cuneiform tablets found at Ras Shamra and Alalakh also indicate its value for making fine furniture and musical instruments.

10:13 ***whatever she asked for:*** As befitting a royal host, ***Solomon*** reciprocated with ***gifts***. The amicable relationship between Solomon and the ***queen of Sheba*** may have culminated in a commercial agreement. Subsequent Jewish, Arabian, and Ethiopian tales of a romantic relationship between them have no foundation in fact.

10:14-29 To further describe Solomon's splendor, the writer builds upon the details of the queen's visit (10:1-13), describing Solomon's wise use of wealth in his palace complex (10:14-21) and concluding with the far-reaching effects of Solomon's wisdom in commercial arrangements (10:22-29).

10:14-15 ***about 25 tons:*** Hebrew *666 talents* [23 metric tons]. The large amount of ***gold*** came from Solomon's various enterprises and taxes; he also levied tolls upon ***merchants and traders*** who passed through his kingdom.

10:16-17 Although such shields were typically designed to accommodate infantry (***large shields***) or archers (***smaller shields***), these shields probably had ceremonial uses (see note on 7:2-5).

10:17
1 Kgs 7:2
[k]*magen* (4043)
‣ 1 Kgs 14:27

10:18
[a]*kisse'* (3678)
‣ Ps 93:2

10:23
1 Kgs 3:12-13; 4:30

10:27
2 Chr 1:15; 9:27

than fifteen pounds. [17]He also made 300 smaller [k]shields of hammered gold, each weighing nearly four pounds. The king placed these shields in the Palace of the Forest of Lebanon.

[18]Then the king made a huge [a]throne, decorated with ivory and overlaid with fine gold. [19]The throne had six steps and a rounded back. There were armrests on both sides of the seat, and the figure of a lion stood on each side of the throne. [20]There were also twelve other lions, one standing on each end of the six steps. No other throne in all the world could be compared with it!

[21]All of King Solomon's drinking cups were solid gold, as were all the utensils in the Palace of the Forest of Lebanon. They were not made of silver, for silver was considered worthless in Solomon's day!

[22]The king had a fleet of trading ships that sailed with Hiram's fleet. Once every three years the ships returned, loaded with gold, silver, ivory, apes, and peacocks.

[23]So King Solomon became richer and wiser than any other king on earth. [24]People from every nation came to consult him and to hear the wisdom God had given him. [25]Year after year everyone who visited brought him gifts of silver and gold, clothing, weapons, spices, horses, and mules.

[26]Solomon built up a huge force of chariots and horses. He had 1,400 chariots and 12,000 horses. He stationed some of them in the chariot cities and some near him in Jerusalem. [27]The king made silver as plentiful in Jerusalem as stone. And valuable cedar timber was as common as the sycamore-fig trees that grow in the foothills of Judah.

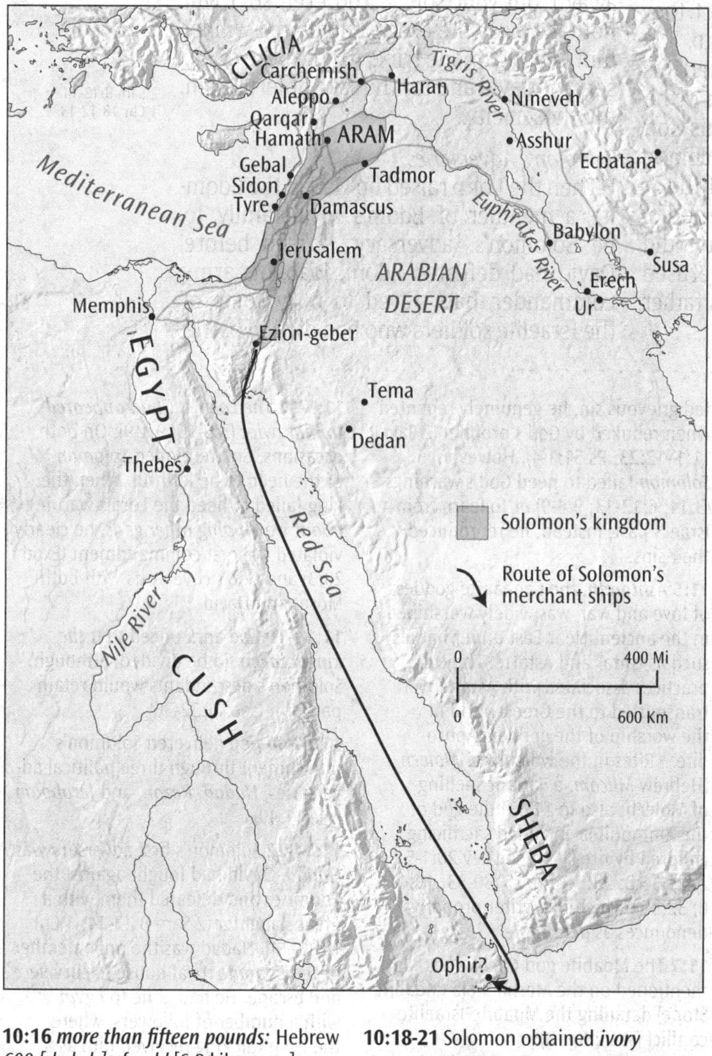

◀ **Solomon's International Presence, 971–931 BC (9:26–10:29).** Solomon built a fleet of trading ships at EZION-GEBER that brought him gold from OPHIR and other exotic goods from faraway lands. Solomon also conducted international business, buying horses and chariots from EGYPT and CILICIA and reselling them to the Arameans and Hittites. Solomon gained such fame throughout the world that even the queen of SHEBA came to visit him.

10:16 ***more than fifteen pounds:*** Hebrew *600 [shekels] of gold* [6.8 kilograms].

10:17 ***nearly four pounds:*** Hebrew *3 minas* [1.8 kilograms].

10:18-21 Solomon obtained *ivory* through commercial ventures with Hiram. Ancient Near Eastern kings often used *lion* figures as symbols of royal power and divine protection of the throne.

10:22 ***fleet of trading ships:*** Literally *fleet of ships of Tarshish*; the Hebrew term designates a type of merchant ship. • Phoenician sailors manned Solomon's fleet, which put out to sea from Ezion-geber (9:26-28; see Isa 23:1). • ***apes, and peacocks*** (or *and baboons*): Archaeology provides ample evidence that kings imported such creatures. Apparently these animals were desired for their novelty and exotic nature and because they reflected conquest of distant lands.

10:26 ***1,400 chariots:*** Prior to Solomon, chariots were not a significant part of Israel's army. In fact, Deut 17:16 condemns kings for accumulating horses rather than relying on God. Although archaeological confirmation of the presence of chariots in Solomon's day is debated, his ***chariot cities*** are commonly identified as Hazor, Megiddo, and Gezer (9:15, 19). The Assyrian king Shalmaneser III reported facing a heavy contingent of enemy chariots at the Battle of Qarqar (853 BC), 2,000 of which were supplied by King Ahab of Israel. • ***horses:*** Or *charioteers;* also in 10:26b.

10:27 ***the foothills of Judah:*** Hebrew *the Shephelah.*

28Solomon's horses were imported from Egypt and from Cilicia; the king's traders acquired them from Cilicia at the standard price. 29At that time chariots from Egypt could be purchased for 600 pieces of silver, and horses for 150 pieces of silver. They were then exported to the kings of the Hittites and the kings of Aram.

Solomon's Decline Amidst Adversaries (11:1-43)

Solomon's Many Wives

11 Now King Solomon loved many foreign women. Besides Pharaoh's daughter, he married women from Moab, Ammon, Edom, Sidon, and from among the Hittites. 2The LORD had clearly instructed the people of Israel, "You must not marry them, because they will turn your hearts to their gods." Yet Solomon insisted on loving them anyway. 3He had 700 wives of royal birth and 300 concubines. And in fact, they did turn his heart away from the LORD.

4In Solomon's old age, they turned his heart to worship other gods instead of being completely faithful to the LORD his God, as his father, David, had been. 5Solomon worshiped Ashtoreth, the goddess of the Sidonians, and Molech, the detestable god of the Ammonites. 6In this way, Solomon did what was evil in the LORD's sight; he refused to follow the LORD completely, as his father, David, had done.

7On the Mount of Olives, east of Jerusalem, he even built a pagan shrine for Chemosh, the detestable god of Moab, and another for Molech, the detestable god of the Ammonites. 8Solomon built such shrines for all his foreign wives to use for burning incense and sacrificing to their gods.

9The LORD was very angry with Solomon, for his heart had turned away from the LORD, the God of Israel, who had appeared to him twice. 10He had warned Solomon specifically about worshiping other gods, but Solomon did not listen to the LORD's command. 11So now the LORD said to him, "Since you have not kept my covenant and have disobeyed my decrees, I will surely tear the kingdom away from you and give it to one of your servants. 12But for the sake of your father, David, I will not do this while you are still alive. I will take the kingdom away from your son. 13And even so, I will not take away the entire kingdom; I will let him be king of one tribe, for the sake of my servant David and for the sake of Jerusalem, my chosen city."

Solomon's Adversaries

14Then the LORD raised up Hadad the Edomite, a member of Edom's royal family, to be Solomon's [b]adversary. 15Years before, David had defeated Edom. Joab, his army commander, had stayed to bury some of the Israelite soldiers who had died in battle.

10:28 2 Chr 1:16; 9:28
10:29 2 Kgs 7:6-7
11:1 Neh 13:23-27
11:2 Exod 23:31-33; 34:12-16; Deut 7:3-4
11:3 2 Sam 5:13-16
11:5 Judg 2:12-14; 10:6; 1 Sam 7:3-4
11:7 Lev 20:2-5; Num 21:27-30; Judg 11:24; 2 Kgs 23:10, 13
11:9 1 Kgs 3:5; 9:2-3
11:10 1 Kgs 6:12; 9:6
11:11 1 Sam 2:30; 1 Kgs 6:11-12; 11:31
11:12 2 Sam 7:15
11:14 [b]*satan* (7854) ‣1 Chr 21:1
11:15 2 Sam 8:13-14; 1 Chr 18:12-13

10:28-29 In addition to his own accumulation, Solomon apparently served as a middle-man, exchanging ***horses*** and ***chariots*** between the Egyptians to the south and the Syrians and Anatolians to the north.

10:28 *Egypt:* Possibly *Muzur,* a district near Cilicia; also in 10:29. • ***Cilicia:*** Hebrew *Kue,* probably another name for Cilicia.

10:29 ***600 pieces of silver:*** Hebrew *600 [shekels] of silver,* about 15 pounds or 6.8 kilograms in weight. • ***150 pieces of silver:*** Hebrew *150 [shekels],* about 3.8 pounds or 1.7 kilograms in weight.

11:1-3 In spite of his God-given wisdom, Solomon blatantly violated the law of Moses with his excessive wealth and many wives (see Exod 34:12-17; Deut 7:3-4; 17:17). Taking wives to form foreign alliances compromised Solomon's spiritual commitment, as predicted, and turned ***his heart away from the LORD.*** The spiritual and political consequences for his people were disastrous (see 11:4-13; 12:4, 16; 2 Kgs 17:5-23; 25:1-23).

11:4-8 ***instead of being completely faithful:*** Although ***David*** had committed grievous sin, he genuinely repented when rebuked by God's prophet (2 Sam 11:1–12:23; Ps 51:1-4). However, ***Solomon*** failed to heed God's warnings (3:14; 6:12-13; 9:4-9) or to learn from Israel's past; instead, he reproduced their sins.

11:5 ***Ashtoreth,*** the Canaanite goddess of love and war, was widely worshiped in the ancient Near East under names such as Ishtar and Astarte. The cult practices associated with Astarte were transmitted to the Greek world in the worship of the goddess Aphrodite. • Rites in the worship of ***Molech*** (Hebrew *Milcom,* a variant spelling of Molech; also in 11:33) the god of the Ammonites, included sacrificing children by fire (11:7; see Lev 20:1-5; 2 Kgs 16:3; 23:5-10; Jer 7:30-33; 19:4-6; 32:35), which the writer properly denounces as ***detestable.***

11:7 The Moabite god ***Chemosh*** is mentioned on the Mesha Stela (Moabite Stone) detailing the Moabite-Israelite conflict (see 2 Kgs 3).

11:7 ***On the Mount of Olives, east of Jerusalem:*** Literally *On the mountain east of Jerusalem.*

11:9-10 ***The LORD . . . had appeared to him twice*** (3:5-15; 9:1-9): On both occasions, God reminded ***Solomon*** of the need to be faithful. When the king failed to heed the Lord's warning ***about worshiping other gods,*** he clearly violated the first commandment (Exod 20:3) and God's covenants with both Moses and David.

11:11-13 God announced that ***the kingdom*** would be divided, although Solomon's descendants would retain part of it (see 11:32-36).

11:14-40 God delivered Solomon's punishment through three political adversaries, ***Hadad, Rezon,*** and ***Jeroboam*** (see 11:40).

11:14-22 Solomon's first adversary was ***Hadad.*** David had fought against the Edomites and defeated them with a great slaughter (2 Sam 8:13-14; 1 Chr 18:13-14). Hadad was the only member of the ***Edomite*** royal house to survive and escape. He had gone to ***Egypt*** with a number of followers, where the Egyptian king received him as a potential ally and ***gave him his wife's sister in marriage.*** When ***David and . . . Joab*** died, Hadad returned to Edom,

11:21
1 Kgs 2:10, 34
11:23
2 Sam 8:3; 10:15-16
11:24
2 Sam 10:7-8, 18
11:26
2 Chr 13:6
11:27
1 Kgs 9:24
11:29
1 Kgs 12:15; 14:2
11:30
1 Sam 15:27-28

While there, they killed every male in Edom. 16Joab and the army of Israel had stayed there for six months, killing them.

17But Hadad and a few of his father's royal officials escaped and headed for Egypt. (Hadad was just a boy at the time.) 18They set out from Midian and went to Paran, where others joined them. Then they traveled to Egypt and went to Pharaoh, who gave them a home, food, and some land. 19Pharaoh grew very fond of Hadad, and he gave him his wife's sister in marriage—the sister of Queen Tahpenes. 20She bore him a son named Genubath. Tahpenes raised him in Pharaoh's palace among Pharaoh's own sons.

21When the news reached Hadad in Egypt that David and his commander Joab were both dead, he said to Pharaoh, "Let me return to my own country."

22"Why?" Pharaoh asked him. "What do you lack here that makes you want to go home?"

"Nothing," he replied. "But even so, please let me return home."

23God also raised up Rezon son of Eliada as Solomon's adversary. Rezon had fled from his master, King Hadadezer of Zobah, 24and had become the leader of a gang of rebels. After David conquered Hadadezer, Rezon and his men fled to Damascus, where he became king. 25Rezon was Israel's bitter adversary for the rest of Solomon's reign, and he made trouble, just as Hadad did. Rezon hated Israel intensely and continued to reign in Aram.

Jeroboam Rebels against Solomon

26Another rebel leader was Jeroboam son of Nebat, one of Solomon's own officials. He came from the town of Zeredah in Ephraim, and his mother was Zeruah, a widow.

27This is the story behind his rebellion. Solomon was rebuilding the supporting terraces and repairing the walls of the city of his father, David. 28Jeroboam was a very capable young man, and when Solomon saw how industrious he was, he put him in charge of the labor force from the tribes of Ephraim and Manasseh, the descendants of Joseph.

29One day as Jeroboam was leaving Jerusalem, the prophet Ahijah from Shiloh met him along the way. Ahijah was wearing a new cloak. The two of them were alone in a field, 30and Ahijah took hold of the new cloak he was wearing and tore it into twelve

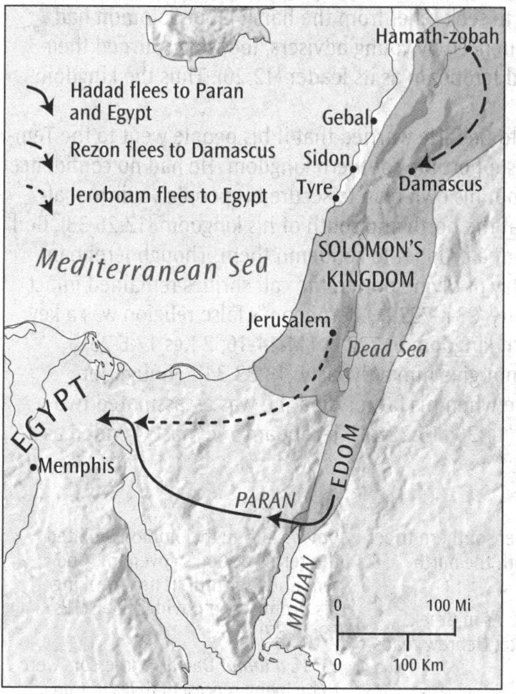

◀ **Solomon's Adversaries (11:14-40).** After Solomon "had turned away from the Lord" (11:9-13), the Lord "raised up" adversaries: Hadad from Edom, who had fled to Midian, then Paran, and on to Egypt during the time of David; Rezon of Aram, who fled from Hamath-zobah to Damascus, where he became king; and Jeroboam from the tribe of Ephraim, who also fled to Egypt until Solomon died.

awaiting an opportunity to retaliate against Israel.

11:20 *raised him:* As in Greek version; Hebrew reads *weaned him.*

11:23-25 Solomon's second adversary was *Rezon*, an Aramean who had served under *King Hadadezer* of Aram-zobah. When *David* had defeated *Hadadezer* (2 Sam 8:3-7), Rezon escaped, gained a group of followers, and went *to Damascus.* He maintained himself there when Solomon campaigned in Hamath-zobah (2 Chr 8:3-4) and eventually *became king* of Damascus. Like Hadad, Rezon remained a bitter enemy of *Israel* and was troublesome to Solomon.

11:26-40 Information about Solomon's third adversary, *Jeroboam son of Nebat*, provides background for the division of the kingdom of Israel (chs 12–14).

11:27-28 *Solomon* noted the work ethic of *Jeroboam* during the repair of the city's structures and *put him in charge.* Jeroboam's status among the laborers may have made him aware of brewing discontent in northern sections of Solomon's kingdom. Jeroboam showed leadership on this occasion, as well as during the empire's division and reorganization of the northern tribes (12:12-19, 25-33). Unfortunately, he did not always use his abilities wisely and later proved unfaithful to the Lord (12:25–13:10; 14:14-16; 2 Kgs 17:21-23).

11:27 *the supporting terraces:* Hebrew *the millo.* The meaning of the Hebrew is uncertain; see note on 9:15.

11:29-39 The meeting between *Jeroboam* and *the prophet Ahijah* set in motion God's judgment on the dynasty of Solomon. *Ahijah* reappears in the account of Jeroboam's sick son (14:1-18). He authored an unpreserved work containing information about Solomon's deeds (2 Chr 9:29).

pieces. [31]Then he said to Jeroboam, "Take
ten of these pieces, for this is what the
LORD, the God of Israel, says: 'I am about
to tear the kingdom from the hand of Solomon, and I will give ten of the tribes to
you! [32]But I will leave him one tribe for the
sake of my servant David and for the sake
of Jerusalem, which I have chosen out of
all the tribes of Israel. [33]For Solomon has
[c]abandoned me and worshiped Ashtoreth,
the goddess of the Sidonians; Chemosh, the
god of Moab; and Molech, the god of the
Ammonites. He has not followed my ways
and done what is pleasing in my sight. He
has not obeyed my decrees and regulations
as David his father did.
[34]" 'But I will not take the entire kingdom from Solomon at this time. For the
sake of my servant David, the one whom I
chose and who obeyed my commands and
decrees, I will keep Solomon as leader for
the rest of his life. [35]But I will take the kingdom away from his son and give ten of the
tribes to you. [36]His son will have one tribe
so that the descendants of David my servant
will continue to reign, shining like a lamp in
Jerusalem, the city I have chosen to be the
place for my name. [37]And I will place you on

11:31 1 Kgs 11:11-12
11:33 1 Kgs 11:5-8; [c]*azab* (5800) ›2 Kgs 17:16
11:35 1 Kgs 12:16
11:36 1 Kgs 15:4; 2 Kgs 8:19; 2 Chr 21:7

JEROBOAM I (11:26–14:20)

1 Kgs 15:6-7, 25-28
2 Chr 10:1–13:22

Jeroboam I (931–910 BC), son of Nebat from the tribe of Ephraim, was the first king of the northern kingdom of Israel. He led the northern ten tribes into the sins that brought about the destruction of the northern kingdom.

Jeroboam began his political career by supervising Solomon's labor forces in the territory of Ephraim and Manasseh (11:26-28). Because Solomon had drifted away from the Lord, God determined to remove the ten northern tribes from the rule of David's descendants. The prophet Ahijah told Jeroboam that the Lord had chosen him to lead those tribes and to give him a lasting dynasty if he was faithful (11:29-40). Solomon apparently caught wind of what had happened and tried to kill Jeroboam, who sought refuge in Egypt (cp. Saul and David, 1 Sam 18:5–20:42).

When Solomon died, his son Rehoboam was immediately proclaimed king in Judah, but the northern tribes had to affirm his kingship separately. Seizing the opportunity, Jeroboam took the northern leaders to Rehoboam to seek relief from the harsh labor Solomon had forced on them (12:1-4). Rehoboam, influenced by young advisers, foolishly spurned their request (12:5-14), so the north appointed Jeroboam as its leader (12:20). Thus the kingdom was divided, as God had promised.

Jeroboam did not remain committed to God. He worried that if his people went to the Temple in Jerusalem to worship, they would support the southern kingdom. He had no confidence in God to secure his reign, so he carried out his own plan to secure his people's spiritual allegiance. He built two gold calf shrines, at the north and south of his kingdom (12:26-33). God was displeased with these shrines and sent a prophet to condemn them. Though Jeroboam initially responded to the prophet's display of divine power, the calf shrines remained intact throughout the northern kingdom's history (931–722 BC). Jeroboam's false religion was a key reason for the destruction of the northern kingdom in 722 BC (14:14-16; 2 Kgs 17:5-23).

Because of Jeroboam's sins, God did not give him a dynasty (13:33-34). Though Jeroboam's son Nadab inherited the throne when his father died, he was assassinated two years later by a usurper named Baasha (14:20; 15:25-31). Jeroboam's "dynasty" ended as a punishment for his sins.

11:29-32 Ahijah's symbolic tearing of his cloak into ***twelve pieces*** and giving ***ten of these pieces*** to ***Jeroboam*** symbolized God's plans for Jeroboam and Israel following Solomon's death (see "Prophetic Sign Acts" at Ezek 4:1-17, p. 1319). ***Ten of the tribes*** would defect; ***one tribe*** (Judah) would remain with Solomon's heir. The twelfth tribe was probably Benjamin (see 12:21). Benjamin consistently acted in tandem with Judah (see 2 Chr 11:3, 23; 14:8; 15:2-9; 17:17). Simeon, the other southern tribe, seems to have allied with the north (2 Chr 15:9; 34:6).

11:33 ***For Solomon has:*** As in Greek, Syriac, and Latin Vulgate; Hebrew reads *For they have.*

11:34-39 Ahijah further described the coming division of the kingdom and delivered God's offer of blessing and perpetuity to Jeroboam, who was required to obey the Lord in order to receive the offer.

11:34 ***For the sake of my servant David:*** Although Solomon violated the terms of God's covenant, God remained faithful in not revoking his promises to David (see also Ps 89:28-37).

11:36 ***a lamp:*** David's successors were to be living representatives of God's covenant with David, and they were to shine as lights of God's grace (15:4; 2 Kgs 8:19; 2 Chr 21:7). They pointed to Jesus, the descendant of David, who is the light of the world (John 1:4-5) and who fulfills God's promises to David (Ezek 34:23-31).

11:38
2 Sam 7:11, 27
11:40
1 Kgs 14:25
2 Chr 12:2
11:41-43
//2 Chr 9:29-31
12:1-24
//2 Chr 10:1–11:4
12:1
Judg 9:1, 6
2 Chr 10:1

the throne of Israel, and you will rule over
all that your heart desires. [38]If you listen to
what I tell you and follow my ways and do
whatever I consider to be right, and if you
obey my decrees and commands, as my servant David did, then I will always be with
you. I will establish an enduring dynasty
for you as I did for David, and I will give Israel to you. [39]Because of Solomon's sin I will
punish the descendants of David—though
not forever.' "

[40]Solomon tried to kill Jeroboam, but he
fled to King Shishak of Egypt and stayed
there until Solomon died.

Summary of Solomon's Reign
1 Kgs 11:41-43 // 2 Chr 9:29-31

[41]The rest of the events in Solomon's reign,
including all his deeds and his wisdom,
are recorded in *The Book of the Acts of Solomon.* [42]Solomon ruled in Jerusalem over
all Israel for forty years. [43]When he died, he
was buried in the City of David, named for
his father. Then his son Rehoboam became
the next king.

2. THE EARLY DIVIDED KINGDOM (12:1–16:14)

The Division of the Nation (12:1-24)

The Northern Tribes Revolt
1 Kgs 12:1-20 // 2 Chr 10:1-19

12 Rehoboam went to Shechem, where
all Israel had gathered to make him
king. [2]When Jeroboam son of Nebat heard
of this, he returned from Egypt, for he had
fled to Egypt to escape from King Solomon.
[3]The leaders of Israel summoned him, and
Jeroboam and the whole assembly of Israel

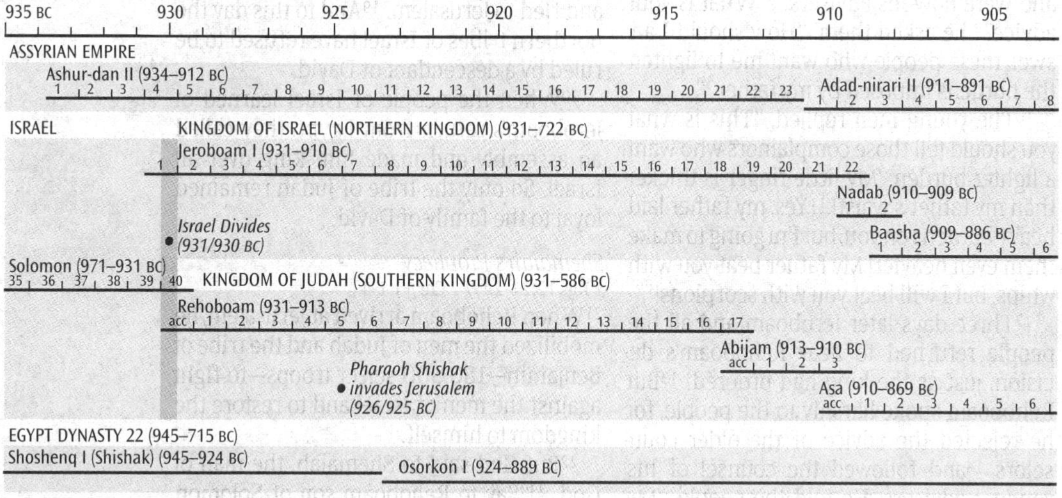

▲**Israel and Judah, 935–903 BC (11:41–15:34).** Each king's regnal years are numbered according to his own system of accounting (see "Chronology: Israel's Monarchy," p. 562). Each king's line on the chart runs from the beginning of the year in which his accession occurred to the end of the year in which he died. • SOLOMON's fortieth and final regnal year began in the fall (the month of Tishri) of 931 BC; his death and the division of the kingdom occurred sometime prior to the spring (the month of Nisan) of 930 BC. • The reign of JEROBOAM I started after that of REHOBOAM, but Jeroboam's first regnal was counted from the previous spring. • Pharaoh SHISHAK of Egypt invaded JERUSALEM during Rehoboam's fifth regnal year (see 14:25-28).

11:38 ***an enduring dynasty:*** Jeroboam had a great opportunity. God promised that if he was faithful and obedient to the Lord, his kingdom would be strong and long-lasting. However, he departed from God (12:25-33; 14:10-18) and set Israel on a destructive spiritual path (2 Kgs 17:21-23).

11:39 David's descendant, Jesus, would later inherit his rightful throne, as stipulated in God's promises to David (2 Sam 7:13, 16-19; Ps 89:35-37), Abraham (Gen 17:1-8; Luke 1:67-79), and Judah (Gen 49:10). He has established a new covenant with God's people, and he will reign ***forever*** (Jer 31:31-36; Ezek 37:22-28; 2 Cor 3:6).

11:40 ***Solomon***, probably aware of impending difficulty, ***tried to kill Jeroboam***. • ***King Shishak of Egypt*** later invaded Judah during the reign of Solomon's son Rehoboam (14:25-26).

11:41-43 The brief closing summary of ***Solomon's reign*** and death is similar to that of his father David (2:10-12). These summaries provide a typical formula for the accounts of succeeding kings. • ***The Book of the Acts of Solomon*** was likely kept in a prophetic center or in palace and Temple archives. It served as a source of information for the author of Kings but is now lost (cp. 14:19, 29). • ***Solomon*** reigned from 971 to 931 BC.

12:1 ***Shechem,*** located in the heart of territory belonging to the northern tribes, had been a strategic site and religious center since the pre-Israelite occupation of Canaan (Gen 12:6-7; 33:18-20), and it became important in Israel as a Levitical city and a city of refuge (Josh 20:7; 21:20; 24:1). ***Rehoboam*** knew that if he wanted to be ***king*** over a united kingdom, he would need the approval and support of the politically and religiously strong northern tribes. Shechem later became the provisional capital of the northern kingdom (12:25). • Rehoboam reigned from 931 to 913 BC (see timeline above).

12:2 ***he returned from Egypt:*** As in Greek version and Latin Vulgate (see also 2 Chr 10:2); Hebrew reads *he lived in Egypt.*

went to speak with Rehoboam. 4"Your father was a hard master," they said. "Lighten
the harsh labor demands and heavy taxes
that your father imposed on us. Then we
will be your loyal subjects."
5Rehoboam replied, "Give me three days
to think this over. Then come back for my
answer." So the people went away.
6Then King Rehoboam discussed the
matter with the older men who had counseled his father, Solomon. "What is your
advice?" he asked. "How should I answer
these people?"
7The older counselors replied, "If you are
willing to be a servant to these people today
and give them a favorable answer, they will
always be your loyal subjects."
8But Rehoboam rejected the advice of the
older men and instead asked the opinion of
the young men who had grown up with him
and were now his advisers. 9"What is your
advice?" he asked them. "How should I answer these people who want me to lighten
the burdens imposed by my father?"
10The young men replied, "This is what
you should tell those complainers who want
a lighter burden: 'My little finger is thicker
than my father's waist! 11Yes, my father laid
heavy burdens on you, but I'm going to make
them even heavier! My father beat you with
whips, but I will beat you with scorpions!' "
12Three days later Jeroboam and all the
people returned to hear Rehoboam's decision, just as the king had ordered. 13But
Rehoboam spoke harshly to the people, for
he rejected the advice of the older counselors 14and followed the counsel of his
younger advisers. He told the people, "My
father laid heavy burdens on you, but I'm
going to make them even heavier! My father
beat you with whips, but I will beat you with
scorpions!"
15So the king paid no attention to the people. This turn of events was the will of the
LORD, for it fulfilled the LORD's message to
Jeroboam son of Nebat through the prophet
Ahijah from Shiloh.
16When all Israel realized that the king
had refused to listen to them, they responded,

"Down with the dynasty of David!
We have no interest in the son of Jesse.
Back to your homes, O Israel!
Look out for your own house,
O David!"

So the people of Israel returned home.
17But Rehoboam continued to rule over the
Israelites who lived in the towns of Judah.
18King Rehoboam sent Adoniram, who
was in charge of the labor force, to restore
order, but the people of Israel stoned him
to death. When this news reached King Rehoboam, he quickly jumped into his chariot
and fled to Jerusalem. 19And to this day the
northern tribes of Israel have refused to be
ruled by a descendant of David.
20When the people of Israel learned of
Jeroboam's return from Egypt, they called
an assembly and made him king over all
Israel. So only the tribe of Judah remained
loyal to the family of David.

Shemaiah's Prophecy
1 Kgs 12:21-24 // 2 Chr 11:1-4

21When Rehoboam arrived at Jerusalem, he
mobilized the men of Judah and the tribe of
Benjamin—180,000 select troops—to fight
against the men of Israel and to restore the
kingdom to himself.
22But God said to Shemaiah, the man of
God, 23"Say to Rehoboam son of Solomon,
king of Judah, and to all the people of Judah
and Benjamin, and to the rest of the people,
24'This is what the LORD says: Do not fight
against your relatives, the Israelites. Go
back home, for what has happened is my
doing!' " So they [d]obeyed the message of

12:4 1 Sam 8:11-18
12:5 1 Kgs 12:12
12:12 1 Kgs 12:5
12:15 Deut 2:30; Judg 14:4; 2 Chr 10:15
12:16 2 Sam 20:1
12:17 1 Kgs 11:13, 36
12:18 2 Sam 20:24
12:19 2 Kgs 17:21
12:20 1 Kgs 11:13, 32
12:21 2 Chr 11:1
12:22 2 Chr 11:2; 12:5-7
12:24 [d]*shama'* (8085) ‣2 Kgs 22:13

12:4 ***harsh labor demands and heavy taxes:*** See 4:7, 22-23; 5:13-18; 9:20-23; 11:27-28.

12:5 ***three days:*** Rehoboam's waiting period to consult his advisers is traditional; the third day was one of final decision (see 2 Kgs 20:4-8). Jesus rose from the grave on the third day (Luke 24:41; 1 Cor 15:4).

12:6-7 ***older men:*** Those who had served under Solomon advised moderation.

12:8-10 ***young men:*** Rehoboam's appointed contemporaries took a hard line and advised the opposite of the older men.

12:11 ***scorpions:*** This was probably a type of whip that contained barbs or nails; the wounds inflicted by this weapon were like a scorpion's sting.

12:12-17 Rehoboam's decision to heed ***the counsel of his younger advisers*** was disastrous; it led the northern tribes to secede, followed by years of intermittent warfare (14:30; 15:7, 32). • ***the will of the LORD:*** God directed these human decisions to fulfill the prophesied judgment against Solomon (11:11-13, 29-39).

12:18 ***Adoniram*** (as in some Greek manuscripts and Syriac version (see also 4:6; 5:14); Hebrew reads *Adoram*) served under both David (2 Sam 20:24) and Solomon (4:6; 5:13-14). His ***death*** by stoning showed the folly of Rehoboam's decision to send the unpopular supervisor of the ***labor force . . . to restore order*** in the north.

12:21-24 Rehoboam resolved ***to restore the kingdom to himself*** by force, but he turned back when confronted with ***the message of the LORD*** through ***Shemaiah***. The term ***man of God*** emphasizes a prophet's relationship to the Lord as his messenger. God's prophets played a leading role in the history of the divided kingdom. Shemaiah apparently authored a history of Rehoboam's reign (2 Chr 12:15).

12:25 Gen 32:30; Judg 8:8, 17
12:27 Deut 12:4-6, 14
12:28 Exod 32:4; 2 Kgs 10:29; 2 Chr 11:15; Hos 8:4-7
12:29 Gen 28:19; Judg 18:27-31
12:30 1 Kgs 13:34; 2 Kgs 17:21
12:31 1 Kgs 13:32; 2 Kgs 17:32; 2 Chr 11:13-15; 13:9
12:32 Lev 23:33-34; Num 29:12

the LORD and went home, as the LORD had commanded.

Jeroboam's Reign in Israel (12:25–14:20)
Jeroboam Makes Gold Calves

25 Jeroboam then built up the city of Shechem in the hill country of Ephraim, and it became his capital. Later he went and built up the town of Peniel.

26 Jeroboam thought to himself, "Unless I am careful, the kingdom will return to the dynasty of David. 27 When these people go to Jerusalem to offer sacrifices at the Temple of the LORD, they will again give their allegiance to King Rehoboam of Judah. They will kill me and make him their king instead."

28 So on the advice of his counselors, the king made two gold calves. He said to the people, "It is too much trouble for you to worship in Jerusalem. Look, Israel, these are the gods who brought you out of Egypt!"

29 He placed these calf idols in Bethel and in Dan—at either end of his kingdom. 30 But this became a great sin, for the people worshiped the idols, traveling as far north as Dan to worship the one there.

31 Jeroboam also erected buildings at the pagan shrines and ordained priests from the common people—those who were not from the priestly tribe of Levi. 32 And Jeroboam instituted a religious festival in Bethel, held on the fifteenth day of the eighth month, in imitation of the annual Festival of Shelters in Judah. There at Bethel he himself offered sacrifices to the calves he had made, and he appointed priests for the pagan shrines he

REHOBOAM (12:1-24)

1 Kgs 14:21-31; 2 Chr 9:31–12:16

Rehoboam (931–913 BC), son of Solomon and an Ammonite woman (14:21), was forty-one when he became king; he reigned for seventeen years. He is remembered for culminating the split of Solomon's kingdom and for being the first king of the southern kingdom of Judah.

When Solomon died (931 BC), Judah immediately proclaimed Rehoboam king. The ten northern tribes resisted him, demanding relief from Solomon's harsh policies (see 12:4; 2 Chr 10:4). The king's mature advisers urged him to agree to their requests, but he rejected their advice and foolishly listened to younger advisers: He told the northerners that he would be much tougher than his father. The northern tribes rebelled and proclaimed Jeroboam, Solomon's former labor official, as their king. Rehoboam went to war, seeking control against the north, but God sent the prophet Shemaiah to tell him this was useless since the split was God's judgment (2 Chr 11:1-4). When he returned, Rehoboam fortified his boundaries (2 Chr 11:5-12).

When Jeroboam established the new apostate religion in the northern kingdom, priests and Levites streamed to the south, where they strengthened the spiritual fiber of the realm and helped to maintain Judah's stability for three years (2 Chr 11:13-17). In the end, however, Rehoboam also promoted idol worship. The people built high places and pagan sanctuaries throughout the land and adopted corrupt religious practices from the heathen nations around them (14:22-24). God stopped supporting Rehoboam, so he was vulnerable when King Shishak of Egypt attacked him (926/925 BC; 14:25; 2 Chr 12:2-3) and removed many precious items from the Temple. Rehoboam replaced Solomon's gold shields with bronze ones (14:27), an act that represented the loss of Judah's glory because of false worship.

12:25-33 Jeroboam's actions in establishing his kingdom are reported in two sections, one on his building activities (12:25), the other on his false shrines and religious practices (12:26-33).

12:25 Both *Shechem* (12:1) and *Peniel* (Hebrew *Penuel,* a variant spelling of Peniel), which Jeroboam built across the Jordan River, were strategic defensive sites against the Arameans.

12:26-27 *Jeroboam* tried to satisfy Israel's spiritual needs and maintain the allegiance of his people by making the worship services in the north both convenient and distinctive.

12:28 *Two gold calves* would strike a responsive chord regarding Israel's history (Exod 32; esp. 32:4). Similar religious practices, associated with the Canaanite god Baal-Hadad, also appealed to the remaining Canaanite population in the northern kingdom. Jeroboam's intentions compromised true worship and caused religious confusion (see 14:9; Hos 8:6). • *to the people:* Literally *to them.*

12:29-30 By placing the *calf idols in Bethel* (the southern part of Israel) and *in Dan* (the far northern section) Jeroboam gave his people two choice sites with long religious traditions (see Gen 12:8; 28:11-19; Judg 18:30-31). Archaeological excavations confirm the existence of a high place—an altar for pagan worship—in Dan. Bethel was where Jacob had his dream (Gen 28:10-22), and it was the resting place of the Ark of the Covenant in the days of the judges (Judg 20:18-28) and a sanctuary in Samuel's time (1 Sam 7:16; 10:3).

12:31 Jeroboam directly violated the law of Moses, which prohibited worship at *pagan shrines* (Deut 12:2-7) and specified that priests were to come only from the *tribe of Levi* (Exod 40:13-15; Num 1:50-53).

12:32-33 Replacing the *Festival of Shelters,* Israel's crowning ceremonial feast in the seventh month, with the *festival in Bethel* also violated the law (Deut 16:13-15). The *imitation* observance one month later during *the eighth month* may have coincided with the end of the Canaanite agricultural year. Jeroboam's

had made. 33So on the fifteenth day of the eighth month, a day that he himself had designated, Jeroboam offered sacrifices on the altar at Bethel. He instituted a religious festival for Israel, and he went up to the altar to burn incense.

A Prophet Denounces Jeroboam

13 At the LORD's command, a man of God from Judah went to Bethel, arriving there just as Jeroboam was approaching the altar to burn incense. 2Then at the LORD's command, he shouted, "O altar, altar! This is what the LORD says: A child named Josiah will be born into the dynasty of David. On you he will sacrifice the priests from the pagan shrines who come here to burn incense, and human bones will be burned on you." 3That same day the man of God gave a sign to prove his message. He said, "The LORD has promised to give this sign: This altar will split apart, and its ashes will be poured out on the ground."

4When King Jeroboam heard the man of God speaking against the altar at Bethel, he pointed at him and shouted, "Seize that man!" But instantly the king's hand became paralyzed in that position, and he couldn't pull it back. 5At the same time a wide crack appeared in the altar, and the ashes poured out, just as the man of God had predicted in his message from the LORD.

6The king cried out to the man of God, "Please ask the LORD your God to restore my hand again!" So the man of God prayed to the LORD, and the king's hand was restored and he could move it again.

7Then the king said to the man of God, "Come to the palace with me and have something to eat, and I will give you a gift."

8But the man of God said to the king, "Even if you gave me half of everything you own, I would not go with you. I would not eat or drink anything in this place. 9For the LORD gave me this command: 'You must not eat or drink anything while you are there, and do not return to Judah by the same way you came.'" 10So he left Bethel and went home another way.

11As it happened, there was an old prophet living in Bethel, and his sons came home and told him what the man of God had done in Bethel that day. They also told their father what the man had said to the king. 12The old prophet asked them, "Which way did he go?" So they showed their father which road the man of God had taken. 13"Quick, saddle the donkey," the old man said. So they saddled the donkey for him, and he mounted it.

14Then he rode after the man of God and found him sitting under a great tree. The old prophet asked him, "Are you the man of God who came from Judah?"

"Yes, I am," he replied.

15Then he said to the man of God, "Come home with me and eat some food."

16"No, I cannot," he replied. "I am not allowed to eat or drink anything here in this place. 17For the LORD gave me this command: 'You must not eat or drink anything while you are there, and do not return to Judah by the same way you came.'"

18But the old prophet answered, "I am a prophet, too, just as you are. And an angel gave me this command from the LORD: 'Bring him home with you so he can have something to eat and drink.'" But the old man was lying to him. 19So they went back together, and the man of God ate and drank at the prophet's home.

13:1 2 Kgs 23:17
13:2 2 Kgs 23:15-16, 20
13:6 Exod 8:8, 28; 9:28 Jer 37:3 Acts 8:24
13:7 1 Sam 9:7 2 Kgs 5:15
13:8 Num 22:18
13:9 Num 22:18; 24:13
13:16 1 Kgs 13:8

false religious practices led to Israel's downfall (2 Kgs 17:22). • Jeroboam's offering of ***sacrifices on the altar at Bethel*** set a bad precedent in spiritual leadership. • ***the fifteenth day of the eighth month:*** This day of the ancient Hebrew lunar calendar occurred in late October or early November, exactly one month after the annual Festival of Shelters in Judah (see Lev 23:34).

13:1-10 The account of the unnamed ***man of God*** who denounced Jeroboam's false altar at Bethel emphasizes the authority of God's word. Like Isaiah's prophecy of Cyrus's coming (Isa 44:28; 45:1) and Micah's prophecy about Bethlehem as the Messiah's birthplace (Mic 5:2), this prophecy gave a distinctive proper name associated with an event long before it happened (2 Kgs 23:15-20). Such prophecies give assurance of God's sovereignty and omniscience (see Isa 42:9).

13:3 In Levitical regulations, ***ashes*** from sacrifices at the prescribed altar were to be taken to a clean place (Lev 1:16; 6:10-11). Because Jeroboam's ***altar . . . split apart, and its ashes . . . poured out,*** the altar and its sacrifices were rendered unclean.

13:4-5 The paralysis of Jeroboam's shoulder and arm and the fulfillment of the prophetic sign concerning the altar confirmed God's omnipotence as well as his direct displeasure with Jeroboam's apostate religion.

13:6 ***hand was restored:*** God showed mercy toward Jeroboam; his restored hand should have reminded Jeroboam that it was still possible to serve God properly.

13:7 ***have something to eat:*** In accordance with ancient Near Eastern custom, the king's seeming gratitude and offer of hospitality also carried implications of approval and fellowship (13:19; see Gen 24:52-54).

13:11-19 Whatever the old prophet's motives were for seeking out the ***man of God,*** he clearly lied about receiving God's message through an angel. The man of God knew that what the ***old prophet*** asked was contrary to the Lord's instructions (13:8-10, 16-17; cp. Gal 1:8).

13:11 ***sons:*** As in Greek version; Hebrew reads ***son.***

13:12 ***So they showed their father:*** As in Greek version; Hebrew reads ***They had seen.***

13:21
1 Sam 13:14
13:24
1 Kgs 20:36
13:31
2 Kgs 23:17-18
13:32
1 Kgs 16:24

[20]Then while they were sitting at the
table, a command from the LORD came to
the old prophet. [21]He cried out to the man
of God from Judah, "This is what the LORD
says: You have defied the word of the LORD
and have disobeyed the command the
LORD your God gave you. [22]You came back
to this place and ate and drank where he
told you not to eat or drink. Because of this,
your body will not be buried in the grave of
your ancestors."
[23]After the man of God had finished eating and drinking, the old prophet saddled
his own donkey for him, [24]and the man of
God started off again. But as he was traveling along, a lion came out and killed him.
His body lay there on the road, with the donkey and the lion standing beside it. [25]People
who passed by saw the body lying in the
road and the lion standing beside it, and
they went and reported it in Bethel, where
the old prophet lived.
[26]When the prophet heard the report, he
said, "It is the man of God who disobeyed
the LORD's command. The LORD has fulfilled his word by causing the lion to attack
and kill him."
[27]Then the prophet said to his sons,
"Saddle a donkey for me." So they saddled
a donkey, [28]and he went out and found
the body lying in the road. The donkey
and lion were still standing there beside
it, for the lion had not eaten the body nor
attacked the donkey. [29]So the prophet laid
the body of the man of God on the donkey
and took it back to the town to mourn over
him and bury him. [30]He laid the body in
his own grave, crying out in grief, "Oh, my
brother!"
[31]Afterward the prophet said to his sons,
"When I die, bury me in the grave where the
man of God is buried. Lay my bones beside
his bones. [32]For the message the LORD told
him to proclaim against the altar in Bethel

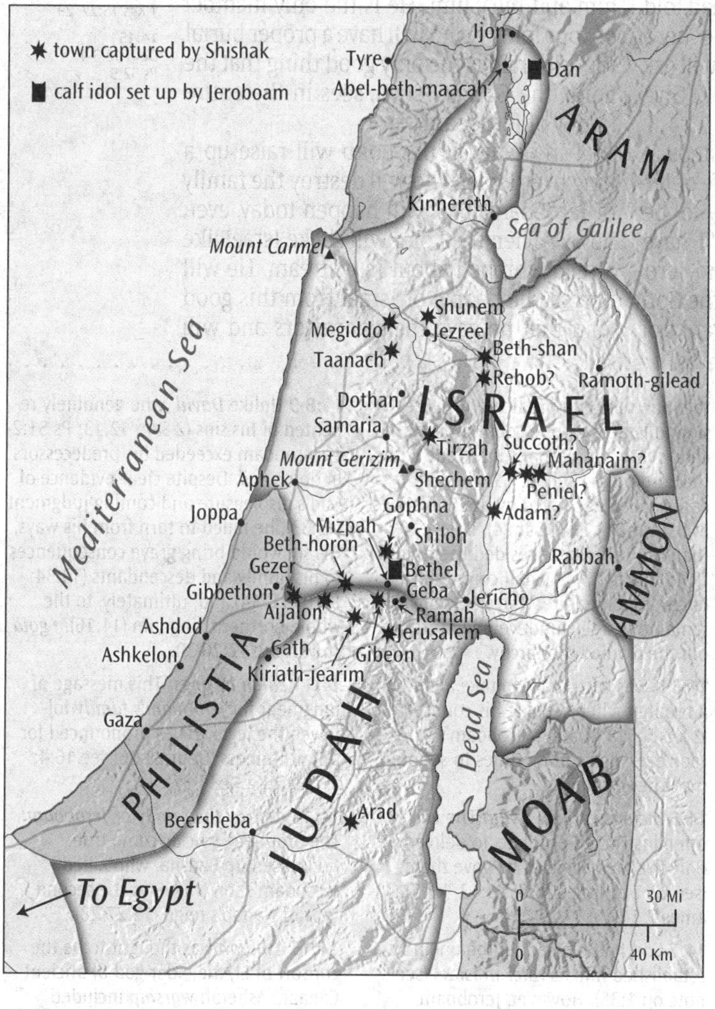

◀ **The Divided Kingdom of Rehoboam and Jeroboam I, 931–910 BC (12:1–14:28).** After the kingdom of Israel divided, Rehoboam remained king of JUDAH while Jeroboam became king of ISRAEL, the ten northern tribes. Jeroboam rebuilt the town of SHECHEM and made it his capital. He also built up the town of PENIEL and tried to keep his people from worshiping at JERUSALEM in Judah by setting up pagan altars at DAN and BETHEL. In 926/925 BC, five years after the division, Pharaoh Shishak I of Egypt came and attacked Jerusalem and many fortified towns in Judah (14:25; 2 Chr 12:1-12). Shishak's campaign also included the territory of Israel; battles are shown at sites listed in Shishak's own annals.

13:20-22 Although the old prophet had lied, God communicated through him.

The severe pronouncement against the *man of God* was that because of his disobedience, he would be denied burial in his ancestral tomb. This death sentence was quickly carried out. Disobedience to the clear command of God is a serious offense (Num 14:21-23; Deut 11:26-28).

13:23-26 The *donkey* did not run away and the *lion* did not eat the man's body, a supernatural event. The *old prophet* immediately understood that God had clearly *fulfilled his word* (13:21-22) by judging disobedience.

13:30 The old prophet probably had a modest *grave.* Such tombs were hewn out of soft limestone in a wadi (a stream bed) near the person's home.

13:32 ***the message . . . will certainly come true:*** The Lord's swift judgment convinced the old prophet that the oracle of judgment pronounced by the man of God against Jeroboam's altar would be fulfilled. The prophecy came true years later during Josiah's reforms

and against the pagan shrines in the towns
of Samaria will certainly come true."
33 But even after this, Jeroboam did not
turn from his evil ways. He continued to
choose priests from the common people.
He appointed anyone who wanted to become a priest for the pagan shrines. 34 This
became a great sin and resulted in the utter
destruction of Jeroboam's dynasty from
the face of the earth.

Ahijah's Prophecy against Jeroboam

14 At that time Jeroboam's son Abijah
became very sick. 2 So Jeroboam told
his wife, "Disguise yourself so that no one
will recognize you as my wife. Then go to
the prophet Ahijah at Shiloh—the man who
told me I would become king. 3 Take him a
gift of ten loaves of bread, some cakes, and
a jar of honey, and ask him what will happen
to the boy."
4 So Jeroboam's wife went to Ahijah's
home at Shiloh. He was an old man now and
could no longer see. 5 But the LORD had told
Ahijah, "Jeroboam's wife will come here,
pretending to be someone else. She will ask
you about her son, for he is very sick. Give
her the answer I give you."
6 So when Ahijah heard her footsteps at
the door, he called out, "Come in, wife of Jeroboam! Why are you pretending to be
someone else?" Then he told her, "I have
bad news for you. 7 Give your husband, Jeroboam, this message from the LORD, the God
of Israel: 'I promoted you from the ranks of
the common people and made you ruler
over my people Israel. 8 I ripped the kingdom away from the family of David and
gave it to you. But you have not been like my
servant David, who obeyed my commands
and followed me with all his heart and always did whatever I wanted. 9 You have done
more evil than all who lived before you. You
have made other gods for yourself and have
made me furious with your gold calves.
And since you have turned your back on me,
10 I will bring disaster on your dynasty and
will destroy every one of your male descendants, slave and free alike, anywhere in
Israel. I will burn up your royal dynasty as
one burns up trash until it is all gone. 11 The
members of Jeroboam's family who die in
the city will be eaten by dogs, and those who
die in the field will be eaten by vultures. I,
the LORD, have spoken.'"
12 Then Ahijah said to Jeroboam's wife,
"Go on home, and when you enter the city,
the child will die. 13 All Israel will mourn for
him and bury him. He is the only member
of your family who will have a proper burial,
for this child is the only good thing that the
LORD, the God of Israel, sees in the entire
family of Jeroboam.
14 "In addition, the LORD will raise up a
king over Israel who will destroy the family
of Jeroboam. This will happen today, even
now! 15 Then the LORD will shake Israel like
a reed whipped about in a stream. He will
uproot the people of Israel from this good
land that he gave their ancestors and will

13:33 1 Kgs 12:31; 2 Chr 13:9
13:34 1 Kgs 14:10; 15:29; 2 Kgs 17:21
14:2 1 Sam 28:7-8; 2 Sam 14:2-3; 2 Chr 18:29
14:3 1 Sam 9:7-8; 2 Kgs 4:42
14:4 1 Sam 3:2-3; 4:15
14:7 1 Kgs 11:28, 31
14:8 1 Kgs 11:33, 38; 15:5
14:9 Exod 34:17; 2 Chr 11:15; Ps 50:17; Ezek 23:35
14:10 Deut 32:36; 1 Kgs 15:29; 21:22; 2 Kgs 9:8-9
14:11 1 Kgs 16:4-7; 21:24
14:12 1 Kgs 14:17
14:14 1 Kgs 15:27, 29
14:15 Deut 12:3-4; Ps 52:5

(2 Kgs 23:15-18). • ***Samaria*** was established as the capital city of Israel during the reign of Omri, first king of Israel's third dynasty (16:24, 29-33). The name *Samaria* sometimes refers to the capital city and sometimes to the northern kingdom in general (2 Kgs 17:24; Amos 6:1). Samaria's mention here reflects the perspective of an author living at a later time. Similar uses of location names elsewhere reflect editorial updating (cp. Gen 23:2 with Josh 14:15; Judg 1:10).

13:33-34 Apparently, ***Jeroboam*** knew what had happened to the man of God, but it did nothing to change his spiritual outlook. Jeroboam's persistently apostate religion, despite God's denunciation of it, doomed his ***dynasty*** to destruction (14:7-11, 15-16; 15:27-30). As succeeding Israelite kings perpetuated his sin, it brought about the complete demise of the northern kingdom (2 Kgs 17:20-23).

14:2 ***Disguise yourself:*** Jeroboam apparently recognized that his sin had separated him from any right to approach God's prophet. He knew that the man who had predicted his accession to Israel's throne could predict the child's fate and perhaps intercede with the Lord on his behalf. • ***Shiloh*** had earlier been destroyed by the Philistines in the time of Eli (1 Sam 4). Before that, the Tabernacle resided there (Josh 18:1; 1 Sam 1:3). A small community once again inhabited the site, which remained largely undeveloped throughout the divided monarchy.

14:3 It was customary to take a ***gift*** to a prophet when seeking his counsel (2 Kgs 5:5; 8:8). King Jeroboam's wife took everyday commodities to supplement her disguise.

14:5 ***the answer I give you:*** The Lord often instructed prophets to deliver only the message that he gave them (see 22:14; Num 22:38; 23:12; Jer 7:2; Amos 7:14-15).

14:7 God had blessed Jeroboam and established him as ***ruler*** in Israel (see note on 1:35). However, Jeroboam abused God's appointment with his false religion.

14:8-9 Unlike ***David,*** who genuinely repented of his sins (2 Sam 12:13; Ps 51:2-4), Jeroboam exceeded his predecessors in doing ***evil.*** Despite clear evidence of God's displeasure and coming judgment (13:33), he failed to turn from his ways. His sin would bring grave consequences to his family and descendants (13:34; 14:10-11, 14) and, ultimately, to the whole northern kingdom (14:16). • ***gold calves:*** see 12:26-30.

14:11 ***eaten by dogs:*** This message of judgment for ***Jeroboam's family*** followed the legal curses pronounced for unfaithfulness (Deut 28:26; see 16:4; 21:23; 2 Kgs 9:35-37).

14:14 ***destroy the family of Jeroboam:*** The prophecy quickly came true. God raised up Baasha, who killed Jeroboam's son Nadab in the second year of Nadab's reign (15:27-28).

14:15 ***Asherah*** was thought to be the consort of El, the elder god of ancient Canaan. Asherah ***worship*** included fertility rites at sacred trees or ***poles;*** it became a chronic sin for God's people

14:16
1 Kgs 12:30

14:17
1 Kgs 15:21, 33; 16:6-9

14:19
1 Kgs 14:29; 15:7, 23, 31; 16:4-7, 14, 20
1 Chr 9:1

14:21, 25-31
//2 Chr 12:9-16

14:21
1 Kgs 11:32, 36
2 Chr 12:13

14:22
Deut 32:21
2 Chr 12:1, 14

14:23
Deut 12:2; 16:22
2 Kgs 17:10
Jer 2:20
Ezek 16:24

scatter them beyond the Euphrates River,
for they have angered the LORD with the
Asherah poles they have set up for worship.
16He will abandon Israel because Jeroboam
sinned and made Israel sin along with him."
17So Jeroboam's wife returned to Tirzah, and the child died just as she walked
through the door of her home. 18And all Israel buried him and mourned for him, as the
LORD had promised through the prophet
Ahijah.
19The rest of the events in Jeroboam's
reign, including all his wars and how he ruled,
are recorded in *The Book of the History of
the Kings of Israel*. 20Jeroboam reigned in Israel twenty-two years. When Jeroboam died,
his son Nadab became the next king.

Rehoboam's Reign in Judah (14:21-31)

1 Kgs 14:25-28 // 2 Chr 12:9-11
1 Kgs 14:29-31 // 2 Chr 12:15-16

21Meanwhile, Rehoboam son of Solomon
was king in Judah. He was forty-one years
old when he became king, and he reigned
seventeen years in Jerusalem, the city the
LORD had chosen from among all the tribes
of Israel as the place to honor his name.
Rehoboam's mother was Naamah, an Ammonite woman.
22During Rehoboam's reign, the people
of Judah did what was evil in the LORD's
sight, provoking his anger with their sin,
for it was even worse than that of their ancestors. 23For they also built for themselves
pagan shrines and set up sacred pillars and

True Success (13:33-34)

1 Kgs 11:38; 12:26-33; 13:1-3; 14:8-11
Deut 6:1-8; 12:4-7
Josh 1:7-8
1 Sam 18:14
2 Kgs 17:13-23
Ps 33:12; 119:1-2; 144:15
Matt 6:33
Luke 10:25-28
1 Jn 5:21

The book of 1 Kings emphasizes the necessity of faithfully worshiping God (see Deut 12:4-7). The author evaluates each king's devotion to God against the precedent set by David (see 11:38; 14:8; 15:3-5, 11). Allowing worship at local pagan shrines is repeatedly singled out for disapproval (see 3:2-4; 11:7).

Each king's reign is introduced with an accession statement followed by a spiritual evaluation. Beginning with Jeroboam I, the kings of Israel (the northern kingdom) uniformly practiced apostate religion and were censured for practicing it (12:31-32; 13:33-34; 15:25-26, 33-34; 16:11-13, 25-26). Of these kings, King Ahab was the most wicked (16:30-33; 21:25-26), and his son Ahaziah closely followed his example and is denounced for his idolatrous ways (22:51-53). Ahaziah's fascination with Baal continued to the end (2 Kgs 1). The kings of the northern kingdom set their people on a course doomed for destruction (2 Kgs 17:21-23). Despite God's repeated efforts to get his people's attention (2 Kgs 17:13-15, 23), they failed to respond, so God invoked the penalties for persistent spiritual infidelity (see 13:33-34).

While two of the kings of Judah (the southern kingdom) receive commendation, two of them are denounced. Rehoboam allowed pagan worship to spread in Judah (14:22-24), while Abijam continued in his father's sins (15:3). Even the good kings, Asa (15:14) and Jehoshaphat (22:43), receive criticism for letting popular local worship sites continue. Failure to give God his rightful place had disastrous results.

God requires complete devotion from his people (Deut 6:4-5; cp. Matt 22:37). True success comes from seeking God and acknowledging him as sovereign (Matt 6:33), to the exclusion of all idols (1 Jn 5:21). While the kings and people of the northern kingdom foolishly pursued their own way, people who instead fear the Lord and live by the standards of God's word will be blessed and find genuine contentment (Ps 33:12; 119:1-2; 144:15). True success is always found in letting God be king of one's life (Matt 6:33).

(15:13; 16:33; 18:19; Deut 16:21; Judg 3:7). • ***the Euphrates River:*** Literally *the river.*

14:17-18 ***Tirzah*** was situated on the road from Shechem to Beth-shan. Noted for its great beauty (Song 6:4), the city was a royal retreat that apparently had become the capital of the northern kingdom (16:6, 8). • ***The child died***, as Ahijah had predicted.

14:19-20 ***all his wars:*** Jeroboam engaged in repeated border skirmishes with Rehoboam (14:30). • ***The Book of the History of the Kings of Israel*** is mentioned seventeen times in 1 Kgs 14:19—2 Kgs 15:31; it includes material that may have originated in official records kept by the court recorder (see 4:3). It was known to the original readers of 1 & 2 Kings but is now lost (see also note on 14:29-31).

14:21-31 Between the opening and closing details about Rehoboam's reign (14:21, 29-31), the account focuses on the deteriorating spiritual experience of God's people in Judah (14:22-24) and on an Egyptian invasion (14:25-28).

14:21 Rather than any city of the northern kingdom, ***the city the LORD had chosen*** was ***Jerusalem.*** • ***Naamah,*** as the queen ***mother***, was highly esteemed in Judah. This role seems to have developed into an official status (15:13), and Judah's queen mothers are often mentioned in connection with the reigning king (see, e.g., Jer 22:26).

14:22 ***the people of Judah did what was evil:*** Although Rehoboam seemed to begin his reign in good spiritual form (2 Chr 11:5-17, 23), he deserted God's standards (2 Chr 12:1).

14:23-24 Solomon had married foreign wives, who led his family into idolatry. Judah, under Rehoboam's leadership, then perpetuated the

Asherah poles on every high hill and under every green tree. [24]There were even male and female shrine prostitutes throughout the land. The people imitated the detestable practices of the pagan nations the LORD had driven from the land ahead of the Israelites.

[25]In the fifth year of King Rehoboam's reign, King Shishak of Egypt came up and attacked Jerusalem. [26]He ransacked the treasuries of the LORD's Temple and the royal palace; he stole everything, including all the gold shields Solomon had made. [27]King Rehoboam later replaced them with bronze [e]shields as substitutes, and he entrusted them to the care of the commanders of the guard who protected the entrance to the royal palace. [28]Whenever the king went to the Temple of the LORD, the guards would also take the shields and then return them to the guardroom.

[29]The rest of the events in Rehoboam's reign and everything he did are recorded in *The Book of the History of the Kings of Judah*. [30]There was constant war between Rehoboam and Jeroboam. [31]When Rehoboam died, he was buried among his ancestors in the City of David. His mother was Naamah, an Ammonite woman. Then his son Abijam became the next king.

Abijam's Reign in Judah (15:1-8)

1 Kgs 15:1-2 // 2 Chr 13:1-2
1 Kgs 15:6-8 // 2 Chr 13:22; 14:1

15 Abijam began to rule over Judah in the eighteenth year of Jeroboam's reign in Israel. [2]He reigned in Jerusalem three years. His mother was Maacah, the daughter of Absalom.

[3]He committed the same sins as his father before him, and he was not faithful to the LORD his God, as his ancestor David had been. [4]But for David's sake, the LORD his God allowed his descendants to continue ruling, shining like a lamp, and he gave Abijam a son to rule after him in Jerusalem. [5]For David had done what was pleasing in the LORD's sight and had obeyed the LORD's commands throughout his life, except in the affair concerning Uriah the Hittite.

[6]There was war between Abijam and Jeroboam throughout Abijam's reign. [7]The rest of the events in Abijam's reign and everything he did are recorded in *The Book of the History of the Kings of Judah*. There was constant war between Abijam and Jeroboam. [8]When Abijam died, he was buried

14:24
Deut 23:17-18
2 Kgs 23:7

14:25
2 Chr 12:2, 9

14:26
1 Kgs 10:16-17; 15:18

14:27
[e]*magen* (4043)
› 2 Chr 14:8

14:30
1 Kgs 12:21; 15:6

15:1-2
//2 Chr 13:1-2

15:3
1 Kgs 11:4

15:4
2 Chr 21:7

15:5
2 Sam 11:2-27
1 Kgs 9:4; 14:8

15:6-8
2 Chr 13:22–14:1

detestable practices of the pagan nations that occupied the land before the Israelites. The spiritual decline of a nation easily follows from debased leadership, which leads to disgrace and destruction (Prov 14:34). • ***Shrine prostitutes*** were not uncommon in Canaan but were prohibited for Israel (see notes on Lev 17:7; Deut 23:17-18). They became a part of Israelite society as the people embraced Canaanite culture.

14:25 ***Shishak*** (Shoshenq I, 945–924 BC), of Egypt's 22nd dynasty, reunited the land of Egypt that was divided during the 21st dynasty. He gave Egypt renewed stability, economic expansion, and military power. His attack on Judah is also recorded by the Chronicler (2 Chr 12:2-4) and is written on the Amon Temple in Thebes (see also notes on 7:2-5; 11:40).

14:26-28 When Rehoboam replaced Solomon's ***gold shields*** with ***bronze shields,*** it reflected the declining spiritual value of Rehoboam's kingdom. The complete destruction of Judah and Jerusalem was avoided only when Rehoboam repented in response to the Lord's word through the prophet Shemaiah (2 Chr 12:5-6, 12).

14:29-31 The closing report concerning ***Rehoboam's reign*** notes his constant strife with ***Jeroboam.*** • ***The Book of the History of the Kings of Judah*** is mentioned 15 times in 1 Kgs 14:29—2 Kgs 24:5 as a source of information on the southern kingdom. This book was known to the original readers of the Book of Kings but is now lost (see also notes on 11:41-43; 14:19-20).

14:31 ***Abijam*** was also known as *Abijah* (see note on 2 Chr 13:1).

15:1-8 The author of 1 & 2 Kings describes the reign of each king of Judah in a typical pattern: the date of his accession in chronological relationship to the current king of the other kingdom (15:1), the length of his reign, the name of his mother (15:2), a spiritual evaluation of his character (15:3-5), details of his reign (15:6-7), sources where further data about him could be found (15:7), where he was buried, and his successor's name (15:8).

15:1 ***Abijam*** (also known as *Abijah*; see note on 2 Chr 13:1) reigned from 913 to 910 BC (see timeline, p. 599).

15:2 Abijam's ***mother was Maacah***, Rehoboam's favorite of his eighteen wives. She was the ***daughter of Absalom*** (Hebrew *Abishalom* [also in 15:10], a variant spelling of Absalom; cp. 2 Chr 11:20). Presumably this Absalom is David's son, though we read in 2 Sam 14:27 that Absalom's daughter was Tamar. Perhaps Maacah was Absalom's granddaughter (the Hebrew can be interpreted either way). Maacah, an idol worshiper, was an evil spiritual influence in Judah (15:13).

15:3-5 Despite Abijam's unfaithfulness, ***God*** remained ***faithful*** to his covenant with David (2 Sam 7:12-16; Ps 89:19-29) and preserved David's line on Judah's throne. Each king that followed David was to be ***a lamp,*** dispensing the light of God's grace (11:36).

15:6 ***Abijam*** inherited the hostility between the northern and southern kingdoms. Like Rehoboam (14:30), he faced ***war*** with ***Jeroboam.*** During one notable battle (2 Chr 13:2b-20), when Abijam and his outnumbered forces were surrounded by northern troops, they cried out to the Lord; God delivered them and enabled them to inflict a severe defeat on Jeroboam. • ***between Abijam and Jeroboam:*** As in a few Hebrew and Greek manuscripts; most Hebrew manuscripts read *between Rehoboam and Jeroboam.*

15:7 ***rest of the events:*** Among other details of ***Abijam's reign,*** the Chronicler tells us that he married fourteen wives and had thirty-eight children (2 Chr 13:21).

15:9-22 //2 Chr 14:2-3; 15:6–16:6
15:11 2 Chr 14:2; 15:17
15:12 Deut 23:17-18; 1 Kgs 22:46; 2 Chr 15:2-5
15:13 1 Kgs 14:24; 2 Chr 15:16-18
15:14 1 Kgs 8:61; 22:43; 2 Kgs 12:3
15:17 Josh 18:25; 2 Chr 16:1-6
15:18 1 Kgs 14:26; 2 Kgs 12:17-18
15:19 2 Chr 16:7
15:22 Josh 18:24; 2 Chr 16:6

in the City of David. Then his son Asa became the next king.

Asa's Reign in Judah (15:9-24)

1 Kgs 15:11-15 // 2 Chr 14:2-3; 15:16-18
1 Kgs 15:16-22 // 2 Chr 16:1-6
1 Kgs 15:23-24 // 2 Chr 16:11-14

9 Asa began to rule over Judah in the twentieth year of Jeroboam's reign in Israel. 10 He
reigned in Jerusalem forty-one years. His
grandmother was Maacah, the daughter of
Absalom.

11 Asa did what was pleasing in the LORD's
sight, as his ancestor David had done. 12 He
banished the male and female shrine prostitutes from the land and got rid of all the
idols his ancestors had made. 13 He even
deposed his grandmother Maacah from
her position as queen mother because she
had made an obscene Asherah pole. He
cut down her obscene pole and burned
it in the Kidron Valley. 14 Although the pagan shrines were not removed, Asa's heart
remained completely faithful to the LORD
throughout his life. 15 He brought into the
Temple of the LORD the silver and gold and
the various items that he and his father had
dedicated.

16 There was constant war between King
Asa of Judah and King Baasha of Israel.
17 King Baasha of Israel invaded Judah and
fortified Ramah in order to prevent anyone
from entering or leaving King Asa's territory in Judah.

18 Asa responded by removing all the silver and gold that was left in the treasuries
of the Temple of the LORD and the royal
palace. He sent it with some of his officials
to Ben-hadad son of Tabrimmon, son of He-
zion, the king of Aram, who was ruling in
Damascus, along with this message:

> 19 "Let there be a treaty between you and
> me like the one between your father
> and my father. See, I am sending you a
> gift of silver and gold. Break your treaty
> with King Baasha of Israel so that he will
> leave me alone."

20 Ben-hadad agreed to King Asa's request
and sent the commanders of his army to
attack the towns of Israel. They conquered
the towns of Ijon, Dan, Abel-beth-maacah,
and all Kinnereth, and all the land of Naphtali. 21 As soon as Baasha of Israel heard what
was happening, he abandoned his project of
fortifying Ramah and withdrew to Tirzah.
22 Then King Asa sent an order throughout
Judah, requiring that everyone, without
exception, help to carry away the building
stones and timbers that Baasha had been
using to fortify Ramah. Asa used these
materials to fortify the town of Geba in Benjamin and the town of Mizpah.

15:9 *Asa* reigned from 910 to 869 BC.

15:10 *forty-one years:* The first ten years of Asa's long reign were peaceful (2 Chr 14:1-7), perhaps due to his father's decisive victory over Jeroboam. • *His grandmother:* Or *The queen mother;* Hebrew reads *His mother* (also in 15:13); compare 15:2.

15:11-13 *did what was pleasing:* In addition to reforms mentioned here, the Chronicler records the positive spiritual influence of God's prophet Azariah upon the king (2 Chr 15:1-7) and Asa's convening of a great assembly to renew the covenant with the Lord (2 Chr 15:9-15). • *shrine prostitutes:* See 14:23-24. Asa's efforts to restrict idolatry and pagan fertility rites even extended to ***Maacah,*** deposing her from her influential role as ***queen mother*** (15:13; 2 Chr 15:16). • The ***Kidron Valley*** became a place for reforming kings of Judah to destroy pagan idols (2 Kgs 23:4-15; 2 Chr 29:16; 30:14).

15:12 *idols:* The Hebrew term (literally *round things*) probably alludes to dung.

15:14-15 Although he allowed the ***pagan shrines*** to remain, ***Asa's heart remained . . . faithful to the LORD.*** The pagan shrines apparently became locations for worshiping the Lord. In his latter days, Asa's spiritual ardor appears to have diminished (2 Chr 16:7-12).

15:16 ***Baasha*** began to reign in Asa's third year (15:33); when Baasha was established, Judah faced renewed hostilities with Israel. ***Asa*** also withstood an attack by Zerah the Ethiopian (2 Chr 14:9-12), who was apparently a commander in the service of Pharaoh Osorkon I (924–889 BC). Asa and his troops won a great victory and took vast plunder from Zerah's forces and from towns in the Negev that probably launched the Egyptian invasion.

15:17 Baasha's southward thrust recaptured towns previously lost to Abijam (2 Chr 13:19), as well as ***Ramah*** in Judah, about four miles north of Jerusalem. This sealed the border, preventing the Israelites from defecting to ***Judah*** and confining Asa to his own territory. Ramah commanded the important north–south and east–west routes in Canaan (Judg 4:5; Isa 10:29; Jer 31:15; 40:1).

15:18-19 ***Ben-hadad . . . the king of Aram*** and his successors were a major factor in Aramean-Israelite relations for many years. Asa's appeal for Ben-hadad's help was reinforced with rich gifts taken from the Temple treasury. Despite previous enmity between the Arameans and Israel (11:23-25; 2 Sam 8:3-12; 2 Chr 8:3-4), Ben-hadad and ***Baasha*** had established a treaty. ***Asa*** understood that the Aramean king's assistance could be purchased for the right price (15:20). When God's prophet Hanani delivered the Lord's rebuke to Asa for approaching Ben-hadad, Asa reacted uncharacteristically and threw him into prison (2 Chr 16:7-10). Asa apparently forgot God's previous intervention on his behalf against Zerah's sizeable army (2 Chr 14:7-8).

15:19 *Let there be a treaty:* As in Greek version; Hebrew reads *There is a treaty.*

15:20-22 As a result of ***King Asa's request,*** the war with Baasha quickly turned to Asa's advantage. ***Ben-hadad*** swiftly captured several sections of northern Israel and secured important northern trade routes, forcing ***Baasha*** to cease operations in ***Ramah*** in order to meet the emergency on his northern frontier. Asa retook Ramah and used its building materials to fortify other strategic border towns against further moves by Baasha.

23The rest of the events in Asa's reign—
the extent of his power, everything he did,
and the names of the cities he built—are
recorded in *The Book of the History of the
Kings of Judah*. In his old age his feet became diseased. 24When Asa died, he was
buried with his ancestors in the City of
David.

Then Jehoshaphat, Asa's son, became the
next king.

Nadab's Reign in Israel (15:25-31)

25Nadab son of Jeroboam began to rule over
Israel in the second year of King Asa's reign
in Judah. He reigned in Israel two years.
26But he did what was evil in the LORD's
sight and followed the example of his father, continuing the sins that Jeroboam had
led Israel to commit.

27Then Baasha son of Ahijah, from the
tribe of Issachar, plotted against Nadab and
assassinated him while he and the Israelite army were laying siege to the Philistine
town of Gibbethon. 28Baasha killed Nadab
in the third year of King Asa's reign in Judah, and he became the next king of Israel.

29He immediately slaughtered all the descendants of King Jeroboam, so that not
one of the royal family was left, just as the
LORD had promised concerning Jeroboam
by the prophet Ahijah from Shiloh. 30This
was done because Jeroboam had provoked
the anger of the LORD, the God of Israel, by
the sins he had committed and the sins he
had led Israel to commit.

31The rest of the events in Nadab's reign
and everything he did are recorded in *The
Book of the History of the Kings of Israel*.

Baasha's Reign in Israel (15:32–16:7)

32There was constant war between King
Asa of Judah and King Baasha of Israel. 33Ba-
asha son of Ahijah began to rule over all
Israel in the third year of King Asa's reign
in Judah. Baasha reigned in Tirzah twenty-
four years. 34But he did what was evil in
the LORD's sight and followed the example
of Jeroboam, continuing the sins that Jeroboam had led Israel to commit.

16 This message from the LORD was delivered to King Baasha by the prophet
Jehu son of Hanani: 2"I lifted you out of the
dust to make you ruler of my people Israel,
but you have followed the evil example of
Jeroboam. You have provoked my anger by
causing my people Israel to sin. 3So now I
will destroy you and your family, just as I destroyed the descendants of Jeroboam son
of Nebat. 4The members of Baasha's family who die in the city will be eaten by dogs,
and those who die in the field will be eaten
by vultures."

5The rest of the events in Baasha's reign
and the extent of his power are recorded
in *The Book of the History of the Kings of
Israel*. 6When Baasha died, he was buried
in Tirzah. Then his son Elah became the
next king.

7The message from the LORD against
Baasha and his family came through the
prophet Jehu son of Hanani. It was delivered because Baasha had done what was
evil in the LORD's sight (just as the family
of Jeroboam had done), and also because
Baasha had destroyed the family of Jeroboam. The LORD's anger was provoked by
Baasha's sins.

Elah's Reign in Israel (16:8-14)

8Elah son of Baasha began to rule over Israel in the twenty-sixth year of King Asa's
reign in Judah. He reigned in the city of Tirzah for two years.

9Then Zimri, who commanded half of
the royal chariots, made plans to kill him.
One day in Tirzah, Elah was getting drunk
at the home of Arza, the supervisor of the

15:23-24 //2 Chr 16:11–17:1
15:25 1 Kgs 14:20
15:26 1 Kgs 12:28-33; 13:33; 14:16
15:27 Josh 19:44; 21:23-24
15:29 1 Kgs 14:9-16
15:31 1 Kgs 14:19
15:32 2 Chr 15:16
16:1 1 Kgs 16:7; 2 Chr 19:2; 20:34
16:2 1 Sam 2:8; 1 Kgs 14:7-9
16:3 1 Kgs 14:10; 15:29; 21:21
16:4 1 Kgs 14:11
16:7 1 Kgs 16:1
16:9 2 Kgs 9:30-33

15:23 *feet became diseased:* The nature of *Asa's* malady is uncertain; the Talmud conjectures that it was gout. During his severe illness, Asa depended only on his physicians rather than seeking the Lord's help (2 Chr 16:12).

15:25-31 The writer of 1 Kings presents Nadab's biography following the standard format (see note on 15:1-8).

15:27-29 *Baasha . . . assassinated . . . Nadab* and *slaughtered all the descendants of . . . Jeroboam*, thus terminating Israel's first dynasty. Baasha's father was named *Ahijah*, who is not to be confused with the prophet who predicted the demise of Jeroboam's dynasty (11:29-39). Baasha's coup d'etat was the first of several in Israel's history (e.g., 16:9-10).

15:30-31 *Jeroboam had provoked* the Lord's condemnation and judgment. His sins were perpetuated by his son Nadab, and Baasha's accession inaugurated a new dynasty that further weakened Israel's spiritual condition (15:34).

15:32-34 *Baasha* established his capital at *Tirzah*, the royal retreat of earlier kings (14:17).

16:1 Like his father *Hanani*, whom Asa had imprisoned (2 Chr 16:10), *Jehu* was a prophet. Also like his father, Jehu would fearlessly deliver the Lord's message anywhere, even if it meant confronting the king.

16:2-4 The Lord charged Baasha with being a murderer (16:7) and with following Jeroboam's idolatry. Because he perpetuated Jeroboam's *evil example*, Baasha and his family would suffer the same consequences (see 14:11).

16:5-7 The ministry of Jehu the prophet apparently covered both Israel and Judah, for he also wrote a history of events in Jehoshaphat's reign that was included in ***The Book of the History of the Kings of Israel*** (cp. 2 Chr 20:34).

16:9-10 Elah's drunkenness in *Tirzah* while his army risked their lives at the

16:11
1 Kgs 15:29

16:13
Deut 32:21
1 Kgs 15:30

16:14
1 Kgs 16:4-7, 20, 28, 30

16:18
1 Sam 31:4-5
2 Sam 17:23

16:19
1 Kgs 12:28

16:20
1 Kgs 16:14, 27

palace. [10]Zimri walked in and struck him down and killed him. This happened in the twenty-seventh year of King Asa's reign in Judah. Then Zimri became the next king.

[11]Zimri immediately killed the entire royal family of Baasha, leaving him not even a single male child. He even destroyed distant relatives and friends. [12]So Zimri destroyed the dynasty of Baasha as the LORD had promised through the prophet Jehu. [13]This happened because of all the sins Baasha and his son Elah had committed, and because of the sins they led Israel to commit. They provoked the anger of the LORD, the God of Israel, with their worthless idols.

[14]The rest of the events in Elah's reign and everything he did are recorded in *The Book of the History of the Kings of Israel.*

3. THE ERA OF ISRAEL'S THIRD DYNASTY (16:15–22:53)

Zimri's Reign in Israel (16:15-20)

[15]Zimri began to rule over Israel in the twenty-seventh year of King Asa's reign in Judah, but his reign in Tirzah lasted only seven days. The army of Israel was then attacking the Philistine town of Gibbethon. [16]When they heard that Zimri had committed treason and had assassinated the king, that very day they chose Omri, commander of the army, as the new king of Israel. [17]So Omri led the entire army of Israel up from Gibbethon to attack Tirzah, Israel's capital. [18]When Zimri saw that the city had been taken, he went into the citadel of the palace and burned it down over himself and died in the flames. [19]For he, too, had done what was evil in the LORD's sight. He followed the example of Jeroboam in all the sins he had committed and led Israel to commit.

[20]The rest of the events in Zimri's reign and his conspiracy are recorded in *The Book of the History of the Kings of Israel.*

Omri's Reign in Israel (16:21-28)

[21]But now the people of Israel were split into two factions. Half the people tried to make Tibni son of Ginath their king, while the other half supported Omri. [22]But Omri's supporters defeated the supporters of Tibni. So Tibni was killed, and Omri became the next king.

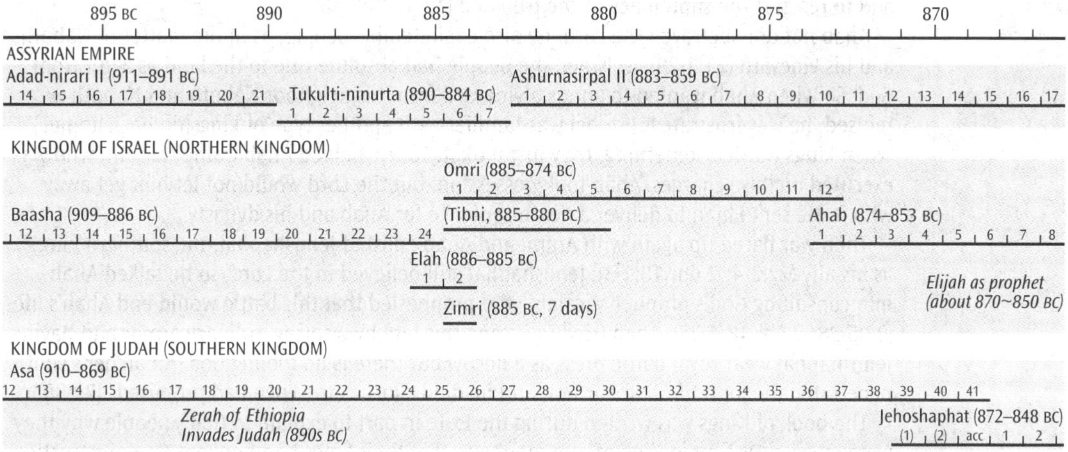

▲ **Israel and Judah, 898–866 BC (16:8–21:29).** ELAH's reign in Israel began in the twenty-sixth year of King ASA's reign in Judah (16:8)—as counted by the scribes of the northern kingdom, who began counting in the year of accession; Asa's years are shown here as counted by the scribes of Judah, who began numbering in the year following accession (see "Chronology: Israel's Monarchy," p. 562). • ZIMRI and TIBNI received no official regnal years for their reigns—Zimri because his reign was only seven days, Tibni because his reign rivaled that of OMRI. • ELIJAH AS PROPHET: See 17:1–19:21. • ZERAH OF ETHIOPIA: See 2 Chr 14:9-13. • JEHOSHAPHAT's reign in Judah began as a co-regency with his father, ASA, during AHAB's fourth year (see 22:41); his actual accession was about two years later when Asa died.

Philistine-controlled city of Gibbethon (16:15) displayed his debased character; he was even less fit to reign than his father, Baasha (see 16:13).

16:11-12 Zimri's execution of all the ***family . . . relatives and friends . . . of Baasha*** was swift and merciless. While ***Zimri*** carried out the Lord's sentence against the ***dynasty of Baasha,*** he doubtless did so for selfish reasons: to keep them from taking revenge on him or using their power or influence to organize their own coup.

16:15-17 Although ***Zimri*** commanded half of the royal chariots (16:9), he was in ***Tirzah*** rather than with the ***army . . . attacking . . . Gibbethon.*** He apparently did not have the respect of the armed forces; they saw his acts as ***treason*** and ***chose*** their commander ***Omri*** as ***the new king of Israel.***

16:18-19 ***burned it down over himself:*** Zimri's cowardice is evident in his suicide in the face of capture.

16:21-22 ***Tibni*** is mentioned only here, and ***Ginath*** is unknown. According to the Greek OT, Tibni received help in his failed bid for power from his brother Joram, and both were ***killed*** in the confrontation with ***Omri.***

[23]Omri began to rule over Israel in the thirty-first year of King Asa's reign in Judah. He reigned twelve years in all, six of them in Tirzah. [24]Then Omri bought the hill now known as Samaria from its owner, Shemer, for 150 pounds of silver. He built a city on it and called the city Samaria in honor of Shemer.

[25]But Omri did what was evil in the LORD's sight, even more than any of the kings before him. [26]He followed the example of Jeroboam son of Nebat in all the sins he had committed and led Israel to commit. The people provoked the anger of the LORD, the God of Israel, with their worthless idols.

[27]The rest of the events in Omri's reign, the extent of his power, and everything he did are recorded in *The Book of the History of the Kings of Israel.* [28]When Omri died, he was buried in Samaria. Then his son Ahab became the next king.

Ahab's Reign in Israel (16:29–22:40)
Ahab's Accession

[29]Ahab son of Omri began to rule over Israel in the thirty-eighth year of King Asa's reign in Judah. He reigned in Samaria twenty-two years. [30]But Ahab son of Omri did what was evil in the LORD's sight, even more than any of the kings before him. [31]And as though it were not enough to follow the example of Jeroboam, he married Jezebel, the daughter

16:24 1 Kgs 13:32
16:25 1 Kgs 14:9; Mic 6:16
16:26 1 Kgs 15:30
16:28 2 Chr 18:1
16:30 1 Kgs 14:9
16:31 Deut 7:3-4; 1 Kgs 11:5; 2 Kgs 10:18; 17:16

AHAB (16:29–22:53)

2 Chr 18:1-34; Mic 6:16

Ahab (874–853 BC), Israel's eighth king, inherited the northern kingdom from his powerful father, Omri (16:27-28). Ahab married Jezebel, daughter of king Ethbaal of Sidon (16:29-31). Under her influence, Ahab began worshiping Baal instead of the Lord.

Ahab had several military successes. He achieved victories over the Arameans (ch 20), and in 853 BC he led a coalition of kings against the Assyrian king Shalmaneser III and defeated him at the battle of Qarqar. However, the OT reports little positive news about Ahab, who was a traitor to God. God raised up the prophet Elijah to confront Ahab and Jezebel's prophets and to reassert the supremacy of the true God (17:1; 18:1-46).

Ahab not only betrayed the Lord, he also exploited his people, as in the matter of Naboth and his vineyard (21:1-29). In Israel, the people had absolute title to the land as a gift from God. So when Ahab wanted to annex a vineyard from his neighbor Naboth and Naboth refused, he was frustrated. Jezebel was familiar with another type of kingship back home. When kings wanted something, they just took it. So she helped Ahab frame Naboth, who was executed on false charges. Ahab took possession, but the Lord would not let him get away with it. He sent Elijah to deliver a death sentence for Ahab and his dynasty.

Then war flared up again with Aram, and Ahab enlisted Jehoshaphat, the southern king, as his ally (22:2-4; 2 Chr 18:1-3). Jehoshaphat still believed in the Lord, so he talked Ahab into consulting God's prophet Micaiah, who prophesied that this battle would end Ahab's life (22:5-28; 2 Chr 18:4-27). Ahab tried to escape this fate by wearing ordinary armor and having Jehoshaphat wear royal battle dress as a decoy, but there is no fooling God. An archer's shot penetrated the joint of Ahab's armor, and he died, "just as the LORD had promised" (22:38).

The book of Kings was written during the Exile in part to explain to God's people why they were in exile. One major line of argument was that their kings had not kept God's instructions in Deut 17:14-20. Ahab was a prime example of such a sinful king.

16:23 ***Omri . . . reigned twelve years in all:*** Omri's son Ahab succeeded him in the seventh year of his reign (cp. 16:29), so Omri's twelve-year rule likely includes about four years of co-regency with Ahab.

16:24 ***Omri*** founded the city of ***Samaria*** and relocated the capital there from Tirzah. Samaria was the capital of Israel until its fall in 722 BC. This site provided Israel with a centrally located and militarily defensible ***hill*** in the northern kingdom, and allowed oversight of the trade routes below. Omri enjoyed his new capital for only six years before his death (16:28). • ***for 150 pounds of silver:*** Hebrew *for 2 talents* [68 kilograms] *of silver.*

16:25-26 ***evil:*** As in the transition from the first to the second dynasties (15:33-34), the new dynastic change did not improve Israel's spiritual climate.

16:27-28 ***the extent of his power:*** Although mentioned only briefly in the OT, ***Omri*** was well known to his contemporaries in surrounding lands. According to the Moabite Stone (Mesha Stela), Omri conquered the territory north of the Arnon River in Moab. Assyrian kings affirmed his importance by calling Israel the "House of Omri." If, as was common in the ancient Near East, Omri arranged the marriage of his son Ahab to Jezebel (the daughter of Ethbaal, king of Tyre and Sidon, 16:31), he may have enjoyed further political and commercial recognition.

16:31-33 The spiritual evaluation of ***Ahab*** is the worst yet among the kings of Israel. Later, Ahab's evil behavior was attributed to his being "under the influence of his wife Jezebel" (21:25). Ahab and Jezebel propagated Canaanite worship rites, leading Israel further from the Lord. Added to Jeroboam's false

[f]*ba'al* (1168)
▸1 Kgs 18:19

16:32
2 Kgs 10:21, 26-27

16:33
1 Kgs 21:25
2 Kgs 13:6

16:34
Josh 6:26

17:1
Judg 12:4
1 Kgs 22:14
Luke 4:25
Jas 5:17

of King Ethbaal of the Sidonians, and he
began to bow down in worship of [f]Baal.
32First Ahab built a temple and an altar for
Baal in Samaria. 33Then he set up an Asherah pole. He did more to provoke the anger
of the LORD, the God of Israel, than any of
the other kings of Israel before him.
34It was during his reign that Hiel, a man
from Bethel, rebuilt Jericho. When he laid
its foundations, it cost him the life of his oldest son, Abiram. And when he completed
it and set up its gates, it cost him the life of
his youngest son, Segub. This all happened
according to the message from the LORD
concerning Jericho spoken by Joshua son
of Nun.

Elijah Fed by Ravens

17 Now Elijah, who was from Tishbe in
Gilead, told King Ahab, "As surely as
the LORD, the God of Israel, lives—the God I
serve—there will be no dew or rain during
the next few years until I give the word!"
2Then the LORD said to Elijah, 3"Go to the
east and hide by Kerith Brook, near where
it enters the Jordan River. 4Drink from the
brook and eat what the ravens bring you, for
I have commanded them to bring you food."
5So Elijah did as the LORD told him and
camped beside Kerith Brook, east of the
Jordan. 6The ravens brought him bread and
meat each morning and evening, and he
drank from the brook. 7But after a while

JEZEBEL (16:31–21:28)

2 Kgs 9:1-37
Rev 2:20

Jezebel, daughter of Ethbaal, king of Sidon (16:31), married King Ahab of Israel, probably to confirm a political alliance between their countries. Jezebel promoted Baal worship and demanded absolute rights for the monarchy.

Jezebel influenced Ahab into establishing Baal worship in Samaria and setting up an Asherah pole (16:30-33). She tried to exterminate God's prophets (18:4) and supported large groups of Baal's prophets in the royal palace (16:19).

Elijah's confrontation with Jezebel and Ahab culminated on Mount Carmel (18:19-40), where Elijah challenged Israel to follow the true God. The Israelites worshiped God and helped Elijah slaughter the false prophets. When Jezebel heard this, she threatened Elijah, and he fled (19:1-2).

Later, Jezebel advised her husband about how to steal Naboth's vineyard. When Naboth wouldn't sell it, Jezebel coldly devised a plan to falsely convict Naboth of cursing God and the king, and he was executed. Ahab seized the vineyard, but God sent Elijah to pronounce judgment on Jezebel and Ahab (21:20-24). Ahab soon died (ch 22), but Jezebel survived through her son Ahaziah's reign. She was later executed when Jehu exterminated the ruling family, and God's sentence against her was fulfilled (2 Kgs 9:30-37).

Jezebel's corrupt influence spread to the southern kingdom of Judah when her daughter Athaliah married Jehoram, King Jehoshaphat's son (see 2 Kgs 8:18, 26-27).

In Rev 2:20, Jezebel's name is used to label a prophetess who seduced the Christians of Thyatira to commit sexual sins and eat things sacrificed to idols. Her name is still used to describe an evil, plotting woman.

worship system, these sins eventually spelled disaster for Israel.

16:34 Despite Joshua's curse against *Jericho* (Josh 6:26-27), the site was occasionally and temporarily occupied prior to being rebuilt by *Hiel* (see Judg 3:13; 2 Sam 10:5; 1 Chr 19:5), as archaeological excavations confirm. Hiel's efforts signify the spiritual defection of Israel. • ***When he laid its foundation . . . Segub:*** An ancient Hebrew scribal tradition reads *He killed his oldest son when he laid its foundations, and he killed his youngest son when he set up its gates.* The Targum (an interpretive Aramaic translation for Jews who did not know Hebrew after the Exile) suggests that Hiel sacrificed his sons as foundation offerings according to pagan practices; others understand the deaths to be from disease or accident. The sentence might be a Hebrew *merism* (using boundaries to indicate everything in between), which would imply that all of Hiel's sons died.

17:1–19:21 The ministry of the prophet Elijah was intimately connected to his own spiritual journey. Elijah confronted Israel's flirtation with the Canaanite storm-god, Baal. As the struggle ensued, Elijah learned of God's power and provision in contrast to Baal's impotence, as demonstrated during Elijah's contest with the prophets of Baal on Mount Carmel (18:1-46). Elijah's subsequent flight from Jezebel led to God's renewal of his prophetic commission at Mount Sinai (19:1-18). Elijah's commission was completed by his successor, Elisha (19:19-21).

17:1 *Elijah* was God's prophet to the northern kingdom during the reigns of the third-dynasty kings *Ahab* (874–853 BC) and Ahaziah (853–852 BC) and into that of Joram (852–841 BC). • Elijah showed his commitment to ***the LORD*** by declaring that he served the living ***God of Israel.*** • Elijah withheld the ***dew*** and ***rain*** as a direct affront to Baal, who supposedly controlled these natural forces. Their absence until God led Elijah to ***give the word*** initiated the contest with Baal that would reach a climax on Mount Carmel (ch 18).

17:2-7 *Kerith Brook* provided a haven for *Elijah* during the divinely instituted drought (see 18:10). The supply of food and water assured Elijah of God's protection. • When Elijah's source of water ***dried up,*** a change of location was necessary.

the brook dried up, for there was no rainfall
anywhere in the land.

The Widow at Zarephath

8Then the LORD said to Elijah, 9"Go and live
in the village of Zarephath, near the city of
Sidon. I have instructed a widow there to
feed you."
10So he went to Zarephath. As he arrived
at the gates of the village, he saw a widow
gathering sticks, and he asked her, "Would
you please bring me a little water in a cup?"
11As she was going to get it, he called to her,
"Bring me a bite of bread, too."
12But she said, "I swear by the LORD your
God that I don't have a single piece of bread
in the house. And I have only a handful of
flour left in the jar and a little cooking oil in
the bottom of the jug. I was just gathering a
few sticks to cook this last meal, and then
my son and I will die."
13But Elijah said to her, "Don't be afraid!
Go ahead and do just what you've said, but
make a little bread for me first. Then use
what's left to prepare a meal for yourself
and your son. 14For this is what the LORD,
the God of Israel, says: There will always be
flour and olive oil left in your containers until the time when the LORD sends rain and
the crops grow again!"
15So she did as Elijah said, and she and
Elijah and her family continued to eat for
many days. 16There was always enough
flour and olive oil left in the containers, just
as the LORD had promised through Elijah.
17Some time later the woman's son became sick. He grew worse and worse, and
finally he died. 18Then she said to Elijah,
"O man of God, what have you done to me?
Have you come here to point out my sins
and kill my son?"
19But Elijah replied, "Give me your son."
And he took the child's body from her arms,
carried him up the stairs to the room where
he was staying, and laid the body on his bed.
20Then Elijah cried out to the LORD, "O LORD
my God, why have you brought tragedy to
this widow who has opened her home to me,
causing her son to die?"
21And he stretched himself out over the
child three times and cried out to the LORD,
"O LORD my God, please let this child's life
return to him." 22The LORD heard Elijah's
prayer, and the life of the child returned,
and he revived! 23Then Elijah brought him
down from the upper room and gave him
to his mother. "Look!" he said. "Your son is
alive!"
24Then the woman told Elijah, "Now I
know for sure that you are a man of God, and
that the LORD truly speaks through you."

17:9 Obad 1:20; Luke 4:26
17:10 Gen 24:17; John 4:7
17:12 2 Kgs 4:2-7
17:21 2 Kgs 4:34; Acts 20:10-12
17:23 Heb 11:35
17:24 John 2:11; 3:1-2; 16:30

17:9-16 Elijah's faith was tested further. At Kerith Brook, God had supplied his needs directly. With these supplies cut off, Elijah now had to depend on a foreign woman's response to a divine test. The account details the setting (17:8-10a), Elijah's test for the widow (17:10b-14), the woman's compliance, and God's reward (17:15-16).

17:9-11 *Zarephath* was in Phoenician territory about seven miles south of *Sidon,* away from Ahab's jurisdiction. Ironically, God provided *Elijah* a place of refuge in Jezebel's homeland, which was associated with worship of Baal. • *So he went:* Elijah again (see 17:5) obeyed the Lord's command. Obedience (1 Sam 15:22; Ps 40:1-6; Isa 1:10-20), trust (Ps 37:3; Prov 3:5-6), and faithfulness (Ps 18:25; 31:25; Rev 2:10) are foundational attributes for successful spiritual service. • God's ongoing provision for Elijah and the *widow* of Zarephath demonstrated God's concern for all people who put him first. • *water . . . bread:* Elijah asked for the basic staples of life, but these were in scarce supply as the drought spread into Phoenician territory.

17:12 *by the LORD your God* (literally *as surely as the LORD your God lives*): The wording reflects Elijah's oath and pronouncement to Ahab (17:1). The Gentile woman's oath does not necessarily claim that the Lord is her god, but it does affirm to Elijah that what she says is the truth.

17:13-14 Despite the woman's dwindling supplies (17:12), ***Elijah*** asked her to serve him before herself and her son. Like the poor widow who gave two small coins (Luke 21:1-4), this woman was asked to give all that she had to the Lord's prophet. True faithfulness means placing God's Kingdom ahead of personal concerns (Matt 6:33).

17:15-16 *She did as Elijah said*, and God rewarded her act of faith. The fresh supply of the widow's daily necessities reminded her of God's faithfulness and goodness (Lam 3:22-24; Phil 4:19).

17:17-24 This narrative begins with the woman's doubts about Elijah (17:17-18) and ends with her acknowledging the authority of God's word as spoken by Elijah (17:24). Ironically, this Gentile widow affirmed God's miraculous power when God's own people, Israel, had forgotten his mighty works.

17:17 *he died:* All attempts to explain away the subsequent miracle fly in the face of the plain statement.

17:18 *my sins:* The widow held to the common idea that suffering and misfortune are always the result of personal sin (see Job 4:7; Luke 13:1-4; John 9:1-3).

17:19 Following ancient Near Eastern custom, Elijah's quarters were probably situated in a separate *room* accessed by an outside stairway. This arrangement maintained the woman's reputation and offered Elijah a measure of privacy.

17:20 *why have you brought tragedy:* Elijah plaintively expressed to God the fear that his presence caused the child's death.

17:21 While it is unclear what life-giving power Elijah was trying to convey by his physical contact with the deceased boy, it is clear that his confidence was in the Lord. Elisha later performed a similar physical ritual when the Lord restored the dead son of the woman from Shunem (2 Kgs 4:32-37).

17:22-24 The miracle of the child's raising rewarded ***Elijah's*** faith and confirmed the mother's initial confidence in God's prophet. Her testimony may indicate that she put her faith in ***the LORD.*** Jesus cited her as an example of God's concern for non-Israelites and as an indication that God's messenger is often more easily received by others

18:1
Jas 5:17-18
18:2
1 Kgs 16:24
18:3
1 Kgs 18:16
18:12
2 Kgs 2:16
Ezek 3:12, 14
Acts 8:39
18:13
1 Kgs 18:3-4

The Contest on Mount Carmel

18 Later on, in the third year of the
drought, the LORD said to Elijah, "Go
and present yourself to King Ahab. Tell him
that I will soon send rain!" 2So Elijah went to
appear before Ahab.
Meanwhile, the famine had become very
severe in Samaria. 3So Ahab summoned
Obadiah, who was in charge of the palace.
(Obadiah was a devoted follower of the
LORD. 4Once when Jezebel had tried to kill
all the LORD's prophets, Obadiah had hidden 100 of them in two caves. He put fifty
prophets in each cave and supplied them
with food and water.) 5Ahab said to Obadiah,
"We must check every spring and valley
in the land to see if we can find enough
grass to save at least some of my horses and
mules." 6So they divided the land between
them. Ahab went one way by himself, and
Obadiah went another way by himself.
7As Obadiah was walking along, he suddenly saw Elijah coming toward him. Obadiah recognized him at once and bowed low
to the ground before him. "Is it really you,
my lord Elijah?" he asked.
8"Yes, it is," Elijah replied. "Now go and
tell your master, 'Elijah is here.' "
9"Oh, sir," Obadiah protested, "what harm
have I done to you that you are sending me
to my death at the hands of Ahab? 10For I
swear by the LORD your God that the king
has searched every nation and kingdom on
earth from end to end to find you. And each
time he was told, 'Elijah isn't here,' King
Ahab forced the king of that nation to swear
to the truth of his claim. 11And now you say,
'Go and tell your master, "Elijah is here." '
12But as soon as I leave you, the Spirit of
the LORD will carry you away to who knows
where. When Ahab comes and cannot find
you, he will kill me. Yet I have been a true
servant of the LORD all my life. 13Has no
one told you, my lord, about the time when

The Old Testament Prophets (17:1–18:46)

1 Kgs 11:29-39; 13:1-32; 14:1-16; 16:2-4; 19:1-21; 20:35-43; 21:17-28; 22:10-28
2 Kgs 17:13-15
2 Tim 4:2-5
1 Pet 1:10-12
2 Pet 1:19-21

God's prophets played a major role in the OT kingdoms of Israel and Judah. They ministered to people's everyday needs, confronted kings and priests over their apostasy, and performed many miracles. They brought announcements of God's coming plans (11:31-32; 17:1), especially messages of judgment (13:1-2; 20:42; 21:20-23; 22:20-22).

Several examples from 1 Kings serve to illustrate the prophets' role. The faithful prophet Nathan rebuked David regarding his sin with Bathsheba (2 Sam 12:1-12), and later he played a crucial role in counteracting Adonijah's attempt to seize his father David's throne (1:5-49). The prophet Ahijah informed Jeroboam that God intended to divide Solomon's kingdom after his death (11:29-39). Later, God used an unnamed prophet to condemn Jeroboam's apostate religion and the altar at Bethel (13:1-10) and to demonstrate the consequences of disobeying the Lord's commission (13:11-32). Ahijah reappeared, announcing the Lord's judgment against Jeroboam and his heirs (14:1-16). The prophet Jehu announced judgment on King Baasha for continuing in Jeroboam's sin (16:2-4). A large portion of 1 Kings is devoted to the prophet Elijah (17–19; 21:17-28), who was God's primary spokesman during King Ahab's reign (though other prophets were also active during this period; see 20:38-43; 22:17-28).

God related to his OT people through his spokesmen, the prophets. Today, many of the prophet's duties are carried out by those who faithfully proclaim God's word (2 Tim 4:2).

than by his own countrymen (Luke 4:24-26). The Scriptures repeatedly mention God's care of widows as illustrating his care for needy people (Exod 22:21; Deut 10:18; 27:19; Ps 68:5; Isa 1:17; Jas 1:27).

18:2 ***Elijah*** continued to obey the Lord's commands (see 17:5, 10), despite the personal danger of appearing ***before Ahab.***

18:3-6 Due to the severity of the continuing drought, ***Ahab*** and ***Obadiah***, his chief officer (cp. 4:6; 16:9), set out to locate sufficient water and grass for the king's horses. These provisions were crucial for military preparedness. Assyrian king Shalmaneser III wrote that Ahab put some 2,000 horse-drawn chariots into the Battle of Qarqar (853 BC). Solomon had also had many horses and chariots (10:26).

18:4 Obadiah's care for ***100*** of ***the LORD's prophets*** may indicate a group of prophets such as had existed since Samuel's time (1 Sam 10:5-18; 19:20, 24). Such groups met together for study and mutual spiritual encouragement and are mentioned several times (2 Kgs 4:1, 38; 9:1). Elijah and Elisha apparently exercised leadership in some of these groups (2 Kgs 2:3-7, 15; 6:1-7).

18:10 ***every nation and kingdom:*** Ancient Near Eastern protocol called for the extradition of fugitives or runaway slaves, as noted in the famous treaty between Pharaoh Ramses II and the Hittite king Hattusilis (see ANET 200b, 203a). But Elijah had not had to seek asylum with a foreign king. God provided for his safety at Kerith Brook (17:3) and with the widow at Zarephath (17:9).

18:12-15 As a true believer, Obadiah recognized that ***the Spirit of the LORD*** operated within God's prophets (Judg 6:34; Ezek 3:12, 14; 11:1). Obadiah feared that the Lord's Spirit would ***carry*** Elijah ***away*** while he was reporting Elijah's whereabouts to ***Ahab***. The king would then interpret his inability to produce Elijah as a sign that he was hiding Elijah, and he would ***kill*** him.

Jezebel was trying to kill the LORD's prophets? I hid 100 of them in two caves and
supplied them with food and water. 14And
now you say, 'Go and tell your master, "Elijah
is here." ' Sir, if I do that, Ahab will certainly
kill me."
15But Elijah said, "I swear by the LORD
Almighty, in whose presence I stand, that I
will present myself to Ahab this very day."
16So Obadiah went to tell Ahab that Elijah
had come, and Ahab went out to meet Elijah.
17When Ahab saw him, he exclaimed, "So, is
it really you, you troublemaker of Israel?"
18"I have made no trouble for Israel," Elijah replied. "You and your family are the
troublemakers, for you have refused to obey
the commands of the LORD and have worshiped the images of Baal instead. 19Now
summon all Israel to join me at Mount Carmel, along with the 450 [g]prophets of [h]Baal
and the 400 [g]prophets of Asherah who are
supported by Jezebel."
20So Ahab summoned all the people of
Israel and the prophets to Mount Carmel.
21Then Elijah stood in front of them and
said, "How much longer will you waver,
hobbling between two opinions? If the
LORD is God, follow him! But if Baal is God,
then follow him!" But the people were completely silent.

18:17 Josh 7:25
18:18 1 Kgs 9:9; 21:25
18:19 Josh 19:26; [g]*nabi'* (5030) ▸2 Chr 34:22; [h]*ba'al* (1168) ▸1 Kgs 18:40
18:21 Josh 24:15; 2 Kgs 17:41

ELIJAH (17:1–19:21)

1 Kgs 21:1-29
2 Kgs 1:1–2:25; 9:36; 10:10, 17
2 Chr 21:12-15
Mal 4:5-6
Matt 11:14; 16:14; 17:1-13; 27:45-49
Mark 6:15; 8:28; 9:2-13; 15:33-36
Luke 1:17; 4:26; 9:28-36
John 1:19-28
Rom 11:1-6
Jas 5:17

Elijah from Tishbe served as prophet of Israel during the reigns of Ahab and Ahaziah (874–852 BC). His name means "my God is Yahweh," and his ministry involved demonstrating that the Lord is the one true God and calling Israel back to the Lord.

Under Ahab and Jezebel, Israel began worshiping Baal, a Canaanite fertility god of storm and rain, so God sent a drought upon Israel (17:1). Elijah hid until the drought ended, and he was sustained by God. During that time, he lived with a widow in Zarephath, a town in Jezebel's home territory of Sidon. The widow's son died, but Elijah prayed for him and he was revived (17:8-24).

In the third year of drought, Elijah challenged Baal's prophets on Mount Carmel to a contest to demonstrate the identity of the true God (18:1-40). The prophets of Baal called on Baal in vain, becoming frantic to induce him to appear, while Elijah made fun of Baal. When it was Elijah's turn, he poured water over his sacrifice and prayed a simple, powerful prayer. Fire immediately consumed the offering. The people of Israel worshiped the Lord and, at Elijah's direction, killed Baal's prophets. Then Elijah prayed for rain, and the drought ended (18:41-46).

Even with such tremendous displays of God's power, Ahab and Jezebel continued to lead Israel astray. Jezebel was furious that her prophets had been killed (19:1-2). She threatened Elijah, who fled to the desert and asked God to take his life. Instead, an angel nourished him until he reached Mount Sinai. Elijah complained that he was the only remaining prophet of the Lord, and his life was at risk. God encouraged him in a quiet voice and with good news, then recommissioned him for service (19:3-18).

Elijah was single-minded in his devotion to the true God. He had an assistant named Elisha whom he trained well. At the end of Elijah's earthly existence, rather than dying, he was caught up into heaven in a chariot of fire (2 Kgs 2:11-12; cp. Gen 5:21-24). Elisha inherited Elijah's prophetic mantle and continued the task of confronting false worship in Israel (see 2 Kgs 2:1–9:13; 13:14-25).

The OT closes with the expectation that Elijah would return before the day of the Lord (Mal 4:5-6), an expectation that John the Baptist fulfilled, at least in part (see Matt 11:14; 17:10-13; Luke 1:17). Elijah appeared with Moses at Jesus' transfiguration (Matt 17:1-13 // Luke 9:28-36). In Rev 11:3-12, one of the two witnesses is either Elijah himself or is modeled after Elijah. Elijah's life illustrates God's kindness and the effectiveness of prayer (Luke 4:25-26; Rom 11:2-6; Jas 5:17-18).

18:16-18 ***troublemakers:*** Although Elijah announced the onset of the drought (17:1), it was *Ahab* and his *family* who brought God's judgment upon Israel by their violations of the covenant and their sponsorship of Baal worship (see Lev 26:19; Deut 28:15, 23; 2 Chr 7:13; Jer 14:1-7; Amos 4:7-8).

18:19-20 ***Mount Carmel*** lies on a ridge dividing the coastal plain of Palestine. The site was known for Canaanite idol worship; an altar to the Lord had also been built there earlier (18:30). It was a natural location for the contest with *Baal*. Although the Septuagint (Greek translation of the OT) may indicate that the prophets of *Asherah* attended the ensuing contest on *Mount Carmel*, the Hebrew text does not (cp. 18:22).

18:19 ***who are supported by Jezebel:*** Literally *who eat at Jezebel's table.*

18:21 The Hebrew word translated *waver* means "to be lame" or "to limp." *Elijah* compared the people's ***hobbling*** between the worship of ***the LORD*** and of *Baal* to a person who limps awkwardly

18:22 1 Kgs 19:10, 14
18:24 1 Sam 7:8; 1 Kgs 18:38
18:26 Ps 115:4-5; Jer 10:5
18:28 Lev 19:28; Deut 14:1
18:30 1 Kgs 19:10, 14
18:31 Josh 4:1-9; 2 Kgs 17:34
18:32 Col 3:17
18:33 Gen 22:9

22Then Elijah said to them, "I am the only
prophet of the LORD who is left, but Baal has
450 prophets. 23Now bring two bulls. The
prophets of Baal may choose whichever one
they wish and cut it into pieces and lay it on
the wood of their altar, but without setting
fire to it. I will prepare the other bull and lay
it on the wood on the altar, but not set fire to
it. 24Then call on the name of your god, and
I will call on the name of the LORD. The god
who answers by setting fire to the wood is
the true God!" And all the people agreed.
25Then Elijah said to the prophets of Baal,
"You go first, for there are many of you.
Choose one of the bulls, and prepare it and
call on the name of your god. But do not set
fire to the wood."
26So they prepared one of the bulls and
placed it on the altar. Then they called on the
name of Baal from morning until noontime,
shouting, "O Baal, answer us!" But there was
no reply of any kind. Then they danced, hobbling around the altar they had made.
27About noontime Elijah began mocking them. "You'll have to shout louder," he
scoffed, "for surely he is a god! Perhaps he
is daydreaming, or is relieving himself. Or
maybe he is away on a trip, or is asleep and
needs to be wakened!"
28So they shouted louder, and following
their normal custom, they cut themselves
with knives and swords until the blood
gushed out. 29They raved all afternoon until the time of the evening sacrifice, but still
there was no sound, no reply, no response.
30Then Elijah called to the people, "Come
over here!" They all crowded around him as
he repaired the altar of the LORD that had
been torn down. 31He took twelve stones,
one to represent each of the tribes of Israel,
32and he used the stones to rebuild the altar in the name of the LORD. Then he dug
a trench around the altar large enough to
hold about three gallons. 33He piled wood
on the altar, cut the bull into pieces, and laid
the pieces on the wood.

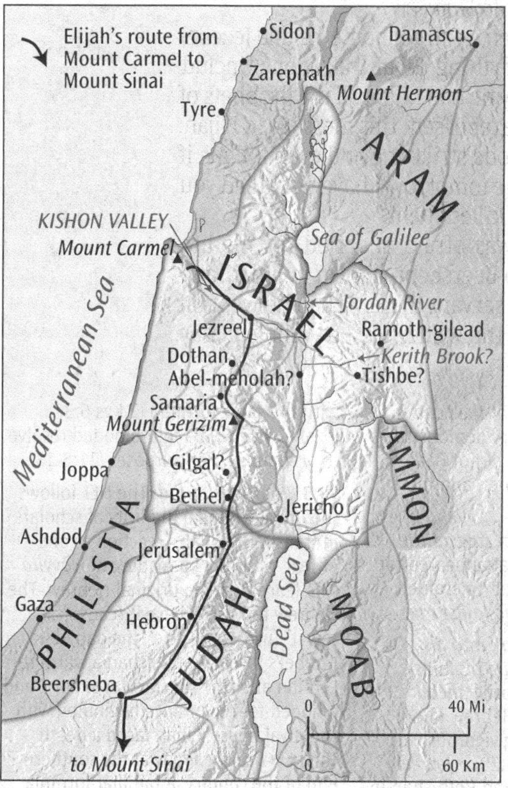

◀ **Elijah the Prophet, about 870 BC** (17:1–19:21). After foretelling of a severe drought throughout the land, Elijah was sent by the Lord to KERITH BROOK, where he was fed by ravens. Later the Lord told Elijah to go live in the Gentile town of ZAREPHATH in the territory of SIDON. After the contest on MOUNT CARMEL between the Lord and Baal, the people killed the prophets of Baal in the KISHON VALLEY near the foot of the mountain. Then Elijah ran ahead of Ahab's chariot all the way to JEZREEL. From there Elijah fled to MOUNT SINAI, leaving his servant in BEERSHEBA and stopping to rest in the wilderness along the way.

from one foot to the other. Elijah may have also been referring to the ritual dance performed by Baal's prophets as they attempted to gain the storm-god's attention (18:26).

18:22 *the only prophet of the LORD:* Obadiah had previously hidden two groups of fifty prophets to protect them from Jezebel's purge (18:4, 13). However, Elijah's public stature must have left him feeling alone in his struggle against false religion (see 19:10, 14); certainly, he did stand alone in confronting the 450 prophets of Baal.

18:23-24 The Lord's presence was attested by *fire* (Exod 9:23; 19:18; 40:38; Deut 4:24; 2 Chr 7:1; Isa 66:15; Amos 7:4), which could have been lightning (cp. Ps 18:12-13; Ezek 1:13-14; Zech 9:14). The contest would demonstrate whether the Canaanite storm-god Baal or the God of Israel was the *true God;* only the true God could *set fire* to *the wood* (cp. Lev 9:24).

18:27 *is relieving himself:* Or *is busy somewhere else,* or *is engaged in business.* Elijah's sarcastic taunts mocked the personification of the gods as having human needs. Egyptian priests awakened their god, then fed, washed, and dressed the idol in fresh clothing. They even put rouge on the idol's face and placed the proper emblem of royalty on it.

18:28-29 *shouted . . . cut themselves . . . raved:* The prophets of Baal demonstrated ecstatic behavior common in ancient pagan religions, but their efforts produced *no response.* Of course, there is only one true God (Deut 4:35; 6:4; Isa 44:8); all other hopes are doomed to failure (Isa 45:22).

18:31-32 The *twelve stones* that Elijah used *to rebuild the altar in the name of the LORD* should have reminded the people that God had a prior claim as the redeemer of all Israel (cp. Josh 4:1-11; see Isa 41:14; 49:26).

18:31 *each of the tribes of Israel:* Literally *each of the tribes of the sons of Jacob to whom the LORD had said, "Your name will be Israel."*

18:32 *three gallons:* Hebrew *2 seahs* [12 liters] *of seed.*

18:33-35 Elijah avoided any hint of deception by dousing the *offering and*

Then he said, "Fill four large jars with water, and pour the water over the offering and the wood."

34After they had done this, he said, "Do the same thing again!" And when they were finished, he said, "Now do it a third time!" So they did as he said, 35and the water ran around the altar and even filled the trench.

36At the usual time for offering the evening sacrifice, Elijah the prophet walked up to the altar and prayed, "O LORD, God of Abraham, Isaac, and Jacob, prove today that you are God in Israel and that I am your servant. Prove that I have done all this at your command. 37O LORD, answer me! Answer me so these people will know that you, O LORD, are God and that you have brought them back to yourself."

38Immediately the fire of the LORD flashed down from heaven and burned up the young bull, the wood, the stones, and the dust. It even licked up all the water in the trench! 39And when all the people saw it, they fell face down on the ground and cried out, "The LORD—he is God! Yes, the LORD is God!"

40Then Elijah commanded, "Seize all the prophets of [i]Baal. Don't let a single one escape!" So the people seized them all, and Elijah took them down to the Kishon Valley and killed them there.

Elijah Prays for Rain

41Then Elijah said to Ahab, "Go get something to eat and drink, for I hear a mighty rainstorm coming!"

42So Ahab went to eat and drink. But Elijah climbed to the top of Mount Carmel and bowed low to the ground and prayed with his face between his knees.

43Then he said to his servant, "Go and look out toward the sea."

The servant went and looked, then returned to Elijah and said, "I didn't see anything."

Seven times Elijah told him to go and look. 44Finally the seventh time, his servant told him, "I saw a little cloud about the size of a man's hand rising from the sea."

Then Elijah shouted, "Hurry to Ahab and tell him, 'Climb into your chariot and go back home. If you don't hurry, the rain will stop you!' "

45And soon the sky was black with clouds. A heavy wind brought a terrific rainstorm, and Ahab left quickly for Jezreel. 46Then the LORD gave special strength to Elijah. He tucked his cloak into his belt and ran ahead of Ahab's chariot all the way to the entrance of Jezreel.

Elijah Flees to Sinai

19 When Ahab got home, he told Jezebel everything Elijah had done, including the way he had killed all the prophets of Baal. 2So Jezebel sent this message to Elijah: "May the gods strike me and even kill me if by this time tomorrow I have not killed you just as you killed them."

3Elijah was afraid and fled for his life. He went to Beersheba, a town in Judah, and he left his servant there. 4Then he went on alone into the wilderness, traveling all day.

18:36 Exod 3:6; 4:5 Num 16:28-32
18:38 Gen 15:17 Lev 9:24; 10:2 2 Kgs 1:12 Job 1:16
18:40 Deut 13:5; 18:20 2 Kgs 10:24 [i]*ba'al* (1168) › 2 Kgs 10:18
18:42 Jas 5:18
18:46 2 Kgs 4:29
19:2 2 Kgs 6:31
19:3 Gen 21:31
19:4 Exod 16:3 Jer 20:14-18 Jon 4:3, 8

the wood with great quantities of water, perhaps taken from the nearby Mediterranean Sea or Kishon River.

18:36 At the appointed time of ***sacrifice*** to the Lord, Elijah prayed. He did not imitate the ecstatic behavior of the prophets of Baal but simply prayed to God in light of his promises to ***Abraham, Isaac, and Jacob*** (Gen 50:24; Exod 3:6, 15; 4:5; Num 32:11; Deut 9:27). • ***and Jacob:*** Literally *and Israel.* The names "Jacob" and "Israel" are often interchanged throughout the OT, referring sometimes to the individual patriarch and sometimes to the nation (see Gen 32:28).

18:37 The call-***answer*** motif appears frequently in the OT, often depicting the petitioner's intimate relationship to the Lord (Job 14:15; Ps 4:1; 91:15; 102:2; Isa 65:24; Jer 33:3).

18:38-39 Whether by lightning-strike or more supernatural means, the Lord sent ***fire*** to consume everything, including ***all the water in the trench.*** This was convincing proof that ***the LORD is God.*** The continuing story demonstrates conclusively that the Lord, not Baal, has control over fire, water, and the weather.

18:41-45 ***The servant . . . saw a little cloud*** on the horizon that appeared to be the size of a hand. Yet it heralded the approach of ***a terrific rainstorm.***

18:46 ***He tucked his cloak into his belt*** (literally *He bound up his loins*) so he could run more easily ***ahead of Ahab's chariot.*** The Hebrew idiom refers to doing anything vigorously or enthusiastically (2 Kgs 4:29). • ***Jezreel*** was between Megiddo and Beth-shan in the southeastern portion of the Valley of Jezreel, about seventeen miles from Mount Carmel.

19:2 Speaking a curse, ***Jezebel*** reinforced her threat to ***kill . . . Elijah*** within a day. Solomon had made a similar declaration regarding his half-brother Adonijah (2:23), and the king of Aram later issued an edict against Elisha with the same formula (2 Kgs 6:31). Jezebel acted with cold-blooded resolve to accomplish her purposes (21:5-15).

19:3 ***Elijah was afraid:*** The NLT follows the Greek OT and a majority of scholars in translating Elijah's reaction as one of fear, proposing a reading of *wayyira'* ("he feared") in the original Hebrew. The Hebrew text as we have it reads, "he saw it" (*wayyare'*)—i.e., the danger in Jezebel's threat. Rather than a warm reception after the spectacular victory, and a hoped-for repentance beginning with the royal house, Elijah faced a death threat. • ***Beersheba*** lay at the southern end of the country. A familiar formula described the limits of the land as "from Dan to Beersheba" (4:25; 2 Sam 24:2).

19:4 Though technically a shrub, the ***broom tree*** can reach a height of ten feet. Its leaves are small, but it provides adequate shade for a weary traveler in ***the wilderness.*** Like Jonah (Jon 4:3), Elijah had successfully carried out his commission, but he felt a sense of defeat with

19:8
Exod 3:1; 4:27; 24:18; 34:28
Deut 9:9
Matt 4:2

19:10
*Rom 11:2-4

19:11
Exod 19:16, 19-20; 24:12
Ezek 1:4

19:12
Job 4:16; 26:14

19:13
Exod 3:6

19:15
2 Kgs 8:7-15

19:16
2 Kgs 2:9, 15; 9:1
[j]*mashakh* (4886)
‣1 Chr 29:22

19:17
2 Kgs 8:12, 29; 9:14; 13:3

19:18
Hos 13:2
*Rom 11:4

He sat down under a solitary broom tree
and prayed that he might die. "I have had
enough, LORD," he said. "Take my life, for I
am no better than my ancestors who have
already died."
5Then he lay down and slept under the
broom tree. But as he was sleeping, an angel
touched him and told him, "Get up and eat!"
6He looked around and there beside his
head was some bread baked on hot stones
and a jar of water! So he ate and drank and
lay down again.
7Then the angel of the LORD came again
and touched him and said, "Get up and eat
some more, or the journey ahead will be too
much for you."
8So he got up and ate and drank, and the
food gave him enough strength to travel
forty days and forty nights to Mount Sinai,
the mountain of God. 9There he came to a
cave, where he spent the night.

The LORD Speaks to Elijah

But the LORD said to him, "What are you doing here, Elijah?"
10Elijah replied, "I have zealously served
the LORD God Almighty. But the people of
Israel have broken their covenant with you,
torn down your altars, and killed every one
of your prophets. I am the only one left, and
now they are trying to kill me, too."
11"Go out and stand before me on the
mountain," the LORD told him. And as Elijah stood there, the LORD passed by, and a
mighty windstorm hit the mountain. It was
such a terrible blast that the rocks were
torn loose, but the LORD was not in the wind.
After the wind there was an earthquake, but
the LORD was not in the earthquake. 12And
after the earthquake there was a fire, but
the LORD was not in the fire. And after the
fire there was the sound of a gentle whisper.
13When Elijah heard it, he wrapped his face
in his cloak and went out and stood at the
entrance of the cave.
And a voice said, "What are you doing
here, Elijah?"
14He replied again, "I have zealously
served the LORD God Almighty. But the
people of Israel have broken their covenant
with you, torn down your altars, and killed
every one of your prophets. I am the only
one left, and now they are trying to kill me,
too."
15Then the LORD told him, "Go back the
same way you came, and travel to the wilderness of Damascus. When you arrive there,
anoint Hazael to be king of Aram. 16Then
[j]anoint Jehu grandson of Nimshi to be king
of Israel, and [j]anoint Elisha son of Shaphat
from the town of Abel-meholah to replace
you as my prophet. 17Anyone who escapes
from Hazael will be killed by Jehu, and
those who escape Jehu will be killed by Elisha! 18Yet I will preserve 7,000 others in
Israel who have never bowed down to Baal
or kissed him!"

the results. • ***no better:*** God's refugee prophet felt that he had accomplished little and would be better off dead.

19:5-7 ***The angel of the LORD*** provided Elijah with precisely what he needed at the moment (17:2-6, 10-12). God often sent an angel to minister to one of his servants (Ps 34:7; Heb 1:14).

19:8 Elijah's determination to go to ***Mount Sinai*** (Hebrew *to Horeb,* another name for Sinai) took him on a journey of approximately 200 miles. The trip would not have required ***forty days and forty nights***, so Elijah may have set a pace that was symbolic of Israel's past. Moses spent forty days on Mount Sinai and Israel subsequently wandered in the wilderness for forty years (Num 14:33-34; Deut 1:2-3). Forty sometimes represented a period of full testing (Gen 7:4; Ps 95:10; Jon 3:4; Matt 4:1-2).

19:9-10 ***a cave*** (literally *the cave*): Some have suggested that Elijah came to the very place where God appeared to Moses (Exod 33:21-23). • ***What are you doing here, Elijah?*** The Lord's question may have a double implication: Why had Elijah come, and did he understand the significance of the spot where he stood? Elijah replied to the former part of the question. Elijah had boldly announced that he was alone in his stand for the Lord (18:22); now, that feeling turned to self-pity.

19:11-12 The powerful physical phenomena that sometimes signal God's presence (Exod 3:2; 19:18; Ps 68:7-8; 114:4; Heb 3:6-7) did not herald God's approach on this occasion. Instead, Elijah sensed God's presence when he heard ***the sound of a gentle whisper.***

19:13-14 ***What are you doing here?*** The Lord repeats his question (see 19:9), and Elijah gives exactly the same response as earlier. Elijah's answer gives no indication that he understood how God was working through all that had happened. Paul makes reference to this interchange in Rom 11:3-4.

19:15-17 ***Go back . . . and travel:*** In loving patience, God renewed his prophet's commission (cp. John 21:15-19). God directed Elijah to retrace his steps back to the place where he had strayed from God's mission; from there he could move forward. • ***Hazael*** and ***Jehu*** both became instruments of God's judgment (2 Kgs 8:7-15; 9:14-37). • ***grandson of Nimshi:*** Hebrew *descendant of Nimshi;* cp. 2 Kgs 9:2, 14, where Jehu is listed as "son of Jehoshaphat, son of Nimshi." • ***Elisha***, Elijah's successor, would bring spiritual discernment and the Lord's further judgment to Israel (2 Kgs 3:10-19; 8:7-15; 9:1–10:31; 13:3, 15-19). • ***Abel-meholah*** was located south of Beth-shan, where the Valley of Jezreel and the Jordan Valley come together (see 4:12; Judg 7:22).

19:18 The Lord corrected Elijah's thinking; the prophet was not alone. Earlier he had forgotten the 100 prophets protected by Obadiah (18:4, 13). Now he learned that there were ***7,000 others*** who remained faithful to the Lord.
• ***bowed down . . . or kissed him:*** These common forms of submission in the ancient Near East (2 Kgs 21:3; Isa 46:6; 60:14; Hos 13:2) are often mentioned in the annals of victorious kings or in the ancient epics. Ashurbanipal reported that on his sixth campaign, an Elamite king kissed his royal feet and tidied up the ground with his beard. In the Mesopotamian creation epic (*Enuma Elish,* V 86), even the great gods bowed down and kissed the feet of Marduk, the victorious head of the pantheon.

The Call of Elisha

[19]So Elijah went and found Elisha son of Shaphat plowing a field. There were twelve teams of oxen in the field, and Elisha was plowing with the twelfth team. Elijah went over to him and threw his cloak across his shoulders and then walked away. [20]Elisha left the oxen standing there, ran after Elijah, and said to him, "First let me go and kiss my father and mother good-bye, and then I will go with you!"

Elijah replied, "Go on back, but think about what I have done to you."

[21]So Elisha returned to his oxen and slaughtered them. He used the wood from the plow to build a fire to roast their flesh. He passed around the meat to the townspeople, and they all ate. Then he went with Elijah as his [k]assistant.

Ben-Hadad Attacks Samaria

20 About that time King Ben-hadad of Aram mobilized his army, supported by the chariots and horses of thirty-two allied kings. They went to besiege Samaria, the capital of Israel, and launched attacks against it. [2]Ben-hadad sent messengers into the city to relay this message to King Ahab of Israel: "This is what Ben-hadad says: [3]'Your silver and gold are mine, and so are your wives and the best of your children!' "

[4]"All right, my lord the king," Israel's king replied. "All that I have is yours!"

[5]Soon Ben-hadad's messengers returned again and said, "This is what Ben-hadad says: 'I have already demanded that you give me your silver, gold, wives, and children. [6]But about this time tomorrow I will send my officials to search your palace and the homes of your people. They will take away everything you consider valuable!' "

[7]Then Ahab summoned all the elders of the land and said to them, "Look how this man is stirring up trouble! I already agreed with his demand that I give him my wives and children and silver and gold."

[8]"Don't give in to any more demands," all the elders and the people advised.

[9]So Ahab told the messengers from Ben-hadad, "Say this to my lord the king: 'I will give you everything you asked for the first time, but I cannot accept this last demand of yours.' " So the messengers returned to Ben-hadad with that response.

[10]Then Ben-hadad sent this message to Ahab: "May the gods strike me and even kill me if there remains enough dust from Samaria to provide even a handful for each of my soldiers."

[11]The king of Israel sent back this answer: "A warrior putting on his sword for battle should not boast like a warrior who has already won."

[12]Ahab's reply reached Ben-hadad and the other kings as they were drinking in their tents. "Prepare to attack!" Ben-hadad commanded his officers. So they prepared to attack the city.

Ahab's Victory over Ben-Hadad

[13]Then a certain prophet came to see King Ahab of Israel and told him, "This is what

19:19 2 Kgs 2:8, 13-14
19:21 [k]*sharath* (8334) ‣Ps 103:21
20:1 1 Kgs 15:18; 2 Kgs 6:24
20:2 2 Chr 16:2
20:7 2 Kgs 5:7
20:10 1 Kgs 19:2; 2 Kgs 6:31
20:11 Prov 27:1

19:19-21 The anointing of ***Elisha*** is an epilogue to the Lord's charge to ***Elijah***. The two other anointings that God assigned to Elijah (19:15-16) were carried out by Elisha instead (2 Kgs 8:7-15; 9:1-10).

19:19 ***Twelve teams of oxen*** would indicate that ***Elisha*** came from a wealthy family. • Elisha understood that Elijah's power from God would come upon him with the prophet's ***cloak***.

19:21 Elisha burned his ***plow*** and ***slaughtered*** his ***oxen*** to signal a complete break from the past in his present calling. From now on, he would serve the Lord. His meal with family and friends may have been a thanksgiving sacrifice to God capped by a communal meal in joyful celebration of God's claim upon Elisha's life. • ***Elisha*** would first serve as Elijah's ***assistant***. Great leaders often begin as good learners. Joshua was Moses' assistant (Exod 24:13) before becoming his successor (Num 27:18-23; Deut 34:9) and assuming command of the forces of Israel (Josh 1:1-9). Later, Elisha had an assistant named Gehazi (2 Kgs 4:12).

20:1 Whether this is ***Ben-hadad*** I or II is unclear. • ***thirty-two allied kings:*** Confederations of kings were common in the ancient Near East. Shalmaneser III recorded Ben-hadad's name as *Hadad-ezer* and reported that he was part of a twelve-king coalition that opposed him in the Battle of Qarqar (853 BC).

20:2-4 Ben-hadad's first delegation of ***messengers*** brought his demand that Israel must agree to surrender both its treasures and people. Ahab capitulated, wanting peace at any cost. He would give up royal treasures and even his family rather than face bloody war with a powerful enemy.

20:7-9 When Ben-hadad's second delegation made even greater demands (see 1 Sam 11:1-2), ***Ahab*** recognized that ***Ben-hadad*** seemed bent on war. Ahab repeated his compliance with Ben-hadad's first ***demand*** but rejected the second. • ***my lord the king:*** Ahab addressed Ben-hadad in polite diplomatic terms, conceding his willingness to accept the Aramean king's rule. Perhaps he hoped that his courteous reply would still avoid military confrontation.

20:10-11 Ben-hadad's third delegation delivered an ultimatum: Surrender or die. His caustic threat to thoroughly plunder ***Samaria*** was reinforced with a curse, an example of the psychological warfare often practiced in the ancient Near East (see 2 Kgs 18:19-35). • Ahab's third reply to Ben-hadad contained proverbial wisdom. The outcome of the conflict was not yet sealed.

20:12 ***Ben-hadad and the other kings . . . were drinking in their tents*** (or *in Succoth;* also in 20:16) in anticipation of ***Ahab's*** capitulation. ***Ahab's reply*** constituted a challenge, and the Aramean officers ***prepared to attack***.

20:13-34 Two distinct battles ensued, one in Samaria (20:13-25) and one at Aphek (20:26-34). The writer included

20:16
1 Kgs 16:9
20:22
2 Sam 11:1

the LORD says: Do you see all these enemy
forces? Today I will hand them all over to
you. Then you will know that I am the LORD."
14Ahab asked, "How will he do it?"
And the prophet replied, "This is what
the LORD says: The troops of the provincial
commanders will do it."
"Should we attack first?" Ahab asked.
"Yes," the prophet answered.
15So Ahab mustered the troops of the
232 provincial commanders. Then he called
out the rest of the army of Israel, some 7,000
men. 16About noontime, as Ben-hadad
and the thirty-two allied kings were still
in their tents drinking themselves into a
stupor, 17the troops of the provincial commanders marched out of the city as the first
contingent.
As they approached, Ben-hadad's scouts
reported to him, "Some troops are coming
from Samaria."
18"Take them alive," Ben-hadad commanded, "whether they have come for peace or for
war."
19But Ahab's provincial commanders
and the entire army had now come out to
fight. 20Each Israelite soldier killed his Aramean opponent, and suddenly the entire
Aramean army panicked and fled. The Israelites chased them, but King Ben-hadad and
a few of his charioteers escaped on horses.
21However, the king of Israel destroyed the
other horses and chariots and slaughtered
the Arameans.
22Afterward the prophet said to King
Ahab, "Get ready for another attack. Begin
making plans now, for the king of Aram will
come back next spring."

Ben-Hadad's Second Attack

23After their defeat, Ben-hadad's officers
said to him, "The Israelite gods are gods of
the hills; that is why they won. But we can

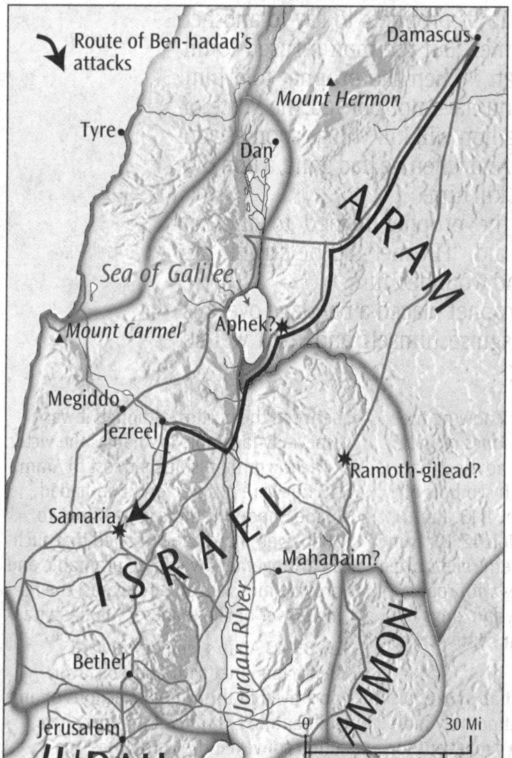

◀ **War between Ahab and Aram (20:1–22:48).** King Ben-hadad of ARAM and his allies tried to besiege SAMARIA, but King Ahab of ISRAEL met them in battle and defeated them. A year later Ben-hadad tried again to defeat Israel at APHEK, believing that the Israelites' gods would be powerless on the plains, but Ahab defeated them again. Despite the warnings of the prophet Micaiah, Ahab, joined by King Jehoshaphat of JUDAH, attacked the Arameans to take back the town of RAMOTH-GILEAD. During the battle Ahab was killed, and his body was taken back to Samaria.

similar details regarding both: (1) pre-battle counsel (20:13-14, 23-25), (2) pre-battle conditions (20:15-16, 26-28), (3) victory for Israel despite the superior numbers of the enemy (20:17-21, 29-30), and (4) post-battle counsel (20:22, 31).

20:13-16 Ahab's forces attacked ***about noontime*** after receiving assurance of victory from an unknown prophet. The Jewish historian Josephus suggested that the prophet was Micaiah (cp. 22:8). The timing of the Israelite attack, during the heat of the day (see Josh 8:14), took the enemy by surprise. ***Ben-hadad and the . . . allied kings*** were still ***drinking***, demonstrating their disdain for Ahab's military capability.

20:17 ***first contingent:*** Ahab apparently sent this small squad to test the enemy. Surprise attacks in the ancient Near East often divided the attacking forces into assault groups designed to launch a pincer movement against the enemy (Judg 7:16; 1 Sam 11:11), to lure the opposing forces into an ambush (Josh 8:15-22), or to draw the enemy to a spot where the attacking army enjoyed a superior position (Judg 4:14-16; 5:19-21).

20:20-22 ***Horses and chariots*** were a key asset in ancient warfare. Ahab's destruction of the major portion of Ben-hadad's striking power was essential to guard against a future incursion. Still, God's ***prophet*** warned that ***the king of Aram*** would return. • ***next spring:*** Literally *at the turn of the year;* similarly in 20:26. The first day of the year in the ancient Hebrew lunar calendar occurred in March or April. Late *spring* and early summer were standard seasons for warfare in the ancient Near East; the forces could count on good weather and a supply of grain from the early harvest.

20:23 The reasoning that Israel had ***gods of the hills*** set the stage for the Lord to show his true identity (20:28). ***Ben-hadad's officers*** had a pagan religious outlook. Perhaps their erroneous view was fostered by traditional knowledge of the Lord's appearance to Israel on Mount Sinai (Exod 19:1-3, 16-18) or of Israel's long-term settlement of the hill country of Canaan (see Josh 10:40; 11:16; Judg 1:19). The Arameans were not aware that God is the Creator and Lord of all the earth (Isa 40:28; 54:5), the only God who alone can save (Isa 45:5, 22).

beat them easily on the plains. 24Only this time replace the kings with field commanders! 25Recruit another army like the one you lost. Give us the same number of horses, chariots, and men, and we will fight against them on the plains. There's no doubt that we will beat them." So King Ben-hadad did as they suggested.

26The following spring he called up the Aramean army and marched out against Israel, this time at Aphek. 27Israel then mustered its army, set up supply lines, and marched out for battle. But the Israelite army looked like two little flocks of goats in comparison to the vast Aramean forces that filled the countryside!

28Then the man of God went to the king of Israel and said, "This is what the LORD says: The Arameans have said, 'The LORD is a god of the hills and not of the plains.' So I will defeat this vast army for you. Then you will know that I am the LORD."

29The two armies camped opposite each other for seven days, and on the seventh day the battle began. The Israelites killed 100,000 Aramean foot soldiers in one day. 30The rest fled into the town of Aphek, but the wall fell on them and killed another 27,000. Ben-hadad fled into the town and hid in a secret room.

31Ben-hadad's officers said to him, "Sir, we have heard that the kings of Israel are merciful. So let's humble ourselves by wearing burlap around our waists and putting ropes on our heads, and surrender to the king of Israel. Then perhaps he will let you live."

32So they put on burlap and ropes, and they went to the king of Israel and begged, "Your servant Ben-hadad says, 'Please let me live!' "

The king of Israel responded, "Is he still alive? He is my brother!"

33The men took this as a good sign and quickly picked up on his words. "Yes," they said, "your brother Ben-hadad!"

"Go and get him," the king of Israel told them. And when Ben-hadad arrived, Ahab invited him up into his chariot.

34Ben-hadad told him, "I will give back the towns my father took from your father, and you may establish places of trade in Damascus, as my father did in Samaria."

Then Ahab said, "I will release you under these conditions." So they made a new treaty, and Ben-hadad was set free.

A Prophet Condemns Ahab

35Meanwhile, the LORD instructed one of the group of prophets to say to another man, "Hit me!" But the man refused to hit the prophet. 36Then the prophet told him, "Because you have not obeyed the voice of the LORD, a lion will kill you as soon as you leave me." And when he had gone, a lion did attack and kill him.

37Then the prophet turned to another man and said, "Hit me!" So he struck the prophet and wounded him.

38The prophet placed a bandage over his eyes to disguise himself and then waited

20:26 2 Kgs 13:17
20:27 Judg 6:3-5; 1 Sam 13:5-8
20:30 1 Kgs 22:25; 2 Chr 18:24
20:31 Gen 37:34
20:34 1 Kgs 15:20
20:35 1 Kgs 13:16-18
20:36 1 Kgs 13:24
20:38 1 Kgs 14:2

20:24-25 Ben-hadad's ***field commanders*** reasoned that with trained military leadership and superiority in manpower and equipment, they would easily defeat Israel on the plains in the next encounter.

20:26 ***Aphek*** was east of the Sea of Galilee in northern Ramoth-gilead. Ben-hadad's officers assumed that this location would favor the Aramean chariots and take away the power of Israel's "gods of the hills."

20:27-30 Despite the Arameans' superior numbers, Israel won another outstanding victory by God's help. All the parties learned that "nothing is impossible with God" (Luke 1:37; see Matt 19:26; Mark 10:27) and that when God is on one's side, the enemy will retreat (Ps 56:9) with staggering losses (Deut 32:30-31; 2 Kgs 19:32-36). Israel could face the foe fearlessly (Ps 3:6; 27:1-3). • God's assurance to Israel through ***the man of God*** showed that this battle was not just for Israel's well-being but for the Lord's glory.

20:31 ***burlap . . . ropes:*** Knowing the ***merciful*** mindset of the ***kings of Israel, . . . Ben-hadad's officers*** advised that they approach Ahab with symbols of humble repentance (Joel 1:13; Jon 3:5-9) and submission (Job 12:18; Lam 1:14). Ancient Near Eastern reliefs often depict captured enemies with ropes around their necks. Assyrian kings boasted of piercing their captives' lips or cheeks with ropes.

20:32-33 ***my brother:*** Ahab spoke to ***Ben-hadad*** in terms that politely indicated the Aramean king's royal authority and Ahab's desire for good relations. Ahab welcomed Ben-hadad ***into his chariot*** to demonstrate his warm reception of the king, yet serving notice that he should recognize ***Ahab*** as his equal. Correspondence and parity agreements between kings of the ancient Near East used the language of brotherhood to express friendship, good relations, or formal equality.

20:34 The ***treaty*** that ***Ahab*** and ***Ben-hadad*** established provided parity between the parties, although it was especially favorable to Ahab as the victor. • ***The towns*** that Israel had lost to Aram (15:20) were restored and Ben-hadad made important ***trade*** concessions to Ahab, who may have reasoned that such an arrangement would be profitable and provide him with an ally against the rising power of Shalmaneser III of Assyria.

20:35-43 Ahab's leniency toward Ben-hadad met with God's disfavor, portrayed in the symbolic actions of an unidentified ***prophet.*** God's prophets often conveyed the Lord's message through symbolic actions (Isa 20:1-6; Jer 27:1-7; Ezek 4:1-3, 9-17; 5:1-4). Ahab had brought judgment upon himself and his people by sparing an untrustworthy enemy rather than trusting further in the Lord.

20:36 ***a lion will kill you:*** A lion was previously the means of divine judgment (13:20-24) and would be so again during the repopulation of Israel following the fall of Samaria (2 Kgs 17:25-26).

20:39 2 Kgs 10:24
20:43 1 Kgs 21:4
21:1 2 Kgs 9:21
21:3 Lev 25:23; Num 36:6-7; Ezek 46:18
21:7 1 Sam 8:14
21:8 2 Sam 11:14; 2 Chr 32:17; Esth 3:12; 8:8
21:10 Exod 22:28; Lev 24:15-16; Acts 6:11

beside the road for the king. 39As the king passed by, the prophet called out to him, "Sir, I was in the thick of battle, and suddenly a man brought me a prisoner. He said, 'Guard this man; if for any reason he gets away, you will either die or pay a fine of seventy-five pounds of silver!' 40But while I was busy doing something else, the prisoner disappeared!"

"Well, it's your own fault," the king replied. "You have brought the judgment on yourself."

41Then the prophet quickly pulled the bandage from his eyes, and the king of Israel recognized him as one of the prophets. 42The prophet said to him, "This is what the LORD says: Because you have spared the man I said must be destroyed, now you must die in his place, and your people will die instead of his people." 43So the king of Israel went home to Samaria angry and sullen.

Naboth's Vineyard

21 Now there was a man named Naboth, from Jezreel, who owned a vineyard in Jezreel beside the palace of King Ahab of Samaria. 2One day Ahab said to Naboth, "Since your vineyard is so convenient to my palace, I would like to buy it to use as a vegetable garden. I will give you a better vineyard in exchange, or if you prefer, I will pay you for it."

3But Naboth replied, "The LORD forbid that I should give you the inheritance that was passed down by my ancestors."

4So Ahab went home angry and sullen because of Naboth's answer. The king went to bed with his face to the wall and refused to eat!

5"What's the matter?" his wife Jezebel asked him. "What's made you so upset that you're not eating?"

6"I asked Naboth to sell me his vineyard or trade it, but he refused!" Ahab told her.

7"Are you the king of Israel or not?" Jezebel demanded. "Get up and eat something, and don't worry about it. I'll get you Naboth's vineyard!"

8So she wrote letters in Ahab's name, sealed them with his seal, and sent them to the elders and other leaders of the town where Naboth lived. 9In her letters she commanded: "Call the citizens together for fasting and prayer, and give Naboth a place of honor. 10And then seat two scoundrels across from him who will accuse him of cursing God and the king. Then take him out and stone him to death."

11So the elders and other town leaders followed the instructions Jezebel had written in the letters. 12They called for a fast and put Naboth at a prominent place before the people. 13Then the two scoundrels came and sat down across from him. And they accused Naboth before all the people, saying, "He cursed God and the king." So he

---

20:39 *seventy-five pounds:* Hebrew *1 talent* [34 kilograms].

20:42-43 ***The LORD*** had apparently told Ahab to put Ben-hadad to death (cp. Josh 6:17-21), but Ahab violated his charge, perhaps viewing the Aramean king as part of the spoils of war (cp. 1 Sam 15:1-23). The ***king of Israel*** would regret his folly: He later faced Ben-hadad in another battle that would cost him his life (22:29-37). Rather than learning from the prophet's rebuke, Ahab went home ***angry and sullen.***

20:42 *destroyed:* The Hebrew term used here refers to the complete consecration of things or people to the Lord, either by destroying them or by giving them as an offering (see Lev 27:28-29; 1 Sam 15:3).

21:1-16 The writer includes another incident in which king Ahab responded in an ***angry and sullen*** manner (20:43; 21:4).

21:1 In addition to his palace in the capital city, ***Ahab*** had a second ***palace . . . in Jezreel.*** Excavations at Jezreel have unearthed a sizeable palace there. • ***Samaria***, which sometimes refers to the capital city, here indicates the whole northern kingdom.

21:2-3 Naboth refused Ahab's generous offer to ***buy*** or ***exchange*** land for his vineyard. While he may have desired to sell, Naboth noted that the law said that inherited property should stay in the family or tribe that originally owned it (Lev 25:23-28; Num 36:7-9). Unlike the kings of the surrounding nations, who could seize whatever property they wished (1 Sam 8:11-17), Ahab was bound by Israel's law.

21:4 *angry and sullen:* Ahab's reaction was the same when he was rebuked by God's prophet (20:43). A sullen attitude can easily arise in a stubborn, self-centered person (21:16, 20, 25-26; see 16:31-32; 18:10, 17; 20:42-43; 22:3, 27-30).

21:7 *I'll get you Naboth's vineyard!* With her ruthless disposition and actions, ***Jezebel*** displayed her cultural upbringing; Canaanite kings did as they pleased (21:8-10, 15, 25; see 19:1-2; 2 Kgs 9:30-31).

21:8-9 *Call the citizens together:* This kind of assembly would normally address sin that could bring divine judgment against the people (see Deut 21:1-9; Josh 7:10-12; 1 Sam 7:1-6). Jezebel convened it to bring false charges against an innocent person.

21:10 ***scoundrels*** (literally *sons of Belial*): The Hebrew term refers to totally evil reprobates (Deut 13:13; Judg 19:22; 1 Sam 10:27; Prov 6:12). Later Jewish writings attributed the name Belial to Satan, a use reflected by Paul in the NT (2 Cor 6:15). • Legally, two witnesses were needed to establish a charge against a person (Deut 19:15; Matt 18:16). The twofold charge of Naboth's blasphemy against God and against the king carried a penalty of death by stoning outside the city (Deut 17:5-6; 22:24). Naboth was apparently put ***to death*** on his own land (see 2 Kgs 9:21-26).

21:13-14 As with Achan (Josh 7:24-26), Naboth's sons were ***stoned to death*** at the same time to prevent the property from passing on to them. Because the charge carried the penalty of state execution (Deut 13:10-11; 17:5) and because Naboth no longer had male heirs, Ahab exercised the royal prerogative of confiscating the property (see 1 Sam 8:14).

was dragged outside the town and stoned to death. 14The town leaders then sent word to Jezebel, "Naboth has been stoned to death."

15When Jezebel heard the news, she said to Ahab, "You know the vineyard Naboth wouldn't sell you? Well, you can have it now! He's dead!" 16So Ahab immediately went down to the vineyard of Naboth to claim it.

17But the LORD said to Elijah, 18"Go down to meet King Ahab of Israel, who rules in Samaria. He will be at Naboth's vineyard in Jezreel, claiming it for himself. 19Give him this message: 'This is what the LORD says: Wasn't it enough that you killed Naboth? Must you rob him, too? Because you have done this, dogs will lick your blood at the very place where they licked the blood of Naboth!' "

20"So, my enemy, you have found me!" Ahab exclaimed to Elijah.

"Yes," Elijah answered, "I have come because you have sold yourself to what is evil in the LORD's sight. 21So now the LORD says, 'I will bring disaster on you and consume you. I will destroy every one of your male descendants, slave and free alike, anywhere in Israel! 22I am going to destroy your family as I did the family of Jeroboam son of Nebat and the family of Baasha son of Ahijah, for you have made me very angry and have led Israel into sin.'

23"And regarding Jezebel, the LORD says, 'Dogs will eat Jezebel's body at the plot of land in Jezreel.'

24"The members of Ahab's family who die in the city will be eaten by dogs, and those who die in the field will be eaten by vultures."

25(No one else so completely sold himself to what was evil in the LORD's sight as Ahab did under the influence of his wife Jezebel. 26His worst outrage was worshiping idols just as the Amorites had done—the people whom the LORD had driven out from the land ahead of the Israelites.)

27But when Ahab heard this message, he tore his clothing, dressed in burlap, and fasted. He even slept in burlap and went about in deep mourning.

28Then another message from the LORD came to Elijah: 29"Do you see how Ahab has humbled himself before me? Because he has done this, I will not do what I promised during his lifetime. It will happen to his sons; I will destroy his dynasty."

Jehoshaphat and Ahab Make an Alliance

1 Kgs 22:2-9 // 2 Chr 18:2-8

22 For three years there was no war between Aram and Israel. 2Then during the third year, King Jehoshaphat of Judah went to visit King Ahab of Israel. 3During the visit, the king of Israel said to his officials, "Do you realize that the town of Ramoth-gilead belongs to us? And yet we've done nothing to recapture it from the king of Aram!"

4Then he turned to Jehoshaphat and asked, "Will you join me in battle to recover Ramoth-gilead?"

Jehoshaphat replied to the king of Israel, "Why, of course! You and I are as one. My troops are your troops, and my horses are your horses." 5Then Jehoshaphat added, "But first let's find out what the LORD says."

6So the king of Israel summoned the

21:19 1 Kgs 22:38; 2 Kgs 9:26
21:20 1 Kgs 18:17; Rom 7:14
21:21 1 Kgs 14:10; 2 Kgs 9:8
21:22 1 Kgs 14:16; 15:29; 16:3
21:23 2 Kgs 9:10, 30-37
21:24 1 Kgs 14:11; 16:4
21:26 Gen 15:16; Lev 18:25-30; 2 Kgs 21:11
21:27 Gen 37:34; 2 Kgs 6:26-30
21:29 1 Kgs 22:38; 2 Kgs 9:25-37; 2 Chr 12:7; 34:27
22:1-28 //2 Chr 18:1-27
22:2 1 Kgs 15:24
22:3 Deut 4:43
22:4 2 Kgs 3:6-8
22:5 2 Kgs 3:11

21:17-22 ***Elijah*** (literally *Elijah the Tishbite;* also in 21:28) delivered the Lord's sentence against ***Ahab*** just as he was about to take possession of the vineyard. Because Ahab was responsible for the death of ***Naboth*** and the seizing of his field, Ahab and his ***family*** would be destroyed. The prophecy concerning Ahab's children would be fulfilled in Jehu's purging of Baal worshipers from Israel (2 Kgs 9:30-37; 10:1-11).

21:23-24 ***Jezebel*** would be killed ***at the plot of land in Jezreel*** (as in several Hebrew manuscripts, Syriac, and Latin Vulgate [see also 2 Kgs 9:26, 36]; most Hebrew manuscripts read *at the city wall*).

21:25-26 The author interrupts his account to reemphasize (see 16:30-34) Ahab's ***evil*** character, to denounce the king's commitment to idolatry, and to condemn his weakness in allowing himself to be ***under the influence of his wife Jezebel.*** Wicked Jezebel would stop at nothing to achieve her own ends (18:4; 19:1-2; 21:5-10, 15). Though arrogant and defiant to the end (2 Kgs 9:30-31), she eventually met her predicted doom (21:23; 2 Kgs 9:32-37).

21:26 ***idols:*** The Hebrew term (literally *round things*) probably alludes to dung.

21:27-29 Ahab was a complex character. Although justly condemned for his evil character, here he repented when the Lord's prophet brought a ***message*** of rebuke (21:27). Because of Ahab's repentance, ***the LORD*** sent ***Elijah*** to postpone the awful sentence against Ahab and instead impose it on his equally wicked sons (2 Kgs 1:17; 9:24-26; 10:1-11).

22:1 ***three years . . . no war:*** During this time, the repeated westward thrusts of the Assyrian king Shalmaneser III (858–824 BC) led to the Battle of Qarqar (853 BC). Shalmaneser's records mention that he faced both Hadadezer (Ben-hadad) and Ahab at that battle. With the Assyrian king temporarily thwarted, old enmities between Aram and Israel flared up again.

22:2-4 ***Jehoshaphat*** and ***Ahab*** were in-laws by the marriage of Ahab's daughter Athaliah to Jehoshaphat's son Jehoram (2 Kgs 8:25-26). However cordial Jehoshaphat may have intended his ***visit*** to be, he quickly became involved in Ahab's plan to occupy Ramoth-gilead. The Assyrian menace prevented Ahab from taking control of this key area that dominated the eastern end of the Plain of Jezreel. Now it needed to be taken by force, and Jehoshaphat placed his ***troops*** and ***horses*** at Ahab's disposal.

22:5-9 In accordance with ancient Near Eastern custom, ***Jehoshaphat*** requested that the two kings determine the will of the Lord before going into battle. Examples of this custom are common in Aramean, Moabite, and Assyrian

22:7 2 Kgs 3:11
22:11 Deut 33:17; 2 Chr 18:10; Zech 1:18-21
22:14 Num 22:18; 24:13; 2 Chr 18:13
22:17 Num 27:17; 1 Kgs 22:33-37; *Matt 9:36; *Mark 6:34
22:19 Isa 6:1; Dan 7:9-10; [a]*tsaba'* (6635) ‣ Ps 24:10
22:22 Judg 9:23; 2 Thes 2:11
22:23 Ezek 14:9
22:24 2 Chr 18:23

prophets, about 400 of them, and asked them, "Should I go to war against Ramoth-gilead, or should I hold back?"

They all replied, "Yes, go right ahead! The Lord will give the king victory."

7But Jehoshaphat asked, "Is there not also a prophet of the LORD here? We should ask him the same question."

8The king of Israel replied to Jehoshaphat, "There is one more man who could consult the LORD for us, but I hate him. He never prophesies anything but trouble for me! His name is Micaiah son of Imlah."

Jehoshaphat replied, "That's not the way a king should talk! Let's hear what he has to say."

9So the king of Israel called one of his officials and said, "Quick! Bring Micaiah son of Imlah."

Micaiah Prophesies against Ahab
1 Kgs 22:10-28 // 2 Chr 18:9-27

10King Ahab of Israel and King Jehoshaphat of Judah, dressed in their royal robes, were sitting on thrones at the threshing floor near the gate of Samaria. All of Ahab's prophets were prophesying there in front of them.
11One of them, Zedekiah son of Kenaanah, made some iron horns and proclaimed, "This is what the LORD says: With these horns you will gore the Arameans to death!"

12All the other prophets agreed. "Yes," they said, "go up to Ramoth-gilead and be victorious, for the LORD will give the king victory!"

13Meanwhile, the messenger who went to get Micaiah said to him, "Look, all the prophets are promising victory for the king. Be sure that you agree with them and promise success."

14But Micaiah replied, "As surely as the LORD lives, I will say only what the LORD tells me to say."

15When Micaiah arrived before the king, Ahab asked him, "Micaiah, should we go to war against Ramoth-gilead, or should we hold back?"

Micaiah replied sarcastically, "Yes, go up and be victorious, for the LORD will give the king victory!"

16But the king replied sharply, "How many times must I demand that you speak only the truth to me when you speak for the LORD?"

17Then Micaiah told him, "In a vision I saw all Israel scattered on the mountains, like sheep without a shepherd. And the LORD said, 'Their master has been killed. Send them home in peace.' "

18"Didn't I tell you?" the king of Israel exclaimed to Jehoshaphat. "He never prophesies anything but trouble for me."

19Then Micaiah continued, "Listen to what the LORD says! I saw the LORD sitting on his throne with all the [a]armies of heaven around him, on his right and on his left.
20And the LORD said, 'Who can entice Ahab to go into battle against Ramoth-gilead so he can be killed?'

"There were many suggestions, 21and finally a spirit approached the LORD and said, 'I can do it!'

22" 'How will you do this?' the LORD asked.

"And the spirit replied, 'I will go out and inspire all of Ahab's prophets to speak lies.'

" 'You will succeed,' said the LORD. 'Go ahead and do it.'

23"So you see, the LORD has put a lying spirit in the mouths of all your prophets. For the LORD has pronounced your doom."

24Then Zedekiah son of Kenaanah walked up to Micaiah and slapped him across the face. "Since when did the Spirit of the LORD leave me to speak to you?" he demanded.

25And Micaiah replied, "You will find out

inscriptions as well as in the OT (1 Sam 23:2-4; 2 Sam 5:19-25). Despite Ahab's misgivings, Jehoshaphat insisted on summoning Micaiah, a genuine ***prophet of the LORD.***

22:10 In the ancient Near East, important business was often conducted ***at the threshing floor*** near the city ***gate.*** David secured the threshing floor of Araunah and built an altar there (2 Sam 24:18-25; 1 Chr 21:26); it later became the site for the Temple in Jerusalem (2 Chr 3:1).

22:13-14 ***The messenger who went to get Micaiah*** warned that he had better ***agree*** with the false ***prophets.*** However, Micaiah promised only that he would faithfully deliver the Lord's word (see Num 22:38; 24:13).

22:15-16 The word *sarcastically* does not occur in the Hebrew text; the NLT simply makes explicit what Ahab sensed in Micaiah's tone of voice (18:27; Job 12:1-2; 16:2).

22:17 Like God himself (Ps 23; Isa 40:10-11), Israel's kings and leaders were charged with care of the people much as a ***shepherd*** cares for his ***sheep*** (Num 27:16-17; Ezek 34:2, 11-16). The motif of the shepherd and the sheep, applied to the coming Messiah (Ezek 34:23-24), was fulfilled in Christ the Good Shepherd (John 10:1-11). Although he laid down his life for the sheep (John 10:14-18; 1 Pet 2:24-25), he still lives (Heb 13:20) and will come again for them (1 Pet 5:4). • ***Their master has been killed:*** Literally *These people have no master.*

22:19-23 Micaiah explained that God had allowed a *lying spirit* of prophecy to mislead Ahab to bring about his death. In his sovereignty, God used the counsel of Ahab's false prophets to accomplish his will.

22:24-25 An indignant ***Zedekiah,*** one of the false prophets, insisted that he and the others were telling the truth. Like Ahab, they would one day find out the real truth when the prophecy against them was fulfilled in Jehu's purge of Baal worship (2 Kgs 10:18-28).

soon enough when you are trying to hide in
some secret room!"
26"Arrest him!" the king of Israel ordered.
"Take him back to Amon, the governor of
the city, and to my son Joash. 27Give them
this order from the king: 'Put this man in
prison, and feed him nothing but bread and
water until I return safely from the battle!' "
28But Micaiah replied, "If you return
safely, it will mean that the LORD has not
spoken through me!" Then he added to
those standing around, "Everyone mark my
words!"

The Death of Ahab
1 Kgs 22:29-37 // 2 Chr 18:28-34

29So King Ahab of Israel and King Jehoshaphat of Judah led their armies against
Ramoth-gilead. 30The king of Israel said to
Jehoshaphat, "As we go into battle, I will disguise myself so no one will recognize me,
but you wear your royal robes." So the king
of Israel disguised himself, and they went
into battle.
31Meanwhile, the king of Aram had issued these orders to his thirty-two chariot
commanders: "Attack only the king of Israel. Don't bother with anyone else!" 32So
when the Aramean chariot commanders
saw Jehoshaphat in his royal robes, they
went after him. "There is the king of Israel!"
they shouted. But when Jehoshaphat called
out, 33the chariot commanders realized he
was not the king of Israel, and they stopped
chasing him.
34An Aramean soldier, however, randomly shot an arrow at the Israelite troops
and hit the king of Israel between the joints
of his armor. "Turn the horses and get me
out of here!" Ahab groaned to the driver of
his chariot. "I'm badly wounded!"
35The battle raged all that day, and the
king remained propped up in his chariot
facing the Arameans. The blood from his
wound ran down to the floor of his chariot,
and as evening arrived he died. 36Just as
the sun was setting, the cry ran through his
troops: "We're done for! Run for your lives!"
37So the king died, and his body was
taken to Samaria and buried there. 38Then
his chariot was washed beside the pool
of Samaria, and dogs came and licked his
blood at the place where the prostitutes
bathed, just as the LORD had promised.
39The rest of the events in Ahab's reign
and everything he did, including the story
of the ivory palace and the towns he built,
are recorded in *The Book of the History of
the Kings of Israel.* 40So Ahab died, and his
son Ahaziah became the next king.

Jehoshaphat's Reign in Judah (22:41-50)
1 Kgs 22:41-50 // 2 Chr 20:31–21:1

41Jehoshaphat son of Asa began to rule over
Judah in the fourth year of King Ahab's
reign in Israel. 42Jehoshaphat was thirty-
five years old when he became king, and he
reigned in Jerusalem twenty-five years. His
mother was Azubah, the daughter of Shilhi.
43Jehoshaphat was a good king, following
the example of his father, Asa. He did what
was pleasing in the LORD's sight. During his
reign, however, he failed to remove all the
pagan shrines, and the people still offered
sacrifices and burned incense there. 44Je-
hoshaphat also made peace with the king
of Israel.
45The rest of the events in Jehoshaphat's
reign, the extent of his power, and the wars
he waged are recorded in *The Book of the
History of the Kings of Judah.* 46He banished from the land the rest of the male

22:27 2 Chr 16:10; 18:25-27
22:28 Deut 18:22
22:29-36 //2 Chr 18:28-34
22:30 2 Chr 35:22
22:31 2 Chr 18:30
22:38 1 Kgs 21:19
22:39 Amos 3:15
22:41-50 //2 Chr 20:31–21:1
22:43 1 Kgs 15:14; 2 Kgs 12:3
22:46 Deut 23:17; 1 Kgs 15:12

22:29-33 Ahab hoped to avoid direct reprisal from Ben-hadad by wearing a ***disguise.*** By urging ***Jehoshaphat*** to ***wear*** his ***royal robes,*** Ahab hoped to escape detection and thwart Micaiah's prophecy.

22:34-36 An Aramean soldier's random ***shot*** fulfilled Micaiah's prophecy about Ahab's death. Ancient armor discovered during excavations in the Near East suggests that the arrow would have found a small unprotected area between the breastplate and the metal platelets that comprised the lower ***armor.*** Although he was ***badly wounded,*** Ahab displayed courage by remaining ***propped up in his chariot*** throughout the course of the day's battle before calling for retreat.

22:34 ***Turn the horses:*** Literally *Turn your hand.*

22:37-38 Elijah's prophecy that ***dogs*** would lick the ***blood*** of Ahab's fallen body (21:19) was fulfilled. • ***his blood at the place where the prostitutes bathed:*** Or *his blood, and the prostitutes bathed [in it];* or *his blood, and they washed his armor.* The meaning of the Hebrew is uncertain.

22:39-40 Excavations at Samaria have disclosed Ahab's ***palace*** and a nearby pool. The description of the palace as ***ivory*** may arise from the ivory-covered furnishings and wall panels. Gleaming white limestone covering the outside of the building also added to the palace's ivory-like luster.

22:39 ***The Book of the History of the Kings of Israel:*** See note on 14:19-20.

22:41-50 This overview provides basic information about Jehoshaphat's twenty-five-year reign as king of Judah. The Chronicler provides more details on Jehoshaphat's good spiritual character that led to religious reforms and the Lord's blessing (2 Chr 17:1–21:1). Including a two-year co-regency with his father, Asa, ***Jehoshaphat*** reigned from 872 to 848 BC (see timeline, p. 609).

22:43-44 Although ***Jehoshaphat*** is remembered as a king who ***did what was pleasing in the LORD's sight,*** his record is blemished by his failure to ***remove all the pagan shrines*** (see 15:14) and by his involvement with Ahab (22:4, 29-32; 2 Chr 19:1-3) and, later, Joram (2 Kgs 3:4-27).

22:43b-53 Verses 22:43b-53 are numbered 22:44-54 in the Hebrew text.

22:46 To Jehoshaphat's credit, he eliminated religious ***prostitutes,*** which,

22:47
2 Sam 8:14
2 Kgs 3:9
22:48
1 Kgs 9:26-28
22:50
2 Chr 21:1
22:52
1 Kgs 15:26

and female shrine prostitutes, who still continued their practices from the days of his father, Asa.

47(There was no king in Edom at that time, only a deputy.)

48Jehoshaphat also built a fleet of trading ships to sail to Ophir for gold. But the ships never set sail, for they met with disaster in their home port of Ezion-geber. 49At one time Ahaziah son of Ahab had proposed to Jehoshaphat, "Let my men sail with your men in the ships." But Jehoshaphat refused the request.

50When Jehoshaphat died, he was buried with his ancestors in the City of David. Then his son Jehoram became the next king.

Ahaziah's Reign in Israel (22:51-53)

51Ahaziah son of Ahab began to rule over Israel in the seventeenth year of King Jehoshaphat's reign in Judah. He reigned in Samaria two years. 52But he did what was evil in the LORD's sight, following the example of his father and mother and the example of Jeroboam son of Nebat, who had led Israel to sin. 53He served Baal and worshiped him, provoking the anger of the LORD, the God of Israel, just as his father had done.

although banned by ***his father, Asa*** (15:12), still existed. Religious prostitution was apparently centered at pagan shrines that his father had not removed (15:14).

22:47 The lack of a ***king in Edom*** may indicate Edom's dependence upon Judah at this time.

22:48-49 Jehoshaphat built this ***fleet of trading ships*** (literally *fleet of ships of Tarshish*) in alliance with Ahaziah (see 2 Chr 20:35-37). Like Solomon, the two kings planned to send a fleet to ***Ophir*** in search of ***gold*** (9:27-28; 10:11). The venture was ill fated; to fulfill a prophetic warning (2 Chr 20:37), the Lord destroyed the fleet before it left port. ***Jehoshaphat*** wisely did not become entangled with ***Ahaziah*** a second time. • ***Ezion-geber*** was Solomon's port city on the Gulf of Aqaba (9:26).

22:51-53 The tragic story of the rule of ***Ahaziah*** in Israel continues in 2 Kgs 1:1-18. He followed in the ***evil*** ways of his parents, Ahab and Jezebel (21:25-26); he worshipped ***Baal*** (2 Kgs 1:2, 16) and supported the state religion instituted by ***Jeroboam*** I (12:28-32). Ahaziah's accession and statement of character provide closure to the account of Ahab in 1 Kings and a smooth transition to the continuing story of the divided kingdom in 2 Kings.

THE SECOND BOOK OF KINGS

The book of 2 Kings is filled with leaders who did not learn from the past. The spiritual failure of these kings brought doom upon themselves and their nation. However, throughout the book are sparkling examples of people who put God and his word first and enjoyed God's covenant promises. Reading their stories inspires us to avoid their mistakes and to enjoy the blessings that God promises to those who love and serve him.

SETTING

The book of 2 Kings continues the story of Israel's divided monarchy, picking up where 1 Kings ends, with Ahaziah reigning over the northern kingdom of Israel and Jehoshaphat ruling in the southern kingdom of Judah. The account traces the fortunes of the two kingdoms to their respective ends—the northern kingdom in 722 BC, the southern kingdom in 586 BC.

This book covers four different periods: (1) the closing years of the northern kingdom's third dynasty (853–841 BC, chs 1–9), (2) the era of the northern kingdom's fourth dynasty (841–752 BC, 10:1–15:12), (3) the era of the northern kingdom's decline and fall (752–722 BC, 15:13–17:41), and (4) the final era of the southern kingdom (722–586 BC, chs 18–25).

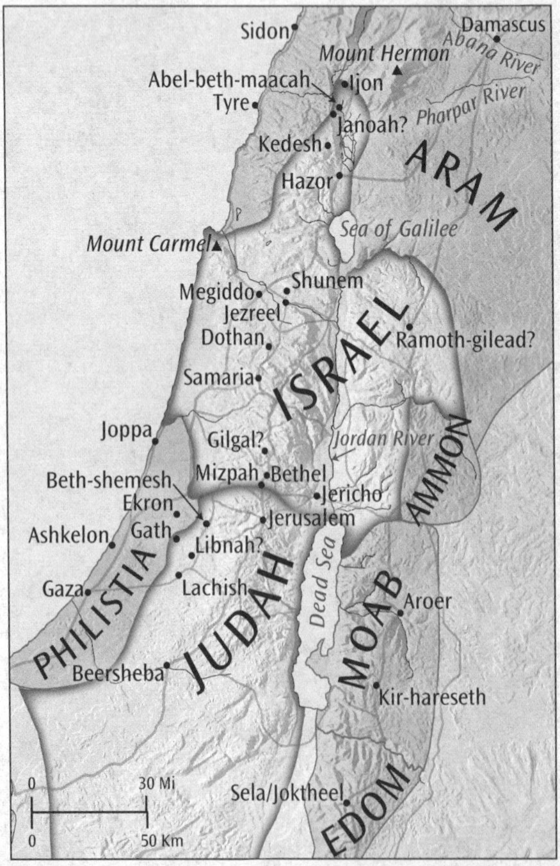

◀ **Key Places in 2 Kings, 853–586 BC.** The book of 2 Kings continues the story of the divided kingdoms of Israel and Judah and their many battles, their sad decline into spiritual idolatry, and their eventual exile to Assyria and Babylon.

ABANA RIVER, PHARPAR RIVER 5:12
AMMON 23:13; 24:2
ARAM 5:1; 6:8; 8:7, 28; 9:14; 12:17; 13:3; 15:37; 16:9; 24:2
BEERSHEBA 12:1; 23:8
BETHEL 2:2, 23; 10:29; 17:28; 23:4, 15-17
BETH-SHEMESH 14:11-13
DAMASCUS 8:7; 14:28; 16:9-11
EDOM 3:8-9; 8:20-22; 14:7, 10; 16:6
GILGAL 2:1; 4:38
JERICHO 2:4, 18; 25:5
JEZREEL 8:29; 9:16-17; 10:11
KIR-HARESETH 3:25
LACHISH 14:19; 18:14
LIBNAH 8:22; 19:8; 23:31; 24:18
MEGIDDO 9:27; 23:29
MIZPAH 25:23-25
MOAB 1:1; 3:4-5; 13:20; 24:2
MOUNT CARMEL 2:25; 4:25
RAMOTH-GILEAD 8:28–9:4
SAMARIA 1:2; 3:1; 6:24; 10:1, 36; 14:23; 17:5-6; 23:19
SHUNEM 4:8-37

The closing years of the northern kingdom's third dynasty included the short reign of Ahaziah in Israel (853–852 BC) and the reign of his younger brother Joram (852–841 BC). The kings reigning in Judah during this time were Jehoshaphat (872–848 BC),[1] Jehoram (853–841 BC), and Ahaziah (841 BC). The Neo-Assyrian Empire was expanding westward at this time, achieving a dominant position that brought stabilization to the area. At the end of this period, the year 841 BC was a crucial year in which the kings of both the northern and southern kingdoms were killed and a new dynasty was inaugurated in the north.

OUTLINE

1:1–17:41
The Divided Monarchy

18:1–25:21
The Last Era of the Southern Kingdom

25:22-30
Historical Appendices

The next period (841–752 BC) covers Israel's fourth dynasty (Jehu–Zechariah, 10:1–15:12), an era marked by both peril and prosperity. Assyrian dominance waned, allowing the Arameans to continue their ruthless campaigns against Israel throughout the days of Jehu (841–814 BC) and his son Jehoahaz (814–798 BC). God eventually raised up a foreign leader (thought to be Adad-nirari III of Assyria, 810–783 BC) who defeated Aram and relieved the pressure on Israel (13:3-5). These circumstances allowed both Israel and Judah to expand their influence. Although hostilities broke out between the two kingdoms for a short time, conditions quickly stabilized under Jeroboam II of Israel (793–753 BC) and Uzziah of Judah (792–740 BC). Their reigns marked an era of unparalleled economic and political prosperity for both kingdoms.

In the third period (753–722 BC), the northern kingdom became unstable and insecure—Jeroboam's son Zechariah reigned only six months (753–752 BC) before he was assassinated by Shallum, and Shallum reigned just one month before being killed by Menahem. Menahem's ten-year reign (752–742 BC) was characterized by spiritual weakness and renewed subservience to the rising power of Assyria. By 743 BC, King Tiglath-pileser of Assyria had made the northern kingdom submit as a vassal state, and in 722 BC the northern kingdom was destroyed.

Meanwhile, the southern kingdom continued to enjoy prosperity during the reign of Jotham (750–732 BC), but after his death, during the reign of his son Ahaz (743–715 BC), Judah was caught up in the swift current of Assyrian expansion. Eventually, Judah also became a vassal of Assyria.

Following the fall of Samaria in 722 BC, a new dynasty rose up in Assyria, and Judah faced the threat of Assyrian supremacy. That era was marked by Manasseh's fifty-five year reign (697–642 BC). Manasseh deliberately reintroduced Canaanite paganism into the spiritual life of Judah, reproducing the very sin that brought God's judgment on the northern kingdom (17:7-17). Even the far-reaching reforms of King Josiah (640–609 BC, 22:1–23:24; 2 Chr 34:1–35:19) did not overcome Judah's entrenched sin (23:26-27).

[1] The overlapping dates of these kings indicate co-regencies; for more information, see "Chronology: Israel's Monarchy," p. 562.

TIMELINE

about 870~850 BC
Elijah as prophet

about 853~798 BC
Elisha as prophet

853–841 BC
Jehoram as king of Judah

853–852 BC
Ahaziah as king of Israel

852–841 BC
Joram as king of Israel

841 BC
Ahaziah (Jehoahaz) as king of Judah

841–835 BC
Athaliah as queen of Judah

841–814 BC
Jehu as king of Israel

835–796 BC
Joash (Jehoash) as king of Judah

814–798 BC
Jehoahaz as king of Israel

798–782 BC
Jehoash as king of Israel

796–767 BC
Amaziah as king of Judah

793–753 BC
Jeroboam II as king of Israel

792–740 BC
Uzziah (Azariah) as king of Judah

753–752 BC
Zechariah as king of Israel

752 BC
Shallum as king of Israel

752–742 BC
Menahem as king of Israel

750–732 BC
Jotham as king of Judah

744–727 BC
Tiglath-pileser III as king of Assyria

743–715 BC
Ahaz as king of Judah

742–740 BC
Pekahiah as king of Israel

740–732 BC
Pekah as king of Israel

about 740~685 BC
Isaiah as prophet

732–722 BC
Hoshea as king of Israel

728–686 BC
Hezekiah as king of Judah

727–722 BC
Shalmaneser V as king of Assyria

722 BC
Assyrians destroy Samaria, end of the kingdom of Israel

721–705 BC
Sargon II as king of Assyria

704–681 BC
Sennacherib as king of Assyria

697–642 BC
Manasseh as king of Judah

680–669 BC
Esarhaddon as king of Assyria

668–626 BC
Ashurbanipal as king of Assyria

642–640 BC
Amon as king of Judah

640–609 BC
Josiah as king of Judah

about 635~622 BC
Zephaniah as prophet

about 627~580 BC
Jeremiah as prophet

610–595 BC
Neco II as pharaoh of Egypt

609 BC
Josiah's death at Megiddo

609 BC
Jehoahaz as king of Judah

609–598 BC
Jehoiakim as king of Judah

605–562 BC
Nebuchadnezzar II as king of Babylon

605 BC
Nebuchadnezzar invades Judah, first deportation

The Babylonians conquered the Assyrians between 612 and 605 BC and took their place as the dominant power. The Babylonians invaded Judah three times (605, 597, 586 BC), destroyed Jerusalem and the Temple, and deported the population.

SUMMARY

The book of 2 Kings is structured around the reigns of the kings of Israel and Judah. The book begins with an accident that caused the death of King Ahaziah of Israel (1:1-18) and with the closing event of Elijah's life, when God took him into heaven (2:1-12). The prophetic mantle passed to Elisha, whose miracles and advice occupy the next several chapters (2:12–8:15; see 9:1-10).

The reigns of kings Jehoram and Ahaziah of Judah (8:16-29) bring the story to the pivotal year of 841 BC, when Jehu's coup led to the deaths of kings Joram and Ahaziah. Jehu also executed Jezebel, the surviving members of Ahab's family, and the officials who worshiped Baal (9:11–10:29). So Jehu's twenty-eight-year reign began (10:30-36). At the same time Athaliah (11:1-20) usurped the throne of Judah and reigned for six years, until those loyal to David's line installed young Joash as king (12:1-21). While Joash, Amaziah, and Uzziah were the kings in Judah, Jehu's dynasty reigned in Israel (11:21–15:12). At the period's high point, the twin kingdoms enjoyed prosperity (14:23–15:7).

The northern kingdom, though, continued to do evil and went into decline. The fourth dynasty ended when Zechariah was assassinated (15:8-12). In its final years, the northern kingdom was in disorder (15:13–17:2), with the short reigns of Shallum, Menahem, Pekahiah, Pekah, and Hoshea. During this time, Jotham and Ahaz were reigning in Judah. Hoshea, Israel's last king (732–722 BC), foolishly placed his confidence in Egypt and rebelled against Assyria, bringing about the capture of Samaria and the end of the northern kingdom in 722 BC (17:3-6). The section closes with an evaluation of the reasons for Israel's fall and an account of Samaria's repopulation (17:7-41).

The book's final section (chs 18–25) deals with the fortunes of Judah, with two kings singled out for particular attention. Hezekiah is remembered for trusting the Lord while under pressure (18:5-6; see 18:13–20:11), and Josiah earns praise for his devotion to the law of the Lord (23:19; see 22:8–23:25). However, even Hezekiah and Josiah made critical mistakes of judgment (20:12-19; 23:29-30; see 2 Chr 35:20-25).

Following Josiah's death, the final kings of Judah did what was evil in the Lord's sight, and the southern kingdom was ravaged and finally destroyed by King Nebuchadnezzar II of Babylon (23:31–25:21). God's prophesied judgment had come (see Jer 38:17-23), and the glorious kingdom of Israel passed into the realm of memory.

The history of the divided monarchy closes with two appended notes, the first dealing with events in Judah after the fall of Jerusalem (25:22-26), and the second with the later release of Jehoiachin in Babylon (25:27-30).

AUTHORSHIP AND DATE

The book of 2 Kings is a continuation of 1 Kings, written by the same author, whose precise identity is unknown. He was well acquainted with sources that enabled him to compose a detailed history of Israel's divided monarchy, and he had insight to evaluate the reasons for

successes and failures on the basis of the people's response to the covenants and standards of Mosaic law. His intimate acquaintance with Judah's later history indicates that he probably lived in or near Jerusalem and was an eyewitness to many of the events that brought about the city's fall. Whether he was still alive to write the final appendix about Jehoiachin's release (561 BC, 25:25-30) is uncertain. If not, these verses were added by someone well acquainted with 2 Kings and of a kindred spirit with the primary writer. A tradition holds that the single author of 1 & 2 Kings was Jeremiah and that he was taken to Babylon during Nebuchadnezzar's return from a campaign in Egypt (about 568 BC) and lived there well into his nineties.

Based on information in the closing chapters, the final composition of 2 Kings most likely took place shortly after the fall of Jerusalem in 586 BC, with the final appendix to the book added shortly after Nebuchadnezzar II's death in 562 BC.

The books of 1 & 2 Kings cover essentially the same time period as 2 Chronicles. Accordingly, there are numerous parallel passages with similar wording. But the authors had different purposes in writing, and these differences can be highlighted by comparing the similarities and the differences in the various parallel passages.

about 605~535 BC
Daniel in Babylon

597 BC
Jehoiachin as king of Judah

Apr 597 BC
Nebuchadnezzar seizes Jerusalem, second deportation

597–586 BC
Zedekiah as king of Judah

about 597~570 BC
Ezekiel as prophet

586 BC
Nebuchadnezzar destroys Jerusalem, third deportation, end of the kingdom of Judah

561 BC
Jehoiachin is released from prison in Babylon

CHRONOLOGY

The books of Kings are filled with chronological information about the kings of Israel and Judah, but none of this information gives us absolute dates. We obtain absolute dates by comparing Israel's records with the records of surrounding nations (Assyria, Babylon, and Egypt) and with astronomical calculations. Remarkable harmony is found among the records, evidence that Israel's records are historically accurate and precise. For more information, see "Chronology: Israel's Monarchy," p. 562.

MEANING AND MESSAGE

Each king of the divided monarchy is evaluated on the basis of his faithfulness or lack of faithfulness to God. Either "he did what was pleasing in the LORD's sight," or "he did what was evil in the LORD's sight."

The kings of Israel were consistently evil. The evaluation of Jehoahaz is typical: "He followed the example of Jeroboam son of Nebat, continuing the sins that Jeroboam had led Israel to commit" (13:2; see 13:11; 14:24; 15:9; 17:2; 24:27). Many of the kings of Judah receive similar censure—for example, "Jehoram followed the example of the kings of Israel and was as wicked as King Ahab" (8:18). Manasseh is condemned for his rampant idolatry and apostasy (21:2-9), an example followed by several kings after him (21:20; 23:32, 37; 24:9, 19).

Several kings of Judah are commended, however, for doing "what was pleasing in the LORD's sight" (12:2; 14:3; 15:3, 34; 18:3; 22:2). The standard of comparison was David, the king with whom God instituted a covenant relationship (see 14:3). Such men were concerned for the upkeep and repair of the Temple (12:6-16; 22:3-7) and for obedience to the precepts of God's word (18:6; 22:8-13; 23:1-3). Some were reformers (12:17-18; 23:4-24). Hezekiah and Josiah receive special commendation, Hezekiah for his trust in the Lord and his honoring of God's word (18:5-6) and Josiah for his high regard for the law of Moses (23:25). The implication is clear. God's people are to live in accord with the high standards of God's

2 Kings . . . is the stuff of tragedy. The nation, chosen by God, saved by God from slavery, settled by God in a land of plenty, loses everything because of its consistent tendency to chase after other gods.

T. R. HOBBS
2 Kings, p. xxvii

word so that they may "do what is pleasing in God's sight" (cp. Ps 119:9-11, 111; 2 Tim 3:16-17).

The prominence given to the final days of the great prophet Elijah (1:3-17; 2:1-11) and to Elisha's spectacular ministry (2:12-25; 3:11-19; 4:1–7:2; 8:1-2) emphasizes the need to proclaim God's words to others (Acts 20:18-21; 2 Tim 2:15; 4:2) so that they may come into covenant relationship with the Lord (2 Cor 3:4-6).

Finally, the failures of even the good kings remind God's people to be faithful to the Lord and to serve him. Then their lives can be filled with good (Ps 84:11; Rom 14:7-8), and when they stand before God for judgment (Rom 14:10-11; 2 Cor 5:10), he will reward and praise them (2 Tim 4:7-8; Rev 2:10; see Matt 25:23).

FURTHER READING

T. R. HOBBS
2 Kings (1985)

PETER LEITHART
1 & 2 Kings (2006)

RICHARD D. PATTERSON AND HERMANN J. AUSTEL
1, 2 Kings in *Expositor's Bible Commentary*, vol. 3 (2009)

DONALD WISEMAN
1 & 2 Kings (1993)

1. THE DIVIDED MONARCHY (1:1–17:41)

The Era of Israel's Third Dynasty (1:1–8:29)

Elijah Confronts King Ahaziah

1 After King Ahab's death, the land of
Moab rebelled against Israel.
2One day Israel's new king, Ahaziah, fell
through the latticework of an upper room
at his palace in Samaria and was seriously
injured. So he sent messengers to the temple of Baal-zebub, the god of Ekron, to ask
whether he would recover.
3But the angel of the LORD told Elijah,
who was from Tishbe, "Go and confront the
messengers of the king of Samaria and ask
them, 'Is there no God in Israel? Why are
you going to Baal-zebub, the god of Ekron,
to ask whether the king will recover? 4Now,
therefore, this is what the LORD says: You
will never leave the bed you are lying on;
you will surely die.'" So Elijah went to deliver the message.
5When the messengers returned to the
king, he asked them, "Why have you returned so soon?"
6They replied, "A man came up to us and
told us to go back to the king and give him
this message. 'This is what the LORD says: Is
there no God in Israel? Why are you sending men to Baal-zebub, the god of Ekron, to
ask whether you will recover? Therefore,
because you have done this, you will never
leave the bed you are lying on; you will
surely die.'"
7"What sort of man was he?" the king demanded. "What did he look like?"
8They replied, "He was a hairy man, and
he wore a leather belt around his waist."
"Elijah from Tishbe!" the king exclaimed.
9Then he sent an army captain with fifty
soldiers to arrest him. They found him sitting on top of a hill. The captain said to him,
"Man of God, the king has commanded you
to come down with us."
10But Elijah replied to the captain, "If I
am a man of God, let fire come down from
[a]heaven and destroy you and your fifty
men!" Then fire fell from [a]heaven and killed
them all.
11So the king sent another captain with
fifty men. The captain said to him, "Man of
God, the king demands that you come down
at once."
12Elijah replied, "If I am a man of God, let
fire come down from heaven and destroy
you and your fifty men!" And again the fire
of God fell from heaven and killed them all.
13Once more the king sent a third captain
with fifty men. But this time the captain

1:1 2 Sam 8:2; 2 Kgs 3:5
1:2 2 Kgs 1:16; 8:7-10; Mark 3:22
1:3 1 Kgs 17:1
1:4 2 Kgs 1:16-17
1:8 Matt 3:4; Mark 1:6
1:10 1 Kgs 18:36-38; Job 1:16; Luke 9:54
[a]*shamayim* (8064) ›2 Chr 30:27

1:1 After *Ahab's death,* the Moabites felt secure enough to declare themselves free of their Israelite overlords (see 3:4-5). The historical notice anticipates the troubles that Israel would experience after the short-lived reign of Ahaziah (see 1 Kgs 22:51).

1:2 *An upper room* or balcony enclosed with *latticework* was common; it allowed for the free flow of air and a degree of privacy, but *latticework* was easily broken. • *Baal-zebub* (*lord of flies*) may be a parody of a Canaanite deity named Baal-zebul (*Baal is prince*). The name of this deity was later used for Satan (see note on Matt 12:24). Ahaziah followed his father Ahab in worshiping Baal.

1:3-4 *The angel of the LORD* does not seem to be a christophany in the book of Kings, as in other OT texts (e.g., Judg 6:11-18). • *Elijah,* who had previously confronted Ahaziah's father, Ahab, had a twofold message for the king: a condemnation for failure to acknowledge that Yahweh, not Baal, is God (see 1 Kgs 18:16-18), and a pronouncement of doom (see 1 Kgs 21:17-24).

1:8 *He was a hairy man:* Or *He was wearing clothing made of hair.*

1:9-10 The arrogant words of the *army captain* contained a contradiction, which *Elijah* pointed out: If Elijah was a *man of God* (i.e., God's prophet), then his authority was from God and to ignore him was to invite peril (Deut 18:15-19). • *Fire* often symbolizes the presence of God in the Scriptures (see Exod 3:1-6; 19:18; cp. 1 Kgs 18:38). • *Fifty soldiers* was a common grouping (1 Kgs 18:4); here it indicates a division within Israel's military organization.

1:11-13 Report of what happened to the previous contingent had apparently reached the king.

1:13-14 In contrast to the first two officers, the third commander *pleaded* for mercy before Elijah and God.

1:15
2 Kgs 1:3
Isa 51:12
Jer 1:17
Ezek 2:6
1:17
2 Kgs 3:1; 8:16
2:1
Gen 5:23-24
1 Kgs 19:16-21
Heb 11:5
2:6
Ruth 1:16
2 Kgs 2:1-2

went up the hill and fell to his knees before
Elijah. He pleaded with him, "O man of God,
please spare my life and the lives of these,
your fifty servants. 14See how the fire from
heaven came down and destroyed the first
two groups. But now please spare my life!"
15Then the angel of the LORD said to Elijah, "Go down with him, and don't be afraid
of him." So Elijah got up and went with him
to the king.
16And Elijah said to the king, "This is what
the LORD says: Why did you send messengers to Baal-zebub, the god of Ekron, to ask
whether you will recover? Is there no God
in Israel to answer your question? Therefore, because you have done this, you will
never leave the bed you are lying on; you
will surely die."
17So Ahaziah died, just as the LORD had
promised through Elijah. Since Ahaziah did
not have a son to succeed him, his brother Joram became the next king. This took place
in the second year of the reign of Jehoram
son of Jehoshaphat, king of Judah.
18The rest of the events in Ahaziah's reign
are recorded in *The Book of the History of
the Kings of Israel.*

Elijah Taken into Heaven

2 When the LORD was about to take Elijah
up to heaven in a whirlwind, Elijah and
Elisha were traveling from Gilgal. 2And Elijah said to Elisha, "Stay here, for the LORD
has told me to go to Bethel."
But Elisha replied, "As surely as the LORD
lives and you yourself live, I will never leave
you!" So they went down together to Bethel.
3The group of prophets from Bethel came
to Elisha and asked him, "Did you know that
the LORD is going to take your master away
from you today?"
"Of course I know," Elisha answered. "But
be quiet about it."
4Then Elijah said to Elisha, "Stay here, for
the LORD has told me to go to Jericho."
But Elisha replied again, "As surely as
the LORD lives and you yourself live, I will
never leave you." So they went on together
to Jericho.
5Then the group of prophets from Jericho came to Elisha and asked him, "Did you
know that the LORD is going to take your
master away from you today?"
"Of course I know," Elisha answered. "But
be quiet about it."
6Then Elijah said to Elisha, "Stay here, for
the LORD has told me to go to the Jordan
River."
But again Elisha replied, "As surely as the
LORD lives and you yourself live, I will never
leave you." So they went on together.
7Fifty men from the group of prophets
also went and watched from a distance as
Elijah and Elisha stopped beside the Jordan

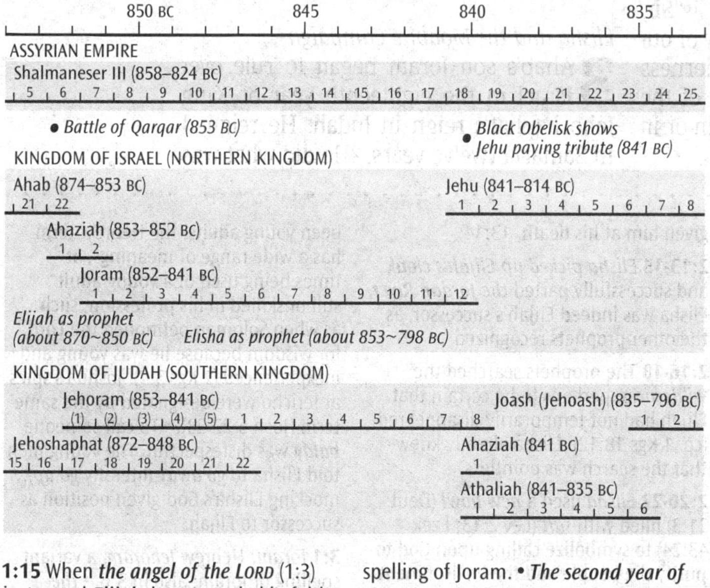

◀ **Israel and Judah, 854–833 BC (1:1–12:3).** Assyrian records help to verify the dates of the kings of Israel. According to these records, AHAB participated in the BATTLE OF QARQAR in 853 BC, and JEHU paid tribute to SHALMANESER III in 841 BC. So, AHAZIAH's two-year reign (1 Kgs 22:51) and JORAM's twelve-year reign (3:1) occurred between these two dates.
• In Judah, JEHORAM became co-regent with his father JEHOSHAPHAT in 853 BC (1:17; 3:1), but his official regnal years were counted from the year of Jehoshaphat's death (8:16-17).
• Jehoram's widow was ATHALIAH, the daughter of Ahab and Jezebel. Athaliah had six official regnal years in Judah's calendar, but in the calendar of the northern kingdom her reign had seven years, corresponding to Jehu's first seven years (see 11:4, apparently written by a northern scribe).

1:15 When *the angel of the LORD* (1:3) instructed *Elijah*, he responded in faithful obedience.

1:16 *Is there no God in Israel?* God's message to Ahaziah remained unchanged (cp. 1:3-4).

1:17 *Joram:* Hebrew *Jehoram,* a variant spelling of Joram. • *The second year of the reign of Jehoram* was 852 BC, during Jehoram's co-regency with his father, *Jehoshaphat* (853–848 BC).

2:1-18 Elijah's translation into heaven transferred the prophetic mantle to Elisha.

2:2-6 *Stay here:* Three times, Elijah urged Elisha to remain behind while he traveled on. Each time, Elisha refused with a solemn vow, determined to be with his master to the end.

River. 8Then Elijah folded his cloak together
and struck the water with it. The river divided, and the two of them went across on
dry ground!
9When they came to the other side, Elijah
said to Elisha, "Tell me what I can do for you
before I am taken away."
And Elisha replied, "Please let me inherit
a double share of your spirit and become
your successor."
10"You have asked a difficult thing," Elijah replied. "If you see me when I am taken
from you, then you will get your request. But
if not, then you won't."
11As they were walking along and talking,
suddenly a chariot of fire appeared, drawn
by horses of fire. It drove between the two
men, separating them, and Elijah was carried by a whirlwind into heaven. 12Elisha
saw it and cried out, "My father! My father!
I see the chariots and charioteers of Israel!"
And as they disappeared from sight, Elisha
tore his clothes in distress.
13Elisha picked up Elijah's cloak, which
had fallen when he was taken up. Then
Elisha returned to the bank of the Jordan
River. 14He struck the water with Elijah's
cloak and cried out, "Where is the LORD, the
God of Elijah?" Then the river divided, and
Elisha went across.
15When the group of prophets from Jericho saw from a distance what happened,
they exclaimed, "Elijah's [b]spirit rests upon
Elisha!" And they went to meet him and
bowed to the ground before him. 16"Sir,"
they said, "just say the word and fifty of our
strongest men will search the wilderness
for your master. Perhaps the [c]Spirit of the
LORD has left him on some mountain or in
some valley."
"No," Elisha said, "don't send them." 17But
they kept urging him until they shamed
him into agreeing, and he finally said, "All
right, send them." So fifty men searched
for three days but did not find Elijah. 18Eli-
sha was still at Jericho when they returned.
"Didn't I tell you not to go?" he asked.

Elisha's First Miracles

19One day the leaders of the town of Jericho
visited Elisha. "We have a problem, my lord,"
they told him. "This town is located in pleasant surroundings, as you can see. But the
water is bad, and the land is unproductive."
20Elisha said, "Bring me a new bowl with
salt in it." So they brought it to him. 21Then
he went out to the spring that supplied the
town with water and threw the salt into it.
And he said, "This is what the LORD says: I
have purified this water. It will no longer
cause death or infertility." 22And the water
has remained pure ever since, just as Elisha
said.
23Elisha left Jericho and went up to Bethel.
As he was walking along the road, a group
of boys from the town began mocking and
making fun of him. "Go away, baldy!" they
chanted. "Go away, baldy!" 24Elisha turned
around and looked at them, and he cursed
them in the name of the LORD. Then two
bears came out of the woods and mauled
forty-two of them. 25From there Elisha
went to Mount Carmel and finally returned
to Samaria.

Elisha and the Moabite Campaign

3 Ahab's son Joram began to rule over
Israel in the eighteenth year of King
Jehoshaphat's reign in Judah. He reigned
in Samaria twelve years. 2He did what was

2:8 Exod 14:21; 1 Kgs 19:19
2:11 2 Kgs 6:17
2:12 2 Kgs 13:14
2:14 2 Kgs 2:8
2:15 [b]*ruakh* (7307) ‣ 2 Kgs 2:16
2:16 1 Kgs 18:12; Acts 8:39; [c]*ruakh* (7307) ‣ Ps 32:2
2:21 Exod 15:25-26; 2 Kgs 4:41; 6:6
2:25 1 Kgs 18:20
3:1 2 Kgs 1:17; 8:16
3:2 1 Kgs 16:30-32; 2 Kgs 10:25-26

2:8 ***Elijah folded his cloak together and struck the water with it:*** Such symbolic actions visually represented God's power (see Exod 14:16, 21, 26-27; 17:8-13; 1 Kgs 11:30-31; Ezek 4:1-17; 5:1-4).

2:9-10 A firstborn son, as the primary heir, inherited ***a double share*** of his father's estate (Deut 21:17); Elisha asked that Elijah's God-given spiritual abilities and privileges might continue to live through him.

2:11 ***Chariot of fire . . . horses of fire . . . whirlwind:*** These things represent God's appearance in mighty power (cp. Isa 66:15). • ***Elijah was carried . . . into heaven,*** like Enoch (Gen 5:24), without dying. Some believe that Enoch and Elijah will reappear at the time of the end (see note on Rev 11:1-13).

2:12 Elijah was Elisha's spiritual ***father*** and personal mentor. Cp. the tribute given him at his death, 13:14.

2:13-15 ***Elisha picked up Elijah's cloak*** and successfully parted ***the Jordan River.*** Elisha was indeed Elijah's successor, as the other prophets recognized.

2:16-18 The prophets searched the ***wilderness,*** perhaps to be certain that Elijah had not temporarily disappeared (cp. 1 Kgs 18:12). Elisha already knew that the search was pointless.

2:20-22 ***Elisha*** used a ***new bowl*** (Deut 21:3) filled with ***salt*** (Lev 2:13; Ezek 43:24) to symbolize calling upon God to purify the people and the environment. Elisha made it clear that the Lord, not he or the ***salt,*** had ***purified this water.***

2:21 ***or infertility:*** Or *or make the land unproductive.* Hebrew reads *or barrenness,* so it can be interpreted either way.

2:23 The ***group of boys*** could have been young adults; the Hebrew term has a wide range of meanings, at times being used of a young adult still unskilled in his profession, such as when Solomon petitioned the Lord for wisdom because he was young and inexperienced (1 Kgs 3:7). Joshua's spies at Jericho were designated by the same term (Josh 6:22-23). • To call someone ***baldy*** was disrespectful. The young men told Elisha to ***go away*** (literally *go up*), mocking Elisha's God-given position as successor to Elijah.

3:1 ***Joram:*** Hebrew *Jehoram,* a variant spelling of Joram; also in 3:6. • ***the eighteenth year of King Jehoshaphat's reign:*** See note on 1:17.

3:2 Ahab apparently erected ***the sacred pillar*** (or ***stela***) ***of Baal*** when instituting Baal worship (see 1 Kgs 16:32-33). Similar stones were also erected to

3:3 1 Kgs 12:28; 14:16
3:4 2 Sam 8:2; Isa 16:1-2
3:5 2 Kgs 1:1
3:7 1 Kgs 22:4
3:11 1 Kgs 19:21; 22:7
3:13 1 Kgs 22:6-11, 22-25
3:15 1 Sam 16:23
3:20 Exod 29:39-40

evil in the LORD's sight, but not to the same extent as his father and mother. He at least tore down the sacred pillar of Baal that his father had set up. [3]Nevertheless, he continued in the sins that Jeroboam son of Nebat had committed and led the people of Israel to commit.

[4]King Mesha of Moab was a sheep breeder. He used to pay the king of Israel an annual tribute of 100,000 lambs and the wool of 100,000 rams. [5]But after Ahab's death, the king of Moab rebelled against the king of Israel. [6]So King Joram promptly mustered the army of Israel and marched from Samaria. [7]On the way, he sent this message to King Jehoshaphat of Judah: "The king of Moab has rebelled against me. Will you join me in battle against him?"

And Jehoshaphat replied, "Why, of course! You and I are as one. My troops are your troops, and my horses are your horses." [8]Then Jehoshaphat asked, "What route will we take?"

"We will attack from the wilderness of Edom," Joram replied.

[9]The king of Edom and his troops joined them, and all three armies traveled along a roundabout route through the wilderness for seven days. But there was no water for the men or their animals.

[10]"What should we do?" the king of Israel cried out. "The LORD has brought the three of us here to let the king of Moab defeat us."

[11]But King Jehoshaphat of Judah asked, "Is there no prophet of the LORD with us? If there is, we can ask the LORD what to do through him."

One of King Joram's officers replied, "Elisha son of Shaphat is here. He used to be Elijah's personal assistant."

[12]Jehoshaphat said, "Yes, the LORD speaks through him." So the kings of Israel, Judah, and Edom went to consult with Elisha.

[13]"Why are you coming to me?" Elisha asked the king of Israel. "Go to the pagan prophets of your father and mother!"

But King Joram of Israel said, "No! For it was the LORD who called us three kings here—only to be defeated by the king of Moab!"

[14]Elisha replied, "As surely as the LORD Almighty lives, whom I serve, I wouldn't even bother with you except for my respect for King Jehoshaphat of Judah. [15]Now bring me someone who can play the harp."

While the harp was being played, the power of the LORD came upon Elisha, [16]and he said, "This is what the LORD says: This dry valley will be filled with pools of water! [17]You will see neither wind nor rain, says the LORD, but this valley will be filled with water. You will have plenty for yourselves and your cattle and other animals. [18]But this is only a simple thing for the LORD, for he will make you victorious over the army of Moab! [19]You will conquer the best of their towns, even the fortified ones. You will cut down all their good trees, stop up all their springs, and ruin all their good land with stones."

[20]The next day at about the time when the morning sacrifice was offered, water suddenly appeared! It was flowing from the direction of Edom, and soon there was water everywhere.

[21]Meanwhile, when the people of Moab heard about the three armies marching against them, they mobilized every man who was old enough to strap on a sword, and they stationed themselves along their border. [22]But when they got up the next morning, the sun was shining across the water, making it appear red to the Moabites—like blood.

pagan deities in Judah (1 Kgs 14:23); such pillars were later purged by Jehu (10:26-27) and Josiah (23:13-15).

3:4-27 The joint war of Israel and Judah against Moab was the setting for one of Elisha's miracles.

3:4-5 The Moabite rebellion (see 1:1) began with the withholding of the ***annual tribute.*** The Moabite Stone (Mesha Stela) records details of Israel's domination of northern Moab in the days of Omri and Ahab, a subservience that continued into the reigns of Ahaziah and Joram.

3:6-7 ***Jehoshaphat***'s ready compliance with ***Joram***'s appeal was typical of his participation in the undertakings of the northern kings (1 Kgs 22:4; 2 Chr 20:35-37). The marriage of Jehoshaphat's son Jehoram to Ahab's daughter Athaliah (2 Chr 18:1; 21:6) heightened Jehoshaphat's entanglement with Israel.

3:8-9 ***The king of Edom . . . joined them:*** Edom was apparently a vassal kingdom to Judah at this time. Later, in the days of Jehoshaphat's son Jehoram, Edom successfully rebelled against Judah (8:20-22). The southern route through Edom avoided strong Moabite fortifications, but it was dangerous because ***water*** was scarce.

3:11-12 ***Is there no prophet of the LORD with us?*** Diviners or prophets often traveled with armies to perceive the divine will. ***Jehoshaphat*** again desired an oracle from a true prophet to learn the Lord's intentions for the battle (cp. 1 Kgs 22:7). However, this time he waited until the campaign had begun before inquiring of the Lord.

3:11 ***He used to be Elijah's personal assistant:*** Literally *He used to pour water on the hands of Elijah.*

3:13-14 Elisha participated because of Jehoshaphat's presence, despite his entanglement with the ***pagan*** Joram.

3:13 ***Why are you coming to me?*** Literally *What is there in common between you and me?*

3:15 ***bring me someone who can play the harp:*** Music stimulated the prophetic spirit (see note on 2 Chr 20:20-21; cp. Ps 49:4). • ***the power:*** Literally *the hand.*

3:18-20 The supply of ***water—a simple thing for the LORD***—was a harbinger of God's enabling the allies to defeat the ***army of Moab.***

23"It's blood!" the Moabites exclaimed. "The three armies must have attacked and killed each other! Let's go, men of Moab, and collect the plunder!"

24But when the Moabites arrived at the Israelite camp, the army of Israel rushed out and attacked them until they turned and ran. The army of Israel chased them into the land of Moab, destroying everything as they went. 25They destroyed the towns, covered their good land with stones, stopped up all the springs, and cut down all the good trees. Finally, only Kir-hareseth and its stone walls were left, but men with slings surrounded and attacked it.

26When the king of Moab saw that he was losing the battle, he led 700 of his swordsmen in a desperate attempt to break through the enemy lines near the king of Edom, but they failed. 27Then the king of Moab took his oldest son, who would have been the next king, and sacrificed him as a burnt offering on the wall. So there was great anger against Israel, and the Israelites withdrew and returned to their own land.

Elisha Helps a Poor Widow

4 One day the widow of a member of the group of prophets came to Elisha and cried out, "My husband who served you is dead, and you know how he feared the LORD. But now a creditor has come, threatening to take my two sons as slaves."

2"What can I do to help you?" Elisha asked. "Tell me, what do you have in the house?"

"Nothing at all, except a flask of olive oil," she replied.

3And Elisha said, "Borrow as many empty jars as you can from your friends and neighbors. 4Then go into your house with your sons and shut the door behind you. Pour olive oil from your flask into the jars, setting each one aside when it is filled."

5So she did as she was told. Her sons kept bringing jars to her, and she filled one after another. 6Soon every container was full to the brim!

"Bring me another jar," she said to one of her sons.

"There aren't any more!" he told her. And then the olive oil stopped flowing.

7When she told the man of God what had happened, he said to her, "Now sell the olive oil and pay your debts, and you and your sons can live on what is left over."

Elisha Helps a Woman in Shunem

8One day Elisha went to the town of Shunem. A wealthy woman lived there, and she urged him to come to her home for a meal. After that, whenever he passed that way, he would stop there for something to eat.

9She said to her husband, "I am sure this man who stops in from time to time is a holy man of God. 10Let's build a small room for him on the roof and furnish it with a bed, a table, a chair, and a lamp. Then he will have a place to stay whenever he comes by."

11One day Elisha returned to Shunem, and he went up to this upper room to rest. 12He said to his servant Gehazi, "Tell the woman from Shunem I want to speak to her." When she appeared, 13Elisha said to Gehazi, "Tell her, 'We appreciate the kind concern you have shown us. What can we do for you? Can we put in a good word for you to the king or to the commander of the army?' "

"No," she replied, "my family takes good care of me."

14Later Elisha asked Gehazi, "What can we do for her?"

3:25 Isa 16:7; Jer 48:31, 36
3:27 Mic 6:7
4:1 Lev 25:39-41, 48; Neh 5:2-5
4:2 1 Kgs 17:12
4:7 1 Kgs 12:22
4:8 Josh 19:18
4:10 Matt 10:41; Rom 12:13

3:24-25 *The army of Israel . . . destroyed the towns.* Elisha's prophecy was fulfilled, although *Kir-hareseth* escaped total destruction. • *destroying everything as they went:* The meaning of the Hebrew is uncertain.

3:26 The reason for the Moabite king's *attempt to break through the enemy lines* might have been to avenge himself against the Edomite king or to escape through a perceived weakness in the allied lines.

3:27 *So there was great anger against Israel:* Or *So Israel's anger was great.* The meaning of the Hebrew is uncertain. The Hebrew phrase translated *great anger* occurs elsewhere to describe the Lord's fury against Israel for covenant violations (Jer 21:5; 32:37; Zech 7:12).

4:1 The widow's ***husband*** had been ***a member of the group of prophets . . . who served*** Elisha (2:3-18; see note on 4:38). • ***take my two sons as slaves:*** The law of Moses allowed a creditor to place a debtor and his children into slavery to work off a debt (Exod 21:2-4; Lev 25:10).

4:4 ***shut the door:*** Elisha was meeting a private need; the miracle was not for public show. • ***Olive oil***, an important staple, had commercial value (see 1 Kgs 5:11; 2 Chr 11:11; Hos 12:1).

4:5-6 Elisha was absent during the miracle so the woman and her son would recognize that the provision was by the Lord's power.

4:8-37 Elisha's dealings with the ***woman*** from ***Shunem*** are presented in two parallel sections (4:8-20, 21-37). ***Shunem*** was a border town in the tribal allotment to Issachar (Josh 19:18).

4:9-10 Because the Shunemite woman recognized that Elisha was a true prophet—***a holy man of God***—she wished to provide hospitality for him during his frequent travels (see Isa 58:7; Heb 13:2; 3 Jn 1:5). • ***A small room . . . on the roof***, reached by an outside stairway, assured privacy for both Elisha and his hosts.

4:11-14 ***Elisha*** wanted to return some favor to his host. • ***his servant Gehazi:*** Gehazi served as an apprentice, as Elisha had served with Elijah (1 Kgs 19:21). It would not be unusual for a prophet to consult with his attendant.

4:16 Gen 18:14
4:21 2 Kgs 4:32

Gehazi replied, "She doesn't have a son, and her husband is an old man."

15"Call her back again," Elisha told him. When the woman returned, Elisha said to her as she stood in the doorway, 16"Next year at this time you will be holding a son in your arms!"

"No, my lord!" she cried. "O man of God, don't deceive me and get my hopes up like that."

17But sure enough, the woman soon became pregnant. And at that time the following year she had a son, just as Elisha had said.

18One day when her child was older, he went out to help his father, who was working with the harvesters. 19Suddenly he cried out, "My head hurts! My head hurts!"

His father said to one of the servants, "Carry him home to his mother."

20So the servant took him home, and his mother held him on her lap. But around noontime he died. 21She carried him up and laid him on the bed of the man of God, then shut the door and left him there. 22She sent a message to her husband: "Send one of the servants and a donkey so that I can hurry to the man of God and come right back."

23"Why go today?" he asked. "It is neither a new moon festival nor a Sabbath."

But she said, "It will be all right."

24So she saddled the donkey and said to the servant, "Hurry! Don't slow down unless I tell you to."

25As she approached the man of God at Mount Carmel, Elisha saw her in the distance. He said to Gehazi, "Look, the woman from Shunem is coming. 26Run out to meet her and ask her, 'Is everything all right with you, your husband, and your child?' "

"Yes," the woman told Gehazi, "everything is fine."

27But when she came to the man of God at the mountain, she fell to the ground

ELISHA (2:1–9:13)

2 Kgs 13:14-21
1 Kgs 19:15-21
Luke 4:27

Elisha the prophet was Elijah's follower and successor in the northern kingdom of Israel during the late 800s BC, a time when the leaders and people of the northern kingdom of Israel turned their backs on God and worshiped the Canaanite god Baal. Ahab and Jezebel, and their descendants who succeeded them on the thrones of both Israel and Judah, were eager worshipers of this false god. Elisha's ministry (853~798 BC) began as King Ahab's reign was ending, and he was an important part of God's strategy to bring down Israel's idol-worshiping leaders.

Elisha started his work as a disciple of Elijah and was the one God chose to take Elijah's place (1 Kgs 19:15-21; 2 Kgs 2:1-18). After Elijah was taken into heaven, Elisha's miracles demonstrated that God's great power was with him.

Elisha's miracles often involved water. He purified the putrid water of a spring near Jericho (2:19-23) and caused an ax head to float (6:1-7). When King Joram's water supply ran out in enemy territory, Elisha predicted ample water supplies (3:4-20). Baal supposedly controlled water, so these signs showed that the LORD, and not Baal, was really in charge.

Elisha displayed God's power by helping people in tangible ways, which the pagan gods never did. He helped a poor woman by miraculously causing her jars to fill with olive oil (4:1-7). He predicted to a woman from Shunem that she would have a son, and brought the boy back to life when he died (4:8-37). He cured an Aramean general named Naaman of leprosy (5:1-19). He provided food for people who needed it (4:38–44).

Elisha was part of God's plan to bring judgment on the Baal-worshiping northern kingdom. God had told Elijah that he was also going to use Jehu from Israel and Hazael of Syria as his tools of judgment (1 Kgs 19:15-18). Elisha anointed both men (8:7-15; 9:1-13), and they brought a violent end to those leaders of Israel who encouraged the worship of Baal.

Elisha's miracles anticipated Jesus' ministry. Jesus also cured lepers (Matt 8:1-4), raised a dead man (John 11:1-44), and provided food (Matt 14:16-21; 15:32-38). Jesus mentioned the healing of Naaman as a precedent for his reaching out to Gentiles, to show that God's mercy is not restricted to Israelites (Luke 4:27).

4:15-16 Cp. similar promises and responses at Gen 18:9-15; Luke 1:6-20.

4:18-20 ***"My head hurts!"*** The boy probably suffered a brain aneurysm. The woman's faith and character were put to the test with the sudden death of her son ***on her lap.***

4:21 ***laid him on the bed of the man of God:*** The woman's action kept her son's death a secret from others and demonstrated her confidence in Elisha's ability to do a miracle.

4:24-26 ***Mount Carmel*** lay about twenty miles northwest of Shunem. The length of the trip and the woman's obvious haste aroused Elisha's suspicion that some tragedy concerning the ***child*** had occurred. • ***"everything is fine":*** The woman brushed off Gehazi's inquiries; she was resolved to deal with no one but Elisha.

before him and caught hold of his feet. Gehazi began to push her away, but the man of God said, "Leave her alone. She is deeply troubled, but the LORD has not told me what it is."

28Then she said, "Did I ask you for a son, my lord? And didn't I say, 'Don't deceive me and get my hopes up'?"

29Then Elisha said to Gehazi, "Get ready to travel; take my staff and go! Don't talk to anyone along the way. Go quickly and lay the staff on the child's face."

30But the boy's mother said, "As surely as the LORD lives and you yourself live, I won't go home unless you go with me." So Elisha returned with her.

31Gehazi hurried on ahead and laid the staff on the child's face, but nothing happened. There was no sign of life. He returned to meet Elisha and told him, "The child is still dead."

32When Elisha arrived, the child was indeed dead, lying there on the prophet's bed.
33He went in alone and shut the door behind him and prayed to the LORD.
34Then he lay down on the child's body, placing his mouth on the child's mouth, his eyes on the child's eyes, and his hands on the child's hands. And as he stretched out on him, the child's body began to grow warm again!
35Elisha got up, walked back and forth across the room once, and then stretched himself out again on the child. This time the boy sneezed seven times and opened his eyes!

36Then Elisha summoned Gehazi. "Call the child's mother!" he said. And when she came in, Elisha said, "Here, take your son!"
37She fell at his feet and bowed before him, overwhelmed with gratitude. Then she took her son in her arms and carried him downstairs.

Elisha Helps Some Prophets

38Elisha now returned to Gilgal, and there was a famine in the land. One day as the group of prophets was seated before him, he said to his servant, "Put a large pot on the fire, and make some stew for the rest of the group."

39One of the young men went out into the field to gather herbs and came back with a pocketful of wild gourds. He shredded them and put them into the pot without realizing they were poisonous.
40Some of the stew was served to the men. But after they had eaten a bite or two they cried out, "Man of God, there's poison in this stew!" So they would not eat it.

41Elisha said, "Bring me some flour." Then he threw it into the pot and said, "Now it's all right; go ahead and eat." And then it did not harm them.

42One day a man from Baal-shalishah brought the man of God a sack of fresh grain and twenty loaves of barley bread made from the first grain of his harvest. Elisha said, "Give it to the people so they can eat."

43"What?" his servant exclaimed. "Feed a hundred people with only this?"

But Elisha repeated, "Give it to the people so they can eat, for this is what the LORD says: Everyone will eat, and there will even be some left over!"
44And when they gave it to the people, there was plenty for all and some left over, just as the LORD had promised.

4:29 Exod 4:17; 7:19; 14:16; 1 Kgs 18:46
4:34 1 Kgs 17:21-23
4:37 Heb 11:35
4:38 2 Kgs 2:1; 8:1
4:41 Exod 15:25; 2 Kgs 2:21-22
4:43 Luke 9:13; John 6:9, 12
4:44 Matt 14:16, 20

4:27 ***caught hold of his feet:*** With this sign of deep respect and supplication, the woman poured out her heart to Elisha (see Matt 28:9; Luke 8:41, 47; 17:16; Rev 1:17).

4:28 The loss of her son undid all the joy she felt at his promised birth and seemed to make that birth a cruel deception.

4:29 ***Get ready to travel:*** Literally *Bind up your loins.* • Elisha instructed Gehazi not to ***talk to anyone along the way***, indicating the seriousness and urgency of the mission. Jesus gave similar instructions when he sent out the seventy-two disciples (Luke 10:4). • Laying Elisha's ***staff on the child's face*** signified the prophet's intention to identify with the boy and claim God's power.

4:31 ***no sign of life:*** Elisha's staff held no magical power; only God is the author of life (Acts 17:25-28).

4:33 ***shut the door:*** Elisha followed the same procedure he had advised the widow to take earlier (4:4). If God were to perform the miracle, it would not be for public display. Only the mother knew of the boy's death and only she needed to know of Elisha's efforts to petition God for the boy's life.

4:34-35 ***lay down on the child's body:*** Elisha's actions and faith in the Lord were similar to Elijah's (1 Kgs 17:17-24).

4:36-37 Again, ***Gehazi*** summoned the woman (4:12, 15), and again, she ***fell at*** Elisha's ***feet*** (4:27), this time ***overwhelmed with gratitude*** rather than anguish.

4:38 Like Bethel (2:3) and Jericho (2:5, 15), ***Gilgal*** was the center for a ***group of prophets*** (2:1). Elisha was the leader of these groups, and thus sat at the head of the table for meals.

4:39-41 The men immediately recognized that the young man's ***wild gourds*** were ***poisonous***; they did not want to be poisoned or to waste the stew during a famine, so they turned to Elisha for help. The ***flour*** was a tangible symbol of God's miraculous provision of food.

4:42-44 ***grain . . . loaves of barley . . . first grain:*** This offering was similar to the first of the crops that were normally presented to God (Lev 23:20) and to the priests (Deut 18:4-5) as their portion. Because of the famine, Elisha shared the offering with all the ***people***. • Elisha's feeding ***a hundred people*** with ***a sack of fresh grain and twenty loaves of barley bread*** anticipated the miraculous ministry of Jesus (Matt 14:15-21; 15:32-38). Nothing is impossible for God (Matt 19:26; Luke 1:37; 18:27).

5:1 Luke 4:27
5:2 2 Kgs 6:23
5:5 1 Sam 9:7-8
5:7 Gen 30:2; 37:29; 1 Kgs 20:7
5:10 John 9:7
5:12 Prov 14:17; 19:11
5:14 Job 33:23-25; Luke 4:27; 5:13
5:15 1 Sam 17:46-47
5:16 Gen 14:22-23; 2 Kgs 3:14

Elisha and the Healing of Naaman

5 The king of Aram had great admiration for Naaman, the commander of
his army, because through him the LORD
had given Aram great victories. But though
Naaman was a mighty warrior, he suffered
from leprosy.
2At this time Aramean raiders had invaded the land of Israel, and among their
captives was a young girl who had been
given to Naaman's wife as a maid. 3One day
the girl said to her mistress, "I wish my master would go to see the prophet in Samaria.
He would heal him of his leprosy."
4So Naaman told the king what the young
girl from Israel had said. 5"Go and visit the
prophet," the king of Aram told him. "I will
send a letter of introduction for you to take
to the king of Israel." So Naaman started
out, carrying as gifts 750 pounds of silver,
150 pounds of gold, and ten sets of clothing.
6The letter to the king of Israel said: "With
this letter I present my servant Naaman. I
want you to heal him of his leprosy."
7When the king of Israel read the letter,
he tore his clothes in dismay and said, "This
man sends me a leper to heal! Am I God, that
I can give life and take it away? I can see that
he's just trying to pick a fight with me."
8But when Elisha, the man of God, heard
that the king of Israel had torn his clothes
in dismay, he sent this message to him:
"Why are you so upset? Send Naaman to me,
and he will learn that there is a true prophet
here in Israel."
9So Naaman went with his horses and
chariots and waited at the door of Elisha's
house. 10But Elisha sent a messenger out to
him with this message: "Go and wash yourself seven times in the Jordan River. Then
your skin will be restored, and you will be
healed of your leprosy."
11But Naaman became angry and stalked
away. "I thought he would certainly come
out to meet me!" he said. "I expected him
to wave his hand over the leprosy and call
on the name of the LORD his God and heal
me! 12Aren't the rivers of Damascus, the
Abana and the Pharpar, better than any of
the rivers of Israel? Why shouldn't I wash
in them and be healed?" So Naaman turned
and went away in a rage.
13But his officers tried to reason with him
and said, "Sir, if the prophet had told you to
do something very difficult, wouldn't you
have done it? So you should certainly obey
him when he says simply, 'Go and wash and
be cured!' " 14So Naaman went down to
the Jordan River and dipped himself seven
times, as the man of God had instructed
him. And his skin became as healthy as the
skin of a young child, and he was healed!
15Then Naaman and his entire party went
back to find the man of God. They stood
before him, and Naaman said, "Now I know
that there is no God in all the world except
in Israel. So please accept a gift from your
servant."
16But Elisha replied, "As surely as the
LORD lives, whom I serve, I will not accept
any gifts." And though Naaman urged him
to take the gift, Elisha refused.

5:1 ***The king of Aram*** was probably Ben-hadad II (860–843 BC). • ***the LORD had given Aram great victories:*** The Lord is sovereign over all nations (Ps 47:8; 99:1-2; Rom 13:1). • ***from leprosy:*** Or *from a contagious skin disease;* the Hebrew word used here and throughout this passage can describe various skin diseases. Naaman's access to society and Gehazi's later social freedom (8:4-5) suggest that the problem was not Hansen's disease but another incurable skin disease (see Lev 13:10-11, 45-46).

5:2-3 During Joram's reign, strained relations between Israel and the Arameans led to incursions by ***Aramean raiders*** into the northern kingdom (see 6:8, 24).

5:5-6 The lavish ***gifts*** and the royal ***letter of introduction***, common practices in the ancient Near East, underscored Naaman's wealth, his value to the Aramean king, and Elisha's reputation. Unlike Ahaziah, who sent his messengers directly to the temple of Baal-zebub in Philistia (1:2), the Aramean king followed diplomatic protocol by sending Naaman first to King Joram.

5:5 ***750 pounds of silver, 150 pounds of gold:*** Hebrew *10 talents* [340 kilograms] *of silver, 6,000 shekels* [68 kilograms] *of gold.*

5:7 ***tore his clothes:*** This action was often a sign of intense agitation (11:4), grief (Gen 37:34; 2 Sam 13:31), or sorrow (6:30; Job 1:20; 2:12). Due to the perennial distrust and hostilities between the Arameans and the Israelites, Joram assumed that the Aramean king was ***trying to pick a fight***, as had occurred in the days of his father Ahab (1 Kgs 20:1-12).

5:8 Elisha had no respect for King Joram (3:14), but he sent the message because of the opportunity for a testimony to the Lord's power.

5:9-12 Rather than receiving Naaman, who came to buy his healing, Elisha left him standing ***at the door*** and communicated with him by ***messenger***. Naaman expected special treatment befitting his station and was disappointed both in Elisha's failure to receive him and at his instructions to ***wash . . . seven times in the Jordan River***, which he considered inferior to the rivers of Aram. Washing in the Jordan would be a visible reminder that only Yahweh, the God of Israel, could heal Naaman.

5:13-14 ***Sir:*** Literally *My father,* a term of respect (2:12; Judg 17:10; 1 Sam 24:11). • ***Naaman*** swallowed his pride. He did ***as the man of God had instructed him*** and experienced God's healing power. Obedience to God brings God's blessings and purity (Ps 119:9-11).

5:15-16 ***No God . . . except in Israel:*** Naaman's physical healing led to spiritual conversion. Like the healed leper in Jesus' parable, Naaman returned to give thanks to his benefactor (Luke 17:15-16). • Naaman offered a gift out of gratitude, but ***Elisha refused***; God's grace and blessings were not to be obtained through money, ***gifts***, or favors (Isa 55:1-5; Rom 2:4; 1 Cor 2:12; Eph 4:8).

[17]Then Naaman said, "All right, but please allow me to load two of my mules with earth from this place, and I will take it back home with me. From now on I will never again offer burnt offerings or sacrifices to any other god except the LORD. [18]However, may the LORD pardon me in this one thing: When my master the king goes into the temple of the god Rimmon to worship there and leans on my arm, may the LORD pardon me when I bow, too."

[19]"Go in peace," Elisha said. So Naaman started home again.

Elisha Confronts Gehazi

[20]But Gehazi, the servant of Elisha, the man of God, said to himself, "My master should not have let this Aramean get away without accepting any of his gifts. As surely as the LORD lives, I will chase after him and get something from him." [21]So Gehazi set off after Naaman.

When Naaman saw Gehazi running after him, he climbed down from his chariot and went to meet him. "Is everything all right?" Naaman asked.

[22]"Yes," Gehazi said, "but my master has sent me to tell you that two young prophets from the hill country of Ephraim have just arrived. He would like 75 pounds of silver and two sets of clothing to give to them."

[23]"By all means, take twice as much silver," Naaman insisted. He gave him two sets of clothing, tied up the money in two bags, and sent two of his servants to carry the gifts for Gehazi. [24]But when they arrived at the citadel, Gehazi took the gifts from the servants and sent the men back. Then he went and hid the gifts inside the house.

[25]When he went in to his master, Elisha asked him, "Where have you been, Gehazi?"

"I haven't been anywhere," he replied.

[26]But Elisha asked him, "Don't you realize that I was there in spirit when Naaman stepped down from his chariot to meet you? Is this the time to receive money and clothing, olive groves and vineyards, sheep and cattle, and male and female servants? [27]Because you have done this, you and your descendants will suffer from Naaman's leprosy forever." When Gehazi left the room, he was covered with leprosy; his skin was white as snow.

Elisha Recovers a Lost Ax Head

6 One day the group of prophets came to Elisha and told him, "As you can see, this place where we meet with you is too small. [2]Let's go down to the Jordan River, where there are plenty of logs. There we can build a new place for us to meet."

"All right," he told them, "go ahead."

[3]"Please come with us," someone suggested.

"I will," he said. [4]So he went with them.

When they arrived at the Jordan, they began cutting down trees. [5]But as one of them was cutting a tree, his ax head fell into the river. "Oh, sir!" he cried. "It was a borrowed ax!"

[6]"Where did it fall?" the man of God asked. When he showed him the place, Elisha cut a stick and threw it into the water at that spot. Then the ax head floated to the surface. [7]"Grab it," Elisha said. And the man reached out and grabbed it.

Elisha Traps the Arameans

[8]When the king of Aram was at war with Israel, he would confer with his officers and say, "We will mobilize our forces at such and such a place."

[9]But immediately Elisha, the man of God, would warn the king of Israel, "Do not go near that place, for the Arameans are planning to mobilize their troops there." [10]So the king of Israel would send word to the place indicated by the man of God. Time and again Elisha warned the king, so that he would be on the alert there.

5:17 Exod 20:24
5:20 2 Kgs 4:11-12, 31, 36
5:22 2 Kgs 5:5
5:26 2 Kgs 5:16
5:27 Exod 4:6; Num 12:10
6:1 2 Kgs 2:3, 5, 7
6:6 Exod 15:25; 2 Kgs 2:21; 4:41
6:9 1 Kgs 20:13, 28; 2 Kgs 6:12

5:17 ***earth from this place:*** Ancient Near Eastern custom identified a nation's god with the soil of the country where he was worshiped; Naaman apparently believed he needed Israelite soil in order to build an altar to properly worship Israel's God.

5:18 The name ***Rimmon*** appears in the name Tabrimmon (1 Kgs 15:18), the father of Ben-hadad I. In Aramean, the god's name is properly Ramman (*the thunderer*), a storm-god noted in Assyrian inscriptions. The spelling *Rimmon* (which means *pomegranate*) may reflect a deliberate pun belittling the deity.

5:22-23 Naaman believed Gehazi's fabricated story to be genuine and was happy to repay Elisha. • ***75 pounds:*** Hebrew *1 talent* [34 kilograms]. • ***take twice as much:*** Hebrew *take 2 talents* [68 kilograms].

5:24 ***the citadel*** (Hebrew *the Ophel*): The Hebrew word means *hill* or *high point in a city.* Citadels were often erected in such places (2 Chr 27:3).

5:25-27 Gehazi could not conceal his deed from Elisha. Gehazi's deception and misuse of his privileged position earned his master's disapproval and the loss of his status as Elisha's servant. But it also brought on him the penalty of ***Naaman's leprosy,*** a sign that Gehazi had traded places with Naaman spiritually as well.

6:1-2 ***logs . . . new place for us to meet:*** The forest areas of the Jordan Valley near Jericho and Gilgal (see 2:1, 4) provided several types of wood for building.

6:5 The Hebrew text indicates that the ***ax head*** was made of iron, quite valuable in a time when few iron tools were available. Because ***it was . . . borrowed,*** the loss was even more acute.

6:8-10 Elisha's ability to know the Aramean king's raiding strategies allowed him to warn Joram of danger. Apparently, the healing of Naaman (5:1-19) had improved relations between Elisha and Joram (see 3:13-14).

6:13
Gen 37:17
6:16
Exod 14:13
2 Chr 32:7
Rom 8:31
6:17
2 Kgs 2:11-12
6:18
Gen 19:11
[d]*palal* (6419)
› 2 Kgs 20:2
6:19
1 Kgs 20:1
2 Kgs 3:1
6:21
1 Sam 24:4, 19; 26:8
6:22
Deut 20:11
2 Chr 28:8-15
Rom 12:20
6:23
2 Kgs 5:2
6:24
1 Kgs 20:1
6:29
Lev 26:29
Deut 28:53-55
6:31
1 Kgs 19:2

11The king of Aram became very upset
over this. He called his officers together
and demanded, "Which of you is the traitor? Who has been informing the king of
Israel of my plans?"
12"It's not us, my lord the king," one of
the officers replied. "Elisha, the prophet
in Israel, tells the king of Israel even the
words you speak in the privacy of your bedroom!"
13"Go and find out where he is," the king
commanded, "so I can send troops to seize
him."
And the report came back: "Elisha is at
Dothan." 14So one night the king of Aram
sent a great army with many chariots and
horses to surround the city.
15When the servant of the man of God
got up early the next morning and went outside, there were troops, horses, and chariots
everywhere. "Oh, sir, what will we do now?"
the young man cried to Elisha.
16"Don't be afraid!" Elisha told him. "For
there are more on our side than on theirs!"
17Then Elisha prayed, "O LORD, open his
eyes and let him see!" The LORD opened the
young man's eyes, and when he looked up,
he saw that the hillside around Elisha was
filled with horses and chariots of fire.
18As the Aramean army advanced toward
him, Elisha [d]prayed, "O LORD, please make
them blind." So the LORD struck them with
blindness as Elisha had asked.
19Then Elisha went out and told them,
"You have come the wrong way! This isn't
the right city! Follow me, and I will take you
to the man you are looking for." And he led
them to the city of Samaria.
20As soon as they had entered Samaria,
Elisha prayed, "O LORD, now open their eyes
and let them see." So the LORD opened their
eyes, and they discovered that they were in
the middle of Samaria.
21When the king of Israel saw them, he
shouted to Elisha, "My father, should I kill
them? Should I kill them?"
22"Of course not!" Elisha replied. "Do we
kill prisoners of war? Give them food and
drink and send them home again to their
master."
23So the king made a great feast for them
and then sent them home to their master.
After that, the Aramean raiders stayed away
from the land of Israel.

Ben-Hadad Besieges Samaria

24Some time later, however, King Ben-hadad
of Aram mustered his entire army and besieged Samaria. 25As a result, there was a
great famine in the city. The siege lasted
so long that a donkey's head sold for eighty
pieces of silver, and a cup of dove's dung
sold for five pieces of silver.
26One day as the king of Israel was walking along the wall of the city, a woman called
to him, "Please help me, my lord the king!"
27He answered, "If the LORD doesn't help
you, what can I do? I have neither food from
the threshing floor nor wine from the press
to give you." 28But then the king asked,
"What is the matter?"
She replied, "This woman said to me:
'Come on, let's eat your son today, then we
will eat my son tomorrow.' 29So we cooked
my son and ate him. Then the next day I
said to her, 'Kill your son so we can eat him,'
but she has hidden her son."
30When the king heard this, he tore his
clothes in despair. And as the king walked
along the wall, the people could see that he
was wearing burlap under his robe next to
his skin. 31"May God strike me and even kill

6:11-14 When the *king of Aram* learned that *Elisha* had the ability to give advance warning to the *king of Israel*, he commanded his men to capture the prophet. • *Dothan* was situated about ten miles north of Samaria. Archaeological excavations have confirmed the city's existence in this period.

6:15 The identity of Elisha's alarmed *servant* is unknown. He was evidently the replacement of Gehazi (5:27).

6:16-17 Elisha asked the Lord to open *the young man's eyes*, revealing an angelic force protecting the city. Angels are active in the affairs of the world (Ps 34:7; Dan 10:20–11:1; Heb 1:7).

6:21 *My father:* Elisha had used this term of respect when addressing Elijah (2:12), as had Naaman's servant when speaking to his master (see note on 5:13-14).

6:23 *great feast:* The Israelites' kind treatment had the result that the Arameans no longer raided Israel. However, it only provided a temporary suspension of hostilities.

6:24-25 So severe was this *famine* that normally unclean things were not only eaten but sold for an exorbitant price. Donkey meat, for example, was forbidden by the laws regarding unclean foods (Lev 11:1-7). • *sold for eighty pieces of silver, and a cup of dove's dung sold for five pieces:* Hebrew *sold for 80 shekels* [2 pounds, or 0.9 kilograms] *of silver, and ¼ of a cab* [0.3 liters] *of dove's dung sold for 5 shekels* [2 ounces, or 57 grams]. *Dove's dung* may be a variety of wild vegetable, but the consumption of dung is known from other sources describing siege conditions (Isa 36:12). The *dove's dung* might also have been used for fuel.

6:26-29 Cannibalism under severe conditions was part of God's curse for unfaithfulness and disobedience (Deut 28:53, 57). It also occurred during the siege that brought about the fall of Jerusalem (Lam 4:9-10).

6:30 When Joram learned of cannibalism in the city, ***he tore his clothes in despair.*** • ***wearing burlap under his robe next to his skin:*** Doing this was an outward sign of mourning.

me if I don't separate Elisha's head from his shoulders this very day," the king vowed.

32 Elisha was sitting in his house with the elders of Israel when the king sent a messenger to summon him. But before the messenger arrived, Elisha said to the elders, "A murderer has sent a man to cut off my head. When he arrives, shut the door and keep him out. We will soon hear his master's steps following him."

33 While Elisha was still saying this, the messenger arrived. And the king said, "All this misery is from the LORD! Why should I wait for the LORD any longer?"

7 Elisha replied, "Listen to this message from the LORD! This is what the LORD says: By this time tomorrow in the markets of Samaria, five quarts of choice flour will cost only one piece of silver, and ten quarts of barley grain will cost only one piece of silver."

2 The officer assisting the king said to the man of God, "That couldn't happen even if the LORD opened the windows of heaven!"

But Elisha replied, "You will see it happen with your own eyes, but you won't be able to eat any of it!"

Lepers Visit the Enemy Camp

3 Now there were four men with leprosy sitting at the entrance of the city gates. "Why should we sit here waiting to die?" they asked each other. 4 "We will starve if we stay here, but with the famine in the city, we will starve if we go back there. So we might as well go out and surrender to the Aramean army. If they let us live, so much the better. But if they kill us, we would have died anyway."

5 So at twilight they set out for the camp of the Arameans. But when they came to the edge of the camp, no one was there! 6 For the Lord had caused the Aramean army to hear the clatter of speeding chariots and the galloping of horses and the sounds of a great army approaching. "The king of Israel has hired the Hittites and Egyptians to attack us!" they cried to one another. 7 So they panicked and ran into the night, abandoning their tents, horses, donkeys, and everything else, as they fled for their lives.

8 When the lepers arrived at the edge of the camp, they went into one tent after another, eating and drinking wine; and they carried off silver and gold and clothing and hid it. 9 Finally, they said to each other, "This is not right. This is a day of good news, and we aren't sharing it with anyone! If we wait until morning, some calamity will certainly fall upon us. Come on, let's go back and tell the people at the palace."

10 So they went back to the city and told the gatekeepers what had happened. "We went out to the Aramean camp," they said, "and no one was there! The horses and donkeys were tethered and the tents were all in order, but there wasn't a single person around!" 11 Then the gatekeepers shouted the news to the people in the palace.

Israel Plunders the Camp

12 The king got out of bed in the middle of the night and told his officers, "I know what has happened. The Arameans know we are starving, so they have left their camp and have hidden in the fields. They are expecting us to leave the city, and then they will take us alive and capture the city."

13 One of his officers replied, "We had better send out scouts to check into this. Let them take five of the remaining horses.

6:32 1 Kgs 18:3-4, 14; Ezek 8:1; 14:1; 20:1
6:33 Isa 8:21
7:2 Gen 7:11; Mal 3:10
7:3 Lev 13:45-46; Num 5:1-4
7:4 2 Kgs 6:24
7:6 2 Sam 5:24; 2 Chr 12:2-3
7:7 Ps 48:4-6; Prov 28:1
7:12 Josh 8:6-12; 2 Kgs 6:25-29

6:31 ***separate Elisha's head from his shoulders:*** Decapitation of one's enemy was frequent (10:6-8; 1 Sam 17:51; 31:9; 2 Sam 4:7-8, 12; 20:22; Matt 14:11) in the ancient Near East. Joram reasoned that the situation stemmed from Elisha's earlier sparing of Ben-hadad's troops (6:22-23). Moreover, Ben-hadad had been after Elisha (6:13), so the prophet's presence had endangered the whole city.

6:32 ***Elisha*** was aware that Joram was sending a ***messenger*** to assassinate him and that the king was not far behind.

6:33 ***And the king said:*** Literally *And he said.* ***The messenger*** might have been delivering the king's words verbatim. • Because the ***misery*** of the siege appeared to be ***from the LORD,*** Joram felt that further prayer for rescue was useless.

7:1 ***This is what the LORD says:*** Despite Joram's pessimism and hostility, Elisha brought a message of hope. ***Tomorrow*** would bring a complete change in conditions, with good products again available. • ***five quarts . . . only one piece of silver:*** Hebrew *1 seah* [6 liters] *of choice flour will cost 1 shekel* [0.4 ounces, or 11 grams]; also in 7:16, 18. • ***ten quarts . . . only one piece of silver:*** Hebrew *2 seahs* [12 liters] *of barley grain will cost 1 shekel* [0.4 ounces, or 11 grams]; also in 7:16, 18. Cp. with the prices in 6:25.

7:2 The disbelief of Joram's ***officer*** would cause him to miss God's blessings.

7:3 These ***four men*** were outcasts because of their condition and remained outside ***the city gates*** (Lev 13:45-46; see Luke 17:11-13). • ***with leprosy:*** Or *with a contagious skin disease.* The Hebrew word used here and throughout this passage can describe various skin diseases.

7:5-7 ***The Hittites*** had settled in the areas just north of Aram and were often in conflict with the Arameans. • ***and Egyptians:*** possibly *and the people of Muzur,* a district near Cilicia in Asia Minor.

7:8-9 The men realized that they needed to share their good fortune with the people in Samaria.

7:10-12 Joram suspected that the Arameans had set a trap, perhaps attempting to lure the Israelites into an ambush. Joshua had used a similar battle tactic in taking the city of Ai (Josh 8:3-23).

7:16 2 Kgs 7:1
7:17 2 Kgs 7:2
7:19 2 Kgs 7:2
8:1 Gen 41:27; 2 Kgs 4:31-35; Ps 105:16; Hag 1:11
8:4 2 Kgs 4:11-12; 5:20-27
8:5 2 Kgs 4:34-35
8:7 2 Kgs 6:24
8:8 1 Kgs 14:3; 19:15
8:11 Luke 19:41

If something happens to them, it will be no worse than if they stay here and die with the rest of us."

14So two chariots with horses were prepared, and the king sent scouts to see what had happened to the Aramean army. 15They went all the way to the Jordan River, following a trail of clothing and equipment that the Arameans had thrown away in their mad rush to escape. The scouts returned and told the king about it. 16Then the people of Samaria rushed out and plundered the Aramean camp. So it was true that five quarts of choice flour were sold that day for one piece of silver, and ten quarts of barley grain were sold for one piece of silver, just as the LORD had promised. 17The king appointed his officer to control the traffic at the gate, but he was knocked down and trampled to death as the people rushed out.

So everything happened exactly as the man of God had predicted when the king came to his house. 18The man of God had said to the king, "By this time tomorrow in the markets of Samaria, five quarts of choice flour will cost one piece of silver, and ten quarts of barley grain will cost one piece of silver."

19The king's officer had replied, "That couldn't happen even if the LORD opened the windows of heaven!" And the man of God had said, "You will see it happen with your own eyes, but you won't be able to eat any of it!" 20And so it was, for the people trampled him to death at the gate!

The Woman from Shunem Returns Home

8 Elisha had told the woman whose son he had brought back to life, "Take your family and move to some other place, for the LORD has called for a famine on Israel that will last for seven years." 2So the woman did as the man of God instructed. She took her family and settled in the land of the Philistines for seven years.

3After the famine ended she returned from the land of the Philistines, and she went to see the king about getting back her house and land. 4As she came in, the king was talking with Gehazi, the servant of the man of God. The king had just said, "Tell me some stories about the great things Elisha has done." 5And Gehazi was telling the king about the time Elisha had brought a boy back to life. At that very moment, the mother of the boy walked in to make her appeal to the king about her house and land.

"Look, my lord the king!" Gehazi exclaimed. "Here is the woman now, and this is her son—the very one Elisha brought back to life!"

6"Is this true?" the king asked her. And she told him the story. So he directed one of his officials to see that everything she had lost was restored to her, including the value of any crops that had been harvested during her absence.

Hazael Murders Ben-Hadad

7Elisha went to Damascus, the capital of Aram, where King Ben-hadad lay sick. When someone told the king that the man of God had come, 8the king said to Hazael, "Take a gift to the man of God. Then tell him to ask the LORD, 'Will I recover from this illness?' "

9So Hazael loaded down forty camels with the finest products of Damascus as a gift for Elisha. He went to him and said, "Your servant Ben-hadad, the king of Aram, has sent me to ask, 'Will I recover from this illness?' "

10And Elisha replied, "Go and tell him, 'You will surely recover.' But actually the LORD has shown me that he will surely die!" 11Elisha stared at Hazael with a fixed gaze

7:13-17 The trail of abandoned articles confirmed the Arameans' ***rush to escape***, and the Israelites ***plundered the Aramean camp***. True to Elisha's prophecy, food supplies were now readily available, and Joram's doubting ***officer*** was ***knocked down and trampled to death***.

7:18-20 The repetition of Elisha's previous conversation with Joram's ***officer*** emphasizes the exact fulfillment of the prophecy.

8:3 ***getting back her house and land:*** Her property might have been held in trust or confiscated.

8:4-5 ***Gehazi***, Elisha's former ***servant***, had gained sufficient social standing to serve ***the king***. Although Joram had often been Elisha's adversary, he apparently wanted to know more about ***the great things*** Elisha had done.

8:6 ***everything . . . was restored:*** Not only did the woman receive her land but Joram made sure that she received all income due to the selling of ***crops that had been harvested during her absence***. Joram, who sometimes displayed less than noble characteristics (3:13-14; 6:31-33), on this occasion showed higher ethical standards than his father Ahab had regarding Naboth's vineyard (1 Kgs 21:1-16).

8:7 Elisha's freedom to visit ***Damascus*** demonstrated the great respect that even Israel's enemies had for him. The visit fulfilled the commission originally given to Elijah (1 Kgs 19:15).

8:8 ***Will I recover?*** Cp. 1:2.

8:9 ***forty camels with the finest products:*** Although gifts were not unusual when inquiring of a prophet (see 1 Sam 9:6-8), Ben-hadad's gifts were lavish, testifying both to his wealth and the esteem he had for Elisha.

8:10 Elisha instructed Hazael to tell the king that he would ***surely recover*** because his illness was not life threatening. Yet Elisha knew that Ben-hadad would ***surely die***.

8:11 ***Elisha stared at Hazael:*** Literally *He stared at him*. • ***Hazael became***

until Hazael became uneasy. Then the man
of God started weeping.
12“What’s the matter, my lord?” Hazael
asked him.
Elisha replied, “I know the terrible things
you will do to the people of Israel. You will
burn their fortified cities, kill their young
men with the sword, dash their little children to the ground, and rip open their
pregnant women!”
13Hazael responded, “How could a nobody like me ever accomplish such great
things?”
Elisha answered, “The LORD has shown me
that you are going to be the king of Aram.”
14When Hazael left Elisha and went back,
the king asked him, “What did Elisha tell
you?”
And Hazael replied, “He told me that you
will surely recover.”
15But the next day Hazael took a blanket,
soaked it in water, and held it over the king’s
face until he died. Then Hazael became the
next king of Aram.

Jehoram’s Reign in Judah
2 Kgs 8:17-22 // 2 Chr 21:5-10
16Jehoram son of King Jehoshaphat of Judah
began to rule over Judah in the fifth year of
the reign of Joram son of Ahab, king of Israel. 17Jehoram was thirty-two years old
when he became king, and he reigned in Jerusalem eight years. 18But Jehoram followed
the example of the kings of Israel and was
as wicked as King Ahab, for he had married
one of Ahab’s daughters. So Jehoram did
what was evil in the LORD’s sight. 19But the
LORD did not want to destroy Judah, for he
had made a covenant with David and promised that his descendants would continue to
rule, shining like a lamp forever.
20During Jehoram’s reign, the Edomites
revolted against Judah and crowned their
own king. 21So Jehoram went with all his
chariots to attack the town of Zair. The
Edomites surrounded him and his chariot
commanders, but he went out at night and
attacked them under cover of darkness. But
Jehoram’s army deserted him and fled to
their homes. 22So Edom has been independent from Judah to this day. The town of
Libnah also revolted about that same time.
23The rest of the events in Jehoram’s reign
and everything he did are recorded in *The
Book of the History of the Kings of Judah.*
24When Jehoram died, he was buried with
his ancestors in the City of David. Then his
son Ahaziah became the next king.

Ahaziah’s Reign in Judah
2 Kgs 8:25-29 // 2 Chr 22:1-6
25Ahaziah son of Jehoram began to rule
over Judah in the twelfth year of the reign
of Joram son of Ahab, king of Israel.
26Ahaziah was twenty-two years old
when he became king, and he reigned in Jerusalem one year. His mother was Athaliah,
a granddaughter of King Omri of Israel.

8:12
2 Kgs 10:32-33; 12:17; 13:3; 15:16
8:13
1 Sam 17:43
2 Sam 9:8
1 Kgs 19:15
8:16-24
//2 Chr 21:5-20
8:17
2 Chr 21:5
8:19
2 Sam 7:12-15
1 Kgs 11:36
8:20
1 Kgs 22:47
2 Kgs 3:9, 26
8:22
Gen 27:39-40
Josh 21:13
8:24
2 Chr 21:20; 22:1
8:25-29
//2 Chr 22:1-6
8:26
2 Kgs 11:1

uneasy: The meaning of the Hebrew is uncertain. • Elisha ***started weeping*** because he foresaw the atrocities that Hazael would commit against God’s people when he became king (8:28; 9:14-15; 10:32-33; 12:17-18; 13:3, 22).

8:13 *a nobody like me:* Literally *a dog.* As scavengers, dogs were held in low esteem in the ancient Near East. King Shalmaneser III of Assyria observed in his annals, “Hazael, son of a nobody, seized the throne.”

8:15 *Hazael became the next king of Aram:* Although Hazael obediently delivered Elisha’s answer to Ben-hadad, ***the next day*** he hastened the fulfillment of Elisha’s prophecy by assassinating the king and taking the throne for himself. Perhaps Hazael falsely reasoned that the prophecy gave him a divine mandate.

8:16 *Jehoram* was co-regent with his father, ***Jehoshaphat,*** for five years before becoming king of ***Judah*** on his own in ***the fifth year of the reign of Joram*** (848 BC; see timeline, p. 631).

8:17 *Jehoram* reigned from 853 to 841 BC, including a five-year co-regency with his father, Jehoshaphat (see timeline, p. 631).

8:18 *evil in the LORD’s sight:* Not only did Jehoram marry Ahab’s daughter Athaliah but he ***followed the example of the kings of Israel*** in worshiping idols. Some have suggested that Ps 45 was composed in honor of the marriage between Jehoram and Athaliah, which joined the royal houses of Judah and Israel (see Ps 45:12; Athaliah was the daughter of Jezebel, the princess of Tyre). While the marriage created temporary harmony between the kingdoms, it brought disastrous spiritual results. Under Athaliah’s influence, Jehoram instituted various false forms of worship (2 Chr 21:11), including worship of Baal (11:17-18).

8:19 Despite Jehoram’s wickedness, God did not ***destroy Judah*** but honored his ***covenant with David*** (2 Sam 7:11-16). • The Lord had promised to preserve David’s descendants on the throne of Judah as a ***shining . . . lamp*** of God’s grace (1 Kgs 11:36). God’s promises to David ultimately find fulfillment in Jesus (Ezek 34:23-31), the light of the world (John 4:1-5).

8:20-21 *the Edomites revolted:* See note on 3:8-9.

8:21 *Jehoram:* Hebrew *Joram,* a variant spelling of Jehoram; also in 8:23, 24. • ***Zair:*** Greek version reads *Seir.* • ***he went out at night and attacked them:*** Or *he went out and escaped.* The meaning of the Hebrew is uncertain.

8:22 The town of ***Libnah*** was located in southwestern Judah, not far from the Philistine border. The Philistines and the Arabians also launched an attack against Jerusalem during Jehoram’s reign; all of Jehoram’s sons except Ahaziah were killed (2 Chr 21:16-17).

8:24 *Jehoram died* of a painful disease of the bowels and was excluded from the royal tombs (2 Chr 21:18-20).

8:25 *twelfth year of the reign of Joram:* The year of Ahaziah’s accession to the throne of Judah (841 BC) was pivotal in ancient Near Eastern history. Before the year was out, both Joram and Ahaziah lay dead, Hazael was confirmed as king of Damascus, and Shalmaneser III of Assyria dominated the region.

8:27 1 Kgs 16:30
8:29 2 Kgs 9:14-15; 2 Chr 22:5-6
9:1 1 Sam 10:1; 16:1; 1 Kgs 1:39; 2 Kgs 8:28
9:3 1 Kgs 19:16
9:6 1 Kgs 19:16
9:7 Deut 32:35; 1 Sam 25:22; 1 Kgs 18:3-4; 21:15, 21; 2 Kgs 10:17
9:9 1 Kgs 14:10; 15:29; 16:3, 11
9:10 1 Kgs 21:23; 2 Kgs 9:35-36
9:13 2 Sam 15:10; 1 Kgs 1:34, 39; Matt 21:8
9:14-15 2 Kgs 8:28-29

27Ahaziah followed the evil example of
King Ahab's family. He did what was evil in
the LORD's sight, just as Ahab's family had
done, for he was related by marriage to the
family of Ahab.
28Ahaziah joined Joram son of Ahab, the
king of Israel, in his war against King Hazael of Aram at Ramoth-gilead. When the
Arameans wounded King Joram in the battle, 29he returned to Jezreel to recover from
the wounds he had received at Ramoth. Because Joram was wounded, King Ahaziah of
Judah went to Jezreel to visit him.

The Era of Israel's Fourth Dynasty (9:1–15:12)

Elisha Anoints Jehu

9 Meanwhile, Elisha the prophet had
summoned a member of the group of
prophets. "Get ready to travel," he told him,
"and take this flask of olive oil with you. Go
to Ramoth-gilead, 2and find Jehu son of Jehoshaphat, son of Nimshi. Call him into a
private room away from his friends, 3and
pour the oil over his head. Say to him, 'This
is what the LORD says: I anoint you to be the
king over Israel.' Then open the door and
run for your life!"
4So the young prophet did as he was told
and went to Ramoth-gilead. 5When he arrived there, he found Jehu sitting around
with the other army officers. "I have a message for you, Commander," he said.
"For which one of us?" Jehu asked.
"For you, Commander," he replied.
6So Jehu left the others and went into the
house. Then the young prophet poured the
oil over Jehu's head and said, "This is what
the LORD, the God of Israel, says: I anoint you
king over the LORD's people, Israel. 7You are
to destroy the family of Ahab, your master.
In this way, I will avenge the murder of my
prophets and all the LORD's servants who
were killed by Jezebel. 8The entire family of
Ahab must be wiped out. I will destroy every
one of his male descendants, slave and free
alike, anywhere in Israel. 9I will destroy the
family of Ahab as I destroyed the families of
Jeroboam son of Nebat and of Baasha son of
Ahijah. 10Dogs will eat Ahab's wife Jezebel
at the plot of land in Jezreel, and no one will
bury her." Then the young prophet opened
the door and ran.
11Jehu went back to his fellow officers,
and one of them asked him, "What did that
madman want? Is everything all right?"
"You know how a man like that babbles
on," Jehu replied.
12"You're hiding something," they said.
"Tell us."
So Jehu told them, "He said to me, 'This is
what the LORD says: I have anointed you to
be king over Israel.'"
13Then they quickly spread out their
cloaks on the bare steps and blew the ram's
horn, shouting, "Jehu is king!"

Jehu Seizes the Throne of Israel

14So Jehu son of Jehoshaphat, son of Nimshi,
led a conspiracy against King Joram. (Now
Joram had been with the army at Ramoth-
gilead, defending Israel against the forces
of King Hazael of Aram. 15But King Joram
was wounded in the fighting and returned
to Jezreel to recover from his wounds.) So
Jehu told the men with him, "If you want me
to be king, don't let anyone leave town and
go to Jezreel to report what we have done."
16Then Jehu got into a chariot and rode
to Jezreel to find King Joram, who was lying there wounded. King Ahaziah of Judah
was there, too, for he had gone to visit him.

8:28-29 Once again, a king of Judah ***joined*** an Israelite king in battle against the Arameans at ***Ramoth-gilead*** (see 1 Kgs 22:1-40). • ***Jezreel*** served as a second capital for Israel during Ahab's reign (1 Kgs 21:1); he retreated there after witnessing Elijah's contest with the prophets of Baal on Mount Carmel (1 Kgs 18:46).

8:29 ***Ramoth:*** Hebrew *Ramah,* a variant spelling of *Ramoth.*

9:1-37 The writer recaps Jehu's coup that instituted the fourth dynasty in Israel in four phases: (1) Elisha sent a member of the prophetic band to the army camp at Ramoth-gilead to anoint Jehu as the next king of Israel (9:1-10); (2) Jehu's men learned of the prophet's visit to their commander and proclaimed Jehu as king (9:11-15); (3) Both Joram and King Ahaziah of Judah were killed (9:16-29); and (4) Jezebel was killed (9:30-37).

9:1-3 Although Jehu received prophetic endorsement of his kingship, his anointing did not signify approval of all his subsequent actions. It did, however, carry a divine charge to execute the house of Ahab as punishment for his wickedness and idolatry (9:8-10).

9:1 ***Get ready to travel:*** Literally *Bind up your loins.*

9:2 This ***Jehoshaphat*** is not to be confused with the former king of Judah, who was the son of Asa.

9:4-10 As the ***young prophet*** carried out his commission, he detailed for Jehu the means for carrying out the divine sentence against the ***family of Ahab*** (see 1 Kgs 21:20-24).

9:11 ***madman:*** God's faithful servants are often disdained as mad by others (see Jer 29:26; Hos 9:7).

9:13 ***The bare steps*** of the house served as a throne and the soldiers' ***cloaks*** as a carpet. Spreading out garments in this fashion was a sign of respect (see Matt 21:8).

9:14-15 ***led a conspiracy:*** Because Jezreel, where Joram was recovering from his wounds, lay about forty-five miles away, Jehu's coup needed to be carried out swiftly and inconspicuously.

9:15 ***Joram:*** Hebrew *Jehoram,* a variant spelling of Joram; also in 9:17, 21, 22, 23, 24.

9:16 While Jehu was receiving the homage of his men as their king, Joram and Ahaziah were still at ***Jezreel*** (8:28-29; 9:14-15).

17The watchman on the tower of Jezreel
saw Jehu and his company approaching, so
he shouted to Joram, "I see a company of
troops coming!"
"Send out a rider to ask if they are coming
in peace," King Joram ordered.
18So a horseman went out to meet Jehu
and said, "The king wants to know if you are
coming in peace."
Jehu replied, "What do you know about
peace? Fall in behind me!"
The watchman called out to the king,
"The messenger has met them, but he's not
returning."
19So the king sent out a second horseman.
He rode up to them and said, "The king
wants to know if you come in peace."
Again Jehu answered, "What do you know
about peace? Fall in behind me!"
20The watchman exclaimed, "The messenger has met them, but he isn't returning
either! It must be Jehu son of Nimshi, for
he's driving like a madman."
21"Quick! Get my chariot ready!" King Joram commanded.
Then King Joram of Israel and King Ahaziah of Judah rode out in their chariots to
meet Jehu. They met him at the plot of land
that had belonged to Naboth of Jezreel.
22King Joram demanded, "Do you come in
peace, Jehu?"
Jehu replied, "How can there be peace as
long as the idolatry and witchcraft of your
mother, Jezebel, are all around us?"
23Then King Joram turned the horses
around and fled, shouting to King Ahaziah,
"Treason, Ahaziah!" 24But Jehu drew his bow
and shot Joram between the shoulders. The
arrow pierced his heart, and he sank down
dead in his chariot.
25Jehu said to Bidkar, his officer, "Throw
him into the plot of land that belonged to
Naboth of Jezreel. Do you remember when
you and I were riding along behind his father,
Ahab? The LORD pronounced this message
against him: 26'I solemnly swear that I will
repay him here on this plot of land, says the
LORD, for the murder of Naboth and his sons
that I saw yesterday.' So throw him out on Naboth's property, just as the LORD said."
27When King Ahaziah of Judah saw what
was happening, he fled along the road to
Beth-haggan. Jehu rode after him, shouting,
"Shoot him, too!" So they shot Ahaziah in his
chariot at the Ascent of Gur, near Ibleam. He
was able to go on as far as Megiddo, but he
died there. 28His servants took him by chariot to Jerusalem, where they buried him with
his ancestors in the City of David. 29Ahaziah
had become king over Judah in the eleventh
year of the reign of Joram son of Ahab.

The Death of Jezebel

30When Jezebel, the queen mother, heard
that Jehu had come to Jezreel, she painted
her eyelids and fixed her hair and sat at a
window. 31When Jehu entered the gate of
the palace, she shouted at him, "Have you
come in peace, you murderer? You're just
like Zimri, who murdered his master!"
32Jehu looked up and saw her at the window and shouted, "Who is on my side?"
And two or three eunuchs looked out at
him. 33"Throw her down!" Jehu yelled. So
they threw her out the window, and her
blood spattered against the wall and on the
horses. And Jehu trampled her body under
his horses' hooves.
34Then Jehu went into the palace and ate
and drank. Afterward he said, "Someone go
and bury this cursed woman, for she is the
daughter of a king." 35But when they went
out to bury her, they found only her skull,
her feet, and her hands.

9:20 2 Sam 18:27
9:21-29 1 Kgs 21:1 //2 Chr 22:7-9
9:22 1 Kgs 16:31; 18:19
9:23 2 Kgs 11:14
9:24 1 Kgs 22:34
9:25 1 Kgs 21:1, 19
9:26 1 Kgs 21:19
9:27 Josh 17:11 Judg 1:27 2 Chr 22:7, 9
9:28 2 Kgs 23:30
9:29 2 Kgs 8:25, 28
9:30 Jer 4:30 Ezek 23:40
9:31 1 Kgs 16:9-20
9:34 1 Kgs 16:30-31

9:21 ***the plot of land that had belonged to Naboth:*** The property Ahab took from Naboth became the location for the demise of Ahab's line, fulfilling Elijah's prophecy (1 Kgs 21:19-24).

9:22-24 The charges against Joram echoed those against his father Ahab and his mother Jezebel (1 Kgs 16:30-33; 21:25-26).

9:23 ***turned the horses around:*** Literally *turned his hands.*

9:27-28 ***The road to Beth-haggan*** led southward along the eastern edge of the Jezreel Valley, past ***Ibleam*** and on to Samaria. • ***Megiddo . . . he died there:*** King ***Ahaziah*** escaped to Samaria, where he was captured and brought to Jehu (2 Chr 22:8-9). The accounts in Chronicles and Kings might be combined to show that although Ahaziah was wounded at ***Gur***, he managed to go on to ***Samaria.*** Later, Jehu's men seized him and brought him to Jehu, where he was put to death. Since the Chronicler associates Ahaziah's capture with Jehu's slaying of Ahab's descendants and some of ***Ahaziah***'s relatives (see 10:1-17), it appears that Ahaziah avoided his pursuers for a time. The account here is greatly compressed, with the writer recording Ahaziah's death and burial before relating further events.

9:30 The narrator returns to events at ***Jezreel.*** Defiant ***Jezebel*** prepared for Jehu's arrival and her impending death by adorning herself, remaining haughty to the end.

9:31 See 1 Kgs 16:9-10, where ***Zimri*** killed ***his master,*** King Elah. Jezebel accused Jehu of being another Zimri, perhaps to remind him that Zimri's quest for power was short lived (1 Kgs 16:15-19).

9:32-33 Jehu showed his violent nature when he ***trampled*** Jezebel's ***body under his horses' hooves.*** • While the Hebrew word translated ***eunuchs*** can refer to emasculated males, it can also refer to high officials.

9:34-37 The scene depicting Jezebel's end brought Elijah's prophecy against the house of Ahab to final fulfillment (1 Kgs 21:21-24; 22:34-38).

9:34 ***Jehu went into the palace*** to dine, a tacit declaration of his assumption of the throne.

9:36 1 Kgs 21:23
9:37 Jer 8:2
10:1 1 Kgs 16:24-25
10:5 Josh 9:8, 11
10:7 Judg 9:5; 2 Kgs 11:1
10:10 1 Kgs 21:29; 2 Kgs 9:7-10

[36]When they returned and told Jehu, he stated, "This fulfills the message from the LORD, which he spoke through his servant Elijah from Tishbe: 'At the plot of land in Jezreel, dogs will eat Jezebel's body. [37]Her remains will be scattered like dung on the plot of land in Jezreel, so that no one will be able to recognize her.' "

Jehu Kills Ahab's Family

10 Ahab had seventy sons living in the city of Samaria. So Jehu wrote letters and sent them to Samaria, to the elders and officials of the city, and to the guardians of King Ahab's sons. He said, [2]"The king's sons are with you, and you have at your disposal chariots, horses, a fortified city, and weapons. As soon as you receive this letter, [3]select the best qualified of your master's sons to be your king, and prepare to fight for Ahab's dynasty."

[4]But they were paralyzed with fear and said, "We've seen that two kings couldn't stand against this man! What can we do?"

[5]So the palace and city administrators, together with the elders and the guardians of the king's sons, sent this message to Jehu: "We are your servants and will do anything you tell us. We will not make anyone king; do whatever you think is best."

[6]Jehu responded with a second letter: "If you are on my side and are going to obey me, bring the heads of your master's sons to me at Jezreel by this time tomorrow." Now the seventy sons of the king were being cared for by the leaders of Samaria, where they had been raised since childhood. [7]When the letter arrived, the leaders killed all seventy of the king's sons. They placed their heads in baskets and presented them to Jehu at Jezreel.

[8]A messenger went to Jehu and said, "They have brought the heads of the king's sons."

So Jehu ordered, "Pile them in two heaps at the entrance of the city gate, and leave them there until morning."

[9]In the morning he went out and spoke to the crowd that had gathered around them. "You are not to blame," he told them. "I am the one who conspired against my master and killed him. But who killed all these? [10]You can be sure that the message of the LORD that was spoken concerning Ahab's family will not fail. The LORD declared through his servant Elijah that this would happen." [11]Then Jehu killed all who were left of Ahab's

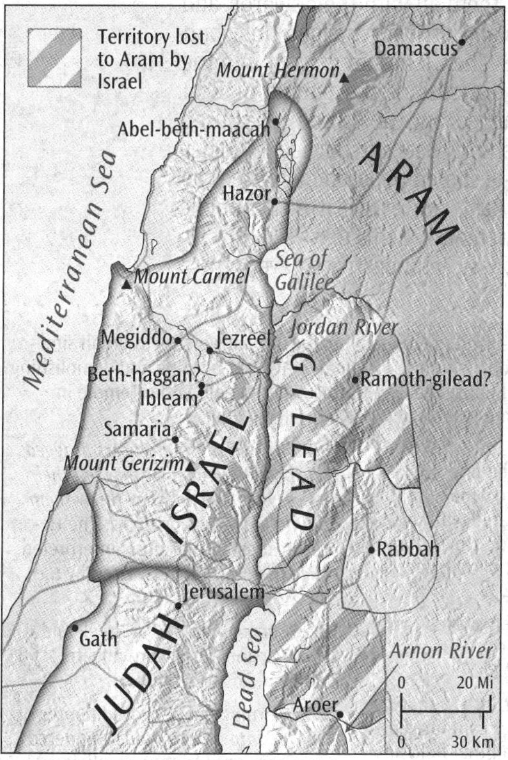

◀ **Jehu's Reign in Israel, 841–814 BC (8:28–10:36).** King Joram of ISRAEL and King Ahaziah of JUDAH went to fight the army of King Hazael of ARAM at RAMOTH-GILEAD in 841 BC (8:28-29). Joram was badly wounded and returned to JEZREEL to recover. While Ahaziah was visiting him, Jehu arrived from Ramoth-gilead and killed Joram. Ahaziah fled for safety but was shot near IBLEAM, and he died in MEGIDDO (9:27). So Jehu began his twenty-eight-year reign in SAMARIA. Hazael, meanwhile, successfully conquered Ramoth-gilead and gained control of all of Israel's territory east of the JORDAN RIVER (10:31-32, as shown on the map).

10:1-27 The writer focuses on two important events of Jehu's reign: his murder of all who might claim Joram's throne (10:1-17), and his execution of the priests of Baal (10:18-27).

10:1 Ahab's *sons* (the term can include grandsons) may have been with Joram at Jezreel temporarily while he was recovering from his wounds (8:29) but had fled to ***Samaria*** to escape Jehu's purge. • ***of the city:*** This reads as in some Greek manuscripts and the Latin Vulgate (see also 10:6); Hebrew reads *of Jezreel.*

10:2-5 Jehu's message pointing out the city's military capacity to protect the surviving members of Ahab's dynasty was actually a declaration of war, and the leaders of Samaria understood it as such. Jehu commanded the main armed forces of Israel, and at Jezreel he had already demonstrated his military power and ruthlessness. The leaders were ***paralyzed with fear*** and agreed to ***do anything*** Jehu instructed them to do.

10:6-7 Decapitation of enemies was a common practice in the ancient Near East (6:31-32; 1 Sam 17:46, 51; cp. Matt 14:11).

10:9-10 ***But who killed all these?*** Jehu claimed that the gruesome deaths were the Lord's will that had been communicated through Elijah (1 Kgs 19:16-17; 21:21-24).

10:11 Jehu also killed all of Ahab's surviving ***relatives*** and associates ***without a single survivor,*** exceeding his divine commission and pursuing a selfish

relatives living in Jezreel and all his important officials, his personal friends, and his
priests. So Ahab was left without a single
survivor.
12 Then Jehu set out for Samaria. Along
the way, while he was at Beth-eked of the
Shepherds, 13 he met some relatives of King
Ahaziah of Judah. "Who are you?" he asked
them.
And they replied, "We are relatives of
King Ahaziah. We are going to visit the sons
of King Ahab and the sons of the queen
mother."
14 "Take them alive!" Jehu shouted to his
men. And they captured all forty-two of
them and killed them at the well of Beth-
eked. None of them escaped.
15 When Jehu left there, he met Jehonadab son of Recab, who was coming to meet
him. After they had greeted each other,
Jehu said to him, "Are you as loyal to me as
I am to you?"
"Yes, I am," Jehonadab replied.
"If you are," Jehu said, "then give me your
hand." So Jehonadab put out his hand, and
Jehu helped him into the chariot. 16 Then
Jehu said, "Now come with me, and see how
devoted I am to the LORD." So Jehonadab
rode along with him.
17 When Jehu arrived in Samaria, he
killed everyone who was left there from
Ahab's family, just as the LORD had promised through Elijah.

Jehu Kills the Priests of Baal

18 Then Jehu called a meeting of all the people of the city and said to them, "Ahab's
worship of [e]Baal was nothing compared
to the way I will worship him! 19 Therefore,
summon all the prophets and worshipers of
Baal, and call together all his priests. See to
it that every one of them comes, for I am going to offer a great sacrifice to Baal. Anyone
who fails to come will be put to death." But
Jehu's cunning plan was to destroy all the
worshipers of Baal.
20 Then Jehu ordered, "Prepare a solemn
assembly to worship Baal!" So they did. 21 He
sent messengers throughout all Israel summoning those who worshiped Baal. They all
came—not a single one remained behind—
and they filled the temple of Baal from one
end to the other. 22 And Jehu instructed the
keeper of the wardrobe, "Be sure that every
worshiper of Baal wears one of these robes."
So robes were given to them.
23 Then Jehu went into the temple of Baal
with Jehonadab son of Recab. Jehu said to
the worshipers of Baal, "Make sure no one
who [f]worships the LORD is here—only those
who worship Baal." 24 So they were all inside
the temple to offer sacrifices and burnt
offerings. Now Jehu had stationed eighty
of his men outside the building and had
warned them, "If you let anyone escape, you
will pay for it with your own life."
25 As soon as Jehu had finished sacrificing the burnt offering, he commanded
his guards and officers, "Go in and kill all
of them. Don't let a single one escape!" So
they killed them all with their swords, and
the guards and officers dragged their bodies outside. Then Jehu's men went into the
innermost fortress of the temple of Baal.
26 They dragged out the sacred pillar used
in the worship of Baal and burned it. 27 They
smashed the sacred pillar and wrecked the
temple of Baal, converting it into a public
toilet, as it remains to this day.
28 In this way, Jehu destroyed every trace

10:13 2 Kgs 8:24, 29; 2 Chr 22:8
10:15 2 Kgs 10:23; Jer 35:6-19
10:17 2 Kgs 9:8
10:18 1 Kgs 16:31-32; [e]*ba'al* (1168) ›2 Kgs 11:18
10:20 Exod 32:5
10:23 [f]*'ebed* (5650) ›Ps 116:16
10:25 1 Sam 22:17; 1 Kgs 18:40
10:26 1 Kgs 14:23; 2 Kgs 3:2

---

quest for power at any cost. The Lord condemned his excesses through the prophet Hosea (Hos 1:4).

10:12-14 The precise location of ***Beth-eked*** is uncertain, but it was in the area of Jenin. • The reply of Ahaziah's ***relatives*** to Jehu sealed their fate. Jehu apparently reasoned that their relation to Ahaziah, hence loosely to the house of Ahab through his daughter Athaliah, could give them some claim on the throne of Israel. In this second round of executions, Jehu again exceeded his commission to terminate Ahab's dynasty.

10:15 Jeremiah portrays ***Jehonadab*** as head of a group of desert nomads who spent their lives in protest against the decadent religion of society (Jer 35). ***Recab*** was a Kenite (1 Chr 2:55). While the nomadic Kenites were concentrated in southern Judah, some lived in Galilee (Judg 4:17; 5:24). Their opposition to the apostasy of the royal house may have led them to welcome Jehu as a rescuer and reformer.

10:18-27 By executing the priests of Baal, Jehu intended to wipe out religious worship associated with the house of Ahab, thereby destroying any sentimental attachment people had with the former dynasty.

10:18-19 Jehu deceptively played to the populace, promising to continue and promote the ***worship of Baal.***

10:25-26 ***innermost fortress . . . sacred pillar:*** Canaanite temples contained a recessed place in the wall that held an image of a sacred stone. The temple of Baal in Samaria contained a sacred altar to Baal and an Asherah pole that Jehu's men destroyed. Josiah's later purge of Baal worship in Judah similarly involved burning and demolishing the Asherah pole in the Temple in Jerusalem (23:6).

10:25 ***the guards and officers dragged their bodies outside:*** Or *they left their bodies lying there;* or *they threw them out into the outermost court.* The Hebrew text can be variously interpreted. • ***the innermost fortress:*** Literally *the city.*

10:26 ***sacred pillar:*** As in Greek and Syriac versions and Latin Vulgate; Hebrew reads *sacred pillars.*

10:27 Turning the destroyed ***temple of Baal . . . into a public toilet*** rendered it unclean, unfit for future religious ceremonies.

10:28-29 Despite extinguishing ***Baal worship from Israel, Jehu*** retained the

10:29 1 Kgs 12:28-30; 13:33-34
10:30 2 Kgs 15:12
10:32 2 Kgs 8:12; 13:22, 25
11:1-21 //2 Chr 22:10–23:21
11:2 2 Kgs 12:1
11:4 2 Kgs 11:19; 2 Chr 23:1
11:5 1 Chr 9:25

of Baal worship from Israel. [29]He did not, however, destroy the gold calves at Bethel and Dan, with which Jeroboam son of Nebat had caused Israel to sin.

[30]Nonetheless the LORD said to Jehu, "You have done well in following my instructions to destroy the family of Ahab. Therefore, your descendants will be kings of Israel down to the fourth generation." [31]But Jehu did not obey the Law of the LORD, the God of Israel, with all his heart. He refused to turn from the sins that Jeroboam had led Israel to commit.

The Death of Jehu

[32]At about that time the LORD began to cut down the size of Israel's territory. King Hazael conquered several sections of the country [33]east of the Jordan River, including all of Gilead, Gad, Reuben, and Manasseh. He conquered the area from the town of Aroer by the Arnon Gorge to as far north as Gilead and Bashan.

[34]The rest of the events in Jehu's reign—everything he did and all his achievements—are recorded in *The Book of the History of the Kings of Israel.*

[35]When Jehu died, he was buried in Samaria. Then his son Jehoahaz became the next king. [36]In all, Jehu reigned over Israel from Samaria for twenty-eight years.

Athaliah Seizes the Throne of Judah
2 Kgs 11:1-3 // 2 Chr 22:10-12

11 When Athaliah, the mother of King Ahaziah of Judah, learned that her son was dead, she began to destroy the rest of the royal family. [2]But Ahaziah's sister Jehosheba, the daughter of King Jehoram, took Ahaziah's infant son, Joash, and stole him away from among the rest of the king's children, who were about to be killed. She put Joash and his nurse in a bedroom to hide him from Athaliah, so the child was not murdered. [3]Joash remained hidden in the Temple of the LORD for six years while Athaliah ruled over the land.

Joash Is Crowned King
2 Kgs 11:4-12 // 2 Chr 23:1-11

[4]In the seventh year of Athaliah's reign, Jehoiada the priest summoned the commanders, the Carite mercenaries, and the palace guards to come to the Temple of the LORD. He made a solemn pact with them and made them swear an oath of loyalty there in the LORD's Temple; then he showed them the king's son.

[5]Jehoiada told them, "This is what you must do. A third of you who are on duty on the Sabbath are to guard the royal palace itself. [6]Another third of you are to stand guard at the Sur Gate. And the final third must stand guard behind the palace guard. These three groups will all guard the palace. [7]The other two units who are off duty on the Sabbath must stand guard for the king at the LORD's Temple. [8]Form a bodyguard around the king and keep your weapons in hand. Kill anyone who tries to break through. Stay with the king wherever he goes."

[9]So the commanders did everything as Jehoiada the priest ordered. The commanders took charge of the men reporting for duty that Sabbath, as well as those who were going off duty. They brought them

---

worship of ***gold calves at Bethel and Dan***, perpetuating the state religion instituted by Jeroboam I (1 Kgs 12:28-30). This would one day lead to the fall of the northern kingdom (17:21-23).

10:30 God fulfilled his promise of a royal line ***to the fourth generation***; four generations of Jehu's descendants reigned as kings of Israel (Jehoahaz, Jehoash, Jeroboam II, and Zechariah).

10:31-33 In response to Jehu's unfaithfulness, ***the LORD began to cut down the size of Israel's territory***, one of the curses for spiritual infidelity to the covenant (Deut 28:25). • The Aramean king ***Hazael*** moved southward, conquering areas ***east of the Jordan River*** north of the border of Moab. The Arameans continued the pressure against Israel throughout the reign of Jehu and into the reign of his son Jehoahaz (12:17-18; 13:3).

11:1-16 ***Athaliah, the mother of King Ahaziah of Judah***, was the daughter of Ahab and Jezebel and the wife of King Jehoram of Judah (8:18, 26). As queen mother, she wielded powerful influence. Unfortunately, it was for evil (8:18, 27; 2 Chr 22:3-4) and included her plans ***to destroy the rest of the royal family*** (see 2 Chr 22:10). The demise of Ahab's family in Samaria was complete, but Athaliah seized power in Judah in a slaughter that mirrored Jehu's slaughter of her family in Samaria.

11:2 ***Jehosheba*** was probably born to ***Jehoram*** (Hebrew *Joram*, a variant spelling of *Jehoram*) by a wife other than Athaliah and was therefore Ahaziah's half-sister (cp. Josephus, *Antiquities* 9.7.1). • The infant ***Joash*** was born to Zibiah of Beersheba (2 Chr 24:1), perhaps a lesser wife of Ahaziah. The baby's birth might therefore have escaped Athaliah's notice.

11:3 Jehosheba's concealment of Joash ***for six years*** was punishable by death if discovered. ***Athaliah ruled over the land*** from 841 to 835 BC.

11:4 ***Jehoiada*** knew that what he was doing was treasonous (11:14), and he was not sure that he could trust the men he was enlisting as his co-conspirators, so he had them ***swear an oath of loyalty*** before he revealed to them the existence of the rightful heir to the throne of Judah. These men went out to the towns of Judah and brought the Levites and heads of families to the Temple in Jerusalem, where they made a covenant with Joash (2 Chr 23:3). • ***The Carite mercenaries***, from the Aegean, served as bodyguards for the king (2 Sam 20:23).

11:5-8 ***Jehoiada*** divided the royal guard into distinctive units: some to guard the young king; others to take up posts at the ***palace***, the ***Sur Gate*** (or Foundation Gate, 2 Chr 23:5), and positions ***behind the palace guard***; and still others to ***stand guard . . . at the LORD's Temple.*** All care was taken to secure the king and the site for his anointing.

all to Jehoiada the priest, [10]and he supplied them with the spears and small shields that had once belonged to King David and were stored in the Temple of the LORD. [11]The palace guards stationed themselves around the king, with their weapons ready. They formed a line from the south side of the Temple around to the north side and all around the altar.

[12]Then Jehoiada brought out Joash, the king's son, placed the crown on his head, and presented him with a copy of God's laws. They anointed him and proclaimed him king, and everyone clapped their hands and shouted, "Long live the king!"

The Death of Athaliah
2 Kgs 11:13-16 // 2 Chr 23:12-15

[13]When Athaliah heard all the noise made by the palace guards and the people, she hurried to the LORD's Temple to see what was happening. [14]When she arrived, she saw the newly crowned king standing in his place of authority by the pillar, as was the custom at times of coronation. The commanders and trumpeters were surrounding him, and people from all over the land were rejoicing and blowing trumpets. When Athaliah saw all this, she tore her clothes in despair and shouted, "Treason! Treason!"

[15]Then Jehoiada the priest ordered the commanders who were in charge of the troops, "Take her to the soldiers in front of the Temple, and kill anyone who tries to rescue her." For the priest had said, "She must not be killed in the Temple of the LORD." [16]So they seized her and led her out to the gate where horses enter the palace grounds, and she was killed there.

Jehoiada's Religious Reforms
2 Kgs 11:17-20 // 2 Chr 23:16-21

[17]Then Jehoiada made a [g]covenant between the LORD and the king and the people that they would be the LORD's people. He also made a covenant between the king and the people. [18]And all the people of the land went over to the temple of [h]Baal and tore it down. They demolished the altars and smashed the idols to pieces, and they killed Mattan the priest of [h]Baal in front of the altars.

Jehoiada the priest stationed guards at the Temple of the LORD. [19]Then the commanders, the Carite mercenaries, the palace guards, and all the people of the land escorted the king from the Temple of the LORD. They went through the gate of the guards and into the palace, and the king took his seat on the royal throne. [20]So all the people of the land rejoiced, and the city was peaceful because Athaliah had been killed at the king's palace.

Overview of Joash's Reign
2 Kgs 11:21–12:3 // 2 Chr 24:1-3

[21]Joash was seven years old when he became king.

12 Joash began to rule over Judah in the seventh year of King Jehu's reign in Israel. He reigned in Jerusalem forty years. His mother was Zibiah from Beersheba. [2]All his life Joash did what was pleasing in the LORD's sight because Jehoiada the priest instructed him. [3]Yet even so, he did

11:10 2 Sam 8:7; 1 Chr 18:7-8
11:12 Exod 25:16; 31:18; 1 Sam 10:24
11:13 2 Chr 23:12
11:14 Gen 37:29; 1 Kgs 1:39; 2 Kgs 9:23
11:17 Josh 24:25; 2 Sam 5:3; 2 Chr 15:12-14; 34:31; [g]*berith* (1285) ‣2 Kgs 23:3
11:18 Deut 12:2-3; 1 Kgs 18:40; [h]*ba'al* (1168) ‣Hos 2:8
11:19 2 Kgs 11:4
11:20 Prov 11:10
11:21 2 Chr 24:1
12:1-21 //2 Chr 24:1-14, 23-27
12:3 2 Kgs 14:4; 15:34-35

11:11-12 With all the *palace guards* in place and *their weapons ready, . . . Jehoiada brought out Joash* before the populace and crowned him *king*. He also presented him *a copy of God's laws* (or *a copy of the covenant*). The king was to receive a copy of the law and make a copy for himself and "read it daily as long as he lives" (Deut 17:18-19). Jehoiada provides a strong contrast with Athaliah's pagan reign.

11:13-14 *The pillar* may be one of the two pillars that Solomon erected at the *Temple* entrance (1 Kgs 7:15-22; 2 Chr 23:13), or the Hebrew term could mean a raised platform set in place for the occasion so that the new king could be seen by all. • Athaliah's cry of *treason* is ironic, considering her own treasonous murders to seize the throne (11:1).

11:15 *Take her to the soldiers in front of the Temple:* Or *Bring her out from between the ranks;* or *Take her out of the Temple precincts.* The meaning of the Hebrew is uncertain.

11:16 Athaliah's death at *the gate where horses enter the palace grounds* is reminiscent of her mother Jezebel's death under the hooves of Jehu's horses (9:33).

11:17 The renewal of the *covenant* was especially important after years of pagan rule. *Covenant* faithfulness accompanied by periodic renewal was mandated in the law (Deut 31:9-13), and Israel observed it at junctures in its history (see 23:1-3; Josh 24).

11:18 The *temple of Baal* may be the temple discovered in Ramat Rahel about three miles south of Jerusalem. As Jehu destroyed Baal worship in the northern kingdom (10:18-27) so the people of Judah *tore . . . down* this pagan temple and executed its priest. • *Jehoiada . . . stationed guards at the Temple* as a precaution against further reprisal by those loyal to Athaliah and her false religion.

11:19-20 *The city was peaceful*—a mark of the kingdom where God and his law are honored (Isa 35:10; 65:18-24; Jer 33:6-16).

11:21–12:21 The reign of Joash is recorded in standard format: accession (11:21–12:3), royal activities (12:4-18), and closing notice (12:19-21). Particular focus is on Joash's efforts to repair the Temple (12:4-16) and his subsequent stripping of the Temple's treasures in the face of an Aramean invasion (12:17-18).

11:21 Verse 11:21 is numbered 12:1 in the Hebrew text. • *Joash:* Hebrew *Jehoash*, a variant spelling of *Joash*.

12:1 Verses 12:1-21 are numbered 12:2-22 in the Hebrew text. • *Joash:* Hebrew *Jehoash*, a variant spelling of *Joash;* also in 12:2, 4, 6, 7, 18. • Joash reigned from 835 to 796 BC.

12:2-3 *Joash*'s indebtedness to *Jehoiada*, the *priest* who *instructed him*, kept him faithful to the Lord while Jehoiada was alive. However, after Jehoiada's death, godless leaders influenced Joash to

12:4
Exod 35:5-9, 22, 29
2 Kgs 22:3-6
1 Chr 29:3-9
12:9
Mark 12:41
Luke 21:1
'aron (0727)
‣1 Chr 28:2
12:13
1 Kgs 7:48-51
12:15
2 Kgs 22:7

not destroy the pagan shrines, and the
people still offered sacrifices and burned
incense there.

Joash Repairs the Temple
2 Kgs 12:4-16 // 2 Chr 24:4-14

[4]One day King Joash said to the priests,
"Collect all the money brought as a sacred offering to the LORD's Temple, whether it is a
regular assessment, a payment of vows, or a
voluntary gift. [5]Let the priests take some of
that money to pay for whatever repairs are
needed at the Temple."

[6]But by the twenty-third year of Joash's
reign, the priests still had not repaired the
Temple. [7]So King Joash called for Jehoiada
and the other priests and asked them, "Why
haven't you repaired the Temple? Don't use
any more money for your own needs. From
now on, it must all be spent on Temple repairs." [8]So the priests agreed not to accept
any more money from the people, and they
also agreed to let others take responsibility
for repairing the Temple.

[9]Then Jehoiada the priest bored a hole in
the lid of a large chest and set it on the right-hand side of the altar at the entrance of the
Temple of the LORD. The priests guarding
the entrance put all of the people's contributions into the chest. [10]Whenever the
chest became full, the court secretary and
the high priest counted the money that had
been brought to the LORD's Temple and put
it into bags. [11]Then they gave the money
to the construction supervisors, who used
it to pay the people working on the LORD's
Temple—the carpenters, the builders, [12]the
masons, and the stonecutters. They also
used the money to buy the timber and the
finished stone needed for repairing the
LORD's Temple, and they paid any other expenses related to the Temple's restoration.

[13]The money brought to the Temple was
not used for making silver bowls, lamp
snuffers, basins, trumpets, or other articles
of gold or silver for the Temple of the LORD.
[14]It was paid to the workmen, who used it for
the Temple repairs. [15]No accounting of this
money was required from the construction

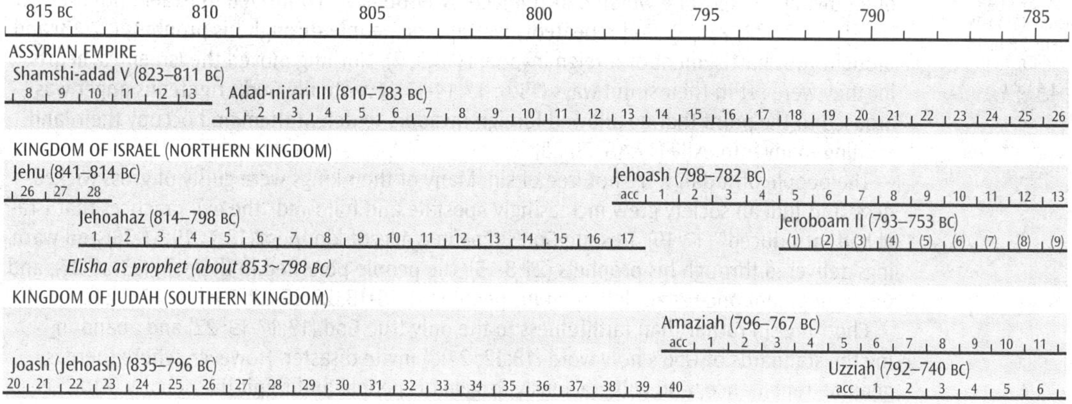

▲**Israel and Judah, 816–784 BC (12:4–14:18).** During this period, both Israel and Judah began practicing long co-regencies between father and son. • In Israel, JEHOASH's reign is recorded as beginning in the thirty-seventh year of JOASH's reign in Judah (13:10), though Joash himself would have called it his thirty-eighth year (as on this diagram). The apparent difference simply reflects two different methods of calculating regnal years in Israel and Judah at this time (see "Chronology: Israel's Monarchy," p. 562). • JEROBOAM II had a total reign of forty-one years in Israel (14:23), although his official accession year did not occur until Jehoash of Israel died (782 BC), so Jeroboam apparently served as co-regent from his father's fifth regnal year. On the timeline, the co-regency years are listed in parentheses. • In Judah, UZZIAH had a total reign of fifty-two years (15:2). His sole reign began in the twenty-seventh year of Jeroboam II (15:1), so he apparently began serving as co-regent with AMAZIAH much earlier; his official regnal years were counted from the start of his co-regency (see, e.g., 15:8, 13, 17, 23, 27).

forsake the Lord and follow Canaanite practices (see 2 Chr 24:17-22). • Joash's failure to ***destroy the pagan shrines*** later became a source of spiritual compromise. Royal tolerance of such shrines in Judah had previously provoked God's anger (1 Kgs 14:23-26) and would do so again in Josiah's day (2 Chr 24:23-24).

12:4-8 Joash ordered the collection of funds from the cities of Judah (2 Chr 24:5) for ***repairs . . . needed at the Temple.*** Such ***money*** would come from special Levitical levies, a census tax (2 Chr 24:9), and voluntary offerings. After some time, ***the priests still had not repaired the Temple.*** So Joash took personal control of the project and put others in charge of the ***repairs*** (see also note on 2 Chr 24:4-8).

12:9-11 Joash's solution for securing and distributing the money for Temple repairs included placing ***a large chest*** at an accessible place to receive ***the people's contributions.*** When Joash informed the people of the need for a tax and voluntary offerings to complete the repairs, they "gladly brought their money and filled the chest with it" (2 Chr 24:9-10). With sufficient funds on hand, the money was given to the ***construction supervisors*** and the repair and restoration of the Temple began.

supervisors, because they were honest and
trustworthy men. 16However, the money
that was contributed for guilt offerings
and sin offerings was not brought into the
LORD's Temple. It was given to the priests
for their own use.

The End of Joash's Reign
2 Kgs 12:17-21 // 2 Chr 24:23-27

17About this time King Hazael of Aram went
to war against Gath and captured it. Then
he turned to attack Jerusalem. 18King Joash
collected all the sacred objects that Jehoshaphat, Jehoram, and Ahaziah, the previous
kings of Judah, had dedicated, along with
what he himself had dedicated. He sent
them all to Hazael, along with all the gold in
the treasuries of the LORD's Temple and the
royal palace. So Hazael called off his attack
on Jerusalem.
19The rest of the events in Joash's reign
and everything he did are recorded in *The
Book of the History of the Kings of Judah.*
20Joash's officers plotted against him and
assassinated him at Beth-millo on the road
to Silla. 21The assassins were Jozacar son of
Shimeath and Jehozabad son of Shomer—
both trusted advisers. Joash was buried
with his ancestors in the City of David. Then
his son Amaziah became the next king.

Jehoahaz's Reign in Israel

13 Jehoahaz son of Jehu began to rule
over Israel in the twenty-third year
of King Joash's reign in Judah. He reigned

12:17
2 Kgs 8:12; 10:32-33
12:18
1 Kgs 15:18
2 Kgs 16:8; 18:15-16
12:20
2 Chr 24:25-27

The Dangers of Sin (13:1-7)

2 Kgs 8:18, 27; 14:23-24; 17:13-23; 18:9-12; 21:8-16; 23:25-27; 24:1-3; 24:19–25:21
Gen 18:20-21
Exod 34:7
Lev 26:14-46
Num 15:30-31
Deut 31:16-18
1 Kgs 8:46-51
Jer 44:2-6

Sinful acts of God's people are prominent in 2 Kings. Words such as *sin, evil,* and *wicked* appear frequently to assert that the kings of both Israel (3:2; 13:2, 11; 14:24; 15:9, 18, 24, 28; 17:2) and Judah (8:18, 27; 21:2, 16, 20; 23:32, 37; 24:9, 19) did "what was evil in the LORD's sight."

The northern kingdom seemed particularly culpable. Its kings were uniformly condemned for their godless ways, and the people willingly followed them (17:16-17, 22). The basic sin of following the apostate worship introduced by Jeroboam I continued in Israel until the end (10:29; 17:21-22; 23:15). God repeatedly warned the people through his prophets (17:13) and brought the chastisement of foreign invaders (13:3, 7). Nothing moved the Israelites' hearts, for they were set in their sinful ways (13:6; 17:14-17). Eventually God's righteous anger was aroused to the point that he allowed foreign invaders to defeat them and occupy their land, sending many into exile (17:18, 20-23).

The people of Judah were not free of sin. Many of their kings were guilty of gross wickedness, and Judean society grew increasingly apostate and followed "the evil practices that Israel had introduced" (17:19). Despite God's repeated acts of kindness (18:7; 19:31-36) and warnings delivered through his prophets (21:8-15), the people persisted in their sin (23:26-27), and God's judgment once again fell upon his people (21:10-15; 23:26-27; 24:1-3; 25:1-21).

Choosing sin rather than faithfulness to the only true God (19:17-19, 22) and abandoning the standards of God's holy word (18:12; 21:8) invite disaster. However, where there is genuine repentance, God will graciously forgive his people and remit the penalty (21:8; see 1 Kgs 8:46-51; 2 Chr 7:14; 33:12-13). How much better to choose to live in faithfulness to God's Word (18:5-6; 23:25; Ps 119:9-11, 33-37; 2 Tim 4:7; Rev 2:10), so that God's blessings (Ps 112:1; 119:1-2; 144:15) might bring good success (18:7; see also 2 Chr 26:4-5; Prov 3:1-10; 2 Cor 3:5). God's people need to give God first place in their lives (1 Kgs 18:21, 36-39; see Deut 6:13; 10:12-13; Mic 6:8; Matt 6:33), pray for God's persevering grace (Ps 19:13), and let the word of God be their guide (Ps 119:9; Col 3:16; 2 Tim 3:16).

12:17 *Hazael,* a perennial oppressor of God's people (8:28; 9:14-15; 10:32-33; 13:3), had assassinated the Aramean king Ben-hadad II and seized the throne (8:15). Hazael's campaign against Israel and Judah probably came after the death of the Assyrian king Shamshi-adad V in 811 BC and before Adad-nirari III (810–783 BC) launched a series of campaigns in 805 BC, leading to the capture of Damascus in 802 BC. Free of Assyria's heavy hand, Hazael could launch a campaign southward. • Whether ***Gath*** is the well-known city of the Philistines (1 Sam 5:8; 6:17) or a Hebrew city otherwise known as Gittaim (2 Sam 4:3; Neh 11:33) is disputed.

12:18 *Sacred objects . . . gold:* Such treasures had been contributed to the Temple earlier by Solomon and Asa (1 Kgs 7:51; 15:15). • ***Hazael*** had already begun the ***attack*** against Jerusalem, and Joash was wounded during the battle (2 Chr 24:25). Paying tribute to ***Hazael*** may have prevented further destruction in the city.

12:20-21 The assassination of the king in 796 BC by some of his own ***officers*** was in reprisal for the murder of Jehoiada's son Zechariah (2 Chr 24:21-22, 25).

12:20 *Beth-millo:* This district lay on a ridge of the eastern hill of Jerusalem in an area known as the City of David, where Solomon installed a series of supporting terraces (1 Kgs 9:15). • ***The road to Silla*** is otherwise unknown.

12:21 *Jozacar:* As in Greek and Syriac versions; Hebrew reads *Jozabad.*

13:1-2 *Jehoahaz* (814–798 BC) began his reign in Israel in the year that King

13:2
1 Kgs 12:26-33
13:3
Judg 2:12-14
2 Kgs 12:17
13:4
Exod 3:7-9
Num 10:9; 21:7-9
13:5
Judg 2:18
Neh 9:27
13:6
1 Kgs 16:33
13:12
2 Kgs 14:8, 15, 28
13:14
2 Kgs 2:12

in Samaria seventeen years. 2But he did what was evil in the LORD's sight. He followed the example of Jeroboam son of Nebat, continuing the sins that Jeroboam had led Israel to commit. 3So the LORD was very angry with Israel, and he allowed King Hazael of Aram and his son Ben-hadad to defeat them repeatedly.

4Then Jehoahaz prayed for the LORD's help, and the LORD heard his prayer, for he could see how severely the king of Aram was oppressing Israel. 5So the LORD provided someone to rescue the Israelites from the tyranny of the Arameans. Then Israel lived in safety again as they had in former days.

6But they continued to sin, following the evil example of Jeroboam. They also allowed the Asherah pole in Samaria to remain standing. 7Finally, Jehoahaz's army was reduced to 50 charioteers, 10 chariots, and 10,000 foot soldiers. The king of Aram had killed the others, trampling them like dust under his feet.

8The rest of the events in Jehoahaz's reign—everything he did and the extent of his power—are recorded in *The Book of the History of the Kings of Israel.* 9When Jehoahaz died, he was buried in Samaria. Then his son Jehoash became the next king.

Jehoash's Reign in Israel

10Jehoash son of Jehoahaz began to rule over Israel in the thirty-seventh year of King Joash's reign in Judah. He reigned in Samaria sixteen years. 11But he did what was evil in the LORD's sight. He refused to turn from the sins that Jeroboam son of Nebat had led Israel to commit.

12The rest of the events in Jehoash's reign and everything he did, including the extent of his power and his war with King Amaziah of Judah, are recorded in *The Book of the History of the Kings of Israel.* 13When Jehoash died, he was buried in Samaria with the kings of Israel. Then his son Jeroboam II became the next king.

Elisha's Final Prophecy

14When Elisha was in his last illness, King Jehoash of Israel visited him and wept over him. "My father! My father! I see the chariots and charioteers of Israel!" he cried.

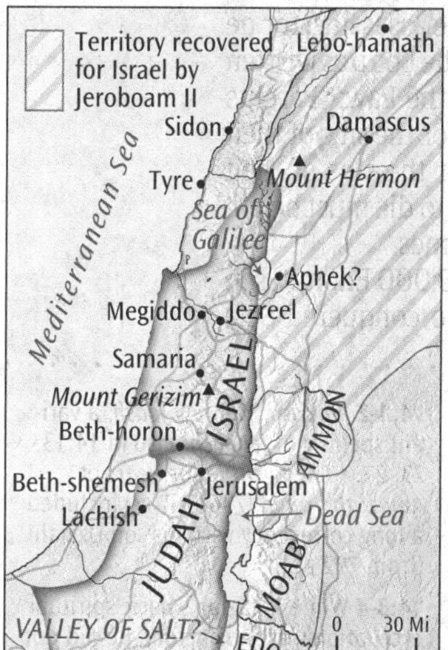

◀ **Israel from Jehoahaz to Jeroboam II, 814–753 BC (13:1–14:29).** King Jehoahaz was repeatedly defeated (13:3) by king Hazael of Aram and his son Ben-hadad, who controlled Gilead during Jehoahaz's reign (814–798 BC). • After winning a decisive battle over the Edomites in the VALLEY OF SALT (14:7), King Amaziah of JUDAH challenged King Jehoash of ISRAEL to fight at BETH-SHEMESH, but Judah was defeated. The army of Israel then marched to JERUSALEM, destroyed much of the wall, and took hostages back to SAMARIA (14:8-14). • Later, Amaziah fled to LACHISH to escape a conspiracy, but he was killed there and buried in Jerusalem (14:19-20). • Jeroboam II (793–753 BC) recovered Israel's territory east of the Jordan (14:25-26, as shown) that Hazael of Aram had conquered during the reign of Jehu, as well as gaining control of Aram itself as far north as LEBO-HAMATH.

Joash of Judah assumed direction of repairs on the Temple (12:6). Because Jehoahaz perpetuated the state religion instituted by Jeroboam I (1 Kgs 12:26-33), his spiritual evaluation was negative.

13:3 ***Hazael,*** who had seized the throne of Aram in Damascus by assassinating his predecessor Ben-hadad II (8:15), continued the oppression of the northern kingdom. • ***Ben-hadad*** apparently served as a commander in Hazael's forces until he succeeded his father as king in 802 BC.

13:4-5 ***Jehoahaz prayed . . . the LORD heard:*** Despite Jehoahaz's poor spiritual condition, God graciously answered his prayer. The Lord graciously answers the earnest prayers of his people (see also 4:32-35; 6:17-20; 19:14-28; 20:2-6; 1 Kgs 3:8-14; 13:4-6; 17:21-23; 18:36-39; Ps 34:4-7; Jas 5:16). • ***provided someone to rescue the Israelites*** (cp. Judg 3:9, 15): Scholars have suggested many possibilities for Israel's rescuer, the most likely being King Adad-nirari III of Assyria, whose westward thrusts brought about the capture of Damascus in 802 BC.

13:6 Despite God's rescue, Israel ***continued to sin,*** eventually resulting in the fall of the northern kingdom (17:21-23; 1 Kgs 14:15-16). • This ***Asherah pole*** (a Canaanite fertility symbol erected by Ahab, 1 Kgs 16:33) had apparently been spared in Jehu's purge of Baal worship (10:26-29).

13:7 Years of Aramean oppression severely ***reduced*** Israel's ***army.*** Only God could save Israel from complete destruction (13:4-5). Ultimately, only God can rescue a helpless and lost humanity (Ps 35:10; Rom 5:6-8).

13:9 ***Jehoash:*** Hebrew *Joash,* a variant spelling of *Jehoash;* also in 13:10, 12, 13, 14, 25.

13:10-13 The narrator atypically combines the accession statement for ***Jehoash*** with the usual closing notice concerning his reign. This arrangement allows him to focus attention on some final details about Elisha (13:14-21) and Israel's continuing problem with Aram (13:22-25) before returning to Jehoash's ***war with King Amaziah of Judah*** in 14:8-14. • ***The Book of the History of the Kings of Israel:*** See note on 1 Kgs 14:19-20.

13:14 Jehoash ***wept over*** Elisha, showing that a faint glow of spiritual consciousness still existed in him. • ***the chariots and charioteers of Israel:*** Jehoash's tribute to Elisha is reminiscent of Elisha's words at Elijah's departure (2:12).

15Elisha told him, "Get a bow and some arrows." And the king did as he was told. 16Elisha told him, "Put your hand on the bow," and Elisha laid his own hands on the king's hands.

17Then he commanded, "Open that eastern window," and he opened it. Then he said, "Shoot!" So he shot an arrow. Elisha proclaimed, "This is the LORD's arrow, an arrow of victory over Aram, for you will completely conquer the Arameans at Aphek."

18Then he said, "Now pick up the other arrows and strike them against the ground." So the king picked them up and struck the ground three times. 19But the man of God was angry with him. "You should have struck the ground five or six times!" he exclaimed. "Then you would have beaten Aram until it was entirely destroyed. Now you will be victorious only three times."

20Then Elisha died and was buried.

Groups of Moabite raiders used to invade the land each spring. 21Once when some Israelites were burying a man, they spied a band of these raiders. So they hastily threw the corpse into the tomb of Elisha and fled. But as soon as the body touched Elisha's bones, the dead man revived and jumped to his feet!

Jehoash and Hazael

22King Hazael of Aram had oppressed Israel during the entire reign of King Jehoahaz. 23But the LORD was gracious and [j]merciful to the people of Israel, and they were not totally destroyed. He pitied them because of his covenant with Abraham, Isaac, and Jacob. And to this day he still has not completely destroyed them or banished them from his presence.

24King Hazael of Aram died, and his son Ben-hadad became the next king. 25Then Jehoash son of Jehoahaz recaptured from Ben-hadad son of Hazael the towns that had been taken from Jehoash's father, Jehoahaz. Jehoash defeated Ben-hadad on three occasions, and he recovered the Israelite towns.

Amaziah's Reign in Judah

2 Kgs 14:1-7 // 2 Chr 25:1-4, 11

14 Amaziah son of Joash began to rule over Judah in the second year of the reign of King Jehoash of Israel. 2Amaziah was twenty-five years old when he became king, and he reigned in Jerusalem twenty-nine years. His mother was Jehoaddin from Jerusalem. 3Amaziah did what was pleasing in the LORD's sight, but not like his ancestor David. Instead, he followed the example of his father, Joash. 4Amaziah did not destroy the pagan shrines, and the people still offered sacrifices and burned incense there.

5When Amaziah was well established as king, he executed the officials who had assassinated his father. 6However, he did not kill the children of the assassins, for he obeyed the command of the LORD as written by Moses in the Book of the Law: "Parents must not be put to death for the sins of their children, nor children for the sins of their parents. Those deserving to die must be put to death for their own crimes."

7Amaziah also killed 10,000 Edomites in the Valley of Salt. He also conquered Sela

13:17 1 Kgs 20:26
13:20 2 Kgs 3:7; 24:2
13:21 Matt 27:52
13:22 2 Kgs 8:12
13:23 Gen 13:16; 17:2-5
2 Kgs 14:27
[j]*rakham* (7355)
› Ps 103:13
13:25 2 Kgs 10:32-33; 14:25
14:1-7 //2 Chr 25:1-4, 11-12
14:4 2 Kgs 12:3
14:5 2 Kgs 12:20
14:6 Deut 24:16
Jer 31:30
Ezek 18:4, 20
14:7 2 Sam 8:13
1 Chr 18:12
2 Chr 25:11
Isa 16:1

13:15-17 ***Elisha laid his own hands on the king's hands:*** This act conveyed spiritual empowerment for the upcoming battle with ***the Arameans at Aphek.*** • ***Aphek*** was situated east of the Sea of Galilee (1 Kgs 20:26), thus the ***eastern window*** faced the place where the battle would take place.

13:18-19 Jehoash failed to act on his knowledge that the arrows signified victory over Aram (13:17). By striking the ground only ***three times,*** he unwittingly limited his own success against the Arameans; final victory came only later in the days of his son Jeroboam II (14:25-28).

13:20-21 Elisha's death provides an opportunity to relate one final story about the prophet. • The ***Moabite raiders*** apparently timed their incursions into Israel to coincide with the early harvest and to precede the summer's heat. • ***The dead man revived*** as his ***body touched Elisha's bones,*** a sign that Elisha's prophecy would come true. Weakened Israel (13:7) would revive and repel the Aramean invaders (13:25; 14:25; cp. Ezek 37:1-14).

13:23 Despite Israel's continued infidelity, God remained faithful to ***his covenant with Abraham*** (Gen 12:1-3; 13:15-17; 15:18-20; 17:6-8). By listing Abraham, ***Isaac, and Jacob,*** the writer emphasizes Israel's spiritual identity with the Lord and its possession of the land of promise (see Gen 50:24; Exod 3:6, 15-16; 6:3, 6-8; Deut 6:10; 9:5; 34:4).

13:24-25 ***Ben-hadad*** son of ***Hazael*** came to the throne of Aram in Damascus in 802 BC, reigning twenty-two years in a declining kingdom. • Adad-nirari III of Assyria inflicted heavy losses against the Arameans (805–802 BC), allowing king ***Jehoash*** of Israel to further decimate this enemy. Fulfilling Elisha's prophecy, Israel ***defeated Ben-hadad on three occasions*** and so recovered the Israelite ***towns.*** Jehoash's limited success provided a springboard for Jeroboam II's full-scale victories over the Arameans (14:25).

14:1-2 ***Jehoash:*** Hebrew *Joash,* a variant spelling of *Jehoash;* also in 14:13, 23, 27. • The ***twenty-nine years*** of ***Amaziah***'s reign (796–767 BC) included a long co-regency with his son Uzziah (from 792 BC).

14:3-4 While Amaziah's basic spiritual evaluation was satisfactory, he did not serve the Lord wholeheartedly as ***his ancestor David*** had (2 Chr 25:2). David continued to be the spiritual standard for evaluating the kings of Judah (16:2; 18:3; 1 Kgs 15:5, 11). Tolerance for long-established ***pagan shrines*** remained a stumbling block for Judah (12:3; 1 Kgs 14:23; 15:14; 22:43).

14:5-6 ***When Amaziah . . . executed*** his father's assassins, he followed the standards of the law concerning ***"Parents . . . crimes"*** (Deut 24:16; see also 2 Chr 25:4) and did not put their ***children*** to death.

14:7 ***10,000 Edomites:*** Amaziah's victory, mentioned only briefly here, is discussed in detail in 2 Chr 25:5-15. De-

14:8-22 //2 Chr 25:17–26:2
14:9 Judg 9:8-15
14:11 Josh 19:35-39
14:13 2 Chr 25:23; Neh 8:16; 12:39
14:14 2 Kgs 12:18
14:15 2 Kgs 13:12-13
14:17 2 Chr 25:25-28
14:19 2 Kgs 12:20
14:20 2 Kgs 9:28
14:21 2 Chr 26:23; Hos 1:1; Matt 1:9
14:23 2 Kgs 13:13; Amos 1:1

and changed its name to Joktheel, as it is called to this day.

Amaziah's War against Jehoash of Israel
2 Kgs 14:8-14 // 2 Chr 25:17-24

8One day Amaziah sent messengers with this challenge to Israel's king Jehoash, the son of Jehoahaz and grandson of Jehu: "Come and meet me in battle!"

9But King Jehoash of Israel replied to King Amaziah of Judah with this story: "Out in the Lebanon mountains, a thistle sent a message to a mighty cedar tree: 'Give your daughter in marriage to my son.' But just then a wild animal of Lebanon came by and stepped on the thistle, crushing it!

10"You have indeed defeated Edom, and you are very proud of it. But be content with your victory and stay at home! Why stir up trouble that will only bring disaster on you and the people of Judah?"

11But Amaziah refused to listen, so King Jehoash of Israel mobilized his army against King Amaziah of Judah. The two armies drew up their battle lines at Beth-shemesh in
Judah. 12Judah was routed by the army of Is-
rael, and its army scattered and fled for home.
13King Jehoash of Israel captured Judah's king, Amaziah son of Joash and grandson of Ahaziah, at Beth-shemesh. Then he marched to Jerusalem, where he demolished 600 feet of Jerusalem's wall, from the Ephraim Gate to
the Corner Gate. 14He carried off all the gold and silver and all the articles from the Temple of the LORD. He also seized the treasures from the royal palace, along with hostages, and then returned to Samaria.

The End of Jehoash's Reign

15The rest of the events in Jehoash's reign and everything he did, including the extent of his power and his war with King Amaziah of Judah, are recorded in *The Book of the History of the Kings of Israel.* 16When Jehoash died, he was buried in Samaria with the kings of Israel. And his son Jeroboam II became the next king.

The End of Amaziah's Reign
2 Kgs 14:17-22 // 2 Chr 25:25–26:2

17King Amaziah of Judah lived for fifteen years after the death of King Jehoash of Is-
rael. 18The rest of the events in Amaziah's reign are recorded in *The Book of the History of the Kings of Judah.*

19There was a conspiracy against Amaziah's life in Jerusalem, and he fled to Lachish. But his enemies sent assassins after him, and they killed him there. 20They brought his body back to Jerusalem on a horse, and he was buried with his ancestors in the City of David.

21All the people of Judah had crowned Amaziah's sixteen-year-old son, Uzziah, as king in place of his father, Amaziah. 22After his father's death, Uzziah rebuilt the town of Elath and restored it to Judah.

Jeroboam II's Reign in Israel

23Jeroboam II, the son of Jehoash, began to rule over Israel in the fifteenth year of King

---

spite granting Amaziah this victory, God chastised him both for hiring Israelite mercenaries and for carrying home Edomite gods and worshiping them. •*The Valley of Salt* was about three miles south of the Dead Sea. • *Sela* is traditionally identified as a site in the rocks and cliffs near Petra in modern Jordan. The capture of this highly defensible location demonstrated that Amaziah's victory was God-given.

14:8 Amaziah's ***challenge to Israel's King Jehoash*** may have been provoked by thoughts of revenge (see 2 Chr 25:13). Perhaps Amaziah had also become overly confident and proud because of his recent victory over Edom. • ***Come and meet me in battle!*** Literally *Come, let us look one another in the face.*

14:9-10 Jehoash's reply came as a parable (see Judg 9:7-15). In essence, Amaziah had as much of a chance of defeating Israel in war as a ***thistle*** trying to make demands against a ***mighty cedar tree.*** Amaziah and Judah would be defeated as easily as a random step would crush the proud ***thistle.***

14:11-12 *Beth-shemesh,* a fortress town fifteen miles west of Jerusalem, was a natural place for the ***battle*** between Israel and Judah. The city history stretched back to when Judah occupied it after the Danites migrated northward (Josh 21:16; see also 1 Sam 6:1-14; 2 Chr 28:18).

14:13-14 *600 feet:* Hebrew *400 cubits* [180 meters]. • The extensive demolition of ***Jerusalem's wall*** and the thorough looting of the city testify to Jehoash's overwhelming victory. Carrying off Temple and palace ***treasures*** and taking ***hostages*** are often noted in the annals of victorious Assyrian kings. See also 12:17-18; 18:13-15; 24:13-14; 25:8-21; 1 Kgs 14:25-26.

14:17-18 Some suggest that Jehoash took Amaziah back to Samaria where he remained captive until Jehoash's death. Subsequently released, Amaziah ruled jointly with his son Uzziah for fifteen years. • ***The Book of the History of the Kings of Judah:*** See note on 1 Kgs 14:29-31.

14:19-20 Like his father Jehoash (12:20-21), Amaziah was killed by ***assassins.*** The Chronicler blames his spiritual infidelity for the ***conspiracy against*** him (2 Chr 25:27). • ***Lachish,*** southwest of Jerusalem, was the site of an important victory by King Sennacherib of Assyria during his invasion of Judah in 701 BC (18:14). It was also seized during Nebuchadnezzar II's advance against Jerusalem in 588 BC (Jer 34:7).

14:21 The fifty-two year reign of ***Uzziah*** (Hebrew *Azariah,* a variant spelling of *Uzziah*) ended in 740 BC; he was ***sixteen*** years old when he became co-regent with his father in 792 BC. Apparently both Jehoash and Amaziah made their sons co-regents before going to war, in order to assure a smooth succession of government.

14:22 *Elath,* built by Solomon (2 Chr 8:17) on the Gulf of Aqaba, provided an important commercial gateway to the Red Sea.

14:23 The ***fifteenth year of King Amaziah's reign in Judah*** marks the beginning of Jeroboam II's independent reign (782 BC). His reign of ***forty-one*** years includes

Amaziah's reign in Judah. Jeroboam reigned
in Samaria forty-one years. 24He did what
was evil in the LORD's sight. He refused to
turn from the sins that Jeroboam son of Nebat had led Israel to commit. 25Jeroboam II
recovered the territories of Israel between
Lebo-hamath and the Dead Sea, just as
the LORD, the God of Israel, had promised
through Jonah son of Amittai, the prophet
from Gath-hepher.
26For the LORD saw the bitter suffering of
everyone in Israel, and that there was no one
in Israel, slave or free, to help them. 27And
because the LORD had not said he would blot
out the name of Israel completely, he used Jeroboam II, the son of Jehoash, to save them.
28The rest of the events in the reign of Jeroboam II and everything he did—including
the extent of his power, his wars, and how
he recovered for Israel both Damascus and
Hamath, which had belonged to Judah—are
recorded in *The Book of the History of the
Kings of Israel*. 29When Jeroboam II died,
he was buried in Samaria with the kings of
Israel. Then his son Zechariah became the
next king.

Uzziah's Reign in Judah
2 Kgs 15:1-3, 5-7 // 2 Chr 26:3-4, 21-23

15 Uzziah son of Amaziah began to
rule over Judah in the twenty-seventh year of the reign of King Jeroboam II

14:24 1 Kgs 15:30
14:25 Deut 3:17; 2 Kgs 13:25; Jon 1:1
14:26 Deut 32:36; 2 Kgs 13:4
14:27 2 Kgs 13:5, 23
15:1 2 Kgs 14:21; 15:13, 17

JEROBOAM II (14:23-29)

2 Kgs 13:13; 14:16; Hos 1:1; Amos 1:1; 7:10-17

Jeroboam II, son of Jehoash, reigned over Israel for 41 years (793–753), longer than any other northern king. He followed the evil example of Jeroboam I (14:23-24). His reign overlapped with those of Amaziah, Uzziah, Jotham, Ahaz, and Hezekiah in Judah.

Jeroboam ruled in Samaria (14:23), where archaeological evidence suggests the opulence of Israel's royal house during his reign. During his era the northern kingdom reached its greatest extent and experienced its greatest prosperity since Solomon. On a human level, an explanation for Israel's newfound prosperity was that Assyria experienced a decline in power during this time, allowing the northern kingdom to expand. The prophet Jonah, however, predicted this prosperity as God's promise (14:25); although Jeroboam's reign came after 150 years of apostasy in the northern kingdom, God still exhibited his faithful love by offering Israel his mercy (14:26-27).

Even so, Jeroboam II was like his earlier (and unrelated) namesake, Jeroboam I, in his wicked character. His reign over Israel produced great wealth, but it was not accompanied by justice. The rich landowners, including Jeroboam II, oppressed the less wealthy and forced small landowners to migrate from their farms to the cities. Extensive government corruption, the people's degenerate spiritual state, economic depression, and political weakness brought about the destruction of the northern kingdom only about thirty years after Jeroboam's reign ended.

God raised up prophets to challenge the leaders and people of Israel during his time. Amos and Hosea prophesied against Israel's vast corruption. Amos was particularly scathing in his attacks on the rich for oppressing the poor, memorably styling the women as "fat cows living in Samaria" (Amos 4:1). He specifically mentions Jeroboam (Amos 7:10-17).

When Jeroboam died, the northern kingdom rapidly declined. In the following years (753–722 BC), six kings ruled in rapid succession, and most of them were assassinated. In 722 BC, Assyria destroyed the northern kingdom and deported its people, thus properly judging the sins of Jeroboam II and other northern kings.

the earlier co-regency with his father (793–782 BC).

14:24 Jeroboam II perpetuated the apostate religion instituted by Jeroboam I (1 Kgs 12:28-33) that led to Israel's demise (17:21-23; 1 Kgs 14:16).

14:25 Israel and Judah apparently lived in harmony at this time so that both kingdoms prospered and ***recovered*** nearly all the territory that Solomon had held (see 2 Chr 26:6-15). • ***Lebo-hamath,*** known from Egyptian and Assyrian inscriptions, lay some forty-five miles north of Damascus in the Beqa' Valley. The extent of Jeroboam's conquests testifies to the northern kingdom's military power. Israel's victories against the Arameans were possible because Aram had been weakened by earlier conquests of Adad-nirari III of Assyria. • ***the Dead Sea:*** Hebrew *the sea of the Arabah.* • ***Jonah*** is the famous ***prophet*** who pronounced the doom of Nineveh but was disappointed when God spared its repentant people (Jon 3:3–4:3).

14:26-28 ***The LORD . . . used Jeroboam II:*** God saw his people's helplessness and remained faithful to the covenant established with Israel's patriarchs (13:23). • ***everything he did:*** The narrator hints at the ***extent*** of Jeroboam's God-given ***power*** and prosperity. The Samaria ostraca also indicate the prosperity of the era. The prophecies of Hosea and Amos show that despite the prosperity during Jeroboam's reign, the Israelites refused to turn to the Lord. • ***to Judah:*** Or *to Yaudi.* The meaning of the Hebrew is uncertain.

14:29 The first sentence is as in some Greek manuscripts; Hebrew lacks ***he was buried in Samaria.***

15:1-3 ***Uzziah:*** Hebrew *Azariah,* a variant spelling of Uzziah; also in 15:6, 7, 8, 17, 23, 27. The name *Uzziah* means

15:5 Lev 13:46
15:8 2 Kgs 14:29
15:10 Amos 7:9
15:12 2 Kgs 10:30
15:13 2 Kgs 15:1, 8
15:16 2 Kgs 8:12; Hos 13:16

of Israel. 2He was sixteen years old when he
became king, and he reigned in Jerusalem
fifty-two years. His mother was Jecoliah
from Jerusalem.
3He did what was pleasing in the LORD's
sight, just as his father, Amaziah, had done.
4But he did not destroy the pagan shrines,
and the people still offered sacrifices and
burned incense there. 5The LORD struck the
king with leprosy, which lasted until the day
he died. He lived in isolation in a separate
house. The king's son Jotham was put in
charge of the royal palace, and he governed
the people of the land.
6The rest of the events in Uzziah's reign
and everything he did are recorded in *The
Book of the History of the Kings of Judah.*
7When Uzziah died, he was buried with his
ancestors in the City of David. And his son
Jotham became the next king.

Zechariah's Reign in Israel

8Zechariah son of Jeroboam II began to
rule over Israel in the thirty-eighth year of
King Uzziah's reign in Judah. He reigned in
Samaria six months. 9Zechariah did what
was evil in the LORD's sight, as his ancestors
had done. He refused to turn from the sins
that Jeroboam son of Nebat had led Israel to
commit. 10Then Shallum son of Jabesh conspired against Zechariah, assassinated him
in public, and became the next king.
11The rest of the events in Zechariah's
reign are recorded in *The Book of the History of the Kings of Israel.* 12So the LORD's
message to Jehu came true: "Your descendants will be kings of Israel down to the
fourth generation."

The Last Years of the Northern Kingdom (15:13–17:41)

Shallum's Reign in Israel

13Shallum son of Jabesh began to rule over Israel in the thirty-ninth year of King Uzziah's
reign in Judah. Shallum reigned in Samaria
only one month. 14Then Menahem son of
Gadi went to Samaria from Tirzah and assassinated him, and he became the next king.
15The rest of the events in Shallum's reign,
including his conspiracy, are recorded in
*The Book of the History of the Kings of
Israel.*

Menahem's Reign in Israel

16At that time Menahem destroyed the
town of Tappuah and all the surrounding
countryside as far as Tirzah, because its

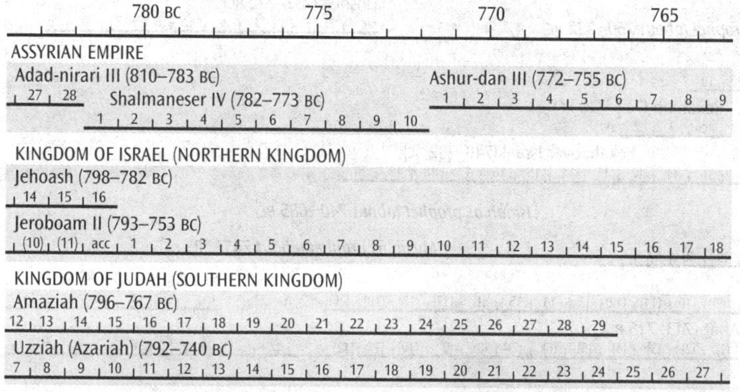

◀ **Israel and Judah, 784–763 BC (14:19–15:12).** JEROBOAM II had his official accession to the throne of Israel in the year his father, JEHOASH, died (14:23); the total count of his years as king includes his co-regency (see timeline, p. 649). • AMAZIAH lived a long life, but his son UZZIAH was actually ruling the kingdom of Judah during most of this time (14:17-21).

Yahweh is my strength. • ***fifty-two years:*** The length of Uzziah's reign (792–740 BC) reflects changed conditions in the early 700s BC. Assyria was in decline and relations between Israel and Judah were cordial. Uzziah's spiritual convictions earned God's blessing so that Judah enjoyed its greatest prosperity since the days of Solomon (2 Chr 26:9-10).

15:4 In spite of his good spiritual evaluation, Uzziah continued to allow worship at the ***pagan shrines*** (14:4).

15:5 Because Uzziah usurped the prerogatives of the priesthood (2 Chr 26:16-21), ***the LORD struck the king with leprosy*** (or *with a contagious skin disease;* the Hebrew word used here and throughout this passage can describe various skin diseases). His son Jotham became co-regent (about 750 BC). While Uzziah's ***isolation*** kept him from public duties, he may have continued to exercise political power. King Tiglath-pileser III of Assyria (744–727 BC), in connection with his first western campaign (744–743 BC), mentioned an opponent named Azariau whom many scholars understand as Uzziah.

15:8-12 Jeroboam II's son ***Zechariah*** was far less capable than his father. Zechariah perpetuated ***the sins that Jeroboam*** [I] . . . ***led Israel to commit.*** God had promised Jehu a royal line ***to the fourth generation*** (10:30); Zechariah's six-month reign fulfilled that promise.

15:10 ***in public:*** Or *at Ibleam.* The meaning of the Hebrew is uncertain.

15:13 ***Jabesh,*** which lay east of the Jordan in northern Gilead, might have been the hometown of ***Shallum,*** whose reign was even shorter than Zechariah's. Shallum was assassinated, as he had done to Zechariah (15:10).

15:14 ***Tirzah*** had been capital of the northern kingdom during Israel's first two dynasties (1 Kgs 14:17; 15:21, 33; 16:8). • ***Menahem*** was an army commander.

15:16 ***Tappuah:*** As in some Greek manuscripts; other Greek manuscripts read *at Ibleam.* Hebrew reads *Tiphsah.* • At ***Tirzah,*** Menahem heard of King Zechariah's assassination by Shallum. Menahem gathered his forces and moved against Samaria. • ***ripped open the pregnant women:*** This horrible wartime practice, noted in Assyrian and Babylonian documents, is also attributed to King Hazael of Aram (8:12). See also Hos 10:14; 13:16; Amos 1:13.

citizens refused to surrender the town.
He killed the entire population and ripped
open the pregnant women.
17Menahem son of Gadi began to rule
over Israel in the thirty-ninth year of King
Uzziah's reign in Judah. He reigned in Samaria ten years. 18But Menahem did what
was evil in the LORD's sight. During his entire reign, he refused to turn from the sins
that Jeroboam son of Nebat had led Israel
to commit.
19Then King Tiglath-pileser of Assyria
invaded the land. But Menahem paid him
thirty-seven tons of silver to gain his support in tightening his grip on royal power.
20Menahem extorted the money from the
rich of Israel, demanding that each of them
pay fifty pieces of silver to the king of Assyria. So the king of Assyria turned from
attacking Israel and did not stay in the land.
21The rest of the events in Menahem's
reign and everything he did are recorded
in *The Book of the History of the Kings of
Israel.* 22When Menahem died, his son Pekahiah became the next king.

Pekahiah's Reign in Israel

23Pekahiah son of Menahem began to rule
over Israel in the fiftieth year of King Uzziah's reign in Judah. He reigned in Samaria
two years. 24But Pekahiah did what was evil
in the LORD's sight. He refused to turn from
the sins that Jeroboam son of Nebat had led
Israel to commit.
25Then Pekah son of Remaliah, the commander of Pekahiah's army, conspired
against him. With fifty men from Gilead, Pekah assassinated the king, along with Argob
and Arieh, in the citadel of the palace at Samaria. And Pekah reigned in his place.
26The rest of the events in Pekahiah's
reign and everything he did are recorded
in *The Book of the History of the Kings of
Israel.*

15:19
1 Chr 5:26

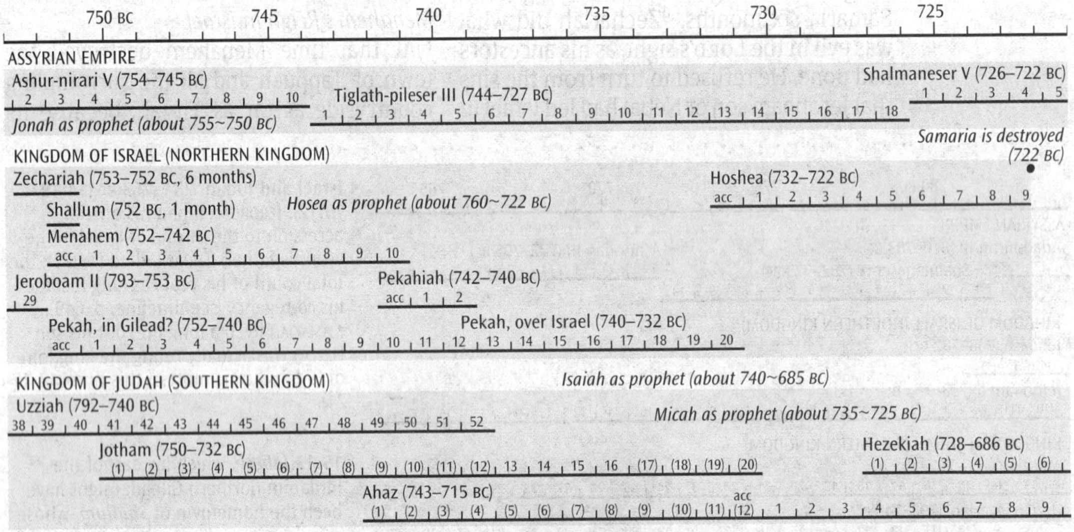

▲**Israel and Judah, 753–721 BC (15:13–18:12).** After the long reign of JEROBOAM II, the kingdom of Israel fell into chaos and disunity for its final quarter century, and orderly succession was replaced by a series of assassinations. SHALLUM assassinated ZECHARIAH son of Jeroboam II, only to be assassinated a month later by MENAHEM, who ruled for ten years. PEKAH appears to have begun ruling Gilead, and he took over the entire kingdom of Israel when he assassinated Menahem's son PEKAHIAH. Pekah's rule likewise ended when HOSHEA assassinated him. Hoshea ruled Israel during its final years of apostasy, siege, and destruction at the hands of the Assyria king SHALMANESER V in 722 BC. • Meanwhile, the kingdom of Judah was characterized by long co-regencies and political stability. For each king, the years in which he was not the primary ruler are shown on the timeline in parentheses. • Concerning the dates for the reign of AHAZ, see notes on 15:32-33; 16:1-2; 17:1.

15:19-20 ***Tiglath-pileser*** (Hebrew *Pul,* another name for *Tiglath-pileser*): The NLT uses the Assyrian (see 15:29; 16:6) form of the name, rather than the Hebrew, which is taken from the Babylonian. Tiglath-pileser III seized the throne of Assyria in 744 BC and provided able leadership until his death in 727 BC. • When Tiglath-pileser launched the western campaign to regain territory held by Aram, Menahem paid him a heavy tribute of ***thirty-seven tons*** (Hebrew *1,000 talents* [34 metric tons]) ***of silver*** to keep him from overrunning Israel. • Although Menahem's name means *comfort,* the unsettled conditions in the northern kingdom provided little consolation for God's people during his reign (752–742 BC). • ***fifty pieces:*** Hebrew *50 shekels* [20 ounces, or 570 grams].

15:23-25 Menahem's son ***Pekahiah*** reigned only ***two years*** before Pekah ***conspired*** to assassinate him. Pekahiah continued the ***sins*** associated with the religious policies initiated by Jeroboam I (1 Kgs 12:26-33). ***Pekah,*** an army commander, had apparently been a rival for the throne for some time.

15:27 2 Kgs 15:32; 16:5 2 Chr 28:6
15:29 2 Kgs 17:6
15:30 2 Kgs 12:20
15:32 2 Chr 27:1 Matt 1:9
15:33-38 //2 Chr 27:1-4, 7-9
15:34 2 Chr 26:4-5
15:36 2 Kgs 15:6; 16:19; 20:20
15:37 2 Kgs 16:5 Isa 7:1

Pekah's Reign in Israel

27Pekah son of Remaliah began to rule over Israel in the fifty-second year of King Uzziah's reign in Judah. He reigned in Samaria twenty years. 28But Pekah did what was evil in the LORD's sight. He refused to turn from the sins that Jeroboam son of Nebat had led Israel to commit.

29During Pekah's reign, King Tiglath-pileser of Assyria attacked Israel again, and he captured the towns of Ijon, Abel-beth-maacah, Janoah, Kedesh, and Hazor. He also conquered the regions of Gilead, Galilee, and all of Naphtali, and he took the people to Assyria as captives. 30Then Hoshea son of Elah conspired against Pekah and assassinated him. He began to rule over Israel in the twentieth year of Jotham son of Uzziah.

31The rest of the events in Pekah's reign and everything he did are recorded in *The Book of the History of the Kings of Israel.*

Jotham's Reign in Judah

2 Kgs 15:32-38 // 2 Chr 27:1-3a, 7-9

32Jotham son of Uzziah began to rule over Judah in the second year of King Pekah's reign in Israel. 33He was twenty-five years old when he became king, and he reigned in Jerusalem sixteen years. His mother was Jerusha, the daughter of Zadok.

34Jotham did what was pleasing in the LORD's sight. He did everything his father, Uzziah, had done. 35But he did not destroy the pagan shrines, and the people still offered sacrifices and burned incense there. He rebuilt the upper gate of the Temple of the LORD.

36The rest of the events in Jotham's reign and everything he did are recorded in *The Book of the History of the Kings of Judah.* 37In those days the LORD began to send King Rezin of Aram and King Pekah of Israel to attack Judah. 38When Jotham died,

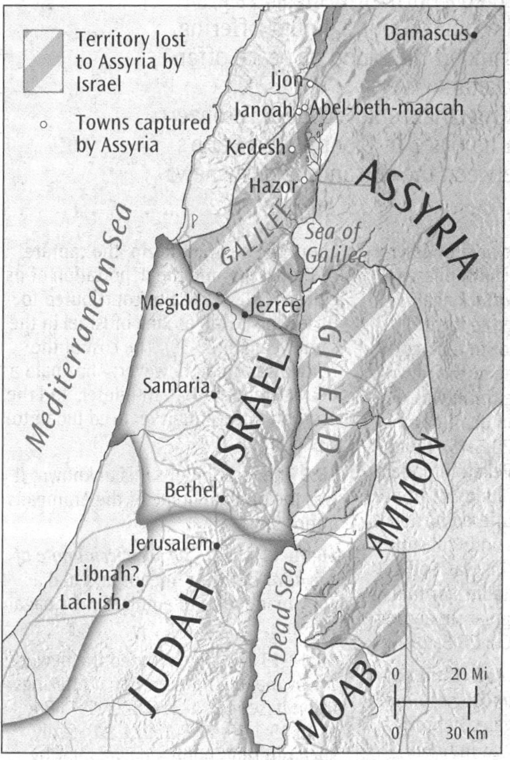

◀ **The Assyrian Empire, 745–612 BC (15:19–20:37).** During the late 700s BC, the power of ASSYRIA grew under the leadership of King Tiglath-pileser III (744–727 BC), and both ISRAEL and JUDAH came under his power. When he invaded Israel, King Menahem of Israel (752–742) began paying him tribute (15:19-20); King Ahaz not long afterward made Judah a vassal of Assyria in seeking protection from Aram and Israel (16:5-9). King Hoshea of Israel (732–722 BC) tried to shake free from paying the heavy annual tribute to Assyria, which led to the destruction of the northern kingdom in 722 BC and the exile of its people. Hezekiah also revolted against Assyria around 705 BC (see note on 18:7-8), which brought the Assyrian invasion of Judah in 701 BC and the Lord's remarkable rescue in response to Hezekiah's faith (see 18:13–19:36).

15:27 ***fifty-second year of King Uzziah's reign:*** The date for Pekah's accession is the final year of Uzziah's reign (740 BC). Because of the standing relationship between Tiglath-pileser and Menahem, Pekah confined his influence to Gilead during Menahem's reign (752–742 BC). With Menahem's death, Pekahiah made Pekah an army commander. This provided Pekah with a broader base of support and gave him opportunity to seize the throne of Israel in 740 BC.

15:29-30 With his second western campaign (734–732 BC), ***Tiglath-pileser . . . attacked Israel again.*** Pekah had allied himself with King Rezin of Aram in an ill-conceived anti-Assyrian coalition (see Isa 9:1). As a result of this invasion, Tiglath-pileser ***captured*** and ***conquered*** much of Israel's northern and eastern territory (see map at left). • Pekah's doomed political policies caused dissension in ***Israel*** that led to his assassination by Hoshea, whose action was probably intended to placate the Assyrian king and preserve the northern kingdom. In his annals, Tiglath-pileser claimed that he put Hoshea on the throne and received his heavy tribute. • The ***twentieth year of Jotham,*** counting from the beginning of his co-regency with his father Uzziah in Judah, was 732 BC, the year of his death (see timeline, facing page).

15:32-33 ***The second year of King Pekah's reign*** reflects the first full year of Jotham's independent reign; he was co-regent with his father for the previous decade. • ***sixteen years:*** From the beginning of his co-regency with his father Uzziah (750 BC) until his son Ahaz became the primary ruler of Judah (735 BC).

15:34-35 Although ***Jotham did what was pleasing in the LORD's sight,*** he allowed worship at ***pagan shrines*** to continue. • ***rebuilt the upper gate of the Temple:*** The prosperity of Uzziah's reign continued during his son Jotham's reign. Jotham built onto Jerusalem's wall at the hill of Ophel and did construction at many Judean sites (2 Chr 27:3-4). He also conquered the rebellious Ammonites (2 Chr 27:5), whom Uzziah had forced into subservience (2 Chr 26:8).

15:37 ***Rezin . . . Pekah:*** See 16:5.

he was buried with his ancestors in the City of David. And his son Ahaz became the next king.

Ahaz's Reign in Judah

2 Kgs 16:1-4 // 2 Chr 28:1-4
2 Kgs 16:19-20 // 2 Chr 28:26-27

16 Ahaz son of Jotham began to rule over Judah in the seventeenth year of King Pekah's reign in Israel. 2Ahaz was twenty years old when he became king, and he reigned in Jerusalem sixteen years. He did not do what was pleasing in the sight of the LORD his God, as his ancestor David had done. 3Instead, he followed the example of the kings of Israel, even sacrificing his own son in the fire. In this way, he followed the detestable practices of the pagan nations the LORD had driven from the land ahead of the Israelites. 4He offered sacrifices and burned incense at the pagan shrines and on the hills and under every green tree.

5Then King Rezin of Aram and King Pekah of Israel came up to attack Jerusalem. They besieged Ahaz but could not conquer him. 6At that time the king of Edom recovered the town of Elath for Edom. He drove out the people of Judah and sent Edomites to live there, as they do to this day.

7King Ahaz sent messengers to King Tiglath-pileser of Assyria with this message: "I am your servant and your vassal. Come up and rescue me from the attacking armies of Aram and Israel." 8Then Ahaz took the silver and gold from the Temple of the LORD and the palace treasury and sent it as a payment to the Assyrian king. 9So the king of Assyria attacked the Aramean capital of Damascus and led its population away as captives, resettling them in Kir. He also killed King Rezin.

10King Ahaz then went to Damascus to meet with King Tiglath-pileser of Assyria. While he was there, he took special note of the altar. Then he sent a model of the altar to Uriah the priest, along with its design in full detail. 11Uriah followed the king's instructions and built an altar just like it, and it was ready before the king returned from Damascus. 12When the king returned, he inspected the altar and made offerings on it. 13He presented a burnt offering and a grain offering, he poured out a liquid offering, and he sprinkled the blood of peace offerings on the altar.

14Then King Ahaz removed the old bronze altar from its place in front of the LORD's Temple, between the entrance and the new

16:1-20 //2 Chr 28:1-27
16:2 2 Kgs 14:3
16:3 Lev 18:21; Deut 12:31; 2 Kgs 17:17; 21:6
16:4 Deut 12:2
16:5 2 Kgs 15:37; 2 Chr 28:5; Isa 7:1-6
16:6 2 Kgs 14:22; 2 Chr 26:2
16:7 2 Kgs 15:29
16:8 2 Kgs 12:17-18; 18:15
16:9 Amos 1:3-5
16:10 Isa 8:2
16:12 2 Chr 26:16, 19
16:14 Exod 40:6; 1 Kgs 8:64

16:1-2 The ***seventeenth year of King Pekah's reign*** was 735 BC. At that time ***Ahaz . . . began to rule:*** He had already been co-regent for eleven years, but now he officially acceded to the throne. This marks the transition from subordination to his father, Jotham (743–735 BC), to a position of reigning in his stead (735–732 BC; see timeline, p. 656). Ahaz presumably had his official accession ceremony following his father's death in 732 BC, so the author of Kings reckons Ahaz's reign of ***sixteen years*** from 731 BC, the year after his father died, to 715 BC (see timeline, p. 656). See also note on 17:1.

16:2-3 Again, ***his ancestor David*** serves as the standard for measuring the spiritual character of Judah's kings (14:3; 1 Kings 15:3, 11). • ***the example of the kings of Israel:*** Ahaz was one of Judah's most wicked kings. He indulged in the apostate religion of Israel and the ***pagan*** practices of other nations to the extent of ***even sacrificing his own son in the fire*** (or *even making his son pass through the fire*; see Jer 19:5; 32:35). Although Levitical regulations prohibited such sacrifices as an abomination detestable to the Lord (Lev 18:10; 20:1-5), the practice was repeated among God's people (Isa 30:33; Jer 7:31) until Josiah's reforms (23:10).

16:5-6 ***Rezin . . . Pekah:*** This alliance between the kings of ***Aram*** and ***Israel*** was intended to free the area of Assyrian dominance under Tiglath-pileser III (15:29-30; Isa 9:1). The ***attack*** against ***Judah*** may have occurred to force Judah into the alliance or to replace the Judean king with one of their own choosing (Isa 7:3-6). The result was captivity and widespread death for the people of Judah (2 Chr 28:5-15). Isaiah reports that Rezin and Pekah intended to install a new king on Judah's throne (Isa 7:3-6). Judah also suffered further attacks by the Edomites and Philistines (2 Chr 28:17-18). All of this was God's will due to Ahaz's detestable spiritual practices, which led to great sin among the people of Judah (2 Chr 28:5, 19).

16:6 ***the king of Edom:*** As in Latin Vulgate; Hebrew reads *Rezin king of Aram.* • ***Edom:*** As in Latin Vulgate; Hebrew reads *Aram.* • ***Edomites:*** As in Greek version, Latin Vulgate, and an alternate reading of the Masoretic Text; the other alternate reads *Arameans.* The NLT translators have chosen to follow the text of several ancient translations, since the town of ***Elath*** is far to the south, nearer to Edom than to Aram.

16:7-9 ***your vassal:*** Literally *your son.* Rather than trusting in God's provision (Isa 7:7-16), ***Ahaz*** petitioned ***Tiglath-pileser*** III of Assyria to ***rescue*** him from his enemies. Tiglath-pileser was successful, and his victory brought about the death of Rezin, the capture of Damascus, and the deportation of its citizens (732 BC). It also contributed to unseating Pekah as king of Israel in the same year (15:29-30). The cost of the rescue was great, however; Ahaz paid a heavy tribute to Tiglath-pileser, and the Assyrian intervention reduced Judah to vassal status.

16:9 The location of ***Kir*** is unknown; it was the original home of the Arameans (Amos 9:7).

16:10-11 ***Ahaz . . . took special note of the altar*** of the Arameans and had a copy made so as to emulate their pagan worship.

16:12-13 ***The king*** initiated the new ***altar*** by making the traditional offerings upon it (see Lev 1–3; 6:8-23; 7:11-34; Num 15:1-10; 28:9-15, 24, 31). Sadly, such offerings upon a pagan altar by a leader devoid of spiritual character constituted a mockery of their deep spiritual meaning.

16:14 Solomon had originally placed the ***bronze altar*** in front of the ***Temple*** (see Exod 40:6; 2 Chr 4:1; 7:7-10). At first, Ahaz positioned his ***new altar*** so that worshipers would come to it before coming to the bronze altar. Then Ahaz had the bronze altar ***placed . . . on the north side*** of the new altar, completely replacing the bronze altar as the center of sacrificial activity.

16:15 Exod 29:38-41
16:17 1 Kgs 7:23, 25, 27
16:20 2 Chr 28:27; 29:1
17:1 2 Kgs 15:30

altar, and placed it on the north side of the
new altar. 15He told Uriah the priest, "Use
the new altar for the morning sacrifices of
burnt offering, the evening grain offering,
the king's burnt offering and grain offering,
and the burnt offerings of all the people, as
well as their grain offerings and liquid offerings. Sprinkle the blood from all the burnt
offerings and sacrifices on the new altar.
The bronze altar will be for my personal
use only." 16Uriah the priest did just as King
Ahaz commanded him.
17Then the king removed the side panels
and basins from the portable water carts.
He also removed the great bronze basin
called the Sea from the backs of the bronze
oxen and placed it on the stone pavement.
18In deference to the king of Assyria, he
also removed the canopy that had been constructed inside the palace for use on the
Sabbath day, as well as the king's outer entrance to the Temple of the LORD.
19The rest of the events in Ahaz's reign
and everything he did are recorded in *The
Book of the History of the Kings of Judah.*
20When Ahaz died, he was buried with his
ancestors in the City of David. Then his son
Hezekiah became the next king.

Hoshea's Reign in Israel

17 Hoshea son of Elah began to rule
over Israel in the twelfth year of King
Ahaz's reign in Judah. He reigned in Sa-

AHAZ (15:38–16:20)

2 Chr 27:9–28:27
Isa 7:1-25

Ahaz (743–715 BC) reigned in Judah during a turbulent period. His father Jotham (15:32-38; 2 Chr 27:1-9) and son Hezekiah (18:1-8) were praised for their obedience to the Lord, but Ahaz was evil, even sacrificing one of his sons to false gods.

Ahaz's reign was marked with conflict. King Pekah of Israel and King Rezin of Aram (Syria) wanted him to join a coalition against Assyria and its ambitious king Tiglath-pileser III, but he refused. So Pekah and Rezin turned against Judah and won substantial victories, which severely frightened Ahaz. Isaiah the prophet encouraged Ahaz to rely on the Lord, but Ahaz refused (Isa 7:1-25).

Revealing his lack of trust in the true God, Ahaz appealed to Tiglath-pileser III for help (16:7-9). The Assyrian king subsequently defeated Syria and killed Rezin in a two-year campaign (734–732 BC). He subdued Israel and incorporated great tracts of Pekah's land into the Assyrian empire (15:29-30). Ahaz made Judah dangerously dependent on Assyria, and Judah effectively became a vassal state.

Ahaz seemed an eager servant of Assyria, because he adopted many religious innovations based on Assyrian models (16:10-18). Ahaz visited Tiglath-pileser III in Damascus, where he saw an Assyrian altar and sent a model of it to Jerusalem, where a similar altar was built, replacing the original bronze altar. Several other Temple alterations also indicate Ahaz's defection from faith in the Lord.

Ahaz illustrates why the people of Judah were finally exiled. He did not comport himself appropriately as a king (Deut 17:14-20), and he did not worship the Lord. He was succeeded by his son Hezekiah (18:1).

16:15-16 Ahaz ordered that standard daily sacrifices (Num 28:1-8) as well as the individual ***offerings*** of the king and ***people*** would be made on the ***new altar*** (literally *the great altar*). Ahaz then restricted the ***bronze altar*** to his ***personal use*** (literally *for seeking/inquiry*), probably to use it for pagan divination. This demand displayed a callous insolence against the Lord and his worship. ***Uriah the priest*** complied with Ahaz's demands (16:10-11, 16), rather than resisting the king.

16:17-18 Because the ***side panels and basins from the . . . water carts*** and the ***Sea*** were made of ***bronze*** (see 1 Kgs 7:25-40), Ahaz might have used them to pay tribute or for some other project. • ***In deference:*** Apparently at the request of ***the king of Assyria,*** Ahaz removed ***the canopy that had been constructed inside the palace for use on the Sabbath day*** (the meaning of the Hebrew is uncertain.) This canopy led to the inner court as well as to the king's private ***entrance to the Temple.*** Judah paid a heavy price in loss of freedom because of Ahaz's trust in the Assyrian king's military intervention on their behalf (16:7-8, 10).

16:19 ***The rest of the events in Ahaz's reign:*** In further rejection of the Lord, Ahaz removed the utensils from the Temple "and broke them into pieces" (2 Chr 28:24). He then closed the Temple and discontinued services there, instead promoting paganism throughout the land (2 Chr 28:25; 29:7). In redefining the worship of Judah so completely, his apostasy was similar to that of Jeroboam I (cp. 3:3; 13:2; 16:2-4; 17:21; 1 Kgs 12:25-33; 16:26; 22:52)

17:1-23 The report of the northern kingdom's fall proceeds in two major sections: (1) events in the reign of Israel's final king, Hoshea, and the circumstances that brought about the capture of Samaria and the deportation of Israel's citizens (17:1-6); (2) the reasons for Israel's collapse and conquest by Assyria—Israel's many sins (17:7-17) that merited God's judgment (17:18-20) and the great sin of Jeroboam I, who laid the foundation for Israel's rampant apostasy (17:21-23).

17:1 ***Hoshea . . . began to rule over Israel*** in 732 BC. • Hoshea's reign is listed

maria nine years. 2He did what was evil in the LORD's sight, but not to the same extent as the kings of Israel who ruled before him.

3King Shalmaneser of Assyria attacked King Hoshea, so Hoshea was forced to pay heavy tribute to Assyria. 4But Hoshea stopped paying the annual tribute and conspired against the king of Assyria by asking King So of Egypt to help him shake free of Assyria's power. When the king of Assyria discovered this treachery, he seized Hoshea and put him in prison.

The Fall of Samaria
2 Kgs 17:5-6 // 2 Kgs 18:9-11

5Then the king of Assyria invaded the entire land, and for three years he besieged the city of Samaria. 6Finally, in the ninth year of King Hoshea's reign, Samaria fell, and the people of Israel were exiled to Assyria. They were settled in colonies in Halah, along the banks of the Habor River in Gozan, and in the cities of the Medes.

7This disaster came upon the people of Israel because they worshiped other gods. They sinned against the LORD their God, who had brought them safely out of Egypt and had rescued them from the power of Pharaoh, the king of Egypt. 8They had followed the practices of the pagan nations the LORD had driven from the land ahead of them, as well as the practices the kings of Israel had introduced. 9The people of Israel had also secretly done many things that were not pleasing to the LORD their God. They built pagan shrines for themselves in all their towns, from the smallest outpost to the largest walled city. 10They set up sacred pillars and Asherah poles at the top of every hill and under every green tree. 11They offered sacrifices on all the hilltops, just like the nations the LORD had driven from the land ahead of them. So the people of Israel had done many evil things, arousing the LORD's anger. 12Yes, they worshiped idols, despite the LORD's specific and repeated warnings.

13Again and again the LORD had sent his prophets and seers to warn both Israel and Judah: "Turn from all your evil ways. Obey my commands and decrees—the entire law that I commanded your ancestors to obey, and that I gave you through my servants the prophets."

14But the Israelites would not listen. They were as stubborn as their ancestors who had

17:3-7
//2 Kgs 18:9-12
17:4
2 Kgs 18:20-21
17:6
Deut 28:64; 29:27-28
2 Kgs 18:11
1 Chr 5:26
Hos 13:16
17:7
Josh 23:15-16
17:8
Lev 18:3
Deut 18:9
17:9
2 Kgs 18:8
17:12
Exod 20:4
17:13
Neh 9:29-30
Jer 7:5-6; 18:11
Acts 7:51-52
17:14
Exod 32:9; 33:3

as beginning in "the twentieth year of Jotham" (15:30) and in ***the twelfth year of King Ahaz's reign in Judah.*** Ahaz apparently co-reigned with Jotham from about 743 BC, when he was twelve years old, but Ahaz's official regnal years were calculated from 731 BC (16:2). Thus the references to Ahaz's reign are in harmony.

17:2 Hoshea's ***evil*** deeds were ***not to the same extent*** as his forebears, though what this means exactly is not explained.

17:3-4 ***King Shalmaneser*** V succeeded his father Tiglath-pileser III in 726 BC. ***Hoshea*** may have reasoned that this leadership change would allow Israel to become independent of Assyrian vassalage. But his withholding of the ***annual tribute*** simply invited Shalmaneser's reprisal. • ***by asking King So of Egypt*** (Or *by asking the king of Egypt at Sais*): Some scholars understand the name *So* as an abbreviation of Pharaoh Osorkon IV (730–715 BC). Others equate *So* with Pharaoh Piankhy (747–716 BC), viewing the biblical name *So* as a Hebraic rendering of one of the names in Piankhy's titulary. Still others suggest that *So* refers to the city of *Sais,* the capital of Pharaoh Tefnakht (727–720 BC). Whatever the identity of this king, it is clear that Hoshea's hope for help from Egypt was misplaced.

17:5-6 ***the king of Assyria:*** Although sources identify Samaria's conqueror as Shalmaneser V of Assyria (726–722 BC), Sargon II (who ruled Assyria 721–705 BC) claimed that he captured the city. Perhaps Sargon was the field commander when Samaria fell and then became king when Shalmaneser died during the year of the siege. • ***invaded the entire land:*** Assyrian military strategy was to devastate the territory surrounding an enemy's primary city before launching a final attack. • ***The ninth year of King Hoshea's reign*** was 722 BC. • ***the people . . . were exiled:*** The Assyrians practiced deportation in order to defuse future rebellions. Sargon also brought other people to Israel to form a mixed population (17:24-25). • ***Halah*** was situated northeast of Nineveh in Assyria. • ***The Habor River*** is a tributary of the Euphrates River in northwestern Assyria. • ***Gozan*** was located on the ***Habor River*** northeast of Haran (Gen 12:4). Assyrian documents from the area list personal names that are clearly Israelite, perhaps reflecting the deportation of the people of Samaria.

17:7 ***sinned against the LORD . . . who had brought them . . . out of Egypt:*** Israel's demise was due to the people's persistent sin of infidelity. Rather than remaining true to their Redeemer, the Israelites ***worshiped other gods.*** • Israel's redemption ***out of Egypt*** is a theme repeated throughout the OT, appearing in the poetic literature (Exod 15:1-18; Ps 77:13-20; 105:26-45; 106:7-12; 114:1-8; Hab 3:3-15), the prophets (Isa 63:11-14; Jer 2:1-8; 32:21-23; Ezek 20:10-12; Mic 6:4), and the historical literature (Josh 3:5; 4:14, 18-24; 1 Sam 12:6).

17:8-13 The catalog of Israel's sins includes numerous ***pagan*** rites and ***practices.*** Whether done in the open or ***secretly,*** God was aware of them all. Many were even initiated by Israel's kings who built ***pagan shrines, sacred pillars, and Asherah poles*** and emulated heathen ***sacrifices*** and idolatry (10:29; 15:18, 28; 1 Kgs 12:28-33; 15:34; 16:30-33). All levels of Israelite society, royalty and commoner alike, persisted in such sins despite denunciation and warning by God's ***prophets,*** which included the writings of Isaiah, Hosea, Amos, and Micah.

17:11 ***arousing the LORD's anger:*** When God becomes angry, he is not vindictive or bad tempered. Instead, human evil angers him because people have rebelled against God and done evil to one another. God responds to human evil with his justice in dealing with sin and evil (see also 13:3; 17:17-18; 21:6; 22:13, 17; 23:26-27; 24:20; Rom 3:23; 6:23; 14:10; 2 Cor 5:10; Col 3:6; 1 Jn 1:8-10).

17:12 ***idols:*** The Hebrew term (literally *round things*) probably alludes to dung.

17:14-15 Like their ***ancestors*** (Deut 10:16; 1 Sam 12:6-9; Ps 106:28), ***the Israelites*** persisted in their infidelity to the Lord (Isa 65:6-7; Amos 2:4; see Acts 7:51-53).

17:15
Exod 24:6-8
Deut 12:30-31; 29:25; 32:21
17:16
1 Kgs 12:28; 16:31
[k]*azab* (5800)
›2 Kgs 22:17
17:17
Lev 19:26
Deut 18:10-12
2 Kgs 3:27; 16:3; 21:6
17:19
1 Kgs 14:22-24
17:21
1 Kgs 11:11, 31; 12:20
17:23
2 Kgs 18:11-12
17:24
2 Kgs 18:34
Ezra 4:2, 10

refused to believe in the LORD their God.
15 They rejected his decrees and the covenant
he had made with their ancestors, and they
despised all his warnings. They worshiped
worthless idols, so they became worthless
themselves. They followed the example of
the nations around them, disobeying the
LORD's command not to imitate them.
16 They [k]rejected all the commands of the
LORD their God and made two calves from
metal. They set up an Asherah pole and
worshiped Baal and all the forces of heaven.
17 They even sacrificed their own sons and
daughters in the fire. They consulted fortune-
tellers and practiced sorcery and sold themselves to evil, arousing the LORD's anger.
18 Because the LORD was very angry with
Israel, he swept them away from his presence. Only the tribe of Judah remained in
the land. 19 But even the people of Judah
refused to obey the commands of the
LORD their God, for they followed the evil
practices that Israel had introduced. 20 The
LORD rejected all the descendants of Israel.
He punished them by handing them over to
their attackers until he had banished Israel
from his presence.
21 For when the LORD tore Israel away
from the kingdom of David, they chose
Jeroboam son of Nebat as their king. But
Jeroboam drew Israel away from following
the LORD and made them commit a great
sin. 22 And the people of Israel persisted in
all the evil ways of Jeroboam. They did not
turn from these sins 23 until the LORD finally
swept them away from his presence, just as
all his prophets had warned. So Israel was
exiled from their land to Assyria, where
they remain to this day.

Foreigners Settle in Israel
24 The king of Assyria transported groups of
people from Babylon, Cuthah, Avva, Hamath,

God's Judgment of His People (17:7-23)

2 Kgs 21:9-16; 23:26-27; 24:20–25:21
Lev 26:27-39
Ps 62:12
Prov 11:31
Hos 11:1-11
Isa 3:10-11
Jer 1:16; 17:10; 23:3-6
Ezek 7:1-9; 33:18-20; 34:17-24; 39:23-24
Amos 3:2
Matt 25:24-30
Luke 12:47-48; 13:6-9
John 5:45-47
Rom 11:5-36
Col 3:23-25
Heb 12:25
Jas 2:12-13
1 Pet 1:17
Rev 2:1–3:22

Although the kings of Israel and Judah had a major role in the history of the divided kingdom, the people also played a part in what occurred. They followed their wicked rulers (3:3; 17:22; 21:9, 11, 16), and it is clear that their own hearts strayed from God (12:3; 14:4; 15:4, 35; 17:9-11; 18:4; 21:9; 22:17). Their participation in the religious practices initiated by Jeroboam I of Israel (10:28-31; 17:21-22) and their worship at the pagan shrines (12:3; 14:4; 15:4, 35; 18:4) were particularly troublesome.

But God's OT people are sometimes portrayed positively. The people of Judah rejoiced over the removal of Athaliah and the installation of Joash as king (11:12, 18-20). At times, the people were instrumental in the succession of kings (14:21; 23:30) or were responsive to godly leadership (11:17; 18:36; 23:1-3, 21-23).

Yet despite God's repeated warnings through his prophets (17:13), the people of both kingdoms became set in their apostasy (17:14-19, 22). So God's righteous wrath burned against them and their leaders, and he brought his threatened judgment upon them (17:22-23; 21:10-15; 22:17; 23:26-27; 24:20; 25:21). God thus acted in accordance with the stipulations in his covenant with them (cp. Lev 26:27-39), even though in love he longed to restore his people (cp. Hos 11:1-11).

Yet God never gave up caring for his people. He rescued them from Sennacherib (18:23–19:37) and promised that a remnant would again thrive in the land (19:30-34). Even the good treatment Jehoiachin received in Babylon (25:27-30) no doubt renewed hope among the repentant of God's people. God promised one day to restore his people from exile and give them fellowship with him in the land once again, ruling over them through his chosen king, the descendant of David (Jer 23:3-6; see also Isa 11:1-16; Rom 11:5-36).

17:16-17 ***all the commands of the LORD:*** The narrator lists specific examples of Israel's disobedience: the ***two calves*** made ***from metal*** erected at Dan and Bethel (1 Kgs 12:28-30), the Canaanite fertility symbol known as ***an Asherah pole*** (13:6; 17:10; 1 Kgs 14:23; 16:33; Mic 5:14), the persistent worship of ***Baal*** (1 Kgs 16:31-33; Hos 2:13; 13:1), and the detestable Molech rites (16:3; Ps 106:37).

17:17 ***sacrificed their own sons and daughters in the fire:*** Or *made their sons and daughters pass through the fire.*

17:18-20 ***the LORD was very angry:*** God's wrath is his righteous response to evil that demands his justice • ***even the people of Judah refused to obey the commands of the LORD:*** This remark foreshadows the eventual fall of the southern kingdom as well (25:1-21).

17:21-23 All of Israel's evil and disobedience were connected to the sins of ***Jeroboam*** I (1 Kgs 12:26-33).

17:21 ***the LORD:*** Literally *he;* cp. 1 Kgs 11:31-32.

17:24-41 The writer appends information concerning later events in Israel, including the repopulation of the land with foreigners and the syncretistic worship that developed among the mixed population.

17:24 Not only were the Israelites exiled to other places held by the Assyrians (17:6), but ***groups of people*** were sent to settle in Israel. By mixing

and Sepharvaim and resettled them in the towns of Samaria, replacing the people of Israel. They took possession of Samaria and lived in its towns. 25But since these foreign settlers did not worship the LORD when they first arrived, the LORD sent lions among them, which killed some of them.

26So a message was sent to the king of Assyria: "The people you have sent to live in the towns of Samaria do not know the religious customs of the God of the land. He has sent lions among them to destroy them because they have not worshiped him correctly."

27The king of Assyria then commanded, "Send one of the exiled priests back to Samaria. Let him live there and teach the new residents the religious customs of the God of the land." 28So one of the priests who had been exiled from Samaria returned to Bethel and taught the new residents how to worship the LORD.

29But these various groups of foreigners also continued to worship their own gods. In town after town where they lived, they placed their idols at the pagan shrines that the people of Samaria had built. 30Those from Babylon worshiped idols of their god Succoth-benoth. Those from Cuthah worshiped their god Nergal. And those from Hamath worshiped Ashima. 31The Avvites worshiped their gods Nibhaz and Tartak. And the people from Sepharvaim even burned their own children as sacrifices to their gods Adrammelech and Anammelech.

32These new residents worshiped the LORD, but they also appointed from among themselves all sorts of people as priests to offer sacrifices at their places of worship. 33And though they worshiped the LORD, they continued to follow their own gods according to the religious customs of the nations from which they came. 34And this is still going on today. They continue to follow their former practices instead of truly worshiping the LORD and obeying the decrees, regulations, instructions, and commands he gave the descendants of Jacob, whose name he changed to Israel.

35For the LORD had made a covenant with the descendants of Jacob and commanded them: "Do not [a]worship any other gods or bow before them or serve them or offer sacrifices to them. 36But worship only the LORD, who brought you out of Egypt with great strength and a powerful arm. Bow down to him alone, and offer sacrifices only to him. 37Be careful at all times to obey the decrees, regulations, instructions, and commands that he wrote for you. You must not worship other gods. 38Do not forget the covenant I made with you, and do not worship other gods. 39You must worship only the LORD your God. He is the one who will rescue you from all your enemies."

40But the people would not listen and continued to follow their former practices. 41So while these new residents worshiped the LORD, they also worshiped their idols. And to this day their descendants do the same.

2. THE LAST ERA OF THE SOUTHERN KINGDOM (18:1–25:21)

Hezekiah's Reign in Judah (18:1–20:21)

Overview of Hezekiah's Reign

2 Kgs 18:2-3 // 2 Chr 29:1-2

18 Hezekiah son of Ahaz began to rule over Judah in the third year of King Hoshea's reign in Israel. 2He was twenty-five years old when he became king, and he

17:29 1 Kgs 12:31; 13:32
17:31 2 Kgs 17:24; 19:37
17:32 1 Kgs 12:31
17:34 Gen 32:28; 35:10
17:35 Exod 20:5; [a]*yare'* (3372) ‣ Ps 86:11
17:37 Deut 5:32
17:38 Deut 4:23; 6:10-12
17:41 Zeph 1:5; Matt 6:24
18:1 2 Chr 28:27
18:2-4 //2 Chr 29:1-2; 31:1

diverse peoples, the Assyrians hoped to have better control of the resulting population and transfer their loyalties to *Assyria*. • *Samaria* became the official name of the new Assyrian province.

17:26-31 ***The king of Assyria*** was Sargon II (721–705 BC). • ***the God of the land . . . has sent lions:*** Religious belief in the ancient Near East held that the tranquility and success of a land was strongly identified with its god and the rites associated with his worship. • ***One of the priests . . . returned to Bethel,*** though his instruction in ***how to worship the LORD*** was doubtless influenced by the religion of Jeroboam I and mixed with paganism. • The ***foreigners also continued to worship their own gods.*** They simply added the worship of Israel's God to the worship of their own gods. Most of the false *gods* mentioned here are unknown. Their names may have been altered by Jewish scribes. • ***Nergal*** was the Mesopotamian god of the underworld. ***Nibhaz and Tartak*** were probably Elamite deities.

17:32-34 ***worshiped the LORD, but . . . continued to follow their own gods:*** Hebrew faith, already blended with the religion of Jeroboam I, was now mixed with many different foreign religious customs. Genuine worship of the Lord virtually disappeared. Only a handful of faithful Israelites remained to respond to Hezekiah's later invitation to come to Judah for the Passover celebration (2 Chr 30:10-19).

17:35-39 According to Israel's ***covenant*** with ***the LORD*** (Exod 20:5; Deut 6:4-15), Israel was to ***worship only the LORD.*** He alone could provide true redemption and ***rescue*** them ***from all . . . enemies.***

17:40-41 ***worshiped the LORD . . . worshiped their idols:*** The reconstituted Samaritan religion was thoroughly syncretistic (an eclectic combination of religions), perhaps explaining why Samaritans were later regarded with suspicion and disdain (see Neh 4:1-2; 10:28-31; John 4:7-9).

18:1-12 The accession statement concerning ***Hezekiah***'s reign (18:1-2) is accompanied by a lengthy evaluation of Hezekiah's spiritual commitment (18:3-7a), followed by background details of the political situation in his time (18:7b-12).

18:1-2 ***the third year of King Hoshea's reign in Israel:*** The date given for ***Hezekiah***'s accession refers to his co-regency with his father, Ahaz. Since Hoshea began his reign in 732 BC, Hezekiah ***began to rule*** in about 728 BC,

18:4 Num 21:8-9; 2 Chr 31:1
18:5-7 //2 Chr 31:20-21
18:5 2 Kgs 19:10; 23:25
18:6 Deut 10:20
18:7 Gen 39:2-3; 1 Sam 18:14
18:8 2 Kgs 17:9; 2 Chr 28:18
18:9-12 //2 Kgs 17:3-7

reigned in Jerusalem twenty-nine years. His
mother was Abijah, the daughter of Zechariah. 3He did what was pleasing in the LORD's
sight, just as his ancestor David had done.
4He removed the pagan shrines, smashed
the sacred pillars, and cut down the Asherah poles. He broke up the bronze serpent
that Moses had made, because the people of
Israel had been offering sacrifices to it. The
bronze serpent was called Nehushtan.

5Hezekiah trusted in the LORD, the God
of Israel. There was no one like him among
all the kings of Judah, either before or after
his time. 6He remained faithful to the LORD
in everything, and he carefully obeyed all the
commands the LORD had given Moses. 7So
the LORD was with him, and Hezekiah was
successful in everything he did. He revolted
against the king of Assyria and refused to
pay him tribute. 8He also conquered the Philistines as far distant as Gaza and its territory,
from their smallest outpost to their largest
walled city.

A Final Note concerning the Fall of Samaria
2 Kgs 18:9-11 // 2 Kgs 17:5-6

9During the fourth year of Hezekiah's reign,
which was the seventh year of King Hoshea's

Obedience and Spiritual Blessings (18:1-8)

2 Kgs 12:6-16; 14:3-6; 18:13–19:36; 20:2-3; 22:1-2; 23:21-25; Exod 19:5; 23:22; Lev 26:3-39; Deut 4:1, 40; 5:29; 6:1-25; 7:9; 11:26-28; 15:10; 28:1-14; Josh 1:8-9; 1 Chr 28:5-9; 2 Chr 26:5; Ps 115:13; Prov 16:7; Isa 1:19; 30:18-26; 66:2-4; Jer 7:3; 17:24-27; 22:15-16; Mal 3:10-12; Mark 13:13; Phil 2:8-9; 2 Tim 4:7-8; Heb 5:8; 10:5-7; 1 Pet 3:9; 1 Jn 2:24; Rev 1:3; 22:7

God requires his people to follow his word, and he rewards spiritual obedience and faithfulness with his blessings (Deut 6:1-25; 11:26-28; Ps 115:13; Isa 30:19-26; 1 Pet 3:9).

Many kings of Judah receive good words from the narrator for doing what was pleasing in the Lord's sight. Joash was personally involved in repairing the Temple (12:6-12). Amaziah is praised for punishing his father Joash's assassins in keeping with the law of Moses (14:5-6). His son Uzziah and his grandson Jotham (15:34) followed in Amaziah's footsteps (15:3). Hezekiah's trust in the Lord brought about the removal of pagan shrines and idolatrous objects (18:3-6; see 20:3). Josiah is commended for having a heart like his ancestor David's, for the many reforms that he instituted, and for his unqualified concern for the law of the Lord (22:1-2; 23:25). Throughout the book of Kings, David's heart for God is held up as the model for godly obedience to the Lord (14:3; 16:2; 18:1-4; 22:1-2; 1 Kgs 14:8).

Although those kings remained faithful to God's laws (1 Kgs 15:14), neither Solomon (1 Kgs 11:6) nor the people followed the Lord completely. In the northern kingdom (Israel), the kings after Jeroboam I consistently perpetuated state-sponsored apostate religion (1 Kgs 15:26; 16:2, 19), incorporating the worship of Baal and other pagan deities (1 Kgs 18:18-21; 21:25; see 11:5). Such disobedience and infidelity earned the Lord's condemnation and judgment throughout the history of the divided kingdom. In the northern kingdom, dynasty after dynasty fell, while the people suffered drought (1 Kgs 17:1-7), famine (1 Kgs 17:12; 18:2), and war (1 Kgs 14:30; 15:6-7, 16, 32; 20:1-34; 22:29-36). They learned all too painfully that although spiritual obedience brings God's blessings (Lev 26:3-13; Deut 6:4-11; 28:1-14), disobedience will occasion his severe judgment (Lev 26:14-39; Num 20:12-13; Deut 28:15-68; 1 Sam 13:13-14; 15:13-23).

The Lord Jesus was obedient in all things (Phil 2:8; Heb 5:8; 10:5-7). God blesses those who have humble and repentant hearts, who live in faithfulness to his word (Isa 66:2-4). Those who follow Jesus' example (Phil 2:12-13), like the kings who followed David's example, can anticipate God's fullest blessings (2 Tim 4:7-8; 1 Jn 2:24).

when he was twelve years old. When Ahaz died in 715 BC, Hezekiah began his sole reign at age ***twenty-five.*** This marks the start of his reign of ***twenty-nine years*** (715–686 BC).

18:2 ***Abijah:*** As in parallel text at 2 Chr 29:1; Hebrew reads *Abi,* a variant spelling of Abijah.

18:3-4 Unlike Ahaz (16:2), Hezekiah compared favorably with ***David.*** Hezekiah destroyed false objects of worship, including the ***pagan shrines . . . sacred pillars, and . . . Asherah poles*** (see 16:3-10; 17:9-11, 19). • Apparently the ***bronze serpent*** used by ***Moses*** (Num 21) had become an object of illicit worship. • ***Nehushtan*** sounds like the Hebrew terms that mean "snake," "bronze," and "unclean thing."

18:5-6 ***Hezekiah trusted in the LORD:*** He was without peer ***among all the kings of Judah.*** Later, Josiah was without equal in upholding the law of Moses (23:25). These two kings were models of piety in times of diminishing spirituality.

18:7-8 Because of Hezekiah's unparalleled spiritual commitment, God blessed him and he was ***successful in everything he did.*** Hezekiah began a series of reforms, including the cleansing, repair, and refurbishing of the Temple (2 Chr 29:3-36); observance of the Passover (2 Chr 30); and the reconstituting of vital worship in Judah (2 Chr 31:1-19). • ***He revolted against the king of Assyria:*** In the ancient Near East, rebellion and the withholding of ***tribute*** usually took place with the change of government; King Sennacherib of Assyria succeeded Sargon II in 704 BC. Assyria's preoccupation with matters in southern Mesopotamia at this time might have emboldened Hezekiah. Assyria's response was to invade Judah in 701 BC (18:13–19:36). • ***He also conquered the Philistines,*** who had been a menace during Ahaz's reign (2 Chr 28:18).

18:9-12 The narrator introduces the fall of Samaria as a reminder that Assyria

reign in Israel, King Shalmaneser of Assyria
attacked the city of Samaria and began a
siege against it. [10]Three years later, during
the sixth year of King Hezekiah's reign and
the ninth year of King Hoshea's reign in Israel, Samaria fell. [11]At that time the king of
Assyria exiled the Israelites to Assyria and
placed them in colonies in Halah, along the
banks of the Habor River in Gozan, and in
the cities of the Medes. [12]For they refused
to listen to the LORD their God and obey
him. Instead, they violated his covenant—all
the laws that Moses the LORD's servant had
commanded them to obey.

Assyria Invades Judah

2 Kgs 18:13 // Isa 36:1 // 2 Chr 32:1

[13]In the fourteenth year of King Hezekiah's
reign, King Sennacherib of Assyria came
to attack the fortified towns of Judah and
conquered them. [14]King Hezekiah sent this
message to the king of Assyria at Lachish:
"I have done wrong. I will pay whatever
tribute money you demand if you will only
withdraw." The king of Assyria then demanded a settlement of more than eleven
tons of silver and one ton of gold. [15]To
gather this amount, King Hezekiah used all
the silver stored in the Temple of the LORD
and in the palace treasury. [16]Hezekiah even
stripped the gold from the doors of the
LORD's Temple and from the doorposts he
had overlaid with gold, and he gave it all to
the Assyrian king.

Sennacherib Threatens Jerusalem

2 Kgs 18:17-25 // Isa 36:2-10 // 2 Chr 32:9-15
2 Kgs 18:26-37 // Isa 36:11-22

[17]Nevertheless, the king of Assyria sent his
commander in chief, his field commander,

18:12 1 Kgs 9:6; Dan 9:6, 10
18:13 2 Chr 32:1; Isa 36:1
18:15 1 Kgs 15:18-19; 2 Kgs 12:18
18:17-37 //2 Chr 32:9-19; //Isa 36:1-22

HEZEKIAH (18:1–20:21)

2 Chr 28:27–32:33; Isa 36:1–39:8

Hezekiah, king of Judah from 728–686 BC, was one of Judah's best kings. Hezekiah's father Ahaz betrayed the Lord, but Hezekiah promoted true worship of God. Reversing the damage done by Ahaz, he repaired the Temple doors, had the Levites sanctify themselves, and reinstated religious ceremonies. He brought sacrifices, restored the priestly Temple service (2 Chr 29), and invited people throughout Judah and Israel to Passover in Jerusalem. After the celebration, he faithfully destroyed pagan worship sites.

Soon after Hezekiah started ruling, the Assyrians under Shalmaneser V and his successor Sargon II defeated the northern kingdom in 722 BC, deported its inhabitants, and brought in foreign residents. When Sargon II died in 705 BC, his son Sennacherib came to power, triggering widespread rebellion. Hezekiah stopped paying the tribute that his father Ahaz had paid (18:7; see 16:7). As a result, in 701 BC Sennacherib invaded Judah. Hezekiah tried to appease the Assyrian by sending a vast tribute payment, but the attempted return to servitude failed and the Assyrian forces threatened Jerusalem and mocked Hezekiah's reliance on the Lord (18:17-35). Hezekiah responded with grieving and supplication. The Lord, speaking through Isaiah the prophet, assured Hezekiah that Sennacherib would not conquer Jerusalem because of Hezekiah's prayers (19:1-34).

Sometime before 701 BC, Hezekiah became seriously ill (20:1-11). Isaiah told him to prepare for death, but Hezekiah turned to the Lord and prayed for healing. The Lord promised him fifteen more years and deliverance from the Assyrians. When he had recovered, Hezekiah unwisely hosted the rebel Babylonian king Merodach-baladan in his palace, showing him the Temple treasures and seeking support from Babylon rather than the Lord. Isaiah predicted that those treasures would be carried off to Babylon (20:12-19).

After the Assyrian threat in 701 BC, Hezekiah's remaining years were peaceful and prosperous; he died in 686 BC and was succeeded by his son Manasseh.

was the prevailing power of the era and that Samaria fell because of Hoshea's apostasy, thus setting the stage for the account of Hezekiah's demonstration of spiritual fiber and God's dealing with him (18:19–19:19).

18:13 The ***fourteenth year*** of Hezekiah's reign was 701 BC. • The annals of ***King Sennacherib of Assyria*** describe this invasion during his third military campaign. He advanced swiftly down the Mediterranean coast through the Phoenician cities and into Philistine territory, then turned inland.

18:14 ***Lachish*** lay southwest of Jerusalem, not far from the Philistine border. • ***I have done wrong*** (literally *I have sinned*). Hezekiah's message to Sennacherib was in well-chosen diplomatic language. • Sennacherib claimed that in addition to the ***eleven tons of silver and one ton of gold*** (Hebrew *300 talents* [10 metric tons] *of silver and 30 talents* [1 metric ton] *of gold*), he received from Hezekiah many jewels and rich treasures as well as Hezekiah's own daughter, the women of his harem, and his male and female singers.

18:15-16 Hezekiah paid a heavy price for refusing to pay tribute money to the king of Assyria. Now, to satisfy Sennacherib's demands he emptied the silver and gold from the ***Temple*** and ***the palace treasury*** (cp. 2 Chr 16:1-9).

18:17 ***sent . . . a huge army:*** In spite of Hezekiah's lavish payment,

18:18
2 Kgs 19:2
Isa 22:15-16, 20

18:26
Ezra 4:7
Dan 2:4

and his chief of staff from Lachish with a
huge army to confront King Hezekiah in Jerusalem. The Assyrians took up a position
beside the aqueduct that feeds water into
the upper pool, near the road leading to the
field where cloth is washed. 18They summoned King Hezekiah, but the king sent
these officials to meet with them: Eliakim
son of Hilkiah, the palace administrator;
Shebna the court secretary; and Joah son of
Asaph, the royal historian.
19Then the Assyrian king's chief of staff
told them to give this message to Hezekiah:

"This is what the great king of Assyria
says: What are you trusting in that
makes you so confident? 20Do you
think that mere words can substitute
for military skill and strength? Who are
you counting on, that you have rebelled
against me? 21On Egypt? If you lean on
Egypt, it will be like a reed that splinters
beneath your weight and pierces your
hand. Pharaoh, the king of Egypt, is
completely unreliable!
22"But perhaps you will say to me, 'We
are trusting in the LORD our God!' But
isn't he the one who was insulted by
Hezekiah? Didn't Hezekiah tear down
his shrines and altars and make everyone
in Judah and Jerusalem worship only at
the altar here in Jerusalem?
23"I'll tell you what! Strike a bargain
with my master, the king of Assyria. I
will give you 2,000 horses if you can
find that many men to ride on them!
24With your tiny army, how can you
think of challenging even the weakest
contingent of my master's troops, even
with the help of Egypt's chariots and
charioteers? 25What's more, do you
think we have invaded your land without
the LORD's direction? The LORD himself
told us, 'Attack this land and destroy it!' "

26Then Eliakim son of Hilkiah, Shebna,
and Joah said to the Assyrian chief of staff,
"Please speak to us in Aramaic, for we understand it well. Don't speak in Hebrew, for the
people on the wall will hear."
27But Sennacherib's chief of staff replied,
"Do you think my master sent this message
only to you and your master? He wants all
the people to hear it, for when we put this
city under siege, they will suffer along with
you. They will be so hungry and thirsty that
they will eat their own dung and drink their
own urine."

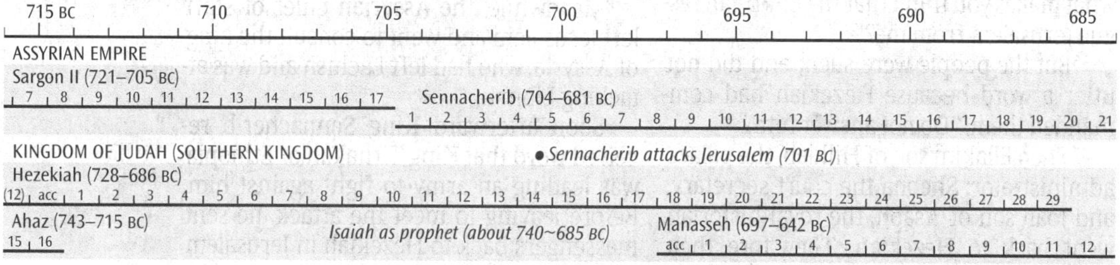

▲ **Kingdom of Judah, 716–684 BC (18:13–21:16).** HEZEKIAH's sole reign began in 715 BC, and his sole reign is used to count his official regnal years (see 18:13). The years of his co-regency, however, are used to date the siege and destruction of Samaria (18:1, 9-10). • SENNACHERIB's attack of Jerusalem in 701 BC is also mentioned in Assyrian records. • MANASSEH's fifty-five-year reign is counted from his accession as co-regent (21:1).

Sennacherib had no intention of being sidetracked from invading Jerusalem. • ***his chief of staff:*** Or *the rabshakeh;* also in 18:19, 26, 27, 28, 37. • ***beside the aqueduct:*** The meeting place of the two delegations is believed to be a location on Jerusalem's northwestern wall; this spot had also served as the meeting place between Isaiah and Ahaz (Isa 7:3-16). • ***washed:*** Or *bleached.*

18:19-22 In earlier days, the term ***great king*** was reserved for the kings of the leading military powers, but it had become a standard epithet for Assyrian kings. • ***What are you trusting in?*** The Assyrian officer asserted that the citizens of Jerusalem, faced with Assyria's overwhelming ***military*** superiority, would be foolish to trust in Hezekiah's words. Similarly, soliciting help from ***Egypt*** would be foolish. Finally, the chief of staff argued that trust ***in the LORD*** would also be misplaced. Perhaps the officer hoped to gain the loyalty of citizens who had worshiped at the ***shrines and altars*** that Hezekiah had destroyed.

18:23-24 The officer next turned to taunting, suggesting that Jerusalem would be unable to field sufficient manpower and strength to withstand even the ***weakest contingent of*** Assyrian ***troops.***

18:25 The chief of staff concluded his argument by claiming that Jerusalem's situation was hopeless because the Assyrians had come at ***the LORD's direction*** to ***destroy*** Judah. To oppose the great king was to oppose God himself!

18:26 Hezekiah's representatives wanted the Assyrian delegation to ***speak . . . in Aramaic,*** the language of diplomacy, so that the ***people*** who were listening would not understand and be discouraged or frightened. • ***in Hebrew:*** Literally *in the dialect of Judah;* also in 18:28.

18:27 ***my master . . . wants all the people to hear:*** The Assyrians used the native tongue of a besieged city as part of their psychological warfare.

28Then the chief of staff stood and
shouted in Hebrew to the people on the
wall, "Listen to this message from the great
king of Assyria! 29This is what the king
says: Don't let Hezekiah deceive you. He
will never be able to rescue you from my
power. 30Don't let him fool you into trusting
in the LORD by saying, 'The LORD will surely
rescue us. This city will never fall into the
hands of the Assyrian king!'

31"Don't listen to Hezekiah! These are the
terms the king of Assyria is offering: Make
peace with me—open the gates and come
out. Then each of you can continue eating
from your own grapevine and fig tree and
drinking from your own well. 32Then I will
arrange to take you to another land like this
one—a land of grain and new wine, bread
and vineyards, olive groves and honey.
Choose life instead of death!

"Don't listen to Hezekiah when he tries
to mislead you by saying, 'The LORD will
rescue us!' 33Have the gods of any other nations ever saved their people from the king
of Assyria? 34What happened to the gods
of Hamath and Arpad? And what about the
gods of Sepharvaim, Hena, and Ivvah? Did
any god rescue Samaria from my power?
35What god of any nation has ever been
able to save its people from my power? So
what makes you think that the LORD can rescue Jerusalem from me?"

36But the people were silent and did not
utter a word because Hezekiah had commanded them, "Do not answer him."

37Then Eliakim son of Hilkiah, the palace
administrator; Shebna the court secretary;
and Joah son of Asaph, the royal historian,
went back to Hezekiah. They tore their
clothes in despair, and they went in to see
the king and told him what the Assyrian
chief of staff had said.

Hezekiah Seeks the LORD's Help

2 Kgs 19:1-19 // Isa 37:1-20

19 When King Hezekiah heard their report, he tore his clothes and put on
burlap and went into the Temple of the LORD.
2And he sent Eliakim the palace administrator, Shebna the court secretary, and the
leading priests, all dressed in burlap, to
the prophet Isaiah son of Amoz. 3They
told him, "This is what King Hezekiah says:
Today is a day of trouble, insults, and disgrace. It is like when a child is ready to be
born, but the mother has no strength to deliver the baby. 4But perhaps the LORD your
God has heard the Assyrian chief of staff,
sent by the king to defy the living God, and
will punish him for his words. Oh, pray for
those of us who are left!"

5After King Hezekiah's officials delivered the king's message to Isaiah, 6the
prophet replied, "Say to your master, 'This is
what the LORD says: Do not be disturbed by
this blasphemous speech against me from
the Assyrian king's messengers. 7Listen! I
myself will move against him, and the king
will receive a message that he is needed at
home. So he will return to his land, where I
will have him killed with a sword.' "

8Meanwhile, the Assyrian chief of staff
left Jerusalem and went to consult the king
of Assyria, who had left Lachish and was attacking Libnah.

9Soon afterward King Sennacherib received word that King Tirhakah of Ethiopia
was leading an army to fight against him.
Before leaving to meet the attack, he sent
messengers back to Hezekiah in Jerusalem
with this message:

18:31 Deut 8:7-9; 1 Kgs 4:25
18:33 2 Kgs 19:12
18:34 2 Kgs 17:24; 19:13
19:1-13 //Isa 37:1-13
19:1 2 Chr 32:20-22
19:2 Isa 1:1
19:4 2 Sam 16:12; 2 Kgs 18:35; Isa 1:9
19:7 2 Kgs 19:37
19:8 2 Kgs 18:14

18:28-30 ***The chief of staff*** ignored the request of Hezekiah's delegation and ***shouted in Hebrew,*** hoping to arouse fear among the people of Jerusalem.

18:31-32a The Assyrian chief of staff then detailed the generous ***terms*** Sennacherib was offering for their surrender. Why die? ***Choose life!***

18:32b-35 ***The LORD will rescue us:*** The chief of staff continued his psychological taunting by asserting that the Lord was just like ***the gods*** of the ***other nations*** and could not save Judah. • ***Arpad*** was a city-state located northwest of Aleppo. Like ***Hamath,*** it was a hub of Aramean activity and is mentioned on other occasions in the OT (see Isa 10:9; Jer 49:23).

18:37 ***tore their clothes in despair:*** This action could have been both a sign of sorrow over the situation in Jerusalem (see 6:30) and an indication of grief over the blasphemous insults of the Assyrian official (see 19:4-6).

19:1 ***Hezekiah*** showed his grief in the same way his representatives had (see Joel 1:13). He wisely went to the ***Temple,*** where he laid bare his soul before God in heartfelt worship and supplication (see Ps 5:7; 48:9-10; 63:1-3).

19:2-3 Leaders often consulted prophets like ***Isaiah*** in emergencies (3:11-12) or before going into battle (1 Kgs 22:8-10); Isaiah was active throughout Hezekiah's reign (20:1, 14). • The term ***a day of trouble*** describes the heart-wrenching distress the king was experiencing because of the blasphemous ***insults and disgrace*** that God and his people were being forced to endure. Hezekiah realized that he and the people were powerless without God's intervention.

19:4 Hezekiah was not denying his own relationship to ***the LORD*** by referring to him as ***your God;*** rather, he was acknowledging God's special call upon Isaiah. • ***the Assyrian chief of staff:*** Or ***the rabshakeh;*** also in 19:8.

19:7 ***I myself will move against him:*** Literally ***I will put a spirit in him.***

19:8 Sennacherib had dispatched his officers and forces to Jerusalem while he was attacking ***Lachish*** (18:14, 17). He had now moved eight miles to the northeast, to ***Libnah.***

19:9 ***King Tirhakah of Ethiopia*** (Hebrew ***of Cush***) would later become pharaoh over Egypt. At this time he was a commander in his brother Shebitku's army.

19:10
2 Kgs 18:5, 30
19:12
2 Kgs 17:6; 18:33
Isa 37:12
19:13
2 Kgs 18:34
19:14-19
//Isa 37:14-20
19:16
1 Kgs 8:29-30
2 Chr 6:40
19:18
Isa 44:9-20
Acts 17:29
19:19
1 Kgs 8:42-43
19:20-37
//Isa 37:21-38
19:21
Lam 2:13
19:22
Exod 5:2
Isa 5:24; 30:10-15

10 "This message is for King Hezekiah of Judah. Don't let your God, in whom you trust, deceive you with promises that Jerusalem will not be captured by the king of Assyria. 11 You know perfectly well what the kings of Assyria have done wherever they have gone. They have completely destroyed everyone who stood in their way! Why should you be any different? 12 Have the gods of other nations rescued them—such nations as Gozan, Haran, Rezeph, and the people of Eden who were in Tel-assar? My predecessors destroyed them all! 13 What happened to the king of Hamath and the king of Arpad? What happened to the kings of Sepharvaim, Hena, and Ivvah?"

14 After Hezekiah received the letter from the messengers and read it, he went up to the LORD's Temple and spread it out before the LORD. 15 And Hezekiah prayed this prayer before the LORD: "O LORD, God of Israel, you are enthroned between the mighty cherubim! You alone are God of all the kingdoms of the earth. You alone created the heavens and the earth. 16 Bend down, O LORD, and listen! Open your eyes, O LORD, and see! Listen to Sennacherib's words of defiance against the living God.

17 "It is true, LORD, that the kings of Assyria have destroyed all these nations. 18 And they have thrown the gods of these nations into the fire and burned them. But of course the Assyrians could destroy them! They were not gods at all—only idols of wood and stone shaped by human hands. 19 Now, O LORD our God, rescue us from his power; then all the kingdoms of the earth will know that you alone, O LORD, are God."

Isaiah Predicts Judah's Deliverance
2 Kgs 19:20-34 // Isa 37:21-35

20 Then Isaiah son of Amoz sent this message to Hezekiah: "This is what the LORD, the God of Israel, says: I have heard your prayer about King Sennacherib of Assyria. 21 And the LORD has spoken this word against him:

"The virgin daughter of Zion
    despises you and laughs at you.
The daughter of Jerusalem
    shakes her head in derision as you flee.

22 "Whom have you been defying and
    ridiculing?
Against whom did you raise your voice?
At whom did you look with such haughty
    eyes?
It was the Holy One of Israel!
23 By your messengers you have defied the
    Lord.
You have said, 'With my many chariots
I have conquered the highest mountains—
    yes, the remotest peaks of Lebanon.
I have cut down its tallest cedars
    and its finest cypress trees.
I have reached its farthest corners
    and explored its deepest forests.

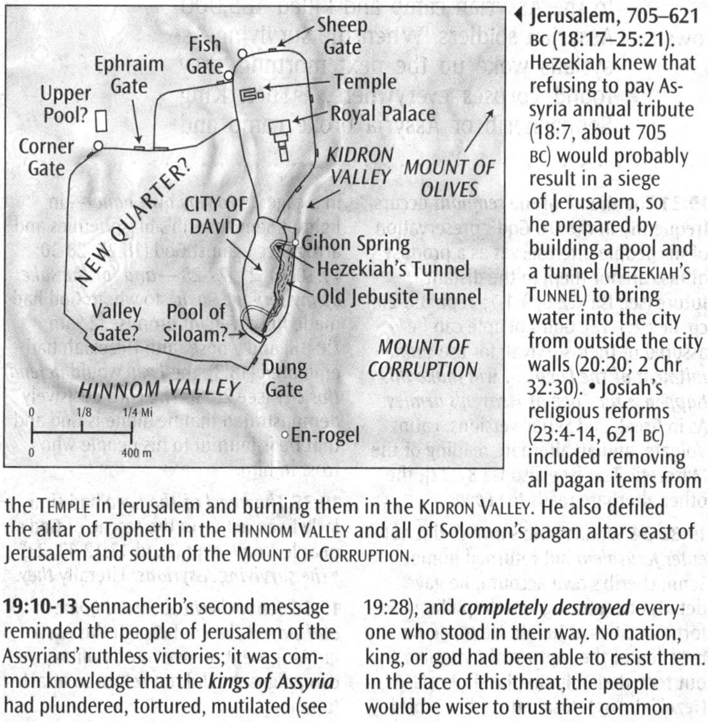

◀ **Jerusalem, 705–621 BC (18:17–25:21).** Hezekiah knew that refusing to pay Assyria annual tribute (18:7, about 705 BC) would probably result in a siege of Jerusalem, so he prepared by building a pool and a tunnel (HEZEKIAH'S TUNNEL) to bring water into the city from outside the city walls (20:20; 2 Chr 32:30). • Josiah's religious reforms (23:4-14, 621 BC) included removing all pagan items from the TEMPLE in Jerusalem and burning them in the KIDRON VALLEY. He also defiled the altar of Topheth in the HINNOM VALLEY and all of Solomon's pagan altars east of Jerusalem and south of the MOUNT OF CORRUPTION.

19:10-13 Sennacherib's second message reminded the people of Jerusalem of the Assyrians' ruthless victories; it was common knowledge that the *kings of Assyria* had plundered, tortured, mutilated (see 19:28), and *completely destroyed* everyone who stood in their way. No nation, king, or god had been able to resist them. In the face of this threat, the people would be wiser to trust their common sense and surrender rather than trust Hezekiah and his deceptive piety.

19:14-19 ***Hezekiah received*** Sennacherib's blasphemous ***letter*** and immediately took it ***to the LORD's Temple.*** His ***prayer*** to God was a lament of praise (19:15) and petition (19:16-19).

19:16-19 Sennacherib's successes were irrelevant because—unlike ***the gods of these nations,*** who were ***not gods at all***—Yahweh was the ***living God.***

19:21-28 The phrase ***virgin daughter*** is often used regarding civic identity (Isa 23:12; 37:22; 47:1; Jer 18:13). Here, the metaphor implies that as a young maiden is rescued from her attacker, so God will rescue Jerusalem. The Lord's answer was delivered as a "taunt song," a common literary form in the ancient Near East that rejoiced over an enemy's humiliation (cp. Isa 14:3-20).

19:23-24 ***highest mountains . . . of Lebanon:*** In his annals, Sennacherib told of scaling high mountain passes and felling Lebanon's great ***trees.*** Sennacherib felt invincible, but he was a mere man, no match for the omniscient Lord of the universe (1 Chr 28:9).

24 I have dug wells in many foreign lands
and refreshed myself with their water.
With the sole of my foot
I stopped up all the rivers of Egypt!'

25 "But have you not heard?
I decided this long ago.
Long ago I planned it,
and now I am making it happen.
I planned for you to crush fortified cities
into heaps of rubble.
26 That is why their people have so little power
and are so frightened and confused.
They are as weak as grass,
as easily trampled as tender green shoots.
They are like grass sprouting on a housetop,
scorched before it can grow lush and tall.

27 "But I know you well—
where you stay
and when you come and go.
I know the way you have raged against me.
28 And because of your raging against me
and your arrogance, which I have heard for myself,
I will put my hook in your nose
and my bit in your mouth.
I will make you return
by the same road on which you came."

29 Then Isaiah said to Hezekiah, "Here is the proof that what I say is true:

"This year you will eat only what grows up by itself,
and next year you will eat what springs up from that.
But in the third year you will plant crops
and harvest them;
you will tend vineyards and eat their fruit.
30 And you who are left in Judah,
who have escaped the ravages of the siege,
will put roots down in your own soil
and will grow up and flourish.
31 For a remnant of my people will spread out from Jerusalem,
a group of survivors from Mount Zion.
The passionate commitment of the LORD of Heaven's Armies
will make this happen!

32 "And this is what the LORD says about the king of Assyria:

"His armies will not enter Jerusalem.
They will not even shoot an arrow at it.
They will not march outside its gates
with their shields
nor build banks of earth against its walls.
33 The king will return to his own country
by the same road on which he came.
He will not enter this city,
says the LORD.
34 For my own honor and for the sake of my servant David,
I will defend this city and protect it."

The LORD Delivers Jerusalem

2 Kgs 19:35-37 // Isa 37:36-38 // 2 Chr 32:21

35 That night the [b]angel of the LORD went out to the Assyrian camp and killed 185,000 Assyrian soldiers. When the surviving Assyrians woke up the next morning, they found corpses everywhere. 36 Then King Sennacherib of Assyria broke camp and

19:25 Isa 10:5-7; 45:5-7
19:26 Ps 129:6-7
19:27 Ps 139:1-4
19:28 2 Kgs 19:33; Ezek 29:4
19:29 Exod 3:12; 2 Kgs 20:8-9
19:30 2 Chr 32:22-23
19:31 Isa 9:7
19:33 2 Kgs 19:28
19:34 1 Kgs 11:12-13; 2 Kgs 20:6
19:35 [b]*mal'ak* (4397) ‣ 2 Chr 32:21
19:36 Jon 1:2

19:25-26 ***I am making it happen:*** All of Sennacherib's great accomplishments were what God had planned for him.

19:27-28 ***I know you well:*** See Ps 44:21; 94:11. • ***hook . . . bit:*** The Assyrian annals mention similar mistreatment of prisoners; the Lord would do to Sennacherib what he and his predecessors had done to those they subjugated.

19:29-30 ***Here is the proof:*** The Lord's message of encouragement included a sign that Jerusalem would be rescued from the siege. The sign was God's provision of food. Because the land had suffered devastation by the Assyrians, the people would need to depend on random crop growth for their survival. The food supply would also remain scarce as the *next year* came. But by *the third year*, there would be a return to regular planting and harvesting.

19:31 The theme of the ***remnant*** occurs frequently in the OT. God's preservation of his people often serves as a promise of his care for them in the distant future (see Isa 4:2-6; 9:1-7; Zeph 3:8-20; cp. Rev 7:1-12). God's people can be assured of their survival, for the ***commitment of the LORD . . . will make this happen.*** • ***the LORD of Heaven's armies:*** As in Greek and Syriac versions, Latin Vulgate, and an alternate reading of the Masoretic Text [see also Isa 37:32]; the other alternate reads *the LORD.*

19:32-34 Sennacherib's ***armies*** did not ***enter Jerusalem*** but returned home. In Sennacherib's own account, he gave details of capturing and despoiling forty-six cities of Judah. He made no mention of the capture of *Jerusalem* but recorded only that he shut up Hezekiah "in Jerusalem . . . like a bird in a cage." • ***For my own honor***—in light of Sennacherib's blasphemies and arrogance against God (18:25, 28-30; 19:10-13, 21, 27-28)—***and for the sake of my servant David***, to whom God had made his covenant promise (2 Sam 7:8-16) and whose faith Hezekiah had emulated (18:3), the ***LORD*** would ***defend this city*** (see 20:6). The Lord decisively demonstrated that he alone is God and that he is faithful to his people who trust in him.

19:35 ***The angel of the LORD*** had similarly been active in the rescue of God's people from Egypt (Exod 12:12-13, 23). • ***the surviving Assyrians:*** Literally *they.*

19:36 ***Sennacherib . . . went home . . . and stayed there:*** Although this Assyrian king went on five more military campaigns, he did not ***return*** to attack Judah.

19:37
Gen 8:4
Ezra 4:2

20:1-11
//2 Chr 32:24-26
//Isa 38:1-8

20:2
[c]*palal* (6419)
‣2 Chr 7:14

20:3
2 Kgs 18:3-6
[d]*zakar* (2142)
‣Ps 22:27

20:5
2 Kgs 19:20
Ps 39:12

20:6
2 Kgs 19:34

returned to his own land. He went home to
his capital of Nineveh and stayed there.
37 One day while he was worshiping in the
temple of his god Nisroch, his sons Adrammelech and Sharezer killed him with their
swords. They then escaped to the land of Ararat, and another son, Esarhaddon, became
the next king of Assyria.

Hezekiah's Sickness and Recovery

2 Kgs 20:1-11 // Isa 38:1-8, 21-22 // 2 Chr 32:24

20 About that time Hezekiah became
deathly ill, and the prophet Isaiah
son of Amoz went to visit him. He gave the
king this message: "This is what the LORD
says: Set your affairs in order, for you are
going to die. You will not recover from this
illness."
2 When Hezekiah heard this, he turned
his face to the wall and [c]prayed to the
LORD, 3 "[d]Remember, O LORD, how I have always been faithful to you and have served
you single-mindedly, always doing what
pleases you." Then he broke down and wept
bitterly.
4 But before Isaiah had left the middle
courtyard, this message came to him from
the LORD: 5 "Go back to Hezekiah, the leader
of my people. Tell him, 'This is what the
LORD, the God of your ancestor David, says: I
have heard your prayer and seen your tears.
I will heal you, and three days from now you
will get out of bed and go to the Temple of
the LORD. 6 I will add fifteen years to your
life, and I will rescue you and this city from
the king of Assyria. I will defend this city

The Sovereignty of God (20:4-6)

2 Kgs 13:4-5; 17:1-6, 18-20; 18:5-7; 19:5-7
Exod 8:22; 9:29
Deut 4:39; 32:8, 39
Josh 2:11
1 Sam 2:6-8
Ps 24:1-2; 84:11; 135:5-12
Isa 40:15-17; 45:7; 46:10
Jer 27:5-7
John 19:11
Rom 9:8-24
1 Cor 1:8-9
Col 1:15-20
Jude 1:24-25

Accounts of God's sovereign power and control permeate the book of Kings. He installed and deposed the kings of Israel and Judah according to his purposes and according to the degree of their obedience.

God displayed his sovereign disposition over the affairs of nations. He permitted successful attacks against his people as punishment for their sins (8:18-22). God was in control when the Assyrians attacked Samaria and brought down the northern kingdom (17:1-6, 18, 20). Hezekiah's successes in Judah are due to the Lord's blessings (18:5-7). God's sovereign hand can be seen in all of the complex international events that happened, just as the Lord had promised, during the reigns of the final kings of Judah (23:26-27).

God also demonstrated his power in his answers to the prayers and petitions of his people. When Elisha prayed, God responded to his faithful prophet's requests. Through Elisha he allowed the woman from Shunem to have a son and later brought him back to life (4:17, 32-35). The Lord graciously answered the prayers of Jehoahaz and provided a deliverer for beleaguered Israel (13:4-5). He honored Hezekiah's prayer for Jerusalem (19:1-7) and for his own life (20:1-6).

God's sovereign hand is in everything. God is in control of the lives of all people (Ps 135:5-12), the universe, and the course of earth's history (Isa 40:15-17; Acts 17:24; Col 1:15-20), directing it to his appointed ends (Isa 46:10; Dan 7:27-28; Matt 24:14-31; Rev 1:7-8). God's people should pray like God's Son: "I want your will to be done, not mine" (Matt 26:39). God's people are challenged to live in harmony with God's will (Rom 12:1-2) and in the strength that he provides (1 Cor 1:8-9). When we live for God's glory (Isa 42:8; Hab 2:14; Jude 1:24-25), whatever happens is also for our good (Ps 84:11; Eph 3:16-19; Col. 1:27; 2 Thes 1:11-12).

19:37 *his sons:* As in Greek version and an alternate reading of the Masoretic Text (see also Isa 37:38); the other alternate reading lacks *his sons.* • ***killed him:*** Although Sennacherib's assassination took place twenty years later in 681 BC, the narrator includes it here to conclude his discussion of the Assyrian king and to point out the irony in his death. He had boasted that no gods were able to rescue the peoples he attacked, yet his god failed to defend him against assassins from his own family! • At Sennacherib's death, his ***son Esarhaddon*** succeeded him and reigned until 669 BC.

20:1-19 ***About that time:*** This general time reference indicates that the order of events is thematic rather than chronological. The episode concerning Merodach-baladan (20:12-19), whom Sennacherib had driven from Babylon before 701 BC, happened earlier than the events of chs 18–19 but after Hezekiah's illness (20:12).

20:1 Since ***Isaiah*** was already active in Hezekiah's reign before Sennacherib moved to take Jerusalem, he was readily available to the king during that emergency (19:2). • ***Set your affairs in order:*** Hezekiah's ***illness*** was terminal.

20:2-3 Unlike Ahab, who went to bed in a royal pout (1 Kgs 21:4), ***Hezekiah . . . turned his face to the wall and prayed.***

20:4 ***the middle courtyard:*** As in Greek version and an alternate reading in the Masoretic Text; the other alternate reads *the middle of the city.*

20:5 Hezekiah's commitment to the Lord compared favorably with that of his ***ancestor David*** (18:3). Just as God had heard David's prayers (Ps 6:8-9; 28:6-7; 31:22; 40:1-2), he would answer Hezekiah's plea.

20:6 When God added more ***years*** to Hezekiah's ***life,*** he also promised to ***defend*** Jerusalem. When Hezekiah reacted to Sennacherib's later invasion (19:14-19) by seeking counsel from Isaiah (19:2), he was following an established precedent.

for my own honor and for the sake of my
servant David.'"
[7]Then Isaiah said, "Make an ointment
from figs." So Hezekiah's servants spread
the ointment over the boil, and Hezekiah
recovered!
[8]Meanwhile, Hezekiah had said to Isaiah,
"What sign will the LORD give to prove that
he will heal me and that I will go to the Temple of the LORD three days from now?"
[9]Isaiah replied, "This is the sign from
the LORD to prove that he will do as he
promised. Would you like the shadow on
the sundial to go forward ten steps or backward ten steps?"
[10]"The shadow always moves forward,"
Hezekiah replied, "so that would be easy.
Make it go ten steps backward instead."
[11]So Isaiah the prophet asked the LORD to
do this, and he caused the shadow to move
ten steps backward on the sundial of Ahaz!

Envoys from Babylon
2 Kgs 20:12-19 // Isa 39:1-8

[12]Soon after this, Merodach-baladan son
of Baladan, king of Babylon, sent Hezekiah
his best wishes and a gift, for he had heard
that Hezekiah had been very sick. [13]Heze-
kiah received the Babylonian envoys and
showed them everything in his treasure-
houses—the silver, the gold, the spices, and
the aromatic oils. He also took them to see
his armory and showed them everything
in his royal treasuries! There was nothing
in his palace or kingdom that Hezekiah
did not show them.
[14]Then Isaiah the prophet went to King
Hezekiah and asked him, "What did those
men want? Where were they from?"
Hezekiah replied, "They came from the
distant land of Babylon."
[15]"What did they see in your palace?" Isaiah asked.
"They saw everything," Hezekiah replied.
"I showed them everything I own—all my
royal treasuries."
[16]Then Isaiah said to Hezekiah, "Listen to
this message from the LORD: [17]The time is
coming when everything in your palace—all
the treasures stored up by your ancestors
until now—will be carried off to Babylon.
Nothing will be left, says the LORD. [18]Some
of your very own sons will be taken away
into exile. They will become eunuchs who
will serve in the palace of Babylon's king."
[19]Then Hezekiah said to Isaiah, "This
message you have given me from the LORD
is good." For the king was thinking, "At least
there will be peace and security during my
lifetime."

Summary of Hezekiah's Reign
2 Kgs 20:20-21 // 2 Chr 32:32-33

[20]The rest of the events in Hezekiah's reign,
including the extent of his power and how
he built a pool and dug a tunnel to bring water into the city, are recorded in *The Book
of the History of the Kings of Judah*. [21]Hez-
ekiah died, and his son Manasseh became
the next king.

Manasseh's Reign in Judah (21:1-18)
2 Kgs 21:1-9 // 2 Chr 33:1-9
2 Kgs 21:17-18 // 2 Chr 33:18-20

21 Manasseh was twelve years old when
he became king, and he reigned
in Jerusalem fifty-five years. His mother
was Hephzibah. [2]He did what was evil in

20:9 Isa 38:7-8
20:11 Josh 10:12-14
20:12-19 //Isa 39:1-8
20:13 2 Chr 32:27
20:17 2 Kgs 24:13; 25:13-15; Jer 52:17-23
20:18 2 Kgs 24:12, 15; 2 Chr 33:11
20:20-21 //2 Chr 32:32-33
20:21 2 Chr 32:33
21:1-10 //2 Chr 33:1-10
21:2 2 Kgs 16:3

• ***for my own honor and for . . . David:*** God reminded Hezekiah of this promise during Sennacherib's invasion (19:34).

20:8 Hezekiah's request for a *sign* as proof of his healing is understandable. He had quickly moved from having an incurable illness to being promised fifteen more years of life. God sometimes provided signs as visible symbols of his intentions (see also 19:29; Gen 9:12-17; Exod 4:1-9; 12:12-13; 31:12-13, 17; 1 Kgs 13:1-3).

20:9 ***Would you like the shadow on the sundial to go forward ten steps or backward ten steps?*** Or *The shadow on the sundial has gone forward ten steps; do you want it to go backward ten steps?*

20:10 ***ten steps backward:*** Such a retreat of the *shadow* was contrary to nature, and the miracle confirmed God's message to Hezekiah.

20:11 ***the sundial:*** Literally *the steps.*

20:12-13 ***Merodach-baladan*** (Hebrew *Berodach-baladan;* see Isa 39:1), a perennial enemy of Assyria, reigned in Babylon from 721 to 710 BC, when Sargon forced him to flee. He ruled again briefly in 703 BC. This visit was probably during his exile; he probably sent ***envoys*** bearing his ***best wishes and a gift*** because he needed an ally against Assyria. • ***There was nothing . . . that Hezekiah did not show them:*** Hezekiah showed ***the Babylonian envoys*** his vast ***treasuries,*** which had not yet been sent to Sennacherib (18:13-16). However, his attempt to impress his visitors was misguided (20:16-18).

20:17 ***everything . . . will be carried off to Babylon:*** The Lord's message through Isaiah predicted the taking of the ***palace . . . treasures*** in Jerusalem to ***Babylon,*** an event that took place in 597–586 BC (24:10-17; 25:1-21).

20:18 ***Some of your very own sons will be taken:*** Hezekiah's son Manasseh was taken as a prisoner to Babylon (2 Chr 33:11-13). This prophecy found ultimate fulfillment in Hezekiah's descendants during the Babylonian deportations of 605 BC (see 24:1 and note; Dan 1:1-7), 597 BC (24:10-12; 2 Chr 36:10), and 586 BC (25:5-7; 2 Chr 36:20; Jer 39:1-7; 52:4-15).

20:20 For more on ***the extent of his power,*** see 18:7-8; 2 Chr 32:27-29.
• In the face of Sennacherib's threat, Hezekiah constructed a 1,777-foot ***tunnel*** (literally *watercourse*) that brought water from outside the city walls into Jerusalem (2 Chr 32:1-5, 30) to a ***pool*** called the Pool of Siloam. An inscription discovered in AD 1880 commemorates this engineering feat.

21:1-2 ***fifty-five years:*** Manasseh's long reign (697–642 BC) certainly cannot be attributed to his faithfulness to the Lord but to the Lord's continued

21:3
Lev 18:25
Deut 12:31; 17:3
1 Kgs 16:29-33
2 Kgs 18:4

21:4
2 Sam 7:13

21:6
Lev 18:21; 19:26, 31
Deut 18:10
2 Kgs 16:3; 17:17
[e]*yidde'oni* (3049)
‣2 Kgs 23:24

21:7
Deut 16:21
1 Kgs 9:3
2 Kgs 23:6

21:8
2 Sam 7:10
2 Kgs 18:11-12
2 Chr 15:2

21:11
Gen 15:16
1 Kgs 21:26
2 Kgs 24:3-4

21:12
Jer 19:3

21:13
Isa 34:11
Amos 7:7-8

21:16
2 Kgs 24:3-4
[f]*dam* (1818)
‣Ps 94:21

21:17-18
//2 Chr 33:18-20

21:18
2 Kgs 21:26

the LORD's sight, following the detestable practices of the pagan nations that the LORD had driven from the land ahead of the Israelites. 3He rebuilt the pagan shrines his father, Hezekiah, had destroyed. He constructed altars for Baal and set up an Asherah pole, just as King Ahab of Israel had done. He also bowed before all the powers of the heavens and worshiped them.

4He built pagan altars in the Temple of the LORD, the place where the LORD had said, "My name will remain in Jerusalem forever." 5He built these altars for all the powers of the heavens in both courtyards of the LORD's Temple. 6Manasseh also sacrificed his own son in the fire. He practiced sorcery and divination, and he consulted with mediums and [e]psychics. He did much that was evil in the LORD's sight, arousing his anger.

7Manasseh even made a carved image of Asherah and set it up in the Temple, the very place where the LORD had told David and his son Solomon: "My name will be honored forever in this Temple and in Jerusalem—the city I have chosen from among all the tribes of Israel. 8If the Israelites will be careful to obey my commands—all the laws my servant Moses gave them—I will not send them into exile from this land that I gave their ancestors." 9But the people refused to listen, and Manasseh led them to do even more evil than the pagan nations that the LORD had destroyed when the people of Israel entered the land.

10Then the LORD said through his servants the prophets: 11"King Manasseh of Judah has done many detestable things. He is even more wicked than the Amorites, who lived in this land before Israel. He has caused the people of Judah to sin with his idols. 12So this is what the LORD, the God of Israel, says: I will bring such disaster on Jerusalem and Judah that the ears of those who hear about it will tingle with horror. 13I will judge Jerusalem by the same standard I used for Samaria and the same measure I used for the family of Ahab. I will wipe away the people of Jerusalem as one wipes a dish and turns it upside down. 14Then I will reject even the remnant of my own people who are left, and I will hand them over as plunder for their enemies. 15For they have done great evil in my sight and have angered me ever since their ancestors came out of Egypt."

16Manasseh also murdered many innocent people until Jerusalem was filled from one end to the other with innocent [f]blood. This was in addition to the sin that he caused the people of Judah to commit, leading them to do evil in the LORD's sight.

17The rest of the events in Manasseh's reign and everything he did, including the sins he committed, are recorded in *The Book of the History of the Kings of Judah.* 18When Manasseh died, he was buried in the palace garden, the garden of Uzza. Then his son Amon became the next king.

---

honoring of his covenant promises (see also 8:19; 19:34; 20:6; 2 Sam 7:11-16). External conditions were largely stable. Though the Assyrian kings Esarhaddon (680–669 BC) and Ashurbanipal (668–626 BC) conducted a number of military campaigns, none was directed against Judah until later in Manasseh's reign, probably around 650–648 BC (see 2 Chr 33:10-13 and notes). Ashurbanipal's attention was on building projects, religious pursuits, and the arts, including a great library. • ***He did what was evil:*** Manasseh was the most wicked of Judah's kings; discussion of his reign focuses on his evil religious practices.

21:3-5 Manasseh's spiritual infidelity included rebuilding local ***pagan shrines*** that his father had destroyed (18:3). He also promoted wicked religious practices associated with the worship of ***Baal and set up an Asherah pole*** (see 18:3; 1 Kgs 16:32) and reintroduced astral worship. God had judged the northern kingdom for these sins (17:16).

21:6 Manasseh's wickedness included participation in the abominable Molech rites and all manner of forbidden cult and occult practices (16:3; see Lev 18:21). • ***also sacrificed his own son in the fire:*** Or *also made his son pass through the fire.* • ***the LORD's . . . anger:*** God responded to Manasseh's detestable religious practices with his righteous judgment, just as he had with the northern kingdom (17:18-20).

21:11 The ***Amorites*** were the pre-Israelite inhabitants of the ***land,*** known for their wickedness. • Manasseh practiced the idolatry of the ***Amorites*** as Ahab had done (1 Kgs 21:26). • ***idols:*** The Hebrew (literally *round things*) probably alludes to dung; also in v 21.

21:12 Based on what had happened to the northern kingdom (17:7-23) and to Ahab's family (9:24-26, 30-37; 10:1-8; 1 Kgs 22:37-38), Manasseh should fully expect God to execute justice against him and the people of ***Judah.***

21:13 ***the same standard . . . the same measure:*** Literally *the same plumb line . . . the same plumb bob.*

21:14-15 ***the remnant:*** Those not killed in God's impending judgment would be at the mercy of their captors. This prophecy was fulfilled when thousands of Judeans were taken into captivity in the Babylonian invasion during the fall of Jerusalem in 586 BC (25:8-21; 2 Chr 36:20; Jer 39:9; 52:15).

21:16 ***innocent blood:*** Beyond his loathsome spiritual ***sin,*** Manasseh was guilty of murder. Jewish tradition holds that Isaiah was one of many prophets that Manasseh put to death.

21:17 ***everything he did:*** The Chronicler records that Manasseh was captured by an Assyrian king, probably when King Ashurbanipal resided in Babylon (about 650–648 BC). This experience humbled Manasseh and brought repentance. After his release, he attempted spiritual reforms, but they were too late in his reign to be effective (2 Chr 33:11-17).

21:18 ***The garden of Uzza*** is otherwise unknown (but see also 21:26). Unlike his father, Hezekiah, who had been buried with honor, Manasseh was not buried in the royal tombs (2 Chr 32:33).

Amon's Reign in Judah (21:19-26)
2 Kgs 21:19-24 // 2 Chr 33:21-25
19Amon was twenty-two years old when he
became king, and he reigned in Jerusalem
two years. His mother was Meshullemeth,
the daughter of Haruz from Jotbah. 20He did
what was evil in the LORD's sight, just as his father, Manasseh, had done. 21He followed the
example of his father, worshiping the same
idols his father had worshiped. 22He abandoned the LORD, the God of his ancestors,
and he refused to follow the LORD's ways.
23Then Amon's own officials conspired
against him and assassinated him in his
palace. 24But the people of the land killed
all those who had conspired against King
Amon, and they made his son Josiah the
next king.
25The rest of the events in Amon's reign
and what he did are recorded in *The Book
of the History of the Kings of Judah.* 26He
was buried in his tomb in the garden of
Uzza. Then his son Josiah became the next
king.

Josiah's Reign in Judah (22:1–23:30)
Josiah Repairs the Temple
2 Kgs 22:1-7 // 2 Chr 34:1-2, 8-11
22 Josiah was eight years old when
he became king, and he reigned
in Jerusalem thirty-one years. His mother
was Jedidah, the daughter of Adaiah from
Bozkath. 2He did what was pleasing in the
LORD's sight and followed the example of
his ancestor David. He did not turn away
from doing what was right.

21:22 2 Kgs 22:17
21:23 2 Kgs 12:20; 14:19
21:26 2 Kgs 21:18
22:1-20 //2 Chr 34:1-2, 8-28
22:1 Josh 15:39

JOSIAH (21:24–23:30)

1 Kgs 13:2
2 Chr 33:25–35:27
Jer 1:1-4; 22:13-23; 25:3; 36:2
Zeph 1:1

Josiah, the sixteenth king of Judah (640–609 BC), was a godly man, unlike his grandfather Manasseh and his father Amon. Josiah "turned to the LORD with all his heart and soul and strength, obeying all the laws of Moses" (23:25).

The kingdom of Judah was grossly idolatrous and wicked during Manasseh's reign (697–642 BC). Despite Manasseh's own repentance toward the end of his reign, conditions continued to worsen under his son Amon (642–640 BC), who was so bad that his own officials assassinated him, and the eight-year-old Josiah was placed on the throne (21:23-24; 22:1; 2 Chr 33:25–34:1).

When Josiah was sixteen, he began "to seek the God of his ancestor David" (2 Chr 34:3). From this point on, he was dedicated to purifying the worship of the people of God. At twenty, Josiah began eradicating pagan places of worship, especially the despised cult center at Bethel. Josiah fulfilled prophecy (1 Kgs 13:1-3) by destroying its altar and burning the bones of pagan priests to desecrate the site (23:15-18).

When Josiah was twenty-six, he organized repairs to the Temple (22:3). In the process, the priest Hilkiah found the Book of the Law and read it to Josiah, who was devastated by its pronouncements against apostasy (22:8-20) and sought more fully to obey God's instructions and to lead the people in worshiping the Lord. He celebrated Passover as the law demanded, destroyed many artifacts used in Baal and sun worship, and eliminated pagan shrines in Judah (23:4-14). In all this, Josiah was apparently supported by the prophets Zephaniah and Jeremiah, who spoke for God during his time.

Josiah was not sensitive to God's voice on one significant occasion, and it cost him his life (23:29-30; 2 Chr 35:20-25). In 609 BC, Pharaoh Neco marched toward Carchemish to reinforce the Assyrian army against Babylon. Josiah delayed Neco at Megiddo, perhaps wanting to support the Babylonians. Neco insisted that the Lord wanted him to fight Babylon, but Josiah attacked him and was killed in battle. Josiah was greatly mourned by Jeremiah and the people of Judah (2 Chr 35:25).

Though Josiah was faithful, the people were not, and once he died, his sons and successors began to turn away from the Lord. In spite of Jeremiah's increased efforts, the people did not repent. The turbulent years that followed Josiah's death ended with the destruction of Jerusalem and the exile of its citizens to Babylon (605–586 BC).

21:19-22 *Amon's* brief reign (642–640 BC) simply perpetuated his father's wickedness. Manasseh's repentance and reforms came too late to have any effect on Amon or on the people of Judah. • ***He abandoned the LORD:*** Amon became a total apostate (see also 2 Chr 33:23).

21:26 Like his father, Manasseh (21:17), Amon was denied burial in the royal tombs and was interred in ***the garden of Uzza.***

22:1-2 *Josiah* ascended the throne of Judah in 640 BC. Like Joash (11:21), he was still a boy when he became king. He was faithful to the Lord, comparing favorably with David, like Asa (1 Kgs 15:11) and Hezekiah (18:3). • ***doing what was right:*** Josiah's conduct met the high standards of the law (Deut 17:11; 28:14).

22:3-4 By ***the eighteenth year of his reign*** (621 BC), Josiah had been devoted to the Lord for ten years (see 2 Chr 34:3-7). • ***Hilkiah the high priest*** was from

22:3
2 Chr 34:8
22:4
2 Kgs 12:4
2 Chr 34:9
22:5
2 Kgs 12:11-14
22:7
2 Kgs 12:15
22:8
Deut 31:24-26
2 Chr 34:14-16
22:11
Josh 7:6
22:12
2 Kgs 25:22
2 Chr 34:20
Jer 26:24
22:13
Deut 29:23-28
[g]*shama'* (8085)
‣Neh 9:16
22:14
2 Chr 34:22
22:16
Dan 9:11
22:17
[h]*'azab* (5800)
‣2 Chr 15:2

3In the eighteenth year of his reign, King
Josiah sent Shaphan son of Azaliah and
grandson of Meshullam, the court secretary, to the Temple of the LORD. He told him,
4"Go to Hilkiah the high priest and have
him count the money the gatekeepers have
collected from the people at the LORD's
Temple. 5Entrust this money to the men
assigned to supervise the Temple's restoration. Then they can use it to pay workers to
repair the Temple of the LORD. 6They will
need to hire carpenters, builders, and masons. Also have them buy the timber and
the finished stone needed to repair the
Temple. 7But don't require the construction supervisors to keep account of the
money they receive, for they are honest and
trustworthy men."

Hilkiah Discovers the Book of the Law
2 Kgs 22:8-20 // 2 Chr 34:14-28

8Hilkiah the high priest said to Shaphan the
court secretary, "I have found the Book of
the Law in the LORD's Temple!" Then Hilkiah
gave the scroll to Shaphan, and he read it.
9Shaphan went to the king and reported,
"Your officials have turned over the money
collected at the Temple of the LORD to the
workers and supervisors at the Temple."
10Shaphan also told the king, "Hilkiah the
priest has given me a scroll." So Shaphan
read it to the king.
11When the king heard what was written
in the Book of the Law, he tore his clothes
in despair. 12Then he gave these orders to
Hilkiah the priest, Ahikam son of Shaphan,
Acbor son of Micaiah, Shaphan the court
secretary, and Asaiah the king's personal
adviser: 13"Go to the Temple and speak to
the LORD for me and for the people and for
all Judah. Inquire about the words written
in this scroll that has been found. For the
LORD's great anger is burning against us because our ancestors have not [g]obeyed the
words in this scroll. We have not been doing everything it says we must do."
14So Hilkiah the priest, Ahikam, Acbor,
Shaphan, and Asaiah went to the New Quarter of Jerusalem to consult with the prophet
Huldah. She was the wife of Shallum son
of Tikvah, son of Harhas, the keeper of the
Temple wardrobe.
15She said to them, "The LORD, the God of
Israel, has spoken! Go back and tell the man
who sent you, 16'This is what the LORD says:
I am going to bring disaster on this city and
its people. All the words written in the scroll
that the king of Judah has read will come
true. 17For my people have [h]abandoned me

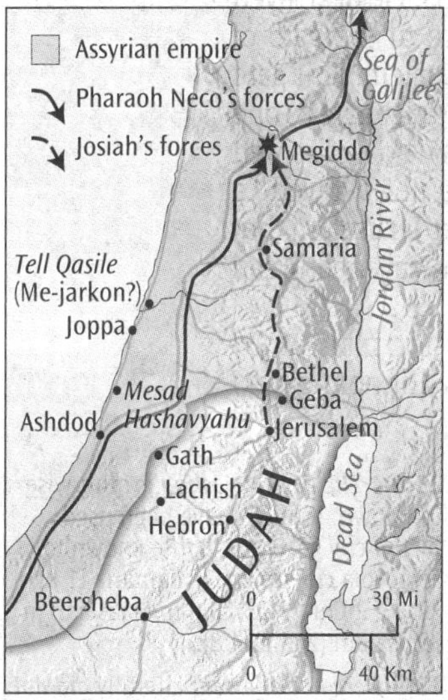

◂ **The Land of Israel during Josiah's Reign, 621–609 BC (23:4-30).** In addition to cleansing idolatry from JERUSALEM in 621 BC (23:4-7, 10-14), Josiah tore down all the pagan altars from GEBA to BEERSHEBA, tore down the altar of Jeroboam I at BETHEL, and removed idolatry from many towns of Samaria (23:8, 15-20). • The map shows Josiah's disastrous attempt, at MEGIDDO in 609 BC (23:29-30), to prevent Pharaoh Neco of Egypt from assisting his allies, the Assyrians, at Haran. Josiah had apparently expanded the area of his rule to the Mediterranean, because Judahite pottery and inscriptions from his time have been found at TELL QASILE and MESAD HASHAVYAHU. Josiah's successes might have emboldened him to confront Pharaoh Neco.

the line of Zadok (1 Chr 9:10-11). Some scholars suggest that this Hilkiah was Jeremiah's father (Jer 1:1). • Apparently the *money* was *collected* in a large chest convenient to the people as they came to the Temple (cp. 12:9).

22:5-7 Josiah's instructions to Shaphan were similar to those given by Joash for restoring the *Temple* during his reign (12:10-15).

22:8-10 The scroll known as ***the Book of the Law*** might have contained all or part of Deuteronomy or even the entire Pentateuch (cp. Deut 31:26). How it had become lost or where it was ***found*** in the ***Temple*** is unknown. ***Shaphan*** reported the momentous discovery immediately and ***read it to the king.***

22:11-13 Like Hezekiah before him (19:1), Josiah ***tore his clothes*** in genuine grief for his own spiritual condition and that of the people of Judah. • ***have not obeyed the words in this scroll:*** The portion that ***Shaphan*** read to Josiah apparently reminded him of God's claim upon his people, the need for faithfulness to the covenant, and the penalties for infidelity (see Deut 28). Recognizing that Judah had failed to obey the law, Josiah rightly feared ***the LORD's great anger.***

22:14 ***the New Quarter:*** Or *the Second Quarter,* a newer section of Jerusalem. Hebrew reads *the Mishneh.* • ***The prophet Huldah . . . was the wife of Shallum:*** Some have suggested that this Shallum was related to Jeremiah (Jer 32:7-12). Huldah's family relationships might have allowed her to serve as a sort of court prophet (see also 2 Chr 34:22-28).

22:15-17 ***The LORD . . . has spoken!*** Like Miriam (Exod 15:20) and Deborah (Judg 4:4), Huldah had the privilege of proclaiming God's will to the people. Huldah confirmed Josiah's fears that God would ***bring disaster*** on Jerusalem because of the people's unfaithfulness and many sins. • ***this city:*** Literally *this place;* also in 22:19, 20.

and offered sacrifices to pagan gods, and I am very angry with them for everything they have done. My anger will burn against this place, and it will not be quenched.'

18"But go to the king of Judah who sent you to seek the LORD and tell him: 'This is what the LORD, the God of Israel, says concerning the message you have just heard: 19You were sorry and humbled yourself before the LORD when you heard what I said against this city and its people—that this land would be cursed and become desolate. You tore your clothing in despair and wept before me in repentance. And I have indeed heard you, says the LORD. 20So I will not send the promised disaster until after you have died and been buried in peace. You will not see the disaster I am going to bring on this city.' "

So they took her message back to the king.

Josiah's Religious Reforms

2 Kgs 23:1-3 // 2 Chr 34:29-32

23 Then the king summoned all the elders of Judah and Jerusalem. 2And the king went up to the Temple of the LORD with all the people of Judah and Jerusalem, along with the priests and the prophets—all the people from the least to the greatest. There the king read to them the entire Book of the Covenant that had been found in the LORD's Temple. 3The king took his place of authority beside the pillar and renewed the [i]covenant in the LORD's presence. He pledged to obey the LORD by keeping all his commands, laws, and decrees with all his heart and soul. In this way, he confirmed all the terms of the [i]covenant that were written in the scroll, and all the people pledged themselves to the [i]covenant.

4Then the king instructed Hilkiah the high priest and the priests of the second rank and the Temple gatekeepers to remove from the LORD's Temple all the articles that were used to worship Baal, Asherah, and all the powers of the heavens. The king had all these things burned outside Jerusalem on the terraces of the Kidron Valley, and he carried the ashes away to Bethel. 5He did away with the idolatrous priests, who had been appointed by the previous kings of Judah, for they had offered sacrifices at the pagan shrines throughout Judah and even in the vicinity of Jerusalem. They had also offered sacrifices to Baal, and to the sun, the moon, the constellations, and to all the powers of the heavens. 6The king removed the Asherah pole from the LORD's Temple and took it outside Jerusalem to the Kidron Valley, where he burned it. Then he ground the ashes of the pole to dust and threw the dust over the graves of the people. 7He also tore down the living quarters of the male and female shrine prostitutes that were inside the Temple of the LORD, where the women wove coverings for the Asherah pole.

8Josiah brought to Jerusalem all the priests who were living in other towns of Judah. He also defiled the pagan shrines, where they had offered sacrifices—all the way from Geba to Beersheba. He destroyed the shrines at the entrance to the gate of Joshua, the governor of Jerusalem. This gate was located to the left of the city gate as one enters the city. 9The priests who had served at the pagan shrines were not allowed to serve at the LORD's altar in Jerusalem, but they were allowed to eat unleavened bread with the other priests.

10Then the king defiled the altar of Topheth in the valley of Ben-Hinnom, so no

22:19 Lev 26:31; Jer 26:6
23:1-3 //2 Chr 34:29-32
23:2 Deut 31:11
23:3 Deut 13:4; 2 Kgs 11:14, 17; [i]*berith* (1285) ›2 Chr 29:10
23:6 2 Chr 34:4
23:7 1 Kgs 14:24; 15:12; 22:46; Ezek 16:16
23:9 Ezek 44:9-14
23:10 Lev 18:21; 1 Kgs 11:7; Jer 7:31-32

22:18-20 God commended Josiah's sorrow and humility in response to the reading of God's word. Although God's judgment was certain, he would withhold it until after Josiah's death.

23:1-2 In the spirit of the instructions of Deuteronomy (Deut 31:10-13) and like Joshua before him (Josh 8:34-35), Josiah ***summoned . . . all the people*** to hear the reading of ***the entire Book of the Covenant.***

23:3 *The king . . . renewed the covenant:* Covenant renewal was observed at several critical points in the history of God's people (see 11:12, 17; Josh 24:1-27; 1 Kgs 8:1-53).

23:4 *remove . . . all the articles:* Josiah eliminated from the Temple detestable items associated with pagan worship. • ***terraces of the Kidron Valley:*** This area, near the Valley of Ben-Hinnom where the loathsome Molech rituals of child sacrifice had been carried out, became a place where ***ashes*** and dead bodies were taken (Jer 26:23). • Taking the ***ashes away to Bethel,*** where Jeroboam had erected one of his cult altars (1 Kgs 12:28-29), would defile the site forever.

23:5-7 Josiah stopped the ***idolatrous priests*** from officiating over pagan rituals. He also demolished the ***living quarters*** of the cult ***prostitutes.*** Manasseh and Amon apparently had allowed the prostitution carried over from Canaanite practices (see 1 Kgs 14:24; 15:12; 22:46) to be practiced within the ***Temple*** itself.

23:8-9 *The gate of Joshua* is otherwise unknown; it might have been used by the city ***governor,*** a title known to refer to a city official in Samaria (1 Kgs 22:26; 2 Chr 18:25) and to Maaseiah in Jerusalem (2 Chr 34:8).

23:9 *were not allowed:* Literally *did not come up.*

23:10 *Topheth* was a precinct in ***the valley of Ben-Hinnom,*** which lay southwest of the city of David and led into the Kidron Valley. The detestable rite of child sacrifice had occurred there. • ***to sacrifice a son or daughter in the fire:*** Or *to make a son or daughter pass through the fire.* • ***Molech*** has been identified with a number of deities (see 1 Kgs 11:5, 7, 33) and with the name of a sacrifice offered to Baal (Jer 7:31-32; 19:5-6; 32:35).

23:12 2 Kgs 21:3-5; 2 Chr 33:4-5; Jer 19:13; Zeph 1:5
23:13 1 Kgs 11:7; Jer 48:7
23:14 Deut 7:5, 25
23:15 1 Kgs 12:28-33
23:16 1 Kgs 13:2, 32
23:17 1 Kgs 13:1-2, 30-31
23:18 1 Kgs 13:11, 31

one could ever again use it to sacrifice a son or daughter in the fire as an offering to Molech. 11He removed from the entrance of the LORD's Temple the horse statues that the former kings of Judah had dedicated to the sun. They were near the quarters of Nathan-melech the eunuch, an officer of the court. The king also burned the chariots dedicated to the sun.

12Josiah tore down the altars that the kings of Judah had built on the palace roof above the upper room of Ahaz. The king destroyed the altars that Manasseh had built in the two courtyards of the LORD's Temple. He smashed them to bits and scattered the pieces in the Kidron Valley. 13The king also desecrated the pagan shrines east of Jerusalem, to the south of the Mount of Corruption, where King Solomon of Israel had built shrines for Ashtoreth, the detestable goddess of the Sidonians; and for Chemosh, the detestable god of the Moabites; and for Molech, the vile god of the Ammonites. 14He smashed the sacred pillars and cut down the Asherah poles. Then he desecrated these places by scattering human bones over them.

15The king also tore down the altar at Bethel—the pagan shrine that Jeroboam son of Nebat had made when he caused Israel to sin. He burned down the shrine and ground it to dust, and he burned the Asherah pole. 16Then Josiah turned around and noticed several tombs in the side of the hill. He ordered that the bones be brought out, and he burned them on the altar at Bethel to desecrate it. (This happened just as the LORD had promised through the man of God when Jeroboam stood beside the altar at the festival.)

Then Josiah turned and looked up at the tomb of the man of God who had predicted these things. 17"What is that monument over there?" Josiah asked.

And the people of the town told him, "It is the tomb of the man of God who came from Judah and predicted the very things that you have just done to the altar at Bethel!"

18Josiah replied, "Leave it alone. Don't disturb his bones." So they did not burn his

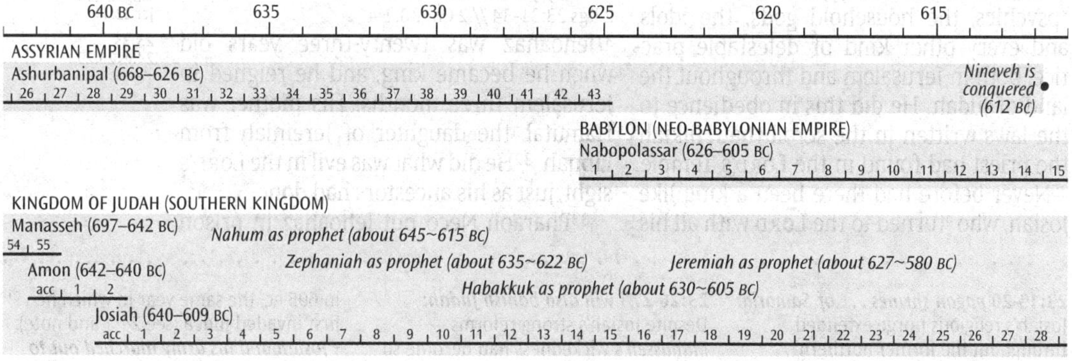

▲ **Kingdom of Judah, 643–611 BC (21:17–23:28).** After MANASSEH's death, AMON's nasty, brutish, and short reign was followed by the long, just, and good reign of JOSIAH. Many of Judah's prophets served during Josiah's reign, calling the people of Judah back to the Lord and warning them of coming judgment. • The reign of Assyrian king ASHURBANIPAL was followed by a quick decline into chaos under a succession of incompetent rulers. NABOPOLASSAR of Babylon took this opportunity to make Babylonia an independent kingdom. Babylon quickly grew into an empire under Nabopolassar's leadership, and in 612 BC the Babylonian army destroyed Assyria's capital Nineveh, ending the Assyrian empire. This series of events demonstrates how quickly empires can rise and fall.

23:11 The ***horse*** was used in ***sun*** worship in the ancient Near East. The Assyrian sun-god Shamash and other deities were depicted riding across the sky in horse-drawn chariots. Archaeological evidence suggests that a solar cult existed in Israel as early as the 800s BC. The cult's popularity likely increased during the reigns of Manasseh and Amon, when it was sponsored by the crown (21:3-5, 21-22). Despite Josiah's reforms, shortly after his death Ezekiel denounced the sun worshipers again for performing their rituals within the inner court of the Temple (Ezek 8:16). • ***the eunuch, an officer of the court:*** The meaning of the Hebrew is uncertain. The term translated *eunuch* can refer not only to those who were physically eunuchs but also to high officials.

23:12 ***upper room of Ahaz:*** Roof-top ***altars*** were used for astral worship (Jer 19:13; Zeph 1:5) and rituals associated with Baal (Jer 32:29). • ***He smashed them to bits:*** Or *He quickly removed them.*

23:13 ***Solomon*** had erected ***the pagan shrines*** because of his many foreign wives (1 Kgs 11:5, 7, 33). • ***Molech:*** Hebrew *Milcom,* a variant spelling of *Molech.*

23:15-17 ***Jeroboam*** had built ***the altar at Bethel*** to encourage Israelites to worship at centers closer to home rather than going to Jerusalem (1 Kgs 12:26-31). Josiah's desecration of the site followed the stipulations of the law (Deut 7:5; 12:3) and fulfilled the earlier prophecy of ***the man of God*** who had denounced ***the altar*** (1 Kgs 13:1-3).

23:16 This verse follows the Greek version; Hebrew lacks ***when Jeroboam stood beside the altar at the festival. Then Josiah turned and looked up at the tomb of the man of God.***

bones or those of the old prophet from Samaria.
[19]Then Josiah demolished all the buildings at the pagan shrines in the towns of
Samaria, just as he had done at Bethel. They
had been built by the various kings of Israel
and had made the LORD very angry. [20]He
executed the priests of the pagan shrines
on their own altars, and he burned human
bones on the altars to desecrate them. Finally, he returned to Jerusalem.

Josiah Celebrates Passover
2 Kgs 23:21-23 // 2 Chr 35:1, 18-19

[21]King Josiah then issued this order to all
the people: "You must celebrate the [j]Pass-
over to the LORD your God, as required in
this Book of the Covenant." [22]There had not
been a Passover celebration like that since
the time when the judges ruled in Israel,
nor throughout all the years of the kings
of Israel and Judah. [23]This Passover was
celebrated to the LORD in Jerusalem in the
eighteenth year of King Josiah's reign.

Josiah's Final Days
2 Kgs 23:28-30 // 2 Chr 35:20–36:1

[24]Josiah also got rid of the mediums and
[k]psychics, the household gods, the idols,
and every other kind of detestable practice, both in Jerusalem and throughout the
land of Judah. He did this in obedience to
the laws written in the scroll that Hilkiah
the priest had found in the LORD's Temple.
[25]Never before had there been a king like
Josiah, who [a]turned to the LORD with all his
heart and soul and strength, obeying all the
laws of Moses. And there has never been a
king like him since.
[26]Even so, the LORD was very [b]angry with
Judah because of all the wicked things Manasseh had done to provoke him. [27]For the
LORD said, "I will also banish Judah from
my presence just as I have banished Israel.
And I will reject my chosen city of Jerusalem and the Temple where my name was to
be honored."
[28]The rest of the events in Josiah's reign
and all his deeds are recorded in *The Book
of the History of the Kings of Judah.*
[29]While Josiah was king, Pharaoh Neco,
king of Egypt, went to the Euphrates River
to help the king of Assyria. King Josiah and
his army marched out to fight him, but King
Neco killed him when they met at Megiddo.
[30]Josiah's officers took his body back in a
chariot from Megiddo to Jerusalem and buried him in his own tomb. Then the people of
the land anointed Josiah's son Jehoahaz and
made him the next king.

Exile of the Kings of Judah (23:31–24:17)
Exile of Jehoahaz
2 Kgs 23:31-34 // 2 Chr 36:2-4

[31]Jehoahaz was twenty-three years old
when he became king, and he reigned in
Jerusalem three months. His mother was
Hamutal, the daughter of Jeremiah from
Libnah. [32]He did what was evil in the LORD's
sight, just as his ancestors had done.
[33]Pharaoh Neco put Jehoahaz in prison

23:19
2 Chr 34:6-7
23:20
2 Kgs 11:18
23:21
Num 9:2-4
Deut 16:2-8
[j]*pesakh* (6453)
›2 Chr 30:18
23:22
2 Chr 35:18-19
23:24
Lev 19:31
Deut 18:10-12
2 Kgs 21:6; 22:8
[k]*yidde'oni* (3049)
›2 Chr 33:6
23:25
2 Kgs 18:5
[a]*shub* (7725)
›2 Chr 15:4
23:26
2 Kgs 21:11-13; 22:15-16
[b]*'ap* (0639)
›Ps 6:1
23:27
2 Kgs 21:13-14
23:28-30
2 Chr 35:20–36:1
23:29
2 Chr 35:20-24
23:30
2 Chr 36:1-4
23:31-34
//2 Chr 36:2-4
23:31
2 Kgs 24:18
Jer 22:11
23:33
2 Kgs 23:29

23:19-20 ***pagan shrines . . . of Samaria:*** Josiah's religious purge extended throughout the former northern kingdom (see also 2 Chr 34:6-7). Josiah's freedom to carry out such reforms testifies to his strength and Assyria's growing weakness (see note on 23:29).

23:19 ***had made the LORD very angry:*** As in Greek and Syriac versions and Latin Vulgate; Hebrew lacks *the LORD* and thus reads *had caused great anger.*

23:21-23 Hezekiah had observed the ***Passover*** with modifications (2 Chr 30:1-4, 13, 23-27). Josiah's ***Passover*** was done in accordance with the strict standards of the law (2 Chr 35:1-19). • ***The eighteenth year*** was the same year in which the Book of the Law was found (22:3, 8).

23:24-25 ***idols:*** The Hebrew term (literally *round things*) probably alludes to dung. • Josiah's commitment to the law brought reforms throughout ***Jerusalem*** and ***Judah.*** His attempts to eradicate ***every other kind of detestable practice*** and his strict observance of the Passover made Josiah greatest among the kings in ***obeying all the laws of Moses.***

23:26-27 ***I will also banish Judah:*** Despite Josiah's strong reforms, ***Manasseh's*** wickedness had become so deeply entrenched among the people that not even Josiah could change their apostate hearts, and the penalties for violation of God's covenant would be applied (Deut 28:15-68).

23:28-30 The closing details of Josiah's reign include a historical notice of his death at the hands of ***Pharaoh Neco*** (see also 2 Chr 35:20-25).

23:29 In 609 BC, ***Pharaoh Neco*** was en route ***to the Euphrates River to help the king of Assyria*** in fighting the Babylonians at Haran, when Josiah ***met*** him ***at Megiddo.*** After the death of Assyrian king Ashurbanipal in 626 BC, Assyrian cities began falling to Nabopolassar (626–605 BC), king of the rising neo-Babylonian power. Nabopolassar captured Nineveh, the capital of Assyria, in 612 BC. The Assyrian forces fled to Haran, where the Babylonians defeated them in 609 BC. Nebuchadnezzar II of Babylon (605–562 BC) later defeated the remaining Assyrians at Carchemish in 605 BC, the same year in which he first invaded Judea (see 24:1 and note). • ***Josiah and his army marched out to fight him:*** Or ***Josiah went out to meet him.*** • ***King Neco:*** Literally *he.*

23:30 The Chronicler reports on the great honor that Josiah received in death (2 Chr 35:24-25).

23:31-34 ***Jehoahaz*** was named Shallum at birth (see note on 1 Chr 3:15); his throne name ***Jehoahaz*** has been discovered among seals from the 600s BC. He was ***twenty-three years old,*** but his brother Jehoiakim was twenty-five (23:36). There is no indication as to why the younger brother was made king. • The ***three months*** of Jehoahaz's reign (in 609 BC) might coincide with the period in which ***Pharaoh Neco*** was attempting to aid the Assyrians (23:29).

23:32 ***He did what was evil in the LORD's sight:*** The entrenched wickedness and apostasy of the times surfaced even in Josiah's own sons (23:32, 37; 24:9, 19). The Lord's intention to judge Judah (23:26-27) was justified and would soon be fulfilled.

23:34
1 Chr 3:15
2 Chr 36:4-8
Jer 22:12
Ezek 19:3-4

23:36–24:6
//2 Chr 36:5-8
Jer 1:3; 26:21

24:1
2 Chr 36:6
Jer 25:1, 9

24:2
2 Kgs 13:20-21; 23:27

24:3
2 Kgs 18:25; 23:26

at Riblah in the land of Hamath to prevent
him from ruling in Jerusalem. He also demanded that Judah pay 7,500 pounds of
silver and 75 pounds of gold as tribute.
[34]Pharaoh Neco then installed Eliakim,
another of Josiah's sons, to reign in place of
his father, and he changed Eliakim's name
to Jehoiakim. Jehoahaz was taken to Egypt
as a prisoner, where he died.

Exile of Jehoiakim
2 Kgs 23:36-37 // 2 Chr 36:5
2 Kgs 24:5-6 // 2 Chr 36:8

[35]In order to get the silver and gold demanded as tribute by Pharaoh Neco, Jehoiakim
collected a tax from the people of Judah, requiring them to pay in proportion to their
wealth.
[36]Jehoiakim was twenty-five years old
when he became king, and he reigned in
Jerusalem eleven years. His mother was
Zebidah, the daughter of Pedaiah from Ru-
mah. [37]He did what was evil in the LORD's
sight, just as his ancestors had done.

24 During Jehoiakim's reign, King
Nebuchadnezzar of Babylon
invaded the land of Judah. Jehoiakim surrendered and paid him tribute for three
years but then rebelled. [2]Then the LORD
sent bands of Babylonian, Aramean, Moabite, and Ammonite raiders against Judah to
destroy it, just as the LORD had promised
through his prophets. [3]These disasters
happened to Judah because of the LORD's
command. He had decided to banish Judah

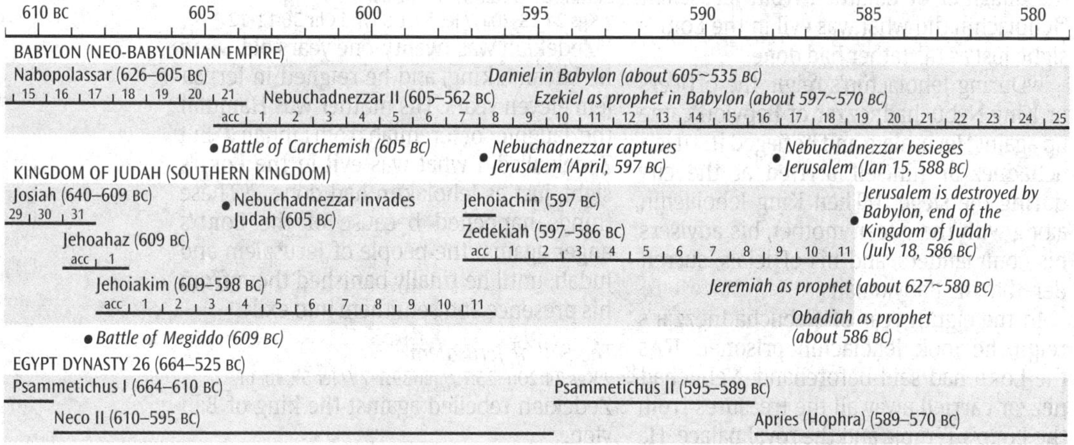

▲ **Kingdom of Judah, 611–579 BC (23:29–25:26).** JOSIAH's reign ended in disaster when Pharaoh NECO II of Egypt killed him at the BATTLE OF MEGIDDO in 609 BC. • The Babylonian victory over Egypt at the BATTLE OF CARCHEMISH (605 BC; see 24:7) cleared the way for NEBUCHADNEZZAR II to invade Judah (24:1); it was during that invasion that DANIEL was taken to Babylon (Dan 1:1-2). Judah became a vassal state, but when JEHOIAKIM rebelled Judah was again raided (24:2). Nebuchadnezzar later arrived in 597 BC, the eighth year of his reign. He besieged Jerusalem, captured it a second time (24:10-12), and took many of its people captive to Babylon (24:13-16), including the prophet EZEKIEL (Ezek 1:1-2). Nebuchadnezzar installed ZEDEKIAH as vassal king of Judah. Zedekiah then rebelled and stopped paying tribute (24:18-20). • Pharaoh APRIES ("HOPHRA") of Egypt was instrumental in forestalling yet another siege of Jerusalem (Jer 37:5), but it only delayed the inevitable (see Jer 44:30). Nebuchadnezzar besieged Jerusalem on Jan 15, 588 BC (25:1-2), captured Jerusalem on July 18, 586 BC, tore down the Temple and the rest of the city beginning on Aug 14, and sent most of its remaining inhabitants into exile (25:3-12). Thus began the period of exile, which lasted until 538 BC (Ezra 1–2).

23:33 ***Riblah*** was a fortified administrative center in Aramean territory about sixty miles northeast of Damascus. • ***to prevent him from ruling:*** The meaning of the Hebrew is uncertain. • ***7,500 pounds of silver and 75 pounds of gold:*** Hebrew *100 talents* [3,400 kilograms] *of silver and 1 talent* [34 kilograms] *of gold.*

23:34 ***Eliakim . . . Jehoiakim:*** Neco continued the Assyrian practice of requiring an oath of loyalty and assigning a new name to the local head of state.

23:36 ***Jehoiakim,*** Jehoahaz's older brother (cp. 23:31), reigned ***eleven years*** (609–598 BC).

23:37 ***did what was evil:*** The record in the book of Jeremiah characterizes Jehoiakim as a total apostate (see Jer 22:13-23; 25:1-14; 26:20-23; 36:1-32).

24:1 In 605 BC, ***Nebuchadnezzar*** commanded forces that defeated the remaining Assyrian army and an Egyptian contingent at Carchemish (see Jer 46:2). While he campaigned in the west, his father, Nabopolassar, died, and Nebuchadnezzar returned home to assume the throne as Nebuchadnezzar II (605–562 BC). When he rejoined his troops, they easily moved down the Mediterranean coast. Sometime during this campaign, he ***invaded the land of Judah*** and took much booty and many captives to Babylon, including Daniel and his three friends (Dan 1:1-7). ***Jehoiakim*** was made a vassal to Nebuchadnezzar and ***paid him tribute for three years.*** When Pharaoh Neco defeated the Babylonians at the Egyptian border in 601 BC, Jehoiakim ***rebelled,*** seizing the opportunity to gain his independence.

24:2 Nebuchadnezzar bided his time between 601 and 598 BC while consolidating his hold on the west, sending various ***raiders*** to harass ***Judah.*** • ***Babylonian:*** Or *Chaldean.*

24:3 ***because of the LORD's command:*** The root of Judah's problems was its

from his presence because of the many sins of Manasseh, 4who had filled Jerusalem with innocent blood. The LORD would not forgive this.

5The rest of the events in Jehoiakim's reign and all his deeds are recorded in *The Book of the History of the Kings of Judah.* 6When Jehoiakim died, his son Jehoiachin became the next king.

7The king of Egypt did not venture out of his country after that, for the king of Babylon captured the entire area formerly claimed by Egypt—from the Brook of Egypt to the Euphrates River.

Exile of Jehoiachin
2 Kgs 24:8-9, 12b-13, 17 // 2 Chr 36:9-10

8Jehoiachin was eighteen years old when he became king, and he reigned in Jerusalem three months. His mother was Nehushta, the daughter of Elnathan from Jerusalem. 9Jehoiachin did what was evil in the LORD's sight, just as his father had done.

10During Jehoiachin's reign, the officers of King Nebuchadnezzar of Babylon came up against Jerusalem and besieged it. 11Nebuchadnezzar himself arrived at the city during the siege. 12Then King Jehoiachin, along with the queen mother, his advisers, his commanders, and his officials, surrendered to the Babylonians.

In the eighth year of Nebuchadnezzar's reign, he took Jehoiachin prisoner. 13As the LORD had said beforehand, Nebuchadnezzar carried away all the treasures from the LORD's Temple and the royal palace. He stripped away all the gold objects that King Solomon of Israel had placed in the Temple. 14King Nebuchadnezzar took all of Jerusalem captive, including all the commanders and the best of the soldiers, craftsmen, and artisans—10,000 in all. Only the poorest people were left in the land.

15Nebuchadnezzar led King Jehoiachin away as a captive to Babylon, along with the queen mother, his wives and officials, and all Jerusalem's elite. 16He also exiled 7,000 of the best troops and 1,000 craftsmen and artisans, all of whom were strong and fit for war. 17Then the king of Babylon installed Mattaniah, Jehoiachin's uncle, as the next king, and he changed Mattaniah's name to Zedekiah.

Zedekiah's Reign and the Fall of Jerusalem (24:18–25:21)

Zedekiah's Reign in Judah
2 Kgs 24:18-20a // Jer 52:1-3a // 2 Chr 36:11-12

18Zedekiah was twenty-one years old when he became king, and he reigned in Jerusalem eleven years. His mother was Hamutal, the daughter of Jeremiah from Libnah. 19But Zedekiah did what was evil in the LORD's sight, just as Jehoiakim had done. 20These things happened because of the LORD's anger against the people of Jerusalem and Judah, until he finally banished them from his presence and sent them into exile.

The Fall of Jerusalem
2 Kgs 24:20b–25:7 // Jer 39:1-7 // Jer 52:3b-11

Zedekiah rebelled against the king of Babylon.

24:4
2 Kgs 21:16
24:6
Jer 22:24-25
24:7
Jer 37:5, 7; 46:2
24:8-17
//2 Chr 36:9-10
24:12
2 Chr 36:10
Jer 24:1; 29:1-2
24:13
1 Kgs 7:48-50
2 Kgs 20:17; 25:13-15
Isa 39:6
24:14
2 Kgs 25:12
Jer 24:1; 52:28
24:17
2 Chr 36:10-13
Jer 37:1
24:18-20
//2 Chr 36:11-13
//Jer 52:1-3
24:20
2 Chr 36:13
Jer 27:12; 38:17, 21-22; 39:1

incorrigible spiritual infidelity. Despite Josiah's reforms, the ***sins of Manasseh*** permeated Judah so that divine judgment was inevitable.

24:4 *innocent blood:* Tradition holds that Manasseh murdered the prophet Isaiah by sawing him in two (cp. Heb 11:37).

24:6 *Jehoiakim died* in 598 BC, either shortly before or during Nebuchadnezzar's second campaign against Jerusalem (Josephus reports that Nebuchadnezzar executed Jehoiakim; see Josephus, *Antiquities* 10.6.3; cp. Jer 22:18-19; 36:30-31).

24:7 *The king of Egypt did not venture out of his country after that* because of Nebuchadnezzar's overwhelming strength. Any hope Judah had of help from Egypt was in vain (see Jer 2:36; 46:2-12; Ezek 29:6, 16). • ***The Brook of Egypt*** has been identified as either the Wadi el-Arish at the edge of the Nile delta, or as Nahal Besor, which lies south of Gaza.

24:8 *Jehoiachin* became king in 597 BC. • ***he reigned in Jerusalem three months:*** cp. Jer 22:28-30.

24:10-12 Faced with the overwhelming forces of ***Nebuchadnezzar***, Jehoiachin ***surrendered.*** • The ***eighth year of Nebuchadnezzar's reign*** was 597 BC. See note on 2 Chr 36:9-10.

24:13 *As the LORD had said beforehand:* See 20:16-17. A greater divine judgment still lay in the future (21:12-15; 22:15-20; 23:26-27). • ***all the treasures:*** In his earlier siege of Jerusalem in 605 BC, Nebuchadnezzar had taken part of the Temple treasures as spoil (2 Chr 36:7; Dan 1:2). He now ***carried away all the treasures.*** Anything left behind on this occasion was taken in his final siege of Jerusalem in 586 BC (25:15). • ***He stripped away:*** Or *He cut apart.*

24:14-16 In addition to ***Jehoiachin***, the prophet Ezekiel was also taken into captivity (Ezek 1:1). Throughout the book of Ezekiel, events in Ezekiel's life are dated in terms of the years since Jehoiachin had been taken captive. • The ***10,000*** taken captive by Nebuchadnezzar likely includes ***7,000 troops, 1,000 craftsmen and artisans***, and a number of administrative officials and leading citizens of Jerusalem. In any case, ***10,000*** is probably a round figure (see also Jer 52:28).

24:17 Like the three kings before him, ***Mattaniah*** received a throne name, ***Zedekiah.*** • ***Jehoiachin's uncle*** (Literally *his uncle*): See 1 Chr 3:15-16.

24:18-20 Zedekiah's reign of ***eleven years*** in Jerusalem (597–586 BC) mirrored Jehoiakim's ***evil*** reign (23:36-37). The Lord was judging Jerusalem and Judah for their sins (see 17:19; 20:16-17; 21:12-15; 22:15-20; 23:26-27). • ***Zedekiah rebelled:*** Zedekiah's rebellion may coincide with an anti-Babylonian alliance spearheaded by Pharaoh Apries of Egypt. When Apries became king of Egypt in about 589 BC, he cherished hopes of recovering Egypt's past glory. Zedekiah appears to have placed his confidence in him (cp. Ezek 17:15-18). Nevertheless, like earlier kings (17:4; 24:1-3), Zedekiah learned that Egypt would be of little help (cp. 18:20-21; Jer 37:3-10; Ezek 29:6-7).

25:1-12 //Jer 39:1-7
25:1 2 Chr 36:17-20 Ezek 21:22; 24:2
25:3 2 Kgs 6:24-25 Lam 4:9-10
25:6 Jer 32:4
25:7 Jer 39:6-7 Ezek 12:13
25:8 Jer 52:12
25:9 2 Chr 36:19 Ps 74:3-8 Amos 2:5
25:10 Neh 1:3
25:11 2 Chr 36:20

25 So on January 15, during the ninth
year of Zedekiah's reign, King Nebuchadnezzar of Babylon led his entire army
against Jerusalem. They surrounded the
city and built siege ramps against its walls.
2Jerusalem was kept under siege until the
eleventh year of King Zedekiah's reign.
3By July 18 in the eleventh year of Zedekiah's reign, the famine in the city had become
very severe, and the last of the food was entirely gone. 4Then a section of the city wall
was broken down, and all the soldiers fled.
Since the city was surrounded by the Babylonians, they waited for nightfall. Then they
slipped through the gate between the two
walls behind the king's garden and headed
toward the Jordan Valley.
5But the Babylonian troops chased the
king and caught him on the plains of Jericho,
for his men had all deserted him and scattered. 6They took him to the king of Babylon
at Riblah, where they pronounced judgment
upon Zedekiah. 7They made Zedekiah watch
as they slaughtered his sons. Then they
gouged out Zedekiah's eyes, bound him in
bronze chains, and led him away to Babylon.

The Temple Destroyed

2 Kgs 25:8-12 // Jer 52:12-16 // Jer 39:8-10
2 Kgs 25:13-21 // Jer 52:17-27

8On August 14 of that year, which was the
nineteenth year of King Nebuchadnezzar's
reign, Nebuzaradan, the captain of the
guard and an official of the Babylonian king,
arrived in Jerusalem. 9He burned down the
Temple of the LORD, the royal palace, and all
the houses of Jerusalem. He destroyed all
the important buildings in the city. 10Then
he supervised the entire Babylonian army
as they tore down the walls of Jerusalem
on every side. 11Nebuzaradan, the captain
of the guard, then took as exiles the rest of

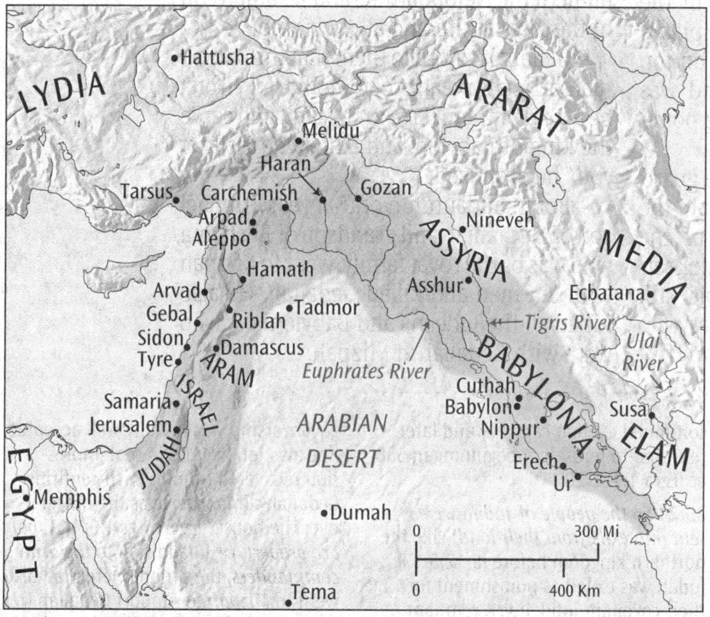

The Babylonian Empire, 610–580 BC (24:1–25:30). By the late 600s BC, BABYLONIA was the dominant power in the Near East, having captured NINEVEH in 612 BC and finally defeating the Assyrian forces at HARAN in 609 BC and CARCHEMISH in 605 BC (see note on 23:29). Nebuchadnezzar II (605–562 BC) carried this forward thrust into JUDAH shortly thereafter (24:1–25:21).

25:1 ***January 15:*** Literally *on the tenth day of the tenth month,* of the ancient Hebrew lunar calendar. A number of events in 2 Kings can be cross-checked with dates in surviving Babylonian records and related accurately to our modern calendar. This day was *January 15,* 588 BC. • ***Siege ramps*** were characteristic of ancient Near Eastern warfare. Attackers built tall earthen *ramps* and towers to give them a more advantageous position (see Jer 52:14; Ezek 21:22).

25:3 ***By July 18 in the eleventh year of Zedekiah's reign:*** Literally *By the ninth day of the [fourth] month* [in the eleventh year of Zedekiah's reign] (cp. Jer 52:6 and note). This day was July 18, 586 BC; also see note on 25:1.

25:4 Using battering rams (Ezek 4:2), ***the Babylonians*** (or *the Chaldeans;* also in 25:13, 25, 26) broke down a section of Jerusalem's ***wall*** and penetrated the city. At ***nightfall,*** King Zedekiah and the remaining troops ***slipped through the gate*** at the southeastern corner of the city into the Kidron Valley, attempting to reach the ***Jordan Valley*** (Hebrew *the Arabah*).

25:5 Zedekiah was overtaken by ***Babylonian*** (or *Chaldean;* also in 25:10, 24) forces on the plains of Jericho.

25:6 ***Riblah,*** formerly an Assyrian administrative center, served as Nebuchadnezzar's battle headquarters, as it had for the Egyptians (23:33).

25:7 ***gouged out Zedekiah's eyes:*** Rebellious leaders were commonly blinded in the ancient Near East. However, Zedekiah's blinding seems especially cruel; the last image he had was of his ***sons*** being ***slaughtered.*** • True to the prophetic word, Zedekiah was taken into captivity, where he died (Jer 32:4-5; 34:3; 52:11; Ezek 12:11-14).

25:8 ***On August 14 of that year:*** Literally *On the seventh day of the fifth month,* of the ancient Hebrew lunar calendar. This day was August 14, 586 BC; also see note on 25:1. • ***Nebuzaradan*** is known from one of Nebuchadnezzar's inscriptions as an important ***official.***

25:9-10 ***destroyed all the important buildings*** (Or *destroyed the houses of all the important people*): The Babylonians destroyed key religious and civic buildings to discourage further resistance or insurrection, and they demolished the city's ***walls,*** leaving Jerusalem defenseless.

25:11-12 The Babylonians took the majority of the population into exile, even some who willingly defected (Jer 39:9; 52:15). • Because ***the poorest people*** were unlikely to cause trouble, they were left behind to work the ***vineyards and fields.***

the people who remained in the city, the defectors who had declared their allegiance to the king of Babylon, and the rest of the population. 12But the captain of the guard allowed some of the poorest people to stay behind in Judah to care for the vineyards and fields.

13The Babylonians broke up the bronze pillars in front of the LORD's Temple, the bronze water carts, and the great bronze basin called the Sea, and they carried all the bronze away to Babylon. 14They also took all the ash buckets, shovels, lamp snuffers, dishes, and all the other bronze articles used for making sacrifices at the Temple. 15Nebuzaradan, the captain of the guard, also took the incense burners and basins, and all the other articles made of pure gold or silver.

16The weight of the bronze from the two pillars, the Sea, and the water carts was too great to be measured. These things had been made for the LORD's Temple in the days of King Solomon. 17Each of the pillars was 27 feet tall. The bronze capital on top of each pillar was 7½ feet high and was decorated with a network of bronze pomegranates all the way around.

18Nebuzaradan, the captain of the guard, took with him as prisoners Seraiah the high priest, Zephaniah the priest of the second rank, and the three chief gatekeepers. 19And from among the people still hiding in the city, he took an officer who had been in charge of the Judean army; five of the king's personal advisers; the army commander's chief secretary, who was in charge of recruitment; and sixty other citizens. 20Nebuzaradan, the captain of the guard, took them all to the king of Babylon at Riblah. 21And there at Riblah, in the land of Hamath, the king of Babylon had them all put to death. So the people of Judah were sent into exile from their land.

3. HISTORICAL APPENDICES (25:22-30)

Gedaliah Governs in Judah

2 Kgs 25:22-26 // Jer 40:7-9; 41:1-3, 17-18

22Then King Nebuchadnezzar appointed Gedaliah son of Ahikam and grandson of Shaphan as governor over the people he had left in Judah. 23When all the army commanders and their men learned that the king of Babylon had appointed Gedaliah as governor, they went to see him at Mizpah. These included Ishmael son of Nethaniah, Johanan son of Kareah, Seraiah son of Tanhumeth the Netophathite, and Jezaniah son of the Maacathite, and all their men.

24Gedaliah vowed to them that the Babylonian officials meant them no harm. "Don't be afraid of them. Live in the land and serve the king of Babylon, and all will go well for you," he promised.

25But in midautumn of that year, Ishmael son of Nethaniah and grandson of Elishama, who was of the royal family, went to Mizpah with ten men and killed Gedaliah. He also killed all the Judeans and Babylonians who were with Gedaliah at Mizpah.

25:12 2 Kgs 24:14; Jer 40:7; 52:16
25:13 1 Kgs 7:15-22; 2 Chr 36:18
25:14 1 Kgs 7:47-50; 2 Chr 24:14
25:17 1 Kgs 7:15-22
25:18 1 Chr 6:14; Ezra 7:1; Jer 29:25-26, 29
25:20 2 Kgs 23:33
25:21 Deut 28:64; 2 Kgs 23:27
25:22-26 //Jer 40:7-9; 41:1-3, 16-18
25:23 Jer 40:7-9
25:25 Jer 41:1-2

25:13-16 The Babylonians *broke up* the Temple furnishings that had been crafted by Huram of Tyre and *all the other bronze articles* (see 1 Kgs 7:13-50) for their own use. The transport of these valuable furnishings to Babylon was a major undertaking; everything of value was carried away (see also Jer 52:17-23).

25:17 *27 feet:* Hebrew *18 cubits* [8.1 meters]. • *7½ feet:* As in parallel texts at 1 Kgs 7:16; 2 Chr 3:15; and Jer 52:22, all of which read *5 cubits* [2.3 meters]; Hebrew reads *3 cubits,* which is 4.5 feet or 1.4 meters. The reading of the Hebrew text might reflect the height of the decorative work adorning the upper part of the *capital* (cp. 1 Kgs 7:17-18).

25:18-20 Instead of deporting key citizens and officials as in the Babylonian invasion of 597 BC (24:14), Nebuchadnezzar had these leaders put to death. Even religious leaders were executed. • Although *Seraiah the high priest* was slain, his son Jehozadak was sent into exile (1 Chr 6:15). Thus the priestly line continued even in captivity and later returned to Jerusalem beginning in 538 BC (Ezra 1:1–2:20).

25:21 *So the people of Judah were sent into exile from their land:* Like the northern kingdom before it (17:5-17), Judah was exiled as punishment for their covenant infidelity. A remnant later returned to the Promised Land in 538 BC (2 Chr 36:22-23; Ezra 1:1–2:20; see also 2 Chr 36:15-21; Jer 25:11; 29:10; Dan 9:2).

25:22-30 Two short appendices describe subsequent events. The first (25:22-26) details the area's reorganization; the second (25:27-30) tells of the later kind treatment accorded King Jehoiachin.

25:22 *Gedaliah*'s father *Ahikam* and grandfather *Shaphan* had been trusted officials during Josiah's reign (22:3, 12). Ahikam had supported Jeremiah during the reign of Jehoiakim (Jer 26:24).

25:23-24 Because *Gedaliah* came from a family experienced in civic affairs, his governorship was initially well accepted (see also Jer 40:1-12). A seal impression recovered from Lachish confirms Gedaliah's importance as the officer "over the house" (see 1 Kgs 4:6; NLT, *palace property*). • In addition to *the army commanders,* the prophet Jeremiah also went to *Mizpah* to support Gedaliah (Jer 40:6). This *Mizpah* was a border town in Benjamin; it had been prominent in Israelite history as a place of religious assembly (1 Sam 7:5-6). • The men listed here held important posts. *Ishmael* was from a prominent family of royal lineage (25:25; Jer 36:12). *Johanan* served Gedaliah faithfully (Jer 40:13-16). The name *Jezaniah* (as in parallel text at Jer 40:8; Hebrew reads *Jaazaniah,* a variant spelling of *Jezaniah.*) occurs on materials recovered from excavations at Tell-en-Nasbeh.

25:25 *in midautumn of that year:* Literally *in the seventh month,* of the ancient Hebrew lunar calendar. This month occurred within the months of October and November 586 BC; also see note on 25:1. • *Gedaliah* had been

25:26
Jer 43:5-7
25:27
2 Kgs 24:12
Jer 52:31-34

26Then all the people of Judah, from the
least to the greatest, as well as the army commanders, fled in panic to Egypt, for they
were afraid of what the Babylonians would
do to them.

Hope for Israel's Royal Line
2 Kgs 25:27-30 // Jer 52:31-34

27In the thirty-seventh year of the exile of
King Jehoiachin of Judah, Evil-merodach
ascended to the Babylonian throne. He
was kind to Jehoiachin and released him
from prison on April 2 of that year. 28He
spoke kindly to Jehoiachin and gave him a
higher place than all the other exiled kings
in Babylon. 29He supplied Jehoiachin with
new clothes to replace his prison garb and
allowed him to dine in the king's presence
for the rest of his life. 30So the Babylonian
king gave him a regular food allowance as
long as he lived.

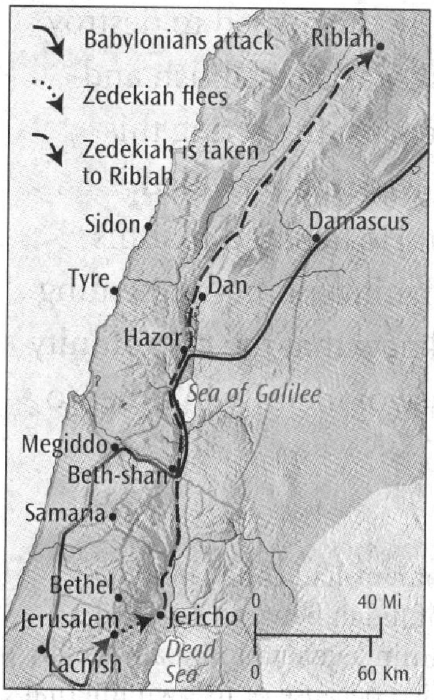

◀ **The Babylonian Invasions of Judah, 605–586 BC (24:1–25:21).** Nebuchadnezzar II invaded Judah on at least three occasions (605, 597, 586 BC) and took plunder from JERUSALEM and captives to Babylon (see 24:1, 10-17; 25:1-21). The map shows Zedekiah's attempted escape to JERICHO, where he was captured, and his trip to RIBLAH, where he faced judgment before Nebuchadnezzar (25:4-7).

warned that *Ishmael* was plotting to assassinate him but was unconvinced (Jer 40:13-16); his trust cost him his life. Ishmael ***also killed*** many ***Judeans and Babylonians,*** fled with many captives, and escaped to Ammon (Jer 41:4-15).

25:26 ***Then all the people of Judah,*** led by Johanan, ***fled in panic to Egypt*** against Jeremiah's counsel (see Jer 42:1–43:7).

25:27-30 ***Evil-merodach*** (Babylonian, *Amel-marduk*, "man of Marduk") succeeded Nebuchadnezzar II at his death and reigned a short time (561–560 BC). • ***He was kind to*** (literally *He raised the head of*) ***Jehoiachin:*** Babylonian annals give details of the rations Jehoiachin received in prison. The narrator's mention of Jehoiachin living in gracious circumstances is perhaps intended to provide hope that God would preserve and restore a repentant people to their land (see 1 Kgs 8:46-53; Isa 35:8-10; 51:11; Jer 29:10-14; Zeph 3:20). • ***on April 2 of that year:*** Literally *on the twenty-seventh day of the twelfth month,* of the ancient Hebrew lunar calendar. This day was April 2, 561 BC; see also note on 25:1.

THE FIRST BOOK OF CHRONICLES

The book of Chronicles was written to inspire hope. Exile had robbed the people of Israel of their wealth, and their return to the land created resentment among their neighbors. Despondency and apathy threatened to destroy them entirely. The Chronicler's task was to establish and validate the people's links with the past. In writing this history, he organized the past in a way that provided meaning and value for the present. He believed that his community, Judea, was critically significant in representing the Kingdom of God. Further, he knew that the community needed to retain its distinctive sense of identity in order to fulfill its purpose.

SETTING

The Babylonians had conquered the kingdom of Judah between 605 and 586 BC. Within a generation, Babylonian power eroded because of its own internal decay (see Dan 5). Meanwhile, to the east, the Persian king Cyrus the Great (559–530 BC) established a new empire that united the Medes and the Persians. In October 539 BC, Babylon fell without

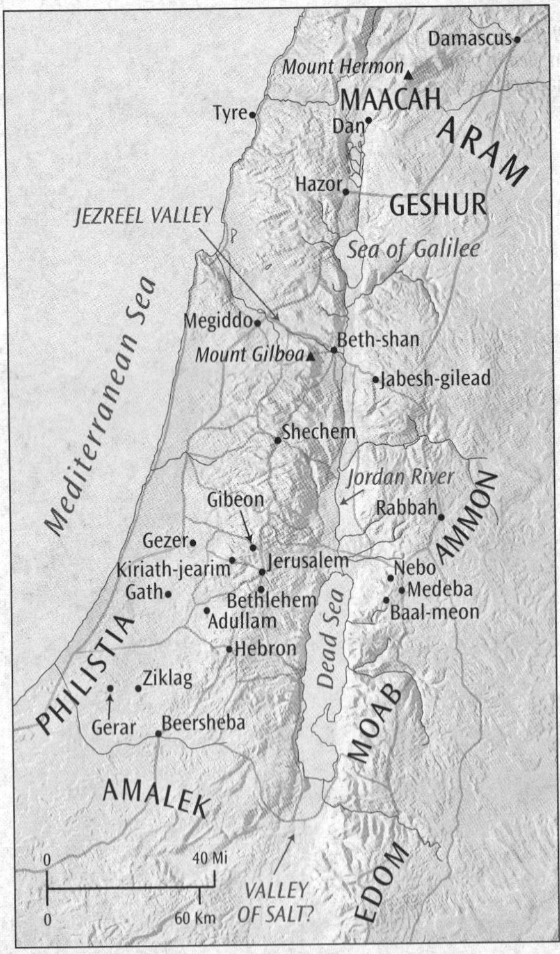

The Land of Israel at the Time of David, about 1000 BC. From Saul's death at the hands of the Philistines on Mount Gilboa to David's victories over Israel's enemies, the land of Israel was the scene of most of the events described in 1 Chronicles.

ADULLAM 11:15
AMALEK, PHILISTIA 18:11
AMMON 18:11; 19:1–20:3
ARAM, DAMASCUS 18:5-6
BETHLEHEM 11:16-18
EDOM 18:11-13
GATH 7:21; 8:13; 13:13; 18:1; 20:5-8
GESHUR 2:23; 3:2
GEZER 14:16; 20:4
GIBEON 9:35; 12:4; 14:16; 16:39; 21:29
HEBRON 11:1, 3; 12:23, 38; 29:27
JERUSALEM 3:4-5; 11:4, 8; 15:3; 20:1; 21:4, 15; 23:25; 28:1; 29:27
JORDAN RIVER 12:15; 19:17
KIRIATH-JEARIM 2:50-53; 13:5-6
MAACAH, MEDEBA 19:7
MOAB 4:22; 8:8; 11:22; 18:2, 11
MOUNT GILBOA 10:1-8
RABBAH 20:1-3
TYRE 14:1; 22:4
VALLEY OF SALT 18:12
ZIKLAG 12:1, 20

resistance, and Cyrus's empire extended westward to include Babylonia (see Dan 5:30-31).

In keeping with his imperial policy, Cyrus provided for the Jewish exiles to return to Judea and establish a province around the city of Jerusalem. The story of this time is told in the books of Ezra and Nehemiah and by the prophets Haggai and Zechariah. The new community faced many struggles as they rebuilt the Temple and later the wall of Jerusalem. The community thus experienced spiritual restoration, physical protection, and a measure of economic independence. Yet there was virtually no hope of political autonomy. The besieged community bore little resemblance to the former kingdom. The people needed a sense of purpose and hope.

The community of Judah also suffered scorn, opposition, and humiliation from surrounding peoples. The people struggled to maintain their identity, faith, and way of life as social and political forces threatened to absorb them completely. The community needed answers concerning its purpose and its future.

The people of Judah faced some profound questions at this time: How could they remain true to their ancestral faith while living under the permanent domination of an imperial power? How could a subordinate people be the people of God? What did the promise of the eternal throne of David mean under these circumstances? One answer, which found expression in later Greek and Roman times (among the "zealots" of the NT era), was a nationalist pressure to rebel and establish independence. Others, recognizing their situation as inescapable, were concerned with the conflict between the political demands of the empire and covenant faithfulness to God. The book of Chronicles was written to address these questions and concerns.

OUTLINE

1:1–9:34
Genealogy of the Nation of Israel

9:35–20:8
Founding of the Kingdom

21:1–29:30
Preparations for the Temple

SUMMARY

The text of 1 Chronicles divides into two distinct sections: the portrayal of Israel's identity through genealogies (chs 1–9) and David's preparing of Jerusalem for the Temple and the rule of Solomon (chs 10–29).

The first chapter of genealogies (ch 1) moves along the line of God's selection of specific people from Adam to Jacob (= Israel). Chapters 2–8 deal with the Israelites from Jacob until the exile to Babylon. This section first details the tribe of Judah (chs 2–4), then discusses the house of David in the central section (ch 3), and finally describes the other tribes of Israel (chs 5–7), including those east of the Jordan River (in Transjordan). At the midpoint in the genealogical lists comes Levi (ch 6), a tribe with central significance. The record continues with the tribe of Benjamin (ch 8), completing the genealogies to the date of writing (see next page), with a list of the chief representatives of the community that returned from exile and began restoring Jerusalem (ch 9).

TIMELINE

1011–971 BC
David as king of Israel

971–931 BC
Solomon as king of Israel

586 BC
Destruction of the Temple in Jerusalem

559–530 BC
Cyrus II as king of Persia

Oct 539 BC
Cyrus II conquers Babylon

538 BC
Cyrus's decree allows exiles to return to Judea

Aug 29–Dec 18, 520 BC
Haggai as prophet

Nov 520–Dec 7, 518 BC
Zechariah as prophet

515 BC
Temple rebuilding is completed

400s BC
Malachi as prophet

458 BC
Ezra travels to Jerusalem

445 BC
Nehemiah travels to Jerusalem

about 400 BC
1–2 Chronicles is written

Saul's genealogy (ch 9) introduces the founding of the monarchy. When Saul died because of his unfaithfulness (ch 10), David became king (chs 11–12). The chapters on David's reign explain his organization of officials and his preparations for the Temple (chs 13–27). The transfer of the Ark of the Covenant to Jerusalem served as a major event in the establishment of David's kingdom (chs 13–16). The remainder of 1 Chronicles traces the steps taken toward building the Temple. These chapters include the identity of the builder (ch 17), the necessary political conditions (chs 18–20), the site (ch 21), the personnel (chs 23–27), the materials, and the plans (chs 22, 28–29). The account of David's reign closes with a great public assembly and Solomon's commissioning as the heir of peace who would build the Temple (chs 28–29).

AUTHORSHIP AND DATE

The book of Chronicles is traditionally ascribed to Ezra, but the author of Chronicles left no clues about his own identity apart from the content of his writings. The Chronicler lived in or near Jerusalem and was an ardent supporter of the Temple and its services. The prominence he gives to the Levites in his writing might suggest that he was among their number. This would explain his access to the material he used to compose his history.

The Chronicler wrote in the latter years of the Persian empire, probably around 400 BC. The genealogy of the descendants of Jehoiachin (3:17-24) suggests a date that is eight generations later than Zerubbabel, who served as governor around 520 BC, during the days of Darius, king of Persia (Zech 1:1; 4:9). The Chronicler probably wrote some time after Nehemiah traveled to Jerusalem in the twentieth year of Artaxerxes (445 BC) to repair the walls of the city (Neh 2:1). Chronicles was not written as late as the Greek period, beginning with Alexander the Great (332 BC), because the writing contains no linguistic or ideological evidence of Greek influence. These considerations give us a date around 400 BC.

Chronicles describes the history of Israel from beginning to "beginning," that is, from the inception of the human existence with Adam, through the destruction of the first commonwealth during the reign of Zedekiah, to the new commencement with the declaration of Cyrus.

SARA JAPHET
1 & 2 Chronicles (2002)

HISTORICAL SITUATION

Little is known about the situation in Judah after Nehemiah, although Nehemiah reveals some of the difficulties of the community. The temptation to marry outside of Israel was great, and mixed marriages remained in the days of Malachi (400s BC; see Mal 2:14-16). Foreign marriages gave access to land and wealth that were not available within the community. The law, which Ezra brought back with him from Babylon, called for adherence to the Temple as the social and economic center of the community. However, this self-sufficiency and exclusivity aroused the ongoing resentment and hostility of the surrounding peoples.

GENRE AND COMPOSITION

The title of the book of Chronicles also defines the genre of the work. In Hebrew, it is "the events of the days"; in other words, it is a history. In the prologue to the Latin translation of Samuel and Kings, Jerome calls Chronicles the *chronikon,* or "annals," a register of events, a record book of ancient times. The Greek translation of the OT (the Septuagint), by contrast, calls this history "the things left out." This

title regarded Chronicles as a secondary complement to Kings, an attitude that would have horrified its author. This work is a unique creation from many different sources.

In writing this history, the Chronicler organized Israel's past in a way that would provide meaning and value for its intended readers. He included genealogies because they answered two critical questions of history: Whose story needed to be told? and, Where did these people live? The Chronicler's work explains why a people with no influence or recognition considered their existence and lifestyle to be of profound significance for the future.

The book of 1 Chronicles covers essentially the same time period as 2 Samuel. Accordingly, there are numerous parallel passages with similar wording. But the authors had different purposes in writing, and these differences can be highlighted by comparing the similarities and the differences in the various parallel passages.

MEANING AND MESSAGE

The significance of God's promise to David (ch 17) occupies the center of the Chronicler's message. When David determined to build a house for God's Ark of the Covenant, Nathan the prophet had a vision informing him that David had it backwards: David would not build a house for God, but God would build a house for David. This house would be a dynasty (17:10-14 // 2 Sam 7:11-14), and the eternal Kingdom of God would come about through David's lineage. Psalm 2 expresses the importance of this promise; God held the nations in derision because they rejected his kingdom and thought that they could establish their own rule. They ignored the fact that God had already anointed his king on Mount Zion, a king who would shatter the nations and receive the earth (God's world) as his inheritance. The Chronicler took this promise very seriously. The Kingdom of God would come through the promised son of David. The community around Jerusalem represented that promised kingdom, the hope of the future.

The Chronicler had a double task. First, he needed to explain why the kingdom of David had failed. Second, he needed to establish that this small struggling state in the mighty Persian empire would become the kingdom that God had promised to David. The explanation for the failure of David's kingdom begins with Saul's failure: God rejected Saul as king over Israel because he was unfaithful. Saul did not obey God, and he violated the covenant to the extent of consulting a medium (10:13). Later kings repeated the essence of Saul's failure: They rebelled against God's covenant, and they sought security from foreign powers and pagan gods rather than from their Rock, the Lord (see Deut 32:4, 15-39).

"Unfaithfulness" is a key word in Chronicles; the Chronicler uses it repeatedly to document the reasons for judgment against the kings of Judah. The rationale for hope, on the other hand, comes from Solomon's prayer at the dedication of the Temple: "Then if my people who are called by my name will humble themselves and pray and seek my face and turn from their wicked ways, I will hear from heaven and will forgive their sins and restore their land" (2 Chr 7:14). This promise reminds the people of the conditions necessary for restoration: humility, prayer, repentance, and healing.

The faithful maintenance of communion with the covenant God in His temple would assure to [the congregation of Israel] the fulfillment of the gracious promises of the covenant, and how falling away into idolatry, on the contrary, would bring misfortune and destruction.

C. F. KEIL
1 & 2 Chronicles

FURTHER READING

LESLIE C. ALLEN
1 & 2 Chronicles (1993)

MARK J. BODA
1 Chronicles in *Cornerstone Biblical Commentary*, vol. 5a (2010)

ANDREW E. HILL
1 & 2 Chronicles (2003)

JOHN H. SAILHAMER
First & Second Chronicles (1983)

MARTIN SELMAN
1 Chronicles (1994)

The book of 1 Chronicles establishes the necessary premises for restoration. The promise to David did not disappear during the Exile; the community that was reestablished in Jerusalem carried the promise. Even the division of the kingdom after Solomon's reign had not put any of the tribes outside of Israel's future. For the Chronicler, all the tribes were present in the restoration, including those of the northern kingdom (9:3). The Chronicler understood Israel as the people of faith, not as a political entity. Israel was not a sovereign nation in his day but a small ethnic province in the mighty empire of Persia. Yet he wanted to show that the unity established by David and Solomon had endured and that the promise made to David gave them hope for the future.

1. GENEALOGY OF THE NATION OF ISRAEL (1:1–9:34)

Founding Ancestors (1:1-34)

From Adam to Noah's Sons

1 The descendants of Adam were Seth,
Enosh, [2]Kenan, Mahalalel, Jared,
[3]Enoch, Methuselah, Lamech, [4]and
Noah.
The sons of Noah were Shem, Ham, and
Japheth.

Descendants of Japheth

[5]The descendants of Japheth were Gomer,
Magog, Madai, Javan, Tubal, Meshech,
and Tiras.
[6]The descendants of Gomer were
Ashkenaz, Riphath, and Togarmah.
[7]The descendants of Javan were Elishah,
Tarshish, Kittim, and Rodanim.

Descendants of Ham

[8]The descendants of Ham were Cush,
Mizraim, Put, and Canaan.
[9]The descendants of Cush were Seba,
Havilah, Sabtah, Raamah, and Sabteca.
The descendants of Raamah were Sheba
and Dedan. [10]Cush was also the ancestor
of Nimrod, who was the first heroic
warrior on earth.
[11]Mizraim was the ancestor of the Ludites,
Anamites, Lehabites, Naphtuhites,
[12]Pathrusites, Casluhites, and the
Caphtorites, from whom the Philistines
came.
[13]Canaan's oldest son was Sidon, the
ancestor of the Sidonians. Canaan
was also the ancestor of the Hittites,
[14]Jebusites, Amorites, Girgashites,
[15]Hivites, Arkites, Sinites, [16]Arvadites,
Zemarites, and Hamathites.

Descendants of Shem

[17]The descendants of Shem were Elam,
Asshur, Arphaxad, Lud, and Aram.
The descendants of Aram were Uz, Hul,
Gether, and Mash.
[18]Arphaxad was the father of Shelah.
Shelah was the father of Eber.
[19]Eber had two sons. The first was named
Peleg (which means "division"), for during
his lifetime the people of the world were
divided into different language groups.
His brother's name was Joktan.
[20]Joktan was the ancestor of Almodad,
Sheleph, Hazarmaveth, Jerah, [21]Hadoram,
Uzal, Diklah, [22]Obal, Abimael, Sheba,
[23]Ophir, Havilah, and Jobab. All these
were descendants of Joktan.
[24]So this is the family line descended from
Shem: Arphaxad, Shelah, [25]Eber, Peleg,
Reu, [26]Serug, Nahor, Terah, [27]and Abram,
later known as Abraham.

1:1-3 Gen 5:1-32; Luke 3:36-38
1:5-7 // Gen 10:2-5
1:8-16 // Gen 10:6-20
1:11 Gen 10:13-18
1:13 Gen 15:19-21
1:17-23 // Gen 10:21-31; 11:10-27; Luke 3:36
1:19 Gen 11:16
1:24 Gen 11:10-26; Luke 3:34-36

1:1–2:2 The Chronicler begins by showing Israel's place among the nations, tracing their line of descent from Adam to Jacob, using material from Genesis.

1:1-4 An overview of the generations between *Adam* and *the sons of Noah* (cp. Gen 5:3-32).

1:4 The second sentence is taken from the Greek version (see also Gen 5:3-32); Hebrew lacks *The sons of Noah were.*

1:5-23 The record of Noah's descendants establishes Abraham's place in history. The ethnic backdrop of the seventy nations of the world provides the context for Israel's history (cp. Gen 10).

1:6 *Riphath:* As in some Hebrew manuscripts and Greek version (see also Gen 10:3); most Hebrew manuscripts read *Diphath.*

1:8 *Mizraim:* Or *Egypt;* also in 1:11.

1:12 *the Caphtorites, from whom the Philistines came:* Hebrew *the Casluhites, from whom the Philistines came, Caphtorites.* See Jer 47:4; Amos 9:7.

1:13 *ancestor of the Hittites:* Hebrew *ancestor of Heth.*

1:17 As in one Hebrew manuscript and some Greek manuscripts (see also Gen 10:23); most Hebrew manuscripts lack *The descendants of Aram were.* • *and Mash:* As in parallel text at Gen 10:23; Hebrew reads *and Meshech.*

1:22 *Obal:* As in some Hebrew manuscripts and Syriac version (see also Gen 10:28); most Hebrew manuscripts read *Ebal.*

1:24-27 The summary of *Shem*'s descendants ends with *Abraham* (cp. Gen 11:10-26).

1:24 *Arphaxad, Shelah:* Some Greek manuscripts read *Arphaxad, Cainan, Shelah.* See notes on Gen 10:24; 11:12-13.

1:28-33 Using the same pattern as the author of Genesis, the Chronicler traces separately the descendants of Abraham

1:29-31 // Gen 25:12-16
1:32-33 // Gen 25:1-4
1:34 Gen 25:25-26; 32:28 Matt 1:2
1:35 Gen 36:4, 19
1:35-37 // Gen 36:10-14
1:38-42 // Gen 36:20-28
1:43-54 // Gen 36:31-43
1:45 Job 2:11

Descendants of Abraham

[28]The sons of Abraham were Isaac and Ishmael. [29]These are their genealogical records:

The sons of Ishmael were Nebaioth (the oldest), Kedar, Adbeel, Mibsam, [30]Mishma, Dumah, Massa, Hadad, Tema, [31]Jetur, Naphish, and Kedemah. These were the sons of Ishmael.

[32]The sons of Keturah, Abraham's concubine, were Zimran, Jokshan, Medan, Midian, Ishbak, and Shuah.

The sons of Jokshan were Sheba and Dedan.

[33]The sons of Midian were Ephah, Epher, Hanoch, Abida, and Eldaah.

All these were descendants of Abraham through his concubine Keturah.

Descendants of Isaac

[34]Abraham was the father of Isaac. The sons of Isaac were Esau and Israel.

Ancestry of the Edomites (1:35-54)

Descendants of Esau

[35]The sons of Esau were Eliphaz, Reuel, Jeush, Jalam, and Korah.

[36]The descendants of Eliphaz were Teman, Omar, Zepho, Gatam, Kenaz, and Amalek, who was born to Timna.

[37]The descendants of Reuel were Nahath, Zerah, Shammah, and Mizzah.

Original Peoples of Edom

[38]The descendants of Seir were Lotan, Shobal, Zibeon, Anah, Dishon, Ezer, and Dishan.

[39]The descendants of Lotan were Hori and Hemam. Lotan's sister was named Timna.

[40]The descendants of Shobal were Alvan, Manahath, Ebal, Shepho, and Onam.

The descendants of Zibeon were Aiah and Anah.

[41]The son of Anah was Dishon.

The descendants of Dishon were Hemdan, Eshban, Ithran, and Keran.

[42]The descendants of Ezer were Bilhan, Zaavan, and Akan.

The descendants of Dishan were Uz and Aran.

Rulers of Edom

[43]These are the kings who ruled in the land of Edom before any king ruled over the Israelites:

Bela son of Beor, who ruled from his city of Dinhabah.

[44]When Bela died, Jobab son of Zerah from Bozrah became king in his place.

[45]When Jobab died, Husham from the land of the Temanites became king in his place.

[46]When Husham died, Hadad son of Bedad became king in his place and ruled from the city of Avith. He was the one who destroyed the Midianite army in the land of Moab.

[47]When Hadad died, Samlah from the city of Masrekah became king in his place.

[48]When Samlah died, Shaul from the city of Rehoboth-on-the-River became king in his place.

[49]When Shaul died, Baal-hanan son of Acbor became king in his place.

[50]When Baal-hanan died, Hadad became king in his place and ruled from the city of Pau. His wife was Mehetabel, the daughter of Matred and granddaughter of Me-zahab. [51]Then Hadad died.

The clan leaders of Edom were Timna, Alvah, Jetheth, [52]Oholibamah, Elah, Pinon, [53]Kenaz, Teman, Mibzar, [54]Magdiel, and Iram. These are the clan leaders of Edom.

apart from Isaac, listing ***the sons of Ishmael*** (1:29-31; cp. Gen 25:12-15) and ***the sons of Keturah*** (1:32-33; cp. Gen 25:1-3) before detailing the descendants in the chosen family line.

1:34–2:2 Isaac's genealogy first lists the descendants of ***Esau*** (1:35-54) and continues with ***Israel*** (the name that God gave to Jacob). The history of Edom is given in three components: ***the sons of Esau*** (1:35-37), ***the descendants of Seir*** (1:38-42), and ***the kings who ruled in Edom*** (1:43-54). This arrangement follows Gen 36.

1:36 *Zepho:* As in many Hebrew manuscripts and a few Greek manuscripts (see also Gen 36:11); most Hebrew manuscripts read *Zephi.* • ***Kenaz, and Amalek, who was born to Timna:*** As in some Greek manuscripts (see also Gen 36:12); Hebrew reads *Kenaz, Timna, and Amalek.*

1:39 *and Hemam:* As in parallel text at Gen 36:22; Hebrew reads *and Homam.*

1:40 *Alvan:* As in many Hebrew manuscripts and a few Greek manuscripts (see also Gen 36:23); most Hebrew manuscripts read *Alian.* • ***Shepho:*** As in some Hebrew manuscripts (see also Gen 36:23); most Hebrew manuscripts read *Shephi.*

1:41 *Hemdan:* As in many Hebrew manuscripts and some Greek manuscripts (see also Gen 36:26); most Hebrew manuscripts read *Hamran.*

1:42 *Akan:* As in many Hebrew and Greek manuscripts (see also Gen 36:27); most Hebrew manuscripts read *Jaakan.* • ***Dishan:*** Hebrew *Dishon;* cp. 1:38 and parallel text at Gen 36:28.

1:43 *before any king ruled over the Israelites:* Or *before an Israelite king ruled over them.*

1:50 *Pau:* As in many Hebrew manuscripts, some Greek manuscripts, Syriac version, and Latin Vulgate (see also Gen 36:39); most Hebrew manuscripts read *Pai.*

1:51-54 The Chronicler lists ***the clan leaders of Edom*** as far as his own sources allowed (see Gen 36:40-43).

1:51 *Alvah:* As in parallel text at Gen 36:40; Hebrew reads *Aliah.*

The Sons of Israel (2:1-2)

2 The sons of Israel were Reuben, Simeon,
Levi, Judah, Issachar, Zebulun, 2 Dan,
Joseph, Benjamin, Naphtali, Gad, and
Asher.

The Royal Family of Judah (2:3–4:23)

From Judah to Azariah

3 Judah had three sons from Bathshua, a
Canaanite woman. Their names were
Er, Onan, and Shelah. But the LORD saw
that the oldest son, Er, was a wicked man,
so he killed him. 4 Later Judah had twin
sons from Tamar, his widowed daughter-
in-law. Their names were Perez and
Zerah. So Judah had five sons in all.
5 The sons of Perez were Hezron and
Hamul.
6 The sons of Zerah were Zimri, Ethan,
Heman, Calcol, and Darda—five in all.
7 The son of Carmi (a descendant of Zimri)
was Achan, who brought disaster on
Israel by taking plunder that had been
set apart for the LORD.
8 The son of Ethan was Azariah.

From Hezron to David

9 The sons of Hezron were Jerahmeel, Ram,
and Caleb.
10 Ram was the father of Amminadab.
Amminadab was the father of Nahshon,
a leader of Judah.
11 Nahshon was the father of Salmon.
Salmon was the father of Boaz.
12 Boaz was the father of Obed.
Obed was the father of Jesse.
13 Jesse's first son was Eliab, his second
was Abinadab, his third was Shimea,
14 his fourth was Nethanel, his fifth was
Raddai, 15 his sixth was Ozem, and his
seventh was David.
16 Their sisters were named Zeruiah and
Abigail. Zeruiah had three sons named
Abishai, Joab, and Asahel. 17 Abigail married a man named Jether, an Ishmaelite,
and they had a son named Amasa.

Other Descendants of Hezron

18 Hezron's son Caleb had sons from his
wife Azubah and from Jerioth. Her sons
were named Jesher, Shobab, and Ardon.
19 After Azubah died, Caleb married
Ephrathah, and they had a son named
Hur. 20 Hur was the father of Uri. Uri was
the father of Bezalel.
21 When Hezron was sixty years old, he
married Gilead's sister, the daughter of
Makir. They had a son named Segub.
22 Segub was the father of Jair, who ruled
twenty-three towns in the land of Gilead.
23 (But Geshur and Aram captured the
Towns of Jair and also took Kenath and
its sixty surrounding villages.) All these
were descendants of Makir, the father
of Gilead.
24 Soon after Hezron died in the town of
Caleb-ephrathah, his wife Abijah gave

2:1-2 // Gen 35:23-26; 46:8-25; Exod 1:1-4; Num 1:2-15; Rev 7:4-8
2:3 Gen 38:2-10
2:4 Gen 38:13-30
2:5-15 // Ruth 4:18-22; Matt 1:3-6
2:7 Josh 7:1
2:10 Num 1:7
2:12 Ruth 4:17; Matt 1:5
2:13 1 Sam 16:6
2:16 1 Sam 26:6; 2 Sam 2:18
2:17 2 Sam 17:25

2:1 ***Israel*** is the name that God gave to Jacob.

2:3–4:23 While the genealogies present the entire people of Israel (2:1-2), David's ancestors in the tribe of Judah receive priority.

2:3-8 The genealogy of Judah is as comprehensive as possible, recording peripheral material as the background to the main line of David's ancestors. Cp. Gen 46:12.

2:3 ***Er*** and ***Onan,*** the first two sons of Judah, were destroyed because of their sin (Gen 38:6-10). The descendants of ***Shelah*** are listed as an appendix at the end of the genealogies of Judah (4:21-23).

2:4-5 The main ancestral line of David descends from ***Perez,*** one of the sons of ***Tamar,*** Judah's ***widowed daughter-in-law.*** • ***Hamul,*** one of Perez's sons, is ignored completely; the Chronicler might not have had information about him.

2:6-8 For the genealogy of ***Zerah,*** cp. Josh 7:1, 17; 1 Kgs 4:31 (Mahol might be another name for Zerah).

2:6 ***Darda:*** As in many Hebrew manuscripts, some Greek manuscripts, and Syriac version (see also 1 Kgs 4:31); most Hebrew manuscripts read *Dara.*

2:7 ***Achan:*** Hebrew *Achar;* cp. Josh 7:1. *Achar* means "disaster." • ***set apart for the LORD:*** The Hebrew term used here refers to the complete consecration of things or people to the Lord, either by destroying them or by giving them as an offering (see Lev 27:28-29; 1 Sam 15:3).

2:9-55 The descendants of Hezron are given down to the time of David, in several sections: the direct line from Hezron to David (2:9-17; cp. Ruth 4:18-22), the other descendants of Hezron (2:18-41), then the descendants of Hezron's son Caleb (2:42-55).

2:9 ***Caleb*** (Hebrew *Kelubai,* a variant spelling of *Caleb;* cp. 2:18) was the most notable immediate descendant of ***Hezron,*** so the author covers his descendants in detail (2:42-55). This ***Caleb*** was apparently not the same individual as Caleb son of Jephunneh, a descendant of Kenaz (see note on 4:13-15).

2:10-17 The passage dedicated to the descendants of ***Ram*** provides a direct line of descent from Ram to ***Jesse,*** then records Jesse's children.

2:11 ***Salmon:*** As in Greek version (see also Ruth 4:20); Hebrew reads *Salma.*

2:14-15 The Chronicler lists ***David*** as the ***seventh*** son of Jesse, while Samuel makes him the eighth (1 Sam 16:6-13; 17:12). Samuel does not provide the names of David's fourth, fifth, or sixth brothers (***Nethanel, Raddai,*** and ***Ozem***). Later, the Chronicler lists a brother named Elihu, who might or might not have been an additional son (see note on 27:18). The number seven (the "perfect" number) perhaps symbolizes that David was chosen by God to rule.

2:18 ***Caleb*** (see note on 2:9) ***had sons from his wife Azubah and from Jerioth:*** Or *Caleb had a daughter named Jerioth from his wife, Azubah.* The meaning of the Hebrew is uncertain.

2:19 ***Ephrathah:*** Hebrew *Ephrath,* a variant spelling of *Ephrathah;* cp. 2:50 and 4:4.

2:20 The Lord chose ***Bezalel,*** a craftsman descended from Hezron, to construct the Tabernacle (see Exod 31:1-2).

2:21-23 Some of the families of ***Gilead,*** listed elsewhere as members of the tribe of Manasseh (cp. Num 32:39-42), also had a connection with the tribe of Judah.

2:23 ***captured the Towns of Jair:*** Or *captured Havvoth-jair.*

2:36 1 Chr 11:41
2:45 Josh 15:55
2:50 1 Chr 4:4
2:55 2 Kgs 10:15

birth to a son named Ashhur (the father
of Tekoa).

Descendants of Hezron's Son Jerahmeel

25 The sons of Jerahmeel, the oldest son of
Hezron, were Ram (the firstborn), Bunah,
Oren, Ozem, and Ahijah. 26 Jerahmeel
had a second wife named Atarah. She
was the mother of Onam.
27 The sons of Ram, the oldest son of
Jerahmeel, were Maaz, Jamin, and Eker.
28 The sons of Onam were Shammai and Jada.
The sons of Shammai were Nadab and
Abishur.
29 The sons of Abishur and his wife Abihail
were Ahban and Molid.
30 The sons of Nadab were Seled and
Appaim. Seled died without children,
31 but Appaim had a son named Ishi. The
son of Ishi was Sheshan. Sheshan had a
descendant named Ahlai.
32 The sons of Jada, Shammai's brother,
were Jether and Jonathan. Jether died
without children, 33 but Jonathan had
two sons named Peleth and Zaza.
These were all descendants of Jerahmeel.
34 Sheshan had no sons, though he did
have daughters. He also had an Egyptian
servant named Jarha. 35 Sheshan gave
one of his daughters to be the wife of
Jarha, and they had a son named Attai.
36 Attai was the father of Nathan.
Nathan was the father of Zabad.
37 Zabad was the father of Ephlal.
Ephlal was the father of Obed.
38 Obed was the father of Jehu.
Jehu was the father of Azariah.
39 Azariah was the father of Helez.
Helez was the father of Eleasah.
40 Eleasah was the father of Sismai.
Sismai was the father of Shallum.
41 Shallum was the father of Jekamiah.
Jekamiah was the father of Elishama.

Descendants of Hezron's Son Caleb

42 The descendants of Caleb, the brother
of Jerahmeel, included Mesha (the
firstborn), who became the father of
Ziph. Caleb's descendants also included
the sons of Mareshah, the father of
Hebron.
43 The sons of Hebron were Korah,
Tappuah, Rekem, and Shema. 44 Shema
was the father of Raham. Raham was
the father of Jorkeam. Rekem was
the father of Shammai. 45 The son of
Shammai was Maon. Maon was the
father of Beth-zur.
46 Caleb's concubine Ephah gave birth to
Haran, Moza, and Gazez. Haran was the
father of Gazez.
47 The sons of Jahdai were Regem, Jotham,
Geshan, Pelet, Ephah, and Shaaph.
48 Another of Caleb's concubines, Maacah,
gave birth to Sheber and Tirhanah. 49 She
also gave birth to Shaaph (the father of
Madmannah) and Sheva (the father of
Macbenah and Gibea). Caleb also had a
daughter named Acsah.
50 These were all descendants of Caleb.

Descendants of Caleb's Son Hur

The sons of Hur, the oldest son of Caleb's
wife Ephrathah, were Shobal (the
founder of Kiriath-jearim), 51 Salma (the
founder of Bethlehem), and Hareph (the
founder of Beth-gader).
52 The descendants of Shobal (the founder
of Kiriath-jearim) were Haroeh, half
the Manahathites, 53 and the families of
Kiriath-jearim—the Ithrites, Puthites,
Shumathites, and Mishraites, from
whom came the people of Zorah and
Eshtaol.
54 The descendants of Salma were the
people of Bethlehem, the Netophathites,
Atroth-beth-joab, the other half of the
Manahathites, the Zorites, 55 and the
families of scribes living at Jabez—the
Tirathites, Shimeathites, and Sucathites.
All these were Kenites who descended
from Hammath, the father of the family
of Recab.

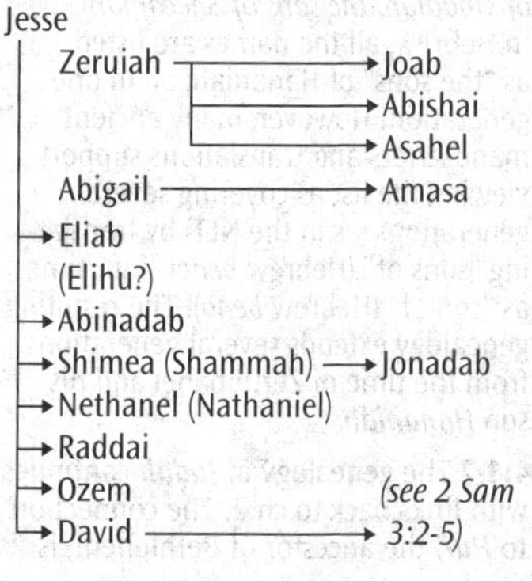

◀ **Jesse's Family** (2:13-17). ZERUIAH and ABIGAIL were apparently David's half-sisters, with a different father (see 2 Sam 17:25). Zeruiah's sons were later a source of consternation for David (see 2 Sam 3:39; 19:22). • ELIAB: See note on 2:14-15; see also 1 Sam 16:6-7; 17:13, 28. • ELIHU might have been another name for Eliab, or he might have been an additional son whose birth-order is unknown (see notes on 2:14-15; 27:18). • SHIMEA: See 2 Sam 13:3, 32; 21:21. • JOAB: See p. 551. • ABISHAI: See p. 547. • ASAHEL: See 11:26; 27:7; 2 Sam 2:18-32; 3:27-30.

2:24 *the father of:* Or *the founder of;* also in 2:42, 45, 49. • *Tekoa* was a small Judean village southeast of Bethlehem (see also 4:5-8).

2:42 *the father of Hebron:* Or *who founded Hebron.* The meaning of the Hebrew is uncertain.

2:55 *the father of the family of Recab:* Or *the founder of Beth-recab.*

Sons of David
1 Chr 3:1-9 // 2 Sam 3:2-5; 5:13-16

3 These are the sons of David who were born in Hebron:

The oldest was Amnon, whose mother was Ahinoam from Jezreel.
The second was Daniel, whose mother was Abigail from Carmel.
2 The third was Absalom, whose mother was Maacah, the daughter of Talmai, king of Geshur.
The fourth was Adonijah, whose mother was Haggith.
3 The fifth was Shephatiah, whose mother was Abital.
The sixth was Ithream, whose mother was Eglah, David's wife.

4 These six sons were born to David in Hebron, where he reigned seven and a half years.

Then David reigned another thirty-three years in Jerusalem. 5 The sons born to David in Jerusalem included Shammua, Shobab, Nathan, and Solomon. Their mother was Bathsheba, the daughter of Ammiel. 6 David also had nine other sons: Ibhar, Elishua, Elpelet, 7 Nogah, Nepheg, Japhia, 8 Elishama, Eliada, and Eliphelet.

9 These were the sons of David, not including his sons born to his concubines. Their sister was named Tamar.

From Solomon to Zedekiah

10 The descendants of Solomon were Rehoboam, Abijah, Asa, Jehoshaphat, 11 Jehoram, Ahaziah, Joash, 12 Amaziah, Uzziah, Jotham, 13 Ahaz, Hezekiah, Manasseh, 14 Amon, and Josiah.
15 The sons of Josiah were Johanan (the oldest), Jehoiakim (the second), Zedekiah (the third), and Jehoahaz (the fourth).
16 The successors of Jehoiakim were his son Jehoiachin and his brother Zedekiah.

Descendants of Jehoiachin

17 The sons of Jehoiachin, who was taken prisoner by the Babylonians, were Shealtiel, 18 Malkiram, Pedaiah, Shenazzar, Jekamiah, Hoshama, and Nedabiah.
19 The sons of Pedaiah were Zerubbabel and Shimei.
The sons of Zerubbabel were Meshullam and Hananiah. (Their sister was Shelomith.) 20 His five other sons were Hashubah, Ohel, Berekiah, Hasadiah, and Jushab-hesed.
21 The sons of Hananiah were Pelatiah and Jeshaiah. Jeshaiah's son was Rephaiah. Rephaiah's son was Arnan. Arnan's son was Obadiah. Obadiah's son was Shecaniah.
22 The descendants of Shecaniah were Shemaiah and his sons, Hattush, Igal, Bariah, Neariah, and Shaphat—six in all.
23 The sons of Neariah were Elioenai, Hizkiah, and Azrikam—three in all.
24 The sons of Elioenai were Hodaviah, Eliashib, Pelaiah, Akkub, Johanan, Delaiah, and Anani—seven in all.

Other Descendants of Judah

4 The descendants of Judah were Perez, Hezron, Carmi, Hur, and Shobal.
2 Shobal's son Reaiah was the father of Jahath. Jahath was the father of Ahumai and Lahad. These were the families of the Zorathites.

3:1-4 // 2 Sam 3:2-5
3:1 1 Sam 25:43
3:2 2 Sam 3:4; 13:20; 14:23
3:4 2 Sam 5:4-5
3:5-8 // 2 Sam 5:14-16 // 1 Chr 14:4-7
3:9 2 Sam 13:1
3:10 1 Kgs 15:1, 8, 24; 2 Chr 13:1; 17:1
3:11 2 Kgs 8:24-25; 11:21; 2 Chr 21:1; 22:11
3:12 2 Kgs 14:1-22; 2 Chr 26:1; 27:1
3:13 2 Kgs 16:1; 18:1; 2 Chr 29:1; 33:1
3:14 2 Kgs 21:19-26
3:15 2 Kgs 23:34
3:22 Ezra 8:2-3
4:1 Num 26:21; 1 Chr 2:3

3:1-24 The genealogy of ***David*** continues the genealogy of Ram (2:10-17), which included David as the seventh son of Jesse (2:15). David's genealogy is divided into three sections: David's sons (3:1-9); the kings of Judah down to ***Jehoiachin*** and ***Zedekiah*** (3:10-16), who were exiled to Babylon; and the descendants of Jehoiachin down to the time of the Chronicler (3:17-23).

3:1-9 The list of David's sons relies on information from Samuel (2 Sam 3:2-5; 5:14-16); the list is divided between ***sons . . . born*** while David ruled ***in Hebron***, and those ***born . . . in Jerusalem***.

3:5 ***Shammua:*** As in Syriac version (see also 14:4; 2 Sam 5:14); Hebrew reads *Shimea*. • ***Bathsheba:*** Hebrew *Bathshua*, a variant spelling of *Bathsheba*.

3:6 ***Elishua:*** As in some Hebrew and Greek manuscripts (see also 14:5-7 and 2 Sam 5:15); most Hebrew manuscripts read *Elishama*. • ***Elpelet:*** Hebrew *Eliphelet;* cp. parallel text at 14:5-7.

3:10-16 The Chronicler lists the kings of Judah in father-to-son progression from Solomon to the Exile.

3:11 ***Jehoram:*** Hebrew *Joram*, a variant spelling of *Jehoram*.

3:12 ***Uzziah:*** Hebrew *Azariah*, a variant spelling of *Uzziah*.

3:15 Only two of the four ***sons of Josiah*** served as kings of Judah. • ***Jehoahaz:*** Hebrew *Shallum*, another name for *Jehoahaz;* cp. note on Jer 22:11.

3:16 ***The successors of Jehoiakim were his son Jehoiachin and his brother Zedekiah:*** Literally *The sons of Jehoiakim were his son Jeconiah* [a variant spelling of *Jehoiachin*] *and his son Zedekiah*. At the very end of the monarchy of Judah, the sequence of kings did not follow the typical pattern of the eldest son succeeding his father.

3:17-23 This portion of the list of David's descendants extends to around 400 BC.

3:17 ***Jehoiachin:*** Hebrew *Jeconiah*, a variant spelling of *Jehoiachin*.

3:21 ***The sons of Hananiah . . . Shecaniah*** (literally *The son of Hananiah [was] Pelatiah and Jeshaiah, the sons of Rephaiah, the sons of Arnan, the sons of Obadiah, the sons of Shecaniah*): In Hebrew, all the names are listed as "the sons" of Hananiah, all in one generation. However, many ancient manuscripts and translations support viewing the list as covering several generations (as in the NLT) by translating "sons of" (Hebrew *beney*, four times) as "son of" (Hebrew *beno*). The resulting genealogy extends several generations from the time of Zerubbabel and his son ***Hananiah***.

4:1-7 The genealogy of ***Judah*** continues, with links back to ch 2. The connection to ***Hur***, the ancestor of Bethlehem, is

4:13
Josh 15:17

3 The descendants of Etam were
Jezreel, Ishma, Idbash, their sister
Hazzelelponi, 4 Penuel (the father of
Gedor), and Ezer (the father of Hushah).
These were the descendants of Hur (the
firstborn of Ephrathah), the ancestor of
Bethlehem.
5 Ashhur (the father of Tekoa) had two
wives, named Helah and Naarah.
6 Naarah gave birth to Ahuzzam, Hepher,
Temeni, and Haahashtari. 7 Helah gave
birth to Zereth, Izhar, Ethnan, 8 and
Koz, who became the ancestor of Anub,
Zobebah, and all the families of Aharhel
son of Harum.
9 There was a man named Jabez who
was more honorable than any of his
brothers. His mother named him Jabez
because his birth had been so painful.
10 He was the one who prayed to the God
of Israel, "Oh, that you would bless me
and expand my territory! Please be with
me in all that I do, and keep me from all
trouble and pain!" And God granted him
his request.
11 Kelub (the brother of Shuhah) was the
father of Mehir. Mehir was the father of
Eshton. 12 Eshton was the father of Beth-
rapha, Paseah, and Tehinnah. Tehinnah
was the father of Ir-nahash. These were
the descendants of Recah.
13 The sons of Kenaz were Othniel and
Seraiah. Othniel's sons were Hathath
and Meonothai. 14 Meonothai was the
father of Ophrah. Seraiah was the father
of Joab, the founder of the Valley of
Craftsmen, so called because they were
craftsmen.
15 The sons of Caleb son of Jephunneh were
Iru, Elah, and Naam. The son of Elah was
Kenaz.
16 The sons of Jehallelel were Ziph, Ziphah,
Tiria, and Asarel.
17 The sons of Ezrah were Jether, Mered,
Epher, and Jalon. One of Mered's
wives became the mother of Miriam,
Shammai, and Ishbah (the father of
Eshtemoa). 18 He married a woman from
Judah, who became the mother of Jered
(the father of Gedor), Heber (the father
of Soco), and Jekuthiel (the father of
Zanoah). Mered also married Bithia, a
daughter of Pharaoh, and she bore him
children.
19 Hodiah's wife was the sister of Naham.
One of her sons was the father of Keilah
the Garmite, and another was the father
of Eshtemoa the Maacathite.
20 The sons of Shimon were Amnon,
Rinnah, Ben-hanan, and Tilon.
The descendants of Ishi were Zoheth and
Ben-zoheth.

Descendants of Judah's Son Shelah

21 Shelah was one of Judah's sons. The
descendants of Shelah were Er (the
father of Lecah); Laadah (the father
of Mareshah); the families of linen
workers at Beth-ashbea; 22 Jokim;
the men of Cozeba; and Joash and
Saraph, who ruled over Moab and
Jashubi-lehem. These names all come
from ancient records. 23 They were the
pottery makers who lived in Netaim and
Gederah. They lived there and worked
for the king.

provided immediately (4:1-4; see 2:19-20, 51-55).

4:3 ***descendants of:*** As in Greek version; Hebrew reads *father of.* The meaning of the Hebrew is uncertain.

4:4 ***the father of:*** Or *the founder of;* also in 4:5, 12, 14, 17, 18, and perhaps other instances where the text reads *the father of.*

4:7 ***Izhar:*** As in an alternate reading in the Masoretic Text (see also Latin Vulgate); the other alternate and the Greek version read *Zohar.*

4:9-20 The exact genealogies of the remaining descendants of Judah are unknown—the Chronicler apparently had incomplete information.

4:9-10 The section on *Jabez* stands independently, allowing the Chronicler to explain the origin of his name; he is not mentioned previously, although Jabez was listed as the name of a town inhabited by some of the descendants of Hur's son Salma (2:55). ***Jabez*** sounds like a Hebrew word meaning "distress" or "pain." He received his name because he caused his mother pain, a fulfillment of the curse on Eve (Gen 3:16). Although his name was a curse, he was ***more honorable than any of his brothers,*** and his prayer changed the outcome of his life. The prayer is poetic; it consists of a plea for blessing followed by requests for prosperity and protection from harm. His last request might mean "keep me from causing trouble and pain." God listened to his prayer and removed his curse.

4:13-15 The name ***Kenaz*** also appears as a descendant of Esau by Eliphaz (Gen 36:11); his descendants are known as the Kenizzites. The Kenizzites lived in the southern part of the land and had affiliations with Judah and Edom. ***Caleb son of Jephunneh*** was a Kenizzite (Num 32:12; Josh 14:6) and had a brother named Kenaz (Josh 15:17), whose family is listed here.

4:13 ***and Meonathai:*** As in some Greek manuscripts and the Latin Vulgate; Hebrew lacks *and Meonothai.*

4:14 ***Joab, the founder of the Valley of Craftsmen:*** Or *Joab, the father of Ge-harashim.*

4:17 ***One of Mered's wives became:*** Or *Jether's wife became;* Hebrew reads *She became.*

4:18 Through Mered's wife ***Bithia, a daughter of Pharaoh,*** the descendants of Judah included children of Egyptian heritage.

4:21-23 Now that Judah's descendants through his wife Tamar have been recorded (2:4–4:20), ***the descendants of Shelah,*** Judah's third son through Bathshua, are listed (see 2:3; Gen 38:2, 5).

Other Tribes of Israel (4:24–5:26)

Descendants of Simeon

24 The sons of Simeon were Jemuel, Jamin,
Jarib, Zohar, and Shaul.
25 The descendants of Shaul were Shallum,
Mibsam, and Mishma.
26 The descendants of Mishma were
Hammuel, Zaccur, and Shimei.
27 Shimei had sixteen sons and six
daughters, but none of his brothers had
large families. So Simeon's tribe never
grew as large as the tribe of Judah.
28 They lived in Beersheba, Moladah, Hazar-
shual, 29 Bilhah, Ezem, Tolad, 30 Bethuel,
Hormah, Ziklag, 31 Beth-marcaboth,
Hazar-susim, Beth-biri, and Shaaraim.
These towns were under their control
until the time of King David. 32 Their
descendants also lived in Etam, Ain,
Rimmon, Token, and Ashan—five towns
33 and their surrounding villages as far
away as Baalath. This was their territory,
and these names are listed in their
genealogical records.
34 Other descendants of Simeon included
Meshobab, Jamlech, Joshah son of
Amaziah, 35 Joel, Jehu son of Joshibiah,
son of Seraiah, son of Asiel, 36 Elioenai,
Jaakobah, Jeshohaiah, Asaiah, Adiel,
Jesimiel, Benaiah, 37 and Ziza son of
Shiphi, son of Allon, son of Jedaiah, son
of Shimri, son of Shemaiah.

38 These were the names of some of the
leaders of Simeon's wealthy clans. Their
families grew, 39 and they traveled to the
region of Gerar, in the east part of the valley, seeking pastureland for their flocks.
40 They found lush pastures there, and the
land was quiet and peaceful.

Some of Ham's descendants had been
living in that region. 41 But during the reign
of King Hezekiah of Judah, these leaders of
Simeon invaded the region and completely
destroyed the homes of the descendants of
Ham and of the Meunites. No trace of them
remains today. They killed everyone who
lived there and took the land for themselves,
because they wanted its good pastureland
for their flocks. 42 Five hundred of these
invaders from the tribe of Simeon went
to Mount Seir, led by Pelatiah, Neariah, Rephaiah, and Uzziel—all sons of Ishi. 43 They
destroyed the few Amalekites who had survived, and they have lived there ever since.

Descendants of Reuben

5 The oldest son of Israel was Reuben.
But since he dishonored his father by
sleeping with one of his father's concubines, his birthright was given to the sons
of his brother Joseph. For this reason, Reuben is not listed in the genealogical records
as the firstborn son. 2 The descendants of
Judah became the most powerful tribe and
provided a ruler for the nation, but the birthright belonged to Joseph.

3 The sons of Reuben, the oldest son of Israel,
were Hanoch, Pallu, Hezron, and Carmi.
4 The descendants of Joel were Shemaiah,
Gog, Shimei, 5 Micah, Reaiah, Baal, 6 and
Beerah. Beerah was the leader of the
Reubenites when they were taken into
captivity by King Tiglath-pileser of
Assyria.

4:28-33 // Josh 19:2-10
4:40 Judg 18:7-10
4:42 Gen 36:8-9
4:43 1 Sam 15:7-8; 30:16-17
5:1 Gen 29:32; 35:22; 48:15-22; 49:4; 1 Chr 2:1
5:2 Gen 49:8-10; Mic 5:2; Matt 2:6
5:3 Gen 46:9; Exod 6:14; Num 26:5
5:6 2 Kgs 15:19

4:24–8:40 After completing the genealogy of Judah's descendants (2:3–4:23), the Chronicler turns to the records for the rest of the sons of Israel (cp. 2:1-2).

4:24-43 ***Simeon*** was Jacob's second son; his tribe's territory was in the southern part of Judah (Josh 19:1-9).

4:24 ***Jemuel:*** As in Syriac version (see also Gen 46:10; Exod 6:15); Hebrew reads *Nemuel.* • ***Zohar:*** As in parallel texts at Gen 46:10 and Exod 6:15; Hebrew reads *Zerah.*

4:33 ***Baalath:*** As in some Greek manuscripts (see also Josh 19:8); Hebrew reads *Baal.*

4:34-43 The list of men described as ***leaders of Simeon's wealthy clans*** (4:34-38) introduces the description of Simeon's geographic expansion (4:38-43). The tribe's expansion involved thirteen family leaders during the days of Hezekiah (late 700s BC) in the area of Gerar. This might have been part of Hezekiah's military action against Philistine territories (2 Kgs 18:8).

4:39 ***Gerar:*** As in Greek version; Hebrew reads *Gedor.* The actual territory is not certain, since Gedor is a common name; the Greek variant *Gerar* would refer to a city in Philistia, to the west of Judah (Gen 10:19).

4:41 ***completely destroyed:*** The Hebrew term used here refers to the complete consecration of things or people to the Lord, either by destroying them or by giving them as an offering (see Lev 27:28-29; 1 Sam 15:3).

5:1-24 Chapter 5 records the genealogies for ***Reuben*** (5:1-10; cp. Gen 46:9), ***Gad*** (5:11-17), and ***Manasseh*** (5:23-24), the tribes of Israel that settled in Transjordan (the area east of the Jordan River).

5:1-2 Although ***Reuben*** was the ***oldest son of Israel*** (*Israel* is the name God gave to Jacob; see Gen 32:28), he did not receive ***his birthright*** because he had sexual relations with his father's concubine (Gen 35:22). Jacob transferred this right to Joseph when he elevated Ephraim and Manasseh to full membership among the tribes (Gen 48:5). This gave Joseph the double portion that traditionally belonged to the firstborn (Deut 21:15-17). As Jacob foresaw, Judah surpassed his brothers and became the forefather of the ruling tribe (Gen 49:8-10). However, Reuben is still listed first (2:1).

5:2 ***and provided a ruler for the nation:*** Or *and from Judah came a prince.*

5:3 ***The sons of Reuben*** are also listed in Gen 46:9; Exod 6:14; Num 26:5-6.

5:4-8 The exact relationship between ***the descendants of Joel*** and the rest of the tribe of Reuben is unknown.

5:6 ***Tiglath-pileser*** (Hebrew *Tilgath-pilneser,* a variant spelling of *Tiglath-pileser;* also in 5:26) was king of Assyria

5:7-8 Num 32:34; Josh 12:2
5:9 Josh 22:8-9
5:10 1 Chr 5:18-21
5:11 Josh 13:11, 24-28
5:16 1 Chr 27:29
5:17 2 Kgs 14:16, 28; 15:5, 32-33
5:18 Num 1:3
5:19 Gen 25:15; 1 Chr 1:31; 5:10
5:20 2 Chr 14:11-13; Ps 9:10
5:22 Josh 23:10; 2 Kgs 15:29; 17:6; 2 Chr 32:8
5:23 Deut 3:9
5:25 Exod 34:15; 2 Kgs 17:7
5:26 2 Kgs 15:19, 29
6:1 Gen 46:11; Exod 6:16-25

7 Beerah's relatives are listed in their genealogical records by their clans: Jeiel (the leader), Zechariah, 8 and Bela son of Azaz, son of Shema, son of Joel.
The Reubenites lived in the area that stretches from Aroer to Nebo and Baal-meon. 9 And since they had so many livestock in the land of Gilead, they spread east toward the edge of the desert that stretches to the Euphrates River.
10 During the reign of Saul, the Reubenites defeated the Hagrites in battle. Then they moved into the Hagrite settlements all along the eastern edge of Gilead.

Descendants of Gad

11 Next to the Reubenites, the descendants of Gad lived in the land of Bashan as far east as Salecah. 12 Joel was the leader in the land of Bashan, and Shapham was second-in-command, followed by Janai and Shaphat.
13 Their relatives, the leaders of seven other clans, were Michael, Meshullam, Sheba, Jorai, Jacan, Zia, and Eber. 14 These were all descendants of Abihail son of Huri, son of Jaroah, son of Gilead, son of Michael, son of Jeshishai, son of Jahdo, son of Buz. 15 Ahi son of Abdiel, son of Guni, was the leader of their clans.

16 The Gadites lived in the land of Gilead, in Bashan and its villages, and throughout all the pasturelands of Sharon. 17 All of these were listed in the genealogical records during the days of King Jotham of Judah and King Jeroboam of Israel.

The Tribes East of the Jordan

18 There were 44,760 capable warriors in the armies of Reuben, Gad, and the half-tribe of Manasseh. They were all skilled in combat and armed with shields, swords, and bows. 19 They waged war against the Hagrites, the Jeturites, the Naphishites, and the Nodabites. 20 They cried out to God during the battle, and he answered their prayer because they trusted in him. So the Hagrites and all their allies were defeated. 21 The plunder taken from the Hagrites included 50,000 camels, 250,000 sheep and goats, 2,000 donkeys, and 100,000 captives. 22 Many of the Hagrites were killed in the battle because God was fighting against them. The people of Reuben, Gad, and Manasseh lived in their land until they were taken into exile.

23 The half-tribe of Manasseh was very large and spread through the land from Bashan to Baal-hermon, Senir, and Mount Hermon. 24 These were the leaders of their clans: Epher, Ishi, Eliel, Azriel, Jeremiah, Hodaviah, and Jahdiel. These men had a great reputation as mighty warriors and leaders of their clans.

25 But these tribes were unfaithful to the God of their ancestors. They worshiped the gods of the nations that God had destroyed. 26 So the God of Israel caused King Pul of Assyria (also known as Tiglath-pileser) to invade the land and take away the people of Reuben, Gad, and the half-tribe of Manasseh as captives. The Assyrians exiled them to Halah, Habor, Hara, and the Gozan River, where they remain to this day.

The Priestly Line (6:1-81)

The High Priests from Aaron to Exile

6 The sons of Levi were Gershon, Kohath, and Merari.
2 The descendants of Kohath included Amram, Izhar, Hebron, and Uzziel.

(744–727 BC); he attacked the tribes of Transjordan during King Pekah's reign (752–732 BC), taking the people *into captivity* (see 5:25-26; 2 Kgs 15:29).

5:7 *Beerah's:* Literally *His.*

5:10 The tribes of Transjordan, including the *Reubenites,* expanded their settlements to the north and east in conjunction with their war with the *Hagrites* in the days of Saul (see 5:18-22; Ps 83:6). Later, the Hagrites were among David's men (see 11:38; 27:31).

5:18-22 The account of the *war against the Hagrites* develops the elements introduced in 5:10. It was a struggle among shepherds over grazing territory. All three tribes were participants; the Chronicler details their prowess, military qualifications, and numbers. With *God . . . fighting against* the enemy, the victory resulted in enormous spoils and total possession of the territory.

5:24 *Epher:* As in Greek version and Latin Vulgate; Hebrew reads *and Epher.*

5:25-26 The tribes of *Reuben, Gad, and the half-tribe of Manasseh* went into permanent exile because of unfaithfulness (see "Covenant Unfaithfulness" at 10:13-14, p. 701).

6:1-81 By its substantial scope and placement in the center of the genealogical lists, this section gives special significance to the priestly tribe of *Levi.*

6:1-48 This section provides the genealogies of the three most significant groups of the tribe of Levi: the high priests (6:1-15), the three clans of Levites (6:16-30), and the singers (6:31-47). Each genealogy begins with an introduction, followed by the list of names.

6:1-15 Verses 6:1-15 are numbered 5:27-41 in the Hebrew text.

6:1 The three *sons of Levi* are introduced, but their actual genealogies are postponed to follow the list of high priests.

6:2-15 After the Exile, the community of Judea, for whom Chronicles was written, needed to establish unequivocally the legitimate ancestry of the priests. This genealogy of *Kohath* established continuity between the ancestors known from the Pentateuch and the later high priests down to the Exile of Judah in 586 BC; other records connected the priests following the Exile with this line (see Ezra 3:2; 7:1-6; Hag 1:1). Not all who served as high priest were included in this listing.

3The children of Amram were Aaron, Moses, and Miriam.
The sons of Aaron were Nadab, Abihu, Eleazar, and Ithamar.
4 Eleazar was the father of Phinehas.
Phinehas was the father of Abishua.
5 Abishua was the father of Bukki.
Bukki was the father of Uzzi.
6 Uzzi was the father of Zerahiah.
Zerahiah was the father of Meraioth.
7 Meraioth was the father of Amariah.
Amariah was the father of Ahitub.
8 Ahitub was the father of Zadok.
Zadok was the father of Ahimaaz.
9 Ahimaaz was the father of Azariah.
Azariah was the father of Johanan.
10 Johanan was the father of Azariah, the high priest at the Temple built by Solomon in Jerusalem.
11 Azariah was the father of Amariah.
Amariah was the father of Ahitub.
12 Ahitub was the father of Zadok.
Zadok was the father of Shallum.
13 Shallum was the father of Hilkiah.
Hilkiah was the father of Azariah.
14 Azariah was the father of Seraiah.
Seraiah was the father of Jehozadak,
15who went into exile when the LORD sent the people of Judah and Jerusalem into captivity under Nebuchadnezzar.

The Clans of the Levites

16The sons of Levi were Gershon, Kohath, and Merari.
17The descendants of Gershon included Libni and Shimei.
18The descendants of Kohath included Amram, Izhar, Hebron, and Uzziel.
19The descendants of Merari included Mahli and Mushi.

The following were the Levite clans, listed according to their ancestral descent:

20The descendants of Gershon included Libni, Jahath, Zimmah, 21Joah, Iddo, Zerah, and Jeatherai.
22The descendants of Kohath included Amminadab, Korah, Assir, 23Elkanah, Abiasaph, Assir, 24Tahath, Uriel, Uzziah, and Shaul.
25The descendants of Elkanah included Amasai, Ahimoth, 26Elkanah, Zophai, Nahath, 27Eliab, Jeroham, Elkanah, and Samuel.
28The sons of Samuel were Joel (the older) and Abijah (the second).
29The descendants of Merari included Mahli, Libni, Shimei, Uzzah, 30Shimea, Haggiah, and Asaiah.

The Temple Musicians

31David assigned the following men to lead
the music at the house of the LORD after the
Ark was placed there. 32They ministered with
music at the Tabernacle until Solomon built
the Temple of the LORD in Jerusalem. They
carried out their work, following all the regulations
handed down to them. 33These are
the men who served, along with their sons:

Heman the musician was from the clan of Kohath. His genealogy was traced back through Joel, Samuel, 34Elkanah, Jeroham, Eliel, Toah, 35Zuph, Elkanah, Mahath, Amasai, 36Elkanah, Joel, Azariah, Zephaniah, 37Tahath, Assir, Abiasaph, Korah, 38Izhar, Kohath, Levi, and Israel.
39Heman's first assistant was Asaph from the clan of Gershon. Asaph's genealogy was traced back through Berekiah, Shimea, 40Michael, Baaseiah, Malkijah, 41Ethni, Zerah, Adaiah, 42Ethan, Zimmah, Shimei, 43Jahath, Gershon, and Levi.
44Heman's second assistant was Ethan from the clan of Merari. Ethan's genealogy was traced back through Kishi, Abdi, Malluch, 45Hashabiah,

6:3 Lev 10:1
6:8 Ezra 7:2
6:14-15 Neh 12:1; Hag 1:1, 14; Zech 6:11
6:19 1 Chr 23:21
6:27 1 Sam 1:1, 20
6:28 1 Sam 8:2; 1 Chr 6:33
6:31 2 Sam 6:17; 1 Chr 15:16-22, 27; 16:4-6

6:10 Most OT scholars agree that the phrase ***the high priest at the Temple built by Solomon in Jerusalem*** belongs in 6:9 (connected to the first *Azariah*) but that the order was transposed through a scribal error. Making this correction yields 12 generations between Aaron and the building of the Temple, which conforms to the date in 1 Kgs 6:1 (480 years is the equivalent of 12 generations of 40 years each in numerical typology). The correction also results in 12 generations between the building of the Temple under Azariah to the rebuilding of the Temple under Jeshua (Ezra 3:2). • ***the Temple:*** Literally *the house.*

6:16-81 Verses 6:16-81 are numbered 6:1-66 in the Hebrew text.

6:16-30 The second introduction of the Levites (6:16-19a) introduces the heads of all the Levitical families (6:19b-30). The list contains the genealogies of ***Gershon*** (6:20-21), ***Kohath*** (6:22-24), ***and Merari*** (6:29-30).

6:16 ***Gershon:*** Hebrew *Gershom,* a variant spelling of *Gershon* (see 6:1); also in 6:17, 20, 43, 62, 71.

6:23 ***Abiasaph:*** Hebrew *Ebiasaph,* a variant spelling of *Abiasaph* (also in 6:37); compare parallel text at Exod 6:24.

6:27 ***and Samuel:*** As in some Greek manuscripts (see also 6:33-34); Hebrew lacks *and Samuel.* When he served under Eli, Samuel assumed a Levitical function (1 Sam 3:1).

6:28 ***Joel:*** As in some Greek manuscripts and the Syriac version (see also 6:33 and 1 Sam 8:2); Hebrew lacks *Joel.*

6:31-47 This genealogy names the lead singers from ***Kohath*** (6:33), ***Gershon*** (6:39), and ***Merari*** (6:44), the chief Levitical families.

6:32 ***the Tabernacle:*** Literally *the Tabernacle, the Tent of Meeting.*

6:33 ***Heman*** held the lead position among David's singers (see Ps 88:TITLE).

6:38 ***Israel*** is the name that God gave to Jacob (Gen 32:28).

6:39 ***Asaph*** wrote several psalms (Pss 50, 73–83). • Hebrew lacks *from the clan of Gershon;* see 6:43.

6:50 1 Chr 6:4-8
6:54 Josh 21:4, 10
6:55-56 Josh 14:13; 15:13
6:58 Josh 10:3
6:61 Josh 21:5; 1 Chr 6:66-70
6:63 Josh 21:7, 34-40
6:64 Num 35:1-8; Josh 21:3, 41-42; 1 Chr 6:57-60
6:66 Josh 21:20-26

Amaziah, Hilkiah, 46Amzi, Bani, Shemer,
47Mahli, Mushi, Merari, and Levi.

48Their fellow Levites were appointed to various other tasks in the Tabernacle, the house of God.

Aaron's Descendants

49Only Aaron and his descendants served as priests. They presented the offerings on the altar of burnt offering and the altar of incense, and they performed all the other duties related to the Most Holy Place. They made atonement for Israel by doing everything that Moses, the servant of God, had commanded them.

50The descendants of Aaron were Eleazar,
Phinehas, Abishua, 51Bukki, Uzzi,
Zerahiah, 52Meraioth, Amariah, Ahitub,
53Zadok, and Ahimaaz.

Territory for the Levites

54This is a record of the towns and territory assigned by means of sacred lots to the descendants of Aaron, who were from the clan of Kohath. 55This territory included Hebron and its surrounding pasturelands in Judah, 56but the fields and outlying areas belonging to the city were given to Caleb son of Jephunneh. 57So the descendants of Aaron were given the following towns, each with its pasturelands: Hebron (a city of refuge), Libnah, Jattir, Eshtemoa, 58Holon, Debir, 59Ain, Juttah, and Beth-shemesh. 60And from the territory of Benjamin they were given Gibeon, Geba, Alemeth, and Anathoth, each with its pasturelands. So thirteen towns were given to the descendants of Aaron. 61The remaining descendants of Kohath received ten towns from the territory of the half-tribe of Manasseh by means of sacred lots.

62The descendants of Gershon received by sacred lots thirteen towns from the territories of Issachar, Asher, Naphtali, and from the Bashan area of Manasseh, east of the Jordan.

63The descendants of Merari received by sacred lots twelve towns from the territories of Reuben, Gad, and Zebulun.

64So the people of Israel assigned all these towns and pasturelands to the Levites. 65The towns in the territories of Judah, Simeon, and Benjamin, mentioned above, were assigned to them by means of sacred lots.

66The descendants of Kohath were given the following towns from the territory of Ephraim, each with its pasturelands: 67Shechem (a city of refuge in the hill country of Ephraim), Gezer, 68Jokmeam, Beth-horon, 69Aijalon, and Gath-rimmon. 70The remaining descendants of Kohath were assigned the towns of Aner and Bileam from the territory of the half-tribe of Manasseh, each with its pasturelands.

71The descendants of Gershon received the towns of Golan (in Bashan) and Ashtaroth from the territory of the half-tribe of Manasseh, each with its pasturelands. 72From the territory of Issachar, they were given Kedesh, Daberath, 73Ramoth, and Anem, each with its pasturelands. 74From the territory of Asher, they received Mashal, Abdon, 75Hukok, and Rehob, each with its pasturelands. 76From the territory of Naphtali, they were given Kedesh in Galilee, Hammon, and Kiriathaim, each with its pasturelands.

77The remaining descendants of Merari received the towns of Jokneam, Kartah, Rimmon, and Tabor from the territory of Zebulun, each with its pasturelands. 78From the territory of Reuben, east of the Jordan River opposite Jericho, they received Bezer (a desert town), Jahaz, 79Kedemoth, and Mephaath, each with its pasturelands. 80And from the territory of Gad, they received Ramoth in Gilead, Mahanaim, 81Heshbon, and Jazer, each with its pasturelands.

6:49 This explanation of the priests' prerogatives introduces the list that follows.

6:50-53 The list of priests from *Aaron* to *Ahimaaz* provides an introduction to the territorial list (6:54-81). The list runs down to David's time, when Ahimaaz served (2 Sam 15:36; 17:17-29; 18:19-29).

6:54-81 The list of Levitical cities is derived from Josh 21, following a geographical logic, with families grouped in defined geographical districts. To show the unity and completeness of Israel, the territorial list presents the Levites as settled in the land to the same extent as the other tribes.

6:57 *were given the following towns, each with its pasturelands: Hebron (a city of refuge):* As in parallel text at Josh 21:13; Hebrew reads *were given the cities of refuge: Hebron, and the following towns, each with its pasturelands.*

6:58 *Holon:* As in Josh 21:15; Masoretic Text reads *Hilez;* other manuscripts read *Hilen.*

6:59 *Ain:* As in parallel text at Josh 21:16; Hebrew reads *Ashan.* • This sentence is translated as in Syriac version (see also Josh 21:16); Hebrew lacks *Juttah.*

6:60 This sentence follows the parallel text at Josh 21:17; Hebrew lacks ***Gibeon.***

6:66-67 *were given the following towns from the territory of Ephraim, each with its pasturelands: Shechem (a city of refuge in the hill country of Ephraim):* As in parallel text at Josh 21:21. Hebrew text reads *were given the cities of refuge: Shechem in the hill country of Ephraim, and the following towns, each with its pasturelands.*

6:77 ***Jokneam, Kartah:*** As in Greek version (see also Josh 21:34); Hebrew lacks ***Jokneam, Kartah.*** • ***Rimmon:*** As in Greek version (see also Josh 19:13); Hebrew reads *Rimmono.*

6:78 *Jahaz:* Hebrew *Jahzah,* a variant spelling of *Jahaz.*

Other Tribes of Israel (7:1–8:40)

Military Roll of Issachar

7 The four sons of Issachar were Tola, Puah, Jashub, and Shimron.
2The sons of Tola were Uzzi, Rephaiah, Jeriel, Jahmai, Ibsam, and Shemuel. Each of them was the leader of an ancestral clan. At the time of King David, the total number of mighty warriors listed in the records of these clans was 22,600.
3The son of Uzzi was Izrahiah. The sons of Izrahiah were Michael, Obadiah, Joel, and Isshiah. These five became the leaders of clans.
4All of them had many wives and many sons, so the total number of men available for military service among their descendants was 36,000.
5The total number of mighty warriors from all the clans of the tribe of Issachar was 87,000. All of them were listed in their genealogical records.

Military Roll of Benjamin

6Three of Benjamin's sons were Bela, Beker, and Jediael.
7The five sons of Bela were Ezbon, Uzzi, Uzziel, Jerimoth, and Iri. Each of them was the leader of an ancestral clan. The total number of mighty warriors from these clans was 22,034, as listed in their genealogical records.
8The sons of Beker were Zemirah, Joash, Eliezer, Elioenai, Omri, Jeremoth, Abijah,
Anathoth, and Alemeth.
9Each of them was the leader of an ancestral clan. The total number of mighty warriors and leaders from these clans was 20,200, as listed in their genealogical records.
10The son of Jediael was Bilhan. The sons of Bilhan were Jeush, Benjamin, Ehud, Kenaanah, Zethan, Tarshish,
and Ahishahar.
11Each of them was the leader of an ancestral clan. From these clans the total number of mighty warriors ready for war was 17,200.
12The sons of Ir were Shuppim and Huppim. Hushim was the son of Aher.

Descendants of Naphtali

13The sons of Naphtali were Jahzeel, Guni, Jezer, and Shillem. They were all descendants of Jacob's concubine Bilhah.

Descendants of Manasseh

14The descendants of Manasseh through his Aramean concubine included Asriel. She also bore Makir, the father of Gilead.
15Makir found wives for Huppim and Shuppim. Makir had a sister named Maacah. One of his descendants was Zelophehad, who had only daughters.
16Makir's wife, Maacah, gave birth to a son whom she named Peresh. His brother's name was Sheresh. The sons
of Peresh were Ulam and Rakem.
17The son of Ulam was Bedan. All these were considered Gileadites, descendants of Makir son of Manasseh.
18Makir's sister Hammoleketh gave birth to Ishhod, Abiezer, and Mahlah.
19The sons of Shemida were Ahian, Shechem, Likhi, and Aniam.

Descendants of Ephraim

20The descendants of Ephraim were Shuthelah, Bered, Tahath, Eleadah,
Tahath,
21Zabad, Shuthelah, Ezer, and Elead. These two were killed trying to

7:1 Gen 46:13
7:2 2 Sam 24:1-9
7:6 1 Chr 8:1-40
7:13 Gen 30:8
7:14 Gen 50:23; Num 26:29-30
7:20 Num 26:35-36

7:1-40 In this chapter, the genealogies of the remaining tribes of Israel are given. • The sections on the tribes of *Issachar, Benjamin,* and *Asher* might have been derived from a military census; the lists are of nearly equal length, emphasize military terminology, record the father's houses, and provide no information on settlements. • The tribes of Zebulun and Dan are omitted entirely, and *Naphtali* has a very brief record (see notes on 7:12, 13).

7:12 The Hebrew text of this verse appears to have been disrupted (something was apparently lost during scribal copying) because no introduction is given for either *Ir* or *Hushim.* The names *Shuppim and Huppim* have parallels in the tribe of Benjamin (8:8, 11; Gen 46:21; Num 26:39). If the Hebrew text was in fact damaged, *Hushim* might be a descendant of Dan (cp. Gen 46:23; Num 26:42).

7:13 In contrast with other genealogies, this abrupt listing of *the sons of Naphtali* includes only the first generation (cp. Gen 46:24; Num 26:48-50). The manuscript of Chronicles might have suffered damage at an early stage of scribal copying, which could also account for the omission of Dan and Zebulun (see note on 7:1-40). It is also possible that the records for Zebulun, Dan, and Naphtali were lost when Tiglath-pileser attacked and exiled these tribes during Pekah's reign (2 Kgs 15:29); in that case, the Chronicler had no records available to include. • *Jahzeel:* As in parallel text at Gen 46:24; Hebrew reads *Jahziel,* a variant spelling of *Jahzeel.* • *Shillem:* As in some Hebrew and Greek manuscripts (see also Gen 46:24; Num 26:49); most Hebrew manuscripts read *Shallum.*

7:14-19 Several difficulties in these verses might indicate that the Hebrew text was damaged (see notes on 7:12, 13): (1) *Maacah* is listed as the sister of *Makir* as well as his wife (7:15-16). (2) *Huppim and Shuppim* were listed earlier with Benjamin (7:12), not *Manasseh.* (3) Those *considered Gileadites* (7:16-17) are rather ambiguously linked to *Gilead,* whose direct descendants are not listed (cp. Num 26:30-33). (4) *The sons of Shemida* are not connected to the genealogy (7:19); Shemida was one of Gilead's descendants (Num 26:32).

7:15 *Makir found wives for:* Or *Makir took a wife from.* The meaning of the Hebrew is uncertain.

7:20-27 The genealogy of *the descendants of Ephraim* includes a story illustrating the circumstances of the tribe's settlement in Canaan (7:21-24). The genealogy ends with *Joshua* son of *Nun,* who led Israel into the Promised Land.

7:22
[a]*'abal* (0056)
‣ Ezra 10:6

7:24
Josh 16:3, 5

7:25-27
Exod 17:9-14; 24:13

7:29
Josh 17:7-11

7:30
Gen 46:17
Num 26:44-46

8:1
Gen 46:21
1 Chr 7:6-12

8:12
Ezra 2:33
Neh 6:2; 7:37; 11:35

8:13
Josh 10:12; 11:22

steal livestock from the local farmers
near Gath. 22Their father, Ephraim,
[a]mourned for them a long time, and
his relatives came to comfort him.
23Afterward Ephraim slept with his wife,
and she became pregnant and gave birth
to a son. Ephraim named him Beriah
because of the tragedy his family had
suffered. 24He had a daughter named
Sheerah. She built the towns of Lower
and Upper Beth-horon and Uzzen-
sheerah.
25The descendants of Ephraim included
Rephah, Resheph, Telah, Tahan, 26Ladan,
Ammihud, Elishama, 27Nun, and Joshua.

28The descendants of Ephraim lived in
the territory that included Bethel and its
surrounding towns to the south, Naaran to
the east, Gezer and its villages to the west,
and Shechem and its surrounding villages
to the north as far as Ayyah and its towns.
29Along the border of Manasseh were the
towns of Beth-shan, Taanach, Megiddo,
Dor, and their surrounding villages. The
descendants of Joseph son of Israel lived in
these towns.

Descendants of Asher

30The sons of Asher were Imnah, Ishvah,
Ishvi, and Beriah. They had a sister
named Serah.
31The sons of Beriah were Heber and
Malkiel (the father of Birzaith).
32The sons of Heber were Japhlet, Shomer,
and Hotham. They had a sister named
Shua.
33The sons of Japhlet were Pasach, Bimhal,
and Ashvath.
34The sons of Shomer were Ahi, Rohgah,
Hubbah, and Aram.
35The sons of his brother Helem were
Zophah, Imna, Shelesh, and Amal.
36The sons of Zophah were Suah,
Harnepher, Shual, Beri, Imrah, 37Bezer,
Hod, Shamma, Shilshah, Ithran, and
Beera.
38The sons of Jether were Jephunneh,
Pispah, and Ara.
39The sons of Ulla were Arah, Hanniel, and
Rizia.
40Each of these descendants of Asher was
the head of an ancestral clan. They were
all select men—mighty warriors and outstanding leaders. The total number of men
available for military service was 26,000, as
listed in their genealogical records.

Descendants of Benjamin

8 Benjamin's first son was Bela, the
second was Ashbel, the third was
Aharah, 2the fourth was Nohah, and
the fifth was Rapha.
3The sons of Bela were Addar, Gera,
Abihud, 4Abishua, Naaman, Ahoah,
5Gera, Shephuphan, and Huram.
6The sons of Ehud, leaders of the clans
living at Geba, were exiled to Manahath.
7Ehud's sons were Naaman, Ahijah, and
Gera. Gera, who led them into exile, was
the father of Uzza and Ahihud.
8After Shaharaim divorced his wives
Hushim and Baara, he had children in
the land of Moab. 9His wife Hodesh gave
birth to Jobab, Zibia, Mesha, Malcam,
10Jeuz, Sakia, and Mirmah. These sons all
became the leaders of clans.
11Shaharaim's wife Hushim had already
given birth to Abitub and Elpaal. 12The
sons of Elpaal were Eber, Misham,
Shemed (who built the towns of Ono and
Lod and their nearby villages), 13Beriah,
and Shema. They were the leaders of the
clans living in Aijalon, and they drove
out the inhabitants of Gath.
14Ahio, Shashak, Jeremoth, 15Zebadiah,
Arad, Eder, 16Michael, Ishpah, and Joha
were the sons of Beriah.
17Zebadiah, Meshullam, Hizki, Heber,

7:22 The *father* of Ezer and Elead is recorded as *Ephraim*, but Ephraim the son of Joseph could not have settled in Canaan after the Exodus. The traditional solution was to imagine an early exodus for the family of Ephraim. Other possibilities are that the name *Ephraim* is a scribal mistake or that *Ephraim* referred to the tribe rather than the son of Joseph who bore the name.

7:23 ***Beriah*** sounds like a Hebrew term meaning "tragedy" or "misfortune."

7:29 ***Beth-shan:*** Hebrew *Beth-shean*, a variant spelling of *Beth-shan*. • ***Israel*** is the name that God gave to Jacob.

7:34 ***The sons of Shomer were Ahi:*** Or *The sons of Shomer, his brother, were*. The meaning of the Hebrew is uncertain.

7:35 ***Helem:*** Possibly another name for *Hotham;* cp. 7:32.

7:37 ***Ithran:*** Possibly another name for *Jether;* cp. 7:38.

8:1-40 The genealogy of ***Benjamin's*** descendants brings the genealogies to a close. The record began with Judah, the tribe of David; it ends with Benjamin, the tribe of Saul.

8:3 ***Gera, Abihud:*** Possibly *Gera the father of Ehud;* cp. 8:6. If so, the second Gera was the first Gera's son. As translated, Bela had two sons named *Gera* (8:3, 5), an unusual situation.

8:6-28 This list reports the militia from the clans of *Ehud* (8:6-7) and *Shaharaim* (8:8-28), who lived in the vicinity of Jerusalem.

8:7 ***Gera, who led them into exile, was the father of Uzza and Ahihud:*** Or *Gera, that is Heglam, was the father of Uzza and Ahihud*. The meaning of the Hebrew is uncertain. This *exile* is unknown; it might have been a voluntary emigration from the territory of Benjamin, perhaps during the period of the judges.

18Ishmerai, Izliah, and Jobab were the
sons of Elpaal.
19Jakim, Zicri, Zabdi, 20Elienai, Zillethai,
Eliel, 21Adaiah, Beraiah, and Shimrath
were the sons of Shimei.
22Ishpan, Eber, Eliel, 23Abdon, Zicri,
Hanan, 24Hananiah, Elam, Anthothijah,
25Iphdeiah, and Penuel were the sons of
Shashak.
26Shamsherai, Shehariah, Athaliah,
27Jaareshiah, Elijah, and Zicri were the
sons of Jeroham.
28These were the leaders of the ancestral
clans; they were listed in their genealogical
records, and they all lived in Jerusalem.
29Jeiel (the father of Gibeon) lived in the
town of Gibeon. His wife's name was
Maacah, 30and his oldest son was named
Abdon. Jeiel's other sons were Zur,
Kish, Baal, Ner, Nadab, 31Gedor, Ahio,
Zechariah, 32and Mikloth, who was the
father of Shimeam. All these families
lived near each other in Jerusalem.

The Family of Saul

33 Ner was the father of Kish.
Kish was the father of Saul.
Saul was the father of Jonathan,
Malkishua, Abinadab, and Esh-baal.
34 Jonathan was the father of Merib-baal.
Merib-baal was the father of Micah.
35 Micah was the father of Pithon, Melech,
Tahrea, and Ahaz.
36 Ahaz was the father of Jadah.
Jadah was the father of Alemeth,
Azmaveth, and Zimri.
Zimri was the father of Moza.
37 Moza was the father of Binea.
Binea was the father of Rephaiah.
Rephaiah was the father of Eleasah.
Eleasah was the father of Azel.
38Azel had six sons: Azrikam, Bokeru,
Ishmael, Sheariah, Obadiah, and Hanan.
These were the sons of Azel.
39Azel's brother Eshek had three sons: the
first was Ulam, the second was Jeush,
and the third was Eliphelet. 40Ulam's
sons were all mighty warriors and
expert archers. They had many sons and
grandsons—150 in all.

All these were descendants of Benjamin.

Israel's Return to Its Inheritance (9:1-34)

Official Records of Israel

9 So all Israel was listed in the genealogical records in *The Book of the Kings of
Israel.*

The Exiles Return to Jerusalem

The people of Judah were exiled to Babylon
because they were unfaithful to the LORD.
2The first of the exiles to return to their
property in their former towns were priests,
Levites, Temple servants, and other Israelites. 3Some of the people from the tribes of
Judah, Benjamin, Ephraim, and Manasseh
came and settled in Jerusalem.

4One family that returned was that of
Uthai son of Ammihud, son of Omri,
son of Imri, son of Bani, a descendant of
Perez son of Judah.
5Others returned from the Shilonite clan,

8:29 Josh 9:3
8:33 1 Sam 9:1; 14:49-50; 1 Chr 9:39-44
8:34 2 Sam 4:4
9:1 1 Chr 5:25
9:2 Ezra 2:43, 58, 70; 8:20; Neh 11:3-22
9:4 Gen 46:12

8:29-32 This list gives the militia that resided at ***Gibeon***, although some of them had moved to ***Jerusalem***.

8:29 ***Jeiel:*** As in some Greek manuscripts (see also 9:35); Hebrew lacks *Jeiel.* • ***the father of:*** Or *the founder of.*

8:30 ***Ner:*** As in some Greek manuscripts (see also 9:36); Hebrew lacks *Ner.*

8:31 ***Zechariah:*** As in parallel text at 9:37; Hebrew reads *Zeker,* a variant spelling of *Zechariah.*

8:32 ***Shimeam:*** As in parallel text at 9:38; Hebrew reads *Shimeah,* a variant spelling of Shimeam.

8:33-40 The Chronicler concludes his record of Benjamin's history with the genealogy of ***Saul***, beginning two generations before Saul and extending through ***Merib-baal*** (=Mephibosheth; see note on 2 Sam 4:4) and down to the families of ***Azel*** and ***Eshek*** (8:38-40). ***Micah*** (8:35) lived in the time of Solomon, and ***Ulam*** (8:39) lived near the end of the kingdom of Judah before the destruction of Jerusalem. Thus, Saul is connected with his larger tribal history and with a noble heritage that carried on throughout the kingdom period.

8:35 ***Tahrea:*** As in parallel text at 9:41; Hebrew reads *Tarea,* a variant spelling of *Tahrea.*

8:36 ***Jadah:*** As in parallel text at 9:42; Hebrew reads *Jehoaddah,* a variant spelling of *Jadah.*

8:37 ***Rephaiah:*** As in parallel text at 9:43; Hebrew reads *Raphah,* a variant spelling of *Rephaiah.*

9:1-34 The Chronicler shows how people and institutions who returned from the Exile had continuity with the past. The Levites and the priests are prominent in this summary of Israel, expressing the Chronicler's view that they were central to the organization of the nation. They were crucial to Israel's function and success as a nation where God was the King. The Chronicler drew upon the records of ancient times as far back as Moses and David (9:19-22) to describe each group's homeland and rank.

9:1 The statement that ***all Israel was listed in the genealogical records*** reveals the crux of the Chronicler's thought, that *all Israel* was represented by the community of Judea in the time of the Chronicler, which had continuity with Israel's past. • ***The Book of the Kings of Israel*** is a source document that the authors of both Kings and Chronicles used but has now been lost (see also note on 1 Kgs 14:19-20). • ***The people of Judah were exiled*** for unfaithfulness, as the other tribes had been (5:25-26; 6:15; see 2 Chr 36:20-21).

9:3-9 ***settled in Jerusalem:*** Jerusalem had always been at the center of all Israel, and people from all the tribes lived there, both before and after the Exile. This statement affirms the inclusion of some members of the northern tribes among those who returned from exile.

9:9
Neh 11:8
9:10
Neh 11:10-14
9:14
Neh 11:15-19
9:17
Ezek 46:1-2
9:20
Num 25:7-13
9:21
1 Chr 26:2, 14
9:25
2 Kgs 11:5, 7
2 Chr 23:8
9:27
1 Chr 23:30-32
9:29
1 Chr 23:29
9:30
Exod 30:23-25
9:32
Lev 24:5-8
9:33
1 Chr 6:31-47; 25:1-31
Ps 134:1

including Asaiah (the oldest) and his
sons.
[6]From the Zerahite clan, Jeuel returned
with his relatives.
In all, 690 families from the tribe of Judah
returned.

[7]From the tribe of Benjamin came Sallu
son of Meshullam, son of Hodaviah, son
of Hassenuah; [8]Ibneiah son of Jeroham;
Elah son of Uzzi, son of Micri; and
Meshullam son of Shephatiah, son of
Reuel, son of Ibnijah.
[9]These men were all leaders of clans, and
they were listed in their genealogical records. In all, 956 families from the tribe of
Benjamin returned.

The Returning Priests

[10]Among the priests who returned were
Jedaiah, Jehoiarib, Jakin, [11]Azariah son
of Hilkiah, son of Meshullam, son of
Zadok, son of Meraioth, son of Ahitub.
Azariah was the chief officer of the
house of God.
[12]Other returning priests were Adaiah
son of Jeroham, son of Pashhur, son of
Malkijah, and Maasai son of Adiel, son
of Jahzerah, son of Meshullam, son of
Meshillemith, son of Immer.
[13]In all, 1,760 priests returned. They were
heads of clans and very able men. They were
responsible for ministering at the house of
God.

The Returning Levites

[14]The Levites who returned were Shemaiah
son of Hasshub, son of Azrikam, son
of Hashabiah, a descendant of Merari;
[15]Bakbakkar; Heresh; Galal; Mattaniah
son of Mica, son of Zicri, son of Asaph;
[16]Obadiah son of Shemaiah, son of Galal,
son of Jeduthun; and Berekiah son of
Asa, son of Elkanah, who lived in the
area of Netophah.
[17]The gatekeepers who returned were
Shallum, Akkub, Talmon, Ahiman, and
their relatives. Shallum was the chief
gatekeeper. [18]Prior to this time, they
were responsible for the King's Gate
on the east side. These men served
as gatekeepers for the camps of the
Levites. [19]Shallum was the son of Kore,
a descendant of Abiasaph, from the
clan of Korah. He and his relatives,
the Korahites, were responsible for
guarding the entrance to the sanctuary,
just as their ancestors had guarded the
Tabernacle in the camp of the LORD.
[20]Phinehas son of Eleazar had been
in charge of the gatekeepers in earlier
times, and the LORD had been with him.
[21]And later Zechariah son of Meshelemiah was responsible for guarding the
entrance to the Tabernacle.

[22]In all, there were 212 gatekeepers in
those days, and they were listed according to
the genealogies in their villages. David and
Samuel the seer had appointed their ancestors because they were reliable men. [23]These
gatekeepers and their descendants, by their
divisions, were responsible for guarding
the entrance to the house of the LORD when
that house was a tent. [24]The gatekeepers
were stationed on all four sides—east, west,
north, and south. [25]Their relatives in the villages came regularly to share their duties for
seven-day periods.

[26]The four chief gatekeepers, all Levites,
were trusted officials, for they were responsible for the rooms and treasuries at the
house of God. [27]They would spend the night
around the house of God, since it was their
duty to guard it and to open the gates every
morning.

[28]Some of the gatekeepers were assigned
to care for the various articles used in worship. They checked them in and out to
avoid any loss. [29]Others were responsible
for the furnishings, the items in the sanctuary, and the supplies, such as choice flour,
wine, olive oil, frankincense, and spices.
[30]But it was the priests who blended the
spices. [31]Mattithiah, a Levite and the oldest
son of Shallum the Korahite, was entrusted
with baking the bread used in the offerings.
[32]And some members of the clan of Kohath
were in charge of preparing the bread to be
set on the table each Sabbath day.

[33]The musicians, all prominent Levites,
lived at the Temple. They were exempt from
other responsibilities since they were on
duty at all hours. [34]All these men lived in
Jerusalem. They were the heads of Levite

9:19 ***Abiasaph:*** Hebrew *Ebiasaph,* a variant spelling of *Abiasaph;* cp. Exod 6:24.

9:21 ***Tabernacle:*** Literally *Tent of Meeting;* see notes on Exod 27:21; 40:2.

9:28-32 ***various articles used in worship:*** See Exod 25:8–30:38.

9:30 The ***priests . . . blended the spices*** for use in the Tabernacle and Temple, and that blend could not be used for secular purposes (Exod 30:34-38).

9:32 ***bread to be set on the table each Sabbath day:*** See Exod 25:23-30.

9:34 The reference to ***Jerusalem*** draws readers back to the beginning (9:3) and defines all Israel in terms of its representatives living in that city. • In detailing the responsibilities of the priests and Levites, the Chronicler's primary focus was ***the heads of Levite families*** (9:10-33).

families and were listed as prominent leaders in their genealogical records.

2. FOUNDING OF THE KINGDOM (9:35–20:8)

Removal of Saul as King (9:35–10:14)

King Saul's Family Tree

35 Jeiel (the father of Gibeon) lived in the
town of Gibeon. His wife's name was
Maacah, 36 and his oldest son was named
Abdon. Jeiel's other sons were Zur,
Kish, Baal, Ner, Nadab, 37 Gedor, Ahio,
Zechariah, and Mikloth. 38 Mikloth was
the father of Shimeam. All these families
lived near each other in Jerusalem.

39 Ner was the father of Kish.
Kish was the father of Saul.
Saul was the father of Jonathan,
Malkishua, Abinadab, and Esh-baal.

40 Jonathan was the father of Merib-baal.
Merib-baal was the father of Micah.

41 The sons of Micah were Pithon, Melech,
Tahrea, and Ahaz.

42 Ahaz was the father of Jadah.
Jadah was the father of Alemeth,
Azmaveth, and Zimri.
Zimri was the father of Moza.

43 Moza was the father of Binea.
Binea's son was Rephaiah.
Rephaiah's son was Eleasah.
Eleasah's son was Azel.

44 Azel had six sons, whose names were
Azrikam, Bokeru, Ishmael, Sheariah,
Obadiah, and Hanan. These were the
sons of Azel.

The Death of King Saul

1 Chr 10:1-14 // 1 Sam 31:1-13

10 Now the Philistines attacked Israel,
and the men of Israel fled before
them. Many were slaughtered on the slopes
of Mount Gilboa. 2 The Philistines closed in
on Saul and his sons, and they killed three
of his sons—Jonathan, Abinadab, and Malkishua. 3 The fighting grew very fierce around
Saul, and the Philistine archers caught up
with him and wounded him.

4 Saul groaned to his armor bearer, "Take
your sword and kill me before these pagan
Philistines come to taunt and torture me."
But his armor bearer was afraid and
would not do it. So Saul took his own sword
and fell on it. 5 When his armor bearer realized that Saul was dead, he fell on his own
sword and died. 6 So Saul and his three sons
died there together, bringing his dynasty to
an end.

7 When all the Israelites in the Jezreel
Valley saw that their army had fled and
that Saul and his sons were dead, they
abandoned their towns and fled. So the Philistines moved in and occupied their towns.

8 The next day, when the Philistines went
out to strip the dead, they found the bodies
of Saul and his sons on Mount Gilboa. 9 So
they stripped off Saul's armor and cut off
his head. Then they proclaimed the good
news of Saul's death before their idols and
to the people throughout the land of Philistia. 10 They placed his armor in the temple of
their gods, and they fastened his head to the
temple of Dagon.

11 But when everyone in Jabesh-gilead
heard about everything the Philistines had
done to Saul, 12 all their mighty warriors
brought the bodies of Saul and his sons
back to Jabesh. Then they buried their
bones beneath the great tree at Jabesh, and
they fasted for seven days.

13 So Saul died because he was unfaithful
to the LORD. He failed to obey the LORD's
command, and he even consulted a medium
14 instead of asking the LORD for guidance.
So the LORD killed him and turned the kingdom over to David son of Jesse.

David Confirmed as King (11:1–12:40)

David Becomes King of All Israel

1 Chr 11:1-3 // 2 Sam 5:1-5

11 Then all Israel gathered before David at Hebron and told him, "We are
your own flesh and blood. 2 In the past, even
when Saul was king, you were the one who
really led the forces of Israel. And the LORD

9:35 1 Chr 8:29-32
9:39 1 Chr 8:33-38
9:41 1 Chr 8:35-37
10:1 1 Sam 31:1-13
10:2 1 Sam 31:2, 4
10:9 1 Sam 31:9
10:13 Lev 19:31; 1 Sam 13:13-14; 15:23; 28:7
10:14 1 Sam 15:28; 1 Chr 12:23
11:1-3 // 2 Sam 5:1-3
11:2 2 Sam 5:2; 7:7

9:35-44 The place of Saul's family in the kingdom has already been established (8:29-40); the repetition of that material provides a transition from the genealogies to the narratives, beginning with the story of Saul's death (ch 10).

9:35 *the father of:* Or *the founder of.*

9:41 This sentence follows the Syriac version and Latin Vulgate (see also 8:35); Hebrew lacks ***and Ahaz.***

9:42 ***Jadah:*** As in some Hebrew manuscripts and Greek version (see also 8:36); most Hebrew manuscripts read *Jarah.*

10:1-14 The narrative of Israel as a kingdom begins with the death of Saul, who failed to fulfill God's purposes for him as king and for Israel as a nation. Saul's death prepares the way for David, whom the Chronicler regarded as the first true king of Israel.

10:6-12 ***Saul and his three sons died . . . bringing his dynasty to an end:*** The Chronicler does not mention Saul's armor bearer or the rest of his troops (see 1 Sam 31:6), emphasizing God's action in removing Saul and replacing him with David (10:14).

11:1-3 ***David*** first became king of Judah ***at Hebron*** and ruled there 7½ years (3:4; 2 Sam 5:5). The Chronicler omits the account of that period (see 2 Sam 2–4) and focuses on David's reign over the entire nation for 33½ years, beginning with his ***covenant . . . with all the elders of Israel*** at Hebron (see 2 Sam 5:1-5).

11:2 ***In the past:*** Or *For some time.*

[b]*ra'ah* (7462)
‣ Ps 23:1
11:3
1 Sam 16:1-13
11:4-9
// 2 Sam 5:6-10
11:4
Josh 15:8, 63
Judg 1:21
11:6
2 Sam 8:16
11:9
2 Sam 3:1
11:10
2 Sam 23:8-39
1 Chr 11:3
11:11
2 Sam 23:8

your God told you, 'You will be the [b]shep-
herd of my people Israel. You will be the
leader of my people Israel.' "
3So there at Hebron, David made a covenant before the LORD with all the elders
of Israel. And they anointed him king of Israel, just as the LORD had promised through
Samuel.

David Captures Jerusalem
1 Chr 11:4-9 // 2 Sam 5:6-10

4Then David and all Israel went to Jerusalem (or Jebus, as it used to be called), where
the Jebusites, the original inhabitants of
the land, were living. 5The people of Jebus
taunted David, saying, "You'll never get in
here!" But David captured the fortress of
Zion, which is now called the City of David.
6David had said to his troops, "Whoever
is first to attack the Jebusites will become
the commander of my armies!" And Joab,
the son of David's sister Zeruiah, was first
to attack, so he became the commander of
David's armies.
7David made the fortress his home, and
that is why it is called the City of David. 8He
extended the city from the supporting terraces to the surrounding area, while Joab
rebuilt the rest of Jerusalem. 9And David became more and more powerful, because the
LORD of Heaven's Armies was with him.

The Three: David's Elite Commanders
1 Chr 11:10-19 // 2 Sam 23:8-17

10These are the leaders of David's mighty
warriors. Together with all Israel, they decided to make David their king, just as the
LORD had promised concerning Israel.
11Here is the record of David's mightiest warriors: The first was Jashobeam the

Covenant Unfaithfulness (10:13-14)

1 Chr 5:25-26
Deut 32:48-51
Josh 7:1-26; 22:20
2 Kgs 23:26; 24:3-4
2 Chr 7:14; 12:1-2, 6-7; 26:16-18; 28:16-25; 29:6-9; 33:1-9, 12-19; 36:14-17
Ezra 9:1-7
Neh 1:8
Isa 1:10-20
Ezek 14:13-14; 15:8; 39:23
Mic 6:6-16
Matt 7:22-23
Luke 12:42-46
2 Tim 2:11-13

The Chronicler needed to explain the failure of Israel as a kingdom. So after establishing the genealogical framework (chs 1–9) he started and ended his narrative by describing the unfaithfulness of Israel's rulers (10:13-14; 2 Chr 36:14).

The rejection of Saul's dynasty (ch 10) exemplified and set the pattern for the rejection of Judah and the Exile that followed. God rejected Saul because of his disobedience and unfaithfulness (10:13-14). Instead of seeking and consulting the Lord, Saul sought and consulted a medium, an act specifically forbidden in the covenant (Deut 18:11-12). God rejected Saul's family from ruling Israel and brought his dynasty to an end (10:6).

Just as it had been with Saul, so it was with the kingdom of Judah: Unfaithfulness brought judgment. When Rehoboam "abandoned the law of the LORD," his unfaithfulness resulted in the invasion by Pharaoh Shishak of Egypt (2 Chr 12:1-2). When Uzziah attempted to act in the role of a priest (2 Chr 26:16-18), his unfaithfulness resulted in his contracting leprosy. When Ahaz sought the assistance of the Assyrian kings, worshiped the gods of Damascus, and actually closed the Temple (2 Chr 28:16-25), his unfaithfulness "aroused the anger of the LORD" (2 Chr 28:25). When Manasseh rebuilt the pagan shrines and promoted false worship in Judah (2 Chr 33:1-9), his unfaithfulness (2 Chr 33:19) led Judah into the sins that later brought about judgment and exile (see 2 Chr 33:22; 2 Kgs 23:26; 24:3). The Chronicler summarized the final demise of Judah as the unfaithfulness of all of its leaders who followed the practices of pagan nations and polluted the Lord's Temple (2 Chr 36:14).

Unfaithfulness to the Lord violates his covenant and alienates an individual or a nation from the Lord. Unfaithfulness results in idolatry, greed, and injustice. Unfaithfulness brings judgment, just as the prophet Micah warned during the time of Ahaz (see Mic 6:9-16).

Avoiding God's judgment does not involve more sacrifices or religiosity (see Isa 1:10-20). Instead, the solution to unfaithfulness is seeking the Lord, becoming faithful to him, and walking humbly with him (2 Chr 7:14; Mic 6:6-8). The way to restore covenant fellowship with God is to repent and seek him. Both Rehoboam (2 Chr 12:6-7) and Manasseh (2 Chr 33:12-19) followed this path, and both of these kings experienced God's mercy. But other unfaithful kings died in their sins, and the unfaithful nation was destroyed.

11:4-9 David's conquest and rebuilding of ***Jerusalem*** established it as the capital city of his reign over all Israel.

11:8 ***the supporting terraces:*** Hebrew *the millo.* The meaning of the Hebrew is uncertain; see note on 1 Kgs 9:15.

11:10-47 This account of ***David's mighty warriors*** demonstrates that David had the support of Israel's best and bravest men, as well as the support of ***all Israel*** (cp. 2 Sam 23:8-39).

11:10 ***just as the LORD had promised:*** David's kingship was God's choice, not David's or the people's (cp. 11:3; 1 Sam 16:11-14).

11:11 ***leader of the Three—the mightiest warriors among David's men:*** As in some Greek manuscripts (see also 2 Sam 23:8); Hebrew reads *leader of the Thirty,* or *leader of the captains.*

Hacmonite, who was leader of the Three—the mightiest warriors among David's men. He once used his spear to kill 300 enemy warriors in a single battle.

12Next in rank among the Three was Eleazar son of Dodai, a descendant of Ahoah. 13He was with David in the battle against the Philistines at Pas-dammim. The battle took place in a field full of barley, and the Israelite army fled. 14But Eleazar and David held their ground in the middle of the field and beat back the Philistines. So the LORD saved them by giving them a great victory.

15Once when David was at the rock near the cave of Adullam, the Philistine army was camped in the valley of Rephaim. The Three (who were among the Thirty—an elite group among David's fighting men) went down to meet him there. 16David was staying in the stronghold at the time, and a Philistine detachment had occupied the town of Bethlehem.

17David remarked longingly to his men, "Oh, how I would love some of that good water from the well by the gate in Bethlehem." 18So the Three broke through the Philistine lines, drew some water from the well by the gate in Bethlehem, and brought it back to David. But David refused to drink it. Instead, he poured it out as an offering to the LORD. 19"God forbid that I should drink this!" he exclaimed. "This water is as precious as the blood of these men who risked their lives to bring it to me." So David did not drink it. These are examples of the exploits of the Three.

The Thirty: David's Mighty Men
1 Chr 11:20-47 // 2 Sam 23:18-39

20Abishai, the brother of Joab, was the leader of the Thirty. He once used his spear to kill 300 enemy warriors in a single battle. It was by such feats that he became as famous as the Three. 21Abishai was the most famous of the Thirty and was their commander, though he was not one of the Three.

22There was also Benaiah son of Jehoiada, a valiant warrior from Kabzeel. He did many heroic deeds, which included killing two champions of Moab. Another time, on a snowy day, he chased a lion down into a pit and killed it. 23Once, armed only with a club, he killed an Egyptian warrior who was 7½ feet tall and whose spear was as thick as a weaver's beam. Benaiah wrenched the spear from the Egyptian's hand and killed him with it. 24Deeds like these made Benaiah as famous as the three mightiest warriors. 25He was more honored than the other members of the Thirty, though he was not one of the Three. And David made him captain of his bodyguard.

26David's mighty warriors also included:

Asahel, Joab's brother;
Elhanan son of Dodo from Bethlehem;
27 Shammah from Harod;
Helez from Pelon;
28 Ira son of Ikkesh from Tekoa;
Abiezer from Anathoth;
29 Sibbecai from Hushah;
Zalmon from Ahoah;
30 Maharai from Netophah;
Heled son of Baanah from Netophah;
31 Ithai son of Ribai from Gibeah (in the land of Benjamin);
Benaiah from Pirathon;
32 Hurai from near Nahale-gaash;
Abi-albon from Arabah;
33 Azmaveth from Bahurim;
Eliahba from Shaalbon;
34 the sons of Jashen from Gizon;
Jonathan son of Shagee from Harar;
35 Ahiam son of Sharar from Harar;
Eliphal son of Ur;
36 Hepher from Mekerah;
Ahijah from Pelon;
37 Hezro from Carmel;
Paarai son of Ezbai;
38 Joel, the brother of Nathan;
Mibhar son of Hagri;
39 Zelek from Ammon;
Naharai from Beeroth, Joab's armor bearer;
40 Ira from Jattir;
Gareb from Jattir;
41 Uriah the Hittite;

11:12 1 Chr 27:4
11:13 2 Sam 23:11-12
11:15 1 Chr 14:9
11:16 1 Sam 10:5
11:22 2 Sam 8:18
11:23 1 Sam 17:7

11:12 *Dodai:* As in parallel text at 2 Sam 23:9 (see also 1 Chr 27:4); Hebrew reads *Dodo,* a variant spelling of *Dodai.*

11:14 *Eleazar and David:* Literally *they.*

11:19 ***This water is as precious as the blood of these men:*** Literally *Shall I drink the lifeblood of these men?*

11:20 *the Thirty:* As in Syriac version; Hebrew reads *the Three;* also in 11:21.

11:22 *two champions:* Or *two sons of Ariel.*

11:23 ***7½ feet:*** Hebrew *5 cubits* [2.3 meters].

11:27 *Shammah from Harod:* As in parallel text at 2 Sam 23:25; Hebrew reads *Shammoth from Haror.*

11:29 *Zalmon:* As in parallel text at 2 Sam 23:28; Hebrew reads *Ilai.*

11:32 *from near Nahale-gaash:* Or *from the ravines of Gaash.* • *Abi-albon:* As in parallel text at 2 Sam 23:31; Hebrew reads *Abiel.*

11:33 *Bahurim:* As in parallel text at 2 Sam 23:31; Hebrew reads *Baharum.*

11:34 *sons of Jashen:* As in parallel text at 2 Sam 23:32; Hebrew reads *sons of Hashem.*

11:35 *son of Sharar:* As in parallel text at 2 Sam 23:33; Hebrew reads *son of Sacar.*

11:37 *Paarai:* As in parallel text at 2 Sam 23:35; Hebrew reads *Naarai.*

12:1 1 Sam 27:2-6
12:2 Judg 3:15; 20:16
12:8 2 Sam 2:18
12:14 Deut 32:30
12:15 Josh 3:15; 4:18
12:18 Judg 3:10; 6:34; 1 Chr 2:17
12:19 1 Sam 29:2-9

Zabad son of Ahlai;
42 Adina son of Shiza, the Reubenite leader
who had thirty men with him;
43 Hanan son of Maacah;
Joshaphat from Mithna;
44 Uzzia from Ashtaroth;
Shama and Jeiel, the sons of Hotham,
from Aroer;
45 Jediael son of Shimri;
Joha, his brother, from Tiz;
46 Eliel from Mahavah;
Jeribai and Joshaviah, the sons of
Elnaam;
Ithmah from Moab;
47 Eliel and Obed;
Jaasiel from Zobah.

Warriors Join David when a Fugitive

12 The following men joined David
at Ziklag while he was hiding from
Saul son of Kish. They were among the
warriors who fought beside David in battle.
2All of them were expert archers, and they
could shoot arrows or sling stones with
their left hand as well as their right. They
were all relatives of Saul from the tribe of
Benjamin. 3Their leader was Ahiezer son
of Shemaah from Gibeah; his brother Joash
was second-in-command. These were the
other warriors:

Jeziel and Pelet, sons of Azmaveth;
Beracah;
Jehu from Anathoth;
4 Ishmaiah from Gibeon, a famous warrior
and leader among the Thirty;
Jeremiah, Jahaziel, Johanan, and Jozabad
from Gederah;
5 Eluzai, Jerimoth, Bealiah, Shemariah, and
Shephatiah from Haruph;
6 Elkanah, Isshiah, Azarel, Joezer, and
Jashobeam, who were Korahites;
7 Joelah and Zebadiah, sons of Jeroham
from Gedor.

8Some brave and experienced warriors
from the tribe of Gad also defected to David
while he was at the stronghold in the wilderness. They were expert with both shield
and spear, as fierce as lions and as swift as
deer on the mountains.

9 Ezer was their leader.
Obadiah was second.
Eliab was third.
10 Mishmannah was fourth.
Jeremiah was fifth.
11 Attai was sixth.
Eliel was seventh.
12 Johanan was eighth.
Elzabad was ninth.
13 Jeremiah was tenth.
Macbannai was eleventh.

14These warriors from Gad were army
commanders. The weakest among them
could take on a hundred regular troops,
and the strongest could take on a thousand! 15These were the men who crossed
the Jordan River during its seasonal flooding at the beginning of the year and drove
out all the people living in the lowlands on
both the east and west banks.

16Others from Benjamin and Judah came
to David at the stronghold. 17David went out
to meet them and said, "If you have come
in peace to help me, we are friends. But if
you have come to betray me to my enemies
when I am innocent, then may the God of
our ancestors see it and punish you."

18Then the Spirit came upon Amasai, the
leader of the Thirty, and he said,

"We are yours, David!
We are on your side, son of Jesse.
Peace and prosperity be with you,
and success to all who help you,
for your God is the one who helps you."

So David let them join him, and he made
them officers over his troops.

19Some men from Manasseh defected
from the Israelite army and joined David
when he set out with the Philistines to fight
against Saul. But as it turned out, the Philistine rulers refused to let David and his men
go with them. After much discussion, they
sent them back, for they said, "It will cost us
our heads if David switches loyalties to Saul
and turns against us."

20Here is a list of the men from Manasseh who defected to David as he was
returning to Ziklag: Adnah, Jozabad, Jediael,
Michael, Jozabad, Elihu, and Zillethai. Each

11:41-47 ***Zabad . . . Jaasiel:*** These warriors, not mentioned in the parallel passage at 2 Sam 23, were from locations east of the Jordan River. David had broad support among all the tribes of Israel as well as among foreigners.

11:47 ***from Zobah:*** Or *the Mezobaite.*

12:1-22 Support for making *David* king did not begin with Saul's demise. When Saul was king and David was a fugitive, *warriors* went to David and eventually became a vast camp of various tribes, representing all of Israel. Even *relatives of Saul* deserted to David and supported him as king (12:2). Of course, David was prudent about such deserters (12:17), making sure they were not traitors who would betray him to Saul. Before David's actual anointing took place at Hebron, the will of the people reflected the will of God that David should become king.

12:4-40 Verses 12:4b-40 are numbered 12:5-41 in the Hebrew text.

commanded 1,000 troops from the tribe of Manasseh. 21They helped David chase down bands of raiders, for they were all brave and able warriors who became commanders in his army. 22Day after day more men joined David until he had a great army, like the army of God.

Warriors Join David in Hebron

23These are the numbers of armed warriors who joined David at Hebron. They were all eager to see David become king instead of Saul, just as the LORD had promised.

24From the tribe of Judah, there were 6,800 warriors armed with shields and spears.
25From the tribe of Simeon, there were 7,100 brave warriors.
26From the tribe of Levi, there were 4,600 warriors. 27This included Jehoiada, leader of the family of Aaron, who had 3,700 under his command. 28This also included Zadok, a brave young warrior, with 22 members of his family who were all officers.
29From the tribe of Benjamin, Saul's relatives, there were 3,000 warriors. Most of the men from Benjamin had remained loyal to Saul until this time.
30From the tribe of Ephraim, there were 20,800 brave warriors, each highly respected in his own clan.
31From the half-tribe of Manasseh west of the Jordan, 18,000 men were designated by name to help David become king.
32From the tribe of Issachar, there were 200 leaders of the tribe with their relatives. All these men understood the signs of the times and knew the best course for Israel to take.
33From the tribe of Zebulun, there were 50,000 skilled warriors. They were fully armed and prepared for battle and completely loyal to David.
34From the tribe of Naphtali, there were 1,000 officers and 37,000 warriors armed with shields and spears.
35From the tribe of Dan, there were 28,600 warriors, all prepared for battle.
36From the tribe of Asher, there were 40,000 trained warriors, all prepared for battle.
37From the east side of the Jordan River—where the tribes of Reuben and Gad and the half-tribe of Manasseh lived—there were 120,000 troops armed with every kind of weapon.

38All these men came in battle array to Hebron with the single purpose of making David the king over all Israel. In fact, everyone in Israel agreed that David should be their king. 39They feasted and drank with David for three days, for preparations had been made by their relatives for their arrival. 40And people from as far away as Issachar, Zebulun, and Naphtali brought food on donkeys, camels, mules, and oxen. Vast supplies of flour, fig cakes, clusters of raisins, wine, olive oil, cattle, sheep, and goats were brought to the celebration. There was great joy throughout the land of Israel.

Establishment of Worship in Jerusalem (13:1–17:27)

The Death of Uzzah

1 Chr 13:1-14 // 2 Sam 6:1-11

13 David consulted with all his officials, including the generals and captains of his army. 2Then he addressed the entire assembly of Israel as follows: "If you approve and if it is the will of the LORD our God, let us send messages to all the Israelites throughout the land, including the priests and Levites in their towns and pasturelands. Let us invite them to come and join us. 3It is time to bring back the Ark of our God, for we neglected it during the reign of Saul."

4The whole assembly agreed to this, for the people could see it was the right thing to do. 5So David summoned all Israel, from the Shihor Brook of Egypt in the south all the way to the town of Lebo-hamath in the north, to join in bringing the Ark of God from Kiriath-jearim. 6Then David and all Israel went to Baalah of Judah (also called Kiriath-jearim) to bring back the Ark of God, which bears the name of the LORD who is enthroned between the cherubim. 7They

12:21 1 Sam 30:1
12:22 Josh 5:13-15
12:23 2 Sam 2:3-4; 1 Chr 10:14; 11:10
12:28 1 Chr 6:8
12:29 2 Sam 2:8-9
12:32 Esth 1:13
12:38 2 Sam 5:1-3; 1 Chr 12:33
12:40 1 Sam 25:18
13:1-4 // 2 Sam 6:1-11
13:3 1 Sam 7:1-2
13:5 1 Sam 6:21; 7:1; 2 Sam 6:1; 1 Kgs 8:65; 1 Chr 15:3
13:6 Josh 15:9; 2 Kgs 19:15

12:23-40 The succession of a king was often a contentious matter, particularly when the new king represented a different family lineage. The gathering of all twelve tribes at Hebron, including some of ***Saul's relatives*** (12:29), to confirm David's rule showed that the animosity of the war among different tribes following Saul's death had been overcome (12:23-37). The Chronicler stresses the unity among the tribes with the declaration that they all, without reservation, had ***the single purpose of making David the king over all Israel*** (12:38).

12:23 ***just as the LORD had promised:*** See note on 11:10.

13:1–17:27 These chapters chronicle the transformation of Jerusalem into the political and religious center of Israel, beginning with David's disastrous attempt to transfer ***the Ark of God from Kiriath-jearim*** to Jerusalem (13:1-14; cp. 2 Sam 6:2-11).

13:1 ***the generals and captains of his army:*** Literally *the commanders of thousands and of hundreds.*

13:6 ***the Ark of God, which bears the name:*** Or *the Ark of God, where the Name is proclaimed—the name.*

13:7 1 Sam 7:1
13:8 1 Chr 15:13-16
13:9 2 Sam 6:6
13:10 Lev 10:2; 1 Chr 15:13, 15
13:13 2 Chr 25:24-25
13:14 1 Chr 26:4-5
14:1-7 // 2 Sam 5:11-16 // 1 Chr 3:5-8
14:1 2 Sam 5:11
14:4 1 Chr 3:5-9
14:8-17 // 2 Sam 5:17-25
14:9 1 Chr 11:15; 14:13
14:13 1 Chr 14:9
14:17 Exod 15:14-16; Deut 2:25
15:1 1 Chr 16:1; 17:1-5

placed the Ark of God on a new cart and brought it from Abinadab's house. Uzzah and Ahio were guiding the cart. 8David and all Israel were celebrating before God with all their might, singing songs and playing all kinds of musical instruments—lyres, harps, tambourines, cymbals, and trumpets.

9But when they arrived at the threshing floor of Nacon, the oxen stumbled, and Uzzah reached out his hand to steady the Ark. 10Then the LORD's anger was aroused against Uzzah, and he struck him dead because he had laid his hand on the Ark. So Uzzah died there in the presence of God.

11David was angry because the LORD's anger had burst out against Uzzah. He named that place Perez-uzzah (which means "to burst out against Uzzah"), as it is still called today.

12David was now afraid of God, and he asked, "How can I ever bring the Ark of God back into my care?" 13So David did not move the Ark into the City of David. Instead, he took it to the house of Obed-edom of Gath. 14The Ark of God remained there in Obed-edom's house for three months, and the LORD blessed the household of Obed-edom and everything he owned.

The LORD Blesses David in Jerusalem

1 Chr 14:1-7 // 2 Sam 5:11-16

14 Then King Hiram of Tyre sent messengers to David, along with cedar timber, and stonemasons and carpenters to build him a palace. 2And David realized that the LORD had confirmed him as king over Israel and had greatly blessed his kingdom for the sake of his people Israel.

3Then David married more wives in Jerusalem, and they had more sons and daughters. 4These are the names of David's sons who were born in Jerusalem: Shammua, Shobab, Nathan, Solomon, 5Ibhar, Elishua, Elpelet, 6Nogah, Nepheg, Japhia, 7Elishama, Eliada, and Eliphelet.

David Conquers the Philistines

1 Chr 14:8-17 // 2 Sam 5:17-25

8When the Philistines heard that David had been anointed king over all Israel, they mobilized all their forces to capture him. But David was told they were coming, so he marched out to meet them. 9The Philistines arrived and made a raid in the valley of Rephaim. 10So David asked God, "Should I go out to fight the Philistines? Will you hand them over to me?"

The LORD replied, "Yes, go ahead. I will hand them over to you."

11So David and his troops went up to Baal-perazim and defeated the Philistines there. "God did it!" David exclaimed. "He used me to burst through my enemies like a raging flood!" So they named that place Baal-perazim (which means "the Lord who bursts through"). 12The Philistines had abandoned their gods there, so David gave orders to burn them.

13But after a while the Philistines returned and raided the valley again. 14And once again David asked God what to do. "Do not attack them straight on," God replied. "Instead, circle around behind and attack them near the poplar trees. 15When you hear a sound like marching feet in the tops of the poplar trees, go out and attack! That will be the signal that God is moving ahead of you to strike down the Philistine army." 16So David did what God commanded, and they struck down the Philistine army all the way from Gibeon to Gezer.

17So David's fame spread everywhere, and the LORD caused all the nations to fear David.

Preparations to Move the Ark

15 David now built several buildings for himself in the City of David. He also prepared a place for the Ark of God and

---

13:9-11 With the death of ***Uzzah***, Israel's celebration abruptly turned to sorrow. Touching the Ark resulted in death because its holiness had been violated (see 15:13).

13:9 ***Nacon:*** As in parallel text at 2 Sam 6:6; Hebrew reads *Kidon.*

13:12 David's response to Uzzah's death might have been an expression of his own inadequacy to bring the Ark to Jerusalem.

14:1-7 Even though the Ark was not present in Jerusalem (13:1-14), God blessed David's palace, his children, and his conquest of the Philistines. God's blessing did not depend on the presence of the Ark. These blessings eventually encouraged David to carry out his original plan to bring the Ark into Jerusalem (15:1-29).

14:1-2 Hiram's generosity provided further evidence of God's purpose in making David king.

14:7 ***Eliada:*** Hebrew *Beeliada,* a variant spelling of *Eliada;* cp. 3:8 and parallel text at 2 Sam 5:16.

14:8-17 News of David's rule ***over all Israel*** catalyzed ***the Philistines*** to attack; they could no longer regard him as subordinate to their patronage, as they had when he ruled only Judah. They attacked through the valley southwest of Jerusalem (see Josh 15:8). David inquired of the Lord before battle, a direct contrast to Saul's inquiring of a medium in seeking help against the Philistines (10:13; see 1 Sam 28).

14:12 David's ***orders to burn*** the Philistine idols conformed to God's instructions (Deut 7:5).

14:14 ***poplar:*** Or *aspen,* or *balsam;* also in 14:15. The exact identification of this tree is uncertain.

15:1-29 Again, David set out to bring ***the Ark of God*** to Jerusalem. This time he made thorough preparations to ensure that the transfer would succeed.

set up a special tent for it. 2Then he commanded, "No one except the Levites may
carry the Ark of God. The LORD has chosen
them to carry the Ark of the LORD and to
serve him forever."
3Then David summoned all Israel to
Jerusalem to bring the Ark of the LORD to
the place he had prepared for it. 4This is the
number of the descendants of Aaron (the
priests) and the Levites who were called together:

5From the clan of Kohath, 120, with Uriel
as their leader.
6From the clan of Merari, 220, with Asaiah
as their leader.
7From the clan of Gershon, 130, with Joel
as their leader.
8From the descendants of Elizaphan, 200,
with Shemaiah as their leader.
9From the descendants of Hebron, 80, with
Eliel as their leader.
10From the descendants of Uzziel, 112,
with Amminadab as their leader.

11Then David summoned the priests, Zadok and Abiathar, and these Levite leaders:
Uriel, Asaiah, Joel, Shemaiah, Eliel, and Amminadab. 12He said to them, "You are the
leaders of the Levite families. You must purify yourselves and all your fellow Levites,
so you can bring the Ark of the LORD, the
God of Israel, to the place I have prepared
for it. 13Because you Levites did not carry
the Ark the first time, the anger of the LORD
our God burst out against us. We failed to
ask God how to move it properly." 14So the
priests and the Levites purified themselves
in order to bring the Ark of the LORD, the
God of Israel, to Jerusalem. 15Then the
Levites carried the Ark of God on their
shoulders with its carrying poles, just as the
LORD had instructed Moses.
16David also ordered the Levite leaders
to appoint a choir of Levites who were
singers and musicians to sing joyful songs
to the accompaniment of harps, lyres, and
cymbals. 17So the Levites appointed Heman
son of Joel along with his fellow Levites:
Asaph son of Berekiah, and Ethan son of
Kushaiah from the clan of Merari. 18The following men were chosen as their assistants:
Zechariah, Jaaziel, Shemiramoth, Jehiel,
Unni, Eliab, Benaiah, Maaseiah, Mattithiah,
Eliphelehu, Mikneiah, and the gatekeepers—Obed-edom and Jeiel.
19The musicians Heman, Asaph, and
Ethan were chosen to sound the bronze
cymbals. 20Zechariah, Aziel, Shemiramoth,
Jehiel, Unni, Eliab, Maaseiah, and Benaiah
were chosen to play the harps. 21Mattithiah,
Eliphelehu, Mikneiah, Obed-edom, Jeiel,
and Azaziah were chosen to play the lyres.
22Kenaniah, the head Levite, was chosen as
the choir leader because of his skill.
23Berekiah and Elkanah were chosen to
guard the Ark. 24Shebaniah, Joshaphat, Nethanel, Amasai, Zechariah, Benaiah, and
Eliezer—all of whom were priests—were chosen to blow the trumpets as they marched
in front of the Ark of God. Obed-edom and
Jehiah were chosen to guard the Ark.

Moving the Ark to Jerusalem
1 Chr 15:25–16:6 // 2 Sam 6:12-19

25Then David and the elders of Israel and
the generals of the army went to the house
of Obed-edom to bring the Ark of the
LORD's Covenant up to Jerusalem with a
great celebration. 26And because God was
clearly helping the Levites as they carried
the Ark of the LORD's Covenant, they sacrificed seven bulls and seven rams.
27David was dressed in a robe of fine
linen, as were all the Levites who carried
the Ark, and also the singers, and Kenaniah
the choir leader. David was also wearing a
priestly garment. 28So all Israel brought up
the Ark of the LORD's Covenant with shouts

15:2 Num 4:15; Deut 10:8
15:3 2 Sam 6:12, 17; 1 Kgs 8:1; 1 Chr 13:5; 15:1, 12
15:4 1 Chr 6:16-30; 12:26
15:11 1 Sam 22:20-23; 1 Kgs 2:26, 35; 1 Chr 12:28
15:12 Exod 19:14-15; 2 Chr 35:6
15:13 1 Chr 13:7
15:15 Exod 25:14
15:16 1 Chr 13:8; 25:1
15:17 1 Chr 25:1
15:24 1 Chr 16:6
15:25–16:3 // 2 Sam 6:12-19
15:25 1 Chr 13:13
15:26 Num 23:1-4, 29

15:1-3 The first attempt to bring ***the Ark*** to Jerusalem (13:1-14) failed because of improper procedure (see 15:13). This time, David prepared a place for the Ark in Jerusalem and organized ***Levites . . . to carry the Ark*** because this was their responsibility (Deut 10:8; 18:5). The ***special tent*** that David prepared for the Ark was not the Tabernacle, which was located at Gibeon at the time (see 16:39; 21:29).

15:7 ***Gershon:*** Hebrew *Gershom,* a variant spelling of *Gershon.*

15:13 See 13:1-10.

15:16-18 This is the first of three lists of Levitical musicians (see 15:19-22; 16:4-6). This list gave the names of the three leaders (***Heman, Asaph,*** and ***Ethan;*** see 6:33-47) along with ***their assistants.***

15:18 ***Zechariah, Jaaziel:*** As in several Hebrew manuscripts and Greek version (see also parallel lists in 15:20; 16:5); Masoretic Text reads *Zechariah ben Jaaziel.*

15:19-22 The second list of Levitical musicians focused on their musical specialties rather than their rank.

15:20 ***harps:*** Hebrew adds *according to Alamoth,* which is probably a musical term. The meaning of the Hebrew is uncertain. *Alamoth* is probably a melody, believed to be sung in the soprano range (related to Hebrew *'almah,* "young woman").

15:21 ***lyres:*** Hebrew adds *according to the Sheminith,* which is probably a musical term. The meaning of the Hebrew is uncertain. *Sheminith* might be related to a term meaning "octave," suggesting a lower vocal range.

15:23 ***were chosen to guard:*** Literally *were chosen as gatekeepers for;* also in 15:24.

15:25 ***the generals of the army:*** Literally *the commanders of thousands.*

15:27 ***a priestly garment:*** Literally *a linen ephod.*

16:1
1 Chr 15:1

16:4
1 Chr 15:2

16:8-22
// Ps 105:1-15

16:8
1 Kgs 8:43
2 Kgs 19:19

16:9
ˢ*zamar* (2167)
‣ Ps 21:13

16:11
Ps 24:6

of joy, the blowing of rams' horns and trumpets, the crashing of cymbals, and loud
playing on harps and lyres.
29 But as the Ark of the LORD's Covenant
entered the City of David, Michal, the daughter of Saul, looked down from her window.
When she saw King David skipping about
and laughing with joy, she was filled with
contempt for him.

16 They brought the Ark of God and
placed it inside the special tent David had prepared for it. And they presented
burnt offerings and peace offerings to God.
2 When he had finished his sacrifices, David
blessed the people in the name of the LORD.
3 Then he gave to every man and woman in
all Israel a loaf of bread, a cake of dates, and
a cake of raisins.
4 David appointed the following Levites
to lead the people in worship before the
Ark of the LORD—to invoke his blessings, to
give thanks, and to praise the LORD, the God
of Israel. 5 Asaph, the leader of this group,
sounded the cymbals. Second to him was
Zechariah, followed by Jeiel, Shemiramoth,
Jehiel, Mattithiah, Eliab, Benaiah, Obed-
edom, and Jeiel. They played the harps and
lyres. 6 The priests, Benaiah and Jahaziel,
played the trumpets regularly before the
Ark of God's Covenant.

David's Song of Praise
1 Chr 16:8-22 // Ps 105:1-15
1 Chr 16:23-33 // Ps 96:1-13
1 Chr 16:34-36 // Ps 106:1, 47-48

7 On that day David gave to Asaph and his
fellow Levites this song of thanksgiving to
the LORD:

8 Give thanks to the LORD and proclaim
his greatness.
Let the whole world know what he has
done.
9 Sing to him; yes, ˢsing his praises.
Tell everyone about his wonderful
deeds.
10 Exult in his holy name;
rejoice, you who worship the LORD.
11 Search for the LORD and for his
strength;
continually seek him.

Seeking the Lord (16:11-13)

1 Chr 10:13-14; 13:3; 16:11-13; 22:19; 28:8-10
2 Chr 6:19-40; 7:14
Ps 27:4-8; 105:4-6
Isa 55:6-7
Jer 29:13-14
Matt 6:31-33
Rom 2:7

The disposition of the heart was a key concern to the Chronicler, who used the vocabulary of "seeking" to express heart disposition. Saul lost the kingdom and his life in part because he sought a medium rather than the Lord (10:13-14). David, by contrast, was a man after the Lord's own heart (1 Sam 13:14).

As king, David's first concern was restoring the Ark of the Covenant, which the Israelites had not sought in the days of Saul (13:3). David failed in his first attempt to bring the Ark to Jerusalem because he and the Levites did not seek to carry the Ark properly (15:13). Undeterred, and with proper preparation, David later brought the Ark to Jerusalem, where Israel celebrated in worship and song. David's song of thanksgiving on that occasion demonstrates a right heart toward the Lord (16:7-36; cp. Ps 105).

The sanctuary and worship there provided a crucial component in seeking the Lord. Once the Ark was situated in the tent prepared for it in Jerusalem, David established a new role for Levites as ministers of music (16:4-6). David consistently exhorted the leaders to "seek the LORD" in building the Temple (22:19; cp. 28:8-10). Solomon's first act to consolidate the kingdom was to gather all the leaders together at the altar at Gibeon in order to seek the Lord (2 Chr 1:6). The Lord met Solomon there to grant him both wisdom and wealth like that of no other king. Later, Solomon completed the Temple and dedicated it as a place for seeking the Lord (2 Chr 6).

Isaiah the prophet urged those waiting for the fulfillment of God's promises to seek God: "Seek the LORD while you can find him. Call on him now while he is near" (Isa 55:6). God's covenant and promise are certain (Isa 55:3), and they are reserved for those who seek the Lord and remember his work of saving his people (Ps 105:4-5).

15:29 The *contempt* of *Michal* (cp. 2 Sam 6:16-23) toward David stands in stark contrast to God's blessing on the celebration (15:26); her description as ***the daughter of Saul*** implies that her attitude mirrored her father's disregard for the Lord (see 1 Sam 10:10-12; 13:7-14; 15:10-23; 28:1-25).

16:1-43 The transfer of the Ark (16:1-3) and the conclusion of the event (16:43) are reported exactly as in Samuel (see 2 Sam 6:17-20). However, between these bookends, the Chronicler elaborates on the celebrations that accompanied the event and on the permanent arrangements for worship (16:4-42). David's psalm of celebration is the central focus of the account (see note on 16:7-36).

16:3 *a cake of dates:* Or *a portion of meat.* The meaning of the Hebrew is uncertain.

16:7-36 David's *song of thanksgiving* is a composite of three psalms: 16:8-22 draws from Ps 105:1-15; 16:23-33 draws from Ps 96:1-13; and 16:34-38 draws from Ps 106:1, 47-48. The composer made several adjustments to the

12 Remember the wonders he has
performed,
his miracles, and the rulings he has
given,
13 you children of his servant Israel,
you descendants of Jacob, his chosen
ones.

14 He is the LORD our God.
His justice is seen throughout the
land.
15 Remember his covenant forever—
the commitment he made to a
thousand generations.
16 This is the covenant he made with
Abraham
and the oath he swore to Isaac.
17 He confirmed it to Jacob as a decree,
and to the people of Israel as a
never-ending covenant:
18 "I will give you the land of Canaan
as your special possession."

19 He said this when you were few in
number,
a tiny group of strangers in Canaan.
20 They wandered from nation to nation,
from one kingdom to another.
21 Yet he did not let anyone oppress
them.
He warned kings on their behalf:
22 "Do not touch my chosen people,
and do not hurt my prophets."

23 Let the whole earth sing to the LORD!
Each day proclaim the good news that
he saves.
24 Publish his glorious deeds among the
nations.
Tell everyone about the amazing
things he does.
25 Great is the LORD! He is most worthy of
praise!
He is to be feared above all gods.
26 The gods of other nations are mere
idols,
but the LORD made the heavens!
27 Honor and majesty surround him;
strength and joy fill his dwelling.

28 O nations of the world, recognize the
LORD,
recognize that the LORD is glorious
and strong.
29 Give to the LORD the glory he deserves!
Bring your offering and come into his
presence.
Worship the LORD in all his holy splendor.
30 Let all the earth tremble before him.
The world stands firm and cannot be
shaken.

31 Let the heavens be glad, and the earth
rejoice!
Tell all the nations, "The LORD reigns!"
32 Let the sea and everything in it shout his
praise!
Let the fields and their crops burst
out with joy!
33 Let the trees of the forest rustle with
praise,
for the LORD is coming to judge the
earth.

34 Give thanks to the LORD, for he is good!
His faithful love endures forever.
35 Cry out, "Save us, O God of our salvation!
Gather and rescue us from among the
nations,
so we can thank your holy name
and rejoice and praise you."

36 Praise the LORD, the God of Israel,
who lives from everlasting to
everlasting!

And all the people shouted "[d]Amen!" and
praised the LORD.

Worship at Jerusalem and Gibeon

37 David arranged for Asaph and his fellow
Levites to serve regularly before the Ark of
the LORD's Covenant, doing whatever needed
to be done each day. 38 This group included
Obed-edom (son of Jeduthun), Hosah, and
sixty-eight other Levites as gatekeepers.
39 Meanwhile, David stationed Zadok the
priest and his fellow priests at the Tabernacle of the LORD at the place of worship in
Gibeon, where they continued to minister
before the LORD. 40 They sacrificed the regular burnt offerings to the LORD each
morning and evening on the altar set aside
for that purpose, obeying everything written in the Law of the LORD, as he had
commanded Israel. 41 David also appointed
Heman, Jeduthun, and the others chosen by
name to give thanks to the LORD, for "his

16:12 Ps 78:43; 103:2
16:14 Ps 48:10
16:16 Gen 17:2; 22:16-18; 26:3
16:17 Gen 35:9-12
16:18 Gen 13:14-17
16:19 Gen 34:30; Deut 7:7
16:21 Gen 12:17; 20:3; Exod 7:15-18
16:22 Gen 20:7
16:23-33 // Ps 96:1-13
16:25 Ps 89:7; 144:3-6
16:26 Lev 19:4; Ps 102:25
16:29 Ps 29:2
16:31 Ps 93:1; 96:10; Isa 44:23; 49:13
16:32 Ps 98:7
16:34-36 // Ps 106:1, 47-48
16:34 Ezra 3:11; Ps 106:1; 136:1; Jer 33:11
16:35 Ps 106:47-48
16:36 Deut 27:15; 1 Kgs 8:15, 56; Neh 8:6; Ps 72:18-19
[d] *'amen* (0543) ➤ Neh 5:13
16:37 2 Chr 8:14
16:38 1 Chr 13:13-14; 26:10
16:39 1 Kgs 3:4; 1 Chr 15:11
16:40 Exod 29:38-42; Num 28:1-8
16:41 1 Chr 6:33; 25:1-6; 2 Chr 5:13

sources to fit this occasion. The Temple did not exist when the Ark was brought to Jerusalem, so the Chronicler says that ***strength and joy fill his dwelling*** (16:27) instead of "his sanctuary" (Ps 96:6) and requires the worshiper to ***come into his presence*** (16:29) instead of "into his courts" (Ps 96:8). The name "Abraham" (Ps 105:9) is also changed to ***Israel*** (16:13) to focus specifically on the nation as the fulfillment of the promises to Abraham. The hymn does not mention the judgment of the earth (Ps 96:10, 13; cp. 16:30, 33) because it was not relevant to the dedication of the Ark.

16:39 ***Gibeon*** served as the central ***place of worship*** until the Temple was built in Jerusalem (see 21:29; 2 Chr 1:3). The personnel ***at the Tabernacle*** had to be reorganized because some of the Levites were permanently transferred to Jerusalem.

16:42
1 Chr 25:7
2 Chr 7:6; 29:27
17:1-15
// 2 Sam 7:1-17
17:4
1 Chr 28:2-3
17:5
Exod 40:2-3
2 Sam 7:6
17:6
2 Sam 7:7

faithful love endures forever." 42They used
their trumpets, cymbals, and other instruments to accompany their songs of praise to
God. And the sons of Jeduthun were appointed as gatekeepers.

43Then all the people returned to their
homes, and David turned and went home to
bless his own family.

The Lord's Covenant Promise to David
1 Chr 17:1-15 // 2 Sam 7:1-17

17 When David was settled in his palace,
he summoned Nathan the prophet.
"Look," David said, "I am living in a beautiful cedar palace, but the Ark of the Lord's
Covenant is out there under a tent!"

2Nathan replied to David, "Do whatever
you have in mind, for God is with you."

3But that same night God said to Nathan,

4"Go and tell my servant David, 'This is
what the Lord has declared: You are not
the one to build a house for me to live in.
5I have never lived in a house, from the
day I brought the Israelites out of Egypt
until this very day. My home has always
been a tent, moving from one place to
another in a Tabernacle. 6Yet no matter
where I have gone with the Israelites, I
have never once complained to Israel's
leaders, the shepherds of my people. I
have never asked them, "Why haven't
you built me a beautiful cedar house?"'

7"Now go and say to my servant David, 'This is what the Lord of Heaven's
Armies has declared: I took you from
tending sheep in the pasture and selected you to be the leader of my people
Israel. 8I have been with you wherever
you have gone, and I have destroyed all
your enemies before your eyes. Now
I will make your name as famous as
anyone who has ever lived on the earth!
9And I will provide a homeland for my
people Israel, planting them in a secure
place where they will never be disturbed.
Evil nations won't oppress them as

The Promise of Dynasty (17:1-15)

1 Chr 5:1-2; 22:6-13; 28:4-7
Gen 49:8-12
Ps 78:67-72; 132:11-12
Amos 9:11-12
Matt 1:1-17; 22:41-46

God promised David that his dynasty would last forever (17:9-14 // 2 Sam 7:11-16). Yet the Chronicler lived at a time when David's dynasty had apparently ended. Although David's line of descent continued (see 3:17-23), no descendant of David had been king since the exile of Judah to Babylon. As a result, Israel's hope for the future was in question. The Chronicler wanted to show that God's promise to David was unconditional and that his throne was "secure forever."

God's selection of David began with his selection of Judah. Reuben (5:1-2) was Jacob's firstborn, but he forfeited his birthright (Gen 49:3-4). Jacob then blessed Joseph with the right of the firstborn (Gen 48) and Judah with the right to rule (Gen 49:8-12; see also Ps 78:67-72). Therefore, the Chronicler's history of Israel begins with Judah (see ch 2), the patriarch of the chosen tribe whose genealogy led to David, the anointed king.

Nathan's prophecy (17:1-15 // 2 Sam 7:1-17) provides the key source text regarding God's promise to continue David's dynasty of kings. The Chronicler emphasizes the grace of God's promise to David (17:13). Even the possibility of exile (22:10-13; 28:7) does not remove the hope of God's promise of a dynasty. The promise would continue for a future time because a future descendant of David would inherit the throne (17:11).

The Chronicler's hope was not directly "messianic" in the strict sense—he was not primarily focused on the arising of an anointed deliverer. His continuing hope in the secure promise to David was that the covenant community would again be led by kings in David's line, and he encouraged the community to look to the future for a new king to improve Israel's condition. The words of Jehoshaphat express the Chronicler's view: "Believe in the Lord your God, and you will be able to stand firm. Believe in his prophets, and you will succeed" (2 Chr 20:20).

With the birth of Jesus, the Son of David, the Chronicler's hope for the community of Israel was finally realized. Matthew's genealogy presents Jesus as the fulfillment of the Chronicler's expectation of a new king (Matt 1:1-17). His kingdom is for all the nations (Isa 49:6), stretching "from sea to sea and from the Euphrates river to the ends of the earth" (Zech 9:10).

16:42 ***to accompany their songs of praise to God:*** Or *to accompany the sacred music;* or *to accompany singing to God.*

17:1-27 The larger section (13:1–17:27) concludes with Nathan's prophecy about David and David's prayer of thanks.

17:1-15 David wanted to build a home for ***the Ark*** that would equal his own ***palace,*** but the Lord designated David's heir, Solomon (ch 22), to build the Temple. Jerusalem was to be the single place of worship for all Israel.

17:1 ***a beautiful cedar palace:*** Literally *a house of cedar.*

17:6 ***leaders:*** As in Greek version (see also 2 Sam 7:7); Hebrew reads *judges.*

they've done in the past, [10]starting from
the time I appointed judges to rule my
people Israel. And I will defeat all your
enemies.
"'Furthermore, I declare that the LORD
will build a house for you—a dynasty of
kings! [11]For when you die and join your
ancestors, I will raise up one of your descendants, one of your sons, and I will
make his kingdom strong. [12]He is the one
who will build a house—a temple—for me.
And I will secure his throne forever. [13]I
will be his father, and he will be my son.
I will never take my favor from him as
I took it from the one who ruled before
you. [14]I will confirm him as king over my
house and my kingdom for all time, and
his throne will be secure forever.'"

[15]So Nathan went back to David and told him everything the LORD had said in this vision.

David's Prayer of Thanks
1 Chr 17:16-27 // 2 Sam 7:18-29

[16]Then King David went in and sat before the LORD and prayed,

"Who am I, O LORD God, and what is my
family, that you have brought me this
far? [17]And now, O God, in addition to
everything else, you speak of giving your
servant a lasting dynasty! You speak
as though I were someone very great,
O LORD God!
[18]"What more can I say to you about
the way you have honored me? You know
what your servant is really like. [19]For
the sake of your servant, O LORD, and
according to your will, you have done all
these great things and have made them
known.
[20]"O LORD, there is no one like you.
We have never even heard of another
God like you! [21]What other nation on
earth is like your people Israel? What
other nation, O God, have you redeemed
from slavery to be your own people? You
made a great name for yourself when
you redeemed your people from Egypt.
You performed awesome miracles and
drove out the nations that stood in their
way. [22]You chose Israel to be your very
own people forever, and you, O LORD,
became their God.
[23]"And now, O LORD, I am your servant;
do as you have promised concerning
me and my family. May it be a promise
that will last forever. [24]And may your
name be established and honored forever so that everyone will say, 'The LORD
of Heaven's Armies, the God of Israel,
is Israel's God!' And may the house of
your servant David continue before you
forever.
[25]"O my God, I have been bold enough
to pray to you because you have revealed
to your servant that you will build a
house for him—a dynasty of kings! [26]For
you are God, O LORD. And you have promised these good things to your servant.
[27]And now, it has pleased you to bless
the house of your servant, so that it will
continue forever before you. For when
you grant a blessing, O LORD, it is an eternal blessing!"

David's Wars (18:1–20:8)

Expansion of the Kingdom
1 Chr 18:1-17 // 2 Sam 8:1-18

18 After this, David defeated and subdued the Philistines by conquering Gath and its surrounding towns. [2]David

17:13 1 Chr 10:14; Heb 1:5
17:16-27 // 2 Sam 7:18-29
17:17 2 Sam 7:19
17:19 2 Sam 7:21, 25; Isa 37:35
17:22 Exod 19:5-6
18:1-13 // 2 Sam 8:1-14

17:10b-14 David had resolved to build a house for the Lord—the Temple. Instead, the Lord would *build a house* for David—*a dynasty of kings.* Establishing David's eternal *dynasty* was the central part of God's plan to establish his rule on earth.

17:12 The construction of the Temple was a central aspect of God's kingdom on earth. Solomon later built the Temple (2 Chr 2–7) and fulfilled this promise.

17:13 The Chronicler made this declaration about Solomon in particular (see 22:9; 28:5-6; cp. 2 Sam 7:14).

17:14 In the parallel at 2 Sam 7:16, God promises to establish David's house, kingdom, and throne, whereas here it is Solomon's. While the books of Samuel and Kings cast David as Israel's ideal king, the Chronicler views Solomon as David's equal. David made all the preparations for building the Temple, but God designated Solomon as the Temple builder. The promise to Israel was secured in the combined reigns of David and Solomon.

17:17 ***You speak as though I were someone very great:*** The meaning of the Hebrew is uncertain.

18:1–20:8 This section recounts David's wars and military achievements, presenting David as the great warrior of Israel's history. This account relates the public and political aspects of David's enemies, but it deals very little with their private affairs. • Three distinct sections reflect accounts in Samuel: (1) the battles in the expansion of the kingdom (18:1-17; see 2 Sam 8:1-16); (2) the battle against the Ammonites (19:1–20:3; see 2 Sam 10:1–11:1; 12:30-31); and (3) the exploits of David's mighty men (20:4-8; see 2 Sam 21:18-22). Each section begins with a chronological transition (***after this***) that loosely joins these events (18:1; 19:1; 20:4).

18:1-17 These war records tell the story of David's expanding kingdom in conquering ***the Philistines*** (18:1), ***Moab*** (18:2), ***Zobah*** (18:3-4), ***Damascus*** (18:5-6), and ***Edom*** (18:12-13); these include records of David's international relations, booty, and tribute (18:7-11). A recurring theme is that ***the LORD made David victorious wherever he went*** (18:6, 13).

18:1 The ***Philistines*** posed a constant threat to David's kingdom (see notes on Josh 13:2; 19:43; Judg 3:3). They

18:11 Num 24:18-20
18:14-17 // 2 Sam 8:15-18
18:15 1 Chr 11:6
19:1-19 // 2 Sam 10:1-19

also conquered the land of Moab, and the
Moabites who were spared became David's
subjects and paid him tribute money.
3David also destroyed the forces of Hadadezer, king of Zobah, as far as Hamath, when
Hadadezer marched out to strengthen his
control along the Euphrates River. 4David
captured 1,000 chariots, 7,000 charioteers,
and 20,000 foot soldiers. He crippled all
the chariot horses except enough for 100
chariots.
5When Arameans from Damascus arrived
to help King Hadadezer, David killed 22,000
of them. 6Then he placed several army garrisons in Damascus, the Aramean capital, and
the Arameans became David's subjects and
paid him tribute money. So the LORD made
David victorious wherever he went.
7David brought the gold shields of Hadadezer's officers to Jerusalem, 8along with
a large amount of bronze from Hadadezer's
towns of Tebah and Cun. Later Solomon
melted the bronze and molded it into the
great bronze basin called the Sea, the pillars, and the various bronze articles used at
the Temple.
9When King Toi of Hamath heard that
David had destroyed the entire army of
King Hadadezer of Zobah, 10he sent his son
Joram to congratulate King David for his
successful campaign. Hadadezer and Toi
had been enemies and were often at war.
Joram presented David with many gifts of
gold, silver, and bronze.
11King David dedicated all these gifts to
the LORD, along with the silver and gold he
had taken from the other nations—from
Edom, Moab, Ammon, Philistia, and Amalek.
12Abishai son of Zeruiah destroyed
18,000 Edomites in the Valley of Salt. 13He
placed army garrisons in Edom, and all the
Edomites became David's subjects. In fact,
the LORD made David victorious wherever
he went.
14So David reigned over all Israel and did
what was just and right for all his people.
15Joab son of Zeruiah was commander of
the army. Jehoshaphat son of Ahilud was the
royal historian. 16Zadok son of Ahitub and
Ahimelech son of Abiathar were the priests.
Seraiah was the court secretary. 17Benaiah
son of Jehoiada was captain of the king's
bodyguard. And David's sons served as the
king's chief assistants.

David Defeats the Ammonites
1 Chr 19:1-19 // 2 Sam 10:1-19

19 Some time after this, King Nahash of
the Ammonites died, and his son Hanun became king. 2David said, "I am going
to show loyalty to Hanun because his father,
Nahash, was always loyal to me." So David
sent messengers to express sympathy to Hanun about his father's death.
But when David's ambassadors arrived
in the land of Ammon, 3the Ammonite commanders said to Hanun, "Do you really think
these men are coming here to honor your
father? No! David has sent them to spy out
the land so they can come in and conquer
it!" 4So Hanun seized David's ambassadors
and shaved them, cut off their robes at the
buttocks, and sent them back to David in
shame.
5When David heard what had happened
to the men, he sent messengers to tell them,
"Stay at Jericho until your beards grow out,
and then come back." For they felt deep
shame because of their appearance.
6When the people of Ammon realized how
seriously they had angered David, Hanun
and the Ammonites sent 75,000 pounds

---

remained entrenched in their coastal settlements; although David conquered ***Gath and its surrounding towns***, a Philistine king remained in Gath at the end of David's reign (1 Kgs 2:39).

18:2-13 David's conquests east of the Jordan River took place in stages. The conquest of ***Moab*** in the south gave David firm control over the plateau north of the Arnon River. David's victory over the Aramean alliance under ***Hadadezer*** brought him into alliance with ***King Toi of Hamath***, an archenemy of Hadadezer (18:9-11). With the defeat of Ammon and the Arameans east of the Jordan, David extended his control over the southern expanses of ***Edom*** and gained access to a southern seaport (18:12-13).

18:3 ***as far as Hamath:*** The meaning of the Hebrew is uncertain.

18:6 The first sentence follows the Greek version and Latin Vulgate (see also 2 Sam 8:6); Hebrew lacks ***several army garrisons***.

18:8 ***Tebah:*** Hebrew reads *Tibhath*, a variant spelling of *Tebah;* cp. parallel text at 2 Sam 8:8.

18:9 ***Toi:*** As in parallel text at 2 Sam 8:9; Hebrew reads *Tou;* also in 18:10.

18:10 ***Joram:*** As in parallel text at 2 Sam 8:10; Hebrew reads *Hadoram*, a variant spelling of *Joram*.

18:14-17 The listing of David's officials demonstrates the greatness of his rule over all of Israel.

18:16 ***Ahimelech:*** As in some Hebrew manuscripts, Syriac version, and Latin Vulgate (see also 2 Sam 8:17); most Hebrew manuscripts read *Abimelech*. • ***Seraiah:*** As in parallel text at 2 Sam 8:17; Hebrew reads *Shavsha*.

18:17 ***of the king's bodyguard:*** Hebrew *of the Kerethites and Pelethites*.

19:1-7 The new Ammonite ruler, ***Hanun***, took exception to Israel's presence so close to his nation. The Ammonites hired Aramean armies from the north, and these combined forces assembled ***at Medeba*** to challenge David's control of Moab's plateau.

19:1 This sentence follows the parallel text at 2 Sam 10:1; Hebrew lacks *Hanun*.

19:6 ***75,000 pounds:*** Hebrew *1,000 talents* [34,000 kilograms].

of silver to hire chariots and charioteers
from Aram-naharaim, Aram-maacah, and
Zobah. 7They also hired 32,000 chariots
and secured the support of the king of Maacah and his army. These forces camped at
Medeba, where they were joined by the Ammonite troops that Hanun had recruited
from his own towns. 8When David heard
about this, he sent Joab and all his warriors to
fight them. 9The Ammonite troops came out
and drew up their battle lines at the entrance
of the city, while the other kings positioned
themselves to fight in the open fields.

10When Joab saw that he would have
to fight on both the front and the rear, he
chose some of Israel's elite troops and
placed them under his personal command
to fight the Arameans in the fields. 11He left
the rest of the army under the command
of his brother Abishai, who was to attack
the Ammonites. 12"If the Arameans are too
strong for me, then come over and help me,"
Joab told his brother. "And if the Ammonites are too strong for you, I will help you.
13Be courageous! Let us fight bravely for our
people and the cities of our God. May the
LORD's will be done."

14When Joab and his troops attacked, the
Arameans began to run away. 15And when
the Ammonites saw the Arameans running,
they also ran from Abishai and retreated into
the city. Then Joab returned to Jerusalem.

16The Arameans now realized that they
were no match for Israel, so they sent
messengers and summoned additional Aramean troops from the other side of the
Euphrates River. These troops were under
the command of Shobach, the commander
of Hadadezer's forces.

17When David heard what was happening, he mobilized all Israel, crossed the
Jordan River, and positioned his troops in
battle formation. Then David engaged the
Arameans in battle, and they fought against
him. 18But again the Arameans fled from
the Israelites. This time David's forces killed
7,000 charioteers and 40,000 foot soldiers,
including Shobach, the commander of their
army. 19When Hadadezer's allies saw that
they had been defeated by Israel, they surrendered to David and became his subjects.
After that, the Arameans were no longer
willing to help the Ammonites.

David Captures Rabbah
1 Chr 20:1-3 // 2 Sam 11:1; 12:29-31

20 In the spring of the year, when kings
normally go out to war, Joab led the
Israelite army in successful attacks against
the land of the Ammonites. In the process
he laid siege to the city of Rabbah. However,
David stayed behind in Jerusalem.

2When David arrived at Rabbah, he removed the crown from the king's head, and
it was placed on his own head. The crown
was made of gold and set with gems, and he
found that it weighed seventy-five pounds.
David took a vast amount of plunder from
the city. 3He also made slaves of the people
of Rabbah and forced them to labor with
saws, iron picks, and iron axes. That is how
David dealt with the people of all the Ammonite towns. Then David and all the army
returned to Jerusalem.

Battles against Philistine Giants
1 Chr 20:4-8 // 2 Sam 21:18-22

4After this, war broke out with the Philistines at Gezer. As they fought, Sibbecai from
Hushah killed Saph, a descendant of the giants, and so the Philistines were subdued.

5During another battle with the Philistines, Elhanan son of Jair killed Lahmi, the
brother of Goliath of Gath. The handle of Lahmi's spear was as thick as a weaver's beam!

19:7 Num 21:30; Josh 13:9, 16
19:14 2 Sam 10:14
19:16 2 Sam 10:15-16
20:1-3 // 2 Sam 11:1; 12:29-31
20:4-8 // 2 Sam 21:15-22
20:5 1 Sam 17:4-7; 2 Sam 21:19; 1 Chr 11:23

19:9-13 The enemy armies drew their battle lines strategically; ***the Ammonites*** positioned themselves so that the city of Medeba could serve as a refuge, while the Israelites also had to deal with a second offensive from ***the Arameans. Joab*** divided his forces to fight on both fronts from a central rallying point.

19:13 Joab knew that the battle was not being waged to gain more territory but to defend the ***people and the cities*** of Israel from invasion (cp. 19:8). • Joab placed his trust in God, knowing that the outcome depended on the Lord's providence.

19:16-19 In the battle against ***the Arameans,*** David accomplished three objectives: He challenged ***Hadadezer's*** supremacy, threw the alliance of the Arameans into disarray, and prevented any possible future alliance between ***the Arameans*** and ***the Ammonites.***

19:16 ***the Euphrates River:*** Literally *the river.* • ***Shobach:*** As in parallel text at 2 Sam 10:16; Hebrew reads *Shophach;* also in 19:18.

20:1-3 This war against the Ammonites was the context of David's sin with Bathsheba (2 Sam 11:2–12:25), which the Chronicler omits.

20:1 ***In the spring of the year:*** Literally *At the turn of the year.* The first day of the year in the ancient Hebrew lunar calendar occurred in March or April.

20:2 ***from the king's head:*** Or *from the head of Milcom* (as in Greek version and Latin Vulgate). Milcom, also called Molech, was the god of the Ammonites. • ***seventy-five pounds:*** Hebrew *1 talent* [34 kilograms].

20:3 ***and forced them to labor with saws, iron picks, and iron axes:*** As in parallel text at 2 Sam 12:31; Hebrew reads *and cut them with saws, iron picks, and saws.*

20:4 ***Saph:*** As in parallel text at 2 Sam 21:18; Hebrew reads *Sippai.* • ***descendant of the giants:*** Hebrew *descendant of the Rephaites;* also in 20:6, 8.

20:5 ***the brother of Goliath:*** See note on 2 Sam 21:19.

21:1-26
// 2 Sam 24:1-25
21:1
[e]*satan* (7854)
‣Job 1:6
21:2
1 Chr 27:23-24
21:3
Deut 1:11
21:5
2 Sam 24:9
21:6
1 Chr 27:24
21:8
2 Sam 12:13
21:9
1 Sam 9:9
2 Sam 24:11
1 Chr 29:29
21:12
2 Sam 24:13
21:13
Ps 51:1; 130:4, 7
21:14
1 Chr 27:24
21:15
Exod 32:14
1 Sam 15:11
Jon 3:10
21:16
1 Kgs 21:27
21:17
2 Sam 7:8
Ps 74:1
21:18
2 Chr 3:1

[6]In another battle with the Philistines at Gath, they encountered a huge man with six fingers on each hand and six toes on each foot, twenty-four in all, who was also a descendant of the giants. [7]But when he defied and taunted Israel, he was killed by Jonathan, the son of David's brother Shimea.

[8]These Philistines were descendants of the giants of Gath, but David and his warriors killed them.

3. PREPARATIONS FOR THE TEMPLE (21:1–29:30)

Designation of the Temple Site (21:1–22:1)

David Takes a Census

1 Chr 21:1-6 // 2 Sam 24:1-9

21 [e]Satan rose up against Israel and caused David to take a census of the people of Israel. [2]So David said to Joab and the commanders of the army, "Take a census of all the people of Israel—from Beersheba in the south to Dan in the north—and bring me a report so I may know how many there are."

[3]But Joab replied, "May the LORD increase the number of his people a hundred times over! But why, my lord the king, do you want to do this? Are they not all your servants? Why must you cause Israel to sin?"

[4]But the king insisted that they take the census, so Joab traveled throughout all Israel to count the people. Then he returned to Jerusalem [5]and reported the number of people to David. There were 1,100,000 warriors in all Israel who could handle a sword, and 470,000 in Judah. [6]But Joab did not include the tribes of Levi and Benjamin in the census because he was so distressed at what the king had made him do.

Judgment for David's Sin

1 Chr 21:7-17 // 2 Sam 24:10-17

[7]God was very displeased with the census, and he punished Israel for it. [8]Then David said to God, "I have sinned greatly by taking this census. Please forgive my guilt for doing this foolish thing."

[9]Then the LORD spoke to Gad, David's seer. This was the message: [10]"Go and say to David, 'This is what the LORD says: I will give you three choices. Choose one of these punishments, and I will inflict it on you.'"

[11]So Gad came to David and said, "These are the choices the LORD has given you. [12]You may choose three years of famine, three months of destruction by the sword of your enemies, or three days of severe plague as the angel of the LORD brings devastation throughout the land of Israel. Decide what answer I should give the LORD who sent me."

[13]"I'm in a desperate situation!" David replied to Gad. "But let me fall into the hands of the LORD, for his mercy is very great. Do not let me fall into human hands."

[14]So the LORD sent a plague upon Israel, and 70,000 people died as a result. [15]And God sent an angel to destroy Jerusalem. But just as the angel was preparing to destroy it, the LORD relented and said to the death angel, "Stop! That is enough!" At that moment the angel of the LORD was standing by the threshing floor of Araunah the Jebusite.

[16]David looked up and saw the angel of the LORD standing between heaven and earth with his sword drawn, reaching out over Jerusalem. So David and the leaders of Israel put on burlap to show their deep distress and fell face down on the ground. [17]And David said to God, "I am the one who called for the census! I am the one who has sinned and done wrong! But these people are as innocent as sheep—what have they done? O LORD my God, let your anger fall against me and my family, but do not destroy your people."

David Builds an Altar

1 Chr 21:18-30 // 2 Sam 24:18-25

[18]Then the angel of the LORD told Gad to instruct David to go up and build an altar to the LORD on the threshing floor of Araunah the Jebusite. [19]So David went up to do what the LORD had commanded him through Gad. [20]Araunah, who was busy

21:1–22:1 This account of the *census* closely parallels 2 Sam 24:1-25 but has an entirely different focus. The Chronicler's account provides the context for the dedication of the altar and the preparations for building the Temple (ch 22).

21:1 *Satan* (or *the adversary*) motivated ***David to take a census*** of his military forces (cp. 2 Sam 24:1). The Chronicler seems to interpret the narrative of Samuel in light of his theology of Satan as the adversary of God and humanity. As God allows Satan to work in the world, Satan unwittingly fulfills God's purposes (cp. 2 Chr 18:3-34; Job 1:6–2:7; Zech 3:1-2; Matt 4:1-11; John 13:27; 1 Cor 5:5; 2 Cor 12:7; 1 Tim 1:20; Rev 20:3, 7-9).

21:7 The note on 2 Sam 24:1 discusses possible reasons why ***God was very displeased with the census.***

21:9 ***Gad*** is later mentioned as having compiled a list of "the events of King David's reign" (29:29).

21:15 ***Araunah:*** As in parallel text at 2 Sam 24:16; Hebrew reads *Ornan*, another name for *Araunah;* also in 21:18-28.

21:16-17 These verses provide a more detailed description of the angel and of David's response than the parallel text (2 Sam 24:17). The sight of the angel carrying out his mission inspired David to plead on behalf of the people.

threshing wheat at the time, turned and
saw the angel there. His four sons, who
were with him, ran away and hid. 21When
Araunah saw David approaching, he left
his threshing floor and bowed before David with his face to the ground.
22David said to Araunah, "Let me buy this
threshing floor from you at its full price.
Then I will build an altar to the LORD there,
so that he will stop the plague."
23"Take it, my lord the king, and use it as
you wish," Araunah said to David. "I will
give the oxen for the burnt offerings, and
the threshing boards for wood to build a
fire on the altar, and the wheat for the grain
offering. I will give it all to you."
24But King David replied to Araunah,
"No, I insist on buying it for the full price.
I will not take what is yours and give it to
the LORD. I will not present burnt offerings
that have cost me nothing!" 25So David gave
Araunah 600 pieces of gold in payment for
the threshing floor.
26David built an altar there to the LORD
and sacrificed burnt offerings and peace offerings. And when David prayed, the LORD
answered him by sending fire from heaven
to burn up the offering on the altar. 27Then
the LORD spoke to the angel, who put the
sword back into its sheath.
28When David saw that the LORD had
answered his prayer, he offered sacrifices
there at Araunah's threshing floor. 29At that
time the [f]Tabernacle of the LORD and the altar of burnt offering that Moses had made
in the wilderness were located at the place
of worship in Gibeon. 30But David was not
able to go there to inquire of God, because
he was terrified by the drawn sword of the
angel of the LORD.

Declaration of the Location of the Temple

22 Then David said, "This will be the
location for the Temple of the LORD
God and the place of the altar for Israel's
burnt offerings!"

Charge to Solomon: Build the Temple (22:2-19)

2So David gave orders to call together the
foreigners living in Israel, and he assigned
them the task of preparing finished stone
for building the Temple of God. 3David provided large amounts of iron for the nails
that would be needed for the doors in the
gates and for the clamps, and he gave more
bronze than could be weighed. 4He also
provided innumerable cedar logs, for the
men of Tyre and Sidon had brought vast
amounts of cedar to David.
5David said, "My son Solomon is still
young and inexperienced. And since the
Temple to be built for the LORD must be a
magnificent structure, famous and glorious
throughout the world, I will begin making
preparations for it now." So David collected
vast amounts of building materials before
his death.
6Then David sent for his son Solomon
and instructed him to build a Temple for
the LORD, the God of Israel. 7"My son, I
wanted to build a Temple to honor the name
of the LORD my God," David told him. 8"But
the LORD said to me, 'You have killed many
men in the battles you have fought. And
since you have shed so much blood in my
sight, you will not be the one to build a Temple to honor my name. 9But you will have a
son who will be a man of peace. I will give
him peace with his enemies in all the surrounding lands. His name will be Solomon,
and I will give [g]peace and quiet to Israel

21:26 Lev 9:24; Judg 6:21
21:29 1 Kgs 3:4; 1 Chr 16:39; [f]*mishkan* (4908) ‣1 Chr 23:26
22:1 1 Chr 21:18-28; 2 Chr 3:1
22:2 1 Kgs 5:17-18; 9:20-21; 2 Chr 2:17-18
22:4 1 Kgs 5:6-10
22:5 1 Kgs 3:7; 1 Chr 29:1
22:7 2 Sam 7:2-3; 1 Chr 17:1-2
22:8 1 Chr 28:3
22:9 2 Sam 12:24-25; 1 Kgs 4:20, 25; [g]*shalom* (7965) ‣Ps 4:8

21:25 ***600 pieces of gold:*** Hebrew *600 shekels of gold,* about 15 pounds or 6.8 kilograms in weight.

21:26–22:1 The census and plague led up to the dedication of ***Araunah's threshing floor*** as the site for the new sanctuary. Typically, ***offerings*** would have been made at ***Gibeon***, where ***the Tabernacle*** was located (see 16:39; 21:29; 2 Chr 1:3). The halting of the plague at the *threshing floor* enabled ***David*** to make offerings there in accordance with the word he received through Gad the seer (21:18). David then designated the new location for the future ***Temple of the LORD God.***

22:2-19 God had promised David that his kingdom would be permanent and that his son would build a temple for the Lord (17:11-12). Now that the site had been chosen (21:18–22:1), David made preparations for ***building the Temple of God.*** He gathered the materials (22:2-5), and he charged both ***Solomon*** (22:6-16) and ***the leaders of Israel*** (22:17-19) with the task of building the Temple after his death.

22:5 While Solomon was ***young and inexperienced*** (see also 29:1; cp. 1 Kgs 3:7; 2 Chr 13:7), David had the wisdom and skill to make ***preparations*** for building ***the Temple;*** David also designed the Temple (28:11-12). Later, God provided Solomon with the wisdom he needed to build the Temple and to govern well (see 2 Chr 1:7-12).

22:8 God did not allow David to build the Temple because he had ***shed so much blood*** (cp. 1 Kgs 5:3-4). David's wars were not unethical, and God had blessed and supported them. However, David had been tainted with a kind of ceremonial uncleanness from the blood he had shed and the deaths he had caused in battle (see 28:3; cp. Gen 4:10-12; Lev 17:3-4; Deut 21:1-9; Matt 27:24-25). Accordingly, he could not build a holy sanctuary for the Lord.

22:9-10 ***Solomon*** sounds like and is probably derived from the Hebrew word for "peace." In fact, he was a ***man of peace,*** free from war and from shedding blood in battle. The ***Temple*** was built during his peaceful reign (see 2 Chr 2–7). • The Hebrew deliberately uses two different words to describe conditions during Solomon's reign: ***peace*** (Hebrew *shalom,* related to Solomon's name), ***and quiet*** (Hebrew *menukhah,* related to the idea of redemption).

22:10 2 Sam 7:13; 1 Chr 17:12
22:11 1 Chr 22:16
22:12 1 Kgs 3:9-12; 2 Chr 1:10
22:13 Josh 1:6-9; 1 Chr 28:7
22:14 1 Chr 22:3; 29:4
22:16 1 Chr 22:11
22:17 1 Chr 28:1-6
22:18 1 Chr 22:9; 23:25
22:19 1 Kgs 8:6, 21; 1 Chr 28:9; 2 Chr 5:7
23:1 1 Chr 28:5; 29:22, 28
23:3 Num 4:3-49; 1 Chr 23:24
23:4 1 Chr 26:29; Ezra 3:8-9
23:5 1 Chr 15:16

during his reign. 10He is the one who will
build a Temple to honor my name. He will
be my son, and I will be his father. And I
will secure the throne of his kingdom over
Israel forever.'
11"Now, my son, may the LORD be with
you and give you success as you follow his directions in building the Temple of the LORD
your God. 12And may the LORD give you wisdom and understanding, that you may obey
the Law of the LORD your God as you rule
over Israel. 13For you will be successful if
you carefully obey the decrees and regulations that the LORD gave to Israel through
Moses. Be strong and courageous; do not be
afraid or lose heart!
14"I have worked hard to provide materials for building the Temple of the
LORD—nearly 4,000 tons of gold, 40,000
tons of silver, and so much iron and bronze
that it cannot be weighed. I have also gathered timber and stone for the walls, though
you may need to add more. 15You have a
large number of skilled stonemasons and
carpenters and craftsmen of every kind.
16You have expert goldsmiths and silver-
smiths and workers of bronze and iron.
Now begin the work, and may the LORD be
with you!"
17Then David ordered all the leaders
of Israel to assist Solomon in this project.
18"The LORD your God is with you," he declared. "He has given you peace with the
surrounding nations. He has handed them
over to me, and they are now subject to the
LORD and his people. 19Now seek the LORD
your God with all your heart and soul. Build
the sanctuary of the LORD God so that you
can bring the Ark of the LORD's Covenant
and the holy vessels of God into the Temple
built to honor the LORD's name."

Organization of the Officials (23:1–26:32)
Duties of the Levites

23 When David was an old man, he
appointed his son Solomon to be
king over Israel. 2David summoned all the
leaders of Israel, together with the priests
and Levites. 3All the Levites who were
thirty years old or older were counted, and
the total came to 38,000. 4Then David said,
"From all the Levites, 24,000 will supervise
the work at the Temple of the LORD. Another
6,000 will serve as officials and judges. 5An-
other 4,000 will work as gatekeepers, and

Temple Worship (22:1-19)

1 Kgs 8:27-53; 2 Chr 5:2-14; 6:41-42; 7:12-16; Ps 48:9; 65:4; 66:13; 138:2; Jer 7:3-11; 11:15; Ezek 8:6-16; 44:1-31; Joel 1:14; 2:17; Hab 2:20; Hag 2:7; John 2:19-22; Eph 2:14-15; 2:20-22; 1 Pet 2:4-5

Throughout the ancient Near East, responsibility for a nation's temple fell to the king. David, the founder of the dynasty of Judah's kings, established Jerusalem as the capital of Israel (2 Sam 5:4-10) and made it the central place of worship. Although Solomon actually built the Temple, David prepared for the building of the Temple and for its liturgy. The Temple, located adjacent to the king's palace, represented God's reign over all creation and all nations: "The LORD is in his holy Temple. Let all the earth be silent before him" (Hab 2:20). The Temple expressed the sovereign and personal relationship between God, his world, and his people. It served to teach Israel about God's exclusive dominion and their total dependence on him.

The Temple established the legitimacy of the human king, who represented divine rule. This role of the Temple was expressed in a psalm celebrating David's restoration of the Ark to Jerusalem (Ps 132:6-12). This psalm was also used at the conclusion of Solomon's prayer of dedication (2 Chr 6:41-42). The kings were charged to devote themselves to God's presence at his resting place in the Temple (22:17-19).

As the representation of God's presence in the world, the Temple found its fulfillment in Christ and the church. Jesus himself signaled the transition from the Temple buildings to his own body as the temple (John 2:19). The disciples began understanding this transition after the resurrection (John 2:21-22). The apostle Paul later described the church as the new sacred space where Jews and Gentiles are reconciled. Using Temple imagery, he described breaking down barriers in the body of Christ, creating one people (Eph 2:14-15). The church stands as a holy temple, resting on the foundation of the apostles and prophets (Eph 2:20-22). It is built from living stones—believers—fashioned together around Jesus Christ, the cornerstone (1 Pet 2:4-5).

22:14 ***nearly 4,000 tons of gold, 40,000 tons of silver:*** Hebrew *100,000 talents* [3,400 metric tons] *of gold, 1,000,000 talents* [34,000 metric tons] *of silver.*

23:1-2 When ***David . . . appointed his son Solomon*** as Israel's king (cp. 1 Kgs 1), David outlined the organizational structure of the kingdom and made all the necessary provisions for the Temple's functioning. • The account of Solomon's coronation continues in chs 28–29; the intervening chapters (23:3–27:24) record in detail the organization of the kingdom.

23:3-5 ***The Levites*** are recorded according to their roles rather than their families. • ***thirty years old or older:*** See note on 23:24-27.

4,000 will praise the LORD with the musical
instruments I have made." [6]Then David divided the Levites into divisions named after
the clans descended from the three sons of
Levi—Gershon, Kohath, and Merari.
[7]The Gershonite family units were defined
by their lines of descent from Libni and
Shimei, the sons of Gershon. [8]Three
of the descendants of Libni were Jehiel
(the family leader), Zetham, and Joel.
[9]These were the leaders of the family
of Libni.
Three of the descendants of Shimei were
Shelomoth, Haziel, and Haran. [10]Four
other descendants of Shimei were
Jahath, Ziza, Jeush, and Beriah. [11]Jahath
was the family leader, and Ziza was next.
Jeush and Beriah were counted as a
single family because neither had many
sons.
[12]Four of the descendants of Kohath were
Amram, Izhar, Hebron, and Uzziel.
[13]The sons of Amram were Aaron and
Moses. Aaron and his descendants
were set apart to dedicate the most
holy things, to offer sacrifices in the
LORD's presence, to serve the LORD, and
to pronounce blessings in his name
forever.
[14]As for Moses, the man of God, his
sons were included with the tribe of
Levi. [15]The sons of Moses were Gershom and Eliezer. [16]The descendants of
Gershom included Shebuel, the family
leader. [17]Eliezer had only one son, Rehabiah, the family leader. Rehabiah had
numerous descendants.
[18]The descendants of Izhar included
Shelomith, the family leader.
[19]The descendants of Hebron included
Jeriah (the family leader), Amariah
(the second), Jahaziel (the third), and
Jekameam (the fourth).
[20]The descendants of Uzziel included
Micah (the family leader) and Isshiah
(the second).
[21]The descendants of Merari included
Mahli and Mushi.
The sons of Mahli were Eleazar and
Kish. [22]Eleazar died with no sons, only
daughters. His daughters married their
cousins, the sons of Kish.
[23]Three of the descendants of Mushi were
Mahli, Eder, and Jerimoth.

[24]These were the descendants of Levi by
clans, the leaders of their family groups, registered carefully by name. Each had to be
twenty years old or older to qualify for service in the house of the LORD. [25]For David
said, "The LORD, the God of Israel, has given
us peace, and he will always live in Jerusalem. [26]Now the Levites will no longer need
to carry the [h]Tabernacle and its furnishings
from place to place." [27]In accordance with
David's final instructions, all the Levites
twenty years old or older were registered
for service.
[28]The work of the Levites was to assist the
priests, the descendants of Aaron, as they
served at the house of the LORD. They also
took care of the courtyards and side rooms,
helped perform the ceremonies of purification, and served in many other ways in
the house of God. [29]They were in charge of
the sacred bread that was set out on the table, the choice flour for the grain offerings,
the wafers made without yeast, the cakes
cooked in olive oil, and the other mixed
breads. They were also responsible to
check all the weights and measures. [30]And
each morning and evening they stood before the LORD to sing songs of thanks and
praise to him. [31]They assisted with the
burnt offerings that were presented to the
LORD on Sabbath days, at new moon celebrations, and at all the appointed festivals.
The required number of Levites served in
the LORD's presence at all times, following
all the procedures they had been given.
[32]And so, under the supervision of the
priests, the Levites watched over the Tabernacle and the Temple and faithfully carried
out their duties of service at the house of
the LORD.

23:6 1 Chr 6:1
23:13 Exod 6:20; 28:1; 30:6-10
23:14 Deut 33:1
23:21 1 Chr 6:19
23:24 Num 10:17, 21; 1 Chr 23:3
23:25 1 Chr 22:18
23:26 Num 4:5, 15; 7:9; Deut 10:8; [h]*mishkan* (4908) ‣Ps 26:8
23:29 Lev 6:20-21; 19:35-36; 24:5-9; 1 Chr 9:29, 32
23:31 Lev 23:2-4; Isa 1:13-14
23:32 Num 1:53; 3:6-9, 38

23:6-23 ***David divided the Levites into divisions*** according to their ancestral families. The number of available clerics far exceeded the requirements for a single Temple; the divisions provided a necessary time-sharing mechanism that enabled all the priests and Levites to serve in the Temple periodically (cp. Luke 1:5, 8).

23:7 ***Libni:*** Hebrew *Ladan* (also in 23:8-9), a variant spelling of *Libni;* cp. 6:17.

23:10 ***Ziza:*** As in Greek version and Latin Vulgate (see also 23:11); Hebrew reads *Zina.*

23:24-27 In the census of 23:3, individuals were counted at age thirty, but the actual registration of the divisions included those ***twenty years old or older*** (cp. Num 1:3). The age of entry into Levitical service apparently varied over time according to need.

23:28-32 ***The work of the Levites was to assist the priests,*** which they accomplished in various ways: maintaining the Temple, setting out the ***sacred bread*** and other offerings, singing, and helping the priests with the sacrifices. These duties were allotted to different family divisions of Levites (23:4-6).

23:32 ***the Tabernacle and the Temple:*** Literally *the Tent of Meeting and the sanctuary.*

24:1 Exod 6:23
24:2 Lev 10:1-2
24:5 1 Chr 24:31
24:6 1 Chr 18:16
24:7 Neh 12:6
24:10 Neh 12:4 Luke 1:5
24:23 1 Chr 23:19

Duties of the Priests

24 This is how Aaron's descendants,
the priests, were divided into groups
for service. The sons of Aaron were Nadab,
Abihu, Eleazar, and Ithamar. 2But Nadab and
Abihu died before their father, and they had
no sons. So only Eleazar and Ithamar were
left to carry on as priests.
3With the help of Zadok, who was a descendant of Eleazar, and of Ahimelech, who
was a descendant of Ithamar, David divided
Aaron's descendants into groups according
to their various duties. 4Eleazar's descendants were divided into sixteen groups and
Ithamar's into eight, for there were more
family leaders among the descendants of
Eleazar.
5All tasks were assigned to the various
groups by means of sacred lots so that no
preference would be shown, for there were
many qualified officials serving God in the
sanctuary from among the descendants of
both Eleazar and Ithamar. 6Shemaiah son
of Nethanel, a Levite, acted as secretary and
wrote down the names and assignments in
the presence of the king, the officials, Zadok the priest, Ahimelech son of Abiathar,
and the family leaders of the priests and
Levites. The descendants of Eleazar and Ithamar took turns casting lots.

7 The first lot fell to Jehoiarib.
The second lot fell to Jedaiah.
8 The third lot fell to Harim.
The fourth lot fell to Seorim.
9 The fifth lot fell to Malkijah.
The sixth lot fell to Mijamin.
10 The seventh lot fell to Hakkoz.
The eighth lot fell to Abijah.
11 The ninth lot fell to Jeshua.
The tenth lot fell to Shecaniah.
12 The eleventh lot fell to Eliashib.
The twelfth lot fell to Jakim.
13 The thirteenth lot fell to Huppah.
The fourteenth lot fell to Jeshebeab.
14 The fifteenth lot fell to Bilgah.
The sixteenth lot fell to Immer.
15 The seventeenth lot fell to Hezir.
The eighteenth lot fell to Happizzez.
16 The nineteenth lot fell to Pethahiah.
The twentieth lot fell to Jehezkel.
17 The twenty-first lot fell to Jakin.
The twenty-second lot fell to Gamul.
18 The twenty-third lot fell to Delaiah.
The twenty-fourth lot fell to Maaziah.

19Each group carried out its appointed
duties in the house of the LORD according
to the procedures established by their ancestor Aaron in obedience to the commands of
the LORD, the God of Israel.

Family Leaders among the Levites

20These were the other family leaders descended from Levi:

From the descendants of Amram, the leader was Shebuel.
From the descendants of Shebuel, the leader was Jehdeiah.
21 From the descendants of Rehabiah, the leader was Isshiah.
22 From the descendants of Izhar, the leader was Shelomith.
From the descendants of Shelomith, the leader was Jahath.
23 From the descendants of Hebron, Jeriah was the leader, Amariah was second, Jahaziel was third, and Jekameam was fourth.
24 From the descendants of Uzziel, the leader was Micah.
From the descendants of Micah, the
leader was Shamir, 25along with
Isshiah, the brother of Micah.
From the descendants of Isshiah, the leader was Zechariah.
26 From the descendants of Merari, the leaders were Mahli and Mushi.
From the descendants of Jaaziah, the leader was Beno.
27 From the descendants of Merari through Jaaziah, the leaders were Beno, Shoham, Zaccur, and Ibri.

24:1-19 The information about the priests' duties includes only their organization into orders and the assignment of their responsibilities by casting lots. The Chronicler does not explain their duties because they had long been solidly established (see Exod 28:1-5; Lev 1–7; Num 6:22-27).

24:1-2 The organization of ***the priests*** into their divisions ***for service*** began with Aaron's sons ***Eleazar and Ithamar;*** all of Israel's priests were descended from these two men.

24:3-6 ***Zadok*** and ***Ahimelech*** were the leaders of the two families of priests during David's time (see 6:8; 18:16; 2 Sam 8:17).

24:7-18 The twenty-four divisions established for the priests continued unchanged for many generations; the order of ***Abijah*** (24:10) is specifically mentioned in Luke 1:5, 8.

24:20-31 ***The other family leaders*** might refer to all those members of the tribe who were not priests yet who had already been documented (see 23:6-23), or it might refer to Levites not mentioned before. However, most of the families were already included in the previous list. Therefore, this list appears to be an independent, supplementary list that complements the previous register of Levites, perhaps bringing the earlier list up to date at a later time.

24:20 ***Shebuel:*** Hebrew *Shubael* (also in 24:20b), a variant spelling of *Shebuel;* cp. 23:16 and 26:24.

24:22 ***Shelomith:*** Hebrew *Shelomoth* (also in 24:22b), a variant spelling of *Shelomith;* cp. 23:18.

24:23 ***From the descendants of Hebron, Jeriah was the leader:*** Literally *From the descendants of Jeriah;* cp. 23:19.

28 From the descendants of Mahli, the leader was Eleazar, though he had no sons.
29 From the descendants of Kish, the leader was Jerahmeel.
30 From the descendants of Mushi, the leaders were Mahli, Eder, and Jerimoth.

These were the descendants of Levi in their
various families. 31 Like the descendants of
Aaron, they were assigned to their duties by means of sacred lots, without regard to age or rank. Lots were drawn in the presence of King David, Zadok, Ahimelech, and the family leaders of the priests and the Levites.

Duties of the Musicians

25 David and the army commanders then appointed men from the families of Asaph, Heman, and Jeduthun to proclaim God's messages to the accompaniment of lyres, harps, and cymbals. Here is a list of their names and their work:

2 From the sons of Asaph, there were Zaccur, Joseph, Nethaniah, and Asarelah. They worked under the direction of their father, Asaph, who proclaimed God's messages by the king's orders.
3 From the sons of Jeduthun, there were Gedaliah, Zeri, Jeshaiah, Shimei, Hashabiah, and Mattithiah, six in all. They worked under the direction of their father, Jeduthun, who proclaimed God's messages to the accompaniment of the lyre, offering thanks and praise to the LORD.
4 From the sons of Heman, there were Bukkiah, Mattaniah, Uzziel, Shubael, Jerimoth, Hananiah, Hanani, Eliathah, Giddalti, Romamti-ezer, Joshbekashah,
Mallothi, Hothir, and Mahazioth. 5 All
these were the sons of Heman, the king's seer, for God had honored him with fourteen sons and three daughters.

6 All these men were under the direction of their fathers as they made music at the house of the LORD. Their responsibilities included the playing of cymbals, harps, and lyres at the house of God. Asaph, Jeduthun, and Heman reported directly to the king.
7 They and their families were all trained in making music before the LORD, and each of them—288 in all—was an accomplished
musician. 8 The musicians were appointed
to their term of service by means of sacred lots, without regard to whether they were young or old, teacher or student.

9 The first lot fell to Joseph of the Asaph clan and twelve of his sons and relatives.
The second lot fell to Gedaliah and twelve of his sons and relatives.
10 The third lot fell to Zaccur and twelve of his sons and relatives.
11 The fourth lot fell to Zeri and twelve of his sons and relatives.
12 The fifth lot fell to Nethaniah and twelve of his sons and relatives.
13 The sixth lot fell to Bukkiah and twelve of his sons and relatives.
14 The seventh lot fell to Asarelah and twelve of his sons and relatives.
15 The eighth lot fell to Jeshaiah and twelve of his sons and relatives.
16 The ninth lot fell to Mattaniah and twelve of his sons and relatives.
17 The tenth lot fell to Shimei and twelve of his sons and relatives.
18 The eleventh lot fell to Uzziel and twelve of his sons and relatives.
19 The twelfth lot fell to Hashabiah and twelve of his sons and relatives.
20 The thirteenth lot fell to Shubael and twelve of his sons and relatives.
21 The fourteenth lot fell to Mattithiah and twelve of his sons and relatives.
22 The fifteenth lot fell to Jerimoth and twelve of his sons and relatives.
23 The sixteenth lot fell to Hananiah and twelve of his sons and relatives.
24 The seventeenth lot fell to Joshbekashah and twelve of his sons and relatives.

24:31 1 Chr 24:5-6
25:1 2 Kgs 3:15; 1 Chr 6:33, 39; 15:16
25:3 1 Chr 16:41-42
25:6 1 Chr 15:16, 19
25:8 1 Chr 26:13

24:31 The Levites were organized according to the same principles as the priests (24:5-6).

25:1-7 The musicians who served at the time of King *David* are listed according to their membership in ***the families of Asaph, Heman, and Jeduthun***.

25:1 ***Asaph:*** See 1 Chr 6:39-40; 15:17-19; 16:5; 2 Chr 29:30; Ezra 2:40-41; Pss 50; 73–83.• ***Heman:*** See 1 Chr 6:33-38; Ps 88. • ***Jeduthun:*** See 1 Chr 16:41-42; 2 Chr 5:12; 35:15; Pss 39; 62; 77.

25:2-3 ***Asaph*** and ***Jeduthun*** . . . ***proclaimed God's messages***, meaning they were prophets as well as musicians.

25:3 This list follows one Hebrew manuscript and some Greek manuscripts (see also 25:17); most Hebrew manuscripts lack ***Shimei***.

25:4 ***Shubael:*** Hebrew *Shebuel*, a variant spelling of *Shubael;* cp. 25:20.

25:8 As with the priests, the order of the musicians by families was decided by ***sacred lots*** so that no preference would be shown (see 24:5, 31).

25:9 The first sentence follows the Greek version; Hebrew lacks ***and twelve of his sons and relatives***.

25:11 ***Zeri:*** Hebrew *Izri*, a variant spelling of *Zeri;* cp. 25:3.

25:14 ***Asarelah:*** Hebrew *Jesarelah*, a variant spelling of *Asarelah;* cp. 25:2.

25:18 ***Uzziel:*** Hebrew *Azarel*, a variant spelling of *Uzziel;* cp. 25:4.

25:22 ***Jerimoth*** Hebrew *Jeremoth*, a variant spelling of *Jerimoth;* cp. 25:4.

25:24 ***Joshbekashah:*** Hebrew *Joshbekasha*, a variant spelling of *Joshbekashah;* cp. 25:4.

25:31
1 Chr 9:33
26:10
1 Chr 16:38
26:13
1 Chr 24:5, 31; 25:8
26:20
1 Chr 26:22, 24; 28:12

25 The eighteenth lot fell to Hanani and twelve of his sons and relatives.
26 The nineteenth lot fell to Mallothi and twelve of his sons and relatives.
27 The twentieth lot fell to Eliathah and twelve of his sons and relatives.
28 The twenty-first lot fell to Hothir and twelve of his sons and relatives.
29 The twenty-second lot fell to Giddalti and twelve of his sons and relatives.
30 The twenty-third lot fell to Mahazioth and twelve of his sons and relatives.
31 The twenty-fourth lot fell to Romamti-ezer and twelve of his sons and relatives.

Duties of the Gatekeepers

26 These are the divisions of the gatekeepers:

From the Korahites, there was
Meshelemiah son of Kore, of the family
of Abiasaph. 2The sons of Meshelemiah
were Zechariah (the oldest), Jediael
(the second), Zebadiah (the third),
Jathniel (the fourth), 3Elam (the fifth),
Jehohanan (the sixth), and Eliehoenai
(the seventh).
4The sons of Obed-edom, also gatekeepers,
were Shemaiah (the oldest), Jehozabad
(the second), Joah (the third), Sacar (the
fourth), Nethanel (the fifth), 5Ammiel
(the sixth), Issachar (the seventh), and
Peullethai (the eighth). God had richly
blessed Obed-edom.
6Obed-edom's son Shemaiah had
sons with great ability who earned positions of great authority in the clan.
7Their names were Othni, Rephael,
Obed, and Elzabad. Their relatives,
Elihu and Semakiah, were also very capable men.
8All of these descendants of Obed-
edom, including their sons and
grandsons—sixty-two of them in all—
were very capable men, well qualified for
their work.
9Meshelemiah's eighteen sons and relatives
were also very capable men.

10Hosah, of the Merari clan, appointed
Shimri as the leader among his sons,
though he was not the oldest. 11His
other sons included Hilkiah (the second),
Tebaliah (the third), and Zechariah
(the fourth). Hosah's sons and relatives,
who served as gatekeepers, numbered
thirteen in all.

12These divisions of the gatekeepers
were named for their family leaders, and
like the other Levites, they served at the
house of the LORD. 13They were assigned by
families for guard duty at the various gates,
without regard to age or training, for it was
all decided by means of sacred lots.
14The responsibility for the east gate went
to Meshelemiah and his group. The north
gate was assigned to his son Zechariah, a
man of unusual wisdom. 15The south gate
went to Obed-edom, and his sons were put
in charge of the storehouse. 16Shuppim and
Hosah were assigned the west gate and the
gateway leading up to the Temple. Guard duties were divided evenly. 17Six Levites were
assigned each day to the east gate, four to
the north gate, four to the south gate, and
two pairs at the storehouse. 18Six were assigned each day to the west gate, four to the
gateway leading up to the Temple, and two
to the courtyard.
19These were the divisions of the gatekeepers from the clans of Korah and
Merari.

Treasurers and Other Officials

20Other Levites, led by Ahijah, were in
charge of the treasuries of the house of God
and the treasuries of the gifts dedicated
to the LORD. 21From the family of Libni in
the clan of Gershon, Jehiel was the leader.
22The sons of Jehiel, Zetham and his brother
Joel, were in charge of the treasuries of the
house of the LORD.
23These are the leaders that descended
from Amram, Izhar, Hebron, and Uzziel:

26:1 The first ancestor of the *gatekeepers* was *Meshelemiah* (called "Shallum" in Ezra 2:42; "Meshullam" in Neh 12:25). • ***Abiasaph:*** As in Greek version (see also Exod 6:24); Hebrew reads *Asaph.*

26:5 ***God had richly blessed Obed-edom,*** who temporarily housed the Ark (13:13-14), by giving him many descendants (26:8).

26:14 ***Meshelemiah:*** Hebrew *Shelemiah,* a variant spelling of *Meshelemiah;* cp. 26:2.

26:16 ***the gateway leading up to the Temple:*** Or *the gate of Shalleketh on the upper road* (also in 26:18). The meaning of the Hebrew is uncertain.

26:18 ***the courtyard:*** Or *the colonnade.* The meaning of the Hebrew is uncertain.

26:20-32 In preparation for Solomon's succession to the throne, David appointed these officials as part of his comprehensive organization of the Levitical orders at the end of his reign. The officers included treasurers, administrators, and judges who were part of the political bureaucracy.

26:21-28 The Levites were in charge of the Lord's treasuries and property (see 2 Chr 24:11; 31:12). Some spoils of war were always dedicated to God (26:26-28).

26:21 ***Libni:*** Hebrew *Ladan,* a variant spelling of *Libni;* cp. 6:17. • ***Jehiel:*** Hebrew *Jehieli* (also in 26:22), a variant spelling of *Jehiel;* cp. 23:8.

24From the clan of Amram, Shebuel
was a descendant of Gershom son
of Moses. He was the chief officer of
the treasuries. 25His relatives through
Eliezer were Rehabiah, Jeshaiah, Joram,
Zicri, and Shelomoth.
26Shelomoth and his relatives were in
charge of the treasuries containing the
gifts that King David, the family leaders,
and the generals and captains and other
officers of the army had dedicated to
the LORD. 27These men dedicated some
of the plunder they had gained in battle to maintain the house of the LORD.
28Shelomoth and his relatives also cared
for the gifts dedicated to the LORD by
Samuel the seer, Saul son of Kish, Abner
son of Ner, and Joab son of Zeruiah. All
the other dedicated gifts were in their
care, too.
29From the clan of Izhar came
Kenaniah. He and his sons were given
administrative responsibilities over
Israel as officials and judges.
30From the clan of Hebron came
Hashabiah. He and his relatives—1,700
capable men—were put in charge of
the Israelite lands west of the Jordan
River. They were responsible for all
matters related to the things of the
LORD and the service of the king in
that area.
31Also from the clan of Hebron came
Jeriah, who was the leader of the Hebronites according to the genealogical
records. (In the fortieth year of David's
reign, a search was made in the records,
and capable men from the clan of Hebron were found at Jazer in the land
of Gilead.) 32There were 2,700 capable
men among the relatives of Jeriah. King
David sent them to the east side of the
Jordan River and put them in charge of
the tribes of Reuben and Gad and the
half-tribe of Manasseh. They were responsible for all matters related to God
and to the king.

Organization of the People (27:1-34)
Military Commanders and Divisions

27 This is the list of Israelite generals
and captains, and their officers, who
served the king by supervising the army divisions that were on duty each month of the
year. Each division served for one month
and had 24,000 troops.

2Jashobeam son of Zabdiel was commander
of the first division of 24,000 troops,
which was on duty during the first
month. 3He was a descendant of Perez
and was in charge of all the army
officers for the first month.
4Dodai, a descendant of Ahoah, was
commander of the second division
of 24,000 troops, which was on duty
during the second month. Mikloth was
his chief officer.
5Benaiah son of Jehoiada the priest was
commander of the third division
of 24,000 troops, which was on duty
during the third month. 6This was the
Benaiah who commanded David's elite
military group known as the Thirty. His
son Ammizabad was his chief officer.
7Asahel, the brother of Joab, was
commander of the fourth division of
24,000 troops, which was on duty during
the fourth month. Asahel was succeeded
by his son Zebadiah.
8Shammah the Izrahite was commander
of the fifth division of 24,000 troops,
which was on duty during the fifth
month.
9Ira son of Ikkesh from Tekoa was
commander of the sixth division
of 24,000 troops, which was on duty
during the sixth month.
10Helez, a descendant of Ephraim from
Pelon, was commander of the seventh
division of 24,000 troops, which was on
duty during the seventh month.
11Sibbecai, a descendant of Zerah from
Hushah, was commander of the eighth
division of 24,000 troops, which was on
duty during the eighth month.

26:26 2 Sam 8:11
26:29 1 Chr 23:4
26:30 1 Chr 27:17
26:31 1 Chr 23:19
27:2 2 Sam 23:8; 1 Chr 11:11-31

26:26 ***the generals and captains:*** Literally *the commanders of thousands and of hundreds.*

26:28 ***Shelomoth:*** Hebrew *Shelomith,* a variant spelling of *Shelomoth.*

26:29 ***were given administrative responsibilities:*** Or *were given outside work;* or *were given work away from the Temple area.*

26:31 ***Jazer*** was a Levitical city (Josh 21:39) that became an administrative center during the monarchy. David and his descendants could depend on the loyalty of the Levites from ***Hebron*** (1 Sam 30:27-31; 2 Sam 2:1-11). • ***Jeriah:*** Hebrew *Jerijah,* a variant spelling of *Jeriah;* cp. 23:19.

27:1-15 David's reserve ***army*** was organized into twelve ***divisions,*** each serving on active duty one ***month*** each year. Their duties probably included protecting the borders, policing, keeping order in conquered territories, manning fortresses, and tending military equipment (horses and chariots). The divisions were not related to Israel's tribal structure; each division contained individuals from various tribes, indicating the integration of the kingdom.

27:1 ***generals and captains:*** Literally *commanders of thousands and of hundreds.*

27:8 ***Shammah:*** Hebrew *Shamhuth,* a variant spelling of *Shammah;* cp. 11:27; 2 Sam 23:25.

27:17 1 Chr 12:28
27:23 2 Sam 24:1
27:24 2 Sam 24:12-15; 1 Chr 21:1-7
27:28 1 Kgs 10:27; 2 Chr 1:15
27:29 1 Chr 5:16
27:31 1 Chr 5:10
27:33 2 Sam 15:12, 32, 37
27:34 1 Kgs 1:7; 1 Chr 11:6; 27:5
28:1 1 Chr 11:10-47; 23:2; 27:1-31

[12]Abiezer from Anathoth in the territory of
Benjamin was commander of the ninth
division of 24,000 troops, which was on
duty during the ninth month.
[13]Maharai, a descendant of Zerah from
Netophah, was commander of the tenth
division of 24,000 troops, which was on
duty during the tenth month.
[14]Benaiah from Pirathon in Ephraim was
commander of the eleventh division
of 24,000 troops, which was on duty
during the eleventh month.
[15]Heled, a descendant of Othniel from
Netophah, was commander of the
twelfth division of 24,000 troops, which
was on duty during the twelfth month.

Leaders of the Tribes

[16]The following were the tribes of Israel
and their leaders:

Tribe	*Leader*
Reuben	Eliezer son of Zicri
Simeon	Shephatiah son of Maacah
[17] Levi	Hashabiah son of Kemuel
Aaron (the priests)	Zadok
[18] Judah	Elihu (a brother of David)
Issachar	Omri son of Michael
[19] Zebulun	Ishmaiah son of Obadiah
Naphtali	Jeremoth son of Azriel
[20] Ephraim	Hoshea son of Azaziah
Manasseh (west)	Joel son of Pedaiah
[21] Manasseh in Gilead (east)	Iddo son of Zechariah
Benjamin	Jaasiel son of Abner
[22] Dan	Azarel son of Jeroham

These were the leaders of the tribes of
Israel.
[23]When David took his census, he did not
count those who were younger than twenty
years of age, because the LORD had promised to make the Israelites as numerous as
the stars in heaven. [24]Joab son of Zeruiah
began the census but never finished it because the anger of God fell on Israel. The
total number was never recorded in King
David's official records.

Administrators and Counselors

[25]Azmaveth son of Adiel was in charge of
the palace treasuries.
Jonathan son of Uzziah was in charge of
the regional treasuries throughout the
towns, villages, and fortresses of Israel.
[26]Ezri son of Kelub was in charge of the
field workers who farmed the king's
lands.
[27]Shimei from Ramah was in charge of the
king's vineyards.
Zabdi from Shepham was responsible for
the grapes and the supplies of wine.
[28]Baal-hanan from Geder was in charge of
the king's olive groves and sycamore-fig
trees in the foothills of Judah.
Joash was responsible for the supplies of
olive oil.
[29]Shitrai from Sharon was in charge of the
cattle on the Sharon Plain.
Shaphat son of Adlai was responsible for
the cattle in the valleys.
[30]Obil the Ishmaelite was in charge of the
camels.
Jehdeiah from Meronoth was in charge of
the donkeys.
[31]Jaziz the Hagrite was in charge of the
king's flocks of sheep and goats.
All these officials were overseers of King David's property.

[32]Jonathan, David's uncle, was a wise
counselor to the king, a man of great insight, and a scribe. Jehiel the Hacmonite
was responsible for teaching the king's
sons. [33]Ahithophel was the royal adviser.
Hushai the Arkite was the king's friend.
[34]Ahithophel was succeeded by Jehoiada
son of Benaiah and by Abiathar. Joab was
commander of the king's army.

Accession of Solomon (28:1–29:30)

David's Address to the Assembly

28 David summoned all the officials
of Israel to Jerusalem—the leaders
of the tribes, the commanders of the army
divisions, the other generals and captains,

27:15 *Heled:* Hebrew *Heldai,* a variant spelling of *Heled;* cp. 11:30; 2 Sam 23:29.

27:16-22 The order of the tribes roughly follows Num 1:5-15: the six sons of Leah, the two sons of Rachel (the "tribe" of Joseph=***Ephraim*** and ***Manasseh***, followed by ***Benjamin***), followed by the two sons of Bilhah (***Dan*** and ***Naphtali***). Changes from the order of that list are that ***Naphtali*** is transferred to his geographical location next to ***Zebulun***, and the tribe of ***Levi*** is inserted at the position of Levi's birth order, with the family of ***Aaron (the priests)*** listed separately. Absent from this list are the two sons of Zilpah (Gad and Asher).

27:18 The name ***Elihu*** might refer to *Eliab* (2:13), or he might have been a different ***brother of David***.

27:24 ***never finished it because:*** Or *never finished it, and yet.*

27:25-31 Ancient kings, including David, acquired large amounts of property for themselves. This list records various aspects of David's estate, including storehouses in Jerusalem and the provinces, property used for agricultural purposes, and various types of livestock.

27:28 ***the foothills of Judah:*** Hebrew *the Shephelah.*

27:32-34 The register of David's officials concludes with this list of influential persons in the king's immediate entourage. • A ***wise counselor to the king*** was probably an intimate confidant.

28:1–29:25 Here the account of Solomon's coronation continues from 23:1-2.

the overseers of the royal property and
livestock, the palace officials, the mighty
men, and all the other brave warriors in
the kingdom. 2David rose to his feet and
said: "My brothers and my people! It was
my desire to build a Temple where the [i]Ark
of the LORD's Covenant, God's footstool,
could rest permanently. I made the necessary preparations for building it, 3but God
said to me, 'You must not build a Temple to
honor my name, for you are a warrior and
have shed much blood.'

4"Yet the LORD, the God of Israel, has chosen me from among all my father's family
to be king over Israel forever. For he has
chosen the tribe of Judah to rule, and from
among the families of Judah he chose my father's family. And from among my father's
sons the LORD was pleased to make me king
over all Israel. 5And from among my sons—
for the LORD has given me many—he [j]chose
Solomon to succeed me on the throne of
Israel and to rule over the LORD's kingdom.
6He said to me, 'Your son Solomon will build
my Temple and its courtyards, for I have chosen him as my son, and I will be his father.
7And if he continues to obey my commands
and regulations as he does now, I will make
his kingdom last forever.'

8"So now, with God as our witness, and in
the sight of all Israel—the LORD's assembly—
I give you this charge. Be careful to obey all
the commands of the LORD your God, so
that you may continue to possess this good
land and leave it to your children as a permanent inheritance.

David's Charge to Solomon

9"And Solomon, my son, learn to know the
God of your ancestors intimately. Worship
and serve him with your whole heart and a
willing mind. For the LORD sees every heart
and knows every plan and thought. If you
seek him, you will find him. But if you forsake him, he will reject you forever. 10So
take this seriously. The LORD has chosen
you to build a Temple as his sanctuary. Be
strong, and do the work."

11Then David gave Solomon the plans
for the Temple and its surroundings, including the entry room, the storerooms,
the upstairs rooms, the inner rooms, and
the inner sanctuary—which was the place
of atonement. 12David also gave Solomon
all the plans he had in mind for the courtyards of the LORD's Temple, the outside
rooms, the treasuries, and the rooms for
the gifts dedicated to the LORD. 13The king
also gave Solomon the instructions concerning the work of the various divisions
of priests and Levites in the Temple of the
LORD. And he gave specifications for the
items in the Temple that were to be used
for worship.

14David gave instructions regarding how
much gold and silver should be used to
make the items needed for service. 15He
told Solomon the amount of gold needed
for the gold lampstands and lamps, and the
amount of silver for the silver lampstands
and lamps, depending on how each would
be used. 16He designated the amount of
gold for the table on which the Bread of the
Presence would be placed and the amount
of silver for other tables.

17David also designated the amount of gold
for the solid gold meat hooks used to handle the sacrificial meat and for the basins,
pitchers, and dishes, as well as the amount

28:2 1 Chr 17:1-2; Ps 132:7; Isa 66:1; [i]*'aron* (0727) ‣Ps 132:8
28:3 1 Chr 17:4; 22:8
28:4 Gen 49:8-10; 1 Sam 16:1-12; 1 Chr 5:2; 17:23, 27
28:5 1 Chr 3:1-9; 14:3-7; 22:9-10; [j]*bakhar* (0977) ‣Ps 78:68
28:6 2 Sam 7:13-14
28:7 1 Chr 22:13
28:9 1 Kgs 8:61; 2 Chr 15:2; Jer 29:13
28:10 1 Chr 22:13
28:11 Exod 25:17-22, 40
28:12 1 Chr 26:20, 28
28:13 1 Chr 23:6; 24:1
28:15 Exod 25:31

David is presented at the pinnacle of his strength as he transfers authority to Solomon (cp. 1 Kgs 1:1–2:9).

28:1 This assembly of *all the officials of Israel* includes all whose names were mentioned in the preceding chapters. • ***the other generals and captains:*** Literally *the commanders of thousands and commanders of hundreds.*

28:2-10 The account of David's first discourse includes a message addressed to his people (28:2-8) and a message to Solomon (28:9-10). The main focus of the address is David's desire for Solomon to ***build a temple.*** In addition, David addressed two other important themes: God's selection of Solomon, and the people's obligation to keep God's commandments.

28:2 David described the Temple as a place where the ***Ark of the LORD's Covenant . . . could rest.*** The term "rest" describes the conquest of the land and the establishment of peace (e.g., Deut 12:9). In the wilderness, the Ark rested at the end of battle (Num 10:35-36). When David brought the Ark to Jerusalem, the Ark's "rest" became permanent, as David expressed in a psalm of worship: "Arise, O LORD, and enter your resting place, along with the Ark, the symbol of your power" (Ps 132:8). God had chosen Mount Zion as his resting place (see "Mount Zion, the City of God" at Ps 48, p. 947).

28:3 See note on 22:8.

28:4-6 ***the LORD . . . has chosen me . . . to be king over Israel forever:*** God's selection of David actually began with Judah (Gen 49:8-12), culminated with David (1 Sam 16:1-13), and continued with Solomon (28:5-6, 10). All subsequent kings reigned by virtue of God's promise to David.

28:9-10 David's message to Solomon did not stress the privileges of being chosen as king but emphasized the responsibilities of assuming the throne. The primary obligation was to ***seek*** the Lord, to ***worship and serve him.*** The Lord also required an unflinching resolve to build the Temple sanctuary.

28:11-21 God gave David the actual ***plans for the Temple*** through divine inspiration (28:19). On other occasions God also provided plans for the Tabernacle in the wilderness (Exod 25:9) and for the future Temple of Ezekiel (Ezek 40:4).

28:12 ***the plans he had in mind:*** Or *the plans of the spirit that was with him.*

28:14-18 This list of vessels legitimized each object in the Temple by

28:18
Exod 25:18-22; 30:1
28:19
1 Chr 28:11-12
28:20
Josh 1:5
1 Chr 22:13
Heb 13:5
28:21
Exod 35:25-35; 36:1-2
29:1
1 Chr 22:5
29:2
1 Chr 22:2-5

of silver for every dish. [18]He designated
the amount of refined gold for the altar of
incense. Finally, he gave him a plan for the
LORD's "chariot"—the gold cherubim whose
wings were stretched out over the Ark of the
LORD's Covenant. [19]"Every part of this plan,"
David told Solomon, "was given to me in writing from the hand of the LORD."
[20]Then David continued, "Be strong and
courageous, and do the work. Don't be
afraid or discouraged, for the LORD God,
my God, is with you. He will not fail you
or forsake you. He will see to it that all the
work related to the Temple of the LORD is
finished correctly. [21]The various divisions
of priests and Levites will serve in the
Temple of God. Others with skills of every
kind will volunteer, and the officials and
the entire nation are at your command."

Gifts for Building the Temple

29 Then King David turned to the
entire assembly and said, "My son
Solomon, whom God has clearly chosen as
the next king of Israel, is still young and
inexperienced. The work ahead of him is
enormous, for the Temple he will build is
not for mere mortals—it is for the LORD God
himself! [2]Using every resource at my command, I have gathered as much as I could for
building the Temple of my God. Now there
is enough gold, silver, bronze, iron, and
wood, as well as great quantities of onyx,
other precious stones, costly jewels, and all
kinds of fine stone and marble.
[3]"And now, because of my devotion to
the Temple of my God, I am giving all of my
own private treasures of gold and silver to
help in the construction. This is in addition

God's Promised Kingdom (28:1-21)

1 Chr 17:9-14
Isa 2:1-4; 60:1-22; 65:17-25
Ezek 37:21-28
Dan 2:31-45; 7:1-28
Mic 4:1-5
Zech 9:9-10; 14:1-21
Matt 4:17; 6:33; 13:11-50; 16:16-19; 18:3-4, 23-35; 19:14, 23-30; 20:1-16; 22:2-14; 25:1-46
Luke 1:30-33
Eph 5:5
Rev 19:1–21:27

God promised that his kingdom would come through David (17:4-14). During his reign, David himself made preparations for the building of the Temple as the focal point of God's kingdom (28:11-19). He also appealed to Israel's leaders to seek the Lord (28:8-10), and he encouraged the community of Israel to "be strong and courageous" in trusting God to provide (28:20-21).

The Chronicler used these words of David to appeal to the citizens of Judea after the Exile to keep the hope of God's kingdom. The Chronicler wanted the people to know that God's promise to David, confirmed to Solomon, was equally confirmed for them. After the Exile, Judah no longer existed as an independent kingdom ruled by the dynasty of David. Instead, Judea stood as a small territory with limited independence under a Persian governor. Yet the community of Judea could experience God's blessing, just as the people had in the days of Hezekiah or Josiah. The Chronicler did not know exactly how God's promise to David would be realized. Yet he had complete trust in God's power, sovereignty, and justice; he knew that God would be faithful to his promise, and his kingdom would eventually rule over all.

Following the time of the Chronicler, it appeared that his hopes were disappointed. The Greeks replaced the Persians as rulers of Israel; their intolerance for the Jewish community of faith reached its zenith in the tyrannical Antiochus (Epiphanes) IV (175–163 BC), who made every effort to destroy Israel's faith and identity, as Daniel had foreseen (Dan 11:21-39). The priestly family of Maccabees resisted Antiochus, restored the Temple, and preserved Judea's identity. But then the community disintegrated under the successors to the Maccabees; Israel fractured into sects (Pharisees, Sadducees, and Essenes) and eventually came under Roman control. When Jesus was born, Roman governors controlled the territory of Israel.

The fulfillment of God's promises to David took place in a way the Chronicler did not anticipate. Jesus was the anointed king, the Messiah from the dynasty of David (Matt 16:16-17). He established his kingdom among his followers. The powers of hell will never prevail against his followers; his kingdom will be forever.

specifically recounting what God had communicated about them through David.

28:18 *for the LORD's "chariot"—the gold cherubim:* Literally *for the gold cherub chariot.* The *cherubim* were various images of composite creatures found in connection with thrones and palaces. Ancient kings sat on cherub thrones. In God's throne room (the Most Holy Place of Israel's sanctuary), *cherubim* atop the Ark of the Covenant served a similar function (see Exod 25:18-22; 2 Sam 6:2; Ps 99:1; cp. Ezek 10:1-22).

28:19 *was given to me in writing from the hand of the LORD:* Or *was written under the direction of the LORD.*

29:1-9 David persuaded the *assembly* of Israel's leaders (28:1) to offer gifts to the Lord for the Temple. David's own generous gift provided an example of the amounts leaders should consider. The Chronicler emphasizes that the heavy expense of building the Temple was not shouldered by Solomon alone; Solomon added to the contributions made by David and the leaders of Israel (see 22:14). • *young and inexperienced:* See note on 22:5.

to the building materials I have already collected for his holy Temple. [4]I am donating
more than 112 tons of gold from Ophir
and 262 tons of refined silver to be used
for overlaying the walls of the buildings
[5]and for the other gold and silver work to
be done by the craftsmen. Now then, who
will follow my example and give offerings
to the LORD today?"

[6]Then the family leaders, the leaders
of the tribes of Israel, the generals and
captains of the army, and the king's administrative officers all gave willingly. [7]For the
construction of the Temple of God, they
gave about 188 tons of gold, 10,000 gold
coins, 375 tons of silver, 675 tons of bronze,
and 3,750 tons of iron. [8]They also contributed numerous precious stones, which were
deposited in the treasury of the house of
the LORD under the care of Jehiel, a descendant of Gershon. [9]The people rejoiced over
the offerings, for they had given freely and
wholeheartedly to the LORD, and King David
was filled with joy.

David's Prayer of Praise

[10]Then David praised the LORD in the presence of the whole assembly:

"O LORD, the God of our ancestor Israel,
may you be praised forever and ever!
[11]Yours, O LORD, is the greatness, the
power, the glory, the victory, and the
majesty. Everything in the heavens and
on earth is yours, O LORD, and this is
your kingdom. We adore you as the one
who is over all things. [12]Wealth and
honor come from you alone, for you
rule over everything. Power and might
are in your hand, and at your discretion people are made great and given
strength.

[13]"O our God, we thank you and
praise your glorious name! [14]But who
am I, and who are my people, that we
could give anything to you? Everything
we have has come from you, and we give
you only what you first gave us! [15]We
are here for only a moment, visitors and
strangers in the land as our ancestors
were before us. Our days on earth are
like a passing shadow, gone so soon
without a trace.

[16]"O LORD our God, even this material
we have gathered to build a Temple to
honor your holy name comes from you!
It all belongs to you! [17]I know, my God,
that you examine our [k]hearts and rejoice
when you find integrity there. You know
I have done all this with good [k]motives,
and I have watched your people offer
their gifts willingly and joyously.

[18]"O LORD, the God of our ancestors Abraham, Isaac, and Israel, make
your people always want to obey you.
See to it that their love for you never
changes. [19]Give my son Solomon the
wholehearted desire to obey all your
commands, laws, and decrees, and to
do everything necessary to build this
Temple, for which I have made these
preparations."

[20]Then David said to the whole assembly,
"Give praise to the LORD your God!" And the
entire assembly praised the LORD, the God
of their ancestors, and they bowed low and
knelt before the LORD and the king.

Solomon Named as King

[21]The next day they brought 1,000 bulls,
1,000 rams, and 1,000 male lambs as burnt
offerings to the LORD. They also brought
liquid offerings and many other sacrifices

29:4 1 Kgs 9:28; 1 Chr 22:14
29:6 1 Chr 27:1, 25; 28:1
29:8 1 Chr 23:8
29:9 1 Kgs 8:61; 2 Cor 9:7
29:11 Rev 5:12-13
29:12 2 Chr 1:12; 20:6
29:15 Lev 25:23; Job 14:2, 10-12
29:17 1 Chr 28:9; [k]*lebab* (3824) ›2 Chr 12:14
29:19 1 Chr 28:9; Ps 72:1
29:20 Josh 22:33
29:21 1 Kgs 8:62-63

29:4 *112 tons of gold:* Hebrew *3,000 talents* [102 metric tons] *of gold.* • ***262 tons of refined silver:*** Hebrew *7,000 talents* [238 metric tons] *of silver.*

29:6 ***the generals and captains of the army:*** Literally *the commanders of thousands and commanders of hundreds.* • Israel's ***leaders*** gave ***willingly***, as had been the case with the Tabernacle (Exod 25:1-7).

29:7 *188 tons of gold:* Hebrew *5,000 talents* [170 metric tons] *of gold.* • ***10,000 gold coins:*** Hebrew *10,000 darics* [a Persian coin] *of gold,* about 185 pounds or 84 kilograms in weight. Persian *darics* were first minted during the reign of King Darius I of Persia (522–486 BC). In describing the Temple gifts presented during the days of Solomon, the Chronicler converted the information of his sources into the equivalents of his own day, just as the NLT converts Hebrew weights and measures to modern equivalents. • ***375 tons of silver:*** Hebrew *10,000 talents* [340 metric tons] *of silver.* • ***675 tons of bronze:*** Hebrew *18,000 talents* [612 metric tons] *of bronze.* • ***3,750 tons of iron:*** Hebrew *100,000 talents* [3,400 metric tons] *of iron.*

29:10-19 David's prayer of praise concluded his addresses at Solomon's coronation. The prayer extols God's ***power*** and the ***glory*** of his ***kingdom***, and it serves to dedicate the offerings given for building the ***Temple***. The prayer is composed of three parts: the doxology (20:10b-13), the presentation and dedication of the offerings (29:14-17), and the petition (29:18-19).

29:10 ***Israel*** is the name that God gave to Jacob (Gen 32:28).

29:18-19 David did not ask God to grant power, victory, or riches, or for the establishment of Solomon's kingdom. Instead he asked God to make the people of Israel, and Solomon in particular, ***always want to obey*** the Lord. Gaining this kind of heart attitude is a gift from the Lord; success and prosperity are secondary.

29:21-25 ***Sacrifices*** followed the speeches and prayers at Solomon's coronation. ***Solomon*** and ***Zadok*** were ***anointed***, and Solomon acceded to the throne. Zadok was not beginning his priestly role but was being dedicated to serve in the Temple itself. (The descendants of Zadok are mentioned in Ezek 40:46; 43:19; 44:15; 48:11.)

29:22
1 Kgs 1:33-34
1 Chr 29:1
[a]*simkhah* (8057)
‣ Job 20:5
[b]*mashakh* (4886)
‣ Ps 45:7

29:25
2 Chr 1:1, 12

29:26-28
// 1 Kgs 2:10-12

29:26
1 Chr 18:14

29:27
2 Sam 5:4-5

29:28
1 Chr 23:1
Acts 13:36

29:29
1 Sam 9:9; 22:5
2 Sam 7:2

on behalf of all Israel. 22They feasted and
drank in the LORD's presence with great
[a]joy that day.
And again they crowned David's son Solomon as their new king. They [b]anointed
him before the LORD as their leader, and
they anointed Zadok as priest. 23So Solomon took the throne of the LORD in place
of his father, David, and he succeeded in
everything, and all Israel obeyed him. 24All
the officials, the warriors, and the sons of
King David pledged their loyalty to King Solomon. 25And the LORD exalted Solomon in
the sight of all Israel, and he gave Solomon
greater royal splendor than any king in
Israel before him.

Summary of David's Reign
1 Chr 29:26-30 // 1 Kgs 2:10-12

26So David son of Jesse reigned over all Israel. 27He reigned over Israel for forty years,
seven of them in Hebron and thirty-three
in Jerusalem. 28He died at a ripe old age,
having enjoyed long life, wealth, and honor.
Then his son Solomon ruled in his place.
29All the events of King David's reign,
from beginning to end, are written in *The
Record of Samuel the Seer, The Record of
Nathan the Prophet,* and *The Record of
Gad the Seer.* 30These accounts include the
mighty deeds of his reign and everything
that happened to him and to Israel and to
all the surrounding kingdoms.

29:26-30 The Chronicler concludes his account of David's reign with a stylized summary, similar in form to those used for all the kings of Israel and Judah (e.g., 1 Kgs 22:41-50). Like Abraham (Gen 25:8) and Isaac (Gen 35:29), ***David . . . died at a ripe old age*** with ***wealth*** and ***honor.***

29:29 The sources used for the chronicles of ***David's reign*** are associated with three prophets, named in the order in which they appear in Chronicles: ***Samuel*** (11:3), ***Nathan*** (ch 17), and ***Gad*** (21:9). The Chronicler had access to various sources in addition to the books of Samuel and Kings (see note on 9:1; see also 1 Kgs 11:41-43; 14:19-20, 29-31).

29:30 The concluding verse extols David by making him the center of the events of his time.

THE SECOND BOOK OF CHRONICLES

The books of Chronicles give purpose and hope to a people whose future appears uncertain. God had promised that David's descendants would have an everlasting kingdom, but the people of Judah had been exiled to Babylon, had returned to Jerusalem, and now lived as Persian subjects. Judah had no king descended from David, and no hope of becoming a kingdom. Yet God's promises are certain, so the Chronicler encouraged the Judeans to hope for the future. The words of King Jehoshaphat capture the spirit of Chronicles: "Listen to me, all you people of Judah

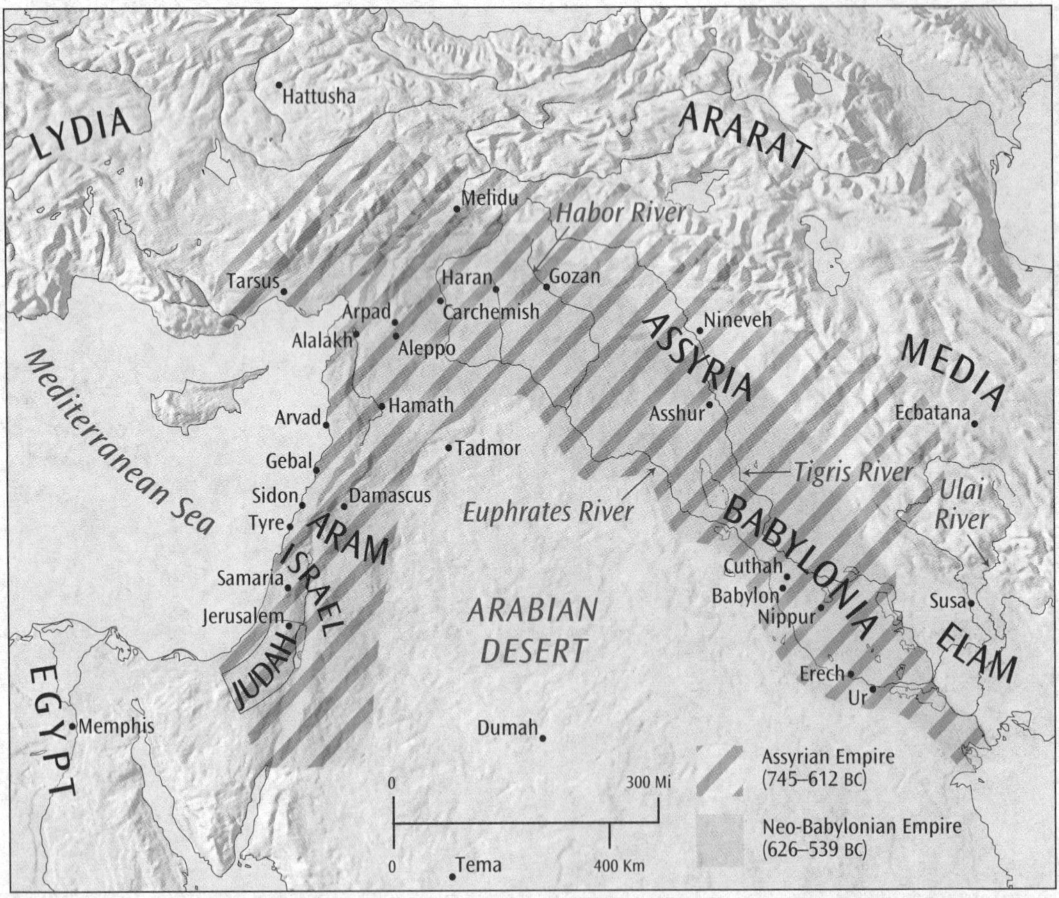

▲ **The Ancient Near East, 1050–550 BC.** Many of the events described in 2 Chronicles were shaped by the rise and fall of the world powers of ancient Near East—EGYPT, ASSYRIA, and BABYLONIA.

ARAM, DAMASCUS 16:2, 7; 24:23-25; 28:5, 23
ASSYRIA 28:16-21; 32:1-22; 33:11
BABYLON 32:31; 33:11; 36:6-20
CARCHEMISH 35:20
EGYPT 1:16-17; 10:2; 12:2, 9; 35:20; 36:3-4
HAMATH, TADMOR 8:4
SAMARIA 18:2; 22:9; 28:8-15
TYRE 2:3

and Jerusalem! Believe in the LORD your God, and you will be able to stand firm. Believe in his prophets, and you will succeed" (20:20).

SETTING

The Babylonian conquest of Judah occurred in 605–586 BC, about two centuries before Chronicles was written (around 400 BC; see 1 Chronicles Introduction, "Authorship and Date," p. 684). To address questions about God's purposes, the Chronicler narrated the past of the Israelites from the earliest times until the destruction of the kingdom of Judah.

The Chronicler was a skilled professional historian. His knowledge of Israel's former glory came through his worship at the Temple, his reading of the Scriptures, and his work as a historian. In his writing, he extensively used the Pentateuch, Samuel, Kings, and many other sources. He selected material from the earlier books and edited it into the order, context, and form that he thought appropriate for his writing purpose. He evaluated his sources, commenting on their meaning and on the significance of the historical events in the earlier texts. By studying the past, he learned about the present and provided hope for the future of faithful people.

OUTLINE

1:1–9:31
Reign of Solomon

10:1–28:27
Israel until the Exile of the North

29:1–36:23
Healing for Israel

The Chronicler was also a sophisticated writer. By carefully selecting his material and reworking it to suit his own purposes, he did not intend to replace or supplement earlier historical writings. Instead, he presumed that his readers were already familiar with his main sources and knew the characters in his books. He made his writings vital to his own time: He evaluated the past from his own vantage point and wrote so that his contemporaries could understand the heritage of the Temple and its worship and the status of God's promises.

SUMMARY

The Chronicler's history focuses on David and Solomon. The promise of the kingdom that God gave to David was confirmed for Solomon (1 Chr 28:4-7), and the Chronicler's account of David and Solomon constitutes almost half of his history (1 Chr 11–29; 2 Chr 1–9). Much of this narrative pertains to the building of the Temple and to providing for the priests.

Solomon's prayer and God's response are central to the Chronicler's account of Solomon (chs 6–7). God responded to Solomon's prayer in a vision that articulated the Chronicler's own theological perspective (7:12-22): God answers the prayers and repentance of his people; he brings judgment upon the disobedient, but he rewards humility and prayer with healing

TIMELINE

971–931 BC
Solomon as king of Israel

967–960 BC
The Temple is built

945–924 BC
Shoshenq I (Shishak) as pharaoh of Egypt

931 BC
The kingdom is divided

931–913 BC
Rehoboam as king of Judah

931–910 BC
Jeroboam I as king of Israel

926/925 BC
Shishak invades Judah

913–910 BC
Abijam as king of Judah

910–869 BC
Asa as king of Judah

909–886 BC
Baasha as king of Israel

about 895 BC
Baasha attacks Judah

874–853 BC
Ahab as king of Israel

872–848 BC
Jehoshaphat as king of Judah

about 870~850 BC
Elijah as prophet

853–841 BC
Jehoram as king of Judah

841 BC
Ahaziah (Jehoahaz) as king of Judah

841–835 BC
Athaliah as queen of Judah

835–796 BC
Joash (Jehoash) as king of Judah

796–767 BC
Amaziah as king of Judah

792–740 BC
Uzziah (Azariah) as king of Judah

750–732 BC
Jotham as king of Judah

744–727 BC
Tiglath-pileser III as king of Assyria

743–715 BC
Ahaz as king of Judah

728–686 BC
Hezekiah as king of Judah

722 BC
End of the northern kingdom of Israel

704–681 BC
Sennacherib as king of Assyria

697–642 BC
Manasseh as king of Judah

642–640 BC
Amon as king of Judah

640–609 BC
Josiah as king of Judah

610–595 BC
Neco II as pharaoh of Egypt

609 BC
Josiah's death at Megiddo, Jehoahaz as king of Judah

609–598 BC
Jehoiakim as king of Judah

605–562 BC
Nebuchadnezzar II as king of Babylon

597 BC
Jehoiachin as king of Judah

Apr 597 BC
Nebuchadnezzar seizes Jerusalem, plunders Temple

597–586 BC
Zedekiah as king of Judah

586 BC
Nebuchadnezzar destroys Jerusalem, exiles the people of Judah, end of the southern kingdom of Judah

559–530 BC
Cyrus II as king of Persia

Oct 539 BC
Cyrus II conquers Babylon

538 BC
Cyrus's decree allows exiles to return to Judea

about 400 BC
▸ 1–2 Chronicles is written

and deliverance. The Chronicler used his sources to explain to his own generation God's rewards and punishments.

After recording the division of the monarchy, the Chronicler focused exclusively on the southern kingdom of Judah. He associated the continuity of the kingdom and Israel's future with two institutions: the dynasty of David and the Temple in Jerusalem. However, the southern kingdom was not always a model of obedience, and the northern kingdom, Israel, sometimes did what was right (e.g., 28:5-15). The Chronicler always saw the northern kingdom as a part of Israel that needed to be restored, and he took special interest in contacts between the north and the south. He did not condemn the northerners for the initial division, but he did blame them for their refusal to return once their grievances were settled.

The Chronicler's portrayal of Judah's kings sometimes departs remarkably from parallel descriptions in the book of Kings, such as with Uzziah, Jotham, and Hezekiah. Although Uzziah was a powerful king who ruled for more than fifty years, he appears as a minor figure in Kings (2 Kgs 15:1-7). In Chronicles, however, Uzziah is depicted as a famous reformer and builder. Although little is said about Jotham in Kings (2 Kgs 15:32-38), his work is portrayed much more extensively in Chronicles. He continued the work of his father Uzziah: He built extensively on the wall of the Ophel, established cities in the hill country of Judah, and built fortresses and towers in the wooded areas (27:3-4). The Chronicler also expands our understanding of Hezekiah, devoting more space to him (29:1–32:33) than to any king except David and Solomon, dealing extensively with Hezekiah's reforms and the restoration of Temple worship, and describing at length how Hezekiah prepared for the Assyrian siege of Jerusalem.

The reigns of Manasseh and Amon follow (ch 33), and their wickedness and idolatry set the stage for Judah's demise. Manasseh experienced his own exile, repentance, and return to Judah—a microcosm of what the Judeans themselves later experienced. Josiah's reign (34:1–35:27) was pleasing to God. But when Josiah died (609 BC), Judah's end soon followed. Within four years, the Babylonians began a series of attacks (605–586 BC) that led to the destruction of Jerusalem and the Temple and the exile of most of the population to Babylon (36:2-21). The covenant unfaithfulness of the people of Judah had come to fruition. Yet the Chronicler included a glimmer of hope, ending his account with the later proclamation of Cyrus in 538 BC that allowed the Jews to return to Judah and rebuild Jerusalem (36:22-23).

CHRONICLES AS HISTORY

Chronicles is an ancient work of history with a distinctive approach. The book of 2 Chronicles covers essentially the same time period as 1 & 2 Kings. And while the Chronicler drew upon the earlier records of Samuel, Kings, and other sources, his own work shows a remarkable independence. He gave detailed attention to military, administrative, and geopolitical affairs in times that were already hundreds of years distant. He frequently added detailed information not found in any surviving sources but evidently available to him.

Archaeology occasionally provides confirmation of administrative and geopolitical reforms discussed by the Chronicler. For example, an inscription has been found in the Siloam Tunnel describing Hezekiah's water project. Most of the time, the evidence has only a broad connection, such as with Uzziah's building activity or agricultural initiatives. The work of the Chronicler is a valuable resource for understanding the history of the times he wrote about.

MEANING AND MESSAGE

The fundamental question for the restoration community that comprised the original audience of Chronicles was its relationship to the Israel of the past. They were no longer an independent nation but a small province in the Persian empire. What validity did God's promises regarding the Temple and the house of David have for a community that had no king, lived under foreign domination, and had only recently rebuilt the Temple destroyed by the Babylonians?

Chronicles presents the period of David and Solomon as an ideal time when all of Israel united in worship at the Temple (7:8). Concern for the correct worship of God dominates the account of David's reign. The restoration of the Ark to Jerusalem and David's military victories provided for the future Temple. David made all the necessary arrangements for the appropriate officials as worship shifted from Gibeon to Jerusalem. To the Chronicler, David's reign offered a paradigm for his own readers: David moved out of being a fugitive from Saul (a condition of exile) and into the functioning community of God. The postexilic community reading Chronicles had undergone a similar transition from exile and could anticipate similar blessings if they were obedient.

The Chronicler regards Solomon's reign as equal to David's, because Solomon brought to fruition David's plans for the Temple and its worship (3:1; 5:1; 7:1). In Chronicles, Solomon enjoys divine blessing and the total support of the people, David appoints Solomon to the throne in a public announcement, and Adonijah's attempted coup is entirely omitted. The Chronicler does not mention Solomon's sins, and he shifts blame for the schism to Jeroboam (13:6-7). Solomon's wealth and international influence reflect his glorious, peaceful, and righteous reign.

The division of Israel into northern and southern kingdoms shows the obvious failure of the kingdom to meet its ideals, but it does not mean that all hope for the kingdom was lost. Obedience still results in God's blessing, and disobedience will be punished. The Chronicler provides a cause for judgment each time calamity occurs, and he also emphasizes the blessings that result from faithfulness. Repentance is always a means of averting, or at least moderating, a threatened judgment. Prophetic warnings are always issued before judgment falls, and the possibility of healing is always present. This pattern provides one of the primary ways that the Chronicler communicates hope for the future in his own time.

With the reign of Hezekiah, the Chronicler offers a solution to the problem of the divided monarchy. Under Ahaz, Judah descended to the same level of disobedience as Israel (28:2, 6), and the kingdom of Israel is presented in a more favorable light. As Israel's leaders confessed their sins (28:13), they indicated that the northerners were

The Chronicler . . . has so connected the historical facts with the attitude of the kings and the people to the Lord and to his law, that they teach how the Lord rewarded fidelity to his covenant with blessing and success both to people and kingdom, but punished with calamity and judgments every faithless revolt from his covenant ordinances.

C. F. KEIL
1 & 2 Chronicles

FURTHER READING

LESLIE C. ALLEN
1 & 2 Chronicles (1993)

MARK J. BODA
2 Chronicles in *Cornerstone Biblical Commentary*, vol. 5a (2010)

RAY DILLARD
2 Chronicles (1987)

ANDREW E. HILL
1 & 2 Chronicles (2003)

JOHN H. SAILHAMER
First & Second Chronicles (1983)

MARTIN SELMAN
2 Chronicles (1994)

ready for restoration. The Chronicler then introduces Hezekiah, distinctively characterizing him as a second Solomon. Hezekiah invited the north to join in the first Passover of his reign, and many responded (30:11); a similar celebration had not been held since Solomon's time (30:26). Hezekiah's Passover provides a model for the restoration of Israel as a unified kingdom.

The Chronicler used his account of Israel's history to teach his readers to regulate their lives and community. He maintained hope for a historical restoration of the promise to David—however remote such a possibility may have seemed in his time. The Chronicler makes it clear that the kingdom of Israel was not a human institution subject to the whims of political expediency. It was God's kingdom, and God would ultimately make it a reality.

1. REIGN OF SOLOMON (1:1–9:31)

Confirmation of Solomon (1:1-17)

Solomon Asks for Wisdom

2 Chr 1:1-13 // 1 Kgs 3:1-15

1 Solomon son of David took firm control
of his kingdom, for the LORD his God
was with him and made him very powerful.
2Solomon called together all the leaders
of Israel—the generals and captains of the
army, the judges, and all the political and
clan leaders. 3Then he led the entire assembly to the place of worship in Gibeon, for
God's Tabernacle was located there. (This
was the Tabernacle that Moses, the LORD's
servant, had made in the wilderness.)
4David had already moved the Ark of God
from Kiriath-jearim to the tent he had prepared for it in Jerusalem. 5But the bronze
altar made by Bezalel son of Uri and grandson of Hur was there at Gibeon in front of
the Tabernacle of the LORD. So Solomon
and the people gathered in front of it to
consult the LORD. 6There in front of the
Tabernacle, Solomon went up to the bronze
altar in the LORD's presence and sacrificed
1,000 burnt offerings on it.
7That night God appeared to Solomon
and said, "What do you want? Ask, and I will
give it to you!"
8Solomon replied to God, "You showed
faithful love to David, my father, and now
you have made me king in his place. 9O LORD
God, please continue to keep your promise
to David my father, for you have made me
king over a people as numerous as the dust
of the earth! 10Give me the wisdom and
knowledge to lead them properly, for who
could possibly govern this great people of
yours?"
11God said to Solomon, "Because your
greatest desire is to help your people, and
you did not ask for wealth, riches, fame, or
even the death of your enemies or a long
life, but rather you asked for wisdom and
knowledge to properly govern my people—
12I will certainly give you the wisdom and
knowledge you requested. But I will also
give you wealth, riches, and fame such as no
other king has had before you or will ever
have in the future!"
13Then Solomon returned to Jerusalem
from the Tabernacle at the place of worship
in Gibeon, and he reigned over Israel.

Solomon's Wealth and Splendor

2 Chr 1:14-17 // 1 Kgs 10:26-29 // 2 Chr 9:25-28

14Solomon built up a huge force of chariots and horses. He had 1,400 chariots and

1:1 1 Kgs 2:12, 46; 1 Chr 29:25
1:2 1 Chr 28:1
1:3 Exod 40:18; 1 Kgs 3:4
1:4 1 Chr 15:25-28
1:5 Exod 31:2; 38:1-7
1:6 1 Kgs 3:4
1:7 1 Kgs 3:5-14
1:8 1 Chr 28:5
1:9 Gen 13:16; 22:17; 2 Sam 7:12-16
1:10 2 Sam 5:2; 1 Kgs 3:9
1:11 1 Kgs 3:11
1:12 1 Chr 29:25; 2 Chr 9:22
1:13 2 Chr 1:3
1:14 1 Kgs 4:26; 9:19; 10:26-29

1:1 David had asked that the Lord be with *Solomon* (1 Chr 22:11) and that Solomon be strong and of good courage (1 Chr 28:20). David also declared that God would make Solomon great, giving strength to all Israel (1 Chr 29:12). Three points about Solomon echo David's blessings: Solomon *took firm control of his kingdom, . . . God was with him*, and God *made him very powerful.*

1:2-6 Solomon's journey to *Gibeon*, reported in 1 Kgs 3:4, is here elaborated. This great public venture was closely associated with Solomon taking the throne. The event included military commanders and *clan leaders.* It took place in Gibeon because the Tabernacle was there, as was the great *bronze altar* where sacrifices were regularly offered.

1:2 *the generals and captains of the army:* Literally *the commanders of thousands and of hundreds.*

1:3 *Tabernacle:* Literally *Tent of Meeting;* also in 1:6, 13. See note on Exod 27:21.

1:5 *was there:* As in Greek version and Latin Vulgate, and some Hebrew manuscripts. Masoretic Text reads *he placed.* • *to consult the LORD:* Literally *to consult him.*

1:7-12 See "Solomon's Wisdom" at 1 Kgs 3:5-14, p. 577.

1:10 Solomon received *wisdom and knowledge* so he could *govern* (Hebrew *shapat*) well. The word *shapat,* often rendered "judge" (e.g., in Judges), can also mean "govern." • *to lead them properly* literally *to go out and come in before this people.*

1:14-17 The illustration of Solomon's wealth and power (expanded on in 9:25-28) comes from the summary of his kingdom in 1 Kgs 10:26-29. In Kings, the summary of Solomon's wealth provided a transition to the negative aspects of Solomon's rule (1 Kgs 11). Here, Solomon's amassing of wealth showed the fulfillment of God's promise (1:12).

1:15 1 Kgs 10:27
2:1 1 Kgs 5:5
2:2 1 Kgs 5:15-16; 2 Chr 2:18
2:3 1 Kgs 5:2-11; 1 Chr 14:1
2:4 Exod 25:30; 29:38-42; 30:7; Num 28:9-10
2:5 Exod 15:11; 1 Chr 16:25
2:6 1 Kgs 8:27; 2 Chr 6:18
2:7 Exod 31:3-5; 1 Chr 22:15; 2 Chr 2:13-15
2:8 2 Chr 9:10-11
2:10 1 Kgs 5:11
2:11 1 Kgs 10:9; 2 Chr 9:8
2:12 2 Chr 2:1; Ps 33:6; 102:25
2:14 1 Kgs 7:14

12,000 horses. He stationed some of them in the chariot cities and some near him in Jerusalem. 15The king made silver and gold as plentiful in Jerusalem as stone. And valuable cedar timber was as common as the sycamore-fig trees that grow in the foothills of Judah. 16Solomon's horses were imported from Egypt and from Cilicia; the king's traders acquired them from Cilicia at the standard price. 17At that time chariots from Egypt could be purchased for 600 pieces of silver, and horses for 150 pieces of silver. They were then exported to the kings of the Hittites and the kings of Aram.

Building the Temple (2:1–7:22)

Preparations for Building the Temple

2 Chr 2:1-18 // 1 Kgs 5:1-18

2 Solomon decided to build a Temple to honor the name of the LORD, and also a royal palace for himself. 2He enlisted a force of 70,000 laborers, 80,000 men to quarry stone in the hill country, and 3,600 foremen.

3Solomon also sent this message to King Hiram at Tyre:

"Send me cedar logs as you did for my father, David, when he was building his palace. 4I am about to build a Temple to honor the name of the LORD my God. It will be a place set apart to burn fragrant incense before him, to display the special sacrificial bread, and to sacrifice burnt offerings each morning and evening, on the Sabbaths, at new moon celebrations, and at the other appointed festivals of the LORD our God. He has commanded Israel to do these things forever.

5"This must be a magnificent Temple because our God is greater than all other gods. 6But who can really build him a worthy home? Not even the highest heavens can contain him! So who am I to consider building a Temple for him, except as a place to burn sacrifices to him?

7"So send me a master craftsman who can work with gold, silver, bronze, and iron, as well as with purple, scarlet, and blue cloth. He must be a skilled engraver who can work with the craftsmen of Judah and Jerusalem who were selected by my father, David.

8"Also send me cedar, cypress, and red sandalwood logs from Lebanon, for I know that your men are without equal at cutting timber in Lebanon. I will send my men to help them. 9An immense amount of timber will be needed, for the Temple I am going to build will be very large and magnificent. 10In payment for your woodcutters, I will send 100,000 bushels of crushed wheat, 100,000 bushels of barley, 110,000 gallons of wine, and 110,000 gallons of olive oil."

11King Hiram sent this letter of reply to Solomon:

"It is because the LORD loves his people that he has made you their king! 12Praise the LORD, the God of Israel, who made the heavens and the earth! He has given King David a wise son, gifted with skill and understanding, who will build a Temple for the LORD and a royal palace for himself.

13"I am sending you a master craftsman named Huram-abi, who is extremely talented. 14His mother is from the tribe of Dan in Israel, and

---

1:14 ***horses:*** Or *charioteers;* also in 1:14b.

1:15 ***the foothills of Judah:*** Hebrew *the Shephelah.*

1:16 ***Egypt:*** Possibly *Muzur,* a district near Cilicia; also in 1:17. If *Egypt* is the correct translation, this verse indicates disobedience by Solomon (see Deut 17:16). However, importing from *Muzur* in Anatolia was not prohibited. • ***Cilicia:*** Hebrew *Kue,* probably another name for Cilicia.

1:17 ***600 pieces of silver:*** Hebrew *600 [shekels] of silver,* about 15 pounds or 6.8 kilograms in weight. • ***150 pieces of silver:*** Hebrew *150 [shekels],* about 3.8 pounds or 1.7 kilograms in weight.

2:1 The *Temple* is immediately introduced as the first priority among Solomon's building projects, although the work actually began in the fourth year of his reign (3:2). Solomon used the intervening years to negotiate with King Hiram (2:3) for materials and skilled workers. • Verse 2:1 is numbered 1:18 in the Hebrew text.

2:2 Verses 2:2-18 are numbered 2:1-17 in the Hebrew text.

2:3 ***Hiram:*** Hebrew *Huram,* a variant spelling of *Hiram;* also in 2:11.

2:5-6 ***a magnificent Temple:*** The greatness of the Temple and the greatness of God were not of the same order, since ***not even the highest heavens can contain*** God.

2:8 The ***cedar*** is *Cedrus libani* ("cedar of Lebanon"), a tree renowned for its beauty, impressive height (sometimes reaching 100 feet), and fragrant wood. Kings from Egypt, Phoenicia, Assyria, Babylon, Persia, and Greece used cedar timber ***from Lebanon*** for building temples and palaces. • ***Red sandalwood*** (or *juniper;* Hebrew reads *algum,* perhaps a variant spelling of *almug;* cp. 9:10-11 and parallel text at 1 Kgs 10:11-12) was used to make supports for the Temple (possibly pillars or balustrades) as well as musical instruments (see 1 Kgs 10:11). Often mentioned in ancient writings, the exact identity of this hard, reddish-brown wood is uncertain.

2:10 ***100,000 bushels of crushed wheat, 100,000 bushels of barley:*** Hebrew *20,000 cors* [3,640 kiloliters] *of crushed wheat, 20,000 cors of barley.* • ***110,000 gallons of wine, and 110,000 gallons of olive oil:*** Hebrew *20,000 baths* [420 kiloliters] *of wine, and 20,000 baths of olive oil.*

2:13-14 The skill and knowledge of ***Huram-abi,*** a ***master*** (literally *wise*) ***craftsman,*** was required for building the Temple. Huram-abi had expertise in

his father is from Tyre. He is skillful at making things from gold, silver, bronze, and iron, and he also works with stone and wood. He can work with purple, blue, and scarlet cloth and fine linen. He is also an engraver and can follow any design given to him. He will work with your craftsmen and those appointed by my lord David, your father.

15 "Send along the wheat, barley, olive oil, and wine that my lord has mentioned. 16 We will cut whatever timber you need from the Lebanon mountains and will float the logs in rafts down the coast of the Mediterranean Sea to Joppa. From there you can transport the logs up to Jerusalem."

17 Solomon took a census of all foreigners in the land of Israel, like the census his father had taken, and he counted 153,600. 18 He assigned 70,000 of them as common laborers, 80,000 as quarry workers in the hill country, and 3,600 as foremen.

Solomon Builds the Temple

2 Chr 3:1-4 // 1 Kgs 6:1-3
2 Chr 3:10-13 // 1 Kgs 6:23-28

3 So Solomon began to build the Temple of the LORD in Jerusalem on Mount Moriah, where the LORD had appeared to David, his father. The Temple was built on the threshing floor of Araunah the Jebusite, the site that David had selected. 2 The construction began in midspring, during the fourth year of Solomon's reign.

3 These are the dimensions Solomon used for the foundation of the Temple of God (using the old standard of measurement). It was 90 feet long and 30 feet wide. 4 The entry room at the front of the Temple was 30 feet wide, running across the entire width of the Temple, and 30 feet high. He overlaid the inside with pure gold.

5 He paneled the main room of the Temple with cypress wood, overlaid it with fine gold, and decorated it with carvings of palm trees and chains. 6 He decorated the walls of the Temple with beautiful jewels and with gold from the land of Parvaim. 7 He overlaid the beams, thresholds, walls, and doors throughout the Temple with gold, and he carved figures of cherubim on the walls.

8 He made the Most Holy Place 30 feet wide, corresponding to the width of the Temple, and 30 feet deep. He overlaid its interior with 23 tons of fine gold. 9 The gold nails that were used weighed 20 ounces each. He also overlaid the walls of the upper rooms with gold.

10 He made two figures shaped like cherubim, overlaid them with gold, and placed them in the Most Holy Place. 11 The total

2:15 2 Chr 2:10
2:16 1 Kgs 5:8-9
2:17 1 Chr 22:2
2:18 2 Chr 2:2
3:1-14 1 Kgs 6:1-29
3:1 1 Chr 21:18
3:4 1 Kgs 6:3
3:5 1 Kgs 6:17
3:7 1 Kgs 6:20-22, 29-35
3:8 Exod 26:33; 1 Kgs 6:16
3:9 1 Chr 28:11
3:10 1 Kgs 6:23-28

---

metals (***gold, silver, bronze, and iron***), in ***stone and wood***, and in textiles (***purple, blue, and scarlet cloth and fine linen***). Similarly, God had chosen Bezalel as the master craftsman of the Tabernacle and had endowed him with wisdom to carry out the work (Exod 31:1-5).

2:16 ***the Mediterranean Sea:*** Literally *the sea.*

2:17-18 The book of Kings explains that all those left from the seven nations were conscripted for labor. Further, no Israelites were conscripted, and Israelites were placed in charge of the ***laborers*** (1 Kgs 9:20-23).

3:1-4a Although in Chronicles ***the Temple*** is the central topic of Solomon's reign, attention to its actual architecture and furnishings is considerably less than that found in Kings (e.g., 1 Kgs 6:2-10).

3:1 While Kings emphasizes the time when ***the Temple*** was built, Chronicles places great emphasis on the Temple's building site and the significance of the location. Geographically, it was ***in Jerusalem on Mount Moriah***, the place ***where the LORD had appeared to David;*** it was ***selected*** under David's authority and it was the sacred place where the plague was stopped at the ***threshing floor of Araunah*** (Hebrew reads *Ornan,* a variant spelling of *Araunah;* cp. 2 Sam 24:16) ***the Jebusite.*** Abraham bound Isaac in the land of ***Moriah*** (Gen 22:2), and tradition associated the Temple Mount as the place where the Lord provided for Abraham (Gen 22:14).

3:2 The book of Kings dates the beginning of the Temple construction in relation to the exodus from Egypt (1 Kgs 6:1). Chronicles consistently omits references to the Exodus, perhaps to emphasize the continuous and abiding bond between the people, the land, and God. • ***in midspring:*** Literally *on the second day of the second month.* This day of the ancient Hebrew lunar calendar occurred in April or May.

3:3 The ***old standard of measurement*** was a cubit equal to 18 inches [46 centimeters]. The new standard was a cubit of approximately 21 inches [53 centimeters]. • ***90 feet long and 30 feet wide:*** Hebrew *60 cubits* [27.6 meters] *long and 20 cubits* [9.2 meters] *wide.*

3:4 ***30 feet wide:*** Hebrew *20 cubits* [9.2 meters] *wide;* also in 3:8, 11, 13. • The measurement of ***30 feet high*** reflects some Greek and Syriac manuscripts, which read *20 cubits* [9.2 meters] *high;* Hebrew reads *120 [cubits] high,* which is 180 feet or 55 meters.

3:5-7 The interior of the Temple was finished with costly materials (see 1 Kgs 6:15-18, 29).

3:6 The gold from ***the land of Parvaim*** was the highest quality. The actual location of this place was unknown by the time of the earliest translators, and might not have been known to the Chronicler either.

3:8 A special area was constructed at the extreme interior of the hall known as ***the Most Holy Place*** (the divine throne room). It might have been a sacred throne space within the long hall, or it might have been a secondary room within the main hall. The dimensions of *the Most Holy Place* were equally ***30 feet*** (20 cubits) in all directions. It might have rested on an elevated platform, as did the shrines of other temples, and a space might have existed between the room and the roof. *The Most Holy Place* was prepared as a repository for the Ark, which contained the terms of the covenant. • ***23 tons:*** Hebrew *600 talents* [20.4 metric tons].

3:9 ***20 ounces:*** Hebrew *50 shekels* [570 grams].

3:10-13 The ***figures shaped like cherubim*** were made of costly wild olive wood and were covered with gold. Similar carvings have been found in Mesopotamia,

3:14 Exod 26:31
3:15 1 Kgs 7:15-20
3:17 1 Kgs 7:21
4:1 Exod 27:1-2; 2 Kgs 16:14
4:2 1 Kgs 7:23-26
4:5 1 Kgs 7:26
4:6 1 Kgs 7:38, 40
4:7 Exod 25:31-40; 1 Kgs 7:49
4:8 1 Kgs 7:48
4:9 1 Kgs 6:36
4:10 1 Kgs 7:39

wingspan of the two cherubim standing side
by side was 30 feet. One wing of the first
figure was 7½ feet long, and it touched the
Temple wall. The other wing, also 7½ feet
long, touched one of the wings of the second
figure. 12 In the same way, the second figure
had one wing 7½ feet long that touched the
opposite wall. The other wing, also 7½ feet
long, touched the wing of the first figure.
13 So the wingspan of the two cherubim side
by side was 30 feet. They stood on their feet
and faced out toward the main room of the
Temple.

14 Across the entrance of the Most Holy
Place he hung a curtain made of fine linen,
decorated with blue, purple, and scarlet
thread and embroidered with figures of
cherubim.

Furnishings for the Temple
2 Chr 3:15–4:5 // 1 Kgs 7:15-26
2 Chr 4:6–5:1 // 1 Kgs 7:38-51

15 For the front of the Temple, he made two
pillars that were 27 feet tall, each topped by
a capital extending upward another 7½ feet.
16 He made a network of interwoven chains
and used them to decorate the tops of the
pillars. He also made 100 decorative pomegranates and attached them to the chains.
17 Then he set up the two pillars at the entrance of the Temple, one to the south of
the entrance and the other to the north. He
named the one on the south Jakin, and the
one on the north Boaz.

4 Solomon also made a bronze altar
30 feet long, 30 feet wide, and 15 feet
high. 2 Then he cast a great round basin,
15 feet across from rim to rim, called the
Sea. It was 7½ feet deep and about 45 feet
in circumference. 3 It was encircled just
below its rim by two rows of figures that
resembled oxen. There were about six oxen
per foot all the way around, and they were
cast as part of the basin.

4 The Sea was placed on a base of twelve
bronze oxen, all facing outward. Three faced
north, three faced west, three faced south,
and three faced east, and the Sea rested on
them. 5 The walls of the Sea were about three
inches thick, and its rim flared out like a cup
and resembled a water lily blossom. It could
hold about 16,500 gallons of water.

6 He also made ten smaller basins for
washing the utensils for the burnt offerings.
He set five on the south side and five on the
north. But the priests washed themselves in
the Sea.

7 He then cast ten gold lampstands according to the specifications that had been
given, and he put them in the Temple. Five
were placed against the south wall, and five
were placed against the north wall.

8 He also built ten tables and placed them
in the Temple, five along the south wall and
five along the north wall. Then he molded
100 gold basins.

9 He then built a courtyard for the priests,
and also the large outer courtyard. He made
doors for the courtyard entrances and overlaid them with bronze. 10 The great bronze
basin called the Sea was placed near the
southeast corner of the Temple.

Syria, and Canaan; such figures were a distinguishing feature of ancient thrones. *Cherubim* were composite creatures signifying the union of royalty (lion) with the highest powers of strength (bull), speed (eagle), and sagacity (human). Ancient temples found in Phoenicia show the throne of the deity supported by two animals. The sides of ancient Canaanite thrones were commonly shaped as cherubs. The cherubs of Solomon's Temple were distinct because they were not designed to serve as a human throne. They were attached to the Ark, which was the footstool to God's throne, with the wings touching in the middle and extending to the walls of the throne room. There was no actual seat to the throne, since none was necessary.

3:11 ***7½ feet:*** Hebrew *5 cubits* [2.3 meters]; also in 3:11b, 12, 15.

3:15-16 The ***two pillars*** set in the porch of ***the Temple*** were made of bronze and were ornately decorated (cp. 1 Kgs 7:15-22).

3:15 *27 feet:* As in Syriac version (see also 1 Kgs 7:15; 2 Kgs 25:17; Jer 52:21), which reads *18 cubits* [8.3 meters]; Hebrew reads *35 cubits,* which is 52.5 feet or 16.5 meters.

3:17 ***Jakin*** probably means "he establishes," which might refer to God's promise regarding the kingdom (see 1 Chr 17:7-14). ***Boaz*** probably means "in him is strength," which might have been a proclamation of trust in God. The gilded reliefs of cherubs, palms, and flowers adorning the doors and walls of the Temple suggest that the pillars were related to the tree of life (Gen 2:9).

4:1 *Solomon:* Or *Huram-abi;* literally *He.* • ***30 feet long, 30 feet wide, and 15 feet high:*** Hebrew *20 cubits* [9.2 meters] *long, 20 cubits wide, and 10 cubits* [4.6 meters] *high.*

4:2-5 The Temple, the house of God, depicted Eden, the Garden of God (cp. Isa 51:3). The massive ***Sea*** that rested on the backs of the ***twelve bronze oxen*** represented either cosmic pre-creation waters or the waters of life that emanated from the Garden of Eden. Divine forces subdue the waters of chaos (Gen 1:2) so that they provide life-giving nourishment for plant, animal, and human life (see Rev 21:1 where the sea is removed forever).

4:2 ***15 feet across . . . 7½ feet deep and about 45 feet in circumference:*** Hebrew *10 cubits* [4.6 meters] *across . . . 5 cubits* [2.3 meters] *deep and 30 cubits* [13.8 meters] *in circumference.*

4:3 ***six oxen per foot:*** Or *20 oxen per meter;* Hebrew reads *10 per cubit.*

4:5 ***three inches:*** Hebrew *a handbreadth* [8 centimeters]. • ***16,500 gallons:*** Hebrew *3,000 baths* [63 kiloliters].

4:6 The ***Sea*** served the same purpose as the bronze washbasin in the Tabernacle (cp. Exod 30:18-19).

4:7 The seven lights of each of the ***ten gold lampstands*** might have represented the Pleiades, a cluster of stars symbolized by seven dots in ancient Mesopotamia (cp. Job 9:9; 38:31; Amos 5:8).

11 Huram-abi also made the necessary washbasins, shovels, and bowls.

So at last Huram-abi completed everything King Solomon had assigned him to make for the Temple of God:

12 the two pillars;
the two bowl-shaped capitals on top of the pillars;
the two networks of interwoven chains that decorated the capitals;
13 the 400 pomegranates that hung from the chains on the capitals (two rows of pomegranates for each of the chain networks that decorated the capitals on top of the pillars);
14 the water carts holding the basins;
15 the Sea and the twelve oxen under it;
16 the ash buckets, the shovels, the meat hooks, and all the related articles.

Huram-abi made all these things of burnished bronze for the Temple of the LORD, just as King Solomon had directed. 17 The king had them cast in clay molds in the Jordan Valley between Succoth and Zarethan. 18 Solomon used such great quantities of bronze that its weight could not be determined.

19 Solomon also made all the furnishings for the Temple of God:

the gold altar;
the tables for the Bread of the Presence;
20 the lampstands and their lamps of solid gold, to burn in front of the Most Holy Place as prescribed;
21 the flower decorations, lamps, and tongs—all of the purest gold;
22 the lamp snuffers, bowls, dishes, and incense burners—all of solid gold;
the doors for the entrances to the Most Holy Place and the main room of the Temple, overlaid with gold.

5 So Solomon finished all his work on the Temple of the LORD. Then he brought all the gifts his father, David, had dedicated—the silver, the gold, and the various articles—and he stored them in the treasuries of the Temple of God.

The Ark Brought to Jerusalem

2 Chr 5:2-14 // 1 Kgs 8:1-11

2 Solomon then summoned to Jerusalem the elders of Israel and all the heads of tribes—the leaders of the ancestral families of Israel. They were to bring the Ark of the LORD's Covenant to the Temple from its location in the City of David, also known as Zion. 3 So all the men of Israel assembled before the king at the annual Festival of Shelters, which is held in early autumn.

4 When all the elders of Israel arrived, the Levites picked up the Ark. 5 The priests and Levites brought up the Ark along with the special tent and all the sacred items that had been in it. 6 There, before the Ark, King Solomon and the entire community of Israel sacrificed so many sheep, goats, and cattle that no one could keep count!

7 Then the priests carried the Ark of the LORD's Covenant into the inner sanctuary of the Temple—the Most Holy Place—and placed it beneath the wings of the cherubim. 8 The cherubim spread their wings over the Ark, forming a canopy over the Ark and its carrying poles. 9 These poles were so long that their ends could be seen from the Temple's main room—the Holy Place—but not from the outside. They are still there to this day. 10 Nothing was in the Ark except

4:11 1 Kgs 7:14, 40
4:12 1 Kgs 7:41; 2 Chr 3:16
4:13 1 Kgs 7:20
4:14 1 Kgs 7:27
4:16 1 Kgs 7:14
4:17-18 1 Kgs 7:47
4:20 Exod 25:31-37
5:1 1 Kgs 7:51
5:2–6:11 //1 Kgs 8:1-21
5:2 2 Sam 6:12; 2 Chr 1:4
5:4 2 Chr 5:7
5:9 1 Kgs 8:8

4:11b-18 Cp. 1 Kgs 7:40b-47, which the Chronicler follows almost verbatim.

4:17 *Zarethan:* As in parallel text at 1 Kgs 7:46; Hebrew reads *Zeredah.*

4:19 The ***Bread of the Presence*** symbolized God's provision for his people. It was placed before ***God*** on ***the tables*** (4:8) as a type of offering, demonstrating that it belonged to God and that Israel's provision came from God's "table." Some of the bread was eaten by the priests (Lev 24:5-9) and the rest was burned; this meal symbolized the covenant meal of fellowship between God and his people (see Exod 24:9-11).

5:1 This verse concludes the section on Temple furnishings, following 1 Kgs 7:51 almost verbatim. • ***the gifts his father, David, had dedicated:*** Just as the spoils taken from Egypt went into building the Tabernacle, the spoils of Israel's enemies built ***the Temple.*** The prophets often portrayed the spoils of other nations as being at Israel's disposal (see Isa 60:10-14; Zech 14:14).

5:3 The dedication of the Temple took place during ***the annual Festival of Shelters, which is held in early autumn*** (literally *at the festival that is in the seventh month*). The *Festival of Shelters* began on the fifteenth day of the seventh month of the ancient Hebrew lunar calendar. This day occurred in late September, October, or early November. This seven-day festival required a pilgrimage to the central place of worship (Deut 16:13-15). The seventh month marked the end of Israel's harvest season, allowing landowners to leave for a week without concern for fields or crops.

5:5 ***the special tent:*** Literally *the Tent of Meeting;* i.e., the tent mentioned in 2 Sam 6:17 and 1 Chr 16:1. "Tent of Meeting" is the name used in Exodus to indicate the function of the Tabernacle (e.g., Exod 33:7). The Tabernacle was the dwelling place of the divine presence (e.g., Exod 25:8-9) and the place where God met with his people through the priests. After the Temple was built, the special tent had no further function.

5:7-8 The giant ***cherubim*** were symbols of the universal and eternal rule of God.

5:9 ***from the Temple's main room—the Holy Place:*** As some Hebrew manuscripts and Greek version (see also 1 Kgs 8:8); Masoretic Text reads *from the Ark in front of the Most Holy Place.* • The Hebrew phrase ***to this day*** might be an idiom meaning *from then on.* The Ark was evidently not in the Temple following the Exile, when the Chronicler wrote.

5:10 Deut 10:2-5; 1 Kgs 8:9; Heb 9:4
5:11 1 Chr 24:1-5
5:12 1 Chr 25:1-4; 2 Chr 7:6
5:13 1 Chr 16:34, 42; 2 Chr 7:3; [a]*halal* (1984) ‣ 2 Chr 20:19; [b]*yadah* (3034) ‣ Ezra 10:1
5:14 1 Kgs 8:11
6:1-11 1 Kgs 8:12-21
6:3 [c]*barak* (1288) ‣ Ezek 34:26
6:6 1 Chr 28:4; 2 Chr 12:13
6:7 1 Chr 28:2
6:8 1 Kgs 5:3
6:11 2 Chr 5:7, 10
6:12-40 //1 Kgs 8:22-53
6:12 Neh 8:4
6:14 Exod 15:11; Deut 3:24; 7:9
6:15 1 Chr 22:9-10

the two stone tablets that Moses had placed in it at Mount Sinai, where the LORD made a covenant with the people of Israel when they left Egypt.

[11]Then the priests left the Holy Place. All the priests who were present had purified themselves, whether or not they were on duty that day. [12]And the Levites who were musicians—Asaph, Heman, Jeduthun, and all their sons and brothers—were dressed in fine linen robes and stood at the east side of the altar playing cymbals, lyres, and harps. They were joined by 120 priests who were playing trumpets. [13]The trumpeters and singers performed together in unison to [a]praise and give [b]thanks to the LORD. Accompanied by trumpets, cymbals, and other instruments, they raised their voices and [a]praised the LORD with these words:

"He is good!
His faithful love endures forever!"

At that moment a thick cloud filled the Temple of the LORD. [14]The priests could not continue their service because of the cloud, for the glorious presence of the LORD filled the Temple of God.

Solomon Praises the LORD
2 Chr 6:1-11 // 1 Kgs 8:12-21

6 Then Solomon prayed, "O LORD, you have said that you would live in a thick cloud of darkness. [2]Now I have built a glorious Temple for you, a place where you can live forever!"

[3]Then the king turned around to the entire community of Israel standing before him and gave this [c]blessing: [4]"Praise the LORD, the God of Israel, who has kept the promise he made to my father, David. For he told my father, [5]'From the day I brought my people out of the land of Egypt, I have never chosen a city among any of the tribes of Israel as the place where a Temple should be built to honor my name. Nor have I chosen a king to lead my people Israel. [6]But now I have chosen Jerusalem as the place for my name to be honored, and I have chosen David to be king over my people Israel.'"

[7]Then Solomon said, "My father, David, wanted to build this Temple to honor the name of the LORD, the God of Israel. [8]But the LORD told him, 'You wanted to build the Temple to honor my name. Your intention is good, [9]but you are not the one to do it. One of your own sons will build the Temple to honor me.'

[10]"And now the LORD has fulfilled the promise he made, for I have become king in my father's place, and now I sit on the throne of Israel, just as the LORD promised. I have built this Temple to honor the name of the LORD, the God of Israel. [11]There I have placed the Ark, which contains the covenant that the LORD made with the people of Israel."

Solomon's Prayer of Dedication
2 Chr 6:12-40 // 1 Kgs 8:22-53
2 Chr 6:41-42 // Ps 132:8-10

[12]Then Solomon stood before the altar of the LORD in front of the entire community of Israel, and he lifted his hands in prayer. [13]Now Solomon had made a bronze platform 7½ feet long, 7½ feet wide, and 4½ feet high and had placed it at the center of the Temple's outer courtyard. He stood on the platform, and then he knelt in front of the entire community of Israel and lifted his hands toward heaven. [14]He prayed,

"O LORD, God of Israel, there is no God
like you in all of heaven and earth. You
keep your covenant and show unfailing
love to all who walk before you in
wholehearted devotion. [15]You have kept
your promise to your servant David, my

5:10 The *Ark* contained only the *tablets* of the covenant (see Exod 25:21; Deut 10:5). The pot of manna Aaron placed in the Ark (Exod 16:33-34) had apparently been lost. • ***Mount Sinai:*** Hebrew *Horeb,* another name for Sinai (see note on Exod 3:1).

5:11-14 The Chronicler complements the dedication of the Temple with a detailed description of a great celebration. He names the three specific orders of ***singers*** and all their kinsmen. The ***120 . . . trumpeters*** apparently included five priests from each of the 24 divisions (1 Chr 24:3-19). The sanctified priests, their standard apparel of ***fine linen robes,*** the musical ***instruments,*** the singers, and the trumpeters were all correctly positioned. When the priests exited, the musicians raised their song, and the ***cloud*** of the ***glorious presence of the LORD filled the Temple.***

6:1-2 The dedication ceremony culminated in Solomon's poetic proclamation that expressed the most basic concept of the Temple. God had chosen to dwell in the ***thick cloud of darkness.*** The dedication of the Temple affirmed God's choice of Israel as his people and his continuous presence in their midst.

6:4-6 Israel as God's people originated at the Exodus, and Israel's history reached a climax when God chose ***David to be king*** and ***Jerusalem*** to be his capital. Both the ***city*** and the dynasty were aspects of God's promise to David (see 1 Chr 28:4; cp. 2 Sam 7:8-17; Ps 2:6-7).

6:10-11 The Chronicler blends ***the covenant*** of Sinai, represented by ***the Ark,*** with the Jerusalem ***Temple*** and the Davidic dynasty; he makes no mention of Israel's exodus from Egypt, only implying it with reference to the Ark. God's covenant relationship with Israel under Solomon and David formed the basis for the community's relationship with God at the time of the Chronicler.

6:13 ***7½ feet long, 7½ feet wide, and 4½ feet high:*** Hebrew *5 cubits* [2.3 meters] *long, 5 cubits wide, and 3 cubits* [1.4 meters] *high.*

father. You made that promise with your
own mouth, and with your own hands
you have fulfilled it today.
16"And now, O LORD, God of Israel,
carry out the additional promise you
made to your servant David, my father.
For you said to him, 'If your descendants
guard their behavior and faithfully
follow my Law as you have done, one
of them will always sit on the throne
of Israel.' 17Now, O LORD, God of Israel,
fulfill this promise to your servant David.
18"But will God really live on earth
among people? Why, even the highest
heavens cannot contain you. How
much less this Temple I have built!
19Nevertheless, listen to my prayer and my
plea, O LORD my God. Hear the cry and
the prayer that your servant is making to
you. 20May you watch over this Temple
day and night, this place where you have
said you would put your name. May you
always hear the prayers I make toward
this place. 21May you hear the humble
and earnest requests from me and your
people Israel when we pray toward this
place. Yes, hear us from heaven where
you live, and when you hear, forgive.
22"If someone wrongs another
person and is required to take an oath
of innocence in front of your altar at
this Temple, 23then hear from heaven
and judge between your servants—the
accuser and the accused. Pay back
the guilty as they deserve. Acquit the
innocent because of their innocence.
24"If your people Israel are defeated by
their enemies because they have sinned
against you, and if they turn back and
acknowledge your name and pray to you
here in this Temple, 25then hear from
heaven and forgive the sin of your people
Israel and return them to this land you
gave to them and to their ancestors.
26"If the skies are shut up and there is
no rain because your people have sinned
against you, and if they pray toward this
Temple and acknowledge your name and
turn from their sins because you have
punished them, 27then hear from heaven
and forgive the sins of your servants,
your people Israel. Teach them to follow
the right path, and send rain on your
land that you have given to your people
as their special possession.
28"If there is a famine in the land or
a plague or crop disease or attacks of
locusts or caterpillars, or if your people's
enemies are in the land besieging their
towns—whatever disaster or disease
there is—29and if your people Israel pray
about their troubles or sorrow, raising
their hands toward this Temple, 30then
hear from heaven where you live, and
forgive. Give your people what their
actions deserve, for you alone know each
human heart. 31Then they will fear you
and walk in your ways as long as they live
in the land you gave to our ancestors.
32"In the future, foreigners who
do not belong to your people Israel
will hear of you. They will come from
distant lands when they hear of your
great name and your strong hand and
your powerful arm. And when they
pray toward this Temple, 33then hear
from heaven where you live, and grant
what they ask of you. In this way, all the
people of the earth will come to know
and fear you, just as your own people
Israel do. They, too, will know that this
Temple I have built honors your name.

6:16
1 Kgs 2:4
2 Chr 7:18
6:18
2 Chr 2:6
6:21
Mic 7:18
6:26
1 Kgs 17:1
6:28
2 Chr 20:9
6:30
1 Sam 16:7
1 Chr 28:9
6:33
2 Chr 7:14

6:18 ***even the highest heavens cannot contain you:*** All creation can be seen as God's true temple—the palace of the divine King (see Isa 66:1-2).

6:21-39 In his covenant with Israel, the Lord established blessings and life as consequences of obedience, and curses and death as consequences of disobedience (Deut 27:11–28:69; 30:15-18). Solomon prayed for God to ***hear . . . and forgive*** when the people failed to keep God's covenant. The seven "if-then" petitions of his prayer represented any future situation that the people of the covenant might encounter. In each case, Solomon described the situation and asked God to intervene to help his people.

6:22-23 Petition 1: Solomon asked for justice to prevail when guilt and innocence cannot easily be determined. An example of such a case would be theft (Exod 22:7-9); the plaintiff and the defendant would both take oaths before God, and the person determined to be guilty would pay double.

6:24-25 Petition 2: Solomon asked God to grant relief in response to repentance when sin causes misfortune. Prayer provides an opportunity for redemption, and God's people experience his pardon through restoration.

6:26-27 Petition 3: Solomon asked that God would guide his people ***to follow the right path*** so that sin would not prevent God's blessing of ***rain*** for the land.

6:28-31 Petition 4: Solomon showed a special sensitivity to human suffering by including both the private ***sorrow*** of those whose pain is hidden and the public distress of those whose pain is apparent. The prayer is personal, appealing to God's knowledge of each individual motive. A further appeal pleads for God's instruction so that the pain of failure might lead the individual to follow God's ways in the future.

6:32-33 Petition 5: Solomon expressed concern for those from other nations who voluntarily joined the society of the covenant when they saw God's blessings on those who obeyed it (Deut 4:6-8). These ***foreigners***, no less than native Israelites, were the object of Solomon's prayer for mercy before God.

6:36
Job 15:14-16
1 Jn 1:8-10

6:40
2 Chr 7:15
Neh 1:6, 11
Ps 17:1

6:41-42
//Ps 132:8-10

34"If your people go out where you
send them to fight their enemies, and if
they pray to you by turning toward this
city you have chosen and toward this
Temple I have built to honor your name,
35then hear their prayers from heaven
and uphold their cause.
36"If they sin against you—and who
has never sinned?—you might become
angry with them and let their enemies
conquer them and take them captive to
a foreign land far away or near. 37But in
that land of exile, they might turn to you
in repentance and pray, 'We have sinned,
done evil, and acted wickedly.' 38If they
turn to you with their whole heart and
soul in the land of their captivity and
pray toward the land you gave to their
ancestors—toward this city you have
chosen, and toward this Temple I have
built to honor your name—39then hear
their prayers and their petitions from
heaven where you live, and uphold their
cause. Forgive your people who have
sinned against you.
40"O my God, may your eyes be open
and your ears attentive to all the prayers
made to you in this place.

41 "And now arise, O LORD God, and
enter your resting place,
along with the Ark, the symbol of
your power.
May your priests, O LORD God, be
clothed with salvation;
may your loyal servants rejoice in
your goodness.
42O LORD God, do not reject the king you
have anointed.
Remember your unfailing love for
your servant David."

God's Name on His Temple (6:20)

2 Chr 6:3-42
Exod 3:13-15
2 Sam 7:12-13
Ps 23:3
1 Pet 2:4-5

In his prayer of dedication, Solomon declared that the Temple was the house where God's name would be present (6:20; cp. 6:5-6). Similarly, according to the Amarna Letters (correspondence between Canaan and Egypt, 1300s BC), the Pharaoh of Egypt had earlier put his name on Jerusalem. God promised David that he would place his own name on the Temple in Jerusalem (1 Chr 17:4-14). When God puts his name in a place, it signifies his possession of it.

For the people of Israel, the Temple embodied the land God promised to them and marked by his name. It was the ultimate symbol of God's relationship with Israel. So Solomon prayed that God would remember his relationship with Israel and hear their prayers at this Temple.

God promised by an oath that David's kingdom would be secure forever. The house God built for David (the royal dynasty) and the house Solomon built for God (the Temple) perpetuated the renown of both God and David. Solomon's prayer uses God's personal name (LORD=*Yahweh;* see Exod 3:13-15) to make the Temple the definitive symbol of Israel's faith. The Temple was the house that fulfilled God's promise to David. It was the chosen place where God's name was called on, the place where the covenant was preserved, and the place where God's name was acknowledged in confession and praise.

The fulfillment of the oath to David is now to be found in the "living temple," the community of God's people. Peter urges believers to come "to Christ, who is the living cornerstone of God's temple. He was rejected by people, but he was chosen by God for great honor. And you are living stones that God is building into his spiritual temple. What's more, you are his holy priests. Through the mediation of Jesus Christ, you offer spiritual sacrifices that please God" (1 Pet 2:4-5). God's name rests on his church as it did on his Temple.

6:34-35 Petition 6: Solomon asked God to hear the prayers of the people when they went out at God's command to ***fight their enemies***.

6:36-39 Petition 7: Solomon's prophetic concern that Israel might be completely exiled is evident in the final petition of his prayer. There were many exiles in the history of Israel, but complete destruction of Jerusalem and its *Temple* were the greatest challenges to faith. Solomon's petitions looked to the Temple as a resource for faith; in a foreign land, the people might remember the chosen place and pray. The mention of land, city, and Temple (6:38) suggests total destruction, not partial exile. The Temple might no longer be present, but the people could still direct their prayers to God in heaven, who would hear and forgive.

6:41-42 Solomon's prayer concludes with the quotation of a psalm (Ps 132:8-10). This prayer was the final part of transferring the Ark to its place in the Temple. Prayers with psalms had also accompanied David's transfer of the Ark to Jerusalem (1 Chr 16:7-36); Solomon's use of a psalm recalls the time when the Ark was first brought to its proper place. • ***God*** is called to *arise,* not to war (cp. Num 10:35), but to his *resting place* in the Temple.

6:42 In harmony with the opening of the prayer (6:15-17), Solomon asks God to ***remember*** his ***unfailing love for . . . David***; this refers to the covenant promise that God made to David (1 Chr 17:4-14; see Isa 55:3).

The Dedication of the Temple
2 Chr 7:4-10 // 1 Kgs 8:62-66

7 When Solomon finished praying, fire
flashed down from heaven and burned
up the burnt offerings and sacrifices, and the
glorious presence of the LORD filled the Temple. 2The priests could not enter the Temple
of the LORD because the glorious presence
of the LORD filled it. 3When all the people of
Israel saw the fire coming down and the glorious presence of the LORD filling the Temple,
they fell face down on the ground and worshiped and praised the LORD, saying,

"He is good!
His faithful love endures forever!"

4Then the king and all the people offered
sacrifices to the LORD. 5King Solomon
offered a sacrifice of 22,000 cattle and
120,000 sheep and goats. And so the king
and all the people dedicated the Temple
of God. 6The priests took their assigned
positions, and so did the Levites who were
singing, "His faithful love endures forever!"
They accompanied the singing with music
from the instruments King David had made
for praising the LORD. Across from the Levites, the priests blew the trumpets, while
all Israel stood.

7Solomon then consecrated the central
area of the courtyard in front of the LORD's
Temple. He offered burnt offerings and the
fat of peace offerings there, because the
bronze altar he had built could not hold all
the burnt offerings, grain offerings, and
sacrificial fat.

8For the next seven days Solomon and all
Israel celebrated the Festival of Shelters. A
large congregation had gathered from as
far away as Lebo-hamath in the north and
the Brook of Egypt in the south. 9On the
eighth day they had a closing ceremony, for
they had celebrated the dedication of the
altar for seven days and the Festival of Shelters for seven days. 10Then at the end of the
celebration, Solomon sent the people home.
They were all joyful and glad because the
LORD had been so good to David and to Solomon and to his people Israel.

The LORD's Response to Solomon
2 Chr 7:11-22 // 1 Kgs 9:1-9

11So Solomon finished the Temple of the
LORD, as well as the royal palace. He completed everything he had planned to do in
the construction of the Temple and the palace. 12Then one night the LORD appeared to
Solomon and said,

"I have heard your prayer and have
chosen this Temple as the place for
making sacrifices. 13At times I might
shut up the heavens so that no rain falls,
or command grasshoppers to devour
your crops, or send plagues among you.
14Then if my people who are called by
my name will humble themselves and
[d]pray and seek my face and turn from
their wicked ways, I will hear from
heaven and will forgive their sins and
restore their land. 15My eyes will be
open and my ears attentive to every
prayer made in this place. 16For I have
chosen this Temple and set it apart to
be holy—a place where my name will be
honored forever. I will always watch over
it, for it is dear to my heart.

17"As for you, if you faithfully follow
me as David your father did, obeying
all my commands, decrees, and
regulations, 18then I will establish the
throne of your dynasty. For I made this
covenant with your father, David, when
I said, 'One of your descendants will
always rule over Israel.'

19"But if you or your descendants
abandon me and disobey the decrees

7:1-10 //1 Kgs 8:54-66
7:1 1 Kgs 8:54; 18:24, 38
7:3 2 Chr 5:13; 20:21
7:4 1 Kgs 8:62-63
7:6 1 Chr 15:16-21; 2 Chr 5:12
7:7 1 Kgs 8:64
7:8 1 Kgs 8:65
7:9 Lev 23:36
7:11-22 //1 Kgs 9:1-9
7:13 2 Chr 6:26-28
7:14 2 Chr 6:37-39; [d]*palal* (6419) ‣ Neh 2:4
7:15 2 Chr 6:20, 40
7:16 2 Chr 7:12
7:18 2 Chr 6:16
7:19 Lev 26:14; Deut 28:15

7:1-3 When the Ark was brought to its place (see 5:13-14), ***the glorious presence of the LORD*** descended on the Temple. The divine glory remained in the Temple, preventing ***the priests*** from entering to perform their service (see "The Glory of God" at Exod 24:15-17, p. 167; "God's Glory with His People" at Ezek 1:1-28, p. 1315).

7:4-6 The offering of ***sacrifices*** was essential to dedicate the dwelling of the Most High on earth; the sacrifices also provided food for the people during the fifteen days of celebration. The numbers of animals sacrificed match those found in 1 Kgs 8:63.

7:8-10 *Lebo-hamath in the north and the Brook of Egypt in the south* marked the boundaries of Israel as promised to the patriarchs (Gen 15:18; Num 34:5, 8; Josh 15:4). The Temple dedication festival preceded the annual Festival of Shelters, which ended on the twenty-second day of the month.

7:8 *the Festival of Shelters:* Literally *the festival* (also in 7:9); see note on 5:3.

7:10 *Then at the end of the celebration:* Literally *Then on the twenty-third day of the seventh month.* This day of the ancient Hebrew lunar calendar occurred in October or early November.

7:13-15 These verses refer directly to Solomon's prayer (see 6:26, 28, 40). God outlined for Solomon the requirements for rescue from judgment. In Solomon's prayer, each case had been addressed separately; in the Lord's answer, the required response is developed more generally and comprehensively. The people need humility, repentance, seeking the Lord, and prayer in order to be healed from their distresses.

7:17-18 God declared to Solomon that God's kingdom is eternal. Where 1 Kgs 9:5 states that one of his descendants will always be on the throne of Israel, the Chronicler says, ***One of your descendants will always rule over Israel.*** In the days of the Chronicler there was no throne in Israel, so his statement alludes to the Messiah (cp. Mic 5:2).

7:19-22 Despite its magnificence, the Temple did become ***an object of mock-***

7:20
Lev 26:33
Deut 28:37; 29:28
1 Kgs 14:15
7:21
Deut 29:24-27
8:1-18
//1 Kgs 9:10-28
8:5
1 Chr 7:24
2 Chr 14:7

and commands I have given you, and
if you serve and worship other gods,
20then I will uproot the people from
this land that I have given them. I will
reject this Temple that I have made holy
to honor my name. I will make it an
object of mockery and ridicule among
the nations. 21And though this Temple
is impressive now, all who pass by will
be appalled. They will ask, 'Why did the
LORD do such terrible things to this land
and to this Temple?'
22"And the answer will be, 'Because
his people abandoned the LORD, the God
of their ancestors, who brought them
out of Egypt, and they worshiped other
gods instead and bowed down to them.
That is why he has brought all these
disasters on them.' "

Achievements of Solomon (8:1–9:31)
Solomon's Projects and Administration
2 Chr 8:1-2 // 1 Kgs 9:10-14
2 Chr 8:3-18 // 1 Kgs 9:17b-28

8 It took Solomon twenty years to build
the LORD's Temple and his own royal
palace. At the end of that time, 2Solomon
turned his attention to rebuilding the towns
that King Hiram had given him, and he settled Israelites in them.
3Solomon also fought against the town
of Hamath-zobah and conquered it. 4He
rebuilt Tadmor in the wilderness and built
towns in the region of Hamath as supply
centers. 5He fortified the towns of Upper
Beth-horon and Lower Beth-horon, rebuilding their walls and installing barred gates.
6He also rebuilt Baalath and other supply
centers and constructed towns where his

God's Plan to Restore (7:13-15)

2 Chr 12:5-12; 14:1-7; 15:1-19; 25:14-28; 26:5, 16; 29:3–31:21; 32:24-26; 33:10-17; 34:3-33
Matt 3:5-12
Rom 5:8-11, 19-21

One of the best known verses in Chronicles lays out God's plan for Israel: "Then if my people who are called by my name will humble themselves and pray and seek my face and turn from their wicked ways, I will hear from heaven and will forgive their sins and restore their land" (7:14). This verse expresses the Chronicler's understanding of how God works with his people. The concept has been described as a "theology of immediate retribution": Each individual experiences the consequences for obedience or failure within his or her own lifetime.

The vocabulary of this verse (humble, pray, turn, seek, heal) appears repeatedly in the Chronicler's writing as he shows this principle operating in the lives of the kings of Judah. The reign of Hezekiah provides one of the most prominent examples. In the very first month of his reign, Hezekiah began to restore the Temple (29:3). He extended an invitation to all Israel (especially northern Israel) to attend the festival at Jerusalem (30:1). When Hezekiah's messengers urged them to turn to the Lord (30:6), many from the north humbled themselves and came to Jerusalem (30:11). So many people arrived that the Judeans could not accommodate them, but those from the north were not ready to observe the Passover. Hezekiah prayed for all the people as they resolved to seek the Lord (30:18-19). The Lord indeed healed the people (30:20), and the festival was extended another seven days (30:23). Hezekiah followed the very principles that Solomon had enunciated in his prayer. Manasseh provides another example of God's redemption at work (33:11-23). His example is an encouragement and exhortation to all.

Those familiar with Chronicles would have understood well the preaching of John the Baptist as he called for repentance and healing (Matt 3:5-12). Failure to repent will result in judgment. But there is no situation beyond the reach of redemption for those willing to humble themselves before God.

ery and ridicule when the people of Israel turned away from the Lord; the Temple was destroyed by the Babylonians in 586 BC.

8:2 The twenty ***towns*** that Solomon had given Hiram in exchange for gold were unsatisfactory to Hiram (1 Kgs 9:11-14); this implies that Hiram gave them back to Solomon, who apparently provided other compensation. • ***Hiram:*** Hebrew *Huram,* a variant spelling of *Hiram;* also in 8:18.

8:3 This verse is the only reference in Chronicles of Solomon's military accomplishments; he was known as a man of peace (1 Chr 22:9). The kingdoms of David and Solomon extended to ***Hamath-zobah*** in the far north on the Orontes River. King Toi, the ruler of Hamath, sought David's support against Hadadezer, king of Zobah (1 Chr 18:9-10). Hadadezer was also referred to as the king of Zobah-Hamath (1 Chr 18:3). Solomon conducted an expedition against this territory to maintain the stability of his kingdom's northern border.

8:4 The Chronicler describes the northern reaches of Solomon's kingdom. ***Tadmor*** later became Palmyra, an oasis city in Syria along the desert trade routes with Mesopotamia, 120 miles northeast of Damascus. It is not mentioned elsewhere in the Bible. At some point, it came to be identified with the list of fortified cities in Solomon's kingdom (cp. 1 Kgs 9:18, where Tamar/Tadmor indicates a city in southeast Judah).

8:5 ***Upper*** and ***Lower Beth-horon*** sit astride a ridge rising from the Valley of Aijalon to the plateau north of Jerusalem. Fortifications protected the route connecting Jerusalem to the major coastal trade route.

8:6 Some cities were used for storage and for military cavalry. Large building

chariots and horses could be stationed. He
built everything he desired in Jerusalem and
Lebanon and throughout his entire realm.
7There were still some people living in the
land who were not Israelites, including the
Hittites, Amorites, Perizzites, Hivites, and
Jebusites. 8These were descendants of the
nations whom the people of Israel had not
destroyed. So Solomon conscripted them
for his labor force, and they serve in the labor force to this day. 9But Solomon did not
conscript any of the Israelites for his labor
force. Instead, he assigned them to serve
as fighting men, officers in his army, commanders of his chariots, and charioteers.
10King Solomon appointed 250 of them to
supervise the people.
11Solomon moved his wife, Pharaoh's
daughter, from the City of David to the new
palace he had built for her. He said, "My
wife must not live in King David's palace, for
the Ark of the LORD has been there, and it is
holy ground."
12Then Solomon presented burnt offerings to the LORD on the altar he had built for
him in front of the entry room of the Temple.
13He offered the sacrifices for the Sabbaths,
the new moon festivals, and the three annual festivals—the Passover celebration, the
Festival of Harvest, and the Festival of Shelters—as Moses had commanded.
14In assigning the priests to their duties,
Solomon followed the regulations of his
father, David. He also assigned the Levites
to lead the people in praise and to assist
the priests in their daily duties. And he assigned the gatekeepers to their gates by
their divisions, following the commands of
David, the man of God. 15Solomon did not
deviate in any way from David's commands
concerning the priests and Levites and the
treasuries.
16So Solomon made sure that all the work
related to building the Temple of the LORD
was carried out, from the day its foundation
was laid to the day of its completion.
17Later Solomon went to Ezion-geber
and Elath, ports along the shore of the Red
Sea in the land of Edom. 18Hiram sent him
ships commanded by his own officers and
manned by experienced crews of sailors.
These ships sailed to Ophir with Solomon's
men and brought back to Solomon almost
seventeen tons of gold.

Visit of the Queen of Sheba
2 Chr 9:1-12 // 1 Kgs 10:1-13

9 When the queen of Sheba heard of Solomon's fame, she came to Jerusalem to
test him with hard questions. She arrived
with a large group of attendants and a great
caravan of camels loaded with spices, large
quantities of gold, and precious jewels.
When she met with Solomon, she talked with
him about everything she had on her mind.
2Solomon had answers for all her questions;
nothing was too hard for him to explain to
her. 3When the queen of Sheba realized how
wise Solomon was, and when she saw the palace he had built, 4she was overwhelmed. She
was also amazed at the food on his tables,
the organization of his officials and their
splendid clothing, the cup-bearers and their
robes, and the burnt offerings Solomon
made at the Temple of the LORD.
5She exclaimed to the king, "Everything
I heard in my country about your achievements and wisdom is true! 6I didn't believe
what was said until I arrived here and saw it
with my own eyes. In fact, I had not heard the

8:8 1 Kgs 4:6; 9:21
8:11 1 Kgs 3:1; 7:8
8:12 2 Chr 4:1
8:13 Exod 23:14-17; 29:38-42; Num 28:3
8:14 1 Chr 24:1; 25:1; 26:1; Neh 12:24, 36
8:17 1 Kgs 9:26; 2 Kgs 14:22
8:18 2 Chr 9:10, 13
9:1 //1 Kgs 10:1-13; Matt 12:42; Luke 11:31

complexes at Hazor, Megiddo, and Gezer contained long rooms divided into three sections with two rows of pillars. They might have been used as stables and storehouses, or they might have provided barracks for a professional army. • ***and horses:*** Or *and charioteers.*

8:11 Solomon's alliance with Egypt through his marriage to Pharaoh's daughter is mentioned repeatedly in Kings (1 Kgs 3:1; 9:16, 24; 11:1). Solomon's ability to marry into the Egyptian royal family shows the extent of his kingdom and international influence. Solomon provided her with a permanent personal residence to show that he regarded her as the most important of his wives. It also preserved the sanctity of ***David's palace,*** probably because Pharaoh's daughter was pagan.

8:13 ***Festival of Harvest:*** Or *Festival of Weeks.*

8:17-18 By discussing Solomon's activities at his kingdom's most northern and southern borders, the Chronicler shows the extent of Solomon's empire. Solomon controlled ***ports*** on ***the Red Sea*** that provided for international trade to the south. • ***Hiram*** was a valuable ally; his people, the Phoenicians of Tyre, had extensive trade networks and were expert mariners, helping ***Solomon*** trade with Ophir. • ***Ophir*** is traditionally thought to be in southwest Arabia (see Gen 10:28-29).

8:17 ***Elath:*** As in Greek version (see also 2 Kgs 14:22; 16:6); Hebrew reads *Eloth,* a variant spelling of Elath. • ***the Red Sea:*** As in parallel text at 1 Kgs 9:26; Hebrew reads *the sea.*

8:18 ***seventeen tons:*** Hebrew *450 talents* [15.3 metric tons].

9:1-2 Although Solomon had long-term economic and political ties with Hiram of Tyre (8:17-18; 9:10-11), the ***queen of Sheba*** visited just once. Ancient Sheba (roughly modern Yemen) was noted for its important female rulers and for a wealthy economy based on trade in frankincense and myrrh. An ancient tradition suggests that the queen of Sheba came from Cush (Ethiopia), perhaps because of Sheba son of Raamah, a descendant of Cush (Gen 10:7; 1 Chr 1:9).

9:3-4 The queen observed the unusual grandeur of Solomon's court, which demonstrated both his wealth and his wisdom.

9:5 ***your achievements:*** Literally *your words.*

9:8
Deut 7:8
1 Chr 28:5; 29:23
2 Chr 2:11

9:10
2 Chr 8:18

9:13-28
//1 Kgs 10:14-28
//2 Chr 1:14-17

9:22
1 Kgs 3:13
2 Chr 1:12

9:25
Deut 17:16
1 Kgs 4:26; 10:26
2 Chr 1:14

9:26
1 Kgs 4:21, 24

half of your great wisdom! It is far beyond what I was told. 7How happy your people must be! What a privilege for your officials to stand here day after day, listening to your wisdom! 8Praise the LORD your God, who delights in you and has placed you on the throne as king to rule for him. Because God loves Israel and desires this kingdom to last forever, he has made you king over them so you can rule with justice and righteousness."

9Then she gave the king a gift of 9,000 pounds of gold, great quantities of spices, and precious jewels. Never before had there been spices as fine as those the queen of Sheba gave to King Solomon.

10(In addition, the crews of Hiram and Solomon brought gold from Ophir, and they also brought red sandalwood and precious jewels. 11The king used the sandalwood to make steps for the Temple of the LORD and the royal palace, and to construct lyres and harps for the musicians. Never before had such beautiful things been seen in Judah.)

12King Solomon gave the queen of Sheba whatever she asked for—gifts of greater value than the gifts she had given him. Then she and all her attendants returned to their own land.

Solomon's Wealth and Splendor

2 Chr 9:13-24 // 1 Kgs 10:14-25
2 Chr 9:25-28 // 1 Kgs 10:26-29 // 2 Chr 1:14-17
2 Chr 9:26 // 1 Kgs 4:21

13Each year Solomon received about 25 tons of gold. 14This did not include the additional revenue he received from merchants and traders. All the kings of Arabia and the governors of the provinces also brought gold and silver to Solomon.

15King Solomon made 200 large shields of hammered gold, each weighing more than 15 pounds. 16He also made 300 smaller shields of hammered gold, each weighing more than 7½ pounds. The king placed these shields in the Palace of the Forest of Lebanon.

17Then the king made a huge throne, decorated with ivory and overlaid with pure gold. 18The throne had six steps, with a footstool of gold. There were armrests on both sides of the seat, and the figure of a lion stood on each side of the throne. 19There were also twelve other lions, one standing on each end of the six steps. No other throne in all the world could be compared with it!

20All of King Solomon's drinking cups were solid gold, as were all the utensils in the Palace of the Forest of Lebanon. They were not made of silver, for silver was considered worthless in Solomon's day!

21The king had a fleet of trading ships manned by the sailors sent by Hiram. Once every three years the ships returned, loaded with gold, silver, ivory, apes, and peacocks.

22So King Solomon became richer and wiser than any other king on earth. 23Kings from every nation came to consult him and to hear the wisdom God had given him. 24Year after year everyone who visited brought him gifts of silver and gold, clothing, weapons, spices, horses, and mules.

25Solomon had 4,000 stalls for his horses and chariots, and he had 12,000 horses. He stationed some of them in the chariot cities, and some near him in Jerusalem. 26He ruled over all the kings from the Euphrates

9:9 ***9,000 pounds:*** Hebrew *120 talents* [4,000 kilograms]. The queen presented Solomon with ***gold*** that equaled the amount he had received from Hiram (cp. 1 Kgs 9:14). • The queen's gift of ***spices***, such as frankincense and myrrh, were used in cosmetics, for embalming, and for religious offerings. High demand and repeated taxation over the long trade route made the spices as valuable as gold in gifts to a king (see Matt 2:11). Solomon was so wealthy that the queen had to give an enormous gift for it to be regarded as significant.

9:10 ***red sandalwood:*** Hebrew *algum wood* (also in 9:11); perhaps a variant spelling of *almug*. Cp. parallel text at 1 Kgs 10:11-12; see also note on 2:8.

9:11 ***steps:*** Or *gateways*. The meaning of the Hebrew is uncertain.

9:13-14 The phrase translated ***each year*** can also refer to one particular year, making it unclear whether ***25 tons*** (Hebrew *666 talents* [23 metric tons]) referred to Solomon's annual income or only to his most profitable year. Solomon also collected taxes from foreign ***traders*** and local ***merchants***. The ***kings of Arabia*** were probably merchant princes who used the routes from Edom to Damascus, while ***the governors of the provinces*** were district officials.

9:15-16 Ornamental and ceremonial ***shields*** were common in ancient Syria and Assyria. Large shields were full-body length and possibly three-sided; small shields, worn on the arm, provided light protection. Guards displayed their shields as ***the king*** went up to the Temple.

9:15 ***more than 15 pounds:*** Hebrew *600 [shekels] of hammered gold* [6.8 kilograms].

9:16 ***more than 7½ pounds:*** Hebrew *300 [shekels] of gold* [3.4 kilograms].

9:17-19 Solomon's ***throne*** was very grand. There were ***six steps***, and the throne might have stood on a platform that made a seventh step; similar Babylonian temple towers were built in seven stages to represent the entire cosmos.

9:21 Solomon's ***fleet of trading ships***, literally *fleet of ships that could sail to Tarshish*, was used to transport cargo. The peculiar shape of these strong ships allowed them to sail long distances in the open sea. • ***Hiram:*** Hebrew *Huram*, a variant spelling of Hiram. • ***and peacocks:*** Or *and baboons*. The meaning of the Hebrew word is uncertain. Solomon was so great that he imported fine goods and exotic animals from the farthest reaches of the known world.

9:25 ***12,000 horses:*** Or *12,000 charioteers*.

9:26 ***the Euphrates River:*** Literally *the river*.

River in the north to the land of the Philistines and the border of Egypt in the south. 27The king made silver as plentiful in Jerusalem as stone. And valuable cedar timber was as common as the sycamore-fig trees that grow in the foothills of Judah. 28Solomon's horses were imported from Egypt and many other countries.

Summary of Solomon's Reign
2 Chr 9:29-31 // 1 Kgs 11:41-43

29The rest of the events of Solomon's reign, from beginning to end, are recorded in *The Record of Nathan the Prophet,* and *The Prophecy of Ahijah from Shiloh,* and also in *The Visions of Iddo the Seer,* concerning Jeroboam son of Nebat. 30Solomon ruled in Jerusalem over all Israel for forty years. 31When he died, he was buried in the City of David, named for his father. Then his son Rehoboam became the next king.

2. ISRAEL UNTIL THE EXILE OF THE NORTH (10:1–28:27)

Reign of Rehoboam (10:1–12:16)

The Northern Tribes Revolt
2 Chr 10:1-19 // 1 Kgs 12:1-20

10 Rehoboam went to Shechem, where all Israel had gathered to make him king. 2When Jeroboam son of Nebat heard of this, he returned from Egypt, for he had fled to Egypt to escape from King Solomon. 3The leaders of Israel summoned him, and Jeroboam and all Israel went to speak with Rehoboam. 4"Your father was a hard master," they said. "Lighten the harsh labor demands and heavy taxes that your father imposed on us. Then we will be your loyal subjects."

5Rehoboam replied, "Come back in three days for my answer." So the people went away.

6Then King Rehoboam discussed the matter with the older men who had counseled

9:27 2 Chr 1:15
9:28 2 Chr 1:16
9:29-31 //1 Kgs 11:41-43
9:30 1 Kgs 11:42-43
9:31 1 Kgs 2:10
10:1–11:14 //1 Kgs 12:1-20
10:2 1 Kgs 11:40

Source	References
The Book of the Kings of Israel	20:34; 33:18; 1 Chr 9:1
The Record of Samuel the Seer	1 Chr 29:29
The Record of Nathan the Prophet	9:29; 1 Chr 29:29
The Record of Gad the Seer	1 Chr 29:29
The Prophecy of Ahijah from Shiloh	9:29; see 10:15; 1 Kgs 11:29-39; 14:1-18; 15:29
The Visions of Iddo the Seer, The Record of Iddo the Seer	9:29; 12:15
The Record of Shemaiah the Prophet	12:15; see 11:2-4; 12:5-8; 1 Kgs 12:22-24
The Commentary of Iddo the Prophet	13:22
The Book of the Kings of Judah and Israel	16:11; 25:26; 28:26; 32:32
The Record of Jehu Son of Hanani	20:34; 19:1-3; 1 Kgs 16:1-4, 7
The Commentary on the Book of the Kings	24:27
The Book of the Kings of Israel and Judah	27:7; 35:27; 36:8
The Vision of the Prophet Isaiah the Son of Amoz	32:32; see 2 Kgs 18:13–20:19; Isa 36:1–39:8
The Record of the Seers	33:19
The Book of Laments	35:25

▲**Sources Consulted by the Chronicler (9:29).** When the Chronicler wrote the book of Chronicles around 400 BC, he worked from primary source documents that had been written earlier in Israel's history. In addition to the sources that are explicitly named, the text of Chronicles contains many other direct citations from Genesis—2 Kings.

9:27 *the foothills of Judah:* Hebrew *the Shephelah.*

9:28 *Egypt:* Possibly *Muzur,* a district near Cilicia. See note on 1:16.

9:29 The Chronicler apparently used prophetic anthologies or annals as part of his source material; the works of individual prophets may have been incorporated into larger collections. These sources no longer exist. ***Nathan*** and ***Ahijah*** were active during the reigns of David and Solomon. ***Iddo*** is otherwise unknown.

9:30 *Solomon* reigned from 971 to 931 BC.

10:1 *Shechem* was in the heart of the territory of the northern tribes; the need for ***Rehoboam*** to go there for confirmation reflects either weak national unity or the comparative strength and influence of the northern tribes.
• ***Rehoboam*** reigned from 931 to 913 BC (see timeline, p. 599).

10:2 ***Jeroboam . . . had fled to Egypt to escape from King Solomon:*** See 1 Kgs 11:26-40. Jeroboam ***returned from Egypt*** at the news of Solomon's death.

10:4 Rehoboam was not powerful enough to enforce taxation over the northern tribes, so they demanded concessions to remain under his rule.

10:6 The ***older men*** of Israel were distinguished from officials, nobles, and guardians (Judg 8:14; 1 Kgs 21:8; 2 Kgs 10:5) who had official government roles. These elders traditionally exercised considerable influence in royal decisions. When Ben-hadad, king of Aram, attacked Samaria, the elders of Samaria were decisive in rejecting his harsh terms of surrender (1 Kgs 20:7-9). Earlier, when Absalom revolted against David, the elders of Israel were influential in critical decisions (2 Sam 17:4, 15; 19:11).

10:15
1 Kgs 11:29-39
10:16
2 Sam 20:1
2 Chr 10:19
10:18
1 Kgs 4:6; 5:14

his father, Solomon. "What is your advice?" he asked. "How should I answer these people?"

7The older counselors replied, "If you are good to these people and do your best to please them and give them a favorable answer, they will always be your loyal subjects."

8But Rehoboam rejected the advice of the older men and instead asked the opinion of the young men who had grown up with him and were now his advisers. 9"What is your advice?" he asked them. "How should I answer these people who want me to lighten the burdens imposed by my father?"

10The young men replied, "This is what you should tell those complainers who want a lighter burden: 'My little finger is thicker than my father's waist! 11Yes, my father laid heavy burdens on you, but I'm going to make them even heavier! My father beat you with whips, but I will beat you with scorpions!' "

12Three days later Jeroboam and all the people returned to hear Rehoboam's decision, just as the king had ordered. 13But Rehoboam spoke harshly to them, for he rejected the advice of the older counselors 14and followed the counsel of his younger advisers. He told the people, "My father laid heavy burdens on you, but I'm going to make them even heavier! My father beat you with whips, but I will beat you with scorpions!"

15So the king paid no attention to the people. This turn of events was the will of God, for it fulfilled the LORD's message to Jeroboam son of Nebat through the prophet Ahijah from Shiloh.

16When all Israel realized that the king had refused to listen to them, they responded,

"Down with the dynasty of David!
We have no interest in the son of Jesse.
Back to your homes, O Israel!
Look out for your own house, O David!"

So all the people of Israel returned home. 17But Rehoboam continued to rule over the Israelites who lived in the towns of Judah.

18King Rehoboam sent Adoniram, who was in charge of the labor force, to restore order, but the people of Israel stoned him to death. When this news reached King Rehoboam, he quickly jumped into his chariot

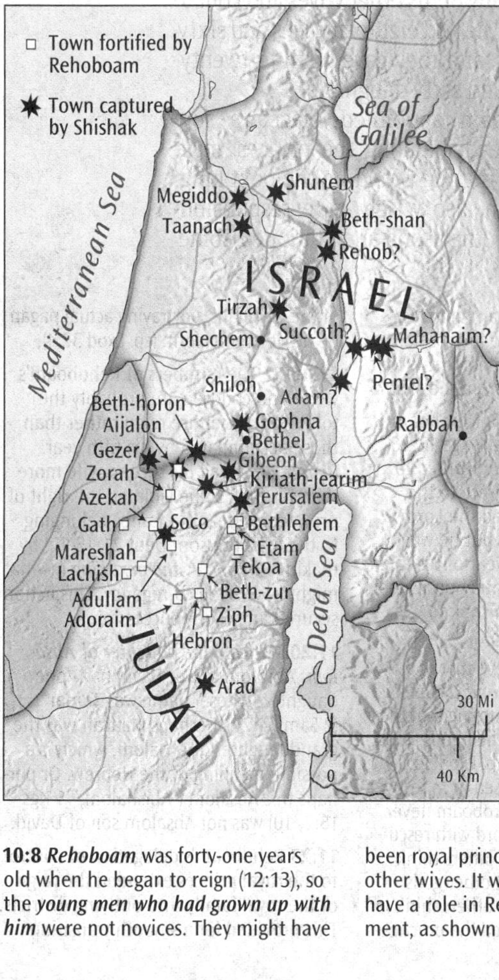

◂ **Rehoboam's Reign in Judah, 931–913 BC (10:1–12:16)** After Solomon's death, Rehoboam rejected the people's plea at Shechem to alleviate their heavy tax burden, so the ten northern tribes broke away from him and formed the northern kingdom of ISRAEL. Rehoboam retained control over the southern kingdom of JUDAH (which included the tribe of Benjamin). Despite Rehoboam's efforts to fortify Judah against attack, King Shishak of Egypt led an extensive military campaign against many of the towns of Israel and Judah, including JERUSALEM. The towns shown as captured are listed in Shishak's own description of the campaign (see note on 12:2-4).

10:8 ***Rehoboam*** was forty-one years old when he began to reign (12:13), so the ***young men who had grown up with him*** were not novices. They might have been royal princes, sons of Solomon's other wives. It was natural for them to have a role in Rehoboam's government, as shown by his promotion of his son Abijah (11:22). Referring to these princes as "young" might have been a comment on the value of their advice, because the young were not viewed as being wise (see Job 12:12).

10:10-11 The words of the younger counselors corresponded with Rehoboam's disposition. They lacked the experience of the elders, but they shared Rehoboam's inclinations and preferences. They delivered their answer in metaphors and rhetoric appropriate to a royal court.

10:14 ***My father laid:*** As in Greek version and many Hebrew manuscripts (see also 1 Kgs 12:14); Masoretic Text reads *I will lay.*

10:16 ***When all Israel realized:*** As in Syriac version, Latin Vulgate, and many Hebrew manuscripts (see also 1 Kgs 12:16); Masoretic Text lacks *realized.* • The people ***responded*** using words that were the converse of a poetic saying the Chronicler had used earlier (1 Chr 12:18); there, the people of the southern tribes of Benjamin and Judah (1 Chr 12:16) showed growing support for ***David.***

10:18 ***Rehoboam*** came to Shechem to be anointed king but barely escaped with his life. His poor understanding of the situation was particularly evident when he sent a civilian official, rather than an army commander, to enforce conscription. • ***Adoniram:*** Hebrew *Hadoram,* a variant spelling of Adoniram; cp. 1 Kgs 4:6; 5:14; 12:18.

and fled to Jerusalem. [19]And to this day the northern tribes of Israel have refused to be ruled by a descendant of David.

Shemaiah's Prophecy
2 Chr 11:1-4 // 1 Kgs 12:21-24

11 When Rehoboam arrived at Jerusalem, he mobilized the men of Judah and Benjamin—180,000 select troops—to fight against Israel and to restore the kingdom to himself.

[2]But the LORD said to Shemaiah, the man of God, [3]"Say to Rehoboam son of Solomon, king of Judah, and to all the Israelites in Judah and Benjamin: [4]'This is what the LORD says: Do not fight against your relatives. Go back home, for what has happened is my doing!' " So they obeyed the message of the LORD and did not fight against Jeroboam.

Establishment of Rehoboam's Reign
[5]Rehoboam remained in Jerusalem and fortified various towns for the defense of Judah. [6]He built up Bethlehem, Etam, Tekoa, [7]Beth-zur, Soco, Adullam, [8]Gath, Mareshah, Ziph, [9]Adoraim, Lachish, Azekah, [10]Zorah, Aijalon, and Hebron. These became the fortified towns of Judah and Benjamin. [11]Rehoboam strengthened their defenses and stationed commanders in them, and he stored supplies of food, olive oil, and wine. [12]He also put shields and spears in these towns as a further safety measure. So only Judah and Benjamin remained under his control.

[13]But all the priests and Levites living among the northern tribes of Israel sided with Rehoboam. [14]The Levites even abandoned their pasturelands and property and moved to Judah and Jerusalem, because Jeroboam and his sons would not allow them to serve the LORD as priests. [15]Jeroboam appointed his own priests to serve at the pagan shrines, where they worshiped the goat and calf idols he had made. [16]From all the tribes of Israel, those who sincerely wanted to worship the LORD, the God of Israel, followed the Levites to Jerusalem, where they could offer sacrifices to the LORD, the God of their ancestors. [17]This strengthened the kingdom of Judah, and for three years they supported Rehoboam son of Solomon, for during those years they faithfully followed in the footsteps of David and Solomon.

Rehoboam's Family
[18]Rehoboam married his cousin Mahalath, the daughter of David's son Jerimoth and of Abihail, the daughter of Eliab son of Jesse. [19]Mahalath had three sons—Jeush, Shemariah, and Zaham.

[20]Later Rehoboam married another cousin, Maacah, the daughter of Absalom. Maacah gave birth to Abijah, Attai, Ziza, and Shelomith. [21]Rehoboam loved Maacah more than any of his other wives and concubines. In all, he had eighteen wives and sixty concubines, and they gave birth to twenty-eight sons and sixty daughters.

[22]Rehoboam appointed Maacah's son Abijah as leader among the princes, making it clear that he would be the next king. [23]Rehoboam also wisely gave responsibilities to his other sons and stationed some

10:19 1 Kgs 12:19
11:1 1 Kgs 12:21
11:2 2 Chr 12:5-7, 15
11:4 2 Chr 10:15; 28:8-11
11:5 2 Chr 8:2-6; 11:23
11:14 Num 35:2-5
11:15 1 Kgs 12:31; 13:33
11:16 2 Chr 15:9
11:17 2 Chr 12:1
11:18 1 Sam 16:6
11:21 Deut 17:17
11:22 Deut 21:15-17

11:1-4 Shemaiah's prophetic intervention averted immediate civil war among Israel's tribes, but the summary of ***Rehoboam*** characterizes his reign as one of continual warfare with Jeroboam (12:15). Civil war characterized the first fifty years of the divided kingdom, until the time of Omri.

11:5-23 The Lord's blessing on Rehoboam is demonstrated in his building activities, the defection of the faithful priests from the north to the south, the migration of the faithful in the north to Jerusalem, and his large family.

11:5-12 ***Rehoboam . . . fortified various towns*** to defend ***Judah*** from east, south, and west, protecting the valleys leading into the Judean hill country and the important crossroads. Rehoboam's first task was to strengthen a minimal but defensible position. The defensive lines made strategic sense against an Egyptian attack, and likely began before the invasion of Pharaoh Shishak (926/925 BC).

11:9 ***Lachish*** formed the pivotal southwestern corner of Rehoboam's fortifications, guarding the road to the coastal highway to the west, a primary route that Egypt could use to attack from the south.

11:13-17 The apostasy that Jeroboam initiated in the north (see 1 Kgs 12:26-33) led ***those who sincerely wanted to worship the LORD*** to emigrate to the south. ***Rehoboam*** followed the Lord faithfully ***for three years***, but he was unfaithful in the fourth year of his reign (12:1). God then immediately punished Rehoboam by sending Shishak to invade from Egypt (12:2-5).

11:15 Some scholars believe that Jeroboam set up the ***goat and calf idols*** as pedestals for the Lord, noting that the Canaanites believed that their gods stood on the backs of animals (cp. Exod 32:5, where the gold calf was used in "a festival to the LORD"). However, Jeroboam never specifically credited the Lord with rescuing Israel (1 Kgs 12:28), so others think he might have meant that other gods stood on the animals. Still others think Jeroboam might have adopted the practice of the Egyptians, portraying actual pagan deities in animal form (cp. Exod 32:4).

11:18-22 The numbers of Rehoboam's wives and children are probably the total from his entire reign rather than those accumulated by his fifth year. ***Rehoboam*** loved his second wife more than his first, so he violated the right of primogeniture (inheritance belonging to the firstborn son, Deut 21:15-17) by making ***Abijah . . . the next king*** in what might have been co-regency. This action secured an orderly succession.

11:20 ***Maacah, the daughter of Absalom:*** Absalom son of David had "one daughter [whose] name was Tamar" (2 Sam 14:27). Perhaps Maacah was the granddaughter of Absalom, which is a possible meaning of the Hebrew. Or perhaps this Absalom ("Abishalom," 1 Kgs 15:2, 10) was not Absalom son of David.

11:23 Rehoboam's delegation of control to the royal princes extended the reign of the royal family into outlying districts. This provided for a smooth transition

12:1 2 Chr 11:17
12:3 2 Chr 16:8; Nah 3:9
12:4 2 Chr 11:5-12
12:5 Deut 28:15; 2 Chr 11:2; 15:2
12:6 Exod 9:27; Dan 9:14
12:7 1 Kgs 21:29; 2 Chr 34:25-27; Ps 78:38
12:8 Deut 28:47-48
12:9-16 //1 Kgs 14:25-31; 2 Chr 9:15-16

of them in the fortified towns throughout the land of Judah and Benjamin. He provided them with generous provisions, and he found many wives for them.

Egypt Invades Judah

2 Chr 12:9-11 // 1 Kgs 14:25-28

12
But when Rehoboam was firmly established and strong, he abandoned
the Law of the LORD, and all Israel followed
him in this sin. 2Because they were unfaithful to the LORD, King Shishak of Egypt came
up and attacked Jerusalem in the fifth
year of King Rehoboam's reign. 3He came
with 1,200 chariots, 60,000 horses, and a
countless army of foot soldiers, including
Libyans, Sukkites, and Ethiopians. 4Shishak
conquered Judah's fortified towns and then
advanced to attack Jerusalem.
5The prophet Shemaiah then met with
Rehoboam and Judah's leaders, who had all
fled to Jerusalem because of Shishak. Shemaiah told them, "This is what the LORD
says: You have abandoned me, so I am abandoning you to Shishak."
6Then the leaders of Israel and the king
humbled themselves and said, "The LORD is
right in doing this to us!"
7When the LORD saw their change of
heart, he gave this message to Shemaiah:
"Since the people have humbled themselves,
I will not completely destroy them and will
soon give them some relief. I will not use
Shishak to pour out my anger on Jerusalem.
8But they will become his subjects, so they
will know the difference between serving
me and serving earthly rulers."
9So King Shishak of Egypt came up and
attacked Jerusalem. He ransacked the treasuries of the LORD's Temple and the royal

God's Purposes in History (11:1-4)

2 Chr 10:1–11:4; 1 Kgs 8:56-61; Job 42:1-6; Ps 115:1-3; Isa 40:9-31; 42:1-17; 55:8-13; Rom 8:26-30; Eph 1:9-14

The Chronicler gives just one explanation for the continued division of the kingdom: Rehoboam and those loyal to him "obeyed the message of the LORD and did not fight against Jeroboam" (11:4). The cause of the division—the irrational response of Rehoboam to the people's request—has already been explained in the previous narrative: "This turn of events was the will of God, for it fulfilled the LORD's message to Jeroboam son of Nebat through the prophet Ahijah from Shiloh" (10:15). Rehoboam could easily have defeated the rebels, but he was deterred by the will of the Lord.

God directs people and events to fulfill his purposes in history. He has no need to explain himself, but he always has a purpose that he is working out; he guides individuals, nations, and events in accord with his will. This philosophy of history remains consistent in the Chronicles and through all biblical history. God works through human actions to bring about results that he has planned and that cannot be explained in any other way except his orchestration.

Obedience to God's will brought positive results for Rehoboam: He fortified cities; he put military leaders, equipment, and food supplies into place; loyal citizens migrated to his territory; and he had a large family. God's will was clear, and the benefit to Rehoboam was obvious, yet the Chronicler could not explain God's purposes. Readers of the book are left to ponder why the kingdom was divided.

The prophet Isaiah declares the mystery of God's ways: "'My thoughts are nothing like your thoughts,' says the LORD. 'And my ways are far beyond anything you could imagine. For just as the heavens are higher than the earth, so my ways are higher than your ways and my thoughts higher than your thoughts'" (Isa 55:8-9). Those who fear God learn not to lean on human understanding, but to follow the word of God even when it is contrary to earthly values.

of power and also made a revolt or attempted coup less likely. Perhaps this was Rehoboam's conscious attempt to avoid troubles that God had promised David's house (2 Sam 12:10-11).

12:1-2 The book of Kings states no theological reason for Egypt's invasion, but the Chronicler does: The Egyptians ***attacked Jerusalem*** because ***Rehoboam*** had ***abandoned*** the covenant and rebelled against ***the LORD***.

12:2-4 ***Shishak,*** also known as Shoshenq I (945–924 BC), ruled a reunited ***Egypt*** and founded the 22nd dynasty. His politically significant campaign in Canaan was recorded on the walls of a temple at Karnak, where more than 150 conquered towns were named. The main objectives of the attack were the conquest of Israel and Judah.

12:3 ***horses:*** Or *charioteers,* or *horsemen.* • ***Sukkites*** are not mentioned elsewhere in the Bible, but are known from Egyptian history as Libyans from the oases of the western desert. • ***and Ethiopians:*** Hebrew *and Cushites.* Shishak was an Ethiopian from southern Egypt.

12:6-7 Shemaiah's speech expresses the elements required in Solomon's prayer at the dedication of the Temple (7:14). ***The leaders of Israel . . . humbled themselves,*** and the wrath of judgment was removed from ***Jerusalem***.

12:9-11 The looting of the royal ***treasuries*** and of the ***Temple*** were the punishment ***Rehoboam*** received for his disobedience. The ***gold shields*** were ritually carried by ***the guard*** accompanying ***the king*** when he moved from the palace to the Temple. The royal processionals lost much of their splendor with

palace; he stole everything, including all
the gold shields Solomon had made. 10King
Rehoboam later replaced them with bronze
shields as substitutes, and he entrusted
them to the care of the commanders of the
guard who protected the entrance to the
royal palace. 11Whenever the king went to
the Temple of the LORD, the guards would
also take the shields and then return them
to the guardroom. 12Because Rehoboam
humbled himself, the LORD's anger was
turned away, and he did not destroy him
completely. There were still some good
things in the land of Judah.

Summary of Rehoboam's Reign
2 Chr 12:15-16 // 1 Kgs 14:29-31

13King Rehoboam firmly established himself in Jerusalem and continued to rule. He
was forty-one years old when he became
king, and he reigned seventeen years in Jerusalem, the city the LORD had chosen from
among all the tribes of Israel as the place to
honor his name. Rehoboam's mother was
Naamah, a woman from Ammon. 14But he
was an evil king, for he did not seek the
LORD with all his [e]heart.

15The rest of the events of Rehoboam's
reign, from beginning to end, are recorded
in *The Record of Shemaiah the Prophet* and
The Record of Iddo the Seer, which are part
of the genealogical record. Rehoboam and
Jeroboam were continually at war with each
other. 16When Rehoboam died, he was buried in the City of David. Then his son Abijah
became the next king.

Reign of Abijah (13:1-22)
Abijah's War with Jeroboam
2 Chr 13:1-2 // 1 Kgs 15:1-2
2 Chr 13:22 // 1 Kgs 15:6-7

13 Abijah began to rule over Judah in
the eighteenth year of Jeroboam's
reign in Israel. 2He reigned in Jerusalem
three years. His mother was Maacah, the
daughter of Uriel from Gibeah.

Then war broke out between Abijah
and Jeroboam. 3Judah, led by King Abijah,
fielded 400,000 select warriors, while Jeroboam mustered 800,000 select troops
from Israel.

4When the army of Judah arrived in the
hill country of Ephraim, Abijah stood on
Mount Zemaraim and shouted to Jeroboam
and all Israel: "Listen to me! 5Don't you realize that the LORD, the God of Israel, made a
lasting covenant with David, giving him and
his descendants the throne of Israel forever?
6Yet Jeroboam son of Nebat, a mere servant
of David's son Solomon, rebelled against
his master. 7Then a whole gang of scoundrels joined him, defying Solomon's son
Rehoboam when he was young and inexperienced and could not stand up to them.

8"Do you really think you can stand
against the kingdom of the LORD that is led
by the descendants of David? You may have
a vast army, and you have those gold calves
that Jeroboam made as your gods. 9But you
have chased away the priests of the LORD
(the descendants of Aaron) and the Levites,
and you have appointed your own priests,
just like the pagan nations. You let anyone
become a priest these days! Whoever comes
to be dedicated with a young bull and seven
rams can become a priest of these so-called
gods of yours!

10"But as for us, the LORD is our God,
and we have not abandoned him. Only the
descendants of Aaron serve the LORD as
priests, and the Levites alone may help them
in their work. 11They present burnt offerings and fragrant incense to the LORD every
morning and evening. They place the Bread
of the Presence on the holy table, and they
light the gold lampstand every evening. We

12:12 2 Chr 12:6-7; 19:3
12:13 1 Kgs 14:21
12:14 2 Chr 19:3; [e]*leb* (3820) ‣Ps 7:9
12:15 1 Kgs 14:29; 2 Chr 9:29; 12:5
12:16 2 Chr 11:20
13:1-2 //1 Kgs 15:1-2; 2 Chr 11:20
13:2 1 Kgs 15:6
13:4 Josh 18:22
13:5 Num 18:19; 2 Sam 7:12-16
13:6 1 Kgs 11:26
13:7 2 Chr 12:13
13:8 1 Kgs 12:28; 2 Chr 11:15
13:9 Exod 29:29-33; 2 Chr 11:14-15; Jer 2:11; 5:7
13:11 Exod 25:30-39; 29:38-39; Lev 24:5-9; 2 Chr 2:4

---

the ***bronze shields*** (cp. 9:15-16), which were safely stored in the huge armory Solomon had built (8:6).

12:12 When ***Rehoboam*** repented, God allowed ***good things*** to remain in Jerusalem: the repentance of the people, their resolve to seek the Lord, and the preservation of worship (see 19:3).

13:1 ***Abijah*** is called Abijam in Kings (e.g., 1 Kgs 15:1). Abijam, possibly the Canaanite form of his name, would mean "my father is *Yam.*" Yam was the Canaanite sea-god prominent in the Baal stories (see note on Job 7:12). *Abijah* means "my father is *Yah,*" the usual short form for Yahweh, the God of Judah. Abijah reigned from 913 to 910 BC.

13:2a ***Maacah:*** As in most Greek manuscripts and Syriac version (see also 11:20-21; 1 Kgs 15:2); Hebrew reads *Micaiah,* a variant spelling of Maacah.

13:2b-3 The ongoing conflict between Rehoboam and ***Jeroboam*** (see 12:15) carried into the reign of ***Abijah.*** Abijah might have been attempting to reunite north and south, as is suggested by his speech (13:5-12). The large numbers of soldiers on each side correspond approximately to David's census (2 Sam 24:9); Israel's double number of soldiers magnifies God's intervention on behalf of Judah (13:14-19).

13:4 ***Mount Zemaraim:*** The town of that name was on the northern border of Benjamin (see Josh 18:22), about five miles northeast of Bethel. Benjamin was a buffer and a battleground between the northern and southern kingdoms.

13:5 ***a lasting covenant:*** Literally *a covenant of salt.* Salt was required with a grain offering (Lev 2:13). The social and religious background for this phrase is unknown. However, salt was used as a preservative and provided an apt metaphor for a permanent covenant.

13:6-7 Abijah's speech castigated the northerners for refusing to support the kingdom of David.

13:8-9 Abijah's speech made two key points about the rebellion of the north: The north rejected the only legitimate king, and they rejected the only legitimate place of worship. The revolt of the northerners, who ***chased away***

13:12 Num 10:8-9
13:13 Josh 8:4-9
13:14 2 Chr 14:11
13:15 2 Chr 14:12
13:18 2 Chr 14:11
13:20 1 Sam 25:38; 1 Kgs 14:20
13:22–14:1 1 Kgs 15:6-8; 2 Chr 24:27
14:2-3 //1 Kgs 15:11-12
14:3 Exod 34:13; Deut 7:5; 1 Kgs 15:12-14
14:5 2 Chr 34:4, 7
14:6 2 Chr 11:5; 15:15
14:7 2 Chr 8:5

are following the instructions of the LORD
our God, but you have abandoned him. 12So
you see, God is with us. He is our leader. His
priests blow their trumpets and lead us into
battle against you. O people of Israel, do not
fight against the LORD, the God of your ancestors, for you will not succeed!"
13Meanwhile, Jeroboam had secretly sent
part of his army around behind the men of
Judah to ambush them. 14When Judah realized that they were being attacked from
the front and the rear, they cried out to the
LORD for help. Then the priests blew the
trumpets, 15and the men of Judah began to
shout. At the sound of their battle cry, God
defeated Jeroboam and all Israel and routed
them before Abijah and the army of Judah.
16The Israelite army fled from Judah, and
God handed them over to Judah in defeat.
17Abijah and his army inflicted heavy losses
on them; 500,000 of Israel's select troops
were killed that day. 18So Judah defeated Israel on that occasion because they trusted
in the LORD, the God of their ancestors.
19Abijah and his army pursued Jeroboam's
troops and captured some of his towns, including Bethel, Jeshanah, and Ephron, along
with their surrounding villages.
20So Jeroboam of Israel never regained
his power during Abijah's lifetime, and finally the LORD struck him down and he
died. 21Meanwhile, Abijah of Judah grew
more and more powerful. He married fourteen wives and had twenty-two sons and
sixteen daughters.
22The rest of the events of Abijah's
reign, including his words and deeds, are
recorded in *The Commentary of Iddo the
Prophet.*

Reign of Asa (14:1–16:14)

Reform and Security

2 Chr 14:1 // 1 Kgs 15:8
2 Chr 14:2-3 // 1 Kgs 15:11-12

14 When Abijah died, he was buried in
the City of David. Then his son Asa
became the next king. There was peace in
the land for ten years. 2Asa did what was
pleasing and good in the sight of the LORD
his God. 3He removed the foreign altars and
the pagan shrines. He smashed the sacred
pillars and cut down the Asherah poles. 4He
commanded the people of Judah to seek
the LORD, the God of their ancestors, and to
obey his law and his commands. 5Asa also
removed the pagan shrines, as well as the
incense altars from every one of Judah's
towns. So Asa's kingdom enjoyed a period
of peace. 6During those peaceful years, he
was able to build up the fortified towns
throughout Judah. No one tried to make war
against him at this time, for the LORD was
giving him rest from his enemies.
7Asa told the people of Judah, "Let us
build towns and fortify them with walls,
towers, gates, and bars. The land is still ours
because we sought the LORD our God, and
he has given us peace on every side." So they
went ahead with these projects and brought
them to completion.

the proper priestly order, is sharply contrasted with "us" (13:10). Most objectionable was the worship of the calves and the role of the unauthorized *priests.*

13:10-11 Abijah's speech portrays him as concerned about the purity of worship at Jerusalem. The account in Kings says nothing of Abijah's devotion (1 Kgs 15:3-4).

13:13-19 The example of God's people turning to him and his helping them, even after the kingdom had been disrupted, provided hope for the original readers in a similar situation.

13:19 The Lord granted the kingdom of Judah a miraculous victory. ***Abijah*** took the territories surrounding ***Bethel, Jeshanah, and Ephron*** from Israel (13:19). Together with Zemaraim (13:4), these towns in the hill country on the northern border of Judah formed a geographical unit (see Josh 18:22-23). The subsequent history of this territorial gain is not known; by the time of Amos (about 760 BC), Bethel was a major pagan shrine in Israel.

13:20 ***Jeroboam*** outlived ***Abijah*** (see 1 Kgs 15:9). The report of his death is included with his defeat, which was typical of vanquished warriors (see 2 Kgs 19:37).

14:1 Verse 14:1 is numbered 13:23 in the Hebrew text. • ***Asa*** reigned from 910 to 869 BC (see timelines, pp. 599, 609).

14:2-15 Verses 14:2-15 are numbered 14:1-14 in the Hebrew text.

14:2-5 At the beginning of his reign, ***Asa . . . removed the foreign altars*** in Judah (14:5). However, he did not remove the pagan shrines from Israel (15:17). These were probably in the cities of the northern kingdom that Asa had inherited from Abijah. Idolatry practiced by other peoples occupying the land plagued Judah throughout its history; this pagan activity might have revived toward the end of Asa's reign more than thirty years later.

14:4 The phrase ***seek the LORD*** is the Chronicler's formula for restoration; it both highlights and critiques Asa's reign (see 15:2, 12-13; 16:12).

14:7-14 Solomon had prayed that the Lord would hear his people when they were led into battle (6:34). In the battle against ***Zerah***, God responded to such a prayer. • "Cushite" (see note on 14:9) might refer to someone from southern Egypt (Nubia) or a Midianite territory northeast of Aqabah (see Num 12:1; Hab 3:7). However, the mention of Libya in 16:8, the size of the battle (comparable to the attack of Shishak against Rehoboam in 12:3), and the location of Mareshah in the west of Judah indicate that Zerah was an Egyptian; he is otherwise unknown. He might have been a Nubian general dispatched by Osorkon I, the Libyan pharaoh who ruled Egypt between the tenth and fourteenth years of Asa (900–897 BC). Another view is that Shishak established a buffer state around Gerar, supported by Nubian mercenaries that invaded Judah. The account, however, only says that Asa and his armies pursued the armies south to ***Gerar*** and took a ***vast amount of plunder***, particularly from the herdsmen living in tents around the cities.

8King Asa had an army of 300,000 warriors from the tribe of Judah, armed with
large shields and spears. He also had an
army of 280,000 warriors from the tribe
of Benjamin, armed with small [f]shields and
bows. Both armies were composed of well-
trained fighting men.

Reform and Security

9Once an Ethiopian named Zerah attacked
Judah with an army of 1,000,000 men and
300 chariots. They advanced to the town
of Mareshah, 10so Asa deployed his armies
for battle in the valley north of Mareshah.
11Then Asa cried out to the LORD his God,
"O LORD, no one but you can help the powerless against the mighty! Help us, O LORD
our God, for we trust in you alone. It is in
your name that we have come against this
vast horde. O LORD, you are our God; do not
let mere men prevail against you!"
12So the LORD defeated the Ethiopians
in the presence of Asa and the army of Judah, and the enemy fled. 13Asa and his army
pursued them as far as Gerar, and so many
Ethiopians fell that they were unable to
rally. They were destroyed by the LORD and
his army, and the army of Judah carried off
a vast amount of plunder.
14While they were at Gerar, they attacked
all the towns in that area, and terror from
the LORD came upon the people there. As a
result, a vast amount of plunder was taken
from these towns, too. 15They also attacked
the camps of herdsmen and captured many
sheep, goats, and camels before finally returning to Jerusalem.

Azariah's Call to Revival

15 Then the Spirit of God came upon
Azariah son of Oded, 2and he went
out to meet King Asa as he was returning
from the battle. "Listen to me, Asa!" he
shouted. "Listen, all you people of Judah
and Benjamin! The LORD will stay with you
as long as you stay with him! Whenever
you seek him, you will find him. But if you
[g]abandon him, he will [g]abandon you. 3For a
long time Israel was without the true God,
without a priest to teach them, and without
the Law to instruct them. 4But whenever
they were in trouble and [h]turned to the

14:8 2 Chr 13:3; [f]*magen* (4043) ‣2 Chr 26:14
14:9 2 Chr 11:8; 12:2-3; 16:8
14:11 2 Chr 13:14, 18
14:12 2 Chr 13:15
14:13 Gen 10:19
14:14 2 Chr 17:10
15:1 2 Chr 20:14; 24:20
15:2 2 Chr 15:4, 15; 20:17; [g]*'azab* (5800) ‣Ps 9:10
15:3 Lev 10:8-11; 1 Kgs 12:28-33; 2 Chr 17:9
15:4 Deut 4:29; [h]*shub* (7725) ‣2 Chr 19:4

ASA (14:1–16:14)

1 Kgs 15:8-24

Asa became the third king (910–869 BC) of the southern kingdom of Judah after the split of Solomon's empire into independent kingdoms. Asa succeeded his father Abijah's brief kingship (913–910 BC), and reigned for 41 years.

In the beginning of his reign, Asa was a good king. He opposed the worship of false gods in the land, destroyed the Asherah pole that his grandmother Maacah had set up, and removed her remaining political influence (15:16; 1 Kgs 15:10).

In these early days, God blessed Asa's reign with military victory and peace. Asa forced out or defeated all who attempted to conquer, divide, or destroy Judah (14:1-8). Asa's most astounding conquest was over an Ethiopian leader named Zerah (14:9-15), who attacked Judah with more than a million troops. Because of Asa's obedience and faithfulness, God gave him a tremendous victory.

Unfortunately, toward the end of his life, Asa's attitude changed: He abandoned his trust in God. Baasha, the king of the northern kingdom, attacked Judah with the support of Ben-hadad, king of Aram, and fortified the city of Ramah. Asa paid the king of Aram to change sides and support him rather than Baasha. This meant that Asa had more confidence in a foreign king than in the Lord. Worse, Asa paid Ben-hadad with gold and silver that he had earlier given to the Temple! Asa's power play worked, and the northern kingdom of Israel had to leave Judah to stave off Ben-hadad's threat from the north. But the prophet Hanani rebuked Asa for his disbelief in God. Infuriated, Asa had Hanani thrown into prison (16:7-10).

For the final years of his reign, Asa became ill with a serious foot disease. "Even with the severity of his disease, he did not seek the LORD's help but turned only to his physicians" (16:12). Yet when Asa died, he was buried with honor in the royal tombs (16:14; 1 Kgs 15:24).

14:9 *an Ethiopian:* Hebrew *a Cushite.* • *an army of 1,000,000 men:* Or *an army of thousands and thousands;* literally *an army of a thousand thousands.*

14:10 *in the valley north of Mareshah:* Or *in the Zephathah Valley near Mareshah.*

14:12 *the Ethiopians:* Hebrew *Cushites;* also in 14:13.

15:1-7 The prophet *Azariah* is unknown outside of this passage. His speech to *King Asa* and the *people of Judah* also served as the Chronicler's own message to the people of Judah following the Exile: *The LORD* will be with his people, he will be found by those who *seek him,* and he will reward their obedience.

15:3-6 The *dark times,* described as resulting from the lack of knowing God (cp. Hos 3:4-5), seem best to fit the period of the judges.

15:5 Judg 5:6
15:6 Matt 24:7
15:7 Josh 1:7, 9
15:8 2 Chr 4:1; 8:12
15:9 2 Chr 11:16
15:11 2 Chr 14:13-15
15:12 2 Chr 23:16
15:13 Exod 22:20; Deut 13:6-9, 15
15:15 2 Chr 14:7
15:16-19 //1 Kgs 15:13-15; 2 Chr 14:2-5

LORD, the God of Israel, and sought him
out, they found him.
5“During those dark times, it was not safe
to travel. Problems troubled the people of
every land. 6Nation fought against nation,
and city against city, for God was troubling
them with every kind of problem. 7But as
for you, be strong and courageous, for your
work will be rewarded.”

Covenant Renewal and Celebration
2 Chr 15:16-18 // 1 Kgs 15:13-15

8When Asa heard this message from Azariah the prophet, he took courage and
removed all the detestable idols from the
land of Judah and Benjamin and in the
towns he had captured in the hill country
of Ephraim. And he repaired the altar of
the LORD, which stood in front of the entry
room of the LORD’s Temple.
9Then Asa called together all the people
of Judah and Benjamin, along with the people of Ephraim, Manasseh, and Simeon who
had settled among them. For many from Israel had moved to Judah during Asa’s reign
when they saw that the LORD his God was
with him. 10The people gathered at Jerusalem in late spring, during the fifteenth year
of Asa’s reign.
11On that day they sacrificed to the LORD
700 cattle and 7,000 sheep and goats from
the plunder they had taken in the battle.
12Then they entered into a covenant to seek
the LORD, the God of their ancestors, with all
their heart and soul. 13They agreed that anyone who refused to seek the LORD, the God
of Israel, would be put to death—whether
young or old, man or woman. 14They shouted
out their oath of loyalty to the LORD with
trumpets blaring and rams’ horns sounding. 15All in Judah were happy about this
covenant, for they had entered into it with
all their heart. They earnestly sought after
God, and they found him. And the LORD gave
them rest from their enemies on every side.
16King Asa even deposed his grandmother Maacah from her position as queen

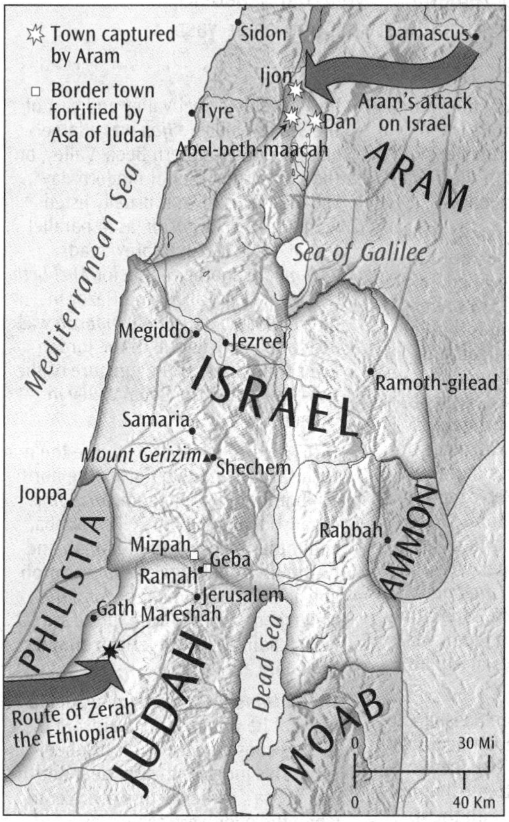

◀ **Asa’s Reign in Judah, 910–869 BC (14:1–16:14).** During King Asa’s reign, Zerah the Ethiopian attacked JUDAH at MARESHAH with a massive army, but Asa defeated Zerah’s forces and drove them from the land. Later, King Baasha of ISRAEL captured the Judean town of RAMAH and prevented anyone from leaving or entering Judah. King Asa bribed King Ben-hadad of ARAM to attack Israel. Ben-hadad captured IJON, DAN, ABEL-BETH-MAACAH, and the store cities of Naphtali. King Baasha of Israel abandoned Ramah, and Asa carried away the building materials to fortify the border towns of GEBA and MIZPAH.

15:5 ***it was not safe to travel:*** Cp. Judg 5:6-8; Zech 8:10.

15:7 The exhortation to ***be strong and courageous*** is a literal quotation of the exhortation that both Moses and Joshua gave Israel when they first entered the land (Deut 31:6-7; Josh 1:6, 9, 18).

15:8-18 The Chronicler described Asa’s response in the precise terms of the prophet’s exhortation, but Asa’s specific actions went far beyond its general directives. As soon as Asa heard the prophetic words, ***he took courage*** in initiating a comprehensive reform, beginning with the removal of the ***detestable idols*** that again infested the land (see 14:5). Full trust in God had won the war against the Cushites, and total renewal of the covenant brought the Promised Land to rest (15:15).

15:8 ***from Azariah the prophet:*** As in Syriac version and Latin Vulgate (see also 15:1); Hebrew reads *from Oded the prophet.* • The ***towns he had captured in the hill country of Ephraim*** were those conquered in his war with Baasha (16:1). There was continuous warfare between Baasha and Asa (see 1 Kgs 15:16).

15:9 ***the people of Ephraim, Manasseh:*** The Chronicler always included the northern tribes in his accounts of spiritual reform (cp. 30:1-11). • The territory of ***Simeon*** was absorbed into ***Judah*** (see map, p. 397).

15:10-15 The ceremony of covenant renewal in the third month was probably during the Festival of Harvest (Pentecost). This great festival brought crowds to the Temple from all the surrounding regions. Disloyalty to the covenant was regarded as treason and carried the ultimate penalty (Deut 17:2-7). The sacrifices were dedicated offerings from the victory over Zerah (14:15).

15:10 ***in late spring:*** Literally *in the third month.* This month of the ancient Hebrew lunar calendar usually occurs within the months of May and June (see chart, “Israel’s Annual Calendar,” p. 145).

15:16 The ***queen mother*** was the first lady of the realm, usually holding the office as long as she lived. When she

mother because she had made an obscene Asherah pole. He cut down her obscene pole, broke it up, and burned it in the Kidron Valley. 17Although the pagan shrines were not removed from Israel, Asa's heart remained completely faithful throughout his life. 18He brought into the Temple of God the silver and gold and the various items that he and his father had dedicated.

19So there was no more war until the thirty-fifth year of Asa's reign.

War with King Baasha of Israel
2 Chr 16:1-6 // 1 Kgs 15:16-22

16 In the thirty-sixth year of Asa's reign, King Baasha of Israel invaded Judah and fortified Ramah in order to prevent anyone from entering or leaving King Asa's territory in Judah.

2Asa responded by removing the silver and gold from the treasuries of the Temple of the LORD and the royal palace. He sent it to King Ben-hadad of Aram, who was ruling in Damascus, along with this message:

3"Let there be a treaty between you and me like the one between your father and my father. See, I am sending you silver and gold. Break your treaty with King Baasha of Israel so that he will leave me alone."

4Ben-hadad agreed to King Asa's request and sent the commanders of his army to attack the towns of Israel. They conquered the towns of Ijon, Dan, Abel-beth-maacah, and all the store cities in Naphtali. 5As soon as Baasha of Israel heard what was happening, he abandoned his project of fortifying Ramah and stopped all work on it. 6Then King Asa called out all the men of Judah to carry away the building stones and timbers that Baasha had been using to fortify Ramah. Asa used these materials to fortify the towns of Geba and Mizpah.

Hanani's Exhortation to King Asa

7At that time Hanani the seer came to King Asa and told him, "Because you have put your trust in the king of Aram instead of in the LORD your God, you missed your chance to destroy the army of the king of Aram. 8Don't you remember what happened to the Ethiopians and Libyans and their vast

16:1-6
//1 Kgs 15:17-22

16:4
Exod 1:11

16:7
1 Kgs 16:1
2 Chr 14:11; 19:2; 32:7-8

16:8
2 Chr 12:3; 13:16, 18; 14:9

---

died, the title passed to the mother of the heir apparent. There is no indication that the *queen mother* held official duties, but she wielded considerable influence. • ***Asherah*** is well known from Canaanite literature as the wife of the god El and the mother of seventy children, including Baal. The image made of her quite possibly had prominent sexual characteristics, a common practice in Canaan. • ***his grandmother:*** Literally *his mother.* The term "mother" can be used generically for any female ancestor. See 11:20, where Maacah is listed as the mother of Abijah (Asa's father).

15:19 ***no more war:*** Literally *no war.* Most translations, including the NLT, add "more" to assist in conveying the probable meaning. But if "no war" is in fact the better reading, ***the thirty-fifth year*** might refer to the thirty-fifth year since the division of the northern and southern kingdoms. That would have been around the time when Zerah the Ethiopian invaded Judah and was defeated by Asa (14:9-15). But see the note on 16:1; see also timeline, p. 609. • The Chronicler inserts chronological notes into his account to divide Asa's reign into periods that show the consequences of his decisions (see 14:1; 15:10; 16:1, 12, 13). The early battles with the north were seen as inconsequential for that period, though the Chronicler was fully aware of them (see 15:8). The first years of ***Asa's reign*** were characterized by divine favor to an obedient king.

16:1-10 Instead of trusting the Lord, Asa relied on foreign powers when Baasha attacked. The Chronicler's theological purpose was to show that disobedience has consequences.

16:1 ***In the thirty-sixth year of Asa's reign:*** According to the book of Kings, ***King Baasha*** (909–886 BC) died in the twenty-sixth year of ***Asa's reign*** (1 Kgs 16:8). One solution is that the Chronicles text might contain transmission errors and should instead read the fifteenth and sixteenth years (about 895 BC) instead of the thirty-fifth (15:19) and ***thirty-sixth*** years of Asa. Another possibility is that the Chronicler counted these years from the division of the kingdom. • ***Ramah*** was located five miles north of Jerusalem near Geba and Mizpah (see 16:6). ***King Baasha*** expanded ***Israel*** deep into the territory of Benjamin, separating important territory from Judah very shortly after the victories of Abijah (13:19).

16:2 To obtain relief from Baasha's aggression, ***Asa*** bribed the Arameans with ***silver and gold from . . . the Temple,*** appealing to an earlier treaty that his father Abijah had made with them.

16:3 ***Let there be a treaty:*** As in Greek version; Hebrew reads *There is a treaty.*

16:4 King ***Ben-hadad*** of Aram (16:2) broke his treaty with Baasha and attacked northern Israel, capturing all the land of ***Naphtali;*** this area included all of Galilee and nearly all of the country north of the Jezreel Valley and east of the Sea of Galilee. • ***Ijon*** was a large village in the southern Beqa' Valley, on the southern border of modern-day Lebanon. This town is usually listed with ***Abel-beth-maacah*** (as in parallel text at 1 Kgs 15:20; Hebrew reads *Abel-maim,* another name for *Abel-beth-maacah*), ***Dan*** (Laish), and Hazor in northern Israel. ***Abel-beth-maacah*** was near a major waterfall of the Jordan River tributaries, at the juncture of the Hula Valley and the Beqa' Valley in Lebanon.

16:6 ***Asa*** drafted laborers to use the materials from ***Ramah*** to fortify the northern border of his kingdom. ***Mizpah*** is usually identified with Tell en-Nasba, about four miles north of Ramah and two miles from Bethel. ***Geba*** was probably located three miles beyond the watershed east of Gibeah, protecting a wadi leading down to Jericho and the sanctuary at Gilgal.

16:7-9 ***Hanani the seer*** announced to Asa that he would suffer war from then on as a consequence of his disobedience. This judgment was a clear antithesis to Asa's earlier victory over Zerah, when the odds were against him but he trusted in the Lord (14:9-13). Just as Asa's previous reliance on the Lord had brought the land peace (14:5), his reliance on military power now destined him to continual warfare.

16:8 ***Ethiopians:*** Hebrew *Cushites.* • ***and charioteers?*** Or *and horsemen?*

16:9
2 Chr 15:17
Prov 15:3
Zech 4:10
16:11–17:1
//1 Kgs 15:23-24
16:12
Jer 17:5
16:14
Gen 50:2
2 Chr 21:19
John 19:39-40
17:1
1 Kgs 15:24
17:2
2 Chr 11:5; 15:8
17:4
1 Kgs 12:28
17:5
2 Chr 18:1

army, with all of their chariots and charioteers? At that time you relied on the LORD,
and he handed them over to you. [9]The eyes
of the LORD search the whole earth in order
to strengthen those whose hearts are fully
committed to him. What a fool you have
been! From now on you will be at war."
[10]Asa became so angry with Hanani for
saying this that he threw him into prison
and put him in stocks. At that time Asa also
began to oppress some of his people.

Summary of Asa's Reign
2 Chr 16:11-14 // 1 Kgs 15:23-24
[11]The rest of the events of Asa's reign, from
beginning to end, are recorded in *The Book
of the Kings of Judah and Israel.* [12]In the
thirty-ninth year of his reign, Asa developed
a serious foot disease. Yet even with the
severity of his disease, he did not seek the
LORD's help but turned only to his physicians.
[13]So he died in the forty-first year of his
reign. [14]He was buried in the tomb he had
carved out for himself in the City of David.
He was laid on a bed perfumed with sweet
spices and fragrant ointments, and the people built a huge funeral fire in his honor.

Reign of Jehoshaphat (17:1–21:1)
Religious and Political Achievements

17 Then Jehoshaphat, Asa's son, became
the next king. He strengthened Judah
to stand against any attack from Israel. [2]He
stationed troops in all the fortified towns
of Judah, and he assigned additional garrisons to the land of Judah and to the towns of
Ephraim that his father, Asa, had captured.
[3]The LORD was with Jehoshaphat because
he followed the example of his father's
early years and did not worship the images
of Baal. [4]He sought his father's God and
obeyed his commands instead of following
the evil practices of the kingdom of Israel.
[5]So the LORD established Jehoshaphat's
control over the kingdom of Judah. All the
people of Judah brought gifts to Jehoshaphat, so he became very wealthy and highly

Trusting in Human Strength (16:1-10)

2 Chr 32:7-8
Deut 13:4
2 Kgs 6:15-18
Ps 20:6-8; 37:3-7; 60:11-12
Prov 11:7-8; 18:10-12
Eccl 3:14
Isa 31:1-5
Jer 17:5-8
Matt 10:26-31
Rom 2:6-11
1 Cor 4:1-5
Rev 2:8-11

Hanani the seer's charge against King Asa of Judah (16:7) is intriguing. Asa regarded the king of Aram as an ally, giving him the treasures of the Temple and palace so he would attack Baasha, king of Israel. However, the prophet Hanani saw in Aram a human foe who would be a nemesis to the kingdom of Judah. Previous battles demonstrate that God was the only ally Asa needed, and God was also the only ally Asa actually had.

Asa's reliance on the king of Aram revealed a much deeper spiritual problem. Asa forgot that "the eyes of the LORD search the whole earth" (16:9; see also Zech 4:10). So when Hanani confronted Asa with the error of his ways, Asa summarily threw the prophet into confinement, and the angry king arbitrarily inflicted cruelties on the people.

Asa provides a sad example of the human propensity to rely on their own tangible resources (see Prov 11:7; Isa 31:1; Jer 17:5-6) and to become angry when corrected. Even those who experience the power of the Lord in a very tangible fashion often have this leaning (16:8). It is much better to rely on the Lord and welcome his direction (cp. Ps 33:18; 37:7; Isa 50:10; Jer 17:7-8; Acts 13:43). Life is a long lesson in trusting God; we might begin by doing what is good and right (14:1), but our legacy is not settled until the last deed is done (see also Rom 2:6-11; 1 Cor 4:1-5). Faithfulness to the kingdom of God must not be compromised by personal ambitions.

16:10 Asa's infidelity to the Lord in relying on power resulted in other sins, including oppression of the prophet and the people.

16:12 Sickness was often seen as punishment for sin (see 21:18-19; 26:20).

16:14 Asa had an honorable burial despite his sins. He had made extravagant preparations for his burial during his lifetime, including a ***tomb he had carved out for himself.*** Asa might have been imitating the pharaohs of Egypt in making these preparations. • The custom of ***a huge funeral fire*** is unknown outside of Chronicles and Jeremiah (cp. Jer 34:5).

17:1 Including a two-year co-regency with his father, Asa, ***Jehoshaphat*** reigned from 872 to 848 BC. • The last years of Asa's reign were characterized by conflicts and oppression, so Jehoshaphat needed to consolidate power within Judah to restore peace and stability. Israel had been an enemy during Asa's days, but Jehoshaphat soon entered into an alliance with Ahab (18:1-2).

17:3-4 For the first time, the Chronicler compares Judah's practices with those of northern Israel, showing his awareness that the Baal cult from Tyre had been introduced into northern worship (see 1 Kgs 16:31-32).

17:3 ***the example of his father's early years:*** Some Hebrew manuscripts read *the example of his father, David.*

17:5-6 The word translated ***gifts*** is usually translated "tribute," such as conquering kings required of their vassals (e.g., Judg 3:15-18), but forced tribute is hardly the sense intended here. The people of Judah voluntarily made Jehoshaphat ***very wealthy.*** As with Uzziah (26:16) and Hezekiah (32:25), riches often result in pride. However, Jehoshaphat ***was deeply committed to*** (literally *His heart was courageous in*) ***the ways of the LORD.*** He was not proud of his own achievements; instead, his courage led him to remove idolatrous worship from the kingdom. ***Jehoshaphat*** established control within his kingdom by practicing righteousness and faithfulness to God.

esteemed. 6He was deeply committed to the ways of the LORD. He removed the pagan shrines and Asherah poles from Judah.

7In the third year of his reign Jehoshaphat sent his officials to teach in all the towns of Judah. These officials included Ben-hail, Obadiah, Zechariah, Nethanel, and Micaiah. 8He sent Levites along with them, including Shemaiah, Nethaniah, Zebadiah, Asahel, Shemiramoth, Jehonathan, Adonijah, Tobijah, and Tob-adonijah. He also sent out the priests Elishama and Jehoram. 9They took copies of the Book of the Law of the LORD and traveled around through all the towns of Judah, teaching the people.

10Then the fear of the LORD fell over all the surrounding kingdoms so that none of them wanted to declare war on Jehoshaphat. 11Some of the Philistines brought him gifts and silver as tribute, and the Arabs brought 7,700 rams and 7,700 male goats.

12So Jehoshaphat became more and more powerful and built fortresses and storage cities throughout Judah. 13He stored numerous supplies in Judah's towns and stationed an army of seasoned troops at Jerusalem. 14His army was enrolled according to ancestral clans.

From Judah there were 300,000 troops
organized in units of 1,000, under
the command of Adnah. 15Next
in command was Jehohanan, who
commanded 280,000 troops. 16Next
was Amasiah son of Zicri, who
volunteered for the LORD's service, with
200,000 troops under his command.
17From Benjamin there were 200,000
troops equipped with bows and shields.
They were under the command of Eliada,
a veteran soldier. 18Next in command
was Jehozabad, who commanded
180,000 armed men.

17:6 2 Chr 15:17
17:7 2 Chr 15:3; 19:8; 35:3
17:8 2 Chr 19:8
17:9 Deut 6:4-9
17:10 2 Chr 14:14
17:11 2 Chr 9:14; 26:8
17:16 Judg 5:2, 9; 1 Chr 29:9

JEHOSHAPHAT (17:1–21:1)

1 Kgs 15:24; 22:1-50
2 Kgs 3:1-27

Jehoshaphat succeeded his father Asa, becoming the fourth king of Judah (872–848 BC). Like Hezekiah and Josiah after him, Jehoshaphat trusted the Lord throughout his life and worked to remove most forms of pagan worship from Israel (17:6).

Jehoshaphat continued his father Asa's religious reforms, but reversed Asa's foreign policy. Jehoshaphat discontinued the war between Judah and Israel over their boundaries (1 Kgs 22:2). To confirm this, he made an alliance with Ahab, had his son Jehoram marry Ahab's daughter Athaliah (18:1-2; 2 Kgs 8:18), and supported the north in its wars against the Arameans (18:3-34; 1 Kgs 22; 2 Kgs 3:4-27). The prophet Jehu rebuked Jehoshaphat for his unwise alliance with Israel (19:1-3), which resulted in his son Jehoram falling under the influence of Ahab and Jezebel. Jehoram and his son Ahaziah turned Judah toward idol worship.

Yet during his reign, Jehoshaphat kept God's worship pure. He closed the temples of prostitution (1 Kgs 22:46) and sent teachers of God's law throughout the land (17:7-9). He also established a system of judges and admonished them to function as the Lord's representatives so that justice might prevail (19:4-11). He appointed Levites, priests, and family heads to handle cases pertaining to the Lord's worship and to negotiate disputes among citizens (17:4-11).

Jehoshaphat also insisted on hearing from a true prophet of the Lord before going to battle. In one of the most stirring OT descriptions of war, Jehoshaphat preached to the army before entering a battle. As a result, God caused the armies from Ammon, Moab, and their allies to turn against each other (ch 20).

Jehoshaphat died when he was about 60 years old and was buried in Jerusalem. His son Jehoram became Judah's next king (21:1).

17:7-9 *Jehoshaphat* carried out the Lord's requirement to know the law (Deut 5:1; 17:18-20), commissioning five royal officers, nine *Levites*, and two *priests* to instruct the people in the book of the covenant. Levites frequently functioned as teachers during the second Temple period as well (Neh 8:7). • Some versions omit *Tob-adonijah;* it appears to be a scribal error of repetition.

17:10-11 The *fear of the LORD* among the *surrounding kingdoms* resulted in *tribute* to Jehoshaphat, an action that was intended to buy peace. Peace is one indicator of divine favor (cp. 14:2-6). • The *Arabs* were probably the desert tribes living south of Judah in territory next to the Philistines.

17:12-19 Jehoshaphat's international status, building enterprises, and army characterized his great rule. Archaeological excavations have revealed a line of highway forts in the Jordan Valley near the Dead Sea dating to his time. • The number of troops in his army—totaling more than a million in Jerusalem—seems unreasonably high. Because the leaders were based on tribal divisions (17:14), it is possible that the term translated as "thousand" (*'alep*) should instead be translated as "squad" or "platoon," a much smaller military unit of perhaps five to fourteen men (see notes on Exod 12:37; Josh 8:3). The totals might also include reserve divisions that served on rotation (see 1 Chr 27:1-15). The number of troops credited to Jehoshaphat is approximately triple those of Abijah (13:3),

17:19
2 Chr 17:2
18:1-27
//1 Kgs 22:1-28
18:1
2 Chr 17:5
18:2
1 Kgs 22:2-35

19 These were the troops stationed in Jerusalem to serve the king, besides those Jehoshaphat stationed in the fortified towns
throughout Judah.

Jehoshaphat and Ahab Make an Alliance
2 Chr 18:2-8 // 1 Kgs 22:2-9

18 Jehoshaphat enjoyed great riches and
high esteem, and he made an alliance
with Ahab of Israel by having his son marry
Ahab's daughter. 2 A few years later he went
to Samaria to visit Ahab, who prepared a
great banquet for him and his officials. They
butchered great numbers of sheep, goats,
and cattle for the feast. Then Ahab enticed
Jehoshaphat to join forces with him to recover Ramoth-gilead.
3 "Will you go with me to Ramoth-gilead?"
King Ahab of Israel asked King Jehoshaphat
of Judah.

Jehoshaphat replied, "Why, of course!
You and I are as one, and my troops are your
troops. We will certainly join you in battle."
4 Then Jehoshaphat added, "But first let's
find out what the LORD says."
5 So the king of Israel summoned the
prophets, 400 of them, and asked them,
"Should we go to war against Ramoth-gilead,
or should I hold back?"
They all replied, "Yes, go right ahead! God
will give the king victory."
6 But Jehoshaphat asked, "Is there not also
a prophet of the LORD here? We should ask
him the same question."
7 The king of Israel replied to Jehoshaphat, "There is one more man who could
consult the LORD for us, but I hate him. He
never prophesies anything but trouble for
me! His name is Micaiah son of Imlah."
Jehoshaphat replied, "That's not the way

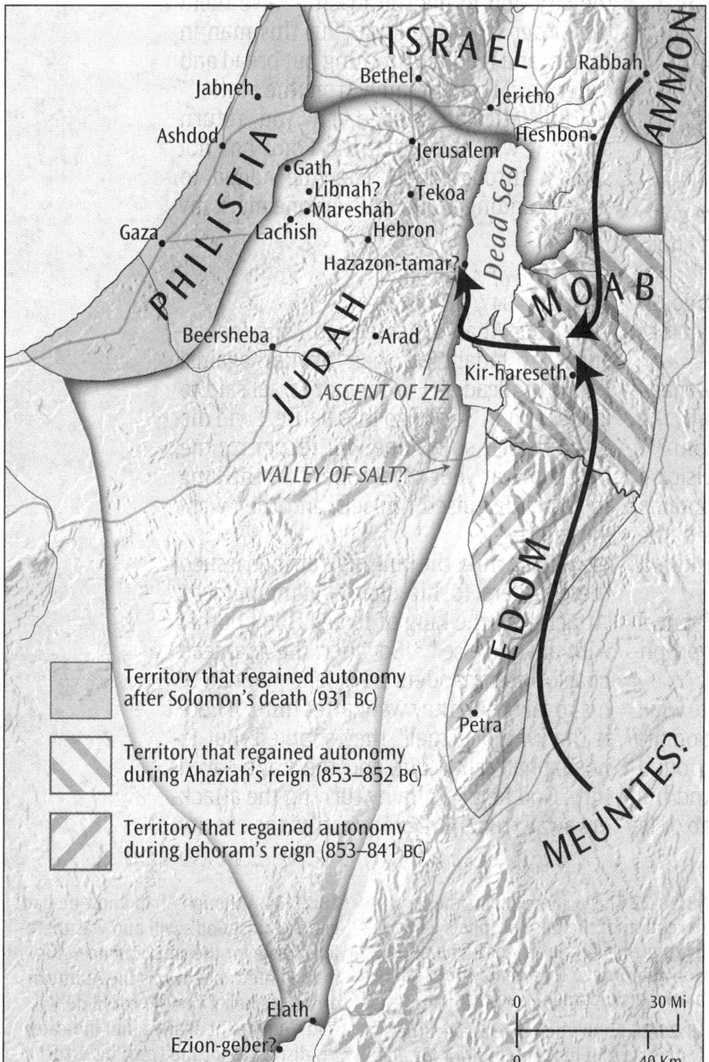

◀ **Judah from Jehoshaphat to Ahaziah, 872–841 BC (17:1–22:9).** During Jehoshaphat's reign, an alliance of MOAB, AMMON, and the MEUNITES declared war on JUDAH and came as far as HAZAZON-TAMAR, but as Jehoshaphat's army advanced to meet them in the wilderness of TEKOA, the alliance panicked and began attacking each other, resulting in a great victory for the people of Judah (20:1-30). • Jehoshaphat's sinful alliance with King Ahaziah of ISRAEL, however, led to the destruction of his fleet of trading ships at EZION-GEBER on the Gulf of Aqaba. • The reign of Jehoram was marked by weakness and decline as EDOM and the town of LIBNAH declared independence from Israel, and the PHILISTINES and Arabs conducted raids on JUDAH and JERUSALEM.

Asa (14:8), Amaziah (25:5), and Uzziah (26:11-15). It is comparable to the number of warriors at the time of David's census (1 Chr 21:5), when soldiers from the northern tribes were counted. A large army was an indication of God's blessing.

18:1-2 Jehoshaphat's ***alliance with Ahab*** led him to compromise his faithfulness to the Lord (see 19:2-3; cp. 2 Cor 6:14-18). The marriage of his son Jehoram (21:1) to ***Ahab's daughter*** Athaliah (22:2) brought Israel's apostasy into Judah (see 21:5-6, 12-13; 22:1-4).

18:5-7 The 400 ***prophets*** were Ahab's "yes-men." ***Jehoshaphat*** wanted instead to hear from ***a prophet of the LORD,*** but Ahab knew in advance that such a prophet would contradict his court prophets.

a king should talk! Let's hear what he has to
say."
8So the king of Israel called one of his officials and said, "Quick! Bring Micaiah son
of Imlah."

Micaiah Prophesies against Ahab
2 Chr 18:9-27 // 1 Kgs 22:10-28

9King Ahab of Israel and King Jehoshaphat
of Judah, dressed in their royal robes, were
sitting on thrones at the threshing floor
near the gate of Samaria. All of Ahab's
prophets were prophesying there in front
of them. 10One of them, Zedekiah son of
Kenaanah, made some iron horns and proclaimed, "This is what the LORD says: With
these horns you will gore the Arameans to
death!"
11All the other prophets agreed. "Yes,"
they said, "go up to Ramoth-gilead and be
victorious, for the LORD will give the king
victory!"
12Meanwhile, the messenger who went
to get Micaiah said to him, "Look, all the
prophets are promising victory for the king.
Be sure that you agree with them and promise success."
13But Micaiah replied, "As surely as the
LORD lives, I will say only what my God says."
14When Micaiah arrived before the king,
Ahab asked him, "Micaiah, should we go to
war against Ramoth-gilead, or should I hold
back?"
Micaiah replied sarcastically, "Yes, go up
and be victorious, for you will have victory
over them!"
15But the king replied sharply, "How many
times must I demand that you speak only the
truth to me when you speak for the LORD?"
16Then Micaiah told him, "In a vision I
saw all Israel scattered on the mountains,
like sheep without a shepherd. And the
LORD said, 'Their master has been killed.
Send them home in peace.' "
17"Didn't I tell you?" the king of Israel
exclaimed to Jehoshaphat. "He never prophesies anything but trouble for me."
18Then Micaiah continued, "Listen to what
the LORD says! I saw the LORD sitting on his
throne with all the armies of heaven around
him, on his right and on his left. 19And the
LORD said, 'Who can entice King Ahab of Israel to go into battle against Ramoth-gilead
so he can be killed?'
"There were many suggestions, 20and finally a spirit approached the LORD and said,
'I can do it!'
" 'How will you do this?' the LORD asked.
21"And the spirit replied, 'I will go out and
inspire all of Ahab's prophets to speak lies.'
" 'You will succeed,' said the LORD. 'Go
ahead and do it.'
22"So you see, the LORD has put a lying
spirit in the mouths of your prophets. For
the LORD has pronounced your doom."
23Then Zedekiah son of Kenaanah walked
up to Micaiah and slapped him across the
face. "Since when did the Spirit of the LORD
leave me to speak to you?" he demanded.
24And Micaiah replied, "You will find out
soon enough when you are trying to hide in
some secret room!"
25"Arrest him!" the king of Israel ordered.
"Take him back to Amon, the governor of
the city, and to my son Joash. 26Give them
this order from the king: 'Put this man in
prison, and feed him nothing but bread and
water until I return safely from the battle!' "
27But Micaiah replied, "If you return
safely, it will mean that the LORD has not
spoken through me!" Then he added to
those standing around, "Everyone mark my
words!"

The Death of Ahab
2 Chr 18:28-34 // 1 Kgs 22:29-37

28So King Ahab of Israel and King Jehoshaphat of Judah led their armies against
Ramoth-gilead. 29The king of Israel said to
Jehoshaphat, "As we go into battle, I will disguise myself so no one will recognize me,
but you wear your royal robes." So the king
of Israel disguised himself, and they went
into battle.
30Meanwhile, the king of Aram had issued
these orders to his chariot commanders:
"Attack only the king of Israel! Don't bother
with anyone else." 31So when the Aramean
chariot commanders saw Jehoshaphat in
his royal robes, they went after him. "There
is the king of Israel!" they shouted. But Jehoshaphat called out, and the LORD saved
him. God helped him by turning the attackers away from him. 32As soon as the chariot

18:13 Num 22:18-20, 35
18:16 Num 27:17; Ezek 34:4-8; *Mark 6:34; Matt 9:36
18:18 Isa 6:1-5; Dan 7:9-10
18:20 Job 1:6
18:22 Ezek 14:9
18:23 Jer 20:2; Mark 14:65; Acts 23:2
18:25 2 Chr 18:8
18:26 2 Chr 16:10
18:28-34 //1 Kgs 22:29-36
18:31 2 Chr 13:14-15

18:15 Ahab understood that Micaiah had not spoken the word of the Lord, perhaps because Micaiah's answer used the same words as that of his rivals, or Micaiah might have been speaking with a sarcastic tone (18:14).

18:16 ***Their master has been killed:*** Literally *These people have no master.*

18:18-22 The vision explains the deception of the false prophets while legitimizing Micaiah's word. The deception guaranteed that Ahab would fall in battle; his judgment was decreed.

18:25-26 Ahab's defiance against the Lord is seen in his contempt for Micaiah, the Lord's prophet.

18:28-34 Although Ahab knew he had gone against God's will and was therefore liable for the consequences, his immediate concern was the Aramean army. His belief that he could defy God's judgment against him indicates his disregard for the Lord; his error was fatal.

19:2
1 Kgs 16:1
2 Chr 18:1, 3; 20:34; 24:18
19:3
2 Chr 12:12; 17:6
19:4
2 Chr 15:8-13
[i]*shub* (7725)
▸2 Chr 36:13
19:5
Deut 16:18
19:6
Lev 19:15
Deut 1:17
19:7
Gen 18:25
Deut 10:17-18; 32:4
19:8
2 Chr 17:8-9
19:10
Deut 17:8
2 Chr 19:2
19:11
1 Chr 28:20
2 Chr 19:8
20:2
Gen 14:7
20:3
1 Sam 7:6
2 Chr 19:3
Ezra 8:21
20:6
Deut 4:39
1 Chr 29:11
20:7
Isa 41:8

commanders realized he was not the king of Israel, they stopped chasing him.

33An Aramean soldier, however, randomly shot an arrow at the Israelite troops and hit the king of Israel between the joints of his armor. "Turn the horses and get me out of here!" Ahab groaned to the driver of the chariot. "I'm badly wounded!"

34The battle raged all that day, and the king of Israel propped himself up in his chariot facing the Arameans. In the evening, just as the sun was setting, he died.

Jehoshaphat Appoints Judges

19 When King Jehoshaphat of Judah arrived safely home in Jerusalem, 2Jehu son of Hanani the seer went out to meet him. "Why should you help the wicked and love those who hate the LORD?" he asked the king. "Because of what you have done, the LORD is very angry with you. 3Even so, there is some good in you, for you have removed the Asherah poles throughout the land, and you have committed yourself to seeking God."

4Jehoshaphat lived in Jerusalem, but he [i]went out among the people, traveling from Beersheba to the hill country of Ephraim, encouraging the people to [i]return to the LORD, the God of their ancestors. 5He appointed judges throughout the nation in all the fortified towns, 6and he said to them, "Always think carefully before pronouncing judgment. Remember that you do not judge to please people but to please the LORD. He will be with you when you render the verdict in each case. 7Fear the LORD and judge with integrity, for the LORD our God does not tolerate perverted justice, partiality, or the taking of bribes."

8In Jerusalem, Jehoshaphat appointed some of the Levites and priests and clan leaders in Israel to serve as judges for cases involving the LORD's regulations and for civil disputes. 9These were his instructions to them: "You must always act in the fear of the LORD, with faithfulness and an undivided heart. 10Whenever a case comes to you from fellow citizens in an outlying town, whether a murder case or some other violation of God's laws, commands, decrees, or regulations, you must warn them not to sin against the LORD, so that he will not be angry with you and them. Do this and you will not be guilty.

11"Amariah the high priest will have final say in all cases involving the LORD. Zebadiah son of Ishmael, a leader from the tribe of Judah, will have final say in all civil cases. The Levites will assist you in making sure that justice is served. Take courage as you fulfill your duties, and may the LORD be with those who do what is right."

Victory over Moab and Ammon

20 After this, the armies of the Moabites, Ammonites, and some of the Meunites declared war on Jehoshaphat. 2Messengers came and told Jehoshaphat, "A vast army from Edom is marching against you from beyond the Dead Sea. They are already at Hazazon-tamar." (This was another name for En-gedi.)

3Jehoshaphat was terrified by this news and begged the LORD for guidance. He also ordered everyone in Judah to begin fasting. 4So people from all the towns of Judah came to Jerusalem to seek the LORD's help.

5Jehoshaphat stood before the community of Judah and Jerusalem in front of the new courtyard at the Temple of the LORD. 6He prayed, "O LORD, God of our ancestors, you alone are the God who is in heaven. You are ruler of all the kingdoms of the earth. You are powerful and mighty; no one can stand against you! 7O our God, did you not drive out those who lived in this land when your people Israel arrived? And did you not give this land forever to the descendants of your friend Abraham? 8Your people settled

---

18:33 *Turn the horses:* Literally *Turn your hand.*

19:1-2 *Jehu* was the *son of Hanani,* the prophet who had rebuked Asa for his reliance on the Arameans (16:7-9). Jehu now chastised Jehoshaphat for his alliance with Ahab. • The word *love* expresses faithfulness to a covenant (see "God's Covenant Love" at Deut 33:3, p. 365). Jehoshaphat's covenant with ***the wicked*** Ahab conflicted with his covenant with the Lord.

19:4-11 In Jehoshaphat's judicial reform, he appointed ***judges*** in the ***fortified towns*** (19:5) and in a central court ***in Jerusalem*** (19:8). He exhorted all the judges to ***think carefully,*** and to ***judge with integrity*** and ***in the fear of the LORD.*** This excluded acting with any ***partiality*** or ***taking of bribes,*** and included warning criminals ***not to sin against the LORD.*** The reform reestablished the law of Deuteronomy (Deut 16:18–17:13).

20:1 *Meunites* (see 1 Chr 4:41): As in some Greek manuscripts (see also 26:7); Hebrew repeats *Ammonites.* The Meunites were a nomadic group living on the southern borders of Judah; their name probably survives as the Arab town of Ma'an, twelve miles southeast of Petra.

20:2 *Edom:* As in one Hebrew manuscript; most Hebrew manuscripts and ancient versions read *Aram.* Translating the word as ***Edom*** is consistent with the Chronicler's later description of the armies (20:10, 22-23) and with the geographical description of the attack from the southeast through ***En-gedi.*** (Aram was northeast of Judah.) • ***the Dead Sea:*** Literally *the sea.*

20:3-12 ***Jehoshaphat*** responded to the news of war with neighboring nations with a prayer of lament, keeping with the ideals of Solomon's prayer (6:24-40).

here and built this Temple to honor your
name. 9They said, 'Whenever we are faced
with any calamity such as war, plague, or
famine, we can come to stand in your presence before this Temple where your name
is honored. We can cry out to you to save us,
and you will hear us and rescue us.'
10"And now see what the armies of Ammon, Moab, and Mount Seir are doing. You
would not let our ancestors invade those
nations when Israel left Egypt, so they went
around them and did not destroy them.
11Now see how they reward us! For they
have come to throw us out of your land,
which you gave us as an inheritance. 12O our
God, won't you stop them? We are powerless against this mighty army that is about
to attack us. We do not know what to do, but
we are looking to you for help."
13As all the men of Judah stood before
the LORD with their little ones, wives, and
children, 14the Spirit of the LORD came
upon one of the men standing there. His
name was Jahaziel son of Zechariah, son of
Benaiah, son of Jeiel, son of Mattaniah, a Levite who was a descendant of Asaph.
15He said, "Listen, all you people of Judah
and Jerusalem! Listen, King Jehoshaphat!
This is what the LORD says: Do not be afraid!
Don't be discouraged by this mighty army,
for the battle is not yours, but God's. 16Tomor-
row, march out against them. You will find
them coming up through the ascent of Ziz
at the end of the valley that opens into the
wilderness of Jeruel. 17But you will not even
need to fight. Take your positions; then stand
still and watch the LORD's victory. He is with
you, O people of Judah and Jerusalem. Do
not be afraid or discouraged. Go out against
them tomorrow, for the LORD is with you!"
18Then King Jehoshaphat bowed low with
his face to the ground. And all the people of
Judah and Jerusalem did the same, worshiping the LORD. 19Then the Levites from the
clans of Kohath and Korah stood to ⁱpraise
the LORD, the God of Israel, with a very loud
shout.
20Early the next morning the army of Judah went out into the wilderness of Tekoa.
On the way Jehoshaphat stopped and said,
"Listen to me, all you people of Judah and Jerusalem! Believe in the LORD your God, and
you will be able to stand firm. Believe in his
prophets, and you will succeed."
21After consulting the people, the king appointed singers to walk ahead of the army,
singing to the LORD and praising him for
his holy splendor. This is what they sang:

"Give thanks to the LORD;
his faithful love endures forever!"

22At the very moment they began to sing
and give praise, the LORD caused the armies
of Ammon, Moab, and Mount Seir to start
fighting among themselves. 23The armies
of Moab and Ammon turned against their
allies from Mount Seir and killed every one
of them. After they had destroyed the army
of Seir, they began attacking each other.
24So when the army of Judah arrived at the
lookout point in the wilderness, all they saw
were dead bodies lying on the ground as far
as they could see. Not a single one of the enemy had escaped.
25King Jehoshaphat and his men went
out to gather the plunder. They found vast
amounts of equipment, clothing, and other
valuables—more than they could carry.
There was so much plunder that it took
them three days just to collect it all! 26On
the fourth day they gathered in the Valley
of Blessing, which got its name that day because the people praised and thanked the
LORD there. It is still called the Valley of
Blessing today.
27Then all the men returned to Jerusalem,
with Jehoshaphat leading them, overjoyed
that the LORD had given them victory over
their enemies. 28They marched into Jerusalem to the music of harps, lyres, and
trumpets, and they proceeded to the Temple of the LORD.
29When all the surrounding kingdoms
heard that the LORD himself had fought
against the enemies of Israel, the fear of
God came over them. 30So Jehoshaphat's
kingdom was at peace, for his God had
given him rest on every side.

Summary of Jehoshaphat's Reign
2 Chr 20:31–21:1 // 1 Kgs 22:41-50

31So Jehoshaphat ruled over the land of Judah. He was thirty-five years old when he

20:9 2 Chr 6:20, 28-30
20:10 Num 20:17-21; 2 Chr 20:1, 22
20:11 Ps 83:12
20:12 Judg 11:27; Ps 25:15; 121:1-2
20:14 2 Chr 15:1; 24:20
20:15 Exod 14:13; 1 Sam 17:47; 2 Chr 32:7-8
20:17 Exod 14:13; 2 Chr 15:2
20:19 ⁱ*halal* (1984) ‣2 Chr 29:30
20:20 Isa 7:9
20:21 1 Chr 16:29, 34, 41; Ps 29:2
20:22 2 Chr 20:10
20:23 Judg 7:22; 1 Sam 14:20
20:27 Neh 12:43
20:29 2 Chr 14:14; 17:10
20:30 2 Chr 14:6-7; 15:15
20:31–21:1 //1 Kgs 22:41-50; 2 Chr 17:6

20:9 *war:* Or *sword of judgment;* or *sword, judgment.*

20:10 ***Mount Seir*** was another name for Edom (see Gen 32:3; note on Gen 25:25).

20:14-17 Following Jehoshaphat's lament, Jahaziel's proclamation of rescue fulfilled the requirements for the speech that a priest was to give before battle (Deut 20:2-4).

20:20-21 The song of the ***appointed singers*** replaced a battle cry. The ***prophets*** were Jahaziel (20:14-17) and the Levitical musicians (20:21), whose musical praise for the battle march was a prophecy, a declaration that God was at the head of the army.

20:25 *clothing:* As in some Hebrew manuscripts and Latin Vulgate; most Hebrew manuscripts read *corpses.*

20:26 *Valley of Blessing:* Hebrew *valley of Beracah.*

20:33 2 Chr 17:6; 19:3
20:34 1 Kgs 16:1, 7
20:35 1 Kgs 22:48-49
20:36 2 Chr 9:21
21:1 1 Kgs 22:50
21:3 2 Chr 11:5
21:5-10 //2 Kgs 8:16-24
21:6 1 Kgs 12:28-30; 2 Chr 18:1

became king, and he reigned in Jerusalem
twenty-five years. His mother was Azubah,
the daughter of Shilhi.
32Jehoshaphat was a good king, following
the ways of his father, Asa. He did what was
pleasing in the LORD's sight. 33During his
reign, however, he failed to remove all the
pagan shrines, and the people never fully
committed themselves to follow the God of
their ancestors.
34The rest of the events of Jehoshaphat's
reign, from beginning to end, are recorded
in *The Record of Jehu Son of Hanani,* which
is included in *The Book of the Kings of
Israel.*
35Some time later King Jehoshaphat of
Judah made an alliance with King Ahaziah
of Israel, who was very wicked. 36Together
they built a fleet of trading ships at the port
of Ezion-geber. 37Then Eliezer son of Doda-
vahu from Mareshah prophesied against
Jehoshaphat. He said, "Because you have allied yourself with King Ahaziah, the LORD
will destroy your work." So the ships met
with disaster and never put out to sea.

21 When Jehoshaphat died, he was buried with his ancestors in the City of
David. Then his son Jehoram became the
next king.

Reign of Jehoram (21:2-20)
The Ruthless Rule of Jehoram
2 Chr 21:5-10 // 2 Kgs 8:17-22

2Jehoram's brothers—the other sons of
Jehoshaphat—were Azariah, Jehiel, Zechariah, Azariahu, Michael, and Shephatiah; all
these were the sons of Jehoshaphat king of
Judah. 3Their father had given each of them
valuable gifts of silver, gold, and costly items,
and also some of Judah's fortified towns.
However, he designated Jehoram as the next
king because he was the oldest. 4But when
Jehoram had become solidly established as
king, he killed all his brothers and some of
the other leaders of Judah.
5Jehoram was thirty-two years old when
he became king, and he reigned in Jerusalem
eight years. 6But Jehoram followed the example of the kings of Israel and was as wicked
as King Ahab, for he had married one of

Holy War (20:20-24)

2 Chr 6:34-35; 20:5-7
Josh 6:1-20; 10:7-15
Judg 7:7-22
2 Kgs 19:14-37
Isa 26:21–27:6
Jon 3:4-10
Matt 16:18
2 Cor 10:3-6
Eph 1:19-23; 6:10-20
Rev 19:11-21

The Arabic term *jihad,* which has become well known in the English language, speaks of a "holy war" in which men fight for God. However, the biblical description of a "holy war" is quite different. A holy war is a conflict where God fights for his people while they trust in him. In these wars, victory does not depend on weapons but on obedience to God.

In a time of war, King Jehoshaphat of Judah proclaimed a fast (20:3) and petitioned God in the typical style of a prayer lament (20:5-12), which included an invocation, a complaint, a confession of trust, and a request. Jehoshaphat and the people reflected their hearts' attitude by bowing low with their faces to the ground (20:18). The image of an army marching into battle headed by a choir giving praise to God (20:21) is amusing, because the battlefield is not usually the place for worship and praise. However, worship is a consistent theme in Chronicles, and war does not change that priority. God rewards acts of trust in him. Worship provides a way to know the will of God, and it invites God to act to save his people.

The divine warrior will conquer all nations (Isa 26:21). The Gospels and Epistles portray Jesus as the conqueror of all the principalities and powers that are arrayed against the kingdom of God (Eph 1:19-21). Finally Jesus will come as the divine conqueror over all temporal and spiritual forces (Rev 19:11). He will bring the ultimate victory of God as king, and worship will be complete: "Praise the LORD! For the Lord our God, the Almighty, reigns" (Rev 19:6).

20:32-33 The comparison of ***Jehoshaphat*** with ***Asa*** is adopted from 1 Kgs 22:43 without alteration.

20:35-37 The Lord destroyed the ***fleet*** to prevent Jehoshaphat's ***alliance with King Ahaziah of Israel*** from prospering.
• ***who was very wicked:*** Or *who made him do what was wicked.*

20:36 ***fleet of trading ships:*** Literally *fleet of ships that could go to Tarshish.*

20:37 ***never put out to sea:*** Literally *never set sail for Tarshish.*

21:2-7 ***Jehoram,*** whose wife was Athaliah, the daughter of Ahab and Jezebel (18:1; 21:6; 22:2), was the first king of David's line to receive a totally negative evaluation. His murders (21:4) seriously threatened the continuation of the dynasty, which was only preserved because of the Lord's own loyal faithfulness to David (21:7). On three other occasions, violence was perpetrated against the royal family that all but ended the dynasty (see 21:17; 22:8-9; 22:10-11).

21:2 ***of Judah:*** Masoretic Text reads *of Israel;* also in 21:4. The author of Chronicles sees Judah as representative of the true Israel. (Some Hebrew manuscripts, Greek and Syriac versions, and Latin Vulgate read *of Judah.*)

21:5 After a three-year co-regency with his father, ***Jehoram*** reigned from 848 to 841 BC.

Ahab's daughters. So Jehoram did what was
evil in the LORD's sight. 7But the LORD did not
want to destroy David's dynasty, for he had
made a covenant with David and promised
that his descendants would continue to rule,
shining like a lamp forever.

8During Jehoram's reign, the Edomites
revolted against Judah and crowned their
own king. 9So Jehoram went out with his
full army and all his chariots. The Edomites
surrounded him and his chariot commanders, but he went out at night and attacked
them under cover of darkness. 10Even so,
Edom has been independent from Judah to
this day. The town of Libnah also revolted
about that same time. All this happened
because Jehoram had abandoned the LORD,
the God of his ancestors. 11He had built pagan shrines in the hill country of Judah and
had led the people of Jerusalem and Judah
to give themselves to pagan gods and to go
astray.

Elijah Warns King Jehoram

12Then Elijah the prophet wrote Jehoram
this letter:

> "This is what the LORD, the God of your
> ancestor David, says: You have not
> followed the good example of your father,
> Jehoshaphat, or your grandfather King
> Asa of Judah. 13Instead, you have been
> as evil as the kings of Israel. You have
> led the people of Jerusalem and Judah to
> worship idols, just as King Ahab did in
> Israel. And you have even killed your own
> brothers, men who were better than you.
> 14So now the LORD is about to strike you,
> your people, your children, your wives,
> and all that is yours with a heavy blow.
> 15You yourself will suffer with a severe
> intestinal disease that will get worse each
> day until your bowels come out."

The Sorry End of Jehoram

16Then the LORD stirred up the Philistines
and the Arabs, who lived near the Ethiopians, to attack Jehoram. 17They marched
against Judah, broke down its defenses,
and carried away everything of value in the
royal palace, including the king's sons and
his wives. Only his youngest son, Ahaziah,
was spared.

18After all this, the LORD struck Jehoram
with the severe intestinal disease. 19The disease grew worse and worse, and at the end
of two years it caused his bowels to come
out, and he died in agony. His people did
not build a great funeral fire to honor him
as they had done for his ancestors.

20Jehoram was thirty-two years old when
he became king, and he reigned in Jerusalem eight years. No one was sorry when he
died. They buried him in the City of David,
but not in the royal cemetery.

Reign of Ahaziah (22:1-9)

2 Chr 22:1-6 // 2 Kgs 8:25-29

22 Then the people of Jerusalem made
Ahaziah, Jehoram's youngest son,
their next king, since the marauding bands
who came with the Arabs had killed all
the older sons. So Ahaziah son of Jehoram
reigned as king of Judah.

2Ahaziah was twenty-two years old when
he became king, and he reigned in Jerusalem one year. His mother was Athaliah, a
granddaughter of King Omri. 3Ahaziah also
followed the evil example of King Ahab's
family, for his mother encouraged him in
doing wrong. 4He did what was evil in the
LORD's sight, just as Ahab's family had done.
They even became his advisers after the
death of his father, and they led him to ruin.

5Following their evil advice, Ahaziah
joined King Joram, the son of King Ahab

21:7 2 Sam 7:11-16; 1 Kgs 11:13
21:8 2 Kgs 8:20; 2 Chr 20:22-23; 21:10
21:11 Lev 20:5; 1 Kgs 11:7
21:12 2 Chr 14:2-5; 17:3-4
21:13 1 Kgs 16:31-33; 2 Chr 21:4, 6, 11
21:15 2 Chr 21:18-19
21:16 2 Chr 17:11; 22:1; 33:11
21:17 2 Chr 25:23
21:18 2 Chr 21:15
21:19 2 Chr 16:14
21:20 2 Chr 24:25; 28:27; Jer 22:18, 28
22:1-6 //2 Kgs 8:25-29
22:1 2 Chr 21:16-17
22:3 2 Chr 21:6-7
22:5 2 Kgs 8:28

21:8-11 *Jehoram's* disobedience caused him to lose the gains that Asa and Jehoshaphat had won. • *the Edomites revolted:* During Solomon's reign, control of the territory of Edom gave Israel access to the rich trade from Arabia. The Edomites had also rebelled before Solomon's death (1 Kgs 11:14-22), and were probably not under Rehoboam's control. They apparently came under Judah's control again following their defeat by Jehoshaphat (20:1-30; cp. 1 Kgs 22:47). • The *town of Libnah* was at the western end of the valley of Elah, on the border of the territory of the Philistines.

21:9 *he went out at night and attacked them:* Or *he went out and escaped.* The meaning of the Hebrew is uncertain.

21:12-15 The letter from *Elijah the prophet* to *Jehoram* announced judgment for his disobedience.

21:16-17 Jehoram's inability to resist the initial revolts of Edom and Libnah (21:8-10) encouraged other attacks on Judah, this time by *the Philistines and the Arabs.* Once again, the royal line was nearly destroyed.

21:16 *the Ethiopians:* Hebrew *the Cushites.*

21:17 *Ahaziah:* Hebrew *Jehoahaz*, a variant spelling of Ahaziah; compare 22:1.

21:18-20 *Jehoram* died after a long and painful bowel disease. He was not given the dignity of an honorary funeral rite (see 16:14), and was buried in disgrace away from the *royal cemetery.*

22:1 *marauding bands who came with the Arabs:* Or *marauding bands of Arabs.*

22:2-4 The queen mother, *Athaliah*, exercised significant influence over the king (see note on 15:16). Athaliah was very much like her mother, Jezebel (see 22:10–23:15; cp. "Jezebel" at 1 Kgs 16:31–21:28, p. 611), and she followed in the footsteps of her grandfather *Omri* (see 1 Kgs 16:21-26).

22:2 *twenty-two:* As in some Greek manuscripts and Syriac version (see also 2 Kgs 8:26); Hebrew reads *forty-two.* • *one year:* Ahaziah, also known as Jehoahaz, reigned briefly over Judah in 841 BC.

22:5-6 *Ramoth-gilead*, a Levitical city in the territory of Gad (Josh 21:38), was located on a major trade route, and was

22:7-9
//2 Kgs 9:21-29

22:8
2 Kgs 10:13-14

22:9
2 Kgs 9:27-28
2 Chr 17:4

22:10–23:21
2 Kgs 11:1-20

23:1
2 Kgs 11:4-20

23:3
2 Sam 7:12
2 Chr 21:7

23:4
1 Chr 9:26

of Israel, in his war against King Hazael of Aram at Ramoth-gilead. When the Arameans wounded Joram in the battle, 6he returned to Jezreel to recover from the wounds he had received at Ramoth. Because Joram was wounded, King Ahaziah of Judah went to Jezreel to visit him.

7But God had decided that this visit would be Ahaziah's downfall. While he was there, Ahaziah went out with Joram to meet Jehu grandson of Nimshi, whom the LORD had appointed to destroy the dynasty of Ahab.

8While Jehu was executing judgment against the family of Ahab, he happened to meet some of Judah's officials and Ahaziah's relatives who were traveling with Ahaziah. So Jehu killed them all. 9Then Jehu's men searched for Ahaziah, and they found him hiding in the city of Samaria. They brought him to Jehu, who killed him. Ahaziah was given a decent burial because the people said, "He was the grandson of Jehoshaphat—a man who sought the LORD with all his heart." But none of the surviving members of Ahaziah's family was capable of ruling the kingdom.

Reign of Joash (22:10–24:27)

Athaliah Seizes the Throne of Judah
2 Chr 22:10-12 // 2 Kgs 11:1-3

10When Athaliah, the mother of King Ahaziah of Judah, learned that her son was dead, she began to destroy the rest of Judah's royal family. 11But Ahaziah's sister Jehosheba, the daughter of King Jehoram, took Ahaziah's infant son, Joash, and stole him away from among the rest of the king's children, who were about to be killed. She put Joash and his nurse in a bedroom. In this way, Jehosheba, wife of Jehoiada the priest and sister of Ahaziah, hid the child so that Athaliah could not murder him. 12Joash remained hidden in the Temple of God for six years while Athaliah ruled over the land.

Joash is Crowned King
2 Chr 23:1-11 // 2 Kgs 11:4-12

23 In the seventh year of Athaliah's reign, Jehoiada the priest decided to act. He summoned his courage and made a pact with five army commanders: Azariah son of Jeroham, Ishmael son of Jehohanan, Azariah son of Obed, Maaseiah son of Adaiah, and Elishaphat son of Zicri. 2These men traveled secretly throughout Judah and summoned the Levites and clan leaders in all the towns to come to Jerusalem. 3They all gathered at the Temple of God, where they made a solemn pact with Joash, the young king.

Jehoiada said to them, "Here is the king's son! The time has come for him to reign! The LORD has promised that a descendant of David will be our king. 4This is what you must do. When you priests and Levites come on duty on the Sabbath, a third of you

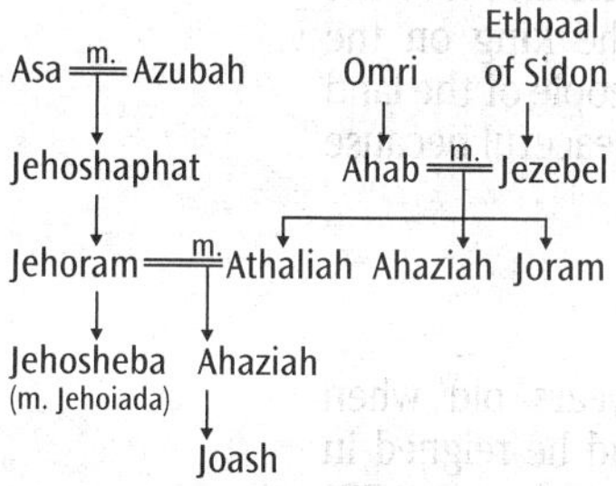

◀ **The Marriage Alliance of Jehoshaphat and Ahab (21:6; 22:2).** The marriage of JEHOSHAPHAT'S son JEHORAM and AHAB'S daughter ATHALIAH cemented the alliance between the northern and the southern kingdoms and brought the evil influence of Israel and SIDON into Judah during the reigns of JEHORAM, his son AHAZIAH, and ATHALIAH (see 21:4, 12-15; 22:2-6). JOASH, influenced by JEHOIADA the priest, broke the cycle of evil.

strategic for ***Aram*** and ***Israel.*** • ***Jezreel,*** at the foot of Mount Gilboa in the plain of Jezreel, became the summer palace of the Israelite kings.

22:5 ***Joram:*** Hebrew *Jehoram,* a variant spelling of Joram; also in 22:6, 7.

22:6 ***Ramoth:*** Hebrew *Ramah,* a variant spelling of *Ramoth.* • ***Ahaziah:*** As in some Hebrew manuscripts, Greek and Syriac versions, and Latin Vulgate (see also 2 Kgs 8:29); most Hebrew manuscripts read *Azariah.*

22:7-9 The death of ***Ahaziah*** was a punishment for his alliance with the king of Israel. The Judahite king who lived by the counsel of the Israelite house of Omri shared their fate and found no refuge there at the time of his death. Ahaziah's infidelity brought David's line almost to the same point as Saul's line, with no one left to assume the throne.

22:7 ***grandson of Nimshi:*** Hebrew *descendant of Nimshi;* cp. 2 Kgs 9:2, 14.

22:8 ***and Ahaziah's relatives:*** As in Greek version (see also 2 Kgs 10:13); Hebrew reads *and sons of the brothers of Ahaziah.*

22:10-12 ***Athaliah*** was never regarded as a legitimate monarch; she was given no royal formula of age or length of reign as were other rulers. Her destruction of ***the rest of Judah's royal family*** concentrated on potential male successors; those who were ineligible to reign, such as ***Ahaziah's sister,*** survived the slaughter. ***Jehosheba*** was Ahaziah's half sister, ***the daughter of King Jehoram*** by a wife other than Athaliah. The ***six years*** of Athaliah's reign were from 841 to 835 BC.

22:11 The first sentence is translated as in the parallel text at 2 Kgs 11:2; Hebrew lacks ***Ahaziah's sister*** and reads *Jehoshabeath* [a variant spelling of *Jehosheba*].

23:1-3 ***Jehoiada . . . made a pact*** or covenant with key military officers, who solicited broad popular support among ***the Levites and clan leaders.*** The content of the people's ***pact with Joash*** was expressed in Jehoiada's declaration that the son of the king must become king.

23:4-6 The most logical time for the coup was at the changing of the Temple guard, when there would be large movements of people. A third of the guards were coming on duty; they were stationed in three locations to perform their regular duties and to watch for any activity from the palace. The remainder of the armed force was stationed in ***the courtyards of the LORD'S Temple,*** providing a human wall to protect the king.

will serve as gatekeepers. 5 Another third will go over to the royal palace, and the final third will be at the Foundation Gate. Everyone else should stay in the courtyards of the LORD's Temple. 6 Remember, only the priests and Levites on duty may enter the Temple of the LORD, for they are set apart as holy. The rest of the people must obey the LORD's instructions and stay outside. 7 You Levites, form a bodyguard around the king and keep your weapons in hand. Kill anyone who tries to enter the Temple. Stay with the king wherever he goes."

8 So the Levites and all the people of Judah did everything as Jehoiada the priest ordered. The commanders took charge of the men reporting for duty that Sabbath, as well as those who were going off duty. Jehoiada the priest did not let anyone go home after their shift ended. 9 Then Jehoiada supplied the commanders with the spears and the large and small shields that had once belonged to King David and were stored in the Temple of God. 10 He stationed all the people around the king, with their weapons ready. They formed a line from the south side of the Temple around to the north side and all around the altar.

11 Then Jehoiada and his sons brought out Joash, the king's son, placed the crown on his head, and presented him with a copy of God's laws. They anointed him and proclaimed him king, and everyone shouted, "Long live the king!"

The Death of Athaliah
2 Chr 23:12-15 // 2 Kgs 11:13-16

12 When Athaliah heard the noise of the people running and the shouts of praise to the king, she hurried to the LORD's Temple to see what was happening. 13 When she arrived, she saw the newly crowned king standing in his place of authority by the pillar at the Temple entrance. The commanders and trumpeters were surrounding him, and people from all over the land were rejoicing and blowing trumpets. Singers with musical instruments were leading the people in a great celebration. When Athaliah saw all this, she tore her clothes in despair and shouted, "Treason! Treason!"

14 Then Jehoiada the priest ordered the commanders who were in charge of the troops, "Take her to the soldiers in front of the Temple, and kill anyone who tries to rescue her." For the priest had said, "She must not be killed in the Temple of the LORD." 15 So they seized her and led her out to the entrance of the Horse Gate on the palace grounds, and they killed her there.

Jehoiada's Religious Reforms
2 Chr 23:16-21 // 2 Kgs 11:17-20

16 Then Jehoiada made a covenant between himself and the king and the people that they would be the LORD's people. 17 And all the people went over to the temple of Baal and tore it down. They demolished the altars and smashed the idols, and they killed Mattan the priest of Baal in front of the altars.

18 Jehoiada now put the priests and Levites in charge of the Temple of the LORD, following all the directions given by David. He also commanded them to present burnt offerings to the LORD, as prescribed by the Law of Moses, and to sing and rejoice as David had instructed. 19 He also stationed gatekeepers at the gates of the LORD's Temple to keep out those who for any reason were ceremonially unclean.

20 Then the commanders, nobles, rulers, and all the people of the land escorted the king from the Temple of the LORD. They went through the upper gate and into the palace, and they seated the king on the royal throne. 21 So all the people of the land rejoiced, and the city was peaceful because Athaliah had been killed.

Overview of Joash's Reign
2 Chr 24:1-3 // 2 Kgs 11:21–12:3

24 Joash was seven years old when he became king, and he reigned in Jerusalem forty years. His mother was Zibiah from Beersheba. 2 Joash did what was pleasing in the LORD's sight throughout the lifetime of Jehoiada the priest. 3 Jehoiada chose two wives for Joash, and he had sons and daughters.

23:6 1 Chr 23:28-32
23:8 1 Chr 24:1
23:15 Neh 3:28
23:17 Deut 13:9
23:18 1 Chr 23:6, 25-31; 2 Chr 5:5
23:19 1 Chr 9:22
23:20 2 Kgs 11:19
24:1-14 //2 Kgs 12:1-16
24:1 2 Kgs 11:21

23:6-7 Because *only the priests and Levites on duty may enter the Temple,* the Levites were required to prevent anyone else from doing so.

23:11 When the seven-year-old *Joash* was anointed and crowned as *king,* he was given a copy of the law, as the law commanded (see Deut 17:18-20). • *a copy of God's laws:* Or *a copy of the covenant.*

23:14 *Take her to the soldiers in front of the Temple:* Or *Bring her out from between the ranks;* or *Take her out of the Temple precincts.* The meaning of the Hebrew is uncertain.

23:16-17 The *covenant* included vows between *the king and the people,* between the Lord and the king, and between the Lord and the people. The vows with the Lord included eliminating the worship of *Baal.*

23:18-19 By arranging for Joash to take the throne, *Jehoiada* the priest restored David's dynasty and reinstituted Temple worship according to *directions given by David.*

24:1 *Joash* reigned from 835 to 796 BC.

24:3 *Jehoiada chose two wives for Joash,* probably to ensure that David's royal line would be replenished with plenty of descendants.

24:4
2 Chr 24:7
[k]*khadash* (2318)
‣ Ps 51:10

24:6
Exod 30:12-16

24:7
2 Chr 21:17

24:9
2 Chr 24:6; 36:22

24:11
2 Kgs 12:10

24:18
Exod 34:12-14
Josh 24:20

24:19
Jer 7:25

24:20
Num 14:41
2 Chr 15:2; 20:14

24:21
Neh 9:26
Matt 23:35

24:22
Gen 9:5

Joash Repairs the Temple

2 Chr 24:4-14 // 2 Kgs 12:4-16

4At one point Joash decided to [k]repair and
restore the Temple of the LORD. 5He summoned the priests and Levites and gave
them these instructions: "Go to all the
towns of Judah and collect the required
annual offerings, so that we can repair the
Temple of your God. Do not delay!" But the
Levites did not act immediately.
6So the king called for Jehoiada the high
priest and asked him, "Why haven't you demanded that the Levites go out and collect
the Temple taxes from the towns of Judah
and from Jerusalem? Moses, the servant of
the LORD, levied this tax on the community
of Israel in order to maintain the Tabernacle of the Covenant."
7Over the years the followers of wicked
Athaliah had broken into the Temple of God,
and they had used all the dedicated things
from the Temple of the LORD to worship the
images of Baal.
8So now the king ordered a chest to be
made and set outside the gate leading to the
Temple of the LORD. 9Then a proclamation
was sent throughout Judah and Jerusalem,
telling the people to bring to the LORD the
tax that Moses, the servant of God, had required of the Israelites in the wilderness.
10This pleased all the leaders and the people, and they gladly brought their money
and filled the chest with it.
11Whenever the chest became full, the
Levites would carry it to the king's officials.
Then the court secretary and an officer of the
high priest would come and empty the chest
and take it back to the Temple again. This
went on day after day, and a large amount
of money was collected. 12The king and Jehoiada gave the money to the construction
supervisors, who hired masons and carpenters to restore the Temple of the LORD. They
also hired metalworkers, who made articles
of iron and bronze for the LORD's Temple.
13The men in charge of the renovation
worked hard and made steady progress.
They restored the Temple of God according
to its original design and strengthened it.
14When all the repairs were finished, they
brought the remaining money to the king
and Jehoiada. It was used to make various
articles for the Temple of the LORD—articles for worship services and for burnt
offerings, including ladles and other articles made of gold and silver. And the burnt
offerings were sacrificed continually in the
Temple of the LORD during the lifetime of Jehoiada the priest.
15Jehoiada lived to a very old age, finally
dying at 130. 16He was buried among the
kings in the City of David, because he had
done so much good in Israel for God and his
Temple.

Joash under Judgment

17But after Jehoiada's death, the leaders of
Judah came and bowed before King Joash
and persuaded him to listen to their advice.
18They decided to abandon the Temple of
the LORD, the God of their ancestors, and
they worshiped Asherah poles and idols instead! Because of this sin, divine anger fell
on Judah and Jerusalem. 19Yet the LORD
sent prophets to bring them back to him.
The prophets warned them, but still the people would not listen.
20Then the Spirit of God came upon Zechariah son of Jehoiada the priest. He stood
before the people and said, "This is what
God says: Why do you disobey the LORD's
commands and keep yourselves from prospering? You have abandoned the LORD, and
now he has abandoned you!"
21Then the leaders plotted to kill Zechariah, and King Joash ordered that they stone
him to death in the courtyard of the LORD's
Temple. 22That was how King Joash repaid
Jehoiada for his loyalty—by killing his son.
Zechariah's last words as he died were,

24:4-8 There is no indication regarding when ***Joash*** first attempted to refurbish ***the Temple.*** However, after the first failure to raise funds, Joash summoned ***Jehoiada*** a second time, in the twenty-third year of his reign (2 Kgs 12:6). The inaction of the priests might have resulted from a disagreement over who should fund the restoration work and who should oversee it. The king censured Jehoiada for his failure to act, and then proposed a plan that put the offering on a more voluntary basis.

24:6 ***Tabernacle of the Covenant:*** Literally *Tent of the Testimony.*

24:12-14 The book of Kings indicates that the funds collected for repairing the Temple were used only for wages (2 Kgs 12:13-14); Chronicles further explains that the funds were used for Temple artifacts only after the repairs were completed.

24:15-16 A lifespan of ***130*** years indicates that ***Jehoiada*** received great blessing by the Lord. Further, his royal burial as a priest-king shows great honor from the people.

24:20-22 ***Jehoiada*** had scrupulously preserved ***the courtyard of the LORD's Temple*** from bloodshed and the dynasty of David from extinction. Yet ironically, ***Zechariah*** his son was murdered in the very place and by the very king, ***Joash,*** who was protected during the coup. Jesus made reference to this murder when he was criticizing the religious leaders (Matt 23:35; Luke 11:51). • ***"May the LORD . . . avenge my death!"*** This prayer for vengeance was similar to those that King David himself had prayed against the injustices done to him by Saul (cp. Ps 5:10; 7:9; 9:19-20; 28:4; 56:7; 139:19; see also "Prayers for Vengeance" at Ps 137, p. 1017).

"May the LORD see what they are doing and avenge my death!"

The End of Joash's Reign

2 Chr 24:23-27 // 2 Kgs 12:17-21

23In the spring of the year the Aramean army marched against Joash. They invaded Judah and Jerusalem and killed all the leaders of the nation. Then they sent all the plunder back to their king in Damascus. 24Although the Arameans attacked with only a small army, the LORD helped them conquer the much larger army of Judah. The people of Judah had abandoned the LORD, the God of their ancestors, so judgment was carried out against Joash.

25The Arameans withdrew, leaving Joash severely wounded. But his own officials plotted to kill him for murdering the son of Jehoiada the priest. They assassinated him as he lay in bed. Then he was buried in the City of David, but not in the royal cemetery. 26The assassins were Jozacar, the son of an Ammonite woman named Shimeath, and Jehozabad, the son of a Moabite woman named Shomer.

27The account of the sons of Joash, the prophecies about him, and the record of his restoration of the Temple of God are written in *The Commentary on the Book of the Kings*. His son Amaziah became the next king.

Reign of Amaziah (25:1–26:2)

Consolidation of Power

2 Chr 25:1-4 // 2 Kgs 14:1-6

25 Amaziah was twenty-five years old when he became king, and he reigned in Jerusalem twenty-nine years. His mother was Jehoaddin from Jerusalem. 2Amaziah did what was pleasing in the LORD's sight, but not wholeheartedly.

3When Amaziah was well established as king, he executed the officials who had assassinated his father. 4However, he did not kill the children of the assassins, for he obeyed the command of the LORD as written by Moses in the Book of the Law: "Parents must not be put to death for the sins of their children, nor children for the sins of their parents. Those deserving to die must be put to death for their own crimes."

Amaziah's War against Edom

2 Chr 25:11 // 2 Kgs 14:7

5Then Amaziah organized the army, assigning generals and captains for all Judah and Benjamin. He took a census and found that he had an army of 300,000 select troops, twenty years old and older, all trained in the use of spear and shield. 6He also paid about 7,500 pounds of silver to hire 100,000 experienced fighting men from Israel.

7But a man of God came to him and said, "Your Majesty, do not hire troops from Israel, for the LORD is not with Israel. He will not help those people of Ephraim! 8If you let them go with your troops into battle, you will be defeated by the enemy no matter how well you fight. God will overthrow you, for he has the power to help you or to trip you up."

9Amaziah asked the man of God, "But what about all that silver I paid to hire the army of Israel?"

The man of God replied, "The LORD is able to give you much more than this!" 10So Amaziah discharged the hired troops and sent them back to Ephraim. This made them very angry with Judah, and they returned home in a great rage.

11Then Amaziah summoned his courage and led his army to the Valley of Salt, where

24:23-27 //2 Kgs 12:17-21
24:24 2 Chr 16:7-8
24:25 2 Kgs 12:20-21
24:27 2 Chr 13:22; 24:12
25:1-4 //2 Kgs 14:1-6
25:2 2 Chr 24:2
25:4 Deut 24:16
25:5 Num 1:3; 2 Chr 26:13
25:8 2 Chr 14:11; 20:6
25:11-12 //2 Kgs 14:7

24:23-26 God could use war to render judgment on Israel just as surely as on any other nation; one of the characteristics of a "holy war" was a small force's defeat of a much larger army (see "Holy War" at 20:20-24, p. 757).

24:23 ***In the spring of the year:*** Literally *At the turn of the year.* The first day of the year in the ancient Hebrew lunar calendar occurred in March or April.

24:25-26 ***Jehoiada*** had received a royal burial (24:15-16), but ***Joash*** was buried in disgrace. • ***son:*** As in Greek version and Latin Vulgate; Hebrew reads *sons.*

24:26 ***Jozacar:*** As in parallel text at 2 Kgs 12:21; Hebrew reads *Zabad.* • ***Shomer:*** As in parallel text at 2 Kgs 12:21; Hebrew reads *Shimrith*, a variant spelling of Shomer.

24:27 ***The Commentary on the Book of the Kings*** that the Chronicler used as a source is no longer available to us (see also 9:29).

25:1 The ***twenty-nine years*** of ***Amaziah***'s reign (796–767 BC) included a long co-regency with his son Uzziah from 792 BC (see timelines, pp. 649, 655). • ***Jehoaddin:*** As in parallel text at 2 Kgs 14:2; Hebrew reads *Jehoaddan*, a variant spelling of Jehoaddin.

25:2 ***but not wholeheartedly:*** See 2 Kgs 14:3-4 for further details.

25:3-4 ***Amaziah . . . executed the officials*** to avenge his father and carry out the justice prescribed in ***the Law.*** • ***"Parents . . . crimes":*** See Deut 24:16.

25:5 ***generals and captains:*** Literally *commanders of thousands and commanders of hundreds.* • The inclusion of ***Benjamin*** in this listing of military officers indicates that this tribe was part of the kingdom of ***Judah*** at that time.

25:6 ***about 7,500 pounds:*** Hebrew *100 talents* [3,400 kilograms]. • Amaziah's force of 300,000 was smaller than Asa's (580,000) or Jehoshaphat's (1,160,000) had been; this might explain Amaziah's desire ***to hire*** additional troops ***from Israel*** (the northern kingdom).

25:7-8 The phrase ***a man of God*** was a way to refer to a prophet (as in Deut 33:1; 1 Sam 2:27; 9:6-10; 1 Kgs 13:1-31). • The kingdom of ***Israel*** was politically foreign and spiritually apostate. Relying on Israel's ***troops*** for military strength would bring spiritual compromise and God's opposition.

25:14 2 Chr 28:23
25:15 2 Chr 25:11-12
25:17-28 //2 Kgs 14:8-20
25:18 Judg 9:8-15
25:19 2 Chr 26:16; 32:25
25:23 2 Chr 21:17
25:24 1 Chr 26:15
25:25 2 Kgs 14:17-22
26:1-4 //2 Kgs 14:21-22; 15:1-3

they killed 10,000 Edomite troops from Seir. [12]They captured another 10,000 and took them to the top of a cliff and threw them off, dashing them to pieces on the rocks below.

[13]Meanwhile, the hired troops that Amaziah had sent home raided several of the towns of Judah between Samaria and Beth-horon. They killed 3,000 people and carried off great quantities of plunder.

[14]When King Amaziah returned from slaughtering the Edomites, he brought with him idols taken from the people of Seir. He set them up as his own gods, bowed down in front of them, and offered sacrifices to them! [15]This made the LORD very angry, and he sent a prophet to ask, "Why do you turn to gods who could not even save their own people from you?"

[16]But the king interrupted him and said, "Since when have I made you the king's counselor? Be quiet now before I have you killed!"

So the prophet stopped with this warning: "I know that God has determined to destroy you because you have done this and have refused to accept my counsel."

Amaziah's War against Jehoash of Israel
2 Chr 25:17-24 // 2 Kgs 14:8-14

[17]After consulting with his advisers, King Amaziah of Judah sent this challenge to Israel's king Jehoash, the son of Jehoahaz and grandson of Jehu: "Come and meet me in battle!"

[18]But King Jehoash of Israel replied to King Amaziah of Judah with this story: "Out in the Lebanon mountains, a thistle sent a message to a mighty cedar tree: 'Give your daughter in marriage to my son.' But just then a wild animal of Lebanon came by and stepped on the thistle, crushing it!

[19]"You are saying, 'I have defeated Edom,' and you are very proud of it. But my advice is to stay at home. Why stir up trouble that will only bring disaster on you and the people of Judah?"

[20]But Amaziah refused to listen, for God was determined to destroy him for turning to the gods of Edom. [21]So King Jehoash of Israel mobilized his army against King Amaziah of Judah. The two armies drew up their battle lines at Beth-shemesh in Judah. [22]Judah was routed by the army of Israel, and its army scattered and fled for home. [23]King Jehoash of Israel captured Judah's king, Amaziah son of Joash and grandson of Ahaziah, at Beth-shemesh. Then he brought him to Jerusalem, where he demolished 600 feet of Jerusalem's wall, from the Ephraim Gate to the Corner Gate. [24]He carried off all the gold and silver and all the articles from the Temple of God that had been in the care of Obed-edom. He also seized the treasures of the royal palace, along with hostages, and then returned to Samaria.

The End of Amaziah's Reign
2 Chr 25:25–26:2 // 2 Kgs 14:17-22

[25]King Amaziah of Judah lived on for fifteen years after the death of King Jehoash of Israel. [26]The rest of the events in Amaziah's reign, from beginning to end, are recorded in *The Book of the Kings of Judah and Israel*.

[27]After Amaziah turned away from the LORD, there was a conspiracy against his life in Jerusalem, and he fled to Lachish. But his enemies sent assassins after him, and they killed him there. [28]They brought his body back on a horse, and he was buried with his ancestors in the City of David.

26 All the people of Judah had crowned Amaziah's sixteen-year-old son, Uzziah, as king in place of his father. [2]After his father's death, Uzziah rebuilt the town of Elath and restored it to Judah.

25:11 The *Valley of Salt* was a perennial battlefield south of the Dead Sea; David had also fought with the Edomites there (2 Sam 8:13; see Ps 60). • Amaziah did not capture the port at Elath (26:2); his conquest was limited to northern Edom.

25:14-15 Conquerors sometimes worshiped the gods of a vanquished nation, wrongly believing that the gods of the defeated people had helped them to victory. ***Amaziah*** held this pagan mindset; he did not believe that the Lord is the only true God (see Isa 40:18-28; 42:8; Jer 10:1-16).

25:17 ***Jehoash:*** Hebrew *Joash*, a variant spelling of *Jehoash;* also in 25:18, 21, 23, 25. • ***Come and meet me in battle:*** Literally *Come, let us look one another in the face.*

25:20 Amaziah's pride was manifested in his failure to seek God. While he seriously overestimated his military capability after defeating Edom, his decision to go to war against Jehoram was actually the result of trusting other gods and of ignoring God's judgment that followed (cp. 18:9-34; 2 Thes 2:11).

25:21 ***Beth-shemesh*** protected the entrance to the Sorek Valley and Jerusalem's access to the coast. Jehoash might have been seeking to cut off Jerusalem's access to trade, or he might have been trying to increase his own access.

25:23 The ***Ephraim Gate*** was on the north side of the city, while ***the Corner Gate*** was on the western wall (see map of Jerusalem, p. 766). • ***600 feet:*** Hebrew *400 cubits* [180 meters].

25:28 ***the City of David:*** As in some Hebrew manuscripts and other ancient versions (see also 2 Kgs 14:20); most Hebrew manuscripts read *the city of Judah*.

26:1-5 The Chronicler gave ***Uzziah*** (called Azariah in Kings) a double introduction (26:1-2, 3-5), quoting two passages found in Kings (2 Kgs 14:21-22; 15:2-3).

26:2 ***Elath:*** As in Greek version (see also 2 Kgs 14:22; 16:6); Hebrew reads *Eloth*, a variant spelling of Elath.

Reign of Uzziah (26:3-23)

Military and Economic Achievements

2 Chr 26:3-4 // 2 Kgs 15:1-3

3Uzziah was sixteen years old when he became king, and he reigned in Jerusalem
fifty-two years. His mother was Jecoliah
from Jerusalem. 4He did what was pleasing in the LORD's sight, just as his father,
Amaziah, had done. 5Uzziah sought God
during the days of Zechariah, who taught
him to fear God. And as long as the king
sought guidance from the LORD, God gave
him success.

6Uzziah declared war on the Philistines
and broke down the walls of Gath, Jabneh,
and Ashdod. Then he built new towns in
the Ashdod area and in other parts of Philistia. 7God helped him in his wars against
the Philistines, his battles with the Arabs of
Gur, and his wars with the Meunites. 8The
Meunites paid annual tribute to him, and
his fame spread even to Egypt, for he had
become very powerful.

9Uzziah built fortified towers in Jerusalem at the Corner Gate, at the Valley Gate,
and at the angle in the wall. 10He also constructed forts in the wilderness and dug
many water cisterns, because he kept great
herds of livestock in the foothills of Judah
and on the plains. He was also a man who
loved the soil. He had many workers who
cared for his farms and vineyards, both on
the hillsides and in the fertile valleys.

11Uzziah had an army of well-trained
warriors, ready to march into battle, unit
by unit. This army had been mustered and
organized by Jeiel, the secretary of the
army, and his assistant, Maaseiah. They
were under the direction of Hananiah, one
of the king's officials. 12These regiments
of mighty warriors were commanded by
2,600 clan leaders. 13The army consisted of
307,500 men, all elite troops. They were prepared to assist the king against any enemy.

14Uzziah provided the entire army with
[a]shields, spears, helmets, coats of mail, bows,

26:5 2 Chr 15:2; 24:2 Dan 1:17
26:6 Isa 14:29
26:7 2 Chr 21:16
26:8 2 Chr 17:11
26:9 2 Chr 25:23 Neh 3:13
26:10 Gen 26:18-21
26:13 2 Chr 25:5
26:14 [a]*magen* (4043) ›Ps 3:3

UZZIAH (26:1-23)

2 Kgs 14:21-22; 15:1-7
Isa 1:1; 6:1
Hos 1:1
Amos 1:1
Zech 14:5

Uzziah, son of King Amaziah and Jecoliah, reigned in Judah for 52 years (792–740 BC; see 2 Kgs 14:21-22; 15:1-7; 2 Chr 26:1-23). He took the throne at age sixteen when his father was assassinated. Uzziah served as a capable, energetic, and well-organized king who pleased the Lord through most of his reign.

During most of Uzziah's reign, Jeroboam II (793–753 BC) ruled in the northern kingdom of Israel. Both kings were successful and brought a period of prosperity to Israel and Judah. Uzziah's long and successful reign defined an era in Judah. Zechariah 14:5 recalls an earthquake that took place during Uzziah's reign. Amos and Hosea both prophesied during his life (Hos 1:1; Amos 1:1), even though most of their oracles were directed toward the northern kingdom. And the prophet Isaiah received his call the year Uzziah died (Isa 1:1; 6:1). Uzziah successfully fought the Philistines, and he built many fortifications in Jerusalem and throughout Judea. He "sought guidance from the LORD" (26:5), and as long as he did, the Lord blessed him in all his undertakings and he prospered.

Uzziah became proud of his many successes and had a sad downfall (26:16). He took upon himself the prerogatives of a priest, entered the holy area of the Temple, and burned incense. The priests tried to stop him from this sin against the Lord, but he angrily rejected their warnings. Because of his disobedience, God struck Uzziah with leprosy and he had to live out the rest of his life in seclusion. Uzziah was buried with his forefathers, but at a distance because of his leprosy (26:23).

26:3 The *fifty-two years* of *Uzziah's* reign (792–740 BC) included a long co-regency with his father, Amaziah (from 792 to 767 BC), and a co-regency with his son Jotham (from 750 to 740 BC; see timeline, p. 656).

26:5 *who taught him to fear God:* As in Syriac and Greek versions; Hebrew reads *who instructed him in divine visions.*

26:6-8 These verses summarize Uzziah's international achievements. His conquests were to the west, south, and southeast, but not to the north, where Jeroboam II's kingdom was powerful (2 Kgs 14:23-29). Uzziah's strategy, with God's guidance (26:7), was to achieve control over the coastal highway and then build towns in the conquered territory.

26:7 *Gur:* As in Greek version; Hebrew reads *Gur-baal.*

26:8 *Meunites:* As in Greek version; Hebrew reads *Ammonites.* Cp. 26:7.

26:9-10 Uzziah repaired damage done to Jerusalem's walls by Jehoash in his campaign against Amaziah; Uzziah might also have repaired damage from the famous earthquake during his time (Amos 1:1; Zech 14:5). Towers and cisterns from excavations in Qumran, Gibeah, Beersheba, and other sites date to this period. • Uzziah was a patron of agriculture, a vital industry for an independent society.

26:10 *the foothills of Judah:* Hebrew *the Shephelah.*

26:11-14 Uzziah's large and well-equipped *army* enabled him to expand and defend his territory. His name has been found on a fragmentary text of

26:16 Deut 32:15; 1 Kgs 13:1-4; 2 Chr 25:19
26:17 1 Chr 6:10
26:18 Exod 30:7-8; Num 16:39-40
26:19 2 Kgs 5:25-27
26:21-23 //2 Kgs 15:5-7
26:22 Isa 1:1

and sling stones. [15]And he built structures
on the walls of Jerusalem, designed by experts to protect those who shot arrows and
hurled large stones from the towers and the
corners of the wall. His fame spread far and
wide, for the LORD gave him marvelous help,
and he became very powerful.

Uzziah's Sin and Punishment
2 Chr 26:21-23 // 2 Kgs 15:5-7

[16]But when he had become powerful, he
also became proud, which led to his downfall. He sinned against the LORD his God
by entering the sanctuary of the LORD's
Temple and personally burning incense
on the incense altar. [17]Azariah the high
priest went in after him with eighty other
priests of the LORD, all brave men. [18]They
confronted King Uzziah and said, "It is not
for you, Uzziah, to burn incense to the LORD.
That is the work of the priests alone, the descendants of Aaron who are set apart for
this work. Get out of the sanctuary, for you
have sinned. The LORD God will not honor
you for this!"

[19]Uzziah, who was holding an incense
burner, became furious. But as he was
standing there raging at the priests before
the incense altar in the LORD's Temple, leprosy suddenly broke out on his forehead.
[20]When Azariah the high priest and all the
other priests saw the leprosy, they rushed
him out. And the king himself was eager to
get out because the LORD had struck him.
[21]So King Uzziah had leprosy until the day
he died. He lived in isolation in a separate
house, for he was excluded from the Temple of the LORD. His son Jotham was put in
charge of the royal palace, and he governed
the people of the land.

[22]The rest of the events of Uzziah's reign,
from beginning to end, are recorded by
the prophet Isaiah son of Amoz. [23]When

Violation of the Sacred (26:16-21)

Gen 2:15-17; 3:1-6; Exod 19:12-13; 31:14-15; Lev 10:1-20; 24:16-17; Num 1:51; 15:32-36; 1 Cor 6:19-20

When King Uzziah entered the Temple to burn incense (26:16), he violated the sanctuary that God had set apart for his own presence. In terms of the function of the Temple, this violation was no trivial matter.

The Temple represented God's sacred presence in creation. So all of its rituals needed to reflect its status as sacred and set apart for God alone. This meant that no one could enter it to make offerings except those anointed for the task. The kings of Israel (unlike kings of other ancient Near Eastern cultures) were excluded from the sacred space because they were only anointed for the secular function of government. The king of Israel was not a priest. He was not God's representative in sacred matters nor (as in other cultures) a god himself. He was a servant of God taken from among his brothers to administer the covenant in the community (Deut 17:18-19).

There can be no violations of God's holy presence, and that included the Temple in Jerusalem. It was a sacred space that he had set apart as his alone (26:16-18). When Uzziah entered the Temple and violated this sacred space, his response was typical of arrogant human hearts (26:16). He assumed that, as king, he had the right to enter God's sacred Temple. But he did not have that right, and he was judged with affliction by a skin disease and separation from daily life. The punishment was appropriate to the arrogance of his sin.

Ever since Eden, humans have attempted to take God's sacred space as their own (Gen 2:15-17; 3:1-6). Uzziah's sacrilege remains an ever-present temptation. Any conduct that fails to glorify God is a violation of that sacred space. All of human history consists of the story of God restoring the entire heavens and earth to be the place of his dwelling. In the new covenant through Jesus Christ, God's sacred space is not limited to a Temple in Jerusalem or any other building; he sets apart for himself the lives of his people who trust in him (1 Cor 6:19-20). In his grace, God has made the people of the new covenant to be his temple on earth (1 Pet 2:4-5), to be the space where his holiness enters creation. History will be complete when all of heaven and earth becomes the temple of God (Isa 65:17-18; Rev 21:1-2).

Tiglath-pileser III of Assyria, identifying *Uzziah* as head of a coalition.

26:15 ***to protect those who shot arrows and hurled large stones:*** Or *to shoot arrows and hurl large stones.*

26:16-18 Uzziah's leprosy was a judgment on the covenant violation of ***burning incense*** within the Temple, an activity reserved exclusively for ***priests*** (Exod 30:7-9; Num 16).

26:19 ***leprosy:*** Or *a contagious skin disease.* The Hebrew word used here and throughout this passage can describe various skin diseases.

26:21 The ***leprosy*** forced ***King Uzziah*** to spend the end of his life in quarantine in ***a separate house*** (literally *a free house*). The significance of this term is not known; it is often interpreted to mean that he was free from the duties of the monarchy. In Ugaritic texts, it seems to be a euphemism for a place of total confinement.

Uzziah died, he was buried with his ancestors; his grave was in a nearby burial field
belonging to the kings, for the people said,
"He had leprosy." And his son Jotham became the next king.

Reign of Jotham (27:1-9)
2 Chr 27:1-3a, 7-9 // 2 Kgs 15:32-38

27 Jotham was twenty-five years old
when he became king, and he
reigned in Jerusalem sixteen years. His
mother was Jerusha, the daughter of Zadok.
2Jotham did what was pleasing in the
LORD's sight. He did everything his father,
Uzziah, had done, except that Jotham did not
sin by entering the Temple of the LORD. But
the people continued in their corrupt ways.
3Jotham rebuilt the upper gate of the
Temple of the LORD. He also did extensive rebuilding on the wall at the hill of Ophel. 4He
built towns in the hill country of Judah and
constructed fortresses and towers in the
wooded areas. 5Jotham went to war against
the Ammonites and conquered them. Over
the next three years he received from them
an annual tribute of 7,500 pounds of silver,
50,000 bushels of wheat, and 50,000 bushels of barley.
6King Jotham became powerful because
he was careful to live in obedience to the
LORD his God.
7The rest of the events of Jotham's reign,
including all his wars and other activities,
are recorded in *The Book of the Kings of*
Israel and Judah. 8He was twenty-five years
old when he became king, and he reigned
in Jerusalem sixteen years. 9When Jotham
died, he was buried in the City of David.
And his son Ahaz became the next king.

Reign of Ahaz (28:1-27)
Transgressions of Ahaz
2 Chr 28:1-4 // 2 Kgs 16:1-4

28 Ahaz was twenty years old when
he became king, and he reigned
in Jerusalem sixteen years. He did not do
what was pleasing in the sight of the LORD,
as his ancestor David had done. 2Instead,
he followed the example of the kings of Israel. He cast metal images for the worship
of Baal. 3He offered sacrifices in the valley
of Ben-Hinnom, even sacrificing his own
sons in the fire. In this way, he followed the
detestable practices of the pagan nations
the LORD had driven from the land ahead
of the Israelites. 4He offered sacrifices and
burned incense at the pagan shrines and on
the hills and under every green tree.

Political and Military Reversals
5Because of all this, the LORD his God allowed the king of Aram to defeat Ahaz
and to exile large numbers of his people
to Damascus. The armies of the king of Israel also defeated Ahaz and inflicted many
casualties on his army. 6In a single day Pekah son of Remaliah, Israel's king, killed
120,000 of Judah's troops, all of them
experienced warriors, because they had

26:23 2 Chr 21:20; 28:27; Isa 6:1
27:1-9 //2 Kgs 15:33-38
27:2 2 Chr 26:16
27:3 2 Chr 33:14; Neh 3:26
27:4 2 Chr 11:5
27:6 2 Chr 26:5
27:7 2 Kgs 15:36
27:8 2 Chr 27:1
28:1-27 //2 Kgs 16:1-20
28:2 Exod 34:17; 2 Chr 22:3
28:3 Lev 18:21; Josh 15:8; 2 Chr 33:2, 6
28:4 2 Chr 28:25
28:5 2 Kgs 16:5; 2 Chr 24:24; Isa 7:1
28:6 2 Kgs 16:5

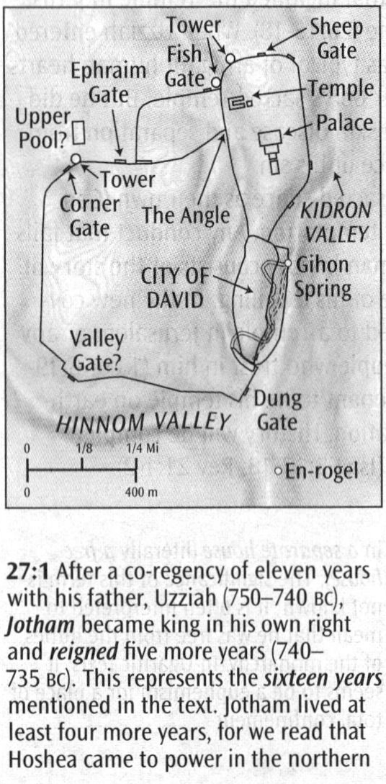

◂ **Fortifications of Jerusalem, 767–643 BC (26:9; 27:3).** Various kings of Judah repaired and augmented the walls of Jerusalem in preparation for attack, including Uzziah (26:9), Jotham (27:3), Hezekiah (32:1-5), and Manasseh following his repentance (33:14).

27:1 After a co-regency of eleven years with his father, Uzziah (750–740 BC), ***Jotham*** became king in his own right and ***reigned*** five more years (740–735 BC). This represents the ***sixteen years*** mentioned in the text. Jotham lived at least four more years, for we read that Hoshea came to power in the northern kingdom "in the twentieth year of Jotham son of Uzziah" (2 Kgs 15:30). But Jotham's son, Ahaz, had already begun a co-regency with Jotham (see note on 2 Kgs 17:1). After Jotham's sixteen official years, Ahaz began to rule in his father's stead (see timeline, p. 656; see also note on 2 Kgs 16:1-2). However, Ahaz presumably had his official accession ceremony following his father's death in 732 BC, so the author of 2 Chronicles reckons Ahaz's official regnal years starting in 731 BC (see 28:1).

27:3-4 Jotham's rebuilding endeavors were like those of his father; he continued the work of restoration begun by Uzziah. He also constructed ***fortresses and towers*** in the forests, providing a network of lookouts and highway defenses within the kingdom and on the frontier.

27:5 Uzziah had received tribute from ***the Ammonites*** (26:8), and Jotham continued to dominate their territory east of the Jordan. The end of these payments after ***three years*** might have been because of Jotham's preoccupation with fighting Israel and Aram (2 Kgs 15:37). • ***7,500 pounds:*** Hebrew *100 talents* [3,400 kilograms]. • ***50,000 bushels of wheat, and 50,000 bushels of barley:*** Hebrew *10,000 cors* [1,820 kiloliters] *of wheat, and 10,000 cors of barley.*

28:1 After a co-regency with his father, Jotham, ***Ahaz*** became king in his own right and ***reigned . . . sixteen years,*** from 731 to 715 BC (see also note on 27:1; 2 Kgs 16:1-2).

28:3-4 ***even sacrificing his own sons in the fire*** (or *even making his sons pass through the fire*): Ahaz was imitating the abominable conduct of the Canaanites (see Deut 12:31; 18:9-10; Jer 7:31; 19:5; 32:35).

28:8 Deut 28:25, 41 2 Chr 11:4
28:9 2 Chr 25:15 Ezra 9:6 Isa 47:6 Rev 18:5
28:10 Lev 25:39
28:11 2 Chr 28:8
28:15 Deut 34:3 2 Kgs 6:22 Prov 25:21-22
28:16 2 Kgs 16:7
28:18 Ezek 16:57

abandoned the LORD, the God of their ancestors. 7Then Zicri, a warrior from Ephraim,
killed Maaseiah, the king's son; Azrikam,
the king's palace commander; and Elkanah, the king's second-in-command. 8The
armies of Israel captured 200,000 women
and children from Judah and seized tremendous amounts of plunder, which they took
back to Samaria.
9But a prophet of the LORD named Oded
was there in Samaria when the army of Israel returned home. He went out to meet
them and said, "The LORD, the God of your
ancestors, was angry with Judah and let you
defeat them. But you have gone too far, killing them without mercy, and all heaven is
disturbed. 10And now you are planning to
make slaves of these people from Judah
and Jerusalem. What about your own sins
against the LORD your God? 11Listen to me
and return these prisoners you have taken,
for they are your own relatives. Watch out,
because now the LORD's fierce anger has
been turned against you!"
12Then some of the leaders of Israel—Azariah son of Jehohanan, Berekiah son of
Meshillemoth, Jehizkiah son of Shallum,
and Amasa son of Hadlai—agreed with this
and confronted the men returning from
battle. 13"You must not bring the prisoners
here!" they declared. "We cannot afford to
add to our sins and guilt. Our guilt is already
great, and the LORD's fierce anger is already
turned against Israel."
14So the warriors released the prisoners
and handed over the plunder in the sight of
the leaders and all the people. 15Then the
four men just mentioned by name came
forward and distributed clothes from the
plunder to the prisoners who were naked.
They provided clothing and sandals to wear,
gave them enough food and drink, and
dressed their wounds with olive oil. They
put those who were weak on donkeys and
took all the prisoners back to their own people in Jericho, the city of palms. Then they
returned to Samaria.

Ahaz Closes the Temple

2 Chr 28:26-27 // 2 Kgs 16:19-20

16At that time King Ahaz of Judah asked the
king of Assyria for help. 17The armies of
Edom had again invaded Judah and taken
captives. 18And the Philistines had raided
towns located in the foothills of Judah and
in the Negev of Judah. They had already captured and occupied Beth-shemesh, Aijalon,
Gederoth, Soco with its villages, Timnah

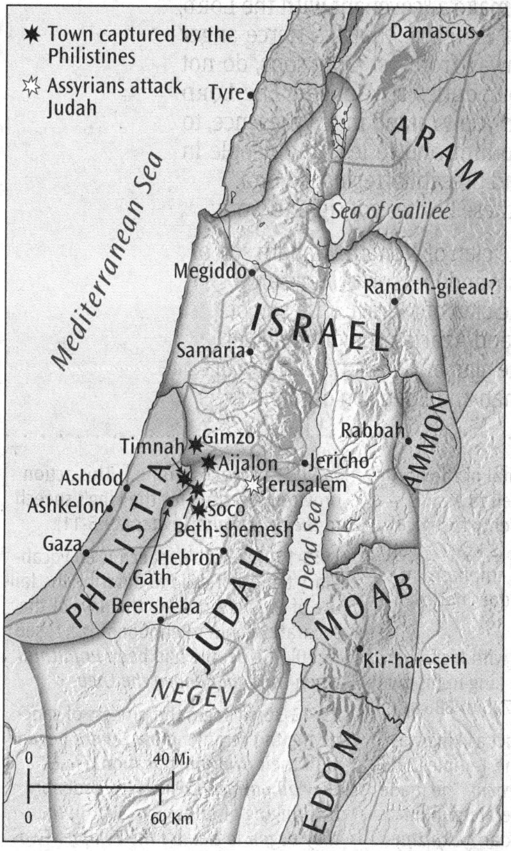

◂ **Ahaz's Reign in Judah, 732–716 BC (28:1-27).** During King Ahaz's reign, the king of ARAM defeated JUDAH and exiled many people to DAMASCUS. The northern kingdom of ISRAEL also defeated Ahaz's army, killed his son, and took many people captive to SAMARIA, although they were later returned to JERICHO. EDOM also attacked Judah and took captives, and the Philistines captured BETH-SHEMESH, AIJALON, SOCO, TIMNAH, and GIMZO. Ahaz asked the king of Assyria for help, but when he arrived, he attacked Judah instead of helping. All of this came, the Chronicler informs us, because of Ahaz's wickedness in turning away from the Lord and serving pagan gods (28:5).

28:9-10 ***you have gone too far:*** Although the Lord was using Israel as a means of punishment toward Judah, the covenant prohibited the enslavement and murder of fellow Israelites (28:10; Lev 25:39-55).

28:11 The Chronicler expresses a positive attitude toward the north with the term ***relatives*** (literally *brothers*).
• ***now the LORD's fierce anger has been turned against you:*** Later, during Ahaz's reign, the kingdom of Israel would be destroyed and exiled (722 BC, 2 Kgs 17:5-23).

28:12 ***Israel:*** Literally *Ephraim*, referring to the northern kingdom of Israel.

28:16 ***Ahaz . . . asked the king of Assyria for help:*** See 2 Kgs 16:7-9 for more details.

28:17-18 The Edomites and ***the Philistines*** were natural enemies ***of Judah***. The towns captured by these armies were all along the ***Aijalon***, Sorek, and Elah valleys in the buffer zone of ***the foothills of Judah*** (Hebrew *the Shephelah*) or ***the Negev***.

with its villages, and Gimzo with its villages. 19The LORD was humbling Judah because of King Ahaz of Judah, for he had encouraged his people to sin and had been utterly unfaithful to the LORD.

20So when King Tiglath-pileser of Assyria arrived, he attacked Ahaz instead of helping him. 21Ahaz took valuable items from the LORD's Temple, the royal palace, and from the homes of his officials and gave them to the king of Assyria as tribute. But this did not help him.

22Even during this time of trouble, King Ahaz continued to reject the LORD. 23He offered sacrifices to the gods of Damascus who had defeated him, for he said, "Since these gods helped the kings of Aram, they will help me, too, if I sacrifice to them." But instead, they led to his ruin and the ruin of all Judah.

24The king took the various articles from the Temple of God and broke them into pieces. He shut the doors of the LORD's Temple so that no one could worship there, and he set up altars to pagan gods in every corner of Jerusalem. 25He made pagan shrines in all the towns of Judah for offering sacrifices to other gods. In this way, he aroused the anger of the LORD, the God of his ancestors.

26The rest of the events of Ahaz's reign and everything he did, from beginning to end, are recorded in *The Book of the Kings of Judah and Israel.* 27When Ahaz died, he was buried in Jerusalem but not in the royal cemetery of the kings of Judah. Then his son Hezekiah became the next king.

3. HEALING FOR ISRAEL (29:1–36:23)

Reign of Hezekiah (29:1–32:33)

Introduction to Hezekiah's Reign

2 Chr 29:1-2 // 2 Kgs 18:2-3

29 Hezekiah was twenty-five years old when he became the king of Judah, and he reigned in Jerusalem twenty-nine years. His mother was Abijah, the daughter of Zechariah. 2He did what was pleasing in the LORD's sight, just as his ancestor David had done.

Restoration of the Temple

3In the very first month of the first year of his reign, Hezekiah reopened the doors of the Temple of the LORD and repaired them. 4He summoned the priests and Levites to meet him at the courtyard east of the Temple. 5He said to them, "Listen to me, you Levites! Purify yourselves, and purify the Temple of the LORD, the God of your ancestors. Remove all the defiled things from the sanctuary. 6Our ancestors were unfaithful and did what was evil in the sight of the LORD our God. They abandoned the LORD and his dwelling place; they turned their backs on him. 7They also shut the doors to the Temple's entry room, and they snuffed out the lamps. They stopped burning incense and presenting burnt offerings at the sanctuary of the God of Israel.

8"That is why the LORD's anger has fallen upon Judah and Jerusalem. He has made them an object of dread, horror, and ridicule, as you can see with your own eyes. 9Because of this, our fathers have been killed in battle, and our sons and daughters and wives have been captured. 10But now I will make a [b]covenant with the LORD, the God of Israel, so that his fierce anger will turn away from us. 11My sons, do not neglect your duties any longer! The LORD has chosen you to stand in his presence, to minister to him, and to lead the people in worship and present offerings to him."

12Then these Levites got right to work:

From the clan of Kohath: Mahath son of Amasai and Joel son of Azariah.
From the clan of Merari: Kish son of Abdi and Azariah son of Jehallelel.
From the clan of Gershon: Joah son of Zimmah and Eden son of Joah.

28:20 1 Chr 5:26
28:21 2 Kgs 16:8-9
28:23 2 Chr 25:14; Jer 44:17-18
28:24 2 Kgs 16:17; 2 Chr 29:7; 30:14; 33:3-5
28:26 2 Kgs 16:19
28:27 2 Kgs 16:20; 2 Chr 24:25
29:1-2 //2 Kgs 18:1-3
29:2 2 Chr 34:2
29:3 2 Chr 28:24; 29:7
29:5 2 Chr 29:15, 34; 35:6
29:6 Ezek 8:16
29:8 Deut 28:25; 2 Chr 24:18; 28:5; Jer 25:9, 18
29:9 2 Chr 28:5-8, 17
29:10 2 Chr 23:16; [b]*berith* (1285) ‣ Ezra 10:3
29:11 Num 3:6; 8:6, 14
29:12 Num 3:19-20; 2 Chr 31:13

28:19 ***of Judah:*** Masoretic Text reads *of Israel;* also in 28:23, 27. The author of Chronicles sees Judah as representative of the true Israel. (Some Hebrew manuscripts and Greek version read *of Judah.*)

28:20-21 ***Tiglath-pileser:*** Hebrew *Tilgath-pilneser,* a variant spelling of Tiglath-pileser.

28:22-23 King Ahaz spurned the Lord by building an altar modeled after one in Damascus (2 Kgs 16:10-16) and by offering ***sacrifices to the gods of Damascus.***

28:24-25 Judah reached its spiritual nadir—a condition similar to exile—under King Ahaz.

28:26 Samaria, the capital of the northern kingdom of Israel, fell to Assyria in 722 BC, during the twenty-first year of Ahaz's reign in Judah (2 Kgs 17:1-6). The Chronicler, with his emphasis on the southern kingdom, does not even mention this event.

29:1 After a co-regency with his father, Ahaz, ***Hezekiah*** became king in his own right and ***reigned*** from 715 to 686 BC.

29:3-4 Hezekiah's first act as king was to repair the doors of the Temple (29:3). The verb used (*yekhazzeqem,* "he made them strong") is a deliberate pun on the name of King Hezekiah (*yekhizqiyahu,* "Yah makes strong"). This action provided a setting for the king's speech to ***the priests and Levites*** (29:5-11).

29:5-11 Hezekiah's speech used vocabulary typical of exile to describe the failure of the nation. As in the days of the separation under Rehoboam (12:1; see 13:10), the people had been ***unfaithful*** when they ***abandoned the LORD.***

29:12-36 To begin the process of sanctifying the Temple, ***these Levites*** began with their own sanctification. First, ***they all purified themselves,*** probably by bringing offerings (cp. 30:15); ***then they began to cleanse the Temple.*** Two

29:15
1 Chr 23:28
2 Chr 29:5; 30:12

29:16
2 Chr 15:16

29:17
2 Chr 29:3

29:19
2 Chr 28:24

29:21
Lev 4:3-14

29:22
Lev 4:18

29:23
Lev 4:15

29:24
Lev 4:26

13 From the family of Elizaphan: Shimri
and Jeiel.
From the family of Asaph: Zechariah
and Mattaniah.
14 From the family of Heman: Jehiel and
Shimei.
From the family of Jeduthun: Shemaiah
and Uzziel.

15 These men called together their fellow
Levites, and they all purified themselves.
Then they began to cleanse the Temple of
the LORD, just as the king had commanded.
They were careful to follow all the LORD's
instructions in their work. 16 The priests
went into the sanctuary of the Temple of
the LORD to cleanse it, and they took out
to the Temple courtyard all the defiled
things they found. From there the Levites
carted it all out to the Kidron Valley.
17 They began the work in early spring, on
the first day of the new year, and in eight
days they had reached the entry room
of the LORD's Temple. Then they purified
the Temple of the LORD itself, which took
another eight days. So the entire task was
completed in sixteen days.

Rededication of the Temple
18 Then the Levites went to King Hezekiah
and gave him this report: "We have cleansed
the entire Temple of the LORD, the altar of
burnt offering with all its utensils, and the
table of the Bread of the Presence with all
its utensils. 19 We have also recovered all the
items discarded by King Ahaz when he was
unfaithful and closed the Temple. They are
now in front of the altar of the LORD, purified and ready for use."
20 Early the next morning King Hezekiah
gathered the city officials and went to the
Temple of the LORD. 21 They brought seven
bulls, seven rams, and seven male lambs as
a burnt offering, together with seven male
goats as a sin offering for the kingdom, for
the Temple, and for Judah. The king commanded the priests, who were descendants
of Aaron, to sacrifice the animals on the altar of the LORD.
22 So they killed the bulls, and the priests
took the blood and sprinkled it on the altar.
Next they killed the rams and sprinkled
their blood on the altar. And finally, they
did the same with the male lambs. 23 The
male goats for the sin offering were then
brought before the king and the assembly
of people, who laid their hands on them.
24 The priests then killed the goats as a sin
offering and sprinkled their blood on the

Apostasy and Renewal (28:1–31:21)

2 Chr 11:13-17; 33:1-20
1 Kgs 21:1-29
Jer 18:7-17
Ezek 16:1-63; 33:10-16
Joel 2:12-32
Luke 19:2-10
1 Cor 6:9-11
1 Tim 1:15-17

During the divided monarchy, the usual distinction was between the apostate northern kingdom and the faithful remnant of Judah. The apostasy of King Ahaz in Judah reversed this pattern. When Jeroboam founded the northern kingdom, the righteous people went to Judah to escape Jeroboam's wickedness (11:13-17). Now Ahaz became like Jeroboam: he made metal images (28:2), worshiped the gods of Damascus (28:23), neglected the Temple (28:24; 29:7, 19), and spread false worship (28:24-25). His apostasy was so great that more righteousness was found in the north than in Judah (28:9-15).

The Chronicler wrote to inspire hope that God would restore Judah. He showed that God is always willing to forgive those who repent. Repentance can make restoration and reconciliation possible, as shown by the northern leaders' response to the prophet who confronted the victorious northern army (28:8-15). The renewal of Judah under Hezekiah also provided a paradigm for restoration and unification, a time that could be compared with Solomon's reign. In the first year of his reign, Hezekiah began to restore the Temple (29:3), and when Hezekiah celebrated the Passover, the glory of Solomon's time was temporarily restored (30:26; cp. 7:8-10).

North and south were brothers, even in time of war. North and south could worship together at the place that God had chosen (30:18-20). Even exile did not bring an end to the covenant community. Healing was possible at any time that the people chose to seek the Lord, whether at the occasion of returning with spoils of war, or reuniting at the Passover festival. The same hope holds true for the church, even when threatened with extinction from persecution or corruption (see Rev 2–3). God's kingdom stands on the solid rock of his promises (see Matt 16:18).

separate acts were required to restore the Temple: purification (the removal of pollution, 29:15-17) and sanctification (the rededication of the Temple for holy worship, 29:20-36).

29:12 ***Kohath . . . Merari . . . Gershon*** were the three sons of Levi; their descendants had become the three main clans of the tribe of Levites (see Exod 6:16).

29:17 ***on the first day of the new year:*** Literally *on the first day of the first month.* This day in the ancient Hebrew lunar calendar occurred in March or early April, 715 BC.

29:21 The ***bulls, . . . rams,*** and ***lambs*** were for the ***burnt offering,*** and the ***male goats*** were for the ***sin offering*** (see Lev 1:1-17; 4:1–5:13).

altar to make atonement for the sins of all Israel. The king had specifically commanded that this burnt offering and sin offering should be made for all Israel.

25King Hezekiah then stationed the Levites at the Temple of the LORD with cymbals, lyres, and harps. He obeyed all the commands that the LORD had given to King David through Gad, the king's seer, and the prophet Nathan. 26The Levites then took their positions around the Temple with the instruments of David, and the priests took their positions with the trumpets.

27Then Hezekiah ordered that the burnt offering be placed on the altar. As the burnt offering was presented, songs of praise to the LORD were begun, accompanied by the trumpets and other instruments of David, the former king of Israel. 28The entire [c]assembly worshiped the LORD as the singers sang and the trumpets blew, until all the burnt offerings were finished. 29Then the king and everyone with him bowed down in worship. 30King Hezekiah and the officials ordered the Levites to [d]praise the LORD with the psalms written by David and by Asaph the seer. So they offered joyous [d]praise and bowed down in worship.

31Then Hezekiah declared, "Now that you have consecrated yourselves to the LORD, bring your sacrifices and thanksgiving offerings to the Temple of the LORD." So the people brought their sacrifices and thanksgiving offerings, and all whose hearts were willing brought burnt offerings, too. 32The people brought to the LORD 70 bulls, 100 rams, and 200 male lambs for burnt offerings. 33They also brought 600 cattle and 3,000 sheep and goats as sacred offerings.

34But there were too few priests to prepare all the burnt offerings. So their relatives the Levites helped them until the work was finished and more priests had been purified, for the Levites had been more conscientious about purifying themselves than the priests had been. 35There was an abundance of burnt offerings, along with the usual liquid offerings, and a great deal of fat from the many peace offerings.

So the Temple of the LORD was restored to service. 36And Hezekiah and all the people rejoiced because of what God had done for the people, for everything had been accomplished so quickly.

Preparations for Passover

30 King Hezekiah now sent word to all Israel and Judah, and he wrote letters of invitation to the people of Ephraim and Manasseh. He asked everyone to come to the Temple of the LORD at Jerusalem to celebrate the Passover of the LORD, the God of Israel. 2The king, his officials, and all the community of Jerusalem decided to celebrate Passover a month later than usual. 3They were unable to celebrate it at the prescribed time because not enough priests could be purified by then, and the people had not yet assembled at Jerusalem.

4This plan for keeping the Passover seemed right to the king and all the people. 5So they sent a proclamation throughout all Israel, from Beersheba in the south to Dan in the north, inviting everyone to come to Jerusalem to celebrate the Passover of the LORD, the God of Israel. The people had not been celebrating it in great numbers as required in the Law.

6At the king's command, runners were sent throughout Israel and Judah. They carried letters that said:

"O people of Israel, return to the LORD,
the God of Abraham, Isaac, and Israel,
so that he will return to the few of us
who have survived the conquest of the
Assyrian kings. 7Do not be like your
ancestors and relatives who abandoned
the LORD, the God of their ancestors, and
became an object of derision, as you

29:25 2 Sam 7:2; 24:11; 1 Chr 25:6; 2 Chr 8:14
29:26 1 Chr 23:5; 2 Chr 5:12
29:27 2 Chr 23:18
29:28 [c]*qahal* (6951) ›2 Chr 30:25
29:29 2 Chr 20:18
29:30 [d]*halal* (1984) ›Ps 22:22
29:31 Exod 35:5, 22
29:34 2 Chr 30:3; 35:11
29:35 Lev 3:16; Num 15:5-10; 2 Chr 29:32
30:2 Num 9:10-11; 2 Chr 30:13, 15
30:3 2 Chr 29:34
30:5 Judg 20:1
30:6 2 Chr 28:20; Esth 8:14; Jer 51:31
30:7 2 Chr 29:8; Ezek 20:13, 18

29:31-36 The purification and rededication of the Temple was followed by individual offerings and sacrifices by the people. • The *thanksgiving offerings* were also called praise offerings, peace offerings, or offerings of well-being (see Lev 3:1-17).

29:34 The Chronicler shows surprise and delight at the people's spontaneity and at the great number of devoted praise offerings consumed as part of the thanksgiving festivities. These things indicated that the Lord himself had prepared the people's hearts for the event, far beyond what the *priests and Levites* had anticipated.

30:1-27 This account of Hezekiah's celebration of *Passover* reflects the Chronicler's concern with the unity of Israel, the spiritual preparedness of the people, and the success of following the formula for restoration given by Solomon at the dedication of the Temple (7:14).

30:2-3 *a month later than usual:* The law made provision for the delayed observance of the *Passover* if an individual inadvertently was ceremonially unclean or was away on a long journey (Num 9:9-11); Hezekiah's Passover followed the spirit if not the letter of those provisions. The delayed Passover provided opportunity for national unity and spiritual renewal.

30:2 *a month later than usual:* Literally *in the second month.* Passover was normally observed in the first month (of the ancient Hebrew lunar calendar).

30:5 Hezekiah dispatched couriers *from Beersheba . . . to Dan*, the traditional designation for the entire nation, including even the now-desolate territories of Israel's northern tribes.

30:6 *Israel* is the name that God gave to Jacob.

30:8 Exod 32:9; 2 Chr 29:10
30:9 Exod 34:6-7; Deut 30:2; Mic 7:18
30:10 2 Chr 36:16
30:11 2 Chr 30:18, 21
30:13 2 Chr 30:2
30:14 2 Chr 28:24; 29:16
30:15 2 Chr 29:34; 30:2-3
30:16 2 Chr 35:10, 15

yourselves can see. 8 Do not be stubborn,
as they were, but submit yourselves to
the LORD. Come to his Temple, which he
has set apart as holy forever. Worship
the LORD your God so that his fierce
anger will turn away from you.
9 "For if you return to the LORD, your
relatives and your children will be
treated mercifully by their captors, and
they will be able to return to this land.
For the LORD your God is gracious and
merciful. If you return to him, he will
not continue to turn his face from you."

Celebration of Passover

10 The runners went from town to town
throughout Ephraim and Manasseh and as
far as the territory of Zebulun. But most of
the people just laughed at the runners and
made fun of them. 11 However, some people
from Asher, Manasseh, and Zebulun humbled themselves and went to Jerusalem.
12 At the same time, God's hand was on the
people in the land of Judah, giving them all
one heart to obey the orders of the king and
his officials, who were following the word
of the LORD. 13 So a huge crowd assembled
at Jerusalem in midspring to celebrate the
Festival of Unleavened Bread. 14 They set to
work and removed the pagan altars from
Jerusalem. They took away all the incense altars and threw them into the Kidron Valley.
15 On the fourteenth day of the second
month, one month later than usual, the
people slaughtered the Passover lamb. This
shamed the priests and Levites, so they purified themselves and brought burnt offerings
to the Temple of the LORD. 16 Then they took
their places at the Temple as prescribed
in the Law of Moses, the man of God. The
Levites brought the sacrificial blood to the
priests, who then sprinkled it on the altar.
17 Since many of the people had not purified themselves, the Levites had to slaughter

God Passing Over (30:1-27)

Exod 12:1-30; 2 Kgs 5:17-19; Matt 15:21-28; John 8:1-11; Rom 3:23-28; 1 Cor 11:27-34; Heb 9:13-15; Jas 5:16

One of King Hezekiah's most important acts in restoring Israel's worship took place when he held a celebration of the Passover. The Passover, a celebration of Israel's redemption from Egypt, was the first festival of Israel's liturgical year (Exod 12:1-2). In seeking to celebrate the Passover, Hezekiah faced a dilemma. The time between the beginning of his renewal and the first month of the year did not allow the priests sufficient time to be prepared and to gather the people (30:2-3). He could not celebrate the Passover at the scheduled time, but he deemed it more important to have the celebration than to hold to the prescribed time.

Hezekiah proceeded with the Passover, holding it a month late (30:15). By deferring the date with the express purpose of allowing time for the people to gather at the Temple in Jerusalem, Hezekiah achieved harmony between Judah and the north and unified the celebration. The precise regulations were less important than ensuring that the Passover was observed, and that all could participate.

Similarly, when the festival began, many of the people were not properly purified, so they were unable to slaughter their own sacrifices as the law required. Again, Hezekiah determined that it was more important for people to participate in the Passover than to meet the precise regulations. Hezekiah prayed for the pilgrims who had no opportunity to be properly prepared; they were not allowed to make the sacrifice in a state of impurity, but they were allowed to participate in the Passover. The right heart attitude and seeking the Lord in prayer brought God's gracious acceptance (30:18-20; cp. 1 Cor 11:27-32).

30:9-11 The northern kingdom had been conquered by the Assyrians (2 Kgs 17:5-28), and many of its people were taken into exile in Assyria. People from other conquered lands now lived there. Most of these foreigners, as well as those Israelites left by the Assyrians, regarded the conquest of Israel as proof that the Lord—the God of Israel—was impotent. They ***laughed*** at the thought of making a pilgrimage ***to Jerusalem*** to honor him.

30:11 ***Some people . . . humbled themselves,*** fulfilling the first criterion in Solomon's formula (7:14).

30:13 ***in midspring:*** Literally *in the second month.* The second month of the ancient Hebrew lunar calendar usually occurs within the months of April and May.

30:14 Several challenges faced Hezekiah before Passover could be observed. Although the Temple had been purified, the city was not pure. The first task of the assembled multitude was to remove all ***pagan altars,*** which they disposed of in the ***Kidron Valley,*** where they could be burned.

30:15 The priests were inadequately prepared for the great number of people who came. The problem might have involved the priests who came from outside the city and had not been a part of the earlier purification. However, the response of the people outstripped that of the professional clerics, to their great shame. • ***On the fourteenth day of the second month, one month later than usual:*** Literally *On the fourteenth day of the second month.* Passover normally began on the fourteenth day of the first month (see Lev 23:5).

30:17-19 A large number of pilgrims who traveled great distances from foreign lands did not have an opportunity to

their Passover lamb for them, to set them apart for the LORD. 18Most of those who came from Ephraim, Manasseh, Issachar, and Zebulun had not purified themselves. But King Hezekiah prayed for them, and they were allowed to eat the [e]Passover meal anyway, even though this was contrary to the requirements of the Law. For Hezekiah said, "May the LORD, who is good, pardon those 19who decide to follow the LORD, the God of their ancestors, even though they are not properly cleansed for the ceremony." 20And the LORD listened to Hezekiah's prayer and healed the people.

21So the people of Israel who were present in Jerusalem joyously celebrated the [f]Festival of Unleavened Bread for seven days. Each day the Levites and priests sang to the LORD, accompanied by loud instruments. 22Hezekiah encouraged all the Levites regarding the skill they displayed as they served the LORD. The celebration continued for seven days. Peace offerings were sacrificed, and the people gave thanks to the LORD, the God of their ancestors.

23The entire assembly then decided to continue the festival another seven days, so they celebrated joyfully for another week. 24King Hezekiah gave the people 1,000 bulls and 7,000 sheep and goats for offerings, and the officials donated 1,000 bulls and 10,000 sheep and goats. Meanwhile, many more priests purified themselves.

25The entire [g]assembly of Judah rejoiced, including the priests, the Levites, [g]all who came from the land of Israel, the foreigners who came to the festival, and all those who lived in Judah. 26There was great joy in the city, for Jerusalem had not seen a celebration like this one since the days of Solomon, King David's son. 27Then the priests and Levites stood and blessed the people, and God heard their prayer from his holy dwelling in [h]heaven.

Hezekiah's Religious Reforms

31 When the festival ended, the Israelites who attended went to all the towns of Judah, Benjamin, Ephraim, and Manasseh, and they smashed all the sacred pillars, cut down the Asherah poles, and removed the pagan shrines and altars. After this, the Israelites returned to their own towns and homes.

2Hezekiah then organized the priests and Levites into divisions to offer the burnt offerings and peace offerings, and to worship and give thanks and praise to the LORD at the gates of the Temple. 3The king also made a personal contribution of animals for the daily morning and evening burnt offerings, the weekly Sabbath festivals, the monthly new moon festivals, and the annual festivals as prescribed in the Law of the LORD. 4In addition, he required the people in Jerusalem to bring a portion of their goods to the priests and Levites, so they could devote themselves fully to the Law of the LORD.

5When the people of Israel heard these requirements, they responded generously by bringing the first share of their grain, new wine, olive oil, honey, and all the produce of their fields. They brought a large quantity—a [i]tithe of all they produced. 6The people who had moved to Judah from Israel, and the people of Judah themselves, brought in the tithes of their cattle, sheep, and goats and a tithe of the things that had been dedicated to the LORD their God, and they piled them up in great heaps. 7They began piling them up in late spring, and the heaps continued to grow until early autumn. 8When Hezekiah and his officials came and saw these huge piles,

30:18 Exod 12:43-49; Num 9:6-10; [e]*pesakh* (6453) ‣2 Chr 35:18
30:21 Exod 12:15; 13:6; [f]*khag* (2282) ‣Ezra 6:22
30:22 2 Chr 32:6; Ezra 10:11
30:23 1 Kgs 8:65
30:24 2 Chr 29:34; 30:3; 35:7-8
30:25 2 Chr 30:11, 18; [g]*qahal* (6951) ‣Ps 22:22
30:26 2 Chr 7:8-10
30:27 Num 6:23; Deut 26:15; 2 Chr 23:18; Ps 68:5; [h]*shamayim* (8064) ‣Job 11:8
31:1 2 Kgs 18:4
31:2 1 Chr 23:28-32; 24:1
31:3 Num 28:1-29; 2 Chr 35:7
31:4 Num 18:8
31:5 Neh 13:12; [i]*ma'aser* (4643) ‣2 Chr 31:12
31:6 Lev 27:30; Deut 14:28

---

receive the proper purification ceremonies and were unfit to participate in the ceremony. Hezekiah allowed the pilgrims to eat the Passover without participating in the sacrificial ritual and in an impure state and prayed that God would accept their worship. Hezekiah was following the formula for restoration (see 7:14).

30:20 God's response to Hezekiah's prayer showed that he is more concerned with the attitude of the heart than with strict attention to ritual details. • ***healed the people:*** Cp. 7:14.

30:21 ***sang to the LORD, accompanied by loud instruments:*** Or *sang to the LORD with all their strength.*

30:25 In this joyful celebration, no one was regarded as a foreigner, and those who had been estranged were reunited.

30:26 No celebration like this had occurred ***since the days of Solomon.*** Hezekiah put into place the conditions for covenant faithfulness equal to those during the time of David and Solomon.

31:1 Following the purification and rededication of the Temple, the city of Jerusalem, and the people, Hezekiah initiated the third stage of his reform, purifying the entire land of pagan objects of worship, not only in Judah, but also in the territories of the north.

31:3-10 Provisions for the Temple came from both the king and his subjects. Israel united in its support of the Temple, and the response was far greater than anticipated or required.

31:6 The ***tithes*** of the animals that ***piled . . . up in great heaps*** might refer to the proceeds from the sale of animals rather than the animals themselves. The law permitted ***the people*** to exchange the yield of the field for money (Deut 14:24-26) and to consume the meat at their homes (Deut 12:15).

31:7 ***in late spring, . . . until early autumn:*** Literally *in the third month . . . until the seventh month.* The third month of the ancient Hebrew lunar calendar usually occurs within the months of May and June; the seventh month usually occurs within September and October.

31:10
1 Chr 6:8-9
Mal 3:10
31:11
1 Kgs 6:5
31:12
[i]*ma'aser* (4643)
‣ Mal 3:8
31:15
Josh 21:9-19
2 Chr 29:12
31:17
1 Chr 23:24
31:19
Lev 25:34
Num 35:2
2 Chr 31:12-15
31:20-21
//2 Kgs 18:5-7
32:1
Isa 36:1–37:37
32:4
2 Kgs 20:20
2 Chr 32:30
32:5
1 Kgs 9:24
2 Kgs 25:4
2 Chr 25:23
32:6
2 Chr 30:22

they thanked the LORD and his people
Israel!
9“Where did all this come from?” Hezekiah asked the priests and Levites.
10And Azariah the high priest, from the
family of Zadok, replied, “Since the people
began bringing their gifts to the LORD's Temple, we have had enough to eat and plenty to
spare. The LORD has blessed his people, and
all this is left over.”
11Hezekiah ordered that storerooms
be prepared in the Temple of the LORD.
When this was done, 12the people faithfully
brought all the [i]tithes and gifts to the Temple. Conaniah the Levite was put in charge,
assisted by his brother Shimei. 13The supervisors under them were Jehiel, Azaziah,
Nahath, Asahel, Jerimoth, Jozabad, Eliel,
Ismakiah, Mahath, and Benaiah. These appointments were made by King Hezekiah
and Azariah, the chief official in the Temple of God.
14Kore son of Imnah the Levite, who was
the gatekeeper at the East Gate, was put in
charge of distributing the voluntary offerings given to God, the gifts, and the things
that had been dedicated to the LORD. 15His
faithful assistants were Eden, Miniamin,
Jeshua, Shemaiah, Amariah, and Shecaniah. They distributed the gifts among the
families of priests in their towns by their
divisions, dividing the gifts fairly among
old and young alike. 16They distributed the
gifts to all males three years old or older, regardless of their place in the genealogical
records. The distribution went to all who
would come to the LORD's Temple to perform their daily duties according to their
divisions. 17They distributed gifts to the
priests who were listed by their families in
the genealogical records, and to the Levites
twenty years old or older who were listed
according to their jobs and their divisions.
18Food allotments were also given to the
families of all those listed in the genealogical records, including their little babies,
wives, sons, and daughters. For they had all
been faithful in purifying themselves.
19As for the priests, the descendants of
Aaron, who were living in the open villages
around the towns, men were appointed by
name to distribute portions to every male
among the priests and to all the Levites
listed in the genealogical records.
20In this way, King Hezekiah handled the
distribution throughout all Judah, doing
what was pleasing and good in the sight of
the LORD his God. 21In all that he did in the
service of the Temple of God and in his efforts to follow God's laws and commands,
Hezekiah sought his God wholeheartedly.
As a result, he was very successful.

Assyria Invades Judah
2 Chr 32:1 // 2 Kgs 18:13 // Isa 36:1

32 After Hezekiah had faithfully
carried out this work, King Sennacherib of Assyria invaded Judah. He laid
siege to the fortified towns, giving orders
for his army to break through their walls.
2When Hezekiah realized that Sennacherib also intended to attack Jerusalem, 3he
consulted with his officials and military
advisers, and they decided to stop the flow
of the springs outside the city. 4They organized a huge work crew to stop the flow of
the springs, cutting off the brook that ran
through the fields. For they said, “Why
should the kings of Assyria come here and
find plenty of water?”
5Then Hezekiah worked hard at repairing all the broken sections of the wall,
erecting towers, and constructing a second
wall outside the first. He also reinforced
the supporting terraces in the City of David
and manufactured large numbers of weapons and shields. 6He appointed military
officers over the people and assembled
them before him in the square at the city
gate. Then Hezekiah encouraged them by

31:10 The people's great generosity is reminiscent of when the Tabernacle was first constructed (Exod 36:3-5).

31:14-19 A great number of Levites, most from provincial towns, were eligible for service. Small groups of them came to Jerusalem on a rotation system for short terms of office (see 1 Chr 24:1-19). All Levites were entitled to portions of the offerings given at the Temple.

32:1-23 The Chronicler summarizes in twenty-three verses the lengthy account of the *siege* against Jerusalem (cp. 2 Kgs 18:17–19:37; Isa 36–38). God's response to the attack of ***King Sennacherib of Assyria*** was a blessing that resulted from Judah's and Hezekiah's faithfulness in seeking the Lord.

32:3-5 Sennacherib's attack did not come as a surprise; Hezekiah provoked it by breaking a treaty (2 Kgs 18:7b, 20). Because water was critical to both attacker and defender in siege warfare, Hezekiah made sure that Sennacherib's army would not have access to the city's water supply. In one of the most famous engineering feats of ancient times, Hezekiah's tunnel connected the fresh waters of the Gihon spring to the pool of Siloam, making water accessible from within the city walls. This famous tunnel is almost one-third of a mile long (approximately 580 yards [530 meters]) and about six feet [2 meters] high. The famous Hezekiah inscription, discovered in the tunnel in 1880, describes how the excavators met to join the two ends. Although much of the tunnel consisted of natural underground aqueducts, it was a tremendous strategy for protecting the citizens of the city.

32:5 ***the supporting terraces:*** Hebrew *the millo.* The meaning of the Hebrew is uncertain; see note on 1 Kgs 9:15.

saying: 7"Be strong and courageous! Don't
be afraid or discouraged because of the
king of Assyria or his mighty army, for
there is a power far greater on our side! 8He
may have a great army, but they are merely
men. We have the LORD our God to help us
and to fight our battles for us!" Hezekiah's
words greatly encouraged the people.

Sennacherib Threatens Jerusalem
2 Chr 32:9-15 // 2 Kgs 18:17-25 // Isa 36:2-10

9While King Sennacherib of Assyria was
still besieging the town of Lachish, he sent
his officers to Jerusalem with this message
for Hezekiah and all the people in the city:

10"This is what King Sennacherib of
Assyria says: What are you trusting in
that makes you think you can survive
my siege of Jerusalem? 11Hezekiah has
said, 'The LORD our God will rescue
us from the king of Assyria.' Surely
Hezekiah is misleading you, sentencing
you to death by famine and thirst!
12Don't you realize that Hezekiah is
the very person who destroyed all
the LORD's shrines and altars? He
commanded Judah and Jerusalem to
worship only at the altar at the Temple
and to offer sacrifices on it alone.

13"Surely you must realize what I and
the other kings of Assyria before me
have done to all the people of the earth!
Were any of the gods of those nations
able to rescue their people from my
power? 14Which of their gods was able
to rescue its people from the destructive
power of my predecessors? What makes
you think your God can rescue you from
me? 15Don't let Hezekiah deceive you!
Don't let him fool you like this! I say it
again—no god of any nation or kingdom
has ever yet been able to rescue his
people from me or my ancestors. How
much less will your God rescue you from
my power!"

16And Sennacherib's officers further
mocked the LORD God and his servant Hezekiah, heaping insult upon insult. 17The king
also sent letters scorning the LORD, the God
of Israel. He wrote, "Just as the gods of all
the other nations failed to rescue their people from my power, so the God of Hezekiah
will also fail." 18The Assyrian officials who
brought the letters shouted this in Hebrew
to the people gathered on the walls of the
city, trying to terrify them so it would be
easier to capture the city. 19These officers
talked about the God of Jerusalem as though
he were one of the pagan gods, made by human hands.

The LORD Delivers Jerusalem
2 Chr 32:21 // 2 Kgs 19:35-37 // Isa 37:36-38

20Then King Hezekiah and the prophet Isaiah son of Amoz cried out in prayer to God
in heaven. 21And the LORD sent an [k]angel
who destroyed the Assyrian army with all
its commanders and officers. So Sennacherib was forced to return home in disgrace
to his own land. And when he entered the
temple of his god, some of his own sons
killed him there with a sword.

22That is how the LORD rescued Hezekiah
and the people of Jerusalem from King Sennacherib of Assyria and from all the others
who threatened them. So there was peace
throughout the land. 23From then on King
Hezekiah became highly respected among
all the surrounding nations, and many gifts
for the LORD arrived at Jerusalem, with valuable presents for King Hezekiah, too.

Hezekiah's Sickness and Recovery
2 Chr 32:24 // 2 Kgs 20:1-2 // Isa 38:1-2

24About that time Hezekiah became deathly
ill. He prayed to the LORD, who healed him
and gave him a miraculous sign. 25But Hezekiah did not respond appropriately to the
kindness shown him, and he became proud.
So the LORD's anger came against him and
against Judah and Jerusalem. 26Then Hezekiah humbled himself and repented of his
pride, as did the people of Jerusalem. So the
LORD's anger did not fall on them during
Hezekiah's lifetime.

27Hezekiah was very wealthy and highly
[a]honored. He built special treasury buildings for his silver, gold, precious stones,

32:7 2 Kgs 6:16; 1 Chr 22:13
32:8 2 Chr 20:17; Jer 17:5
32:9-19 //2 Kgs 18:17-35; //Isa 36:2-20
32:12 2 Chr 31:1
32:13 2 Kgs 18:33-35
32:14 Isa 10:9-11
32:17 2 Chr 32:14
32:20-21 //2 Kgs 19:35-37; //Isa 37:36-38
32:21 [k]*mal'ak* (4397) ‣Job 33:23
32:23 2 Sam 8:10
32:24-33 //2 Kgs 20:1-21; //Isa 37:21-38; 38:1-8
32:25 2 Chr 24:18; 26:16
32:26 Jer 26:18-19
32:27 [a]*kabod* (3519) ‣Ps 4:2

32:10-19 The Assyrian king's threats clarified the critical issues for the people of Jerusalem. The real question was whether or not to trust in God. The enemy king suggested that Hezekiah could not be trusted (32:11-12) because he had offended the Lord by tearing down God's shrines and altars. However, just the opposite was true. This reform was Hezekiah's greatest act of faithfulness to the Lord. The question came down to whether God could be trusted against the power of Assyria (32:11-15).

32:18 ***in Hebrew:*** Literally *in the dialect of Judah.*

32:21 The fate of ***Sennacherib*** is reported similarly to the account in Kings (see 2 Kgs 19:35-37).

32:22-23 The Chronicler's conclusion provides a fitting end to the story: The disaster for Assyria resulted in domestic peace for Judah, and both ***the LORD*** and ***Hezekiah*** received honor from other nations.

32:26 The humble repentance of both Hezekiah and the people pleased God, so ***the LORD's anger did not fall on them during Hezekiah's lifetime.***

32:27-30 Hezekiah's wealth marked him as a king like Solomon.

32:29 1 Chr 29:12
32:30 1 Kgs 1:33; 2 Kgs 20:20
32:31 Deut 8:16; 2 Kgs 20:12; 2 Chr 32:24; Isa 38:7-8; 39:1
32:32 [b]*khazon* (2377) ‣ Prov 29:18
33:1-10 //2 Kgs 21:1-10
33:2 2 Chr 28:3
33:3 Deut 16:21; 2 Kgs 23:5-6; 2 Chr 31:1
33:4 2 Chr 7:16; 28:24
33:5 2 Chr 4:9
33:6 Lev 19:31; 20:27; 2 Chr 28:3; [c]*yidde'oni* (3049) ‣ Isa 8:19
33:8 2 Sam 7:10
33:11 Deut 28:36; 2 Chr 36:6
33:12 2 Chr 32:26
33:13 Ezra 8:23; Dan 4:25, 32
33:14 1 Kgs 1:33; 2 Chr 27:3; Neh 3:3

and spices, and for his shields and other
valuable items. [28]He also constructed many
storehouses for his grain, new wine, and
olive oil; and he made many stalls for his
cattle and pens for his flocks of sheep and
goats. [29]He built many towns and acquired
vast flocks and herds, for God had given
him great wealth. [30]He blocked up the upper spring of Gihon and brought the water
down through a tunnel to the west side of
the City of David. And so he succeeded in
everything he did.
[31]However, when ambassadors arrived
from Babylon to ask about the remarkable
events that had taken place in the land, God
withdrew from Hezekiah in order to test
him and to see what was really in his heart.

Summary of Hezekiah's Reign
2 Chr 32:32-33 // 2 Kgs 20:20-21

[32]The rest of the events in Hezekiah's reign
and his acts of devotion are recorded in *The*
[b]*Vision of the Prophet Isaiah Son of Amoz,*
which is included in *The Book of the Kings*
of Judah and Israel. [33]When Hezekiah
died, he was buried in the upper area of the
royal cemetery, and all Judah and Jerusalem
honored him at his death. And his son Manasseh became the next king.

Reign of Manasseh (33:1-20)
Idolatrous Abominations
2 Chr 33:1-9 // 2 Kgs 21:1-9

33 Manasseh was twelve years old
when he became king, and he
reigned in Jerusalem fifty-five years. [2]He
did what was evil in the LORD's sight, following the detestable practices of the pagan
nations that the LORD had driven from the
land ahead of the Israelites. [3]He rebuilt the
pagan shrines his father, Hezekiah, had broken down. He constructed altars for the
images of Baal and set up Asherah poles.
He also bowed before all the powers of the
heavens and worshiped them.
[4]He built pagan altars in the Temple of
the LORD, the place where the LORD had said,
"My name will remain in Jerusalem forever."
[5]He built these altars for all the powers of
the heavens in both courtyards of the LORD's
Temple. [6]Manasseh also sacrificed his own
sons in the fire in the valley of Ben-Hinnom.
He practiced sorcery, [c]divination, and witchcraft, and he consulted with mediums and
psychics. He did much that was evil in the
LORD's sight, arousing his anger.
[7]Manasseh even took a carved idol he had
made and set it up in God's Temple, the very
place where God had told David and his son
Solomon: "My name will be honored forever
in this Temple and in Jerusalem—the city I
have chosen from among all the tribes of Israel. [8]If the Israelites will be careful to obey
my commands—all the laws, decrees, and
regulations given through Moses—I will not
send them into exile from this land that I
set aside for your ancestors." [9]But Manasseh led the people of Judah and Jerusalem
to do even more evil than the pagan nations
that the LORD had destroyed when the people of Israel entered the land.

Humility and Restoration
2 Chr 33:18-20 // 2 Kgs 21:17-18

[10]The LORD spoke to Manasseh and his
people, but they ignored all his warnings.
[11]So the LORD sent the commanders of the
Assyrian armies, and they took Manasseh
prisoner. They put a ring through his nose,
bound him in bronze chains, and led him
away to Babylon. [12]But while in deep distress, Manasseh sought the LORD his God
and sincerely humbled himself before
the God of his ancestors. [13]And when he
prayed, the LORD listened to him and was
moved by his request. So the LORD brought
Manasseh back to Jerusalem and to his kingdom. Then Manasseh finally realized that
the LORD alone is God!
[14]After this Manasseh rebuilt the outer

32:31 The details of the visit by the Babylonian envoys is recorded more fully in 2 Kgs 20:12-20. The Chronicler provides a commentary on God's purposes in that visit.

33:1-20 *Manasseh* ruled *fifty-five years* (697-642 BC), longer than any other king in Judah. The years of his reign included a co-regency with his father, Hezekiah, from 697 to 686 BC (see timeline, p. 665). Such a long reign was usually a sign of blessing, even though Manasseh *did what was evil in the LORD's sight.* So the Chronicler tells of his humiliation, repentance, and restoration of worship in Judah.

33:6 *also sacrificed his own sons in the fire:* Or *also made his sons pass through the fire.* See note on 28:3-4.

33:7 The *carved idol* was an image of Asherah (see 2 Kgs 21:7).

33:11 A nose ring caused not only pain but complete humiliation. Assyrian records portray such treatment of their prisoners.

33:12-17 The book of Kings does not mention Manasseh's repentance, telling only of the promise of judgment resulting from his wicked deeds (see 2 Kgs 21:10-16). Chronicles tells the good things he did after he repented, following his father Hezekiah's example. However, Manasseh's actions were unable to turn the hearts of the people back to the Lord or to avert God's judgment on Judah (33:17).

33:12 Manasseh's response followed the requirements of Solomon's prayer at the dedication of the Temple (7:14).

33:13 Manasseh's experience was a microcosm of what the nation would experience: Exile and bondage brought on by apostasy, then repentance and returning to the Lord.

33:14-17 Manasseh might have been repairing damage done to the walls

wall of the City of David, from west of the Gihon Spring in the Kidron Valley to the Fish Gate, and continuing around the hill of Ophel. He built the wall very high. And he stationed his military officers in all of the fortified towns of Judah. [15]Manasseh also removed the foreign gods and the idol from the LORD's Temple. He tore down all the altars he had built on the hill where the Temple stood and all the altars that were in Jerusalem, and he dumped them outside the city. [16]Then he restored the altar of the LORD and sacrificed peace offerings and thanksgiving offerings on it. He also encouraged the people of Judah to worship the LORD, the God of Israel. [17]However, the people still sacrificed at the pagan shrines, though only to the LORD their God.

[18]The rest of the events of Manasseh's reign, his prayer to God, and the words the seers spoke to him in the name of the LORD, the God of Israel, are recorded in *The Book of the Kings of Israel*. [19]Manasseh's prayer, the account of the way God answered him, and an account of all his sins and unfaithfulness are recorded in *The Record of the Seers*. It includes a list of the locations where he built pagan shrines and set up Asherah poles and idols before he humbled himself and repented. [20]When Manasseh died, he was buried in his palace. Then his son Amon became the next king.

Reign of Amon (33:21-25)
2 Chr 33:21-25 // 2 Kgs 21:19-24

[21]Amon was twenty-two years old when he became king, and he reigned in Jerusalem two years. [22]He did what was evil in the LORD's sight, just as his father, Manasseh, had done. He worshiped and sacrificed to all the idols his father had made. [23]But unlike his father, he did not humble himself before the LORD. Instead, Amon sinned even more.

[24]Then Amon's own officials conspired against him and assassinated him in his palace. [25]But the people of the land killed all those who had conspired against King Amon, and they made his son Josiah the next king.

Reign of Josiah (34:1–35:27)
Josiah Repairs the Temple
2 Chr 34:1-2, 8-11 // 2 Kgs 22:1-7

34 Josiah was eight years old when he became king, and he reigned in Jerusalem thirty-one years. [2]He did what was pleasing in the LORD's sight and followed the example of his ancestor David. He did not turn away from doing what was right.

[3]During the eighth year of his reign, while he was still young, Josiah began to seek the God of his ancestor David. Then in the twelfth year he began to purify Judah and Jerusalem, destroying all the pagan shrines, the Asherah poles, and the carved idols and cast images. [4]He ordered that the altars of Baal be demolished and that the incense altars which stood above them be broken down. He also made sure that the Asherah poles, the carved idols, and the cast images were smashed and scattered over the graves of those who had sacrificed to them. [5]He burned the bones of the pagan priests on their own altars, and so he purified Judah and Jerusalem.

[6]He did the same thing in the towns of Manasseh, Ephraim, and Simeon, even as far as Naphtali, and in the regions all around them. [7]He destroyed the pagan altars and the Asherah poles, and he crushed the idols into dust. He cut down all the incense altars throughout the land of Israel. Finally, he returned to Jerusalem.

[8]In the eighteenth year of his reign, after he had purified the land and the Temple, Josiah appointed Shaphan son of Azaliah, Maaseiah the governor of Jerusalem, and Joah son of Joahaz, the royal historian, to repair the Temple of the LORD his God. [9]They gave Hilkiah the high priest the money that had been collected by the Levites who served as gatekeepers at the Temple of God. The gifts were brought by people from Manasseh, Ephraim, and from all the remnant of Israel, as well as from all Judah, Benjamin, and the people of Jerusalem.

33:15 2 Chr 33:3-7
33:17 2 Chr 32:12
33:18-20 //2 Kgs 21:17-18
33:19 2 Chr 33:3, 13
33:21-25 //2 Kgs 21:19-24
33:23 2 Chr 33:12, 19
33:24 2 Chr 25:27
34:1-2 //2 Kgs 22:1-2
34:2 2 Chr 29:2
34:3 1 Kgs 13:2; 2 Chr 15:2; 33:17, 22
34:4 Exod 32:20; 2 Kgs 23:4-5, 11
34:5 1 Kgs 13:2; 2 Kgs 23:20
34:6 2 Kgs 23:15, 19
34:7 2 Chr 31:1
34:8-13 //2 Kgs 22:3-7
34:9 2 Chr 30:10, 18; 35:8

when he was taken captive. His religious reforms were similar to Hezekiah's but incomplete; Josiah later removed the Temple altars that Manasseh built (2 Kgs 23:12).

33:18 *The Book of the Kings of Israel* is a record that no longer exists.

33:19 *The Record of the Seers:* Or *The Record of Hozai.* This record no longer exists.

33:21 *Amon*'s short reign was from 642 to 640 BC.

33:24 The political forces that brought about *Amon's* assassination are not indicated, but they might have been instigated by Egypt when Assyria's declining power provided opportunity.

34:1 *Josiah*'s reign of *thirty-one years* was from 640 to 609 BC.

34:3 ***Josiah began to seek the God of his ancestor David*** when he was just sixteen. He initiated his own acts of reform when he reached age twenty.

34:6 By Josiah's twelfth year as king (628 BC), the Assyrian empire had largely disintegrated. During this time, the north of Israel was virtually deserted, making it possible for Josiah to extend his influence and control into ***Manasseh, Ephraim, and Simeon, even as far as Naphtali.*** • ***in the regions:*** As in Syriac version. Hebrew reads *in their temples*, or *in their ruins*. The meaning of the Hebrew is uncertain.

34:11
2 Chr 33:4-7
34:12
1 Chr 25:1
34:13
Neh 4:10
34:14-28
//2 Kgs 22:8-20
34:14
2 Chr 34:9
34:19
Josh 7:6
34:21
2 Chr 29:8

10 He entrusted the money to the men assigned to supervise the restoration of the
LORD's Temple. Then they paid the workers
who did the repairs and renovation of the
Temple. 11 They hired carpenters and builders, who purchased finished stone for the
walls and timber for the rafters and beams.
They restored what earlier kings of Judah
had allowed to fall into ruin.
12 The workers served faithfully under the
leadership of Jahath and Obadiah, Levites
of the Merarite clan, and Zechariah and
Meshullam, Levites of the Kohathite clan.
Other Levites, all of whom were skilled musicians, 13 were put in charge of the laborers
of the various trades. Still others assisted as
secretaries, officials, and gatekeepers.

Hilkiah Discovers the Book of the Law
2 Chr 34:14-28 // 2 Kgs 22:8-20

14 While they were bringing out the money
collected at the LORD's Temple, Hilkiah the
priest found the Book of the Law of the LORD
that was written by Moses. 15 Hilkiah said to
Shaphan the court secretary, "I have found
the Book of the Law in the LORD's Temple!"
Then Hilkiah gave the scroll to Shaphan.
16 Shaphan took the scroll to the king
and reported, "Your officials are doing
everything they were assigned to do. 17 The
money that was collected at the Temple of
the LORD has been turned over to the supervisors and workmen." 18 Shaphan also told
the king, "Hilkiah the priest has given me a
scroll." So Shaphan read it to the king.
19 When the king heard what was written
in the Law, he tore his clothes in despair.
20 Then he gave these orders to Hilkiah, Ahikam son of Shaphan, Acbor son of Micaiah,
Shaphan the court secretary, and Asaiah the
king's personal adviser: 21 "Go to the Temple
and speak to the LORD for me and for all the
remnant of Israel and Judah. Inquire about

MANASSEH (32:33–33:20)

2 Kgs 20:21–21:18; 23:26; 24:3
Jer 15:4

Manasseh, the thirteenth king of Judah (697–642 BC), had a long but notoriously wicked reign (33:1-20; 2 Kgs 21:1-18). His parents were the godly king Hezekiah and his wife Hephzibah (2 Kgs 20:21–21:1).

In 697 BC, Manasseh became co-ruler with his father Hezekiah at age twelve (33:1). In 686 BC, Hezekiah died and Manasseh became sole monarch. He reigned a total of 55 years (2 Kgs 21:1), longer than any other king in Judah or Israel. Regrettably, he was the most wicked of all the kings of Judah. He rebuilt the high places for pagan worship; he encouraged the worship of Baal, the sun, moon, and stars; and he even burnt his son as a child sacrifice (2 Kgs 21:2-9; see 2 Kgs 23:10; Jer 7:31). He allowed divination and sorcery in Judah and "murdered many innocent people until Jerusalem was filled . . . with innocent blood" (2 Kgs 21:16; 24:3-4).

Surviving Assyrian records note that Manasseh provided men to transport timber from Lebanon to Nineveh for the Assyrian king Esarhaddon (680–669 BC), and he paid tribute to King Ashurbanipal (668–626 BC) after an Assyrian military campaign in Egypt in 667 BC. Manasseh served Assyria more faithfully than he served the Lord.

Because of Manasseh's tremendous sin, God determined to "wipe away the people of Jerusalem as one wipes a dish and turns it upside down" (2 Kgs 21:13). However, Manasseh repented late in life. The Assyrian army captured him, put a hook through his nose, and exiled him to Babylon (33:10-13). There Manasseh turned to the Lord. God heard his prayers, restored him as king, and blessed the rest of his reign as Manasseh sought to restore proper worship of God alone (33:14-17).

Sadly, Manasseh's sins had infected the people of Judah (33:17), and God did not reverse his determination to judge the kingdom (2 Kgs 23:26; 24:3). This indicates just how seriously Manasseh had sinned. Even Jeremiah, 100 years later, announced: "Because of the wicked things Manasseh son of Hezekiah, king of Judah, did in Jerusalem, I will make my people an object of horror to all the kingdoms of the earth" (Jer 15:4). The destruction of Jerusalem and its Temple and the exile of Judah's people followed.

When Manasseh died in 642 BC at age 67, he was buried in his own garden (2 Kgs 21:18), rather than with highly regarded leaders such as Jehoiada and Hezekiah (24:16; 32:33).

34:12-13 That ***musicians*** supervised the construction shows how important it was for *Levites* to be in charge of this work. Other ancient texts note that music was a common element of construction projects.

34:14-18 The discovery of ***the Book of the Law of the LORD*** was one of the rewards for faithfulness. • The book ***that was written by Moses*** was probably Deuteronomy. It might have been neglected and lost during the apostasies of Manasseh or Amon.

34:20 ***Acbor son of Micaiah:*** As in parallel text at 2 Kgs 22:12; Hebrew reads *Abdon son of Micah.*

the words written in the scroll that has been
found. For the LORD's great anger has been
poured out on us because our ancestors
have not obeyed the word of the LORD. We
have not been doing everything this scroll
says we must do."
22So Hilkiah and the other men went to
the New Quarter of Jerusalem to consult
with the [d]prophet Huldah. She was the wife
of Shallum son of Tikvah, son of Harhas,
the keeper of the Temple wardrobe.
23She said to them, "The LORD, the God
of Israel, has spoken! Go back and tell the
man who sent you, 24'This is what the LORD
says: I am going to bring disaster on this
city and its people. All the curses written in
the scroll that was read to the king of Judah
will come true. 25For my people have abandoned me and offered sacrifices to pagan
gods, and I am very angry with them for
everything they have done. My anger will
be poured out on this place, and it will not
be quenched.'
26"But go to the king of Judah who sent
you to seek the LORD and tell him: 'This is
what the LORD, the God of Israel, says concerning the message you have just heard:
27You were sorry and humbled yourself before God when you heard his words against
this city and its people. You humbled yourself and tore your clothing in despair and
wept before me in repentance. And I have
indeed heard you, says the LORD. 28So I will
not send the promised disaster until after
you have died and been buried in peace.
You yourself will not see the disaster I am
going to bring on this city and its people.' "
So they took her message back to the
king.

Josiah's Religious Reforms
2 Chr 34:29-32 // 2 Kgs 23:1-3

29Then the king summoned all the elders of
Judah and Jerusalem. 30And the king went
up to the Temple of the LORD with all the
people of Judah and Jerusalem, along with
the priests and the Levites—all the people from the greatest to the least. There
the king read to them the entire Book of
the Covenant that had been found in the
LORD's Temple. 31The king took his place
of authority beside the pillar and renewed
the covenant in the LORD's presence. He
pledged to obey the LORD by keeping all his
commands, laws, and decrees with all his
heart and soul. He promised to obey all the
terms of the covenant that were written in
the scroll. 32And he required everyone in
Jerusalem and the people of Benjamin to
make a similar pledge. The people of Jerusalem did so, renewing their covenant with
God, the God of their ancestors.
33So Josiah removed all detestable idols
from the entire land of Israel and required
everyone to worship the LORD their God.
And throughout the rest of his lifetime, they
did not turn away from the LORD, the God of
their ancestors.

Josiah Celebrates Passover
2 Chr 35:1, 18-19 // 2 Kgs 23:21-23

35 Then Josiah announced that the
Passover of the LORD would be celebrated in Jerusalem, and so the Passover
lamb was slaughtered on the fourteenth
day of the first month. 2Josiah also assigned
the priests to their duties and encouraged
them in their work at the Temple of the
LORD. 3He issued this order to the Levites,
who were to teach all Israel and who had
been set apart to serve the LORD: "Put the
holy Ark in the Temple that was built by Solomon son of David, the king of Israel. You
no longer need to carry it back and forth
on your shoulders. Now spend your time
serving the LORD your God and his people
Israel. 4Report for duty according to the
family divisions of your ancestors, following the directions of King David of Israel
and the directions of his son Solomon.

34:22 [d]*nebi'ah* (5031) ‣Neh 6:14
34:24 Deut 28:15-68; 2 Chr 36:14-20
34:25 2 Chr 33:3
34:27 2 Chr 12:7; 32:26
34:29-32 //2 Kgs 23:1-3
34:30 Neh 8:1-3
34:31 2 Chr 23:16; 29:10
34:33 2 Kgs 23:3; 2 Chr 34:3-7
35:1 Exod 12:6; Num 9:3; 2 Kgs 23:21-22
35:2 2 Chr 29:11
35:3 1 Chr 23:26; 2 Chr 17:7-9; Neh 8:7
35:4 1 Chr 9:10-13; 2 Chr 8:14

34:22 *the New Quarter:* Or *the Second Quarter,* a newer section of Jerusalem. Hebrew reads *the Mishneh.* • *son of Tikvah, son of Harhas:* As in parallel text at 2 Kgs 22:14; Hebrew reads *son of Tokhath, son of Hasrah.*

34:24 *the curses written in the scroll:* See Deut 27:14-26; 28:15-68. Curses in a covenant stipulate what will happen to those who are unfaithful to the covenant, as Israel and Judah were in their covenant with the Lord. These curses included exile. • *this city:* Literally *this place;* also in 34:27, 28.

34:27-28 King Josiah did not die in peace; he was killed by Pharaoh Neco II of Egypt (35:20-25). However, Josiah was *buried in peace,* meaning that the city of Jerusalem was at peace and exile did not come during Josiah's reign. His repentant spirit averted immediate disaster.

34:29-32 Renewal of the covenant was the most significant event in Josiah's reform.

35:1 *the fourteenth day of the first month:* This day in the ancient Hebrew lunar calendar was April 5, 622 BC.

35:3 The *holy Ark* might have been removed from *the Temple* during the apostasy of Manasseh or Amon.

35:4-6 The assignments of the priests and Levites mirrored the *directions* of *David* and *Solomon* (8:14-15; 1 Chr 24–26). The Passover animal was typically slaughtered by the offerer (Deut 16:5-6). However, because the offerers did not have time to purify themselves, Josiah continued the practice Hezekiah had begun of having the Levites slaughter the Passover animals (see 30:13-20). In Josiah's time, the large number of participants also might have caused logistical problems.

35:6
2 Chr 29:5, 15; 35:1
35:8
2 Chr 31:13
35:9
2 Chr 31:12
35:10
2 Chr 35:4-5
35:11
2 Chr 29:22, 34; 35:1, 6
35:13
Exod 12:8-9
Lev 6:25
35:15
1 Chr 25:1; 26:12-19
35:17
Exod 12:15
2 Chr 30:21
35:18-19
//2 Kgs 23:21-23
[e]*pesakh* (6453)
‣ Ezra 6:19
35:20–36:1
//2 Kgs 23:28-30
35:22
Judg 5:19
2 Chr 18:29; 35:21

5“Then stand in the sanctuary at the place appointed for your family division and help the families assigned to you as they bring their offerings to the Temple. 6Slaughter the Passover lambs, purify yourselves, and prepare to help those who come. Follow all the directions that the LORD gave through Moses.”

7Then Josiah provided 30,000 lambs and young goats for the people’s Passover offerings, along with 3,000 cattle, all from the king’s own flocks and herds. 8The king’s officials also made willing contributions to the people, priests, and Levites. Hilkiah, Zechariah, and Jehiel, the administrators of God’s Temple, gave the priests 2,600 lambs and young goats and 300 cattle as Passover offerings. 9The Levite leaders—Conaniah and his brothers Shemaiah and Nethanel, as well as Hashabiah, Jeiel, and Jozabad—gave 5,000 lambs and young goats and 500 cattle to the Levites for their Passover offerings.

10When everything was ready for the Passover celebration, the priests and the Levites took their places, organized by their divisions, as the king had commanded. 11The Levites then slaughtered the Passover lambs and presented the blood to the priests, who sprinkled the blood on the altar while the Levites prepared the animals. 12They divided the burnt offerings among the people by their family groups, so they could offer them to the LORD as prescribed in the Book of Moses. They did the same with the cattle. 13Then they roasted the Passover lambs as prescribed; and they boiled the holy offerings in pots, kettles, and pans, and brought them out quickly so the people could eat them.

14Afterward the Levites prepared Passover offerings for themselves and for the priests—the descendants of Aaron—because the priests had been busy from morning till night offering the burnt offerings and the fat portions. The Levites took responsibility for all these preparations.

15The musicians, descendants of Asaph, were in their assigned places, following the commands that had been given by David, Asaph, Heman, and Jeduthun, the king’s seer. The gatekeepers guarded the gates and did not need to leave their posts of duty, for their Passover offerings were prepared for them by their fellow Levites.

16The entire ceremony for the LORD’s Passover was completed that day. All the burnt offerings were sacrificed on the altar of the LORD, as King Josiah had commanded. 17All the Israelites present in Jerusalem celebrated Passover and the Festival of Unleavened Bread for seven days. 18Never since the time of the prophet Samuel had there been such a [e]Passover. None of the kings of Israel had ever kept a [e]Passover as Josiah did, involving all the priests and Levites, all the people of Jerusalem, and people from all over Judah and Israel. 19This [e]Passover celebration took place in the eighteenth year of Josiah’s reign.

The Death of Josiah
2 Chr 35:20-27 // 2 Kgs 23:28-30a

20After Josiah had finished restoring the Temple, King Neco of Egypt led his army up from Egypt to do battle at Carchemish on the Euphrates River, and Josiah and his army marched out to fight him. 21But King Neco sent messengers to Josiah with this message:

“What do you want with me, king of
Judah? I have no quarrel with you today!
I am on my way to fight another nation,
and God has told me to hurry! Do not
interfere with God, who is with me, or he
will destroy you.”

22But Josiah refused to listen to Neco, to whom God had indeed spoken, and he would not turn back. Instead, he disguised himself and led his army into battle on the plain of Megiddo. 23But the enemy archers hit King Josiah with their arrows and wounded him. He cried out to his men, “Take me from the battle, for I am badly wounded!”

35:7-9 The Passover sacrifice required ***lambs and young goats*** (Exod 12:21). The ***cattle*** were an additional offering. The totals ***Josiah provided*** along with the contributions of others were nearly double the offerings in Hezekiah’s time (see 30:24), yet less than the offerings at the dedication of the Temple (see 7:5).

35:13 The Levites ***brought*** the food ***out quickly***, observing the element of haste required in the Passover (Exod 12:11).

35:18 This ***Passover*** included a greater number of participants than the one Hezekiah had observed (see note at 35:7-9). In this Passover, ***the priests and Levites*** took a prominent and proper role, as Josiah had specifically required (35:15-16; cp. 30:3, 15).

35:20-24 The narrative jumps from Josiah’s eighteenth year (622 BC) to the year of his death (609 BC). The decline of the Assyrian empire brought Egypt and Babylon, two great powers that had long been subject to Assyria, into conflict with each other. ***King Neco of Egypt***, who had allied with Assyria to resist Babylonian expansion, asked Josiah to allow free passage of his army. Josiah’s interception might have been the result of a coalition with Babylon, or it might have been his own attempt to establish independence from Egypt. Josiah’s death was caused by his disobedience to a divine oracle delivered by a Gentile king.

35:20 ***Josiah and his army marched out to fight him:*** Or *Josiah went out to meet him.*

24 So they lifted Josiah out of his chariot
and placed him in another chariot. Then
they brought him back to Jerusalem, where
he died. He was buried there in the royal
cemetery. And all Judah and Jerusalem
mourned for him. 25 The prophet Jeremiah
composed funeral songs for Josiah, and to
this day choirs still sing these sad songs
about his death. These songs of sorrow have
become a tradition and are recorded in *The
Book of Laments.*
26 The rest of the events of Josiah's reign
and his acts of devotion (carried out according to what was written in the Law of the
LORD), 27 from beginning to end—all are recorded in *The Book of the Kings of Israel
and Judah.*

Exile of the Kings of Judah (36:1-10)

Exile of Jehoahaz

2 Chr 36:1-4 // 2 Kgs 23:30b-34

36 Then the people of the land took Josiah's son Jehoahaz and made him
the next king in Jerusalem.
2 Jehoahaz was twenty-three years old
when he became king, and he reigned in Jerusalem three months.
3 Then he was deposed by the king of
Egypt, who demanded that Judah pay 7,500
pounds of silver and 75 pounds of gold as
tribute.
4 The king of Egypt then installed Eliakim,
the brother of Jehoahaz, as the next king of
Judah and Jerusalem, and he changed Eliakim's name to Jehoiakim. Then Neco took
Jehoahaz to Egypt as a prisoner.

Reign of Jehoiakim

2 Chr 36:5 // 2 Kgs 23:36-37
2 Chr 36:8 // 2 Kgs 24:5-6

5 Jehoiakim was twenty-five years old when
he became king, and he reigned in Jerusalem
eleven years. He did what was evil in the
sight of the LORD his God.
6 Then King Nebuchadnezzar of Babylon
came to Jerusalem and captured it, and he
bound Jehoiakim in bronze chains and led
him away to Babylon. 7 Nebuchadnezzar
also took some of the treasures from the
Temple of the LORD, and he placed them in
his palace in Babylon.
8 The rest of the events in Jehoiakim's
reign, including all the evil things he did
and everything found against him, are recorded in *The Book of the Kings of Israel
and Judah.* Then his son Jehoiachin became the next king.

Exile of Jehoiachin

2 Chr 36:9-10 // 2 Kgs 24:8-9, 12b-13, 17

9 Jehoiachin was eighteen years old when he
became king, and he reigned in Jerusalem
three months and ten days. Jehoiachin did
what was evil in the LORD's sight.
10 In the spring of the year King Nebuchadnezzar took Jehoiachin to Babylon.
Many treasures from the Temple of the
LORD were also taken to Babylon at that
time. And Nebuchadnezzar installed Jehoiachin's uncle, Zedekiah, as the next king in
Judah and Jerusalem.

Zedekiah's Reign and the Fall of Jerusalem (36:11-21)

Reign of Zedekiah

2 Chr 36:11-12 // 2 Kgs 24:18-20a // Jer 52:1-3a

11 Zedekiah was twenty-one years old when
he became king, and he reigned in Jerusalem eleven years. 12 He did what was evil
in the sight of the LORD his God, and he refused to humble himself when the prophet
Jeremiah spoke to him directly from the

35:25 Jer 22:10-13; Lam 4:20; Zech 12:11
36:1 Jer 22:11
36:2-4 //2 Kgs 23:31-34
36:4 Jer 22:10, 12
36:5-8 //2 Kgs 23:36–24:6
36:5 Jer 22:13-19
36:6 2 Kgs 24:1; 2 Chr 33:11; Jer 22:19-20
36:7 2 Kgs 24:13
36:8 2 Kgs 24:5
36:9-10 //2 Kgs 24:8-17
36:10 Jer 37:1
36:11-16 //2 Kgs 24:18-20; //Jer 52:1-3
36:12 2 Chr 33:23; Jer 21:3-7

35:25 ***Jeremiah*** held ***Josiah*** in high esteem (see Jer 22:15-16; cp. Jer 22:10). ***The Book of Laments*** was lost; it is not related to the Book of Lamentations.

36:1-4 ***Jehoahaz,*** also known as Shallum (see Jer 22:11 and note), was not Josiah's oldest son (1 Chr 3:15), and the reason he was chosen as king is not explained. Pharaoh Neco immediately intervened and established Jehoahaz's older brother ***Eliakim*** in his place and renamed him ***Jehoiakim.***

36:2 ***Jehoahaz:*** Hebrew *Joahaz,* a variant spelling of Jehoahaz; also in 36:4. • Jehoahaz's reign of ***three months*** was in 609 BC.

36:3 ***7,500 pounds of silver and 75 pounds of gold:*** Hebrew *100 talents* [3,400 kilograms] *of silver and 1 talent* [34 kilograms] *of gold.*

36:5 ***Jehoiakim*** reigned from 609 to 598 BC. • ***He did what was evil:*** Jeremiah characterized his reign as one of self-aggrandizement and injustice (Jer 22:13-17).

36:6 ***Jehoiakim*** was ***bound:*** See note on 2 Kgs 24:6.

36:7 ***palace:*** Or *temple.*

36:9-10 The Chronicler limits his record of Jehoiachin's short reign to his exile and payment of tribute from the Temple instruments. The capture of Jehoiachin is described in the *Babylonian Chronicle:* "In the seventh year (of Nebuchadnezzar), the month of Kislev, the king of Akkad mustered his troops, marched to [the land west of the Jordan], and encamped against the city of Judah, and on the second day of the month of Adar he seized the city and captured the king." Jehoiachin was thus taken captive on March 16, 597 BC. He was taken to Babylon about a month later. • Jehoiachin remained a captive in Babylon for thirty-seven years (see 2 Kgs 25:27; Jer 52:31).

36:9 ***eighteen:*** As in one Hebrew manuscript, some Greek manuscripts, and Syriac version (see also 2 Kgs 24:8); most Hebrew manuscripts read *eight.*

36:10 ***In the spring of the year:*** Literally *At the turn of the year.* The first day of this year in the ancient Hebrew lunar calendar was April 13, 597 BC. • ***uncle:*** As in parallel text at 2 Kgs 24:17; Hebrew reads *brother,* or *relative.*

36:11-14 Although ***Jeremiah*** repeatedly urged ***Zedekiah*** to submit to the Babylonians rather than look for help from Egypt (Jer 25:1-11; 27:1-22; 34:1-22; 37:1–38:28), Zedekiah ***refused to humble himself*** and ***rebelled,*** violating his oath.

36:11 ***Zedekiah*** reigned from 597 to 586 BC.

36:13
2 Chr 30:8
Jer 52:3
Ezek 17:15
[f]*shub* (7725)
‣Job 36:10

36:15
Jer 7:13; 25:3-4

36:16
2 Chr 30:10
Ezra 5:12
Prov 1:24-32
Jer 5:12-13

36:17-20
//2 Kgs 25:1-21
//Jer 52:4-27

36:18
2 Chr 36:7, 10

36:19
2 Kgs 25:9
Jer 52:13

36:20
2 Kgs 25:11
Jer 27:7

36:21
Lev 25:4; 26:33-34
Jer 29:10
[g]*shabbath* (7676)
‣Neh 13:15

36:22-23
//Ezra 1:1-3

36:22
Isa 44:28
Jer 29:10

LORD. [13]He also rebelled against King Nebuchadnezzar, even though he had taken an oath of loyalty in God's name. Zedekiah was a hard and stubborn man, refusing to [f]turn to the LORD, the God of Israel.

[14]Likewise, all the leaders of the priests and the people became more and more unfaithful. They followed all the pagan practices of the surrounding nations, desecrating the Temple of the LORD that had been consecrated in Jerusalem.

[15]The LORD, the God of their ancestors, repeatedly sent his prophets to warn them, for he had compassion on his people and his Temple. [16]But the people mocked these messengers of God and despised their words. They scoffed at the prophets until the LORD's anger could no longer be restrained and nothing could be done.

The Fall of Jerusalem

[17]So the LORD brought the king of Babylon against them. The Babylonians killed Judah's young men, even chasing after them into the Temple. They had no pity on the people, killing both young men and young women, the old and the infirm. God handed all of them over to Nebuchadnezzar. [18]The king took home to Babylon all the articles, large and small, used in the Temple of God, and the treasures from both the LORD's Temple and from the palace of the king and his officials. [19]Then his army burned the Temple of God, tore down the walls of Jerusalem, burned all the palaces, and completely destroyed everything of value. [20]The few who survived were taken as exiles to Babylon, and they became servants to the king and his sons until the kingdom of Persia came to power.

[21]So the message of the LORD spoken through Jeremiah was fulfilled. The land finally enjoyed its [g]Sabbath rest, lying desolate until the seventy years were fulfilled, just as the prophet had said.

Restoration under Cyrus (36:22-23)

2 Chr 36:22-23 // Ezra 1:1-4

[22]In the first year of King Cyrus of Persia, the LORD fulfilled the prophecy he had given through Jeremiah. He stirred the heart of Cyrus to put this proclamation in writing and to send it throughout his kingdom:

[23]"This is what King Cyrus of Persia says:

"The LORD, the God of heaven, has
given me all the kingdoms of the earth.
He has appointed me to build him a
Temple at Jerusalem, which is in Judah.
Any of you who are the LORD's people
may go there for this task. And may the
LORD your God be with you!"

36:13 ***an oath of loyalty in God's name:*** The vassal oath imposed on him was probably similar to those known from Assyrian treaties, sworn in the name of the vassal's god.

36:17 ***Babylonians:*** Or *Chaldeans.*

36:19 ***destroyed everything of value:*** Or *destroyed all the valuable articles from the Temple.* The Temple was destroyed in August 586 BC (see 2 Kgs 25:8; Jer 52:12).

36:21 The length of the captivity had been predicted by ***Jeremiah*** (Jer 25:11-12; 29:10). • ***The land finally enjoyed its Sabbath rest:*** See Lev 26:34-35, 43, where the punishment for disobedience is exile; the land is left unused for all the Sabbaths of which it had been deprived. The land's time of rest was also a preparation for the time of restoration. See note on Ezra 6:15. • ***the prophet:*** That is, Jeremiah.

36:22-23 Chronicles concludes with the verses that form the introduction to Ezra. ***King Cyrus of Persia*** permitted the community of Judah to experience a new exodus, as proclaimed by the prophet Isaiah (Isa 40:1-11). • ***The first year*** of Cyrus's reign over Babylon was 538 BC. • ***the prophecy . . . through Jeremiah:*** See Jer 25:11-12; 29:10.

THE HISTORICAL BACKGROUND OF

Israel's Exile and Return

The period of the Exile (605–539 BC) was a time of great disaster and despair for Israel. But after exile came an era of hope as the Jews returned to their land and the community of Israel was reborn (538–400 BC). The setting of Israel's experience was not an obscure corner of the world. Rather, Israel lived among the superpowers of the ancient Near East: the Neo-Babylonian empire, the Persian empire, and Egypt. Israel's history intersected at vital points with world history, for Israel was a real and vital part of the ancient Near East. These points of contact and overlap help to illustrate the authenticity, validity, and reliability of the biblical writers' presentation of this time of death and rebirth.

THE BEGINNING OF EXILE 605–586 BC

In 605 BC, Babylon's king Nebuchadnezzar II (605–562 BC) defeated the remnants of the Assyrian military and forced Assyria's Egyptian allies to flee from the eastern shore of the Mediterranean. These events are clearly recorded in the Babylonian Chronicle, a series of cuneiform Babylonian tablets covering roughly the years 745–100 BC (see COS 1.137). The Babylonian Chronicle includes reports from the first eleven years of Nebuchadnezzar's reign and military excursions (605–594 BC). These documents illuminate the setting in which the biblical accounts of Nebuchadnezzar's invasions of Judah (605–586 BC) took place (see 2 Kgs 24–25).

The biblical report of skilled Israelites being taken into captivity by the Babylonians (see 2 Kgs 25:8-12; cp. Dan 1:1-5) reflects a common practice by

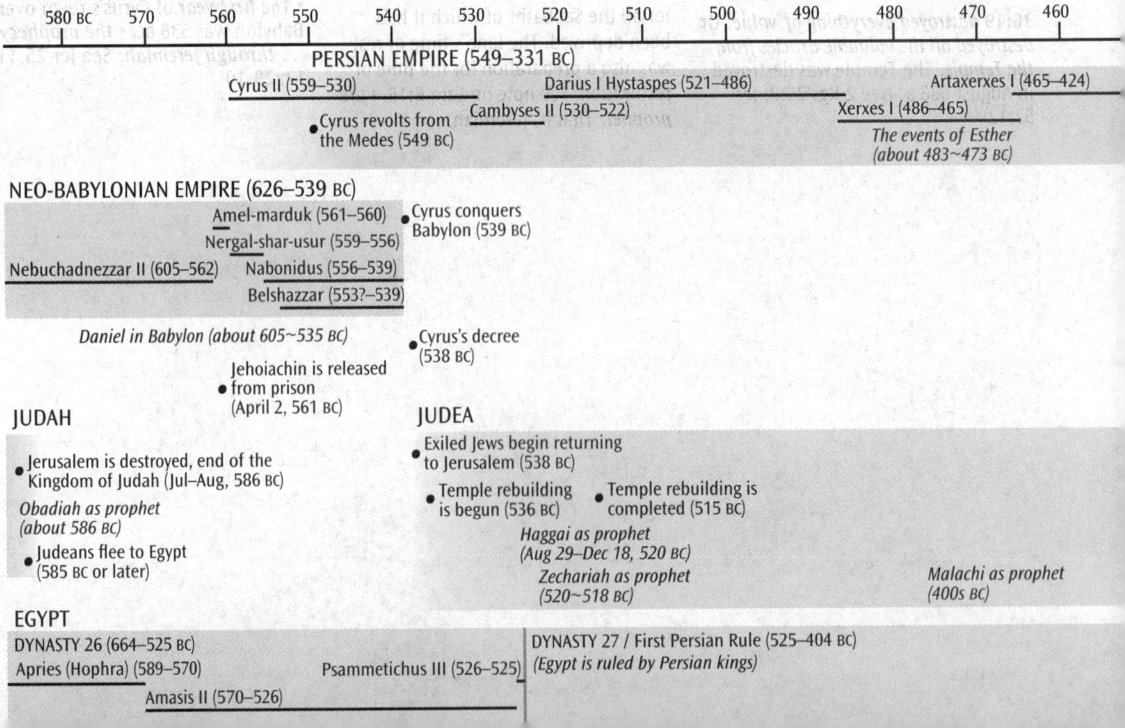

conquerors. Assyrian kings had redeployed skilled captives into the Assyrian military, economic, political, religious, and social structures. Skilled craftsmen were valued highly in the ancient Near East. Babylonian ration tablets (records of food distribution) record the capture and use of sailors, leaders, musicians, carpenters, monkey keepers, and guards. The Neo-Babylonians were looking for such highly qualified people to strengthen their own empire.

Some of the elite who had been taken into exile prospered, such as Daniel (Dan 1:17, 21) and Mordecai (Esth 10:1-3). Babylonian documents describe the benefits accorded to Jehoiachin and his sons when he was kindly released by Evil-merodach (561 BC; cp. 2 Kgs 25:27-30). According to the Murashu Archives, some of the Jewish Murashu family became bankers and brokers in Babylon, and they succeeded during the Exile and beyond. But not all Jews in exile were at the top of the structures of society; so Daniel prayed for the end of the Exile and for God to restore his people again (Dan 9).

THE REMNANT IN JUDAH 586–581 BC

Jeremiah 40–43 describes religious, political, and military confusion in the land of Judah soon after the fall of Jerusalem. Some of the people and places mentioned in the biblical record of this era are also mentioned in other historical documents and artifacts. Gedaliah, the governor appointed by Nebuchadnezzar, is mentioned on seals and *bullae* (seal impressions) that have been found and dated to this era. According to the biblical record, Mizpah was Gedaliah's headquarters (2 Kgs 25:23-25), and archaeology provides supporting evidence by indicating that Mizpah underwent repairs and expansion at about this time. Gedaliah was assassinated, and his assassin was backed by Baalis, king of Ammon (Jer 40:14), who is referred to on a seal from this era. Jeremiah's scribe, Baruch, also appears on *bullae* from this time (see "Baruch" at Jer 45:1-5, p. 1283). These examples of historical confirmation of the details of Scripture illuminate our understanding of the Jewish remnant community.

When Gedaliah had been killed, the remnant community in Judah fled to Egypt, taking Jeremiah with them and stopping at Tahpanhes in Egypt (see

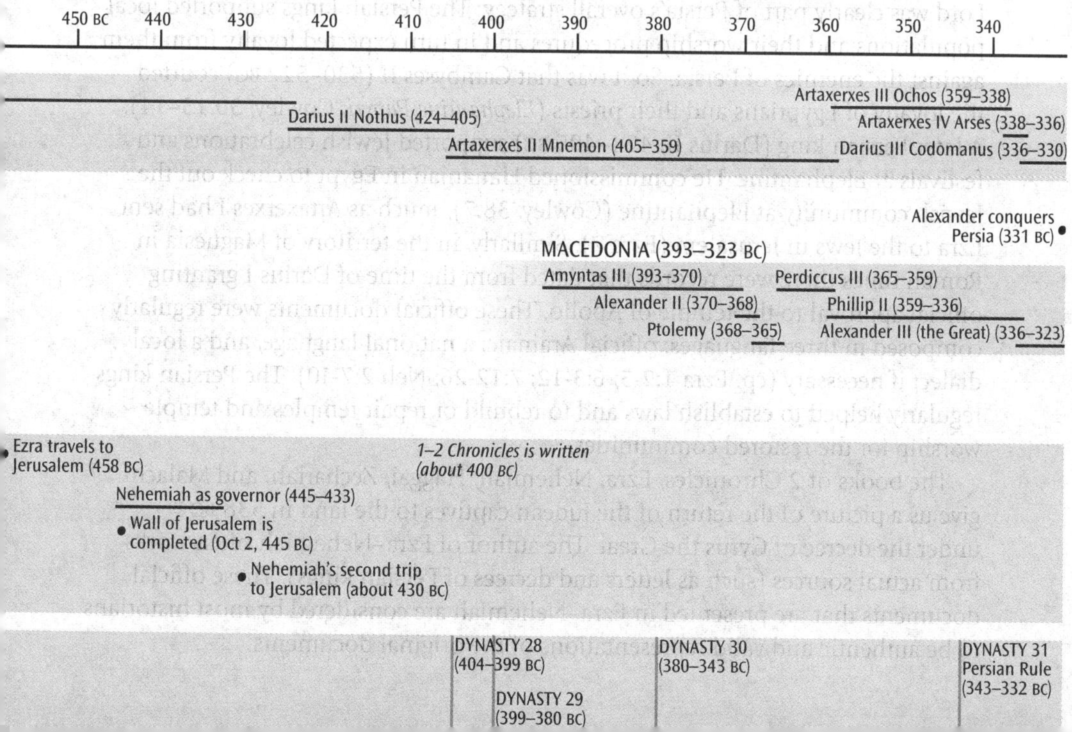

2 Kgs 25:22-26; Jer 40:7–44:30). The death of Pharaoh Hophra amidst the violent rise to power of Amasis II (570 BC) is probably referred to in Jer 44:30. Jeremiah's assertion that Nebuchadnezzar would invade Egypt was perhaps fulfilled in 568 BC, when Amasis II resisted Nebuchadnezzar in the area (ANET 308).

THE EXILE IN BABYLON 586–538 BC

Israel's human travail in exile was shared by numerous other ancient Near Eastern peoples conquered by Assyria and Babylon. In addition, Herodotus's history recounts the exile and resettlement of peoples by both Greek and Persian authorities (e.g., Herodotus, *Histories* 5.15, 30; 7.80–81). Exile was not uncommon.

Unfortunately, the period of Judah's exile is poorly documented. There is no running historical narrative for the period 586 to 538 BC. The books of Daniel and Ezekiel provide some insight into this period, however, and their records harmonize well with what is known from Babylonian sources. For example, we now know about the erratic rule of Nabonidus, the last king of Babylon (556–539 BC), who spent the last years of his reign in Teima in Arabia. He had become obsessed with worship of the moon god and thereby alienated the powerful priesthood of Marduk (see COS 2.123A, 2.123B; ANET 560–562). Nabonidus thus failed to administer Babylonia, leaving it in the hand of his son Belshazzar, mentioned in Daniel 5 as *de facto* king (see note on Dan 5:7). His actions helped assure the fall of Babylon to Cyrus the Great in 539 BC.

THE RETURN FROM EXILE 538–400 BC

Cyrus's conquest of Babylon in 539 BC is recorded in the Cyrus Cylinder (COS 2.124; ANET 315). We find there a record of the decree that he issued concerning the exiles of Judea, among many other peoples and national groups who were permitted to return to their ancestral lands and rebuild their temples. Cyrus was looked upon as "a ruler who revives" the dead "corpses" of nations taken to Babylon (cp. Ezek 37). He wisely created goodwill toward his many peoples by dealing respectfully and kindly with them by returning their religious artifacts used in worshiping their gods (see COS 2.124).

The foreign policy of permitting the Jews to return to Judea and worship the Lord was clearly part of Persia's overall strategy: The Persian kings supported local populations and their worship procedures and in turn expected loyalty from them against the enemies of Persia. So it was that Cambyses II (530–522 BC) courted the loyalty of Egyptians and their priests (*Elephantine Papyri*; Cowley, 30.13–14). A later Persian king (Darius II, 424–405 BC) supported Jewish celebrations and festivals at Elephantine. He commissioned Hananiah in Egypt to check out the Jewish community at Elephantine (Cowley, 38.7), much as Artaxerxes I had sent Ezra to the Jews in Jerusalem (Ezra 7). Similarly, in the territory of Magnesia in Roman times there were records that dated from the time of Darius I granting official approval to the temple of Apollo. These official documents were regularly composed in three languages: official Aramaic, a national language, and a local dialect if necessary (cp. Ezra 1:2-5; 6:3-12; 7:12-26; Neh 2:7-10). The Persian kings regularly helped to establish laws and to rebuild or repair temples and temple worship for the restored communities.

The books of 2 Chronicles, Ezra, Nehemiah, Haggai, Zechariah, and Malachi give us a picture of the return of the Judean captives to the land in 538 BC under the decree of Cyrus the Great. The author of Ezra–Nehemiah often works from actual sources (such as letters and decrees of Persian kings). These official documents that are presented in Ezra–Nehemiah are considered by most historians to be authentic and valid representations of the original documents.

The book of Esther, meanwhile, provides a glimpse of a Jewish community that had chosen to remain in exile (see Esth 1:3; 3:7). Several helpful extrabiblical sources give insights into this postexilic era as well (including the Babylonian Chronicles, the Cyrus Cylinder, the Behistun Inscriptions, administrative tablets in Elamite cuneiform, other Aramaic documents, ostraca from Elephantine in Egypt, the Wadi Daliyeh papyri from Palestine, and historians Ctesias, Herodotus, and Xenophon).

Nehemiah returned to Judea in 445 BC, successfully rebuilt the walls of Jerusalem, and effectively organized the community. His status as cup-bearer to the king (Artaxerxes I) has long been recognized as a position of high honor (cp. Herodotus, *Histories* 3.34). The letter of safe conduct granted to Nehemiah (Neh 2:7) is paralleled by a roughly contemporary letter from a Persian satrap for his military staff officer who is granted travel protection from Babylonia to Damascus and Egypt.

CONCLUSION

The particular context in which Israel's exile occurred gave the experience a unique and special purpose for Israel and for the world. The Exile of 586–538 BC was more than merely a time of great disaster and despair for Israel; it was a covenantal and theological lesson, an event driven by the covenant that also included great expectations. In the Exile and return, the people of Israel experienced judgment, humiliation, repentance, restoration, and hope.

PRIMARY SOURCES

HERODOTUS
The Histories, trans. Aubrey de Selincourt (2003)

[COS] WILLIAM W. HALLO AND K. LAWSON YOUNGER, EDS.
The Context of Scripture (2003)

[ANET] JAMES B. PRITCHARD
Ancient Near Eastern Texts Relating to the Old Testament (1969)

ARTHUR E. COWLEY
Aramaic Papyri of the Fifth Century BC (1923)

FURTHER READING

DAVID M. HOWARD, JR. AND MICHAEL A. GRISANTI, EDS.
Giving the Sense: Understanding and Using Old Testament Historical Texts (2004)

K. A. KITCHEN
On the Reliability of the Old Testament (2006)

RALPH W. KLEIN
Israel in Exile (1979)

JOAN OATES
Babylon (1986)

IAIN PROVAN, V. PHILIPS LONG, AND TREMPER LONGMAN III
A Biblical History of Israel (2003)

LEON J. WOOD
A Survey of Israel's History (1986)

EDWIN M. YAMAUCHI
Persia and the Bible (1990)

THE BOOK OF EZRA

Ezra recounts God's marvelous work in bringing many Israelites back to Jerusalem after seventy years of exile in Babylon. The book highlights the restored community's struggle to resist pagan influences, to rebuild the Temple, and to deal with sin in the lives of those who chose to follow the world's values rather than God's. In Ezra we see how God provides for and protects those who trust in him and faithfully obey his word.

SETTING

About 130 years before Ezra came to Jerusalem in 458 BC, God punished Judah's persistent wickedness by sending the Babylonians to destroy the city, demolish the Temple, and take thousands into exile (see 2 Kgs 25). While in exile in Babylon, the Israelites were able to build homes, have gardens, and live a fairly good life with some religious freedom (Jer 29:4-5). Some attained positions of power (Dan 3, 6).

God had promised to return his people to the holy land after seventy years (2 Chr 36:21; Jer 25:12; 29:10). About 559 BC, the Persian prince Cyrus II subdued the Medes and fused them into what would become the Persian empire. Then, in 539 BC, the Persians defeated the Babylonians,

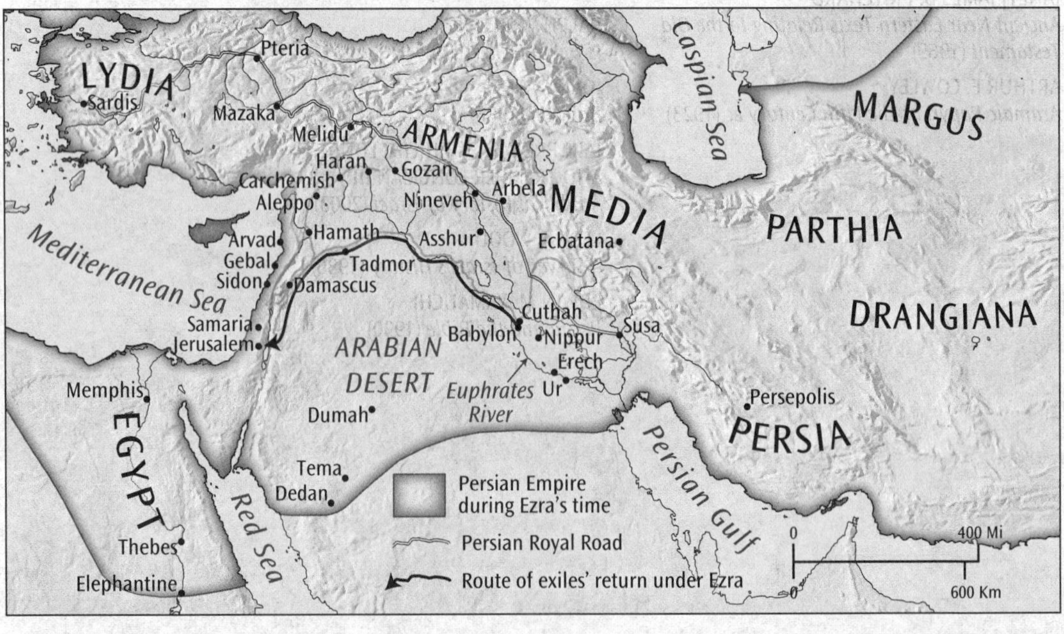

▲**The Persian Empire of Cyrus II, 539–530 BC.** After conquering the Babylonian empire in 539 BC, King Cyrus II of PERSIA (559–530 BC) allowed exiled peoples, including the Jews, to return from BABYLON to their homelands (1:1–2:70; 7:1–8:36). Many of the places shown do not appear in the Old Testament but are known from other sources during Ezra's time.

BABYLON 1:11; 4:12; 7:6; 7:9
ECBATANA, MEDIA 6:2
ERECH, SUSA 4:9
PERSIA 1:1-2
SAMARIA 4:10, 17
SIDON 3:7

paving the way for this promise to be fulfilled. In 538 BC, Cyrus began to allow the Jewish people to leave Babylon. Sheshbazzar led the first group of exiles in the return to their homeland (1:1-8).

When the people of Israel and Judah had been deported to foreign lands, the Assyrians and Babylonians had settled other conquered peoples in the land of Israel. The returning Jewish exiles found these foreigners inhabiting the land that they sought to reclaim and rebuild. These foreigners claimed to worship the same God as the Jews, but they actually advocated a "melting pot" religion that combined pagan and Jewish ideas and practices. These foreigners wanted to worship with the returning Jews, who recognized the spiritual compromise that would entail (4:3). The Jews refused the foreigners any part in their community. As a result, the Jewish community experienced severe opposition from the foreigners living in the land. Although this stand led to many years of conflict and a delay in Temple reconstruction, the Exile had taught the Jews that compromising the purity of their faith would yield worse results.

OUTLINE

1:1–6:22
The People Return to Rebuild the Temple

7:1–10:44
Ezra Returns to Teach God's Law

When Ezra arrived in Jerusalem several decades later, he found that some of the Israelites had compromised their faith by marrying foreigners. God had expressly forbidden such marriage (see Deut 7:3-4; Josh 23:12-13) because it would inevitably lead to adopting pagan religious beliefs (9:1-2). If not confessed and rectified (9:13-15; 10:14), this sin would surely bring God's judgment. Therefore, in accordance with the word of God, Ezra led the people to renew their covenant with God and to separate themselves from the pagans (10:1-11).

CHRONOLOGICAL SUMMARY

Ezra retraces events in Judah from 538 to about 450 BC.

538–536 BC. After Cyrus's decree allowing Jews to return to their homeland (538 BC, 1:1-4), a group of about 50,000 returnees set out to restore worship in Jerusalem, where they reestablished the Jewish community, built a new altar (1:5–3:6), and began rebuilding the Temple (3:7-13). These Jews refused to compromise their beliefs by joining together with local unbelievers to rebuild the Temple. Before long, all progress in their rebuilding effort stopped because of local opposition (4:1-5).

520–516 BC. Almost two decades later, God used the prophets Haggai and Zechariah to motivate his people to continue rebuilding the Temple (5:1–6:12). The Jews responded, and while official letters were sent to and from the royal Persian court, the Temple was completed in 515 BC without further interference (see also Hag 1:2-6; Zech 4:9; 6:12-15; 8:9).

486–445 BC. Ezra reports on later opposition the Jews experienced during their initial attempt to rebuild the city and its walls (4:6-23).

TIMELINE

605–562 BC
Nebuchadnezzar II as king of Babylon

605 BC
Nebuchadnezzar first invades Judah

about 605~535 BC
Daniel in Babylon

586 BC
Nebuchadnezzar destroys Jerusalem, takes people of Judah into exile

559–530 BC
Cyrus II as king of Persia

553?–539 BC
Belshazzar as regent of Babylon (for Nabonidus)

Oct 539 BC
Cyrus II conquers Babylon

538 BC
Cyrus's decree allows exiles to return to Judea, Sheshbazzar leads the first group of exiles to Jerusalem

Oct 537 BC
Temple rebuilding begins

530–522 BC
Cambyses II as king of Persia

521–486 BC
Darius I as king of Persia

Aug 29–Dec 18, 520 BC
Haggai as prophet

Sept 21, 520 BC
Temple rebuilding resumes

Nov 520–Dec 7, 518 BC
Zechariah as prophet

515 BC
Temple rebuilding is completed

486–465 BC
Xerxes I (Ahasuerus) as king of Persia

479~478 BC
Esther becomes queen of Persia

465–424 BC
Artaxerxes I as king of Persia

458 BC
Ezra travels to Jerusalem

445 BC
Nehemiah travels to Jerusalem

445–433 BC
Nehemiah as governor of Judea

Oct 2, 445 BC
Jerusalem's wall is completed

400s BC
Malachi as prophet

458 BC. Ezra traveled to Jerusalem to administer government affairs (7:1-26). As he began his official duties, Ezra learned that some people were not following the laws of Moses but were marrying unbelievers and defiling Israel. After Ezra interceded for God's mercy, he led an official judicial investigation of this matter. Many Israelites repented of their sins and divorced their pagan wives (9:1–10:44).

445 BC. Nehemiah arrived in Jerusalem and succeeded in rebuilding its walls amid much opposition and difficulty (see Neh 1–7).

AUTHORSHIP

In Jewish tradition, Ezra and Nehemiah are considered a single book written by Ezra. As a scribe, Ezra would have had access to many of the official documents included in the book. Some also maintain that Ezra wrote Chronicles because the last verses in 2 Chronicles (2 Chr 36:22-23) are very similar to the first verses in Ezra (1:1-3). The books have common vocabulary and similar theological viewpoints. Still, many recent scholars reject this conclusion on the grounds that the linguistic and theological differences between Chronicles and Ezra—Nehemiah far outweigh the similarities.

LANGUAGE AND SOURCES

Most of the OT was written in Hebrew. However, the book of Ezra contains two sections written in Aramaic (4:8–6:18 and 7:12-26), the common language of the Persian empire. The six official documents in these sections are: Rehum's letter to King Artaxerxes (4:8-16), Artaxerxes' letter to Rehum (4:17-22), Tattenai's letter to King Darius (5:6-17), Cyrus's decree to build the Temple in Jerusalem (6:3-5), Darius's letter to Tattenai (6:6-12), and Artaxerxes' letter to Ezra (7:12-26). The authentic character of these documents helps verify the truthfulness of Ezra's account. They also demonstrate how God used pagan officials to accomplish his sovereign plan.

Ezra also includes several documents written in Hebrew: the decree of Cyrus (1:2-4); a list of Temple vessels (1:9-11); a list of the Israelites who returned to Jerusalem first (2:1-69); a list of those who returned with Ezra (8:1-14); a list of treasures Ezra brought to Jerusalem with him (8:26-27); and a list of the men who divorced pagan wives (10:18-44). These lists assured the Jewish people that Ezra kept accurate records. Only the original holy objects would be used in the Temple, only those on the official list of Israelites could worship at the Temple, and only the men who divorced pagan wives would be included in the holy people of God. By including these details, Ezra took great care to distinguish between what was holy and what was not.

[Ezra] calls us back to a renewed obedience to God's Word, a fresh realization of the power of prayer, and wholehearted commitment to the work of God.

S. K. EVERS
Doing a Great Work (1996)

MEANING AND MESSAGE

The people of God felt helpless as they returned to Jerusalem from exile in Babylon. They faced the threat of robbers on their long trip back to Jerusalem, opposition to their presence in Jerusalem from neighboring states and foreigners who had settled there, inability to influence Persian government policies, and the enormous task of rebuilding a nation in ruins. How could they follow God when so many things were out of their control? Ezra focuses on four key themes to explain how God accomplishes his will in the lives of his people.

1. *Everything that happens results from God's sovereign control over Israel's history.* Just as God had foretold (Isa 44:28–45:1; Jer 29:10), he moved Cyrus to allow the Jews to return to Jerusalem after seventy years of exile (1:1-4). Later, God promised that treasures from other nations would flow to Jerusalem to rebuild the Temple (Hag 2:7-8); this happened (6:6-12) because God changed Darius's heart (6:22). Later, when Ezra came to Jerusalem, God's gracious hand moved Artaxerxes to give Ezra everything he needed (7:6). It was God who protected the Jews from attack as they traveled to Jerusalem (8:22, 31). Ezra recognized that the future of the nation was in God's hand (9:6-15). Only a believer who is convinced that God is sovereign over this world will be able to remain faithful to God in the midst of conflict, difficulty, and discouragement.

2. *God's people must be pure and separate from sinfulness in this world.* As a priest from the line of Aaron (7:1-5), Ezra was strong in his conviction regarding separateness. So were the early returnees who refused to cooperate with the local pagan people (4:1-5). While this led to many years of frustration and conflict, the people knew that they could not compromise the purity of their faith and still remain the people of God. When Ezra returned to Jerusalem, this commitment was not evident among those living there (9:1-2). Ezra recognized the crisis (9:3-15) and led the people to renew their covenant with God and to separate themselves from these pagan people (10:1-11).

3. *Following God's word is of primary importance.* As a scribe, Ezra was determined to study and obey the law of God and to teach it to others (7:10). Ezra repeatedly explained his decisions by pointing to God's instructions in Scripture. The king of Persia had instructed Ezra to teach and enforce the Mosaic laws (7:14, 23-25), and that is exactly what Ezra did (e.g., 8:35; 9:1–10:15).

4. *Intercessory prayer invites God's compassion and power.* Ezra's prayer of confession (9:6-15) is a model of humility in seeking God's grace. Ezra knew that these sinful people would not be moved by a sternly worded sermon condemning them. Instead, he tore his clothes, wept, and mourned over the sinfulness of the nation. God powerfully used his confession to pierce the hearts of the people, and a great revival took place (9:6–10:15). In a similar manner, Ezra had earlier taught those who were returning to Jerusalem with him to fast and pray for safety on their journey because only God could protect them from attack (8:21-23)—and so he did (8:31-32).

God's recurrent action in Israel's history proved to the postexilic community that they represented the continuation of God's redemptive plan. . . . In God's providence this was a step in the preparation for the New Testament transition to the church under the new covenant.

M. BRENEMAN
Ezra, Nehemiah, Esther (1993)

FURTHER READING

M. BRENEMAN
Ezra, Nehemiah, Esther (1993)

F. CHARLES FENSHAM
The Books of Ezra and Nehemiah (1982)

DEREK KIDNER
Ezra & Nehemiah (1979)

GARY V. SMITH
Ezra-Nehemiah in *Cornerstone Biblical Commentary*, vol. 5b (2010)

1. THE PEOPLE RETURN TO REBUILD THE TEMPLE (1:1–6:22)

God Brings Back the Exiles (1:1–2:70)

King Cyrus Permits the Exiles to Return

Ezra 1:1-4 // 2 Chr 36:22-23

1 In the first year of King Cyrus of Persia,
the LORD fulfilled the prophecy he had
given through Jeremiah. He stirred the heart
of Cyrus to put this proclamation in writing
and to send it throughout his kingdom:

2“This is what King Cyrus of Persia says:
“The LORD, the God of heaven, has given
me all the kingdoms of the earth. He has
appointed me to build him a Temple at
Jerusalem, which is in Judah. 3Any of you
who are his people may go to Jerusalem in
Judah to rebuild this Temple of the LORD,
the God of Israel, who lives in Jerusalem.
And may your God be with you!
4Wherever this Jewish remnant is found,
let their neighbors contribute toward
their expenses by giving them silver
and gold, supplies for the journey, and
livestock, as well as a voluntary offering
for the Temple of God in Jerusalem.”

5Then God stirred the hearts of the
priests and Levites and the leaders of the
tribes of Judah and Benjamin to go to Jerusalem to rebuild the Temple of the LORD.
6And all their neighbors assisted by giving
them articles of silver and gold, supplies for
the journey, and livestock. They gave them
many valuable gifts in addition to all the
voluntary offerings.

7King Cyrus himself brought out the articles that King Nebuchadnezzar had taken
from the LORD’s Temple in Jerusalem and
had placed in the temple of his own gods.

1:1-3 //2 Chr 36:22-23
1:1 Jer 25:11-12; 29:10-14
1:2 Isa 44:28; 45:1-13
1:3 Dan 6:26
1:5 2 Chr 36:22
1:7 2 Kgs 24:13; 25:13-16; 2 Chr 36:7-18; Ezra 6:5

CYRUS II, THE GREAT (1:1-11)

Ezra 3:7; 4:1-5; 5:6-17; 6:14-15
2 Chr 36:22-23
Isa 44:28–45:13; 48:14-16
Dan 6:28; 10:1

Cyrus II, the Great, king of Persia (559–530 BC), founded the great Persian empire. From ancient Near Eastern texts, we know that he was king of Persia when it was a small nation. His father was king of Persia, and his mother was the daughter of the king of the Medes. Cyrus conquered the Medes in 549 BC and combined the two nations into one. He conquered Lydia in Asia Minor in 547 BC, then turned to the east and brought Parthia and part of India into the Persian empire. Finally, on October 29, 539 BC, Cyrus conquered the city of Babylon and brought Babylonia into his empire (see Dan 5:30-31).

After conquering Babylon, Cyrus issued a decree (found on the Cyrus Cylinder) that allowed Jewish people to return home. The part of this decree dealing with the Jews has been recorded in 2 Chr 36:22-23 and Ezra 1:1-3. Cyrus commissioned the Jews to rebuild their temple and society.

Isaiah named Cyrus as Judah’s future deliverer (Isa 44:28–45:13) and even called him the Lord’s anointed (Isa 45:1, Hebrew *mashiakh,* “messiah”). Israel regarded Cyrus as called and empowered by God to free them. Cyrus was not the Messiah, but what he did served as an example of what the Messiah, Jesus Christ, would later do in setting God’s people free from servitude.

1:1-3 The first three verses of Ezra appear almost verbatim in 2 Chr 36:22-23, suggesting continuity between the books.

1:1 The ***first year*** of Cyrus’s reign over Babylon was 538 BC. ***King Cyrus*** II reigned over ***Persia*** from 559 to 530 BC. Cyrus and his Persian forces defeated the city of Babylon in October, 539 BC, just as Daniel had predicted (Dan 5). • ***the prophecy . . . through Jeremiah:*** God had promised to return his people after seventy years in exile (see Jer 25:11-12; 29:10). • God’s power over the ***heart*** and mind of this pagan king moved him to enact the decree that follows (see also Isa 13:17; 41:2, 25; Jer 50:9). God is sovereign, even when rulers and nations do not recognize his authority (Isa 10:5, 12-14).

1:2 Though Cyrus speaks of ***the LORD, the God of heaven,*** Cyrus actually was a Zoroastrian. His proclamation, written in Hebrew, was probably political propaganda to gain Jewish support for his rule. In a similar statement to the Babylonians, Cyrus claimed to worship their chief god, Marduk. However, his words here do reflect that God had ***appointed*** him ***to build him a Temple at Jerusalem*** (see Isa 44:28; 45:1, 13). He might have learned of such prophecies from Daniel, who served in his court as a high government official (see Dan 6; 9; 10, where Cyrus is apparently referred to by his Median name, Darius). God had long planned to raise up Cyrus and give him a vision to restore worship at Jerusalem (Isa 44:28; 45:13; 48:14-15).

1:3 ***Any of you who are his people may go:*** The Assyrians and Babylonians had ruled their empires by deporting people and spreading them out in cities throughout their empires. The Persians, by contrast, returned exiled people to their homelands, expecting the returned people to be thankful, obey the Persians, and pay their taxes.

1:4 Cyrus was probably not urging Babylonian ***neighbors*** of the ***Jewish remnant*** to help the Hebrews. Rather, he was encouraging Jews who had decided to stay in Babylon to help their countrymen who were returning to Jerusalem.

1:5-6 As he had done with the heart of Cyrus (1:1), ***God stirred the hearts*** of Israel’s leaders. • Very few ***priests*** and ***Levites*** actually responded (see 2:36-42). Most of the people who did respond were from two tribes, ***Judah*** and ***Benjamin.*** Persian documents show that many Jews stayed in Babylon, where they had homes, businesses, and relatives. A dangerous four-month trip back to the desolate city of Jerusalem, now inhabited by foreigners, was not an inviting choice compared to their comfortable life in Babylon. It was much easier to give ***many valuable gifts*** and ***voluntary offerings*** to those who did return.

1:7 Many ***articles . . . from the LORD’s Temple*** had been taken to Babylon (see 2 Chr 36:7; Dan 1:2). By putting these

1:8
Ezra 5:14-16
2:1-70
//Neh 7:6-73
2:1
2 Kgs 24:14-16; 25:11
2 Chr 36:20
2:2
Neh 7:7
2:5-6
Neh 7:10-11

8Cyrus directed Mithredath, the treasurer of Persia, to count these items and present them to Sheshbazzar, the leader of the exiles returning to Judah. 9This is a list of the items that were returned:

gold basins	30
silver basins	1,000
silver incense burners	29
10 gold bowls	30
silver bowls	410
other items	1,000

11In all, there were 5,400 articles of gold and silver. Sheshbazzar brought all of these along when the exiles went from Babylon to Jerusalem.

Exiles Who Returned with Zerubbabel

2 Here is the list of the Jewish exiles of the provinces who returned from their captivity. King Nebuchadnezzar had deported them to Babylon, but now they returned to Jerusalem and the other towns in Judah where they originally lived. 2Their leaders were Zerubbabel, Jeshua, Nehemiah, Seraiah, Reelaiah, Mordecai, Bilshan, Mispar, Bigvai, Rehum, and Baanah.

This is the number of the men of Israel who returned from exile:

3 The family of Parosh	2,172
4 The family of Shephatiah	372
5 The family of Arah	775
6 The family of Pahath-moab (descendants of Jeshua and Joab)	2,812
7 The family of Elam	1,254
8 The family of Zattu	945
9 The family of Zaccai	760
10 The family of Bani	642
11 The family of Bebai	623
12 The family of Azgad	1,222
13 The family of Adonikam	666
14 The family of Bigvai	2,056

ZERUBBABEL (2:1–6:22)

Neh 7:7
Hag 1:1–2:23
Zech 4:1-14
Matt 1:12

Zerubbabel, a Babylonian-born Jew, returned to Judea in 538 BC as governor of Jerusalem under Persian rule. In 539 BC, Cyrus king of Persia declared that Jews captured and exiled from Judah might return to their homeland, and Zerubbabel led one of the first groups of those who returned.

Zerubbabel returned with the mission of rebuilding the Temple, and he constructed the altar first. Sacrifice could begin again once the Holy Place was restored. However, the community of Judea soon ran into opposition from the people in the land, who effectively shut down construction. The Judeans were distracted from the project until the preaching of Haggai and Zechariah encouraged them to begin working again. Zerubbabel was instrumental in leading and organizing the Temple rebuilding effort, which took about six years (520–515 BC).

Exuberant hope surrounded Zerubbabel, who was a direct descendant of King David (3:2; 1 Chr 3:17-19). Zechariah and Haggai both describe Zerubbabel in messianic terms as the one chosen by God to bring restoration to Israel (Hag 2:21-23; Zech 4:6-7). But Zerubbabel soon disappears from the biblical narrative without explanation. This early governor of Judea was not the Messiah. Jesus Christ, one of Zerubbabel's descendants (Matt 1:12), would later assume that glorious position.

items in his pagan temple, ***Nebuchadnezzar*** had attempted to show his god's power over the Hebrew God. However, God had promised the return of all the stolen items (see Jer 27:16-22). The items from the Temple were holy utensils, acceptable to God for worship and very valuable to the returning worshipers.

1:8 ***Sheshbazzar, the leader of the exiles returning to Judah*** (literally *Sheshbazzar, the prince of Judah*): Sheshbazzar was the Persian-appointed governor of Judah who laid the foundation of the Temple (5:14-16). Some believe that Zerubbabel (3:2, 8) was the same person with a new name (cp. Dan 1:7). However, both names are Babylonian, so it is more likely that these two leaders worked together on the Temple foundation and that Zerubbabel later took over as governor when Sheshbazzar died.

1:9-11 ***5,400 articles of gold and silver:*** The numbers listed total only 2,499 items. A parallel account, in the apocryphal book *1 Esdras* 2:13-15, lists 5,469 items, while a list in the Jewish historian Josephus's *Antiquities* 11.15 lists 5,220 objects. Ezra's shortened list illustrates the kind of items included but does not include every item. Keeping track of consecrated utensils reduced the possibility of confusing these sacred items with the pagan utensils used in the worship of other gods.

1:9 ***silver incense burners:*** The meaning of this Hebrew word is uncertain.

2:1-70 This chapter is the first of Ezra's major digressions from the main story line. The returning exiles needed to keep track of who the true Jews were so that the community could maintain its identity (by knowing whom they could marry) and theological purity (by knowing who could worship at the Temple). This list is not an initial list (cp. Neh 7:6-73) of all the Jews who returned to Jerusalem but a slightly later list (after Sheshbazzar had died) of people who had settled in their towns.

2:2 ***Jeshua*** (a variant spelling of *Joshua*), son of Jehozadak (3:2, 8), from the line of Aaron, was the high priest (Hag 1:1; Zech 3:1). The ***Nehemiah*** mentioned here is not the person who later built the walls of Jerusalem, nor is this ***Mordecai*** the famous relative of Esther.

2:3-20 ***The family of:*** In the ancient Near East, an individual's identity was

15 The family of Adin 454
16 The family of Ater
(descendants of Hezekiah) 98
17 The family of Bezai 323
18 The family of Jorah 112
19 The family of Hashum 223
20 The family of Gibbar 95
21 The people of Bethlehem 123
22 The people of Netophah 56
23 The people of Anathoth 128
24 The people of Beth-azmaveth 42
25 The people of Kiriath-jearim,
Kephirah, and Beeroth 743
26 The people of Ramah and Geba . . . 621
27 The people of Micmash 122
28 The people of Bethel and Ai. 223
29 The citizens of Nebo 52
30 The citizens of Magbish 156
31 The citizens of West Elam. 1,254
32 The citizens of Harim 320
33 The citizens of Lod, Hadid, and Ono . 725
34 The citizens of Jericho 345
35 The citizens of Senaah. 3,630

36 These are the priests who returned from exile:
The family of Jedaiah (through
the line of Jeshua) 973
37 The family of Immer 1,052
38 The family of Pashhur 1,247
39 The family of Harim 1,017

40 These are the Levites who returned from exile:
The families of Jeshua and Kadmiel
(descendants of Hodaviah) 74
41 The singers of the family of Asaph . 128
42 The gatekeepers of the families of
Shallum, Ater, Talmon, Akkub,
Hatita, and Shobai 139

43 The descendants of the following Temple servants returned from exile:
Ziha, Hasupha, Tabbaoth,
44 Keros, Siaha, Padon,
45 Lebanah, Hagabah, Akkub,
46 Hagab, Shalmai, Hanan,
47 Giddel, Gahar, Reaiah,
48 Rezin, Nekoda, Gazzam,
49 Uzza, Paseah, Besai,
50 Asnah, Meunim, Nephusim,
51 Bakbuk, Hakupha, Harhur,
52 Bazluth, Mehida, Harsha,
53 Barkos, Sisera, Temah,
54 Neziah, and Hatipha.

55 The descendants of these servants of King Solomon returned from exile:
Sotai, Hassophereth, Peruda,
56 Jaalah, Darkon, Giddel,
57 Shephatiah, Hattil, Pokereth-hazzebaim,
and Ami.

58 In all, the Temple servants and the descendants of Solomon's servants numbered 392.

59 Another group returned at this time
from the towns of Tel-melah, Tel-harsha, Kerub, Addan, and Immer. However, they could
not prove that they or their families were descendants of Israel.
60 This group included
the families of Delaiah, Tobiah, and Nekoda—
a total of 652 people.
61 Three families of priests—Hobaiah,
Hakkoz, and Barzillai—also returned. (This
Barzillai had married a woman who was a descendant of Barzillai of Gilead, and he had
taken her family name.)
62 They searched
for their names in the genealogical records,
but they were not found, so they were

2:36 1 Chr 24:7-18
2:38 1 Chr 9:12
2:39 1 Chr 24:8
2:40 Neh 12:24
2:43 1 Chr 9:2
2:55-57 Neh 7:57-60
2:61 2 Sam 17:27
2:62 Num 3:10; 16:39-40 Ezra 2:59

closely connected to the question, "Who are your father and your family?" Ultimately, the priests were identified as the sons of Aaron. If this link could not be verified, they were barred from service (2:61-62). Others were identified by a well-known elder in their group.

2:21-35 *The people of . . . The citizens of:* Some of the returnees were identified by their towns of origin. Apparently, not all knew their genealogical histories or had large families with renowned leaders. Most of the cities mentioned were concentrated in a relatively small area in the vicinity of Jerusalem.

2:24 *Beth-azmaveth:* As in parallel text at Neh 7:28; Hebrew reads *Azmaveth.*

2:25 *Kiriath-jearim:* As in some Hebrew manuscripts and Greek version (see also Neh 7:29); Hebrew reads *Kiriath-arim.*

2:31 *of West Elam:* Or *of the other Elam.*

2:36-42 *the priests . . . the Levites:* Only seventy-four Levites returned to Jerusalem—a very low number. Ezra later worked hard to get thirty-eight more to come with him (see note on 8:18).

2:41-42 The *singers* played instruments and sang for worship at the Temple (1 Chr 25; Pss 73–83) while the *gatekeepers* regulated the Temple gates and storehouses (1 Chr 9:26-27; 2 Chr 23:19; Neh 12:25). • *Asaph* was one of the three Levites David had appointed to conduct music at the Temple (1 Chr 16:5, 7), and he wrote a collection of psalms (Pss 50, 73–83). His *family* carried on his work (1 Chr 25:1-7).

2:43-54 The *Temple servants* were probably descendants of the Gibeonites (Josh 9:23-27). They assisted the Levites (8:20) by carrying water and wood and by sweeping floors.

2:46 *Shalmai:* As in an alternate reading of the Masoretic Text (see also Neh 7:48); the other alternate reads *Shamlai.*

2:55-58 The *descendants* of the *servants of King Solomon* are connected with the Temple servants (2:43-54). Their names might indicate their responsibilities: e.g., ***Hassophereth*** ("the scribe") probably kept inventories, and ***Pokereth-hazzebaim*** ("gazelle-hunter") likely hunted game.

2:59-60 Some returnees believed in Israel's God but had no genealogical records to *prove* that they were Israelites. Without this information, the other Israelites did not know whether to treat them as brothers and intermarry with them or to treat them as outsiders. The genealogies in 1 Chr 1–9 illustrate how carefully many family histories were kept.

2:61-63 *were not found:* The lack of a genealogy was problematic for three families (2:61-62). They were excluded

2:63 Exod 28:30; Lev 2:3, 10
2:64 Neh 7:66-67
2:69 Ezra 8:25-34
2:70 Neh 7:73
3:1 Neh 7:73; 8:1
3:2 Lev 1:1-17; 6:8-13; Deut 12:5-6; 1 Chr 3:17-20; Ezra 2:2; Neh 12:1, 8; Hag 1:1; Zech 6:11
3:3 Num 28:1-8

disqualified from serving as priests. 63The governor told them not to eat the priests' share of food from the sacrifices until a priest could consult the LORD about the matter by using the Urim and Thummim—the sacred lots.

64So a total of 42,360 people returned to Judah, 65in addition to 7,337 servants and 200 singers, both men and women. 66They took with them 736 horses, 245 mules, 67435 camels, and 6,720 donkeys.

68When they arrived at the Temple of the LORD in Jerusalem, some of the family leaders made voluntary offerings toward the rebuilding of God's Temple on its original site, 69and each leader gave as much as he could. The total of their gifts came to 61,000 gold coins, 6,250 pounds of silver, and 100 robes for the priests.

70So the priests, the Levites, the singers, the gatekeepers, the Temple servants, and some of the common people settled in villages near Jerusalem. The rest of the people returned to their own towns throughout Israel.

Faithfulness Brings Opposition (3:1–4:23)
The Altar Is Rebuilt in Jerusalem

3 In early autumn, when the Israelites had settled in their towns, all the people assembled in Jerusalem with a unified purpose. 2Then Jeshua son of Jehozadak joined his fellow priests and Zerubbabel son of Shealtiel with his family in rebuilding the altar of the God of Israel. They wanted to sacrifice burnt offerings on it, as instructed in the Law of Moses, the man of God. 3Even though the people were afraid of the local residents, they rebuilt the altar at its old site. Then they began to sacrifice

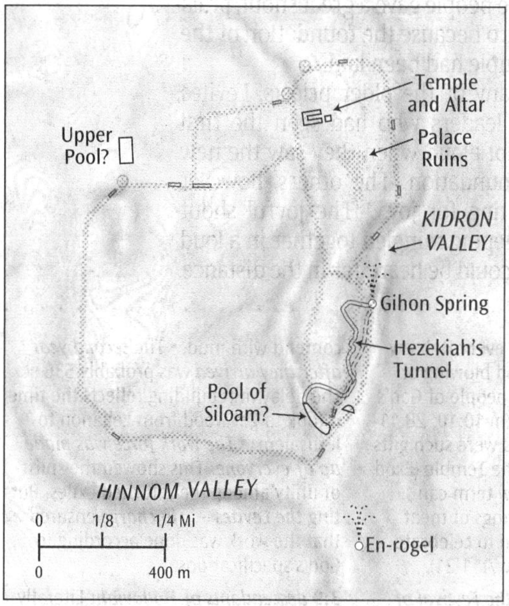

◀ **Jerusalem at the Time of Zerubbabel, 520–515 BC** (3:1–6:15). When the first wave of exiles returned to Jerusalem in 538 BC, the altar was rebuilt first, and the daily sacrifices were resumed. Construction of the new Temple began in the spring of 536 BC, and the foundation was quickly laid, but work was soon halted due to opposition. The work was resumed in 520 BC and completed in 515 BC. When Ezra arrived with the second wave of exiles in 458 BC, he brought with him many furnishings and funds for the newly rebuilt Temple (7:21-24; 8:24-34). The wall of Jerusalem remained in ruins until 445 BC, when it was rebuilt under Nehemiah's leadership (Neh 1:1–7:3).

from priestly privileges or responsibilities until the high priest received divine direction through the use of ***the Urim and Thummim*** to determine the will of God (see Exod 28:30; Num 27:21). Although using *the Urim and Thummim* resembled throwing dice or drawing straws, when done by the priest, the result was a divine decision rather than blind chance.

2:64-66 ***42,360 people:*** This number, which does not match the total of individuals (28,774) listed in 2:3-42, might include children. • The large number of ***servants*** and animals shows that some of the Jews who returned were wealthy.

2:68-69 As when the Tabernacle was built (Exod 25:2-7; 35:4-9) and the Temple was renovated (2 Kings 12), the people gave ***voluntary offerings*** to finance this effort. These funds supplemented the provincial grant by Darius (6:8) and gifts from Israelites who stayed in Babylon (1:6). Each ***gave as much as he could*** based on his resources.

2:69 ***61,000 gold coins:*** Hebrew *61,000 darics of gold,* about 1,100 pounds or 500 kilograms in weight. Each daric was worth a month's wages for a professional soldier. • ***6,250 pounds:*** Hebrew *5,000 minas* [3,000 kilograms]. Each mina weighed 20 ounces and was equal to 60 shekels of silver; each shekel was worth an average worker's monthly wages.

3:1–4:5 After resettling in various towns in Judah, the community turned to restoring the worship of God at Jerusalem. They quickly rebuilt the altar and began regular sacrifices in time to celebrate the Jewish festivals (3:4), and then they began the more difficult task of rebuilding the Temple itself (3:8). Soon they faced opposition from local foreigners (4:1-5).

3:1 ***In early autumn:*** Literally *In the seventh month.* The year is not specified, so it may have been during Cyrus's first year (538 BC) or second year (537 BC). The seventh month of the ancient Hebrew lunar calendar occurred within the months of September/October 538 BC and October/November 537 BC. Festivals during the seventh month included the Festival of Trumpets (see Lev 23:23-25), the Day of Atonement (see Lev 16), and the Festival of Shelters (see Lev 23:34-36).

3:2 ***Jeshua*** (Hag 1:1; Zech 3:1) was the high priest (Neh 12:1). However, Ezra never used this title (2:2; 3:2; 4:3; 5:2), which suggests that the title was given after the Temple was completed (6:15). • ***Jehozadak:*** Hebrew *Jozadak,* a variant spelling of Jehozadak; also in 3:8. • ***Zerubbabel*** served as the Persian-appointed governor of Judah (Hag 1:1), most likely after the death of Sheshbazzar (see note on 1:8). He was the grandson of King Jehoiachin of Judah (1 Chr 3:17).

3:3 The ***local residents*** were foreigners resettled from abroad by the Assyrian king Esarhaddon (680–669 BC) after the people of the northern kingdom of Israel were exiled in 722 BC (2 Kgs 17:24-40). Some had moved into the Jerusalem area during Judah's

burnt offerings on the altar to the LORD each morning and evening.

4They celebrated the Festival of Shelters as prescribed in the Law, sacrificing the number of burnt offerings specified for each day of the festival. 5They also offered the regular burnt offerings and the offerings required for the new moon celebrations and the annual festivals as prescribed by the LORD. The people also gave voluntary offerings to the LORD. 6Fifteen days before the Festival of Shelters began, the priests had begun to sacrifice burnt offerings to the LORD. This was even before they had started to lay the foundation of the LORD's Temple.

Foundation of the Temple Is Celebrated

7Then the people hired masons and carpenters and bought cedar logs from the people of Tyre and Sidon, paying them with food, wine, and olive oil. The logs were brought down from the Lebanon mountains and floated along the coast of the Mediterranean Sea to Joppa, for King Cyrus had given permission for this.

8The construction of the Temple of God began in midspring, during the second year after they arrived in Jerusalem. The work force was made up of everyone who had returned from exile, including Zerubbabel son of Shealtiel, Jeshua son of Jehozadak and his fellow priests, and all the Levites. The Levites who were twenty years old or older were put in charge of rebuilding the LORD's Temple. 9The workers at the Temple of God were supervised by Jeshua with his sons and relatives, and Kadmiel and his sons, all descendants of Hodaviah. They were helped in this task by the Levites of the family of Henadad.

10When the builders completed the foundation of the LORD's Temple, the priests put on their robes and took their places to blow their trumpets. And the Levites, descendants of Asaph, clashed their cymbals to praise the LORD, just as King David had prescribed. 11With praise and thanks, they sang this song to the LORD:

"He is so good!
    His faithful love for Israel endures
        forever!"

Then all the people gave a great shout, praising the LORD because the foundation of the LORD's Temple had been laid.

12But many of the older priests, Levites, and other leaders who had seen the first Temple wept aloud when they saw the new Temple's foundation. The others, however, were shouting for joy. 13The joyful shouting and weeping mingled together in a loud noise that could be heard far in the distance.

3:4 Exod 23:16; Num 29:12; Neh 8:14
3:5 Exod 29:38, 42; Num 28:11-14; 29:39
3:7 1 Kgs 5:9-11; 2 Chr 2:10-16; Ezra 1:2; 6:3
3:8 Num 4:3; Ezra 3:2; 4:2
3:9 Ezra 2:40
3:10 1 Chr 6:31; 25:1
3:11 1 Chr 16:34, 41; 2 Chr 7:3; Neh 12:24, 40; Ps 106:1
3:12 Hag 2:3

---

seventy-year exile. A pagan altar might have been erected on the site, and it needed to be torn down before the new one, dedicated to the Lord, could be built. • *at its old site* (Literally *on its foundations*): It was important to place the altar at the exact sacred spot where Solomon's altar had been to connect with the authentic worship carried on before the Exile. • Daily *morning and evening* sacrifices (see Exod 29:38-42; Num 28:3-8) dedicated the day to God.

3:4 The seven-day *Festival of Shelters . . . prescribed in the Law* (Lev 23:33-36; Num 29:12-38; Deut 16:13-16) reminded the people of God's guidance and care during the forty years the nation spent in tents during the wilderness journey from Egypt to the Promised Land. This festival was especially significant to those who had just experienced a similar journey from a foreign land, living in tents as they walked to the Promised Land.

3:5-6 The catalog of sacrifices, offered even before the Temple's foundation was laid, showed the people's enthusiasm for faithfully worshiping God at every opportunity. They did everything exactly as they were instructed in the law. • The *new moon celebrations* took place on the first day of every Hebrew month; the sacrifices and blowing of trumpets reminded the people of God's covenant with them (Num 10:10; 28:11-15). • *Voluntary offerings* were such gifts as money for building the Temple (Exod 35:29; 36:3). The Hebrew term can also refer to peace offerings of meat or bread that were eaten to celebrate fellowship with God (Lev 7:11-21).

3:6 *Fifteen days before the Festival of Shelters began:* Literally *On the first day of the seventh month.* This day in the ancient Hebrew lunar calendar occurred in September or October. *The Festival of Shelters* began on the fifteenth day of the seventh month.

3:7 *Tyre and Sidon:* Few tall and straight trees grew in the dry climate of Judah, and those that had grown in Israel had already been cut down. Therefore, skilled laborers were hired in countries that had tall trees (see also 1 Chr 22:1-5; 2 Chr 2:7-16). • *the Mediterranean Sea:* Literally *the sea.*

3:8 *in midspring:* Literally *in the second month.* This month in the ancient Hebrew lunar calendar occurred within the months of April and May 536 BC. In midspring, the dry season was beginning and workers would not have to contend with mud. • The *second year after they arrived* was probably 536 BC. The delay in rebuilding reflects the time it took to get wood from Lebanon to Jerusalem. • *The work force was made up of everyone:* This showed the spirit of unity among the returned exiles. Putting *the Levites . . . in charge* ensured that the work was done according to God's specifications.

3:9 *descendants of Hodaviah:* Literally *sons of Judah* (Hebrew *bene-yehudah*); *bene* might also be read here as the proper name Binnui, and *yehudah* is probably another name for *Hodaviah.* Cp. 2:40; Neh 7:43; *1 Esdras* 5:58.

3:10-11 The music at this dedication ceremony sounded similar to the singing when Solomon first brought the Ark into the Temple (2 Chr 5:12-13). Both events caused the worshipers to give *praise and thanks . . . to the LORD* for his faithful covenant love and goodness. • *Asaph:* See note on 2:41-42. • *as King David had prescribed:* See 1 Chr 25:1-7.

3:12 Those who *wept aloud* either were disappointed that the foundation of the Temple wasn't as wonderful as the old one had been (cp. Hag 2:3) or were deeply moved with joy at seeing the Temple of the Lord restored.

4:1 Ezra 4:7-10
4:2 2 Kgs 17:32; 19:37
4:3 Ezra 1:1-4; 6:3-5 Neh 2:20
4:4 Ezra 3:3
4:6 Esth 1:1 Dan 9:1
4:7 2 Kgs 18:26 Isa 36:11 Dan 2:4

Opposition to Rebuilding the Temple

4 The enemies of Judah and Benjamin
heard that the exiles were rebuilding a
Temple to the LORD, the God of Israel. 2 So
they approached Zerubbabel and the other
leaders and said, "Let us build with you, for
we worship your God just as you do. We
have sacrificed to him ever since King Esarhaddon of Assyria brought us here."

3 But Zerubbabel, Jeshua, and the other
leaders of Israel replied, "You may have no
part in this work. We alone will build the
Temple for the LORD, the God of Israel, just
as King Cyrus of Persia commanded us."

4 Then the local residents tried to discourage and frighten the people of Judah to keep
them from their work. 5 They bribed agents
to work against them and to frustrate their
plans. This went on during the entire reign
of King Cyrus of Persia and lasted until
King Darius of Persia took the throne.

Later Opposition to Rebuilding the Walls

6 Years later when Xerxes began his reign,
the enemies of Judah wrote a letter of accusation against the people of Judah and
Jerusalem.

7 Even later, during the reign of King Artaxerxes of Persia, the enemies of Judah, led

Purity and Identity (4:1-5)

Ezra 5:11; 9:1–10:11
Gen 27:46–28:5
Exod 19:4-6; 34:15-16
Lev 19:2
Deut 7:3-4
Josh 23:12-13
1 Kgs 11:1-5
Mal 2:15
1 Cor 6:15-20
2 Cor 6:14-18
2 Tim 2:21-22
1 Pet 2:9-10

One of Ezra's main purposes in writing was to remind the Jews who had returned to Jerusalem of their need to remain pure in their beliefs and commitments. When Ezra arrived in Jerusalem, he found that the people had intermarried with pagan foreigners, even though doing so was not permitted in God's law (see Deut 7:3-4; Josh 23:12-13). As a result, their identity as God's holy nation was in danger of disintegrating (9:1-2).

In order to impress on his readers the need for separation from these foreigners, Ezra recounts how those who first returned to Jerusalem refused to cooperate with the pagan people living around them (4:1-5). These people claimed to worship the same God, but they actually worshiped several gods in addition to Israel's God. If the Jews had joined with these people, they soon would have compromised their beliefs and become ungodly, just as Israel had done before the Exile (see Exod 34:15-16; 1 Kgs 11:1-5; 2 Kgs 16:3). The leaders of Israel understood the danger of accommodating these foreigners. They learned from their ancestors' experience and refused to compromise the purity of their faith for the sake of peace. They carefully followed God's instructions in everything they did (3:2, 9; 6:18). If they were going to identify themselves as "the servants of the God of heaven and earth" (5:11), they would need to please and serve him and no other gods.

God is holy, and he made the covenant with Israel to establish a holy nation (Exod 19:4-6; Lev 19:2). Israel's identity as God's people required purity in worship and in social relationships (10:1-11). Similarly, believers today are identified as God's holy people (1 Pet 2:9), a title that speaks of theological purity. Paul admonished the Corinthians to refrain from marrying unbelievers—for Christ and Satan have no fellowship. Righteousness and unrighteousness do not mix (2 Cor 6:14-15). The people of God must be separate by not touching unclean things and not marrying unbelievers (2 Cor 6:16-18).

4:1 ***Judah and Benjamin:*** Most of the exiles who had returned were from these two tribes of Israel (1:5).

4:2 ***King Esarhaddon of Assyria*** (680–669 BC) had deported the people of Israel to foreign lands and had relocated other conquered peoples to the land of Israel during the reign of King Manasseh in Judah. These foreigners had learned about the Lord when they entered the land of Israel but had also continued to worship their old gods (2 Kgs 17:27-34, 40-41).

4:3 The key political, religious, and tribal leaders spoke with a unified voice against the foreigners' proposal, which would have opened the door for their idolatrous beliefs. The Jews did not want to make the same mistake as their ancestors, who were sent into exile as a result of worshiping the false gods of the Canaanites. • ***as King Cyrus of Persia commanded us:*** See 1:2-4.

4:4 Realizing that they would have no way to influence an established Jewish community (4:1-3), the foreigners took hostile measures to neutralize the growing political power of the Israelites.

4:5 The people paid a heavy price for their uncompromising commitment to holiness. • ***during the entire reign of King Cyrus:*** Until 530 BC. • ***Darius*** I reigned 521–486 BC. Work on the Temple was not finished until 515 BC (see 6:15).

4:6-23 These verses are a parenthetical discussion of later opposition to Jewish rebuilding efforts. The account actually belongs with much later events in the reign of Xerxes (486–465 BC) and Artaxerxes I (465–424 BC), but it is included here because it fits with the theme of opposition. Chronologically, 4:6 fits between chs 6 and 7, while 4:7-23 fits before Neh 1.

4:6 ***Xerxes:*** Hebrew *Ahasuerus,* another name for Xerxes. He reigned 486–465 BC and was Esther's husband.

4:7 ***Artaxerxes*** [I] reigned 465–424 BC. The exact date of these events is unknown, but they might have occurred around the same time as an Egyptian revolt in 448 BC (a few years before Artaxerxes sent Nehemiah to Jerusalem in 445 BC). If so, ***the enemies of Judah*** and Artaxerxes probably thought that the Jews would revolt as the Egyptians

by Bishlam, Mithredath, and Tabeel, sent
a letter to Artaxerxes in the Aramaic language, and it was translated for the king.
8 Rehum the governor and Shimshai the
court secretary wrote the letter, telling King
Artaxerxes about the situation in Jerusalem.
9 They greeted the king for all their colleagues—the judges and local leaders, the
people of Tarpel, the Persians, the Babylonians, and the people of Erech and Susa (that
is, Elam). 10 They also sent greetings from the
rest of the people whom the great and noble
Ashurbanipal had deported and relocated
in Samaria and throughout the neighboring
lands of the province west of the Euphrates
River. 11 This is a copy of their letter:

"To King Artaxerxes, from your loyal
subjects in the province west of the
Euphrates River.
12 "The king should know that the
Jews who came here to Jerusalem from
Babylon are rebuilding this rebellious
and evil city. They have already laid
the foundation and will soon finish
its walls. 13 And the king should know
that if this city is rebuilt and its walls
are completed, it will be much to your
disadvantage, for the Jews will then
refuse to pay their tribute, customs,
and tolls to you.
14 "Since we are your loyal subjects and
do not want to see the king dishonored
in this way, we have sent the king this
information. 15 We suggest that a search
be made in your ancestors' records,
where you will discover what a rebellious
city this has been in the past. In fact, it
was destroyed because of its long and
troublesome history of revolt against
the kings and countries who controlled
it. 16 We declare to the king that if this
city is rebuilt and its walls are completed,
the province west of the Euphrates River
will be lost to you."

17 Then King Artaxerxes sent this reply:

"To Rehum the governor, Shimshai the
court secretary, and their colleagues
living in Samaria and throughout the
province west of the Euphrates River.
Greetings.
18 "The letter you sent has been
translated and read to me. 19 I ordered
a search of the records and have found
that Jerusalem has indeed been a hotbed
of insurrection against many kings. In
fact, rebellion and revolt are normal
there! 20 Powerful kings have ruled
over Jerusalem and the entire province
west of the Euphrates River, receiving
tribute, customs, and tolls. 21 Therefore,
issue orders to have these men stop
their work. That city must not be rebuilt
except at my express command. 22 Be
diligent, and don't neglect this matter,
for we must not permit the situation to
harm the king's interests."

23 When this letter from King Artaxerxes
was read to Rehum, Shimshai, and their colleagues, they hurried to Jerusalem. Then,
with a show of strength, they forced the
Jews to stop building.

4:8 Ezra 5:6
4:12 Ezra 5:3, 9
4:13 Ezra 7:24; Neh 5:4
4:18 Neh 8:8
4:20 1 Kgs 4:21, 24; 1 Chr 18:3; Ezra 4:13

had. • *Aramaic* was the international diplomatic language of the Persian empire.

4:8–6:18 The original text of 4:8–6:18 is in Aramaic.

4:9 Adding greetings from an assortment of key political figures and local ethnic leaders would give credibility to the letter's accusations and ensure that the message would have maximum political weight. • ***Judges*** were trusted court officials who knew the Persian laws. • Having the support of people from the Mesopotamian cities of Babylon and ***Erech*** and the Persian city of ***Susa*** would make the case against the Jews more persuasive.

4:10 ***Ashurbanipal*** (Aramaic *Osnappar,* another name for *Ashurbanipal,* 668–626 BC) ***had deported*** people from other conquered lands into the lands of Israel and Aram (see 2 Kgs 17:24-41). • The city of ***Samaria*** was the former capital of the northern kingdom of Israel. • ***the province west of the Euphrates River*** (literally *the province beyond the river;* also in 4:11, 16, 17, 20) included Syria, Israel, and Judah.

4:11-22 Ezra includes a copy in Aramaic of the letter sent to Artaxerxes and his reply.

4:13 A ***tribute*** was an annual fixed tax, ***customs*** were probably sales taxes, and ***tolls*** were probably charges for using roads. Previous rulers had collected considerable revenue from the region (4:20; cp. 1 Kgs 10:14-15).

4:14 ***Since we are your loyal subjects:*** Literally *Since we eat the salt of the palace.* This was a metaphor for taking an oath of loyalty to the king. • The letter's authors claimed that their only interest was to preserve the honor of the king, but they were actually grasping for power and political advantage over the Jews.

4:15-16 The Persians had access to Babylonian ***records,*** which described Jerusalem's revolts against Nebuchadnezzar (see 2 Kgs 24:1-7). • The claim that the Persians would lose the whole ***province west of the Euphrates*** (see note on 4:10) was an exaggeration: The Jews actually comprised a small minority in that province.

4:18 The letter was ***translated*** from Aramaic to Persian, the king's native language.

4:19-20 King Jehoiakim (609–598 BC) had rebelled against Babylon in about 601 BC, and King Zedekiah (597–586 BC) had rebelled in about 588 BC (see 2 Kgs 25:2).

4:21 ***except at my express command:*** Work on the walls remained stopped until 445 BC, when Nehemiah, Artaxerxes' cup-bearer, gained his permission to resume reconstruction (see Neh 2:1-6).

4:23 A military unit probably ***forced the Jews to stop building*** and enforced the king's wishes. Part of the rebuilt wall might have been torn down at this time (cp. Neh 1:3). • This verse ends the parenthetical section that began in 4:6.

4:24
Hag 1:1, 15
Zech 1:1

5:1
Ezra 6:14
Hag 1:1
Zech 1:1

5:2
Ezra 3:2

5:3
Ezra 1:3; 5:6, 9, 17; 6:6, 13

5:4
Ezra 5:10

5:5
Ezra 7:6, 28
Ps 33:18

5:11
1 Kgs 6:1-38
2 Chr 3:1-2

God Overcomes Opposition (4:24–6:22)

The Rebuilding Resumes

24So the work on the Temple of God in Jerusalem had stopped, and it remained at a
standstill until the second year of the reign
of King Darius of Persia.

5 At that time the prophets Haggai and
Zechariah son of Iddo prophesied to the
Jews in Judah and Jerusalem. They prophesied in the name of the God of Israel who
was over them. 2Zerubbabel son of Shealtiel
and Jeshua son of Jehozadak responded by
starting again to rebuild the Temple of God
in Jerusalem. And the prophets of God were
with them and helped them.
3But Tattenai, governor of the province
west of the Euphrates River, and Shethar-
bozenai and their colleagues soon arrived
in Jerusalem and asked, "Who gave you permission to rebuild this Temple and restore
this structure?" 4They also asked for the
names of all the men working on the Temple. 5But because their God was watching
over them, the leaders of the Jews were not
prevented from building until a report was
sent to Darius and he returned his decision.

Tattenai's Letter to King Darius

6This is a copy of the letter that Tattenai the
governor, Shethar-bozenai, and the other officials of the province west of the Euphrates
River sent to King Darius:

7"To King Darius. Greetings.
8"The king should know that we went
to the construction site of the Temple of
the great God in the province of Judah. It
is being rebuilt with specially prepared
stones, and timber is being laid in its
walls. The work is going forward with
great energy and success.
9"We asked the leaders, 'Who gave
you permission to rebuild this Temple
and restore this structure?' 10And we
demanded their names so that we could
tell you who the leaders were.
11"This was their answer: 'We are the
servants of the God of heaven and earth,

King of Persia	Dates	References
Cyrus II, the Great	559–530 BC	Ezra 1:1-8; 2 Chr 36:22-23; Isa 44:28–45:13; 48:14-15; Dan 1:21
Cyrus II conquers Babylon	*Oct 539 BC*	Dan 5:25-31
Cambyses II	530–522 BC	
Darius I	521–486 BC	Ezra 4:24–6:15; Hag 1:1; Zech 1:1
Xerxes I (Ahasuerus)	486–465 BC	Ezra 4:6; Esth 1:1–10:3
Artaxerxes I	465–424 BC	Ezra 4:7-23; 7:1-21; Neh 1:1; 5:14; 13:6
Darius II	424–405 BC	
Artaxerxes II	405–359 BC	
Artaxerxes III	359–338 BC	
Bogoas	338–336 BC	
Darius III	336–330 BC	
Alexander the Great conquers Persia	*331 BC*	Dan 8:5-7

▲ **The Kings of Persia (Ezra 4:5-7)**

4:24–5:5 Ezra now returns to telling about the building of the Temple in 520–515 BC.

4:24 ***The second year of the reign of King Darius of Persia*** was 520 BC. The narrative started in 4:1-5 is resumed at 4:24. The events of the following verses occurred approximately sixteen years after the events up through 4:5.

5:1 ***Haggai*** first prophesied on August 29, 520 BC (Hag 1:1). ***Zechariah*** began prophesying about two months later (Zech 1:1). The books of Haggai and Zechariah record their messages (see also 6:14).

5:2 The Jewish leaders had not led by faith (see Hag 1:1, 12). Now God's Spirit stirred them up (Hag 1:14), and they obeyed by getting to work. • ***Zerubbabel son of Shealtiel . . . Jeshua son of Jehozadak*** (Aramaic *Jozadak*, a variant spelling of *Jehozadak*): See note on 3:2. Zerubbabel and Jeshua figure prominently in the books of Haggai and Zechariah.

5:3 ***the province west of the Euphrates River:*** Literally *the province beyond the river;* also in 5:6. • ***Who gave you permission?*** Unlike the hostile opposition recorded in ch 4, this seems to have been a routine inquiry to make sure that everything was done according to official requirements.

5:5 ***God was watching over them:*** All credit goes to God's sovereign control of events, not to any human leader or prophet. God had promised that the ruins would be rebuilt (Isa 44:26).

5:6-17 Ezra includes a copy in Aramaic of Tattenai's letter to King Darius. Unlike the letter of 4:11-16, this letter was a straightforward inquiry into the validity of the Jews' activity.

5:6 ***other officials:*** A Persian term for *inspectors* or *investigators.*

5:8 ***the great God:*** This title was a Persian way of referring to an important high deity; it does not indicate that the provincial authorities believed in Israel's God. • Following the pattern of Solomon's Temple (1 Kgs 6:36), after every three rows of ***prepared stones,*** a layer of ***timber*** was ***laid in its walls*** (see 6:4) to reduce potential damage from earthquakes.

5:11 ***the God of heaven:*** This title would be understood by the Persians: He was the universal high God, not an insignificant local deity. • ***a great king of Israel:*** Solomon (see 1 Kgs 5–8).

and we are rebuilding the Temple that was built here many years ago by a great king of Israel. 12But because our ancestors angered the God of heaven, he abandoned them to King Nebuchadnezzar of Babylon, who destroyed this Temple and exiled the people to Babylonia. 13However, King Cyrus of Babylon, during the first year of his reign, issued a decree that the Temple of God should be rebuilt. 14King Cyrus returned the gold and silver cups that Nebuchadnezzar had taken from the Temple of God in Jerusalem and had placed in the temple of Babylon. These cups were taken from that temple and presented to a man named Sheshbazzar, whom King Cyrus appointed as governor of Judah. 15The king instructed him to return the cups to their place in Jerusalem and to rebuild the Temple of God there on its original site. 16So this Sheshbazzar came and laid the foundations of the Temple of God in Jerusalem. The people have been working on it ever since, though it is not yet completed.'

17"Therefore, if it pleases the king, we request that a search be made in the royal archives of Babylon to discover whether King Cyrus ever issued a decree to rebuild God's Temple in Jerusalem. And then let the king send us his decision in this matter."

Darius Approves the Rebuilding

6 So King Darius issued orders that a search be made in the Babylonian archives, which were stored in the treasury. 2But it was at the fortress at Ecbatana in the province of Media that a scroll was found. This is what it said:

"Memorandum:

3"In the first year of King Cyrus's reign, a decree was sent out concerning the Temple of God at Jerusalem.

"Let the Temple be rebuilt on the site where Jews used to offer their sacrifices, using the original foundations. Its height will be ninety feet, and its width will be ninety feet. 4Every three layers of specially prepared stones will be topped by a layer of timber. All expenses will be paid by the royal treasury. 5Furthermore, the gold and silver cups, which were taken to Babylon by Nebuchadnezzar from the Temple of God in Jerusalem, must be returned to Jerusalem and put back where they belong. Let them be taken back to the Temple of God."

6So King Darius sent this message:

"Now therefore, Tattenai, governor of the province west of the Euphrates River, and Shethar-bozenai, and your colleagues and other officials west of the Euphrates River—stay away from there! 7Do not disturb the construction of the Temple of God. Let it be rebuilt on its original site, and do not hinder the governor of Judah and the elders of the Jews in their work.

8"Moreover, I hereby decree that you are to help these elders of the Jews as they rebuild this Temple of God. You must pay the full construction costs, without delay, from my taxes collected in the province west of the Euphrates River so that the work will not be interrupted.

9"Give the priests in Jerusalem whatever is needed in the way of young bulls, rams, and male lambs for the burnt offerings presented to the God of

5:12 2 Kgs 24:2, 10; 25:1, 8-11; 2 Chr 36:6-20
5:13 Ezra 1:1-8
5:14 Ezra 1:7-8, 11; 5:16; 6:3-5; Dan 5:2
5:17 Ezra 6:1-2
6:1 Ezra 5:17
6:3 Ezra 3:10
6:4 1 Kgs 6:36
6:6 Ezra 5:3; 6:13

5:12 ***Nebuchadnezzar of Babylon:*** Literally *Nebuchadnezzar the Chaldean.* • ***destroyed this Temple and exiled the people:*** See 2 Kgs 25:9-17.

5:13 ***King Cyrus*** of Persia is here identified as the king ***of Babylon*** because Persia had conquered the Babylonian empire in 539 BC. • ***a decree:*** See 1:1-4.

5:14-15 The Jews provided detailed information that the Persians could check for accuracy (see 1:7-11).

5:16 Most likely, ***Sheshbazzar*** began the work and Zerubbabel finished it (see note on 1:8).

6:2 The ***fortress at Ecbatana,*** the king's summer home, was located about 300 miles northeast of Babylon. This suggests that Cyrus wrote the scroll in the summer of 538 BC. • ***Media*** was a mountainous area north of Persia and east of Assyria (see map, Ezra Introduction, p. 786). This area is now inhabited by the Kurds (descendants of the Medes). • Texts introduced by the term ***Memorandum*** tended to be summaries that listed the main facts of an event for the royal archives (cp. 1:9-10).

6:3 This ***decree*** is recorded in 1:2-4. • The Temple's ***height will be ninety feet, and its width will be ninety feet:*** Hebrew *Its height will be 60 cubits* [27.6 meters], *and its width will be 60 cubits.* It is commonly held that this verse should be emended to read: "Its height will be 30 cubits [45 feet, or 13.8 meters], its length will be 60 cubits [90 feet, or 27.6 meters], and its width will be 20 cubits [30 feet, or 9.2 meters]"; cp. 1 Kgs 6:2. The emendation regarding the width is supported by the Syriac version. The emendations would make these measurements match those of Solomon's Temple (1 Kgs 6:2, 17, 20). But the larger measurements given here might represent the maximum size that the Persians would fund.

6:4 ***Every three layers . . . timber:*** See note on 5:8. • ***All expenses will be paid by the royal treasury.*** Although it seems surprising that the Persians would do this, it was consistent with Persian practice elsewhere (e.g., at Sais and Elephantine in Egypt, and at Ur in Mesopotamia). Such generosity was designed to ensure loyalty to Persia.

6:6 ***the province west of the Euphrates River:*** Literally *the province beyond the river;* also in 6:6b, 8, 13.

6:8 ***You must pay the full construction costs:*** This command fulfilled God's promise through Haggai (Hag 2:7).

6:10 Ezra 7:23
6:11 Ezra 7:26; Dan 2:5; 3:29
6:12 Deut 12:4-5, 11; 1 Kgs 9:2-3
6:13 Ezra 6:6
6:14 Ezra 5:1-2; 6:12; 7:1, 7-9, 11; Zech 4:9
6:16 1 Kgs 8:63; 2 Chr 7:5
6:17 Ezra 8:35
6:18 Num 3:6; 1 Chr 23:6; 2 Chr 35:4-5
6:19 Exod 12:6; [a]*pesakh* (6453) ‣ Ezek 45:21
6:20 2 Chr 29:34; 30:15-17; 35:11
6:21 Num 9:6-7, 10-14; Ezra 9:1-15; Neh 9:2
6:22 Exod 12:15; Ezra 1:1; 7:27; [b]*khag* (2282) ‣ Ps 81:3

heaven. And without fail, provide them
with as much wheat, salt, wine, and olive
oil as they need each day. [10]Then they
will be able to offer acceptable sacrifices
to the God of heaven and pray for the
welfare of the king and his sons.
[11]"Those who violate this decree in
any way will have a beam pulled from
their house. Then they will be tied to
it and flogged, and their house will
be reduced to a pile of rubble. [12]May
the God who has chosen the city of
Jerusalem as the place to honor his name
destroy any king or nation that violates
this command and destroys this Temple.
"I, Darius, have issued this decree. Let
it be obeyed with all diligence."

The Temple Is Dedicated

[13]Tattenai, governor of the province west of
the Euphrates River, and Shethar-bozenai
and their colleagues complied at once with
the command of King Darius. [14]So the Jewish elders continued their work, and they
were greatly encouraged by the preaching
of the prophets Haggai and Zechariah son
of Iddo. The Temple was finally finished, as
had been commanded by the God of Israel
and decreed by Cyrus, Darius, and Artaxerxes, the kings of Persia. [15]The Temple was
completed on March 12, during the sixth
year of King Darius's reign.
[16]The Temple of God was then dedicated with great joy by the people of Israel,
the priests, the Levites, and the rest of
the people who had returned from exile.
[17]During the dedication ceremony for the
Temple of God, 100 young bulls, 200 rams,
and 400 male lambs were sacrificed. And
12 male goats were presented as a sin offering for the twelve tribes of Israel. [18]Then
the priests and Levites were divided into
their various divisions to serve at the Temple of God in Jerusalem, as prescribed in
the Book of Moses.

Passover Is Celebrated

[19]On April 21 the returned exiles celebrated [a]Passover. [20]The priests and Levites
had purified themselves and were ceremonially clean. So they slaughtered the
Passover lamb for all the returned exiles,
for their fellow priests, and for themselves.
[21]The Passover meal was eaten by the people of Israel who had returned from exile
and by the others in the land who had
turned from their immoral customs to worship the LORD, the God of Israel. [22]Then
they celebrated the [b]Festival of Unleavened
Bread for seven days. There was great joy
throughout the land because the LORD had
caused the king of Assyria to be favorable
to them, so that he helped them to rebuild
the Temple of God, the God of Israel.

6:9 *the God of heaven:* See note on 5:11.

6:10 *pray for the welfare of the king and his sons:* In the Cyrus Cylinder (a Persian account of Cyrus's defeat of Babylon), King Cyrus requests, "May all the gods whom I have resettled in their sacred cities ask [the Babylonian gods] Bel and Nebo daily for a long life for me" (see 1:1-4).

6:11-12 *Those who violate this decree:* Inscriptions and official decrees often included curses on those who opposed the will of the king (cp. Dan 2:5). • The Aramaic translated *they will be tied to it and flogged* might mean that the person would be executed by being impaled on the beam, rather than merely being disciplined. • *a pile of rubble:* Literally *a dunghill.*

6:14 *the prophets Haggai and Zechariah:* See note on 5:1.

6:15 *on March 12:* Literally *on the third day of the month Adar,* of the ancient Hebrew lunar calendar. A number of events in Ezra can be cross-checked with dates in surviving Persian records and related accurately to our modern calendar. This day was March 12, 515 BC. Thus Israel's second Temple was finished approximately seventy years after its destruction by Nebuchadnezzar in 586 BC. Herod the Great remodeled and expanded this Temple at the time of Christ. The Temple stood for approximately 585 years until the Roman army of Titus destroyed it in AD 70.

6:17 *12 male goats . . . a sin offering:* This blood sacrifice brought God's forgiveness for unintentional sins, ceremonial uncleanness, or thoughtless wrong acts (Lev 4–5). Similar sacrifices were offered when Moses dedicated the Tabernacle (Num 7) and when Solomon dedicated the first Temple (2 Chr 7:1, 4). • *for the twelve tribes of Israel:* Although most returnees were from Judah and Benjamin (1:5; 4:1), people from the priestly tribe of Levi are also mentioned (1:5; 2:40, 70). It is also likely that there were returnees from some of the ten northern tribes of Israel. Even if all tribes were not physically represented, the twelve sacrifices emphasized the desire for God to maintain his covenant relationship with all Israel.

6:18 *prescribed in the Book of Moses:* See Exod 29; Lev 8; Num 3. The Temple personnel operated according to the organization instituted by David (1 Chr 23–27). • This verse concludes the Aramaic section that began in 4:8.

6:19 *On April 21:* Literally *On the fourteenth day of the first month,* of the ancient Hebrew lunar calendar. This day was April 21, 515 BC; also see note on 6:15. • The *Passover* celebration commemorates God's sparing of the firstborn of each family that put blood on the doorposts of their home (Exod 12–13). This occasion was the first time any of these people had celebrated a joyous national festival.

6:20 *purified themselves:* They acted in accord with the law of Moses (see Lev 9; Num 8; 2 Chr 29).

6:21 *and by the others in the land who had turned from their immoral customs:* The exclusion of foreigners in 4:1-5 was due to their pagan religious practices, not their ethnicity (see also 9:1-2).

6:22 Passover was the beginning of the seven-day *Festival of Unleavened Bread* (see Exod 12:15-20; Lev 23:6-8), a time of feasting in remembrance of the unleavened bread eaten when Israel left Egypt. • *the LORD had caused:* Although Darius I was the powerful king of a vast empire, God directed his heart to help *rebuild the Temple of God.* • King Darius of Persia is here identified as *the king of Assyria* because Persia had conquered the Babylonian empire, which included the earlier Assyrian empire.

2. EZRA RETURNS TO TEACH GOD'S LAW (7:1–10:44)

God Brings Ezra to Jerusalem (7:1–8:36)

Ezra Is Introduced

7 Many years later, during the reign of King Artaxerxes of Persia, there was a man named Ezra. He was the son of Seraiah, son of Azariah, son of Hilkiah, 2son of Shallum, son of Zadok, son of Ahitub, 3son of Amariah, son of Azariah, son of Meraioth, 4son of Zerahiah, son of Uzzi, son of Bukki, 5son of Abishua, son of Phinehas, son of Eleazar, son of Aaron the high priest. 6This Ezra was a scribe who was well versed in the Law of Moses, which the LORD, the God of Israel, had given to the people of Israel. He came up to Jerusalem from Babylon, and the king gave him everything he asked for, because the gracious hand of the LORD his God was on him. 7Some of the people of Israel, as well as some of the priests, Levites, singers, gatekeepers, and Temple servants, traveled up to Jerusalem with him in the seventh year of King Artaxerxes' reign.

8Ezra arrived in Jerusalem in August of that year. 9He had arranged to leave Babylon on April 8, the first day of the new year, and he arrived at Jerusalem on August 4, for

7:1 1 Chr 6:9-14; Ezra 7:12, 21; 8:1–10:44; Neh 8:1-18
7:6 Ezra 7:10-11, 21-28; Neh 8:9, 13
7:7 Ezra 8:1-20
7:9 Ezra 7:6

EZRA THE SCRIBE (7:1–10:44)

Neh 8:1-18; 12:1, 26, 36

Ezra was a priest and scribe (7:11-12; cp. Neh 8:2, 9) of the high priestly line of Zadok (7:1-5). He was a leader in Judah following the Jews' return from exile. As a scribe, Ezra was not just a copyist but a disciplined student of God's laws (7:6) who was qualified to teach, preach, and interpret the Scriptures.

As an important official who assisted the king with Jewish affairs in the Persian empire, Ezra visited Jerusalem about 458 BC, bringing articles for the Temple and the mission of establishing God's laws and the laws of Persia. One of his first reforms was to confront the sin of intermarriage with non-believers (9:1–10:44). Later, after the city walls were rebuilt in 445 BC (Neh 6:15), Ezra led the community to obey God's law more fully (Neh 8:13-15).

Ezra honored God through his handling of finances. The Persian king trusted Ezra's judgment (7:15-18) and allowed him to ask for more money when needed (7:21-22). Ezra gave others the responsibility for financial affairs whenever he could and required strict financial integrity of them (8:24-30). He identified certain financial resources as holy and belonging to God.

Ezra humbled himself before God when the people began their journey (8:21-23), when he found out about their unholy marriages (9:5-15), and when he gathered those who must divorce their unbelieving wives (10:6). He always recognized that God's gracious hand—not his own ability or wisdom—enabled good things to happen (7:6, 9, 28; 8:18, 22, 31; 9:8-9). He studied and lived by God's word and taught others to follow what God revealed (7:10). He was a teacher and servant-leader, not a self-important official who lorded it over other people.

Ezra's piety and dedication through prayer and fasting put his reforming zeal in proper spiritual perspective. He set the pattern for life in the postexilic Jewish community, making God's word and worship central priorities.

7:1-5 Ezra highlights his standing by listing his own genealogy through Zadok, priest under Solomon (1 Kgs 2:35), all the way back to ***Aaron the high priest***, Moses' brother. This list is clearly abbreviated: It has only sixteen generations from Aaron to eighty years after the Exile, while 1 Chr 6:3-15 has twenty-three generations from Aaron to the Exile.

7:1 ***Many years later:*** Ezra arrived in Jerusalem in 458 BC (7:7-8), about fifty-seven years after the dedication of the second Temple. Ezra has been recording events that occurred before his time, but now he begins to record his own history. • ***Artaxerxes*** I reigned 465–424 BC. • ***son:*** Or *descendant;* see 1 Chr 6:14. In biblical genealogies, the Hebrew word translated *son* often means *descendant.* • ***Seraiah*** was high priest under Zedekiah; he was executed by Nebuchadnezzar in 586 BC (2 Kgs 25:18-21).

7:3 ***son of Meraioth:*** Or *descendant of Meraioth;* see 1 Chr 6:6-10.

7:5 ***the high priest:*** Or *the first priest.*

7:6 ***Ezra*** came from ***Babylon,*** where there was still a substantial and prosperous Jewish community. • The Hebrew term translated *scribe* is sometimes translated as "secretary." It describes an educated and reliable individual who transcribed and interpreted official documents. Accordingly, many scholars think that Ezra functioned like a "Secretary of State for Jewish Affairs" in the Persian government. Here, however, the emphasis is on his scribal role of studying and teaching from the five Books of Moses.

7:8 ***in August:*** Literally *in the fifth month.* This month in the ancient Hebrew lunar calendar occurred within the months of August and September 458 BC.

7:9 ***on April 8, the first day of the new year:*** Hebrew *on the first day of the first month,* of the ancient Hebrew lunar calendar. This day was April 8, 458 BC; also see note on 6:15. Ezra and his entourage did not actually leave until April 19, 458 BC (8:31). In those intervening 11 days, he organized the group and assembled it at the Ahava Canal, searched for more Levites, and proclaimed a fast. • ***on August 4:*** Hebrew *on the first day of the fifth month,* of the ancient Hebrew lunar calendar. This day was August 4, 458 BC; also see note on 6:15.

7:10 Neh 8:1
7:12 Ezek 26:7; Dan 2:37, 47
7:14 Ezra 7:15, 28
7:16 1 Chr 29:6; Ezra 8:25
7:17 Num 15:4-13; Deut 12:4-11
7:20 Ezra 6:4

the gracious hand of his God was on him.
10This was because Ezra had determined to
study and obey the Law of the LORD and to
teach those decrees and regulations to the
people of Israel.

Artaxerxes Outlines Ezra's Responsibilities

11King Artaxerxes had given a copy of the
following letter to Ezra, the priest and scribe
who studied and taught the commands and
decrees of the LORD to Israel:

12"From Artaxerxes, the king of kings, to
Ezra the priest, the teacher of the law of
the God of heaven. Greetings.

13"I decree that any of the people
of Israel in my kingdom, including the
priests and Levites, may volunteer to
return to Jerusalem with you. 14I and
my council of seven hereby instruct you
to conduct an inquiry into the situation
in Judah and Jerusalem, based on your
God's law, which is in your hand. 15We
also commission you to take with you
silver and gold, which we are freely
presenting as an offering to the God of
Israel who lives in Jerusalem.

16"Furthermore, you are to take any
silver and gold that you may obtain from
the province of Babylon, as well as the
voluntary offerings of the people and the
priests that are presented for the Temple
of their God in Jerusalem. 17These
donations are to be used specifically for
the purchase of bulls, rams, male lambs,
and the appropriate grain offerings
and liquid offerings, all of which will
be offered on the altar of the Temple
of your God in Jerusalem. 18Any silver
and gold that is left over may be used in
whatever way you and your colleagues
feel is the will of your God.

19"But as for the cups we are
entrusting to you for the service of the
Temple of your God, deliver them all
to the God of Jerusalem. 20If you need
anything else for your God's Temple or
for any similar needs, you may take it
from the royal treasury.

Temple Dedication (6:14-22)

Exod 40:1-38; 1 Kgs 7:51–9:9; Zech 4:1-10; Hag 1:8; 2:7-8; Rev 21:1-27

The dedication of Israel's second Temple on March 12, 515 BC, was the most significant event in the lives of those who returned from Babylonian exile. Now they could worship and praise God in the same way their ancestors had worshiped before the Exile, and God's requirements for covenant relationship with him could be fulfilled. The high priest could go into God's presence to sprinkle the blood once a year on the Day of Atonement for the nation's sins. After seventy years of estrangement from God, the covenant community was now restored.

This joyous event did not come without difficulty. With God's help, the returned exiles overcame sixteen years of opposition from the people who had inhabited their land and from Persian officials. Although their enemies made every attempt to discourage them, the Israelites completed the job of rebuilding the Temple and reestablishing worship through patience, persistence, and strong prophetic encouragement (5:1-5; 6:14).

The dedication of the Temple demonstrates that God can accomplish his will through a small group of people who set their priorities on pleasing him and who trust him to provide the resources to fulfill his promises (6:8; Hag 2:7-8). Instead of focusing on what little they had, the people of God trusted in what he could provide. They were dedicated to glorifying God and maintaining their relationship with him. God proved that he was sovereignly in control of nations and could change the hearts of the leaders of those nations to accomplish his will (5:5; 6:6-10, 22).

• To make the 800-mile journey in four months, Ezra's party would have walked an average of about ten miles per day, five days per week. Ezra knew that his success was attributable only to *the gracious hand of his God* (see also 7:6, 28; 8:22, 31).

7:10 *Ezra* had three life goals: (1) *to study* God's word, (2) to *obey* what God said, and (3) to *teach . . . the people of Israel.* He allowed God's word to transform his character and behavior so that he could influence the lives of others.

7:11-26 In this *letter,* King Artaxerxes granted Ezra the power and responsibility to evaluate the situation in Jerusalem (7:14), present freewill offerings to God (7:15-20), obtain supplies and finances from local authorities (7:21-24), and institute judicial reforms (7:25-26). • The original text of 7:12-26 is in Aramaic.

7:12 *God of heaven:* See note on 5:11.

7:14 *I and my council of seven:* The Greek historian Xenophon knew of this council (Xenophon, *Anabasis* 1.6.4-5), and Esth 1:14 lists the names of the seven princes of Xerxes, Artaxerxes' father. • *your God's law:* The word translated *law* in this verse is the Aramaic word *dath* rather than the Hebrew *torah* (7:10), suggesting that a Persian wrote this letter (7:11-26).

7:15 *who lives in Jerusalem:* God's Temple was located there. Artaxerxes probably thought that he was helping rebuild the house of Jerusalem's local deity (cp. 1 Kgs 8:27; Ps 24:1).

7:16 Like Cyrus (1:4, 6), Artaxerxes allowed Jews in Babylon to send freewill offerings to Jerusalem. A sizeable sum was collected from the king and his council as well as from Jewish contributors (8:25-27).

[21]"I, Artaxerxes the king, hereby send this decree to all the treasurers in the province west of the Euphrates River: 'You are to give Ezra, the priest and teacher of the law of the God of heaven, whatever he requests of you. [22]You are to give him up to 7,500 pounds of silver, 500 bushels of wheat, 550 gallons of wine, 550 gallons of olive oil, and an unlimited supply of salt. [23]Be careful to provide whatever the God of heaven demands for his Temple, for why should we risk bringing God's anger against the realm of the king and his sons? [24]I also decree that no priest, Levite, singer, gatekeeper, Temple servant, or other worker in this Temple of God will be required to pay tribute, customs, or tolls of any kind.'

[25]"And you, Ezra, are to use the wisdom your God has given you to appoint magistrates and judges who know your God's laws to govern all the people in the province west of the Euphrates River. Teach the law to anyone who does not know it. [26]Anyone who refuses to obey the law of your God and the law of the king will be punished immediately, either by death, banishment, confiscation of goods, or imprisonment."

Ezra Praises the Lord

[27]Praise the LORD, the God of our ancestors, who made the king want to beautify the Temple of the LORD in Jerusalem! [28]And praise him for demonstrating such unfailing love to me by honoring me before the king, his council, and all his mighty nobles! I felt encouraged because the gracious hand of the LORD my God was on me. And I gathered some of the leaders of Israel to return with me to Jerusalem.

Exiles Who Returned with Ezra

8 Here is a list of the family leaders and the genealogies of those who came with me from Babylon during the reign of King Artaxerxes:

[2] From the family of Phinehas: Gershom.
From the family of Ithamar: Daniel.
From the family of David: Hattush, [3]a descendant of Shecaniah.
From the family of Parosh: Zechariah and 150 other men were registered.
[4] From the family of Pahath-moab: Eliehoenai son of Zerahiah and 200 other men.
[5] From the family of Zattu: Shecaniah son of Jahaziel and 300 other men.
[6] From the family of Adin: Ebed son of Jonathan and 50 other men.
[7] From the family of Elam: Jeshaiah son of Athaliah and 70 other men.
[8] From the family of Shephatiah: Zebadiah son of Michael and 80 other men.
[9] From the family of Joab: Obadiah son of Jehiel and 218 other men.
[10] From the family of Bani: Shelomith son of Josiphiah and 160 other men.
[11] From the family of Bebai: Zechariah son of Bebai and 28 other men.
[12] From the family of Azgad: Johanan son of Hakkatan and 110 other men.
[13] From the family of Adonikam, who came later: Eliphelet, Jeuel, Shemaiah, and 60 other men.
[14] From the family of Bigvai: Uthai, Zaccur, and 70 other men.

Ezra's Journey to Jerusalem

[15]I assembled the exiles at the Ahava Canal, and we camped there for three days while I went over the lists of the people and the priests who had arrived. I found that not

7:21 Ezra 7:6
7:25 Exod 18:21-25; Deut 16:18; Ezra 7:6, 10
7:26 Ezra 6:11-12
7:27= Ezra 6:22
7:28 Ezra 9:9
8:1 Ezra 7:7
8:3 Ezra 2:3
8:15 Ezra 8:21, 31

7:21-22 The items listed were typically used as offerings in worship (cp. Exod 27:20; 29:2; Lev 2:4, 13; 14:10; Num 28:7). • ***the province west of the Euphrates River:*** Literally *the province beyond the river;* also in 7:25. • ***7,500 pounds:*** Hebrew *100 talents* [3,400 kilograms]. • ***500 bushels:*** Hebrew *100 cors* [18.2 kiloliters]. • ***550 gallons of wine, 550 gallons of olive oil:*** Hebrew *100 baths* [2.1 kiloliters] *of wine, 100 baths of olive oil.*

7:23 ***the God of heaven:*** This is the title by which the Jews had referred to the Lord (5:11-12) and that Cyrus had used (1:2). The Persian king probably believed, like others in the ancient Near East, that each country's god or gods controlled their territory. Artaxerxes did not want to ***risk bringing God's anger against the realm of the king*** and undermine the peace of his empire by failing to provide for the God of Jerusalem (7:19) the worship that he required.

7:24 The tax exemptions given to Temple personnel in Jerusalem were similar to the conciliatory gestures made to those in other nations.

7:25-26 Ezra was to teach ***God's laws*** and govern the area occupied by the Jews in accordance with God's laws and ***the law of the king***—i.e., Persian civil law.

8:1-14 This ***list of the family leaders*** designates those who stepped out in faith and traveled with Ezra back to Jerusalem to join the Jewish community there. It lists fifteen families represented by 1,515 men. Including women and children, the total could have been around 5,000 people.

8:5 ***Zattu:*** As in some Greek manuscripts (see also *1 Esdras* 8:32); Hebrew lacks *Zattu.*

8:10 ***Bani:*** As in some Greek manuscripts (see also *1 Esdras* 8:36); Hebrew lacks *Bani.*

8:13 ***who came later:*** Or *who were the last of his family.*

8:14 ***Zaccur:*** As in Greek and Syriac versions and an alternate reading of the Masoretic Text; the other alternate reads *Zabbud.*

8:15 The ***Ahava Canal*** came off the Euphrates River near Babylon. • ***not one***

8:17 Ezra 2:43-54
8:20 Ezra 2:43
8:21 2 Chr 20:3; Ezra 8:15, 31; Ps 27:11; Isa 58:3, 5
8:22 2 Chr 15:2; Ezra 7:6, 9, 28
8:23 2 Chr 33:13
8:25 Ezra 7:15-16
8:28 Lev 21:6-8; 22:2-3; Isa 52:11
8:29 Ezra 8:33-34
8:31 Ezra 7:9
8:32 Neh 2:11
8:33 Ezra 8:30

one Levite had volunteered to come along.
16 So I sent for Eliezer, Ariel, Shemaiah, Elnathan, Jarib, Elnathan, Nathan, Zechariah,
and Meshullam, who were leaders of the
people. I also sent for Joiarib and Elnathan,
who were men of discernment. 17 I sent
them to Iddo, the leader of the Levites at Ca-
siphia, to ask him and his relatives and the
Temple servants to send us ministers for the
Temple of God at Jerusalem.
18 Since the gracious hand of our God
was on us, they sent us a man named Sherebiah, along with eighteen of his sons and
brothers. He was a very astute man and a
descendant of Mahli, who was a descendant of Levi son of Israel. 19 They also sent
Hashabiah, together with Jeshaiah from the
descendants of Merari, and twenty of his
sons and brothers, 20 and 220 Temple servants. The Temple servants were assistants
to the Levites—a group of Temple workers
first instituted by King David and his officials. They were all listed by name.
21 And there by the Ahava Canal, I gave
orders for all of us to fast and humble ourselves before our God. We prayed that he
would give us a safe journey and protect
us, our children, and our goods as we traveled. 22 For I was ashamed to ask the king
for soldiers and horsemen to accompany us
and protect us from enemies along the way.
After all, we had told the king, "Our God's
hand of protection is on all who worship
him, but his fierce anger rages against those
who abandon him." 23 So we fasted and earnestly prayed that our God would take care
of us, and he heard our prayer.
24 I appointed twelve leaders of the
priests—Sherebiah, Hashabiah, and ten
other priests—25 to be in charge of transporting the silver, the gold, the gold bowls,
and the other items that the king, his council, his officials, and all the people of Israel
had presented for the Temple of God. 26 I
weighed the treasure as I gave it to them
and found the totals to be as follows:

24 tons of silver,
7,500 pounds of silver articles,
7,500 pounds of gold,
27 20 gold bowls, equal in value to 1,000
gold coins,
2 fine articles of polished bronze, as
precious as gold.

28 And I said to these priests, "You and
these treasures have been set apart as holy
to the LORD. This silver and gold is a voluntary offering to the LORD, the God of our
ancestors. 29 Guard these treasures well until
you present them to the leading priests, the
Levites, and the leaders of Israel, who will
weigh them at the storerooms of the LORD's
Temple in Jerusalem." 30 So the priests and
the Levites accepted the task of transporting these treasures of silver and gold to the
Temple of our God in Jerusalem.
31 We broke camp at the Ahava Canal on
April 19 and started off to Jerusalem. And
the gracious hand of our God protected us
and saved us from enemies and bandits
along the way. 32 So we arrived safely in Jerusalem, where we rested for three days.
33 On the fourth day after our arrival,
the silver, gold, and other valuables were
weighed at the Temple of our God and entrusted to Meremoth son of Uriah the priest
and to Eleazar son of Phinehas, along with
Jozabad son of Jeshua and Noadiah son of

Levite had volunteered: Only a few Levites had come earlier with Sheshbazzar (2:40). It is unclear why so few Levites returned to Jerusalem.

8:16-17 The Hebrew term translated *men of discernment* refers to those who could interpret and explain the Torah. These men were probably respected because of their expertise in Scripture (cp. Neh 8:8-9). Ezra commissioned them to use their influence to recruit more Levites.

8:18 ***the gracious hand of our God:*** Ezra, his leaders, and Iddo all took action to rectify the problem, but ultimately everything was accomplished because of God's grace. Only thirty-eight Levites (including the leaders) and 220 Temple servants responded. • ***Israel*** is the name that God gave to Jacob (Gen 32:28).

8:20 ***first instituted by King David and his officials:*** See 1 Chr 24–26.

8:21 ***fast and humble ourselves:*** Ezra recognized the need to look to God for the protection, safety, and health of 5,000 people going 800 miles on foot. Robbers might be hiding in the hills, there was danger in crossing rivers, and people could get sick.

8:22 ***ashamed:*** Ezra had openly proclaimed his faith in God's ability to protect the Israelites on their journey. Asking the king for help now would suggest that Ezra did not really believe in God's ability to provide. • ***horsemen:*** Or *charioteers.*

8:23 ***fasted . . . prayed:*** In the OT, fasting often accompanied prayer as a demonstration of need before God (1 Kgs 21:9; 2 Chr 20:3; Neh 1:4; Dan 9:3).

8:25 The items that the leaders were *in charge of transporting* included offerings for the Temple and sacrifices. Because these gifts belonged to God and were holy (8:28), it was necessary that the priests care for them.

8:26-27 The Persians and supportive Jews had given an enormous amount of money. It was a huge risk to transport it without a royal escort. • ***24 tons:*** Hebrew *650 talents* [22 metric tons]. • ***7,500 pounds:*** Hebrew *100 talents* [3,400 kilograms]. • ***1,000 gold coins:*** Hebrew *1,000 darics,* about 19 pounds or 8.6 kilograms in weight.

8:31-32 ***We broke camp . . . on April 19:*** Literally *on the twelfth day of the first month,* of the ancient Hebrew lunar calendar. This day was April 19, 458 BC; also see note on 6:15. It took twelve days to get organized, to encourage some Levites to join them, and to pray for God's protection before Ezra could actually get the people moving toward Jerusalem (see 7:9).

Binnui—both of whom were Levites. 34Ev-
erything was accounted for by number and
weight, and the total weight was officially
recorded.
35Then the exiles who had come out of
captivity sacrificed burnt offerings to the
God of Israel. They presented twelve bulls
for all the people of Israel, as well as ninety-
six rams and seventy-seven male lambs.
They also offered twelve male goats as a sin
offering. All this was given as a burnt offering to the LORD. 36The king's decrees were
delivered to his highest officers and the governors of the province west of the Euphrates
River, who then cooperated by supporting
the people and the Temple of God.

Ezra Intercedes for the Holy Race (9:1–10:44)

Ezra's Prayer concerning Pagan Intermarriage

9 When these things had been done, the
Jewish leaders came to me and said,
"Many of the people of Israel, and even some
of the priests and Levites, have not kept
themselves separate from the other peoples living in the land. They have taken up
the detestable practices of the Canaanites,
Hittites, Perizzites, Jebusites, Ammonites,
Moabites, Egyptians, and Amorites. 2For the
men of Israel have married women from
these people and have taken them as wives
for their sons. So the holy race has become
polluted by these mixed marriages. Worse
yet, the leaders and officials have led the
way in this outrage."
3When I heard this, I tore my cloak and
my shirt, pulled hair from my head and
beard, and sat down utterly shocked. 4Then
all who trembled at the words of the God of
Israel came and sat with me because of this
outrage committed by the returned exiles.
And I sat there utterly appalled until the
time of the evening sacrifice.
5At the time of the sacrifice, I stood up
from where I had sat in mourning with my
clothes torn. I fell to my knees and lifted my
hands to the LORD my God. 6I prayed,

"O my God, I am utterly ashamed; I
blush to lift up my face to you. For
our sins are piled higher than our
heads, and our guilt has reached to
the heavens. 7From the days of our
ancestors until now, we have been
steeped in sin. That is why we and our
kings and our priests have been at the
mercy of the pagan kings of the land.
We have been killed, captured, robbed,
and disgraced, just as we are today.
8"But now we have been given a brief
moment of grace, for the LORD our God
has allowed a few of us to survive as a
remnant. He has given us security in this
holy place. Our God has brightened our
eyes and granted us some relief from our
slavery. 9For we were slaves, but in his
unfailing love our God did not abandon
us in our slavery. Instead, he caused
the kings of Persia to treat us favorably.
He revived us so we could rebuild the

8:35 Ezra 2:1; 6:17
8:36 Ezra 7:21
9:1 Exod 23:28; Lev 18:24-30; Deut 20:17
9:2 Exod 34:16
9:3 Neh 1:4
9:4 Exod 29:38-39
9:5 Exod 9:29, 33
9:6 2 Chr 28:9; Rev 18:5
9:9 Exod 1:11-14; Neh 9:36-37; Ps 106:45-46

8:35 ***sacrificed burnt offerings:*** For many of the Jews who came to Jerusalem with Ezra, this was probably the first sacrifice they had ever offered. It would have been a moving spiritual experience for them to confess their sins and dedicate their lives to God in this way. For details on the burnt offering, see Lev 1.

8:36 ***the province west of the Euphrates River:*** Literally *the province beyond the river.*

9:1–10:44 Ezra confronted the problem of intermarriage with idolatrous foreigners. The Jewish leaders had allowed this practice, though the early settlers had committed to keep separate from pagan influences (4:1-5). Ezra interceded on behalf of the nation and helped those convicted of their sins to make things right.

9:1-2 The events that follow took place approximately four months after Ezra's arrival (cp. 7:9; 10:9). • Intermarriage with pagan foreigners was dangerous because Israelites could end up worshiping other gods and accepting ***the detestable practices of*** other religions (cp. 4:1-5; Deut 7:1-4). • ***the holy race has become polluted:*** Literally *the holy seed has intermingled itself.* Because Israel was a holy covenant nation (Exod 19:6), it was not to be involved with pagan practices (Lev 19:2-4; 20:6-8, 22-26). Therefore, the people were to avoid marriages with those who could influence Israelites to embrace such practices. When the religious and political ***leaders and officials*** intermarried with foreigners, they were in danger of leading others astray and destroying the unique identity of Israel as a holy people.

9:3 ***utterly shocked:*** Cp. Gen 37:34; 2 Kgs 22:11; Job 1:20.

9:4 ***The time of the evening sacrifice*** was around 3:00 p.m.

9:5 Ezra's inner humility before God was consistent with his falling on his ***knees.*** His outstretched ***hands*** demonstrated his pleading with God to intervene.

9:6-15 Ezra's prayer provides a model for intercessory prayer (cp. Neh 1:5-11; Dan 9:4-19). It includes confessing sin (9:6-7), remembering God's past grace (9:8-9), admitting that the people have ignored God (9:10-12), and recognizing their unworthiness (9:13-15).

9:6 ***I am utterly ashamed . . . our sins are piled higher than our heads:*** Although he was not one of the offending parties, Ezra personally identified with his people (see "Community Identity" at Lev 4:3, 13-21, p. 199).

9:7 Ezra forthrightly summarizes Israel's past history. The people and their leaders had sinned and were justly punished. • ***just as we are today:*** The effects of Israel's punishment were still evident in Jerusalem at this time.

9:8-9 God's abundant ***grace*** and ***unfailing love*** should affect how people respond to him (cp. Deut 30:1-5). After all that God had done for the ***remnant,*** it was shameful that they were so ready to betray him. • ***the kings of Persia to treat us favorably:*** Babylon and Assyria had tortured and exiled their enemies (2 Kgs 17, 25), but Persia treated exiled

9:12 Deut 7:3
9:14 Deut 9:7-8, 13-14
9:15 Neh 9:33-34; Ps 130:3; Dan 9:7-11
10:1 2 Chr 20:9; Dan 9:20; [c]*yadah* (3034) ‣Neh 1:6

Temple of our God and repair its ruins.
He has given us a protective wall in
Judah and Jerusalem.
10 "And now, O our God, what can
we say after all of this? For once again
we have abandoned your commands!
11 Your servants the prophets warned
us when they said, 'The land you are
entering to possess is totally defiled by
the detestable practices of the people
living there. From one end to the other,
the land is filled with corruption.
12 Don't let your daughters marry their
sons! Don't take their daughters as
wives for your sons. Don't ever promote
the peace and prosperity of those
nations. If you follow these instructions,
you will be strong and will enjoy the
good things the land produces, and
you will leave this prosperity to your
children forever.'
13 "Now we are being punished
because of our wickedness and our
great guilt. But we have actually been
punished far less than we deserve, for
you, our God, have allowed some of us to
survive as a remnant. 14 But even so, we
are again breaking your commands and
intermarrying with people who do these
detestable things. Won't your anger
be enough to destroy us, so that even
this little remnant no longer survives?
15 O LORD, God of Israel, you are just. We
come before you in our guilt as nothing
but an escaped remnant, though in such
a condition none of us can stand in your
presence."

The People Confess Their Sin

10 While Ezra prayed and made this
[c]confession, weeping and lying face
down on the ground in front of the Temple
of God, a very large crowd of people from Israel—men, women, and children—gathered

Marriage and Divorce (9:1–10:44)

Deut 7:1-6; Josh 2:1-14; 6:23-25; Judg 3:3-7; 14:1-9; Ruth 4:1-22; 1 Kgs 11:1-8; 2 Kgs 17:7-17; 1 Cor 7:10-16; 2 Cor 6:14-15; Heb 11:31

God had warned his people not to intermarry with unbelieving foreigners (Deut 7:1-6). The sin was not that they married people from another country or race but that they married people committed to another religion. Moses had married a Cushite woman (Num 12:1), and other foreigners had joined Israel through marriage, notably Rahab the Canaanite (Josh 2:6; Heb 11:31) and Ruth the Moabite (Ruth 4). These women embraced faith in the Lord, and they were blessed. On the other hand, Solomon had taken many foreign wives, and their devotion to other religions led him into idolatry, just as the Lord had warned (1 Kgs 11:1-5).

The marriage covenant is sacred, but it was even more important for Israel to remain faithful to the Lord's covenant with them as a people. Mixed marriages would produce children who were not fully committed to Israel's faith, having been influenced by their mothers' idolatrous beliefs. This compromise would lead Israel right back to where they were before the Exile—to wholesale unfaithfulness to God and wholehearted embracing of false religions (see Judg 3:3-7; 14:1-9; 1 Kgs 11:1-8; 2 Kgs 17:7-17).

Ezra's solution is not prescriptive for believers today. In the new covenant under Christ, the faith of a believer sanctifies his or her marriage and children, so marriage to an unbeliever does not threaten the identity or purity of God's people (1 Cor 7:14-16). The apostle Paul realized that divorce might occur when believers and unbelievers married, but he did not encourage believers in that situation to seek a divorce (1 Cor 7:10-13). Certainly, the wise policy to avoid these problems is to heed Paul's advice not to marry an unbeliever in the first place. God's people need to remain separated from what is unholy: "How can righteousness be a partner with wickedness? How can light live with darkness? What harmony can there be between Christ and the devil? How can a believer be a partner with an unbeliever?" (2 Cor 6:14-15). But those who are married to an unbeliever today have God's assurance that he can use that difficult situation for his glory (see also 1 Pet 3:1-2).

people kindly and returned them to their homelands (see 1:1-3). • ***protective wall:*** This phrase refers to God's presence protecting the nation of Judah, not the physical walls of Jerusalem, which were rebuilt several years later by Nehemiah.

9:11-12 ***Your servants the prophets warned us:*** God had clearly revealed what he expected from his people (see Deut 7:3-4; Mal 2:10-12) and had promised great blessings if they followed his covenant stipulations (see Lev 26:1-13; Deut 28:1-14; Jer 32:36–33:18; Ezek 37:15-28; Hos 14:1-8).

9:14 ***Won't your anger be enough to destroy us?*** The sin of intermarriage with non-believers was so serious that they had no hope of survival if they did not repent.

9:15 ***you are just:*** God's anger with sin is based on his justice and holiness.

10:1 Ezra's genuine mourning in response to his people's sin moved many of them to join him.

and wept bitterly with him. 2Then Shecaniah son of Jehiel, a descendant of Elam, said to Ezra, "We have been unfaithful to our God, for we have married these pagan women of the land. But in spite of this there is hope for Israel. 3Let us now make a [d]covenant with our God to divorce our pagan wives and to send them away with their children. We will follow the advice given by you and by the others who respect the commands of our God. Let it be done according to the Law of God. 4Get up, for it is your duty to tell us how to proceed in setting things straight. We are behind you, so be strong and take action."

5So Ezra stood up and demanded that the leaders of the priests and the Levites and all the people of Israel swear that they would do as Shecaniah had said. And they all swore a solemn oath. 6Then Ezra left the front of the Temple of God and went to the room of Jehohanan son of Eliashib. He spent the night there without eating or drinking anything. He was still in [e]mourning because of the unfaithfulness of the returned exiles.

7Then a proclamation was made throughout Judah and Jerusalem that all the exiles should come to Jerusalem. 8Those who failed to come within three days would, if the leaders and elders so decided, forfeit all their property and be expelled from the assembly of the exiles.

9Within three days, all the people of Judah and Benjamin had gathered in Jerusalem. This took place on December 19, and all the people were sitting in the square before the Temple of God. They were trembling both because of the seriousness of the matter and because it was raining. 10Then Ezra the priest stood and said to them: "You have committed a terrible sin. By marrying pagan women, you have increased Israel's guilt. 11So now confess your sin to the LORD, the God of your ancestors, and do what he demands. Separate yourselves from the people of the land and from these pagan women."

12Then the whole assembly raised their voices and answered, "Yes, you are right; we must do as you say!" 13Then they added, "This isn't something that can be done in a day or two, for many of us are involved in this extremely sinful affair. And this is the rainy season, so we cannot stay out here much longer. 14Let our leaders act on behalf of us all. Let everyone who has a pagan wife come at a scheduled time, accompanied by the leaders and judges of his city, so that the fierce anger of our God concerning this affair may be turned away from us."

15Only Jonathan son of Asahel and Jahzeiah son of Tikvah opposed this course of action, and they were supported by Meshullam and Shabbethai the Levite.

16So this was the plan they followed. Ezra selected leaders to represent their families, designating each of the representatives by name. On December 29, the leaders sat down to investigate the matter. 17By March 27, the first day of the new year, they had finished dealing with all the men who had married pagan wives.

Those Guilty of Intermarriage

18These are the priests who had married pagan wives:

From the family of Jeshua son of Jehozadak and his brothers: Maaseiah, Eliezer, Jarib, and Gedaliah. 19They vowed to divorce their wives, and they each acknowledged

10:2 Ezra 9:2; 10:11; Neh 13:27
10:3 Deut 7:2-3; 2 Chr 34:31; [d]*berith* (1285) ‣Isa 42:6
10:5 Neh 5:12; 13:25
10:6 Deut 9:18; [e]*'abal* (0056) ‣Neh 1:4
10:9 1 Sam 12:17-18; Ezra 9:4
10:11 Lev 26:40; Ezra 10:3
10:14 2 Chr 29:10; 30:8
10:19 Lev 5:15

10:2 ***Shecaniah*** was the first person brave enough to publicly admit that he had been ***unfaithful*** to God. Admission of guilt gives the ***hope*** of forgiveness for sin.

10:3 A ***covenant*** is a binding agreement, in this case specifically ***to divorce . . . pagan wives*** that the people of Israel had inappropriately married. By taking this action, they would renew their commitment to the Sinai covenant.
• Women were generally given custody of their ***children*** when a marriage failed (cp. Hagar and Ishmael, Gen 21:14).

10:4 ***it is your duty:*** As an expert in the law (see 7:10), Ezra was responsible for leading the people to a God-honoring solution to the problem of intermarriage. Because the law of Moses did not contain explicit directions for divorcing pagan wives, Ezra needed to develop a plan consistent with the requirements of Scripture and fair to the participants.

10:5 The ***solemn oath*** involved both a promise to take action and a self-imposed curse for failure to do what was promised (see Ruth 1:16-17; 1 Sam 14:24-28).

10:6 ***He spent the night:*** As in parallel text at *1 Esdras* 9:2; Hebrew reads *He went.*

10:8 ***if the leaders and elders so decided:*** It was reasonable for Ezra to add this exception clause because it might simply be impossible for some people to come to Jerusalem to participate in settling this matter.

10:9 ***on December 19:*** Literally *on the twentieth day of the ninth month,* of the ancient Hebrew lunar calendar. This day was December 19, 458 BC; also see note on 6:15. The cold and wet weather made an outdoor meeting uncomfortable.

10:15 It is unclear why these four people ***opposed*** the plan. Perhaps they wanted a stricter penalty, or perhaps they or members of their families did not want to divorce their foreign wives. That there were only four dissenters shows the overwhelming support the policy had gained among the rest of the exiles. Sadly, a few years later, a similar problem of intermarriage with pagan wives created another crisis within the community (Neh 9–10).

10:16 ***On December 29:*** Literally *On the first day of the tenth month,* of the ancient Hebrew lunar calendar. This day was December 29, 458 BC; also see note on 6:15.

10:17 ***By March 27, the first day of the new year:*** Literally *By the first day of the first month,* of the ancient Hebrew lunar calendar. This day was March 27, 457 BC; also see note on 6:15.

10:18 ***Jehozadak:*** Hebrew *Jozadak,* a variant spelling of Jehozadak.

10:44 Ezra 10:3

their guilt by offering a ram as a guilt offering.
20From the family of Immer: Hanani and Zebadiah.
21From the family of Harim: Maaseiah, Elijah, Shemaiah, Jehiel, and Uzziah.
22From the family of Pashhur: Elioenai, Maaseiah, Ishmael, Nethanel, Jozabad, and Elasah.

23These are the Levites who were guilty: Jozabad, Shimei, Kelaiah (also called Kelita), Pethahiah, Judah, and Eliezer.
24This is the singer who was guilty: Eliashib.

These are the gatekeepers who were guilty: Shallum, Telem, and Uri.

25These are the other people of Israel who were guilty:
From the family of Parosh: Ramiah, Izziah, Malkijah, Mijamin, Eleazar, Hashabiah, and Benaiah.
26From the family of Elam: Mattaniah, Zechariah, Jehiel, Abdi, Jeremoth, and Elijah.
27From the family of Zattu: Elioenai, Eliashib, Mattaniah, Jeremoth, Zabad, and Aziza.
28From the family of Bebai: Jehohanan, Hananiah, Zabbai, and Athlai.
29From the family of Bani: Meshullam, Malluch, Adaiah, Jashub, Sheal, and Jeremoth.
30From the family of Pahath-moab: Adna, Kelal, Benaiah, Maaseiah, Mattaniah, Bezalel, Binnui, and Manasseh.
31From the family of Harim: Eliezer, Ishijah, Malkijah, Shemaiah, Shimeon,
32Benjamin, Malluch, and Shemariah.
33From the family of Hashum: Mattenai, Mattattah, Zabad, Eliphelet, Jeremai, Manasseh, and Shimei.
34From the family of Bani: Maadai, Amram,
Uel, 35Benaiah, Bedeiah, Keluhi, 36Vaniah,
Meremoth, Eliashib, 37Mattaniah,
Mattenai, and Jaasu.
38From the family of Binnui: Shimei,
39Shelemiah, Nathan, Adaiah,
40Macnadebai, Shashai, Sharai, 41Azarel,
Shelemiah, Shemariah, 42Shallum,
Amariah, and Joseph.
43From the family of Nebo: Jeiel, Mattithiah, Zabad, Zebina, Jaddai, Joel, and Benaiah.

44Each of these men had a pagan wife, and some even had children by these wives.

10:25 ***Hashabiah:*** As in parallel text at *1 Esdras* 9:26; Hebrew reads *Malkijah.*

10:37-38 ***Jaasu. From the family of Binnui:*** As in Greek version; Hebrew reads *Jaasu,* [38]*Bani, Binnui.*

10:44 ***and some even had children by these wives:*** Or *and they sent them away with their children.* The meaning of the Hebrew is uncertain. The couples who had children had probably married before Ezra came back to Jerusalem; even they were not excused from the decree.

THE BOOK OF NEHEMIAH

Nehemiah left a comfortable job as an assistant to the king of Persia in order to help the demoralized people of Jerusalem. His new work involved motivating the people to rebuild the city's walls in spite of their neighbors' opposition. Nehemiah's work was not just with bricks and mortar. He also mediated a financial crisis, initiated religious reforms with the help of Ezra the scribe, and reorganized civic responsibilities in Jerusalem. Nehemiah demonstrated that with faith, prayer, integrity, and God's help, God's servants can succeed.

SETTING

After the Jews had spent several decades in exile in Babylon, God caused the Persian king Cyrus to decree in 538 BC that they could return to their homeland to rebuild their sacred Temple (Ezra 1:2-4). About 50,000 people returned to Jerusalem at that time. After arriving, they built an altar and joyfully worshiped God (Ezra 3:1-13).

When they started rebuilding the rest of the Temple, the Jews were threatened by local people who had settled in the city. These opponents turned the Persian authorities against the Jews (Ezra 4:1-5). After fifteen years of frustration, work on the Temple finally began again during the reign of Darius I (521–486 BC), primarily through the prophetic encouragement of Haggai and Zechariah (Ezra 5:1-5). This time, the Persians fully supported the rebuilding of the Temple (Ezra 6:1-12).

About sixty years later, in 458 BC, Ezra the scribe brought a group of several thousand pilgrims back to Jerusalem (Ezra 7:1–8:36). Before long, he learned that some of the leaders and priests had married wives who did not worship Israel's God. Ezra saw this as a threat to the unity and purity of the nation, and he knew it would eventually cause God to punish the people with another exile from the land (Ezra 9:1-15).

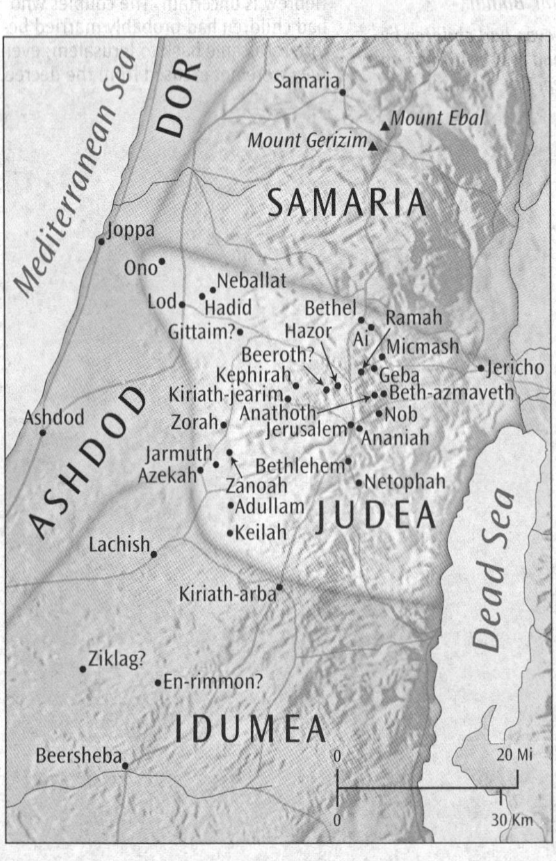

Judea during Nehemiah's Time, 445–433 BC. By the time Nehemiah traveled to JERUSALEM in 445 BC, two earlier waves of Jews had already returned to JUDAH from exile in Babylon (538 and 458 BC). The towns that Nehemiah lists as being repopulated by Jews (see 7:26-38; 11:25-36) show that Judea's borders were somewhat reduced from those of the kingdom of Judah before the exile to Babylon (cp. map, p. 767).

After Ezra's emotional prayer confessing their sin, some of the others agreed that the intermarriage was wrong.

Ezra did not solve all the problems in Jerusalem. The people still did not have a secure city with rebuilt walls and gates. Numerous enemies still opposed their presence in Jerusalem. They needed a strong civic leader who could help them preserve the independence, economic vitality, security, and sanctity of Jerusalem. God sent a new leader, Nehemiah, to address these issues.

SUMMARY

The book of Nehemiah traces events from around 445 BC, the twentieth year of Artaxerxes I (2:1), until after 432 BC, the thirty-second year of Artaxerxes (13:6-7).

Nehemiah was the cup-bearer of king Artaxerxes of Persia (1:11). When Nehemiah heard about the ruined condition of Jerusalem (1:1-3), he earnestly prayed for God's help. God's answer came through Artaxerxes, who sent Nehemiah to Judah to rebuild the walls of Jerusalem (3:1-32). Nehemiah organized and motivated the people and led them with courage and integrity through times of resistance from outside enemies (4:1-23; 6:1-14) and conflict within the community (5:1-19). Despite strong opposition (6:1-4), under Nehemiah's leadership the people rebuilt the walls of Jerusalem in just fifty-two days (6:15).

Following the completion of the walls, the account focuses on religious reforms led by Ezra and Nehemiah (7:73b–10:39). At the annual Festival of Shelters, Ezra read from the books of Moses to the crowd (8:5-8), resulting in a revival and a long prayer of confession (9:5-37). During this revival, the Israelites committed not to intermarry with foreigners and not to profane the Sabbath (10:28-39).

The book's final section (11:1–13:31) describes Nehemiah's civic efforts to resettle more people in Jerusalem (11:1-36), to dedicate the walls of Jerusalem (12:27-43), and to organize the gatekeepers and Temple storeroom attendants (12:44–13:5). The final chapter records how Nehemiah returned to Jerusalem after a time of absence (13:6-7). When he arrived, he took measures to ensure the purity of the Temple, and he again confronted the people concerning the Sabbath and intermarriage with people who worshiped other gods (13:10-28).

OUTLINE

1:1–7:73a
Nehemiah's Work to Rebuild the Walls of Jerusalem

7:73b–10:39
Ezra's Teaching of the Law Brings Covenant Renewal

11:1–13:31
Nehemiah Reorganizes Jerusalem and Institutes Further Reforms

AUTHORSHIP

The book itself does not identify its author. The Talmud (*Baba Batra* 15a) says that Ezra wrote both Ezra and Nehemiah, and this is the most likely possibility. Chapters 8–10 were probably from Ezra's own memoirs. Ezra also

TIMELINE

Oct 539 BC
Cyrus II conquers Babylon

538 BC
Cyrus's decree allows exiles to return to Judea

486–465 BC
Xerxes I (Ahasuerus) as king of Persia

479~478 BC
Esther becomes queen of Persia

465–424 BC
Artaxerxes I as king of Persia

458 BC
Ezra travels to Jerusalem

445 BC
Nehemiah's first trip to Jerusalem

445–433 BC
Nehemiah as governor of Judea

Oct 2, 445 BC
Jerusalem's wall is completed

432 BC
Nehemiah returns to Persia

about 430 BC
Nehemiah's second trip to Jerusalem

400s BC
Malachi as prophet

apparently depended on Nehemiah's memoirs. Chapters 1–7 and 11–13 might originally have been Nehemiah's report to the Persian court about his reconstruction progress in Jerusalem. Ezra adapted and arranged this material to fit his purpose when he wrote Ezra—Nehemiah.

Nehemiah shares several characteristics with Ezra. Both Ezra (chs 1–6) and Nehemiah (chs 1–7) describe the return of exiles to Jerusalem to complete a rebuilding project. Both books contain stories of neighbors opposing rebuilding efforts. Most importantly, both Nehemiah and Ezra show how hard work and God's help enabled the people to complete the construction of important structures in Jerusalem. Both books also tell of spiritual reforms in which the community listened to God's word, repented of past failures, and instituted religious and social reforms (chs 8–10; Ezra 9–10).

Several events in Nehemiah have parallels in Ezra that are told in similar ways. There are stories about those who opposed the rebuilding (6:1-14; Ezra 4:1-23), processionals to celebrate dedications (12:31-43; Ezra 6:16-18), and similar reforms (13:15-29; Ezra 9–10). Like Ezra, Nehemiah has lists of names (3:1-32; 7:6-73; 10:1-27; 11:1–12:26) and at least one parenthetical section (7:6–10:39) followed by the resumption of a previous account (11:1-4). These factors lead many biblical scholars to believe that one author wrote both Ezra and Nehemiah.

MEANING AND MESSAGE

Prayer. Nehemiah based his service on prayer. He earnestly prayed for God to rescue the people from their despised situation, and God answered by sending Nehemiah (1:1–2:8). When foreigners opposed restoring the walls of Jerusalem, Nehemiah asked God to judge them (4:4-5; 6:14). Nehemiah prayed for divine support when he dealt with people who were driving fellow Jews into slavery (6:14), those who were not tithing (13:14), and people who were not keeping the Sabbath (13:22). Prayer provided the power to accomplish God's will. Six times Nehemiah repeated a refrain asking the Lord to "remember" Nehemiah or his opponents (5:19; 6:14; 13:14, 22, 29, 31).

Nehemiah was a genuine leader, an excellent administrator, and a man of prayer. . . . Nehemiah's single-mindedness of purpose, attention to detail, and dependence on God were combined in a man who can simply be labeled as a servant of God.

M. BRENEMAN
Ezra, Nehemiah, Esther, p. 59

God's Providence. The book of Nehemiah emphasizes that God sovereignly controls the lives of individuals and nations. God is great and awesome, able to restore people from exile (1:8-9), to promote one of his servants to be the king's cup-bearer and later the governor of a province (1:11; 2:8, 18), and to give success in rebuilding the walls (2:20; 6:16). God protects his people (4:4-5, 9, 20) and frustrates the plans of the wicked (4:14-15). The same God who created heaven and earth (9:6), called Abram from Ur, and gave the land to Israel (9:7-8) was able to accomplish his will through Nehemiah.

Dedication to God's Word. The authoritative law of Moses contained God's instructions on how his people should live. God had made a "covenant of unfailing love with those who love him and obey his commands" (1:5). However, his people had not obeyed the instructions God gave to Moses (1:7-9), so they were in danger of God's punishment. Ezra read from the law of Moses (8:1-3) to restore the nation. In response, some of the people dedicated themselves to following the law by separating themselves from unbelievers (10:28), keeping the Sabbath, and giving their tithe for the Levites (10:29-39; 12:44).

Courage against Opposition. Nehemiah was courageous in dealing with opposition. Sanballat, Geshem, and Tobiah opposed the rebuilding of Jerusalem's walls (2:10) and mocked the work of God's people (2:19; 4:1-3). In addition, Arabs, Ammonites, and people from Ashdod plotted to attack the builders (4:7-9, 11; 6:1-14). Nehemiah responded to this opposition by posting guards and praying for God's help (4:6-23). Nehemiah also confronted internal conflict from members of the community who abused the poor (5:1-13), who married foreigners (9:1-2; 10:28-30; 13:23-28), and who did not tithe or keep the Sabbath holy (10:31-39; 13:10-22). Nehemiah's courage and prayer enabled him to succeed in addressing these problems.

FURTHER READING

M. BRENEMAN
Ezra, Nehemiah, Esther (1993)

F. CHARLES FENSHAM
The Books of Ezra and Nehemiah (1982)

DEREK KIDNER
Ezra & Nehemiah (1979)

GARY V. SMITH
Ezra-Nehemiah in *Cornerstone Biblical Commentary*, vol. 5b (2010)

1:1 Neh 2:1; 10:1; Esth 1:2; Dan 8:2; Zech 7:1
1:2 Neh 7:2
1:3 Neh 2:3, 17; 7:6
1:4 //Ezra 9:3; 10:1; [a]*'abal* (0056) ›Isa 3:26
1:5 Exod 20:6; Neh 4:14; 9:32
1:6 2 Chr 29:6; Ezra 10:1; Dan 9:20; [b]*yadah* (3034) ›Ps 7:17
1:7 Deut 28:14; Dan 9:5
1:8 Lev 26:33
1:9 Deut 12:5; 30:2-4
1:10 Exod 32:11; Deut 9:29
1:11 Gen 40:21; Neh 1:6

1. NEHEMIAH'S WORK TO REBUILD THE WALLS OF JERUSALEM (1:1–7:73a)

1 These are the memoirs of Nehemiah
son of Hacaliah.

Nehemiah's Concern for Jerusalem

In late autumn, in the month of Kislev, in
the twentieth year of King Artaxerxes'
reign, I was at the fortress of Susa. [2]Hanani,
one of my brothers, came to visit me with
some other men who had just arrived from
Judah. I asked them about the Jews who had
returned there from captivity and about
how things were going in Jerusalem.
[3]They said to me, "Things are not going
well for those who returned to the province
of Judah. They are in great trouble and disgrace.
The wall of Jerusalem has been torn
down, and the gates have been destroyed
by fire."
[4]When I heard this, I sat down and wept.
In fact, for days I [a]mourned, fasted, and
prayed to the God of heaven. [5]Then I said,
"O LORD, God of heaven, the great and
awesome God who keeps his covenant of
unfailing love with those who love him
and obey his commands, [6]listen to my
prayer! Look down and see me praying
night and day for your people Israel. I
[b]confess that we have sinned against
you. Yes, even my own family and I have
sinned! [7]We have sinned terribly by not
obeying the commands, decrees, and
regulations that you gave us through
your servant Moses.
[8]"Please remember what you
told your servant Moses: 'If you are
unfaithful to me, I will scatter you
among the nations. [9]But if you return to
me and obey my commands and live by
them, then even if you are exiled to the
ends of the earth, I will bring you back
to the place I have chosen for my name
to be honored.'
[10]"The people you rescued by your
great power and strong hand are your
servants. [11]O Lord, please hear my
prayer! Listen to the prayers of those of
us who delight in honoring you. Please

1:1–2:20 Upon hearing about Jerusalem's ruined condition, Nehemiah prayed for God's grace (1:1-11) and asked the king to send him to Jerusalem (2:1-8). When he arrived, he challenged the people to rebuild the city's wall (2:11-20).

1:1 ***the memoirs of Nehemiah:*** See Nehemiah Introduction, "Authorship," p. 809. • ***In late autumn, in the month of Kislev, in the twentieth year:*** Hebrew *In the month of Kislev of the twentieth year.* A number of dates in the book of Nehemiah can be cross-checked with dates in surviving Persian records and related accurately to our modern calendar. This month of the ancient Hebrew lunar calendar occurred within the months of November and December 446 BC. The *twentieth year* probably refers to the reign of King Artaxerxes I; cp. 2:1; 5:14. • ***Artaxerxes*** I reigned over Persia from 465 to 424 BC. • ***The fortress of Susa*** was the Persian king's winter palace.

1:2 ***Hanani*** might have been one of Nehemiah's blood ***brothers;*** this word in Hebrew can also mean "fellow countryman" (e.g., Deut 1:16, "fellow Israelite"). • ***the Jews who had returned:*** See Ezra 2:64-65; 8:1-14.

1:3 ***The wall of Jerusalem has been torn down:*** This probably refers to a recent setback in Jerusalem (see Ezra 4:6-23), not to the Babylonian conquest in 586 BC. • ***disgrace:*** Foreigners could gloat about the destroyed city, using it as evidence that Israel's God was too weak to protect it (cp. Joel 2:17; Mic 7:8-10).

1:4 Nehemiah fervently ***mourned, fasted, and prayed*** for about four months (cp. 1:1; 2:1), deeply concerned for Jerusalem.

1:5-11 Nehemiah's prayer includes praise (1:5), confession (1:6-7), remembrance of God's promises (1:8-9), and petition (1:10-11). Nehemiah recognized that Israel's current situation was not a failure of God's ***covenant of unfailing love.*** Israel's persistent sin had brought about the punishments entailed in the covenant.

1:6 ***I confess that we have sinned:*** Like Ezra (Ezra 9:5-15) and Daniel (Dan 9:4-19), Nehemiah identified with the sins of his people, made no excuses, and accepted both his individual responsibility and the responsibility of the larger covenant group that had sinned against God.

1:8-9 Nehemiah recalls God's curse on sin and his promise of restoration (Deut 4:25-31; 30:1-5). • ***The place . . . for my name to be honored*** was Jerusalem.

1:10 Nehemiah alludes to God's long-standing covenant relationship with the Israelites: He had ***rescued*** them in the Exodus (Deut 9:29) and made them his ***servants.***

1:11 ***today by making the king favorable to me*** (literally *today in the sight of this man*): Nehemiah knew God could

grant me success today by making the
king favorable to me. Put it into his heart
to be kind to me."

In those days I was the king's cup-bearer.

Nehemiah Goes to Jerusalem

2 Early the following spring, in the month
of Nisan, during the twentieth year of
King Artaxerxes' reign, I was serving the
king his wine. I had never before appeared
sad in his presence. 2So the king asked me,
"Why are you looking so sad? You don't look
sick to me. You must be deeply troubled."

Then I was terrified, 3but I replied, "Long
live the king! How can I not be sad? For the
city where my ancestors are buried is in
ruins, and the gates have been destroyed
by fire."

4The king asked, "Well, how can I help
you?"

With a [c]prayer to the God of heaven, 5I replied, "If it please the king, and if you are
pleased with me, your servant, send me to Judah to rebuild the city where my ancestors
are buried."

6The king, with the queen sitting beside
him, asked, "How long will you be gone?
When will you return?" After I told him how
long I would be gone, the king agreed to my
request.

7I also said to the king, "If it please the
king, let me have letters addressed to the
governors of the province west of the Euphrates River, instructing them to let me travel
safely through their territories on my way to
Judah. 8And please give me a letter addressed
to Asaph, the manager of the king's forest,

2:1 Ezra 7:1; Neh 1:1, 11
2:2 Prov 15:13
2:3 Neh 1:3; Dan 2:4
2:4 Neh 1:4; [c]*palal* (6419) ‣Neh 4:9
2:6 Neh 13:6
2:7 Ezra 7:21; 8:36; Neh 2:9
2:8 Eccl 2:5-6

NEHEMIAH (1:1–7:73)

Neh 8:9-10; 10:1–13:31

Nehemiah was a powerful leader of God's people living in Judea following the Exile. Nehemiah improved the morale and strength of God's people in the midst of their difficulties. Before Nehemiah returned to Judea, he was cup-bearer to the Persian king, Artaxerxes I (465–424 BC). The cup-bearer brought the king his wine (tasting it first to make sure it wasn't poisoned) and was his trusted confidant and adviser. Nehemiah was moved with compassion when he heard reports about Jerusalem's sad state and asked the king's permission to return to Judea to help his people. The king made him governor of the province of Judea for twelve years to aid his fellow Jews and rebuild the walls of Jerusalem (1:1–2:8). Nehemiah had the support of the Persian king, but he faced opposition from the inhabitants of the land. These people were Samaritans, people of mixed heritage who lived in the north. Nehemiah showed great courage and skill as he successfully helped the people of Judea rebuild the walls that protected Jerusalem.

Nehemiah had a strong personal faith, as seen by his prayers (1:4-11; 2:4) and his confidence in divine guidance and help (2:8, 18, 20). He advocated economic justice (ch 5). He rebuked a few rich Judeans who were exploiting a food shortage by exacting high interest from their poorer brothers, and he provided an example of better conduct.

Nehemiah was vitally concerned about the people's faithfulness, and he individually confronted men who had married pagan women (13:23-29). He had a strong interest in maintaining Temple worship, and he led the Jewish community to pledge to support Temple personnel and provide offerings (10:1, 32-39). He also reformed Sabbath observance (13:15-22).

Although there were still problems at the end of his tenure in Jerusalem (13:1-31), Nehemiah was a forceful leader (13:25) who restored a national and religious identity to the Jewish settlers in a period of political and economic weakness.

influence the king's ***heart*** to ***be kind*** to Nehemiah. • As ***cup-bearer*** Nehemiah tasted the king's wine to make sure it was not poisoned, which provided him daily access to King Artaxerxes.

2:1 ***Early the following spring:*** Literally *In the month of Nisan.* This month of the ancient Hebrew lunar calendar occurred within the months of April and May 445 BC. • ***King Artaxerxes:*** See note on 1:1. • ***never . . . sad in his presence:*** A servant was not to let his personal life interfere with serving the king.

2:2 Nehemiah ***was terrified*** because he had let his sadness show, and he did not know how the king would respond if he told him the reason for his sorrow (King Artaxerxes had previously ordered that Jerusalem not be rebuilt, Ezra 4:21-22). Nehemiah was not putting on an act; his deep mourning showed despite his best efforts to conceal it.

2:3 Nehemiah affirmed his loyalty with the customary ***long live the king*** (cp. Dan 2:4), yet he did not deny his sadness.

2:4 ***With a prayer:*** The king was subject to ***the God of heaven,*** and Nehemiah needed God's guidance and provision as he made his request.

2:5 ***send me to Judah to rebuild the city:*** Artaxerxes' openness to this proposal seems surprising in light of Jerusalem's history of rebellions against Persia (Ezra 4:17-23). The king might have viewed Nehemiah's plan as a way to solidify his own control over a troubled area of his empire.

2:6 ***How long will you be gone?*** (see 5:14): Nehemiah probably requested a short period of time initially, later asking for an extension.

2:7 ***the province west of the Euphrates River:*** Literally *the province beyond the river;* also in 2:9.

2:9
Ezra 8:22
Neh 2:7
2:10
Neh 2:19; 4:1-3
2:13
Neh 1:3; 3:13
2:14
2 Kgs 20:20
Neh 3:15

instructing him to give me timber. I will need
it to make beams for the gates of the Temple
fortress, for the city walls, and for a house for
myself." And the king granted these requests,
because the gracious hand of God was on me.
9When I came to the governors of the
province west of the Euphrates River, I delivered the king's letters to them. The king, I
should add, had sent along army officers and
horsemen to protect me. 10But when Sanballat the Horonite and Tobiah the Ammonite
official heard of my arrival, they were very
displeased that someone had come to help
the people of Israel.

Nehemiah Inspects Jerusalem's Wall

11So I arrived in Jerusalem. Three days later,
12I slipped out during the night, taking only
a few others with me. I had not told anyone
about the plans God had put in my heart for
Jerusalem. We took no pack animals with us
except the donkey I was riding. 13After dark
I went out through the Valley Gate, past the
Jackal's Well, and over to the Dung Gate to
inspect the broken walls and burned gates.
14Then I went to the Fountain Gate and to
the King's Pool, but my donkey couldn't get
through the rubble. 15So, though it was still
dark, I went up the Kidron Valley instead,
inspecting the wall before I turned back
and entered again at the Valley Gate.
16The city officials did not know I had
been out there or what I was doing, for I
had not yet said anything to anyone about
my plans. I had not yet spoken to the Jewish leaders—the priests, the nobles, the

God Works through Prayer (1:4-11)

Neh 2:4-5; 4:4-5, 9
Gen 24:10-20
Judg 15:18-20
Ezra 9:6-15
Ps 18:1-30; 22:4-5, 24; 30:2-3; 31:22; 34:4; 40:1-2; 81:7; 106:1-48; 107:6-7, 13-14; 116:1; 118:5
Dan 9:4-19
Jon 2:1-10
Acts 4:24-31
Jas 5:16-18

Prayer is essential for anyone who desires to live a godly life and carry out an effective ministry. In response to Jerusalem's disgraceful condition, Nehemiah spent four months in intensive intercessory prayer (cp. 1:1; 2:1). His prayers included praising God for his power and covenant love, confessing the nation's sins, and calling on God to act (1:4-11; cp. Ezra 9:6-15; Dan 9:4-19). Nehemiah based his prayer for Jerusalem in 1:5-11 on God's "covenant of unfailing love with those who love him and obey his commands" (1:5). The Israelites had not obeyed the instructions God gave to Moses (1:7), resulting in the exile of the nation as God had warned. However, Nehemiah was firmly convinced that God would keep his promise to restore the nation if the people repented (1:8-9; see Deut 4:25-31; 30:1-5).

When God presented an opening for Nehemiah to approach the Persian king about returning to Jerusalem, Nehemiah immediately prayed for God's guidance (2:4). He knew that only God could change the king's heart. Later, Nehemiah made a practical and balanced response to threats against those building the wall by posting guards and rallying the people, all while praying for God's protection and strength (4:4-5, 9; 6:9, 14). He needed God's help and blessing then and in the future as he confronted people who acted improperly.

When Nehemiah returned to Jerusalem after a brief visit to Persia, he found that some Jews were not contributing their tithe (13:10-12), some were not keeping the Sabbath (13:22), and some had married unbelievers (13:29-31). When confronting these people about their sin, Nehemiah prayed for God to have compassion on him and remember what he had done. Nehemiah knew that he had to depend on God's power to change people's hearts.

2:8 ***Temple fortress*** might refer to the Tower of Hananel or the Tower of the Hundred. • ***the gracious hand of God was on me:*** Nehemiah knew that ***the king granted these requests*** because God was sovereignly guiding the king to do so.

2:9 Because Nehemiah was a government official, he had an armed escort of ***officers and horsemen*** (or *charioteers*) for his trip to Jerusalem (cp. Ezra 8:22).

2:10 Some of the local, non-Jewish officials ***were very displeased*** because rebuilding the walls of Jerusalem would change the balance of political power in favor of the Jews. • ***Sanballat*** was the main leader of opposition to Nehemiah's rebuilding efforts. • ***the Horonite:*** He was probably from Upper or Lower Horon (Beth-horon, Josh 16:3), approximately 12 miles [19 kilometers] northwest of Jerusalem. Sanballat's name might indicate that he was a descendant of the Assyrian people imported by Sargon II after the fall of Samaria (2 Kgs 17:24). A document discovered in Egypt indicates that he eventually became governor of Samaria in 408 BC.

2:12-15 Nehemiah needed firsthand knowledge of the condition of the walls to present credible ***plans*** for their reconstruction and to rally the labor he would need. He conducted his survey secretly ***after dark*** to avoid detection by his opponents. His inspection covered only the southern part of the city.

2:13 ***Jackal's Well*** (or *Serpent's Well*) might have been En-rogel, a water source located about 400 yards [365 meters] south of the city, or the pool of Siloam, which is filled by water flowing through Hezekiah's meandering, serpentine tunnel. • The ***Dung Gate*** (called the "Gate of Broken Pots" in Jer 19:2) at the southern end of the western wall (see 3:13) led to the Hinnom Valley, where inhabitants of the city threw their garbage.

2:14 The ***King's Pool*** was either the pool of Siloam or another pool southeast of the city; both were created from the overflow of the Gihon Spring (see 2 Kgs 20:20).

2:15 ***the Kidron Valley:*** Literally *the valley*.

2:16-17 Nehemiah kept his inspection and rebuilding plans secret from both the Persian and ***Jewish leaders***

officials, or anyone else in the administration. 17But now I said to them, "You know
very well what trouble we are in. Jerusalem
lies in ruins, and its gates have been destroyed by fire. Let us rebuild the wall of
Jerusalem and end this disgrace!" 18Then I
told them about how the gracious hand of
God had been on me, and about my conversation with the king.
They replied at once, "Yes, let's rebuild
the wall!" So they began the good work.
19But when Sanballat, Tobiah, and Geshem the Arab heard of our plan, they
scoffed contemptuously. "What are you
doing? Are you rebelling against the king?"
they asked.
20I replied, "The God of heaven will help
us succeed. We, his servants, will start rebuilding this wall. But you have no share,
legal right, or historic claim in Jerusalem."

Rebuilding the Walls of Jerusalem

3 Then Eliashib the high priest and the
other priests started to rebuild at the
Sheep Gate. They dedicated it and set up its
doors, building the wall as far as the Tower
of the Hundred, which they dedicated, and
the Tower of Hananel. 2People from the
town of Jericho worked next to them, and
beyond them was Zaccur son of Imri.
3The Fish Gate was built by the sons of
Hassenaah. They laid the beams, set up
its doors, and installed its bolts and bars.
4Meremoth son of Uriah and grandson of
Hakkoz repaired the next section of wall.
Beside him were Meshullam son of Berekiah and grandson of Meshezabel, and then
Zadok son of Baana. 5Next were the people
from Tekoa, though their leaders refused to
work with the construction supervisors.
6The Old City Gate was repaired by Joiada

2:17 Neh 1:3
2:19 Neh 6:6
2:20 Ezra 4:3; Neh 2:4
3:1 Neh 3:20, 32; 6:1; 7:1; 12:39; 13:28; Jer 31:38
3:2 Neh 7:36
3:3 Neh 12:39
3:6 Neh 12:39

The Wall of Jerusalem (3:1-32)

Neh 1:2-4; 2:10-20; 4:1-23; 6:1-16
Ps 51:16-18
Isa 22:5; 26:1-3
Rev 21:10-27

The wall of Jerusalem had great political, social, and religious significance for the people of Judah (see 2:10, 19; 4:1-15; 6:1-14). The destroyed wall was a shameful reminder that God had destroyed the city, fulfilling the covenant curses because of the people's sin (1:2, 6-8; 2:17). Consequently, the rebuilt wall would be a sign of God's blessing and proof that God was bringing the promised restoration to his covenant people. Israel's enemies knew that if the wall was rebuilt, the Jews would gain political power, security, and self-determination, and so they opposed it fiercely.

Unfortunately, we are unable fully to reconstruct the Jerusalem of Nehemiah's day and the location of his walls. Many of the landmarks mentioned in Nehemiah were destroyed during Herod the Great's renovations some 400 years later (37–4 BC), and today only limited excavation is permitted in Jerusalem. Many scholars now believe that Nehemiah's restoration project included only the wall around the City of David on the eastern hill.

The speed and success of the reconstruction is a witness to all believers that with God's help, his people can accomplish amazing things (2:18; 4:14-15, 20; 6:16).

to prevent opposition from being organized. ***But now*** Nehemiah was effectively positioned to lead the rebuilding effort. • ***what trouble we are in:*** The broken walls brought ***disgrace*** on the city and reflected negatively on God; Jerusalem certainly did not look like the "city of the great King" (Ps 48:2).

2:18 Evidence of God's clear involvement (2:8) is a strong motivator in any project. Nehemiah had God's guidance, the king's permission, the necessary letters to procure lumber, and a plan to lead the project. So the people enthusiastically agreed to begin working.

2:19 Nehemiah's enemies immediately ***scoffed*** and tried to stop progress. These opponents were dangerous because of their potential ability to discourage the people and undermine Nehemiah's credibility. • ***Are you rebelling against the king?*** This serious charge could bring death (see also Ezra 4:6-23).

2:20 The title ***God of heaven*** communicated to Persian audiences that Israel's true God was not a minor local deity. Nehemiah remained focused on obeying his sovereign by building the walls.

3:1-32 This summary of the people who rebuilt the walls of Jerusalem moves in a circle around the city, starting at the northeast corner and moving west, then south, east, and north.

3:1-5 The rebuilding of the walls and gates around the northern section of the city was divided into eight work groups.

3:1 ***Eliashib the high priest,*** the grandson of Jeshua (12:10), led the priests in working on the northern wall around the Temple. • ***The Sheep Gate*** was where the people brought in their sheep on their way to sacrifice at the Temple. • ***The Tower of the Hundred*** and ***the Tower of Hananel*** were two major military towers along the northern wall (12:39; Jer 31:38; Zech 14:10).

3:3 At the ***Fish Gate,*** people sold fish from the Sea of Galilee and the Mediterranean Sea.

3:4 ***Meremoth:*** See Ezra 8:33. • ***Meshullam*** had given his daughter in marriage to a son of Tobiah (6:18; see also 10:20).

3:5 The ***leaders*** of ***Tekoa*** might have been influenced by Geshem (2:19), who controlled the area south of Tekoa.

3:6-8 These verses describe work done on the walls and gates on the western side of Jerusalem. Even people from outside the city and people having wealth or more delicate occupations participated.

3:6 ***The Old City Gate*** (or ***The Mishneh Gate,*** or ***The Jeshanah Gate***): The oldest part of Jerusalem sat on an eastern hill that ran north to the Temple Mount.

3:8
Neh 3:31-32; 12:38
3:9
Neh 3:12, 17
3:11
Neh 12:38
3:12
Neh 3:9
3:13
Neh 2:13
3:14
Neh 2:13
3:15
2 Kgs 25:4-5
Neh 2:14; 12:37
3:16
2 Kgs 20:20
Neh 2:14; 3:9, 12, 17

son of Paseah and Meshullam son of Besodeiah. They laid the beams, set up its doors, and installed its bolts and bars. 7 Next to them were Melatiah from Gibeon, Jadon from Meronoth, people from Gibeon, and people from Mizpah, the headquarters of the governor of the province west of the Euphrates River. 8 Next was Uzziel son of Harhaiah, a goldsmith by trade, who also worked on the wall. Beyond him was Hananiah, a manufacturer of perfumes. They left out a section of Jerusalem as they built the Broad Wall.

9 Rephaiah son of Hur, the leader of half the district of Jerusalem, was next to them on the wall. 10 Next Jedaiah son of Harumaph repaired the wall across from his own house, and next to him was Hattush son of Hashabneiah. 11 Then came Malkijah son of Harim and Hasshub son of Pahath-moab, who repaired another section of the wall and the Tower of the Ovens. 12 Shallum son of Hallohesh and his daughters repaired the next section. He was the leader of the other half of the district of Jerusalem.

13 The Valley Gate was repaired by the people from Zanoah, led by Hanun. They set up its doors and installed its bolts and bars. They also repaired the 1,500 feet of wall to the Dung Gate.

14 The Dung Gate was repaired by Malkijah son of Recab, the leader of the Beth-hakkerem district. He rebuilt it, set up its doors, and installed its bolts and bars.

15 The Fountain Gate was repaired by Shallum son of Col-hozeh, the leader of the Mizpah district. He rebuilt it, roofed it, set up its doors, and installed its bolts and bars. Then he repaired the wall of the pool of Siloam near the king's garden, and he rebuilt the wall as far as the stairs that descend from the City of David. 16 Next to him was Nehemiah son of Azbuk, the leader of half the district of Beth-zur. He rebuilt the wall from a place across from the tombs of David's family as far as the water reservoir and the House of the Warriors.

17 Next to him, repairs were made by a group of Levites working under the supervision of Rehum son of Bani. Then came Hashabiah, the leader of half the district of Keilah, who supervised the building of the wall on behalf of his own district. 18 Next down the line were his countrymen led by

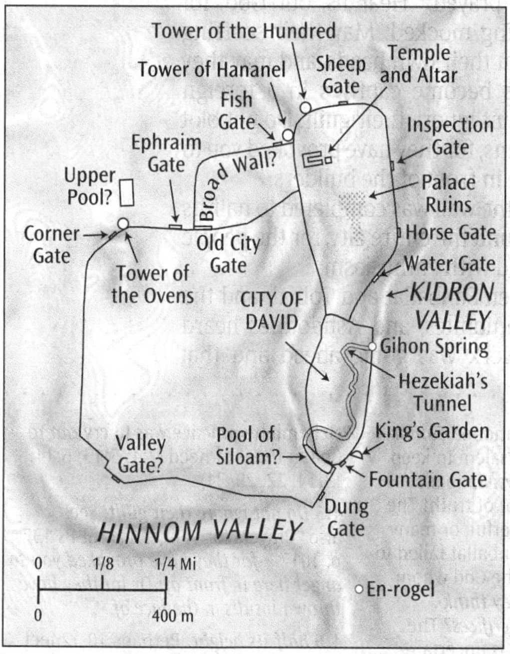

◀ **The Rebuilding of Jerusalem, 445 BC** (3:1–7:15). The walls of Jerusalem had lain in ruins since the destruction of Jerusalem in 586 BC. Under Nehemiah's leadership, the inhabitants of Judea rebuilt the entire wall in only 52 days during the fall of 445 BC.

3:7 ***Gibeon*** and ***Mizpah*** were about six miles [10 kilometers] north of Jerusalem. • ***the province west of the Euphrates River:*** Literally *the province beyond the river.*

3:8 ***They left out a section of Jerusalem as they built the Broad Wall:*** Or *They fortified Jerusalem up to the Broad Wall.* The *Broad Wall* was located in the newer, western section of the city.

3:9-13 Nehemiah wisely assigned people to work near their homes both to motivate them to do good work and to save them traveling time.

3:11 The ***Tower of the Ovens*** on the western wall of the city might have been a place to bake bread or to burnish pottery (Jer 19:1-2).

3:13 ***Zanoah*** was a village about thirteen miles [21 kilometers] southwest of Jerusalem. • ***1,500 feet:*** Hebrew *1,000 cubits* [450 meters].

3:14-15 These verses focus on the reconstruction of the southern tip of the city where the Hinnom Valley and Kidron Valley meet.

3:14 The ***Beth-hakkerem district*** might have been about two miles [3.2 kilometers] south of Jerusalem (at modern Ramat Rachel) or five miles [8 kilometers] west (at modern Ain Karem).

3:15 The ***Mizpah district*** was about six miles [10 kilometers] north of Jerusalem. • ***Shallum:*** As in Syriac version; Hebrew reads *Shallun.* • ***pool of Siloam:*** Hebrew *pool of Shelah,* another name for the *pool of Siloam.* • The ***king's garden*** was a lush area south of the pool of Siloam near where the Kidron and Hinnom Valleys meet, possibly at the King's Pool (2:14).

3:16-32 These verses describe the building of the new eastern wall.

3:16 The ***district of Beth-zur*** was located just north of Hebron. • The ***tombs of David's family*** might refer to where King David was buried (1 Kgs 2:10; 11:43; 2 Chr 21:20; Acts 2:29), and the ***House of the Warriors*** might have been a tomb for David's mighty men (2 Sam 23:8-39).

Binnui son of Henadad, the leader of the other half of the district of Keilah.

[19]Next to them, Ezer son of Jeshua, the leader of Mizpah, repaired another section of wall across from the ascent to the armory near the angle in the wall. [20]Next to him was Baruch son of Zabbai, who zealously repaired an additional section from the angle to the door of the house of Eliashib the high priest. [21]Meremoth son of Uriah and grandson of Hakkoz rebuilt another section of the wall extending from the door of Eliashib's house to the end of the house.

[22]The next repairs were made by the priests from the surrounding region. [23]After them, Benjamin and Hasshub repaired the section across from their house, and Azariah son of Maaseiah and grandson of Ananiah repaired the section across from his house. [24]Next was Binnui son of Henadad, who rebuilt another section of the wall from Azariah's house to the angle and the corner. [25]Palal son of Uzai carried on the work from a point opposite the angle and the tower that projects up from the king's upper house beside the court of the guard. Next to him were Pedaiah son of Parosh, [26]with the Temple servants living on the hill of Ophel, who repaired the wall as far as a point across from the Water Gate to the east and the projecting tower. [27]Then came the people of Tekoa, who repaired another section across from the great projecting tower and over to the wall of Ophel.

[28]Above the Horse Gate, the priests repaired the wall. Each one repaired the section immediately across from his own house. [29]Next Zadok son of Immer also rebuilt the wall across from his own house, and beyond him was Shemaiah son of Shecaniah, the gatekeeper of the East Gate. [30]Next Hananiah son of Shelemiah and Hanun, the sixth son of Zalaph, repaired another section, while Meshullam son of Berekiah rebuilt the wall across from where he lived. [31]Malkijah, one of the goldsmiths, repaired the wall as far as the housing for the Temple servants and merchants, across from the Inspection Gate. Then he continued as far as the upper room at the corner. [32]The other goldsmiths and merchants repaired the wall from that corner to the Sheep Gate.

Opposition to the Rebuilding

4 Sanballat was very angry when he learned that we were rebuilding the wall. He flew into a rage and mocked the Jews, [2]saying in front of his friends and the Samarian army officers, "What does this bunch of poor, feeble Jews think they're doing? Do they think they can build the wall in a single day by just offering a few sacrifices? Do they actually think they can make something of stones from a rubbish heap—and charred ones at that?"

[3]Tobiah the Ammonite, who was standing beside him, remarked, "That stone wall would collapse if even a fox walked along the top of it!"

[4]Then I prayed, "Hear us, our God, for we are being mocked. May their scoffing fall back on their own heads, and may they themselves become captives in a foreign land! [5]Do not ignore their guilt. Do not blot out their sins, for they have provoked you to anger here in front of the builders."

[6]At last the wall was completed to half its height around the entire city, for the people had worked with enthusiasm.

[7]But when Sanballat and Tobiah and the Arabs, Ammonites, and Ashdodites heard that the work was going ahead and that

3:19 2 Chr 26:9; Neh 3:15-16
3:20 Neh 3:1
3:22 Neh 12:28
3:24 Neh 3:19
3:25 Jer 32:2
3:26 Neh 7:46; 8:1, 3; 11:21
3:27 Neh 3:5
3:28 2 Kgs 11:16; 2 Chr 23:15; Jer 31:40
3:31 Neh 3:1, 8
3:32 Neh 3:1; 12:39
4:1 Neh 2:10, 19
4:3 Neh 2:10
4:4 Ps 79:12; 123:3-4
4:5 Ps 69:27-28; Jer 18:23

3:18 *Binnui:* As in a few Hebrew manuscripts, some Greek manuscripts, and Syriac version (see also 3:24; 10:9); most Hebrew manuscripts read *Bavvai.*

3:24 The *angle and the corner* refers to an unidentified turn in the wall.

3:25-26 The *tower that projects up from the king's upper house* and the *court of the guard* might refer to a royal complex on the *hill of Ophel,* just south of the Temple area.

3:28-32 This final group of workers connected the repairs to the *Sheep Gate,* where the work had started (3:1). • *Horse Gate:* See also 2 Chr 23:15; Jer 31:40. • *East Gate:* See also 1 Chr 26:14, 17; 2 Chr 31:14; Ezek 10:19; 40:21-22.

4:1-6 Verses 4:1-6 are numbered 3:33-38 in the Hebrew text.

4:2 The Persians had stationed *Samarian army officers* in Jerusalem to keep peace. • *poor, feeble Jews:* Sanballat's mockery had an element of truth: The Jews were not rich, powerful, or many in number. However, Sanballat failed to realize the strength of the God whom the Jews served. • *Do they think . . . by just offering a few sacrifices?* The meaning of the Hebrew is uncertain. Sanballat might have been mocking a sudden increase in sacrifices at the Temple as the Israelites dedicated their work to the Lord. • *rubbish . . . charred:* When fire destroyed Jerusalem (586 BC), it heated the stones, causing some to crack and crumble. The people used these stones to restore the walls.

4:4 Nehemiah prayed intensely for God to stop those who opposed God's will. Nehemiah's practice was to cry out to God in times of need (2:4; 5:19; 6:14; 13:14, 22, 29, 31).

4:5 *Do not ignore their guilt:* See also "Prayers for Vengeance" at Ps 137, p. 1017. • *for they have provoked you to anger here in front of:* Or *for they have thrown insults in the face of.*

4:6 *half its height:* Perhaps 10-12 feet [3.0-3.7 meters] tall, since some scholars speculate that the original wall was 20-24 feet [6.0-7.3 meters] high.

4:7-23 Verses 4:7-23 are numbered 4:1-17 in the Hebrew text.

4:7 Israel's enemies from the north (*Sanballat*), the south (*Arabs*), the east (*Ammonites*), and the west (*Ashdodites*) were enraged by the speed and success of Jerusalem's reconstruction, which

4:9 [d]palal (6419) ‣Ps 32:6
4:13 Neh 4:9, 17-18
4:14 Num 14:9 Deut 1:29-30 2 Sam 10:12
4:15 2 Sam 17:14

the gaps in the wall of Jerusalem were being repaired, they were furious. [8]They all made plans to come and fight against Jerusalem and throw us into confusion. [9]But we [d]prayed to our God and guarded the city day and night to protect ourselves.

[10]Then the people of Judah began to complain, "The workers are getting tired, and there is so much rubble to be moved. We will never be able to build the wall by ourselves."

[11]Meanwhile, our enemies were saying, "Before they know what's happening, we will swoop down on them and kill them and end their work."

[12]The Jews who lived near the enemy came and told us again and again, "They will come from all directions and attack us!" [13]So I placed armed guards behind the lowest parts of the wall in the exposed areas. I stationed the people to stand guard by families, armed with swords, spears, and bows.

[14]Then as I looked over the situation, I called together the nobles and the rest of the people and said to them, "Don't be afraid of the enemy! Remember the Lord, who is great and glorious, and fight for your brothers, your sons, your daughters, your wives, and your homes!"

[15]When our enemies heard that we knew of their plans and that God had frustrated them, we all returned to our work on the wall. [16]But from then on, only half my men worked while the other half stood guard with spears, shields, bows, and coats of mail. The leaders stationed themselves behind the people of Judah [17]who were building the wall. The laborers carried on their work with one hand supporting their load and one hand holding a weapon. [18]All the builders

Dealing with Conflict (4:1-23)

Neh 2:19-20; 5:1-13; 6:1-14; 13:4-28
Gen 13:5-13; 26:12-35
Exod 32:1-35
1 Sam 7:3-8
2 Sam 12:1-31; 19:41-43
2 Chr 20:1-37; 34:3-7
Ps 140:1-2
Prov 13:10; 17:14, 19; 25:8; 26:17, 21; 29:22
Hab 1:3
Acts 23:6-11
2 Cor 7:5-6
Eph 6:10-18
Phil 2:3
1 Tim 6:4
2 Tim 2:14, 23-26
Titus 2:15
Jas 3:13-18

Nehemiah faced both external and internal opposition to all that God was directing him to do. External opposition came from foreigners such as Sanballat, Geshem, and Tobiah. They fiercely opposed the rebuilding of Jerusalem's walls (2:10) and mocked Nehemiah's leadership (2:19; 4:1-3). The opposition gradually grew to include other Arabs, Ammonites, and people from Ashdod, who plotted to attack the builders (4:7-9, 11). To meet this opposition, Nehemiah posted guards, prayed for God's help, developed an emergency warning system, and kept working (4:6-23). Israel's frustrated enemies made several attempts to disgrace or kill Nehemiah (6:1-14). However, Nehemiah had the wisdom to avoid or frustrate their plots while focusing on the task God had given him.

Nehemiah also faced internal problems. Wealthy Jews were mistreating the poor by charging high interest (5:1-13). Jews had married foreigners who worshiped other gods (9:1-2; 10:28-30; 13:23-28). Many were not tithing or keeping the Sabbath holy (10:31-39; 13:10-22). Confronting these problems required a firm commitment to the principles explained in Scripture, boldness in insisting that people follow these divine instructions, and compassion in restoring people to fellowship after the confrontation. Finally, he had to oppose the high priest Eliashib, who had allowed Tobiah to use one of the Temple storerooms (13:4-9).

In each of these cases, Nehemiah courageously followed the example of earlier leaders such as Moses, who opposed the worship of the gold calf (Exod 32); Samuel, who opposed those involved with Baal worship (1 Sam 7:3-8); Nathan, who opposed David's sins (2 Sam 12); and Jehoshaphat, who trusted in God to defeat a much stronger enemy (2 Chr 20). Like these earlier men of God, Nehemiah took a stand for what was right instead of letting those for whom he was responsible go their own ways. He refused to be discouraged or intimidated by internal difficulties or external threats against him. He consistently depended on God for wisdom and for blessing on his work.

threatened these opponents' political power in the region.

4:9 ***we prayed . . . and guarded:*** This wise approach to the threat involved both relying on God and doing what was needed.

4:11 The relentless psychological attack of Israel's *enemies* was having a negative effect on morale.

4:12 ***They will come from all directions and attack us!*** The meaning of the Hebrew is uncertain. Jews from the surrounding areas might have been exhorting the people working in Jerusalem to return to their villages to avoid being killed in an attack.

4:13 Nehemiah countered by positioning ***armed guards*** near the most vulnerable ***parts of the wall.*** He also made sure opponents outside the wall could see the forces ready to defend the city.

4:14 The strongest motivation for hope was Israel's ***great and glorious*** God, who had delivered his people from mighty nations before (cp. 2 Chr 32:7-8; see Exod 14:13-14; Deut 8:1-3; 20:3; Josh 10:25). Another motivation was to protect their own families and properties.

4:15 Nehemiah gave the credit to *God* (see also 2:20; 6:16), who ***had frustrated them*** through the prayers of the people, the 24-hour patrol, the open display of force, and the confidence in God's protection.

had a sword belted to their side. The trumpeter stayed with me to sound the alarm.
19Then I explained to the nobles and officials and all the people, "The work is very
spread out, and we are widely separated
from each other along the wall. 20When you
hear the blast of the trumpet, rush to wherever it is sounding. Then our God will fight
for us!"
21We worked early and late, from sunrise
to sunset. And half the men were always
on guard. 22I also told everyone living outside the walls to stay in Jerusalem. That
way they and their servants could help with
guard duty at night and work during the
day. 23During this time, none of us—not I,
nor my relatives, nor my servants, nor the
guards who were with me—ever took off our
clothes. We carried our weapons with us at
all times, even when we went for water.

Nehemiah Defends the Oppressed

5 About this time some of the men and
their wives raised a cry of protest
against their fellow Jews. 2They were saying, "We have such large families. We need
more food to survive."
3Others said, "We have mortgaged our
fields, vineyards, and homes to get food during the famine."
4And others said, "We have had to borrow money on our fields and vineyards
to pay our taxes. 5We belong to the same
family as those who are wealthy, and our
children are just like theirs. Yet we must sell
our children into slavery just to get enough
money to live. We have already sold some of
our daughters, and we are helpless to do anything about it, for our fields and vineyards
are already mortgaged to others."
6When I heard their complaints, I was
very angry. 7After thinking it over, I spoke
out against these nobles and officials. I told
them, "You are hurting your own relatives
by charging interest when they borrow
money!" Then I called a public meeting to
deal with the problem.
8At the meeting I said to them, "We are
doing all we can to redeem our Jewish relatives who have had to sell themselves to
pagan foreigners, but you are selling them
back into slavery again. How often must we
redeem them?" And they had nothing to say
in their defense.
9Then I pressed further, "What you are
doing is not right! Should you not walk in
the fear of our God in order to avoid being
mocked by enemy nations? 10I myself, as
well as my brothers and my workers, have
been lending the people money and grain,
but now let us stop this business of charging interest. 11You must restore their fields,
vineyards, olive groves, and homes to them
this very day. And repay the interest you
charged when you lent them money, grain,
new wine, and olive oil."
12They replied, "We will give back everything and demand nothing more from
the people. We will do as you say." Then
I called the priests and made the nobles
and officials swear to do what they had
promised.
13I shook out the folds of my robe and
said, "If you fail to keep your promise, may

4:20 Exod 14:14; Deut 1:30
5:1-2 Lev 25:35; Deut 15:7
5:4 Ezra 4:13; 7:24
5:5 Gen 37:27; Lev 25:39
5:7 Exod 22:25; Lev 25:36
5:8 Lev 25:48
5:12 Ezra 10:5; Neh 10:31
5:13 Neh 8:6; Acts 18:6

4:18-19 Through the ***trumpeter***, Nehemiah could ***sound the alarm*** to direct workers to any portion of the wall that might be attacked.

4:20 ***our God will fight for us!*** Drawing on Israel's ancient holy war tradition (Exod 14:14; Deut 1:30; 20:4; Josh 10:14; 23:10), Nehemiah encouraged the people that victory was certain if they trusted in the Lord.

4:23 Nehemiah and the other leaders were not elitists who relaxed while others toiled. • ***We carried . . . went for water:*** Or *Each carried his weapon in his right hand.* Hebrew reads *Each his weapon the water.* The meaning of the Hebrew is uncertain.

5:1-13 Although severe financial problems threatened to derail the wall's completion (5:1-5), Nehemiah worked out a solution (5:6-13).

5:2 Some farmers had diverted their efforts from raising crops to building the wall, leaving their ***large families*** in need of ***food to survive.*** Someone had to feed their families, or they would have to stop work on the wall and go home to work in their fields.

5:3 Some small landowners had ***mortgaged*** everything to survive. The ***famine*** made the problem worse because grain was scarce and the price of food naturally increased.

5:4 ***to pay our taxes:*** Despite the famine, the Persians did not cancel the onerous royal tribute due at harvest time.

5:5 ***we must sell our children into slavery:*** See Exod 21:1-11. These families were desperate to survive.

5:6-7 Nehemiah was ***very angry,*** but he controlled himself, thought it over, and then ***spoke out*** in order to resolve the conflict rather than make it worse (see Jas 1:19-20).

5:9 ***walk in the fear of our God:*** See Lev 25:35-43. • ***avoid being mocked:*** See also 1:3; 2:19; 4:1-3.

5:10 ***I myself . . . have been lending:*** Nehemiah and his associates were evidently making loans without burdening people. Nehemiah's example was the solution: to give financial help without pushing people further into debt by ***charging interest*** (see Deut 15:7-11).

5:11 Nehemiah demanded that the rich lenders ***restore their fields*** and ***repay the interest*** (literally ***the hundredth part***), which they should not have collected (see also Exod 22:25; Lev 25:35-37). The literal *hundredth part* suggests that the interest was one percent per month, lower than the twenty percent annual rate found in some documents of that time, or the sixty percent annual rate charged at Elephantine in Egypt. But even a relatively low rate of interest violated God's covenant.

5:12 ***made the nobles and officials swear:*** Both God and the community would hold them accountable.

e'amen (0543)
‣Neh 8:6

5:14
Neh 1:1; 13:6

5:15
Neh 5:9

5:17
1 Kgs 18:19

5:18
1 Kgs 4:22-23
2 Thes 3:8

5:19
Neh 13:14, 22, 31

6:1
Neh 3:1, 3

6:2
1 Chr 8:12

6:6
Neh 2:19

6:10
Jer 36:5

6:13
Neh 6:6

God shake you like this from your homes and from your property!"

The whole assembly responded, "eAmen," and they praised the LORD. And the people did as they had promised.

14For the entire twelve years that I was governor of Judah—from the twentieth year to the thirty-second year of the reign of King Artaxerxes—neither I nor my officials drew on our official food allowance. 15The former governors, in contrast, had laid heavy burdens on the people, demanding a daily ration of food and wine, besides forty pieces of silver. Even their assistants took advantage of the people. But because I feared God, I did not act that way.

16I also devoted myself to working on the wall and refused to acquire any land. And I required all my servants to spend time working on the wall. 17I asked for nothing, even though I regularly fed 150 Jewish officials at my table, besides all the visitors from other lands! 18The provisions I paid for each day included one ox, six choice sheep or goats, and a large number of poultry. And every ten days we needed a large supply of all kinds of wine. Yet I refused to claim the governor's food allowance because the people already carried a heavy burden.

19Remember, O my God, all that I have
done for these people, and bless me for it.

Continued Opposition to Rebuilding

6 Sanballat, Tobiah, Geshem the Arab, and the rest of our enemies found out that I had finished rebuilding the wall and that no gaps remained—though we had not yet set up the doors in the gates. 2So Sanballat and Geshem sent a message asking me to meet them at one of the villages in the plain of Ono.

But I realized they were plotting to harm me, 3so I replied by sending this message to them: "I am engaged in a great work, so I can't come. Why should I stop working to come and meet with you?"

4Four times they sent the same message, and each time I gave the same reply. 5The fifth time, Sanballat's servant came with an open letter in his hand, 6and this is what it said:

"There is a rumor among the surrounding nations, and Geshem tells me it is true, that you and the Jews are planning to rebel and that is why you are building the wall. According to his reports, you plan to be their king. 7He also reports that you have appointed prophets in Jerusalem to proclaim about you, 'Look! There is a king in Judah!'

"You can be very sure that this report will get back to the king, so I suggest that you come and talk it over with me."

8I replied, "There is no truth in any part of your story. You are making up the whole thing."

9They were just trying to intimidate us, imagining that they could discourage us and stop the work. So I continued the work with even greater determination.

10Later I went to visit Shemaiah son of Delaiah and grandson of Mehetabel, who was confined to his home. He said, "Let us meet together inside the Temple of God and bolt the doors shut. Your enemies are coming to kill you tonight."

11But I replied, "Should someone in my position run from danger? Should someone in my position enter the Temple to save his life? No, I won't do it!" 12I realized that God had not spoken to him, but that he had uttered this prophecy against me because Tobiah and Sanballat had hired him. 13They were hoping to intimidate me and make me

5:14-19 This section describes Nehemiah's consistent policy of servant leadership and personal generosity.

5:14 This is the first mention of Nehemiah's status as *governor,* a position not mentioned when the king first sent Nehemiah to Jerusalem. • Persia's government officials usually *drew* an ***official food allowance*** from the local population, but Nehemiah and his associates instead purchased food out of their regular pay. • ***from the twentieth year to the thirty-second year of the reign of King Artaxerxes:*** That is, 445–433 BC.

5:15 ***The former governors*** were probably Nehemiah's immediate predecessors, not Sheshbazzar (Ezra 1:8, about ninety years earlier) or Zerubbabel (Hag 1:1, about eighty years earlier). • ***forty pieces:*** Hebrew *40 shekels* [1 pound, or 456 grams].

5:19 Nehemiah's prayer for God to ***remember*** and ***bless*** him was a sign of his dependence on God.

6:1-19 With the financial crisis solved (ch 5), the narrative returns to how the enemies of rebuilding tried to intimidate or eliminate Nehemiah.

6:2 ***at one of the villages:*** As in Greek version; Hebrew reads *at Kephirim.* • The ***plain of Ono,*** located near Lod (Ezra 2:33), was probably a neutral site west of Jerusalem, where Nehemiah would have been unprotected.

6:6-7 ***planning to rebel . . . you plan to be their king:*** Those who had opposed the restoration of the Temple had used similar tactics (see Ezra 4). • At times in Israel's history, ***prophets*** did play a role in establishing a new king (cp. 1 Sam 9:16; 2 Kgs 9). • ***Geshem:*** Hebrew *Gashmu,* a variant spelling of *Geshem.*

6:9 ***So I continued the work with even greater determination:*** As in Greek version; Hebrew reads *But now to strengthen my hands.*

6:11 A good leader would not ***run from danger*** but would stand as an example to his people.

sin. Then they would be able to accuse and
discredit me.

14 Remember, O my God, all the evil
things that Tobiah and Sanballat have
done. And remember Noadiah the
[f]prophet and all the [f]prophets like her
who have tried to intimidate me.

The Builders Complete the Wall

15 So on October 2 the wall was finished—
just fifty-two days after we had begun.
16 When our enemies and the surrounding
nations heard about it, they were frightened
and humiliated. They realized this work had
been done with the help of our God.
17 During those fifty-two days, many letters went back and forth between Tobiah
and the nobles of Judah. 18 For many in Judah had sworn allegiance to him because
his father-in-law was Shecaniah son of
Arah, and his son Jehohanan was married to
the daughter of Meshullam son of Berekiah.
19 They kept telling me about Tobiah's good
deeds, and then they told him everything I
said. And Tobiah kept sending threatening
letters to intimidate me.

7 After the wall was finished and I had set
up the doors in the gates, the gatekeepers, singers, and Levites were appointed. 2 I
gave the responsibility of governing Jerusalem to my brother Hanani, along with
Hananiah, the commander of the fortress,
for he was a faithful man who feared God
more than most. 3 I said to them, "Do not
leave the gates open during the hottest part
of the day. And even while the gatekeepers are on duty, have them shut and bar
the doors. Appoint the residents of Jerusalem to act as guards, everyone on a regular
watch. Some will serve at sentry posts and
some in front of their own homes."

Nehemiah Registers the People

4 At that time the city was large and spacious, but the population was small, and
none of the houses had been rebuilt. 5 So my
God gave me the idea to call together all the
nobles and leaders of the city, along with
the ordinary citizens, for registration. I had
found the genealogical record of those who
had first returned to Judah. This is what
was written there:

6 Here is the list of the Jewish exiles of
the provinces who returned from their
captivity. King Nebuchadnezzar had
deported them to Babylon, but now they
returned to Jerusalem and the other
towns in Judah where they originally
lived. 7 Their leaders were Zerubbabel,
Jeshua, Nehemiah, Seraiah, Reelaiah,
Nahamani, Mordecai, Bilshan, Mispar,
Bigvai, Rehum, and Baanah.

This is the number of the men of Israel
who returned from exile:

8 The family of Parosh	2,172
9 The family of Shephatiah	372
10 The family of Arah	652
11 The family of Pahath-moab (descendants of Jeshua and Joab)	2,818
12 The family of Elam	1,254
13 The family of Zattu	845
14 The family of Zaccai	760
15 The family of Bani	648
16 The family of Bebai	628
17 The family of Azgad	2,322
18 The family of Adonikam	667
19 The family of Bigvai	2,067

6:14 Neh 13:29; Ezek 13:17
[f]*nebi'ah* (5031) ▸ Ps 51:TITLE

6:15 Neh 4:1-2

6:16 Neh 2:10; 4:1, 7

7:1 Neh 6:1, 15

7:2 Neh 1:2; 10:23

7:6-73 //Ezra 2:1-70

7:7 Ezra 2:2

6:15-16 ***on October 2:*** Literally *on the twenty-fifth day of the month Elul,* of the ancient Hebrew lunar calendar. This day was October 2, 445 BC.; also see note on 1:1. • ***just fifty-two days:*** Everyone realized that ***the help of our God*** was what made such success possible (see also 1:11; 2:8, 18, 20; 4:15, 20).

7:1 ***the wall was finished:*** The actual dedication of the wall is reported in 12:27-34. • The ***Levites*** usually assisted with caring for the Temple area, including guarding its gates.

7:2 ***my brother Hanani:*** See note on 1:2. • ***a faithful man who feared God:*** Hanani displayed two leadership characteristics favored by Nehemiah and God (see also 5:9, 15; Dan 6:4; Luke 16:10-12; 1 Pet 5:12).

7:3 ***Do not leave the gates open during the hottest part of the day:*** Or *Keep the gates of Jerusalem closed until the sun is hot.* The ***gatekeepers*** were apparently supposed to close the gates during the time in the afternoon when people were resting and were not prepared to defend the city from attack. Elsewhere, similar language refers to the portion of the day when the sun is the hottest and people retreat inside (Gen 18:1; 2 Sam 4:5).

7:4-5 Most people lived in the country near their fields, so ***the population*** of Jerusalem ***was small.*** Apparently, a ***registration*** would encourage more people to settle in and near Jerusalem (7:73).

7:6 ***Jewish exiles . . . returned to Jerusalem and the other towns:*** These lists were not complete (the individual numbers do not add up to the total number in 7:66), but they were the best records available to verify who truly was a Jew.

7:7 ***Their leaders:*** Sheshbazzar (see Ezra 1:8) is omitted here and in Ezra 2:2, suggesting that both lists were developed after the people had settled in their towns and after Sheshbazzar had died. • ***Seraiah, Reelaiah, . . . Mispar, . . . Rehum:*** As in parallel text at Ezra 2:2; Hebrew reads *Azariah, Raamiah, . . . Mispereth, Nehum.*

7:8-38 ***the family of:*** This list is similar to that in Ezra 2:3-35, with some differences in names and the number of people in each family. People were listed by family (7:8-25) and by the town where they settled (7:26-38). Most of the towns were north of Jerusalem.

7:15 ***Bani:*** As in parallel text at Ezra 2:10; Hebrew reads *Binnui.*

7:39 Ezra 2:36-39
7:43 Ezra 2:40-42
7:46 Ezra 2:43-54
7:57 Ezra 2:55-57
7:63 Ezra 2:61

20 The family of Adin 655
21 The family of Ater (descendants of Hezekiah) 98
22 The family of Hashum 328
23 The family of Bezai 324
24 The family of Jorah 112
25 The family of Gibbar 95
26 The people of Bethlehem and Netophah 188
27 The people of Anathoth. 128
28 The people of Beth-azmaveth 42
29 The people of Kiriath-jearim, Kephirah, and Beeroth 743
30 The people of Ramah and Geba . . 621
31 The people of Micmash. 122
32 The people of Bethel and Ai 123
33 The people of West Nebo. 52
34 The citizens of West Elam 1,254
35 The citizens of Harim. 320
36 The citizens of Jericho 345
37 The citizens of Lod, Hadid, and Ono 721
38 The citizens of Senaah 3,930

39 These are the priests who returned from exile:
The family of Jedaiah (through the line of Jeshua) 973
40 The family of Immer 1,052
41 The family of Pashhur. 1,247
42 The family of Harim. 1,017

43 These are the Levites who returned from exile:
The families of Jeshua and Kadmiel (descendants of Hodaviah) 74
44 The singers of the family of Asaph 148
45 The gatekeepers of the families of Shallum, Ater, Talmon, Akkub, Hatita, and Shobai 138

46 The descendants of the following Temple servants returned from exile:
Ziha, Hasupha, Tabbaoth,
47 Keros, Siaha, Padon,
48 Lebanah, Hagabah, Shalmai,
49 Hanan, Giddel, Gahar,
50 Reaiah, Rezin, Nekoda,
51 Gazzam, Uzza, Paseah,
52 Besai, Meunim, Nephusim,
53 Bakbuk, Hakupha, Harhur,
54 Bazluth, Mehida, Harsha,
55 Barkos, Sisera, Temah,
56 Neziah, and Hatipha.

57 The descendants of these servants of King Solomon returned from exile:
Sotai, Hassophereth, Peruda,
58 Jaalah, Darkon, Giddel,
59 Shephatiah, Hattil, Pokereth-hazzebaim, and Ami.

60 In all, the Temple servants and the descendants of Solomon's servants numbered 392.

61 Another group returned at this time from the towns of Tel-melah, Tel-harsha, Kerub, Addan, and Immer. However, they could not prove that they or their families were descendants of Israel.
62 This group included the families of Delaiah, Tobiah, and Nekoda—a total of 642 people.
63 Three families of priests—Hobaiah, Hakkoz, and Barzillai—also returned. (This Barzillai had married a woman who was a descendant of Barzillai of Gilead, and he had taken her family name.) 64 They searched for their names in the genealogical records, but they were not found, so they were disqualified from serving as priests.
65 The governor told them not to eat the priests' share of food from the sacrifices until a priest could consult the LORD about the matter by using the Urim and Thummim—the sacred lots.
66 So a total of 42,360 people returned to Judah, 67 in addition to 7,337 servants and 245 singers, both men and women.

7:24 ***Jorah:*** As in parallel text at Ezra 2:18; Hebrew reads *Hariph.*

7:25 ***Gibbar:*** As in parallel text at Ezra 2:20; Hebrew reads *Gibeon.*

7:33 ***of West Nebo:*** Or *of the other Nebo.*

7:34 ***of West Elam:*** Or *of the other Elam.*

7:39-60 Nehemiah wanted to be sure that only legitimate *priests* and *Levites* served in God's Temple.

7:43 ***Hodaviah:*** As in parallel text at Ezra 2:40; Hebrew reads *Hodevah.*

7:47 ***Siaha:*** As in parallel text at Ezra 2:44; Hebrew reads *Sia.*

7:52 ***Nephusim:*** As in parallel text at Ezra 2:50; Hebrew reads *Nephushesim.*

7:54 ***Bazluth:*** As in parallel text at Ezra 2:52; Hebrew reads *Bazlith.*

7:57 ***Hassophereth, Peruda:*** As in parallel text at Ezra 2:55; Hebrew reads *Sophereth, Perida.*

7:58 ***Jaalah:*** As in parallel text at Ezra 2:56; Hebrew reads *Jaala.*

7:59 ***Ami:*** As in parallel text at Ezra 2:57; Hebrew reads *Amon.*

7:60 The ***descendants of Solomon's servants*** apparently assisted the Levites by carrying wood or sweeping the floor (cp. Ezra 2:55-58). They might have been Gibeonites (Josh 9:23-27; 1 Chr 9:35-44) or war captives (Num 31:30-47).

7:61-62 ***they could not prove that they . . . were descendants of Israel:*** They had no genealogical records. • ***Addan:*** As in parallel text at Ezra 2:59; Hebrew reads *Addon.*

7:65 ***Urim and Thummim . . . sacred lots:*** See notes on Exod 28:30; Lev 8:8; Deut 33:8; 1 Sam 14:41.

7:66 The total number *42,360* agrees with Ezra 2:64, but the numbers for the families listed total only 31,089. The individual numbers for each family might not include young children, or the list might simply be incomplete.

68 They took with them 736 horses,
245 mules, 69 435 camels, and 6,720
donkeys.
70 Some of the family leaders gave
gifts for the work. The governor gave to
the treasury 1,000 gold coins, 50 gold
basins, and 530 robes for the priests.
71 The other leaders gave to the treasury
a total of 20,000 gold coins and some
2,750 pounds of silver for the work.
72 The rest of the people gave 20,000
gold coins, about 2,500 pounds of silver,
and 67 robes for the priests.
73 So the priests, the Levites, the
gatekeepers, the singers, the Temple
servants, and some of the common
people settled near Jerusalem. The rest
of the people returned to their own
towns throughout Israel.

2. EZRA'S TEACHING OF THE LAW BRINGS COVENANT RENEWAL (7:73b–10:39)

Ezra Reads the Law

8 In October, when the Israelites had
settled in their towns, 8:1 all the people
assembled with a unified purpose at the
square just inside the Water Gate. They
asked Ezra the scribe to bring out the Book
of the Law of Moses, which the LORD had
given for Israel to obey.
2 So on October 8 Ezra the priest brought
the Book of the Law before the assembly,
which included the men and women and all
the children old enough to understand. 3 He
faced the square just inside the Water Gate
from early morning until noon and read
aloud to everyone who could understand.
All the people listened closely to the Book
of the Law.
4 Ezra the scribe stood on a high wooden
platform that had been made for the occasion. To his right stood Mattithiah, Shema,
Anaiah, Uriah, Hilkiah, and Maaseiah. To
his left stood Pedaiah, Mishael, Malkijah,
Hashum, Hashbaddanah, Zechariah, and Meshullam. 5 Ezra stood on the platform in full
view of all the people. When they saw him
open the book, they all rose to their feet.
6 Then Ezra praised the LORD, the great
God, and all the people chanted, "[g]Amen!
[g]Amen!" as they lifted their hands. Then
they [h]bowed down and worshiped the LORD
with their faces to the ground.
7 The Levites—Jeshua, Bani, Sherebiah,
Jamin, Akkub, Shabbethai, Hodiah, Maaseiah, Kelita, Azariah, Jozabad, Hanan, and
Pelaiah—then instructed the people in
the Law while everyone remained in their
places. 8 They read from the Book of the Law
of God and clearly explained the meaning
of what was being read, helping the people
understand each passage.

7:70 Neh 8:9
7:73 Ezra 3:1
8:1 2 Chr 34:15; Ezra 7:6; Neh 3:26
8:2 Lev 23:24; Deut 31:9-12
8:6 Exod 4:31; Neh 5:13; 1 Tim 2:8
[g]*'amen* (0543) ▸Ps 41:13
[h]*khawah* (7812) ▸Ps 29:2
8:7 Lev 10:11; Deut 33:10

7:68 This verse is as in some Hebrew manuscripts (see also Ezra 2:66); most Hebrew manuscripts lack this verse. Verses 7:69-73 are numbered 7:68-72 in the Hebrew text.

7:70-72 *Some of the family leaders gave gifts* as their forefathers had done when sacred buildings were built (Exod 25:2-7; 35:4-9; 2 Kgs 12). This money supplemented gifts by Israelites who stayed in Babylon (Ezra 1:6) and by the Persian kings (Ezra 6:8). • ***1,000 gold coins:*** Hebrew *1,000 darics of gold,* about 19 pounds or 8.6 kilograms in weight.

7:71 *20,000 gold coins:* Hebrew *20,000 darics of gold,* about 375 pounds or 170 kilograms in weight; also in 7:72. • *2,750 pounds:* Hebrew *2,200 minas* [1,300 kilograms].

7:72 *2,500 pounds:* Hebrew *2,000 minas* [1,200 kilograms].

7:73a ***their own towns throughout Israel:*** Each family settled in the land that had been inhabited by their ancestors before the Exile.

7:73b–10:39 This section, perhaps originally a part of Ezra's personal memoirs, describes how Ezra's teaching of God's law brought renewal of the people's commitment to serve God and follow his instructions. Spiritual revival accompanied the civic work of Ezra and Nehemiah.

7:73b ***In October:*** Literally *in the seventh month.* This month of the ancient Hebrew lunar calendar occurred within the months of October and November 445 BC. The first day of the seventh month marked the Festival of Trumpets (Lev 23:23-25).

8:1 The *Water Gate* was located toward the middle of the eastern wall of Jerusalem, south of the Temple and east of the palace ruins (3:26; 12:37). There was plenty of open space so no one would be excluded.

8:2 *on October 8:* Literally *on the first day of the seventh month,* of the ancient Hebrew lunar calendar. This day was October 8, 445 BC; also see note on 1:1. The people came together on this day to celebrate the Festival of Trumpets (Lev 23:24-25), which marked the beginning of a new year in the postexilic calendar.

8:3 The timeframe *from early morning until noon* provided about six hours for reading and interpreting (8:7-8). • *understand* (see also 8:2, 8, 12): This was not just a ritual reading of the law. It included explanations, insight, and application.

8:4 These thirteen people were apparently community leaders. Some might have helped Ezra roll the scroll as he read.

8:5 The people *all rose to their feet* out of respect for God's word (Job 29:8). Apparently, they stood the whole time Ezra was reading.

8:6 *Ezra praised the LORD:* See also 1:5; 9:32; Deut 10:17; Jer 32:18; Dan 9:4. • *Amen!* A statement of agreement (see 5:13). Lifting hands (Ps 28:2) and bowing in humble worship were signs of reverence for God and submission to his word.

8:7-9 The *Levites* always had the role of teaching people God's word (Deut 33:10; Mal 2:5-6). In this case, they probably ***explained the meaning*** of the Hebrew Scriptures to smaller groups of people in Aramaic. Most of the people spoke Aramaic, the language of Babylon, rather than Hebrew as their first language. Jewish leaders eventually translated large portions of the Hebrew Bible into Aramaic, allowing people to read and study the Bible in a language they understood.

8:9 Deut 12:7, 12; Neh 8:2
8:10 Deut 26:11-13; Esth 9:22
8:12 Neh 8:7-8, 10
8:14 Lev 23:34, 40, 42
8:16 2 Kgs 14:13; Neh 8:1; 12:39; Jer 32:29

9 Then Nehemiah the governor, Ezra the priest and scribe, and the Levites who were interpreting for the people said to them, "Don't mourn or weep on such a day as this! For today is a sacred day before the LORD your God." For the people had all been weeping as they listened to the words of the Law.

10 And Nehemiah continued, "Go and celebrate with a feast of rich foods and sweet drinks, and share gifts of food with people who have nothing prepared. This is a sacred day before our Lord. Don't be dejected and sad, for the joy of the LORD is your strength!"

11 And the Levites, too, quieted the people, telling them, "Hush! Don't weep! For this is a sacred day." 12 So the people went away to eat and drink at a festive meal, to share gifts of food, and to celebrate with great joy because they had heard God's words and understood them.

The Festival of Shelters

13 On October 9 the family leaders of all the people, together with the priests and Levites, met with Ezra the scribe to go over the Law in greater detail. 14 As they studied the Law, they discovered that the LORD had commanded through Moses that the Israelites should live in shelters during the festival to be held that month. 15 He had said that a proclamation should be made throughout their towns and in Jerusalem, telling the people to go to the hills to get branches from olive, wild olive, myrtle, palm, and other leafy trees. They were to use these branches to make shelters in which they would live during the festival, as prescribed in the Law.

16 So the people went out and cut branches and used them to build shelters on the roofs of their houses, in their courtyards, in the courtyards of God's Temple,

The Centrality of God's Word (8:1–10:39)

Neh 13:1-3; Exod 24:7; 34:1; Deut 4:2; 6:4-9; 31:9-13; Josh 1:7-8; 1 Sam 15:22; Ps 1:2-3; 19:7-9; 119:9, 15, 97, 105; Isa 55:10-11; Matt 5:17-19; 13:3-23; 24:35; 2 Tim 3:14-17

In the fall of 445 BC, Nehemiah finished rebuilding the wall of Jerusalem. Just five days later, on the first day of the seventh month, the settlers in Judah came together to celebrate the Festival of Trumpets (see chart, "Israel's Festivals," p. 235). During and after the festival, Ezra read from the Law, and as the people listened they mourned and wept, for they realized they had not obeyed God's law. They confessed their sins, studied God's word to learn what he required, and obeyed what they learned. The Book of the Law of Moses transformed Jewish life and social behavior during Ezra's and Nehemiah's ministries in Judea.

These events provide a dramatic reminder that God's word is central to the lives of his people. God's word provides the essential guide to life or death (Gen 2:16-17), and his promises prove true (e.g., Gen 17:15-21; 18:10-14). God's word was written in stone (Exod 34:1) and was to be taught to children (Deut 6:7), worn on the hands and forehead, and written on the doorpost (Deut 6:8-9), so that people would constantly be reminded of what God had said. God's instructions were to be read to the people every seven years so that people would remember to fear God (Deut 31:9-13). Success depended on meditating on God's word and following it (Josh 1:7-8; Ps 1:2; 119:15). Obedience was far more important than giving a sacrifice (1 Sam 15:22).

God's word is perfect. It has the power to restore, make wise, and give joy (Ps 19:7-9). Godly individuals love God's word (Ps 119:97). It sheds light on their paths (Ps 119:105) and keeps them from sin (Ps 119:9). God's word accomplishes its purpose (Isa 55:11) and remains relevant forever (Matt 5:17-19; 24:35; 2 Tim 3:14-17).

8:9-10 *Ezra the priest and scribe:* See note on Ezra 7:6. • ***Don't mourn or weep . . . today is a sacred day:*** God touched the people's hearts, prompting them to regret their failures to keep God's laws. While weeping is an appropriate response to sin (see Ezek 9:4; Luke 6:21), Ezra and Nehemiah encouraged the people to rejoice at what God had done. Because this New Year's festival was to be a time of joy (Num 29:1-6), weeping would have destroyed the spirit of the day.

8:10 *Nehemiah:* Literally *he.* • ***Rich foods*** such as meat were eaten only on a special occasion. • ***Sweet drinks*** referred to unfermented juice, in contrast to the vinegar of the common laborer (see Ruth 2:14). • It is right to ***share*** with those who have need (see Deut 15:11; Job 29:16; Prov 31:20; Matt 6:2-3; Acts 4:34-35).

8:13 *On October 9:* Literally *On the second day,* of the seventh month of the ancient Hebrew lunar calendar. This day was October 9, 445 BC; also see notes on 1:1 and 8:2.

8:14 *that month:* Literally *in the seventh month.* This month of the ancient Hebrew lunar calendar usually occurs within the months of September and October. See Lev 23:39-43.

8:15 *wild olive:* Or *pine;* literally *oil tree.* • ***make shelters in which they would live during the festival:*** The Festival of Shelters commemorated that the people of Israel had lived in tents during their wilderness journey (Lev 23:33-43; see also Num 29:12-39; Deut 16:13-15).

8:16 *The Ephraim Gate* might have been located on the north side of Jerusalem, facing toward the northern tribes of Ephraim (see 12:39).

or in the squares just inside the Water Gate
and the Ephraim Gate. 17So everyone who
had returned from captivity lived in these
shelters during the festival, and they were
all filled with great joy! The Israelites had
not celebrated like this since the days of
Joshua son of Nun.
18Ezra read from the Book of the Law of
God on each of the seven days of the festival. Then on the eighth day they held a
solemn assembly, as was required by law.

The People Confess Their Sins

9 On October 31 the people assembled
again, and this time they fasted and
dressed in burlap and sprinkled dust on
their heads. 2Those of Israelite descent separated themselves from all foreigners as
they confessed their own sins and the sins
of their ancestors. 3They remained standing in place for three hours while the Book
of the Law of the LORD their God was read
aloud to them. Then for three more hours
they confessed their sins and worshiped
the LORD their God. 4The Levites—Jeshua,
Bani, Kadmiel, Shebaniah, Bunni, Sherebiah,
Bani, and Kenani—stood on the stairway of
the Levites and cried out to the LORD their
God with loud voices.
5Then the leaders of the Levites—Jeshua,
Kadmiel, Bani, Hashabneiah, Sherebiah,
Hodiah, Shebaniah, and Pethahiah—called
out to the people: "Stand up and praise the
LORD your God, for he lives from everlasting
to everlasting!" Then they prayed:

"May your glorious name be praised!
May it be [i]exalted above all blessing and
praise!
6"You alone are the LORD. You made
the skies and the heavens and all the
stars. You made the earth and the seas
and everything in them. You preserve
them all, and the angels of heaven
worship you.
7"You are the LORD God, who chose
Abram and brought him from Ur of the
Chaldeans and renamed him Abraham.
8When he had proved himself faithful,
you made a covenant with him to give
him and his descendants the land of the
Canaanites, Hittites, Amorites, Perizzites,
Jebusites, and Girgashites. And you have
done what you promised, for you are
always true to your word.
9"You saw the misery of our ancestors
in Egypt, and you heard their cries from
beside the Red Sea. 10You displayed
miraculous signs and wonders against
Pharaoh, his officials, and all his people,
for you knew how arrogantly they were
treating our ancestors. You have a
glorious reputation that has never been
forgotten. 11You divided the sea for your
people so they could walk through on dry
land! And then you hurled their enemies
into the depths of the sea. They sank like
stones beneath the mighty waters. 12You
led our ancestors by a pillar of cloud
during the day and a pillar of fire at night
so that they could find their way.

8:17
2 Chr 7:8; 8:13; 30:21
8:18
Lev 23:36
Num 29:35
Deut 31:11
9:1
1 Sam 4:12
Ezra 8:23
Neh 8:2
Job 2:12
9:2
Ezra 10:11
Neh 13:3
9:3
Neh 8:3
9:4
Neh 8:7
9:5
[i]*rum* (7311)
›Ps 30:1
9:6
Gen 1:1
Deut 6:4
2 Kgs 19:15
Ps 103:20
Col 1:16-17
9:7
Gen 11:31; 12:1;
15:7; 17:5
9:8
Gen 15:6, 18-21
Josh 21:43-45
9:9
Exod 14:10-14
9:10
Exod 3:7; 5:2; 9:16
9:11
Exod 14:21; 15:1,
5, 10
9:12
Exod 13:21-22
9:13
Exod 19:11, 18-20
Ps 19:7-9
[i]*torah* (8451)
›Job 22:22

8:17 *since the days of Joshua* (Hebrew *Jeshua*, a variant spelling of *Joshua*): Although Israel had observed this festival on numerous occasions (1 Kgs 8:2; 2 Kgs 23:22; 2 Chr 7:8-10; 30:26; 35:18; Ezra 3:4), this was an exceptional celebration.

8:18 *Ezra read from the Book of the Law of God:* The law was to be read every seven years at the Festival of Shelters (Deut 31:10-12). It reminded the people of the covenant stipulations and of God's past acts of grace.

9:1 *On October 31:* Literally *On the twenty-fourth day of that same month,* the seventh month of the ancient Hebrew lunar calendar. This day was October 31, 445 BC; also see notes on 1:1 and 8:2.

9:2 *Those of Israelite descent separated themselves from all foreigners as they confessed their own sins:* This sentence might allude to the problem of intermarriage with foreigners, as narrated in Ezra 9–10.

9:3 *They confessed their . . . sins* after hearing God's word (cp. 8:1-9, 13-14, 18). • *for three hours:* Literally *for a quarter of a day.*

9:5b-37 This long prayer confesses the nation's sins and praises God for his compassion throughout history (cp. Pss 105–106, 135–136). It prompted listeners to confess their own unfaithfulness and to call on God to be compassionate and forgive their sins.

9:5b-6 The Levites' prayer praised God for his *glorious* reputation, his sole divinity, his creation of the universe, his providential care for life on *earth,* and his worship by *angels.* Putting the focus on God brought Israel's present circumstances into proper perspective.

9:7-8 God's actions with *Abram*—calling him (Gen 12:1-3; 15:7), giving him a new name and identity (Gen 17:5), making a covenant with him (Gen 15:6-21; 17:4-5), and fulfilling his promises of land and descendants (Gen 15:18-21)—demonstrated God's faithfulness and inspired confidence about what God would do in the future.

9:9 God had paid attention to his people's *misery* under foreign domination (Exod 2:23-25; 3:7; 14:10-14), which was analogous to their present situation (9:32-37). • *Red Sea:* Literally *sea of reeds.*

9:10-11 *You have a glorious reputation:* In the Exodus, God had demonstrated his character with plagues, parting the sea, and defeating the arrogant Egyptian army (Exod 15:5, 9-10, 19).

9:12-21 This prayer reminded the people of God's miraculous direction of Israel in the wilderness (Exod 13:21-22), his personal appearance at *Mount Sinai* to reveal his covenant laws through Moses (see Exod 19–20), and his faithfulness in providing *bread . . . and water* (see Exod 16:4; 17:1-6). Despite all of that, Israel's *ancestors* had been *proud and stubborn* and *refused to obey* (see Exod 32; Num 14:4). Yet in his grace, God remained faithful and had compassion (see Exod 34:6) and provided his Spirit to direct and teach them (cp. Exod 33:2; Num 11:17).

13"You came down at Mount Sinai and spoke to them from heaven. You gave them regulations and [j]instructions that were just, and decrees and commands that were good. 14You instructed them concerning your holy Sabbath. And you commanded them, through Moses your servant, to obey all your commands, decrees, and instructions.

15"You gave them bread from heaven when they were hungry and water from the rock when they were thirsty. You commanded them to go and take possession of the land you had sworn to give them.

16"But our ancestors were proud and stubborn, and they [k]paid no attention to your commands. 17They refused to obey and did not remember the miracles you had done for them. Instead, they became stubborn and appointed a leader to take them back to their slavery in Egypt! But you are a God of forgiveness, gracious and merciful, [a]slow to become angry, and rich in unfailing love. You did not abandon them, 18even when they made an idol shaped like a calf and said, 'This is your god who brought you out of Egypt!' They committed terrible blasphemies.

19"But in your great mercy you did not abandon them to die in the wilderness. The pillar of cloud still led them forward by day, and the pillar of fire showed them the way through the night. 20You sent your good Spirit to instruct them, and you did not stop giving them [b]manna from heaven or water for their thirst. 21For forty years you sustained them in the wilderness, and they lacked nothing. Their clothes did not wear out, and their feet did not swell!

22"Then you helped our ancestors conquer kingdoms and nations, and you placed your people in every corner of the land. They took over the land of King Sihon of Heshbon and the land of King Og of Bashan. 23You made their descendants as numerous as the stars in the sky and brought them into the land you had promised to their ancestors.

24"They went in and took possession of the land. You subdued whole nations before them. Even the Canaanites, who inhabited the land, were powerless! Your people could deal with these nations and their kings as they pleased. 25Our ancestors captured fortified cities and fertile land. They took over houses full

9:14
Exod 16:23; 20:8
9:15
Exod 16:4, 14-15; 17:6
Num 20:7-13
Deut 1:8, 21
Josh 1:2-4
9:16
Deut 31:27
Neh 9:10, 29
[k]*shama'* (8085)
‣ Eccl 7:21
9:17
Exod 34:6-7
Num 14:4
Ps 78:11
[a]*'arek 'appayim* (0750, 0639)
‣ Ps 86:15
9:18
Exod 32:4-8, 31
9:19
Neh 9:12, 27, 31
9:20
Num 11:17
Neh 9:15, 30
Isa 63:11-14
[b]*man* (4478)
‣ Ps 78:24
9:21
Deut 2:7
9:22
Num 21:21-35
Deut 2:26–3:11
9:23
Gen 15:5
9:24
Josh 18:1; 21:43
9:25
Num 13:27
Deut 3:5; 6:11; 32:15
1 Kgs 8:66

Confidence in God (9:6-31)

God gave Nehemiah favor in the eyes of a mighty Persian king so that the king responded favorably to all of Nehemiah's requests (1:11; 2:8, 18). Nehemiah then had the confidence to present his bold plan to rebuild the walls of Jerusalem, and the people of Jerusalem responded positively, believing that God was able to give them success in rebuilding the walls (2:20) and to protect them from their enemies (4:4-5, 9). They confidently continued with their work in spite of opposition because they knew that God fights for his people and frustrates the plans of the wicked (4:14-15, 20). When the walls of Jerusalem were finished, Nehemiah recognized that the entire difficult project was completed only because of God's help (6:16).

The book of Nehemiah vividly demonstrates that God is all-powerful and able to accomplish his will, both in individual lives and in nations. Nehemiah's prayer in ch 9 focuses on praising God for his sovereign and powerful acts: God created the heavens and earth (9:6), called Abram from Ur, and gave the land to Israel (9:7-8, 22-25). The miraculous signs in Egypt, the parting of the Red Sea, and the provision of guidance, food, and water in the wilderness all demonstrate God's power over man and nature to provide for his people (9:9-15).

The Lord had sent the Israelites into exile after generations of persistent sin (9:26-27). Now he was fulfilling part of his promise to restore them (1:8-9). Nehemiah had the confidence to pray and lead because he knew that everything that happened was part of God's sovereign plan. This same confidence in God's sovereignty led Abram to leave Ur and by faith go to an unknown land (Gen 12:1-3; Heb 11:8-10), caused Rahab to trust in God (Josh 2:9-14; Heb 11:31), and prompted Hezekiah not to give in to the demands of the Assyrian king Sennacherib (2 Kgs 18–19). Confidence comes when people believe that God will keep his promises and complete the work he has started in their lives (Phil 1:6).

Neh 1:8-9, 11; 2:8, 18, 20; 4:4-5, 9, 14-15, 20; 6:16
Gen 12:1-4
Josh 1:10-18; 2:9-14
2 Kgs 18:1–19:37
Ps 4:5; 9:10; 37:3; 40:3; 44:6-7; 56:3-12; 112:1-9
Prov 3:5-12; 16:20; 28:1, 25
Isa 26:3
Heb 11:8-10, 31
1 Jn 4:17

9:22 ***placed . . . in every corner of the land:*** The meaning of the Hebrew is uncertain.

9:24 ***You subdued whole nations:*** See Josh 6–12.

9:25 Cp. Deut 6:10-11; 8:6-10. • ***they were full and grew fat:*** Prosperity proved to include spiritual danger (see Deut 8:11-20).

of good things, with cisterns already dug
and vineyards and olive groves and fruit
trees in abundance. So they ate until
they were full and grew fat and enjoyed
themselves in all your blessings.
26“But despite all this, they were
disobedient and rebelled against
you. They turned their backs on your
Law, they killed your prophets who
warned them to return to you, and they
committed terrible blasphemies. 27So
you handed them over to their enemies,
who made them suffer. But in their time
of trouble they cried to you, and you
heard them from heaven. In your great
mercy, you sent them liberators who
rescued them from their enemies.
28“But as soon as they were at peace,
your people again committed evil in
your sight, and once more you let their
enemies conquer them. Yet whenever
your people turned and cried to you
again for help, you listened once more
from heaven. In your wonderful mercy,
you rescued them many times!
29“You warned them to return to
your Law, but they became proud
and obstinate and [c]disobeyed your
commands. They did not follow your
regulations, by which people will find life
if only they obey. They stubbornly turned
their backs on you and refused to listen.
30In your love, you were patient with them
for many years. You sent your Spirit, who
warned them through the prophets. But
still they wouldn’t listen! So once again
you allowed the peoples of the land to
conquer them. 31But in your great mercy,
you did not destroy them completely or
abandon them forever. What a gracious
and merciful God you are!
32“And now, our God, the great and
mighty and awesome God, who keeps
his covenant of unfailing love, do not let
all the hardships we have suffered seem
insignificant to you. Great trouble has
come upon us and upon our kings and
leaders and priests and prophets and
ancestors—all of your people—from
the days when the kings of Assyria first
triumphed over us until now. 33Every
time you punished us you were being
just. We have sinned greatly, and you
gave us only what we deserved. 34Our
kings, leaders, priests, and ancestors
did not obey your Law or listen to
the warnings in your commands and
laws. 35Even while they had their
own kingdom, they did not serve you,
though you showered your goodness
on them. You gave them a large, fertile
land, but they refused to turn from
their wickedness.
36“So now today we are slaves in
the land of plenty that you gave our
ancestors for their enjoyment! We are
slaves here in this good land. 37The
lush produce of this land piles up in the
hands of the kings whom you have set
over us because of our sins. They have
power over us and our livestock. We
serve them at their pleasure, and we are
in great misery.”

The People Agree to Obey

38The people responded, “In view of all this,
we are making a solemn promise and putting it in writing. On this sealed document
are the names of our leaders and Levites
and priests.”

10 The document was ratified and
sealed with the following names:

The governor:
Nehemiah son of Hacaliah, and also
Zedekiah.
2The following priests:
Seraiah, Azariah, Jeremiah, 3Pashhur,
Amariah, Malkijah, 4Hattush, Shebaniah,
Malluch, 5Harim, Meremoth, Obadiah,

9:26 Judg 2:11; 1 Kgs 14:9; 2 Chr 36:16
9:27 Judg 2:14, 16, 18
9:28 Judg 3:11; Ps 106:43
9:29 Lev 18:5; Zech 7:11; *ᶜkhata’* (2398) ›Ps 41:4
9:30 2 Kgs 17:13; Neh 9:20
9:31 Neh 9:17; Jer 4:27
9:32 2 Kgs 15:19, 29; 17:3-6
9:33 Gen 18:25; Jer 12:1
9:35 Deut 28:45-47
9:36 Deut 28:48
9:37 Deut 28:33

9:26-27 The prayer recounts the pattern in the book of Judges (see Judg 2:11-23).

9:28-31 The people did not learn from mistakes made in the period of the judges (9:26-27), and the same pattern of disobedience emerged during the subsequent monarchy (cp. 2 Kgs 17). Despite the nation’s persistent disobedience (9:29), God was persistent in his *love,* patience, compassion, and guidance through the *Spirit* and *through the prophets.*

9:32-37 *And now:* The prayer moves to the current situation, petitioning *the great . . . God*—who has *unfailing love*—for continued love and mercy to his people in their present difficult situation (9:32). The leaders recognized God’s justice in punishing them for their sins (9:33-35), and they lamented their enslavement under the Persians (9:36-37).

9:38–10:39 *The people,* embracing the prayer, renewed their dedication to God and his word. They signed their names to indicate their commitment (9:38–10:27) and took an oath to live by the covenant (10:28-39).

9:38 Verse 9:38 is numbered 10:1 in the Hebrew text. • *In view of all this:* Or *In spite of all this.* • *making a solemn promise . . . putting it in writing:* These actions indicate a serious vow of faithfulness to the covenant. The *sealed document* had legal standing.

10:1-39 Verses 10:1-39 are numbered 10:2-40 in the Hebrew text.

10:1-27 The eighty-four names included *the governor: Nehemiah* (10:1), and a group of *priests* (10:2-8; cp. 12:1-7), *Levites* (10:9-13; cp. 9:4-5; 12:8-9), and *leaders* (10:14-27; cp. 3:4-31).

10:8-9 Neh 12:1
10:28 Ezra 2:36-58; Neh 9:2
10:29 Neh 5:12
10:30 Exod 34:16; Deut 7:3
10:31 Exod 23:10-11; Lev 25:1-7; Deut 15:1-2; Neh 13:15-22
10:32 Exod 30:11-16; Matt 17:24
10:33 Lev 23:1-44; 24:5-7
10:34 Neh 11:1; 13:31
10:35 Exod 23:19; Deut 26:2
10:36 Exod 13:2
10:37 Lev 23:17; 27:30; Neh 13:5, 9
10:38 Num 18:26; Neh 13:12-13

6 Daniel, Ginnethon, Baruch, 7 Meshullam,
Abijah, Mijamin, 8 Maaziah, Bilgai, and
Shemaiah. These were the priests.

9 The following Levites:
Jeshua son of Azaniah, Binnui from
the family of Henadad, Kadmiel,
10 and their fellow Levites: Shebaniah,
Hodiah, Kelita, Pelaiah, Hanan, 11 Mica,
Rehob, Hashabiah, 12 Zaccur, Sherebiah,
Shebaniah, 13 Hodiah, Bani, and Beninu.

14 The following leaders:
Parosh, Pahath-moab, Elam, Zattu, Bani,
15 Bunni, Azgad, Bebai, 16 Adonijah, Bigvai,
Adin, 17 Ater, Hezekiah, Azzur, 18 Hodiah,
Hashum, Bezai, 19 Hariph, Anathoth,
Nebai, 20 Magpiash, Meshullam, Hezir,
21 Meshezabel, Zadok, Jaddua, 22 Pelatiah,
Hanan, Anaiah, 23 Hoshea, Hananiah,
Hasshub, 24 Hallohesh, Pilha, Shobek,
25 Rehum, Hashabnah, Maaseiah, 26 Ahiah,
Hanan, Anan, 27 Malluch, Harim, and
Baanah.

The Vow of the People

28 Then the rest of the people—the priests, Levites, gatekeepers, singers, Temple servants, and all who had separated themselves from the pagan people of the land in order to obey the Law of God, together with their wives, sons, daughters, and all who were old enough to understand—
29 joined their leaders and bound themselves with an oath. They swore a curse on themselves if they failed to obey the Law of God as issued by his servant Moses. They solemnly promised to carefully follow all the commands, regulations, and decrees of the LORD our Lord:

30 "We promise not to let our daughters marry the pagan people of the land, and not to let our sons marry their daughters.

31 "We also promise that if the people of the land should bring any merchandise or grain to be sold on the Sabbath or on any other holy day, we will refuse to buy it. Every seventh year we will let our land rest, and we will cancel all debts owed to us.

32 "In addition, we promise to obey the command to pay the annual Temple tax of one-eighth of an ounce of silver for the care of the Temple of our God.
33 This will provide for the Bread of the Presence; for the regular grain offerings and burnt offerings; for the offerings on the Sabbaths, the new moon celebrations, and the annual festivals; for the holy offerings; and for the sin offerings to make atonement for Israel. It will provide for everything necessary for the work of the Temple of our God.

34 "We have cast sacred lots to determine when—at regular times each year—the families of the priests, Levites, and the common people should bring wood to God's Temple to be burned on the altar of the LORD our God, as is written in the Law.

35 "We promise to bring the first part of every harvest to the LORD's Temple year after year—whether it be a crop from the soil or from our fruit trees.
36 We agree to give God our oldest sons and the firstborn of all our herds and flocks, as prescribed in the Law. We will present them to the priests who minister in the Temple of our God.
37 We will store the produce in the storerooms of the Temple of our God. We will bring the best of our flour and other grain offerings, the best of our fruit, and the best of our new wine and olive oil. And we promise to bring to the Levites a tenth of everything our land produces, for it is the Levites who collect the tithes in all our rural towns.

38 "A priest—a descendant of Aaron—will be with the Levites as they receive

---

10:28 ***separated themselves from the pagan people:*** See 9:2; cp. Ezra 9–10.

10:29 ***swore a curse on themselves if they failed to obey the Law:*** Cp. Lev 26:14-35; Deut 28:15-62.

10:30-39 Although the community had committed itself broadly to all the instructions in the law of Moses, some specific issues were being addressed in this commitment. These issues related to maintaining the purity of the community and worship at the Temple.

10:30 Cp. Ezra 9–10.

10:31 Ceasing trade on the Sabbath was necessary for covenant faithfulness (cp. 13:15-22; see Exod 16:29; 20:8-11; 31:15; Num 15:32-36; Amos 8:5). • ***Every seventh year:*** See Exod 23:10-11; Lev 25:2-7; Deut 15:1-3.

10:32 ***tax of one-eighth of an ounce of silver:*** Hebrew *tax of ⅓ of a shekel* [4 grams] (see Exod 30:11-16).

10:33 ***Bread of the Presence:*** See Lev 24:5-9; Num 28:1-8. • ***everything necessary:*** With the money from the annual tax, priests could purchase the animals for daily sacrifices and maintain the ***Temple*** complex (cp. 2 Kgs 12:11-12).

10:34 Because the fire ***on the altar*** burned continually (Lev 6:12), a good deal of wood was used. The Gibeonites provided it at an earlier time (Josh 9:27), but now it was a joint responsibility.

10:35-37 Offerings from the community provided food for ***the priests*** and ***Levites***, who had no allocations of agricultural land and no means of providing for themselves. These provisions came from ***the first part of every harvest*** (see Exod 23:19; 34:26; Num 18:12-13; Deut 26:1-11), the redemption money of five shekels paid for the ***oldest sons*** and the ***firstborn*** of all the ***herds and flocks*** (see Exod 13:13; 34:20; Num 18:15-17), as well as ***a tenth of everything*** (see Num 18:21-24; Deut 14:22-29).

10:37-39 The ***Levites*** collected the tithes ***in all . . . rural towns*** and sent a tenth of that collection to the Temple in Jerusalem (see Num 18:25-32).

these tithes. And a tenth of all that is collected as tithes will be delivered by the Levites to the Temple of our God and placed in the storerooms. 39The people and the Levites must bring these offerings of grain, new wine, and olive oil to the storerooms and place them in the sacred containers near the ministering priests, the gatekeepers, and the singers.

"We promise together not to neglect the Temple of our God."

3. NEHEMIAH REORGANIZES JERUSALEM AND INSTITUTES FURTHER REFORMS (11:1–13:31)

The Resettlement of People in Jerusalem

11 The leaders of the people were living in Jerusalem, the holy city. A tenth of the people from the other towns of Judah and Benjamin were chosen by sacred lots to live there, too, while the rest stayed where they were. 2And the people commended everyone who volunteered to resettle in Jerusalem.

3Here is a list of the names of the provincial officials who came to live in Jerusalem. (Most of the people, priests, Levites, Temple servants, and descendants of Solomon's servants continued to live in their own homes in the various towns of Judah, 4but some of the people from Judah and Benjamin resettled in Jerusalem.)

From the tribe of Judah:

Athaiah son of Uzziah, son of Zechariah, son of Amariah, son of Shephatiah, son of Mahalalel, of the family of Perez. 5Also Maaseiah son of Baruch, son of Col-hozeh, son of Hazaiah, son of Adaiah, son of Joiarib, son of Zechariah, of the family of Shelah. 6There were 468 descendants of Perez who lived in Jerusalem—all outstanding men.

7From the tribe of Benjamin:

Sallu son of Meshullam, son of Joed, son of Pedaiah, son of Kolaiah, son of Maaseiah, son of Ithiel, son of Jeshaiah. 8After him were Gabbai and Sallai and a total of 928 relatives. 9Their chief officer was Joel son of Zicri, who was assisted by Judah son of Hassenuah, second-in-command over the city.

10From the priests:

Jedaiah son of Joiarib; Jakin; 11and Seraiah son of Hilkiah, son of Meshullam, son of Zadok, son of Meraioth, son of Ahitub, the supervisor of the Temple of God. 12Also 822 of their associates, who worked at the Temple. Also Adaiah son of Jeroham, son of Pelaliah, son of Amzi, son of Zechariah, son of Pashhur, son of Malkijah, 13along with 242 of his associates, who were heads of their families. Also Amashsai son of Azarel, son of Ahzai, son of Meshillemoth, son of Immer, 14and 128 of his outstanding associates. Their chief officer was Zabdiel son of Haggedolim.

15From the Levites:

Shemaiah son of Hasshub, son of Azrikam, son of Hashabiah, son of Bunni. 16Also Shabbethai and Jozabad, who were in charge of the work outside the Temple of God. 17Also Mattaniah son of Mica, son of Zabdi, a descendant of Asaph, who led in thanksgiving and prayer. Also Bakbukiah, who was Mattaniah's assistant, and Abda son of Shammua, son of Galal, son of Jeduthun. 18In all, there were 284 Levites in the holy city.

19From the gatekeepers:

Akkub, Talmon, and 172 of their associates, who guarded the gates.

20The other priests, Levites, and the rest of the Israelites lived wherever their family inheritance was located in any of the towns of Judah. 21The Temple servants, however, whose leaders were Ziha and Gishpa, all lived on the hill of Ophel.

22The chief officer of the Levites in Jerusalem was Uzzi son of Bani, son of Hashabiah, son of Mattaniah, son of Mica, a descendant of Asaph, whose family served as singers at God's Temple. 23Their daily responsibilities were carried out according to the terms of a royal command.

10:39 Deut 12:6; Neh 13:10-11
11:1 Neh 7:4; 10:34; 11:18; Isa 48:2
11:3-19 //1 Chr 9:1-17; Ezra 2:43-57; Neh 7:57-59; 11:20
11:18 Neh 11:1, 3
11:21 Neh 3:26
11:22 Neh 11:9, 14, 17

11:1-36 The narrative returns to the issue of repopulating the secure city of Jerusalem (see 7:1-5). The list of names roughly parallels the list in 1 Chr 9:2-17.

11:1-2 *Sacred lots* were probably the Urim and Thummim (10:34; Josh 7:14, 16-18; 14:2).

11:4 *Perez* was one of Judah's sons (Gen 38:29).

11:5 *of the family of Shelah:* Literally *son of the Shilonite.*

11:14 *his outstanding associates:* As in Greek version; Hebrew reads *their outstanding associates.*

11:16 *The work outside the Temple* probably included collecting tithes from people and caring for the tithes in storehouses (10:37-39; see also 1 Chr 26:29).

11:17 *a descendant of Asaph:* David had chosen Asaph and his sons to provide music for the Temple worship (1 Chr 25:1-8). They took up this role again when the new Temple was built.

11:21 *The hill of Ophel* was high ground just south of the Temple (3:26). It provided an ideal location to house those who worked in the Temple.

11:25
Josh 13:9, 17; 14:15

12:1
Ezra 2:1-2

12:8
Ezra 2:2
Neh 11:17

24 Pethahiah son of Meshezabel, a descendant of Zerah son of Judah, was the royal adviser in all matters of public administration.

25 As for the surrounding villages with their open fields, some of the people of Judah lived in Kiriath-arba with its settlements, Dibon with its settlements, and Jekabzeel with its villages. 26 They also lived in Jeshua, Moladah, Beth-pelet, 27 Hazar-shual, Beersheba with its settlements, 28 Ziklag, and Meconah with its settlements. 29 They also lived in En-rimmon, Zorah, Jarmuth, 30 Zanoah, and Adullam with their surrounding villages. They also lived in Lachish with its nearby fields and Azekah with its surrounding villages. So the people of Judah were living all the way from Beersheba in the south to the valley of Hinnom.

31 Some of the people of Benjamin lived at Geba, Micmash, Aija, and Bethel with its settlements. 32 They also lived in Anathoth, Nob, Ananiah, 33 Hazor, Ramah, Gittaim, 34 Hadid, Zeboim, Neballat, 35 Lod, Ono, and the Valley of Craftsmen. 36 Some of the Levites who lived in Judah were sent to live with the tribe of Benjamin.

A List of Authentic Priests

12 Here is the list of the priests and Levites who returned with Zerubbabel son of Shealtiel and Jeshua the high priest:

Seraiah, Jeremiah, Ezra,
2 Amariah, Malluch, Hattush,
3 Shecaniah, Harim, Meremoth,
4 Iddo, Ginnethon, Abijah,
5 Miniamin, Moadiah, Bilgah,
6 Shemaiah, Joiarib, Jedaiah,
7 Sallu, Amok, Hilkiah, and Jedaiah.
These were the leaders of the priests and their associates in the days of Jeshua.

8 The Levites who returned with them were Jeshua, Binnui, Kadmiel, Sherebiah, Judah, and Mattaniah, who with his associates was in charge of the songs of thanksgiving. 9 Their associates, Bakbukiah and Unni, stood opposite them during the service.

10 Jeshua the high priest was the father of Joiakim.
Joiakim was the father of Eliashib.
Eliashib was the father of Joiada.
11 Joiada was the father of Johanan.
Johanan was the father of Jaddua.

12 Now when Joiakim was high priest, the family leaders of the priests were as follows:

Meraiah was leader of the family of Seraiah.
Hananiah was leader of the family of Jeremiah.
13 Meshullam was leader of the family of Ezra.
Jehohanan was leader of the family of Amariah.
14 Jonathan was leader of the family of Malluch.
Joseph was leader of the family of Shecaniah.
15 Adna was leader of the family of Harim.
Helkai was leader of the family of Meremoth.

11:24 The *royal adviser* informed the king of events in Jerusalem and notified Jewish officials of the king's *public administration* of Persian policies.

11:30 *all the way from Beersheba . . . to the valley of Hinnom:* Earlier descriptions of places where people settled concentrated on areas north of Jerusalem (3:1-32; 11:31-36); this list (11:25-30) reflects progressive expansion of places where Jewish people lived as they occupied many of their preexilic towns, both north and south of Jerusalem.

11:35 *and the Valley of Craftsmen:* Or *and Ge-harashim.*

12:1-26 These lists of priests and Levites include a list of those who originally returned from exile with Zerubbabel (12:1-9), a chronological list of high priests (12:10-11), and the priests and Levites who served at the time of Joiakim, the high priest at the time of Nehemiah and Ezra (12:12-26).

12:1-9 ***priests and Levites who returned with Zerubbabel . . . and Jeshua:*** See Ezra 1:1-5. Only those who could prove their priestly lineage could serve at the Temple, so it was important to maintain an accurate genealogical record of these families.

12:3 *Harim:* Hebrew *Rehum;* cp. 7:42; 12:15; Ezra 2:39.

12:4 *Ginnethon:* As in some Hebrew manuscripts and Latin Vulgate (see also 12:16); most Hebrew manuscripts read *Ginnethoi.*

12:5 *Miniamin, Moadiah:* Hebrew *Mijamin, Maadiah;* cp. 12:17.

12:7 ***leaders of the priests:*** Cp. Ezra 2:36-39. • ***Jeshua*** was the high priest in Jerusalem when the people returned from captivity shortly after 538 BC (Ezra 2:2; 3:2, 8; 4:3). He was still serving in 520 BC when Haggai and Zechariah encouraged the people to finish building the Temple (Ezra 5:1; Hag 1:1; Zech 3:1).

12:8-9 ***Their associates . . . stood opposite:*** To provide antiphonal singing (12:24; Ezra 3:1-11).

12:10-11 ***Joiakim*** probably served in the early years of Ezra's service. • ***Eliashib*** and ***Joiada*** served during Nehemiah's time (3:1; 13:4, 28). • ***Johanan*** (Hebrew *Jonathan;* cp. 12:22): An Aramaic papyrus document from a Jewish colony that settled in Elephantine, Egypt (about 410 BC) and Josephus (*Antiquities* 11.5.4, AD 93) both mention Johanan serving after Nehemiah's time.

12:12-21 This list was probably compiled ***when Joiakim was high priest*** (12:12) to verify the legitimacy of the priests and Levites who were in office. Except for the omission of Hattush (see 12:2), this list contains the same names as 12:1-7.

12:14 *Malluch:* As in Greek version (see also 10:4; 12:2); Hebrew reads *Malluchi.* • *Shecaniah:* As in many Hebrew manuscripts, some Greek manuscripts, and Syriac version (see also 12:3); most Hebrew manuscripts read *Shebaniah.*

12:15 *Meremoth:* As in some Greek manuscripts (see also 12:3); Hebrew reads *Meraioth.*

16 Zechariah was leader of the family of Iddo.
Meshullam was leader of the family of Ginnethon.
17 Zicri was leader of the family of Abijah.
There was also a leader of the family of Miniamin.
Piltai was leader of the family of Moadiah.
18 Shammua was leader of the family of Bilgah.
Jehonathan was leader of the family of Shemaiah.
19 Mattenai was leader of the family of Joiarib.
Uzzi was leader of the family of Jedaiah.
20 Kallai was leader of the family of Sallu.
Eber was leader of the family of Amok.
21 Hashabiah was leader of the family of Hilkiah.
Nethanel was leader of the family of Jedaiah.

22A record of the Levite families was
kept during the years when Eliashib, Joiada,
Johanan, and Jaddua served as high priest.
Another record of the priests was kept
during the reign of Darius the Persian. 23A
record of the heads of the Levite families
was kept in *The Book of History* down to the
days of Johanan, the grandson of Eliashib.
24These were the family leaders of the Levites: Hashabiah, Sherebiah, Jeshua, Binnui,
Kadmiel, and other associates, who stood
opposite them during the ceremonies of
praise and thanksgiving, one section responding to the other, as commanded by
David, the man of God. 25This included Mattaniah, Bakbukiah, and Obadiah.

Meshullam, Talmon, and Akkub were the
gatekeepers in charge of the storerooms
at the gates. 26These all served in the days
of Joiakim son of Jeshua, son of Jehozadak,
and in the days of Nehemiah the governor
and of Ezra the priest and scribe.

The Joyous Dedication of Jerusalem's Walls

27For the dedication of the new wall of Jerusalem, the Levites throughout the land were
asked to come to Jerusalem to assist in the
ceremonies. They were to take part in the
joyous occasion with their songs of [d]thanks-
giving and with the music of cymbals, harps,
and lyres. 28The singers were brought together from the region around Jerusalem
and from the villages of the Netophathites.
29They also came from Beth-gilgal and the
rural areas near Geba and Azmaveth, for
the singers had built their own settlements
around Jerusalem. 30The priests and Levites
first purified themselves; then they purified
the people, the gates, and the wall.

31I led the leaders of Judah to the top of
the wall and organized two large choirs to
give [e]thanks. One of the choirs proceeded
southward along the top of the wall to the
Dung Gate. 32Hoshaiah and half the leaders of Judah followed them, 33along with
Azariah, Ezra, Meshullam, 34Judah, Benjamin, Shemaiah, and Jeremiah. 35Then
came some priests who played trumpets,
including Zechariah son of Jonathan, son
of Shemaiah, son of Mattaniah, son of Micaiah, son of Zaccur, a descendant of Asaph.
36And Zechariah's colleagues were Shemaiah, Azarel, Milalai, Gilalai, Maai, Nethanel,
Judah, and Hanani. They used the musical
instruments prescribed by David, the man
of God. Ezra the scribe led this procession.
37At the Fountain Gate they went straight
up the steps on the ascent of the city wall
toward the City of David. They passed the
house of David and then proceeded to the
Water Gate on the east.

38The second choir giving thanks went
northward around the other way to meet

12:24 Neh 11:17
12:25 1 Chr 26:15-16
12:26 Neh 8:9
12:27 1 Chr 15:16, 28
[d]*todah* (8426) ‣Neh 12:31
12:28 1 Chr 9:16
12:30 Neh 13:22, 30
12:31 Neh 2:13; 3:13-14
[e]*todah* (8426) ‣Ps 26:7
12:37 Neh 2:14; 3:15, 26
12:38 Neh 3:8, 11

12:17 ***There was also a leader:*** The Hebrew text lacks the name of this family leader.

12:20 ***Sallu:*** Hebrew *Sallai;* cp. 12:7.

12:22 ***Darius the Persian*** is probably Darius II, who reigned 424–405 BC, or possibly Darius III, who reigned 336–330 BC.

12:23 ***grandson:*** Literally *descendant;* cp. 12:10-11.

12:24 ***Binnui:*** Hebrew *ben* ("son of"), which should probably be read here as the proper name *Binnui;* cp. Ezra 3:9 and the note there.

12:26 ***Jehozadak:*** Hebrew *Jozadak,* a variant spelling of *Jehozadak.*

12:27-43 ***The dedication of the new wall*** probably happened shortly after its completion (6:15-19). This account probably came from Nehemiah's personal memoirs.

12:27-29 Since few ***Levites*** had returned to live in Jerusalem (see Ezra 2:40-42; 8:15-19), all those ***throughout the land*** were recruited to create two impressive choirs and orchestras. • ***Netophathites*** were from near Bethlehem (1 Chr 2:54). • ***Beth-gilgal*** was near Jericho. • ***Geba*** and ***Azmaveth*** were in the territory of Benjamin.

12:30 The dedication ceremony required that ***the priests and Levites*** be ***purified*** and ready to enter the Temple area (see Exod 19:10; Num 8:5-7).

12:31-37 This impressive march ***proceeded southward*** (literally *to the right*) ***along the top of the wall to the Dung Gate*** at the southern end of the city (3:13-14). Then the procession continued north on the wall along the east side of the city, past the ruins of ***the house of David*** and up to the ***Water Gate*** (3:26; 8:1) near the Temple.

12:35 Long, slender, metal ***trumpets*** were played for festive, joyous occasions (1 Chr 13:8; 15:23; 16:6, 42; Ezra 3:10) by the descendants ***of Asaph*** (see note on 11:17).

12:38-39 ***The second choir . . . went northward*** (literally *to the left*), up the western wall past the ***Broad Wall*** (3:8), the ***Old City Gate*** (or *the Mishneh Gate,*

12:39 Neh 3:1, 3, 6, 25, 31-32; 8:16 Jer 31:38
12:44 Neh 13:4-5, 12-13
12:45 1 Chr 25:1-8; 26:1-32
12:46 2 Chr 29:30
12:47 Num 18:21-29
13:1 Deut 23:3-5 Neh 13:23
13:2 Num 22:3-11
13:3 Neh 9:2; 10:28
13:4 Neh 6:17-19; 12:44
13:5 Num 18:21

them. I followed them, together with the other half of the people, along the top of the wall past the Tower of the Ovens to the Broad Wall, 39 then past the Ephraim Gate to the Old City Gate, past the Fish Gate and the Tower of Hananel, and on to the Tower of the Hundred. Then we continued on to the Sheep Gate and stopped at the Guard Gate.

40 The two choirs that were giving thanks then proceeded to the Temple of God, where they took their places. So did I, together with the group of leaders who were with me. 41 We went together with the trumpet-playing priests—Eliakim, Maaseiah, Miniamin, Micaiah, Elioenai, Zechariah, and Hananiah—42 and the singers—Maaseiah, Shemaiah, Eleazar, Uzzi, Jehohanan, Malkijah, Elam, and Ezer. They played and sang loudly under the direction of Jezrahiah the choir director.

43 Many sacrifices were offered on that joyous day, for God had given the people cause for great joy. The women and children also participated in the celebration, and the joy of the people of Jerusalem could be heard far away.

Provisions for Temple Worship

44 On that day men were appointed to be in charge of the storerooms for the offerings, the first part of the harvest, and the tithes. They were responsible to collect from the fields outside the towns the portions required by the Law for the priests and Levites. For all the people of Judah took joy in the priests and Levites and their work. 45 They performed the service of their God and the service of purification, as commanded by David and his son Solomon, and so did the singers and the gatekeepers. 46 The custom of having choir directors to lead the choirs in hymns of praise and thanksgiving to God began long ago in the days of David and Asaph. 47 So now, in the days of Zerubbabel and of Nehemiah, all Israel brought a daily supply of food for the singers, the gatekeepers, and the Levites. The Levites, in turn, gave a portion of what they received to the priests, the descendants of Aaron.

Nehemiah's Various Reforms

13 On that same day, as the Book of Moses was being read to the people, the passage was found that said no Ammonite or Moabite should ever be permitted to enter the assembly of God. 2 For they had not provided the Israelites with food and water in the wilderness. Instead, they hired Balaam to curse them, though our God turned the curse into a blessing. 3 When this passage of the Law was read, all those of foreign descent were immediately excluded from the assembly.

4 Before this had happened, Eliashib the priest, who had been appointed as supervisor of the storerooms of the Temple of our God and who was also a relative of Tobiah, 5 had converted a large storage room and placed it at Tobiah's disposal. The room had previously been used for storing the grain offerings, the frankincense, various articles for the Temple, and the tithes of grain, new wine, and olive oil (which were prescribed for the Levites, the singers, and the gatekeepers), as well as the offerings for the priests.

---

or *the Jeshanah Gate;* see 3:6), and the ***Fish Gate*** (3:3), then across the northern side of the wall until it came to the ***Sheep Gate*** (3:1) on the northeast corner of the Temple. • The ***Guard Gate*** might be the Inspection Gate (3:31). • ***Ephraim Gate:*** See note on 8:16.

12:43 This community celebration included everyone. God was the true source of their ***great joy*** because his power had enabled them to accomplish the huge task of rebuilding the walls. Psalm 147 might have been written for this occasion.

12:44-47 ***On that day,*** the day of the dedication of the wall (12:44; 13:1), ***men were appointed*** to take care of the tithes and gifts given for the physical needs of the priests and Levites. Their duties were ***to collect*** the gifts of the people for the priests and Levites (10:32-39; see also Exod 30:11-16; 38:25-26), to perform ***the service of their God*** (probably sacrifices; see Lev 1–5), and to oversee ***the service of purification*** of those people who were unclean. They also purified pans, knives, and clothing used in Temple worship as described in Lev 11–15 (1 Chr 23:28).

12:46 ***David*** had given instructions for ordering the music at the Temple (1 Chr 23–26), and he had put ***Asaph,*** along with Heman and Jeduthun, in charge of the music (1 Chr 25:2-5).

12:47 From the time of the first returnees to Jerusalem ***in the days of Zerubbabel*** in 538 BC (Ezra 3:1) until the time of ***Nehemiah*** around 445 BC, Israelites brought food for those working at the Temple. Most of the ***Levites*** lived in cities around the country; they collected the tithe and brought a tenth of what they received to the Temple in Jerusalem to support its ministry (see 10:38-39).

13:1-3 On the ***same day*** the Temple workers were appointed (12:44), the text from Deut 23:3-6 was read. It said that ***no Ammonite or Moabite should ever be permitted to enter the assembly of God*** (see Deut 23:3-6). Nehemiah later discovered (13:4-14) that these teachings were no longer being observed.

13:4-14 ***Eliashib the priest*** (see 12:10, 22; 13:28) had stopped following the practice of excluding the Ammonites and Moabites (13:1), and the people quit giving their tithes to the Levites (13:10-12). Now, Nehemiah corrected these problems.

13:4-5 ***Eliashib***'s family intermarried with the families of Sanballat (13:28) and ***Tobiah.*** Both of these men were enemies of the Jewish community (2:10, 19; 4:1). Tobiah's use of the storeroom meant there was less room to store tithes and gifts for the Temple workers (cp. 10:39; 13:10-12; 2 Chr 31:11) and less space for supplies needed to conduct regular worship at the Temple (Lev 2).

6I was not in Jerusalem at that time, for I had returned to King Artaxerxes of Babylon in the thirty-second year of his reign, though I later asked his permission to return. 7When I arrived back in Jerusalem, I learned about Eliashib's evil deed in providing Tobiah with a room in the courtyards of the Temple of God. 8I became very upset and threw all of Tobiah's belongings out of the room. 9Then I demanded that the rooms be purified, and I brought back the articles for God's Temple, the grain offerings, and the frankincense.

10I also discovered that the Levites had not been given their prescribed portions of food, so they and the singers who were to conduct the worship services had all returned to work their fields. 11I immediately confronted the leaders and demanded, "Why has the Temple of God been neglected?" Then I called all the Levites back again and restored them to their proper duties. 12And once more all the people of Judah began bringing their tithes of grain, new wine, and olive oil to the Temple storerooms.

13I assigned supervisors for the storerooms: Shelemiah the priest, Zadok the scribe, and Pedaiah, one of the Levites. And I appointed Hanan son of Zaccur and grandson of Mattaniah as their assistant. These men had an excellent reputation, and it was their job to make honest distributions to their fellow Levites.

> 14Remember this good deed, O my
> God, and do not forget all that I have
> faithfully done for the Temple of my God
> and its services.

Nehemiah Confronts the People's Sin

15In those days I saw men of Judah treading out their winepresses on the [f]Sabbath. They were also bringing in grain, loading it on donkeys, and bringing their wine, grapes, figs, and all sorts of produce to Jerusalem to sell on the [f]Sabbath. So I rebuked them for selling their produce on that day. 16Some men from Tyre, who lived in Jerusalem, were bringing in fish and all kinds of merchandise. They were selling it on the Sabbath to the people of Judah—and in Jerusalem at that!

17So I confronted the nobles of Judah. "Why are you profaning the Sabbath in this evil way?" I asked. 18"Wasn't it just this sort of thing that your ancestors did that caused our God to bring all this trouble upon us and our city? Now you are bringing even more wrath upon Israel by permitting the Sabbath to be desecrated in this way!"

19Then I commanded that the gates of Jerusalem should be shut as darkness fell every Friday evening, not to be opened until the Sabbath ended. I sent some of my own servants to guard the gates so that no merchandise could be brought in on the Sabbath day. 20The merchants and tradesmen with a variety of wares camped outside Jerusalem once or twice. 21But I spoke sharply to them and said, "What are you doing out here, camping around the wall? If you do this again, I will arrest you!" And that was the last time they came on the Sabbath. 22Then I commanded the Levites to purify themselves and to guard the gates in order to preserve the holiness of the Sabbath.

> Remember this good deed also, O my
> God! Have compassion on me according
> to your great and unfailing love.

23About the same time I realized that some of the men of Judah had married women from Ashdod, Ammon, and Moab.

13:6 Neh 5:14
13:7 Neh 13:5
13:9 2 Chr 29:5, 15-19
13:10 Neh 10:37; 12:28-29
13:12 Neh 10:37-39; 12:44
13:13 Neh 7:2
13:14 Neh 5:19; 13:22, 31
13:15 Exod 20:8-11; 34:21
Neh 13:21
[f]*shabbath* (7676)
‣ Isa 56:2
13:17 Neh 13:11, 15
13:18 Jer 17:21
13:19 Lev 23:32
13:21 Neh 13:15
13:22 Neh 13:14, 31
13:23 Ezra 9:2
Neh 10:30

13:6 Nehemiah had returned to Persia after twelve years of service in Jerusalem (445–433 BC). The text does not say how long he stayed there, but it was probably no longer than a year or two. When he arrived back in Jerusalem, he found Tobiah living in the Temple storeroom (13:1-5). • ***King Artaxerxes*** of Persia is here identified as the king ***of Babylon*** because Persia had conquered the Babylonian empire. The ***thirty-second year*** of Artaxerxes was 433 BC.

13:8-9 ***I became very upset. . . . I demanded:*** When people rejected God's instructions, Nehemiah refused to be silent. • Everything associated with the Temple had to be ***purified*** and consecrated to God. The clothes that the priests and Levites wore (Exod 29), the priests themselves (Lev 8–9), the Temple building and altars (Lev 16:15-33), and all the holy things (1 Chr 23:28) were purified (cp. 2 Chr 29:5, 15-19).

13:10-12 With Tobiah using the storeroom, there had been no place to store tithes to feed the Levites and Temple singers (Num 18:21-24; see notes on 12:44-45, 47). They had to farm outside of Jerusalem (12:28-29) to support themselves and could not serve in the Temple.

13:13 ***These men had an excellent reputation:*** Cp. Acts 6:1-6.

13:14 Because he stood up for God, Nehemiah asked God to ***remember*** his deeds and not abandon him in his time of need. Perhaps he experienced opposition from those he had corrected. See similar refrains in 13:22, 29, 31.

13:15-31 Nehemiah instituted two additional reforms to restore proper Sabbath observance (13:15-22) and proper marriage practices (13:23-31). These two sections have similar structures: Nehemiah discovered a problem, corrected the problem, and asked God for his blessing.

13:15-16 Normal work was to cease ***on the Sabbath*** in order to keep it holy (Exod 20:8-11; 31:14-17; 35:2-3; Jer 17:19-27).

13:19 ***as darkness fell every Friday evening:*** Literally *on the day before the Sabbath.* The Sabbath began at sunset on *Friday evening* and lasted until sunset on Saturday evening.

13:22 ***Have compassion on me:*** Nehemiah's prayer implies that he felt the pressure of this unpopular decision. He knew that God's ***unfailing love,*** not his own popularity, would sustain him.

13:25 Deut 25:2; Neh 10:29-30; 13:11, 17
13:26 1 Kgs 3:13; 11:1-8; 2 Chr 1:12
13:27 Ezra 10:2; Neh 13:23
13:28 Neh 2:10, 19
13:29 Num 25:13; Neh 6:14
13:30 Neh 10:30
13:31 Neh 10:34; 13:14, 22

24Furthermore, half their children spoke
the language of Ashdod or of some other
people and could not speak the language
of Judah at all. 25So I confronted them and
called down curses on them. I beat some of
them and pulled out their hair. I made them
swear in the name of God that they would
not let their children intermarry with the
pagan people of the land.
26"Wasn't this exactly what led King
Solomon of Israel into sin?" I demanded.
"There was no king from any nation who
could compare to him, and God loved him
and made him king over all Israel. But even
he was led into sin by his foreign wives.
27How could you even think of committing
this sinful deed and acting unfaithfully
toward God by marrying foreign women?"
28One of the sons of Joiada son of Eliashib the high priest had married a daughter of Sanballat the Horonite, so I banished him from my presence.

29Remember them, O my God, for they
have defiled the priesthood and the
solemn vows of the priests and Levites.

30So I purged out everything foreign and
assigned tasks to the priests and Levites,
making certain that each knew his work. 31I
also made sure that the supply of wood for
the altar and the first portions of the harvest were brought at the proper times.

Remember this in my favor, O my God.

13:23-24 The earlier marriage reforms (9:2; 10:28; Ezra 9:1–10:44) had not lasted. The children's inability to speak Hebrew (***the language of Judah***) was disastrous because they could not read or understand the Scriptures.

13:25 When Nehemiah ***called down curses on them,*** it was because the parents avoided Hebrew and did not teach their children the language of the Hebrew Bible. A curse called on God to remove his blessing on people. • ***I beat some of them and pulled out their hair:*** Apparently, some of the men did not accept Nehemiah's rebuke at first, so he ***made them swear in the name of God*** not to intermarry with pagans.

13:26-27 ***King Solomon*** had led the nation ***into sin by his foreign wives*** (1 Kgs 11). If intermarriage with pagans was allowed to continue, the same apostasy would overtake the community. Nehemiah would not let that happen.

13:28 Even the family of ***the high priest,*** who were supposed to be Israel's spiritual leaders, had participated in the sin of intermarriage with unbelieving foreigners (cp. Lev 21:14). Nehemiah ***banished*** the offender, stripping him of status and removing his rights in the Jewish community.

13:29 ***Remember them, O my God:*** Many would probably resent Nehemiah's aggressive attack on intermarriage in the family of the high priest. So he prayed for God's judgment to fall on these spiritual leaders who ***defiled the priesthood.***

13:30-31 These final verses summarize Nehemiah's reform. The emphasis on ***making certain*** and making ***sure*** shows that Nehemiah checked to see that the people did what they agreed to. He held people accountable for their commitments and did not allow for half-hearted reform.

THE BOOK OF ESTHER

Esther's rags-to-riches drama illustrates how a woman with wisdom, courage, and willingness can affect the lives of thousands. With a praying community of supporters, and with God providentially working in the background, Esther accepted her role and put her life on the line to save others.

SETTING

The book of Esther describes events during the reign of King Xerxes of Persia (486–465 BC). In a previous generation (538 BC), Sheshbazzar had led about 50,000 people back from captivity in Babylonia (Ezra 1:1-5; 2:64-67). But many Jewish families, including Esther's, had stayed behind.

During Xerxes' reign, the Persian empire was near its peak. Xerxes and his military had accomplished great things, such as conquering Egypt. Wealth from taxes poured into the Persian capital of Susa, and Xerxes oversaw the construction of a luxurious new palace at Persepolis. However, Xerxes was a cruel king who ruled with tyrannical force. Esther entered Xerxes' court and was chosen to be his queen. Her challenge was to serve God and her people in time of crisis while being the faithful wife of a pagan king.

SUMMARY

When King Xerxes gave a lavish banquet for key leaders of Persia, Queen Vashti refused to show off her beauty, so Xerxes deposed her and searched for a new queen (1:1–2:4). Mordecai's cousin Esther was chosen (2:5-18).

Mordecai became a palace official. One day, he uncovered a plot against the king and reported it through Esther. Mordecai also refused to bow to Haman, Xerxes' highest official, which led to Haman's vindictive plot to kill all the Jews in the empire (2:19–3:15).

As the Jewish community prayed (4:16), Esther endangered her own life, approached the king, and invited him and Haman to a feast (4:1-17).

Haman had built a pole so that he could impale Mordecai (5:14), but King Xerxes made Haman honor Mordecai in the streets of the city, a bitter humiliation (6:1-14). Then Esther revealed Haman's plot as a personal attack. Haman was impaled on his own pole (7:1-10).

King Xerxes then allowed the Jewish people to defend themselves (8:1-14). The

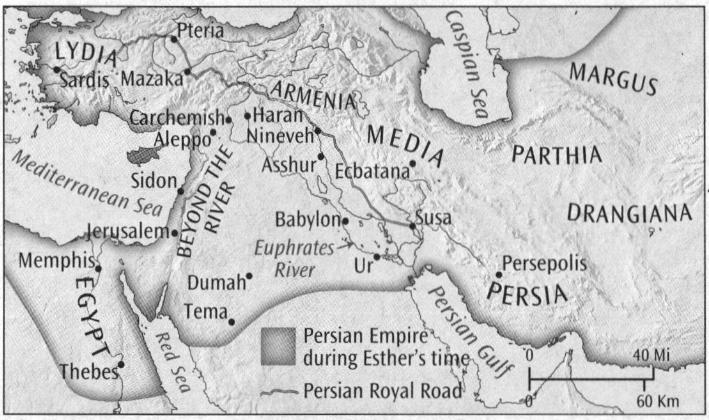

◀ **The Empire of Xerxes I, 486–465 BC.** During Esther's time, Xerxes I was king of the vast Persian empire. The map shows the major towns and some of the provinces over which Xerxes ruled (1:1). The region of Judea was part of the Persian province "BEYOND THE RIVER," which consisted of the area from the EUPHRATES RIVER west to the MEDITERRANEAN SEA (see note on Ezra 4:10).

Jews rejoiced, Mordecai was promoted, and Haman's sons were executed (9:1-17). The Jewish people then defended themselves successfully and celebrated God's marvelous deliverance at the first festival of Purim.

AUTHOR & DATE

The text of Esther does not indicate who wrote the book or when it was written. Some early church fathers thought that Ezra wrote Esther, but Clement of Alexandria suggested Mordecai. Since there are many Persian words in the book and there is no Greek influence, the book was probably written between 460 BC (i.e., after the conclusion of Xerxes I's reign) and 331 BC (i.e., before the rise of the Greek empire under Alexander the Great).

OUTLINE

1:1–2:18
Xerxes Replaces His Queen

2:19–3:15
Haman Plots to Destroy the Jews

4:1–5:14
Mordecai and Esther Counter Haman's Plot

6:1–7:10
The King Honors Mordecai and Executes Haman

8:1–9:19
Rescue for the Jews

9:20-32
The Festival of Purim

10:1-3
The Greatness of Xerxes and Mordecai

PURPOSE

The book of Esther was written to explain to a Jewish audience how the festival of Purim originated. Purim was to be an annual remembrance of how God delivered his people from death (9:20-22), similar to their deliverance during the exodus from Egypt.

GENRE: HISTORY OR FICTION?

The book of Esther is a biographical narrative similar to the narrative of Joseph (Gen 37–48) and the book of Ruth. Some question whether this story is history. They allege that (a) the decree for widespread extermination of the Jews by a Persian king is implausible; (b) the slaughter of 75,000 enemies in one day by the Jews is implausible; (c) since only Persians were queens, Esther would never have been chosen; and (d) the large number of improbable coincidences suggests that this is fiction.

On the other hand, the historical accuracy of the book is supported because (a) the book uses authentic Persian names, titles, and customs; (b) elsewhere God works behind the scenes to use improbable coincidences to his glory (e.g., Gen 37–48; Ruth 1–4); (c) Esther hid her identity as a Jew until long after she became queen; and (d) kings do not usually oppose the slaughter of their enemies, which Haman said the Jews were. These factors testify to the authenticity and historical character of the book.

ADDITIONS TO THE BOOK OF ESTHER

The Hebrew text of Esther is defined by a strong and consistent Hebrew manuscript tradition. Nevertheless, the Targums and Midrash (interpretation and commentary on the Hebrew OT), the Greek OT, the Latin

TIMELINE

559–530 BC
Cyrus II as king of Persia

Oct 539 BC
Cyrus II conquers Babylon

538 BC
Cyrus's decree allows exiles to return to Judea

486–465 BC
Xerxes I (Ahasuerus) as king of Persia

about 483~473 BC
The events in the book of Esther take place

465–424 BC
Artaxerxes I as king of Persia

458 BC
Ezra travels to Jerusalem

445–433 BC
Nehemiah as governor of Judea

The author of Esther wanted his readers to see the mystery of God's hand in history. He chose to show how human decision and action are the instrumentation of divine purpose.

M. BRENEMAN
Ezra, Nehemiah, Esther (1993)

Vulgate, and Josephus (a first-century Roman Jewish historian) all have many additional stories that are not included in the Hebrew text but were composed later. The longer additions mention God numerous times, whereas the Hebrew text does not. None of the additions contain authoritative original information; some just repeat information, some contradict information in the Hebrew version of Esther, and others are based on the imagination of later authors. Instead of inserting these additions where they fit chronologically and making them look like an authentic part of the story, Jerome, who translated and edited the Latin Vulgate, wisely collected them together at the end of the OT in the Deuterocanonical (or, Apocryphal) books that are included in Roman Catholic and Orthodox translations.

FURTHER READING

JOYCE G. BALDWIN
Esther (1984)

A. B. LUTER AND B. C. DAVIS
God Behind the Seen: Exposition of the Books of Ruth and Esther (1995)

KAREN H. JOBES
Esther (1999)

M. ROBERTS
Ezra, Nehemiah, Esther (1993)

GARY V. SMITH
Esther in *Cornerstone Biblical Commentary*, vol. 5b (2010)

MEANING AND MESSAGE

Although the book of Esther never mentions God, its central purpose is to demonstrate that God works providentially to take care of his people. God used Xerxes' drunken arrogance to elevate Esther to a position of influence (chs 1–2). Haman's evil plans to kill the Jews were brought back on his own head through a series of unique and ironic circumstances, and the day of execution became a day of joy for God's people. The book of Esther reminds us that God providentially directs believers and unbelievers alike to accomplish his will.

1. XERXES REPLACES HIS QUEEN (1:1–2:18)

Xerxes' Rule over His Own House Is Challenged (1:1-22)

The King's Banquet

1 These events happened in the days of
King Xerxes, who reigned over 127 provinces stretching from India to Ethiopia. [2]At
that time Xerxes ruled his empire from his
royal throne at the fortress of Susa. [3]In the
third year of his reign, he gave a banquet
for all his nobles and officials. He invited
all the military officers of Persia and Media
as well as the princes and nobles of the provinces. [4]The celebration lasted 180 days—a
tremendous display of the opulent wealth
of his empire and the pomp and splendor
of his majesty.

[5]When it was all over, the king gave a banquet for all the people, from the greatest to
the least, who were in the fortress of Susa.
It lasted for seven days and was held in the
courtyard of the palace garden. [6]The courtyard was beautifully decorated with white
cotton curtains and blue hangings, which
were fastened with white linen cords and
purple ribbons to silver rings embedded in
marble pillars. Gold and silver couches stood
on a mosaic pavement of porphyry, marble,
mother-of-pearl, and other costly stones.
[7]Drinks were served in gold goblets of
many designs, and there was an abundance
of royal wine, reflecting the king's generosity. [8]By edict of the king, no limits were
placed on the drinking, for the king had

1:1 Ezra 4:6; Esth 8:9-10; Dan 8:2
1:2 Neh 1:1
1:3 Esth 2:18
1:5 Esth 7:7-8
1:6 Ezek 23:41; Amos 6:4
1:7 Esth 2:18

1:1 *Xerxes:* Hebrew *Ahasuerus*, another name for *Xerxes;* also throughout the book of Esther. *Xerxes* reigned 486–465 BC. The name *Xerxes* comes from the Greek transliteration of the Persian *Xshayarshan*, which the Hebrew text renders *'akhashwerosh* (*Ahasuerus*). His father, Darius I (521–486 BC), was king when Haggai and Zechariah encouraged the people of Judah to finish building the Temple in Jerusalem (see Ezra 4:24–6:22; Hag 1:1; Zech 1:1). • *127 provinces:* Xerxes reigned over a vast empire *stretching from India to Ethiopia* (Hebrew *to Cush*).

1:2 *The fortress of Susa* was the king's winter capital during the cold months.

1:4 ***The celebration lasted 180 days:*** Officials probably took turns attending different events planned during this six-month period of ***celebration***, thus maintaining the nation's military and infrastructure throughout the celebration. • This ***tremendous display*** of ***pomp and splendor*** was designed to impress others with the king's greatness; it also illustrates Xerxes' pride.

1:5 A second, briefer ***banquet*** allowed members of every level of society (***from the greatest to the least***) to experience the king's majestic wealth. Because of the large numbers of people who could attend, this continuous open house reception was held outdoors in the paved ***courtyard of the palace garden***.

1:6 ***White*** and ***blue*** (or ***violet***) were royal colors. Even the ***mosaic pavement*** was exquisitely opulent.

1:8 ***no limits were placed on the drinking:*** Often guests would drink only when the Persian king bade them with a toast (see Xenophon, *Cyropaedia* 8.8.18); at this banquet people were able to drink without restraint.

1:10
Judg 16:25
Dan 5:1-4

1:13
1 Chr 12:32

1:19
Esth 8:8
Dan 6:8, 15

1:22
Esth 3:12; 8:9-10

2:1
Esth 1:19-20; 7:10

2:3
Esth 2:8-9, 15

instructed all his palace officials to serve
each man as much as he wanted.
[9]At the same time, Queen Vashti gave a
banquet for the women in the royal palace
of King Xerxes.

Queen Vashti Deposed

[10]On the seventh day of the feast, when
King Xerxes was in high spirits because of
the wine, he told the seven eunuchs who attended him—Mehuman, Biztha, Harbona,
Bigtha, Abagtha, Zethar, and Carcas—[11]to
bring Queen Vashti to him with the royal
crown on her head. He wanted the nobles
and all the other men to gaze on her beauty,
for she was a very beautiful woman. [12]But
when they conveyed the king's order to
Queen Vashti, she refused to come. This
made the king furious, and he burned
with anger.
[13]He immediately consulted with his wise
advisers, who knew all the Persian laws and
customs, for he always asked their advice.
[14]The names of these men were Carshena,
Shethar, Admatha, Tarshish, Meres, Marsena,
and Memucan—seven nobles of Persia and
Media. They met with the king regularly and
held the highest positions in the empire.
[15]"What must be done to Queen Vashti?"
the king demanded. "What penalty does the
law provide for a queen who refuses to obey
the king's orders, properly sent through his
eunuchs?"
[16]Memucan answered the king and his
nobles, "Queen Vashti has wronged not only
the king but also every noble and citizen
throughout your empire. [17]Women everywhere will begin to despise their husbands
when they learn that Queen Vashti has refused to appear before the king. [18]Before
this day is out, the wives of all the king's nobles throughout Persia and Media will hear
what the queen did and will start treating
their husbands the same way. There will be
no end to their contempt and anger.
[19]"So if it please the king, we suggest that
you issue a written decree, a law of the Persians and Medes that cannot be revoked. It
should order that Queen Vashti be forever
banished from the presence of King Xerxes,
and that the king should choose another
queen more worthy than she. [20]When this
decree is published throughout the king's
vast empire, husbands everywhere, whatever their rank, will receive proper respect
from their wives!"
[21]The king and his nobles thought this
made good sense, so he followed Memucan's counsel. [22]He sent letters to all parts
of the empire, to each province in its own
script and language, proclaiming that every
man should be the ruler of his own home
and should say whatever he pleases.

Esther Is Chosen to Be Queen (2:1-18)

2 But after Xerxes' anger had subsided, he
began thinking about Vashti and what
she had done and the decree he had made.
[2]So his personal attendants suggested, "Let
us search the empire to find beautiful young
virgins for the king. [3]Let the king appoint
agents in each province to bring these beautiful young women into the royal harem at the
fortress of Susa. Hegai, the king's eunuch in
charge of the harem, will see that they are
all given beauty treatments. [4]After that, the
young woman who most pleases the king
will be made queen instead of Vashti." This

1:9 Since *Vashti* means *the best, desired, beloved,* this is possibly the title for a favored wife rather than her actual name. Ancient Greek historians refer to her as *Amestris* (e.g., Herodotus, *Histories* 7.114). Her son, Artaxerxes I, became king of Persia (465–424 BC) after Xerxes' death (see Ezra 4:7-23; 6:14; 7:1, 7, 11-26; 8:1; Neh 1:1; 2:1; 5:14; 13:6).

1:10 ***Xerxes was in high spirits:*** He was probably fairly drunk and apt to do something foolish. • ***Eunuchs*** were servants who had been castrated because their roles brought them into frequent contact with the women of the royal harem.

1:11 ***she was a very beautiful woman:*** The king wanted to display one of his prized possessions.

1:12 ***she refused to come:*** The queen's refusal is not explained. Perhaps she feared the drunken king would humiliate her in some way. • ***This made the king furious:*** The king's anger was probably heightened by his drunken state and by his humiliation before his male friends.

1:13 The king did not react immediately but ***consulted with his wise advisers,*** following his normal custom of checking with Persian legal advisers to see what could be done about his disobedient wife (1:15).

1:15 ***What penalty does the law provide:*** In his humiliation, the king no doubt wanted to punish Vashti to the fullest extent.

1:16-18 ***Queen Vashti has wronged:*** The adviser ***Memucan*** did not quote Persian law as precedent to guide the king's decision. His impetuous advice to the king turned Vashti's action into a potential crime by all women.

1:17 ***Women everywhere will begin to despise their husbands:*** Fear of consequences rather than facts or law motivated the council's decision.

1:19 ***issue a written decree . . . that cannot be revoked:*** The written decree would become unalterable law that could not be changed (8:8; Dan 6:8, 12).

1:22 The decree was published in each region ***in its own script and language*** so that the decree would be understood by every language group in the vast Persian empire. • ***every man should be the ruler of his own home:*** It was already the cultural norm throughout the ancient Near East at that time that men ruled their houses. The decree added legal enforcement of the custom. • ***and should say whatever he pleases:*** Or *and should speak in the language of his own people.*

advice was very appealing to the king, so he
put the plan into effect.
[5]At that time there was a Jewish man in
the fortress of Susa whose name was Mordecai son of Jair. He was from the tribe of
Benjamin and was a descendant of Kish and
Shimei. [6]His family had been among those
who, with King Jehoiachin of Judah, had been
exiled from Jerusalem to Babylon by King
Nebuchadnezzar. [7]This man had a very beautiful and lovely young cousin, Hadassah, who
was also called Esther. When her father and
mother died, Mordecai adopted her into his
family and raised her as his own daughter.
[8]As a result of the king's decree, Esther,
along with many other young women, was
brought to the king's harem at the fortress of
Susa and placed in Hegai's care. [9]Hegai was
very impressed with Esther and treated her
kindly. He quickly ordered a special menu
for her and provided her with beauty treatments. He also assigned her seven maids
specially chosen from the king's palace, and
he moved her and her maids into the best
place in the harem.
[10]Esther had not told anyone of her nationality and family background, because
Mordecai had directed her not to do so. [11]Ev-
ery day Mordecai would take a walk near
the courtyard of the harem to find out about
Esther and what was happening to her.
[12]Before each young woman was taken to
the king's bed, she was given the prescribed
twelve months of beauty treatments—six
months with oil of myrrh, followed by six
months with special perfumes and ointments. [13]When it was time for her to go to
the king's palace, she was given her choice
of whatever clothing or jewelry she wanted
to take from the harem. [14]That evening she
was taken to the king's private rooms, and
the next morning she was brought to the
second harem, where the king's wives lived.
There she would be under the care of Shaashgaz, the king's eunuch in charge of the
concubines. She would never go to the king
again unless he had especially enjoyed her
and requested her by name.
[15]Esther was the daughter of Abihail,
who was Mordecai's uncle. (Mordecai had
adopted his younger cousin Esther.) When
it was Esther's turn to go to the king, she accepted the advice of Hegai, the eunuch in
charge of the harem. She asked for nothing
except what he suggested, and she was admired by everyone who saw her.
[16]Esther was taken to King Xerxes at the
royal palace in early winter of the seventh
year of his reign. [17]And the king loved Esther
more than any of the other young women.
He was so delighted with her that he set
the royal crown on her head and declared
her queen instead of Vashti. [18]To celebrate
the occasion, he gave a great banquet in Esther's honor for all his nobles and officials,
declaring a public holiday for the provinces
and giving generous gifts to everyone.

2. HAMAN PLOTS TO DESTROY THE JEWS (2:19–3:15)

Mordecai's Loyalty to the King

[19]Even after all the young women had
been transferred to the second harem and

2:5 Esth 3:2-6
2:6 2 Kgs 24:14-15
2:7-8 Esth 2:15
2:9 Esth 2:3, 12
2:10 Esth 2:20
2:15 Esth 9:29
2:17 Esth 1:11
2:18 Esth 1:3-8

2:6 ***His family:*** Literally *He.* Since King Jehoiachin was *exiled* in 597 BC (2 Kgs 24:6-16), over 100 years earlier, it was probably one of Mordecai's ancestors who was part of the group taken into Babylonian captivity. • ***Jehoiachin:*** Hebrew *Jeconiah,* a variant spelling of Jehoiachin.

2:7 ***Hadassah*** is a Hebrew name that means *myrtle;* ***Esther*** is a Persian name that means *star.*

2:9 ***ordered a special menu . . . beauty treatments:*** Hegai knew the king's taste and singled out the best prospects for special attention. • Hegai assigned ***seven*** of the best assistants to Esther, indicating that he thought she was one of the very best candidates for becoming the queen.

2:10 Probably Mordecai had already experienced some prejudice against Jews. Esther's Jewish background would later become the key to her exposing Haman's terrible plot.

2:12 The ***twelve months*** of preparation no doubt involved training in court customs as well as ***beauty treatments,*** but the focus here is on physical beauty.

2:14 ***to the second harem:*** Or *to another part of the harem.* Each woman would spend one night with the king in his bedroom and then live essentially as a widow the rest of her life unless the king remembered her name and called for her. The women in the second harem lived an easy life in a luxurious setting ***under the care of Shaashgaz, the king's eunuch.***

2:15 ***Hegai*** apparently knew the king's preferences, so he was able to give Esther good ***advice,*** which she wisely ***accepted*** and followed.

2:16 ***in early winter:*** Literally *in the tenth month, the month of Tebeth.* A number of dates in the book of Esther can be cross-checked with dates in surviving Persian records and related accurately to our modern calendar. This month of the ancient Hebrew lunar calendar occurred within the months of December 479 BC and January 478 BC.

2:17 ***he set the royal crown on her head:*** Now Esther had access to the king's heart as his favored wife. She was now in a place where God could use her to impact the thoughts and actions of the king.

2:18 ***he gave a great banquet in Esther's honor:*** Now the king honored his wife instead of putting her on display (cp. 1:11). • ***declaring a public holiday:*** The Hebrew word translated "public holiday" (*hanakhah*) is related to the verb that means "rest" (*nukh*). The book as a whole describes how the Jewish people obtained rest from the threats of their enemies (see 9:16-22).

2:19 ***Even after all the young women had been transferred to the second harem:*** The meaning of the Hebrew is uncertain. Since the queen had been chosen, those in waiting would join the other concubines. • ***and Mordecai had become a palace official:*** Literally *and Mordecai was sitting in the gate of the king.* Court cases were decided and much official business was conducted

2:20 Esth 2:10
2:21 Esth 1:10; 6:2
2:22 Esth 6:1-2
2:23 Esth 10:2
3:1 Esth 3:10; 5:11
3:2 Esth 5:9
3:3 Esth 3:2
3:5 Esth 5:9
3:6 Ps 83:4

Mordecai had become a palace official,
[20]Esther continued to keep her family background and nationality a secret. She was still following Mordecai's directions, just as she did when she lived in his home.
[21]One day as Mordecai was on duty at the king's gate, two of the king's eunuchs, Bigthana and Teresh—who were guards at the door of the king's private quarters—became angry at King Xerxes and plotted to assassinate him.
[22]But Mordecai heard about the plot and gave the information to Queen Esther. She then told the king about it and gave Mordecai credit for the report.
[23]When an investigation was made and Mordecai's story was found to be true, the two men were impaled on a sharpened pole. This was all recorded in *The Book of the History of King Xerxes' Reign*.

Mordecai Will Not Honor Haman

3 Some time later King Xerxes promoted Haman son of Hammedatha the Agagite over all the other nobles, making him the most powerful official in the empire.
[2]All the king's officials would bow down before Haman to show him respect whenever he passed by, for so the king had commanded. But Mordecai refused to bow down or show him respect.
[3]Then the palace officials at the king's gate asked Mordecai, "Why are you disobeying the king's command?"
[4]They spoke to him day after day, but still he refused to comply with the order. So they spoke to Haman about this to see if he would tolerate Mordecai's conduct, since Mordecai had told them he was a Jew.

Haman's Plot against the Jews

[5]When Haman saw that Mordecai would not bow down or show him respect, he was filled with rage.
[6]He had learned of Mordecai's nationality, so he decided it was not enough to lay hands on Mordecai alone. Instead, he looked for a way to destroy all the Jews throughout the entire empire of Xerxes.

ESTHER (2:7-20)

Esth 4:4–5:8; 7:1–9:32

Esther was queen of Persia during the reign of Xerxes I (486–465 BC). She was a woman of the *Diaspora* ("scattering"), descended from Jews who had been scattered among the nations at the time of the Exile. Her family had not returned to the land of Judah, as some Jews had (see Ezra 1–2), but had chosen to stay in the land of Persia, like many others. Noting how important her cousin Mordecai was in the Persian government makes us guess that her family had grown rich and comfortable.

Esther was an orphan and was raised by her cousin Mordecai, who became a minor official in the Persian government in Susa. She became queen after King Xerxes became displeased with Queen Vashti for refusing to attend a banquet when commanded to do so (1:11-12).

After Esther's coronation, she discreetly won Xerxes' confidence by informing him of an assassination plot (2:21-23). This later enabled her to rescue her people from a massacre planned by Haman, a high official to the king. Through her wise advice and brave action, Esther exposed Haman, he was executed, and the Jewish people were rescued. The Jewish Festival of Purim was instituted to celebrate these events.

at the gate. There he was able to hear about the plot against the king (2:21-23).

2:20 ***keep her family background and nationality a secret:*** That this is mentioned twice (see also 2:10) indicates how important it was for the rest of the story. • With humility, ***she was still following Mordecai's directions.*** She did not become conceited and forget her people or the family that raised her.

2:21 ***Bigthana*** (Hebrew *Bigthan;* cp. 6:2) might be the Bigtha of 1:10, one of the king's seven eunuchs. He and ***Teresh*** guarded the king's bedroom, so it would not have been hard for them to carry out their plot if they hadn't been discovered.

2:22 ***gave the information to Queen Esther:*** The quickest, safest way for the information to get to the king was through the queen. • Although Esther could have promoted herself by taking credit for this information, she ***gave Mordecai credit for the report,*** an important point later in the story (6:1-3).

2:23 ***impaled on a sharpened pole*** (literally *hanged on a tree,* or *hanged on wood*): This phrase has traditionally been translated *hanged on a gallows,* but inscriptions from ancient Persia show that impalement was a standard form of execution. Xerxes' father, Darius I, claimed to have impaled 3,000 Babylonians when he conquered Babylon. Sometimes criminals were executed first and then displayed on a stake, as with the execution of Haman's sons (9:5-14). • ***This was all recorded:*** Mordecai was not rewarded until much later (6:1-14). • While various records of Xerxes' reign have been found, the particular book mentioned here no longer exists.

3:1-15 ***Haman***'s hatred for Mordecai develops into a plot to kill all the Jewish people.

3:2 It was a common custom to ***bow down*** before a superior (e.g., Gen 33:3). Since Mordecai served at the large gate to the palace and ***Haman*** entered the king's court through that gate, there were many opportunities for Mordecai to break the king's command and not bow before Haman.

3:6 Haman was not interested in justice; he wanted revenge. He was determined to do everything in his power to crush Mordecai, including exterminating his entire people—the Jews.

7So in the month of April, during the twelfth year of King Xerxes' reign, lots were cast in Haman's presence (the lots were called *purim*) to determine the best day and month to take action. And the day selected was March 7, nearly a year later.

8Then Haman approached King Xerxes and said, "There is a certain race of people scattered through all the provinces of your empire who keep themselves separate from everyone else. Their laws are different from those of any other people, and they refuse to obey the laws of the king. So it is not in the king's interest to let them live. 9If it please the king, issue a decree that they be destroyed, and I will give 10,000 large sacks of silver to the government administrators to be deposited in the royal treasury."

10The king agreed, confirming his decision by removing his signet ring from his finger and giving it to Haman son of Hammedatha the Agagite, the enemy of the Jews. 11The king said, "The money and the people are both yours to do with as you see fit."

12So on April 17 the king's secretaries were summoned, and a decree was written exactly as Haman dictated. It was sent to the king's highest officers, the governors of the respective provinces, and the nobles of each province in their own scripts and languages. The decree was written in the name of King Xerxes and sealed with the king's signet ring. 13Dispatches were sent by swift messengers into all the provinces of the empire, giving the order that all Jews—young and old, including women and children—must be killed, slaughtered, and annihilated on a single day. This was scheduled to happen on March 7 of the next year. The property of the Jews would be given to those who killed them.

14A copy of this decree was to be issued as law in every province and proclaimed to all peoples, so that they would be ready to do their duty on the appointed day. 15At the king's command, the decree went out by swift messengers, and it was also proclaimed in the fortress of Susa. Then the king and Haman sat down to drink, but the city of Susa fell into confusion.

3. MORDECAI AND ESTHER COUNTER HAMAN'S PLOT (4:1–5:14)

Mordecai Requests Esther's Help

4 When Mordecai learned about all that had been done, he tore his clothes, put on burlap and ashes, and went out into the

3:7 Esth 9:24-26
3:8 Ezra 4:12-15; Acts 16:20-21
3:10 Gen 41:42; Esth 8:2
3:12 1 Kgs 21:8; Esth 8:8-10
3:13 Esth 8:9-14; 9:2, 7-10, 17
3:14 Esth 4:8; 8:13-14
3:15 Esth 8:15
4:1 2 Sam 1:11; Esth 3:8-10; Ezek 27:30; Jon 3:4-9

3:7 ***in the month of April:*** Literally *in the first month, the month of Nisan.* This month of the ancient Hebrew lunar calendar occurred within the months of April and May 474 BC; also see note on 2:16. • ***lots were cast . . . (the lots were called purim):*** Throwing the *purim* was like throwing dice. The Hebrews used lots from time to time to understand God's will (Lev 16:8-10; Neh 10:34). Persian astrologers used *purim* in the first month of the year to determine which days that year would bring good fortune. • ***March 7, nearly a year later:*** As in 3:13, which reads *the thirteenth day of the twelfth month, the month of Adar;* Hebrew reads *in the twelfth month,* of the ancient Hebrew lunar calendar. The date selected was March 7, 473 BC; see also note on 2:16.

3:8 ***who keep themselves separate:*** Jews intermarried within tight-knit communities and resisted integration into the larger culture. • ***Their laws are different:*** They had a unique set of laws (eating and religious customs) and were to be separate from the sinful customs of the people around them (Lev 14:42-45; 15:31; 19:2, 26-37). • ***they refuse to obey the laws of the king:*** This accusation, which is false in general, probably refers to Mordecai's refusal to bow to Haman. • ***So it is not in the king's interest to let them live:*** Haman played on the king's fears and interests as Memucan had done in 1:16. Intolerance toward any particular group of people ran against the general Persian tendency to be respectful of other people's cultural and religious differences.

3:9 ***10,000 large sacks:*** Hebrew *10,000 talents,* about 375 tons or 340 metric tons in weight. Haman tipped his hand by offering to bribe the king with a large sum of *silver,* which should have made the king suspicious of Haman's motives. The value of the proposed gift is so astronomical that Haman may have been exaggerating to show his intended generosity.

3:10-11 ***The king agreed*** with no inquiry. The king is presented as someone very irresponsible and easily manipulated. By ***removing his signet ring,*** the king gave up his control over official policies; by ***giving it to Haman,*** he signified that Haman had complete authority to seal the decree. • ***the enemy of the Jews:*** The narrator's new title for Haman is an ominous note regarding his power to persecute the Jews (see also 8:1; 9:10, 24). • ***The money and the people are both yours:*** It may appear that the king did not want the bribe, but 4:7 suggests that Haman did give the money. The king was following a customary protocol to make the bribe and his greed less obvious (cp. Gen 23:10-16). For the sake of public appearance the king pretended not to be interested in the money, but in reality he was.

3:12 ***So on April 17:*** Literally *On the thirteenth day of the first month,* of the ancient Hebrew lunar calendar. This day was April 17, 474 BC; see also note on 2:16. Haman's choice of the day before the Jewish Passover began (see Exod 12:6) was probably calculated to terrorize and demoralize the Jews. But as at the Exodus, God would deliver the Jews miraculously from a tyrant who was trying to destroy them.

3:13 The phrase ***killed, slaughtered, and annihilated*** is repeated with ironic effect in 8:11 and 9:5. • ***on March 7 of the next year:*** Literally *on the thirteenth day of the twelfth month, the month of Adar,* of the ancient Hebrew lunar calendar. The date selected was March 7, 473 BC; see also note on 2:16. Haman's "lucky day" that was chosen by casting lots (3:7) was eleven months after the decree, by God's providence, giving time to overcome the decree. • ***The property of the Jews would be given to those who killed them:*** Haman ingeniously bribed the would-be executioners.

3:14-15 ***This decree*** carried the full weight of Xerxes' royal authority. • The foolish ***king*** and wicked ***Haman*** celebrated this occasion, but the people of ***the fortress of Susa*** were perplexed, bewildered, and confused at such a ruthless and unjust decree.

4:7 Esth 3:9
4:8 Esth 3:14-15
4:11 Esth 5:1-2; 6:4; 8:4 Dan 2:9

city, crying with a loud and bitter wail. 2He went as far as the gate of the palace, for no one was allowed to enter the palace gate while wearing clothes of mourning. 3And as news of the king's decree reached all the provinces, there was great mourning among the Jews. They fasted, wept, and wailed, and many people lay in burlap and ashes.

4When Queen Esther's maids and eunuchs came and told her about Mordecai, she was deeply distressed. She sent clothing to him to replace the burlap, but he refused it. 5Then Esther sent for Hathach, one of the king's eunuchs who had been appointed as her attendant. She ordered him to go to Mordecai and find out what was troubling him and why he was in mourning. 6So Hathach went out to Mordecai in the square in front of the palace gate.

7Mordecai told him the whole story, including the exact amount of money Haman had promised to pay into the royal treasury for the destruction of the Jews. 8Mordecai gave Hathach a copy of the decree issued in Susa that called for the death of all Jews. He asked Hathach to show it to Esther and explain the situation to her. He also asked Hathach to direct her to go to the king to beg for mercy and plead for her people. 9So Hathach returned to Esther with Mordecai's message.

10Then Esther told Hathach to go back and relay this message to Mordecai: 11"All the king's officials and even the people in the provinces know that anyone who appears before the king in his inner court without being invited is doomed to die unless the king holds out his gold scepter. And the king has not called for me to come to him for thirty days." 12So Hathach gave Esther's message to Mordecai.

13Mordecai sent this reply to Esther: "Don't think for a moment that because you're in the palace you will escape when all other Jews are killed. 14If you keep quiet at a time like this, deliverance and relief for

Ethnic Hatred (3:1-9)

Gen 46:33-34
Deut 7:1-6; 23:3-8
Matt 15:22-28
Luke 4:27
Acts 10:34-35
Rom 9:1–11:36
Gal 3:26-29
Eph 2:14

Haman hated Mordecai because Mordecai would not bow down as everyone else did when Haman passed by (3:1-5). Haman despised a man with integrity who would not obey laws that were against his own convictions. This personal hatred of Mordecai the Jew became a murderous desire to destroy all Jews (3:6). His charge against the Jewish people was what he hated in Mordecai: They did not assimilate with other people, they had unique laws and customs, and they did not obey some of the laws of the king (3:8). No other example of ethnic hatred in Scripture (e.g., Gen 46:33-34) is comparable to the hatred expressed by Haman.

Selfish pride, a desire to maintain power, and hatred for those who stand in the way have often been the basis for the persecution of racial or religious groups. Many people have died through the centuries because of such hatred. The Spanish Inquisition (1400s) and the recent Holocaust in Nazi Germany (1930s–40s) were other terrible attempts to wipe the Jewish people off the face of the earth. Today also, religious and ethnic hatred can lead to diabolical plans.

God disapproves of such hatred against any ethnic or religious group, and those who attempt to carry out such plots will eventually be held accountable by God (see Exod 20:5; Deut 30:7; Ps 21:7-11; 34:19-21; 44:7). God has saved the Jewish people and defeated their enemies, for God is faithful to all his promises (see Rom 9–11). He will similarly preserve his church through all persecution (see Matt 16:18; Rom 8:26-39).

4:1 Mordecai's dramatic response showed extreme grief and mourning (see 2 Sam 1:11; Ezra 9; Jon 3:5-9).

4:2 ***no one was allowed:*** The king did not want to hear all the sorry stories of misfortune and people pleading for mercy.

4:3 ***great mourning among the Jews:*** In these reports of lamenting, God's name is not mentioned, but the lamenting and fasting implies crying out in prayer for God to intervene and save his people (Exod 2:23-25; Ezra 9:5-15; Dan 9:1-19).

4:8 ***A copy of the decree*** with the king's seal would prove to Esther the seriousness of the situation. • ***to beg for mercy:*** Mordecai gave Esther no reasons to present to the king, only an appeal to the king's mercy and Esther's influence on him on behalf of her own people.

4:11 ***anyone who appears . . . without being invited is doomed to die:*** Access to the king was strictly controlled by his guards to prevent unwanted guests from wasting the king's time with petty requests. Since these were the official rules of the court, the danger to Esther's life was enormous. Apparently she ruled out requesting an audience with the king through a messenger, possibly because she would have to tell the messenger why she wanted to talk to the king. • ***has not called for me to come to him for thirty days:*** Esther had no guarantee of the king's favorable response.

4:12 ***Hathach:*** As in Greek version; Hebrew reads *they.*

4:13-14 ***Don't think . . . you will escape:*** Mordecai did not back down and did not excuse her because of the danger, and he reminded her that it would be more dangerous for her to say nothing to the king. • ***deliverance and relief for the Jews will arise from some other place:*** Mordecai knew God's promises and realized that God would not allow his chosen people to be annihilated (see Gen 12:3; 22:18; 28:14; Isa 60:1-5).

the Jews will arise from some other place, but you and your relatives will die. Who knows if perhaps you were made queen for just such a time as this?"

15Then Esther sent this reply to Mordecai: 16"Go and gather together all the Jews of Susa and fast for me. Do not eat or drink for three days, night or day. My maids and I will do the same. And then, though it is against the law, I will go in to see the king. If I must die, I must die." 17So Mordecai went away and did everything as Esther had ordered him.

Esther's First Banquet for the King

5 On the third day of the fast, Esther put on her royal robes and entered the inner court of the palace, just across from the king's hall. The king was sitting on his royal throne, facing the entrance. 2When he saw Queen Esther standing there in the inner court, he welcomed her and held out the gold scepter to her. So Esther approached and touched the end of the scepter.

3Then the king asked her, "What do you want, Queen Esther? What is your request? I will give it to you, even if it is half the kingdom!"

4And Esther replied, "If it please the king, let the king and Haman come today to a banquet I have prepared for the king."

5The king turned to his attendants and said, "Tell Haman to come quickly to a banquet, as Esther has requested." So the king and Haman went to Esther's banquet.

6And while they were drinking wine, the king said to Esther, "Now tell me what you really want. What is your request? I will give it to you, even if it is half the kingdom!"

7Esther replied, "This is my request and deepest wish. 8If I have found favor with the king, and if it pleases the king to grant my request and do what I ask, please come with Haman tomorrow to the banquet I will prepare for you. Then I will explain what this is all about."

Haman's Plan to Kill Mordecai

9Haman was a happy man as he left the banquet! But when he saw Mordecai sitting at the palace gate, not standing up or trembling nervously before him, Haman became furious. 10However, he restrained himself and went on home.

Then Haman gathered together his friends and Zeresh, his wife, 11and boasted to them about his great wealth and his many children. He bragged about the honors the king had given him and how he had been promoted over all the other nobles and officials.

12Then Haman added, "And that's not all! Queen Esther invited only me and the king himself to the banquet she prepared for us. And she has invited me to dine with her and the king again tomorrow!" 13Then he added, "But this is all worth nothing as long as I see Mordecai the Jew just sitting there at the palace gate."

14So Haman's wife, Zeresh, and all his friends suggested, "Set up a sharpened pole that stands seventy-five feet tall, and in the morning ask the king to impale Mordecai on it. When this is done, you can go on your merry way to the banquet with the king." This pleased Haman, and he ordered the pole set up.

4:16 2 Chr 20:3
5:1 Esth 4:11, 16; 6:4
5:2 Esth 4:11; 8:4
5:3 Esth 5:6; 7:2; Mark 6:23; Luke 18:41
5:5 Esth 6:14
5:6 Esth 5:3; 7:2
5:8 Esth 6:14; 7:3; 8:5
5:9 Esth 3:2, 5
5:10 Esth 6:13
5:14 Esth 5:10; 6:4; 7:9-10

• ***perhaps you were made queen for just such a time as this:*** Esther's rise to power at this precise time was not just a lucky chance of fate—her position as Xerxes' favored wife and queen was a role that God had given her to influence history for the Jewish people.

4:16 *fast for me:* Esther was convinced, but she wanted as many Jews as possible to pray that God would intervene to save her life. • ***Do not eat or drink for three days, night or day:*** A total *fast* without any food or water often lasted only one day (Lev 16:29-31; Judg 20:26). The three-day length was consistent with the seriousness of the situation and the absolute need for God's intervention. • ***though it is against the law, I will go in to see the king:*** In spite of the danger, she determined that she must act for the sake of her people. • ***If I must die, I must die:*** She, like Mordecai, was a person of character who would do what was right in spite of personal danger.

5:2 ***he welcomed her and held out the gold scepter to her:*** She was not killed for entering the king's presence without an invitation (4:11, 16).

5:3 ***I will give it to you, even if it is half the kingdom!*** This conventional idiom meant the king would be generous toward her request. The king did not want anything to prevent Esther from speaking the full truth.

5:4 *If it please the king:* Esther showed proper deference (cp. 1:12).

5:8 *please come . . . tomorrow:* It was a customary protocol not to appear anxious about asking for a favor or negotiating an agreement. The delay provided opportunity for Xerxes to discover Mordecai's act of loyalty, which led to the foiling of Haman's plot (see 6:1-14).

5:9-14 This brief interlude emphasizes the depth of Haman's hatred for Mordecai.

5:9 *Mordecai*'s fasting had ended and he was back at the *gate* operating in his official capacity. ***Not standing up or trembling*** was an even stronger refusal to show Haman honor (cp. 3:2-6).

5:14 *A sharpened pole* was a common device of execution (see also 2:23; Gen 40:19, 22; Josh 8:29). The Hebrew term has traditionally been translated *gallows*, but see the note on 2:23. • ***Seventy-five feet*** (Hebrew *50 cubits* [22.5 meters]) is unusually high, but Haman wanted to make an example out of Mordecai, with everyone viewing his dead body. The number might be a hyperbole for effect—*50 cubits* is an obviously round number—or it might reflect a stake placed high atop the city wall for public viewing.

4. THE KING HONORS MORDECAI AND EXECUTES HAMAN (6:1–7:10)

Haman Must Honor Mordecai

6 That night the king had trouble sleeping, so he ordered an attendant to bring
the book of the history of his reign so it
could be read to him. 2In those records he
discovered an account of how Mordecai had
exposed the plot of Bigthana and Teresh,
two of the eunuchs who guarded the door
to the king's private quarters. They had plotted to assassinate King Xerxes.
3"What reward or recognition did we
ever give Mordecai for this?" the king
asked.
His attendants replied, "Nothing has been
done for him."
4"Who is that in the outer court?" the
king inquired. As it happened, Haman had
just arrived in the outer court of the palace
to ask the king to impale Mordecai on the
pole he had prepared.
5So the attendants replied to the king,
"Haman is out in the court."
"Bring him in," the king ordered. 6So Haman came in, and the king said, "What should
I do to honor a man who truly pleases me?"
Haman thought to himself, "Whom
would the king wish to honor more than
me?" 7So he replied, "If the king wishes to
honor someone, 8he should bring out one of
the king's own royal robes, as well as a horse
that the king himself has ridden—one with
a royal emblem on its head. 9Let the robes
and the horse be handed over to one of the
king's most noble officials. And let him
see that the man whom the king wishes to
honor is dressed in the king's robes and led
through the city square on the king's horse.
Have the official shout as they go, 'This is
what the king does for someone he wishes
to honor!' "
10"Excellent!" the king said to Haman.
"Quick! Take the robes and my horse, and do
just as you have said for Mordecai the Jew,
who sits at the gate of the palace. Leave out
nothing you have suggested!"
11So Haman took the robes and put them
on Mordecai, placed him on the king's own
horse, and led him through the city square,
shouting, "This is what the king does for
someone he wishes to honor!" 12Afterward
Mordecai returned to the palace gate, but
Haman hurried home dejected and completely humiliated.
13When Haman told his wife, Zeresh, and
all his friends what had happened, his wise
advisers and his wife said, "Since Mordecai—this man who has humiliated you—is
of Jewish birth, you will never succeed in
your plans against him. It will be fatal to continue opposing him."
14While they were still talking, the king's
eunuchs arrived and quickly took Haman to
the banquet Esther had prepared.

Haman Is Exposed and Executed

7 So the king and Haman went to Queen
Esther's banquet. 2On this second occasion, while they were drinking wine, the king
again said to Esther, "Tell me what you want,
Queen Esther. What is your request? I will
give it to you, even if it is half the kingdom!"
3Queen Esther replied, "If I have found
favor with the king, and if it pleases the
king to grant my request, I ask that my life
and the lives of my people will be spared.
4For my people and I have been sold to
those who would kill, slaughter, and annihilate us. If we had merely been sold as

6:1 Esth 2:21-23; 10:2; Dan 6:18
6:2 Esth 2:21-22
6:4 Esth 4:11; 5:14
6:6 Esth 6:7, 9, 11
6:8 1 Kgs 1:33
6:9 Gen 41:43
6:12 2 Sam 15:30; Esth 7:8; Jer 14:3
6:13 Esth 5:10, 14
6:14 Esth 5:5-8
7:2 Esth 5:3, 6
7:3 Esth 5:7-8; 8:5
7:4 Esth 3:9; 4:7

6:1 ***the king had trouble sleeping:*** God was working to protect Esther and Mordecai. • ***the book of the history of his reign:*** Ancient kings kept royal annals of their reigns.

6:2 Providentially, the king's servant happened to open the royal annals to the page describing ***how Mordecai had exposed the plot*** (2:21-23).

6:3 ***What reward or recognition did we ever give Mordecai?*** The Persian kings were known for generosity to their supporters, so the king was probably surprised that ***nothing*** had ***been done.***

6:4-6 Just as the king was pondering what to do to honor Mordecai, ***Haman*** arrived to seek Mordecai's death. With great irony, the narrator recounts the king's consulting with him about how to reward Mordecai. • ***impale . . . on the pole:*** See note on 2:23.

6:7-9 Haman delighted in public acclaim and recognition. He wanted to be honored as the king, to wear kingly attire, and to ride the king's horse; in other words, he wanted to be king for a day. • Haman thought another ***one of the king's most noble officials*** would honor him through the streets of Susa. Instead, Haman himself would fill that role for Mordecai (6:10).

6:10-12 ***do just as you have said for Mordecai the Jew:*** With utter shock at this complete reversal, Haman could do nothing but obey the king's command, right down to the last detail.

6:13 ***Since Mordecai—this man who has humiliated you—is of Jewish birth, you will never succeed in your plans:*** Haman's wife and friends could see that this was more than just a series of coincidences. The text does not explain why Zeresh and the advisers felt that the fact of Mordecai's Jewish heritage would necessarily mean that Haman's plans would not succeed.

7:3-4 ***my life and the lives of my people:*** The statement that someone wanted to kill the queen and her family must have surprised and shocked the king. • ***my people and I have been sold:*** Esther carefully referred to the huge price Haman had paid the king to approve the decree (3:8-11). She also used the exact terminology of Haman's decree when she said that its purpose was to ***kill, slaughter, and annihilate*** (cp. 3:13). • ***If we had merely been sold as slaves, I could remain quiet:*** Esther humbly justifies her request as due to the severity of the attack on her and her people.

slaves, I could remain quiet, for that would be too trivial a matter to warrant disturbing the king."

5"Who would do such a thing?" King Xerxes demanded. "Who would be so presumptuous as to touch you?"

6Esther replied, "This wicked Haman is our adversary and our enemy." Haman grew pale with fright before the king and queen. 7Then the king jumped to his feet in a rage and went out into the palace garden.

Haman, however, stayed behind to plead for his life with Queen Esther, for he knew that the king intended to kill him. 8In despair he fell on the couch where Queen Esther was reclining, just as the king was returning from the palace garden.

The king exclaimed, "Will he even assault the queen right here in the palace, before my very eyes?" And as soon as the king spoke, his attendants covered Haman's face, signaling his doom.

9Then Harbona, one of the king's eunuchs, said, "Haman has set up a sharpened pole that stands seventy-five feet tall in his own courtyard. He intended to use it to impale Mordecai, the man who saved the king from assassination."

"Then impale Haman on it!" the king ordered. 10So they impaled Haman on the pole he had set up for Mordecai, and the king's anger subsided.

5. RESCUE FOR THE JEWS (8:1–9:19)

Xerxes' Decree to Help the Jews

8 On that same day King Xerxes gave the property of Haman, the enemy of the Jews, to Queen Esther. Then Mordecai was brought before the king, for Esther had told the king how they were related. 2The king took off his signet ring—which he had taken back from Haman—and gave it to Mordecai. And Esther appointed Mordecai to be in charge of Haman's property.

3Then Esther went again before the king, falling down at his feet and begging him with tears to stop the evil plot devised by Haman the Agagite against the Jews. 4Again the king held out the gold scepter to Esther. So she rose and stood before him.

5Esther said, "If it please the king, and if I have found favor with him, and if he thinks it is right, and if I am pleasing to him, let there be a decree that reverses the orders of Haman son of Hammedatha the Agagite, who ordered that Jews throughout all the king's provinces should be destroyed. 6For how can I endure to see my people and my family slaughtered and destroyed?"

7Then King Xerxes said to Queen Esther and Mordecai the Jew, "I have given Esther the property of Haman, and he has been impaled on a pole because he tried to destroy the Jews. 8Now go ahead and send a message to the Jews in the king's name, telling them whatever you want, and seal it with the king's signet ring. But remember that whatever has already been written in the king's name and sealed with his signet ring can never be revoked."

9So on June 25 the king's secretaries were summoned, and a decree was written exactly as Mordecai dictated. It was sent to the Jews and to the highest officers, the governors, and the nobles of all the 127 provinces stretching from India to Ethiopia. The decree was written in the scripts and languages of all the peoples of the empire,

7:6 Esth 3:10
7:8 Esth 1:6
7:9 Esth 5:14
7:10 Esth 9:25; Ps 7:16; 94:23
8:1 Esth 2:7; 7:6
8:2 Esth 3:10
8:4 Esth 4:11; 5:2
8:5 Esth 3:13; 5:7-8; 7:3
8:6 Esth 3:13; 7:4; 9:1
8:7 Esth 7:10
8:8 Esth 1:19; 3:12; 8:2, 9-10, 14; Dan 6:15
8:9 Esth 1:1, 2, 22; 3:12

7:5 *Who would do such a thing?* The king could hardly believe what he was hearing and could not imagine someone trying to do this atrocious thing. He asks for no details about Esther's accusations, assuming they were all true (cp. 3:10).

7:6-7 *Esther* finally identified *this wicked Haman* as the *enemy*. • ***Haman grew pale with fright:*** With this surprising and aggressive accusation by the queen and the evident *rage* of the king, Haman's doom suddenly became apparent.

7:8 ***he fell on the couch where Queen Esther was reclining:*** A major mistake, for no one should touch the queen, much less be on the same couch with her. • ***Will he even assault the queen . . . before my very eyes?*** This exaggerated rhetorical question implicates Haman with the worst possible motives.

7:9 *seventy-five feet:* Hebrew *50 cubits* [22.5 meters]. See note on 5:14. • ***He intended to use it to impale Mordecai:*** Harbona, one of the king's seven eunuchs (1:10), was apparently no friend of Haman and was already aware of Haman's plot. • ***impale Haman on it!*** This great reversal of fortunes demonstrates the guiding hand of God. Regarding impalement, see note on 2:23.

8:1 Just as Haman had promised the wealth of the Jews to those who would kill them (3:13), ***Xerxes gave the property of Haman, the enemy of the Jews, to Queen Esther.***

8:2 The *signet ring* that Haman had used to seal the decree to destroy the Jewish people (3:10) was now given to the Jewish person he had most wanted to destroy.

8:3 *Esther* probably expected the king to reverse Haman's decree right after he was killed, but that did not happen. This time she was much more insistent on raising the issue of Haman's plot against her people.

8:5 Esther was asking for the unusual favor of reversing a law signed with the king's seal. • ***the orders of Haman:*** Esther diplomatically avoided suggesting any responsibility on the king's part.

8:7 ***impaled on a pole:*** See note on 2:23.

8:8 According to Persian law, ***whatever has already been written . . . can never be revoked*** (see Esth 1:19; Dan 6:8, 12; cp. Ps 148:6). However, a new decree with the king's royal seal could give different or competing directions.

8:9 ***on June 25:*** Literally *on the twenty-third day of the third month, the month of Sivan,* of the ancient Hebrew lunar calendar. This day was June 25, 474 BC; see also note on 2:16. The details of writing and sending the new decree

8:11 Esth 3:13; 9:2, 10
8:12 Esth 3:13; 9:1
8:13 Esth 3:14
9:1 Esth 3:13; 8:11-12; 9:17
9:2 Esth 8:11, 17; 9:15-18
9:3 Esth 8:17
9:5 Esth 3:13
9:10 Esth 5:11; 8:11
9:12 Esth 7:2

including that of the Jews. [10]The decree was written in the name of King Xerxes and sealed with the king's signet ring. Mordecai sent the dispatches by swift messengers, who rode fast horses especially bred for the king's service.

[11]The king's decree gave the Jews in every city authority to unite to defend their lives. They were allowed to kill, slaughter, and annihilate anyone of any nationality or province who might attack them or their children and wives, and to take the property of their enemies. [12]The day chosen for this event throughout all the provinces of King Xerxes was March 7 of the next year.

[13]A copy of this decree was to be issued as law in every province and proclaimed to all peoples, so that the Jews would be ready to take revenge on their enemies on the appointed day. [14]So urged on by the king's command, the messengers rode out swiftly on fast horses bred for the king's service. The same decree was also proclaimed in the fortress of Susa.

[15]Then Mordecai left the king's presence, wearing the royal robe of blue and white, the great crown of gold, and an outer cloak of fine linen and purple. And the people of Susa celebrated the new decree. [16]The Jews were filled with joy and gladness and were honored everywhere. [17]In every province and city, wherever the king's decree arrived, the Jews rejoiced and had a great celebration and declared a public festival and holiday. And many of the people of the land became Jews themselves, for they feared what the Jews might do to them.

The Victory of the Jews

9 So on March 7 the two decrees of the king were put into effect. On that day, the enemies of the Jews had hoped to overpower them, but quite the opposite happened. It was the Jews who overpowered their enemies. [2]The Jews gathered in their cities throughout all the king's provinces to attack anyone who tried to harm them. But no one could make a stand against them, for everyone was afraid of them. [3]And all the nobles of the provinces, the highest officers, the governors, and the royal officials helped the Jews for fear of Mordecai. [4]For Mordecai had been promoted in the king's palace, and his fame spread throughout all the provinces as he became more and more powerful.

[5]So the Jews went ahead on the appointed day and struck down their enemies with the sword. They killed and annihilated their enemies and did as they pleased with those who hated them. [6]In the fortress of Susa itself, the Jews killed 500 men. [7]They also killed Parshandatha, Dalphon, Aspatha, [8]Poratha, Adalia, Aridatha, [9]Parmashta, Arisai, Aridai, and Vaizatha—[10]the ten sons of Haman son of Hammedatha, the enemy of the Jews. But they did not take any plunder.

[11]That very day, when the king was informed of the number of people killed in the fortress of Susa, [12]he called for Queen

---

purposely match the account of sending out the original decree in 3:12. • *to Ethiopia:* Hebrew *to Cush.*

8:11 *The king's decree* did not permit the Jewish people to start a war but to defend themselves and plunder the property of those who attacked them (reversing the decree in 3:13). • The phrase ***kill, slaughter, and annihilate*** is an ironic repetition of the words in Haman's original edict (3:13; see also 9:5).

8:12 ***March 7 of the next year:*** Literally *the thirteenth day of the twelfth month, the month of Adar,* of the ancient Hebrew lunar calendar. The date selected was March 7, 473 BC; see also note on 2:16. This date was nearly a year after Haman's original decree was published (3:12).

8:13 The Hebrew word translated ***to take revenge*** could also mean *to establish justice.* In situations where civil government could not exercise authority over all the parties involved in a conflict, this law would allow people who were attacked to establish justice by redressing wrongs committed against them.

8:15 Just as the city of *Susa* had been in great confusion after Haman's original decree (3:15), now there was great rejoicing by all—they understood the injustice of the original decree and the justice of the new one.

8:17 ***many . . . became Jews themselves:*** That is, they became proselytes of Judaism.

9:1 ***on March 7:*** Literally *on the thirteenth day of the twelfth month, the month of Adar,* of the ancient Hebrew lunar calendar. This day was March 7, 473 BC; see also note on 2:16. • When that fateful day arrived, there were many ***enemies of the Jews*** who wanted to carry out Haman's wishes.

9:3-4 People saw that *Mordecai* was the man in charge, so they knew it would not be wise to oppose him.

9:5 ***They killed and annihilated their enemies:*** It was not an attack on defenseless people or a ruthless uncontrolled killing spree, but a victorious self-defense against their attackers. The phrase used here repeats the terminology of Haman's original decree (3:12).

9:6 Although most people ***in the fortress of Susa itself*** supported Mordecai, ***the Jews killed 500 men,*** a mini-revolt that probably consisted of killing Haman's relatives and close supporters.

9:7-10 ***They also killed . . . the ten sons of Haman:*** Now everything that Haman had boasted about (5:11) was gone, even his ten sons.

9:10 ***But they did not take any plunder:*** Although taking plunder from those who attacked was permitted (8:11), the Jews did not want anything to do with the defiled wealth of Haman's sons. Many years earlier, Abram had refused his portion of the plunder from the king of Sodom (Gen 14:21-23).

9:12 If the king had been disturbed by the high numbers, he would not have allowed another day of fighting (9:14-15). It seems more likely that the

Esther. He said, "The Jews have killed
500 men in the fortress of Susa alone, as
well as Haman's ten sons. If they have done
that here, what has happened in the rest of
the provinces? But now, what more do you
want? It will be granted to you; tell me and
I will do it."
13Esther responded, "If it please the king,
give the Jews in Susa permission to do again
tomorrow as they have done today, and let
the bodies of Haman's ten sons be impaled
on a pole."
14So the king agreed, and the decree was
announced in Susa. And they impaled the
bodies of Haman's ten sons. 15Then the
Jews at Susa gathered together on March 8
and killed 300 more men, and again they
took no plunder.
16Meanwhile, the other Jews throughout
the king's provinces had gathered together
to defend their lives. They gained relief
from all their enemies, killing 75,000 of
those who hated them. But they did not take
any plunder. 17This was done throughout
the provinces on March 7, and on March 8
they rested, celebrating their victory with a
day of feasting and gladness. 18(The Jews at
Susa killed their enemies on March 7 and
again on March 8, then rested on March 9,
making that their day of feasting and gladness.) 19So to this day, rural Jews living in
remote villages celebrate an annual festival
and holiday on the appointed day in late
winter, when they rejoice and send gifts of
food to each other.

6. THE FESTIVAL OF PURIM (9:20-32)

20Mordecai recorded these events and sent
letters to the Jews near and far, throughout
all the provinces of King Xerxes, 21calling on
them to celebrate an annual festival on these
two days. 22He told them to celebrate these
days with feasting and gladness and by giving gifts of food to each other and presents
to the poor. This would commemorate a
time when the Jews gained relief from their
enemies, when their sorrow was turned into
gladness and their mourning into joy.
23So the Jews accepted Mordecai's proposal and adopted this annual custom.
24Haman son of Hammedatha the Agagite,
the enemy of the Jews, had plotted to crush
and destroy them on the date determined
by casting lots (the lots were called *purim*).
25But when Esther came before the king, he
issued a decree causing Haman's evil plot
to backfire, and Haman and his sons were
impaled on a sharpened pole. 26That is why
this celebration is called Purim, because it
is the ancient word for casting lots.

So because of Mordecai's letter and because of what they had experienced, 27the
Jews throughout the realm agreed to inaugurate this tradition and to pass it on to
their descendants and to all who became
Jews. They declared they would never fail
to celebrate these two prescribed days at
the appointed time each year. 28These days
would be remembered and kept from generation to generation and celebrated by every
family throughout the provinces and cities

9:13 Esth 8:11
9:15 Esth 9:10
9:16 Esth 9:2
9:17-18 Esth 9:1-2, 21
9:19 Neh 8:10; Esth 9:20-31
9:24 Esth 3:1, 6-7
9:25 Esth 3:6-15; 7:4-10; Ps 7:16
9:26 Esth 3:7; 9:20
9:27 Esth 8:17; 9:20-21

king was astonished that there were so many people who followed Haman and opposed the new regime directed by Mordecai. He was thinking of the political stability of the empire.

9:13 Possibly Esther knew that some of the people in Susa who had attacked Jews on the first day had gotten away and would be planning additional attacks to avenge the death of Haman. • ***impaled on a pole:*** See note on 2:23.

9:14 ***So the king agreed, and the decree was announced in Susa:*** It was not in the king's interest for there to be warring parties within the palace plotting to kill one another.

9:15 ***March 8:*** Literally *the fourteenth day of the month of Adar,* of the ancient Hebrew lunar calendar. This day was March 8, 473 BC; see also note on 2:16. • Once ***again,*** the Jews took the high moral ground and ***took no plunder*** from their enemies, though it was legally permitted (8:11; 9:10).

9:16 ***75,000*** seems like quite a large number. The Old Greek translation has 15,000 and the Targum has 10,107 men. The Hebrew word translated *thousands* can also indicate an extended family or lineage, so it is possible that 75 *extended families* were killed (see notes on Exod 12:37; Judg 5:8).

9:17 ***on March 7, and on March 8:*** Literally *on the thirteenth day of the month of Adar, and on the fourteenth day they rested.* These days were March 7 and 8, 473 BC; see also note on 2:16. • ***they rested, celebrating their victory with a day of feasting and gladness:*** God is not mentioned, but surely they thanked God on this day for their rescue. This was the beginning of a new festival, later called Purim (9:19-32).

9:18 ***killed their enemies on March 7 and again on March 8, then rested on March 9:*** Literally *killed their enemies on the thirteenth day and the fourteenth day, and then rested on the fifteenth day,* of the Hebrew month of Adar.

9:19 The ***annual festival and holiday*** of Purim celebrates God's blessing of peace from their enemies (see Deut 25:19; Josh 21:44; 1 Sam 7:11-14). The narrator reports that the festival was celebrated ***to this day.*** Now, more than 2,400 years later, it is still celebrated annually by Jewish people. • ***in late winter:*** Literally *on the fourteenth day of the month of Adar.* This day of the ancient Hebrew lunar calendar occurs in February or March. It is still the day on which Purim is celebrated. • The exchange of ***gifts of food*** demonstrated the unity of the people and their care for one another and helped them to spread an atmosphere of joy for everyone celebrating the festival.

9:21 ***on these two days:*** Literally *on the fourteenth and fifteenth days of Adar,* of the Hebrew lunar calendar.

9:23-26a These verses summarize the events leading to the Festival of Purim. • ***impaled on a pole:*** See note on 2:23.

9:26b-28 This paragraph justifies ***Purim*** as an approved Jewish ***festival*** even though Moses did not authorize it along with other festival days.

9:29
Esth 2:15; 9:20-21
9:30
Esth 1:1
9:31
Esth 4:3
10:1
Isa 24:15
10:2
Esth 2:23; 8:15; 9:4
10:3
Gen 41:43-44
Neh 2:10

of the empire. This Festival of Purim would
never cease to be celebrated among the Jews,
nor would the memory of what happened
ever die out among their descendants.
29Then Queen Esther, the daughter of Abihail, along with Mordecai the Jew, wrote
another letter putting the queen's full
authority behind Mordecai's letter to establish the Festival of Purim. 30Letters wishing
peace and security were sent to the Jews
throughout the 127 provinces of the empire
of Xerxes. 31These letters established the
Festival of Purim—an annual celebration of
these days at the appointed time, decreed
by both Mordecai the Jew and Queen Esther.
(The people decided to observe this festival,
just as they had decided for themselves and
their descendants to establish the times of
fasting and mourning.) 32So the command
of Esther confirmed the practices of Purim,
and it was all written down in the records.

7. THE GREATNESS OF XERXES AND MORDECAI (10:1-3)

10 King Xerxes imposed a tribute
throughout his empire, even to the
distant coastlands. 2His great achievements and the full account of the greatness
of Mordecai, whom the king had promoted,
are recorded in *The Book of the History of
the Kings of Media and Persia.* 3Mordecai
the Jew became the prime minister, with authority next to that of King Xerxes himself.
He was very great among the Jews, who
held him in high esteem, because he continued to work for the good of his people
and to speak up for the welfare of all their
descendants.

Purim (9:1-32)

Ps 37:23; 91:1-16
Prov 16:9, 33
Rom 8:28
1 Pet 3:12

The festival of Purim is the only OT festival not established by Moses (see chart, "Israel's Festivals," p. 235). Its name is derived from a word that means *lots* or *dice* (Hebrew *purim,* derived from Akkadian *puru*). It was a common practice in the ancient world to cast *purim* to determine whether God favored a particular course of action: A good number would indicate God's approval, a bad number his disapproval. Near the king's throne room at Susa in Persia, archaeologists found a small four-sided object with a number engraved on each side. A similar die inscribed with the word *pur* dates to the 800s BC. In the book of Esther, the Persian astrologers used *purim* to establish the best time to slaughter the Jews (3:7).

On the fateful day—March 7, 473 BC—God miraculously rescued his people from certain death, even as he had rescued the nation from Egypt at the Passover. Mordecai and Esther therefore formalized an annual celebration of God's rescue so that all future generations would remember what God had accomplished (9:28). The festival was widely celebrated thereafter among Jews (see *2 Maccabees* 15:36; Josephus, *Antiquities* 11.6.13; perhaps John 5:1).

When God rescued his chosen people, the day for Jewish execution turned into a day of holy vengeance and was followed by a day of celebration. Today, Jewish people fast and pray to commemorate Esther's fasting. This fast is then followed by Purim, which is celebrated on the fourteenth day of the month of Adar (cp. the note on 9:19). On this joyous holiday they read Esther (with loud *boo*s for Haman and *hooray*s for Mordecai) and have a time of feasting and rejoicing, with gifts for friends and for the poor. It is a celebration of how God providentially worked to care for his people so that they were not exterminated (9:1-17) and of how God continues to care for, provide for, and save his people (see also Gen 45:5; Ps 37:23; 91; Prov 16:9, 33; Dan 2:21; Acts 1:6-7; 2:22-23; 4:28-30; 17:25-27; Rom 8:28; 1 Pet 3:12).

9:29-32 The *letter* that *Queen Esther . . . wrote* provided further official endorsement to Mordecai's proposal (9:20-23).

10:1-2 *King Xerxes imposed a tribute:* Persian taxes on the provinces were heavy. This burden supported the Persian government's free spending.

10:2 ***The Book of the History of the Kings of Media and Persia*** was the Persian royal annals. While many ancient Persian records have survived, this reference to ***the greatness of Mordecai*** has not been found in any records excavated thus far.

10:3 *Mordecai the Jew* did not brag about himself as Haman did (5:11-12), but this righteous man who continually looked out for the good of others was rewarded with a high government position (***prime minister***) and the high esteem of his people (***He was very great among the Jews***).

INTRODUCTION TO THE BOOKS OF POETRY AND WISDOM

"The wisdom literature is exciting, because it deals directly with life."

R. E. Murphy, *The Tree of Life: An Exploration of Biblical Wisdom Literature*, p. ix

"The final test of wisdom and character is the quality of community it engenders, a community of peace and righteousness whose arms can stretch wide enough to welcome the Kingdom of Peace."

W. P. Brown, *Character in Crisis: A Fresh Approach to the Wisdom Literature of the Old Testament*, p. 164

The books of wisdom and poetry (Job—Song of Songs) make a distinctive contribution to the canon of Scripture. The books of law and history (Genesis—Esther) present a narrative of God's interaction in Israel's past and express God's will to his people in the form of commands. The prophets (Isaiah—Malachi) boldly speak in the name of God. In comparison, the books of wisdom and poetry have a more experiential tone. In these books, humans express their joyful and troubled prayers to God (Psalms), offer wise advice for healthy living (Proverbs), struggle with the apparent unfairness of life (Job and Ecclesiastes), and celebrate God's creation of male and female (Song of Songs). Though these books are presented more from a human perspective than other parts of Scripture, God's voice speaks clearly and authoritatively.

SETTING

The OT books of poetry are set throughout the history of Israel from the time of Abraham (around 2000 BC) to the end of the OT period, several hundred years before Christ (around 400 BC).

The book of Job seems to be set during a very early period of time, perhaps before Abraham (though it might have been composed much later—see Job Introduction, "Author and Date of Composition," pp. 853–854).

The book of Psalms contains poems from as early as the time of Moses (Ps 90) and as late as the postexilic period, perhaps even as late as the last books of the OT (Pss 126, 137). The largest single group of psalms is associated with the sweet songster of Israel—David, who reigned around 1000 BC.

As for Proverbs, Ecclesiastes, and Song of Songs, their superscriptions all associate them with Solomon, the third king of Israel (971–931 BC), although portions of these books were compiled later (e.g., Prov 25–29 was compiled during the reign of Hezekiah, 728–686 BC). For more about the date and composition of each book, see that book's introduction.

THE BOOKS OF POETRY

The poetic books consist almost completely of poetry. The only non-poetic passages are found in Ecclesiastes and in the prologue and epilogue of Job. Hebrew poetry is a highly literary type of writing. Though these writings were composed in a historical context, they were written in such a way that any reader would have an easy time applying them to life. For instance, when we read Psalm 51, which was composed (according to its title) after Nathan confronted David about his sin with Bathsheba, we can apply it to our own lives as we express our repentance toward God. Similarly, the poetical form of Job makes us see that Job's struggle with undeserved suffering has implications for our own thinking about the apparent unfairness of life.

Poetry not only informs the intellect, it stimulates the imagination, arouses emotions, and appeals to the reader's will. Poetry addresses the whole person and shows that God is interested in more than just our brains. He wants to capture our hearts as well.

Poetry is compressed language. A poem says a lot using only a few words. As a result, poems should be the object of reflection and meditation—skimming is possible, but it is not a very productive way of reading poetry. Poetry is a less precise but more vivid manner of writing. Ambiguity is to be expected and often preserves a sense of the mystery of God.

Extensive use of imagery and metaphors in poetry provides a way to say a lot with a few words. Think how much the sentence, "The LORD is my shepherd" (Ps 23:1), communicates about who God is, how we relate to him, and how the psalmist feels toward him. It would take a page of prose to even begin to capture what is communicated here. Good readers of poetry must grow experienced at unpacking imagery.

The Poetry of Each Book

The Psalms and Song of Songs are good examples of lyric poetry—that is, poetry that expresses the internal thoughts and feelings of the poet. These books are written in a way that allows readers to imagine themselves as the speaker. That is why Christians find the psalms such a wonderful resource for their own prayers. It is also why the Song of Songs can be an inspiration to

husbands and wives to praise the beauty of their spouse.

Job, on the other hand, is narrative and poetic dialogue. It tells a story about an innocent man who suffers and who ultimately encounters God, and it records an extended discussion between Job and his "friends" about the meaning of Job's suffering. The poetic form of the book of Job makes it easier for readers to identify with that story and learn lessons for themselves.

Proverbs and Ecclesiastes are didactic poetry—i.e., their aim is to teach. They both are interested in teaching a wise way to live. Proverbs uses poetry to give very practical advice about how to speak and act in the right way at the right time. Ecclesiastes wants to remind us that we cannot find ultimate meaning "under the sun"; Ecclesiastes keeps us from reading Proverbs in an overly optimistic manner, as if we could control and conquer life on our own resources.

Hebrew poetry occurs in other OT books as well. For instance, the books of the Pentateuch (Genesis—Deuteronomy) contain poems similar to psalms except that they are tied to specific historical occasions. For example, while Psalm 98 celebrates God's victories in general, Exodus 15 praises God for the defeat of the Egyptians at the Red Sea. The books of prophecy (Isaiah—Malachi) also utilize poetry to communicate their messages of judgment and salvation.

Literary Features of Hebrew Poetry

Hebrew poetry is identified by *parallelism*, a high frequency of *figurative language*, and a number of other secondary literary devices.

Parallelism. The normal unit of Hebrew poetry is the couplet of two parallel lines, although other formats do occur. *Parallelism* refers to the echoing effect between the clauses in a verse. Sometimes a verse sounds like it is saying the same thing two or more times. Psalm 131:1, for instance, might seem repetitive as the psalmist denies being prideful:

LORD, my heart is not proud;
my eyes are not haughty.
I don't concern myself with
matters too great
or too awesome for me.

However, a closer reading shows a progression: the psalmist begins by denying pride in his core personality ("heart"), then his demeanor ("eyes"), and finally in terms of his thoughts and actions.

For more on Hebrew parallelism, see Proverbs Introduction, "Genre and Style," pp. 1026–1027.

Figurative Language. Hebrew poetry uses figurative language very expressively. Its simplicity of form combines intensity of feeling and pictorial power, and allows great play of imagination. Metaphors, figures of speech, and word images communicate ideas and feelings in an intense, colorful way.

Acrostics. From time to time in the Psalms and in other poetic books we find *acrostics*. An acrostic is a poem in which every verse or every line in a stanza begins with a successive letter of the Hebrew alphabet (see Pss 9–10; 111; 112; 119; Prov 31:10-31; Lam 1–4). This literary device may have aided memorization, and it certainly imparts a sense of completeness and closure to the poem.

The acrostic form is just one of many different types of acoustic and word plays that Hebrew poets utilized as they wrote these poems. Unfortunately, it is impossible to fully represent these powerful literary devices in an English translation. The most important ones, however, are discussed in the study materials.

THE BOOKS OF WISDOM

In addition to being poetry, Job through Song of Songs can also be described as "wisdom literature," literature that was written to impart wisdom. Wisdom is not the same as intelligence or knowledge. Knowledge is a mastery of facts and ideas, and intelligence is the ability to gain that mastery. By contrast, wisdom is the ability to live life well. It is the ability to know the right time to say or do something, and it includes the proper expression of emotions in relationship to circumstances.

Proverbs is the most explicit of these books in its purpose of imparting wisdom—it clearly states as its purpose to make its readers wise (Prov 1:1-7). Ecclesiastes and Job contain the struggles of wise men as they seek to understand God's ways in the world; as we grapple with the same issues, we can gain wisdom. Song of Songs gives us God's wisdom in the important area of love and physical intimacy. The book of Psalms is the one book in this group that is not explicitly and pervasively concerned with wisdom, though there are many psalms that are classified as wisdom psalms (e.g., Pss 1, 37, 119; see "Wisdom Psalms," p. 937).

It is interesting to read the accounts of Joseph (Gen 37–50) and Daniel (Dan 1–6) in the light of wisdom literature. Both Joseph and Daniel illustrate the principles of wisdom in their words and actions. In the NT, the book of James is comparable to Proverbs both in its practical advice and in its understanding that wisdom comes "from above" (Jas 3:17).

PLACE IN THE HEBREW BIBLE: THE "WRITINGS"

The Hebrew Bible has a different order from the English Bible. In the English Bible, the books of poetry and wisdom appear between the books of history (Joshua—Esther) and the books of prophecy (Isaiah—Malachi). The Hebrew Bible has a different arrangement. It is divided into three parts: The "Torah" (Genesis—Deuteronomy) is the same as in the English Bible; but then the "Prophets" and the "Writings" both include some books that we would identify as historical and some that we would identify as prophetic. (See Old Testament Introduction, "The Canon of the Old Testament," pp. 4-5.)

In the Hebrew Bible, all of the poetic books are found in the third section, the "Writings." The first book in the Writings is the Psalms; Jesus even refers to this entire third section by the name "Psalms" (Luke 24:44). Then comes Job, followed by Proverbs. In the middle of the Writings are five books called the *Megilloth* ("Five Scrolls"), which include Song of Songs and Ecclesiastes. Each of the books in the *Megilloth* is associated with a Jewish festival—Song of Songs is associated with Passover, Ecclesiastes with the Festival of Weeks.

INTERPRETATION

The nature of Hebrew poetry and wisdom should remind the modern reader to consider a number of important interpretive principles.

The poet's message is given using only a few well-chosen words, written in a condensed style. This style requires the reader to avoid skimming the words; rather, we should take the time to reflect and meditate on how and what the poem says.

The poet has also carefully structured the poem so there are interesting echoes within a poem (see "Parallelism," facing page). Much of what a Hebrew poem says is in the relationships and parallels. Careful reading will discern these relationships and reveal their meaning.

The books of poetry use figurative language extensively. Particularly common are metaphors that compare two things that are essentially unlike each other except in some striking way (e.g., "The LORD is my shepherd," Ps 23:1). Metaphors call on the reader to reflect on the relationship between the two parts of the image. What is the poet trying to teach by making such comparisons? (See also "Metaphorical language," p. A35.)

While parallelism and imagery are two of the most important and frequently occurring poetic devices in the biblical poet's literary arsenal, there are a host of others. Many of these are lost in translations, so the study materials point out some of the most important.

It is important to remember that a poem is not only conveying information to its readers but also arousing their emotions and stimulating their imaginations. We should use both our minds and our hearts to read biblical poetry and wisdom.

The poets and wise teachers of Israel were not interested only in the internal life—they wrote so that we would live in ways that please God. Therefore, it is important for us as readers to ask the question, "What does this passage tell me about how God wants me to obey him?"

MEANING AND MESSAGE

The poetry and wisdom of the OT, like the books of law, history, and prophecy, are the word of God. However, in the books of poetry and wisdom, God speaks to us through the reflections, meditations, and prayers of human beings.

- The Psalms are the prayers of God's people, but their prayers provide authoritative descriptions of the true God and models for future prayers.
- The Song of Songs is a love poem, expressing the romantic desire that an unnamed man and an unnamed woman feel toward each other. In it, we learn the shape of God-pleasing romantic love in the context of marriage.
- Proverbs and Ecclesiastes describe the advice that fathers give their children (see Prov 1–9; Eccl 12:12), but that advice comes with God's own authority.
- Finally, the book of Job reports the human struggle to come to grips with suffering; here God speaks both through the human conversations and, at the end of the book, directly.

As the books of poetry and wisdom express the hearts of their human authors, they express God's own heart and thoughts. We see this most clearly in Jesus, who embodies what the human authors of these books expressed—a heart of devotion, human struggle, worship, and wisdom. As we read these books, God himself walks with us (see John 1:14; Heb 4:14-16).

FURTHER READING

ROBERT ALTER
The Art of Biblical Poetry (1981)

C. HASSELL BULLOCK
An Introduction to the Old Testament Poetic Books (1988)

DEREK KIDNER
The Wisdom of Proverbs, Job and Ecclesiastes (1985)

ERNEST C. LUCAS
Exploring the Old Testament: A Guide to Psalms and Wisdom Literature (2004)

ROLAND E. MURPHY
The Tree of Life: An Exploration of Biblical Wisdom Literature (2002)

LELAND RYKEN AND TREMPER LONGMAN III
A Complete Literary Guide to the Bible (1993)

THE BOOK OF JOB

When suffering comes to us, we often ask why. The book of Job examines the suffering of one man who suffered precisely because he was blameless. His friends supposed that Job was guilty of some unknown sin. They tried to persuade him to repent, but Job did not accept their pat explanations. Finally, God appeared, but he did not give Job the answers he sought. Instead, God confronted him, changed his perspective, and blessed him.

SETTING

The book of Job unfolds early in the patriarchal age, before Israel became a nation. Job's wealth, like Abraham's, was in livestock and slaves (1:3; 42:12; see Gen 12:16; 32:5). He was his family's priest, as was a common practice before the law of Moses (1:5; 42:8; see Gen 4:4; 8:20; 12:7-8; 13:18; 15:9-10; 26:25; 33:20; 35:1-6; 46:1). During Job's time, the Sabeans and Chaldeans were nomadic raiders (1:15, 17), not important political and economic powers as in the late monarchical period (cp. Isa 45:14; Joel 3:8). The money was called the *kesitah,* which was used during the patriarchal age (42:11; see Gen 33:19; Josh 24:32). Only those who lived before the flood (Gen 1–6) and the patriarchs (Abraham, Isaac, and Jacob) matched or exceeded Job's longevity (42:16; see Gen 5:3-32; 25:7; 35:28; 47:28; 50:26). With Job, we return to the beginning of history, when mortals first struggled to know God and understand the world.

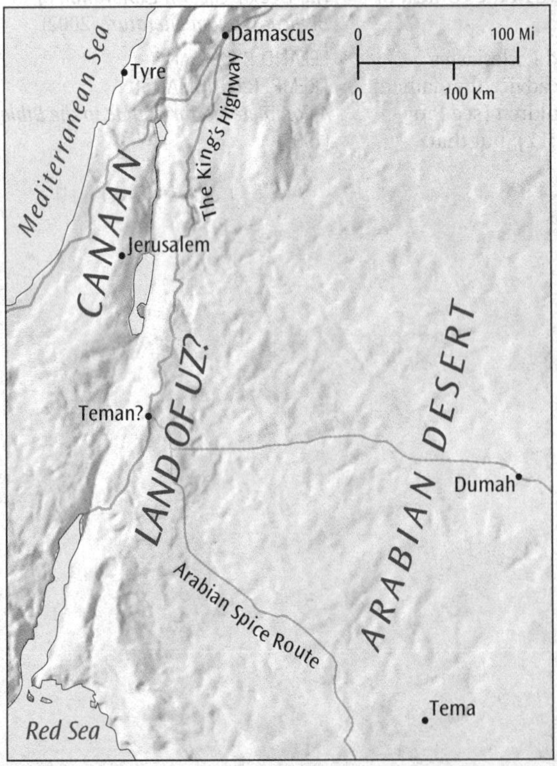

SUMMARY

The prose introduction to the book of Job (chs 1–2) provides the heavenly perspective on Job's suffering and sets the context for the human dialogue that forms the body of the work. Job was a righteous man whom God allowed Satan to test. In the heavenly courtroom, Satan argued that if God removed his blessings from Job, he would "surely curse you to your face" (1:11).

◂ The Setting of Job.
The book of Job is set in the LAND OF UZ, probably ancient Edom (see note 1:1), around the time of the patriarchs (around 2000 BC). • Eliphaz the Temanite (2:11; 4:1; 15:1; 22:1; 42:7, 9) was probably from TEMAN.
DUMAH Gen 25:14; Josh 15:52; 1 Chr 1:30
TEMA Job 6:19; Gen 25:15; Isa 21:14; Jer 25:23
TEMAN Gen 36:11, 15, 34, 42; Jer 49:7, 20; Ezek 25:13; Amos 1:12; Obad 1:9

Instead, Job responded, "Praise the name of the LORD!" (1:21). "Should we accept only good things from the hand of God and never anything bad?" (2:10). Satan lost his challenge to Job's righteousness.

The story leaves the court of heaven and enters the council of humans as three of Job's friends come to sympathize with him. Their silent, seven-day vigil is apparently a genuine attempt to console Job (2:11-13). However, when Job breaks his silence with a bitter complaint (ch 3), his counselors begin to criticize and condemn him. In three rounds of debate (chs 4–27), their rhetoric varies from innuendo to blatant accusation. Job's friends argue that since God is righteous, he rewards each person according to what that person has done; therefore, Job's suffering must be the just punishment for some evil he has committed. To each of their speeches, Job responds by insisting that he is innocent and that his suffering is undeserved and unfair.

After the three rounds of dialogue between Job and his friends, a poetic interlude praises God as the sole source of wisdom (ch 28). When Job has made his final statement about his misery and his righteousness (chs 29–31), his three friends give up on him, saying that he is too self-righteous (32:1). Elihu (a new voice) then renews the human struggle to explain Job's suffering (chs 32–37). Finally, God arrives to challenge Job (chs 38–41). Instead of hearing Job's case, God demands answers and demonstrates his own power and sovereignty through the questions he poses. Job responds with repentance and acknowledges that he does not have the right to question God (42:1-6).

In the final prose section (42:7-17), God reaffirms Job's righteousness and faithfulness, pronounces judgment on Job's friends, and pours out final blessings on Job.

OUTLINE

1:1–2:13
Prologue: The Testing of Righteous Job

3:1–37:24
Dialogues about Suffering

38:1–42:6
The LORD Challenges Job

42:7-17
Epilogue: The LORD Vindicates Job

JOB AS HISTORY

The heavenly setting of the book's opening and closing tempts the modern reader to cast the book of Job as something like a parable. The poetic dialogues also suggest that it is something more than just a dry historical record. But history can be described in flights of poetry just as well as in plodding narrative (cp. Exod 14:21-31; 15:1-12; Pss 78; 105). The biblical record clearly suggests that the account of Job is historical (see "Setting," facing page). Ezekiel and James later referred to Job as an example of righteousness and endurance (Ezek 14:14, 20; Jas 5:11).

AUTHOR AND DATE OF COMPOSITION

The authorship and composition of Job is a riddle. Although the story has a patriarchal setting (around 2000 BC), the date of its composition appears to be much later. Commentators have suggested dates that range from the

TIMELINE

3300–2200 BC
Early Bronze Age

2000–1500 BC
Middle Bronze Age

2166 / 1990 BC*
Abraham is born

2091 / 1915 BC
Abraham moves to Canaan

around 2000 BC
▸ Job lives in Uz

1446 / 1270 BC
Israel leaves Egypt (the Exodus), moves to Mount Sinai
The covenant at Sinai

* *The two dates harmonize with the traditional "early" chronology and a more recent "late" chronology of the Exodus. All dates are approximate. Please see "Chronology: Abraham to Joshua," p. 118.*

era of Israel's wilderness wanderings (Exodus—Numbers) to the era following the return from exile (Ezra—Nehemiah). The final composition of Job probably took place during the monarchy (1–2 Kings), when other wisdom materials such as Proverbs and Ecclesiastes were being accumulated.

Even if we accept that Job was a historical character, we still do not know who the author was, where he lived, or what level of society he came from. The author appears to have been a sage who was skilled in the use of proverbs (e.g., 4:2; 6:5-6), rhetorical questions (e.g., 21:29), and the art of eloquence. He also knew about plant and animal life, foreign culture, and antiquity, including the patriarchal period.

The book cannot be dated with certainty by reference to (1) events or people mentioned or implied in the book (the earliest reference to Job is during the Exile, in Ezek 14:14, 20); (2) theological ideas in the book that point to distinct dates; or (3) textual relationship to other material in the OT (e.g., cp. 3:3-10; Jer 20:14-18). Job may even have been edited over a period of time by a number of different people.

Job's friends . . . keep on saying that everything in the universe fits into everything else, as if there were anything comforting about a number of nasty things all fitting into each other. . . . If prosperity is regarded as the reward of virtue, it will be regarded as the symptom of virtue. Men will leave off the heavy task of making good men successful. They will adopt the easier task of making out successful men [to be] good.

G. K. CHESTERTON
"Introduction to the Book of Job"

LITERARY CHARACTERISTICS

Ancient Parallels to Job. There are several parallels to the book of Job in ancient Near Eastern literature:

- The Canaanite "Legend of King Keret" tells of a king who loses his family in a series of natural disasters; his god El restores his family.[1]
- The Egyptian document "Dispute over Suicide" (2000s BC) tells of a man who considers suicide and hopes that someone will take up his case with the heavenly council. Job wishes he had never been born, but he never considers suicide.[2]
- Also from Egypt, the story "Protests of the Eloquent Peasant" (2200s BC) tells of a robbery victim who is not treated justly. At first he is polite, but as he keeps returning to present his case, his language becomes increasingly strident. His appeal is not to his god but to local authorities.[3]
- From Babylonia, the story "I Will Praise the Lord of Wisdom" tells of a high-ranking, pious man who was struck down with illness and suffered the mockery of friends. Unlike Job, this man believed that he had committed some accidental sin, perhaps something that he never thought was wrong. Rather than maintain his innocence, he acknowledges his guilt and begs for mercy. His god restores his fortunes after a series of exorcisms that bring healing. In gratitude, he concludes with a long hymn of praise to his god, Marduk.[4]
- Also from Babylonia, the "Babylonian Theodicy" follows the same dialogue form that the book of Job uses: The sufferer complains, and his friends respond with rebukes. The arguments on both sides are remarkably similar to those in Job.[5] Yet we also see key differences: (1) The "Babylonian Theodicy" is polytheistic, whereas Job is monotheistic; (2) its sufferer threatens to abandon his faith and give up obedience, even if he does end with a petition to his god and goddess. Job remains committed to the Lord throughout (e.g., 13:15-16).

[1] James B. Pritchard, ed., *Ancient Near Eastern Texts Relating to the Old Testament* [*ANET*], 3rd ed. [Princeton: Princeton University Press, 1969], 142–149. [2] *ANET*, 405–407. [3] *ANET*, 407–410. [4] *ANET*, 434–437. [5] *ANET*, 601–604.

Relationship to Israel's Wisdom Literature. The book of Job has the flavor of other OT wisdom literature. Job's friends follow lines of thought spelled out in Deuteronomy, Chronicles, and Proverbs. They argue that wisdom and righteousness lead to life and prosperity, while folly and wickedness lead to death and failure. Job joins the author of Ecclesiastes in questioning the simplistic, universal application of this doctrine. In effect, Job says, "Let's be realistic. Sometimes no one can explain suffering, so give me the benefit of the doubt and show me some sympathy."

MEANING AND MESSAGE

Though the book of Job does not clarify the meaning of suffering, it demonstrates that suffering is not necessarily God's retribution for sin. Job does not get an answer as to why bad things happen to good people, and neither do we. It is not the purpose of the book to explain suffering.

The central conflict of the book is between the integrity of the Creator and the integrity of a man. Heaven and earth appear to be at odds. It is too easy simply to line up with Job's three friends in denying Job's innocence. We can appeal to various NT passages that deny that any human is righteous (e.g., Rom 3:10, 23; Luke 18:19), but Job's righteousness is genuine and thorough. However, his obsession with his own rectitude sometimes borders on self-righteousness. He grows so adamant in defending his integrity that he seems ready to defy God. Job's three friends set out a view of God that is more orthodox, at least on the surface. These counselors are more than weak, imaginary straw men; they accurately develop most of the biblical ways of explaining suffering. Their theology is excellent, but their presumptuous applications go sour. They insist on a *quid pro quo* view of retribution, in which all the good and evil that people experience is directly related to what they have earned or deserved.

The book works within the basic commitments of OT Israel's faith. Job and all of the other speakers take seriously the covenantal ideas of blessing and cursing (Lev 26; Deut 28) and of sowing and reaping in this life (Ps 34:11-22; Gal 6:7; 1 Pet 3:10). They don't even consider solutions from outside the scope of biblical revelation (e.g., metaphysical dualism, polytheistic tensions, materialistic naturalism, deism, gnosticism, or stoicism). Instead, the book's speakers explore only biblical answers for the meaning of suffering as (1) punishment for sin (e.g., 4:7-9); (2) the inevitable lot of mortals, who tend toward sin (e.g., 15:14-16); (3) God's disciplinary work (e.g., 5:17-18; 33:15-28; 36:8-15; see Prov 3:11; Heb 12:2-13); (4) part of God's mysterious plan (11:7-8; 37:19, 23); or (5) a test imposed on earth to satisfy a heavenly dispute (e.g., 1:6-12).

Since life "under the sun" (see Ecclesiastes) is an arena too small to provide answers to all the great questions, the writer looks to the courts of heaven for a divine dimension to what takes place on earth. But the answer is not disclosed even there. Why did God entertain Satan's challenge in the first place?

In the end, God defends Job's innocence and rejects easy explanations of suffering. God also rejects Job's demands for an explanation. Since Job could not possibly understand the whole universe, he should not demand an explanation of how his suffering fits into that order. The world cannot be explained in terms that humans can fully understand.

> *The author of the book of Job knows what people think, what people say in whispers.*
>
> CHRISTIAN DUQUOC
> *Job and the Silence of God*

The book of Job thus offers a complex picture of God. Rather than deciding that he does not have to prove anything to Satan, "God chooses to get an open victory over Satan for his own glory."[6] God does not even explain his role to Job. Instead, God challenges Job's right to question the integrity of divine justice (40:8).

The way to live through calamities is not just to keep a stiff upper lip but to bow reverently before God and trust his sovereign goodness. In the day of calamity, humans properly respond to God by worshiping him and blessing him for the wisdom and justice of his ways, regardless of how harsh the pain or dark the confusion. God's holy purposes for human suffering are sometimes hidden. Yet in the end, Job draws closer to God through his suffering: "I had only heard about you before, but now I have seen you with my own eyes" (Job 42:5).

[6] Piper, John. "Job: Reverent in Suffering [Job 1:1–2:10]," Sermon, Bethlehem Baptist Church. Minneapolis, Minn., 1985.

FURTHER READING

ROBERT L. ALDEN
Job (1993)

FRANCIS I. ANDERSON
Job: An Introduction and Commentary (1976)

PAUL CIHOLAS
Consider My Servant Job (1998)

AUGUST H. KONKEL
Job in *Cornerstone Biblical Commentary*, vol. 6 (2006)

DAVID L. MCKENNA
Job (1986)

PROLOGUE: THE TESTING OF RIGHTEOUS JOB (1:1–2:13)

Job's Integrity (1:1-5)

1 There once was a man named Job who
lived in the land of Uz. He was blameless—a man of complete integrity. He feared
God and stayed away from evil. 2He had
seven sons and three daughters. 3He owned
7,000 sheep, 3,000 camels, 500 teams of
oxen, and 500 female donkeys. He also had
many servants. He was, in fact, the richest
person in that entire area.

4Job's sons would take turns preparing
feasts in their homes, and they would also
invite their three sisters to celebrate with
them. 5When these celebrations ended—
sometimes after several days—Job would
purify his children. He would get up early
in the morning and offer a burnt offering
for each of them. For Job said to himself,
"Perhaps my children have sinned and have
cursed God in their hearts." This was Job's
regular practice.

Satan Tests Job the First Time (1:6-22)

The Heavenly Council Meets

6One day the members of the [a]heavenly
court came to present themselves before
the LORD, and the [b]Accuser, Satan, came
with them. 7"Where have you come from?"
the LORD asked Satan.

Satan answered the LORD, "I have been
patrolling the earth, watching everything
that's going on."

1:1
Gen 6:9; 17:1; 22:12
Exod 18:21
Job 28:28
Jer 25:20
Lam 4:21
Ezek 14:14
Jas 5:11

1:2
Job 42:13

1:3
Job 42:12

1:5
Gen 8:20
1 Kgs 21:10-11
Job 8:4; 42:8

1:6
Job 38:7
[a]*ben 'elohim* (1121, 0430)
›Job 2:1
[b]*satan* (7854)
›Job 1:9

1:7
1 Pet 5:8

1:1–2:13 God and Satan agree to a test that would bring about Job's troubles and confirm his integrity (1:20-21; 2:10). None of the book's characters ever learn of this heavenly council.

1:1 The opening phrase, ***There once was a man***, can introduce either a parable (2 Sam 12:1) or history (1 Sam 25:2). • ***Job*** is also mentioned in Ezek 14:14, 20 and Jas 5:11. • ***Uz*** is east of the Jordan, either in Edom to the south (Gen 36:28; 1 Chr 1:42; Jer 25:19-20; Lam 4:21) or in Aram to the north (Gen 10:23; 22:21; 1 Chr 1:17, 42). Job was not an Israelite—he lived before the nation was born and outside its later territory. • Job was morally ***blameless—a man of complete integrity*** (1:8; 2:3; see Ps 25:21; 37:37; Prov 2:7; 20:11; 29:10). He did not claim to be perfect or sinless (6:24; 7:21; see also Eccl 7:20; Rom 3:23; 1 Jn 1:8), but he was righteous; his suffering did not result from guilt. He ***feared God*** (see Ps 111:10; Prov 1:7; 9:10; 2 Cor 7:1) and did not appeal to any of the ancient Near Eastern gods (9:8; 23:13; 31:26-28).

1:2-3 Job was prosperous in ***sons, daughters***, livestock, and ***servants*** (cp. Gen 30:43; Deut 7:13; Ps 107:38). • Numbers such as ***seven*** and ***three*** (and ***7,000*** and ***3,000***) indicate the completeness of the blessing Job experienced (see 42:13; see also Ps 127:3-5; 128:3). • ***the richest person in that entire area:*** The figures that catalogue Job's wealth might not be exact, but they are realistic for a wealthy man of that time (cp. Nabal's wealth, 1 Sam 25:2).

1:5 Ritual washing and changing garments were common ways for individuals to ***purify*** themselves before offering a sacrifice (Gen 35:2; Exod 19:10, 14). • The common time for conscientious piety was ***early in the morning*** (see Gen 22:3; Ps 5:3; Mark 1:35). • ***cursed:*** The Hebrew term *barak* (literally *blessed*) is used here as a euphemism for cursing (cp. 1:11; 2:5, 9; 1 Kgs 21:10, 13; Ps 10:3). Job was concerned that his children might have committed this capital crime (Lev 24:10-16; 1 Kgs 21:9-13; cp. Job 1:11; 2:5, 9). Job understood that sinful attitudes in people's ***hearts*** constitute sin (Jer 17:9-10; Mark 7:21-23).

1:6-7 The ***members of the heavenly court*** (literally *the sons of God*) are heavenly beings; they may be either holy angels or rebellious demons (Gen 6:2, 4). They join God in his deliberations, including at creation (Gen 1:26) and in his rule over creation (Gen 3:22; Job 1:6; 2:1; 1 Kgs 22:19-22; Dan 3:13, 17, 23, 25; 7:9-14; Ps 82:1; 89:5, 7-8). • ***the Accuser, Satan*** (Hebrew *the satan;* similarly throughout this chapter): See "Satan, the Adversary," facing page). The account remains unclear as to whether Satan usually ***came with*** other members of the heavenly court to make a report or whether he was intruding as Job's adversary. • ***Where have you come from?*** The question was God's sovereign demand for a report from a subordinate (see Gen 3:9). • Satan was not ***patrolling*** to implement God's judgments (cp. 1 Chr 21:1-14; 2 Kgs 19:35 // Isa 37:36; Ezek 1:5-9) but to oppose God's purposes (2 Tim 2:26; 1 Pet 5:8).

1:8
Num 12:7
Josh 1:2, 7
Job 1:1; 42:7-8
1:9
[c]*satan* (7854)
›Job 1:12
1:10
Job 29:2-6; 31:25
1:11
Job 2:5; 19:21
1:12
[d]*satan* (7854)
›Job 2:2
1:15
Job 6:19
1:16
Gen 19:24
Lev 10:2
Num 11:1-3
1:17
Gen 11:28, 31

8 Then the LORD asked Satan, "Have you
noticed my servant Job? He is the finest man
in all the earth. He is blameless—a man of
complete integrity. He fears God and stays
away from evil."
9 [c]Satan replied to the LORD, "Yes, but Job
has good reason to fear God. 10 You have always put a wall of protection around him
and his home and his property. You have
made him prosper in everything he does.
Look how rich he is! 11 But reach out and
take away everything he has, and he will
surely curse you to your face!"
12 "All right, you may test him," the LORD
said to [d]Satan. "Do whatever you want with
everything he possesses, but don't harm
him physically." So [d]Satan left the LORD's
presence.

Satan Strikes Job's Household

13 One day when Job's sons and daughters
were feasting at the oldest brother's house,
14 a messenger arrived at Job's home with
this news: "Your oxen were plowing, with
the donkeys feeding beside them, 15 when
the Sabeans raided us. They stole all the animals and killed all the farmhands. I am the
only one who escaped to tell you."
16 While he was still speaking, another
messenger arrived with this news: "The fire
of God has fallen from heaven and burned
up your sheep and all the shepherds. I am
the only one who escaped to tell you."
17 While he was still speaking, a third
messenger arrived with this news: "Three
bands of Chaldean raiders have stolen your
camels and killed your servants. I am the
only one who escaped to tell you."
18 While he was still speaking, another
messenger arrived with this news: "Your
sons and daughters were feasting in their
oldest brother's home. 19 Suddenly, a powerful wind swept in from the wilderness
and hit the house on all sides. The house collapsed, and all your children are dead. I am
the only one who escaped to tell you."

Satan, the Adversary (1:6–2:7)

Num 22:22, 32
1 Chr 21:1
Zech 3:1-4
Matt 4:1-10; 12:24; 13:19, 38-39; 16:23
Mark 1:13; 4:15
Luke 4:6; 10:17-20; 11:15; 22:3, 31
John 8:44; 12:31; 13:2, 27; 16:11
Acts 13:9-10; 26:17-18
Rom 16:20
1 Cor 7:5
2 Cor 2:10-11; 4:4; 6:15; 11:13-15
1 Thes 3:5
2 Thes 2:2-12
Heb 2:14
Jas 4:7
1 Pet 5:8
1 Jn 2:13-14; 3:12; 5:18
Rev 12:3, 9; 20:2, 10

The book of Job includes "the satan" among the heavenly court (1:6; 2:1). The Hebrew word *satan* refers to an adversary or an accuser in court (chs 1–2; see Zech 3:1). God sometimes appoints angels as adversaries for righteous judgment and opposition to evildoers (e.g., Num 22:22, 32, where the verb *satan* is translated "block"; see also 1 Kgs 22:19-23; 1 Cor 5:5). The OT hints at the accuser's demonic character, but between the times of the OT and the NT, Satan became identified with the serpent in Eden (see *Wisdom of Solomon* 2:24). The NT refers to the chief demon as "(the) Satan" (Rev 20:2), along with numerous other names such as the devil (Matt 4:1-10), the tempter (1 Thes 3:5), Beelzeboul, the ruler of demons (see notes on Matt 12:24; Luke 11:15), the evil one (Matt 13:19, 38; 1 Jn 2:13-14; 3:12; 5:18), Beliar (see note on 2 Cor 6:15), the deceiver (Rev 12:9), the great seven-headed dragon and serpent of old (Rev 12:3, 9; 20:2), a murderer, and the father of lies (John 8:44).

Satan incited David's census (1 Chr 21:2; cp. 2 Sam 24:1), tempted and betrayed Jesus (Mark 1:13; 4:15; John 13:27), desired to test Peter as he had tested Job (Luke 22:31), enslaved sinners (Acts 26:18), and deceitfully opposed God's people (1 Cor 7:5; 2 Cor 11:14; 2 Thes 2:28). The adversary of God's people will be overcome in the end, when God defeats and imprisons him (Rev 12:9; 20:2).

1:8 ***my servant:*** This title was used for the patriarchs (Gen 26:24; Exod 32:13), the prophets (2 Kgs 17:13; Jer 7:25; Zech 1:6), and David (e.g., 2 Sam 7; Ps 18:1; 36:1). • ***He is blameless . . . fears God:*** See note on 1:1.

1:9-11 ***Job has good reason*** (Hebrew *khinnam;* see notes on 2:3; 9:17) ***to fear God:*** The wisdom tradition links piety with prosperity. Satan went a step further by suggesting that Job's piety was contingent upon his affluence.

1:10 ***wall of protection:*** See 1 Sam 25:16; Ps 5:12; 34:7; Zech 2:5; cp. Isa 5:5.

1:11-12 ***reach out . . . test him . . . Do whatever you want:*** Satan was God's agent; the hand he put forth was the Lord's as well as Satan's, for here they acted against everything Job possessed and later against Job himself (2:5-6). • Job later cursed the day of his birth (3:1, 8), but he did not *curse* God (31:30), even when his distraught wife urged him to do so (2:9). • God allowed Satan to test Job to prove that Satan's cynicism was incorrect (1 Cor 10:11; see Jas 1:13; cp. Luke 22:31-32; John 19:11).

1:13-19 These attacks destroyed the blessings enumerated in 1:2-3; Job was left alone with the four ominous messengers who came to report and a wife who offered misguided counsel. • The repetition of ***while he was still speaking*** emphasizes the relentlessness of the attacks (see Jer 51:31). The repetition of ***I am the only one who escaped to tell you*** emphasizes the total obliteration of Job's resources.

1:15 The ***Sabeans*** were marauding bandit tribes from the desert (cp. Judg 6:3). By the 700s BC, the southern Sabeans would become a national power that traded in gold, precious stones, perfume, and slaves (Ps 72:10; Isa 43:3; 45:14; 60:6; Jer 6:20).

1:16 The ***fire of God . . . from heaven*** (20:26) might have been lightning (Lev 10:2; 1 Kgs 18:38; 2 Kgs 1:10-14), wildfire (Num 11:1-3), or volcanic activity (Gen 19:24).

1:19 That the ***wind . . . hit the house on all sides*** suggests that Job and his children were settled farmers living in houses rather than nomads living in tents.

Job Responds to the Disaster
20Job stood up and tore his robe in grief.
Then he shaved his head and fell to the
ground to worship. 21He said,

"I came naked from my mother's womb,
and I will be naked when I leave.
The LORD gave me what I had,
and the LORD has taken it away.
Praise the name of the LORD!"

22In all of this, Job did not sin by blaming
God.

Satan Tests Job the Second Time (2:1-10)
The Heavenly Council Meets
2 One day the members of the [e]heavenly
court came again to present themselves
before the LORD, and the Accuser, Satan,
came with them. 2"Where have you come
from?" the LORD asked [f]Satan.
[f]Satan answered the LORD, "I have been
patrolling the earth, watching everything
that's going on."
3Then the LORD asked Satan, "Have you
noticed my servant Job? He is the finest
man in all the earth. He is blameless—a
man of complete integrity. He fears God
and stays away from evil. And he has maintained his integrity, even though you urged
me to harm him without cause."
4[g]Satan replied to the LORD, "Skin for
skin! A man will give up everything he has
to save his life. 5But reach out and take away
his health, and he will surely curse you to
your face!"

Satan Strikes Job's Body
6"All right, do with him as you please," the
LORD said to Satan. "But spare his life." 7So
Satan left the LORD's presence, and he struck
Job with terrible boils from head to foot.

Job Responds to His Illness
8Job scraped his skin with a piece of broken
pottery as he sat among the ashes. 9His wife
said to him, "Are you still trying to maintain
your integrity? Curse God and die."
10But Job replied, "You talk like a foolish
woman. Should we accept only good things
from the hand of God and never anything
bad?" So in all this, Job said nothing wrong.

Job's Three Comforters Mourn with Him (2:11-13)
11When three of Job's friends heard of the
tragedy he had suffered, they got together
and traveled from their homes to comfort
and console him. Their names were Eliphaz
the Temanite, Bildad the Shuhite, and Zophar the Naamathite. 12When they saw Job
from a distance, they scarcely recognized
him. Wailing loudly, they tore their robes
and threw dust into the air over their heads

1:20 Gen 37:29, 34
1:21 1 Sam 2:7-8; Job 2:10; Eccl 5:15; 1 Tim 6:7
1:22 Job 2:10
2:1 Job 1:6-8; [e]*ben 'elohim* (1121, 0430) ▸Job 38:7
2:2 [f]*satan* (7854) ▸Job 2:4
2:3 Job 27:5-6
2:4 [g]*satan* (7854) ▸Ps 109:6
2:5 Job 1:11
2:7 Deut 28:35; Job 7:5; 13:28
2:8 Job 42:6; Jer 6:26; Ezek 27:30; Jon 3:6; Matt 11:21
2:10 Job 1:21-22; Ps 39:1
2:12 Josh 7:6; Job 1:20; Lam 2:10; Ezek 27:30

1:20 Job *tore his robe* and *shaved his head;* both were common Near East rituals that demonstrated *grief.* These actions sometimes substituted for self-mutilation as a physical response to shock, horror, or bad news (2:12; Gen 37:29, 34; Judg 11:35; Jer 16:6; Ezek 7:18; Amos 8:10). • He *fell to the ground,* not to wail in despair, but *to worship* in hope (1 Pet 5:6).

2:1-3 This scene is an exact repetition of the scene presented in 1:6-8.

2:1 *the members of the heavenly court:* Literally *the sons of God.* • *Satan:* Hebrew *and the satan;* similarly throughout this chapter.

2:3 The phrase *without cause* (Hebrew *khinnam*) is a wordplay on Satan's question in 1:9. See also 9:17 and note.

2:5-7 *reach out . . . do . . . as you please . . . left the LORD's presence:* See 1:11-12 and note.

2:5 *take away his health* (literally *strike his flesh and bones*): Bones were thought to be the seat of health.

2:6 *spare* (literally *guard/watch over*): God ironically made Satan responsible for guarding Job's *life* (cp. 10:13-14; 13:27; 33:11).

2:7 This term for *terrible boils* was used for any inflamed, running sores (Exod 9:10; Lev 13:18-20; Deut 28:27, 35).

2:8 Job might have *scraped his skin* to relieve itching; the Greek OT says that it was "to scrape away the pus." • *The ashes* might refer to a place where lepers were quarantined, but Job was probably demonstrating his grief and dismay (30:19; Gen 18:27; 2 Sam 12:16; Isa 58:5; Jon 3:6).

2:9 Job's *wife* first summarized the essence of Job's temptation by echoing God's words (2:3); Job was trying to *maintain* his *integrity.* In her frustration and anguish, however, she then counseled Job to *curse God* and thus unknowingly fulfill Satan's prediction (1:11; 2:5).

2:10 Job's acceptance of *bad* as well as *good things* from God's hand demonstrates his righteousness and faith (cp. 1:21; 2 Sam 12:16-20; Luke 22:42). • By saying *nothing wrong,* Job controlled his tongue (Prov 13:3; 21:23; see Jas 3:2).

2:11 It might have taken several months for *Job's friends* (see note on 6:14-27) to hear of his afflictions (see 7:3). • The text implies that Job's friends were Edomites, a people who were famous for their wisdom (Jer 49:7; Obad 1:8). • *Eliphaz the Temanite* was probably a descendant of Esau's grandson Teman (Gen 36:10-11, 15); his land was located in Edom (Ezek 25:13; Amos 1:11-12). • The *Bil-* element in *Bildad* would remind Hebrew readers of names like *Bilhan,* a descendant of Esau (Gen 36:27; 1 Chr 1:42). The *-dad* element would remind them of names like *Bedad,* father of the Edomite king *Hadad* (Gen 36:35; 1 Chr 1:46). • *Shuhite:* No place named Shuah is known, but Abraham's son Shuah was sent to "a land in the east" (Gen 25:1, 6; 1 Chr 1:32; see note on 1:2-3). • The Greek OT lists *Zophar* instead of Zepho as one of Esau's grandsons (Gen 36:11, 15; 1 Chr 1:36). A *Naamathite* might reside in a town named Naamah, but no such location is known. Two OT women are named Naamah, but neither is a likely ancestor of Zophar (Gen 4:22; 1 Kgs 14:21).

2:12 *they scarcely recognized him:* This expression indicates the extreme suffering Job had experienced (cp. Isa 52:14; 53:3). • Job's friends mourned by *wailing loudly,* just as they would have done for a dead man. • *tore their robes:* See note on 1:20. • Throwing *dust* sometimes expressed anger or disdain (2 Sam 16:13; Acts 22:23), but here it signaled mourning (see Josh 7:6; 1 Sam 4:12; Neh 9:1; Lam 2:10).

2:13 Gen 50:10; Ezek 3:15
3:3 Jer 20:14
3:8 Job 41:1, 10, 25
3:9 Job 41:18
3:11 Job 10:18-19
3:13 Job 14:10-15; 19:25-27

to show their grief. 13Then they sat on the ground with him for seven days and nights. No one said a word to Job, for they saw that his suffering was too great for words.

DIALOGUES ABOUT SUFFERING (3:1–37:24)

Job Curses the Day of His Birth (3:1-26)

3 At last Job spoke, and he cursed the day of his birth. 2He said:

3 "Let the day of my birth be erased,
and the night I was conceived.
4 Let that day be turned to darkness.
Let it be lost even to God on high,
and let no light shine on it.
5 Let the darkness and utter gloom claim
that day for its own.
Let a black cloud overshadow it,
and let the darkness terrify it.
6 Let that night be blotted off the
calendar,
never again to be counted among the
days of the year,
never again to appear among the
months.
7 Let that night be childless.
Let it have no joy.
8 Let those who are experts at cursing—
whose cursing could rouse Leviathan—
curse that day.
9 Let its morning stars remain dark.
Let it hope for light, but in vain;
may it never see the morning light.
10 Curse that day for failing to shut my
mother's womb,
for letting me be born to see all this
trouble.

11 "Why wasn't I born dead?
Why didn't I die as I came from the
womb?
12 Why was I laid on my mother's lap?
Why did she nurse me at her breasts?
13 Had I died at birth, I would now be at
peace.
I would be asleep and at rest.
14 I would rest with the world's kings and
prime ministers,
whose great buildings now lie in
ruins.

Job's Complaint (3:1-26; 6:1–7:21)

Gen 4:13-14; Exod 14:10-14; 16:2-18; Num 14:27-37; 2 Sam 6:8; 1 Kgs 19:3-18; Ps 38:1-22; 39:10-13; 44:1-26; 73:1-17; Eccl 2:17-18; Jer 20:14-18; Jon 4:1-11; Mal 3:14-18; Matt 27:46; John 6:41-59; 1 Cor 10:1-10; Eph 5:20; Phil 2:14; 4:4; 1 Thes 5:16; Jas 5:9-13

Job complained mightily and earned God's rebuke for it, yet God ultimately confirmed his righteousness. Job's fundamental complaint was that God did not allow him a fair hearing to demonstrate his innocence before God and man. Job's friends attacked Job for trying to vindicate himself, but God upheld Job's innocence. God rebuked Job for his overreaching self-defense with its implied criticism of God's fairness. In a gracious but firm act of self-revelation, God rebuked Job and shifted his focus away from his troubles and toward God (chs 38–41).

In general, the Bible depicts complaining as wrong. For example, God judged the Israelites for grumbling about their hardships in the wilderness (Num 14:27-37). Nonetheless, God affirmed Job and rejected those who tried to stop him from complaining (42:7-8).

Scripture admonishes us to rejoice and give thanks in all situations (Eph 5:20; Phil 4:4; 1 Thes 5:16-18). If we want to complain in prayer, we should follow the pattern of the psalms, which lead us past ourselves and back to God. Scripture calls us to endure through suffering and to persist in prayer (Jas 5:10, 13). Job's positive example (Jas 5:11) is not so much in how he responded to his troubles or to his comforters but in how he responded to God (40:4-5; 42:1-6).

2:13 Job's friends ***sat on the ground*** to identify with Job's suffering (see 2:8 and note). • The standard period for mourning the death of a notable person or for acknowledging other disastrous news was ***seven days and nights*** (Gen 50:10; 1 Sam 31:13; see also Ezek 3:14-15).

3:1-26 Job's outburst did not mean that his integrity had cracked under the strain (42:7-8; Jas 5:11). Elijah and Jeremiah, both godly men, used the same hyperbolic language (1 Kgs 19:4; Jer 20:14-18).

3:1-10 ***Job spoke*** and thus put at risk his refusal to sin with his mouth (1:21; 2:10). • Job ***cursed the day of his birth*** in great detail. However, his words sound more like pitiful complaints. Job didn't curse God as his creator, but he lamented the conditions of his existence.

3:5 Job longed for the sinister ***darkness*** of the underworld (Exod 10:22; Prov 4:19; Joel 2:2) and the ***gloom*** of death (10:21-22; 38:17) to ***claim*** the ***day*** of his birth.

3:8 The expression ***experts at cursing*** refers to professional cursers such as Balaam (Num 22–24). • The identification of ***Leviathan*** is disputed, ranging from an earthly creature to a mythical sea monster in ancient literature. See note on 7:12.

3:9 Venus and Mercury, the ***morning stars***, herald the dawn (38:7).

3:10 ***shut my mother's womb:*** Closing or opening the womb sometimes refers to conception (Gen 16:2; 20:18; 29:31; 30:22; 1 Sam 1:5-6), but here it refers to birth (see also 38:8).

3:11-24 Job's language turns from curse to lamentation. Job alternates between repugnance for life and a romance with death. Seven times (see note on 1:2-3), Job laments his situation by asking ***why*** (3:11, 12, 16, 20, 23; see Ps 10:1; 22:1; Jer 20:18; Lam 5:20).

3:14 The dead were thought to continue their identities and social status after death. Perhaps Job wanted ***the world's kings and prime ministers*** to acknowledge his own princely status (1:3).

15 I would rest with princes, rich in gold,
whose palaces were filled with silver.
16 Why wasn't I buried like a stillborn child,
like a baby who never lives to see the light?
17 For in death the wicked cause no trouble,
and the weary are at rest.
18 Even captives are at ease in death,
with no guards to curse them.
19 Rich and poor are both there,
and the slave is free from his master.

20 "Oh, why give light to those in misery,
and life to those who are bitter?
21 They long for death, and it won't come.
They search for death more eagerly than for hidden treasure.
22 They're filled with joy when they finally die,
and rejoice when they find the grave.
23 Why is life given to those with no future,
those God has surrounded with difficulties?
24 I cannot eat for sighing;
my groans pour out like water.
25 What I always feared has happened to me.
What I dreaded has come true.
26 I have no peace, no quietness.
I have no rest; only trouble comes."

First Round of Speeches (4:1–14:22)
Eliphaz Responds to Job

4 Then Eliphaz the Temanite replied to Job:

2 "Will you be patient and let me say a word?
For who could keep from speaking out?
3 "In the past you have encouraged many people;
you have strengthened those who were weak.
4 Your words have supported those who were falling;
you encouraged those with shaky knees.
5 But now when trouble strikes, you lose heart.
You are terrified when it touches you.
6 Doesn't your reverence for God give you confidence?
Doesn't your life of integrity give you hope?

7 "Stop and think! Do the innocent die?
When have the upright been destroyed?
8 My experience shows that those who plant trouble
and cultivate evil will harvest the same.
9 A breath from God destroys them.
They vanish in a blast of his anger.
10 The lion roars and the wildcat snarls,
but the teeth of strong lions will be broken.
11 The fierce lion will starve for lack of prey,
and the cubs of the lioness will be scattered.

12 "This truth was given to me in secret,
as though whispered in my ear.
13 It came to me in a disturbing vision at night,
when people are in a deep sleep.
14 Fear gripped me,
and my bones trembled.

3:21 Rev 9:6
3:23 Job 19:6, 8, 12; Ps 88:8; Lam 3:7
3:24 Job 6:7; 33:20; Ps 42:3-4
3:25 Job 9:28; 30:15
3:26 Job 7:13-14
4:2 Job 32:18-20
4:3 Job 29:21, 25
4:5 Job 6:14; 19:21
4:6 Job 1:1; Prov 3:26
4:7-8 Job 8:20; Ps 37:25; Prov 22:8; Gal 6:7-8
4:9 Job 15:30; Isa 30:33; 2 Thes 2:8
4:11 Job 5:4; Ps 34:10
4:12 Job 26:14; 33:15-18

3:15 ***rich in gold, whose palaces were filled with silver:*** This might refer to treasure-filled tombs, but it more likely refers to the futile hoarding of wealth that ends in death (as in 3:14).

3:20 Job equated *light* with *life* (33:30; see John 1:4; 8:12). • *Bitter* might mean "short tempered" (Judg 18:25), "enraged" (2 Sam 17:8), "in deep anguish" (7:11; Prov 31:6), or "discontented" (1 Sam 1:10; 22:2).

3:21 People in misery *long for death* with the desperation of those who dig for *hidden treasure.*

4:1–14:22 This section begins three rounds of speeches by each of Job's three comforters, each with a response from Job (4:1–27:23). In this first round, Job's friends exhort him to seek God so that he can again enjoy prosperity.

4:1-2 *Eliphaz the Temanite* (see note on 2:11) was the most prominent and probably the oldest of Job's friends; his speeches are longer and more ornate than the others. • ***who could keep from speaking out?*** Eliphaz mimicked the urgency of a prophetic revelation (4:12-16; see Jer 20:9; Amos 3:8).

4:3-4 *People . . . who were weak* were depressed and suffered from low morale (Isa 13:7; 35:3; Ezek 7:17).

4:7 Job probably counted his children among the *innocent* dead (1:5), and even Eliphaz must have known that innocent blood is sometimes shed (cp. Deut 19:10; Prov 6:17; Jer 7:6).

4:8 The *harvest* metaphor illustrates the scriptural principle that behavior merits judgment (Prov 22:8; Hos 8:7; Rom 2:9-11; Gal 6:7-8). The NT describes the final judgment as a harvest (Matt 13:39). Jesus rejected simplistic attempts to analyze people's lives by this principle (Luke 13:4; John 9:1-3).

4:9 ***They vanish in a blast of his anger:*** Eliphaz understood the wind of 1:19 as divine judgment (cp. Isa 40:7; Hos 13:15).

4:12-16 Eliphaz posed as a prophet, implying that God spoke to him *in secret* (Num 12:6); later God did speak to him, but not to affirm his counsel (42:7).

4:13 Eliphaz probably referred to the God-induced *sleep* associated with prophetic vision (33:15; Gen 15:12; Num 12:6; Isa 29:10).

4:14 *Fear* is common in God's presence (Gen 15:12; Dan 8:17-18; 10:8-10), but God tells his people not to be afraid (Gen 15:1; 26:24; Isa 40:9; 44:8). • Eliphaz's *bones trembled* like those of a prophet with terrible news to deliver (Jer 23:9; Hab 3:16).

4:17
Job 9:2; 35:10
4:19
Gen 2:7; 3:19
Job 10:9; 15:15; 22:16
4:20
Job 14:2, 20; 20:7
4:21
Job 8:22
5:1
Job 15:15
5:2
Prov 12:16; 27:3
[h]qin'ah (7068)
‣ Prov 3:31
5:3
Job 24:18
5:5
Job 18:8-10; 31-8
5:7
Job 14:1

15 A spirit swept past my face,
and my hair stood on end.
16 The spirit stopped, but I couldn't see its shape.
There was a form before my eyes.
In the silence I heard a voice say,
17 'Can a mortal be innocent before God?
Can anyone be pure before the Creator?'

18 "If God does not trust his own angels
and has charged his messengers with foolishness,
19 how much less will he trust people made of clay!
They are made of dust, crushed as easily as a moth.
20 They are alive in the morning but dead by evening,
gone forever without a trace.
21 Their tent-cords are pulled and the tent collapses,
and they die in ignorance.

5 1 "Cry for help, but will anyone answer you?
Which of the angels will help you?
2 Surely resentment destroys the fool,
and [h]jealousy kills the simple.
3 I have seen that fools may be successful for the moment,
but then comes sudden disaster.
4 Their children are abandoned far from help;
they are crushed in court with no one to defend them.
5 The hungry devour their harvest,
even when it is guarded by brambles.
The thirsty pant after their wealth.
6 But evil does not spring from the soil,
and trouble does not sprout from the earth.
7 People are born for trouble
as readily as sparks fly up from a fire.

8 "If I were you, I would go to God
and present my case to him.

Material Reward (4:7-9)

Job 11:6; 19:5
Gen 13:2
1 Kgs 10:23
Ps 49:16-20; 73:1-28
Prov 14:20; 18:11; 28:11
Eccl 5:10-20
Jer 17:11
Zeph 1:18
Matt 27:57
Mark 4:19; 10:17-25
Luke 6:24-25; 16:10-31
1 Tim 6:17
Jas 1:2-4, 9; 5:1
1 Jn 2:16
3 Jn 1:2

It was a common OT belief that righteous people would always prosper materially. Some hold this view today. The problem with this theology is that it can induce false guilt and accusations when prosperity does not come. Job's friends accepted this traditional theological view. They said that Job's troubles stood as evidence against him (19:5). They claimed that his suffering was punishment for sin (4:7-9) and pointed out that Job's penalty was probably less than he deserved (11:6). However, God's analysis of Job's life proved this idea to be false (42:7-8). God testified to his special relationship with Job and restored Job's good reputation as God's servant. He even restored Job's fortune (42:10-17).

Material well-being is not necessarily in opposition to spiritual blessing (cp. 3 Jn 1:2). Once we equate blessings with material gain, however, "the worries of this life, the lure of wealth, and the desire for other things" tend to crowd out our attention to spiritual blessings (Mark 4:19; Luke 6:25). We might even come to prefer physical stimulation, a craving for everything we see, and self-esteem based on what we own (even if we still owe many payments on it). This worldview is not Christian but characterizes worldly people (1 Jn 2:15-17).

Instead, we should regard hardships as occasions for spiritual growth (Jas 1:2-4). Job's suffering moved him from complaint to renewed humility that acknowledged God's righteous power (40:4-5; 42:2-6).

4:15 *A spirit* (or *wind;* also in 4:16) ***swept past my face:*** Wind is a physical display of God's powerful presence (38:1; Nah 1:3; Acts 2:2; cp. 1 Kgs 19:11). • ***my hair stood on end:*** Or *its wind sent shivers up my spine.*

4:17 As the characters in the book repeatedly acknowledge, no one is truly ***innocent*** or ***pure*** (see 9:2; 15:14; 25:4; 35:7) because all are depraved (Ps 14:3; 53:3; Rom 3:10-11). Eliphaz used these terms to mean that human beings are sinful creatures and God is the sinless Creator. Job and God used them to mean that Job had faithfully carried out the duties inherent in his relationship with God. Job and Eliphaz never agreed on the meaning of these terms. Later, God said that Eliphaz had spoken inaccurately (42:7).

4:18-21 The concept that ***God does not trust his own angels*** and that he ***charged his messengers with foolishness*** is otherwise unknown (but see Gen 6:1-4).

4:21 A ***tent*** was a common symbol for mortal life (Isa 38:12; 2 Cor 5:1; cp. Eccl 12:6).

5:1 ***The angels*** (literally *the holy ones*), probably a reference back to 4:18, are called "holy ones" because of their proximity to God, not because they were morally perfect (15:15; Dan 4:14; 8:13; Zech 14:5).

5:4 The ***court*** (literally *the gate*) was the site of legal and commercial deliberations in which Job had participated (29:7; see Deut 21:19-21; Ruth 4:1-11).

5:5 ***even when it is guarded by brambles:*** The meaning of the Hebrew for this phrase is uncertain.

5:8 To ***go to God*** meant lodging a formal appeal with God for assistance, counsel, or vindication, sometimes by way of repentance (Amos 5:4, 6) and possibly through a prophetic oracle (Gen 25:22; 1 Sam 9:9; 1 Kgs 22:8). • Job wanted to ***present*** his ***case*** to God (13:3, 15, 18; 23:3-8), and later he attempted to do so (chs 29–31).

9 He does great things too marvelous to
understand.
He performs countless miracles.
10 He gives rain for the earth
and water for the fields.
11 He gives prosperity to the poor
and protects those who suffer.
12 He frustrates the plans of schemers
so the work of their hands will not
succeed.
13 He traps the wise in their own
cleverness
so their cunning schemes are
thwarted.
14 They find it is dark in the daytime,
and they grope at noon as if it were
night.
15 He rescues the poor from the cutting
words of the strong,
and rescues them from the clutches of
the powerful.
16 And so at last the poor have hope,
and the snapping jaws of the wicked
are shut.

17 "But consider the [i]joy of those corrected
by God!
Do not despise the discipline of the
Almighty when you sin.
18 For though he wounds, he also
bandages.
He strikes, but his hands also heal.
19 From six disasters he will rescue you;
even in the seventh, he will keep you
from evil.
20 He will save you from death in time of
famine,
from the power of the sword in time
of war.
21 You will be safe from slander
and have no fear when destruction
comes.
22 You will laugh at destruction and
famine;
wild animals will not terrify you.
23 You will be at peace with the stones of
the field,
and its wild animals will be at peace
with you.
24 You will know that your home is safe.
When you survey your possessions,
nothing will be missing.
25 You will have many children;
your descendants will be as plentiful
as grass!
26 You will go to the grave at a ripe old age,
like a sheaf of grain harvested at the
proper time!

27 "We have studied life and found all this
to be true.
Listen to my counsel, and apply it to
yourself."

Job Responds to Eliphaz

6 Then Job spoke again:

2 "If my misery could be weighed
and my troubles be put on the scales,
3 they would outweigh all the sands of the
sea.
That is why I spoke impulsively.
4 For the Almighty has struck me down
with his arrows.
Their poison infects my spirit.
God's terrors are lined up against me.
5 Don't I have a right to complain?
Don't wild donkeys bray when they
find no grass,
and oxen bellow when they have no
food?
6 Don't people complain about unsalted
food?
Does anyone want the tasteless white
of an egg?

5:9
Job 9:10; 37:14, 16;
42:3

5:10
Job 36:27-29; 37:6-11
Ps 65:9

5:11
Job 22:29; 36:7

5:13
*1 Cor 3:19

5:14
Deut 28:29

5:16
Ps 107:42

5:17
Ps 94:12
Heb 12:5-11
'ashrey (0835)
›Ps 1:1

5:18
Deut 32:39
Isa 30:26
Hos 6:1

5:20
Ps 33:19; 144:10

5:23
Isa 11:6-9; 65:25

5:24
Job 8:6

5:26
Gen 15:15
Job 42:17
Prov 9:11

6:2
Job 31:6

6:3
Job 23:2

6:4
Job 16:13; 21:20;
30:15
Ps 38:2

6:5
Job 39:5-8

5:9-16 Eliphaz's doxology praised God as the wonder-working Creator and Sustainer of the universe (5:9-10) and as the righteous Judge who brings down the powerful and lifts up the poor (5:11-16).

5:9-10 Job's region depended upon *rain* rather than irrigation (see 36:27-28).

5:13 God *traps the wise* in the cleverness of their words (Prov 12:13). Paul alluded to this verse in his rejection of worldly wisdom (1 Cor 1:19).

5:17 ***the discipline of the Almighty:*** See Deut 8:5; Prov 3:11-12; Rev 3:19.

5:19-26 ***six disasters . . . even in the seventh:*** This wisdom formula reflects a sense of completeness (cp. Prov 30:15-31). • This list reflects Mosaic covenant blessings and curses (Lev 26; Deut 28). Eliphaz thought that people in right relationship with God would be free from *famine* (5:20, 22; see Lev 26:4-5, 10; Deut 28:4-6, 8, 11-12), *war* (i.e., death, 5:20) and the *destruction* it causes (5:21, 22; see Lev 26:6-8; Deut 28:7, 48), and *slander.* They will even be *at peace* with *wild animals* (5:23; see Lev 26:6) and *the stones of the field.* This peace might indicate fertile rather than stony fields (2 Kgs 3:19, 25; Matt 13:5), or it might symbolize wider harmony with the natural world (see Ps 91:11-12).

5:24 ***nothing will be missing:*** See Deut 28:11-12; cp. 1:6-19.

5:25 ***descendants . . . as plentiful as grass:*** See Gen 22:17; Lev 26:9; Deut 28:4, 11-12.

6:1–7:21 Job's response attacks his counselors (ch 6) and challenges God (ch 7). He excuses his passionate words by referencing the depths of his misery (6:2-3; 7:11). Job says that Eliphaz has failed to offer comfort or sympathy as a friend, having chosen instead to haggle over stale theological precepts.

6:3-4 In the OT, *arrows* are associated with supernatural peril, pestilence, and destructive ills (7:20; 16:12-13; Deut 32:23-24, 42; Ps 7:12-13; 38:2; 64:7; 91:5-6; Lam 2:4; 3:12-13; Ezek 5:16).

6:6 ***the tasteless white of an egg?*** Or *the tasteless juice of the mallow plant?* Job's riddle-like complaint probably refers both to Eliphaz's weak counsel and the detestable situation God had allowed him to endure.

6:9 1 Kgs 19:4
6:10 Job 23:11-12
6:11 Job 21:4
6:13 Job 26:2-3
6:14 Job 1:5; 4:5
6:15 Jer 15:18
6:17 Job 24:19
6:19 Gen 25:15; Job 1:15; Isa 21:14
6:20 Jer 14:3
6:26 Job 8:2
6:27 Job 22:9; 24:9; Joel 3:3; Nah 3:10; 2 Pet 2:3
6:29 Job 13:18; 27:5-6; 42:1-6
6:30 Job 12:11
7:1 Lev 25:50; Job 14:6, 14
7:4 Deut 28:67; Job 7:13-14

7 My appetite disappears when I look at it;
I gag at the thought of eating it!
8 "Oh, that I might have my request,
that God would grant my desire.
9 I wish he would crush me.
I wish he would reach out his hand
and kill me.
10 At least I can take comfort in this:
Despite the pain,
I have not denied the words of the
Holy One.
11 But I don't have the strength to endure.
I have nothing to live for.
12 Do I have the strength of a stone?
Is my body made of bronze?
13 No, I am utterly helpless,
without any chance of success.

14 "One should be kind to a fainting friend,
but you accuse me without any fear of
the Almighty.
15 My brothers, you have proved as
unreliable as a seasonal brook
that overflows its banks in the spring
16 when it is swollen with ice and
melting snow.
17 But when the hot weather arrives, the
water disappears.
The brook vanishes in the heat.
18 The caravans turn aside to be refreshed,
but there is nothing to drink, so they
die.
19 The caravans from Tema search for this
water;
the travelers from Sheba hope to find it.
20 They count on it but are disappointed.
When they arrive, their hopes are
dashed.
21 You, too, have given no help.
You have seen my calamity, and you
are afraid.
22 But why? Have I ever asked you for a
gift?
Have I begged for anything of yours
for myself?
23 Have I asked you to rescue me from my
enemies,
or to save me from ruthless people?
24 Teach me, and I will keep quiet.
Show me what I have done wrong.
25 Honest words can be painful,
but what do your criticisms
amount to?
26 Do you think your words are convincing
when you disregard my cry of
desperation?
27 You would even send an orphan into
slavery
or sell a friend.
28 Look at me!
Would I lie to your face?
29 Stop assuming my guilt,
for I have done no wrong.
30 Do you think I am lying?
Don't I know the difference between
right and wrong?

7 1 "Is not all human life a struggle?
Our lives are like that of a hired
hand,
2 like a worker who longs for the shade,
like a servant waiting to be paid.
3 I, too, have been assigned months of
futility,
long and weary nights of misery.
4 Lying in bed, I think, 'When will it be
morning?'
But the night drags on, and I toss till
dawn.
5 My body is covered with maggots and
scabs.
My skin breaks open, oozing with pus.

6:9 At one time, both Moses and Elijah wished that God would *kill* them (Num 11:15; 1 Kgs 19:4).

6:14-27 Job and his friends might have been bound by a covenant of loyalty and faithfulness (Hebrew *khesed;* see Gen 21:23; Exod 15:13; 1 Chr 16:34) that made them like brothers (6:14-15), protectors (6:21-23), and trusted friends (6:27).

6:14 ***but you accuse me without any fear of the Almighty:*** Or *or he might lose his fear of the Almighty.* Job accused his counselors of violating their covenant with him.

6:19 The city of ***Tema*** in the northern Arabian desert was at the junction of roads from Damascus to Mecca and from the Persian Gulf to Aqaba (Isa 21:14; Jer 25:23). It might have been named after one of Ishmael's descendants (Gen 25:15). It was not the same as Teman, Eliphaz's home in Edom (see note on 2:11). • ***Sheba,*** located in southwest Arabia, was a market city for precious commodities (Ps 72:10, 15; Isa 60:6; Jer 6:20; Ezek 27:22-23; 38:13).

6:27 ***even send an orphan into slavery*** (literally *even gamble over an orphan*): Job, the former protector of orphans (31:17, 21), used a proverbial example of his counselors' hard-heartedness toward the defenseless (see 17:5).

6:30 ***Don't I know the difference between right and wrong?*** (literally *Can't my palate discern malice?*): Job might have been echoing his earlier comment about a tasteless, revolting diet (6:6-7; see note on 6:6).

7:1 ***Human life*** has been a ***struggle*** since the Fall (Gen 3:17; 5:29; Eccl 1:2, 13-14; 2:11, 17; Rom 8:20-22).

7:2 A ***worker*** was ***to be paid*** at the end of each day (Lev 19:13; Deut 24:15; see Matt 29:8), though this did not always happen (Jer 22:13; Mal 3:5; Jas 5:4).

7:3 Job's trial might already have gone on for ***months.*** • The Hebrew term (*'amal*) that runs throughout Job is translated as "*misery*/miserable" (3:20; 7:3; 11:16; 16:2; 20:22) or as "trouble" (3:10; 4:8; 5:6, 7; 15:35).

7:5 Job's reference to ***maggots*** signified mortality (25:6) and the rampant corruption of Sheol (17:14; 21:26; 24:20; see Isa 14:11).

Job Cries Out to God

6 "My days fly faster than a weaver's
shuttle.
They end without hope.
7 O God, remember that my life is but a
breath,
and I will never again feel happiness.
8 You see me now, but not for long.
You will look for me, but I will be
gone.
9 Just as a cloud dissipates and vanishes,
those who [j]die will not come back.
10 They are gone forever from their
home—
never to be seen again.

11 "I cannot keep from speaking.
I must express my anguish.
My bitter [k]soul must complain.
12 Am I a sea monster or a dragon
that you must place me under guard?
13 I think, 'My bed will comfort me,
and sleep will ease my misery,'
14 but then you shatter me with dreams
and terrify me with visions.
15 I would rather be strangled—
rather die than suffer like this.
16 I hate my life and don't want to go on
living.
Oh, leave me alone for my few
remaining days.

17 "What are people, that you should make
so much of us,
that you should think of us so often?
18 For you examine us every morning
and test us every moment.
19 Why won't you leave me alone,
at least long enough for me to
swallow!
20 If I have sinned, what have I done to you,
O watcher of all humanity?
Why make me your target?
Am I a burden to you?
21 Why not just forgive my sin
and take away my guilt?
For soon I will lie down in the dust and
die.
When you look for me, I will be gone."

Bildad Responds to Job

8 Then Bildad the Shuhite replied to Job:

2 "How long will you go on like this?
You sound like a blustering wind.
3 Does God twist justice?
Does the Almighty twist what is right?
4 Your children must have sinned against
him,
so their punishment was well
deserved.
5 But if you pray to God
and seek the favor of the Almighty,

7:7 Job 7:16; 9:25; Ps 78:39
7:8 Job 7:21; 20:9
7:9 [j]*she'ol* (7585) ‣Job 17:16
7:10 Ps 103:16
7:11 [k]*nepesh* (5315) ‣Ps 6:3
7:13 Job 7:4; Ps 6:6
7:16 Job 6:9; 7:7; 9:21; 10:1
7:17 Job 22:2; Heb 2:6
7:20 Job 35:3, 6
7:21 Job 10:9, 14
8:3 Gen 18:25; Deut 32:4; 2 Chr 19:7; Job 34:10, 12; 36:23; Rom 3:5
8:4 Job 1:5, 18-19
8:5 Job 5:17-27

7:6-21 Job cried out to God, complaining that life was too brief (7:6-10). This complaint contrasts ironically with his earlier desire that God end it all (6:9).

7:7 Those who call upon *God* to *remember* are typically seeking covenant mercy (Ps 35:6; 106:4). • Job's declaration that *life is but a breath* (Hebrew *ruakh*) meant either that he was one breath away from death or that his life was like a passing wind (Ps 39:9, 11).

7:8 ***You see me now, but not for long:*** The Greek OT omitted this verse to avoid the implication that God would be unable to see Job in Sheol (see note on 7:9).

7:9 ***who die*** (literally *who go down to Sheol*): This is the first explicit mention of Sheol in Job. It is described as a place of rest from earthly pressures and distinctions (3:13-19) and as a dark dwelling place (10:21-22; 17:13) deep in the earth (11:8) that is covered in dust (17:16). It is the destiny of all the living (30:23) from which no one can return (10:21; see Gen 37:25; 2 Sam 12:12).

7:11 ***I cannot keep from speaking:*** Job echoed Eliphaz's inability to refrain from words (4:2).

7:12 The ***sea monster*** (Hebrew *yam*) and ***dragon*** (Hebrew *tannin*) represent chaotic opposition to God's orderly creation. In Canaanite mythology, Yam was the primordial sea god and Tannin was a sea monster (Jer 51:34) or a mythological deity of chaos (Ps 74:13-14). This kind of chaos is also represented in Job as *Leviathan* (3:8; Isa 27:1) or *Rahab* (9:13; 26:12; Isa 51:9). The Lord is sovereign over the sea and all that it represents (26:12; 38:8-11; Ps 89:9-10; Jer 5:22).

7:13-14 Job's sickbed ***dreams*** and ***visions*** echoed those of Eliphaz (4:12-16).

7:16 ***for my few remaining days:*** Literally *for my days are a vapor* (Hebrew *hebel*); see "*Hebel,* 'Vapor'" at Eccl 1:2, p. 1073.

7:17-18 ***that you should make so much of us:*** Cp. Ps 8:4-5, which treats the same thoughts positively. • ***examine*** (Hebrew *paqad*): In Ps 8:5, the same term means "to honor or care for"; Job used the term ironically, meaning "to be pestered" (cp. "attacked," Isa 26:14).

7:19 ***Won't you leave me alone*** (literally *How long will you not look away from me*): Job sought the opposite of the watchful care that faithful people usually seek (Num 6:25; Ps 27:9; 69:17; 80:3, 7, 19; Lam 1:9). • ***to swallow:*** This is equivalent to "a chance to catch my breath."

7:20 ***watcher of all humanity:*** Rather than praising God for his goodness expressed in watchfulness (Deut 32:10; Ps 25:21; Prov 24:12), Job blamed God for hostile surveillance, which actually characterizes Satan's activity (1:7). • ***Why*** is from the language of lament (see note on 3:11-24). • ***your target:*** See 6:4; Lam 3:12.

8:1 Like Eliphaz, ***Bildad the Shuhite*** (see 2:11) believed that Job's sufferings were God's retribution (8:3-6, 13; see 4:7-8; 5:2-3). This counselor revered the wisdom of the past (8:8-10; see 4:7, 27) and addressed Job with a mixture of instruction (8:3-6, 8-10; see 4:12-21; 5:9-16) and encouragement (8:5-7, 20-22; see 4:6; 5:19-26). His point was that Job should quit blustering. He advised Job to repent and allow God's justice to bring about restoration (8:1-7).

8:2 ***How long?*** Bildad's question might be an ironic parody of Job's question in 7:19.

8:3-4 According to Bildad, ***God*** does not ***twist justice,*** so the death of Job's children proved that they had ***sinned against*** God. Bildad divided people into the blameless (Hebrew *tam,* 8:20a; see 1:1) and the secretly wicked (Hebrew *khanep,* 8:13b). He believed that they could be differentiated by watching what God did to them.

8:6 Job 22:27 Ps 7:6
8:7 Job 42:12
8:8 Deut 4:32; 32:7 Job 15:18
8:13 Ps 9:17
8:15 Job 27:18 Ps 49:11
8:16 Ps 37:35; 80:11
8:19 Job 20:4-5
8:21 Ps 126:1-2; 132:16
8:22 Job 8:15 Ps 132:18
9:2 Job 4:17; 25:4
9:3 Job 10:2; 40:2
9:5 Job 26:6-14
9:6 Isa 2:19, 21; 13:13 Hag 2:6 Heb 12:26
9:7 Isa 13:10
9:8 Gen 1:1 Ps 77:19; 104:2 Isa 40:22
9:9 Job 38:31-32 Amos 5:8
9:11 Job 23:8-9

6 and if you are pure and live with integrity,
he will surely rise up and restore your happy home.
7 And though you started with little,
you will end with much.

8 "Just ask the previous generation.
Pay attention to the experience of our ancestors.
9 For we were born but yesterday and know nothing.
Our days on earth are as fleeting as a shadow.
10 But those who came before us will teach you.
They will teach you the wisdom of old.

11 "Can papyrus reeds grow tall without a marsh?
Can marsh grass flourish without water?
12 While they are still flowering, not ready to be cut,
they begin to wither more quickly than grass.
13 The same happens to all who forget God.
The hopes of the godless evaporate.
14 Their confidence hangs by a thread.
They are leaning on a spider's web.
15 They cling to their home for security, but it won't last.
They try to hold it tight, but it will not endure.
16 The godless seem like a lush plant growing in the sunshine,
its branches spreading across the garden.
17 Its roots grow down through a pile of stones;
it takes hold on a bed of rocks.
18 But when it is uprooted,
it's as though it never existed!
19 That's the end of its life,
and others spring up from the earth to replace it.

20 "But look, God will not reject a person of integrity,
nor will he lend a hand to the wicked.
21 He will once again fill your mouth with laughter
and your lips with shouts of joy.
22 Those who hate you will be clothed with shame,
and the home of the wicked will be destroyed."

Job Responds to Bildad

9 Then Job spoke again:
2 "Yes, I know all this is true in principle.
But how can a person be declared innocent in God's sight?
3 If someone wanted to take God to court,
would it be possible to answer him even once in a thousand times?
4 For God is so wise and so mighty.
Who has ever challenged him successfully?

5 "Without warning, he moves the mountains,
overturning them in his anger.
6 He shakes the earth from its place,
and its foundations tremble.
7 If he commands it, the sun won't rise
and the stars won't shine.
8 He alone has spread out the heavens
and marches on the waves of the sea.
9 He made all the stars—the Bear and Orion,
the Pleiades and the constellations of the southern sky.
10 He does great things too marvelous to understand.
He performs countless miracles.

11 "Yet when he comes near, I cannot see him.
When he moves by, I do not see him go.

8:7 ***you will end with much:*** Bildad's words were more true than he realized (42:12; cp. 5:19-26).

8:8-10 Bildad made the case for traditional wisdom by appealing to ancient tradition and history (Deut 4:32; Jer 18:13).

8:9 ***born but yesterday and know nothing:*** Bildad suggested that Job's generation was either born too late to be acquainted with ancient wisdom or was too young to have accumulated it.

8:11 ***Papyrus reeds grow*** as high as ten to fifteen feet.

8:12-13 To ***forget God*** does not mean to have a lapse of memory but to act as if God did not exist (see Ps 10:4; 14:1; Zeph 1:12) or cannot see (see 22:13-17; Ps 94:7).

8:16-17 In this parable, a ***plant*** with ***roots*** that ***grow down through a pile of stones*** gains stability by becoming entwined with the rocks.

9:1-35 Job responded to Bildad by describing God's cosmic and judicial power. His speech sounds like a complicated legal case, with a summons and response (9:3b, 14-16, 19b, 32), the possibility of self-incrimination (9:20), an arbiter (9:33-34), an accusatory question (9:12b), a legal sentence (9:22), and a declaration of guilt (9:28b-30).

9:3 ***If someone wanted to take God to court:*** Or *If God wanted to take someone to court.* Job later expressed the wish to meet God in court (13:3, 15, 23; 23:4).

9:5-6 When God ***moves the mountains*** and when the ***foundations*** of the earth ***tremble***, it is a sign of his presence as lawgiver (Exod 19:18), judge (Jer 4:24), or rescuer (Ps 18:7; Isa 13:13; 29:6).

9:9 The ***Bear*** (also at 38:32) is commonly identified as Arcturus but might also refer to the constellations of Ursa Minor or Leo. • The ***Pleiades*** is a group of seven stars (38:31; Amos 5:8).

12 If he snatches someone in death, who
can stop him?
Who dares to ask, 'What are you
doing?'
13 And God does not restrain his anger.
Even the monsters of the [a]sea are
crushed beneath his feet.

14 "So who am I, that I should try to answer
God
or even reason with him?
15 Even if I were right, I would have no
defense.
I could only plead for mercy.
16 And even if I summoned him and he
responded,
I'm not sure he would listen to me.
17 For he attacks me with a storm
and repeatedly wounds me without
cause.
18 He will not let me catch my breath,
but fills me instead with bitter sorrows.
19 If it's a question of strength, he's the
strong one.
If it's a matter of justice, who dares to
summon him to court?
20 Though I am innocent, my own mouth
would pronounce me guilty.
Though I am blameless, it would prove
me wicked.

21 "I am innocent,
but it makes no difference to me—
I despise my life.
22 Innocent or wicked, it is all the same to
God.
That's why I say, 'He destroys both the
blameless and the wicked.'
23 When a plague sweeps through,
he laughs at the death of the innocent.
24 The whole earth is in the hands of the
wicked,
and God blinds the eyes of the judges.
If he's not the one who does it, who is?

25 "My life passes more swiftly than a
runner.
It flees away without a glimpse of
happiness.
26 It disappears like a swift papyrus boat,
like an eagle swooping down on its
prey.
27 If I decided to forget my complaints,
to put away my sad face and be
cheerful,
28 I would still dread all the pain,
for I know you will not find me
innocent, O God.
29 Whatever happens, I will be found
guilty.
So what's the use of trying?
30 Even if I were to wash myself with soap
and clean my hands with lye,
31 you would plunge me into a muddy ditch,
and my own filthy clothing would
hate me.

32 "God is not a mortal like me,
so I cannot argue with him or take
him to trial.
33 If only there were a mediator
between us,
someone who could bring us together.
34 The mediator could make God stop
beating me,
and I would no longer live in terror of
his punishment.
35 Then I could speak to him without fear,
but I cannot do that in my own
strength.

Job Pleads with God

10 1 "I am disgusted with my life.
Let me complain freely.
My bitter soul must complain.
2 I will say to God, 'Don't simply condemn
me—
tell me the charge you are bringing
against me.
3 What do you gain by oppressing me?
Why do you reject me, the work of
your own hands,
while smiling on the schemes of the
wicked?
4 Are your eyes like those of a human?
Do you see things only as people see
them?

9:12 Job 10:7; 11:10; Isa 45:9
9:13 Job 26:12; Ps 89:10; [a]*rahab* (7293) ›Job 26:12
9:15 Job 8:5; 10:15
9:17 Job 16:12, 14
9:18 Job 27:2
9:20 Job 9:15, 29
9:21 Job 1:1; 7:16
9:22 Eccl 9:2-3
9:24 Job 12:6, 17; 16:11
9:25 Job 7:6-7
9:26 Hab 1:8
9:28 Job 3:25; 7:21; 10:14
9:29 Ps 37:33
9:30 Job 31:7; Jer 2:22
9:32 1 Sam 2:25; Rom 9:20
9:33 1 Sam 2:25
9:34 Ps 39:10
10:1 1 Kgs 19:4; Job 7:11, 16
10:2 Job 9:29
10:3 Job 9:22-24; 10:8; 19:6; 21:16; 22:18
10:4 1 Sam 16:7; Job 9:12; 36:26

9:13 *monsters of the sea* (literally *the helpers of Rahab*): Job personified demonic powers as creatures like this mythical sea monster that represents chaos in ancient literature (26:12; Ps 89:11; Isa 51:9).

9:17 *with a storm:* Perhaps the words translated "with a storm" (*bis'arah)* is a double entendre with *besa'arah* ("for a hair"; i.e., "for the littlest thing"), which would parallel *without cause* (Hebrew *khinnam;* see notes on 1:9-11; 2:3).

9:18 *catch my breath:* See note on 7:19.

9:20 *it:* Or *he.*

9:21 Job was indeed *innocent* (1:1, 7; 2:3), and he maintained this claim throughout the debate (23:11-12; 27:5; 31:1-40).

9:23 *plague:* Or *disaster.*

9:28 The word *you* makes it clear that this is a prayer, although the phrase *O God* is not explicit in the Hebrew.

9:30 *wash myself:* Job spoke of cleansing himself with the strongest *soap* to represent ridding himself of all sin (1:5; cp. Ps 26:6; Matt 27:24).

9:31 The *muddy ditch* (literally *pit*) can refer to the place of the dead (17:14; 33:18), so it might allude to the defilement of death. • The *filthy clothing* of guilt contrasts with the clean clothes of acquittal (Zech 3:3-5; see Isa 61:10; 64:6; Rev 19:8).

9:32-33 A *mediator* would not judge God and man but would work to *bring* them *together* (see 16:19-21).

10:8 Job 9:22; Ps 119:73
10:9 Job 4:19; 7:21; 33:6
10:12 Job 33:4
10:13 Job 23:13
10:14 Job 9:28
10:15 Job 6:29; Isa 3:11
10:16 Job 5:9
10:17 Job 16:8
10:18 Job 3:11-13
10:20 Job 7:19; 14:1
10:21 Ps 23:4; 88:12

5 Is your lifetime only as long as ours?
Is your life so short
6 that you must quickly probe for my guilt
and search for my sin?
7 Although you know I am not guilty,
no one can rescue me from your hands.
8 " 'You formed me with your hands; you made me,
yet now you completely destroy me.
9 Remember that you made me from dust—
will you turn me back to dust so soon?
10 You guided my conception
and formed me in the womb.
11 You clothed me with skin and flesh,
and you knit my bones and sinews together.
12 You gave me life and showed me your unfailing love.
My life was preserved by your care.
13 " 'Yet your real motive—
your true intent—
14 was to watch me, and if I sinned,
you would not forgive my guilt.
15 If I am guilty, too bad for me;
and even if I'm innocent, I can't hold my head high,
because I am filled with shame and misery.
16 And if I hold my head high, you hunt me like a lion
and display your awesome power against me.
17 Again and again you witness against me.
You pour out your growing anger on me
and bring fresh armies against me.
18 " 'Why, then, did you deliver me from my mother's womb?
Why didn't you let me die at birth?
19 It would be as though I had never existed,
going directly from the womb to the grave.
20 I have only a few days left, so leave me alone,
that I may have a moment of comfort
21 before I leave—never to return—
for the land of darkness and utter gloom.
22 It is a land as dark as midnight,
a land of gloom and confusion,
where even the light is dark as midnight.' "

The Righteous Suffer (9:33-35)

Job 14:13; 19:25-27; Gen 4:4-8; 26:17-33; 31:38-42; 37:2-36; 39:1-20; Exod 1:8-11; 1 Sam 18:10-11, 28-29; 19:10; 22:1-19; 1 Kgs 21:1-15; 2 Chr 24:20-22; Isa 54:17; Jer 11:18-21; 26:1-23; 38:1-13; Matt 23:29-37; John 5:24; 15:20; Acts 6:8–7:60; Rom 8:17-18, 26-39; Heb 12:1-13; 1 Pet 4:12-16

The book of Job invites us to examine the basis of our faith in God. Job's loss of possessions and family members and the alienation of his friends shook his faith to its foundation. However, he kept his faith by trusting in God, and he gave the lie to Satan's accusations.

Even in his complaints, Job acknowledged that only God could provide the answers he needed. When Job wished for death, it was to gain relief until God could deal with him under more favorable conditions (14:13). When Job desired a mediator (9:33-35), it was to facilitate finding favor with God. When Job complained that God didn't listen, it was because he knew that his answers had to come from God (19:25-27). That is the very essence of faith.

Sin does bring suffering, but Satan's accusation that suffering people must have sinned is not necessarily true (Isa 54:17; Rom 8:1). Some today blindly follow Job's friends in equating godliness with blessing. But at its root, this equation expresses unbelief because it refuses to realize that "what we suffer now is nothing compared to the glory he will reveal to us later" (Rom 8:18). As the apostle Paul reminds us, "We must also share his suffering" (Rom 8:17).

We are not meant to know or understand everything (see Gen 2:17; Deut 29:29; Acts 1:7; 1 Thes 5:1-2). Some things are for God alone to comprehend and direct according to his sovereign will. Our response should be to accept in faith what he sends us. Even when we suffer, we can trust God (see Rom 8:26-39).

10:8-11 A succession of images describes God's role in creating Job. • ***You formed me with your hands . . . made me from dust:*** This was how a potter made a vessel (Isa 45:9; Jer 18:1-12). Although the potter has incontestable sovereignty over his clay (Isa 45:9; Jer 18:5-12; Rom 9:20-25), Job was questioning God. • ***back to dust:*** This common motif in Job represents the temporary nature of life (4:19; 7:9-10, 21; 14:1-2, 10; see Gen 3:19). • ***You guided my conception and formed me in the womb:*** The Hebrew terminology (literally *You poured me out like milk and curdled me like cheese*) evokes graphic images of a newborn baby still covered with the creamy substance called vernix.

10:20-22 Earlier, Job had painted a fairly pleasant picture of Sheol (3:13-19); now he describes it as a ***land of darkness and utter gloom*** (see also 7:9-10; 14:7-22).

Zophar Responds to Job

11 Then Zophar the Naamathite replied to Job:

2 "Shouldn't someone answer this torrent of words?
Is a person proved innocent just by a lot of talking?
3 Should I remain silent while you babble on?
When you mock God, shouldn't someone make you ashamed?
4 You claim, 'My beliefs are pure,'
and 'I am clean in the sight of God.'
5 If only God would speak;
if only he would tell you what he thinks!
6 If only he would tell you the secrets of wisdom,
for true wisdom is not a simple matter.
Listen! God is doubtless punishing you far less than you deserve!

7 "Can you solve the mysteries of God?
Can you discover everything about the Almighty?
8 Such knowledge is higher than the [b]heavens—
and who are you?
It is deeper than the underworld—
what do you know?
9 It is broader than the earth
and wider than the sea.
10 If God comes and puts a person in prison
or calls the court to order, who can stop him?
11 For he knows those who are false,
and he takes note of all their sins.
12 An empty-headed person won't become wise
any more than a wild donkey can bear a human child.

13 "If only you would prepare your heart
and lift up your hands to him in prayer!
14 Get rid of your sins,
and leave all iniquity behind you.
15 Then your face will brighten with innocence.
You will be strong and free of fear.
16 You will forget your misery;
it will be like water flowing away.
17 Your life will be brighter than the noonday.
Even darkness will be as bright as morning.
18 Having hope will give you courage.
You will be protected and will rest in safety.
19 You will lie down unafraid,
and many will look to you for help.
20 But the wicked will be blinded.
They will have no escape.
Their only hope is death."

Job Responds to Zophar

12 Then Job spoke again:
2 "You people really know everything, don't you?
And when you die, wisdom will die with you!
3 Well, I know a few things myself—
and you're no better than I am.
Who doesn't know these things you've been saying?
4 Yet my friends laugh at me,
for I call on God and expect an answer.
I am a just and [c]blameless man,
yet they laugh at me.
5 People who are at ease mock those in trouble.
They give a push to people who are stumbling.
6 But robbers are left in peace,
and those who provoke God live in safety—
though God keeps them in his power.
7 "Just ask the animals, and they will teach you.
Ask the birds of the sky, and they will tell you.

11:2 Job 8:2; 15:2
11:3 Job 17:2; 21:3
11:4 Job 6:10; 10:7
11:6 Job 22:5
11:7 Job 33:12-13; 36:26; 37:5
11:8 Job 22:12; 38:17
[b]*shamayim* (8064) ‣Job 26:11
11:10 Job 9:12
11:11 Job 34:21-25
11:12 Ps 62:9
11:13 Ps 78:8; 88:9
11:14 Job 22:23
11:15 Ps 27:3; 46:2
11:16 Job 22:11; Isa 65:16
11:17 Ps 37:6
11:19 Lev 26:6; Zeph 3:13
11:20 Deut 28:65; Job 6:9; 34:22
12:2 Job 17:10
12:3 Job 13:2
12:4 Job 6:29; 17:6; 30:1, 9-10
[c]*tamim* (8549) ‣Ps 15:2
12:6 Job 9:24; 21:7-9

11:1 *Zophar the Naamathite* (see note on 2:11), the most severe of Job's three friends, dealt only with the issue of sin.

11:2-3 *this torrent of words:* Verbosity is characteristic of fools (Prov 10:8, 14) and sinners (Prov 10:19), but Job was innocent. • *mock God:* Zophar viewed Job's words about God's justice as sinfully sarcastic (10:2-7, 13-15).

11:4 *My beliefs are pure:* Job was not defining doctrine but defending his own integrity.

11:5-6 *punishing you . . . less than you deserve:* Zophar believed that calamity indicated divine retribution for sins (cp. 34:36).

11:7 No one can *discover everything about the Almighty* (literally *find out the limits of the Almighty*), who is beyond the limits of the heavens, underworld, land, and sea (11:8-9).

11:8 *than the underworld:* Hebrew *than Sheol.* See note on 7:9.

11:12 *any more than a wild donkey can bear a human child:* Or *any more than a wild male donkey can bear a tame colt.* The Hebrew can be translated either way.

11:13-14 Zophar laid out three conditions for restoration (11:15): (1) *prepare your heart,* in an inward act that is not just a ritual; (2) *lift up your hands,* a symbolic gesture of prayer, appeal (Exod 9:29; Prov 1:24; Isa 1:15), or surrender; (3) *leave all iniquity,* not by sacrifice and remorse, but by quitting the sin (cp. Heb 11:6; Jas 4:8; 5:16).

12:1–14:22 In his longest speech thus far, Job addresses not only Zophar's remarks but the entire first round of speeches.

12:7-9 A switch from *you* (plural in 12:2-3) to *you* (singular here) probably indicates that Job is directing his comments to Zophar.

12:9 Isa 41:20
12:10 Job 33:4; 34:3
12:12 Job 32:7
12:13 Job 9:4; 11:6
12:14 Job 19:10; Isa 25:2
12:15 Gen 7:11-24; Deut 11:17; 1 Kgs 8:35
12:16 Job 13:7, 9; 37:7
12:17 Job 3:14
12:18 Ps 116:16
12:19 Job 34:24-28
12:20 Job 32:9
12:21 Job 12:18; 34:19; Ps 107:40
12:22 Dan 2:22; 1 Cor 4:5

8 Speak to the earth, and it will instruct you.
Let the fish in the sea speak to you.
9 For they all know
that my disaster has come from the hand of the LORD.
10 For the life of every living thing is in his hand,
and the breath of every human being.
11 The ear tests the words it hears
just as the mouth distinguishes between foods.
12 Wisdom belongs to the aged,
and understanding to the old.

13 "But true wisdom and power are found in God;
counsel and understanding are his.
14 What he destroys cannot be rebuilt.
When he puts someone in prison, there is no escape.
15 If he holds back the rain, the earth becomes a desert.
If he releases the waters, they flood the earth.
16 Yes, strength and wisdom are his;
deceivers and deceived are both in his power.
17 He leads counselors away, stripped of good judgment;
wise judges become fools.
18 He removes the royal robe of kings.
They are led away with ropes around their waist.
19 He leads priests away, stripped of status;
he overthrows those with long years in power.
20 He silences the trusted adviser
and removes the insight of the elders.
21 He pours disgrace upon princes
and disarms the strong.

22 "He uncovers mysteries hidden in darkness;
he brings light to the deepest gloom.

Counselors (12:17)

Job 2:9-10; 4:8; 16:2; 2 Sam 17:1-23; 1 Kgs 12:3-17; 22:15-28; Prov 1:5; 9:9; 11:14; 12:15; 15:2-4, 22-23; 19:20; 20:18; 24:6; 25:11; 27:9; Isa 9:6; 28:29; 50:4; Luke 19:12-27; Rom 8:14; Eph 4:29; Col 2:3

The book of Proverbs teaches that many counselors are good because they provide safety (Prov 11:14; 24:6) and improve our odds of success (Prov 15:22). The book of Job shows that counselors can also mislead, even when their theology is orthodox (12:17; see 26:3; 38:2; 42:3).

Job's comforters repeatedly elaborated on the biblical principle of sowing and reaping, which was deeply embedded in the covenant (Lev 26; Deut 28; Prov 1:31; 22:8; Hos 8:7; Gal 6:7-8). We can't simply reject their words because much of what they said is correct teaching about God's nature and his ways of working with human beings. However, Job's friends misapplied this principle (see 4:8). They didn't look at Job's life, point out where he had sown evil, and then threaten divine judgment. Instead, they ignored Job's faithful pattern of life, focused on his torment, and concluded that he was reaping the effects of sin. God eventually called these counselors liars, reminding us that even the most orthodox theology must be rightly applied in order to please God and build up others (Prov 15:2-4, 23; 25:11; Isa 50:4; Eph 4:29).

While it is good to weigh advice from various sources, we must compare the counsel of others with what we believe to be right before God (see, e.g., Acts 20:22; 21:4, 11, 13). God might use human counselors to help us define his will, but God himself guides us. Jesus Christ is our "Wonderful Counselor" (Isa 9:6; see Isa 28:29), who embodies "all the treasures of wisdom and knowledge" (Col 2:3). We must be led by God's Spirit (Rom 8:14).

12:7-8 ***ask the animals . . . birds . . . earth . . . fish:*** Job believed that the reason for his misery was obvious and that even nature would understand it (Prov 6:6). Later, God directed Job's attention to the animal kingdom to convince Job that he did not understand (chs 38–40).

12:9 ***that my disaster:*** Literally *that this.* • ***from the hand of the LORD:*** This is the only place in the dialogues (chs 3–27; 29–37) that the Hebrew *Yahweh* ("the LORD") is used. For Job, the dispute was not about who caused his misery but why it happened.

12:11 ***the mouth distinguishes between foods:*** See 6:6-7.

12:12 ***Wisdom belongs to the aged:*** Job's friends defended this opinion (8:8-10; 15:10; 32:6-9), but Job questioned it (12:20).

12:17 ***stripped of good judgment:*** The NLT adds "of good judgment" for clarity. In this image, God metaphorically strips leaders of their abilities. It could also refer to being stripped of the symbols of office or to becoming naked captives (12:18-19).

12:18 When God ***removes the royal robe of kings,*** he takes away the symbols of their authority (cp. 19:9). It could also be translated as "God loosens the bonds of kings," referring to the bondage they have imposed on others.

12:19 The ***priests*** are figuratively ***stripped of status*** (the NLT adds "of status" for clarity) or are actually stripped of priestly robes; they might even be naked captives (12:18).

12:21 ***pours disgrace upon princes:*** Cp. Ps. 107:40. • ***disarms*** (literally *looses the belt of*): The ***strong*** are no longer girded for battle.

12:22 ***uncovers mysteries*** (literally *uncovers the deeps*): This phrase might allude to Zophar's words that God's knowledge is "deeper than the underworld" (11:8). • ***darkness . . . deepest gloom:*** The OT often describes God as dwelling in darkness (1 Kgs 8:12; 2 Chr 6:1) and as manifesting himself through darkness (2 Sam 22:10, 12; Ps 18:9, 11), as when he gave the law at Sinai (Deut 4:11; 5:22-23) or when he comes in judgment (Zeph 1:15).

23 He builds up nations, and he destroys
them.
He expands nations, and he abandons
them.
24 He strips kings of understanding
and leaves them wandering in a
pathless wasteland.
25 They grope in the darkness without a
light.
He makes them stagger like
drunkards.

Job Wants to Argue His Case

13 1 "Look, I have seen all this with my
own eyes
and heard it with my own ears, and
now I understand.
2 I know as much as you do.
You are no better than I am.
3 As for me, I would speak directly to the
Almighty.
I want to argue my case with God
himself.
4 As for you, you smear me with lies.
As physicians, you are worthless
quacks.
5 If only you could be silent!
That's the wisest thing you could do.
6 Listen to my charge;
pay attention to my arguments.
7 "Are you defending God with lies?
Do you make your dishonest
arguments for his sake?
8 Will you slant your testimony in his
favor?
Will you argue God's case for him?
9 What will happen when he finds out
what you are doing?
Can you fool him as easily as you fool
people?
10 No, you will be in trouble with him
if you secretly slant your testimony in
his favor.
11 Doesn't his majesty terrify you?
Doesn't your fear of him overwhelm
you?
12 Your platitudes are as [d]valuable as ashes.
Your defense is as fragile as a clay pot.
13 "Be silent now and leave me alone.
Let me speak, and I will face the
consequences.
14 Yes, I will take my life in my hands
and say what I really think.
15 God might kill me, but I have no other
[e]hope.
I am going to argue my case with him.
16 But this is what will save me—I am not
godless.
If I were, I could not stand before him.
17 "Listen closely to what I am about to say.
Hear me out.
18 I have prepared my case;
I will be proved innocent.
19 Who can argue with me over this?
And if you prove me wrong, I will
remain silent and die.

Job Asks How He Has Sinned

20 "O God, grant me these two things,
and then I will be able to face you.
21 Remove your heavy hand from me,
and don't terrify me with your
awesome presence.
22 Now summon me, and I will answer!
Or let me speak to you, and you reply.
23 Tell me, what have I done wrong?
Show me my rebellion and my sin.
24 Why do you turn away from me?
Why do you treat me as your enemy?
25 Would you terrify a leaf blown by the
wind?
Would you chase dry straw?
26 "You write bitter accusations against me
and bring up all the sins of my youth.
27 You put my feet in stocks.
You examine all my paths.
You trace all my footprints.

12:23 Isa 9:3
12:24 Job 12:20
13:2 Job 12:3
13:3 Job 13:22; 23:4
13:4 Ps 119:69; Jer 23:32
13:5 Prov 17:28
13:7 Job 27:4
13:10 Job 32:21
13:11 Job 31:23
13:12 Job 15:3; [d]*mashal* (4912) ‣Ps 78:2
13:13 Job 13:5
13:15 Job 7:6; 27:5; 34:21-23; [e]*yakhal* (3176) ‣Ps 33:18
13:18 Job 9:21; 23:4
13:19 Job 7:21; Isa 50:8
13:21 Job 9:34; Ps 39:10
13:22 Job 14:15
13:24 Job 19:11; 33:10; Ps 13:1
13:25 Lev 26:36
13:26 Job 9:18; Ps 25:7
13:27 Job 33:11

12:23-24 Cp. Dan 2:21. • ***strips kings of understanding:*** See 12:18; cp. Dan 4:23, 32-33. • ***He . . . leaves them wandering in a pathless wasteland*** like the princes in Ps 107:40 (see 12:21).

12:25 Perhaps foolish counsel made the kings ***stagger like drunkards*** (12:17; see Isa 19:14); it resulted from "drinking" God's wrath (Ps 75:8; Jer 25:15-27).

13:1-2 Job appealed to experience, as his comforters had done (3:12-17; 5:2).

13:7-10 ***defending God with lies:*** False witnesses were forbidden even if speaking on God's behalf (Exod 20:16).

13:12 *Ashes* are worthless (cp. Isa 44:20).

13:15 ***but I have no other hope:*** An alternate reading in the Masoretic Text reads *but I hope in him.*

13:20-21 Job had contemplated finding an arbiter to ***remove*** God's ***heavy hand*** (9:33-34). Eliphaz had urged Job to accept God's chastening (5:17).

13:22-23 Job wanted God to ***summon*** him, and then Job would ***answer*** in his own defense; or Job would ***speak to*** God, and then God would ***reply*** to substantiate the charges against Job. Since God did not take the first option, Job initiated the second one (13:23). Eventually, God did summon Job (38:1-3; 40:1-2), and Job was unable to reply (40:3-5).

13:24 ***Why?*** See note on 3:11-24. • God can ***turn away*** in wrath (Deut 31:18; Isa 54:8; Jer 33:5) or refuse to show friendship (Ps 30:7; 69:17; 102:2). • Job, perhaps playing on his own name (*'iyyob*), denied that he was God's ***enemy*** (*'oyeb*).

13:25 In the OT, ***dry straw*** is a common image for what can be blown away ("chaff," Ps 83:13; Isa 40:24; Jer 13:24) or burned (Exod 15:7; Isa 47:14; Mal 4:1; see also "dry grass," Isa 5:24; 33:11), or for what is weak (41:20-21) and trifling (Isa 41:2).

13:27 See notes on 7:17-20; 14:3.

14:1
Job 5:7
Eccl 2:23
14:2
Job 8:9
14:3
Ps 143:2; 144:3
14:4
Job 15:14; 25:4
14:5
Job 21:21
14:10
Job 13:19
14:11
Isa 19:5
14:13
Isa 26:20
14:16
Job 10:6; 31:4; 34:21
Prov 5:21
14:17
Deut 32:32-34
14:18
ᶠ*tsur* (6697)
‣Ps 18:46
14:19
Job 7:6
14:20
Job 20:7; 34:20
14:21
Eccl 9:5
15:2
Job 6:26

28 I waste away like rotting wood,
like a moth-eaten coat.

14 1 "How frail is humanity!
How short is life, how full of trouble!
2 We blossom like a flower and then wither.
Like a passing shadow, we quickly disappear.
3 Must you keep an eye on such a frail creature
and demand an accounting from me?
4 Who can bring purity out of an impure person?
No one!
5 You have decided the length of our lives.
You know how many months we will live,
and we are not given a minute longer.
6 So leave us alone and let us rest!
We are like hired hands, so let us finish our work in peace.

7 "Even a tree has more hope!
If it is cut down, it will sprout again
and grow new branches.
8 Though its roots have grown old in the earth
and its stump decays,
9 at the scent of water it will bud
and sprout again like a new seedling.

10 "But when people die, their strength is gone.
They breathe their last, and then where are they?
11 As water evaporates from a lake
and a river disappears in drought,
12 people are laid to rest and do not rise again.
Until the heavens are no more, they will not wake up
nor be roused from their sleep.

13 "I wish you would hide me in the grave
and forget me there until your anger has passed.
But mark your calendar to think of me again!
14 Can the dead live again?
If so, this would give me hope through all my years of struggle,
and I would eagerly await the release of death.
15 You would call and I would answer,
and you would yearn for me, your handiwork.
16 For then you would guard my steps,
instead of watching for my sins.
17 My sins would be sealed in a pouch,
and you would cover my guilt.

18 "But instead, as mountains fall and crumble
and as ᶠrocks fall from a cliff,
19 as water wears away the stones
and floods wash away the soil,
so you destroy people's hope.
20 You always overpower them, and they pass from the scene.
You disfigure them in death and send them away.
21 They never know if their children grow up in honor
or sink to insignificance.
22 They suffer painfully;
their life is full of trouble."

Second Round of Speeches (15:1–21:34)
Eliphaz Responds to Job

15 Then Eliphaz the Temanite replied:
2 "A wise man wouldn't answer with such empty talk!
You are nothing but a windbag.
3 The wise don't engage in empty chatter.
What good are such words?
4 Have you no fear of God,
no reverence for him?

14:1-2 The *flower* is an image of life's brevity (Ps 90:5-6; 103:15-16; Isa 40:6-7). • A *shadow* passes swiftly (1 Chr 29:15; Ps 102:11).

14:3 ***keep an eye on:*** Job lamented God's relentless surveillance (7:8, 17-20; 10:6, 14; 13:27).

14:12 ***do not rise again:*** Job himself did not have even the minimal evidence of resurrection found in the OT (2 Kgs 13:21; Isa 26:19; Dan 12:2; cp. Job 19:25). • Job was not focusing on the end of the universe when *the heavens* will be ***no more*** (Ps 102:25-26; Isa 34:4; 51:6; Heb 1:10-12) but on the eternity of the heavens (Ps 148:6; cp. Ps 72:5, 7, 17; 89:29, 37). His phrase refers to the permanency of death.

14:13 Since the grave is a permanent abode (14:10-12, see 3:13-19; 7:6-10; 10:20-22), Job could not even fulfill his request of 13:20-21 by hiding temporarily *in the grave* (Hebrew *in Sheol*).

14:16 ***guard my steps:*** Here, Job refers to God's providential care (10:12) rather than to his surveillance (13:27; 14:3).

14:17 If *sins* are ***sealed in a pouch*** they do not await a time of reckoning (Deut 32:34-35; Hos 13:12)—they are hidden forever. Job was requesting acquittal.

14:22 Job no longer saw Sheol as a haven (3:17-19; 14:13-17). The OT usually depicts the dead as being without feeling (Ps 88:12; Eccl 9:5; cp. Isa 50:11; 66:24); the doctrine that the dead *suffer painfully* is clearer in the NT (Luke 16:23, 28; Rev 14:11).

15:1–21:34 In this second round of speeches, Job's friends focus on the fate of the wicked and imply that Job's condition shows he has sinned.

15:2-3 ***You are nothing but a windbag*** (literally *You fill your belly with the east wind*): Since the east wind was hot, it might represent heated (Exod 14:21; Hos 13:15; Jon 4:8) or violent (27:21; Jer 18:17) speech.

15:4 ***Have you no fear of God?*** See note on 1:1.

5 Your sins are telling your mouth what to say.
Your words are based on clever deception.
6 Your own mouth condemns you, not I.
Your own lips testify against you.

7 "Were you the first person ever born?
Were you born before the hills were made?
8 Were you listening at God's secret council?
Do you have a monopoly on wisdom?
9 What do you know that we don't?
What do you understand that we do not?
10 On our side are aged, gray-haired men
much older than your father!

11 "Is God's comfort too little for you?
Is his gentle word not enough?
12 What has taken away your reason?
What has weakened your vision,
13 that you turn against God
and say all these evil things?
14 Can any mortal be pure?
Can anyone born of a woman be just?
15 Look, God does not even trust the angels.
Even the heavens are not absolutely pure in his sight.
16 How much less pure is a corrupt and sinful person
with a thirst for wickedness!

17 "If you will listen, I will show you.
I will answer you from my own experience.
18 And it is confirmed by the reports of wise men
who have heard the same thing from their fathers—
19 from those to whom the land was given
long before any foreigners arrived.

20 "The wicked writhe in pain throughout their lives.
Years of trouble are stored up for the ruthless.
21 The sound of terror rings in their ears,
and even on good days they fear the attack of the destroyer.
22 They dare not go out into the darkness
for fear they will be murdered.
23 They wander around, saying, 'Where can I find bread?'
They know their day of destruction is near.
24 That dark day terrifies them.
They live in distress and anguish,
like a king preparing for battle.
25 For they shake their fists at God,
defying the Almighty.
26 Holding their strong shields,
they defiantly charge against him.

27 "These wicked people are heavy and prosperous;
their waists bulge with fat.
28 But their cities will be ruined.
They will live in abandoned houses
that are ready to tumble down.
29 Their riches will not last,
and their wealth will not endure.
Their possessions will no longer
spread across the horizon.

15:5 Job 5:12-13
15:6 Job 9:20
15:7 Job 38:4, 21; Prov 8:25
15:8 Rom 11:34
15:9 Job 12:3; 13:2
15:10 Job 12:12
15:11 Job 6:10
15:12 Job 36:13
15:14 Job 14:4; 25:4; Prov 20:9; Eccl 7:20
15:15 Job 4:18; 25:5
15:16 Job 34:7; Ps 14:1, 3
15:18 Job 8:8
15:21 Job 18:11; 20:21, 25
15:22 Job 15:30; 19:29; 27:14
15:25 Job 36:9
15:27 Ps 73:7; 119:70
15:29 Job 27:16-17

15:6 ***Your own mouth condemns you:*** Job feared that this would happen (9:20; see Matt 26:65).

15:7-8 When the Lord himself later issued a similar challenge, Job found it convicting (38:1-11).

15:8 The book's readers know about ***God's secret council*** (1:6-12; 2:1-6; see 1 Kgs 22:19-20; Ps 89:5-7), but Job and his company did not.

15:9-10 ***Aged, gray-haired men*** claim a monopoly on wisdom (8:8-10; 12:20; see 12:2).

15:12 ***What has weakened your vision*** (Or *Why do your eyes flash with anger;* Hebrew reads *Why do your eyes blink*): This sentence might be a metaphor for unbelief, or it could indicate winking like a schemer or blinking in disbelief.

15:14 ***Can any mortal be pure?*** Eliphaz repeated himself (4:17-19) and Job (7:17; 14:4). • ***anyone born of a woman:*** Both "mortal" and "born of woman" imply weakness.

15:15 ***the angels:*** Literally *the holy ones.* • The ***heavens,*** traditionally associated with purity (Exod 24:10), were ***not absolutely pure;*** they had been defiled, perhaps by rebellious angels (1:6-7).

15:17-19 ***before any foreigners arrived:*** Eliphaz's contempt for foreign ideas is ironic because wisdom literature has a more international flavor than is characteristic of other OT writings.

15:20-35 ***The wicked*** also suffer everything that happened to Job (see 1:16-19)—attacks by marauders (15:21), loss of possessions (15:29), crumbled houses (15:28), and fire (15:30, 34).

15:21 Although Eliphaz generalized the ***terror*** that the wicked experience, Job had undergone similar experiences (3:25; 6:4; 9:34; 13:11, 21; 23:15; 27:20; 30:15). Bildad (18:11, 14) and Zophar (20:25) spoke of more terror to come. • The Sabeans and Chaldeans were examples of ***the destroyer*** (1:13-17), but this could refer to any destructive agent (1:18-19). Destroyers might be agents of Satan (1 Cor 10:10; Rev 9:11) or divine agents that punish wickedness (Exod 12:23; 2 Sam 24:16; 2 Chr 32:21; Acts 12:23; Heb 11:28). Eliphaz meant the latter.

15:22 ***for fear they will be murdered*** (literally *he is marked for the sword*): The wicked might be killed by murder or by the sword of God's wrath.

15:23 ***They wander around, saying, "Where can I find bread?":*** The Greek version reads *He is appointed to be food for a vulture.* Like the wicked (15:20), Job either experienced hunger (see 15:27) or (following the Greek OT) had been "appointed to be food for a vulture," which would parallel "marked for the sword" (15:22).

15:25 Job had complained earlier that God was treating him like a formidable foe (7:23; 13:24).

15:30
Job 4:9; 5:14; 22:20
15:31
Isa 59:4
15:32
Job 18:16; 22:16
15:34
Job 8:22
15:35
Ps 7:14
Isa 59:4
16:2
Job 13:4; 21:34
16:3
Job 6:26
16:4
Ps 22:7; 109:25
16:6
Job 9:27-28
16:7
Job 7:3; 16:20; 19:13-15
16:8
Job 10:17; 19:20
16:9
Job 13:24; 33:10
16:10
Job 30:12
16:12
Job 7:20; 9:17
16:13
Job 6:4; 19:12
16:14
Job 9:17
Joel 2:7
16:15
Gen 37:34
Job 30:19
Ps 69:11
Jon 3:8
16:16
Job 16:20; 24:17
16:17
Job 27:4
16:19
Job 19:25-27; 31:2

30 "They will not escape the darkness.
The burning sun will wither their shoots,
and the breath of God will destroy them.
31 Let them no longer fool themselves by trusting in empty riches,
for emptiness will be their only reward.
32 Like trees, they will be cut down in the prime of life;
their branches will never again be green.
33 They will be like a vine whose grapes are harvested too early,
like an olive tree that loses its blossoms before the fruit can form.
34 For the godless are barren.
Their homes, enriched through bribery, will burn.
35 They conceive trouble and give birth to evil.
Their womb produces deceit."

Job Responds to Eliphaz

16 Then Job spoke again:
2 "I have heard all this before.
What miserable comforters you are!
3 Won't you ever stop blowing hot air?
What makes you keep on talking?
4 I could say the same things if you were in my place.
I could spout off criticism and shake my head at you.
5 But if it were me, I would encourage you.
I would try to take away your grief.
6 Instead, I suffer if I defend myself,
and I suffer no less if I refuse to speak.
7 "O God, you have ground me down
and devastated my family.
8 As if to prove I have sinned, you've reduced me to skin and bones.
My gaunt flesh testifies against me.
9 God hates me and angrily tears me apart.
He snaps his teeth at me
and pierces me with his eyes.
10 People jeer and laugh at me.
They slap my cheek in contempt.
A mob gathers against me.
11 God has handed me over to sinners.
He has tossed me into the hands of the wicked.

12 "I was living quietly until he shattered me.
He took me by the neck and broke me in pieces.
Then he set me up as his target,
13 and now his archers surround me.
His arrows pierce me without mercy.
The ground is wet with my blood.
14 Again and again he smashes against me,
charging at me like a warrior.
15 I wear burlap to show my grief.
My pride lies in the dust.
16 My eyes are red with weeping;
dark shadows circle my eyes.
17 Yet I have done no wrong,
and my prayer is pure.

18 "O earth, do not conceal my blood.
Let it cry out on my behalf.
19 Even now my witness is in heaven.
My advocate is there on high.

15:30 ***The burning sun*** (literally *The flame*) might be the scorching sun or a flame of judgment from God (15:34, see Num 16:31-35; Ps 106:17-18; Ezek 20:47). • The ***breath of God*** might be a desert wind or a more direct theophany (a manifestation of God's presence) that caused the burning of 15:34.

15:34 The flame of judgment (15:30) will ***burn*** the unjust gain of the ***godless***.

16:4 Job might have wanted to ***shake*** his ***head*** in mockery or in horror (2 Kgs 19:21; Ps 22:7; 109:25; Isa 37:22; Jer 18:16; Lam 2:15; Matt 27:39).

16:7 Job's ***family*** here means his extended household, including his servants (1:15-19).

16:9-10 ***jeer and laugh at me:*** Job was the subject of mockery (cp. Ps 35:21; Isa 57:4; Lam 2:16; 3:46). • To ***slap*** the ***cheek*** was less an act of violence (Ps 3:7; Mic 5:1) than an insult (1 Kgs 22:24; Isa 50:6; Lam 3:30; Matt 26:67).

16:12 ***took me by the neck:*** This might refer to a wild animal with its prey (see 16:9), but it is more likely a military image that signaled defeat (Gen 49:8; Ps 18:40).

16:13 ***pierce me:*** Literally *pierce my kidneys.* • ***my blood:*** Literally *my gall.* The picture is of wounds to vital organs.

16:14 ***Again and again he smashes against me:*** It is as if Job represented a fortress that needed to be neutralized. • Job saw God as a ***warrior*** (cp. Exod 15:3; Ps 24:8) who did not defend him or offer him salvation (Jer 20:11; Zeph 3:17) but attacked him as though he were dangerous (6:12; see Isa 42:13).

16:15 Since Job insisted on his innocence, his wearing ***burlap*** (literally *I sewed on burlap*) was a sign of mourning, not penitence. Perhaps it was attached to indicate that he would never remove it because he could never be consoled (Gen 37:34-35). • ***My pride lies in the dust*** (literally *I have buried my horn in the dust*): A horn symbolized dignity and power (1 Sam 2:1; Ps 75:4-5; 89:17, 24; 92:10; 112:9; 148:14); cutting it off inflicted degrading humiliation (Ps 75:10; Jer 48:25; Zech 1:12).

16:17 ***done no wrong*** (or *done no violence;* Hebrew *lo'-khamas*): If ***violence*** is the meaning, Job was possibly denying that he was a formidable warrior who should be attacked (16:12-14; see also Isa 59:6; Jon 3:8). • Contrary to Eliphaz's charge (15:4-5) and Bildad's assumption (8:6), Job's prayer was ***pure*** because he was innocent (Gen 20:5; Isa 59:3).

16:18-22 Job expected his suffering to prove fatal (7:7, 21; 10:20-22); he pleaded with God to reveal his innocence even if he died first.

16:18 Job's ***blood*** would ***cry out*** that he had been innocent and that he had suffered undeservedly (cp. Gen 4:10-11; Isa 26:21; Ezek 24:7-8).

16:19-21 ***my witness is in heaven:*** Job wished for a benevolent third party who would ***mediate*** between him and God (see 9:32-35). Job wanted an

20 My friends scorn me,
but I pour out my tears to God.
21 I need someone to mediate between God
and me,
as a person mediates between friends.
22 For soon I must go down that road
from which I will never return.

Job Defends His Innocence

17 1 "My spirit is crushed,
and my life is nearly snuffed out.
The grave is ready to receive me.
2 I am surrounded by mockers.
I watch how bitterly they taunt me.
3 "You must defend my innocence, O God,
since no one else will stand up for me.
4 You have closed their minds to
understanding,
but do not let them triumph.
5 They betray their friends for their own
advantage,
so let their children faint with hunger.
6 "God has made a mockery of me among
the people;
they spit in my face.
7 My eyes are swollen with weeping,
and I am but a shadow of my former
self.
8 The virtuous are horrified when they
see me.
The innocent rise up against the
ungodly.
9 The righteous keep moving forward,
and those with clean hands become
stronger and stronger.

10 "As for all of you, come back with a
better argument,
though I still won't find a wise man
among you.
11 My days are over.
My hopes have disappeared.
My heart's desires are broken.
12 These men say that night is day;
they claim that the darkness is light.
13 What if I go to the grave
and make my bed in darkness?
14 What if I call the grave my father,
and the maggot my mother or my
sister?
15 Where then is my hope?
Can anyone find it?
16 No, my hope will go down with me to the
[g]grave.
We will rest together in the dust!"

Bildad Responds to Job

18 Then Bildad the Shuhite replied:
2 "How long before you stop talking?
Speak sense if you want us to answer!
3 Do you think we are mere animals?
Do you think we are stupid?
4 You may tear out your hair in anger,
but will that destroy the earth?
Will it make the rocks tremble?

5 "Surely the light of the wicked will be
snuffed out.
The sparks of their fire will not glow.
6 The light in their tent will grow dark.
The lamp hanging above them will be
quenched.
7 The confident stride of the wicked will
be shortened.
Their own schemes will be their
downfall.
8 The wicked walk into a net.
They fall into a pit.
9 A trap grabs them by the heel.
A snare holds them tight.

16:22 Job 3:13
17:1 Ps 88:3-4
17:2 Job 12:4; 17:6
17:3 Ps 119:122
17:4 Job 12:20
17:5 Job 11:20
17:6 Job 30:9-10
17:8 Job 22:19
17:9 Job 22:30
17:10 Job 12:2
17:11 Job 7:6
17:13 Job 3:13
17:14 Job 21:26
17:15 Job 7:6
17:16 Job 3:17; 21:33
[g]*she'ol* (7585) ›Job 26:6
18:3 Ps 73:22
18:5 Job 21:17
18:6 Job 12:25
18:8 Job 22:10

advocate from heaven (16:19; cp. Zech 3:1) who would eventually stand on the earth (19:25; cp. 1 Sam 24:15; John 14:16, 26; 15:26; 16:7; 1 Jn 2:1).

17:1 *My spirit is crushed:* This can refer to a properly contrite attitude (Ps 51:17), but more often it connotes an unbearably sad heart (Prov 18:14).

17:2 *surrounded by mockers:* Laments typically describe mockery as the response of the wicked to the distress of the righteous (Ps 22:7; 69:10-12; 89:50-52). In wisdom literature, mockery is directed against the right behavior (Prov 1:22; 9:7).

17:3-5 *defend my innocence, O God* (literally *please keep my pledge with yourself*): A pledge (Hebrew *'erabon*) can be a deposit guaranteeing payment (Gen 38:17-20; Exod 22:26-27; Deut 24:10-14; see Prov 20:16; 27:13), so this might suggest atonement. It might also be another reference to Job's desire for an advocate to plead his case (see note on 16:19-21).

17:6 To *spit in* someone's *face* was even more insulting than a slap (16:10) because spit made the person unclean (Num 12:14).

17:8-9 Some scholars view these verses as being out of place, but perhaps Job was ironically quoting his opponents' words.

17:10-16 Job gave up on his comforters (6:15-21; 13:4-5; 16:2-3; cp. 12:2) and believed he would die a hopeless death.

17:13 *to the grave* (Hebrew *to Sheol*): The realm of the dead was visualized as a house (30:23; Ps 49:11; Eccl 12:5).

17:14 *my father . . . mother . . . sister:* This bitter parody of a family reunion in a graveyard shows how Job envisioned his impending death.

17:16 *the grave* (literally *the bars of Sheol*): Sheol—the abode of the dead—was seen as having a barred gate, allowing no escape.

18:2-3 *How long before you stop talking?* Bildad addressed Job in the plural, perhaps meaning "people like you."

18:5 *The light of the wicked will be snuffed out* could be a metaphor for a life of confused darkness (Prov 4:19); more likely, it indicates an early death (Prov 13:9; 24:20).

18:7 The *stride* that is *shortened* is the opposite of walking and running in the blessed life (Prov 4:12).

18:8-10 A series of hunting devices illustrates the biblical principle of retribution (see note on 34:11).

18:11
Job 15:21; 18:18
18:14
Job 8:22; 15:21
18:16
Job 15:30, 32
Isa 5:24
Hos 9:1-16
Amos 2:9
18:17
Job 24:20
Ps 34:16
Prov 10:7
18:18
Job 5:14; 27:21-23
18:19
Job 27:14-15
Isa 14:22
Jer 22:30
18:20
Jer 50:27
Obad 1:12
19:5
Ps 35:26; 38:16; 55:12-13
19:6
Job 16:11; 18:8-10; 27:2
Ps 66:11
19:7
Job 30:20, 24
Hab 1:2
19:8
Job 3:23; 30:26
Lam 3:7, 9
19:9
Job 12:17, 19
Ps 89:39, 44
Lam 5:16
19:10
Job 7:6; 12:14; 24:20
19:11
Job 13:24; 16:9
19:12
Job 16:13; 30:12
19:13
Job 16:7, 20
Ps 69:8; 88:8, 18
19:14
Job 19:19
19:19
Ps 38:11; 55:12-13

10 A noose lies hidden on the ground.
A rope is stretched across their path.
11 "Terrors surround the wicked
and trouble them at every step.
12 Hunger depletes their strength,
and calamity waits for them to stumble.
13 Disease eats their skin;
death devours their limbs.
14 They are torn from the security of their homes
and are brought down to the king of terrors.
15 The homes of the wicked will burn down;
burning sulfur rains on their houses.
16 Their roots will dry up,
and their branches will wither.
17 All memory of their existence will fade from the earth;
no one will remember their names.
18 They will be thrust from light into darkness,
driven from the world.
19 They will have neither children nor grandchildren,
nor any survivor in the place where they lived.
20 People in the west are appalled at their fate;
people in the east are horrified.
21 They will say, 'This was the home of a wicked person,
the place of one who rejected God.' "

Job Responds to Bildad

19 Then Job spoke again:
2 "How long will you torture me?
How long will you try to crush me with your words?
3 You have already insulted me ten times.
You should be ashamed of treating me so badly.
4 Even if I have sinned,
that is my concern, not yours.
5 You think you're better than I am,
using my humiliation as evidence of my sin.
6 But it is God who has wronged me,
capturing me in his net.
7 "I cry out, 'Help!' but no one answers me.
I protest, but there is no justice.
8 God has blocked my way so I cannot move.
He has plunged my path into darkness.
9 He has stripped me of my honor
and removed the crown from my head.
10 He has demolished me on every side, and I am finished.
He has uprooted my hope like a fallen tree.
11 His fury burns against me;
he counts me as an enemy.
12 His troops advance.
They build up roads to attack me.
They camp all around my tent.
13 "My relatives stay far away,
and my friends have turned against me.
14 My family is gone,
and my close friends have forgotten me.
15 My servants and maids consider me a stranger.
I am like a foreigner to them.
16 When I call my servant, he doesn't come;
I have to plead with him!
17 My breath is repulsive to my wife.
I am rejected by my own family.
18 Even young children despise me.
When I stand to speak, they turn their backs on me.
19 My close friends detest me.
Those I loved have turned against me.

18:11-13 Bildad applies the biblical principle of retribution (18:8-10) to Job, as do Eliphaz (15:21-23) and Zophar (20:25).

18:13 *death devours:* Isaiah later reversed the figure and saw the Lord as swallowing up death (Isa 25:8; see 1 Cor 15:54).

18:15 The image of *burning sulfur* recalls the fate of Sodom and Gomorrah (Gen 19:24) and suggests the fate of all the wicked (Ps 11:6; Rev 19:20; 21:8).

18:17 Being forgotten by those who come later is a familiar curse against the wicked (see 18:19; Ps 34:16; 109:13; Prov 10:7).

18:19 This curse of childlessness (see 18:16; Ps 109:13; Isa 14:21-22) and Bildad's earlier cruelty (8:4) show that he regarded Job's condition as the just reward for his wickedness (1:18-19).

18:20 *in the west . . . in the east:* These phrases might refer to people from times past and times to come or to people from various places.

18:21 Bildad kept implying that Job had *rejected God* (15:4, 13, 25).

19:3 The number *ten* did not represent a specific count but an indefinite large number (e.g., Gen 31:7; Lev 26:26; Num 14:22; Dan 1:20).

19:6 Job was convinced that justice had been delayed (19:7) and that *God* had *wronged* him (19:8-12). Later, Elihu (34:12) and God himself (40:2) disagreed. • *capturing me in his net* (Or *for I am like a city under siege*): Job might have been responding to Bildad's accusation (18:8-10).

19:7 *Help!* (literally *Violence!*): Cp. Jer 20:8; Hab 1:2-3. • *no one answers:* See Ps 22:2; Lam 3:8; Hab 1:2-3.

19:8 *blocked my way:* See 3:23; 13:27; Ps 88:8; Lam 3:7, 9.

19:9 *stripped me of my honor:* See 12:17-19; 29:7-14, 20.

19:17 *my own family:* Job might have been referring to his tribal line, his parents, his own children, or his siblings.

19:19 *Those I loved have turned against me:* See 2:11; also 6:14-15, 21-23, 27; cp. Ps 41:9; 55:12-14, 20.

20 I have been reduced to skin and bones
and have escaped death by the skin of
my teeth.
21 "Have mercy on me, my friends, have
mercy,
for the hand of God has struck me.
22 Must you also persecute me, like God
does?
Haven't you chewed me up enough?
23 "Oh, that my words could be recorded.
Oh, that they could be inscribed on a
monument,
24 carved with an iron chisel and filled
with lead,
engraved forever in the rock.
25 "But as for me, I know that my
[h]Redeemer lives,
and he will stand upon the earth at
last.
26 And after my body has decayed,
yet in my body I will see God!
27 I will see him for myself.
Yes, I will see him with my own eyes.
I am overwhelmed at the thought!
28 "How dare you go on persecuting me,
saying, 'It's his own fault'?
29 You should fear punishment yourselves,
for your attitude deserves
punishment.
Then you will know that there is
indeed a judgment."

Zophar Responds to Job

20 Then Zophar the Naamathite replied:

2 "I must reply
because I am greatly disturbed.
3 I've had to endure your insults,
but now my spirit prompts me to reply.
4 "Don't you realize that from the
beginning of time,
ever since people were first placed on
the earth,
5 the triumph of the wicked has been
short lived
and the [i]joy of the godless has been
only temporary?
6 Though the pride of the godless reaches
to the heavens
and their heads touch the clouds,
7 yet they will vanish forever,
thrown away like their own dung.
Those who knew them will ask,
'Where are they?'
8 They will fade like a dream and not be
found.
They will vanish like a vision in the
night.
9 Those who once saw them will see them
no more.
Their families will never see them
again.
10 Their children will beg from the poor,
for they must give back their stolen
riches.
11 Though they are young,
their bones will lie in the dust.
12 "They enjoyed the sweet taste of
wickedness,
letting it melt under their tongue.
13 They savored it,
holding it long in their mouths.
14 But suddenly the food in their bellies
turns sour,
a poisonous venom in their stomach.

19:20 Job 33:21; Ps 102:5; Lam 4:8
19:21 Job 1:11
19:22 Ps 69:26
19:23 Isa 30:8; Jer 36:2
19:25 Job 16:19; Ps 78:35; Isa 43:14; Jer 50:34; [h]*go'el* (1350) ‣ Ps 19:14
19:26 Matt 5:8; 1 Cor 13:12; 1 Jn 3:2
19:28 Job 19:22
19:29 Job 22:4; Ps 9:7; Eccl 12:14
20:3 Job 19:3
20:5 Job 8:12-13; Ps 37:35-36; [i]*simkhah* (8057) ‣ Ps 16:11
20:6 Isa 14:13-14; Obad 1:3-4
20:7 Job 4:20; 7:10; 8:18; 14:20
20:8 Job 18:18; Ps 73:20; 90:5
20:9 Job 7:8, 10; 8:18
20:10 Job 5:4; 27:16-17
20:11 Job 13:26
20:12 Job 15:16

19:20 ***escaped death by the skin of my teeth:*** This is an idiom for a narrow escape; the Hebrew could also mean that Job was reduced to a skeleton with a toothy skull.

19:21 The *hand of God* had *struck* Job through the permission he gave to Satan (1:11; 2:5).

19:22 *persecute* (literally *pursue*): Job complained that God had tracked him like a hunter (10:16) or a warrior (16:13).

19:23 Job wanted his *words . . . inscribed on a monument,* not in a book; Job desired a permanent record of his claim to innocence in response to Bildad's assertion that he would be forgotten (18:17).

19:25 Job's faith in a *Redeemer* could find fulfillment only in Christ; the same was true of his request for an advocate (9:33) and a witness in heaven (16:19). The term "Redeemer" (Hebrew *go'el*) comes from both criminal and civil law. An individual could redeem or avenge wrongful bloodshed (Num 35:12-18) or redeem lost property, perhaps by buying back a slave or marrying the heir's widow (Lev 25:25, 47-49; 27:11-13; Ruth 3:13). The OT knew the Lord as redeemer (Exod 6:6; Ps 19:14; 103:4; Prov 23:10-11; Isa 43:1 ["ransomed"]; 54:5); NT believers know the Redeemer as the Lord Jesus Christ (Eph 1:7, 14; Heb 9:12; 1 Pet 1:18). Job wanted his Redeemer to declare his innocence (see 1:1 and note).

19:26 ***yet in my body I will see God!*** Or *without my body I will see God.* The meaning of the Hebrew is uncertain. Job had faith that he would be vindicated even if death came first.

19:27 ***I will see him for myself:*** The thought is the same as the psalmist's in "when I awake" (Ps 17:15). For Job, this hope could only be fulfilled in seeing God at the end of time (Matt 5:8; 1 Cor 13:12; 1 Jn 3:2; Rev 1:7) in transformed flesh (1 Cor 15:43-53; Phil 3:21).

19:29 Given the biblical principles against bearing false witness (13:7-11; see Matt 7:1-2; Jas 4:11-12), Job warned his friends that they should fear God's judgment. They did eventually face his judgment, but they also received mercy (42:7-8).

20:1 ***Zophar the Naamathite:*** See note on 2:11.

20:7 ***thrown away like their own dung:*** Cp. 1 Kgs 14:9-11; 2 Kgs 9:36-37; Ps 83:10; Jer 8:1-2.

20:10 Because ***stolen riches*** are ill-gotten, they provide no lasting benefit (20:18-21; Ps 109:10).

20:16 Deut 32:24, 33
20:17 Deut 32:13-14; Job 29:6
20:18 Job 20:10, 15
20:19 Job 24:2-4; 35:9
20:20 Eccl 5:13-15
20:21 Job 15:29
20:22 Job 5:5
20:23 Num 11:18-20, 33; Ps 78:30-31
20:24 Isa 24:18; Amos 5:19
20:25 Job 16:13; 18:11, 14
20:26 Job 15:30; 18:18; Ps 21:9
20:27 Deut 31:28
20:28 Deut 28:31; Job 21:30
20:29 Job 27:13; 31:2-3

15 They will vomit the wealth they
swallowed.
God won't let them keep it down.
16 They will suck the poison of cobras.
The viper will kill them.
17 They will never again enjoy streams of
olive oil
or rivers of milk and honey.
18 They will give back everything they
worked for.
Their wealth will bring them no joy.
19 For they oppressed the poor and left
them destitute.
They foreclosed on their homes.
20 They were always greedy and never
satisfied.
Nothing remains of all the things they
dreamed about.
21 Nothing is left after they finish gorging
themselves.
Therefore, their prosperity will not
endure.

22 "In the midst of plenty, they will run into
trouble
and be overcome by misery.
23 May God give them a bellyful of
trouble.
May God rain down his anger upon
them.
24 When they try to escape an iron weapon,
a bronze-tipped arrow will pierce
them.
25 The arrow is pulled from their back,
and the arrowhead glistens with
blood.
The terrors of death are upon them.
26 Their treasures will be thrown into
deepest darkness.
A wildfire will devour their goods,
consuming all they have left.
27 The heavens will reveal their guilt,
and the earth will testify against them.
28 A flood will sweep away their house.
God's anger will descend on them in
torrents.
29 This is the reward that God gives the
wicked.
It is the inheritance decreed by God."

Job Responds to Zophar

21 Then Job spoke again:
2 "Listen closely to what I am saying.
That's one consolation you can
give me.

The Afterlife (19:25-27)

Job 3:13-22; 7:9; 10:19; 11:8; 14:13-17; 17:13-16; 26:6; 33:18, 22, 30
Gen 49:33
Num 16:33
Deut 18:11; 32:22
1 Sam 2:6; 28:11-15
1 Kgs 17:20-22
2 Kgs 4:32-35
Ps 6:5; 16:10-11; 17:15; 18:4-5; 30:3; 49:15; 86:13; 88:11; 139:8; 141:7
Prov 1:12; 15:11
Isa 14:11; 26:19; 38:18
Ezek 26:20
Matt 22:31-32
Rom 8:23
1 Cor 15:50-58
Phil 3:21

What did Job's original readers believe about life after death? Writers in the OT describe the realm of the dead as a place beneath the earth's surface to which people descend (Ezek 26:20). Sometimes they are swallowed alive (Num 16:31-33; Ps 55:15), but generally they are dragged down by the cords of death (Ps 18:4-5) to be consumed (24:19; Num 16:30; Ps 49:14; 141:7; Isa 5:14; 14:11). In the OT, the afterlife is generally regarded as a gloomy, hopeless place of no return (7:9; Isa 38:18).

In Job, the key images of the realm of the dead are dark and dusty Sheol (11:8; 14:13; 17:13, 16; 24:19; 26:6), a pit fouled with the filth of decomposition (Hebrew *shakhat;* see 9:31; 17:14; 33:18, 22, 24, 28, 30), and the grave (Hebrew *qeber;* see 3:22; 5:26; 10:19; 17:1; 21:32; 27:15).

The OT does give occasional hints of deliverance from the grave (see 1 Sam 2:6; Ps 16:10-11; 30:3; 49:15; 56:13; 73:24-26; 86:13; 139:7-10; Isa 26:19). These intimations give Job the hope that Sheol might relieve him of his troubles (3:13-22; 14:13-17) and that a redeemer might justify him even after death (19:25-26). But only the NT gives the full promise of redemption from death (1 Cor 15:50-58).

20:14-16 ***poisonous venom . . . cobras . . . viper:*** In the end, the wicked are no longer deadly to others (Matt 3:7; Rom 3:13) but only to themselves (Prov 23:29-35).

20:17 The ***streams of olive oil*** and ***rivers of milk and honey*** signify superabundant blessing (Exod 5:19; Deut 27:3; Joel 3:18).

20:20 Like the grave or death (Prov 27:20; 30:15-16), the wicked are ***always greedy and never satisfied*** (Eccl 5:19; Isa 57:20-21; Hab 2:5).

20:24 The wicked cannot escape trouble (cp. Isa 24:17-18; Jer 15:2-3; Amos 5:19; 9:1-2). When they try to escape one threat, they fall victim to another.

20:25 ***terrors of death:*** Although the words "of death" are not in the Hebrew, they are implied because ***the arrowhead glistens with blood*** (literally *with gall*), indicating a deadly hit on a vital organ (6:4; 16:13; Ps 7:12).

20:26 Images such as ***deepest darkness*** and ***wildfire*** are often associated with God's presence (Deut 4:11; 5:22-23; Heb 12:18) and especially with his judgment (Exod 9:23-24; 10:21-29).

20:27 ***heavens . . . will testify:*** Cp. Deut 4:26; 30:19; 31:28.

21:2 Job's friends insisted that they were delivering God's own message of comfort (15:11), but Job found no comfort in their words (16:2), so he asked for the ***consolation*** of their attentive silence (see 13:5).

3 Bear with me, and let me speak.
After I have spoken, you may resume mocking me.
4 "My complaint is with God, not with people.
I have good reason to be so impatient.
5 Look at me and be stunned.
Put your hand over your mouth in shock.
6 When I think about what I am saying, I shudder.
My body trembles.
7 "Why do the wicked prosper,
growing old and powerful?
8 They live to see their children grow up and settle down,
and they enjoy their grandchildren.
9 Their homes are safe from every fear,
and God does not punish them.
10 Their bulls never fail to breed.
Their cows bear calves and never miscarry.
11 They let their children frisk about like lambs.
Their little ones skip and dance.
12 They sing with tambourine and harp.
They celebrate to the sound of the flute.
13 They spend their days in prosperity,
then go down to the grave in peace.
14 And yet they say to God, 'Go away.
We want no part of you and your ways.
15 Who is the Almighty, and why should we obey him?
What good will it do us to pray?'
16 (They think their prosperity is of their own doing,
but I will have nothing to do with that kind of thinking.)
17 "Yet the light of the wicked never seems to be extinguished.
Do they ever have trouble?
Does God distribute sorrows to them in anger?
18 Are they driven before the wind like straw?
Are they carried away by the storm like chaff?
Not at all!
19 " 'Well,' you say, 'at least God will punish their children!'
But I say he should punish the ones who sin,
so that they understand his judgment.
20 Let them see their destruction with their own eyes.
Let them drink deeply of the anger of the Almighty.
21 For they will not care what happens to their family
after they are dead.
22 "But who can teach a lesson to God,
since he judges even the most powerful?
23 One person dies in prosperity,
completely comfortable and secure,
24 the picture of good health,
vigorous and fit.
25 Another person dies in bitter poverty,
never having tasted the good life.
26 But both are buried in the same dust,
both eaten by the same maggots.
27 "Look, I know what you're thinking.
I know the schemes you plot against me.
28 You will tell me of rich and wicked people
whose houses have vanished because of their sins.
29 But ask those who have been around,
and they will tell you the truth.
30 Evil people are spared in times of calamity
and are allowed to escape disaster.

21:4 Job 6:11; 7:11
21:5 Job 29:9; 40:4
21:6 Ps 55:5
21:7 Ps 73:3; Jer 12:1
21:8 Ps 17:14
21:9 Job 12:6; Ps 73:5
21:13 Job 36:11
21:14 Job 22:17
21:15 Job 22:17; 34:9
21:17 Job 18:5-6
21:18 Job 13:25; Ps 1:4; 35:5; 83:13; Isa 17:13
21:19 Exod 20:5; Ezek 18:4
21:20 Isa 51:17; Jer 25:15; Rev 14:10
21:22 Job 36:22; Ps 82:1; Isa 40:13-14; Rom 11:34
21:26 Job 3:13; 20:11; 24:20
21:28 Job 1:3
21:30 Job 20:29; Prov 16:4; Rom 2:5; 2 Pet 2:9

21:6 ***When I think about what I am saying:*** Job was dismayed by his horrible task of complaining against God (13:3, 15-16, 22; 23:1-5) and discussing his terrors (6:4; 27:20; 30:15). • ***My body trembles:*** This reaction resembles that of Habakkuk (Hab 1:5; 3:16), Ezekiel (Ezek 3:14), and Daniel (Dan 8:27; 10:8-9).

21:8 In spite of assertions by Eliphaz (5:4), Bildad (18:19), and Zophar (20:10), Job noted that the wicked enjoy ***children*** and ***grandchildren***, which should be the reward of the righteous (Prov 17:6) but was apparently not going to be his own reward (1:18-19; but see 42:13-16).

21:13 ***to the grave:*** Hebrew *to Sheol.* See note on 7:9.

21:17 ***light of the wicked never seems to be extinguished:*** Job countered Bildad (18:5-6, 18) and standard wisdom (Prov 13:9; 20:20; 24:20; see God's remarks, Job 38:15).

21:19 ***you say:*** Job was quoting and rebutting his friends' arguments. • ***God will punish their children:*** These were the words of Eliphaz (5:4) and Zophar (20:10), but Job thought God ***should punish the ones who sin*** (see Ezek 18:19-20).

21:22 The rhetorical answer is that no one ***can teach a lesson to God*** (Isa 40:13-14; 45:9; Rom 11:34; 1 Cor 2:16). • The ***most powerful*** might refer to angels or demons (1 Cor 6:3; 2 Pet 2:4; Jude 1:6; Rev 20:1-3) or, more likely, to the powerful on earth (34:17-19).

21:24 ***vigorous and fit*** (literally *the marrow of his bones [is] moist*): Bones were thought to be the seat of health (see note on 2:5).

21:25 ***in bitter poverty:*** Job repeatedly complained about the apparent futility of existence (3:20; 7:11; 9:18; 10:1).

21:26 ***eaten by the same maggots:*** Cp. 17:14; Isa 14:11; see Job 19:26.

21:28 ***houses have vanished because of their sins:*** Job was echoing Bildad (8:22), Eliphaz (15:34), and Zophar (20:26).

21:33 Job 3:19, 22; 17:16; 24:24
21:34 Job 16:2
22:2 Job 35:7 Luke 17:10
22:4 Job 14:3
22:5 Job 11:6; 15:5
22:6 Exod 22:26 Deut 24:6, 17 Job 24:3, 9; 31:19-20 Ezek 18:16
22:7 Job 31:31 Matt 10:42
22:8 Job 9:24; 15:19
22:9 Job 6:27; 24:3, 21
22:12 Job 11:7-9
22:13 Ps 10:11; 64:5; 94:7 Isa 29:15
22:14 Job 26:9
22:16 Job 14:14; 15:32 Matt 7:26-27
22:17 Job 21:14-15
22:18 Job 12:6; 21:16
22:19 Ps 58:10; 107:42
22:20 Job 15:30

31 No one criticizes them openly
or pays them back for what they have done.
32 When they are carried to the grave,
an honor guard keeps watch at their tomb.
33 A great funeral procession goes to the cemetery.
Many pay their respects as the body is laid to rest,
and the earth gives sweet repose.
34 "How can your empty clichés comfort me?
All your explanations are lies!"

Third Round of Speeches (22:1–26:14)
Eliphaz Responds to Job

22 Then Eliphaz the Temanite replied:
2 "Can a person do anything to help God?
Can even a wise person be helpful to him?
3 Is it any advantage to the Almighty if you are righteous?
Would it be any gain to him if you were perfect?
4 Is it because you're so pious that he accuses you
and brings judgment against you?
5 No, it's because of your wickedness!
There's no limit to your sins.

6 "For example, you must have lent money to your friend
and demanded clothing as security.
Yes, you stripped him to the bone.
7 You must have refused water for the thirsty
and food for the hungry.
8 You probably think the land belongs to the powerful
and only the privileged have a right to it!
9 You must have sent widows away empty-handed
and crushed the hopes of orphans.
10 That is why you are surrounded by traps
and tremble from sudden fears.
11 That is why you cannot see in the darkness,
and waves of water cover you.

12 "God is so great—higher than the heavens,
higher than the farthest stars.
13 But you reply, 'That's why God can't see what I am doing!
How can he judge through the thick darkness?
14 For thick clouds swirl about him, and he cannot see us.
He is way up there, walking on the vault of heaven.'

15 "Will you continue on the old paths
where evil people have walked?
16 They were snatched away in the prime of life,
the foundations of their lives washed away.
17 For they said to God, 'Leave us alone!
What can the Almighty do to us?'
18 Yet he was the one who filled their homes with good things,
so I will have nothing to do with that kind of thinking.

19 "The righteous will be happy to see the wicked destroyed,
and the innocent will laugh in contempt.
20 They will say, 'See how our enemies have been destroyed.
The last of them have been consumed in the fire.'

21 "Submit to God, and you will have peace;
then things will go well for you.

21:33 ***the earth gives sweet repose:*** Job viewed death as a relief (3:17-18).

21:34 They told *lies* about Job (13:4) and about God (42:7).

22:1–26:14 In this third round of speeches, Job's friends explicitly accuse Job of being among the wicked and sharing their fate.

22:2-3 Eliphaz did not understand that God would *gain* pleasure from Job's righteousness (1:8; 2:3), as he does from every righteous person (1 Chr 29:17; Ps 147:10-11; Prov 11:1, 20; 12:22). God would also gain glory from Job's steadfast faith, which emphasized the lie behind Satan's challenge (1:9-12; 2:4-6). • Job steadfastly claimed that he was *perfect* (23:10-12), as did God himself (1:1, 8; 2:3).

22:6 Demanding ***clothing as security*** for ***lent money*** was forbidden by the law and condemned by the prophets (Exod 22:26-27; Deut 24:10-13; Ezek 18:7-8; Amos 2:8). In contrast, Job had provided clothing for the poor (31:19-20).

22:9 The OT gives Israel the responsibility of caring for ***widows*** and ***orphans*** (Deut 10:18; 14:29) and repeatedly condemns their neglect as the worst of social evils (Exod 22:22-24; Deut 27:19). Job agreed that it was wicked (24:3, 21) but claimed that he was innocent (29:12-13; 31:16-18, 21).

22:12-14 ***That's why:*** Job had not claimed that ***God can't see,*** but others have (Ps 10:11; 73:11; 94:7).

22:18 ***I will have nothing to do with that kind of thinking:*** Eliphaz threw Job's words back at him (21:16b).

22:19-20 ***The righteous will be happy to see the wicked destroyed:*** They will be glad to see justice done and injustices avenged (see also Ps 58:10-11; Rev 19:1-4). Eliphaz's sentiment neglected God's desire that sinful people repent (see Ezek 33:11).

22 Listen to his [i]instructions,
and store them in your heart.
23 If you return to the Almighty, you will be restored—
so clean up your life.
24 If you give up your lust for money
and throw your precious gold into the river,
25 the [k]Almighty himself will be your treasure.
He will be your precious silver!
26 "Then you will take delight in the Almighty
and look up to God.
27 You will pray to him, and he will hear you,
and you will fulfill your vows to him.
28 You will succeed in whatever you choose to do,
and light will shine on the road ahead of you.
29 If people are in trouble and you say, 'Help them,'
God will save them.
30 Even sinners will be rescued;
they will be rescued because your hands are pure."

Job Responds to Eliphaz

23 Then Job spoke again:
2 "My complaint today is still a bitter one,
and I try hard not to groan aloud.
3 If only I knew where to find God,
I would go to his court.
4 I would lay out my case
and present my arguments.
5 Then I would listen to his reply
and understand what he says to me.
6 Would he use his great power to argue with me?
No, he would give me a fair hearing.
7 Honest people can reason with him,
so I would be forever acquitted by my judge.
8 I go east, but he is not there.
I go west, but I cannot find him.
9 I do not see him in the north, for he is hidden.
I look to the south, but he is concealed.

10 "But he knows where I am going.
And when he tests me, I will come out as pure as gold.
11 For I have stayed on God's paths;
I have followed his ways and not turned aside.
12 I have not departed from his commands,
but have treasured his words more than daily food.
13 But once he has made his decision, who can change his mind?
Whatever he wants to do, he does.
14 So he will do to me whatever he has planned.
He controls my destiny.
15 No wonder I am so terrified in his presence.
When I think of it, terror grips me.
16 God has made me sick at heart;
the Almighty has terrified me.

22:22 Job 6:10; 23:12; Prov 2:6; [i]*torah* (8451) ›Ps 1:2
22:23 Job 8:5; 11:14; Isa 19:22; Zech 1:3
22:24 Job 31:24-25
22:25 [k]*shadday* (7706) ›Job 37:23
22:26 Job 27:10; Ps 37:4; Isa 58:14
22:27 Job 33:26; 34:28; Isa 58:9
22:28 Job 11:17; Ps 112:4
22:29 Job 5:11; Matt 23:12; Jas 4:6; 1 Pet 5:5
22:30 Job 42:7-8; Ps 18:20; 24:3-4
23:2 Job 6:2-3; 7:11
23:4 Job 13:18
23:6 Job 9:4
23:7 Job 13:3, 16
23:8 Job 9:11
23:10 Job 7:18; Ps 7:9; 11:5
23:11 Job 31:7; Ps 17:5; 44:18
23:12 Job 6:10
23:16 Deut 20:3; Jer 51:46

22:22 The term *instructions* (Hebrew *torah,* "law," Deut 17:11), used in Job only here, frequently refers to the Pentateuch (Genesis—Deuteronomy). • ***Listen . . . store:*** See Deut 4:1-2; 6:6-9; Ps 119:11; Prov 2:1-9. Job had done this (23:12).

22:23 ***return to the Almighty:*** Bildad (8:5-6) and Zophar (11:13-14) had already misapplied this biblical principle (Isa 55:6-7; Hos 14:1-2; Zech 1:3; Acts 26:20), and now Eliphaz also misapplies it.

22:24 ***precious gold*** (literally *Ophir*): Ophir was probably located in southern Arabia (see 1 Kgs 9:28; 22:48). The gold of Ophir was the standard in fine gold (Isa 13:12); queens wore it at weddings (Ps 45:9).

22:25 God promises to be his people's ***treasure*** (Ps 16:5; Isa 33:6; Matt 19:21; Mark 10:21); although they possess nothing, they will be rich (2 Cor 6:10; Jas 2:5).

22:27 Ironically, Job ***will pray,*** God ***will hear,*** and Eliphaz will reap the benefits (42:8). • ***you will fulfill your vows:*** Vows were often stimulated by repentance and forgiveness (Hos 14:2; Jon 1:16; 2:9) and when seeking divine intervention (Judg 11:29-40; 1 Sam 1; Ps 22:25; 61:5, 8; 116:14, 18). Vows are binding (Num 30:2; Deut 23:23; Ps 22:25; 61:5, 8; 116:14, 18; Eccl 5:4-5).

22:29 This difficult text probably conveys the effectiveness of a righteous man's prayer. The principle (Ps 34:15, 17; 145:18; Prov 15:8, 29; Jas 5:16) is illustrated throughout Scripture (see, e.g., Gen 18:23-32; 19:29; 20:7, 17; 32:28; Exod 9:28-32; 17:11; 32:10-14; Rom 5:19).

23:2 Job dropped the doubt he had expressed earlier (9:14-20, 32) and here expressed confidence that he could successfully present his ***complaint.***

23:4 ***present my arguments:*** Job wanted to make his ***case*** with God (13:3, 18, 22; 16:21; 31:35); Abraham pled directly with God regarding Sodom (Gen 18:25-32), and Moses did the same for Israel (Exod 32:12-13; Num 14:13-19).

23:6-7 Earlier, Job had believed that God was too strong for him to summon (9:19), so he had requested an arbiter (9:33-34) and asked God not to terrify him (13:21). Here he expressed more hope that God would grant him ***a fair hearing.*** • ***acquitted:*** Job did not want to be pardoned as a guilty man but to be declared innocent (13:18; see Ps 17:2-3; 26:1-3).

23:10 ***tests me:*** Job did not want the kind of chastising that would cleanse him like a refiner's fire (Prov 17:3; Zech 13:9; Mal 3:2-3). He wanted an examination that would prove that he had been as ***pure as gold*** and did not need to amend his life (22:23).

23:13-14 No one can ***change*** God's ***mind*** (9:12-13; 11:10; 12:14; 34:29; Num 23:19-20; Jas 1:17).

23:15-17 ***terrified in his presence:*** See Ps 24:14; 77:3; 88:16; 119:120. • Job had complained earlier of being plunged into ***darkness*** (19:8); Eliphaz (15:22; 22:1) and Bildad (18:6, 18) ascribed this fate to the wicked.

23:17 Job 10:18-19; 19:8
24:1 Isa 2:12; Jer 46:10
24:2 Deut 19:14; 27:17
24:3 Exod 22:26; Deut 24:17
24:4 Job 29:16; 30:25; Prov 14:31; Amos 8:4
24:5 Job 39:5-8; Ps 104:23
24:7 Exod 22:26
24:8 Lam 4:5
24:9 Job 6:27
24:12 Job 9:23-24
24:14 Ps 10:8; Mic 2:1
24:15 Prov 7:9
24:16 Exod 22:2; Matt 6:19
24:17 Ps 91:5
24:18 Job 5:3; 22:11, 16; 27:20
24:19 Job 6:16-17; 21:13
24:20 Job 18:17; 19:10; 21:26; Prov 10:7; Isa 49:15; Dan 4:14

17 Darkness is all around me;
thick, impenetrable darkness is everywhere.

Job Asks Why the Wicked Are Not Punished

24 1 "Why doesn't the Almighty bring the wicked to judgment?
Why must the godly wait for him in vain?
2 Evil people steal land by moving the boundary markers.
They steal livestock and put them in their own pastures.
3 They take the orphan's donkey
and demand the widow's ox as security for a loan.
4 The poor are pushed off the path;
the needy must hide together for safety.
5 Like wild donkeys in the wilderness,
the poor must spend all their time looking for food,
searching even in the desert for food for their children.
6 They harvest a field they do not own,
and they glean in the vineyards of the wicked.
7 All night they lie naked in the cold,
without clothing or covering.
8 They are soaked by mountain showers,
and they huddle against the rocks for want of a home.

9 "The wicked snatch a widow's child from her breast,
taking the baby as security for a loan.
10 The poor must go about naked, without any clothing.
They harvest food for others while they themselves are starving.
11 They press out olive oil without being allowed to taste it,
and they tread in the winepress as they suffer from thirst.
12 The groans of the dying rise from the city,
and the wounded cry for help,
yet God ignores their moaning.

13 "Wicked people rebel against the light.
They refuse to acknowledge its ways or stay in its paths.
14 The murderer rises in the early dawn
to kill the poor and needy;
at night he is a thief.
15 The adulterer waits for the twilight,
saying, 'No one will see me then.'
He hides his face so no one will know him.
16 Thieves break into houses at night
and sleep in the daytime.
They are not acquainted with the light.
17 The black night is their morning.
They ally themselves with the terrors of the darkness.

18 "But they disappear like foam down a river.
Everything they own is cursed,
and they are afraid to enter their own vineyards.
19 The grave consumes sinners
just as drought and heat consume snow.
20 Their own mothers will forget them.
Maggots will find them sweet to eat.

24:1 ***bring . . . to judgment*** (literally *set times*): The times for God's judgment are set (Eccl 3:17; 8:6; Dan 2:21; Luke 21:22-24), but they are not known to us (Acts 1:7). They will be revealed at the proper moment (1 Tim 6:15; 1 Thes 5).

24:2-17 This inventory of criminal behaviors focuses first on crimes against the weak (24:2-12) and then on the criminals themselves (24:13-17).

24:2 The law, wisdom literature, and prophecy all condemned the ***moving*** of ***boundary markers*** (Deut 19:14; 27:17; Prov 22:28; 23:10; see note on Hos 5:10).

24:3 The law did not allow seizing necessary belongings as ***security*** or collateral ***for a loan*** (22:6-9; Deut 24:6, 10-13, 17-21).

24:6 ***glean in the vineyards of the wicked:*** Job was depicting the desperate condition of the poor. If their fields had been stolen like Naboth's vineyard (24:2; see 1 Kgs 21), the poor would harvest for the thieving owners what should have been their own crops; instead of owning the whole crop, they would get just the leftover pickings for themselves. Perhaps the point is that the poor were forced to glean from the fields of wicked people who left no gleanings (Lev 19:10; 23:22), instead of being able to glean from the righteous, who leave something for the poor (Lev 19:9-10; 23:22; Ruth 2).

24:7 Unjust lenders sometimes left debtors ***without clothing or covering***, which they had seized as collateral on loans (22:6; Exod 22:26-27; Deut 24:11-13; Amos 2:8).

24:9 ***widow's child . . . security for a loan:*** See 2 Kgs 4:1; Neh 5:1-5; Matt 18:25.

24:11 ***without being allowed to taste it:*** These words, which are not in the original text, are implied by the parallel with *starving* and ***suffer from thirst.*** • To force workers to ***tread in the winepress as they suffer from thirst*** violates the principle of letting workers enjoy some of the produce they are harvesting (see Deut 25:4; cp. 2 Tim 2:6).

24:12 ***ignores their moaning:*** It appeared to Job that contrary to God's own character (Exod 2:23-24; Ps 12:5), God neither relieved the plight of the wronged (24:2-12) nor hindered the wicked from harming their victims (24:13-17).

24:18-24 These sentiments appear to oppose Job's observations, so some scholars suggest that they were the words of Bildad or Zophar. However, Job might have been pronouncing curses on the wicked, sarcastically quoting his friends' views, or saying that the fate of the wicked presented by Eliphaz (5:2-7; 15:17-25), Bildad (8:8-19; 18:5-21), and Zophar (20:4-29) also overtakes the righteous (21:23-26).

24:19 ***The grave:*** Hebrew *Sheol.* See note on 7:9.

No one will remember them.
Wicked people are broken like a tree in the storm.
21 They cheat the woman who has no son to help her.
They refuse to help the needy widow.
22 "God, in his power, drags away the rich.
They may rise high, but they have no assurance of life.
23 They may be allowed to live in security, but God is always watching them.
24 And though they are great now, in a moment they will be gone like all others, cut off like heads of grain.
25 Can anyone claim otherwise?
Who can prove me wrong?"

Bildad Responds to Job

25 Then Bildad the Shuhite replied:

2 "God is powerful and dreadful.
He enforces peace in the heavens.
3 Who is able to count his heavenly army?
Doesn't his light shine on all the earth?
4 How can a mortal be innocent before God?
Can anyone born of a woman be pure?
5 God is more glorious than the moon; he shines brighter than the stars.
6 In comparison, people are maggots; we [a]mortals are mere worms."

Job Responds to Bildad

26 Then Job spoke again:

2 "How you have helped the powerless!
How you have saved the weak!
3 How you have enlightened my stupidity!
What wise advice you have offered!
4 Where have you gotten all these wise sayings?
Whose spirit speaks through you?
5 "The dead tremble—
those who live beneath the waters.
6 The [b]underworld is naked in God's presence.
The place of destruction is uncovered.
7 God stretches the northern sky over empty space and hangs the earth on nothing.
8 He wraps the rain in his thick clouds, and the clouds don't burst with the weight.
9 He covers the face of the moon, shrouding it with his clouds.
10 He created the horizon when he separated the waters;
he set the boundary between day and night.
11 The foundations of [c]heaven tremble;
they shudder at his rebuke.
12 By his power the sea grew calm.
By his skill he crushed the [d]great sea monster.
13 His Spirit made the heavens beautiful, and his power pierced the gliding serpent.
14 These are just the beginning of all that he does,
merely a whisper of his power.
Who, then, can comprehend the thunder of his power?"

24:21 Job 22:9
24:22 Job 9:4; 12:6
24:23 Job 11:11; 12:6
24:24 Job 14:21; Ps 37:10
24:25 Job 6:28; 27:4
25:2 Job 9:4; 16:19; 31:2; 36:5; 37:23
25:4 Job 4:17; 9:2
25:5 Job 15:15; 31:26
25:6 Job 7:17; [a]*ben 'adam* (1121, 0120) ‣Job 35:8
26:2 Ps 71:9
26:5 Job 3:13; Ps 88:10
26:6 [b]*she'ol* (7585) ‣Ps 16:10
26:7 Job 9:8
26:8 Job 37:11; Prov 30:4
26:9 Job 22:14; Ps 97:2; 105:39
26:10 Job 38:1-11, 19-20, 24; Prov 8:29
26:11 [c]*shamayim* (8064) ‣Ps 11:4
26:12 [d]*rahab* (7293) ‣Ps 87:4
26:13 Job 9:8; Isa 27:1
26:14 Job 36:29; 37:4-5

25:4 Eliphaz had said that it is nearly impossible to ***be innocent*** or ***pure*** (4:17-19; 15:14-16), and then only after suffering (22:21-23). Bildad claimed that only the totally blameless could hope to be pure (8:20).

26:2 Job's friends had not ***helped*** him (12:2; 16:4). Bildad's denial that acquittal was possible hit Job's most sensitive nerve (10:1-7; 13:3, 13-19; 16:18-21; 19:23-27; 23:2-7).

26:4 Eliphaz (4:15), Zophar (20:3), and Elihu (32:18; 33:4) all claimed to be prompted by the proper ***spirit*** (see Jer 29:8-9; 1 Cor 12:10; 1 Jn 4:1).

26:5-6 ***The underworld*** (Hebrew *Sheol*), the abode of all the dead, is located ***beneath the waters*** of the sea. • ***The place of destruction*** (Hebrew *Abaddon*) existed specifically for the wicked.

26:7 The Hebrew *tsapon* ("north," Gen 3:14) sometimes refers to the ***northern*** mountain of the Canaanite gods (the Canaanite equivalent of Olympus; see note on 37:22); here the NLT understands it to refer to the ***sky***, stretched out ***over empty space*** (see Gen 1:6-8; Ps 104:2-3; Isa 40:22-23).

26:9 ***covers the face of the moon:*** Or *covers his throne*, or *covers the view of his throne.* If God's throne was in view, he might use clouds to shroud his lofty abode (Ps 104:3-13; Amos 9:6).

26:10 ***created the horizon:*** See Gen 1:6-10; Ps 104:6-9; Prov 8:29.

26:11 Mountains at the edge of the horizon might be the ***foundations*** [or "pillars," Judg 16:25-26] ***of heaven*** or the earth (9:6). They were thought to reach from below the waters of the sea (Jon 2:6) and up to the clouds to support the vaults of heaven.

26:12 ***the sea grew calm*** (cp. Exod 14:21; Mark 4:39): Or *the sea was stirred up* (cp. Isa 51:15; Jer 31:35). In either interpretation, God performed a miracle on behalf of his people. • ***crushed the great sea monster*** (Hebrew *Rahab,* a mythical sea monster that represents chaos in ancient literature): God's dominance over the sea demythologized popular beliefs about the sea's divinity. See also Ps 74:13-14; 89:9-10; Isa 27:1; 51:9-10.

26:13 ***His Spirit*** (or ***wind***): God's authority clears the skies after a storm (26:12). • The ***gliding serpent*** corresponds to Yam and Rahab (see notes on 7:12; 26:12); it provides background for the image of Satan as a dragon (Isa 27:1; also Ps 74:13-14; see Gen 3:15; Rom 16:20; Rev 12:9; 20:2).

27:1 Job 29:1
27:2 Job 9:18; 16:11
27:3 Job 32:8; 33:4
27:4 Job 6:28; 33:3
27:6 Job 2:3; 13:18
27:8 Job 8:13; 11:20
27:9 Job 35:12-13; Prov 1:27-28; Isa 1:15
27:10 Job 22:26-27
27:13 Job 15:20; 20:29
27:14 Job 20:18-21
27:15 Ps 78:64

Job's Final Speeches (27:1–31:40)

Job Speaks of Human Wisdom

27 Job continued speaking:

2 "I vow by the living God, who has
taken away my rights,
by the Almighty who has embittered
my soul—
3 As long as I live,
while I have breath from God,
4 my lips will speak no evil,
and my tongue will speak no lies.
5 I will never concede that you are right;
I will defend my integrity until I die.
6 I will maintain my innocence without
wavering.
My conscience is clear for as long as
I live.

7 "May my enemy be punished like the
wicked,
my adversary like those who do evil.
8 For what hope do the godless have when
God cuts them off
and takes away their life?
9 Will God listen to their cry
when trouble comes upon them?
10 Can they take delight in the Almighty?
Can they call to God at any time?
11 I will teach you about God's power.
I will not conceal anything concerning
the Almighty.
12 But you have seen all this,
yet you say all these useless things
to me.

13 "This is what the wicked will receive
from God;
this is their inheritance from the
Almighty.
14 They may have many children,
but the children will die in war or
starve to death.
15 Those who survive will die of a plague,
and not even their widows will mourn
them.

16 "Evil people may have piles of money
and may store away mounds of clothing.
17 But the righteous will wear that
clothing,
and the innocent will divide that
money.

Job's Innocence (27:5-6)

Job 1:1, 8-11; 2:3-5; 4:6; 9:33-34; 13:18; 14:16-17; 15:14; 19:25-26; 23:10; 25:4; 42:7-8
1 Kgs 8:46
Ps 25:7; 37:37; 51:17
Ezek 4:14
Rom 3:10, 23, 25; 4:4-5; 6:23
1 Cor 5:7; 13:12
2 Cor 4:18

Job's comforters could not stomach the idea that any human could be truly innocent (4:17-19; 15:14-16; 25:4-6). Job's claim to innocence also seems to conflict with the biblical teaching that "no one is righteous—not even one. . . . All fall short of God's glorious standard" (Rom 3:10, 23). Was Job right in proclaiming his innocence?

Eliphaz and the others talked right past Job. When they denied that Job could be right or pure, they were referring to the absolute qualitative difference between the creature and the Creator, but Job was not claiming absolute purity. He acknowledged his youthful sins (13:26) and was aware of his need to have his sins and his guilt covered (14:16-17).

Nonetheless, Job repeatedly claimed to be a man of integrity and innocence in his relationship with God (13:14-18; 23:10-12; 27:3-6; 31:1-40). Even Eliphaz acknowledged that Job's life was upright (4:6). Job's faith made him doggedly pursue an audience with God and tenaciously believe in God's justice despite his immediate experience. Job kept looking for his Redeemer (19:25). Although God's justice might require a mediator (9:33-35), and it might not be evident before death (19:26), it guaranteed Job's acquittal. No calamity would separate Job from the love of God, even if he did not yet know that this love came in Christ Jesus (Rom 8:35, 39). Job lived "by believing and not by seeing" (2 Cor 5:7; see also Rom 8:24; 1 Cor 13:12; 2 Cor 4:18; Heb 11:1-2; 1 Pet 1:6-8).

When held up to the light of Christ's absolute righteousness, Job stands with all of us as a sinner. Job was not justified by his deeds but by his faith, and on that basis God declared that Job was "blameless—a man of complete integrity" (1:1, 8; 2:3; 42:7-8). God does the same for us when we, like Job, put our complete trust in him (see Rom 4:4-5; Jas 2:23).

27:1 ***Job continued speaking***, no longer responding to the three friends but returning to the themes of his opening statement (3:1-26).

27:2 The Bible permits a ***vow by the living God*** (Ruth 3:13; 1 Sam 20:21; 25:26; 1 Kgs 17:1; 18:15; Jer 4:2), although sometimes it is done foolishly or falsely (1 Sam 14:39, 45; Jer 5:2). • Elihu later criticized Job for saying that God had ***taken away*** his ***rights*** (34:5). • ***embittered . . . soul*** (7:11; 10:1; 21:25): Cp. Naomi (Ruth 1:20-21) and the widow from Shunem after the loss of her son (2 Kgs 4:27).

27:5-6 Job considered it profane and reprehensible to ***concede that*** his friends were right. Condemning the innocent, as they were doing to him, was an abomination (Exod 23:7; Prov 6:16-19; 17:15).

27:9-23 Some interpreters see a new speech here and ascribe it to Zophar because otherwise Zophar has no speech in this cycle (see also note on 28:1-28).

18 The wicked build houses as fragile as a
spider's web,
as flimsy as a shelter made of
branches.
19 The wicked go to bed rich
but wake to find that all their wealth
is gone.
20 Terror overwhelms them like a flood,
and they are blown away in the
storms of the night.
21 The east wind carries them away, and
they are gone.
It sweeps them away.
22 It whirls down on them without mercy.
They struggle to flee from its power.
23 But everyone jeers at them
and mocks them.

A Hymn to God's Wisdom

28 1 "People know where to mine silver
and how to refine gold.
2 They know where to dig iron from the
earth
and how to smelt copper from rock.
3 They know how to shine light in the
darkness
and explore the farthest regions of
the earth
as they search in the dark for ore.
4 They sink a mine shaft into the earth
far from where anyone lives.
They descend on ropes, swinging back
and forth.
5 Food is grown on the earth above,
but down below, the earth is melted
as by fire.
6 Here the rocks contain precious lapis
lazuli,
and the dust contains gold.
7 These are treasures no bird of prey can
see,
no falcon's eye observe.
8 No wild animal has walked upon these
treasures;
no lion has ever set his paw there.
9 People know how to tear apart flinty
rocks
and overturn the roots of mountains.
10 They cut tunnels in the rocks
and uncover precious stones.
11 They dam up the trickling streams
and bring to light the hidden
treasures.

12 "But do people know where to find
wisdom?
Where can they find understanding?
13 No one knows where to find it,
for it is not found among the living.
14 'It is not here,' says the ocean.
'Nor is it here,' says the sea.
15 It cannot be bought with gold.
It cannot be purchased with silver.
16 It's worth more than all the gold of
Ophir,
greater than precious onyx or lapis
lazuli.
17 Wisdom is more valuable than gold and
crystal.
It cannot be purchased with jewels
mounted in fine gold.
18 Coral and jasper are worthless in trying
to get it.
The price of wisdom is far above
rubies.
19 Precious peridot from Ethiopia cannot
be exchanged for it.
It's worth more than the purest gold.

20 "But do people know where to find
wisdom?
Where can they find understanding?
21 It is hidden from the eyes of all
humanity.
Even the sharp-eyed birds in the sky
cannot discover it.
22 Destruction and Death say,
'We've heard only rumors of where
wisdom can be found.'

23 "God alone understands the way to
wisdom;
he knows where it can be found,
24 for he looks throughout the whole
earth
and sees everything under the
heavens.

27:18 Job 8:15
27:19 Job 7:8, 21
27:20 Job 15:21; 20:8
27:21 Job 7:10; 18:18; 20:8; 21:18
27:22 Job 11:20 Jer 13:14 Ezek 5:11; 24:14
28:5 Ps 104:14
28:9 Deut 8:15; 32:13
28:12 Job 28:23, 28
28:17 Prov 8:10; 16:16
28:18 Prov 8:11
28:19 Prov 8:19
28:20 Job 28:23, 28
28:22 Job 26:6
28:23 Prov 8:22-36
28:24 Ps 33:13-14 Prov 15:3

27:18 ***spider's web:*** As in Greek and Syriac versions (see also 8:14); Hebrew reads *a moth*.

28:1-28 This section is a self-contained speech. No speaker is listed, so it could be a continuation of the preceding words (either Job's or Zophar's; see note on 27:9-23). However, some consider this a poetic interlude by the author of Job that sums up the argument to this point, emphasizes the failure of human wisdom, and lays the foundation for the Lord's speeches.

28:5 Miners ***melted*** rock by burning a ***fire*** in a mine for days or even weeks to melt out the ore. Some alternated fire with cold water to split the rocks.

28:13 Wisdom does not originate ***among the living***. God is the source of true wisdom (28:23-28).

28:16-19 The metals, gemstones, and glass listed here were precious in the ancient world, but the speaker says that wisdom is much more precious than wealth. • ***from Ethiopia:*** Hebrew *from Cush*.

28:22 ***Destruction:*** Hebrew *Abaddon* (see note on 26:5-6).

28:23-27 When God ***looks throughout the whole earth*** (28:23), he sees his own wisdom expressed in his creation. God later showcased his wisdom for Job when he took him on a cosmic tour (Job 38–41).

28:25 Job 12:15; 38:8-11; Ps 135:7
28:26 Job 37:3, 6, 11-12; 38:25
28:28 Ps 111:10; Prov 1:7; 9:10
29:1 Job 27:1
29:3 Job 11:17
29:6 Deut 32:13; Ps 81:16
29:9 Job 21:5; 29:21
29:11 Job 4:3-4
29:12 Job 24:4, 9; 31:16-17, 21; 34:28
29:13 Job 31:19-20
29:14 Job 27:5-6; Ps 132:9; Isa 59:17; 61:10; Eph 6:14
29:16 Prov 29:7
29:17 Ps 3:7
29:19 Jer 17:8; Hos 14:5
29:20 Gen 49:24; Ps 18:34
29:21 Job 29:9
29:25 Job 1:3; 4:4; 16:5; 31:37
30:1 Job 12:4

25 He decided how hard the winds should blow
and how much rain should fall.
26 He made the laws for the rain
and laid out a path for the lightning.
27 Then he saw wisdom and evaluated it.
He set it in place and examined it thoroughly.
28 And this is what he says to all humanity:
'The fear of the Lord is true wisdom;
to forsake evil is real understanding.' "

Job Speaks of Former Blessings

29 Job continued speaking:

2 "I long for the years gone by
when God took care of me,
3 when he lit up the way before me
and I walked safely through the darkness.
4 When I was in my prime,
God's friendship was felt in my home.
5 The Almighty was still with me,
and my children were around me.
6 My cows produced milk in abundance,
and my groves poured out streams of olive oil.

7 "Those were the days when I went to the city gate
and took my place among the honored leaders.
8 The young stepped aside when they saw me,
and even the aged rose in respect at my coming.
9 The princes stood in silence
and put their hands over their mouths.
10 The highest officials of the city stood quietly,
holding their tongues in respect.

11 "All who heard me praised me.
All who saw me spoke well of me.
12 For I assisted the poor in their need
and the orphans who required help.
13 I helped those without hope, and they blessed me.
And I caused the widows' hearts to sing for joy.
14 Everything I did was honest.
Righteousness covered me like a robe,
and I wore justice like a turban.
15 I served as eyes for the blind
and feet for the lame.
16 I was a father to the poor
and assisted strangers who needed help.
17 I broke the jaws of godless oppressors
and plucked their victims from their teeth.

18 "I thought, 'Surely I will die surrounded by my family
after a long, good life.
19 For I am like a tree whose roots reach the water,
whose branches are refreshed with the dew.
20 New honors are constantly bestowed on me,
and my strength is continually renewed.'

21 "Everyone listened to my advice.
They were silent as they waited for me to speak.
22 And after I spoke, they had nothing to add,
for my counsel satisfied them.
23 They longed for me to speak as people long for rain.
They drank my words like a refreshing spring rain.
24 When they were discouraged, I smiled at them.
My look of approval was precious to them.
25 Like a chief, I told them what to do.
I lived like a king among his troops
and comforted those who mourned.

Job Speaks of Present Anguish

30 1 "But now I am mocked by people younger than I,
by young men whose fathers are not worthy to run with my sheepdogs.

28:28 *fear of the Lord* (see note on 1:1; Hebrew, *'adonay*): In Job, this name for God appears only here, which might be one argument for understanding ch 28 as the narrator's own poem (see note on 28:1-28).

29:1–31:40 Job contrasts his former happiness, honor, and wealth (ch 29) with his loss of social dignity and divine friendship (ch 30). He concludes his speech with wide-ranging oaths of innocence (ch 31).

29:2 Although elsewhere Job uses the Hebrew *shamar* to describe what he perceived as God's oppressive surveillance (10:14; 13:27; 14:16), here it refers to God's kindly *care* ("watch(es) over," Ps 121:3-8).

29:7 The *city gate* was a town's administrative center (see Ruth 4:1-2, 11).

29:14 Job described his *righteousness* in royal terms. A *robe* is a common biblical image for righteousness (Ps 132:9; Isa 59:17; 61:10; Rom 13:14; Rev 19:8).

29:16 Job actively searched out and *assisted strangers who needed help*.

29:18 *after a long, good life* (literally *after I have counted my days like sand*): Job thought the length of his years would signify God's blessing, like the great number of Abraham's offspring (Gen 15:5; 32:12) or the abundance of Joseph's supplies in Egypt (Gen 41:49).

29:25 In the past, Job had *comforted those who mourned* (4:3-4). This verse is a prophetic mandate closely associated with the work of the Messiah (Isa 40:1; 61:1-3; Luke 4:18-19; cp. 2 Cor 1:3-4).

2 A lot of good they are to me—
those worn-out wretches!
3 They are gaunt with hunger
and flee to the deserts,
to desolate and gloomy wastelands.
4 They pluck wild greens from among the bushes
and eat from the roots of broom trees.
5 They are driven from human society,
and people shout at them as if they were thieves.
6 So now they live in frightening ravines,
in caves and among the rocks.
7 They sound like animals howling among the bushes,
huddled together beneath the nettles.
8 They are nameless fools,
outcasts from society.

9 "And now they mock me with vulgar songs!
They taunt me!
10 They despise me and won't come near me,
except to spit in my face.
11 For God has cut my bowstring.
He has humbled me,
so they have thrown off all restraint.
12 These outcasts oppose me to my face.
They send me sprawling
and lay traps in my path.
13 They block my road
and do everything they can to destroy me.
They know I have no one to help me.
14 They come at me from all directions.
They jump on me when I am down.
15 I live in terror now.
My honor has blown away in the wind,
and my prosperity has vanished like a cloud.

16 "And now my life seeps away.
Depression haunts my days.
17 At night my bones are filled with pain,
which gnaws at me relentlessly.
18 With a strong hand, God grabs my shirt.
He grips me by the collar of my coat.
19 He has thrown me into the mud.
I'm nothing more than dust and ashes.

20 "I cry to you, O God, but you don't answer.
I stand before you, but you don't even look.
21 You have become cruel toward me.
You use your power to persecute me.
22 You throw me into the whirlwind
and destroy me in the storm.
23 And I know you are sending me to my death—
the destination of all who live.

24 "Surely no one would turn against the needy
when they cry for help in their trouble.
25 Did I not weep for those in trouble?
Was I not deeply grieved for the needy?
26 So I looked for good, but evil came instead.
I waited for the light, but darkness fell.
27 My heart is troubled and restless.
Days of suffering torment me.
28 I walk in gloom, without sunlight.
I stand in the public square and cry for help.
29 Instead, I am considered a brother to jackals
and a companion to owls.

30:9 Job 12:4; 17:6; Ps 69:11-12
30:10 Num 12:14; Deut 25:9; Isa 50:6; Matt 26:67
30:11 Ruth 1:21; Ps 88:7
30:12 Job 19:12; Ps 140:4-5; Isa 3:5
30:15 Job 3:25; 7:9; 31:23; Ps 55:3-5; Hos 13:3
30:16 Ps 22:14; 42:4
30:17 Job 30:30
30:19 Ps 69:2, 14
30:20 Job 19:7
30:21 Job 16:9, 14
30:22 Job 9:17; 10:3; 27:21
30:23 Job 3:19; 9:22; 10:8
30:24 Job 19:7
30:26 Job 3:25-26; 19:8; Jer 8:15
30:28 Job 19:7; Ps 38:6; 42:9; 43:2
30:29 Mic 1:8

30:2-3 In the past, the most honorable members of society spoke well of Job (29:11); now, the least honorable mocked him (30:1) and spit in his face (30:10). Cp. Ps 35:15; 69:12; Mark 14:65; 15:17-20.

30:5-6 ***live in frightening ravines, in caves and among the rocks:*** The wretched life of Job's mockers resembled Israel's situation under Midianite oppression (Judg 6:2), David's life as he fled from Saul (1 Sam 22:1-2), and Elijah's life as he awaited the Lord's instruction (1 Kgs 17:3-8).

30:9 ***They taunt me!*** See also 17:6; cp. Ps 69:12; Lam 3:14, 63.

30:10 ***won't come near me:*** See also 19:13-15; cp. Ps 88:8; Prov 19:7; Matt 26:56. • To *spit in* someone's *face* was to display revulsion or contempt (Deut 25:9; Isa 50:6; Matt 26:67; 27:30; Mark 14:65).

30:12-14 The series of images presented here is drawn from a military advance against a fortified city. Job had already used this image for God's attack on him (19:10-12). • The word translated *traps* might refer to siege ramps raised against a city's walls.

30:15 ***terror:*** See also 6:4; 7:14; cp. Ps 88:15.

30:18 ***God grabs . . . the collar of my coat:*** The Hebrew in this verse is difficult to translate; it could mean that Job feels like he's in a chokehold and is about to be thrown into the mud (cp. 30:19).

30:19 ***dust and ashes:*** Earlier, Job was sitting "among the ashes" in anguish (2:8); later, he would "sit in dust and ashes to show . . . repentance" (42:6).

30:20-21 ***you don't answer:*** This was Job's frequent complaint (7:20-21; 10:14-17; 13:25-28; 16:9-14; 19:6-9).

30:22 Job felt tossed ***into the whirlwind*** and blown about like worthless straw or chaff (9:17; 21:18; 27:21; Ps 1:4; Isa 17:13).

30:28 Before his testing began, Job had been respected in ***the public square*** (29:7-10, 21-25); he helped others who were in need (29:11-17).

30:29 ***I am considered:*** Job might have been expressing what he thought of himself, how others viewed him, or both. • By claiming that he was ***a brother to jackals and a companion to owls,*** Job might have been describing himself as in the throes of lament (Mic 1:8). Jackals were associated with desolation or ruin (see Ps 63:10; Isa 13:22; 34:13; 35:7; Jer 9:11; 10:22; 49:33; 51:37; Lam 5:18; Ezek 13:4; Mal 1:3).

30:30 Job 2:7; Ps 102:3
31:1 2 Sam 11:2-4; Matt 5:28
31:2 Job 20:29
31:3 Job 18:12; 21:30
31:4 2 Chr 16:9; Job 14:16; 28:24; 34:21; Prov 5:21
31:6 Job 6:2-3; Isa 26:7
31:7 Job 23:11
31:8 Lev 26:16; Job 20:18
31:10 Deut 28:30; Jer 8:10
31:11 Deut 22:24
31:12 Job 15:30
31:13 Deut 24:14-15
31:15 Job 10:3
31:16 Exod 22:22-24; Job 20:19
31:17 Job 22:7-9; 29:12
31:19 Job 22:6
31:20 Job 29:13
31:22 Job 38:15
31:23 Job 13:11; 31:3

30 My skin has turned dark,
and my bones burn with fever.
31 My harp plays sad music,
and my flute accompanies those who weep.

Job Rests His Case, Claiming Innocence

31 1 "I made a covenant with my eyes
not to look with lust at a young woman.
2 For what has God above chosen for us?
What is our inheritance from the Almighty on high?
3 Isn't it calamity for the wicked
and misfortune for those who do evil?
4 Doesn't he see everything I do
and every step I take?

5 "Have I lied to anyone
or deceived anyone?
6 Let God weigh me on the scales of justice,
for he knows my integrity.
7 If I have strayed from his pathway,
or if my heart has lusted for what my eyes have seen,
or if I am guilty of any other sin,
8 then let someone else eat the crops I have planted.
Let all that I have planted be uprooted.

9 "If my heart has been seduced by a woman,
or if I have lusted for my neighbor's wife,
10 then let my wife belong to another man;
let other men sleep with her.
11 For lust is a shameful sin,
a crime that should be punished.
12 It is a fire that burns all the way to hell.
It would wipe out everything I own.

13 "If I have been unfair to my male or female servants
when they brought their complaints to me,
14 how could I face God?
What could I say when he questioned me?
15 For God created both me and my servants.
He created us both in the womb.

16 "Have I refused to help the poor,
or crushed the hopes of widows?
17 Have I been stingy with my food
and refused to share it with orphans?
18 No, from childhood I have cared for orphans like a father,
and all my life I have cared for widows.
19 Whenever I saw the homeless without clothes
and the needy with nothing to wear,
20 did they not praise me
for providing wool clothing to keep them warm?

21 "If I raised my hand against an orphan,
knowing the judges would take my side,
22 then let my shoulder be wrenched out of place!
Let my arm be torn from its socket!
23 That would be better than facing God's judgment.
For if the majesty of God opposes me,
what hope is there?

30:30 The *skin* of a person who lived in comfortable circumstances was protected from the sun and wind; *dark* skin indicated physical and social decline (Lam 4:8; 5:10).

31:1-40 Job called down curses on himself if he were guilty of the accusations made against him. Except for his mention of idolatry (31:26-27), Job addressed his fidelity to God in terms of the second half of the Ten Commandments, summarized by the command to "love your neighbor as yourself" (Lev 19:18; Rom 13:9).

31:1 Job's *covenant with* his *eyes* included a self-cursing oath (cp. Matt 5:28-29). Perhaps lust of the eyes was at the head of Job's list because the eye is the first instrument of sin (Gen 3:6). • To ***look with lust at a young woman*** violates the spirit of the seventh (Deut 5:18, see Matt 5:27-28), and potentially the tenth (Deut 5:21), commandment.

31:5-8 If Job had ***lied to anyone*** as part of a business deal, it would violate the eighth commandment (Deut 5:19); if it occurred in court, it would violate the ninth (Deut 5:20). This sin would merit fiery judgment (Rev 21:8). • If Job ***lusted for what*** his ***eyes*** had ***seen***, he would violate the tenth commandment (Deut 5:21). • ***then let someone else eat:*** This was a self-curse.

31:9-10 Whether she *seduced* him or he waited for her (24:15-16), if Job ***lusted for*** his ***neighbor's wife*** he would break the seventh (Deut 5:18, Matt 5:27-28) and tenth (Deut 5:21) commandments. • ***belong to:*** Literally *grind for*. This might refer to servitude (Exod 11:5) or to sexual intercourse.

31:11 The Hebrew term *zimmah* (***shameful sin***) is associated with sexual crimes such as incest ("wicked act," Lev 18:17), gang-rape ("terrible crime," Judg 20:6), and prostitution (Ezek 23:49).

31:12 ***to hell*** (Hebrew *to Abaddon;* see note on 26:5-6): The association of ***fire*** with hell or the grave is rare in the OT (cp. Deut 32:22).

31:13-15 ***unfair to . . . servants:*** This might refer to violations of the fourth commandment (Deut 5:12-15). • ***God created both me and my servants:*** Job extended the implications of being created in God's image to the poor (Prov 14:31; 22:2) and even to slaves.

31:21 ***knowing the judges would take my side:*** Job was respected and regarded as a member of the elite class (29:7-10).

31:22-23 If an ***arm*** was used in sinful action (31:21), having it ***torn from its socket*** would be a fitting punishment and ***better than facing God's judgment*** (cp. Matt 5:28-30).

24 "Have I put my trust in money
or felt secure because of my gold?
25 Have I gloated about my wealth
and all that I own?

26 "Have I looked at the sun shining in the skies,
or the moon walking down its silver pathway,
27 and been secretly enticed in my heart
to throw kisses at them in worship?
28 If so, I should be punished by the judges,
for it would mean I had denied the God of heaven.

29 "Have I ever rejoiced when disaster struck my enemies,
or become excited when harm came their way?
30 No, I have never sinned by cursing anyone
or by asking for revenge.

31 "My servants have never said,
'He let others go hungry.'
32 I have never turned away a stranger
but have opened my doors to everyone.

33 "Have I tried to hide my sins like other people do,
concealing my guilt in my heart?
34 Have I feared the crowd
or the contempt of the masses,
so that I kept quiet and stayed indoors?

35 "If only someone would listen to me!
Look, I will sign my name to my defense.
Let the Almighty answer me.
Let my accuser write out the charges against me.
36 I would face the accusation proudly.
I would wear it like a crown.
37 For I would tell him exactly what I have done.
I would come before him like a prince.

38 "If my land accuses me
and all its furrows cry out together,
39 or if I have stolen its crops
or murdered its owners,
40 then let thistles grow on that land instead of wheat,
and weeds instead of barley."

Job's words are ended.

Elihu's Speeches (32:1–37:24)
Elihu Responds to Job's Friends

32 Job's three friends refused to reply
further to him because he kept insisting on his innocence.
2Then Elihu son of Barakel the Buzite, of
the clan of Ram, became angry. He was angry because Job refused to admit that he
had sinned and that God was right in punishing him. 3He was also angry with Job's
three friends, for they made God appear to
be wrong by their inability to answer Job's
arguments. 4Elihu had waited for the others to speak to Job because they were older
than he. 5But when he saw that they had no
further reply, he spoke out angrily. 6Elihu
son of Barakel the Buzite said,

31:24 Job 22:23-25; Mark 10:23
31:25 Ps 62:10
31:30 Job 5:3; Rom 12:14
31:31 Job 22:7
31:34 Prov 29:25
31:35 Job 19:7; 27:7; 30:20, 24, 28; 35:14; Ps 26:1
31:37 Job 1:3; 29:25; 31:4
31:38 Job 24:2, 6, 10-12
31:40 Isa 5:6
32:1 Job 10:7; 13:18; 31:6; 33:9
32:2 Gen 22:21
32:6 Job 15:10

31:24 ***Have I put my trust in . . . my gold:*** Job left the consequence of this oath unstated because the if-then pattern was now established (31:5-23). He rejected Eliphaz's implied judgment (22:24-25; see Ps 52:7; 62:10; 1 Tim 6:10, 17).

31:25 ***gloated about my wealth:*** See Deut 8:17-18; cp. Isa 10:12-14; Dan 4:28-30; Hos 12:8.

31:26-28 Like adultery (cp. 31:1, 9-12), worshiping the sun and moon was a capital crime. Both were sins of the eye that enticed the heart, and both types of sin were tried before judges.

31:26 ***Have I looked at the sun . . . or the moon:*** This oath denies violation (cp. Jer 8:2; 44:17; Ezek 8:16; Acts 7:43) of the first commandment (Deut 5:7; see Deut 4:19; 17:2-7).

31:27 ***secretly enticed in my heart:*** See 31:9. • ***throw kisses at them in worship:*** Cp. 1 Kgs 19:18; Hos 13:2.

31:28 In Israel, *the judges* (see 31:11) were to punish idol worship by execution (Deut 17:2-7). • Denying *the God of heaven* violated the first commandment (Deut 5:7).

31:29-30 ***rejoiced when disaster struck my enemies:*** See Prov 24:17-18; cp. 2 Sam 16:5-8. • ***Cursing anyone*** violated the spirit of the sixth commandment (Deut 5:17; see Matt 5:21-22). • It was against God's will to ask ***for revenge*** (Matt 5:43-44; Rom 12:14; Jas 3:6-10; 1 Pet 3:9).

31:31-32 ***never turned away a stranger:*** The OT values hospitality (Gen 18:1-13; 19:2-3; Judg 19:20-21), and the NT commands it (Matt 25:35; Rom 12:13; 1 Tim 3:2; Heb 13:2; 1 Pet 4:9).

31:35 ***sign my name:*** Job wanted to make the proceedings official (19:23-24).

31:36 ***face the accusation proudly*** (literally *carry it on my shoulder;* cp. Exod 28:12; Isa 22:22): He would take full responsibility for his actions.

31:37 A ***prince*** who had been wrongly accused had the right to ***come before*** his king to make an appeal.

31:38 The *land* was the chief witness to crimes committed upon it (20:27; see Gen 4:10; cp. Jas 5:4).

31:40 ***let thistles grow:*** Job's curse on himself echoed God's primal curse on Adam (Gen 3:17-18; cp. Isa 7:25; Zeph 2:9).

32:1–37:24 Having completed three cycles of speeches between Job and his three friends, we now hear from a new voice. Elihu has not been previously introduced, but he is a young man who has listened to everything the others have said.

32:1 ***Job's three friends*** (see 2:11) failed to comfort him (6:14-30; 13:4; 16:2; 19:21; 42:10).

32:2 ***the Buzite:*** Buz had connections with Aram (Gen 22:21) and Arabia (Jer 25:23), as did *Uz* (1:1). • Elihu repeatedly stated that he was ***angry;*** he probably regarded his anger as righteous zeal (Ps 69:9).

32:3 ***God:*** As in ancient Hebrew scribal tradition; the Masoretic Text reads *Job.*

32:8 Job 33:4; 38:36 Prov 2:6 1 Cor 2:11
32:11 Prov 18:17
32:13 Jer 9:23
32:21 Lev 19:15 Job 13:8, 10; 34:19
33:3 Job 6:28; 27:4; 36:4
33:4 Job 10:3; 27:3; 32:8
33:5 Job 33:32
33:7 Job 13:22
33:9 Job 7:21; 9:21; 10:7, 14; 13:23; 16:17
33:10 Job 13:23-24
33:11 Job 13:27
33:13 Job 40:2 Isa 45:9
33:14 Job 40:5 Ps 62:11
33:15 Job 4:12-17

"I am young and you are old,
so I held back from telling you what
I think.
7 I thought, 'Those who are older should
speak,
for wisdom comes with age.'
8 But there is a spirit within people,
the breath of the Almighty within them,
that makes them intelligent.
9 Sometimes the elders are not wise.
Sometimes the aged do not
understand justice.
10 So listen to me,
and let me tell you what I think.

11 "I have waited all this time,
listening very carefully to your
arguments,
listening to you grope for words.
12 I have listened,
but not one of you has refuted Job
or answered his arguments.
13 And don't tell me, 'He is too wise for us.
Only God can convince him.'
14 If Job had been arguing with me,
I would not answer with your kind of
logic!
15 You sit there baffled,
with nothing more to say.
16 Should I continue to wait, now that you
are silent?
Must I also remain silent?
17 No, I will say my piece.
I will speak my mind.
18 For I am full of pent-up words,
and the spirit within me urges me on.
19 I am like a cask of wine without a vent,
like a new wineskin ready to burst!
20 I must speak to find relief,
so let me give my answers.
21 I won't play favorites
or try to flatter anyone.
22 For if I tried flattery,
my Creator would soon destroy me.

Elihu Presents His Case against Job

33 1 "Listen to my words, Job;
pay attention to what I have
to say.
2 Now that I have begun to speak,
let me continue.
3 I speak with all sincerity;
I speak the truth.
4 For the Spirit of God has made me,
and the breath of the Almighty gives
me life.
5 Answer me, if you can;
make your case and take your stand.
6 Look, you and I both belong to God.
I, too, was formed from clay.
7 So you don't need to be afraid of me.
I won't come down hard on you.

8 "You have spoken in my hearing,
and I have heard your very words.
9 You said, 'I am pure; I am without sin;
I am innocent; I have no guilt.
10 God is picking a quarrel with me,
and he considers me his enemy.
11 He puts my feet in the stocks
and watches my every move.'

12 "But you are wrong, and I will show you
why.
For God is greater than any human
being.
13 So why are you bringing a charge against
him?
Why say he does not respond to
people's complaints?
14 For God speaks again and again,
though people do not recognize it.
15 He speaks in dreams, in visions of the
night,

32:4-7 Elihu's deference to elders followed a well-known principle (see also 12:12; 15:10; Lev 19:32; 1 Tim 5:1; 1 Pet 5:5).

32:8-9 The *spirit* (or *Spirit;* also in 32:18) *within people* might not be the prophetic Spirit that Elihu later appeals to (33:14-15), as Eliphaz had done (4:12-17; cp. 32:18-20). This spirit might simply exist by virtue of creation (33:4; Gen 2:7; Acts 17:25).

32:15-16 As translated, the phrase *you sit there . . . you are silent* is addressed to Job's friends. An alternate translation is *they sit there . . . they are silent,* in which case Elihu is speaking to Job about his friends.

32:18-20 The length of Elihu's speech (chs 32–37) demonstrates that he truly was *full of pent-up words.* • Elihu probably thought *the spirit* (Hebrew *ruakh*) *within* him was prophetic urgency (32:8, 19-20; Ps 39:3), but the reader might find him full of *wind* (Hebrew *ruakh;* see note on 15:2-3). • Like Zophar, Elihu *must speak to find relief* (cp. 20:2).

33:1 *Listen:* Elihu begged to be heard (33:1; 34:2, 16), which is what Job had also sought (13:6).

33:5 By inviting Job to *make* his *case,* Elihu acted as though he were God, or at least the arbiter that Job had been seeking (9:32-35).

33:7 *you don't need to be afraid of me* (literally *my terror shall not make you afraid*): God's terrors (6:4; 7:14; 9:34; 13:21; 23:15) had been thrown in Job's face by Eliphaz (15:21, 24; 22:10), Bildad (18:11, 14), and Zophar (20:25). • Elihu promised not to *come down hard on* Job, but later he broke his word (34:7-9, 33-37).

33:9 *You said:* Job claimed to be *pure* and *without sin,* using various terms (9:21; 10:6-7; 11:4; 13:23-24; 15:14-16; 16:17; 31:1-40).

33:11 Job frequently complained about God's surveillance (7:20; 10:14; 13:27); he wanted relief from having his *every move* scrutinized (14:16; 29:2).

33:13 Job's central complaint was that God *does not respond* (9:16; 19:7; 23:2-7).

33:15 *He speaks in dreams:* See, e.g., Gen 15:12; 20:3; 31:24; 40:1–41:36; Dan 2:1-45; Joel 2:28; Acts 16:9-10.

when deep sleep falls on people
as they lie in their beds.
16 He whispers in their ears
and terrifies them with warnings.
17 He makes them turn from doing wrong;
he keeps them from pride.
18 He protects them from the grave,
from crossing over the river of death.

19 "Or God disciplines people with pain on
their sickbeds,
with ceaseless aching in their bones.
20 They lose their appetite
for even the most delicious food.
21 Their flesh wastes away,
and their bones stick out.
22 They are at death's door;
the angels of death wait for them.

23 "But if an ᵉangel from heaven appears—
a special messenger to intercede for
a person
and declare that he is upright—
24 he will be gracious and say,
'Rescue him from the grave,
for I have found a ransom for his life.'
25 Then his body will become as healthy as
a child's,
firm and youthful again.
26 When he prays to God,
he will be accepted.
And God will receive him with joy
and restore him to good standing.
27 He will declare to his friends,
'I sinned and twisted the truth,
but it was not worth it.
28 God rescued me from the grave,
and now my life is filled with light.'

29 "Yes, God does these things
again and again for people.
30 He rescues them from the grave
so they may enjoy the light of life.
31 Mark this well, Job. Listen to me,
for I have more to say.
32 But if you have anything to say, go ahead.
Speak, for I am anxious to see you
justified.
33 But if not, then listen to me.
Keep silent and I will teach you
wisdom!"

Elihu Accuses Job of Arrogance

34 Then Elihu said:
2 "Listen to me, you wise men.
Pay attention, you who have
knowledge.
3 Job said, 'The ear tests the words it hears
just as the mouth distinguishes
between foods.'
4 So let us discern for ourselves what is
right;
let us learn together what is good.
5 For Job also said, 'I am innocent,
but God has taken away my rights.
6 I am innocent, but they call me a liar.
My suffering is incurable, though I
have not sinned.'

7 "Tell me, has there ever been a man like
Job,
with his thirst for irreverent talk?
8 He chooses evil people as companions.
He spends his time with wicked men.
9 He has even said, 'Why waste time
trying to please God?'

10 "Listen to me, you who have
understanding.
Everyone knows that God doesn't sin!
The Almighty can do no wrong.

33:16 Job 36:10, 15
33:18 Job 33:24, 28, 30
33:19 Job 30:17
33:20 Job 3:24; 6:7 Ps 107:18
33:21 Job 16:8; 19:20 Ps 22:17
33:23 ᵉ*mal'ak* (4397) ›Ps 34:7
33:24 Isa 38:17
33:26 Job 22:26-27; 34:28
33:27 2 Sam 12:13 Luke 15:21 Rom 6:21
33:28 Job 22:28
33:29 Eph 1:11 Phil 2:13
33:33 Ps 34:11
34:3 Job 12:11
34:5 Job 27:2; 33:9
34:7 Job 15:16
34:9 Job 21:15; 35:3

33:18 ***from crossing over the river of death:*** This phrase may also be translated *from passing* [i.e., *dying*] *by the sword.* Both translations fit the context (cp. 36:12).

33:22 ***angels of death wait for them:*** Cp. Exod 12:23; 2 Sam 24:16; 1 Cor 10:10.

33:23 An ***angel from heaven*** would ***intercede,*** taking the role of the mediator Job longed for (see 5:1; 9:33-34; 16:18-21).

33:24 The ***ransom*** is ultimately ***found*** in Christ (Matt 20:28; Rom 3:24-25; 1 Tim 2:6; 1 Pet 1:18-19).

33:26 ***God will receive him with joy:*** Cp. Num 6:24-26; Ps 67:1; Acts 2:28; Jude 1:24.

33:27 ***but it was not worth it:*** Greek version reads *but he* [God] *did not punish me as my sin deserved* (cp. 11:6).

33:32 For Elihu to say that he was ***anxious to see*** Job ***justified*** sounds ironic; he had entered the discussion in the first place "because Job refused to admit that he had sinned" (32:1-5).

34:3-4 ***ear tests . . . mouth distinguishes:*** Elihu echoed Job's earlier complaint about the other counselors' weak argument regarding the "wisdom of the aged" (12:11-12; see 6:30; Heb 5:14).

34:5-6 Job had claimed to be ***innocent:*** See 9:20-21; 13:18; 27:6.

34:6 Eliphaz had accused Job of being a ***liar*** (15:5), fulfilling Job's earlier worry (6:28-29). • ***My suffering*** (literally *My arrow*): For the link with the Lord's arrows, see 6:4; 16:13; Jer 10:19; 15:18; 30:12, 15; Lam 3:12; Mic 1:9; Nah 3:19.

34:9 Elihu later repeated this accusation (35:3; cp. Ps 73:13; Zeph 1:12; Mal 3:14), but he misrepresented Job's words (9:22-23; 21:15). Job had actually condemned those who held this view (21:14-16).

34:10-15 The passage attaches three ideas to the truth that God can do no wrong (34:10, 12): (1) God pays back all people according to their behavior (34:11); (2) as the Creator, God is not answerable to anyone (34:13); and (3) every living being depends upon God for its existence, and God can withdraw that gift without doing anything wrong (34:14-15; cp. Rom 9:19-29).

34:11 ***according to their deeds:*** Cp. Ps 62:12; Prov 24:12; Jer 32:19; Ezek 33:20; Matt 16:27; Rom 2:6; Gal 6:7-8; 1 Pet 1:17. The ultimate harvest will take place at the end of time (2 Cor 5:10; Rev 2:23; 20:52; 22:12).

34:11 Ps 62:12; Prov 24:12; Matt 16:27; Rom 2:6; 2 Cor 5:10; Rev 22:12
34:15 Gen 3:19; 7:21; Job 9:22; 10:9
34:17 Job 40:8
34:19 Deut 10:17; Acts 10:34; Rom 2:11; Gal 2:6; Eph 6:9; 1 Pet 1:17
34:20 Exod 12:29; Job 12:19; 36:20
34:21 Prov 5:21; 15:3
34:22 Ps 139:11-12; Amos 9:2-3
34:24 Job 12:19
34:25 Job 34:11, 20
34:27 1 Sam 15:11
34:28 Exod 22:23; Job 5:15; 22:27; 35:9
34:30 Job 34:17
34:35 Job 35:16
34:36 Job 22:15; Ps 17:3; 26:2
35:2 Job 2:9
35:3 Job 9:30-31; 34:9

11 He repays people according to their
deeds.
He treats people as they deserve.
12 Truly, God will not do wrong.
The Almighty will not twist justice.
13 Did someone else put the world in his
care?
Who set the whole world in place?
14 If God were to take back his spirit
and withdraw his breath,
15 all life would cease,
and humanity would turn again to
dust.

16 "Now listen to me if you are wise.
Pay attention to what I say.
17 Could God govern if he hated justice?
Are you going to condemn the
almighty judge?
18 For he says to kings, 'You are wicked,'
and to nobles, 'You are unjust.'
19 He doesn't care how great a person
may be,
and he pays no more attention to the
rich than to the poor.
He made them all.
20 In a moment they die.
In the middle of the night they pass
away;
the mighty are removed without
human hand.

21 "For God watches how people live;
he sees everything they do.
22 No darkness is thick enough
to hide the wicked from his eyes.
23 We don't set the time
when we will come before God in
judgment.
24 He brings the mighty to ruin without
asking anyone,
and he sets up others in their place.
25 He knows what they do,
and in the night he overturns and
destroys them.
26 He strikes them down because they are
wicked,
doing it openly for all to see.
27 For they turned away from following him.
They have no respect for any of his
ways.
28 They cause the poor to cry out, catching
God's attention.
He hears the cries of the needy.
29 But if he chooses to remain quiet,
who can criticize him?
When he hides his face, no one can find
him,
whether an individual or a nation.
30 He prevents the godless from ruling
so they cannot be a snare to the
people.

31 "Why don't people say to God, 'I have
sinned,
but I will sin no more'?
32 Or 'I don't know what evil I have done—
tell me.
If I have done wrong, I will stop at
once'?

33 "Must God tailor his justice to your
demands?
But you have rejected him!
The choice is yours, not mine.
Go ahead, share your wisdom with us.
34 After all, bright people will tell me,
and wise people will hear me say,
35 'Job speaks out of ignorance;
his words lack insight.'
36 Job, you deserve the maximum penalty
for the wicked way you have talked.
37 For you have added rebellion to your sin;
you show no respect,
and you speak many angry words
against God."

Elihu Reminds Job of God's Justice

35 Then Elihu said:
2 "Do you think it is right for you to
claim,
'I am righteous before God'?
3 For you also ask, 'What's in it for me?
What's the use of living a righteous
life?'

4 "I will answer you
and all your friends, too.

34:17 The implied answer was that *God* could not *govern if he hated justice* (cp. Rom 3:4-7; 7:7, 13; 9:14; Gal 2:17; 6:14). • Later, God also asked if Job was *going to condemn the almighty judge* (40:8).

34:19 *doesn't care how great a person may be:* Impartiality flows from God's justice (Acts 10:34; Rom 2:11; Gal 2:6; Eph 6:9; Col 3:25; 1 Pet 1:17).

34:22 The *wicked* might try to hide in *darkness* (Jer 23:24), but they will fail (Ps 139:11-12; cp. Amos 9:2-3). God brings everything to light (1 Cor 4:5).

34:23 *We don't set the time:* Elihu rejected Job's wish for a quick (21:19), published time of *judgment* (24:1).

34:24 God knows everything *without asking anyone* (34:25). • *sets up others in their place:* Dan 2:21; 5:28-30.

34:26 When God renders justice *openly*, it leads to proper fear among the wicked (Deut 21:21; 1 Tim 5:20) and to public rejoicing among the righteous (cp. Exod 14:30-31).

34:31 *Why don't people say?* Elihu was indirectly asking, "Job, why won't you admit it?"

34:36 *deserve the maximum penalty:* Zophar had also said that Job was being punished less than he deserved (11:6).

35:4-8 Elihu attempted to answer his

5 Look up into the sky,
and see the clouds high above you.
6 If you sin, how does that affect God?
Even if you sin again and again,
what effect will it have on him?
7 If you are good, is this some great gift to him?
What could you possibly give him?
8 No, your sins affect only people like yourself,
and your good deeds also affect only [f]humans.

9 "People cry out when they are oppressed.
They groan beneath the power of the mighty.
10 Yet they don't ask, 'Where is God my Creator,
the one who gives songs in the night?
11 Where is the one who makes us smarter than the animals
and wiser than the birds of the sky?'
12 And when they cry out, God does not answer
because of their pride.
13 But it is wrong to say God doesn't listen,
to say the Almighty isn't concerned.
14 You say you can't see him,
but he will bring justice if you will only wait.
15 You say he does not respond to sinners with anger
and is not greatly concerned about wickedness.
16 But you are talking nonsense, Job.
You have spoken like a fool."

36

Elihu continued speaking:
2 "Let me go on, and I will show you the truth.
For I have not finished defending God!
3 I will present profound arguments
for the righteousness of my Creator.
4 I am telling you nothing but the truth,
for I am a man of great knowledge.

5 "God is mighty, but he does not despise anyone!
He is mighty in both power and understanding.
6 He does not let the wicked live
but gives justice to the afflicted.
7 He never takes his eyes off the innocent,
but he sets them on thrones with kings
and exalts them forever.
8 If they are bound in chains
and caught up in a web of trouble,
9 he shows them the reason.
He shows them their sins of pride.
10 He gets their attention
and commands that they [g]turn from evil.

11 "If they listen and obey God,
they will be blessed with prosperity throughout their lives.
All their years will be pleasant.
12 But if they refuse to listen to him,
they will be killed by the sword
and die from lack of understanding.
13 For the godless are full of resentment.
Even when he punishes them,
they refuse to cry out to him for help.
14 They die when they are young,
after wasting their lives in immoral living.
15 But by means of their suffering, he rescues those who suffer.
For he gets their attention through adversity.

16 "God is leading you away from danger, Job,
to a place free from distress.
He is setting your table with the best food.
17 But you are obsessed with whether the godless will be judged.
Don't worry, judgment and justice will be upheld.

35:5 Job 11:7-8
35:6 Job 7:20; Prov 8:36; Jer 7:19
35:7 Job 22:2-3; Prov 9:12; Luke 17:10; Rom 11:35
35:8 [f]*ben 'adam* (1121, 0120) ‣Ps 8:4
35:9 Exod 2:23
35:10 Job 27:10; Ps 42:8; 149:5; Acts 16:25
35:11 Ps 94:12; Jer 32:33
35:12 Prov 1:28
35:13 Job 27:9; Isa 1:15; Jer 11:11; Jas 4:3
35:14 Job 31:35; Ps 37:5-6
35:16 Job 34:35; 38:2
36:3 Job 8:3; 37:23
36:4 Job 33:3; 37:16
36:5 Ps 22:24; 69:33; 102:17
36:6 Job 5:15; 8:22; 34:26
36:7 Ps 33:18; 34:15; 113:8
36:9 Job 15:25
36:10 2 Kgs 17:13; Job 33:16; 36:21; Jon 3:8; [g]*shub* (7725) ‣Ps 22:27
36:12 Job 4:21; 15:22
36:15 Job 36:10
36:17 Job 34:33; Jon 4:4, 9

own question (35:2), but his *answer* did not add to what Zophar (11:8-9), Eliphaz (22:12), Bildad (25:5-6), and Job (9:8-10) had already said. Elihu failed to recognize that all sin wrongs God (Gen 39:9; Matt 25:41-46; cp. Prov 19:17).

35:13-14 These verses can also be translated as follows: [13]*Indeed, God does not listen to their empty plea; / the Almighty is not concerned. / [14]How much less will he listen when you say you do not see him, / and that your case is before him and you're waiting for justice.*

35:15-16 Elihu echoed and then rejected Job's words (9:24; 12:6-10; 21:7-15, 17). • ***wickedness:*** As in Greek and Latin versions; the meaning of this Hebrew word is uncertain.

35:16 Elihu echoed his earlier accusation (34:35); later, God would agree (38:2).

36:4 *I am a man of great knowledge* (literally *one who is perfect in knowledge is with you*): Elihu was probably claiming to be completely sincere or saying that his logic was flawless.

36:7 The biblical principle that God ***never takes his eyes off the innocent*** (2 Chr 16:9; Ps 33:18; 34:15; 1 Pet 3:12) answered Job's frustration about divine surveillance (7:17-21).

36:11 *If they listen and obey God, they will be blessed:* This is a valid biblical principle of repentance (see 11:13-19; 22:21-25; Deut 4:30; Jer 7:23; 26:13).

36:12 *they will be killed by the sword:* Or *they will cross the river* [of death] (cp. 33:18). • ***die from lack of understanding:*** See also 4:21; Prov 5:23; 10:21.

36:16-20 The meaning of the Hebrew in this passage is uncertain.

36:20 Job 34:20, 25
36:21 Ps 66:18
36:22 Job 35:11
36:23 Job 8:3
36:24 Ps 59:16
36:26 Job 11:7-9; 37:23 Ps 90:2; 102:24, 27
36:27 Job 5:10; 37:6, 11 Ps 147:8
36:29 Job 26:14; 37:11, 16
36:31 Job 37:13 Acts 14:17
36:32 Job 37:11-12, 15
36:33 Job 37:2
37:2 Job 36:33
37:5 Job 5:9; 26:14 Rom 11:33
37:6 Job 36:27; 38:22
37:7 Job 12:14 Ps 109:27
37:8 Job 38:40 Ps 104:21-22
37:9 Job 9:9 Jer 30:23
37:10 Job 38:29 Ps 147:17
37:11 Job 36:27, 29; 37:15
37:12 Ps 148:8
37:13 Exod 9:18-19 1 Kgs 18:45 Job 38:26
37:16 Job 36:4; 37:5, 14, 23

18 But watch out, or you may be seduced by wealth.
Don't let yourself be bribed into sin.
19 Could all your wealth
or all your mighty efforts
keep you from distress?
20 Do not long for the cover of night,
for that is when people will be destroyed.
21 Be on guard! Turn back from evil,
for God sent this suffering
to keep you from a life of evil.

Elihu Reminds Job of God's Power

22 "Look, God is all-powerful.
Who is a teacher like him?
23 No one can tell him what to do,
or say to him, 'You have done wrong.'
24 Instead, glorify his mighty works,
singing songs of praise.
25 Everyone has seen these things,
though only from a distance.

26 "Look, God is greater than we can understand.
His years cannot be counted.
27 He draws up the water vapor
and then distills it into rain.
28 The rain pours down from the clouds,
and everyone benefits.
29 Who can understand the spreading of the clouds
and the thunder that rolls forth from heaven?
30 See how he spreads the lightning around him
and how it lights up the depths of the sea.
31 By these mighty acts he nourishes the people,
giving them food in abundance.
32 He fills his hands with lightning bolts
and hurls each at its target.
33 The thunder announces his presence;
the storm announces his indignant anger.

37 1 "My heart pounds as I think of this.
It trembles within me.
2 Listen carefully to the thunder of God's voice
as it rolls from his mouth.
3 It rolls across the heavens,
and his lightning flashes in every direction.
4 Then comes the roaring of the thunder—
the tremendous voice of his majesty.
He does not restrain it when he speaks.
5 God's voice is glorious in the thunder.
We can't even imagine the greatness of his power.

6 "He directs the snow to fall on the earth
and tells the rain to pour down.
7 Then everyone stops working
so they can watch his power.
8 The wild animals take cover
and stay inside their dens.
9 The stormy wind comes from its chamber,
and the driving winds bring the cold.
10 God's breath sends the ice,
freezing wide expanses of water.
11 He loads the clouds with moisture,
and they flash with his lightning.
12 The clouds churn about at his direction.
They do whatever he commands
throughout the earth.
13 He makes these things happen either to punish people
or to show his unfailing love.

14 "Pay attention to this, Job.
Stop and consider the wonderful miracles of God!
15 Do you know how God controls the storm
and causes the lightning to flash from his clouds?
16 Do you understand how he moves the clouds
with wonderful perfection and skill?
17 When you are sweltering in your clothes
and the south wind dies down and everything is still,

36:18 ***But watch out, or you may be seduced by wealth:*** Or *But don't let your anger lead you to mockery.*

36:19 ***Could all your wealth:*** Or *Could all your cries for help.*

36:31 The Hebrew *yadin* can mean *he governs* or ***he nourishes,*** which parallels ***food in abundance*** (38:26; Ps 65:9-13; 104:13-15, 27-28). The more common meaning for *yadin* is "judge," which would mean that God does all things to bless his people and judge his enemies (37:11-13; 38:22-23; see Gen 6:17; 19:24; Exod 9:23-25; Josh 10:11-14; 1 Sam 12:18).

36:33 ***the storm announces his indignant anger*** (36:29; 37:2; 2 Sam 22:14): Or *even the cattle know when a storm is coming.* The meaning of the Hebrew is uncertain. Cp. 37:8.

37:2 The OT often associates ***thunder*** with ***God's voice*** (36:29, 33; 37:5; 38:1; Exod 19:16-19; Ps 104:7).

37:7 ***everyone stops working . . . watch his power:*** The ending of the agricultural work season gave people time to meditate on God's providential control.

37:13 The same act by God can serve more than one function, such as storms that both destroy enemies and give God's people victory (Josh 10; Judg 4; 1 Sam 7:10-11; Ps 18:7-15; 105:32-33).

37:17 The hot ***south wind*** caused the ***sweltering*** conditions.

18 he makes the skies reflect the heat like a
bronze mirror.
Can you do that?
19 "So teach the rest of us what to say to
God.
We are too ignorant to make our own
arguments.
20 Should God be notified that I want to
speak?
Can people even speak when they are
confused?
21 We cannot look at the sun,
for it shines brightly in the sky
when the wind clears away the clouds.
22 So also, golden splendor comes from the
mountain of God.
He is clothed in dazzling splendor.
23 We cannot imagine the power of the
[h]Almighty;
but even though he is just and
righteous,
he does not destroy us.
24 No wonder people everywhere fear him.
All who are wise show him reverence."

THE LORD CHALLENGES JOB (38:1–42:6)

The Lord Challenges Job a First Time (38:1–40:5)

The Lord's Challenge

38 Then the Lord answered Job from
the whirlwind:
2 "Who is this that questions my wisdom
with such ignorant words?
3 Brace yourself like a man,
because I have some questions for
you,
and you must answer them.
4 "Where were you when I laid the
foundations of the earth?
Tell me, if you know so much.
5 Who determined its dimensions
and stretched out the surveying line?
6 What supports its foundations,
and who laid its cornerstone
7 as the morning stars sang together
and all the [i]angels shouted for joy?
8 "Who kept the sea inside its boundaries
as it burst from the womb,
9 and as I clothed it with clouds
and wrapped it in thick darkness?
10 For I locked it behind barred gates,
limiting its shores.
11 I said, 'This far and no farther will you
come.
Here your proud waves must stop!'
12 "Have you ever commanded the
morning to appear
and caused the dawn to rise in the
east?
13 Have you made daylight spread to the
ends of the earth,
to bring an end to the night's
wickedness?
14 As the light approaches,
the earth takes shape like clay pressed
beneath a seal;
it is robed in brilliant colors.
15 The light disturbs the wicked
and stops the arm that is raised in
violence.
16 "Have you explored the springs from
which the seas come?
Have you explored their depths?
17 Do you know where the gates of death
are located?
Have you seen the gates of utter
gloom?
18 Do you realize the extent of the earth?
Tell me about it if you know!
19 "Where does light come from,
and where does darkness go?
20 Can you take each to its home?
Do you know how to get there?

37:18 Job 9:8-9; Ps 104:2; Isa 44:24; 45:12; Jer 10:12
37:23 Job 8:3; Isa 63:9; [h]*shadday* (7706) ▸Job 40:2
37:24 Job 5:13; Matt 10:28; 11:25; 1 Cor 1:26
38:1 Job 40:6
38:2 Job 35:16; 42:3
38:3 Job 40:7; 42:4
38:4 Job 15:7; Ps 104:5; Prov 8:29; 30:4
38:7 Job 1:6; [i]*ben 'elohim* (1121, 0430) ▸Ps 29:1
38:8 Gen 1:9
38:10 Gen 1:9; Ps 33:7; Prov 8:29; Jer 5:22
38:13 Job 34:25-26; John 1:5
38:15 Job 5:14; Ps 10:15; 37:17
38:16 Gen 7:11; 8:2; Prov 8:24, 28
38:17 Job 28:24; 33:22; Ps 9:13
38:20 Job 26:10

37:20 *speak when they are confused?* Or *speak without being swallowed up?* Punishment as severe as death might result from contesting God's judgment (see notes at 13:14).

37:22 *the mountain of God* (or *from the north;* or *from the abode;* Hebrew *from Zaphon*): In the literature of the ancient city of Ugarit, Zaphon was the northern mountainous abode of Baal; here it figuratively refers to God's lofty home in the heavens (see Isa 14:13-14).

37:23 *cannot imagine the power of the Almighty:* Cp. 11:7; 26:14; Rom 11:33; 1 Tim 6:16. • *he is just and righteous:* Cp. 9:4, 19; 12:13; Ps 62:11; 66:3; 93:1; 99:4.

38:1–42:6 Finally, *the Lord answered Job.* In this final section, the Lord challenges Job's overreaching self-defense with a display of his works that remind Job of God's transcendent greatness.

38:1–40:5 God challenges Job, who acknowledges his inability to judge the moral world by demonstrating his ignorance of the natural world's cosmic (38:4-21) and meteorological elements (38:22-38), animals, and birds (38:39–39:30).

38:1-3 God challenged Job from out of the *whirlwind.* The OT commonly associates storms with God's presence (2 Kgs 2:1, 11; Ezek 1:4; Nah 1:3). Job finally had an audience with God (13:22-23).

38:2 *questions my wisdom:* God's accusation sounds like a charge made by Eliphaz (15:2) and Elihu (34:35; 35:16) to which Job eventually admitted guilt (42:3).

38:7 The *morning stars* are personified in parallel construction with *the angels* (literally *the sons of God*; 1:6; 2:1).

38:10-11 *locked it behind barred gates:* The sea is depicted as a dangerous creature kept under control.

38:14 *it is robed in brilliant colors:* Or *its features stand out like folds in a robe.* The rising sun brings out the colors, shapes, and textures of things.

38:21
Job 15:7
38:22
Exod 9:18
Job 37:6
Isa 30:30
Ezek 13:11, 13
Rev 16:21
38:24
Job 26:10
38:26
Job 36:27
38:27
Ps 104:13-14
38:29
Job 37:10
Ps 147:16-17
38:31
Job 9:9
Amos 5:8
38:34
Job 36:27-28
38:35
Job 36:32; 37:3
38:36
Job 32:8
Ps 51:6
Eccl 2:26
38:39
Job 37:8
Ps 104:21
38:41
Ps 147:9
Luke 12:24
39:1
Deut 14:5
39:5
Job 6:5; 11:12; 24:5
39:6
Job 24:5
Jer 2:24
39:9
Num 23:22
Deut 33:17
Ps 92:10

21 But of course you know all this!
For you were born before it was all
created,
and you are so very experienced!

22 "Have you visited the storehouses of the
snow
or seen the storehouses of hail?
23 (I have reserved them as weapons for the
time of trouble,
for the day of battle and war.)
24 Where is the path to the source of light?
Where is the home of the east wind?

25 "Who created a channel for the torrents
of rain?
Who laid out the path for the lightning?
26 Who makes the rain fall on barren land,
in a desert where no one lives?
27 Who sends rain to satisfy the parched
ground
and make the tender grass spring up?

28 "Does the rain have a father?
Who gives birth to the dew?
29 Who is the mother of the ice?
Who gives birth to the frost from the
heavens?
30 For the water turns to ice as hard as rock,
and the surface of the water freezes.

31 "Can you direct the movement of the
stars—
binding the cluster of the Pleiades
or loosening the cords of Orion?
32 Can you direct the sequence of the
seasons
or guide the Bear with her cubs across
the heavens?
33 Do you know the laws of the universe?
Can you use them to regulate the
earth?

34 "Can you shout to the clouds
and make it rain?
35 Can you make lightning appear
and cause it to strike as you direct?
36 Who gives intuition to the heart
and instinct to the mind?
37 Who is wise enough to count all the
clouds?
Who can tilt the water jars of heaven
38 when the parched ground is dry
and the soil has hardened into clods?

39 "Can you stalk prey for a lioness
and satisfy the young lions' appetites
40 as they lie in their dens
or crouch in the thicket?
41 Who provides food for the ravens
when their young cry out to God
and wander about in hunger?

39

1 "Do you know when the wild
goats give birth?
Have you watched as deer are born in
the wild?
2 Do you know how many months they
carry their young?
Are you aware of the time of their
delivery?
3 They crouch down to give birth to their
young
and deliver their offspring.
4 Their young grow up in the open fields,
then leave home and never return.

5 "Who gives the wild donkey its
freedom?
Who untied its ropes?
6 I have placed it in the wilderness;
its home is the wasteland.
7 It hates the noise of the city
and has no driver to shout at it.
8 The mountains are its pastureland,
where it searches for every blade of
grass.

9 "Will the wild ox consent to being
tamed?
Will it spend the night in your stall?
10 Can you hitch a wild ox to a plow?
Will it plow a field for you?

. . . .

38:21 ***you were born before it was all created:*** Cp. Prov 8:25. This sarcasm resembles that of Eliphaz (15:7).

38:22-23 ***Snow*** and ***hail*** are kept in divine ***storehouses*** such as those for the deep seas and winds (Ps 33:7; 135:7; Jer 10:13; 51:16). God uses these elements as ***weapons*** (36:32; Isa 30:30; Ezek 13:11-13; Rev 16:21) in the storms he sends on ***the day of battle and war*** (e.g., Josh 10:11; Judg 5:20-21; 1 Sam 7:10).

38:24-27 The ***east wind*** blows off the desert to scorch crops (Gen 41:6, 23, 27; Jer 4:11; Jon 4:8) and dry up seas (Exod 14:21; Isa 11:15). It is an arid contrast to ***the torrents of rain*** that cause flooding. • Beneficial ***rain to satisfy the parched ground*** (Ps 104:10-11; 107:35; Isa 35:7; 58:11) stands in contrast to both scorching winds (38:24) and flooding rains (38:25).

38:31-32 ***Pleiades . . . Orion . . . the Bear with her cubs:*** See note on 9:9.

38:36 ***heart . . . mind:*** These words can also be translated *ibis . . . rooster.* The Egyptians thought the ibis was wise about the flooding of the Nile, the most important seasonal event in Egypt; and Israel's rabbis thought the rooster could forecast rain or that its crow distinguished day from night. The idea would then be *Who taught the ibis and the rooster?* See also Ps 51:6; Prov 2:6; Jas 1:5, 17.

39:5-7 ***wild donkey . . . hates*** (literally *scorns*) ***the noise of the city:*** This is the first in a series of animals that scorn others who are their inferiors in some way (cp. 39:18, 22; 41:29). These images illustrate how God scorns the opposition of a man like Job (see Ps 2:4).

39:9-12 Now extinct and already rare by Moses' time, the ***wild ox*** was the most powerful land animal in early Canaan. This OT symbol of strength (Num 23:22; 24:8; Deut 33:17; Ps 29:6; 92:10) was never ***tamed*** (cp. Gen 1:28; 9:2; Ps 8:5-6).

11 Given its strength, can you trust it?
Can you leave and trust the ox to do your work?
12 Can you rely on it to bring home your grain
and deliver it to your threshing floor?

13 "The ostrich flaps her wings grandly,
but they are no match for the feathers of the stork.
14 She lays her eggs on top of the earth,
letting them be warmed in the dust.
15 She doesn't worry that a foot might crush them
or a wild animal might destroy them.
16 She is harsh toward her young,
as if they were not her own.
She doesn't care if they die.
17 For God has deprived her of wisdom.
He has given her no understanding.
18 But whenever she jumps up to run,
she passes the swiftest horse with its rider.

19 "Have you given the horse its strength
or clothed its neck with a flowing mane?
20 Did you give it the ability to leap like a locust?
Its majestic snorting is terrifying!
21 It paws the earth and rejoices in its strength
when it charges out to battle.
22 It laughs at fear and is unafraid.
It does not run from the sword.
23 The arrows rattle against it,
and the spear and javelin flash.
24 It paws the ground fiercely
and rushes forward into battle when the ram's horn blows.
25 It snorts at the sound of the horn.
It senses the battle in the distance.
It quivers at the captain's commands
and the noise of battle.

26 "Is it your wisdom that makes the hawk soar
and spread its wings toward the south?
27 Is it at your command that the eagle rises
to the heights to make its nest?
28 It lives on the cliffs,
making its home on a distant, rocky crag.
29 From there it hunts its prey,
keeping watch with piercing eyes.
30 Its young gulp down blood.
Where there's a carcass, there you'll find it."

40 Then the LORD said to Job,
2 "Do you still want to argue with the [j]Almighty?
You are God's critic, but do you have the answers?"

Job Responds to the LORD

3 Then Job replied to the LORD,

4 "I am nothing—how could I ever find the answers?
I will cover my mouth with my hand.
5 I have said too much already.
I have nothing more to say."

The LORD Challenges Job a Second Time (40:6–42:6)

The LORD Challenges Job Again

6 Then the LORD answered Job from the whirlwind:

7 "Brace yourself like a man,
because I have some questions for you,
and you must answer them.

8 "Will you discredit my justice
and condemn me just to prove you are right?
9 Are you as strong as God?
Can you thunder with a voice like his?
10 All right, put on your glory and splendor,
your honor and majesty.

39:16 Lam 4:3
39:20 Jer 8:16; Joel 2:5
39:21 Jer 8:6
39:27 Jer 49:16; Obad 1:4
39:29 Job 9:26
39:30 Matt 24:28; Luke 17:37
40:2 Job 9:3; 10:2; 13:3; 23:4; 31:35; 33:13
[j]*shadday* (7706) ‣Ps 68:14
40:4 Job 21:5; 29:9
40:5 Job 9:3, 15
40:6 Job 38:1
40:7 Job 38:3; 42:4
40:8 Job 10:3, 7; 13:18; 27:2, 6; Rom 3:4
40:9 Job 37:5
40:10 Ps 93:1; 104:1

39:13-18 In the ancient Near East, the *ostrich* had a reputation as a bird that God had *deprived* of *wisdom.*

39:14-16 The ostrich is a symbol of neglect for her *young* (Lam 4:3) because she (1) *lays her eggs on top of the earth;* (2) appears to leave her eggs to *die* when a predator approaches them (although she is probably attempting to lure the predator away from the nest); and (3) lays her eggs with several other hens in one nest, so most of the eggs are *not her own.*

39:18 *passes* (literally *scorns*) *the swiftest horse with its rider:* See 39:7, 22; 41:29.

39:24 The *ram's horn* was sounded in combat to call for the charge (Josh 6:4-6).

39:30 *Where there's a carcass, there you'll find it*—feeding on the remains (Ezek 39:17-19; Matt 24:28; Luke 17:37).

40:1-2 The Greek OT omits this conclusion to God's first speech.

40:3-5 Job's brief and humble response does not acknowledge guilt, but it does admit his insignificance (40:4). He had previously thought that he could approach God like a prince (31:37) or even cross-examine him (13:22-23).

40:4 *I am nothing* (cp. 42:6): Job was not repenting from sin; like Abraham, he recognized his unworthiness (Gen 18:27). • Job had asked his comforters to *cover* their *mouth* to acknowledge shock (21:5); here he does so himself in reaction to his own rash words.

40:5 Job had *nothing more to say;* he had no further charges against God, nor would he make a rebuttal.

40:6-7 The Lord repeated his earlier challenge (see 38:1-3).

40:8 Job's words (10:7; 27:2; 31:35-37) had angered Elihu (32:2; 34:5); now God himself challenged them.

40:11 Isa 2:12; 42:25; Dan 4:37; Nah 1:6, 8
40:12 Isa 13:11; 63:3
40:13 Isa 2:10-12
40:19 Job 40:15; 41:33
41:1 Job 3:8; Ps 74:14; 104:26; Isa 27:1
41:2 2 Kgs 19:28; Isa 37:29
41:10 Job 3:8
41:11 Exod 19:5; Deut 10:14; Ps 24:1; 50:12; Rom 11:35; 1 Cor 10:26

11 Give vent to your anger.
Let it overflow against the proud.
12 Humiliate the proud with a glance;
walk on the wicked where they stand.
13 Bury them in the dust.
Imprison them in the world of the dead.
14 Then even I would praise you,
for your own strength would save you.

15 "Take a look at Behemoth,
which I made, just as I made you.
It eats grass like an ox.
16 See its powerful loins
and the muscles of its belly.
17 Its tail is as strong as a cedar.
The sinews of its thighs are knit
tightly together.
18 Its bones are tubes of bronze.
Its limbs are bars of iron.
19 It is a prime example of God's handiwork,
and only its Creator can threaten it.
20 The mountains offer it their best food,
where all the wild animals play.
21 It lies under the lotus plants,
hidden by the reeds in the marsh.
22 The lotus plants give it shade
among the willows beside the stream.
23 It is not disturbed by the raging river,
not concerned when the swelling
Jordan rushes around it.
24 No one can catch it off guard
or put a ring in its nose and lead it
away.

41

1 "Can you catch Leviathan with a
hook
or put a noose around its jaw?
2 Can you tie it with a rope through the
nose
or pierce its jaw with a spike?
3 Will it beg you for mercy
or implore you for pity?
4 Will it agree to work for you,
to be your slave for life?
5 Can you make it a pet like a bird,
or give it to your little girls to play
with?
6 Will merchants try to buy it
to sell it in their shops?
7 Will its hide be hurt by spears
or its head by a harpoon?
8 If you lay a hand on it,
you will certainly remember the battle
that follows.
You won't try that again!
9 No, it is useless to try to capture it.
The hunter who attempts it will be
knocked down.
10 And since no one dares to disturb it,
who then can stand up to me?
11 Who has given me anything that I need
to pay back?
Everything under heaven is mine.

12 "I want to emphasize Leviathan's limbs
and its enormous strength and
graceful form.
13 Who can strip off its hide,
and who can penetrate its double layer
of armor?
14 Who could pry open its jaws?
For its teeth are terrible!
15 Its scales are like rows of shields
tightly sealed together.
16 They are so close together
that no air can get between them.
17 Each scale sticks tight to the next.
They interlock and cannot be
penetrated.

40:11-12 Job could not do God's work of humbling the proud (Isa 2:11-12, 17; Jas 4:6; 1 Pet 5:5-6) apart from God's authority (Mal 4:3; Rom 16:20).

40:15-24 Following a list of natural animals (39:1-30), God described Behemoth (40:15-24) and Leviathan (41:1-34) as creatures that man cannot tame. Job couldn't tame the wild donkey or ox (39:5-12), let alone Behemoth and Leviathan (40:15-24), but God created them and could control them, and Job had to acknowledge it (41:2). • The identification of *Behemoth* is disputed, ranging from an earthly creature to a mythical sea monster in ancient literature. Here it seems to be a natural creature: (1) It is an animal that God *made*, just as he made Job (40:15); (2) it is not a dreadful predator but *eats grass like an ox* (40:15); and (3) it is in a poem describing God's creation of the natural order, rather than in a mythological story of the world's formation. Most commentators identify Behemoth with the hippopotamus, a huge, grass-eating animal (40:15-19) that lies in the river among the lotus plants and reeds (40:21). Like the wild ox, Behemoth is powerful (40:16-18, 24; 39:11), yet is essentially peaceful (40:20-23).

40:21 *lotus plants:* Or *bramble bushes;* also in 40:22.

41:1-8 Verses 41:1-8 are numbered 40:25-32 in the Hebrew text.

41:1 The identification of *Leviathan* is disputed, ranging from an earthly creature to a mythical sea monster in ancient literature (see also 3:8; Ps 74:14; 104:26; Isa 27:1). Unlike the peaceful Behemoth (40:15-24), Leviathan was menacing. Most commentators identify Leviathan with the crocodile, with its terrible jaws (41:14) and armored hide (41:15-17, 23), thrashing the water (41:31-32). But Leviathan is a fire-breathing dragon (41:18-21) that wraps its coils around the sun to cause an eclipse (3:8-9). The background for Leviathan is the seven-headed sea monster that represents chaos in ancient Near Eastern mythology. In the biblical record, this unruly maritime monster is a frequent biblical image for chaos and wickedness, whose head the Lord crushes (Ps 74:14; Isa 27:1; cp. Job 9:13; 26:12; Ps 89:9-10; Isa 30:7; 51:9). Later in the Bible, Satan is linked to the ancient serpent (Gen 3) and unruly dragon (Rev 12:9; 20:2), whose head Christ and his followers crush (Rom 16:20).

41:9-34 Verses 41:9-34 are numbered 41:1-26 in the Hebrew text.

41:13 *its double layer of armor?* As in Greek version; Hebrew reads *its bridle?* (41:1-2, 8-9).

18 "When it sneezes, it flashes light!
Its eyes are like the red of dawn.
19 Lightning leaps from its mouth;
flames of fire flash out.
20 Smoke streams from its nostrils
like steam from a pot heated over
burning rushes.
21 Its breath would kindle coals,
for flames shoot from its mouth.

22 "The tremendous strength in
Leviathan's neck
strikes terror wherever it goes.
23 Its flesh is hard and firm
and cannot be penetrated.
24 Its heart is hard as rock,
hard as a millstone.
25 When it rises, the mighty are afraid,
gripped by terror.
26 No sword can stop it,
no spear, dart, or javelin.
27 Iron is nothing but straw to that creature,
and bronze is like rotten wood.
28 Arrows cannot make it flee.
Stones shot from a sling are like bits
of grass.
29 Clubs are like a blade of grass,
and it laughs at the swish of javelins.
30 Its belly is covered with scales as sharp
as glass.
It plows up the ground as it drags
through the mud.

31 "Leviathan makes the water boil with its
commotion.
It stirs the depths like a pot of
ointment.
32 The water glistens in its wake,
making the sea look white.
33 Nothing on earth is its equal,
no other creature so fearless.
34 Of all the creatures, it is the proudest.
It is the king of beasts."

Job Responds to the LORD

42 Then Job replied to the LORD:
2 "I know that you can do anything,
and no one can stop you.
3 You asked, 'Who is this that questions
my wisdom with such ignorance?'
It is I—and I was talking about things I
knew nothing about,
things far too wonderful for me.
4 You said, 'Listen and I will speak!
I have some questions for you,
and you must answer them.'
5 I had only heard about you before,
but now I have seen you with my own
eyes.
6 I take back everything I said,
and I sit in dust and ashes to show my
repentance."

EPILOGUE: THE LORD VINDICATES JOB (42:7-17)

The LORD's Verdict

7 After the LORD had finished speaking to
Job, he said to Eliphaz the Temanite: "I am
angry with you and your two friends, for
you have not spoken accurately about me,
as my servant Job has. 8 So take seven bulls
and seven rams and go to my servant Job
and offer a burnt offering for yourselves.
My servant Job will pray for you, and I will
accept his prayer on your behalf. I will not
treat you as you deserve, for you have not
spoken accurately about me, as my servant
Job has." 9 So Eliphaz the Temanite, Bildad
the Shuhite, and Zophar the Naamathite
did as the LORD commanded them, and the
LORD accepted Job's prayer.

The LORD Restores Job

10 When Job prayed for his friends, the LORD
restored his fortunes. In fact, the LORD gave
him twice as much as before! 11 Then all his
brothers, sisters, and former friends came

41:18 Job 3:9
41:33 Job 40:19
41:34 Job 28:8
42:2 Gen 18:14; Matt 19:26
42:3 Job 38:2; Ps 40:5; 131:1; 139:6
42:4 Job 38:3; 40:7
42:5 Job 26:14; Isa 6:5
42:7 Job 40:3-5
42:8 Job 1:5; 22:30; Jas 5:16
42:10 Ps 14:7; 85:1-3; 126:1-6
42:11 Job 2:11; 19:13

42:1-6 Job understood the message of God's speeches: ***I know that you can do anything.*** Nothing is too hard for God (Gen 18:14; Jer 32:17; Matt 19:26) and nothing can stop his plan (23:13; Isa 14:27; 46:10). Job realized how unlike God he was.

42:5 ***now I have seen you:*** Up to this point, Job had not seen God (see 23:8); now, like Isaiah, he had been in God's presence and was overwhelmed by God's holiness (Isa 6:1).

42:7 ***Eliphaz the Temanite*** was the spokesman for the friends, which probably indicates his seniority (see note on 2:11). Eliphaz had falsely implied that his advice originated in prophetic visions (4:12-16); now God did speak to him, but not to affirm his message. • Unlike his three friends (cp. 13:7-10), Job had ***spoken accurately*** about God. Job's blunt questions were better suited to arriving at the truth about God than the friends' superficial orthodox doctrine.

42:8-9 The Lord made Job the mediator that Job had hoped to find for himself (9:33; 16:19-21; 19:25) and that Elihu desired to be (chs 32–37). • ***go to my servant Job:*** God wanted Job's friends to be reconciled with Job before they presented their offerings (Matt 5:23-24). • ***My servant Job will pray for you;*** he had also prayed for his children (1:5; cp. Jas 5:16; 1 Jn 5:16). • When ***the LORD accepted Job's prayer,*** it ironically fulfilled Eliphaz's promise (22:26-30).

42:10 Job's ***fortunes*** probably included his health (42:16-17). God created humans in order to bless them, not curse them. • ***twice as much:*** See note on 42:16.

42:11 Although Job was restored, he still needed to be ***consoled*** and ***comforted*** for the loss of his children. Following Job's own earlier practice (4:4; 16:5), his family and ***former friends*** took up where the three other friends left off (2:11; cp. 2 Cor 7:6). • The ***gift of money*** (Hebrew *a kesitah;* the value or weight of the *kesitah* is no longer known) was not so much charity to provide a financial basis for Job's restored fortune as it was to honor and seek the favor of an

42:12
Job 1:3, 10; 8:7
1 Tim 6:17

42:17
Gen 15:15; 25:8

and feasted with him in his home. And
they consoled him and comforted him because of all the trials the LORD had brought
against him. And each of them brought him
a gift of money and a gold ring.
12So the LORD blessed Job in the second
half of his life even more than in the beginning. For now he had 14,000 sheep, 6,000
camels, 1,000 teams of oxen, and 1,000
female donkeys. 13He also gave Job seven
more sons and three more daughters. 14He
named his first daughter Jemimah, the second Keziah, and the third Keren-happuch.
15In all the land no women were as lovely as
the daughters of Job. And their father put
them into his will along with their brothers.
16Job lived 140 years after that, living to
see four generations of his children and
grandchildren. 17Then he died, an old man
who had lived a long, full life.

Understanding Job (42:7)

Job 1:1, 8; 2:3; 5:17-18; 19:25-27; 33:15-28; 36:8-15; 38:2; 40:8
Prov 3:11
Heb 12:7, 10
Jas 5:11

For as long as people have read Job's story, they have struggled with the tension between the positive and negative aspects of Job's character. The book's approval of Job in the opening prologue is unequivocal (1:1, 8; 2:3), yet we later hear God interrogate Job: "Who is this that questions my wisdom with such ignorant words?" (38:2). "Will you discredit my justice and condemn me just to prove you are right?" (40:8).

God's questions have led various interpreters to accuse Job of talking too much and even of confusing God's work with the work of Satan. Some contemporary interpretations side with Job's counselors in blaming Job for his suffering. Still others follow Eliphaz (5:17-27) and Elihu (33:15-33; 36:7-17) in arguing that Job's suffering was God's loving and sanctifying chastisement. Even the faithful are not exempt from that (Heb 12:6-12; see Prov 3:11-12), but this explanation flies in the face of the rationale given in the book's opening verses.

Job suffered because God wanted to prove Job's integrity to Satan. God's own judgment of Job's life was positive from start to finish (1:1, 8; 2:3; 42:7). This perspective carries through to the NT, where Job is shown as an example of endurance that we should imitate (Jas 5:11). To understand Job, we need to see his reactions as normal. He does not stand like a rock in reverent stoicism as though he were unaffected by his trials. Neither does he trumpet heroic defiance of his troubles, as though they could never get him down. He reacts in a natural human way. Job rages, protests, moans, and even vacillates between confidence and despair, but he never gives up. He does not curse God, and he does not make a false confession of guilt in the hope that God will then let up on him. Although Job could not understand his situation, he knows that his answer will be found in God (19:25-27).

influential man (e.g., Prov 18:16), and perhaps even to assuage disfavor (e.g., Gen 32:20; 33:10; 43:11; 1 Sam 25:27). • A *gold ring* was worn in a woman's nose (Gen 24:47; Prov 11:22; Isa 3:21) or on the ears of either men or women (Gen 35:4; Exod 32:2-3; Judg 8:24).

42:12 When God *blessed* Job, it ironically fulfilled Bildad's promise (8:7).

42:14 The beautiful names of Job's new daughters spoke of Job's renewed and pleasant good fortunes. • ***Jemimah*** means "soft-voiced turtledove" (see Song 2:14). • ***Keziah*** means "cassia" or "cinnamon flower" (see Ps 45:8). • ***Keren-happuch*** means "horn of antimony," which refers to a lustrous container for cosmetics.

42:15 ***their father put them into his will:*** Daughters normally inherited only when there were no male heirs (Num 27; 36). Perhaps Job's unusual action expressed his superabundant prosperity; only a wealthy man could afford to pass some of his wealth to the families into which his daughters would marry.

42:16 *140 years* was twice the normal life span (Ps 90:10). If the analogy of double restoration holds (42:10), Job might have been 70 already and then lived another 140 years. A lifespan of 210 years would not be out of keeping with the patriarchal setting of the book (see Gen 25:7; 35:28; 47:28; 50:26; Deut 34:7; Josh 24:29). • ***living to see four generations of his children and grandchildren:*** Job's blessing extended to watching his multigenerational family grow (Gen 50:23; Ps 128:6).

42:17 Like Abraham and Isaac, who also died at a ripe old age (Gen 25:8; 35:29), Job *lived a long, full life,* fulfilling Eliphaz's promise (5:26), which was based on God's general promise (Deut 6:2; Ps 91:16). • At the end of the book, the Greek OT adds a note declaring that Job will rise from the dead at the resurrection. It goes on to provide information about where and when Job and his descendants lived.

THE BOOK OF PSALMS

The Lord Jesus and the apostles loved the book of Psalms and quoted from it; beyond that, they lived out of it. These ancient prayers and praises of Israel are also God's inspired word. The psalms provide a bridge to cross between the Old and New Testaments, and the themes addressed in the psalms find further development in the NT. Jesus connects with the dynasty of David in its mission, its disappointments, and its failures. Where David's dynasty has failed, Jesus gives hope. His sinlessness, his identification with the suffering of the members of David's dynasty, his perfect obedience, and his exaltation open up new perspectives on the many questions raised in the Psalter. Yet we are still living by faith; the hope of the book of Psalms, that God's people will completely fulfill his purposes and that all nations will submit to the Messiah, still remains for the future (see 1 Cor 15:25-27).

BACKGROUND

The psalms, like all Scripture, are inspired and given by God (2 Tim 3:16). And yet, each psalm originated with a human author as a prayer or praise to the Lord. The psalms are diverse, composed as the responses of God's people to him. The psalms include laments, psalms of praise, wisdom, thanksgiving, reflections on God's mighty acts, celebrations of God's revelation, and worship.

The book of Psalms reflects a long process of collection. For a thousand years, poets wrote these poems while people recited and collected them. The Temple liturgy encouraged both the collection and the writing of psalms. Gradually editors incorporated smaller collections into larger collections, shaping five collections into the one book of Psalms.

SUMMARY

The first two psalms serve as an introduction to the entire Psalter (the book of Psalms). Psalm 1 introduces the Lord's instruction in wisdom, while Ps 2 introduces God's rule over a rebellious, sinful world. In Ps 1, the person of God's choice is godly and wise, delights in God, lives by divine instruction, and is not influenced by evildoers. Psalm 2 speaks of the rebellion of the nations and of the wicked, the judgment of rebellious nations, and the protection of the godly.

Reading Ps 1 in the context of the entire Psalter raises three questions: (1) Is there forgiveness for sins? (2) Why do the godly suffer? and (3) Why do the wicked prosper? Reading Ps 2 in the context of the Psalter raises two similar questions: (1) Why do the nations prosper? and (2) Why were the

kings of David's line not victorious? The psalmists wrestle with these questions and offer different perspectives. Some of the poets quietly accept their problems, while others wrestle with God, question him, or become exasperated. New questions and issues develop out of their dialogues with God.

THE COMPOSITION OF THE PSALMS

The process of editing the Psalter into one book took place over time and was completed following the exile to Babylon. There are several markers of editorial activity:

1. The editors placed Pss 1 and 2 as an introduction to the whole book of Psalms. Both psalms give an idealized portrayal: Psalm 1 is a portrayal of the ideal godly person who lives by God's instruction. Psalm 2 portrays the Messiah, the ideal king of Israel. The rest of the Psalter develops and deepens these portrayals, while at the same time expressing how neither the people of God nor their king were able to fulfill God's ideals and bring about the happiness and peace of God's kingdom. The Psalter therefore testifies to Jesus as the ideal godly man and king of Israel, the Messiah who alone has pleased God and by whom alone redemption, happiness, and peace are secure.

2. Individual psalms were collected in units. The editors arranged these smaller groupings of psalms into five larger collections: Book One (Pss 1–41, with a doxology and double Amen in 41:13), Book Two (Pss 42–72, with a doxology and double Amen in 72:19), Book Three (Pss 73–89, with a doxology and double Amen in 89:52), Book Four (Pss 90–106, with a doxology and Amen in 106:48), and Book Five (Pss 107–150, without a doxology).

3. Books One (Pss 1–41) and Two (Pss 42–72) form the first stage of the collection. The shift from David (Pss 3–32, 34–41) in Book One to collections of psalms in Book Two (the sons of Korah, Pss 42–49; Asaph, Ps 50; David, Pss 51–65, 68–70; Solomon, Ps 72) reveals a thematic shift from David as the sole model and teacher to other perspectives opened by these psalms. At the end of Book Two, the editor comments, "This ends the prayers of David son of Jesse" (72:20). This comment remained in place even when Books Three, Four, and Five (with additional psalms of David) were added to the collection.

4. The addition of Book Three (Pss 73–89) marks the second stage. Book Three shares with Book Two its preference of the name *Elohim* for God (Pss 42–83) and its diversity of collections (Asaph, Pss 73–83; sons of Korah, Pss 84–85, 87–88; David, Ps 86). Psalm 73 breaks the spell cast by the magnificent vision of the messianic kingdom in Ps 72, as it questions God's justice and power. This issue comes to a head again in Ps 89, the last psalm of Book Three.

OUTLINE

Pss 1–41
Book One

Pss 42–72
Book Two

Pss 73–89
Book Three

Pss 90–106
Book Four

Pss 107–150
Book Five

TIMELINE

2091 / 1915 BC
Abraham moves to Canaan

1876 / 1661 BC
Jacob moves to Egypt

1446 / 1270 BC
Israel leaves Egypt (the Exodus)
The covenant at Sinai

1406 / 1230 BC
Israel enters Canaan

1011–971 BC
David as king of Israel

971–931 BC
Solomon as king of Israel

931 BC
The kingdom is divided

722 BC
End of the Northern Kingdom of Israel

586 BC
End of the Southern Kingdom of Judah

538 BC
Cyrus's edict of return, exiles return to Judea

Oct 537 BC
Temple rebuilding begins

515 BC
Temple rebuilding is completed

250~200 BC
The OT is translated into Greek

5. The psalms of Book Four (Pss 90–106) wrestle with questions raised at the time of the Exile, when it seemed that God's covenant with David had been dissolved (see Ps 89). Several psalms encourage individual growth in character and godliness (Pss 91–92) in response to the crisis. Most psalms in this collection present God as the true and faithful king whose kingdom extends to every part of creation (Pss 93–100). He still loves the people, the flock of his pasture (Ps 100), but they have to listen to him (Pss 95, 100). He is the source of forgiveness, and his compassion assures the exilic community that the Lord still cares for his people. The review of redemptive history from creation to the Exile (Pss 104–106) explains both God's wisdom and Israel's folly as a framework for understanding the Exile. The benediction of Ps 106:48 is included in 1 Chr 16:36 and might indicate that Book Four was completed in the postexilic era (when Chronicles was compiled).

6. Book Five (Pss 107–150) was then added to the Psalter. It includes a number of smaller collections: the *Egyptian Hallel* (Pss 111–118, including three hallelujah hymns, Pss 111–113, and the *Great Hallel,* Pss 114–118), the *Torah psalm* (Ps 119), the *Songs of Ascents* (Pss 120–134), eight psalms of David (Pss 138–145), and five concluding hallelujah hymns (Pss 146–150). Book Five sets out the thematic progression of affliction, lament, God's rescue, and praise. The opening psalm (Ps 107) begins this pattern, and its final verse (107:43) points to the importance of wisdom in discerning God's ways. Psalm 119, the longest psalm, celebrates the wisdom of God and the word of God. The Lord's historic care for Israel in the wilderness (Pss 114–118, 135–136) prepares exilic and postexilic Israel to read David's final prayers (Pss 138–145) in a new way: David looks forward to the full coming of God's kingdom (Ps 145). The hallelujah psalms affirm the truthfulness of this hope (Ps 146–150).

7. Additions appear to have been made to already-existing psalms. This may explain the prayer for the restoration of Zion (51:18-19) and for God's blessing on Jerusalem (69:34-36). Changes in the circumstances of God's people may have occasioned the addition of new lines in each case.

8. The available manuscripts reveal some flexibility in the organization and titles of the psalms. Both the Hebrew and Greek editions of the Psalter contain 150 psalms, but with differing divisions and numbering as well as differences regarding which psalms have titles. The Greek text combines both Pss 9–10 and Pss 114–115 into one psalm each, but it splits both Pss 116 and 147 into two. Differences between the Hebrew and English numbering are indicated in the notes.

By the time of Jesus Christ, the Psalter was well known as the book of Psalms (Luke 20:42; Acts 1:20). It was part of the third section of the Hebrew canon, called the Writings (Luke 24:44; see Old Testament Introduction, "The Canon of the Old Testament," p. 4).

The Psalter, taken on its own terms, is not so much a liturgical library, storing up standard literature for cultic requirements, as a hospitable house, well lived in, where most things can be found and borrowed after some searching, and whose first occupants have left on it everywhere the imprint of their experiences and the stamp of their characters.

DEREK KIDNER
Psalms 1–72, p. 18

AUTHORS

Many of the psalms are associated with David, but not all of them; less than half (seventy-three of them) are connected with him. Others are connected with Asaph (Pss 50, 73–83), the sons of Korah (Pss 42–49, 84–85, 87), Solomon (Pss 72, 127), Heman (Ps 88), Ethan (Ps 89), and Moses (Ps 90).

Of the 116 psalms with a title (see "Psalm Titles," below), most identify a person. The person named may be the author, but not necessarily. The Hebrew preposition *le* before the name (often translated "of") can mean "for," "dedicated to," "concerning," "to," or "by." So, *ledawid* (often translated "of David") could be interpreted as "for David," "dedicated to David," "concerning David," or "by David." While many psalms "of David" may have been written by him, there are several reasons for caution. The titles occasionally have two names, such as David and Jeduthun or Asaph (Pss 39, 62, 77). It is possible that the other individual was the actual author of the psalm. Furthermore, the psalms whose titles connect them with an episode of David's life (Pss 3, 7, 18, 34, 51, 52, 54, 56, 57, 59, 60, 63, 142) provide little or no specific connection with those episodes. For example, the title in Ps 51 connects the psalm with David's sin and Nathan's rebuke. The psalm speaks of sin, forgiveness, and a broken spirit, but any mention of the specifics of the sin is notoriously absent. In addition, several psalms "of David" seem to assume the existence of the Temple, which was not constructed until after David's death (see Ps 5:7; 122:TITLE; 138:2). Similarly, the title of Ps 30 connects David with the dedication of the Temple, and Ps 69 does not seem to fit with what is known of David's life. Finally, some textual traditions vary in the mention of David in the heading (e.g., Pss 122, 124). It is possible, therefore, that *ledawid* should be understood in many cases as meaning "for/dedicated to/concerning David" rather than "by David." Such psalms evoke his persona as the chief representative of the dynasty of David without implying that he himself was the author of the psalm. Still, there are many psalms that could have been authored by David himself.

LITERARY ISSUES

The title *Psalms* for the collection comes from the Greek word *psalmos* ("song"; see Luke 24:44; 20:42), which translates the Hebrew *mizmor*, a word frequently found in the titles of individual psalms (e.g., see Ps 3:TITLE, "psalm"). The word *mizmor* is related to a verb meaning "to play a stringed instrument." The psalms were originally accompanied by instruments and were part of the oral tradition of Israel before they were collected into groupings. The Hebrew title of the Psalter is *tehillim* ("praises"), a word that is related to the expression *hallelujah* ("praise Yahweh").

Psalm Titles. The psalm titles, or short superscriptions accompanying most of the psalms, give information such as the author (see above), the type of psalm (e.g., song, prayer), a musical notation, a notation on the use of the psalm, a historical context, or a dedication. Much of the information is not well understood. As a result, many scholars do not place much emphasis on the psalm titles in the interpretation of the psalms.

In the Hebrew text, the psalm titles are typically numbered as verse 1. As a result, the verse numbers through the entire psalm differ from the numbers in the NLT and most English translations.

Interlude (Hebrew Selah*).* This word is found seventy-one times in the book of Psalms. The meaning of the word is uncertain, though it is probably a musical or literary term. In the NLT it is consistently rendered *Interlude*.

The theological richness of the psalms emerges out of a profound knowledge of God rooted in relationship.

PETER C. CRAIGIE
Psalms 1–50, p. 40

Groupings of the Psalms. The psalms can be grouped in a number of ways:

- By the names they use for God: *Yahweh* ("the LORD," Pss 1–41) and *Elohim* ("God," Pss 42–72).
- By the names in the titles: David (Pss 3–32, 34–41, etc.), the sons of Korah (Pss 42–49, 84–85, 87–88), and Asaph (Pss 50, 73–83).
- By genre (see below).
- Many of the psalms are in collections within the Psalter: e.g., the Songs of Ascents (Pss 120–134). Other collections were recognized in Jewish tradition, such as the Egyptian Hallel (Pss 113–118) and the hallelujah hymns (Pss 146–150).
- By thematic connections, such as God's kingship (Pss 93–100), or the storyline from creation to the Exile (Pss 104–106).

Genres of the Psalms. The psalm titles often designate the genre of a psalm. The most frequent genre designation in a psalm's title is "psalm" (Hebrew *mizmor*), a song originally accompanied by stringed instruments. Less frequent are the words *maskil* ("psalm, a chant": Pss 32, 42, 44–45, 52–55, 74, 88, 89), *miktam* ("psalm, a chant": Pss 16, 56–60), *shir* ("song": Pss 45, 120–135), *shiggayon* ("psalm," a generic or musical term: Ps 7), *tepillah* ("prayer": Pss 17, 86, 90) and *tehillah* ("psalm of praise": Ps 145), *higgayon* ("meditation," meaning unknown: Ps 9:16), and *todah* (psalm of thanksgiving: Ps 100).

In addition to the genre identifications that are found in the Hebrew text, the psalms may also be divided into three main categories:

1. Wisdom or instructional psalms (Pss 1, 15, 24, 33, 34, 37, 73, 90, 107);
2. Psalms of lament (most psalms in books I—III), which can be subdivided into individual laments and community laments;
3. Hymns of praise or thanksgiving (Pss 8, 19, 29, 65, 67, 114), which can similarly be divided into individual and community hymns.

The psalms of praise include several subgenres, including "royal" psalms about the king (Pss 2, 45, 72, 89, 110); psalms ascribing kingship to the Lord (Pss 93, 95–99); hymns about creation (Pss 19, 29, 104); and hymns about Zion (Pss 46, 48, 84, 87).

Another way of reading the psalms is based on the movement in many psalms from instruction to a problem and from a problem to a renewal in commitment and character. The Psalter as a collection of five books is largely instructional in nature. It is "instruction" (*torah,* "law," 1:2) and has the purpose of teaching God's people how to live.

The Psalter . . . promises Christ's death and resurrection so clearly—and pictures his kingdom and the condition and nature of all Christendom—that it might well be called a little Bible. In it is comprehended most beautifully and briefly everything that is in the entire Bible.

MARTIN LUTHER
Word and Sacrament

THE PSALMS IN ISRAEL'S WORSHIP

The collection of 150 lyric poems known as the Psalter contains much information on music-making in ancient Israel. The majority of psalms are songs of praise, thanksgiving, prayer, and repentance. There are also historic odes that relate great national events (for example, Ps 30, "a song at the dedication of the Temple," and Ps 137, which portrays the sufferings of the Jews in captivity). Such psalms played a role in the life of the community; however, the exact nature of that role is uncertain.

MEANING AND MESSAGE

The psalms provide windows into the souls of the ancient saints who wrote them. Their theological reflections are not easy or simple-

minded, but the psalmists' faith, when tried, is purified. The psalms model depth of character, wisdom, honesty, and authenticity. They prepare God's people for the coming of Jesus Christ as the perfect Adam (human) and as the king, the descendant of David who has absolute integrity.

The prayers in the Psalter are more than models to be imitated: They are God's instructions for righteous living, part of his *torah* ("instruction"; see Pss 1, 19, 119). God teaches who he is, what he has done, and what he expects from his people. The psalms are God-centered, instructing God's people to be like God, to receive his correction, and to discern error in themselves. Through the psalms, God encourages his people individually and as communities to worship him vibrantly. The psalms and their musical accompaniments bear witness about God to the world.

The psalmists reflected on the transitory nature of life, on suffering, and on the many kinds of adversity that human beings experience. As the psalmists faced alienation and pain, they longed for God's presence, provision, and protection (e.g., Ps 23), and for a lasting glory. Even the psalms connected with David often reveal a humble, rather than a victorious, David—a humiliated David more often than a glorious and royal David. The psalmists lived in a world full of alienation, and they longed for redemption. They experienced shame, and they trusted in the Lord to vindicate them with his glorious presence.

The Psalter illustrates the failures of Israel and of David's dynasty. The best of the godly Israelites and of the Davidic kings were unable to bring in the condition of happiness and peace that Pss 1 and 2 speak of (see also Ps 72). The psalms are God's exhortation to each person to cultivate wisdom, to trust in him, to live by grace, and to have hope in the coming one who would bring God's blessings to a needy world.

Jesus and the apostles understood Jesus' life and ministry in light of the psalms (see Matt 13:34-35; 21:16, 42; 23:39; John 2:17; 15:25; 19:24, 28, 36; Acts 2:22-35; 4:11; 13:32-38; Rom 15:3; 1 Cor 15:25-27; Eph 4:7-10; 1 Pet 2:7). Jesus entered the world of humans and lived out the patterns found in the psalms, including humiliation, suffering, death, vindication, and glory. He is the only human being who has completely pleased God (Ps 1). He is the Messiah and King (Ps 2) who has become our means of redemption, happiness, and peace.

FURTHER READING

LESLIE C. ALLEN
Psalms 101–150 (2002)

JAMES MONTGOMERY BOICE
Psalms (1994)

PETER C. CRAIGIE
Psalms 1–50 (1983)

MARK D. FUTATO
Psalms in *Cornerstone Biblical Commentary*, vol. 7 (2009)

DEREK KIDNER
Psalms 1–72, 73–150 (1973, 1975)

MARVIN E. TATE
Psalms 51–100 (1990)

GERALD H. WILSON
Psalms, Volume 1 (2002)

1. BOOK ONE (PSS 1–41)

PSALM 1

1 Oh, the [a]joys of those who do not
follow the advice of the wicked,
or stand around with sinners,
or join in with mockers.
2 But they delight in the [b]law of the LORD,
[c]meditating on [b]it day and night.
3 They are like trees planted along the
riverbank,
bearing fruit each season.
Their leaves never wither,
and they prosper in all they do.

4 But not the wicked!
They are like worthless chaff,
scattered by the wind.
5 They will be condemned at the time of
judgment.
Sinners will have no place among the
godly.
6 For the LORD watches over the path of
the godly,
but the path of the wicked leads to
destruction.

PSALM 2

1 Why are the nations so angry?
Why do they waste their time with
futile plans?
2 The [d]kings of the earth prepare for
battle;
the rulers plot together
against the LORD
and against his anointed one.

1:1
Ps 26:5
Prov 4:14
[a]*'ashrey* (0835)
‣ Ps 32:1

1:2
Ps 25:5; 119:13-16
[b]*torah* (8451)
‣ Ps 19:7
[c]*hagah* (1897)
‣ Ps 35:28

1:3
Jer 17:7-8

1:4
Ps 35:4-5
Isa 17:12-13

1:5
Ps 5:5; 9:7-8; 89:5, 7

1:6
Ps 9:5-6; 11:6
2 Tim 2:19

2:1
Ps 21:11; 46:6
Acts 4:25-26

Book One (Pss 1–41) Book One reveals God's purpose in the world, God's order in creation, and the significance of wisdom. It issues an invitation to dwell on the mountain of the Lord and gives insights into the psalmist's life and struggles.

Pss 1–8 Psalms 1 and 8 form an *inclusio* (set of literary bookends) that describes what God expects of the ideal person (cp. Pss 19, 33, 104, 145), contrasts the godly person with the wicked, and extols the godly person's dignity. Jesus the Messiah (Ps 2)—the sovereign Lord (Heb 2:6-8; see 1 Cor 15:27) and perfection of humanity—embodies this ideal.

Pss 1–2 The first two psalms are an introduction to the entire Psalter. Psalm 1 introduces the Lord's instruction in wisdom, while Ps 2 introduces God's rule over a rebellious, sinful world. Together, these psalms invite people to leave the way of folly that leads to destruction and to enter the way of God that leads to wisdom and salvation. The NT affirms that God will rule the nations through Jesus Christ, his appointed agent (Heb 1:5; Rev 12:5; 19:15).

Ps 1 This wisdom psalm sets the tone for the whole Psalter. The psalmist strongly contrasts the happiness of the godly with the condemnation of the wicked; in the end, the way of wisdom will triumph. This idealization of the godly person (as in Ps 8) highlights the Lord's expectations of his people and especially of the coming Messiah (Ps 2). The people of Israel did not live up to this ideal, and neither did the kings of David's dynasty. Not even the best of them could bring in the triumph of righteousness described in Pss 1, 2, and 72. In the NT, the apostles' use of the Psalter to describe the life and ministry of Jesus the Messiah confirms that Jesus alone fulfills the ideal of the godly person presented in the psalms. Only Jesus could please God and secure redemption, happiness, and peace. Psalm 1 introduces the hopeful anticipation of the final hallelujah (Ps 150), when the Lord will remove all evil from his creation and prosper his children.

1:1-2 The Lord gives true happiness to all who reject evil and delight in him.

1:1 ***Oh, the joys:*** This Hebrew term (*'ashrey*) is used twenty-six times in Psalms. Some translations render it as "blessed," but a different term (*barak*) is used in contexts of blessing (5:12; 45:2; 107:38). • The godly do not permit themselves to live under the influence of sinners. Those who do not fear the Lord are ***wicked*** (36:1); they are the enemies of those who love God, those who do right, and the poor and oppressed (see 10:2-13; 37:14). The wicked might appear pious (50:16) and sometimes enjoy temporary prosperity (37:35), but sorrow (32:10) and destruction (1:4-6) await them when their deeds catch up with them (9:16). • Those who go astray (25:8) in rebellion against the Lord (78:17) are ***sinners;*** they commit heinous crimes such as adultery and murder (cp. Ps 51). • ***join in with:*** This expression (literally *sit in the seat of*) depicts a life in bondage to sin (cp. 1:2; 26:3-7; Deut 6:7). • ***Mockers*** hate the Lord, scorn his wisdom, and insult anyone who attempts to correct them (Prov 9:7-8). They seek only the "wisdom" that justifies their actions. These brash people have little regard for the Lord, his plans, or his children (see 86:14; 119:51, 69, 78, 85, 122). These three terms (wicked, sinners, mockers) apply to all kinds of ungodly people.

1:2 The *law* (Hebrew *torah*) ***of the LORD*** is the full revelation of God's instructions (see note on Deut 4:44). • ***Meditating*** is a process of inner reflection that can be positive (1:2; 63:6; 77:12; 143:5) or negative (see 2:1; 38:12). The Lord's word is the object of godly meditation (119:48). • ***Day and night*** includes all times, whether one is walking, standing, sitting, or sleeping (see Deut 6:7).

1:3-5 The future belongs to the godly.

1:3 Well-watered ***trees*** endure and bear abundant fruit (cp. Jer 17:8).

1:4 The coming time of judgment (1:5) will carry off ***the wicked*** and their deeds (35:5; 83:13; Isa 17:13; see note on Jer 13:24).

1:5 The wicked cannot abide the scrutiny of the Lord's ***judgment;*** they are already ***condemned*** (see 5:5; 7:6; 101:7).

1:6 The Lord's care for the righteous and the demise of the wicked both demonstrate the Lord's principle of retribution (see Gal 6:7-10). The brief and futile lives of the wicked will end, whereas the Lord and his saints will triumph (see 9:5, 6, 18; 10:16; 37:20; 73:27; 92:9; cp. 142:4; Isa 57:1). • The godly (see 5:12; 14:5) are joyful (1:1) because ***the LORD*** protects and cares for them, hears them when they cry out for justice, and secures their future (see 121:3-4). • A person's ***path*** is his life and character.

Ps 2 This royal psalm pertains to the Lord's appointment of a king descended from David. It celebrates the mission of all the kings in David's line, and it introduces the hope of an ideal ruler who will accomplish the Lord's goal of bringing all nations into submission (2:11) or to destruction (2:9). The NT identifies Jesus as this descendant (see Acts 13:33; 1 Cor 15:25-27; Heb 1:5; 5:5; Rev 19:15).

2:1-3 Their futile paths lead to death (1:4, 6), but fallen human beings unite in opposing the true God and his Messiah.

2:1 ***plans:*** The Hebrew verb rendered "meditate" in 1:2 here suggests an attitude of opposing the Lord in speech (Isa 59:13) or in thought (38:12; Prov 24:2).

2:2 ***The kings*** hate the Lord's established order in the world, so they desire to be independent of him (see 36:4). They scheme about dominating the Lord's people (31:13; see 83:1-4). Their goal is to subvert the Lord's rule in the world by overthrowing ***his anointed***

2:2 Ps 48:4-6; 74:18, 23 ^d^*melek* (4428) ‣Ps 5:2
2:5 Ps 76:7; 78:49-50
2:6 Ps 3:4; 45:6; 48:1-2
2:7 *Acts 13:32-33 *Heb 1:5-6; 5:5
2:9 Rev 2:26-27; 12:5; 19:15

3 "Let us break their chains," they cry,
"and free ourselves from slavery to
God."
4 But the one who rules in heaven laughs.
The Lord scoffs at them.
5 Then in anger he rebukes them,
terrifying them with his fierce fury.
6 For the Lord declares, "I have placed my
chosen king on the throne
in Jerusalem, on my holy mountain."
7 The king proclaims the LORD's decree:
"The LORD said to me, 'You are my son.
Today I have become your Father.
8 Only ask, and I will give you the nations
as your inheritance,
the whole earth as your possession.
9 You will break them with an iron rod
and smash them like clay pots.' "
10 Now then, you kings, act wisely!
Be warned, you rulers of the earth!

Royal Psalms (Ps 2)

Pss 18, 20, 21, 45, 61, 72, 89, 101, 110, 132, 144

The *royal psalms* all have some reference to the king, the nature of his rule, and his relationship to God. Psalms 2, 18, 20, 21, 45, 61, 72, 89, 101, 110, 132, and 144 are usually regarded as the royal psalms. Belief in God's kingship is the foundation of the royal psalms (Ps 2). Each king in David's dynasty served as messianic agent—i.e., he represented God's kingship. As God's representative, the Davidic king was expected to uphold the qualities of justice, righteousness, faithfulness, and peace (72:1-3).

The royal psalms express the hope and aspirations of the dynasty of David. But with its corruption and failure, the dynasty came to an apparent end (89:38-45). Yet hope remained alive for the future of a king descended from David who would serve as God's agent. The royal psalms maintain this hope for a king whose perfect obedience would guarantee the continuity of David's dynasty and the perpetual benefits of his reign. In this sense, the royal psalms may also be called *messianic psalms* in that they express hope in messianic agent, an ideal king descended from David. Jesus stated that the psalmists wrote of him (Luke 24:44), and other NT writers affirmed the identification of Jesus as the Messiah. Some of the most significant links are as follows:

- Psalm 2 is associated with Israel's king, the descendant of David. Nevertheless, it speaks of a universal vindication and rule that far transcends even David's or Solomon's reigns (see Acts 13:33; Heb 1:5; 5:5).
- Psalm 45 is a marriage psalm for one of the Davidic kings, possibly Solomon, yet it speaks of a permanent rule (45:6).
- Psalm 110 is the most frequently quoted messianic psalm (see Matt 22:43-45; Acts 2:34-35; Heb 1:13; 5:5-10; 6:20; 7:21). It speaks of the privileges, universal victory, and continuing priesthood of David and his successors. Such language would be hyperbole, and possibly misleading, except for its fulfillment in Jesus. In contrast to the angels who are privileged to stand in God's presence (Luke 1:19), Christ the Son sits in the place of power and authority over all things at God's right hand (Heb 1:13).

one (or *his messiah*); the Lord chose the kings of David's dynasty to establish his kingdom throughout the earth. The NT confirms that Jesus, the appointed and anointed Son of God (Acts 4:26; 13:33; Heb 1:5; 5:5), fulfills the role in which these earlier kings failed.

2:3 ***break their chains:*** These kings believe that acknowledging the true God and his chosen ruler will result in their enslavement (Isa 28:22; 52:2; cp. Lam 3:7; Rom 1:1; 1 Cor 7:22; Titus 1:1).

2:4-6 The Lord finds the human threat insignificant. He provided a solution long before their rebellion. He will end their agitation through the appointment of a human agent, a descendant of David's line who will rule the nations.

2:4 ***rules in heaven:*** The Lord's place in the universe is so certain that he *scoffs* at humans who boast that they can rebel against his power and authority (see 37:13; 59:8).

2:6 ***my chosen king:*** The Lord establishes his anointed ruler. • ***in Jerusalem:*** Hebrew *on Zion.* See "Mount Zion, the City of God" at Ps 48, p. 947.

2:7-9 The Lord adopted ***the king*** of David's dynasty to conquer rebellious ***nations*** by force (see 89:26-27).

2:7 ***my son*** (or *Son*). ***Today I have become your Father*** (or *Today I reveal you as my son*): People in the ancient Near East commonly accepted a father-son relationship between gods and kings. In Israel, the Lord adopted kings as his sons. God set David apart as his most excellent and exalted son (89:27). All descendants of David were the Lord's representatives or agents. As an eternal member of the Godhead (John 1:1) and a descendant of David (Acts 13:33; Heb 1:5; 5:5), Jesus is the true Son of God.

2:8 In an example of the suzerain-vassal relationship between the Lord and Israel's king (see Deuteronomy Introduction, "Literary Form," p. 314), the Lord invites the king to ***ask*** for favors (see 21:2, 4). • All nations will be subject to David's descendant, the Messiah.

2:9 The Lord gives his anointed ruler the power to conquer the nations as his inheritance (Isa 11:4; Rev 2:27; 12:5; 19:15), breaking their rebellion, resistance, and independence. • ***break:*** Greek version reads *rule.* Cp. Rev 2:27.

2:10 It pleases the Lord when his people submit to him and seek his protection. The wise accept the Lord's rebuke and desire to repent.

11 Serve the LORD with reverent fear,
and rejoice with trembling.
12 Submit to God's royal son, or he will
become angry,
and you will be destroyed in the midst
of all your activities—
for his anger flares up in an instant.
But what joy for all who take refuge
in him!

PSALM 3

A psalm of David, regarding the time David fled from his son Absalom.

1 O LORD, I have so many enemies;
so many are against me.
2 So many are saying,
"God will never rescue him!"
Interlude
3 But you, O LORD, are a [e]shield
around me;
you are my glory, the one who holds
my head high.
4 I cried out to the LORD,
and he answered me from his holy
mountain. *Interlude*
5 I lay down and slept,
yet I woke up in safety,
for the LORD was watching over me.
6 I am not afraid of ten thousand
enemies
who surround me on every side.
7 Arise, O LORD!
Rescue me, my God!
Slap all my enemies in the face!
Shatter the teeth of the wicked!
8 Victory comes from you, O LORD.
May you bless your people.
Interlude

PSALM 4

For the choir director: A psalm of David, to be accompanied by stringed instruments.

1 Answer me when I call to you,
O God who declares me innocent.
Free me from my troubles.
Have mercy on me and hear my prayer.
2 How long will you people ruin my
[f]reputation?
How long will you make groundless
accusations?
How long will you continue your lies?
Interlude
3 You can be sure of this:
The LORD set apart the godly for
himself.
The LORD will answer when I call to
him.
4 Don't sin by letting anger control you.
Think about it overnight and remain
silent. *Interlude*
5 [g]Offer sacrifices in the right spirit,
and trust the LORD.

2:11 Ps 5:7; 119:119-120 Heb 12:28
2:12 Ps 5:11; 34:8; 34:22 Rev 6:15-17
3:1 Ps 69:4
3:2 Ps 22:7-8; 71:11
3:3 Ps 27:5-6; 28:7; 62:7
[e]*magen* (4043) ‣Ps 7:10
3:4 Ps 4:3; 34:4; 99:9
3:5 Lev 26:6 Prov 3:24-26
3:6 Ps 27:3; 118:10-13
3:8 Isa 43:11
4:1 Ps 3:4; 17:6; 18:6, 18-19; 25:16
4:2 Ps 31:6, 18; 69:7-10, 19-20
[f]*kabod* (3519) ‣Ps 24:7
4:3 Ps 6:8-9; 17:6; 31:23; 50:5; 135:4
4:4 Ps 77:6 Eph 4:26
4:5 Ps 37:3, 5; 50:14
[g]*zabakh* (2076) ‣Ps 51:17
4:6 Num 6:25-26 Job 7:7; 9:25 Ps 80:3, 7, 19

2:11-12 *rejoice:* Rulers must welcome the Son as their true and only King. • ***Submit to God's royal son*** (or *Submit to God's royal Son,* or *kiss the son*; the meaning of the Hebrew is uncertain): Kissing was an expression of submission (Hos 13:2). • The Lord gives *joy* to all who fear him (1:1-2) and trust him (18:30; 34:22; 119:1-3).

Pss 3–7 This group of psalms moves readers from the orderly world of Pss 1–2 to a disoriented one. The Lord's anointed cries out while facing enemies, ferocious opposition, evil schemes, and the Lord's apparent distance.

Ps 3 This psalm laments that the expectations raised by Pss 1–2 have not been met. But even when beset by enemies, godly people need not question the Lord's just dealings. Rather, they can confidently trust his goodness and expect God to rescue them.

3:TITLE This sad episode in David's life (see 2 Sam 15–18) helps readers keep the promises of Ps 2 in perspective. The Lord granted victory to his anointed king (Ps 2), but the manner and timing of this victory remained in God's hands.

3:1-2 The psalmist's *many enemies* speak brashly (4:6; 40:15; see notes on 2:3; 12:4) and question the Lord's ability to rescue (10:11; 22:7-8; 71:10). Their words haunt him because it seems that the Lord will not answer his prayer. • These enemies wield great power (cp. 2:1-3); unlike Ps 2, this psalm does not resolve the crisis.

3:2 ***Interlude:*** Hebrew *Selah*. The meaning of this word is uncertain, though it is probably a musical or literary term. It is rendered *Interlude* throughout the Psalms.

3:3-4 The psalmist's eyes turn from his enemies to the Lord.

3:3 The psalmist contrasts the contention of his enemies (3:2) with the Lord's provision. The Lord is a *shield* for his people; he turns their defeat and shame into victory and *glory* (see notes on 4:2; 27:6; 140:7).

3:5 By refocusing on the Lord (3:3-4) in the midst of his crisis, the psalmist can rest, confident of his *safety* (see note on 4:8). The Lord cares for his servant; he protects him and keeps his mind and heart from fear (37:17; 54:4; 119:116; 145:14; see note on 121:4).

3:6 The psalmist's peaceful confidence in the Lord's protection and care shields him from evil and gives him a new sense of reality (23:4; 27:1, 3; 46:1; 56:4, 11; 91:5-6; 118:6).

3:7-8 The psalmist does not seek revenge; instead, he waits for the Lord's vengeance (see note on Ps 94). • ***Arise:*** The psalmist calls upon the Lord to take action now.

Ps 4 This individual lament includes a prayer for rescue (4:1), a rebuke of the adversary (4:2-3), an exhortation to the godly (4:4-5), and an expression of confidence (4:6-8).

4:1 Waiting for the Lord's ***answer*** allows for growth in patience and for the refinement of living faith (38:15).

4:2 The opponents of the godly place their hope in delusions, treachery, and idolatry. • ***my reputation*** (or *my glory*): The honor of the psalmist, or possibly of the Lord, is at stake.

4:4 Angry feelings are not sinful, but ***letting anger control you*** leads to sin (see 37:7-8; cp. Eph 4:26-27, 31-32). • Instead of acting on their emotions, the godly ***think about*** their circumstances ***overnight.*** They might be disturbed as they sleep, but silence opens their hearts to trust in the Lord (4:5).

4:5 ***Offer sacrifices in the right spirit:*** Redirecting emotions toward the Lord prevents a godly individual from doing too much self-reflection (40:6-8; 51:17).

4:7
Ps 97:11-12
Acts 14:17

4:8
Lev 25:18
Deut 12:10
Job 11:19
Ps 3:5; 16:9
[h]*shalom* (7965)
‣ Ps 29:11

5:1
Ps 54:2

5:2
Ps 84:3
[i]*melek* (4428)
‣ Ps 24:9

5:3
Ps 88:13; 130:5

5:4
Ps 11:5; 34:16; 92:15

5:5
Ps 1:5; 11:5; 45:7; 75:4

5:6
Ps 52:4-5; 55:23

5:7
Ps 69:13; 115:11, 13

5:8
Ps 27:11; 31:1, 3

5:9
*Rom 3:13
Luke 11:44

6 Many people say, "Who will show us
better times?"
Let your face smile on us, LORD.
7 You have given me greater joy
than those who have abundant
harvests of grain and new wine.
8 In [h]peace I will lie down and sleep,
for you alone, O LORD, will keep me safe.

PSALM 5

For the choir director: A psalm of David, to be accompanied by the flute.

1 O LORD, hear me as I pray;
pay attention to my groaning.
2 Listen to my cry for help, my [i]King and
my God,
for I pray to no one but you.
3 Listen to my voice in the morning, LORD.
Each morning I bring my requests to
you and wait expectantly.
4 O God, you take no pleasure in
wickedness;
you cannot tolerate the sins of the
wicked.
5 Therefore, the proud may not stand in
your presence,
for you hate all who do evil.
6 You will destroy those who tell lies.
The LORD detests murderers and
deceivers.
7 Because of your unfailing love, I can
enter your house;
I will worship at your Temple with
deepest awe.
8 Lead me in the right path, O LORD,
or my enemies will conquer me.
Make your way plain for me to follow.
9 My enemies cannot speak a truthful
word.
Their deepest desire is to destroy
others.
Their talk is foul, like the stench from an
open grave.
Their tongues are filled with flattery.

Title of the Messiah	Reference in Psalms	Applied to Jesus
Messiah (Anointed One)	2:2	Matt 16:16; Acts 4:24-30; 13:33
Son of God	2:7, 12	Matt 3:17; 17:5; Acts 13:33; Rom 1:4; Heb 1:5; 5:5
Sovereign King	8:4-6	1 Cor 15:27; Heb 2:8
Suffering Servant	22:1-31	Matt 27:35, 46; Mark 15:34; John 19:24
Faithful Servant	40:6-8; 69:1-36	John 2:17; Rom 15:3; Heb 10:7
Victorious King	68:18	Eph 4:8
Exalted Lord	110:1	Matt 22:41-45; Acts 2:32-36; Heb 1:10-13
Royal High Priest	110:4	Heb 5:6; 7:17, 21
Precious Stone	118:22	Matt 21:42; Mark 12:10-11; Luke 20:17; Acts 4:11; 1 Pet 2:7
Blessed King	118:26	Matt 21:9; 23:39; Mark 11:9; Luke 13:35; 19:38; John 12:13

▲ **Messiah in the Psalms** (2:2). In the NT, the writers of the Gospels, Acts, the Letters, and the book of Revelation strongly connect Jesus with the Psalter. Jesus completes David's dynasty. Although the earlier kings failed, there is now hope. Jesus' sinlessness, his identification with Israel's kings, his perfect obedience, and his exaltation open up new perspectives on the many questions raised in the Psalter. We are still living by faith. The hope of the Psalter is that all nations will submit to God's king, the Messiah (cp. 1 Cor 15:25-27).

4:6 ***your face*** (or ***the light of your face***)**:** The psalmist seeks God's favor and peace (Num 6:25-26), which can transform darkness into light (see 27:1). Confident trust in the Lord is an antidote to anger, resentment, jealousy, and materialism.

4:8 ***Peace*** comes from God's blessing and protection (4:6; see 37:11).

Ps 5 This morning prayer (5:3) expresses unwavering confidence in the Lord's help and protection. The psalmist asks for and awaits God's response (5:1-3). He describes the schemes of the wicked in detail but does not get lost in his circumstances. The psalmist also knows that the wicked cannot coexist with God (5:4-6, 9; see 1:5). He keeps returning to the Lord (5:7-8, 10; see 5:1-3), and then he prays for the godly community (5:10-12; see 3:8b).

5:1-2 The request ***hear me*** appears in several prayers as a call for God's attention during a time of trouble (39:12; 84:8; 143:1), as does ***pay attention*** (17:1; 54:2; 130:2). The needy ask their God, "Are you listening?"

5:3 The psalmist begins and ends each day with prayer, awaiting new expressions of God's fidelity and goodness (143:8). • ***wait expectantly:*** The psalmist does not demand God's grace but places hope in it (see Mic 7:7; Hab 2:1).

5:5 ***the proud:*** Mockers (see note on 1:1), the wicked (73:3; 75:4), and the arrogant (10:2) use their mouths to twist truth and challenge the faith of the godly. • The Lord allows only the godly into his ***presence*** (see 1:5). His holiness and justice do not tolerate oppression or those ***who do evil.*** • ***you hate:*** The Lord rejects proud sinners (see also 11:5).

5:7 God promises his ***unfailing love***—his covenant goodness and faithfulness—to his people (see 25:6; 69:16; Lam 3:32). • ***your house:*** The godly long to come into God's presence with reverence and awe (see Heb 12:28).

5:8 God guides those who are obedient, submissive, and patient in waiting for him to ***lead,*** provide, and protect them (27:11; 43:3; 143:10), not those who expect God simply to endorse their own decisions. • Following ***the right path*** of wisdom leads to the Lord (27:11; 61:2; 139:24).

5:9-10 The psalmist again describes the vile acts of the wicked, who cannot stand in God's presence.

5:9 ***with flattery:*** Greek version reads *with lies.* Cp. Rom 3:13, where Paul quotes from this verse in his description of the depravity of all people.

10 O God, declare them guilty.
Let them be caught in their own traps.
Drive them away because of their many sins,
for they have rebelled against you.
11 But let all who take refuge in you rejoice;
let them sing joyful praises forever.
Spread your protection over them,
that all who love your name may be filled with joy.
12 For you bless the godly, O LORD;
you surround them with your shield of love.

PSALM 6

For the choir director: A psalm of David, to be accompanied by an eight-stringed instrument.

1 O LORD, don't rebuke me in your [j]anger
or discipline me in your rage.
2 Have compassion on me, LORD, for I am weak.
Heal me, LORD, for my bones are in agony.
3 I am sick at [k]heart.
How long, O LORD, until you restore me?
4 Return, O LORD, and rescue me.
[a]Save me because of your unfailing love.
5 For the dead do not remember you.
Who can praise you from the grave?
6 I am worn out from sobbing.
All night I flood my bed with weeping,
drenching it with my tears.
7 My vision is blurred by grief;
my eyes are worn out because of all my enemies.
8 Go away, all you who do evil,
for the LORD has heard my weeping.
9 The LORD has heard my [b]plea;
the LORD will answer my prayer.
10 May all my enemies be disgraced and terrified.
May they suddenly turn back in shame.

PSALM 7

A psalm of David, which he sang to the LORD concerning Cush of the tribe of Benjamin.

1 I come to you for protection, O LORD my God.
Save me from my persecutors—
rescue me!
2 If you don't, they will maul me like a lion,
tearing me to pieces with no one to rescue me.
3 O LORD my God, if I have done wrong
or am guilty of injustice,
4 if I have betrayed a friend
or plundered my enemy without cause,

5:10 Ps 9:16; 36:12
5:11 Ps 2:12; 12:7; 64:10; Isa 65:13
5:12 Ps 29:11; 32:7, 10
6:1 Ps 2:5; 38:1; [j]*'ap* (0639) ‣Prov 27:4
6:2 Ps 22:14
6:3 Ps 38:8; 90:13; John 12:27; [k]*nepesh* (5315) ‣Ps 19:7; [a]*yasha'* (3467) ‣Ps 34:18
6:4 Ps 17:13
6:5 Ps 30:9; Isa 38:18
6:6 Ps 42:3; 69:3
6:7 Ps 31:9
6:9 [b]*tekhinnah* (8467) ‣Ps 55:1
6:10 Ps 71:24; 73:19
7:1 Ps 11:1; 31:1, 14-15
7:2 Ps 17:12; 57:4
7:3 1 Sam 24:11
7:4 1 Sam 24:7; 26:9
7:6 Ps 138:7
7:8 Ps 18:20; 35:24; 96:13

5:10 The psalmist prays for the justice and retribution that God promised against the wicked (1:6)—those who have *rebelled against* the Lord. • The wicked lay *traps* to kill (38:12) or deceive (140:4-5).

5:11 A blessing rests on *all who take refuge in* God (see 18:30). • Joy and praise make good companions. The godly *rejoice* when they see evidence of God's rescue. They *sing joyful praises* as a new song (see 33:3). When the Lord restores peace to this world, puts down evil, and rewards the righteous, they will have lasting *joy* (9:2-4; 53:6; 90:14-15; 118:24). • The children of God, who find refuge in him, *love* his *name*. To love his name is to love his very character.

5:12 The psalmist extends his concern beyond himself to all the *godly*. • A *shield*, here an image of God's protection, deflects spears and arrows from its bearer.

Ps 6 The occasion for this lament might have been sickness or a mental or spiritual depression from which the psalmist sought healing.

6:TITLE *to be accompanied by an eight-stringed instrument:* Literally *with stringed instruments; according to the sheminith.*

6:1-3 The psalmist asks for God's favor and restoration at a difficult time.

6:1 *don't rebuke me . . . or discipline me:* The psalmist does not explicitly connect God's discipline with sin here (cp. 39:8-11), but it might be implied.

6:2-3 In his longing for God's response to his prayer, the psalmist grew physically *weak* (6:6; see 77:3; 119:81; 142:1-3; see also Ps 101). Fasting might have played a part in his *agony*, but this is not mentioned.

6:4-5 The experience was so painful that the psalmist might as well have been *dead*, or perhaps he feared for his life.

6:5 *from the grave?* Hebrew *from Sheol?* In the OT, Sheol is the abode of the dead. It is not necessarily associated with punishment.

6:6-7 The psalmist is exhausted to the depths of his being from the anguish of his spiritual distance from the Lord (31:9; 22:1; 31:10; 102:5). • When *eyes* dim, the body is failing (see 13:3; 31:9; 38:10; Matt 6:22).

6:8-10 In a closing note of triumph, the psalmist reasserts his confidence in the Lord.

Ps 7 This psalm consists of a lament (7:1-2), an oath of innocence (7:3-5), an appeal to God's justice (7:6-9), an affirmation of God's just kingship (7:10-16), and a concluding hymn of praise (7:17).

7:TITLE *Cush*, an unknown person *of the tribe of Benjamin,* remained hostile to David.

7:1 *Persecutors* (a common term for "enemies") intentionally seek out people in order to destroy them (31:15; 56:1-2; 71:11; 143:3).

7:2 *Like a lion,* a wicked enemy relentlessly and violently pursues its prey (10:9; 17:12; 22:13, 21; 35:17; 57:4), but God promises victory (91:13).

7:3-5 The psalmist swears to his innocence, making himself vulnerable to scrutiny (7:9).

7:3 The psalmist does not claim to be without sin, but he knows that he does not deserve the brutal attacks of his opponents (see 35:7).

7:9
Ps 11:4-5; 94:23
Jer 11:20
Rev 2:23
[c]*leb* (3820)
‣Ps 28:7

7:10
Ps 97:10-11; 125:4
[d]*magen* (4043)
‣Ps 28:7

7:11
Ps 50:6; 90:9
[e]*shapat* (8199)
‣Ps 9:4

7:12
Deut 32:41
Ezek 33:9

7:13
Ps 18:14; 45:5; 64:7

7:14
Job 15:34-35
Isa 59:4
Jas 1:15

7:15
Ps 57:6

7:16
Esth 9:24-25
Ps 140:9, 11

7:17
Ps 9:2; 66:1-2, 4; 71:15-16
[f]*yadah* (3034)
‣Ps 30:12
[g]*'elyon* (5945)
‣Ps 46:4

8:1
Ps 57:5; 113:4; 148:13

5 then let my enemies capture me.
Let them trample me into the ground
and drag my honor in the dust.
Interlude

6 Arise, O LORD, in anger!
Stand up against the fury of my enemies!
Wake up, my God, and bring justice!
7 Gather the nations before you.
Rule over them from on high.
8 The LORD judges the nations.
Declare me righteous, O LORD,
for I am innocent, O Most High!
9 End the evil of those who are wicked,
and defend the righteous.
For you look deep within the mind and [c]heart,
O righteous God.
10 God is my [d]shield,
saving those whose hearts are true
and right.
11 God is an honest [e]judge.
He is angry with the wicked every day.
12 If a person does not repent,
God will sharpen his sword;
he will bend and string his bow.
13 He will prepare his deadly weapons
and shoot his flaming arrows.
14 The wicked conceive evil;
they are pregnant with trouble
and give birth to lies.
15 They dig a deep pit to trap others,
then fall into it themselves.
16 The trouble they make for others
backfires on them.
The violence they plan falls on their
own heads.

17 I will [f]thank the LORD because he is just;
I will sing praise to the name of the
LORD [g]Most High.

PSALM 8

For the choir director: A psalm of David, to be accompanied by a stringed instrument.

1 O LORD, our Lord, your majestic name
fills the earth!
Your glory is higher than the heavens.

Notation	References*
Interlude *(Selah)*	3:2, 4, 8; etc.
Accompanied by stringed instruments	Pss 4, 6, 54, 55, 61, 67, 76
Accompanied by the flute	Ps 5
An eight-stringed instrument	Pss 6, 12
Accompanied by a stringed instrument	Pss 8, 81, 84
Sung to the tune "Death of the Son"	Ps 9
Sung to the tune "Doe of the Dawn"	Ps 22
Sung to the tune "Lilies"	Pss 45, 69
Sung by soprano voices (*'alamoth*)	Ps 46
Sung to the tune "Dove on Distant Oaks"	Ps 56
Sung to the tune "Do Not Destroy!"	Pss 57–59, 75
Sung to the tune "Lily of the Testimony"	Ps 60
Sung to the tune "Lilies of the Covenant"	Ps 80
Sung to the tune "The Suffering of Affliction"	Ps 88

* All full-psalm listings refer to Psalm titles

▲**Musical Notations in the Psalms (Ps 5).** These musical notations are not well understood.

7:5 ***trample:*** Cp. 44:5; 60:12; 91:13; 108:13. • ***into the ground . . . in the dust:*** Disgrace and shame can lead to death and the grave (143:3; see 13:3-4).

7:6-9 With this appeal to God for justice in the world, the psalmist also submits to God's examination.

7:6 God's judgment brings *justice,* despite the chaos created by adversaries (see 7:11).

7:8 The judgment is against the defendants (the nations) and in favor of the *righteous* plaintiff (the psalmist; see 43:1). • Although not *innocent* of all sin, the psalmist is a person of authentic integrity (see 15:2; 25:21; 41:12; 78:72; cp. Job 1:1, 8; 9:20, 22).

7:9 God examines ***the mind and heart*** of each person (see 11:3-4; 26:2; 139:1, 23).

7:10-13 The psalmist moves from his own situation (7:1-9) to speak for all the godly who long for redemption (7:10-16). He depicts God as the righteous King who vindicates his subjects when they cry out for rescue.

7:11 The ***honest*** Lord cannot be bought or bribed, nor does he abuse his power (9:4; cp. 82:1-8).

7:12-13 ***sword . . . bow . . . deadly weapons . . . flaming arrows:*** As the Divine Warrior, *God* (literally *he*) takes the offensive on behalf of himself and his people.

7:14 ***Evil*** begins with small words or steps, and gives ***birth*** to increasingly worse deeds as time goes on (see Isa 59:4-5).

7:17 ***I will thank . . . sing praise:*** The laments in Pss 3–7 usually move from lament to praise, as does the Psalter as a whole. • ***Most High:*** This is an ancient designation for God (see note on 91:1). • God is *just* and reliable, so his order prevails in this world.

Ps 8 Psalm 8 opens the second segment of Book One (Pss 8–14). The psalmist celebrates God's creation and the dignity of the ideal human being (see Ps 1). Instead of the world of enemies, wicked people, and distorted justice that is presented in Pss 3–7, this psalm promotes an image of the world as God originally created it. A weary person can envision a place of dignity in God's world.

8:TITLE ***to be accompanied by a stringed instrument:*** Hebrew *according to the gittith.*

8:1 The ***LORD*** (Hebrew *Yahweh*), the covenant God of Israel (Exod 3:15), also holds the title of ***Lord*** (Hebrew *'adonay*), the king of the earth. • The word translated ***majestic*** (sometimes translated "mighty") can describe kings (136:18), heroes (16:3), mountains (76:4), or waves breaking on the seashore (93:4).

2 You have taught children and infants
to tell of your strength,
silencing your enemies
and all who oppose you.
3 When I look at the night sky and see the
work of your fingers—
the moon and the stars you set in
place—
4 what are mere mortals that you should
think about them,
[h]human beings that you should care
for them?
5 Yet you made them only a little lower
than God
and crowned them with glory and
honor.
6 You gave them charge of everything you
made,
putting all things under their
authority—
7 the flocks and the herds
and all the wild animals,
8 the birds in the sky, the fish in the sea,
and everything that swims the ocean
currents.

9 O LORD, our Lord, your majestic name
fills the earth!

PSALM 9

For the choir director: A psalm of David, to be sung to the tune "Death of the Son."

1 I will praise you, LORD, with all my heart;
I will tell of all the marvelous things
you have done.
2 I will be filled with joy because of you.
I will sing praises to your name,
O Most High.

3 My enemies retreated;
they staggered and died when you
appeared.
4 For you have judged in my favor;
from your throne you have [i]judged
with fairness.

8:2 Matt 21:16
8:3 Ps 89:11; 136:9
8:4 Job 7:17; Ps 144:3; Heb 2:6-8; [h]*ben 'adam* (1121, 0120) ‣Ps 80:17
8:5 Ps 21:5; 82:6; 103:4
8:6 Gen 1:26, 28; *1 Cor 15:27
9:1 Ps 26:7; 86:12
9:2 Ps 66:2, 4; 92:1; 104:34
9:3 Ps 27:2; 56:9
9:4 Ps 47:8; 140:12; 1 Pet 2:23; [i]*shapat* (8199) ‣Ps 75:7
9:5 Ps 69:28; 119:21
9:6 Ps 34:16; 40:15

While all are awe-inspiring and mighty, the created order pales in comparison with the Lord. • A person's ***name*** embodies his reputation. • ***The earth*** and ***the heavens*** reveal the Lord's splendor. All creation worships and praises the Lord (66:4; 113:3; 145:21).

8:2 ***to tell of your strength:*** Greek version reads *to give you praise.* Cp. Matt 21:16. • ***silencing:*** The loud noise of the oppressors contrasts with the praise of God. In the end, the praise of God will overwhelm the sound of evil (31:18; 63:11; 101:5; 143:12). • Those who ***oppose*** God seethe with vindictive anger (2:1-3; 44:16; cp. 149:6-7).

8:3-5 In light of God's awesome glory, it might seem that people would be insignificant to him. However, he has ***crowned them with glory and honor*** and placed them over all creation.

8:3 The nations around Israel worshiped heavenly objects as deities. The sun, ***moon,*** and ***stars*** are indeed immense and glorious, but they are merely ***the work of your fingers,*** a reason to praise the Almighty.

8:4 ***what are mere mortals that you should think about them, / human beings that you should care for them?*** Literally *what is man that you should think of him, / the son of man* (or *son of Adam*) *that you should care for him?* See also 144:3. • ***human beings*** (literally *son of Adam*): The Hebrew idiom *son of man* (or *son of Adam*) means a human being. Through the influence of Dan 7:13-14, it became a title with divine overtones in the NT. See Heb 2:6-8, where this passage is quoted.

8:5 ***Yet you made them only a little lower than God:*** Or *Yet you made them only a little lower than the angels;* Hebrew reads *Yet you made him* [i.e., man] *a little lower than Elohim.* Humans bear God's image; the Lord has endowed humans with dignity and charged them to rule (Gen 1:26-27). Hebrews 2:6-8 applies these words to Jesus Christ, the ideal human who fully realized God's purposes. • ***them:*** Literally *him* (i.e., man).

8:6 ***gave them*** (literally *him,* i.e., man) ***charge of everything:*** The psalmist is still referring to humans in general. Paul applies these words to Jesus as the perfect man who has made the created order—even death (1 Cor 15:25-27)—subject to God and his glory. The NT connects these themes of creation and salvation with Jesus Christ (John 1:1-2, 14; Col 1:16).

8:7-8 ***Wild animals,*** including ***birds*** and ***fish,*** remind readers of God's creation of the animal world in Gen 1. Contrary to beliefs among Israel's neighbors in the ancient Near East, animals are not sacred.

Pss 9–10 This hymn celebrates the Lord's kingship and victory over evil. It might also serve as a response to the laments of Pss 3–7. Some believe that Pss 9 and 10 should be read together as one psalm in two parts because Ps 9 includes a title and Ps 10 does not, and although several letters are missing or inverted, the two psalms connect as an acrostic of the Hebrew alphabet (see note on Ps 25; other such alphabetic acrostics are Pss 25, 34, 37, 111–112, 119, 145). The ancient Greek and Latin translations treat Pss 9 and 10 as one.

9:TITLE This psalm was originally ***sung to the tune "Death of the Son,"*** but that tune is no longer known. So also with the tunes mentioned in Pss 22, 45, 56–60, 69, 75, and 80.

9:1 The verb translated ***praise*** is translated "thank" in 7:17, suggesting a close connection between Pss 7 and 9 (see 7:17; 8:1-2). ***With all my heart*** expresses the psalmist's deep devotion and commitment (86:12; 111:1; 119:10; 138:1). • ***I will tell:*** These stories educate the next generation (78:4; 145:4); when they are not remembered, a generation might easily depart from the Lord (78:11, 32). • The ***marvelous things*** include the Lord's judgments on the enemies of his people (9:4) and his care for the oppressed (9:9). The wonders in creation, in redemption, and in revelation reveal his character and show his power (89:5; 111:4; 119:18, 27). His powerful manifestations evoke public praise (9:1; 26:7; 75:1).

9:2 ***filled with joy . . . sing praises:*** The psalmist often connects joy with praises, as one leads to the other (5:11-12; 32:11; 67:4; 90:14; 92:4). • ***Most High:*** See note on 91:1.

9:3-6 The psalmist celebrates God's judgment of the wicked, which is a testimony to the Lord's reliable promise to establish his kingdom on earth (1:6; Ps 2).

9:3 ***retreated . . . staggered:*** The Lord overpowers even powerful ***enemies*** (see 27:2). Israel also experienced judgment when it resisted the Lord (107:12).

9:4 The ***throne*** represents the Lord's royal authority.

9:7
Ps 10:16; 89:14-15
9:8
Ps 96:13
[j]*tsedeq* (6664)
‣Ps 23:3
9:9
Ps 18:2; 37:39; 59:9, 16-17
9:10
Ps 37:28; 91:14; 94:14
[k]*'azab* (5800)
‣Ps 22:1
9:11
Ps 76:2; 105:1
9:12
Gen 9:5-6
Ps 72:14
9:13
Ps 30:3; 38:19; 86:13
9:14
Ps 13:5; 20:5; 35:9; 51:12; 106:2
9:15
Ps 7:15; 35:8
9:16
[a]*mishpat* (4941)
‣Ps 33:5
9:17
Ps 49:14; 50:22
9:18
Ps 9:12; 62:5; 71:5
9:19
Num 10:35
2 Chr 14:11
9:20
Ps 62:9
10:1
Ps 13:1; 22:1; 55:1
10:2
Ps 7:15; 9:16; 73:6, 8

5 You have rebuked the nations and
destroyed the wicked;
you have erased their names forever.
6 The enemy is finished, in endless ruins;
the cities you uprooted are now
forgotten.
7 But the LORD reigns forever,
executing judgment from his throne.
8 He will judge the world with [j]justice
and rule the nations with fairness.
9 The LORD is a shelter for the oppressed,
a refuge in times of trouble.
10 Those who know your name trust in you,
for you, O LORD, do not [k]abandon
those who search for you.
11 Sing praises to the LORD who reigns in
Jerusalem.
Tell the world about his unforgettable
deeds.
12 For he who avenges murder cares for the
helpless.
He does not ignore the cries of those
who suffer.

13 LORD, have mercy on me.
See how my enemies torment me.
Snatch me back from the jaws of
death.
14 Save me so I can praise you publicly at
Jerusalem's gates,
so I can rejoice that you have
rescued me.
15 The nations have fallen into the pit they
dug for others.
Their own feet have been caught in
the trap they set.
16 The LORD is known for his [a]justice.
The wicked are trapped by their own
deeds. *Quiet Interlude*

17 The wicked will go down to the grave.
This is the fate of all the nations who
ignore God.
18 But the needy will not be ignored
forever;
the hopes of the poor will not always
be crushed.

19 Arise, O LORD!
Do not let mere mortals defy you!
Judge the nations!
20 Make them tremble in fear, O LORD.
Let the nations know they are merely
human. *Interlude*

PSALM 10

1 O LORD, why do you stand so far away?
Why do you hide when I am in
trouble?
2 The wicked arrogantly hunt down the
poor.

9:5 God created the heavens and the earth with a word (Gen 1), and he can bring ***nations*** to an end with a word (see 2:5). Evil and those who do evil will come to an absolute end (109:13; Rev 21:4; see note on 69:28).

9:7-10 The godly do not put their hope in corruptible human government but in God's everlasting rule of ***justice*** and ***fairness*** (see Pss 96–100).

9:9 The Lord provides ***shelter*** in dangerous circumstances and ***refuge*** from powerful and oppressive people. The Psalter includes many similar images of the Lord, such as fortress (18:2; 31:2), refuge (59:16-17), rock (18:2; 42:9), strength (18:1), and strong tower (144:2). These images occur frequently in the royal prayers (see 9:9; 18:30). • Even ***oppressed***, afflicted, and marginalized people (10:17; 74:21) can enjoy divine protection. • The ***times of trouble*** (10:1; 20:1) stand in contrast with appointed times when the Lord openly bestows his favor upon the afflicted (69:13; 102:13; see 107:6).

9:10 Alienation from the Lord might be part of an individual's experience (22:1; 42:9; 119:8), yet the psalms affirm that the Lord will not ***abandon*** his people (16:10; 37:25, 28).

9:11-12 Recognition that the Lord's judgment falls on some of the wicked (9:3-6) and that God promises to judge all evil (9:7-10) motivates praise. The psalmist calls on the godly community to join him.

9:11 The psalm writers often connect the idea that God ***reigns*** (or *sits,* or *is enthroned*) with a place, such as heaven (2:4; see 47:9), ***Jerusalem*** (Hebrew *Zion;* also in 9:14), "between the cherubim" (80:1; 99:1), "on high" (113:5), or "at the right hand" (110:1). Since the Lord rules the ***world,*** all people must know of ***his unforgettable deeds*** of salvation (see 9:1; 64:9; 66:16; 105:1).

9:12 The Lord ***avenges*** and saves his servants (18:46) by righteously judging his enemies on earth (58:11). The godly do not seek revenge; they wait for the Lord to vindicate them (94:1-2; Deut 32:35; Rom 12:19).

9:13 The psalmist returns from a vision of the glorious future to the reality of facing his ***enemies*** (9:3). • The ***jaws*** (literally *gates)* are a vivid image of the powerful grip of ***death*** (see 13:3-4).

9:14 ***Jerusalem's gates*** provide an intentional contrast to "the gates of death" (see note on 9:13).

9:16 ***Quiet Interlude:*** Hebrew *Higgayon Selah.* The meaning of this phrase is uncertain.

9:17 ***to the grave:*** Hebrew *to Sheol.* See note on 6:5.

9:18 Hope requires waiting for the Lord's rescue or justice (25:3, 5, 21). The godly find hope, rest, and quietness as they await the Lord (see 1:6; 27:14).

9:19-20 The psalmist ends his lament with a prayer for the Lord's intervention and divine vengeance. • ***mere mortals . . . merely human:*** Humans who have received authority and glory sometimes become oppressive and assume glory for themselves (see 8:4; 10:18).

Ps 10 The lament of Ps 9:13-20 continues in Ps 10 (see note on Pss 9–10), but the mood changes from confident assertion to anguished questioning. The psalmist prays for rescue, believing that the Lord, as a just king, takes care of the needy.

10:1 The opening questions set the mood. The Lord does not seem to hear the prayers of his people (22:1, 19; see 2 Kgs 4:27; Isa 1:15).

10:2-11 Wicked and oppressive people might prosper, leaving ugly consequences. Evil can be as dramatic as the psalmist portrays it here, or it could be more subtle.

10:2 ***The wicked*** brazenly defy God with their acts and speech (17:10; 31:18;

Let them be caught in the evil they
plan for others.
3 For they brag about their evil desires;
they praise the greedy and curse the
LORD.
4 The wicked are too proud to seek God.
They seem to think that God is dead.
5 Yet they succeed in everything they do.
They do not see your punishment
awaiting them.
They sneer at all their enemies.
6 They think, "Nothing bad will ever
happen to us!
We will be free of trouble forever!"
7 Their mouths are full of cursing, lies,
and threats.
Trouble and evil are on the tips of
their tongues.
8 They lurk in ambush in the villages,
waiting to murder innocent people.
They are always searching for helpless
victims.
9 Like lions crouched in hiding,
they wait to pounce on the helpless.
Like hunters they capture the helpless
and drag them away in nets.
10 Their helpless victims are crushed;
they fall beneath the strength of the
wicked.
11 The wicked think, "God isn't watching us!
He has closed his eyes and won't even
see what we do!"

12 Arise, O LORD!
Punish the wicked, O God!
Do not ignore the helpless!
13 Why do the wicked get away with
despising God?
They think, "God will never call us to
account."
14 But you see the trouble and grief they
cause.
You take note of it and punish them.
The helpless put their trust in you.
You defend the orphans.
15 Break the arms of these wicked, evil
people!
Go after them until the last one is
destroyed.
16 The LORD is king [b]forever and ever!
The godless nations will vanish from
the land.
17 LORD, you know the hopes of the helpless.
Surely you will hear their cries and
comfort them.
18 You will bring justice to the orphans and
the oppressed,
so mere people can no longer terrify
them.

PSALM 11

For the choir director: A psalm of David.

1 I trust in the LORD for protection.
So why do you say to me,
"Fly like a bird to the mountains for
safety!
2 The wicked are stringing their bows
and fitting their arrows on the
bowstrings.
They shoot from the shadows
at those whose hearts are right.
3 The foundations of law and order have
collapsed.
What can the righteous do?"

4 But the LORD is in his holy Temple;
the LORD still rules from [c]heaven.

10:3 Ps 49:6; 94:3-4
10:4 Ps 14:1; 36:1-2
10:5 Ps 28:5; 52:7
10:6 Ps 30:6-7; 49:11
10:7 Ps 59:12; 73:8; 140:3 *Rom 3:14
10:8 Ps 11:2; 94:6-7
10:9 Ps 10:2; 17:12; 59:3; 140:5
10:11 Ps 10:4
10:12 Ps 9:12; 17:7
10:14 Ps 9:12; 22:9-11; 37:5
10:15 Ps 37:17; 140:11
10:16 Deut 8:20 Ps 29:10 [b]*'olam* (5769) ‣ Ps 30:12
10:17 Ps 9:18; 34:15; 145:19
10:18 Ps 9:9; 74:21; 146:9 Isa 29:20
11:1 Ps 121:1-2
11:2 Ps 7:12; 64:3-4
11:3 Ps 82:5
11:4 Ps 34:15-16; 103:19 [c]*shamayim* (8064) ‣ Ps 19:1

59:12; 73:8; 123:4). Although the Lord will deal with them (31:23), they disturb the righteous (see 5:4-6) prior to their condemnation and judgment.

10:3 Unlike those who have ***evil desires***, the godly wait for justice (10:17).

10:4 ***God is dead:*** See 10:11; 14:1.

10:6-7 Despite their evil ways (5:9; 28:3; Rom 3:14), the wicked expect a future ***free of trouble*** such as the righteous will enjoy. • ***cursing, lies, and threats:*** Greek version reads *cursing and bitterness.* Cp. Rom 3:14.

10:8 The wicked rely on outright violence (11:5; 37:32) and deception (Prov 12:6; 23:27-28).

10:12-15 With confidence that the wicked will be held responsible for their deeds and that the Lord will care for the helpless, the psalmist prays intensely for rescue from evil.

10:14 Because the Lord cares for the afflicted, he will ***take note*** and ***punish*** evildoers (see 72:14; 116:15).

10:15 The psalmist strongly invokes a curse as he prays (see "Prayers for Vengeance" at Ps 137, p. 1017). • ***Arms*** represent an ability to wage war (18:34; 44:3).

10:16 As the true and just ***king***, God will bring the wicked to an end, as he promises (1:6).

10:17-18 The psalmist expresses his confidence in the Lord.

10:18 ***Mere people*** (see note on 8:4) misuse their power and enslave the very people God wants them to serve (see 9:19-20; Luke 22:25-26).

Ps 11 The psalmist affirms his faith in the righteous God. Even though the world appears hopelessly chaotic, both the godly and the wicked can count on God's justice. The godly can depend on him as a refuge and shelter.

11:1 God provides ***protection*** (or *refuge;* see 5:11; 9:9; 25:20) when the foundations of justice collapse. • The ***mountains*** provide another place of refuge (see 121:1; see note on 30:6-7).

11:2-3 In the inevitable battle between the evil and the godly, the wicked cannot tolerate the righteous, so they victimize them. This seems to leave the godly with nothing but questions.

11:2 The ***wicked*** live in the ***shadows*** and create gloom for the godly (82:5; 139:11; 143:3; Prov 4:19).

11:3 The wicked create a world of darkness (see 82:5).

11:4 The righteous King ***rules from heaven***, where his throne is untouched by human corruption (see

11:5 Gen 22:1; Ps 5:5
11:6 Jer 4:11-12; Ezek 38:22
11:7 Ps 7:9-11; 17:15; 33:5
12:1 Mic 7:1-2
12:2 Ps 28:3; 41:6; Jer 9:8; Rom 16:18
12:3 Ps 55:21; 73:8-9
12:5 Ps 3:7; 34:6; 35:10
12:6 Ps 19:8-10; 119:140; Prov 30:5
12:7 Ps 37:28; 97:10
12:8 Ps 55:10-11
13:1 Job 13:24; Ps 44:24; 89:46
13:2 Ps 42:4-5, 9

He watches everyone closely,
examining every person on earth.
5 The LORD examines both the righteous
and the wicked.
He hates those who love violence.
6 He will rain down blazing coals and
burning sulfur on the wicked,
punishing them with scorching
winds.
7 For the righteous LORD loves justice.
The virtuous will see his face.

PSALM 12

For the choir director: A psalm of David, to be accompanied by an eight-stringed instrument.

1 Help, O LORD, for the godly are fast
disappearing!
The faithful have vanished from the
earth!
2 Neighbors lie to each other,
speaking with flattering lips and
deceitful hearts.
3 May the LORD cut off their flattering lips
and silence their boastful tongues.
4 They say, "We will lie to our hearts'
content.
Our lips are our own—who can stop us?"
5 The LORD replies, "I have seen violence
done to the helpless,
and I have heard the groans of the poor.
Now I will rise up to rescue them,
as they have longed for me to do."
6 The LORD's promises are pure,
like silver refined in a furnace,
purified seven times over.
7 Therefore, LORD, we know you will
protect the oppressed,
preserving them forever from this
lying generation,
8 even though the wicked strut about,
and evil is praised throughout the land.

PSALM 13

For the choir director: A psalm of David.

1 O LORD, how long will you forget me?
Forever?
How long will you look the other way?
2 How long must I struggle with anguish
in my soul,

The Poor and Needy (Ps 10)

Ps 9:18; 10:2; 12:5; 22:1-31; 34:1-22; 35:10; 37:14; 40:17; 41:1; 49:2; 68:10; 69:33; 70:5; 72:2-4, 12-13; 74:21; 82:3-4; 107:41; 109:16, 22, 31; 132:15; 140:12

The poor and needy are oppressed, persecuted people. They hunger and thirst for righteousness, but are deprived of it by the structures of society or the rapacious people around them (14:6; 37:14; 109:16). In their distress, they take refuge in the Lord (see 107:4-9), and they cry out to the Lord (25:16-18; 74:19; 76:9), who has promised to care for them (1:6). They have faith in him and wait hopefully for the Lord to appear and bring justice (1:18; 70:5).

One psalmist confessed that he had cried out to the Lord all his life (88:15). Much of life might be lived in anguish (90:15; see Ps 102). Affliction might be a form of discipline that gives training in righteousness (119:71, 75). The psalms testify that the Lord hears the cry of the poor (10:17-18; 12:5; 22:24; 34:6; 35:10; 74:21-23; 82:4; 86:1; 107:41; 109:22, 31; 113:5-7; 140:12) and that they will be satisfied (22:26; 132:15). Then the godly will rejoice (34:2; 69:32).

Like the Lord, the messianic king brings justice to his afflicted people (72:2, 4, 12), yet he confesses that he, too, is needy (40:17). The Davidic kings before Christ did not bring ultimate justice. Jesus identifies with our human situation (Isa 53:4, 7); he is the hope of those who recognize their poverty and their need (see Matt 5:3-12).

2:4). He examines everyone and sees everything that happens on earth (see 14:2-3).

11:5 ***hates:*** See 5:4-6; Prov 6:16-18. • Wicked deeds result in destruction and ***violence*** (58:2; 73:6; 74:20).

11:6 God rained ***blazing coals*** and ***burning sulfur*** on Sodom and Gomorrah (Gen 19) as symbols of judgment (18:8; 120:4; 140:10).

11:7 The godly are assured of the Lord's favorable presence when they ***see his face*** (see 23:6).

Ps 12 This community lament seeks the Lord's help against the prevalence of evil. Because of the Lord's answer, the godly can face the future knowing that God protects them.

12:TITLE ***to be accompanied by an eight-stringed instrument:*** Hebrew *according to the sheminith.*

12:1-4 Evil becomes so pervasive that the godly pray for rescue (Isa 57:1; Mic 7:2; cp. 1:6; 37:20; 58:7; 104:35).

12:3 ***May the LORD cut off:*** See "Prayers for Vengeance" at Ps 137, p. 1017.

12:4 The words ***they say*** reveal the character of the wicked. They deceive and overpower the godly and arrogantly question the Lord's purposes.

12:6 The godly can rely on the ***LORD's promises,*** but not on the lies of the wicked (12:2-4). • ***Seven times*** means totally or completely.

12:7-8 The godly know that the Lord cares, even though the wicked continue to oppress them. The Lord sees the corrupt and foolish people who praise evildoers (see 9:19-20; 14:2-6).

Ps 13 The psalmist's piercing cry for help becomes a confident song of hope.

13:1-2 ***how long?*** The fourfold repetition expresses agitation and deep anguish (79:5).

13:2 A sense of ***anguish*** and ***sorrow*** closes off any perspective of hope (6:3). Unless the Lord answers the psalmist's prayers (22:1), death seems inescapable,

with sorrow in my heart every day?
How long will my enemy have the upper hand?

3 Turn and answer me, O LORD my God!
Restore the sparkle to my eyes, or I will die.
4 Don't let my enemies gloat, saying, "We have defeated him!"
Don't let them rejoice at my downfall.

5 But I trust in your unfailing love.
I will rejoice because you have rescued me.
6 I will sing to the LORD
because he is good to me.

PSALM 14

Ps 14:1-7 // Ps 53:1-6

For the choir director: A psalm of David.

1 Only fools say in their hearts,
"There is no God."
They are corrupt, and their actions are evil;
not one of them does good!
2 The LORD looks down from heaven
on the entire human race;
he looks to see if anyone is truly wise,
if anyone seeks God.
3 But no, all have turned away;
all have become corrupt.
No one does good,
not a single one!
4 Will those who do evil never learn?
They eat up my people like bread
and wouldn't think of praying to the LORD.
5 Terror will grip them,
for God is with those who obey him.
6 The wicked frustrate the plans of the oppressed,
but the LORD will protect his people.

7 Who will come from Mount Zion to rescue Israel?
When the LORD restores his people,
Jacob will shout with joy, and Israel will rejoice.

PSALM 15

A psalm of David.

1 Who may worship in your sanctuary, LORD?
Who may enter your presence on your holy hill?
2 Those who lead [d]blameless lives and do what is right,
speaking the truth from sincere hearts.
3 Those who refuse to gossip
or harm their neighbors
or speak evil of their friends.
4 Those who despise flagrant sinners,
and honor the faithful followers of the LORD,
and keep their promises even when it hurts.
5 Those who lend money without charging interest,
and who cannot be bribed to lie about the innocent.
Such people will stand firm forever.

13:3 Ezra 9:8; Job 33:29-30; Ps 5:1
13:4 Ps 25:2; 38:16
13:5 Ps 9:14; 52:8
13:6 Ps 116:7
14:1-7 //Ps 53:1-6
14:1 Ps 10:4; 53:1; *Rom 3:10-12
14:2 Ps 33:13-15; 102:19
14:3 Ps 58:3; 143:2
14:4 Isa 64:7
14:6 Ps 9:9; 40:17
14:7 Job 42:10; Ps 53:6; 85:1-2
15:1 Ps 24:3; 27:5-6
15:2 Ps 24:4; Eph 4:25; [d]*tamim* (8549) ‣Ps 18:25
15:3 Exod 23:1; Ps 28:3
15:4 Judg 11:35; Acts 28:10
15:5 Exod 22:25; 23:8; Deut 16:19

torturous, and slow (6:6; 32:3; 55:4; 61:2; 102:5; 116:3). The psalmist hardly knows how to pray; he longs for God's redemption (25:17-18; 31:10; 38:8; 39:2).

13:3-4 Only the Lord can bring enlightenment and relief. The psalmist longs for the Lord's vindication so that his foes will not rejoice.

13:3 The psalmist's affliction feels like death (22:15; 55:4; 88:15; 94:17; 116:3).

13:5-6 The psalmist no longer hears the ridicule of his foes. Instead, because of his trust in the Lord, he is full of joy.

Ps 14 This wisdom psalm contains some characteristics of lament and prophetic speech. The ideals of Ps 8 have run aground on the reality of foolish human attitudes and sinful actions. With the exception of vv 5-6, this psalm parallels Ps 53.

14:1-3 Paul uses phrases from the Greek translation of this passage in his description of the depravity of all people (Rom 3:10-12).

14:1 Also known as *fools,* the wicked speak to themselves, think, scheme (10:4, 6, 11), and make claims; however, because they do not heed God's revelation, they possess no understanding (14:1; 39:8; 53:1; 74:18; 74:22).

14:2-3 From ***heaven*** (33:13; 80:14; 102:19), the Lord sees the wicked, who stand out as vile sinners (11:3-5). The ***entire human race*** lacks wisdom and fails to live up to the glory originally given to them (10:4-11; see Rom 1–3).

14:3 ***have become corrupt:*** Greek version reads *have become useless.* Cp. Rom 3:12.

14:4 The evil live at the expense of others (27:2; 44:11; 53:4; see Isa 5:8) and have no reverence or knowledge of God (79:6).

14:5 Though the wicked perish (1:5-6), ***God is with*** the godly.

14:7 The psalmist prays for the renewal of God's relationship with his people. • ***Jacob*** is a synonym for ***Israel*** (see Gen 35:9-10).

Pss 15–19 The psalms in this section affirm integrity and purity (17:15; 18:20-26; 19:13-14). They refer to people as dwelling in God's presence (16:9-11; 17:15) and as not being shaken (15:5; 16:8).

Ps 15 In this wisdom poem, the psalmist contrasts the lifestyle of the godly with the actions of fools (Ps 14). The questions in this psalm invite readers to examine themselves and to look away from problems with the wicked. The question of who dwells in God's presence leads into a description of godly character qualities (cp. 24:3-6; Isa 33:14-16).

15:1 Only the godly may reside in the Lord's ***presence*** (5:4). As his guests, they experience his hospitality and protection. • ***sanctuary*** (or ***tent***): In David's time, God's sanctuary was a tent (the Tabernacle; see 1 Sam 21:6; 2 Sam 6:17; 7:6; 12:20; 1 Chr 6:32).

15:2 The godly speak truthfully and act faithfully in their relationships. Unlike the wicked, they are open and transparent (12:2-4).

15:5 The Lord prohibited Israel from ***charging interest*** to people in need (Exod 22:25-27). • The assurance of

16:1
Ps 7:1; 17:8
[e]*'el* (0410)
‣Ps 17:6

16:2
Ps 73:25

16:3
Ps 101:6; 119:63

16:4
Exod 23:13
Josh 23:7
Ps 32:10; 106:37-38

16:6
Ps 78:55
Jer 3:19

16:7
Ps 73:24; 77:6

16:8
Ps 27:8; 73:23; 110:5; 123:1-2

16:10
Ps 49:15; 86:13
*Acts 2:25-28; 13:35
[f]*she'ol* (7585)
‣Ps 49:14

16:11
Ps 36:7-8
[g]*simkhah* (8057)
‣Ps 30:11

17:1
Ps 61:1; 88:2; 142:6

17:2
Ps 98:8-9; 99:4; 103:6

17:3
Job 23:10
Ps 26:1-2; 39:1; 66:10
Jer 50:20

17:4
Ps 10:5-11; 119:9, 101

17:5
Ps 18:36; 37:30-31; 44:18

17:6
[h]*'el* (0410)
‣Ps 36:7

PSALM 16
A psalm of David.

1 Keep me safe, O [e]God,
for I have come to you for refuge.

2 I said to the LORD, "You are my Master!
Every good thing I have comes from
you."
3 The godly people in the land
are my true heroes!
I take pleasure in them!
4 Troubles multiply for those who chase
after other gods.
I will not take part in their sacrifices
of blood
or even speak the names of their gods.

5 LORD, you alone are my inheritance, my
cup of blessing.
You guard all that is mine.
6 The land you have given me is a pleasant
land.
What a wonderful inheritance!

7 I will bless the LORD who guides me;
even at night my heart instructs me.
8 I know the LORD is always with me.
I will not be shaken, for he is right
beside me.

9 No wonder my heart is glad, and I
rejoice.
My body rests in safety.
10 For you will not leave my soul among the
[f]dead
or allow your holy one to rot in the
grave.
11 You will show me the way of life,
granting me the [g]joy of your presence
and the pleasures of living with you
forever.

PSALM 17
A prayer of David.

1 O LORD, hear my plea for justice.
Listen to my cry for help.
Pay attention to my prayer,
for it comes from honest lips.
2 Declare me innocent,
for you see those who do right.

3 You have tested my thoughts and
examined my heart in the night.
You have scrutinized me and found
nothing wrong.
I am determined not to sin in what I
say.
4 I have followed your commands,
which keep me from following cruel
and evil people.
5 My steps have stayed on your path;
I have not wavered from following
you.

6 I am praying to you because I know you
will answer, O [h]God.
Bend down and listen as I pray.
7 Show me your unfailing love in
wonderful ways.

God's presence keeps the godly from destruction (16:8; 46:5; 125:1). Their circumstances might shake them temporarily, but they ultimately ***stand firm*** (30:6; 94:18; 112:6).

Ps 16 In this psalm of confidence, the poet moves quickly from a short petition (16:1), to expressions of passionate commitment to God and his people (16:2-6), to a conclusion of confident praise (16:7-11).

16:TITLE ***A psalm:*** Hebrew *miktam.* This may be a literary or musical term.

16:1 The psalmist feels *safe* because the Lord alone offers security (16:5-6), guidance (16:7-8), and the joy of his presence (16:9-11).

16:2 ***I said to the LORD:*** The various writers of the psalms pray, lament, and praise the Lord throughout the Psalter, and the Lord answers them (see 12:5-6).

16:4 The psalmist dissociates himself from ungodly worship, rituals, and words (see 15:3-5).

16:5 The ***cup of blessing*** represents God's provision for all the psalmist's needs (23:5; see 116:13; cp. 75:8; Isa 51:17).

16:6 The ***land*** is God's gift for his people (Deut 18:8).

16:7-8 God's instruction brings life (16:11; see 5:8; 23:1-3; 32:8; 73:24). • The psalmist so deeply depends on the Lord for strength and joy that he senses that God is ***right beside*** him (16:11; see 73:23; 109:31; 110:1, 5; 121:5). • Peter quoted 16:8-11 in his sermon on the day of Pentecost (Acts 2:25-28).

16:9-11 Knowing that not even death can separate him from the Lord strengthens the psalmist's confidence. He fears a separation (see 13:3-4), but he remains confident of seeing the Lord (see 11:7).

16:9 ***and I rejoice:*** Greek version reads *and my tongue shouts his praises.* Cp. Acts 2:26.

16:10 The psalmist expresses his confidence that life continues beyond death. The apostles applied this text to the resurrection of Jesus (Acts 2:25-33; 13:35). • ***among the dead:*** Hebrew *in Sheol.* See note on 6:5. • ***your holy one:*** Or *your Holy One*; see 86:2.

16:11 ***You will show me the way of life, / granting me the joy of your presence:*** Greek version reads *You have shown me the way of life, / and you will fill me with the joy of your presence.* Cp. Acts 2:28. • ***with you:*** See 16:7-8; 110:1.

Ps 17 The psalmist pleads for God's protection and vindication, affirms his own integrity, and prays that the Lord will prevail against his fierce enemies.

17:1 ***comes from honest lips:*** Deception characterizes the wicked. The godly reject such deceit as a failure of character and pray for rescue from such people (5:6; 43:1; 120:2). They love honesty, truth, and integrity (15:2-3; 24:4; 101:7).

17:3-5 The psalmist declares his innocence (17:1) and commits himself to integrity by being open to God's examination.

17:3 Though he is not perfect, the psalmist commits himself to the Lord. He does not want to *sin* through deception, flattery, or gossip (see 10:7; 15:2-3; 17:1).

17:6-9 This prayer for God's care returns to the petition begun in 17:1-2 for redemption from evil.

By your mighty power you rescue
those who seek refuge from their
enemies.
8 Guard me as you would guard your own
eyes.
Hide me in the shadow of your
wings.
9 Protect me from wicked people who
attack me,
from murderous enemies who
surround me.
10 They are without pity.
Listen to their boasting!
11 They track me down and
surround me,
watching for the chance to throw me
to the ground.
12 They are like hungry lions, eager to tear
me apart—
like young lions hiding in ambush.
13 Arise, O LORD!
Stand against them, and bring them
to their knees!
Rescue me from the wicked with your
sword!
14 By the power of your hand, O LORD,
destroy those who look to this world
for their reward.
But satisfy the hunger of your treasured
ones.
May their children have plenty,
leaving an inheritance for their
descendants.
15 Because I am righteous, I will see you.
When I awake, I will see you face to
face and be satisfied.

PSALM 18

Ps 18:1-50 // 2 Sam 22:1-51

For the choir director: A psalm of David, the servant of the LORD. He sang this song to the LORD on the day the LORD rescued him from all his enemies and from Saul. He sang:

1 I love you, LORD;
you are my strength.
2 The LORD is my rock, my fortress, and
my savior;
my God is my rock, in whom I find
protection.
He is my shield, the power that saves me,
and my place of safety.
3 I called on the LORD, who is worthy of
praise,
and he saved me from my enemies.
4 The ropes of death entangled me;
floods of [i]destruction swept over me.
5 The grave wrapped its ropes around me;
death laid a trap in my path.
6 But in my distress I cried out to the LORD;
yes, I prayed to my God for help.
He heard me from his sanctuary;
my cry to him reached his ears.
7 Then the earth quaked and trembled.
The foundations of the mountains
shook;
they quaked because of his anger.
8 Smoke poured from his nostrils;
fierce flames leaped from his mouth.
Glowing coals blazed forth from him.
9 He opened the heavens and came down;
dark storm clouds were beneath his
feet.

17:8 Deut 32:10; Ruth 2:12; Ps 36:7; 91:1, 4
17:10 1 Sam 2:3; Ps 31:18; 73:7-8
17:11 Ps 37:14; 88:17
17:12 Ps 7:2; 10:9
17:13 Ps 22:20
17:14 Ps 73:3-7
17:15 Ps 4:6-7; 16:11; 140:13
18:TITLE //2 Sam 22:1-51
18:1 Ps 59:17
18:2 1 Sam 2:2; Ps 19:14; 28:1; 59:9, 11; 71:3; 75:10; 144:2
18:3 Num 10:9; Ps 34:6; 96:4
18:4 Ps 69:1-2; 116:3; 124:2-5
[i]*beliya'al* (1100) › Ps 101:3
18:5 Ps 116:3
18:6 Ps 3:4; 34:15
18:7 Ps 114:4, 6-7
18:9 Exod 20:21; Ps 97:2; 144:5

17:8 *as you would guard your own eyes* (literally *as the pupil of your eye*): This metaphor expresses God's care and affection for the psalmist (see Deut 32:10). • The *shadow of* God's *wings* is a place of his protection from enemies and adversity (36:7; 57:1; 61:4; 63:7; 91:4).

17:13-14 The psalmist confidently prays for the Lord's victory, knowing that God possesses more power than the evildoers. The psalmist finds his joy in the Lord's inheritance (16:5), whereas the wicked search for joy in this world.

17:15 *see you face to face:* The psalmist does not allow temporary concerns raised by adversaries to stand in the way of his experiencing a real and lasting relationship with the Lord.

Ps 18 This royal drama of divine rescue (also found with minor variations in 2 Sam 22) encourages readers who are following the laments and requests for rescue in Pss 16 and 17. The psalmist describes the dramatic nature of God's rescue in three different ways (18:7-15, 16-19, 30-36). The psalm also extends hope that a future Son of David will be totally victorious over evil (18:43-50; cp. Ps 2).

18:TITLE David was a faithful *servant of the LORD*, charged with the responsibility of establishing God's kingdom on earth (see 78:70; 132:10; 144:10). • The Lord *rescued* David *from all his enemies* when he enabled David to conquer them (see 2 Sam 8:1-14).

18:2 A *shield* is an image of protection, salvation, and victory (7:10; 18:2, 30, 35; 84:11; 91:4; 115:9, 10, 11; 119:114; 144:2). It evokes a response of trust, waiting, and godly confidence.

18:3 God deserves praise for his greatness and faithfulness (48:1; 96:4; 145:3).

18:5 *The grave:* Hebrew *Sheol.* See note on 6:5.

18:6 God dwells in *his sanctuary*, the heavenly temple (102:19; see 14:2-3). He knows everything, sees everyone, and will vindicate the godly (see 11:3-7).

18:7-15 The psalmist depicts the Lord's descent from heaven to earth with phenomena such as earthquakes, flames, smoke, darkness, and rain. Creation shudders at God's marvelous coming as the Divine Warrior (see 97:2-5) and Judge (see 50:1-6).

18:7 The destabilization of the whole *earth* will be a means of God's judgment (77:17-18; 96:9; 97:4; 99:1; 104:32; Isa 29:6; Mic 1:3-4; Nah 1:2-6; Hag 2:7, 21).

18:8 *his nostrils . . . his mouth:* The psalmist likens God to an angry person or a fierce creature (see Job 41:12-22). • The terrifying images of *smoke, flames,* and *glowing coals* express God's wrath against sin.

18:9-11 The Lord's sovereignty extends over all of nature (see 104:2-4; 148:5-6).

18:10
Ps 80:1; 99:1
18:12
Ps 97:2; 104:1-2
18:13
Ps 29:3; 104:7-8
18:14
Ps 144:6
18:15
Exod 15:8
Ps 106:9
18:16
Ps 144:7
18:17
Ps 35:10
18:18
Ps 16:8; 59:16
18:19
Ps 31:8; 37:23; 41:1, 11; 118:5
18:20
Ps 7:8; 24:4
18:21
2 Chr 34:33
Ps 37:34; 119:33, 102-103

10 Mounted on a mighty angelic being, he flew,
soaring on the wings of the wind.
11 He shrouded himself in darkness,
veiling his approach with dark rain clouds.
12 Thick clouds shielded the brightness around him
and rained down hail and burning coals.
13 The LORD thundered from heaven;
the voice of the Most High resounded
amid the hail and burning coals.
14 He shot his arrows and scattered his enemies;
his lightning flashed, and they were greatly confused.
15 Then at your command, O LORD,
at the blast of your breath,
the bottom of the sea could be seen,
and the foundations of the earth were laid bare.
16 He reached down from heaven and rescued me;
he drew me out of deep waters.
17 He rescued me from my powerful enemies,
from those who hated me and were too strong for me.
18 They attacked me at a moment when I was in distress,
but the LORD supported me.
19 He led me to a place of safety;
he rescued me because he delights in me.
20 The LORD rewarded me for doing right;
he restored me because of my innocence.
21 For I have kept the ways of the LORD;
I have not turned from my God to follow evil.
22 I have followed all his regulations;
I have never abandoned his decrees.
23 I am blameless before God;
I have kept myself from sin.
24 The LORD rewarded me for doing right.
He has seen my innocence.

Salvation in the Psalms (Ps 18)

Ps 3:7-8; 6:4; 7:10; 14:7; 16:9-11; 17:7; 18:17-20, 27-28, 46-48; 20:6; 22:4-5; 25:4-14; 27:1; 31:1-2, 15-16; 32:1-5; 33:18-19; 34:6-7, 17-19; 40:16-17; 43:5; 46:1-11; 62:1-8; 70:4-5; 72:12-14; 80:1-19; 91:1-16; 98:1-3; 107:1-43; 121:1-8; 149:4

The psalmists experienced God's salvation (see 32:1-5) as rescue from evil in the world. They were well acquainted with grief (69:18). It seemed to them that God had abandoned them and that the wicked took advantage of the apparent injustice to ridicule the godly (3:2; 71:11).

While waiting for rescue, the psalmists had faith that the Lord was with them, keeping guard over them (Pss 46, 121), and would not abandon them (16:10; 94:14; see also 7:10; 31:2; 62:6-7; 144:2). The psalmists cried out for rescue, knowing that they were completely dependent on the Lord (31:15; 35:17; 69:13).

God graciously rescues his needy servants and answers their prayers (20:6, 9; 28:8; 34:6, 18; 40:13; 76:9; 107; 145:19; 149:4). When the Lord rescues his people, he receives glory through their thanksgiving, praise, and testimony (50:15; 79:9; 85:9). God's mighty acts are recorded in Scripture so that his people will praise him for what he has done and trust him to rescue them.

The Psalter encourages the godly to identify themselves with these stories of salvation. For example, in Ps 18 the psalmist describes his anguish, his lament, and the Lord's salvation (18:17, 19, 20, 43, 48) in such a manner that all the humble are invited to look to the Lord in hope (72:12). The Lord has rescued the psalmist, and the Lord will save his people again.

Salvation excludes the wicked (69:27; 119:155), who ridicule those whose hope is in the Lord's rescue (22:8). They may call to the Lord in their hour of judgment, but he will not rescue them (18:27; 50:22; 78:22). Hope in God's salvation requires a life of faith (119:123) and love of the Lord (60:5; 108:6). Such faith casts out fear (34:4) because the Lord does what is right (71:2).

The Lord Jesus came to save sinners. He ministered to the needy and the marginalized, though he died under oppression. He rescues people from themselves, from Satan, from death, and from adversity. He has the power to vindicate the faithful, judge sinners, and completely save all of God's children. He will renew all things, while excluding the wicked from his everlasting salvation.

18:10 ***a mighty angelic being*** (Hebrew *a cherub*): See notes on 1 Chr 28:18; 2 Chr 3:10-13.

18:12 ***and burning coals:*** Or *and lightning bolts;* also in 18:13.

18:19 Because God loves and ***delights in*** the psalmist (see 18:1), he will save him (37:23; 41:11; 91:14-16).

18:20-24 The psalmist affirms that loyalty is rewarded. He puts his trust in the Lord (see 16:1) and commits himself to living with integrity (see Pss 1, 15, 24; see also 19:12-14).

18:21 ***kept the ways of the LORD:*** The psalmist faithfully obeys God's instructions (see 25:8-10). • ***not turned . . . to follow evil:*** The psalmist rejects the way of folly (see Pss 1, 14) and chooses the way of wisdom (see Pss 1, 15).

25 To the faithful you show yourself
faithful;
to those with [j]integrity you show
integrity.
26 To the pure you show yourself pure,
but to the wicked you show yourself
hostile.
27 You rescue the humble,
but you humiliate the proud.
28 You light a lamp for me.
The LORD, my God, lights up my
darkness.
29 In your strength I can crush an army;
with my God I can scale any wall.

30 God's way is perfect.
All the LORD's promises prove true.
He is a shield for all who look to him
for protection.
31 For who is God except the LORD?
Who but our God is a solid rock?
32 God arms me with strength,
and he makes my way perfect.
33 He makes me as surefooted as a deer,
enabling me to stand on mountain
heights.
34 He trains my hands for battle;
he strengthens my arm to draw a
bronze bow.
35 You have given me your shield of victory.
Your right hand supports me;
your help has made me great.
36 You have made a wide path for my feet
to keep them from slipping.

37 I chased my enemies and caught them;
I did not stop until they were
conquered.
38 I struck them down so they could not
get up;
they fell beneath my feet.
39 You have armed me with strength for
the battle;
you have subdued my enemies under
my feet.
40 You placed my foot on their necks.
I have destroyed all who hated me.
41 They called for help, but no one came to
their rescue.
They even cried to the LORD, but he
refused to answer.
42 I ground them as fine as dust in the wind.
I swept them into the gutter like dirt.
43 You gave me victory over my accusers.
You appointed me ruler over nations;
people I don't even know now
serve me.
44 As soon as they hear of me, they submit;
foreign nations cringe before me.
45 They all lose their courage
and come trembling from their
strongholds.

46 The LORD lives! Praise to my [k]Rock!
May the God of my salvation be
exalted!
47 He is the God who pays back those who
harm me;
he subdues the nations under me
48 and rescues me from my enemies.
You hold me safe beyond the reach of my
enemies;
you save me from violent opponents.
49 For this, O LORD, I will praise you among
the nations;
I will sing praises to your name.
50 You give great victories to your king;
you show unfailing love to your
anointed,
to David and all his descendants
forever.

18:25 Ps 62:12; Matt 5:7; [j]*tamim* (8549) ›Ps 19:7
18:27 Ps 72:12; 101:5; Prov 6:16-19
18:28 Job 18:6; Ps 27:1
18:29 Ps 118:10-12; 2 Cor 12:9
18:30 Ps 12:6; 19:7
18:31 Deut 32:31, 39; Ps 62:2; 86:8-10
18:32 Isa 45:5
18:33 Deut 32:13; Hab 3:19
18:35 Ps 33:20; 63:8; 119:117
18:36 Ps 31:8; 66:9
18:37 Ps 44:5
18:38 Ps 36:12; 47:3
18:40 Ps 21:12; 94:23
18:41 Ps 50:22
18:42 Ps 83:13
18:43 2 Sam 3:1; Ps 89:27; Isa 55:5
18:44 Ps 66:3
18:46 [k]*tsur* (6697) ›Ps 27:5
18:47 Ps 47:3; 94:1-2; 144:2
18:48 Ps 3:7; 27:5-6
18:49 Ps 108:1; *Rom 15:9
18:50 Ps 21:1; 28:8; 89:4

18:25-29 The *faithful* God remains true to his character. He loves faithfulness, blamelessness, and purity, and he hates the perverse (see 1:6).

18:26 The *pure* have clean hands (see 18:20-24). • ***to the wicked you show yourself hostile:*** The Lord knows each person's character, and he justly responds to them in kind.

18:27 ***proud:*** The Lord hates pride (101:5; 131:1; see Prov 6:16-17; 21:4; 30:13).

18:28 ***light a lamp:*** The Lord renews the psalmist's life, helping him overcome the *darkness* of adversity (see 112:4; 119:105).

18:29 ***scale any wall:*** God helps his servants fight their battles.

18:30-36 The psalmist experiences God's rescue and provision of victory.

18:30 ***perfect:*** God's character has integrity (see 18:26). • God ***promises*** to protect his people, and he does so. • Seeking God's ***protection*** entails trust and faith. Regardless of his feelings or external circumstances, the psalmist makes a deep commitment to the Lord. He experiences joy (5:11; 64:10) as he awaits the Lord's rescue (57:1).

18:32-34 The psalmist's victories come from the Lord. He completely depends on God.

18:36 A ***wide path*** represents freedom and safety (see 4:8; 119:35).

18:37-42 With help from the Divine Warrior, the psalmist experienced victory over his enemies.

18:40 Placing a ***foot*** on the ***necks*** of the enemy represents total victory (see Josh 10:23-26).

18:43-45 With God's victorious help, the psalmist achieved military and political success, thus fulfilling the history of David's dynasty (Ps 2). The previous laments find some resolution in this psalm.

18:46-50 The psalmist again reflects on the Lord's victories. God's marvelous rescue and the king's victory are cause for celebration.

18:47 God vindicates his servant and so fulfills his mission (Ps 2; see 47:3; 144:2).

18:49 The psalmist's vision of ***praise . . . among the nations*** motivated Paul in his mission to the Gentiles (Rom 15:9).

18:50 God appointed David, his ***anointed*** ruler, to bring order into God's world (see Ps 2). Both ***David*** and ***his descendants*** received this responsibility.

19:1 Gen 1:6-8; Rom 1:19-20; [a]*shamayim* (8064) ‣Ps 50:6
19:2 Ps 74:16
19:4 *Rom 10:18
19:6 Ps 113:3
19:7 Ps 23:3; 36:9; 111:7; 119:98-100, 142, 160; [b]*torah* (8451) ‣Ps 40:8; [c]*tamim* (8549) ‣Ps 119:1; [d]*nepesh* (5315) ‣Ps 23:3
19:8 Ps 12:6; 119:128
19:9 Ps 119:138, 142
19:10 Ps 119:127
19:11 Ps 17:4; Prov 29:18-19
19:12 Ps 51:1-2; 90:8; 139:23-24
19:13 Ps 25:11; 32:2
19:14 Ps 18:2; 104:34; [e]*go'el* (1350) ‣Isa 41:14
20:1 Ps 46:7, 11
20:2 Ps 3:4; 110:2
20:3 Ps 51:19; Acts 10:4

PSALM 19

For the choir director: A psalm of David.

1 The [a]heavens proclaim the glory of God.
The skies display his craftsmanship.
2 Day after day they continue to speak;
night after night they make him known.
3 They speak without a sound or word;
their voice is never heard.
4 Yet their message has gone throughout
the earth,
and their words to all the world.

God has made a home in the heavens for
the sun.
5 It bursts forth like a radiant bridegroom
after his wedding.
It rejoices like a great athlete eager to
run the race.
6 The sun rises at one end of the heavens
and follows its course to the other end.
Nothing can hide from its heat.

7 The [b]instructions of the LORD are [c]perfect,
reviving the [d]soul.
The decrees of the LORD are trustworthy,
making wise the simple.
8 The commandments of the LORD are
right,
bringing joy to the heart.
The commands of the LORD are clear,
giving insight for living.
9 Reverence for the LORD is pure,
lasting forever.
The laws of the LORD are true;
each one is fair.
10 They are more desirable than gold,
even the finest gold.
They are sweeter than honey,
even honey dripping from the comb.
11 They are a warning to your servant,
a great reward for those who obey
them.

12 How can I know all the sins lurking in
my heart?
Cleanse me from these hidden faults.
13 Keep your servant from deliberate sins!
Don't let them control me.
Then I will be free of guilt
and innocent of great sin.

14 May the words of my mouth
and the meditation of my heart
be pleasing to you,
O LORD, my rock and my [e]redeemer.

PSALM 20

For the choir director: A psalm of David.

1 In times of trouble, may the LORD answer
your cry.
May the name of the God of Jacob
keep you safe from all harm.
2 May he send you help from his sanctuary
and strengthen you from Jerusalem.
3 May he remember all your gifts
and look favorably on your burnt
offerings. *Interlude*

Ps 19 God's wisdom is manifest in heaven (19:1-4), in nature (19:4-6), in his instruction (19:7-11), and in the life of the psalmist (19:12-14). Like Ps 8, this hymn uses creation to motivate reflection—it is a peaceful oasis after the drama of the lament and victory psalms. The psalm begins with creation as a source of wisdom, then moves to God's word as the perfect source of wisdom, and ends with the human need for redemption.

19:1-4 The created order is an arena of God's wisdom, and the heavens are the place of God's dwelling (2:4; see 8:1; 57:5; 89:6; 115:3). From heaven, God observes humanity (11:4; 14:2; 33:13; 53:2; 80:14; 102:19) and comes to the rescue of his servants (18:6-8, 13; 20:6; 57:3; 76:8; 144:5). The heavens remain unaffected by human failures and rebellions (see 2:1-4). They display God's qualities of fidelity, righteousness (36:5; 50:6; 57:10; 85:11; 89:2, 5; 97:6; 108:4), and wisdom (136:5; see 119:89-90). The heavens reveal the Lord's glory (see 19:1) and give evidence of his presence and handiwork.

19:1 The *glory of God* refers to the splendor or manifest presence of the Creator (113:4). • ***God*** (Hebrew *'el*): *El* is an ancient designation for God that signifies his creative power (see note on Gen 1:1).

19:3-4 God's wisdom does not need to be spoken. Through creation, it is seen, felt, and experienced. Paul applied this text to condemn Israel for its lack of receptivity to Jesus Christ (Rom 10:18). • ***They speak without a sound or word; their voice is never heard:*** Or *There is no speech or language where their voice is not heard.* The Hebrew can be translated either way. • The *sun* is part of God's creation, but it is not a deity, as people of other nations in the ancient Near East commonly believed.

19:7-11 God's *instructions* to humans reveal his character and wisdom. God's instruction is precious and pleasant (119:103). It nourishes the person (Prov 16:24; 24:14) and is of more value than objects of human worth (81:13-16).

19:12-14 The psalmist knows his faults, so he prays to remain faithful and commits himself to the Lord.

19:13 An individual who commits *deliberate sins* does so with an insolent (86:14) or arrogant (119:21, 69) attitude. • The ***great sin*** is rebellion (see 32:1).

19:14 ***words of my mouth . . . meditation of my heart:*** The psalmist desires to please God in everything he says and thinks (see Luke 6:45; Rom 12:1-2).

Pss 20–24 This sequence of psalms expresses the experience of moving from confidence and commitment (Pss 20–21), through anguish and abandonment (Ps 22), and finally to comfort, insight, and hope (Pss 23–24).

Ps 20 This royal prayer for God's victory (20:1-5) leads to confidence in God's rescue (20:6-8) and a communal request for God's response (20:9).

20:1-5 The community prays for the king's protection and victory.

20:1 The term *God of Jacob* affectionately expresses God's ancient relationship with his people (see 24:6; 46:7, 11; 75:9; 76:6; 81:1, 4; 84:8; 94:7; 114:7; 146:5). • ***keep you safe from all harm:*** See 59:1-2.

20:2 ***Jerusalem:*** Hebrew *Zion.* See "Mount Zion, the City of God" at Ps 48, p. 947.

20:3 ***Gifts*** and ***burnt offerings*** express submission to the Lord (cp. 40:6).

4 May he grant your heart's desires
and make all your plans succeed.
5 May we shout for joy when we hear of
your victory
and raise a victory banner in the name
of our God.
May the LORD answer all your prayers.
6 Now I know that the LORD rescues his
anointed king.
He will answer him from his holy
heaven
and rescue him by his great power.
7 Some nations boast of their chariots and
horses,
but we boast in the name of the LORD
our God.
8 Those nations will fall down and collapse,
but we will rise up and stand firm.
9 Give victory to our king, O LORD!
Answer our cry for help.

PSALM 21

For the choir director: A psalm of David.

1 How the king rejoices in your strength,
O LORD!
He shouts with joy because you give
him victory.
2 For you have given him his heart's
desire;
you have withheld nothing he
requested. *Interlude*
3 You welcomed him back with success
and prosperity.
You placed a crown of finest gold on
his head.
4 He asked you to preserve his life,
and you granted his request.
The days of his life stretch on
forever.
5 Your victory brings him great honor,
and you have clothed him with
splendor and majesty.
6 You have endowed him with eternal
blessings
and given him the joy of your
presence.
7 For the king trusts in the LORD.
The unfailing love of the Most High
will keep him from stumbling.
8 You will capture all your enemies.
Your strong right hand will seize all
who hate you.
9 You will throw them in a flaming
furnace
when you appear.
The LORD will consume them in his
anger;
fire will devour them.
10 You will wipe their children from the
face of the earth;
they will never have descendants.
11 Although they plot against you,
their evil schemes will never succeed.
12 For they will turn and run
when they see your arrows aimed at
them.
13 Rise up, O LORD, in all your power.
With music and singing we [f]celebrate
your mighty acts.

PSALM 22

For the choir director: A psalm of David, to be sung to the tune "Doe of the Dawn."

1 My God, my God, why have you
[g]abandoned me?

20:4 Ps 21:2; 145:19
20:5 1 Sam 1:17; Ps 9:14; 60:4
20:6 Ps 28:8; 41:11; Isa 58:9
20:7 2 Chr 32:8; Ps 33:16-17
20:9 Ps 17:6
21:1 Ps 59:16-17
21:2 Ps 37:4
21:4 Ps 61:6; 91:16; 133:3
21:5 Ps 8:5; 96:6
21:7 Ps 112:6; 125:1
21:8 Isa 10:10
21:9 Lam 2:2; Mal 4:1
21:11 Ps 2:1-3
21:12 Ps 7:12-13; 18:40
21:13 Ps 59:16; 81:1; [f]*zamar* (2167) ‣Ps 27:6
22:1 *Matt 27:46; *Mark 15:34; [g]*'azab* (5800) ‣Ps 27:10

20:4-5 *make all your plans succeed . . . answer all your prayers:* These requests could be those stated in 21:3-6 (cp. 27:4).

20:5 Troops carried a *victory banner* to battle, under which they gathered and roused one another to action (see Isa 11:10, 12).

20:6-8 An individual member of the community (20:1-5) responds with a word of assurance and confidence in God's help.

20:6 God chose *his anointed king* to be his ruler (see 2:7).

20:7 *chariots and horses:* These were instruments of war (see 33:16-17; 76:6; 147:10; Isa 30:16; 31:1-3).

Ps 21 God's people thank him for giving victory to the king.

21:2 The king has experienced *his heart's desire*—God's protection and blessing (see 20:5; see also 2:8).

21:3-6 The king returned victorious from battle and received honor from the people. His greatest honor came from God, who gave him blessings, life, and his presence.

21:3 *success and prosperity:* See Prov 10:6.

21:4 God offers a rich quality of *life* (61:6-7; 91:14-16; 128:4-6) characterized by his presence (16:11; 23:6; 27:4; 36:9), joy (16:11), goodness (23:6; 34:14-15), and protection (41:2; 61:7).

21:6 God's *eternal blessings* also bring fullness of life in the present (see Ps 133).

21:7 The king enjoyed victory not because of his strength or intrinsic goodness but because God honored his faith.

21:8-12 As long as even a single enemy opposed the king's authority, God's kingdom was not fully present. This prayer requests victory over all evil in the world.

21:9 The *flaming furnace* and *fire* portray the severity of God's judgment on the wicked. In the OT, this image often refers to hell (11:6; 18:8; 50:3; 68:2; 78:21; 79:5; 80:16; 89:46; 97:3; 104:4; 140:10; see Isa 66:24).

21:10 *children . . . descendants:* Evil will end when God destroys all opposition to himself (109:13; cp. 18:50; 22:30-31; 25:13; 102:28).

21:13 *Rise up* (or *be exalted,* as in 57:5, 11; 108:5) expresses communal praise and joy in God's greatness and *power.*

Ps 22 All previous laments pale in comparison with this outcry against the enemy and God's abandonment. The psalm contains two main sections: the lament (22:1-21) and praise for

22:2 Ps 42:3; 88:1
22:3 Ps 99:9; 148:14
22:6 Job 25:6; Ps 31:11; Isa 41:14; 49:7
22:7 Isa 53:3; Matt 27:39; Mark 15:29-30
22:8 Matt 27:43
22:9 Ps 71:5-6
22:10 Isa 46:3
22:11 Ps 72:12
22:13 Ps 17:12
22:14 Job 30:16; Ps 31:9-10
22:15 Ps 38:10; 104:29; *John 19:28

Why are you so far away when I groan
for help?
2 Every day I call to you, my God, but you
do not answer.
Every night you hear my voice, but I
find no relief.

3 Yet you are holy,
enthroned on the praises of Israel.
4 Our ancestors trusted in you,
and you rescued them.
5 They cried out to you and were saved.
They trusted in you and were never
disgraced.

6 But I am a worm and not a man.
I am scorned and despised by all!
7 Everyone who sees me mocks me.
They sneer and shake their heads,
saying,
8 "Is this the one who relies on the LORD?
Then let the LORD save him!
If the LORD loves him so much,
let the LORD rescue him!"

9 Yet you brought me safely from my
mother's womb
and led me to trust you at my mother's
breast.
10 I was thrust into your arms at my birth.
You have been my God from the
moment I was born.

11 Do not stay so far from me,
for trouble is near,
and no one else can help me.
12 My enemies surround me like a herd of
bulls;
fierce bulls of Bashan have hemmed
me in!
13 Like lions they open their jaws
against me,
roaring and tearing into their prey.
14 My life is poured out like water,
and all my bones are out of joint.
My heart is like wax,
melting within me.
15 My strength has dried up like sunbaked
clay.
My tongue sticks to the roof of my
mouth.
You have laid me in the dust and left
me for dead.

Psalms of Suffering (Ps 22)

Pss 16, 40, 69, 102, 109; Isa 42:1-9; 52:13–53:12; Matt 27:46; Luke 23:34; Heb 10:5-10

The four psalms of suffering (also called "Passion Psalms"; Pss 16, 22, 40, 69) address the deep distress experienced by God's servant.

Psalm 22 is the most remarkable of the psalms of suffering. In this psalm, God's servant suffers though he is righteous. There is no suggestion of any sin, so the psalmist's suffering appears completely unjustified. There is no prayer for vengeance (see Ps 137) despite bitter persecution, like the sinless Christ (2 Cor 5:21) who even prayed for his executioners (Luke 23:34). Jesus recited part of Ps 22 when he was on the cross (22:1; see Matt 27:46), and the psalm has other noteworthy connections with the crucifixion (e.g., 22:6-8, 14-18).

The other psalms of suffering are also associated with Jesus Christ. Psalm 16:10 anticipates Christ's triumph over death (cp. Acts 2:24-31). Psalm 40:6-8 foreshadows the self-giving, redemptive work of Christ (Heb 10:5-10). Psalm 60 refers to isolation as resulting from commitment to God's cause (69:8-9). It anticipates the part Judas played in what was fundamentally God's work in Christ (69:25-26; 109:8; Isa 53:10; Acts 1:20).

redemption (22:22-31), which leads naturally to Ps 23. The apostles saw in this psalm an expression of the sufferings of Jesus Christ, who ultimately fulfilled the purpose of David's humiliation, rejection by people, and divine abandonment (Matt 27:35, 39, 43, 46; Mark 15:34; John 19:23-24, 28; Heb 2:12).

22:1-21 The psalmist alternates between reflections on his present dire circumstances and memories of the Lord's past faithfulness; he ends with a prayer for rescue.

22:1-2 A deep sense of alienation from God overwhelms the psalmist (see 10:1).

22:3 God, the *holy* King, is set apart from all his creation, but he chooses to reveal himself to Israel. • God greatly desires that his people offer *praises* to him.

22:6-8 Both the Lord and people reject the psalmist. He vividly describes his anguish (22:1-2); he lives like a lowly animal.

22:7 Everyone *mocks* the psalmist's confidence in the Lord (see 3:2; Matt 27:43), which shames him (44:13-14; 74:10; 89:50; 109:25).

22:9-11 The psalmist reflects on his past relationship with God (see 22:3-5). The Lord has been his very life.

22:9 The Lord took care of the psalmist before he could do anything for himself (see 71:6; 139:13).

22:12-18 The psalmist returns to expressing his anguish and suffering (see 22:1-2, 6-8). His trouble comes from human beings who act like beasts.

22:12 *Bashan,* a region known for its herds and vegetation, produced strong *bulls* (68:30).

22:14 The psalmist's sense of being *poured out like water* expresses a meaningless, transitory existence that leaves him depleted.

22:15 Facing adversity is as horrible as dying of thirst (see 137:6). • Jesus may have had this verse in mind when he said, "I am thirsty" (John 19:28).

16 My enemies surround me like a pack of dogs;
an evil gang closes in on me.
They have pierced my hands and feet.
17 I can count all my bones.
My enemies stare at me and gloat.
18 They divide my garments among themselves
and throw dice for my clothing.
19 O LORD, do not stay far away!
You are my strength; come quickly to my aid!
20 Save me from the sword;
spare my precious life from these dogs.
21 Snatch me from the lion's jaws
and from the horns of these wild oxen.
22 I will proclaim your name to my brothers and sisters.
I will [h]praise you among your [i]assembled people.
23 Praise the LORD, all you who fear him!
Honor him, all you descendants of Jacob!
Show him reverence, all you descendants of Israel!
24 For he has not ignored or belittled the suffering of the needy.
He has not turned his back on them,
but has listened to their cries for help.
25 I will praise you in the great [j]assembly.
I will fulfill my vows in the presence of those who worship you.
26 The poor will eat and be satisfied.
All who seek the LORD will praise him.
Their hearts will rejoice with everlasting joy.
27 The whole earth will [k]acknowledge the LORD and [a]return to him.
All the families of the nations will bow down before him.
28 For royal power belongs to the LORD.
He rules all the nations.
29 Let the rich of the earth feast and worship.
Bow before him, all who are mortal,
all whose lives will end as dust.
30 Our children will also serve him.
Future generations will hear about the wonders of the Lord.
31 His righteous acts will be told to those not yet born.
They will hear about everything he has done.

PSALM 23
A psalm of David.

1 The LORD is my [b]shepherd;
I have all that I need.

22:16 Ps 59:6-7; John 20:25
22:18 *Matt 27:35; *Mark 15:24; *Luke 23:34; *John 19:23-24
22:19 Ps 22:11; 70:5
22:20 Ps 35:17; 37:14
22:21 Ps 34:4; 118:5; 120:1
22:22 *Heb 2:12; [h]*halal* (1984) ‣Ps 109:30; [i]*qahal* (6951) ‣Ps 22:25
22:23 Ps 33:8; 86:12
22:24 Ps 27:9; 31:22
22:25 Ps 35:18; 40:9-10; [j]*qahal* (6951) ‣Ps 26:5
22:26 Ps 40:16; 69:32; 107:9
22:27 [k]*zakar* (2142) ‣Ps 115:12; [a]*shub* (7725) ‣Isa 55:7
22:28 Ps 47:6-8
22:30 Ps 102:18, 28
23:1 John 10:11; [b]*ro'eh* (7462) ‣Ps 78:72

22:16 The wild *pack of dogs* represents fierce and unscrupulous people.

22:17-18 ***I can count all my bones:*** The psalmist's enemies have utterly shamed him by taking his garments (see 6:2). Jesus also suffered this disgrace (see Matt 27:35). • ***stare at me and gloat:*** Enemies make the psalmist the object of their scorn (see 35:24, 26; 38:16; 55:3; cp. 59:10). • ***throw dice:*** Literally *cast lots.* The casting of lots was sometimes a way for godly people to find God's direction (Lev 16:8; Num 27:21; Acts 1:24-26). Here, the lots are thrown simply as a game of chance. The soldiers threw dice for Jesus' clothing after the crucifixion (Matt 27:35; Mark 15:24; Luke 23:34; John 19:24).

22:19-21 The psalmist faces his troubles by praying for God's rescue. Only the Lord has the strength to ward off *dogs, lions,* and *oxen.*

22:20 The *sword* makes evident the lethal intent of the enemy.

22:22-24 The psalmist praises the Lord and calls for the godly to join him. He tells of God's goodness to the needy, including himself.

22:22 ***I will proclaim your name:*** The writer to the Hebrews ascribes these words to Jesus (Heb 2:12). • ***my brothers and sisters:*** The literal reading in the Hebrew is *my brothers.* In the NT quotation, the Greek translation picks up the broader meaning as "my brothers and sisters."

22:23 The godly respond with awe (see 22:25).

22:24 Unlike his response to the wicked (see 21:8-12), God cares about the needy and hears their prayers (51:17; 69:33; 102:17).

22:25-31 The psalmist vows to praise the Lord, the great King of the earth (22:27-28) who cares for the needy. God alone deserves praise.

22:25 The ***great assembly*** might include all nations (22:27; 26:12; 35:18).

22:26 God knows his people's needs and addresses them (63:5; 81:16; 103:5; 107:9; 132:15; 145:16; 147:14).

22:27 ***families of the nations:*** All clans and tribes of humanity (see Gen 12:3; Rev 5:9-10) will live in submission to the Lord (96:1-3; see note on 2:8; see also Pss 2; 72; Isa 2:2-4; 1 Cor 15:25-27).

22:28 The universal kingdom belongs to God alone (Obad 1:21).

22:29 The Lord invites all people, *rich* and poor (22:26), to the banquet as long as they *worship* him.

22:30 ***Future generations*** will join those from the past who praised the Lord (22:3-5). The descendants of the godly will receive blessings (22:30-31), unlike the offspring of the wicked (21:10).

22:31 The Lord's *acts* of redemption (40:9; 50:6; 71:15, 16, 24; 97:6) demonstrate that he is *righteous* (see 4:1). His righteousness provides the character required for rule, judicial decisions, and relationships. This virtue leads to harmony and order (see 50:6).

Pss 23–28 These psalms develop the importance of integrity (25:4-7, 12-14, 21; 26:6, 11; 27:7-12), God's shepherding care (23:1; 28:9), God's guidance (23:2-3; 25:5; 27:11), God's goodness (23:6; 25:7-8; 27:13), and living in his house (23:6; 26:8; 27:4, 8).

Ps 23 This psalm of trust and confidence in the Lord has been a favorite of God's people for generations. It expresses assurance of God's presence in the midst of adversity. It evokes images of the Good Shepherd (23:1-3; see Ezek 34:12; John 10:11) and of the messianic banquet (23:5-6; see Isa 25:6; Rev 19:9).

23:1-3 People in the ancient Near East commonly viewed their rulers as shepherds.

23:1 The Lord promises to take care of his children (34:9-10; Isa 51:14). He demonstrated this ability to Israel in the wilderness (Deut 2:7) and in the Promised Land (Deut 8:9).

23:2
Ps 46:4
Ezek 34:14
Rev 7:17

23:3
Ps 5:8; 19:7; 85:13
[c]*nepesh* (5315)
‣Ps 25:1
[d]*tsedeq* (6664)
‣Ps 35:28

23:4
Ps 27:1; 107:14

23:5
Ps 16:5; 78:19; 92:10

23:6
Ps 25:6-7, 10; 27:4-6

24:1
Ps 89:11
*1 Cor 10:26
[e]*'erets* (0776)
‣Ps 47:2

24:3
Ps 15:1; 65:4

2 He lets me rest in green meadows;
he leads me beside peaceful
streams.
3 He renews my [c]strength.
He guides me along [d]right paths,
bringing honor to his name.
4 Even when I walk
through the darkest valley,
I will not be afraid,
for you are close beside me.
Your rod and your staff
protect and comfort me.
5 You prepare a feast for me
in the presence of my enemies.
You honor me by anointing my head
with oil.
My cup overflows with blessings.
6 Surely your goodness and unfailing love
will pursue me
all the days of my life,
and I will live in the house of the LORD
forever.

PSALM 24

A psalm of David.

1 The [e]earth is the LORD's, and everything
in it.
The world and all its people belong
to him.
2 For he laid the earth's foundation on the
seas
and built it on the ocean depths.

3 Who may climb the mountain of the
LORD?

God's Presence (Ps 24:3-6)

Ps 4:6; 13:1; 21:6; 27:9; 44:3, 24; 67:1; 69:17; 88:14; 89:46; 102:2; 104:29; 143:7

Scripture writers often express the desire to experience God's close presence. In the experience of intimacy, God's rich goodness and love (21:6; 44:3) are all that people need (4:6). The absence of God's presence is distressing and damaging.

The poets of Israel often spoke of God's face as a way of expressing his presence or absence. They sought his face (24:6; 27:8; 105:4; 119:58). When his face shone or was turned toward his people, they experienced his presence in blessing, provision, and protection (67:1). God's hiding his face from his people was a picture of divine abandonment (13:1; 27:9; 44:24; 69:17; 88:14; 89:46; 102:2; 104:29; 143:7), as if God were not seeing or hearing them (10:11; 11:1; 42:3). The absence of God creates dismay, shame, and chaos, and may cause death (30:7; 44:24; 104:29).

The psalmists prayed for God's presence as they requested a change in their circumstances (31:16; 67:1; 69:17; 80:3, 7, 19) or as they reflected on answers to prayer (see 44:3). The godly long to be invited into God's presence (11:7; 16:9-11; 17:15). His presence alone satisfies their deepest longing (17:15; see Prov 16:15) and gives them lasting pleasure (1:2; 111:2; see also 22:8; 37:4; 40:6, 8; 43:4; 73:25). Everything about God delights them.

God's favor and goodness are experienced in his presence (23:6). God is the true good of the godly (16:2; 73:1), and he protects them (84:11). Hence, God's goodness and his Temple are closely linked (65:4). God shows his goodness by manifesting his presence (27:13; 31:19; 34:8, 10; 86:17; 103:5), and he satisfies his needy people (107:9; 116:7, 12). Goodness may be synonymous with God's unfailing love (23:6; 25:7; 69:16). In connection with the land or crops, goodness is understood as blessing, abundance, and prosperity (4:6; 21:3; 65:11; 68:10; 85:12; 106:5; 122:9; 128:2). God's goodness and presence promote health and vitality in his people (34:12-22).

23:2 Sheep *rest* after they have eaten their fill (Zeph 3:13; see Isa 11:7; cp. Isa 13:20; 27:10). • The Lord *leads* the sheep for their own benefit (see 5:8). • Sheep only drink from still water, so the shepherd seeks out *peaceful streams* for his flock.

23:3 Cp. 19:7; the Lord's word *renews my strength.* • The Lord *guides* by rescuing his people from evil (23:4-5; see 31:3), bringing them back to himself (5:8; 61:2), caring (48:14; 139:10), ruling (67:4), counseling (73:24), protecting (78:53; 107:30; 143:11), and instructing them in wisdom (27:11; see Prov 4:11). • The Lord's *name* guarantees the relationship; he guards his reputation against any accusation of his abandoning his people or allowing them to sin (see 25:11; 31:3; 106:8; 143:11).

23:4 *darkest valley:* Or *dark valley of death.* • The shepherd used his *rod* and *staff* to fend off danger.

23:5 A *feast* demonstrates the Lord's care and mercy toward his people (see 22:26, 29). Although *enemies* can watch, they cannot trouble the guests. • The ritual of *anointing* the *head with oil* showed guests *honor* (92:9-11), hospitality, and refreshment (104:15; 133:2).

23:6 The Lord expresses his *unfailing love* through the *goodness* of his presence and other benefits that he alone provides (69:16; 86:17; 109:21; see 18:6; 61:4). He actively bestows care that is greater than the temporary trials imposed by enemies (7:1).

Ps 24 The shepherd of Ps 23, who is also the King of the whole world, takes possession of Zion.

24:1-2 The kingdom belongs to the Creator, the Great King (cp. 22:27).

24:1 The Lord created and now rules the *earth* and *everything in it* (see 1 Cor 10:25-26). He sees *all its people* (33:14), regardless of their status (49:1-2).

24:2 God created everything in an orderly and stable manner (see 89:11; 102:25; 104:5).

24:3-6 The citizens of the King's realm include all who seek him. The Lord invites them to enter his presence.

Who may stand in his holy place?
4 Only those whose hands and hearts are pure,
who do not worship idols
and never tell lies.
5 They will receive the LORD's blessing
and have a right relationship with God their savior.
6 Such people may seek you
and worship in your presence, O God of Jacob. *Interlude*

7 Open up, ancient gates!
Open up, ancient doors,
and let the King of [f]glory enter.
8 Who is the King of glory?
The LORD, strong and mighty;
the LORD, invincible in battle.
9 Open up, ancient gates!
Open up, ancient doors,
and let the [g]King of glory enter.
10 Who is the King of glory?
The LORD of [h]Heaven's Armies—
he is the King of glory. *Interlude*

PSALM 25

A psalm of David.

1 O LORD, I give my [i]life to you.
2 I trust in you, my God!
Do not let me be disgraced,
or let my enemies rejoice in my defeat.
3 No one who trusts in you will ever be disgraced,
but disgrace comes to those who try to deceive others.

4 Show me the right path, O LORD;
point out the road for me to follow.
5 Lead me by your [j]truth and teach me,
for you are the God who saves me.
All day long I put my hope in you.
6 Remember, O LORD, your compassion
and [k]unfailing love,
which you have shown from long ages past.
7 Do not remember the rebellious sins of my youth.
Remember me in the light of your unfailing love,
for you are merciful, O LORD.

8 The LORD is good and does what is right;
he shows the proper path to those who go astray.
9 He leads the [a]humble in doing right,
teaching [a]them his way.
10 The LORD leads with unfailing love and faithfulness
all who keep his covenant and obey his demands.

11 For the honor of your name, O LORD,
forgive my many, many sins.
12 Who are those who fear the LORD?
He will show them the path they should choose.
13 They will live in prosperity,
and their children will inherit the land.
14 The LORD is a friend to those who fear him.
He teaches them his covenant.

24:4 Matt 5:8
24:5 Deut 11:26-27
24:6 Ps 27:8
24:7 [f]*kabod* (3519) ‣Ps 145:5
24:8 Exod 15:3, 6
24:9 Matt 21:5; [g]*melek* (4428) ‣Ps 33:16
24:10 [h]*tsaba'* (6635) ‣Ps 80:19
25:1 [i]*nepesh* (5315) ‣Ps 34:2
25:3 Isa 49:22-23
25:4 Ps 5:8; 86:11
25:5 Ps 24:5; 40:1; [j]*'emeth* (0571) ‣Ps 26:3
25:6 Ps 103:17; [k]*khesed* (2617) ‣Ps 51:1
25:7 Job 13:26; Ps 51:1
25:8 Ps 86:5
25:9 Ps 23:3; 32:8; [a]*'anaw* (6035) ‣Ps 37:11
25:10 Ps 40:11; 103:17-18
25:11 Ps 79:9
25:13 Ps 37:11; 69:36

24:3 These questions invite readers to look away from their problems with the wicked and to examine themselves (see 15:1). • God's ***holy place*** is the holy ***mountain***, a reference both to Jerusalem and to heaven.

24:4 Those with pure ***hands*** have not shed blood or injured relationships between people (see 9:12; 15:2-5). • Those with pure ***hearts*** commit themselves fully to the Lord, as evidenced in strength of character, transparency, and selflessness (51:10; 73:1; see Matt 5:8).

24:10 ***The LORD of Heaven's Armies*** reigns from his home, the Temple in Jerusalem (84:3-5). He excludes sin and sinners (24:3-6) but protects all who dwell in Zion.

Ps 25 This psalm is a Hebrew acrostic poem; each verse begins with a successive letter of the Hebrew alphabet. This individual lament includes instruction in wisdom and a community lament; it begins and ends with an affirmation of trust in the Lord (25:1-3, 15-22). The psalmist prays for guidance (25:4-7) and encourages the godly to practice a lifestyle of wisdom (25:12-14). In addition to the enemies who trouble him, the psalmist confesses his sins (25:7, 11, 18) as part of his anguish. Trust develops with understanding God's character: He is compassionate, faithful, and good (25:8-10).

25:1-3 The psalmist expresses confidence that the godly will be vindicated and his enemies will not succeed (see 25:15-22).

25:1 The psalmist commits himself to the Lord instead of to idols (see 24:3-4).

25:2 Enemies would ***rejoice*** by singing a victory song.

25:4-7 In this prayer for guidance, compassion, and forgiveness, the psalmist turns to the Lord for instruction in wisdom. He confesses his past failures and acknowledges that his hope lies with his merciful Savior.

25:4-6 The ***right path***, the path of wisdom (see 5:8), means being open to instruction that leads to life (27:11; 43:3; 73:24; 119:12).

25:5 Biblical ***hope*** does not mean wishing for an event to turn out favorably. Hope trusts the Lord's will and gives the courage to face disappointments (33:22; 130:5).

25:6 ***compassion:*** See also 51:1; 57:1; 103:8.

25:8-10 The Lord keeps his people close to himself.

25:11 The psalmist again asks forgiveness for his ***many sins*** (25:7; 32:1-5). The sins of Israel's kings demonstrated the weaknesses inherent in David's dynasty and the reasons for its failure in OT Israel (see Ps 89).

25:12-15 Those who fear the Lord will receive further instruction and experience God's presence (25:14) and blessing (25:13).

25:13 ***prosperity:*** See 23:6. • ***inherit the land:*** Unlike the wicked, who will perish (1:6), the godly have a secure future. In the end, God will bless them, and their blessings will endure (see 37:9, 11, 22, 29, 34; Isa 57:13; Matt 5:5).

25:15 Ps 31:4; 123:2; 141:8
25:16 Ps 69:16
25:17 Ps 40:12; 107:6
25:18 Ps 31:7; 103:3
25:19 Ps 3:1; 9:13
25:20 Ps 25:2; 86:2
25:21 Ps 25:3; 41:12
26:1 Ps 7:8; 13:5 Heb 10:23
26:2 Ps 7:9; 139:23
26:3 Ps 1:2; 48:9 [b]*'emeth* (0571) ‣Ps 86:11
26:4 Ps 1:1
26:5 Ps 1:1; 31:6; 139:21 [c]*qahal* (6951) ‣Ps 89:5
26:6 Ps 43:3-4
26:7 Ps 9:1 [d]*todah* (8426) ‣Ps 42:4
26:8 Ps 27:4 [e]*mishkan* (4908) ‣Ps 43:3
26:9 Ps 28:3
26:11 Ps 26:1; 69:18
26:12 Ps 22:22; 27:11; 40:2
27:1 Ps 18:28; 118:6, 14
27:3 Ps 3:6-7

15 My eyes are always on the LORD,
for he rescues me from the traps of
my enemies.

16 Turn to me and have mercy,
for I am alone and in deep distress.
17 My problems go from bad to worse.
Oh, save me from them all!
18 Feel my pain and see my trouble.
Forgive all my sins.
19 See how many enemies I have
and how viciously they hate me!
20 Protect me! Rescue my life from them!
Do not let me be disgraced, for in you
I take refuge.
21 May integrity and honesty protect me,
for I put my hope in you.

22 O God, ransom Israel
from all its troubles.

PSALM 26

A psalm of David.

1 Declare me innocent, O LORD,
for I have acted with integrity;
I have trusted in the LORD without
wavering.
2 Put me on trial, LORD, and
cross-examine me.
Test my motives and my heart.
3 For I am always aware of your unfailing
love,
and I have lived according to your
[b]truth.
4 I do not spend time with liars
or go along with hypocrites.
5 I hate the [c]gatherings of those who do
evil,
and I refuse to join in with the wicked.
6 I wash my hands to declare my
innocence.
I come to your altar, O LORD,
7 singing a song of [d]thanksgiving
and telling of all your wonders.
8 I love your sanctuary, LORD,
the place where your glorious
presence [e]dwells.

9 Don't let me suffer the fate of sinners.
Don't condemn me along with
murderers.
10 Their hands are dirty with evil schemes,
and they constantly take bribes.
11 But I am not like that; I live with integrity.
So redeem me and show me mercy.
12 Now I stand on solid ground,
and I will publicly praise the LORD.

PSALM 27

A psalm of David.

1 The LORD is my light and my salvation—
so why should I be afraid?
The LORD is my fortress, protecting me
from danger,
so why should I tremble?
2 When evil people come to devour me,
when my enemies and foes attack me,
they will stumble and fall.
3 Though a mighty army surrounds me,
my heart will not be afraid.
Even if I am attacked,
I will remain confident.

25:15-22 The psalmist expresses confidence in the Lord, commits to a life of integrity, and prays for rescue.

25:15 ***the traps of my enemies:*** See 5:9-10; 31:4; 140:5; Prov 3:26.

25:17-18 The psalmist can find no relief (see 4:1; 13:1-2) as his ***problems go from bad to worse.*** He associates his anguish with sin, but he does not elaborate on the nature of his sin (see 25:7, 11).

25:19-20 Knowing that the Lord hates violent people (see 11:5), the psalmist pleads with God to deal with these ***enemies.***

25:21 Just as it opened, the psalm closes with a commitment of trust and ***hope*** (see 9:18; 25:5).

Ps 26 In this individual lament, the psalmist prays for redemption on the basis of his own innocence and the Lord's justice.

26:1-3 The psalmist opens himself to divine examination of his life, especially in the areas of his character and devotion.

26:3 For God's ***truth*** to become part of one's character requires a habitual commitment.

26:4-5 Because of his devotion to the Lord (26:1-3), the psalmist dissociates himself from evil people (see 1:1).

26:6-8 The psalmist demonstrates his loyalty to the Lord through pious rituals, praise, and acknowledgment of the Lord's presence in the Temple.

26:6 Ritual purity required the worshiper to ***wash*** his ***hands,*** symbolic of separation from evil and evildoers (see 73:13). • The ***altar*** symbolizes God's presence (43:4).

26:8 The ***sanctuary*** symbolized the manifest ***presence*** of the Lord (see 18:6).

26:9 ***Don't let me suffer:*** The end of the godly cannot be the same as that of the wicked.

26:12 The psalmist's footing on ***solid ground*** represents salvation (cp. 143:10). • ***publicly:*** Or *in the great assembly* at the Temple (26:6-8; 22:25).

Ps 27 This psalm mixes two genres—a psalm of confidence (27:1-6) and an individual lament (27:7-14)—held together by the theme of longing for the Lord's presence. The psalmist focuses on the Lord; his circumstances are secondary. The strength of the psalmist's faith is expressed in his openness to the Lord's instruction, timing, and priorities.

27:1-3 The psalmist acknowledges the Lord at the center of his life (27:1). Because of God's presence, he engages his adversaries with confidence. They cannot intimidate him or penetrate his inner security.

27:1 ***Light*** expresses the Lord's goodness (27:13; see 4:6; 23:6; 31:19; 38:10; 43:3; 56:13).

27:2 The psalmist's enemies seek to ***devour*** him by living at his expense (see note on 14:4).

27:3 ***remain confident:*** See 25:2; 26:1.

4 The one thing I ask of the LORD—
the thing I seek most—
is to live in the house of the LORD all the days of my life,
delighting in the LORD's perfections
and meditating in his Temple.
5 For he will conceal me there when troubles come;
he will hide me in his sanctuary.
He will place me out of reach on a high [f]rock.
6 Then I will hold my head high
above my enemies who surround me.
At his sanctuary I will offer sacrifices with shouts of joy,
singing and [g]praising the LORD with music.

7 Hear me as I pray, O LORD.
Be merciful and answer me!
8 My heart has heard you say, "Come and talk with me."
And my heart responds, "LORD, I am coming."
9 Do not turn your back on me.
Do not reject your servant in anger.
You have always been my helper.
Don't leave me now; don't abandon me,
O God of my salvation!
10 Even if my father and mother
[h]abandon me,
the LORD will hold me close.
11 Teach me how to live, O LORD.
Lead me along the right path,
for my enemies are waiting for me.
12 Do not let me fall into their hands.
For they accuse me of things I've never done;
with every breath they threaten me with violence.
13 Yet I am confident I will see the LORD's goodness
while I am here in the land of the living.

14 Wait patiently for the LORD.
Be brave and courageous.
Yes, wait patiently for the LORD.

PSALM 28

A psalm of David.

1 I pray to you, O LORD, my rock.
Do not turn a deaf ear to me.
For if you are silent,
I might as well give up and die.
2 Listen to my prayer for mercy
as I cry out to you for help,
as I lift my hands toward your holy sanctuary.

3 Do not drag me away with the wicked—
with those who do evil—
those who speak friendly words to their neighbors
while planning evil in their hearts.
4 Give them the punishment they so richly deserve!
Measure it out in proportion to their wickedness.
Pay them back for all their evil deeds!
Give them a taste of what they have done to others.
5 They care nothing for what the LORD has done
or for what his hands have made.
So he will tear them down,
and they will never be rebuilt!

6 Praise the LORD!
For he has heard my cry for mercy.

27:4 Ps 23:6; 26:8
27:5 Ps 17:8; 31:20
[f]*tsur* (6697) ‣Ps 31:2
27:6 Ps 13:6; 107:22
[g]*zamar* (2167) ‣Ps 30:12
27:7 Ps 13:3
27:8 Ps 105:4
27:9 Ps 6:1; 40:17; 69:17; 94:14
27:10 Isa 40:11; 49:15
[h]*'azab* (5800) ‣Prov 4:6
27:11 Ps 5:8; 25:4; 86:11
27:12 Ps 35:11 Matt 26:60 Acts 9:1
27:13 Ps 116:9; 142:5 Isa 38:11
27:14 Ps 31:24; 37:34
28:1 Ps 18:2; 35:22; 83:1; 88:4-5
28:2 Ps 141:2 Lam 2:19 1 Tim 2:8
28:3 Ps 26:9-10; 55:21; 62:4 Jer 9:8
28:4 Ps 62:12 2 Tim 4:14 Rev 18:6
28:5 Isa 5:12
28:6 Ps 116:1

27:4-6 Searching for and enjoying the Lord's presence provides the psalmist's foundation for confidence and security. He lives in the assurance of God's protection and looks forward to offering sacrifices of thanksgiving and praise (see 18:6).

27:5 ***sanctuary*** (or ***tabernacle***): This early shrine was the Israelites' place of worship before the Temple was constructed.

27:6 ***hold my head high:*** A sign of victory. • The granting of the request of 27:4 prompts ***sacrifices with shouts of joy.***

27:7-12 The psalmist requests the Lord's mercy, presence, and instruction. God is the psalmist's greatest good; enemies and other circumstances are peripheral.

27:7-8 Unlike the wicked (10:4), who only want a temporary advantage (78:34-36), the godly search for the Lord as a thirsty person searches for water in the desert (63:1; 105:4; 119:2, 10; Matt 6:33). They act wisely (34:10, 14) while waiting for the Lord to resolve their crisis (34:4; 69:6; 77:2; 119:58).

27:13-14 The psalmist expresses confidence and hope in the Lord's presence. To live in faith means to ***wait patiently*** in recognition of the Lord's goodness. Such a life is not always pleasant for the godly (42:2-3, 43:5), but their future is secure (37:9; 130:7; see 9:18).

Ps 28 In this individual lament, the psalmist pleads for justice and mercy. He expresses confidence in the Lord's strength and faithfulness, and he intercedes for the Lord's people.

28:1-2 The psalmist urges the Lord to listen; his urgency flows out of the tension between his deep relationship with the Lord and the adversity he faces.

28:1 ***if you are silent:*** The psalmist appeals to the Lord to take action (35:22; 50:3; 83:1; 109:1).

28:2 It was common to ***lift*** up one's ***hands*** in a gesture of devoted prayer (63:4; 134:2).

28:3-5 The psalmist curses his enemies, asking God for retribution and vindication.

28:5 The wicked do not acknowledge the difference between the sacred and the common, so they have no respect for the Lord's creation, redemption, or revelation.

28:6-8 The psalmist anticipates rescue because of his confidence in the Lord's justice.

28:7
Ps 13:5-6; 16:9; 40:3; 59:17
[i]*magen* (4043)
▸Ps 84:9
[j]*leb* (3820)
▸Ps 86:12

28:8
Ps 20:6

28:9
Deut 9:29; 32:9
Ps 33:12; 80:1
Isa 40:11

29:1
1 Chr 16:28-29
Ps 96:7-9
[k]*ben 'el* (1121, 0410)
▸Ps 89:6

29:2
[a]*khawah* (7812)
▸Isa 46:6

29:4
Ps 68:33

29:5
Isa 2:13

29:6
Deut 3:9
Ps 114:4

29:8
Num 13:26

29:10
Gen 6:17
Ps 10:16

29:11
Ps 28:8; 37:11; 68:35
Isa 40:29
[b]*shalom* (7965)
▸Ps 34:14

30:1
Ps 25:2; 35:19, 24; 118:28; 145:1
[c]*rum* (7311)
▸Ps 34:3

30:2
Ps 6:2; 88:13

30:3
Ps 28:1; 86:13

30:4
Ps 97:12; 149:1

7 The LORD is my strength and [i]shield.
I trust him with all my [j]heart.
He helps me, and my [j]heart is filled with joy.
I burst out in songs of thanksgiving.

8 The LORD gives his people strength.
He is a safe fortress for his anointed king.
9 Save your people!
Bless Israel, your special possession.
Lead them like a shepherd,
and carry them in your arms forever.

PSALM 29

A psalm of David.

1 Honor the LORD, you [k]heavenly beings;
honor the LORD for his glory and strength.
2 Honor the LORD for the glory of his name.
[a]Worship the LORD in the splendor of his holiness.

3 The voice of the LORD echoes above the sea.
The God of glory thunders.
The LORD thunders over the mighty sea.
4 The voice of the LORD is powerful;
the voice of the LORD is majestic.
5 The voice of the LORD splits the mighty cedars;
the LORD shatters the cedars of Lebanon.
6 He makes Lebanon's mountains skip like a calf;
he makes Mount Hermon leap like a young wild ox.
7 The voice of the LORD strikes
with bolts of lightning.
8 The voice of the LORD makes the barren wilderness quake;
the LORD shakes the wilderness of Kadesh.
9 The voice of the LORD twists mighty oaks
and strips the forests bare.
In his Temple everyone shouts, "Glory!"

10 The LORD rules over the floodwaters.
The LORD reigns as king forever.
11 The LORD gives his people strength.
The LORD blesses them with [b]peace.

PSALM 30

A psalm of David. A song for the dedication of the Temple.

1 I will [c]exalt you, LORD, for you rescued me.
You refused to let my enemies triumph over me.
2 O LORD my God, I cried to you for help,
and you restored my health.
3 You brought me up from the grave, O LORD.
You kept me from falling into the pit of death.

4 Sing to the LORD, all you godly ones!
Praise his holy name.

28:7 ***my strength and shield:*** The Lord protects the psalmist (see 59:9, 17).

28:9 The poem closes with intercession for the Lord's people. • ***Bless Israel, your special possession:*** Literally *Bless your inheritance.* See 29:11; 133:3.

Ps 29 This nature hymn in praise of the Creator declares that the Lord holds all power over nature. God uses the same unsurpassed strength to care for his people.

29:1-2 The psalmist issues a call to ***honor*** the Lord for his power (cp. 96:7-8). • ***you heavenly beings*** (literally *you sons of God*): Angels or deities who, some believed, held special powers. The psalmist did not believe in other deities but called on people who thought they were real to look to the Lord as the only God.

29:3-9 The word translated *voice* (Hebrew *qol*) can also mean "noise" (1 Kgs 1:45) or "thunder" (Joel 3:16). The Lord's voice is awe-inspiring, and it dominates whatever rumblings people might attribute to other deities.

29:3 ***God*** (Hebrew *'el*): See note on 19:1.

29:5 The ***cedars of Lebanon*** were known for their size and quality (see Isa 2:13).

29:6 ***Lebanon's mountains*** and ***Hermon*** are high mountains to the north of Israel. • The Lord can cause even immense ***mountains*** to shake at his command (see 114:4). • ***Mount Hermon:*** Hebrew *Sirion,* another name for Mount Hermon.

29:8 The ***wilderness of Kadesh*** was located south of Judah. God's voice can be heard throughout the land, from the north (29:6) to the south.

29:9 ***twists mighty oaks:*** Or *causes the deer to writhe in labor.* The meaning of the Hebrew is uncertain.

29:10 The image of powerful ***flood-waters*** connects with the Genesis flood (Gen 6:17). The Lord ***reigns as king*** over the whole created order; no one contests his kingdom.

29:11 The ruler of nature ***blesses*** his people ***with peace*** (see 28:8-9; 37:11; 133:3).

Ps 30 This individual thanksgiving psalm opens in praise to the Lord for his salvation (30:1-3), then contrasts God's favor with his anger (30:4-7), and ends with a transformation from mourning to dancing (30:8-12).

30:TITLE Perhaps *David* wrote this psalm in advance ***for the dedication of the Temple,*** making his own experience representative of the nation's.

30:1-3 The psalmist praises God for his triumph over adversity, which he likens to salvation from the grave.

30:1 ***I will exalt you*** is a call to lift up the Lord's name in praise and thanksgiving (34:3; 81:1; 99:5, 9; 107:32; 118:28; 145:1; see Exod 15:1; Isa 25:1). • ***you rescued me:*** God pulled the psalmist from death (30:3). • In his justice and care, God ***refused to let*** the psalmist's ***enemies triumph*** (see 26:9; 27:12; 28:3; 31:8).

30:3 ***from the grave:*** Hebrew *from Sheol.* See note on 6:5.

30:4 The godly should celebrate the Lord's acts of rescue with song and ***praise*** (33:21; 97:12; 103:1; 105:3; 145:21).

5 For his anger lasts only a moment,
but his favor lasts a lifetime!
Weeping may last through the night,
but joy comes with the morning.

6 When I was prosperous, I said,
"Nothing can stop me now!"
7 Your favor, O LORD, made me as secure
as a mountain.
Then you turned away from me, and I
was shattered.
8 I cried out to you, O LORD.
I begged the Lord for mercy, saying,
9 "What will you gain if I die,
if I sink into the grave?
Can my dust praise you?
Can it tell of your faithfulness?
10 Hear me, LORD, and have mercy on me.
Help me, O LORD."

11 You have turned my mourning into
joyful dancing.
You have taken away my clothes of
mourning and clothed me with [d]joy,
12 that I might [e]sing praises to you and not
be silent.
O LORD my God, I will [f]give you thanks
[g]forever!

PSALM 31

For the choir director: A psalm of David.

1 O LORD, I have come to you for
protection;
don't let me be disgraced.
Save me, for you do what is right.
2 Turn your ear to listen to me;
rescue me quickly.
Be my [h]rock of protection,
a fortress where I will be safe.
3 You are my rock and my fortress.
For the honor of your name, lead me
out of this danger.
4 Pull me from the trap my enemies set
for me,
for I find protection in you alone.
5 I entrust my spirit into your hand.
Rescue me, LORD, for you are a
faithful God.

6 I hate those who worship worthless
idols.
I trust in the LORD.
7 I will be glad and rejoice in your
unfailing love,
for you have seen my troubles,
and you care about the anguish of my
soul.
8 You have not handed me over to my
enemies
but have set me in a safe place.

9 Have mercy on me, LORD, for I am in
distress.
Tears blur my eyes.
My body and soul are withering away.
10 I am dying from grief;
my years are shortened by sadness.
Sin has drained my strength;
I am wasting away from within.
11 I am scorned by all my enemies
and despised by my neighbors—
even my friends are afraid to come
near me.
When they see me on the street,
they run the other way.
12 I am ignored as if I were dead,
as if I were a broken pot.
13 I have heard the many rumors
about me,
and I am surrounded by terror.
My enemies conspire against me,
plotting to take my life.

14 But I am trusting you, O LORD,
saying, "You are my God!"

30:5 Ps 103:9; 118:1
30:6 Ps 10:6
30:7 Ps 104:29
30:9 Ps 6:5
30:10 Ps 4:1; 27:7, 9
30:11 Jer 31:4, 13
[d]*simkhah* (8057)
‣Ps 51:8
30:12 Ps 44:8; 57:8; 108:1
[e]*zamar* (2167)
‣Ps 33:2
[f]*yadah* (3034)
‣Ps 32:5
[g]*'olam* (5769)
‣Ps 44:8
31:1-4 //Ps 71:1-3
31:1 Ps 25:2; 143:1
31:2 Ps 71:3; 86:1; 102:2
[h]*tsur* (6697)
‣Ps 61:2
31:3 Ps 18:2; 23:2-3
31:4 Ps 25:15
31:5 Luke 23:46
Acts 7:59
31:6 Jon 2:8-9
31:7 Ps 10:14; 90:14
31:8 Deut 32:30
31:9 Ps 32:3; 38:3-4; 102:4
31:10 Ps 13:2
31:11 Ps 38:11; 88:8, 18
Isa 53:3
31:12 Ps 88:5
31:13 Jer 20:10
Matt 27:1
31:14 Ps 140:6; 143:9

30:6-7 ***Nothing can stop me now!*** The psalmist confesses his presumptuous attitude (cp. 32:3-4). • ***secure as a mountain:*** In the psalms, this phrase creates a powerful image of stability and of God's control (see 11:1; 18:7; 36:6; 46:2; 72:3; 76:4; 83:14; 97:5; 114:4, 6; 125:2). • ***I was shattered:*** The absence of God's favor destroys the security of the proud (cp. 104:27-30).

30:8-12 The psalmist faced death (also in 30:1-3)—perhaps literally, perhaps figuratively. But when he turned to the Lord, the Lord rescued him and turned his ***mourning into joyful dancing.*** Only God's favor can permanently and powerfully overcome human failure and the depths of despair.

Ps 31 The psalmist encourages the godly to find refuge in the Lord and wait for his salvation. Despite having had a death-like experience, he testifies to the Lord's faithfulness. This psalm foreshadows the suffering of Jesus (Luke 23:46).

31:1-5 The Lord offers refuge to anyone who comes to him for protection. The psalmist trusts in and submits to the Lord. See also 71:1-3.

31:2 The psalmist issues an urgent call for the Lord to pay attention to his desperate situation (71:2; 88:2; 102:2).

31:5 ***I entrust my spirit into your hand:*** Whether he lives or dies, the psalmist will trust his Lord. Jesus uttered these words on the cross just before he died (Luke 23:46).

31:6-8 Trust in the Lord requires confidence that he has our best interests at heart.

31:8 A ***safe place*** literally means a broad place, in contrast to a "narrow" or constricted place of distress (see 18:19).

31:9-13 In this prayer for mercy, the psalmist wedges a description of the intensity of suffering and the pain of rejection between two affirmations of trust (31:6, 14).

31:10 ***wasting away from within:*** This is a powerful description of how despair takes a toll on our physical well-being.

31:14-18 Hope does not confide in frail and changeable human beings but only in the Lord. The sufferer entrusts himself to God while waiting for the Lord's justice.

31:15 Ps 143:9
31:16 Num 6:24-26
31:17 Ps 25:2-3, 20
31:18 1 Sam 2:3
31:20 Job 5:21; Ps 27:5; 31:13
31:21 Ps 17:7
31:22 Ps 145:19; Lam 3:54-56
31:23 Deut 32:40-41; Ps 37:28
31:24 Ps 27:14
32:1 [i]*'ashrey* (0835) ‣ Ps 34:8; [j]*pesha'* (6588) ‣ Ps 32:5; [k]*nasa'* (5375) ‣ Ps 32:5
32:2 Ps 85:2; *Rom 4:7-8; [a]*ruakh* (7307) ‣ Ps 51:11
32:3 Ps 31:10; 39:2
32:4 Ps 22:15; 39:10
32:5 Lev 26:40; Ps 38:18; 1 Jn 1:9; [b]*yadah* (3034) ‣ Ps 49:18; [c]*pesha'* (6588) ‣ Ps 51:3; [d]*nasa'* (5375) ‣ Ps 85:2
32:6 Ps 69:13; Isa 43:2; [e]*palal* (6419) ‣ Ps 72:15
32:7 Ps 31:20; 40:3; 121:7
32:8 Ps 25:8; 33:18-19

15 My future is in your hands.
Rescue me from those who hunt me
down relentlessly.
16 Let your favor shine on your servant.
In your unfailing love, rescue me.
17 Don't let me be disgraced, O LORD,
for I call out to you for help.
Let the wicked be disgraced;
let them lie silent in the grave.
18 Silence their lying lips—
those proud and arrogant lips that
accuse the godly.

19 How great is the goodness
you have stored up for those who fear
you.
You lavish it on those who come to you
for protection,
blessing them before the watching
world.
20 You hide them in the shelter of your
presence,
safe from those who conspire against
them.
You shelter them in your presence,
far from accusing tongues.

21 Praise the LORD,
for he has shown me the wonders of
his unfailing love.
He kept me safe when my city was
under attack.
22 In panic I cried out,
"I am cut off from the LORD!"
But you heard my cry for mercy
and answered my call for help.

23 Love the LORD, all you godly ones!
For the LORD protects those who are
loyal to him,
but he harshly punishes the arrogant.
24 So be strong and courageous,
all you who put your hope in the LORD!

PSALM 32

A psalm of David.

1 Oh, what [i]joy for those
whose [j]disobedience is [k]forgiven,
whose sin is put out of sight!
2 Yes, what joy for those
whose record the LORD has cleared
of guilt,
whose [a]lives are lived in complete
honesty!
3 When I refused to confess my sin,
my body wasted away,
and I groaned all day long.
4 Day and night your hand of discipline
was heavy on me.
My strength evaporated like water in
the summer heat. *Interlude*

5 Finally, I [b]confessed all my sins to you
and stopped trying to hide my guilt.
I said to myself, "I will confess my
[c]rebellion to the LORD."
And you [d]forgave me! All my guilt is
gone. *Interlude*

6 Therefore, let all the godly [e]pray to you
while there is still time,
that they may not drown in the
floodwaters of judgment.
7 For you are my hiding place;
you protect me from trouble.
You surround me with songs of
victory. *Interlude*

8 The LORD says, "I will guide you along
the best pathway for your life.
I will advise you and watch over you.

31:15 ***My future is in your hands:*** To relinquish control of timing is one way to express submission.

31:17 The psalmist, who did not deserve to be ***disgraced,*** invokes the principle of retribution (see note on 1:6). • ***in the grave:*** Hebrew *in Sheol.*

31:19-24 The psalmist thanks the Lord for answering his prayer (31:1-18) and rescuing him.

31:19-20 Since the godly are under the Lord's protection and shelter, evil has no power over them.

31:21-22 ***Praise the LORD:*** The psalmist expresses his joy at the experience of God's goodness and love. Throughout his ordeal, the Lord has cared for him.

31:23-24 Out of his own pain and renewed awareness of the Lord's goodness, the psalmist turns to others who suffer. He holds out the promise of God's loving care for those who persevere in hoping for the Lord.

Ps 32 This wisdom psalm of confession and thanksgiving encourages and exhorts the godly to learn from the psalmist's experience of sin, denial, confession, and forgiveness. This psalm was one of the seven psalms of penitence used in the early church (also Pss 6, 38, 51, 102, 130, 143).

32:TITLE ***psalm:*** Hebrew *maskil.* This may be a literary or musical term.

32:1-2 The Lord's forgiveness restores people to fellowship with him, clears them of ***guilt,*** and gives them great ***joy.*** Paul quoted this text when explaining justification by faith alone (Rom 4:4-8).

32:2 ***of guilt:*** Greek version reads *of sin.* Cp. Rom 4:7.

32:3-5 The psalmist acknowledges his own sin (see 19:12-13; 25:7, 11, 15-22) and his resistance to confessing sin. The Lord pressed him hard until he confessed his guilt.

32:4 The psalmist attributes his suffering directly to the Lord's ***hand of discipline*** (cp. 38:2; 39:10).

32:5 God has forgiven the ***guilt*** and ***rebellion*** of 32:1. The Lord's nature is to reconcile and forgive (78:38; 85:2; 130:4), but he requires confession and repentance.

32:6 The ***godly*** will learn from the psalmist's experience to pray for forgiveness before it is too late.

32:7 The Lord promises to be his people's ***hiding place*** (31:20). Instead of being overwhelmed by terror (31:13), the psalmist is surrounded by ***songs of victory.***

32:8 God interrupts the psalmist's teaching with a message that invites the godly to receive the Lord's wisdom (see 5:8; 23:3; 25:4-6).

9 Do not be like a senseless horse or mule
that needs a bit and bridle to keep it
under control."

10 Many sorrows come to the wicked,
but unfailing love surrounds those
who trust the LORD.
11 So rejoice in the LORD and be glad, all
you who obey him!
Shout for joy, all you whose hearts are
pure!

PSALM 33

1 Let the godly sing for joy to the LORD;
it is fitting for the pure to praise
him.
2 Praise the LORD with melodies on the
lyre;
[f]make music for him on the ten-
stringed harp.
3 Sing a new song of praise to him;
play skillfully on the harp, and sing
with joy.
4 For the word of the LORD holds true,
and we can trust everything he does.
5 He loves whatever is just and [g]good;
the unfailing love of the LORD fills the
earth.
6 The LORD merely spoke,
and the heavens were created.
He breathed the word,
and all the stars were born.
7 He assigned the sea its boundaries
and locked the oceans in vast
reservoirs.
8 Let the whole world fear the LORD,
and let everyone stand in awe of him.
9 For when he spoke, the world began!
It appeared at his command.
10 The LORD frustrates the plans of the
nations
and thwarts all their schemes.
11 But the LORD's plans stand firm
forever;
his intentions can never be shaken.
12 What joy for the nation whose God is the
LORD,
whose people he has chosen as his
inheritance.

13 The LORD looks down from heaven
and sees the whole human race.
14 From his throne he observes
all who live on the earth.
15 He made their hearts,
so he understands everything
they do.
16 The best-equipped army cannot save a
[h]king,
nor is great strength enough to save
a warrior.
17 Don't count on your warhorse to give you
victory—
for all its strength, it cannot save you.

18 But the LORD watches over those who
fear him,
those who [i]rely on his unfailing love.
19 He rescues them from death
and keeps them alive in times of
famine.

20 We put our hope in the LORD.
He is our help and our shield.
21 In him our hearts rejoice,
for we trust in his holy name.
22 Let your unfailing love surround us,
LORD,
for our hope is in you alone.

32:10 Ps 16:4; Prov 16:20; Rom 2:9-10
33:1 Ps 32:11; 147:1
33:2 Ps 92:3; [f]*zamar* (2167) ‣ Ps 47:7
33:3 Ps 96:1; 98:1; Rev 5:9
33:4 Ps 19:8
33:5 Ps 11:7; 119:64; [g]*mishpat* (4941) ‣ Ps 37:30
33:6 Gen 1:6-7; Ps 148:5; Heb 11:3
33:7 Exod 15:8; Job 38:8-11
33:8 Ps 67:7; 96:9
33:9 Gen 1:3; Ps 148:5
33:10 Ps 2:1-4; Isa 8:9-10; 19:3
33:12 Exod 19:5; Ps 144:15
33:16 Ps 44:6; 147:10; [h]*melek* (4428) ‣ Ps 47:2
33:17 Ps 20:7; Prov 21:31
33:18 Ps 34:15; [i]*yakhal* (3176) ‣ Ps 42:11
33:19 Ps 37:19
33:20 Ps 115:9; Isa 8:17

32:9 The *senseless* person is not wise. Rejecting the Lord's counsel ruins life and makes one like an animal (see Isa 1:3; Jas 3:3).

32:10 Difficulties common to all of life will ensnare the wicked, whereas the Lord promises to protect the godly with his care.

Ps 33 This hymn of creation (see also Pss 8, 19, 104, 145) might be a continuation of Ps 32. It exhorts readers to praise God (33:1-3), to recognize the power of his word in creation (33:4-7), and to fear the Creator (33:8-11). It offers hope to forgiven sinners (Ps 32) that they can live a new life in the fear of the Lord and under divine protection.

33:1-3 The psalmist exhorts *the godly* to praise the Lord *with melodies,* with *a new song,* and with *skillfully*-played music.

33:4-7 God's *word* displays his character and his power.

33:7 The nations surrounding Israel thought that the *sea* had divine power, but it is under God's control, within *boundaries* that he set (see 104:8-10).

33:8-11 *Fear* of the Lord begins with awe for God and for his powerful word. His word created everything and continues to order and sustain creation. He *frustrates* the plans of people who oppose his plans.

33:8 The power of the Lord extends to all the nations (see Ps 2; 96:1-3).

33:10 The *plans* and *schemes* of the mighty will not prevail, except by God's will (see Isa 8:9-10).

33:11 God's word still orders creation and will do so *forever.* • God's *intentions* are marvelous (40:5; 92:5).

33:12 People who fear God are *chosen as his inheritance* (see 33:13-19); this excludes rebellious people (78:62).

33:13-19 From the heavens, the Lord searches out and cares for anyone who fears him (see 14:2-3).

33:16-17 *army . . . great strength . . . warhorse:* Even military might is under God's control (see 33:10-11; Eccl 9:11). • *strength:* See note on 33:22.

33:18 God *watches over* all who live by his counsel (32:8). He protects, rescues, and remains close to them (34:15-22).

33:20-22 The godly respond to this magnificent vision of God's power in creation and in the affairs of the world with an affirmation of trust, commitment, joy, and hope as they pray and wait for God's rescue.

33:22 Using a play on words, the psalmist contrasts his people's sure *hope* (Hebrew *yakhal*) in the Lord with the supposed strength (33:17; Hebrew *khayil*) of the horses of the wicked.

34:1 Ps 71:6 Eph 5:20
34:2 Jer 9:24 [j]nepesh (5315) ›Ps 35:9
34:3 [k]rum (7311) ›Ps 57:5
34:5 Ps 36:9
34:7 Dan 6:22 [a]mal'ak (4397) ›Ps 78:49
34:8 1 Pet 2:3 [b]'ashrey (0835) ›Ps 41:1
34:9 Ps 23:1; 31:23
34:10 Ps 84:11
34:11 Ps 111:10
34:12 1 Pet 3:10-12
34:13 Jas 1:26 1 Pet 2:22
34:14 Ps 37:27 Rom 14:18-19 Heb 12:14 [c]shalom (7965) ›Ps 119:165
34:15 Job 36:7 Ps 33:18-19
34:16 Ps 9:6; 109:15
34:18 Ps 51:17; 145:18 Isa 57:15 [d]yasha' (3467) ›Ps 67:2
34:19 Ps 71:20 Prov 24:16
34:21 Ps 94:23
34:22 Ps 71:23

PSALM 34

A psalm of David, regarding the time he pretended to be insane in front of Abimelech, who sent him away.

1 I will praise the LORD at all times.
I will constantly speak his praises.
2 [j]I will boast only in the LORD;
let all who are helpless take heart.
3 Come, let us tell of the LORD's greatness;
let us [k]exalt his name together.

4 I prayed to the LORD, and he answered me.
He freed me from all my fears.
5 Those who look to him for help will be radiant with joy;
no shadow of shame will darken their faces.
6 In my desperation I prayed, and the LORD listened;
he saved me from all my troubles.
7 For the [a]angel of the LORD is a guard;
he surrounds and defends all who fear him.

8 Taste and see that the LORD is good.
Oh, the [b]joys of those who take refuge in him!
9 Fear the LORD, you his godly people,
for those who fear him will have all they need.
10 Even strong young lions sometimes go hungry,
but those who trust in the LORD will lack no good thing.

11 Come, my children, and listen to me,
and I will teach you to fear the LORD.
12 Does anyone want to live a life
that is long and prosperous?
13 Then keep your tongue from speaking evil
and your lips from telling lies!
14 Turn away from evil and do good.
Search for [c]peace, and work to maintain it.

15 The eyes of the LORD watch over those who do right;
his ears are open to their cries for help.
16 But the LORD turns his face against those who do evil;
he will erase their memory from the earth.
17 The LORD hears his people when they call to him for help.
He rescues them from all their troubles.
18 The LORD is close to the brokenhearted;
he [d]rescues those whose spirits are crushed.

19 The righteous person faces many troubles,
but the LORD comes to the rescue each time.
20 For the LORD protects the bones of the righteous;
not one of them is broken!

21 Calamity will surely overtake the wicked,
and those who hate the righteous will be punished.
22 But the LORD will redeem those who serve him.
No one who takes refuge in him will be condemned.

Ps 34 This psalm is a Hebrew acrostic poem; each verse begins with a successive letter of the Hebrew alphabet. The acrostic is missing one letter (*waw*) and has an additional verse at the end (34:22). This wisdom psalm includes a thanksgiving hymn (34:1-7) that celebrates the Lord's care for and protection of godly sufferers. It also includes an invitation to wisdom (34:8-14) and an exposition of wisdom concerning the Lord's care for the needy and the suffering of the wicked (34:15-22).

34:TITLE *Abimelech* is another name for Achish (see 1 Sam 21:10-15). The body of the psalm makes no explicit connection to this event.

34:1-3 The psalmist exhorts the ***helpless*** to join him in praise.

34:5-6 The psalmist narrates his experiences of answered prayer.

34:7 The ***angel of the LORD*** represented the Lord's presence during the wilderness journey. He protected Israel from the forces of Egypt (Exod 14:19-20), and he will guard all the godly (91:11).

34:8-14 The godly encourage everyone to seek wisdom, to fear the Lord, and to place themselves under the protection of the Lord's angel.

34:9-10 Fear of the Lord includes reverence and respect, and it motivates a life of wisdom (see Prov 1:7; 9:10).

34:11-13 Wisdom contains three components: fearing the Lord (34:11), doing good (34:14), and rejecting evil (34:13).

34:11 Anyone who listens, even ***children***, can become wise followers of God.

34:12-16 Peter quotes this passage in his instructions for peaceful living (1 Pet 3:10-12).

34:13 Godly people control their words; ***speaking evil*** and ***telling lies*** are foolish (see 10:7; cp. 17:1).

34:14 The way of ***peace*** leads to harmony and order, whereas *evil* destroys them (see 37:11).

34:15-16 The Lord distinguishes between wise and foolish people; he shows his concern for the wise by rescuing them from trouble (34:15, 17-20), but he destroys the foolish (34:16, 21).

34:18 Those who are ***brokenhearted*** possess a spirit of deep contrition and dependence on the Lord. God accepts this spirit as a proper sacrifice (51:17). The wicked hate the brokenhearted (109:16), but the Lord heals them (147:3; see Isa 57:15; 61:1).

34:19-22 The godly might suffer, but the Lord will reward them in the end. Similarly, the wicked might prosper for a time, but ultimately they will perish (1:6; 34:15-16).

34:20 ***Bones*** represent a person's entire being (see 6:2). • ***not one of them is broken:*** John applied this statement to Jesus at the crucifixion (John 19:36).

PSALM 35

A psalm of David.

1 O LORD, oppose those who oppose me.
Fight those who fight against me.
2 Put on your armor, and take up your shield.
Prepare for battle, and come to my aid.
3 Lift up your spear and javelin
against those who pursue me.
Let me hear you say,
"I will give you victory!"
4 Bring shame and disgrace on those trying to kill me;
turn them back and humiliate those who want to harm me.
5 Blow them away like chaff in the wind—
a wind sent by the angel of the LORD.
6 Make their path dark and slippery,
with the angel of the LORD pursuing them.
7 I did them no wrong, but they laid a trap for me.
I did them no wrong, but they dug a pit to catch me.
8 So let sudden ruin come upon them!
Let them be caught in the trap they set for me!
Let them be destroyed in the pit they dug for me.

9 Then [e]I will rejoice in the LORD.
I will be glad because he rescues me.
10 With every bone in my body I will praise him:
"LORD, who can compare with you?
Who else rescues the helpless from the strong?
Who else protects the helpless and poor from those who rob them?"

11 Malicious witnesses testify against me.
They accuse me of crimes I know nothing about.
12 They repay me evil for good.
I am sick with despair.
13 Yet when they were ill, I grieved for them.
I denied myself by fasting for them,
but my prayers returned unanswered.
14 I was sad, as though they were my friends or family,
as if I were grieving for my own mother.
15 But they are glad now that I am in trouble;
they gleefully join together against me.
I am attacked by people I don't even know;
they slander me constantly.
16 They mock me and call me names;
they snarl at me.

17 How long, O Lord, will you look on and do nothing?
Rescue me from their fierce attacks.
Protect my life from these lions!
18 Then I will thank you in front of the great assembly.
I will praise you before all the people.
19 Don't let my treacherous enemies rejoice over my defeat.
Don't let those who hate me without cause gloat over my sorrow.
20 They don't talk of peace;
they plot against innocent people who mind their own business.
21 They shout, "Aha! Aha!
With our own eyes we saw him do it!"

22 O LORD, you know all about this.
Do not stay silent.
Do not abandon me now, O Lord.
23 Wake up! Rise to my defense!
Take up my case, my God and my Lord.
24 Declare me not guilty, O LORD my God,
for you give justice.
Don't let my enemies laugh about me in my troubles.
25 Don't let them say, "Look, we got what we wanted!
Now we will eat him alive!"

35:1 Ps 56:1-2; Isa 49:25
35:2 Ps 91:4
35:3 Ps 62:2
35:4 Ps 40:14; 70:2-3
35:5 Job 21:18; Ps 1:4; 83:13; Isa 29:5
35:6 Ps 73:18; Jer 23:12
35:7 Ps 69:4; 109:3
35:8 Ps 9:15; Isa 47:11; 1 Thes 5:3
35:9 Isa 61:10; Luke 1:47; [e]*nepesh* (5315) ▸Ps 42:1
35:10 Exod 15:11-12; Ps 18:17; 37:14
35:11 Ps 27:12
35:12 Ps 38:20; John 10:32
35:13 Job 30:25; Ps 69:10
35:16 Lam 2:16
35:17 Ps 13:1; 22:20-21; Hab 1:13
35:18 Ps 22:23, 25
35:19 Ps 13:4; 38:16, 19; 69:4; *John 15:25
35:21 Ps 22:13; 40:15
35:22 Exod 3:7; Ps 10:14
35:24 Ps 9:4; 43:1
35:25 Ps 56:1; Lam 2:16

Ps 35 In this lament, the Lord's troubled servant calls for God to see his circumstances and vindicate him.

35:4-10 The psalmist longs for the Lord's salvation. The language seems vindictive, but it arises from a desire for justice and for the Lord to care for the needy and oppressed.

35:6 A *path* that is *dark and slippery* suggests instability and untimely doom under the Lord's judgment (see 69:23; 73:18; 82:5; 107:10; 143:3). • The *angel of the LORD* is an agent of judgment as well as salvation.

35:10 Nothing in the universe can *compare* with the Lord (see 86:8; 89:6, 8; Isa 40:18, 25).

35:11-18 The psalmist presents the Lord with the reasons for his suffering. Evil has many faces. He is tired and worn out, and he knows that only the Lord can help him.

35:11 *Malicious witnesses* want nothing but violence (see 11:4-6; 54:3).

35:16 The psalmist's attackers *snarl* to express their bitter envy.

35:19-25 In this prayer for vindication, the psalmist's crisis looms so large that a resolution must be found in the Lord. The psalmist has taken the high road, believing that vengeance belongs to the Lord. God's patience hardens the hearts of the wicked and gives them reasons to justify their evil lifestyle.

35:19 John applied this claim of innocence (see also 69:4) to Jesus (John 15:25).

35:21, 25 *Aha! . . . Look!* Both words translate the same expression of glee (Hebrew *he'akh*).

35:26
Ps 38:16; 40:14
35:27
Ps 40:16; 70:4; 149:4-5
35:28
Ps 51:14-15
[f]*hagah* (1897)
‣ Ps 37:30
[g]*tsedeq* (6664)
‣ Ps 45:7
36:1
*Rom 3:18
36:3
Ps 10:7
Jer 4:22
36:4
Prov 4:16
Isa 65:2
Mic 2:1
36:5
Ps 57:10; 103:11; 108:4
36:6
Ps 104:14-15; 145:16-17
Rom 11:33
36:7
Ruth 2:12
Ps 91:4; 139:17-18
[h]*elohim* (0430)
‣ Ps 40:17
36:8
Isa 25:6
Rev 22:1
36:9
1 Pet 2:9
36:12
Ps 140:10
37:1
Ps 73:3
Prov 3:31
37:2
Job 14:2
Ps 90:5-6
37:3
Deut 30:20
Ps 62:8
Isa 40:11

26 May those who rejoice at my troubles
be humiliated and disgraced.
May those who triumph over me
be covered with shame and dishonor.
27 But give great joy to those who came to
my defense.
Let them continually say, "Great is the
LORD,
who delights in blessing his servant
with peace!"
28 Then I will [f]proclaim your [g]justice,
and I will praise you all day long.

PSALM 36

For the choir director: A psalm of David, the servant of the LORD.

1 Sin whispers to the wicked, deep within
their hearts.
They have no fear of God at all.
2 In their blind conceit,
they cannot see how wicked they
really are.
3 Everything they say is crooked and
deceitful.
They refuse to act wisely or do good.
4 They lie awake at night, hatching sinful
plots.
Their actions are never good.
They make no attempt to turn from
evil.

5 Your unfailing love, O LORD, is as vast as
the heavens;
your faithfulness reaches beyond the
clouds.
6 Your righteousness is like the mighty
mountains,
your justice like the ocean depths.
You care for people and animals alike,
O LORD.
7 How precious is your unfailing love,
O [h]God!
All humanity finds shelter
in the shadow of your wings.
8 You feed them from the abundance of
your own house,
letting them drink from your river of
delights.
9 For you are the fountain of life,
the light by which we see.

10 Pour out your unfailing love on those
who love you;
give justice to those with honest hearts.
11 Don't let the proud trample me
or the wicked push me around.
12 Look! Those who do evil have fallen!
They are thrown down, never to rise
again.

PSALM 37

A psalm of David.

1 Don't worry about the wicked
or envy those who do wrong.
2 For like grass, they soon fade away.
Like spring flowers, they soon wither.

3 Trust in the LORD and do good.
Then you will live safely in the land
and prosper.

35:26-28 The psalmist calls on the Lord to judge the wicked and to rescue the godly and bring them joy.

Ps 36 This lament contrasts the world of folly devised by the wicked with the world of wisdom created and sustained by the Lord. The wicked care only about themselves, whereas the Lord cares for all of creation. He will intervene to bring about justice in his world. The righteous will enjoy his protection, but the wicked will perish.

36:1-4 Fools despise what is wise and good as they pursue evil.

36:1 ***no fear of God:*** Paul includes this phrase in his description of the depravity of all people (Rom 3:18).

36:5-9 As the source of wisdom, the Lord is reliable and incomparable. His faithful care extends to all parts of the created order.

36:5-6 God's all-encompassing goodness surpasses that of the created order. God graciously meets his people's practical needs.

36:6-9 All creatures live by God's grace (1 Tim 4:10).

36:7-8 God invites ***all humanity*** to the banquet in his ***house*** (cp. Prov 9:1-6).

36:9 ***Light*** represents salvation and celebration (18:25-29; 27:1; cp. 35:6).

36:10-11 Since God's wisdom extends to all of creation, it protects the godly.

36:12 The psalmist remains confident that the disorder caused by the wicked (36:1-4) will end when they meet their demise.

Ps 37 This psalm is a Hebrew acrostic poem; each stanza begins with a successive letter of the Hebrew alphabet. It elaborates on the problems posed in Ps 36: How should the godly respond to the reality of evil? When will the Lord bring justice? Why does he permit the wicked to destroy his created order? Psalm 37 offers clear responses that reduce the tensions of life (37:1-9, 34) and promise that the meek will have a future (37:10-11, 39-40). The alternating contrast between the godly and the wicked emphasizes the futility of folly (37:12-24, 27-33). The personal observations of the psalmist add a human touch (37:25-26, 35-38). He encourages viewing the inheritance of the land from a long-range perspective: The earth belongs to the Lord, who will give it to those he blesses—the lowly and godly who trust in him, put their hope in him, and follow him (see 37:9, 11, 22, 29, 34; see also Isa 57:13; Matt 5:5).

37:1-9 The wise respond to evil by trusting in the Lord. Trust includes five dimensions: (1) renouncing irritability and envy (37:1-2); (2) delighting in the Lord (37:3-4); (3) submitting to the Lord (37:5-6); (4) practicing patience in hope (37:7); and (5) avoiding anger (37:8-9).

37:1 ***envy:*** The jealous desire to have what others enjoy leads to further sin (73:3; Prov 3:31; Jas 1:14-15; 4:1-2).

37:2 Finite existence is part of the human condition (see 90:5-6; 92:7; 102:4, 11; 103:15; 129:6; Isa 40:7-8).

37:3-4 The antidote to irritability and envy (37:1) is trust in the Lord.

37:3 To ***do good*** means cultivating a devotion to wisdom (see 34:14; Prov 3:5-7).

4 Take delight in the LORD,
and he will give you your heart's
desires.
5 Commit everything you do to the LORD.
Trust him, and he will help you.
6 He will make your innocence radiate like
the dawn,
and the justice of your cause will
shine like the noonday sun.

7 Be still in the presence of the LORD,
and wait patiently for him to act.
Don't worry about evil people who
prosper
or fret about their wicked schemes.

8 Stop being angry!
Turn from your rage!
Do not lose your temper—
it only leads to harm.
9 For the wicked will be destroyed,
but those who trust in the LORD will
possess the land.

10 Soon the wicked will disappear.
Though you look for them, they will
be gone.
11 The lowly will possess the land
and will live in peace and prosperity.

12 The wicked plot against the godly;
they snarl at them in defiance.
13 But the Lord just laughs,
for he sees their day of judgment
coming.

14 The wicked draw their swords
and string their bows
to kill the poor and the oppressed,
to slaughter those who do right.
15 But their swords will stab their own
hearts,
and their bows will be broken.

16 It is better to be godly and have little
than to be evil and rich.
17 For the strength of the wicked will be
shattered,
but the LORD takes care of the godly.

18 Day by day the LORD takes care of the
innocent,
and they will receive an inheritance
that lasts forever.
19 They will not be disgraced in hard times;
even in famine they will have more
than enough.

20 But the wicked will die.
The LORD's enemies are like flowers
in a field—
they will disappear like smoke.

21 The wicked borrow and never repay,
but the godly are generous givers.
22 Those the LORD blesses will possess the
land,
but those he curses will die.

23 The LORD directs the steps of the godly.
He delights in every detail of their lives.
24 Though they stumble, they will never fall,
for the LORD holds them by the hand.

25 Once I was young, and now I am old.
Yet I have never seen the godly
abandoned
or their children begging for bread.
26 The godly always give generous loans to
others,
and their children are a blessing.

27 Turn from evil and do good,
and you will live in the land forever.
28 For the LORD loves justice,
and he will never abandon the godly.

He will keep them safe forever,
but the children of the wicked will die.

37:4 Ps 145:19; Isa 58:14
37:5 Ps 55:22; Prov 16:3; 1 Pet 5:7
37:6 Isa 58:8, 10; Mic 7:9
37:7 Ps 40:1; 62:5; Jer 12:1
37:8 Eph 4:31; Col 3:8
37:9 Ps 25:13; Isa 60:21
37:10 Job 24:24
37:11 Matt 5:3, 5; ˈ*anaw* (6035) ‣Ps 147:6
37:12 Ps 35:16
37:13 Ps 2:4
37:14 Ps 11:2; 35:10
37:15 Ps 9:16; 46:9
37:16 Prov 15:16; 16:8
37:17 Job 38:15; Ps 10:15
37:19 Job 5:20; Ps 33:18-19
37:20 Ps 68:2; 73:27; 102:3
37:22 Job 5:3; Prov 3:33
37:23 1 Sam 2:9; Ps 40:2; 147:11
37:24 Ps 145:14; 147:6; Prov 24:15-16
37:25 Isa 41:17; Heb 13:5
37:26 Ps 37:21
37:27 Ps 34:14

37:4 To *take delight in the LORD* means aligning with the Lord's way in order to enjoy him.

37:6 *Justice* occurs when the Lord's will triumphs and the godly experience his rescue (Isa 45:8; 51:5-6; 58:8, 10-11).

37:7 *Be still:* We should let the Lord be God rather than taking matters into our own hands.

37:8 Irritability and anger quickly corrode character.

37:9-11 The wicked will not *possess the land;* those who *trust in the LORD* will. The Lord promises an inheritance because he is committed to caring for his people.

37:11 The Lord is the author of *peace* (85:10)—he brings peace to a chaotic world (29:11; 37:11; 85:8; 147:14). His wisdom guides *the lowly* into the way of peace (119:165; Matt 5:5).

37:12-17 *The wicked* seek to destroy the Lord's order, but he defeats them.

37:12-13 The wicked *snarl* to express their bitter envy. They plot to bring an end to the godly, but the Lord derides them because they cannot succeed (2:4).

37:14-15 The weapons of the wicked will turn against them (cp. 7:12-13).

37:16 Being wise with modest means is *better* than having prosperity and power (Prov 15:16; 16:8, 19; 17:1; 28:6) and being wicked.

37:18-20 The Lord cares for the blameless in this life and for eternity, but the wicked will perish.

37:20 *Smoke* depicts the temporary nature of life (68:2; 102:3).

37:21 To *borrow and never repay* is a behavior of a crooked lifestyle. • *Generous givers* freely share what they freely receive from the Lord (see 111:5; 112:5).

37:23-24 The rectitude and strength of a godly person's life comes from the Lord (see Prov 4:12; 14:15; 16:9; 20:24).

37:25-26 The Lord does not abandon his children or their descendants.

37:27-33 The *godly* are wise; they do good and reject evil. The Lord cares for them, protecting them and ensuring

37:28 Ps 11:7; 21:10
37:29 Ps 37:9, 18
37:30 [j]hagah (1897) ‣Ps 38:12 [k]mishpat (4941) ‣Ps 48:11
37:31 Ps 40:8 Isa 51:7
37:32 Ps 10:8; 37:14
37:33 2 Pet 2:9
37:34 Ps 27:14; 37:9
37:35 Job 5:3
37:38 Ps 1:1; 73:19
37:39 Ps 3:8; 9:9

29 The godly will possess the land
and will live there forever.

30 The godly [j]offer good counsel;
they teach [k]right from wrong.
31 They have made God's law their own,
so they will never slip from his path.

32 The wicked wait in ambush for the godly,
looking for an excuse to kill them.
33 But the LORD will not let the wicked
succeed
or let the godly be condemned when
they are put on trial.

34 Put your hope in the LORD.
Travel steadily along his path.
He will honor you by giving you the land.
You will see the wicked destroyed.

35 I have seen wicked and ruthless people
flourishing like a tree in its native soil.
36 But when I looked again, they were gone!
Though I searched for them, I could
not find them!

37 Look at those who are honest and good,
for a wonderful future awaits those
who love peace.
38 But the rebellious will be destroyed;
they have no future.

39 The LORD rescues the godly;
he is their fortress in times of trouble.
40 The LORD helps them,
rescuing them from the wicked.
He saves them,
and they find shelter in him.

Wisdom Psalms (Ps 37)

Pss 1, 14, 25, 34, 39, 49, 73, 78, 90–91, 111–112, 127–128, 131, 133, 139

Some psalms are called wisdom psalms because they make a case for the primary importance of wisdom or instruct readers in dealing with questions, issues, and doubts that arise in life (see Pss 1, 14, 25, 34, 37, 39, 49, 73, 78, 90, 91, 111, 112, 127, 128, 131, 133, 139). Many other psalms contain elements of wisdom teaching (see Pss 18, 27, 31, 32, 40, 62, 92, 94, 107, 144, 146).

In the ancient Near East, wisdom had to do with ordering life and society, pleasing God and other people, and carefully observing life, society, and nature. In Israel, wisdom shares these concerns but is distinct in the centrality it gives to fear of the Lord. God alone is the center and focus of life (76:7), and proper fear of him opens the path of wisdom (111:10). Fear of the Lord is a disposition of absolute submission to and trust in the Lord (40:3; 112:7; 115:11), which leads to purity of life (19:9). Psalm 34 defines the fear of the Lord as a search for abundant life (34:12) that begins with seeking the Lord (34:4).

The way of wisdom is the way of godliness. Psalm 1 invites all readers of the Psalter to delight in God, his revelation, and the lifestyle that results from his care for the wise. The lives of the godly demonstrate inner consistency, growth, and beauty as they increasingly reflect God's righteousness and justice, love and fidelity, compassion and grace. They practice godliness from the heart—from the inside out.

Wisdom enlarges a person's perspective on life. A wise person desires to see life from God's point of view. This search means living in submission and trust under the sovereign King who maintains the order and harmony of creation. Seeking God encourages an orderly and peaceful life (104:24; 139:14) and motivates obedience (19:7; 25:12; 51:6; 112:1; 119:98). The wise imitate God, and their lives are full of joy even when they are suffering hardship. They praise the Lord amidst all circumstances of life (22:23, 25). They face life confidently because the Lord is with them (23:4; 27:1, 3; 33:18; 49:5; 91:1-16).

In contrast to the way of the wise is the way of the fool, or the wicked. Such people perceive themselves as powerful and continually boast of their accomplishments. They do not accept limitations. They brag, oppress, steal, and deprive others of their happiness. They have no fear of the Lord (36:1; 55:19). The poets of Israel repeatedly warned the people to be wary of the path of folly, lest God's judgment overtake the foolish (2:10-11; 33:8; 64:9; 94:8).

Jesus Christ came into the world as God in the flesh. He embodies all the qualities of wisdom. Through him, we can walk in the way of wisdom since he suffered for our sins (Col 2:2-3).

that they receive their rightful portion of ***the land*** as their inheritance. The ***wicked*** might try to ***ambush*** the ***godly***, but they will not succeed.

37:30 ***The godly*** base their ***counsel*** on the Lord's wisdom.

37:31 ***They have made God's law their own:*** The godly internalize God's wisdom and instructions (see 119:11; Jer 24:7; 31:31-34).

37:35-36 The ***wicked*** might appear to be ***flourishing like a tree*** (cp. 52:8; 92:12-13), but they eventually die and are forgotten (37:2).

37:39-40 The Lord provides strength for his people.

PSALM 38

A psalm of David, asking God to remember him.

1 O LORD, don't rebuke me in your anger
or discipline me in your rage!
2 Your arrows have struck deep,
and your blows are crushing me.
3 Because of your anger, my whole body is sick;
my health is broken because of my sins.
4 My guilt overwhelms me—
it is a burden too heavy to bear.
5 My wounds fester and stink
because of my foolish sins.
6 I am bent over and racked with pain.
All day long I walk around filled with grief.
7 A raging fever burns within me,
and my health is broken.
8 I am exhausted and completely crushed.
My groans come from an anguished heart.
9 You know what I long for, Lord;
you hear my every sigh.
10 My heart beats wildly, my strength fails,
and I am going blind.
11 My loved ones and friends stay away,
fearing my disease.
Even my own family stands at a distance.
12 Meanwhile, my enemies lay traps to kill me.
Those who wish me harm make plans to ruin me.
All day long they [a]plan their treachery.

13 But I am deaf to all their threats.
I am silent before them as one who cannot speak.
14 I choose to hear nothing,
and I make no reply.
15 For I am waiting for you, O LORD.
You must answer for me, O Lord my God.
16 I prayed, "Don't let my enemies gloat over me
or rejoice at my downfall."
17 I am on the verge of collapse,
facing constant pain.
18 But I confess my sins;
I am deeply sorry for what I have done.
19 I have many aggressive enemies;
they hate me without reason.
20 They repay me evil for good
and oppose me for pursuing good.
21 Do not abandon me, O LORD.
Do not stand at a distance, my God.
22 Come quickly to help me,
O Lord my savior.

PSALM 39

For Jeduthun, the choir director: A psalm of David.

1 I said to myself, "I will watch what I do
and not sin in what I say.
I will hold my tongue
when the ungodly are around me."
2 But as I stood there in silence—
not even speaking of good things—
the turmoil within me grew worse.
3 The more I thought about it,
the hotter I got,
igniting a fire of words:
4 "LORD, remind me how brief my time on earth will be.

38:1 Ps 6:1
38:2 Job 6:4; Ps 32:4
38:3 Ps 6:2; 31:9-10; Isa 1:5-6
38:4 Ezra 9:6
38:5 Ps 69:5
38:6 Ps 35:14
38:7 Ps 102:3-4
38:8 Job 3:24; Ps 22:1
38:9 Ps 10:17
38:10 Ps 6:7; 31:10
38:12 Ps 35:20; 54:3; 140:5; [a]*hagah* (1897) ‣ Ps 63:6
38:15 Ps 17:6
38:16 Ps 13:4; 35:26
38:17 Ps 13:2
38:18 2 Cor 7:9-10
38:19 Ps 18:17; 35:19
38:20 Ps 35:12; 1 Jn 3:12
38:21 Ps 22:19; 35:22
38:22 Ps 22:19; 40:13, 17
39:1 Ps 34:13; 141:3; Jas 3:2, 5-12
39:4 Ps 78:39; 90:12; 103:14-15

Ps 38 This lament and prayer for healing is an acrostic that uses the twenty-two letters of the Hebrew alphabet. The psalmist's suffering is associated with his unconfessed sin. He confesses his sin and entrusts his case to the Lord.

38:TITLE ***asking God to remember him:*** The meaning of this phrase is uncertain (also in 70:TITLE).

38:1-17 These verses form a prelude to the psalmist's confession (38:18) and describe his woeful condition.

38:1-4 The psalmist's ***sins*** had triggered the Lord's ***anger*** and ***rage,*** resulting in the ***arrows*** and ***blows*** of ***discipline*** and ***rebuke;*** as a result, his ***whole body is sick.***

38:3 Sin can lead to sickness and even death (1 Cor 11:30). Whether the psalmist actually felt physically ill or his sickness was a metaphor for emotional turmoil, he knew that it came from God and threatened his life (see 32:3; 39:10).

38:4 The psalmist's ***burden*** results from sin (see 40:12; 41:4; cp. Gen 4:13).

38:5-8 The severity of God's punishment brings anguish that affects every part of the psalmist's being.

38:9-12 The psalmist longs for a restored relationship with God, but he feels alienated. He finds himself lost and alone as his friends disappear.

38:13 The psalmist suffers quietly before his opponents (see Isa 53:7).

38:15 The Lord alone will resolve the conflict (9:18; 27:14; 37:9, 34).

38:17-20 No longer able to endure his suffering and teetering ***on the verge of collapse*** (cp. 15:5), the psalmist confesses his sin (see 32:5).

38:19 That the psalmist's enemies hate him ***without reason*** compounds his pain.

38:22 Asking the Lord to act quickly in times of great need is common in the Psalter (22:19; 31:2; 40:13; 69:17; 70:1; 71:12; 79:8; 102:2; 141:1; 143:7). However, wisdom and experience teach that God's people must often wait for him to act (27:14; 37:7; Isa 8:17; 40:31).

Ps 39 This prayer for rescue reflects the psalmist's discouragement, which comes from having a limited perspective on his situation.

39:TITLE ***Jeduthun*** was a levitical singer appointed by David along with Asaph (1 Chr 9:16; 16:38; 25:1).

39:1-3 Suffering in ***silence*** only intensifies the psalmist's anguish, pain, and inner ***turmoil.***

39:4-6 Because of his suffering and sin, the psalmist concludes that life is meaningless and fleeting (see Job 7:7-10; Isa 40:6-8). He had expected a wicked life to have those qualities (see

Remind me that my days are
numbered—
how fleeting my life is.
5 You have made my life no longer than
the width of my hand.
My entire lifetime is just a moment
to you;
at best, each of us is but a [b]breath."
Interlude
6 We are merely moving shadows,
and all our busy rushing ends in
[c]nothing.
We heap up wealth,
not knowing who will spend it.
7 And so, Lord, where do I put my hope?
My only hope is in you.
8 Rescue me from my rebellion.
Do not let fools mock me.
9 I am silent before you; I won't say a word,
for my punishment is from you.
10 But please stop striking me!
I am exhausted by the blows from
your hand.
11 When you discipline us for our sins,
you consume like a moth what is
precious to us.
Each of us is but a breath.
Interlude
12 Hear my prayer, O LORD!
Listen to my cries for help!
Don't ignore my tears.
For I am your guest—
a traveler passing through,
as my ancestors were before me.
13 Leave me alone so I can smile again
before I am gone and exist no more.

PSALM 40

For the choir director: A psalm of David.

1 I waited patiently for the LORD to help me,
and he turned to me and heard my cry.
2 He lifted me out of the pit of despair,
out of the mud and the mire.
He set my feet on solid ground
and steadied me as I walked along.
3 He has given me a new song to sing,
a hymn of praise to our God.
Many will see what he has done and be
amazed.
They will put their trust in the LORD.

4 Oh, the joys of those who trust the LORD,
who have no confidence in the proud
or in those who worship idols.
5 O LORD my God, you have performed
many wonders for us.
Your plans for us are too numerous
to list.
You have no equal.
If I tried to recite all your wonderful
deeds,
I would never come to the end of them.

6 You take no delight in sacrifices or
offerings.
Now that you have made me listen, I
finally understand—
you don't require burnt offerings or
sin offerings.
7 Then I said, "Look, I have come.
As is written about me in the
Scriptures:
8 I take joy in doing your will, my God,
for your [d]instructions are written on
my heart."

9 I have told all your people about your
justice.
I have not been afraid to speak out,
as you, O LORD, well know.
10 I have not kept the good news of your
justice hidden in my heart;
I have talked about your faithfulness
and saving power.

39:5 Job 14:2; Ps 62:9; 89:47; 144:4
[b]*hebel* (1892) ‣Ps 39:6
39:6 Ps 127:2; Luke 12:20; 1 Pet 1:24
[c]*hebel* (1892) ‣Eccl 1:2
39:8 Ps 51:9; 79:4, 9
39:9 Job 2:10
39:10 Job 9:34; Ps 32:4
39:11 Job 13:27-28; Ps 90:7; 2 Pet 2:16
39:12 Ps 102:1; Heb 11:13; 1 Pet 2:11
39:13 Job 10:20; 14:6
40:1 Ps 27:14; 34:15
40:2 Ps 27:5; 69:1-2; Jer 38:6
40:3 Ps 32:7; 33:3; 64:9
40:4 Ps 84:12
40:5 Job 5:9; Ps 136:4; 139:17-18; Isa 55:8
40:6-8 1 Sam 15:22; Jer 7:22-23; Mic 6:6-8; *Heb 10:5-7
40:8 Ps 37:31; John 4:34; Rom 7:22
[d]*torah* (8451) ‣Ps 119:1
40:9 Ps 22:25; 119:13
40:10 Ps 89:1; Acts 20:20, 27

37:2, 20; 103:15-16), but now whether a person is godly or not seems to be irrelevant.

39:4-5 ***how fleeting my life is:*** This perspective comes out of suffering (see 78:39; 89:47-48; 90:3-10). The human ***lifetime*** is but a ***moment*** to God (90:4), as temporary as a ***breath*** (see 39:11; 144:4).

39:8 The idea that ***rebellion*** brings on suffering is a common thread in Pss 32, 38–41.

39:9-11 The psalmist links suffering with God's ***discipline***, assuming that it is ***punishment*** for his sin.

39:11 The Lord uses ***discipline*** to correct his children (38:1, 3, 7; 40:12; see Prov 3:11-12; Heb 12:5-6).

39:12 A ***guest*** (or ***foreigner***) had no rights of land ownership (see Lev 25:23). The patriarchs had lived as guests in Canaan (105:23).

39:13 Unlike the psalmist's earlier request that God stay close to him (38:21-22), his present desire for God to ***leave*** him ***alone*** echoes Job's disposition (Job 7:17-19).

Ps 40 This psalm includes a thanksgiving song (40:1-10) followed by a lament (40:11-17). The thanksgiving song includes the reason for the thanksgiving (40:1-5), an affirmation of commitment (40:6-8), and a public testimony of God's character (40:7-10). The lament concerns the psalmist's troubles because of his sins (40:11-12) and is followed by two prayers for vindication (40:13-15, 17).

40:1-5 The psalmist thanks the Lord for his rescue and testifies that God can be trusted.

40:6 The Lord delights in the attitude and character of the person making an offering more than in the offering itself. • ***Now that you have made me listen, I finally understand:*** Greek version reads *You have given me a body.* In Heb 10:5-7, the writer quotes from the Greek version of 40:6-8. He casts the words as something Jesus said as he left heaven and came into the world.

40:7 ***As is written about me in the Scriptures:*** Moses had recorded God's requirements for Israel's kings in Deut 17:14-15.

I have told everyone in the great
assembly
of your unfailing love and
faithfulness.
11 LORD, don't hold back your tender
mercies from me.
Let your unfailing love and
faithfulness always protect me.
12 For troubles surround me—
too many to count!
My sins pile up so high
I can't see my way out.
They outnumber the hairs on my head.
I have lost all courage.
13 Please, LORD, rescue me!
Come quickly, LORD, and help me.
14 May those who try to destroy me
be humiliated and put to shame.
May those who take delight in my
trouble
be turned back in disgrace.
15 Let them be horrified by their shame,
for they said, "Aha! We've got him
now!"
16 But may all who search for you
be filled with joy and gladness in you.
May those who love your salvation
repeatedly shout, "The LORD is
great!"
17 As for me, since I am poor and needy,
let the Lord keep me in his thoughts.
You are my helper and my savior.
O my [e]God, do not delay.

PSALM 41

For the choir director: A psalm of David.

1 Oh, the [f]joys of those who are kind to the
poor!
The LORD rescues them when they are
in trouble.
2 The LORD protects them
and keeps them alive.
He gives them prosperity in the land
and rescues them from their enemies.
3 The LORD nurses them when they are
sick
and restores them to health.
4 "O LORD," I prayed, "have mercy on me.
Heal me, for I have [g]sinned against
you."
5 But my enemies say nothing but evil
about me.
"How soon will he die and be
forgotten?" they ask.
6 They visit me as if they were my friends,
but all the while they gather gossip,
and when they leave, they spread it
everywhere.
7 All who hate me whisper about me,
imagining the worst.
8 "He has some fatal disease," they say.
"He will never get out of that bed!"
9 Even my best friend, the one I trusted
completely,
the one who shared my food, has
turned against me.
10 LORD, have mercy on me.
Make me well again, so I can pay them
back!
11 I know you are pleased with me,
for you have not let my enemies
triumph over me.
12 You have preserved my life because I am
innocent;
you have brought me into your
presence forever.
13 Praise the LORD, the God of Israel,
who lives from everlasting to
everlasting.
[h]Amen and [h]amen!

40:11 Ps 61:7
40:12 Ps 18:5; 38:4; 73:26; 116:3
40:13-17 //Ps 70:1-5
40:14 Ps 35:4, 26; 70:2-3
40:16 Ps 35:27; 70:4
40:17 Ps 70:5
[e]*'elohim* (0430) ‣Ps 85:4
41:1 Ps 37:19; 82:3-4; Prov 14:21
[f]*'ashrey* (0835) ‣Ps 84:5
41:2 Ps 37:22, 28
41:4 Ps 6:2; 51:4; 103:3
[g]*khata'* (2398) ‣Ps 119:11
41:5 Ps 38:12
41:6 Ps 12:2
41:7 Ps 56:5
41:9 Job 19:19; Ps 55:12-13, 20; Jer 20:10; *Mark 14:18; *John 13:18
41:10 Ps 9:13
41:11 Ps 25:2; 37:23-24; 147:11
41:12 Job 36:7; Ps 21:6; 37:17
41:13 Ps 72:18-19; 106:48
[h]*'amen* (0543) ‣Isa 65:16

40:11 The psalmist prays that the Lord will be true to his character when answering this plea for mercy.

40:12-17 The psalmist is troubled both by his adversities and his own *sins* and prays for rescue. • This passage is repeated almost verbatim as Ps 70.

Ps 41 In this wisdom psalm, the psalmist prays for healing (41:4, 10), laments his distress (41:5-9), and expresses confidence in the Lord's blessing (41:1-3, 11-12).

41:1 The *poor* who suffer hardship have special protection under God's law (Lev 14:21; 19:10); they receive God's justice and godly rule (72:13; 82:3-4). The word translated *poor* is often a synonym for the godly (113:7; see Zeph 3:12).

41:3 *when they are sick:* This illness might be physical or spiritual (see 6:2; Ps 38).

41:4 The psalmist applies the blessing to himself (41:12). Apparently he has taken care of the poor (41:1), but he has sinned against the Lord in other ways. Out of his pain, he cries for healing while confessing his sin. The Lord alone can grant the restoration that brings true joy (30:2; 107:20-21).

41:5-9 The psalmist's enemies disguise themselves as friends, while his friends openly become his enemies.

41:5 *How soon will he die?* The psalmist's opponents regard his suffering as a divine judgment (cp. 1:6).

41:9 *the one who shared my food:* Eating together was a sign of unity (Acts 2:42). Refusing to eat with someone indicated hostility (1 Cor 5:11). Jesus experienced the same kind of betrayal (John 13:1, 18).

41:11-12 The psalmist knows that the Lord has forgiven him and will bless him.

41:13 This doxology closes Book One (Pss 1–41). Cp. 106:48.

Book Two (Pss 42–72) Book Two includes psalms by many authors: eighteen psalms of David (Pss 51–65, 68–70), eight psalms of the descendants of Korah (Pss 42–49), one psalm ascribed to Asaph (Ps 50), one to Solomon (Ps 72), and several with no author credited. See Psalms Introduction, "The Composition of the Psalms," p. 901.

42:1 Ps 63:1
[i]*nepesh* (5315)
‣Ps 57:1
42:2 Ps 43:4; 84:2; 143:6
Jer 10:10
Rom 9:26
42:3 Ps 79:10; 80:5
Joel 2:17
42:4 Job 30:16
Ps 100:4
Isa 30:29
[j]*todah* (8426)
‣Ps 50:23
42:5 Ps 38:6; 77:3
Lam 3:24
42:6 Ps 61:2
*Mark 14:34
42:7 Ps 88:7
Jon 2:3

2. BOOK TWO (PSS 42–72)

PSALM 42

For the choir director: A psalm of the descendants of Korah.

1 As the deer longs for streams of water,
so [i]I long for you, O God.
2 I thirst for God, the living God.
When can I go and stand before him?
3 Day and night I have only tears for food,
while my enemies continually taunt me, saying,
"Where is this God of yours?"

4 My heart is breaking
as I remember how it used to be:
I walked among the crowds of worshipers,
leading a great procession to the house of God,
singing for joy and [j]giving thanks
amid the sound of a great celebration!

5 Why am I discouraged?
Why is my heart so sad?
I will put my hope in God!
I will praise him again—
my Savior and 6my God!

Now I am deeply discouraged,
but I will remember you—
even from distant Mount Hermon, the source of the Jordan,
from the land of Mount Mizar.
7 I hear the tumult of the raging seas
as your waves and surging tides sweep over me.

Questions and Doubt (Pss 42–43)

Ps 2:1; 4:2; 6:3; 10:1; 11:3; 13:1-6; 22:1; 35:17; 44:23-24; 53:6; 60:9-10; 68:16; 73–74; 77:8-9; 79:5; 80:4, 12; 82:2; 83:2; 85:5-6; 88:14; 89:1-52; 90:11, 13; 94:3-4, 16, 20; 101:2; 108:10-11; 114:5-6; 119:82, 84; 137:4; 147:17

The psalmists are not afraid to ask questions and express doubts. These questions clarify life issues. The intensity of the mood or the significance of an issue can be judged by the number of questions asked. For example, the psalmist of 4:2 asks three questions of his adversaries, and there are five questions in 13:1-2. The psalms with the greatest number of questions raise some of the most significant issues, such as God's perceived abandonment (Pss 42–43, 74, 89) and the prosperity of the wicked (Ps 73).

Questions about God ask whether the Lord is the true God (94:9-10; 121:1) and why he seems to have abandoned the godly (77:7). Questions call attention to the success of the wicked (10:13), the impotence of the godly (11:3), the election of Zion (68:16), the power of God (114:5-6; 147:17), the folly of the nations (2:1), and the issue of injustice (82:2). The psalmists question, examine, challenge, doubt, and occasionally despair over God's seeming lack of concern.

Questions may also lead to praise and worship: "Who can list the glorious miracles of the LORD? Who can ever praise him enough?" (106:2). The question, "Who will come from Mount Zion to rescue Israel?" (53:6) calls attention to the answer: The Lord rescues his people. For many questions, the implied answer brings praise to the Lord: "Whom have I in heaven but you? I desire you more than anything on earth" (73:25; 89:8). Questions may also express wonder at God's grace (8:4; 130:3; 144:3). Asking good questions can be the beginning of a dialogue with the Lord that leads us along the path of wisdom and results in worship and praise.

Pss 42–43 These psalms, like Pss 9 and 10, form a unit comprising a lament with a bittersweet refrain of hope (42:5, 11; 43:5). In many Hebrew manuscripts these two psalms are combined as one. The historical context is uncertain; these psalms might be the voice of God's people in exile, confessing their loyalty to God as he punishes them for their prevailing apostasy. The psalmist longs for such fellowship with God as he enjoyed in Jerusalem (42:4); his memories only make him more discouraged. As the psalmist cries out to God, he recalls God's love and faithfulness (42:8), which moves him to plead for vindication (43:1-4).

42:TITLE *psalm:* Hebrew *maskil.* This may be a literary or musical term. • ***The descendants of Korah*** were members of a Levitical choir appointed by David to serve as Temple singers (see 1 Chr 6:22-38; 9:19-34; 2 Chr 20:19). Their ancestor Korah was the apostate who had rebelled against Moses and whom the earth swallowed up (Exod 6:24; Num 16).

42:1-4 The psalmist's longing for God comes from being geographically distant from the Temple as he remembers the past. • The verb translated ***longs*** is found only here and in Joel 1:20 ("cry out"); in both cases it refers to extreme ***thirst*** in a waterless desert (see 63:1; 143:6; see also 84:2).

42:3 Having ***tears for food*** speaks of great grief (80:5; 102:9; see 6:6; 56:8; 126:5; 119:136). • The wicked try to hold God to their timetable and deny his power to intervene.

42:4 The psalmist recalls ***leading a great procession*** as a member of the Levitical choir, possibly during the high holy days.

42:5-6 The psalmist encourages himself with questions and answers.

42:5 The psalmist feels depressed, but it does not incapacitate him. He remembers that the living God is his ***Savior.*** This verse is repeated in 42:11 and 43:5.

42:6 ***Mount Hermon*** is a high mountain range northeast of Israel. The ***source of the Jordan*** is by Dan at the foot of Mount Hermon. • ***Mount Mizar*** might be a peak in the Mount Hermon range.

42:7 The ***raging seas, waves,*** and ***surging tides*** conjure images of God's wrath (see 88:7).

8 But each day the LORD pours his
unfailing love upon me,
and through each night I sing his songs,
praying to God who gives me life.

9 "O God my rock," I cry,
"Why have you forgotten me?
Why must I wander around in grief,
oppressed by my enemies?"
10 Their taunts break my bones.
They scoff, "Where is this God of
yours?"

11 Why am I discouraged?
Why is my heart so sad?
I will [k]put my hope in God!
I will praise him again—
my Savior and my God!

PSALM 43

1 Declare me innocent, O God!
Defend me against these ungodly
people.
Rescue me from these unjust liars.
2 For you are God, my only safe haven.
Why have you tossed me aside?
Why must I wander around in grief,
oppressed by my enemies?
3 Send out your light and your truth;
let them guide me.
Let them lead me to your holy mountain,
to the [a]place where you live.
4 There I will go to the altar of God,
to God—the source of all my joy.
I will praise you with my harp,
O God, my God!

5 Why am I discouraged?
Why is my heart so sad?
I will put my hope in God!
I will praise him again—
my Savior and my God!

PSALM 44

For the choir director: A psalm of the descendants of Korah.

1 O God, we have heard it with our own
ears—
our ancestors have told us
of all you did in their day,
in days long ago:
2 You drove out the pagan nations by your
power
and gave all the land to our ancestors.
You crushed their enemies
and set our ancestors free.
3 They did not conquer the land with their
swords;
it was not their own strong arm that
gave them victory.
It was your right hand and strong arm
and the blinding light from your face
that helped them,
for you loved them.

4 You are my King and my God.
You command victories for Israel.
5 Only by your power can we push back
our enemies;
only in your name can we trample
our foes.
6 I do not trust in my bow;
I do not count on my sword to save me.
7 You are the one who gives us victory over
our enemies;
you disgrace those who hate us.
8 O God, we give glory to you all day long
and [b]constantly praise your name.
Interlude

9 But now you have tossed us aside in
dishonor.
You no longer lead our armies to battle.

42:8 Job 35:10; Ps 16:7; 57:3; 77:6; 149:4-5
42:9 Ps 17:9; 38:6
42:11 [k]*yakhal* (3176) › Ps 119:43
43:1 1 Sam 24:15; Ps 26:1; 35:24
43:2 Ps 42:9; 44:9
43:3 Ps 36:9; 84:1; [a]*mishkan* (4908) › Ps 46:4
43:4 Ps 26:6; 33:2
44:1 Exod 12:26-27
44:2 Ps 78:55; 80:8
44:3 Deut 4:37; Josh 24:12; Ps 77:15
44:4 Ps 74:12
44:5 Ps 60:12
44:7 Ps 53:5; 136:24
44:8 Ps 30:12; 34:2; [b]*olam* (5769) › Ps 90:2
44:9 Ps 43:2; 60:10; 74:1

42:8 The psalmist sees rays of hope. A life oriented to God includes *songs* of joy and *praying* for justice and vindication (42:9-10; 43:1-4).

42:9-10 The psalmist brings his many doubts, discouragements, and questions directly to God.

43:1-4 The psalmist turns to the Lord for rescue from his troubles, for guidance, for restoration, and for vindication.

43:2 *tossed me aside:* Other psalms similarly ask whether God has rejected his people (44:9, 23; 60:1, 10; 74:1; 77:7; 88:14; 89:38; 108:11).

43:3 In this prayer for God's redemption, *light* and *truth* are viewed as guides (see 18:25-29; 27:1; 85:10-13; 89:14-18; see also 119:105; John 3:19; Eph 5:8; 1 Thes 5:5-7). • The Temple on the *mountain* in Jerusalem symbolized God's *holy* presence among his people (15:1; 43:3; 99:5, 9; 132:7).

43:5 This verse is repeated in 42:5, 11.

Ps 44 This national lament after defeat in battle continues the tone of the previous two psalms, including reflecting on an unspecified moment in Israel's history and calling on God for salvation. The people recite God's past acts of rescue (44:1-3), acknowledge God's power to save (44:4-8), describe their humiliation in exile (44:9-16), claim their innocence and lament the injustice of their current situation (44:17-22), and cry for vindication (44:23-26).

44:TITLE *psalm:* Hebrew *maskil.* This may be a literary or musical term.

44:1 *we have heard . . . of all you did:* The story of redemption encompasses the story of God's favor and power in his past acts of rescue (see 78:1-4; see also Pss 105–106).

44:2 God *drove out the pagan nations* during the conquests recorded in Joshua.

44:3 Though the Israelites used *swords* and other weapons (44:6), they would have lost their battles without the *light* of the Lord's favor (see 18:25-29; 27:1; 89:15).

44:4-8 God's people feel confident about his mighty acts; he was with them in the past, and he is their king in the present.

44:4 *Israel:* Literally *for Jacob.* The names "Jacob" and "Israel" are often interchanged throughout the Old Testament, referring sometimes to the individual patriarch and sometimes to the nation.

44:9-16 The people have experienced defeat (44:9-12), so they understand suffering and disgrace (44:13-16).

10 You make us retreat from our enemies
and allow those who hate us to
plunder our land.
11 You have butchered us like sheep
and scattered us among the nations.
12 You sold your precious people for a
pittance,
making nothing on the sale.
13 You let our neighbors mock us.
We are an object of scorn and derision
to those around us.
14 You have made us the butt of their jokes;
they shake their heads at us in scorn.
15 We can't escape the constant humiliation;
shame is written across our faces.
16 All we hear are the taunts of our
mockers.
All we see are our vengeful enemies.
17 All this has happened though we have
not forgotten you.
We have not violated your covenant.
18 Our hearts have not deserted you.
We have not strayed from your path.
19 Yet you have crushed us in the jackal's
desert home.
You have covered us with darkness
and death.
20 If we had forgotten the name of our God
or spread our hands in prayer to
foreign gods,
21 God would surely have known it,
for he knows the secrets of every
heart.
22 But for your sake we are killed every day;
we are being slaughtered like sheep.
23 Wake up, O Lord! Why do you sleep?
Get up! Do not reject us forever.
24 Why do you look the other way?
Why do you ignore our suffering and
oppression?
25 We collapse in the dust,
lying face down in the dirt.
26 Rise up! Help us!
Ransom us because of your unfailing
love.

PSALM 45

For the choir director: A love song to be sung to the tune "Lilies." A psalm of the descendants of Korah.

1 Beautiful words stir my heart.
I will recite a lovely poem about the
king,
for my tongue is like the pen of a
skillful poet.

2 You are the most handsome of all.
Gracious words stream from your
lips.
God himself has blessed you forever.
3 Put on your sword, O mighty warrior!
You are so glorious, so majestic!
4 In your majesty, ride out to victory,
defending truth, humility, and justice.
Go forth to perform awe-inspiring
deeds!
5 Your arrows are sharp, piercing your
enemies' hearts.
The nations fall beneath your feet.

6 Your throne, O God, endures forever and
ever.
You rule with a scepter of justice.
7 You love [c]justice and hate evil.
Therefore God, your God, has
[d]anointed you,
pouring out the oil of joy on you more
than on anyone else.
8 Myrrh, aloes, and cassia perfume your
robes.
In ivory palaces the music of strings
entertains you.

44:10 Josh 7:8, 12; Ps 89:41
44:11 Deut 4:27; 28:64; Ps 106:27; Ezek 20:23-24
44:12 Isa 52:3-4
44:13 Ps 79:4; 80:6
44:14 Ps 109:25; Jer 24:9
44:17 Ps 119:61, 83, 109, 141, 153, 176
44:18 Job 23:11; Ps 119:51, 157
44:19 Job 3:5; Ps 51:8
44:20 Ps 81:9
44:22 Isa 53:7; *Rom 8:36
44:23 Ps 7:6; 77:7; 78:65
44:24 Job 13:24; Ps 42:9; 88:14
44:25 Ps 119:25
45:2 Ps 21:6; Luke 4:22
45:4 Rev 6:2
45:5 Ps 120:4; Isa 5:28
45:6 Ps 93:2; 98:8-9; *Heb 1:8-9
45:7 Ps 11:7; 21:6; 33:5; [c]*tsedeq* (6664) ‣ Ps 97:2; [d]*mashakh* (4886) ‣ Ps 89:20
45:8 Song 1:3; 4:13-14

44:11 ***scattered us among the nations:*** This probably refers to the Exile (see 51:18-19; 89:38-51; 106:40-47; 137).

44:22 Paul quotes this verse as a parenthetical aside in his list of things that cannot separate us from Christ's love (Rom 8:36).

44:23-26 In the end, God's people can turn to the Lord and trust him for rescue. Their petition for God to remedy their situation is as strong as their lament about God's rejection.

44:23 ***Wake up:*** Biblical authors often call for God's attention in a crisis (35:23; 44:23; 73:20; 80:2; Mark 4:38).

Ps 45 This psalm celebrates a royal wedding; it might have been sung on many occasions and not just at one wedding. As God's representative, the king carried the responsibility of dispensing justice and maintaining order in God's world (see Ps 2).

45:TITLE The *tune "Lilies"* is no longer known (see also Ps 69). • ***psalm:*** Hebrew *maskil*. This may be a literary or musical term.

45:2 This general description of the king's symbolic status anticipates his permanent legacy (45:16). That the Lord has ***blessed*** him and charged him to bear God's attributes is symbolized by his ***handsome*** appearance and ***gracious words***.

45:3-5 The psalmist expounds on the royal splendor the king showed when fighting his enemies.

45:3 Glory and majesty belong to the Lord (96:6; 111:3).

45:4 As God's agent of ***truth, humility, and justice*** (see 72:1-2, 4, 7), the king can carry out ***awe-inspiring deeds*** (65:5; 96:4).

45:6-9 The king is like a god among humans; he is anointed by God, he has received a mighty throne, and he dispenses justice as he rules forever. • The writer to the Hebrews applies 45:6-7 to Jesus as he argues that the Son is greater than the angels (Heb 1:8-9).

45:6 ***Your throne, O God:*** Or *Your divine throne*. • ***Justice*** characterizes God's ***rule***, as it should characterize the king's administration.

45:8 Fine spices mixed with oil create distinctive perfumes. • The king's ***palaces*** were wood paneled with ivory inlays (cp. Amos 3:15; 6:4).

9 Kings' daughters are among your noble
women.
At your right side stands the queen,
wearing jewelry of finest gold from
Ophir!
10 Listen to me, O royal daughter; take to
heart what I say.
Forget your people and your family
far away.
11 For your royal husband delights in your
beauty;
honor him, for he is your lord.
12 The princess of Tyre will shower you
with gifts.
The wealthy will beg your favor.
13 The bride, a princess, looks glorious
in her golden gown.
14 In her beautiful robes, she is led to the
king,
accompanied by her bridesmaids.
15 What a joyful and enthusiastic procession
as they enter the king's palace!
16 Your sons will become kings like their
father.
You will make them rulers over many
lands.
17 I will bring honor to your name in every
generation.
Therefore, the nations will praise you
forever and ever.

PSALM 46

For the choir director: A song of the descendants of Korah, to be sung by soprano voices.

1 God is our refuge and strength,
always ready to help in times of trouble.
2 So we will not fear when earthquakes
come
and the mountains crumble into the
sea.
3 Let the oceans roar and foam.
Let the mountains tremble as the
waters surge! *Interlude*
4 A river brings joy to the city of our God,
the sacred [e]home of the [f]Most High.
5 God dwells in that city; it cannot be
destroyed.
From the very break of day, God will
protect it.
6 The nations are in chaos,
and their kingdoms crumble!
God's voice thunders,
and the earth melts!
7 The LORD of Heaven's Armies is here
among us;
the God of Israel is our fortress.
Interlude
8 Come, see the glorious works of the LORD:
See how he brings destruction upon
the world.
9 He causes wars to end throughout the
earth.
He breaks the bow and snaps the spear;
he burns the shields with fire.
10 "Be still, and know that I am God!
I will be honored by every nation.
I will be honored throughout the
world."
11 The LORD of Heaven's Armies is here
among us;
the God of Israel is our fortress.
Interlude

45:9 1 Kgs 2:19; 9:28; Song 6:8; Isa 13:12
45:10 Deut 21:13
45:12 Ps 72:10-11
45:13 Isa 61:10
45:14 Esth 2:13; Song 1:4; Ezek 16:9-13
45:17 Ps 138:4; Mal 1:11
46:1 Deut 4:7; Ps 9:9; 14:6; 62:7-8; 145:18
46:2 Ps 18:7; 23:4; 82:5
46:4 Ps 87:3; Rev 3:12; 22:1; [e]*mishkan* (4908) ‣Ps 74:7; [f]*elyon* (5945) ‣Ps 47:2
46:5 Isa 12:6; 41:14; Ezek 43:7; Luke 1:54
46:6 Ps 2:1; Mic 1:4
46:7 Num 14:9; 2 Chr 13:12; Ps 9:9
46:8 Ps 66:5; Isa 61:4; Jer 51:43
46:9 Isa 2:4; 9:5; Mic 4:3
46:10 Ps 100:3; Isa 2:11, 17
47:1 Ps 98:8-9; 106:47

45:9 Marriages often sealed diplomatic connections between kings; the *women* became part of the harem (see 1 Kgs 11:1-3).

45:10-12 The bride is a representative of the king. Powerful people and nations try to gain her favor in order to get close to the king. This is a great honor, and she is encouraged to give herself fully to her new position.

45:12 *The princess of Tyre:* Literally *The daughter of Tyre.* Israel traded with Tyre, a powerful city-state. The noblest woman of the city bears a wedding gift to her counterpart, the new queen, who represents an honored kingdom.

Ps 46 This psalm of Zion celebrates God's special presence in Jerusalem (see also Pss 48, 76, 87, 122), inviting confidence in the Lord because the citizens of Zion enjoy his protection.

46:TITLE *sung by soprano voices:* Hebrew *according to 'alamoth* ("maidens"; see also note on 1 Chr 15:20). In worship, a choir or a group of instrumentalists performed this hymn.

46:1-3 Even when faced with natural disasters, the citizens of Zion express no fear.

46:4-6 The strong city where *God dwells* protects its inhabitants. They enjoy the *river* flowing inside the city. This river contrasts with the turbulent waters (the powers of the nations) outside the city.

46:4 Like the streams flowing through Eden, this *river* brings the water of life, restoration, and healing (36:8-9; see Gen 2:10; Ezek 47; Rev 22:2).

46:5 *From the very break of day:* In the ancient Near East, enemies attacked cities during the day; even during the most dangerous times, the Lord *will protect* the place where his name dwells.

46:6 People and *nations* live *in chaos,* characterized by opportunism (83:2), busyness (39:6), and noise. Psalmists also used this word to describe the snarling of dogs (59:6, 14) and the groaning of the needy (77:3). These people shake, totter, and *crumble,* unlike the city of God (cp. 15:5). In contrast, when the godly feel disturbed, they cry out for God's help (42:5, 11; 43:5; 55:17).

46:7 This refrain reminds readers of the identity of the God of Zion. • *among us:* Hebrew *'immanu,* part of the name Immanuel, "God with us" (Isa 7:14; 8:8; Matt 1:23). • *God of Israel:* Literally *of Jacob;* also in 46:11. See note on 44:4.

46:8-9 This invitation to trust in the Lord offers a perspective on God's interactions with human powers.

46:8 Israel saw the Lord's *glorious works* in the wilderness (107:24; 111:2), but the wicked, who have no concern for them (28:5), are left desolate (73:19).

46:10 A message directly from the Lord confirms the authenticity of the

47:2 Deut 7:21
[g]'elyon (5945) ‣Ps 50:14
[h]melek (4428) ‣Prov 16:12
[i]'erets (0776) ‣Ps 97:5
47:3 Ps 18:47
47:4 1 Pet 1:4
47:5 Ps 68:18, 25, 33; 98:6
47:6 Ps 68:4
47:7 [j]zamar (2167) ‣Ps 66:2
47:8 1 Chr 16:31
47:9 Ps 72:11; 89:18; 97:9 Isa 49:7, 23 Rom 4:11-12
48:1 1 Chr 16:25 Ps 87:1; 96:4; 145:3 Zech 8:3
48:2 Ps 50:2 Lam 2:15 Matt 5:35
48:3 Ps 46:7
48:4 2 Sam 10:6-19
48:5 Exod 15:15
48:6 Isa 13:8
48:8 Ps 87:5
48:9 Ps 26:3; 40:10
48:10 Josh 7:9 Isa 41:10 Mal 1:11
48:11 Ps 97:8 [k]mishpat (4941) ‣Ps 103:6

PSALM 47

For the choir director: A psalm of the descendants of Korah.

1 Come, everyone! Clap your hands!
Shout to God with joyful praise!
2 For the LORD [g]Most High is awesome.
He is the great [h]King of all the [i]earth.
3 He subdues the nations before us,
putting our enemies beneath our feet.
4 He chose the Promised Land as our inheritance,
the proud possession of Jacob's descendants, whom he loves.
Interlude

5 God has ascended with a mighty shout.
The LORD has ascended with trumpets blaring.
6 Sing praises to God, sing praises;
sing praises to our King, sing praises!
7 For God is the King over all the earth.
[j]Praise him with a psalm.
8 God reigns above the nations,
sitting on his holy throne.
9 The rulers of the world have gathered together
with the people of the God of Abraham.
For all the kings of the earth belong to God.
He is highly honored everywhere.

PSALM 48

A song. A psalm of the descendants of Korah.

1 How great is the LORD,
how deserving of praise,
in the city of our God,
which sits on his holy mountain!
2 It is high and magnificent;
the whole earth rejoices to see it!
Mount Zion, the holy mountain,
is the city of the great King!
3 God himself is in Jerusalem's towers,
revealing himself as its defender.

4 The kings of the earth joined forces
and advanced against the city.
5 But when they saw it, they were stunned;
they were terrified and ran away.
6 They were gripped with terror
and writhed in pain like a woman in labor.
7 You destroyed them like the mighty ships of Tarshish
shattered by a powerful east wind.

8 We had heard of the city's glory,
but now we have seen it ourselves—
the city of the LORD of Heaven's Armies.
It is the city of our God;
he will make it safe forever.
Interlude

9 O God, we meditate on your unfailing love
as we worship in your Temple.
10 As your name deserves, O God,
you will be praised to the ends of the earth.
Your strong right hand is filled with victory.
11 Let the people on Mount Zion rejoice.
Let all the towns of Judah be glad
because of your [k]justice.

---

psalmist's vision (see also 12:5-6; 32:8). • ***know that I am God:*** The Lord will do what he promises (Isa 45:3; 49:23; 60:16). • God will be exalted (Ps 47; Isa 6:1); he will judge the nations and rescue his people (see 57:11; 89:13; 108:5-6; 118:16).

Ps 47 This psalm celebrates God's kingship over all the earth; it tells of God's victory in dealing with Israel and the nations. Both Israel (47:3-4) and the nations (47:9) participate in God's kingdom.

47:1-2 As the sovereign king over the nations, God requires praise.

47:1 People ***clap*** their ***hands*** in praise and recognition of marvelous deeds (47:3-4; see 98:8; Isa 55:12; cp. Nah 3:19).

47:3-4 The Lord made Israel victorious, especially under David (see 18:40-50). God's mighty deeds of redemption manifest his love for Israel.

47:4 ***Jacob's descendants:*** Jacob was the father of all Israelites (Gen 32:28); the name Jacob often represents the nation of Israel. • God ***loves*** and commits himself to Jacob (see 78:68; 127:2; see Rom 11:28).

47:5-6 The psalmist portrays the Lord as returning to heaven, having accomplished his victories. For a portrayal of his descent, see 18:9-16.

47:5 ***trumpets:*** Or *ram's horns* (see 81:3). At times, ram's horns were sounded in celebration (98:5-6; 2 Kgs 11:14; 1 Chr 15:28).

47:7 People from ***all the earth*** (see 96:1-3) will worship God. • ***psalm:*** Hebrew *maskil.* This may be a literary or musical term.

Ps 48 This song of Zion (see also Pss 46, 76, 87, 122) explicitly views Jerusalem (Zion) as the city of the Great King where the godly find protection (48:1-3). God rules from Zion in faithfulness, righteousness, and justice, and he inspires his subjects with confidence and joy (48:9-11). They commit themselves to seeing the glory of Zion for themselves so that they can tell the next generation about it (48:8, 12-14).

48:2 ***Mount Zion, the holy mountain:*** Or *Mount Zion, in the far north;* Hebrew reads *Mount Zion, the heights of Zaphon.* The meaning of the Hebrew is uncertain.

48:3 God dwells in Zion to protect it from all enemies (see 46:5).

48:7 The ***ships of Tarshish,*** built for long voyages, represent human accomplishment (see also 2 Chr 9:21; Isa 2:16). Their destruction might be the event mentioned in 1 Kgs 22:48.

48:9-11 The psalmist joyfully celebrates the Lord's presence in the midst of the community, reflecting on the faithfulness, righteousness, and justice of God's rule.

12 Go, inspect the city of Jerusalem.
Walk around and count the many
towers.
13 Take note of the fortified walls,
and tour all the citadels,
that you may describe them
to future generations.
14 For that is what God is like.
He is our God forever and ever,
and he will guide us until we die.

PSALM 49

For the choir director: A psalm of the descendants of Korah.

1 Listen to this, all you people!
Pay attention, everyone in the world!
2 High and low,
rich and poor—listen!
3 For my words are wise,
and my thoughts are filled with insight.
4 I listen carefully to many proverbs
and solve riddles with inspiration
from a harp.
5 Why should I fear when trouble comes,
when enemies surround me?
6 They trust in their wealth
and boast of great riches.
7 Yet they cannot redeem themselves
from death
by paying a ransom to God.
8 Redemption does not come so easily,
for no one can ever pay enough
9 to live forever
and never see the grave.
10 Those who are wise must finally die,
just like the foolish and senseless,
leaving all their wealth behind.
11 The grave is their eternal home,
where they will stay forever.
They may name their estates after
themselves,
12 but their fame will not last.
They will die, just like animals.
13 This is the fate of fools,
though they are remembered as being
wise. *Interlude*
14 Like sheep, they are led to the [a]grave,
where death will be their shepherd.
In the morning the godly will rule over
them.
Their bodies will rot in the [a]grave,
far from their grand estates.
15 But as for me, God will redeem my life.
He will snatch me from the power of
the grave. *Interlude*
16 So don't be dismayed when the wicked
grow rich
and their homes become ever more
splendid.
17 For when they die, they take nothing
with them.
Their wealth will not follow them into
the grave.
18 In this life they consider themselves
fortunate
and are [b]applauded for their success.
19 But they will die like all before them
and never again see the light of day.
20 People who boast of their wealth don't
understand;
they will die, just like animals.

PSALM 50

A psalm of Asaph.

1 The LORD, the Mighty One, is God,
and he has spoken;
he has summoned all humanity
from where the sun rises to where it
sets.

48:13 Ps 78:5-7
48:14 Ps 23:4; Isa 58:11
49:1 Ps 33:8; 78:1
49:3 Ps 37:30; 119:130
49:4 Num 12:8; 2 Kgs 3:15; Ps 78:2
49:5 Ps 23:4; 27:1
49:6 Ps 52:7; Mark 10:24-25
49:7 Job 36:18
49:8 Matt 16:26
49:9 Ps 22:29; 89:48
49:10 Ps 39:6; Luke 12:20-21
49:11 Deut 3:14; Ps 10:6
49:13 Jer 17:11
49:14 Ps 9:17; Dan 7:18; Mal 4:3; 1 Cor 6:2; Rev 2:26
[a]*she'ol* (7585) ‣Ps 89:48
49:15 Ps 16:10-11
49:16 Ps 37:7
49:17 Ps 17:14; 1 Tim 6:7
49:18 Ps 10:3; Luke 12:19
[b]*yadah* (3034) ‣Ps 86:12
49:19 Job 33:29-30
49:20 Ps 49:12
50:1 Josh 22:22; Ps 113:3

48:12-13 ***Jerusalem:*** Hebrew *Zion.* • ***towers . . . fortified walls . . . citadels:*** These structures provide a visual tour of Zion's strength.

48:14 No one is like God (35:10; 71:19; 86:8; 89:6, 8; 113:5; see Isa 40:18, 25). He is the shepherd King (95:7) who ***will guide*** (see 5:8; 23:2) the sheep of his flock (77:20).

Ps 49 In this wisdom psalm, a wise teacher warns against enemies, whom he portrays as living a rich lifestyle and caring only for themselves (49:5-9). They cannot keep anyone alive, least of all themselves, even in their memories (49:10-12). Like fattened animals, they are led to slaughter (49:14-20).

49:1-4 The wisdom teacher invites everyone to the hall of wisdom; he promises to instruct with a proverb and a riddle.

49:2 Anyone who will ***listen*** can gain wisdom (Prov 1:5, 8, 33).

49:4 The teacher used both ***proverbs*** and ***riddles*** for instruction in wisdom (see Prov 1:5-6).

49:5-8 If enemies who live for material rewards cannot sustain themselves, how can they give life to others?

49:7 ***they cannot redeem themselves from death:*** Or *no one can redeem the life of another.* The Hebrew can be translated either way.

49:11-12 The teacher brings wisdom through irony. Everyone dies, and even those with ***estates*** named after them will be forgotten.

49:13-15 The teachers of false wisdom cannot rescue themselves from death. Only God has that power.

49:13 ***though they are remembered as being wise:*** The meaning of the Hebrew is uncertain.

49:14 The teachers of false wisdom will go ***to the grave*** (Hebrew *Sheol;* also in 49:15) and to ***death*** in the underworld. See note on 6:5.

49:16-20 The ***wicked*** might have rich, luxurious lives, but they forget that they cannot avoid death.

Ps 50 God appears as judge to remind the godly and the ungodly in turn that outward performance of sacrificial rituals and recitation of the law are worthless without thankfulness, repentance, and justice.

50:1-3 The whole universe must pay attention when ***God approaches*** to bring justice into the world.

50:2
Deut 33:2
Ps 48:2; 80:1

50:3
Ps 18:12-13
Dan 7:10

50:4
Deut 4:26; 32:1
Isa 1:2

50:5
Exod 24:7

50:6
Ps 75:7; 96:13; 97:6
[c]*shamayim* (8064)
‣ Ps 108:4

50:8
Ps 40:6

50:9
Ps 69:31

50:10
Ps 104:24

50:12
Exod 19:5

50:13
Hos 6:6

50:14
Deut 23:21
Hos 14:2
Rom 12:1
Heb 13:15
[d]*elyon* (5945)
‣ Ps 78:35

2 From Mount Zion, the perfection of
beauty,
God shines in glorious radiance.
3 Our God approaches,
and he is not silent.
Fire devours everything in his way,
and a great storm rages around him.
4 He calls on the heavens above and earth
below
to witness the judgment of his
people.
5 "Bring my faithful people to me—
those who made a covenant with me
by giving sacrifices."
6 Then let the [c]heavens proclaim his
justice,
for God himself will be the judge.
Interlude

7 "O my people, listen as I speak.
Here are my charges against you,
O Israel:
I am God, your God!
8 I have no complaint about your sacrifices
or the burnt offerings you constantly
offer.
9 But I do not need the bulls from your
barns
or the goats from your pens.
10 For all the animals of the forest are mine,
and I own the cattle on a thousand hills.
11 I know every bird on the mountains,
and all the animals of the field are
mine.
12 If I were hungry, I would not tell you,
for all the world is mine and
everything in it.
13 Do I eat the meat of bulls?
Do I drink the blood of goats?
14 Make thankfulness your sacrifice to God,
and keep the vows you made to the
[d]Most High.
15 Then call on me when you are in trouble,
and I will rescue you,
and you will give me glory."

Mount Zion, the City of God (Ps 48)

Ps 14:7; 50:2; 51:18; 53:6; 65:1; 68:16; 76:2; 78:68; 87:2, 5; 102:21; 125:1; 128:5; 132:13; 133:3; 135:21; 147:12
2 Sam 5:7
1 Kgs 8:1
Isa 1:27; 2:3; 3:16-17, 26; 4:3-5; 8:18; 10:12, 24, 32; 16:1; 24:23; 29:8; 30:19; 31:4, 9; 33:20; 37:22, 32; 40:9; 41:27; 52:1-2; 60:14; 62:1; 64:10
Jer 26:18; 51:35
Lam 2:13
Joel 2:32; 3:16-17
Amos 1:2
Obad 1:21
Mic 3:12; 4:2
Zeph 3:14, 16
Zech 1:14, 17; 2:7; 8:2-3; 9:9
Heb 12:22
Rev 14:1

Zion is the Hebrew name for the mountain in Jerusalem where the Temple was located (see 2 Sam 5:7; see also 2 Chr 3:1). On the one hand, Zion is synonymous with Jerusalem, and the NLT often translates *Zion* as "Jerusalem" (69:35; 87:2; 97:8; 132:13). Zion is the actual city of Jerusalem that was destroyed in 586 BC (see 79:1; 102:13; 126:1; 137:1) and again in AD 70.

On the other hand, Zion is the city of God that transcends geographical location. Zion is God's universal kingdom, pictured as the city in which he dwells (74:2; 76:2; 84:7; 135:21; see Isa 26). The prophets and poets of Israel speak of the city of God as being more extensive than the physical city. The citizens of this city come from Judah, Israel, and the nations (see 87:5-6; Heb 12:22-24). It is on a high mountain (48:2) at the center of God's kingdom on earth (99:2; 132:13), and his throne is in Zion (see note on 9:11). Therefore, godly prayers and praise focus on Zion (53:6; 65:1; 137:1; 147:12; 149:2) and redemption is sought there (14:7; 20:2; 50:2; 53:6; 133:3).

Zion is also symbolic of God's protection and blessings (51:18; 128:5; 134:3; see Pss 46; 48). Anyone who trusts in the Lord is as secure as Mount Zion (125:1), but those who reject the Lord also reject Zion and have no future (129:5-8). Zion is the mother of all the nations (87:4-6). Members of the Davidic dynasty are the legitimate heirs who rule over Zion as agents to establish God's universal kingdom (2:6; 110:2).

The NT likewise speaks of a heavenly Jerusalem, the spiritual home of those from all nations who have been reborn through faith in Jesus Christ (Gal 4:24-26; Heb 12:22-24; Rev 3:12; 21:2-4). The book of Hebrews speaks of Zion as the mother city. Abraham sought it in faith (Heb 11:10), and all men and women of faith are its citizens (Heb 12:22-24). Because the Lord knows no geographical limitations (1 Kgs 8:27), the true Zion he inhabits is in the hearts of all who worship him (22:3).

50:4-6 The Lord is coming to bring righteousness. This hope encourages his ***faithful people,*** but those who have been unfaithful will not experience blessing when ***the heavens above and the earth below*** testify against them (cp. Deut 30:19; 31:28; 32:1; Isa 1:2). The Lord comes to restore order to the world (5:8; 22:31; 33:5; 40:9; 50:6; 71:16; 97:6).

50:7-13 The psalmist delivers a message against those who regard the sacrificial rituals as more important than having a proper heart attitude.

50:9 Unlike pagan gods, God does ***not need*** food; instead, he wants his people to serve him with a right heart (50:14-15).

50:10 ***I own the cattle on a thousand hills:*** God has no needs; he possesses everything.

50:14 ***Thankfulness*** means looking beyond self-interest to express gratitude for God's blessings (see 51:15-17; 54:6).
• True ***sacrifice*** requires offering one's self to the glory of God (50:23; Rom 12:1-2).

50:15 God's response to his people's cry is to ***rescue*** them.

16 But God says to the wicked:
"Why bother reciting my decrees
and pretending to obey my covenant?
17 For you refuse my discipline
and treat my words like trash.
18 When you see thieves, you approve of them,
and you spend your time with adulterers.
19 Your mouth is filled with wickedness,
and your tongue is full of lies.
20 You sit around and slander your brother—
your own mother's son.
21 While you did all this, I remained silent,
and you thought I didn't care.
But now I will rebuke you,
listing all my charges against you.
22 Repent, all of you who forget me,
or I will tear you apart,
and no one will help you.
23 But giving [e]thanks is a sacrifice that truly honors me.
If you keep to my path,
I will reveal to you the salvation of God."

PSALM 51

For the choir director: A psalm of David, regarding the time Nathan the [f]prophet came to him after David had committed adultery with Bathsheba.

1 Have mercy on me, O God,
because of your [g]unfailing love.
Because of your great compassion,
blot out the stain of my sins.
2 Wash me clean from my guilt.
Purify me from my sin.
3 For I recognize my [h]rebellion;
it haunts me day and night.
4 Against you, and you alone, have I sinned;
I have done what is evil in your sight.
You will be proved right in what you say,
and your judgment against me is just.
5 For I was born a sinner—
yes, from the moment my mother conceived me.
6 But you desire honesty from the womb,
teaching me wisdom even there.

7 Purify me from my sins, and I will be clean;
wash me, and I will be whiter than snow.
8 Oh, give me back my [i]joy again;
you have broken me—
now let me rejoice.
9 Don't keep looking at my sins.
Remove the stain of my guilt.
10 [j]Create in me a clean heart, O God.
[k]Renew a loyal spirit within me.
11 Do not banish me from your presence,
and don't take your Holy [a]Spirit from me.

50:16 Isa 29:13
50:17 Neh 9:26
50:18 Rom 1:32
50:21 Eccl 8:11
50:22 Ps 9:17
50:23 [e]*todah* (8426) ‣Ps 100:4
51:TITLE [f]*nabi'* (5030) ‣Ps 74:9
51:1 [g]*khesed* (2617) ‣Ps 57:10
51:2 Jer 33:8; 1 Jn 1:7-9
51:3 Isa 59:12; [h]*pesha'* (6588) ‣Ps 103:12
51:4 *Rom 3:4
51:5 Eph 2:1-3
51:7 Isa 1:18
51:8 [i]*simkhah* (8057) ‣Ps 97:11
51:10 [j]*bara'* (1254) ‣Ps 148:5; [k]*khadash* (2318) ‣Ps 103:5
51:11 Eph 4:30; [a]*ruakh* (7307) ‣Ps 104:30

50:16-21 This message is against the wicked, who only pretend to listen to God.

50:17 ***my discipline . . . my words:*** The wicked may observe rituals, but they reject more important matters such as justice, mercy, and faithfulness (cp. Matt 23:23-24).

50:21 Because he is patient, God ***remained silent.***

50:22-23 The wicked will experience God's justice, while the godly will see God's everlasting salvation.

50:22 God ***will tear*** the wicked ***apart*** like a lion tearing its prey (Isa 5:29; 31:4; Ezek 19:3; cp. Ps 7:2; 22:13).

Pss 51–65 These psalms of David share a common thread in their reflection on the experience of evil. In Ps 51, the psalmist confesses the evil he has done and asks God's forgiveness. Psalms 52–64 lament specific evils that David experienced. A song of praise (Ps 65) brings David's laments to an end.

Ps 51 This moving prayer for restoration asks for God's favor, mercy, forgiveness, and cleansing. Out of a broken spirit, the psalmist confesses and accepts responsibility for his sin (51:3-6), then petitions God to remove his guilt and renew him inwardly (51:7-12). The psalmist then recommits himself to a lifestyle of wisdom and joy in the service of God and others (51:13-17).

51:TITLE ***regarding the time Nathan . . . Bathsheba:*** See 2 Sam 11:1-27. The text of the psalm contains no explicit reference to this event.

51:1-2 The repentant offender has nothing to offer God. He needs God's favor, mercy, forgiveness, and blessing before he can experience renewal and restoration.

51:1 A prayer for God's ***mercy*** and kindness is part of the genre of lament. Sometimes the plea comes from the psalmist's acknowledgment of his weakness and sin, as here (see also 6:2; 9:13; 25:16; 31:9; 41:4, 10). At other times, it arises from the psalmist's commitment to the Lord (see 26:11; 27:7; 119:29, 58, 132). In each case, God's mercy brings an inner renewal.

51:2 ***Wash me . . . Purify me:*** The psalmist prays for cleansing and release from the ***guilt*** of his sin (51:7; see 26:6; Isa 1:16, 18; 4:4).

51:3-6 The psalmist accepts the consequences of his sin against God. He knows that there is nothing good in him unless God renews his life.

51:4 ***Against . . . you alone:*** This is hyperbole—the psalmist knows he also ***sinned*** against human beings (2 Sam 11:2-4, 15-17), but his offense against God is more important. He expects God to rebuke him and will accept whatever verdict God renders (see Rom 3:4). • ***and your judgment against me is just:*** Greek version reads *and you will win your case in court.* Cp. Rom 3:4, where Paul quotes the Greek translation of this verse.

51:5 ***I was born a sinner:*** The psalmist is not making excuses but is acknowledging the depth of his sinfulness. From the time we are ***conceived,*** we all share in the human condition of sinfulness.

51:6 ***from the womb:*** Or *from the heart;* Hebrew reads *in the inward parts.*

51:7 ***Purify me from my sins*** (literally *Purify me with the hyssop branch*; see Exod 12:22; Lev 14:4; John 19:29; Heb 9:19): The psalmist depends on God to purify and renew him (see Isa 1:18).

51:8 Regaining ***joy*** is a gracious gift from God. • ***you have broken me:*** The psalmist's whole being feels broken (6:2; cp. 34:20).

51:10-12 God's Spirit renews and recreates the human spirit.

51:10 ***A loyal spirit*** yields the inner qualities of constancy and perseverance.

51:13
Ps 22:27
51:14
2 Sam 12:9
Ps 9:14; 25:5; 71:15
51:16
1 Sam 15:22
Ps 40:6
51:17
Ps 34:18
[b]*zebakh* (2077)
‣ Prov 21:27
51:18
Isa 51:3
51:19
Ps 4:5; 66:13, 15
52:1
Ps 94:4
52:2
Ps 5:9; 57:4; 59:7
52:3
Ps 36:4; 58:3
Jer 9:4-5
52:4
Ps 120:3
52:5
Prov 2:22
Isa 22:18-19
52:6
Job 22:19
Ps 40:3
52:8
Ps 13:5; 128:3
Jer 11:16
52:9
Ps 30:12; 54:6
53:1-6
//Ps 14:1-7

12 Restore to me the joy of your salvation,
and make me willing to obey you.
13 Then I will teach your ways to rebels,
and they will return to you.
14 Forgive me for shedding blood, O God
who saves;
then I will joyfully sing of your
forgiveness.
15 Unseal my lips, O Lord,
that my mouth may praise you.

16 You do not desire a sacrifice, or I would
offer one.
You do not want a burnt offering.
17 The [b]sacrifice you desire is a broken spirit.
You will not reject a broken and
repentant heart, O God.
18 Look with favor on Zion and help her;
rebuild the walls of Jerusalem.
19 Then you will be pleased with sacrifices
offered in the right spirit—
with burnt offerings and whole burnt
offerings.
Then bulls will again be sacrificed on
your altar.

PSALM 52

For the choir director: A psalm of David, regarding the time Doeg the Edomite said to Saul, "David has gone to see Ahimelech."

1 Why do you boast about your crimes,
great warrior?
Don't you realize God's justice
continues forever?
2 All day long you plot destruction.
Your tongue cuts like a sharp razor;
you're an expert at telling lies.
3 You love evil more than good
and lies more than truth. *Interlude*
4 You love to destroy others with your
words,
you liar!
5 But God will strike you down once and
for all.
He will pull you from your home
and uproot you from the land of the
living. *Interlude*
6 The righteous will see it and be amazed.
They will laugh and say,
7 "Look what happens to mighty warriors
who do not trust in God.
They trust their wealth instead
and grow more and more bold in their
wickedness."

8 But I am like an olive tree, thriving in the
house of God.
I will always trust in God's unfailing
love.
9 I will praise you forever, O God,
for what you have done.
I will trust in your good name
in the presence of your faithful people.

PSALM 53

Ps 53:1-6 // Ps 14:1-7

For the choir director: A meditation; a psalm of David.

1 Only fools say in their hearts,
"There is no God."
They are corrupt, and their actions are evil;
not one of them does good!

51:11 ***your Holy Spirit:*** Or *your spirit of holiness.* Only the power of the Holy Spirit can change the human will to make it "loyal" (51:10) and "willing to obey" (51:12).

51:13 As he learns from his sin and its consequences, the psalmist wants to ***teach*** others.

51:14 ***shedding blood:*** This idiom includes any injustice, not just homicide (9:12; 58:10; see 2 Sam 11:14-26; cp. Isa 1:15-17).

51:18-19 ***rebuild the walls of Jerusalem:*** These verses were probably added as a prayer for national restoration after the Exile (see Pss 42–43); the entire community in exile identified with the spirit of the psalm.

51:19 ***Sacrifices offered in the right spirit*** come from a heart that is right with God and with others (see 15:2-5; 24:3-6; 50:14; Matt 5:23-24).

Ps 52 Wicked people use words to destroy relationships and communities. They foolishly think that they can be heroes by their words (52:1-4), but their fate suddenly overtakes them (52:5-7). In contrast, the godly renew their commitment to the Lord (52:8-9) and find their future secure in him.

52:TITLE ***psalm:*** Hebrew *maskil.* This may be a literary or musical term. • This psalm refers to an incident in 1 Sam 21:1-10; 22:9-10. The accuser, ***Doeg the Edomite,*** is a paradigm of evil.

52:1-4 Liars foolishly deceive themselves by thinking that they can be heroes by their words. They believe themselves innocent of any charges of evildoing, though they love evil and cause destruction. Those who speak curses, sarcasm, bitterness, arrogant boasting, and deceptions (31:18; 34:13; 59:7, 12; 120:2-3; 140:3, 9) bring about chaos, alienation, and destruction (Jas 3:5). Their sharp words cut like swords and daggers (55:21; 57:4; 64:3), the fangs of a snake (140:3), or a ***razor.***

52:3 Deceptive speech changes one's character.

52:5-7 God's judgment on the wicked will come suddenly and forcibly. The godly rejoice in God's justice, not in the misfortunes of the wicked.

52:5 God ***will strike*** the wicked ***down*** like a pagan altar, idol, or unclean vessel (Exod 34:13; Lev 11:35; 2 Kgs 10:27).

52:6 In Hebrew, the verbs here translated ***see*** and ***be amazed*** sound almost alike.

52:8-9 The psalmist commits himself to a life of trust in the Lord. • An ***olive tree*** lives a long time when cared for (1:3; 128:3). The psalmist desires to be close to the Lord, his Savior and the source of his blessing (18:6; 23:6).

Ps 53 This psalm parallels Ps 14, differing only in verse 5.

53:TITLE ***A meditation; a psalm:*** Hebrew *according to makhalath; a maskil.* These may be literary or musical terms.

53:1-3 Paul uses the Greek translation of this passage in his description of the depravity of all people (Rom 3:10-12).

2 God looks down from heaven
on the entire human race;
he looks to see if anyone is truly wise,
if anyone seeks God.
3 But no, all have turned away;
all have become corrupt.
No one does good,
not a single one!
4 Will those who do evil never learn?
They eat up my people like bread
and wouldn't think of praying to God.
5 Terror will grip them,
terror like they have never known
before.
God will scatter the bones of your
enemies.
You will put them to shame, for God
has rejected them.

6 Who will come from Mount Zion to
rescue Israel?
When God restores his people,
Jacob will shout with joy, and Israel
will rejoice.

PSALM 54

For the choir director: A psalm of David, regarding the time the Ziphites came and said to Saul, "We know where David is hiding." To be accompanied by stringed instruments.

1 Come with great power, O God, and
rescue me!
Defend me with your might.
2 Listen to my prayer, O God.
Pay attention to my plea.
3 For strangers are attacking me;
violent people are trying to kill me.
They care nothing for God.
Interlude

4 But God is my helper.
The Lord keeps me alive!
5 May the evil plans of my enemies be
turned against them.
Do as you promised and put an end
to them.

6 I will sacrifice a voluntary offering to
you;
I will praise your name, O LORD,
for it is good.
7 For you have rescued me from my
troubles
and helped me to triumph over my
enemies.

PSALM 55

For the choir director: A psalm of David, to be accompanied by stringed instruments.

1 Listen to my prayer, O God.
Do not ignore my [c]cry for help!
2 Please listen and answer me,
for I am overwhelmed by my
troubles.
3 My enemies shout at me,
making loud and wicked threats.
They bring trouble on me
and angrily hunt me down.

4 My heart pounds in my chest.
The terror of death assaults me.
5 Fear and trembling overwhelm me,
and I can't stop shaking.
6 Oh, that I had wings like a dove;
then I would fly away and rest!
7 I would fly far away
to the quiet of the wilderness.
Interlude

8 How quickly I would escape—
far from this wild storm of hatred.

9 Confuse them, Lord, and frustrate their
plans,
for I see violence and conflict in the
city.

53:2 Ps 33:13-15
53:3 Rom 3:10, 12
53:5 Lev 26:17, 36; Ps 44:7; Jer 6:30; 8:1-2; Ezek 6:5
53:6 Ps 14:7
54:1 2 Chr 20:6; Ps 20:1
54:3 1 Sam 20:1; Ps 36:1; 40:14; 86:14; 140:1, 4
54:4 Ps 37:24, 40
54:6 Ps 50:14
54:7 Ps 34:6; 59:10
55:1 Ps 27:9; 61:1; [c]*tekhinnah* (8467) ›Ps 119:170
55:2 1 Sam 1:16; Ps 77:3; 86:6-7; Isa 38:14
55:3 2 Sam 16:7-8; Ps 17:9; 71:11
55:4 Ps 116:3
55:5 Job 21:6
55:6 Job 3:13
55:8 Isa 4:6
55:9 Jer 6:7

53:3 *have become corrupt:* Greek version reads *have become useless.* Cp. Rom 3:12.

53:5 *scatter the bones:* Israel's *enemies* would suffer shameful defeat and lack the peaceful rest of a decent burial (see note on Gen 49:29-33; cp. Ps 141:7; 2 Kgs 9:10; Jer 8:1-2; Ezek 6:5).

Ps 54 In this individual lament, occasioned by violent and godless people (54:3), the psalmist turns to God in prayer and maintains his focus on God's help (54:4). He prays for God to save him from evil and to judge his enemies (54:5, 7).

54:TITLE *psalm:* Hebrew *maskil.* This may be a literary or musical term. • The psalm refers to the account of 1 Sam 23:19-20, when the *Ziphites* were bent on violence.

54:3 The *strangers* were alienated from the covenant community (see 109:11; Prov 5:10). • Proud and *violent people* hold no regard for God or for other people (see 35:11, 25; 86:14; Prov 11:16).

54:6-7 In anticipation of God's response, the mood of the psalm changes from gloom to thanksgiving.

54:6 A *voluntary offering* is a sacrifice of praise (see "Grain Offering" and "Peace Offering" in chart, "Israel's Sacrifices," p. 197). Sacrifices of praise are the kind of offering God most desires (see 50:14-15, 23).

Ps 55 The psalmist is faced with adversaries whose leader is a former friend (55:12-14), and he is overwhelmed with anguish. He turns to the Lord in prayer and commits himself to the Lord for redress (55:22-23). Jesus experienced similar suffering when his friend (Judas) betrayed him. He also experienced the answer to the psalmist's prayer: (1) by taking the place of the wicked and receiving their judgment (Isa 53:7-9), and (2) by committing himself to the Father, who rescued (Luke 23:46) and rewarded him (Isa 53:10-12).

55:TITLE *psalm:* Hebrew *maskil.* This may be a literary or musical term.

55:1-3 The occasion for this prayer is an attack by an enemy.

55:4-8 In the experience of deep anguish, the psalmist confesses that his adversity has become unbearable and he seeks an escape.

55:11 Ps 5:9; 10:7
55:12-13 Ps 41:9
55:14 Ps 42:4
55:15 Num 16:30, 33; Ps 64:7
55:16 Ps 57:2-3
55:17 Ps 5:3; 88:13; 141:2; Dan 6:10; Acts 3:1
55:18 Ps 103:4
55:19 Ps 36:1; 93:2
55:20 Num 30:2; Ps 7:3-4; 89:34
55:21 Ps 12:2; 28:3; Prov 5:3-4
55:22 Ps 37:5; 112:6; 1 Pet 5:7
55:23 Ps 5:6; 56:3-4; 73:18
56:1 Ps 17:9; 35:1, 25
56:3 Ps 11:1; 56:10-11
56:4 Ps 118:6; Heb 13:6
56:5 Ps 41:7; 2 Pet 3:15-16
56:6 Ps 17:11; 59:3
56:7 Ps 36:12; 55:23
56:8 Ps 39:12; 139:3; Mal 3:16
56:9 Ps 41:11; 118:6; Rom 8:31

10 Its walls are patrolled day and night
against invaders,
but the real danger is wickedness
within the city.
11 Everything is falling apart;
threats and cheating are rampant in
the streets.
12 It is not an enemy who taunts me—
I could bear that.
It is not my foes who so arrogantly
insult me—
I could have hidden from them.
13 Instead, it is you—my equal,
my companion and close friend.
14 What good fellowship we once enjoyed
as we walked together to the house
of God.

15 Let death stalk my enemies;
let the grave swallow them alive,
for evil makes its home within them.

16 But I will call on God,
and the LORD will rescue me.
17 Morning, noon, and night
I cry out in my distress,
and the LORD hears my voice.
18 He ransoms me and keeps me safe
from the battle waged against me,
though many still oppose me.
19 God, who has ruled forever,
will hear me and humble them.
Interlude
For my enemies refuse to change their
ways;
they do not fear God.

20 As for my companion, he betrayed his
friends;
he broke his promises.
21 His words are as smooth as butter,
but in his heart is war.
His words are as soothing as lotion,
but underneath are daggers!

22 Give your burdens to the LORD,
and he will take care of you.
He will not permit the godly to slip
and fall.
23 But you, O God, will send the wicked
down to the pit of destruction.
Murderers and liars will die young,
but I am trusting you to save me.

PSALM 56

For the choir director: A psalm of David, regarding the time the Philistines seized him in Gath. To be sung to the tune "Dove on Distant Oaks."

1 O God, have mercy on me,
for people are hounding me.
My foes attack me all day long.
2 I am constantly hounded by those who
slander me,
and many are boldly attacking me.
3 But when I am afraid,
I will put my trust in you.
4 I praise God for what he has promised.
I trust in God, so why should I be
afraid?
What can mere mortals do to me?

5 They are always twisting what I say;
they spend their days plotting to
harm me.
6 They come together to spy on me—
watching my every step, eager to
kill me.
7 Don't let them get away with their
wickedness;
in your anger, O God, bring them
down.

8 You keep track of all my sorrows.
You have collected all my tears in your
bottle.
You have recorded each one in your
book.

9 My enemies will retreat when I call to
you for help.
This I know: God is on my side!
10 I praise God for what he has promised;
yes, I praise the LORD for what he has
promised.
11 I trust in God, so why should I be afraid?
What can mere mortals do to me?

55:12-20 The psalmist's enemy was once a *friend*; memories of that close relationship bring him pain (see 31:11).

55:15 *let the grave:* Hebrew *let Sheol* (see note on 6:5). See "Prayers for Vengeance" at Ps 137, p. 1017.

55:19-21 God is good and faithful, but the psalmist's enemies and so-called friend are deceitful and wicked.

55:22-23 The psalmist commits all his cares *to the LORD.*

55:23 To *die young* means that one fails to experience God's full blessing (cp. Prov 3:2, 16).

Ps 56 This individual lament moves from petition to confidence two times (56:1-4, 5-13).

56:TITLE *A psalm:* Hebrew *miktam.* This may be a literary or musical term. • David was *seized* by *Philistines* concerned about his loyalties and brought before King Achish (1 Sam 21:10-15).

56:4 *mere mortals:* Or *mere flesh,* in contrast to the immortal and infinitely more powerful God (see Isa 2:22).

56:5-7 The psalmist specifies his charge against his attackers as he prays for their evil to cease.

56:8 The psalmist makes a play on the Hebrew words translated *sorrows* (Hebrew *nod*) and *bottle* (Hebrew *no'd*). The word translated "sorrows" can also be translated "wanderings."

56:11 *mere mortals* (Hebrew *'adam*): The psalm also uses two other words for man: *'enosh* ("people," 56:1) and *basar* ("mere mortals," 56:4). All express the ideas of mortality and finitude.

12 I will fulfill my vows to you, O God,
and will offer a sacrifice of thanks for your help.
13 For you have rescued me from death;
you have kept my feet from slipping.
So now I can walk in your presence, O God,
in your life-giving light.

PSALM 57

For the choir director: A psalm of David, regarding the time he fled from Saul and went into the cave. To be sung to the tune "Do Not Destroy!"

1 Have mercy on me, O God, have mercy!
[d]I look to you for protection.
I will hide beneath the shadow of your wings
until the danger passes by.
2 I cry out to God Most High,
to God who will fulfill his purpose for me.
3 He will send help from heaven to rescue me,
disgracing those who hound me.
Interlude
My God will send forth his unfailing love and faithfulness.
4 I am surrounded by fierce lions
who greedily devour human prey—
whose teeth pierce like spears and arrows,
and whose tongues cut like swords.
5 Be [e]exalted, O God, above the highest heavens!
May your glory shine over all the earth.
6 My enemies have set a trap for me.
I am weary from distress.
They have dug a deep pit in my path,
but they themselves have fallen into it.
Interlude
7 My heart is confident in you, O God;
my heart is confident.
No wonder I can sing your praises!
8 Wake up, my heart!
Wake up, O lyre and harp!
I will wake the dawn with my song.
9 I will thank you, Lord, among all the people.
I will sing your praises among the nations.
10 For your [f]unfailing love is as high as the heavens.
Your faithfulness reaches to the clouds.
11 Be exalted, O God, above the highest heavens.
May your glory shine over all the earth.

PSALM 58

For the choir director: A psalm of David, to be sung to the tune "Do Not Destroy!"

1 Justice—do you rulers know the meaning of the word?
Do you judge the people fairly?
2 No! You plot injustice in your hearts.
You spread violence throughout the land.
3 These wicked people are born sinners;
even from birth they have lied and gone their own way.
4 They spit venom like deadly snakes;
they are like cobras that refuse to listen,

56:12 Ps 50:14-15
56:13 Job 33:30; Ps 33:19; 86:13; 116:8-9
57:1 Ruth 2:12; Ps 36:7; 91:4; Isa 26:20; [d]*nepesh* (5315) ‣Ps 62:1
57:2 Ps 138:8
57:3 Ps 18:16; 25:10; 56:2; 144:5, 7
57:4 Ps 58:6; 64:3; Prov 30:13-14
57:5 Ps 108:5; [e]*rum* (7311) ‣Ps 89:16
57:6 Ps 10:9; 35:7; 140:5; Prov 26:27
57:7-11 //Ps 108:1-5
57:8 Ps 16:9; 30:12; 150:3
57:10 Ps 36:5; [f]*khesed* (2617) ‣Ps 103:4
58:1 Ps 82:2
58:2 Ps 94:20
58:3 Ps 53:3; Isa 48:8
58:4 Deut 32:33; Ps 81:11; 140:3

56:13 The *light* of God's goodness and salvation will replace the darkness of *death* (see 18:25-29; 27:1).

Ps 57 The psalmist's cry for mercy and protection quickly turns into an affirmation of trust and confidence in the Lord (57:1-4). When the wicked fall into their own traps (57:6), the psalmist will praise the Lord (57:7-10).

57:TITLE *A psalm:* Hebrew *miktam.* This may be a literary or musical term. • ***David . . . fled from Saul and went into the cave:*** See 1 Sam 22:1 or 24:1-8.

57:1 ***shadow of your wings:*** As a bird protects its young, God protects the one who trusts in him (see 17:8).

57:2 ***God Most High*** (Hebrew *'elohim-'elyon*) is a generic title for God, who is more powerful than all real or imagined supernatural beings (see 91:1; 97:9; Gen 14:18-22). • ***who will fulfill his purpose:*** Or *who will end my [trouble],* or *who deals kindly with me.*

57:3-4 These verses are a prayer for rescue from powerful enemies. The metaphor of ***fierce lions*** describes human enemies; the psalmist feels unable to escape them without God's intervention (see also 35:11-21; 124:6).

57:5 This verse is repeated in 57:11 and 108:5. • God's ***glory***—his manifest presence that excludes all evil (8:1; 19:1-4; 24:7)—will fill the whole created order (Isa 6:3).

57:7-11 This section is repeated with a few modifications in 108:1-5.

57:7-8 The poet is ***confident*** that God will end the night of evil (cp. 56:13).

57:10-11 God's glory extends to the whole universe, as will praise for his ***unfailing love*** and ***faithfulness.***

Ps 58 The administration of justice is a mark of good government. God expects nothing less from his people. The psalmist condemns Israel's leaders for abusing their power, and he calls on the Lord to rain down his curses upon the wicked. The demonstration of divine justice will reassure the godly that God is just.

58:TITLE *A psalm:* Hebrew *miktam.* This may be a literary or musical term.

58:1-5 The administrators of justice were furthering their own interests rather than those of the needy. The absence of justice gradually resulted in a violent society.

58:1 ***rulers*** (or *gods*): This designation was used for high officials and administrators of ***justice*** (82:1, 6). Elsewhere, it might refer to angelic creatures (89:7) or to the gods of the nations (82:1; Dan 11:36).

58:3 All human beings are ***born sinners*** (see 51:5); however, whereas the ***wicked*** indulge their sinful nature, the godly fight against it (Rom 7:19-23; Jas 4:1-10).

58:4 ***Venom*** here means poisonous speech (see 140:3).

58:6 Job 4:10; Ps 3:7
58:7 Josh 7:5; Ps 64:3; 112:10
58:8 Job 3:16
58:9 Job 27:21; Ps 118:12; Prov 10:25
58:10 Ps 32:11; 64:10; 68:22-23; 91:8
58:11 Ps 9:8; 18:20; Luke 6:23, 35
59:1 Ps 20:1; 143:9
59:2 Ps 14:4; 28:3; 94:16; 139:19
59:3 Ps 7:3-4; 56:6; 69:4
59:4 Ps 35:19, 23
59:5 Ps 9:5; 84:8; Jer 18:23
59:7 Job 22:13; Ps 10:11; 73:11; 94:4-7
59:8 Ps 2:4; 37:13
59:9 Ps 9:9
59:10 Ps 54:7
59:11 Deut 4:9; Ps 106:27; 144:6
59:12 Ps 10:7; Prov 12:13; Zeph 3:11
59:13 Ps 83:18; 104:35
59:14 Ps 59:6

5 ignoring the tunes of the snake
charmers,
no matter how skillfully they play.
6 Break off their fangs, O God!
Smash the jaws of these lions, O LORD!
7 May they disappear like water into
thirsty ground.
Make their weapons useless in their
hands.
8 May they be like snails that dissolve into
slime,
like a stillborn child who will never
see the sun.
9 God will sweep them away, both young
and old,
faster than a pot heats over burning
thorns.
10 The godly will rejoice when they see
injustice avenged.
They will wash their feet in the blood
of the wicked.
11 Then at last everyone will say,
"There truly is a reward for those who
live for God;
surely there is a God who judges justly
here on earth."

PSALM 59

For the choir director: A psalm of David, regarding the time Saul sent soldiers to watch David's house in order to kill him. To be sung to the tune "Do Not Destroy!"

1 Rescue me from my enemies, O God.
Protect me from those who have
come to destroy me.
2 Rescue me from these criminals;
save me from these murderers.
3 They have set an ambush for me.
Fierce enemies are out there waiting,
LORD,
though I have not sinned or offended
them.
4 I have done nothing wrong,
yet they prepare to attack me.
Wake up! See what is happening and
help me!
5 O LORD God of Heaven's Armies, the God
of Israel,
wake up and punish those hostile
nations.
Show no mercy to wicked traitors.
Interlude
6 They come out at night,
snarling like vicious dogs
as they prowl the streets.
7 Listen to the filth that comes from their
mouths;
their words cut like swords.
"After all, who can hear us?" they
sneer.
8 But LORD, you laugh at them.
You scoff at all the hostile nations.
9 You are my strength; I wait for you to
rescue me,
for you, O God, are my fortress.
10 In his unfailing love, my God will stand
with me.
He will let me look down in triumph
on all my enemies.
11 Don't kill them, for my people soon
forget such lessons;
stagger them with your power, and
bring them to their knees,
O Lord our shield.
12 Because of the sinful things they say,
because of the evil that is on their lips,
let them be captured by their pride,
their curses, and their lies.
13 Destroy them in your anger!
Wipe them out completely!
Then the whole world will know
that God reigns in Israel.
Interlude
14 My enemies come out at night,
snarling like vicious dogs
as they prowl the streets.
15 They scavenge for food
but go to sleep unsatisfied.

58:6 The psalmist calls on God to ***break*** the destructive power of the wicked.

58:7 ***Make their weapons useless in their hands:*** Or *Let them be trodden down and wither like grass.* The meaning of the Hebrew is uncertain.

58:8 When moving over dry ground, ***snails*** dry up.

58:9-10 God's judgment will come suddenly. The certainty of vindication brings joy to the godly.

58:11 Vindication is the reward of ***those who live for God.***

Ps 59 The psalmist laments the power of enemies who conspire with other nations.

59:TITLE ***A psalm:*** Hebrew *miktam.* This may be a literary or musical term. • ***the time Saul sent soldiers to watch David's house:*** See 1 Sam 19:11-18.

59:1-2 ***Protect me*** (or *place me on high*): When surrounded by evil, the godly pray for God to set them apart for himself and protect them.

59:4-5 The psalmist asks God to show the treacherous, deceptive, and ***wicked traitors*** no mercy (see 25:2).

59:6-8 The wicked threaten like ***vicious dogs,*** but the Lord responds with scorn.

59:11-13 The psalmist prays that the wicked will be forced to endure the same agonizing pain they have caused.

59:13 ***in Israel:*** Literally *in Jacob.* See note on 44:4.

59:14-16 The wicked will go ***unsatisfied,*** but the psalmist will praise the Lord's ***power*** and ***unfailing love.***

59:15 ***but go to sleep unsatisfied:*** Or *and growl if they don't get enough.* The meaning of the Hebrew is uncertain.

16 But as for me, I will sing about your
power.
Each morning I will sing with joy
about your unfailing love.
For you have been my refuge,
a place of safety when I am in distress.
17 O my Strength, to you I sing praises,
for you, O God, are my refuge,
the God who shows me unfailing love.

PSALM 60

For the choir director: A psalm of David useful for teaching, regarding the time David fought Aram-naharaim and Aram-zobah, and Joab returned and killed 12,000 Edomites in the Valley of Salt. To be sung to the tune "Lily of the Testimony."

1 You have rejected us, O God, and broken
our defenses.
You have been angry with us; now
restore us to your favor.
2 You have shaken our land and split it
open.
Seal the cracks, for the land trembles.
3 You have been very hard on us,
making us drink wine that sent us
reeling.
4 But you have raised a banner for those
who fear you—
a rallying point in the face of attack.
Interlude
5 Now rescue your beloved people.
Answer and save us by your power.
6 God has promised this by his holiness:
"I will divide up Shechem with joy.
I will measure out the valley of
Succoth.
7 Gilead is mine,
and Manasseh, too.
Ephraim, my helmet, will produce my
warriors,
and Judah, my scepter, will produce
my kings.
8 But Moab, my washbasin, will become
my servant,
and I will wipe my feet on Edom
and shout in triumph over Philistia."
9 Who will bring me into the fortified
city?
Who will bring me victory over Edom?
10 Have you rejected us, O God?
Will you no longer march with our
armies?
11 Oh, please help us against our enemies,
for all human help is useless.
12 With God's help we will do mighty
things,
for he will trample down our foes.

PSALM 61

For the choir director: A psalm of David, to be accompanied by stringed instruments.

1 O God, listen to my cry!
Hear my prayer!
2 From the ends of the earth,
I cry to you for help
when my heart is overwhelmed.
Lead me to the towering [g]rock of safety,
3 for you are my safe refuge,
a fortress where my enemies cannot
reach me.
4 Let me live forever in your sanctuary,
safe beneath the shelter of your
wings! *Interlude*

59:16 Ps 21:13; 46:1; 101:1
59:17 Ps 59:9-10
60:1 Ps 44:9; 79:5; 80:3
60:2 2 Chr 7:14; Ps 18:7
60:3 Ps 66:12
60:5-12 //Ps 108:6-13
60:6 Gen 33:17; Josh 17:7; Ps 89:35
60:7 Gen 49:10; Deut 33:17; Josh 13:31
60:8 2 Sam 8:1-2, 14
60:9 Ps 44:9
60:10 Ps 60:1
60:11 Ps 146:3
60:12 Num 24:15-19; Ps 44:5; 118:16
61:1 Ps 64:1; 86:6
61:2 Ps 18:2; 77:3; [g]*tsur* (6697) › Ps 62:7
61:3 Ps 62:7; Prov 18:10
61:4 Ps 17:8; 23:6; 27:4; 91:4

Ps 60 The psalmist laments a national defeat and cries out to God for rescue.

60:TITLE ***A psalm:*** Hebrew *miktam.* This may be a literary or musical term. • ***useful for teaching:*** This psalm was taught to young people as part of their education. • ***regarding the time:*** See 2 Sam 8:13-14. • ***Aram-naharaim*** and ***Aram-zobah*** refer to the Arameans of northwest Mesopotamia and Syria (see note on Gen 24:10). • The ***tune "Lily of the Testimony"*** is unknown today.

60:1-4 When God's people experience his discipline, they affirm their loyalty and await God's answer.

60:3 ***wine*** (Hebrew *yayin*) ***that sent us reeling:*** *Yayin,* the generic Hebrew term meaning "wine," is often associated with drunkenness (2 Sam 13:28; Isa 5:11; 28:7-8; cp. Ps 104:15; Deut 14:26; Isa 55:1); it symbolized God's judgment of the wicked (75:8; Jer 51:7).

60:4 God ***raised a banner*** over his people to serve as ***a rallying point*** and as a source of pride and confidence. • The ***fear*** of God that leads to wisdom (111:10) is not weakness; it provides the perspective and strength required to do what is right.

60:5-12 This section is repeated verbatim in 108:6-13.

60:5 The psalmist prays for rescue based on the special relationship between God and his people.

60:6-8 The Lord responds with a message of promise. He shares his land with his people as spoils of war.

60:6 ***by his holiness:*** Or *in his sanctuary.* • ***Shechem*** and ***Succoth*** represent Israel's heartland.

60:9 Destroying a defeated invader's capital (***the fortified city***) would help to ensure that they would not attack again. The capital of ***Edom*** was Bozrah, located to the southeast of Israel. Only God could grant ***victory.***

Pss 61–63 In these royal prayers, the psalmist longs for God's presence. All three psalms concern themselves with the king's security.

Ps 61 The lamenting psalmist petitions God to protect him and lead him into his presence (61:4-5). He prays for God to extend and protect the king's rule and makes vows to praise God.

61:2 ***the ends of the earth:*** This expression has the connotation of a cry that comes from a place far away from God. • The psalmist's ***heart is overwhelmed*** with deep anguish.

61:4 The poet longs for God's presence and seeks entrance into God's home on earth for divine protection and care. To be received into God's ***sanctuary*** (literally *tent*) is the greatest good (see 15:1; 23:6; 24:3-6). The Hebrew word translated *sanctuary* recalls the Tabernacle and the tent that David built for the Ark (1 Chr 15:1). See also note on John 1:14. • The ***shelter of your wings*** symbolizes God's protection and care (see 9:9; 17:8).

61:5
Ps 56:12
Mal 2:5; 4:2

61:7
Ps 40:11; 41:12

61:8
Ps 30:4; 65:1; 71:22

62:1
Ps 33:20
nepesh (5315)
‣Ps 63:5

62:2
Ps 37:39; 59:17; 89:26

62:3
Isa 30:13

62:4
Ps 4:2; 28:3

62:7
Ps 46:1
tsur (6697)
‣Ps 73:26

62:8
Ps 42:4
Lam 2:19

62:9
Isa 40:15

62:10
Ps 49:6
Isa 61:8
Mark 10:25
Luke 12:15
1 Tim 6:10

5 For you have heard my vows, O God.
You have given me an inheritance
reserved for those who fear your
name.
6 Add many years to the life of the king!
May his years span the generations!
7 May he reign under God's protection
forever.
May your unfailing love and
faithfulness watch over him.
8 Then I will sing praises to your name
forever
as I fulfill my vows each day.

PSALM 62

For Jeduthun, the choir director: A psalm of David.

1 [h]I wait quietly before God,
for my victory comes from him.
2 He alone is my rock and my salvation,
my fortress where I will never be
shaken.

3 So many enemies against one man—
all of them trying to kill me.
To them I'm just a broken-down wall
or a tottering fence.
4 They plan to topple me from my high
position.
They delight in telling lies about me.
They praise me to my face
but curse me in their hearts.
Interlude

5 Let all that I am wait quietly before God,
for my hope is in him.
6 He alone is my rock and my salvation,
my fortress where I will not be shaken.
7 My victory and honor come from God
alone.
He is my refuge, a [i]rock where no
enemy can reach me.
8 O my people, trust in him at all times.
Pour out your heart to him,
for God is our refuge. *Interlude*

9 Common people are as worthless as a
puff of wind,
and the powerful are not what they
appear to be.
If you weigh them on the scales,
together they are lighter than a breath
of air.

10 Don't make your living by extortion
or put your hope in stealing.
And if your wealth increases,
don't make it the center of your life.

11 God has spoken plainly,
and I have heard it many times:

Trust in the Lord (Ps 62)

Ps 5:11; 7:1; 9:9; 11:1; 18:30-36; 22:4-5, 8-9; 25:1-3, 20; 26:1; 28:7; 31:1-6, 19; 34:8-10, 22; 37:3-9, 34, 40; 40:1-4; 46:1; 55:23; 56:3-4, 11; 57:1; 59:16; 62:8; 64:10; 78:7; 84:12; 86:2; 112:7; 115:9-11; 119:42; 125:1; 130:5-6; 141:8
Prov 3:5; 22:19
Isa 26:4; 40:31
Jer 17:7
Heb 10:35

The Lord's loving character leads people to trust in him (13:5; 21:7; 32:10; 52:8; 143:8; 17:7; 36:7). His name and reputation also encourage people's trust (9:10; 20:7; 33:21). The godly reject idolatry and any commitment that detracts from their absolute trust in the Lord (31:6, 14; 44:6; 49:6, 13; 52:7).

For the godly, every adversity in life is an occasion for growth in trust (9:9; 25:2; 46:1; 55:23; 57:1; 59:16; 62:8; 78:7). They are not afraid of life (56:3-4, 11; 112:7) but grow more confident (112:7; 119:42; 125:1). David confides that he trusted in the Lord when he was still a nursing child (22:9-10). Trust in the Lord is a form of wisdom that focuses on the Lord (141:8), the rejection of folly and evil, and the pursuit of the Lord's way (31:19; 37:3, 5; 115:11).

The Lord rescues, cares for, and rewards his people who trust in him (7:1; 16:1; 25:20; 26:1; 31:1-2, 4, 19; 34:22; 37:40; 86:2). They are blessed (2:12; 22:4-5, 8; 34:8; 40:4; 84:12) as they long for God's redemption (37:7, 34; 38:15; 40:1; 119:84, 166; 130:5-6). Faith in the Lord gives reason to rejoice and praise the Lord (5:11; 18:30-36; 28:7; 40:3; 56:4; 64:10).

61:5 ***you have heard my vows:*** The psalmist's vows might also be a part of ceremonial sacrifices (66:13-15; 76:11; 116:14, 18). He praises and thanks God for his rescue. • The ***inheritance*** refers to the promise of the land (see Ps 60), the sacredness of the Temple, the joy of God's presence (119:111), or any similar reward (16:6; 37:9, 11, 18, 22, 29, 34; 127:3).

Ps 62 This psalm expresses confidence in the king and offers prayer for him. The king rests in God despite his difficulties. Although his deceptive and powerful adversaries push hard against him, he remains undaunted. He encourages himself and his people to trust in God and to see their human adversaries from God's perspective, where they appear frail, fleeting, and deceptive (62:9).

62:TITLE ***Jeduthun:*** See 1 Chr 25:1; also in Pss 39 and 77.

62:3-4 The enemies desire to topple the king with lies and cunning.

62:4 ***My high position*** refers to the royal throne.

62:5-8 The psalmist encourages himself and others to place their hope in God.

62:9-12 Unlike God, humans are transient beings. Even when they thrive, their prosperity is fleeting.

62:9 ***not what they appear to be:*** People often try to look stronger and better than they are.

62:10 The crime of ***extortion*** means using intimidation and threats to make others give up what is theirs, while ***stealing*** is taking what belongs to others.

Power, O God, belongs to you;
12 unfailing love, O Lord, is yours.
Surely you repay all people
according to what they have done.

PSALM 63

A psalm of David, regarding a time when David was in the wilderness of Judah.

1 O God, you are my God;
I earnestly search for you.
My soul thirsts for you;
my whole body longs for you
in this parched and weary land
where there is no water.
2 I have seen you in your sanctuary
and gazed upon your power and glory.
3 Your unfailing love is better than life
itself;
how I praise you!
4 I will praise you as long as I live,
lifting up my hands to you in prayer.
5 You satisfy [j]me more than the richest
feast.
I will praise you with songs of joy.
6 I lie awake thinking of you,
[k]meditating on you through the night.
7 Because you are my helper,
I sing for joy in the shadow of your
wings.
8 I cling to you;
your strong right hand holds me
securely.
9 But those plotting to destroy me will
come to ruin.
They will go down into the depths of
the earth.
10 They will die by the sword
and become the food of jackals.
11 But the king will rejoice in God.
All who trust in him will praise him,
while liars will be silenced.

PSALM 64

For the choir director: A psalm of David.

1 O God, listen to my complaint.
Protect my life from my enemies'
threats.
2 Hide me from the plots of this evil mob,
from this gang of wrongdoers.
3 They sharpen their tongues like swords
and aim their bitter words like arrows.
4 They shoot from ambush at the innocent,
attacking suddenly and fearlessly.
5 They encourage each other to do evil
and plan how to set their traps in
secret.
"Who will ever notice?" they ask.
6 As they plot their crimes, they say,
"We have devised the perfect plan!"
Yes, the human heart and mind are
cunning.
7 But God himself will shoot them with
his arrows,
suddenly striking them down.
8 Their own tongues will ruin them,
and all who see them will shake their
heads in scorn.
9 Then everyone will be afraid;
they will proclaim the mighty acts of
God
and realize all the amazing things he
does.

62:12 Job 34:11; Matt 16:27; *Rom 2:6
63:1 Ps 42:2; 84:2
63:2 Ps 27:4
63:3 Ps 69:16
63:4 Ps 28:2; 104:33
63:5 Ps 36:8; 71:23; [j]*nepesh* (5315) ‣Ps 86:4
63:6 Ps 4:4; 16:7; 42:8; [k]*hagah* (1897) ‣Ps 77:12
63:8 Ps 18:35
63:9 Ps 40:14; 55:15
63:11 Deut 6:13; Isa 45:23
64:2 Ps 56:6; 59:2
64:3 Ps 140:3
64:4 Ps 10:8; 11:2
64:5 Ps 140:5
64:7 Ps 7:12-13; 9-3
64:8 Prov 18:6-7

62:11-12 Strength and *unfailing love* remain in balance only in God. He cares for his people by ridding the world of evildoers (see 1:6).

Ps 63 The king longs for God's presence so vividly that he eats, drinks, and sees God's goodness. Though worn out and harassed by the wicked, the king sees God, and this animates him with praise. God becomes his life (63:3), while the wicked perish (63:9).

63:1 Together, *soul* and *whole body* refer to a person's entire being. • *parched and weary land:* When David was living in the desert, he also found himself in a spiritual wasteland, separated from God's people and the sanctuary.

63:2 The psalmist remembers that he had found God to be present in his *sanctuary* (see 18:6; 61:4; 62:5, 11-12).

63:3 *better than life itself:* The highest quality of life is found in relationship with God (see 4:7; 63:5; Prov 16:8).

63:6-8 The psalmist reflects and meditates on God's presence *through the night*. In the absence of light, God is the light. The quietness of the night and the longing for dawn provide time to focus on the true significance of life with the Lord.

63:6 *Meditating* on God requires focused awareness, concentration, thought, and reflection (see 1:2).

63:9 The wicked were *plotting to destroy* the psalmist's life through deception and lies, but they would meet their end. • The *depths of the earth* refers to the place of the dead.

63:10 Wild *jackals* are associated with desolation and abandonment (Isa 13:20-22; 34:10-15; Jer 9:11; 49:33; 51:37; Lam 5:18; Mal 1:3). The wicked will not receive honor in death; their bodies will be left to scavenging animals (Eccl 6:3; Jer 22:18-19; 36:29-30).

63:11 Those who truly *trust in* God are loyal to him.

Ps 64 This lament decries the destructive plots and arrogant attitude of the wicked (64:1-6). The psalmist turns to God in prayer and takes heart in God's justice because whatever the wicked do will be undone by the righteous judge. The godly will rejoice and grow in wisdom as they reflect on God's mighty acts.

64:1-6 These verses form a prayer for rescue from bold and powerful liars.

64:3 *their tongues . . . bitter words:* Liars use their speech to kill. This description might also refer to practicing magic.

64:6 The enemies create a *perfect plan* to harm the innocent without getting caught. • Human beings will sink to unthinkable depths with evil words, acts, or plans (83:3; see Jer 17:9).

64:7-10 What God does is righteous. God undoes what is wicked and pays the wicked back with what they planned for others.

64:10
Ps 11:1; 25:20; 32:11
65:1
Ps 86:9; 116:18
65:2
Isa 66:23
65:3
Ps 40:12
Heb 9:14
[a]*kapar* (3722)
‣Ps 78:38
65:4
Ps 4:3; 33:12; 36:8
65:5
Ps 45:4; 48:10
65:6
Ps 93:1; 95:4
65:7
Ps 89:9
Isa 17:12-13
Matt 8:26
65:8
Ps 139:9-10
65:9
Ps 104:13-14, 24
65:12
Job 38:26-27
65:13
Ps 98:8; 144:13
Isa 30:23; 55:12
66:2
[b]*zamar* (2167)
‣Ps 71:22
66:3
Ps 18:44; 47:2
66:4
Ps 22:27; 67:4
66:5
Ps 46:8
66:6
Exod 14:21
Ps 105:43

10 The godly will rejoice in the LORD
and find shelter in him.
And those who do what is right
will praise him.

PSALM 65

For the choir director: A song. A psalm of David.

1 What mighty praise, O God,
belongs to you in Zion.
We will fulfill our vows to you,
2 for you answer our prayers.
All of us must come to you.
3 Though we are overwhelmed by our sins,
you [a]forgive them all.
4 What joy for those you choose to bring near,
those who live in your holy courts.
What festivities await us
inside your holy Temple.

5 You faithfully answer our prayers with awesome deeds,
O God our savior.
You are the hope of everyone on earth,
even those who sail on distant seas.
6 You formed the mountains by your power
and armed yourself with mighty strength.
7 You quieted the raging oceans
with their pounding waves
and silenced the shouting of the nations.
8 Those who live at the ends of the earth
stand in awe of your wonders.
From where the sun rises to where it sets,
you inspire shouts of joy.

9 You take care of the earth and water it,
making it rich and fertile.
The river of God has plenty of water;
it provides a bountiful harvest of grain,
for you have ordered it so.
10 You drench the plowed ground with rain,
melting the clods and leveling the ridges.
You soften the earth with showers
and bless its abundant crops.
11 You crown the year with a bountiful harvest;
even the hard pathways overflow with abundance.
12 The grasslands of the wilderness
become a lush pasture,
and the hillsides blossom with joy.
13 The meadows are clothed with flocks of sheep,
and the valleys are carpeted with grain.
They all shout and sing for joy!

PSALM 66

For the choir director: A song. A psalm.

1 Shout joyful praises to God, all the earth!
2 [b]Sing about the glory of his name!
Tell the world how glorious he is.
3 Say to God, "How awesome are your deeds!
Your enemies cringe before your mighty power.
4 Everything on earth will worship you;
they will sing your praises,
shouting your name in glorious songs."
Interlude

5 Come and see what our God has done,
what awesome miracles he performs for people!
6 He made a dry path through the Red Sea,
and his people went across on foot.
There we rejoiced in him.

Ps 65 This psalm recounts the reasons why all people should praise and revere God for his almighty power and merciful care for his universe.

65:1-3 Praise is the appropriate response to God's majestic deeds in redemption (65:3-5) and in nature (65:5-13).

65:1 God alone deserves *praise* and is worthy to have *vows* made to him.

65:2 *All of us* means all humans.

65:3 *you forgive:* God graciously removes the guilt of sin (see 32:5).

65:4 *those you choose to bring near:* This includes people from Israel and from other nations. • Only those whom God sees as blameless *live in* his *holy courts* (Pss 15, 24). • At the *Temple*, God's earthly palace, all nations can gather to experience God's holy presence. No structure can separate humans from God (see Rev 21:22).

65:6-7 God brought order to *the mountains*, the *raging oceans*, and the *pounding waves* (see 95:4-5; 104:6-9). • The psalmist compares the chaotic forces of nature with the rebellion of the *nations* (see Ps 2; 33:6-11; 46:6).

65:8 All over the world (Job 38:13; see Ps 50:1-3 and note), people should *stand in awe of* the Lord.

65:9-13 The created order provides clear evidence of God's power (65:6-8). He shows his love by maintaining nature. Everything praises the Lord as all the parts fit together harmoniously.

65:9 The *river of God* and all rivers demonstrate God's victorious power and goodness through the order in nature and the regularity of the harvests (see 1:3; 36:8; 46:4; Ezek 47:6-12; Zech 14:8; Rev 22:1).

65:13 Nature bursts out in praise of the Creator (see 79:13; 96:11-13; 148:3-5, 7-12; Isa 55:12-13).

Ps 66 This anonymous psalm includes two hymns (66:1-12, 13-20) that praise God for his redemption.

66:1-4 The psalmist exhorts nature to join in a mighty chorus to praise God's glory, name, and power.

66:2 The *glory of his name* represents the perfection of God's character.

66:3 God conquers his *enemies* (see 18:44; 59:11; 81:15).

66:5-7 The story of the Exodus and God's victory over the sea evokes responses of astonishment (66:5) and worship (66:6). God works *miracles . . . for people* in order to redeem them for himself.

66:6 *Red Sea:* Literally *the sea.*

7 For by his great power he rules forever.
He watches every movement of the nations;
let no rebel rise in defiance. *Interlude*

8 Let the whole world bless our God
and loudly sing his praises.
9 Our lives are in his hands,
and he keeps our feet from stumbling.
10 You have tested us, O God;
you have purified us like silver.
11 You captured us in your net
and laid the burden of slavery on our backs.
12 Then you put a leader over us.
We went through fire and flood,
but you brought us to a place of great abundance.
13 Now I come to your Temple with burnt offerings
to fulfill the vows I made to you—
14 yes, the sacred vows that I made
when I was in deep trouble.
15 That is why I am sacrificing burnt offerings to you—
the best of my rams as a pleasing aroma,
and a sacrifice of bulls and male goats. *Interlude*

16 Come and listen, all you who fear God,
and I will tell you what he did for me.
17 For I cried out to him for help,
praising him as I spoke.
18 If I had not confessed the sin in my heart,
the Lord would not have listened.
19 But God did listen!
He paid attention to my prayer.
20 Praise God, who did not ignore my prayer
or withdraw his unfailing love from me.

PSALM 67

For the choir director: A song. A psalm, to be accompanied by stringed instruments.

1 May God be merciful and bless us.
May his face smile with favor on us. *Interlude*

2 May your ways be known throughout the earth,
your [c]saving power among people everywhere.
3 May the nations praise you, O God.
Yes, may all the nations praise you.
4 Let the whole world sing for joy,
because you govern the nations with justice
and guide the people of the whole world. *Interlude*

5 May the nations praise you, O God.
Yes, may all the nations praise you.
6 Then the earth will yield its harvests,
and God, our God, will richly bless us.
7 Yes, God will bless us,
and people all over the world will fear him.

PSALM 68

For the choir director: A song. A psalm of David.

1 Rise up, O God, and scatter your enemies.
Let those who hate God run for their lives.

66:7 Ps 11:4; 140:8; 145:13
66:9 Ps 30:3
66:10 Ps 17:3; Zech 13:9; 1 Pet 1:6-7
66:11 Lam 1:13
66:12 Ps 18:19; Isa 43:2; 51:23
66:13 Ps 22:25; Eccl 5:4
66:14 Ps 18:6
66:15 Num 6:14; Ps 51:19
66:16 Ps 34:11; 71:15, 24
66:18 Job 36:21; Ps 18:41; Isa 1:15; Jas 4:3
66:19 Ps 116:1-2
66:20 Ps 22:24
67:1 Num 6:25; Ps 4:6; 80:3, 7, 19
67:2 Acts 18:25; Titus 2:11; [c]*yeshu'ah* (3444) ‣Ps 74:12
67:3 Ps 66:4
67:4 Ps 96:10, 13
67:5 Ps 22:27
67:6 Lev 26:4; Ezek 34:27
67:7 Ps 33:8
68:1 Num 10:35

66:7 God's ***power*** brings redemption. The same word occurs in 65:6 for God's power in creation (see also 80:2).

66:8-10 The orderly lives of the redeemed reflect the order of God's world. The Lord protects them from evil and purifies them.

66:9 God guides his people into wisdom and away from folly (17:5; 37:31; 121:3).

66:10 ***You have tested us, O God:*** As the silversmith heats ***silver*** to remove the dross, God's discipline removes sin from his people (see 12:6).

66:11 God decrees and permits the many trying circumstances his people experience.

66:12 ***Then you put a leader over us:*** Or *You made people ride over our heads.* This expression possibly refers to a foreign ruler who kept the Israelites in submission.

66:15 Vows often included sacrifices of thanksgiving, including ***burnt offerings*** (see 20:3; 40:6; 50:8; 51:19).

66:16-20 The private testimony in the conclusion of the psalm parallels the public praise of its opening (66:1-4).

66:18 Confession leads to restoration (see 32:5).

Ps 67 In this anonymous prayer for God's blessing, the psalmist addresses the knowledge and worship of God among the nations (cp. 64:9; 65:8). The prayer requests that God's name be kept holy and that his kingdom come (cp. Matt 6:9-13).

67:1-2 This prayer is based on the priestly blessing found in Num 6:24-26. God's goodness to Israel affects his reputation among the nations (see 96:1-3).

67:3 God's international reputation leads to his praise among the ***nations*** (see 138:4), whose turmoil and rebelliousness will cease when they join Israel in praise of God. • One God rules over all, and the nations will give thanks for God's just rule (see 67:4).

67:4 God brings the ultimate ***justice*** that human beings desire (96:10; 98:9).

67:6-7 Bountiful ***harvests*** are evidence of God's blessing (Gen 26:12; Isa 30:23). • ***all over the world:*** See 2:8; 96:1-3. • All ***will fear him,*** joining with Israel to acknowledge the God of Israel.

Ps 68 This prayer for God's victorious rule traces God's march from Sinai to Zion (68:7, 16-18, 24). He rescued the nation of Israel from Egypt, guided it through the wilderness, brought it into the Promised Land, and established his kingdom. He is a caring and victorious God, whose nature is unchanging. Therefore, the godly hope and rejoice in the prospect of God's universal dominion.

68:2
Ps 37:20
Isa 9:18
Hos 13:3
Mic 1:4

68:4
Ps 40:3; 68:33

68:5
Deut 10:18; 26:15

68:7
Exod 13:21

68:8
Exod 19:18
Judg 5:4-5

68:9
Deut 11:11

68:11
Exod 15:20

68:13
Gen 49:14

68:14
Josh 10:10
[d]*shadday* (7706)
▸Ps 91:1

68:15
Ps 36:6

68:17
Deut 33:2
Dan 7:10

68:18
*Eph 4:8

2 Blow them away like smoke.
Melt them like wax in a fire.
Let the wicked perish in the presence of God.
3 But let the godly rejoice.
Let them be glad in God's presence.
Let them be filled with joy.
4 Sing praises to God and to his name!
Sing loud praises to him who rides the clouds.
His name is the LORD—
rejoice in his presence!
5 Father to the fatherless, defender of widows—
this is God, whose dwelling is holy.
6 God places the lonely in families;
he sets the prisoners free and gives them joy.
But he makes the rebellious live in a sun-scorched land.

7 O God, when you led your people out from Egypt,
when you marched through the dry wasteland, *Interlude*
8 the earth trembled, and the heavens poured down rain
before you, the God of Sinai,
before God, the God of Israel.
9 You sent abundant rain, O God,
to refresh the weary land.
10 There your people finally settled,
and with a bountiful harvest, O God,
you provided for your needy people.

11 The Lord gives the word,
and a great army brings the good news.
12 Enemy kings and their armies flee,
while the women of Israel divide the plunder.
13 Even those who lived among the sheepfolds found treasures—
doves with wings of silver
and feathers of gold.
14 The [d]Almighty scattered the enemy kings
like a blowing snowstorm on Mount Zalmon.
15 The mountains of Bashan are majestic,
with many peaks stretching high into the sky.
16 Why do you look with envy, O rugged mountains,
at Mount Zion, where God has chosen to live,
where the LORD himself will live forever?
17 Surrounded by unnumbered thousands of chariots,
the Lord came from Mount Sinai into his sanctuary.
18 When you ascended to the heights,
you led a crowd of captives.
You received gifts from the people,
even from those who rebelled against you.
Now the LORD God will live among us there.

68:1-3 These verses form a prayer for God to *rise up* and *scatter* his *enemies,* as he did when Israel entered the Promised Land (cp. Num 10:35-36; Josh 6–12).

68:2 Both *smoke* and *wax* represent a transitory existence (22:12-18; 37:20; 102:3).

68:3 The lot of *the godly* contrasts with that of the wicked (see 1:6).

68:4-6 The psalmist praises God's powerful and compassionate reign.

68:4 *him who rides the clouds:* This is an ancient description of Baal, a Canaanite deity. The psalmist applies it to *the LORD* as the true "Rider of the Clouds" (see 68:33; 104:3). God wields power over the clouds and the rain.

68:5 God, the *father* of all marginalized and needy people, shows them compassion and protects their rights (see 10:14, 18; 69:33; 82:3). • Like his *dwelling,* the Lord *is holy.* The supreme example of the holy God coming down to rescue humanity is Jesus Christ.

68:6 God released Israel from slavery in Egypt (Exod 20:2; see Ps 69:33), and he still *sets the prisoners free.* • The *sun-scorched* desert represents alienation from God and separation from blessing.

68:8-10 The *earth trembled* as in an earthquake (see Exod 19:18). • *the heavens poured down rain:* Wells in the desert and rain showers in Canaan supplied an abundance of water.

68:11 *a great army* (or *a host of women*) *brings:* The Hebrew suggests women singers caroling *the good news* of victory (see 68:25; Exod 15:20).

68:13 The seminomadic pastoral people *who lived among the sheepfolds* were surprised to receive *silver* and *gold* carvings from the battle.

68:14 *The Almighty* (Hebrew *Shaddai*) is an ancient designation for God (see 91:1; Gen 17:1). • The identification of *Mount Zalmon* is uncertain; it was possibly a mountain in Bashan (see 68:15).

68:15 *Bashan* is a plateau northeast of Jerusalem and east of the Sea of Galilee that was known for its woods and pastureland (see 22:12; Isa 2:13). The *mountains* might have included Mount Hermon to the north of the plateau or Mount Zalmon, which might be Jebel ed-Druze on the east.

68:16 *Why do you look with envy?* Bashan is physically much more impressive than the mountains around Jerusalem, but it was not the home of the Lord. Only Mount Zion enjoyed the privilege of providing God's dwelling place.

68:17 *Chariots,* the ultimate weapon of the armed forces in the psalmist's day, are an image of the Lord's power to grant victory (20:7; 44:3).

68:18 *When you ascended to the heights:* The Most High established his reign victoriously in Zion. • *a crowd of captives . . . gifts:* This is an image of a victorious ruler leading the victory march after battle. Paul applied this image to Jesus Christ (Eph 4:8-13).

19 Praise the Lord; praise God our savior!
For each day he carries us in his arms.
Interlude
20 Our God is a God who saves!
The Sovereign LORD rescues us from death.
21 But God will smash the heads of his enemies,
crushing the skulls of those who love their guilty ways.
22 The Lord says, "I will bring my enemies down from Bashan;
I will bring them up from the depths of the sea.
23 You, my people, will wash your feet in their blood,
and even your dogs will get their share!"
24 Your procession has come into view, O God—
the procession of my God and King as he goes into the sanctuary.
25 Singers are in front, musicians behind;
between them are young women playing tambourines.
26 Praise God, all you people of Israel;
praise the LORD, the source of Israel's life.
27 Look, the little tribe of Benjamin leads the way.
Then comes a great throng of rulers from Judah
and all the rulers of Zebulun and Naphtali.
28 Summon your might, O God.
Display your power, O God, as you have in the past.
29 The kings of the earth are bringing tribute
to your Temple in Jerusalem.
30 Rebuke these enemy nations—
these wild animals lurking in the reeds,
this herd of bulls among the weaker calves.
Make them bring bars of silver in humble tribute.
Scatter the nations that delight in war.
31 Let Egypt come with gifts of precious metals;
let Ethiopia bow in submission to God.
32 Sing to God, you kingdoms of the earth.
Sing praises to the Lord.
Interlude
33 Sing to the one who rides across the ancient heavens,
his mighty voice thundering from the sky.
34 Tell everyone about God's power.
His majesty shines down on Israel;
his strength is mighty in the heavens.
35 God is awesome in his sanctuary.
The God of Israel gives power and strength to his people.

Praise be to God!

PSALM 69

For the choir director: A psalm of David, to be sung to the tune "Lilies."

1 Save me, O God,
for the floodwaters are up to my neck.
2 Deeper and deeper I sink into the mire;
I can't find a foothold.
I am in deep water,
and the floods overwhelm me.
3 I am exhausted from crying for help;
my throat is parched.
My eyes are swollen with weeping,
waiting for my God to help me.

68:19 Ps 55:22; 65:5; Isa 46:4
68:20 Ps 56:13
68:21 Ps 110:6; Hab 3:13
68:22 Amos 9:1-3
68:23 1 Kgs 21:19; Ps 58:10; Jer 15:3
68:24 Ps 63:2
68:25 Exod 15:20; Judg 11:34; 1 Chr 13:8
68:26 Deut 33:28; Ps 22:22-23; 26:12
68:28 Ps 29:11; 44:4
68:29 Ps 72:10
68:30 Ps 89:10
68:31 Isa 19:19-21; 45:14
68:32 Ps 102:21-22
68:33 Ps 18:10; 29:4
68:35 Deut 10:17; Ps 29:11; 47:2
69:2 Jon 2:3
69:3 Ps 6:6; 119:82, 123; Isa 38:14

68:19-20 The Divine Warrior cares for his people like a shepherd; the people praise him.

68:19 Like a caring father or a shepherd, God ***carries*** his people ***in his arms*** (see 55:22; 68:5-6).

68:21 ***God will smash the heads of his enemies:*** Cp. Gen 3:15.

68:22 God will deal with all ***enemies***, whether from high places (represented by ***Bashan***) or low (***the depths of the sea***).

68:24-27 A great company joins together in the pilgrimage to Zion.

68:28-31 The people pray for God's success and for victory over the enemy nations (68:1-3).

68:29 The conquered ***kings*** will bring gifts to the Lord.

68:30 Hostile and rebellious people delight in warfare and insurrection (see 2:1-3).

68:31 ***of precious metals:*** Or ***of rich cloth.*** • ***Ethiopia:*** Hebrew *Cush.*

68:32-35 The psalmist calls for the people to praise God, who is victorious over his enemies.

68:32 The term ***kingdoms of the earth*** includes all nations and power structures.

68:34 When the Lord demonstrates his ***power, majesty,*** and ***strength*** against the nations, he strengthens his people (see 68:28; 96:4-6).

Pss 69–72 These last four psalms of Book Two contrast with the psalms describing God's mighty acts in creation and in redemption, capped by God's march to Zion (Pss 65–68). Psalms 69–71 portray the king's anguish, and Ps 72 responds with a prayer for God to bless the king.

Ps 69 In this individual lament, the poet expresses his vulnerability, humiliation, and overwhelming pain, asking God to vindicate him for the sake of the righteous.

69:TITLE ***to the tune "Lilies":*** Psalm 45 also notes this tune, but Ps 45 celebrates the glory of kingship, whereas Ps 69 is the cry of a tired king who feels abandoned by the Lord.

69:1-2 The psalmist sees himself as almost drowning but still surviving chaotic forces and alienation from God (see 42:7; 69:14, 15; Isa 8:8).

69:4
Ps 35:11; 59:3
*John 15:25

69:5
Ps 44:21
[e]*'iwweleth* (0200)
‣ Prov 12:23

69:6
2 Sam 12:14

69:8
Ps 31:11; 38:11

69:9
*John 2:17
*Rom 15:3

69:12
Job 30:9

69:13
Ps 32:6
Isa 49:8
2 Cor 6:2

69:14
Ps 144:7

69:15
Num 16:33
Ps 124:4-5

69:16
Ps 25:16; 51:1; 63:3

69:18
Ps 49:15; 119:134

69:19
Ps 22:6-7
Isa 53:3

69:21
*Matt 27:48
*John 19:29

69:23
*Rom 11:9-10

69:25
Matt 23:38
Luke 13:35
*Acts 1:20

69:26
2 Chr 28:9
Isa 53:4

4 Those who hate me without cause
outnumber the hairs on my head.
Many enemies try to destroy me with lies,
demanding that I give back what I didn't steal.

5 O God, you know how [e]foolish I am;
my sins cannot be hidden from you.
6 Don't let those who trust in you be ashamed because of me,
O Sovereign LORD of Heaven's Armies.
Don't let me cause them to be humiliated,
O God of Israel.
7 For I endure insults for your sake;
humiliation is written all over my face.
8 Even my own brothers pretend they don't know me;
they treat me like a stranger.

9 Passion for your house has consumed me,
and the insults of those who insult you have fallen on me.
10 When I weep and fast,
they scoff at me.
11 When I dress in burlap to show sorrow,
they make fun of me.
12 I am the favorite topic of town gossip,
and all the drunks sing about me.

13 But I keep praying to you, LORD,
hoping this time you will show me favor.
In your unfailing love, O God,
answer my prayer with your sure salvation.
14 Rescue me from the mud;
don't let me sink any deeper!
Save me from those who hate me,
and pull me from these deep waters.
15 Don't let the floods overwhelm me,
or the deep waters swallow me,
or the pit of death devour me.

16 Answer my prayers, O LORD,
for your unfailing love is wonderful.
Take care of me,
for your mercy is so plentiful.
17 Don't hide from your servant;
answer me quickly, for I am in deep trouble!
18 Come and redeem me;
free me from my enemies.

19 You know of my shame, scorn, and disgrace.
You see all that my enemies are doing.
20 Their insults have broken my heart,
and I am in despair.
If only one person would show some pity;
if only one would turn and comfort me.
21 But instead, they give me poison for food;
they offer me sour wine for my thirst.

22 Let the bountiful table set before them become a snare
and their prosperity become a trap.
23 Let their eyes go blind so they cannot see,
and make their bodies shake continually.
24 Pour out your fury on them;
consume them with your burning anger.
25 Let their homes become desolate
and their tents be deserted.
26 To the one you have punished, they add insult to injury;
they add to the pain of those you have hurt.

69:4 John applied this lament to Jesus (John 15:25).

69:5-6 The psalmist confesses his *sins* and prays that God's response to him will encourage others in similar conditions to place their hope in the Lord.

69:7-12 Mistreated and abandoned by family, friends, and community, the psalmist turns to the Lord for comfort, relief (69:13-18), and redress (69:22-28).

69:9 Though the psalmist concerns himself with God and all that is holy, *insults* have been his earthly reward. This verse was later applied to Jesus' anger at the Temple's money changers (John 2:17) and to his undeserved suffering (Rom 15:3).

69:10-12 When the psalmist denies himself normal comforts to seek God in prayer, the wicked ridicule him.

69:13-18 The psalmist's only recourse is to pray for rescue and relief from his enemies.

69:19-21 Alone and misunderstood, the psalmist confesses that he cannot bear his doubts. His heart has been broken by his problems.

69:21 *poison:* Or *gall,* a bitter substance. • *sour wine for my thirst:* This description applies to Jesus' suffering (Matt 27:34, 48; Luke 23:36; John 19:28-29).

69:22-28 See "Prayers for Vengeance" at Ps 137, p. 1017.

69:22-23 The psalmist wants God to transfer his suffering (69:3) to his enemies. Paul applied these words to the unbelieving Jews of his day (Rom 11:9-10).

69:22 *Let the bountiful table set before them become a snare /and their prosperity become a trap:* Greek version reads *Let their bountiful table set before them become a snare, / a trap that makes them think all is well. / Let their blessings cause them to stumble, / and let them get what they deserve.* Cp. Rom 11:9, where Paul quotes from the Greek translation of this verse.

69:23 *and make their bodies shake continually:* Greek version reads *and let their backs be bent forever.* Cp. Rom 11:10, where Paul quotes from the Greek translation.

69:25 Peter quoted this verse after the death of Judas Iscariot (Acts 1:20).

27 Pile their sins up high,
and don't let them go free.
28 Erase their names from the Book of Life;
don't let them be counted among the righteous.
29 I am suffering and in pain.
Rescue me, O God, by your saving power.
30 Then I will praise God's name with singing,
and I will honor him with thanksgiving.
31 For this will please the LORD more than sacrificing cattle,
more than presenting a bull with its horns and hooves.
32 The humble will see their God at work and be glad.
Let all who seek God's help be encouraged.
33 For the LORD hears the cries of the needy;
he does not despise his imprisoned people.
34 Praise him, O heaven and earth,
the seas and all that move in them.
35 For God will save Jerusalem
and rebuild the towns of Judah.
His people will live there
and settle in their own land.
36 The descendants of those who obey him will inherit the land,
and those who love him will live there in safety.

PSALM 70

For the choir director: A psalm of David, asking God to remember him.

1 Please, God, rescue me!
Come quickly, LORD, and help me.
2 May those who try to kill me
be humiliated and put to shame.
May those who take delight in my trouble
be turned back in disgrace.
3 Let them be horrified by their shame,
for they said, "Aha! We've got him now!"
4 But may all who search for you
be filled with joy and gladness in you.
May those who love your salvation
repeatedly shout, "God is great!"
5 But as for me, I am poor and needy;
please hurry to my aid, O God.
You are my helper and my savior;
O LORD, do not delay.

PSALM 71

1 O LORD, I have come to you for protection;
don't let me be disgraced.
2 Save me and rescue me,
for you do what is right.
Turn your ear to listen to me,
and set me free.
3 Be my rock of safety
where I can always hide.
Give the order to save me,
for you are my rock and my fortress.
4 My God, rescue me from the power of the wicked,
from the clutches of cruel oppressors.
5 O Lord, you alone are my hope.
I've trusted you, O LORD, from childhood.
6 Yes, you have been with me from birth;
from my mother's womb you have cared for me.
No wonder I am always praising you!
7 My life is an example to many,
because you have been my strength and protection.
8 That is why I can never stop praising you;
I declare your glory all day long.

69:28 Exod 32:32-33; Luke 10:20; Rev 3:5; 13:8; 20:15
69:30 Ps 28:7; 50:14-15
69:31 Ps 50:13-14
69:32 Ps 22:26; 34:2
69:34 Ps 148:1-13
69:35 Ps 147:2; Isa 44:26
69:36 Ps 25:13
70:1-5 //Ps 40:13-17
70:2 Ps 35:4, 26
71:1 Ps 25:2-3; 31:1-3
71:2 Ps 17:6; 31:1
71:3 Deut 33:27; Ps 18:2
71:5 Ps 22:9-11; Jer 17:7, 17
71:6 Ps 22:9-10; 34:1; Isa 46:3
71:7 Ps 61:3

69:28 ***Erase their names from the Book of Life:*** Cp. 1:5-6; 9:5; Rev 3:5; 20:15; 21:22-27.

69:29-33 The psalmist prays that his pain will turn to praise.

69:31 Making a vow often included a sacrifice (20:3; 51:19; cp. 50:13-14; 51:16).

69:32-33 ***despise:*** See 22:24; cp. Matt 25:36; Heb 13:3.

69:34-36 The psalmist prays for Zion, offering a new petition from a new circumstance. He applies the prayer (69:1-33) to the desperate condition of Judah (see 51:18-19).

69:35 ***Jerusalem:*** Hebrew *Zion.* See "Mount Zion, the City of God" at Ps 48, p. 947.

69:36 God's people ***will inherit the land*** because the wicked will perish (see 37:8-9).

Ps 70 This psalm, nearly identical to 40:13-17, contains an urgency (70:1, 5) that fits with the surrounding psalms (cp. 69:17; 71:12).

70:TITLE ***asking God to remember him:*** The meaning of this phrase is unknown (also found in 38:TITLE).

Ps 71 This untitled lament by an aging believer is more of a confession of confidence and hope than the cry of someone abandoned by God. The psalmist experienced God's power and protection in his youth (71:5-8) and now prays for rescue from the adversaries who stalk him in his old age (71:9-13). Even in the midst of his peril, he continues to tell of God's past faithfulness and looks forward with hope to a time when he can testify to the next generation that God is faithful and righteous.

71:1-4 The poet has learned to acknowledge God as the reliable rock who will do what is right toward him and his oppressors. See also 31:1-3.

71:5-6 The psalmist has *trusted* God throughout his life (see 22:9).

71:9
Ps 92:14
71:10
Matt 27:1
71:11
Ps 3:2; 7:2
71:12
Ps 22:9-11
71:13
Ps 35:4, 26
71:15
Ps 35:28; 40:5
71:16
Ps 106:2
71:18
Ps 22:31; 78:4, 6
71:19
Deut 3:24
Ps 35:10; 57:10
Luke 1:49
71:20
Ps 23:4; 60:3-4; 119:25
Hos 6:2
71:22
Ps 33:2; 89:18; 147:7
[f]*zamar* (2167)
‣Ps 92:1

9 And now, in my old age, don't set me
aside.
Don't abandon me when my strength
is failing.
10 For my enemies are whispering
against me.
They are plotting together to kill me.
11 They say, "God has abandoned him.
Let's go and get him,
for no one will help him now."

12 O God, don't stay away.
My God, please hurry to help me.
13 Bring disgrace and destruction on my
accusers.
Humiliate and shame those who want
to harm me.
14 But I will keep on hoping for your help;
I will praise you more and more.
15 I will tell everyone about your
righteousness.
All day long I will proclaim your
saving power,
though I am not skilled with words.
16 I will praise your mighty deeds,
O Sovereign LORD.
I will tell everyone that you alone are
just.
17 O God, you have taught me from my
earliest childhood,
and I constantly tell others about the
wonderful things you do.
18 Now that I am old and gray,
do not abandon me, O God.
Let me proclaim your power to this new
generation,
your mighty miracles to all who come
after me.

19 Your righteousness, O God, reaches to
the highest heavens.
You have done such wonderful things.
Who can compare with you, O God?
20 You have allowed me to suffer much
hardship,
but you will restore me to life again
and lift me up from the depths of the
earth.
21 You will restore me to even greater honor
and comfort me once again.
22 Then I will praise you with music on the
harp,
because you are faithful to your
promises, O my God.
I will [f]sing praises to you with a lyre,
O Holy One of Israel.

Music in Ancient Israel (Ps 71:22-23)

Gen 4:21
Exod 28:34-35
2 Sam 6:5
2 Chr 7:6

The earliest nomadic peoples made music. The first musician mentioned in the Bible is "Jubal . . . the first of all who play the harp and flute" (Gen 4:21). Music and sound were significant from the beginning of Israel's worship in the Tabernacle. In Exodus 28:34-35, Aaron's robe is described as having bells attached to the lower hem that sounded as he entered the Holy Place. In the OT, the first liturgical music mentioned is in the narrative of the transfer of the Ark—David and the Israelites sang, played instruments, and danced to the glory of the Lord (2 Sam 6:5).

This music bore little resemblance to the stately ceremony of Solomon's Temple that is described later (2 Chr 7:1-6). Singers and musicians for the Temple worship were chosen from the tribe of Levi (1 Chr 25:1, 7). They rotated their participation in the weekday, Sabbath, and high holy day services.

David is recognized as inventing the musical instruments used in the Temple (2 Chr 7:6). In the postexilic era, the Levitical singers that are mentioned were the descendants of Asaph, the singing-master appointed by David (Ezr 2:41; Neh 7:44; 11:22-23). From passages such as these, we understand that liturgical music and organization originated in David's time.

71:9-18 The aging believer turns to the Lord for hope. As questions from his adversaries get under his skin and his own strength fails, he asks God to answer his prayers. He does not seek answers to prayer for himself but so that he can tell the story to the next generation.

71:9 The poet prays for continued fellowship with God (see 9:10; 51:11). In his weakness, he needs the Lord's strength even more (see 143:7).

71:10 In their *plotting*, the psalmist's enemies take counsel and scheme together (2:2; 21:11; 31:13; 35:4; 63:9-10).

71:14 The psalmist contrasts his own goodness with his enemies' evil; he centers his life in the Lord, even during hard times (see 9:17-18; 27:13-14).

71:15 ***though I am not skilled with words:*** Or *though I cannot count it.* The Hebrew can be translated either way.

71:19-21 God's righteous character provides encouragement and strength in the midst of suffering. The wounded psalmist confesses faith in God's ability to transform his misery and weakness into abundant life.

71:20 ***lift me up from the depths:*** The psalmist hopes for the renewal of an abundant earthly *life.* This later became grounds for belief in the resurrection of the dead.

71:21 Being assured of God's *comfort* also assures the poet of God's presence, care, and goodness (23:4, 6; 86:17). God's comfort enhances the psalmist's sense of being alive (see 119:50).

23 I will shout for joy and sing your
praises,
for you have ransomed me.
24 I will tell about your righteous deeds
all day long,
for everyone who tried to hurt me
has been shamed and humiliated.

PSALM 72

A psalm of Solomon.

1 Give your love of justice to the king,
O God,
and righteousness to the king's son.
2 Help him judge your people in the right
way;
let the poor always be treated fairly.
3 May the mountains yield prosperity for
all,
and may the hills be fruitful.
4 Help him to defend the poor,
to rescue the children of the needy,
and to crush their oppressors.
5 May they fear you as long as the sun
shines,
as long as the moon remains in the
sky.
Yes, forever!

6 May the king's rule be refreshing like
spring rain on freshly cut grass,
like the showers that water the earth.
7 May all the godly flourish during his reign.
May there be abundant prosperity
until the moon is no more.
8 May he reign from sea to sea,
and from the Euphrates River to the
ends of the earth.
9 Desert nomads will bow before him;
his enemies will fall before him in
the dust.
10 The western kings of Tarshish and other
distant lands
will bring him tribute.
The eastern kings of Sheba and Seba
will bring him gifts.
11 All kings will bow before him,
and all nations will serve him.

12 He will rescue the poor when they cry to
him;
he will help the oppressed, who have
no one to defend them.
13 He feels pity for the weak and the needy,
and he will rescue them.
14 He will redeem them from oppression
and violence,
for their lives are precious to him.

15 Long live the king!
May the gold of Sheba be given to him.
May the people always [g]pray for him
and bless him all day long.

71:23 Ps 5:11; 103:4
71:24 Ps 35:28; 71:13
72:1 1 Kgs 3:9
72:2 Ps 82:3; Isa 9:7; 11:2-5
72:3 Isa 9:5-6; Mic 4:3-4; Zech 9:10
72:4 Isa 11:4
72:5 Ps 89:36-37
72:6 Deut 32:2; Ps 65:10; Hos 6:3
72:7 Ps 92:12
72:8 Exod 23:31; Zech 9:10
72:9 Isa 49:23; Mic 7:17
72:10 Ps 45:12; 68:29; Isa 42:4, 10; 60:6
72:11 Ps 86:9; 138:4; Isa 49:23
72:12 Job 29:12
72:14 Ps 116:15
72:15 Isa 60:6
[g]*palal* (6419) ‣Isa 45:20

71:22-24 As he awaits God's rescue, the psalmist prepares himself to declare with instruments and voice that God is faithful and righteous.

Ps 72 This royal psalm closes Book Two, with 72:18-20 functioning as an epilogue to all of Book Two. The psalmist reflects on the prospects of David's royal line and on Zion (see Pss 46, 48). He prays that Israel's kings will be good and prosperous, extending the Lord's blessing on his people throughout the whole earth. The surpassing righteousness and dominion sought in this prayer foreshadow the coming of Jesus, the Son of David.

72:1-7 The blessings of justice create a balance in nature, resulting in harmony, prosperity, and fertility.

72:1 *love of justice . . . righteousness:* Kings in the ancient Near East were expected to represent justice; the standard for Israel's kings was much higher because the Lord was their model.

72:3 The administration of justice transforms the earth into fruitfulness, abundance, harmony, and goodness (see Isa 32:16-17).

72:4 A just ruler will ***defend the poor*** against injustice, ***rescue*** them from violence, and bring ***their oppressors*** to account for their wrongdoing.

72:5 ***May they fear you:*** In Hebrew, this clause seems to be a response to the enforcement of justice. The Greek version reads *May they endure,* which makes this a prayer for longevity (21:4; 72:15, 17).

72:6-7 The administration of justice is ***refreshing like spring rain,*** enabling the ***godly*** to ***flourish*** (see Isa 45:8) like flowers. • ***until the moon is no more:*** This phrase means forever (see 89:36-37).

72:8-11 The anointed king will rule over the whole world. Even hostile nations will submit to him. In the ancient Near East, bearing gifts to the king acknowledged his success and his reputation (see 1 Kgs 10).

72:8-9 ***from sea to sea:*** This phrase represents the whole world. • Solomon's kingdom extended ***from the Euphrates River*** (literally *the river*) in the east to the Philistine territory in the west (1 Kgs 4:21; see Ps 80:8-11; 89:19-25), where the Mediterranean Sea appeared to be at ***the ends of the earth*** (see 2:8). Everyone ***will bow before*** this king, including the ***desert nomads*** (72:9), ***his enemies,*** and all the kings of the world (see Mic 7:17).

72:10 ***The western kings of Tarshish*** came from a major colony in the western basin of the Mediterranean. ***The eastern kings of Sheba*** came from an area in southern Arabia, home of the queen of Sheba (1 Kgs 10). • ***Seba*** was probably located somewhere south of Egypt, perhaps on the western shore of the Red Sea across from Sheba. • The ***gifts*** offered to the king represented a tribute and a token of submission.

72:11 ***All kings*** and ***all nations*** must submit to the messianic king. The hope expressed in Ps 2:10-11 will be realized (see 96:1-3; 1 Cor 15:25) when other leaders and peoples ***bow before*** and ***serve*** this king.

72:12-14 The anointed king will rescue the needy. He is not only the judge but also a father to the poor (10:14, 17; 68:5).

72:12 To ***rescue the poor*** means to bring an end to the rule of their oppressors.

72:13 Like a father, the king ***feels pity*** for those in need (see Mal 3:17).

72:15-17 The just kingdom will be long-lasting and universal. The summary combines the themes of abundance of crops, longevity, tribute of the nations, and the prayer of the nations.

72:15 The ***people*** will ***bless him,*** fulfilling God's promise to Abraham (Gen 12:3; see Ps 133:3).

72:16
Job 5:25
72:17
Gen 12:3; 22:18
Ps 89:36
72:18
Exod 15:11
Ps 41:13; 77:14
72:19
Num 14:20-21
Neh 9:5
73:1
Ps 24:3-4; 51:10
Matt 5:8
73:2
Ps 94:18
73:3
Ps 37:1, 7
Jer 12:1
73:5
Job 21:9-10
73:6
Ps 109:18
73:7
Job 15:27-28
Ps 17:10
73:8
Ps 1:1; 17:10
Jude 1:16
73:11
Job 22:13
73:12
Ps 49:6
73:13
Job 21:15; 34:9
Ps 26:6

16 May there be abundant grain throughout
the land,
flourishing even on the hilltops.
May the fruit trees flourish like the trees
of Lebanon,
and may the people thrive like grass
in a field.
17 May the king's name endure forever;
may it continue as long as the sun
shines.
May all nations be blessed through him
and bring him praise.

18 Praise the LORD God, the God of Israel,
who alone does such wonderful
things.
19 Praise his glorious name forever!
Let the whole earth be filled with his
glory.
Amen and amen!

20 (This ends the prayers of David son of
Jesse.)

3. BOOK THREE (PSS 73–89)

PSALM 73

A psalm of Asaph.

1 Truly God is good to Israel,
to those whose hearts are pure.
2 But as for me, I almost lost my footing.
My feet were slipping, and I was
almost gone.
3 For I envied the proud
when I saw them prosper despite their
wickedness.
4 They seem to live such painless lives;
their bodies are so healthy and strong.
5 They don't have troubles like other
people;
they're not plagued with problems
like everyone else.
6 They wear pride like a jeweled necklace
and clothe themselves with cruelty.
7 These fat cats have everything
their hearts could ever wish for!
8 They scoff and speak only evil;
in their pride they seek to crush
others.
9 They boast against the very heavens,
and their words strut throughout the
earth.
10 And so the people are dismayed and
confused,
drinking in all their words.
11 "What does God know?" they ask.
"Does the Most High even know what's
happening?"
12 Look at these wicked people—
enjoying a life of ease while their
riches multiply.

13 Did I keep my heart pure for nothing?
Did I keep myself innocent for no
reason?

72:16 ***the trees of Lebanon:*** Lebanon was renowned for its lumber (see note on 2 Chr 2:8).

72:18-19 This doxology concludes Book Two of the Psalter.

72:20 This parenthetical note ends Book Two, which consists mostly of ***prayers of David***. Books Three to Five were probably compiled after Book Two; they include additional psalms of David (Pss 86, 101, 103, 108–110, 122, 124, 131, 133, 138–145).

Book Three (Pss 73–89) Book Three begins with the problem of inequity in the world: The wicked enjoy prosperity while the righteous suffer. Psalm 73 also prepares readers to contemplate the collapse of David's dynasty, which forms the context for the end of Book Three (Ps 89). • Book Three consists of two collections: (1) psalms by Asaph that focus on the restoration of God's people and the judgment of his enemies (Pss 73–83); and (2) psalms by the "Sons of Korah" (Pss 84–89).

Pss 73–75 The apparent prosperity of the wicked (Ps 73) and God's apparent rejection of his people (Ps 74) raise questions about his justice. God is sovereign over the whole world, and he determines the time for judgment (Ps 75).

Ps 73 This wisdom psalm (see "Wisdom Psalms" at Ps 37, p. 937) examines the injustice of the prosperity of the wicked. The psalmist affirms that God is good to the godly but his own experience differs (73:2-12). Nearly overcome by his doubts (73:13-16), the psalmist meets the Lord in the sanctuary and gains a perspective that stretches beyond his life and renews his confidence in God (73:17-26). His disturbing doubts stir a greater passion for truth. He knows that he can trust God and that God will rescue him (73:27-28).

73:TITLE ***Asaph*** was a Levitical singer appointed by David (1 Chr 6:39); his descendants were singers and instrumentalists (1 Chr 15:16-17). Many of the psalms of Asaph (Pss 50, 73–83) were probably written by Asaph's descendants at a later time in Israel's history (e.g., Ps 74).

73:1 People ***whose hearts are pure*** are renewed by God's Spirit (51:10), commit themselves to lives of godliness, keep away from anything that is sinful, and enjoy God's presence (see 24:3-4 and notes).

73:2-3 The poet sees the prosperity of the wicked as unfair (see 72:7) and resents it. • The psalmist's ***feet were slipping*** from the way of wisdom and godliness (see 17:5; 37:31), but God kept him from falling off the trail entirely (38:16; 66:9; 94:18; 121:3). • ***when I saw them prosper:*** Cp. 72:3, 7.

73:4-12 The psalmist presents a caricature of the bliss of the wicked (cp. Ps 1).

73:6 The proud adorn themselves with ***pride*** and ***cruelty*** rather than wisdom (Prov 1:9).

73:9 The proud ***boast***, claiming that they own everything and are not subject to anyone (see 2:1-3).

73:13-17 Recognizing the ramifications of his discouragement and doubt, the psalmist turns to the Lord and receives special insight.

73:13-14 These rhetorical questions expect a discouraging "yes" for an answer. The psalmist wonders if godliness has become a meaningless ritual (see Mal 3:14-15). • ***My heart*** refers to his whole being. • The psalmist's ***pain*** comes from discipline and rebuke (39:11; Prov 1:23, 25; 12:1).

14 I get nothing but trouble all day long;
every morning brings me pain.
15 If I had really spoken this way to others,
I would have been a traitor to your people.
16 So I tried to understand why the wicked prosper.
But what a difficult task it is!
17 Then I went into your sanctuary, O God,
and I finally understood the destiny of the wicked.
18 Truly, you put them on a slippery path
and send them sliding over the cliff to destruction.
19 In an instant they are destroyed,
completely swept away by terrors.
20 When you arise, O Lord,
you will laugh at their silly ideas
as a person laughs at dreams in the morning.
21 Then I realized that my heart was bitter,
and I was all torn up inside.
22 I was so foolish and ignorant—
I must have seemed like a senseless animal to you.
23 Yet I still belong to you;
you hold my right hand.
24 You guide me with your counsel,
leading me to a glorious destiny.
25 Whom have I in heaven but you?
I desire you more than anything on earth.
26 My health may fail, and my spirit may grow weak,
but God remains the [h]strength of my heart;
he is mine forever.
27 Those who desert him will perish,
for you destroy those who abandon you.
28 But as for me, how good it is to be near God!
I have made the [i]Sovereign LORD my shelter,
and I will tell everyone about the wonderful things you do.

PSALM 74
A psalm of Asaph.

1 O God, why have you rejected us so long?
Why is your anger so intense against the sheep of your own pasture?
2 Remember that we are the people you chose long ago,
the tribe you redeemed as your own special possession!
And remember Jerusalem, your home here on earth.
3 Walk through the awful ruins of the city;
see how the enemy has destroyed your sanctuary.
4 There your enemies shouted their victorious battle cries;
there they set up their battle standards.
5 They swung their axes
like woodcutters in a forest.
6 With axes and picks,
they smashed the carved paneling.
7 They burned your sanctuary to the ground.
They defiled the [j]place that bears your name.
8 Then they thought, "Let's destroy everything!"
So they burned down all the places where God was worshiped.
9 We no longer see your miraculous signs.
All the [k]prophets are gone,
and no one can tell us when it will end.

73:14 Ps 38:5-6; 118:18
73:16 Eccl 7:15; 8:16-17
73:17 Ps 27:4
73:19 Num 16:21; Isa 47:11
73:22 Eccl 3:18
73:24 Ps 32:8; 48:14
73:26 Ps 16:5; 38:10
[h]*tsur* (6697) ‣Ps 78:35
73:27 Ps 37:20
73:28 Ps 40:5; 71:7; Heb 10:22
[i]*'adonay Yahweh* (0136, 3068) ‣Isa 61:1
74:1 Deut 29:20; Ps 44:9; 89:46
74:2 Deut 32:6, 9; Ps 68:16
74:3 Ps 79:1; Isa 61:4
74:5 Jer 46:22
74:7 2 Kgs 25:9
[j]*mishkan* (4908) ‣Ps 78:60
74:8 Ps 83:4
74:9 Lev 24:16; Ps 78:43
[k]*nabi'* (5030) ‣Isa 8:3

73:15-16 If the psalmist had verbalized his suspicions about the futility of godly living, he would have discouraged God's people and given God's enemies an opportunity to blaspheme (cp. John 13:20). Instead, the psalmist internalizes the problem and reflects on it.

73:17-20 At this time, God's *sanctuary* was the Temple in Jerusalem. There, in God's presence, the psalmist receives special insight (cp. 18:6). • God deals with the *wicked* over the long term. He waits patiently and gives them time to repent (Ezek 33:11; 2 Pet 3:9); those who do not repent will get what they deserve.

73:21-22 The psalmist's feelings about the prosperity of the wicked had given him a ***bitter*** spirit.

73:24 The Lord leads the godly through their troubles and changes their misery into splendor.

73:25-26 Nothing ***in heaven*** or ***on earth*** is better than being near God.

Ps 74 The psalmist laments the destruction of the Temple in Jerusalem (586 BC) with vivid imagery, questions, fresh memories, and a direct appeal for the Lord to act (74:19-23).

74:TITLE ***psalm:*** Hebrew *maskil.* This may be a literary or musical term.

74:1-2 In the aftermath of Jerusalem's fall, it seemed that God had forgotten his special covenant relationship with his people.

74:1 God ***rejected*** his people because their sin aroused his anger (106:34-46). • Like a tender shepherd, God cares for his people, ***the sheep of*** his ***pasture*** (Ps 23; 100:3).

74:2 The Lord ***chose*** and ***redeemed*** Israel from Egypt in the Exodus (cp. Exod 15:13). • ***your own special possession:*** This is another expression for "your people" (28:9; 78:62; 94:14; 106:40). • ***Jerusalem:*** Hebrew *Mount Zion.* See "Mount Zion, the City of God" at Ps 48, p. 947.

74:3-8 Like a guide, the psalmist points out to the Lord what took place during the destruction of Jerusalem in 586 BC.

74:10
Ps 44:16
74:11
Ps 59:13
74:12
Ps 44:4
[a]*yeshu'ah* (3444)
‣ Isa 30:15
74:13
Exod 14:21
74:15
Exod 14:21-22; 17:5-6
74:16
Gen 1:14-18
Ps 136:7-8
74:17
Gen 8:22
Acts 17:26
74:18
Deut 32:6
Ps 39:8; 74:10
74:20
Gen 17:7
Ps 106:45
74:21
Ps 35:10
Isa 41:17
74:22
Ps 43:1
74:23
Ps 65:7
75:1
Ps 44:1; 71:17
75:3
1 Sam 2:8
Ps 46:6
75:5
Ps 94:4
75:7
1 Sam 2:7
[b]*shapat* (8199)
‣ Ps 82:1
75:9
Ps 40:10
75:10
Ps 89:17; 148:14

10 How long, O God, will you allow our
enemies to insult you?
Will you let them dishonor your name
forever?
11 Why do you hold back your strong right
hand?
Unleash your powerful fist and
destroy them.
12 You, O God, are my king from ages past,
bringing [a]salvation to the earth.
13 You split the sea by your strength
and smashed the heads of the sea
monsters.
14 You crushed the heads of Leviathan
and let the desert animals eat him.
15 You caused the springs and streams to
gush forth,
and you dried up rivers that never
run dry.
16 Both day and night belong to you;
you made the starlight and the sun.
17 You set the boundaries of the earth,
and you made both summer and
winter.

18 See how these enemies insult you,
LORD.
A foolish nation has dishonored your
name.
19 Don't let these wild beasts destroy your
turtledoves.
Don't forget your suffering people
forever.

20 Remember your covenant promises,
for the land is full of darkness and
violence!
21 Don't let the downtrodden be
humiliated again.
Instead, let the poor and needy praise
your name.

22 Arise, O God, and defend your cause.
Remember how these fools insult you
all day long.
23 Don't overlook what your enemies have
said
or their growing uproar.

PSALM 75

For the choir director: A psalm of Asaph. A song to be sung to the tune "Do Not Destroy!"

1 We thank you, O God!
We give thanks because you are near.
People everywhere tell of your
wonderful deeds.

2 God says, "At the time I have planned,
I will bring justice against the wicked.
3 When the earth quakes and its people
live in turmoil,
I am the one who keeps its
foundations firm. *Interlude*

4 "I warned the proud, 'Stop your
boasting!'
I told the wicked, 'Don't raise your fists!
5 Don't raise your fists in defiance at the
heavens
or speak with such arrogance.' "
6 For no one on earth—from east or west,
or even from the wilderness—
should raise a defiant fist.
7 It is God alone who [b]judges;
he decides who will rise and who will
fall.
8 For the LORD holds a cup in his hand
that is full of foaming wine mixed
with spices.
He pours out the wine in judgment,
and all the wicked must drink it,
draining it to the dregs.

9 But as for me, I will always proclaim
what God has done;
I will sing praises to the God of Jacob.
10 For God says, "I will break the strength
of the wicked,
but I will increase the power of the
godly."

74:12 ***my king from ages past:*** The psalmist acknowledges God's power and his historical bond with Israel (5:2; 44:4; 84:3).

74:14 The identification of ***Leviathan*** is disputed, ranging from an earthly creature to a mythical sea monster in ancient literature (see 104:26; Job 3:8; 41:1, 12, 22, 31; Isa 27:1). Here, its multiple ***heads*** point to the mythical monster.

74:15 ***springs and streams to gush forth:*** God provided water in the desert for his people (see 68:8-9; Exod 17:6); he ***dried up*** the Red Sea (Exod 14:21) and the Jordan River (Josh 3:17).

74:16 ***starlight:*** Or *moon;* Hebrew reads *light.*

74:19-23 The poet urges God to act.

Ps 75 This hymn of thanksgiving includes two direct messages from God that provide assurance of his justice (75:2-3, 10). The Lord rebukes arrogant people who defy him, promising to forcibly humble them (75:4-8). Together, the community and the psalmist respond with thanksgiving for God's character (75:1, 9).

75:2-8 The Lord will bring justice in his own time.

75:4-5 ***The wicked*** arrogantly defy ***the heavens***—the dwelling place of God. Through their ***boasting*** they insist that they are wiser than God.

75:6 No creature has the right to rebel against its Creator. • ***should raise a defiant fist:*** Literally *should lift.*

75:7-8 The Lord alone is the Judge, with the power to exalt and humble (see 1 Sam 2:7; Luke 1:52).

PSALM 76

For the choir director: A psalm of Asaph. A song to be accompanied by stringed instruments.

1 God is honored in Judah;
his name is great in Israel.
2 Jerusalem is where he lives;
Mount Zion is his home.
3 There he has broken the fiery arrows of the enemy,
the shields and swords and weapons of war. *Interlude*

4 You are glorious and more majestic
than the everlasting mountains.
5 Our boldest enemies have been plundered.
They lie before us in the sleep of death.
No warrior could lift a hand against us.
6 At the blast of your breath, O God of Jacob,
their horses and chariots lay still.

7 No wonder you are greatly feared!
Who can stand before you when your anger explodes?
8 From heaven you sentenced your enemies;
the earth trembled and stood silent before you.
9 You stand up to judge those who do evil, O God,
and to rescue the oppressed of the earth. *Interlude*

10 Human defiance only enhances your glory,
for you use it as a weapon.
11 Make vows to the LORD your God, and keep them.
Let everyone bring tribute to the Awesome One.
12 For he breaks the pride of princes,
and the kings of the earth fear him.

PSALM 77

For Jeduthun, the choir director: A psalm of Asaph.

1 I cry out to God; yes, I shout.
Oh, that God would listen to me!
2 When I was in deep trouble,
I searched for the Lord.
All night long I prayed, with hands lifted toward heaven,
but my soul was not comforted.
3 I think of God, and I moan,
overwhelmed with longing for his help. *Interlude*

4 You don't let me sleep.
I am too distressed even to pray!
5 I think of the good old days,
long since ended,
6 when my nights were filled with joyful songs.
I search my soul and ponder the difference now.
7 Has the Lord rejected me forever?
Will he never again be kind to me?
8 Is his unfailing love gone forever?
Have his promises permanently failed?
9 Has God forgotten to be gracious?
Has he slammed the door on his compassion? *Interlude*

10 And I said, "This is my fate;

76:2 Ps 48:2-3; 132:13; 135:21
76:3 Ps 46:9
76:5 Isa 10:12
76:6 Exod 15:1, 21
76:7 Ps 89:7; Nah 1:6; Rev 6:17
76:8 1 Chr 16:30
76:9 Ps 9:7-9; 72:4
76:10 Exod 9:16; Rom 9:17
77:2 Job 11:13; Ps 50:15; 88:9; Isa 26:9, 16
77:3 Ps 43:5; 61:2; 142:2-3
77:5 Ps 143:5
77:6 Ps 42:8
77:8 Ps 89:49
77:9 Ps 25:6

Ps 76 This psalm appears to celebrate a victory. The victory might have been recent, such as over the Assyrians (see note on 76:TITLE; see also Isa 37); or the psalm might be recalling God's great acts of rescue in the past.

76:TITLE ***to be accompanied by stringed instruments:*** Greek version reads *for the Assyrian.*

76:1-3 God's victory over Zion's enemies foreshadows his worldwide victory over all his enemies.

76:2 ***Jerusalem:*** Hebrew *Salem,* another name for Jerusalem (see Gen 14:18).

76:3 God brings an end to the attacks of his enemies (see 46:9).

76:4-6 The psalmist praises God for his achievement and for his ***glorious*** majesty.

76:4 The victorious king's splendor, glory, and majesty are greater than anything in the created order (8:1; 29:4; 111:3). • ***than the everlasting mountains:*** As in Greek version; Hebrew reads *than mountains filled with beasts of prey.*

76:7-9 The needy await their victorious God, while the wicked stand in fear of him.

76:7 The word translated *feared* (Hebrew *nora'*) is a wordplay on the word translated "glorious" in 76:4 (Hebrew *na'or*).

76:10 ***for you use it as a weapon:*** The meaning of the Hebrew is uncertain.

Ps 77 The psalmist laments that God has turned away from him, even though he feels innocent. He reflects on his situation (77:3, 6, 12) and finds hope (see 25:5) in remembering God's past deeds (77:11).

77:1-3 The ***night*** provides a special opportunity for prayer and meditation (77:6, 11; see 6:6; 16:7; 17:3; 30:5; 63:6; 119:55, 62, 148).

77:3 ***I think of God:*** God's people inevitably face difficult times, but recalling his mighty acts at the beginning of their relationship assures them of God's commitment. • Feeling ***overwhelmed,*** the psalmist is unable to deal with the crisis (142:3; 143:4).

77:4-6 As the psalmist meditates at night, he feels so disturbed that he cannot sleep or speak. He has pleasant memories of the past, but he cannot look beyond the present moment into the future.

77:7-9 The psalmist questions his status before God.

77:7 Feeling ***rejected*** (see 43:2), the psalmist asks if the situation is permanent.

the Most High has turned his hand
against me."
11 But then I recall all you have done,
O LORD;
I remember your wonderful deeds of
long ago.
12 They are constantly in my [c]thoughts.
I cannot stop thinking about your
mighty works.

13 O God, your ways are holy.
Is there any god as mighty as you?
14 You are the God of great wonders!
You demonstrate your awesome
power among the nations.
15 By your strong arm, you [d]redeemed your
people,
the descendants of Jacob and Joseph.
Interlude

16 When the Red Sea saw you, O God,
its waters looked and trembled!
The sea quaked to its very depths.
17 The clouds poured down rain;
the thunder rumbled in the sky.
Your arrows of lightning flashed.
18 Your thunder roared from the
whirlwind;
the lightning lit up the world!
The earth trembled and shook.
19 Your road led through the sea,
your pathway through the mighty
waters—
a pathway no one knew was there!
20 You led your people along that road like
a flock of sheep,
with Moses and Aaron as their
shepherds.

PSALM 78
A psalm of Asaph.

1 O my people, listen to my instructions.
Open your ears to what I am saying,
2 for I will speak to you in a [e]parable.
I will teach you hidden lessons from our
past—
3 stories we have heard and known,
stories our ancestors handed down
to us.
4 We will not hide these truths from our
children;
we will tell the next generation
about the glorious deeds of the LORD,
about his power and his mighty
wonders.
5 For he issued his laws to Jacob;
he gave his instructions to Israel.
He commanded our ancestors
to teach them to their children,
6 so the next generation might know
them—
even the children not yet born—
and they in turn will teach their own
children.
7 So each generation should set its hope
anew on God,
not forgetting his glorious miracles
and obeying his commands.
8 Then they will not be like their
ancestors—
stubborn, rebellious, and unfaithful,
refusing to give their hearts to God.

9 The warriors of Ephraim, though armed
with bows,
turned their backs and fled on the
day of battle.
10 They did not keep God's covenant
and refused to live by his instructions.
11 They forgot what he had done—
the great wonders he had shown
them,
12 the miracles he did for their ancestors
on the plain of Zoan in the land of
Egypt.

77:11 Exod 15:11; Ps 86:8
77:12 [c]*hagah* (1897) › Ps 143:5
77:13 Exod 15:11; Ps 86:8
77:15 Exod 6:6; Deut 9:29; [d]*ga'al* (1350) › Ps 103:4
77:16 Exod 14:21
77:17 Ps 68:33
77:18 Judg 5:4
77:19 Hab 3:15
77:20 Exod 6:26; 13:21; Ps 78:52; Isa 63:11-13
78:2 *Matt 13:34-35; [e]*mashal* (4912) › Prov 1:1
78:3 Ps 44:1
78:4 Deut 11:19; Ps 22:30
78:5 Deut 6:4-9
78:6 Deut 11:19; Ps 102:18
78:7 Deut 4:2, 9; Josh 22:5
78:8 Exod 32:9; Ezek 20:18
78:10 2 Kgs 18:12
78:11 Ps 106:13
78:12 Num 13:22; Isa 19:11

77:10-12 The memories of God's mighty works in the past fill the psalmist's mind.

77:10 The psalmist fears that God's ***hand*** of protection (44:3; 77:15; Exod 6:6) and favor (16:7-8; 110:1) is now ***against*** him for no apparent reason.

77:13-15 This central section of the poem reflects on God as the holy and powerful redeemer.

77:16 ***the Red Sea:*** Literally *the waters.* The Canaanites attributed divine power to the sea, but God is the one who made the sea and uses it for his own purposes.

Ps 78 This wisdom psalm exhorts the people to learn wisdom and faithfully pass it on.

78:TITLE ***psalm:*** Hebrew *maskil.* This may be a literary or musical term.

78:1-8 The prologue is an invitation to learn wisdom.

78:2 The psalmist recites Israel's story (78:5-72) ***in a parable*** in order to teach wisdom and insight. • Jesus quoted this verse to explain why he taught in parables (Matt 13:35).

78:3-4 This story of what God has done should be told from generation to generation (see Deut 6:20-25; Prov 4:1-4).

78:5-6 The telling of the story should motivate God's people to obey what he ***commanded*** (Deut 6:4-9).

78:7-8 God holds ***each generation*** responsible for its own response, which should be to maintain faith and ***hope*** (see 9:18; 27:14) and avoid being ***stubborn, rebellious, and unfaithful*** (see Deut 9:6-7; 10:16; 30:6; 31:27).

78:9-11 ***Ephraim,*** the second son of Joseph, received a special blessing from Jacob (Gen 48:15-20; 49:22-26; Deut 33:13-17). The land that his descendants received included fertile valleys and strategic roads (Judg 8:2). However, the people of Ephraim did not live in obedience to God's gracious covenant.

78:12-16 The focus shifts from Ephraim (78:9-11) to Israel as a whole as the psalmist reflects on God's power in Egypt (see 81:4-7) and in the wilderness.

78:12 ***The miracles*** are the ten plagues against Egypt that God performed during Israel's captivity (Exod 7–12).

13 For he divided the sea and led them
through,
making the water stand up like walls!
14 In the daytime he led them by a cloud,
and all night by a pillar of fire.
15 He split open the rocks in the wilderness
to give them water, as from a gushing
spring.
16 He made streams pour from the rock,
making the waters flow down like a
river!

17 Yet they kept on sinning against him,
rebelling against the Most High in the
desert.
18 They stubbornly tested God in their
hearts,
demanding the foods they craved.
19 They even spoke against God himself,
saying,
"God can't give us food in the
wilderness.
20 Yes, he can strike a rock so water gushes
out,
but he can't give his people bread and
meat."
21 When the LORD heard them, he was
furious.
The fire of his wrath burned against
Jacob.
Yes, his anger rose against Israel,
22 for they did not believe God
or trust him to care for them.
23 But he commanded the skies to open;
he opened the doors of heaven.
24 He rained down [f]manna for them to eat;
he gave them bread from heaven.
25 They ate the food of angels!
God gave them all they could hold.
26 He released the east wind in the heavens
and guided the south wind by his
mighty power.
27 He rained down meat as thick as dust—
birds as plentiful as the sand on the
seashore!
28 He caused the birds to fall within their
camp
and all around their tents.
29 The people ate their fill.
He gave them what they craved.
30 But before they satisfied their craving,
while the meat was yet in their
mouths,
31 the anger of God rose against them,
and he killed their strongest men.
He struck down the finest of Israel's
young men.

32 But in spite of this, the people kept
sinning.
Despite his wonders, they refused to
trust him.
33 So he ended their lives in failure,
their years in terror.
34 When God began killing them,
they finally sought him.
They repented and took God
seriously.
35 Then they remembered that God was
their [g]rock,
that God [h]Most High was their
redeemer.
36 But all they gave him was lip service;
they lied to him with their tongues.
37 Their hearts were not loyal to him.
They did not keep his covenant.
38 Yet he was merciful and [i]forgave their
sins
and did not destroy them all.
Many times he held back his anger
and did not unleash his fury!
39 For he remembered that they were
merely mortal,
gone like a breath of wind that never
returns.

40 Oh, how often they rebelled against him
in the wilderness
and grieved his heart in that dry
wasteland.
41 Again and again they tested God's
patience
and provoked the Holy One of Israel.
42 They did not remember his power
and how he rescued them from their
enemies.

78:13 Exod 14:21; 15:8
78:14 Exod 13:21
78:15 Exod 17:5-6; *1 Cor 10:4
78:16 Num 20:8, 10-11
78:17 Heb 3:16
78:18 Num 11:4-5; *1 Cor 10:9-10
78:19 Exod 16:3; Num 21:5
78:20 Num 20:11
78:21 Num 11:1
78:22-23 Heb 3:19
78:23 Mal 3:10
78:24 Exod 16:4; *John 6:30-31; [f]*man* (4478) ‣Exod 16:15
78:26 Num 11:31
78:27 Exod 16:13; Ps 105:40
78:29 Num 11:19-20
78:31 Num 11:33-34
78:32 Num 14:11
78:33 Num 14:29, 34-35
78:34 Hos 5:15
78:35 Deut 9:26; 32:4; [g]*tsur* (6697) ‣Ps 89:26; [h]*'elyon* (5945) ‣Ps 82:6
78:36 Exod 32:7-8; Ezek 33:31
78:38 Exod 34:5-6; Num 14:18-20; [i]*kapar* (3722) ‣Ps 79:9
78:39 Job 7:16-17; Jas 4:14
78:41 2 Kgs 19:22
78:42 Judg 8:34

78:13 God *divided the sea* when Israel crossed through the Red Sea (see Exod 14–15).

78:14 God used a *cloud* and a *pillar of fire* to guide and protect Israel in the wilderness (Exod 13:21-22).

78:17-31 Israel rebelled in the wilderness despite God's abundant provision.

78:23-25 Abundance comes through *the doors of heaven* (Gen 8:2; 2 Kgs 7:2; Mal 3:10). • Israel ate *manna* for forty years in the wilderness (Exod 16:31-36; John 6:31).

78:26-31 God powerfully satisfied the people's desires, but they did not respond with gratitude or faith. Therefore, God exercised his justice.

78:32-39 Israel's rebellion resulted in God's judgment, but even their short-lived and insincere repentance motivated God to exercise forbearance.

78:33 An entire generation died in the wilderness (Num 14:22-23, 28-35).

78:34-39 Israel's continued existence, in spite of the people's rebellion and unbelief (78:7-8), was due to God's compassion.

78:34 *They repented:* This demonstration of zeal was not sincere.

78:35-39 The Israelites *remembered* the right doctrine (9:9; 91:1), but they did not allow God to change their *hearts* (Lev 26:41). • *God Most High:* Hebrew *'el-'elyon.*

78:40-55 The Israelites *rebelled* even though the Lord had rescued them from powerful plagues.

78:43
Exod 7:3
78:44
Exod 7:20
Ps 105:29
78:45
Exod 8:6, 24
Ps 105:30-31
78:46
Exod 10:14
ʾarbeh (0697)
‣ Prov 30:27
78:47
Exod 9:23-25
Ps 105:32
78:48
Exod 9:19
78:49
Exod 15:7
[k]*malʾak* (4397)
‣ Ps 91:11
78:51
Exod 12:29-30
Ps 105:36
78:52
Ps 77:20
78:53
Exod 14:19-20, 27-28
78:54
Exod 15:17
78:55
Josh 23:4-5
Ps 44:1-2; 105:10-11
78:58
Lev 26:1
Deut 32:16, 21
78:59
Lev 26:30
Deut 32:19
78:60
1 Sam 4:11
[a]*mishkan* (4908)
‣ Exod 25:9

43 They did not remember his miraculous
signs in Egypt,
his wonders on the plain of Zoan.
44 For he turned their rivers into blood,
so no one could drink from the
streams.
45 He sent vast swarms of flies to consume
them
and hordes of frogs to ruin them.
46 He gave their crops to caterpillars;
their harvest was consumed by
[j]locusts.
47 He destroyed their grapevines with hail
and shattered their sycamore-figs
with sleet.
48 He abandoned their cattle to the hail,
their livestock to bolts of lightning.
49 He loosed on them his fierce anger—
all his fury, rage, and hostility.
He dispatched against them
a band of destroying [k]angels.
50 He turned his anger against them;
he did not spare the Egyptians' lives
but ravaged them with the plague.
51 He killed the oldest son in each Egyptian
family,
the flower of youth throughout the
land of Egypt.
52 But he led his own people like a flock of
sheep,
guiding them safely through the
wilderness.
53 He kept them safe so they were not
afraid;
but the sea covered their enemies.
54 He brought them to the border of his
holy land,
to this land of hills he had won for
them.
55 He drove out the nations before them;
he gave them their inheritance by lot.
He settled the tribes of Israel into
their homes.
56 But they kept testing and rebelling
against God Most High.
They did not obey his laws.
57 They turned back and were as faithless
as their parents.
They were as undependable as a
crooked bow.
58 They angered God by building shrines to
other gods;
they made him jealous with their
idols.
59 When God heard them, he was very
angry,
and he completely rejected Israel.
60 Then he abandoned his [a]dwelling at
Shiloh,

God's Anger (Ps 78:18-64)

Ps 2:5-9, 12; 6:1; 7:6, 11-13; 21:9; 27:9; 30:5; 38:1-10; 74:1; 79:5-6; 80:4; 85:2-7; 86:15; 90:9-11; 95:8-11; 102:10-11; 103:8-9; 106:21-43; 110:5-7; 145:8
Isa 64:9-12
Lam 5:19-22
Rom 2:5-11
Eph 5:6
Rev 6:15-17; 11:18; 19:11-16

The psalmists understood Israel's exodus from Egypt as an object lesson about God's anger (78:18-64). God expressed his anger against the Egyptians while sparing his people (78:49-50). But Israel became the object of his wrath during the wilderness journey, when the people provoked the Lord to anger through their rebelliousness (78:31; 106:29, 32; see Rom 2:5). God took an oath that that rebellious generation would not enter his place of rest (95:8-11), and they died in the wilderness. But he restrained his wrath (78:38) and did not destroy Israel as it deserved.

The Lord is just and righteous in his judgment (7:11); he is patient and slow to anger (86:15; 103:8; 145:8). The wicked have stirred up God's wrath and deserve his judgment (see 2:5, 12; 21:9; 56:7; 59:13; 69:24; 79:6; see also Rom 1:18). The purpose of his wrath is to remove evildoers and extend his kingdom. Evil must come to an end, and the wicked must perish for the godly to inherit the earth (Ps 37).

God's people experience his wrath when they sin. The experience, though painful, is brief in comparison to their joy in God's mercy and goodness (30:5). He will not be angry forever (103:9). God's wrath brings death (106:23), but his forgiveness and mercy restore his people (see 85:2-7).

God is love, and he loves people with justice and holiness. In love for us, he poured out his anger on Jesus Christ (Rom 3:25; 5:9). Jesus received the full brunt of God's wrath so that he could atone for our sins and reconcile us to God. He saves his people (1 Jn 2:2) and rules from heaven at God's right hand (Heb 2:17). Jesus is now the agent of God's wrath against the wicked (2:5-9; 110:5-7; Eph 5:6; Rev 6:15-17; 11:18; 19:11-16).

78:51 *throughout the land of Egypt:* Literally *in the tents of Ham.*

78:56-64 Israel's rebellion desecrated the Promised Land. The people built *shrines* to false gods and worshiped *idols* (78:58) during the period of the judges (e.g., Judg 2:11; 3:7; 17–18).

78:60 God *abandoned his dwelling at Shiloh* because of the people's idol worship (1 Sam 4:11; Jer 7:12).

the Tabernacle where he had lived
among the people.
61 He allowed the Ark of his might to be
captured;
he surrendered his glory into enemy
hands.
62 He gave his people over to be butchered
by the sword,
because he was so angry with his own
people—his special possession.
63 Their young men were killed by fire;
their young women died before
singing their wedding songs.
64 Their priests were slaughtered,
and their widows could not mourn
their deaths.
65 Then the Lord rose up as though waking
from sleep,
like a warrior aroused from a
drunken stupor.
66 He routed his enemies
and sent them to eternal shame.
67 But he rejected Joseph's descendants;
he did not choose the tribe of
Ephraim.
68 He [b]chose instead the tribe of Judah,
and Mount Zion, which he loved.
69 There he built his sanctuary as high as
the heavens,
as solid and enduring as the earth.
70 He chose his servant David,
calling him from the sheep pens.
71 He took David from tending the ewes
and lambs
and made him the shepherd of Jacob's
descendants—
God's own people, Israel.
72 He [c]cared for them with a true heart
and led them with skillful hands.

PSALM 79
A psalm of Asaph.

1 O God, pagan nations have conquered
your land,
your special possession.
They have defiled your holy Temple
and made Jerusalem a heap of ruins.
2 They have left the bodies of your servants
as food for the birds of heaven.
The flesh of your godly ones
has become food for the wild animals.
3 Blood has flowed like water all around
Jerusalem;
no one is left to bury the dead.
4 We are mocked by our neighbors,
an object of scorn and derision to
those around us.

5 O LORD, how long will you be angry with
us? Forever?
How long will your jealousy burn like
fire?
6 Pour out your wrath on the nations that
refuse to acknowledge you—
on kingdoms that do not call upon
your name.
7 For they have devoured your people Israel,
making the land a desolate
wilderness.
8 Do not hold us guilty for the sins of our
ancestors!
Let your compassion quickly meet our
needs,
for we are on the brink of despair.

9 Help us, O God of our salvation!
Help us for the glory of your name.
Save us and [d]forgive our sins
for the honor of your name.
10 Why should pagan nations be allowed to
scoff,
asking, "Where is their God?"
Show us your vengeance against the
nations,

78:61 1 Sam 4:17
78:62 Judg 20:21; 1 Sam 4:10
78:63 Num 11:1; Jer 7:34; 16:9
78:64 1 Sam 22:18
78:65 Isa 42:13
78:66 1 Sam 5:6
78:68 Ps 87:1-2; [b]*bakhar* (0977) ‣ Ps 135:4
78:69 1 Kgs 6:1-38
78:70 1 Sam 16:10-12
78:71 2 Sam 5:2; 7:8; 1 Chr 11:2
78:72 1 Kgs 9:4; [c]*ra'ah* (7462) ‣ Isa 40:11
79:1 Ps 74:2-7; Jer 26:18; Lam 1:10
79:2 Deut 28:26; Jer 7:33; 16:4
79:3 Jer 14:16
79:4 Ps 44:13
79:5 Ps 74:1, 9-10; Zeph 3:8
79:6 Jer 10:25; 2 Thes 1:8
79:7 Ps 53:4
79:8 Ps 106:6; 142:6; Isa 26:5; 64:9
79:9 2 Chr 14:11; Jer 14:7; [d]*kapar* (3722) ‣ Prov 16:6
79:10 Ps 115:2

78:67 ***The tribe of Ephraim*** was not completely ***rejected***, but God favored Judah (78:68).

78:68-69 In the choice of ***Mount Zion*** instead of Shiloh as God's ***sanctuary*** on earth, God moved from the north to the south (see Ps 69).

78:70-72 The God who had turned against his ***own people*** (78:62) chose ***David***, a shepherd (Gen 46:34; 1 Sam 16:10-11), to become their ***shepherd*** (78:52; cp. 23:1).

Ps 79 This lament describes the occasion of Jerusalem's fall in 586 BC. The early history of Israel's rebellions described in Ps 78 provoked God's wrath, resulting in the desolation of Zion described here as the defilement of the Temple and the disgraced bodies that littered the landscape. The psalmist then prays for forgiveness and rescue (79:8-9), as well as for God to pay back the nation's enemies (79:12-13). Other psalms lamenting the Exile include Pss 42–44, 102, 107, 126, 137.

79:1-4 The poet laments the desecration of the Temple and the success of the enemy.

79:1 ***your special possession:*** This phrase might refer to the ***land***, the ***Temple*** (see 61:5), or the people (see 79:2; 78:71).

79:5-8 The intensity of God's judgment surprises the people; they cry out in despair for compassion, forgiveness, and relief. Verses 6-7 are repeated almost verbatim in Jer 10:25.

79:6 The repentant among God's people ask him not to vent his anger on them but on their wicked and unrepentant enemies.

79:7 ***devoured your people Israel:*** Literally *devoured Jacob.* See note on 44:4.

79:8 The people's accumulation of past ***sins*** contributed to the Exile (2 Kgs 17:7-23; 24:3-4); however, the people perished because of their own sins (Jer 31:30; Ezek 18:20).

79:9-11 The people ask God to rescue them. Although Israel's sins caused the tragedy, the ***pagan nations*** must also be held responsible for the bloodshed.

79:12 Gen 4:15; Ps 74:10, 18, 22
79:13 Ps 74:1; 95:7; 100:3; Isa 43:21
80:1 Exod 25:22; Ps 23:1; 77:20
80:2 Ps 35:23
80:3 Num 6:24-26; Ps 31:16; 60:1; Lam 5:21
80:4 Ps 79:5; 84:8
80:5 Ps 42:3; 102:9
80:6 Ps 44:13; 79:4
80:8 2 Chr 20:7; Ps 44:2; Isa 5:2, 7; Jer 2:21; 11:17; Ezek 17:6, 23; Amos 9:15
80:9 Exod 23:28; Isa 5:2; Hos 14:5
80:11 Ps 72:8
80:12 Ps 89:40; Isa 5:5
80:13 Jer 5:6
80:16 2 Chr 36:19; Ps 39:11; Jer 52:13
80:17 Ps 89:21; [e]*ben 'adam* (1121, 0120) ‣Ps 90:3

for they have spilled the blood of your
servants.
11 Listen to the moaning of the prisoners.
Demonstrate your great power by
saving those condemned to die.

12 O Lord, pay back our neighbors seven
times
for the scorn they have hurled at you.
13 Then we your people, the sheep of your
pasture,
will thank you forever and ever,
praising your greatness from
generation to generation.

PSALM 80

For the choir director: A psalm of Asaph, to be sung to the tune "Lilies of the Covenant."

1 Please listen, O Shepherd of Israel,
you who lead Joseph's descendants
like a flock.
O God, enthroned above the cherubim,
display your radiant glory
2 to Ephraim, Benjamin, and Manasseh.
Show us your mighty power.
Come to rescue us!

3 Turn us again to yourself, O God.
Make your face shine down upon us.
Only then will we be saved.
4 O LORD God of Heaven's Armies,
how long will you be angry with our
prayers?
5 You have fed us with sorrow
and made us drink tears by the
bucketful.
6 You have made us the scorn of
neighboring nations.
Our enemies treat us as a joke.

7 Turn us again to yourself, O God of
Heaven's Armies.
Make your face shine down upon us.
Only then will we be saved.
8 You brought us from Egypt like a
grapevine;
you drove away the pagan nations and
transplanted us into your land.
9 You cleared the ground for us,
and we took root and filled the land.
10 Our shade covered the mountains;
our branches covered the mighty
cedars.
11 We spread our branches west to the
Mediterranean Sea;
our shoots spread east to the
Euphrates River.
12 But now, why have you broken down our
walls
so that all who pass by may steal our
fruit?
13 The wild boar from the forest
devours it,
and the wild animals feed on it.

14 Come back, we beg you, O God of
Heaven's Armies.
Look down from heaven and see our
plight.
Take care of this grapevine
15 that you yourself have planted,
this son you have raised for yourself.
16 For we are chopped up and burned by
our enemies.
May they perish at the sight of your
frown.
17 Strengthen the man you love,
the [e]son of your choice.

79:12 The Exile resulted in national suffering and in individual searching for the Lord. • *pay back:* See 1:6; 94:2; Jer 32:18. • The expression *seven times* signifies something complete. • Israel's *neighbors* included Edom, Moab, and Ammon (see 137:7; 2 Kgs 24:2; Obad 1:1-21).

Ps 80 This psalm of lament might originate with the remnant of the northern kingdom after its fall in 722 BC. The people call on God as their Shepherd and as the God of Heaven's Armies in the hope that he will return to them and restore them. They remember the Exodus and their special relationship with the Lord and conclude with an expression of renewed commitment to him (80:18).

80:TITLE *The tune "Lilies of the Covenant"* is unknown today.

80:1-3 The psalmist urgently calls upon the Lord to act.

80:1-2 God is the *Shepherd of Israel:* See also 23:1; 28:9; 78:52-53. • *radiant glory . . . power:* These expressions (145:11) refer to God's manifest presence.

80:3 This verse is repeated (with an increasing crescendo) in 80:7, 19.

80:4-7 The people cry out for rescue from the shame of their recent defeat. The enemy's victory is less devastating, however, than the knowledge that they themselves are objects of God's wrath.

80:6 *the scorn:* As in Syriac version; Hebrew reads *the strife.*

80:8-11 Israel has a glorious past, beginning with its redemption from Egypt.

80:8-9 Israel had been a prosperous *grapevine* (Gen 1:28; Gal 5:22-23) that God *transplanted* into the land of Canaan at the time of the conquest. However, the people forgot the source of their prosperity and chose to do evil (Isa 5:1-7; Hos 10:1).

80:10-11 Solomon's kingdom had extended *west to the Mediterranean Sea* and *east to the Euphrates River* (literally *west to the sea, . . . east to the river*; see 72:8-9; 89:25; 1 Kgs 4:21).

80:12 *broken down our walls:* God no longer defended Israel (Isa 5:5).

80:13 The surrounding nations were ceremonially unclean, like a *wild boar* or vicious *wild animals.*

80:15 Israel was the *son* that God had brought out of Egypt (see Hos 11:1) and *planted* in the Holy Land.

80:16-19 The community prays for God to change their desperate situation and restore them. They are still the Lord's chosen people.

80:17 The *son of your choice* was probably the northern kingdom of Israel, although it might allude to the king of David's dynasty (110:1).

18 Then we will never abandon you again.
Revive us so we can call on your name
once more.
19 Turn us again to yourself, O LORD God of
[f]Heaven's Armies.
Make your face shine down upon us.
Only then will we be saved.

PSALM 81

For the choir director: A psalm of Asaph, to be accompanied by a stringed instrument.

1 Sing praises to God, our strength.
Sing to the God of Jacob.
2 Sing! Beat the tambourine.
Play the sweet lyre and the harp.
3 Blow the ram's horn at new moon,
and again at full moon to call a
[g]festival!
4 For this is required by the decrees of
Israel;
it is a regulation of the God of Jacob.
5 He made it a law for Israel
when he attacked Egypt to set us
free.

I heard an unknown voice say,
6 "Now I will take the load from your
shoulders;
I will free your hands from their
heavy tasks.
7 You cried to me in trouble, and I saved
you;
I answered out of the thundercloud
and tested your faith when there was
no water at Meribah. *Interlude*
8 "Listen to me, O my people, while I give
you stern warnings.
O Israel, if you would only listen
to me!
9 You must never have a foreign god;
you must not bow down before a false
god.
10 For it was I, the LORD your God,
who rescued you from the land of
Egypt.
Open your mouth wide, and I will fill
it with good things.
11 "But no, my people wouldn't listen.
Israel did not want me around.
12 So I let them follow their own stubborn
desires,
living according to their own ideas.
13 Oh, that my people would listen to me!
Oh, that Israel would follow me,
walking in my paths!
14 How quickly I would then subdue their
enemies!
How soon my hands would be upon
their foes!
15 Those who hate the LORD would cringe
before him;
they would be doomed forever.
16 But I would feed you with the finest
wheat.
I would satisfy you with wild honey
from the rock."

PSALM 82

A psalm of Asaph.

1 God presides over heaven's court;
he [h]pronounces judgment on the
heavenly beings:
2 "How long will you hand down unjust
decisions
by favoring the wicked? *Interlude*
3 "Give justice to the poor and the orphan;
uphold the rights of the oppressed
and the destitute.

80:18
Ps 71:20
Isa 50:5

80:19
[f]*tsaba'* (6635)
‣Ps 103:21

81:1
Ps 46:1; 59:16; 66:1; 95:1-2

81:2
Ps 108:2; 144:9; 149:3

81:3
Lev 23:24
Num 10:10
[g]*khag* (2282)
‣Isa 30:29

81:5
Exod 11:4

81:6
Isa 9:4; 10:27

81:7
Exod 2:23; 17:5-7; 19:19
Ps 50:15; 95:8

81:8
Ps 50:7

81:9
Exod 20:3
Isa 43:12

81:10
Exod 20:2
Ps 78:25; 103:5

81:11
Exod 32:1

81:12
Acts 7:42
Rom 1:24, 26

81:13
Deut 5:29
Isa 48:18
Jer 7:23

81:14
Ps 47:3
Amos 1:8

81:16
Deut 32:13-14

82:1
Ps 58:11
Isa 3:13
[h]*shapat* (8199)
‣Prov 31:9

82:2
Deut 1:17
Ps 58:1-2
Prov 18:5

82:3
Deut 24:17

Ps 81 This warning message invites Israel to worship only the Lord and to enjoy the fullness of his blessing.

81:TITLE ***to be accompanied by a stringed instrument:*** Hebrew *according to the gittith.*

81:1-3 As a prelude to the message of warning, the psalmist invites Israel to contemplate their God in song and dance.

81:2 An Israelite ***tambourine*** was a hand drum—a round frame covered with a skin, used as a percussion instrument during festivities, often to accompany dancing (68:25; 149:3; 150:4). • The ***sweet lyre*** and ***the harp,*** both stringed instruments, are the instruments most frequently mentioned in the psalms (e.g., 33:2; 57:8; 71:22; 150:3).

81:3 The ***ram's horn*** mustered armies and announced special holy days (47:5; 98:6). • ***new moon:*** The first day of the lunar month marked ***a festival.***

81:4-5 The festival, a time to celebrate and listen to the Lord, took place at God's appointed time.

81:5 ***for Israel:*** Literally *for Joseph.* The tribes of Ephraim and Manasseh (the sons of Joseph) are used here to refer to the entire nation of Israel.

81:6-7 The Lord heard Israel's cry in Egypt and rescued them from oppressive slavery.

81:8-10 God pleads with his people to remember the covenant and the Ten Commandments.

81:10 God emphasizes that he and no one else ***rescued*** Israel. • The nation should ***open*** its ***mouth wide*** to take in God's word (cp. Deut 8:3; Ezek 3:1).

81:11-16 The Lord helps Israel to understand that their failure was not because of his weakness.

81:13-14 God wants to give his children his goodness, but only if they ***listen*** (Isa 1:18-19; 28:12; 48:18-19; see Deut 6:3). • God promises to ***subdue*** the ***enemies*** (Deut 9:3) of those who walk the ***paths*** of obedience and loyalty. He will also richly feed his people (Isa 1:19).

Ps 82 God condemns those who mistreat the helpless.

82:1 ***God presides*** and stands ready to render ***judgment*** (see Isa 3:13). • ***heaven's court:*** See Job 1:6. • ***heavenly beings:*** See notes on 29:1-2; 58:1.

82:2 Since justice marks God's reign (89:4), he opposes ***favoring the wicked.*** So the psalmist is perplexed and cries out to God for justice (82:3-4, 8).

82:4 Job 29:12
82:6 *John 10:34
[i]*elyon* (5945)
‣Ps 91:1
82:7 Ps 49:12; 83:11
82:8 Ps 2:8; 12:5
Rev 11:15
83:1 Ps 28:1; 109:1
83:2 Ps 2:1; 81:15
Isa 17:12
83:3 Ps 31:20
83:4 Esth 3:5-6
83:5 Ps 2:2
83:6 Gen 25:12-16
2 Chr 20:1, 10
Ps 137:7
83:7 1 Sam 4:1; 15:2
2 Chr 20:10
Ezek 27:2-3, 9
83:9 Judg 4:22-23
83:11 Judg 7:25; 8:21
83:12 2 Chr 20:11
83:14 Deut 32:22
Isa 9:18
83:15 Job 9:17
Ps 58:9
83:16 Ps 109:29
83:18 Ps 59:13
Isa 45:21

4 Rescue the poor and helpless;
deliver them from the grasp of evil people.
5 But these oppressors know nothing;
they are so ignorant!
They wander about in darkness,
while the whole world is shaken to the core.
6 I say, 'You are gods;
you are all children of the [i]Most High.
7 But you will die like mere mortals
and fall like every other ruler.' "

8 Rise up, O God, and judge the earth,
for all the nations belong to you.

PSALM 83

A song. A psalm of Asaph.

1 O God, do not be silent!
Do not be deaf.
Do not be quiet, O God.
2 Don't you hear the uproar of your enemies?
Don't you see that your arrogant enemies are rising up?
3 They devise crafty schemes against your people;
they conspire against your precious ones.
4 "Come," they say, "let us wipe out Israel as a nation.
We will destroy the very memory of its existence."
5 Yes, this was their unanimous decision.
They signed a treaty as allies against you—
6 these Edomites and Ishmaelites;
Moabites and Hagrites;
7 Gebalites, Ammonites, and Amalekites;
and people from Philistia and Tyre.
8 Assyria has joined them, too,
and is allied with the descendants of Lot. *Interlude*
9 Do to them as you did to the Midianites
and as you did to Sisera and Jabin at the Kishon River.
10 They were destroyed at Endor,
and their decaying corpses fertilized the soil.
11 Let their mighty nobles die as Oreb and Zeeb did.
Let all their princes die like Zebah and Zalmunna,
12 for they said, "Let us seize for our own use
these pasturelands of God!"
13 O my God, scatter them like tumbleweed,
like chaff before the wind!
14 As a fire burns a forest
and as a flame sets mountains ablaze,
15 chase them with your fierce storm;
terrify them with your tempest.
16 Utterly disgrace them
until they submit to your name,
O LORD.
17 Let them be ashamed and terrified forever.
Let them die in disgrace.
18 Then they will learn that you alone are
called the LORD,
that you alone are the Most High,
supreme over all the earth.

82:5 The unjust ***oppressors*** cannot bring or restore order. ***They wander about in darkness***, unmoved by circumstances even when the whole world order falls apart around them (cp. 11:3).

82:6-7 The ***gods*** (see notes on 29:1-2; 58:1), ***like mere mortals***, cannot escape the judgment common to human rulers. Jesus quoted from this passage in John 10:34.

82:8 The ***nations belong to*** God; he will take over the realms formerly ruled by local deities and give them to his people, just as he did with the Promised Land.

Ps 83 This community lament asks God for rescue and victory. The terse poetry suggests difficult times. A powerful coalition desires to destroy Israel (83:1-4) and allies itself against God (83:5-8). Recalling the fate of others who came against Israel (83:9-12), the psalmist prays that the same will happen to these enemies (83:13-16) so that God will receive honor among them (83:17-18). It is unclear whether this psalm arose out of a specific historical instance of opposition by these nations, or if it is a poetic collage of nations representing Israel's enemies.

83:1-4 The enemy has successfully intimidated God's people, so the poet prays that the Lord will hear and act.

83:5-8 ***signed a treaty:*** The ***allies*** agreed to fight against God and his people. The nations that are named in the alliance were situated around Israel and Judah.

83:6-7 The ***Edomites***, descendants of Esau, were located to the southeast of Judah (see Gen 25:30; 32:3; 36:1-8). • ***Ishmaelites*** were desert-dwelling descendants of Hagar. • ***Moabites*** and ***Ammonites*** descended from Lot; both were located to the east of Israel and Judah. • The ***Hagrites*** were possibly located north of the Ammonites (1 Chr 5:10).

83:7 The ***Gebalites*** probably came from Gebal/Byblos on the coast of Lebanon. • The ***Amalekites*** were located south of Israel in the Negev. • ***Philistia*** was southwest of Judah, by the Mediterranean Sea. • ***Tyre*** was a port city on the Mediterranean, northwest of Israel.

83:8 ***Assyria*** was northeast of Israel and north of the Persian Gulf. • The ***descendants of Lot*** were the Moabites and the Ammonites (83:6-7).

83:9-18 The psalmist prays that God will miraculously destroy the new coalition as he did three other enemies; doing so would bring him glory.

83:9-11 The ***Midianites***, ruled by ***Zebah*** and ***Zalmunna*** and led by ***Oreb and Zeeb***, were Israel's enemy in the days of Gideon (Judg 7:1–8:5). Barak's coalition defeated ***Sisera and Jabin*** (Judg 4).

83:12 The coalition's motivation for wiping out Israel was to acquire the land (see Jer 3:19).

83:13 ***tumbleweed . . . chaff:*** This dry plant material easily blows away (see Isa 17:13).

83:14-15 ***fire . . . fierce storm . . . tempest:*** These are images of God's manifestation in judgment (see note on 18:7-15; Isa 29:6).

PSALM 84

For the choir director: A psalm of the descendants of Korah, to be accompanied by a stringed instrument.

1 How lovely is your dwelling place,
O LORD of Heaven's Armies.
2 I long, yes, I faint with longing
to enter the courts of the LORD.
With my whole being, body and soul,
I will shout joyfully to the living God.
3 Even the sparrow finds a home,
and the swallow builds her nest and
raises her young
at a place near your altar,
O LORD of Heaven's Armies, my King
and my God!
4 What joy for those who can live in your
house,
always singing your praises.
Interlude
5 What [j]joy for those whose strength
comes from the LORD,
who have set their minds on a
pilgrimage to Jerusalem.
6 When they walk through the Valley of
Weeping,
it will become a place of refreshing
springs.
The autumn rains will clothe it with
blessings.
7 They will continue to grow stronger,
and each of them will appear before
God in Jerusalem.
8 O LORD God of Heaven's Armies, hear my
prayer.
Listen, O God of Jacob. *Interlude*
9 O God, look with favor upon the king,
our [k]shield!
Show favor to the one you have
anointed.
10 A single day in your courts
is better than a thousand anywhere
else!
I would rather be a gatekeeper in the
house of my God
than live the good life in the homes of
the wicked.
11 For the LORD God is our sun and our
[a]shield.
He gives us grace and glory.
The LORD will withhold no good thing
from those who do what is right.
12 O LORD of Heaven's Armies,
what [b]joy for those who trust in you.

PSALM 85

For the choir director: A psalm of the descendants of Korah.

1 LORD, you poured out blessings on your
land!
You restored the fortunes of Israel.
2 You [c]forgave the guilt of your people—
yes, you covered all their sins.
Interlude
3 You held back your fury.
You kept back your blazing anger.

84:1 Ps 27:4
84:2 Ps 42:1-2; 63:1
84:3 Ps 43:4
84:4 Ps 65:4
84:5 Ps 81:1 [j]*'ashrey* (0835) ‣Ps 84:12
84:6 Ps 107:35
84:7 Isa 40:31
84:9 Ps 115:9-11 [k]*magen* (4043) ‣Ps 84:11
84:10 Ps 27:4
84:11 Ps 2:12 [a]*magen* (4043) ‣Ps 89:18
84:12 Ps 28:7 [b]*'ashrey* (0835) ‣Ps 94:12
85:1 Jer 30:18
85:2 Ps 32:1 Jer 31:33-34 [c]*nasa'* (5375) ‣Ps 99:8
85:3 Ps 78:38

Ps 84 The psalmist expresses his deep spiritual longing for God's presence. He faints with longing as he reflects on the Temple and on pilgrims making the journey to Jerusalem (84:1-7). He prays for himself and for the community (84:8-9). The conclusion of the psalm (84:10-12) clarifies that the Temple represents God—the psalmist truly longs for God's presence. He knows that God's goodness is greater than life and that only God can give his people favor and honor (84:10-11).

84:TITLE ***to be accompanied by a stringed instrument:*** Hebrew *according to the gittith.*

84:1-4 The psalmist is far from the Temple. He turns toward it in hopeful reflection.

84:3 The poet envies the birds that have nesting places in and around the Temple.

84:4 The priests and Temple personnel lived in the Temple.

84:5-7 The pilgrimage to Jerusalem reenacted the Exodus, when God marvelously provided for his people (see 78:15-16; 105:41). The psalmist imagines the pains of travel turning to the joy of arrival.

84:5 Travelers needed ***strength*** to meet the challenges of ***pilgrimage*** by foot along unpaved paths, in all kinds of weather and with the possibility of assaults.

84:6 The ***Valley of Weeping*** (or *Valley of Poplars;* Hebrew reads *valley of Baca*) probably refers to the anguish that lonely pilgrims endured (see 23:4), rather than to an actual location. • ***refreshing springs . . . autumn rains:*** Even when pilgrims feel totally exhausted, the prospect of drawing near to the Lord renews their spirits (cp. Isa 35:6-10; 41:18-20; 43:17-20; 49:10).

84:7 ***Jerusalem:*** Hebrew *Zion.* See "Mount Zion, the City of God" at Ps 48, p. 947.

84:9 Both kings and priests were ***anointed*** to dedicate them for service (see 132:17; Exod 28:41; 1 Sam 9:16; 16:1-13; cp. Isa 61:1; Acts 10:38).

84:10 The psalmist viewed being in God's presence as much ***better than*** being ***anywhere else.***

84:11 Some people worshiped the ***sun*** as a god, but the true God provides all that anyone needs.

Ps 85 The psalmist leads the postexilic community in lament and prayer for full redemption. He ponders God's past rescue of Israel from exile (85:1-3), longs for greater evidence of God's goodness, and leads the community in prayer for full restoration (85:4-7). God responds with a message of peace (85:8-9), and the psalm concludes with a lyrical outburst at the grandeur of God's salvation (85:10-13).

85:1-5 Though the psalmist gratefully acknowledges God's goodness, he also asks God whether his wrath will last forever.

85:1 God ***restored the fortunes*** of Israel by bringing the nation back from exile (see 14:7; 126:1). • ***of Israel:*** Literally *of Jacob.* See note on 44:4.

85:2 When God ***forgave the guilt*** of ***their sins,*** he gave the people the possibility of fellowship with him (see 32:5).

85:4
Ps 80:3, 7
[d]*'elohim* (0430)
‣ Ps 85:8
85:5
Ps 74:1; 79:5; 80:4
85:8
[e]*'el* (0410)
‣ Isa 42:5
85:9
John 1:14
85:10
Prov 3:3
Isa 32:17
85:12
Ps 84:11
Jas 1:17
86:2
Ps 4:3; 25:20
86:4
[f]*nepesh* (5315)
‣ Ps 103:1
86:5
Ps 103:8; 130:4
86:6
Ps 55:1
86:7
Ps 50:14-15
86:8
Exod 15:11
Deut 3:24
86:9
Isa 66:23
Rev 15:3-4
86:10
Deut 32:39
Isa 44:6, 8
Mark 12:29
1 Cor 8:4
86:11
Ps 25:5
Jer 32:39
[g]*'emeth* (0571)
‣ Ps 119:142
[h]*yare'* (3372)
‣ Ps 112:1
86:12
Ps 111:1
[i]*lebab* (3824)
‣ Ps 141:4
[j]*yadah* (3034)
‣ Ps 100:4
86:13
Ps 30:3
86:14
Ps 54:3

4 Now restore us again, O [d]God of our
salvation.
Put aside your anger against us once
more.
5 Will you be angry with us always?
Will you prolong your wrath to all
generations?
6 Won't you revive us again,
so your people can rejoice in you?
7 Show us your unfailing love, O LORD,
and grant us your salvation.

8 I listen carefully to what [e]God the LORD
is saying,
for he speaks peace to his faithful
people.
But let them not return to their
foolish ways.
9 Surely his salvation is near to those who
fear him,
so our land will be filled with his
glory.

10 Unfailing love and truth have met
together.
Righteousness and peace have kissed!
11 Truth springs up from the earth,
and righteousness smiles down from
heaven.
12 Yes, the LORD pours down his blessings.
Our land will yield its bountiful
harvest.
13 Righteousness goes as a herald before
him,
preparing the way for his steps.

PSALM 86

A prayer of David.

1 Bend down, O LORD, and hear my prayer;
answer me, for I need your help.
2 Protect me, for I am devoted to you.
Save me, for I serve you and trust you.
You are my God.
3 Be merciful to me, O Lord,
for I am calling on you constantly.
4 Give [f]me happiness, O Lord,
for I give myself to you.
5 O Lord, you are so good, so ready to
forgive,
so full of unfailing love for all who ask
for your help.
6 Listen closely to my prayer, O LORD;
hear my urgent cry.
7 I will call to you whenever I'm in trouble,
and you will answer me.

8 No pagan god is like you, O Lord.
None can do what you do!
9 All the nations you made
will come and bow before you, Lord;
they will praise your holy name.
10 For you are great and perform
wonderful deeds.
You alone are God.

11 Teach me your ways, O LORD,
that I may live according to your
[g]truth!
Grant me purity of heart,
so that I may [h]honor you.
12 With all my [i]heart I will [j]praise you,
O Lord my God.
I will give glory to your name forever,
13 for your love for me is very great.
You have rescued me from the depths
of death.

14 O God, insolent people rise up
against me;
a violent gang is trying to kill me.
You mean nothing to them.

85:6-7 This prayer for renewal is based on God's ***unfailing love*** for his people.

85:8-9 When *God the LORD* speaks, ***his faithful people*** listen. He promises them ***peace***, meaning wholeness and well-being (see 37:11). They fear the Lord and know that he and ***his salvation*** are ***near*** to them. • The Lord does not tolerate ***foolish ways***, such as those that resulted in the Exile.

85:10-13 In the glorious world of renewal and salvation, all the qualities of God's care—***love, truth, righteousness***, and ***peace***—come together and transform the created order into something new (see Isa 32:15-20).

85:13 ***Righteousness*** is like a messenger preparing the world for God's coming in response to the prayers of his people (85:4-7; 89:14).

Ps 86 The psalmist invokes God's help and praises his character in a lament prompted by the presence of evil (86:14, 17). All people will worship the gracious and almighty God (86:8-10). To this end, the poet commits himself to a lifestyle of ethical integrity (86:11) and praising the Lord (86:12-13). The last stanza contrasts the qualities of evil people with those of the Lord (86:14-17).

86:TITLE This is the only psalm connected with ***David*** in Book Three.

86:1-4 God's devoted servant prays for mercy. The psalmist sees himself as a member of the covenant community and as a citizen of the world.

86:5-7 The psalmist appeals to God to remain true to his character, which is the basis for hope.

86:5 The psalmist recounts the catalog of divine perfections (Exod 34:6-7), especially God's willingness to forgive sin (see 32:5; 85:2; 145:7-10).

86:8-10 ***All the nations*** must submit themselves to the Lord and worship him (45:17; 117:1; 148:7-11).

86:11 The poet responds to the Lord by seeking faithful instruction in the ***truth***. • An individual with ***purity of heart*** has integrity and wholeness (see 73:1).

86:12-13 In anticipation of God's rescue, the psalmist praises him and trusts in his goodness.

86:13 *of death:* Hebrew *of Sheol.* See note on 6:5.

86:14-17 The arrogant exist both inside and outside the community. The psalmist asks for a vision of God's character; God is so great that just a glimpse of his goodness will shut the mouths of the wicked.

15 But you, O Lord,
are a God of compassion and mercy,
[k]slow to get angry
and filled with unfailing love and faithfulness.
16 Look down and have mercy on me.
Give your strength to your servant;
save me, the son of your servant.
17 Send me a sign of your favor.
Then those who hate me will be put to shame,
for you, O LORD, help and comfort me.

PSALM 87

A song. A psalm of the descendants of Korah.

1 On the holy mountain
stands the city founded by the LORD.
2 He loves the city of Jerusalem
more than any other city in Israel.
3 O city of God,
what glorious things are said of you!
Interlude

4 I will count [a]Egypt and Babylon among
those who know me—
also Philistia and Tyre, and even
distant Ethiopia.
They have all become citizens of
Jerusalem!
5 Regarding Jerusalem it will be said,
"Everyone enjoys the rights of
citizenship there."
And the Most High will personally
bless this city.
6 When the LORD registers the nations, he
will say,
"They have all become citizens of
Jerusalem." *Interlude*

7 The people will play flutes and sing,
"The source of my life springs from
Jerusalem!"

PSALM 88

For the choir director: A psalm of the descendants of Korah. A song to be sung to the tune "The Suffering of Affliction." A psalm of Heman the Ezrahite.

1 O LORD, God of my salvation,
I cry out to you by day.
I come to you at night.
2 Now hear my prayer;
listen to my cry.
3 For my life is full of troubles,
and death draws near.
4 I am as good as dead,
like a strong man with no strength left.
5 They have left me among the dead,
and I lie like a corpse in a grave.
I am forgotten,
cut off from your care.
6 You have thrown me into the lowest pit,
into the darkest depths.
7 Your anger weighs me down;
with wave after wave you have
engulfed me. *Interlude*

8 You have driven my friends away
by making me repulsive to them.
I am in a trap with no way of escape.
9 My eyes are blinded by my tears.
Each day I beg for your help, O LORD;
I lift my hands to you for mercy.
10 Are your wonderful deeds of any use to
the dead?
Do the dead rise up and praise you?
Interlude

86:15 [k]*'arek 'appayim* (0750, 0639) ‣Ps 103:8
86:16 Ps 68:35
86:17 Ps 112:10; 118:13; 119:122
87:1 Ps 78:68-69 Isa 28:16
87:2 Ps 78:67-68
87:3 Ps 46:4; 48:8 Isa 60:1
87:4 Ps 45:12; 68:31 Isa 19:23-25 [a]*rahab* (7293) ‣Ps 89:10
87:5 Ps 48:8
87:6 Isa 4:2-4
87:7 Ps 36:9
88:1 Ps 22:2 Luke 18:7
88:2 Ps 18:6; 86:1
88:3 Ps 107:18; 116:3
88:4 Ps 28:1
88:5 Ps 31:12 Isa 53:8
88:6 Ps 32:4; 69:15; 143:3 Lam 3:55
88:7 Ps 42:7
88:8 Job 19:19; 30:10 Ps 31:11
88:9 Job 11:13 Ps 6:7; 22:2
88:10 Ps 6:5

86:15 God has *mercy* on his people (51:1); he is gracious (25:6), ***slow to get angry*** (103:8; 145:8), and ***filled with unfailing love and faithfulness*** (Hebrew *khesed* and *'emeth*; 143:1). This verse repeats a theme first expressed in Exod 34:7; Num 14:18 (cp. 103:8; 145:8; Neh 9:17; Joel 2:13; Jon 4:2).

Ps 87 This psalm envisions Jerusalem as the city of God where all the nations are citizens.

87:1 Jerusalem was Israel's capital and the location of the Temple, God's earthly palace (see Ps 84).

87:2 This verse reads literally *He loves the gates of Zion more than all the dwellings of Jacob.* See note on 44:4.

87:4 As great as Zion is, it will be even greater when it becomes an international city where believers from all the nations have citizenship. • ***Egypt:*** Hebrew *Rahab*, the name of a mythical sea monster that represents chaos in ancient literature. The name is used here as a poetic name for Egypt (Isa 30:7). In other passages Rahab refers to the sea monsters themselves (89:10; see Job 9:13). • God keeps a record of all who confess him as their Lord (Dan 7:10; Rev 13:8). • ***Ethiopia:*** Hebrew *Cush.*

87:5-6 ***Jerusalem*** (Hebrew *Zion*) becomes the international city where all God's children are ***citizens.***

87:7 ***will play flutes:*** Or *will dance.*

Ps 88 In this lament, the psalmist sees himself as cast out from God's presence. At first, he calls on the Lord. When he finds no relief from his suffering, he presents three charges against God (88:6-7, 8-12, 13-17).

88:TITLE ***psalm:*** Hebrew *maskil.* This may be a literary or musical term. • ***Heman the Ezrahite*** might be a sage from Solomon's time (1 Kgs 4:31), a descendant of Judah (1 Chr 2:6), or a member of the Levitical family charged with singing at the Temple (1 Chr 15:17; 2 Chr 5:12).

88:1-5 The psalmist calls on the ***LORD*** for ***salvation.***

88:3 ***death:*** Hebrew *Sheol*, the place of the dead.

88:6-7 In his first charge, the psalmist blames the Lord for his demise. God's overpowering anger did not make sense. • The phrase ***the darkest depths*** implies the place of the dead (143:3; see Lam 3:6) or the depths of the sea (68:22; 69:1-2).

88:8-12 In his second charge, the psalmist claims that God has isolated him and caused his loneliness (cp. 31:11; 38:11). Loneliness was a curse in a culture where relationships were more important than personal achievement.

88:12 Job 10:20-21
88:13 Ps 5:3; 119:147
88:14 Job 13:24; Ps 13:1
88:15 Job 6:4
88:17 Ps 22:12, 16
88:18 Job 19:13; Ps 31:11; 38:11
89:1 Ps 40:10; 59:16
89:2 Ps 36:5
89:3 Ps 132:11; Isa 9:7; Luke 1:31-33
89:4 2 Sam 7:16; Isa 9:7; Luke 1:33; [b]*zera'* (2233) ‣Isa 53:10
89:5 [c]*qahal* (6951) ‣Ps 149:1
89:6 Ps 29:1; 96:4; [d]*ben 'el* (1121, 0410) ‣Hos 1:10
89:7 Ps 47:2; 96:4

11 Can those in the grave declare your
unfailing love?
Can they proclaim your faithfulness
in the place of destruction?
12 Can the darkness speak of your
wonderful deeds?
Can anyone in the land of
forgetfulness talk about your
righteousness?
13 O LORD, I cry out to you.
I will keep on pleading day by day.
14 O LORD, why do you reject me?
Why do you turn your face from me?
15 I have been sick and close to death since
my youth.
I stand helpless and desperate before
your terrors.
16 Your fierce anger has
overwhelmed me.
Your terrors have paralyzed me.
17 They swirl around me like floodwaters
all day long.
They have engulfed me completely.
18 You have taken away my companions
and loved ones.
Darkness is my closest friend.

PSALM 89

A psalm of Ethan the Ezrahite.

1 I will sing of the LORD's unfailing love
forever!
Young and old will hear of your
faithfulness.
2 Your unfailing love will last forever.
Your faithfulness is as enduring as the
heavens.
3 The LORD said, "I have made a covenant
with David, my chosen servant.
I have sworn this oath to him:
4 'I will establish your [b]descendants as
kings forever;
they will sit on your throne from now
until eternity.'" *Interlude*
5 All heaven will praise your great
wonders, LORD;
[c]myriads of angels will praise you for
your faithfulness.
6 For who in all of heaven can compare
with the LORD?
What [d]mightiest angel is anything like
the LORD?
7 The highest angelic powers stand in awe
of God.

The Exile in the Psalms (Ps 89)

Ps 107:1-22; 126:1-6; Lev 26:27-45; Deut 28:36-37, 63-68; 30:1-5; 2 Kgs 17:5-23; 24:1–25:21; Ezra 5:12; Isa 5:13; 27:13; 52:1-12; 59:10; Jer 2:37; 3:18; 4:13; Ezek 6:9; 20:41; 37:1-14; Amos 5:11; Mic 6:14-15

Israel's kings repeatedly rebelled against God, and the people of Israel sinned and broke their covenant with him. God therefore declared that he would bring the curses of the covenant upon them and their nation (see Deut 28:15-68; cp., e.g., Isa 59:10; Jer 4:13; Amos 5:11; Mic 6:14-15). In his wrath, God sent the Assyrian and Babylonian armies to execute this sentence, and all but a few of the Israelites were taken into exile (see 2 Kgs 24:1–25:21).

The Exile shaped many of the psalms; we see its impact working behind the scenes in their images and themes. The grief, anguish, and confusion of the Exile are distilled into several questions that the psalmist addresses: How long will God's wrath last (89:46)? Does God understand human frailty (89:47-48)? Is God true to his nature (89:49)? Is God just in not avenging his people (89:50-51)? Has God abandoned David's royal line (89:38-39)?

These questions were on the minds of God's people during and after the Exile. Some of their doubts raise questions concerning God's ability to rule. Rather than dismissing these questions, wise readers listen, reflect, and study the answers that Scripture gives. The definitive answer came in the Lord Jesus Christ (see Isa 52:1–54:17; Luke 1:46-55, 67-79; 4:18-19; Rom 6:6, 16-22; Heb 12:22-24). However, those who experienced the Exile could only dimly foresee his coming. They asked these hard questions and lived without clear answers.

88:11 *in the place of destruction?* Hebrew *in Abaddon?*

88:13-17 In his third charge, the psalmist accuses the Lord of rejecting him. The force and apparent cruelty of the psalmist's suffering overwhelm him.

88:18 The psalmist restates his second and first charges.

Ps 89 Book Three (Pss 73–89) begins and ends with weighty questions. Though Ps 89 begins with a praise-filled account of how the Lord exalted the throne of David (89:1-37), the psalmist protests the Lord's apparent rejection of his covenant with David (89:38-51; see 2 Sam 7:8-16).

89:TITLE *psalm:* Hebrew *maskil.* This may be a literary or musical term.
• *Ethan the Ezrahite* was a wise man (see 88:TITLE and note; 1 Kgs 4:31).

89:1 God's *unfailing love* gives reason to celebrate *forever.*

89:3-4 The psalmist restates God's covenant with David (see also 89:19-37).

89:3 The Lord has *sworn* by his own holiness (89:35; see 110:4).

89:5-8 God is the absolute standard of *faithfulness*, commitment, and order. The angelic beings and the heavens testify to his constancy.

89:5 Praise for God's greatness (see 8:1) comes from the inhabitants of *heaven* who witness his *faithfulness.*

89:6 *mightiest angel:* Literally *son of God* (see note on 29:1-2).

He is far more awesome than all who
surround his throne.
8 O LORD God of Heaven's Armies!
Where is there anyone as mighty as
you, O LORD?
You are entirely faithful.
9 You rule the oceans.
You subdue their storm-tossed waves.
10 You crushed the great [e]sea monster.
You scattered your enemies with your
mighty arm.
11 The heavens are yours, and the earth is
yours;
everything in the world is yours—you
created it all.
12 You created north and south.
Mount Tabor and Mount Hermon
praise your name.
13 Powerful is your arm!
Strong is your hand!
Your right hand is lifted high in
glorious strength.
14 Righteousness and justice are the
foundation of your throne.
Unfailing love and truth walk before
you as attendants.
15 Happy are those who hear the joyful call
to worship,
for they will walk in the light of your
presence, LORD.
16 They rejoice all day long in your
wonderful reputation.
They [f]exult in your righteousness.
17 You are their glorious strength.
It pleases you to make us strong.
18 Yes, our [g]protection comes from the LORD,
and he, the Holy One of Israel, has
given us our king.
19 Long ago you spoke in a vision to your
faithful people.
You said, "I have raised up a warrior.
I have selected him from the common
people to be king.
20 I have found my servant David.
I have [h]anointed him with my holy oil.
21 I will steady him with my hand;
with my powerful arm I will make
him strong.
22 His enemies will not defeat him,
nor will the wicked overpower him.
23 I will beat down his adversaries before
him
and destroy those who hate him.
24 My faithfulness and unfailing love will
be with him,
and by my authority he will grow in
power.
25 I will extend his rule over the sea,
his dominion over the rivers.
26 And he will call out to me, 'You are my
Father,
my God, and the [i]Rock of my
salvation.'
27 I will make him my firstborn son,
the mightiest king on earth.
28 I will love him and be kind to him forever;
my covenant with him will never end.
29 I will preserve an heir for him;
his throne will be as endless as the
days of heaven.
30 But if his descendants forsake my
instructions
and fail to obey my regulations,
31 if they do not obey my decrees
and fail to keep my commands,
32 then I will punish their sin with the rod,
and their disobedience with beating.
33 But I will never stop loving him
nor fail to keep my promise to him.
34 No, I will not break my covenant;
I will not take back a single word I said.

89:8 Ps 35:10; 71:19
89:9 Ps 65:7; 107:29
89:10 Ps 18:14; [e]*rahab* (7293) ‣Isa 30:7
89:11 Gen 1:1; 1 Chr 29:11; Ps 24:1
89:12 Josh 12:1; 19:22
89:13 Ps 118:16
89:14 Ps 97:2
89:15 Num 10:10
89:16 [f]*rum* (7311) ‣Ps 99:2
89:17 Ps 44:3; 75:10; 148:14
89:18 Ps 47:9; [g]*magen* (4043) ‣Prov 2:7
89:19 2 Sam 17:10; 1 Kgs 11:34
89:20 1 Sam 16:13; *Acts 13:22; [h]*mashakh* (4886) ‣Isa 61:1
89:22 2 Sam 7:10-11
89:23 2 Sam 7:9
89:26 2 Sam 7:14; 1 Chr 22:10; [i]*tsur* (6697) ‣Ps 92:15
89:27 Ps 2:7; 72:11; Rev 19:16
89:29 Isa 9:7; Jer 33:17
89:30 2 Sam 7:14
89:33 2 Sam 7:15

89:9-13 In this hymn, the psalmist celebrates God's comprehensive and powerful sovereignty over nature.

89:9-10 ***the great sea monster:*** The Hebrew term *Rahab* refers to a mythical sea monster that represents chaos in ancient literature (see 87:4 and note). The Lord rules over all parts of the created order, including evil. • ***You scattered your enemies:*** The Lord will crush (Luke 1:51) evil powers that oppose him (2:1-3). • ***with your mighty arm:*** This phrase represents God's strength (89:13).

89:12 ***Mount Tabor*** was in northern Israel. ***Mount Hermon*** formed the extreme northern border of the nation.

89:14-18 God rules wisely over creation. The qualities of ***righteousness, justice,*** and faithfulness fit the profile of a wise ruler. The ***happy*** people who live under his rule enjoy his ***protection.***

89:15-16 Those who are wise ***worship*** God, ***walk*** in his ***light, rejoice*** in their relationship with him, and ***exult in*** his character.

89:17-18 The Lord protects his people with the same power by which he established the created order.

89:19-37 The Lord chose David as his son and as king of Israel (see 2:4-6; 2 Sam 7:8-16) to provide protection for his people.

89:20 ***I have anointed him:*** This is the verb from which *anointed one* (Hebrew *messiah*) is derived.

89:26-29 The Lord adopted David as his ***son,*** appointed him as his commander over the nations, and promised to support him ***forever.*** Verse 26 recalls a verse from David's song of praise (2 Sam 22:47).

89:27 David would be the most eminent of earthly kings. The Hebrew word translated ***mightiest*** is the same as the designation for God as "Most High" (*'elyon*).

89:29 The Lord writes his faithfulness in ***heaven,*** on the canvas of his universe (see 89:2). He records his commitment to the dynasty of David in the same way.

89:30-37 The Lord disciplines but does not reject his erring children. He foresees violation of trust and subsequent punishment, but he commits himself to uphold the covenant. His fidelity to David corresponds to his faithfulness to the created order.

89:34 Num 23:19 Jer 33:20-21
89:36 Ps 72:5
89:38 1 Chr 28:9
89:39 Ps 78:59
89:40 Lam 2:2, 5
89:42 Ps 13:2; 80:6
89:43 Ps 44:10
89:44 Ezek 28:7
89:45 Ps 44:15-16
89:46 Ps 13:1; 79:5
89:47 Ps 39:5-6
89:48 [i]*she'ol* (7585) ‣Ps 116:3
89:49 2 Sam 7:15
89:51 Ps 74:9-10, 18, 22
89:52 Ps 41:13; 106:48
90:1 Deut 33:27 Rev 21:3
90:2 Ps 102:24-25, 27 [k]*'olam* (5769) ‣Ps 92:8
90:3 Job 34:14-15 [a]*ben 'adam* (1121, 0120) ‣Isa 56:2
90:4 Ps 39:5 2 Pet 3:8
90:5 Isa 40:6
90:6 Ps 92:7

35 I have sworn an oath to David,
and in my holiness I cannot lie:
36 His dynasty will go on forever;
his kingdom will endure as the sun.
37 It will be as eternal as the moon,
my faithful witness in the sky!"
Interlude

38 But now you have rejected him and cast
him off.
You are angry with your anointed king.
39 You have renounced your covenant with
him;
you have thrown his crown in the
dust.
40 You have broken down the walls
protecting him
and ruined every fort defending him.
41 Everyone who comes along has robbed
him,
and he has become a joke to his
neighbors.
42 You have strengthened his enemies
and made them all rejoice.
43 You have made his sword useless
and refused to help him in battle.
44 You have ended his splendor
and overturned his throne.
45 You have made him old before his time
and publicly disgraced him.
Interlude

46 O LORD, how long will this go on?
Will you hide yourself forever?
How long will your anger burn like
fire?
47 Remember how short my life is,
how empty and futile this human
existence!
48 No one can live forever; all will die.
No one can escape the power of the
[i]grave. *Interlude*

49 Lord, where is your unfailing love?
You promised it to David with a
faithful pledge.
50 Consider, Lord, how your servants are
disgraced!
I carry in my heart the insults of so
many people.
51 Your enemies have mocked me, O LORD;
they mock your anointed king
wherever he goes.

52 Praise the LORD forever!
Amen and amen!

4. BOOK FOUR (PSS 90–106)

PSALM 90

A prayer of Moses, the man of God.

1 Lord, through all the generations
you have been our home!
2 Before the mountains were born,
before you gave birth to the earth and
the world,
from [k]beginning to [k]end, you are God.

3 You turn people back to dust, saying,
"Return to dust, you [a]mortals!"
4 For you, a thousand years are as a
passing day,
as brief as a few night hours.
5 You sweep people away like dreams that
disappear.
They are like grass that springs up in
the morning.
6 In the morning it blooms and flourishes,
but by evening it is dry and withered.

89:35 ***holiness:*** The Lord is wholly distinct from the created order (22:3); his character is totally pure. He does as he pleases (115:3), and he chooses to be faithful (89:1; 115:1); therefore, he ***cannot lie.***

89:38 ***You are angry:*** The harshness of God's wrath perplexes the psalmist.

89:40 ***broken down the walls:*** The Lord's people are completely vulnerable.

89:42 Although the Lord promised to strengthen David, he secretly ***strengthened*** David's ***enemies.***

89:46-47 The psalmist wonders if he will live to see the end of the Lord's ***anger.*** Our lifetimes are ***short,*** like a day in the Lord's sight (90:4, 10).

89:48 ***of the grave:*** Hebrew *of Sheol.* See note on 6:5.

89:50 The phrase ***your servants*** refers to the community loyal to the Lord.

89:52 This doxology concludes all of Book Three (Pss 73–89); it is not intended to be read as part of Ps 89. It stands in stark contrast to the anguish and questioning of Ps 89. Cp. 41:13; 106:48.

Book Four (Pss 90–106) Book Four can be understood as a poetic response to the problem of the Exile and the apparent suspension of David's royal line (see Ps 89). The response is that the Lord rules over the created order; his kingdom overcomes all chaos, anarchy, and confusion.

Ps 90 Although the Lord's people have made their home in him for generations, their sin widens the gap between them and their infinite Lord. The Lord's wrath against a person's sin might last a lifetime and yet be only a taste of his displeasure with sin. This lamentable situation calls the community to seek the Lord's light. Taking the first step means seeking restoration with the Lord on the basis of his compassion and love (90:13-14). He alone makes his servants glad and blesses their future generations (90:16-17).

90:TITLE ***Moses*** led God's people from slavery in Egypt to Mount Sinai, where he received the law and established God's covenant with Israel. • ***the man of God:*** Moses enjoyed a special relationship with God (Deut 33:1).

90:1-2 The Lord becomes the ***home*** of the godly; he has provided shelter for countless ***generations.*** The word translated *home* is not used frequently in the Psalter. It describes a place of safety where the Lord meets his needy people and cares for them (68:5; 71:3).

90:2 The Lord is the eternal God. • The Lord ***gave birth to the earth*** by creating it.

90:3-6 Unlike God, humans are mortal and transitory.

7 We wither beneath your anger;
we are overwhelmed by your fury.
8 You spread out our sins before you—
our secret sins—and you see them all.
9 We live our lives beneath your wrath,
ending our years with a groan.

10 Seventy years are given to us!
Some even live to eighty.
But even the best years are filled with
pain and trouble;
soon they disappear, and we fly away.
11 Who can comprehend the power of your
anger?
Your wrath is as awesome as the fear
you deserve.
12 Teach us to realize the brevity of life,
so that we may grow in wisdom.

13 O LORD, come back to us!
How long will you delay?
Take pity on your servants!
14 Satisfy us each morning with your
unfailing love,
so we may sing for joy to the end of
our lives.
15 Give us gladness in proportion to our
former misery!
Replace the evil years with good.
16 Let us, your servants, see you work
again;
let our children see your glory.
17 And may the Lord our God show us his
approval
and make our efforts successful.
Yes, make our efforts successful!

PSALM 91

1 Those who live in the shelter of the
[b]Most High
will find rest in the shadow of the
[c]Almighty.
2 This I declare about the LORD:
He alone is my refuge, my place of safety;
he is my God, and I trust him.
3 For he will rescue you from every trap
and protect you from deadly disease.
4 He will cover you with his feathers.
He will shelter you with his wings.
His faithful promises are your armor
and protection.
5 Do not be afraid of the terrors of the
night,
nor the arrow that flies in the day.
6 Do not dread the disease that stalks in
darkness,
nor the disaster that strikes at midday.
7 Though a thousand fall at your side,
though ten thousand are dying
around you,
these evils will not touch you.
8 Just open your eyes,
and see how the wicked are punished.

9 If you make the LORD your refuge,
if you make the Most High your shelter,
10 no evil will conquer you;
no plague will come near your home.
11 For he will order his [d]angels
to protect you wherever you go.
12 They will hold you up with their hands
so you won't even hurt your foot on a
stone.
13 You will trample upon lions and cobras;
you will crush fierce lions and
serpents under your feet!

14 The LORD says, "I will rescue those who
love me.

90:9 Ps 78:33
90:10 Ps 78:39; Eccl 12:2-7
90:11 Ps 76:7
90:12 Ps 39:4
90:13 Deut 32:36
90:14 Ps 36:8; 103:5; Jer 31:14
90:15 Ps 31:10; 86:4
90:16 Ps 44:1
90:17 Ps 27:4; Isa 26:12
91:1 Isa 25:4; 32:2; [b]*'elyon* (5945) ›Ps 97:9; [c]*shadday* (7706) ›Joel 1:15
91:2 Ps 18:2; 142:5; Jer 16:19
91:3 2 Chr 20:9; Ps 124:7
91:4 Ps 35:2; 57:1; 63:7
91:5 Job 5:19-23; Ps 23:4
91:6 Job 5:22
91:8 Ps 37:34
91:10 Prov 12:21
91:11 Ps 34:7; *Matt 4:6; *Luke 4:9-11; [d]*mal'ak* (4397) ›Ps 103:20
91:13 Judg 14:6; Luke 10:19

90:7-10 Sinners cannot escape God's wrath because the Lord sees their *sins*. Their fleeting *lives* are filled with afflictions.

90:9-10 A *groan* of sorrow (Ezek 2:10) sums up a life spent in facing the consequences of sin. • Humans cause *trouble* (see 10:6) and receive *pain* in return.

90:11-12 In the search for wisdom, no one *can comprehend* the Lord (see Isa 40:13). The appropriate human response to the Lord is godly *fear* (see 60:4). The Lord alone can *teach* humans to follow the path of *wisdom* (25:4-6).

90:13-17 The psalmist prays for the Lord's favor and restoration.

90:13 The phrase *your servants* refers to the community of those loyal to the Lord.

90:15 The psalmist calls upon the Lord to *give* the people *gladness* to replace their mourning (see 92:4-5).

90:16 The *children* represent future generations in contrast to the generations past (90:1).

90:17 Humans waste their *efforts* unless the Lord makes them *successful* (44:3).

Ps 91 This wisdom psalm expresses confidence in the Almighty God, who provides a shelter for those who take refuge in him. They receive redemption, life, and glory from the Lord, who loves and cares for those who seek him.

91:1-2 The Lord is an ancient *shelter* (see 90:1), open to those who seek *refuge* in him.

91:1 The *Most High* is an ancient title that expresses the Lord's exalted status (Gen 14:19) as the ruler and protector of the godly.

91:3-4 The psalmist invites the godly to trust in the Lord and find protection in him.

91:3 God protects the godly from *deadly disease* and even a destructive word.

91:4 The *armor* might refer to a body shield, while *protection* refers to a small shield worn on the arm. • *wings:* See note on 17:8.

91:5-8 The godly should *not be afraid*, because the Lord watches over them. These promises do not guarantee an escape from trouble, but they create an expectation of the Lord's goodness.

91:6 The reference to *disease* represents any kind of affliction.

91:9-13 The poet again invites the godly to seek refuge in the Lord and enjoy the benefits of divine protection.

91:11 *he will order his angels:* Satan cited these words when he tempted Jesus (Matt 4:6; Luke 4:10-11), but God makes this promise for those who obey him (91:14), not for those who arrogantly test him (Matt 4:4, 7).

91:14-16 The godly can trust the Lord's protection and provision.

91:15
1 Sam 2:30
Ps 50:15
John 12:26

92:1
[e]*zamar* (2167)
‣ Ps 138:1

92:3
1 Sam 10:5
1 Chr 13:8
Neh 12:27

92:5
Ps 40:5; 139:17
Rom 11:33

92:6
Ps 73:22

92:7
Ps 37:38

92:9
Ps 37:20; 68:1

92:8
[f]*olam* (5769)
‣ Ps 100:5

92:10
Ps 23:5; 75:10

92:11
Ps 54:7

92:14
Isa 37:31
John 15:2

92:15
Rom 9:14
[g]*tsur* (6697)
‣ Ps 144:1

93:1
Ps 65:6; 96:10; 97:1;
99:1; 104:1
Isa 51:9

I will protect those who trust in my
name.
15 When they call on me, I will answer;
I will be with them in trouble.
I will rescue and honor them.
16 I will reward them with a long life
and give them my salvation."

PSALM 92

A psalm. A song to be sung on the Sabbath Day.

1 It is good to give thanks to the LORD,
to [e]sing praises to the Most High.
2 It is good to proclaim your unfailing love
in the morning,
your faithfulness in the evening,
3 accompanied by the ten-stringed harp
and the melody of the lyre.

4 You thrill me, LORD, with all you have
done for me!
I sing for joy because of what you
have done.
5 O LORD, what great works you do!
And how deep are your thoughts.
6 Only a simpleton would not know,
and only a fool would not understand
this:
7 Though the wicked sprout like weeds
and evildoers flourish,
they will be destroyed forever.
8 But you, O LORD, will be exalted [f]forever.
9 Your enemies, LORD, will surely perish;
all evildoers will be scattered.
10 But you have made me as strong as a
wild ox.
You have anointed me with the finest
oil.
11 My eyes have seen the downfall of my
enemies;
my ears have heard the defeat of my
wicked opponents.
12 But the godly will flourish like palm
trees
and grow strong like the cedars of
Lebanon.
13 For they are transplanted to the LORD's
own house.
They flourish in the courts of our God.
14 Even in old age they will still produce
fruit;
they will remain vital and green.
15 They will declare, "The LORD is just!
He is my [g]rock!
There is no evil in him!"

PSALM 93

1 The LORD is king! He is robed in majesty.
Indeed, the LORD is robed in majesty
and armed with strength.
The world stands firm
and cannot be shaken.

91:14 Those who *love* the Lord will obey him (Deut 30:20; 1 Jn 5:3) and seek his protection (91:1; 145:18).

91:15 The Lord promises to ***answer*** the prayers of his people. • The Psalter often speaks of people honoring the Lord (50:15); here, God promises to ***honor*** the godly who risk everything for his sake (62:7; 71:21; 84:11).

91:16 A ***long life*** on earth represents just a small part of the Lord's goodness and eternal friendship (23:6).

Ps 92 Thanksgiving and praise open this psalm. The Lord—the Most High—is faithful and just in discerning between the godly and the wicked. The godly will enjoy a glorious, vigorous future, while the wicked will perish. The wise see and understand the Lord's works as they reveal his justice (92:6-7, 11, 15). The wicked, like grass, are quickly destroyed (92:7-10).

92:TITLE *on the Sabbath Day:* Jewish tradition assigned one psalm to each day of the week: Sunday (Ps 24), Monday (Ps 48), Tuesday (Ps 82), Wednesday (Ps 94), Thursday (Ps 81), Friday (Ps 93), and the Sabbath (Ps 92). This is the only psalm that indicates this use in its title.

92:1-3 The psalmist offers praise and thanksgiving for God's unfailing love and faithfulness.

92:4-7 Fools perish because they do not understand the Lord's marvelous works and eternal plans.

92:4-5 The Lord acts and the psalmist responds in praise (92:4). God's acts spring from his thoughts (92:5).

92:5-6 The Lord's ***thoughts*** do not make sense to the ***simpleton*** or the ***fool***, the immoral person who desires no wisdom (Prov 1:22; 10:23).

92:7 Even when the ungodly seem to grow luxuriantly (73:3-5), they have no future (92:9; see 1:6; 90:5-6; Isa 40:6-8).

92:8-10 The glory of the Lord provides the reason for the poet's renewed strength and glory, and for the imminent defeat of the enemy.

92:8 The transcendent Lord stays above the world of human experience. From this *exalted* place, he rules and judges (7:7), celebrates his victories (68:18; see Ps 47), comes to rescue the needy (102:19), brings an end to the wicked (92:7-8), and receives praise (148:1).

92:10 *as strong as a wild ox:* The Lord allows the psalmist to share his exaltation (92:8), thus ensuring victory.

92:11-15 The psalmist understands the Lord's mighty acts. He shares in the glory of the wise of heart.

92:12 Carvings of ***palm trees*** (1 Kgs 6:29, 32, 35; 7:36) adorned the Temple, and builders made rich use of ***cedars*** (1 Kgs 5:6). The trees represent the godly, who are planted in the very courts of the Temple.

92:13 The Temple area consisted of ***the LORD's own house*** and the ***courts*** that surrounded it.

92:15 *There is no evil in him!* The Lord is consistently just; he rightly judges everyone (see Zeph 3:5).

Pss 93-100 These psalms challenge the doubts created by the Exile (see Ps 89) and answer the questions asked in Ps 90:11, 13. The Lord has established a kingdom (Ps 93) that is characterized by the punishment of the wicked (Ps 94), reverent obedience among his people (Ps 95), justice for the poor (Ps 96), celebration in Zion (Ps 97), salvation for Israel (Ps 98), holiness (Ps 99), and praise (Ps 100).

Ps 93 The everlasting Lord gloriously establishes his kingship (cp. Pss 47, 99–100).

93:1 *robed in majesty:* The Lord stands victorious both before and after battle (see 45:3).

2 Your [h]throne, O LORD, has stood from
time immemorial.
You yourself are from the everlasting
past.
3 The floods have risen up, O LORD.
The floods have roared like thunder;
the floods have lifted their pounding
waves.
4 But mightier than the violent raging of
the seas,
mightier than the breakers on the
shore—
the LORD above is mightier than
these!
5 Your royal laws cannot be changed.
Your reign, O LORD, is holy forever and
ever.

PSALM 94

1 O LORD, the God of vengeance,
O God of vengeance, let your glorious
justice shine forth!
2 Arise, O judge of the earth.
Give the proud what they deserve.
3 How long, O LORD?
How long will the wicked be allowed
to gloat?
4 How long will they speak with
arrogance?
How long will these evil people boast?
5 They crush your people, LORD,
hurting those you claim as your own.
6 They kill widows and foreigners
and murder orphans.
7 "The LORD isn't looking," they say,
"and besides, the God of Israel doesn't
care."
8 Think again, you fools!
When will you finally catch on?
9 Is he deaf—the one who made your ears?
Is he blind—the one who formed your
eyes?
10 He punishes the nations—won't he also
punish you?
He knows everything—doesn't he also
know what you are doing?
11 The LORD knows people's thoughts;
he knows they are worthless!
12 [i]Joyful are those you discipline, LORD,
those you teach with your
instructions.
13 You give them relief from troubled times
until a pit is dug to capture the wicked.
14 The LORD will not reject his people;
he will not abandon his special
possession.
15 Judgment will again be founded on
justice,
and those with virtuous hearts will
pursue it.
16 Who will protect me from the wicked?
Who will stand up for me against
evildoers?
17 Unless the LORD had helped me,
I would soon have settled in the
silence of the grave.
18 I cried out, "I am slipping!"
but your unfailing love, O LORD,
supported me.
19 When doubts filled my mind,
your comfort gave me renewed hope
and cheer.

93:2 Lam 5:19 [h]*kisse'* (3678) ‣Ps 103:19
93:3 Ps 98:7-8
93:4 Ps 65:7
93:5 Ps 19:7; 1 Cor 3:17
94:1 Deut 32:35; Isa 35:4; Nah 1:2; Rom 12:19
94:4 Ps 31:18; 52:1
94:6 Isa 10:2
94:9 Exod 4:11; Prov 20:12
94:10 Ps 44:2
94:11 *1 Cor 3:20
94:12 Deut 8:5; Heb 12:5-6 [i]*'ashrey* (0835) ‣Ps 106:3
94:14 1 Sam 12:22; Rom 11:2
94:15 Isa 42:3; Mic 7:9
94:16 Num 10:35; Isa 33:10
94:17 Ps 124:1-2
94:19 Isa 57:18; 66:13

93:3-4 God's victory over natural chaos gives the psalmist confidence that the Lord will also defeat his present enemies (cp. Jer 46:8; 47:2).

93:5 Through his stable rule and ***royal laws***, the Lord orders the world. • ***Your reign*** (literally *your house*): The *house* from which God reigns might be the Lord's heavenly palace or the earthly Temple.

Ps 94 This plea for the Lord's justice includes both communal and individual expressions of lament (94:1-7, 16-23). The psalmist gives voice to the pain and suffering caused by the wicked, but he also depicts the comfort and stability of the Lord's protection. He calls on the Lord to avenge the needy against the arrogant and foolish, he rebukes such people for their folly (94:8-11), and he pronounces a blessing on the wise (94:12-15).

94:1-7 After the community falls victim to the *wicked* (94:5-7), they pray that the Lord will render *justice* (see 7:11; 9:12).

94:2 Just as the Lord's enemies rise up against him and his people (3:7; 93:3), he must *arise* and make retribution against the enemy (see 79:12; Isa 65:6).

94:6 ***widows . . . foreigners . . . orphans:*** The Lord's law protects needy people (Deut 24:17; 27:19), but they remain vulnerable in society.

94:7 The wicked think that they can get away with their vile acts and speech, foolishly assuming that God ***isn't looking*** or ***doesn't care.*** • ***of Israel:*** Literally *of Jacob.* See note on 44:4.

94:8-11 The psalmist rebukes human folly.

94:9 It is preposterous that those with *ears* and *eyes* would imagine their Creator to be ***deaf*** and ***blind***.

94:10 ***punishes:*** This word also carries the idea of "warns" (2:10), "disciplines" (6:1; 94:12), or "instructs" (16:7). The Lord disciplines his people to purify their character (Prov 3:11-12; Heb 12:6-11). He punishes his enemies by giving them what they deserve (1:6; Rom 6:23).

94:11 While the Lord's thoughts are deep, ***people's thoughts*** are ***worthless*** (cp. 92:5; 1 Cor 3:20).

94:12-15 True to his nature, the Lord rewards those who live by his wise instruction (see note on 1:2) and makes them happy according to his promises.

94:13 God's *relief* includes his comfort and rescue.

94:14 Even when it seems that he has, ***the LORD will not reject his people.***

94:16-23 The psalmist's prayer resumes (see 94:1-7) with a desperate cry for the Lord's justice; it concludes with the hopeful expectation that evil will end.

94:16 Only God has the power to ***stand up*** to the wicked (see 2:2).

94:18-19 The psalmist's experience of *slipping* contrasts with God's promise to stand with him (94:12-13; see 15:5; 93:1).

94:20
Ps 58:2

94:21
Exod 23:7
Matt 27:4
[j]*dam* (1818)
‣ Ezek 33:4

94:22
Ps 59:9; 71:7

94:23
Ps 7:16; 140:9, 11

95:2
Mic 6:6-8

95:4
Ps 135:5-6

95:5
Gen 1:9-10

95:7-11
*Heb 3:7-11, 15; 4:7

95:8
Exod 17:7
Num 20:13
Deut 6:16

95:9
Num 14:22

95:10
Acts 7:36; 13:18
Heb 3:10, 17

95:11
Deut 1:35
*Heb 4:3, 5

20 Can unjust leaders claim that God is on
their side—
leaders whose decrees permit
injustice?
21 They gang up against the righteous
and condemn the innocent to [j]death.
22 But the LORD is my fortress;
my God is the mighty rock where I
hide.
23 God will turn the sins of evil people back
on them.
He will destroy them for their sins.
The LORD our God will destroy them.

PSALM 95

1 Come, let us sing to the LORD!
Let us shout joyfully to the Rock of
our salvation.
2 Let us come to him with thanksgiving.
Let us sing psalms of praise to him.
3 For the LORD is a great God,
a great King above all gods.
4 He holds in his hands the depths of the
earth
and the mightiest mountains.
5 The sea belongs to him, for he made it.
His hands formed the dry land, too.

6 Come, let us worship and bow down.
Let us kneel before the LORD our maker,
7 for he is our God.
We are the people he watches over,
the flock under his care.

If only you would listen to his voice today!
8 The LORD says, "Don't harden your
hearts as Israel did at Meribah,
as they did at Massah in the
wilderness.
9 For there your ancestors tested and tried
my patience,
even though they saw everything I did.
10 For forty years I was angry with them,
and I said,
'They are a people whose hearts turn
away from me.
They refuse to do what I tell them.'
11 So in my anger I took an oath:
'They will never enter my place of
rest.' "

The Creator-King (Pss 93–100)

Pss 8, 19, 28–29, 33, 89, 104
Gen 1:1–2:4
Eccl 12:1-7, 13-14
Isa 40:25-28; 43:15; 44:24; 51:13
Jer 10:16
Acts 4:23-31
Col 3:10

The Psalter portrays Israel's view of God as the Creator, the great King over the world of nature and nations. God created and established the world, and he rules over it (95:4-5; 96:10; see 24:2; 78:69). The whole of creation is his handiwork. The Creator governs and cares for all that he made.

Several psalms celebrate the manifestation of God's glory in creation (Pss 8, 19, 29, 33, 89, and 104). Psalm 8 centers on God's endowing human beings with splendor and vesting them as his rulers in creation. Psalm 19 encourages reflection on creation in order to cultivate wisdom. Psalm 29 reveals God's power in the world and the stability of his creation. Psalm 33 exalts God's governance, order, and wisdom in creation and fosters the importance of wisdom. Psalm 89 lays the foundation of God's covenant with David on his commitment to creation (89:9-18).

Psalms 93–100 anticipate the worldwide dominion of God. When he comes into the world, he brings harmony and peace. The earth already belongs to him, and the Creator has demonstrated his power in history. Psalm 104 is a creation hymn that reworks the six days of creation into a marvelous lyric in praise of God's wisdom.

The psalms call upon all nations to acknowledge and praise God and to show their acceptance of his sovereign rule over all nations (see 9:11; 47:1-2, 7-9; 66:8; 67; 117:1).

Ps 95 This call to worship urges the people to respond to the Lord, the Shepherd, and to follow him faithfully. The previous generation, who refused to obey, did not receive the blessings of the Promised Land.

95:3-5 The Lord is the *great King* over the whole universe.

95:3 ***above all gods:*** The psalmist refutes idolatry and paganism (96:4-6; 135:15-18; see also Isa 46:5-7).

95:4-5 The whole created order owes its existence to the sovereign Lord alone—not to various gods.

95:6-7 The great King cares for his people as a shepherd cares for his *flock* (Isa 40:11). • The *LORD our maker,* the Creator of heaven and earth, also made a people for himself (Isa 45:9-12; 51:12-16).

95:8-11 If people want to enter into the Lord's rest, they need to respond immediately (see Heb 3:7–4:11).

95:8 To ***harden your hearts*** means to be stubborn and resist the Lord's grace (see Num 20:2-13; see also Matt 13:3-23; John 12:37-43; Eph 4:17-32; Heb 3:6-19; 4:6-11).

95:9 Israel's ***ancestors . . . saw*** the wonders of the Lord, but they foolishly did not try to grasp their significance (see 92:5-6).

95:11 The generation of Israel that wandered in the wilderness for forty years failed to enter the ***place of rest*** that Israel enjoyed after the conquest of the land (1 Kgs 8:56; see Deut 12:9). The Lord promised them the land and gave it to them (Isa 28:12), but they did not obey him (Isa 28:1). The warning reminds every generation of the need to obey in faith. • The rest that God provides includes peace, provision, and protection (132:14-18). The author of Hebrews challenged a new generation to enter the rest provided by Jesus Christ (Heb 3:7–4:13).

PSALM 96

Ps 96:1-13 // 1 Chr 16:23-33

1 Sing a new song to the LORD!
Let the whole earth sing to the LORD!
2 Sing to the LORD; praise his name.
Each day proclaim the good news that
he saves.
3 Publish his glorious deeds among the
nations.
Tell everyone about the amazing
things he does.
4 Great is the LORD! He is most worthy of
praise!
He is to be feared above all gods.
5 The gods of other nations are mere idols,
but the LORD made the heavens!
6 Honor and majesty surround him;
strength and beauty fill his sanctuary.

7 O nations of the world, recognize the
LORD;
recognize that the LORD is glorious
and strong.
8 Give to the LORD the glory he deserves!
Bring your offering and come into his
courts.
9 Worship the LORD in all his holy splendor.
Let all the earth tremble before him.
10 Tell all the nations, "The LORD reigns!"
The world stands firm and cannot be
shaken.
He will judge all peoples fairly.

11 Let the heavens be glad, and the earth
rejoice!
Let the sea and everything in it shout
his praise!
12 Let the fields and their crops burst out
with joy!
Let the trees of the forest rustle with
praise
13 before the LORD, for he is coming!
He is coming to judge the earth.
He will judge the world with justice,
and the nations with his truth.

PSALM 97

1 The LORD is king!
Let the earth rejoice!
Let the farthest coastlands be glad.
2 Dark clouds surround him.
[k]Righteousness and justice are the
foundation of his throne.
3 Fire spreads ahead of him
and burns up all his foes.
4 His lightning flashes out across the
world.
The earth sees and trembles.
5 The mountains melt like wax before the
LORD,
before the Lord of all the [a]earth.
6 The heavens proclaim his
righteousness;
every nation sees his glory.
7 Those who worship idols are disgraced—

96:1-13 //1 Chr 16:23-33
96:2 Ps 71:15
96:3 Ps 145:12
96:5 1 Chr 16:26; Isa 42:5
96:6 Ps 104:1
96:8 Ps 115:1
96:9 1 Chr 16:29; 2 Chr 20:21
96:10 Ps 58:11; 67:4; 93:1
96:11 Ps 97:1; 98:7; Isa 49:13
96:12 Isa 35:1; 44:23; 55:12-13
97:1 Ps 96.10-11
97:2 Exod 19:9; Deut 4:11; 1 Kgs 8:12; Ps 18:11; 89:14
[k]*tsedeq* (6664) ‣ Ps 119:75
97:3 Heb 12:29
97:5 Josh 3:11; Amos 9:5
[a]*'erets* (0776) ‣ Isa 65:17
97:6 Ps 50:6

Ps 96 This psalm establishes the Lord's universal kingship (see Ps 93) and prepares for the coming of the Lord to bring justice and righteousness into the world. The psalmist invites everyone to worship the Lord (96:1-3), the glorious Creator of all the earth (96:4-6), because worship is due to him alone (96:7-9). The universe joins in praise as the righteous Judge establishes a new order (96:10-13). • This psalm (along with 105:1-15; 106:1, 47-48) is included in David's song of praise recorded in 1 Chr 16.

96:1 Three psalms open with the exhortation to ***sing a new song*** (Pss 96, 98, 149); the song celebrates the Lord's universal kingship (see 33:3).

96:4-6 The gods of the nations are as nothing before the glorious and majestic Creator of the earth.

96:4 ***Great is the LORD! . . . most worthy of praise:*** With this refrain, the poet exalts the Lord over all the gods (95:3) and nations (99:2). He inspires awe more than anyone or anything else (76:7, 12; 89:7; 99:3; 111:9). He is beyond human possession or comprehension. The story of what he does to redeem his people causes them to praise him.

96:5 The ***LORD made the heavens,*** an even greater task than creating the earth. The ***idols,*** made by human hands (115:4), created nothing.

96:6 ***Honor and majesty:*** The Lord is glorious (96:6; 104:1; 148:13), and so are his works in nature (8:1) and in redemption (111:3; 145:5).

96:7 ***nations of the world*** (literally ***families of the nations***): Families and clans represent subdivisions of the nations (see Gen 12:3). • The nations must respond to the Lord's glory (8:1; 19:1-4; 24:7).

96:8 The ***courts*** of God's sanctuary were usually off-limits to non-Jewish people. In this psalm the nations of the world—the non-Jews—are invited in (65:4; 84:2, 10; 100:4; 116:19; 135:2; Isa 1:12).

96:9 Worshipers should ***tremble*** in awe (96:4; see 18:7-15; 97:4) at the ***splendor*** of the Lord's majesty and holiness (Heb 12:25).

96:10 The Lord's coming means the end of injustice. He rules fairly (9:8; 96:13; 98:9) and inaugurates an era of harmony and order not experienced since Eden. • The Lord's reign over ***the world*** is founded on "the strong pillars of righteousness and justice" (89:14), so it ***cannot be shaken*** (cp. 11:3).

96:11-13 The psalmist exhorts the created order to respond with joy to the news of the Lord's coming. Cp. a similar theme in 98:7-9.

96:12 All of nature will experience renewal in God's presence (65:13; 72:6, 16; Isa 44:23; 55:12; Rom 8:21-22).

Ps 97 God is greatly exalted over the gods and over all the earth. Awe-inspiring phenomena accompany his coming. Even the created order is visibly affected and the wicked perish, but the people of Zion love his coming and rejoice.

97:1 The ***farthest coastlands*** represent the most remote parts of the world.

97:2-4 ***Dark clouds . . . Fire . . . lightning:*** This language shows that the Lord is coming in judgment (see note on 18:7-15).

97:5-7 The created order stirs at the coming of its King. He alone deserves worship.

97:6 As the Lord enters the world, the testimony of his righteousness resounds from above (50:6). • ***Every nation*** will view the open display of the Lord's ***glory*** (see 8:1; 19:1-4a; 24:7; Isa 40:5).

97:7 Jer 10:14 *Heb 1:6
97:8 Zeph 3:14
97:9 Exod 18:11 Ps 83:18; 95:3 [b]*elyon* (5945) ‣Isa 14:14
97:10 Dan 3:28 Rom 12:9
97:11 Job 22:28 [c]*simkhah* (8057) ‣Prov 10:28
97:12 Ps 32:11
98:1 Exod 15:6 Isa 52:10
98:3 Luke 1:54, 72
98:4 Ps 100:1
98:6 Num 10:10 2 Chr 15:14
98:7 Ps 24:1; 96:11
98:9 Ps 96:10, 13
99:1 Exod 25:22 1 Sam 4:4
99:2 [d]*rum* (7311) ‣Ps 99:5
99:3 Deut 28:58 Josh 24:19 1 Sam 2:2
99:4 Ps 17:2
99:5 [e]*rum* (7311) ‣Ps 118:28
99:6 Exod 15:25 1 Sam 7:9

all who brag about their worthless
gods—
for every god must bow to him.
8 Jerusalem has heard and rejoiced,
and all the towns of Judah are glad
because of your justice, O LORD!
9 For you, O LORD, are [b]supreme over all
the earth;
you are exalted far above all gods.

10 You who love the LORD, hate evil!
He protects the lives of his godly
people
and rescues them from the power of
the wicked.
11 Light shines on the godly,
and [c]joy on those whose hearts are
right.
12 May all who are godly rejoice in the LORD
and praise his holy name!

PSALM 98

A psalm.

1 Sing a new song to the LORD,
for he has done wonderful deeds.
His right hand has won a mighty victory;
his holy arm has shown his saving
power!
2 The LORD has announced his victory
and has revealed his righteousness to
every nation!
3 He has remembered his promise to love
and be faithful to Israel.
The ends of the earth have seen the
victory of our God.
4 Shout to the LORD, all the earth;
break out in praise and sing for joy!
5 Sing your praise to the LORD with the
harp,
with the harp and melodious song,
6 with trumpets and the sound of the
ram's horn.
Make a joyful symphony before the
LORD, the King!

7 Let the sea and everything in it shout his
praise!
Let the earth and all living things join in.
8 Let the rivers clap their hands in glee!
Let the hills sing out their songs of joy
9 before the LORD.
For the LORD is coming to judge the
earth.
He will judge the world with justice,
and the nations with fairness.

PSALM 99

1 The LORD is king!
Let the nations tremble!
He sits on his throne between the
cherubim.
Let the whole earth quake!
2 The LORD sits in majesty in Jerusalem,
[d]exalted above all the nations.
3 Let them praise your great and awesome
name.
Your name is holy!
4 Mighty King, lover of justice,
you have established fairness.
You have acted with justice
and righteousness throughout Israel.
5 [e]Exalt the LORD our God!
Bow low before his feet, for he is holy!
6 Moses and Aaron were among his priests;
Samuel also called on his name.

97:7 At the Lord's coming, when *every god must bow* to him, those who worship other gods will face their own folly (see 95:3-5).

97:8-12 *Jerusalem* (Hebrew *Zion*) rejoices at the news of the Lord's coming, for he brings justice and rescues the upright of heart.

97:11 The godly people of integrity (see Prov 2:7, 21; 3:32; 11:6, 11; 14:2), *whose hearts are right,* maintain a relationship with the Lord and with others (94:15; 125:4). The wicked plan the downfall of the godly (11:2), but the Lord rescues them (11:1; 36:10). Then the sorrows of the godly turn to joy and praise (32:11; 64:10; 111:1; 119:7).

Ps 98 This psalm celebrates the Lord's kingship. The Lord is Israel's true King, its champion and savior. His people sing a new song celebrating his victorious power and faithfulness to them. The Lord displays his righteous rule to all the nations throughout the earth, which will culminate in a worldwide kingdom of justice (98:2, 9). Consequently, all the earth must worship and rejoice together because the Lord is coming (98:4-6).

98:2-3 The Lord makes known his righteousness and faithfulness (see also Isa 52:10).

98:4-6 The psalmist invites the whole earth to worship the King (see 96:1).

98:6 The Temple musicians used *trumpets* to call people together for meetings (cp. 81:3).

98:7-9 The created order is personified as rejoicing at the coming of the righteous Judge (see 93:3-4; 96:11-13).

Ps 99 The psalmist calls the nations to worship the Lord, the king of the earth who rules from Zion (see note on Ps 93).

99:1-5 The Lord is the holy and righteous King (Isa 6:1-5). Mount Zion, the location of the Lord's Temple, metaphorically stands as the highest point on earth (113:4; Isa 2:2; 6:1). From this summit, the Great King (47:2) can see, rule over, and receive praise from all nations and peoples.

99:1 It is fitting to *tremble* and *quake* in response to the Lord's holiness (see 96:9). • The *throne between the cherubim* refers to the cover of the Ark of the Covenant (Exod 25:17-22).

99:2 *Jerusalem:* Hebrew *Zion.* See "Mount Zion, the City of God" at Ps 48, p. 947.

99:4 The qualities of the Lord's rule include strength, *justice,* love, *fairness,* and *righteousness* (see 93:4; 97:2, 6-7, 12; 98:2-3, 9; 138:6). • *Israel:* Literally *Jacob.* See note on 44:4.

99:6-8 God showed favor by responding to his people in the past, while holding sinners accountable.

99:6 *Moses* and *Samuel* were great models and leaders who had prayed on behalf of the Lord's people (Exod 32:31-32; 1 Sam 12:23).

They cried to the LORD for help,
and he answered them.
7 He spoke to Israel from the pillar of cloud,
and they followed the laws and
decrees he gave them.
8 O LORD our God, you answered them.
You were a [f]forgiving God to them,
but you punished them when they
went wrong.

9 Exalt the LORD our God,
and worship at his holy mountain in
Jerusalem,
for the LORD our God is holy!

PSALM 100

A psalm of thanksgiving.

1 Shout with joy to the LORD, all the earth!
2 Worship the LORD with gladness.
Come before him, singing with joy.
3 Acknowledge that the LORD is God!
He made us, and we are his.
We are his people, the sheep of his
pasture.
4 Enter his gates with [g]thanksgiving;
go into his courts with praise.
[h]Give thanks to him and praise his
name.
5 For the LORD is good.
His unfailing love continues [i]forever,
and his faithfulness continues to each
generation.

PSALM 101

A psalm of David.

1 I will sing of your love and justice, LORD.
I will praise you with songs.
2 I will be careful to live a blameless life—
when will you come to help me?
I will lead a life of integrity
in my own home.
3 I will refuse to look at
anything [j]vile and vulgar.
I hate all who deal crookedly;
I will have nothing to do with them.
4 I will reject perverse ideas
and stay away from every evil.
5 I will not tolerate people who slander
their neighbors.
I will not endure conceit and pride.

6 I will search for faithful people
to be my companions.
Only those who are above reproach
will be allowed to serve me.
7 I will not allow deceivers to serve in my
house,
and liars will not stay in my presence.
8 My daily task will be to ferret out the
wicked
and free the city of the LORD from
their grip.

PSALM 102

A prayer of one overwhelmed with trouble, pouring out problems before the LORD.

1 LORD, hear my prayer!
Listen to my plea!
2 Don't turn away from me
in my time of distress.
Bend down to listen,
and answer me quickly when I call
to you.
3 For my days disappear like smoke,
and my bones burn like red-hot coals.
4 My heart is sick, withered like grass,
and I have lost my appetite.
5 Because of my groaning,
I am reduced to skin and bones.
6 I am like an owl in the desert,
like a little owl in a far-off wilderness.

99:7 Exod 33:9; Num 12:5
99:8 Num 14:20; [f]*nasa'* (5375) ‣Hos 14:2
100:1 Ps 98:4
100:2 Deut 28:47
100:3 1 Kgs 18:39; Ezek 34:30-31; Mark 14:27; John 10:11
100:4 Ps 95:2; 96:2; [g]*todah* (8426) ‣Ps 107:22; [h]*yadah* (3034) ‣Ps 109:30
100:5 Ps 25:8; 119:90; [i]*'olam* (5769) ‣Ps 110:4
101:1 Ps 89:1; 145:7
101:3 [j]*beliya'al* (1100) ‣Prov 6:12
101:4 Prov 11:20
101:5 Ps 50:20; Prov 6:16-19
101:6 Ps 119:1
101:8 Ps 46:4; 75:10; 118:10-12
102:1 Exod 2:23; 1 Sam 9:16
102:2 Ps 69:17
102:3 Job 30:30; Jas 4:14
102:5 Lam 4:8

99:7 The Lord spoke to Moses and Aaron from ***the pillar of cloud*** (Exod 33:9; Num 12:5-6), and for a time, the people responded to the revelation.

Ps 100 This psalm calls all nations to come to Jerusalem to worship the Lord and acknowledge his goodness to Israel.

100:3 ***and we are his:*** As in an alternate reading in the Masoretic Text; the other alternate and some ancient versions read ***and not we ourselves. The LORD*** is the one who determines who ***his people*** are. • ***the sheep of his pasture:*** God will guide and protect his people (23:1, 4).

100:4 ***Gates*** and ***courts*** were part of the Temple in Jerusalem.

Ps 101 This hymn expresses a commitment to live with integrity and to avoid evil. Jesus meets this ideal.

101:2 ***in my own home*** (literally *in my house*): This commitment to ***integrity*** might refer to private life at home. Some interpreters view ***my house*** as referring to the king's palace; the commitment would then refer to the policies of his administration. • Leading a ***life of integrity*** means choosing a wise lifestyle.

101:4-5 The psalmist hates what the Lord hates (Prov 6:16-19; see Ps 5:5; 11:4-5). • ***Perverse ideas*** come from corrupt human hearts (18:26).

101:6 The psalmist surrounds himself with people who are also committed to integrity (101:2).

101:7-8 The psalmist commits himself to ridding his ***house*** and ***the city of the LORD***—representing the entire kingdom—of all evil.

Ps 102 A frail and afflicted human being prays for the Lord's compassion on Jerusalem and for his presence with its inhabitants.

102:1-2 The psalmist appeals to the Lord not to ***turn away*** (or ***hide your face***). Israel experienced his turning his face away during their exile.

102:3 ***Smoke*** is an image of transitory life (37:20; 68:2). • The psalmist's ***bones*** represent his whole being (see 6:2; 34:19-22).

102:4 ***Like*** dried ***grass***, the psalmist senses his life ebbing away.

102:5 ***skin and bones:*** The psalmist has wasted away because of his anguish (see 102:9; 109:24).

102:6 The ***owl*** was associated with ruin and desolation (Isa 34:11, 15).

102:7
Ps 77:4
102:8
2 Sam 16:5
Isa 65:15
Luke 23:11
Acts 26:11
102:12
Exod 3:15
Lam 5:19
102:13
Isa 60:10
Zech 1:12
102:15
1 Kgs 8:41-42
102:16
Isa 60:1-2
102:17
Neh 1:6
102:18
Deut 31:19
1 Cor 10:11
102:19
Deut 26:15
102:21
Zech 8:20-23
102:22
Ps 86:9
102:24
Isa 38:10
102:25-27
Gen 1:1
*Heb 1:10-12
102:26
Matt 24:35
2 Pet 3:10
Rev 20:11
102:27
Mal 3:6
Jas 1:17
103:1
Ps 33:21; 104:1
[k]*nepesh* (5315)
▸Ps 119:20

7 I lie awake,
lonely as a solitary bird on the roof.
8 My enemies taunt me day after day.
They mock and curse me.
9 I eat ashes for food.
My tears run down into my drink
10 because of your anger and wrath.
For you have picked me up and
thrown me out.
11 My life passes as swiftly as the evening
shadows.
I am withering away like grass.

12 But you, O LORD, will sit on your throne
forever.
Your fame will endure to every
generation.
13 You will arise and have mercy on
Jerusalem—
and now is the time to pity her,
now is the time you promised to help.
14 For your people love every stone in her
walls
and cherish even the dust in her streets.
15 Then the nations will tremble before the
LORD.
The kings of the earth will tremble
before his glory.
16 For the LORD will rebuild Jerusalem.
He will appear in his glory.
17 He will listen to the prayers of the
destitute.
He will not reject their pleas.

18 Let this be recorded for future
generations,
so that a people not yet born will
praise the LORD.
19 Tell them the LORD looked down
from his heavenly sanctuary.
He looked down to earth from heaven
20 to hear the groans of the prisoners,
to release those condemned to die.
21 And so the LORD's fame will be
celebrated in Zion,
his praises in Jerusalem,
22 when multitudes gather together
and kingdoms come to worship the
LORD.

23 He broke my strength in midlife,
cutting short my days.
24 But I cried to him, "O my God, who lives
forever,
don't take my life while I am so
young!
25 Long ago you laid the foundation of the
earth
and made the heavens with your
hands.
26 They will perish, but you remain forever;
they will wear out like old clothing.
You will change them like a garment
and discard them.
27 But you are always the same;
you will live forever.
28 The children of your people
will live in security.
Their children's children
will thrive in your presence."

PSALM 103
A psalm of David.

1 Let all that [k]I am praise the LORD;
with my whole heart, I will praise his
holy name.

102:7-8 The psalmist cannot sleep (see 63:6-8). Like a ***bird on the roof,*** he feels isolated from both friends (see 88:8) and ***enemies.***

102:10 The psalmist blames the Lord for his troubles.

102:11 The psalmist's existence seems empty and transitory (102:4; 109:23; 144:4).

102:12-17 The topic changes from the psalmist's miseries to the Lord's glory. A vision of the Lord's compassionate kingship gives him confidence in Zion's future.

102:12 ***forever . . . to every generation:*** The frailty of humans (102:3-11) contrasts with the permanence of the Lord.

102:13 ***Jerusalem:*** Hebrew *Zion;* also in 102:16. • ***Now is the time*** for the Lord to restore Jerusalem from exile (see 75:2; Jer 29:10; Dan 9:1-19).

102:15-16 When the Lord arises (102:13), ***the nations will tremble*** with fear because they will see ***his glory*** (see 8:1; 19:1-4a; 24:7). The rebuilding of Zion and the Temple portray God's glory and fulfill this promise. An even greater fulfillment will come with the New Jerusalem (Rev 21).

102:17 The people of Israel were ***destitute*** (or *naked*) during the Exile.

102:18-22 The Lord will have mercy; Jews and Gentiles alike will worship him.

102:18 ***Let this be recorded:*** The written record stands as a memorial to the Lord's goodness.

102:19 The ***heavenly sanctuary*** refers to God's holy place on high (see 92:8-10).

102:22 The ***multitudes***—both Jews and Gentiles—will join in the worship of the Lord (see 96:7, 9; 106:48; Isa 2:2-4; 43:10-13; 57:15; 60:3-7).

102:23-28 Although the psalmist suffers in the present, he bases his hope for the future on the Lord's past faithfulness.

102:24 The psalmist draws a contrast between his days (102:23) and God's years (cp. 90:4).

102:25-27 In contrast with the permanence of the Creator, the created order ***will wear out like*** a piece of ***clothing*** (see Isa 40:28). • The writer to the Hebrews describes this passage as having been addressed to Jesus, the Son (Heb 1:10-12).

102:28 The Lord's ***presence*** provides the basis for the security and happiness of his ***people*** (23:6).

Ps 103 This psalm celebrates the Lord's perfection, compassion, forgiveness, and goodness. The structure of the psalm is an acrostic poem, with one verse for each letter in the Hebrew alphabet (see also Pss 9–10, 25, 34, 37, 38, 111, 112, 119, 145).

103:1-6 The psalmist offers praise for the Lord's goodness.

2 Let all that I am praise the LORD;
may I never forget the good things he
does for me.
3 He forgives all my sins
and heals all my diseases.
4 He [a]redeems me from death
and crowns me with [b]love and tender
mercies.
5 He fills my life with good things.
My youth is [c]renewed like the eagle's!

6 The LORD gives righteousness
and [d]justice to all who are treated
unfairly.
7 He revealed his character to Moses
and his deeds to the people of Israel.
8 The LORD is compassionate and merciful,
[e]slow to get angry and filled with
unfailing love.
9 He will not constantly accuse us,
nor remain angry forever.
10 He does not punish us for all our sins;
he does not deal harshly with us, as
we deserve.
11 For his unfailing love toward those who
fear him
is as great as the height of the heavens
above the earth.
12 He has removed our [f]sins as far from us
as the east is from the west.
13 The LORD is like a father to his children,
tender and [g]compassionate to those
who fear him.
14 For he knows how weak we are;
he remembers we are only dust.
15 Our days on earth are like grass;
like wildflowers, we bloom and die.
16 The wind blows, and we are gone—
as though we had never been here.
17 But the love of the LORD remains forever
with those who fear him.
His salvation extends to the children's
children
18 of those who are faithful to his
covenant,
of those who obey his
commandments!

19 The LORD has made the heavens his
[h]throne;
from there he rules over everything.

20 Praise the LORD, you [i]angels,
you mighty ones who carry out his
plans,
listening for each of his commands.
21 Yes, praise the LORD, you [j]armies of
angels
who [k]serve him and do his will!
22 Praise the LORD, everything he has
created,
everything in all his kingdom.

Let all that I am praise the LORD.

PSALM 104

1 Let all that I am praise the LORD.

O LORD my God, how great you are!
You are robed with honor and majesty.
2 You are dressed in a robe of light.
You stretch out the starry curtain of the
heavens;
3 you lay out the rafters of your home in
the rain clouds.
You make the clouds your chariot;
you ride upon the wings of the wind.

103:3
Exod 34:7

103:4
Ps 49:15
[a]*ga'al* (1350)
‣ Ps 107:2
[b]*khesed* (2617)
‣ Prov 3:3

103:5
Isa 40:31
[c]*khadash* (2318)
‣ Ps 104:30

103:6
[d]*mishpat* (4941)
‣ Ps 106:3

103:7
Exod 33:13

103:8
Num 14:18
Jon 3:10–4:10
[e]*'arek 'appayim* (0750, 0639)
‣ Ps 145:8

103:9
Ps 30:5
Isa 57:16

103:10
Lam 3:22

103:11
Ps 36:5

103:12
[f]*pesha'* (6588)
‣ Prov 10:12

103:13
Mal 3:17
[g]*rakham* (7355)
‣ Ps 116:5

103:14
Gen 3:19
Isa 40:6-8

103:15
Jas 1:10-11

103:18
Deut 7:9

103:19
[h]*kisse'* (3678)
‣ Prov 16:12

103:20
[i]*mal'ak* (4397)
‣ Ps 148:2

103:21
[j]*tsaba'* (6635)
‣ Isa 6:5
[k]*sharath* (8334)
‣ Isa 61:6

103:1-2 ***Let all that I am praise the LORD:*** Psalms 103 and 104 each open and close with this commitment (103:1-2, 22; 104:1, 35; see also 146:1).

103:7-8 The Lord *revealed* himself *to Moses* in distinctive ways that ensured his relationship with his people (see Exod 34:6-7; Num 14:18).

103:9 If the Lord were to *constantly accuse* or *remain angry forever,* no one would be left (see Isa 54:7-8; 57:16).

103:11-12 The Lord's *love* and forgiveness are infinite and complete.

103:13 ***The LORD is like a father to his children:*** This analogy forms the basis for Jesus' teaching about God's fatherhood (see Matt 5:43-48; 6:1; 10:19-20; 12:50; Luke 6:36; 12:29-32; John 8:31-59; 15:1-8; see also 2 Sam 7:14; Jer 3:19; 31:9; Mal 1:6; 2 Cor 6:16-18).

103:14-16 The Lord compassionately cares for frail humans (see 37:2; 90:5; 92:7; 102:4; Isa 40:6-8).

103:17-19 ***the love of the LORD remains forever:*** The Lord's kingdom is everlasting, so he commits himself to his people across many generations.

103:18 To *obey* God means to be *faithful* and loyal to him.

103:20-21 The psalmist exhorts the Lord's angels, his servants and messengers, to praise the Lord.

103:22 God's *kingdom* extends over all things, so all things are called to praise the Lord. • The concluding phrase takes us back to 103:1-2.

Ps 104 This creation hymn (see also Pss 8, 33, 145) exalts God's goodness and majesty. The psalmist reflects on the present world, the original creation, and a future new creation. He sees both creations as marvelously and wisely made (cp. 139:14), as the work of the Lord's Spirit (104:30; Gen 1:2; 2 Cor 3:6).

104:1 ***Let all that I am praise the LORD:*** Pss 103 and 104 each open and close with this commitment to praise (103:1-2, 22; 104:1, 35). • ***how great you are!*** This acclamation expresses praise for rescue (see also 35:27; 40:16; 70:4).

104:2-4 The psalmist interacts with two of the days of creation (see Gen 1:1-8), when God created the heavens and light.

104:3 This poetic portrayal envisions *the clouds* as beams that support heaven.

104:4 ***The winds are your messengers; / flames of fire are your servants:*** Greek version reads *He sends his angels like the winds, / his servants like flames of fire.* Cp. Heb 1:7, where the Greek version is quoted. • Wind and lightning are seen as divine *messengers.* The Lord uses weather phenomena as he desires (77:17-18; 78:26; 135:7; 148:5-6). • The psalmist interacts with day three of creation (Gen 1:9-13). The Lord is master of water and earth.

104:2 Dan 7:9
104:3 Ps 18:10; Amos 9:6
104:4 *Heb 1:7
104:5 Job 38:4
104:6 Gen 1:2
104:7 Ps 18:15; 29:3
104:9 Job 38:10-11; Jer 5:22
104:10 Isa 41:18
104:12 Matt 8:20
104:14 Gen 1:29-30
104:15 Judg 9:13; Prov 31:6; Eccl 10:19; Luke 7:46
104:17 Lev 11:19
104:18 Lev 11:5; Prov 30:26
104:19 Gen 1:14

4 The winds are your messengers;
flames of fire are your servants.
5 You placed the world on its foundation
so it would never be moved.
6 You clothed the earth with floods of water,
water that covered even the mountains.
7 At your command, the water fled;
at the sound of your thunder, it hurried away.
8 Mountains rose and valleys sank
to the levels you decreed.
9 Then you set a firm boundary for the seas,
so they would never again cover the earth.

10 You make springs pour water into the ravines,
so streams gush down from the mountains.
11 They provide water for all the animals,
and the wild donkeys quench their thirst.
12 The birds nest beside the streams
and sing among the branches of the trees.
13 You send rain on the mountains from your heavenly home,
and you fill the earth with the fruit of your labor.
14 You cause grass to grow for the livestock
and plants for people to use.
You allow them to produce food from the earth—
15 wine to make them glad,
olive oil to soothe their skin,
and bread to give them strength.
16 The trees of the LORD are well cared for—
the cedars of Lebanon that he planted.
17 There the birds make their nests,
and the storks make their homes in the cypresses.
18 High in the mountains live the wild goats,
and the rocks form a refuge for the hyraxes.
19 You made the moon to mark the seasons,
and the sun knows when to set.

Praise Psalms (Ps 103)

Pss 9, 18, 32, 34, 46–48, 93, 96–99, 113, 116, 124, 129, 136, 138

The Hebrew title of the book of Psalms means "Praises," and that title accurately defines a large number of the psalms. God is praised for his nature and for his great acts in creation and history. Praise psalms were written for individual use and for the community.

Individual praise (Pss 9, 18, 32, 34, 116, 138). It was customary in Temple worship to give verbal thanks before the whole assembly whenever a vow-offering or a thank-offering was made (see, e.g., 22:22-26; 66:13-20; 116:17-19). Such opportunities for personal praise and testimony must have added warmth and significance to worship. Each act of rescue and every experience of God's mercy became part of the cumulative, ongoing story of salvation. Worship was not simply a recital of God's deeds in earlier centuries.

Communal praise (Pss 103, 113, 124, 129, 136). When the community gathered, they praised the Lord in song for his acts in history (Ps 103) or for a specific recent manifestation of his mercy (Pss 124, 129). In Ps 103, the psalmist praises God for his mercy to each individual (103:1-5) and to the whole community (103:6-14). The frailty of humanity contrasts with God's constancy (103:15-18); his universal and absolute rule merits universal praise (103:19-22).

104:6 At first, *water* covered the earth.

104:7 The Lord created dry ground on day three of creation (Gen 1:9-13).

104:8 The earth originates in God's will.

104:9-10 The Lord reigns over all bodies of water, including those on land. He replaced chaotic waters with order and abundance, and the earth became a splendid place for animals and humans, with water refreshing the ground, the birds, and the animals.

104:9 The Lord *set a firm boundary for the seas* to protect the land. God's sovereignty over sea and land was an argument against the existence of Baal, whom the Canaanites celebrated as victorious over the waters (see Ps 29).

104:11-18 The psalmist celebrates animal, plant, and human life, as well as the Lord's abundant provision for all of it (Gen 1:9-30).

104:14 *people to use:* People are the managers of the created order, and they receive nourishment from the work of their hands.

104:15 While both can be misused (cp. Prov 21:17), the Lord provides *wine* and *olive oil* as gifts to enhance life. Life is sustained by basic food, represented by *bread*.

104:17-18 The *storks* migrated from northern Europe and resided in Palestine during the winter. • *hyraxes* (or *coneys*, or *rock badgers*): These animals are about the size of a rabbit and live in rocky places.

104:19-23 The psalmist rejoices in the order of night and day, marking day four of creation (Gen 1:14-19). This cycle gives all creatures an opportunity to live.

104:19 *the moon to mark the seasons:* Ancient Israel based its calendar on the cycles of the moon (see chart, p. 145). • *the sun knows when to set:* This is a poetic description from the perspective of normal observation. The sun goes down at a regular time every evening.

20 You send the darkness, and it becomes
night,
when all the forest animals prowl
about.
21 Then the young lions roar for their prey,
stalking the food provided by God.
22 At dawn they slink back
into their dens to rest.
23 Then people go off to their work,
where they labor until evening.

24 O LORD, what a variety of things you
have made!
In wisdom you have made them all.
The earth is full of your creatures.
25 Here is the ocean, vast and wide,
teeming with life of every kind,
both large and small.
26 See the ships sailing along,
and Leviathan, which you made to
play in the sea.

27 They all depend on you
to give them food as they need it.
28 When you supply it, they gather it.
You open your hand to feed them,
and they are richly satisfied.
29 But if you turn away from them, they
panic.
When you take away their breath,
they die and turn again to dust.
30 When you give them your [a]breath, life is
created,
and you [b]renew the face of the earth.

31 May the glory of the LORD continue
forever!
The LORD takes pleasure in all he has
made!
32 The earth trembles at his glance;
the mountains smoke at his touch.

33 I will sing to the LORD as long as I live.
I will praise my God to my last breath!
34 May all my thoughts be pleasing to him,
for I rejoice in the LORD.
35 Let all sinners vanish from the face of
the earth;
let the wicked disappear forever.

Let all that I am praise the LORD.

Praise the LORD!

PSALM 105

Ps 105:1-15 // 1 Chr 16:8-22

1 Give thanks to the LORD and proclaim
his greatness.
Let the whole world know what he
has done.
2 Sing to him; yes, sing his praises.
Tell everyone about his wonderful
deeds.
3 Exult in his holy name;
rejoice, you who worship the LORD.
4 Search for the LORD and for his strength;
continually seek him.
5 Remember the wonders he has
performed,
his miracles, and the rulings he has
given,

104:20 Isa 45:7; 56:9
104:22 Job 37:8
104:23 Gen 3:19
104:24 Ps 40:5; 65:9 Jer 10:12; 51:15
104:26 Job 41:1
104:27 Ps 136:25
104:29 Gen 3:19
104:30 Ezek 37:9
[a]*ruakh* (7307) ‣ Eccl 12:7
[b]*khadash* (2318) ‣ Isa 61:4
104:31 Gen 1:31
104:32 Exod 19:18 Judg 5:5
104:35 Ps 37:10; 59:13
105:1-15 //1 Chr 16:8-22
105:2 Ps 98:5
105:3 Ps 33:21
105:4 Ps 27:8

104:20-23 Cycles of ***darkness*** and ***dawn*** mark the days on earth. • Some creatures live nocturnally, while others become active during the day.

104:24-26 The Lord's works testify to his wisdom. All parts fit together—land and sea, night and day, land creatures and sea creatures. The Lord's wisdom makes life orderly and wonderful.

104:25 The ***ocean, . . . teeming with life of every kind*** (see Gen 1:20-21), exemplifies the Lord's creative activities.

104:26 ***ships sailing:*** Commercial vessels engaged in sea trade were one of the wonders of the ancient Near East (see Isa 2:16; 23:1, 3). • The identification of ***Leviathan*** is disputed, ranging from an earthly creature to a mythical sea monster in ancient literature. The psalmist says that this feared creature is nothing but the Lord's pet.

104:27-30 All life depends on the gracious sustenance of the Lord of life and death (cp. Matt 6:11).

104:29-30 ***When you give them your breath:*** Or *When you send your Spirit.* Life on earth is only possible as the Lord's gift, symbolized by his breath (Hebrew *ruakh,* "breath, wind, spirit"). The Lord's Spirit is the agent of renewal (Isa 32:15-20).

104:31-35 The psalmist moves from describing the known creation to anticipating the new creation, when the Lord will renew the created order into a world without sinners.

104:31 The Lord reveals his presence in the created order (see 8:1; 19:1-4; 24:7) and takes ***pleasure*** in his new creation (see Isa 65:19).

104:32 The trembling ***earth*** and the smoking ***mountains*** represent the Lord's coming in judgment against sinners and salvation for his faithful people (see 18:7-15).

104:35 The Lord will remove all forms of evil that defile his creation. • The concluding phrase takes us back to 104:1 (see also 103:1-2, 22; 146:1).

Ps 105 This hymn praises the Lord's faithfulness to Abraham and his descendants in all their journeys—from Ur to Canaan (105:12), to Egypt (105:17, 23), through the wilderness (105:37, 41), and back to Canaan (105:44). All of this fulfilled the Lord's promise to Abraham (105:9, 42), which was the basis for Israel's very existence. Joseph, whose suffering was changed into glory, is a paradigm of encouragement for Israel (105:16-25). • Verses 1-15 (along with 96:1-13; 106:1, 47-48) are included in David's song of praise recorded in 1 Chr 16.

105:1-5 The poet begins with the exhortation, ***Give thanks*** (see also 106:1; 107:1; 118:1; 136:1). The other psalms continue with the refrain, "for he is good!" The rest of Ps 105 tells of God's goodness.

105:6-11 The story of Israel is based on the Lord's commitment to Abraham. Even when a question arises about the future of God's covenant with David (Ps 89), God's covenant with Abraham stands, as does the spiritual bond

105:7 Isa 26:9
105:8 Gen 22:16-18; Deut 7:9; Luke 1:72
105:10 Gen 28:13-15; Josh 23:4
105:11 Gen 13:15; 15:18
105:12 Gen 23:4; 34:30; Heb 11:9
105:14 Gen 12:17; 35:5
105:16 Lev 26:26; Isa 3:1; Ezek 4:16
105:17 Gen 37:28, 36; Acts 7:9
105:19 Ps 66:10
105:20 Gen 41:14
105:22 ᶜ*zaqen* (2205) ‣Ps 107:32
105:24 Exod 1:7, 9
105:25 Exod 1:8; Acts 7:19
105:26 Exod 3:10; Num 16:5
105:27 Ps 78:43-51
105:28 Exod 10:22
105:29 Exod 7:20-21
105:30 Exod 8:6
105:31 Exod 8:16, 21
105:32 Exod 9:23
105:36 Exod 12:29-30
105:37 Exod 12:33, 35-36

6 you children of his servant Abraham,
you descendants of Jacob, his chosen ones.

7 He is the LORD our God.
His justice is seen throughout the land.
8 He always stands by his covenant—
the commitment he made to a thousand generations.
9 This is the covenant he made with Abraham
and the oath he swore to Isaac.
10 He confirmed it to Jacob as a decree,
and to the people of Israel as a never-ending covenant:
11 "I will give you the land of Canaan
as your special possession."

12 He said this when they were few in number,
a tiny group of strangers in Canaan.
13 They wandered from nation to nation,
from one kingdom to another.
14 Yet he did not let anyone oppress them.
He warned kings on their behalf:
15 "Do not touch my chosen people,
and do not hurt my prophets."

16 He called for a famine on the land of Canaan,
cutting off its food supply.
17 Then he sent someone to Egypt ahead of them—
Joseph, who was sold as a slave.
18 They bruised his feet with fetters
and placed his neck in an iron collar.
19 Until the time came to fulfill his dreams,
the LORD tested Joseph's character.
20 Then Pharaoh sent for him and set him free;
the ruler of the nation opened his prison door.
21 Joseph was put in charge of all the king's household;
he became ruler over all the king's possessions.
22 He could instruct the king's aides as he pleased
and teach the king's ᶜadvisers.

23 Then Israel arrived in Egypt;
Jacob lived as a foreigner in the land of Ham.
24 And the LORD multiplied the people of Israel
until they became too mighty for their enemies.
25 Then he turned the Egyptians against the Israelites,
and they plotted against the LORD's servants.

26 But the LORD sent his servant Moses,
along with Aaron, whom he had chosen.
27 They performed miraculous signs among the Egyptians,
and wonders in the land of Ham.
28 The LORD blanketed Egypt in darkness,
for they had defied his commands to let his people go.
29 He turned their water into blood,
poisoning all the fish.
30 Then frogs overran the land
and even invaded the king's bedrooms.
31 When the LORD spoke, flies descended on the Egyptians,
and gnats swarmed across Egypt.
32 He sent them hail instead of rain,
and lightning flashed over the land.
33 He ruined their grapevines and fig trees
and shattered all the trees.
34 He spoke, and hordes of locusts came—
young locusts beyond number.
35 They ate up everything green in the land,
destroying all the crops in their fields.
36 Then he killed the oldest son in each Egyptian home,
the pride and joy of each family.

37 The LORD brought his people out of Egypt, loaded with silver and gold;

between God and Israel, Abraham's descendants.

105:8 The *covenant* is the Lord's irrevocable oath to be the Father of Abraham and his descendants (see Gen 12:1-9; 15:1-21).

105:11 God promised *the land of Canaan* to Abraham's descendants as their *special possession*, where they could live as God's people (105:44-45; Gen 12:7; 15:7-21).

105:12-15 The Lord protected Israel's patriarchs.

105:15 Abraham was one of the nation's *prophets* (Gen 20:7).

105:16-22 These verses tell the story of Joseph (see Gen 37–41).

105:19 *his dreams:* Literally *his word.* • *tested Joseph's character:* See Gen 39:6-12.

105:23-25 These verses tell the story of Israel's affliction in Egypt (see Exod 1:1-14).

105:23 Egypt (Hebrew *mitsrayim*) was in *the land of Ham* (see map, p. 39).

105:26-36 The psalmist recounts the story of Moses and the plagues in Egypt (Exod 7:20–12:30).

105:37-45 The Exodus and the conquest of Canaan fulfilled God's promise to Abraham, Isaac, and Jacob (105:9-10). Unlike Ps 78, the poet recites the Lord's goodness without commenting on Israel's history of rebellion (cp. Ps 106).

105:37 *not one . . . stumbled:* The Lord protected all of his people (cp. 9:3).

and not one among the tribes of Israel even stumbled.
38 Egypt was glad when they were gone,
for they feared them greatly.
39 The LORD spread a cloud above them as a covering
and gave them a great fire to light the darkness.
40 They asked for meat, and he sent them quail;
he satisfied their hunger with manna—bread from heaven.
41 He split open a rock, and water gushed out
to form a river through the dry wasteland.
42 For he remembered his sacred promise
to his servant Abraham.
43 So he brought his people out of Egypt with joy,
his chosen ones with rejoicing.
44 He gave his people the lands of pagan nations,
and they harvested crops that others had planted.
45 All this happened so they would follow his decrees
and obey his instructions.

Praise the LORD!

PSALM 106

Ps 106:1, 47-48 // 1 Chr 16:34-36

1 Praise the LORD!

Give thanks to the LORD, for he is good!
His faithful love endures forever.
2 Who can list the glorious miracles of the LORD?
Who can ever praise him enough?
3 There is [d]joy for those who deal [e]justly with others
and always do what is right.

4 Remember me, LORD, when you show favor to your people;
come near and rescue me.
5 Let me share in the prosperity of your chosen ones.
Let me rejoice in the joy of your people;
let me praise you with those who are your heritage.

6 Like our ancestors, we have sinned.
We have done wrong! We have acted wickedly!
7 Our ancestors in Egypt
were not impressed by the LORD's miraculous deeds.
They soon forgot his many acts of kindness to them.
Instead, they rebelled against him at the Red Sea.
8 Even so, he saved them—
to defend the honor of his name
and to demonstrate his mighty power.
9 He commanded the Red Sea to dry up.
He led Israel across the sea as if it were a desert.
10 So he rescued them from their enemies
and redeemed them from their foes.
11 Then the water returned and covered their enemies;
not one of them survived.
12 Then his people [f]believed his promises.
Then they sang his praise.
13 Yet how quickly they forgot what he had done!
They wouldn't wait for his counsel!
14 In the wilderness their desires ran wild,
testing God's patience in that dry wasteland.

105:39 Neh 9:12; Isa 4:5
105:40 Num 11:31; John 6:31
105:41 Exod 17:6; Ps 78:15; 1 Cor 10:4
105:43 Exod 15:1
105:44 Deut 6:10-11; Josh 13:7
105:45 Deut 4:40
106:1 1 Chr 16:34, 41; Ps 100:4-5; 105:1
106:3 Ps 15:2; [d]*'ashrey* (0835) ‣Prov 3:13; [e]*mishpat* (4941) ‣Prov 12:5
106:4 Ps 44:3
106:5 Ps 1:3; 118:15
106:6 2 Chr 30:7; Ezra 9:7; Neh 1:7; Zech 1:4
106:7 Judg 3:7
106:8 Ezek 20:9
106:9 Exod 14:21; Isa 63:11-13
106:11 Exod 15:5
106:12 [f]*'aman* (0539) ‣Ps 119:66
106:14 Num 11:4

105:39 The Lord's presence was as evident to all as a *fire* in the *darkness* (Exod 13:22).

105:42-45 The story of redemption is also the story of the Lord's faithfulness.

105:44 Canaan was a land of *pagan nations* (see 111:6). The psalmist might also be reflecting on God's promise to Abraham (Gen 24:60) regarding the lands given to Isaac (Gen 26:3).

105:45 The Lord planned for Israel to testify about him by obeying him; Israel was to be his model people.

Ps 106 The Israelite community in exile confessed the Lord's goodness and justice and their own historic sinfulness. From the humble state of exile, they pleaded for redemption and restoration, asking to be gathered back from all the places the Lord had scattered them in his wrath. The psalm does not end in despair but with the memory of the Lord's former mercy and the hope that his mercy will be renewed (106:44-48). Israel failed, but the Lord is constant.
• Verses 1, 47-48 (along with 96:1-13; 105:1-15) are included in David's song of praise recorded in 1 Chr 16.

106:1 ***Praise the LORD!*** This refrain (Hebrew *haleluyah*) characterizes four small subgroups in the psalms: 104–106, 111–113, 115–117, 146–150.

106:2-3 Wise people who practice justice and righteousness receive encouragement to proclaim the Lord's great acts.

106:4-5 The poet prays individually for the Lord's favor before leading the community confession that follows.

106:6-13 The community joins together to confess their sins and their ancestors' many acts of unbelief.

106:6 The story of Israel's redemption encompasses their sinful response from the days of the *ancestors* to the present (106:43). The themes of sin and divine wrath both open and close Book Four (90:1-9; 106:6, 23, 43).

106:7 ***at the Red Sea:*** Literally *at the sea, the sea of reeds.* See note on Exod 13:18.

106:9 ***Red Sea:*** Literally *sea of reeds;* also in 106:22. See Exod 14:15-31.

106:13 ***They wouldn't wait:*** God's impatient people did not trust him to work according to his will (e.g., see Exod 15:24; 16:2-3; 17:1-3; Num 14:26-45; 21:4-9).

106:15 Ps 78:29-31
106:16 Num 16:1-3
106:17 Deut 11:6
106:18 Num 16:35
106:19 Acts 7:41
106:20 Jer 2:11; Rom 1:23
106:21 Deut 10:21
106:22 Ps 105:27
106:23 Exod 32:10-14
106:24 Num 13:31–14:3; Jer 3:19
106:26 Num 14:29; Heb 3:11
106:28 Num 25:1-3; Hos 9:10
106:30 Num 25:7-13
106:32 Exod 17:7; Num 20:13; Ps 78:40
106:34 Judg 1:21, 27-36
106:37 2 Kgs 17:17
106:39 Hos 4:12
106:40 Judg 2:12-14

15 So he gave them what they asked for,
but he sent a plague along with it.
16 The people in the camp were jealous of Moses
and envious of Aaron, the LORD's holy priest.
17 Because of this, the earth opened up;
it swallowed Dathan
and buried Abiram and the other rebels.
18 Fire fell upon their followers;
a flame consumed the wicked.

19 The people made a calf at Mount Sinai;
they bowed before an image made of gold.
20 They traded their glorious God
for a statue of a grass-eating bull.
21 They forgot God, their savior,
who had done such great things in Egypt—
22 such wonderful things in the land of Ham,
such awesome deeds at the Red Sea.
23 So he declared he would destroy them.
But Moses, his chosen one, stepped between the LORD and the people.
He begged him to turn from his anger and not destroy them.

24 The people refused to enter the pleasant land,
for they wouldn't believe his promise to care for them.
25 Instead, they grumbled in their tents
and refused to obey the LORD.
26 Therefore, he solemnly swore
that he would kill them in the wilderness,
27 that he would scatter their descendants among the nations,
exiling them to distant lands.

28 Then our ancestors joined in the worship of Baal at Peor;
they even ate sacrifices offered to the dead!
29 They angered the LORD with all these things,
so a plague broke out among them.
30 But Phinehas had the courage to intervene,
and the plague was stopped.
31 So he has been regarded as a righteous man
ever since that time.

32 At Meribah, too, they angered the LORD,
causing Moses serious trouble.
33 They made Moses angry,
and he spoke foolishly.

34 Israel failed to destroy the nations in the land,
as the LORD had commanded them.
35 Instead, they mingled among the pagans
and adopted their evil customs.
36 They worshiped their idols,
which led to their downfall.
37 They even sacrificed their sons
and their daughters to the demons.
38 They shed innocent blood,
the blood of their sons and daughters.
By sacrificing them to the idols of Canaan,
they polluted the land with murder.
39 They defiled themselves by their evil deeds,
and their love of idols was adultery in the LORD's sight.

40 That is why the LORD's anger burned against his people,
and he abhorred his own special possession.

106:15 ***he sent a plague:*** See Exod 32:35; Num 11:33.

106:16-18 The people became ***jealous*** because they presumed to have the same privileges as God's appointed priests (see Num 16:1-35). • ***the earth opened up:*** See Num 16:28-33.

106:19-23 ***they bowed before an image:*** The people forgot their Savior and committed the sin of idolatry (see Exod 32:1-6).

106:19 ***at Mount Sinai:*** Hebrew *at Horeb,* another name for Sinai.

106:22 ***The land of Ham*** is Egypt.

106:24-25 The people disobeyed God's command when they ***refused to enter the pleasant land*** (the Promised Land; see Jer 3:19). • ***they wouldn't believe his promise:*** See Num 13:25–14:12.

106:26-27 God's judgment when Israel refused to obey was death and exile (Num 14:26-30). The occasion for these severe judgments seems to have been disobeying God's word (106:24-25) and provoking the Lord's wrath (106:28-46).

106:28-39 Israel's idolatry outside of the land came with them into their land. Their nature did not change; they continued to provoke the Lord to anger by their actions.

106:28 ***the worship of Baal at Peor:*** See Num 25:3; Deut 4:3.

106:30-33 ***Phinehas,*** who executed a flagrantly apostate Israelite man (Num 25:3-8), is an even better model of ***a righteous*** man than ***Moses,*** who failed ***at Meribah*** (Num 20:11-13).

106:33 ***They made Moses angry:*** Literally *They embittered his spirit.* As a result, ***he spoke foolishly*** and disobeyed the Lord (see Num 20:12).

106:34 Israel continued to disobey the word of the Lord while living in the Promised Land. Rather than destroying the nations, Israel accepted them and their ways (see Judg 2:1-3, 11-15; 3:5-6).

106:37 Pagan gods were ***demons*** (see Deut 32:17).

106:39 Idolatry, like ***adultery,*** defiles God's people (see Lev 18:24; Hos 5:3).

106:40-46 The psalmist returns to the Babylonian exile (106:26-27). The Lord judged Israel severely, but he also restrained his wrath, remembering the covenant he had made with Abraham.

106:40 God ***abhorred*** Israel's sin, as he does all sin.

41 He handed them over to pagan nations,
and they were ruled by those who hated them.
42 Their enemies crushed them
and brought them under their cruel power.
43 Again and again he rescued them,
but they chose to rebel against him,
and they were finally destroyed by their sin.
44 Even so, he pitied them in their distress
and listened to their cries.
45 He remembered his covenant with them
and relented because of his unfailing love.
46 He even caused their captors
to treat them with kindness.

47 Save us, O LORD our God!
Gather us back from among the nations,
so we can thank your holy name
and rejoice and praise you.
48 Praise the LORD, the God of Israel,
who lives from everlasting to everlasting!
Let all the people say, "Amen!"

Praise the LORD!

5. BOOK FIVE (PSS 107–150)

PSALM 107

1 Give thanks to the LORD, for he is good!
His faithful love endures forever.
2 Has the LORD [g]redeemed you? Then speak out!
Tell others he has [g]redeemed you
from your enemies.
3 For he has gathered the exiles from many lands,
from east and west,
from north and south.

4 Some wandered in the wilderness,
lost and homeless.
5 Hungry and thirsty,
they nearly died.
6 "LORD, help!" they cried in their trouble,
and he rescued them from their distress.
7 He led them straight to safety,
to a city where they could live.
8 Let them praise the LORD for his great love
and for the wonderful things he has done for them.
9 For he satisfies the thirsty
and fills the hungry with good things.
10 Some sat in darkness and deepest gloom,
imprisoned in iron chains of misery.
11 They rebelled against the words of God,
scorning the counsel of the Most High.
12 That is why he broke them with hard labor;
they fell, and no one was there to help them.

106:41 Neh 9:27
106:43 Judg 6:6; Ps 81:12
106:45 Lev 26:42
106:46 2 Chr 30:9; Ezra 9:9
106:47-48 //1 Chr 16:35-36
107:1 Ps 106:1
107:2 Isa 35:9-10; [g]*ga'al* (1350) ‣Isa 43:1
107:3 Neh 1:9; Ps 106:47; Ezek 20:34
107:4 Josh 5:6
107:7 Jer 31:9
107:9 Matt 5:6; Luke 1:53
107:10 Mic 7:8-9; Luke 1:79
107:11 Num 15:31

106:43-44 When Israel was *finally destroyed,* the destruction was not complete. The Lord *pitied them,* so he left a remnant.

106:45 *He remembered . . . and relented:* Unlike Israel, the Lord is faithful to his *covenant* (105:8).

106:46 As harsh as the Exile was, the Lord still protected his people (see 2 Kgs 25:27-29).

106:47 *Gather us back:* The community prays for restoration from exile (see 102:19-22; 107:3; see also Isa 11:12; 40:11; 43:5; 54:7; 56:8; 66:18).

106:48 This doxology concludes Book Four (cp. 41:13; 89:52). • *from everlasting to everlasting!* The reference to God's eternal nature links to the opening of Book Four (Ps 90:1-2). • *Let all the people say, "Amen!":* The Hebrew word *'amen* means "It is true." The godly accept the Lord's will in exile and his promise to be their God.

Book Five (Pss 107–150) This final book of the Psalter was shaped in the context of Israel's return from exile in Babylon. God's sovereign power and loving faithfulness to his covenant people were demonstrated as he restored and exalted them. The uncertainty in Book Four about the future of David's royal line (see 89:38) finds positive resolution in Book Five. The psalms of David occur in greater number in this final book than they do in Books Three and Four, and David is remembered for the covenant he received and for his devotion to the Lord (e.g., Ps 132). Thus, there remains the prospect of a coming King. Book Five contains two early liturgical collections: the "Egyptian Hallel" (Pss 113–118) and the "Great Hallel" (Pss 120–136; *hallel* means "praise"). The Great Hallel is largely made up of a collection known as the "Songs of Ascents" or "Pilgrim Psalms" (Pss 120–134). The Psalter then returns to its roots with a collection of David's psalms dominated by lament (Pss 138–145), followed by a section of praise to conclude the whole book of Psalms (Pss 146–150).

Ps 107 This psalm is a hymn of praise to God the Redeemer. After an introduction exhorting the redeemed to praise God for his goodness (107:1-3), the poet brings together four case studies of people whom the Lord redeemed from adversity (107:4-32). He then sums up the Lord's sovereignty (107:33-42) and concludes with an invitation to discern God's unfailing love in all areas of life (107:43).

107:2 The *redeemed* might be all who came out of exile.

107:3 *exiles:* People came from all nations where the people of Israel and Judah had been scattered.

107:4-9 Those who were lost in the *wilderness* thank God for his rescue. The wilderness might be a metaphor for leaving the path of wisdom (1:1; Prov 4:10-15).

107:6 The psalmist does not specify the occasion of his *trouble* and *distress.* The generic nature of the adversity permits readers in a variety of circumstances to identify with the laments.

107:7-8 God *led them* like a shepherd (see 23:1). • Verse 8 is a refrain that is repeated in 107:15, 21, 31.

107:10-16 The psalmist calls for thanksgiving and praise from people in despair over the consequences of their rebellion.

107:11 God's *counsel* includes his instruction and will.

107:12 Exhausted by their *hard labor* (Lam 5:13), the people *fell.* While this

107:14 Ps 116:16; Acts 12:7
107:16 Isa 45:1-2
107:17 Isa 65:6-7; Ezek 24:23
107:18 Job 33:19-22; Ps 9:13; 88:3
107:20 2 Kgs 20:5; Matt 8:8
107:22 Lev 7:12; Ps 9:11; 50:14; 73:28; 118:17; h*todah* (8426) ‣Jer 30:19
107:25 Ps 93:3-4
107:29 Matt 8:26; Luke 8:24
107:32 Ps 22:22, 25; Isa 25:1; i*zaqen* (2205) ‣Ps 119:100
107:34 Gen 19:24-25
107:35 Isa 35:6-7; 41:18
107:37 2 Kgs 19:29; Amos 9:14
107:38 Gen 12:2; Exod 1:7
107:42 Job 22:19; Ps 52:6; Rom 3:19
107:43 Ps 64:9; Jer 9:12; Hos 14:9

13 "LORD, help!" they cried in their trouble,
and he saved them from their distress.
14 He led them from the darkness and deepest gloom;
he snapped their chains.
15 Let them praise the LORD for his great love
and for the wonderful things he has done for them.
16 For he broke down their prison gates of bronze;
he cut apart their bars of iron.

17 Some were fools; they rebelled
and suffered for their sins.
18 They couldn't stand the thought of food,
and they were knocking on death's door.
19 "LORD, help!" they cried in their trouble,
and he saved them from their distress.
20 He sent out his word and healed them,
snatching them from the door of death.
21 Let them praise the LORD for his great love
and for the wonderful things he has done for them.
22 Let them offer sacrifices of hthanksgiving
and sing joyfully about his glorious acts.

23 Some went off to sea in ships,
plying the trade routes of the world.
24 They, too, observed the LORD's power in action,
his impressive works on the deepest seas.
25 He spoke, and the winds rose,
stirring up the waves.
26 Their ships were tossed to the heavens
and plunged again to the depths;
the sailors cringed in terror.
27 They reeled and staggered like drunkards
and were at their wits' end.
28 "LORD, help!" they cried in their trouble,
and he saved them from their distress.
29 He calmed the storm to a whisper
and stilled the waves.
30 What a blessing was that stillness
as he brought them safely into harbor!
31 Let them praise the LORD for his great love
and for the wonderful things he has done for them.
32 Let them exalt him publicly before the congregation
and before the ileaders of the nation.

33 He changes rivers into deserts,
and springs of water into dry, thirsty land.
34 He turns the fruitful land into salty wastelands,
because of the wickedness of those who live there.
35 But he also turns deserts into pools of water,
the dry land into springs of water.
36 He brings the hungry to settle there
and to build their cities.
37 They sow their fields, plant their vineyards,
and harvest their bumper crops.
38 How he blesses them!
They raise large families there,
and their herds of livestock increase.

39 When they decrease in number and become impoverished
through oppression, trouble, and sorrow,
40 the LORD pours contempt on their princes,
causing them to wander in trackless wastelands.
41 But he rescues the poor from trouble
and increases their families like flocks of sheep.
42 The godly will see these things and be glad,
while the wicked are struck silent.
43 Those who are wise will take all this to heart;
they will see in our history the faithful love of the LORD.

might be expected of the wicked (9:3; 27:2), it was unlike the Israelites' flight from Egypt (105:37).

107:17-22 Fools who received what they deserved but were rescued from death offer thanksgiving to the Lord.

107:20 The Lord creates (Gen 1:3) and sustains the universe (Heb 1:3) simply by speaking (147:18); when he speaks, people are also *healed* (Matt 8:8).

107:23-32 Sailors give thanks to the Lord when he saves them from the chaos and peril of the sea.

107:25-29 The same God who speaks and brings about the sailors' distress can also calm the storm with just a word (cp. Jon 1:4; Matt 8:26).

107:32 This call for public praise expands the refrains in 107:21-22 and 107:31.

107:33-42 These two sections (107:33-38, 39-42) expand the theme of the Lord's sovereignty over things that humans cannot control.

107:33-35 The Lord can choose to make the earth fertile or barren (74:15; Isa 35:6-7).

107:38 God's presence can be seen in the abundance of his people's *families* and *herds* (127:3; 133:3; cp. 109:8).

107:39 People often *become impoverished* when their rulers practice *oppression*.

107:40 In his *contempt* for human rulers, the Lord rectifies their corruption on earth.

107:41 The large *families* of *the poor* are evidence of God's blessing.

107:42-43 Justice prevails in God's world (1:6), and Israel's history demonstrates God's faithful love.

PSALM 108

A song. A psalm of David.

1 My heart is confident in you, O God;
no wonder I can sing your praises
with all my heart!
2 Wake up, lyre and harp!
I will wake the dawn with my song.
3 I will thank you, LORD, among all the
people.
I will sing your praises among the
nations.
4 For your unfailing love is higher than the
ʲheavens.
Your faithfulness reaches to the
clouds.
5 Be exalted, O God, above the highest
heavens.
May your glory shine over all the
earth.
6 Now rescue your beloved people.
Answer and save us by your power.
7 God has promised this by his holiness:
"I will divide up Shechem with joy.
I will measure out the valley of
Succoth.
8 Gilead is mine,
and Manasseh, too.
Ephraim, my helmet, will produce my
warriors,
and Judah, my scepter, will produce
my kings.
9 But Moab, my washbasin, will become
my servant,
and I will wipe my feet on Edom
and shout in triumph over Philistia."
10 Who will bring me into the fortified
city?
Who will bring me victory over
Edom?
11 Have you rejected us, O God?
Will you no longer march with our
armies?
12 Oh, please help us against our enemies,
for all human help is useless.
13 With God's help we will do mighty
things,
for he will trample down our foes.

PSALM 109

For the choir director: A psalm of David.

1 O God, whom I praise,
don't stand silent and aloof
2 while the wicked slander me
and tell lies about me.
3 They surround me with hateful words
and fight against me for no reason.
4 I love them, but they try to destroy me
with accusations
even as I am praying for them!
5 They repay evil for good,
and hatred for my love.
6 They say, "Get an evil person to turn
against him.
Send an ᵏaccuser to bring him to trial.
7 When his case comes up for judgment,
let him be pronounced guilty.
Count his prayers as sins.
8 Let his years be few;
let someone else take his position.
9 May his children become fatherless,
and his wife a widow.
10 May his children wander as beggars
and be driven from their ruined
homes.
11 May creditors seize his entire estate,
and strangers take all he has earned.
12 Let no one be kind to him;
let no one pity his fatherless children.
13 May all his offspring die.
May his family name be blotted out in
a single generation.
14 May the LORD never forget the sins of his
fathers;
may his mother's sins never be erased
from the record.
15 May the LORD always remember these
sins,
and may his name disappear from
human memory.

108:1-5 //Ps 57:7-11
108:4 Ps 113:4; ʲ*shamayim* (8064) ‣Isa 14:12
108:6-13 //Ps 60:5-12
108:11 Ps 44:9
109:1 Ps 83:1
109:2 Ps 52:4; 120:2
109:3 Ps 69:4
109:4 Ps 38:20
109:5 John 7:7
109:6 Zech 3:1; ᵏ*satan* (7854) ‣Zech 3:1
109:7 Prov 28:9
109:8 *Acts 1:20
109:9 Exod 22:24
109:11 Isa 1:7
109:12 Isa 9:17
109:14 Neh 4:5; Isa 65:6-7
109:15 Jer 16:17

Ps 108 This psalm combines two excerpts from David's other psalms (cp. 57:5, 7-11; 60:5-12).

108:7 ***by his holiness:*** Or *in his sanctuary.*

Ps 109 The psalmist begins this lament with a general charge against his accusers: They do evil in return for good (109:1-5). At the end of the psalm, he turns to the Lord in prayer, asking for his protection (109:21-25) and vengeance (109:26-31).

109:1 The psalmist sees no evidence that God cares (see 28:1).

109:4-5 The psalmist's acts of kindness and godliness (see 35:12-14) have only met with stubborn opposition and expressions of hatred.

109:6-19 The NLT translates these verses as the words of the psalmist's accusers; Hebrew lacks ***They say,*** which makes it unclear who is speaking.

109:8-11 Family members of those guilty of capital crimes often died with the perpetrator (Num 16:1-33; Josh 7:1-25) or had their property confiscated (1 Kgs 21:13-16).

109:8 The wicked person apparently held a ***position*** of leadership. Peter referred to this psalm in regard to Judas Iscariot (Acts 1:20-26).

109:13 If one's ***family name*** was ***blotted out***, it meant there was no ***offspring*** to carry on the family name or remember its history (see Prov 10:7).

109:14 Children inherit the sinful nature of their parents (51:5; Exod 20:5; Eph 2:3). The speaker wants the Lord to punish the perpetrator for the guilt of family members who went before him (cp. Matt 23:35-36).

109:16 Ps 37:32
109:17 Matt 7:2
109:18 Ps 73:6
109:19 Ezek 7:27
109:20 Isa 3:11; 2 Tim 4:14
109:21 Ps 25:11; Ezek 36:22
109:22 Ps 40:17; Prov 18:14
109:24 Heb 12:12
109:26 Ps 119:86
109:28 2 Sam 16:11-12
109:29 Job 8:22; Ps 35:26
109:30 Ps 35:18; [a]*yadah* (3034) ‣Ps 136:1; [b]*halal* (1984) ‣Ps 113:1
109:31 Ps 16:8; 37:33
110:1 *Matt 22:44; *Mark 12:36; 14:62; *Luke 20:42; *Acts 2:34; *Heb 1:13
110:2 Ps 45:6; Dan 7:13-14
110:3 Judg 5:2; Ps 96:9

16 For he refused all kindness to others;
he persecuted the poor and needy,
and he hounded the brokenhearted
to death.
17 He loved to curse others;
now you curse him.
He never blessed others;
now don't you bless him.
18 Cursing is as natural to him as his
clothing,
or the water he drinks,
or the rich food he eats.
19 Now may his curses return and cling to
him like clothing;
may they be tied around him like a
belt."
20 May those curses become the LORD's
punishment
for my accusers who speak evil of me.
21 But deal well with me, O Sovereign LORD,
for the sake of your own reputation!
Rescue me
because you are so faithful and good.
22 For I am poor and needy,
and my heart is full of pain.
23 I am fading like a shadow at dusk;
I am brushed off like a locust.
24 My knees are weak from fasting,
and I am skin and bones.
25 I am a joke to people everywhere;
when they see me, they shake their
heads in scorn.

26 Help me, O LORD my God!
Save me because of your unfailing
love.
27 Let them see that this is your doing,
that you yourself have done it, LORD.
28 Then let them curse me if they like,
but you will bless me!
When they attack me, they will be
disgraced!
But I, your servant, will go right on
rejoicing!
29 May my accusers be clothed with
disgrace;
may their humiliation cover them like
a cloak.
30 But I will [a]give repeated thanks to the
LORD,
[b]praising him to everyone.
31 For he stands beside the needy,
ready to save them from those who
condemn them.

PSALM 110
A psalm of David.

1 The LORD said to my Lord,
"Sit in the place of honor at my right
hand
until I humble your enemies,
making them a footstool under your
feet."

2 The LORD will extend your powerful
kingdom from Jerusalem;
you will rule over your enemies.
3 When you go to war,
your people will serve you willingly.
You are arrayed in holy garments,
and your strength will be renewed
each day like the morning dew.

109:16 The defendant committed capital crimes and did not exercise even basic decency.

109:18 *Cursing* is the accused person's whole way of life.

109:20 The psalmist appeals to the principle of retribution (see 94:23).

109:21-25 Vulnerable and miserable, the psalmist appeals to his Lord for help. The accusations have killed his inner spirit and even his physical stamina.

109:21 The Lord's *reputation* is at stake. If the wicked triumph, others could think that the Lord is also wicked and be drawn to that wickedness (1:1).

109:23 A *shadow at dusk* suggests a transitory, empty existence (102:11; 144:4); a single *locust* could easily be *brushed off* one's clothing.

109:26-31 These verses form a prayer for God's presence and for vindication. The psalmist wants everyone to see that he is vindicated by the Lord, not by any human agent.

109:28 The Lord's *servant* demonstrates loyalty and obedience.

109:29 The psalmist had been accused of being clothed with curses (109:18); now he asks that his accusers be ***clothed with disgrace*** and ***humiliation***.

Ps 110 Jesus and the apostles cite this psalm to explain Jesus' unique ministry and status as the Messiah (Matt 22:43-45; Acts 2:32-36). It reaffirms God's covenant with David and gives hope for the future (see 2 Sam 7:8-16).

110:1 The king of Israel had the great privilege of being the Lord's adopted son (Ps 2; 1 Chr 22:10), but he fell (Ps 89). This decree restores and heightens his position. • ***The LORD:*** Hebrew *Yahweh,* the name of God (see Exod 3:6-14; 6:2-8; 20:2). • ***My Lord*** (Hebrew *'adoni*) means "my master" or "my superior." The psalmist viewed God's messianic ruler as his superior. The NT frequently cites this psalm to validate Jesus' claim to be the Messiah (Matt 22:44-45; Mark 12:36-37; Luke 20:42-44; Acts 2:34-35; Heb 1:13). • The Lord's ***right hand*** represents his authority, strength, presence, and benefits. The Lord chose the descendant of David and raised him up to be close to him (80:17). Jesus claimed this position for himself (Matt 26:64; Mark 14:62; 16:19; Luke 22:69), and the apostles announced that Jesus, having ascended to heaven, sits at the right hand of the Father (Acts 2:33; 5:31; 7:55-56; Rom 8:34; Eph 1:20; Col 3:1; Heb 1:3; 8:1; 10:12; 12:2). • Ancient Near Eastern kings were sometimes portrayed as placing their feet on the backs of their conquered ***enemies*** as on a ***footstool*** (see Heb 10:12-13).

110:2-3 The ***kingdom*** will expand and increase, beginning from Jerusalem, until all enemies are conquered. • ***Jerusalem:*** Hebrew *Zion.* See "Mount Zion, the City of God" at Ps 48, p. 947.

4 The LORD has taken an oath and will not
break his vow:
"You are a priest [c]forever in the order
of Melchizedek."
5 The Lord stands at your right hand to
protect you.
He will strike down many kings when
his anger erupts.
6 He will punish the nations
and fill their lands with corpses;
he will shatter heads over the whole
earth.
7 But he himself will be refreshed from
brooks along the way.
He will be victorious.

PSALM 111

1 Praise the LORD!

I will thank the LORD with all my heart
as I meet with his godly people.
2 How amazing are the deeds of the LORD!
All who delight in him should ponder
them.
3 Everything he does reveals his glory and
majesty.
His righteousness never fails.
4 He causes us to remember his wonderful
works.
How gracious and merciful is our LORD!
5 He gives food to those who fear him;
he always remembers his covenant.
6 He has shown his great power to his
people
by giving them the lands of other
nations.
7 All he does is just and good,
and all his commandments are
trustworthy.
8 They are forever true,
to be obeyed faithfully and with
integrity.
9 He has paid a full ransom for his people.
He has guaranteed his covenant with
them forever.
What a holy, awe-inspiring name he
has!
10 Fear of the LORD is the foundation of
true [d]wisdom.
All who obey his commandments will
grow in wisdom.
Praise him forever!

PSALM 112

1 Praise the LORD!

How joyful are those who [e]fear the LORD
and delight in obeying his commands.
2 Their children will be successful
everywhere;

110:4
*Heb 5:6; 7:17, 21
[c]*'olam* (5769)
‣Ps 119:44

110:5
Ps 2:5, 12; 16:8
Rom 2:5
Rev 6:17

111:1
Ps 138:1

111:2
Ps 92:5

111:3
Ps 96:6; 145:5

111:4
Ps 86:15; 103:8

111:5
Matt 6:31-33

111:7
Ps 19:7-9
Rev 15:3-4

111:8
Isa 40:8
Matt 5:18

111:9
Ps 99:3
Luke 1:68

111:10
Prov 1:7, 9; 3:4-5; 9:10
[d]*khokmah* (2451)
‣Prov 13:10

112:1
Ps 119:16
[e]*yare'* (3372)
‣Jon 1:9

112:2
Ps 25:13

112:3
Prov 3:16-17; 8:18

112:4
Job 11:17
Ps 97:11

110:4 The Lord had made an unbreakable *oath* and covenant, so his apparent rejection of David's dynasty (89:38) in the Exile had led to a crisis. The placement of Ps 110 in Book Five reaffirms the future of the dynasty: David's descendant must conform to God's standard of integrity (Ps 101). His ministry will be transformed as he serves under God's kingship (Pss 93–100). • *You are a priest forever:* The role of God's messianic ruler changes. The priestly kingship of David and his descendants extended to serving as patrons of the Temple. David had the Ark brought to Jerusalem (2 Sam 6:15) and arranged for the Temple service (1 Chr 6:31-48; 15:11-26; 16:4-42; 23:4-32; 25:1). Solomon supervised the Temple construction (1 Kgs 5–7). Even so, Israel's kingship was separate from its priesthood. In the messianic kingdom, the king would also minister as priest, as *Melchizedek*, king of Salem (Gen 14:18), had done. The NT develops the ministry of Jesus Christ as a fulfillment of this new order (see Heb 5:6-10; 6:20–7:25).

110:5-7 The new priestly role of David's descendant does not rescind his old role as conquering ruler. He must still bring the nations under his rule (110:2-3; see Ps 2).

110:5-6 *at your right hand:* This position brings help and protection (see 16:7-8; 108:13). • The Lord *will strike down* rebellious *kings*. Rebellion against the Lord is a capital offense (Ps 2; Rom 6:23).

110:7 God's messianic ruler obtains victory as a vigorous person, as if he had received nourishment *from brooks along the way* (110:3).

Pss 111–117 The refrain *Praise the LORD!* (Hebrew *halelu yah*) characterizes this group of psalms.

Ps 111 This psalm is a Hebrew acrostic poem; after the introductory note of praise, each line begins with a successive letter of the Hebrew alphabet. • This wisdom psalm contains many references to the works of the Lord that reveal his character. God is righteous, gracious, compassionate, faithful, just, trustworthy, upright, holy, and awe-inspiring (111:3, 4, 7, 8, 9). God's character gives hope in the covenant relationship (111:5). He rescued Israel from Egypt (111:9), gave them the land (111:6), and provides for his people (111:5). However, God demands that the beneficiaries of this relationship also be people of righteousness and integrity.

111:1-5 The godly praise God and delight themselves in his great works. His mighty acts reflect his righteousness, grace, and compassion (see 116:5-7). All who submit themselves to him experience his glory.

111:5 God takes care of his people's needs, even providing *food*. He *remembers his covenant* with Abraham (see 105:8-11).

111:6-8 Giving Israel *the lands of other nations* was *just and good* because the Lord was executing his justice on those he dispossessed and showing grace to the Israelites. However, if the Israelites do not live *faithfully and with integrity*, they will also be dispossessed. The Lord's people must reflect his character.

111:9 The people of the Exodus generation went free because of God's grace.

111:10 *True wisdom* is the source of life (Prov 3:18; 9:11; Eccl 7:12); it begins with the *fear of the LORD* (Prov 9:10).

Ps 112 This psalm is a Hebrew acrostic poem; after the introductory note of praise, each line begins with a successive letter of the Hebrew alphabet. • The psalm reiterates the themes of wisdom and the fear of the Lord (Ps 111). The wise have reason to be happy (112:1-5) and vigorous (112:6-10).

112:1-5 The fear of the Lord leads to a life of wisdom that honors God and blesses the family and community. The godly joyfully imitate God; their obedience is not slavish.

112:2-3 *successful:* All will know the *children* of *godly people* (see 127:4) because the godly leave a legacy for their children (see 1:3; cp. Matt 6:20).

112:5
Ps 37:21, 26
112:6
Ps 15:5; 55:22
112:7
Ps 56:4
112:8
Ps 56:10-11
112:9
Ps 148:14
*2 Cor 9:9
112:10
Matt 8:12
Luke 13:28
113:1
Ps 135:1
[f]*halal* (1984)
‣ Ps 119:164
113:2
Dan 2:20
113:3
Ps 50:1
113:4
Ps 8:1; 97:9; 99:2
113:5
Ps 89:6; 103:19
113:6
Ps 11:4
Isa 57:15
113:7
1 Sam 2:8
113:8
Job 36:7
113:9
1 Sam 2:5
Ps 68:6
Isa 54:1
114:1
Exod 13:3
114:2
Exod 19:6; 29:45-46
Ps 78:68-69
114:3
Exod 14:21
Josh 3:13-14, 16

an entire generation of godly people
will be blessed.
3 They themselves will be wealthy,
and their good deeds will last forever.
4 Light shines in the darkness for the godly.
They are generous, compassionate,
and righteous.
5 Good comes to those who lend money
generously
and conduct their business fairly.
6 Such people will not be overcome by evil.
Those who are righteous will be long
remembered.
7 They do not fear bad news;
they confidently trust the LORD to
care for them.
8 They are confident and fearless
and can face their foes triumphantly.
9 They share freely and give generously to
those in need.
Their good deeds will be remembered
forever.
They will have influence and honor.
10 The wicked will see this and be
infuriated.
They will grind their teeth in anger;
they will slink away, their hopes
thwarted.

PSALM 113

1 [f]Praise the LORD!

Yes, [f]give praise, O servants of the LORD.
[f]Praise the name of the LORD!
2 Blessed be the name of the LORD
now and forever.
3 Everywhere—from east to west—
praise the name of the LORD.
4 For the LORD is high above the nations;
his glory is higher than the heavens.

5 Who can be compared with the LORD
our God,
who is enthroned on high?
6 He stoops to look down
on heaven and on earth.
7 He lifts the poor from the dust
and the needy from the garbage
dump.
8 He sets them among princes,
even the princes of his own people!
9 He gives the childless woman a family,
making her a happy mother.

Praise the LORD!

PSALM 114

1 When the Israelites escaped from
Egypt—
when the family of Jacob left that
foreign land—
2 the land of Judah became God's
sanctuary,
and Israel became his kingdom.

3 The Red Sea saw them coming and
hurried out of their way!
The water of the Jordan River turned
away.

112:4-5 The godly imitate God by being ***generous, compassionate, and righteous*** (51:1; 111:1-10; 2 Cor 9:9). They ***lend money*** to the poor without charging interest (15:5; 112:9; Exod 22:25).

112:6 The honesty and compassion of the wise keeps them from stumbling (15:5; 37:23-24), ensuring that they ***will be long remembered*** (Prov 10:7).

112:8 Because the godly joyfully expect God to prevail and rescue them, they ***face their foes triumphantly*** (59:10; 112:4; 118:7).

112:9 Paul quotes this verse in his instructions about generous giving (2 Cor 9:9).

112:10 The ***wicked . . . grind their teeth in anger*** out of their bitter envy (35:16; 37:12). The vigor and reputation of the godly cause conflict with those who want them dead. • The wicked ***will slink away*** out of fear and shame.

Pss 113–118 These psalms form what is known as the "Egyptian Hallel" (*hallel* means "praise") because Jews use the collection in the celebration of Passover, which was instituted at the beginning of the exodus from Egypt. Psalms 113–114 are recited before the Passover meal and Pss 115–118 afterward.

Ps 113 This hymn of praise exalts the greatness of the Lord's name and glory. God is greatly exalted and glorious in heaven (113:4); he also stoops down to take care of the lowly and needy on earth (113:5-9).

113:1-3 ***The name of the LORD*** (Hebrew *Yahweh;* see Exod 3:15) reveals his being, character, and reputation. He is exalted in time (***now and forever***) and in space (***from east to west***).

113:4 The Lord's glory reaches to the ***heavens*** (57:5, 11; 99:2; 108:5; 138:6; Isa 6:1; 57:15) and throughout the world of human relationships.

113:5-9 The incomparable Lord intimately involves himself in caring for people on earth.

113:6 The Lord ***stoops*** to the world's level to be directly involved with his people (see 138:6; Phil 2:6-8).

113:7-8a These phrases are a quotation from Hannah's prayer of praise (1 Sam 2:8-9a).

113:9 A ***childless woman*** was customarily treated with disdain (Gen 16:4); the Lord has the power to make her ***a happy mother***, as he made Sarah (Gen 21:2), Rebekah (Gen 25:21), Rachel (Gen 30:23), and Hannah (1 Sam 1:20). • God's greatness and goodness provide ample reason to ***praise*** him.

Ps 114 This lyrical celebration of the Lord's power in nature recalls Israel's beginning as a nation at the Exodus (114:1-2) and upon their entry to the Promised Land (114:3-6). It promotes reverence for the God of Jacob (114:7-8).

114:1-2 At the time of Israel's exodus from Egypt and their entrance into the Promised Land, Israel was one holy ***kingdom*** (Exod 19:5-6). • The separate references to ***the land of Judah*** and ***Israel*** indicate that the psalm was composed after the kingdom was divided (1 Kgs 12:16-17; cp. 1 Sam 11:8; 1 Kgs 1:35), and probably after the Exile. The ***land of Judah became God's sanctuary*** because the people worshiped God; his Tabernacle and later his Temple were located there.

114:3-4 ***The Red Sea:*** Literally *the sea;* also in 114:5. • ***hurried out of their way!*** The waters divided for Israel to escape Egypt (77:17-18; Exod 14). • ***The Jordan River turned away*** when Israel arrived

4 The mountains skipped like rams,
the hills like lambs!
5 What's wrong, Red Sea, that made you
hurry out of their way?
What happened, Jordan River, that
you turned away?
6 Why, mountains, did you skip like rams?
Why, hills, like lambs?

7 Tremble, O earth, at the presence of the
Lord,
at the presence of the God of Jacob.
8 He turned the rock into a pool of
water;
yes, a spring of water flowed from
solid rock.

PSALM 115

1 Not to us, O LORD, not to us,
but to your name goes all the glory
for your unfailing love and
faithfulness.
2 Why let the nations say,
"Where is their God?"
3 Our God is in the heavens,
and he does as he wishes.
4 Their idols are merely things of silver
and gold,
shaped by human hands.
5 They have mouths but cannot speak,
and eyes but cannot see.
6 They have ears but cannot hear,
and noses but cannot smell.
7 They have hands but cannot feel,
and feet but cannot walk,
and throats but cannot make a
sound.
8 And those who make idols are just like
them,
as are all who trust in them.

9 O Israel, trust the LORD!
He is your helper and your shield.
10 O priests, descendants of Aaron, trust
the LORD!
He is your helper and your shield.
11 All you who fear the LORD, trust the LORD!
He is your helper and your shield.

12 The LORD [g]remembers us and will
bless us.
He will bless the people of Israel
and bless the priests, the descendants
of Aaron.
13 He will bless those who fear the LORD,
both great and lowly.

14 May the LORD richly bless
both you and your children.
15 May you be blessed by the LORD,
who made heaven and earth.
16 The heavens belong to the LORD,
but he has given the earth to all
humanity.
17 The dead cannot sing praises to the
LORD,
for they have gone into the silence of
the grave.
18 But we can praise the LORD
both now and forever!

Praise the LORD!

PSALM 116

1 I love the LORD because he hears my voice
and my prayer for mercy.

114:4 Ps 29:5-6; Hab 3:6
114:5 Hab 3:8
114:7 Ps 96:9
114:8 Exod 17:5-6; Deut 8:15
115:1 Ps 29:2; Isa 48:11; Ezek 36:22, 32
115:2 Ps 42:3; 79:10
115:3 Ps 103:19; 135:6; Dan 4:35
115:4-11 //Ps 135:15-20
115:5 Jer 10:5
115:8 Ps 135:18
115:9 Ps 33:20; 62:8
115:11 Ps 103:11; 135:20
115:12 Ps 98:3; [g]*zakar* (2142) ▸Ps 119:55
115:13 Ps 128:1, 4
115:14 Deut 1:11
115:15 Gen 1:1; 14:19
115:16 Ps 8:6; 89:11
115:17 Ps 6:5; 31:17
115:18 Ps 113:2
116:1 Ps 18:1; 66:19

to cross over (see Josh 3). • ***skipped like rams:*** God's presence caused the mountains to quake (Exod 19:16-20).

114:8 The Lord miraculously provided for his people in hard times after the Exile, just as he had done in the wilderness after the Exodus.

Ps 115 In this hymn of thanksgiving for God's blessings, the community ascribes all glory to the name of the Lord, who is the true source of hope and blessing. Meanwhile, those who trust in idols are greatly disappointed. The blessing of the Creator of heaven and earth extends to future generations (115:14), and especially to the priesthood (115:12).

115:1-3 The community confesses their faith that God will rescue them for the glory of his name.

115:2-3 ***Where is their God?*** People deny God's presence or power when he does not act as they think he should (cp. 14:1; 42:3, 10). However, ***God is in the heavens***—he has all power, authority, and knowledge. He ***does as he wishes,*** not what people think he should do. He works out his plans in accord with his will (Eph 1:11) and acts in his own time and in ways he chooses.

115:4-11 This entire section is repeated in 135:15-20. • Unlike the Lord (95:3-5), ***idols*** cannot do anything; they are good for nothing.

115:8 Worshiping idols leads one astray and corrupts those ***who trust in them*** (Isa 44:20).

115:9-11 ***Israel . . . priests . . . you who fear the LORD:*** The psalmist calls on all those in the God-fearing community to commit their ways to the living God. The threefold address assures them that the Lord is their true ***helper*** and ***shield*** (cp. 118:2-4).

115:12-13 The groups named in 115:9-11 receive assurance of the Lord's blessing, regardless of their social status (see 113:8).

115:14-15 The psalmist blesses (107:37-38, 41) all who trust in and fear the Lord. The Creator will care for the families of those who fear him. • ***who made heaven and earth:*** This statement speaks of the Lord's all-encompassing power in creation.

115:16-18 ***The heavens belong to the LORD:*** God's exaltation begins in heaven (113:4), far above the gods of the nations. Of course, the earth also belongs to him (47:9; 95:4). • The ***dead*** cannot participate in God's blessings. The living ***praise*** God in thanksgiving for his blessings (79:13).

Ps 116 This hymn of thanksgiving rejoices in God's character and in rescue from death (116:1-11). It gives an assurance of God's protection in life and reminds the godly that the Lord watches over them even at death. The psalmist commits to living as God's servant and resolves to honor him publicly (116:12-19).

116:1-4 The psalmist praises the Lord for answering his prayers and rescuing him from death.

116:1 ***I love the LORD:*** This unique opening expresses affection for and commit-

116:2 Ps 17:6; 31:2
116:3 Ps 18:4-6
[h]*she'ol* (7585) ‣ Ps 139:8
116:4 Ps 22:20; 118:5
116:5 Exod 34:6
[i]*rakham* (7355) ‣ Isa 30:18
116:6 Ps 142:6
116:7 Ps 13:6; Matt 11:29
116:8 Ps 49:15; 56:13
116:10 *2 Cor 4:13
116:12 2 Chr 32:25; 1 Thes 3:9
116:14 Ps 22:25; 50:14
116:15 Ps 72:14
116:16 [j]*'ebed* (5650) ‣ Ps 119:65
117:1 *Rom 15:11
117:2 Ps 100:5
118:1 Ps 136:1-26
118:2 Ps 115:9
118:5 Ps 18:19; 120:1
118:6 Job 19:27; *Heb 13:6
118:7 Ps 54:7

2 Because he bends down to listen,
I will pray as long as I have breath!
3 Death wrapped its ropes around me;
the terrors of the [h]grave overtook me.
I saw only trouble and sorrow.
4 Then I called on the name of the LORD:
"Please, LORD, save me!"
5 How kind the LORD is! How good he is!
So [i]merciful, this God of ours!
6 The LORD protects those of childlike faith;
I was facing death, and he saved me.
7 Let my soul be at rest again,
for the LORD has been good to me.
8 He has saved me from death,
my eyes from tears,
my feet from stumbling.
9 And so I walk in the LORD's presence
as I live here on earth!
10 I believed in you, so I said,
"I am deeply troubled, LORD."
11 In my anxiety I cried out to you,
"These people are all liars!"
12 What can I offer the LORD
for all he has done for me?
13 I will lift up the cup of salvation
and praise the LORD's name for
saving me.
14 I will keep my promises to the LORD
in the presence of all his people.

15 The LORD cares deeply
when his loved ones die.
16 O LORD, I am your [j]servant;
yes, I am your [j]servant, born into your
household;
you have freed me from my chains.
17 I will offer you a sacrifice of
thanksgiving
and call on the name of the LORD.
18 I will fulfill my vows to the LORD
in the presence of all his people—
19 in the house of the LORD
in the heart of Jerusalem.

Praise the LORD!

PSALM 117

1 Praise the LORD, all you nations.
Praise him, all you people of the earth.
2 For he loves us with unfailing love;
the LORD's faithfulness endures
forever.

Praise the LORD!

PSALM 118

1 Give thanks to the LORD, for he is good!
His faithful love endures forever.
2 Let all Israel repeat:
"His faithful love endures forever."
3 Let Aaron's descendants, the priests,
repeat:
"His faithful love endures forever."
4 Let all who fear the LORD repeat:
"His faithful love endures forever."

5 In my distress I prayed to the LORD,
and the LORD answered me and set
me free.
6 The LORD is for me, so I will have no fear.
What can mere people do to me?
7 Yes, the LORD is for me; he will help me.
I will look in triumph at those who
hate me.

---

ment to the Lord (see 18:1; Deut 6:5) on the basis of what the Lord has done.

116:2 Because the Lord responds to the cry of his people (107:41; 113:6-8), the psalmist now strongly believes in prayer.

116:3 ***of the grave:*** Hebrew *of Sheol.* See note on 6:5. • It isn't clear if the psalmist's crisis was a literal near-death experience or if he was using the term figuratively.

116:4 This is the first of three times that the psalmist calls on the Lord's ***name*** (i.e., reputation).

116:5-7 The gracious, righteous, and compassionate Lord (see 111:1-5) rescued and gave rest to the psalmist.

116:6 People with ***childlike faith*** readily receive his wisdom and instruction (19:7-11; Matt 18:3-4).

116:8-11 The psalmist's near-death crisis made him more aware of life and of walking before the Lord. Though he had been in anguish, the Lord was faithful. However, ***people are all liars.***

116:9 ***I walk in the LORD's presence:*** The psalmist already lived with integrity, but since his experience of deep distress, he now enjoys open fellowship with the Lord (see 56:13; cp. Job 42:5).

116:10 ***I believed in you:*** Paul quotes this phrase in 2 Cor 4:13.

116:12-14 The Lord's gracious gifts are so great that the psalmist can do nothing to repay his debt. Keeping his promises publicly demonstrates his gratitude. • ***All he has done for*** the psalmist includes answers to prayer, rescue, and life. • The ***cup of salvation*** overflows with God's blessings (23:5), unlike the cup of judgment (75:8). • The psalmist makes ***promises*** ("vows," 116:18) to praise the Lord publicly (116:17-18).

116:15-19 No one lives or dies outside of God's will. Having been given a second chance at life, the poet readily commits himself to the Lord with renewed acts of public devotion.

Ps 117 This psalm, the shortest in the Psalter, invites ***all . . . people of the earth*** to ***praise the LORD*** because of his ***unfailing love*** and enduring ***faithfulness.***

117:1 Paul quotes this verse to show that Gentiles would eventually praise the God of Israel (Rom 15:11).

Ps 118 With an exultant testimony, the psalmist gives thanks for the Lord's goodness and encourages others to trust in his faithful love (118:1-4, 29). This poem is the last of the Egyptian Hallel (Pss 113–118).

118:2-4 ***Israel . . . Aaron's descendants . . . all who fear the LORD:*** These three groups represent the whole of the covenant community (cp. 115:9-11; 135:19-20).

118:5-9 The Lord alone is the psalmist's helper.

118:6-7 ***The LORD is for me:*** Cp. Rom 8:31; Heb 13:6. • God's presence cancels out the need to fear ***mere people*** (56:11). The psalmist joyfully expects God's rescue (59:10; 112:8).

8 It is better to take refuge in the LORD
than to trust in people.
9 It is better to take refuge in the LORD
than to trust in princes.

10 Though hostile nations surrounded me,
I destroyed them all with the
authority of the LORD.
11 Yes, they surrounded and attacked me,
but I destroyed them all with the
authority of the LORD.
12 They swarmed around me like bees;
they blazed against me like a
crackling fire.
But I destroyed them all with the
authority of the LORD.
13 My enemies did their best to kill me,
but the LORD rescued me.
14 The LORD is my strength and my song;
he has given me victory.
15 Songs of joy and victory are sung in the
camp of the godly.
The strong right arm of the LORD has
done glorious things!
16 The strong right arm of the LORD is
raised in triumph.
The strong right arm of the LORD has
done glorious things!
17 I will not die; instead, I will live
to tell what the LORD has done.
18 The LORD has punished me severely,
but he did not let me die.

19 Open for me the gates where the
righteous enter,
and I will go in and thank the LORD.
20 These gates lead to the presence of the
LORD,
and the godly enter there.
21 I thank you for answering my prayer
and giving me victory!

22 The stone that the builders rejected
has now become the cornerstone.
23 This is the LORD's doing,
and it is wonderful to see.
24 This is the day the LORD has made.
We will rejoice and be glad in it.
25 Please, LORD, please save us.
Please, LORD, please give us success.
26 Bless the one who comes in the name of
the LORD.
We bless you from the house of the
LORD.
27 The LORD is God, shining upon us.
Take the sacrifice and bind it with
cords on the altar.
28 You are my God, and I will praise you!
You are my God, and I will [k]exalt you!

29 Give thanks to the LORD, for he is good!
His faithful love endures forever.

PSALM 119

Aleph (א)

1 Joyful are people of [a]integrity,
who follow the [b]instructions of the
LORD.
2 Joyful are those who obey his laws
and search for him with all their
hearts.
3 They do not compromise with evil,
and they walk only in his paths.

118:8 2 Chr 32:7-8; Isa 57:13
118:10 Ps 18:40
118:12 Deut 1:44
118:14 Exod 15:2; Isa 12:2
118:15 Ps 89:13; Luke 1:51
118:18 Jer 31:18; 1 Cor 11:32; 2 Cor 6:9
118:19 Isa 26:2
118:22 *Matt 21:42; *Mark 12:10-11; *Luke 20:17; *Acts 4:11; *1 Pet 2:7
118:23 *Matt 21:42; *Mark 12:11
118:26 *Matt 21:9; *Mark 11:9; *Luke 13:35; 19:38; *John 12:13
118:27 1 Pet 2:9
118:28 Exod 15:2; Isa 25:1; [k]*rum* (7311) ‣Prov 14:34
119:1 Prov 11:20; 13:6; [a]*tamim* (8549) ‣Ps 119:80; [b]*torah* (8451) ‣Ps 119:18
119:2 Deut 4:29; 10:12; 11:13; 30:2

118:8-9 Trusting in the Lord is better than placing confidence in even the most powerful human leaders (118:6; 146:3).

118:10-12 Strength comes in the name of the Lord, declared by the threefold mention of the attackers, the Lord's name, and victory. • Even when hostile people *blazed . . . like a crackling fire*, the Lord caused them to subside like burning thorns (see Isa 9:18; 10:17).

118:14-18 The psalmist celebrates the victory of the Lord's *strong right arm*, which kept him from death.

118:17-21 God has restored the psalmist from death to life, so he praises the Lord publicly (cp. 116:6, 12-19).

118:22-24 The psalmist sees his own salvation as the beginning of a new day in which the Lord will do great things.

118:22 The *cornerstone* (or *keystone*) of a building or an arch gives the structure its shape and foundation. It is the most important of all the stones. The Lord chooses and places this stone for his sanctuary (Isa 28:16). Jesus referred to himself as this cornerstone (Matt 21:42; Mark 12:10-11; Luke 20:17; see Acts 4:11; Eph 2:20; 1 Pet 2:6-7).

118:24 ***This is the day the LORD has made:*** The day of the Lord's victory has already arrived, although its completion awaits another day (118:25).

118:25-29 The psalmist concludes with prayer and thanksgiving, anticipating an even greater revelation of God's victory and rescue.

118:26 The ***one who comes in the name of the LORD*** brings the Lord's complete victory (see 118:10-12). • During Jesus' triumphant entry into Jerusalem, the crowds called out various blessings, including phrases taken from this verse (Matt 21:9; Mark 11:9; Luke 19:38; John 12:13). Jesus himself quoted this passage as he wept over Jerusalem (Matt 23:39; Luke 13:35).

Ps 119 This psalm is a Hebrew acrostic poem; there are twenty-two stanzas, one for each successive letter of the Hebrew alphabet. Each of the eight verses within each stanza begins with the Hebrew letter named in its heading. Psalm 119 combines elements of wisdom, lament, praise, thanksgiving, and confession. Eight Hebrew words are used frequently, translated as "instructions," "laws," "words," "regulations," "statutes," "commands," "decrees," "commandments," and "promises." Together, these words encourage love for and obedience to God's instructions, as found in the Scriptures (see 2 Tim 3:14-17). The expression of deep commitment to these instructions unifies the psalm.

119:1-8 *Aleph* (א): God, the author of these *instructions,* commands that his followers live by them. The psalmist prays to be given the grace to live by that revelation.

119:1-4 The wise are happy. They are *people of integrity* (see 84:11) who *follow* the path of divine instruction. They *obey* God's revelation and *search* for it *with all their hearts* (see 27:7; 119:10, 45, 94, 155), but they reject all forms of evil. Cp. 1:1-2.

119:4 Deut 4:13
119:5 2 Chr 7:17; Prov 4:26
119:8 Ps 71:9, 18
119:9 1 Kgs 8:25; 2 Chr 6:16
119:11 Luke 2:19, 51; [c]*khata'* (2398) ‣Isa 1:4
119:13 Ps 40:9
119:15 Isa 58:2
119:18 [d]*torah* (8451) ‣Ps 119:34
119:19 1 Chr 29:15; Heb 11:8-9, 13
119:20 Ps 42:1-2; [e]*nepesh* (5315) ‣Prov 13:4
119:21 Deut 27:26; Ps 37:22
119:25 Ps 44:25
119:28 Ps 22:14; 1 Pet 5:10
119:31 Deut 11:22
119:33 1 Chr 22:12; Ezek 44:24
119:34 [f]*torah* (8451) ‣Ps 119:97
119:35 Ps 25:4; 112:1

4 You have charged us
to keep your commandments carefully.
5 Oh, that my actions would consistently
reflect your decrees!
6 Then I will not be ashamed
when I compare my life with your
commands.
7 As I learn your righteous regulations,
I will thank you by living as I should!
8 I will obey your decrees.
Please don't give up on me!

Beth (ב)

9 How can a young person stay pure?
By obeying your word.
10 I have tried hard to find you—
don't let me wander from your
commands.
11 I have hidden your word in my heart,
that I might not [c]sin against you.
12 I praise you, O LORD;
teach me your decrees.
13 I have recited aloud
all the regulations you have given us.
14 I have rejoiced in your laws
as much as in riches.
15 I will study your commandments
and reflect on your ways.
16 I will delight in your decrees
and not forget your word.

Gimel (ג)

17 Be good to your servant,
that I may live and obey your word.
18 Open my eyes to see
the wonderful truths in your
[d]instructions.
19 I am only a foreigner in the land.
Don't hide your commands from me!
20 [e]I am always overwhelmed
with a desire for your regulations.
21 You rebuke the arrogant;
those who wander from your
commands are cursed.
22 Don't let them scorn and insult me,
for I have obeyed your laws.
23 Even princes sit and speak against me,
but I will meditate on your decrees.
24 Your laws please me;
they give me wise advice.

Daleth (ד)

25 I lie in the dust;
revive me by your word.
26 I told you my plans, and you answered.
Now teach me your decrees.
27 Help me understand the meaning of
your commandments,
and I will meditate on your wonderful
deeds.
28 I weep with sorrow;
encourage me by your word.
29 Keep me from lying to myself;
give me the privilege of knowing your
instructions.
30 I have chosen to be faithful;
I have determined to live by your
regulations.
31 I cling to your laws.
LORD, don't let me be put to shame!
32 I will pursue your commands,
for you expand my understanding.

He (ה)

33 Teach me your decrees, O LORD;
I will keep them to the end.
34 Give me understanding and I will obey
your [f]instructions;
I will put them into practice with all
my heart.
35 Make me walk along the path of your
commands,

119:4 To ***keep*** God's ***commandments*** means to guard them by obeying them.

119:9-16 *Beth* (ב): The psalmist is determined to pursue purity and encourages the cultivation of wisdom through God's principles (119:9) and instructions (119:10-16).

119:9 A ***young person*** tends toward foolishness (Prov 22:15) and can easily make mistakes that destroy his life (Prov 7:6-23). Youth is also the best time to develop personal discipline and pursue wisdom (see 34:11; Prov 1:4). • To ***stay pure*** means to remain uncorrupted by wickedness and sin and to develop the integrity of life defined in Ps 15.

119:10 The student asks God the teacher to discipline him so that he will not ***wander.***

119:14 God's wisdom is far greater than any ***riches*** humans seek (119:72, 127; Prov 3:14-15).

119:15 The way of wisdom includes meditating on God's ***ways*** (see 119:1, 3). The wise reflect on the implications of God's word.

119:17-24 *Gimel* (ג): Like a ***foreigner*** in hostile territory, God's ***servant*** needs God's guidance.

119:17-18 The psalmist seeks to please the Lord with a full and obedient life of praise (118:17; 119:25, 77, 116, 144, 175). Only the Lord can remove his adversaries and enable him to ***see*** the wonderful truths found in God's instructions.

119:20-21 The ***arrogant*** are probably those who mock the psalmist (119:22-23).

119:23-24 Those who ***meditate*** on God's instructions receive ***wise advice*** from them.

119:25-32 *Daleth* (ד): Though the poet feels anguish and sorrow, he entreats the Lord to revive him because he wants to obey the Lord. Suffering and death may result from the Lord's chastening (118:17-18; 119:67, 71, 75), but his instruction revives the weary soul (see 119:12).

119:29 ***lying to myself:*** Self-deception is a fruit of sinful human nature (Jer 17:9); it leads to folly. • Access to God's word is a ***privilege***, not a right.

119:33-40 *He* (ה): As a student, the poet asks his teacher, God, to renew life and to transform disgrace into righteousness.

for that is where my happiness is
found.
36 Give me an eagerness for your laws
rather than a love for money!
37 Turn my eyes from worthless things,
and give me life through your word.
38 Reassure me of your promise,
made to those who fear you.
39 Help me abandon my shameful ways;
for your regulations are good.
40 I long to obey your commandments!
Renew my life with your goodness.

Waw (ו)

41 LORD, give me your unfailing love,
the salvation that you promised me.
42 Then I can answer those who taunt me,
for I trust in your word.
43 Do not snatch your word of truth
from me,
for your regulations are my only [g]hope.
44 I will keep on obeying your instructions
[h]forever and ever.
45 I will walk in freedom,
for I have devoted myself to your
commandments.
46 I will speak to kings about your laws,
and I will not be ashamed.
47 How I delight in your commands!
How I love them!
48 I honor and love your commands.
I meditate on your decrees.

Zayin (ז)

49 Remember your promise to me;
it is my only hope.
50 Your promise revives me;
it comforts me in all my troubles.
51 The proud hold me in utter contempt,
but I do not turn away from your
instructions.
52 I meditate on your age-old regulations;
O LORD, they comfort me.
53 I become furious with the wicked,
because they reject your instructions.
54 Your decrees have been the theme of my
songs
wherever I have lived.
55 I [i]reflect at night on who you are,
O LORD;
therefore, I obey your instructions.
56 This is how I spend my life:
obeying your commandments.

Heth (ח)

57 LORD, you are mine!
I promise to obey your words!
58 With all my heart I want your blessings.
Be merciful as you promised.
59 I pondered the direction of my life,
and I turned to follow your laws.
60 I will hurry, without delay,
to obey your commands.
61 Evil people try to drag me into sin,
but I am firmly anchored to your
instructions.
62 I rise at midnight to thank you
for your just regulations.
63 I am a friend to anyone who fears you—
anyone who obeys your
commandments.
64 O LORD, your unfailing love fills the
earth;
teach me your decrees.

Teth (ט)

65 You have done many good things for [j]me,
LORD,
just as you promised.
66 I [k]believe in your commands;
now teach me good judgment and
knowledge.
67 I used to wander off until you
disciplined me;
but now I closely follow your word.
68 You are good and do only good;
teach me your decrees.
69 Arrogant people smear me with lies,
but in truth I obey your
commandments with all my heart.

119:36 Luke 12:15; Heb 13:5
119:37 Ps 71:20; Isa 33:15
119:38 2 Sam 7:25
119:43 [g]*yakhal* (3176) ‣ Ps 119:114
119:44 [h]*'olam* (5769) ‣ Ps 119:89
119:45 John 8:32
119:46 Matt 10:18; Acts 26:1-2
119:48 Josh 1:8
119:50 Rom 15:4
119:51 Job 23:11; Jer 20:7
119:52 Ps 103:18
119:53 Exod 32:19; Neh 13:25; Matt 21:12-13
119:55 Ps 42:8; 63:6; 92:2; Acts 16:25; [i]*zakar* (2142) ‣ Ps 137:1
119:57 Deut 33:9; Ps 16:5
119:58 Ps 41:4
119:59 Mark 14:72; Luke 15:17
119:61 Ps 140:5
119:63 Ps 101:6
119:64 Ps 33:5
119:65 [j]*'ebed* (5650) ‣ Ps 119:124
119:66 Phil 1:9; [k]*'aman* (0539) ‣ Prov 14:15
119:67 Jer 31:18-19; Heb 12:5-11
119:68 Ps 86:5; 125:4

119:36 The *love for money* can lead to sin (cp. Exod 18:21; 1 Tim 3:1-5; 6:10).

119:37 *through your word:* Some manuscripts read *in your ways.*

119:41-48 *Waw* (ו): The psalmist prays that God's word would continue to be the source of his *love* and *salvation.*

119:41-43 The psalmist asks to be saved from enemies who speak harshly (see 42:10; 44:16; 89:50-51; 102:8).

119:44-46 The psalmist is determined to obey the Lord.

119:47-48 The psalmist finds *delight* in God's word in spite of pain (119:92, 143).

119:49-56 *Zayin* (ז): The psalmist asks God to *remember* his word as the psalmist also remembers God's word and his name. Remembrance expresses devotion.

119:52 The *age-old regulations* are the Torah (God's "instructions" or "law"), a term that refers to the books of Genesis—Deuteronomy. See Introduction to the Pentateuch, "Literary Genres," p. 12.

119:57-64 *Heth* (ח): The psalmist seeks God's favor and *unfailing love.* Although surrounded by evildoers, he remains a loyal servant of the Lord.

119:61 *Evil people try to drag* him *into sin,* but the psalmist's memory of God's word keeps him standing firm (see 119:16).

119:64 God's goodness *fills the earth;* the whole created order provides evidence of his goodness (see Isa 6:3; 11:9).

119:65-72 *Teth* (ט): The psalmist describes himself as a penitent sinner who gratefully accepts the Lord's discipline.

119:65-68 *Good judgment and knowledge* come from wisdom (111:10). • The psalmist admits that he *used to wander off* like a stray sheep (119:176). • *you disciplined me:* See 119:25-29. • *You are good and do only good:* God's character is perfect (97:2; Jas 1:17; 1 Jn 1:5).

119:70
Ps 17:10
Isa 6:10
Jer 5:28
119:72
Prov 8:10-11, 19
119:73
Job 31:15
Ps 139:15-16
119:74
Ps 35:27
119:75
Heb 12:10
[a]*tsedeq* (6664)
‣ Ps 119:123
119:78
Jer 50:32
119:80
[b]*tamim* (8549)
‣ Prov 11:20
119:82
Isa 38:14
Lam 2:11
119:84
Rev 6:10
119:85
Ps 35:19; 57:6
Jer 18:22
119:89
Isa 40:8
Matt 24:35
1 Pet 1:25
[c]*'olam* (5769)
‣ Ps 119:142
119:90
Ps 89:1-2; 148:6
119:91
Jer 31:35
119:95
Ps 40:14
Isa 32:7
119:97
[d]*torah* (8451)
‣ Ps 119:113
119:98
Deut 4:6
119:100
Job 32:7-9
[e]*zaqen* (2205)
‣ Prov 31:23

70 Their hearts are dull and stupid,
but I delight in your instructions.
71 My suffering was good for me,
for it taught me to pay attention to
your decrees.
72 Your instructions are more valuable to me
than millions in gold and silver.

Yodh (י)

73 You made me; you created me.
Now give me the sense to follow your
commands.
74 May all who fear you find in me a cause
for joy,
for I have put my hope in your word.
75 I know, O LORD, that your regulations are
[a]fair;
you disciplined me because I
needed it.
76 Now let your unfailing love comfort me,
just as you promised me, your servant.
77 Surround me with your tender mercies
so I may live,
for your instructions are my delight.
78 Bring disgrace upon the arrogant people
who lied about me;
meanwhile, I will concentrate on your
commandments.
79 Let me be united with all who fear you,
with those who know your laws.
80 May I be [b]blameless in keeping your
decrees;
then I will never be ashamed.

Kaph (כ)

81 I am worn out waiting for your rescue,
but I have put my hope in your word.
82 My eyes are straining to see your
promises come true.
When will you comfort me?
83 I am shriveled like a wineskin in the
smoke,
but I have not forgotten to obey your
decrees.
84 How long must I wait?
When will you punish those who
persecute me?
85 These arrogant people who hate your
instructions
have dug deep pits to trap me.
86 All your commands are trustworthy.
Protect me from those who hunt me
down without cause.
87 They almost finished me off,
but I refused to abandon your
commandments.
88 In your unfailing love, spare my life;
then I can continue to obey your laws.

Lamedh (ל)

89 Your [c]eternal word, O LORD,
stands firm in heaven.
90 Your faithfulness extends to every
generation,
as enduring as the earth you created.
91 Your regulations remain true to this
day,
for everything serves your plans.
92 If your instructions hadn't sustained
me with joy,
I would have died in my misery.
93 I will never forget your commandments,
for by them you give me life.
94 I am yours; rescue me!
For I have worked hard at obeying
your commandments.
95 Though the wicked hide along the way
to kill me,
I will quietly keep my mind on your
laws.
96 Even perfection has its limits,
but your commands have no limit.

Mem (מ)

97 Oh, how I love your [d]instructions!
I think about them all day long.
98 Your commands make me wiser than
my enemies,
for they are my constant guide.
99 Yes, I have more insight than my
teachers,
for I am always thinking of your laws.
100 I am even wiser than my [e]elders,
for I have kept your commandments.

119:73-80 *Yodh* (י): In this prayer for comfort and compassion, the psalmist commits himself to his Creator, who has afflicted him. He wants God to pay back his enemies for the wrongs they have done. He also prays to receive the gift of life. He not only prays for himself but also considers the whole community of the godly, asking that God's answers to prayer would encourage them.

119:73-76 As God's child, the psalmist asks for divine wisdom.

119:81-88 *Kaph* (כ): The psalmist is ***worn out*** from ***waiting*** for the Lord, but his ***hope*** is in God's future ***rescue***.

119:85-88 God's word is ***trustworthy***, in contrast to the deceptions of the enemies ***who hunt*** the psalmist ***down without cause*** (see 119:78).

119:89-96 *Lamedh* (ל): The stability of God's wisdom gives understanding. God's word provides order and a framework for living, even when under pressure from adversaries.

119:95 The ***wicked*** intended to ***kill*** the psalmist, but destruction (1:6) was their own fate.

119:96 ***Even perfection has its limits:*** Humans cannot fully understand God's ways (see Eccl 3:11).

119:97-104 *Mem* (מ): The instruction and wisdom of God through his word are far superior to the best that human teachers can offer.

119:97-102 ***make me wiser:*** God's word provides wisdom and perspective. God is the true source of wisdom.

101 I have refused to walk on any evil path,
so that I may remain obedient to your word.
102 I haven't turned away from your regulations,
for you have taught me well.
103 How sweet your words taste to me;
they are sweeter than honey.
104 Your commandments give me understanding;
no wonder I hate every false way of life.

Nun (נ)

105 Your word is a lamp to guide my feet
and a light for my path.
106 I've promised it once, and I'll promise it again:
I will obey your righteous regulations.
107 I have suffered much, O LORD;
restore my life again as you promised.
108 LORD, accept my offering of praise,
and teach me your regulations.
109 My life constantly hangs in the balance,
but I will not stop obeying your instructions.
110 The wicked have set their traps for me,
but I will not turn from your commandments.
111 Your laws are my treasure;
they are my heart's delight.
112 I am determined to keep your decrees
to the very end.

Samekh (ס)

113 I hate those with divided loyalties,
but I love your [f]instructions.
114 You are my refuge and my shield;
your word is my source of [g]hope.
115 Get out of my life, you evil-minded people,
for I intend to obey the commands of my God.
116 LORD, sustain me as you promised, that I may live!
Do not let my hope be crushed.
117 Sustain me, and I will be rescued;
then I will meditate continually on your decrees.
118 But you have rejected all who stray from your decrees.
They are only fooling themselves.
119 You skim off the wicked of the earth like scum;
no wonder I love to obey your laws!
120 I tremble in fear of you;
I stand in awe of your regulations.

Ayin (ע)

121 Don't leave me to the mercy of my enemies,
for I have done what is just and right.
122 Please guarantee a blessing for me.
Don't let the arrogant oppress me!
123 My eyes strain to see your rescue,
to see the [h]truth of your promise fulfilled.
124 I am your [i]servant; deal with me in unfailing love,
and teach me your decrees.
125 Give discernment to me, your servant;
then I will understand your laws.
126 LORD, it is time for you to act,
for these evil people have violated your instructions.
127 Truly, I love your commands
more than gold, even the finest gold.
128 Each of your commandments is right.
That is why I hate every false way.

Pe (פ)

129 Your laws are wonderful.
No wonder I obey them!
130 The teaching of your word gives light,
so even the simple can understand.
131 I pant with expectation,
longing for your commands.
132 Come and show me your mercy,
as you do for all who love your name.
133 Guide my steps by your word,
so I will not be overcome by evil.
134 Ransom me from the oppression of evil people;
then I can obey your commandments.
135 Look upon me with love;
teach me your decrees.

119:102 Deut 17:20; Josh 23:6
119:103 Ps 19:10
119:105 Prov 3:6; 6:23
119:108 Hos 14:2; Heb 13:15
119:110 Ps 91:3; 140:5
119:111 Deut 33:4; Matt 6:21; Luke 12:34
119:113 1 Kgs 18:21; Jas 1:8; 4:8; [f]*torah* (8451) ‣Ps 119:174
119:114 Ps 31:20; 61:4; [g]*yakhal* (3176) ‣Ps 130:7
119:115 Ps 6:8; 139:19; Matt 7:23
119:116 Ps 25:2, 20; 31:1, 17; Rom 5:5; 9:33; Phil 1:20
119:117 Ps 12:5; Prov 29:25
119:119 Isa 1:22, 25; Ezek 22:18-19
119:120 Job 4:14; Hab 3:16
119:121 2 Sam 8:15; Job 29:14
119:123 [h]*tsedeq* (6664) ‣Isa 11:4
119:124 Ps 51:1; 106:45; 109:26; [i]*'ebed* (5650) ‣Prov 11:29
119:126 Jer 18:23; Ezek 31:11
119:128 Ps 19:8
119:130 Prov 6:23
119:131 Ps 42:1
119:133 Ps 19:13
119:134 Ps 142:6
119:135 Num 6:25; Ps 67:1

119:103-104 Wisdom is preferable to even the finest food (19:10; 81:16). • The psalmist had already rejected the delusion offered by the way of folly (see 119:18, 78, 86, 163).

119:105-112 *Nun* (נ): The psalmist's devotion to God's word comes from within his being (119:112) and guides his external life.

119:105-106 The Lord's ***word is a lamp*** that provides perspective, hope, and guidance in darkness (18:25-29; 119:130). Even more, this ***light*** gives life (Prov 6:23).

119:108-112 ***offering of praise:*** This Hebrew expression is unique in the OT (cp. 50:23). • The psalmist is vulnerable to his opponents because of his commitment to a wise life.

119:113-120 *Samekh* (ס): The psalmist declares his hatred of evil and his love for God and his ways.

119:113 The godly hate the wicked and their deeds (5:4-6; cp. Ezek 33:11).

119:121-128 *Ayin* (ע): The servant of the Lord strains to endure the evil around him. He boldly petitions the Lord to rescue him immediately!

119:125 Simply possessing God's law does not provide any benefits. The psalmist knows that only as the Lord gives ***discernment*** will he ***understand*** it.

119:129-136 *Pe* (פ): The psalmist prays earnestly for God to speak to him as he suffers from his adversities.

119:136 Jer 9:1, 18; 14:17 Lam 3:48
119:137 Ezra 9:15 Jer 12:1 Dan 9:7, 14
119:139 Ps 69:9
119:140 Ps 12:6
119:141 Ps 22:6
119:142 [j]*'olam* (5769) ‣ Eccl 3:11 [k]*'emeth* (0571) ‣ Ps 119:151
119:144 Ps 19:9
119:146 Ps 3:7
119:147 Ps 108:2
119:151 Ps 34:18 Isa 50:8 [a]*'emeth* (0571) ‣ Ps 119:160
119:152 Luke 21:33
119:154 Ps 35:1 Mic 7:9
119:156 2 Sam 24:14
119:158 Ps 139:21
119:160 [b]*'emeth* (0571) ‣ Prov 16:6
119:162 1 Sam 30:16 Isa 9:3
119:163 Ps 31:6 Prov 13:5
119:164 [c]*halal* (1984) ‣ Ps 135:3
119:165 Prov 3:23 1 Jn 2:10 [d]*shalom* (7965) ‣ Ps 122:6
119:166 Gen 49:18

136 Rivers of tears gush from my eyes
because people disobey your
instructions.

Tsadhe (צ)

137 O LORD, you are righteous,
and your regulations are fair.
138 Your laws are perfect
and completely trustworthy.
139 I am overwhelmed with indignation,
for my enemies have disregarded your
words.
140 Your promises have been thoroughly
tested;
that is why I love them so much.
141 I am insignificant and despised,
but I don't forget your
commandments.
142 Your justice is [j]eternal,
and your instructions are [k]perfectly
true.
143 As pressure and stress bear down on
me,
I find joy in your commands.
144 Your laws are always right;
help me to understand them so I may
live.

Qoph (ק)

145 I pray with all my heart; answer me,
LORD!
I will obey your decrees.
146 I cry out to you; rescue me,
that I may obey your laws.
147 I rise early, before the sun is up;
I cry out for help and put my hope in
your words.
148 I stay awake through the night,
thinking about your promise.
149 In your faithful love, O LORD, hear my
cry;
let me be revived by following your
regulations.
150 Lawless people are coming to
attack me;
they live far from your instructions.
151 But you are near, O LORD,
and all your commands are [a]true.
152 I have known from my earliest days
that your laws will last forever.

Resh (ר)

153 Look upon my suffering and rescue me,
for I have not forgotten your
instructions.
154 Argue my case; take my side!
Protect my life as you promised.
155 The wicked are far from rescue,
for they do not bother with your
decrees.
156 LORD, how great is your mercy;
let me be revived by following your
regulations.
157 Many persecute and trouble me,
yet I have not swerved from your laws.
158 Seeing these traitors makes me sick at
heart,
because they care nothing for your
word.
159 See how I love your commandments,
LORD.
Give back my life because of your
unfailing love.
160 The very essence of your words is [b]truth;
all your just regulations will stand
forever.

Shin (ש)

161 Powerful people harass me without
cause,
but my heart trembles only at your
word.
162 I rejoice in your word
like one who discovers a great
treasure.
163 I hate and abhor all falsehood,
but I love your instructions.
164 I will [c]praise you seven times a day
because all your regulations are just.
165 Those who love your instructions have
great [d]peace
and do not stumble.
166 I long for your rescue, LORD,
so I have obeyed your commands.
167 I have obeyed your laws,
for I love them very much.

119:137-144 *Tsadhe* (צ): God is righteous, and his word is right and just, especially in contrast to the deceptions of the wicked.

119:139 The psalmist's *indignation* (cp. 69:9) comes from seeing the wicked disregard God's word.

119:141 The psalmist is greatly troubled by his oppressors (see 119:143; cp. Isa 53).

119:145-152 *Qoph* (ק): The psalmist prays to the Lord at night. Although God appears to be distant, he is nearby.

119:145-148 ***I pray*** and ***I cry out*** translate the same Hebrew verb. • ***I rise early*** and ***I stay awake*** translate the same Hebrew verb.

119:150-151 ***Coming to attack me*** (or *are coming near to me*) is a Hebrew wordplay on ***but you are near***. The wicked remain far from God's instructions, whereas the psalmist stays near, so he does not need to fear.

119:153-160 *Resh* (ר): This petition for *life* can be found throughout Ps 119, but it is concentrated in this stanza.

119:161-168 *Shin* (ש): The psalmist looks beyond his adversaries to the peace of God. This perspective allows him to praise God throughout the day.

119:161-164 ***my heart trembles . . . I rejoice:*** Fear, trembling, and joy mark the psalmist's devotion to God. • God's word is a ***treasure***. • In the OT, *seven* signifies wholeness.

168 Yes, I obey your commandments and
laws
because you know everything I do.

Taw (ת)

169 O LORD, listen to my cry;
give me the discerning mind you
promised.
170 Listen to my [e]prayer;
rescue me as you promised.
171 Let praise flow from my lips,
for you have taught me your decrees.
172 Let my tongue sing about your word,
for all your commands are right.
173 Give me a helping hand,
for I have chosen to follow your
commandments.
174 O LORD, I have longed for your rescue,
and your [f]instructions are my
delight.
175 Let me live so I can praise you,
and may your regulations help me.
176 I have wandered away like a lost sheep;
come and find me,
for I have not forgotten your
commands.

PSALM 120

A song for pilgrims ascending to Jerusalem.

1 I took my troubles to the LORD;
I cried out to him, and he answered
my prayer.
2 Rescue me, O LORD, from liars
and from all deceitful people.
3 O deceptive tongue, what will God do to
you?
How will he increase your
punishment?
4 You will be pierced with sharp arrows
and burned with glowing coals.

5 How I suffer in far-off Meshech.
It pains me to live in distant Kedar.
6 I am tired of living
among people who hate peace.
7 I search for peace;
but when I speak of peace, they want
war!

PSALM 121

A song for pilgrims ascending to Jerusalem.

1 I look up to the mountains—
does my help come from there?
2 My help comes from the LORD,
who made heaven and earth!

3 He will not let you stumble;
the one who watches over you will not
slumber.
4 Indeed, he who watches over Israel
never slumbers or sleeps.

5 The LORD himself watches over you!
The LORD stands beside you as your
protective shade.
6 The sun will not harm you by day,
nor the moon at night.

7 The LORD keeps you from all harm
and watches over your life.
8 The LORD keeps watch over you as you
come and go,
both now and forever.

119:168 Ps 139:3; Prov 5:21
119:169 Ps 18:6
119:170 Ps 22:20; 31:2; 140:6; [e]*tekhinnah* (8467) ▸Jer 36:7
119:171 Isa 2:3; Mic 4:2
119:172 Ps 51:14
119:173 Josh 24:22; Ps 37:24
119:174 [f]*torah* (8451) ▸Isa 5:24
119:175 Isa 55:3
119:176 Isa 53:6; Luke 15:4
120:1 Ps 18:6; 102:2
120:2 Ps 52:4; Prov 12:22
120:4 Ps 140:10
120:5 Gen 10:2; 25:13; Jer 2:10; 49:28
120:7 Ps 55:21; 109:4
121:2 Ps 115:15; 124:8
121:3 Ps 66:9; 127:1
121:5 Ps 91:4
121:6 Isa 49:10; Rev 7:16
121:7 Ps 91:10-12

119:169-176 *Taw* (ת): God's servant petitions the Lord one final time; he still feels like a lost sheep.

119:176 God, the Great Shepherd, seeks out his *lost sheep* (23:1; Luke 15:4-6).

Pss 120–134 These short, appealing songs were sung during pilgrims' journeys to Jerusalem for the national festivals three times per year (Deut 16:16). The title of these psalms includes the Hebrew word for stairs, which some take to mean "ascending to Jerusalem." These psalms (sometimes called the Songs of Ascents) take the reader on a pilgrimage to Jerusalem to praise God for his goodness to Israel throughout history.

Ps 120 This short, individual lament expresses the psalmist's trust that the Lord will deal with deceptive evildoers. It also laments living as a stranger among hateful liars. The psalmist's picture of his life in a foreign land might have been a reality as he set out for Jerusalem, or it might depict his feelings and concerns as he begins his pilgrimage. Overwhelmed with injustice, he trusts God and looks forward to arriving in the Lord's presence.

120:1-2 The psalmist is surrounded by *liars*, so he makes his lament *to the LORD*, the only one who can help him.

120:3-4 The psalmist dialogues with the liars who surround him. He feels reassured that the Lord will judge them. • The Divine Warrior (see 7:12-13; 11:4-6) will throw *sharp arrows* and *glowing coals* on the liars.

120:5-7 The psalmist feels the anguish of alienation, isolation, and perpetual conflict.

120:5 *Meshech* was a Japhethite territory far to the north of Canaan. *Kedar* was an Ishmaelite territory in Arabia. Violent people lived in both locations. Meshech was the home of a famous slave trade (Ezek 27:13; cp. Exod 21:16) and Kedar of renowned warriors (Isa 21:16-17). These places can be understood as representative of the apostate, violent land where the psalmist suffered.

120:6-7 *peace:* See 37:11; 122:6-9; 125:5; 128:6.

Ps 121 The leader of the group of pilgrims uses word pictures to assure the group of the Lord's presence during the journey.

121:1 *The mountains* were known for their idolatrous worship (Deut 12:2), and Israel was enticed to the hilltop shrines (Hos 4:13). This verse can be understood as a rhetorical question expecting a negative answer: The gods of the hilltop shrines cannot rescue anyone. Others understand the mountains to be a symbol of the Lord's strength (95:4). In that case, the question would be interpreted literally (*Where does my help come from?*), with the answer given in the next verse.

121:4-6 The Creator (121:2) is the guardian of Israel. • God *stands beside* Israel, supporting and caring for the godly (see 16:7-8). • Both the *sun* and the *moon* were regarded as deities in the ancient Near East, but the Creator limits their power. They, too, praise the Lord (148:3).

121:4 God *watches over* his own, even and especially when they face many troubles (12:5, 7; 69:29; 91:14; 146:9).

122:1 Isa 2:3; Zech 8:21
122:3 Ps 48:13
122:4 Deut 16:16
122:5 Deut 17:8; 2 Chr 19:8
122:6 Ps 102:14; [g]*shalom* (7965) › Prov 3:17
122:7 Isa 62:6
122:8 Ps 133:1
123:1 Ps 11:4; 141:8
123:2 Mal 1:6
123:3 Neh 4:4; Ps 4:1; 51:1; 79:4; 119:22
123:4 Ps 79:4
124:1 Ps 94:17; 129:1
124:3 Ps 56:1; 57:3
124:4 Ps 18:16; 69:2
124:7 Ps 91:3; 141:10; Prov 6:5
124:8 Gen 1:1; Ps 121:2
125:1 Ps 46:5

PSALM 122

A song for pilgrims ascending to Jerusalem. A psalm of David.

1 I was glad when they said to me,
"Let us go to the house of the LORD."
2 And now here we are,
standing inside your gates, O Jerusalem.
3 Jerusalem is a well-built city;
its seamless walls cannot be breached.
4 All the tribes of Israel—the LORD's people—
make their pilgrimage here.
They come to give thanks to the name of the LORD,
as the law requires of Israel.
5 Here stand the thrones where judgment is given,
the thrones of the dynasty of David.

6 Pray for [g]peace in Jerusalem.
May all who love this city prosper.
7 O Jerusalem, may there be peace within your walls
and prosperity in your palaces.
8 For the sake of my family and friends,
I will say,
"May you have peace."
9 For the sake of the house of the LORD our God,
I will seek what is best for you,
O Jerusalem.

PSALM 123

A song for pilgrims ascending to Jerusalem.

1 I lift my eyes to you,
O God, enthroned in heaven.
2 We keep looking to the LORD our God for his mercy,
just as servants keep their eyes on their master,
as a slave girl watches her mistress for the slightest signal.
3 Have mercy on us, LORD, have mercy,
for we have had our fill of contempt.
4 We have had more than our fill of the scoffing of the proud
and the contempt of the arrogant.

PSALM 124

A song for pilgrims ascending to Jerusalem. A psalm of David.

1 What if the LORD had not been on our side?
Let all Israel repeat:
2 What if the LORD had not been on our side
when people attacked us?
3 They would have swallowed us alive
in their burning anger.
4 The waters would have engulfed us;
a torrent would have overwhelmed us.
5 Yes, the raging waters of their fury
would have overwhelmed our very lives.

6 Praise the LORD,
who did not let their teeth tear us apart!
7 We escaped like a bird from a hunter's trap.
The trap is broken, and we are free!
8 Our help is from the LORD,
who made heaven and earth.

PSALM 125

A song for pilgrims ascending to Jerusalem.

1 Those who trust in the LORD are as secure as Mount Zion;
they will not be defeated but will endure forever.

Ps 122 Jerusalem is here idealized as the city of God, the city of David, and the city of faith. A group of people on a pilgrimage joyfully arrive in the city (122:1-2). The poet sings an ode to Jerusalem (122:3-5) and prays for the city's peace (122:6-9).

122:1 The central sanctuary was the ***house of the LORD.*** This phrase originally referred to the Tabernacle (Exod 23:19; 34:26).

122:2 Several psalms celebrate or look forward to being ***inside*** the ***gates*** of the city (9:14; 87:2; 100:4; 118:19).

122:3-5 Jerusalem is a metaphor for God's heavenly dwelling. David was the archetype for God's chosen rulers.

122:3 In the time of David and Solomon, ***Jerusalem*** was renowned as a place of security (1 Kgs 10:6-7).

122:4 Each of the people of ***Israel*** belonged to one of the tribes, and all of the ***tribes*** belonged to the Lord. • To ***give thanks*** is to present an offering acceptable to the Lord (50:14, 23; 100:4; 118:19). • ***as the law requires of Israel:*** See Exod 23:17; Deut 16:16.

122:5 ***the thrones where judgment is given:*** In the eras of ***David*** and Solomon (1 Kgs 3:28), Jerusalem was the home of wisdom and justice; it would be so again (Isa 9:7).

122:6-9 Prayers for the ***peace*** of Jerusalem are motivated by love of family and God's sanctuary.

Ps 123 This lament on the psalmist's lowly position expresses vivid trust in the Lord (123:1-2). The psalmist prays for God's favor on the community, as the reality of evil surrounds them (123:3-4). The poet looks beyond Jerusalem (Ps 122) to God's throne ***in heaven.***

Ps 124 This thanksgiving song describes what might happen if the Lord were not present with his people.

124:1-2 The negative rhetorical questions emphasize the positive idea that the ***LORD*** was indeed on their side.

124:4-5 ***the raging waters of their fury:*** The enemies could have ***overwhelmed*** the Israelites and wiped them out if the Lord had not been with his people (cp. 69:15; Jer 46:8).

124:6-8 The enemies of God's people, like lions or bears who ***tear*** their prey with their ***teeth*** (see 57:4; Prov 28:15), had their mouths shut by the Lord (Dan 6:22).

Ps 125 The psalmist expresses the community's confidence in the Lord's protection (125:1-2) and prays for peace (125:3-5).

2 Just as the mountains surround
Jerusalem,
so the LORD surrounds his people,
both now and forever.
3 The wicked will not rule the land of the
godly,
for then the godly might be tempted
to do wrong.
4 O LORD, do good to those who are good,
whose hearts are in tune with you.
5 But banish those who turn to crooked
ways, O LORD.
Take them away with those who do
evil.

May Israel have peace!

PSALM 126
A song for pilgrims ascending to Jerusalem.

1 When the LORD brought back his exiles
to Jerusalem,
it was like a dream!
2 We were filled with laughter,
and we sang for joy.
And the other nations said,
"What amazing things the LORD has
done for them."
3 Yes, the LORD has done amazing things
for us!
What joy!

4 Restore our fortunes, LORD,
as streams renew the desert.
5 Those who plant in tears
will harvest with shouts of joy.
6 They weep as they go to plant their seed,
but they sing as they return with the
harvest.

PSALM 127
A song for pilgrims ascending to Jerusalem. A psalm of Solomon.

1 Unless the LORD builds a house,
the work of the builders is wasted.
Unless the LORD protects a city,
guarding it with sentries will do no
good.
2 It is useless for you to work so hard
from early morning until late at
night,
anxiously working for food to eat;
for God gives rest to his loved ones.

3 Children are a gift from the LORD;
they are a reward from him.
4 Children born to a young man
are like arrows in a warrior's hands.
5 How joyful is the man whose quiver is
full of them!
He will not be put to shame when he
confronts his accusers at the city
gates.

PSALM 128
A song for pilgrims ascending to Jerusalem.

1 How joyful are those who fear the LORD—
all who follow his ways!
2 You will enjoy the fruit of your labor.
How joyful and prosperous you will
be!
3 Your wife will be like a fruitful
grapevine,
flourishing within your home.
Your children will be like vigorous young
olive trees
as they sit around your table.

125:2 Ps 121:8; Zech 2:5
125:3 1 Sam 24:10; Prov 22:8; Isa 14:5
125:4 Ps 7:10; 94:15; 119:68
125:5 Gal 6:16
126:1 Jer 29:14
126:2 Job 8:21; Ps 51:14
126:3 Isa 25:9
126:4 Isa 35:6; 43:19
126:5 Ps 80:5; Gal 6:9
127:1 Ps 78:69
127:2 Gen 3:17; Job 11:18-19; Eccl 5:12
127:3 Deut 28:4
128:1 Ps 112:1; 119:3
128:2 Eccl 8:12
128:3 Ps 52:8

125:2 ***surrounds:*** God guards and protects like a wall of fire (Zech 2:5).

125:3 The ***godly might be tempted*** through peer pressure and cultural domination.

125:4-5 People who reject the straight path of the upright are fools (Prov 2:12-15). God pours out his goodness on the godly (see 122:6-9).

Ps 126 This hymn celebrates Israel's return from exile (126:1-3). The psalmist prays for full restoration (126:4-6).

126:1-3 The Lord brought about Israel's restoration from exile, just as he had brought Israel out of Egypt (114:1). The restoration transformed the weeping of the Lord's people into ***laughter*** and showed the Lord's character to the ***nations*** (9:11; 64:9; Isa 12:4). • ***Jerusalem:*** Hebrew *Zion* (see "Mount Zion, the City of God" at Ps 48, p. 947).

126:4-6 The prophets had spoken of the restoration as a time when the wilderness would change into the Garden of Eden (Isa 51:3; Ezek 47); the reality fell far short of paradise. Here the restoration community prays for full redemption (see Hag 2:19). • ***as streams renew the desert:*** The seasonal rains filled the dry river beds (*wadis*), and the land turned green again. The prayer looks for a similar transformation of Israel's ***fortunes***, a fulfillment of the imagery of the "Second Exodus" in Isaiah (see "The Second Exodus" at Isa 52:11-12, p. 1185). • The ***harvest*** represents God's full restoration.

Ps 127 Blessing and protection come from God. Without his presence, there is no success (127:1-2). This is particularly true for children, who are God's gift (127:3-5).

127:1-2 ***Unless:*** These conditional sentences emphasize the positive idea that the Lord will protect the city (cp. 124:1-2). • Human effort is futile unless the Lord blesses it (see 44:3). • ***from early morning until late at night:*** This depicts an aggressive and competitive lifestyle. • God's ***loved ones*** enjoy a quiet night's sleep (3:5; 4:8).

127:3-5 ***Children*** are one of God's blessings. The words translated "children" (Hebrew *banim*) and "builders" (*bonim*, 127:1) form a wordplay. Having children builds a family.

127:4-5 ***like arrows:*** God uses children to protect the reputation of his people against the wicked (cp. 120:4; 7:12-13).

Ps 128 The godly, who fear the Lord, will know true happiness (128:1-2). The Lord is with them (see 127:1-2), building their home life (128:3-4) and blessing them across the generations (128:5-6).

128:1-2 Enjoying ***the fruit*** of one's ***labor*** means gaining benefit from whatever work one does.

128:3 Like ***vigorous young olive trees,*** children are saplings filled with potential. Olive oil symbolizes God's blessing (104:15; Num 18:12; Jer 31:12; Hag 2:19).

128:5
Ps 122:9; 134:3
128:6
Gen 48:11
129:1
Exod 1:11
129:2
Jer 15:20
Matt 16:18
129:5
Ps 71:13
Mic 4:11
129:6
2 Kgs 19:26
Ps 37:2
129:8
Ruth 2:4
Ps 118:26
130:1
Ps 42:7; 69:2
130:2
2 Chr 6:40
Ps 28:2; 64:1
130:3
Ps 76:7; 86:5
130:4
Exod 34:7
130:5
Ps 40:1
Isa 8:17
130:6
Ps 63:6
130:7
Ps 103:4; 131:3
[h]*yakhal* (3176)
‣Ps 131:3
130:8
Luke 1:68
131:1
Rom 12:16
131:2
Ps 62:1

4 That is the LORD's blessing
for those who fear him.
5 May the LORD continually bless you from
Zion.
May you see Jerusalem prosper as
long as you live.
6 May you live to enjoy your
grandchildren.
May Israel have peace!

PSALM 129

A song for pilgrims ascending to Jerusalem.

1 From my earliest youth my enemies have
persecuted me.
Let all Israel repeat this:
2 From my earliest youth my enemies have
persecuted me,
but they have never defeated me.
3 My back is covered with cuts,
as if a farmer had plowed long
furrows.
4 But the LORD is good;
he has cut me free from the ropes of
the ungodly.
5 May all who hate Jerusalem
be turned back in shameful defeat.
6 May they be as useless as grass on a
rooftop,
turning yellow when only half
grown,
7 ignored by the harvester,
despised by the binder.
8 And may those who pass by
refuse to give them this blessing:
"The LORD bless you;
we bless you in the LORD's name."

PSALM 130

A song for pilgrims ascending to Jerusalem.

1 From the depths of despair, O LORD,
I call for your help.
2 Hear my cry, O Lord.
Pay attention to my prayer.
3 LORD, if you kept a record of our sins,
who, O Lord, could ever survive?
4 But you offer forgiveness,
that we might learn to fear you.
5 I am counting on the LORD;
yes, I am counting on him.
I have put my hope in his word.
6 I long for the Lord
more than sentries long for the dawn,
yes, more than sentries long for the
dawn.
7 O Israel, [h]hope in the LORD;
for with the LORD there is unfailing
love.
His redemption overflows.
8 He himself will redeem Israel
from every kind of sin.

PSALM 131

A song for pilgrims ascending to Jerusalem. A psalm of David.

1 LORD, my heart is not proud;
my eyes are not haughty.
I don't concern myself with matters too
great
or too awesome for me to grasp.
2 Instead, I have calmed and quieted myself,
like a weaned child who no longer
cries for its mother's milk.

128:4-6 God will ***continually bless*** all who fear him (133:3) from his dwelling in ***Zion*** (20:2; 50:2; 110:2), no matter where they live. • ***grandchildren:*** God's blessings extend from generation to generation for the faithful (79:12-13; 89:1; 100:4-5; 103:17-19).

Ps 129 The psalmist briefly reviews Israel's history of trouble (129:1-2) and redemption (129:3-4). He concludes with curses against the enemies and blessings on the godly (129:5-6).

129:1-2 Israel's ***earliest youth*** as a nation was during its sojourn in Egypt.

129:3-4 ***the LORD is good:*** He rescued Israel from Egypt, from many enemy attacks, and from the Babylonian exile.

129:5 ***Jerusalem:*** Hebrew *Zion* (see "Mount Zion, the City of God" at Ps 48, p. 947).

129:6-8 ***Grass on a rooftop*** had shallow roots and would scorch easily. A crop was ***ignored by the harvester*** when the yield was low. The enemies who had sown hurt among God's people would gain little.

Ps 130 Beginning with himself as a representative of the community, the psalmist cries for God's mercy (130:1-3) out of deep distress. He places his hope in the Lord (130:4-6), knowing that the Lord will rescue when and as he chooses. Based on this confidence, the psalmist invites Israel to wait for the Lord (130:7-8).

130:1-3 A ***cry*** from ***the depths*** is from a place of deep distress (cp. 69:2, 14; Isa 51:10; Ezek 27:34). Out of the frailty of his being, the psalmist prays for divine favor.

130:3 The psalmist knows that his ***sins*** make him guilty and deserving of God's judgment.

130:4-6 The good news comes in God's readiness to forgive sinners. His grace encourages people to fear him and hope in him.

130:5 God's ***word*** imparts ***hope*** (119:42-43, 49; 147:11).

130:7-8 ***Israel*** is invited to ***hope in the LORD*** (9:18; 27:14; 131:3) because the Lord pays the costly price for ***redemption*** and covers whatever ***sin*** separates humans from him (see also 111:9; Exod 6:6-8; 2 Sam 7:23-24; Isa 43:1-4; Titus 2:14; Heb 9:12; 1 Pet 1:18).

Ps 131 Out of his contentment in the Lord, the psalmist invites Israel to seek their rest in God (131:3).

131:1 The ***heart*** represents the whole being (see 27:8). • God hates arrogance, which is a foolish way of life (Prov 6:16-19). • The psalmist does not trouble himself with matters that properly belong to the Lord.

131:2 The psalmist ***calmed and quieted*** himself, surrendering his ambitions and taming his ego (Gal 2:20). • ***like a weaned child:*** The psalmist sees himself as a contented child.

Yes, like a weaned child is my soul
within me.

3 O Israel, [i]put your hope in the LORD—
now and always.

PSALM 132

A song for pilgrims ascending to Jerusalem.

1 LORD, remember David
and all that he suffered.
2 He made a solemn promise to the LORD.
He vowed to the Mighty One of Israel,
3 "I will not go home;
I will not let myself rest.
4 I will not let my eyes sleep
nor close my eyelids in slumber
5 until I find a place to build a house for
the LORD,
a sanctuary for the Mighty One of
Israel."

6 We heard that the Ark was in Ephrathah;
then we found it in the distant
countryside of Jaar.
7 Let us go to the sanctuary of the LORD;
let us worship at the footstool of his
throne.
8 Arise, O LORD, and enter your resting place,
along with the [j]Ark, the symbol of
your power.
9 May your priests be clothed in godliness;
may your loyal servants sing for joy.
10 For the sake of your servant David,
do not reject the king you have
anointed.
11 The LORD swore an oath to David
with a promise he will never take back:
"I will place one of your descendants
on your throne.
12 If your descendants obey the terms of
my covenant
and the laws that I teach them,
then your royal line
will continue forever and ever."
13 For the LORD has chosen Jerusalem;
he has desired it for his home.
14 "This is my resting place forever," he said.
"I will live here, for this is the home I
desired.
15 I will bless this city and make it
prosperous;
I will satisfy its poor with food.
16 I will clothe its priests with godliness;
its faithful servants will sing for joy.
17 Here I will increase the power of David;
my anointed one will be a light for my
people.
18 I will clothe his enemies with shame,
but he will be a glorious king."

PSALM 133

A song for pilgrims ascending to Jerusalem. A psalm of David.

1 How wonderful and pleasant it is
when brothers live together in
harmony!
2 For harmony is as precious as the
anointing oil
that was poured over Aaron's head,
that ran down his beard
and onto the border of his robe.
3 Harmony is as refreshing as the dew
from Mount Hermon
that falls on the mountains of Zion.
And there the LORD has pronounced his
blessing,
even life everlasting.

131:3
Ps 130:7
[i]*yakhal* (3176)
‣Isa 51:5

132:2
Gen 49:24
Isa 49:26

132:4
Prov 6:4

132:5
Acts 7:46

132:6
Gen 35:19
1 Sam 7:1; 17:12

132:7
1 Chr 28:2
Ps 5:7; 99:5

132:8-10
//2 Chr 6:41-42

132:8
Num 10:35
Ps 78:61
[j]*'aron* (0727)
‣Jer 3:16

132:9
Ps 149:5

132:11
2 Sam 7:12-16
2 Chr 6:16
*Acts 2:30

132:12
Luke 1:32

132:13
Ps 78:68

132:14
Matt 23:21

132:15
Ps 107:9

133:2
Exod 30:25, 30
Lev 8:12

133:3
Deut 4:48

Ps 132 This psalm celebrates the Lord's faithfulness to David. When David wanted to bring the Ark into Jerusalem (132:1-5), the Lord granted the request and made Jerusalem his earthly home (132:6-10). The choice of Jerusalem marked God's election of David's line (132:11-13), of Zion (132:14-17), and of the priesthood (132:9, 16).

132:2 ***the Mighty One of Israel:*** Literally *of Jacob;* also in 132:5. See note on 44:4.

132:6-10 These verses form a recollection of David's moving the Ark of the Covenant to Jerusalem (2 Sam 6:1-15) and of the Lord's oath to David (2 Sam 7:4-16).

132:6 *Ephrathah* is Bethlehem (Gen 35:19; 48:7). • ***Jaar*** is the singular form of the plural "Jearim." The Ark was at Kiriath-jearim for twenty years in Samuel's time (1 Sam 7:1-2).

132:8-10 These verses are a quotation from Solomon's prayer at the dedication of the Temple (2 Chr 6:41-42).

132:9 The ***priests*** were to exhibit righteousness in their lives (132:16; Mal 2:6).

132:11-12 The ***LORD swore an oath to David*** (2 Sam 7:4-16): God's ***promise*** is unconditional, but the covenant is not (***If . . . then***). Those who break God's covenant can expect the discipline of God's judgment (see 89:30-37).

132:13-17 The psalmist recounts the selection of Jerusalem and of the priests.

132:13 ***Jerusalem:*** Hebrew *Zion* (see "Mount Zion, the City of God" at Ps 48, p. 947).

132:17 ***anointed one:*** The ruler God chose and established (see Pss 1–8) would never cease to provide ***light for*** the Lord's ***people.*** This light would burn continually (see 1 Kgs 11:36; 2 Kgs 8:19).

132:18 The adversaries will be humiliated, in contrast to the ***glorious king*** (132:9, 16).

Ps 133 In this wisdom psalm (see Ps 1), peaceful and harmonious relationships manifest the presence of God.

133:1-2 The psalmist tells of the joy of consecrated relationships.

133:1 ***Brothers*** are related by blood, by profession, or by commitment.

133:2 The ***anointing oil*** was the oil used to ordain and consecrate Aaron for service in his office (see Exod 29:7). • ***head . . . beard . . . border of his robe:*** The oil consecrated Aaron completely.

133:3 The ***dew*** represents the richness of divine blessings; in Jerusalem, it comes from moist winds from the Mediterranean Sea. ***Mount Hermon,*** which is capped with snow, is a place of abundant moisture. • A ***blessing*** is God's life-giving power, a guarantee of his

134:1
Deut 10:8
1 Chr 9:33
2 Chr 29:11
134:2
Ps 28:2
1 Tim 2:8
134:3
Ps 124:8; 128:5
135:2
Ps 116:19
135:3
Ps 68:4; 100:5
[k]*halal* (1984)
‣ Ps 147:12
135:4
Exod 19:5
Deut 7:6; 10:15
1 Pet 2:9
[a]*bakhar* (0977)
‣ Isa 40:20
135:5
Ps 48:1; 97:9
135:6
Ps 115:3
135:7
Job 38:25-26
Jer 51:16
Zech 10:1
135:8
Ps 78:51
135:9
Deut 6:22
135:10
Ps 136:17-21
135:11
Num 21:33-35
Josh 12:7-24
135:12
Ps 78:55
135:13
Exod 3:15
Ps 102:12
135:14
Deut 32:36
Ps 106:45
135:15-20
//Ps 115:4-11
135:20
Ps 118:4

PSALM 134

A song for pilgrims ascending to Jerusalem.

1 Oh, praise the LORD, all you servants of
the LORD,
you who serve at night in the house of
the LORD.
2 Lift up holy hands in prayer,
and praise the LORD.

3 May the LORD, who made heaven and
earth,
bless you from Jerusalem.

PSALM 135

1 Praise the LORD!

Praise the name of the LORD!
Praise him, you who serve the LORD,
2 you who serve in the house of the LORD,
in the courts of the house of our God.

3 [k]Praise the LORD, for the LORD is good;
celebrate his lovely name with music.
4 For the LORD has [a]chosen Jacob for
himself,
Israel for his own special treasure.

5 I know the greatness of the LORD—
that our Lord is greater than any other
god.
6 The LORD does whatever pleases him
throughout all heaven and earth,
and on the seas and in their depths.
7 He causes the clouds to rise over the
whole earth.
He sends the lightning with the rain
and releases the wind from his
storehouses.

8 He destroyed the firstborn in each
Egyptian home,
both people and animals.
9 He performed miraculous signs and
wonders in Egypt
against Pharaoh and all his people.
10 He struck down great nations
and slaughtered mighty kings—
11 Sihon king of the Amorites,
Og king of Bashan,
and all the kings of Canaan.
12 He gave their land as an inheritance,
a special possession to his people
Israel.

13 Your name, O LORD, endures forever;
your fame, O LORD, is known to every
generation.
14 For the LORD will give justice to his
people
and have compassion on his
servants.

15 The idols of the nations are merely
things of silver and gold,
shaped by human hands.
16 They have mouths but cannot speak,
and eyes but cannot see.
17 They have ears but cannot hear,
and noses but cannot smell.
18 And those who make idols are just like
them,
as are all who trust in them.

19 O Israel, praise the LORD!
O priests—descendants of Aaron—
praise the LORD!
20 O Levites, praise the LORD!
All you who fear the LORD, praise the
LORD!
21 The LORD be praised from Zion,
for he lives here in Jerusalem.

Praise the LORD!

provision and protection (5:12; 41:2), secured by his presence (21:6; 67:1). Even the other nations will ultimately be blessed (Ps 67; 72:17). Zion is the focal point of God's blessing (134:3; 147:13). • God gives *life everlasting* to human beings.

Ps 134 In the last of the pilgrims' songs (Pss 120–134), the travelers call the Temple workers to praise the Lord. In return, they will receive a much-anticipated blessing.

134:1-2 Those *who serve at night* were the priests and Levites (see also 135:2).

134:3 ***Jerusalem:*** Hebrew *Zion* (see "Mount Zion, the City of God" at Ps 48, p. 947).

Ps 135 God, the Creator and the Lord of history, "made heaven and earth" (134:3). He deserves praise because, unlike idols, he redeems his people.

135:4 The synonyms ***Jacob*** and ***Israel*** include all twelve tribes. The Lord cherishes his chosen people. They are his ***treasure*** out of all the kingdoms of the world (Exod 19:5-6).

135:5 The Lord is superior to any real or imagined supernatural being (see 95:3-5; 115:4-8).

135:6 God is sovereign over the whole created order—he ***does whatever pleases him.*** • The phrase ***heaven and earth*** refers to all of creation.

135:7 The psalmist tells of God's sovereignty over the weather (Ps 29; 77:17-18; 78:26; 104:4; 147:8-9; 148:5-6).

135:8-12 The Lord was sovereign over the Exodus and the conquest of the Promised Land.

135:8-11 In the tenth and culminating plague against Egypt, God ***destroyed the firstborn*** of each family. • The ***miraculous signs and wonders*** are the ten plagues (see Exod 7–11; Deut 4:34; Neh 9:10).

135:13-18 The Lord's name and character stand in contrast to idols.

135:15-20 This entire section is repeated in 115:4-11.

135:15-18 Idols corrupt the thinking because they are ***merely things*** made by humans; they cannot ***speak, see, hear,*** or ***smell*** (Isa 41:22-24; 44:9, 18; Rom 1:21-23).

135:19-21 The groups named here comprised the covenant community (see 115:9-11).

PSALM 136

1 [b]Give thanks to the LORD, for he is good!
His faithful love endures forever.
2 Give thanks to the God of gods.
His faithful love endures forever.
3 Give thanks to the Lord of lords.
His faithful love endures forever.

4 Give thanks to him who alone does
mighty miracles.
His faithful love endures forever.
5 Give thanks to him who made the
heavens so skillfully.
His faithful love endures forever.
6 Give thanks to him who placed the earth
among the waters.
His faithful love endures forever.
7 Give thanks to him who made the
heavenly lights—
His faithful love endures forever.
8 the sun to rule the day,
His faithful love endures forever.
9 and the moon and stars to rule the night.
His faithful love endures forever.

10 Give thanks to him who killed the
firstborn of Egypt.
His faithful love endures forever.
11 He brought Israel out of Egypt.
His faithful love endures forever.
12 He acted with a strong hand and
powerful arm.
His faithful love endures forever.
13 Give thanks to him who parted the Red
Sea.
His faithful love endures forever.
14 He led Israel safely through,
His faithful love endures forever.
15 but he hurled Pharaoh and his army into
the Red Sea.
His faithful love endures forever.
16 Give thanks to him who led his people
through the wilderness.
His faithful love endures forever.
17 Give thanks to him who struck down
mighty kings.
His faithful love endures forever.
18 He killed powerful kings—
His faithful love endures forever.
19 Sihon king of the Amorites,
His faithful love endures forever.
20 and Og king of Bashan.
His faithful love endures forever.
21 God gave the land of these kings as an
inheritance—
His faithful love endures forever.
22 a special possession to his servant Israel.
His faithful love endures forever.

23 He remembered us in our weakness.
His faithful love endures forever.
24 He saved us from our enemies.
His faithful love endures forever.
25 He gives food to every living thing.
His faithful love endures forever.
26 Give thanks to the God of heaven.
His faithful love endures forever.

PSALM 137

1 Beside the rivers of Babylon, we sat and
wept
as we [c]thought of Jerusalem.
2 We put away our harps,
hanging them on the branches of
poplar trees.
3 For our captors demanded a song from us.
Our tormentors insisted on a joyful
hymn:
"Sing us one of those songs of
Jerusalem!"
4 But how can we sing the songs of the LORD
while in a pagan land?

5 If I forget you, O Jerusalem,
let my right hand forget how to play
the harp.
6 May my tongue stick to the roof of my
mouth

136:1 1 Chr 16:41; 2 Chr 20:21; Ps 107:1
[b]*yadah* (3034) ‣ Dan 9:4
136:2 Deut 10:17
136:4 Ps 72:18
136:5 Prov 3:19
136:6 Ps 24:2
136:7 Ps 74:16
136:8 Gen 1:16
136:10 Exod 12:29; Ps 78:51
136:11 Exod 12:51; 13:3; Deut 9:29
136:12 Deut 4:34; Ps 44:3
136:13 Exod 14:21; Ps 78:13
136:14 Ps 106:9
136:16 Exod 13:18; Deut 8:15
136:17 Ps 135:10-12
136:21 Josh 12:1
136:22 Isa 41:8; 45:4
136:23 Ps 9:12; 106:45
136:24 Judg 6:9
136:25 Ps 104:27; 145:15
136:26 2 Chr 36:23; Ezra 3:11
137:1 Neh 1:4; Ezek 1:1, 3
[c]*zakar* (2142) ‣ Isa 64:9
137:2 Ezek 26:13
137:3 2 Chr 29:27; Neh 12:46

Ps 136 This is the last of the Great Hallel psalms (Pss 120–136; see note on Book Five at Ps 107). It distinctively repeats the refrain ***His faithful love endures forever*** in every verse. The hymn is framed by a call to praise (136:1-3, 26). It proclaims the Lord as the Creator of all and the Redeemer of Israel, both in the distant (136:10-22) and in the recent past (136:23-24).

136:1-3 The psalmist invites the community to praise the Lord, who is good and full of love, the true Lord of humanity. Verse 1 alludes to the poetic expression in 2 Chr 5:13.

136:10-22 The psalmist recounts the early history of Israel's redemption.

136:13 ***Red Sea:*** Literally *sea of reeds;* also in 136:15. See note on Exod 13:18.

136:23-24 The psalmist relates the recent history of Israel's redemption, although the circumstances are not specified.

136:25 The Lord provides for all of his creatures.

136:26 The phrase ***God of heaven*** is an exilic and postexilic designation for the Lord; it is found in Ezra (Ezra 1:2; 5:11, 12; 6:9, 10; 7:12; etc.), Nehemiah (Neh 1:5; 2:4, 20; etc.), and Daniel (Dan 2:18, 19, 37, 44).

Ps 137 In response to the pain of exile (137:1-4), the psalmist resolves to remember Jerusalem even though the memories cause him pain (137:4-6). He also writes an astounding imprecation, or prayer for vengeance (137:7-9).

137:1 ***Jerusalem:*** Hebrew *Zion;* also in 137:3 (see "Mount Zion, the City of God" at Ps 48, p. 947).

137:2-4 Because the music of Jerusalem was tied to the joys of life in the Promised Land, the Exile removed any occasion for singing joyous songs. The Babylonians wanted the Judeans to sing and dance for them, but the exiles' grief made doing so either distasteful or impossible. The songs celebrating the Lord speak of his power and goodness, but his people were filled with doubts and questions. They hung their harps in trees, perhaps signifying the death of their joy under God's curse (Deut 21:23).

137:6
Ezek 3:26
137:7
Jer 49:7-22
Ezek 25:12-14
Obad 1:10-14
137:8
Isa 13:1-22; 47:1-15
Jer 50:1-46; 51:1-64
138:1
Ps 95:3; 96:4; 111:1
[d]*zamar* (2167)
‣Ps 146:2
138:2
Ps 5:7
138:3
Ps 28:7; 46:1; 118:5

if I fail to remember you,
if I don't make Jerusalem my greatest
joy.
7 O LORD, remember what the Edomites did
on the day the armies of Babylon
captured Jerusalem.
"Destroy it!" they yelled.
"Level it to the ground!"
8 O Babylon, you will be destroyed.
Happy is the one who pays you back
for what you have done to us.
9 Happy is the one who takes your babies
and smashes them against the
rocks!

PSALM 138

A psalm of David.

1 I give you thanks, O LORD, with all my
heart;
I will [d]sing your praises before the gods.
2 I bow before your holy Temple as I
worship.
I praise your name for your unfailing
love and faithfulness;
for your promises are backed
by all the honor of your name.
3 As soon as I pray, you answer me;
you encourage me by giving me
strength.

Prayers for Vengeance (Ps 137)

Ps 3:7; 9:19-20; 10:15; 12:3; 41:10; 55:15; 69:22-28; 79:6; 109:6-20; 110:5-6
2 Chr 24:22
Neh 4:5
Isa 61:2
Jer 11:20-23; 18:19-23; 51:35
Lam 1:22; 3:64-66
Luke 4:19
Acts 1:20
Rom 11:9-10
Rev 6:10

The psalmists sometimes asked the Lord to execute vengeance against their adversaries. It was not unusual for a psalmist to pray for the violent destruction of his enemies as a manifestation of divine justice.

How does one defend this kind of prayer? Is this a form of Jewish or Christian *jihad* (an Arabic word meaning "striving," sometimes meaning "holy war")? In contrast with *jihad,* the psalmist called on God, not humans, to act.

Divine justice is defined in Ps 1:6: The Lord loves the righteous and destroys the wicked. The wicked are subversive, corrupt, and thoroughly committed to evil; they live in opposition to God and to everything that God does. The wicked shake the foundations of God's kingdom, of ethics, and of society.

Prayers for termination of the wicked arose out of the psalmists' concern with justice and righteousness and out of their confidence in God. They argued that evil is inconsistent with God's nature and that the removal of evil is the only way for his kingdom to thrive. The poets of Israel did not simply invoke God's judgment on anyone with whom they could not get along. God charges the gods and their followers with the evil of injustice in Ps 82 and holds all humans accountable to his divine standard of justice and righteousness. These were also the standards that guided the psalmists.

The psalmists were intimately acquainted with grief. They had suffered and been oppressed and marginalized by bullies, leaders, and kings from inside and outside of Israel. Their prayers were full of faith and hope, asking how long the Lord would tolerate their suffering and confessing that the Lord alone could rescue them from evil. They expressed deep longing for his redemption. Through these prayers for justice and vindication, the godly may rest in peace as they await God's rescue. By the principle of retribution, they asked the Lord to inflict upon the wicked the suffering that they had endured (5:10; 6:10; 7:9; 8:2; 9:19-20; 28:4; 37:8-10, 36; 56:7; 104:35; 137:9; 139:19).

Prayers for the end of evil are appropriate as long as God is recognized as arbiter, judge, and executor. Do we truly see evil as evil, or do we perceive it merely as an inconvenience? The prayer for the coming of God's kingdom implies the removal of evil. The cruelty inflicted on the wicked has been transformed through the cruel crucifixion of Jesus Christ. Jesus will judge and bring an end to evil (see Rev 19:11-21). Christians are to love as Christ loved (John 13:34), pray for their enemies, and forgive them (Matt 5:38-48; Col 3:13).

137:5-6 The psalmist pledges his loyalty to ***Jerusalem,*** the city at the center of God's reign and the location of fellowship with him.

137:7-9 The poet witnessed the betrayal of God's people from Judah by ***the Edomites,*** so he curses Edom. The long rivalry between Edom and Judah came to a head during Judah's last days, when the Edomites handed the Judeans over to the Babylonians (Obad 1:10-11) and rejoiced in Jerusalem's fall. • This prayer for vengeance is shocking (see "Prayers for Vengeance," above).

Pss 138–145 In this final collection of psalms of David, praise and wisdom psalms (Pss 138–139, 145) form a frame around five poems of lament (Pss 140–144).

Ps 138 In this wisdom psalm, the Lord is presented as the God of gods. He rescued his people and has a perfect plan for them as individuals. The nations will join Israel in glorifying God.

138:1-3 The Lord receives praise before the gods of the nations.

4 Every king in all the earth will thank you, LORD,
for all of them will hear your words.
5 Yes, they will sing about the LORD's ways,
for the glory of the LORD is very great.
6 Though the LORD is great, he cares for the humble,
but he keeps his distance from the proud.
7 Though I am surrounded by troubles,
you will protect me from the anger of my enemies.
You reach out your hand,
and the power of your right hand saves me.
8 The LORD will work out his plans for my life—
for your faithful love, O LORD, endures forever.
Don't abandon me, for you made me.

PSALM 139

For the choir director: A psalm of David.

1 O LORD, you have examined my heart
and know everything about me.
2 You know when I sit down or stand up.
You know my thoughts even when I'm far away.
3 You see me when I travel
and when I rest at home.
You know everything I do.
4 You know what I am going to say
even before I say it, LORD.
5 You go before me and follow me.
You place your hand of blessing on my head.
6 Such knowledge is too wonderful for me,
too great for me to understand!
7 I can never escape from your Spirit!
I can never get away from your presence!
8 If I go up to heaven, you are there;
if I go down to the [e]grave, you are there.
9 If I ride the wings of the morning,
if I dwell by the farthest oceans,
10 even there your hand will guide me,
and your strength will support me.
11 I could ask the darkness to hide me
and the light around me to become night—
12 but even in darkness I cannot hide from you.
To you the night shines as bright as day.
Darkness and light are the same to you.
13 You made all the delicate, inner parts of my body
and knit me together in my mother's womb.
14 Thank you for making me so wonderfully complex!
Your workmanship is marvelous—how well I know it.
15 You watched me as I was being formed in utter seclusion,
as I was woven together in the dark of the womb.
16 You saw me before I was born.
Every day of my life was recorded in your book.
Every moment was laid out
before a single day had passed.
17 How precious are your thoughts about me, O God.
They cannot be numbered!

138:4 Ps 102:15
138:6 Ps 101:5; 113:4-7 Prov 3:34 Jas 4:6
138:7 Exod 15:12 Ezra 9:8-9 Ps 20:6; 23:4; 71:20
138:8 Job 10:3 Ps 27:9; 71:9 Phil 1:6
139:1 Ps 44:21
139:2 Ps 94:11
139:3 Job 14:16
139:4 Heb 4:13
139:5 Ps 34:7
139:6 Job 42:3 Rom 11:33
139:7 Jer 23:24
139:8 Prov 15:11 Amos 9:2-4 [e]she'ol (7585) › Prov 5:5
139:10 Ps 23:2-3
139:11 Job 22:13
139:12 Job 34:22 Dan 2:22 1 Jn 1:5
139:13 Ps 119:73
139:15 Job 10:8-10 Eccl 11:5
139:16 Job 14:5 Ps 56:8
139:17 Ps 40:5

138:4-5 As the Lord's ***glory*** fills the earth, the world's population must willingly submit to him. ***Every king*** (cp. Ps 2) will join the community of praise as they hear ***the LORD's ways*** of truth and love.

138:6-8 The exalted God takes care of the humble (138:6), especially his servant the psalmist (138:7-8).

138:6 God's holiness and excellence are ***great,*** beyond the scope of humanity (see 99:2; 113:4; Isa 6:1; 57:15).

138:8 The psalmist expresses confidence in the Lord's ***plans,*** which are perfect, and prays for God's continued involvement. The psalmist sees himself as part of God's plans (see 9:10; 139:14).

Ps 139 In this wisdom psalm, the psalmist opens every aspect of his being, character, behavior, and speech to God's examination. As hard as life is, he wants to ensure his own growth in wisdom so that he does not come under God's judgment of the wicked (141:5; 142:3; 143:8, 10; 144:3-4). Further, the poet recognizes that he cannot escape from the Lord. His sense of stress disappears when he considers the Lord's loving care for him, even before birth (139:13-18). He then invites the Lord to continue examining him as he walks in the path of wisdom (139:23-24).

139:1-6 The Lord knows the psalmist well; God has examined him thoroughly, in an inescapable examination that is painful at times (Job 7:17-19).

139:2 The phrase ***sit down or stand up*** refers to daily activities (cp. Deut 6:6-9).

139:3-6 The Lord's omniscience and omnipotence provide comfort to the godly, but they imprison the hearts of the wicked (2:3).

139:6 The Lord's ***wonderful*** understanding lies beyond the psalmist's ability to comprehend (see Judg 13:18).

139:7-12 The psalmist expresses his awe at the Lord's omnipresence.

139:8 ***down to the grave*** (Hebrew *to Sheol*): God has total access to his entire creation—even the most hard-to-reach places. See note on 6:5.

139:9 ***ride the wings of the morning:*** This poetic expression describes traveling eastward, as far as the sunrise, if that were possible. • ***the farthest oceans:*** This expression takes the traveler in the opposite direction, far to the west.

139:13 The ***delicate, inner parts*** of the ***body*** include a person's very being. • Even when hidden in his ***mother's womb,*** the psalmist was guided by the Lord.

139:17 ***How precious are your thoughts about me*** (or *How precious to me are your thoughts*): God's investigation reveals loving care. Fellowship with the Lord provides riches beyond description.

139:19 Isa 11:4
139:20 Exod 20:7; Deut 5:11
139:23 Ps 26:2
139:24 Ps 5:8; 16:11; 143:10
140:1 Ps 17:13
140:2 Ps 56:6; Prov 6:14; Isa 59:4
140:3 Rom 3:13; Jas 3:8
140:4 Ps 71:4
140:5 Job 18:9; Ps 35:7; 57:6
140:7 Ps 28:8; 144:10

18 I can't even count them;
they outnumber the grains of sand!
And when I wake up,
you are still with me!

19 O God, if only you would destroy the wicked!
Get out of my life, you murderers!
20 They blaspheme you;
your enemies misuse your name.
21 O LORD, shouldn't I hate those who hate you?
Shouldn't I despise those who oppose you?
22 Yes, I hate them with total hatred,
for your enemies are my enemies.

23 Search me, O God, and know my heart;
test me and know my anxious thoughts.
24 Point out anything in me that offends you,
and lead me along the path of everlasting life.

PSALM 140

For the choir director: A psalm of David.

1 O LORD, rescue me from evil people.
Protect me from those who are violent,
2 those who plot evil in their hearts
and stir up trouble all day long.
3 Their tongues sting like a snake;
the venom of a viper drips from their lips. *Interlude*

4 O LORD, keep me out of the hands of the wicked.
Protect me from those who are violent,
for they are plotting against me.
5 The proud have set a trap to catch me;
they have stretched out a net;
they have placed traps all along the way. *Interlude*

6 I said to the LORD, "You are my God!"
Listen, O LORD, to my cries for mercy!
7 O Sovereign LORD, the strong one who rescued me,

The Heart (Ps 139)

Ps 7:9; 9:1; 13:2; 14:1; 16:7-9; 17:3; 19:8; 20:4; 21:2; 22:14, 26; 24:4; 26:2; 27:3, 14; 28:3, 7; 33:21; 34:17-18; 37:4; 38:8, 10; 51:10, 17; 55:4, 21; 57:7; 58:2; 61:2; 62:4, 8-10; 64:6; 69:20; 73:1, 7, 13, 21, 26; 78:8, 37; 81:12; 84:2; 86:12; 89:50; 95:8, 10; 102:4; 108:1; 109:22; 111:1; 119:70, 111, 145; 131:1; 138:1; 140:2; 147:3

The Hebrew words *leb* and *lebab* (both meaning "heart") are hard to translate because they rarely refer to the physical human heart. Rather, the heart is the center of one's being, an image for a person's thought life, reflections, and will. The story of the heart reveals a person's commitment and direction in life.

The hearts of the wicked are cunning and scheming (58:2; 64:6; 140:2). They are deceptive, hypocritical (28:3; 41:6; 55:21; 62:4), lacking in integrity, greedy, and jealous (10:3; 62:10; 141:4). As time goes on, they become more arrogant (14:1; 101:5; 131:1), callous, and stubborn (17:10; 73:7; 78:8; 81:12; 95:8, 10; 119:70). Their only commitment is to themselves (78:37); their destructive way of life (5:9; 101:4) leads to their own destruction.

The psalmists openly confess their sorrow, trouble, anguish, and despair (13:2; 22:14; 25:17; 38:8, 10; 40:12; 55:4; 61:2; 69:20; 73:21, 26; 109:22; 143:4; 147:3). Through their pain, their hearts grow. They pray intensely (62:8; 119:80, 145), long for God (84:2), trust in him (28:7), and open their hearts to God's examination (7:9; 17:3; 26:2; 139:1-6, 23). Their commitment does not waver, and their lives are pure (24:4; 51:10; 73:1, 13) and contented (131:1), even when broken.

As their broken hearts (34:17-18; 51:17) are healed by the Lord (147:3), they become strong, confident (27:3, 14; 31:24; 57:7; 108:1; 112:7-8; 138:3), and vital (22:26; 69:32; 119:32). In the end, the Lord gives them the desires of their hearts (20:4; 21:2; 37:4) and then satisfies them. This fills the godly with joy and praise (4:7; 9:1; 13:5; 16:7, 9; 19:8; 30:12; 33:21; 86:12; 89:50; 102:4; 104:15; 105:3; 111:1; 119:7, 111; 138:1).

139:19-24 The psalmist's sense of awe leads him to consider the wicked and to reflect on himself. The Lord, as the examiner of all people, judges the wicked for their destructive acts and speech; thus, the psalmist prays that he will not be among them.

139:21 ***I hate:*** Rejection of evil is a mark of wisdom (see 1:1; 5:4-6).

139:23-24 The psalmist's prayer against the wicked leads him also to reflect on himself; he does not presume that he is righteous. This prayer has been repeated by believers over the centuries.

139:24 The *path* of wisdom leads to *everlasting life* (see 1:6; Prov 4:18; 6:23).

Ps 140 In this individual lament, the psalmist artistically sketches God's enemies with all their evil intents. He prays for the Lord's protection and rescue with confidence in God's strength and justice. He foresees the evil as being judged by fire (140:9-11) and himself as being vindicated and dwelling in the Lord's presence (140:13).

140:1-3 The psalmist prays for the Lord to rescue him from wicked people.

140:3 ***sting like a snake . . . a viper:*** These creatures depict the wicked as very corrupt people (see Prov 23:32; Isa 14:29; Rom 3:13).

140:4-5 The psalmist asks for divine protection (see Ps 121), praying that the Lord will keep him safe from the many schemes of the wicked.

140:7 The expression *Sovereign LORD* comes from combining the name *Yahweh* with the title *Adonai* (Master). See also 68:20; 69:6; 71:16; 73:28; 109:21; 140:7; 141:8.

you protected me on the day of
battle.
8 LORD, do not let evil people have their
way.
Do not let their evil schemes succeed,
or they will become proud.
Interlude
9 Let my enemies be destroyed
by the very evil they have planned
for me.
10 Let burning coals fall down on their heads.
Let them be thrown into the fire
or into watery pits from which they
can't escape.
11 Don't let liars prosper here in our land.
Cause great disasters to fall on the
violent.
12 But I know the LORD will help those they
persecute;
he will give justice to the poor.
13 Surely righteous people are praising your
name;
the godly will live in your presence.

PSALM 141

A psalm of David.

1 O LORD, I am calling to you. Please hurry!
Listen when I cry to you for help!
2 Accept my prayer as incense offered to
you,
and my upraised hands as an evening
offering.
3 Take control of what I say, O LORD,
and guard my lips.
4 Don't let [f]me drift toward evil
or take part in acts of wickedness.
Don't let me share in the delicacies
of those who do wrong.
5 Let the godly strike me!
It will be a kindness!
If they correct me, it is soothing medicine.
Don't let me refuse it.
But I pray constantly
against the wicked and their deeds.
6 When their leaders are thrown down
from a cliff,
the wicked will listen to my words and
find them true.
7 Like rocks brought up by a plow,
the bones of the wicked will lie
scattered without burial.
8 I look to you for help, O Sovereign LORD.
You are my refuge; don't let them
kill me.
9 Keep me from the traps they have set
for me,
from the snares of those who do wrong.
10 Let the wicked fall into their own nets,
but let me escape.

PSALM 142

A psalm of David, regarding his experience in the cave. A prayer.

1 I cry out to the LORD;
I plead for the LORD's mercy.
2 I pour out my complaints before him
and tell him all my troubles.
3 When I am overwhelmed,
you alone know the way I should turn.
Wherever I go,
my enemies have set traps for me.
4 I look for someone to come and help me,
but no one gives me a passing thought!
No one will help me;
no one cares a bit what happens to me.
5 Then I pray to you, O LORD.
I say, "You are my place of refuge.
You are all I really want in life.
6 Hear my cry,
for I am very low.
Rescue me from my persecutors,
for they are too strong for me.

140:8 Ps 112:10
140:9 Esth 9:25; Ps 7:16
140:10 Ps 11:6; 21:9; Matt 3:10
140:11 Ps 34:21
140:12 Ps 9:4; 35:10
140:13 Ps 16:11; 17:15; 97:12
141:1 Ps 70:5
141:2 Exod 29:41; 30:8; Rev 5:8; 8:3-4
141:3 Ps 39:1; Prov 13:3; 21:23
141:4 Ps 119:36; Prov 23:6; Mal 3:15
[f]*leb* (3820) ▸Prov 21:4
141:5 Ps 23:5; Prov 9:8; 19:25; 27:6; Gal 6:1
141:7 Ps 53:5
141:8 Ps 11:1
141:9 Ps 91:3
141:10 Ps 35:8
142:1 Ps 30:8; 77:1
142:3 Ps 140:5
142:4 Ps 88:8; Jer 30:17
142:5 Ps 91:2, 9
142:6 Ps 18:17; 79:8

140:9-11 The psalmist prays for God's judgment on the wicked.

140:10 The poet wants *fire* to descend on his enemies, and he wants them thrown into *pits* so they can never attack again. The language foreshadows the NT teaching on hell (Matt 5:22, 29-30; 10:28; 18:9; Mark 9:43-47; Luke 12:5; Jas 3:6; 2 Pet 2:4).

Ps 141 The psalmist prays for rescue and wisdom, and he envisions the end of evil. The principle of retribution (141:10) unifies the psalm.

141:1-2 The psalmist prays urgently for rescue. He does not have at hand either *incense* or an *evening offering* (Exod 29:38-39), but his prayers and devotion are the reality that those elements represent (cp. Isa 1:13; Rev 5:8). • *Upraised hands* are a posture of prayer (28:2; 88:9; 143:6; Exod 9:29; 1 Tim 2:8).

141:3-5 Wisdom sometimes requires protection from oneself. One could say or think things that lead to the evil path (Prov 13:3; 21:23). • Wisdom opens itself to correction from *godly* people (see Prov 3:11; 9:8; 15:31; 19:25).

141:7 *scattered without burial:* Literally *scattered at the mouth of Sheol.* See note on 6:5.

Ps 142 The psalmist faces severe persecution, so he cries to the Lord, and the Lord will rescue him.

142:TITLE *psalm:* Hebrew *maskil.* This may be a literary or musical term. • *regarding his experience in the cave:* See note on 57:TITLE.

142:1-3 Though *overwhelmed* by his persecutors (142:6), the psalmist looks to the Lord for wisdom.

142:3-4 The psalmist reaches a point of despair (see 77:3), and the Lord cares for him in his distress. The psalmist commits himself to the Lord's wisdom (see Ps 139) but laments his entrapment by the wicked (5:9-10; 140:5; 141:9; 142:3).

142:5 Though he is alone, the psalmist's trust remains in the Lord, who is his *life* (see 9:9; 16:5; 27:13).

142:6-7 Though overwhelmed by loneliness and trouble, the psalmist focuses on the Lord's goodness and protection.

142:7 Ps 13:6
143:1 Ps 140:6
143:2 Job 14:3; 22:4
143:3 Lam 3:6
143:4 Lam 3:11
143:5 Ps 77:5, 10-11
[g]*hagah* (1897) ‣Josh 1:8
143:6 Ps 63:1
143:7 Ps 69:17; 88:4
143:8 Ps 32:8
143:9 Ps 59:1
143:10 Neh 9:20 Ps 23:3; 119:12
143:12 Ps 54:5; 116:16
144:1 Ps 18:2
[h]*tsur* (6697) ‣Isa 26:4
144:3 Ps 8:4
144:4 Job 8:9; 14:2 Ps 39:11; 109:23
144:5 Ps 18:9 Isa 64:1
144:6 Hab 3:11 Zech 9:14
144:7 Ps 18:44; 69:1, 14
144:8 Deut 32:40 Ps 12:2; 41:6 Isa 44:20

7 Bring me out of prison
so I can thank you.
The godly will crowd around me,
for you are good to me."

PSALM 143
A psalm of David.

1 Hear my prayer, O LORD;
listen to my plea!
Answer me because you are faithful
and righteous.
2 Don't put your servant on trial,
for no one is innocent before you.
3 My enemy has chased me.
He has knocked me to the ground
and forces me to live in darkness like
those in the grave.
4 I am losing all hope;
I am paralyzed with fear.
5 I remember the days of old.
I [g]ponder all your great works
and think about what you have done.
6 I lift my hands to you in prayer.
I thirst for you as parched land thirsts
for rain. *Interlude*

7 Come quickly, LORD, and answer me,
for my depression deepens.
Don't turn away from me,
or I will die.
8 Let me hear of your unfailing love each
morning,
for I am trusting you.
Show me where to walk,
for I give myself to you.
9 Rescue me from my enemies, LORD;
I run to you to hide me.
10 Teach me to do your will,
for you are my God.
May your gracious Spirit lead me forward
on a firm footing.
11 For the glory of your name, O LORD,
preserve my life.
Because of your faithfulness, bring
me out of this distress.
12 In your unfailing love, silence all my
enemies
and destroy all my foes,
for I am your servant.

PSALM 144
A psalm of David.

1 Praise the LORD, who is my [h]rock.
He trains my hands for war
and gives my fingers skill for battle.
2 He is my loving ally and my fortress,
my tower of safety, my rescuer.
He is my shield, and I take refuge in him.
He makes the nations submit to me.

3 O LORD, what are human beings that you
should notice them,
mere mortals that you should think
about them?
4 For they are like a breath of air;
their days are like a passing shadow.

5 Open the heavens, LORD, and come down.
Touch the mountains so they billow
smoke.
6 Hurl your lightning bolts and scatter
your enemies!
Shoot your arrows and confuse them!
7 Reach down from heaven and rescue me;
rescue me from deep waters,
from the power of my enemies.
8 Their mouths are full of lies;
they swear to tell the truth, but they
lie instead.

He knows that the Lord alone is his Redeemer, so he offers his praise.

142:7 His experience of confinement and duress is like being in ***prison*** (see 107:10).

Ps 143 In this lament, the psalmist feels overwhelmed by constant harassment from his foes, so he turns to the Lord's love, righteousness, and faithfulness. He remembers God's acts in the past and yearns for the renewal of the Lord's love. He opens himself to God's wisdom because he knows that instruction will lead to life.

143:1-2 The psalmist prays for God's love and mercy.

143:2 All people are guilty before God (Rom 3:20-24).

143:3-4 ***I am losing all hope:*** The psalmist confesses his desperation as his life slips away under oppressive and ruthless foes.

143:5-6 Remembering God's acts from the past reassures the psalmist of God's faithfulness (42:4; 63:6; 77:3, 6; 119:55).

143:6 The psalmist's ***thirst*** is a deep longing for God's redemption (see 42:1-2).

143:7-10 The psalmist petitions the Lord for a renewal of his love.

143:7 The psalmist experiences ***depression.*** He feels that he is dying from anguish (31:10; 119:87), exhausted (39:10; 71:9; 119:81), fainting with longing (84:2), and overwhelmed by the weariness of life (90:7, 9).

143:8-10 The psalmist prays for wisdom (see 5:8; 25:4-6; Ps 138; 143:10). • ***your gracious Spirit:*** The Spirit brings God's goodness (see 23:6).

143:11 To ***preserve*** means in this case to restore from despair (80:19; 85:6; 138:7).

143:12 A prayer for vindication and renewal of life concludes the psalm.

Ps 144 This lament begins with an exclamation of love for the Lord. The community then reflects on the transitory nature of life (144:3-4). The psalmist prays for divine intervention and anticipates victory (144:5-11). A new song (144:9-10) and a prayer for rescue (144:11) open up the theme of the Lord's blessing through his provisions and protection (144:12-15).

144:1-2 The psalmist's descriptive names for the Lord reveal his deep love for him.

144:2 ***the nations:*** Some manuscripts read *my people.*

144:3-4 ***what are human beings?*** The same question in 8:4-6 elicits the answer that humans are mere mortals but are also glorious rulers. The psalmist depicts humans as having a transitory, empty existence (see 90:3, 7-10; 102:11; 109:23; 146:4).

144:5-8 The psalmist prays for God's intervention against his ***enemies*** (cp. 18:7-19).

9 I will sing a new song to you, O God!
I will sing your praises with a
ten-stringed harp.
10 For you grant victory to kings!
You rescued your servant David from
the fatal sword.
11 Save me!
Rescue me from the power of my
enemies.
Their mouths are full of lies;
they swear to tell the truth, but they
lie instead.

12 May our sons flourish in their youth
like well-nurtured plants.
May our daughters be like graceful pillars,
carved to beautify a palace.
13 May our barns be filled
with crops of every kind.
May the flocks in our fields multiply by
the thousands,
even tens of thousands,
14 and may our oxen be loaded down
with produce.
May there be no enemy breaking
through our walls,
no going into captivity,
no cries of alarm in our town squares.
15 Yes, joyful are those who live like this!
Joyful indeed are those whose God is
the LORD.

PSALM 145

A psalm of praise of David.

1 I will exalt you, my God and King,
and praise your name forever and ever.
2 I will praise you every day;
yes, I will praise you forever.
3 Great is the LORD! He is most worthy of
praise!
No one can measure his greatness.

4 Let each generation tell its children of
your mighty acts;
let them proclaim your power.
5 I will meditate on your majestic,
[i]glorious splendor
and your wonderful miracles.
6 Your awe-inspiring deeds will be on
every tongue;
I will proclaim your greatness.
7 Everyone will share the story of your
wonderful goodness;
they will sing with joy about your
righteousness.
8 The LORD is merciful and compassionate,
[j]slow to get angry and filled with
unfailing love.
9 The LORD is good to everyone.
He showers compassion on all his
creation.
10 All of your works will thank you, LORD,
and your faithful followers will praise
you.
11 They will speak of the glory of your
kingdom;
they will give examples of your power.
12 They will tell about your mighty deeds
and about the majesty and glory of
your reign.
13 For your kingdom is an everlasting
kingdom.
You rule throughout all generations.

The LORD always keeps his promises;
he is gracious in all he does.
14 The LORD helps the fallen
and lifts those bent beneath their loads.
15 The eyes of all look to you in hope;
you give them their food as they need it.
16 When you open your hand,
you satisfy the hunger and thirst of
every living thing.
17 The LORD is righteous in everything he
does;
he is filled with kindness.
18 The LORD is close to all who call on him,
yes, to all who call on him in truth.
19 He grants the desires of those who fear
him;
he hears their cries for help and
rescues them.

144:9
Ps 40:3
144:10
2 Sam 18:7
Ps 140:7
144:11
Ps 12:2
Isa 44:20
144:12
Ps 92:12-14
Prov 3:9-10
Song 4:4; 7:4
144:14
2 Kgs 25:11
Isa 24:11
Jer 14:2
145:3
Rom 11:33
145:4
Isa 38:19
145:5
Ps 119:27
[i]*kabod* (3519)
‣Prov 11:16
145:6
Deut 10:21; 32:3
145:7
Ps 51:14
Isa 63:7
145:8
Exod 34:6
[j]*'arek 'appayim* (0750, 0639)
‣Prov 14:29
145:9
Ps 100:5
Nah 1:7
Matt 19:17
Mark 10:18
145:10
Ps 19:1; 68:26
145:12
Ps 105:1
Isa 2:10, 19, 21
145:13
2 Pet 1:11
145:15
Ps 104:27
145:18
Deut 4:7
John 4:24
145:19
Ps 10:17
Prov 15:29

144:12-15 This prayer for the Lord's blessing brings the laments of Pss 140–144 to a close. It offers a vision of God's provision and protection (see Ps 127), not only for the psalmist, but for his descendants and those of all the godly.

144:12 The psalmist compares *sons* and *daughters* to plants and pillars, which are images of strength and beauty.

144:13-14 ***no enemy . . . no cries of alarm:*** These images depict peace and security.

Ps 145 This psalm is a Hebrew acrostic poem; each verse (including 13b) begins with a successive letter of the Hebrew alphabet. This hymn of praise is the last in this collection of the psalms of David (Pss 138–145). Praise continues in the last five psalms (Pss 146–150). This psalm celebrates the Lord as King of all (145:1-3, 10-13). God's actions reveal his royal qualities (145:4-7). He cares for all creatures (145:14-17) and for those who fear him (145:18-20).

145:1-3 Praise to God, the Great King who reigns over all other rulers (see 47:2).

145:4-7 This litany praises God's character and mighty deeds. *Each generation* will continue to testify to God's power (22:30).

145:5 ***I will meditate:*** Some manuscripts read *They will speak.*

145:8-9 God consistently demonstrates his character toward ***all his creation*** (see 136:25).

145:10-13 These verses form a description of the Lord's kingdom.

145:13 The last two lines of 145:13 are not found in many of the ancient manuscripts.

145:14-20 The Lord cares for his creatures.

145:20 Ps 31:23; 37:38
145:21 Ps 71:8; 150:6
146:1 Ps 103:1
146:2 Ps 63:4; 104:33
[k]*zamar* (2167)
‣Ps 147:1
146:3 Ps 60:11
146:4 Ps 33:10; 104:29
Eccl 12:7
146:5 Ps 71:5
146:6 Acts 14:15
146:7 Ps 68:6
146:8 Matt 9:30
John 9:7
146:9 Exod 22:21
Lev 19:34
Deut 10:18
146:10 Ps 10:16
147:1 Ps 33:1; 135:3
[a]*zamar* (2167)
‣Ps 149:3
147:2 Isa 11:12; 56:8
Ezek 39:28
147:4 Gen 15:5
Isa 40:26
147:5 Ps 98:1
Isa 40:28
147:6 [b]*'anaw* (6035)
‣Ps 149:4
147:8 Job 5:10; 26:8; 38:26
147:9 Job 38:41
Ps 104:27
147:10 1 Sam 16:7
Ps 33:17
147:12 [c]*halal* (1984)
‣Ps 150:1

20 The LORD protects all those who love
him,
but he destroys the wicked.

21 I will praise the LORD,
and may everyone on earth bless his
holy name
forever and ever.

PSALM 146

1 Praise the LORD!

Let all that I am praise the LORD.
2 I will praise the LORD as long as I live.
I will [k]sing praises to my God with my
dying breath.
3 Don't put your confidence in powerful
people;
there is no help for you there.
4 When they breathe their last, they
return to the earth,
and all their plans die with them.
5 But joyful are those who have the God of
Israel as their helper,
whose hope is in the LORD their God.
6 He made heaven and earth,
the sea, and everything in them.
He keeps every promise forever.
7 He gives justice to the oppressed
and food to the hungry.
The LORD frees the prisoners.
8 The LORD opens the eyes of the blind.
The LORD lifts up those who are weighed
down.
The LORD loves the godly.
9 The LORD protects the foreigners
among us.
He cares for the orphans and
widows,
but he frustrates the plans of the
wicked.

10 The LORD will reign forever.
He will be your God, O Jerusalem,
throughout the generations.

Praise the LORD!

PSALM 147

1 Praise the LORD!

How good to [a]sing praises to our God!
How delightful and how fitting!
2 The LORD is rebuilding Jerusalem
and bringing the exiles back to Israel.
3 He heals the brokenhearted
and bandages their wounds.
4 He counts the stars
and calls them all by name.
5 How great is our Lord! His power is
absolute!
His understanding is beyond
comprehension!
6 The LORD supports the [b]humble,
but he brings the wicked down into
the dust.

7 Sing out your thanks to the LORD;
sing praises to our God with a harp.
8 He covers the heavens with clouds,
provides rain for the earth,
and makes the grass grow in
mountain pastures.
9 He gives food to the wild animals
and feeds the young ravens when they
cry.
10 He takes no pleasure in the strength of a
horse
or in human might.
11 No, the LORD's delight is in those who
fear him,
those who put their hope in his
unfailing love.
12 Glorify the LORD, O Jerusalem!
[c]Praise your God, O Zion!

145:20 The Lord cares for those *who love him* and fear him. God-fearers love the Lord and find refuge in him (5:11); they seek him as their only true Savior (40:16; 70:4). They will experience a grand future (69:36), as well as God's peace (119:165).

Pss 146–150 The Psalter ends with five hallelujah psalms, so named because each begins and ends with *Praise the LORD!* (Hebrew *halelu-yah*).

Ps 146 The call to praise (146:1-2) leads into a warning against folly and false confidence (146:3-4). The psalm concludes with a blessing for all who place their hope in the Lord (146:5-7).

146:1 This verse is reminiscent of 103:1, 2, 22; 104:1, 35.

146:5-7 *the God of Israel:* Literally *of Jacob.* See note on 44:4; see also 20:1.

146:8-9 The fourfold repetition of the name of *the LORD* emphasizes that only he heals, unburdens, loves, and protects.

146:10 *Jerusalem:* Hebrew *Zion* (see "Mount Zion, the City of God" at Ps 48, p. 947).

Ps 147 The psalmist calls for the Lord to be praised for restoring and blessing Zion, caring for the poor, displaying his power over nature, and revealing himself to his people.

147:1 This verse is a call to worship.

147:2-6 The psalmist recalls the restoration of Jerusalem and the Lord's afflicted exiles.

147:4-5 The Lord created the heavens.
• *He counts the stars:* God's people can feel secure in knowing that the Lord attends to every detail of his creation; he knows all that belongs to him.

147:6 God measures out his justice on the poor and on the wicked (55:22; 140:12; 145:14; 146:7).

147:7-11 Human achievements fail to impress the God who commands nature; rather, he takes pleasure in those who fear him.

147:8 God holds sovereign power over the weather (77:17-18; 78:26; 104:4; 148:5-6).

147:10-11 *human might:* Any physical or intellectual achievement is a gift from the Lord, just like the *strength of a horse.* These gifts are a reason to praise the Lord, not to boast (Jer 9:23-24).

13 For he has strengthened the bars of your gates
and blessed your children within your walls.
14 He sends peace across your nation
and satisfies your hunger with the finest wheat.
15 He sends his orders to the world—
how swiftly his word flies!
16 He sends the snow like white wool;
he scatters frost upon the ground like ashes.
17 He hurls the hail like stones.
Who can stand against his freezing cold?
18 Then, at his command, it all melts.
He sends his winds, and the ice thaws.
19 He has revealed his words to Jacob,
his decrees and regulations to Israel.
20 He has not done this for any other nation;
they do not know his regulations.

Praise the LORD!

PSALM 148

1 Praise the LORD!

Praise the LORD from the heavens!
Praise him from the skies!
2 Praise him, all his [d]angels!
Praise him, all the armies of heaven!
3 Praise him, sun and moon!
Praise him, all you twinkling stars!
4 Praise him, skies above!
Praise him, vapors high above the clouds!
5 Let every [e]created thing give praise to the LORD,
for he issued his command, and they came into being.
6 He set them in place forever and ever.
His decree will never be revoked.
7 Praise the LORD from the earth,
you creatures of the ocean depths,
8 fire and hail, snow and clouds,
wind and weather that obey him,
9 mountains and all hills,
fruit trees and all cedars,
10 wild animals and all livestock,
small scurrying animals and birds,
11 kings of the earth and all people,
rulers and judges of the earth,
12 young men and young women,
old men and children.

13 Let them all praise the name of the LORD.
For his name is very great;
his glory towers over the earth and heaven!
14 He has made his people strong,
honoring his faithful ones—
the people of Israel who are close to him.

Praise the LORD!

PSALM 149

1 Praise the LORD!

Sing to the LORD a new song.
Sing his praises in the [f]assembly of the faithful.
2 O Israel, rejoice in your Maker.
O people of Jerusalem, exult in your King.
3 Praise his name with dancing,
[g]accompanied by tambourine and harp.
4 For the LORD delights in his people;
he crowns the [h]humble with victory.
5 Let the faithful rejoice that he honors them.
Let them sing for joy as they lie on their beds.
6 Let the praises of God be in their mouths,
and a sharp sword in their hands—
7 to execute vengeance on the nations
and punishment on the peoples,

147:13 Neh 3:3; 7:3
147:14 Deut 32:14
147:15 Job 37:12
147:19 Deut 33:3-4; Mal 4:4
147:20 Deut 4:7-8; Ps 79:6
148:1 Ps 102:19
148:2 Ps 103:20-21; [d]*mal'ak* (4397) ‣Zech 3:1
148:4 Gen 1:7; Deut 10:14
148:5 Gen 1:1; [e]*bara'* (1254) ‣Eccl 12:1
148:6 Job 38:33
148:7 Gen 1:21; Ps 74:13; Hab 3:10
148:9 Isa 44:23; 49:13; 55:12
148:13 Ps 8:1; 113:4; Rev 5:12
148:14 Deut 10:21; 1 Sam 2:1; Eph 2:17
149:1 Ps 33:3; 89:5; [f]*qahal* (6951) ‣Joel 2:16
149:2 Judg 8:23; Ps 47:6
149:3 Exod 15:20; [g]*zamar* (2167) ‣1 Chr 16:9
149:4 Ps 35:27; [h]*'anaw* (6035) ‣Prov 3:34
149:5 Job 35:10

147:13 The *bars* of the city *gates* symbolize defenses against enemies. • God *blessed* his people by empowering them with safety, prosperity, peace, and provisions (see 133:3).

147:15-18 Simply by speaking *his command,* the Lord can change the season from unbearable winter to refreshing spring (see 147:8; 148:5-6).

147:17 *like stones:* Literally *like bread crumbs.*

147:19-20 *words . . . decrees . . . regulations:* The Lord gave powerful words to Israel so that they might obey him (105:45).

Ps 148 This psalm calls for the whole created order to praise the Lord because he has honored his faithful people.

148:1 During Jesus' triumphant entry into Jerusalem, the crowds called out various blessings, including a phrase taken from this verse (Matt 21:9; Mark 11:10; Luke 19:38).

148:6 The created order is stable because of the Lord's word (see 33:9).

148:8 In the ancient Near East, people viewed different gods as having control over separate aspects of nature. The Lord, however, reigns sovereign over all natural phenomena; all the parts of creation are his servants, bringing praise to him through their obedience (77:17-18; 104:4; 135:7; 147:8, 15-18; Num 11:31). • *clouds:* Or *mist,* or *smoke.*

148:11-12 The psalmist calls all humans to offer praise to God, regardless of status, age, or gender.

148:13-14 Universal praise of the Lord is fitting because he is glorious, and he has blessed his people (see 147:13; Isa 46:13; Eph 3:10). • ***His faithful ones*** are his trusting and devoted servants (86:2).

Ps 149 This hymn of praise celebrates the Lord's victory. He is the *Maker* of Israel (149:1-2) and the victorious *King* who shares his glory with his faithful ones (149:3-9).

149:2 ***Jerusalem:*** Hebrew *Zion* (see "Mount Zion, the City of God" at Ps 48, p. 947).

149:4 God's people, whom the world ignores and despises, will be vindicated (Matt 19:30). The ***humble*** will experience ***victory*** over their oppressors and persecutors (see Isa 61:3).

149:6 Ps 66:17
150:1 ʾhalal (1984) ▸Prov 27:2
150:2 Deut 3:24
150:3 Ps 98:6
150:4 Isa 38:20
150:5 1 Chr 13:8; 15:16
150:6 Ps 145:21

8 to bind their kings with shackles
and their leaders with iron chains,
9 to execute the judgment written against them.
This is the glorious privilege of his faithful ones.

Praise the LORD!

PSALM 150

1 ʾPraise the LORD!

ʾPraise God in his sanctuary;
ʾpraise him in his mighty heaven!
2 Praise him for his mighty works;
praise his unequaled greatness!
3 Praise him with a blast of the ram's horn;
praise him with the lyre and harp!
4 Praise him with the tambourine and dancing;
praise him with strings and flutes!
5 Praise him with a clash of cymbals;
praise him with loud clanging cymbals.
6 Let everything that breathes sing praises to the LORD!
Praise the LORD!

Instrument	References	Explanation
Stringed Instruments (**minnim, Ps 150:4*****)***		
Harp or Lyre (*kinnor*)	Ps 81:2; 1 Sam 10:5; 16:16, 23; 2 Sam 6:5; Isa 5:12	The *kinnor,* the most frequently mentioned musical instrument in the Bible, was a hand-held harp or lyre. The strings were made of sheep gut, and the sounding box was at the bottom of the instrument.
Harp (*nebel*)	Ps 57:8; 2 Sam 6:5; 1 Kgs 10:12; Neh 12:27; Amos 5:23	The *nebel* was a larger and louder instrument than the *kinnor.* It was probably shaped like a bottle, with the belly-shaped sounding box on the bottom.
Ten-stringed Harp (*nebel ʿasor*)	Ps 33:2; 92:3; 144:9	The *nebel ʿasor* is often identified with the Phoenician zither, which had ten strings.
Wind Instruments		
Ram's horn (*shofar*)	Ps 98:6; 150:3; 2 Sam 6:15; 15:10; 1 Kgs 1:34; 2 Kgs 9:13; 1 Chr 15:28; 2 Chr 15:14	The *shofar,* mentioned in the Bible more than any other Hebrew instrument, is the only instrument of ancient Israel that survives and is still used in Jewish liturgy. The early *shofar* was simply a hollowed ram's horn. Later shofars might have mouthpieces added, and some are straightened with a bend near the bell of the horn. The *shofar* was used for signaling important events, not for playing music.
Flute (*ʿugab*)	Ps 150:4; Gen 4:21; Job 21:12; 30:31	The *ʿugab* was a type of flute. Its only sacred use is recorded in Ps 150:4.
Trumpet (*khatsotsirah*)	Ps 98:6; Num 10:1-10; 1 Chr 15:28; 2 Chr 15:14; Hos 5:8	The *khatsotsirah* was a sort of trumpet. Similar instruments were known in Egypt, Assyria, the Hittite Empire, and Greece. The *khatsotsirah* became an important part of the Temple service.
Flute or Oboe (*khalil*)	Jer 48:36; 1 Sam 10:5; Isa 5:12	The *khalil* was similar to the Greek *aulos,* a primitive oboe (see Matt 9:23; 1 Cor 14:7; Rev 18:22). The *khalil* had a double-reed mouthpiece and probably produced a shrill, penetrating sound.
Percussion Instruments		
Castanet (*menaʿanʿim*)	2 Sam 6:5	The *menaʿanʿim* was probably a form of the Egyptian *sistrum,* a loud metal rattle, made from rods and loose rings that rattled.
Bells (*paʿamonim*)	Exod 28:33-34; 39:25-26	The *paʿamonim* were bells attached to the hem of the priest's garment.
Tambourine or Hand Drum (*tof*)	Ps 81:2; Exod 15:20; 1 Sam 10:5; 2 Sam 6:5	The *tof* was a loud hand drum used in merrymaking. A wooden or metal hoop was covered with the skin of a ram or goat and was played with the hand.
Cymbals (*tseltselim* and *metsiltayim*)	Ps 150:5; 2 Sam 6:5; 1 Chr 13:8; 15:19	The *tseltselim* and *metsiltayim* were cymbals, probably played in a pair by one musician. The cymbals were used as signals for the singing to begin and between the sections of the psalms.
Cymbal (*shalish*)	1 Sam 18:6	The *shalish* might have been a type of cymbal or rattle.

Source: *Tyndale Bible Dictionary,* "Musical Instruments" (Tyndale House Publishers, 2001). Used by permission.

▲ **Musical Instruments in Israel (Ps 150).**

149:6-9 Vengeance is the Lord's business (see 2:3; 94:1; 102:20; 142:7; 146:7).

Ps 150 Everything that breathes is commanded to ***praise*** the Lord as he deserves. The whole Psalter describes the greatness of the Lord, so this psalm is a fitting conclusion.

150:1 The phrase ***mighty heaven*** alludes to Gen 1 and to God's glorious work in filling the emptiness.

150:3-5 The psalmist calls all people to praise God with instruments and dancing. • ***flutes:*** These wind instruments are not mentioned as being used in Temple worship. • ***clanging cymbals:*** Temple musicians clapped two bronze bowls together as percussion instruments.

150:6 ***Praise the LORD:*** This refrain is a fitting conclusion to the entire book of Psalms.

THE BOOK OF PROVERBS

Each day, life confronts us with many decisions. The book of Proverbs is a compass that helps us navigate the murky waters of life. It provides wisdom, instructions for living, and guidance for achieving strong character. Proverbs tells us how to succeed in any situation by remaining calm-headed in a crisis, patient when pressed, gentle when challenged, and firm when confronted with temptation. Above all, Proverbs shows us that the source of all wisdom is a right relationship with God.

SETTING

Proverbs is ancient Israel's anthology of wise sayings, advice, instructions, and warnings. The book is structured as a manual for a young man launching his career. The son appears to be at an age when he would be entering a profession, and some of the proverbs seem intended to help a young man get along in his career.

While Proverbs is Israel's anthology, it is not only for the people of Israel but for everyone. The book contains just a few references to Israel's specific ideas and institutions, such as the covenant, Israel's redemptive history (e.g., the Exodus), and its formal religious institutions (such as sacrifice and atonement). Proverbs supplements Israel's formal religion with practical advice.

Proverbs is a collection of sayings from various times and social contexts. Many individual proverbs find their primary setting in the royal court, addressing matters such as how to act in front of a king. Some proverbs have a family setting and best fit an agricultural context. Others pertain to the world of commerce, trade, and business. Proverbs offers wisdom and guidance for success in all the spheres of life that a young man in ancient Israel might face. Yet it is also timeless, with significant application to readers today.

SUMMARY

The collection of Proverbs has two major sections: the opening discourses (1:1–9:18) and the wise sayings (10:1–31:31). The opening discourses are talks that a father gives to his son. Occasionally, a figure named Wisdom breaks in to add her perspective (1:20-33; 8:1–9:13).

The second part of the book contains several collections of wise sayings. These proverbs cover a wide range of topics; most frequently mentioned are wealth and poverty, planning, laziness, prostitutes, hard work, relationships, pride, and humility.

GENRE AND STYLE

In the ancient Near East, wise sayings were collected into books such as Proverbs to consult when guidance was needed in a situation. The

sayings were intended to guide people to a correct course of action. In Israel as in neighboring nations, the purpose of these collections was to educate the young and give them direction for living well. Evidence suggests that Babylonian and Egyptian wisdom collections formed the curriculum of schools.

A proverb expresses an insight, observation, or piece of advice that has been popularly accepted as general truth. A proverb is a saying so universally accepted that uttering the right proverb at the appropriate time is often all it takes to resolve a discussion.

Proverbs is also a book of poetry. Its compact language holds a lot of content in few words. It is literature that rewards reflective time and meditation on its rich nuances.

One important characteristic of Hebrew poetry is parallelism, an echoing or matching effect between parts of the same line:

> The king is pleased with words from righteous lips;
> he loves those who speak honestly (16:13).

The parallelism in this example is synonymous—the second part of the parallelism continues and sharpens the thought of the first part. Some proverbs are antithetical, meaning that the first and second parts are opposites:

> A wise woman builds her home,
> but a foolish woman tears it down with her own hands (14:1).

Other proverbs make comparisons; some of these are informally referred to as "better-than" sayings:

> Better to have little, with fear for the LORD,
> than to have great treasure and inner turmoil (15:16).

Many proverbs teach through poetic imagery. For example, vinegar and smoke are both irritants:

> Lazy people irritate their employers,
> like vinegar to the teeth or smoke in the eyes (10:26).

A handful of proverbs are repeated within the book. These are identified in the notes with parallel slash marks: (e.g., 14:12 // 16:25).

OUTLINE

1:1-7
Introduction

1:8–9:18
Lectures of a Father to a Son

10:1–22:16
Proverbs of Solomon

22:17–24:22
The Thirty Sayings of the Wise

24:23-34
More Sayings of the Wise

25:1–29:27
More Proverbs of Solomon

30:1-33
The Sayings of Agur

31:1-9
The Sayings of King Lemuel

31:10-31
A Virtuous and Capable Wife

AUTHORS AND EDITORS

The Proverbs anthology was begun by "Solomon, David's son, king of Israel" (1:1), its most prominent and prolific contributor and editor. Solomon was a wise king, thanks to God's gift (1 Kgs 3:5-15). He collected

TIMELINE

about 2400s BC
Earliest Egyptian proverbs

about 1200s BC
Egyptian Instruction of Amenemope

971–931 BC
Solomon as king of Israel, writes proverbs

728–686 BC
Hezekiah as king of Judah, collects proverbs

Biblical wisdom invites us to ponder the nuances and complexities of life; it invites us to become wise.

R. C. VAN LEEUWEN
"Proverbs" in *A Complete Literary Guide to the Bible*, p. 266

Proverbs' guiding belief is that the human intellect—wisdom—founded on fear of God and tutored in traditional teachings, is the prime virtue of character, and as such is the necessary (and almost sufficient) means for creating a life of success—materially, physically, socially, and morally.

M. V. FOX
Proverbs 1–9, p. 3

proverbs and composed his own (1 Kgs 4:29-32). But he was not the last one to edit the collection or to add to it. Material written by later teachers was added. For example, 200 years after Solomon, "the advisers of King Hezekiah of Judah" collected additional proverbs of Solomon and added them to the anthology (25:1). Other composers or editors mentioned in Proverbs include Agur (30:1), Lemuel (31:1), and "the wise" (22:17; 24:23). Some of the sayings are influenced by neighboring nations, such as the "thirty sayings" of the wise (22:17–24:22, especially 22:20), which appear to have borrowed heavily from an Egyptian writing called *The Instruction of Amenemope* (1200s BC). The collection of Proverbs was edited to its final form several hundred years after Solomon's time, late in the history of Israel. Of course, it was ultimately authored by God through several of Israel's wise teachers.

READERS

Proverbs 1:8–9:18 contains a series of discourses from a father to a son (and, in 1:20-33 and 8:1-36, from a woman called Wisdom to the young man). There is some debate as to whether this was a biological son or an apprentice since the recipient of the Egyptian *Instruction of Amenemope* was an apprentice. However, the presence of the "mother" in Proverbs (e.g., 1:8) suggests a biological son.

Much of the material is more appropriate for young males than for women (such as warnings to avoid immoral women), yet Proverbs has a much broader audience than just young men. Its purpose is to teach wisdom to people (1:2), both to the simple (1:4) and to the wise (1:5). Proverbs is addressed to everyone—but not everyone will receive it (1:7).

MEANING AND MESSAGE

Proverbs is a book of practical wisdom for the affairs of life. It often takes the form of a father teaching his son, who receives instruction for an enriched life. As he walks the path of life, the son will come to crossroads where he must make decisions about which way to go.

Beyond its original audience, Proverbs helps us to make right choices today. The book of Proverbs instructs the reader that there are rewards for wise behavior and punishments for foolish behavior. While these rewards motivate us to heed instruction, they are not universal promises. Proverbs offers principles that are generally true. For example, a person who works hard and has integrity is likely to have more material resources than a lazy and shiftless person. However, the lazy person might inherit wealth, and a hard worker might lose wealth when exploited by a corrupt government official. (This disjunction between righteousness and material reward is a major theme of Ecclesiastes and Job.) Rather than guaranteeing a favorable outcome, wisdom gives us generally true principles for life decisions.

On the surface, the advice of Proverbs sometimes seems to contradict itself, but careful reading reveals the circumstances to which each piece of advice applies. Should we answer a fool's arguments? Or should we be silent when we realize that we are arguing with a fool (26:4-5)? It depends. We find the same thing with English aphorisms. On some occasions "Look before you leap" applies; other times we are reminded that "He who hesitates is lost." Contradictory sayings might

FURTHER READING

DEREK KIDNER
Proverbs (1964)

PAUL KOPTAK
Proverbs (2003)

TREMPER LONGMAN III
Proverbs (2006)

GEORGE M. SCHWAB
Proverbs in *Cornerstone Biblical Commentary*, vol. 7 (2009)

BRUCE K. WALTKE
Proverbs 1:1–15:29 (2004)
Proverbs 15:30–31:31 (2005)

both be true in different situations. Proverbs are not laws; they offer general advice and guidance. The truly wise person knows when to apply a particular proverb and when not to.

The wisdom of Proverbs is practical, but the sayings contain much more than good advice. The message of Proverbs is that real wisdom is based on relationship with God, the true source of all wisdom. This message is expressed in 1:7, "Fear of the LORD is the foundation of true knowledge." Proverbs invokes a fundamental spiritual choice because there is no true wisdom apart from a living relationship with God.

1:1
1 Kgs 4:32
Prov 25:1
Eccl 1:1; 12:9
[a]*mashal* (4912)
‣Prov 1:6

1:3
Prov 2:9; 19:20

1:4
Prov 2:10-11; 8:5, 12

1:5
Prov 9:9; 14:6
Eccl 9:1

1:6
[b]*mashal* (4912)
‣Prov 10:1

1:7
Prov 9:10; 15:33
Eccl 12:13

1:8-9
Prov 6:20

1:10
Ps 1:1
Prov 7:21; 13:20

1:11
Prov 1:18

1. INTRODUCTION (1:1-7)

Superscription

1 These are the [a]proverbs of Solomon,
David's son, king of Israel.

Preface and Motto: The Purpose of Proverbs

2 Their purpose is to teach people wisdom
and discipline,
to help them understand the insights
of the wise.
3 Their purpose is to teach people to live
disciplined and successful lives,
to help them do what is right, just, and
fair.
4 These proverbs will give insight to the
simple,
knowledge and discernment to the
young.

5 Let the wise listen to these proverbs and
become even wiser.
Let those with understanding receive
guidance
6 by exploring the meaning in these
[b]proverbs and parables,
the words of the wise and their
riddles.

7 Fear of the LORD is the foundation of
true knowledge,
but fools despise wisdom and
discipline.

2. LECTURES OF A FATHER TO A SON (1:8–9:18)

A Father's Exhortation: Acquire Wisdom

8 My child, listen when your father
corrects you.
Don't neglect your mother's instruction.
9 What you learn from them will crown
you with grace
and be a chain of honor around your
neck.

10 My child, if sinners entice you,
turn your back on them!
11 They may say, "Come and join us.
Let's hide and kill someone!
Just for fun, let's ambush the innocent!
12 Let's swallow them alive, like the grave;
let's swallow them whole, like those
who go down to the pit of death.
13 Think of the great things we'll get!
We'll fill our houses with all the stuff
we take.

1:1 *Solomon* is the foremost authority on Israelite wisdom (see 1 Kgs 3:1-28; 4:32). Many *proverbs* are rightly ascribed to Solomon, but he did not write all of them (see 22:17; 24:23; 25:1; 30:1; 31:1).

1:2-7 This prologue explains the purpose of the book and identifies the different readers to whom it is addressed.

1:2-3 *Wisdom* is practical knowledge that involves ethical choices. Words such as *right, just,* and *fair* are associated with biblical wisdom. Gaining wisdom involves *discipline*, an active, intentional training of energy toward wisdom and away from folly. The book of Proverbs encourages us to resist our natural sinful tendencies towards wrong behavior.

1:4 The *simple* are like empty containers. Wisdom and folly compete to fill their minds and hearts (see 9:1-18).

1:6 Proverbs help the wise person to understand *riddles.* Here the Hebrew word (*khidoth*) indicates enigmas or paradoxes—difficult sayings that require interpretation (cp. Judg 14:14).

1:7 *Fear of the LORD* recognizes total dependence on God for everything, including knowledge and wisdom (9:10). It is not just a mental attitude but involves service, love, and obeying God's laws (see Deut 10:12-13). Fear of the Lord is the basis of all *knowledge.* How can we understand life without knowing the most fundamental truth about it—that it is God's creation?

1:8–9:18 *My child* (Literally *My son;* also in 1:10, 15): Like other wisdom literature of the ancient Near East, much of chs 1–9 is a *father's* (and occasionally, a *mother's*) instruction to a son. Because the son is being trained to follow in his father's profession, much of the teaching concerns the son's occupation. The NLT usually translates the term as *child,* since the lessons are applicable to both sons and daughters.

1:8-19 There are two paths (1:15) in the book of Proverbs: a wise, just way and a foolish, evil way. The parents represent the wise way and encourage their child to follow it.

1:9 *crown you . . . chain of honor:* Ornaments often represent wisdom and its rewards (see also 3:22; 4:9). This imagery inspires readers to pursue wisdom with diligence.

1:10-19 The father warns his child not to join a gang of *sinners* in their plan to pounce on the *innocent,* for their evil actions will rebound on themselves (see 28:10; Ps 9:15; 35:8). The evil way is a path of violence and robbery.

1:12 *like the grave:* Hebrew *like Sheol.* In the OT, Sheol is the abode of the dead. It is not necessarily associated with punishment.

14 Come, throw in your lot with us;
we'll all share the loot."
15 My child, don't go along with them!
Stay far away from their paths.
16 They rush to commit evil deeds.
They hurry to commit murder.
17 If a bird sees a trap being set,
it knows to stay away.
18 But these people set an ambush for
themselves;
they are trying to get themselves
killed.
19 Such is the fate of all who are greedy for
money;
it robs them of life.

Wisdom Shouts in the Streets

20 Wisdom shouts in the streets.
She cries out in the public square.
21 She calls to the crowds along the main
street,
to those gathered in front of the city
gate:
22 "How long, you simpletons,
will you insist on being simpleminded?
How long will you mockers relish your
mocking?
How long will you fools hate
knowledge?
23 Come and listen to my counsel.
I'll share my heart with you
and make you wise.
24 "I called you so often, but you wouldn't
come.
I reached out to you, but you paid no
attention.
25 You ignored my advice
and rejected the correction I offered.
26 So I will laugh when you are in trouble!
I will mock you when disaster
overtakes you—
27 when calamity overtakes you like a
storm,
when disaster engulfs you like a
cyclone,
and anguish and distress overwhelm
you.
28 "When they cry for help, I will not
answer.
Though they anxiously search for me,
they will not find me.
29 For they hated knowledge
and chose not to fear the LORD.

1:15 Ps 1:1; 119:101 Prov 4:14
1:16 Isa 59:7 *Rom 3:15-17
1:19 Prov 15:27
1:20 Prov 8:1-5; 9:3
1:22 Prov 9:4; 14:15
1:23 Joel 2:28
1:24 Isa 65:12; 66:4
1:25 2 Chr 36:16 Ps 107:11
1:26 Ps 2:4
1:27 Prov 10:25
1:28 Job 27:9 Ps 18:41 Ezek 8:18 Zech 7:13
1:29 Job 21:14

Fear of the LORD (1:7)

Prov 3:7; 8:13; 9:10; 10:27; 14:2, 26-27; 15:16, 33; 19:23; 22:4
Job 28:28
Ps 14:1; 111:10
Eccl 12:13
Isa 11:1-2; 33:6

The main theme of Proverbs can be summed up in just ten words that appear near the beginning of the book: "Fear of the LORD is the foundation of true knowledge" (1:7). *Fear* implies respect, awe, and (at times) knee-knocking terror. It also acknowledges that everything, including knowledge and wisdom, comes from total dependence on God. The fear of the Lord leads people toward humility and away from pride (3:7; 15:33). With such an attitude, readers of Proverbs are more apt to listen to God than to their own independent judgment.

Fear of the Lord recognizes God's central place in the order of the world. God is the Creator and Master of all things. This is why Ps 14:1 labels those who reject God as "fools." Those who fear the Lord receive wisdom because they begin to understand that everything is under God's rule and in his service. This is more than just an attitude; it is a way of living that takes into account God's power and authority and our ultimate accountability to him.

Wisdom is closely connected with a proper relationship with God—both require choices in line with God's character (see 14:2; Job 28:28; Eccl 12:13). Do you want wisdom? Then you must enter into a relationship with the one who has all wisdom (see 1 Cor 1–2; Col 2:3).

1:17-19 Birds will not go into an obvious *trap*, but *greedy* people will. By resorting to violence and robbery, they will be violently robbed of *life*. They might be killed in the attempt or executed when caught. Even if sinners prosper until the end of their lives, they will find judgment in death, but the righteous will be in God's presence (see Ps 1).

1:20-33 The author personifies wisdom as a woman (the Hebrew noun translated wisdom, *khokmah*, is grammatically feminine) and encourages his son to embrace her (see 3:18; 8:1–9:6).

1:22 Three main words in Proverbs describe those who lack God's wisdom. *Simpletons* (Hebrew *pethim*) have not hardened themselves against God's wisdom and are most open to correction (see 1:4). *Fools* (Hebrew *kesilim*) have heard God's wisdom but resist it. *Mockers* (Hebrew *latsonim*) not only resist wisdom but ridicule it.

1:23 Wisdom invites all three groups (1:22) to *come* so she can make them *wise*. An intimate relationship with Wisdom means entering an intimate relationship with God, the foundation of true knowledge (1:7; see Job 28).

1:24-27 *You ignored my advice*—i.e., the call of God himself (see Ps 14). God calls to us through creation (Ps 8; Rom 1:18-20) and Scripture (2 Tim 3:16-17; 2 Pet 1:20-21).

1:28 *I will not answer:* If a person has not sought wisdom before calamity strikes, it is often too late to learn.

1:29-30 *they hated knowledge:* There is no middle ground in the language of Proverbs. One either loves and embraces Wisdom or hates and rejects her.

1:30
Ps 81:11

1:31
Job 4:8
Prov 5:22; 22:8

1:32
Jer 2:19

1:33
Ps 23:4
Prov 3:24-26

2:1
Prov 3:1; 4:10

2:4
Prov 3:14
Matt 13:44

2:6
Job 32:8
Jas 1:5

2:7
[c]*magen* (4043)
› Prov 30:5

2:8
1 Sam 2:9

2:9
Prov 8:20

2:10
Prov 14:33; 22:18

2:11
Ps 82:5
Prov 6:22

2:14
Prov 10:23
Hab 1:15

30 They rejected my advice
and paid no attention when I
corrected them.
31 Therefore, they must eat the bitter fruit
of living their own way,
choking on their own schemes.
32 For simpletons turn away from me—to
death.
Fools are destroyed by their own
complacency.
33 But all who listen to me will live in peace,
untroubled by fear of harm."

The Benefits of Wisdom

2 1 My child, listen to what I say,
and treasure my commands.
2 Tune your ears to wisdom,
and concentrate on understanding.
3 Cry out for insight,
and ask for understanding.
4 Search for them as you would for silver;
seek them like hidden treasures.
5 Then you will understand what it means
to fear the LORD,
and you will gain knowledge of God.
6 For the LORD grants wisdom!
From his mouth come knowledge and
understanding.
7 He grants a treasure of common sense to
the honest.
He is a [c]shield to those who walk with
integrity.
8 He guards the paths of the just
and protects those who are faithful
to him.

9 Then you will understand what is right,
just, and fair,
and you will find the right way to go.
10 For wisdom will enter your heart,
and knowledge will fill you with joy.
11 Wise choices will watch over you.
Understanding will keep you safe.
12 Wisdom will save you from evil people,
from those whose words are twisted.
13 These men turn from the right way
to walk down dark paths.
14 They take pleasure in doing wrong,
and they enjoy the twisted ways of
evil.

Wisdom (2:1-22)

Prov 1:7; 6:6-8; 12:1; 30:24-28
Deut 1:13-18; 4:5-8; 34:9
1 Kgs 3:1-28
Job 12:12; 28:20-28
Ps 19:7; 90:12; 107:43; 119:98
Eccl 2:12-16; 7:4-19
Isa 11:1-2
Jer 9:23-24; 10:12
Hos 14:9
Matt 11:19
Luke 7:35
1 Cor 3:18-20
Jas 1:5; 3:13-17
Rev 7:12

Wisdom helps us to know how to act and speak in different situations. It provides the ability to avoid problems as well as the skill to handle them when they arise. Wisdom goes beyond simple intelligence. Proverbs notes that even animals such as ants, rock badgers, locusts, and lizards (30:24-28) are wise. This is not because they have great intelligence but because they know how to navigate life skillfully.

The foundation of wisdom is God himself. No wisdom exists apart from fear of the Lord (1:7). Wisdom is closely connected to righteousness and remains distant from evil. According to Proverbs, wisdom is gained through observation and experience (6:6-8), from instruction based on tradition (22:17-21), in learning from mistakes (12:1), and finally, but most importantly, through divine revelation (1:7).

In 1 Cor 1–2, Paul contrasts the "wisdom" of the world (which he calls foolishness) with the wisdom of Christ. Paul also says of Jesus, "In him lie hidden all the treasures of wisdom and knowledge" (Col 2:3).

1:31 Evil people suffer the consequences of their own actions (see 1:15-19); God will ensure that sinners receive their proper punishment (see Matt 25:44-46; Heb 10:29; 2 Pet 2:9).

1:33 Truly wise people are ***untroubled by fear.*** They know that God is in control, and wisdom guides them in dealing with every situation.

2:1-22 The father urges his son to seek wisdom. It will protect him from evil men and from the dangers of promiscuous women. The son must seek wisdom, while understanding that it is a gift from God.

2:1 ***My child:*** Literally *My son.* See note on 1:8–9:18. • To ***treasure my commands*** means to give attention to them and obey them; they allow us to live to the fullest.

2:2-3 ***wisdom . . . insight . . . understanding:*** All three words point toward skills needed to navigate life's difficulties.

2:4 Searching for ***silver*** or ***hidden treasures*** would be undertaken with urgency, excitement, and anticipation of reward (cp. Matt 13:44; Luke 15:8-10).

2:5 The quest for true wisdom leads to God. Wisdom is impossible without fear of the Lord (1:7).

2:6 ***The LORD grants wisdom*** to those who learn it from the Scriptures, which come ***from his mouth*** (2 Tim 3:16; 2 Pet 1:20-21). It is impossible to become wise through empirical observation alone.

2:7-8 Here, ***common sense*** is intuitive understanding built through listening to God's words and observing his world. God ***is a shield*** who ***guards*** and ***protects*** those who live in relationship with him.

2:10 ***Wisdom will enter your heart,*** becoming an integral part of life. Rather than occasionally doing wise things, the wise person consistently makes wise choices. • ***Knowledge*** brings ***joy*** because it helps people live successfully.

2:12-15 Wisdom discerns when ***words are twisted*** to represent what is wrong as being right. The ***right way*** leads to life, the ***wrong*** way to death (1:10-19; 2:18-19; 5:5-6; 9:1-6, 13-18). • ***dark paths:*** In the NT, darkness represents the realm of evil, while light represents the realm of God's goodness (Matt 4:16; 5:14-16; John 1:14; Rom 2:19).

15 Their actions are crooked,
and their ways are wrong.
16 Wisdom will save you from the immoral woman,
from the seductive words of the promiscuous woman.
17 She has abandoned her husband
and ignores the covenant she made before God.
18 Entering her house leads to death;
it is the road to the grave.
19 The man who visits her is doomed.
He will never reach the paths of life.
20 Follow the steps of good men instead,
and stay on the paths of the righteous.
21 For only the godly will live in the land,
and those with integrity will remain in it.
22 But the wicked will be removed from the land,
and the treacherous will be uprooted.

Trusting in the Lord

3 1 My child, never forget the things I have taught you.
Store my commands in your heart.
2 If you do this, you will live many years,
and your life will be satisfying.
3 Never let [d]loyalty and kindness leave you!
Tie them around your neck as a reminder.
Write them deep within your heart.
4 Then you will find favor with both God and people,
and you will earn a good reputation.
5 Trust in the Lord with all your heart;
do not depend on your own understanding.
6 Seek his will in all you do,
and he will show you which path to take.
7 Don't be impressed with your own wisdom.
Instead, fear the Lord and turn away from evil.
8 Then you will have healing for your body
and strength for your bones.
9 Honor the Lord with your wealth
and with the best part of everything you produce.
10 Then he will fill your barns with grain,
and your vats will overflow with good wine.
11 My child, don't reject the Lord's discipline,
and don't be upset when he corrects you.
12 For the Lord corrects those he loves,
just as a father corrects a child in whom he delights.
13 [e]Joyful is the person who finds wisdom,
the one who gains understanding.
14 For wisdom is more profitable than silver,
and her wages are better than gold.
15 Wisdom is more precious than rubies;
nothing you desire can compare with her.

2:15 Ps 125:5
2:16 Prov 6:24; 23:27
2:17 Mal 2:14-15
2:18 Prov 7:27
2:20 Prov 13:20
2:21 Ps 37:9, 29
2:22 Ps 37:37-38; Prov 10:30
3:2 Ps 91:16; 119:93; Prov 9:11
3:3 Prov 6:21; 7:3; 2 Cor 3:3; [d]*khesed* (2617) ‣Lam 3:22
3:4 Prov 8:35; Luke 2:52
3:5 Prov 22:19
3:6 1 Chr 28:9; Prov 16:3
3:7 Job 1:1; 28:28; Prov 4:21; 8:13; 16:6
3:9 Exod 23:19; Mal 3:10
3:11 Job 5:17; *Heb 12:5-6
3:13 Job 28:17; [e]*'ashrey* (0835) ‣Prov 14:21
3:14 Prov 8:10, 19
3:16 Prov 3:2; 22:4

2:16 Wisdom keeps a young man from an ***immoral woman***, helping him to resist her flattering, ***seductive words***. Wisdom includes emotional maturity, restraint, and the ability to assess the purpose of someone's speech.

2:17 By pursuing another man, an immoral woman has ***abandoned her husband***. Her marriage ***covenant . . . before God*** included vows of faithfulness (cp. Mal 2:14-16).

2:18-19 Adultery ***leads . . . to the grave*** (literally *to the spirits of the dead*). It betrays a fundamental covenant with one's spouse and with God (see also Gen 39:2-9; Mal 2:14).

2:20-22 Those who make wise choices ***will live in the land;*** those who do not will be evicted. God gave the land of Israel to his people, but they could only stay in it if they followed God's commands (Deut 28:9-11, 64-68). If they broke his law (Exod 20:14; Deut. 5:18), they were expelled (586 BC; see 2 Kgs 25; 2 Chr 36:15-21).

3:1-12 The Lord blesses those who trust him and seek his will. His correction benefits those who follow him.

3:1 ***My child:*** Literally *My son;* also in 3:11, 21. See note on 1:8–9:18. • To ***store*** God's ***commands in your heart*** means not just memorizing them but making them an integral part of life and acting on them.

3:2 Those who obey God's laws are more likely to ***live many years;*** wickedness generally has negative physical and psychological consequences. However, evil people sometimes outlive righteous people (Eccl 7:15-18).

3:3 ***Loyalty and kindness*** reflect the intimate and wholehearted commitment of God's covenant relationship with his people (see Deut 6:8-9). • ***write them:*** For a parallel command, see 7:3.

3:5-6 On the path of wisdom, God himself guides us by the wisdom embodied in his word.

3:8 ***Healing*** and ***strength*** mean enjoying physical vitality as God's reward for following wisdom's way.

3:9-10 God receives ***honor*** and blesses his people when they recognize him as the source of all they have and when they give him the ***best part of everything*** they ***produce*** (Gen 4:3-5; 18:6; Exod 34:36; Num 18:12, 29).

3:11-12 ***The Lord's discipline*** can take the form of hardships, disappointments, and frustrations (see Heb 12:4-6). Like a good ***father***, God's purpose is to make us wise, good, and happy. • ***just as a father corrects a child in whom he delights:*** Greek version reads *and he punishes those he accepts as his children.* Cp. Heb 12:6.

3:13 ***Wisdom*** and ***understanding*** provide skill for living and handling life's problems.

3:14-15 ***Wisdom*** is worth more than ***precious*** metals and jewels. It leads to relationship with God, the ultimate joy-giver (see 2:1-8).

3:17
[f]*shalom* (7965)
‣Prov 12:20
3:19
Prov 8:27-28
3:20
Gen 7:11
3:21
Prov 4:21
3:22
Deut 32:47
Prov 1:9; 4:22
3:23
Prov 4:12; 10:9
3:24
Job 5:21; 11:19
Ps 3:5
Prov 1:33; 6:22
3:25
Ps 91:5
3:27
Deut 24:15
Rom 13:8
3:29
Prov 14:22
3:30
Prov 26:17
Rom 12:18
3:31
Ps 37:1
Prov 24:1
[g]*qana'* (7065)
‣Prov 14:30
3:32
Ps 25:14
3:33
Deut 11:28
Job 8:6
Mal 2:2
3:34
*Jas 4:6
*1 Pet 5:5
[h]*'anaw* (6035)
‣Isa 29:19
4:1
Prov 1:8
4:4
Prov 3:1; 4:10; 9:11
4:5
Prov 4:7; 16:16
4:6
Prov 2:11
2 Thes 2:10
[i]*'azab* (5800)
‣Jer 2:13
4:7
Prov 23:23

16 She offers you long life in her right hand,
and riches and honor in her left.
17 She will guide you down delightful paths;
all her ways are [f]satisfying.
18 Wisdom is a tree of life to those who
embrace her;
happy are those who hold her tightly.

19 By wisdom the LORD founded the earth;
by understanding he created the
heavens.
20 By his knowledge the deep fountains of
the earth burst forth,
and the dew settles beneath the night
sky.

21 My child, don't lose sight of common
sense and discernment.
Hang on to them,
22 for they will refresh your soul.
They are like jewels on a necklace.
23 They keep you safe on your way,
and your feet will not stumble.
24 You can go to bed without fear;
you will lie down and sleep soundly.
25 You need not be afraid of sudden
disaster
or the destruction that comes upon
the wicked,
26 for the LORD is your security.
He will keep your foot from being
caught in a trap.

27 Do not withhold good from those who
deserve it
when it's in your power to help them.
28 If you can help your neighbor now, don't
say,
"Come back tomorrow, and then I'll
help you."

29 Don't plot harm against your neighbor,
for those who live nearby trust you.

30 Don't pick a fight without reason,
when no one has done you harm.

31 Don't [g]envy violent people
or copy their ways.
32 Such wicked people are detestable to the
LORD,
but he offers his friendship to the
godly.

33 The LORD curses the house of the wicked,
but he blesses the home of the upright.

34 The LORD mocks the mockers
but is gracious to the [h]humble.

35 The wise inherit honor,
but fools are put to shame!

A Father's Wise Advice

4 1 My children, listen when your father
corrects you.
Pay attention and learn good
judgment,
2 for I am giving you good guidance.
Don't turn away from my instructions.
3 For I, too, was once my father's son,
tenderly loved as my mother's only
child.

4 My father taught me,
"Take my words to heart.
Follow my commands, and you will
live.
5 Get wisdom; develop good judgment.
Don't forget my words or turn away
from them.
6 Don't [i]turn your back on wisdom, for she
will protect you.
Love her, and she will guard you.
7 Getting wisdom is the wisest thing you
can do!
And whatever else you do, develop
good judgment.

3:18 The *tree of life* alludes to the original tree in the Garden of Eden (Gen 2:9).

3:19-20 God's *wisdom* created harmony in the universe. Having wisdom means living in conformity with principles embedded in creation.

3:21-26 This passage enumerates the benefits of *common sense* and *discernment,* which are fruits of wisdom.

3:27-28 A wise person is a kind and helpful *neighbor.* Proverbs strongly emphasizes helping the financially needy (11:24; 28:27; 29:7, 14).

3:29 Because we have frequent contact with *those who live nearby,* we must not take advantage of them.

3:30 While it is impossible to avoid all conflict, we are not to *pick a fight.*

3:31-32 The *violent* will ultimately be punished for their ways (1:18-32), even if they seem to have an enviable position in the world (11:16).The wise will not *envy* them, because they are *detestable to the LORD.* God's *friendship* is of far greater benefit than anything the violent achieve.

3:34 The Greek version reads *The LORD opposes the proud / but favors the humble.* Cp. Jas 4:6; 1 Pet 5:5.

4:1 *My children:* Literally *My sons.* See note on 1:8–9:18. • Discourses in chs 1–9 often begin with the call to *listen* (cp. 1:8, 23; 2:1; 4:20-21; 5:1-2; 6:20-23; 7:1-3). • *when your father corrects you:* The children have reason to listen, because they have made mistakes.

4:2 Wise people navigate life's difficulties successfully because they have heeded *good guidance.*

4:3 *my father's son . . . my mother's only child:* In Proverbs, both parents give instruction in wisdom. This involvement of both parents is unique among the traditions of the ancient Near East.

4:4 *my commands:* The words that describe the father's teaching are used elsewhere in Scripture for God's law. Fathers represent God to their children; the instruction of wise fathers conforms to God's law.

4:5 In the OT, to *forget* means more than not to remember; it is failure to obey.

4:6 *she:* In Proverbs, *wisdom* is sometimes personified as a woman (see 1:20-33; 8:1–9:6).

8 If you prize wisdom, she will make you
great.
Embrace her, and she will honor you.
9 She will place a lovely wreath on your
head;
she will present you with a beautiful
crown."

10 My child, listen to me and do as I say,
and you will have a long, good life.
11 I will teach you wisdom's ways
and lead you in straight paths.
12 When you walk, you won't be held back;
when you run, you won't stumble.
13 Take hold of my instructions; don't let
them go.
Guard them, for they are the key to life.

14 Don't do as the wicked do,
and don't follow the path of evildoers.
15 Don't even think about it; don't go that
way.
Turn away and keep moving.
16 For evil people can't sleep until they've
done their evil deed for the day.
They can't rest until they've caused
someone to stumble.
17 They eat the food of wickedness
and drink the wine of violence!

18 The way of the righteous is like the first
gleam of dawn,
which shines ever brighter until the
full light of day.
19 But the way of the wicked is like total
darkness.
They have no idea what they are
stumbling over.

20 My child, pay attention to what I say.
Listen carefully to my words.
21 Don't lose sight of them.
Let them penetrate deep into your
heart,
22 for they bring life to those who find
them,
and healing to their whole body.

23 Guard your heart above all else,
for it determines the course of your
life.

24 Avoid all perverse talk;
stay away from corrupt speech.

25 Look straight ahead,
and fix your eyes on what lies before
you.
26 Mark out a straight path for your feet;
stay on the safe path.
27 Don't get sidetracked;
keep your feet from following evil.

Avoid Immoral Women

5 1 My son, pay attention to my wisdom;
listen carefully to my wise counsel.
2 Then you will show discernment,
and your lips will express what you've
learned.

3 For the lips of an immoral woman are as
sweet as honey,
and her mouth is smoother than oil.

4:8 Prov 3:18
4:10 Prov 2:1; 9:11; 10:27; 22:4
4:13 Prov 3:18, 21
4:14 Ps 1:1; Prov 1:15
4:16 Ps 36:4; Mic 2:1
4:18 2 Sam 23:4; Dan 12:3
4:19 Job 18:5; Isa 59:9-10
4:20 Prov 2:1; 5:1
4:21 Prov 3:21; 7:1
4:22 Prov 3:8, 22
4:23 Luke 6:45
4:24 Job 11:14
4:25 Job 31:1
4:26 Heb 12:13
4:27 Deut 5:32; 28:14
5:1 Prov 4:20
5:3 Ps 55:21; Prov 5:20; 7:5

4:7-8 *Wisdom* often, though not always, brings relational and material prosperity.

4:9 *A lovely wreath* and a *beautiful crown* represent wisdom's rewards (see also 1:9 and 3:22).

4:10-19 The father again lays two paths before his children, encouraging them to avoid evil with its horrible consequences and to embrace good with its promise of blessing.

4:10 *My child:* Literally *My son;* also in 4:20. See note on 1:8–9:18. • Not every wise person lives longer than every evil person, but obedience and wise living make *long, good life* much more likely (see also 5:1-14, 21-23; 23:29-35; cp. Eccl 2:12-17).

4:11-12 *Wisdom's . . . paths* are *straight* (nondeceptive), while those of a fool are crooked (2:15). • *When you walk . . . run:* The wise reach their goals more quickly and efficiently.

4:16 The wicked stay up at night to plan evil (Ps 36:4; Mic 2:1).

4:17 To *eat . . . wickedness* and *drink . . . violence* means that those attributes are at the very center of someone's life. Just as we eat and drink to stay alive, evil people sustain themselves by committing evil acts.

4:18-19 *Light* stands for wisdom and righteousness, and *darkness* stands for foolishness and wickedness (see Eccl 2:12-14). Light brings actions into the open; darkness hides them. Righteous people have nothing to hide, while the wicked try to hide what they do and end up *stumbling over* obstacles in the dark (see Matt 4:16; 5:14-16; John 1:14; Rom 2:19).

4:20-27 The wise walk the path of life with eyes straight ahead.

4:20-21 *pay attention:* See also 1:8, 23; 2:1; 5:1-2; 7:1-3; 8:1. The child is to let these teachings transform his personality, represented by his *heart.* A lifelong commitment to follow wisdom requires a change of heart.

4:22 *Life* and *healing* are rewards for following the wise instructions of the father (see 4:10).

4:23 In the OT, the *heart* represents the center of emotions, thinking, and reasoning (e.g., Gen 6:5; Deut 4:29; Ps 131:1). The heart is crucial in the battle between wisdom and foolishness, between righteousness and evil (see Matt 5:8; 13:15; John 12:40; Rom 6:17).

4:24 Because a person's words originate in the heart, Proverbs teaches extensively about speech. One of the most basic lessons is to avoid *perverse* or *corrupt* speech, later defined as lies, slander, gossip, and rumor (6:12; 17:4; 18:8).

5:1-23 These instructions on embracing one's wife and avoiding immoral women were originally addressed to young men just beginning their professional careers (see also 2:16-22; 7:1-27). This topic is also popular in ancient Egyptian wisdom writing.

5:1-2 Paying *attention* to instruction results in *discernment*—the ability to tell a right action from a wrong one. These instructions are vitally important when dealing with an immoral woman.

5:3-4 The *lips* of the immoral woman seem sweet and enticing but are actually bitter and deadly. Sexual activity

5:4 Ps 57:4; Eccl 7:26
5:5 Prov 2:18; 7:27; [j]*she'ol* (7585) ‣Prov 23:14
5:6 2 Pet 2:14
5:7 Prov 7:24
5:8 Prov 7:25; 9:14
5:12 Prov 1:22, 25
5:13 Prov 1:8
5:16 Prov 5:18
5:18 Eccl 9:9; Mal 2:14
5:19 Song 4:5; 7:3
5:20 Prov 2:16; 5:3
5:21 Job 14:16; Ps 119:168
5:22 Num 32:23

4 But in the end she is as bitter as poison,
as dangerous as a double-edged sword.
5 Her feet go down to death;
her steps lead straight to the [j]grave.
6 For she cares nothing about the path to life.
She staggers down a crooked trail and doesn't realize it.

7 So now, my sons, listen to me.
Never stray from what I am about to say:
8 Stay away from her!
Don't go near the door of her house!
9 If you do, you will lose your honor
and will lose to merciless people all you have achieved.
10 Strangers will consume your wealth,
and someone else will enjoy the fruit of your labor.
11 In the end you will groan in anguish
when disease consumes your body.
12 You will say, "How I hated discipline!
If only I had not ignored all the warnings!
13 Oh, why didn't I listen to my teachers?
Why didn't I pay attention to my instructors?
14 I have come to the brink of utter ruin,
and now I must face public disgrace."

15 Drink water from your own well—
share your love only with your wife.
16 Why spill the water of your springs in the streets,
having sex with just anyone?
17 You should reserve it for yourselves.
Never share it with strangers.

18 Let your wife be a fountain of blessing for you.
Rejoice in the wife of your youth.
19 She is a loving deer, a graceful doe.
Let her breasts satisfy you always.
May you always be captivated by her love.
20 Why be captivated, my son, by an immoral woman,
or fondle the breasts of a promiscuous woman?

21 For the LORD sees clearly what a man does,
examining every path he takes.
22 An evil man is held captive by his own sins;
they are ropes that catch and hold him.

Marriage and Sexuality (5:15-20)

Prov 2:16-22; 6:20-35; 7:1-27; Gen 2:18-25; Jer 5:7-11; Hos 2:20; Mal 2:14-16; Matt 19:4-6; 22:30; 1 Cor 6:15-20; Heb 13:4

In Proverbs, the wise teacher frequently warns naive young men to avoid the temptations of sexual expression outside of marriage (2:16-22; 5:1-23; 6:20–7:27). While a young man might find other women physically attractive and seductive, the consequences of acting on these temptations are dire: His family and professional aspirations might be destroyed. Proverbs teaches young men to cultivate a strong relationship with their own wives. They are counseled to have healthy marital sex rather than sleeping with other women (5:15-20). Although Proverbs was originally written to instruct young men, women readers can think in the same categories and consider the same important issues.

From the beginning of Scripture, marriage is sacred, and appropriate sexual expression is an important part of marriage (Gen 2:23-25). The Fall created a rupture in all relationships, first between God and humans, and then between husband and wife (Gen 3). The division between Adam and Eve was expressed in terms of their sexuality; they could no longer stand naked in the garden without feeling shame. Proverbs urges young men and women to reclaim the beauty of marital love and guard its sanctity as God, the wise Creator, intended it.

often begins with a kiss, and flattering words can entice a man.

5:5-6 A relationship with an immoral woman leads *to death* (Hebrew *to Sheol*), as does a relationship with the woman named Folly (see 9:13-18).

5:9-10 An illicit relationship can be tempting, but it eventually brings shame. If the woman is a prostitute, the young man will have to pay her and thus lose income. If the woman is another man's wife, he might have to pay her husband (see Lev 20:10).

5:11 Some sexually transmitted diseases were well known in the ancient Near East. Leviticus 15:1-15 describes what is probably gonorrhea; other texts from Mesopotamia describe "the disease of intercourse" and the "disease of Ishtar" (goddess of love) with the physical symptoms of venereal diseases.

5:15-18 To *drink* from one's own *well* (see also Song 4:12, 15) is to enjoy sexual relations within marriage. Rather than expend sexual energy on immoral women, a man should cultivate a healthy sexual relationship with his wife. Sex is not to be shared with *strangers.* This honors marriage (Gen 2:22-25) and keeps the seventh commandment (Exod 20:14 and Deut 5:18).

5:15 Literally *Drink water from your own cistern, / flowing water from your own well.*

5:16 Literally *Why spill your springs in the streets, / your streams in the city squares?*

5:19 *deer:* cp. Song 4:5.

5:21-23 Even if a man keeps an illicit relationship secret from his family and society, nothing is hidden from *the LORD.* Adultery is a sin against God (Gen 39:8-9).

5:22 Habitual sins are like *ropes that catch and hold* people.

23 He will die for lack of self-control;
he will be lost because of his great
foolishness.

Lessons for Daily Life

6

1 My child, if you have put up security
for a friend's debt
or agreed to guarantee the debt of a
stranger—
2 if you have trapped yourself by your
agreement
and are caught by what you said—
3 follow my advice and save yourself,
for you have placed yourself at your
friend's mercy.
Now swallow your pride;
go and beg to have your name erased.
4 Don't put it off; do it now!
Don't rest until you do.
5 Save yourself like a gazelle escaping
from a hunter,
like a bird fleeing from a net.

6 Take a lesson from the ants, you
lazybones.
Learn from their ways and become
wise!
7 Though they have no prince
or governor or ruler to make them
work,
8 they labor hard all summer,
gathering food for the winter.
9 But you, lazybones, how long will you
sleep?
When will you wake up?
10 A little extra sleep, a little more slumber,
a little folding of the hands to rest—
11 then poverty will pounce on you like a
bandit;
scarcity will attack you like an armed
robber.

12 What are [k]worthless and wicked people
like?
They are constant liars,
13 signaling their deceit with a wink of the
eye,
a nudge of the foot, or the wiggle of
fingers.
14 Their perverted hearts plot evil,
and they constantly stir up trouble.
15 But they will be destroyed suddenly,
broken in an instant beyond all hope
of healing.

16 There are six things the LORD hates—
no, seven things he detests:
17 haughty eyes,
a lying tongue,
hands that kill the innocent,
18 a heart that plots evil,
feet that race to do wrong,
19 a false witness who pours out lies,
a person who sows discord in a
family.

20 My son, obey your father's commands,
and don't neglect your mother's
instruction.
21 Keep their words always in your heart.
Tie them around your neck.
22 When you walk, their counsel will lead
you.
When you sleep, they will protect you.
When you wake up, they will advise
you.
23 For their command is a lamp
and their instruction a light;
their corrective discipline
is the way to life.
24 It will keep you from the immoral
woman,
from the smooth tongue of a
promiscuous woman.

5:23 Job 4:21; 36:12; Prov 10:21
6:1 Prov 11:15; 17:18; 20:16; 22:26; 27:13
6:5 Ps 91:3; 124:7
6:6 Prov 10:26; 13:4; 30:24-25
6:8 Prov 10:5
6:10 //Prov 24:33
6:12 [k]*beliya'al* (1100) ‣Prov 19:28
6:13 Ps 35:19; Prov 10:10
6:14 Prov 6:19; Mic 2:1
6:15 2 Chr 36:16; Prov 24:22; Jer 19:11
6:16-19 Gen 6:5; Prov 1:16; 6:14; 19:5, 9; 21:4; 24:2; 28:17; Isa 1:15
6:21 Prov 3:3
6:22 Prov 3:23
6:23 Ps 119:105; Prov 13:9
6:24 Prov 2:16; 5:3

5:23 ***He will die:*** Young men must exercise ***self-control*** because death can result from acting on sexual desire for what is forbidden.

6:1-5 ***My child:*** Literally *My son.* See note on 1:8–9:18. • To secure the ***debt*** of another person is to guarantee it with one's own possessions. Whether to earn a ***friend's*** goodwill or to turn a profit from ***a stranger*** (cp. Exod 22:25; Lev 25:36-37; Deut 23:19-20), the risk is too great to take; it could lead to financial ruin. This message is repeated in 11:15; 17:18; 20:16; 22:26; 27:13.

6:3-5 ***save yourself:*** The danger of ruin is so great that escaping the situation is almost a matter of life and death, as highlighted by the images of animals caught in a trap.

6:6-11 Lazy people sleep rather than make necessary provisions (see also 24:33-34). They are the opposite of self-motivated and industrious ***ants.*** • ***Extra sleep . . . more slumber*** sarcastically expresses a lazy person's ambition.

6:10-11 // 24:33-34 The result of laziness is ***poverty.*** It will come suddenly and ruthlessly, ***like a bandit*** or ***an armed robber.***

6:12-15 ***eye . . . foot . . . fingers . . . hearts:*** The different parts of a worthless person's body describe overall character, not just an occasional foolish act.

6:13 ***wink . . . nudge . . . wiggle:*** These behaviors were signals used while trying to deceive the innocent.

6:15 Even if wicked people seem to prosper, they will ***suddenly*** be punished.

6:16-19 The first line gives a number followed by a second line that increases that number by one. This device (called *number parallelism*) introduces a list of items and often, as here, draws attention to the climactic final item (see also 30:15-23).

6:19 A ***false witness*** perverts the truth in court or in everyday conversation.

6:20-35 This passage emphasizes the life-threatening risk of sleeping with another man's wife (see also 1:8, 23; 2:16-22; 5:1-23; 7:1-27).

6:24-25 The ***immoral woman*** uses ***smooth*** talk and physical ***beauty*** to appeal to the vanity of young men.

6:25 2 Kgs 9:30 Matt 5:28
6:26 Prov 5:9-10; 29:3
6:29 Ezek 18:6
6:31 Ezek 22:1-4
6:32 Prov 7:7, 22-23; 9:15-18
6:34 Prov 11:4; 27:4 Song 8:6
7:1 Prov 2:1; 4:1
7:2 Deut 32:10 Ps 17:8 Prov 4:4; 9:11
7:3 Deut 6:8 Prov 3:3; 6:21
7:5 Prov 6:24
7:7 Prov 1:22; 6:32
7:8 Prov 7:12
7:9 Job 24:15
7:10 Gen 38:14-15
7:11 Prov 9:13
7:12 Prov 23:28
7:16 Prov 31:22 Ezek 27:7

25 Don't lust for her beauty.
Don't let her coy glances seduce you.
26 For a prostitute will bring you to poverty,
but sleeping with another man's wife
will cost you your life.
27 Can a man scoop a flame into his lap
and not have his clothes catch on fire?
28 Can he walk on hot coals
and not blister his feet?
29 So it is with the man who sleeps with
another man's wife.
He who embraces her will not go
unpunished.

30 Excuses might be found for a thief
who steals because he is starving.
31 But if he is caught, he must pay back
seven times what he stole,
even if he has to sell everything in his
house.
32 But the man who commits adultery is an
utter fool,
for he destroys himself.
33 He will be wounded and disgraced.
His shame will never be erased.
34 For the woman's jealous husband will be
furious,
and he will show no mercy when he
takes revenge.
35 He will accept no compensation,
nor be satisfied with a payoff of any
size.

Another Warning about Immoral Women

7 1 Follow my advice, my son;
always treasure my commands.
2 Obey my commands and live!
Guard my instructions as you guard
your own eyes.
3 Tie them on your fingers as a reminder.
Write them deep within your heart.

4 Love wisdom like a sister;
make insight a beloved member of
your family.
5 Let them protect you from an affair with
an immoral woman,
from listening to the flattery of a
promiscuous woman.

6 While I was at the window of my house,
looking through the curtain,
7 I saw some naive young men,
and one in particular who lacked
common sense.
8 He was crossing the street near the
house of an immoral woman,
strolling down the path by her house.
9 It was at twilight, in the evening,
as deep darkness fell.
10 The woman approached him,
seductively dressed and sly of heart.
11 She was the brash, rebellious type,
never content to stay at home.
12 She is often in the streets and markets,
soliciting at every corner.
13 She threw her arms around him and
kissed him,
and with a brazen look she said,
14 "I've just made my peace offerings
and fulfilled my vows.
15 You're the one I was looking for!
I came out to find you, and here you
are!
16 My bed is spread with beautiful blankets,
with colored sheets of Egyptian linen.
17 I've perfumed my bed
with myrrh, aloes, and cinnamon.

6:26 Sleeping with a ***prostitute*** has bad consequences, but ***sleeping with another man's wife*** is even worse. Her husband will seek revenge (6:34-35), and God is watching in judgment. • ***to poverty:*** Literally *to a loaf of bread.*

6:27-29 ***walk on hot coals:*** Of course ***his feet*** will ***blister.*** The consequences are horrible.

6:30-31 ***Seven times*** is probably a way of saying *a great amount* since the law never stipulated such high repayment (see Exod 22:1, 4, 9).

6:32-35 A thief might be punished severely even if he had a reason for his actions, but his punishment is nothing compared to an adulterer's, who has no excuse for his crime. A ***jealous husband*** will seek the full punishment provided by law, which is death (Deut 22:22).

7:1-27 This is the last of four sections in chs 1–9 that warn against the dangers of promiscuous women (see also 2:16-22; 5:1-23; 6:20-35).

7:2 ***as you guard your own eyes*** (literally *as the pupil of your eye*): That is, with great care.

7:3 The OT uses the phrase ***tie . . . on your fingers as a reminder*** for something that needs to be remembered, most notably God's commands (Deut 6:8; 11:18). • The NLT's ***write them deep within your heart*** reflects the Hebrew idiom *write them on the tablet of your heart* (see also 3:3). Only obedience that comes from the heart will last.

7:4 In Hebrew, ***sister*** is a term of endearment that expresses intimacy (see Song 4:9-10).

7:5 Loving wisdom will leave no room for a ***promiscuous woman,*** whose arsenal includes ***flattery*** that appeals to a young man's vanity.

7:6-23 The young man's father tells a story to illustrate his teaching about immoral women.

7:6-7 ***Naive young men,*** not yet set in their ways, are still open to correction. With each foolish act, they move closer to becoming fools.

7:9 Foolish actions are often associated with ***darkness*** (see 4:18-19; Eccl 2:13-14).

7:10 The woman, ***seductively dressed,*** looks good on the outside but inside is full of trouble.

7:12 Prostitutes commonly solicited business in public areas such as ***markets*** and at ***every corner*** of busy ***streets*** (e.g., Gen 38:13-16).

7:14 The immoral woman's observance of religious ritual makes her look good on the surface, but her immoral behavior reveals a corrupt heart.

7:16-17 Her emphasis on her ***bed*** and exotic perfumes (***myrrh, aloes, and cinnamon***) is explicitly sexual (cp. Song 4:13-14).

18 Come, let's drink our fill of [a]love until
morning.
Let's enjoy each other's caresses,
19 for my husband is not home.
He's away on a long trip.
20 He has taken a wallet full of money with
him
and won't return until later this
month."

21 So she seduced him with her pretty
speech
and enticed him with her flattery.
22 He followed her at once,
like an ox going to the slaughter.
He was like a stag caught in a trap,
23 awaiting the arrow that would pierce
its heart.
He was like a bird flying into a snare,
little knowing it would cost him his
life.

24 So listen to me, my sons,
and pay attention to my words.
25 Don't let your hearts stray away toward
her.
Don't wander down her wayward path.
26 For she has been the ruin of many;
many men have been her victims.
27 Her house is the road to the grave.
Her bedroom is the den of death.

Wisdom Calls for a Hearing

8 1 Listen as Wisdom calls out!
Hear as understanding raises her
voice!
2 On the hilltop along the road,
she takes her stand at the crossroads.
3 By the gates at the entrance to the town,
on the road leading in, she cries aloud,
4 "I call to you, to all of you!
I raise my voice to all people.
5 You simple people, use good judgment.
You foolish people, show some
understanding.
6 Listen to me! For I have important things
to tell you.
Everything I say is right,
7 for I speak the truth
and detest every kind of deception.
8 My advice is wholesome.
There is nothing devious or crooked
in it.
9 My words are plain to anyone with
understanding,
clear to those with knowledge.
10 Choose my instruction rather than silver,
and knowledge rather than pure gold.
11 For wisdom is far more valuable than
rubies.
Nothing you desire can compare
with it.

12 "I, Wisdom, live together with good
judgment.
I know where to discover knowledge
and discernment.
13 All who fear the LORD will hate evil.
Therefore, I hate pride and arrogance,
corruption and perverse speech.
14 Common sense and success belong
to me.
Insight and strength are mine.
15 Because of me, kings reign,
and rulers make just decrees.
16 Rulers lead with my help,
and nobles make righteous judgments.

17 "I love all who love me.
Those who search will surely find me.

7:18 [a]*dod* (1730) ›Song 1:2
7:21 Prov 5:3; 6:24
7:23 Eccl 9:12
7:24 Prov 4:1
7:25 Prov 5:8
7:27 Prov 2:18; 9:18
8:1 Prov 1:20-21
8:5 Prov 1:4, 22, 32
8:9 Prov 3:13; 14:6
8:11 Prov 3:14-15; 16:16; 20:15
8:12 Prov 1:4; 8:5
8:13 Prov 3:7; 6:12; 15:9
8:14 Prov 1:25; 2:7
8:17 1 Sam 2:30; Ps 91:14; Prov 2:4-5; 4:6; John 14:21

7:18 ***let's drink our fill of love:*** cp. Song 5:1.

7:20 ***until later this month:*** Literally *until the moon is full.*

7:21-23 The naive young man's foolish actions might ***cost him his life*** (see 5:11; 6:32-35).

7:24-27 The father reasserts the point of his lesson: While an adulteress might look good and a relationship with her is enticing, harm or even death will result.

7:27 ***to the grave:*** Hebrew *to Sheol.* See note on 1:12.

8:1–9:18 The first part of Proverbs climaxes when the son encounters two women. Both invite the young man, and the reader with him, into an intimate relationship. The young man and the reader must decide between the woman named Wisdom, personifying the true wisdom of God (8:1–9:6), and the woman named Folly (9:13-18), representing the wisdom of the world (1 Cor 1:18–2:16). Both women's houses are on "the heights overlooking the city" (9:3, 14), suggesting ancient temples; the choice is thus between the true God and false gods.

8:1-2 ***Wisdom calls out*** openly and publicly, appealing to all and offering them her gift of wisdom. Like a prophet, she wants all to respond to her words.

8:2 The ***hilltop*** and ***crossroads*** provide maximum public access to all who pass by.

8:3 In ancient Near Eastern cities, the city ***gates*** had built-in chambers for conducting legal proceedings and business transactions. It was an appropriate place for Wisdom to make her appeal to the most people.

8:6-9 Wisdom is associated with ***truth, understanding,*** and ***knowledge,*** which are ***right, wholesome, plain,*** and ***clear.*** Wisdom detests ***deception,*** which is ***devious*** and crooked (cp. 1:2-7; 6:16-19).

8:10-11 ***Choose:*** An ethical choice must be made between seeking money or valuables and seeking wisdom, which is far more valuable.

8:12 ***Good judgment, knowledge,*** and ***discernment*** are only available to those who have ***Wisdom.***

8:13 Those who choose wisdom, i.e., those who ***fear the LORD*** (see 1:7; 9:10), will not speak in ways that harm others or bend the truth.

8:15-16 The best ***rulers*** choose wisdom to guide them (e.g., 1 Kgs 3:16-28).
• ***and nobles make righteous judgments:*** Some Hebrew manuscripts and Greek version read *and nobles are judges over the earth.*

8:18 Ps 112:3; Prov 3:16; 22:4; Matt 6:33; Jas 2:5
8:19 Prov 3:14; 10:20
8:20 Ps 23:3; 25:4
8:21 Prov 3:16
8:22 Job 28:27
8:23 John 17:5, 24
8:24 Job 38:16
8:25 Ps 90:2
8:27 Job 26:10; Prov 3:19
8:29 Job 38:6, 10; Ps 104:9
8:32 Ps 119:1-2; Prov 5:7; 29:18
8:33 Prov 4:1
8:34 Ps 27:4; Prov 3:13, 18; Jas 1:22
8:35 Prov 3:4; 4:22; 12:2; John 17:3
8:36 Prov 1:31-32; 5:12; 15:32
9:1 Eph 2:20-22; 1 Pet 2:5
9:2 Matt 22:4
9:3 Prov 1:20; 8:1-2; Matt 22:3
9:4 Ps 19:7; Prov 8:5
9:5 Song 5:1; Isa 55:1; John 6:27
9:6 Prov 9:11; 16:22
9:7 Prov 23:9

18 I have riches and honor,
as well as enduring wealth and justice.
19 My gifts are better than gold, even the purest gold,
my wages better than sterling silver!
20 I walk in righteousness,
in paths of justice.
21 Those who love me inherit wealth.
I will fill their treasuries.

22 "The LORD formed me from the beginning,
before he created anything else.
23 I was appointed in ages past,
at the very first, before the earth began.
24 I was born before the oceans were created,
before the springs bubbled forth their waters.
25 Before the mountains were formed,
before the hills, I was born—
26 before he had made the earth and fields
and the first handfuls of soil.
27 I was there when he established the heavens,
when he drew the horizon on the oceans.
28 I was there when he set the clouds above,
when he established springs deep in the earth.
29 I was there when he set the limits of the seas,
so they would not spread beyond their boundaries.
And when he marked off the earth's foundations,
30 I was the architect at his side.
I was his constant delight,
rejoicing always in his presence.
31 And how happy I was with the world he created;
how I rejoiced with the human family!

32 "And so, my children, listen to me,
for all who follow my ways are joyful.
33 Listen to my instruction and be wise.
Don't ignore it.
34 Joyful are those who listen to me,
watching for me daily at my gates,
waiting for me outside my home!
35 For whoever finds me finds life
and receives favor from the LORD.
36 But those who miss me injure themselves.
All who hate me love death."

9

1 Wisdom has built her house;
she has carved its seven columns.
2 She has prepared a great banquet,
mixed the wines, and set the table.
3 She has sent her servants to invite everyone to come.
She calls out from the heights overlooking the city.
4 "Come in with me," she urges the simple.
To those who lack good judgment, she says,
5 "Come, eat my food,
and drink the wine I have mixed.
6 Leave your simple ways behind, and begin to live;
learn to use good judgment."

7 Anyone who rebukes a mocker will get an insult in return.
Anyone who corrects the wicked will get hurt.
8 So don't bother correcting mockers;
they will only hate you.
But correct the wise,
and they will love you.

8:22-25 *formed me from the beginning . . . I was appointed in ages past:* God's wisdom has always existed. His wisdom is here personified, but wisdom itself is not a person. Wisdom does not exist outside of God; wisdom is an expression of his character and nature. Unlike pagan gods, God needs no outside counselor to give him instructions (see Isa 40:13-14). Jesus is the apex of God's wisdom (see Col 1:15-17; 2:3).

8:27-29 God used his wisdom to establish the created order, so wisdom can tell us how the world works and testifies to God's greatness.

8:30 *architect:* God's wisdom guided the shaping of creation, bringing order out of chaos.

8:32-36 *my children:* Literally *my sons.* See note on 1:8–9:18. • Wisdom offers great rewards to those who *listen to* and *follow* wisdom.

8:35-36 *Life* is the ultimate reward for the wise, while rejecting wisdom results in *death.* These verses point to eternal life and death (see Luke 23:43; 1 Cor 15).

9:1-6 The invitation to join *Wisdom* for a lavish meal is met by a competing invitation in 9:13-18.

9:1 The number *seven* can denote grandeur or fullness, so the seven *columns* represent the grandeur of Wisdom's *house,* the place where it dwells.

9:2 In the ancient Near East, *a great banquet* would accompany a marriage, a military victory, or the making of a treaty. Wisdom's celebration marks the beginning of a committed relationship with the hearer.

9:3 Throughout the ancient Near East, temples were built on *the heights overlooking the city.* A commitment to wisdom involves a commitment to the Lord (contrast 9:14).

9:4 Wisdom makes her appeal especially to *the simple* and *those who lack good judgment* because they have not yet decided between wisdom and folly. See 9:16, where Folly mimics and then perverts Wisdom's words.

9:6 Wisdom gives people the ability to navigate life successfully.

9:7-9 These verses seem to create an awkward break between the invitations of Wisdom and Folly, but perhaps the purpose is to caution that, in contrast with inviting the simple (9:4), inviting *mockers* and *the wicked* is futile at best. Such people have already chosen

9 Instruct the wise,
and they will be even wiser.
Teach the righteous,
and they will learn even more.
10 Fear of the LORD is the foundation of wisdom.
Knowledge of the Holy One results in good judgment.
11 Wisdom will multiply your days
and add years to your life.
12 If you become wise, you will be the one to benefit.
If you scorn wisdom, you will be the one to suffer.

Folly Calls for a Hearing

13 The woman named Folly is brash.
She is ignorant and doesn't know it.
14 She sits in her doorway
on the heights overlooking the city.
15 She calls out to men going by
who are minding their own business.
16 "Come in with me," she urges the simple.
To those who lack good judgment, she says,
17 "Stolen water is refreshing;
food eaten in secret tastes the best!"
18 But little do they know that the dead are there.
Her guests are in the depths of the grave.

3. PROVERBS OF SOLOMON (10:1–22:16)

10 The [b]proverbs of Solomon:

A wise child brings joy to a father;
a foolish child brings grief to a mother.

2 Tainted wealth has no lasting value,
but right living can save your life.
3 The LORD will not let the godly go hungry,
but he refuses to satisfy the craving of the wicked.
4 Lazy people are soon poor;
hard workers get rich.
5 A wise youth harvests in the summer,
but one who sleeps during harvest is a disgrace.
6 The godly are showered with blessings;
the words of the wicked conceal violent intentions.
7 We have happy memories of the godly,
but the name of a wicked person rots away.
8 The wise are glad to be instructed,
but babbling fools fall flat on their faces.
9 People with integrity walk safely,
but those who follow crooked paths will slip and fall.
10 People who wink at wrong cause trouble,
but a bold reproof promotes peace.
11 The words of the godly are a life-giving fountain;
the words of the wicked conceal violent intentions.
12 Hatred stirs up quarrels,
but love makes up for all [c]offenses.
13 Wise words come from the lips of people with understanding,
but those lacking sense will be beaten with a rod.

9:9
Prov 1:5
9:10
Job 28:28
Ps 111:10
Prov 1:7
9:11
Prov 3:1-2; 10:27
9:12
Job 22:2
9:13
Prov 5:6; 7:11
9:16
//Prov 9:4
9:17
Prov 20:17
9:18
Prov 7:27
10:1
Prov 15:20; 17:25; 29:15
[b]*mashal* (4912)
‣ Prov 25:1
10:2
Prov 11:4; 21:6
10:3
Ps 34:9-10; 37:25
Matt 6:33
10:4
Prov 13:4
10:6
Prov 28:20
10:7
Ps 9:5-6
10:8
Prov 9:8
Matt 7:24
10:9
Prov 3:21-26
Isa 33:15-16
10:10
Prov 6:13
10:11
Prov 13:14; 18:4
10:12
Prov 17:9
1 Cor 13:4-7
*1 Pet 4:8
[c]*pesha'* (6588)
‣ Prov 10:19
10:13
Prov 10:31; 26:3
10:14
Prov 9:9; 13:3; 18:7
Jas 3:2, 5
10:15
Ps 52:7
Prov 18:11; 19:7

their path and respond to Wisdom's advice with violence. By contrast, ***the wise*** appreciate corrective advice; they welcome it and benefit from it.

9:10-12 ***Fear of the LORD:*** See note on 1:7.

9:13-18 The woman named Folly also invites ***the simple*** and ***those who lack good judgment*** to join her for the banquet she has prepared. Her invitation and advice are antithetical to Wisdom's (9:1-6).

9:13 ***The woman named Folly is brash:*** Fools talk boldly and without shame but have nothing intelligent to say.

9:14 ***On the heights overlooking the city*** was the traditional location for a temple. Folly personifies false gods and goddesses that compete for the affection and loyalty of God's people (contrast 9:2-3).

9:17 Like Wisdom, Folly has prepared a banquet for her guests (cp. 9:2-5). However, this meal is dishonest and perverse.

9:18 Folly's dinner ***guests*** end up ***in the depths of the grave*** (Hebrew *in Sheol*), in contrast to the reward for Wisdom's *guests* (see 9:6).

10:1–22:16 This long section is called ***The proverbs of Solomon.*** It consists mostly of brief bits of advice and observation. These sayings make heavy use of ***antithetical parallelism*** to contrast wisdom and righteousness with folly and wickedness. The arrangement of these proverbs appears to be essentially random, as in Egyptian and Mesopotamian wisdom literature. Some proverbs are repeated (see 6:10-11 and 24:33-34; 14:12 and 16:25; 18:8 and 26:22; 19:24 and 26:15; 20:16 and 27:13; 21:9 and 25:24; 22:3 and 27:12). Sometimes a group of proverbs shares a similar theme (e.g., 16:1-11).

10:1 ***child:*** Literally *son.* See note on 1:8–9:18. • The ***joy*** or ***grief*** of godly parents reflects the degree of their child's obedience to principles of wisdom.

10:2 ***tainted wealth . . . right living:*** The book of Proverbs promotes good behavior over having money (see also 11:18; 13:11, 22).

10:3 This proverb can be misused if outward results are regarded as a barometer of godliness. Job's three friends, for example, wrongly reasoned that Job must have sinned to earn his suffering (see Job 22:6-11; "Material Reward" at Job 4:7-9, p. 861).

10:4-5 ***Lazy people*** are foolish, while

10:16 Prov 11:18-19
10:17 Prov 6:23
10:18 Prov 26:24
10:19 Job 11:2; Prov 18:21; Eccl 5:3; Jas 3:2; [d]*pesha'* (6588) ‣Prov 17:19
10:20 Prov 8:19
10:21 Prov 5:23; 10:11
10:22 Gen 24:35; 26:12; Deut 8:18; Prov 8:21
10:23 Prov 15:21
10:24 Ps 145:19; Prov 15:8; Matt 5:6
10:25 Ps 15:1-5; Prov 12:3; Matt 7:24-25
10:27 Ps 55:23; Prov 3:2; 9:11; 14:27

14 Wise people treasure knowledge,
but the babbling of a fool invites disaster.

15 The wealth of the rich is their fortress;
the poverty of the poor is their destruction.

16 The earnings of the godly enhance their lives,
but evil people squander their money on sin.

17 People who accept discipline are on the pathway to life,
but those who ignore correction will go astray.

18 Hiding hatred makes you a liar;
slandering others makes you a fool.

19 Too much talk leads to [d]sin.
Be sensible and keep your mouth shut.

20 The words of the godly are like sterling silver;
the heart of a fool is worthless.

21 The words of the godly encourage many,
but fools are destroyed by their lack of common sense.

22 The blessing of the Lord makes a person rich,
and he adds no sorrow with it.

23 Doing wrong is fun for a fool,
but living wisely brings pleasure to the sensible.

24 The fears of the wicked will be fulfilled;
the hopes of the godly will be granted.

25 When the storms of life come, the wicked are whirled away,
but the godly have a lasting foundation.

26 Lazy people irritate their employers,
like vinegar to the teeth or smoke in the eyes.

27 Fear of the Lord lengthens one's life,
but the years of the wicked are cut short.

Speaking (9:13-18)

Prov 7:21-22; 8:7-9; 10:11, 18; 11:13; 14:5, 25; 15:4, 23; 16:23-24; 17:28; 18:4, 21; 20:20; 25:11; 26:17, 23-26; 27:2, 5; Matt 12:33-37; Jas 3:1-12

As children we heard, "Sticks and stones may break my bones, but words will never hurt me." Proverbs presents another viewpoint—that words have the power of life and death (18:21). The words contained in lies (14:5, 25), arguments (26:17), insults (20:20), slander (10:18), gossip (11:13), rumors (18:8), flattery (7:21-22), and bragging (26:23; 27:2) can all be death-dealing.

Proverbs repeatedly emphasizes that foolish people speak foolish words. They are represented by "the woman named Folly" (9:13-18), who lies and deceives to harm her hearers. Words reflect the condition of the heart (16:23; 18:4). While someone might attempt to conceal an evil heart by using pleasant words (26:23), a person's true character will surface in the end (26:24-26). The words of fools not only harm others; these words ultimately injure those who speak them. This is what James had in mind when he said that the tongue is full of wickedness that can ruin your whole life (Jas 3:6).

In contrast, wise people speak the life-giving words (10:11) represented by Wisdom (8:7-9). Wise people use their words sparingly (17:28) and are usually gentle (15:4; 16:24). However, a wise person also knows the right time to speak the right words (15:23; 25:11) and realizes that, at times, even harsh criticism is necessary (27:5). Proverbs wisely reminds its readers to pay close attention both to what they say and to how and when they say it.

hard workers are wise (see also 10:26; 26:13-16).

10:7 ***the name of a wicked person rots away:*** In ancient Israel, as is still true today in the Middle East, honor and shame were powerful motivators.

10:9 ***Paths*** are a metaphor for life (see 1:15).

10:10 To ***wink at wrong*** suggests approving of bad behavior rather than confronting it. • ***but a bold reproof promotes peace:*** As in Greek version; Hebrew reads *but babbling fools fall flat on their faces.* The NLT translators assume that the original text is reflected in the Greek version. The second line in the Hebrew text may have been copied by mistake from 10:8.

10:11 As a ***fountain*** provides water that sustains life, ***the words of the godly*** give life to those who hear them. In contrast, the ***violent intentions*** concealed in ***the words of the wicked*** bring death (see also 10:6; Jas 3:1-12).

10:13 ***beaten with a rod:*** People ***lacking sense*** will bring harm upon themselves through what they say. Concerning physical discipline, see 23:13-14.

10:15 Although ***wealth*** can be a ***fortress*** against trouble, money can also create trouble (13:8) and can provide false security (18:10-11).

10:17 Wise people are not afraid to have their thinking or behavior corrected—they ***accept discipline*** as an opportunity to grow in wisdom.

10:19 Those who ***talk too much*** show their ignorance and get in trouble (see also 10:17; 13:3; 17:28).

10:20 ***Words*** are an expression of the ***heart.***

10:25 ***The wicked*** might enjoy the material blessings of life, but only temporarily, in contrast with ***the godly.*** Jesus also expressed this reality (Matt 7:24-27).

28 The hopes of the godly result in
[e]happiness,
but the expectations of the wicked
come to nothing.
29 The way of the LORD is a stronghold to
those with integrity,
but it destroys the wicked.
30 The godly will never be disturbed,
but the wicked will be removed from
the land.
31 The mouth of the godly person gives
wise advice,
but the tongue that deceives will be
cut off.
32 The lips of the godly speak helpful words,
but the mouth of the wicked speaks
perverse words.

11

1 The LORD detests the use of
dishonest scales,
but he delights in accurate weights.

2 [f]Pride leads to disgrace,
but with humility comes wisdom.

3 Honesty guides good people;
dishonesty destroys treacherous people.

4 Riches won't help on the day of judgment,
but right living can save you from
death.

5 The godly are directed by honesty;
the wicked fall beneath their load of
sin.

6 The godliness of good people rescues
them;
the ambition of treacherous people
traps them.

7 When the wicked die, their hopes die
with them,
for they rely on their own feeble
strength.

8 The godly are rescued from trouble,
and it falls on the wicked instead.

9 With their words, the godless destroy
their friends,
but knowledge will rescue the
righteous.

10 The whole city celebrates when the
godly succeed;
they shout for joy when the wicked die.

11 Upright citizens are good for a city and
make it prosper,
but the talk of the wicked tears it
apart.

12 It is foolish to belittle one's neighbor;
a sensible person keeps quiet.

13 A gossip goes around telling secrets,
but those who are trustworthy can
keep a confidence.

14 Without wise leadership, a nation falls;
there is safety in having many
advisers.

15 There's danger in putting up security for
a stranger's debt;
it's safer not to guarantee another
person's debt.

16 A gracious woman gains [g]respect,
but ruthless men gain only wealth.

17 Your kindness will reward you,
but your cruelty will destroy you.

18 Evil people get rich for the moment,
but the reward of the godly will last.

19 Godly people find life;
evil people find death.

20 The LORD detests people with crooked
hearts,
but he delights in those with
[h]integrity.

21 Evil people will surely be punished,
but the children of the godly will go
free.

22 A beautiful woman who lacks discretion
is like a gold ring in a pig's snout.

10:28 Prov 11:7, 23
[e]*simkhah* (8057)
› Prov 15:23

10:29 Prov 21:15

10:30 Ps 37:29

10:31 Prov 11:20

10:32 Prov 6:12
Eccl 12:10

11:1 Deut 25:13-16
Prov 16:11

11:2 Prov 16:18; 29:23
[f]*zadon* (2087)
› Prov 13:10

11:3 Prov 13:6; 22:12

11:4 Prov 10:2
Ezek 7:19

11:5 Prov 3:6; 5:22

11:6 Ps 7:15-16; 9:15

11:7 Prov 10:28

11:10 Prov 28:12

11:13 Lev 19:16
Prov 19:11; 20:19

11:14 Prov 15:22; 20:18

11:15 Prov 6:1; 27:13

11:16 Prov 31:28, 30
[g]*kabod* (3519)
› Prov 25:2

11:17 Matt 5:7; 25:34-36

11:19 Prov 19:23; 21:16;
Rom 6:23
Jas 1:15

11:20 Prov 13:6
[h]*tamim* (8549)
› Prov 28:10

11:21 Prov 16:5

11:23 Prov 10:28
Rom 2:8-9

11:25 Matt 5:7
2 Cor 9:6-7

11:26 Job 29:13

10:30 This proverb connects with God's covenant promises to Israel (see Deut 28:1-14, 63-68). Such connections are rare in the book of Proverbs (see Proverbs Introduction, "Setting," p. 1026).

11:1 Here, honest practices are applied to the business world (see also 16:11; 20:10, 23; Lev 19:35-37; Deut 25:13-15; Ezek 45:10; Hos 12:7-8; Mic 6:11). • *Scales* were often made of two metal bowls suspended from a crossbar. The unit of currency, the *shekel,* comes from the verb meaning "to weigh" (see Amos 8:5-6).

11:2 *Pride* is dishonest self-promotion, whereas *humility* is an honest assessment of one's strengths and weaknesses.

11:4 *Right living,* which flows from wisdom, is more important than *riches.* Nothing is wrong with *riches* (10:15, 22; 14:24) that are gained properly (cp. 13:11; 21:6; 22:16).

11:10 Our actions, whether *godly* or *wicked,* affect *the whole city* (cp. Eccl 8:9-13).

11:13 This perspective on *a gossip* is repeated in 20:19.

11:14 The future of an entire *nation* depends on wisdom.

11:15 This message is repeated in 6:1-5; 17:18; 20:16; 22:26; 27:13.

11:16 *Respect* is the great and lasting reward of being *gracious,* while *wealth* is the lesser and temporary prize of being *ruthless* (see also 10:2; 11:18).

11:21 *Godly* behavior has positive consequences for the next generation.

11:22 *Discretion* is the ability to tell right from wrong, the beautiful from the ugly, and good taste from bad taste.

23 The godly can look forward to a reward,
while the wicked can expect only
judgment.

24 Give freely and become more wealthy;
be stingy and lose everything.

25 The generous will prosper;
those who refresh others will
themselves be refreshed.

26 People curse those who hoard their
grain,
but they bless the one who sells in
time of need.

27 If you search for good, you will find
favor;
but if you search for evil, it will find
you!

28 Trust in your money and down you go!
But the godly flourish like leaves in
spring.

29 Those who bring trouble on their
families inherit the wind.
The fool will be a [i]servant to the wise.

30 The seeds of good deeds become a tree
of life;
a wise person wins friends.

31 If the righteous are rewarded here on
earth,
what will happen to wicked sinners?

12

1 To learn, you must love discipline;
it is stupid to hate correction.

2 The LORD approves of those who are
good,
but he condemns those who plan
wickedness.

3 Wickedness never brings stability,
but the godly have deep roots.

4 A worthy wife is a crown for her
husband,
but a disgraceful woman is like cancer
in his bones.

5 The plans of the godly are [j]just;
the advice of the wicked is
treacherous.

6 The words of the wicked are like a
murderous ambush,
but the words of the godly save lives.

7 The wicked die and disappear,
but the family of the godly stands
firm.

8 A sensible person wins admiration,
but a warped mind is despised.

9 Better to be an ordinary person with a
[k]servant
than to be self-important but have no
food.

10 The godly care for their animals,
but the wicked are always cruel.

11 A hard worker has plenty of food,
but a person who chases fantasies has
no sense.

12 Thieves are jealous of each other's loot,
but the godly are well rooted and bear
their own fruit.

13 The wicked are trapped by their own
words,
but the godly escape such trouble.

14 Wise words bring many benefits,
and hard work brings rewards.

15 Fools think their own way is right,
but the wise listen to others.

16 A fool is quick-tempered,
but a wise person stays calm when
insulted.

17 An honest witness tells the truth;
a false witness tells lies.

11:27 Ps 7:15
11:28 Ps 1:2-3; 92:12 / Jer 17:7-8 / Mark 10:24-25 / 1 Tim 6:17
11:29 Prov 14:19; 15:27 / [i]*'ebed* (5650) ›Prov 12:9
11:30 Prov 3:18 / Jas 5:20
11:31 2 Sam 22:21 / *1 Pet 4:18
12:1 Prov 1:5; 9:9; 25:12
12:2 Prov 3:4; 8:35-36
12:3 Ps 15:1-5 / Prov 10:25; 11:5
12:4 Prov 14:1; 21:9; 27:15; 31:10
12:5 Prov 16:23 / Matt 12:34; 15:18 / [j]*mishpat* (4941) ›Prov 21:15
12:6 Ps 35:11 / Prov 14:3; 31:8
12:7 Prov 11:21; 14:11 / Matt 7:24-27
12:8 Eccl 8:1
12:9 Luke 14:11 / [k]*'ebed* (5650) ›Prov 17:2
12:10 Gen 33:13
12:11 Prov 9:6; 14:23-24
12:12 Prov 1:10-19; 11:25
12:13 Prov 11:8; 13:5; 25:18
12:14 Prov 12:24; 13:11 / Isa 3:10
12:15 Prov 14:12; 16:2
12:16 Prov 19:11; 29:11
12:17 Prov 12:13; 25:18

11:23 ***The wicked*** might prosper and ***the godly*** might suffer in the short term, but the future will right this imbalance.

11:24-26 ***Generous*** people who ***give freely*** to others ***will prosper,*** but those who ***hoard*** their money will lose it (see 28:27; 2 Cor 9:6-9).

11:28 ***Money*** can be a blessing from God, but it is uncertain. ***The godly*** trust in God and ***flourish*** (see Ps 1).

11:30 ***a wise person wins friends:*** Or *and those who win souls are wise.*

11:31 The implied answer is that ***wicked sinners*** will be punished on earth. • Greek version reads *If the righteous are barely saved, / what will happen to godless sinners?* Cp. 1 Pet 4:18.

12:4 Elsewhere in Proverbs a ***crown*** symbolizes wealth (14:24), long life (16:31), and grandchildren (17:6). • ***cancer*** (literally *rot*): A ***disgraceful*** wife is a deep and life-threatening problem.

12:7 ***The wicked*** might prosper momentarily, but they do not last. ***The family of the godly stands firm*** for generations.

12:8 To be ***sensible*** means to act only after reflecting on the consequences. A ***warped mind*** acts on impulse.

12:9 Reality is more important than appearance.

12:11 This proverb is repeated but with a different conclusion in 28:19.

12:12 The instability of ***thieves*** can produce violent behavior at any moment. By contrast, ***the godly are well rooted:*** Their relationships are stable even under duress.

12:15 ***Fools*** fail to realize what ***the wise*** know—that listening is the way to learn.

12:16 Keeping a level head allows a ***wise person*** to think clearly and avoid reactions that could cause a fight.

12:17 The message of this proverb is repeated in 14:5.

18 Some people make cutting remarks,
but the words of the wise bring
healing.

19 Truthful words stand the test of time,
but lies are soon exposed.

20 Deceit fills hearts that are plotting evil;
joy fills hearts that are planning
[a]peace!

21 No harm comes to the godly,
but the wicked have their fill of
trouble.

22 The LORD detests lying lips,
but he delights in those who tell the
truth.

23 The wise don't make a show of their
knowledge,
but fools broadcast their [b]foolishness.

24 Work hard and become a leader;
be lazy and become a slave.

25 Worry weighs a person down;
an encouraging word cheers a
person up.

26 The godly give good advice to their
friends;
the wicked lead them astray.

27 Lazy people don't even cook the game
they catch,
but the diligent make use of
everything they find.

28 The way of the godly leads to life;
that path does not lead to death.

13

1 A wise child accepts a parent's
discipline;
a mocker refuses to listen to
correction.

2 Wise words will win you a good meal,
but treacherous people have an
appetite for violence.

3 Those who control their tongue will have
a long life;
opening your mouth can ruin
everything.

4 Lazy [c]people want much but get little,
but [c]those who work hard will prosper.

5 The godly hate lies;
the wicked cause shame and disgrace.

6 Godliness guards the path of the
blameless,
but the evil are misled by sin.

7 Some who are poor pretend to be rich;
others who are rich pretend to be poor.

8 The rich can pay a ransom for their lives,
but the poor won't even get
threatened.

9 The life of the godly is full of light and
joy,
but the light of the wicked will be
snuffed out.

10 [d]Pride leads to conflict;
those who take advice are [e]wise.

11 Wealth from get-rich-quick schemes
quickly disappears;
wealth from hard work grows over
time.

12 Hope deferred makes the heart sick,
but a dream fulfilled is a tree of life.

13 People who despise advice are asking for
trouble;
those who respect a command will
succeed.

14 The instruction of the wise is like a life-
giving fountain;
those who accept it avoid the snares
of death.

15 A person with good sense is respected;
a treacherous person is headed for
destruction.

16 Wise people think before they act;
fools don't—and even brag about their
foolishness.

17 An unreliable messenger stumbles into
trouble,
but a reliable messenger brings
healing.

12:18
Ps 57:4
Prov 8:6-7; 15:4

12:19
Prov 19:9

12:20
Prov 2:10; 26:24-26
[a]*shalom* (7965)
‣ Eccl 3:8

12:21
Ps 121:7
Prov 1:33
1 Pet 3:13

12:22
Eccl 5:2
Isa 19:21

12:23
Prov 10:14; 13:16
[b]*'iwweleth* (0200)
‣ Prov 14:17

12:24
Prov 12:11; 14:11;
22:29

12:25
Prov 15:13; 17:22

12:26
Prov 6:21; 12:15;
18:15

12:27
Prov 10:4; 13:4

12:28
Prov 8:35; 9:11
Ezek 18:9, 20
Rom 5:21

13:1
Prov 10:1; 15:12, 20

13:3
Prov 18:7, 21; 20:19;
21:23
Jas 3:2

13:4
[c]*nepesh* (5315)
‣ Isa 26:8

13:5
Prov 3:35

13:6
Prov 6:15

13:7
Prov 11:24
Luke 12:20-21
2 Cor 6:10
Jas 2:5

13:9
Job 18:5; 29:3
Prov 4:18; 24:20

13:10
[d]*zadon* (2087)
‣ Prov 21:24
[e]*khokmah* (2451)
‣ Prov 14:6

13:13
2 Chr 36:16

13:14
Ps 18:5
Prov 10:11

13:15
Prov 3:4

13:16
Prov 12:23

13:17
Prov 25:13

12:26 ***The godly give good advice to their friends:*** Or *The godly are cautious in friendship;* or *The godly are freed from evil.* The meaning of the Hebrew is uncertain.

13:1 ***A wise child accepts a parent's discipline*** (Literally *A wise son accepts his father's discipline*): Gaining wisdom requires ***discipline*** and ***correction.***

13:3 Having ***control*** of the ***tongue*** demonstrates wisdom (see Jas 3:1-12).

13:7 Appearances do not always reflect reality.

13:8 Money can be a blessing or a curse (see 3:9-10; 21:6).

13:9 ***snuffed out:*** Cp. 20:20; 24:20.

13:15 ***a treacherous person is headed for destruction:*** As in Greek version; Hebrew reads *the way of the treacherous is lasting.*

13:17 Oral messages were the primary form of communication, so an ***unreliable messenger*** delivering the wrong message could incite all kinds of ***trouble.***

13:18
Prov 15:5, 32
13:20
Prov 2:20
13:21
Ps 32:10
Prov 11:31
Isa 3:10
13:22
Ezra 9:12
Ps 37:25
Prov 28:8
13:24
Prov 19:18; 22:15; 23:13
13:25
Ps 34:10
Prov 10:3
14:1
Prov 31:10-27
14:3
Prov 12:6
14:5
Prov 6:19; 12:17
Rev 3:14
14:6
[f]*khokmah* (2451)
‣Prov 16:16
14:7
Prov 23:9
14:8
Prov 15:28
14:11
Prov 12:7
14:12
//Prov 16:25
Rom 6:21
14:13
Eccl 2:1-2
14:14
Prov 1:31; 12:14, 21
14:15
[g]*'aman* (0539)
‣Isa 28:16
14:16
Prov 22:3

18 If you ignore criticism, you will end in
poverty and disgrace;
if you accept correction, you will be
honored.

19 It is pleasant to see dreams come true,
but fools refuse to turn from evil to
attain them.

20 Walk with the wise and become wise;
associate with fools and get in
trouble.

21 Trouble chases sinners,
while blessings reward the
righteous.

22 Good people leave an inheritance to
their grandchildren,
but the sinner's wealth passes to the
godly.

23 A poor person's farm may produce much
food,
but injustice sweeps it all away.

24 Those who spare the rod of discipline
hate their children.
Those who love their children care
enough to discipline them.

25 The godly eat to their hearts' content,
but the belly of the wicked goes
hungry.

14

1 A wise woman builds her home,
but a foolish woman tears it
down with her own hands.

2 Those who follow the right path fear the
LORD;
those who take the wrong path
despise him.

3 A fool's proud talk becomes a rod that
beats him,
but the words of the wise keep them
safe.

4 Without oxen a stable stays clean,
but you need a strong ox for a large
harvest.

5 An honest witness does not lie;
a false witness breathes lies.

6 A mocker seeks [f]wisdom and never
finds it,
but knowledge comes easily to those
with understanding.

7 Stay away from fools,
for you won't find knowledge on their
lips.

8 The prudent understand where they are
going,
but fools deceive themselves.

9 Fools make fun of guilt,
but the godly acknowledge it and seek
reconciliation.

10 Each heart knows its own bitterness,
and no one else can fully share its joy.

11 The house of the wicked will be destroyed,
but the tent of the godly will flourish.

12 There is a path before each person that
seems right,
but it ends in death.

13 Laughter can conceal a heavy heart,
but when the laughter ends, the grief
remains.

14 Backsliders get what they deserve;
good people receive their reward.

15 Only simpletons [g]believe everything
they're told!
The prudent carefully consider their
steps.

16 The wise are cautious and avoid danger;
fools plunge ahead with reckless
confidence.

13:20 We are influenced by those we *associate with.*

13:23 Hard work does not always bring prosperity (cp. 10:4-6; 12:11; 13:4) because *injustice* occurs in the world.

13:24 Physical punishment is sometimes necessary to motivate instruction. Love will lead to *discipline* in whatever form is most effective, whereas refusal to discipline one's child is a sign of laziness (see also 19:18; 23:13-14; 29:17).

14:1 Building or tearing down the *home* is a metaphor for strengthening or weakening one's family.

14:2 The *path* is a metaphor for life and conduct (see 2:13, 20; 3:6; 4:11; 6:23). • *fear the LORD:* See 1:7.

14:3 A *fool's* word can be used against him.

14:4 It's easy to keep a *stable . . . clean* if it is empty, but a farmer without an *ox* has no *harvest.*

14:5 *Honest* speech and *lies* both flow from deep within a person's character. Cp. 12:17.

14:9 *The godly acknowledge* their mistakes and sins, leading to change and *reconciliation.* Fools defend themselves by making *fun of guilt.*

14:10 No one can fully understand the emotions of another (cp. Ps 103:14; Isa 63:9; Nah 1:7; Rom 8:27). *Bitterness* and *joy* are at opposite ends of the emotional spectrum; this poetic device of referring to polar opposites (*merism*) covers the whole range in between.

14:11 Although a *house* is typically more stable than a *tent,* wickedness destroys and tears down, while godliness builds up (14:1).

14:12 // 16:25 The right choice is not always the one that *seems right* on the surface (see Matt 7:13-14).

14:13 A person's outward demeanor might not reflect what is in the *heart.*

14:14 *Backsliders* foolishly act against what they know to be good and right and wise.

14:16 *The wise are cautious:* Literally *The wise fear.*

17 Short-tempered people do [h]foolish
things,
and schemers are hated.

18 Simpletons are clothed with foolishness,
but the prudent are crowned with
knowledge.

19 Evil people will bow before good people;
the wicked will bow at the gates of the
godly.

20 The poor are despised even by their
neighbors,
while the rich have many "friends."

21 It is a sin to belittle one's neighbor;
[i]blessed are those who help the poor.

22 If you plan to do evil, you will be lost;
if you plan to do good, you will receive
unfailing love and faithfulness.

23 Work brings profit,
but mere talk leads to poverty!

24 Wealth is a crown for the wise;
the [j]effort of fools yields only
[j]foolishness.

25 A truthful witness saves lives,
but a false witness is a traitor.

26 Those who fear the LORD are secure;
he will be a refuge for their children.

27 Fear of the LORD is a life-giving fountain;
it offers escape from the snares of
death.

28 A growing population is a king's glory;
a prince without subjects has nothing.

29 People with understanding [k]control their
anger;
a hot temper shows great foolishness.

30 A peaceful heart leads to a healthy body;
[a]jealousy is like cancer in the bones.

31 Those who oppress the poor insult their
Maker,
but helping the poor honors him.

32 The wicked are crushed by disaster,
but the godly have a refuge when they
die.

33 Wisdom is enshrined in an
understanding heart;
wisdom is not found among fools.

34 Godliness makes a nation [b]great,
but sin is a disgrace to any people.

35 A king rejoices in wise servants
but is angry with those who disgrace
him.

15

1 A gentle answer deflects anger,
but harsh words make tempers
flare.

2 The tongue of the wise makes
knowledge appealing,
but the mouth of a fool belches out
foolishness.

3 The LORD is watching everywhere,
keeping his eye on both the evil and
the good.

4 Gentle words are a tree of life;
a deceitful tongue crushes the spirit.

5 Only a fool despises a parent's discipline;
whoever learns from correction is
wise.

6 There is treasure in the house of the godly,
but the earnings of the wicked bring
trouble.

14:17
Prov 14:29
[h]*'iwweleth* (0200)
‣ Prov 14:24

14:20
Prov 19:4, 7

14:21
Ps 41:1
Prov 11:12
[i]*'ashrey* (0835)
‣ Prov 28:14

14:22
Prov 12:2

14:24
[j]*'iwweleth* (0200)
‣ Prov 15:14

14:25
Prov 14:5

14:26
Prov 19:23

14:27
Prov 13:14

14:29
Prov 16:32; 19:11
Jas 1:19
[k]*'arek 'appayim* (0750, 0639)
‣ Prov 15:18

14:30
[a]*qin'ah* (7068)
‣ Prov 24:19

14:31
Ps 12:5
Prov 17:5; 22:16

14:32
2 Cor 1:9

14:34
[b]*rum* (7311)
‣ Isa 6:1

14:35
Matt 24:45

15:1
Judg 8:1-3
Prov 15:18; 25:10, 15

15:2
Prov 12:23; 15:28

15:3
Job 31:4; 34:21
Heb 4:13

15:5
Prov 13:1

15:6
Prov 8:21

15:7
Prov 10:13

15:8
Prov 21:27
Isa 1:11

14:17 *Short-tempered people* do not anticipate consequences before expressing anger. *Schemers* reflect, but they, too, are *hated* because of the evil that they do.

14:18 *are clothed with foolishness:* Or *inherit foolishness.* One's true nature and heart attitude will eventually show in one's demeanor.

14:20 This proverb might commend having neither too little nor too much (30:7-9).

14:21 *blessed are those who help the poor:* See also 3:27-28; 11:24; 28:27; 29:7, 14.

14:24 This proverb states a general principle, even though *fools* sometimes have *wealth* (10:2; 11:18), and poverty is not always the result of *foolishness* (cp. 13:23; 16:8).

14:28 The well-being and growth of the people, not wealth or military victory, are the true signs of a *king's* success.

14:29 Wise people can *control* their emotions and express them appropriately.

14:30 *A peaceful heart* has resolved its inner tensions. Freedom from intense, stressful emotions is beneficial to physical health.

14:31 Wise people help *the poor* (cp. 11:24-26; 28:27; see Lev 19:9-10; Deut 15:11; 24:10-15; Isa 3:14-15; Jer 2:34; see also Jas 2:1-13). • *insult their Maker:* See also 17:5.

14:32 Proverbs hints at life after death infrequently. Some scholars think this verse refers to God's granting courage to face death with dignity and serenity.

14:33 *wisdom is not:* As in Greek and Syriac versions; Hebrew lacks *not.*

14:34 A great *nation* is not defined by wealth, power, or military victories (14:28) but by *godliness.*

15:1 Moderating emotions and suiting them to the context helps others listen to what we say without reacting.

15:2 A *wise* teacher presents lessons in an attractive way. Crude belching describes the ugly teaching of a *fool.*

15:3 Knowing that *the LORD is watching everywhere* is motivation for wise behavior.

15:5 *parent's:* Literally *father's.* • Wisdom requires learning from *correction.*

15:6 God blesses the *godly* with wealth (10:22; cp. 10:15 and 14:24). *The wicked* may also gain wealth, but it will bring *trouble* rather than blessing (11:4, 18; 13:11; 21:6; 22:16).

15:9
Prov 11:20
15:11
1 Sam 16:7
2 Chr 6:30
Job 26:6
Acts 1:24
15:12
Prov 9:7; 13:1; 19:25; 24:9
15:13
Prov 17:22
Eccl 8:1
15:14
Prov 18:15
[c]*'iwweleth* (0200)
‣Prov 15:21
15:16
Ps 37:16
Prov 16:8
1 Tim 6:6
15:17
Prov 17:1
15:18
Prov 14:29; 16:28; 26:21
Eccl 10:4
[d]*'arek 'appayim* (0750, 0639)
‣Prov 16:32
15:20
Prov 10:1; 29:3; 30:17
15:21
Eph 5:15
[e]*'iwweleth* (0200)
‣Prov 17:12
15:22
Prov 11:14
15:23
Prov 25:11
[f]*simkhah* (8057)
‣Prov 21:15

7 The lips of the wise give good advice;
the heart of a fool has none to give.

8 The LORD detests the sacrifice of the wicked,
but he delights in the prayers of the upright.

9 The LORD detests the way of the wicked,
but he loves those who pursue godliness.

10 Whoever abandons the right path will be severely disciplined;
whoever hates correction will die.

11 Even Death and Destruction hold no secrets from the LORD.
How much more does he know the human heart!

12 Mockers hate to be corrected,
so they stay away from the wise.

13 A glad heart makes a happy face;
a broken heart crushes the spirit.

14 A wise person is hungry for knowledge,
while the fool feeds on [c]trash.

15 For the despondent, every day brings trouble;
for the happy heart, life is a continual feast.

16 Better to have little, with fear for the LORD,
than to have great treasure and inner turmoil.

17 A bowl of vegetables with someone you love
is better than steak with someone you hate.

18 A hot-tempered person starts fights;
a [d]cool-tempered person stops them.

19 A lazy person's way is blocked with briers,
but the path of the upright is an open highway.

20 Sensible children bring joy to their father;
foolish children despise their mother.

21 [e]Foolishness brings joy to those with no sense;
a sensible person stays on the right path.

22 Plans go wrong for lack of advice;
many advisers bring success.

23 Everyone [f]enjoys a fitting reply;
it is wonderful to say the right thing at the right time!

Anger (14:29)

Prov 12:16; 15:1, 18; 16:14, 32; 17:14; 19:11-12, 19; 22:24-25; 27:4
Gen 4:3-8; 49:5-7
1 Sam 18:8-11
1 Kgs 21:3-16
Ps 7:11-13; 30:5; 37:8
Eccl 7:9
Jon 4:1-11
Nah 1:2-3
Matt 5:22
Rom 9:22; 12:19
Eph 4:26-27, 31-32
Col 3:8
1 Tim 2:8
Titus 1:7
Jas 1:19-21

Wise people do not fly off the handle in anger. "People with understanding control their anger; a hot temper shows great foolishness" (14:29). Because anger can cloud judgment, it is vitally important for the wise to reflect on their actions before responding (14:16).

Although Proverbs comments on anger only in a negative light, Scripture overall does not portray all anger as bad. Many Psalms express anger (e.g., Ps 77), and Jesus demonstrated anger as he threw the money changers out of the Temple (Mark 11:15-17; John 2:13-16). Though it is often hard to tell the two apart, people must learn to distinguish righteous anger from unrighteous anger. Unrighteous anger is only concerned to protect or promote oneself (e.g., Gen 4:3-8; 1 Sam 18:8-9; 1 Kgs 21:3-4; 2 Kgs 5:11; 2 Chr 25:10; Jon 4:1-11), whereas righteous anger reflects God's hatred of evil and love of justice (e.g., Exod 32:1-35; Num 11:1, 10; see also Nah 1:3; Rom 9:22). The wise person reads the circumstances and discerns whether and to what degree to express anger (see also 22:24; Eccl 7:9; Matt 5:22; Rom 12:19; Eph 4:26-27, 31; Jas 1:19-20).

15:8 God looks beyond the outward actions of *sacrifice* and *prayers* to see if they reflect the heart's attitude (see also 21:27; Ps 40:6-8; Mic 6:6-8).

15:11 *Death and Destruction* (Hebrew *Sheol and Abaddon*), personify the destiny of the dead. *Sheol* is the abode of the dead; *Abaddon* is a synonym for Sheol that has an added implication of punishment. • God knows all *secrets* (see Ps 139:1-12).

15:12 *Mockers* cannot become *wise* because they keep criticism at a distance (cp. 10:17; 13:1, 10).

15:13 What people feel affects how they present themselves (cp. 15:30).

15:14 Whether we enjoy *knowledge* or *trash* reveals whether we are on the path of wisdom or of folly.

15:15 Personality affects our outlook on life.

15:16 A healthy *fear for the LORD* counteracts *inner turmoil* and brings inner peace. • *Better to have little:* See also 16:8.

15:17 This *better than* proverb shows the relative value of wealth. A substantial meal (*steak*) is good, but *love* is better.

15:18 Controlling one's emotions is a sign of wisdom (see also Jas 1:19-20).

15:19 A *lazy person* can find all kinds of obstacles (e.g., a path *blocked with briers*) to avoid work (see 10:4, 26; 12:11, 14; 13:4; 14:4).

15:22 An individual might not think of all the angles of a problem; a wise person invites *advice* from *many advisers*.

24 The path of life leads upward for the
wise;
they leave the grave behind.

25 The LORD tears down the house of the
proud,
but he protects the property of
widows.

26 The LORD detests evil plans,
but he delights in pure words.

27 Greed brings grief to the whole family,
but those who hate bribes will live.

28 The heart of the godly thinks carefully
before speaking;
the mouth of the wicked overflows
with evil words.

29 The LORD is far from the wicked,
but he hears the prayers of the
righteous.

30 A cheerful look brings joy to the heart;
good news makes for good health.

31 If you listen to constructive criticism,
you will be at home among the wise.

32 If you reject discipline, you only harm
yourself;
but if you listen to correction, you
grow in understanding.

33 Fear of the LORD teaches wisdom;
humility precedes honor.

16

1 We can make our own plans,
but the LORD gives the right
answer.

2 People may be pure in their own eyes,
but the LORD examines their motives.

3 Commit your actions to the LORD,
and your plans will succeed.

4 The LORD has made everything for his
own purposes,
even the wicked for a day of disaster.

5 The LORD detests the proud;
they will surely be punished.

6 Unfailing love and [g]faithfulness make
[h]atonement for sin.
By fearing the LORD, people avoid evil.

7 When people's lives please the LORD,
even their enemies are at peace with
them.

8 Better to have little, with godliness,
than to be rich and dishonest.

9 We can make our plans,
but the LORD determines our steps.

10 The king speaks with divine wisdom;
he must never judge unfairly.

11 The LORD demands accurate scales and
balances;
he sets the standards for fairness.

12 A [i]king detests wrongdoing,
for his [j]rule is built on justice.

13 The king is pleased with words from
righteous lips;
he loves those who speak honestly.

14 The anger of the king is a deadly threat;
the wise will try to appease it.

15 When the king smiles, there is life;
his favor refreshes like a spring rain.

16 How much better to get [k]wisdom than
gold,
and good judgment than silver!

15:25
Ps 68:5; 146:9
15:27
Exod 23:8
15:28
Prov 10:19, 32
15:29
Ps 145:18-19
15:33
Prov 1:7
16:2
Prov 21:2
16:3
Ps 37:5; 55:22
Prov 3:6
16:4
Job 38:23
Eccl 3:11
Isa 43:7
16:5
Prov 6:16-17; 8:13;
11:21
16:6
Prov 8:13; 14:27
[g]*'emeth* (0571)
‣ Isa 38:3
[h]*kapar* (3722)
‣ Dan 9:24
16:7
2 Chr 17:10
16:9
Ps 37:23
Prov 16:1; 19:21;
20:24
Jer 10:23
16:10
1 Kgs 3:28
16:11
Prov 11:1
16:12
Prov 25:5
[i]*melek* (4428)
‣ Prov 19:12
[j]*kisse'* (3678)
‣ Prov 20:28
16:13
Prov 14:35
16:14
Prov 19:12
16:15
Job 29:23
16:16
Prov 8:10, 19
[k]*khokmah* (2451)
‣ Prov 17:24

15:24 A wise person avoids death by choosing *the path of life.* • *the grave:* Hebrew *Sheol.* See note on 1:12.

15:25 The *proud* think that they are self-sufficient. *Widows* in the ancient Near East were just the opposite—completely vulnerable and without means of support or protection.

15:29 The heart behind *prayers* determines whether God hears them.

15:30 Just as how we feel affects our demeanor (see 15:13), what we experience (such as another person's *cheerful look* or *good news*) can affect how we feel.

15:33 *Fear of the LORD* fosters *humility* because proper regard for God counteracts our delusions of self-sufficiency.

16:1 *Our own plans* will come to fruition only if God allows (see also 16:9, 33; Jas 4:13-16).

16:2 God's moral evaluation is what counts (see Gen 8:21; 1 Sam 13:14; 16:6-7; Luke 16:15). This proverb is repeated almost verbatim in 21:2.

16:3 God must affirm our *plans* (16:1), so it makes sense to ask his help in accomplishing our goals (see Jas 4:13-16).

16:4 *The wicked* will have trouble in this life and in death. Nothing is outside of God's control (see also Rom 9:10-24; 2 Pet 2:9).

16:5 God *detests the proud,* who refuse to commit their ways to the Lord (16:3) and mistakenly believe that they can accomplish their plans on their own (16:1).

16:6 God's *unfailing love and faithfulness* are foundational in his covenant relationship with Israel (see Exod 15:13; 34:6-7; Num 14:18-19; Deut 7:9-11).

16:8 *Better to have little:* See also 15:16.

16:10-15 This series of sayings reflects on *the king,* who represents God's power on earth.

16:10 *Divine wisdom* refers to divinely inspired guidance that helps the king make judgments (e.g., 1 Kgs 3:28; see also Ps 72:2).

16:11 The message of this proverb is stated four times in the collection (cp. 11:1; 20:10, 23).

16:12-13 These proverbs presuppose a wise, godly *king* (see Isa 9:6-7). Many of Israel's kings loved wrongdoing and hated truth (e.g., Ahab in 1 Kgs 21).

16:14-15 *The king* is powerful, so people are wise to avoid his *anger* and gain his *favor.*

16:16 *Wisdom* and *good judgment* may lead to wealth, but wealth cannot buy wisdom.

16:18 Jer 49:16
16:19 Isa 57:15
16:20 Ps 2:12; 34:8 Jer 17:7
16:21 Prov 16:23
16:23 Ps 37:30 Prov 15:18, 28
16:24 Prov 4:22; 15:26; 17:22; 24:13
16:25 Prov 14:12
16:27 Prov 6:14, 18 Jas 3:6
16:29 Prov 1:10
16:31 Prov 20:29
16:32 Prov 19:11
[a]*'arek 'appayim* (0750, 0639)
›Joel 2:13
17:1 Prov 15:17

17 The path of the virtuous leads away
from evil;
whoever follows that path is safe.

18 Pride goes before destruction,
and haughtiness before a fall.

19 Better to live humbly with the poor
than to share plunder with the proud.

20 Those who listen to instruction will
prosper;
those who trust the LORD will be
joyful.

21 The wise are known for their
understanding,
and pleasant words are persuasive.

22 Discretion is a life-giving fountain to
those who possess it,
but discipline is wasted on fools.

23 From a wise mind comes wise speech;
the words of the wise are persuasive.

24 Kind words are like honey—
sweet to the soul and healthy for the
body.

25 There is a path before each person that
seems right,
but it ends in death.

26 It is good for workers to have an
appetite;
an empty stomach drives them on.

27 Scoundrels create trouble;
their words are a destructive blaze.

28 A troublemaker plants seeds of strife;
gossip separates the best of
friends.

29 Violent people mislead their
companions,
leading them down a harmful path.

30 With narrowed eyes, people plot evil;
with a smirk, they plan their
mischief.

31 Gray hair is a crown of glory;
it is gained by living a godly life.

32 Better to be [a]patient than powerful;
better to have self-control than to
conquer a city.

33 We may throw the dice,
but the LORD determines how they
fall.

17 1 Better a dry crust eaten in peace
than a house filled with
feasting—and conflict.

Wealth and Poverty (16:8, 16)

Prov 3:9-10, 15-16; 10:15, 22; 11:4, 18, 28; 13:8, 11; 14:24; 15:6, 16-17; 23:4-5; 28:27; 29:7, 14
Deut 6:10-13; 8:10-11
1 Sam 2:7
Ps 37:16
Eccl 5:10-17
1 Tim 6:10

The book of Proverbs devotes many sayings to wealth and poverty. In isolation, they might seem in tension or even contradictory, but they are really individual snapshots of a broad truth—that God blesses the wise with wealth (3:9-10, 15-16; 10:22), making life's difficulties more manageable (10:15), while foolish behavior leads to poverty. Laziness is frequently singled out as leading to poverty (26:13-15). The book of Proverbs readily acknowledges that some wicked fools are wealthy, but it also reminds us that this kind of wealth will not last long (11:18; 13:11). Poverty can sometimes result from injustice (13:23) rather than foolishness, and wealth sometimes comes from injustice and dishonesty (16:8). Those who have wealth need to use it wisely, which includes generosity to those in need (28:27; 29:7, 14).

The benefits of wealth are limited. Occasionally, wealth produces problems rather than solving them (11:4; 13:8). Because wisdom can help where wealth cannot, wisdom is much more important than money (15:16-17; 16:8, 16).

All things being equal, the godly will be rewarded with material blessings and the opportunity to be generous. However, things are not always equal. Sometimes wealth does not go to the deserving (see Eccl 9:11), nor does it necessarily produce satisfaction (see Eccl 2:17-23; 5:10-17). In fact, money can be detrimental to faith (1 Tim 6:10; Jas 2:1-13). When a choice must be made between godliness and money, the wise will choose godliness.

16:18 The *pride* of those who resist God and stubbornly rely on their own strength (16:5) is self-destructive and foolish because, apart from God's help, no one has the resources required for life.

16:25 // 14:12 The life choices that seem right and obvious from a human perspective will lead us to death if we are not following God's priorities (see Matt 7:13-14).

16:27-29 ***Scoundrels, a troublemaker,*** and ***violent people*** all disrupt relationships, creating ***trouble*** with their ***harmful*** actions.

16:31 ***Godly*** people grow in wisdom as they grow older, so their ***gray hair is a crown*** (cp. 4:9; 12:4; 17:6).

16:32 Patience and ***self-control*** are far more valuable than brute force.

16:33 ***We may throw the dice*** (Literally *We may cast lots*): These dice were not for gambling but a means commissioned by God to determine his will (Exod 28:30; see also Josh 14:2; 1 Sam 10:17-27; 14:40-43).

2 A wise [b]servant will rule over the
master's disgraceful son
and will share the inheritance of the
master's children.

3 Fire tests the purity of silver and gold,
but the LORD tests the heart.

4 Wrongdoers eagerly listen to gossip;
liars pay close attention to slander.

5 Those who mock the poor insult their
Maker;
those who rejoice at the misfortune of
others will be punished.

6 Grandchildren are the crowning glory of
the aged;
parents are the pride of their children.

7 Eloquent words are not fitting for a fool;
even less are lies fitting for a ruler.

8 A bribe is like a lucky charm;
whoever gives one will prosper!

9 Love prospers when a fault is forgiven,
but dwelling on it separates close
friends.

10 A single rebuke does more for a person
of understanding
than a hundred lashes on the back of
a fool.

11 Evil people are eager for rebellion,
but they will be severely punished.

12 It is safer to meet a bear robbed of her
cubs
than to confront a fool caught in
[c]foolishness.

13 If you repay good with evil,
evil will never leave your house.

14 Starting a quarrel is like opening a
floodgate,
so stop before a dispute breaks out.

15 Acquitting the guilty and condemning
the innocent—
both are detestable to the LORD.

16 It is senseless to pay tuition to educate a
fool,
since he has no heart for learning.

17 A friend is always loyal,
and a brother is born to help in time
of need.

18 It's poor judgment to guarantee another
person's debt
or put up security for a friend.

19 Anyone who loves to quarrel loves [d]sin;
anyone who trusts in high walls
invites disaster.

20 The crooked heart will not prosper;
the lying tongue tumbles into trouble.

21 It is painful to be the parent of a fool;
there is no joy for the father of a rebel.

22 A cheerful heart is good medicine,
but a broken spirit saps a person's
strength.

23 The wicked take secret bribes
to pervert the course of justice.

24 Sensible people keep their eyes glued on
[e]wisdom,
but a fool's eyes wander to the ends of
the earth.

25 Foolish children bring grief to their father
and bitterness to the one who gave
them birth.

26 It is wrong to punish the godly for being
good
or to flog leaders for being honest.

27 A truly wise person uses few words;
a person with understanding is even-
tempered.

17:2
[b]*'ebed* (5650)
▸Prov 30:10

17:3
1 Chr 29:17
Ps 26:2

17:4
Prov 1:10; 16:29

17:5
Job 31:29
Prov 14:31; 24:17

17:6
Gen 48:11
Prov 13:22

17:7
Prov 12:22; 24:7

17:8
Prov 21:14
Isa 1:23
Amos 5:12

17:9
Prov 10:12
Jas 5:20

17:12
Prov 29:9
Hos 13:8
[c]*'iwweleth* (0200)
▸Prov 22:15

17:13
Ps 109:5
Prov 13:21
Jer 18:20

17:14
Prov 20:3; 25:8

17:15
Exod 23:7
Prov 24:24
Isa 5:23

17:17
Ruth 1:16
Prov 18:24

17:18
Prov 6:1; 11:15; 22:26

17:19
Prov 13:2; 16:18;
29:22-23
[d]*pesha'* (6588)
▸Prov 28:13

17:20
Jas 3:8

17:21
Prov 10:1; 17:25;
19:13

17:22
Prov 15:13

17:23
Exod 23:8

17:24
Eccl 2:14
[e]*khokmah* (2451)
▸Prov 29:3

17:2 Wisdom is so much more important than privilege that if children act like fools, a *wise servant* will rise to prominence over the household.

17:3 The Lord's refining *fire* (see Ps 66:10; Jer 9:7; Mal 3:2-3) separates what is precious from the impurities in a person's *heart* (cp. 16:2; 21:2; 27:21).

17:4 Lies (6:16-19; 14:5, 25; 25:18), *gossip* (11:13; 18:8), and *slander* (10:18) distort reality for malicious purposes.

17:5 To make fun of what God created is to mock God.

17:6 Only those who have been blessed with a long life live to become grandparents, and the continuation of the family line is a sign of God's blessing (see Gen 12:1-3). • *parents:* Literally *fathers.* This proverb applies to both fathers and mothers.

17:9 Maintaining a good relationship with another person means forgiving rather than dwelling on faults.

17:10 The wise will listen to a mild *rebuke* and act on good advice. Even harsh correction (*a hundred lashes*) will not change a fool.

17:11 *Rebellion* flows from the inner character of *evil people* who defy the punishment that will follow.

17:12 This saying cautions those who try to teach fools. *A fool caught in foolishness* will react with anger and violence.

17:14 *opening a floodgate:* Once a quarrel starts, it is very difficult to stop it; *a dispute* should be avoided if at all possible (see 10:12; 15:18; 16:28; 20:3; 22:10; 26:21).

17:18 The essence of this message is repeated in 6:1-5; 11:15; 20:16; 22:26; 27:13.

17:19 *high walls:* Foolish confidence in the ability to win a fight emboldens people to engage in disastrous arguments.

17:24 Wisdom is not a natural quality but must be pursued. *Sensible people* persistently cultivate wisdom, but *a fool's eyes* cannot stay focused.

17:25 *Foolish children:* Literally *A foolish son.* This proverb is equally true of foolish sons and foolish daughters. See note on 1:22.

17:25 Prov 10:1
17:26 Prov 18:5
17:27 Prov 10:19; Jas 1:19
17:28 Job 13:5
18:2 Prov 12:23
18:4 Prov 20:5
18:5 Prov 17:15; 24:23
18:6 Prov 10:14; 13:3
18:10 2 Sam 22:2; Ps 18:2; 61:3; 91:2; Prov 29:25
18:11 Prov 10:15
18:12 Prov 11:2; 16:18; 29:23
18:13 Prov 20:25; John 7:51
18:15 Prov 15:14
18:16 Gen 32:20; 1 Sam 25:27
18:18 Prov 16:33
18:20 Prov 12:14
18:21 Prov 13:3; Matt 12:37

28 Even fools are thought wise when they
keep silent;
with their mouths shut, they seem
intelligent.

18 1 Unfriendly people care only about
themselves;
they lash out at common sense.

2 Fools have no interest in understanding;
they only want to air their own
opinions.

3 Doing wrong leads to disgrace,
and scandalous behavior brings
contempt.

4 Wise words are like deep waters;
wisdom flows from the wise like a
bubbling brook.

5 It is not right to acquit the guilty
or deny justice to the innocent.

6 Fools' words get them into constant
quarrels;
they are asking for a beating.

7 The mouths of fools are their ruin;
they trap themselves with their lips.

8 Rumors are dainty morsels
that sink deep into one's heart.

9 A lazy person is as bad as
someone who destroys things.

10 The name of the LORD is a strong fortress;
the godly run to him and are safe.

11 The rich think of their wealth as a strong
defense;
they imagine it to be a high wall of
safety.

12 Haughtiness goes before destruction;
humility precedes honor.

13 Spouting off before listening to the facts
is both shameful and foolish.

14 The human spirit can endure a sick body,
but who can bear a crushed spirit?

15 Intelligent people are always ready to
learn.
Their ears are open for knowledge.

16 Giving a gift can open doors;
it gives access to important people!

17 The first to speak in court sounds right—
until the cross-examination begins.

18 Flipping a coin can end arguments;
it settles disputes between powerful
opponents.

19 An offended friend is harder to win back
than a fortified city.
Arguments separate friends like a
gate locked with bars.

20 Wise words satisfy like a good meal;
the right words bring satisfaction.

21 The tongue can bring death or life;
those who love to talk will reap the
consequences.

Bribes (17:8, 23)

Prov 15:27; 18:16; 21:14; 28:21; 29:4; Exod 23:8; Deut 10:17; 16:19; 1 Sam 8:1-3; Ps 15:5; 26:9-11; Eccl 7:7; Isa 1:23; 5:23; 33:14-16; Amos 5:12; Mic 3:9-12; 7:3; Matt 28:11-15; Acts 24:24-26

Like other teachings in the book of Proverbs, the teaching on bribery seems contradictory. Bribes are condemned as perverting justice (15:27; 17:23). Yet bribes can be used for good purposes and may even be encouraged (17:8; 18:16; 21:14).

These proverbs can all ring true when applied to the right circumstances, which seem to be connected to the reason for which a bribe or gift is given. If someone gives a bribe so that a judge will condemn an innocent person or set a guilty person free, then it is an evil bribe (see Exod 23:8; Deut 10:17; 16:19; 27:25; Ps 15:5). However, if a bribe helps an innocent person to find justice or serves some good purpose, then it seems to be allowable. An example of the latter from modern times might be a "gift" to a foreign immigration official that expedites the processing of a visa for a missionary.

18:4 Words flow from one's character as water bubbles up from the earth (see also 10:20; 12:23; 16:23; cp. Jas 3:10-12).

18:8 // 26:22 ***Rumors*** may be delicious to hear and repeat, but they are deadly.

18:10-11 In a troubled world, only ***the LORD*** can save. The rich might believe ***their wealth*** is ***a strong defense***, but the power of money is limited (11:4; 13:8).

18:12 ***Haughtiness*** cultivates pride. It leads to failure because it does not allow for change in the face of criticism. ***Humility*** learns from others and leads to the ***honor*** of success.

18:14 A spiritual or emotional problem (***a crushed spirit***) can be more trying than a physical one (***sick body***).

18:16 See "Bribes" at 17:8, above.

18:17 It is important to hear both sides of a dispute. Only fools jump to conclusions and rush to judgment; the wise take time to discern.

18:18 ***Flipping a coin*** (literally ***Casting lots***): Casting lots was a valid way of seeking God's will (Num 27:21; Josh 18:6-10). The Lord determined how the lots would fall (see note on 16:33).

18:21 ***Life*** and ***death:*** The wise speak thoughtfully (10:19; 11:12; 12:23) because they know that what we say has ***consequences*** (13:3; 14:3).

22 The man who finds a wife finds a
treasure,
and he receives favor from the LORD.

23 The poor plead for mercy;
the rich answer with insults.

24 There are "friends" who destroy each
other,
but a real friend sticks closer than a
brother.

19 1 Better to be poor and honest
than to be dishonest and a fool.

2 Enthusiasm without knowledge is no
good;
haste makes mistakes.

3 People ruin their lives by their own
foolishness
and then are angry at the LORD.

4 Wealth makes many "friends";
poverty drives them all away.

5 A false witness will not go unpunished,
nor will a liar escape.

6 Many seek favors from a ruler;
everyone is the friend of a person
who gives gifts!

7 The relatives of the poor despise them;
how much more will their friends
avoid them!
Though the poor plead with them,
their friends are gone.

8 To acquire wisdom is to love oneself;
people who cherish understanding
will prosper.

9 A false witness will not go unpunished,
and a liar will be destroyed.

10 It isn't right for a fool to live in luxury
or for a slave to rule over princes!

11 Sensible people control their temper;
they earn respect by overlooking
wrongs.

12 The [f]king's anger is like a lion's roar,
but his favor is like dew on the grass.

13 A foolish child is a calamity to a father;
a quarrelsome wife is as annoying as
constant dripping.

14 Fathers can give their sons an
inheritance of houses and wealth,
but only the LORD can give an
understanding wife.

15 Lazy people sleep soundly,
but idleness leaves them hungry.

16 Keep the commandments and keep your
life;
despising them leads to death.

17 If you help the poor, you are lending to
the LORD—
and he will repay you!

18 Discipline your children while there is
hope.
Otherwise you will ruin their lives.

19 Hot-tempered people must pay the
penalty.
If you rescue them once, you will have
to do it again.

20 Get all the advice and instruction you can,
so you will be wise the rest of your life.

21 You can make many plans,
but the LORD's purpose will prevail.

22 Loyalty makes a person attractive.
It is better to be poor than dishonest.

23 Fear of the LORD leads to life,
bringing security and protection
from harm.

24 Lazy people take food in their hand
but don't even lift it to their mouth.

18:22 Prov 12:4; 19:14; 31:10-31
18:23 Prov 19:7; Jas 2:3
19:1 Prov 20:7; 28:6
19:3 Isa 8:21
19:4 Prov 14:20
19:5 Exod 23:1; Deut 19:16-19; Prov 19:9
19:6 Prov 18:16; 29:26
19:7 Ps 38:11; Prov 18:23
19:8 Prov 16:20
19:9 Prov 19:5
19:10 Prov 26:1; Eccl 10:6-7
19:11 Prov 14:29; 16:32
19:12 Gen 27:28; Prov 16:14-15; [f]*melek* (4428) › Eccl 8:2
19:13 Prov 17:25; 21:9, 19
19:14 Prov 18:22; 2 Cor 12:14
19:15 Prov 6:9; 16:26; 24:33
19:16 Prov 16:17; Luke 10:28; 11:28
19:17 Deut 15:7; Prov 14:31; 28:27; Luke 6:38
19:18 Prov 13:24
19:20 Prov 4:1; 8:33; 12:15
19:21 Ps 33:10-11; Prov 16:1, 9
19:23 Ps 25:13; Prov 14:27; 1 Tim 4:8
19:24 //Prov 26:15

18:23 God will punish the powerful who disparage ***the poor;*** wise people care for the needy (11:24; 28:27; 29:7, 14).

18:24 Some people who present themselves as ***"friends"*** are not. The wise see beyond pretense, discerning ***a real friend*** from false friends by how they act in adverse circumstances.

19:1 It is ***better to be . . . honest,*** though ***poor,*** because wealth gained by ***dishonest*** means is short lived (10:2) and will not preserve one from harm (11:4; see also 15:16-17; 16:8, 16; 17:1; 22:1; 28:6).

19:2 Rushing into things without understanding is dangerous.

19:3 Rather than acknowledge wrong choices and actions, fools blame ***the LORD.***

19:5 God will make sure that liars are punished (see 12:17, 19; 14:5, 25; 19:9).

19:8 It is in our self-interest ***to acquire wisdom*** because ***understanding*** helps us ***prosper.***

19:9 The reference to a ***false witness*** (see also 19:5) reminds us of the ninth commandment (Exod 20:16).

19:12 A ***lion's roar*** is a frightening prelude to life-threatening violence (cp. 20:2). ***Dew on the grass*** is soothing and contributes to growth (see 16:14-15).

19:13-14 ***child:*** Literally ***son;*** also in 19:27. • No choice for a son is more important than a good wife (cp. 31:10-31); a poor choice brings agony (see 10:1; 11:22; 12:4b; 21:9, 19; 25:24; 27:15-17). The wise man will look to ***the LORD*** to ***give an understanding wife.***

19:16 Keeping God's ***commandments*** (i.e., the law of Moses) protects one's ***life*** (see Deut 28:15-68).

19:18 Growing in wisdom requires ***discipline*** for everyone, including ***children*** (see 10:17; 13:1, 10; 15:31-32; 17:10). Discipline sometimes includes physical punishment (13:24; 22:15; 23:13-14).

19:24 // 26:15 This proverb is a humorous comment on the foolishness of being ***lazy*** (see also 10:4-6, 26; 12:11, 27; 13:4; 15:19; 18:9).

19:25 Prov 9:7-8; 21:11
19:26 Prov 20:20; 28:24
19:28 Job 15:16
[g]*beliya'al* (1100)
› Deut 13:13
19:29 Prov 9:12; 10:13; 26:3
20:1 Prov 31:4
Isa 5:22; 56:12
20:2 1 Kgs 2:23
Prov 8:36; 19:12
20:3 Prov 14:29; 16:32; 19:11
20:5 Prov 18:4
20:7 Ps 37:26; 112:2
20:8 Prov 20:26
20:9 2 Chr 6:36
Job 14:4
20:10 Prov 11:1; 20:23
20:11 Matt 7:16
20:12 Exod 4:11
20:13 Prov 6:9-11; 19:15; 24:32-34
20:17 Prov 9:17-18
20:18 Prov 15:22; 24:6
Luke 14:31
20:19 Prov 11:13

25 If you punish a mocker, the
simpleminded will learn a lesson;
if you correct the wise, they will be all
the wiser.

26 Children who mistreat their father or
chase away their mother
are an embarrassment and a public
disgrace.

27 If you stop listening to instruction, my
child,
you will turn your back on
knowledge.

28 A [g]corrupt witness makes a mockery of
justice;
the mouth of the wicked gulps down
evil.

29 Punishment is made for mockers,
and the backs of fools are made to be
beaten.

20

1 Wine produces mockers; alcohol
leads to brawls.
Those led astray by drink cannot be
wise.

2 The king's fury is like a lion's roar;
to rouse his anger is to risk your life.

3 Avoiding a fight is a mark of honor;
only fools insist on quarreling.

4 Those too lazy to plow in the right
season
will have no food at the harvest.

5 Though good advice lies deep within the
heart,
a person with understanding will
draw it out.

6 Many will say they are loyal friends,
but who can find one who is truly
reliable?

7 The godly walk with integrity;
blessed are their children who follow
them.

8 When a king sits in judgment, he weighs
all the evidence,
distinguishing the bad from the good.

9 Who can say, "I have cleansed my heart;
I am pure and free from sin"?

10 False weights and unequal measures—
the LORD detests double standards of
every kind.

11 Even children are known by the way they
act,
whether their conduct is pure, and
whether it is right.

12 Ears to hear and eyes to see—
both are gifts from the LORD.

13 If you love sleep, you will end in
poverty.
Keep your eyes open, and there will be
plenty to eat!

14 The buyer haggles over the price, saying,
"It's worthless,"
then brags about getting a bargain!

15 Wise words are more valuable
than much gold and many rubies.

16 Get security from someone who
guarantees a stranger's debt.
Get a deposit if he does it for
foreigners.

17 Stolen bread tastes sweet,
but it turns to gravel in the mouth.

18 Plans succeed through good counsel;
don't go to war without wise advice.

19 A gossip goes around telling secrets,
so don't hang around with chatterers.

19:25 *A mocker* is beyond help (see notes on 1:22; 21:11). A leader should still *punish* him because *the simpleminded will learn a lesson.*

19:26 See Exod 20:12; 21:15, 17.

20:1 Too much *alcohol* clouds a person's judgment. The OT is not against drinking *wine* in moderation (3:10; 9:5; Ps 104:14-15), but it adamantly opposes excessive drinking (21:17; 23:29-35; 31:4-5).

20:2 A *lion's roar* is a frightening prelude to life-threatening violence (cp. 20:2). Queen Esther was willing to *rouse* the king's *anger* and *risk* her *life* (Esth 7:1-10).

20:6 True *friends* are *reliable* even in difficulties.

20:8 The *king* should be the epitome of wisdom and justice.

20:9 Wise people recognize their own weaknesses. Pride prohibits people from seeing their faults (6:17-18; 11:2; 13:10; 15:33; 16:18; 18:12; see also 1 Jn 1:8-10).

20:10 *False weights and unequal measures:* Literally *A stone and a stone, an ephah and an ephah.* Merchants, for example, should not cheat their customers by using false weights to weigh out grain (cp. 11:1; 16:11; 20:23).

20:12 The ability to observe and learn from experience is a divine gift.

20:13 Laziness leads to *poverty* (see 10:4-6, 26; 12:11; 13:4; 14:4; 15:19; 18:9; 19:15, 24; 20:4).

20:14 Sellers must see past a buyer's words to avoid being cheated.

20:16 // 27:13 A wise lender gets *security* or *a deposit* on a loan. A *stranger* was an Israelite unknown to a lender, who required security. Proverbs warns the wise to avoid borrowing altogether (see 6:1-2). • *for foreigners:* An alternate reading in the Masoretic Text is *for a promiscuous woman.* • This proverb is repeated verbatim in 27:13, and its message is repeated in 6:1-5; 11:15; 17:18; 22:26.

20:19 This perspective on the *gossip* is repeated in 11:13.

20 If you insult your father or mother,
your light will be snuffed out in total
darkness.

21 An inheritance obtained too early in life
is not a blessing in the end.

22 Don't say, "I will get even for this
wrong."
Wait for the LORD to handle the
matter.

23 The LORD detests double standards;
he is not pleased by dishonest scales.

24 The LORD directs our steps,
so why try to understand everything
along the way?

25 Don't trap yourself by making a rash
promise to God
and only later counting the cost.

26 A wise king scatters the wicked like
wheat,
then runs his threshing wheel over
them.

27 The LORD's light penetrates the human
spirit,
exposing every hidden motive.

28 Unfailing love and faithfulness protect
the king;
his [h]throne is made secure through
love.

29 The glory of the young is their strength;
the gray hair of experience is the
splendor of the old.

30 Physical punishment cleanses away evil;
such discipline purifies the heart.

21

1 The king's heart is like a stream of
water directed by the LORD;
he guides it wherever he pleases.

2 People may be right in their own eyes,
but the LORD examines their heart.

3 The LORD is more pleased when we do
what is right and just
than when we offer him sacrifices.

4 Haughty eyes, a proud [i]heart,
and evil actions are all sin.

5 Good planning and hard work lead to
prosperity,
but hasty shortcuts lead to poverty.

6 Wealth created by a lying tongue
is a vanishing mist and a deadly trap.

7 The violence of the wicked sweeps them
away,
because they refuse to do what is just.

8 The guilty walk a crooked path;
the innocent travel a straight road.

9 It's better to live alone in the corner of
an attic
than with a quarrelsome wife in a
lovely home.

10 Evil people desire evil;
their neighbors get no mercy from
them.

11 If you punish a mocker, the
simpleminded become wise;
if you instruct the wise, they will be
all the wiser.

12 The Righteous One knows what is going
on in the homes of the wicked;
he will bring disaster on them.

20:20 Exod 21:17; Lev 20:9; Prov 30:11; Matt 15:4
20:22 Ps 27:14; Prov 24:28-29; Matt 5:39; Rom 12:17
20:23 Prov 11:1; 20:10
20:24 Ps 37:23; Prov 16:9
20:25 Eccl 5:4-5
20:26 Prov 20:8
20:27 1 Cor 2:11
20:28 Prov 29:14; [h]*kisse'* (3678) ‣ Prov 29:14
20:29 Prov 16:31
21:1 Ezra 6:21, 22
21:2 Prov 16:2; 24:11-12; Luke 16:15
21:3 Prov 15:8; Isa 1:11; Mic 6:6-8
21:4 Prov 6:17; 30:13; Luke 11:34; [i]*leb* (3820) ‣ Jer 17:9
21:5 Prov 10:4; 28:22
21:6 Prov 10:2; 13:11
21:10 Prov 2:14
21:11 Prov 19:25
21:13 Luke 16:19-31; Jas 2:13; 1 Jn 3:17

. . . .

20:21 An *inheritance* gained *early in life* is likely to be spent long before death, leaving nothing to live on.

20:22 See also Rom 12:17-21.

20:23 The message of this proverb is presented in three other proverbs (cp. 11:1; 16:11; 20:10).

20:24 God's role in guiding *our steps* is clear (see 16:1, 9, 33). We do not need to *understand* why things happen, but we should not lose hope, for God is in control.

20:25 *Counting the cost* is particularly important when making a *promise to God* (see Judg 11:29-40; Eccl 5:4-6).

20:26 A *king* represents God on earth, so he should support the godly and punish *the wicked.*

20:27 *The LORD's light penetrates the human spirit:* Or *The human spirit is the LORD's light.* God sees deep into people's hearts (see 16:2).

20:28 God's *unfailing love* and *faithfulness* are closely connected to his covenant with his people (see Exod 34:5-7; Deut 7:7-9). The king represents God on earth, so God will *protect* him (see 2 Sam 7).

20:30 *Physical punishment cleanses away evil:* The meaning of the Hebrew is uncertain (see 13:24; 22:15; 23:13-14).

21:1 A *king* was the most powerful individual in an ancient nation, and it seemed that he could do as he pleased. However, God directs the *heart* of the king.

21:2 This proverb is repeated almost verbatim in 16:2.

21:3 God is not *pleased* with worship unless godly actions flow from a godly heart (see Ps 40:6-8; Mic 6:6-8).

21:4 Demeanor (*eyes*), character (*heart*), and *actions* are all significant. God hates pride (see 6:17-18; 11:2; 13:10; 15:33; 16:18; 18:12).

21:6 *mist and a deadly trap:* As in Greek version; Hebrew reads *mist for those who seek death.*

21:8 The *crooked path* of foolishness ends with death; the *straight road* of wisdom leads to life.

21:9 // 25:24 A marriage that looks good on the outside (*in a lovely home*) is unrewarding if it is filled with quarrels (see also 21:19; 25:24; 27:15-17; cp. 11:22; 12:4b).

21:10 *Evil people* do not just act evil; they are evil. No appeal will persuade them to act otherwise.

21:11 The *simpleminded* learn by seeing *a mocker* punished (see 1:22; 19:25). *The wise* do not need the threat of punishment because they already desire wisdom.

21:12 *The Righteous One:* Or *The righteous man.* God sees what *the wicked* do in the privacy of their *homes* and will

21:14
Prov 17:8; 19:6
21:15
Prov 10:29
[j]*mishpat* (4941)
‣Isa 30:18
[k]*simkhah* (8057)
‣Isa 29:19
21:16
Ps 49:14
21:17
Prov 23:19-21
21:18
Prov 11:8
Isa 43:3-4
21:19
Prov 21:9
21:20
Job 20:15, 18
Prov 8:21
21:21
Matt 5:6
21:22
2 Sam 5:6-9
Prov 24:5
Eccl 9:15-16
21:23
Prov 12:13; 13:3
Jas 3:2
21:24
Ps 1:1
Prov 1:22
[a]*zadon* (2087)
‣Jer 49:16
21:25
Prov 13:4
21:27
Prov 15:8
[b]*zebakh* (2077)
‣Isa 1:11
21:30
Isa 8:9; 14:27
Acts 5:38-39
21:31
Ps 20:7
Isa 31:1-3
1 Cor 15:57
22:2
Job 31:15
Prov 14:31
22:3
Prov 14:16; 27:12
22:4
Prov 3:16; 4:4
22:5
Prov 15:19

13 Those who shut their ears to the cries of the poor
will be ignored in their own time of need.

14 A secret gift calms anger;
a bribe under the table pacifies fury.

15 [j]Justice is a [k]joy to the godly,
but it terrifies evildoers.

16 The person who strays from common sense
will end up in the company of the dead.

17 Those who love pleasure become poor;
those who love wine and luxury will never be rich.

18 The wicked are punished in place of the godly,
and traitors in place of the honest.

19 It's better to live alone in the desert
than with a quarrelsome, complaining wife.

20 The wise have wealth and luxury,
but fools spend whatever they get.

21 Whoever pursues righteousness and unfailing love
will find life, righteousness, and honor.

22 The wise conquer the city of the strong
and level the fortress in which they trust.

23 Watch your tongue and keep your mouth shut,
and you will stay out of trouble.

24 Mockers are proud and haughty;
they act with boundless [a]arrogance.

25 Despite their desires, the lazy will come to ruin,
for their hands refuse to work.

26 Some people are always greedy for more,
but the godly love to give!

27 The [b]sacrifice of an evil person is detestable,
especially when it is offered with wrong motives.

28 A false witness will be cut off,
but a credible witness will be allowed to speak.

29 The wicked bluff their way through,
but the virtuous think before they act.

30 No human wisdom or understanding or plan
can stand against the LORD.

31 The horse is prepared for the day of battle,
but the victory belongs to the LORD.

22

1 Choose a good reputation over great riches;
being held in high esteem is better than silver or gold.

2 The rich and poor have this in common:
The LORD made them both.

3 A prudent person foresees danger and takes precautions.
The simpleton goes blindly on and suffers the consequences.

4 True humility and fear of the LORD
lead to riches, honor, and long life.

5 Corrupt people walk a thorny, treacherous road;
whoever values life will avoid it.

punish them for their sins. Alternatively, *the righteous one* might refer to the insight of any righteous individual.

21:15 God is just, so he will reward the innocent and punish the wicked. No wonder *the godly* love justice while the wicked fear it.

21:16 Those who have *common sense* can avoid life's dangers.

21:17 The expenses of *wine and luxury* prevent people from amassing their resources—they spend rather than save.

21:18 *The wicked* will fall prey to the traps they set for others (26:27; see also 11:8).

21:19 ***It's better to live alone:*** Cp. 21:9; 25:24.

21:20 See also 3:9-10, 15-16; 10:15, 16, 22; 14:24.

21:21 ***Righteousness*** and ***unfailing love*** are character traits associated with Israel's covenant with God (see Exod 34:5-7; Deut 7:9-11). The covenant promised ***life*** and ***honor*** to those who obeyed God's law (Deut 28:1-14).

21:22 A ***wise*** military strategist can devise ways to defeat stronger forces. This makes wisdom superior to raw power (cp. Eccl 7:12; 9:13-18).

21:24 ***Mockers:*** See 1:25-27; 9:7-9. Also see note on 1:22.

21:26 Generosity is a trait of ***the godly***, while stinginess is characteristic of fools (29:7, 14). Paradoxically, the more you give, the more you get (11:24).

21:30-31 ***Human wisdom*** is impotent if it stands ***against the LORD*** (see 16:1, 3, 9, 33). Similarly, military power (represented by ***the horse***) is impotent without the Lord's blessing.

22:1 A wise person will never compromise his reputation in pursuit of money.

22:2 Remembering that ***the LORD made them both*** helps prevent the exploitation of ***the poor***.

22:3 // 27:12 The theme of taking ***precautions*** is found in several proverbs (14:8, 15; 21:29).

22:4 ***Fear of the LORD*** (see 1:7; 9:10) goes hand in hand with ***humility***. A humble person knows that he is not the center of the universe. Humility is more valuable than wealth (16:19; see also 11:2; 15:33; 18:12).

22:5 Living by deceit is dangerous; ***corrupt people*** never know when their treachery will be discovered or backfire.

6 Direct your children onto the right path,
and when they are older, they will not leave it.

7 Just as the rich rule the poor,
so the borrower is servant to the lender.

8 Those who plant injustice will harvest disaster,
and their reign of terror will come to an end.

9 Blessed are those who are generous,
because they feed the poor.

10 Throw out the mocker, and fighting goes, too.
Quarrels and insults will disappear.

11 Whoever loves a pure heart and gracious speech
will have the king as a friend.

12 The LORD preserves those with knowledge,
but he ruins the plans of the treacherous.

13 The lazy person claims, "There's a lion out there!
If I go outside, I might be killed!"

14 The mouth of an immoral woman is a dangerous trap;
those who make the LORD angry will fall into it.

15 A youngster's heart is filled with ᶜfoolishness,
but physical discipline will drive it far away.

16 A person who gets ahead by oppressing the poor
or by showering gifts on the rich will end in poverty.

4. THE THIRTY SAYINGS OF THE WISE (22:17–24:22)

17 Listen to the words of the wise;
apply your heart to my instruction.
18 For it is good to keep these sayings in your heart
and always ready on your lips.
19 I am teaching you today—yes, you—
so you will trust in the LORD.
20 I have written thirty sayings for you,
filled with advice and knowledge.
21 In this way, you may know the truth
and take an accurate report to those who sent you.

22 Don't rob the poor just because you can,
or exploit the needy in court.
23 For the LORD is their defender.
He will ruin anyone who ruins them.

24 Don't befriend angry people
or associate with hot-tempered people,
25 or you will learn to be like them
and endanger your soul.

26 Don't agree to guarantee another person's debt
or put up security for someone else.
27 If you can't pay it,
even your bed will be snatched from under you.

22:6 Eph 6:4
22:7 Jas 2:6
22:8 Job 4:8; Prov 24:16
22:9 Prov 19:17; Luke 14:13; 2 Cor 9:6
22:10 Prov 24:9
22:11 Ps 24:4; Prov 14:35; Matt 5:8
22:13 Rom 12:11
22:14 Eccl 7:26
22:15 Prov 13:24; 23:14; ᶜ*iwweleth* (0200) ‣ Prov 26:4
22:16 Prov 14:31; 28:3
22:17 Prov 5:1
22:22 Zech 7:10; Mal 3:5
22:24 Prov 29:22
22:26 Prov 6:1-5

22:7 This is a warning against being a *borrower;* other proverbs warn against guaranteeing others' debts (6:1-2; 20:16).

22:8 The Greek version includes an additional proverb: *God blesses a man who gives cheerfully, / but his worthless deeds will come to an end.* Paul quotes this additional proverb in 2 Cor 9:7.

22:11 Even a wicked ruler wants advisers who have a *pure heart*—i.e., who are completely loyal—and who can communicate with *gracious speech.*

22:12 This proverb reminds the wise (*those with knowledge*) that *the LORD* is in control.

22:13 Of the many proverbs on laziness (10:4-6, 26; 12:11; 13:4; 14:4; 15:19; 18:9; 19:15, 24; 20:4, 13; 21:25; 26:13), this is among the funniest. Lazy people will come up with any outlandish excuse for not working.

22:14 *An immoral woman*, using flattery and seduction, tries to *trap* a young man to commit sin.

22:15 Wisdom is learned, not inherited or innate. It takes *discipline,* sometimes *physical,* to change *foolishness* into wisdom.

22:16 *A person . . . gets ahead* by hard work, not by exploiting the poor or bribing *the rich* (cp. 22:29).

22:17–24:22 This section is ascribed to a group called *the wise.* Who they were is unknown. There is a reference to *thirty sayings* (22:20), and the wisdom sayings that follow can be divided into thirty sections that are similar to an Egyptian composition called the *Instruction of Amenemope,* which is also divided into thirty chapters.

22:17-21 As with the prologue that opens the book of Proverbs (1:2-7) and the introductions to the individual discourses (see 1:8-9; 2:1-11), this section begins with an encouragement to *listen.* This wisdom is more than good practical advice—its purpose is to inspire *trust in the LORD.*

22:20 *thirty sayings* (or *excellent sayings;* the meaning of the Hebrew is uncertain): Early scribes noticed that the Hebrew word for *thirty* has been written in an unusual form (*shlshwm*) rather than the usual form (*shlyshym*). All the early translations of the OT (e.g., Greek Septuagint, Latin Vulgate, Syriac Peshitta) read it as *thirty.* Nonetheless, some prefer to translate the word as *excellent sayings.*

22:22-23 Saying 1: God defends the weak, including the *poor.* Those who are well off are responsible to be generous to the poor (11:24-26; 21:13; 22:9, 16; 28:27).

22:24-25 Saying 2: *befriend . . . associate:* See note on 13:20. An *angry . . . hot-tempered* person is unable to control his emotions and expresses his anger at inappropriate times.

22:26-27 Saying 3: See note on 6:1-5. The message of this proverb is also repeated in 11:15; 17:18; 20:16; 27:13.

22:28
Deut 19:14; 27:17
22:29
1 Kgs 10:8; 11:28
23:2
Prov 23:20
23:3
Ps 141:4
23:4
Prov 15:27; 28:20
Matt 6:19
1 Tim 6:9
23:6
Ps 141:4
Prov 1:15; 4:14; 23:1
23:9
Prov 1:7
23:10
Deut 19:14
Prov 22:28
Jer 22:3
Zech 7:10
23:12
Prov 22:17
23:13
Prov 13:24; 19:18
1 Cor 5:5
23:14
[d]*she'ol* (7585)
‣Isa 38:18
23:15
Prov 15:20; 27:11; 29:3

28 Don't cheat your neighbor by moving the
ancient boundary markers
set up by previous generations.

29 Do you see any truly competent workers?
They will serve kings
rather than working for ordinary
people.

23 1 While dining with a ruler,
pay attention to what is put
before you.
2 If you are a big eater,
put a knife to your throat;
3 don't desire all the delicacies,
for he might be trying to trick you.

4 Don't wear yourself out trying to get rich.
Be wise enough to know when to quit.
5 In the blink of an eye wealth disappears,
for it will sprout wings
and fly away like an eagle.

6 Don't eat with people who are stingy;
don't desire their delicacies.
7 They are always thinking about how
much it costs.
"Eat and drink," they say, but they
don't mean it.
8 You will throw up what little you've eaten,
and your compliments will be wasted.

9 Don't waste your breath on fools,
for they will despise the wisest advice.

10 Don't cheat your neighbor by moving the
ancient boundary markers;
don't take the land of defenseless
orphans.
11 For their Redeemer is strong;
he himself will bring their charges
against you.

12 Commit yourself to instruction;
listen carefully to words of knowledge.

13 Don't fail to discipline your children.
They won't die if you spank them.
14 Physical discipline
may well save them from [d]death.

15 My child, if your heart is wise,
my own heart will rejoice!
16 Everything in me will celebrate
when you speak what is right.

Children and Parents (22:6, 15)

Prov 1:8-9; 3:1-2; 4:1-4; 10:1; 11:21, 29; 12:7; 13:22; 14:1; 15:20; 17:21, 25; 19:18, 26; 20:7, 20; 23:13-14; 29:15, 17; 30:11-14, 17
Deut 5:16; 6:1-9, 20-25; 7:3-6
Ps 78:1-8; 103:13; 127:1–128:6
Mark 7:9-13
Luke 1:17; 18:29-30
Eph 6:1-4

Much of the teaching in Proverbs takes the form of a father's or mother's instruction. Wise children bring great joy to their parents, while foolish children cause them much grief (10:1; 15:20). This observation motivates parents to guide their children into wisdom (17:21, 25) and encourages children to pay attention to this instruction (19:26; 20:20).

When children need discipline, parents should not shirk their responsibility, because the consequences are dangerous to the child (19:18; 22:6, 15; 23:13-14). Parents are also instructed to teach through the example of their own wise and godly behavior (11:21; 12:7; 13:22; 20:7), and children must show godly parents the respect that is due them (20:20; 30:11-14, 17). Parents are to instruct their children in the ways of the Lord (Deut 7:4-9) and to inform them about his great deeds in history (Ps 78:1-8). This knowledge will lead children to obedience and blessing.

Psalms 127–128 describe a family that is flourishing because of its dependence on the Lord. The book of Proverbs affirms the power and impact of a strong, cohesive family that loves and follows God. The book has strong warnings for those who would disrupt a family (6:19; 11:29), and it heaps great praise on those who build up the family (14:1).

22:28 Saying 4: Property was marked by stones set up as ***boundary markers;*** it was a great offense to move these ancient markers of real estate (see also 23:10; Deut 19:14).

22:29 Saying 5: Those who hone their skills and work hard will have the best jobs and work for the best people.

23:1-3 Saying 6: Many proverbs address young men in government service. A ruler's rich fare might tempt a novice to overindulge through lack of self-control. But he will be vulnerable when sated.

23:4-5 Saying 7: Riches can be God's blessing (3:9-10, 15-16; 10:22), but there are other things in life that are more important.

23:6-8 Saying 8: Proverbs puts a high premium on generosity (11:24-26; 21:13; 22:9).

23:7 ***They are always thinking about how much it costs:*** The meaning of the Hebrew is uncertain.

23:9 Saying 9: ***Fools*** ignore ***advice*** (cp. 9:7-12; 10:18), so the wise do not ***waste*** their ***breath*** (see Matt 7:6).

23:10-11 Saying 10: The wise avoid unfair business practices and illegitimate gains (see 22:28), knowing that the Lord will judge wrongdoing. • ***Redeemer:*** Or *redeemer.* The NLT is probably correct in capitalizing the word *Redeemer* and identifying him with God, although a human redeemer might be intended.

23:12 Saying 11: ***listen carefully:*** Learning is the way to improve (see 10:17; 13:1, 10; 15:24, 31-32; 17:10; 19:24).

23:13-14 Saying 12: See 19:18; 29:17. • ***from death:*** Hebrew *from Sheol.* See note on 1:12.

23:15-16 Saying 13: A wise parent ***will rejoice*** in a ***wise . . . child*** (see 10:1). • ***My child:*** Literally *My son;* also in 23:19. See note on 1:8–9:18.

[17] Don't envy sinners,
but always continue to fear the LORD.
[18] You will be rewarded for this;
your hope will not be disappointed.

[19] My child, listen and be wise:
Keep your heart on the right course.
[20] Do not carouse with drunkards
or feast with gluttons,
[21] for they are on their way to poverty,
and too much sleep clothes them in rags.

[22] Listen to your father, who gave you life,
and don't despise your mother when she is old.
[23] Get the truth and never sell it;
also get wisdom, discipline, and good judgment.
[24] The father of godly children has cause for joy.
What a pleasure to have children who are wise.
[25] So give your father and mother joy!
May she who gave you birth be happy.

[26] O my son, give me your heart.
May your eyes take delight in following my ways.
[27] A prostitute is a dangerous trap;
a promiscuous woman is as dangerous as falling into a narrow well.
[28] She hides and waits like a robber,
eager to make more men unfaithful.

[29] Who has anguish? Who has sorrow?
Who is always fighting? Who is always complaining?
Who has unnecessary bruises? Who has bloodshot eyes?
[30] It is the one who spends long hours in the taverns,
trying out new drinks.
[31] Don't gaze at the wine, seeing how red it is,
how it sparkles in the cup, how smoothly it goes down.
[32] For in the end it bites like a poisonous snake;
it stings like a viper.
[33] You will see hallucinations,
and you will say crazy things.
[34] You will stagger like a sailor tossed at sea,
clinging to a swaying mast.
[35] And you will say, "They hit me, but I didn't feel it.
I didn't even know it when they beat me up.
When will I wake up
so I can look for another drink?"

24

[1] Don't envy evil people
or desire their company.
[2] For their hearts plot violence,
and their words always stir up trouble.

[3] A house is built by wisdom
and becomes strong through good sense.
[4] Through knowledge its rooms are filled
with all sorts of precious riches and valuables.

[5] The wise are mightier than the strong,
and those with knowledge grow stronger and stronger.
[6] So don't go to war without wise guidance;
victory depends on having many advisers.

[7] Wisdom is too lofty for fools.
Among leaders at the city gate, they have nothing to say.

[8] A person who plans evil
will get a reputation as a troublemaker.
[9] The schemes of a fool are sinful;
everyone detests a mocker.

[10] If you fail under pressure,
your strength is too small.

23:17 Ps 37:1; 73:3 Prov 24:1, 14, 19
23:19 Prov 23:26
23:21 Prov 21:17
23:22 Prov 1:8; 30:17
23:23 Prov 4:7; 18:15
23:24 Prov 10:1
23:26 Prov 3:1; 4:4
23:29 Isa 5:11, 22
23:35 Isa 56:12
24:1 Ps 1:1; 37:1 Prov 1:15; 23:17; 24:19
24:2 Ps 10:7 Jer 22:17
24:5 Prov 21:22
24:6 Prov 11:14; 20:18
24:7 Prov 14:6; 17:16, 24
24:8 Prov 6:14; 14:22 Rom 1:30
24:10 Job 4:5 Heb 12:3

23:17-18 Saying 14: Sometimes ***sinners*** prosper, but the wise will see that *to fear the LORD* is what ultimately rewards (see 1:7).

23:19-21 Saying 15: Discipline is necessary for living a wise and balanced life. Overindulgence in drink (***drunkards***, see also 23:29-35), food (***gluttons***, see also 23:1-3), or ***sleep*** (see also 10:5; 19:15) results in ***poverty***.

23:22-25 Saying 16: This saying is an exhortation to pursue the wisdom that a godly ***father*** and ***mother*** provide. Unlike other ancient Near East wisdom texts, Proverbs attributes wisdom to both ***father*** and ***mother*** (1:8; 6:20).

23:24 ***to have children who are wise:*** Literally *to have a wise son.*

23:26-28 Saying 17: Falling for a ***promiscuous woman*** is a ***trap***, not a source of benefit. Proverbs repeatedly emphasizes avoiding sexual relations outside of marriage (see 5:1-23; 6:20-35; 7:1-27).

23:29-35 Saying 18: This extended saying portrays the foolishness of the person who overindulges in alcohol (see 20:1).

24:1-2 Saying 19: See 1:8-19.

24:3-4 Saying 20: See 14:11.

24:5-6 Saying 21: See 21:22. • ***The wise are mightier than the strong:*** As in Greek version; Hebrew reads *A wise man is strength.*

24:7 Saying 22: Rulers should be wise (see 8:5-6).

24:8-9 Saying 23: Fools are alienated from the community because of their evil actions.

24:10 Saying 24: A wise person has emotional self-control and strength ***under pressure*** (e.g., Dan 1:8-16; 3:1-18).

24:11
Ps 82:4
24:12
*Rom 2:6
24:13
Ps 19:10
Prov 25:16
24:14
Prov 2:10
24:17
Ps 35:15
Rom 11:18-21
24:19
Job 15:31
Prov 13:9; 24:1
ᵉ*qana'* (7065)
‣Joel 2:18
24:21
Rom 13:4
1 Pet 2:17
24:24
Prov 17:15
24:28
Prov 25:18
24:29
Prov 20:22
Matt 5:39
24:30
Prov 6:6-11
24:31
Prov 6:10-11; 12:24; 23:21

11 Rescue those who are unjustly sentenced
to die;
save them as they stagger to their
death.
12 Don't excuse yourself by saying, "Look,
we didn't know."
For God understands all hearts, and
he sees you.
He who guards your soul knows you
knew.
He will repay all people as their
actions deserve.

13 My child, eat honey, for it is good,
and the honeycomb is sweet to the
taste.
14 In the same way, wisdom is sweet to your
soul.
If you find it, you will have a bright
future,
and your hopes will not be cut short.

15 Don't wait in ambush at the home of the
godly,
and don't raid the house where the
godly live.
16 The godly may trip seven times, but they
will get up again.
But one disaster is enough to
overthrow the wicked.

17 Don't rejoice when your enemies fall;
don't be happy when they stumble.
18 For the LORD will be displeased with you
and will turn his anger away from
them.

19 Don't fret because of evildoers;
don't ᵉenvy the wicked.
20 For evil people have no future;
the light of the wicked will be snuffed
out.

21 My child, fear the LORD and the king.
Don't associate with rebels,
22 for disaster will hit them suddenly.
Who knows what punishment will come
from the LORD and the king?

5. MORE SAYINGS OF THE WISE (24:23-34)

23 Here are some further sayings of the wise:

It is wrong to show favoritism when
passing judgment.
24 A judge who says to the wicked, "You are
innocent,"
will be cursed by many people and
denounced by the nations.
25 But it will go well for those who convict
the guilty;
rich blessings will be showered on
them.

26 An honest answer
is like a kiss of friendship.

27 Do your planning and prepare your
fields
before building your house.

28 Don't testify against your neighbors
without cause;
don't lie about them.
29 And don't say, "Now I can pay them back
for what they've done to me!
I'll get even with them!"

30 I walked by the field of a lazy person,
the vineyard of one with no common
sense.
31 I saw that it was overgrown with nettles.
It was covered with weeds,
and its walls were broken down.
32 Then, as I looked and thought about it,
I learned this lesson:
33 A little extra sleep, a little more slumber,
a little folding of the hands to rest—
34 then poverty will pounce on you like a
bandit;
scarcity will attack you like an armed
robber.

24:11-12 Saying 25: The wise do what they can to prevent injustice and suffering (e.g., Job 29:12-17).

24:13-14 Saying 26: Both ***honey*** and ***wisdom*** are sweet. Wisdom improves the ***soul,*** enhancing opportunities for the ***future.*** • ***My child:*** Literally *My son;* also in 24:21. See note on 1:8–9:18.

24:15-16 Saying 27: Those who are godly will not allow a setback to keep them down. • ***Seven times*** is symbolic for "many times."

24:17-18 Saying 28: This saying leads to Jesus' call to love our ***enemies*** (Matt 5:43-48).

24:19-20 Saying 29: ***Don't envy*** the apparent prosperity of ***the wicked*** (see 24:1-2), because their success is fleeting. • ***snuffed out:*** Cp. 13:9; 20:20.

24:21-22 Saying 30: ***The king*** is associated with ***the LORD,*** reflecting his power and sovereignty on the earth (see 1 Sam 12; Ps 2).

24:23-34 This addendum to the thirty sayings ***of the wise*** (22:17–24:22) includes five ***further sayings.***

24:23-25 Saying 1: Truthfulness in rendering ***judgment*** is a hallmark of wisdom (see 6:19; 12:17; 19:28; 24:28-29; 25:18).

24:26 Saying 2: A true friend does not cover up problems but honestly points out areas for improvement. A wise person welcomes the correction of a friend.

24:27 Saying 3: A wise person establishes a source of income before spending money on himself.

24:28-29 Saying 4: The truth should not be bent, not even for revenge (see 6:19; 12:17; 14:25; 19:28; 24:23-24; 25:18).

24:30-34 Saying 5: Laziness and love for ***sleep*** lead to ***poverty*** (see 10:4-5, 26; 12:11; 13:4; 15:19; 18:9; 19:15, 24; 20:4, 13).

24:33-34 // 6:10-11 This example of laziness repeats one of the proverbs presented earlier.

6. MORE PROVERBS OF SOLOMON (25:1–29:27)

25 These are more [f]proverbs of Solomon, collected by the advisers of King Hezekiah of Judah.

2 It is God's [g]privilege to conceal things
and the king's [g]privilege to discover them.

3 No one can comprehend the height of heaven, the depth of the earth,
or all that goes on in the king's mind!

4 Remove the impurities from silver,
and the sterling will be ready for the silversmith.
5 Remove the wicked from the king's court,
and his reign will be made secure by justice.

6 Don't demand an audience with the king
or push for a place among the great.
7 It's better to wait for an invitation to the head table
than to be sent away in public disgrace.
Just because you've seen something,
8 don't be in a hurry to go to court.
For what will you do in the end
if your neighbor deals you a shameful defeat?

9 When arguing with your neighbor,
don't betray another person's secret.
10 Others may accuse you of gossip,
and you will never regain your good reputation.

11 Timely advice is lovely,
like golden apples in a silver basket.

12 To one who listens, valid criticism
is like a gold earring or other gold jewelry.

13 Trustworthy messengers refresh like snow in summer.
They revive the spirit of their employer.

14 A person who promises a gift but doesn't give it
is like clouds and wind that bring no rain.

15 Patience can persuade a prince,
and soft speech can break bones.

16 Do you like honey?
Don't eat too much, or it will make you sick!

17 Don't visit your neighbors too often,
or you will wear out your welcome.

18 Telling lies about others
is as harmful as hitting them with an ax,
wounding them with a sword,
or shooting them with a sharp arrow.

19 Putting confidence in an unreliable person in times of trouble
is like chewing with a broken tooth or walking on a lame foot.

20 Singing cheerful songs to a person with a heavy heart
is like taking someone's coat in cold weather
or pouring vinegar in a wound.

21 If your enemies are hungry, give them food to eat.
If they are thirsty, give them water to drink.
22 You will heap burning coals of shame on their heads,
and the LORD will reward you.

23 As surely as a north wind brings rain,
so a gossiping tongue causes anger!

25:1 Prov 1:1
[f]*mashal* (4912)
‣ Prov 26:7

25:2 Deut 29:29
Ezra 6:1
Rom 11:33
[g]*kabod* (3519)
‣ Isa 4:2

25:4 Ezek 22:18
Mal 3:2-3

25:8 Prov 17:14

25:11 Prov 15:23

25:12 Prov 15:31; 20:12

25:13 Prov 13:17

25:15 Prov 15:1
Eccl 10:4

25:16 Prov 25:27

25:18 Ps 57:4
Prov 12:18; 24:28
Jer 9:8

25:19 Job 6:15

25:21 Exod 23:4-5
2 Kgs 6:22
2 Chr 28:15
Matt 5:44

25:22 *Rom 12:20

25:23 Prov 13:3; 26:20

25:1–29:27 During the reign of ***King Hezekiah*** (728–686 BC), wise men (***advisers***) collected these ***proverbs of Solomon*** and added them to the collection.

25:2-3 This warning reminds young men entering royal service that some things cannot be understood, including the king's sometimes mysterious reasoning (e.g., 2 Sam 11:14-25; 24:3).

25:4-5 As ***silver*** is ready for use once it is refined of impurities, ***the king's court*** can do ***justice*** when ***wicked*** people are removed. A little bit of evil can spoil much good (Eccl 10:1).

25:6-7a To gain ***an audience with the king***, a wise person will practice humility instead of pride (cp. Matt 20:20-28).

25:7b-8 Rash actions often result in shame.

25:9-10 See 11:13; 20:19.

25:11-12 ***Timely advice*** and ***valid criticism*** are precious, beautiful, and rare (see also 15:23; 26:7, 9), and should be welcome (see 10:17; 13:1, 10; 15:24, 31-32; 17:10).

25:13 ***Snow*** would be a welcome relief in Israel's hot, dry summers (cp. 26:1); ***trustworthy messengers*** refresh ***their employer*** by enabling him or her to plan for the future.

25:14 In Israel, ***rain*** is rare. When rain does not follow the appearance of storm ***clouds***, it is like the disappointment caused by someone who gives empty ***promises***. Cp. Jude's description of false teachers (Jude 1:12).

25:16-17 ***Honey*** in moderation is tasty and healthy (24:13-14); ***too much*** will cause vomiting. This principle can be applied to other areas of life; for example, it is good to ***visit your neighbors***, but not ***too often***.

25:18 Lying can have deadly consequences (see 6:16-19; 14:5, 25).

25:20 ***pouring vinegar in a wound:*** As in Greek version; Hebrew reads ***pouring vinegar on soda***.

25:21-22 Contrary to expectation, compassion toward an enemy is more effective than anger (see Rom 12:20).

25:24 Prov 21:9
25:25 Prov 15:30
25:26 Ezek 32:2; 34:18
25:27 Prov 25:16; 27:2
25:28 2 Chr 32:5 Prov 16:32
26:1 1 Sam 12:17
26:2 Num 23:8 2 Sam 16:12
26:3 Ps 32:9 Prov 10:13
26:4 Prov 23:9; 29:9 [h]*'iwweleth* (0200) ›Prov 26:5
26:5 [i]*'iwweleth* (0200) ›Ps 69:5
26:7 [j]*mashal* (4912) ›Eccl 12:9
26:11 Exod 8:15 *2 Pet 2:22
26:12 Prov 3:7; 29:20

24 It's better to live alone in the corner of
an attic
than with a quarrelsome wife in a
lovely home.

25 Good news from far away
is like cold water to the thirsty.

26 If the godly give in to the wicked,
it's like polluting a fountain or
muddying a spring.

27 It's not good to eat too much honey,
and it's not good to seek honors for
yourself.

28 A person without self-control
is like a city with broken-down walls.

26 1 Honor is no more associated with
fools
than snow with summer or rain with
harvest.

2 Like a fluttering sparrow or a darting
swallow,
an undeserved curse will not land on
its intended victim.

3 Guide a horse with a whip, a donkey with
a bridle,
and a fool with a rod to his back!

4 Don't answer the [h]foolish arguments of
fools,
or you will become as foolish as they
are.

5 Be sure to answer the [i]foolish arguments
of fools,
or they will become wise in their own
estimation.

6 Trusting a fool to convey a message
is like cutting off one's feet or
drinking poison!

7 A [j]proverb in the mouth of a fool
is as useless as a paralyzed leg.

8 Honoring a fool
is as foolish as tying a stone to a
slingshot.

9 A proverb in the mouth of a fool
is like a thorny branch brandished by
a drunk.

10 An employer who hires a fool or a
bystander
is like an archer who shoots at random.

11 As a dog returns to its vomit,
so a fool repeats his foolishness.

12 There is more hope for fools
than for people who think they are wise.

Laziness versus Hard Work (24:30-34)

Prov 6:6-11; 10:4-6, 26; 12:11, 24, 27; 13:4, 11; 14:4, 23; 15:19; 18:9; 19:15; 21:5, 25; 26:13-16; 28:19; 31:10-31
Gen 2:15
Exod 23:12
Eccl 2:18-26; 4:5-6; 5:12; 9:10; 11:4-6
Acts 20:35
Rom 12:11
Eph 4:28
1 Thes 4:11-12
2 Thes 3:10-15

Proverbs equates lazy people with the foolish; their lack of productivity leads to poverty and death (6:6-10; 10:26; 15:19; 18:9; 19:15, 24; 20:4; 21:25; 22:13; 24:30-34; 26:13-16). By contrast, diligent people are seen as wise; their activities lead to wealth and life (10:4-6; 12:11; 13:4; 14:4; 20:13; 31:10-27). Proverbs isn't afraid to poke fun at lazy people. They are sarcastically compared to a door that swings back and forth (26:14), and their empty excuses are subjected to parody (e.g., 22:13).

The theme of laziness arises in the contrast between the two women, Wisdom and Folly (9:1-18). The virtuous woman of ch 31 reflects the industriousness of Wisdom (31:16-18). While it is true that ultimate meaning and fulfillment do not come from hard work (Eccl 2:17-26), the lazy are still condemned (Eccl 4:5-6). God created Adam and Eve and put them in the Garden to tend it, not just to sit back and enjoy it (Gen 2:15). Proverbs and the whole of Scripture support the truth that work is not a result of the Fall but rather is a dignified and important part of creation.

25:24 // 21:9 ***It's better to live alone:*** Cp. 21:9, 19.

25:26 A ***spring*** or ***fountain*** that yields fresh water gives life. When ***godly*** people allow ***the wicked*** to dominate them, what was life-giving becomes deadly.

25:27-28 The wise have self-control and cannot easily be dominated.

26:1 It is not fitting to give ***honor*** to ***fools.***

26:2 Curses and blessings can have real effect (see Gen 27:1-41; 48:8-9, 15-20; Num 6:23-27), but an ***undeserved curse*** has no effect.

26:3 A ***fool*** is like a dumb animal that can only be guided by brute force (see 10:13; 14:3).

26:4-5 Proverbs are often context sensitive. Whether or not to ***answer the foolish arguments of fools*** depends on what kind of fool and what kind of situation.

26:7 A ***fool*** might know a ***proverb*** but not be able to use it correctly. Cp. 26:9.

26:9 A ***proverb*** misapplied by ***a fool*** might actually cause harm. Cp. 26:7.

26:10 ***A fool or a bystander*** might easily be lazy (see 10:4-6) or incompetent (see 26:6-7). ***An employer*** should beware!

26:11 Even when ***foolishness*** brings terrible consequences, ***a fool*** persists in it (17:10; see also 2 Pet 2:22).

26:12 ***Fools*** have ***hope*** because they might recognize their folly and seek advice. However, those ***who think they are wise*** will remain ignorant.

13 The lazy person claims, "There's a lion
on the road!
Yes, I'm sure there's a lion out there!"

14 As a door swings back and forth on its
hinges,
so the lazy person turns over in bed.

15 Lazy people take food in their hand
but don't even lift it to their mouth.

16 Lazy people consider themselves smarter
than seven wise counselors.

17 Interfering in someone else's argument
is as foolish as yanking a dog's ears.

18 Just as damaging
as a madman shooting a deadly
weapon
19 is someone who lies to a friend
and then says, "I was only joking."

20 Fire goes out without wood,
and quarrels disappear when gossip
stops.

21 A quarrelsome person starts fights
as easily as hot embers light charcoal
or fire lights wood.

22 Rumors are dainty morsels
that sink deep into one's heart.

23 Smooth words may hide a wicked heart,
just as a pretty glaze covers a clay pot.

24 People may cover their hatred with
pleasant words,
but they're deceiving you.
25 They pretend to be kind, but don't
believe them.
Their hearts are full of many evils.
26 While their hatred may be concealed by
trickery,
their wrongdoing will be exposed in
public.

27 If you set a trap for others,
you will get caught in it yourself.
If you roll a boulder down on others,
it will crush you instead.

28 A lying tongue hates its victims,
and flattering words cause ruin.

27 1 Don't brag about tomorrow,
since you don't know what the
day will bring.

2 Let someone else [k]praise you, not your
own mouth—
a stranger, not your own lips.

3 A stone is heavy and sand is weighty,
but the resentment caused by a fool is
even heavier.

4 Anger is cruel, and [a]wrath is like a flood,
but jealousy is even more dangerous.

5 An open rebuke
is better than hidden love!

6 Wounds from a sincere friend
are better than many kisses from an
enemy.

7 A person who is full refuses honey,
but even bitter food tastes sweet to
the hungry.

8 A person who strays from home
is like a bird that strays from its nest.

9 The heartfelt counsel of a friend
is as sweet as perfume and incense.

10 Never abandon a friend—
either yours or your father's.

26:13 Prov 22:13
26:14 Prov 6:9
26:15 //Prov 19:24
26:17 Prov 3:30; 20:3
26:18-19 Prov 24:12, 28
26:20 Prov 16:28; 22:10; 24:28
26:21 Prov 15:18; 29:22
26:22 //Prov 18:8
26:23 Luke 11:39
26:24 Ps 41:6; Prov 12:20
26:27 Ps 7:15
26:28 Prov 28:23
27:1 Luke 12:19-20; Jas 4:13-16
27:2 Prov 25:27; 2 Cor 10:12, 18; [k]*halal* (1984) ‣Prov 28:4
27:4 Prov 6:34; [a]*'ap* (0639) ‣Prov 29:8
27:5 Prov 25:12
27:6 Ps 141:5; Matt 26:49
27:10 1 Kgs 12:6; 2 Chr 10:6-8; Prov 17:17; 18:24

26:13-16 *The lazy person:* See 6:6-11; 10:4-5; 15:19; 22:13.

26:15 // 19:24 This is a humorous comment on the foolishness of being *lazy*.

26:17 The wise avoid getting involved in other people's arguments (cp. 26:21).

26:18-19 Lies are extremely dangerous because they lead people to act on false information. Liars cannot cover up later by claiming that they were *only joking* (see 6:16-19; 14:5, 25; 25:18).

26:20-21 A *gossip* and a *quarrelsome person* are both like fuel to the *fire* of trouble and discord.

26:22 // 18:8 *Rumors* may be delicious to hear and repeat, but they are deadly.

26:23-26 People sometimes hide evil attitudes and wicked intentions through flattery. In the end, the true *hatred* of smooth talkers will *be exposed*.

• *Smooth:* As in Greek version; Hebrew reads *Burning*.

26:25 *many evils:* Literally *seven evils* (see notes on 9:1; 24:15-16).

26:27 People usually receive the bad consequences they intend for others (see 1:17-19).

27:1 We should plan (24:27), but our plans succeed only when God so wills (16:1, 3, 33; Jas 4:13-16). Only fools think that they control the future.

27:2 The Hebrew word translated *praise* comes from the same root as "brag" in 27:1. Bragging (self-praise) is foolish.

27:3 Fools cause *heavy . . . resentment* by their foolish words and actions.

27:4 *Anger* is bad but can be countered with a gentle answer (15:1). *Jealousy* is harder to resolve (6:34-35).

27:5 A *rebuke* improves life by correcting harmful behavior (13:1; 14:6). *Hidden*, unexpressed *love* has no value.

27:6 *Wounds from a . . . friend* are from a loving rebuke (27:5). They are *better than* flattery (*many kisses*) from an enemy who intends to harm rather than help.

27:7 Even the best teaching (*honey*) will be refused if offered at the wrong time. The key to real learning is the receptivity of the student.

27:8 *A person who* forsakes his family and *strays from home* will more likely find trouble than whatever he was seeking (e.g., Luke 15:11-16).

27:9 Nothing is more encouraging than *heartfelt counsel* from an intimate *friend* (see also 27:6).

27:10 In a crisis, one might need

27:11
Prov 10:1; 23:15
27:12
//Prov 22:3
27:13
//Prov 20:16
27:15
Prov 19:13
27:18
Luke 12:42-44
1 Cor 9:7
2 Tim 2:6
27:20
Prov 30:15-16
Eccl 1:8-11
Hab 2:5
27:21
Prov 17:3
Zech 13:9
Luke 6:26
27:22
Prov 23:35; 26:11
Jer 5:3
27:23
Ezek 34:12
John 10:3
28:1
Lev 26:17, 36
28:2
1 Kgs 16:8-28
2 Kgs 15:8-15
28:3
Matt 18:28
28:4
Rom 1:32
Eph 5:11
[b]*halal* (1984)
‣Prov 31:30
28:5
Ps 92:6-7
Prov 2:9

When disaster strikes, you won't have to
ask your brother for assistance.
It's better to go to a neighbor than to a
brother who lives far away.

11 Be wise, my child, and make my heart
glad.
Then I will be able to answer my
critics.

12 A prudent person foresees danger and
takes precautions.
The simpleton goes blindly on and
suffers the consequences.

13 Get security from someone who
guarantees a stranger's debt.
Get a deposit if he does it for
foreigners.

14 A loud and cheerful greeting early in the
morning
will be taken as a curse!

15 A quarrelsome wife is as annoying
as constant dripping on a rainy day.
16 Stopping her complaints is like trying to
stop the wind
or trying to hold something with
greased hands.

17 As iron sharpens iron,
so a friend sharpens a friend.

18 As workers who tend a fig tree are
allowed to eat the fruit,
so workers who protect their
employer's interests will be
rewarded.

19 As a face is reflected in water,
so the heart reflects the real person.

20 Just as Death and Destruction are never
satisfied,
so human desire is never satisfied.

21 Fire tests the purity of silver and gold,
but a person is tested by being praised.

22 You cannot separate fools from their
foolishness,
even though you grind them like grain
with mortar and pestle.

23 Know the state of your flocks,
and put your heart into caring for your
herds,
24 for riches don't last forever,
and the crown might not be passed to
the next generation.
25 After the hay is harvested and the new
crop appears
and the mountain grasses are
gathered in,
26 your sheep will provide wool for clothing,
and your goats will provide the price
of a field.
27 And you will have enough goats' milk for
yourself,
your family, and your servant girls.

28 1 The wicked run away when no
one is chasing them,
but the godly are as bold as lions.

2 When there is moral rot within a nation,
its government topples easily.
But wise and knowledgeable leaders
bring stability.

3 A poor person who oppresses the poor
is like a pounding rain that destroys
the crops.

4 To reject the law is to [b]praise the wicked;
to obey the law is to fight them.

5 Evil people don't understand justice,
but those who follow the LORD
understand completely.

immediate assistance, so it is important to have friends close by and neighbors who can help.

27:11 *my child:* Literally *my son.* Fairly or not, parents are evaluated by their children's public behavior.

27:12 // 22:3 The theme of taking ***precautions*** is found in several proverbs (14:8, 15; 21:29).

27:13 // 20:16 *for foreigners:* As in Greek and Latin versions (see also 20:16); Hebrew reads *for a promiscuous woman.* See note on 20:16, where this proverb is repeated verbatim. Its message is also repeated in 6:1-5; 11:15; 17:18; 22:26.

27:14 It is important to speak appropriately for the circumstances (cp. 15:23).

27:15 *A quarrelsome wife:* Cp. 19:13; 21:9, 19; 25:24.

27:17 *iron sharpens iron:* Wisdom comes from interaction, often critical, with a good *friend* (see 27:6, 9).

27:18 An *employer* values loyal *workers* who ***protect their employer's interests.*** Wise employers give their workers incentives to be loyal, such as allowing them to *eat the fruit* (see Deut 25:4; 1 Cor 9:7-10; 1 Tim 5:17-18).

27:20 *Death and Destruction:* Hebrew *Sheol and Abaddon.* See note on 15:11. • ***Human desire is never satisfied*** by money, power, or pleasure.

27:21 *A person* who avoids conceit in response to praise demonstrates *purity* of character (cp. 17:3). • ***by being praised:*** Or *by flattery.*

27:22 *Foolishness* is deeply engrained in the character of a fool.

27:23-27 Agricultural property can provide food and clothing from generation to generation; these resources require continuous labor and attention or, like *riches,* they disappear.

28:1 *The wicked* experience God's curse for breaking his covenant (see Lev 26:14-17, 36-37).

28:2 *Wise . . . leaders* rule justly and effectively (8:15-16).

28:4 Without *law,* chaos results and the wicked flourish.

28:5 *Evil people* seek gain by breaking the law. ***Justice*** ensures that they are punished and the righteous are rewarded.

6 Better to be poor and honest
than to be dishonest and rich.

7 Young people who obey the law are
wise;
those with wild friends bring shame
to their parents.

8 Income from charging high interest
rates
will end up in the pocket of someone
who is kind to the poor.

9 God detests the prayers
of a person who ignores the law.

10 Those who lead good people along an
evil path
will fall into their own trap,
but the [c]honest will inherit good
things.

11 Rich people may think they are wise,
but a poor person with discernment
can see right through them.

12 When the godly succeed, everyone is
glad.
When the wicked take charge, people
go into hiding.

13 People who conceal their [d]sins will not
prosper,
but if they confess and turn from
them, they will receive mercy.

14 [e]Blessed are those who fear to do wrong,
but the stubborn are headed for
serious trouble.

15 A wicked ruler is as dangerous to the
poor
as a roaring lion or an attacking bear.

16 A ruler with no understanding will
oppress his people,
but one who hates corruption will
have a long life.

17 A murderer's tormented conscience will
drive him into the grave.
Don't protect him!

18 The blameless will be rescued from
harm,
but the crooked will be suddenly
destroyed.

19 A hard worker has plenty of food,
but a person who chases fantasies
ends up in poverty.

20 The trustworthy person will get a rich
reward,
but a person who wants quick riches
will get into trouble.

21 Showing partiality is never good,
yet some will do wrong for a mere
piece of bread.

22 Greedy people try to get rich quick
but don't realize they're headed for
poverty.

23 In the end, people appreciate honest
criticism
far more than flattery.

24 Anyone who steals from his father and
mother
and says, "What's wrong with that?"
is no better than a murderer.

25 Greed causes fighting;
trusting the LORD leads to prosperity.

26 Those who trust their own insight are
foolish,
but anyone who walks in wisdom is
safe.

28:6 Prov 19:1
28:7 Prov 23:20
28:8 Exod 22:25; Deut 23:19-20
28:9 Ps 66:18; 109:7; Prov 15:8
28:10 Prov 26:27; Heb 6:12; [c]*tamim* (8549) ‣Gen 6:9
28:11 Prov 26:12
28:12 Eccl 10:5-6
28:13 Ps 32:1-11; 1 Jn 1:6-9; [d]*pesha'* (6588) ‣Isa 53:5
28:14 Rom 2:5; [e]*'ashrey* (0835) ‣Isa 30:18
28:15 Prov 19:12; Matt 2:16; 1 Pet 5:8
28:16 Eccl 10:16; Isa 3:12
28:17 Gen 9:6; Exod 21:14
28:19 Prov 12:11
28:20 Matt 25:21
28:21 Ezek 13:19
28:24 Prov 19:26; 20:20
28:26 Prov 3:5

28:6 Virtue is more valuable than material wealth. This proverb is repeated with a slightly different conclusion in 19:1.

28:7 ***their parents:*** Literally *their father.* This proverb applies to both fathers and mothers.

28:8 The law prohibited charging needy Israelites interest on loans (Exod 22:25; Lev 25:36; Deut 23:19). The rich were instructed to lend generously to the poor (3:27-28; 11:24; 28:27; 29:7, 14).

28:9 ***A person who ignores the law*** shows no fear of the Lord (1:7), the lawgiver. That person's prayers are hypocritical—why should God listen to them?

28:12 ***When the wicked take charge:*** See also 28:28.

28:13 The wise admit their mistakes and sins and pursue correction (see Ps 32:1-5).

28:14 ***those who fear to do wrong:*** Or *those who fear the LORD;* literally *those who fear.*

28:15 A ***wicked ruler*** will not help the ***poor*** because his rule is not just. Like a ***roaring lion or an attacking bear,*** he destroys their lives.

28:17 ***tormented conscience:*** See 1 Sam 25:31; Rom 2:15; 13:5; cp. Heb 10:22. • ***Don't protect him!*** Murder is such a serious offense that a fine could not replace the death penalty (see Num 35:32).

28:19 This proverb is repeated but with a different conclusion in 12:11.

28:20 ***quick riches:*** Wealth must be earned ethically, or it will cause harm and will not last (see 13:11, cp. 10:2; 11:18; 13:22; 21:6).

28:21 Rendering a wrong verdict based on a bribe is evil (17:23; 22:16).

28:23 The wise desire ***honest criticism*** of their faults so they can improve (10:17; 13:1, 10; 15:24, 31-32).

28:24 Callous children who exploit their parents are wicked (see Exod 20:12).

28:25 Those who are greedy fight to control circumstances so as to gain riches. ***Trusting the LORD*** allows the wise to face life calmly and, ironically, to experience ***prosperity.***

28:26 The one ***who walks in wisdom*** listens to the advice of others; ***those who trust their own insight*** show themselves ***foolish.***

27 Whoever gives to the poor will lack
nothing,
but those who close their eyes to
poverty will be cursed.

28 When the wicked take charge, people go
into hiding.
When the wicked meet disaster, the
godly flourish.

29

1 Whoever stubbornly refuses to
accept criticism
will suddenly be destroyed beyond
recovery.

2 When the godly are in authority, the
people rejoice.
But when the wicked are in power,
they groan.

3 The man who loves [f]wisdom brings joy
to his father,
but if he hangs around with
prostitutes, his wealth is wasted.

4 A just king gives stability to his nation,
but one who demands bribes
destroys it.

5 To flatter friends
is to lay a trap for their feet.

6 Evil people are trapped by sin,
but the righteous escape, shouting
for joy.

7 The godly care about the rights of the
poor;
the wicked don't care at all.

8 Mockers can get a whole town agitated,
but the wise will calm [g]anger.

9 If a wise person takes a fool to court,
there will be ranting and ridicule but
no satisfaction.

10 The bloodthirsty hate blameless
people,
but the upright seek to help them.

11 Fools vent their anger,
but the wise quietly hold it back.

12 If a ruler pays attention to liars,
all his advisers will be wicked.

13 The poor and the oppressor have this in
common—
the LORD gives sight to the eyes of
both.

14 If a king judges the poor fairly,
his [h]throne will last forever.

15 To discipline a child produces [i]wisdom,
but a mother is disgraced by an
undisciplined child.

16 When the wicked are in authority, sin
flourishes,
but the godly will live to see their
downfall.

17 Discipline your children, and they will
give you peace of mind
and will make your heart glad.

18 When people do not accept [j]divine
guidance, they run wild.
But whoever obeys the law is joyful.

19 Words alone will not discipline a
servant;
the words may be understood, but
they are not heeded.

20 There is more hope for a fool
than for someone who speaks without
thinking.

21 A servant pampered from childhood
will become a rebel.

22 An [k]angry person starts fights;
a hot-tempered person commits all
kinds of sin.

23 Pride ends in humiliation,
while humility brings honor.

24 If you assist a thief, you only hurt
yourself.

28:27
Prov 11:24; 19:17

29:1
1 Sam 2:25
2 Chr 36:16
Prov 1:24-31; 13:18; 15:31-32

29:2
Esth 8:15-16
Prov 11:10; 28:12, 28

29:3
Prov 6:26; 10:1; 28:7
Luke 15:13
[f]*khokmah* (2451)
▸ Prov 29:15

29:4
Prov 8:15; 15:27; 29:14

29:5
Ps 5:9

29:7
Ps 41:1
Prov 31:8-9

29:8
Prov 11:11; 16:14
[g]*'ap* (0639)
▸ Prov 29:22

29:10
1 Jn 3:12

29:12
1 Kgs 12:14

29:13
Ps 13:3

29:14
Ps 72:4
Prov 16:12
[h]*kisse'* (3678)
▸ Isa 6:1

29:15
[i]*khokmah* (2451)
▸ Eccl 1:16

29:16
Ps 37:34-38

29:18
Exod 32:25
Ps 1:1-2; 119:2-3
[j]*khazon* (2377)
▸ Isa 29:7

29:20
Prov 26:12
Jas 1:19

29:22
[k]*'ap* (0639)
▸ Isa 12:1

29:23
Prov 15:33; 22:4
Dan 4:30-31
Matt 23:12
Jas 4:6

29:24
Lev 5:1

28:28 ***When the wicked take charge:*** See also 28:12.

29:3 A man's ***wisdom*** affects his parents (10:1; 15:20; 17:21). • ***Prostitutes*** cost money and a man's ***wealth is*** rapidly ***wasted*** on them.

29:4 A ***just king*** looks out for the rights of others; a ruler who accepts ***bribes*** uses his office for personal gain (see also 17:23; 22:16; 28:21).

29:5 Flattery is usually ***a trap*** to taking advantage of someone (7:21-22; 26:23).

29:10 ***The bloodthirsty hate blameless people, but the upright seek to help them:*** Or *The bloodthirsty hate blameless people, and they seek to kill the upright;* literally *The bloodthirsty hate blameless people; as for the upright, they seek their life.*

29:11 ***Wise*** people learn to control their emotions; they remain calm even under stress.

29:13 ***The oppressor*** should be motivated to treat ***the poor*** more humanely because God created them ***both*** (see also 3:27; 11:24; 28:27; 29:7).

29:15 ***Wisdom*** is not instinctive—it must be taught.

29:18 The wise ***accept divine guidance*** from God's law, the guide to his will.

29:19 In some instances, physical ***discipline*** might need to accompany instructions (see 13:24; 22:15; 23:13-14).

29:23 See 6:17-18; 11:2; 13:10; 15:33; 16:18-19; 18:12; 19:20; 22:4.

29:24 ***You are sworn to tell the truth:*** See Lev 5:1.

You are sworn to tell the truth, but you
dare not testify.

25 Fearing people is a dangerous trap,
but trusting the LORD means
safety.

26 Many seek the ruler's favor,
but justice comes from the LORD.

27 The righteous despise the unjust;
the wicked despise the godly.

7. THE SAYINGS OF AGUR (30:1-33)

30 The sayings of Agur son of Jakeh
contain this message.

I am weary, O God;
I am weary and worn out, O God.
2 I am too stupid to be human,
and I lack common sense.
3 I have not mastered human wisdom,
nor do I know the Holy One.

4 Who but God goes up to heaven and
comes back down?
Who holds the wind in his fists?
Who wraps up the oceans in his cloak?
Who has created the whole wide
world?
What is his name—and his son's name?
Tell me if you know!

5 Every word of God proves true.
He is a [a]shield to all who come to him
for protection.
6 Do not add to his words,
or he may rebuke you and expose you
as a liar.

7 O God, I beg two favors from you;
let me have them before I die.
8 First, help me never to tell a lie.
Second, give me neither poverty nor
riches!
Give me just enough to satisfy my
needs.
9 For if I grow rich, I may deny you and say,
"Who is the LORD?"
And if I am too poor, I may steal and
thus insult God's holy name.

10 Never slander a [b]worker to the employer,
or the person will curse you, and you
will pay for it.

11 Some people curse their father
and do not thank their mother.
12 They are pure in their own eyes,
but they are filthy and unwashed.
13 They look proudly around,
casting disdainful glances.
14 They have teeth like swords
and fangs like knives.
They devour the poor from the earth
and the needy from among humanity.

15 The leech has two suckers
that cry out, "More, more!"

There are three things that are never
satisfied—
no, four that never say, "Enough!":
16 the grave,
the barren womb,
the thirsty desert,
the blazing fire.

17 The eye that mocks a father
and despises a mother's instructions
will be plucked out by ravens of the
valley
and eaten by vultures.

18 There are three things that amaze me—
no, four things that I don't understand:

29:25 Gen 12:11-13; Luke 12:4
29:26 Isa 49:4
29:27 Ps 69:4; 139:21-22; Matt 10:22; 24:9
30:2 Job 42:3-6; Ps 49:10
30:4 Exod 15:10; Job 26:8; 38:8-9; Ps 24:2; 68:18; 135:7; Isa 45:18; Rev 19:12
30:5 Ps 3:3; 12:6; 18:30; 84:11; Prov 2:7-8
[a]*magen* (4043) ‣Isa 21:5
30:6 Deut 4:2; 12:32; Rev 22:18
30:8 Matt 6:11
30:9 Deut 8:12; 31:20; Neh 9:25; Hos 13:6
30:10 Eccl 7:21
[b]*'ebed* (5650) ‣Isa 42:1
30:11 Exod 21:17; Prov 20:20
30:14 Job 29:17; Ps 14:4
30:15 Prov 27:20
30:17 Gen 9:22

29:25 ***Fearing people is a dangerous trap:*** See 1:7; Luke 12:4-5.

30:1a This superscription probably refers to the whole of ch 30. • ***son of Jakeh contain this message:*** Or *son of Jakeh from Massa;* or *son of Jakeh, an oracle.* Apart from this reference, Agur and Jakeh are unknown. If Massa was the home of ***Agur***, then he was a non-Israelite (the tribe of Massa is known from Assyrian texts). See note on 31:1-9.

30:1b-3 Agur expresses his ignorance (cp. Ps 73:22, where the psalmist calls himself a *senseless animal*). The first step toward wisdom is acknowledging what we do not know. • ***I am weary, O God; I am weary and worn out, O God:*** The Hebrew can also be translated *The man declares this to Ithiel, to Ithiel and to Ucal.* A man named Ithiel is mentioned in Neh 11:7; Ucal is unknown.

30:4-6 In contrast to Agur's ignorance and powerlessness stands the strength and wisdom of ***God*** (cp. Ps 18:30). This is good news to Agur, who understands that God is ***a shield to all who come to him for protection.***

30:7-9 Agur requests ***two favors*** from God: that God will help him not to ***lie*** (cp. 6:16-19; 14:5, 25; 25:18; 26:18-19) and that he not be given too much or too little. It is not sinful to be rich (3:9-10, 15-16; 10:15, 22) or poor (3:27; 11:24; 28:27; 29:7, 14), but Agur wisely wanted to avoid the pitfalls of both.

30:11-14 These verses summarize the character traits that wise people despise. Fools dishonor their parents (10:1; 20:20; Exod 20:12; Deut 5:16), deceive themselves (8:7), think they are ***pure*** when they are ***filthy*** (20:9), are proud (6:17-18; 11:2; 13:10; 15:33; 16:18; 18:12; 19:20; 29:23), wound others with their words (***teeth like swords,*** see 25:18), and harm the poor (3:27; 11:24; 28:27; 29:7, 14).

30:15-16 ***two suckers that cry out, "More, more!"*** Literally *two daughters who cry out, "Give, give!"* • The number parallelism (***three . . . no, four***) is a device for presenting a list of poetic examples. This list shows powers that are insatiable and often dangerous. See also 30:18-19, 21-23, 29-31.

30:16 ***the grave*** (Hebrew *Sheol*): See 27:20 and note on 1:12. • ***barren womb:*** Women who are unable to have children might be restless and dissatisfied. • The ***thirsty desert*** and ***fire*** consume whatever is offered them.

30:17 People who are callous toward their parents will meet a violent end (see 10:1; 19:26; 28:24; 29:3; 30:11).

30:20 Prov 5:6
30:25 Prov 6:6
30:27 ᶜ*arbeh* (0697) ‣Joel 1:4
30:32 Job 21:5; 40:4 Mic 7:16
30:33 Prov 10:12; 29:22
31:2 1 Sam 1:11 Isa 49:15
31:3 Deut 17:17 1 Kgs 11:1-2 Prov 5:8-9
31:4 Prov 20:1 Eccl 10:16-17 Isa 5:22-23 Hos 4:11
31:5 Deut 16:19 Prov 17:15
31:8 Job 29:12-17 Ps 82:3-5 Isa 58:9-10

19 how an eagle glides through the sky,
how a snake slithers on a rock,
how a ship navigates the ocean,
how a man loves a woman.

20 An adulterous woman consumes a man,
then wipes her mouth and says,
"What's wrong with that?"

21 There are three things that make the earth tremble—
no, four it cannot endure:
22 a slave who becomes a king,
an overbearing fool who prospers,
23 a bitter woman who finally gets a husband,
a servant girl who supplants her mistress.

24 There are four things on earth that are small but unusually wise:
25 Ants—they aren't strong,
but they store up food all summer.
26 Hyraxes—they aren't powerful,
but they make their homes among the rocks.
27 ᶜLocusts—they have no king,
but they march in formation.
28 Lizards—they are easy to catch,
but they are found even in kings' palaces.

29 There are three things that walk with stately stride—
no, four that strut about:
30 the lion, king of animals, who won't turn aside for anything,
31 the strutting rooster,
the male goat,
a king as he leads his army.

32 If you have been a fool by being proud or plotting evil,
cover your mouth in shame.

33 As the beating of cream yields butter
and striking the nose causes bleeding,
so stirring up anger causes quarrels.

8. THE SAYINGS OF KING LEMUEL (31:1-9)

31 The sayings of King Lemuel contain this message, which his mother taught him.

2 O my son, O son of my womb,
O son of my vows,
3 do not waste your strength on women,
on those who ruin kings.

4 It is not for kings, O Lemuel, to guzzle wine.
Rulers should not crave alcohol.
5 For if they drink, they may forget the law
and not give justice to the oppressed.
6 Alcohol is for the dying,
and wine for those in bitter distress.
7 Let them drink to forget their poverty
and remember their troubles no more.

8 Speak up for those who cannot speak for themselves;
ensure justice for those being crushed.

Pride Versus Humility (29:23)

Prov 10:17; 11:2; 12:15; 15:5; 22:4
1 Kgs 3:5-14
2 Chr 26:14-20
Matt 5:5; 11:29; 18:4; 21:5
Luke 18:9-14
Rom 12:16
Eph 4:2
Phil 2:3
Jas 1:21; 3:13; 4:10
1 Pet 5:5-6

Wise people are humble, not proud. Humility is demonstrated when a person recognizes a mistake, listens to another's correction (10:17; 12:1), and learns life's lessons. It is hard for the proud to accept this discipline. Pride puts self first and does not allow the cracks and flaws to show in public. However, truly humble people acknowledge that others have something to teach them about life. To be truly wise, we must begin with fear of the Lord (1:7), which recognizes that we have everything to learn from God and nothing to teach him.

Learning from our own mistakes and observing the mistakes of others provides an avenue to wisdom and puts us on the road to life. Only a humility that acknowledges weaknesses and failings will allow this kind of instruction to work its benefits in our lives (see 11:2; 15:33; 16:18).

30:18-19 See note on 30:15-16. The writer stands amazed at how one thing moves on another.

30:20 The writer expresses horror at sex outside of marriage.

30:21-23 See note on 30:15-16. This proverb lists ***four*** injustices that ***make the earth tremble*** (cp. Rom 8:20-22). • ***who prospers*** (literally *who is full of bread*): In the ancient Near East as in much of the non-industrialized world today, having adequate food (bread) was a sign of prosperity.

30:24-28 Another example of number parallelism (see note on 30:15-16). Here, small, insignificant animals are surprisingly powerful and resourceful.

30:26 ***Hyraxes:*** Or *Coneys*, or *Rock badgers.*

30:29-31 See note on 30:15-16.

31:1-9 ***of King Lemuel contain this message:*** Or *of Lemuel, king of Massa;* or *of King Lemuel, an oracle.* Lemuel, like Agur, might have been from Massa (see note on 30:1a). Lemuel's mother's teaching encourages him to control his lusts (particularly for women and alcohol) so that he might reign justly. • Apart from this passage, Lemuel is unknown.

31:2-3 The admonition not to ***waste*** energy on lust for ***women*** echoes earlier warnings (5:1-23; 6:20-35; 7:1-27).

31:4-7 Too much ***wine*** numbs the senses. A king needs his wits about him and should not overindulge in ***alcohol.***

9 Yes, speak up for the poor and helpless,
and see that they [d]get justice.

9. A VIRTUOUS AND CAPABLE WIFE (31:10-31)

10 Who can find a virtuous and capable wife?
She is more precious than rubies.
11 Her husband can trust her,
and she will greatly enrich his life.
12 She brings him good, not harm,
all the days of her life.

13 She finds wool and flax
and busily spins it.
14 She is like a merchant's ship,
bringing her food from afar.
15 She gets up before dawn to prepare breakfast for her household
and plan the day's work for her servant girls.

16 She goes to inspect a field and buys it;
with her earnings she plants a vineyard.
17 She is energetic and strong,
a hard worker.
18 She makes sure her dealings are profitable;
her lamp burns late into the night.

19 Her hands are busy spinning thread,
her fingers twisting fiber.
20 She extends a helping hand to the poor
and opens her arms to the needy.
21 She has no fear of winter for her household,
for everyone has warm clothes.
22 She makes her own bedspreads.
She dresses in fine linen and purple gowns.
23 Her husband is well known at the city gates,
where he sits with the other civic [e]leaders.
24 She makes belted linen garments
and sashes to sell to the merchants.

25 She is clothed with strength and dignity,
and she laughs without fear of the future.
26 When she speaks, her words are wise,
and she gives instructions with kindness.
27 She carefully watches everything in her household
and suffers nothing from laziness.

28 Her children stand and bless her.
Her husband praises her:
29 "There are many virtuous and capable women in the world,
but you surpass them all!"

30 Charm is deceptive, and beauty does not last;
but a woman who fears the LORD will be greatly [f]praised.
31 Reward her for all she has done.
Let her deeds publicly declare her praise.

31:9 Lev 19:15; Isa 1:17; [d]*shapat* (8199) ▸Eccl 3:17
31:10 Ruth 3:11; Prov 12:4; 19:14
31:13 1 Tim 2:9-10
31:15 Rom 12:11
31:20 Deut 15:11; Eph 4:28
31:23 [e]*zaqen* (2205) ▸Exod 12:21
31:26 Prov 10:31
31:27 Prov 19:15
31:30 Prov 22:4; [f]*halal* (1984) ▸Jer 20:13
31:31 Prov 11:16

31:8-9 Rather than opening his mouth to drink wine (31:4-7), the king should ***speak up*** on behalf of the defenseless.

31:10-31 Proverbs ends with a powerful poem celebrating the virtuous wife. This section comprises a Hebrew acrostic poem; each verse begins with a successive letter of the Hebrew alphabet. This arrangement gives an impression of completeness and provides the student with an aid for learning.

31:10-12 No one can ***find a virtuous and capable wife*** without God's help (18:22). Such a woman, like wisdom, is ***more precious than rubies*** (cp. 3:15).

31:13-15 This wife works to provide food and clothing for her family.

31:16-18 An excellent wife is engaged in commercial enterprises outside her home.

31:19-21 A virtuous wife is generous to the poor, another characteristic of wise people (11:24-26; 21:13; 22:9, 16, 22-23; 28:27).

31:21 ***warm:*** As in Greek and Latin versions; Hebrew reads *scarlet.*

31:22-24 A capable wife's industriousness enables her husband to distinguish himself among community leaders. In ancient Israel, ***civic leaders*** met at the ***city gates*** to conduct trials and make decisions.

31:25-27 The noble wife's character exemplifies wisdom. She is cool headed as she faces future uncertainties. She gives advice in a winsome way.

31:28-29 Those most important to the woman testify to her character, abilities, and achievements.

31:30-31 The book concludes where it began, by affirming the ultimate importance of the fear of ***the LORD*** (see 1:7). A woman's character is more important than her physical ***beauty.***

Themes in Proverbs.

Theme	Selected Proverbs
Anger / Temper	12:16; 14:17, 29; 15:1, 18; 19:11, 19; 21:14; 22:24-25; 29:8, 22; 30:33
Arguing / Quarrels	3:30; 10:12; 13:10; 15:18; 16:28; 17:14; 17:19; 18:19; 20:3; 21:19; 22:10; 25:8; 26:4-5, 17, 20-21; 29:22; 30:33
Bad Company / Associations	4:14-19; 13:20; 14:7; 16:19; 20:19; 22:5, 24-25; 23:6-8, 20-21; 24:1-2, 21-22
Bribes	15:27; 17:8, 23; 18:16; 21:14; 28:21; 29:4
Cheating	11:1; 16:8; 20:23; 22:28; 23:10; 28:8
Children	1:8-9; 3:1-2; 4:1-4; 10:1; 13:22; 15:20; 17:21, 25; 19:18, 26; 20:7; 22:6, 15; 23:13-14; 29:15, 17
Correction / Confrontation	1:8; 1:20-33; 3:11-12; 4:1; 9:7-8; 10:17; 12:1; 13:1, 18; 15:5, 12, 32; 17:12; 25:12; 27:17; 28:23
Counsel / Advice	1:20-33; 5:1-2; 6:20-23; 7:1-2; 10:31; 11:14; 12:5, 26; 13:13; 15:7, 22; 19:20; 20:5, 18; 23:9; 27:9
Envy	3:31; 14:30; 23:17; 24:1-2, 19-20
Faithfulness	3:3; 11:13; 14:22; 16:6; 17:17; 19:22; 20:6, 28; 23:26-28; 25:13, 19; 28:20
Fear of the LORD	1:7; 2:1-5; 3:7-8; 8:13; 9:10; 10:27; 14:2, 26-27; 15:16, 33; 16:6; 19:23; 22:4; 23:17-18; 24:21; 28:14; 29:25; 31:30
Flattery	7:4-5, 21; 26:28; 28:23; 29:5
Fools and Foolishness	1:7, 22, 32; 8:5; 9:13-18; 10:8, 18, 23; 11:29; 12:15-16, 23; 13:16, 19-20; 14:7-9, 16-18, 29; 15:5, 14; 17:10, 16, 24, 28; 18:2, 13; 19:3; 20:3; 21:20; 22:15; 26:1-12; 28:26; 29:11; 30:32
Friendship	3:32; 11:30; 12:26; 14:20; 16:28; 17:9, 17; 18:19, 24; 19:4, 6-7; 20:6; 22:11, 24; 24:26; 27:6, 9-10; 27:17; 28:7; 29:5
Generosity / Giving	3:9-10, 27-28; 11:24-25; 21:26; 22:9; 23:6; 25:14, 21-22; 28:27
Good Judgment	1:4; 3:21-26; 4:1-7; 5:1-2; 9:1-6, 10; 14:8, 15; 21:5; 22:3; 23:23; 27:12
Goodness	2:20; 3:27; 11:3, 6, 17, 27, 30; 12:2; 13:22; 14:14, 19, 22; 15:3; 17:13, 26; 20:8; 28:10, 21; 31:10-12
Gossip	6:16, 19; 10:12; 11:9, 12-13; 16:27-28; 17:4, 9; 18:8; 20:19; 25:9-10, 23; 26:20-22
Greed	1:18-19; 15:16, 27; 21:26; 22:1; 25:16; 27:20; 28:6, 8, 22, 25; 29:4
Happiness	3:18; 8:32-36; 10:28; 12:25; 15:13, 15, 30; 16:20; 17:22; 23:25; 24:17; 28:20; 29:18
Harmony / Peace	1:33; 10:10; 11:12; 12:20; 14:30; 16:7; 17:1; 29:17
Haste	18:13; 19:2; 21:5; 25:8; 28:20, 22; 29:20
Hating	6:16-19; 8:13; 9:8; 10:12, 18; 13:5, 24; 14:17; 15:17; 26:24, 26, 28; 28:16; 29:10
Honesty / Integrity	2:7; 11:1, 3, 20; 12:19, 22; 14:25; 16:13; 19:1; 20:7, 10; 24:26, 28; 28:6, 13, 23
Humility	3:34; 11:2; 12:15; 13:10; 15:5, 33; 16:19; 18:12; 22:4; 29:23
Justice	2:8-9; 8:20; 12:5; 13:23; 16:10-12; 17:15, 23, 26; 18:5; 19:28; 21:3, 7, 15; 22:8, 22; 24:11; 25:5; 28:5; 29:4, 26-27; 31:8-9

Theme	Selected Proverbs
Kindness	3:3; 11:17; 16:24; 26:25; 28:8; 31:26
Knowledge	1:4-7; 2:3-6, 10-12; 8:9-12; 9:10; 10:14; 11:9; 12:23; 14:6-7, 18; 15:2, 14; 18:15; 19:2, 27; 22:12; 23:12; 24:3-5; 28:2
Laziness	6:6-11; 10:4-5, 26; 12:11, 24, 27; 13:4, 11; 14:23; 15:19; 18:9; 19:15, 24; 20:4, 13; 21:5, 25; 24:30-34; 26:13-16; 28:19
Loans / Debt	6:1-5; 11:15; 17:18; 20:16; 22:7, 26-27; 27:13
Love	3:11-12; 7:4; 8:17, 21; 9:8; 10:12; 13:24; 14:22; 15:9, 17; 16:6; 17:9, 17; 18:19, 24; 19:8; 20:28; 21:17, 21; 27:5-6, 9-10; 29:3
Lying	6:16-19; 10:31; 12:19-22; 13:5; 14:25; 17:7, 20; 19:9; 21:6, 28; 25:18; 26:18-19, 24; 26:28; 28:13; 30:5-8
Marriage	5:18; 12:4; 18:22; 19:13-14; 31:10-11
Mercy	11:16-17; 18:23; 19:17; 21:10; 28:13
Mocking / Scorn	3:34; 9:7-8, 12; 13:1; 14:6; 15:12; 17:5; 19:25; 21:24; 22:10; 24:9; 29:8; 30:17
Money	1:19; 3:14; 10:16; 11:28; 20:15; 22:1
Obedience	1:8-9; 3:1-2; 4:1-13, 20-22; 5:1-2; 6:20-23; 7:1-3; 10:17; 19:16; 23:22; 28:4, 7; 29:18
Parents	1:8-9; 4:1-4; 10:1; 15:20; 17:21, 25; 19:26; 20:20; 30:11-12, 17
Poverty	10:15; 13:8; 15:16; 16:8; 28:27; 29:7, 14
Pride	8:13; 11:2; 13:10; 16:18-19; 18:12; 21:4, 24; 22:4; 26:12; 29:23; 30:32
Revenge	6:34; 20:22; 24:28-29; 25:21-22
Righteousness	3:33; 4:18; 11:11, 30-31; 13:21; 14:2; 15:8, 19, 29; 16:13; 21:12, 21; 29:6, 10, 27
Self-Control	14:29; 16:32; 19:11; 23:1-3; 25:28
Sexuality	5:3-23; 6:20-35; 7:4-27; 22:14; 23:26-28; 30:20-23; 31:3
Speaking	10:11; 15:4, 23; 16:23-24; 18:4, 21; 26:23
Stealing	6:30-31; 22:22; 28:24; 29:24; 30:7-9
Strength	3:7-8; 10:29; 11:7; 17:22; 18:10-11; 20:29; 21:22; 24:3, 5; 24:10; 30:25; 31:17, 25
Temptation	1:10; 4:23-27; 10:9; 11:5-6; 14:12, 16, 22; 15:3; 16:6, 17; 19:21; 21:15; 28:26; 29:6
Trust in the LORD	3:5-6; 11:28; 16:20; 20:24; 21:22, 31; 22:17-19; 28:25-26; 29:25; 30:4-5; 31:11
Understanding	2:2-7; 3:5; 14:6, 29, 33; 15:32; 16:21; 17:10, 27; 18:2; 19:8; 20:5; 21:30; 28:16
Wealth / Prosperity	3:9-10; 10:2-4, 15, 22; 11:4, 25, 28; 13:7-8, 11, 22; 14:20, 24; 15:6, 16-17; 16:20; 18:11; 19:4; 20:21; 21:5-6; 22:4, 7, 16; 23:4-5; 28:11, 19-20, 22, 25; 30:8-9
Wickedness	3:31-33; 4:14-19; 5:22-23; 6:12-15; 10:6-7, 24-30; 11:10-11; 12:5-7, 10; 17:23; 21:7, 29; 26:23-26; 28:4; 29:7, 12
Wisdom	1:7; 2:6; 3:13-20; 4:5-13; 5:1-2; 8:1–9:6, 10-12; 11:2; 14:33; 15:33; 16:16; 17:24; 18:4; 19:8; 24:3, 7; 24:14; 28:26; 30:24-28
Working	6:6-11; 10:4-6; 12:11, 24, 27; 13:4; 14:4, 23; 21:5; 22:29; 27:23-27; 28:19; 31:10-31

THE BOOK OF ECCLESIASTES

Ecclesiastes challenges us to think deeply about very basic questions. Life and all it contains appears to be a meaningless vapor, here today and gone tomorrow. Even so, life need not be without purpose. Ecclesiastes recommends wisdom, righteous living, finding purpose in remembering our Creator, and keeping God's commands. Then we can experience joy in the life God has given us.

SETTING

When Israel was in its golden years of peace after David had established his empire, Solomon devoted time and energy to enhancing culture. Rather than expanding or simply defending Israel's borders, he advanced his nation culturally with material prosperity and profound literature. In 1 Kings, we learn of Solomon's great accomplishments in international commerce and diplomacy, agriculture, and the building of cities, fortresses, and the Temple.

Rather than warring against and alienating other nations, Solomon engaged them and their literature and incorporated their modes of cultural expression into Israel's relationship with the Lord God. Solomon's failures are well known, but he accomplished a great deal with his God-given wisdom. Eventually, after his kingdom was split in two, the prophets came in waves to inform the people of the basic legal requirements of successfully managing God's holy nation. During his reign, Solomon fulfilled these legal duties, and he embellished them with his instructions on managing life wisely.

SUMMARY

The book of Ecclesiastes is a discourse or set of discourses exploring the value of life and all it contains and what people should do. The collection is bound by the editor's very brief prologue (1:1) and his epilogue and conclusion (12:9-14). Within this framework are the words of "the Teacher" (Hebrew *Qoheleth,* which is how most commentators refer to him). This book explores a wide range of topics, such as time, work, wisdom, pleasure, and injustice, and repeatedly returns to the theme of the book: Life and all it contains are *hebel* (see "*Hebel,* 'Vapor'" at 1:2, p. 1073). Ecclesiastes also discusses how humans should deal with these circumstances in a world that is under God's sovereign rule. This aspect of the book's message is summed up by the editor at the close of the book: "Here now is my final conclusion: Fear God and obey his commands, for this is everyone's duty. God will judge us for everything we do, including every secret thing, whether good or bad" (12:13-14).

It is only when one loves life and the world so much that without them everything would be gone, that one can believe in the resurrection and the new world.

DIETRICH BONHOEFFER
Letters and Papers from Prison, p. 157

AUTHOR AND RECIPIENTS

In the book of Ecclesiastes, the main speaker is Solomon (see 1:1, 12, 16; 2:7, 9), whose speech is framed within the opening and closing comments of the editor who recorded it (1:1; 12:9-14). This editor speaks highly of Solomon as the wise Teacher and adds a bit of his own helpful advice.

The book's speaker is introduced as the king of Israel and as "the Teacher" (Hebrew *Qoheleth,* literally [the one who] *gathers an assembly or congregation*). This idea is expressed in the Greek title of the book, Ecclesiastes (from Greek *ekklēsia,* "assembly, congregation"). David and Solomon addressed an assembly of their royal court or tribal representatives at various times (see 1 Chr 28:1–29:20; 2 Chr 5:2–7:7). We are also told that many kings and their ambassadors came to hear Solomon speak because of his wisdom (1 Kgs 4:24; 10:23). Perhaps the content of Ecclesiastes was delivered publicly on one or more of these occasions.

OUTLINE

1:1
Prologue

1:2–12:8
The Teacher's Lecture

12:9-14
Epilogue and Conclusion

ECCLESIASTES AS WISDOM LITERATURE

Ecclesiastes is one of the OT wisdom books, along with Proverbs and Job. Wisdom literature emphasizes the role of the individual in pleasing God beyond the requirements of the law. The instructions in these books identify ways for God's people to be successful as individuals, and in so doing to enhance the general success of Israelite society. The Teacher in Ecclesiastes speaks of wisdom as a general understanding of how God and the world work, learned through lifelong investigation. The conclusions to his research are the subject of his lecture.

MEANING AND MESSAGE

In this discourse, the Teacher addresses the broadest and most significant question of life: Is anything ultimately meaningful? As a momentary shadow or a fleeting breath, how can our lives have meaning? The Teacher contextualizes this philosophical matter within the real world of government and everyday life through which administrators and ordinary citizens must navigate.

The Teacher's message is unified, and the editor summarizes its implications (12:13-14). Life and all it contains is fleeting and apparently fraught with futility. Everything in this world is temporary, and life's frustrations could lead to the conclusion that it is meaningless. What we do doesn't last, and we can't find meaning in the world itself. We will soon die and be forgotten, so we should remember how short our lives are and enjoy them while we can. These realities of a fallen world need not engender despair. We also live in a world that is ruled by God, and it has meaning and purpose in reference to him. We should keep his commands and live to please him because we will soon stand before him for judgment.

The wisdom of Ecclesiastes is in coping with and even thriving in this life despite its brevity and apparent futility. Although we cannot comprehend all of God's actions or the purpose of our lives, Ecclesiastes assures us that our sovereign God has a strong hand in all that happens, both positive and tragic. Those who trust God will take the apparent futility of life as an incentive to diligently and wisely achieve what they can while they are alive and to enjoy God's good gifts in the process.

Ecclesiastes . . . defends the life of faith in a generous God by pointing to the grimness of the alternative.

MICHAEL EATON
Ecclesiastes, p. 44

FURTHER READING

MICHAEL A. EATON
Ecclesiastes (1983)

DANIEL C. FREDERICKS
Coping with Transience: Ecclesiastes on Brevity in Life (1993)

DEREK KIDNER
The Message of Ecclesiastes (1984)

TREMPER LONGMAN III
Ecclesiastes in *Cornerstone Biblical Commentary*, vol. 6 (2006)

ROLAND MURPHY
Ecclesiastes (1992)

ROGER N. WHYBRAY
Ecclesiastes (1989)

1. PROLOGUE (1:1)

1 These are the words of the Teacher, King David's son, who ruled in Jerusalem.

2. THE TEACHER'S LECTURE (1:2–12:8)

Everything Is Meaningless

2"[a]Everything is [a]meaningless," says the Teacher, "completely [a]meaningless!"

3What do people get for all their hard work under the sun? 4Generations come and generations go, but the earth never changes. 5The sun rises and the sun sets, then hurries around to rise again. 6The wind blows south, and then turns north. Around and around it goes, blowing in circles. 7Rivers run into the sea, but the sea is never full. Then the water returns again to the rivers and flows out again to the sea. 8Everything is wearisome beyond description. No matter how much we see, we are never satisfied. No matter how much we hear, we are not content.

9History merely repeats itself. It has all been done before. Nothing under the sun is truly new. 10Sometimes people say, "Here is something new!" But actually it is old; nothing is ever truly new. 11We don't remember what happened in the past, and in future generations, no one will remember what we are doing now.

The Teacher Speaks: The Futility of Wisdom

12I, the Teacher, was king of Israel, and I lived in Jerusalem. 13I devoted myself to search for understanding and to explore by wisdom everything being done under heaven. I soon discovered that God has dealt a tragic existence to the human race. 14I observed everything going on under the sun, and really, it is all [b]meaningless—like chasing the wind.

15 What is wrong cannot be made right.
What is missing cannot be recovered.

16I said to myself, "Look, I am [c]wiser than any of the kings who ruled in Jerusalem before me. I have greater [c]wisdom and knowledge than any of them." 17So I set out to learn everything from wisdom to madness and folly. But I learned firsthand that pursuing all this is like chasing the wind.

18 The greater my wisdom, the greater my grief.
To increase knowledge only increases sorrow.

The Futility of Pleasure

2 I said to myself, "Come on, let's try pleasure. Let's look for the 'good things' in life." But I found that this, too, was [d]meaningless. 2So I said, "Laughter is silly. What good does it do to seek pleasure?" 3After much thought, I decided to cheer myself with wine. And while still seeking wisdom, I clutched at foolishness. In this way, I tried to experience the only happiness most people find during their brief life in this world.

4I also tried to find meaning by building huge homes for myself and by planting beautiful vineyards. 5I made gardens and parks,

1:1 Eccl 1:12; 12:8-10
1:2 Ps 39:5-6; 62:9; [a]*hebel* (1892) ▸Eccl 1:14
1:3 Eccl 2:11; 3:9; 5:16
1:4 Ps 104:5; 119:90
1:8 Prov 27:20
1:9 Eccl 2:12; 3:15
1:11 Eccl 2:16; 9:5
1:12 Eccl 1:1; 7:27; 12:8-10
1:13 Eccl 3:10-11; 8:17
1:14 Eccl 2:11; 4:4; 6:9; [b]*hebel* (1892) ▸Eccl 2:1
1:15 Eccl 7:13
1:16 1 Kgs 3:10-12; 4:29-34; [c]*khokmah* (2451) ▸Isa 11:2
1:17 Eccl 2:12; 7:25
1:18 Eccl 12:12
2:1 Eccl 7:4, 6; 8:15; [d]*hebel* (1892) ▸Eccl 3:19
2:2 Prov 14:15
2:3 Eccl 6:12; 8:15
2:4 1 Kgs 7:1-12
2:5 Neh 2:8; Song 4:16; 5:1
2:6 Neh 2:14; 3:15-16

1:1 *the Teacher:* Hebrew *Qoheleth;* this term is rendered "the Teacher" throughout this book (see also 1:2, 12; 7:27; 12:8-10). Ecclesiastes never uses the Teacher's name, but ***King David's son*** probably refers to Solomon (see also 1:12, 16; 2:4-9).

1:2-11 The Teacher begins by observing that each natural and historical activity is accentuated by its circular repetitive rhythm of coming and going, being and not being. This can lead to the despairing cry that ***everything is meaningless.*** The Teacher moves rapidly from subject to subject and finishes this section with the topic he started with, using a literary pattern that mirrors the circularity he describes in nature and in human history.

1:2 ***Everything is meaningless . . . completely meaningless*** (literally *vapor of vapors, everything is vapor*): Wherever "meaningless" occurs in this book, the Hebrew word *hebel* ("breath, vapor") is behind it. The Teacher's conclusion is that everything is a transitory and meaningless vapor.

1:3 The Hebrew idiom ***under the sun*** is used twenty-nine times in Ecclesiastes. The NLT sometimes renders it with expressions such as "here on earth" (2:18) or "in this world" (2:20). It suggests a view of life that is earthbound rather than reflecting God's perspective.

1:4 ***Generations come*** and ***go,*** and individual lives seem to pass away without significance.

1:7-8 ***the sea is never full . . . we are never satisfied:*** This image introduces the unfulfilling nature of life.

1:11 ***no one will remember:*** We cannot count on anyone remembering anything that we think we have achieved.

1:12–2:26 The Teacher explores the relationships among wisdom, work, and pleasure.

1:13 ***God has dealt a tragic existence:*** The grim realities of human experience remind us of the Fall in Eden (Gen 3). Ecclesiastes does not dodge depressing descriptions of death, oppression, and loneliness; it meets them head-on and incorporates them into realistic conclusions.

1:14 ***like chasing the wind:*** Just as the wind quickly comes and goes, so does life.

2:1-11 The Teacher dismisses the pursuit of pleasure for its own sake as hollow. Even great achievements are a vapor.

2:1-2 Seeking ***pleasure*** for its own sake only ends in ***silly . . . laughter.***

2:3 The Teacher understood that trying to ***cheer*** himself ***with wine*** was ***foolishness,*** but he did it ***while still seeking wisdom***—i.e., during his attempt to understand how ***to experience . . . happiness.*** This proved to be empty (2:11). • ***brief life in this world:*** The totality of human experience is "a breath."

2:4-8 Solomon's building achievements were as small as porches and gates and as large as entire cities (see 1 Kgs 9:15-19). These projects, meant primarily for his own pleasure, included the palace and its accompanying buildings (see 1 Kgs 7:1-12).

2:4 Solomon's ***vineyards*** are mentioned in Song 8:11-12.

2:7
Gen 14:14; 15:3
1 Kgs 4:23
2:8
1 Kgs 9:28; 10:10, 14
2:9
1 Chr 29:25
Eccl 1:16
2:10
Eccl 3:22; 5:18; 6:2; 9:9
2:11
Eccl 1:3, 14; 2:22; 3:9; 5:16

filling them with all kinds of fruit trees. [6]I
built reservoirs to collect the water to irrigate my many flourishing groves. [7]I bought
slaves, both men and women, and others
were born into my household. I also owned
large herds and flocks, more than any of the
kings who had lived in Jerusalem before me.
[8]I collected great sums of silver and gold,
the treasure of many kings and provinces.
I hired wonderful singers, both men and
women, and had many beautiful concubines.
I had everything a man could desire!
[9]So I became greater than all who had
lived in Jerusalem before me, and my wisdom never failed me. [10]Anything I wanted,
I would take. I denied myself no pleasure. I
even found great pleasure in hard work, a
reward for all my labors. [11]But as I looked
at everything I had worked so hard to
accomplish, it was all so meaningless—like

Hebel, "Vapor" (1:2)

Deut 32:21
2 Kgs 17:15
Job 7:16
Ps 63:9; 78:33; 94:11; 144:4
Prov 21:6
Isa 30:7; 49:4; 57:13

The key word in Ecclesiastes is the Hebrew word *hebel* ("vapor," translated "meaningless" in 1:2). This word expresses the core of the Teacher's judgment concerning life in this world.

At root, *hebel* means physical "breath" or "vapor." *Hebel* is used 78 times in the OT, but in only three instances is the physical meaning clearly intended (see Ps 63:9; Prov 21:6; Isa 57:13). In the other 75 instances, the word is used metaphorically to describe what is incomprehensible, futile, meaningless, false, or insubstantial. The term is often used to describe the insubstantiality, unreality, and worthlessness of false gods (Deut 32:21; 2 Kgs 17:15; Isa 30:7). In this sense, *hebel* is the opposite of "glory"—the substantial, weighty, and lasting presence of God (see "The Glory of God" at Exod 24:15-17, p. 167). Sometimes the word *hebel* stands for the way life is fleeting and momentary, like vapor (Job 7:16; Ps 144:4). In other cases, it refers to the meaninglessness and frustration of life (Ps 78:33; 94:11; Isa 49:4).

There is a long tradition of understanding *hebel* in Ecclesiastes as meaning "vanity," not in the sense of thinking too highly of one's self, but in the sense of experiencing life as futile and without purpose or meaning. The ancient Greek translation of the OT used the word *mataiotēs,* which means "emptiness" or "futility." The Latin Vulgate then translated *hebel* with the Latin word *vanitas,* which means "purposelessness, pointlessness, hollowness, worthlessness." From the Vulgate comes the long-standing tradition of translating the word as "vanity" in English. Most translators today understand the word *hebel* in this sense: Life on earth has no apparent purpose or meaning, and all that we do is futile.

Some translators, however, understand *hebel* in Ecclesiastes to be referring primarily to the transitory impermanence of life. Vapor has no permanence or weight. This translation leads to a different understanding of Ecclesiastes: Life is not so much meaningless and futile as it is impermanent and fleeting. Many phrases in Ecclesiastes allude to the fleeting nature of human life and its efforts. In the NT, a similar thought can be found in James 4:13-15. The understanding of *hebel* as "impermanence" in Ecclesiastes has merit in explaining the book coherently; it is, however, a minority view among scholars.

The NLT translates *hebel* in Ecclesiastes as "meaningless" to summarize what the term means in this book. However, while reading Ecclesiastes, it is helpful to keep in mind the root of the word ("breath" or "vapor") that stands behind the metaphors and can help flesh out the concept.

The brevity, frustration, and apparent meaninglessness of life can be depressing. This discouragement should motivate us toward working more wisely and diligently and enjoying life while we can. We have all observed the apparent absurdity of life's tragedies, such as the success of a wicked fool or unchecked injustice. But these things come into proportion when we remember God's sovereignty, because "God will judge us for everything we do, including every secret thing, whether good or bad" (12:14).

2:7 Solomon's ***slaves, . . . large herds, and flocks*** were numerous, and caring for them consumed vast resources (1 Kgs 4:22-23; 9:20-21).

2:8 ***silver and gold . . . kings and provinces:*** Solomon ruled from the Fertile Crescent (north and east of Israel) to the border of Egypt in the south. His wealth in precious metals came from trade, gifts from admiring rulers of other nations, and taxes from lands he held within his empire (1 Kgs 4:21; 9:28; 10:14, 22-25; 1 Chr 29:4; 2 Chr 9:26-27). • ***many beautiful concubines:*** Solomon had 700 wives and 300 concubines by the end of his reign (1 Kgs 11:3).

2:9 ***I became greater:*** Cp. 1 Kgs 10:23. • Solomon's ***wisdom*** enabled his successful rise in power and prosperity (see 1 Kgs 3:2-14; 4:20-34).

2:10 ***I even found great pleasure in hard work:*** The Teacher introduces a significant, repetitive theme: Joy comes from wise and rigorous work (5:12, 18-20).

2:11 ***meaningless . . . nothing really worthwhile:*** Accomplishment only brings hopelessness and discouragement because the accomplishment itself has no lasting meaning (2:18-23).

chasing the wind. There was nothing really
worthwhile anywhere.

The Wise and the Foolish

[12]So I decided to compare wisdom with foolishness and madness (for who can do this
better than I, the king?). [13]I thought, "Wisdom is better than foolishness, just as light
is better than darkness. [14]For the wise can
see where they are going, but fools walk in
the dark." Yet I saw that the wise and the
foolish share the same fate. [15]Both will die.
So I said to myself, "Since I will end up the
same as the fool, what's the value of all my
wisdom? This is all so meaningless!" [16]For
the wise and the foolish both die. The wise
will not be remembered any longer than
the fool. In the days to come, both will be
forgotten.

[17]So I came to hate life because everything done here under the sun is so
troubling. Everything is meaningless—like
chasing the wind.

The Futility of Work

[18]I came to hate all my hard work here on
earth, for I must leave to others everything
I have earned. [19]And who can tell whether
my successors will be wise or foolish? Yet
they will control everything I have gained
by my skill and hard work under the sun.
How meaningless! [20]So I gave up in despair,
questioning the value of all my hard work
in this world.

[21]Some people work wisely with knowledge and skill, then must leave the fruit of
their efforts to someone who hasn't worked
for it. This, too, is meaningless, a great tragedy. [22]So what do people get in this life for
all their hard work and anxiety? [23]Their
days of labor are filled with pain and grief;
even at night their minds cannot rest. It is
all meaningless.

[24]So I decided there is nothing better
than to enjoy food and drink and to find satisfaction in work. Then I realized that these
pleasures are from the hand of God. [25]For
who can eat or enjoy anything apart from
him? [26]God gives wisdom, knowledge, and
joy to those who please him. But if a sinner
becomes wealthy, God takes the wealth away
and gives it to those who please him. This,
too, is meaningless—like chasing the wind.

A Time for Everything

3 [1] For everything there is a season,
a time for every activity under
heaven.
[2] A time to be born and a time to die.
A time to plant and a time to harvest.
[3] A time to kill and a time to heal.
A time to tear down and a time to
build up.
[4] A time to cry and a time to laugh.
A time to grieve and a time to dance.
[5] A time to scatter stones and a time to
gather stones.
A time to embrace and a time to turn
away.
[6] A time to search and a time to quit
searching.
A time to keep and a time to throw
away.

2:12 Eccl 1:9-10, 17; 7:25
2:13 Eccl 7:11-12, 19
2:14 Ps 49:10; Eccl 9:2-3
2:15 Eccl 2:16; 6:8, 11
2:16 Eccl 1:11; 2:14; 9:5
2:17 Eccl 4:2
2:18 Ps 39:6; 49:10
2:21 Eccl 2:18; 4:4
2:22 Eccl 1:3
2:23 Job 5:7; 14:1
2:24 Eccl 3:22; 5:18; 9:7
2:26 Job 27:16-17; 32:8; Eccl 1:14
3:1 Eccl 3:17; 8:6
3:2 Heb 9:27
3:4 Exod 15:20; Ps 126:2; Rom 12:15
3:7 Amos 5:13
3:8 Ps 101:3-8; [e]*shalom* (7965) ›Isa 9:6
3:9 Eccl 1:3; 2:11; 5:16
3:10 Eccl 1:13; 2:26
3:11 Eccl 8:17; Rom 11:33; [h]*'olam* (5769) ›Eccl 12:5

2:12-23 The Teacher now looks at the value of wisdom (2:12-17) and hard work (2:18-23). These, too, are "meaningless" (2:17).

2:12 ***who can do this better than I, the king?*** The meaning of the Hebrew is uncertain. No one after the Teacher will have any better perspective for comparing wisdom and folly because nothing new will be done under the sun (1:9-10).

2:13-14 ***Wisdom is better than foolishness:*** Wisdom has value in navigating life successfully. It cannot, however, save one from the *fate* of death or provide meaning (2:15-16).

2:15-16 If ***both*** the wise and the foolish ***will die,*** what advantage is there in being wise? Since the lives of both wise and foolish people are fleeting, the conclusion is that all is meaningless. • ***both will be forgotten:*** Those who follow us will not remember us or our accomplishments, so our efforts will come to nothing (cp. 1:11; 9:13-16).

2:17-20 The Teacher ***came to hate life*** because of its griefs (1:18), toils (2:18), and apparent futility (2:19-20).

2:19 ***Foolish,*** destructive ***successors*** are more of a threat to wise accomplishments than wise successors, but since the Teacher couldn't ***tell*** what kind of successors he would have, his accomplishments were ***meaningless*** to him. Solomon's immediate successor—his son Rehoboam—turned out to be foolish (see 1 Kgs 12:1-20).

2:21 ***work wisely with knowledge and skill:*** Skill in work is an expression of wisdom (e.g., see Exod 31:1-5). • ***leave the fruit . . . to someone who hasn't worked for it:*** A person who has little personal investment tends to waste it or take foolish risks.

2:24-26 Though life "under the sun" (1:3) is like a vapor (2:23, "meaningless"), we should enjoy God's good gifts of food, work, and wisdom.

2:24 ***pleasures are from . . . God:*** No one should discount God's gifts, including the basic enjoyment of food and work. If God did not give them, they would not be available. We can be thankful and satisfied.

2:25 ***apart from him?*** As in Greek and Syriac versions; Hebrew reads *apart from me?*

2:26 If a ***sinner becomes wealthy,*** it is meaningless to him because ***God takes the wealth away.***

3:1-8 ***For everything there is a season, a time for every activity under heaven:*** Wisdom recognizes that everything has its own season—in human activities as in the realm of nature (see 1:3-7). A wise person will determine the appropriate time to pursue any activity (8:5). The opportunity is fleeting (Eph 5:16; Col 4:5).

3:2-8 We have no control over when we are ***born*** or when we ***die*** (8:8), but it is our responsibility to live wisely between those events. • ***plant and . . . harvest:*** Wise agricultural decisions must be made in the natural seasons. • In ancient Israel, the times to ***kill***

7 A time to tear and a time to mend.
A time to be quiet and a time to speak.
8 A time to love and a time to hate.
A time for war and a time for [e]peace.

9 What do people really get for all their
hard work? 10 I have seen the burden God
has placed on us all. 11 Yet God has made
everything beautiful for its own time. He
has planted [f]eternity in the human heart, but
even so, people cannot see the whole scope
of God's work from beginning to end. 12 So
I concluded there is nothing better than to
be happy and enjoy ourselves as long as we
can. 13 And people should eat and drink and
enjoy the fruits of their labor, for these are
gifts from God.

14 And I know that whatever God does is
final. Nothing can be added to it or taken
from it. God's purpose is that people should
fear him. 15 What is happening now has happened before, and what will happen in the
future has happened before, because God
makes the same things happen over and
over again.

The Injustices of Life

16 I also noticed that under the sun there is
evil in the courtroom. Yes, even the courts
of law are corrupt! 17 I said to myself, "In due
season God will [g]judge everyone, both good
and bad, for all their deeds."

18 I also thought about the human condition—how God proves to people that they
are like animals. 19 For people and animals
share the same fate—both breathe and both
must die. So people have no real advantage
over the animals. How [h]meaningless! 20 Both
go to the same place—they came from dust
and they return to dust. 21 For who can prove
that the human spirit goes up and the spirit
of animals goes down into the earth? 22 So I
saw that there is nothing better for people
than to be happy in their work. That is why
we are here! No one will bring us back from
death to enjoy life after we die.

4 Again, I observed all the oppression
that takes place under the sun. I saw the
tears of the oppressed, with no one to comfort them. The oppressors have great power,
and their victims are helpless. 2 So I concluded that the dead are better off than the
living. 3 But most fortunate of all are those
who are not yet born. For they have not seen
all the evil that is done under the sun.

4 Then I observed that most people are
motivated to success because they envy their
neighbors. But this, too, is [i]meaningless—like
chasing the wind.

5 "Fools fold their idle hands,
leading them to ruin."

3:12 Eccl 2:24
3:13 Eccl 5:19
3:14 Eccl 8:12-13; 12:13
3:15 Eccl 1:9; 6:10
3:16 Eccl 4:1; 5:8; 8:9
3:17 Ps 96:13; 98:9; Matt 16:27; Rom 2:6-10; [g]*shapat* (8199) ‣Isa 1:26
3:18 Ps 49:12, 20; 73:22
3:19 Eccl 9:12; [h]*hebel* (1892) ‣Eccl 4:4
3:20 Gen 3:19; Eccl 12:7
3:21 Eccl 12:7
3:22 Eccl 2:24
4:1 Eccl 3:16; 5:8; Isa 5:7
4:2 Job 3:11-26; Eccl 2:17
4:3 Eccl 6:3
4:4 Eccl 1:14; 2:21; [i]*hebel* (1892) ‣Eccl 5:7
4:5 Prov 6:10; 24:33; Isa 9:20

. . . .

included capital punishment and war. • In times of mourning, people in the Near East would often ***tear*** their clothes. • There is ***a time to hate,*** even for God (Ps 5:5; 11:5).

3:9-14 Even though every activity has an appropriate occasion (3:1-8), only God can truly know what that occasion is (3:9-11). Mortals must be content with uncertainty and trust the sovereign God who gives enjoyment to those who work wisely and righteously.

3:9 ***get for . . . hard work?*** See 3:12-13.

3:10 ***the burden God has placed on us all:*** God intensified the severity of our labor following humankind's rebellion against him (Gen 3:17-19). This burden is not so great that we cannot enjoy our work and its fruits (3:11-13).

3:11 ***God has made everything beautiful for its own time:*** We can sometimes see this beauty in our work and in the world, but many times ***people cannot see:*** God reserves for himself the understanding of how everything fits together (cp. Rom 8:22-28). • God has ***planted eternity,*** an awareness of the infinite, within each of us—enough for us to be in awe of him who is infinite and eternal, and enough to hope for eternal life after death.

3:12-13 ***be happy and enjoy:*** Though life and work can be burdensome, the Teacher repeats his conclusion from 2:24.

3:14 Knowing that ***whatever God does is final*** is a reason to ***fear him***—to trust and revere God and respect all that he does.

3:15 ***The same things happen over and over again:*** The repetitiveness of history (1:9-10) is part of God's sovereign plan.

3:16–5:7 This section comments on a variety of topics, including justice, humans and animals, oppression, moderation, companionship, politics, and worship.

3:16 ***courtroom*** (literally ***the place of justice***): In Israel, local court proceedings were held at the city gates, where the city's elders sat to hear and adjudicate legal matters (e.g., see Ruth 4:1-12).

3:17 ***In due season God will judge:*** Human injustices (3:16) are temporary and will be righted by God's justice. The narrator repeats this point to close the entire book (12:14).

3:19 ***both breathe:*** Or ***both have the same spirit.*** • With respect to breathing and dying, ***people have no real advantage over the animals,*** but we have other advantages (e.g., see Gen 1:26-28).

3:20 ***from dust . . . to dust:*** The Teacher refers to God's judgment against human rebellion in Eden (see Gen 3:19).

3:21 ***the human spirit goes up:*** Cp. 12:7.

3:22 ***happy in their work:*** Work now stands alone as a source of enjoyment, apart from food and drink (cp. 2:24-25; 3:12-13).

4:1 ***all the oppression:*** Abuse is rampant at many levels in society—in family, religion, the workplace, government, and foreign powers.

4:2 Where oppression reigns, ***the dead are better off than the living.*** Those who have died are no longer mistreated.

4:4 ***Most people are motivated to success*** by a competitive drive. Since the fruits of these efforts have no intrinsic value, the Teacher recommends that moderation (4:5-6) replace envy.

4:5-6 ***Fools*** do not even try to succeed and end up impoverished. Others frantically devote ***two handfuls***—all their time and effort—to ***hard work*** in pursuit of fleeting wealth that they will have no time to enjoy (cp. Prov 23:4-5). Wise people practice moderation and contentment (***quietness***).

6 And yet,

"Better to have one handful with
quietness
than two handfuls with hard work
and chasing the wind."

The Advantages of Companionship

7 I observed yet another example of something meaningless under the sun. 8 This is
the case of a man who is all alone, without
a child or a brother, yet who works hard to
gain as much wealth as he can. But then he
asks himself, "Who am I working for? Why
am I giving up so much pleasure now?" It is
all so meaningless and depressing.
9 Two people are better off than one, for
they can help each other succeed. 10 If one
person falls, the other can reach out and
help. But someone who falls alone is in real
trouble. 11 Likewise, two people lying close
together can keep each other warm. But
how can one be warm alone? 12 A person
standing alone can be attacked and defeated, but two can stand back-to-back and
conquer. Three are even better, for a triple-
braided cord is not easily broken.

The Futility of Political Power

13 It is better to be a poor but wise youth than
an old and foolish king who refuses all advice. 14 Such a youth could rise from poverty
and succeed. He might even become king,
though he has been in prison. 15 But then
everyone rushes to the side of yet another
youth who replaces him. 16 Endless crowds
stand around him, but then another generation grows up and rejects him, too. So it is
all meaningless—like chasing the wind.

Approaching God with Care

5 As you enter the house of God, keep
your ears open and your mouth shut. It
is evil to make mindless offerings to God.
2 Don't make rash promises, and don't be
hasty in bringing matters before God. After
all, God is in heaven, and you are here on
earth. So let your words be few.
3 Too much activity gives you restless
dreams; too many words make you a fool.
4 When you make a promise to God, don't
delay in following through, for God takes
no pleasure in fools. Keep all the promises
you make to him. 5 It is better to say nothing than to make a promise and not keep
it. 6 Don't let your mouth make you sin. And
don't defend yourself by telling the Temple messenger that the promise you made
was a mistake. That would make God angry,
and he might wipe out everything you have
achieved.
7 Talk is cheap, like daydreams and other
useless activities. Fear God instead.

The Futility of Wealth

8 Don't be surprised if you see a poor person being oppressed by the powerful and if
justice is being miscarried throughout the
land. For every official is under orders from
higher up, and matters of justice get lost in
red tape and bureaucracy. 9 Even the king
milks the land for his own profit!
10 Those who love money will never have
enough. How meaningless to think that
wealth brings true happiness! 11 The more
you have, the more people come to help
you spend it. So what good is wealth—except perhaps to watch it slip through your
fingers!

4:6 Prov 15:16-17; 16:8
4:8 Prov 27:20; Eccl 1:8; 2:21; 5:10
4:11 1 Kgs 1:1-4
4:13 Eccl 7:19; 9:15
4:14 Gen 41:14, 41-43
4:16 Eccl 1:14
5:1 Exod 3:5; 30:18-20; 1 Sam 15:22; Prov 15:8; 21:27; Isa 1:12
5:2 Num 30:2-16; Prov 10:19; 20:25; Matt 6:7
5:4 Num 30:2; Ps 50:14; 66:13-14; 76:11
5:5 Prov 20:25; Acts 5:4
5:6 Lev 4:2, 22; Num 15:25
5:7 Eccl 3:14; 12:13; *hebel* (1892) ‣ Eccl 6:2
5:8 Ps 12:5; Eccl 4:1; Ezek 18:18; 1 Pet 4:12
5:10 Eccl 2:10-11
5:11 Eccl 2:9
5:12 Prov 3:24

4:7-8 This solitary man is a case study of the principle expressed in 4:6.

4:9-12 ***Two people are better off than one:*** The solitary man (4:8) brings to mind the advantages of partnerships for business and for personal well-being.

4:13-14 ***It is better to be . . . wise:*** Wisdom is valuable for its practical benefits.

4:15-16 As with everything else, a ruler's popularity is only temporary and fleeting, like *the wind.*

4:15 ***another youth:*** Literally *the second youth.*

4:16 ***Endless crowds stand around him:*** Literally *There is no end to all the people, to all those who are before them.*

5:1 Though the *house of God* provides opportunity for reverent words and measured promises, it is primarily a place for listening. • Verse 5:1 is numbered 4:17 in the Hebrew text.

5:2-20 Verses 5:2-20 are numbered 5:1-19 in the Hebrew text.

5:3 ***Too much activity . . . too many words:*** Moderation should characterize our efforts and words (cp. Prov 10:19).

5:4-5 ***Keep all the promises you make to him:*** This is virtually a direct quote from the law (Deut 23:21-23; see also Prov 12:22; 20:25). Vows to God were voluntary, but once they were made, it was obligatory to keep them.

5:7 ***Fear God:*** Reverence for God is the foundation for worthwhile words and useful activities (see 12:1; Prov 1:7).

5:8-9 The meaning of the Hebrew in verses 8 and 9 is uncertain. The NLT understands these verses to mean that ***bureaucracy*** brings oppression rather than justice, all the way up to the king (see also 1 Sam 8:11-18). This should not be surprising because that is how bureaucracies tend to function. Others interpret the verses to mean that the king and his officials provide oversight to restrain injustice and oppression. The former view is more in keeping with the realistic perspective of the Teacher. • ***For every official is under orders from higher up, and matters of justice get lost in red tape and bureaucracy. Even the king milks the land for his own profit!*** Or *For one official watches over another, and higher officials are over them. The land benefits from a king who cultivates the field.* This alternate translation suggests the second, more positive interpretation mentioned above.

5:10 Because we are created as spiritual and not just physical beings, possessions and *wealth* can never completely satisfy us.

5:12 ***People who work hard sleep well:*** Hard work and moderation yield the

5:13 Eccl 6:2
5:15 Job 1:21; Ps 49:17; 1 Tim 6:7
5:16 Prov 11:29; Eccl 1:3; 2:11; 3:9
5:17 Eccl 2:23
5:18 Eccl 2:10, 24
5:19 2 Chr 1:12; Eccl 3:13; 6:2
6:1 Eccl 5:13
6:2 1 Kgs 3:13; Ps 17:14; 73:7; [k]*hebel* (1892) ‣Eccl 7:6
6:3 Job 3:16; Eccl 4:3; Isa 14:20; Matt 26:24
6:6 Eccl 2:14
6:7 Prov 16:26
6:8 Eccl 2:15

12 People who work hard sleep well,
whether they eat little or much. But the rich
seldom get a good night's sleep.
13 There is another serious problem I have
seen under the sun. Hoarding riches harms
the saver. 14 Money is put into risky investments that turn sour, and everything is lost.
In the end, there is nothing left to pass on
to one's children. 15 We all come to the end
of our lives as naked and empty-handed as
on the day we were born. We can't take our
riches with us.
16 And this, too, is a very serious problem. People leave this world no better off
than when they came. All their hard work
is for nothing—like working for the wind.
17 Throughout their lives, they live under a
cloud—frustrated, discouraged, and angry.
18 Even so, I have noticed one thing, at
least, that is good. It is good for people to
eat, drink, and enjoy their work under the
sun during the short life God has given
them, and to accept their lot in life. 19 And it
is a good thing to receive wealth from God
and the good health to enjoy it. To enjoy
your work and accept your lot in life—this
is indeed a gift from God. 20 God keeps such
people so busy enjoying life that they take
no time to brood over the past.

6 There is another serious tragedy I
have seen under the sun, and it weighs
heavily on humanity. 2 God gives some people great wealth and honor and everything
they could ever want, but then he doesn't
give them the chance to enjoy these things.
They die, and someone else, even a stranger,
ends up enjoying their wealth! This is [k]mean-
ingless—a sickening tragedy.
3 A man might have a hundred children
and live to be very old. But if he finds no
satisfaction in life and doesn't even get a
decent burial, it would have been better
for him to be born dead. 4 His birth would
have been meaningless, and he would have
ended in darkness. He wouldn't even have
had a name, 5 and he would never have seen
the sun or known of its existence. Yet he
would have had more peace than in growing up to be an unhappy man. 6 He might
live a thousand years twice over but still not
find contentment. And since he must die
like everyone else—well, what's the use?
7 All people spend their lives scratching for food, but they never seem to have
enough. 8 So are wise people really better
off than fools? Do poor people gain anything by being wise and knowing how to act
in front of others?

Enjoying God's Gifts (5:18-20)

Eccl 2:24-25; 3:12-13, 22; 4:6; 6:9; 8:15; 9:7-9; 11:7-12; Isa 22:13; 56:12; Luke 12:19-20; Phil 4:4; Col 2:20-22; Jas 1:2; 4:13-16

The conclusion of many of the Teacher's reflections is that we are responsible for enjoying life because it is God's gift (see 2:24-25; 3:12-13, 22; 4:6; 5:18; 6:9; 8:15; 9:7-9; 11:7-12). One tradition in Christianity states that "The chief end of man is to glorify God and enjoy him forever" (*Westminster Shorter Catechism,* Question 1). The NT similarly encourages us to be joyful in all things, including trials and challenges (Phil 4:4; Jas 1:2).

Although there are conditions in which it would seemingly be better not to be alive, life is meant to be enjoyed with laughing, dancing, love, and peace. It is especially worth living when old age and death challenge that joy (9:4, 9; 11:7-9; 12:1). We are to enjoy our food, drink, health, proper clothes, our loving spouse, children, daily work, and entertainment. Only when we treat the things of life and their enjoyment as ends in themselves are they deterrents to happiness. The Teacher speaks strongly against the pursuit of pleasure for its own sake as foolish and without profit (2:1, 2; 7:2, 4, 6; 10:16-19; see also Isa 22:13; 56:12; Luke 12:19-20).

It may be surprising to hear such joy in a book that acknowledges such intense tragedy and frustration. But it is exactly this balance of joy and sorrow that characterizes the wise person who reflects on all of life and understands its complexities in a fallen world.

formula for a peaceful, productive life. Pursuing wealth leads to unnecessary anxieties (5:3).

5:13-14 *Hoarding riches . . . everything is lost:* Possessions are transitory and can be lost for any number of reasons.

5:16-17 Working simply to gain possessions is *like working for the wind;* it leads to being *frustrated, discouraged, and angry.*

5:18-20 The prescription for enjoying life is repeated: We should enjoy our food, drink, and work and appreciate them as gifts from God.

6:1-2 This "unfortunate man" parable resembles 4:7-8 and 5:13-17. It is *a sickening tragedy* when someone succeeds but then cannot *enjoy these things.* Such a person has missed out on the only available benefit of success.

6:3-6 *a hundred children and . . . be very old:* Such honors as virility and old age amount to nothing if life is not enjoyable or does not end well (*a decent burial*). The *darkness* of being *born dead* is preferable to a discontented life.

6:7 People never seem to be satisfied with what they have, no matter how much it is (cp. 5:10).

6:8-9 *are wise people really better off . . . being wise?* Yes, as long as they *enjoy* and are content with what the Lord has provided.

9 Enjoy what you have rather than desiring what you don't have. Just dreaming
about nice things is meaningless—like chasing the wind.

The Future—Determined and Unknown

10 Everything has already been decided.
It was known long ago what each person
would be. So there's no use arguing with
God about your destiny.
11 The more words you speak, the less
they mean. So what good are they?
12 In the few days of our meaningless lives,
who knows how our days can best be spent?
Our lives are like a shadow. Who can tell
what will happen on this earth after we are
gone?

Wisdom for Life

7

1 A good reputation is more valuable
than costly perfume.
And the day you die is better than the
day you are born.
2 Better to spend your time at funerals
than at parties.
After all, everyone dies—
so the living should take this to heart.
3 Sorrow is better than laughter,
for sadness has a refining influence
on us.
4 A wise person thinks a lot about death,
while a fool thinks only about having
a good time.

5 Better to be criticized by a wise person
than to be praised by a fool.
6 A fool's laughter is quickly gone,
like thorns crackling in a fire.
This also is [a]meaningless.

7 Extortion turns wise people into
fools,
and bribes corrupt the heart.

8 Finishing is better than starting.
Patience is better than pride.

9 Control your temper,
for anger labels you a fool.

10 Don't long for "the good old days."
This is not wise.

11 Wisdom is even better when you have
money.
Both are a benefit as you go through
life.
12 Wisdom and money can get you almost
anything,
but only wisdom can save your life.

13 Accept the way God does things,
for who can straighten what he has
made crooked?
14 Enjoy prosperity while you can,
but when hard times strike, realize
that both come from God.
Remember that nothing is certain in
this life.

The Limits of Human Wisdom

15 I have seen everything in this meaningless
life, including the death of good young people and the long life of wicked people. 16 So
don't be too good or too wise! Why destroy
yourself? 17 On the other hand, don't be
too wicked either. Don't be a fool! Why die
before your time? 18 Pay attention to these
instructions, for anyone who fears God will
avoid both extremes.

6:9 Eccl 1:14; 11:9
6:10 Job 9:32; 40:2; Isa 45:9
6:11 Hos 12:1
7:1 Prov 22:1; Eccl 4:2; 7:8
7:2 Ps 90:12; Eccl 2:16; 9:2-3
7:5 Ps 141:5; Prov 13:18; 15:31-32
7:6 [a]*hebel* (1892) › Eccl 8:10
7:7 Exod 23:8; Deut 16:19; Prov 17:23
7:8 Prov 16:32
7:9 Prov 14:17; Jas 1:19
7:11 Prov 8:10-11
7:12 Prov 3:18; 8:35
7:13 Eccl 1:15; 3:11; 8:17
7:14 Deut 8:5; 26:11; Eccl 3:22; 9:7; 11:9
7:15 Eccl 6:12; 8:12-14; 9:9
7:16 Rom 12:3
7:17 Ps 55:23; Prov 10:27
7:18 Eccl 3:14; 5:7; 8:12-13
7:20 Ps 143:2; Rom 3:23

6:10–7:22 God's sovereign rule over ***everything*** is sobering, but it is ultimately a source of hope.

6:10 ***Everything has already been decided:*** Cp. Rom 8:29; Eph 1:5, 11. • ***It was known long ago what each person would be:*** Cp. Ps 139:15-16. • ***no use arguing with God about your destiny:*** Cp. Rom 9:20-24.

6:11 ***more words . . . the less they mean:*** Cp. Prov 10:19; 17:28.

6:12 ***who knows? Who can tell?*** These questions have already been answered. Our ***days can best be spent*** in wise living and in enjoying our work and God's gifts (2:13-14, 24; 3:22; 5:18). ***What will happen on this earth*** is what has already happened (1:9, 10; 3:15). • ***like a shadow:*** Cp. Ps 39:4-6; 90:3-6, 10-12; 109:23; 144:4.

7:1-4 These proverbs are similar to the sayings in the book of Proverbs.

7:1 The effort to pursue luxuries such as ***costly perfume*** is better spent seeking a ***good reputation*** for wisdom and righteousness (Prov 22:1; 28:6). • ***the day you die is better than the day you are born:*** There is a sense of relief when the troubles of life are over. The difficulties of life can make one look forward to the peace of death (1:18; 2:22; 4:2-3; 12:1).

7:2-6 Frivolous merry-making is foolish when wisdom demands sobriety about death (see also 2:12-13).

7:3-4 ***refining influence:*** Thinking soberly ***about death*** leads us to see the severity of God's curse on sin and convinces us of the need to enjoy life wisely (9:10).

7:5-6 Being ***praised by a fool*** and enjoying ***a fool's laughter*** are short-lived and worthless. Being ***criticized by a wise person*** can lead to real gain (Prov 17:10).

7:8 ***Finishing*** a project by exercising ***patience*** is ***better than starting*** a project with the ***pride*** of boastful words.

7:9 ***anger labels you a fool:*** Cp. Prov 14:29; 29:11; see "Anger" at Prov 14:29, p. 1047.

7:11-12 ***Wisdom*** and ***money*** are powerful means to bring us ***benefit.*** • ***but only wisdom can save your life:*** See 7:17; Prov 10:2; 11:4.

7:13 God's sovereign acts are irresistible; it is useless to counter or avoid his purposes.

7:14 Enjoying ***prosperity*** is beneficial, but such gifts are fleeting. The wise person accepts God's sovereign hand in everything (cp. Phil 4:11-13).

7:16 However hard we work, we could always do more, and we can ***destroy*** ourselves in the process.

7:17 ***don't be too wicked either:*** Wicked foolishness can lead to an early death (e.g., 1 Sam 25).

7:18 ***will avoid both extremes:*** Or ***will follow them both.***

7:21
[b]*shama'* (8085)
‣Isa 42:24
7:24
Job 11:7; 37:23
Rom 11:33
7:25
Eccl 1:17
7:26
Prov 5:3-5; 22:14
7:28
1 Kgs 11:3
7:29
Gen 1:27
8:1
Exod 34:29-30
8:2
[c]*melek* (4428)
‣Isa 33:22
8:6
Eccl 3:1, 17, 22
8:7
Eccl 6:12; 9:12
8:8
Deut 20:5-8
Ps 49:7-9
Eccl 8:13
8:9
Eccl 4:1, 16; 5:8
8:10
[d]*hebel* (1892)
‣Eccl 9:9
8:11
Exod 34:6
Ps 86:15
Rom 2:4-5
2 Pet 3:9
8:12
Deut 4:40
Ps 37:11
Prov 1:33
Eccl 7:15
Isa 3:10
8:13
Eccl 6:12; 8:8
Isa 3:11
8:14
Job 21:7
Ps 73:3, 12
Eccl 7:15
Jer 12:1
Mal 3:15
8:15
Eccl 2:24; 3:12-13;
5:18; 9:7

19One wise person is stronger than ten
leading citizens of a town!
20Not a single person on earth is always
good and never sins.
21Don't eavesdrop on others—you may
[b]hear your servant curse you. 22For you know
how often you yourself have cursed others.
23I have always tried my best to let wisdom guide my thoughts and actions. I said
to myself, "I am determined to be wise." But
it didn't work. 24Wisdom is always distant
and difficult to find. 25I searched everywhere, determined to find wisdom and to
understand the reason for things. I was determined to prove to myself that wickedness
is stupid and that foolishness is madness.
26I discovered that a seductive woman is
a trap more bitter than death. Her passion
is a snare, and her soft hands are chains.
Those who are pleasing to God will escape
her, but sinners will be caught in her snare.
27"This is my conclusion," says the Teacher.
"I discovered this after looking at the matter
from every possible angle. 28Though I have
searched repeatedly, I have not found what I
was looking for. Only one out of a thousand
men is virtuous, but not one woman! 29But I
did find this: God created people to be virtuous, but they have each turned to follow
their own downward path."

8 1How wonderful to be wise,
to analyze and interpret things.
Wisdom lights up a person's face,
softening its harshness.

Obedience to the King
2Obey the [c]king since you vowed to God that
you would. 3Don't try to avoid doing your duty,
and don't stand with those who plot evil, for
the king can do whatever he wants. 4His command is backed by great power. No one can
resist or question it. 5Those who obey him
will not be punished. Those who are wise
will find a time and a way to do what is right,
6for there is a time and a way for everything,
even when a person is in trouble.
7Indeed, how can people avoid what they
don't know is going to happen? 8None of us
can hold back our spirit from departing.
None of us has the power to prevent the day
of our death. There is no escaping that obligation, that dark battle. And in the face of
death, wickedness will certainly not rescue
the wicked.

The Wicked and the Righteous
9I have thought deeply about all that goes
on here under the sun, where people have
the power to hurt each other. 10I have seen
wicked people buried with honor. Yet they
were the very ones who frequented the Temple and are now praised in the same city
where they committed their crimes! This,
too, is [d]meaningless. 11When a crime is not
punished quickly, people feel it is safe to do
wrong. 12But even though a person sins a
hundred times and still lives a long time, I
know that those who fear God will be better
off. 13The wicked will not prosper, for they
do not fear God. Their days will never grow
long like the evening shadows.
14And this is not all that is meaningless in
our world. In this life, good people are often
treated as though they were wicked, and
wicked people are often treated as though
they were good. This is so meaningless!
15So I recommend having fun, because
there is nothing better for people in this
world than to eat, drink, and enjoy life. That

7:19 ***One wise person:*** E.g., see 9:14-15; 2 Sam 20:15-22.

7:20 ***Not a single person . . . always good and never sins:*** Cp. 1 Kgs 8:46; Prov 20:9; Rom 3:23.

7:22 It is right to forgive and be gracious toward others' indiscretions or slips of the tongue.

7:23-25 ***it didn't work:*** The Teacher was not able ***to find*** the ***wisdom*** that he sought or ***the reason for things***. Such reasons are hidden in the mind of God (3:11; 8:17).

7:26 ***a seductive woman:*** Literally *a woman;* cp. Prov 5:1-23; 6:20–7:27.

7:28 The NLT adds the phrase ***is virtuous*** (based on 7:29) to give the sense of the verse. Virtue is extremely rare: In his own experience, the Teacher found only a few men, and no women, with that quality.

7:29 After much searching, the Teacher ***did find*** that humanity's ***downward path*** from God's created order (Gen 1:27-28; 2:23-25; 3:1-19) was repeated by Adam and Eve's descendants (cp. Rom 3:10-18, 23).

8:1 ***softening its harshness:*** Anxiety, anger, sorrow, and frustration can harden one's face, but the enjoyment of life and wisdom will lighten it.

8:2 ***since you vowed to God that you would:*** Cp. 5:2-6; 1 Kgs 2:41-43.

8:3-4 Plotting against ***the king*** is futile because he has ***great power*** and can ***do whatever he wants.***

8:6 ***there is a time . . . for everything:*** Those who are wise will be ready when an opportune time appears (see 3:1-8; Eph 5:16).

8:7-8 Since our strength, goodness, and wisdom cannot forestall calamity, turning to ***wickedness*** would ***certainly*** be futile.

8:9-11 In this world, injustice often prevails. The apparent success of the ***wicked*** can be frustrating.

8:10 ***and are now praised:*** As in some Hebrew manuscripts and Greek version; many Hebrew manuscripts read *and are forgotten.*

8:12-13 Injustice is momentary and does not upset God's plans for justice (3:16-17; 12:14). In reality, wickedness does not pay.

8:15 The Teacher's conclusion is familiar (2:24-25; 3:12-13, 22; 5:18-20; 6:9). In spite of tragedies and hard labor, we can enjoy life and be happy. • In Hebrew, the word translated ***having fun*** means finding enjoyment in our daily activities, not pursuing pleasure or entertainment for its own sake.

way they will experience some happiness
along with all the hard work God gives them
under the sun.
16In my search for wisdom and in my observation of people's burdens here on earth,
I discovered that there is ceaseless activity,
day and night. 17I realized that no one can
discover everything God is doing under the
sun. Not even the wisest people discover
everything, no matter what they claim.

Death Comes to All

9 1This, too, I carefully explored: Even
though the actions of godly and wise people are in God's hands, no one knows whether
God will show them favor. 2The same destiny
ultimately awaits everyone, whether righteous or wicked, good or bad, ceremonially
clean or unclean, religious or irreligious.
Good people receive the same treatment as
sinners, and people who make promises to
God are treated like people who don't.
3It seems so tragic that everyone under
the sun suffers the same fate. That is why
people are not more careful to be good. Instead, they choose their own mad course,
for they have no hope. There is nothing
ahead but death anyway. 4There is hope
only for the living. As they say, "It's better to
be a live dog than a dead lion!"
5The living at least know they will die,
but the dead know nothing. They have no
further reward, nor are they remembered.
6Whatever they did in their lifetime—loving,
hating, envying—is all long gone. They no
longer play a part in anything here on earth.
7So go ahead. Eat your food with joy, and
drink your wine with a happy heart, for God
approves of this! 8Wear fine clothes, with a
splash of cologne!
9Live happily with the woman you love
through all the [e]meaningless days of life
that God has given you under the sun. The
wife God gives you is your reward for all your
earthly toil. 10Whatever you do, do well. For
when you go to the grave, there will be no
work or planning or knowledge or wisdom.
11I have observed something else under
the sun. The fastest runner doesn't always
win the race, and the strongest warrior
doesn't always win the battle. The wise
sometimes go hungry, and the skillful are
not necessarily wealthy. And those who are
educated don't always lead successful lives.
It is all decided by chance, by being in the
right place at the right time.
12People can never predict when hard
times might come. Like fish in a net or birds in
a trap, people are caught by sudden tragedy.

Thoughts on Wisdom and Folly

13Here is another bit of wisdom that has impressed me as I have watched the way our
world works. 14There was a small town with
only a few people, and a great king came
with his army and besieged it. 15A poor,
wise man knew how to save the town, and
so it was rescued. But afterward no one
thought to thank him. 16So even though wisdom is better than strength, those who are
wise will be despised if they are poor. What
they say will not be appreciated for long.

17 Better to hear the quiet words of a wise
person
than the shouts of a foolish king.
18 Better to have wisdom than weapons of
war,
but one sinner can destroy much that
is good.

10 1 As dead flies cause even a bottle of
perfume to stink,
so a little foolishness spoils great
wisdom and honor.

2 A wise person chooses the right road;
a fool takes the wrong one.

8:16 Eccl 1:13-14
9:1 Deut 33:3; Eccl 9:6; 10:14
9:2 Job 9:22; Eccl 2:14; 3:19; 6:6; 7:2
9:3 Eccl 1:17; 8:11; 9:2
9:5 Job 14:21; Ps 88:12; Eccl 1:11; 2:16; 8:10; Isa 26:14
9:6 Eccl 2:10; 3:22
9:7 Eccl 2:24
9:8 2 Sam 12:20; Ps 23:5
9:9 Eccl 6:12; 7:15
[e]*hebel* (1892) › Eccl 11:8
9:10 Gen 37:35; Job 21:13; Eccl 9:5; 11:6; Rom 12:11; Col 3:23
9:11 Deut 8:17-18; 1 Sam 6:9; 2 Chr 20:15; Ps 76:5; Amos 2:14-15; Zech 4:6
9:12 Eccl 8:7; Isa 24:18; Hos 9:8; Luke 21:34-35
9:15 2 Sam 20:22; Eccl 2:16; 4:13; 8:10
9:16 Prov 21:22; Eccl 7:12, 19
9:17 Eccl 7:5; 10:12
9:18 Josh 7:1-26; 2 Kgs 21:2-17; Eccl 9:16
10:1 1 Cor 5:6

8:16–9:12 Another generalization from lifelong observation is that death appears to be meaningless. Why do some die and others live longer? God's sovereign decision in this matter is unpredictable (7:13-14).

8:16-17 A person could spend night and day looking for the answers to every question, but the reasons for *everything* will not be apparent. God's justice, for example, will always be mysterious.

9:1 ***No one knows whether God will show them favor:*** There is no guarantee that righteousness will be rewarded in this life (cp. 3:17-22; 8:10-15; 12:14).

9:2 The *destiny* all people share is death. • ***good or bad:*** As in Greek and Syriac versions and Latin Vulgate; Hebrew lacks *or bad.*

9:3 ***That is why people are not . . . good:*** When punishments, including death, are delayed, people continue *their own mad course,* perhaps intensifying their sin and foolishness.

9:4-6 The hope for enjoyment is only as alive as the one who is hoping. In this sense, it is better to be alive (cp. 6:3; 7:1).

9:7-10 Though death is inevitable, enjoying life is beneficial.

9:10 ***to the grave:*** Hebrew *to Sheol.* In the OT, Sheol is the abode of the dead. It is not necessarily associated with punishment.

9:11 ***decided by chance:*** We cannot control the outcome (cp. 7:13).

9:13-18 This poor man's particular wise action was effective. Wisdom is better than power, strength, or weapons (see 4:13; 7:9, 19; 10:4), yet the worthy are not always honored, and even the wise are forgotten (see 2:16; 4:16).

9:18–10:1 ***one sinner can destroy . . . a little foolishness spoils:*** Sin and foolishness can undo a lot of good in a very short time.

10:2-3 These two proverbs show the stupidity of *fools.* They choose wrongly,

10:3 Prov 13:16; 18:2
10:4 1 Sam 25:24-33; Prov 25:15; Eccl 8:3
10:6 Esth 3:1; Prov 28:12; 29:2
10:7 Esth 6:8; Prov 19:10
10:8 Ps 7:15; Prov 26:27; Amos 5:19
10:11 Ps 58:45; Jer 8:17
10:12 Prov 10:14, 32; 22:11
10:14 Prov 15:2; Eccl 5:3; 6:12; 7:14; 8:7
10:16 Isa 3:4-5, 12; 5:11
10:18 Prov 24:30-34
10:19 Judg 9:13; Ps 104:15; Eccl 2:3; 7:12
10:20 Exod 22:28; 2 Kgs 6:12; Luke 12:3; Acts 23:5

3 You can identify fools
just by the way they walk down the
street!

4 If your boss is angry at you, don't quit!
A quiet spirit can overcome even great
mistakes.

The Ironies of Life

5There is another evil I have seen under
the sun. Kings and rulers make a grave
mistake 6when they give great authority to
foolish people and low positions to people
of proven worth. 7I have even seen servants
riding horseback like princes—and princes
walking like servants!

8 When you dig a well,
you might fall in.
When you demolish an old wall,
you could be bitten by a snake.
9 When you work in a quarry,
stones might fall and crush you.
When you chop wood,
there is danger with each stroke of
your ax.
10 Using a dull ax requires great strength,
so sharpen the blade.
That's the value of wisdom;
it helps you succeed.

11 If a snake bites before you charm it,
what's the use of being a snake
charmer?

12 Wise words bring approval,
but fools are destroyed by their own
words.
13 Fools base their thoughts on foolish
assumptions,
so their conclusions will be wicked
madness;
14 they chatter on and on.

No one really knows what is going to
happen;
no one can predict the future.
15 Fools are so exhausted by a little work
that they can't even find their way
home.

16 What sorrow for the land ruled by a
servant,
the land whose leaders feast in the
morning.
17 Happy is the land whose king is a noble
leader
and whose leaders feast at the proper
time
to gain strength for their work, not to
get drunk.

18 Laziness leads to a sagging roof;
idleness leads to a leaky house.

19 A party gives laughter,
wine gives happiness,
and money gives everything!

20 Never make light of the king, even in
your thoughts.
And don't make fun of the powerful,
even in your own bedroom.
For a little bird might deliver your
message
and tell them what you said.

and everything they do shows that they are foolish.

10:4 A ***boss*** can be anyone in authority.

10:5-7 The unjust and destructive delegation of ***authority*** to those incapable of using it wisely is a ***grave mistake***. Favoritism, nepotism, extortion, and bribery can place the most reckless fools in the most powerful positions.

10:7 ***servants riding . . . princes walking:*** Cp. Prov 19:10.

10:8-9 Every activity requires wisdom. Wisdom is evident in the safety precautions taken by those engaged in every profession, yet there is always a degree of risk.

10:10 ***wisdom . . . helps you succeed:*** In all occupations, there are tools that must be kept in good order to be most efficient. Simply sharpening the blade of ***a dull ax*** can be a significant act of wisdom for those whose livelihood depends on it.

10:11 One purpose of charming ***a snake*** is to keep it from biting, but a ***snake charmer*** risks being bitten before it is charmed. Some occupations are so hazardous that the wise do not engage in them at all.

10:12 ***Fools are destroyed by*** such things as foolish promises, getting caught in false testimony, and making the wrong people angry (see 5:6; Prov 17:20; 18:6-7; 19:5, 9).

10:14 ***they chatter on and on:*** Fools are always talking about nothing (see 5:3; 6:11; Prov 10:19; 17:28). • ***no one can predict the future:*** The wise will not waste time in foolish talking nor suffer its consequences (see Jas 4:13-16).

10:15-20 The audience for this speech might have been an assembly of government workers. How should one rule when power and wealth invite a lack of accountability?

10:15 ***Fools*** are so unaccustomed to ***work*** that when they actually try to work, they become ***exhausted***.

10:16-17 ***A servant*** (or ***a child***) lacks leadership skills. • ***feast at the proper time:*** Wise ***leaders*** take their leisure only after the work is finished, not ***in the morning*** before work has even started. Lazy leaders weaken a society or organization.

10:18 Delay in repairing a ***roof*** leads to drooping rafters and eventually to the ruin of the home (see Prov 12:27; 20:4). Corruption in government has a similar effect (10:15-16).

10:19 ***money gives everything:*** It is the way to get what you want or need in this world (cp. 7:11-12).

10:20 It is often a mystery how someone knows what we have said. The best way to control our reputation is to control our ***thoughts***.

The Uncertainties of Life

11

1 Send your grain across the seas,
and in time, profits will flow
back to you.
2 But divide your investments among
many places,
for you do not know what risks might
lie ahead.
3 When clouds are heavy, the rains come
down.
Whether a tree falls north or south, it
stays where it falls.
4 Farmers who wait for perfect weather
never plant.
If they watch every cloud, they never
harvest.

5 Just as you cannot understand the path
of the wind or the mystery of a tiny baby
growing in its mother's womb, so you cannot understand the activity of God, who
does all things.
6 Plant your seed in the morning and
keep busy all afternoon, for you don't know
if profit will come from one activity or another—or maybe both.

Advice for Young and Old

7 Light is sweet; how pleasant to see a new
day dawning.
8 When people live to be very old, let them
rejoice in every day of life. But let them also
remember there will be many dark days.
Everything still to come is [f]meaningless.
9 Young people, it's wonderful to be young!
Enjoy every minute of it. Do everything you
want to do; take it all in. But remember that
you must give an account to God for everything you do. 10 So refuse to worry, and
keep your body healthy. But remember that
youth, with a whole life before you, is meaningless.

12

Don't let the excitement of youth
cause you to forget your [g]Creator.
Honor him in your youth before you grow
old and say, "Life is not pleasant anymore."
2 Remember him before the light of the sun,
moon, and stars is dim to your old eyes, and
rain clouds continually darken your sky. 3 Remember him before your legs—the guards
of your house—start to tremble; and before
your shoulders—the strong men—stoop. Remember him before your teeth—your few
remaining servants—stop grinding; and before your eyes—the women looking through
the windows—see dimly.
4 Remember him before the door to life's
opportunities is closed and the sound of
work fades. Now you rise at the first chirp-
ing of the birds, but then all their sounds
will grow faint.
5 Remember him before you become fearful of falling and worry about danger in the
streets; before your hair turns white like an
almond tree in bloom, and you drag along
without energy like a dying grasshopper,
and the caperberry no longer inspires sexual desire. Remember him before you near
the grave, your [h]everlasting home, when the
mourners will weep at your funeral.
6 Yes, remember your Creator now while
you are young, before the silver cord of life
snaps and the golden bowl is broken. Don't
wait until the water jar is smashed at the
spring and the pulley is broken at the well.
7 For then the dust will return to the earth,
and the [i]spirit will return to God who gave it.

11:1 Isa 32:20; Gal 6:9
11:2 1 Tim 6:18-19
11:5 Ps 139:13-16; John 3:8
11:6 Eccl 9:10
11:7 Eccl 6:5; 7:11
11:8 Eccl 9:7; 12:1; [f]*hebel* (1892) ›Eccl 12:8
11:9 Eccl 3:17; 12:14; Rom 14:10
11:10 2 Cor 7:1; 2 Tim 2:22
12:1 Deut 8:18; 2 Sam 19:35; [g]*bara'* (1254) ›Isa 40:28
12:5 Gen 50:10; Job 17:13; Jer 9:17; [h]*'olam* (5769) ›Isa 45:17
12:7 Gen 3:19; Job 34:14; Ps 104:29; Eccl 3:20-21; Isa 57:16; Zech 12:1; Luke 23:46; Acts 7:59; [i]*ruakh* (7307) ›Isa 4:4

11:1-6 All profitable activity involves risk. We must act as wisely as we can and trust God for the result.

11:1-2 We should invest rather than hoard our resources, even if we cannot control the results.

11:1 ***Send your grain . . . profits will flow back to you:*** Or *Give generously, / for your gifts will return to you later.* Hebrew reads *Throw your bread on the waters, / for after many days you will find it again.*

11:2 ***among many places:*** Literally *among seven or even eight.* The Hebrew idiom implies a large number.

11:3 ***clouds . . . rains:*** Sometimes we can be reasonably certain of what will happen. • ***a tree . . . stays where it falls:*** Our actions sometimes yield irrevocable consequences.

11:5 ***Just as . . . mother's womb:*** Some manuscripts read *Just as you cannot understand how breath comes to a tiny baby in its mother's womb.* • ***The activity of God*** is often unpredictable and mysterious. Our job is to work when we have the opportunity to do so (see Prov 12:11; 24:27).

11:9 ***Young people*** (literally *Young man*) are encouraged to enjoy their youth to the fullest. They should also ***remember*** that they will ***give an account to God*** and should therefore avoid foolish behavior.

11:10 ***Youth,*** like life itself, is beneficial and enjoyable but ultimately ***meaningless,*** a fleeting vapor that passes away without apparent significance or lasting purpose.

12:1-7 This beautiful prose poem, which uses many metaphors in Hebrew, describes the torturous deterioration of aging (in continuation of 11:7-10).

12:1-2 ***Don't . . . forget your Creator:*** Reverence for God can give wisdom (Prov 1:7) and guidance as to what will be beneficial in this life and pleasing to God at the judgment (12:13-14). It is better to ***remember*** God when young, when wisdom can make a real difference in life's results.

12:3 The NLT translates the Hebrew metaphors (***guards . . . strong men . . . servants . . . women***) and also provides an interpretation of these poetic elements (***legs . . . shoulders . . . teeth . . . eyes***).

12:5 The ***caperberry*** was well known in the ancient Near East as an aphrodisiac.

12:6 The ***silver cord*** and the ***golden bowl,*** like human life, are very valuable. • The body is like a common earthen ***jar*** that is fragile and soon broken (cp. Isa 29:16; Jer 19:1, 10-11; 22:28; 2 Cor 4:7).

12:7 ***the dust will return to the earth:*** See Gen 2:7; 3:19. • That ***the spirit will return to God who gave it*** hints at belief in an afterlife (cp. 3:21; see "The Afterlife" at Job 19:25-27, p. 877).

12:8
[j]*hebel* (1892)
‣Isa 49:4

12:9
1 Kgs 4:32
[k]*mashal* (4912)
‣Ezek 24:3

12:13
Deut 4:2; 6:2; 10:12

12:14
Rom 2:16
1 Cor 4:5

8 “[j]Everything is [j]meaningless,” says the
Teacher, “completely [j]meaningless.”

3. EPILOGUE AND CONCLUSION (12:9-14)

9 Keep this in mind: The Teacher was considered wise, and he taught the people
everything he knew. He listened carefully
to many [k]proverbs, studying and classifying
them. 10 The Teacher sought to find just the
right words to express truths clearly.
11 The words of the wise are like cattle
prods—painful but helpful. Their collected
sayings are like a nail-studded stick with
which a shepherd drives the sheep.
12 But, my child, let me give you some further advice: Be careful, for writing books is
endless, and much study wears you out.
13 That’s the whole story. Here now is my
final conclusion: Fear God and obey his commands, for this is everyone’s duty. 14 God
will judge us for everything we do, including
every secret thing, whether good or bad.

12:8 This nearly verbatim repetition of 1:2 sums up the Teacher’s conclusion.

12:9-14 This coda by the editor (see “Author and Recipients” in the Introduction) expresses the editor’s respect for the Teacher, exhorts readers to apply his teaching, and gives the editor’s own conclusion from studying the Teacher (12:13-14).

12:9 Even as king (1:1), the Teacher found time to study wisdom. He collected and arranged proverbs (see also 1 Kgs 4:29-34; Prov 1:1; 10:1; 25:1).

12:10 ***sought to find just the right words to express truths clearly:*** Or *sought to write what was upright and true.*

12:11 ***cattle prods . . . nail-studded stick:*** Painful lessons are sometimes required to direct us into paths that we would rather not take. • ***a shepherd*** (Or *one Shepherd*): This word is possibly an allusion to God as the shepherd of his people (Ps 23:1; Isa 40:11). The sentence might also just be comparing ***the words of the wise*** to the work that any shepherd does in taking care of his flock.

12:12 ***my child:*** Literally *my son.* • A moderate approach to writing and studying wisdom leaves enough time to apply it and enjoy its fruits.

12:13-14 The editor’s ***conclusion*** from studying the Teacher’s work is to ***fear God*** (see 3:14; 5:7; 7:18; 8:12-13), which includes the need to ***obey his commands***, because everything we do will be judged (see 11:9; 2 Cor 5:10; Heb 9:27).

THE BOOK OF SONG OF SONGS

The Song of Songs is romantic poetry at its best. It portrays two passionate lovers who revel in the emotional and physical pleasures of human intimacy. The book was misunderstood in the past as being only an allegory of the relationship between God and the church, but is now accepted as celebrating the profound love between a man and a woman, providing a refreshingly realistic and wholesome treatment of human sexuality without being a how-to manual. The book never mentions God, but it bears witness that the Creator has graciously provided his human creatures with the good gifts of sexuality and intimate love.

SETTING

As a song of mutual human love, the Song of Songs is unique in the Bible. It is composed of the speeches of its characters, primarily an unnamed young man and an unnamed young woman. There is no narrator. Though the subject matter is not unique in the OT, the intense and exclusive focus on it certainly is. Other ancient Near Eastern literature, primarily Egyptian, has similar songs of admiration and intense desire in which the lover's physical attributes are extolled and direct invitations to enjoy them are given.

The Song of Songs is associated with Solomon, David's son and the third king of Israel (see "Authorship," below; see also 1:1). Solomon is also mentioned in a few of the poems, both negatively and positively. The motivation of the author was apparently to celebrate God's good gift of love and sexuality.

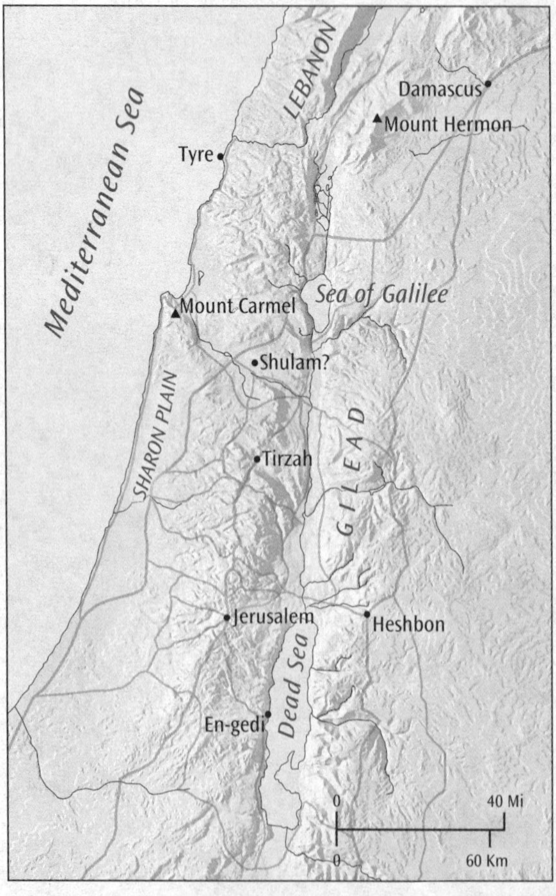

The Setting of the Song of Songs.
The Song of Songs is traditionally understood as having been written in Jerusalem by King Solomon (971–931 BC). Many of the places mentioned in the Song are shown.

DAMASCUS 7:4
EN-GEDI 1:14
GILEAD 4:1; 6:5
HESHBON 7:4
JERUSALEM 1:4-5; 2:7, 14; 3:5, 10-11; 5:1, 8, 16; 6:4, 12; 8:4
LEBANON 3:9; 4:8, 11, 15; 5:15; 7:4
MOUNT CARMEL 7:5
MOUNT HERMON 4:8
PLAIN OF SHARON 2:1
SHULAM 6:13
TIRZAH 6:4

TITLE

The Song is entitled "The Song of Songs" or "The Song of Solomon" because the opening phrase in the original language is literally "The Song of Songs of Solomon." Sometimes it is called "Canticles" after its Latin title. The phrase "Song of Songs" means that we are about to study the song that is more wonderful than any other.

AUTHORSHIP

The superscription (first line of text) calls the work, literally, "The Song of Songs of Solomon." Many take this to mean that Solomon wrote the book in its entirety.

One difficulty with viewing Solomon as the only author is that some of the Hebrew words appear to be foreign loanwords from Aramaic and Persian, which would presumably have come from a later era than that of Solomon, when the Aramaic and Persian cultures were more widespread. However, it is possible that these words were in use during Solomon's era. Furthermore, Solomon was the first truly cosmopolitan king of Israel, so it is not surprising that he would use foreign loanwords.

Another problem with accepting Solomon as the sole author is that he was not a good example of godly love—it was precisely his love for many foreign women that led him away from the Lord (1 Kgs 11:1-13). In fact, the only positive reference to Solomon in the Song is in 3:6-11, while 8:11-12 presents him negatively and 1:5 is neutral. It is possible that Solomon did not compose the entire Song, but only part of it—especially if the Song is viewed as a poetic anthology. In this view, Solomon's authorship of the Song might be similar to his authorship in the book of Proverbs and David's authorship in the Psalms. On the other hand, Solomon might have written of himself in a self-deprecating tone.

INTERPRETING THE SONG

Serious study of the Song of Songs requires a humble, open spirit because of two very significant matters that are usually straightforward in other biblical books but are very obscure here: (1) It is difficult to find a story line in these eight chapters, and (2) if the Song is a story, it is not easy to identify the main characters and their relationships.

Early Interpretation (up to the 1800s). We have no written records of people's understanding of the Song until AD 100, long after the book was written, and even then we have only brief statements. The earliest comments from this time, provided by Rabbi Aqiba, demonstrate Judaism's ambivalence about the message of the Song. The rabbi famously stated: "Whoever sings the Song of Songs with a tremulous voice in a banquet hall and [so] treats it as a sort of ditty has no share in the world to come." Some people clearly understood the Song's imagery as sexual. Aqiba censured this interpretation of the Song, even damning those who held it. In his declaration that "the Song of Songs is the Holy of Holies," Aqiba indicated his understanding of the book as an allegory. This view represents

All the ages are not worth the day on which the Song of Songs was given to Israel; for all the Writings are holy, but the Song of Songs is the Holy of Holies.

RABBI AQIBA, about AD 100

the predominant Jewish interpretation of the Song from Aqiba's time through the mid-1800s. The man and the woman are not seen as a real man and woman, but as representing God and Israel. As an example of this interpretation, the Aramaic *Targum* (interpretive paraphrase) of the Song presents it as the story of God's relationship with Israel from the Exodus to the future reign of the Messiah.

Early Christian interpreters, such as Origen (AD 185–253) and Jerome (AD 347–420) adopted the allegorical interpretation, but identified the man as Jesus Christ and the woman as the individual Christian or the church as a whole. The details of the Song were also made to fit the allegory. For example, Cyril of Alexandria proposed that the sachet of myrrh lying between the woman's breasts (1:13) was a picture of Christ, who spans the OT and the NT.

For many centuries the synagogue and the church continued to accept this interpretation. In Jewish circles it sometimes took a philosophical or mystical turn, as in the work of Levi ben Gershom, a Jewish philosopher of the 1200s who was influenced by Aristotle. He believed that the man represented "active intelligence" and the woman "passive intelligence," and that their union as described in the Song signified mystical ecstasy.

Although details varied, the allegorical approach dominated interpretation until the 1800s. We find it in Catholic writers as well as in great Reformation statements by such interpreters as John Calvin, the Westminster Assembly, and John Wesley.

Recent Interpretations (1800s to the Present). In the 1800s the allegorical interpretation began to lose followers. It became increasingly clear that the only reason to deny the Song's obvious references to sexuality was the deep-seated but unbiblical idea that physical love and spiritual life are polar opposites. This idea came more from Greek philosophy than from the Bible itself. The Bible text itself never suggests that the images of the Song were intended as anything but sensual and romantic.

The 1800s also recovered much from the ancient cultures of Egypt and Mesopotamia. Egypt produced love poetry similar to the Song that could only be understood as human love poetry. There was thus a decisive shift from allegorical interpretation to an understanding of the Song as love poetry. Today there is virtually universal agreement that the Song speaks God's wisdom into an important area of our lives as human beings: It affirms and celebrates God's good gift of love and sexuality in the context of marriage.

No composition of comparable size in world literature has provoked and inspired such volume and variety of comment and interpretation as the biblical Song of Songs.

M. H. POPE
Song of Songs, p. 17

The Song as a Love Story. Many scholars understand these poems as a drama telling a story, either about two lovers or about a woman and two men. If only a couple is present, the characters are usually understood to be King Solomon and a young woman, and the entire poem is their conversation with each other. If it is a triangle, there is a second man whom the woman loves. In this case, Solomon is trying to force the woman to leave her true lover and enter his harem, but she remains faithful and true to her lover.

The main drawbacks of the dramatic perspective are: (1) There is no narrator to guide the reading of the story, and (2) there are many different possible stories, and every interpreter seems to see a different story.

The Song as a Two-Character Drama. Some interpreters understand the Song as a drama of King Solomon's love affair with a woman. According to this view, the entire poem is a conversation between Solomon and the woman he loves more than all of the other queens and concubines in his possession. The storyline could then be something like the following:[1]

Act One: The Lovers' Mutual Affection (1:2–2:7)
Act Two: Mutual Seeking and Finding (2:8–3:5)
Act Three: The Marriage (3:6–5:1)
Act Four: Love Disdained but Won Again (5:2–6:9)
Act Five: The Attractive Yet Humble Princess (6:10–8:4)
Act Six: Love in the Woman's Native Home (8:5-14)

If there was a favored woman in Solomon's life, the Scriptures suggest that she was Pharaoh's daughter, whom he married very early (1 Kgs 3:1; 7:8; 9:24; 11:1), not the working woman from the king's flocks and vineyards who is pictured here. Furthermore, this song of true love is not very credible if the woman was one of the scores of Solomon's women who are clearly mentioned in 6:8. If this romance between Solomon and the woman was of such deep sincerity, why did Solomon add another 860 women to his harem afterwards?

The Song as a Three-Character Drama. Noting the difficulties with the two-character storyline, several recent scholars have become convinced that the Song actually describes a three-character drama. This would suggest a more complicated plot in which the woman actually loves a shepherd, not the king. The unfortunate woman finds herself in Solomon's harem as a concubine, probably because she is unable to pay a debt of one thousand pieces of silver, which she owes as caretaker of the king's vineyards (8:11-12). She is unable to pay because her angry brothers have forced her first to take care of vineyards other than her own (1:6). So even though she is in the very close and potentially intimate presence of the king in the city palace (1:12), her passionate thoughts are set intently on her love for a common shepherd in the countryside (1:7). This fervent affection drives her to escape with her true love into the country where they declare their mutual love to one another in marriage. Three separations of the couple are recounted in the song, proving that the agony of isolation from each other is just as intense as their ecstasy when together. After the woman escapes and lives with her shepherd husband, she is able to hire caretakers to harvest her crop and pay off the debt to Solomon. Now she and her beloved are forever free to continue living and loving together in the countryside (8:12-14).

From this perspective, the Song could be outlined as follows:

1. *Superscription* (1:1)
2. *The Woman's Predicament with Solomon* (1:2-14)
   - *Her Desire to Be Rescued* (1:2-4)
   - *Her Searching Heart* (1:5-11)
   - *Her Choice: King or Shepherd?* (1:12-14)
3. *Their Prenuptial Relationship* (1:15–3:5)
   - *Mutual Admiration* (1:15–2:7)
   - *An Excursion in the Country* (2:8-15)
   - *Separated and Searching Again* (2:16–3:5)

Know, my brother, that you will find great differences in interpretation of the Song of Songs. In truth they differ because the Song of Songs resembles locks to which the keys have been lost.

RABBI SAADIA, AD 882–942

[1] See F. Delitzsch, *The Song of Songs.*

4. *Their Wedding and Consummation* (3:6–5:1)
    - *Solomon Graces Their Wedding* (3:6-11)
    - *The Consummation* (4:1–5:1)
5. *Her Nightmare: Separation and Searching* (5:2–6:3)
    - *The Trauma of Interrupted Love* (5:2-6a)
    - *Another Search for Her Lover* (5:6b-16)
    - *Their Love No Longer Interrupted* (6:1-3)
6. *Their Stimulating Marriage* (6:4–8:10)
    - *She Is Her Husband's Delight* (6:4–7:9)
    - *He Gives His Wife Pleasure* (7:10–8:7)
    - *Protective Brothers* (8:8-10)
7. *Free from Debt, Free to Love* (8:11-14)

The Song as an Anthology of Love Poetry. Some scholars have concluded that approaching the Song as a drama would impose a story on the book that is not really there. These interpreters believe that the Song of Songs is an anthology of love poems that do not tell a story, but rather evoke a mood. The poems use imagery to express the poets' understanding of human sexuality. In this way, the Song is similar to the book of Psalms, except that all the poems have to do with love between a man and a woman.

From this perspective, the Song of Songs is composed of some twenty love poems that are bound together by consistency of characters, refrains, repeated images, and other poetic binding devices:

Superscription (1:1)
1. *The Woman's Pursuit* (1:2-4)
2. *Dark But Beautiful* (1:5-6)
3. *An Invitation to a Tryst* (1:7-11)
4. *Intimate Fragrances* (1:12-14)
5. *Outdoor Love* (1:15-17)
6. *Flowers and Trees* (2:1-7)
7. *Spring, the Time for Love* (2:8-17)
8. *Seeking and (Not) Finding* (3:1-5)
9. *A Royal Wedding Procession* (3:6-11)
10. *The Man's Sensuous Description of the Woman* (4:1–5:1)
11. *To Search and (Not) Find, Once Again* (5:2–6:3)
12. *Like an Army with Banners* (6:4-10)
13. *Surprise in the Walnut Grove* (6:11-12)
14. *The Dance of the Woman of Shulam* (6:13–7:9)
15. *Back to the Garden* (7:10-13)
16. *Yearning for Love* (8:1-4)
17. *Like a Seal* (8:5-7)
18. *Protecting the Sister* (8:8-10)
19. *Who Owns the Vineyard?* (8:11-12)
20. *Lingering Desire* (8:13-14)

The main criticism of viewing the Song as merely a poetic anthology is that the Song exhibits a greater unity and development than is usual for such a collection. There is repetition and development of poetic themes, and there seems to be growth in the couple's relationship. Those who view the Song as a story or drama would argue that the

anthology view fails to take this into account. Even if the Song is not a story per se, it certainly seems to have a structure and coherence that transcends the individual stanzas of poetry. However, those who view it as an anthology rather than a story generally do take into account the unity and development in the Song. They view the Song like a concerto or symphony in which themes repeat and build, without actually providing a narrative or plot.

Conclusion. All of the interpretive approaches have their challenges. The approach in these study notes is (1) to point out different elements in the book that might contribute to a storyline or to our understanding of its structure as an anthology, and (2) to discuss the possible meaning of individual scenes and images.

MARRIAGE IN THE SONG

The man and woman in the Song of Songs speak in the most romantic terms, describing sensuous longings and alluding to an intimate physical relationship. However, they are never explicitly described as married, leading some readers to suggest that the Song is an example of unmarried love in the Bible. Such a reading ignores obvious allusions to the true marriage relationship between the man and the woman. The language of some of the passages clearly indicates that the couple is married. For example, the man occasionally refers to the woman as his "bride" (e.g., 4:8-12).

Even more importantly, viewing the couple as unmarried though sexually intimate does not take into account the context of the Song in the whole of Scripture, including the law found in the Pentateuch. In the context of ancient Israel, it is impossible to believe that this couple is not married when engaged in such an intimate relationship. A study of the books of OT history (Gen 39), law (Exod 20:14), and other wisdom literature (Prov 5–7) makes it clear that sexual relations were only tolerated within the legal commitment of marriage. The couple, accordingly, should be understood as being married, at least in those passages where they are found in intimate embrace.

Though the Song itself does not address it, other passages of Scripture explain how marriage is a picture of God's relationship with his people (see Jer 2:1-2; Hos 1–3; Eph 5:21-33; Rev 19:6-8).

MEANING AND MESSAGE

Many people have questioned whether the Song of Songs, with its overtly sensual imagery, belongs in Holy Scripture, but this poem is a wonderful celebration of one of God's good and holy gifts. The Bible does not envision human beings as intangible souls temporarily encased in a body; rather, body and soul are two terms that emphasize different aspects of a single entity. The body is important, and sexuality is good and precious when enjoyed within marriage.

Human Intimacy. Intense love and the appropriateness of voicing that love in words of physical attraction and fulfillment is the central theme of the song. Yet it is clear that the lovers' relationship is not only physical. They are friends and desire to be with each other for more than sexual reasons. Their total relationship includes their sensual enjoyment of each other.

God's action of creating us as sexual beings was no accident or compromise. . . . It should not be considered obscene that at least one book of the Bible be dedicated to the celebration of one of the central realities of our creaturehood.

G. LLOYD CARR
The Song of Solomon

FURTHER READING

G. LLOYD CARR
The Song of Solomon (1984)

DUANE GARRETT AND PAUL R. HOUSE
Song of Songs/Lamentations (2004)

TREMPER LONGMAN III
Song of Songs (2001)
Song of Songs in *Cornerstone Biblical Commentary*, vol. 6 (2006)

I. PROVAN
Ecclesiastes/Song of Songs (2001)

Sexual intimacy has always been a critical issue for individuals and for the community. Numerous biblical passages recount the beauty and dangers of sex, as well as the practical implications of its appropriate and inappropriate expressions. As human love poetry, the Song plays a crucial role in the Bible. Love and its physical expression are major aspects of the human experience, and God has spoken through the Song to encourage us and warn us about the power of sexuality in our lives. Here we have wonderful wisdom from God describing the beauty of a wholesome sexual relationship between a woman and a man. According to the Song, marital love should be mutual, exclusive, complete, and beautiful. The book encourages intimate, passionate love between a man and a woman who have committed themselves to each other.

1 This is Solomon's song of songs, more wonderful than any other.

Young Woman

2 Kiss me and kiss me again,
for your [a]love is sweeter than wine.
3 How fragrant your cologne;
your name is like its spreading fragrance.
No wonder all the young women love you!
4 Take me with you; come, let's run!
The king has brought me into his bedroom.

Young Women of Jerusalem

How happy we are for you, O king.
We praise your [b]love even more than wine.

1:1 1 Kgs 4:32
1:2 Song 1:4; 4:10
[a]*dod* (1730) ›Song 1:4
1:3 Eccl 7:1; Song 4:10; John 12:3
1:4 Ps 45:14-15
[b]*dod* (1730) ›Song 4:10

1:1 This verse is the source of the English title of the book. Formally, it is a superscription that functions as the title page of the book, providing the genre (song) and a connection with the probable author of some or all of the book (see Song of Songs Introduction, "Title," p. 1085). The NLT rightly understands *song of songs* as a Hebrew superlative, so this song is the highest, best, or most sublime, which probably means that it is ***more wonderful than any other*** of Solomon's 1,005 songs (see 1 Kgs 4:32).

1:2-14 The headings identifying the speakers are not in the original text, though the Hebrew usually gives clues by means of the gender of the person speaking. • The Song begins with the woman's expression of desire for intimate union with the man she loves. In the Song, the woman is frequently the one who initiates relationship. The members of the chorus (identified in the NLT as "Young Women of Jerusalem") affirm her choice of this man. • According to the three-character dramatic interpretation, the Song opens by explaining the woman's predicament. The king is about to take her into his palace, but her true passions lie with her shepherd lover. The woman hopes that her lover will rescue her from the king's presence (1:4).

1:2 ***Kiss me and kiss me again:*** The woman longs for the touch and taste of kisses from her true love. From the very start we find that the young woman and the man share a strong attraction. Their relationship is one of mutual respect and loving concern. • Love is a sensual experience in the Song. The taste of ***love is sweeter than wine,*** a rich and sensuous liquid; love, like wine, also leaves its partaker slightly light-headed.

1:3 The ***fragrance*** of the man's ***cologne*** suggests sweet smells of love, indicating that the woman wants to get physically closer to him. • ***all the young women love you:*** The young man's allure is not only physical. He has an excellent reputation—the chorus of women expresses their respect and adoration for him in 1:4. By highlighting the attention he receives from other women, the woman makes it clear that her love is not blind, and that she feels fortunate to be the one whose love the man returns.

1:4 ***Take me with you:*** The two lovers are very active throughout the Song, traveling through the hills, to the city, and out to the country. This time the woman invites the man to take her away with him, and urgently expresses her desire (***let's run!***). According to the three-character dramatic view, they may be running to escape the king, who has brought the young woman into his palace. • ***The king has brought me into his bedroom*** (literally *into his rooms*): A common interpretation of this clause is that the woman is anticipating an intimate relationship with King Solomon. However, though a literal Hebrew translation indicates that she has been brought into Solomon's *rooms,* it does not specify which rooms she was taken into. Nor does the Hebrew imply that it was her personal desire. • The text changes here from the second person ("you") to the third person ("his"), which might indicate that two different men are involved—one being spoken to, the other being spoken about. In that case, it is possible that the woman desires to run because she does not want to be the king's concubine. • If the Song is a collection of love songs without a narrative thread, it is not problematic for the lover to be identified here as ***the king*** and later as a shepherd (e.g., 1:7): (1) The language may or may not be intended literally; (2) these titles, consistent with other ancient Middle Eastern love poetry, may reflect the woman's view of her lover at a particular time (e.g., by indicating that he is a king in her eyes); or (3) different poems may refer to different couples. • The woman frequently addresses the young women of Jerusalem (e.g., 2:7; 3:5). They are portrayed as close, trusted friends who are fond of the woman and responsive to her requests. She often confides in them about her lover, and they commend the couple from their outside perspective (e.g., 5:1, 9). • ***O king*** is not in the Hebrew; its addition reflects the view that the young man is the king rather than a shepherd.

1:5
Song 2:7, 14; 4:3; 5:8; 6:4

1:6
Ps 69:8
Song 8:11

1:7
Song 2:16; 3:1-4; 8:13

1:8
Song 5:9; 6:1

1:9
2 Chr 1:16-17

1:10
Gen 24:53
Song 5:13

1:12
Song 4:13-14
Mark 14:3

1:13
Ps 45:8
John 19:39

1:14
1 Sam 23:29
Song 4:13

1:15
Song 1:16; 2:10, 13; 4:1

Young Woman
How right they are to adore you.

5 I am dark but beautiful,
O women of Jerusalem—
dark as the tents of Kedar,
dark as the curtains of Solomon's tents.
6 Don't stare at me because I am dark—
the sun has darkened my skin.
My brothers were angry with me;
they forced me to care for their vineyards,
so I couldn't care for myself—my own vineyard.

7 Tell me, my love, where are you leading your flock today?
Where will you rest your sheep at noon?
For why should I wander like a prostitute
among your friends and their flocks?

Young Man
8 If you don't know, O most beautiful woman,
follow the trail of my flock,
and graze your young goats by the shepherds' tents.
9 You are as exciting, my darling,
as a mare among Pharaoh's stallions.
10 How lovely are your cheeks;
your earrings set them afire!
How lovely is your neck,
enhanced by a string of jewels.
11 We will make for you earrings of gold
and beads of silver.

Young Woman
12 The king is lying on his couch,
enchanted by the fragrance of my perfume.
13 My lover is like a sachet of myrrh
lying between my breasts.
14 He is like a bouquet of sweet henna blossoms
from the vineyards of En-gedi.

Young Man
15 How beautiful you are, my darling,
how beautiful!
Your eyes are like doves.

1:5-11 If the Song is a three-character drama and the shepherd is her lover, the couple was apart while she was in the king's palace, and in this passage she wants to be sure of where to find him when she leaves there. On two occasions, she is frantic about losing him again (3:1-4; 5:2-8). At other times, her concern is more subtle (2:14).

1:5-6 The woman's ***dark*** skin color has nothing to do with her race; her complexion has been ***darkened*** by ***the sun***. Even so, she retains her self-respect and asserts her beauty. She is wholesome-looking from tending ***vineyards*** and goats (see also 1:8). • Solomon had caretakers of his fields, vineyards, herds, and flocks; the herders lived in ***dark*** goats'-hair ***tents***.

1:6 ***my own vineyard:*** The NLT interprets ***vineyard*** as a metaphor for the woman's own body (cp. 2:15; 7:12). In ancient Near Eastern societies, brothers protected sisters from premature intimate relationships with men. The woman's protest reflects her belief that she is ready for love (see also 8:8-12, the only other mention of the brothers). • The dramatic view takes ***vineyard*** literally: The brothers' abuse had resulted in the woman's inability to take care of the vineyards for which she was personally responsible. She found herself in Solomon's harem because she had not been able to pay Solomon the money she owed him (8:11, 12).

1:7-8 ***leading your flock:*** In the dramatic view, the woman's lover and his friends are literal shepherds, not a line of work or the company that one would associate with King Solomon at any time in his life. • ***like a prostitute*** (literally *like a veiled woman*): Prostitutes wore veils to hide their identities (Gen 38:14-16). Since the woman has been claimed by Solomon as a concubine, she has reason to shroud herself and avoid being obvious. She wants to avoid having to ask everyone around her for the location of someone she loves (cp. 3:3; 5:6-7). She wants to find him privately during the resting period at ***noon*** so they can enjoy the time together.

1:8 The man's first words in this poem lovingly pacify the woman's anxiety by giving directions to where she should meet him. • The man desires to be with her and tells her to come under the guise of a goatherd, following the ***trail of*** his ***flock***.

1:9 The shepherd frequently calls the woman ***darling*** (literally *companion*) to show his respect for her as a partner and friend as well as a lover (1:15; 2:2, 10, 13; 4:1, 7; 5:2; 6:4). • In the ancient Near East, a charge of horsemen on ***stallions*** was sometimes diverted by letting loose a ***mare*** in heat. This so distracted the attacking horses that they broke the charge. Similarly, the woman's beauty drives other men to distraction.

1:10-11 The woman's beauty is enhanced by her jewelry. This beauty deserves to be even further ornamented, so the man says that even more jewelry will be provided for her (cp. Matt 13:12).

1:12-14 In the dramatic view, it appears that although the woman is physically in the king's palace (1:4, 12), her heart is with her shepherd lover (1:13-14). • In the anthology view, this is a short poem on intimate fragrances.

1:12 The meaning of the word translated ***couch*** is uncertain, and the word ***lying*** is not found in the Hebrew, so the king and the woman could be lying together on a couch or bed, or simply sitting at a table in one of the palace rooms. • The interpretation that sees the Song as a collection of love songs is not concerned with whether the man is literally a king (see note on 1:4).

1:13 ***Myrrh*** is extracted from the branches of a fragrant shrub that did not grow in Israel, but was imported from Arabia and India at extravagant cost. The ***sachet*** is a little packet of sweet-smelling myrrh. The woman's desire for intimacy is expressed by comparing her ***lover*** to the sachet ***lying between*** her ***breasts***. • According to the three-character dramatic view, the woman is with the king in one of his palace rooms, but the fragrance of myrrh between her breasts fondly reminds her of her shepherd lover who is truly there, closer to her heart than the king.

1:14 The woman thirsts for the sincere love of her man the way a traveler would thirst for the water of ***En-gedi***, an oasis in the wilderness west of the Dead Sea. • ***Henna*** is an aromatic shrub from the region around En-gedi; its blossoms were used for red hair dye.

1:15–2:7 The couple exchange adoring descriptions of each other that honor her incomparable beauty and praise his stalwart protection and provision for her.

1:15 The comparison of the woman's ***eyes*** with ***doves*** (see also 4:1; 5:12) is not clear. The metaphor may be commenting on their color or on a softness of expression.

Young Woman

16 You are so handsome, my love,
pleasing beyond words!
The soft grass is our bed;
17 fragrant cedar branches are the
beams of our house,
and pleasant smelling firs are the
rafters.

Young Woman

2 1 I am the spring crocus blooming on
the Sharon Plain,
the lily of the valley.

Young Man

2 Like a lily among thistles
is my darling among young women.

Young Woman

3 Like the finest apple tree in the
orchard
is my lover among other young men.
I sit in his delightful shade
and taste his delicious fruit.
4 He escorts me to the banquet hall;
it's obvious how much he loves me.
5 Strengthen me with raisin cakes,
refresh me with apples,
for I am weak with love.
6 His left arm is under my head,
and his right arm embraces me.

7 Promise me, O women of Jerusalem,
by the gazelles and wild deer,
not to awaken love until the time is
right.

8 Ah, I hear my lover coming!
He is leaping over the mountains,
bounding over the hills.
9 My lover is like a swift gazelle
or a young stag.
Look, there he is behind the wall,
looking through the window,
peering into the room.

10 My lover said to me,
"Rise up, my darling!
Come away with me, my fair one!
11 Look, the winter is past,
and the rains are over and gone.
12 The flowers are springing up,
the season of singing birds has come,
and the cooing of turtledoves fills
the air.
13 The fig trees are forming young fruit,
and the fragrant grapevines are
blossoming.

1:17 1 Kgs 6:9-10; 2 Chr 3:5; Jer 22:14; Ezek 41:16
2:1 Isa 33:9; 35:2; Hos 14:5
2:3 Song 8:5
2:4 Ps 63:2-5; Song 1:4
2:5 Song 5:8; 7:8
2:6 Prov 4:8; Song 8:3
2:7 Gen 49:21; Song 3:5; 5:8; 8:14; Hab 3:19
2:8 Song 2:17; Isa 52:7
2:9 Judg 5:28; Prov 6:5; Song 2:17; 3:5; 8:14
2:12 Gen 15:9; Ps 74:19
2:13 Matt 24:32

1:16-17 ***grass is our bed . . . branches are the beams . . . firs are the rafters:*** The lovers imagine that their luxurious surroundings of grass and overhanging trees are their house. She does not need the royal, palatial surroundings of a king since these God-created natural surroundings are more than enough for her and her true lover. • In a number of the poems the countryside is the place of happy intimacy. The man and the woman make their bed in the great outdoors and enjoy each other's company.

2:1-7 In this short poem, the man and the woman exchange compliments. Using metaphors of flowers and trees, they describe the nature of their loving relationship, emphasizing his role as protector and provider. • The poem ends (2:6) with the man and the woman in an intimate embrace.

2:1-2 ***I am the spring crocus blooming on the Sharon Plain:*** Traditionally rendered *I am the rose of Sharon;* Sharon Plain is a region in the coastal plain of Palestine. • ***the lily of the valley:*** The Hebrew shows the woman's modesty and humility, as she claims to be but one flower among many in Sharon and in the expansive valleys of Israel. • The man affirms her comparison to a lily, but says that her beauty is far from common; she is ***a lily among thistles.*** • ***my darling*** (literally *my companion*): They are in love, and they are also friends.

2:3 As she is the finest of small, beautiful flowers, he is like a larger and stronger ***apple tree.*** An apple tree is a sensuous image in the ancient Near East because of its delicious ***fruit*** and pleasant fragrance. In the intense heat of the Middle Eastern climate, a tree's ***shade*** is more than refreshing; it can be life-saving (cp. Jon 4:6; Matt 13:32).

2:4 ***He escorts me to the banquet hall:*** Dropping the image of the apple tree, the woman now speaks of the man as her provider at a feast. • ***it's obvious how much he loves me:*** Literally *His banner over me is "Love."* He likes to tell others how much he loves her.

2:5-6 The woman's love is intense, his love overwhelming. • If the Song is an anthology, the couple can be seen as married, and lovemaking is seen as so physically exhausting that she grows faint and calls for the sustenance of ***raisin cakes*** and ***apples.*** These foods were considered aphrodisiacs in the ancient Near East. • ***Strengthen me:*** She now depends on him to revive her with the fruit of the earlier image—he is the apple tree, so he can provide apples for her renewed strength. • ***His left arm is under my head:*** He tenderly supports her with his embrace as they lie together (see also 8:3).

2:7 ***Promise me . . . by the gazelles and wild deer:*** This plea is obviously important to the Song; it is repeated in 3:5 and 8:4, and a promise is requested. When a promise was made, witnesses were needed, and the wild animals were the only witnesses present. These graceful animals suggest a romantic pastoral setting. • ***not to awaken love until the time is right:*** Or *not to awaken love until it is ready.* As in 8:8-9, virginity is praised. The woman warns the women of Jerusalem to be cautious and not to hurry love.

2:8-17 In this poem, the woman anticipates the arrival of her lover. She describes the passing of winter and the coming of spring, a time of floral fragrance and new beginnings. She and her lover are in their country garden, a place of intimacy, though even here there is a hint of threat (2:15).

2:8-10 The man ardently desires to be in the woman's presence. He finally arrives at his lover's home and takes her into the romantic countryside during the new, budding spring. • The woman compares the man to a ***gazelle,*** a fast, sleek animal that easily overcomes obstacles to reach its destination.

2:10-13 In the Middle East, winter is the rainy season of clouds, gloom, and cold. When ***winter is past, and the rains are over and gone,*** the stimulating and invigorating sights, sounds, and smells of spring energize romantic feelings. • ***the season of singing birds:*** Or *the season of pruning vines.*

2:14 Song 5:2; 6:9; Jer 48:28
2:15 Judg 15:4-5; Song 2:13
2:16 Song 4:5; 6:2-3; 7:10
2:17 Song 2:8-9; 4:6
3:1 Song 1:7; 5:6
3:2 Jer 5:1
3:3 Song 5:7
3:4 Song 8:2
3:5 //Song 2:7
3:6 Exod 13:21-22; Song 1:13; 4:12-14; Rev 5:8; 18:13

Rise up, my darling!
Come away with me, my fair one!"

Young Man

14 My dove is hiding behind the rocks,
behind an outcrop on the cliff.
Let me see your face;
let me hear your voice.
For your voice is pleasant,
and your face is lovely.

Young Women of Jerusalem

15 Catch all the foxes,
those little foxes,
before they ruin the vineyard of love,
for the grapevines are
blossoming!

Young Woman

16 My lover is mine, and I am his.
He browses among the lilies.
17 Before the dawn breezes blow
and the night shadows flee,
return to me, my love, like a gazelle
or a young stag on the rugged
mountains.

Young Woman

3 1 One night as I lay in bed, I yearned
for my lover.
I yearned for him, but he did not
come.
2 So I said to myself, "I will get up and
roam the city,
searching in all its streets and
squares.
I will search for the one I love."
So I searched everywhere but did not
find him.
3 The watchmen stopped me as they made
their rounds,
and I asked, "Have you seen the one
I love?"
4 Then scarcely had I left them
when I found my love!
I caught and held him tightly,
then I brought him to my mother's
house,
into my mother's bed, where I had
been conceived.
5 Promise me, O women of Jerusalem,
by the gazelles and wild deer,
not to awaken love until the time is
right.

Young Women of Jerusalem

6 Who is this sweeping in from the
wilderness
like a cloud of smoke?
Who is it, fragrant with myrrh and
frankincense
and every kind of spice?

2:14 In the dramatic view, the couple is playing a game of hide-and-seek in which she is teasing him; he resorts to simply pleading for her to appear, for even playful separation from her is too frustrating for him. • *The rocks* are a metaphor for separation that the man wants to overcome to be with her.

2:15 The *foxes* may represent threats to the relationship. These threats are not identified; they could be the normal ups and downs of love, rival suitors, or anything else that might keep the couple from enjoying one another. • In the dramatic view, the woman's responsibilities as a vinedresser are still in mind. She is probably instructing the vinedressers who cared for her *vineyard* and received two hundred pieces of silver from her in 8:12. The alarm about catching the foxes may be understood in terms of the woman's personal interest in maintaining the value of her vineyards; eventually, she needs to pay Solomon the lease. If the foxes' hole-digging ruins the *grapevines,* she will be further in debt.

2:16–3:5 In the dramatic view, the woman has already been separated from her lover and is horrified by the notion that she will not see him soon. One night, her worries drive her from bed to search frantically for him; she finds him and takes him to see her mother.

2:16-17 ***He browses . . . like a gazelle:*** The woman has so identified her lover with the strength and speed of a gazelle that she portrays his delay as grazing in the country. • Alternatively, the lover, in the guise of a gazelle, grazes ***among the lilies*** that possibly represent the woman, suggesting the intimate association of the couple. The woman is often likened to a garden (see also 4:12, 15-16; 5:1; 6:2). • ***return to me:*** Her longing to see him in the evening is intensifying by the hour. • ***on the rugged mountains:*** Or *on the hills of Bether.*

3:2 The poem is partly about a lover's being willing and able to overcome all obstacles in order to be with the beloved. • Since the women of Jerusalem are mentioned frequently (3:5), ***the city*** is probably Jerusalem. ***Searching in all its streets and squares*** was an ambitious effort. • The king of Israel would probably not be outside in the city at night, and if he had his sixty-man entourage with him (3:7-8), she would find him easily. Rather, the woman appears to be looking for a common man in common places.

3:3 ***The watchmen*** of ancient towns or cities were roughly equivalent to police. Guardians of social custom and law, they were posted on the city walls to look out for attack and to assure that any traffic in or out of the city was not threatening. • The woman may have been ***stopped*** because she was not a resident of the city and was not recognized. It was not considered appropriate for a woman to be out alone at night. The scene accentuates the strong desire that the woman must have felt toward the man as she ignored social conventions and safety considerations.

3:5 ***not to awaken love until the time is right:*** Or *not to awaken love until it is ready.* See note on 2:7.

3:6-11 According to the three-character dramatic interpretation, Solomon's humility and generosity show in his attending this wedding of a woman who preferred a common shepherd's love over his. With Solomon in attendance, this ordinary wedding becomes a magnificent ceremony. • If the Song is an anthology, this poem describes what appears to be Solomon's wedding procession. People are amazed by the opulence of his carriage and the power represented by his entourage. All of this reflects on the significance of marriage in the same way that expensive and beautiful wedding dresses and tuxedos do in modern marriages.

7 Look, it is Solomon's carriage,
surrounded by sixty heroic men,
the best of Israel's soldiers.
8 They are all skilled swordsmen,
experienced warriors.
Each wears a sword on his thigh,
ready to defend the king against an attack in the night.
9 King Solomon's carriage is built
of wood imported from Lebanon.
10 Its posts are silver,
its canopy gold;
its cushions are purple.
It was decorated with love
by the young women of Jerusalem.

Young Woman

11 Come out to see King Solomon,
young women of Jerusalem.
He wears the crown his mother gave him
on his wedding day,
his most joyous day.

Young Man

4 1 You are beautiful, my darling,
beautiful beyond words.
Your eyes are like doves
behind your veil.
Your hair falls in waves,
like a flock of goats winding down the slopes of Gilead.
2 Your teeth are as white as sheep,
recently shorn and freshly washed.
Your smile is flawless,
each tooth matched with its twin.
3 Your lips are like scarlet ribbon;
your mouth is inviting.
Your cheeks are like rosy pomegranates
behind your veil.
4 Your neck is as beautiful as the tower of David,
jeweled with the shields of a thousand heroes.
5 Your breasts are like two fawns,
twin fawns of a gazelle grazing
among the lilies.
6 Before the dawn breezes blow
and the night shadows flee,
I will hurry to the mountain of myrrh
and to the hill of frankincense.
7 You are altogether beautiful, my darling,
beautiful in every way.

8 Come with me from Lebanon, my bride,
come with me from Lebanon.
Come down from Mount Amana,
from the peaks of Senir and Hermon,
where the lions have their dens
and leopards live among the hills.

9 You have captured my heart,
my treasure, my bride.
You hold it hostage with one glance of your eyes,
with a single jewel of your necklace.
10 Your ᶜlove delights me,
my treasure, my bride.
Your ᶜlove is better than wine,
your perfume more fragrant than spices.

3:8 Ps 45:3; 91:5; Jer 50:9
3:11 Isa 62:5
4:1 Song 1:15; 5:12; 6:5, 7
4:3 Song 5:13, 16; 6:7
4:4 Neh 3:19; Ps 48:3, 12; Song 7:4
4:5 Song 2:16; 6:2-3; 7:3
4:6 Song 2:17; 4:14
4:8 Deut 3:9; 1 Kgs 4:33; 1 Chr 5:23; Song 5:1; Isa 62:5
4:9 Song 5:1; Ezek 16:11
4:10 ᶜ*dod* (1730) ‣Song 4:16

3:9-10 The materials out of which *King Solomon's carriage* was made befit his wealth and power, including the same expensive Lebanese wood that was used in building the Temple (1 Kgs 5:5-6). • *decorated with love by the young women of Jerusalem:* Beyond all his splendor, Solomon was admired and served with love, even by his servants.

3:11 This is the only explicit mention of a *wedding* in the Song. The woman is called a "bride" in 4:8-12; 5:1. • *Jerusalem:* Hebrew *Zion;* see "Zion" at Isa 60:1-22, p. 1195.

4:1–5:1 The consummation of the marriage is now expressed. • This poem is the first "descriptive poem" in the book (see also 5:10-16; 6:4-6; 7:2-8). Scholars commonly refer to these poems by the Arabic term *wasf* ("description"); these poems are similar in form to songs sung at modern Arabic weddings. These sensuous poems are preludes to sexual intimacy. In their descriptions of physical beauty, they often move—as this one does—from the head downward.

4:1 *my darling* (see note on 1:9): The man is about to consummate his love with the one who is his friend as well as lover (see also 4:7). • *like a flock of goats winding down the slopes of Gilead:* Middle Eastern goats are very dark, if not black. The woman's hair flows over and down her lighter veil.

4:2 *Your smile is flawless, each tooth matched with its twin:* Literally *Not one is missing; each has a twin.* Her teeth are matched on both sides, with none missing. In an age when dental care was not what it is today, a woman with all her teeth was quite a prize!

4:3 *Pomegranates* have a *rosy* appearance and are one of the most lush of Middle Eastern fruits.

4:4 A slender *neck* held high is a sign of confidence and dignity as well as beauty. The *tower of David* is not mentioned elsewhere in Scripture.

4:5 *Your breasts are like two fawns . . . grazing among the lilies:* The comparison can be seen in terms of physical softness, firmness, beauty, and roundness.

4:6 After mention of the breasts in the previous verse, the man's exclamation that he wants to hurry to the *mountain of myrrh* and *hill of frankincense* is easily understood as his desire to be intimately close to this beautiful woman.

4:8 *Come down:* Or *Look down.* • *Mount Amana, Senir,* and *Hermon* are the three northernmost peaks in Israel and the highest point on the border with *Lebanon.* They represent the height of the couple's ecstasy, from which they must at times descend.

4:9 *my treasure* (literally *my sister;* also in 4:10, 12): The man calls the woman his *sister* to emphasize their relationship as loving companions and his role as her protector (see note on 8:8). This sounds strange to modern ears, but it does not suggest an incestuous relationship. Ancient Near Eastern love poetry often uses the language of brother and sister to refer to two people in love.

4:10-11 *wine . . . nectar . . . honey . . . milk:* The woman is compared with much that is smooth, sweet, and sensuous. Her love and their kissing within

4:11 Gen 27:27; Prov 24:13-14; Hos 14:6
4:12 Gen 2:8-15; 29:3; Prov 5:15-18
4:14 Exod 30:23; Song 1:12; 4:6; John 19:39
4:15 Zech 14:8; John 4:10, 14; 7:38
4:16 Song 1:13; 2:3; 5:1; 6:2; [d]*dod* (1730) ›Song 7:12
5:1 Prov 9:5; Song 1:13; 4:9; 6:2; Isa 55:1; John 3:29
5:2 Song 2:14; 4:9; 6:9
5:3 Gen 19:2; Luke 11:7
5:5 Song 5:13
5:6 Prov 1:28; Song 3:1; 5:2; 6:1

11 Your lips are as sweet as nectar, my bride.
Honey and milk are under your tongue.
Your clothes are scented
like the cedars of Lebanon.

12 You are my private garden, my treasure, my bride,
a secluded spring, a hidden fountain.
13 Your thighs shelter a paradise of pomegranates
with rare spices—
henna with nard,
14 nard and saffron,
fragrant calamus and cinnamon,
with all the trees of frankincense, myrrh, and aloes,
and every other lovely spice.
15 You are a garden fountain,
a well of fresh water
streaming down from Lebanon's mountains.

Young Woman

16 Awake, north wind!
Rise up, south wind!
Blow on my garden
and spread its fragrance all around.
Come into your garden, my [d]love;
taste its finest fruits.

Young Man

5 1 I have entered my garden, my treasure, my bride!
I gather myrrh with my spices
and eat honeycomb with my honey.
I drink wine with my milk.

Young Women of Jerusalem

Oh, lover and beloved, eat and drink!
Yes, drink deeply of your love!

Young Woman

2 I slept, but my heart was awake,
when I heard my lover knocking and calling:
"Open to me, my treasure, my darling,
my dove, my perfect one.
My head is drenched with dew,
my hair with the dampness of the night."

3 But I responded,
"I have taken off my robe.
Should I get dressed again?
I have washed my feet.
Should I get them soiled?"

4 My lover tried to unlatch the door,
and my heart thrilled within me.
5 I jumped up to open the door for my love,
and my hands dripped with perfume.
My fingers dripped with lovely myrrh
as I pulled back the bolt.
6 I opened to my lover,
but he was gone!
My heart sank.
I searched for him
but could not find him anywhere.
I called to him,
but there was no reply.

the lavish fragrance around them is nearing the ultimate delight for this bridegroom.

4:12 ***private garden . . . secluded spring . . . hidden fountain*** (literally *locked garden . . . locked spring . . . sealed fountain*): This affirmation of her purity and virginity accentuates his exclusive and privileged position (see Prov 5:15 for similar imagery). The images of spring and fountain evoke thoughts of the most intimate parts of a woman's body.

4:13-14 The man's description of his lover now focuses on the most exquisite place of delight between her ***thighs.***

4:16 ***Come into your garden, my love; taste its finest fruits:*** Finally, the woman invites the man to enter her and experience her now-unlocked body in all its sensual perfection. • The man had poetically affirmed the woman's chastity (4:12). However, she is totally and exclusively committed to him, so she reveals her treasures and invites him into the garden.

5:1 ***I have entered my garden . . . myrrh with my spices . . . honeycomb with my honey . . . wine with my milk:*** In penetrating the garden, the man finds that there is no limit to what he can enjoy. They are ecstatic over finally unlocking the vast enjoyment of intercourse. • ***my treasure:*** Literally *my sister;* also in 5:2. See note on 4:9. • ***drink deeply of your love!*** The young women of Jerusalem encourage the couple to enjoy their sexual union to the fullest; there can be no guilt or shame in the deepest pleasure between husband and wife.

5:2–6:3 One verse earlier, the couple are fully enjoying their intimate union. Now the woman feels the torment of separation. In the dramatic interpretation, the woman has been separated from the man twice before and has searched for him (1:4-7; 3:1-4). This last time, the separation takes place in her dreams—it is only a nightmare. Her dream seems to extend to 6:3, given the natural flow of questions and answers between the woman and the young women of Jerusalem. • If the Song is an anthology, these poems explore love rather than giving accounts of actual events. This poem reminds us that an intimate relationship is not always easy or perfectly satisfying.

5:2 ***I slept, but my heart was awake:*** This is an apt definition of a dream; she was physically asleep, but emotionally and psychologically awake. • ***my lover knocking . . . "Open to me":*** Opening doors is a metaphor for sexual activity in the ancient Near East (see also 8:9). By describing the man as knocking at the door and requesting entry, the poem suggests that the man is requesting sexual union. He awaits permission; he does not presume.

5:4-6 ***My lover tried to unlatch the door, and my heart thrilled:*** The man persists in his attempts to arouse the woman, and she eventually responds positively to his overtures. However, by the time she responds, he has given up or become otherwise occupied. This is a powerful poetic picture of the struggles of two lovers to be sexually intimate with each other.

7 The night watchmen found me
as they made their rounds.
They beat and bruised me
and stripped off my veil,
those watchmen on the walls.

8 Make this promise, O women of
Jerusalem—
If you find my lover,
tell him I am weak with love.

Young Women of Jerusalem

9 Why is your lover better than all others,
O woman of rare beauty?
What makes your lover so special
that we must promise this?

Young Woman

10 My lover is dark and dazzling,
better than ten thousand others!
11 His head is finest gold,
his wavy hair is black as a raven.
12 His eyes sparkle like doves
beside springs of water;
they are set like jewels
washed in milk.
13 His cheeks are like gardens of spices
giving off fragrance.
His lips are like lilies,
perfumed with myrrh.
14 His arms are like rounded bars of gold,
set with beryl.
His body is like bright ivory,
glowing with lapis lazuli.
15 His legs are like marble pillars
set in sockets of finest gold.
His posture is stately,
like the noble cedars of Lebanon.
16 His mouth is sweetness itself;
he is desirable in every way.
Such, O women of Jerusalem,
is my lover, my friend.

Young Women of Jerusalem

6 1 Where has your lover gone,
O woman of rare beauty?
Which way did he turn
so we can help you find him?

Young Woman

2 My lover has gone down to his
garden,
to his spice beds,
to browse in the gardens
and gather the lilies.
3 I am my lover's, and my lover is mine.
He browses among the lilies.

Young Man

4 You are beautiful, my darling,
like the lovely city of Tirzah.
Yes, as beautiful as Jerusalem,
as majestic as an army with billowing
banners.
5 Turn your eyes away,
for they overpower me.
Your hair falls in waves,
like a flock of goats winding down the
slopes of Gilead.
6 Your teeth are as white as sheep
that are freshly washed.
Your smile is flawless,
each tooth matched with its twin.
7 Your cheeks are like rosy pomegranates
behind your veil.

5:7 Song 3:3
5:8 Song 2:5, 7; 3:5
5:9 Song 1:8; 6:1
5:10 1 Sam 16:12; Ps 45:2
5:12 Song 1:15; 4:1
5:13 Song 2:1; 5:5; 6:2
5:14 Exod 24:10; 28:18, 20; Job 28:16; Isa 54:11; Ezek 1:16; Dan 10:6
5:15 1 Kgs 4:33; Song 7:4
5:16 2 Sam 1:23; Song 7:9
6:1 Song 1:8; 5:6
6:2 Song 1:7; 2:1; 4:16; 5:1, 13
6:3 Song 2:16; 4:5; 7:10
6:4 1 Kgs 14:17; Ps 48:2; 50:2; Song 1:15; 6:10
6:5 Song 4:1
6:6-7 Song 4:2-3

5:7 ***The night watchmen . . . beat and bruised me:*** The watchmen who were protectors in 3:3 now become demonized characters in her dream (5:2). What they do describes how she feels—pummeled and wounded. • ***stripped off my veil:*** She feels that she has lost her dignity.

5:8-9 The woman enlists the young women of Jerusalem to help her find her ***lover.*** They ask her to describe him, and this leads into the second descriptive poem (*wasf*) of the Song (see note on 4:1–5:1).

5:8 ***I am weak with love:*** The woman's trauma is an image for her love sickness (cp. 2:5).

5:10-16 This extended portrayal of the ***lover*** in the Song emphasizes his worth to the woman.

5:10 ***dark and dazzling:*** He is radiantly healthy and deeply tanned.

5:11-15 The woman describes the man as a statue made of ***gold, ivory, lapis lazuli,*** and ***marble pillars,*** suggesting that he is god-like in appearance, since statues of deities were composed of such precious metals in antiquity (Exod 32:1-4; 1 Kgs 12:28; Dan 2:32-33; 3:1).

5:12 For the description of ***eyes . . . like doves,*** see note on 1:15.

5:13 ***His cheeks are like gardens of spices*** because they were covered by the full beard that was worn by all men of that culture. This beard would have been perfumed.

5:14 The man's body is portrayed as beautiful and precious. • ***Beryl*** is an olive-green gem. • ***Lapis lazuli*** is a blue gem.

5:15 ***Lebanon*** was to the north of Israel and contained legendary cedar trees that were large, ***stately,*** and pleasantly fragrant.

5:16 The woman ends her description with an indication of her desire to kiss him.

6:1-3 The conversation that ends this poem indicates that it is not an actual event. The dream ends as the young women of Jerusalem ask the woman where her man has gone. The woman tells them not to concern themselves with finding him—he is back in bed with her, enjoying his ***garden*** with its ***spice beds*** and ***lilies,*** a description of sexual intimacy.

6:4-10 The man again describes the physical beauty of the woman. He repeats parts of the description from ch 4 almost verbatim, showing the same high regard for his wife.

6:4 ***Tirzah*** was a city-state as early as Joshua's time; it eventually became great enough to be the capital of the northern kingdom (Josh 12:24; 1 Kgs 15:33). The town's name means "pleasant." • ***Jerusalem*** was the capital of David's and Solomon's united kingdom and after that, the most important city of Judah.

6:6 ***Your smile is flawless, each tooth matched with its twin:*** Literally *Not one is missing; each has a twin.* See note on 4:2.

6:8
1 Kgs 11:3
Song 1:3

6:9
Gen 30:13
Song 2:14; 5:2

6:10
Job 31:26
Song 6:4
Matt 17:2
Rev 1:16

6:11
Song 4:13; 7:12

6:13
Gen 32:2
Judg 21:21
2 Sam 17:24

7:1
Ps 45:13

7:3
Song 4:5

7:4
Num 21:26
Song 4:4

7:5
Isa 35:2

8 Even among sixty queens
and eighty concubines
and countless young women,
9 I would still choose my dove, my perfect one—
the favorite of her mother,
dearly loved by the one who bore her.
The young women see her and praise her;
even queens and royal concubines
sing her praises:
10 "Who is this, arising like the dawn,
as fair as the moon,
as bright as the sun,
as majestic as an army with billowing banners?"

Young Woman
11 I went down to the grove of walnut trees
and out to the valley to see the new spring growth,
to see whether the grapevines had budded
or the pomegranates were in bloom.
12 Before I realized it,
my strong desires had taken me to the chariot of a noble man.

Young Women of Jerusalem
13 Return, return to us, O maid of Shulam.
Come back, come back, that we may see you again.

Young Man
Why do you stare at this young woman of Shulam,
as she moves so gracefully between two lines of dancers?

7

1 How beautiful are your sandaled feet,
O queenly maiden.
Your rounded thighs are like jewels,
the work of a skilled craftsman.
2 Your navel is perfectly formed
like a goblet filled with mixed wine.
Between your thighs lies a mound of wheat
bordered with lilies.
3 Your breasts are like two fawns,
twin fawns of a gazelle.
4 Your neck is as beautiful as an ivory tower.
Your eyes are like the sparkling pools in Heshbon
by the gate of Bath-rabbim.
Your nose is as fine as the tower of Lebanon
overlooking Damascus.
5 Your head is as majestic as Mount Carmel,
and the sheen of your hair radiates royalty.
The king is held captive by its tresses.

6:8-9 If the Song were an allegory of the Lord's love for his people, it would provide a very weak parallel, since Solomon's excesses in marrying do a poor job of picturing God's love and faithfulness (see 1 Kgs 11:1-13). • ***sixty queens:*** Many of Solomon's wives were obtained by marrying into international treaties (see 1 Kgs 11:1-3, 8). • ***Concubines*** were wives who had secondary status, lower than a wife but higher than a slave. Concubines were acquired by war, debt repayment, or purchase. • In the anthology view, the reference to *queens* and *concubines* simply means that the woman herself is more desirable than all other women.

6:9 ***sing her praises:*** Literally *called her blessed.* If the Song is a drama, the woman has left Solomon's harem, and the singing took place in the past, when the woman was still there.

6:10 The poem ends as it began in 6:4: The woman's majesty, like an ***army with billowing banners*** in full display, makes the knees knock and the heart flutter.

6:11 ***I went down:*** There is ambiguity over who is speaking here. The NLT presents it as the beginning of the young woman's speech, though it could just as plausibly be a continuation of the young man's. The trip to the ***walnut*** grove is a poetic way of expressing desire for a romantic meeting.

6:12 ***to the chariot of a noble man:*** Or *to the royal chariots of my people,* or *to the chariots of Amminadab.* The meaning of the Hebrew is uncertain. Desire leads to the union of the man and the woman. There may be support here for Solomon being the husband, though this description could be a metaphor for the joys of romance (cp. 1:16-17).

6:13–7:9 An interaction between the young women of Jerusalem and the man introduces his last major description of the woman's beauty and his desire to hold her (see note on 4:1–5:1).

6:13 Verse 6:13 is numbered 7:1 in the Hebrew text. • ***Return:*** Or *turn around.* • ***Shulam:*** The place is not known, though some have identified it with *Shunem* (1 Kgs 1:3; 2 Kgs 4:11-12). ***Maid of Shulam*** (Hebrew *shulammith*) might be a wordplay on the name Solomon (Hebrew *shelomoh*). It would then be equivalent to saying "Solomon's maiden." • ***as she moves so gracefully between two lines of dancers?*** Or *as you would at the movements of two armies?* Or *as you would at the dance of Mahanaim?* The meaning of the Hebrew is uncertain. The man praises the woman's grace and beauty to everyone.

7:1-13 Verses 7:1-13 are numbered 7:2-14 in the Hebrew text.

7:1 The man now praises the woman's dancing ***feet*** and then ascends her sensuous body to her flowing ***hair*** (7:1-5). • This ***queenly maiden*** (literally *prince's daughter*) might or might not be from a royal family, but she is as fine as royalty.

7:2 ***Between your thighs lies a mound of wheat*** (literally *Your belly is like a mound of wheat*): The man is either describing the woman's smoothly rounded abdomen or her pubic mound.

7:4 ***ivory tower:*** See note on 4:4. • ***sparkling pools in Heshbon by the gate of Bath-rabbim:*** The pools of Heshbon, formed by a brook, can still be seen today near the ruins of Heshbon on the east coast of the Dead Sea. • The ***tower of Lebanon*** is probably a metaphor for Mount Hermon, a high mountain that overlooks the valley of ***Damascus,*** the capital of Syria. The majestic beauty of the woman's nose rises above her other facial features.

7:5-6 ***Mount Carmel*** is a high mountain range on the Mediterranean coast. • ***your hair radiates royalty*** (literally *your hair is as purple threads*): Purple was an expensive color to produce, so it was the exclusive property of royalty.

6 Oh, how beautiful you are!
How pleasing, my love, how full of delights!
7 You are slender like a palm tree,
and your breasts are like its clusters of fruit.
8 I said, "I will climb the palm tree
and take hold of its fruit."
May your breasts be like grape clusters,
and the fragrance of your breath like apples.
9 May your kisses be as exciting as the best wine,
flowing gently over lips and teeth.

Young Woman

10 I am my lover's,
and he claims me as his own.
11 Come, my love, let us go out to the fields
and spend the night among the wildflowers.
12 Let us get up early and go to the vineyards
to see if the grapevines have budded,
if the blossoms have opened,
and if the pomegranates have bloomed.
There I will give you my [e]love.
13 There the mandrakes give off their fragrance,
and the finest fruits are at our door,
new delights as well as old,
which I have saved for you, my lover.

Young Woman

8 1 Oh, I wish you were my brother,
who nursed at my mother's breasts.
Then I could kiss you no matter who was watching,
and no one would criticize me.
2 I would bring you to my childhood home,
and there you would teach me.
I would give you spiced wine to drink,
my sweet pomegranate wine.
3 Your left arm would be under my head,
and your right arm would embrace me.
4 Promise me, O women of Jerusalem,
not to awaken love until the time is right.

Young Women of Jerusalem

5 Who is this sweeping in from the desert,
leaning on her lover?

Young Woman

I aroused you under the apple tree,
where your mother gave you birth,
where in great pain she delivered you.
6 Place me like a seal over your heart,
like a seal on your arm.
For love is as strong as death,
its jealousy as enduring as the grave.
Love flashes like fire,
the brightest kind of flame.
7 Many waters cannot quench love,
nor can rivers drown it.
If a man tried to buy love
with all his wealth,
his offer would be utterly scorned.

The Young Woman's Brothers

8 We have a little sister
too young to have breasts.
What will we do for our sister
if someone asks to marry her?

7:6 Song 1:15-16
7:8 Song 2:5
7:9 Prov 23:31; Song 5:16
7:10 Ps 45:11; Song 2:16; 6:3
7:12 Song 6:11; [e]*dod* (1730) ‣Ezek 16:8
7:13 Gen 30:14; Song 2:3; 4:13, 16
8:2 Song 3:4
8:3 Song 2:6
8:4 Song 2:7; 3:5
8:5 Song 2:3; 3:6
8:6 Prov 6:34; Isa 49:16; Jer 22:24; Hag 2:23
8:8 Ezek 16:7

7:7-8 The husband describes their love-making. He ascends her body and caresses her ***breasts***.

7:9 The man compares the woman's love and her *kisses* to *wine* in that they are delightful and make one light-headed (see 1:2). • ***over lips and teeth:*** As in Greek and Syriac versions and Latin Vulgate; Hebrew reads *over lips of sleepers*.

7:11-12 The woman suggests that they go together to check on the status of the vineyards and make love while there. • ***among the wildflowers:*** Or *in the villages*.

7:13 ***Mandrakes*** (Hebrew *duda'im*) were a Middle Eastern aphrodisiac (see Gen 30:14-16); the roots of the plant resemble a human torso. The word is a play on *my lover* (Hebrew *dodi*). • ***at our door:*** All sexual pleasures are available to them now, and she will share with him the ***delights*** she has ***saved*** for him alone. • ***new . . . old:*** She has in mind the sexual expressions they have already experienced, and new ones as well.

8:1-4 The woman expresses her desire to be with the man and in his embrace.

8:1 If he were her brother she could kiss him publicly; romantic kisses were not appropriate in public, but kisses between blood relatives were acceptable.

8:2-3 ***bring you to my childhood home*** (literally *to my mother's house*): Cp. 3:4. • ***there you would teach me:*** Or *there she will teach me*; or *there she bore me*.

8:4 ***Promise me:*** For the third time, the woman encourages the young women of Jerusalem to retain their virginity (see 2:7; 3:5). The virtue of virginity is confirmed in 8:8-9. • ***not to awaken love until the time is right:*** Or *not to awaken love until it is ready*.

8:5 ***I aroused you under the apple tree:*** The apple tree is a symbol of fertility because it is fruit-bearing (see 2:3, 5; 7:8). • ***where your mother gave you birth:*** Mentioning his mother may be a subtle way of suggesting procreation as a fruit of sexual love (cp. 8:2).

8:6 ***seal over your heart . . . on your arm:*** In ancient Israel a seal was used for identification or to show ownership by pressing the face of a ring into soft wax. The wife wants her husband to mark her with his identity, privately upon her heart, and publicly upon her arm as well. • ***love is as strong as death:*** Though death is inevitable, the bond of love is resolute, unshakable, and broken only in death. • ***its jealousy:*** Or *its passion*. The energy of jealousy moves to protect an exclusive relationship such as that of husband and wife or between God and his people (Nah 1:2; Zech 1:14-17). • ***as the grave:*** Hebrew *as Sheol* (see note on Ps 6:5).

8:8-10 In the midst of a passionate exchange of romantic compliments and commitments, here again is strong praise for sexual abstinence until marriage.

8:8 ***We have a little sister:*** The wife's brothers express concern for their sister's chastity. According to ancient Near Eastern custom, they are the

8:9 1 Kgs 6:15
8:11 Eccl 2:4; Song 1:6; 2:3; 8:12; Isa 7:23; Matt 21:33
8:13 Song 1:7; 2:14
8:14 Song 2:7, 9, 17; 4:6

9 If she is a virgin, like a wall,
we will protect her with a silver tower.
But if she is promiscuous, like a
swinging door,
we will block her door with a cedar
bar.

Young Woman

10 I was a virgin, like a wall;
now my breasts are like towers.
When my lover looks at me,
he is delighted with what he sees.

11 Solomon has a vineyard at Baal-hamon,
which he leases out to tenant farmers.
Each of them pays a thousand pieces of
silver
for harvesting its fruit.
12 But my vineyard is mine to give,
and Solomon need not pay a thousand
pieces of silver.
But I will give two hundred pieces
to those who care for its vines.

Young Man

13 O my darling, lingering in the gardens,
your companions are fortunate to
hear your voice.
Let me hear it, too!

Young Woman

14 Come away, my love! Be like a gazelle
or a young stag on the mountains of
spices.

Beauty in Nature (7:10-13)

Song 2:8-17; 4:12–5:1; 6:2-3; 6:11-12; Gen 2:1-9; Ps 8:3-8; 19:1-6; 96:5-6; Matt 6:26-30

God's original commission to man and woman was for them to enjoy and wisely manage God's creation (Gen 1:26-28; see also 1 Kgs 3:9; 4:32-33). The couple in the Song of Songs enjoy nature within their own Garden of Eden as they enjoy each other. The mystique of nature draws the couple deep into the country in their escapades, and provides them with the environment in which their love is the most rustic, and at the same time, the most exotic and exhilarating.

In the Song of Songs, sexual intimacy takes place in the countryside (2:8-17; 4:12–5:1; 6:2-3, 11-12), a place of pleasant fragrances and secluded meeting places. The garden, vineyard, and orchard create intimate and pleasant settings and evoke a romantic mood.

The couple uses extensive metaphors from nature to describe each other's physical attributes and their arousing effects. Their portrayal of each other forces them to use illustrations from God's exquisite creation. God's creation provides them with pictures that express their greatest pleasures and delights in each other. In a similar manner, God's creation provides pictures of his own goodness, justice, and love for his people.

protectors of their sister's sexuality until her marriage.

8:9 ***wall:*** There appear to be two metaphorical meanings for this term: (1) The prepubescent girl's chest is like a wall (see 8:10); and (2) until she is married, she should be abstinent, impenetrable like a wall. • ***protect her with a silver tower:*** Towers were used as lookouts for protecting the city; a silver one would be more prominent and impregnable. If the woman is already a wall, having kept her virginity, they will honor and reinforce her resolve. • On the other hand, a ***swinging door*** indicates promiscuity. The brothers will force her to restrain herself.

8:10 ***I was a virgin, like a wall:*** The woman affirms that she was chaste in preparation for marriage. • ***now . . . like towers:*** The woman describes herself in the language of desirability (cp. 4:4; 7:4, 8) and challenges her brothers' perception of her as immature.

8:11-14 In the dramatic view, the wife's dilemma concerning the vineyard of 1:6 is finally resolved: She has managed to bring in the lease money from her vineyard in Baal-hamon, so she can pay Solomon and her hired harvesters. • If the passage is purely poetic, its main message is that love may not be bought, even by a powerful king like Solomon.

8:11 ***Baal-hamon*** is not otherwise mentioned in the Bible. However "Balamon" occurs in later literature as a place in northern Israel; it may be the same place. • ***a thousand pieces of silver*** (Hebrew *1,000 shekels of silver*): There are different denominations of shekels in the OT, so the exact price cannot be determined, but the vineyard was a large one.

8:13 The scene has changed from that of the lease payment to the more familiar and pleasant ***gardens.*** • ***your companions:*** It appears that the wife may be talking with her friends. Her man is gently jealous and wants her to himself.

8:14 ***Come away, my love!*** She invites him to follow her, and he chases her with all the robust and exhilarating speed of ***a gazelle*** (see 2:8-10). • ***mountains of spices:*** Cp. 4:6.

INTRODUCTION TO THE
BOOKS OF THE PROPHETS

Then Jesus took them through the writings of Moses and all the prophets,
explaining from all the Scriptures the things concerning himself.
LUKE 24:27

Each of the prophets of the Old Testament, from Moses (around 1400 BC) to Malachi (around 400 BC), communicated God's messages to Israel and Judah. God directly commissioned the prophets to their task, and the Holy Spirit empowered their work. Their job was to confront God's people with their sin, to show them the inevitable consequences of judgment that would flow from their continuing to break God's covenant with them, and to communicate a hopeful future for God's people that would extend beyond judgment. The prophets show us our need for a savior and consistently point us to Christ.

SETTING

From the beginning of God's relationship with people, there were prophets who enjoyed a "face-to-face" relationship with him, starting with Abraham and including Moses, Samuel, and David. But the "classical" era of prophecy covers the later periods of the history of Israel and Judah—the divided monarchy, the Exile, and the period of return from exile. This era began with Elijah, who prophesied during Ahab's reign (874–853 BC; see 1 Kgs 17–19), and it stretched down to Malachi, who prophesied in the 400s BC. It was during this period that the books of Israel's prophets were written. The earlier "writing prophets," such as Amos and Hosea (700s BC), warned the people of their sin, urged them to repent, and pointed ahead to inevitable judgment if they refused. By the time of Jeremiah and Ezekiel (late 600s–early 500s), the coming judgment was already inevitable and the prophets were more focused on explaining the causes for the judgment and speaking of a future beyond judgment. The postexilic prophets such as Haggai (520 BC), Zechariah (about 520–518 BC), and Malachi (400s BC) confronted a discouraged and tempted people and called them back to careful and joyous obedience to their covenant Lord.

THE TASK OF THE PROPHET

Emissaries of the Lord, Israel's King

The prophets were mediators of the covenant relationship between God and his people. That covenant, like other ancient treaties, contained blessings for obedience and curses for disobedience. In the ancient world, when such treaties were broken, the Great King would send emissaries to warn the vassals. The warnings would be introduced with, "This is what [name of the king] says . . ." (see 1 Kgs 20:5). The prophets, likewise, were emissaries of the Lord, and they used the same formula to introduce God's messages. These messages detailed God's charges, urged Israel to return to obedience, and warned them of coming judgment if they did not.

Israel was almost always in rebellion against the Lord. As a result, the true prophets seem "too negative" to modern ears. But just as there is no cure for an infection until it has been identified and eradicated, so also with people's rebellion against the Lord their God. The true prophets were trying to help Israel by warning them of disaster. By contrast, those who spoke "nice things" (Isa 30:10) were false prophets, because they communicated the false idea that people could continue sinning and yet still enjoy God's blessings.

Messengers for the Lord

The Lord promised to place his words in the mouths of his prophets, which they in turn would communicate to God's people (see Deut 18:18). In their role as God's messengers, the prophets followed in the footsteps of Moses, the archetypal prophet, who spoke with the Lord "face to face" (Deut 34:10) and told God's people what God had said (Exod 4:11-16). But the prophets did not merely take dictation for God. They entered

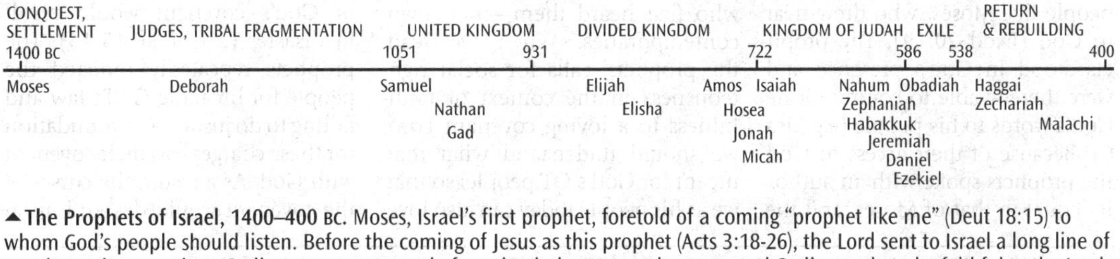

▲ **The Prophets of Israel, 1400–400 BC.** Moses, Israel's first prophet, foretold of a coming "prophet like me" (Deut 18:15) to whom God's people should listen. Before the coming of Jesus as this prophet (Acts 3:18-26), the Lord sent to Israel a long line of prophets who gave them God's messages, warned of coming judgment, and encouraged God's people to be faithful to the Lord.

into God's heart, sharing his anger and his grief, his sense of rejection, and his continuing passionate love for his people. Through the prophets we get a glimpse of the complexity and depth of God's person that is not duplicated elsewhere in the Bible.

Intercessors before the Lord

Not only did the prophets bring God's word to Israel, they also brought the people's response to God and interceded on their behalf (see, e.g., Amos 7:1-6), just as Abraham, Moses, and Samuel had done (see Gen 20:7; Exod 32:9-14, 30-35; 1 Sam 7:5-10). The prophets were not neutral parties that delivered messages from a safe distance. They were personally involved in the communication process, often in ways that were costly (e.g., Isa 20; Ezek 24:15-27). One characteristic of the false prophets was their inability to intercede on behalf of the people (Jer 27:18). Their claim to be ambassadors for God was shown to be false because they could not successfully speak on Israel's behalf to the Lord.

THE CHARACTERISTICS OF A TRUE PROPHET

I knew you before I formed you in your mother's womb. Before you were born I set you apart and appointed you as my prophet to the nations.

Jeremiah 1:5

In Deuteronomy, Moses lays out the basic characteristics of a true prophet of the Lord. In Deut 18:15-22 he speaks about the coming of a future prophet like himself, but the characteristics of that future prophet also apply to all true prophets of the Lord. Prophets were to be Israelites (Deut 18:15) whose messages were in agreement with God's word (Deut 13:5) and whose predictions came true (Deut 18:21-22). Prophets were also to be people like Moses, who drew near to God (Exod 20:19). The prophets stood in God's presence and were thereby able to communicate God's words to his people (e.g., Isa 6). Because of their access to God, the prophets spoke with an authority equal to that of Moses, and the people were responsible for listening to their messages (Deut 18:19).

Prophecy is closely associated with the outpouring of the Spirit (see Num 11:25, 29; 1 Sam 10:9-13; Joel 2:28-29). The fulfillment of Joel's prophecy occurred on the Day of Pentecost, when the Spirit was poured out on all who believed the message (Acts 2). They then prophesied and were empowered by the Spirit for the task of carrying to the world God's message of salvation in Jesus Christ. All who follow Christ are called to communicate his message to those around us. As we testify to the Lord, the Spirit gives us the power to communicate God's truth faithfully to a rebellious world (Acts 1:8).

INTERPRETATION

The prophets have a queer way of talking, like people who, instead of proceeding in an orderly manner, ramble off from one thing to the next, so that you cannot make head or tail of them or see what they are getting at.

Martin Luther[1]

The OT prophecies are sometimes hard to interpret (cp. Num 12:6-8; Isa 6:9-10). God spoke through the prophets in visions, dreams, and riddles. Some of those prophecies were clear and unambiguous (e.g., Mic 5:2; cp. Matt 2:3-6). Yet who would have anticipated when Isaiah spoke of "God . . . with us" (Isa 7:14) that God would take on human flesh (John 1:14)? Or that the glorious "son of man" (Dan 7:13) would come "not to be served but to serve others and to give his life as a ransom for many" (Matt 20:28)?

The messages of the prophets must be understood first of all on their own terms. Many of their messages addressed specific situations in Israel and Judah, so it is imperative first to understand what the prophets were saying to those who first heard them—their own contemporaries. When we read the prophets' calls for social righteousness in the context of faithfulness to a loving covenant Lord, we should understand what that meant for God's OT people, so that we as his people today can also love and serve him faithfully. When we read the prophets' stirring promises of a glorious future, we must understand those promises first from their own timeframe, not our own. The more we can see things from the perspective of an OT Israelite, the better we will be able to understand the meaning and significance of the prophets' messages.

It is also important to remember that the books of prophecy, like the rest of Scripture, have Christ as their central focus and theme (Luke 24:44-49). To attempt to understand them apart from Christ would be to misunderstand them. We must read the prophets and hear their messages in the light of all that God has done in Christ. The central interpretive principle of the OT prophets is that their message points toward Christ and the glories that would follow his sufferings (Luke 24:26, 44; Acts 3:18-21; 1 Pet 1:10-12). In other words, the heart of their messages is not simply social action, morality, or predicting the future, but the Good News about Jesus Christ.

Although we have a "better covenant with God, based on better promises" through Jesus Christ (Heb 8:6), we have much to learn from the OT prophets and their messages. We too often live at odds with God's character, and we may find ourselves aptly rebuked by the prophets' condemnations. We may also be comforted by their proclamation of hope. Our hope, like OT Israel's, rests in the coming of a new Israel, Jesus Christ, the perfect law-keeper who frees us from the condemnation and death that we deserve. The prophets show us our need for such a savior. By anticipating what this savior would be like, they consistently point us to Christ.

THE MESSAGE OF THE PROPHETS

The prophets repeatedly warned the people that their constant breaches of God's covenant would result in disaster (2 Chr 36:15-16). The prophets repeatedly indicted the people for breaking God's law and failing to do justice. The foundation for these charges was their covenant with God. As a result, the curses of the covenant would descend upon

[1] Cited by Gerhard von Rad, *Old Testament Theology*, vol. 2 (1965), p. 33

them, and they would be exiled from the land, just as Moses had warned (Deut 28:64-68).

The prophets also spoke of hope for the future. Judgment and exile would not be the end of the story for God's people. Because of the Lord's merciful character, and for the honor of his name, he would bring them back. After judgment and exile, he would restore them and bless them. In spite of their sins, God would purify his people, establish his sanctuary among them, and live with them forever (Ezek 37:27-28).

The prophets did not speak only to Israel and Judah; they also addressed the nations, Israel's neighbors. These messages warned of judgment for harming God's people (see Gen 12:1-3). An assault against Israel was an assault against the Lord. During the dark days of the Exile, these messages encouraged God's people: If God was still committed to judging those who had harmed his people, there was still a future for them. These messages also reminded them that the Lord is the God of the whole world, and all nations will ultimately bow before him.

Not all of the messages to other nations were negative. The prophets anticipated a time when the nations would turn to Israel's God in repentance and faith and be incorporated into God's family (e.g., Isa 2:2; Zech 8:20-23). Though the movement of the nations to join Israel and worship Israel's God had been a mere trickle down through Israel's history, in the last days it would turn into a flood as the Lord brought the nations at last to bow before him. These promises have begun to be fulfilled through Christ and the church, as the book of Acts so eloquently describes.

THE ULTIMATE PROPHET

The anticipation of a prophet like Moses (Deut 18:15) did not simply point forward to a line of individual prophets in Israel's history. Supremely, it represents the hope of a single, climactic prophet. The NT makes clear that the expectation of a new prophet like Moses found its fulfillment in Jesus Christ. At his transfiguration, Jesus shone with divine glory, and God's voice from heaven declared, "This is my dearly loved Son, who brings me great joy. Listen to him" (Matt 17:5). The divine command, "Listen to him," repeats Deut 18:15—God was identifying Jesus as the prophet like Moses. At that event, Jesus' appearance was transformed and glorious, just as Moses' face had shone (Exod 34:29-35; cp. 2 Cor 3:7-18). Peter later made this same identification when he pointed to Christ as the climactic fulfillment of this expectation of a prophet like Moses (Acts 3:22). Stephen made the same connection while addressing the Jewish high council (Acts 7:37).

The promise of a prophet like Moses should have opened the hearts of the Jewish people to expect and welcome Jesus' coming, but instead it did the opposite—many of them rejected the promised Messiah (see Matt 13:10-17; Rom 9–11).

In the past, God spoke through the prophets, but now he has spoken once and for all through his Son (Heb 1:1-2). In Christ we have the ultimate revelation of God and his plan, and in Christ we have the ultimate intercessor with the Father for us humans. In the past, God sent Moses as the mediator of his covenant, but as great as Moses was, he was merely a servant in God's house. Jesus is the Son (Heb 3:5-6), the mediator of the new and final covenant (Heb 8:6). He comes with a message of judgment for those who will not repent, but he has grace and mercy for all who come to the Father through him. He intercedes for us before the Father's throne, and he invites people from all nations—men and women, young and old—to receive the blessings of the new covenant. In him, and through him, we are able to enter God's presence and dwell with him forever.

FURTHER READING

O. PALMER ROBERTSON
The Christ of the Prophets (2004)

D. BRENT SANDY
Plowshares & Pruning Hooks: Rethinking the Language of Biblical Prophecy and Apocalyptic (2002)

WILLEM A. VANGEMEREN
Interpreting the Prophetic Word (1990)

MICHAEL J. WILLIAMS
The Prophet and His Message: Reading Old Testament Prophecy Today (2003)

THE BOOK OF ISAIAH

Can God rescue us from the problems we face? Can he save us from oppressive world powers? Can he break the power of our sin and help us deal with its consequences? Throughout this book—which provides a vision of the loving greatness and holiness of God—Isaiah answers these questions with a resounding yes! The prophet's words sometimes overwhelm us with their beauty. At other times, his piercing words reveal our sin and drive us to our knees. Isaiah's own ministry began with the kind of vision that convicts the human heart, motivating us to trust in our Creator alone for forgiveness, restoration, and purpose in life.

SETTING

By the time of King Uzziah's death (740 BC), the southern kingdom of Judah faced a major crisis. The empire of Assyria, dormant for nearly fifty years, was now on the move again. Assyria's conquest reached southwestward from its homeland in what is now northern Iraq toward its ultimate destination, Egypt. The small nations of the Mediterranean coast, including Israel and Judah, stood in Assyria's path. Assyria took Galilee and much of Israel's territory east of the Jordan River. But Assyria would be

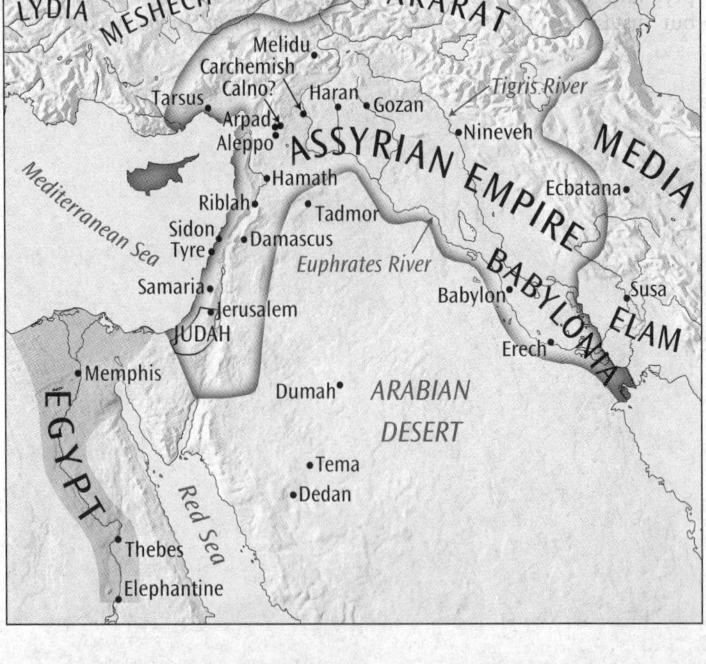

The World of Isaiah's Time, about 745–701 BC. When Isaiah was living and prophesying in Jerusalem, Assyria was the major power in the region and the major threat to the kingdom of Judah—a threat that came to a head in 701 BC during the reign of King Hezekiah (see 36:1–37:38).

ARARAT 37:38
ARPAD, CALNO, CARCHEMISH 10:9
ASSYRIA 7:17-20; 10:5-34; 19:23-25; 30:31-33; 36:1–37:38; 52:4
BABYLON 13:1-22; 21:1-10; 39:1-8
DAMASCUS 7:1-9; 8:4; 9:12; 17:1-3
EGYPT 19:1-25; 20:3-6; 30:1-7; 31:1-3; 43:17; 45:14; 49:12
ELAM, MEDIA 11:11; 21:2
HAMATH 10:9; 11:11; 36:19
HARAN 37:12
JERUSALEM, JUDAH 1:1; 2:1-3; 7:1-4; 11:12-13; 18:7; 22:1-14; 25:10; 27:13; 29:1-3; 36:1-2; 37:8-10; 37:31-33; 59:20
MEMPHIS 19:13
NINEVEH 37:37
SAMARIA 7:9; 8:4; 9:8-9; 10:9-11; 28:1-4
TYRE, SIDON 23:1-18

satisfied only with total control of Israel, Judah, and all the other smaller nations in the area.

While Judah's King Uzziah was still alive, Judah was able to ignore the crisis. Uzziah had a strong army (2 Chr 26:11-15). Overall, Uzziah was a good and effective king, and his people hoped that he could somehow save the nation from the Assyrians. When Uzziah died, however, ungodly rulers succeeded him. During this crisis of leadership, God gave Isaiah the vision that launched his ministry for the next forty years (6:1-13).

Assyria, meanwhile, pushed steadily southward along the coast of the Mediterranean, conquering one small nation after another. During this time, Judah's policy on Assyria oscillated between appeasement and confrontation. The prophet Isaiah brought a much-needed message: God is absolutely dependable, and it is utter folly to trust in anything or anyone other than God.

OUTLINE

1:1–12:6
The Lord, the Holy One of Israel

13:1–23:18
The Day of the Lord

24:1–27:13
The "Little Apocalypse"

28:1–33:24
Threats of Judgment

34:1–35:10
Message about the Future

36:1–39:8
The Lord Rescues Jerusalem

40:1–66:24
God's Glorious Kingdom

Unfortunately, Isaiah's central message was not always heeded. Around 734 BC, Israel formed a coalition with Syria to stand against Assyria. When King Ahaz of Judah refused to join this alliance, Israel and Syria attacked Judah in order to force Ahaz to join them. Faced with this crisis, Ahaz foolishly chose not to trust God (7:1-12). Instead, Ahaz called the Assyrians to rescue him (2 Chr 28:16-21). Although the king of Assyria did come to the rescue, defeating Syria and Israel, he also attacked Ahaz and placed a heavy burden of taxation on Judah. Just a few years later (722 BC), Assyria defeated the kingdom of Israel again and sent most of its people into exile (2 Kgs 17:5-18).

In 701 BC, during King Hezekiah's reign, Assyria again invaded Judah. This time, Judah relied on God's faithfulness, and as promised, God rescued the nation from the Assyrian army (37:21-36).

Regrettably, God's people did not remain faithful to him. As a result, God eventually allowed Judah to be overcome by Assyria's successor, Babylon (605–586 BC). What would Judah's destruction and exile to Babylon mean in terms of God's absolute reliability, which Isaiah had proclaimed? Isaiah answered this as well: God would indeed punish Judah's wickedness. He would also preserve a remnant that one day would return to the holy land. This return would not be due to any faithfulness on their part; it would be an act of God's grace.

Upon returning from exile (538 BC, see Ezra 1:1-4), the people were again tempted to wickedness, this time by the paganism that had taken root in their homeland during their absence. Isaiah showed that the gracious God who rescued them is also the holy God who demanded their obedience, righteousness, and exclusive devotion.

TIMELINE

792–740 BC
Uzziah (Azariah) as king of Judah

750–732 BC
Jotham as king of Judah

744–727 BC
Tiglath-pileser III as king of Assyria

740–732 BC
Pekah as king of Israel

about 740~685 BC
▸ **Isaiah as prophet**

743–715 BC
Ahaz as king of Judah

about 735~725 BC
Micah as prophet

732–722 BC
Hoshea as king of Israel

728–686 BC
Hezekiah as king of Judah

726–722 BC
Shalmaneser V as king of Assyria

722 BC
Samaria is destroyed by Assyria, end of the northern kingdom of Israel

721–705 BC
Sargon II as king of Assyria

704–681 BC
Sennacherib as king of Assyria

697–642 BC
Manasseh as king of Judah

680–669 BC
Esarhaddon as king of Assyria

668–626 BC
Ashurbanipal as king of Assyria

586 BC
Nebuchadnezzar destroys Jerusalem, end of the southern kingdom of Judah

559–530 BC
Cyrus II as king of Persia

Oct 539 BC
Cyrus II conquers Babylon

538 BC
Cyrus's decree of return, exiles return to Judea

SUMMARY

Chapters 1–39 cover the period during Isaiah's active ministry, from the death of Uzziah (740 BC) to 701 BC. The introduction (chs 1–5) contrasts Judah's present state of sin and injustice with the blessed existence in God's presence that they had originally been called to. This comparison raises a question: How can the present corruption ever be transformed into glory, purity, and fruitfulness? The prophet answers in ch 6, as he recounts his own renewal and calling as an example of how a change could take place nationwide. If Judah wanted to experience such renewal, however, it needed to turn from its sinful ways and learn to trust God. Throughout chs 13–35 the prophet uses a variety of literary forms and life situations to confirm that God is the only truly trustworthy one; relying on any of the surrounding nations in place of God represents extreme foolishness. Isaiah brackets this message with two historical accounts of experiences with Assyria: King Ahaz's experience in chs 7–12, and King Hezekiah's in chs 36–39. When Ahaz failed to trust God, disaster resulted. By contrast, his son Hezekiah trusted God, and a great rescue occurred. Hezekiah, however, also had times of weakness (39:1-8), setting the stage for Judah's later defeat and exile by Babylon.

Chapters 40–55 address the questions that would arise during Judah's exile to Babylon in 586 BC. Does the Exile mean that God was defeated, either by the Babylonians or by Judah's sin? Has God's will for Judah been frustrated, and is he helpless to do anything about it? In chs 40–48, Isaiah shows that God is infinitely superior to any idol-god, and his people will be the proof of this when God rescues them out of Babylon's ultimately helpless hands. In chs 49–55, the prophet addresses the deeper question of Judah's sin. Just as God rescued Judah from Babylon, he also intends to rescue a remnant of the people from the enslaving power of sin; he will accomplish it through the death of his servant.

Chapters 56–66 address Judah's experience following the end of their exile in 539 BC. God had rescued a remnant from exile as promised; now they needed to be pure, righteous, and holy. God's servants must not continue to walk in darkness and corruption, for those attitudes and actions had led to exile in the first place. As Isaiah speaks of rescue from sin, the light of God's own holy and righteous character dawns in his people. As a result, all the nations that Israel once trusted in place of God will now come to Jerusalem to learn God's ways from Israel.

[In studying Isaiah] I have soared into the heavens and seen the glory of God, and with new eyes I have seen this world and my own place in it. The view has been breathtaking.

BARRY WEBB
The Message of Isaiah, p. 12

AUTHOR

The book of Isaiah addresses three different historical situations, two of them beyond the prophet's own lifetime. As a result, some critical scholars have argued that the prophet Isaiah could not have written the entire book, a view that has prevailed since the mid-1800s. However, if we assume the reality of God's inspiration, predictive prophecy is a reality, so it should not present a problem that parts of the book address what was in the future for Isaiah. Furthermore, the book displays a remarkable literary unity. When Jesus and NT authors quote from the book of Isaiah, they consistently claim that they are referring to what the prophet Isaiah said (e.g., see Matt 8:17; 12:17-21; Luke 3:4-6; Acts 8:28-35; Rom 10:16).

DATE OF WRITING

It seems likely from the historical references in chs 6–39 that these materials were recorded at various times throughout the thirty-eight

years between Uzziah's death in 740 BC and Sennacherib's retreat from Jerusalem in 701 BC. Because of the simpler, meditative, and reflective lyrical style of chs 40–66, it seems probable that a period of time elapsed between 701 BC and the writing of these chapters. We do not know when Isaiah died, but tradition dates his death during the period of the sole reign of Manasseh (686–642 BC). It is thus possible that some fifteen years elapsed between the writing of chs 1–39 and the writing of chs 40–66.

The preaching of Isaiah represents the theological high-water mark of the whole Old Testament. . . . Not one of the other prophets approaches Isaiah in intellectual vigor, or, more particularly, in the magnificent sweep of his ideas.

GERHARD VON RAD
The Message of the Prophets, p. 118

LITERARY GENRES

There is a rich array of sub-genres within the book of Isaiah. Notable among them are (1) judgment speeches that warn the nation of Israel that God will punish them for their sins (9:8-21); (2) prophecies of woe that lament the approaching death of the nation (5:8-30; 29:1-12; 31:1-9); (3) parables that teach a lesson through an analogy (5:1-8; 27:2-6); (4) trial speeches to prove a case (41:21-29); (5) salvation prophecies of hope for the future (2:1-5; 32:1-20; 60:1-22); (6) hymns of praise to God for his faithfulness (12:1-6; 26:1-6); (7) prophecies against foreign nations (15:1–16:14; 23:1-18); (8) prophecies of a coming king, the Messiah (9:1-7; 11:1-9); (9) servant songs about one who would suffer for the sins of others (42:1-9; 52:12–53:12); and (10) historical narratives (36:1-22; 39:1-8).

MEANING AND MESSAGE

The book of Isaiah could be called the Bible in miniature. It has more overtones of the NT than any other OT book. Isaiah gives us a complete picture of God as unique and *transcendent* (beyond our experience). Yet the holy and exalted God reveals himself and desires to be *Immanuel* ("God is with us," 7:14). Therefore, the transcendent God is also *immanent* (nearby). God's nearness prepares Isaiah's readers to receive God *incarnate* (in the flesh), Jesus Christ, who is truly the Immanuel (see Matt 1:23).

Isaiah tackles the foolishness of idolatry head on. He exposed the folly of trying to capture God in any created thing or trying to manipulate God to our own ends. The only way to receive the blessings God wants to pour out upon us is through our surrender and trust. However, the human spirit stubbornly opposes this. We would rather trust anything or anyone other than God, who is beyond our control. Those who stubbornly refuse to submit themselves to the true God and turn instead to false gods become estranged from God and face his judgment.

The prophet tells the story of God's judgment on his sinful people through exile. However, God graciously returns to his people and declares that he will not cast them away altogether. Instead, he will purify and preserve a remnant that will glorify him among the nations and demonstrate that he alone is the true and living God.

The kingdom of God, centered in a new Zion (new Jerusalem), populated by a new community of the faithful, and ruled by God's righteous servant, the Messiah, will be built on the power of love rather than on the power of oppression and injustice. Only the righteous can belong to this new community. The same grace that rescues God's people from the consequences of their sin also produces in them obedience to his will. As a result, they will glorify God and transform the world.

FURTHER READING

ROBERT B. CHISHOLM, JR.
Handbook on the Prophets (2003)

J. ALEC MOTYER
Isaiah (1999)

JOHN N. OSWALT
Isaiah (2003)

WILLEM A. VANGEMEREN
Interpreting the Prophetic Word (1988)

LARRY L. WALKER
Isaiah in *Cornerstone Biblical Commentary*, vol. 8 (2005)

HERBERT M. WOLF
Interpreting Isaiah (1985)

1. THE LORD, THE HOLY ONE OF ISRAEL (1:1–12:6)

Superscription (1:1)

1 These are the visions that Isaiah son of
Amoz saw concerning Judah and Jerusalem. He saw these visions during the years when Uzziah, Jotham, Ahaz, and Hezekiah were kings of Judah.

Messages of Judgment and Salvation (1:2–2:22)

A Message for Rebellious Judah

2 Listen, O heavens! Pay attention, earth!
This is what the LORD says:
"The children I raised and cared for
have rebelled against me.
3 Even an ox knows its owner,
and a donkey recognizes its master's
care—
but Israel doesn't know its master.
My people don't recognize my care
for them."
4 Oh, what a [a]sinful nation they are—
loaded down with a burden of guilt.
They are evil people,
corrupt children who have rejected
the LORD.
They have despised the Holy One of
Israel
and turned their backs on him.
5 Why do you continue to invite
punishment?
Must you rebel forever?
Your head is injured,
and your heart is sick.
6 You are battered from head to foot—
covered with bruises, welts, and
infected wounds—
without any soothing ointments or
bandages.
7 Your country lies in ruins,
and your towns are burned.
Foreigners plunder your fields before
your eyes
and destroy everything they see.

1:1
2 Kgs 15:1, 13; 16:1; 18:1
Isa 2:1; 40:9

1:2
Deut 32:1
Isa 65:2
Jer 3:22
Mic 1:2

1:3
Jer 8:7; 9:3, 6

1:4
Isa 1:28; 5:24; 14:20
[a]*khata'* (2398)
‣ Lam 3:39

1:5
Isa 31:6; 33:24

1:6
Ps 38:3

1:7
Lev 26:33
Jer 44:6

ISAIAH THE PROPHET (1:1)

2 Kgs 19:1–20:19
2 Chr 26:22; 32:20, 32
Matt 3:3; 4:14-16; 8:17; 12:17-21; 13:14-15; 15:7-9
Mark 1:2-3; 7:6-7
Luke 3:4-6; 4:17-19
John 1:23; 12:38-41
Acts 8:28-34; 28:25-27
Rom 9:27-29; 10:15-16, 20-21; 15:12
Gal 4:27

Isaiah was a Judean prophet during the reigns of Uzziah, Jotham, Ahaz, and Hezekiah. He had a long ministry (about 740~685 BC). He was the son of Amoz (1:1) and was possibly related to King Amaziah. He lived in Jerusalem, was well educated, and had deep insight into human nature. As Judah's political and religious counselor, he had access to kings and was apparently the court historian (2 Chr 26:22; 32:32). Isaiah's wife was called a "prophetess" (see note on 8:3); their sons were Shear-jashub (7:3) and Maher-shalal-hash-baz (8:3).

Isaiah opposed social and political evil at all social levels. He censured fortune-tellers and exhorted everyone to obey God's covenant. He rebuked kings for their willfulness and indifference, and he denounced wealthy, influential people who ignored their responsibilities. Isaiah opposed Canaanite idolatry and insincere religious observances (1:10-17; 29:13), declaring that only a righteous remnant would survive (6:13). He foretold the coming Messiah, the peaceful prince of God's kingdom (11:1-11; cp. 9:6-7) who was also an obedient, suffering servant (53:3-12). The book of Isaiah has more overtones of the NT than any other OT book and is frequently cited by NT authors.

1:1 *These are the visions* (literally *The vision*): This term introduces the book as a unified whole, covering Isaiah's prophecies over a period of some fifty-five years (about 740~685 BC). • ***Isaiah son of Amoz:*** Beyond this, nothing is known of Isaiah's family background. • ***Jerusalem,*** the capital city of ***Judah,*** was the center of Isaiah's ministry. However, some of his prophecies also relate to the northern kingdom, Israel (referred to as Samaria and Ephraim, 9:8-21; 28:1-13), which fell in 722 BC (see 2 Kgs 17). • ***Uzziah, Jotham, Ahaz, and Hezekiah:*** These kings reigned from 792 to 686 BC.

1:2 ***heavens . . . earth:*** All of creation is called to witness the trial that God convened against Judah (cp. Deut 31:28; 32:1).

1:3 ***an ox knows its owner:*** Not so with Judah. Yet despite their rebellion, God still graciously addressed them as ***my people.***

1:4 The term ***Holy One of Israel*** is frequently used in Isaiah as a title for the Lord. God is the righteous and just King of heaven and earth (6:3-5), the incomparable God (40:25), and the Redeemer of his people (43:14). It was a terrible and foolish sin for Judah to reject him.

1:5 God sent famine, war, disease, and death as ***punishment.*** In most cases, however, God wanted to change stubborn behavior rather than simply to punish. • As a result of their persistent rebellion, the people's ***head is injured*** and their ***heart is sick.*** The nation was wounded physically from Assyrian aggression, while spiritually they were defiled and overtaken by sin (64:6).

1:6 ***without any soothing ointments or bandages:*** Judah's national condition was like the body of an injured person who had not received medical care.

1:7 ***country . . . towns:*** By 701 BC, the Assyrians had destroyed the infrastructure, taken cities, and ravaged the fields (see 64:10). This fulfilled Isaiah's prophetic word (6:11-13). Those who survived this Assyrian onslaught would know by experience to heed later warnings of exile to Babylon (39:6-7). God does what he says he will do, so the warning of God's judgment on all the nations is certain.

1:9
Isa 10:20-22; 11:11, 16
*Rom 9:29
1:10
Ezek 16:46
Rev 11:8
1:11
Jer 6:20
Mal 1:10
[b]*zebakh* (2077)
‣ Hos 6:6
1:13
1 Chr 23:31
1:14
Isa 43:24

8 Beautiful Jerusalem stands abandoned
like a watchman's shelter in a
vineyard,
like a lean-to in a cucumber field after
the harvest,
like a helpless city under siege.
9 If the LORD of Heaven's Armies
had not spared a few of us,
we would have been wiped out like
Sodom,
destroyed like Gomorrah.

10 Listen to the LORD, you leaders of
"Sodom."
Listen to the law of our God, people of
"Gomorrah."
11 "What makes you think I want all your
[b]sacrifices?"
says the LORD.
"I am sick of your burnt offerings of
rams
and the fat of fattened cattle.
I get no pleasure from the blood
of bulls and lambs and goats.
12 When you come to worship me,
who asked you to parade through my
courts with all your ceremony?
13 Stop bringing me your meaningless
gifts;
the incense of your offerings
disgusts me!
As for your celebrations of the new
moon and the Sabbath
and your special days for fasting—
they are all sinful and false.
I want no more of your pious
meetings.
14 I hate your new moon celebrations and
your annual festivals.
They are a burden to me. I cannot
stand them!

Religious Hypocrisy (1:11-15)

Isa 29:13-15; 48:1-2; 58:2-7; 65:3-5
Ps 50:16-23; 55:20-21
Prov 15:8; 21:27; 26:23
Jer 7:4-10; 12:2
Ezek 14:1-3; Hos 8:13
Amos 5:21-24
Mic 3:11
Zech 7:5-6
Mal 2:13-14
Matt 6:1-18; 7:21; 23:1-36
Luke 12:1-3
Rom 2:1-3
2 Tim 3:1-5
Titus 1:15-16
Jas 1:21-27
1 Pet 2:1
1 Jn 2:4, 9; 4:20

Isaiah preached to what seemed to be a very religious people. They fasted, said prayers, celebrated holy days, and brought their sacrifices to Jerusalem. Yet God rejected these practices. Why? These acts had value—the Lord himself had prescribed them! Yet the people's worship was not from the heart, and it was not accompanied by the personal holiness and social justice that God requires (Lev 19:13-17). The people of Judah had fallen into the trap of religious hypocrisy.

Religious hypocrisy can result from selective obedience, from lip service to God's law without changes of heart and life to back it up. People who parade their piety for others to see often have little desire to truly obey God. Many years after Isaiah, Jesus confronted this kind of hypocrisy in the Pharisees. He challenged them to be better doers of God's *whole* revelation rather than just the parts that brought them acclaim (Matt 23:1-36, especially Matt 23:23). The apostles Paul and James also distinguished between mere religiosity and true spirituality (1 Cor 3:1-23; Jas 1:21–2:13). Jesus' rebuke of the Pharisees also serves as a warning to us: We are not to be like them (see also Matt 6:1-18; 1 Pet 2:1). Instead, Jesus calls us to be authentic before God and with others, to obey his entire word, and to go beyond mere formalism and appearance in our devotion to God.

1:8 ***Beautiful Jerusalem*** (Hebrew *The daughter of Zion*): Zion, one of the hills on which Jerusalem stands, often served as a synonym for Jerusalem. Zion carried with it the notion of God's presence (Ps 46), his protection of his people, and Jerusalem's resistance to enemy forces. Now, however, the opposite was true. Jerusalem had become weak, ***like a helpless city under siege*** and like an ***abandoned . . . shelter*** or ***lean-to***.

1:9 ***The LORD of Heaven's Armies*** refers to the millions of angels that are at the Lord's command (see 2 Kgs 6:16-17; Matt 26:53). At the Exodus, Moses described God as a warrior fighting for his people (Exod 15:1-21). Ironically, in Isaiah's day, God fought against Judah because of their wickedness (1:24; 3:1-5). • ***a few of us:*** Greek version reads *a few of our children.* Cp. Rom 9:29.

1:10 ***Listen to*** (literally *listen to the word of*) ***the LORD:*** In this context, *listen* means to respond in obedience to ***the law*** (or *teaching;* Hebrew *torah*) ***of our God*** (see 2:3; 5:24). • ***leaders . . . people:*** All levels of society were guilty. • Like ***Sodom*** and ***Gomorrah***, Jerusalem had come under divine judgment for its rebellion against God's laws. Jerusalem might have been utterly destroyed like those cities were it not for God's grace (1:9; see Gen 19).

1:11-15 The people had so offended God through their sin that he took ***no pleasure*** any more in their ***sacrifices***. The Lord wanted Judah to stop the religious exercises he had commanded them to do rather than to continue them in a manner that was ***sinful and false*** (1:13). Ritual is never an acceptable substitute for true godliness.

1:13 The ***incense*** that accompanied ***offerings*** was intended as a sweet fragrance to the Lord (see Exod 30:7-8), but when offered with hypocrisy it was a nauseating stench and an abomination to God. • While the Lord had ordered ***special days for fasting*** at the Temple (Lev 16:31; 23:32; Num 29:7), they were ruined by the guilt of Judah's sin (see 58:1-7; Matt 6:16-18). • ***pious meetings:*** These holy days were associated with the new moon and other festivals (see Lev 23).

1:14 ***New moon celebrations*** occurred on the first day of each lunar month (Num 28:11-15) and included sacrifices, feasting, and rest from work. • The ***annual festivals*** were the festivals of Passover, Harvest, Trumpets, and Shelters (Num 28:16–29:39; Deut 16:1-17).

15 When you lift up your hands in prayer, I
will not look.
Though you offer many prayers, I will
not listen,
for your hands are covered with the
blood of innocent victims.
16 Wash yourselves and be clean!
Get your sins out of my sight.
Give up your evil ways.
17 Learn to do good.
Seek justice.
Help the oppressed.
Defend the cause of orphans.
Fight for the rights of widows.

18 "Come now, let's settle this,"
says the LORD.
"Though your sins are like scarlet,
I will make them as white as snow.
Though they are red like crimson,
I will make them as white as wool.
19 If you will only obey me,
you will have plenty to eat.
20 But if you turn away and refuse to listen,
you will be devoured by the sword of
your enemies.
I, the LORD, have spoken!"

Unfaithful Jerusalem

21 See how Jerusalem, once so faithful,
has become a prostitute.
Once the home of justice and
righteousness,
she is now filled with murderers.
22 Once like pure silver,
you have become like worthless slag.
Once so pure,
you are now like watered-down wine.
23 Your leaders are rebels,
the companions of thieves.
All of them love bribes
and demand payoffs,
but they refuse to defend the cause of
orphans
or fight for the rights of widows.

24 Therefore, the Lord, the LORD of
Heaven's Armies,
the Mighty One of Israel, says,
"I will take revenge on my enemies
and pay back my foes!
25 I will raise my fist against you.
I will melt you down and skim off your
slag.
I will remove all your impurities.
26 Then I will give you good [c]judges again
and wise counselors like you used to
have.
Then Jerusalem will again be called the
Home of Justice
and the Faithful City."
27 Zion will be restored by justice;
those who repent will be revived by
righteousness.
28 But rebels and sinners will be completely
destroyed,
and those who desert the L[illegible]
consumed.

29 You will be ashamed of your idol
worship
in groves of sacred oaks.

1:15 Isa 59:2; Amos 5:21-24; Mic 3:4
1:16 Ps 26:6; Isa 52:11; Jer 25:5
1:17 Jer 22:3
1:18 Ps 51:7; Isa 43:26; 44:22; Rev 7:14
1:19 Deut 30:15-16
1:20 Isa 3:25
1:21 Jer 2:20
1:23 Exod 23:8; Jer 5:28; Ezek 22:7; Mic 7:3
1:24 Isa 35:4; 49:26
1:25 Ezek 22:19-22; Mal 3:3
1:26 Isa 33:5; Zech 8:3
[c]*shapat* (8199) ›Isa 33:22
1:28 Ps 9:5; 2 Thes 1:8-9
1:29 Isa 65:3

1:15 ***I will not look . . . I will not listen:*** The Lord does not respond to ***prayer*** offered from a life of persistent wickedness. In this case, God charged the people with perverting his laws in order to practice violent injustice toward *innocent victims.*

1:16 ***Wash . . . and be clean!*** The people were defiled by their sin and the uncleanness of their sacrifices. To be clean in God's eyes, they needed to change their behavior, get rid of their *sins*, and *give up* their *evil ways* (see also 1:18).

1:17 Seeking ***justice*** means upholding God's standards of fairness and advancing the rights of the ***oppressed, orphans,*** and ***widows***—those who are weak and marginalized in society (see also Jer 7:5-7; 22:3; Zech 7:10; Matt 23:23; 25:31-46; Jas 1:27).

1:18 God called his people to *come* and *settle* their dispute so that he could restore his covenant relationship with them. This required Judah to make a decision between obeying or turning away (1:19-20). Isaiah says their *sins* ***are like scarlet; . . . they are red like crimson,*** the color of blood, which Judah had unjustly shed (1:15). • ***white as snow . . . white as wool:*** The people would be radically transformed—cleansed, purified, and made holy (see also Ps 51:7; Dan 7:9).

1:19-20 Repentance leads to life, whereas resisting God's will and turning away from him results in death (see Deut 11:26-28; 28:1-62).

1:20 ***I, the LORD, have spoken!*** This statement marks the solemnity of what God has just promised. The phrase is used eleven times in Isaiah.

1:21 The image of ***Jerusalem*** as ***a prostitute*** represents Judah's unfaithfulness to God (see Jer 3:6-14; Ezek 16:25-26; Hos 1–3).

1:24 ***The LORD of Heaven's Armies, the Mighty One of Israel*** was usually Israel's protector (31:5). However, in this context, God was coming to ***take revenge*** against his own people, who by their wickedness had become his ***enemies*** and ***foes.***

1:25 ***I will raise my fist against you:*** God, normally Israel's protector, would become their attacker. However, he had a purpose beyond punishment. • ***I will melt you down. . . . I will remove all your impurities:*** God would use the Exile to remove the wicked from among his people and to refine those who would return.

1:26 The restoration of the community would be marked by new leaders who uphold justice rather than perverting it (see 1:23). ***Jerusalem*** would ***again*** be pure silver (see 1:22), ***the Home of Justice and the Faithful City.***

1:27 Here, ***Zion*** refers to the remnant community. Only ***those who repent*** would receive God's salvation and purification and would dwell in his presence. Zion was required to be the bastion of ***justice*** and ***righteousness,*** for God loves righteousness. God expected the covenant community to reflect the holy standards he cares about.

1:29-30 The rebels (1:28), who practiced idolatry ***in groves of sacred oaks*** and

1:31
Isa 5:24; 33:11-14; 66:24
Matt 3:12

2:1-4
//Mic 4:1-3

2:3
Isa 51:4-5
Luke 24:47

2:4
Isa 32:17-18
Hos 2:18

2:5
Isa 58:1; 60:1-2, 19-20
1 Jn 1:5, 7

2:6
Deut 31:17
2 Kgs 1:2; 16:7-8

You will blush because you worshiped
in gardens dedicated to idols.
30 You will be like a great tree with
withered leaves,
like a garden without water.
31 The strongest among you will disappear
like straw;
their evil deeds will be the spark that
sets it on fire.
They and their evil works will burn up
together,
and no one will be able to put out the
fire.

The Lord's Future Reign in the Restored City
Isa 2:2-4 // Mic 4:1-3

2 This is a vision that Isaiah son of Amoz
saw concerning Judah and Jerusalem:
2 In the last days, the mountain of the
Lord's house
will be the highest of all—
the most important place on earth.
It will be raised above the other hills,
and people from all over the world
will stream there to worship.
3 People from many nations will come
and say,
"Come, let us go up to the mountain of
the Lord,
to the house of Jacob's God.
There he will teach us his ways,
and we will walk in his paths."
For the Lord's teaching will go out from
Zion;
his word will go out from Jerusalem.
4 The Lord will mediate between
nations
and will settle international disputes.
They will hammer their swords into
plowshares
and their spears into pruning hooks.
Nation will no longer fight against
nation,
nor train for war anymore.

A Warning of Judgment
5 Come, descendants of Jacob,
let us walk in the light of the Lord!
6 For the Lord has rejected his people,
the descendants of Jacob,

---

in gardens dedicated to idols, would become like drought-stricken oaks and gardens. They would lack the nourishing vitality of the true God's presence. Those who followed the Canaanite fertility religion of Baal treated gardens and trees as sacred, believing that they brought blessings. Instead, they brought spiritual death.

2:1 ***vision*** (literally *word*): This heading (see 1:1) likely introduces the revelation of chs 2–12. The main focus of this section is on ***Judah,*** but a handful of passages expand that focus to include the nations in general (2:2-4), humanity at large (2:6-22), Syria and the northern kingdom of Israel (chs 7–9), and the Assyrians (ch 10).

2:2-4 God's gracious salvation would one day extend beyond Israel and Judah. This would prompt the nations to come to Zion, not in battle but to be blessed there and live by the rules of God's kingdom. Isaiah encouraged Judah to look at the benefits that the nations would enjoy. He wanted to stimulate the people of Judah (2:5) to jealousy and provoke them to follow the Lord so that they would not be left out in that day. This section is repeated almost verbatim in Mic 4:1-3.

2:2 In the OT, the expression ***the last days*** is a general reference to the future era (see Jer 49:39; Ezek 38:16; Hos 3:5); in the NT, it is used to refer to the period that began with the coming of the Lord Jesus (Heb 1:2) and more specifically to the period immediately preceding the end of the present age (2 Pet 3:3). • ***The mountain of the Lord's house*** referred to the Temple Mount. This location symbolized God's glorious exaltation (see 6:1) and his kingdom on earth. Isaiah's focus on God's exalted and supreme kingship flows out of his famous vision of God (ch 6). • Far from being a narrow nationalistic dream, Isaiah's prophetic hope extended beyond Judah and Jerusalem to include ***people from all over the world.***

2:3 Human society will undergo changes as people conform to God's revelation and follow his ***ways*** and ***paths.*** • Judah received the revelation (***teaching . . . word***) but did not obey it (1:10-15); however, the nations will be ready to do God's will.

2:4 The kingdom of God is evident when conflict and violence end, and it is always characterized by peace (Rom 14:17). People will cooperate willingly or they will be forced to end their hostilities (Ps 46:9). The nations will submit to divine arbitration rather than go to war (see 1:18-20). • The words ***mediate*** and ***settle*** refer to God's acts here, but later verses show the Messiah as the executor of justice (11:3-4). When this takes place, ***war*** will cease, and the ***nations*** will change their instruments of war into agricultural tools. • ***swords into plowshares:*** Cp. Joel 3:10, where the nations are exhorted to hammer their plowshares into swords.

2:5–4:1 Isaiah condemned Israel's and Judah's arrogance and self-exaltation, warning them that only God was to be exalted. All attempts by humans to lift themselves up will actually result in humiliation.

2:5-22 The prophet threatened judgment and scoffed at human pride. All human structures (religious, economic, military, social) will come under divine scrutiny and be found deficient on the day of the Lord—that final day in history when God will judge the wicked once and for all (1 Cor 1:8; 1 Thes 5:2; 2 Thes 2:2; 2 Pet 3:10; Rev 20:7-15). At times, the prophets also used the term the "day of the Lord" (or others like it, such as "that day") to refer to special instances of God's judgment upon wickedness during the course of history (see 13:6, 9; Ezek 13:5; 30:3; Obad 1:15). On the day of the Lord, God alone will be exalted, while all human wickedness and pride will be struck down. The glorious day of God's coming will fill wicked and arrogant humans with terror (2:10, 19, 21).

2:5 ***Come . . . let us walk:*** Walking in God's ***light*** (his revelation) will lead to glorious participation in his kingdom (see 60:1; 1 Jn 1:7). God is the only light that overcomes the darkness of sin and evil (9:2). People cannot generate such light in and of themselves (59:9) but must walk in the light God provides, as they trust him and live in obedience to his will (50:10). • The phrase ***descendants of Jacob*** alludes to Israel's special historic relationship with the Lord as well as their history of sinfulness and rebellion (see 14:1; 48:1).

2:6 The Lord had ***rejected his people*** to discipline them (8:17). While not

because they have filled their land with
practices from the East
and with sorcerers, as the
Philistines do.
They have made alliances with
pagans.
7 Israel is full of silver and gold;
there is no end to its treasures.
Their land is full of warhorses;
there is no end to its chariots.
8 Their land is full of idols;
the people worship things they have
made
with their own hands.
9 So now they will be humbled,
and all will be brought low—
do not forgive them.
10 Crawl into caves in the rocks.
Hide in the dust
from the terror of the LORD
and the glory of his majesty.
11 Human pride will be brought down,
and human arrogance will be
humbled.
Only the LORD will be exalted
on that day of judgment.
12 For the LORD of Heaven's Armies
has a day of reckoning.
He will punish the proud and mighty
and bring down everything that is
exalted.
13 He will cut down the tall cedars of
Lebanon
and all the mighty oaks of
Bashan.
14 He will level all the high mountains
and all the lofty hills.
15 He will break down every high tower
and every fortified wall.
16 He will destroy all the great trading
ships
and every magnificent vessel.
17 Human pride will be humbled,
and human arrogance will be brought
down.
Only the LORD will be exalted
on that day of judgment.

18 Idols will completely disappear.
19 When the LORD rises to shake the earth,
his enemies will crawl into holes in
the ground.
They will hide in caves in the rocks
from the terror of the LORD
and the glory of his majesty.
20 On that day of judgment they will
abandon the gold and silver idols
they made for themselves to
worship.
They will leave their gods to the rodents
and bats,
21 while they crawl away into caverns
and hide among the jagged rocks in
the cliffs.
They will try to escape the terror of the
LORD
and the glory of his majesty
as he rises to shake the earth.
22 Don't put your trust in mere humans.
They are as frail as breath.
What good are they?

2:7 Deut 17:16
2:8 Ps 115:4-8; Isa 10:11; 17:8; 44:17
2:9 Neh 4:5; Isa 5:15
2:10 2 Thes 1:9; Rev 6:15-16
2:11 Isa 13:11
2:12 Job 40:11-12; Mal 4:1
2:13 Isa 10:33-34; Zech 11:2
2:16 1 Kgs 10:22; Isa 23:1, 14
2:18 Isa 21:9; Mic 1:7
2:19 Ps 18:7; Hag 2:6-7; Heb 12:26
2:20 Isa 30:22
2:21 Isa 2:10, 19
2:22 Ps 8:4; 144:3-4; 146:3; Jer 17:5; Jas 4:14

permanent, the rejection seriously threatened their expectations of a glorious future. • ***sorcerers:*** These practitioners of pagan religion were expressly banned from Israel (Deut 18:10-11). • The ***Philistines*** were Israel's ancient enemies (9:12; 11:14; 14:29, 31).

2:7-8 Isaiah pointed out all the things that people substitute for the true God: material achievements and securities (***silver . . . treasures***), military strength (***warhorses . . . chariots***), and objects of affection (***idols***). Such wealth and military strength characterized the reign of King Uzziah (2 Chr 26:6-21). Elsewhere, Isaiah pointed out the sheer folly of worshiping anything that is ***made with*** one's ***own hands*** (see 44:9-20; 45:16).

2:10 In the day of God's judgment, people will seek refuge in ***caves in the rocks,*** natural hiding places in the rocky land of Judah, rather than repent in humility before almighty God. Kings and leaders as well as slaves and free persons will seek protection from judgment (see also Rev 6:15). • The ***terror of the LORD*** refers to God's unbridled wrath against wickedness that will be revealed on the day of the Lord's judgment (see note on 2:5-22). The prophecy shifts from Israel (2:5-6) to humanity at large. The Lord is against anything and anyone that exalts and trusts in human structures and beliefs rather than in God (2:11-12, 22).

2:11-12 A key theme in Isaiah is that the Lord will be ***exalted*** and humble people will be restored (57:15), while ***proud and mighty*** people are ***humbled*** (26:5). • The ***day of judgment*** and the "day of reckoning" are also called the "day of the LORD" (see note on 2:5-22). There are seven such references in chs 2–4 (2:11, 17, 20; 3:6, 18; 4:1, 2).

2:13-16 The prophet used several images of human strength to elaborate on 2:11-12.

2:13 The ***cedars of Lebanon*** were prized trees used in the construction of Solomon's Temple and palace (1 Kgs 5:6) and other important buildings (Ezra 3:7). They represented wealth and power (2 Chr 25:18; Ps 92:12; 104:16), yet these mighty trees were as nothing before the Lord (10:34; 33:9; see the boast of Sennacherib in 37:24). • The ***oaks of Bashan*** were also an image of strength and splendor (Ezek 27:6); they, too, will disappoint (33:9; Nah 1:4; Zech 11:2).

2:16 ***all the great trading ships:*** Hebrew *every ship of Tarshish*; see 23:1. • ***every magnificent vessel:*** Ornate sea-going vessels were a sign of prosperity.

2:17 The ***day of judgment*** is the "day of the LORD" (see 13:4-13).

2:20-21 Animals such as ***rodents and bats*** lead a shadowy, subterranean existence. Those who worship idols will become like them in attempting to escape the Lord's judgment.

2:22 The judgment prophecy of 2:6-21 is set between two related exhortations: to trust the Lord (2:5) and not to put trust in human beings (2:22). • Human strength is temporary, ***frail as breath*** (see Ps 90).

3:1 Lev 26:26 Ezek 4:16
3:2 Isa 9:14-15
3:4 Eccl 10:16
3:5 Isa 9:19 Jer 9:3-8 Mic 7:3-6
3:7 Ezek 34:4
3:8 Isa 1:7; 6:11; 9:17; 65:3, 5
3:9 Gen 13:13 Prov 8:36
3:10 Deut 28:1-14
3:11 Deut 28:15-68
3:12 Isa 9:16
3:13 Hos 4:1 Mic 6:2
3:14 Job 24:9, 14 Ps 10:9; 14:4 Ezek 18:12; 20:35-36 Jas 2:6
3:15 Ps 94:5

Messages of Woe and of Hope (3:1–5:30)

Judgment against Judah

3 1 The Lord, the LORD of Heaven's
Armies,
will take away from Jerusalem and
Judah
everything they depend on:
every bit of bread
and every drop of water,
2 all their heroes and soldiers,
judges and prophets,
fortune-tellers and elders,
3 army officers and high officials,
advisers, skilled craftsmen, and
astrologers.

4 I will make boys their leaders,
and toddlers their rulers.
5 People will oppress each other—
man against man,
neighbor against neighbor.
Young people will insult their elders,
and vulgar people will sneer at the
honorable.

6 In those days a man will say to his brother,
"Since you have a coat, you be our leader!
Take charge of this heap of ruins!"
7 But he will reply,
"No! I can't help.
I don't have any extra food or clothes.
Don't put me in charge!"

8 For Jerusalem will stumble,
and Judah will fall,
because they speak out against the LORD
and refuse to obey him.
They provoke him to his face.
9 The very look on their faces gives them
away.
They display their sin like the people
of Sodom
and don't even try to hide it.
They are doomed!
They have brought destruction upon
themselves.

10 Tell the godly that all will be well for
them.
They will enjoy the rich reward they
have earned!
11 But the wicked are doomed,
for they will get exactly what they
deserve.

12 Childish leaders oppress my people,
and women rule over them.
O my people, your leaders mislead you;
they send you down the wrong
road.

13 The LORD takes his place in court
and presents his case against his
people!
14 The LORD comes forward to pronounce
judgment
on the elders and rulers of his
people:
"You have ruined Israel, my vineyard.
Your houses are filled with things
stolen from the poor.
15 How dare you crush my people,
grinding the faces of the poor into
the dust?"
demands the Lord, the LORD of
Heaven's Armies.

3:1-12 These verses continue the subject of judgment against Israel's leadership (see 1:23-25). The removal of leadership at all levels would allow the mob to gain control. Chaos and famine would turn Judah and Jerusalem into a social wasteland.

3:1 ***take away . . . bread . . . water:*** God had long ago warned of famine, with its horrible conditions that sometimes led to desperate acts, as one possible judgment for wickedness (Lev 26:26-29).

3:2-3 Regardless of their status, all military, civil, judicial, and religious leaders would be removed in the day of judgment (39:7; 2 Kgs 24:14-16). God would eventually give his people good leaders again (1:26) but not diviners and others who used pagan forms of revelation (47:9, 12-13; see Deut 18:10-12).

3:4 Conditions would be so severe that ***boys*** and ***toddlers*** would qualify as candidates for office. By this, Isaiah either meant that adult leaders would be so decimated that only children would be left alive to assume the role or simply that the new leaders would be as immature, unwise, strong willed, and inexperienced as children.

3:6-7 Things would be so bad (a ***heap of ruins***) that no one would want to take leadership. The people would become so desperate that anyone providing ***food or clothes*** (3:6) could be the leader of the people. In fact, however, no one would have food or clothing (see 4:1).

3:8-9 The failure of human strength and societal organization can be a form of divine judgment. • ***to his face:*** The people of Judah had become bold in their wickedness ***like the people of Sodom*** (3:9; see also 1:9-10).

3:9 ***The very look on their faces:*** At this time people boldly displayed their rebellion against God.

3:10 The ***godly***—the righteous remnant—will receive God's rewards (see 40:10).

3:11 The ***wicked*** who practice and execute injustice will receive God's just punishment.

3:13 The Lord is both the prosecutor and the supreme judge in this trial against his people.

3:14 ***elders and rulers:*** Wickedness and abuse by ungodly and incompetent leadership thwarts God's purpose for his people (see also 3:12). Therefore, leaders come under more severe judgment because they bear responsibility for the welfare of those under them. • ***my vineyard:*** See the Song of the Vineyard (5:1-7).

3:15 The Lord cares for ***the poor.*** These were the marginalized and oppressed (see 1:17), but God is their protector (see 25:4). God called for his people to share his concern for the poor, but the Israelites were exploiting them to gain wealth (see 3:14).

A Warning to Jerusalem

16 The LORD says, "Beautiful Zion is haughty:
craning her elegant neck,
flirting with her eyes,
walking with dainty steps,
tinkling her ankle bracelets.
17 So the Lord will send scabs on her head;
the LORD will make beautiful Zion
bald."

18 On that day of judgment
the Lord will strip away everything
that makes her beautiful:
ornaments, headbands, crescent
necklaces,
19 earrings, bracelets, and veils;
20 scarves, ankle bracelets, sashes,
perfumes, and charms;
21 rings, jewels,
22 party clothes, gowns, capes, and purses;
23 mirrors, fine linen garments,
head ornaments, and shawls.

24 Instead of smelling of sweet perfume,
she will stink.
She will wear a rope for a sash,
and her elegant hair will fall out.
She will wear rough burlap instead of
rich robes.
Shame will replace her beauty.
25 The men of the city will be killed with
the sword,
and her warriors will die in battle.
26 The gates of Zion will weep and [d]mourn.
The city will be like a ravaged woman,
huddled on the ground.

4 In that day so few men will be left that
seven women will fight for each man,
saying, "Let us all marry you! We will provide our own food and clothing. Only let us
take your name so we won't be mocked as
old maids."

A Promise of Restoration

2 But in that day, the [e]branch of the LORD
will be beautiful and [f]glorious;
the fruit of the land will be the pride and
glory
of all who survive in Israel.
3 All who remain in Zion
will be a holy people—
those who survive the destruction of
Jerusalem
and are recorded among the living.
4 The Lord will wash the filth from
beautiful Zion
and cleanse Jerusalem of its bloodstains
with the hot [g]breath of fiery judgment.
5 Then the LORD will provide shade for
Mount Zion
and all who assemble there.
He will provide a canopy of cloud during
the day
and smoke and flaming fire at night,
covering the glorious land.

3:16 Isa 4:4
3:18 Judg 8:21
3:24 Esth 2:12; Isa 15:3; 22:12; 1 Pet 3:3
3:25 Isa 1:20; 65:12
3:26 Jer 14:2; Lam 2:10; [d]*'abal* (0056) ‣Isa 66:10
4:1 Isa 13:12; 54:4
4:2 Isa 11:1-5; 52:13; 53:2; Jer 23:5-6; Zech 3:8; 6:12; [e]*tsemakh* (6780) ‣Isa 11:1; [f]*kabod* (3519) ‣Isa 6:3
4:3 Isa 28:5; Luke 10:20
4:4 [g]*ruakh* (7307) ‣Isa 11:2
4:5 Num 9:15-23

3:16–4:1 This passage applies the prophet's teaching on arrogance (see 2:11-12) to the people of Jerusalem. An alternate understanding is that this passage applies specifically to the women of Jerusalem (see note on 3:16).

3:16 The dramatic descriptions show how the people of Jerusalem loved their refined way of life. They openly displayed their proud self-reliance, power, and prestige. • ***Beautiful Zion:*** Or *The women of Zion* (with corresponding changes to plural forms through verse 24); Hebrew reads *The daughters of Zion;* also in 3:17. See "Zion" at 60:1-22, p. 1195.

3:17-25 In a reversal of fortune, the affluent and proud people of Jerusalem would suffer disgrace. Some of their ***ornaments*** (3:18) likely were amulets to keep evil away, but they could not ward off the calamity of judgment. These items of beauty were status symbols and represented financial security.

3:24 ***Shame will replace her beauty:*** As in Dead Sea Scrolls; Masoretic Text reads *because instead of beauty.*

3:25 ***The men . . . will die in battle:*** Part of the city's hopeless destitution would be the deaths of the men.

4:1 During Isaiah's ministry, Jerusalem's population was so decimated through war, famine, and disease (3:1-3; 6:13; 14:30; 22:2; 37:4) that there were ***few men*** left, creating an absence of leadership (see 3:1-12). Even worse conditions lay ahead with the approaching war between Judah and the alliance of Syria and Israel in 734–732 BC (2 Chr 28) and eventually the conquest and fall of Jerusalem (605–586 BC).

4:2-6 In bold contrast to the desperate picture of 3:16–4:1, this prophecy of salvation and hope (see also 2:2-4) promised cleansing, consecration, and the renewal of God's presence with the remnant. The imagery in 4:5-6 alludes to Israel's exodus from Egypt, when a pillar of cloud and of fire guided and protected them. Israel's restoration from exile would be a second exodus.

4:2 ***The branch*** (or *the Branch*) in this context probably refers to the remnant that would constitute Israel's new beginning after the Exile (see 6:13). Some also understand it as representing the ideal descendant of David, the Messiah (see 11:1; Jer 23:5; 33:15-16; Zech 3:8; 6:12). • A ***beautiful and glorious*** transformation from shame and disgrace (3:17-25) to fertility and beauty would manifest God's presence and blessing among the remnant (4:6). • ***The fruit of the land,*** nature itself, would also be transformed from desolation to glory. Elsewhere, Isaiah described the future circumstances as resembling the Garden of Eden (see 51:3; 65:22). The message of renewal finds its ultimate fulfillment in the new creation (see Rom 8:19-27; 2 Cor 5:17; Gal 6:15; Eph 2:15; 4:24; Rev 21:22-27). • Those *who survive in Israel*—the remnant—would be the true citizens of Zion.

4:3 To be ***holy*** was the requirement for citizenship in ***Zion,*** where God dwells in his glorious majesty (see 6:3; Heb 12:14). • The remnant would have their names ***recorded among the living*** in the Book of Life (Exod 32:32; Dan 12:1; Mal 3:16; Rev 3:5; 20:12).

4:4 God's ***judgment*** has a purifying effect on his covenant people (see Mal 3:3). Justice must be satisfied before restoration can be offered. • ***from beautiful Zion:*** Or *from the women of Zion;* literally *from the daughters of Zion.*

4:5 The references to a ***canopy of cloud . . . and smoke and flaming fire*** recall God's continuous presence and protection during the exodus from Egypt (Exod 13:21-22; 14:21-22).

4:6
Ps 27:5
Isa 25:4; 32:1-2

5:1
Ps 80:8-9
Jer 12:10
Matt 21:33
Mark 12:1
Luke 20:9

5:2
Jer 2:21
Matt 21:19
Mark 11:13
Luke 13:6

5:4
Jer 7:25-26
Matt 23:37

5:5
Ps 80:12
Lam 1:15
Luke 21:24
Rev 11:2

5:6
Isa 24:3
Jer 14:1-22; 25:11

5:8
Jer 22:13-17
Mic 2:2

5:9
Isa 6:11-12
Matt 23:38

5:10
Hag 1:6; 2:16

6 It will be a shelter from daytime heat
and a hiding place from storms and rain.

The Song of the Vineyard

5 1 Now I will sing for the one I love
a song about his vineyard:
My beloved had a vineyard
on a rich and fertile hill.
2 He plowed the land, cleared its stones,
and planted it with the best vines.
In the middle he built a watchtower
and carved a winepress in the nearby rocks.
Then he waited for a harvest of sweet grapes,
but the grapes that grew were bitter.

3 Now, you people of Jerusalem and Judah,
you judge between me and my vineyard.
4 What more could I have done for my vineyard
that I have not already done?
When I expected sweet grapes,
why did my vineyard give me bitter grapes?
5 Now let me tell you
what I will do to my vineyard:
I will tear down its hedges
and let it be destroyed.
I will break down its walls
and let the animals trample it.
6 I will make it a wild place
where the vines are not pruned and the ground is not hoed,
a place overgrown with briers and thorns.
I will command the clouds
to drop no rain on it.

7 The nation of Israel is the vineyard of
the LORD of Heaven's Armies.
The people of Judah are his pleasant garden.
He expected a crop of justice,
but instead he found oppression.
He expected to find righteousness,
but instead he heard cries of violence.

Judah's Guilt and Judgment

8 What sorrow for you who buy up house
after house and field after field,
until everyone is evicted and you live
alone in the land.
9 But I have heard the LORD of Heaven's Armies
swear a solemn oath:
"Many houses will stand deserted;
even beautiful mansions will be empty.
10 Ten acres of vineyard will not produce
even six gallons of wine.

4:6 *shelter* (literally *shadow;* see 32:2): God's protection would keep the remnant safe from enemies and from the destruction he would bring on the wicked (33:14-16).

5:1-30 The prophet pronounced judgment through song (5:1-7) and prophecies of woe (5:8-30). Although Israel's future condition would be one of purity and fellowship with God (4:2-6), that future cannot ignore the present sinful condition of the people and their leaders.

5:1-7 The Song of the Vineyard expresses in poetic form God's indictment of the wicked leadership that had ruined his vineyard, Israel. Like some wisdom literature, it presents readers with an account of a puzzling situation (5:1-2) before giving its spiritual significance (5:3-7). The theme of the vineyard's transformation is found again in ch 27 and in Jesus' teaching (Matt 21:33; Mark 12:1).

5:1 The *one I love* refers to the Lord; the prophet was singing this song on the Lord's behalf. • At first, the song sounds like a love song, but by 5:3 readers realize it is actually a complaint. • On Israel as God's *vineyard,* see also 3:14; Matt 21:33-46; John 15:1-17.

5:2 The Lord gave the best care to his vineyard, preparing and nursing it as an expert agriculturalist. He watched over it with great attentiveness, planting the ***best vines***—ones that had the potential for abundant ***sweet grapes.*** God had great expectations of Israel as his people (see Exod 19:5-6), so the ***bitter*** grapes they produced—their unrighteous deeds—were useless and disappointing (cp. Gal 5:22-23).

5:3-4 Clearly, the Lord had graciously done everything possible for the vineyard. He was not to blame for the bitter grapes. • ***you judge:*** Isaiah wanted the audience to condemn the vineyard before he revealed that in fact they were the vineyard (5:7) This rhetorical tactic is similar to the one Nathan used to confront David (2 Sam 12:1-5).

5:5-6 The Lord promised to make his ***vineyard,*** Israel, a desolate place because it was fit only for destruction. Later, Isaiah prophesied the gracious, glorious transformation of Israel from desolation to fruitful vitality (see 55:13).

5:6 The withholding of ***rain*** was at times a divine judgment (Deut 28:23-24; Hag 1:11; 2:16). It was especially devastating to a society that depended heavily on agriculture.

5:7 The identification of ***Israel*** as ***the vineyard*** is a surprise that resolves the riddle of this passage. • Here, a powerful play on Hebrew words indicted Israel. The Lord expected ***justice*** (Hebrew *mishpat*) but saw only ***oppression*** (*mispakh*) of the needy. Instead of ***righteousness*** (*tsedaqah*), there were ***cries of violence*** (*tse'aqah*) against the poor (see 1:21-23).

5:8-23 This section contains six pronouncements of ***sorrow***—six threats of dreadful judgment (5:8, 11, 18, 20, 21, 22). The sorrows identify some of the "bitter grapes" produced by the vineyard of Israel (5:1-7; see note on 5:2).

5:8-10 ***What sorrow:*** The first threat of judgment was against oppressive greed. Properties (***house . . . and field***) were being taken by illegal means. The new owners were thugs who used every avenue to enrich themselves at the expense of the poor (see 1 Kgs 21:1-29; Amos 2:6-7).

5:10 ***Ten acres:*** Literally *A ten yoke,* that is, the area of land plowed by ten teams of oxen in one day. • ***six gallons:*** Hebrew *a bath* [21 liters]. • ***Ten baskets***

Ten baskets of seed will yield only one
basket of grain."
11 What sorrow for those who get up early
in the morning
looking for a drink of alcohol
and spend long evenings drinking wine
to make themselves flaming drunk.
12 They furnish wine and lovely music at
their grand parties—
lyre and harp, tambourine and flute—
but they never think about the LORD
or notice what he is doing.
13 So my people will go into exile far away
because they do not know me.
Those who are great and honored will
starve,
and the common people will die of
thirst.
14 The grave is licking its lips in
anticipation,
opening its mouth wide.
The great and the lowly
and all the drunken mob will be
swallowed up.
15 Humanity will be destroyed, and people
brought down;
even the arrogant will lower their eyes
in humiliation.
16 But the LORD of Heaven's Armies will be
exalted by his justice.
The holiness of God will be displayed
by his righteousness.
17 In that day lambs will find good pastures,
and fattened sheep and young goats
will feed among the ruins.
18 What sorrow for those who drag their
sins behind them
with ropes made of lies,
who drag wickedness behind them
like a cart!
19 They even mock God and say,
"Hurry up and do something!
We want to see what you can do.
Let the Holy One of Israel carry out his
plan,
for we want to know what it is."
20 What sorrow for those who say
that evil is good and good is evil,
that dark is light and light is dark,
that bitter is sweet and sweet is bitter.
21 What sorrow for those who are wise in
their own eyes
and think themselves so clever.
22 What sorrow for those who are heroes at
drinking wine
and boast about all the alcohol they
can hold.
23 They take bribes to let the wicked go
free,
and they punish the innocent.
24 Therefore, just as fire licks up stubble
and dry grass shrivels in the flame,
so their roots will rot
and their flowers wither.
For they have rejected the [h]law of the
LORD of Heaven's Armies;
they have despised the word of the
Holy One of Israel.
25 That is why the LORD's anger burns
against his people,

5:11
Prov 23:29-30
Isa 28:1, 3, 7-8

5:12
Ps 28:5

5:13
Isa 1:3; 3:3
Hos 4:6

5:14
Prov 30:16

5:15
Isa 2:11

5:16
Isa 33:5, 10

5:17
Isa 29:23
Zeph 2:6

5:18
Jer 23:10-14

5:19
2 Pet 3:3-4

5:20
Job 17:12
Prov 17:15
Matt 6:22-23
Luke 11:34-35

5:21
Prov 3:7
Rom 12:16
1 Cor 3:18-20

5:22
Isa 5:11; 56:12
Hab 2:15

5:23
Ps 94:21
Mic 3:11
Jas 5:6

5:24
Isa 9:18-19; 30:12
[h]*torah* (8451)
▸Hab 1:4

5:25
2 Kgs 22:13, 17
Isa 9:12, 17, 21; 10:4;
66:15

---

of seed . . . one basket: Hebrew *A homer* [5 bushels or 182 liters] *of seed will yield only an ephah* [20 quarts or 22 liters]. As with drought (5:5-6), the reduction of crops was at times a divine judgment (see Hag 1:6, 9; 2:16).

5:11-17 ***What sorrow:*** The second threat of judgment concerned indulgent lifestyles. The language throughout this section indicates a life of corruption.

5:12 Self-indulgent and contented, these people ***never think about the LORD.*** They were too busy enjoying their drunken parties to reflect on why things went bad in the first place, such as why God sent no rain, or why they lost a battle.

5:13 Israel and Judah would ***go into exile*** to Assyria (722 BC) and Babylon (586 BC). • The people did not respond to the Lord because they did not ***know*** him (see 1:3). They likely knew about him, but their behavior showed that they did not know him in any intimate way.

5:14 The ***grave*** (Hebrew *Sheol*) represented the place of the dead in ancient Near Eastern thinking (see note on 14:9).

5:16 God's kingship is by definition just and righteous, and he will be ***exalted by his justice.*** At his exaltation, oppressors will be condemned (see 1:21-23).

5:17 ***young goats:*** As in Greek version; Hebrew reads *strangers.*

5:18-19 ***What sorrow:*** The third threat of judgment was against mockers, who openly treated God's authority with contempt.

5:18 God's ***ropes*** were "ropes of kindness and love" for Israel (Hos 11:4).

5:19 The people challenged God to ***hurry up and do something*** to prove that he really exists and is in control of this world. The verb ***hurry up*** translates two Hebrew verbs: *maher* ("be quick") and *khush* ("be speedy"). The same Hebrew words are used in the name *Maher-shalal-hash-baz* (see 8:1; 10:6). • God's ***plan*** was revealed to Isaiah. Little did the people know that God's purposes would turn against them.

5:20 ***What sorrow:*** The fourth threat of judgment was against a lack of integrity. • ***evil is good . . . dark is light . . . bitter is sweet:*** This twisted way of looking at life corrupts God's holy order.

5:21 ***What sorrow:*** The fifth threat of judgment concerned the folly of self-deception.

5:22-24 ***What sorrow:*** The sixth threat of judgment was against the indulgent lifestyle of the wicked.

5:24 The image of rotting ***roots*** reflects human transience (cp. 11:1; 27:6; 37:31). • To despise the Lord's ***word*** means to ignore it, to live without regard for keeping it. Such an attitude toward God's revelation leads to folly and ruin (Prov 1:30; 5:12; 15:5).

5:25 ***mountains tremble:*** God's wrath against sinners is often expressed as the shaking of the earth's foundations (13:13; 23:11; 24:18-19; 29:6; 54:10).

5:26
Isa 13:2-3
5:27
Joel 2:7-8
5:28
Ps 7:12-13
Jer 4:13
5:29
Isa 42:22
Zeph 3:3
5:30
Isa 8:22; 17:12
Jer 4:23-28; 6:23
Joel 2:10
6:1
2 Kgs 15:7
Isa 1:1
John 12:41
[i]*rum* (7311)
‣ Exod 15:2
[j]*kisse'* (3678)
‣ Isa 9:7
6:2
Rev 4:8
[k]*sarap* (8314)
‣ Isa 6:6
6:3
Ps 72:19
Rev 4:8
[a]*kabod* (3519)
‣ Isa 40:5
6:5
Jer 9:3-8; 51:57
Luke 5:8

and why he has raised his fist to crush
them.
The mountains tremble,
and the corpses of his people litter
the streets like garbage.
But even then the LORD's anger is not
satisfied.
His fist is still poised to strike!

26 He will send a signal to distant nations
far away
and whistle to those at the ends of the
earth.
They will come racing toward Jerusalem.
27 They will not get tired or stumble.
They will not stop for rest or sleep.
Not a belt will be loose,
not a sandal strap broken.
28 Their arrows will be sharp
and their bows ready for battle.
Sparks will fly from their horses' hooves,
and the wheels of their chariots will
spin like a whirlwind.
29 They will roar like lions,
like the strongest of lions.
Growling, they will pounce on their
victims and carry them off,
and no one will be there to rescue them.
30 They will roar over their victims on that
day of destruction
like the roaring of the sea.
If someone looks across the land,
only darkness and distress will be seen;
even the light will be darkened by
clouds.

Isaiah's Cleansing and Call (6:1-13)

6 It was in the year King Uzziah died that
I saw the Lord. He was sitting on a [i]lofty
[j]throne, and the train of his robe filled the
Temple. 2Attending him were mighty [k]sera-
phim, each having six wings. With two
wings they covered their faces, with two they
covered their feet, and with two they flew.
3They were calling out to each other,

"Holy, holy, holy is the LORD of Heaven's
Armies!
The whole earth is filled with his [a]glory!"

4Their voices shook the Temple to its foundations, and the entire building was filled
with smoke.
5Then I said, "It's all over! I am doomed,
for I am a sinful man. I have filthy lips, and
I live among a people with filthy lips. Yet I

God's appearance in judgment or salvation in natural phenomena such as smoke, darkness, lightning, and earthquake is called a theophany (see 6:1-4, 6; 13:13; Exod 19:18-19; Ps 18:7-15; Mic 1:3-4; Rev 8:5; 16:17-18; 18:21-22).

5:26 The *signal* was a banner raised on a long pole and often placed on a high hill (see also 13:2; 18:3; 30:17). The expression ***signal to distant nations*** is common in Isaiah and might be a call for participation in battle (as here) or in salvation (11:10, 12; 49:22; 62:10). • ***Distant nations*** refers to the Assyrians and Babylonians, who served as instruments of God's judgment on Israel (722 BC) and on Judah (586 BC). They were the "wild animals" (5:5) called in to trample the vineyard (5:1-7). They would fiercely attack Israel and Judah, not letting up until God's judgment was complete (5:27-30).

5:30 *day of destruction* (literally *that day;* see note on 2:5-22). • In OT prophecy, ***darkness*** represents the experience of God's alienation, wrath, and judgment (see also 8:22), while light stands for his holy presence (see especially 60:2, 19).

6:1-13 Isaiah's marvelous vision of God as King on his throne served as a pivotal event in the life of the prophet. The historical circumstances surrounding this event can be interpreted in two ways: (1) Some see ch 6 as Isaiah's original call to ministry, meaning that chs 1–5 and 7–12 fit into the reign of Ahaz, who came to rule after the death of Uzziah (6:1). If this were so, why was Isaiah's call not at the beginning of the book? Perhaps his call was put in ch 6 for literary reasons, serving as a conclusion to chs 1–5 and an introduction to chs 7–12. The prophet's own transformation and commissioning symbolizes the entire nation's need for conversion if it wants to fulfill its mandate to be God's light to the world. (2) Others understand chs 1–12 as chronological; Isaiah's call in ch 6 would then serve as a recommissioning of the prophet to minister in a new way in a different period (the time of Ahaz) when his words would be rejected. Those who hold this interpretation point to 2:7-9; 3:16-24; and 5:8-14, contending that these passages reflect a time of prosperity, military strength, pride, and splendor; these conditions existed during Uzziah's reign but not during Ahaz's reign.

6:1 At the time that ***King Uzziah died*** in 740 BC, the Assyrians had begun to reassert their dominance in the ancient Near East. It marked the beginning of an era dominated by major world powers—Assyria, then Babylonia, Persia, Greece, and Rome. • ***I saw the Lord:*** "Lord" (Hebrew *'adonay*) is used to describe human rulers as well as God. God is the supreme King. • ***on a lofty throne:*** The apostle John also had a vision of God's heavenly throne (see Rev 4:2; 7:10; 21:5). • If just the ***train of*** the Lord's ***robe filled the Temple,*** how great and majestic must have been the robe itself and the one wearing it.

6:2 The ***mighty seraphim*** are heavenly beings not mentioned elsewhere in Scripture (but see also Rev 4:6-9; 15:8). The Hebrew term might suggest an association with fire. They ***covered their faces*** so as not to look on God.

6:3 The triple usage of the word ***holy*** emphasizes the absolute separateness of the Lord. • ***The whole earth is filled:*** Because there is no verb in the Hebrew, two slightly different translations of the seraphim's proclamation are possible. It could be that the ***earth,*** though defiled, is currently ***filled with his glory*** in creation. Or, it could mean that the earth *will* be filled with the glory of the Lord when he establishes his kingship on the earth in the future. Either way, the Lord's glorious presence will one day dwell more fully on earth, despite humanity's sinfulness and the power of wicked nations. God's glory was further revealed in the incarnation of the Son (John 12:41; 2 Cor 3:18; 4:4-7).

6:5 ***It's all over! I am doomed:*** The prophet felt unworthy of the vision. He was painfully aware of his personal uncleanness (***sinful . . . filthy lips***) when compared to the holiness of God. Isaiah knew that he was unworthy to speak the pure word of God, as were his people.

have seen the King, the LORD of Heaven's
[b]Armies."
[6]Then one of the [c]seraphim flew to me
with a burning coal he had taken from the altar with a pair of tongs. [7]He touched my lips
with it and said, "See, this coal has touched
your lips. Now your guilt is removed, and
your sins are forgiven."
[8]Then I heard the Lord asking, "Whom
should I send as a messenger to this people?
Who will go for us?"
I said, "Here I am. Send me."
[9]And he said, "Yes, go, and say to this
people,

'Listen carefully, but do not understand.
Watch closely, but learn nothing.'
[10] Harden the hearts of these people.
Plug their ears and shut their eyes.
That way, they will not see with their
eyes,
nor hear with their ears,
nor understand with their hearts
and turn to me for healing."

[11]Then I said, "Lord, how long will this
go on?"
And he replied,

"Until their towns are empty,
their houses are deserted,
and the whole country is a wasteland;
[12] until the LORD has sent everyone away,
and the entire land of Israel lies
deserted.
[13] If even a tenth—a remnant—survive,
it will be invaded again and burned.
But as a terebinth or oak tree leaves a
stump when it is cut down,
so Israel's stump will be a holy seed."

God's Plan vs. Human Counsel (7:1–11:16)
Crisis: A Message for Ahaz

7 When Ahaz, son of Jotham and grandson of Uzziah, was king of Judah, King
Rezin of Syria and Pekah son of Remaliah,
the king of Israel, set out to attack Jerusalem. However, they were unable to carry out
their plan.
[2]The news had come to the royal court
of Judah: "Syria is allied with Israel against
us!" So the hearts of the king and his people trembled with fear, like trees shaking in
a storm.

[b]*tsaba'* (6635)
‣Isa 13:4

6:6
[c]*sarap* (8314)
‣Isa 14:29

6:7
Isa 40:2
Jer 1:9
1 Jn 1:7

6:9
*Matt 13:15
*Luke 8:10
Rom 11:8

6:10
Jer 5:21
*Mark 4:12
*John 12:40
*Acts 28:26-27

6:11
Lev 26:31
Mic 3:12

6:12
Jer 4:29

6:13
Ezra 9:2
Job 14:7
Isa 11:1

7:1
2 Kgs 15:25, 37; 16:1

7:2
Isa 7:13; 8:12

6:7 ***your guilt is removed, and your sins are forgiven:*** The prophet's experience of forgiveness anticipated Israel's national need for forgiveness and cleansing (43:25; 44:22; see note on 39:6-7).

6:8 ***Who will go for us?*** The Lord spoke in the presence of his angels, the heavenly council (see also 1 Kgs 22:19-22; Jer 23:18, 22). • ***Here I am:*** The prophet was so overcome by the grace of God in cleansing him that he willingly committed himself to a lifetime of ministry.

6:9-10 For these verses, the Greek version reads *And he said, "Go and say to this people, / 'When you hear what I say, you will not understand. / When you see what I do, you will not comprehend.' / For the hearts of these people are hardened, / and their ears cannot hear, and they have closed their eyes—/ so their eyes cannot see, / and their ears cannot hear, / and their hearts cannot understand, / and they cannot turn to me and let me heal them."* Cp. Matt 13:14-15; Mark 4:12; Luke 8:10; Acts 28:26-27, all of which quote from the Greek version.

6:9 ***do not understand . . . learn nothing:*** The prophet's words brought out the heart response of his audience. The people were so sunk in sin that when they heard the truth it did not bring them closer to God but actually drove them away (Ahaz, ch 7). Yet the truth had to be declared. Jesus also applied this principle in his own preaching (Matt 13:14-15; Luke 8:10; 19:42; John 12:40; see also Acts 28:26-27; Rom 11:8).

6:10 Isaiah was God's agent to stimulate blindness and deafness in the wicked and sight and hearing in the godly (see also 29:9-10, 18; 35:5; 42:7, 16-19; 43:8; 56:10; 59:10). • ***turn to me for healing:*** The Lord was ready to heal those who truly repented, but not those who merely wanted to avoid judgment while holding on to their sinful ways.

6:11 ***how long . . . until . . . the whole country is a wasteland:*** During the prophet's ministry from 740 to 701 BC, the nation was plagued by wars, famines, and other forms of devastation.

6:13 Even if ***a tenth—a remnant—survive,*** the judgment would continue until nearly all were destroyed. The prophet often spoke of near extermination or decimation (9:18-21; 10:20; 22:4; 48:19; 51:18) but maintained the hope of a remnant who would make a new beginning (7:21-22; 29:23; 37:31; 44:26; 49:19; 54:1). • ***Israel's stump will be a holy seed:*** The stump represents a remnant of holy people (see 4:2-3) whose new leader would be pleasing to the Lord (11:1).

7:1–39:8 In this long section of the book, the nation of Israel was confronted with a vision of God, similar to how Isaiah was confronted in ch 6.

7:1–12:6 The historical context of these prophecies involved Assyria's rise to power and the alliance between Syria and Israel as enemies of Judah (7:1-2; see 2 Kgs 16:5). Assyria became God's rod to punish Syria, Israel, and Judah (chs 7–10). See map on 2 Kgs 15:19–20:37, p. 657.

7:1-25 At one point in his reign, Ahaz found himself in a crisis. The leaders of Syria and Israel attacked Judah. They planned to replace Ahaz and force Judah to join them in their resistance against Assyria. Ahaz responded by calling Assyria in to help him (2 Kgs 16:7-10), thus refusing Isaiah's challenge to trust the Lord instead (7:12). Although the Assyrians squelched the alliance of Syria and Israel, leading to the eventual downfall of both those nations, they also soon set their sights on total domination of Judah.

7:1 ***Rezin*** was king of ***Syria*** (Hebrew *Aram;* also in 7:2, 4, 5, 8). Damascus was Syria's capital city. • ***Pekah*** was king of Israel 740–732 BC. He was a renowned warrior (2 Chr 28:5-8). • Pekah and Rezin began to ***attack Jerusalem*** while Jotham was king (740–732 BC), and they intensified their efforts during the early years of young King Ahaz (2 Kgs 15:37; 16:5).

7:2 ***Israel:*** Literally *Ephraim,* referring to the northern kingdom of *Israel;* also in 7:5, 8, 9, 17. • ***hearts . . . trembled with fear:*** In contrast, Ahaz's son King Hezekiah faced the Assyrians some thirty years later with great faith (701 BC; see 37:6-7, 14-20).

7:4 Exod 14:13; Isa 10:24; 30:15; 35:4; Lam 3:26
7:7 Isa 8:10
7:8 Isa 17:1-3
7:9 2 Chr 20:20; Isa 30:12-14
7:11 2 Kgs 19:29; Isa 37:30; 38:7-8
7:14 Isa 8:8, 10; *Matt 1:23

3 Then the LORD said to Isaiah, "Take your son Shear-jashub and go out to meet King Ahaz. You will find him at the end of the aqueduct that feeds water into the upper pool, near the road leading to the field where cloth is washed.
4 Tell him to stop worrying. Tell him he doesn't need to fear the fierce anger of those two burned-out embers, King Rezin of Syria and Pekah son of Remaliah.
5 Yes, the kings of Syria and Israel are plotting against him, saying,
6 'We will attack Judah and capture it for ourselves. Then we will install the son of Tabeel as Judah's king.'
7 But this is what the Sovereign LORD says:

"This invasion will never happen;
it will never take place;
8 for Syria is no stronger than its capital,
Damascus,
and Damascus is no stronger than its
king, Rezin.
As for Israel, within sixty-five years
it will be crushed and completely
destroyed.
9 Israel is no stronger than its capital,
Samaria,
and Samaria is no stronger than its
king, Pekah son of Remaliah.
Unless your faith is firm,
I cannot make you stand firm."

The Sign of Immanuel

10 Later, the LORD sent this message to King Ahaz:
11 "Ask the LORD your God for a sign of confirmation, Ahaz. Make it as difficult as you want—as high as heaven or as deep as the place of the dead."
12 But the king refused. "No," he said, "I will not test the LORD like that."
13 Then Isaiah said, "Listen well, you royal family of David! Isn't it enough to exhaust human patience? Must you exhaust the patience of my God as well?
14 All right then, the Lord himself will give you the sign. Look!

Fearing People (7:1-25)

Isa 41:10; 51:7-8, 12-13; 54:4; 57:11; Num 14:1-12; 21:34-35; Josh 1:9; 2 Kgs 16:5-18; 2 Chr 28:16-23; Ps 23:4; Prov 29:25; Jer 10:5; 30:10; 46:27-28

One of the purposes of Isaiah's prophecy was to highlight the contrast between faith and fear. We see Ahaz as an example of fear (7:1-25). We then see Hezekiah as an imperfect example of faith (see ch 37). Isaiah himself provides a better example of faith (ch 8). Finally, God's servant stands as the ideal example of faith (42:1-7; 50:4-7).

Ahaz trembled when he heard that Syria and Israel had allied against him (7:2). The Lord encouraged him to be a man of faith, because without faith he could not expect the Lord's protection (7:9). However, Ahaz refused to trust the Lord. Rather, he turned to the Assyrians for help. As a result, the Lord became a trap for him, as for all Israel and Judah, rather than a source of safety (8:11-15). God can be a stumbling stone (8:14) for those who look elsewhere for peace and security.

Combining the fear, or worship, of the Lord with the worship of human beings, institutions, or idols is called *syncretism*. Syncretism is a deceptive trap. Isaiah presents the Lord as the incomparable one (see 40:18) who does not tolerate syncretism (17:10; 57:11). Those who do not commit themselves wholly to God will live in fear of others. Ultimately, they will live lives filled with dread.

7:3 *Shear-jashub* is a symbolic name meaning *a remnant will return* (see 10:21). • The ***aqueduct*** was a place where political negotiations took place later during Hezekiah's reign (see 36:2). • ***washed:*** Or *bleached.*

7:4 ***he doesn't need to fear:*** This was a "fear not" prophecy (common in Isaiah) in which the Lord assured his people of his presence and purpose. • ***two burned-out embers:*** If Ahaz had God's perspective, he would have seen that Rezin and Pekah were minor threats who were about to be extinguished.

7:6 The *son of Tabeel,* otherwise unknown, was obviously sympathetic to Israel's and Syria's resistance against Assyria.

7:8 The Assyrian kings Esarhaddon and Ashurbanipal had Israel resettled with people from other places *within sixty-five years* (by 670 BC; see 2 Kgs 17:24-34). • Damascus was ***crushed and completely destroyed*** by 732 BC, and Samaria was crushed by 722 BC.

7:9 The last sentence is a play on two Hebrew words: If you do not have faith (*ta'aminu*), you will not stand firm (*te'amenu*). Firm trust in the Lord is utterly essential, especially for a leader of God's people (see also 2 Chr 20:20), and it must be firmly acted upon in order to demonstrate that it exists. Ahaz and his contemporaries trusted their enemy (Assyria) rather than God. By contrast, Hezekiah later demonstrated his faith in the Lord in a similar context (see chs 36–38).

7:11 A ***sign of confirmation*** would be performed before Ahaz's eyes as a token of God's truthfulness. His son Hezekiah would also receive such a sign (see 37:30). • ***as deep as the place of the dead:*** Hebrew *as deep as Sheol.* See note on Ps 6:5.

7:12 ***I will not test the LORD like that:*** Despite this seemingly pious response (based on Deut 6:16), Ahaz was most likely already in negotiations with the Assyrians and had already decided whom he would trust for rescue in this war.

7:14 ***virgin*** (Hebrew *'almah*): Or *young woman.* • This prophecy received its ultimate fulfillment in the birth of Jesus Christ (Matt 1:18-24). Yet it is likely that it also had a partial fulfillment in Isaiah's day, either with the birth of godly king Hezekiah, Ahaz's son, or with the birth of one of Isaiah's children. The

The virgin will conceive a child! She will give
birth to a son and will call him Immanuel
(which means 'God is with us'). 15By the time
this child is old enough to choose what is
right and reject what is wrong, he will be eating yogurt and honey. 16For before the child
is that old, the lands of the two kings you
fear so much will both be deserted.
17"Then the LORD will bring things on
you, your nation, and your family unlike anything since Israel broke away from Judah.
He will bring the king of Assyria upon you!"
18In that day the LORD will whistle for
the army of southern Egypt and for the
army of Assyria. They will swarm around
you like flies and bees. 19They will come
in vast hordes and settle in the fertile areas
and also in the desolate valleys, caves, and
thorny places. 20In that day the Lord will
hire a "razor" from beyond the Euphrates
River—the king of Assyria—and use it to
shave off everything: your land, your crops,
and your people.
21In that day a farmer will be fortunate
to have a cow and two sheep or goats left.
22Nevertheless, there will be enough milk
for everyone because so few people will
be left in the land. They will eat their fill of
yogurt and honey. 23In that day the lush vineyards, now worth 1,000 pieces of silver, will
become patches of briers and thorns. 24The
entire land will become a vast expanse of
briers and thorns, a hunting ground overrun by wildlife. 25No one will go to the
fertile hillsides where the gardens once
grew, for briers and thorns will cover them.
Cattle, sheep, and goats will graze there.

The Coming Assyrian Invasion

8 Then the LORD said to me, "Make a
large signboard and clearly write this
name on it: Maher-shalal-hash-baz." 2I asked
Uriah the priest and Zechariah son of Jebere-
kiah, both known as honest men, to witness
my doing this.
3Then I slept with my [d]wife, and she became pregnant and gave birth to a son. And
the LORD said, "Call him Maher-shalal-hash-
baz. 4For before this child is old enough to
say 'Papa' or 'Mama,' the king of Assyria will
carry away both the abundance of Damascus and the riches of Samaria."
5Then the LORD spoke to me again and
said, 6"My care for the people of Judah is
like the gently flowing waters of Shiloah,
but they have rejected it. They are rejoic-

7:15 Isa 8:4
7:17 1 Kgs 12:16-17; Isa 10:5-6
7:18 Isa 5:26
7:19 Jer 16:16
7:20 Isa 8:7; 10:5, 15; 24:1; Ezek 5:1-4
7:21 Jer 39:10
8:1 Isa 30:8; Hab 2:2
8:2 2 Kgs 16:10-11, 15-16
8:3 [d]*nebi'ah* (5031) › Jer 6:13
8:4 Isa 7:8-9, 16
8:6 Isa 7:1; 30:12

similar sequence of the verbs in 7:14 and 8:3 (***conceive . . . give birth . . . call***) and the link between Immanuel and Maher-shalal-hash-baz in 8:5-10 suggest that Immanuel and Maher-shalal-hash-baz were the same person; see note on 8:5-10. • The name ***Immanuel (which means 'God is with us')*** symbolized God's presence and protection. God was with Judah during the attack by the alliance of Syria and Israel (734 BC), in the Assyrian crisis (701 BC), and throughout their prolonged existence until their fall in 586 BC. The kingdom of Israel fell during the time of Isaiah (722 BC). The assurance "I am with you" remained significant even in the exilic and postexilic periods (41:10; 43:2, 5). The greatest assurance ultimately came in Jesus Christ, the incarnate Son of God (Matt 1:23; see also Rev 12:5).

7:15-16 ***By the time this child is old enough:*** The crisis involving the alliance of Syria and Israel against Judah was in 734 BC; by 732 BC Damascus, capital of Syria, was destroyed, and the northern kingdom, Israel, was defeated. • ***choose what is right and reject what is wrong:*** This was to happen by the age of 12, when a child was held responsible as an adult. In 722 BC, Israel went into exile. • ***he will be eating yogurt*** (or *curds;* also in 7:22) ***and honey:*** The land would be so depopulated that these delicacies would be available to all.

7:17 ***Israel broke away from Judah*** in 931 BC (see 1 Kgs 12:19-20). • ***will bring the king of Assyria upon you:*** Ahaz called Assyria in to help (2 Kgs 16:8-9), but Assyria turned against him and made Judah a vassal state.

7:18-25 The repetition of ***in that day*** referred to the yet future day of the Lord (see note on 2:5-22). Judah would experience the judgment already announced by Isaiah as a foretaste of an even greater judgment to come: exile in Babylon (586–538 BC).

7:19 Locations such as ***desolate valleys, caves, and thorny places*** were places of refuge for the desperate (see 2:10). However, Judah's enemies would find them there.

7:20 ***the Euphrates River:*** Literally *the river.* • ***shave off everything: your land, your crops, and your people*** (literally *shave off the head, the hair of the legs, and the beard*): In the ancient Near East, forced shaving was an act of disgrace (see 2 Sam 10:4-5). Here it was a metaphor for the despoiling of the country.

7:23-25 Farmers faced near total disaster. Fertile agricultural fields (***lush vineyards***) would revert to wild grazing lands dominated by worthless plants (***briers and thorns;*** see 5:6).

7:23 ***1,000 pieces of silver:*** Hebrew *1,000 shekels of silver,* about 25 pounds or 11.4 kilograms in weight.

8:1 ***Maher-shalal-hash-baz*** means "Swift to plunder and quick to carry away"; see note on 5:19. The words apply both to Judah's enemies (8:4) and to Judah itself (8:7-8). They had trusted Assyria in place of God, and now Assyria would turn on them and all but destroy them. God was with them (*Immanuel;* see 7:14), but his presence would be destructive if they refused to trust in him (see 8:14).

8:3 ***my wife:*** Literally *the prophetess.* • Like the name *Immanuel* (7:14), ***Maher-shalal-hash-baz*** is symbolic. It is possible that this child was the partial fulfillment of the Immanuel prophecy as well (see note on 7:14). The ultimate fulfillment of the Immanuel prophecy occurred with the birth of Jesus (Matt 1:22-23).

8:4 ***before this child is old enough:*** See also 7:16. • ***Damascus*** and ***Samaria*** were ruined and destroyed in 732 BC, fulfilling this verse along with 7:8, 19-20.

8:5-10 This prophecy connects the sign of Maher-shalal-hash-baz with the sign of Immanuel (8:8, 10; see note on 7:14).

8:6 ***The gently flowing waters of Shiloah*** supplied Jerusalem with water. Here they represent God's loving presence and provision (see Ps 46:4). • Ahaz ***rejected*** the sign and the promise of God's protection. He was not a man of faith (7:9), and now ***the people*** were following in his footsteps by placing their

8:7
Isa 17:12-13
Amos 8:8; 9:5
8:8
Isa 7:14; 10:6; 30:28
8:9
Dan 2:34-35
8:11
Ezek 2:8; 3:14
8:12
Isa 7:2
*1 Pet 3:13-15
8:13
Num 20:12
Isa 5:16; 29:23
8:14
Isa 25:4
Ezek 11:16
Luke 2:34
*Rom 9:33
*1 Pet 2:8
8:15
Isa 28:13
Luke 20:18
Rom 9:32
8:16
Isa 50:4
Dan 12:4
8:17
Deut 31:17
Isa 30:18; 54:8
Hab 2:3
8:18
*Heb 2:13

ing over what will happen to King Rezin
and King Pekah. 7 Therefore, the Lord will
overwhelm them with a mighty flood from
the Euphrates River—the king of Assyria
and all his glory. This flood will overflow
all its channels 8 and sweep into Judah until it is chin deep. It will spread its wings,
submerging your land from one end to the
other, O Immanuel.

9 "Huddle together, you nations, and be
terrified.
Listen, all you distant lands.
Prepare for battle, but you will be crushed!
Yes, prepare for battle, but you will be
crushed!
10 Call your councils of war, but they will be
worthless.
Develop your strategies, but they will
not succeed.
For God is with us!"

A Call to Trust the Lord

11 The Lord has given me a strong warning
not to think like everyone else does. He said,

12 "Don't call everything a conspiracy, like
they do,
and don't live in dread of what
frightens them.
13 Make the Lord of Heaven's Armies holy
in your life.
He is the one you should fear.
He is the one who should make you
tremble.
14 He will keep you safe.
But to Israel and Judah
he will be a stone that makes people
stumble,
a rock that makes them fall.
And for the people of Jerusalem
he will be a trap and a snare.
15 Many will stumble and fall,
never to rise again.
They will be snared and captured."
16 Preserve the teaching of God;
entrust his instructions to those who
follow me.
17 I will wait for the Lord,
who has turned away from the
descendants of Jacob.
I will put my hope in him.

18 I and the children the Lord has given
me serve as signs and warnings to Israel

hope in Assyria to save them from ***King Rezin and King Pekah*** (Hebrew *and the son of Remaliah*; 7:7-8, 16). • ***They are rejoicing over what will happen to:*** Or *They are rejoicing because of.*

8:7 The ***mighty flood from the Euphrates River*** (literally *the river*) represents the invading Assyrian army (see Jer 47:2). The river would ***overflow all its channels*** when the Assyrians marched deep into Judah. This stood as a frightening contrast with the gently flowing waters of Shiloah (8:6).

8:8 ***chin deep:*** Judah barely survived the Assyrian assaults in 701 BC (see chs 36–37). • ***submerging your land from one end to the other:*** From north to south, Judah was nearly devastated, except for the city of Jerusalem (see 1:8-9; chs 36–37). • ***Immanuel:*** Despite their failure to trust him and the disaster it brought, God was still with his people (see 7:14).

8:9-10 God's plan to rescue his stubborn people would ultimately be fulfilled. God planned to destroy Assyria, just as he does every other proud nation that rejects him or boasts in its own power.

8:10 ***God is with us:*** Hebrew *Immanuel!* See 7:14; 8:8.

8:11-15 This text reveals the heart of Isaiah's message. The issue was fear of the Lord versus fear of people (see 7:9; 8:6). When an individual fears people, the Lord becomes a trap and destruction is certain (cp. Prov 29:25). For those who fear the Lord, he becomes a sanctuary; their salvation is assured.

8:12 People regarded Isaiah's message of non-involvement with Assyria as treasonous, part of a ***conspiracy.*** But Isaiah was not trying to play political games; rather, he proclaimed God's message. • ***What frightens them*** was the alliance of Syria and Israel attacking Judah (see 7:1, 4).

8:13 To ***make the Lord . . . holy*** meant giving him first place in life and acknowledging that nothing is greater than he is. • ***Fear*** of God means reverencing him as God (Prov 1:7). The people of Judah were not to fear Israel and Syria or the Assyrians (7:9; 10:24).

8:14 ***He will keep you safe*** (literally *he will be a sanctuary*): God is a place of refuge. • ***stone . . . stumble . . . rock . . . fall:*** By trusting Assyria rather than God, the people of ***Jerusalem*** would find themselves in ***a trap and a snare*** as the Assyrians turned against them. For those who trust in the Lord, however, he is faithful and strong (28:16; see Ps 118:22-23; Luke 2:34; Rom 9:32-33; 1 Pet 2:6-8).

8:16-17 The command to preserve Isaiah's teaching suggests that it was harshly received by his contemporaries, who might have wanted to snuff it out (see note on 8:12). Faithful disciples safely preserved the prophet's messages.

8:16 ***instructions*** (Hebrew *torah*): The Torah defined Israel's covenant relationship with God, but the people were quick to forget (see also 1:10).

8:17 ***I will wait for the Lord . . . I will put my hope in him:*** Isaiah's message against Syria, Israel, and Assyria would be proven true in the historical events that followed. The fulfillment would further encourage the godly to await the final downfall of all ungodly power structures (see 8:9-10). Waiting for the Lord requires submission, prayer, hope, and faith (see 25:9; 26:8; 33:2), resulting in a quiet spirit and a renewal of inner strength (40:31). The book of Hebrews applies these words to Jesus Christ (Heb 2:13). • God had ***turned away;*** the people of Israel and Judah were alienated from the Lord because of their sin.

8:18 ***I and the children the Lord has given me*** (see the application to Jesus Christ in Heb 2:13): The names of the prophet Isaiah and his children carried significance as ***signs and warnings.*** Shear-jashub (*a remnant will return;* 7:3) was a sign of God's faithfulness to Judah. Maher-shalal-hash-baz (*swift to plunder and quick to carry away*) signified the destruction of Damascus and Samaria (8:1-4) and the desolation of faithless Judah (8:5-8). The name of Isaiah (*Yahweh is salvation*) itself signifies that salvation is from the Lord alone. These three names also represent major themes in the book: the remnant, the desolation of Judah, and salvation.

from the LORD of Heaven's Armies who
dwells in his Temple on Mount Zion.
19 Someone may say to you, "Let's ask the
mediums and those who consult the [e]spir-
its of the dead. With their whisperings and
mutterings, they will tell us what to do." But
shouldn't people ask God for guidance?
Should the living seek guidance from the
dead?
20 Look to God's instructions and teachings! People who contradict his word are
completely in the dark. 21 They will go from
one place to another, weary and hungry.
And because they are hungry, they will rage
and curse their king and their God. They
will look up to heaven 22 and down at the
earth, but wherever they look, there will be
trouble and anguish and dark despair. They
will be thrown out into the darkness.

Hope in the Messiah

9 Nevertheless, that time of darkness and
despair will not go on forever. The land
of Zebulun and Naphtali will be humbled,
but there will be a time in the future when
Galilee of the Gentiles, which lies along the
road that runs between the Jordan and the
sea, will be filled with glory.

2 The people who walk in darkness
will see a great light.
For those who live in a land of deep
darkness,
a light will shine.
3 You will enlarge the nation of Israel,
and its people will rejoice.
They will rejoice before you
as people rejoice at the harvest
and like warriors dividing the plunder.
4 For you will break the yoke of their
slavery
and lift the heavy burden from their
shoulders.
You will break the oppressor's rod,
just as you did when you destroyed
the army of Midian.
5 The boots of the warrior
and the uniforms bloodstained by war
will all be burned.
They will be fuel for the fire.
6 For a child is born to us,
a son is given to us.
The government will rest on his
shoulders.
And he will be called:
Wonderful Counselor, Mighty God,
Everlasting Father, Prince of [f]Peace.
7 His government and its peace
will never end.
He will rule with fairness and justice
from the [g]throne of his ancestor
David
for all eternity.
The passionate commitment of the LORD
of Heaven's Armies
will make this happen!

8:19
Lev 20:6
1 Sam 28:8
2 Kgs 21:6
Isa 19:3; 30:2
[e]*yidde'oni* (3049)
‣Isa 19:3

8:20
Mic 3:6
Luke 16:29

8:22
Isa 5:30
Jer 13:16
Amos 5:18, 20
Zeph 1:14-15

9:1
2 Kgs 15:29
2 Chr 16:4

9:2
*Matt 4:15-16

9:3
Isa 26:15; 35:10;
66:10

9:4
Isa 49:26

9:6
Deut 10:17
Neh 9:32
Isa 7:14; 26:3, 12
Matt 28:18
1 Cor 15:25
[f]*shalom* (7965)
‣Isa 59:8

9:7
Dan 2:44
Luke 1:32-33
[g]*kisse'* (3678)
‣Isa 66:1

Immanuel (*God is with us*) embodies all of these themes, along with the idea that Judah would be protected if only it would trust in the Lord.

8:19-22 Isaiah contrasts his counsel with that of his ungodly contemporaries. Isaiah's message gives light, whereas the message of the spiritists led to darkness and death. • ***Mediums*** used various means of divination, including summoning the dead, in the attempt to determine the future (see 19:3). God had banned these useless activities (47:9; Deut 18:9-11).

8:20 God gave ***instructions and teachings*** through the law and through his prophets, such as Isaiah (see 8:16).

9:1-7 Beyond destruction there is hope. In the Messiah's kingdom, the darkness would give way to great light, which was to dawn in Galilee and reach the whole nation, and then the whole world. The Messiah's rule would be marked by the vindication of the oppressed and the end of all oppression. He would bring justice and righteousness forever in a kingdom of peace.

9:1 Verse 9:1 is numbered 8:23 in the Hebrew text. • ***Zebulun and Naphtali*** were northern tribes in Israel (Judg 6:35). They were ***humbled*** by the Assyrian invaders under Tiglath-pileser III in 734 and 732 BC. In Jesus' lifetime, this prophecy was connected with his coming out of Galilee (Matt 4:14-16). • ***Galilee of the Gentiles*** was the region of Israel between the Sea of Galilee and the Mediterranean Sea. It was heavily influenced—culturally, religiously, and politically—by the surrounding Gentile nations.

9:2 Verses 9:2-21 are numbered 9:1-20 in the Hebrew text. • ***a land of deep darkness:*** Greek version reads *a land where death casts its shadow.* Cp. Matt 4:16.

9:4 The people experienced the rule of other nations as a ***yoke of . . . slavery*** and a ***heavy burden*** (Jer 30:8). • ***oppressor's rod:*** In 10:5, the Assyrians are called "the rod of [the Lord's] anger." Just as God's anger will cease, so will Assyria's oppression of Judah (14:5). • The Lord had ***destroyed the army of Midian*** through Gideon (see Judg 6:35; 7:22-25).

9:5 Burning the ***boots*** and ***uniforms*** marked the end of the need for instruments of war.

9:6 ***a child is born to us, a son is given to us:*** This child, the Messiah, would be David's descendant (11:1). • ***he will be called:*** These names can be read as four throne names, signifying the nature of the child's rule: (1) The ***Wonderful Counselor*** (or ***Wonderful, Counselor***) conforms to God's wisdom (11:1; 25:1; 28:29; 40:13), unlike the counselors of Judah (1:26; 3:3). (2) ***Mighty God*** is an affirmation of the Messiah's divine nature. (3) He cares for his children as the ***Everlasting Father,*** the father whose care continues forever (cp. 22:21; 63:16). (4) The ***Prince of Peace*** is a leader who brings peace. • Alternatively, the four names could be collapsed into two: (1) "A Wonderful Counselor [is] the Mighty God"; and (2) "the Everlasting Father [is] a Prince of Peace" (on his nature, see 11:1-9). • Jesus Christ, the Son of David (Matt 1:1; Luke 1:32; see also Isa 7:14; 8:3, 18), will bring in the kingdom of his peace (Rev 19).

9:7 Like Ahaz, this ruler will be a descendant of ***David.*** Unlike Ahaz and the rulers of Jerusalem (1:21-23), he would trust God and rule with justice and righteousness (11:1-3). Jesus the Messiah reigns for all eternity (Luke 1:32-33).

9:9 Isa 7:8-9
9:12 Ps 79:7
9:13 Jer 5:3; Hos 7:10
9:14 Isa 19:15; Rev 18:8
9:16 Matt 15:14
9:17 Amos 8:13; Matt 12:34
9:18 Mal 4:1
9:19 Joel 2:3; Mic 7:2, 6
9:20 Isa 8:21-22; 49:26

The Lord's Anger: Judgment against Israel

8 The Lord has spoken out against Jacob;
his judgment has fallen upon Israel.
9 And the people of Israel and Samaria,
who spoke with such pride and arrogance,
will soon know it.
10 They said, "We will replace the broken bricks of our ruins with finished stone,
and replant the felled sycamore-fig trees with cedars."

11 But the LORD will bring Rezin's enemies against Israel
and stir up all their foes.
12 The Syrians from the east and the Philistines from the west
will bare their fangs and devour Israel.
But even then the LORD's anger will not be satisfied.
His fist is still poised to strike.

13 For after all this punishment, the people will still not repent.
They will not seek the LORD of Heaven's Armies.
14 Therefore, in a single day the LORD will destroy both the head and the tail,
the noble palm branch and the lowly reed.
15 The leaders of Israel are the head,
and the lying prophets are the tail.
16 For the leaders of the people have misled them.
They have led them down the path of destruction.
17 That is why the Lord takes no pleasure in the young men
and shows no mercy even to the widows and orphans.
For they are all wicked hypocrites,
and they all speak foolishness.
But even then the LORD's anger will not be satisfied.
His fist is still poised to strike.

18 This wickedness is like a brushfire.
It burns not only briers and thorns
but also sets the forests ablaze.
Its burning sends up clouds of smoke.
19 The land will be blackened
by the fury of the LORD of Heaven's Armies.
The people will be fuel for the fire,
and no one will spare even his own brother.
20 They will attack their neighbor on the right
but will still be hungry.
They will devour their neighbor on the left
but will not be satisfied.
In the end they will even eat their own children.

Trusting the Lord (8:16-20)

Isa 2:22; 7:4-9; 12:1-2; 26:2-3, 12; 32:17-18; 35:4; 40:9-11, 28-31; 51:12; Jer 14:22; Lam 3:22-27

After Isaiah saw a vision of God's goodness and glory (ch 6), he looked at life with a renewed perspective on God's righteousness and exaltation. The prophet saw that mere humans prove untrustworthy (2:22); the Lord alone is holy and to be feared. The prophet led his family and disciples to wait for and hope in the Lord alone (8:16-17).

Isaiah's trust in the Lord represents the spirit of the "new community." God's children come out of Israel, Judah, and the Gentile nations. They live in awe of the Lord (29:23) and are not afraid (see 7:4; 35:4; 40:9), knowing that the Lord will be with them (51:12). They respond in praise because they trust in him (12:1-2). The faithful might feel the effects of God's judgment on his enemies as they await the Lord's salvation. Yet they find new strength day by day (40:31). They see themselves as citizens of God's city, Zion, even while living with contemporaries who do not believe as they do (26:2).

In all this, Isaiah anticipates the coming servant, the Messiah (49:1-7). The lifestyle of trusting the Lord brings true and lasting inner peace (26:3, 12; 32:17-18).

9:8-12 This prophecy of judgment was against the northern kingdom of Israel. Despite God's message that the Assyrians would crush them (chs 7–8), the people of Samaria were foolishly confident that they could withstand the siege.

9:9 ***of Israel:*** Literally *of Ephraim,* referring to the northern kingdom of Israel.

9:10 In their proud confidence, Israel thought it would replace whatever was lost with more expensive items (see 2:13-16; also Amos 5:11).

9:11 ***Rezin's enemies*** were the Assyrians (7:4, 17; 8:4). Rezin was king of Syria (see 7:1-25).

9:12 ***Syrians:*** Hebrew *Arameans.*

9:13-17 God's punishment was intended to bring repentance, not destruction; but Israel was apostate and refused to *repent* or *seek* the Lord.

9:17 Even ***widows and orphans,*** ordinarily objects of God's compassion (1:17, 23; 10:2), became objects of his wrath when they were unrepentant.

9:18-21 Following the decimation of leadership, civil war would destroy the nation like an out-of-control ***brushfire.***

9:20 ***eat their own children:*** Or *eat their own arms.*

21 Manasseh will feed on Ephraim,
Ephraim will feed on Manasseh,
and both will devour Judah.
But even then the LORD's anger will not
be satisfied.
His fist is still poised to strike.

10 1 What sorrow awaits the unjust
judges
and those who issue unfair laws.
2 They deprive the poor of justice
and deny the rights of the needy
among my people.
They prey on widows
and take advantage of orphans.
3 What will you do when I punish you,
when I send disaster upon you from a
distant land?
To whom will you turn for help?
Where will your treasures be safe?
4 You will stumble along as prisoners
or lie among the dead.
But even then the LORD's anger will not
be satisfied.
His fist is still poised to strike.

Judgment against Assyria

5 "What sorrow awaits Assyria, the rod of
my anger.
I use it as a club to express my anger.
6 I am sending Assyria against a godless
nation,
against a people with whom I am angry.
Assyria will plunder them,
trampling them like dirt beneath its
feet.
7 But the king of Assyria will not
understand that he is my tool;
his mind does not work that way.
His plan is simply to destroy,
to cut down nation after nation.
8 He will say,
'Each of my princes will soon be a
king.
9 We destroyed Calno just as we did
Carchemish.
Hamath fell before us as Arpad did.
And we destroyed Samaria just as we
did Damascus.
10 Yes, we have finished off many a
kingdom
whose gods were greater than those in
Jerusalem and Samaria.
11 So we will defeat Jerusalem and her gods,
just as we destroyed Samaria with
hers.' "

12 After the Lord has used the king of Assyria to accomplish his purposes on Mount
Zion and in Jerusalem, he will turn against
the king of Assyria and punish him—for he
is proud and arrogant. 13 He boasts,

"By my own powerful arm I have done
this.
With my own shrewd wisdom I
planned it.

9:21 Isa 5:25
10:1 Ps 94:20; Isa 59:14
10:2 Isa 1:23; 5:23
10:3 Isa 13:6; Luke 19:43-44
10:4 Isa 34:3; 66:16
10:5 Isa 13:5; Jer 51:20
10:6 Isa 5:25, 29; 9:17-19
10:7 Gen 50:20; Mic 4:11-12; Acts 2:23-24
10:9 2 Kgs 16:9; 2 Chr 35:20; Amos 6:2
10:10 2 Kgs 19:17-18
10:12 2 Kgs 19:31; Jer 50:18
10:13 2 Kgs 19:22-24; Isa 37:24-27; Ezek 28:4; Dan 4:30

9:21 *Manasseh* and *Ephraim* represent the northern kingdom as its largest tribes. The two largest tribes of Israel and ***Judah*** fought amongst themselves. This is probably a reference to the war between Judah and the alliance of Syria and Israel, which is commonly called the Syro-Ephraimite War (7:1-12). In that conflict, brothers savagely fought against brothers (2 Chr 28).

10:1-4 This prophecy was directed against Judah's leaders, who used their positions to enrich themselves at the people's expense.

10:1 *Sorrow* introduces a threat of divine judgment.

10:3 The implied answer to Isaiah's rhetorical questions was that there would be no one to turn to when God punished Judah. • *Disaster* came first *from* the ***distant land*** of Assyria and later from Babylon.

10:5–11:16 The primacy of the Lord's moral law was established in 9:8–10:4; this passage works out the implications of the law: (1) Assyria was only a tool in God's hands and was therefore as liable to judgment by God as any other nation (10:5-19, 28-34); (2) those among God's people who trusted in him and obeyed his covenant would be rescued (10:20-27); and (3) God would establish his kingdom on earth (11:1-16).

10:5-19 This judgment was pronounced on Assyria because of their ruthless destruction of nations (10:7), blasphemous boasting (10:12), oppression (10:13-14), and self-perceived autonomy (10:15).

10:5 The Assyrians were God's instrument (***rod . . . club***) in judging Syria, Israel, and Judah, but they would not go unpunished for their own wickedness.

10:6 Despite their privileged calling as God's covenant people, Judah had become a ***godless nation,*** making them the object of God's anger (10:4). • The word ***plunder*** translates both the Hebrew words *shalal* and *baz,* recalling the name *Maher-shalal-hash-baz* (see 5:19; 8:1, 3, 5-10).

10:7 ***will not understand:*** The Assyrians did not realize they were following God's intended purpose to punish Israel and Judah. Because they went about savagely killing and looting other nations of their own accord, God would also hold them guilty.

10:9 ***We destroyed:*** By 717 BC, the regions to the north of Judah were firmly in Assyrian hands. ***Calno,*** in northern Syria (referred to as *Calneh* in Amos 6:2), fell to the Assyrian king Tiglath-pileser III in 738 BC. ***Carchemish,*** on the Euphrates River, was taken by King Sargon II in 717 BC. ***Hamath,*** on the Orontes River, was subjugated in 738 and 720 BC. ***Arpad*** was located south of Calno. ***Samaria*** and ***Damascus,*** the capitals of Israel and Syria, were taken in 732 and 722 BC, respectively (7:8; 8:4).

10:10 ***whose gods were greater than those in Jerusalem and Samaria:*** Assyria made a similar argument in 36:19-20; 37:12.

10:11 Assyria ***destroyed Samaria*** under Shalmaneser V and Sargon II in 722 BC (2 Kgs 17:3-6). If Samaria and Judah worshiped the same God, and Assyria had already defeated Samaria, the king of Assyria could expect to defeat Judah also.

10:12 Any royal power that exalts itself against the Lord, the Great King, is ***proud and arrogant*** (see 2:11-12) and will be crushed.

10:13 ***my own powerful arm . . . my own shrewd wisdom*** (cp. 10:5): God alone is all-powerful and wise. He plans the future, and he determines which

10:15
Isa 10:5; 29:16
Jer 51:20
Rom 9:20-21

10:17
Isa 27:4; 30:33; 31:9; 33:12; 37:23
Jer 4:4

10:19
Isa 21:17

10:20
Isa 17:7-8

10:22
Isa 28:22
*Rom 9:27-28

10:24
Exod 5:14-16

10:25
Isa 17:14

10:26
Exod 14:16, 27
Judg 7:25
Isa 37:36-38

10:27
Isa 14:25

10:28
1 Sam 13:2, 5; 14:2

10:29
Josh 18:25; 21:17
1 Sam 10:26

I have broken down the defenses of
nations
and carried off their treasures.
I have knocked down their kings like
a bull.
14 I have robbed their nests of riches
and gathered up kingdoms as a
farmer gathers eggs.
No one can even flap a wing against me
or utter a peep of protest."

15 But can the ax boast greater power than
the person who uses it?
Is the saw greater than the person
who saws?
Can a rod strike unless a hand moves it?
Can a wooden cane walk by itself?
16 Therefore, the Lord, the LORD of
Heaven's Armies,
will send a plague among Assyria's
proud troops,
and a flaming fire will consume its
glory.
17 The LORD, the Light of Israel, will be a fire;
the Holy One will be a flame.
He will devour the thorns and briers
with fire,
burning up the enemy in a single
night.
18 The LORD will consume Assyria's glory
like a fire consumes a forest in a
fruitful land;
it will waste away like sick people in
a plague.
19 Of all that glorious forest, only a few
trees will survive—
so few that a child could count them!

Hope for the LORD's People

20 In that day the remnant left in Israel,
the survivors in the house of Jacob,
will no longer depend on allies
who seek to destroy them.
But they will faithfully trust the LORD,
the Holy One of Israel.
21 A remnant will return;
yes, the remnant of Jacob will return
to the Mighty God.
22 But though the people of Israel are as
numerous
as the sand of the seashore,
only a remnant of them will return.
The LORD has rightly decided to
destroy his people.
23 Yes, the Lord, the LORD of Heaven's Armies,
has already decided to destroy the
entire land.

24 So this is what the Lord, the LORD of
Heaven's Armies, says: "O my people in
Zion, do not be afraid of the Assyrians when
they oppress you with rod and club as the
Egyptians did long ago.
25 In a little while
my anger against you will end, and then my
anger will rise up to destroy them."
26 The
LORD of Heaven's Armies will lash them
with his whip, as he did when Gideon triumphed over the Midianites at the rock of
Oreb, or when the LORD's staff was raised to
drown the Egyptian army in the sea.

27 In that day the LORD will end the
bondage of his people.
He will break the yoke of slavery
and lift it from their shoulders.

28 Look, the Assyrians are now at Aiath.
They are passing through Migron
and are storing their equipment at
Micmash.
29 They are crossing the pass
and are camping at Geba.

nations will rise to power and which will be defeated.

10:15 ***ax . . . saw . . . rod . . . wooden cane:*** Such instruments are only as good as ***the person who uses*** them. Assyria considered itself independent of the ***hand*** of God, but their conquests were made possible only by his permission and to serve his purposes (10:5).

10:16 The fulfillment of this prophecy was in 701 BC, when 185,000 Assyrian troops were killed by ***plague*** and ***flaming fire*** (see 37:36).

10:20-27 In the midst of Assyrian oppression, there was hope for the remnant. This passage develops more fully the meaning of Shear-jashub, ***a remnant will return*** (10:21; see 7:3; 8:18).

10:20 ***left . . . the survivors:*** A remnant from Jerusalem barely survived, but their safety was secure because God promised to preserve them (see 1:8-9; 4:2; 6:13; 37:31-32). • All these wars would teach the Israelite remnant to ***no longer depend on allies*** such as Assyria. Instead, they would ***faithfully trust*** in the Lord (see 8:13; 17:7).

10:21 ***A remnant will return:*** Hebrew *Shear-jashub;* see 7:3; 8:18. A small fraction of the people would remain, and an even smaller part would return to the Lord.

10:22-23 Greek version reads *only a remnant of them will be saved. / For he will carry out his sentence quickly and with finality and righteousness; / for God will carry out his sentence upon all the world with finality.* Cp. Rom 9:27-28, which quotes from the Greek version.

10:22 God had similarly promised descendants ***as numerous as the sand of the seashore*** to Abraham (Gen 22:17). • ***rightly decided to destroy:*** God's decision was a just response to the people's persistent wickedness.

10:24-34 God assured his people of his presence and purpose (see note on 7:4).

10:24 ***as the Egyptians did long ago:*** See Exod 1:8–2:25.

10:26 ***Gideon triumphed over the Midianites:*** See Judg 7:25.

10:27 Israel's ***bondage*** ended in 539 BC with a new exodus from exile. • The last sentence is translated from the Greek version; Hebrew reads *The yoke will be broken, / for you have grown so fat.*

10:28-34 ***Look, the Assyrians are now at Aiath:*** The march described in 10:29-32 is a poetic account of Assyria's defeat.

Fear strikes the town of Ramah.
All the people of Gibeah, the hometown of Saul,
are running for their lives.
30 Scream in terror,
you people of Gallim!
Shout out a warning to Laishah.
Oh, poor Anathoth!
31 There go the people of Madmenah, all fleeing.
The citizens of Gebim are trying to hide.
32 The enemy stops at Nob for the rest of that day.
He shakes his fist at beautiful Mount Zion, the mountain of Jerusalem.
33 But look! The Lord, the LORD of Heaven's Armies,
will chop down the mighty tree of Assyria with great power!
He will cut down the proud.
That lofty tree will be brought down.
34 He will cut down the forest trees with an ax.
Lebanon will fall to the Mighty One.

A Branch from David's Line

11 1 Out of the stump of David's family will grow a shoot—
yes, a new [h]Branch bearing fruit from the old root.
2 And the [i]Spirit of the LORD will rest on him—
the [i]Spirit of [j]wisdom and understanding,
the [i]Spirit of counsel and might,
the [i]Spirit of knowledge and the fear of the LORD.
3 He will delight in obeying the LORD.
He will not judge by appearance
nor make a decision based on hearsay.
4 He will give [k]justice to the poor
and make fair decisions for the exploited.
The earth will shake at the force of his word,

10:30 Josh 21:18; 1 Sam 25:44
10:32 Isa 19:16; Zech 2:9
10:33 Isa 37:24; Ezek 31:2-3; Amos 2:9
11:1 Jer 23:5; Rev 5:5; [h]*netser* (5342) ‣Jer 23:5
11:2 Isa 61:1; Matt 3:16; John 1:32; Eph 1:17; [i]*ruakh* (7307) ‣Isa 26:9; [j]*khokmah* (2451) ‣Jer 9:23
11:3 John 2:24-25
11:4 Isa 30:28; 2 Thes 2:8; [k]*tsedeq* (6664) ‣Isa 45:8

The Remnant (11:10-16)

Isa 1:8-9; 4:1-3; 6:13; 10:19-22; 27:12-13; 28:5; 37:31-32; 46:3-4; 2 Kgs 19:31; 2 Chr 36:20; Ezra 9:14; Jer 6:9; 23:3-4; 31:7-8; Amos 5:15; Mic 2:12; 4:6-7; 5:7-8; 7:18; Zeph 3:11-13

The theme of the remnant is integral to Isaiah's vision of the new order. The desolation of all things would bring an end to one era, while the salvation of the remnant opens up the new world.

When he judged his OT people, the Lord saved a small community to be the core of a new beginning (1:9; 37:4, 31-32). Because the population had been decimated, it was a very small beginning. This new beginning is depicted as a branch (4:2), a stump (6:13), a community of the poor and needy (25:4), or handpicked grain (27:12-13). The Lord promised that this small community would swell into a huge multitude that comes out of both Israel and the Gentile nations (27:6; 60:3).

In Isaiah, the exiles represent the whole remnant community from the prophet's day until the coming of the Lord Jesus. The prophecy calls on the remnant to leave their world of separation from God and his blessings to walk in the light of the new order—with life, peace, joy, and reconciliation—and to return home to Zion, the city of God. These faithful people hear and believe the good news that God is coming to reward them (3:10; 40:10). They have repented of their rebelliousness and have put their trust in the Lord (10:21; 31:6).

The places follow a route from the north down to Jerusalem. Upon arriving at Jerusalem, the Assyrians were forced to retreat. God was with Jerusalem, and eventually Assyria would be utterly destroyed. This passage might foretell Sennacherib's invasion in 701 BC (see chs 36–37), but it could just as well describe an earlier or later invasion.

10:34 ***with an ax. Lebanon will fall to the Mighty One:*** Or *with an ax / as even the mighty trees of Lebanon fall.*

11:1-16 The kingdom of the Messiah, first introduced in 9:1-7, is now considered in more detail. Isaiah challenged the Israelites about why they would trust in any of the nations when God had far better plans in mind.

11:1 ***the stump of David's family:*** Hebrew *the stump of the line of Jesse.* Jesse was King David's father. • ***stump . . . shoot . . . new Branch . . . from the old root:*** This new growth refers to the continuity of David's royal family line despite its virtual cessation during the Exile (see also 6:13; 39:7; Rev 22:16). The new growth from the old roots would not be like the former frail and unjust descendants of David (see 4:2). Jesus, the Messiah, is the final fulfillment.

11:2 ***The Spirit of the LORD will rest on*** the Messiah. The succession of David's line is guaranteed by the Spirit. The Messiah's coming would bring justice and righteousness (11:4), peace (11:8), and the extension of the Kingdom to the nations (11:10; see also 32:15-16). • The promised Messiah would have great *wisdom and understanding,* like Solomon, as well as *knowledge and the fear of the LORD* (1 Kgs 3:28; 4:29; Prov 1:1-7; 2:6-7). • ***The Spirit of counsel and might*** alludes to 9:6. The Messiah will be full of wisdom and will have the power to execute his righteous rule.

11:3 ***obeying the LORD:*** Literally *the fear of the LORD,* as in 11:2 (see Prov 1:7).

11:4 ***The poor and . . . the exploited*** would receive the justice due to them, which the wicked leaders of Judah had previously withheld. • ***the force of his word:*** Literally *the scepter of his mouth* (see Ps 2:9; Rev 19:15).

11:6
Isa 65:25
11:9
Job 5:23
Isa 45:6
Ezek 34:25
Hos 2:18
Hab 2:14
11:10
Luke 2:32
John 3:14-15
*Rom 15:12
11:11
Isa 60:9; 66:19-20
Zech 10:10
11:12
Isa 11:10
Zeph 3:10
11:13
Jer 3:18
Ezek 37:16-17, 22
11:15
Isa 51:10

and one breath from his mouth will
destroy the wicked.
5 He will wear righteousness like a belt
and truth like an undergarment.

6 In that day the wolf and the lamb will
live together;
the leopard will lie down with the
baby goat.
The calf and the yearling will be safe
with the lion,
and a little child will lead them all.
7 The cow will graze near the bear.
The cub and the calf will lie down
together.
The lion will eat hay like a cow.
8 The baby will play safely near the hole of
a cobra.
Yes, a little child will put its hand in a
nest of deadly snakes without harm.
9 Nothing will hurt or destroy in all my
holy mountain,
for as the waters fill the sea,
so the earth will be filled with people
who know the LORD.

10 In that day the heir to David's throne
will be a banner of salvation to all the
world.
The nations will rally to him,
and the land where he lives will be a
glorious place.

11 In that day the Lord will reach out his
hand a second time
to bring back the remnant of his
people—
those who remain in Assyria and
northern Egypt;
in southern Egypt, Ethiopia, and Elam;
in Babylonia, Hamath, and all the
distant coastlands.
12 He will raise a flag among the nations
and assemble the exiles of Israel.
He will gather the scattered people of
Judah
from the ends of the earth.

13 Then at last the jealousy between Israel
and Judah will end.
They will not be rivals anymore.
14 They will join forces to swoop down on
Philistia to the west.
Together they will attack and plunder
the nations to the east.
They will occupy the lands of Edom and
Moab,
and Ammon will obey them.
15 The LORD will make a dry path through
the gulf of the Red Sea.
He will wave his hand over the
Euphrates River,
sending a mighty wind to divide it into
seven streams
so it can easily be crossed on foot.

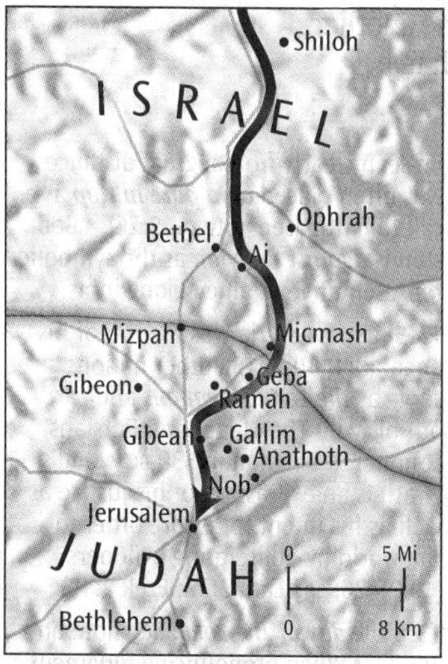

◀ **Assyria at the Doorstep (Isa 10:28-34).** Isaiah foresees Assyria's advance southward through JUDAH toward JERUSALEM (shown by the heavy black arrow; see note on 10:28-34).

11:5 By virtue of the righteous character of the Messiah, his reign will be characterized by justice, ***righteousness***, and truth, in contrast to the conditions of Jerusalem described in 1:21.

11:6 ***In that day*** means *in the coming age of the Messiah*. The prophecy that follows received partial fulfillment in Isaiah's day or shortly thereafter. The final fulfillment is found in the coming of the Messiah to inaugurate and then fully establish the age to come.

11:9 ***Nothing will hurt or destroy:*** There will be no evildoers, corruption, or sin on God's ***holy mountain*** (Zion).

11:10 ***the heir to David's throne:*** Literally *the root of Jesse* (11:1; Rev 5:5; 22:16). • The Messiah will bring ***salvation to all the world*** (2:1-5). Members of other ***nations*** will even serve as priests and Levites (66:20-21), but only if they repent and believe in the true God. • The Greek version of this verse reads *In that day the heir to David's throne* [literally *the root of Jesse*] *will come, / and he will rule over the Gentiles. / They will place their hopes on him.* Cp. Rom 15:12, which quotes from the Greek version.

11:11 The first time ***the Lord*** reached ***out his hand*** was at the Exodus; the ***second time*** will occur in the future when the Messiah gathers Gentiles (11:10) and his own people who live among the Gentile nations (11:11). The Exodus remained the paradigm of hope for those in exile (see 11:16; 35:8; 40:3; 43:19-20; 48:21). • The ***remnant of his people*** included Israelites who survived the Assyrian and Babylonian invasions and were sent into exile. • ***in southern Egypt, Ethiopia:*** Hebrew *in Pathros, Cush.* • ***in Babylonia:*** Hebrew *in Shinar.*

11:13 ***jealousy between Israel*** (literally *Ephraim,* referring to the northern kingdom of Israel) ***and Judah:*** The two kingdoms had become enemies during Judah's war with the alliance of Syria and Israel (see 7:1-12). In the future, they would cooperate in joint military expeditions.

11:14 ***Philistia to the west:*** The Philistines were Israel's historic enemy. • ***The nations to the east*** included the Edomites, Moabites, and Ammonites. All foes would be vanquished.

11:15-16 ***will make a dry path through the gulf of the Red Sea:*** Literally *will destroy the tongue of the sea of Egypt.* Using imagery from Israel's past Exodus, Isaiah encouraged his listeners by promising that God would bring his people out of Assyria the way he brought them out of Egypt (Exod 14:29–15:18; see also Rev 16:12). • ***the Euphrates River:*** Literally *the river.*

16 He will make a highway for the remnant
of his people,
the remnant coming from Assyria,
just as he did for Israel long ago
when they returned from Egypt.

Songs of Praise for Salvation (12:1-6)

12 1 In that day you will sing:
"I will praise you, O LORD!
You were [a]angry with me, but not any more.
Now you comfort me.
2 See, God has come to save me.
I will trust in him and not be afraid.
The LORD GOD is my strength and my song;
he has given me victory."
3 With joy you will drink deeply
from the fountain of salvation!
4 In that wonderful day you will sing:
"Thank the LORD! Praise his name!
Tell the nations what he has done.
Let them know how mighty he is!
5 Sing to the LORD, for he has done
wonderful things.
Make known his praise around the
world.
6 Let all the people of Jerusalem shout his
praise with joy!
For great is the Holy One of Israel who
lives among you."

2. THE DAY OF THE LORD (13:1–23:18)

A Message about Babylon

13 Isaiah son of Amoz received this message concerning the destruction of Babylon:

2 "Raise a signal flag on a bare hilltop.
Call up an army against Babylon.
Wave your hand to encourage them
as they march into the palaces of the
high and mighty.
3 I, the LORD, have dedicated these
soldiers for this task.
Yes, I have called mighty warriors to
express my anger,
and they will rejoice when I am
exalted."
4 Hear the noise on the mountains!
Listen, as the vast armies march!
It is the noise and shouting of many
nations.
The LORD of Heaven's [b]Armies has
called this [b]army together.
5 They come from distant countries,
from beyond the farthest horizons.
They are the LORD's weapons to carry
out his anger.
With them he will destroy the whole
land.
6 Scream in terror, for the day of the LORD
has arrived—
the time for the Almighty to
destroy.
7 Every arm is paralyzed with fear.
Every heart melts,
8 and people are terrified.
Pangs of anguish grip them,
like those of a woman in labor.
They look helplessly at one another,
their faces aflame with fear.

11:16 Exod 14:29; Isa 19:23
12:1 Isa 40:1; [a]*'ap* (0639) ‣Hab 3:8
12:2 Ps 118:14; Isa 26:4
12:3 Jer 2:13; John 4:10; 7:37-38
12:4 Ps 145:4
12:5 Ps 98:1; Isa 44:23
12:6 Isa 54:1; Zeph 3:14, 15-17
13:1 Jer 50:1–51:64
13:2 Isa 45:1-3
13:3 Joel 3:11
13:4 Isa 5:30; [b]*tsaba'* (6635) ‣Amos 4:13
13:5 Isa 5:26
13:6 Isa 34:2, 8; Ezek 30:3; Amos 5:18
13:7 Ezek 21:7
13:8 Isa 21:3; 26:17

12:1-6 The prophet's personal song of praise for God's salvation closes the meditations on trust in chs 7–12. God will prove himself trustworthy in his promises to rescue his people even though they initially refused to trust him. The song anticipates chs 40–66 with its themes of salvation, forgiveness, praise, joy, and the nations.

12:1 God's *comfort* is the main subject of chs 40–66.

12:2 God's promise *to save* includes reconciliation (1:18), participation (11:10), cleansing and protection (4:3-6), peace and confidence (32:16-17), and restoration (11:6-9). • ***LORD GOD*** (Hebrew *Yah Yahweh*): The first word is an abbreviation of the second. • ***The LORD GOD is my strength and my song:*** See Exod 15:2; Ps 118:14.

12:3 God's *salvation* is like a deep and unending source of water that provides life (see also 41:18; Ps 87:7).

12:4-5 ***Tell the nations what he has done:*** The story of salvation must be told, even beyond the community of Israel (Ps 67:2; 70:4; 98:2).

12:6 See Ps 48:1; 96:4; 99:2. • ***Jerusalem:*** Hebrew *Zion.*

13:1–23:18 This section contains prophecies of judgment against the nations. By including a prophecy against Judah and Jerusalem (22:1-25) in the midst of prophecies against the pagan nations, Isaiah emphasized that Israel's identity as God's people would not protect them from God's punishment when they sinned as the other nations do.

13:1 At the time of this prophecy, Assyria was the major power. Isaiah anticipated the rise of Babylon as an even crueler kingdom that would destroy Judah and Jerusalem (39:6-7; chs 46–47). The universal language of 13:1–14:23 suggests that in this context, Babylon represents all wicked and arrogant nations in the same way that "Babylon the Great" does in the book of Revelation (Rev 18). Therefore, while this description of Babylon's fall applies to the fall of historic Babylon in 539 BC, it also applies until the final judgment against the ultimate kingdom of evil (Rev 19).

13:2 A *signal flag* or banner that could be seen clearly from a great distance was often placed ***on a bare hilltop*** as a call to battle (see note on 5:26). • God stands ***against Babylon*** as the symbolic representative of all evil kingdoms.

13:5 Just as Assyria was the rod of his anger (9:4; 10:5, 15), other nations serve as ***the LORD's weapons*** and carry out his will. The Medes and Persians conquered Babylon in 539 BC. • God's wrath is an expression of his justice as well as his intent to restore order to the world by obliterating evildoers (10:25-26; see Lam 2:22; Ezek 7:19).

13:6 ***the day of the LORD:*** See note on 2:5-22. • When pronouncing judgment that is still in the future, the prophets sometimes spoke as though it had already ***arrived.*** This emphasized the urgency of turning back to God (Ezek 30:3; Joel 1:15; 3:14; Obad 1:15; Zeph 1:7).

13:8 ***pangs . . . like those of a woman in labor:*** The day of the Lord (see note on 2:5-22) brings sudden and overpowering pain and fear for the wicked (see also Jer 30:6; Hos 13:13; Mic 4:9, 10; 5:3).

13:9 Isa 66:15-16
13:10 *Matt 24:29 *Mark 13:24-25
13:11 Dan 5:22-23
13:12 Isa 6:11-12
13:13 Hag 2:6
13:14 1 Kgs 22:17 Matt 9:36
13:15 Jer 51:3-4
13:16 Ps 137:8-9 Hos 10:14
13:17 Jer 51:11
13:18 2 Chr 36:17
13:19 Gen 19:24 Rev 18:16-17, 19
13:20 Jer 51:37-43

9 For see, the day of the LORD is coming—
the terrible day of his fury and fierce anger.
The land will be made desolate,
and all the sinners destroyed with it.
10 The heavens will be black above them;
the stars will give no light.
The sun will be dark when it rises,
and the moon will provide no light.

11 "I, the LORD, will punish the world for its evil
and the wicked for their sin.
I will crush the arrogance of the proud
and humble the pride of the mighty.
12 I will make people scarcer than gold—
more rare than the fine gold of Ophir.
13 For I will shake the heavens.
The earth will move from its place
when the LORD of Heaven's Armies
displays his wrath
in the day of his fierce anger."

14 Everyone in Babylon will run about like a hunted gazelle,
like sheep without a shepherd.
They will try to find their own people
and flee to their own land.
15 Anyone who is captured will be cut down—
run through with a sword.
16 Their little children will be dashed to death before their eyes.
Their homes will be sacked, and their wives will be raped.

17 "Look, I will stir up the Medes against Babylon.
They cannot be tempted by silver
or bribed with gold.
18 The attacking armies will shoot down
the young men with arrows.
They will have no mercy on helpless babies
and will show no compassion for children."

19 Babylon, the most glorious of kingdoms,
the flower of Chaldean pride,
will be devastated like Sodom and Gomorrah
when God destroyed them.
20 Babylon will never be inhabited again.
It will remain empty for generation after generation.
Nomads will refuse to camp there,
and shepherds will not bed down their sheep.

The Day of the Lord (13:4-12)

Isa 2:10-22; 4:1-6
Ezek 30:1-5
Joel 1:13-15; 2:1-11, 28-32; 3:9-16
Amos 5:18-24
Obad 1:15-16
Zeph 1:2-18
Mal 4:1-5
1 Cor 1:8; 5:5
1 Thes 5:2
2 Thes 2:2
2 Tim 1:18
2 Pet 3:10
Rev 20:1-15

On the day of the Lord, God will manifest his awe-inspiring lordship over creation. When God comes in glory, humans will experience terror (2:10, 19, 21) because all human support structures (religious, economic, military, social) will come under his scrutiny. God alone will be exalted, while all merely human endeavors will be brought down.

The day of the Lord is a time of retribution when God judges his enemies in wrath and fury, whether they come out of Israel, Judah, Syria, Assyria, or Babylon (see chs 7–10; 13–24; 34; 63:1-6). The ungodly receive the punishment they deserve, while the righteous enter into their full salvation (3:9-11; 4:2-4).

The full meaning of the day of the Lord extends beyond a specific time and place. Even when the prophet singles out a particular nation, that nation symbolizes something more significant (see 34:1-17). For example, Babylon (chs 13–14; 46–47) stands for any power independent of God.

The day of the Lord provides assurance to God's people that God is sovereign in judging nations and people throughout human history until the last battle and the final judgment (Rev 18:21; 19:2; 20:11).

13:10 Cosmic upheaval and darkness are common images for the day of the Lord (see note on 2:5-22), a time of God's judgment (see also Ezek 32:7-8; Joel 2:10, 31; 3:15; Matt 24:29; Mark 13:24; Rev 6:12-13; 8:12; cp. Isa 30:26).

13:11 ***punish the world:*** See note on 13:1; see also Rev 20:11.

13:12 Solomon's imported ***gold*** came from ***Ophir*** (1 Kgs 9:28).

13:13 God ***will shake the heavens. The earth will move:*** Cosmic upheaval will accompany God's coming in judgment (see note on 5:25; see also Hag 2:7, 21; Heb 12:26-27; Rev 16:17-18; 18:21-22).

13:16 These terrible acts of war would be perpetrated against Babylon, itself a cruel conquering power (see also Ps 137:8-9; Jer 6:11-12; Nah 3:10).

13:17 The Lord is sovereign and controls history. He can ***stir up*** kingdoms to execute his will. • The ***Medes*** from northwestern Iran joined Persian King Cyrus in fighting ***against Babylon*** in 539 BC.

13:19-22 This picture of ***Babylon*** as a perpetually haunted ruin contrasts with its magnificence at its peak (see Dan 4:29-30).

13:20 ***Babylon will never be inhabited again:*** Babylon, often a symbol of idolatry, immorality, imperialism, and oppression in Scripture, will one day come completely to an end (see Rev 18:2; 19:2).

21 Desert animals will move into the ruined
city,
and the houses will be haunted by
howling creatures.
Owls will live among the ruins,
and wild goats will go there to dance.
22 Hyenas will howl in its fortresses,
and jackals will make dens in its
luxurious palaces.
Babylon's days are numbered;
its time of destruction will soon arrive.

Consolation for Israel

14 But the LORD will have mercy on the
descendants of Jacob. He will choose
Israel as his special people once again. He
will bring them back to settle once again
in their own land. And people from many
different nations will come and join them
there and unite with the people of Israel.
2The nations of the world will help the
LORD's people to return, and those who
come to live in their land will serve them.
Those who captured Israel will themselves
be captured, and Israel will rule over its enemies.

A Taunt for Babylon's King

3In that wonderful day when the LORD gives
his people rest from sorrow and fear, from
slavery and chains, 4you will taunt the king
of Babylon. You will say,

"The mighty man has been destroyed.
Yes, your insolence is ended.
5 For the LORD has crushed your wicked
power
and broken your evil rule.
6 You struck the people with endless
blows of rage
and held the nations in your angry grip
with unrelenting tyranny.
7 But finally the earth is at rest and quiet.
Now it can sing again!
8 Even the trees of the forest—
the cypress trees and the cedars of
Lebanon—
sing out this joyous song:
'Since you have been cut down,
no one will come now to cut us down!'
9 "In the place of the dead there is
excitement
over your arrival.
The spirits of world leaders and mighty
kings long dead
stand up to see you.
10 With one voice they all cry out,
'Now you are as weak as we are!
11 Your might and power were buried with
you.
The sound of the harp in your palace
has ceased.
Now maggots are your sheet,
and worms your blanket.'
12 "How you are fallen from ᶜheaven,
O shining star, son of the morning!
You have been thrown down to the earth,
you who destroyed the nations of the
world.

13:21 Isa 34:11-15; Zeph 2:14
14:1 Ps 102:13; Isa 41:8-9; 49:13, 15; Zech 2:11-12
14:2 Isa 45:14; Dan 7:18, 27
14:3 Ezra 9:8-9; Jer 30:10
14:4 Hab 2:6
14:6 Isa 47:6
14:7 Ps 98:1-9
14:8 Isa 55:12
14:10 Ezek 32:21
14:11 Isa 5:14
14:12 Luke 10:18; Rev 9:1
ᶜshamayim (8064) ▸Isa 34:4

14:1-2 This message for Israel separates two prophecies of judgment against Babylon (13:1-22; 14:3-23).

14:1 The Hebrew word here translated ***mercy*** draws from the imagery of a woman's maternal care for her child to illustrate God's merciful love for his people (see also 49:15; 66:13). • God had initially chosen Israel as his ***special people*** when he called Abraham (see 41:8; Gen 12:1-3). Although their status did not change during the Exile, they faced God's wrath like any other wicked nation because they had rejected him. • ***settle once again in their own land:*** This promise began to be fulfilled in 538 BC (see Ezra 1). • ***People from many different nations*** would join Israel as the people of God (see also 2:3-4; 11:11-12; 19:18-25; 60:1-14). • ***the people of Israel:*** Literally *the house of Jacob.* The names "Jacob" and "Israel" are often interchanged throughout the Old Testament, referring sometimes to the individual patriarch and sometimes to the nation.

14:2 Just as Israel was subject to the Lord, so the ***nations of the world*** would submit themselves to the Lord through Israel (45:14; 49:7, 23; 60:12, 14; 66:23). • The oppressed nation of Israel ***will rule over its enemies,*** assuming a position of power and favor with God.

14:3-23 This taunting song for the king of Babylon is in the form of a funeral dirge (cp. Rev 18).

14:3 God ***gives . . . rest*** (i.e., *relief;* 28:12; see Deut 25:19; 2 Sam 7:11) ***from*** the ***sorrow and fear, . . . slavery and chains*** Israel experienced under foreign oppressors (see 9:4).

14:4 A ***taunt*** is a mocking comparison in song form. In this instance, the king of Babylon is compared to a dead man entering the world of the dead. • ***insolence:*** As in the Dead Sea Scrolls; the meaning of the Masoretic Text is uncertain.

14:7-8 The land and people will be ***at rest and quiet*** because the oppression has ended and the king of Babylon has died. • The whole creation will join in praise, able to ***sing again*** (see also 42:11; 44:23; see Rom 8:22).

14:9 The Babylonians saw the ***place of the dead*** (Hebrew *Sheol;* also in 14:15) as a place of no return. • ***stand up*** (literally *get up from their thrones*): The thrones reflect the Babylonian concept of the life hereafter as a continuation of the same mode of existence as the present life. It appears that the other kings are honoring the great king of Babylon, but the next verses tell a different story.

14:10 ***weak as we are:*** The Babylonian king had no power over anyone after death and was unable to leave *Sheol.* The Israelites will mock this great king who on earth appeared to have no weaknesses.

14:11 Babylon's ***might and power*** and ***the sound of the harp*** were ended, and its magnificence was destroyed (see also Rev 18:22). • ***Maggots*** and ***worms*** symbolized death and decomposition (66:24). • ***were buried with you:*** Literally *were brought down to Sheol.*

14:12 ***fallen from heaven, O shining star:*** These words allude to the Canaanite story of the god Helel's rebellion against the god El (chief deity of the

14:13 Ezek 28:2
14:14 2 Thes 2:4
d'elyon (5945) ‣Lam 3:38
14:15 Matt 11:23 Luke 10:15
14:19 Isa 5:25
14:20 Job 18:19 Ps 21:10
14:21 Exod 20:5 Isa 13:16
14:23 Isa 13:6; 34:11
14:24 Job 23:13 Isa 46:11
14:25 Isa 9:4 Nah 1:13
14:26 Isa 23:9
14:27 Exod 15:12 Isa 43:13 Dan 4:31, 35

13 For you said to yourself,
'I will ascend to heaven and set my throne above God's stars.
I will preside on the mountain of the gods
far away in the north.
14 I will climb to the highest heavens
and be like the dMost High.'
15 Instead, you will be brought down to the place of the dead,
down to its lowest depths.
16 Everyone there will stare at you and ask,
'Can this be the one who shook the earth
and made the kingdoms of the world tremble?
17 Is this the one who destroyed the world
and made it into a wasteland?
Is this the king who demolished the world's greatest cities
and had no mercy on his prisoners?'
18 "The kings of the nations lie in stately glory,
each in his own tomb,
19 but you will be thrown out of your grave
like a worthless branch.
Like a corpse trampled underfoot,
you will be dumped into a mass grave
with those killed in battle.
You will descend to the pit.
20 You will not be given a proper burial,
for you have destroyed your nation
and slaughtered your people.
The descendants of such an evil person
will never again receive honor.
21 Kill this man's children!
Let them die because of their father's sins!
They must not rise and conquer the earth,
filling the world with their cities."

22 This is what the LORD of Heaven's Armies says:
"I, myself, have risen against Babylon!
I will destroy its children and its children's children,"
says the LORD.
23 "I will make Babylon a desolate place of owls,
filled with swamps and marshes.
I will sweep the land with the broom of destruction.
I, the LORD of Heaven's Armies, have spoken!"

A Message about Assyria

24 The LORD of Heaven's Armies has sworn this oath:
"It will all happen as I have planned.
It will be as I have decided.
25 I will break the Assyrians when they are in Israel;
I will trample them on my mountains.
My people will no longer be their slaves
nor bow down under their heavy loads.
26 I have a plan for the whole earth,
a hand of judgment upon all the nations.
27 The LORD of Heaven's Armies has spoken—
who can change his plans?
When his hand is raised,
who can stop him?"

Canaanite pantheon) and his fall from heaven. Some see the fall of the king of Babylon here as symbolizing the fall of Satan (see Ezek 28; Luke 10:18; Rev 12:9). However, there is little to suggest that Isaiah understood it in that way. He was thinking of the historical king of Babylon. • ***son of the morning:*** The battle took place under the early morning sun. The Latin Vulgate translates the term as *Lucifer* (*morning star*), a name for Satan in Christian tradition, but the Hebrew text makes no apparent reference here to Satan.

14:13 ***on the mountain of the gods far away in the north:*** Or *on the heights of Zaphon.* • This verse alludes to the Canaanite belief that the chief god El and the other gods were enthroned on Mount Zaphon, a northern mountain (see Ps 48:2; for a NT application, see Matt 11:23; Luke 10:15).

14:14 ***Most High:*** See Gen 14:19-22.

14:15-17 This is a restatement of 14:9-11. The dead spirits inhabiting ***the place of the dead*** will be startled and amazed that the Babylonian king, who ruled the world with his merciless might, has absolutely no power in death.

14:18-20 The absence of ***a proper burial*** was a sign of great shame and dishonor. Unlike other kings, the king of Babylon would be disgraced in judgment.

14:21 As another sign of disgrace, the king of Babylon would have no children to provide a future legacy. • ***because of their father's sins:*** God looks at individuals in relationship to their families and their people. Here, the Babylonian king's children had joint responsibility for their father's actions (see also Deut 5:9-10).

14:22-23 Isaiah summarized the previous taunt (14:3-21) with this prophecy, spoken in the first person. God decrees the destruction and desolation of Babylon.

14:24-27 This prophecy resumes declaring judgment on Assyria (see ch 10). The placement of this prophecy after the judgment against Babylon suggests close connections between Assyria and Babylon.

14:24 ***I have planned . . . I have decided:*** No nation can either diminish or resist God's plans to bring judgment against Assyria or his plans in general. The prophets understood and communicated God's plan so that his people could respond appropriately.

14:25 This prophecy told what would happen when Sennacherib attacked Hezekiah some years later in 701 BC (see chs 36–37).

14:26 The Lord's power over Assyria is just one example of his sovereignty over ***the whole earth.***

A Message about Philistia

28This message came to me the year King Ahaz died:

29 Do not rejoice, you Philistines,
that the rod that struck you is broken—
that the king who attacked you is dead.
For from that snake a more poisonous snake will be born,
a [e]fiery serpent to destroy you!
30 I will feed the poor in my pasture;
the needy will lie down in peace.
But as for you, I will wipe you out with famine
and destroy the few who remain.
31 Wail at the gates! Weep in the cities!
Melt with fear, you Philistines!
A powerful army comes like smoke from the north.
Each soldier rushes forward eager to fight.

32What should we tell the Philistine messengers? Tell them,

"The LORD has built Jerusalem;
its walls will give refuge to his oppressed people."

A Message about Moab

15 This message came to me concerning Moab:

In one night the town of Ar will be leveled,
and the city of Kir will be destroyed.
2 Your people will go to their temple in Dibon to mourn.
They will go to their sacred shrines to weep.
They will wail for the fate of Nebo and Medeba,
shaving their heads in sorrow and cutting off their beards.
3 They will wear burlap as they wander the streets.
From every home and public square will come the sound of wailing.
4 The people of Heshbon and Elealeh will cry out;
their voices will be heard as far away as Jahaz!
The bravest warriors of Moab will cry out in utter terror.
They will be helpless with fear.
5 My heart weeps for Moab.
Its people flee to Zoar and Eglath-shelishiyah.
Weeping, they climb the road to Luhith.
Their cries of distress can be heard all along the road to Horonaim.
6 Even the waters of Nimrim are dried up!
The grassy banks are scorched.
The tender plants are gone;
nothing green remains.
7 The people grab their possessions
and carry them across the Ravine of Willows.
8 A cry of distress echoes through the land of Moab
from one end to the other—
from Eglaim to Beer-elim.
9 The stream near Dibon runs red with blood,
but I am still not finished with Dibon!
Lions will hunt down the survivors—
both those who try to escape
and those who remain behind.

14:28 2 Kgs 16:20
14:29 [e]*sarap* (8314) ‣Ezek 10:5
14:30 Isa 8:21; 11:4
14:31 Jer 1:14
14:32 Ps 87:1, 5; Isa 25:4
15:1 Isa 11:4; Jer 48:1; Ezek 25:8-11
15:2 Jer 48:37
15:3 Isa 22:4; Jer 48:38; Jon 3:6-8
15:5 Jer 48:5
15:6 Jer 48:34; Joel 1:10-12
15:9 2 Kgs 17:25; Jer 50:17

14:28 *King Ahaz died* in 715 BC.

14:29 The *king who attacked* Philistia was probably Ahaz (14:28). • ***a more poisonous snake:*** This probably refers to one of the later Assyrian kings, either Sennacherib (701 BC), Esarhaddon (680 BC), or Ashurbanipal (668 BC).

14:31 The advancing army, probably Assyria, would stir up clouds of dust ***like smoke*** that were ominously visible in ***the north.***

14:32 ***The LORD has built Jerusalem*** (Hebrew *Zion*; see 1:8): God was fully willing and capable of defending Judah, and he did not want the kingdom to make alliances with nations such as the Philistines to protect themselves from the invading Assyrians.

15:1–16:14 This message of judgment and lament concerned Moab's fall. The extensive references to Moabite place names indicate that Isaiah was thoroughly familiar with Moab.

15:1 ***Moab*** was Judah's enemy, situated on the eastern side of the Dead Sea. • ***In one night:*** Destruction would be sudden and decisive.

15:2 In the ancient Near East, actions such as ***shaving*** or ***cutting off their beards*** revealed deep sorrow (see Jer 48:37).

15:4 ***Heshbon*** was the former capital of Sihon (Num 21:23-26). • ***Elealeh*** was located close to Heshbon. • ***Jahaz*** was between Heshbon and the Arnon River (see Jer 48:34).

15:5 ***My heart weeps for Moab:*** The prophet joined in the lament to express the greatness of Moab's pain. • ***Zoar*** was in the southeastern area of the Dead Sea (Gen 14:2; 19:23).

15:6 Identification of the ***waters of Nimrim*** is uncertain (see also Jer 48:34). • ***dried up . . . scorched . . . tender plants:*** For the theme of natural resources drying up as a form of judgment, see note on 24:4.

15:7-8 The precise locations of the ***Ravine of Willows*** and of ***Eglaim*** and ***Beer-elim*** are uncertain.

15:9 ***Dibon:*** As in the Dead Sea Scrolls, some Greek manuscripts, and Latin Vulgate. The Masoretic Text reads *Dimon* (also in 15:9b), which is a play on the word translated *blood* (Hebrew *dam*). • ***blood:*** Apparently many people from Moab had already been killed, but their judgment had only begun.

16:1 2 Kgs 3:4; 14:7 Isa 42:11
16:2 Num 21:13-14
16:4 Isa 9:4; 54:14
16:6 Jer 48:29 Zeph 2:8, 10
16:7 2 Kgs 3:25 Jer 48:31
16:8 Num 32:38 Isa 15:4 Jer 48:32
16:9 Jer 48:32
16:10 Job 24:11 Isa 24:7-8 Jer 48:33 Amos 5:17
16:11 Isa 15:5; 63:15
16:12 1 Kgs 18:26-29 Jer 48:35

16

1 Send lambs from Sela as tribute
to the ruler of the land.
Send them through the desert
to the mountain of beautiful Zion.
2 The women of Moab are left like
homeless birds
at the shallow crossings of the Arnon
River.
3 "Help us," they cry.
"Defend us against our enemies.
Protect us from their relentless attack.
Do not betray us now that we have
escaped.
4 Let our refugees stay among you.
Hide them from our enemies until the
terror is past."

When oppression and destruction have
ended
and enemy raiders have disappeared,
5 then God will establish one of David's
descendants as king.
He will rule with mercy and truth.
He will always do what is just
and be eager to do what is right.

6 We have heard about proud Moab—
about its pride and arrogance and rage.
But all that boasting has disappeared.
7 The entire land of Moab weeps.
Yes, everyone in Moab mourns
for the cakes of raisins from Kir-
hareseth.
They are all gone now.
8 The farms of Heshbon are abandoned;
the vineyards at Sibmah are deserted.
The rulers of the nations have broken
down Moab—
that beautiful grapevine.
Its tendrils spread north as far as the
town of Jazer
and trailed eastward into the
wilderness.
Its shoots reached so far west
that they crossed over the Dead Sea.

9 So now I weep for Jazer and the
vineyards of Sibmah;
my tears will flow for Heshbon and
Elealeh.
There are no more shouts of joy
over your summer fruits and harvest.
10 Gone now is the gladness,
gone the joy of harvest.
There will be no singing in the vineyards,
no more happy shouts,
no treading of grapes in the winepresses.
I have ended all their harvest joys.
11 My heart's cry for Moab is like a lament
on a harp.
I am filled with anguish for Kir-
hareseth.
12 The people of Moab will worship at their
pagan shrines,
but it will do them no good.
They will cry to the gods in their temples,
but no one will be able to save them.

13 The LORD has already said these things
about Moab in the past. 14 But now the LORD
says, "Within three years, counting each
day, the glory of Moab will be ended. From

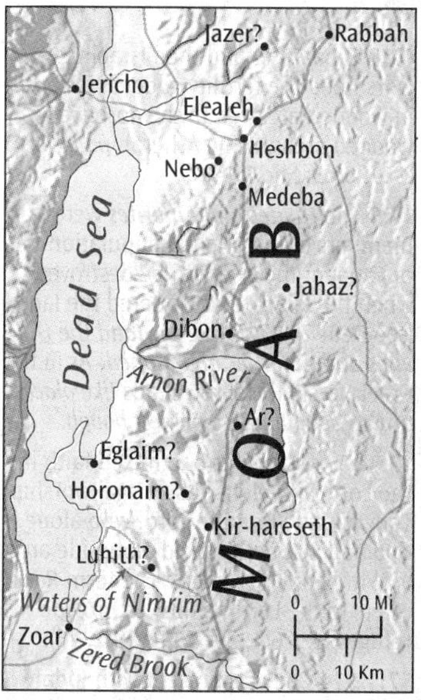

◀ **Moab's Doom, around 715 BC** (Isa 15:1–16:14). The map shows many of the places mentioned in this prediction of an invasion of MOAB; the exact occasion of this invasion is unknown.

16:1-4 A request for asylum.

16:1 Moab was known for its sheep (see 2 Kgs 3:4). The *lambs* were sent as tribute to Judah in recognition of Judah's sovereignty over Moab. • *Sela* (*the cliff*), an unknown remote site, was apparently where the Moabites escaped *through the desert.*

16:3-4 *Do not betray us . . . Hide them:* Moab's situation would become so dire that they would beg for asylum in other lands.

16:4-5 This prophecy of salvation spoke of the future of David's dynasty. • Activities such as *oppression and destruction* would cease with the end of Moabite hostilities (see 2 Kgs 13:20).

16:5 God would *establish one of David's descendants as king* (see also 9:7; 11:1-5, 10-12).

16:6-11 The response to Moab's request for asylum (16:1-4).

16:6 The Moabites' hardened state of *pride and arrogance and rage* and *boasting* prevented them from humbling themselves before God.

16:8 The *vineyards at Sibmah* were located by the Moabite city of *Heshbon.* • Moab was like a luxuriant vine that extends far and wide, but Israel's beautiful vine reached to the ends of the earth (27:6). • The location of *Jazer* is unknown. • *the Dead Sea:* Literally *the sea.*

16:11 *Kir-hareseth:* Hebrew *Kir-heres,* a variant spelling of Kir-hareseth.

16:12 The hilltops were sites for pagan shrines (see 15:2). • *no one will be able to save them,* including the idols the Moabites called on for protection (see 40:18-19; 44:18-19).

16:14 *Within three years, counting each day* (literally *Within three years, as a servant bound by contract would count them*; see also 21:16): A man who had sold himself into servitude for a period of time would calculate how much time remained right down to the final day. This verse refers to events that are

its great population, only a few of its people
will be left alive."

A Message about Damascus and Israel

17 This message came to me concerning Damascus:

"Look, the city of Damascus will
disappear!
It will become a heap of ruins.
2 The towns of Aroer will be deserted.
Flocks will graze in the streets and lie
down undisturbed,
with no one to chase them away.
3 The fortified towns of Israel will also be
destroyed,
and the royal power of Damascus will
end.
All that remains of Syria
will share the fate of Israel's departed
glory,"
declares the LORD of Heaven's
Armies.

4 "In that day Israel's glory will grow dim;
its robust body will waste away.
5 The whole land will look like a grainfield
after the harvesters have gathered the
grain.
It will be desolate,
like the fields in the valley of Rephaim
after the harvest.
6 Only a few of its people will be left,
like stray olives left on a tree after the
harvest.
Only two or three remain in the highest
branches,
four or five scattered here and there
on the limbs,"
declares the LORD, the God of Israel.
7 Then at last the people will look to their
Creator
and turn their eyes to the Holy One
of Israel.
8 They will no longer look to their idols for
help
or worship what their own hands
have made.
They will never again bow down to their
Asherah poles
or worship at the pagan shrines they
have built.
9 Their largest cities will be like a deserted
forest,
like the land the Hivites and Amorites
abandoned
when the Israelites came here so long ago.
It will be utterly desolate.
10 Why? Because you have turned from the
God who can save you.
You have forgotten the Rock who can
hide you.
So you may plant the finest grapevines
and import the most expensive
seedlings.
11 They may sprout on the day you set them
out;
yes, they may blossom on the very
morning you plant them,
but you will never pick any grapes from
them.
Your only harvest will be a load of
grief and unrelieved pain.

17:1 Isa 10:9; 25:2
17:2 Zeph 2:6
17:3 Isa 8:4; Hos 9:11
17:4 Isa 10:3, 16
17:5 Jer 51:33
17:6 Deut 4:27; Isa 24:13; 27:12
17:7 Isa 10:20; Hos 6:1
17:8 Exod 34:13; Isa 27:9; 30:22
17:10 Deut 32:4, 18, 30-31; Isa 30:29; 62:11
17:11 Hos 10:13

unknown. • *The glory of Moab will be ended,* probably because of the Assyrian conquest of Moab (late 700s BC). • *only a few of its people will be left alive:* Though decimated by war, the Moabites still existed during Nehemiah's time (Neh 13:23).

17:1–20:6 This section contains prophecies of judgment against Damascus, Israel, Ethiopia, and Egypt. The scene moves from the crisis of 734 BC (the alliance of Syria and Israel—see note on 7:1-25) to the Assyrian crisis in 701 BC (see chs 36–37).

17:1 *Damascus,* the ringleader in the alliance of Syria and Israel against Judah (see note on 7:1-25), fell when the Assyrian king Tiglath-pileser III invaded in 732 BC.

17:2 *The towns of Aroer* were east of the Dead Sea (see 2 Kgs 10:32-33). • *Flocks will graze in the streets:* The city would be useless for any other purpose.

17:3 The strategic *fortified towns of Israel* (literally *Ephraim,* referring to the northern kingdom of Israel) were the pride of Israel, but they could not resist God's purposes. • *Syria:* Hebrew *Aram.*

17:4-11 The vision shifts from Damascus (17:1-3) to the northern kingdom of Israel; Damascus and Israel were allies in the war against Judah (see note on 7:1-25), and both were later destroyed by Assyria.

17:4 *Israel's* (literally *Jacob's;* see note on 14:1) *glory will grow dim:* God will judge all human pride. • Israel's *robust body will waste away* like a person who is ill.

17:5 The *valley of Rephaim* was a fertile valley in Judah; however, it looked bare after each harvest.

17:6 Although *the God of Israel* judged the wickedness of Israel, he was still its God.

17:7 The *people* referred to here are either Israelites or humanity at large. • *look . . . turn their eyes:* They will again put their trust in the Lord.

17:8 Canaanites and then Israelites worshiped the fertility goddess *Asherah* in wooded areas or, in the absence of wooded areas, using Asherah *poles* (see 27:9; 65:3; Mic 5:14).

17:9 The *Hivites and Amorites* were members of the original population of Canaan; they were to be destroyed when the Israelites conquered the land (see Deut 20:17). • *like the land the Hivites and Amorites abandoned:* As in the Greek version; Hebrew reads *like places of the wood and the highest bough.*

17:10 The Israelites had mixed faith in the Lord with elements of Baal worship. They *turned from* the Lord, who alone is God and will not be held alongside an idol in people's hearts. • The term *Rock* refers to the Lord's ability to provide refuge (see 26:4; 30:29; Ps 18:2, 46).

17:12-14 God was present with Judah during the crisis.

17:12 At times, the *sea* represents opposition to God (see Job 7:12; 26:12; Ps 46:3; 93:3).

17:12 Jer 6:23
17:13 Ps 1:4; Isa 29:5
17:14 2 Kgs 19:35; Isa 41:11-12
18:1 Isa 20:3-5; Ezek 30:4, 6, 9; Zeph 2:12
18:2 Exod 2:3; 2 Chr 12:2-4; Isa 18:7
18:3 Ps 49:1; Mic 1:2
18:5 Isa 26:21; Ezek 17:6-10
18:6 Isa 56:9; Ezek 39:17-20; Rev 19:17-21
18:7 Zech 14:16-17
19:1 Josh 2:11; Ps 104:3; Jer 43:12; Matt 26:64
19:2 Judg 7:22; Matt 10:21, 36

12 Listen! The armies of many nations
roar like the roaring of the sea.
Hear the thunder of the mighty forces
as they rush forward like thundering waves.
13 But though they thunder like breakers on a beach,
God will silence them, and they will run away.
They will flee like chaff scattered by the wind,
like a tumbleweed whirling before a storm.
14 In the evening Israel waits in terror,
but by dawn its enemies are dead.
This is the just reward of those who plunder us,
a fitting end for those who destroy us.

A Message about Ethiopia

18 1 Listen, Ethiopia—land of fluttering sails
that lies at the headwaters of the Nile,
2 that sends ambassadors
in swift boats down the river.

Go, swift messengers!
Take a message to a tall, smooth-skinned people,
who are feared far and wide
for their conquests and destruction,
and whose land is divided by rivers.

3 All you people of the world,
everyone who lives on the earth—
when I raise my battle flag on the mountain, look!
When I blow the ram's horn, listen!
4 For the LORD has told me this:
"I will watch quietly from my dwelling place—
as quietly as the heat rises on a summer day,
or as the morning dew forms during the harvest."
5 Even before you begin your attack,
while your plans are ripening like grapes,
the LORD will cut off your new growth with pruning shears.
He will snip off and discard your spreading branches.
6 Your mighty army will be left dead in the fields
for the mountain vultures and wild animals.
The vultures will tear at the corpses all summer.
The wild animals will gnaw at the bones all winter.

7 At that time the LORD of Heaven's Armies will receive gifts
from this land divided by rivers,
from this tall, smooth-skinned people,
who are feared far and wide for their conquests and destruction.
They will bring the gifts to Jerusalem,
where the LORD of Heaven's Armies dwells.

A Message about Egypt

19 This message came to me concerning Egypt:

Look! The LORD is advancing against Egypt,
riding on a swift cloud.
The idols of Egypt tremble.
The hearts of the Egyptians melt with fear.

2 "I will make Egyptian fight against Egyptian—
brother against brother,
neighbor against neighbor,
city against city,
province against province.

17:13 ***God will silence them:*** The Lord is sovereign over the nations, as he is over the sea (Ps 65:7).

17:14 ***In the evening . . . by dawn:*** Despite frightening circumstances, Israel can have confidence in the Lord's ability to save quickly (see 37:36-38).

18:1 ***Ethiopia*** (Hebrew *Cush*) was at the southern extremity of the kingdom of Egypt. At the time, Egypt was ruled by the dynasty of the Ethiopian Piankhi. • ***land of fluttering sails:*** (Or *land of many locusts;* literally *land of whirring wings.*

18:3 Both the ***battle flag*** and ***ram's horn*** were used to marshal and send signals to armies in battle (see note on 5:26; see also Judg 3:27; 6:34; 2 Sam 2:28).

18:4 The Lord is untroubled by human activities; he watches ***quietly from*** his ***dwelling place*** and acts in his own time (see Ps 2:1-4).

18:5 ***your plans are ripening:*** Ethiopia had made every effort to form alliances to protect itself against Assyria, but its alliance with Judah would not help.

18:7 Conquered or weaker nations were often forced to pay tribute to a dominant king in the region (see 16:1; 2 Kgs 3:4-5). The Ethiopians would come bringing ***gifts*** to honor the Lord for his defeat of the Assyrians (see also 2 Chr 32:23). • ***to Jerusalem:*** Hebrew *to Mount Zion.*

19:1–20:6 See also Jer 46; Ezek 29–32.

19:1-10 Egypt was vulnerable, depending on the Nile for food, fish, and industry. When the Lord struck the Nile, Egypt would be in dire straits, and their gods would not be able to help.

19:1 ***Riding on a swift cloud*** shows God's sovereignty and power over creation (Ps 104:3). He is coming in judgment against Judah's enemies (see Deut 33:26; Ps 18:9-10; 68:4; 97:2-3). • ***The idols of Egypt tremble*** because they are weak and impotent, unable to help (see 40:18; 45:16; 46:1).

19:2 Egypt had a history of civil wars that ravaged the country. Egypt's fragile unity was breaking apart.

3 The Egyptians will lose heart,
and I will confuse their plans.
They will plead with their idols for
wisdom
and call on spirits, mediums, and
those who consult the [f]spirits of the
dead.
4 I will hand Egypt over
to a hard, cruel master.
A fierce king will rule them,"
says the Lord, the LORD of Heaven's
Armies.

5 The waters of the Nile will fail to rise
and flood the fields.
The riverbed will be parched and dry.
6 The canals of the Nile will dry up,
and the streams of Egypt will stink
with rotting reeds and rushes.
7 All the greenery along the riverbank
and all the crops along the river
will dry up and blow away.
8 The fishermen will lament for lack of
work.
Those who cast hooks into the Nile
will groan,
and those who use nets will lose heart.
9 There will be no flax for the harvesters,
no thread for the weavers.
10 They will be in despair,
and all the workers will be sick at heart.

11 What fools are the officials of Zoan!
Their best counsel to the king of Egypt
is stupid and wrong.
Will they still boast to Pharaoh of their
wisdom?
Will they dare brag about all their
wise ancestors?
12 Where are your wise counselors, Pharaoh?
Let them tell you what God plans,
what the LORD of Heaven's Armies is
going to do to Egypt.
13 The officials of Zoan are fools,
and the officials of Memphis are
deluded.
The leaders of the people
have led Egypt astray.
14 The LORD has sent a spirit of foolishness
on them,
so all their suggestions are wrong.
They cause Egypt to stagger
like a drunk in his vomit.
15 There is nothing Egypt can do.
All are helpless—
the head and the tail,
the noble palm branch and the lowly
reed.

16In that day the Egyptians will be as weak
as women. They will cower in fear beneath
the upraised fist of the LORD of Heaven's Armies. 17Just to speak the name of Israel will
terrorize them, for the LORD of Heaven's Armies has laid out his plans against them.
18In that day five of Egypt's cities will follow the LORD of Heaven's Armies. They will
even begin to speak Hebrew, the language
of Canaan. One of these cities will be Heliopolis, the City of the Sun.
19In that day there will be an altar to the
LORD in the heart of Egypt, and there will be
a monument to the LORD at its border. 20It
will be a sign and a witness that the LORD
of Heaven's Armies is worshiped in the
land of Egypt. When the people cry to the
LORD for help against those who oppress
them, he will send them a savior who will

19:3 Isa 8:19
[f]*yidde'oni* (3049)
‣ Lev 19:31
19:4 Isa 20:4
Ezek 29:19
19:5 Ezek 30:12
19:6 Exod 7:18
19:7 Isa 23:3
19:9 Prov 7:16
19:11 Gen 41:38-39
1 Kgs 4:30
Acts 7:22
19:12 Rom 9:17
19:13 Jer 2:16
19:14 Isa 3:12
19:15 Isa 9:14-15
19:16 Jer 51:30
Heb 10:31
19:17 Dan 4:35
19:18 Isa 45:23; 65:16
19:19 Gen 28:18
Josh 22:10, 26-27
19:20 Isa 43:3, 11; 45:15, 21; 49:25

19:3 ***Idols . . . spirits, mediums, and those who consult the spirits of the dead*** were called upon in an attempt to ward off impending destruction (see 8:19-22; 47:12-13).

19:4 ***hard, cruel master:*** In 671 BC, the Assyrian king Esarhaddon invaded Egypt and destroyed the royal city of Memphis. In 663 BC, Ashurbanipal attacked and destroyed Thebes (see Nah 3:8-10).

19:5 The ***waters of the Nile*** were Egypt's lifeline. Any disturbance in the regular pattern of flooding affected the whole nation. In ancient Egypt, the Nile was considered to be a god. However, the true God could easily dry it up.

19:9 There was ***no flax*** or ***thread:*** The drought crippled the linen industry.

19:11-15 The prophet taunted the leaders and wise men of Egypt, who were helpless to avert tragedy.

19:11 ***Zoan*** was the capital of Egypt, located in the Nile delta (see Num 13:22). • ***officials . . . best counsel:*** The king depended on the strategies and counsel of wise men (19:12; see Gen 41:39-40). • The officials of Zoan were known for ***all their wise ancestors***, and Egypt liked to ***brag about*** them.

19:12 ***Where are your wise counselors:*** Cp. 1 Cor 1:20.

19:13 ***Memphis*** (Hebrew *Noph*) was an ancient capital in Egypt located south of the Nile delta. It was destroyed by Esarhaddon in 671 BC.

19:15 ***There is nothing Egypt can do:*** No leader, idol, or conventional wisdom can stand against God's judgment. • ***The head and the tail*** represented all of Egypt's leaders from the greatest to the least important (see 9:14-15).

19:16 An ***upraised fist*** (literally *waving the hand*) was a threatening motion. • ***LORD of Heaven's Armies:*** See note on 1:9.

19:18 ***five of Egypt's cities:*** This is probably just a way of saying "a number of cities" (see also 17:6; 30:17). • Jews living in Egypt after the destruction of Jerusalem spoke Hebrew, here called the ***language of Canaan.*** • ***will be Heliopolis, the City of the Sun*** (or *will be the City of Destruction*; Gen 41:50; Ezek 30:17-18): This city was devoted to Re, the sun god. At a time when Judah was resisting the Lord, Isaiah envisioned the Egyptians following the Lord.

19:19-25 The new Egypt would receive a place in God's purposes together with Assyria and Israel.

19:19 This ***altar*** or ***monument*** refers either to the temple that was built by Jews at Elephantine in Egypt (500 BC), to some other Jewish place of worship, or perhaps to a memorial the Egyptians constructed in devotion to the Lord.

19:20 The altar (19:19) would be ***a sign and a witness*** of the Egyptians' religious

19:21 Isa 56:7
19:22 Deut 32:39; Isa 27:13; 45:14; Heb 12:11
19:23 Isa 11:16
19:25 Hos 2:23
20:1 1 Sam 5:1; 2 Kgs 18:17
20:2 1 Sam 19:24; Mic 1:8
20:3 Isa 8:18; 43:3
20:4 Isa 19:4; 47:2-3
20:5 Jer 9:23-24
20:6 Isa 10:3; 30:3-5, 7
21:1 Isa 13:20-22; Zech 9:14
21:2 Isa 33:1; Jer 49:34
21:3 Ps 48:6; 1 Thes 5:3

rescue them. 21 The LORD will make himself
known to the Egyptians. Yes, they will know
the LORD and will give their sacrifices and
offerings to him. They will make a vow to
the LORD and will keep it. 22 The LORD will
strike Egypt, and then he will bring healing.
For the Egyptians will turn to the LORD, and
he will listen to their pleas and heal them.
23 In that day Egypt and Assyria will be
connected by a highway. The Egyptians
and Assyrians will move freely between
their lands, and they will both worship God.
24 And Israel will be their ally. The three will
be together, and Israel will be a blessing to
them. 25 For the LORD of Heaven's Armies
will say, "Blessed be Egypt, my people.
Blessed be Assyria, the land I have made.
Blessed be Israel, my special possession!"

A Message about Egypt and Ethiopia

20 In the year when King Sargon of Assyria sent his commander in chief
to capture the Philistine city of Ashdod, 2 the
LORD told Isaiah son of Amoz, "Take off the
burlap you have been wearing, and remove
your sandals." Isaiah did as he was told and
walked around naked and barefoot.
3 Then the LORD said, "My servant Isaiah
has been walking around naked and barefoot for the last three years. This is a sign—a
symbol of the terrible troubles I will bring
upon Egypt and Ethiopia. 4 For the king of
Assyria will take away the Egyptians and
Ethiopians as prisoners. He will make them
walk naked and barefoot, both young and
old, their buttocks bared, to the shame of
Egypt. 5 Then the Philistines will be thrown
into panic, for they counted on the power
of Ethiopia and boasted of their allies in
Egypt! 6 They will say, 'If this can happen to
Egypt, what chance do we have? We were
counting on Egypt to protect us from the
king of Assyria.' "

A Message about Babylon

21 This message came to me concerning Babylon—the desert by the sea:

Disaster is roaring down on you from
the desert,
like a whirlwind sweeping in from the
Negev.
2 I see a terrifying vision:
I see the betrayer betraying,
the destroyer destroying.
Go ahead, you Elamites and Medes,
attack and lay siege.
I will make an end
to all the groaning Babylon caused.
3 My stomach aches and burns with pain.
Sharp pangs of anguish are upon me,
like those of a woman in labor.
I grow faint when I hear what God is
planning;
I am too afraid to look.

connection with Israel (see 19:24, 25). • God answers the prayers of those who *cry to the LORD for help.* • The Lord is *a savior;* he would protect the Egyptians even as he protected Jerusalem from the Assyrians.

19:22 ***strike Egypt:*** The Hebrew verb used here is the same as the one used for the tenth plague (Exod 12:13, 23, 27), bringing up associations of what God did during the Exodus. • The Lord, who brings a plague, can also ***bring healing.*** • ***he will listen to their pleas and heal them:*** This expresses a covenantal relationship between the Lord and Egypt (see 65:24).

19:23 Traditionally, ***Egypt and Assyria*** were enemies of one another and of Israel. They were idolatrous to the core, but they would leave behind their enmity and their idols to ***worship*** the true ***God.*** • In the rugged terrain of the ancient Near East, a ***highway*** provided a means for safe, easy travel and trade (see 11:16; 35:8; 40:3; 62:10).

19:24 ***Israel will be a blessing*** in fulfillment of God's promise to Abraham (Gen 12:3).

19:25 Two designations usually reserved for Israel, ***my people*** and ***the land I have made*** (see 29:22; 32:18), are applied here to foreign nations. The Lord promised to regard those from the nations who turn to him as his ***special possession*** (63:17).

20:1-5 Ashdod's reliance on Egypt and Ethiopia was useless. As a complement to his words, Isaiah walked about exposed and barefoot, a symbolic action for what God would do.

20:1 ***Sargon of Assyria*** is Sargon II (721–705 BC). • ***Ashdod,*** one of the five Philistine cities that rebelled against Assyria in 713 BC, was captured by Assyria in 711 BC.

20:2 Prophets characteristically wore ***burlap*** or other rough clothing as a sign of mourning over the sins of the people (see 2 Kgs 1:8; Mark 1:6). • ***naked:*** That is, exposed in some way, possibly even completely nude.

20:3-4 This symbolic event took place some ***three years*** before the fall of Ashdod (see 20:2). Through it, Isaiah became an object lesson for the people (see 8:18). • ***Ethiopia:*** Hebrew *Cush;* also in 20:5. • ***Ethiopians:*** Hebrew *Cushites.*

20:5-6 Philistia's downfall was a warning to the people of Judah, who also relied on Egypt and other alliances rather than on God.

21:1 ***concerning Babylon—the desert by the sea:*** Literally *concerning the desert by the sea.* This description of Babylon was perhaps an ironic way to say that the land was physically lush but spiritually desolate. • ***Disaster . . . from the desert:*** Literally *from the desert, from the terrifying land* (cp. Deut 8:15).

21:2 ***I see:*** The prophet personalized Babylon's experience, which intensifies his poetry, as does the terse language and the repetition of similar sounds, such as ***the betrayer betraying*** (Hebrew *habboged boged*) and ***the destroyer destroying*** (Hebrew *hashoded shoded;* also in 33:1). • The ***Elamites*** (Hebrew *'elam*) lived to the northeast of Babylon. Along with the Medes, they were archrivals of the Babylonians. • ***I will make an end to all the groaning Babylon caused:*** Babylon had caused groaning by attacking and enslaving many nations. It is likely that the ***Elamites and Medes*** played a part in the overthrow of Babylon in 539 BC (21:9).

21:3 ***I grow faint . . . I am too afraid:*** Through his vision, Isaiah experienced the terror of the Babylonian people (see also Dan 8:27; 10:16-17).

4 My mind reels and my heart races.
I longed for evening to come,
but now I am terrified of the dark.

5 Look! They are preparing a great feast.
They are spreading rugs for people to sit on.
Everyone is eating and drinking.
But quick! Grab your [g]shields and prepare for battle.
You are being attacked!

6 Meanwhile, the Lord said to me,
"Put a watchman on the city wall.
Let him shout out what he sees.
7 He should look for chariots
drawn by pairs of horses,
and for riders on donkeys and camels.
Let the watchman be fully alert."

8 Then the watchman called out,
"Day after day I have stood on the watchtower, my lord.
Night after night I have remained at my post.
9 Now at last—look!
Here comes a man in a chariot
with a pair of horses!"
Then the watchman said,
"Babylon is fallen, fallen!
All the idols of Babylon
lie broken on the ground!"
10 O my people, threshed and winnowed,
I have told you everything the LORD of Heaven's Armies has said,
everything the God of Israel has told me.

A Message about Edom

11This message came to me concerning
Edom:

Someone from Edom keeps calling to me,
"Watchman, how much longer until morning?
When will the night be over?"
12 The watchman replies,
"Morning is coming, but night will soon return.
If you wish to ask again, then come back and ask."

A Message about Arabia

13This message came to me concerning
Arabia:

O caravans from Dedan,
hide in the deserts of Arabia.
14 O people of Tema,
bring water to these thirsty people,
food to these weary refugees.
15 They have fled from the sword,
from the drawn sword,
from the bent bow
and the terrors of battle.

16The Lord said to me, "Within a year,
counting each day, all the glory of Kedar
will come to an end. 17Only a few of its courageous archers will survive. I, the LORD, the
God of Israel, have spoken!"

A Message about Jerusalem

22 This message came to me concerning Jerusalem—the Valley of Vision:

21:4 Deut 28:67
21:5 Jer 51:39, 57; [g]*magen* (4043) ‣Ezek 23:24
21:7 Isa 21:9
21:8 Hab 2:1
21:9 Isa 46:1; Jer 50:2; Rev 14:8
21:10 Jer 51:33
21:11 Gen 32:3
21:13 Jer 49:8
21:14 Gen 25:13-15
21:15 Isa 13:14-15
21:16 Ps 120:5; Isa 16:14
21:17 Isa 10:19
22:1 Jer 21:13; Joel 3:12, 14

21:7 The *riders* were messengers who reported what had taken place on the battlefield.

21:8 ***the watchman:*** As in the Dead Sea Scrolls and Syriac version; Masoretic Text reads *a lion.*

21:9 ***Babylon is fallen, fallen:*** Assyrian king Sennacherib destroyed the city of Babylon in 689 BC. The final fall of Babylon was in 539 BC. In Scripture, ***Babylon*** represents all the ungodly power structures of this world (see note on 13:19-22), including nations and kingdoms that do not submit to God and his word. The apostle John gave hope with his prophecy that all Babylons will fall (Rev 14:8; 18:2). • ***All the idols of Babylon lie broken:*** False gods could not save the Babylonians (see 46:1-2).

21:10 ***O my people:*** The focus shifted back to the people of Judah. • Judah would be oppressed (***threshed and winnowed***) by the Babylonians, but Babylon, too, would fall. • ***I have told you everything:*** The prophet had been faithful in his duty to report what the Lord revealed to him.

21:11-17 These two prophecies pertain to Edom and Arabia, located in the territory between Babylon and Israel. These outlying regions suffered under Assyrian domination, and like Judah, they would not be able to rest under Babylon's oppressive regime.

21:11-12 ***message . . . concerning Edom:*** Hebrew *Dumah,* which means "silence" or "stillness." It is a wordplay on the word *Edom.* Edom was an oasis in the northern desert of Arabia. • ***from Edom*** (Hebrew *from Seir,* another name for Edom): Seir was the mountainous area of Edom. • ***how much longer until morning:*** Edom's suffering would be a long ordeal. The Assyrians were dominant in the ancient Near East during the 700s and 600s BC.

21:12 ***Morning is coming,*** but it would mark the beginning of another oppressive era. Because the Babylonians were on the horizon, ***night will soon return.***

21:13-17 Cp. Jer 49:28-33.

21:13 ***Dedan*** was a tribe in Arabia (see Ezek 27:20; 38:13). • ***Caravans*** would ***hide in the deserts of Arabia*** from attacks by the Assyrians and Babylonians, both of whom harassed the Arabian tribes (see 21:1-10; Jer 49:28-29).

21:14 ***Tema*** was an oasis in Arabia on a main trade route from Babylon.

21:15 Assyrian weapons of war such as ***the drawn sword*** and ***the bent bow*** were highly advanced compared to the primitive weapons used by desert peoples.

21:16 ***Within a year, counting each day:*** Literally *Within a year, as a servant bound by contract would count it.* Some ancient manuscripts read *Within three years.* See note on 16:14. • ***Kedar*** was an Arabian tribe that had great wealth and possessions (see 60:7; Ezek 27:21).

21:17 ***Only a few . . . will survive:*** Cp. 10:22; 14:30; 16:14; 24:6, 13; 37:32.

22:1-25 This message addresses the Assyrian siege of Jerusalem in 701 BC

22:2
Isa 23:7
Jer 14:18
Lam 2:20
22:3
Isa 21:15
22:4
Jer 9:1
22:5
Isa 37:3
Lam 2:2
22:6
Isa 21:2
22:8
1 Kgs 7:2; 10:17
22:11
2 Kgs 20:20; 25:4
22:12
Isa 32:11
Joel 1:13
Mic 1:16
22:13
Isa 5:11, 22; 56:12
*1 Cor 15:32
22:14
Isa 65:6-7

What is happening?
Why is everyone running to the
rooftops?
2 The whole city is in a terrible uproar.
What do I see in this reveling city?
Bodies are lying everywhere,
killed not in battle but by famine and
disease.
3 All your leaders have fled.
They surrendered without resistance.
The people tried to slip away,
but they were captured, too.
4 That's why I said, "Leave me alone to
weep;
do not try to comfort me.
Let me cry for my people
as I watch them being destroyed."

5 Oh, what a day of crushing defeat!
What a day of confusion and terror
brought by the Lord, the LORD of
Heaven's Armies,
upon the Valley of Vision!
The walls of Jerusalem have been broken,
and cries of death echo from the
mountainsides.
6 Elamites are the archers,
with their chariots and charioteers.
The men of Kir hold up the shields.
7 Chariots fill your beautiful valleys,
and charioteers storm your gates.
8 Judah's defenses have been stripped away.
You run to the armory for your
weapons.
9 You inspect the breaks in the walls of
Jerusalem.
You store up water in the lower pool.
10 You survey the houses and tear some
down
for stone to strengthen the walls.
11 Between the city walls, you build a
reservoir
for water from the old pool.
But you never ask for help from the One
who did all this.
You never considered the One who
planned this long ago.

12 At that time the Lord, the LORD of
Heaven's Armies,
called you to weep and mourn.
He told you to shave your heads in
sorrow for your sins
and to wear clothes of burlap to show
your remorse.
13 But instead, you dance and play;
you slaughter cattle and kill sheep.
You feast on meat and drink wine.
You say, "Let's feast and drink,
for tomorrow we die!"

14 The LORD of Heaven's Armies has revealed this to me: "Till the day you die, you
will never be forgiven for this sin." That is

(see chs 36–37; 2 Kgs 18:17–19:37) and perhaps the people's preparation for the subsequent Babylonian siege in 588–586 BC.

22:1-4 The prophet rebukes the people for their excitement over the Assyrian retreat (701 BC). They did not foresee that the Babylonian army would complete in 586 BC what the Assyrians failed to do, namely, the destruction of Jerusalem.

22:1 ***concerning Jerusalem—the Valley of Vision*** (literally *concerning the Valley of Vision*): The meaning of the Hebrew phrase is uncertain. Assuming that it refers to Jerusalem (see 22:5), it is ironic: Jerusalem sits atop a hill, and visions were not typically thought to originate in a *valley.* Similarly, Jerusalem was proud of its self-perceived religious *vision*, but its inhabitants were spiritually blind (see 6:10; 42:18).

22:2 The ***reveling city*** was full of feasting and drinking (22:13; see 23:7; 32:13), probably in response to the Assyrian retreat. Now a new threat approaches—the Babylonian siege (586 BC). • The people died ***not in battle but by famine and disease.*** Siege warfare left the inhabitants of the city cut off from needed agricultural resources and in a terrible sanitation and health crisis.

22:3 ***Leaders*** might try to flee, but they would not escape (see 2 Kgs 25:4-6).

22:4 ***Leave me alone to weep:*** Isaiah mourned the victims and the decimation of his people (see 6:13).

22:5-8 The defeat of Judah would be a manifestation of the yet-future "day of the Lord" (see note on 2:5-22). Jerusalem would be impotent in the day of disaster.

22:5 Jerusalem's ***walls*** were ***broken*** by the invading Babylonians, who breached them with battering rams (2 Kgs 25:4).

22:6 ***Elamites:*** Elam was to the east of Babylon and would later play a role in Babylon's defeat (see 21:2; also Jer 49:34-39). • The actual location of ***Kir*** is unknown (see also Amos 1:5).

22:7 The Kidron and Hinnom ***valleys*** were located to the east and south of Jerusalem.

22:8-11 The inhabitants of Jerusalem planned for war by counting weapons, checking walls, and preparing a water supply. However, the people did not consider God's plans (see 13:1–14:23). Although Hezekiah was very prominent in these efforts, the second person verbs are plural. Isaiah was apparently not singling out Hezekiah, as he did Hezekiah's father Ahaz (7:1-4).

22:8 ***to the armory:*** Literally *to the House of the Forest;* see 1 Kgs 7:2-5. This magnificent building was both an armory and a storage place for valuables (see 39:2; 1 Kgs 7:2-6).

22:9 ***Jerusalem*** (literally *the city of David*): Calling Jerusalem "the city of David" evokes memories of Israel's greatest king and God's blessing upon him and the nation (see also 60:14). • ***You store up water in the lower pool:*** Hezekiah expended great energy in ensuring a constant supply of water (see 22:11; 2 Kgs 20:20).

22:12-14 Judah's feasting and disobedience resulted in a prophecy of judgment. • Verse 13 is quoted in 1 Cor 15:32.

22:14 ***you will never be forgiven for this sin:*** The people of Judah added sin upon sin to the point that God would justly condemn them. This foreshadowed the Exile; although it took place in 586 BC, Isaiah was already anticipating it in 701 BC.

the judgment of the Lord, the LORD of Heaven's Armies.

15 This is what the Lord, the LORD of Heav-
en's Armies, said to me: "Confront Shebna,
the palace administrator, and give him this
message:

16 "Who do you think you are,
    and what are you doing here,
  building a beautiful tomb for yourself—
    a monument high up in the rock?
17 For the LORD is about to hurl you away,
      mighty man.
    He is going to grab you,
18 crumple you into a ball,
    and toss you away into a distant,
      barren land.
  There you will die,
    and your glorious chariots will be
      broken and useless.
    You are a disgrace to your master!

19 "Yes, I will drive you out of office," says
the LORD. "I will pull you down from your
high position. 20 And then I will call my servant Eliakim son of Hilkiah to replace you.
21 I will dress him in your royal robes and
will give him your title and your authority.
And he will be a father to the people of Jerusalem and Judah. 22 I will give him the key
to the house of David—the highest position
in the royal court. When he opens doors,
no one will be able to close them; when he
closes doors, no one will be able to open
them. 23 He will bring honor to his family
name, for I will drive him firmly in place
like a nail in the wall. 24 They will give him
great responsibility, and he will bring honor
to even the lowliest members of his family."

25 But the LORD of Heaven's Armies also
says: "The time will come when I will pull
out the nail that seemed so firm. It will
come out and fall to the ground. Everything
it supports will fall with it. I, the LORD, have
spoken!"

A Lament for Tyre

23 This message came to me concerning Tyre:

  Weep, O ships of Tarshish,
    for the harbor and houses of Tyre are
      gone!
  The rumors you heard in Cyprus
    are all true.
2 Mourn in silence, you people of the coast
    and you merchants of Sidon.
  Your traders crossed the sea,
3   sailing over deep waters.
  They brought you grain from Egypt
    and harvests from along the Nile.
  You were the marketplace of the world.

22:16 2 Chr 16:14; Matt 27:60
22:18 Job 18:18
22:19 Ezek 17:24
22:20 Isa 36:3
22:21 Gen 45:8
22:23 Job 36:7; Zech 10:4
22:25 Esth 9:24-25; Isa 46:11
23:1 Josh 19:29; Ezek 26:1—28:19
23:2 Isa 47:5
23:3 Ezek 27:3-25

22:15-25 Shebna and Eliakim were two royal officials in King Hezekiah's court (see 2 Kgs 18:18; 19:2). Apparently assuming that death at the hands of the Assyrians was inevitable, Shebna planned for an ostentatious burial place (22:16). Although the rebuke of Shebna preceded Assyria's siege of Jerusalem in 701 BC (see 22:19-21; 36:3), it connects well with the admonitions of 22:1-13 regarding the ensuing Babylonian siege.

22:15 The actions of ***Shebna*** represent among the populace a lack of confidence in God's ability to rescue Jerusalem from the Assyrian attack. • A ***palace administrator*** held the highest possible position in the royal court (see 22:21-22).

22:16 Shebna was ***building a beautiful tomb . . . a monument.*** This lavish burial place was intended to last for centuries.

22:18 ***toss you away into a distant, barren land:*** Shebna would not find a resting place or have a memorial (cp. 14:11-20). • ***your glorious chariots:*** In his high position, Shebna had lived in luxury.

22:19-20 ***drive you out of office:*** Shebna (22:15) was demoted to court secretary by the time of Jerusalem's siege, when ***Eliakim*** (22:20) was the palace administrator (36:3). Eliakim was a true ***servant*** of the Lord.

22:21 A leader is like ***a father to the people*** when he truly cares for them and addresses their needs. In contrast, Shebna was concerned only for himself.

22:22 ***The key to the house of David*** represents a high position of honor in the royal court (see also Rev 3:7). • ***When he opens doors . . . when he closes doors:*** The officer with ***the highest position*** has sole authority in giving access to the king (cp. Matt 16:19).

22:24 A literal translation of this verse would read *They will hang on him all the glory of his father's house: its offspring and offshoots, all its lesser vessels, from the bowls to all the jars.*

22:25 ***I will pull out the nail:*** Even godly Eliakim would not be able to save Judah or David's dynasty from God's judgment. The people of Judah would go into exile more than a century later (39:6-7).

23:1-18 Tyre was a prosperous seaport northwest of Israel. The relationship between Judah and Tyre went back to the time of David and Solomon (1 Kgs 5:8-9). Tyre, with its proximity to plentiful forests and to the Mediterranean Sea, was one of the commercial centers of the ancient Near East. Its fleets were renowned, and its colonies brought it great prestige and riches. The city came under repeated attack by the Assyrians, Babylonians, and Macedonians, and it fell to Alexander the Great in 332 BC. Isaiah not only prophesied the end of Tyre but by implication warned all whose wealth and earthly securities lead to pride instead of dependence on God (see 2:12-16; Matt 11:21).

23:1 The ***ships of Tarshish*** plied the sea between the Phoenician coast and the port of Tarshish in Spain (see 2:16; 23:6). • ***rumors you heard in Cyprus*** (Hebrew *Kittim;* also in 23:12): Cyprus was the last port of call for sailors coming home from Spain before the final leg of their journey to Tyre.

23:2 ***Sidon*** was a Phoenician port to the north of Tyre. • Tyre's commercial network of ***traders*** was extensive.

23:3 ***Egypt:*** Hebrew *Shihor,* a branch of the Nile River. • Fish, agricultural produce, flax, and linen were all ***harvests from along the Nile*** (see ch 19). • Tyre was known as ***the marketplace of the world,*** comparable to modern cities like New York, Hong Kong, or London.

23:4 Gen 10:15, 19; Jer 47:4
23:7 Isa 32:13
23:9 Isa 5:13; Dan 4:37
23:11 Isa 50:2; Zech 9:3-4
23:12 Rev 18:22
23:13 Isa 13:21
23:15 Jer 25:11
23:18 Isa 60:5-9; Zech 14:20

4 But now you are put to shame, city of Sidon,
for Tyre, the fortress of the sea, says,
"Now I am childless;
I have no sons or daughters."
5 When Egypt hears the news about Tyre,
there will be great sorrow.
6 Send word now to Tarshish!
Wail, you people who live in distant lands!
7 Is this silent ruin all that is left of your once joyous city?
What a long history was yours!
Think of all the colonists you sent to distant places.

8 Who has brought this disaster on Tyre,
that great creator of kingdoms?
Her traders were all princes,
her merchants were nobles.
9 The LORD of Heaven's Armies has done it
to destroy your pride
and bring low all earth's nobility.
10 Come, people of Tarshish,
sweep over the land like the flooding Nile,
for Tyre is defenseless.
11 The LORD held out his hand over the sea
and shook the kingdoms of the earth.
He has spoken out against Phoenicia,
ordering that her fortresses be destroyed.
12 He says, "Never again will you rejoice,
O daughter of Sidon, for you have been crushed.
Even if you flee to Cyprus,
you will find no rest."

13 Look at the land of Babylonia—
the people of that land are gone!
The Assyrians have handed Babylon over
to the wild animals of the desert.
They have built siege ramps against its walls,
torn down its palaces,
and turned it to a heap of rubble.
14 Wail, O ships of Tarshish,
for your harbor is destroyed!

15 For seventy years, the length of a king's
life, Tyre will be forgotten. But then the city
will come back to life as in the song about
the prostitute:

16 Take a harp and walk the streets,
you forgotten harlot.
Make sweet melody and sing your songs
so you will be remembered again.

17 Yes, after seventy years the LORD will revive Tyre. But she will be no different than
she was before. She will again be a prostitute to all kingdoms around the world.
18 But
in the end her profits will be given to the
LORD. Her wealth will not be hoarded but
will provide good food and fine clothing for
the LORD's priests.

3. THE "LITTLE APOCALYPSE" (24:1–27:13)

The Day of the LORD

24 1 Look! The LORD is about to
destroy the earth
and make it a vast wasteland.

23:4 Part of the great port city of Tyre was on an island. The island city was a ***fortress of the sea***, but it fell in 332 BC. • ***I am childless; I have no sons or daughters:*** This metaphor was a judgment on Tyre's colonial ports around the Mediterranean Sea. In the ancient world, to reach old age without having children was considered a terrible fate (see 49:21; 54:1).

23:5 ***Egypt*** depended on the ships from Tyre for the export of its products (see 23:3).

23:8 The Lord had ***brought this disaster on Tyre*** (23:9). • Through commercial links, Tyre had created wealth for itself and its trading partners; in this sense, Tyre was a ***great creator of kingdoms***.

23:10 The meaning of the Hebrew in this verse is uncertain. • ***Sweep over the land like the flooding Nile:*** This difficult phrase means either (1) that the sailors who had returned from Tarshish were being invited to loot ruined Tyre; or (2) that the people of Tarshish were forced to move back to their agricultural fields to make their living (instead of trading) now that Tyre had been destroyed.

23:11 ***Phoenicia*** (Hebrew *Canaan*) was the region north of Israel. Tyre and Sidon were its main cities.

23:13 ***Babylonia*** (or ***Chaldea***) was stripped and looted by the Assyrians under Sennacherib (689 BC); eventually it rose to be a mighty empire once again.

23:15-18 There was hope for Tyre.

23:17 Metaphorically, Tyre was ***a prostitute*** because of its indifferent willingness to sell anything to anyone (cp. Rev 17:2; 18:3, 12-13).

23:18 Even though Tyre's earnings came from unrighteous commerce, the ***profits will be given to the LORD*** rather than being squandered. • There will be ***good food and fine clothing for the LORD's priests***. The theme of the wealth of the nations being brought to the Lord in Jerusalem is more fully developed in 60:5-11; 61:6.

24:1–27:13 This section is often referred to as the "Little Apocalypse" because of its similarities to the book of Revelation. In these chapters Isaiah takes readers out of the present into a vision of the future world. The universal imagery of the Little Apocalypse makes it difficult to assign the events described to any precise historical situation. That means that these chapters cannot be used to outline a sequence of events or create a historical blueprint for the future. Instead, the imagery is intended to create an impressionistic drama of an unfolding world that is both like and unlike the present. The combination of aspects of the old era with aspects of the new era (for instance, people of Zion will all be righteous [new], but still long for their redemption [old]) is consistent with the NT concept of the future age breaking into and overlapping with the present evil age (2 Cor 4:4; Gal 1:4). Peter, for example, wrote of believers as living in the last days (1 Pet 1:12; 2 Pet 3:3) even though the last day remains yet future (2 Pet 3:10).

24:1-23 Here the judgments described in chs 13–23 are extended to the creation at large.

He devastates the surface of the earth
and scatters the people.
2 Priests and laypeople,
servants and masters,
maids and mistresses,
buyers and sellers,
lenders and borrowers,
bankers and debtors—none will be
spared.
3 The earth will be completely emptied
and looted.
The LORD has spoken!

4 The earth mourns and dries up,
and the crops waste away and wither.
Even the greatest people on earth
waste away.
5 The earth suffers for the sins of its people,
for they have twisted God's
instructions,
violated his laws,
and broken his everlasting covenant.
6 Therefore, a curse consumes the earth.
Its people must pay the price for their
sin.
They are destroyed by fire,
and only a few are left alive.
7 The grapevines waste away,
and there is no new wine.
All the merrymakers sigh and mourn.
8 The cheerful sound of tambourines is
stilled;
the happy cries of celebration are
heard no more.
The melodious chords of the harp are
silent.
9 Gone are the joys of wine and song;
alcoholic drink turns bitter in the
mouth.
10 The city writhes in chaos;
every home is locked to keep out
intruders.
11 Mobs gather in the streets, crying out for
wine.
Joy has turned to gloom.
Gladness has been banished from the
land.
12 The city is left in ruins,
its gates battered down.
13 Throughout the earth the story is the
same—
only a remnant is left,
like the stray olives left on the tree
or the few grapes left on the vine after
harvest.

14 But all who are left shout and sing for joy.
Those in the west praise the LORD's
majesty.
15 In eastern lands, give glory to the LORD.
In the lands beyond the sea, praise the
name of the LORD, the God of Israel.
16 We hear songs of praise from the ends
of the earth,
songs that give glory to the Righteous
One!

But my heart is heavy with grief.
Weep for me, for I wither away.
Deceit still prevails,
and treachery is everywhere.
17 Terror and traps and snares will be
your lot,
you people of the earth.
18 Those who flee in terror will fall into a
trap,
and those who escape the trap will be
caught in a snare.

24:5
Gen 3:17
Num 35:33-34
24:6
Zech 5:3-4
24:7
Joel 1:10, 12
24:8
Jer 16:9
24:9
Isa 5:11, 22
24:11
Isa 32:13
24:12
Isa 45:2
24:13
Isa 17:6
24:14
Isa 12:6; 52:8
24:15
Isa 42:4, 10, 12
24:16
Isa 11:12; 28:5
24:18
Gen 7:10-12
Ps 46:2

24:1 ***destroy the earth and make it a vast wasteland:*** There is a play here on the Hebrew words *baqaq* (*destroy*) and *balaq* (*make a wasteland*). The devastation will begin with Judah and be extended to the whole world (see 1 Pet 4:17). • All ***the earth*** will be destroyed, ***the people*** as well as national political structures.

24:4-13 All humanity is guilty (Rom 3:23) and under condemnation (see 59:1-15). Judgment is likened to a failed grape harvest that brings drinking and feasting to a halt.

24:4 ***earth . . . dries up . . . crops waste away and wither:*** The prophets often used the imagery of a drought to get the attention of people who live off the land (see also Jer 23:10; Joel 1:12; Amos 1:2).

24:5 Isaiah was probably referring to the ***everlasting covenant*** that God made with all humanity through Noah (Gen 9:8-17). The prophet saw a parallel with the wickedness in his day and the wickedness of the pre-flood world.

24:6 The effect of sin is so great that no earthly thing or action can adequately atone for it. Hope ultimately lies in God himself. God has reconciled the world to himself in Christ (Col 1:19-20).

24:7 ***Merrymakers*** will ***sigh and mourn*** because they are dependent on wine for pleasure.

24:8 ***Tambourines*** and ***melodious chords of the harp*** represent good times (see 5:12; Rev 18:22).

24:10 ***city writhes in chaos:*** With normal levels of urban disarray being raised to chaotic and dangerous disorder, people will be forced to seek refuge in ***locked*** homes.

24:11 ***Gladness has been banished from the land,*** not by edict, but because there is no reason to celebrate.

24:13 ***stray olives left on the tree:*** The remnant will include godly people both from Israel (see 17:6) and from other nations. • The theme of the ***remnant*** is common in Isaiah (10:22; 14:30; 16:14; 24:6; 37:32).

24:14-16 In spite of wailing and ruin, the sound of praise is heard from all directions. Even while still experiencing the pain of the devastation of the old world, the godly will respond with joyous expectation for the new world.

24:16 ***But my heart is heavy with grief:*** The prophets were well acquainted with the emotional pain brought on by the sin of their people and its consequences (see 15:5; 21:4; Jer 15:10; Mic 1:8). • Although aspects of the new world are present, the ***deceit*** of the old world ***still prevails*** for a time.

24:18 No one can ***escape*** the day of the Lord (see notes on 2:5-22; Amos 5:18). • ***Destruction falls like rain from***

24:19 Num 16:31-32
24:20 Isa 19:14; 43:27; 66:24
24:21 Ps 76:12
24:22 Isa 10:4
24:23 Mic 4:7
Heb 12:22
Rev 21:23
25:1 Exod 15:2
Ps 40:5
Eph 1:11
25:2 Isa 17:1
25:4 Isa 32:2
25:5 Jer 51:54-56
25:6 Isa 2:2-4
25:8 Ps 69:9
Isa 65:19
*1 Cor 15:54-55
1 Pet 4:14
Rev 21:4
25:9 Isa 30:18; 35:1-2, 10; 40:9

Destruction falls like rain from the
heavens;
the foundations of the earth shake.
19 The earth has broken up.
It has utterly collapsed;
it is violently shaken.
20 The earth staggers like a drunk.
It trembles like a tent in a storm.
It falls and will not rise again,
for the guilt of its rebellion is very
heavy.

21 In that day the LORD will punish the
gods in the heavens
and the proud rulers of the nations
on earth.
22 They will be rounded up and put in
prison.
They will be shut up in prison
and will finally be punished.
23 Then the glory of the moon will wane,
and the brightness of the sun will fade,
for the LORD of Heaven's Armies will
rule on Mount Zion.
He will rule in great glory in
Jerusalem,
in the sight of all the leaders of his
people.

The Mountain of the LORD

25 1 O LORD, I will honor and praise
your name,
for you are my God.
You do such wonderful things!
You planned them long ago,
and now you have accomplished them.
2 You turn mighty cities into heaps of
ruins.
Cities with strong walls are turned to
rubble.
Beautiful palaces in distant lands
disappear
and will never be rebuilt.
3 Therefore, strong nations will declare
your glory;
ruthless nations will fear you.
4 But you are a tower of refuge to the poor,
O LORD,
a tower of refuge to the needy in
distress.
You are a refuge from the storm
and a shelter from the heat.
For the oppressive acts of ruthless people
are like a storm beating against a wall,
5 or like the relentless heat of the
desert.
But you silence the roar of foreign nations.
As the shade of a cloud cools
relentless heat,
so the boastful songs of ruthless
people are stilled.

6 In Jerusalem, the LORD of Heaven's
Armies
will spread a wonderful feast
for all the people of the world.
It will be a delicious banquet
with clear, well-aged wine and choice
meat.
7 There he will remove the cloud of gloom,
the shadow of death that hangs over
the earth.
8 He will swallow up death forever!
The Sovereign LORD will wipe away
all tears.
He will remove forever all insults and
mockery
against his land and people.
The LORD has spoken!

9 In that day the people will proclaim,
"This is our God!
We trusted in him, and he saved us!
This is the LORD, in whom we trusted.
Let us rejoice in the salvation he
brings!"

---

the heavens (literally *the floodgates of heaven are opened*): The imagery is like the flood in Noah's time (see notes on 24:5; Gen 7:11-12; 8:2). • ***the foundations of the earth shake:*** An earthquake is characteristic of a *theophany,* a physical manifestation of God's presence (see note on 5:25; see also 6:4; 13:13; 19:1).

24:21 The phrase translated *gods* (Hebrew *tseba' hammarom,* "armed host of the heavens") might refer to pagan gods represented by the stars. It might also refer to the angels or even demons (Rev 12:4, 9). Judgment will extend to all parts of creation (13:13; 34:5; see Eph 6:11-12).

24:22 *put in prison . . . punished:* See also 2 Pet 2:4; Rev 9:2, 11; 17:8.

25:1-12 The second part of the Little Apocalypse (see note on 24:1–27:13) describes praise for God's judgment (25:1-5, 11-12) and salvation (25:6-9).

25:1-5 Isaiah here praises God for protecting the needy (see 12:1-6).

25:3 Assyria and Egypt were ***strong . . . ruthless nations,*** but in the future they will exalt God rather than their own power.

25:6-8 The banquet is a symbol of God's providing richly for all those who will receive his gracious invitation (Rev 3:20-21; 19:9).

25:6 *In Jerusalem:* Literally *On this mountain* (also in 25:10)—that is, the mountain of the Lord (see 2:2; 24:23): This does not refer to a geographical city but to Zion, the eternal city of God (see 1:8, 27).

25:8 *He will swallow up death forever* (Greek version reads *Death is swallowed up in victory;* cp. 1 Cor 15:54): Isaiah's hope was God's power over sin and sin's devastating results. In the NT this promise is realized in Jesus Christ (1 Cor 15:54). • The Lord's presence will be a source of eternal comfort; he will ***wipe away all tears*** (see Rev 21:4).

25:9-12 The new community of God's people will respond in joy and faith. When the enemy is defeated, God's people will be free forever.

10 For the LORD's hand of blessing will rest
on Jerusalem.
But Moab will be crushed.
It will be like straw trampled down
and left to rot.
11 God will push down Moab's people
as a swimmer pushes down water
with his hands.
He will end their pride
and all their evil works.
12 The high walls of Moab will be
demolished.
They will be brought down to the
ground,
down into the dust.

The City of the LORD

26 In that day, everyone in the land of
Judah will sing this song:

Our city is strong!
We are surrounded by the walls of
God's salvation.
2 Open the gates to all who are righteous;
allow the faithful to enter.
3 You will keep in perfect peace
all who trust in you,
all whose thoughts are fixed on you!
4 Trust in the LORD always,
for the LORD GOD is the eternal [h]Rock.
5 He humbles the proud
and brings down the arrogant city.
He brings it down to the dust.
6 The poor and oppressed trample it
underfoot,
and the needy walk all over it.
7 But for those who are righteous,
the way is not steep and rough.
You are a God who does what is right,
and you smooth out the path ahead
of them.
8 LORD, we show our trust in you by
obeying your laws;
our [i]heart's desire is to glorify your
name.
9 All night long I search for you;
in the morning [j]I earnestly seek for
God.
For only when you come to judge the
earth
will people learn what is right.
10 Your kindness to the wicked
does not make them do good.
Although others do right, the wicked
keep doing wrong
and take no notice of the LORD's
majesty.
11 O LORD, they pay no attention to your
upraised fist.
Show them your eagerness to defend
your people.
Then they will be ashamed.
Let your fire consume your enemies.
12 LORD, you will grant us peace;
all we have accomplished is really
from you.
13 O LORD our God, others have ruled us,
but you alone are the one we worship.
14 Those we served before are dead and
gone.
Their departed spirits will never
return!

25:11 Isa 16:6
25:12 Isa 26:5
26:1 Isa 12:1; 60:18
26:2 Isa 45:25
26:3 Isa 57:19
26:4 Isa 50:10
[h]*tsur* (6697) ‣Isa 51:1
26:6 Isa 29:19
26:7 Ps 25:4-5; Isa 42:16
26:8 Isa 12:4
[i]*nepesh* (5315) ‣Gen 1:20
26:9 Ps 63:1; 77:2; Hos 5:15
[j]*ruakh* (7307) ‣Isa 28:6
26:10 Isa 22:12-13; John 5:37-38
26:11 Isa 10:17; 66:15, 24
26:13 Isa 2:8

25:10 *on Jerusalem:* Literally *on this mountain;* see note on 25:6. • ***Moab*** (see 15:1–16:14) here represents the nations under judgment, those who trust only themselves (see 34:5-17). • ***like straw trampled down:*** The people would be helpless and dying in the most degrading circumstances.

25:11 Isaiah used the image of a ***swimmer*** forcibly kept under ***water*** to illustrate that ***Moab's people*** are hopelessly doomed and their human pride will be conquered.

26:1-21 This section of the Little Apocalypse (see note on 24:1–27:13) is a song of praise and a prayer for redemption.

26:1-6 The new community of God's people is likened to the citizens of a city, securely held together by the Lord. They are righteous, faithful, peaceful, and trusting.

26:1 ***Our city*** refers to Zion, the eternal city of God, where the Lord is present to protect and bless his people (see 1:8, 27; see also Ps 46). Zion stands in direct contrast to the "mighty cities" of the nations (25:2; 26:5), which are helpless and are brought down to "ruins." • The ***walls of God's salvation*** protectively enclose his people; no one can hurt them again.

26:2 ***Open*** access is given to ***all who,*** like God and his Messiah, ***are righteous*** and ***faithful.*** The citizens of true Zion are committed to the Lord.

26:3 A ***perfect peace,*** marked by harmony, quietness, and confidence, is a benefit of the new creation.

26:5 The ***proud*** and ***arrogant*** are often characterized as exalting themselves (see 2:11-12), whereas God ***humbles*** them.

26:6 Justice finally occurs when ***the needy walk all over*** the ruins of the city where the proud have perished.

26:7-21 The godly pray for the end of oppression and the full establishment of God's kingdom. Isaiah encouraged the godly to persevere as they wait for their final vindication and the resurrection of the body.

26:7 God will do ***what is right*** for those who walk in his way, even if they have to suffer a while longer (see 24:16). One day, they will experience harmony and integrity (see Prov 2:8-9; 15:19).

26:8 ***we show our trust*** (see 26:3-4; literally ***we wait for you***): Waiting involves trust in the Lord and longing for his redemption. • People express their commitment to God ***by obeying*** his ***laws;*** mere lip service is not sufficient.

26:9 ***I search . . . I earnestly seek:*** Cp. Ps 63:1.

26:10 God has shown ***kindness to the wicked.*** Although they deserve judgment (see also Rom 2:4; 2 Pet 3:9), he has been patient and forbearing and has blessed them. However, time will run out one day.

26:11 An ***upraised fist*** expresses anger and the threat of judgment (see note on 19:16-17). • ***Fire*** was often an image for God's judgment.

26:15 Isa 54:2
26:16 Hos 5:15
26:17 John 16:21
26:18 Isa 33:11
26:19 Ezek 37:1-14; Dan 12:2; Eph 5:14
26:20 Ps 30:5
26:21 Job 16:18; Mic 1:3; Jude 1:14
27:1 Job 3:8; Ps 74:14
27:2 Ps 80:8
27:3 John 10:28
27:4 2 Sam 23:6; Isa 33:12
27:5 Job 22:21; Isa 25:4
27:6 Isa 35:1-2; 37:31
27:7 Isa 10:12, 17

You attacked them and destroyed them,
and they are long forgotten.
15 O LORD, you have made our nation great;
yes, you have made us great.
You have extended our borders,
and we give you the glory!

16 LORD, in distress we searched for you.
We prayed beneath the burden of your discipline.
17 Just as a pregnant woman
writhes and cries out in pain as she gives birth,
so were we in your presence, LORD.
18 We, too, writhe in agony,
but nothing comes of our suffering.
We have not given salvation to the earth,
nor brought life into the world.
19 But those who die in the LORD will live;
their bodies will rise again!
Those who sleep in the earth
will rise up and sing for joy!
For your life-giving light will fall like dew
on your people in the place of the dead!

20 Go home, my people,
and lock your doors!
Hide yourselves for a little while
until the LORD's anger has passed.
21 Look! The LORD is coming from heaven
to punish the people of the earth for their sins.
The earth will no longer hide those who have been killed.
They will be brought out for all to see.

The Vineyard of the LORD

27 In that day the LORD will take his terrible, swift sword and punish Leviathan, the swiftly moving serpent, the coiling, writhing serpent. He will kill the dragon of the sea.

2 "In that day,
sing about the fruitful vineyard.
3 I, the LORD, will watch over it,
watering it carefully.
Day and night I will watch so no one can harm it.
4 My anger will be gone.
If I find briers and thorns growing,
I will attack them;
I will burn them up—
5 unless they turn to me for help.
Let them make peace with me;
yes, let them make peace with me."
6 The time is coming when Jacob's
descendants will take root.
Israel will bud and blossom
and fill the whole earth with fruit!

7 Has the LORD struck Israel
as he struck her enemies?
Has he punished her
as he punished them?

26:15 This verse is a confident expression of thanks for God's blessings. In Isaiah's time, during King Hezekiah's prosperous reign, the ***borders*** of the ***nation*** of Israel were ***extended,*** and people gave glory to God for his great deeds.

26:16 While waiting for God's salvation (26:1), the godly were ***in distress*** and longed for their vindication. They ***prayed beneath the burden*** of God's ***discipline.*** In Hezekiah's time, Judah was in distress when Sennacherib attacked and destroyed the whole nation except for Jerusalem.

26:17 The imagery of ***a pregnant woman*** in childbirth describes the nation's pain when Assyrian king Sennacherib attacked it in 701 BC (see 37:3).

26:18 Only God can give ***salvation*** and bring ***life*** (see 59:9-15).

26:19 ***those who die . . . will live:*** There is hope for the remnant. Some hold the minimal interpretation that this means the people would be restored to the land after the Exile (see Ezek 37:11-12) or that the Lord would preserve Jerusalem (see 29:4, 6-8). More likely it refers to the resurrection of the body from the grave (see 25:7-8). The OT has little to say about the resurrection, but this text anticipates fuller development in the NT (see 1 Cor 15:12-58).

26:20 God will punish the wicked, so the godly should ***go home*** and stay out of the way.

26:21 The wicked retain power now, but their oppressive rule will end in the day of the Lord's wrath, when he will ***punish*** them ***for their sins.***

27:1 The identification of ***Leviathan*** is disputed, ranging from an earthly creature to a mythical sea monster in ancient literature. Israel adapted this imagery to refer to evil powers that oppose God. Leviathan's death symbolizes the end of evil, Satan, the demonic, and the dominion of forces hostile to God (see 51:9; Ps 74:14; 104:7-9, 26; see also the serpent in Gen 3; Rev 12; 13; 16:13; 20:2, 10).

27:2-6 The Song of the Fruitful Vineyard, in which the vineyard represents God's people (cp. 5:1-7).

27:3 God identifies himself as ***the LORD*** of the covenant to assure his people that what he says and does is reliable (see Exod 6:2-3). The phrase is used many times throughout Isaiah. • ***watch . . . watering . . . watch:*** The Lord will provide even greater care and protection for his ultimate vineyard than he did for Israel, his first vineyard (see 5:1-2).

27:5 God expects all his people to ***turn to*** him and to trust him ***for help.*** • ***Let them make peace with me*** is God's offer of reconciliation for his people.

27:6 ***Jacob's descendants will take root*** and the remnant will increase (37:31; cp. 5:24; 14:30; for application to the Messiah, see 11:1, 10). • ***fill the whole earth:*** The fulfillment of this prophecy extends beyond the restoration of Israel from exile to the second coming of the Lord Jesus. It includes all the righteous children of God—Jews and Gentiles—who suffer but remain obedient as they wait for the fullness of redemption (see 26:18; John 15:1-8).

27:7-11 Isaiah reminded readers of the reasons for the Exile and judgment: Israel's sinfulness, God's righteous judgment, and the absence of divine compassion.

27:7 Despite being God's covenant people, Israel was ***struck*** and ***punished*** like any other wicked nation. However, Israel was not completely destroyed; a remnant remained.

8 No, but he exiled Israel to call her to
account.
She was exiled from her land
as though blown away in a storm from
the east.
9 The LORD did this to purge Israel's
wickedness,
to take away all her sin.
As a result, all the pagan altars will be
crushed to dust.
No Asherah pole or pagan shrine will
be left standing.
10 The fortified towns will be silent and
empty,
the houses abandoned, the streets
overgrown with weeds.
Calves will graze there,
chewing on twigs and branches.
11 The people are like the dead branches of
a tree,
broken off and used for kindling
beneath the cooking pots.
Israel is a foolish and stupid nation,
for its people have turned away from
God.
Therefore, the one who made them
will show them no pity or mercy.

12 Yet the time will come when the LORD
will gather them together like handpicked
grain. One by one he will gather them—
from the Euphrates River in the east to the
Brook of Egypt in the west. 13 In that day the
great trumpet will sound. Many who were
dying in exile in Assyria and Egypt will return to Jerusalem to worship the LORD on
his holy mountain.

4. THREATS OF JUDGMENT (28:1–33:24)

Woe on Samaria

28 1 What sorrow awaits the proud
city of Samaria—
the glorious crown of the drunks of
Israel.
It sits at the head of a fertile valley,
but its glorious beauty will fade like
a flower.
It is the pride of a people
brought down by wine.
2 For the Lord will send a mighty army
against it.
Like a mighty hailstorm and a
torrential rain,
they will burst upon it like a surging flood
and smash it to the ground.
3 The proud city of Samaria—
the glorious crown of the drunks of
Israel—
will be trampled beneath its enemies'
feet.
4 It sits at the head of a fertile valley,
but its glorious beauty will fade like
a flower.
Whoever sees it will snatch it up,
as an early fig is quickly picked and
eaten.

5 Then at last the LORD of Heaven's Armies
will himself be Israel's glorious crown.
He will be the pride and joy
of the remnant of his people.
6 He will give a [k]longing for justice
to their judges.
He will give great courage
to their warriors who stand at the gates.

27:9 Isa 17:8; Dan 11:35
27:11 Deut 32:18, 28; Isa 43:1, 7
27:12 Deut 30:3-4; Isa 11:11
27:13 Zech 14:16; Matt 24:31; Rev 11:15
28:2 Isa 8:7; 30:28; Nah 1:8
28:4 Hos 9:10; Nah 3:12
28:5 Isa 41:16; 62:3
28:6 2 Chr 32:6-8; Isa 11:2; 25:4; 32:16
[k]*ruakh* (7307) ›Isa 32:15

27:8 The Assyrians *exiled* large numbers of citizens from the northern kingdom of Israel when Samaria fell in 722 BC. The Babylonians exiled many from Judah from 605 to 586 BC. • Storms *from the east* were known for their destructive effects (see Job 27:21; 38:24; Jer 4:11).

27:9 God's justice requires him to punish sin. That punishment is designed to correct behavior and to purify. Being conquered and exiled was *to purge Israel's* (literally *Jacob's;* see note on 14:1) *wickedness* and *to take away all her sin* (see Rom 11:27). • This was to be the end of *all the pagan* worship in Israel, including the incense altars and the poles that were used in worshiping the goddess *Asherah.*

27:10 Places previously associated with human power and accomplishment would be ruined to the extent that animals would *graze* in them.

27:11 *The people* were outside of God's covenantal care; they foolishly *turned away* from him.

27:12 *Yet:* God's withholding of mercy from Israel (27:11) will be temporary. • *from the Euphrates River* (literally *the river*) . . . *to the Brook of Egypt:* God's remnant will return from Assyria and Egypt to the territory that God promised to Abraham (Gen 15:18; see 1 Kgs 4:21).

27:13 The *great trumpet* was used to gather the people (see Matt 24:31).

28:1–33:24 This section is connected by a series of six threats of judgment or woes (cp. 5:8-23). Apart from the initial address to Samaria in 28:1-6, the remainder of the section is addressed to Judah, especially because of their inclination to trust Egypt to rescue them from Assyria (30:2).

28:1-29 The glory of Samaria, capital of the northern kingdom of Israel, is here contrasted with the glory of the Lord. This section represents the first of the six woes (*What sorrow . . .*).

28:1 The first two lines can be literally translated, *What sorrow awaits the crowning glory of the drunks of Ephraim,* referring to *Samaria,* capital of the northern kingdom of Israel. • The *drunks of Israel* epitomized pride, spiritual complacency, and scorn for God and his commands. • Unlike Jerusalem, Samaria was in a *fertile valley.*

28:2 *the LORD will send:* The covenant God will act against his own people, whose behavior had effectively disqualified them as God's people (see Hos 1:9). • The *mighty army* is that of the Assyrians, who destroyed Samaria in 722 BC.

28:3 *The proud city of Samaria—the glorious crown of the drunks of Israel:* Literally *The crowning glory of the drunks of Ephraim;* see note on 28:1.

28:5-6 In the future, after God's judgment has purged his people, he will restore a righteous remnant, transforming the desires and character of his people. Samaria will no longer be the source of Israel's pride; instead, they will glory in the Lord, their true *crown.*

28:7
Hab 2:15-16

28:8
Jer 48:26

28:9
Heb 5:12-13

28:10
Neh 9:30

28:11
Isa 33:19
*1 Cor 14:21

28:12
Jer 6:16
Matt 11:28-29

28:13
Matt 21:44

28:14
Isa 28:22

28:15
Isa 28:18

28:16
Ps 118:22
Matt 21:42
Acts 4:11
*Rom 9:33; 10:11
Eph 2:20
*1 Pet 2:6
[a]*'aman* (0539)
▸Isa 53:1

28:17
Isa 61:8
Amos 7:7-9

28:18
Isa 28:15

7 Now, however, Israel is led by drunks
who reel with wine and stagger with alcohol.
The priests and prophets stagger with alcohol
and lose themselves in wine.
They reel when they see visions
and stagger as they render decisions.
8 Their tables are covered with vomit;
filth is everywhere.
9 "Who does the LORD think we are?" they ask.
"Why does he speak to us like this?
Are we little children,
just recently weaned?
10 He tells us everything over and over—
one line at a time,
one line at a time,
a little here,
and a little there!"
11 So now God will have to speak to his people
through foreign oppressors who speak a strange language!
12 God has told his people,
"Here is a place of rest;
let the weary rest here.
This is a place of quiet rest."
But they would not listen.
13 So the LORD will spell out his message for them again,
one line at a time,
one line at a time,
a little here,
and a little there,
so that they will stumble and fall.
They will be injured, trapped, and captured.

Judgment on Jerusalem

14 Therefore, listen to this message from the LORD,
you scoffing rulers in Jerusalem.
15 You boast, "We have struck a bargain to cheat death
and have made a deal to dodge the grave.
The coming destruction can never touch us,
for we have built a strong refuge made of lies and deception."
16 Therefore, this is what the Sovereign LORD says:
"Look! I am placing a foundation stone in Jerusalem,
a firm and tested stone.
It is a precious cornerstone that is safe to build on.
Whoever [a]believes need never be shaken.
17 I will test you with the measuring line of justice
and the plumb line of righteousness.
Since your refuge is made of lies,
a hailstorm will knock it down.
Since it is made of deception,
a flood will sweep it away.
18 I will cancel the bargain you made to cheat death,
and I will overturn your deal to dodge the grave.
When the terrible enemy sweeps through,
you will be trampled into the ground.

28:7-13 The focus returns to the lamentable present situation in Israel (and Judah). The leaders and people will be ensnared by their own schemes.

28:7 The *priests and prophets* led the people astray. • Intoxicating beverages such as *wine* and *alcohol* were prohibited for priests while fulfilling their duties (Lev 10:9).

28:9-10 The people had become hardened to God's revelation (1 Cor 14:21; see note on 28:13).

28:11 *God will have to speak* through circumstances such as hardship, exile, and death in order to get through to his hardened people. • *a strange language:* In the NT, Paul applied this text to the spiritual gift of tongues as a sign of judgment to unbelievers (see 1 Cor 14:21-22).

28:12 Had *his people* listened, God's revelation would have led them to rest (see 48:18-19). *But they would not listen* because of their hard hearts (65:12).

28:13 *one line at a time, one line at a time, a little here, and a little there:* The Hebrew here is difficult to understand. The words might be intentional nonsense to illustrate the point that the people were so spiritually blind that God's clearest revelation was nonsense to them (see 6:9-10).

28:14-22 The focus shifts specifically to *Jerusalem.* The leaders of Judah are accused of being as blind as those in the northern kingdom of Israel.

28:15 *cheat death* (literally *have made a covenant with death*) . . . *dodge the grave* (Hebrew *Sheol;* also in 28:18): There are two interpretive possibilities: (1) The people had sold themselves to the Canaanite god of death, Mot, in return for his supposed protection. (2) The prophet was being sarcastic; the people thought their various political and economic moves guaranteed their personal security, but they had actually destroyed themselves. • *lies and deception:* The leaders did not think of themselves as deceptive, but they were.

28:16 The Lord himself is the reliable *foundation stone in Jerusalem* (Hebrew *in Zion*), *a precious cornerstone* of the true city of God. There would be real hope in Jerusalem if the leaders and the people would only turn to him. If they would trust in God, they would be secure in the most terrible storm or the most devastating earthquake (see 8:14; Ps 118:22; Matt 7:24-27; 21:42; see the application to Jesus Christ, Rom 9:33; 10:11; 1 Cor 3:11; Eph 2:20; 1 Pet 2:4-7). • Greek version reads *Look! I am placing a stone in the foundation of Jerusalem* [literally *Zion*], */ a precious cornerstone for its foundation, chosen for great honor. / Anyone who trusts in him will never be disgraced.* Cp. Rom 9:33; 28:6; 1 Pet 2:6, all of which quote from the Greek version.

28:17 The Lord judges people on their works, which reveal the presence or absence of living faith (for *justice* and *righteousness,* see 1:21-23).

19 Again and again that flood will come,
morning after morning,
day and night,
until you are carried away."

This message will bring terror to your
people.
20 The bed you have made is too short to
lie on.
The blankets are too narrow to cover
you.
21 The LORD will come as he did against the
Philistines at Mount Perazim
and against the Amorites at Gibeon.
He will come to do a strange thing;
he will come to do an unusual deed:
22 For the Lord, the LORD of Heaven's
Armies,
has plainly said that he is determined
to crush the whole land.
So scoff no more,
or your punishment will be even
greater.

23 Listen to me;
listen, and pay close attention.
24 Does a farmer always plow and never sow?
Is he forever cultivating the soil and
never planting?
25 Does he not finally plant his seeds—
black cumin, cumin, wheat, barley,
and emmer wheat—
each in its proper way,
and each in its proper place?
26 The farmer knows just what to do,
for God has given him understanding.
27 A heavy sledge is never used to thresh
black cumin;
rather, it is beaten with a light stick.
A threshing wheel is never rolled on
cumin;
instead, it is beaten lightly with a flail.
28 Grain for bread is easily crushed,
so he doesn't keep on pounding it.
He threshes it under the wheels of a cart,
but he doesn't pulverize it.
29 The LORD of Heaven's Armies is a
wonderful teacher,
and he gives the farmer great wisdom.

Woe on Jerusalem

29 1 "What sorrow awaits Ariel, the
City of David.
Year after year you celebrate your
feasts.
2 Yet I will bring disaster upon you,
and there will be much weeping and
sorrow.
For Jerusalem will become what her
name Ariel means—
an altar covered with blood.
3 I will be your enemy,
surrounding Jerusalem and attacking
its walls.
I will build siege towers
and destroy it.
4 Then deep from the earth you will speak;
from low in the dust your words will
come.
Your voice will whisper from the ground
like a ghost conjured up from the grave.

5 "But suddenly, your ruthless enemies
will be crushed
like the finest of dust.
Your many attackers will be driven away
like chaff before the wind.
Suddenly, in an instant,
6 I, the LORD of Heaven's Armies, will
act for you
with thunder and earthquake and great
noise,
with whirlwind and storm and
consuming fire.

28:19 Ps 88:15
28:21 2 Sam 5:20; Luke 19:41-44
28:22 Isa 10:22-23; 28:14
28:27 Amos 1:3
28:29 Rom 11:33
29:1 2 Sam 5:9
29:2 Isa 3:26
29:3 Lam 2:5; Luke 19:43-44
29:4 Isa 8:19
29:5 Isa 17:13-14; 41:15-16; 1 Thes 5:3
29:6 Matt 24:7; Mark 13:8; Luke 21:11; Rev 11:13, 19; 16:18

28:20 ***The bed. . . . The blankets:*** The leaders were ill-prepared for God's coming in judgment.

28:21 ***as he did . . . at Mount Perazim:*** See 2 Sam 5:20. • God had rescued Israel through a hailstorm ***at Gibeon*** (Josh 10:10-12), but now he would turn against them.

28:23 ***Listen to me:*** The analogy that follows was written as a wisdom poem, with Isaiah calling on his audience to pay careful attention and to discern what is right.

28:24-29 ***A farmer*** knows that there are right and wrong ways to do things, but the leaders of Judah were not that intelligent.

28:27-28 The Lord has a variety of means (***a heavy sledge . . . a light stick***) for accomplishing his purposes. There are degrees of judgment.

28:28 ***he doesn't keep on pounding it:*** This process would end; after judgment would come redemption.

28:29 ***wonderful teacher*** (or ***counselor;*** see 9:6): God's people should learn wisdom about God's ways, as the farmer has done.

29:1-14 After having pronounced judgment on Samaria (ch 28), Isaiah now pronounces judgment on Jerusalem. This is the second of the six woes (***What sorrow . . .***).

29:1-8 In the Assyrian siege, the Lord would be fighting against Jerusalem, but he would force the Assyrians to abandon Jerusalem in his own time.

29:1-2 ***Ariel*** sounds like a Hebrew term that means "hearth" or "***altar.***" It was another name for Mount Zion (29:8); it probably means ***altar of God.***

29:3 The Lord himself would come against Jerusalem, ***surrounding*** and ***attacking*** it.

29:4 God's goal was to destroy the sinful pride of the people of Jerusalem. Their voice would rise as if ***from the grave.*** Through the Assyrians, God would humble his people, but he would not abandon them.

29:6 ***will act for you*** (literally ***you will be visited***): God would bring rescue for his people. • ***thunder and earthquake . . . storm and consuming fire:*** These phenomena indicate a theophany (see note on 5:25).

29:7
Zech 12:9
[b]*khazon* (2377)
‣Jer 14:14
29:8
Isa 54:17
29:9
Isa 51:17
29:10
*Rom 11:8
2 Thes 2:9-12
29:11
Dan 12:4
Matt 13:11
29:13
Ezek 33:31
*Mark 7:6-7
29:14
Isa 44:25
*1 Cor 1:19
29:15
Ps 10:11, 13
Isa 47:10
29:16
Isa 45:9
Rom 9:20-21
29:18
Isa 32:3
29:19
Isa 14:30, 32
Matt 5:5
Jas 2:5
[c]*'anaw* (6035)
‣Zeph 2:3
[d]*simkhah* (8057)
‣Isa 55:12
29:21
Amos 5:10, 12

7 All the nations fighting against Jerusalem
will vanish like a dream!
Those who are attacking her walls
will vanish like a [b]vision in the night.
8 A hungry person dreams of eating
but wakes up still hungry.
A thirsty person dreams of drinking
but is still faint from thirst when
morning comes.
So it will be with your enemies,
with those who attack Mount Zion."

9 Are you amazed and incredulous?
Don't you believe it?
Then go ahead and be blind.
You are stupid, but not from wine!
You stagger, but not from liquor!
10 For the LORD has poured out on you a
spirit of deep sleep.
He has closed the eyes of your
prophets and visionaries.

11 All the future events in this vision are
like a sealed book to them. When you give
it to those who can read, they will say, "We
can't read it because it is sealed." 12 When
you give it to those who cannot read, they
will say, "We don't know how to read."

13 And so the Lord says,
"These people say they are mine.
They honor me with their lips,
but their hearts are far from me.
And their worship of me
is nothing but man-made rules
learned by rote.
14 Because of this, I will once again astound
these hypocrites
with amazing wonders.
The wisdom of the wise will pass away,
and the intelligence of the intelligent
will disappear."

Woe on Judah

15 What sorrow awaits those who try to
hide their plans from the LORD,
who do their evil deeds in the dark!
"The LORD can't see us," they say.
"He doesn't know what's going on!"
16 How foolish can you be?
He is the Potter, and he is certainly
greater than you, the clay!
Should the created thing say of the one
who made it,
"He didn't make me"?
Does a jar ever say,
"The potter who made me is stupid"?

A Message of Hope

17 Soon—and it will not be very long—
the forests of Lebanon will become a
fertile field,
and the fertile field will yield
bountiful crops.
18 In that day the deaf will hear words read
from a book,
and the blind will see through the
gloom and darkness.
19 The [c]humble will be filled with fresh [d]joy
from the LORD.
The poor will rejoice in the Holy One
of Israel.
20 The scoffer will be gone,
the arrogant will disappear,
and those who plot evil will be killed.
21 Those who convict the innocent
by their false testimony will
disappear.

29:7 ***Jerusalem:*** Hebrew *Ariel* (see note on 29:1-2). • The Assyrians' sudden lifting of the siege came ***like a dream . . . like a vision in the night***. God would save Judah and judge Assyria.

29:8-12 Jerusalem's blindness kept its people from understanding God's plan.

29:8 Like a ***hungry*** or ***thirsty person,*** the Assyrians could taste the victory over Jerusalem. Yet they never became victorious.

29:10 ***a spirit of deep sleep:*** The people's folly was reinforced by God's judgment on them (cp. Rom 1:24-32; 11:8); they had no perception of reality. • ***Prophets*** were also sometimes called ***visionaries.*** Neither the people nor their prophets would understand what God was doing (6:9-10).

29:13 ***These people*** used pious-sounding language in their prayers and talk (see Matt 15:8; Mark 7:6-7), but they did not truly ***honor*** God. • In ***their hearts,*** they were not committed to the Lord at all. • In ***their worship,*** they followed ***man-made rules*** and regulations rather than God's word. • ***And their worship of me is nothing but man-made rules learned by rote:*** Greek version reads *Their worship is a farce, / for they teach man-made ideas as commands from God.* Cp. Mark 7:7.

29:14 Human ***wisdom . . . intelligence . . . will disappear*** (see 1 Cor 1:19). The prophet had already spoken of the failure of Egypt's wise men (19:11-12); even Judah's wise men would blunder.

29:15-24 This threat of coming judgment is the third of the six woes (see note on 28:1–33:24). It begins with judgment but moves to a vision of creation being renewed and of the wicked coming to an end.

29:15 ***Their plans*** might refer to the advice that royal counselors were giving Hezekiah, who at first attempted to free himself from Assyria by making alliances with Egypt (715 or 701 BC).• The people were conspiring to commit ***evil deeds*** in secret, but God saw everything.

29:16 ***Potter . . . clay:*** The Lord's sovereignty is beyond challenge. Scripture does not discourage questions to God, but there is no place for resistance to God's will (see 10:15; 45:9; 64:8; Rom 9:20). • ***He didn't make me:*** Such claims against God demonstrate a total unwillingness to recognize God's intimate involvement with every aspect of a person's life.

29:17 ***The forests of Lebanon*** are usually an image of luxuriant growth (see 2:13; 14:8), but here they represent desolation.

29:18 The people were ***deaf*** and ***blind*** in heart and spirit (see 6:10; 42:18; 43:8). Yet humanity and all of creation would be renewed (see 35:1-5).

29:21 The ***false testimony*** that led to the oppression of the poor through

A similar fate awaits those who use
trickery to pervert justice
and who tell lies to destroy the
innocent.

22 That is why the LORD, who redeemed Abraham, says to the people of Israel,

"My people will no longer be ashamed
or turn pale with fear.
23 For when they see their many children
and all the blessings I have given them,
they will recognize the holiness of the
Holy One of Israel.
They will stand in awe of the God of
Jacob.
24 Then the wayward will gain
understanding,
and complainers will accept
instruction.

Woe on Judah: A Worthless Treaty with Egypt

30 1 "What sorrow awaits my
rebellious children,"
says the LORD.
"You make plans that are contrary to
mine.
You make alliances not directed by my
Spirit,
thus piling up your sins.
2 For without consulting me,
you have gone down to Egypt for help.
You have put your trust in Pharaoh's
protection.
You have tried to hide in his shade.
3 But by trusting Pharaoh, you will be
humiliated,
and by depending on him, you will be
disgraced.
4 For though his power extends to Zoan
and his officials have arrived in Hanes,
5 all who trust in him will be ashamed.
He will not help you.
Instead, he will disgrace you."

6 This message came to me concerning the
animals in the Negev:

The caravan moves slowly
across the terrible desert to
Egypt—
donkeys weighed down with riches
and camels loaded with treasure—
all to pay for Egypt's protection.
They travel through the wilderness,
a place of lionesses and lions,
a place where vipers and poisonous
snakes live.
All this, and Egypt will give you nothing
in return.
7 Egypt's promises are worthless!
Therefore, I call her ᵉRahab—
the Harmless Dragon.

A Warning for Rebellious Judah

8 Now go and write down these words.
Write them in a book.
They will stand until the end of time
as a witness
9 that these people are stubborn rebels
who refuse to pay attention to the
LORD's instructions.
10 They tell the seers,
"Stop seeing visions!"
They tell the prophets,
"Don't tell us what is right.
Tell us nice things.
Tell us lies.
11 Forget all this gloom.
Get off your narrow path.
Stop telling us about your
'Holy One of Israel.'"

29:22
Isa 41:8

29:24
Isa 30:21; 41:20

30:1
Isa 8:11-12

30:2
Isa 8:19; 31:1

30:3
Isa 36:6
Jer 42:18, 22

30:4
Isa 19:11

30:5
Isa 31:3
Jer 2:36

30:6
Deut 8:15

30:7
Isa 51:9
ᵉ*rahab* (7293)
‣ Isa 51:9

30:8
Isa 8:1

30:9
Isa 24:5; 28:15; 30:1

30:10
1 Kgs 22:8, 13
Jer 6:14
Ezek 13:7
Amos 2:12
2 Tim 4:3-4

30:11
Job 21:14

trickery in the courts of Isaiah's era would end. Because of God's work in their hearts, the people would turn from their sinful behavior of the past.

29:22-24 The prophecy of woe, which began at 29:15, now ends with a prophecy of salvation.

29:22 ***Abraham*** was the father of all Israel (see Gen 12:1-3; see also Gal 3:29). • ***Israel:*** Literally *Jacob.* See note on 14:1. • Rescued from human abuse and God's judgment, the people would ***no longer be ashamed;*** their disgrace resulted from the apparent failure of what they had trusted (see Ps 71:1; 1 Pet 2:6).

30:1-33 After threatening Judah with judgment because of their stubbornness and their reliance on Egypt (30:1-17), God again committed himself to deal compassionately with his people and to break the power of their enemies.

30:1-5 This prophecy was against Judah's dependence on Egypt. It is the fourth of the six woes (see note on 28:1–33:24).

30:1 The wisdom of the people of Judah was ***not directed by*** God's ***Spirit*** (cp. 11:2); instead, they had formed ***alliances*** that God did not approve of. Although the Assyrian attack on Jerusalem was overwhelming, making an alliance with Egypt demonstrated that the leaders of Judah depended on human resources for their protection rather than on God. Fortunately, Hezekiah later had a change of heart (see chs 36–37).

30:4 ***Zoan:*** See note on 19:11. The location of ***Hanes*** is uncertain.

30:6-7 This taunt was against those who were busy trying to please the Egyptians in order to get Egypt's military support.

30:6 Caravans moved from Judah through ***the Negev*** and the Sinai Peninsula to Egypt to avoid the main coast road that was under Assyrian control. It was a dangerous region, filled with ***lions*** and ***poisonous snakes.*** People would risk their lives to make a worthless alliance. • Being ***weighed down with riches*** might refer to money being sent to Egypt to buy that nation's help.

30:7 ***Harmless Dragon:*** Literally *Rahab who sits still.* Rahab is the name of a mythical sea monster that represents chaos in ancient literature. It is used here as a poetic name for Egypt. In an ancient mythology, Rahab was the enemy of the good gods and was depicted in fearsome terms, somewhat like a giant

30:12 Isa 5:24; 59:13
30:13 Isa 26:21; 29:5
30:14 Ps 2:9; Jer 19:10-11
30:15 Isa 28:12; 32:17; f*yasha'* (3467) ‣Isa 33:22
30:16 Isa 31:1, 3
30:17 Deut 28:25; 32:30
30:18 Isa 25:9; 2 Pet 3:9, 15; g*rakham* (7355) ‣Isa 49:10; h*mishpat* (4941) ‣Isa 51:4; i*'ashrey* (0835) ‣Job 5:17
30:19 Isa 25:8; 65:24

12 This is the reply of the Holy One of Israel:

"Because you despise what I tell you
and trust instead in oppression and lies,
13 calamity will come upon you suddenly—
like a bulging wall that bursts and falls.
In an instant it will collapse
and come crashing down.
14 You will be smashed like a piece of pottery—
shattered so completely that
there won't be a piece big enough
to carry coals from a fireplace
or a little water from the well."

15 This is what the Sovereign LORD,
the Holy One of Israel, says:
"Only in returning to me
and resting in me will you be [f]saved.
In quietness and confidence is your strength.
But you would have none of it.
16 You said, 'No, we will get our help from Egypt.
They will give us swift horses for riding into battle.'
But the only swiftness you are going to see
is the swiftness of your enemies chasing you!
17 One of them will chase a thousand of you.
Five of them will make all of you flee.
You will be left like a lonely flagpole on a hill
or a tattered banner on a distant mountaintop."

Blessings for the LORD's People

18 So the LORD must wait for you to come to him
so he can show you his love and [g]compassion.
For the LORD is a [h]faithful God.
[i]Blessed are those who wait for his help.

19 O people of Zion, who live in Jerusalem,
you will weep no more.

The Holy One of Israel (29:17-24)

Isa 1:4; 6:1-5; 10:17, 20; 12:6; 17:7; 29:19, 23; 30:15; 31:1; 37:23; 40:22-26; 41:14, 17-20; 43:1-4, 10-21; 45:11-12; 48:17-18; 49:7; 54:4-5; 55:5; 57:15; Ps 71:22-23; 78:41; Prov 9:10; Jer 50:29; 51:5; Ezek 39:7-8; Hos 11:8-9; Hab 3:3-6; John 6:66-69; Acts 2:27; 13:35; Rev 16:5-7

The Holy One of Israel is a key phrase in Isaiah. The Holy One is the King (6:5), the righteous and just one (26:7), the incomparable God (40:25), and the Redeemer of his people (41:14). Anyone coming to the Holy One must worship him in reverence and in awe. The Holy One identifies himself with Mount Zion, called holy because it is his symbolic dwelling place (see 18:7; 24:23; 27:13; 56:7; 60:1-22).

The Holy One stands apart from all his creation because he is morally perfect. Sinful people (1:4) cannot dwell with him. God's holiness requires ritual purity and moral perfection. As a consuming fire, God purges away anything that does not conform to his holy will (33:14).

The Holy One sets aside a remnant for himself (4:2-3; 6:13). He washes away their filth and commits to be present with them (12:6), his own redeemed people (35:8-9; 62:12). The good news is that the Holy One is also the Redeemer (49:7). He demonstrates his holy power (52:10) as he comes to the aid of sinful and weak humans, rescues them from the exile that their sin creates, and opens up the new creation for them.

crocodile (see 27:1; 51:9; Job 41:1-34). By saying that Egypt was *harmless*, the prophet meant that it would be of no help to Judah.

30:8-11 God instructed the prophet to write down the vision for future generations. The present generation was rebellious; they rejected God's word in favor of the false prophets' fantasies (see 8:16-17).

30:11 *Stop telling us:* The people of Judah did not want to be confronted about sin or judgment. • *Holy One of Israel:* See note on 1:4.

30:12-17 Judgment would suddenly overtake the people of Judah because they were content with their fantasy world, and they refused God's path to rest and quietness.

30:12 The whole society accepted *oppression and lies.* People reinforced each other's delusions, so it was considered acceptable to trust that Egypt would protect them from Assyria, even though that was a lie. It was also considered legitimate to oppress the poor by legally taking their land.

30:15 The people of Judah needed to repent of their sinful ways (30:12-14), *returning* to the Lord, in order to be rescued. • Trust in the Lord would bring *quietness and confidence,* unlike their frantic negotiations with Egypt.

30:16 Judah's reliance on Egypt to supply *swift horses* (see Ps 33:17) amounted to a rejection of God's help and threatened to bring about its fall.

30:17 *One . . . Five:* This curse is the opposite of God's blessing for obedience (Lev 26:8; Deut 32:30). • The Assyrians had dominated the rest of the land of Judah, leaving Jerusalem isolated *like a lonely flagpole on a hill.*

30:18-33 This prophecy of salvation includes promises that directed Israel's attention away from their present adversity to the glorious future awaiting the children of God.

30:18 *A faithful God* would restore righteous order to the world by punishing the wicked and rescuing his people from them (see 1:27; see Ps 96:10-12). • God blesses *those who wait;* faithful people do not rush ahead of him to solve their own problems but instead rely on his power and goodness.

30:19 This was probably a challenge and promise to Hezekiah during the Assyrian siege of Jerusalem (see chs 36–37). If he would just trust in God,

He will be gracious if you ask for help.
He will surely respond to the sound of your cries.
20 Though the Lord gave you adversity for food
and suffering for drink,
he will still be with you to teach you.
You will see your teacher with your own eyes.
21 Your own ears will hear him.
Right behind you a voice will say,
"This is the way you should go,"
whether to the right or to the left.
22 Then you will destroy all your silver idols
and your precious gold images.
You will throw them out like filthy rags,
saying to them, "Good riddance!"

23 Then the LORD will bless you with rain
at planting time. There will be wonderful
harvests and plenty of pastureland for
your livestock. 24 The oxen and donkeys
that till the ground will eat good grain, its
chaff blown away by the wind. 25 In that day,
when your enemies are slaughtered and
the towers fall, there will be streams of water flowing down every mountain and hill.
26 The moon will be as bright as the sun, and
the sun will be seven times brighter—like
the light of seven days in one! So it will be
when the LORD begins to heal his people
and cure the wounds he gave them.

27 Look! The LORD is coming from far away,
burning with anger,
surrounded by thick, rising smoke.
His lips are filled with fury;
his words consume like fire.
28 His hot breath pours out like a flood
up to the neck of his enemies.
He will sift out the proud nations for destruction.
He will bridle them and lead them away to ruin.
29 But the people of God will sing a song of joy,
like the songs at the holy [j]festivals.
You will be filled with joy,
as when a flutist leads a group of pilgrims
to Jerusalem, the mountain of the LORD—
to the Rock of Israel.
30 And the LORD will make his majestic voice heard.
He will display the strength of his mighty arm.
It will descend with devouring flames,
with cloudbursts, thunderstorms, and huge hailstones.
31 At the LORD's command, the Assyrians will be shattered.
He will strike them down with his royal scepter.
32 And as the LORD strikes them with his rod of punishment,
his people will celebrate with tambourines and harps.
Lifting his mighty arm, he will fight the Assyrians.
33 Topheth—the place of burning—
has long been ready for the Assyrian king;
the pyre is piled high with wood.
The breath of the LORD, like fire from a volcano,
will set it ablaze.

Woe on Judah: The Futility of Relying on Egypt

31 1 What sorrow awaits those who look to Egypt for help,
trusting their horses, chariots, and charioteers

30:20 Ps 80:5
30:21 Isa 35:8-9
30:22 Exod 32:2, 4
30:23 Ps 65:9-13
30:24 Matt 3:12
30:25 Isa 41:18
30:26 Isa 33:24; Hos 6:1-2; Rev 21:23; 22:5
30:27 Isa 66:15
30:28 2 Kgs 19:28; Isa 8:7-8; 2 Thes 2:8
30:29 [j]*khag* (2282) ‣Amos 8:10
30:31 Isa 31:8
30:32 1 Sam 18:6; Jer 31:4
30:33 Gen 19:24; Isa 34:9
31:1 Ps 20:7; Isa 10:17; Hos 11:9; Hab 1:12

his people would *weep no more.* • The Lord cares for the needs of his people; when they *ask* for something, he will *surely respond.*

30:20 *adversity for food and suffering for drink:* A city under enemy siege for a long time would eventually be overcome by starvation and disease. God did not intend that this disaster should destroy the people of Jerusalem, rather that it would be a tool to *teach* them.

30:21 The people's *own ears will hear* and follow God's instructions (see 6:9-10; 29:18; 35:5).

30:22 One aspect of Hezekiah's reforms was to remove *silver idols* and other idolatry of Ahaz's era and to call the people back to the worship of the God of Israel (2 Chr 29; 2 Kgs 18:4-5).

30:23-24 The people of Judah would again enjoy covenant blessings rather than curses (see Lev 26:4).

30:26 The Lord who struck his people would also *heal* them *and cure the wounds he gave them.*

30:27-33 In this prophecy of judgment against the nations, Isaiah foretold that Assyria's power would be broken by God's strong arm, not by the Egyptians.

30:28 *like a flood up to the neck:* Assyria's destruction would be as devastating as their invasion of Judah (see 8:8).

30:30 *His mighty arm* presents an image of strength that echoes God's victory over the Egyptians in the Exodus (63:12; see Exod 15:6). • *devouring flames . . . huge hailstones:* Such phenomena are associated with God's appearance in a theophany (see note on 5:25).

30:31 *royal scepter:* The Lord, the true King, would be victorious over the threatening Assyrian king.

30:32 *tambourines and harps:* Instruments formerly silenced in judgment (24:8) would again be used by God's people; this time, the people would celebrate the Lord's goodness rather than becoming spiritually complacent (see 5:12).

30:33 *Topheth* was a pagan altar in the valley of Ben-Hinnom outside Jerusalem where child sacrifices were offered to the Ammonite god Molech by *burning* (2 Kgs 23:9-10).

31:1-3 Isaiah delivered another vision regarding Judah's negotiations with Egypt, which probably took place in 705–701 BC. During that time, the conquering Assyrians were on the move,

31:2 Num 23:19; Jer 44:29; Rom 16:27
31:3 Jer 15:6; Ezek 28:9
31:4 Isa 42:13
31:5 Deut 32:11; Ps 91:4
31:6 Isa 55:7; Jer 3:10, 14, 22
31:7 Isa 2:20
31:8 Isa 10:12; 14:2
31:9 Isa 13:2
32:1 Jer 23:5; Ezek 37:24; Zech 9:9
32:2 Isa 25:4; 35:6
32:4 Isa 29:24
32:5 1 Sam 25:25; 1 Kgs 21:13; Ps 14:1
32:6 Isa 10:2; 59:7, 13
32:7 Isa 5:23; Jer 5:26-28; Mic 7:3
32:8 2 Cor 9:6-11

and depending on the strength of
human armies
instead of looking to the LORD,
the Holy One of Israel.
2 In his wisdom, the LORD will send great
disaster;
he will not change his mind.
He will rise against the wicked
and against their helpers.
3 For these Egyptians are mere humans,
not God!
Their horses are puny flesh, not
mighty spirits!
When the LORD raises his fist against
them,
those who help will stumble,
and those being helped will fall.
They will all fall down and die together.

4 But this is what the LORD has told me:

"When a strong young lion
stands growling over a sheep it has
killed,
it is not frightened by the shouts and
noise
of a whole crowd of shepherds.
In the same way, the LORD of Heaven's
Armies
will come down and fight on Mount
Zion.
5 The LORD of Heaven's Armies will hover
over Jerusalem
and protect it like a bird protecting
its nest.
He will defend and save the city;
he will pass over it and rescue it."

6 Though you are such wicked rebels, my
people, come and return to the LORD. 7 I
know the glorious day will come when each
of you will throw away the gold idols and silver images your sinful hands have made.

8 "The Assyrians will be destroyed,
but not by the swords of men.
The sword of God will strike them,
and they will panic and flee.
The strong young Assyrians
will be taken away as captives.
9 Even the strongest will quake with terror,
and princes will flee when they see
your battle flags,"
says the LORD, whose fire burns in Zion,
whose flame blazes from Jerusalem.

Israel's Ultimate Deliverance

32 1 Look, a righteous king is coming!
And honest princes will rule
under him.
2 Each one will be like a shelter from the
wind
and a refuge from the storm,
like streams of water in the desert
and the shadow of a great rock in a
parched land.
3 Then everyone who has eyes will be able
to see the truth,
and everyone who has ears will be
able to hear it.
4 Even the hotheads will be full of sense
and understanding.
Those who stammer will speak out
plainly.
5 In that day ungodly fools will not be
heroes.
Scoundrels will not be respected.
6 For fools speak foolishness
and make evil plans.
They practice ungodliness
and spread false teachings about the
LORD.
They deprive the hungry of food
and give no water to the thirsty.
7 The smooth tricks of scoundrels are evil.
They plot crooked schemes.
They lie to convict the poor,
even when the cause of the poor is
just.
8 But generous people plan to do what is
generous,
and they stand firm in their
generosity.

threatening Judah. At first, Hezekiah tried political and military means to avert being totally conquered (see 2 Kgs 18:13-16).

31:1 ***What sorrow:*** This is the fifth of the six woes (see note on 28:1–33:24). • ***looking to the LORD*** implies seeking his guidance with a worshipful attitude (see Deut 4:29; Ps 105:3-4).

31:4-9 This prophecy concerned God's protection of Jerusalem and its rescue from the Assyrians.

31:9 ***princes will flee:*** This was fulfilled when Sennacherib fled to Nineveh after God destroyed 185,000 troops (see 37:36-37). • God himself was the ***fire*** or ***flame*** that would devour Assyria.

32:1 ***a righteous king:*** The Messiah (11:1); the emphasis now is on righteous and wise leadership (Prov 8:20). • In Isaiah's day, ***honest princes*** were few and far between (see 3:1-6; 28:7-19).

32:2 ***like a shelter . . . a refuge:*** The same words were also used to describe God's protection (25:4) and his provision of life-giving water (41:18; 43:19-20). The leaders would serve as God's agents in blessing his people.

32:5 Only foolish people value ***fools*** and ***scoundrels*** as ***heroes*** (see also 19:11, 13; 32:6-8).

32:6 Because they do not care about God's standards of justice and righteousness, fools have no regard for those who are ***hungry*** or ***thirsty*** (see 1:17; 58:7, 10).

32:7 ***smooth tricks . . . crooked schemes:*** See Prov 6:12, 18; 16:27; 24:8-9.

9 Listen, you women who lie around in
ease.
Listen to me, you who are so smug.
10 In a short time—just a little more than a
year—
you careless ones will suddenly begin
to care.
For your fruit crops will fail,
and the harvest will never take place.
11 Tremble, you women of ease;
throw off your complacency.
Strip off your pretty clothes,
and put on burlap to show your grief.
12 Beat your breasts in sorrow for your
bountiful farms
and your fruitful grapevines.
13 For your land will be overgrown with
thorns and briers.
Your joyful homes and happy towns
will be gone.
14 The palace and the city will be deserted,
and busy towns will be empty.
Wild donkeys will frolic and flocks will
graze
in the empty forts and watchtowers
15 until at last the [k]Spirit is poured out
on us from heaven.
Then the wilderness will become a
fertile field,
and the fertile field will yield
bountiful crops.
16 Justice will rule in the wilderness
and righteousness in the fertile field.
17 And this righteousness will bring peace.
Yes, it will bring quietness and
confidence forever.
18 My people will live in safety, quietly at
home.
They will be at rest.
19 Even if the forest should be destroyed
and the city torn down,
20 the LORD will greatly bless his people.
Wherever they plant seed, bountiful
crops will spring up.
Their cattle and donkeys will graze
freely.

Woe on Assyria

33 1 What sorrow awaits you Assyrians,
who have destroyed others
but have never been destroyed
yourselves.
You betray others,
but you have never been betrayed.
When you are done destroying,
you will be destroyed.
When you are done betraying,
you will be betrayed.
2 But LORD, be merciful to us,
for we have waited for you.
Be our strong arm each day
and our salvation in times of trouble.
3 The enemy runs at the sound of your
voice.
When you stand up, the nations flee!
4 Just as caterpillars and locusts strip the
fields and vines,
so the fallen army of Assyria will be
stripped!
5 Though the LORD is very great and lives
in heaven,
he will make Jerusalem his home of
justice and righteousness.

32:9 Isa 28:23; 47:8
32:10 Isa 5:5-6
32:11 Isa 22:12; 47:2
32:13 Isa 5:5-6, 10, 17
32:14 Isa 24:12
32:15 Ps 107:35 Isa 11:2 Joel 2:28 [k]*ruakh* (7307) ›Isa 61:1
32:16 Isa 33:5
32:17 Isa 2:4 Rom 14:17 Jas 3:18
32:18 Hos 2:18-23
32:20 Isa 30:23
33:1 Jer 25:12-14 Hab 2:8
33:2 Isa 25:9; 40:10
33:3 Jer 25:30-31
33:5 Ps 97:9

32:9-15 This prophecy of judgment was against the complacent women of Jerusalem. God's promises regarding the future did not justify continuing in sin.

32:9 The women of Jerusalem *lie around in ease.* Complacent in their high standard of life and low standard of morality, they put their trust in wealth and status to maintain their way of life.

32:10 *In a short time:* Assyria's siege of Jerusalem (701 BC) was looming.

32:11 *Burlap* was worn *to show . . . grief,* especially when mourning (see Ps 30:11). The Assyrian conquest of the farmlands of Judah and most of its cities (except Jerusalem) would cause rich people in the large cities to mourn.

32:14 Jerusalem was eventually destroyed, but by the Babylonians, not the Assyrians (for a prediction of this, see 39:1-8). • *the empty forts:* Hebrew *the Ophel.*

32:15 The *Spirit* would transform the nation into a godly community and bring in an era of justice and righteousness (see also Joel 2:28-32). The Spirit is connected to the Messiah (11:1) and the servant (42:1; 61:1). • *wilderness . . . bountiful crops:* When the people are transformed, nature will be too.

32:17 Being right with God and humans *will bring peace* (Hebrew *shalom;* see 26:3; 48:18; 52:7; cp. Jas 3:18). Peace is more than the absence of conflict. It includes personal wholeness and does not depend on outside circumstances (see also Rom 5:1).

32:18 Living *in safety* and feeling *at rest* were blessings of Israel's covenant with the Lord (see Lev 26:5-6), but the people's sin had previously brought curses rather than blessings (cp. 32:9-11).

32:19 *the forest . . . the city:* The godly would remain secure even with evidence of God's judgment all around them.

33:1 This was the sixth threat of woe (see note on 28:1–33:24). • *What sorrow awaits you Assyrians, who have destroyed others:* Literally *What sorrow awaits you, O destroyer.* The Hebrew text does not specifically name Assyria as the object of the prophecy in this chapter. However, Isaiah undoubtedly had Assyria in mind; they were the *destroyer* most immediately at hand when the prophecy was written. The prophecy applies, however, to any who seek to destroy God's people; this included, but was not limited to, the Babylonians (see chs 13–14). • *When you are done betraying:* Wicked nations often break political agreements with other nations when these contracts are no longer to their own advantage.

33:2 The godly community prayed for God to *be merciful* in response to the promise of 30:18. • *we have waited for you:* See note on 8:17.

33:5 *Jerusalem:* Hebrew *Zion;* also in 33:14.

33:6 Ps 112:1-3; Isa 51:6
33:7 2 Kgs 18:18, 37
33:9 Isa 10:34; 24:4; 35:2
33:10 Ps 12:5; Isa 2:19
33:12 2 Sam 23:6-7; Isa 10:17
33:13 Isa 49:1
33:14 Isa 1:28; 30:27; Heb 12:29
33:15 Ps 24:3-4; Isa 58:6-11; Zeph 3:11-13
33:16 Isa 25:4; 49:10

6 In that day he will be your sure foundation,
providing a rich store of salvation,
wisdom, and knowledge.
The fear of the LORD will be your
treasure.

7 But now your brave warriors weep in
public.
Your ambassadors of peace cry in
bitter disappointment.
8 Your roads are deserted;
no one travels them anymore.
The Assyrians have broken their peace
treaty
and care nothing for the promises
they made before witnesses.
They have no respect for anyone.
9 The land of Israel wilts in mourning.
Lebanon withers with shame.
The plain of Sharon is now a wilderness.
Bashan and Carmel have been
plundered.

10 But the LORD says: "Now I will stand up.
Now I will show my power and might.
11 You Assyrians produce nothing but dry
grass and stubble.
Your own breath will turn to fire and
consume you.
12 Your people will be burned up
completely,
like thornbushes cut down and tossed
in a fire.
13 Listen to what I have done, you nations
far away!
And you that are near, acknowledge
my might!"

14 The sinners in Jerusalem shake with fear.
Terror seizes the godless.
"Who can live with this devouring fire?"
they cry.
"Who can survive this all-consuming
fire?"
15 Those who are honest and fair,
who refuse to profit by fraud,
who stay far away from bribes,
who refuse to listen to those who plot
murder,
who shut their eyes to all enticement
to do wrong—
16 these are the ones who will dwell on
high.
The rocks of the mountains will be
their fortress.
Food will be supplied to them,
and they will have water in abundance.

God's Just and Righteous Kingdom (32:16-17)

Isa 1:16-20, 24-28; 5:7, 16; 9:7; 11:2-5; 13:11; 16:5; 28:6; 32:1-2, 15-17; 59:18; 61:8
Gen 18:17-19, 25
Lev 19:15
Deut 1:16-17; 16:18-20; 17:8-13; 32:4
Ps 36:5-9; 89:14; 119:75
Prov 21:3
Eccl 12:14
Lam 3:25-39
Ezek 34:15-16; 36:22-36; 37:24-27
Amos 5:21-24
Mic 6:6-8
Zech 7:9-10
Matt 5:6, 10, 20
Luke 1:74-75
Acts 17:30-31
2 Pet 3:11-14

The Lord's justice (*mishpat*) is part of his divine order. A world without justice is a place where people set aside the order planned by the Creator. Since the Lord is the Creator, it follows that his rule will be just and righteous. His Messiah will usher in a just world (9:7; 11:2-5; 16:5; 32:1-2), and his Spirit will transform the world into a place of justice, righteousness, and peace (32:15-17). This is good news for the poor and needy (25:4), whose rights have been denied by the powerful of society.

The theme of God's just and righteous kingdom runs throughout all of Isaiah. This theme explains the prophecies of judgment, which condemn the leaders and people for their injustice. It also explains the prophecies against the nations because of their oppressive, proud, and unjust ways. Justice is central, and humans are condemned for failing to uphold God's justice (28:17; 29:21).

Isaiah does not define justice and injustice; he illustrates it with examples (e.g., 1:17, 21-23; 5:7-23; 32:6, 7). Justice is relating rightly to God and dealing fairly with fellow human beings. It is closely related to righteousness and faithfulness (1:21; Zech 7:9).

God's retribution is just, because people get no worse than they deserve (3:9-11; 13:11; 59:18). In fact, they often get better than they deserve, because God pours out his just judgment on a willing substitute, whose death calls people to turn away from their sin and live by God's righteousness (Rom 6:22-23; 1 Pet 3:18). When God's kingdom is fully established, the world, too, will be just and righteous (1:26; 28:6; 2 Pet 3:13).

33:8 ***care nothing for the promises they made before witnesses:*** As in Dead Sea Scrolls; Masoretic Text reads *care nothing for the cities.*

33:9 ***Sharon, Bashan,*** and ***Carmel*** were all fertile areas. Their desolation represents the destruction Assyria had inflicted on ***Israel.***

33:11 In most passages, the ***Assyrians*** were turning other nations into worthless ***dry grass and stubble*** (see 17:13; 29:5; 40:24; 41:2). Here, ironically, they get a taste of their own medicine.

33:14 ***The godless*** were people who lived without regard for God and his law. • The image of a ***devouring fire*** came from God's judgment of offenders during the wilderness journey (Exod 24:17; Deut 4:24). God still expects people to worship him with reverence and awe (Heb 12:29).

33:15 A godly life provides evidence that an individual truly knows God (see Col 3:5-17; Jas 2:14-18; 1 Pet 1:14-16; 1 Jn 1:5-6).

17 Your eyes will see the king in all his
splendor,
and you will see a land that stretches
into the distance.
18 You will think back to this time of terror,
asking,
"Where are the Assyrian officers
who counted our towers?
Where are the bookkeepers
who recorded the plunder taken from
our fallen city?"
19 You will no longer see these fierce,
violent people
with their strange, unknown language.

20 Instead, you will see Zion as a place of
holy festivals.
You will see Jerusalem, a city quiet and
secure.
It will be like a tent whose ropes are taut
and whose stakes are firmly fixed.
21 The LORD will be our Mighty One.
He will be like a wide river of protection
that no enemy can cross,
that no enemy ship can sail upon.
22 For the LORD is our [a]judge,
our lawgiver, and our [b]king.
He will care for us and [c]save us.
23 The enemies' sails hang loose
on broken masts with useless tackle.
Their treasure will be divided by the
people of God.
Even the lame will take their share!
24 The people of Israel will no longer say,
"We are sick and helpless,"
for the LORD will forgive their sins.

5. MESSAGE ABOUT THE FUTURE (34:1–35:10)

A Message for the Nations

34 1 Come here and listen, O nations of
the earth.
Let the world and everything in it hear
my words.
2 For the LORD is enraged against the
nations.
His fury is against all their armies.
He will completely destroy them,
dooming them to slaughter.
3 Their dead will be left unburied,
and the stench of rotting bodies will
fill the land.
The mountains will flow with their
blood.
4 The [d]heavens above will melt away
and disappear like a rolled-up scroll.
The stars will fall from the sky
like withered leaves from a grapevine,
or shriveled figs from a fig tree.

5 And when my sword has finished its
work in the heavens,
it will fall upon Edom,
the nation I have marked for
destruction.
6 The sword of the LORD is drenched with
blood
and covered with fat—
with the blood of lambs and goats,
with the fat of rams prepared for
sacrifice.
Yes, the LORD will offer a sacrifice in the
city of Bozrah.
He will make a mighty slaughter in
Edom.
7 Even men as strong as wild oxen will
die—
the young men alongside the veterans.
The land will be soaked with blood
and the soil enriched with fat.
8 For it is the day of the LORD's revenge,
the year when Edom will be paid back
for all it did to Israel.
9 The streams of Edom will be filled with
burning pitch,
and the ground will be covered with
fire.

33:17 Isa 6:5
33:18 1 Cor 1:20
33:19 Deut 28:49-50; Isa 28:11
33:20 Ps 46:5
33:21 Isa 48:18
33:22 Isa 49:25-26; Zech 9:9; Jas 4:12
[a]*shapat* (8199) ▸Jer 11:20
[b]*melek* (4428) ▸Isa 43:15
[c]*yasha'* (3467) ▸Isa 43:12
33:24 Mic 7:18-19; 1 Jn 1:7-9
34:1 Deut 32:1
34:2 Isa 26:20-21
34:4 Joel 2:31; *Matt 24:29; *Mark 13:24-25; 2 Pet 3:10; Rev 6:12-14
[d]*shamayim* (8064) ▸Isa 51:6
34:6 Isa 63:1
34:7 Ps 68:30
34:8 Isa 13:6; 63:4
34:9 Deut 29:23

33:17-24 This vision is about God's reign in Zion.

33:17 ***The king*** is the human representative (32:1) of the Great King, God himself (33:22). • The ***land*** belonging to God's people would appear to be without borders because the foreign enemies had been judged (54:3).

33:18 ***Assyrian officers*** brought great terror to Judah when the Assyrians defeated various cities around Jerusalem (2 Kgs 18:13).

33:19 The ***strange, unknown language*** was the tongue of Assyria and later of Babylon (see 28:11).

33:24 ***The people of Israel*** were the people of Zion (cp. 33:20; see note on 1:27). • ***sick . . . the LORD will forgive their sins:*** See note on 1:5-6; see also 43:25.

34:1-17 This prophecy of judgment was against the nations at the terrifying "day of the Lord" (see note on 2:5-22; see also 63:1-6).

34:2 ***completely destroy:*** The Hebrew term used here refers to the complete consecration of things or people to the LORD, either by destroying them or by giving them as an offering; similarly in 34:5. See Lev 27:28-29.

34:3 It was a disgrace for a corpse to remain ***unburied.***

34:4 ***The heavens . . . stars:*** See also 13:10; Joel 2:30-31; Matt 24:29; Mark 13:24-25; 2 Pet 3:10-13; Rev 6:13-14.

34:5 ***Edom*** here represents what all the nations would experience, just as Moab was singled out in ch 25.

34:6 ***Bozrah*** was a city in Edom, southeast of the Dead Sea.

34:8 ***The LORD's revenge*** refers to God's wrathful but righteous vengeance against his enemies and the oppressors of his people on the day of the Lord (see note on 2:5-22). • ***Edom will be paid back:*** There will be retribution for Edom's crimes against Judah (see also Ps 137:7; Lam 4:21; Obad; Mal 1:3-5). Edom, with its history of treachery, would come to an end. • ***to Israel:*** Hebrew *to Zion.*

34:9 Edom's judgment was similar to the judgment of Sodom and Gomorrah (Gen 19:24; see also Jer 49:17-18).

34:10 Isa 1:31; Ezek 29:11; Mal 1:3-4; Rev 14:11; 19:3
34:11 Lam 2:8
34:13 Jer 9:11; 10:22
34:14 Isa 13:21
34:16 Isa 40:5
34:17 Jer 13:25
35:1 Isa 41:18-19; 51:3; 55:12-13
35:2 Isa 25:9; 60:13; 66:14
35:3 Job 4:3-4; Heb 12:12
35:4 Ps 145:19
35:5 John 9:6-7
35:6 Luke 7:19-21; 11:14; John 7:38; Acts 3:7-8

10 This judgment on Edom will never end;
the smoke of its burning will rise forever.
The land will lie deserted from generation to generation.
No one will live there anymore.
11 It will be haunted by the desert owl and the screech owl,
the great owl and the raven.
For God will measure that land carefully;
he will measure it for chaos and destruction.
12 It will be called the Land of Nothing,
and all its nobles will soon be gone.
13 Thorns will overrun its palaces;
nettles and thistles will grow in its forts.
The ruins will become a haunt for jackals
and a home for owls.
14 Desert animals will mingle there with hyenas,
their howls filling the night.
Wild goats will bleat at one another among the ruins,
and night creatures will come there to rest.
15 There the owl will make her nest and lay her eggs.
She will hatch her young and cover them with her wings.
And the buzzards will come,
each one with its mate.

16 Search the book of the LORD,
and see what he will do.
Not one of these birds and animals will be missing,
and none will lack a mate,
for the LORD has promised this.
His Spirit will make it all come true.
17 He has surveyed and divided the land
and deeded it over to those creatures.
They will possess it forever,
from generation to generation.

Hope for Restoration

35 1 Even the wilderness and desert
will be glad in those days.
The wasteland will rejoice and
blossom with spring crocuses.
2 Yes, there will be an abundance of flowers
and singing and joy!
The deserts will become as green as the mountains of Lebanon,
as lovely as Mount Carmel or the plain of Sharon.
There the LORD will display his glory,
the splendor of our God.
3 With this news, strengthen those who have tired hands,
and encourage those who have weak knees.
4 Say to those with fearful hearts,
"Be strong, and do not fear,
for your God is coming to destroy your enemies.
He is coming to save you."
5 And when he comes, he will open the eyes of the blind
and unplug the ears of the deaf.
6 The lame will leap like a deer,
and those who cannot speak will sing for joy!
Springs will gush forth in the wilderness,
and streams will water the wasteland.
7 The parched ground will become a pool,
and springs of water will satisfy the thirsty land.
Marsh grass and reeds and rushes will flourish
where desert jackals once lived.

34:10 See also Rev 14:11; 19:3.

34:11-14 Wild animals, night birds, and hostile plants with ***thorns*** and ***nettles*** created an eerie environment. • The identification of some of these birds is uncertain, but they inhabited wild and deserted places and many were considered unclean (Deut 14:11-18).

34:12 The meaning of the Hebrew is uncertain.

34:14 ***night creatures:*** Hebrew *Lilith*, possibly a reference to a mythical demon of the night.

34:16 ***Search the book of the LORD:*** Isaiah's prophecy was God's witness to the truthfulness of his word. • The power of the ***Spirit*** enacts the Lord's decrees, assuring that all prophecy comes together to be fulfilled as God promised.

35:1-10 God will come to vindicate and transform his people. Instead of being deaf, blind, and lame (see 6:10), the people will be pure, holy, and redeemed.

35:1 God's land would become like a ***wasteland***, spiritually desolate and physically exiled. However, God would turn the desert into a garden (see also 32:15), taking his people from exile to glory.

35:2 ***Lebanon . . . Mount Carmel . . . Sharon:*** There will be a reversal of earlier judgments (see 2:13; 10:34; 29:17; 33:9). • ***glory . . . splendor of our God:*** See also 6:3; 40:5.

35:3 ***Tired hands*** and ***weak knees*** express discouragement and anxiety (see Heb 12:12).

35:4 ***do not fear:*** The Lord here assures his people of his presence and purpose (see also 7:4; 10:24; 40:9; 43:1; 44:2; 54:4). • The essence of the good news is that ***God is coming*** to save his people (see also 40:9; 52:7; 62:11). God's coming brings spiritual transformation as well as rescue from ***enemies***.

35:5 ***eyes . . . ears:*** There will be a transformation from spiritual blindness and deafness to understanding and knowing God (6:10; 29:18; 32:3; 42:7; see also Luke 7:22; Acts 26:18).

35:6 The ***lame . . . those who cannot speak:*** All handicaps will be removed (see Matt 11:5; 12:22; Mark 7:37; Acts 3:7-8).

8 And a great road will go through that
once deserted land.
It will be named the Highway of
Holiness.
Evil-minded people will never travel
on it.
It will be only for those who walk in
God's ways;
fools will never walk there.
9 Lions will not lurk along its course,
nor any other ferocious beasts.
There will be no other dangers.
Only the redeemed will walk on it.
10 Those who have been ransomed by the
LORD will return.
They will enter Jerusalem singing,
crowned with everlasting joy.
Sorrow and mourning will disappear,
and they will be filled with joy and
gladness.

6. THE LORD RESCUES JERUSALEM (36:1–39:8)

Assyria Invades Judah
Isa 36:1 // 2 Kgs 18:13 // 2 Chr 32:1

36 In the fourteenth year of King Hezekiah's reign, King Sennacherib of Assyria came to attack the fortified towns of Judah and conquered them.

Sennacherib Threatens Jerusalem
Isa 36:2-10 // 2 Kgs 18:17-25 // 2 Chr 32:9-15
Isa 36:11-22 // 2 Kgs 18:26-37

2Then the king of Assyria sent his chief
of staff from Lachish with a huge army to
confront King Hezekiah in Jerusalem. The
Assyrians took up a position beside the aqueduct that feeds water into the upper pool,
near the road leading to the field where
cloth is washed.
3These are the officials who went out to
meet with them: Eliakim son of Hilkiah,
the palace administrator; Shebna the court
secretary; and Joah son of Asaph, the royal
historian.
4Then the Assyrian king's chief of staff
told them to give this message to Hezekiah:

"This is what the great king of Assyria
says: What are you trusting in that makes
you so confident? 5Do you think that mere
words can substitute for military skill and
strength? Who are you counting on, that
you have rebelled against me? 6On Egypt?
If you lean on Egypt, it will be like a reed
that splinters beneath your weight and
pierces your hand. Pharaoh, the king of
Egypt, is completely unreliable!
7"But perhaps you will say to me,

35:8 Matt 7:13-14
35:9 Isa 51:10
35:10 Rev 21:4
36:1-22 //2 Kgs 18:13-37 //2 Chr 32:9-19
36:3 Isa 22:15, 20
36:4 2 Kgs 18:19
36:5 2 Kgs 18:7
36:6 Ps 146:3; Ezek 29:6-7
36:7 Deut 12:2-5; 2 Kgs 18:4-5

35:8 The imagery of the ***great road*** recalls Israel's crossing through the Red Sea (51:10). • Only holy and undefiled people will share ***the Highway of Holiness.*** God's goal in salvation is that humans will share in his character and act as he does (see Eph 5:1-2; 1 Pet 2:21).

35:10 ***Jerusalem*** (Hebrew *Zion*): The prophecy extends beyond the return of Israel from exile to the final establishment of God's kingdom on earth. It will be characterized by ***joy and gladness*** and the absence of ***sorrow and mourning*** (see also 25:7; 51:11; Rev 21:4).

36:1–39:8 Jerusalem's rescue from King Sennacherib of Assyria is a focal point of chs 1–39. The Lord promised to rescue his people by remaining present with Jerusalem (see 7:14) and by maintaining a remnant (see note on 10:21). Even though much of the country was desolate and the population decimated because of their foolish alliance with Assyria (chs 7–8), the Lord preserved his people from total conquest through Hezekiah, a godly king. Hezekiah faced the same test that Ahaz did, a test of trust (note the recurrence of words for *trust* in the Assyrian officer's challenge in ch 36). But Hezekiah has learned the lessons taught in chs 13–35 and, at least initially, he passed the test. This narrative is duplicated in 2 Kgs 18:13–20:19 (see map, p. 657).

36:1 ***The fourteenth year of King Hezekiah's reign*** was 701 BC, a nearly catastrophic year. ***King Sennacherib of Assyria*** ruled from 704–681 BC. Hezekiah, like many other kings under Assyrian vassalage, had reasserted his independence in 704 BC when Sennacherib came to the throne in troubled circumstances. By 701 BC, the Assyrian king was ready to punish Hezekiah. Sennacherib recorded having ***conquered*** forty-six fortified cities and many villages, and having taken 200,146 captives. Hezekiah responded by attempting to appease Sennacherib (see 2 Kgs 18:14-16), but it was too late.

36:2 ***his chief of staff:*** Or *the rabshakeh;* also in 36:4, 11, 12, 22. • ***Lachish*** was a city overlooking the low-lying hills to the west of Jerusalem. It had to be taken before the final attack on Jerusalem could be launched. • ***the aqueduct that feeds water into the upper pool:*** This was a pool on the north side of Jerusalem, not the Gihon spring in the Kidron valley (see map, p. 667). • Isaiah had met Ahaz on this same ***road leading to the field where cloth is washed*** some thirty-three years earlier (see 7:3). At that time he had challenged Ahaz to trust God. However, Ahaz trusted Assyria instead, and this desperate situation was a result. Now the challenge to trust God came from mocking, foreign lips (see 28:11-13). • ***washed:*** Or *bleached.*

36:3 ***Eliakim*** eventually advanced in rank, while ***Shebna*** was demoted (see 22:15-24).

36:4-22 The Assyrian chief of staff attempted to use intimidation to negotiate a settlement without bloodshed. In his first speech (36:4-10), he rightly argued against Egypt's ability to rescue but wrongly charged Hezekiah with misplaced trust in the Lord. Strikingly, the Assyrian did not see the contest as being between the gods of Assyria and the Lord but rather between Sennacherib—***the great king***—and the Lord.

36:4 ***Great king*** is a title similar to *emperor.*

36:5 ***Who are you counting on:*** Judah had asked Egypt to help them (see 30:1-5).

36:6 ***Egypt . . . is completely unreliable:*** Isaiah argued the same case, pointing to the Lord as the only reliable source of help (31:1-3, 7; 39:7). • A kind of ***reed*** that breaks easily grows near the Nile (see Ezek 29:6-7).

36:7 ***We are trusting in the LORD our God:*** Ironically, the Assyrian chief of staff knew about and played on Isaiah's message (26:4; 36:15; 37:10). • Hezekiah showed his zeal for the Lord by tearing ***down*** the pagan ***shrines and***

36:9 Isa 20:5
36:10 1 Kgs 13:18
36:11 Ezra 4:7; Dan 2:4
36:13 2 Chr 32:18
36:14 Isa 37:10
36:16 Zech 3:10
36:19 2 Kgs 17:6; Isa 10:9-11; 37:11-13; Jer 49:23
36:20 1 Kgs 20:23, 28
37:1-13 //2 Kgs 19:1-13
37:3 Isa 22:5; 26:17-18

'We are trusting in the LORD our God!' But isn't he the one who was insulted by Hezekiah? Didn't Hezekiah tear down his shrines and altars and make everyone in Judah and Jerusalem worship only at the altar here in Jerusalem?

8 "I'll tell you what! Strike a bargain with my master, the king of Assyria. I will give you 2,000 horses if you can find that many men to ride on them! 9 With your tiny army, how can you think of challenging even the weakest contingent of my master's troops, even with the help of Egypt's chariots and charioteers? 10 What's more, do you think we have invaded your land without the LORD's direction? The LORD himself told us, 'Attack this land and destroy it!' "

11 Then Eliakim, Shebna, and Joah said to the Assyrian chief of staff, "Please speak to us in Aramaic, for we understand it well. Don't speak in Hebrew, for the people on the wall will hear."

12 But Sennacherib's chief of staff replied, "Do you think my master sent this message only to you and your master? He wants all the people to hear it, for when we put this city under siege, they will suffer along with you. They will be so hungry and thirsty that they will eat their own dung and drink their own urine."

13 Then the chief of staff stood and shouted in Hebrew to the people on the wall, "Listen to this message from the great king of Assyria! 14 This is what the king says: Don't let Hezekiah deceive you. He will never be able to rescue you. 15 Don't let him fool you into trusting in the LORD by saying, 'The LORD will surely rescue us. This city will never fall into the hands of the Assyrian king!'

16 "Don't listen to Hezekiah! These are the terms the king of Assyria is offering: Make peace with me—open the gates and come out. Then each of you can continue eating from your own grapevine and fig tree and drinking from your own well. 17 Then I will arrange to take you to another land like this one—a land of grain and new wine, bread and vineyards.

18 "Don't let Hezekiah mislead you by saying, 'The LORD will rescue us!' Have the gods of any other nations ever saved their people from the king of Assyria? 19 What happened to the gods of Hamath and Arpad? And what about the gods of Sepharvaim? Did any god rescue Samaria from my power? 20 What god of any nation has ever been able to save its people from my power? So what makes you think that the LORD can rescue Jerusalem from me?"

21 But the people were silent and did not utter a word because Hezekiah had commanded them, "Do not answer him."

22 Then Eliakim son of Hilkiah, the palace administrator; Shebna the court secretary; and Joah son of Asaph, the royal historian, went back to Hezekiah. They tore their clothes in despair, and they went in to see the king and told him what the Assyrian chief of staff had said.

Hezekiah Seeks the LORD's Help

Isa 37:1-20 // 2 Kgs 19:1-19

37 When King Hezekiah heard their report, he tore his clothes and put on burlap and went into the Temple of the LORD. 2 And he sent Eliakim the palace administrator, Shebna the court secretary, and the leading priests, all dressed in burlap, to the prophet Isaiah son of Amoz. 3 They told him, "This is what King Hezekiah says: Today is

---

altars (2 Kgs 18:4), but the Assyrians mistakenly thought Hezekiah had angered God in the process.

36:8 At this time, cavalry mounted on ***horses*** was the newest military technology. The Assyrian chief of staff was mocking the Judeans because he knew that Judah had no trained ***men*** who knew how ***to ride***.

36:10 ***The LORD himself told us:*** It was common for a king to claim the approval of a deity in destroying other kingdoms. This claim was consistent with Isaiah's prophecy in 10:5-6.

36:11 ***Aramaic*** was the lingua franca used throughout the Assyrian empire, understood by the elite but not by the common people of Judah. • ***Hebrew:*** Literally *the dialect of Judah;* also in 36:13.

36:13-20 In the Assyrian chief of staff's second speech, he claimed that his nation's gods were more powerful (see 10:9-10) than the God of Judah. God's ability to rescue his people was at stake. In the ensuing drama, the Lord shocked the Assyrian with his power (37:36-37).

36:14 ***Don't let Hezekiah deceive you:*** This public accusation against Hezekiah was intended to undermine the people's confidence in him.

36:15 Hezekiah demonstrated a strong faith ***in the LORD,*** unlike Ahaz (ch 7). Hezekiah's faith would bring ***rescue,*** whereas Ahaz's lack of faith brought him trouble (see 7:9).

36:16-17 The Assyrian was tempting the people of Jerusalem with provisions that the Lord had promised to provide his obedient people (see 1:19; 37:30-35; Deut 8:7-9). It was a tempting offer, but a counterfeit. And it covered up the reality of exile that would have followed (36:17).

36:19 The populations of ***Hamath and Arpad*** (see note on 10:9) had been relocated to Samaria, where the new local deities were ***the gods of Sepharvaim*** (2 Kgs 17:24). The logic of the argument made sense to an Assyrian. If the Assyrian gods defeated all the gods of the other nations and the God of the Israelite nation of Samaria, would they not also defeat the God of Judah?

37:1 Hezekiah responded to the threats by seeking the Lord's favor. • The king ***tore his clothes and put on burlap*** as a sign of mourning and prayer.

a day of trouble, insults, and disgrace. It is
like when a child is ready to be born, but the
mother has no strength to deliver the baby.
4But perhaps the LORD your God has heard
the Assyrian chief of staff, sent by the king
to defy the living God, and will punish him
for his words. Oh, pray for those of us who
are left!"

5After King Hezekiah's officials delivered the king's message to Isaiah, 6the
prophet replied, "Say to your master, 'This is
what the LORD says: Do not be disturbed by
this blasphemous speech against me from
the Assyrian king's messengers. 7Listen! I
myself will move against him, and the king
will receive a message that he is needed at
home. So he will return to his land, where I
will have him killed with a sword.'"

8Meanwhile, the Assyrian chief of staff
left Jerusalem and went to consult the king
of Assyria, who had left Lachish and was attacking Libnah.

9Soon afterward King Sennacherib received word that King Tirhakah of Ethiopia
was leading an army to fight against him.
Before leaving to meet the attack, he sent
messengers back to Hezekiah in Jerusalem
with this message:

10"This message is for King Hezekiah of
Judah. Don't let your God, in whom you
trust, deceive you with promises that
Jerusalem will not be captured by the
king of Assyria. 11You know perfectly
well what the kings of Assyria have done
wherever they have gone. They have
completely destroyed everyone who
stood in their way! Why should you be
any different? 12Have the gods of other
nations rescued them—such nations as
Gozan, Haran, Rezeph, and the people
of Eden who were in Tel-assar? My
predecessors destroyed them all! 13What
happened to the king of Hamath and the
king of Arpad? What happened to the
kings of Sepharvaim, Hena, and Ivvah?"

14After Hezekiah received the letter
from the messengers and read it, he went
up to the LORD's Temple and spread it out
before the LORD. 15And Hezekiah prayed
this prayer before the LORD: 16"O LORD
of Heaven's Armies, God of Israel, you are
enthroned between the mighty cherubim!
You alone are God of all the kingdoms of
the earth. You alone created the heavens
and the earth. 17Bend down, O LORD, and listen! Open your eyes, O LORD, and see! Listen
to Sennacherib's words of defiance against
the living God.

18"It is true, LORD, that the kings of Assyria have destroyed all these nations.
19And they have thrown the gods of these
nations into the fire and burned them.
But of course the Assyrians could destroy
them! They were not gods at all—only idols
of wood and stone shaped by human hands.
20Now, O LORD our God, rescue us from his
power; then all the kingdoms of the earth
will know that you alone, O LORD, are God."

Isaiah Predicts Jerusalem's Rescue
Isa 37:21-35 // 2 Kgs 19:20-34

21Then Isaiah son of Amoz sent this message to Hezekiah: "This is what the LORD,
the God of Israel, says: Because you prayed
about King Sennacherib of Assyria, 22the
LORD has spoken this word against him:

"The virgin daughter of Zion
despises you and laughs at you.

37:4 Isa 1:9; 10:20-22
37:6 Isa 7:4; 35:4
37:11 Isa 10:9-11
37:12 Gen 11:31; 2 Kgs 17:6; Acts 7:2
37:14-20 //2 Kgs 19:14-19
37:16 Exod 25:22; Ps 80:1; 86:10; Jer 10:12
37:18 2 Kgs 15:29; 1 Chr 5:26
37:19 Isa 17:8
37:20 1 Kgs 18:36-37; Isa 33:22; Ezek 36:23
37:22 Lam 2:13; Zeph 3:14

37:4 ***perhaps . . . God has heard the Assyrian chief of staff*** (or *the rabshakeh*) . . . ***defy the living God:*** Hezekiah's hope was not based on Judah's or his own goodness, or the presence of the Temple in Jerusalem; instead, it was based on God responding to Assyria's blasphemy.

37:5-7 God answered that he would deal with the Assyrians and rescue the remnant of his people from their distress (see 63:9).

37:7 ***I myself will move against him:*** Literally *I will put a spirit in him.*

37:8 ***Assyrian chief of staff:*** Or *the rabshakeh.* • ***Libnah*** was a city on the Philistine plain near Lachish. Sennacherib was preparing to fight both Egypt and Jerusalem when he sent word to Hezekiah.

37:9 ***King Tirhakah of Ethiopia*** (Hebrew *of Cush*) was then the ruler of Egypt.

37:12 The argument was that Judah's god, like ***the gods of other nations*** already conquered by Assyria, would be unable to save Judah (see also 36:18-20). • ***Gozan, Haran, Rezeph, . . . Eden,*** and ***Tel-assar*** were cities in Mesopotamia.

37:14-20 When he received Sennacherib's boastful threat, Hezekiah returned to the Temple and prayed for rescue. His prayer stands in contrast to Ahaz's response to danger decades earlier (see ch 7).

37:16 ***God of Israel:*** Hezekiah was not taken in by the false claims of Sennacherib that the Lord was powerless. In his prayer, Hezekiah acknowledged that, because the Lord is the Creator, he is ***God of all the kingdoms of the earth.*** The Lord is sovereign over all kingdoms. • The ***mighty cherubim*** were located in the Temple atop the Ark of the Covenant, which was God's throne in his Temple (see note on Lev 16:2; Ps 80:1; 99:1).

37:20 ***you alone, O LORD, are God*** (as in Dead Sea Scrolls, see also 2 Kgs 19:19; Masoretic Text reads *you alone are the LORD*): Hezekiah was concerned for the Lord's reputation, which Sennacherib had impugned. Hezekiah recognized that if the Lord defeated the Assyrians and their gods, his holy name would be glorified among all the nations of the world (cp. Exod 9:16; 14:4, 17-18; Josh 2:9-11; 1 Sam 4:7-8).

37:21 ***Because you prayed:*** Prayer is powerful; it moved God's heart and was part of the reason why the Lord answered with this message of hope.

37:22 ***The virgin daughter of Zion:*** Jerusalem is personified as a young woman who mocks the Assyrian king (see also 3:26).

37:23
Isa 5:15, 21
Ezek 39:7
Hab 1:12
37:24
Isa 14:8
37:26
Isa 25:2
Acts 2:23; 4:27-28
37:27
Ps 129:6
Isa 40:7
37:28
Ps 139:1
37:29
Isa 30:28
Ezek 38:4
37:30
Lev 25:5, 11-12
37:31
Isa 10:20; 27:6
37:32
//2 Kgs 19:31

The daughter of Jerusalem
shakes her head in derision as you flee.
23 "Whom have you been defying and ridiculing?
Against whom did you raise your voice?
At whom did you look with such haughty eyes?
It was the Holy One of Israel!
24 By your messengers you have defied the Lord.
You have said, 'With my many chariots
I have conquered the highest mountains—
yes, the remotest peaks of Lebanon.
I have cut down its tallest cedars
and its finest cypress trees.
I have reached its farthest heights
and explored its deepest forests.
25 I have dug wells in many foreign lands
and refreshed myself with their water.
With the sole of my foot,
I stopped up all the rivers of Egypt!'

26 "But have you not heard?
I decided this long ago.
Long ago I planned it,
and now I am making it happen.
I planned for you to crush fortified cities
into heaps of rubble.
27 That is why their people have so little power
and are so frightened and confused.
They are as weak as grass,
as easily trampled as tender green shoots.
They are like grass sprouting on a housetop,
scorched before it can grow lush and tall.
28 "But I know you well—
where you stay
and when you come and go.
I know the way you have raged against me.
29 And because of your raging against me
and your arrogance, which I have heard for myself,
I will put my hook in your nose
and my bit in your mouth.
I will make you return
by the same road on which you came."

30 Then Isaiah said to Hezekiah, "Here is the proof that what I say is true:

"This year you will eat only what grows up by itself,
and next year you will eat what springs up from that.
But in the third year you will plant crops
and harvest them;
you will tend vineyards and eat their fruit.
31 And you who are left in Judah,
who have escaped the ravages of the siege,
will put roots down in your own soil
and grow up and flourish.
32 For a remnant of my people will spread out from Jerusalem,
a group of survivors from Mount Zion.

37:23 ***Whom . . . Against whom:*** Sennacherib's speech was not so much an insult against Judah as it was against the Lord.

37:24 Isaiah seems to be familiar with the typical royal Assyrian boasts, including that they possessed ***the highest mountains.*** These words sound very much like those found in the annals of the Assyrian kings inscribed on the walls of their temples.

37:25 ***I have dug wells . . . I stopped up all the rivers of Egypt:*** Sennacherib's boasts demonstrate his attitude of independence. However, the Lord alone is sovereign over nature (42:15; 43:19; 44:27). • This verse is as in Dead Sea Scrolls (see also 2 Kgs 19:24); Masoretic Text lacks *in many foreign lands.*

37:26 ***I planned for you to crush . . . into heaps of rubble:*** Assyria was God's agent of destruction, but the Assyrians did not realize that they were only a tool in God's hand (see ch 10), fulfilling what God had planned long before (14:24-27).

37:27 ***like grass sprouting on a housetop, scorched:*** As in Dead Sea Scrolls and some Greek manuscripts (see also 2 Kgs 19:26); most Hebrew manuscripts read *like a terraced field.*

37:28 ***you have raged against me:*** Assyria was utterly hostile to the Lord, which brought them even greater condemnation.

37:29 ***my hook . . . my bit:*** The Assyrians would be led away like animals, just as they had led so many of their captives away.

37:30-35 In this prophecy of salvation, Isaiah assured Hezekiah that Jerusalem would be spared and that the remnant was under God's protection. The names of Isaiah and his sons anticipated God's rescue (see 7:1–11:16). The book's record of God's presence and rescue provided assurance that the Lord would always have a remnant that he will protect and rescue.

37:30 ***This year . . . next year . . . the third year:*** Because of the Assyrian siege and its destruction of agriculture, the people of Judah would not be able to plant and harvest as usual. The promise that life would resume after the siege assured them that God was with them and would provide as they carried out their everyday activities. They needed to develop their trust in God over a period of three calendar years in the confident expectation (*waiting,* 30:15, 18) that God's word would be true. Perhaps the point was that after rescue from the Assyrians, it would be too late in the present year for fall planting. They would have to wait until fall in the second year to plant again, and they would reap their first crop in the spring and summer of the third year.

37:32 ***The passionate commitment*** of God includes his energetic zeal to keep his promise, the best guarantee his people could ever have (see also 9:7).

The passionate commitment of the LORD
of Heaven's Armies
will make this happen!

33 "And this is what the LORD says about the
king of Assyria:

" 'His armies will not enter Jerusalem.
They will not even shoot an arrow at it.
They will not march outside its gates
with their shields
nor build banks of earth against its
walls.
34 The king will return to his own country
by the same road on which he came.
He will not enter this city,'
says the LORD.
35 'For my own honor and for the sake of
my servant David,
I will defend this city and protect it.' "

The LORD Rescues Jerusalem
Isa 37:36-38 // 2 Kgs 19:35-37 // 2 Chr 32:21

36 That night the angel of the LORD went out
to the Assyrian camp and killed 185,000
Assyrian soldiers. When the surviving Assyrians woke up the next morning, they
found corpses everywhere. 37 Then King
Sennacherib of Assyria broke camp and
returned to his own land. He went home to
his capital of Nineveh and stayed there.
38 One day while he was worshiping in the
temple of his god Nisroch, his sons Adrammelech and Sharezer killed him with their
swords. They then escaped to the land of Ararat, and another son, Esarhaddon, became
the next king of Assyria.

Hezekiah's Sickness and Recovery
Isa 38:1-8 // 2 Kgs 20:1-11 // 2 Chr 32:24

38 About that time Hezekiah became
deathly ill, and the prophet Isaiah
son of Amoz went to visit him. He gave the
king this message: "This is what the LORD
says: 'Set your affairs in order, for you are
going to die. You will not recover from this
illness.' "
2 When Hezekiah heard this, he turned
his face to the wall and prayed to the
LORD, 3 "Remember, O LORD, how I have always been [e]faithful to you and have served
you single-mindedly, always doing what
pleases you." Then he broke down and wept
bitterly.
4 Then this message came to Isaiah from
the LORD: 5 "Go back to Hezekiah and tell
him, 'This is what the LORD, the God of
your ancestor David, says: I have heard your
prayer and seen your tears. I will add fifteen
years to your life, 6 and I will rescue you and
this city from the king of Assyria. Yes, I will
defend this city.
7 " 'And this is the sign from the LORD to
prove that he will do as he promised: 8 I will
cause the sun's shadow to move ten steps
backward on the sundial of Ahaz!' " So the
shadow on the sundial moved backward
ten steps.

Hezekiah's Poem of Praise
Isa 38:21-22 // 2 Kgs 20:7-8

9 When King Hezekiah was well again, he
wrote this poem:

37:35
2 Kgs 20:6
Isa 48:9, 11

37:36
//2 Kgs 19:35
Isa 10:12, 33-34

37:37
Gen 10:11
Jon 3:3
Zeph 2:13

37:38
Gen 8:4

38:1-8
//2 Kgs 20:1-11
2 Chr 32:24-26

38:3
2 Kgs 18:5-6
Neh 13:14
Ps 6:6-8
[e]'*emeth* (0571)
‣ Dan 10:21

38:5
2 Kgs 18:2, 13

38:6
Isa 31:5

38:7
Isa 7:11, 14

38:8
2 Kgs 20:9-11

37:33 ***armies . . . arrow . . . shields . . . banks of earth:*** Despite their advanced military technology and great power, the Assyrians would not succeed against Jerusalem.

37:35 ***for the sake of my servant David:*** God had promised David a perpetual dynasty (see 9:6-7; 2 Sam 7:8-17).

37:36 ***The angel of the LORD*** was a special heavenly agent through whom God worked on earth. Often his role was to communicate special messages (see Gen 16:7-14), but sometimes he brought judgment (see 2 Sam 24:16). • ***killed 185,000 Assyrian soldiers:*** The Lord began to fulfill what he had repeatedly promised—rescue of Jerusalem and judgment of Assyria (see 10:16, 33-34; 30:31; 31:8). • ***the surviving Assyrians:*** Literally *they.*

37:38 ***One day:*** Sennacherib was probably killed in 681 BC, about twenty years after his withdrawal from Jerusalem. • ***Esarhaddon*** was King of Assyria from 680–669 BC. It is ironic that Sennacherib, who mocked the Lord, was killed by his sons in ***the temple of his god.***

38:1-9 The story of Hezekiah's healing connects Hezekiah's extension of life with Jerusalem's relief from the Assyrians. The events of this story took place before Jerusalem's rescue from the Assyrians but were placed in a thematic rather than chronological order (see notes on 38:6; 2 Kgs 20:1-19). One theme is the importance of prayer (see 37:14-20; 38:2-3). The Lord does listen! Hezekiah had learned the lesson of trust that his father, Ahaz, refused. As a result, Judah and Jerusalem were spared total destruction by the Assyrians. Yet Hezekiah was not the Messiah, the Son of David promised in 7:14; 9:1-7; 11:1-16; 16:5; 32:1, and 33:17-22. Thus, these accounts of his failure and mortality (chs 38–39) prepare the reader for the revelation of the true Messiah that follows (chs 40–66).

38:1 ***About that time*** (literally *in those days*): This is a very general time statement. Hezekiah's illness and subsequent healing probably preceded Jerusalem's rescue (chs 36–37), even though Isaiah places it afterward. Merodach-baladan's reign in Babylon (39:1) ended before Sennacherib's invasion in 701 BC. The order in the text indicates a connection between these two events (see 38:6).

38:3 ***I have always been faithful to you:*** Hezekiah's heart was right with the Lord for most of his reign (2 Kgs 18:1-5), although his dependence on Egypt was a time of weakness when he did not act faithfully (31:1-9).

38:5 ***the God of your ancestor David:*** Hezekiah faithfully walked in David's footsteps (see 37:35; 38:1-22).

38:6 ***I will rescue you . . . I will defend this city:*** This promise refers to the rescue of Jerusalem (chs 36–37); it also provides a greater context for understanding Hezekiah's sickness and healing. Just as Hezekiah received another fifteen years, Jerusalem also received a temporary reprieve (see ch 39).

38:8 ***the sundial:*** Literally *the steps.*

38:9-20 Hezekiah's poem contains both lament (38:9-14) and praise (38:15-20), although the praise is distinctly muted until the final verse.

38:10 Ps 102:24; 107:18
38:11 Ps 27:13
38:12 Job 4:20; 2 Cor 5:1
38:13 Job 10:16
38:14 Job 7:11; Ps 119:123; Ezek 7:16
38:16 Ps 39:13; 119:71, 75
38:17 Isa 43:25; Jer 31:34; Jon 2:6
38:18 Ps 6:5
[f]*she'ol* (7585) ‣ Hos 13:14
38:19 Ps 78:5-7; 119:175
38:20 Ps 33:1-3; 116:17-19; 146:2
38:21 2 Kgs 20:7-8
39:1-8 //2 Kgs 20:12-19
39:2 2 Kgs 18:15-16; 2 Chr 32:25, 31
39:3 Jer 5:15

10 I said, "In the prime of my life,
must I now enter the place of the dead?
Am I to be robbed of the rest of my years?"
11 I said, "Never again will I see the LORD GOD
while still in the land of the living.
Never again will I see my friends
or be with those who live in this world.
12 My life has been blown away
like a shepherd's tent in a storm.
It has been cut short,
as when a weaver cuts cloth from a loom.
Suddenly, my life was over.
13 I waited patiently all night,
but I was torn apart as though by lions.
Suddenly, my life was over.
14 Delirious, I chattered like a swallow or a crane,
and then I moaned like a mourning dove.
My eyes grew tired of looking to heaven for help.
I am in trouble, Lord. Help me!"
15 But what could I say?
For he himself sent this sickness.
Now I will walk humbly throughout my years
because of this anguish I have felt.
16 Lord, your discipline is good,
for it leads to life and health.
You restore my health
and allow me to live!
17 Yes, this anguish was good for me,
for you have rescued me from death
and forgiven all my sins.
18 For the [f]dead cannot praise you;
they cannot raise their voices in praise.
Those who go down to the grave
can no longer hope in your faithfulness.
19 Only the living can praise you as I do today.
Each generation tells of your
faithfulness to the next.
20 Think of it—the LORD is ready to heal me!
I will sing his praises with instruments
every day of my life
in the Temple of the LORD.

21 Isaiah had said to Hezekiah's servants, "Make an ointment from figs and spread it over the boil, and Hezekiah will recover."
22 And Hezekiah had asked, "What sign will prove that I will go to the Temple of the LORD?"

Envoys from Babylon
Isa 39:1-8 // 2 Kgs 20:12-19

39 Soon after this, Merodach-baladan son of Baladan, king of Babylon, sent Hezekiah his best wishes and a gift. He had heard that Hezekiah had been very sick and that he had recovered.
2 Hezekiah was delighted with the Babylonian envoys and showed them everything in his treasure-houses—the silver, the gold, the spices, and the aromatic oils. He also took them to see his armory and showed them everything in his royal treasuries! There was nothing in his palace or kingdom that Hezekiah did not show them.
3 Then Isaiah the prophet went to King Hezekiah and asked him, "What did those men want? Where were they from?"
Hezekiah replied, "They came from the distant land of Babylon."

38:10 *enter the place of the dead?* (literally *enter the gates of Sheol?*): This image comes from an ancient idea that people enter death through gates (see 14:9). OT believers did not understand the afterlife as the NT reveals it. It was a shadowy place where all the dead were together and where no praise of God existed (see 38:18; also Ps 88:10; 115:17).

38:11 Hezekiah lamented that if he died, he would not enjoy fellowship with God, his family, and his friends.

38:12 These images depicted the brevity of life (cp. 2 Cor 5:1).

38:15 ***I will walk humbly:*** Hezekiah might have previously taken his life and good health for granted. Now he recognized that these gifts from the Lord can be withdrawn at any time.

38:16 God's restoration of Hezekiah's ***health*** also symbolized the restoration from exile that Judah would experience in the future.

38:18 *the dead* (Hebrew *Sheol*) *cannot praise you:* See note on 38:10. • People can experience ***hope*** when they remember God's ***faithfulness*** in the past (see 25:1).

38:21-22 Hezekiah received a sign, reminiscent of another sign the prophet had offered Ahaz (7:11). Ahaz and Hezekiah were two bookends to a long story. Ahaz represented the ungodly king and Hezekiah the godly king. The former brought disaster on his people, while the latter rescued his people (but see ch 39).

38:22 Hezekiah could not ***go to the Temple*** with an infection (see Lev 13), so going to the Temple signifies restored health.

39:1-8 Hezekiah was exemplary in godliness, prayer, and care for the people of Jerusalem. But he failed the Lord by parading his financial and military strength before the envoys from Babylon.

39:1 *Merodach-baladan,* the king of Babylon (722–710 and 704–703 BC), planned to rebel against Assyria and sought help from Hezekiah. His envoys visited after ***Hezekiah had been very sick*** and had recovered but before Sennacherib's final attack in 701 BC.

39:2 *silver . . . aromatic oils . . . his armory:* Showing these treasures demonstrated to Babylon's envoys that Hezekiah had the resources to be a worthy ally.

4“What did they see in your palace?”
asked Isaiah.
“They saw everything,” Hezekiah replied.
“I showed them everything I own—all my
royal treasuries.”
5Then Isaiah said to Hezekiah, “Listen to
this message from the LORD of Heaven’s Armies: 6‘The time is coming when everything
in your palace—all the treasures stored up
by your ancestors until now—will be carried
off to Babylon. Nothing will be left,’ says the
LORD. 7‘Some of your very own sons will be
taken away into exile. They will become
eunuchs who will serve in the palace of Babylon’s king.’ ”
8Then Hezekiah said to Isaiah, “This message you have given me from the LORD is
good.” For the king was thinking, “At least
there will be peace and security during my
lifetime.”

7. GOD’S GLORIOUS KINGDOM (40:1–66:24)

The Good News of Salvation (40:1–48:22)

Comfort for God’s People

40 1“Comfort, comfort my people,”
says your God.
2“Speak tenderly to Jerusalem.
Tell her that her sad days are gone
and her sins are pardoned.
Yes, the LORD has punished her twice over
for all her sins.”

3Listen! It’s the voice of someone shouting,
“Clear the way through the wilderness
for the LORD!
Make a straight highway through the
wasteland
for our God!
4Fill in the valleys,
and level the mountains and hills.
Straighten the curves,
and smooth out the rough places.
5Then the [g]glory of the LORD will be
revealed,
and all people will see it together.
The LORD has spoken!”

6A voice said, “Shout!”
I asked, “What should I shout?”
“Shout that people are like the grass.
Their beauty fades as quickly
as the flowers in a field.

39:5
1 Sam 15:16
39:6
2 Kgs 24:13
Jer 20:5
39:7
Dan 1:2-7
39:8
2 Chr 34:28
40:1
Isa 49:13
2 Cor 1:4
40:2
Isa 53:5-6, 11
Zech 9:12
40:3
Mal 3:1
*Matt 3:3
*Mark 1:3
*Luke 3:4
*John 1:23
40:4
Ezek 17:24
*Luke 3:5
40:5
Hab 2:14
*Luke 3:6
[g]*kabod* (3519)
‣ Ezek 10:18
40:6
Job 14:2
1 Pet 1:24

39:6-7 ***carried off to Babylon:*** This prophecy was given before the prophecy of the rescue of Jerusalem (37:35). Although this pronouncement of judgment and exile comes as a surprise ending to the story of Hezekiah, the exile of both Israel and Judah had been in the background from the beginning (10:3-4, 20-23). The Lord had promised that he would spare Judah and Jerusalem when the Assyrians attacked in 701 BC, but he had clearly revealed to Isaiah that worse things would come if they did not change their ways. God had demonstrated the truth of his sovereignty and trustworthiness in his defeat of the Assyrians, but that did not mean the people had changed. The only way the promises of 2:1-5 and 4:2-6 were going to be realized was through the fires of judgment (4:4). Until the burning coal of exile was applied to the nation’s unclean lips (6:5-7), their mission to the nations would fail.

40:1–66:24 The rest of Isaiah provides a message of comfort and a revelation of God’s character and his purposes for Israel. As 39:6-7 predicted, Judah would experience judgment and exile after the time of Isaiah. Throughout chs 40–66, Isaiah prophesied from the vantage point of the Exile having already become a reality. Therefore, the Babylonian exile provides the background for understanding these chapters.

40:1–55:13 This section announces the good news of God’s coming salvation. The Lord is coming to vindicate his own and to judge his enemies. Salvation would be accomplished through the arrival, suffering, and exaltation of the Lord’s servant—the Messiah, Jesus Christ.

40:1-31 This chapter introduces chs 40–66. In this section, ***comfort*** refers to the result of God’s merciful way of dealing with people in the age to come. It includes encouragement, strength, and acceptance. God wants to rescue his people (40:1-11) and is more than able to do so (40:12-26). The exiles needed to believe God’s promises and wait on him for their rescue (40:27-31; see also 30:15-18).

40:2 ***Speak tenderly:*** The prophet’s message was to encourage Jerusalem with the good news of his forgiveness, reconciliation, and restoration. • From the prophetic perspective, Israel’s ***sad days are gone*** because the Exile is over. • ***punished her twice over for all her sins:*** Israel experienced the full brunt of God’s wrath (51:19-23; cp. 61:7).

40:3-5 There is now a shift from the general announcement of the good news to the specific expectation of God’s coming. The good news (40:1-2) is grounded in God himself. Isaiah portrayed the Lord as coming on a highway through the desert (see ch 35), although the imagery is here reversed: In ch 35, the people were traveling to Zion, toward the Lord. Here, the Lord is coming toward his people (see also 52:8, where the two images are brought together). • Greek version reads *He is a voice shouting in the wilderness, / “Prepare the way for the LORD’s coming! / Clear a road for our God! / Fill in the valleys, / and level the mountains and hills. / And then the glory of the LORD will be revealed, / and all people will see the salvation sent from God. / The LORD has spoken!”* Cp. Matt 3:3; Mark 1:3; Luke 3:4-6, all of which quote from the Greek version.

40:3 ***the voice of someone shouting:*** In Mal 3:1 this person (possibly the Elijah of Mal 4:5) was God’s messenger who prepared the way for God’s coming. In the Gospels, this announcer was identified with John the Baptist (Matt 3:3; Mark 1:3; Luke 3:4; John 1:23). • ***Clear the way . . . Make a straight highway:*** The announcer’s message would expedite God’s coming (see 35:8). As God made a way for Israel through the Red Sea (43:16), so a way would be opened up for the Lord (see 52:11-12).

40:5 The future revelation of God’s glory would include the return of Judah from exile but would also go beyond it. The NT confirmed that the revelation of God’s glory came in Jesus Christ (John 1:14; Heb 1:3). • ***The LORD has spoken:*** The coming salvation and judgment would certainly occur because the Lord, who keeps his word, had declared it (see 1:20; 58:14).

40:6-8 All humanity is mortal and fleeting. By contrast, God persists in his plans and succeeds. Time does not limit him from carrying out his will (see 14:24). • This verse is quoted in 1 Pet 1:24-25.

40:6 ***Shout:*** So that all can hear. • ***People*** are not worthy of the revelation of God’s glory because they are mortal.

40:7
Jas 1:10-11
1 Pet 1:24
40:8
Matt 5:18
*1 Pet 1:25
40:10
Isa 59:16
Rev 22:12
40:11
Ezek 34:12-14, 23, 31
John 10:11, 14-16
[h]*ra'ah* (7462)
›Jer 3:15
40:12
Isa 48:13
40:13
*Rom 11:34
*1 Cor 2:16
40:14
Col 2:3
40:17
Isa 29:7
40:18
Exod 8:10
Isa 46:5
Mic 7:18
40:19
Ps 115:4-8
Hab 2:18-19

7 The grass withers and the flowers fade
beneath the breath of the LORD.
And so it is with people.
8 The grass withers and the flowers fade,
but the word of our God stands
forever."

9 O Zion, messenger of good news,
shout from the mountaintops!
Shout it louder, O Jerusalem.
Shout, and do not be afraid.
Tell the towns of Judah,
"Your God is coming!"
10 Yes, the Sovereign LORD is coming in
power.
He will rule with a powerful arm.
See, he brings his reward with him as
he comes.
11 He will [h]feed his flock like a shepherd.
He will carry the lambs in his arms,
holding them close to his heart.
He will gently lead the mother sheep
with their young.

The LORD Has No Equal

12 Who else has held the oceans in his
hand?
Who has measured off the heavens
with his fingers?
Who else knows the weight of the earth
or has weighed the mountains and
hills on a scale?
13 Who is able to advise the Spirit of the
LORD?
Who knows enough to give him
advice or teach him?
14 Has the LORD ever needed anyone's
advice?
Does he need instruction about what
is good?
Did someone teach him what is right
or show him the path of justice?

15 No, for all the nations of the world
are but a drop in the bucket.
They are nothing more
than dust on the scales.
He picks up the whole earth
as though it were a grain of
sand.
16 All the wood in Lebanon's forests
and all Lebanon's animals would not
be enough
to make a burnt offering worthy of
our God.
17 The nations of the world are worth
nothing to him.
In his eyes they count for less than
nothing—
mere emptiness and froth.

18 To whom can you compare God?
What image can you find to resemble
him?
19 Can he be compared to an idol formed
in a mold,
overlaid with gold, and decorated
with silver chains?

40:7 ***The breath of the LORD*** refers to God's spoken words of judgment (see 4:4).

40:8 ***the word of our God stands forever:*** All of God's words (his plans as well as the written word) will succeed. God might frustrate human expectations, but everything will happen according to his wise plan (see 14:24; 55:8-11; see also Matt 25:34).

40:9-11 God is the good news. Although he comes like a warrior to rescue his people with power, he also holds them tenderly as a shepherd.

40:9 ***O Zion, messenger of good news, shout from the mountaintops! Shout it louder, O Jerusalem:*** Or *O messenger of good news, shout to Zion from the mountaintops! Shout it louder to Jerusalem.* • ***God is coming*** to save and restore human beings (see also 35:4; Rev 22:12).

40:10 The Lord's ***rule*** is not like that of the unjust and powerless rulers whom he will judge. It is compassionate, just, righteous, and powerful. • ***with a powerful arm:*** God manifested his power in events such as the defeat of the Egyptians (63:12), the judgment of his enemies (30:30; 48:14; 51:9), and the rescue of his people (59:16).

40:11 Isaiah used the familiar biblical metaphor of a ***shepherd*** to speak of God's care for his people (see also 49:10; Ps 23:1; Jer 3:15; 23:4; Ezek 34:11-17; Matt 2:6; John 10:1-18).

40:12-17 Against the backdrop of Israel's questions (spoken by the prophet), the Lord affirmed that he is the incomparable God, a wise and sovereign creator who rules over the nations.

40:12-13 These rhetorical questions evoke the answer "No one!" God alone created all that exists. He will judge creation (24:17), and he alone can and will restore creation through his salvation. • ***Who is able to advise the Spirit of the LORD?*** Greek version reads *Who can know the LORD's thoughts?* Cp. Rom 11:34; 1 Cor 2:16.

40:15 God is sovereign over ***all the nations of the world*** and over their human power structures. In comparison to God, they are almost ***nothing.*** This included the Babylonian empire, which was merely a tool in God's hand. • ***whole earth:*** Literally *coastlands* or *islands.*

40:16 Lebanon was prized for its abundance of wood and its wildlife (see 2:13-16; Ps 104:16-17).

40:17 The nations, including their leaders (40:23), pagan structures (41:24, 29; 44:9-11), and all enemies of God's people (41:11-12), are ***worth nothing*** apart from God.

40:18 ***To whom . . . What image:*** Earlier in the book, idolatry was shown to be ridiculous (16:12; 37:16-19). Chapters 40–48 open up a much more extensive argument against idolatry. Idols are symbolic representations of gods and, at times, other religious concepts. Those who worship them don't recognize the implication that they are man-made trinkets. Idols are powerless (41:7, 22-24; 48:14), give a false sense of security (42:17), delude people (44:20), and lead to severe disappointment (42:17; 45:16, 20). They cannot help those who care for them. In fact, they are so weak that they fall down (40:20; 41:7). In the end, idols compete for God's glory (42:8) and take away human dignity (44:9; see also 41:21-29). • The Lord, the true God, is incomparable (see 40:25; 46:5; Ps 86:8; 89:6); no one could ***resemble him.***

20 Or if people are too poor for that,
they might at least [i]choose wood that
won't decay
and a skilled craftsman
to carve an image that won't fall
down!

21 Haven't you heard? Don't you
understand?
Are you deaf to the words of God—
the words he gave before the world
began?
Are you so ignorant?
22 God sits above the circle of the earth.
The people below seem like
grasshoppers to him!
He spreads out the heavens like a curtain
and makes his tent from them.
23 He judges the great people of the world
and brings them all to nothing.
24 They hardly get started, barely taking
root,
when he blows on them and they
wither.
The wind carries them off like chaff.

25 "To whom will you compare me?
Who is my equal?" asks the Holy One.

26 Look up into the heavens.
Who created all the stars?
He brings them out like an army, one
after another,
calling each by its name.
Because of his great power and
incomparable strength,
not a single one is missing.

27 O Jacob, how can you say the LORD does
not see your troubles?
O Israel, how can you say God ignores
your rights?
28 Have you never heard?
Have you never understood?
The LORD is the everlasting God,
the [j]Creator of all the earth.
He never grows weak or weary.
No one can measure the depths of his
understanding.
29 He gives power to the weak
and strength to the powerless.
30 Even youths will become weak and tired,
and young men will fall in exhaustion.
31 But those who trust in the LORD will find
new strength.
They will soar high on wings like
eagles.
They will run and not grow weary.
They will walk and not faint.

God's Help for Israel

41 1 "Listen in silence before me, you
lands beyond the sea.
Bring your strongest arguments.
Come now and speak.
The court is ready for your case.

2 "Who has stirred up this king from the
east,
rightly calling him to God's service?
Who gives this man victory over many
nations
and permits him to trample their
kings underfoot?

40:20 Isa 46:7
[i]*bakhar* (0977)
‣Isa 43:10
40:21 Isa 51:13
Rom 1:19
40:22 Ps 104:2
40:23 Ps 107:40
Jer 25:18-27
40:24 Isa 17:13
40:26 Ps 147:4
Isa 42:5
40:27 Job 34:5-6
Isa 54:8
40:28 Ps 90:2; 147:5
Rom 11:33
[j]*bara'* (1254)
‣Isa 43:15
40:29 Jer 31:25
40:30 Jer 9:21
40:31 2 Cor 4:8-10, 16
Heb 12:3
41:1 Hab 2:20
Zech 2:13
41:2 2 Chr 36:23
Isa 46:11

40:20 ***image that won't fall down:*** This is a sarcastic remark; it would be embarrassing if the idol did not even have the power to remain standing (see 40:18; 41:7; 1 Sam 5:4).

40:21 Idolaters fail to discern who God is or to respond wisely to him. The godly in Israel would ***understand*** and see the hand of God in the unfolding story of redemption, which includes both exile and restoration (41:20).

40:22 ***God sits*** enthroned as King over all ***the earth*** (see 6:1; Ps 2:4; 80:1; 99:1; 102:12; 113:5). God is so immense and awesome that humans are ***like grasshoppers*** in comparison. • Belief in God as creator of ***the heavens*** and earth contradicts the popular Babylonian and Egyptian belief that the sun, moon, and stars represent gods. • ***like a curtain . . . his tent:*** See also Ps 104:2.

40:23 ***great people:*** God is unimpressed by human power and fame.

40:25 ***The Holy One*** is a shortened form of "the Holy One of Israel," a common designation for God in Isaiah (see note on 1:4; also 10:17; Ps 22:3; 43:15).

40:26 ***Look up into the heavens:*** Just as God directed Abraham to look into the sky (Gen 15:5), he also directed Israel to look to the stars for encouragement (see also 51:2-3). The cosmos bears witness to God's ***great power and incomparable strength.*** The Strong One is able to strengthen the weak (40:27-31; see Ps 147:5).

40:27 ***does not see your troubles . . . ignores your rights:*** The coming exile, a period when God's powerful presence and rescue would not be seen, would prompt questions (see also 49:14; 54:7; Lam 5:20-22).

40:28 ***heard . . . understood:*** Cp. 40:21. • ***the everlasting God, the Creator of all the earth:*** Creation reveals God's power and wisdom. He is also the Creator of the age to come, a world of righteousness, justice, and peace (45:8; 48:6-7; 65:17-18). • ***He never grows weak or weary:*** God is not susceptible to human limitations.

40:29 ***The weak*** in this context are those who face persecution or oppression (such as the Babylonian exile); the Lord is their only recourse (see 49:4-5; 50:4; Ps 68:9; 119:28).

40:31 ***trust in the LORD:*** See note on 8:17; see also 33:2; 49:23; 51:5. • ***like eagles:*** This powerful image of rescue reminded readers of the Exodus event of long ago (Exod 19:4; Deut 32:10-12; see also Ps 103:5).

41:1-7 The Lord here invited the nations to a trial where he would prove that he alone is God. They were defenseless as he declared that a ***king from the east*** (41:2) would crush Babylon, opening the way for Israel to return.

41:1 The nations coming together for a trial have to ***listen in silence*** to the presentation of God's arguments. • ***Bring your strongest arguments:*** Literally *let them find new strength,* a play on 40:31. • God invited the nations to ***come . . . and speak,*** challenging them to refute his case.

41:2 ***This king from the east*** was Cyrus, the Persian king who conquered

41:4
Isa 44:7; 48:12
Rev 1:8, 17-18; 22:13

41:5
Josh 5:1
Ezek 26:15-16

41:6
Joel 3:9-11

41:8
Isa 51:2
Jas 2:23

41:9
Deut 7:6
Isa 11:11

41:10
Deut 31:6
Ps 89:13
Rom 8:31

41:11
Isa 29:5, 7-8

41:12
Job 20:7-9

41:13
Isa 45:1

41:14
Isa 43:14
[k]*go'el* (1350)
‣ Isa 44:6

41:15
Mic 4:13

41:16
Isa 35:10

41:17
Isa 30:19; 42:16; 44:3

With his sword, he reduces armies to
dust.
With his bow, he scatters them like
chaff before the wind.
3 He chases them away and goes on safely,
though he is walking over unfamiliar
ground.
4 Who has done such mighty deeds,
summoning each new generation
from the beginning of time?
It is I, the Lord, the First and the Last.
I alone am he."
5 The lands beyond the sea watch in fear.
Remote lands tremble and mobilize
for war.
6 The idol makers encourage one another,
saying to each other, "Be strong!"
7 The carver encourages the goldsmith,
and the molder helps at the anvil.
"Good," they say. "It's coming along
fine."
Carefully they join the parts together,
then fasten the thing in place so it
won't fall over.

8 "But as for you, Israel my servant,
Jacob my chosen one,
descended from Abraham my friend,
9 I have called you back from the ends of
the earth,
saying, 'You are my servant.'
For I have chosen you
and will not throw you away.
10 Don't be afraid, for I am with you.
Don't be discouraged, for I am your
God.
I will strengthen you and help you.
I will hold you up with my victorious
right hand.
11 "See, all your angry enemies lie there,
confused and humiliated.
Anyone who opposes you will die
and come to nothing.
12 You will look in vain
for those who tried to conquer you.
Those who attack you
will come to nothing.
13 For I hold you by your right hand—
I, the Lord your God.
And I say to you,
'Don't be afraid. I am here to help you.
14 Though you are a lowly worm, O Jacob,
don't be afraid, people of Israel, for I
will help you.
I am the Lord, your [k]Redeemer.
I am the Holy One of Israel.'
15 You will be a new threshing instrument
with many sharp teeth.
You will tear your enemies apart,
making chaff of mountains.
16 You will toss them into the air,
and the wind will blow them all
away;
a whirlwind will scatter them.
Then you will rejoice in the Lord.
You will glory in the Holy One of
Israel.

17 "When the poor and needy search for
water and there is none,
and their tongues are parched from
thirst,

Babylon in 539 BC and permitted the Jews to return to their land and rebuild Jerusalem (538 BC; Ezra 1:1-4). Isaiah's prophecies about Cyrus (see 44:28–45:13; 48:14-15) encouraged Israel to look to the Lord as sovereign over all of human history, including the actions of great kings. • ***Who gives this man victory over many nations?*** As victorious as the conquering Cyrus was, he was still subject to the Lord.

41:4 ***each new generation from the beginning of time:*** God is sovereign over all things. From the beginning he has unfolded each stage of history according to his plan. • In the book of Revelation, Jesus identifies himself as the Alpha and the Omega, ***the First and the Last***, the Beginning and the End (Rev 1:8, 17; 2:8; 21:6; 22:13). • ***I alone am he:*** The Lord alone is God (see also 43:10, 13; 46:4; 48:12; Deut 32:39). Jesus used similar expressions for himself (see John 6:35; 8:12, 24; 9:5; 10:7, 9, 11, 14; 11:25; 14:6; 15:1, 5).

41:5-7 This taunt against idolatry (see note on 40:18) was a response to God's raising up of Cyrus; the nations hope to find protection in their idols.

41:6 ***Be strong!*** The nations put their hope in things that have no strength, objects made by human craftsmen.

41:8-16 These two prophecies of salvation for God's servant Israel (41:8-13, 14-16) prepare for the first of the suffering servant songs (see note on 42:1-4).

41:8 The servant—here the nation of Israel—was God's ***chosen one***, whose calling was grounded in God's purposes. • ***Abraham my friend:*** The phrase in Hebrew could mean *Abraham who loves me* or *Abraham whom I love*. See also Jas 2:23.

41:9 ***I have chosen you*** restates 41:8 to emphasize God's commitment and faithfulness to his people Israel, who had not been faithful to him. • ***not throw you away:*** Because of the Exile, the people felt that God had rejected them (see 49:21; 54:6). However, God had good purposes for them.

41:10 ***I am with you:*** The promise of God's presence (see 7:14) is central to the Bible. Because God is present, his people do not need to fear (see also 43:1-2, 5). • ***I am your God:*** The Lord used the language of the covenant to affirm that he is their God and that they are his people (see also Jer 7:23; 31:1, 33; Ezek 14:11; 36:28; 37:27; Zech 8:8). • ***hold you . . . my victorious right hand:*** The Lord used language reminiscent of the Exodus (cp. Exod 15:6) to encourage Israel (see also 41:13; 63:12).

41:13 ***Don't be afraid:*** See note on 7:4.

41:14 In exile, Israel was in a ***lowly*** state. • God is the ***Redeemer.*** He works mightily to rescue and restore people from sin and its consequences (for Israel, the Exile; for application to Jesus, see Luke 2:38; 21:28; Rom 3:24; 1 Cor 1:30; Gal 4:5; Eph 1:1-14; Titus 2:14; Heb 9:12).

41:16 When the grain is thrown into ***the wind***, the chaff is blown away. Likewise, Israel's enemies appeared to be strong but would easily be driven off.

then I, the LORD, will answer them.
I, the God of Israel, will never abandon them.
18 I will open up rivers for them on the high plateaus.
I will give them fountains of water in the valleys.
I will fill the desert with pools of water.
Rivers fed by springs will flow across the parched ground.
19 I will plant trees in the barren desert—
cedar, acacia, myrtle, olive, cypress, fir, and pine.
20 I am doing this so all who see this miracle
will understand what it means—
that it is the LORD who has done this,
the Holy One of Israel who created it.

21 "Present the case for your idols,"
says the LORD.
"Let them show what they can do,"
says the King of Israel.
22 "Let them try to tell us what happened long ago
so that we may consider the evidence.
Or let them tell us what the future holds,
so we can know what's going to happen.
23 Yes, tell us what will occur in the days ahead.
Then we will know you are gods.
In fact, do anything—good or bad!
Do something that will amaze and frighten us.
24 But no! You are less than nothing and can do nothing at all.
Those who choose you pollute themselves.

25 "But I have stirred up a leader who will come from the north.
I have called him by name from the east.
I will give him victory over kings and princes.
He will trample them as a potter treads on clay.
26 "Who told you from the beginning that this would happen?
Who predicted this,
making you admit that he was right?
No one said a word!
27 I was the first to tell Zion,
'Look! Help is on the way!'
I will send Jerusalem a messenger with good news.
28 Not one of your idols told you this.
Not one gave any answer when I asked.
29 See, they are all foolish, worthless things.
All your idols are as empty as the wind.

The LORD's Chosen Servant

42 1 "Look at my [a]servant, whom I strengthen.
He is my chosen one, who pleases me.
I have put my Spirit upon him.
He will bring justice to the nations.
2 He will not shout
or raise his voice in public.
3 He will not crush the weakest reed
or put out a flickering candle.
He will bring justice to all who have been wronged.
4 He will not falter or lose heart
until justice prevails throughout the earth.

41:18 Ps 107:35; Isa 30:25
41:19 Isa 55:13
41:20 Job 12:7-9
41:22 Isa 43:9; 45:21
41:23 Jer 10:5; John 13:19
41:24 1 Cor 8:4
41:25 Jer 50:3; Mic 7:10
41:26 Isa 44:7
41:27 Isa 40:9
41:28 Isa 63:5
41:29 Hab 2:18-19
42:1-4 *Matt 12:18-21
42:1 Isa 11:2; 53:11; Matt 3:17; 12:18; [a]*'ebed* (5650) ›Isa 53:11
42:3 Ps 72:2, 4
42:4 Isa 24:15; 66:19

41:18 ***rivers . . . fountains . . . pools of water . . . springs:*** These images would strike a responsive chord in an agrarian culture. They also suggest that rescue from the Exile would be a second exodus (cp. Exod 15:27; 17:6).

41:21-29 This trial scene develops the Lord's case against idolatry. Idols are nothing but a human creation, whereas God is the Creator of all things. Idols cannot speak, act, accomplish anything, or save their worshipers.

41:21 ***the King of Israel:*** Literally *the King of Jacob.* See note on 14:1. See also 6:5; 43:15; 44:6.

41:25 ***I have stirred up a leader:*** The God who had planned the Exile through Babylon had already planned for Israel's restoration from exile through Cyrus (see note on 41:2; see also 13:17). • Although Persia is located to the *east,* rough terrain required those traveling to Israel and Judah to enter *from the north.* • ***I will give him victory . . . He will trample them:*** As Babylon was sent to trample Assyria, so Persia would trample Babylon.

41:26 Idols and false gods could not predict the future.

41:27 The ***messenger with good news*** told of God's coming to rescue his people (see 40:9). • ***'Look! Help is on the way!':*** Or *'Look! They are coming home.'*

42:1-4 The ***servant*** here is not the people Israel (as in 41:8-28 and elsewhere in chs 41–48; see 49:5-6) but is a royal figure who accomplishes his mission with care for people, especially for those who are hurting. The passage is the first of four songs about this servant (42:1-4; 49:1-13; 50:4-11; 52:13–53:12). He brings in an era of universal justice. For the connection of the servant with Jesus Christ, see Matt 12:18-21.

42:1 ***who pleases me:*** God used similar language at Jesus' baptism (Matt 3:17). • ***I have put my Spirit upon him:*** Any leader might be called a servant, but the presence of the Spirit suggests a king of David's line or a prophet like Moses (see Num 11:17, 24-29). • Establishing *justice* is the responsibility of a king (see 9:6-7; Ps 72:1). • This king's mission will be a greater mission *to the nations* than simply governing the small nation of Judah.

42:2 ***shout or raise his voice:*** The royal servant will have calm confidence in his message and calling from God (see also 11:1-5).

42:3 The royal servant will be gentle with the oppressed and discouraged (see 3:15; 41:17).

42:4 ***distant lands:*** The nations long for *justice* and for ***instruction*** on bringing it about. In this regard the servant is like Moses, to whom the law was given. However, the servant is greater in that

42:5 Job 33:4; Ps 104:2; Isa 45:18; Acts 17:25
[b]*'el* (0410) ‣Exod 3:6
42:6 Jer 23:5-6; Luke 2:32
[c]*berith* (1285) ‣Isa 55:3
42:7 Isa 35:5; 61:1
42:8 Exod 3:15; 20:3-5
42:9 Isa 48:3, 6
42:10 Ps 33:3
42:13 Isa 59:17; 66:14-16
42:15 Ezek 38:19-20
42:16 Ps 94:14; Isa 40:4; Luke 1:78-79; Eph 5:8
42:17 Ps 97:7; Isa 44:9, 11
42:18 Isa 35:5
42:20 Jer 6:10

Even distant lands beyond the sea will
wait for his instruction."
5 [b]God, the LORD, created the heavens and
stretched them out.
He created the earth and everything
in it.
He gives breath to everyone,
life to everyone who walks the earth.
And it is he who says,
6 "I, the LORD, have called you to
demonstrate my righteousness.
I will take you by the hand and guard
you,
and I will give you to my people, Israel,
as a symbol of my [c]covenant with
them.
And you will be a light to guide the
nations.
7 You will open the eyes of the blind.
You will free the captives from prison,
releasing those who sit in dark
dungeons.

8 "I am the LORD; that is my name!
I will not give my glory to anyone else,
nor share my praise with carved idols.
9 Everything I prophesied has come true,
and now I will prophesy again.
I will tell you the future before it
happens."

A Song of Praise to the LORD

10 Sing a new song to the LORD!
Sing his praises from the ends of the
earth!
Sing, all you who sail the seas,
all you who live in distant coastlands.
11 Join in the chorus, you desert towns;
let the villages of Kedar rejoice!
Let the people of Sela sing for joy;
shout praises from the mountaintops!
12 Let the whole world glorify the LORD;
let it sing his praise.
13 The LORD will march forth like a mighty
hero;
he will come out like a warrior, full
of fury.
He will shout his battle cry
and crush all his enemies.

14 He will say, "I have long been silent;
yes, I have restrained myself.
But now, like a woman in labor,
I will cry and groan and pant.
15 I will level the mountains and hills
and blight all their greenery.
I will turn the rivers into dry land
and will dry up all the pools.
16 I will lead blind Israel down a new path,
guiding them along an unfamiliar way.
I will brighten the darkness before them
and smooth out the road ahead of them.
Yes, I will indeed do these things;
I will not forsake them.
17 But those who trust in idols,
who say, 'You are our gods,'
will be turned away in shame.

Israel's Failure to Listen and See

18 "Listen, you who are deaf!
Look and see, you blind!
19 Who is as blind as my own people, my
servant?
Who is as deaf as my messenger?
Who is as blind as my chosen people,
the servant of the LORD?
20 You see and recognize what is right
but refuse to act on it.
You hear with your ears,
but you don't really listen."

21 Because he is righteous,
the LORD has exalted his glorious law.

---

he extends justice beyond Israel to all the nations. • ***Even distant lands beyond the sea will wait for his instruction:*** Greek version reads *And his name will be the hope of all the world.* Compare Matt 12:21.

42:6 *my people, Israel . . . my covenant with them* (literally *a covenant for the people*): It is also possible that "the people" referred to all the peoples/nations of the earth (see 49:6). • ***light to guide the nations:*** See also 51:4; Acts 13:47.

42:7 The servant will open the *eyes of the* spiritually *blind* (see 6:10; 29:18) and *free the* spiritual *captives from the prison* of sin, in addition to those who were captive in the Babylonian exile (see 61:1 with Luke 4:18).

42:8-9 *I am the LORD:* As Creator of the world, and as the only one who can bring about the things he predicts, the Lord alone is glorious and worthy of *praise.*

42:10-11 The various geographical regions represent the extremes of human habitation. The whole earth is called to praise God for his commitment to redeem humanity. • ***Kedar*** and ***Sela*** (42:11; see also 16:1; 21:16-17) were representative desert sites.

42:13 *a mighty hero . . . a warrior:* The background of this theme is God's victory at the Red Sea during the Exodus (Exod 15:3). • God will be victorious over *all his enemies* in order to rescue his people (51:9; 63:1-6; see also Ps 54:7; 108:9; 112:8).

42:14 *I have long been silent . . . restrained myself:* Israel had experienced God's absence in the Exile, which came about because of their idolatrous ways (57:11-13; 2 Kgs 17:6-24). The godly will pray for God's presence and renewed involvement in their situation (64:12), and the Lord will answer their prayers because of his commitment to their redemption (62:1, 6).

42:18-20 The Israelites who refused to listen to what God said and to understand what they saw God doing in history were rendered spiritually *blind* and *deaf* (see 6:9-10). They had knowledge of the truth through God's word and the prophets, but their closed minds refused to act upon it.

42:21 *exalted his glorious law:* God's word is a witness to his righteous rule (see 1:10).

22 But his own people have been robbed
and plundered,
enslaved, imprisoned, and trapped.
They are fair game for anyone
and have no one to protect them,
no one to take them back home.

23 Who will hear these lessons from the past
and see the ruin that awaits you in the future?

24 Who allowed Israel to be robbed and hurt?
It was the LORD, against whom we sinned,
for the people would not walk in his path,
nor would they [d]obey his law.

25 Therefore, he poured out his fury on them
and destroyed them in battle.
They were enveloped in flames,
but they still refused to understand.
They were consumed by fire,
but they did not learn their lesson.

The Savior of Israel

43 1 But now, O Jacob, listen to the LORD who created you.
O Israel, the one who formed you says,
"Do not be afraid, for I have [e]ransomed you.
I have called you by name; you are mine.

2 When you go through deep waters,
I will be with you.
When you go through rivers of difficulty,
you will not drown.
When you walk through the fire of oppression,
you will not be burned up;
the flames will not consume you.

3 For I am the LORD, your God,
the Holy One of Israel, your Savior.
I gave Egypt as a ransom for your freedom;
I gave Ethiopia and Seba in your place.

4 Others were given in exchange for you.
I traded their lives for yours
because you are precious to me.
You are honored, and I love you.

5 "Do not be afraid, for I am with you.
I will gather you and your children
from east and west.

6 I will say to the north and south,
'Bring my sons and daughters back to Israel
from the distant corners of the earth.

7 Bring all who claim me as their God,
for I have made them for my glory.
It was I who created them.'"

8 Bring out the people who have eyes but are blind,
who have ears but are deaf.

9 Gather the nations together!
Assemble the peoples of the world!
Which of their idols has ever foretold such things?
Which can predict what will happen tomorrow?
Where are the witnesses of such predictions?
Who can verify that they spoke the truth?

10 "But you are my witnesses, O Israel!" says the LORD.
"You are my servant.
You have been [f]chosen to know me,
believe in me,
and understand that I alone am God.
There is no other God—
there never has been, and there never will be.

42:22 Isa 24:18
42:24 Isa 48:18
[d]*shama'* (8085) ‣Dan 9:10
42:25 Isa 5:25; Hos 7:9
43:1 Isa 44:2, 21-24; 45:3-4
[e]*ga'al* (1350) ‣Isa 63:9
43:2 Deut 31:6, 8; Dan 3:25, 27
43:3 Exod 20:2; Isa 43:11
43:4 Isa 63:9
43:5 Isa 49:12; Jer 30:10-11
43:6 Ps 107:3; 2 Cor 6:17-18
43:7 Ps 100:3; Isa 46:13; Eph 2:10
43:8 Ezek 12:2
43:9 Isa 41:22, 26
43:10 [f]*bakhar* (0977) ‣Exod 18:25

42:22-25 Throughout its history, Israel's sin (42:24) made Israel ***fair game*** for foreign oppressors. Many nations, Assyria and Babylon in particular, became instruments God used to pour ***out his fury*** (42:25) on his rebellious people.

42:25 Generation after generation of Israelites ***did not learn their lesson,*** even when God disciplined them through military defeat.

43:1-7 In this promise of salvation, the Lord addressed his plundered people in the first person.

43:1 ***the LORD who created you:*** The language of creation (see note on 40:28) was now applied to God's formation of the nation Israel. • ***I have ransomed you:*** At the Exodus, when God brought his people out of bondage. Similarly, God planned to bring his people out of exile and back into their land. Ultimately, Jesus gave his life as a ransom for all humanity (Matt 20:28; 1 Tim 2:6; Heb 9:15) • ***I have called you by name; you are mine:*** Despite having faced his wrath, the people of Israel are still God's chosen people.

43:2 Conquering forces could be compared to flooding ***rivers*** (see 8:8). • ***I will be with you:*** God is committed to being with his people to protect and care for them (see 7:14; 41:10; 43:5; 45:14). • Israel experienced God's judgment as ***the fire of oppression*** during the Exile.

43:3 ***Holy One of Israel:*** See note on 1:4. • ***Ethiopia:*** Hebrew *Cush.*

43:7 One of God's purposes in restoring his people was to display his ***glory*** to the watching world.

43:8-13 The Lord here called on Israel, his blind servant, to be his star witness in a mock trial against idols and false gods. Israel knew that the Lord alone is God, and the people had experienced his salvation.

43:10 ***you are my witnesses:*** By their very presence in exile, Israel was evidence that God is truly God. He predicted the Exile long beforehand, and now it had come to pass. God alone is the true God because he speaks and acts and controls all of history. Idols and false gods could do none of these things. Israel would later become even greater evidence because God had also predicted their redemption (43:11-12).

43:11
Hos 13:4
43:12
Ps 81:9
[g]*yasha'* (3467)
‣Isa 45:20
43:13
Job 9:12
Ps 90:2
43:14
Isa 41:14
43:15
Isa 44:6
[h]*bara'* (1254)
‣Isa 65:17
[i]*melek* (4428)
‣Ezek 37:22
43:16
Exod 14:21-22
Josh 3:15-16
Ps 77:19
43:17
Ps 76:5-6
43:18
Jer 16:14
43:19
Deut 8:15
2 Cor 5:17
Rev 21:5
43:20
Isa 41:17-18
2 Pet 2:9
43:21
Ps 102:18
43:22
Mic 6:3
43:23
Exod 30:34
Mal 1:6-8
43:24
Jer 6:20
Mal 2:17
43:25
Isa 55:7
Jer 31:34
Ezek 36:22
43:26
Isa 1:18; 43:9
43:28
Lam 2:2, 6
Ezek 5:15
[j]*kherem* (2764)
‣Mal 4:6
44:1
Jer 30:10
44:2
Deut 32:15

11 I, yes I, am the LORD,
and there is no other Savior.
12 First I predicted your rescue,
then I [g]saved you and proclaimed it to the world.
No foreign god has ever done this.
You are witnesses that I am the only God,"
says the LORD.
13 "From eternity to eternity I am God.
No one can snatch anyone out of my hand.
No one can undo what I have done."

The LORD's Promise of Victory

14 This is what the LORD says—your Redeemer, the Holy One of Israel:

"For your sakes I will send an army
against Babylon,
forcing the Babylonians to flee in
those ships they are so proud of.
15 I am the LORD, your Holy One,
Israel's [h]Creator and [i]King.
16 I am the LORD, who opened a way
through the waters,
making a dry path through the sea.
17 I called forth the mighty army of Egypt
with all its chariots and horses.
I drew them beneath the waves, and they drowned,
their lives snuffed out like a
smoldering candlewick.
18 "But forget all that—
it is nothing compared to what I am going to do.
19 For I am about to do something new.
See, I have already begun! Do you not see it?
I will make a pathway through the wilderness.
I will create rivers in the dry
wasteland.
20 The wild animals in the fields will
thank me,
the jackals and owls, too,
for giving them water in the desert.
Yes, I will make rivers in the dry
wasteland
so my chosen people can be refreshed.
21 I have made Israel for myself,
and they will someday honor me
before the whole world.
22 "But, dear family of Jacob, you refuse to
ask for my help.
You have grown tired of me, O Israel!
23 You have not brought me sheep or goats
for burnt offerings.
You have not honored me with
sacrifices,
though I have not burdened and wearied you
with requests for grain offerings and
frankincense.
24 You have not brought me fragrant
calamus
or pleased me with the fat from
sacrifices.
Instead, you have burdened me with
your sins
and wearied me with your faults.
25 "I—yes, I alone—will blot out your sins
for my own sake
and will never think of them again.
26 Let us review the situation together,
and you can present your case to
prove your innocence.
27 From the very beginning, your first
ancestor sinned against me;
all your leaders broke my laws.
28 That is why I have disgraced your priests;
I have decreed complete [j]destruction
for Jacob
and shame for Israel.

44

1 "But now, listen to me, Jacob my servant,
Israel my chosen one.
2 The LORD who made you and helps you
says:
Do not be afraid, O Jacob, my servant,
O dear Israel, my chosen one.

43:14-21 The Lord assured Israel of its coming redemption from Babylon; the redemption would be modeled on Israel's past redemption from Egypt and would be greater in some ways (43:18).

43:14 ***Babylonians:*** Or *Chaldeans.*

43:18 God did not want the Israelites to ***forget*** the exodus from Egypt. However, they needed to look forward in faith to the spectacular event that was about to occur rather than dwelling on the past.

43:21 One purpose of redemption is to ***honor*** God through the praises of the redeemed (see 1 Pet 2:9).

43:22 Israel's history of rebellion had led them into crisis after crisis, yet their rebellion was so great that they stubbornly refused ***to ask*** God for ***help.*** When they did pray, their wickedness often caused their prayers not to be heard (1:15).

43:25 God ***alone*** can and does ***blot out . . . sins,*** no matter how many or how great (see also 44:22).

43:27 ***leaders:*** God held Israel's and Judah's kings especially responsible for leading the nation into sin (see 2 Kgs 21).

43:28 ***complete destruction:*** The Hebrew term used here refers to the complete consecration of things or people to the LORD, either by destroying them or by giving them as an offering.

44:1-5 The promise of salvation extended the usefulness of sinful Israel to another generation (44:3). The past was bleak (see 43:22-28), but the future would be a glorious new era transformed by the Spirit.

44:2 ***Israel:*** Hebrew *Jeshurun,* a term of endearment for Israel.

3 For I will pour out water to quench your thirst
and to irrigate your parched fields.
And I will pour out my Spirit on your descendants,
and my blessing on your children.
4 They will thrive like watered grass,
like willows on a riverbank.
5 Some will proudly claim, 'I belong to the LORD.'
Others will say, 'I am a descendant of Jacob.'
Some will write the LORD's name on their hands
and will take the name of Israel as their own."

The Foolishness of Idols

6 This is what the LORD says—Israel's King and [k]Redeemer, the LORD of Heaven's Armies:

"I am the First and the Last;
there is no other God.
7 Who is like me?
Let him step forward and prove to you his power.
Let him do as I have done since ancient times
when I established a people and explained its future.
8 Do not tremble; do not be afraid.
Did I not proclaim my purposes for you long ago?
You are my witnesses—is there any other God?
No! There is no other Rock—not one!"

9 How foolish are those who manufacture idols.
These prized objects are really worthless.
The people who worship idols don't know this,
so they are all put to shame.
10 Who but a fool would make his own god—
an idol that cannot help him one bit?
11 All who worship idols will be disgraced
along with all these craftsmen—mere humans—
who claim they can make a god.
They may all stand together,
but they will stand in terror and shame.

12 The blacksmith stands at his forge to make a sharp tool,
pounding and shaping it with all his might.
His work makes him hungry and weak.
It makes him thirsty and faint.
13 Then the wood-carver measures a block of wood
and draws a pattern on it.
He works with chisel and plane
and carves it into a human figure.
He gives it human beauty
and puts it in a little shrine.
14 He cuts down cedars;
he selects the cypress and the oak;
he plants the pine in the forest
to be nourished by the rain.
15 Then he uses part of the wood to make a fire.
With it he warms himself and bakes his bread.
Then—yes, it's true—he takes the rest of it
and makes himself a god to worship!
He makes an idol
and bows down in front of it!
16 He burns part of the tree to roast his meat
and to keep himself warm.
He says, "Ah, that fire feels good."
17 Then he takes what's left
and makes his god: a carved idol!
He falls down in front of it,
worshiping and praying to it.
"Rescue me!" he says.
"You are my god!"

18 Such stupidity and ignorance!
Their eyes are closed, and they cannot see.
Their minds are shut, and they cannot think.
19 The person who made the idol never stops to reflect,
"Why, it's just a block of wood!
I burned half of it for heat
and used it to bake my bread and roast my meat.

44:3 Isa 61:9; Joel 2:28
44:6 Isa 41:21; 45:5-6, 21; Rev 1:8, 17; [k]*go'el* (1350) ‣Isa 44:24
44:7 Isa 41:22
44:8 Deut 4:35, 39; Isa 30:29
44:9 Ps 97:7
44:10 Jer 10:5; Hab 2:18; Acts 19:26
44:12 Isa 40:19; 41:7
44:13 Ps 115:5-7; Isa 41:7
44:15 2 Chr 25:14
44:17 1 Kgs 18:26, 28; Isa 45:20
44:18 Ps 81:12; Isa 6:9-10; 29:10; Jer 10:8, 14
44:19 Deut 27:15

44:3 The restoration theme is connected with God's promise to *pour out* the *Spirit* (see also 32:15-17; Joel 2:28-32; Acts 2:16-18). • ***on your descendants . . . children:*** The next generation of Israelites offered hope.

44:6-20 This passage uses the form of a trial speech to press God's argument that disgrace comes to all who trust in idols and false gods.

44:15-17 ***he uses part of the wood to make a fire . . . he takes the rest of it and makes himself a god to worship:*** This description of the process of making an idol drips with sarcasm and ridicule at the stupidity of the foolish idol worshipers (see also 44:19).

44:18-19 ***Their minds are shut:*** Idol worshipers cannot see the irony in using one part of a log to warm themselves and another part of the same log to be their god.

44:20
Ps 102:9
Hos 4:12
44:21
Isa 44:1-2; 46:8; 49:15
44:22
Ps 51:1, 9
Isa 55:7
Acts 3:19
1 Pet 1:18-19
44:23
Ps 69:34; 98:7-8
44:24
Isa 40:22
[a]*go'el* (1350)
‣Isa 54:5
44:25
1 Cor 1:20, 27
44:26
Jer 32:15, 44
44:27
Isa 50:2
44:28
2 Chr 36:22-23
Isa 14:32
45:1
Ps 73:23
Jer 51:11, 20, 24
45:2
Ps 107:16
Isa 40:4
Jer 51:30
45:3
Isa 49:1
45:4
Isa 43:1
Acts 17:23
45:5
Ps 18:39
Isa 44:8
45:6
Mal 1:11

How can the rest of it be a god?
Should I bow down to worship a piece of wood?"
20 The poor, deluded fool feeds on ashes.
He trusts something that can't help him at all.
Yet he cannot bring himself to ask,
"Is this idol that I'm holding in my hand a lie?"

Restoration for Jerusalem

21 "Pay attention, O Jacob,
for you are my servant, O Israel.
I, the LORD, made you,
and I will not forget you.
22 I have swept away your sins like a cloud.
I have scattered your offenses like the morning mist.
Oh, return to me,
for I have paid the price to set you free."

23 Sing, O heavens, for the LORD has done this wondrous thing.
Shout for joy, O depths of the earth!
Break into song,
O mountains and forests and every tree!
For the LORD has redeemed Jacob
and is glorified in Israel.

24 This is what the LORD says—
your [a]Redeemer and Creator:
"I am the LORD, who made all things.
I alone stretched out the heavens.
Who was with me
when I made the earth?
25 I expose the false prophets as liars
and make fools of fortune-tellers.
I cause the wise to give bad advice,
thus proving them to be fools.
26 But I carry out the predictions of my prophets!
By them I say to Jerusalem, 'People will live here again,'
and to the towns of Judah, 'You will be rebuilt;
I will restore all your ruins!'
27 When I speak to the rivers and say, 'Dry up!'
they will be dry.
28 When I say of Cyrus, 'He is my shepherd,'
he will certainly do as I say.
He will command, 'Rebuild Jerusalem';
he will say, 'Restore the Temple.' "

Cyrus, the LORD's Chosen One

45 1 This is what the LORD says to Cyrus, his anointed one,
whose right hand he will empower.
Before him, mighty kings will be paralyzed with fear.
Their fortress gates will be opened,
never to shut again.
2 This is what the LORD says:

"I will go before you, Cyrus,
and level the mountains.
I will smash down gates of bronze
and cut through bars of iron.
3 And I will give you treasures hidden in the darkness—
secret riches.
I will do this so you may know that I am the LORD,
the God of Israel, the one who calls you by name.

4 "And why have I called you for this work?
Why did I call you by name when you did not know me?
It is for the sake of Jacob my servant,
Israel my chosen one.
5 I am the LORD;
there is no other God.
I have equipped you for battle,
though you don't even know me,
6 so all the world from east to west
will know there is no other God.
I am the LORD, and there is no other.

44:21-22 The Lord promised to forgive Israel's sins.

44:23 All creation is called to celebrate God's redemption of Israel (cp. 1:2).

44:24–45:8 The Lord alone is sovereign over history. He raised up Cyrus of Persia to execute judgment on Babylon and restore Israel to the Holy Land.

44:25 ***False prophets*** and ***fortune-tellers*** used forbidden forms of divination to try to predict the future. Eventually God would expose them as deluded liars (see 3:2; 9:15; 47:13; Deut 18:10-11).

44:27 The sudden depletion of natural resources at times indicates a divine judgment (see 42:15; cp. 43:20). Here, however, God's ability to ***dry up*** streams with just a word illustrates his power to do what he said he would do through Cyrus of Persia.

44:28 ***He is my shepherd:*** Cyrus went beyond simply permitting the Jews to return to their homeland. He facilitated a major restoration project to ***rebuild Jerusalem*** and ***restore the Temple*** (see 45:13; Ezra 1:2-4; 6:3-5).

45:1 ***anointed one:*** This designation, commonly reserved for David or the Messiah, is here applied to Cyrus. Cyrus was anointed in the sense that he was selected to fulfill a special mission. This title was never used of any other foreign ruler (cp. 1 Sam 10:1; Rom 13:1). • ***whose right hand he will empower:*** The Lord would give Cyrus victory over Babylon (see 43:14).

45:2 ***the mountains:*** As in Dead Sea Scrolls and Greek version; Masoretic Text reads *the swellings.*

45:3 ***so you may know:*** Cyrus's victories provided factual proof that the Lord has the power to fulfill his plans, whereas idols and false gods do not (see 41:21-29).

45:4-5 ***I call you by name:*** Cyrus did not ***know*** the Lord, but the Lord knew him. Isaiah predicted the rescuer Cyrus by name 150 years in advance. This prophecy would prove to the exiles that the Lord is indeed God and that he knows the future.

7 I create the light and make the
darkness.
I send good times and bad times.
I, the LORD, am the one who does
these things.
8 "Open up, O heavens,
and pour out your [b]righteousness.
Let the earth open wide
so salvation and righteousness can
sprout up together.
I, the LORD, created them.

9 "What sorrow awaits those who argue
with their Creator.
Does a clay pot argue with its maker?
Does the clay dispute with the one who
shapes it, saying,
'Stop, you're doing it wrong!'
Does the pot exclaim,
'How clumsy can you be?'
10 How terrible it would be if a newborn
baby said to its father,
'Why was I born?'
or if it said to its mother,
'Why did you make me this way?' "

11 This is what the LORD says—
the Holy One of Israel and your
Creator:
"Do you question what I do for my
children?
Do you give me orders about the work
of my hands?
12 I am the one who made the earth
and created people to live on it.
With my hands I stretched out the
heavens.
All the stars are at my command.
13 I will raise up Cyrus to fulfill my
righteous purpose,
and I will guide his actions.
He will restore my city and free my
captive people—
without seeking a reward!
I, the LORD of Heaven's Armies, have
spoken!"

Future Conversion of Gentiles

14 This is what the LORD says:

"You will rule the Egyptians,
the Ethiopians, and the Sabeans.
They will come to you with all their
merchandise,
and it will all be yours.
They will follow you as prisoners in
chains.
They will fall to their knees in front of
you and say,
'God is with you, and he is the only God.
There is no other.' "

15 Truly, O God of Israel, our Savior,
you work in mysterious ways.
16 All craftsmen who make idols will be
humiliated.
They will all be disgraced together.
17 But the LORD will save the people of Israel
with [c]eternal salvation.
Throughout [c]everlasting ages,
they will never again be humiliated
and disgraced.

18 For the LORD is God,
and he created the heavens and earth
and put everything in place.
He made the world to be lived in,
not to be a place of empty chaos.
"I am the LORD," he says,
"and there is no other.
19 I publicly proclaim bold promises.
I do not whisper obscurities in some
dark corner.
I would not have told the people of Israel
to seek me
if I could not be found.
I, the LORD, speak only what is true
and declare only what is right.

20 "Gather together and come,
you fugitives from surrounding
nations.
What fools they are who carry around
their wooden idols
and [d]pray to gods that cannot [e]save!

45:7
Ps 104:20
Amos 3:6

45:8
Ps 72:6; 85:11
Isa 61:11
[b]*tsedeq* (6664)
▸Isa 62:2

45:9
Rom 9:20-21

45:12
Neh 9:6
Jer 27:5

45:13
2 Chr 36:22-23
Isa 52:3

45:14
Isa 14:1-2; 49:23
1 Cor 14:25

45:16
Isa 44:11

45:17
Isa 51:6
Rom 11:26
[c]*'olam* (5769)
▸Isa 51:11

45:18
Gen 1:2, 26
Ps 115:16
Isa 42:5

45:19
2 Chr 15:2
Isa 43:12
Jer 29:13-14

45:20
Isa 44:18-19; 46:6-7
Jer 10:5
[d]*palal* (6419)
▸Jer 32:16
[e]*yasha'* (3467)
▸Isa 45:22

45:7 ***light . . . darkness . . . good times and bad times:*** Everything is under God's control.

45:9-13 The Lord confronts those who question his right to use a pagan king to achieve his purposes. He, the Creator, is free and sovereign in his activities. He promised to bring his people back to their land, and he would use anyone he chose to accomplish that purpose.

45:9-11 ***pot . . . its maker . . . baby . . . its father:*** It is ridiculous for a creature to question the wisdom of its creator.

45:14 ***Egyptians . . . Ethiopians*** (Hebrew *Cushites*) *. . .* ***Sabeans:*** Israel's restoration would bring them a new sovereignty. Foreign nations would honor God, and because they recognized God's special blessing on his people, they would also want to honor his people.

45:17 Israel would never again be ***humiliated and disgraced,*** oppressed, harassed, or abused. The finality of these declarations suggests that this promise will be fulfilled at the end of time.

45:18-25 Salvation is from the Lord alone. He is the creator, the revealer, and the executor of his will in human history. He promised to establish a new era of salvation and righteousness (see 45:8). Every human being will submit to God, either willingly or unwillingly (45:23-24).

45:18 Ancient pagan people viewed the world as ***a place of empty chaos.*** However, God's purposes are good, and he made the world from the beginning as a place to be ***lived in*** with him in harmony.

45:19 ***of Israel:*** Literally *of Jacob.* See note on 14:1.

21 Consult together, argue your case.
Get together and decide what to say.
Who made these things known so long ago?
What idol ever told you they would happen?
Was it not I, the LORD?
For there is no other God but me,
a righteous God and Savior.
There is none but me.
22 Let all the world look to me for [f]salvation!
For I am God; there is no other.
23 I have sworn by my own name;
I have spoken the truth,
and I will never go back on my word:
Every knee will bend to me,
and every tongue will confess allegiance to me."
24 The people will declare,
"The LORD is the source of all my righteousness and strength."
And all who were angry with him
will come to him and be ashamed.
25 In the LORD all the generations of Israel will be justified,
and in him they will boast.

Babylon's False Gods

46 1 Bel and Nebo, the gods of Babylon,
bow as they are lowered to the ground.
They are being hauled away on ox carts.
The poor beasts stagger under the weight.
2 Both the idols and their owners are bowed down.
The gods cannot protect the people,
and the people cannot protect the gods.
They go off into captivity together.

3 "Listen to me, descendants of Jacob,
all you who remain in Israel.
I have cared for you since you were born.
Yes, I carried you before you were born.
4 I will be your God throughout your lifetime—
until your hair is white with age.
I made you, and I will care for you.
I will carry you along and save you.

5 "To whom will you compare me?
Who is my equal?
6 Some people pour out their silver and gold
and hire a craftsman to make a god from it.
Then they bow down and [g]worship it!
7 They carry it around on their shoulders,
and when they set it down, it stays there.
It can't even move!
And when someone prays to it, there is no answer.
It can't rescue anyone from trouble.

8 "Do not forget this! Keep it in mind!
Remember this, you guilty ones.
9 Remember the things I have done in the past.
For I alone am God!
I am God, and there is none like me.
10 Only I can tell you the future
before it even happens.
Everything I plan will come to pass,
for I do whatever I wish.
11 I will call a swift bird of prey from the east—
a leader from a distant land to come and do my bidding.
I have said what I would do,
and I will do it.

45:21 Isa 43:3, 11; 44:7; Mark 12:32
45:22 Num 21:8-9; Isa 52:10; Mic 7:7; ᶠ*yasha'* (3467) ›Isa 51:8
45:23 *Rom 14:11; Phil 2:10-11
45:25 Isa 53:11
46:1 Isa 21:9; Jer 50:2; 51:44
46:2 Jer 43:12-13
46:3 Isa 10:21-22
46:4 Ps 71:18
46:5 Isa 40:18, 25
46:6 Isa 44:12-17; ᵍ*khawah* (7812) ›Isa 66:23
46:7 Isa 40:20; Jer 10:5
46:10 Isa 41:26-27; 42:9; Acts 5:39
46:11 Num 23:19

45:22 ***Let all the world look to me:*** All humanity needs to seek the Lord, the true God who created all things, while he may be found (55:6). • In God there is ***salvation***, the only hope for all of humanity (45:8).

45:23 God's words are always true. God's swearing by his ***own name*** reinforces the certainty that he will ***never go back on*** his ***word*** (see also 14:24; 54:9; 62:8; Heb 6:13). • ***Every knee . . . every tongue:*** At the end of time all nations will submit to his authority, whether willingly or unwillingly (see Rom 14:11; 1 Cor 15:25-27; Phil 2:10-11). • ***will confess allegiance to me:*** Literally *will confess;* Greek version reads *will confess and give praise to God.* Cp. Rom 14:11.

45:24 In this context, ***the people*** are all who turn to the Lord for salvation, even those from foreign nations (45:22).

45:25 ***justified:*** Literally *righteous* (see also 45:8, 24).

46:1-2 This taunt was against the self-contradiction of Babylonian religion (see note on 14:4).

46:1 ***Marduk-bel*** was the most important god in the Babylonian pantheon. ***Bel*** (similar to "Baal") designated lordship. • ***Nebo*** (*Nabu, Nebu*), the patron deity of Babylonian scribes, was thought to be the son of Marduk-bel. • Instead of being paraded in glory at a Babylonian festival, these gods would be ***hauled away on ox carts*** and disposed of, rejected by the Babylonian people.

46:3 Those ***who remain in Israel*** referred to the remnant that would be left alive after the destruction of Jerusalem in 586 BC. • The Lord, the Creator of humanity, cares for and carries his people (contrast the Babylonian idols that must be ***carried*** instead). • ***since you were born . . . before you were born:*** The Lord chose Israel even before they were a nation (see also 49:5).

46:8-13 Many of the exiles would be completely discouraged and not believe the prediction of God's rescue. God challenged this unbelief.

46:10 God knows ***the future before it even happens;*** he has comprehensive control over all events, and all his acts match his words (41:4, 26). He is the First and the Last (44:6; 48:12).

46:11 The ***swift bird of prey from the east*** refers to Cyrus, the Persian king (see note on 41:2).

12 "Listen to me, you stubborn people
who are so far from doing right.
13 For I am ready to set things right,
not in the distant future, but right now!
I am ready to save Jerusalem
and show my glory to Israel.

Prediction of Babylon's Fall

47 1 "Come down, virgin daughter of
Babylon, and sit in the dust.
For your days of sitting on a throne
have ended.
O daughter of Babylonia, never again
will you be
the lovely princess, tender and delicate.
2 Take heavy millstones and grind flour.
Remove your veil, and strip off your
robe.
Expose yourself to public view.
3 You will be naked and burdened with
shame.
I will take vengeance against you
without pity."
4 Our Redeemer, whose name is the LORD
of Heaven's Armies,
is the Holy One of Israel.
5 "O beautiful Babylon, sit now in
darkness and silence.
Never again will you be known as the
queen of kingdoms.
6 For I was angry with my chosen people
and punished them by letting them
fall into your hands.
But you, Babylon, showed them no mercy.
You oppressed even the elderly.
7 You said, 'I will reign forever as queen of
the world!'
You did not reflect on your actions
or think about their consequences.
8 "Listen to this, you pleasure-loving
kingdom,
living at ease and feeling secure.
You say, 'I am the only one, and there is
no other.
I will never be a widow or lose my
children.'
9 Well, both these things will come upon
you in a moment:
widowhood and the loss of your
children.
Yes, these calamities will come upon you,
despite all your witchcraft and magic.
10 "You felt secure in your wickedness.
'No one sees me,' you said.
But your 'wisdom' and 'knowledge' have
led you astray,
and you said, 'I am the only one, and
there is no other.'
11 So disaster will overtake you,
and you won't be able to charm it away.
Calamity will fall upon you,
and you won't be able to buy your way
out.
A catastrophe will strike you suddenly,
one for which you are not prepared.
12 "Now use your magical charms!
Use the spells you have worked at all
these years!
Maybe they will do you some good.
Maybe they can make someone afraid
of you.
13 All the advice you receive has made you
tired.
Where are all your astrologers,
those stargazers who make predictions
each month?
Let them stand up and save you from
what the future holds.

46:12 Zech 7:11-12
46:13 Isa 51:5; 61:3
47:1 Jer 48:18
47:2 Gen 24:65; 1 Cor 11:5
47:3 Isa 63:4
47:5 Lam 2:10; Dan 2:37
47:6 Deut 28:50; Zech 1:15
47:7 Rev 18:7
47:8 Isa 22:13; 32:9, 11; Rev 18:7
47:9 Isa 13:16; 1 Thes 5:2-3; Rev 18:8, 10, 23
47:10 Ps 52:7; Isa 5:21; Ezek 8:12
47:11 Jer 51:8, 43
47:13 Isa 8:19

46:12 Formerly, Israel cared little for *doing right* (literally *righteousness;* see also 58:2; 59:9).

46:13 The good news for Israel was that God was coming to ***set things right*** (literally *I will bring my righteousness near;* see 40:9; 51:5). • ***Jerusalem:*** Hebrew *Zion.* • ***show my glory to Israel:*** Unlike a craftsman who bestows material splendor on an idol (44:13), the Lord bestows true dignity on his people.

47:1–48:22 Two conclusions can be drawn from the preceding evidence that the Lord alone is God: (1) Babylon's great pride is foolishness (47:1-15); (2) Israel needs to pay attention to the word of the Lord (48:1-22).

47:1-4 In this taunt against Babylon, the queen of nations is humiliated, forced to work as a servant girl.

47:1 To ***sit in the dust*** was a way of expressing humiliation. • ***Babylonia:*** or *Chaldea;* also in 47:5.

47:3 God's ***vengeance*** against those who oppose him and those who oppress his people (see 34:8) will bring justice to the world by purging it of wickedness.

47:5-11 Babylon's confidence and arrogance were well known (see 14:13-17; see Dan 4:30). All of this nation's charms, magic, and wisdom were useless against the disaster decreed for it.

47:6 The people of Israel had provoked God's wrath, prompting him to use Babylon to punish them. Now wicked Babylon itself would be punished.

47:8 ***I am the only one, and there is no other:*** This was a claim to divinity (cp. 45:5; 47:10). Only the Lord can make such a claim. For any created thing, including a nation, to utter this is the height of hubris. • To be a ***widow or*** to ***lose*** one's ***children*** was a disgrace.

47:9 ***Witchcraft and magic*** were commonly used in an attempt to ward off evil and to secure a happy future.

47:10 In this context, ***'wisdom'*** and ***'knowledge'*** probably refer sarcastically to the pseudo-knowledge gained through occult practices, which actually *led* Babylon away from the truth and into disaster (47:11).

47:12-15 In the face of calamity, Babylon would turn to occult practices for help, but it would not find help.

47:13 Babylon was advanced in astronomy, which the ***astrologers*** and ***stargazers*** used as a form of divination (see Dan 2:2, 10; 5:7).

47:14 Jer 51:30, 32, 58; Nah 1:10
47:15 Rev 18:11
48:1 Isa 45:23
48:2 Rom 2:17
48:3 Josh 21:45; Isa 42:9
48:4 Ezek 2:4
48:5 Jer 44:15-18
48:6 Isa 43:19
48:8 Deut 9:7, 24; Ps 58:3
48:9 Ps 103:8-10
48:10 1 Kgs 8:51; Ezek 22:18-22
48:11 Deut 32:26-27; Ps 106:8; Isa 42:8
48:12 Deut 32:39; Rev 1:17
48:13 Ps 102:25
48:14 Jer 50:21-29
48:15 Isa 41:2; 45:1-2

14 But they are like straw burning in a fire;
they cannot save themselves from the flame.
You will get no help from them at all;
their hearth is no place to sit for warmth.
15 And all your friends,
those with whom you've done business since childhood,
will go their own ways,
turning a deaf ear to your cries.

God's Stubborn People: A Call to Respond

48 1 "Listen to me, O family of Jacob,
you who are called by the name of Israel
and born into the family of Judah.
Listen, you who take oaths in the name of the LORD
and call on the God of Israel.
You don't keep your promises,
2 even though you call yourself the holy city
and talk about depending on the God of Israel,
whose name is the LORD of Heaven's Armies.
3 Long ago I told you what was going to happen.
Then suddenly I took action,
and all my predictions came true.
4 For I know how stubborn and obstinate you are.
Your necks are as unbending as iron.
Your heads are as hard as bronze.
5 That is why I told you what would happen;
I told you beforehand what I was going to do.
Then you could never say, 'My idols did it.
My wooden image and metal god commanded it to happen!'
6 You have heard my predictions and seen them fulfilled,
but you refuse to admit it.
Now I will tell you new things,
secrets you have not yet heard.
7 They are brand new, not things from the past.
So you cannot say, 'We knew that all the time!'
8 "Yes, I will tell you of things that are entirely new,
things you never heard of before.
For I know so well what traitors you are.
You have been rebels from birth.
9 Yet for my own sake and for the honor of my name,
I will hold back my anger and not wipe you out.
10 I have refined you, but not as silver is refined.
Rather, I have refined you in the furnace of suffering.
11 I will rescue you for my sake—
yes, for my own sake!
I will not let my reputation be tarnished,
and I will not share my glory with idols!

Freedom from Babylon

12 "Listen to me, O family of Jacob,
Israel my chosen one!
I alone am God,
the First and the Last.
13 It was my hand that laid the foundations of the earth,
my right hand that spread out the heavens above.
When I call out the stars,
they all appear in order."

14 Have any of your idols ever told you this?
Come, all of you, and listen:
The LORD has chosen Cyrus as his ally.
He will use him to put an end to the empire of Babylon
and to destroy the Babylonian armies.

15 "I have said it: I am calling Cyrus!
I will send him on this errand and will help him succeed.

48:1-22 The Lord here calls on Israel to forsake her historic rebelliousness and listen to what he says. The Hebrew word translated *listening* is often synonymous with *obeying* or acting upon what is heard.

48:1-11 This prophecy is a *disputation,* a speech in which the prophet argues a set of points against his audience.

48:1-2 Israel was religious but not truly committed to the Lord.

48:1 ***Jacob . . . Judah:*** Although Isaiah's normal focus was on Judah, here he addressed all the tribes of Israel.

48:3 The Lord had forewarned Israel of *what was going to happen* in the Exile.

48:6-7 Even though Israel had repeatedly failed to believe God's past predictions, here he revealed *new things* that were *not yet heard.* Specifically, God revealed that Babylon would fall and Israel would be restored.

48:10 The Exile was a *furnace of suffering* (cp. Deut 4:20) through which God *refined* Israel.

48:11 ***I will not let my reputation be tarnished:*** Israel's exile raised questions among the nations about the Lord's character and reputation. The nations would not have perceived that Israel's wicked character led to the Exile. Instead they would have viewed it as a failure of Israel's God to protect his people and their land (see 36:19-20; 37:12; Ezek 36:19-26).

48:12-22 This final trial speech reviews the arguments of chs 40–48 and announces the final conclusion.

48:14 ***chosen Cyrus*** (literally *him*) ***as his ally:*** See 44:28; 45:1-2. • ***Babylonian:*** Or *Chaldean.*

48:15 ***I will send him*** and ***will help him succeed:*** Cyrus would humiliate Babylon and liberate Israel (45:1-4).

16 Come closer, and listen to this.
From the beginning I have told you
plainly what would happen."

And now the Sovereign LORD and his
Spirit
have sent me with this message.
17 This is what the LORD says—
your Redeemer, the Holy One of Israel:
"I am the LORD your God,
who teaches you what is good for you
and leads you along the paths you
should follow.
18 Oh, that you had listened to my
commands!
Then you would have had peace
flowing like a gentle river
and righteousness rolling over you
like waves in the sea.
19 Your descendants would have been like
the sands along the seashore—
too many to count!
There would have been no need for your
destruction,
or for cutting off your family name."

20 Yet even now, be free from your captivity!
Leave Babylon and the Babylonians.
Sing out this message!
Shout it to the ends of the earth!
The LORD has redeemed his servants,
the people of Israel.
21 They were not thirsty
when he led them through the desert.
He divided the rock,
and water gushed out for them to
drink.
22 "But there is no peace for the wicked,"
says the LORD.

The Servant of the LORD (49:1–55:13)

The LORD's Servant Commissioned

49 1 Listen to me, all you in distant
lands!
Pay attention, you who are far away!
The LORD called me before my birth;
from within the womb he called me
by name.
2 He made my words of judgment as sharp
as a sword.
He has hidden me in the shadow of
his hand.
I am like a sharp arrow in his quiver.
3 He said to me, "You are my servant,
Israel,
and you will bring me glory."
4 I replied, "But my work seems so
useless!
I have spent my strength for nothing
and to [h]no purpose.
Yet I leave it all in the LORD's hand;
I will trust God for my reward."

48:16 Isa 45:19
48:17 Ps 32:8; Isa 41:14
48:18 Deut 5:29; 32:29; Ps 119:165; Amos 5:24
48:19 Gen 22:17
48:20 Isa 52:9; Jer 31:10-11
48:21 Ps 78:15-16
49:2 Isa 51:16; Heb 4:12; Rev 1:16
49:4 [h]*hebel* (1892) ‣Jon 2:8

48:16 ***I have told you plainly:*** God's promises are clear, though not always specific as to manner and time. • ***now the Sovereign LORD and his Spirit have sent me with this message:*** The identity of the one who is sent is unclear. Isaiah might be referring to himself as a Spirit-inspired prophet who spoke the very words of God to Israel. The connection with the Spirit suggests that it refers to the promised servant, the Messiah. • The presence of the Spirit assures the servant's success.

48:18 ***Peace*** and ***righteousness*** will be established when the kingdom of God comes in its fullness (see 66:12). • ***like a gentle river . . . like waves:*** An abundance of comforting peace and overflowing resources of righteousness (cp. Amos 5:24) could have been Israel's if its people had only listened to God.

48:19 ***Your descendants . . . like the sands:*** This would fulfill God's covenant to Abraham (Gen 22:17); by contrast, the Israelites were nearly wiped out in the Exile (see 44:26).

48:20 ***Leave Babylon:*** See also 52:11-12; 55:12. • ***the Babylonians:*** Or *the Chaldeans.* • ***the people of Israel:*** Literally *his servant, Jacob.* See note on 14:1.

48:21 ***not thirsty . . . rock . . . water gushed:*** These reminders of God's provision in the Exodus provide a fitting summary of what he would do to rescue Israel from captivity in Babylon (see Num 20:11).

48:22 This refrain, ***no peace for the wicked*** (also 57:21), continues the sharp divide between the godly and the wicked (see 66:24). Peace speaks of God's kingdom, from which the wicked are excluded.

49:1–55:13 God intended to rescue the Israelites from exile. However, the question remained: How could sinful Israel again become the servant of the Holy One? God would make a way for Israel's sin to be atoned and for their fellowship with him to be restored. That way would be the promised servant, who would come for Israel and for all peoples. This servant was introduced in 42:1-9, but in this passage he becomes the central focus.

49:1-13 This has traditionally been regarded as the second of four suffering servant songs (see note on 42:1-4). The suffering role of the promised servant becomes increasingly clear (see also 50:4-9; 52:13–53:12).

49:1 ***distant lands:*** The servant's ministry would extend beyond Israel (see 42:4, 10, 12; 51:5; 60:9; 66:19). • ***called me before my birth . . . from within the womb . . by name:*** The promised servant's prophetic call was similar to the call of Jeremiah (see Jer 1:5; see also Gal 1:15). It was not a general call but a very specific, personal one (see also 43:1; 45:3-4).

49:2 ***my words of judgment:*** The servant's mission would be prophetic (see 11:4; Eph 6:17; Heb 4:12; Rev 1:16; 2:12, 16; 19:15).

49:3 The suffering ***servant*** would come out of ***Israel*** (see 41:8) and would himself be the true Israel. He would serve as both king (42:1) and prophet (49:1), anointed with the Spirit of God (61:1) and commissioned (48:16) as a faithful witness to God's purposes (43:12; 48:20). In his mission toward both Israel and the other nations (49:6), he would suffer rejection and disgrace while being faithful, unlike the nation of Israel (see 50:4-9). His suffering would be on behalf of God's chosen people. Jesus became the ultimate fulfillment of the suffering servant (see note on 52:13–53:12).

49:4 ***my work seems so useless . . . to no purpose:*** Even though people stubbornly refuse his message, the servant would reach out to them. • ***I will trust***

49:5 Isa 12:2
49:6 Ps 37:28; Acts 13:47; 26:23
49:7 Ps 22:6-8; Isa 53:3
49:8 Ps 69:13; Isa 44:26; 2 Cor 6:2
49:9 Isa 42:7; Luke 4:18
49:10 Ps 23:2; Rev 7:16; ʾrakham (7355) › Isa 49:13
49:11 Isa 40:4

5 And now the LORD speaks—
the one who formed me in my
mother's womb to be his servant,
who commissioned me to bring Israel
back to him.
The LORD has honored me,
and my God has given me strength.
6 He says, "You will do more than restore
the people of Israel to me.
I will make you a light to the Gentiles,
and you will bring my salvation to the
ends of the earth."
7 The LORD, the Redeemer
and Holy One of Israel,
says to the one who is despised and
rejected by the nations,
to the one who is the servant of rulers:
"Kings will stand at attention when you
pass by.
Princes will also bow low
because of the LORD, the faithful one,
the Holy One of Israel, who has
chosen you."

Promises of Israel's Restoration

8 This is what the LORD says:

"At just the right time, I will respond to
you.
On the day of salvation I will help
you.
I will protect you and give you to the
people
as my covenant with them.
Through you I will reestablish the land
of Israel
and assign it to its own people
again.
9 I will say to the prisoners, 'Come out in
freedom,'
and to those in darkness, 'Come into
the light.'
They will be my sheep, grazing in green
pastures
and on hills that were previously
bare.
10 They will neither hunger nor thirst.
The searing sun will not reach them
anymore.
For the LORD in his ʾmercy will lead
them;
he will lead them beside cool waters.
11 And I will make my mountains into level
paths for them.
The highways will be raised above the
valleys.

God's Servant (49:1-7)

Isa 41:8-10; 42:1-4, 19-20; 43:10; 44:1-5, 21-22; 52:7; 52:13–53:12; 61:1-3; Lev 25:42, 55; 1 Kgs 11:36; 2 Kgs 9:7; Ps 89:20-29; 113:1; Jer 30:10; 33:20-22, 26; 46:27-28; Ezek 28:25; 34:23-24; 37:24-25; Zech 3:8; Matt 12:15-21; Acts 2:18; 2 Tim 2:24

Isaiah deals with the theme of God's servant in chs 40–66. The servant proclaims the new order of justice and righteousness to the world (42:3-4). He serves as God's instrument to prepare the world for God's coming (52:7).

Who is the Lord's servant? Isaiah identifies the servant with Israel (41:8; 44:1-2), who serves as God's witness (43:10) and as a light to the Gentiles. Yet Israel could not fulfill this mission: Israel was deaf, blind (42:19), and in need of God's forgiveness (44:21-22). Israel failed again and again. By contrast, God's servant faithfully witnesses, proclaims, and waits for the coming redemption (61:1-3; 62:1-5). He represents the godly in Israel. Isaiah portrays him as an obedient individual who suffers. The servant is God's faithful witness to humanity and stands in opposition to the idolatrous practices of paganism.

One Israelite in particular was perfectly faithful and suffered on behalf of others: Jesus Christ fulfilled the role of the righteous servant. By his suffering, God's benefits came to many, including other nations (see Acts 26:23). In union and fellowship with him, the apostles ministered as servants of Jesus Christ to both Jews and Gentiles (Acts 13:47; 26:17).

Though Israel first received the message of the servant, this message is still relevant for all who have faith in Jesus Christ. They share in the mission of the servant and fulfill the role of God's servants in the world (e.g., Rom 14:4; Col 1:7; 4:12; 1 Tim 4:6; 2 Tim 2:24).

God: Despite discouragement and suffering, the servant would continue to discharge his duty faithfully, trusting God for the outcome. God promised to ***reward*** the servant's faithfulness (see also 40:10; 50:8).

49:6 ***a light to the Gentiles:*** As the Messiah, the servant's mission would have a worldwide reach (see 11:10, 12; 42:6). The apostle Paul explained his apostolic mission to the Gentiles on the basis of this prophecy (Acts 13:47; 26:23).

49:7 The promised servant would be ***despised and rejected by the nations*** (see 52:14–53:5) as well as by his own people (see also 50:6-7; 53:8-9). • ***Kings*** and ***princes will bow low*** to express respect and humility before the servant (see also 52:15), whom God will exalt after he has suffered. God is ***faithful*** to his servant.

49:8 God acts at ***just the right time*** to accomplish his purposes (Acts 1:7; 2 Cor 6:2). Israel returned to ***reestablish the land of Israel*** after the Exile. The land was restored and the city rebuilt beginning with Cyrus's edict (44:26-28). • ***I will respond to you:*** Greek version reads *I heard you.* Cp. 2 Cor 6:2.

49:10-11 Like a shepherd, the Lord in his ***mercy will lead*** the returning exiles ***beside cool waters;*** he promised to comfort them and tend to their needs (see also 40:11; Ps 23:1). • ***level paths . . . highways:*** The Lord would open up the way of salvation.

12 See, my people will return from far away,
from lands to the north and west,
and from as far south as Egypt."
13 Sing for joy, O heavens!
Rejoice, O earth!
Burst into song, O mountains!
For the LORD has comforted his people
and will have ᶦcompassion on them in their suffering.
14 Yet Jerusalem says, "The LORD has deserted us;
the Lord has forgotten us."
15 "Never! Can a mother forget her nursing child?
Can she feel no love for the child she has borne?
But even if that were possible,
I would not forget you!
16 See, I have written your name on the palms of my hands.
Always in my mind is a picture of Jerusalem's walls in ruins.
17 Soon your descendants will come back,
and all who are trying to destroy you will go away.
18 Look around you and see,
for all your children will come back to you.
As surely as I live," says the LORD,
"they will be like jewels or bridal ornaments for you to display.
19 "Even the most desolate parts of your abandoned land
will soon be crowded with your people.
Your enemies who enslaved you
will be far away.
20 The generations born in exile will return and say,
'We need more room! It's crowded here!'
21 Then you will think to yourself,
'Who has given me all these descendants?
For most of my children were killed,
and the rest were carried away into exile.
I was left here all alone.
Where did all these people come from?
Who bore these children?
Who raised them for me?'"
22 This is what the Sovereign LORD says:
"See, I will give a signal to the godless nations.
They will carry your little sons back to you in their arms;
they will bring your daughters on their shoulders.
23 Kings and queens will serve you
and care for all your needs.
They will bow to the earth before you
and lick the dust from your feet.
Then you will know that I am the LORD.
Those who trust in me will never be put to shame."
24 Who can snatch the plunder of war from the hands of a warrior?
Who can demand that a tyrant let his captives go?
25 But the LORD says,
"The captives of warriors will be released,
and the plunder of tyrants will be retrieved.
For I will fight those who fight you,
and I will save your children.
26 I will feed your enemies with their own flesh.
They will be drunk with rivers of their own blood.

49:12 Isa 43:5-6
49:13 Isa 54:1, 7-8, 10; Rev 12:12; ᶦ*rakham* (7355) ‣Isa 54:8
49:16 Song 8:6; Isa 62:6
49:18 Isa 45:23; 61:10; Luke 15:22-24
49:19 Isa 1:7; Zech 10:10
49:20 Isa 54:1-3
49:21 Lam 1:1
49:22 Isa 11:10, 12; 14:2
49:23 Ps 25:3; 72:9; Isa 60:14, 16
49:25 Jer 50:33-34
49:26 Isa 14:4; Ezek 39:7

49:12 The remnant would come from the *north* (i.e., from Babylon and Persia; see note on 41:25), from the *west* by sea, and *from as far south as Egypt* (as in the Dead Sea Scrolls, which read *from the region of Aswan*, which is in southern Egypt; Masoretic Text reads *from the region of Sinim*).

49:13 This hymn of praise is in response to the salvation that the servant would make possible. • *comforted his people:* See note on 40:1-31.

49:14 Although the prophet announced cause for rejoicing (49:8-13), the exiles continued to ponder the calamity that came upon them when Babylon invaded the land, destroyed *Jerusalem* (Hebrew *Zion*), and carried the people of Judah into exile where they felt *deserted* and *forgotten*.

49:18 *like jewels or bridal ornaments:* As a wedding calls for festivity and public display, so God's restoration of Israel would be an open act for all to see (see also 61:10).

49:19-21 The population explosion would reach beyond Israel to include the members of foreign nations who turn to the Lord (see 56:6-8; Rev 7:9). • *more room:* The expanded population would require space far beyond the traditional boundaries of the land of Israel (see also Zech 2:4).

49:22 *carry your little sons . . . your daughters:* The mighty rulers of the nations, some of whom had previously killed children in Israel, would aid in their return to Zion (see also 60:3-9). Elsewhere Isaiah envisioned people of foreign nations streaming to Zion to worship the Lord (see 2:2-4).

49:23 *you will know that I am the LORD:* The stunning role-reversal—kings and queens serving the lowly exiles upon their return—would reveal God's power to do the unimaginable (see also 60:16). • The godly would experience temporary disgrace in the Exile but would not ultimately *be put to shame*, as the idolaters and ungodly were.

49:24 *Who can snatch . . . Who can demand:* The people considered it nearly impossible that they would be rescued from their oppressors. • *a tyrant:* As in Dead Sea Scrolls, Syriac version, and Latin Vulgate (also see 49:25); Masoretic Text reads *a righteous person*.

49:25 The Lord is like a warrior who *will fight* to protect his children, as promised to Abraham (Gen 12:3; see also 54:15).

49:26 *of Israel:* Literally *of Jacob;* see note on 14:1.

50:1 Deut 32:30 Isa 59:2 Jer 3:8 [k]*kerithuth* (3748) ›Jer 3:1
50:2 Gen 18:14 Exod 14:21 Josh 3:16
50:3 Rev 6:12
50:4 Ps 5:3 Jer 31:25
50:5 Matt 26:39 John 8:29; 14:31; 15:10 Acts 26:19 Heb 5:8
50:6 Matt 26:67 Mark 15:19 Luke 22:63
50:7 Ezek 3:8-9 Luke 9:51
50:8 Rom 8:33-34
50:9 Isa 54:17
50:10 Eph 5:8
50:11 Isa 65:13-15

All the world will know that I, the
LORD,
am your Savior and your Redeemer,
the Mighty One of Israel."

50 This is what the LORD says:
"Was your mother sent away
because I [k]divorced her?
Did I sell you as slaves to my
creditors?
No, you were sold because of your sins.
And your mother, too, was taken
because of your sins.
2 Why was no one there when I came?
Why didn't anyone answer when I
called?
Is it because I have no power to rescue?
No, that is not the reason!
For I can speak to the sea and make it
dry up!
I can turn rivers into deserts covered
with dying fish.
3 I dress the skies in darkness,
covering them with clothes of
mourning."

The LORD's Faithful Servant

4 The Sovereign LORD has given me his
words of wisdom,
so that I know how to comfort the
weary.
Morning by morning he wakens me
and opens my understanding to his
will.
5 The Sovereign LORD has spoken to me,
and I have listened.
I have not rebelled or turned away.
6 I offered my back to those who beat me
and my cheeks to those who pulled
out my beard.
I did not hide my face
from mockery and spitting.

7 Because the Sovereign LORD helps me,
I will not be disgraced.
Therefore, I have set my face like a stone,
determined to do his will.
And I know that I will not be put to
shame.
8 He who gives me justice is near.
Who will dare to bring charges
against me now?
Where are my accusers?
Let them appear!
9 See, the Sovereign LORD is on my side!
Who will declare me guilty?
All my enemies will be destroyed
like old clothes that have been eaten
by moths!

10 Who among you fears the LORD
and obeys his servant?
If you are walking in darkness,
without a ray of light,
trust in the LORD
and rely on your God.
11 But watch out, you who live in your own
light
and warm yourselves by your own fires.

50:1-3 This disputation shows that God was not forced to give Israel up, and therefore he could take the nation back as his people if he desired.

50:1 God was not at fault for the people's problems; it was their sin that brought about their exile (see also 59:1-15). • Jerusalem—the mother city of Judah (Ps 87:5-6)—was destroyed, and the people of Judah were ***taken*** into exile in 586 BC.

50:2 ***Why didn't anyone answer:*** The people had not responded to God's repeated call to trust in him and repent of their sins. They were deaf and stubborn (see 6:9-10; 29:18; 35:5; 42:18-19). • The Lord ***came*** and ***called*** the people through the prophets (see also 65:1-3). • ***Is it because I have no power to rescue?*** God was fully able to rescue Israel and Judah from the Assyrians and Babylonians, but he first had to deal justly with his people's sinfulness (see 59:1). • ***speak to the sea and make it dry:*** This was an allusion to the parting of the Red Sea during the exodus from Egypt (Exod 14:21-22).

50:3 Phenomena such as ***darkness*** and ***clothes of mourning*** were associated with the day of the Lord (13:10; see note on 2:5-22). The mention of darkness might allude to the plague of darkness in Egypt (Exod 10:21).

50:4-11 This is the third of four servant songs (see note on 42:1-4). The faithful and suffering servant portrays an ideal Israel; the image was realized in Jesus Christ.

50:4 The Lord, who never grows weary (40:28), sends the servant with good news (see 40:28-31) to ***comfort*** those who are ***weary*** (see note on 40:1-31).

50:6 ***beat me . . . pulled out my beard . . . mockery and spitting:*** These connections with the experience of Jesus at his crucifixion are too close to be coincidental—Jesus is the true suffering servant (see Matt 27:27-31).

50:7 Externally, the servant would be ***disgraced*** and ***put to shame,*** but within himself he would calmly await God's vindication (see 29:22; 54:4; 61:7). • ***set my face like a stone:*** The servant would be determined to do God's will (see Luke 9:51).

50:8 ***He who gives me justice is near:*** God vindicates those who suffer for doing his will (see note on 49:4). Vindication is an act of God by which he exalts those who have been wrongly disgraced and strikes down the wicked, self-exalted, and arrogant (see also 2 Thes 1:6-9). • ***bring charges . . . my accusers:*** Confidence in God's vindication removes fear and bolsters faith (see Rom 8:31-34).

50:9 ***Who will declare me guilty?*** The implied answer to this rhetorical question is, "No one!" This answer foreshadows the NT understanding of justification (see Rom 8:31-35).

50:10-11 This is a call for response to the servant's ministry.

50:10 The test of whether or not an individual ***fears the LORD*** is how he or she responds to God's righteous ***servant.*** The same idea is present in Jesus' claim that no one can come to the Father except through him (John 14:6). • Those who ***trust in the LORD*** have great hope for the future (see 12:2).

50:11 ***warm yourselves by your own fires:*** Spiritually complacent people are

This is the reward you will receive
from me:
You will soon fall down in great
torment.

A Call to Trust the Lord

51 1 "Listen to me, all who hope for
deliverance—
all who seek the Lord!
Consider the [a]rock from which you were
cut,
the quarry from which you were
mined.
2 Yes, think about Abraham, your ancestor,
and Sarah, who gave birth to your
nation.
Abraham was only one man when I
called him.
But when I blessed him, he became a
great nation."

3 The Lord will comfort Israel again
and have pity on her ruins.
Her desert will blossom like Eden,
her barren wilderness like the garden
of the Lord.
Joy and gladness will be found there.
Songs of thanksgiving will fill the air.

4 "Listen to me, my people.
Hear me, Israel,
for my law will be proclaimed,
and my [b]justice will become a light to
the nations.
5 My mercy and justice are coming soon.
My salvation is on the way.
My strong arm will bring justice to the
nations.
All distant lands will look to me
and [c]wait in hope for my powerful
arm.
6 Look up to the [d]skies above,
and gaze down on the earth below.
For the [d]skies will disappear like smoke,
and the earth will wear out like a
piece of clothing.
The people of the earth will die like flies,
but my salvation lasts forever.
My righteous rule will never end!

7 "Listen to me, you who know right from
wrong,
you who cherish my law in your
hearts.
Do not be afraid of people's scorn,
nor fear their insults.
8 For the moth will devour them as it
devours clothing.
The worm will eat at them as it eats
wool.
But my righteousness will last forever.
My [e]salvation will continue from
generation to generation."

9 Wake up, wake up, O Lord! Clothe
yourself with strength!
Flex your mighty right arm!
Rouse yourself as in the days of old
when you slew [f]Egypt, the dragon of
the Nile.
10 Are you not the same today,
the one who dried up the sea,
making a path of escape through the
depths
so that your people could cross over?
11 Those who have been ransomed by the
Lord will return.
They will enter Jerusalem singing,
crowned with [g]everlasting joy.
Sorrow and mourning will disappear,
and they will be filled with joy and
gladness.

51:1
Gen 17:15-17
[a]*tsur* (6697)
▸Exod 33:22

51:2
Gen 12:1
Heb 11:11

51:3
Gen 2:8
Isa 41:19

51:4
Ps 78:1
Isa 42:4
[b]*mishpat* (4941)
▸Isa 56:1

51:5
Isa 46:13
[c]*yakhal* (3176)
▸Lam 3:21

51:6
Ps 102:25-26
Matt 24:35
2 Pet 3:10
[d]*shamayim* (8064)
▸Isa 55:9

51:7
Ps 37:30-31
Matt 5:11
Acts 5:40-41

51:8
Isa 14:11
[e]*yeshu'ah* (3444)
▸Isa 59:1

51:9
Deut 4:34
[f]*rahab* (7293)
▸Job 9:13

51:10
Exod 14:21-22
Isa 63:11-12

51:11
Isa 61:7
Rev 7:17; 21:4; 22:3
[g]*'olam* (5769)
▸Dan 12:2

unresponsive toward God. Though they have comfort and security now, they ***will soon fall down in great torment*** (see 66:24).

51:1-8 This prophecy calls for trust in the Lord. Each of its three units begins with the phrase, ***Listen to me*** (51:1, 4, 7).

51:1 ***The rock*** and ***the quarry*** represent Abraham and Sarah (51:2).

51:2 ***Abraham . . . became a great nation:*** The exiled community had decreased in number. They needed to have faith that God could restore them again to a healthy and thriving population.

51:3 ***comfort Israel:*** Hebrew *Zion;* also in 51:16; see note on 40:1. • ***Eden . . . the garden of the Lord:*** God's salvation will one day reestablish conditions like those in which human beings first lived (see Gen 2–3).

51:4 ***my law . . . my justice:*** The work of the servant will prosper because justice will be the rule in God's kingdom on earth (see 42:1-4). • ***a light to the nations:*** The nations will receive the Lord and his revelation (see also 42:6; 49:6; 60:1-3; 66:19-23; Matt 4:15-16; Luke 2:32; John 1:4-9; 12:35-50; Acts 13:47).

51:5 God is ***strong*** enough to crush his enemies and rescue his people, such as when he rescued Israel in the Exodus (see 51:9; Exod 6:6; 15:16).

51:6 ***die like flies:*** The wicked will die in great multitudes on the day of God's judgment.

51:7 ***cherish my law in your hearts:*** Beyond simply knowing God's word, the Lord desires for his people to internalize, treasure, and obey it (see also Ps 37:31; Jer 31:33). • Those who obey the Lord often endure ***scorn*** and ***insults*** (see also Matt 5:10-12).

51:9-10 ***Wake up, wake up:*** God does not sleep; this prayer is for God to act immediately to save his people (see 52:1; see especially God's military garb in 59:17). • ***in the days of old:*** The exodus from Egypt was an act of redemption that displayed God's power as he made ***a path of escape*** (51:10) for his people (see also 11:15). • ***you slew Egypt, the dragon of the Nile:*** Literally *you slew Rahab; you pierced the dragon.* Rahab is the name of a mythical sea monster that represents chaos in ancient literature. It is used here as a poetic name for Egypt; also see note on 30:7.

51:11 ***Jerusalem:*** Hebrew *Zion.*

51:12 Ps 118:6; 1 Pet 1:24
51:13 Deut 8:11; Job 9:8
51:14 Isa 49:10
51:15 Ps 107:25
51:16 Exod 33:22; Deut 18:18
51:17 Jer 25:15
51:18 Ps 142:4
51:20 Isa 66:15; Jer 14:16
51:21 Isa 29:9
51:22 Jer 50:34
51:23 Jer 25:15-17, 26, 28
52:1 Exod 28:2, 40; Neh 11:1; Isa 48:2; 61:10; Rev 21:2, 27
52:3 Ps 44:12; Isa 63:4

12 "I, yes I, am the one who comforts you.
So why are you afraid of mere humans,
who wither like the grass and disappear?
13 Yet you have forgotten the LORD, your Creator,
the one who stretched out the sky like a canopy
and laid the foundations of the earth.
Will you remain in constant dread of human oppressors?
Will you continue to fear the anger of your enemies?
Where is their fury and anger now?
It is gone!
14 Soon all you captives will be released!
Imprisonment, starvation, and death will not be your fate!
15 For I am the LORD your God,
who stirs up the sea, causing its waves to roar.
My name is the LORD of Heaven's Armies.
16 And I have put my words in your mouth
and hidden you safely in my hand.
I stretched out the sky like a canopy
and laid the foundations of the earth.
I am the one who says to Israel,
'You are my people!' "

17 Wake up, wake up, O Jerusalem!
You have drunk the cup of the LORD's fury.
You have drunk the cup of terror,
tipping out its last drops.
18 Not one of your children is left alive
to take your hand and guide you.
19 These two calamities have fallen on you:
desolation and destruction, famine and war.
And who is left to sympathize with you?
Who is left to comfort you?
20 For your children have fainted and lie in the streets,
helpless as antelopes caught in a net.
The LORD has poured out his fury;
God has rebuked them.
21 But now listen to this, you afflicted ones
who sit in a drunken stupor,
though not from drinking wine.
22 This is what the Sovereign LORD,
your God and Defender, says:
"See, I have taken the terrible cup from your hands.
You will drink no more of my fury.
23 Instead, I will hand that cup to your tormentors,
those who said, 'We will trample you into the dust
and walk on your backs.' "

Rescue for Jerusalem

52 1 Wake up, wake up, O Zion!
Clothe yourself with strength.
Put on your beautiful clothes, O holy city of Jerusalem,
for unclean and godless people will enter your gates no longer.
2 Rise from the dust, O Jerusalem.
Sit in a place of honor.
Remove the chains of slavery from your neck,
O captive daughter of Zion.
3 For this is what the LORD says:
"When I sold you into exile,
I received no payment.
Now I can redeem you
without having to pay for you."

51:13 ***you have forgotten the LORD:*** The Lord will never forget Israel (see 44:21; 49:15), so they should not forget him. • The ***Creator*** of the world also created the nation Israel (see note on 40:28).

51:14 The Exile brought such brutal conditions as ***imprisonment, starvation, and death.***

51:15 ***I am the LORD:*** The Lord uses this formula to identify himself as the covenant God and to assure his people of the truth of his word and the reliability of his actions (see 27:3-4; see 51:16).

51:16 ***my words in your mouth:*** The focus shifted back to the servant. • ***stretched out:*** As in Syriac version (see also 51:13); Hebrew reads *planted.* • ***to Israel:*** Hebrew *to Zion* (see note on 1:8). • ***You are my people:*** Israel was the covenant community.

51:17-23 The prophet called the people of Israel to be done with their past and to anticipate God's future for them.

51:17 ***Wake up, wake up:*** Israel used these words in a prayer to the Lord (51:9). Israel's problems were not the result of God's slowness to act; rather the people were slow to believe God's promises. • ***the cup of the LORD's fury:*** The Lord will appropriately measure out his judgment; those who fall under his judgment must figuratively drink from his wrath (see also Matt 26:39).

51:19 ***Who is left to comfort you?*** As in Dead Sea Scrolls and Greek, Latin, and Syriac versions; Masoretic Text reads *How can I comfort you?*

51:20 ***children have fainted:*** A sad commentary on Jerusalem's desolation is provided in Lam 1:13, 22; 2:11-12, 19.

51:22 God would be the ***Defender*** of Israel as he was when Assyria besieged Jerusalem (38:6).

51:23 The ***tormentors*** were the Babylonians who brought about destruction, war, and famine (51:19).

52:1 This second call to ***wake up*** (see 51:17) was in preparation for a glorious future. • ***holy city:*** The new city would be holy because its citizens would be holy (see 4:3). • ***enter your gates no longer:*** Things that are ***unclean*** will not be permitted to enter the holy city (see Rev 21:27 and note).

52:3 ***I sold you into exile . . . Now I can redeem you:*** The Lord was fully in control when he gave his people into the hands of their enemies. Likewise, he remained fully in control and could redeem them if he chose to do so.

4This is what the Sovereign LORD says:
"Long ago my people chose to live in Egypt.
Now they are oppressed by Assyria. 5What
is this?" asks the LORD. "Why are my people
enslaved again? Those who rule them shout
in exultation. My name is blasphemed
all day long. 6But I will reveal my name to
my people, and they will come to know its
power. Then at last they will recognize that
I am the one who speaks to them."

7 How beautiful on the mountains
are the feet of the messenger who
brings good news,
the good news of peace and salvation,
the news that the God of Israel reigns!
8 The watchmen shout and sing with joy,
for before their very eyes
they see the LORD returning to
Jerusalem.
9 Let the ruins of Jerusalem break into
joyful song,
for the LORD has comforted his people.
He has redeemed Jerusalem.
10 The LORD has demonstrated his holy
power
before the eyes of all the nations.
All the ends of the earth will see
the victory of our God.

11 Get out! Get out and leave your
captivity,
where everything you touch is
unclean.
Get out of there and purify yourselves,
you who carry home the sacred
objects of the LORD.
12 You will not leave in a hurry,
running for your lives.
For the LORD will go ahead of you;
yes, the God of Israel will protect you
from behind.

The LORD's Suffering Servant

13 See, my servant will prosper;
he will be highly exalted.
14 But many were amazed when they saw
him.
His face was so disfigured he seemed
hardly human,
and from his appearance, one would
scarcely know he was a man.
15 And he will startle many nations.
Kings will stand speechless in his
presence.
For they will see what they had not been
told;
they will understand what they had
not heard about.

52:5 Ezek 36:20, 23; *Rom 2:24
52:7 Ps 93:1; *Rom 10:15
52:8 Isa 62:6
52:9 Ps 98:4; Isa 61:4
52:10 Ps 98:1-3; Luke 3:6
52:11 Isa 1:16; *2 Cor 6:17; 2 Tim 2:19
52:12 Exod 12:11, 33; 14:19-20; Isa 26:7
52:13 Phil 2:9
52:14 Ps 22:6-7
52:15 *Rom 15:21

52:4 ***in Egypt . . . oppressed by Assyria:*** The exodus from exile would be like Israel's past exodus from Egypt.

52:5 The oppressors would *shout in exultation* because they believed they had conquered not only Israel but also its God. • ***My name is blasphemed all day long*** (Greek version reads *The Gentiles continually blaspheme my name because of you;* cp. Rom 2:24): The condition of God's people affects God's reputation in the eyes of the watching world (see 37:6, 23; 48:11).

52:6 Just as God did to Moses before the Exodus (Exod 3:15), he *will reveal* himself in the coming rescue from exile.

52:7-12 This is a poetic description of God's promise to rescue his people from the alienation their sin created. The imagery is of a besieged city waiting for word that its hero has defeated the enemy armies. Paul applies these words to the proclamation of the Good News of the Lord Jesus (Rom 10:15).

52:7 ***How beautiful on the mountains:*** See Nah 1:15; Rom 10:15. • The ***good news*** goes beyond proclaiming an end to the Exile; it also points to the ***peace and salvation*** of the age to come (54:13-14; see 40:9-10; 41:27). • ***of Israel:*** Hebrew *of Zion;* (see note on 1:8).

52:8 ***The watchmen*** were those looking for the news of Zion's redemption. • ***the LORD returning to Jerusalem*** (Hebrew *Zion*): The sin of the city's inhabitants had driven God away.

52:10 ***victory of our God:*** The rescue of God's people from disgrace foreshadows an even greater victory when God will reign victoriously to ***the ends of the earth*** (note the many similarities with Ps 98:1-3).

52:11-12 This is an exhortation to leave the captivity of sin (see 48:20 on leaving physical captivity in Babylon). See also 2 Cor 6:17; 2 Tim 2:19.

52:11 Here the imagery of leaving the ***unclean*** enemy city encourages the people to ***purify*** themselves by turning away from all known sin. Those who ***carry home the sacred objects of the LORD*** need to be pure.

52:12 ***not leave in a hurry:*** At the time of the Exodus the people had to leave quickly (see Exod 12:11, 31-36). Isaiah drew this contrast to emphasize the newness of God's plan. • ***protect you from behind:*** See Exod 13:21; 14:19-20.

52:13–53:12 This is the fourth of four passages that speak about the promised servant (see note on 42:1-4). The Hebrew poem is carefully constructed in five three-line stanzas. It begins with the servant's exaltation (52:13), proceeds to the humiliation (52:14–53:9), and ends with his exaltation (53:10-12). The faithful servant's suffering would bring reconciliation between God and humans. The Lord Jesus perfectly fulfilled this prophecy (see ch 40; Matt 8:17; Acts 8:30-35; Rom 10:15-17; 15:21; 1 Pet 2:24-25).

52:13 ***prosper . . . be highly exalted:*** The servant would be wise and successful, set apart with the great and noble. Similar terms describe God in 6:1 and 57:15.

52:14-15 Despite the servant's greatness, the actual way he would appear on earth would shock people.

52:14 ***were amazed:*** No one expected that the rescuer would suffer and die. • ***him:*** As in Syriac version; Hebrew reads *you.*

52:15 ***Startle*** (or *cleanse*) ***many nations:*** They would be amazed that a rescuer would appear so weak and helpless and would ***stand speechless.*** • What ***they will see*** and what ***they will understand*** will be in complete contrast to anything they had previously imagined. • ***For they will see what they had not been told; they will understand what they had not heard about:*** Greek version reads *Those who have never been told about him will see, / and those who have never heard of him will understand.* Cp. Rom 15:21.

53:1
*John 12:38
*Rom 10:16
h'aman (0539)
›Jon 3:5
53:2
Isa 11:1
53:3
Ps 22:6
Luke 18:31-33
John 1:10-11
53:4
*Matt 8:17
1 Pet 2:24
53:5-6
Rom 4:25
1 Cor 15:3
Heb 5:8; 9:28
1 Pet 2:24-25
ipesha' (6588)
›Amos 5:12
53:7
Matt 27:12-14
Luke 23:9
53:8
*Acts 8:32-33

53 1 Who has hbelieved our message?
To whom has the LORD
revealed his powerful arm?
2 My servant grew up in the LORD's
presence like a tender green shoot,
like a root in dry ground.
There was nothing beautiful or majestic
about his appearance,
nothing to attract us to him.
3 He was despised and rejected—
a man of sorrows, acquainted with
deepest grief.
We turned our backs on him and looked
the other way.
He was despised, and we did not care.
4 Yet it was our weaknesses he carried;
it was our sorrows that weighed him
down.
And we thought his troubles were a
punishment from God,
a punishment for his own sins!
5 But he was pierced for our irebellion,
crushed for our sins.
He was beaten so we could be whole.
He was whipped so we could be healed.
6 All of us, like sheep, have strayed away.
We have left God's paths to follow our
own.
Yet the LORD laid on him
the sins of us all.
7 He was oppressed and treated harshly,
yet he never said a word.
He was led like a lamb to the slaughter.
And as a sheep is silent before the
shearers,
he did not open his mouth.
8 Unjustly condemned,
he was led away.

The Second Exodus (52:11-12)

Isa 35:8-10; 42:14-16; 43:18-21; 44:3-4; 48:20-21; 49:9-12; 58:8-12
Jer 31:2-17
Joel 3:17-21
Luke 1:78-79
John 7:38; 15:19
2 Cor 5:17; 6:17-18
Eph 5:8
Col 1:13
Heb 13:12-14
Rev 7:16

Exodus stands as a prominent theme in Isaiah. Israel's return from exile would, like the exodus from Egypt, restore the people of Israel to the land. Just as they had left Egypt many years before, the people of Israel would leave Babylon (48:20-21). This time they would have to be cleansed (52:11) and would not rush their departure (52:12).

The second exodus would be "new" (43:19), not merely a duplication of the first Exodus. Both the experience in exile and the journey are likened to a desert (see 35:1) from which the Lord would bring rescue. He prepares a road through the desert (43:19), transforms the desert into a watering hole with vegetation and animals (43:18-20), removes obstacles along the way (42:16; 49:11), guides his people through the desert (42:16; 58:11; 63:13), feeds them (49:10), protects them from the desert heat (49:10), and strengthens them (58:11). He changes the experience of the exiles from sorrow to great joy (51:3) and pours out his Spirit on them (44:3-4).

An "exodus" continues today—an exodus from sin and death through Christ's death and the power of his resurrection. The Holy Spirit enables us to live in newness of life and to serve God with joy as we await the coming of his kingdom in all its fullness.

53:1 *our message:* The identity of the speaker has been debated—the main possibilities are (1) a faithful remnant of Israel, and (2) Isaiah himself. Most likely, Isaiah the prophet was speaking for and with Israel. • ***powerful arm:*** God's strength, so dramatically described in the previous chapters (see 50:2; 51:5, 9; 52:10), would actually manifest itself in weakness and apparent helplessness through the servant's humiliation and exaltation (see 1 Cor 1:27-30). • This verse is quoted in John 12:38 and Rom 10:16.

53:2 ***a tender green shoot . . . in dry ground:*** Such a plant is vulnerable to extinction (cp. 37:27). It can hardly stay alive for itself, let alone provide anything for anyone else. • ***nothing beautiful or majestic:*** The servant appeared to have no greatness or self-evident royal splendor (see 52:13-15). • ***nothing to attract us to him:*** People like their leaders to be physically attractive and personally charismatic. The servant would be neither.

53:3 ***a man of sorrows, acquainted with deepest grief*** (or *a man of pains, acquainted with illness*): The servant would fully experience the effects of sin and the Fall. • ***we did not care:*** Because people would fail to see how such a weak, insignificant person could do anything beneficial for them, they would be unconcerned about his suffering.

53:4 ***Yet it was our weaknesses he carried; it was our sorrows:*** These phrases can also be rendered *Yet it was our sicknesses he carried; / it was our diseases* (cp. Matt 8:17). The callous world would assume that the servant somehow brought his suffering on himself, never realizing that he was suffering for them. • ***troubles . . . punishment:*** These descriptions of the servant's humiliation contrast with the descriptions of his exaltation (see note on 52:13).

53:5 ***he was pierced:*** See also Zech 12:10. • ***crushed . . . beaten . . . whipped:*** These were typically punishments for crimes. Sin is a crime against God. • ***be whole:*** Hebrew *shalom*, usually translated "peace." *Shalom* means to experience wholeness in body, in mind, and in relationships with others. The servant would be injured so that humanity can be whole and healthy in all aspects of life (see also 57:18). We do not need to suffer divine condemnation for our sins because the servant has already done so (see Gal 1:4).

53:6 ***strayed away . . . left God's paths:*** These are metaphors for sin (see also Rom 3:10-18).

53:7-8 The Ethiopian eunuch was reading this passage when Philip met him (Acts 8:32-33).

53:7 See 1 Pet 2:21-25 for the fulfillment of this prophecy in Jesus Christ.

53:8 ***Unjustly condemned, he was led away:*** Greek version reads *He was humiliated and received no justice.*

No one cared that he died without
descendants,
that his life was cut short in
midstream.
But he was struck down
for the rebellion of my people.
9 He had done no wrong
and had never deceived anyone.
But he was buried like a criminal;
he was put in a rich man's grave.

10 But it was the LORD's good plan to crush
him
and cause him grief.
Yet when his life is made an offering for
sin,
he will have many [j]descendants.
He will enjoy a long life,
and the LORD's good plan will prosper
in his hands.
11 When he sees all that is accomplished by
his anguish,
he will be satisfied.
And because of his experience,
my righteous [k]servant will make it
possible
for many to be counted righteous,
for he will bear all their sins.
12 I will give him the honors of a victorious
soldier,
because he exposed himself to death.
He was counted among the rebels.
He bore the sins of many and
interceded for rebels.

Future Glory for Jerusalem

54

1 "Sing, O childless woman,
you who have never given birth!
Break into loud and joyful song,
O Jerusalem,
you who have never been in labor.
For the desolate woman now has more
children
than the woman who lives with her
husband,"
says the LORD.
2 "Enlarge your house; build an addition.
Spread out your home, and spare no
expense!
3 For you will soon be bursting at the
seams.
Your descendants will occupy other
nations
and resettle the ruined cities.

4 "Fear not; you will no longer live in shame.
Don't be afraid; there is no more
disgrace for you.
You will no longer remember the shame
of your youth
and the sorrows of widowhood.

53:9
Matt 27:57-60
*1 Pet 2:22
Rev 14:5

53:10
Lev 5:2-6
Ps 22:30
John 1:29
[j]*zera'* (2233)
‣Jer 33:26

53:11
John 10:14-18
Rom 5:18-19
[k]*'ebed* (5650)
‣Exod 20:10

53:12
Matt 26:38-39, 42
*Mark 15:27
*Luke 22:37
2 Cor 5:21
Phil 2:9-11
1 Pet 2:24

54:1
Isa 62:4
*Gal 4:27

54:3
Gen 28:14
Isa 14:1-2

Cp. Acts 8:33. • ***Unjustly condemned:*** The servant will be given no legal protection or proper defense. • ***No one cared that he died without descendants, that his life was cut short in midstream:*** Or *As for his contemporaries, / who cared that his life was cut short in midstream?* Greek version reads *Who can speak of his descendants? / For his life was taken from the earth.* Cp. Acts 8:33. • ***cut short in midstream:*** To die in midlife was understood to be God's judgment.

53:9 ***no wrong . . . never deceived anyone:*** See 1 Pet 2:21-25. • ***in a rich man's grave:*** Literally *he was with the rich in his death* (see Matt 27:57-61). Although the Bible often considers riches as a blessing from God, it regularly condemns the rich as crooked and oppressive. The point here might be ironic: This good man would be buried with oppressors.

53:10-12 The final stanza of the poem first explains why the servant suffered and was treated unjustly in the place of others; it then explains what the result of that obedience would be.

53:10 The servant's *grief* would accomplish a greater good; the forgiveness and reconciliation of sinful humanity. Note also God's *good plan* to prosper and exalt the servant. • ***when his life is made an offering for sin:*** The suffering of the servant provided a substitute for others, just as the animal sacrifices in the Temple did. • Having ***many descendants*** and enjoying a ***long life*** are rewards for godly and wise living (see Prov 3:2; 17:6; 20:7). Because the servant left his fate in his God's hands, he would receive eternal rewards from the God who vindicates the righteous (see Phil 2:9-11).

53:11 ***his experience*** (literally *his knowledge*): This clearly does not refer to intellectual knowledge but to all that the servant would experience in his obedience, suffering, and intimate relationship with God. • The servant's ***righteous*** obedience enables people to be put right with God (see Gen 15:6; Rom 5:18-19), ***for he will bear all their sins.***

53:12 ***the honors:*** See Phil 2:9-11. • ***He was counted among the rebels:*** *Rebels* (Hebrew *poshe'im*) is a stronger word than *sinners* and is a key word in Isaiah. It refers to those who are in willful defiance of a lawful authority, in this case, God. This phrase is quoted in Luke 22:37; see also note on Mark 15:27. • ***interceded for rebels:*** The servant would pray for sinners in the midst of his suffering (see Exod 32:30; Luke 23:34).

54:1–55:13 This is an invitation to participate in the restoration to God's favor made possible through the ministry of the promised servant.

54:1-17 Salvation flows from the vindication of the suffering servant. The promises mentioned here go beyond the return from Babylonian exile and apply to the coming of Jesus Christ, the extension of the kingdom to the church, the benefits of the second coming of Jesus Christ as the bridegroom of the church, and the new Jerusalem.

54:1-3 The prophet encourages Jerusalem, likened to a barren woman, to rejoice because its fate was rapidly changing. She would have so many children that she would outgrow her home (see Gal 4:27).

54:1 In the ancient world, a ***woman*** who had ***never given birth*** after being married for a time would be ashamed. Isaiah compares ***Jerusalem*** to a barren woman who rejoices at the long-awaited blessing of children (see Gal 4:27).

54:3 Israel's ***descendants*** (cp. 53:10) would ***occupy other nations*** in fulfillment of God's promise to Abraham (Gen 22:17) and to Jacob (Gen 28:14). • As desolation took place (6:11; 14:21), the people of God would inherit the earth and ***resettle the ruined cities*** (51:6; 52:10; 65:17; see also Matt 5:5; Rom 4:13).

54:5 Hos 2:19 ^a go'el (1350) ‣Isa 60:16
54:6 Isa 62:4
54:7 Isa 11:12
54:8 Isa 49:10, 13; 60:10 ^b rakham (7355) ‣Lam 3:32
54:9 Gen 9:9-11 Ezek 39:29
54:10 2 Sam 23:5 Ps 89:34; 102:25-26
54:11 Isa 28:16
54:13 Isa 66:12 Jer 31:34 *John 6:45
54:14 Isa 9:4, 7
54:15 Isa 41:11-16
54:17 Isa 29:8
55:1 Ps 63:1 Lam 5:4 Matt 10:8 John 4:14; 7:37 Rev 3:18; 21:6; 22:17

5 For your Creator will be your husband;
the LORD of Heaven's Armies is his name!
He is your [a]Redeemer, the Holy One of Israel,
the God of all the earth.
6 For the LORD has called you back from your grief—
as though you were a young wife abandoned by her husband,"
says your God.
7 "For a brief moment I abandoned you,
but with great compassion I will take you back.
8 In a burst of anger I turned my face away for a little while.
But with everlasting love I will have [b]compassion on you,"
says the LORD, your Redeemer.
9 "Just as I swore in the time of Noah
that I would never again let a flood cover the earth,
so now I swear
that I will never again be angry and punish you.
10 For the mountains may move
and the hills disappear,
but even then my faithful love for you will remain.
My covenant of blessing will never be broken,"
says the LORD, who has mercy on you.

11 "O storm-battered city,
troubled and desolate!
I will rebuild you with precious jewels
and make your foundations from lapis lazuli.
12 I will make your towers of sparkling rubies,
your gates of shining gems,
and your walls of precious stones.
13 I will teach all your children,
and they will enjoy great peace.
14 You will be secure under a government that is just and fair.
Your enemies will stay far away.
You will live in peace,
and terror will not come near.
15 If any nation comes to fight you,
it is not because I sent them.
Whoever attacks you will go down in defeat.
16 "I have created the blacksmith
who fans the coals beneath the forge
and makes the weapons of destruction.
And I have created the armies that destroy.
17 But in that coming day
no weapon turned against you will succeed.
You will silence every voice
raised up to accuse you.
These benefits are enjoyed by the servants of the LORD;
their vindication will come from me.
I, the LORD, have spoken!

Invitation to the LORD's Salvation

55 1 "Is anyone thirsty?
Come and drink—
even if you have no money!

54:5 ***Creator . . . husband:*** The Lord committed himself to the abandoned woman (his people in exile) as her maker (44:24; see note on 40:28) and husband (see also 62:4-5; Hos 2:19-20). • ***LORD of Heaven's Armies:*** See note on 1:9. • The ***Redeemer*** transforms misery into freedom and fulfillment (see note on 41:14).

54:7-8 The pain of separation would be ***brief*** compared to the depth of the renewal of love and ***compassion.*** • The Lord ***abandoned*** Israel in exile ***for a little while*** because of the people's sins. • ***everlasting love:*** The Lord is eternally committed to his people, making the seventy-year punishment of exile seem short indeed (see 25:1; Hos 2:1).

54:9 The Exile was similar in both drama and trauma to the flood ***in the time of Noah.*** In both instances, people sinned grievously against the Lord, but the Lord renewed his commitment to creation (after Noah's flood) and to his people (after the Exile).

54:10 God's ***faithful love*** for his people endures despite their unfaithfulness. • God's ***covenant of blessing*** was the assurance of his presence, resulting in wholeness, blessing, and protection. It replaces the shame and disgrace of the Exile (see Ezek 34:25; 37:26).

54:11-17 This is a vision of the renewed Jerusalem as a city under God's protection, a place of peace and righteousness (see 59:21–60:22). This section forms the background of John's vision of the new Jerusalem (Rev 21:10-21).

54:11 The Lord himself would ***rebuild*** the ***city*** (see Heb 11:10). • ***Lapis lazuli*** is a semi-precious stone.

54:13 ***I will teach:*** Jesus alluded to this verse in John 6:45. • ***They will enjoy great peace,*** the benefits of God's presence and protection (53:5; see 48:17-18; 54:10).

54:14 Jerusalem would again be a righteous city, ***secure under a government that is just and fair*** (see 1:26).

54:15 God gives assurance that no ***nation*** can ***defeat*** his people. The Lord has promised to protect them, just as he had promised Abraham (Gen 12:3; see 49:25).

54:17 ***no weapon . . . will succeed . . . accuse you . . . vindication:*** God will protect his people in war and in the courtroom. • ***These benefits are enjoyed by the servants of the LORD:*** Only the true children of God—people who come out of Israel and the nations—will enjoy the promised blessings of the age to come that God establishes.

55:1-13 This final chapter of the prophecies of comfort (chs 40–55) summarizes the section's prominent themes: blessing, covenant, witness, word, nations, glory, forgiveness, and joy.

55:1 ***thirsty . . . wine or milk:*** The invitation to eat and drink is similar to Wisdom's call in Prov 9:5. The image promises the slaking of thirst not only by water but also by more costly items such as wine and milk. John applied a

Come, take your choice of wine or milk—
it's all free!
2 Why spend your money on food that
does not give you strength?
Why pay for food that does you no
good?
Listen to me, and you will eat what is
good.
You will enjoy the finest food.

3 "Come to me with your ears wide
open.
Listen, and you will find life.
I will make an everlasting [c]covenant with
you.
I will give you all the unfailing love I
promised to David.
4 See how I used him to display my power
among the peoples.
I made him a leader among the
nations.
5 You also will command nations you do
not know,
and peoples unknown to you will
come running to obey,
because I, the LORD your God,
the Holy One of Israel, have made you
glorious."

6 Seek the LORD while you can find him.
Call on him now while he is near.
7 Let the wicked change their ways
and banish the very thought of doing
wrong.
Let them [d]turn to the LORD that he may
have mercy on them.
Yes, turn to our God, for he will forgive
generously.

8 "My thoughts are nothing like your
thoughts," says the LORD.
"And my ways are far beyond anything
you could imagine.
9 For just as the [e]heavens are higher than
the earth,
so my ways are higher than your
ways
and my thoughts higher than your
thoughts.

10 "The rain and snow come down from the
heavens
and stay on the ground to water the
earth.
They cause the grain to grow,
producing seed for the farmer
and bread for the hungry.
11 It is the same with my word.
I send it out, and it always produces
fruit.
It will accomplish all I want it to,
and it will prosper everywhere I
send it.
12 You will live in [f]joy and peace.
The mountains and hills will burst
into song,
and the trees of the field will clap
their hands!
13 Where once there were thorns, cypress
trees will grow.
Where nettles grew, myrtles will
sprout up.
These events will bring great honor to
the LORD's name;
they will be an everlasting sign of his
power and love."

55:2 Ps 22:26; Eccl 6:2
55:3 *Acts 13:34; [c]*berith* (1285) ‣Jer 31:31
55:5 Zech 8:22
55:6 Ps 32:6; 2 Cor 6:1-2
55:7 Isa 1:16; 44:22; [d]*shub* (7725) ‣Jer 5:3
55:8 Isa 65:2
55:9 Ps 103:11; [e]*shamayim* (8064) ‣Isa 65:17
55:10 2 Cor 9:10
55:11 Isa 46:10
55:12 1 Chr 16:33; Jer 29:11; [f]*simkhah* (8057) ‣Isa 61:7
55:13 Jer 33:9

similar theme to Jesus Christ (John 4:14; 6:27, 35; 7:37; Rev 21:6; 22:17). • ***it's all free:*** Reconciliation with God is for anyone and has no cost.

55:2 ***Listen to me . . . eat what is good:*** Responding positively to God satisfies one's spiritual, social, and physical being (see 1:19; 58:13-14; Prov 4:10).

55:3 ***Come to me. . . . Listen . . . find life:*** Those who respond obediently to God's word find eternal life (see also 55:11). • ***an everlasting covenant . . . I promised to David:*** King David received a special covenant from God, a promise to preserve his kingly line (see 2 Sam 7:15-16). David's dynasty was eternally confirmed in the kingship of the Messiah, Jesus Christ (see 9:6-7; 11:1-16; Acts 2:22-36; 13:34).

55:6-9 The prophet calls for a response while the time is right.

55:6 ***while you can find him:*** When God graciously extends an invitation to salvation, people must respond (65:1; Jer 29:13-14; Hos 5:6; 10:12). Those who do not seek him at such times risk never having the opportunity again.

55:7 ***Let the wicked change . . . turn to the LORD:*** True conversion demands a change of how we live in favor of God's requirements (see 1:16-17; 30:15; 59:20). • ***have mercy on them:*** God's compassion reaches out to the needy and finds them where they are. • ***he will forgive generously:*** Forgiveness of sin is foundational to the good news of redemption (see Eph 1:7; Col 1:14; see also Ps 32:1; 86:5; 99:8; 103:2-5).

55:8-9 ***My thoughts are nothing like your thoughts:*** God's plans are marvelous (Ps 92:5; cp. Ps 94:11). God's creatures, including humans, can never fully understand the Creator's thoughts, but his revelation through his messengers gives great insight and knowledge of some of the things he will do.

55:10-11 The Creator not only sends rain and snow but also his *word* (Hebrew *dabar*). In this context, *dabar* means his *will* or *plan* (see 14:24; 40:8). God's written word, as an expression of God's plan, accomplishes his purposes. God is effective in whatever he does (see 14:26-27; 46:10).

55:12-13 The prophet encourages his people to forget the past, to leave Babylon, and to accept the perspective of the coming age.

55:12 *Joy* is found in being redeemed from bondage. • Godly people experience an inner *peace* not known to the wicked (48:22). • ***mountains and hills . . . trees of the field:*** Creation participates in the freedom of the children of God (44:23; 49:11, 13; see Rom 8:19-23).

55:13 Redemption is like the transformation from desert to forest (see also 35:1; 41:19; 60:13). • ***great honor to the LORD's name:*** God's glory will be more and more visible to humanity as his redemption takes effect.

56:1
Ps 98:2
Isa 1:17; 42:6
Rom 3:26
[g]*mishpat* (4941)
‣Mic 3:1

56:2
Exod 31:13-17
Ps 119:1-2
Ezek 20:12, 20
[h]*ben 'adam* (1121, 0120)
‣Jer 49:18
[i]*shabbath* (7676)
‣Jer 17:21

56:3
Acts 8:27, 36-39

56:5
Isa 2:2-3; 26:1; 62:2

56:6
Isa 60:10; 61:5

56:7
Isa 65:25
Mic 4:1-2
*Matt 21:13
*Mark 11:17
*Luke 19:46
Rom 12:1
Heb 13:15

56:8
John 10:16

56:9
Jer 12:9

56:10
Jer 14:13-14
Ezek 3:17

The Servants of the LORD (56:1–66:24)

Blessings for All Nations

56 This is what the LORD says:
"Be [g]just and fair to all.
Do what is right and good,
for I am coming soon to rescue you
and to display my righteousness
among you.
2 Blessed are all those
who are careful to do this.
Blessed are [h]those who honor my
[i]Sabbath days of rest
and keep themselves from doing
wrong.

3 "Don't let foreigners who commit
themselves to the LORD say,
'The LORD will never let me be part of
his people.'
And don't let the eunuchs say,
'I'm a dried-up tree with no children
and no future.'
4 For this is what the LORD says:
I will bless those eunuchs
who keep my Sabbath days holy
and who choose to do what pleases me
and commit their lives to me.
5 I will give them—within the walls of my
house—
a memorial and a name
far greater than sons and daughters
could give.
For the name I give them is an
everlasting one.
It will never disappear!

6 "I will also bless the foreigners who
commit themselves to the LORD,
who serve him and love his name,
who worship him and do not desecrate
the Sabbath day of rest,
and who hold fast to my covenant.
7 I will bring them to my holy mountain of
Jerusalem
and will fill them with joy in my house
of prayer.
I will accept their burnt offerings and
sacrifices,
because my Temple will be called a
house of prayer for all nations.
8 For the Sovereign LORD,
who brings back the outcasts of
Israel, says:
I will bring others, too,
besides my people Israel."

Judgment on Sinful Leaders

9 Come, wild animals of the field!
Come, wild animals of the forest!
Come and devour my people!
10 For the leaders of my people—
the LORD's watchmen, his shepherds—
are blind and ignorant.
They are like silent watchdogs
that give no warning when danger
comes.

56:1–66:24 This last major division of the book of Isaiah brings together themes from chs 1–39 (sin, justice and righteousness, responsibility, vengeance and vindication) and chs 40–55 (salvation, the age to come).

56:1-8 This section summarizes chs 1–55 with an invitation to the outcasts to participate in God's redemption.

56:1 ***Be just and fair:*** A key aspect of the message of chs 1–39 is the call for justice in relationship with others and God. True godliness comes only through having character that is shaped by the character of God, which only happens by understanding and consistently applying God's word. • ***I am coming soon:*** This statement summarizes the message of chs 40–55, that the Lord is creating a world of harmony, peace, restoration, vindication, and the removal of enemies (46:13).

56:2 ***Blessed:*** Cp. 30:18; 32:20; see also Ps 1:1; 119:1; Matt 5:3. • The ***Sabbath,*** as a sign of the covenant (Exod 31:13-17), is God's gift to his people; it belongs to this age as well as to the age to come (56:4, 6; 58:13-14; see Heb 4:1-13).

56:3-7 The blessing (56:2) would extend to eunuchs and to the Gentiles.

56:3 ***Foreigners who commit themselves to the LORD*** would become full participants in the covenant community. Previously, their participation had been carefully regulated (Deut 23:3, 7-8). • ***eunuch:*** In the past, an emasculated person was excluded from the community (Deut 23:1). Both eunuchs and foreigners had no share in Israel's holiness and were considered marginal to God's kingdom. In the age to come, God would bring to the center those who had previously been marginalized (cp. Matt 20:16).

56:4 The ***Sabbath*** is a sign of the covenant (Exod 31:13-17).

56:5 ***within the walls of my house:*** Those previously excluded would have a place in God's presence. • ***a memorial and a name:*** Everlasting existence in God's presence is better than the blessing of physical descendants.

56:6 The essential ingredient for covenant fellowship is *love* for God (Deut 6:5; 30:20; Matt 22:34-38). • Keeping the ***Sabbath*** is a sign of keeping the ***covenant*** itself (see Exod 31:13-17).

56:7 ***burnt offerings and sacrifices:*** God had previously rejected sinful Israel's expressions of piety (1:11-13) but would welcome offerings from righteous Gentiles or foreigners. Nationality is worth little without true piety. • ***a house of prayer for all nations:*** The Lord would open the doors of the Temple to all nations (see 2:2-4). Jesus rebuked the people for desecrating the Temple and for preventing it from functioning as the house of prayer (Matt 21:13; Mark 11:17; Luke 18:46).

56:8 The ***outcasts of Israel*** were those dispersed among the nations as the result of the Exile (see also 11:12). • The ***others*** would be eunuchs and Gentiles (56:3-7; see also 57:19; John 10:16).

56:9–57:13 This is a reflection on the prevalence of evil among God's people; they were greedy (56:9-12), hostile to the righteous (57:1-2), and idolatrous (57:3-13).

56:9 ***Wild animals*** are here a metaphor for the hostile nations surrounding Judah.

56:10 The leaders of Israel failed to guide and protect God's people from the sins that led to the Exile. • ***sleeping and dreaming:*** See 29:10.

They love to lie around, sleeping and
dreaming.
11 Like greedy dogs, they are never
satisfied.
They are ignorant shepherds,
all following their own path
and intent on personal gain.
12 "Come," they say, "let's get some wine
and have a party.
Let's all get drunk.
Then tomorrow we'll do it again
and have an even bigger party!"

57 1 Good people pass away;
the godly often die before their
time.
But no one seems to care or wonder
why.
No one seems to understand
that God is protecting them from the
evil to come.
2 For those who follow godly paths
will rest in peace when they die.

Idolatrous Worship Condemned

3 "But you—come here, you witches'
children,
you offspring of adulterers and
prostitutes!
4 Whom do you mock,
making faces and sticking out your
tongues?
You children of sinners and liars!
5 You worship your idols with great passion
beneath the oaks and under every
green tree.
You sacrifice your children down in the
valleys,
among the jagged rocks in the cliffs.
6 Your gods are the smooth stones in the
valleys.
You worship them with liquid
offerings and grain offerings.
They, not I, are your inheritance.
Do you think all this makes me happy?
7 You have committed adultery on every
high mountain.
There you have worshiped idols
and have been unfaithful to me.
8 You have put pagan symbols
on your doorposts and behind your
doors.
You have left me
and climbed into bed with these
detestable gods.
You have committed yourselves to them.
You love to look at their naked bodies.
9 You have given olive oil to Molech
with many gifts of perfume.
You have traveled far,
even into the world of the dead,
to find new gods to love.
10 You grew weary in your search,
but you never gave up.
Desire gave you renewed strength,
and you did not grow weary.
11 "Are you afraid of these idols?
Do they terrify you?
Is that why you have lied to me
and forgotten me and my words?
Is it because of my long silence
that you no longer fear me?
12 Now I will expose your so-called good
deeds.
None of them will help you.
13 Let's see if your idols can save you
when you cry to them for help.
Why, a puff of wind can knock them
down!
If you just breathe on them, they fall
over!

56:11 Jer 22:17; Mic 3:5, 11
56:12 Luke 12:19-20
57:1 2 Kgs 22:19-20; Ps 12:1
57:3 Matt 16:4
57:5 Ps 106:37-38; Jer 2:20; 7:31
57:6 Jer 7:18; Hab 2:19
57:7 Ezek 16:16, 28
57:8 Ezek 23:18
57:9 Ezek 23:16, 40
57:10 Jer 2:25
57:11 Ps 50:21; Prov 29:25; Jer 2:32
57:12 Mic 3:1-4
57:13 Ps 37:3, 9; Jer 30:14

56:11 ***ignorant shepherds:*** Israel's leaders did not know how to rule in a godly way (see also Ezek 34:1-6). By contrast, the Lord is the faithful Shepherd of his people (40:11). • ***all following their own path:*** They had no concern for God or his standards of godly leadership (see also 53:6). • ***personal gain:*** Contrast 33:15.

57:1-2 This is a lament for the righteous who suffer in a wicked society.

57:1 ***the evil to come:*** Judgment that would come on the wicked nations. • ***protecting them:*** At times, God allows the godly to *die* in order to protect them from harsher times to come.

57:2 The wicked would not be able to *rest in peace* (57:21).

57:3 ***witches' children . . . adulterers and prostitutes:*** Baal religion, which flourished in Israel before the Exile (see 1:21-23), included lewd sexual practices.

57:4 ***Mock . . . sticking out your tongues:*** The wicked oppressed the righteous by their insults (57:1-2; see also 28:9, 14).

57:5 ***beneath the oaks and under every green tree:*** Tree groves were commonly used as places of pagan worship (see 1:29-30). • ***sacrifice your children:*** The horrible practice of child sacrifice was occasionally practiced in Israel (see Ps 106:37-38).

57:6 ***Liquid offerings and grain offerings*** were believed to satisfy the basic needs of the gods and thus to earn their favor.

57:8 ***climbed into bed:*** The people of Israel had a sickening commitment to the fertility religions, which included sex as part of their rituals.

57:9 ***to Molech:*** Or *to the king,* depending on how the Hebrew word is vocalized. • ***into the world of the dead:*** Hebrew *into Sheol.*

57:11 The people were living in fear of false gods instead of fearing the Lord (see 8:12-13).

57:12 The Lord did not consider the people's ***so-called good deeds*** (literally *righteousness;* see 59:16) to be truly righteous.

57:13 ***your idols . . . fall over:*** See note on 40:18. • ***inherit the land:*** The Hebrew word translated *land* can also signify the whole earth (see Ps 25:13; 37:9, 11, 22, 29, 34; Matt 5:5). • ***my holy mountain:*** God's servants will enjoy God's presence in Zion (see 2:2; 56:7).

57:14
Isa 62:10
57:15
Deut 33:27
Ps 34:18
Isa 66:1
57:16
Mic 7:18
57:17
Isa 1:4
57:18
Isa 53:5; 61:1-3
57:19
Isa 26:12
Acts 2:39
Eph 2:17
Heb 13:15
57:20
Job 18:5-14
57:21
Isa 48:22
58:2
Isa 29:13
Jer 7:9-10
Titus 1:16
58:3
Zech 7:5-6
Luke 18:9-12
58:4
1 Kgs 21:9-10

But whoever trusts in me will inherit the
land
and possess my holy mountain."

God Forgives the Repentant

14 God says, "Rebuild the road!
Clear away the rocks and stones
so my people can return from
captivity."
15 The high and lofty one who lives in
eternity,
the Holy One, says this:
"I live in the high and holy place
with those whose spirits are contrite
and humble.
I restore the crushed spirit of the humble
and revive the courage of those with
repentant hearts.
16 For I will not fight against you forever;
I will not always be angry.
If I were, all people would pass away—
all the souls I have made.
17 I was angry,
so I punished these greedy people.
I withdrew from them,
but they kept going on their own
stubborn way.
18 I have seen what they do,
but I will heal them anyway!
I will lead them.
I will comfort those who mourn,
19 bringing words of praise to their lips.
May they have abundant peace, both
near and far,"
says the LORD, who heals them.
20 "But those who still reject me are like the
restless sea,
which is never still
but continually churns up mud and
dirt.
21 There is no peace for the wicked,"
says my God.

True and False Worship

58 1 "Shout with the voice of a
trumpet blast.
Shout aloud! Don't be timid.
Tell my people Israel of their sins!
2 Yet they act so pious!
They come to the Temple every day
and seem delighted to learn all
about me.
They act like a righteous nation
that would never abandon the laws of
its God.
They ask me to take action on their
behalf,
pretending they want to be
near me.
3 'We have fasted before you!' they say.
'Why aren't you impressed?
We have been very hard on ourselves,
and you don't even notice it!'

"I will tell you why!" I respond.
"It's because you are fasting to please
yourselves.
Even while you fast,
you keep oppressing your
workers.
4 What good is fasting
when you keep on fighting and
quarreling?
This kind of fasting
will never get you anywhere with me.
5 You humble yourselves
by going through the motions of
penance,
bowing your heads
like reeds bending in the wind.
You dress in burlap
and cover yourselves with ashes.
Is this what you call fasting?
Do you really think this will please the
LORD?

57:14-21 The Lord here promises to be present with the humble, to heal them, and to grant them his peace. The promise extends to all the citizens of Zion, both Jews and Gentiles. The Holy One comes to the humble with an all-inclusive offer of salvation, while dealing justly with the wicked.

57:15 Even though God is ***the high and lofty one,*** he promises to dwell with the humble.

57:18 ***I will heal them anyway:*** Salvation is by God's grace (see 19:22; 30:26; 53:5).

57:19 ***words of praise:*** God's redemption should bring a response of praise from its recipients. • ***both near and far:*** Both Gentiles and Jews are included (see 56:3; John 10:16; Eph 2:17).

57:20 ***restless sea . . . never still:*** Those who live in constant opposition to God (see Ps 46:3, 6; 93:3-4) do not enjoy inner quiet because they are not at peace with God (30:15; 32:17). • ***churns up mud and dirt:*** Their activity has little productivity (see Ps 40:2).

57:21 ***no peace:*** Contrast 57:2; see also 48:22.

58:1-4 This is a charge against religious Israelites who were pleased with themselves because of their religious activities.

58:1 ***Israel:*** Literally *Jacob.* See note on 14:1.

58:2 ***they act so pious*** (literally *they seek me*): They may have been truly committed to a religious form, but they failed to truly meet God in their religious activities.

58:3 ***Fasting*** should be a time of self-deprivation in order to focus on God and pleasing him (Lev 16:29; see Zech 7:5). However, these people were only interested in pleasing themselves and continuing in their sins.

58:5 This is a satirical portrayal of the people's fasting as mere external piety without repentance and righteous acts. Ritualistic and insincere fasting is nothing but pomp. • Wearing ***burlap*** and ***ashes*** are expressions of sorrow and mourning. • ***please the LORD:*** The people erroneously believed that the Lord would bless them, if only they performed the right rituals.

6 "No, this is the kind of fasting I want:
Free those who are wrongly imprisoned;
lighten the burden of those who work
for you.
Let the oppressed go free,
and remove the chains that bind people.
7 Share your food with the hungry,
and give shelter to the homeless.
Give clothes to those who need them,
and do not hide from relatives who
need your help.

8 "Then your salvation will come like the
dawn,
and your wounds will quickly heal.
Your godliness will lead you forward,
and the glory of the LORD will protect
you from behind.
9 Then when you call, the LORD will answer.
'Yes, I am here,' he will quickly reply.

"Remove the heavy yoke of oppression.
Stop pointing your finger and
spreading vicious rumors!
10 Feed the hungry,
and help those in trouble.
Then your light will shine out from the
darkness,
and the darkness around you will be
as bright as noon.
11 The LORD will guide you continually,
giving you water when you are dry
and restoring your strength.
You will be like a well-watered garden,
like an ever-flowing spring.
12 Some of you will rebuild the deserted
ruins of your cities.
Then you will be known as a rebuilder
of walls
and a restorer of homes.

13 "Keep the Sabbath day holy.
Don't pursue your own interests on
that day,
but enjoy the Sabbath
and speak of it with delight as the
LORD's holy day.
Honor the Sabbath in everything you do
on that day,
and don't follow your own desires or
talk idly.
14 Then the LORD will be your delight.
I will give you great honor
and satisfy you with the inheritance I
promised to your ancestor Jacob.
I, the LORD, have spoken!"

Warnings against Sin

59 1 Listen! The LORD's arm is not too
weak to [j]save you,
nor is his ear too deaf to hear you call.
2 It's your sins that have cut you off from
God.
Because of your sins, he has turned
away
and will not listen anymore.
3 Your hands are the hands of murderers,
and your fingers are filthy with sin.
Your lips are full of lies,
and your mouth spews corruption.

4 No one cares about being fair and honest.
The people's lawsuits are based on lies.
They conceive evil deeds
and then give birth to sin.
5 They hatch deadly snakes
and weave spiders' webs.
Whoever falls into their webs will die,
and there's danger even in getting
near them.

58:6 Neh 5:10-12
58:7 Deut 22:1-4; Ezek 18:7, 16; Matt 25:35; Luke 3:11; Heb 13:2
58:8 Ps 85:13; Jer 30:17
58:10 Deut 15:7
58:11 Ps 107:9; Song 4:15; John 4:14; 7:37-38
58:12 Ezek 36:10; Amos 9:11
58:13 Jer 17:21-27
58:14 Deut 32:13
59:1 Jer 32:17; [j]*yasha'* (3467) ›Jer 17:14
59:2 Isa 1:15; Ezek 8:18
59:3 Jer 2:30, 34; Hos 4:2
59:4 Ps 7:14
59:5 Job 8:14

58:6-7 True fasting creates an awareness of injustice and oppression and prompts the practitioner to reach out to help the needy in their struggles (see 42:7; Matt 25:35-36; Jas 1:27).

58:8 ***your salvation*** (literally *your light*): The light of the coming age (see 42:6-7; 60:1-3) will *dawn* on those who turn fully to the Lord. The night of divine judgment and oppression will be over. • ***your wounds:*** The nation of Israel was wounded when they were conquered and sent into exile. • ***protect you from behind:*** See also 52:12.

58:9 ***the LORD will answer:*** Cp. 1:15; see also 19:22. • ***Stop . . . spreading vicious rumors:*** God calls for an end to acts and words that destroy relationships (see Prov 6:12-14).

58:10 ***your light . . . as bright as noon:*** God would rescue and vindicate his people (see Job 11:17; Ps 37:6).

58:12 ***a rebuilder of walls:*** Nehemiah would later fulfill this promise (see Neh 2:17).

58:13 Like the practice of fasting, ***the Sabbath*** was intended to be an expression of self-denial and worship. It consists of delighting in the Lord, trusting him to provide for one's needs while abstaining from work, and living in obedience to his will.

58:14 As people *honor* God through obedience, they themselves will be honored by God. • ***the inheritance I promised to your ancestor Jacob:*** The promised inheritance includes living with many descendants in the holy land and enjoying God's presence, blessing, and protection (Gen 31:3; 35:9-12).

59:1-20 The Lord alone can and will usher in his salvation. Like a warrior, he will break into the world to avenge himself on his enemies and to vindicate his holy people.

59:1-8 The people complained that the Lord could not rescue them, but the real problem was that they had not repented (59:20) and were still living in sin.

59:1 ***not too weak:*** The delay in their rescue could not be attributed to an inherent weakness in the Lord.

59:2 ***your sins . . . cut you off:*** The Israelites, like all people (Rom 3:15-17), had sinned, which resulted in alienation from God (*he has turned away*).

59:4 ***being fair and honest:*** Israel did not practice these qualities that are part of God's nature and that he expects from people (1:21; see 25:1).

59:5-6 The images of ***deadly snakes*** and ***spiders' webs*** represent plans designed to destroy others' lives and relationships.

59:6 Jer 6:7
59:7-8 Prov 1:16; Mark 7:21-22; *Rom 3:15-17
59:8 [k]*shalom* (7965) ‣Zech 8:19
59:9 Isa 5:30
59:10 Deut 28:29; Lam 3:6
59:11 Ezek 7:16
59:12 Ezra 9:6; Hos 5:5
59:13 Matt 10:33; Titus 1:16
59:14 Hab 1:4
59:15 Isa 1:21-23; 5:23
59:16 Ezek 22:30
59:17 Eph 6:14

6 Their webs can't be made into clothing,
and nothing they do is productive.
All their activity is filled with sin,
and violence is their trademark.
7 Their feet run to do evil,
and they rush to commit murder.
They think only about sinning.
Misery and destruction always
follow them.
8 They don't know where to find [k]peace
or what it means to be just and
good.
They have mapped out crooked roads,
and no one who follows them knows
a moment's [k]peace.

9 So there is no justice among us,
and we know nothing about right
living.
We look for light but find only
darkness.
We look for bright skies but walk in
gloom.
10 We grope like the blind along a wall,
feeling our way like people without
eyes.
Even at brightest noontime,
we stumble as though it were dark.
Among the living,
we are like the dead.
11 We growl like hungry bears;
we moan like mournful doves.
We look for justice, but it never comes.
We look for rescue, but it is far away
from us.
12 For our sins are piled up before God
and testify against us.
Yes, we know what sinners we are.
13 We know we have rebelled and have
denied the LORD.
We have turned our backs on our
God.
We know how unfair and oppressive we
have been,
carefully planning our deceitful lies.
14 Our courts oppose the righteous,
and justice is nowhere to be found.
Truth stumbles in the streets,
and honesty has been outlawed.
15 Yes, truth is gone,
and anyone who renounces evil is
attacked.

The LORD looked and was displeased
to find there was no justice.
16 He was amazed to see that no one
intervened
to help the oppressed.
So he himself stepped in to save them
with his strong arm,
and his justice sustained him.
17 He put on righteousness as his body
armor
and placed the helmet of salvation on
his head.
He clothed himself with a robe of
vengeance
and wrapped himself in a cloak of
divine passion.
18 He will repay his enemies for their evil
deeds.
His fury will fall on his foes.
He will pay them back even to the
ends of the earth.

Salvation (59:15b-21)

Isa 49:8; 61:1-3; Ps 27:1; Hab 3:13; Luke 4:18-21; John 3:16-17; 12:47; Acts 4:11-12; 10:34-36; 16:30-31; Rom 1:16-17; 10:9-13; 2 Cor 5:18-21; Eph 2:8-10; Titus 2:11-13; Heb 9:27-28; 1 Pet 3:18-21; Rev 7:9-10

Salvation involves all aspects of existence. The word *salvation* occurs in the book of Isaiah together with *righteousness* to signify a harmonious order where injustice, disgrace, and mourning are absent (45:8; 51:8). Isaiah's name means *Yahweh is salvation* (see note on 8:18). He calls on people to turn away from their many false saviors to the only true Savior and protector.

The good news in Isaiah is that the Lord is coming to restore his people (40:10). Babylon will fall, and the anguish and humiliation of the exiles will end. Chapters 1–39 anticipate this message, while chs 40–66 clearly describe it.

The history of redemption comes in three stages: First, God restored Israel from exile. Second, Jesus Christ came, bringing the Good News of salvation through his death and resurrection (61:1-3; Luke 4:18-21; Acts 10:36). Finally, Jesus will return to inaugurate his everlasting kingdom (Matt 26:64; Heb 9:28).

59:7-8 Paul quotes from these verses in his description of the depravity of all people (Rom 3:15-17). • ***Misery and destruction:*** The people lamented being victims of oppression (51:19), yet they were oppressors themselves.

59:9-15 Israel's history of rebellion was well established. The prophet here confesses the nation's sins and laments that they could not apprehend the light of God's salvation.

59:10 ***people without eyes:*** See 6:10; Deut 28:29.

59:11-14 The people ***growl*** and ***moan*** with longing for redemption, finally coming to terms with their sinfulness.

59:15-17 The Lord goes out as a warrior intent on achieving victory against the wicked (cp. Eph 6:14).

59:18 ***repay his enemies:*** The Lord will dole out righteous retribution on the whole earth. His justice requires people to be judged for the evil they have done (see also 3:9-11; 13:9).

19 In the west, people will respect the name
of the LORD;
in the east, they will glorify him.
For he will come like a raging flood tide
driven by the breath of the LORD.
20 "The Redeemer will come to Jerusalem
to buy back those in Israel
who have turned from their sins,"
says the LORD.

21 "And this is my covenant with them,"
says the LORD. "My Spirit will not leave
them, and neither will these words I have
given you. They will be on your lips and on
the lips of your children and your children's
children forever. I, the LORD, have spoken!

Future Glory for Jerusalem

60
1 "Arise, Jerusalem! Let your light
shine for all to see.
For the glory of the LORD rises to
shine on you.
2 Darkness as black as night covers all the
nations of the earth,
but the glory of the LORD rises and
appears over you.
3 All nations will come to your light;
mighty kings will come to see your
radiance.

4 "Look and see, for everyone is coming
home!
Your sons are coming from distant
lands;
your little daughters will be carried
home.
5 Your eyes will shine,
and your heart will thrill with joy,
for merchants from around the world
will come to you.
They will bring you the wealth of
many lands.
6 Vast caravans of camels will converge on
you,
the camels of Midian and Ephah.
The people of Sheba will bring gold and
frankincense
and will come worshiping the LORD.
7 The flocks of Kedar will be given to you,
and the rams of Nebaioth will be
brought for my altars.
I will accept their offerings,
and I will make my Temple glorious.

8 "And what do I see flying like clouds to
Israel,
like doves to their nests?
9 They are ships from the ends of the
earth,
from lands that trust in me,
led by the great ships of Tarshish.
They are bringing the people of Israel
home from far away,
carrying their silver and gold.
They will honor the LORD your God,
the Holy One of Israel,
for he has filled you with splendor.

10 "Foreigners will come to rebuild your
towns,
and their kings will serve you.
For though I have destroyed you in my
anger,
I will now have mercy on you through
my grace.
11 Your gates will stay open day and night
to receive the wealth of many lands.

59:19 Isa 30:28
59:20 Ezek 18:30-31; Acts 2:38-39; *Rom 11:26-27
59:21 Isa 44:3; Jer 31:31-34
60:1 Eph 5:14
60:2 Col 1:13
60:3 Isa 2:3
60:5 Ps 34:5; Isa 61:6
60:9-10 Ps 72:10; Isa 49:22-23
60:11 Isa 26:2

59:19 ***In the west . . . in the east:*** I.e., in all parts of the world. • ***For he will come like a raging flood tide driven by the breath of the LORD:*** Or *When the enemy comes like a raging flood tide, / the Spirit of the LORD will drive him back.*

59:20 ***The Redeemer will come to Jerusalem to buy back those in Israel who have turned from their sins:*** Literally *The Redeemer will come to Zion / to buy back those in Jacob / who have turned from their sins.* Greek version reads *The one who rescues will come on behalf of Zion, / and he will turn Jacob away from ungodliness.* Cp. Rom 11:26, which quotes from the Greek version.

59:21 The members of the new community have the ***Spirit,*** and they know and practice God's word (see also Ezek 36:24-28). The Lord promises to regenerate the ***children*** by his Spirit and bring them into the covenant of obedience and love for the Lord (Joel 2:28; Acts 2:39).

60:1-3 God will come to be with his people and will transform Zion's destiny from the ***darkness as black as night*** caused by sin and judgment.

60:3 The transformation of ***all nations*** and ***mighty kings*** will be so radical that all kingdoms will take notice and be drawn to God through his people (see also Rev 21:24).

60:5-7 Zion's losses from warfare will be restored by ***the wealth of many lands;*** foreign nations will be eager to make a contribution (60:11; 61:6; 66:12; see Rev 21:26).

60:6 ***Midian and Ephah*** were Midianite tribes located southeast of Israel. • ***Sheba*** was a region in southern Arabia (see 1 Kgs 10:1-2) famed for ***frankincense*** (Jer 6:20). • These were real nations—the restoration would be a historical reality, not just an idealistic vision. Many nations would submit themselves to and worship ***the LORD.***

60:7 ***Kedar*** was a tribe in Arabia (21:16-17). • ***Nebaioth*** was an Ishmaelite tribe. • ***I will make my Temple glorious:*** The glory of God will be even more evident than it was in Solomon's Temple (see 6:1-5; Hag 2:9; Rev 21:11, 22).

60:9 ***filled you with splendor:*** See Rev 21:26.

60:10-16 Those who previously oppressed the people of God will one day participate in restoring the holy city (see 2:2-4; 19:18-25; Neh 2:8; Amos 9:12).

60:10 ***their kings will serve you:*** God's people who were previously humiliated (2:11) will be exalted.

60:11 There are two likely reasons for why the ***gates*** are not closed at night (see also Rev 21:25): (1) So much traffic will be coming into the city (60:8-10) that the gates will need to be open. (2) The citizens of Zion will no longer need to fear enemies because the Lord is

60:12 Zech 14:17
60:14 Isa 1:26; 14:1-2 Rev 3:9
60:15 Isa 65:18 Jer 30:17-19
60:16 Isa 43:3, 11; 63:16 [a]go'el (1350) Isa 63:16
60:18 Isa 26:1
60:19 Isa 9:2 Zech 2:5 Rev 21:23; 22:5
60:20 Rev 21:4

The kings of the world will be led as
captives
in a victory procession.
12 For the nations that refuse to serve you
will be destroyed.

13 "The glory of Lebanon will be yours—
the forests of cypress, fir, and pine—
to beautify my sanctuary.
My Temple will be glorious!
14 The descendants of your tormentors
will come and bow before you.
Those who despised you
will kiss your feet.
They will call you the City of the LORD,
and Zion of the Holy One of Israel.

15 "Though you were once despised and
hated,
with no one traveling through you,
I will make you beautiful forever,
a joy to all generations.
16 Powerful kings and mighty nations
will satisfy your every need,
as though you were a child
nursing at the breast of a queen.
You will know at last that I, the LORD,
am your Savior and your [a]Redeemer,
the Mighty One of Israel.
17 I will exchange your bronze for gold,
your iron for silver,
your wood for bronze,
and your stones for iron.
I will make peace your leader
and righteousness your ruler.
18 Violence will disappear from your land;
the desolation and destruction of war
will end.
Salvation will surround you like city
walls,
and praise will be on the lips of all
who enter there.

19 "No longer will you need the sun to shine
by day,
nor the moon to give its light by night,
for the LORD your God will be your
everlasting light,
and your God will be your glory.
20 Your sun will never set;
your moon will not go down.

Zion (60:1-22)

Isa 1:21-26; 4:2-3; 7:14; 33:20; 40:9; 46:13; 65:17-19
Ps 2:6; 48:1-14
Jer 31:6-12
Lam 2:1-18
Mic 3:9-12
Zeph 3:14-17
Heb 12:22-24
Rev 14:1-5; 21:1-27

When David first conquered the city of Jerusalem, he captured "the fortress of Zion" and named it "the City of David" (2 Sam 5:7, 9). Later, when Solomon built the Temple in Jerusalem, the site was poetically called Mount Zion (Ps 68:16; 76:2).

In Isaiah, Zion is a theological name for Jerusalem, the city of God. Zion symbolizes God's presence and protection for his people, their resilience and victory against enemies, and the resulting peace (Ps 46). Zion is a place of security, tranquility, and rest (33:20). In essence, Zion is wherever God and his people are (60:1-22; 65:17-19). Zion proclaims the good news (40:9) that God comes to redeem his people and bring them back to his presence (46:13). The citizens of Zion are all washed, purified, and holy (4:2-3).

Zion also has a moral dimension. Because the Lord is already present among his people, they must live according to his ways. Chief characteristics of the Lord's city are trust, justice, righteousness, and commitment. The Lord does not tolerate impurity, uncleanness, idolatry, injustice, or unrighteousness (1:21-26). All of Zion's citizens must live by God's revelation; disobedience is subject to judgment. Only those who repent can be citizens of Zion (see 1:16-17). God's people are the objects of his salvation and purification (Isaiah, "Yahweh is salvation"), and he is committed to being present with them (Immanuel, "God is with us," 7:14).

In many Christian hymns, Zion is used to refer to the ultimate kingdom of God.

their protector (60:18); the nations that remain will be serving the Lord and his people (60:9, 12).

60:12 In the coming age, *nations* that refuse to obey God *will be destroyed*.

60:13 The *Temple* was God's *sanctuary*, the symbol of his presence on earth. Believers now are the temple of God by the indwelling Spirit (1 Cor 3:16). We still await the fullness of God's presence (Rev 21:22).

60:15 *beautiful forever . . . a joy to all generations:* This would be radical change from the conditions of the Exile in Babylon. Fulfillments of this prophecy include the Jews' restoration from exile, the coming of Jesus Christ, and the inclusion of the Gentiles in the church. The final fulfillment awaits the glorious second coming of Jesus Christ, which will usher in the New Jerusalem.

60:16 *of Israel:* Literally *of Jacob.* See note on 14:1.

60:17-20 These verses portray Zion's future grandeur (cp. Rev 21:10–22:4).

60:17 *gold . . . silver . . . bronze . . . iron:* These metals are for adornment and strength (cp. 54:11; Rev 21:15-21).
• *Peace* and *righteousness* will bring harmony and blessing among people and with God.

60:18 *praise will be on the lips of all who enter there* (literally *they will call your gates "praise"*): Entrance into the city of *salvation* will be through the metaphorical gates of praise to the Lord for his great salvation.

60:19-20 Natural sources of light such as *the sun* and *the moon* will be as nothing in comparison to the brightness of God's presence (see also 9:2; 30:26; Zech 2:5; Rev 21:23-24).

For the LORD will be your everlasting
light.
Your days of mourning will come to
an end.
21 All your people will be righteous.
They will possess their land forever,
for I will plant them there with my own
hands
in order to bring myself glory.
22 The smallest family will become a
thousand people,
and the tiniest group will become a
mighty nation.
At the right time, I, the LORD, will
make it happen."

Good News for the Oppressed

61 1 The [b]Spirit of the [c]Sovereign LORD
is upon me,
for the LORD has [d]anointed me
to bring good news to the poor.
He has sent me to comfort the
brokenhearted
and to proclaim that captives will be
released
and prisoners will be freed.
2 He has sent me to tell those who mourn
that the time of the LORD's favor has
come,
and with it, the day of God's anger
against their enemies.
3 To all who mourn in Israel,
he will give a crown of beauty for
ashes,
a joyous blessing instead of mourning,
festive praise instead of despair.
In their righteousness, they will be like
great oaks
that the LORD has planted for his own
glory.
4 They will rebuild the ancient ruins,
repairing cities destroyed long ago.
They will [e]revive them,
though they have been deserted for
many generations.
5 Foreigners will be your servants.
They will feed your flocks
and plow your fields
and tend your vineyards.
6 You will be called priests of the LORD,
[f]ministers of our God.
You will feed on the treasures of the
nations
and boast in their riches.
7 Instead of shame and dishonor,
you will enjoy a double share of honor.
You will possess a double portion of
prosperity in your land,
and everlasting [g]joy will be yours.

8 "For I, the LORD, love justice.
I hate robbery and wrongdoing.
I will faithfully reward my people for
their suffering
and make an everlasting covenant
with them.
9 Their descendants will be recognized
and honored among the nations.
Everyone will realize that they are a
people
the LORD has blessed."

10 I am overwhelmed with joy in the LORD
my God!
For he has dressed me with the
clothing of salvation
and draped me in a robe of
righteousness.
I am like a bridegroom in his wedding
suit
or a bride with her jewels.

60:21 Ps 37:22; Jer 31:28
60:22 Isa 51:2
61:1-2 Isa 49:8-9; *Luke 4:18-19
61:1 [b]*ruakh* (7307) ‣Isa 63:10; [c]*'adonay Yahweh* (0136, 3068) ‣Ezek 2:4; [d]*mashakh* (4886) ‣Exod 40:9
61:3 Ps 23:5; Jer 17:7-8
61:4 Ezek 36:33; Amos 9:14; [e]*khadash* (2318) ‣Lam 5:21
61:5 Isa 14:2
61:6 Isa 66:21; [f]*sharath* (8334) ‣Jer 33:22
61:7 Zech 9:12; [g]*simkhah* (8057) ‣1 Kgs 1:40
61:8 Gen 17:7; Isa 5:16
61:9 Isa 44:3
61:10 Isa 51:3; 52:1

60:21 The citizens of Zion will be ***righteous,*** enjoying a right relationship with God and with others (Rev 21:27). • ***their land:*** Or *the entire earth* (54:5; 62:7; 65:17; 66:22).

60:22 ***I, the LORD:*** The Lord identifies himself as the covenant God of Israel. His identity ensures that he ***will make it happen*** (see 27:3-4).

61:1-3 The servant here proclaims the good news that his ministry will restore Zion. The Lord Jesus applied these words to his own mission (Luke 4:18-19).

61:1 The presence of God's ***Spirit*** ensures the success of the servant's mission (see 11:1-5; 42:1). • The servant will restore and heal the marginalized ***poor*** and the ***brokenhearted*** (see 25:4). • ***and prisoners will be freed:*** Greek version reads *and the blind will see.* Cp. Luke 4:18.

61:2 ***to tell those who mourn that the time of the LORD's favor has come:*** Or *to proclaim the acceptable year of the LORD,* which is the day of God's salvation (see 49:8). • ***the day of God's anger:*** God now turns his wrath against the enemies of his people. It will be a day of righteous vengeance (see 34:8; 63:3-4).

61:3 Putting ***ashes*** on one's head was a sign of ***mourning*** (note the reversal of the judgment stated in 3:16-25). Mourning would be replaced by joy. The words translated ***crown of beauty*** and ***ashes*** form a wordplay in Hebrew. • ***joyous blessing*** (literally *oil of gladness*): A face covered with oil was a sign of blessing and well-being (see Ps 45:8; 133:2). • The remnant would start out as small offshoots but would grow into ***great oaks*** (see 60:21). • ***in Israel:*** Hebrew *in Zion.*

61:6 ***priests . . . ministers:*** The nation would fulfill its original calling (Exod 19:6).

61:7 The people had suffered God's wrath for their sins (40:2); now they would receive ***a double share*** of God's blessing.

61:8 Those who belong to the community of God's people are to imitate the character of God, who loves ***justice*** (see Mic 6:8) and hates ***wrongdoing*** (33:15).

61:9 ***Their descendants:*** The covenant will be effective from generation to generation. • ***The LORD has blessed*** them in fulfillment of his promise to Abraham (Gen 12:1-2; see 65:23).

61:10 ***clothing of salvation . . . robe of righteousness:*** With great joy God will clothe his people with the benefits of his salvation and righteousness (see 51:5; 56:1), ***like a bridegroom . . . or a bride*** (see 49:18; 62:5; Jer 2:32; 7:34; 16:9; 25:10; 33:11).

62:1 Isa 46:13
62:2 Isa 56:5
[h]*tsedeq* (6664) › Zeph 2:3
62:3 Zech 9:16; 1 Thes 2:19
62:4 Isa 54:6-7; Jer 32:41; Zeph 3:17-18
62:5 Isa 65:19
62:6 Jer 14:21; Ezek 33:7
62:7 Luke 18:1-8
62:9 Isa 65:13, 21-23
62:10 Isa 11:10
62:11 Isa 49:6; Zech 9:9; *Matt 21:5; Rev 22:12
62:12 Deut 7:6; 1 Pet 2:9

11 The Sovereign LORD will show his justice
to the nations of the world.
Everyone will praise him!
His righteousness will be like a garden in
early spring,
with plants springing up everywhere.

Isaiah's Prayer for Jerusalem

62 1 Because I love Zion,
I will not keep still.
Because my heart yearns for Jerusalem,
I cannot remain silent.
I will not stop praying for her
until her righteousness shines like the
dawn,
and her salvation blazes like a
burning torch.
2 The nations will see your [h]righteousness.
World leaders will be blinded by your
glory.
And you will be given a new name
by the LORD's own mouth.
3 The LORD will hold you in his hand for
all to see—
a splendid crown in the hand of God.
4 Never again will you be called "The
Forsaken City"
or "The Desolate Land."
Your new name will be "The City of
God's Delight"
and "The Bride of God,"
for the LORD delights in you
and will claim you as his bride.
5 Your children will commit themselves to
you, O Jerusalem,
just as a young man commits himself
to his bride.
Then God will rejoice over you
as a bridegroom rejoices over his
bride.
6 O Jerusalem, I have posted watchmen on
your walls;
they will pray day and night,
continually.
Take no rest, all you who pray to the
LORD.
7 Give the LORD no rest until he completes
his work,
until he makes Jerusalem the pride of
the earth.
8 The LORD has sworn to Jerusalem by his
own strength:
"I will never again hand you over to
your enemies.
Never again will foreign warriors come
and take away your grain and new wine.
9 You raised the grain, and you will eat it,
praising the LORD.
Within the courtyards of the Temple,
you yourselves will drink the wine you
have pressed."
10 Go out through the gates!
Prepare the highway for my people to
return!
Smooth out the road; pull out the
boulders;
raise a flag for all the nations to see.
11 The LORD has sent this message to every
land:
"Tell the people of Israel,
'Look, your Savior is coming.
See, he brings his reward with him as
he comes.' "
12 They will be called "The Holy People"
and "The People Redeemed by the
LORD."
And Jerusalem will be known as "The
Desirable Place"
and "The City No Longer Forsaken."

62:1-12 The servant here commits himself to proclaiming the good news continuously until the glory of Zion is realized.

62:2 The real beauty and *glory* of God's people would not be seen in earthly treasures or a rebuilt city but would shine forth from their *righteousness.* Others would be drawn by this divine gift. • A *new name* reflects the change in Zion's status (see 62:4).

62:4 ***The Forsaken City:*** Hebrew *Azubah,* which means "forsaken." In the Exile, the Lord abandoned his people to the judgment they deserved (54:7). • ***The Desolate Land:*** Hebrew *Shemamah,* which means "desolate." • ***The City of God's Delight:*** Hebrew *Hephzibah,* which means "my delight is in her." • ***The Bride of God:*** Hebrew *Beulah,* which means "married." The people will be "married" to the Lord—an appropriate image for the close covenant relationship (54:5; Hos 1–3).

62:6-7 The *watchmen* probably represent the prophets. • ***they will pray day and night:*** They will continually seek the full restoration and blessing of Zion, unlike the destructive watchmen of 56:10.

62:8 The Lord swore an oath just as he did when he had *sworn* an oath to Noah (Gen 8:20–9:17), to Abraham (Gen 22:16; see also Luke 1:73; Heb 6:13), and to David (Ps 89:3). • ***I will never again hand you over:*** In order to punish and purge a remnant from his people, God had intentionally brought in the Assyrians and Babylonians to decimate them (see 6:12-13). He would never do this again.

62:9 The people would eat and drink the fruit of their labor (65:13, 22; see Lev 23:39-40; Deut 14:22-26). This is the opposite of what happened when God judged them (see Deut 28:38-40; Amos 5:11; Mic 6:14-15).

62:10-12 This call to prepare for God's coming salvation combines elements from all parts of Isaiah: the proclamation (the signal or banner, see 5:26), the preparation of the road (40:3; 57:14), the coming of God with his reward (40:5, 9-10), and the holy and redeemed citizenry (35:8-10).

62:10 ***highway:*** See also 40:3; 57:14. • A ***flag for all the nations to see*** is a signal that directs foreigners to come to Zion for God's salvation. Earlier, a similar signal was used to call for the nations to attack Judah (5:26).

62:11 ***Tell the people of Israel:*** Literally *Tell the daughter of Zion;* see also Matt 21:5.

Judgment against the LORD's Enemies

63 1 Who is this who comes from
Edom,
from the city of Bozrah,
with his clothing stained red?
Who is this in royal robes,
marching in his great strength?

"It is I, the LORD, announcing your
salvation!
It is I, the LORD, who has the power to
save!"

2 Why are your clothes so red,
as if you have been treading out grapes?

3 "I have been treading the winepress
alone;
no one was there to help me.
In my anger I have trampled my enemies
as if they were grapes.
In my fury I have trampled my foes.
Their blood has stained my clothes.
4 For the time has come for me to avenge
my people,
to ransom them from their oppressors.
5 I was amazed to see that no one
intervened
to help the oppressed.
So I myself stepped in to save them with
my strong arm,
and my wrath sustained me.
6 I crushed the nations in my anger
and made them stagger and fall to the
ground,
spilling their blood upon the earth."

Praise for the LORD's Rescue

7 I will tell of the LORD's unfailing love.
I will praise the LORD for all he has done.
I will rejoice in his great goodness to
Israel,
which he has granted according to his
mercy and love.
8 He said, "They are my very own people.
Surely they will not betray me again."
And he became their Savior.
9 In all their suffering he also suffered,
and he personally rescued them.
In his love and mercy he [i]redeemed
them.
He lifted them up and carried them
through all the years.
10 But they rebelled against him
and grieved his Holy [j]Spirit.
So he became their enemy
and fought against them.

11 Then they remembered those days of old
when Moses led his people out of
Egypt.
They cried out, "Where is the one who
brought Israel through the sea,
with Moses as their shepherd?
Where is the one who sent his Holy
Spirit
to be among his people?
12 Where is the one whose power was
displayed
when Moses lifted up his hand—
the one who divided the sea before them,
making himself famous forever?
13 Where is the one who led them through
the bottom of the sea?
They were like fine stallions
racing through the desert, never
stumbling.
14 As with cattle going down into a
peaceful valley,
the Spirit of the LORD gave them rest.
You led your people, LORD,
and gained a magnificent reputation."

63:1
Jer 49:13
Amos 1:12
Zeph 3:17

63:2
Rev 19:13, 15

63:3
Isa 22:5
Mic 7:10

63:4
Jer 51:6

63:5
Isa 52:10; 59:16

63:7
1 Kgs 8:66
Ps 25:6-7; 86:5
Eph 2:4

63:8
Exod 6:7

63:9
Exod 23:20-23
Judg 10:16
[i]*ga'al* (1350)
›Jer 31:11

63:10
Ps 78:40
Acts 7:51
Eph 4:30
[j]*ruakh* (7307)
›Mic 2:7

63:11
Num 11:17, 25, 29
Isa 51:9-10

63:12
Exod 6:6; 14:21-22

63:13
Jer 31:9

63:14
Josh 21:44

63:1-6 The judgment of Edom typifies God's judgment of all the nations (see also 34:5-15).

63:1 The Lord's robes are *stained red* with blood (63:3; cp. Rev 19:13). • The name *Bozrah* (Hebrew *botsrah*) is a wordplay on the verb *batsar* ("gather grapes").

63:2 The term *red* (Hebrew *'adom*) is a wordplay on the name *Edom.*

63:4 ***the time . . . to avenge my people:*** See note on 34:8. • ***to ransom:*** See note on 43:1.

63:6 ***made them stagger:*** The wicked nations would be forced to drink from the intoxicating cup of God's wrath (49:26; 51:17, 21).

63:7-14 The prophet reflects on Israel's past, how God showed his unfailing love and how his people alternatively rebelled against him, suffered hardship, returned to the Lord, and experienced his blessing.

63:7 ***unfailing love . . . all he has done . . . his great goodness:*** The whole history of God's care for his people demonstrates his compassion, provision, and protection.

63:8 ***They are my very own people:*** God's possession of and commitment to his people was central to the covenant (see 43:1). • ***they will not betray me:*** The Lord expected his own people to honor their relationship with him, unlike the nations, whose story is a history of treachery (Gen 3–11). But Israel, too, betrayed their God (63:10). • ***their Savior:*** God rescued and protected his people (see 43:3).

63:9 ***he also suffered:*** God identified with his suffering people, and their suffering brought him grief. Later, Jesus suffered on behalf of all humanity. • ***and he personally*** (literally *and the angel of his presence*) ***rescued them:*** E.g., see Exod 12:25-33; 14:10-31; 23:20-23.

63:10 ***But they rebelled:*** See also 1:2; 1:4; 59:1-15; Pss 78; 106. • Persistent disobedience and unbelief ***grieved his Holy Spirit*** (Ps 106:33; Matt 12:32; Mark 3:29). • ***he became their enemy:*** Examples include Israel's period of wandering in the wilderness (see the book of Numbers), the period of the judges (see the book of Judges), and the period leading up to the Exile (see the book of Jeremiah).

63:14 God *gave* his people *rest* after he brought them into the Promised Land (see 63:9; Josh 1:13; 22:4; 23:1).

Prayer for Mercy and Pardon

15 LORD, look down from heaven;
look from your holy, glorious home,
and see us.
Where is the passion and the might
you used to show on our behalf?
Where are your mercy and
compassion now?
16 Surely you are still our Father!
Even if Abraham and Jacob would
disown us,
LORD, you would still be our Father.
You are our [k]Redeemer from ages past.
17 LORD, why have you allowed us to turn
from your path?
Why have you given us stubborn
hearts so we no longer fear you?
Return and help us, for we are your
servants,
the tribes that are your special
possession.
18 How briefly your holy people possessed
your holy place,
and now our enemies have destroyed it.
19 Sometimes it seems as though we never
belonged to you,
as though we had never been known
as your people.

64 1 Oh, that you would burst from the
heavens and come down!
How the mountains would quake in
your presence!
2 As fire causes wood to burn
and water to boil,
your coming would make the nations
tremble.
Then your enemies would learn the
reason for your fame!
3 When you came down long ago,
you did awesome deeds beyond our
highest expectations.
And oh, how the mountains quaked!
4 For since the world began,
no ear has heard
and no eye has seen a God like you,
who works for those who wait for
him!
5 You welcome those who gladly do good,
who follow godly ways.
But you have been very angry with us,
for we are not godly.
We are constant sinners;
how can people like us be saved?
6 We are all infected and impure with sin.
When we display our righteous
deeds,
they are nothing but filthy rags.
Like autumn leaves, we wither and fall,
and our sins sweep us away like the
wind.
7 Yet no one calls on your name
or pleads with you for mercy.
Therefore, you have turned away from us
and turned us over to our sins.
8 And yet, O LORD, you are our Father.
We are the clay, and you are the potter.
We all are formed by your hand.
9 Don't be so angry with us, LORD.
Please don't [a]remember our sins
forever.
Look at us, we pray,
and see that we are all your people.
10 Your holy cities are destroyed.
Zion is a wilderness;
yes, Jerusalem is a desolate ruin.
11 The holy and beautiful Temple
where our ancestors praised you
has been burned down,
and all the things of beauty are
destroyed.
12 After all this, LORD, must you still refuse
to help us?
Will you continue to be silent and
punish us?

63:15 Ps 80:14
63:16 Isa 41:8; Jer 31:20; [k]*go'el* (1350) ›Jer 50:34
63:17 Num 10:36; Isa 29:13-14
63:18 Ps 74:3-7
63:19 Lam 3:43-45
64:1 Exod 19:18; Judg 5:5; Nah 1:5
64:2 Ps 99:1
64:3 Ps 65:5; 66:5
64:4 Isa 40:31; *1 Cor 2:9
64:6 Ps 90:5-6; Isa 1:30; 30:22
64:7 Deut 31:18; Isa 1:15
64:8 Ps 100:3; Isa 45:9
64:9 Mic 7:18; [a]*zakar* (2142) ›Jer 15:15
64:11 Ps 74:3-7
64:12 Ps 83:1

63:15–64:12 The prophet's reflections on the past (63:7-14) inspire him to pray that God would now rescue his people as he has done before.

63:16 ***our Father:*** God's fatherhood and his commitment to his children are much more important and secure than national ancestry (see 9:6; 64:8; Deut 32:6; Ps 68:5; Mal 2:10; Matt 6:9-15; Rom 8:15-17). • ***Jacob:*** Literally *Israel;* see note on 14:1.

63:17 The prophet understands that God has the power to keep his people faithful, so he asks, ***why have you allowed us to turn from your path?*** • ***Return and help us:*** God likewise has the power to call his people back to himself (Ezek 36:25-27) and to defeat all their enemies.

63:18 The ***people*** were supposed to be ***holy,*** but their lack of holiness had led to destruction. • The ***holy place*** was the Temple, which the Babylonians destroyed in 586 BC (64:11; 2 Kgs 25:1-21).

63:19 Israel was constantly turning from God and then being punished by him.

64:1 In the Hebrew text this verse is included in 63:19.

64:2-12 Verses 64:2-12 are numbered 64:1-11 in Hebrew text.

64:4 Paul quotes this verse in 1 Cor 2:9.

64:5-6 ***constant sinners . . . infected and impure with sin:*** See also 59:1-15. The only hope for salvation and transformation is through Jesus Christ (see Rom 7:25–8:11).

64:7 ***you have turned away from us:*** See 1:15; 30:20; 59:2. • ***turned us over*** (as in Greek, Syriac, and Aramaic versions; Hebrew reads *melted us*) ***to our sins:*** Because the people were so bent on sinning, God left them to perish in their sinful ways (see Rom 1:24).

64:8 ***clay . . . potter:*** See also 29:16; 45:9; Rom 9:20-21.

64:10 ***holy cities:*** All the cities of Judah were considered holy to God. However, the Temple in the host city of Jerusalem was the most holy place.

Judgment and Final Salvation

65 The LORD says,
"I was ready to respond, but no one
asked for help.
I was ready to be found, but no one
was looking for me.
I said, 'Here I am, here I am!'
to a nation that did not call on my name.
2 All day long I opened my arms to a
rebellious people.
But they follow their own evil paths
and their own crooked schemes.
3 All day long they insult me to my face
by worshiping idols in their sacred
gardens.
They burn incense on pagan altars.
4 At night they go out among the graves,
worshiping the dead.
They eat the flesh of pigs
and make stews with other forbidden
foods.
5 Yet they say to each other,
'Don't come too close or you will
defile me!
I am holier than you!'
These people are a stench in my nostrils,
an acrid smell that never goes away.

6 "Look, my decree is written out in front
of me:
I will not stand silent;
I will repay them in full!
Yes, I will repay them—
7 both for their own sins
and for those of their ancestors,"
says the LORD.
"For they also burned incense on the
mountains
and insulted me on the hills.
I will pay them back in full!
8 "But I will not destroy them all,"
says the LORD.
"For just as good grapes are found among
a cluster of bad ones
(and someone will say, 'Don't throw
them all away—
some of those grapes are good!'),
so I will not destroy all Israel.
For I still have true servants there.
9 I will preserve a remnant of the people
of Israel
and of Judah to possess my land.
Those I choose will inherit it,
and my servants will live there.
10 The plain of Sharon will again be filled
with flocks
for my people who have searched
for me,
and the valley of Achor will be a place
to pasture herds.

11 "But because the rest of you have
forsaken the LORD
and have forgotten his Temple,
and because you have prepared feasts to
honor the god of Fate
and have offered mixed wine to the
god of Destiny,
12 now I will 'destine' you for the sword.
All of you will bow down before the
executioner.
For when I called, you did not answer.
When I spoke, you did not listen.
You deliberately sinned—before my very
eyes—
and chose to do what you know I
despise."

65:1-2
*Rom 10:20-21
65:3
Job 2:5
65:4
Lev 11:7
65:5
Matt 9:11
Luke 18:9-12
65:6
Ps 50:3, 21
Isa 42:14
65:7
Jer 13:25
Ezek 20:27-28
Hos 2:13
65:9
Amos 9:11-15
65:10
Josh 7:24
Isa 33:9
65:11
Isa 1:4, 28
65:12
2 Chr 36:15-16
Prov 1:24

65:1–66:24 Here the Lord responds to the prayer in 63:7–64:12. These chapters also conclude the book of Isaiah.

65:1-2 The Lord opened up every opportunity for the people of Israel to seek him (55:6; 58:2), but they did not. • ***I was ready to respond . . . to a rebellious people:*** Greek version reads *I was found by people who were not looking for me. / I showed myself to those who were not asking for me. / All day long I opened my arms to them, / but they were disobedient and rebellious.* Cp. Rom 10:20-21, which quotes from the Greek version. • ***to a nation that did not call on my name:*** or *to a nation that did not bear my name.*

65:3 ***Sacred gardens*** were a part of the fertility religion of Baal (see note on 1:29-30).

65:4 ***worshiping the dead:*** God had banned the practice of necromancy (consulting dead spirits; see 8:19-22; 47:9; Deut 18:9-11). • ***the flesh of pigs . . . other forbidden foods:*** See 66:3-4; Lev 11:7; Deut 14:3, 8.

65:5 ***you will defile me! I am holier than you!*** The people of Israel used the language of ritual purification, as stated in the laws of Moses, yet they practiced rites influenced by paganism. Because of this hypocrisy, they were a ***stench*** in God's ***nostrils*** (see 1:10-15).

65:6 ***my decree is written out*** (or *their sins are written out;* literally *it stands written*): God is fully committed to carry out his plan. • The godly had asked whether the Lord would ***stand silent*** forever (64:12). God answered that he would not but would deal with the wicked before restoring the righteous remnant.

65:7 The people of Israel practiced their pagan religion at sacred shrines on ***mountains*** and ***hills*** (see 1 Kgs 14:23; Hos 4:13).

65:8-16 The Lord planned to spare and reward a remnant of righteous people.

65:9 ***Those I choose:*** See note on 41:8. • ***remnant of the people of Israel:*** Literally *remnant of Jacob.* See note on 14:1.

65:10 ***Sharon*** was a fertile and beautiful marshy region southwest of Mount Carmel (see 33:9). The ***valley of Achor*** in the vicinity of Jericho was associated with the curse on Achan (Josh 7:24-26); it would be transformed into a place of blessing (Hos 2:15). These western and eastern regions might represent the renewal of the whole land.

65:11 ***Fate*** and ***Destiny*** are names of pagan gods (*Gad, Meni*) that were thought to bring fortune and determine one's destiny.

65:12 ***'destine':*** This verb (Hebrew *manithi*) is a wordplay on Meni (65:11). However, God alone controls human and national destinies.

65:13 Isa 5:13
65:14 Matt 8:12; Luke 13:28
65:15 Jer 24:9
65:16 Isa 45:23; [b]'amen (0543) ›Jer 11:5
65:17 2 Cor 5:17; 2 Pet 3:13; [c]bara' (1254) ›Mal 2:10; [d]shamayim (8064) ›Jer 23:24; [e]'erets (0776) ›Isa 66:22
65:18 Ps 98:1-9; Isa 35:10
65:19 Jer 32:41; Rev 7:17
65:20 Eccl 8:12-13
65:21 Amos 9:14
65:23 Isa 61:9
65:24 Ps 91:15; Dan 10:12
65:25 Gen 3:14; Isa 11:6-7, 9

13 Therefore, this is what the Sovereign
LORD says:
"My servants will eat,
but you will starve.
My servants will drink,
but you will be thirsty.
My servants will rejoice,
but you will be sad and ashamed.
14 My servants will sing for joy,
but you will cry in sorrow and despair.
15 Your name will be a curse word among
my people,
for the Sovereign LORD will destroy
you
and will call his true servants by
another name.
16 All who invoke a blessing or take an oath
will do so by the God of [b]truth.
For I will put aside my anger
and forget the evil of earlier days.
17 "Look! I am [c]creating new [d]heavens and
a new [e]earth,
and no one will even think about the
old ones anymore.
18 Be glad; rejoice forever in my creation!
And look! I will create Jerusalem as a
place of happiness.
Her people will be a source of joy.
19 I will rejoice over Jerusalem
and delight in my people.
And the sound of weeping and crying
will be heard in it no more.
20 "No longer will babies die when only a
few days old.
No longer will adults die before they
have lived a full life.
No longer will people be considered old
at one hundred!
Only the cursed will die that young!
21 In those days people will live in the
houses they build
and eat the fruit of their own vineyards.
22 Unlike the past, invaders will not take
their houses
and confiscate their vineyards.
For my people will live as long as trees,
and my chosen ones will have time to
enjoy their hard-won gains.
23 They will not work in vain,
and their children will not be doomed
to misfortune.
For they are people blessed by the LORD,
and their children, too, will be blessed.
24 I will answer them before they even call
to me.
While they are still talking about their
needs,
I will go ahead and answer their
prayers!
25 The wolf and the lamb will feed together.
The lion will eat hay like a cow.
But the snakes will eat dust.
In those days no one will be hurt or
destroyed on my holy mountain.
I, the LORD, have spoken!"

The New Order (65:17-25)

Isa 11:1; 24:14-16; 25:7-8; 26:19; 30:26; 43:18-19; 60:18-19; 62:2; Jer 23:7-8; 31:10-14; 2 Cor 3:6-11; 5:17; Heb 12:18-24; Rev 21:1–22:21

Isaiah differentiates the *old order,* the present world of human powers and pressures, from the *new order,* a new creation where justice and harmony triumph.

The old order—defiled and condemned—evokes memories of weeping (65:19), death (65:20, 23), oppression and violence (65:21-22), and the absence of God (65:24). The old order contrasts with the new (43:18-19; 48:6; 62:2; 65:17). Every judgment by God reduces human power structures and pride. When the Lord acts in a redemptive way, he restructures the world under his kingship.

Isaiah's vision of the new order centers on the Lord as the Great King in his holiness and glory (6:1-5). God's people experience aspects of the new order in this life, such as God's comfort (40:1), salvation (45:22), joy (24:14-15), righteousness (24:16), peace (26:3), divine blessing, and protection. Other dimensions lie beyond our experience: the end of death (25:7-8); the resurrection (26:19); the cessation of enmity, corruption, and evil (60:18; 65:25); the full enjoyment of God's presence (30:26; 60:19); and God's uncontested rule in his eternal kingdom (see Rev 21–22).

65:13-15 The contrast between the wicked (addressed as *you*) and God's *servants* pertains to all areas of life. God punishes the wicked but blesses those who truly serve him (see 65:17-25).

65:15 The new *name* given to the faithful represents a new identity and a deeper relationship with the Lord (see also 62:2).

65:16 *evil of earlier days:* Cp. Rev 21:4.

65:17 The *new heavens* and *new earth* will be a place of righteousness (see also 2 Pet 3:13; Rev 21). Paul described those who believe in Christ as already being part of the new creation (see 2 Cor 5:17; Gal 6:15).

65:18-19 *Jerusalem* here symbolizes God's eternal kingdom (Rev 21:1-4).

65:24 God will be present with his people (see also 19:22; 30:19; contrast 1:15; 59:2).

65:25 *The snakes* represent evil (27:1; Gen 3).

66 This is what the LORD says:
"Heaven is my [f]throne,
and the earth is my footstool.
Could you build me a temple as good as
that?
Could you build me such a resting
place?
2 My hands have made both heaven and
earth;
they and everything in them are mine.
I, the LORD, have spoken!

"I will bless those who have humble and
contrite hearts,
who tremble at my word.
3 But those who choose their own ways—
delighting in their detestable sins—
will not have their offerings accepted.
When such people sacrifice a bull,
it is no more acceptable than a human
sacrifice.
When they sacrifice a lamb,
it's as though they had sacrificed a dog!
When they bring an offering of grain,
they might as well offer the blood of
a pig.
When they burn frankincense,
it's as if they had blessed an idol.
4 I will send them great trouble—
all the things they feared.
For when I called, they did not answer.
When I spoke, they did not listen.
They deliberately sinned before my very
eyes
and chose to do what they know
I despise."

5 Hear this message from the LORD,
all you who tremble at his words:
"Your own people hate you
and throw you out for being loyal to
my name.
'Let the LORD be honored!' they scoff.
'Be joyful in him!'
But they will be put to shame.
6 What is all the commotion in the city?
What is that terrible noise from the
Temple?
It is the voice of the LORD
taking vengeance against his
enemies.

7 "Before the birth pains even begin,
Jerusalem gives birth to a son.
8 Who has ever seen anything as strange
as this?
Who ever heard of such a thing?
Has a nation ever been born in a single
day?
Has a country ever come forth in a
mere moment?
But by the time Jerusalem's birth pains
begin,
her children will be born.
9 Would I ever bring this nation to the
point of birth
and then not deliver it?" asks the
LORD.
"No! I would never keep this nation from
being born,"
says your God.

10 "Rejoice with Jerusalem!
Be glad with her, all you who love her
and all you who [g]mourn for her.
11 Drink deeply of her glory
even as an infant drinks at its
mother's comforting breasts."
12 This is what the LORD says:
"I will give Jerusalem a river of peace and
prosperity.
The wealth of the nations will flow
to her.
Her children will be nursed at her
breasts,
carried in her arms, and held on her
lap.
13 I will comfort you there in
Jerusalem
as a mother comforts her child."

66:1
Ps 11:4
Matt 5:34-35
John 4:20-21
*Acts 7:49-50
[f]*kisse'* (3678)
›Ezek 1:26

66:2
Ps 34:18
Matt 5:3-4
Luke 18:13-14

66:4
Prov 1:31-32; 10:24
Jer 7:13, 30

66:5
Ps 38:20
Matt 5:10-12
Luke 13:17
John 9:34

66:6
Joel 3:7

66:9
Isa 37:3

66:10
Ps 122:6
Rom 15:10
[g]*'abal* (0056)
›Dan 10:2

66:12
Isa 60:5

66:13
2 Cor 1:4

66:1 ***my throne . . . my footstool:*** God's kingdom extends over all creation (see 40:22; Matt 5:34-35). • ***a temple . . . a resting place:*** Because the entire universe is God's dwelling place, humans cannot limit him to a building (see 1 Kgs 8:27). • Stephen quoted 66:1-2a in his last sermon (Acts 7:49-50).

66:2 God is pleased to dwell with ***those who have humble and contrite hearts*** (57:15; Ps 51:17). • ***they and everything in them are mine:*** As in Greek, Latin, and Syriac versions; Hebrew reads *these things are.* • ***who tremble at my word:*** The humble and contrite submit themselves to God's will, whereas the arrogant resist it.

66:3 ***delighting in their detestable sins:*** Literally *delighting in abominations,* which refers to pagan worship practices. • ***sacrifice a bull . . . blessed an idol:*** Wicked people brought sacrifices as prescribed by the law, but their sin rendered those sacrifices equivalent to pagan offerings (see 1:11-17).

66:6 ***terrible noise from the Temple:*** This parallels the situation described in Ezek 9 when God's executioner began to destroy the wicked people of Jerusalem. • ***vengeance against his enemies:*** God would deal out retribution to the disobedient members of his own people. They were his enemies because of their persistent sin and rejection of God.

66:7 ***birth pains . . . give birth to a son:*** See 9:6-7; 54:1-3.

66:8 ***by the time . . . her children will be born:*** A miraculous repopulation of Zion would occur (see 49:19-20; 54:1-3; contrast 1:8-9). • ***Jerusalem's:*** Hebrew *Zion's.*

66:9 The Lord promised that he would surely recreate his holy nation.

66:12 ***a river:*** The people, who lost *peace and prosperity* in the Exile, would receive it back abundantly (see 48:18).

66:13 ***I will comfort you:*** See note on 40:1-31.

66:14
Prov 3:8
Zech 10:7

66:16
Ezek 38:22

66:17
Lev 11:7

66:19
1 Chr 16:24
Isa 42:12

66:20
Isa 2:2-3; 43:5-6; 49:22; 52:11; 60:4

66:21
Isa 61:6
1 Pet 2:5, 9

66:22
John 10:27-29
2 Pet 3:13
Rev 21:1
[h]*'erets* (0776)
›Gen 1:1

66:23
Isa 27:13
[i]*khawah* (7812)
›Zech 14:16

66:24
Isa 1:31
Dan 12:2
*Mark 9:48

14 When you see these things, your heart
will rejoice.
You will flourish like the grass!
Everyone will see the LORD's hand of
blessing on his servants—
and his anger against his enemies.
15 See, the LORD is coming with fire,
and his swift chariots roar like a
whirlwind.
He will bring punishment with the fury
of his anger
and the flaming fire of his hot rebuke.
16 The LORD will punish the world by fire
and by his sword.
He will judge the earth,
and many will be killed by him.

17"Those who 'consecrate' and 'purify'
themselves in a sacred garden with its idol
in the center—feasting on pork and rats and
other detestable meats—will come to a terrible end," says the LORD.
18"I can see what they are doing, and
I know what they are thinking. So I will
gather all nations and peoples together,
and they will see my glory.
19I will perform a sign among them. And I will send
those who survive to be messengers to the
nations—to Tarshish, to the Libyans and Lydians (who are famous as archers), to Tubal
and Greece, and to all the lands beyond the
sea that have not heard of my fame or seen
my glory. There they will declare my glory
to the nations.
20They will bring the remnant of your people back from every nation.
They will bring them to my holy mountain
in Jerusalem as an offering to the LORD.
They will ride on horses, in chariots and
wagons, and on mules and camels," says the
LORD.
21"And I will appoint some of them to
be my priests and Levites. I, the LORD, have
spoken!

22 "As surely as my new heavens and [h]earth
will remain,
so will you always be my people,
with a name that will never disappear,"
says the LORD.
23 "All humanity will come to [i]worship me
from week to week
and from month to month.
24 And as they go out, they will see
the dead bodies of those who have
rebelled against me.
For the worms that devour them will
never die,
and the fire that burns them will
never go out.
All who pass by
will view them with utter horror."

66:14 ***flourish like the grass:*** Contrast 40:7; 64:6. • God's ***enemies*** included the disobedient from the foreign nations and from within Israel (see 61:2; 66:6).

66:15-16 ***the LORD is coming with fire:*** See note on 5:25. God will appear with furious judgment against his enemies (see Ps 7:13). By contrast, he will reveal his glory to his people (see 40:5, 10). • God ***will judge*** all creation as a part of the process of renewing ***the earth*** (see 24:1-4; 65:17).

66:17 Apostates who ***'consecrate' and 'purify' themselves*** through idolatrous practices are an abomination to God (cp. 1:28-31; 65:4).

66:18-23 When God reveals his glory to all people, the nations join in God's plan of redemption; they can even serve as priests and Levites before him. The godly from all nations last from generation to generation as they serve the living God.

66:19 The ***sign*** is the proclamation of God's glory among the nations (66:20). God will establish a righteous and faithful new people consisting of godly Gentiles together with faithful Israelites (Rev 15:3-4; see also Acts 2). • ***Libyans:*** As in some Greek manuscripts, which read *Put* [that is, *Libya*]; Hebrew reads *Pul*. • ***Lydians:*** Hebrew *Lud*. • ***Greece:*** Hebrew *Javan*.

66:21 That some of the Gentiles would serve as ***priests and Levites*** signifies the removal of God's distinction between Hebrews and Gentiles (see 56:7; see also Gal 6:15; Eph 4:11-13).

66:22 ***always be my people:*** God's promise to Abraham was secure (Gen 17:7; see also Gal 3:8, 14). • ***a name that will never disappear:*** The identity of this new people will last forever (see 59:21).

66:24 Isaiah gives a final warning of the severity of God's judgment. The book begins and ends with the condemnation of ***those who have rebelled*** (see 1:2-4). • The judgment of God on wicked humans will generate ***utter horror*** because such people will have no hope and no relief from suffering (see also Matt 5:22; 25:41; Mark 9:47-48; Rev 20:11-15).

THE BOOK OF JEREMIAH

God called Jeremiah to warn the kingdom of Judah of its impending destruction. When Jeremiah began preaching, Judah was relatively prosperous, free, and secure, but the kingdom's fortunes changed dramatically as Nebuchadnezzar II of Babylon asserted his power in the region. Judah suffered under his heavy hand for twenty years before he destroyed the city of Jerusalem and exiled its citizens to Babylon. Throughout these events, Jeremiah warned of judgment and destruction while distinctively recording his own experience of the pain and conflict these announcements brought. As God passionately and tenderly begged his people to return to him and receive salvation, Jeremiah beautifully conveyed God's promise to restore Israel as his people.

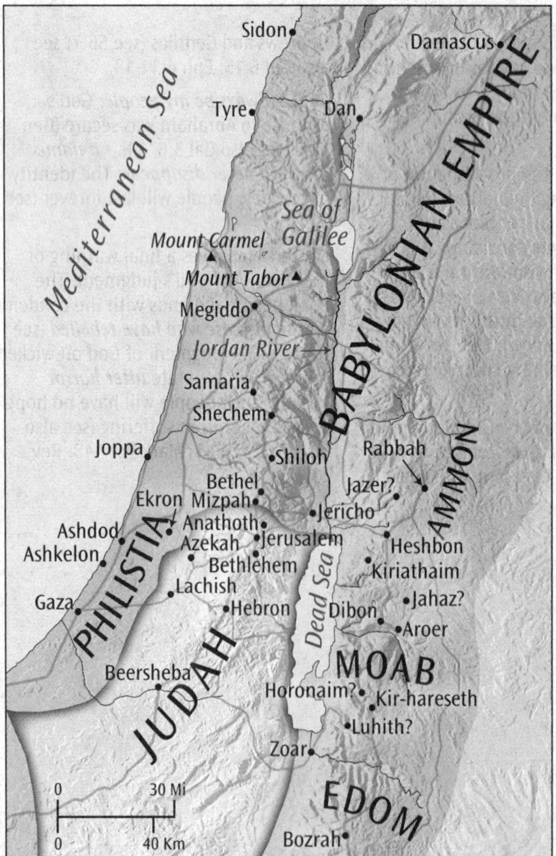

SETTING

During the decades before Jeremiah's birth, Assyria dominated the ancient Near East, including Egypt for a time. King Manasseh of Judah became an Assyrian vassal, swore allegiance to the Assyrian deities, and worshiped idols (see 2 Kgs 21:1-7) for most of his long reign (686–642 BC). As a result, the kingdom of Judah became a spiritual

◂ **Israel and Judah during Jeremiah's Ministry, about 605 BC.** Between 612 and 605 BC, the Babylonians conquered the Assyrians, beat back the Egyptians, and gained decisive control of the region. Thereafter the kingdom of Judah experienced Babylon's crushing hand until 586 BC, when Jerusalem was destroyed. Most of Jeremiah's prophecies came 605–586 BC.

Ammon, Rabbah 25:21; 27:3; 40:11-14; 41:10-15; 49:1-6
Anathoth 1:1; 11:21-23; 32:6-15
Philistia 25:20; 47:1-7
Azekah, Lachish 34:7
Bethel 48:13
Bethlehem 41:17
Moab 25:21; 27:3; 40:11; 48:1-47
Damascus 49:23-27
Dan 4:15; 8:16
Edom 25:21; 27:3; 40:11; 49:7-22
Jericho 39:5; 52:8
Mizpah 40:6–41:14
Mount Carmel, Mount Tabor 46:18
Samaria, Shechem 23:13; 31:5; 41:5
Shiloh 7:12-15; 26:4-9; 41:5
Sidon, Tyre 27:3; 47:4

wasteland (but see 2 Chr 33:10-17). Manasseh's son Amon followed his father's negative example during his brief reign (2 Kgs 21:21). When some of the palace servants in Jerusalem assassinated Amon (2 Kgs 21:23-24), his eight-year-old son, Josiah, was quickly crowned king of Judah.

Josiah served the Lord and rejected his father's and grandfather's support of paganism. In the twelfth year of his reign, he decreed that pagan idols and altars should be destroyed (2 Chr 34:3-7). In his eighteenth year on the throne, he funded the repair of the Temple so that the priests and people of Judah could participate in worshiping the one true God (2 Chr 34:8). During these repairs, the Book of the Law, which had been forgotten during Manasseh's reign, was recovered. It so clearly described Judah's sins in Jeremiah's time that its teachings became a significant basis for Jeremiah's prophetic ministry.

Jeremiah was born into a priestly family in the small town of Anathoth, a few miles north of Jerusalem. He was familiar with the history of God's relationship with Israel and with the covenant God had made with Israel under Moses. That knowledge was enhanced by the recovery of the Book of the Law. Jeremiah's ministry began about 627 BC, soon after the Book of the Law was found.

Josiah's death in battle with the Egyptians in 609 BC (2 Kgs 23:29) spelled the end of revival in Judah and the beginning of the end of the nation. Between 612 and 605 BC, the Babylonians crushed the Assyrians and beat back the Egyptians; Judah's security and prosperity ended as the Babylonians gained control of the region. Between 605 and 586 BC, King Nebuchadnezzar of Babylon attacked, subjugated, and finally destroyed the kingdom of Judah and the city of Jerusalem.

During this time, Judah's kings remained apostate from the Lord and refused to heed Jeremiah's warnings. Josiah's son, King Jehoiakim (609–598 BC), renewed pagan worship in Judah and relied on the Egyptians for support against the Babylonians; he was violently antagonistic to Jeremiah's messages. His son Jehoiachin reigned for only three months at the beginning of 597 BC. When the Babylonians defeated Judah in April 597 BC, they replaced Jehoiachin with his uncle, Zedekiah (597–586 BC), who reigned as a vassal of Babylon.

Zedekiah is depicted as weak and indecisive. He respected Jeremiah and often asked him for advice, but he lacked the courage to follow the Lord.

OUTLINE

1:1-3
Superscription

1:4-19
Jeremiah's Call and First Visions

2:1–20:18
Jeremiah's Early Ministry

21:1–28:17
Messages of Judgment

29:1-32
Messages to the Exiles in Babylon

30:1–33:26
Messages of Hope

34:1–39:18
Jerusalem's Destruction

40:1–44:30
After the Destruction of Jerusalem

45:1-5
A Message for Baruch

46:1–51:64
Messages for the Nations

52:1-34
Historical Appendix: Judgment on Jerusalem

TIMELINE

697–642 BC
Manasseh as king of Judah

about 645~615 BC
Nahum as prophet

642–640 BC
Amon as king of Judah

640–609 BC
Josiah as king of Judah

about 635~622 BC
Zephaniah as prophet

about 630 / 605 BC
Habakkuk as prophet

about 627~580 BC
Jeremiah as prophet

612 BC
Nineveh is conquered by Babylon

610–595 BC
Neco II as pharaoh of Egypt

609 BC
Jehoahaz as king of Judah; taken prisoner to Egypt

609–598 BC
Jehoiakim as king of Judah

605–562 BC
Nebuchadnezzar II as king of Babylon

605 BC
Battle of Carchemish

605 BC
Nebuchadnezzar first invades Judah

about 605~535 BC
Daniel in Babylon

597 BC
Jehoiachin as king of Judah

April 597 BC
Nebuchadnezzar captures Jerusalem, takes Jehoiachin and others to Babylon

about 593~570 BC
Ezekiel as prophet in Babylon

597–586 BC
Zedekiah as king of Judah

586 BC
Nebuchadnezzar destroys Jerusalem, takes people of Judah into exile, end of the southern kingdom of Judah

around 586 BC
Obadiah as prophet

585 BC or later
Judah's remaining people flee to Egypt

April 2, 561 BC
Jehoiachin is released from prison

559–530 BC
Cyrus II as king of Persia

Oct 539 BC
Cyrus II conquers Babylon

538 BC
Cyrus's decree of return, exiles return to Judea
Sheshbazzar leads first group of exiles to Jerusalem
Zerubbabel as governor of Judea

Instead, Zedekiah followed the advice of his administrators and broke his covenant to serve the Babylonian king. As a result, the Babylonians laid siege to Jerusalem in January 588 BC. In July 586 BC they finally broke through the walls of Jerusalem, destroyed the Temple, and razed the city. Most of the people in Jerusalem were taken captive to Babylon, though a remnant remained in Judah—including Jeremiah, who recorded what happened to the remnant community during the days following Jerusalem's destruction.

SUMMARY

Chapter 1 (627 BC) tells how God chose Jeremiah as his messenger.

Chapters 2–20 (627~605 BC) establish the dynamic pattern of relationships among God, Jeremiah, and the people of Judah. Through Jeremiah, God severely criticized pagan worship in Judah, warned of invasion from the north, and pronounced severe punishment. In chs 11–20, Jeremiah learns more about God's purposes.

Chapters 21–29 (605~593 BC) focus on verbal battles that Jeremiah had with Judah's kings, priests, and other prophets. Jeremiah's messages include scathing criticisms of these vicious leaders.

Chapters 30–33 (596~588 BC) provide a bright spot as they emphasize the possibility of restoration for the people of Judah and envision a new covenant to enrich the relationship between God and his people. The vision reaches into the future and announces a "righteous descendant" (33:15) who will bring salvation.

Chapters 34–45 (605~580 BC) tell of the Babylonian siege of Jerusalem, the breach of the city walls, and the complete destruction of the Temple, the city of Jerusalem, and the kingdom of Judah. Chapters 34–36 make it clear that the destruction was the result of Judah's having broken its covenant with the Lord. Jeremiah then describes what occurred after the Babylonians left Judah (586~580 BC): Gedaliah the governor was assassinated, and the remaining people of Judah fled to Egypt despite Jeremiah's warning not to.

Chapters 46–51 (605~593 BC) are an anthology of God's judgments on Judah's neighbors. All the nations, large and small, were to be punished for their idolatry and for their cruelty to God's chosen people. A few nations were promised divine help in the future. Israel was promised deliverance from exile and restoration in the Promised Land.

Chapter 52 (586~561 BC) describes the last days of Jerusalem, essentially repeating 2 Kgs 24:18–25:30.

AUTHORSHIP AND DATE

In the fourth year of King Jehoiakim's reign (605 BC), Jeremiah dictated a scroll to Baruch and had it delivered to the king (36:1-26). The king destroyed this scroll, but Jeremiah and Baruch rewrote the messages and "added much more!" (36:32). The contents of this second scroll probably make up Jer 2–20. Much of the rest of the book of Jeremiah appears to have been written later and added to the growing anthology. The book includes events down to Jeremiah's arrival in Egypt, so it seems likely that the book was essentially complete by 580 BC.

MANUSCRIPTS

Two very different texts of Jeremiah have been preserved. The first is the Hebrew Masoretic Text, which underlies nearly all English

translations of Jeremiah. The other Hebrew text was the basis of the Greek translation (the Septuagint or LXX), which was produced by Jewish scholars in Alexandria, Egypt about 250 BC. The Septuagint text is about 2,700 words shorter than the Hebrew Masoretic Text, and it rearranges some of the material. This provides evidence for two different collections of messages, one having been finalized among the Babylonian exiles, the other among the Egyptian refugees.

LITERARY FEATURES

The Messenger System. The text of Jeremiah is dominated by a structure of communication called a "messenger system," common in the royal governments of the ancient Near East. It is still used today. The king, emperor, or ruler of a country selected a person to deliver verbal and written messages to leaders of other countries. The messenger, often called a herald, carried the authority of his ruler as he delivered the royal message. The recipient accepted or rejected the message and sent back a reply with the messenger. If the recipient rejected the message, he might abuse the messenger and prepare for war (see 2 Sam 10:1-19). The messenger would report back to his ruler, who would decide how to punish the rebellious recipient.

Judicial Framework. Most of the messages in Jeremiah feature a judicial framework and vocabulary. The courtroom setting is established early in the book with the Lord's statement, "I will bring my case against you. . . . I will even bring charges against your children's children in the years to come" (2:9). The Lord assumes the roles of plaintiff, judge, and executioner. As plaintiff, he makes Jeremiah his advocate in bringing charges and evidence of sin against the leaders and the people. As judge, God makes Jeremiah the prosecutor. After the defendants express their arguments, the Lord pronounces the sentence and then carries it out.

Narratives. In Jeremiah, historical narratives focus on incidents involving Jeremiah and others. The prophet deals with kings, officials, priests, prophets, and the common people in times of crisis. The book also includes many autobiographical narratives that include the Lord speaking with Jeremiah. Often narrative sections end with the pronouncement of a decree, usually in poetic form.

MEANING AND MESSAGE

A battle raged in OT Israel between pagan idol worship and worship of the Lord. Jeremiah repeatedly reminded the Israelites that their covenant with the Lord required that they give him true, heartfelt, and exclusive devotion. In a pivotal passage (10:1-16), Jeremiah clearly contrasts the foolishness of idolatry with the majesty, glory, purity, and power of the God of Israel.

The people of Jerusalem and Judah thus faced a major conflict. If they continued to worship pagan idols, they would lose their holy city and Temple, their loved ones, and their wealth and freedom. The people tried to escape their predicament through defiance, arrogance, and anger, but the events of war soon plunged them into utter despair and death. Even then, they seemed unable to choose another course of action. To cease believing in the magical power of idols and rituals and to give up the allure and excitement of pagan festivals and sexual

Jeremiah is unusual among the Hebrew prophets because of the extent to which he revealed his personal feelings. Whereas others delivered their oracles without disclosing much of their inner selves, Jeremiah effectively lays bare the turbulent emotions of a man selected somewhat against his will to be God's spokesman to his generation.

R. K. HARRISON
Jeremiah, p. 34

freedom seemed too great a loss. The possibility that the Temple and Jerusalem might be destroyed was unthinkable. So only a few repented.

With passionate pleas, often couched in "if . . . then" sentences, the Lord offered a way back to his gracious salvation. If the people would earnestly and completely remove the vicious and salacious practices of idolatry from their lives, submit to the Lord without reservation, and fulfill his ethical requirements, then the Lord would cease being angry and accept them as his people again. Even when the calamities of ruin, death, and exile became a reality, the Lord promised to preserve a remnant that would serve him. He promised to bring the captives back to their homeland and grant them peace and prosperity.

The brightest description of God's mercies is found in 30:1–33:26, where a new covenant and a new king are promised. Instead of "uprooting and tearing down," he would "plant and rebuild" (1:10; 31:28). However, only a few repented in Jeremiah's days. In all of this, the prophet Jeremiah experienced a deep tension between the Lord's command (1:17-19) and his own desires. The Lord's command was "Go . . . and tell," whereas the prophet desired to keep peace with his neighbors (see 20:8-9). He felt a deep solidarity with his people, and the terrible words of judgment and destruction he was called to pronounce cut deeply into his own soul. More than any other OT prophet, Jeremiah let us see his heart as he struggled to obey (15:16-18; cp. Matt 26:36-42).

FURTHER READING

J. ANDREW DEARMAN
Jeremiah, Lamentations (2002)

R. K. HARRISON
Jeremiah & Lamentations (1973)

ELMER A. MARTENS
Jeremiah in *Cornerstone Biblical Commentary*, vol. 8 (2006)

J. A. THOMPSON
The Book of Jeremiah (1980)

1. SUPERSCRIPTION (1:1-3)

1 These are the words of Jeremiah son
of Hilkiah, one of the priests from the
town of Anathoth in the land of Benjamin.
2The LORD first gave messages to Jeremiah
during the thirteenth year of the reign of
Josiah son of Amon, king of Judah. 3The
LORD's messages continued throughout the
reign of King Jehoiakim, Josiah's son, until
the eleventh year of the reign of King Zedekiah, another of Josiah's sons. In August of
that eleventh year the people of Jerusalem
were taken away as captives.

2. JEREMIAH'S CALL AND FIRST VISIONS (1:4-19)

4The LORD gave me this message:

5 "I knew you before I formed you in your
mother's womb.
Before you were born I set you apart
and appointed you as my prophet to
the nations."

6"O Sovereign LORD," I said, "I can't speak
for you! I'm too young!"

7The LORD replied, "Don't say, 'I'm too
young,' for you must go wherever I send
you and say whatever I tell you. 8And don't
be afraid of the people, for I will be with
you and will protect you. I, the LORD, have
spoken!" 9Then the LORD reached out and
touched my mouth and said,

"Look, I have put my words in your
mouth!

1:1 2 Chr 36:12, 21; Ezra 1:1; Jer 3:6; 36:2; Dan 9:2; Matt 2:17; 16:14; 27:9
1:2 1 Kgs 13:2; 2 Kgs 21:24
1:3 2 Kgs 23:34; Jer 25:1; 39:2
1:5 Ps 139:15-16; Isa 49:1, 5; Jer 25:15-26
1:6 Exod 4:10
1:7 Ezek 2:3-4
1:8 Jer 15:20; Ezek 2:6

1:1-19 Jeremiah's call is presented as a conversation; God spoke as a king to Jeremiah. Jeremiah's objections show that he understood himself clearly. God responded to his objections with promises and compelling visions.

1:2-3 Jehoahaz and Jehoiachin are both missing from this list of kings. Neither of them reigned for longer than three months, and only a limited number of events are mentioned after the fall of Jerusalem. • The ***thirteenth year of the reign of Josiah*** was 627 BC. • ***In August:*** Literally *In the fifth month* of the ancient Hebrew lunar calendar. A number of events in Jeremiah can be cross-checked with dates in surviving Babylonian records and related accurately to our modern calendar. The fifth month in the eleventh year of Zedekiah's reign occurred within the months of August and September 586 BC. Also see 52:12 and note.

1:4-5 In his first *message* from the Lord, Jeremiah learned three important truths about God: his knowledge of all things, including individuals; his ability to choose individuals for specific tasks even before they come into existence; and his willingness to extend his authority to the people he calls. • God *set* Jeremiah *apart* to perform a special task and granted him the official status of a *prophet* when he *appointed* Jeremiah to that task. • Jeremiah's ministry extended to the *nations*. Although he traveled away from the kingdom of Judah only three times (see 13:4-7; 43:7-8), his written materials have been read worldwide.

1:6 Jeremiah was *young* (probably a teenager).

1:7-8 God urged Jeremiah to look beyond himself to the importance of the task he was called to fulfill. He had to meet God's requirements for a royal messenger, which included willingness to travel and the faithful delivery of the Lord's messages.

1:9 When God placed his *words* in Jeremiah's *mouth*, he granted the prophet the status of an official royal messenger, including the ability to speak authoritatively in public.

1:9
Exod 4:11-16
Deut 18:18
1:10
Isa 44:26-28
Jer 24:6; 31:28
2 Cor 10:4
1:11
Jer 24:3
Amos 7:8
1:12
Deut 32:35
1:13
Ezek 11:3, 7
Zech 4:2
1:14
Isa 41:25
Jer 4:6; 10:22
1:15
Isa 22:7
Jer 9:11; 25:9
1:16
Isa 2:8; 37:19
Jer 7:9; 10:3-5; 19:4
1:17
Ezek 2:6; 3:16-18

10 Today I appoint you to stand up
against nations and kingdoms.
Some you must uproot and tear down,
destroy and overthrow.
Others you must build up
and plant."

11 Then the LORD said to me, "Look, Jeremiah! What do you see?"
And I replied, "I see a branch from an almond tree."
12 And the LORD said, "That's right, and
it means that I am watching, and I will certainly carry out all my plans."
13 Then the LORD spoke to me again and
asked, "What do you see now?"
And I replied, "I see a pot of boiling water,
spilling from the north."
14 "Yes," the LORD said, "for terror from
the north will boil out on the people of this
land. 15 Listen! I am calling the armies of the
kingdoms of the north to come to Jerusalem. I, the LORD, have spoken!

"They will set their thrones
at the gates of the city.
They will attack its walls
and all the other towns of Judah.
16 I will pronounce judgment
on my people for all their
evil—
for deserting me and burning incense to
other gods.
Yes, they worship idols made with
their own hands!
17 "Get up and prepare for action.
Go out and tell them everything I tell
you to say.
Do not be afraid of them,
or I will make you look foolish in front
of them.

JEREMIAH (1:1-10)

Jer 13:1-14; 18:1-12; 19:1–20:6; 24:1-10; 26:1–29:32; 32:1-15; 36:1–44:30
2 Chr 35:25; 36:12, 21
Dan 9:2
Matt 16:14; 27:9

Jeremiah, a prophet in Jerusalem before its destruction in 586 BC, was born in Anathoth, near Jerusalem, during Manasseh's reign. Jeremiah's father was Hilkiah of Benjamin. Jeremiah, a vivid OT personality, is sometimes called the "weeping prophet" because he shared his personal struggles as he delivered God's messages.

Jeremiah received his calling as a prophet during the thirteenth year of Josiah's reign (627 BC). At first, Jeremiah retreated from his call (1:6), but God assured Jeremiah that he would be told what to say, and that God would guide and protect him despite opposition (1:7-8, 18-19).

Jeremiah warned the people of Judah to repent in order to avoid exile. They had broken God's covenant, primarily through idolatry (10:1-16), and as a result, they were subject to the covenant curses (Deut 27–28). They rejected God's invitation, so Jeremiah later delivered messages of God's inevitable judgment.

Jeremiah was particularly hated by Judah's leaders. Most of Jeremiah's speeches were made to kings Jehoiakim and Zedekiah. Jehoiakim held Jeremiah in contempt and tried to silence him. Zedekiah secretly sought Jeremiah's advice, but bowed to his administrators when they wanted to silence the prophet. God's word could not be silenced, however, and the promised judgment came in 586 BC. Jerusalem was sacked, the Temple was destroyed, and Judah's leaders were killed or exiled to Babylon.

Nebuchadnezzar, king of Babylon, knew of Jeremiah and was favorably disposed toward him (39:11-12). As a result, the captain of the Babylonian army allowed Jeremiah to stay with the remnant in Judah. Jeremiah counseled those who remained behind to submit to Babylon, even when Judean terrorists killed Gedaliah. The Judeans rejected Jeremiah's advice and fled to Egypt. Jeremiah accompanied them, and little more is ever heard about Jeremiah. According to tradition, he was stoned to death by Jewish exiles in Tahpanhes, Egypt.

Jeremiah suffered continual rejection, imprisonment, and physical abuse during his life, but his ministry was not entirely negative. He foretold that the Exile would be temporary (25:1-14) and that God would establish a new covenant with his people (31:31-34). This promise was fulfilled in Jesus Christ (Luke 22:20).

1:11-12 The *almond tree* is the first plant to flower, usually in late January or early February. The Hebrew word translated "watching" (*shoqed*) sounds like the word translated "almond tree" (*shaqed*). The Lord wanted Jeremiah to know that he was always ***watching*** him (see also Ps 121:3-8).

1:13-14 Like a flood of ***boiling water,*** invading armies would bring ***terror*** to the people of Judah. Although Babylon was due east of Judah, the desert between them required that the Babylonian army attack Judah ***from the north.***

1:17 Jeremiah was ***afraid*** of looking ***foolish*** as the Lord's messenger (see Jeremiah Introduction, "Literary Features: The Messenger System," p. 1207). In reality, it would be foolish of Jeremiah to refuse to do as God commanded.

[18] For see, today I have made you strong
like a fortified city that cannot be captured,
like an iron pillar or a bronze wall.
You will stand against the whole land—
the kings, officials, priests, and people of Judah.
[19] They will fight you, but they will fail.
For I am with you, and I will take care of you.
I, the LORD, have spoken!"

3. JEREMIAH'S EARLY MINISTRY (2:1–20:18)

The LORD's Case against His People

2 The LORD gave me another message. He said, [2]"Go and shout this message to Jerusalem. This is what the LORD says:

"I remember how eager you were to please me
as a young bride long ago,
how you loved me and followed me
even through the barren wilderness.
[3] In those days Israel was holy to the LORD,
the first of his children.
All who harmed his people were declared guilty,
and disaster fell on them.
I, the LORD, have spoken!"

[4]Listen to the word of the LORD, people of Jacob—all you families of Israel! [5]This is what the LORD says:

"What did your ancestors find wrong with me
that led them to stray so far from me?
They worshiped worthless idols,
only to become worthless themselves.
[6] They did not ask, 'Where is the LORD
who brought us safely out of Egypt
and led us through the barren wilderness—
a land of deserts and pits,
a land of drought and death,
where no one lives or even travels?'
[7] "And when I brought you into a fruitful land
to enjoy its bounty and goodness,
you defiled my land and
corrupted the possession I had promised you.
[8] The priests did not ask,
'Where is the LORD?'
Those who taught my word ignored me,
the rulers turned against me,
and the prophets spoke in the name of Baal,
wasting their time on worthless idols.
[9] Therefore, I will bring my case against you,"
says the LORD.
"I will even bring charges against your children's children
in the years to come.
[10] "Go west and look in the land of Cyprus;
go east and search through the land of Kedar.
Has anyone ever heard of anything as strange as this?

1:19 Jer 1:8; 20:11
2:2 Isa 58:1; Jer 11:6; Ezek 16:8
2:3 Exod 19:5-6; Deut 7:6; 14:2; Isa 41:11; Jer 30:16
2:5 2 Kgs 17:15; Jer 8:19; Mic 6:3
2:6 Deut 8:15; 32:10
2:7 Deut 8:7-9; 11:10-12; Jer 3:2; 16:18
2:8 Jer 10:21; 23:13; Hab 2:18; Mal 2:6-7
2:9 Ezek 20:35-36
2:10 Ps 120:5; Isa 23:12; 37:19; Jer 49:28

1:18 A *fortified city* could hold out for a long time against a siege, often until the besieging army left to deal with a crisis elsewhere in the empire.

1:19 *I, the LORD, have spoken:* This statement has the force of a royal decree (see note on 2:2).

2:1-13 Jeremiah used images of marriage, infidelity, and divorce to represent Judah's spiritual apostasy.

2:2 *This is what the LORD says:* This and similar statements were equivalent to an official seal or a stamp of authority on a document. In many inscriptions of royal messages from the ancient Near East, the ruler stated that the message came from him and carried his authority. • The image of Israel as a *bride* had been used since the days of Hosea (about 760–722 BC; Hos 2:2-19; see also Isa 54:6-8; 62:5). The concept is later applied to the redeemed community in heaven (Rev 19:7; 21:2, 9). • *long ago:* Following the exodus from Egypt, the Israelites were symbolically married to God when they agreed to a covenant relationship (Exod 19:8; 24:7, 8; Deut 5:27; Ezek 16:8). • *eager . . . to please* (Hebrew *khesed*): The Israelites made a commitment of loyalty to the covenant Lord (see Deut 5:29).

2:3 *Israel was holy* because the Lord had separated her from other nations to be his special *people* and reflect his character (Exod 19:5-6; Lev 19:1-37; 22:31-33). • *first of his children:* Literally *the firstfruits of his harvest.* Mosaic law required the people to offer the first portion of every harvest to the Lord (Exod 23:16, 19; 34:22, 26; Lev 2:12, 14; 23:10, 17, 20; Num 18:12; 28:26; Deut 18:4; 26:10; Zech 14:20). The people who made the covenant with God at Mount Sinai pledged their full commitment to the one true God. In return, the Lord protected them and punished their enemies during their journey to Canaan.

2:5 The Israelites *worshiped worthless idols,* so their lives were ruled by delusions.

2:6 By not seeking *the LORD,* Israel's ancestors showed that they had lost interest in their history. To them, the God of Israel was a delusion. They were only interested in the sensual excitement of the moment.

2:7 *defiled . . . corrupted:* See Deut 4:25-28.

2:8 Instead of teaching the people about the Lord, the leaders taught them about *Baal.*

2:9 *Therefore* often indicates that the Lord was about to issue a decree (e.g., 5:14; 6:21). • The Hebrew word translated *bring my case* can mean "strive" or "contend." In addition, it might indicate combat, as in a fight or a battle, a verbal quarrel, or a legal argument in court. Because the leaders of the nation (2:8) failed to direct the people to him, the Lord was going to present his case against them. He was setting up a court in which he would be the plaintiff and the all-powerful Judge (Ezek 20:35, 36; Mic 6:2). Jeremiah was a messenger, prosecutor, and advocate for the plaintiff.

2:10 *Cyprus:* Hebrew *Kittim.* • *Kedar,* an Arabic tribe descended from Ishmael, lived in the desert area east of the Jordan River Valley (see note at 49:28-33; see also Isa 21:16).

2:11 Ps 106:20; Rom 1:23, 25
2:13 Ps 36:9; Jer 17:13; John 4:14; [a]'azab (5800) ‣Ezek 9:9
2:15 Jer 4:7
2:16 Jer 44:1; Hos 9:6
2:17 Deut 32:10; Jer 4:18
2:18 Josh 13:3; Isa 30:2
2:19 Ps 36:1; Isa 3:9; Jer 3:8; 5:24; Hos 11:7; Amos 8:10
2:20 Lev 26:13; Deut 12:2; Isa 57:5; Jer 3:2, 6; 17:2
2:21 Exod 15:17; Ps 80:8; Isa 5:2, 4
2:22 Jer 4:14

11 Has any nation ever traded its gods for
new ones,
even though they are not gods at all?
Yet my people have exchanged their
glorious God
for worthless idols!
12 The heavens are shocked at such a thing
and shrink back in horror and dismay,"
says the LORD.
13 "For my people have done two evil
things:
They have [a]abandoned me—
the fountain of living water.
And they have dug for themselves
cracked cisterns
that can hold no water at all!

The Results of Israel's Sin

14 "Why has Israel become a slave?
Why has he been carried away as
plunder?
15 Strong lions have roared against him,
and the land has been destroyed.
The towns are now in ruins,
and no one lives in them anymore.
16 Egyptians, marching from their cities of
Memphis and Tahpanhes,
have destroyed Israel's glory and
power.
17 And you have brought this upon
yourselves
by rebelling against the LORD your
God,
even though he was leading you on
the way!
18 "What have you gained by your alliances
with Egypt
and your covenants with Assyria?
What good to you are the streams of the
Nile
or the waters of the Euphrates River?
19 Your wickedness will bring its own
punishment.
Your turning from me will shame
you.
You will see what an evil, bitter thing it is
to abandon the LORD your God and
not to fear him.
I, the Lord, the LORD of Heaven's
Armies, have spoken!
20 "Long ago I broke the yoke that
oppressed you
and tore away the chains of your
slavery,
but still you said,
'I will not serve you.'
On every hill and under every green
tree,
you have prostituted yourselves by
bowing down to idols.
21 But I was the one who planted you,
choosing a vine of the purest stock—
the very best.
How did you grow into this corrupt
wild vine?
22 No amount of soap or lye can make you
clean.
I still see the stain of your guilt.
I, the Sovereign LORD, have spoken!

2:11 No pagan nation ***traded its gods*** for those of another nation. Although the pagan nations all worshiped the same nature deities (by different names), each nation remained loyal to its own god. Only Israel was disloyal. • ***their glorious God:*** Literally *their glory.*

2:12 ***The heavens*** and the earth are often portrayed as witnesses to events among humans (see 51:48; Deut 32:1, 43; 1 Chr 16:31; Ps 96:11; Isa 1:2; 44:23; 49:13).

2:13 The Israelites foolishly did ***two evil things:*** They ***abandoned*** the Lord, their true source of life, and they began to worship false gods that could not help them. • A ***fountain of living*** [i.e., running] ***water*** that flows throughout the year, even in drought, is a rare treasure (Ps 36:9; John 4:14). • The ***cisterns*** the Israelites dug after they entered Canaan were holes in the ground that were lined with plaster. These crude tanks collected water that drained from roofs in wet weather and provided water through the dry summers. The water could become putrid and dangerous to drink, and the plaster often cracked, letting the water drain out.

2:14-22 This historical review of Israel's sin further emphasizes the folly, violence, arrogance, and despair of turning away from the true God to worship false pagan gods.

2:14 The Israelites had been rescued from slavery in Egypt, but they became slaves again in Jeremiah's time through their covenants with Egypt and Assyria (2:18).

2:15 Jeremiah portrays the Assyrians who destroyed the northern kingdom (2 Kgs 17:5-23; Nah 2:11-12) as ***lions.***

2:16 Another enemy, the ***Egyptians,*** invaded from the south to pick up the pieces (50:17; 2 Kgs 23:29-37). • ***Memphis*** (Hebrew *Noph*) and ***Tahpanhes,*** Egypt's major cities near the mouth of the Nile, were famous for their wealth.

2:18 Israel's ***alliances with Egypt*** and ***covenants with Assyria*** (2 Kgs 15:19–19:37) provided no benefits, only sorrow. Neither the ***Nile*** (Hebrew *Shihor,* a branch of the Nile River) in Egypt nor ***the Euphrates*** (literally *the river*) in Assyria ever helped Israel (Isa 30:1-3; Hos 5:13).

2:19 The decision to ***abandon the LORD*** brought further ***punishment*** and ***shame*** on Israel's people (Isa 3:9; Hos 5:5).

2:20-21 ***Long ago:*** Lessons from Israel's history concerning the Israelites' rescue from ***slavery*** in Egypt had little effect, and the people of Israel defiantly refused to ***serve*** God (Exod 19:8; 34:15; Lev 26:13; Deut 12:2; Josh 24:16; Judg 10:16; Isa 57:5, 7). • ***you have prostituted yourselves:*** This metaphor was especially apt regarding the Israelites' ***bowing down to idols.*** The Israelites backed their defiant words with rebellious behavior. They repeatedly worshiped fertility deities in hopes of good crops and green pastures. Their rituals were useless because the Lord is the one who had ***planted*** the Israelites in Canaan, and he creates life and fertility.

2:22 The metaphor changes from a planted vine to a dirty cloth that ***soap or lye*** cannot wash ***clean.*** However hard the Israelites scrubbed, their ***guilt*** was still apparent (cp. Isa 1:18). • ***I . . . have spoken:*** See note at 2:2.

Israel, an Unfaithful Wife

23 "You say, 'That's not true!
I haven't worshiped the images of
Baal!'
But how can you say that?
Go and look in any valley in the land!
Face the awful sins you have done.
You are like a restless female camel
desperately searching for a mate.
24 You are like a wild donkey,
sniffing the wind at mating time.
Who can restrain her lust?
Those who desire her don't need to
search,
for she goes running to them!
25 When will you stop running?
When will you stop panting after
other gods?
But you say, 'Save your breath.
I'm in love with these foreign gods,
and I can't stop loving them now!'

26 "Israel is like a thief
who feels shame only when he gets
caught.
They, their kings, officials, priests, and
prophets—
all are alike in this.
27 To an image carved from a piece of
wood they say,
'You are my father.'
To an idol chiseled from a block of stone
they say,
'You are my mother.'
They turn their backs on me,
but in times of trouble they cry out
to me,
'Come and save us!'
28 But why not call on these gods you have
made?
When trouble comes, let them save
you if they can!
For you have as many gods
as there are towns in Judah.
29 Why do you accuse me of doing wrong?
You are the ones who have rebelled,"
says the LORD.
30 "I have punished your children,
but they did not respond to my
discipline.
You yourselves have killed your prophets
as a lion kills its prey.

31 "O my people, listen to the words of the
LORD!
Have I been like a desert to Israel?
Have I been to them a land of
darkness?
Why then do my people say, 'At last we
are free from God!
We don't need him anymore!'
32 Does a young woman forget her
jewelry?
Does a bride hide her wedding dress?
Yet for years on end
my people have forgotten me.

33 "How you plot and scheme to win your
lovers.
Even an experienced prostitute could
learn from you!
34 Your clothing is stained with the blood
of the innocent and the poor,
though you didn't catch them
breaking into your houses!
35 And yet you say,
'I have done nothing wrong.
Surely God isn't angry with me!'
But now I will punish you severely
because you claim you have not
sinned.

2:23 Prov 30:12; Jer 7:31; 9:14
2:25 Deut 32:16; Jer 14:10; 18:12
2:26 Jer 48:27
2:27 Isa 26:16; Jer 18:17
2:28 Deut 32:37; 2 Kgs 17:30-31; Isa 45:20; Jer 11:12-13
2:29 Dan 9:11
2:30 Neh 9:26; Isa 1:5; Jer 5:3; 7:28; 26:20-24
2:31 Deut 32:15; Isa 45:19
2:32 Isa 17:10; Jer 3:21; Hos 8:14
2:34 2 Kgs 21:16; Jer 7:6; 19:4
2:35 Jer 25:31; 1 Jn 1:8, 10

2:23–3:5 Instead of acting like a faithful wife, Israel behaved like a wild animal in heat (2:23-25), a thief (2:26-30), and a prostitute (2:31–3:5).

2:23 The people protested that it was ***not true*** that they were ***Baal*** worshipers (cp. 2:25). Archaeologists have found small plaques showing an Asherah (female goddess) and a male god resembling Baal, but their inscriptions bear the name of the Lord (*Yahweh*). Baal worship was apparently sometimes disguised as worship of Israel's God.

2:25 The Israelites confessed to the Baal worship that they had earlier denied (2:23), thus revealing the true state of their hearts.

2:26 Israel's leaders felt no ***shame*** for the evil they did; any contrition they expressed in the face of God's punishment stemmed from selfishness, not repentance (Ps 78:34-37).

2:27 These idols of a ***father*** and ***mother*** probably represented Baal and Asherah. • ***in times of trouble they cry out:*** See, e.g., Judg 10:10; Isa 26:16; Hos 5:15.

2:28 The Israelites were foolishly devoted to ***many gods*** (11:13; Deut 32:37; Judg 10:14; 2 Kgs 17:30-31), who were all powerless to help them. • Jeremiah addressed the individual tribe of ***Judah***, the people standing before him.

2:30 ***killed your prophets:*** See 26:20-23.

2:31 The Lord's anger turned to an appeal. He questioned why the Israelites considered life in obedience to him a ***desert*** of death and deprivation (Num 21:5), full of the evil and terror of ***darkness*** (Job 24:17; 1 Jn 1:5-6).

2:32 For centuries, the Israelites had ***forgotten*** the Lord, their husband (13:25; Ps 106:21; Hos 8:14).

2:33-34 The Israelites would ***plot and scheme*** with their ***lovers***, their neighbors with powerful armies, by making treaties to gain the protection that the Lord had already promised them. God considered this an act of prostitution that left a stain of ***blood*** on Israel's character. Like their pagan neighbors, Israel now crushed its own ***innocent*** and ***poor*** (7:6; 2 Kgs 21:16; 24:4).

2:35 Israel's sinful condition was evident in the people's arrogant retort. They claimed that they were innocent, and that God was needlessly ***angry*** with them. God responded to the people's denial of guilt by decreeing that he would be severe in his punishment and that he would not tolerate their denial of wrongdoing (Prov 23:13; Mal 2:17, 3:8; 1 Jn 1:8, 10).

2:36
2 Chr 28:16, 20-21
Hos 12:1

2:37
Jer 37:7-10

3:1
Deut 24:4
Jer 4:1
Ezek 16:26, 28-29
Zech 1:3
[b]*shalakh* (7971)
‣Jer 3:8

3:2
Deut 12:2
Jer 2:7, 20
Ezek 16:25

3:3
Lev 26:19
Jer 6:15; 14:3-6

36 First here, then there—
you flit from one ally to another
asking for help.
But your new friends in Egypt will let
you down,
just as Assyria did before.
37 In despair, you will be led into exile
with your hands on your heads,
for the LORD has rejected the nations
you trust.
They will not help you at all.

3 1 "If a man [b]divorces a woman
and she goes and marries someone
else,
he will not take her back again,
for that would surely corrupt the land.
But you have prostituted yourself with
many lovers,
so why are you trying to come back
to me?"
says the LORD.
2 "Look at the shrines on every hilltop.
Is there any place you have not been
defiled
by your adultery with other gods?
You sit like a prostitute beside the road
waiting for a customer.
You sit alone like a nomad in the desert.
You have polluted the land with your
prostitution
and your wickedness.
3 That's why even the spring rains have
failed.

The Broken Covenant (2:1–3:10)

Jer 2:3; 3:1; 4:4; 22:8-9; 31:31-34
Exod 6:7
Ezek 16:1-63
Hos 2:2-13; 3:1; 4:1–5:15

A central issue in the Lord's relationship with the Israelite people was whether the covenant made at Sinai (see Exod 20:1–24:11), which the people of Israel had broken, was still valid. In the politics of the ancient Near East, covenant agreements were common. When one of the partners in a covenant broke the terms of the agreement, the result was usually war.

The Sinai Covenant was unique because the Lord was one of the covenant partners. Patterned after secular covenants, the covenant required the Lord and Israel to seal the covenant with solemn oaths of faithfulness (Exod 24:1-11; Deut 29–30; Josh 8:30-35; 24:1-28). The Lord always remained faithful to his covenant commitment, but the Israelite people repeatedly broke the covenant as Canaanite polytheism lured them away from the Lord. They broke the laws banning the worship of idols, engaged in immoral sex rituals, and ignored God's requirements for righteousness.

For centuries, the Israelites swung back and forth between worship of the Lord God and worship of Baal. Whenever they repented and returned to the Lord, he mercifully took them back into the covenant relationship. However, by the mid-700s BC, the Israelites of the northern kingdom of Israel had become so determined in their idol worship that the Lord let the Assyrians destroy the kingdom and take many people into captivity.

At the time of Jeremiah's ministry, over 100 years later, Judah was headed down the same road. In Jer 2–3, Jeremiah likened this tragedy to the break-up of a marriage relationship, much as Hosea had pictured it earlier for Israel (Hos 1–2). Israel's bond with the Lord is portrayed as a marriage in which the bride forsook her husband and took up with other lovers. The Lord charged Israel with violating the marriage bond by being a prostitute (3:1), and he warned the nation to return to the Lord or face destruction. The Lord was also like a father whose relationship with his son had been broken because the son had turned his back on him. God could no longer say of the Israelites, "I will be their God, and they will be my people" (31:33; see also Exod 6:7; Hos 1:9).

Just as breaking the covenant had cost the northern kingdom its existence, so it later destroyed the southern kingdom of Judah. Jerusalem was torn apart, and the Temple was destroyed. This punishment cut deeply and painfully into God's heart. The ever-merciful Lord promised a new covenant to replace the broken Sinai Covenant (31:31-34).

2:36 Judah, in its unfaithfulness to the Lord, chose unreliable and unfaithful allies. The leaders sought political help from neighbors such as *Egypt*—as false a friend as *Assyria* had been a century before.

3:1-5 *Adultery* was solid grounds for divorce (Deut 24:1-2; Hos 2:1-5; 9:1). Judah committed spiritual adultery, smugly assuming that God would have no objections (Ezek 16:26; Zech 1:3).

3:1 The law prohibited a man from marrying a woman he had previously divorced who had then married another man (Deut 24:1-4). A woman who had *many lovers* was even less likely to be received back. • ***prostituted:*** See note on 2:20-21.

3:2 As the Lord's bride (see 2:2), Israel was not supposed to commit *adultery with other gods.*

3:3 The Lord did not condone the *shameless* behavior of the people. He had already brought on a drought, and their sexual rituals had no effect against it (14:3-6; Lev 26:19; Zeph 3:5).

For you are a brazen prostitute and
completely shameless.
4 Yet you say to me,
'Father, you have been my guide since
my youth.
5 Surely you won't be angry forever!
Surely you can forget about it!'
So you talk,
but you keep on doing all the evil
you can."

Judah Follows Israel's Example

6During the reign of King Josiah, the LORD
said to me, "Have you seen what fickle Israel has done? Like a wife who commits
adultery, Israel has worshiped other gods
on every hill and under every green tree. 7I
thought, 'After she has done all this, she will
return to me.' But she did not return, and
her faithless sister Judah saw this. 8She saw
that I [c]divorced faithless Israel because of
her adultery. But that treacherous sister Judah had no fear, and now she, too, has left
me and given herself to prostitution. 9Israel
treated it all so lightly—she thought nothing
of committing adultery by worshiping idols
made of wood and stone. So now the land
has been polluted. 10But despite all this, her
faithless sister Judah has never sincerely returned to me. She has only pretended to be
sorry. I, the LORD, have spoken!"

Hope for Wayward Israel

11Then the LORD said to me, "Even faithless
Israel is less guilty than treacherous Judah!
12Therefore, go and give this message to Israel. This is what the LORD says:

"O Israel, my faithless people,
come home to me again,
for I am merciful.
I will not be angry with you forever.
13 Only acknowledge your guilt.
Admit that you rebelled against the
LORD your God
and committed adultery against him
by worshiping idols under every green
tree.
Confess that you refused to listen to my
voice.
I, the LORD, have spoken!

14 "Return home, you wayward children,"
says the LORD,
"for I am your master.
I will bring you back to the land of
Israel—
one from this town and two from that
family—
from wherever you are scattered.
15 And I will give you [d]shepherds after my
own heart,
who will [d]guide you with knowledge
and understanding.

3:4 Ps 71:17
3:6 Jer 17:2; Ezek 23:4-10
3:7 Ezek 16:47
3:8 Isa 50:1; Ezek 16:46-47; 23:11; [c]*kerithuth* (3748) ‣ Ezek 44:22
3:9 Isa 57:6; Jer 2:7, 27
3:10 Jer 12:2
3:11 Ezek 16:51
3:12 Ps 86:15; Jer 31:20; 33:26
3:13 Deut 12:2; 30:1-3; Jer 14:20
3:14 Jer 50:4-5; Hos 2:19
3:15 Jer 23:4; Acts 20:28; [d]*ro'eh* (7462) ‣ Ezek 34:2

3:4-5 Instead of confessing their sins, the people tried to cover them over with sweet *talk*. However, God saw through their deception. They were inadvertently correct that he would not *be angry forever* (Ps 103:9; Isa 57:16; Mal 1:6); though he promised to vent his wrath (4:7).

3:6-10 The Lord had been addressing the kingdom of Judah as "Israel" (2:1–3:5), emphasizing their identity as his people. Now the Lord distinguishes between *Israel*, the northern kingdom that had been destroyed (2 Kgs 17), and the kingdom of *Judah*. Since the people of the southern kingdom had learned nothing from the fate of the northern kingdom, they were doomed to experience the same fate. • *Josiah* (640–609 BC) promoted a return to historic faith and practice in 621 BC (2 Chr 34:29-33).

3:7-8 King Josiah's reforms failed to reach many of the common people. The love of idol worship common in northern Israel also continued among the farmers and shepherds of Judah. They failed to learn from the fate of the northern tribes, and even surpassed their practice of *adultery* (see note on 2:20; see also Ezek 16:47-48).

3:8 *divorced:* See 2 Kgs 17:23.

3:9 *land has been polluted:* As a result of Israel's apostasy, fertile fields no longer produced crops and sheep did not graze on green grass (Isa 57:6).

3:10 Like the northern tribes of Israel, the people of Judah did not see anything immoral about idol worship; they treated the Lord's objections lightly. The people did not really repent, but *pretended* to do so under the pressure of Josiah's authority (2 Chr 34:32). Their religion was tainted with deception (12:2; Hos 7:14).

3:11–4:2 The Lord appealed to Israel to repent, return, and be reconciled to him (contrast 2:1–3:10). Israel had sinned and had received its punishment. Now the people of Judah were sinning even more brazenly than their northern kin, and they ignored the lesson the Lord had taught Israel (Ezek 16:51-52). But it was still not too late to repent and become the *blessing to the nations* (4:1-2) that God intended them to be (Gen 12:3).

3:12 *Therefore:* See note on 2:9. • *to Israel:* Literally *toward the north.* • In this decree, the Lord calls the survivors of the *faithless* Israel of a century before to *come home.* God's solid, underlying character is *merciful,* and he desires to extend salvation and restoration (12:15; 31:20; 33:26; 2 Kgs 17:6; Ps 86:15).

3:13 *acknowledge your guilt . . . Admit that you rebelled . . . Confess that you refused to listen:* Through these three elements of repentance, the people could demonstrate their willingness to receive the Lord's salvation and restoration (Lev 26:40; Deut 30:1-5).

3:14 *Return home:* The Lord had spoken to all Israel as a husband to an adulterous wife, but now he refers to Israel as *wayward children.* The Lord would bring selected exiles back to the Promised Land (31:6, 32; Hos 2:19-20; Rom 11:5). • *to the land of Israel:* Hebrew *to Zion* (see "Mount Zion, the City of God" at Ps 48, p. 947).

3:15 If the people of Israel repented, the Lord wanted to give them more than just the land. He also promised to provide leaders (*shepherds*) who would *guide* them *with knowledge and understanding* (23:4, 31; Ezek 34:11; Acts 20:28; Eph 4:11).

3:16
Isa 65:17
[e]*'aron* (0727)
‣Gen 50:26

3:17
Jer 12:15-16; 16:19; 17:12
Ezek 43:7

3:18
Isa 11:13; 60:9
Jer 16:14-15; 31:8; 50:4-5
Hos 1:11
Amos 9:15

3:19
Ps 16:6
Isa 63:16

3:20
Isa 48:8

3:21
Isa 15:2
Jer 2:32

3:22
Hos 6:1; 14:4

3:23
Ps 3:8; 121:1-2
Jer 17:14

3:25
Ezra 9:7
Jer 22:21

4:1
Jer 7:3, 7; 35:15
Joel 2:12

4:2
Gen 22:18
Deut 10:20
Isa 65:16
Jer 9:24
1 Cor 1:31
Gal 3:8

16 "And when your land is once more filled
with people," says the LORD, "you will no
longer wish for 'the good old days' when you
possessed the [e]Ark of the LORD's Covenant.
You will not miss those days or even remember them, and there will be no need to
rebuild the Ark. 17 In that day Jerusalem will
be known as 'The Throne of the LORD.' All
nations will come there to honor the LORD.
They will no longer stubbornly follow their
own evil desires. 18 In those days the people of Judah and Israel will return together
from exile in the north. They will return to
the land I gave their ancestors as an inheritance forever.

19 "I thought to myself,
'I would love to treat you as my own children!'
I wanted nothing more than to give you this beautiful land—
the finest possession in the world.
I looked forward to your calling me 'Father,'
and I wanted you never to turn from me.
20 But you have been unfaithful to me, you people of Israel!
You have been like a faithless wife who leaves her husband.
I, the LORD, have spoken."

21 Voices are heard high on the windswept mountains,
the weeping and pleading of Israel's people.
For they have chosen crooked paths
and have forgotten the LORD their God.
22 "My wayward children," says the LORD,
"come back to me, and I will heal your wayward hearts."

"Yes, we're coming," the people reply,
"for you are the LORD our God.
23 Our worship of idols on the hills
and our religious orgies on the mountains
are a delusion.
Only in the LORD our God
will Israel ever find salvation.
24 From childhood we have watched
as everything our ancestors worked for—
their flocks and herds, their sons and daughters—
was squandered on a delusion.
25 Let us now lie down in shame
and cover ourselves with dishonor,
for we and our ancestors have sinned
against the LORD our God.
From our childhood to this day
we have never obeyed him."

4

1 "O Israel," says the LORD,
"if you wanted to return to me, you could.
You could throw away your detestable idols
and stray away no more.
2 Then when you swear by my name, saying,
'As surely as the LORD lives,'
you could do so
with truth, justice, and righteousness.

3:16 When Judah was decimated and Jerusalem was destroyed, the land was nearly empty of people. But in the future, the devastated land would ***once more*** be ***filled with people.*** Its inhabitants would not dwell on the past or need the ***Ark*** to remind them of God's presence (23:3; Isa 49:19; 65:17).

3:17 In the future, the city of ***Jerusalem*** would be a global center of worship called ***The Throne of the LORD,*** and people from ***nations*** around the earth would renounce their rebellion (7:24; Deut 29:19; Isa 60:9).

3:18 ***Judah and Israel*** would be among the people flowing to Jerusalem. The Lord would mercifully bring them ***from exile*** and once again settle them in the Promised Land (31:8; Isa 11:13; Ezek 37:16-22; Hos 1:11; Amos 9:15).

3:19-20 ***But:*** This transitional word emphasizes the contrast between what the Lord ***wanted*** and the actual situation. The Lord ***would love to treat*** his people as his precious ***children,*** but he could not. The covenant marriage between God and his people had been ruptured by the ***faithless wife.*** The Lord could not overlook this sin (Isa 48:8).

3:21–4:2 The people, held captive in Assyria, cried out that they had repented of their sins. However, their words were insincere, and the Lord rejected their plea. God was telling his people that if they were really going to turn back to him, they had to abandon the altars on the hills where they had worshiped idols and purge their religion of every trace of idolatry.

3:22-24 The Lord heard the touching prayer of devotion; the people affirmed their acceptance of ***the LORD*** as their ***God*** (31:7; Ps 121:1-2; 38:18).
• The people even confessed that they had worshiped ***idols*** and engaged in ***religious orgies.*** They admitted that all this was a ***delusion*** (11:13; 14:20; Hos 9:10) and acknowledged that ***salvation*** is found only in ***the LORD.*** Their ***ancestors*** had ***squandered*** their wealth by killing their animals and children in honor of Baal.

3:22 The Lord did not forget his ***children.*** Out of the depths of his being, he called them to ***come back*** so that he could ***heal*** them. He desired to set aside his anger and pour forth his love (30:17; 33:6; Hos 6:1; 14:4).

4:1 The Lord saw that despite their lovely prayer, the people did not intend to ***throw away*** their ***idols*** or change their lifestyle (15:19; Joel 2:12).

4:2 ***As surely as the LORD lives:*** The correct attitude when offering a prayer of confession and making oaths reflects ***truth, justice, and righteousness. Truth*** means that the inner attitudes and thoughts of those praying match the words they utter. ***Justice*** means living by the laws of the Lord, who will judge the earth. ***Righteousness*** means that people relate to others in accordance with the Lord's Spirit and the moral standards he has established. This kind of prayer requires a radical transformation of people's inner lives and outer lifestyle (Gen 22:18; Deut 10:20; Ps 72:18; Isa 48:1; 1 Cor 1:31). If the Israelites

Then you would be a blessing to the
nations of the world,
and all people would come and praise
my name."

Coming Judgment against Judah

3 This is what the LORD says to the people of
Judah and Jerusalem:

"Plow up the hard ground of your hearts!
Do not waste your good seed among
thorns.
4 O people of Judah and Jerusalem,
surrender your pride and power.
Change your hearts before the LORD,
or my anger will burn like an
unquenchable fire
because of all your sins.

5 "Shout to Judah, and broadcast to
Jerusalem!
Tell them to sound the alarm
throughout the land:
'Run for your lives!
Flee to the fortified cities!'
6 Raise a signal flag as a warning for
Jerusalem:
'Flee now! Do not delay!'
For I am bringing terrible destruction
upon you
from the north."

7 A lion stalks from its den,
a destroyer of nations.
It has left its lair and is headed your way.
It's going to devastate your land!
Your towns will lie in ruins,
with no one living in them anymore.
8 So put on clothes of mourning
and weep with broken hearts,
for the fierce anger of the LORD
is still upon us.

9 "In that day," says the LORD,
"the king and the officials will tremble
in fear.
The priests will be struck with horror,
and the prophets will be appalled."
10 Then I said, "O Sovereign LORD,
the people have been deceived by
what you said,
for you promised peace for Jerusalem.
But the sword is held at their
throats!"

11 The time is coming when the LORD will
say
to the people of Jerusalem,
"My dear people, a burning wind is
blowing in from the desert,
and it's not a gentle breeze useful for
winnowing grain.
12 It is a roaring blast sent by me!
Now I will pronounce your
destruction!"

13 Our enemy rushes down on us like storm
clouds!
His chariots are like whirlwinds.
His horses are swifter than eagles.
How terrible it will be, for we are
doomed!
14 O Jerusalem, cleanse your heart
that you may be saved.
How long will you harbor
your evil thoughts?
15 Your destruction has been announced
from Dan and the hill country of
Ephraim.

4:3 Hos 10:12; Matt 13:7, 22
4:4 Deut 10:16; Isa 30:27; Jer 9:25-26; 21:12; Mark 9:43, 48; Rom 2:28-29
4:5 Josh 10:20; Jer 6:1; Hos 8:1
4:6 Jer 1:14-15; 6:1, 22
4:7 Isa 1:7; 6:11; Jer 2:15; 5:6; 25:9, 38
4:8 Isa 5:25; 10:4; Jer 30:24
4:9 Jer 48:41
4:10 2 Thes 2:11
4:11 Jer 51:1; Ezek 17:10; Hos 13:15
4:13 Deut 28:49; Isa 66:15; Lam 4:19
4:14 Isa 1:16; Jer 13:27; Jas 4:8
4:15 Jer 6:19

returned to the Lord in this way, the people would be blessed, and their influence would flow out as a ***blessing*** to all ***the nations of the world.*** Their changed lives would cause people of the world to *come* and join in a chorus of *praise* to God's *name.*

4:3-18 These verses bring the kingdom of ***Judah*** and its capital, ***Jerusalem,*** to center stage in God's courtroom. The Lord decreed that he would judge Jerusalem at the hands of the Babylonians.

4:3 Sinners must intentionally face their rebellion and change their ways through confession and repentance (Hos 10:12; cp. Matt 13:1-9).

4:4 To deal with their sin, the people needed to give up the ***pride*** and ***power*** that were so precious to them (Deut 10:16; 30:6; Amos 5:6; Mark 9:43; Rom 2:28; Col 2:11). • ***surrender your pride and power. Change your hearts before the LORD:*** Literally *circumcise yourselves to the LORD, and take away the foreskins of your heart.* Circumcision was a covenant sign of submission to God.

4:5-6 God was opening the pot of boiling water (see 1:13-14) and pouring out a cruel army upon the people (8:14; 50:2; Josh 10:20; Isa 62:10). • ***Jerusalem:*** Hebrew *Zion.*

4:7 The coming army of Babylonian soldiers was like a cruel and vicious ***lion*** (see 2:15). With power and savagery, it would wipe out everything, leaving houses empty and in ***ruins*** (25:9, 38; 50:17; 2 Kgs 24:1; Isa 1:7; 6:11; Ezek 26:7-10; Dan 7:4).

4:8 The Israelites were in trouble with the Lord and needed to make things right with him. Putting an army in the field or organizing guerrilla bands would be futile. Instead, Jeremiah called for the people to repent by ***mourning*** and by weeping with ***broken hearts*** (Isa 22:12). By using the pronoun ***us,*** the prophet seems to include himself in the need for repentance (see 10:24).

4:9 The impact of the foreign invasion would show Judah's leaders that they were not as invincible as they believed (48:41; Isa 22:3-5).

4:10 Jeremiah was confused and offended because he and ***the people*** thought that God had promised ***peace for Jerusalem.*** However, these promises were false prophecies (6:14; 14:13; 23:16-17).

4:11-12 The Lord's ***people*** would soon feel the ***burning wind*** and ***roaring blast*** of God's judgment (13:24; Hos 13:15).

4:13 Like his countrymen, Jeremiah was fearful when he heard that the invasion from the north had begun (Deut 28:49; Isa 5:28; Lam 4:19; Hos 8:1; Hab 1:8).

4:14-15 Jeremiah still hoped that his people would ***cleanse*** their ***heart,*** get rid of their ***evil thoughts,*** and make a clean break with idolatry. Otherwise, they would face God's judgment (4:1; 6:19; 13:27; 50:17; Prov 1:22; Isa 1:16; Jas 4:8).

4:16
Jer 5:15
Ezek 21:22
4:17
2 Kgs 25:1
Jer 5:23
4:18
Jer 2:17-19
4:19
Isa 21:3; 22:4
Hab 3:16
4:20
Jer 10:20
Ezek 7:26
4:22
Jer 5:21; 10:8; 13:23
Rom 16:19
4:23
Gen 1:2
Isa 24:19
4:24
Isa 5:25
Ezek 38:20
4:25
Jer 9:10; 12:4
Zeph 1:3
4:26
Jer 9:10
4:27
Jer 5:10, 18; 12:11-12; 30:11; 46:28
4:28
Num 23:19
Isa 5:30; 50:3
Jer 23:20; 30:24
Hos 4:3
Joel 2:30-31
4:29
Isa 2:19-21
Jer 16:16
4:30
2 Kgs 9:30
Jer 22:20, 22
Ezek 23:9-10, 22, 40
4:31
Isa 1:15; 42:14
Jer 13:21
Lam 1:17
5:1
Gen 18:26, 32
2 Chr 16:9

16 "Warn the surrounding nations
and announce this to Jerusalem:
The enemy is coming from a distant land,
raising a battle cry against the towns of Judah.
17 They surround Jerusalem like watchmen around a field,
for my people have rebelled against me,"
says the LORD.
18 "Your own actions have brought this upon you.
This punishment is bitter, piercing you to the heart!"

Jeremiah Weeps for His People

19 My heart, my heart—I writhe in pain!
My heart pounds within me! I cannot be still.
For I have heard the blast of enemy trumpets
and the roar of their battle cries.
20 Waves of destruction roll over the land,
until it lies in complete desolation.
Suddenly my tents are destroyed;
in a moment my shelters are crushed.
21 How long must I see the battle flags
and hear the trumpets of war?
22 "My people are foolish
and do not know me," says the LORD.
"They are stupid children
who have no understanding.
They are clever enough at doing wrong,
but they have no idea how to do right!"

Jeremiah's Vision of Coming Disaster

23 I looked at the earth, and it was empty and formless.
I looked at the heavens, and there was no light.
24 I looked at the mountains and hills,
and they trembled and shook.
25 I looked, and all the people were gone.
All the birds of the sky had flown away.
26 I looked, and the fertile fields had become a wilderness.
The towns lay in ruins,
crushed by the LORD's fierce anger.

27 This is what the LORD says:
"The whole land will be ruined,
but I will not destroy it completely.
28 The earth will mourn
and the heavens will be draped in black
because of my decree against my people.
I have made up my mind and will not change it."
29 At the noise of charioteers and archers,
the people flee in terror.
They hide in the bushes
and run for the mountains.
All the towns have been abandoned—
not a person remains!
30 What are you doing,
you who have been plundered?
Why do you dress up in beautiful clothing
and put on gold jewelry?
Why do you brighten your eyes with mascara?
Your primping will do you no good!
The allies who were your lovers
despise you and seek to kill you.
31 I hear a cry, like that of a woman in labor,
the groans of a woman giving birth to her first child.
It is beautiful Jerusalem
gasping for breath and crying out,
"Help! I'm being murdered!"

The Sins of Judah

5 1 "Run up and down every street in Jerusalem," says the LORD.
"Look high and low; search throughout the city!

4:17-18 The foreign armies already surrounded the capital city. The impending attack was due to the people's rebellion against the Lord.

4:19-21 When Jeremiah ***heard . . . trumpets*** and the ***battle cries*** of the invaders who brought ***desolation,*** he realized that his own family and other people he knew were being killed or left homeless. Jeremiah could not escape the effects of God's judgment even though he was faithfully serving the Lord (9:1, 19; 10:19-20; 20:9; 2 Kgs 25:11; 2 Chr 36:20; Ps 42:7; Isa 15:5; 16:11; 21:3; 22:4; Ezek 7:26).

4:23-26 In Jeremiah's vision, ***the LORD's fierce anger*** took precedence over his creative love (10:10; 12:4; Isa 5:25; 24:19; Ezek 38:20; Zeph 1:3). He was undoing the order of creation (see Gen 1:2-3).

4:28 At funerals in Hebrew society, it was customary for people to ***mourn*** and be ***draped in black*** (cp. Isa 5:30; 50:3). The Lord had determined the people's guilt, and he promised to be true to his word (5:10; 30:11, 24; Isa 5:30; 46:10, 11).

4:29 ***flee . . . hide . . . run:*** Panic gripped the people of Judah in reaction to the horrors of war. Their arrogance and smug confidence disappeared (see 6:23-24).

4:30 Strangely, some people acted as if nothing serious were happening. They tried to ignore the enemy, but their future was bleak. The enemy would ***kill*** them (22:20, 22; 2 Kgs 9:30; Isa 22:13; Lam 1:2, 19; Ezek 23:9, 10, 22, 40-42).

4:31 The people in Jerusalem felt such intense anguish that Jeremiah likened their pain to the agony of a woman ***giving birth to her first child.*** Like such women, ***beautiful Jerusalem*** (literally ***the daughter of Zion***) was desperate (13:21; 23:23; 30:6; Isa 1:15; 42:14; Lam 1:17).

5:1-2 A ***just*** person lives according to God's laws and deals with other people accordingly. An ***honest person*** is dependable, truthful, and faithful to God.

If you can find even one just and honest
person,
I will not destroy the city.
2 But even when they are under oath,
saying, 'As surely as the LORD lives,'
they are still telling lies!"

3 LORD, you are searching for honesty.
You struck your people,
but they paid no attention.
You crushed them,
but they refused to be corrected.
They are determined, with faces set like
stone;
they have refused to repent.

4 Then I said, "But what can we expect
from the poor?
They are ignorant.
They don't know the ways of the LORD.
They don't understand God's laws.
5 So I will go and speak to their leaders.
Surely they know the ways of the
LORD
and understand God's laws."
But the leaders, too, as one man,
had thrown off God's yoke
and broken his chains.
6 So now a lion from the forest will attack
them;
a wolf from the desert will pounce on
them.
A leopard will lurk near their towns,
tearing apart any who dare to venture
out.
For their rebellion is great,
and their sins are many.

7 "How can I pardon you?
For even your children have turned
from me.
They have sworn by gods that are not
gods at all!
I fed my people until they were full.
But they thanked me by committing
adultery
and lining up at the brothels.
8 They are well-fed, lusty stallions,
each neighing for his neighbor's wife.
9 Should I not punish them for this?" says
the LORD.
"Should I not avenge myself against
such a nation?

10 "Go down the rows of the vineyards and
destroy the grapevines,
leaving a scattered few alive.
Strip the branches from the vines,
for these people do not belong to the
LORD.
11 The people of Israel and Judah
are full of treachery against me,"
says the LORD.
12 "They have lied about the LORD
and said, 'He won't bother us!
No disasters will come upon us.
There will be no war or famine.
13 God's prophets are all windbags
who don't really speak for him.
Let their predictions of disaster fall
on themselves!' "

14 Therefore, this is what the LORD God of Heaven's Armies says:

"Because the people are talking like this,
my messages will flame out of your
mouth
and burn the people like kindling wood.
15 O Israel, I will bring a distant nation
against you,"
says the LORD.

5:2 Titus 1:16
5:3 Jer 7:26, 28; 8:5; 19:15; Ezek 3:8; Zeph 3:2; *shub* (7725) ▸Jer 15:19
5:4 Isa 27:11; Jer 4:22; Hos 4:6
5:5 Jer 2:20; Mic 3:1
5:6 Jer 30:14-15; Hos 13:7; Hab 1:8
5:7 Deut 32:21; Josh 23:7; Jer 2:11; Zeph 1:5; Gal 4:8
5:8 Jer 13:27; 29:23; Ezek 22:11
5:9 Jer 9:9
5:10 Jer 4:27
5:11 Jer 3:6-7
5:12 2 Chr 36:16; Jer 43:1-4
5:13 Jer 14:13, 15
5:14 Jer 23:29
5:15 Deut 28:49; Isa 5:26; 28:11

Jeremiah did not find either justice or honesty. Although he put people ***under oath***, their claims of innocence were false. Their behavior showed that they had perjured themselves (4:2; 7:9; Gen 18:23-32; Isa 48:1; Ezek 22:30; Titus 1:15-16).

5:3 Even when ***crushed*** by the disaster of war, the people ignored God and ***refused to repent*** of their sins (Isa 9:13).

5:4-5 Jeremiah searched for an economic reason behind Jerusalem's rebellion, but found that the ***leaders***, despite their advantages, were as rebellious as the uneducated ***poor***. • A wooden ***yoke*** was placed on the neck of a farm animal, with ***chains*** attached to a plow or another implement for working the fields (cp. 27:2-12; Ps 2:3).

5:6 The Babylonians would attack like a ***lion***, a ***wolf***, and a ***leopard***. These ferocious beasts were capable of destroying human life. The people's ***rebellion*** and ***sins*** were very serious to the Lord (4:7; 30:14-15; Ps 104:20; Ezek 22:27; Hos 13:7; Hab 1:8; Zeph 3:3).

5:7-8 These verses list the evidence of sins the people had committed, including rejection of the Lord, submission to pagan deities, and sexual misbehavior (7:9; 12:16; Num 25:1-3; Deut 32:21; Josh 23:7; Zeph 1:5; Gal 4:8). Idolatry and adultery were closely connected in Israel because both represented the breach of an exclusive covenant.

5:9 The Lord regarded the people's sins as worthy of punishment (9:9; 13:27; 29:23; Ezek 22:11).

5:10-13 The Lord delivered a decree to destroy Judah's ***vineyards***, which probably represented Judah itself (see Isa 5:1-7; 27:2-6). The people were ignoring the Lord. They did not belong to him as his children, and he could not overlook the ***treachery*** of their love for idols (3:6; 4:27; 7:27).

5:12-13 Even with the enemy looming on the northern horizon, the people thought that nothing bad would happen to them (14:13; Isa 47:8). They did not respect ***God's prophets*** (literally ***the prophets***), either. • Some interpreters end the people's quote with 5:12 and attribute 5:13 to the Lord. The ***windbags*** would then refer to false prophets.

5:14-19 The approaching army was probably that of Babylon, which attacked Jerusalem in 605 BC. The Lord called the Babylonians to carry out the punishment he had promised (see Deut 28:15-62).

5:15 The Babylonian language was a Semitic ***language*** like Hebrew, but the Israelites did not ***understand*** it.

5:16
Isa 5:28; 13:18
5:17
Lev 26:16
Deut 28:31, 33
Jer 8:16
Hos 8:14
5:19
Deut 28:48; 29:24-26
1 Kgs 9:8-9
Jer 16:10-13
5:21
Isa 43:8
Ezek 12:2
Matt 13:15
Mark 8:18
5:22
Deut 28:58
Job 38:8-11
Ps 104:9; 119:120
Jer 2:19; 10:7
5:23
Ps 78:8
Jer 4:17
5:24
Gen 8:22
Ps 147:8
Joel 2:23
Matt 5:45

"It is a mighty nation,
an ancient nation,
a people whose language you do not know,
whose speech you cannot understand.
16 Their weapons are deadly;
their warriors are mighty.
17 They will devour the food of your harvest;
they will devour your sons and daughters.
They will devour your flocks and herds;
they will devour your grapes and figs.
And they will destroy your fortified towns,
which you think are so safe.

18"Yet even in those days I will not blot
you out completely," says the LORD. 19"And
when your people ask, 'Why did the LORD
our God do all this to us?' you must reply,
'You rejected him and gave yourselves to foreign gods in your own land. Now you will
serve foreigners in a land that is not your
own.'

A Warning for God's People

20 "Make this announcement to Israel,
and say this to Judah:
21 Listen, you foolish and senseless people,
with eyes that do not see
and ears that do not hear.
22 Have you no respect for me?
Why don't you tremble in my presence?
I, the LORD, define the ocean's sandy shoreline
as an everlasting boundary that the waters cannot cross.
The waves may toss and roar,
but they can never pass the boundaries I set.
23 But my people have stubborn and rebellious hearts.
They have turned away and abandoned me.
24 They do not say from the heart,
'Let us live in awe of the LORD our God,
for he gives us rain each spring and fall,
assuring us of a harvest when the time is right.'

The Basis of God's Judgment (5:1-9)

Jer 2:7-13; 3:8-11; 6:10-21; 7:16-29; 8:9-13; 11:6-14; 17:1-4; 22:1-9; 23:10-12; 34:8-20
Exod 20:2-17
Lev 19:18
Deut 5:6-21; 6:5
Matt 19:19; 22:37
Mark 12:30-31
Luke 10:27
1 Cor 13:13

Throughout Scripture, the one true God is the highest authority, and his laws are set out both as positive commands and as negative prohibitions. The positive side can be summed up in two basic laws: "You must love the LORD your God with all your heart, all your soul, and all your strength" (Deut 6:5; Matt 22:37; Mark 12:30; Luke 10:27), and "Love your neighbor as yourself" (Lev 19:18; Matt 19:19; Mark 12:31; Luke 10:27). These two basic laws are reflected in the positive laws in the Ten Commandments (Exod 20:2-17; Deut 5:6-21): "I am the LORD your God. . . . Observe the Sabbath day. . . . Honor your father and mother." Each command opens a door to the expression of "faith, hope, and love" (1 Cor 13:13).

The negative prohibitions set up a boundary between good and evil. Primary among these laws are the two that Jeremiah highlights: "You must not have any other god but me" (Exod 20:3), and "You must not make for yourself an idol of any kind or an image. . . . You must not bow down to them or worship them" (Exod 20:4-5). These prohibited behaviors violate the fundamental commands to love the Lord and one's neighbor.

In the book of Jeremiah, these laws lie behind the evaluation of the Israelites' conduct as well as the conduct of any ruler, group of people, or individual in any time or place. Those who violate these laws reject the one true God, resulting in disastrous natural consequences and in decrees of divine judgment.

5:16-17 The soldiers of the well-trained and well-equipped Babylonian army treated their victims viciously and destroyed everything of value in the lands they conquered (cp. Hab 1:6-10).

5:18-19 The Lord comforted Jeremiah with the knowledge that the destruction would not be total, and he prepared the prophet to respond to those who wondered why the Lord would bring such severe judgment upon them.

5:20-21 ***to Israel:*** Literally *to the house of Jacob.* The names "Jacob" and "Israel" are often interchanged throughout the Old Testament, referring sometimes to the individual patriarch and sometimes to the nation. • To be ***foolish*** is to engage in rash and immoral behavior that ignores consequences. • ***senseless:*** Literally *no heart.* When "heart" is used in a negative sense, it means that a person or group does not desire to do moral acts and so disdains the intelligent behavior that is pleasing to God. • The people's ***ears*** and ***eyes*** functioned (see note on 6:10), but they stubbornly shut out the true meaning of what they heard and saw (Isa 6:9; Ezek 12:2; Mark 8:18).

5:22 The people should at least ***respect*** the Lord for his power and ***tremble*** at the thought of his unleashing that power against them. If even the mighty sea was unable to ***pass the boundaries*** the Lord had ***set*** for it, surely the rebellion of little Jerusalem would fail.

5:23-25 The people falsely thought that they could do without the Lord, who provided ***rain*** for their crops (Deut 11:14). This ***wickedness*** caused them to lose ***wonderful blessings*** and ***good things*** (3:3).

25 Your wickedness has deprived you of
these wonderful blessings.
Your sin has robbed you of all these
good things.
26 "Among my people are wicked men
who lie in wait for victims like a
hunter hiding in a blind.
They continually set traps
to catch people.
27 Like a cage filled with birds,
their homes are filled with evil plots.
And now they are great and rich.
28 They are fat and sleek,
and there is no limit to their wicked
deeds.
They refuse to provide justice to orphans
and deny the rights of the poor.
29 Should I not punish them for this?" says
the LORD.
"Should I not avenge myself against
such a nation?
30 A horrible and shocking thing
has happened in this land—
31 the prophets give false prophecies,
and the priests rule with an iron hand.
Worse yet, my people like it that way!
But what will you do when the end
comes?

Jerusalem's Last Warning

6 1 "Run for your lives, you people of
Benjamin!
Get out of Jerusalem!
Sound the alarm in Tekoa!
Send up a signal at Beth-hakkerem!
A powerful army is coming from the
north,
coming with disaster and destruction.
2 O Jerusalem, you are my beautiful and
delicate daughter—
but I will destroy you!
3 Enemies will surround you, like
shepherds camped around the city.
Each chooses a place for his troops to
devour.
4 They shout, 'Prepare for battle!
Attack at noon!'
'No, it's too late; the day is fading,
and the evening shadows are falling.'
5 'Well then, let's attack at night
and destroy her palaces!' "
6 This is what the LORD of Heaven's
Armies says:
"Cut down the trees for battering rams.
Build siege ramps against the walls of
Jerusalem.
This is the city to be punished,
for she is wicked through and
through.
7 She spouts evil like a fountain.
Her streets echo with the sounds of
violence and destruction.
I always see her sickness and sores.
8 Listen to this warning, Jerusalem,
or I will turn from you in disgust.
Listen, or I will turn you into a heap of
ruins,
a land where no one lives."
9 This is what the LORD of Heaven's
Armies says:
"Even the few who remain in Israel
will be picked over again,
as when a harvester checks each vine a
second time
to pick the grapes that were missed."

Judah's Constant Rebellion

10 To whom can I give warning?
Who will listen when I speak?
Their ears are closed,
and they cannot hear.

5:25 Jer 2:17; 4:18
5:26 Ps 10:9; Jer 18:22; Hab 1:15
5:28 Deut 32:15; Isa 1:23; Jer 7:6; 22:3; Zech 7:10
5:29 Mal 3:5
5:30 Jer 23:14; Hos 6:10
5:31 Jer 14:14; Ezek 13:6; Mic 2:11
6:1 Neh 3:14; Jer 1:14; 4:6
6:2 Deut 28:56; Jer 4:31
6:3 2 Kgs 25:1; Jer 4:17; 12:10; Luke 19:43
6:4 Jer 6:23; 15:8
6:5 Isa 32:14; Jer 52:13
6:6 Deut 20:19-20; Jer 22:17; 32:24
6:7 Jer 20:8; 30:12-13; Ezek 7:11, 23; Jas 3:10-12
6:8 Jer 17:23; Ezek 23:18; Hos 9:12
6:9 Jer 8:3; 16:16; 49:9; Obad 1:5-6
6:10 Jer 7:26; 20:8; Acts 7:51

5:26-28 Among the people of Jerusalem were ***wicked men*** who grew ***fat and sleek*** by oppressing ***orphans and . . . the poor*** (7:6).

5:29-31 The people's sins (5:26-28) fully justified the Lord's punishment, but the religious leaders committed several more. The ***prophets*** told lies and called them ***prophecies*** from the Lord (14:14; Ezek 13:6). The ***priests,*** assigned to do servant tasks, had become tyrants who dominated the people ***with an iron hand.*** Amazingly, the people approved of their leaders' new roles, even though this situation left them unprepared for the doom descending upon them (Mic 2:11).

6:1-9 The invasion from the ***north,*** probably by the Babylonians in 605 BC, was moving toward the kingdom of Judah. As the Lord's messenger, Jeremiah had the duty of arousing the people so that they could find shelter.

6:1 Jeremiah's parents lived in the tribal area of ***Benjamin,*** a narrow strip of land oriented east to west a few miles north of ***Jerusalem.*** Amos had lived in ***Tekoa,*** about twelve miles south of Jerusalem (Amos 1:1). • ***Beth-hakkerem*** was about three miles south of Jerusalem, overlooking Bethlehem.

6:2-5 ***Jerusalem:*** Literally *Daughter of Zion.* • Jeremiah portrayed the commanding officers of the invading army as ***shepherds*** who led their flocks of soldiers to camp ***around the city.*** The initial plan was to strike the city walls ***at noon,*** when the attackers could see their work. But the people in the city were so weakened that the ***attack at night*** was just as effective (see 2 Kgs 25:1-4).

6:6-7 The Lord was orchestrating the attack by the Babylonians. He instructed the invading enemy to construct ***battering rams*** for breaking through the ***walls,*** and to build dirt ramps against the walls for easy access (32:24).

6:8 Even at this late hour, the purpose of the Lord's accusations was to make the people ***listen*** and turn back to him.

6:9 Little time remained for the people to turn back to the one true God. The survivors of the invasion would be like leftover ***grapes*** on vines; God, the ***harvester,*** would track down the survivors to ensure that everyone in Israel experienced this punishment.

6:10-15 In a series of rhetorical questions, Jeremiah, the messenger-prosecutor, revealed his love for the

6:11
Job 32:18-19
Jer 7:20; 9:21; 15:6; 20:9

6:12
Deut 28:30
Jer 8:10; 15:6; 38:22

6:13
Isa 56:11; 57:17
Jer 22:17
Mic 3:5, 11
gnabi' (5030)
›Jer 7:25

6:14
//Jer 8:11
Ezek 13:10

6:15
Jer 3:3; 8:12

6:16
Jer 18:15; 31:21
Mal 4:4
*Matt 11:29

6:17
Isa 21:11; 58:1
Jer 25:4
Ezek 3:17

6:19
Isa 1:2
Jer 8:9

6:20
Ps 40:6; 50:7-9
Isa 1:11; 60:6; 66:3
Amos 5:21

6:21
Isa 8:14; 9:14-17
Jer 9:21-22; 13:16

6:22
Jer 1:15; 10:22; 50:41-43

6:23
Isa 5:30
Jer 4:29; 50:42

They scorn the word of the LORD.
They don't want to listen at all.
11 So now I am filled with the LORD's fury.
Yes, I am tired of holding it in!
"I will pour out my fury on children
playing in the streets
and on gatherings of young men,
on husbands and wives
and on those who are old and gray.
12 Their homes will be turned over to their
enemies,
as will their fields and their wives.
For I will raise my powerful fist
against the people of this land,"
says the LORD.
13 "From the least to the greatest,
their lives are ruled by greed.
From gprophets to priests,
they are all frauds.
14 They offer superficial treatments
for my people's mortal wound.
They give assurances of peace
when there is no peace.
15 Are they ashamed of their disgusting
actions?
Not at all—they don't even know how
to blush!
Therefore, they will lie among the
slaughtered.
They will be brought down when I
punish them,"
says the LORD.

Judah Rejects the LORD's Way

16 This is what the LORD says:
"Stop at the crossroads and look around.
Ask for the old, godly way, and walk
in it.
Travel its path, and you will find rest for
your souls.
But you reply, 'No, that's not the road
we want!'
17 I posted watchmen over you who said,
'Listen for the sound of the alarm.'
But you replied,
'No! We won't pay attention!'
18 "Therefore, listen to this, all you nations.
Take note of my people's situation.
19 Listen, all the earth!
I will bring disaster on my people.
It is the fruit of their own schemes,
because they refuse to listen to me.
They have rejected my word.
20 There's no use offering me sweet
frankincense from Sheba.
Keep your fragrant calamus imported
from distant lands!
I will not accept your burnt offerings.
Your sacrifices have no pleasing
aroma for me."
21 Therefore, this is what the LORD says:
"I will put obstacles in my people's
path.
Fathers and sons will both fall over them.
Neighbors and friends will die
together."

An Invasion from the North

22 This is what the LORD says:
"Look! A great army coming from the
north!
A great nation is rising against you
from far-off lands.
23 They are armed with bows and spears.
They are cruel and show no mercy.

people; he then expressed his disbelief when the people responded with scorn. After presenting evidence of sins committed by the people from the lowest level of society to the highest, the prophet transmitted a divine decree. The future tense of his indictment suggests that the message was given before the invasion.

6:10 The people could literally ***hear,*** because their retorts were filled with ***scorn,*** but they did not take the Lord's message seriously (cp. Acts 7:51).

6:11-12 Jeremiah shared the Lord's ***fury*** toward the people; he could not contain his feelings.

6:13 The people were so ***ruled by greed*** that they sought gain even by violent methods (cp. Prov 1:11-19; see also Isa 56:11; Mic 3:5, 11). The religious leaders were ***frauds;*** they did not function as their titles indicated they should.

6:14 The sinful condition of God's people was the ***mortal wound*** that warranted God's judgment. Instead of calling for repentance, the religious leaders gave the people unfounded ***assurances of peace*** (23:17; Ezek 13:10).

6:16-21 The Lord again appealed to the people to repent and warned them of the terrible consequences that awaited them if they refused.

6:16 Following ***the old, godly way*** of God's laws (Mal 4:4) would lead to ***rest for*** the people's ***souls*** (cp. Matt 11:29).

6:17 Prophets were the Lord's ***watchmen*** (25:4; Isa 58:1; Ezek 3:17).

6:18-19 All the ***nations*** would know that ***disaster*** had come upon the Lord's people because they had ***rejected*** his ***word*** (19:3; Prov 1:31; Isa 1:2).

6:20 The offerings of expensive ***frankincense*** and ***fragrant*** perfumes were repulsive to the Lord because of his people's rebellion (7:21-23; Exod 30:23; Ps 40:6; 50:7-9; Isa 1:11; 43:24; 66:3; Amos 5:21; Mic 6:6-7).

6:22-30 This dialogue between Jeremiah and the Lord probably took place at the beginning of the Babylonian invasion in 605 BC. In these three poems, Jeremiah declares the Lord's message (6:22-23), identifies with his people's fear, and urges them to repent quickly (6:24-26). He then receives a heart-to-heart message from the Lord (6:27-30).

6:22-23 The Lord reminded the people that the impending invasion was not fictitious; the soldiers had real ***bows and spears*** (Isa 13:18). • ***sound like a roaring sea:*** The sound of tens of thousands of soldiers with cavalry and chariots must have been terrifying (Isa 5:27-30). • ***beautiful Jerusalem:*** Literally *daughter of Zion*.

They sound like a roaring sea
as they ride forward on horses.
They are coming in battle formation,
planning to destroy you, beautiful
Jerusalem.”
24 We have heard reports about the
enemy,
and we wring our hands in fright.
Pangs of anguish have gripped us,
like those of a woman in labor.
25 Don’t go out to the fields!
Don’t travel on the roads!
The enemy’s sword is everywhere
and terrorizes us at every turn!
26 Oh, my people, dress yourselves in
burlap
and sit among the ashes.
Mourn and weep bitterly, as for the loss
of an only son.
For suddenly the destroying armies
will be upon you!
27 “Jeremiah, I have made you a tester of
metals,
that you may determine the quality of
my people.
28 They are the worst kind of rebel,
full of slander.
They are as hard as bronze and iron,
and they lead others into corruption.
29 The bellows fiercely fan the flames
to burn out the corruption.
But it does not purify them,
for the wickedness remains.
30 I will label them ‘Rejected Silver,’
for I, the LORD, am discarding them.”

Jeremiah Speaks at the Temple

7 The LORD gave another message to Jeremiah. He said, 2“Go to the entrance of
the LORD’s Temple, and give this message to
the people: ‘O Judah, listen to this message
from the LORD! Listen to it, all of you who
worship here! 3This is what the LORD of
Heaven’s Armies, the God of Israel, says:
“ ‘Even now, if you quit your evil ways, I
will let you stay in your own land. 4But don’t
be fooled by those who promise you safety
simply because the LORD’s Temple is here.
They chant, “The LORD’s Temple is here! The
LORD’s Temple is here!” 5But I will be merciful only if you stop your evil thoughts and
deeds and start treating each other with justice; 6only if you stop exploiting foreigners,
orphans, and widows; only if you stop your
murdering; and only if you stop harming
yourselves by worshiping idols. 7Then I will
let you stay in this land that I gave to your
ancestors to keep forever.
8“ ‘Don’t be fooled into thinking that you
will never suffer because the Temple is here.
It’s a lie! 9Do you really think you can steal,
murder, commit adultery, lie, and burn incense to Baal and all those other new gods of
yours, 10and then come here and stand before me in my Temple and chant, “We are
safe!”—only to go right back to all those evils
again? 11Don’t you yourselves admit that
this Temple, which bears my name, has become a den of thieves? Surely I see all the
evil going on there. I, the LORD, have spoken!
12“ ‘Go now to the place at Shiloh where I
once put the Tabernacle that bore my name.

6:24 Isa 28:19; Jer 4:19-21
6:25 Jer 12:12; 14:18
6:26 Jer 4:8; 25:34; Amos 8:10; Mic 1:10; Zech 12:10
6:27 Jer 1:18; 15:20
6:28 Ezek 22:18
6:29 Jer 15:19
6:30 Ps 119:119; Isa 1:22
7:2 Jer 17:19
7:3 Jer 4:1; 18:11; 26:13
7:4 Mic 3:11
7:5 Isa 1:19; Jer 21:12; 22:3
7:6 Exod 22:21-24; Deut 6:14-15; 8:19; Jer 5:28; 13:10
7:7 Deut 4:40
7:9 Exod 20:3; Jer 11:13, 17; 19:4
7:10 Ezek 23:39
7:11 Isa 56:7; Jer 29:23; *Matt 21:13; *Mark 11:17; *Luke 19:46
7:12 Josh 18:1, 10; Jer 26:6
7:13 Jer 15:1

6:26 Jeremiah advised the people to put on ***burlap and sit among the ashes*** to show remorse for their sin and to beg for God’s mercy (Isa 58:5; Amos 8:10; Jon 3:6; Mic 1:10).

6:27-30 The Lord interrupted Jeremiah’s lamentation and brought him back to his commissioned task. God depicted the prophet as a silversmith working with raw ore. The refining process was going to reveal that the silver content of the ore was so small as to be worthless.

6:27 ***of metals:*** As in Greek version; Hebrew reads *of my people a fortress.* • Jeremiah’s prophetic task was at odds with the empathy that he felt for his ***people.*** Like a metalworker, he was to direct the fire of criticism on the people to ***determine*** their ***quality*** in the light of God’s standards.

6:28 The people’s dross was spiritual; it included rebellion against God, ***slander*** of other people, a ***hard*** and stubborn attitude, and a disposition to ***lead others into corruption*** (Ezek 22:18).

6:29 To expose their wickedness, God was fanning the ***flames*** with the ***bellows*** of his judgment. But no valuable silver appeared; only the dross of ***wickedness*** remained (Zech 13:9; Mal 3:3).

6:30 The people, the ***Rejected Silver,*** must be thrown away (Isa 1:22).

7:1-15 Jeremiah disabused the people of their belief that God’s ***Temple*** would guarantee their safety (cp. 26:1-6).

7:1-2 The people were probably at ***the entrance of the LORD’s Temple*** for one of the annual festivals (see also 17:19; 26:2).

7:3-4 Pagans believed that a symbol was identical with what it represented, so in the paganized worship of Jeremiah’s day, the Temple *was* God’s heavenly house. It would be ridiculous to think that enemies could destroy it. To reinforce that idea, the people vigorously repeated a chant, ***The LORD’s Temple is here.*** However, ***the LORD of Heaven’s Armies*** needed no earthly house (2 Sam 7:6-7; 1 Kgs 8:27); whatever security the Israelites obtained from the Temple came from the Lord himself, and only on his terms (1 Kgs 6:12).

7:5-7 Idol worship had harmed the people—spiritually, because idols were delusions; socially, because their behavior destroyed fellowship; and politically, because they did not think foreign armies could conquer them. Unless the people changed, they had no future in the Promised Land (Exod 22:21-24; Deut 4:40; 6:14-15).

7:8-10 ***steal, murder, commit adultery, lie:*** The people’s behavior violated most of the Ten Commandments (Exod 20:3-7, 13-17). • ***burn incense . . . chant:*** Israel’s relationship with God did not depend on any magical, ritual connection with him. It depended on their keeping the terms of his covenant. The things they were doing violated the terms of that relationship and denied the Lord’s holy character.

7:11 ***a den of thieves:*** See 5:29-31; Matt 21:13; Mark 11:17; Luke 19:46.

7:14 1 Kgs 9:7; Jer 7:4, 12
7:15 2 Kgs 17:23
7:16 Jer 11:14; 15:1
7:18 Deut 32:16; Jer 11:17; 44:17
7:19 Job 35:6; Jer 9:19
7:20 Jer 8:13
7:21 Isa 1:11; Jer 6:20; 14:12; Hos 8:13; Amos 5:21
7:22 1 Sam 15:22; Ps 51:16; Hos 6:6
7:23 Exod 15:26; 19:5-6; Lev 26:12; Deut 6:3; Isa 3:10
7:24 Ps 81:11; Jer 11:8; Ezek 20:8, 13, 16, 21
7:25 [h]*nabi'* (5030) ›Hos 9:7
7:26 Jer 16:12; 17:23; Matt 23:32
7:27 Isa 65:12; Jer 26:2; Ezek 2:7
7:28 Jer 11:10
7:29 Isa 15:2; 22:12; Jer 6:30; 14:19; 16:6; Mic 1:16
7:30 2 Kgs 21:4; 2 Chr 33:4-5, 7; Jer 32:34

See what I did there because of all the wickedness of my people, the Israelites. 13While
you were doing these wicked things, says
the LORD, I spoke to you about it repeatedly,
but you would not listen. I called out to
you, but you refused to answer. 14So just as
I destroyed Shiloh, I will now destroy this
Temple that bears my name, this Temple
that you trust in for help, this place that I
gave to you and your ancestors. 15And I will
send you out of my sight into exile, just as I
did your relatives, the people of Israel.'

Judah's Persistent Idolatry

16"Pray no more for these people, Jeremiah.
Do not weep or pray for them, and don't beg
me to help them, for I will not listen to you.
17Don't you see what they are doing throughout the towns of Judah and in the streets
of Jerusalem? 18No wonder I am so angry!
Watch how the children gather wood and
the fathers build sacrificial fires. See how
the women knead dough and make cakes
to offer to the Queen of Heaven. And they
pour out liquid offerings to their other idol
gods! 19Am I the one they are hurting?" asks
the LORD. "Most of all, they hurt themselves,
to their own shame."

20So this is what the Sovereign LORD says:
"I will pour out my terrible fury on this
place. Its people, animals, trees, and crops
will be consumed by the unquenchable fire
of my anger."

21This is what the LORD of Heaven's Armies, the God of Israel, says: "Take your
burnt offerings and your other sacrifices
and eat them yourselves! 22When I led your
ancestors out of Egypt, it was not burnt offerings and sacrifices I wanted from them.
23This is what I told them: 'Obey me, and I
will be your God, and you will be my people.
Do everything as I say, and all will be well!'

24"But my people would not listen to me.
They kept doing whatever they wanted, following the stubborn desires of their evil
hearts. They went backward instead of forward. 25From the day your ancestors left
Egypt until now, I have continued to send
my servants, the [h]prophets—day in and day
out. 26But my people have not listened to
me or even tried to hear. They have been
stubborn and sinful—even worse than their
ancestors.

27"Tell them all this, but do not expect
them to listen. Shout out your warnings,
but do not expect them to respond. 28Say
to them, 'This is the nation whose people
will not obey the LORD their God and who refuse to be taught. Truth has vanished from
among them; it is no longer heard on their
lips. 29Shave your head in mourning, and
weep alone on the mountains. For the LORD
has rejected and forsaken this generation
that has provoked his fury.'

The Valley of Slaughter

30"The people of Judah have sinned before
my very eyes," says the LORD. "They have set
up their abominable idols right in the Temple that bears my name, defiling it. 31They

7:12-15 God had allowed the Philistines to capture the Ark of the Covenant and destroy the Tabernacle at Shiloh when the people tried to use the Ark as a magical talisman (1 Sam 4:1-11). In the same way, he would allow the Babylonians to destroy the Temple.

7:12 ***Shiloh*** was a hill located halfway between Shechem and Jerusalem. The ***Tabernacle*** had been set up there after the conquest of Canaan led by Joshua (Josh 18:1, 6-19; Judg 18:31). It remained the center of worship for the tribes of Israel until Shiloh was destroyed about 1045 BC by the Philistine army (see 26:6; Ps 78:60).

7:13-15 ***of Israel:*** Literally *of Ephraim,* referring to the northern kingdom of Israel. • The people of the northern kingdom had previously done what Judah was now doing. God had sent many prophets who ***spoke*** and ***called out*** to them (2 Kgs 17:22-23; 2 Chr 36:15-16), but they ***would not listen*** and ***refused to answer.*** The Lord had spared Jerusalem and the Temple when the northern tribes were taken into exile by the Assyrians in 722 BC; this time, the Temple would be destroyed.

7:16 The Lord commanded Jeremiah not to ***pray . . . for these people*** because it would not do any good (15:1; cp. Exod 32:10; Deut 9:14).

7:17-18 Pagan worship had become a family affair; each member of a family provided some part of the ritual. The object of their worship was Asherah, the ***Queen of Heaven,*** the mother goddess of the Canaanites with her family of deities (see 44:17-19 and notes).

7:19 God's law was made for human benefit. Those who refused to follow his instructions ***hurt themselves*** (cp. Mark 2:27).

7:20-23 The people's ***offerings*** and ***sacrifices*** meant nothing to the Lord if disobedience ruled in their hearts. Their sacrifices did not manipulate God into doing something he would rather not do. Rather, they embodied the people's trust in God's gracious forgiveness. When the people tried to use the sacrificial system to manipulate God while living self-serving lives, it only infuriated him (Isa 1:10-16; Amos 5:21-27). Obedience to God allows for a personal relationship between God and his people that provides the basis for a wonderful future (Hos 6:6).

7:24-26 Throughout their history, the Israelites had rejected the messages of the Lord's ***prophets*** (2 Chr 36:15; Mark 12:1-10).

7:27-29 The Lord instructed Jeremiah to continue to proclaim his messages even though the people of Judah had totally rejected the Lord and would not listen (cp. Ezek 2:7). The appropriate action for Jeremiah to take was to ***shave*** his ***head,*** mourn, and ***weep alone on the mountains*** (cp. Job 1:20).

7:30–8:3 This message decreed death for the people of Judah. It was finally fulfilled in the destruction of Jerusalem (586 BC).

7:30-34 The ***valley of Ben-Hinnom*** began on the west side of Jerusalem and continued around the south side. This narrow, steep-sided valley opened into the Kidron Valley and was the city's combined garbage dump and graveyard. The

have built pagan shrines at Topheth, the
garbage dump in the valley of Ben-Hinnom,
and there they burn their sons and daughters in the fire. I have never commanded
such a horrible deed; it never even crossed
my mind to command such a thing! 32 So
beware, for the time is coming," says the
LORD, "when that garbage dump will no
longer be called Topheth or the valley of
Ben-Hinnom, but the Valley of Slaughter.
They will bury the bodies in Topheth until there is no more room for them. 33 The
bodies of my people will be food for the vultures and wild animals, and no one will be
left to scare them away. 34 I will put an end
to the happy singing and laughter in the
streets of Jerusalem. The joyful voices of
bridegrooms and brides will no longer be
heard in the towns of Judah. The land will
lie in complete desolation.

8 "In that day," says the LORD, "the enemy will break open the graves of the
kings and officials of Judah, and the graves
of the priests, prophets, and common people of Jerusalem. 2 They will spread out their
bones on the ground before the sun, moon,
and stars—the gods my people have loved,
served, and worshiped. Their bones will not
be gathered up again or buried but will be
scattered on the ground like manure. 3 And
the people of this evil nation who survive
will wish to die rather than live where I will
send them. I, the LORD of Heaven's Armies,
have spoken!

Deception by False Prophets

4 "Jeremiah, say to the people, 'This is what
the LORD says:

" 'When people fall down, don't they get
up again?
When they discover they're on the
wrong road, don't they turn back?
5 Then why do these people stay on their
self-destructive path?
Why do the people of Jerusalem
refuse to turn back?
They cling tightly to their lies
and will not turn around.
6 I listen to their conversations
and don't hear a word of truth.
Is anyone sorry for doing wrong?
Does anyone say, "What a terrible
thing I have done"?
No! All are running down the path of sin
as swiftly as a horse galloping into
battle!
7 Even the stork that flies across the sky
knows the time of her migration,
as do the turtledove, the swallow, and
the crane.
They all return at the proper time
each year.
But not my people!
They do not know the LORD's laws.

8 " 'How can you say, "We are wise because
we have the word of the LORD,"
when your teachers have twisted it by
writing lies?
9 These wise teachers will fall
into the trap of their own foolishness,

7:31 2 Kgs 23:10; Ps 106:38; Jer 19:5
7:32 Jer 19:6-7
7:33 Deut 28:26; Ps 79:2; Jer 12:9
7:34 Isa 1:7; 24:7; Jer 4:27; 16:9; Ezek 26:13; Hos 2:11
8:1 Ezek 6:5
8:2 2 Kgs 23:5; Jer 22:19; 36:30; Zeph 1:5; Acts 7:42
8:3 Deut 30:1, 4; Job 3:21-22; Jon 4:3; Rev 9:6
8:4 Prov 24:16; Mic 7:8
8:6 Job 39:21-25; Ps 14:2; Ezek 22:30; Mal 3:16; Rev 9:20
8:7 Prov 6:6-8; Song 2:12
8:8 Jer 4:22; Rom 1:22; 2:17
8:9 Jer 6:15; 1 Cor 1:27

bodies of the poor who were murdered or died of disease were dumped there, and child sacrifice (a practice totally abhorrent to the Lord; see 2 Chr 28:3; 33:6) was performed there. The valley was also known as ***Topheth*** (2 Kgs 23:10; Isa 30:33), perhaps referring to the ritual drums (Hebrew *top*) or to the sacrificial fires (*tap*) that were used there. In the NT it is called Gehenna, and Jesus compared hell to the fire that burned continuously in that valley (see notes on Matt 5:22; 18:9). Before long, it would be known as ***the Valley of Slaughter,*** because the siege and destruction of Jerusalem (588–586 BC) would fill the valley to overflowing with the bodies of the slain.

8:1-2 Scattering the ***bones*** of the dead was the ultimate act of contempt for a defeated nation. Jerusalem's favorite pagan deities—***the sun, moon, and stars***—would be unable to prevent it from happening.

8:4-17 These three short poems were probably delivered during Jehoiakim's reign.

8:4-7 These verses itemize the evidence of Judah's sins. The people had fallen into idolatrous ritual sex and followed the ways of idol worship. They remained in their delusions because their minds and hearts were trapped by ***lies,*** a term that is often applied to idols (5:3, 6; 7:24; 9:6; Prov 24:16; Isa 44:20; Amos 5:2; Mic 7:8).

8:6 The Lord, who can ***listen to*** everything (cp. Luke 12:3), heard the people even when they talked in private. Not ***a word*** correlated with reality, and no one was ***sorry for doing wrong.*** Like ***a horse galloping into battle*** with no thought of death or danger, they did not consider the consequences of their sins.

8:7 ***stork . . . turtledove . . . swallow . . . crane:*** The identification of some of these birds is uncertain. The Creator gave certain birds the ability to navigate the sky from summer nesting places to winter feeding grounds, and they always follow those instincts precisely. By contrast, the people of Israel ignored God's revelations and the covenant laws he had established.

8:8-13 The people protested God's judgment because they possessed ***the word of the LORD.*** God condemned them because they did not put his word into practice (cp. Matt 7:26; Jas 1:22-25).

8:8 The ***teachers,*** highly valued in the government and in the Temple, included priests and non-priestly Levites. They were experts in explaining the Sinai covenant, and they were honored for their knowledge of covenant doctrine and the fine points of the legal system related to it. Now they were promoting the pagan viewpoints of King Jehoiakim and his officials as an updated ***word of the LORD*** (cp. note on 2:23). The Lord called these new doctrines ***lies.***

8:9-10 The phrase ***wise teachers*** is sarcastic—the Lord called their teachings ***foolishness*** and exposed their motivation as ***greed*** (cp. Job 28:28). This sin ruled the lives of the ***prophets and priests,*** making all of them ***frauds.***

8:10
Deut 28:30
Isa 56:11
Jer 6:12-13
8:11
Jer 6:14; 14:13-14
Lam 2:14
Ezek 13:10
8:12
Deut 32:35
Isa 3:9; 9:14
Zeph 3:5
8:13
Matt 21:19
8:14
Deut 29:18
Ps 69:21
Jer 3:25; 4:5; 9:15; 14:20
Matt 27:34
8:15
Jer 14:19
8:16
Judg 5:22
8:17
Num 21:6
Deut 32:24
Ps 58:4-5
8:19
Deut 32:21
Ps 31:6
8:21
Jer 4:19; 9:1; 14:17
Joel 2:6
Nah 2:10
8:22
Gen 37:25
Jer 14:19; 30:13; 46:11

for they have rejected the word of the
Lord.
Are they so wise after all?
10 I will give their wives to others
and their farms to strangers.
From the least to the greatest,
their lives are ruled by greed.
Yes, even my prophets and priests are
like that.
They are all frauds.
11 They offer superficial treatments
for my people's mortal wound.
They give assurances of peace
when there is no peace.
12 Are they ashamed of these disgusting
actions?
Not at all—they don't even know how
to blush!
Therefore, they will lie among the
slaughtered.
They will be brought down when I
punish them,
says the Lord.
13 I will surely consume them.
There will be no more harvests of figs
and grapes.
Their fruit trees will all die.
Whatever I gave them will soon be gone.
I, the Lord, have spoken!'

14 "Then the people will say,
'Why should we wait here to die?
Come, let's go to the fortified towns and
die there.
For the Lord our God has decreed our
destruction
and has given us a cup of poison to drink
because we sinned against the Lord.
15 We hoped for peace, but no peace came.
We hoped for a time of healing, but
found only terror.'

16 "The snorting of the enemies' warhorses
can be heard
all the way from the land of Dan in
the north!
The neighing of their stallions makes the
whole land tremble.
They are coming to devour the land
and everything in it—
cities and people alike.
17 I will send these enemy troops among
you
like poisonous snakes you cannot
charm.
They will bite you, and you will die.
I, the Lord, have spoken!"

Jeremiah Weeps for Sinful Judah

18 My grief is beyond healing;
my heart is broken.
19 Listen to the weeping of my people;
it can be heard all across the land.
"Has the Lord abandoned Jerusalem?"
the people ask.
"Is her King no longer there?"
"Oh, why have they provoked my anger
with their carved idols
and their worthless foreign gods?"
says the Lord.

20 "The harvest is finished,
and the summer is gone," the people
cry,
"yet we are not saved!"

21 I hurt with the hurt of my people.
I mourn and am overcome with
grief.
22 Is there no medicine in Gilead?
Is there no physician there?
Why is there no healing
for the wounds of my people?

8:10b-12 These verses repeat 6:13-15.

8:13 Having presented the evidence (see note on 8:4-7), the Lord now decreed the punishment of the elite sinners. They would be consumed, along with the land's produce. • ***I, the Lord, have spoken:*** The Lord placed his authority behind his decree (see note at 2:2).

8:14-15 These people had heard Jeremiah publicly deliver the decree of the Lord; they now realized that they deserved their punishment because they had ***sinned against the Lord.*** Though their doom was sealed, they still did not seek forgiveness for their sins.

8:16 See 6:22-23 and note.

8:18–9:26 The priests in the Temple expertly memorized and repeated carefully crafted prayers as rituals in the Temple worship. Repeating the precise wording of the prayers was thought to be very important; failure to do so drained the prayers of their perceived magical power. The character of the priests who uttered the prayers was considered of minor importance. The same was true of lamentations. In contrast, Jeremiah's prayers and lamentations were spontaneous and involved him to the depths of his being.

8:19 ***Jerusalem:*** Hebrew *Zion.*

8:20 Instead of confessing their sin, the people surrendered to despair. The ***harvest*** time of their salvation was ***gone*** and they were ***not saved.***

8:21-22 Jeremiah empathized with the suffering of his people. The closeness between the Lord and his prophet means that sometimes the first-person pronouns refer to the Lord as well—the Lord also hurts ***with the hurt*** of his ***people*** (cp. Matt 23:37).

8:22 The ***medicine in Gilead*** consisted of sticky sap that oozed from cuts made in the trunks or branches of small evergreen trees in the highlands east of the Jordan River. Merchants who sold this resin to the people claimed that it had healing powers. • Jeremiah saw the people's need for God to heal their deep spiritual sickness. The people saw only the physical manifestations of God's judgment against them and refused to acknowledge that their spiritual rebellion was the source of their problems. The African-American spiritual "There Is a Balm in Gilead" points to Jesus as the ultimate balm for our souls.

9 1 If only my head were a pool of water
and my eyes a fountain of tears,
I would weep day and night
for all my people who have been
slaughtered.
2 Oh, that I could go away and forget my
people
and live in a travelers' shack in the
desert.
For they are all adulterers—
a pack of treacherous liars.

Judgment for Disobedience

3 "My people bend their tongues like bows
to shoot out lies.
They refuse to stand up for the truth.
They only go from bad to worse.
They do not know me,"
says the LORD.

4 "Beware of your neighbor!
Don't even trust your brother!
For brother takes advantage of brother,
and friend slanders friend.
5 They all fool and defraud each other;
no one tells the truth.
With practiced tongues they tell lies;
they wear themselves out with all their
sinning.
6 They pile lie upon lie
and utterly refuse to
acknowledge me,"
says the LORD.

7 Therefore, this is what the LORD of
Heaven's Armies says:
"See, I will melt them down in a crucible
and test them like metal.
What else can I do with my people?
8 For their tongues shoot lies like
poisoned arrows.
They speak friendly words to their
neighbors
while scheming in their heart to kill
them.
9 Should I not punish them for this?" says
the LORD.
"Should I not avenge myself against
such a nation?"

10 I will weep for the mountains
and wail for the wilderness pastures.
For they are desolate and empty of life;
the lowing of cattle is heard no more;
the birds and wild animals have all fled.

11 "I will make Jerusalem into a heap of
ruins," says the LORD.
"It will be a place haunted by jackals.
The towns of Judah will be ghost towns,
with no one living in them."

12 Who is wise enough to understand all
this? Who has been instructed by the LORD
and can explain it to others? Why has the
land been so ruined that no one dares to
travel through it?

13 The LORD replies, "This has happened
because my people have abandoned my instructions; they have refused to obey what
I said. 14 Instead, they have stubbornly followed their own desires and worshiped the

9:1 Jer 8:18; 13:17
9:2 Ps 55:6-7; 120:5-6
9:3 Ps 64:3; Isa 59:4; Jer 9:8; Hos 4:1
9:4 Gen 27:35; Prov 10:18; Jer 12:6
9:5 Mic 6:12
9:6 Jer 5:27; 11:10; 13:10; John 3:19-20
9:7 Isa 1:25; Jer 6:27; Mal 3:3
9:8 Ps 28:3; Jer 5:26
9:9 Isa 1:24; Jer 5:9, 29
9:10 Jer 4:24-25; 12:4; Ezek 14:15; 29:11; 33:28; Hos 4:3
9:11 Isa 25:2; 34:13; Jer 26:9
9:12 Ps 107:43; Jer 23:10, 16; Hos 14:9
9:13 2 Chr 7:19-20; Ps 89:30; Jer 5:19; 22:9
9:14 Jer 2:8; 7:24; 11:8; Rom 1:21-24; 1 Pet 1:18

9:1 Verse 9:1 is numbered 8:23 in the Hebrew text.

9:2-26 Verses 9:2-26 are numbered 9:1-25 in the Hebrew text.

9:2 Jeremiah wanted to run away and build a ***shack in the desert*** to blot the reality of war from his memory (Ps 55:6-8). He understood that his people were ***adulterers*** and ***liars*** who deserved their punishment, but he did not want to be in Jerusalem to watch it happen.

9:3-16 The heavenly court was still in session (see notes on 2:9; 4:3-18); the divine Judge lectured the people about the charges facing them and justified the severity of the verdict. Jeremiah interrupted the Lord's speech twice to respond to the Lord's messages (9:10, 12).

9:3 The Lord did not scold Jeremiah for his outburst. Instead, the Lord recited the guilty charges against his people. • The comparison with ***bows*** indicates that the people's ***lies*** were deliberately aimed to harm their targets.

9:4-6 The ***lie*** of idolatry (see note on 5:7-8) was at the root of an entire culture of deceit. • The word ***brother,*** as a synonym for ***neighbor,*** indicates that even the closest relationships were polluted with fraud.

9:7-9 The Lord announced that he would place the people in the ***crucible*** of affliction (6:27-30; Isa 1:25). The three rhetorical questions challenged Jeremiah or anyone else to suggest a possible alternative to the Lord's actions or to explain why they were not justified. • ***with my people:*** Literally *with the daughter of my people;* Greek version reads *with the evil daughter of my people.*

9:10 It is unclear whether these words were uttered by the Lord or by Jeremiah (cp. note on 8:21-22). If the words belong to the Lord, they indicate that he pronounced judgment from a broken heart. If they come from Jeremiah, they show the depths of pain in his heart as he delivered the Lord's decree. The prophet faced the difficult task of separating his patriotism and empathy for the people from his identity as the Lord's messenger.

9:11 The Lord clearly spoke these words, counterbalancing the deep emotion of 9:10 with a further declaration of judgment.

9:12 It is unclear who asks these three questions. It might be the people or Jeremiah. The first two questions express frustration that the Lord's message about the religious and political situation made no sense—the Lord's words seemed too harsh and too extreme. The third question reveals anger that the land had been desolated. The questioner seems to ask where to find the wisdom and goodness of the Lord in what was happening.

9:13-14 The Lord answered the questions (9:12) by repeating what he had said before. The people caused the destruction of city, towns, and land. They rejected the Lord's covenant instructions and deliberately disobeyed his commands. They became dedicated idol worshipers because ***their ancestors taught them*** to worship ***images of Baal,*** the Canaanite god of storm and fertility.

9:15
Deut 29:18
Jer 8:14; 23:15
9:16
Lev 26:33
Deut 28:64
Jer 13:24; 44:27
Ezek 5:2, 12
9:17
Amos 5:16
9:18
Jer 14:17
9:19
Deut 28:29
2 Chr 35:25
Jer 4:13; 7:15, 29
9:21
2 Chr 36:17
Jer 6:11; 18:21
9:22
Ps 83:10
Isa 5:25
Jer 8:2; 16:4
9:23
1 Kgs 20:10-11
Ps 49:6-9
Eccl 9:11
Ezek 28:3-7
[i]*khokmah* (2451)
‣Exod 36:1
9:24
Exod 34:6-7
Ps 36:5, 7; 44:8
Isa 61:8
Mic 7:18
*1 Cor 1:31
2 Cor 10:17
Gal 6:14
9:26
Lev 26:41
Jer 25:23
Ezek 44:7
Rom 2:28

images of Baal, as their ancestors taught
them. 15So now, this is what the LORD of
Heaven's Armies, the God of Israel, says:
Look! I will feed them with bitterness and
give them poison to drink. 16I will scatter
them around the world, in places they and
their ancestors never heard of, and even
there I will chase them with the sword until
I have destroyed them completely."

Weeping in Jerusalem

17 This is what the LORD of Heaven's
Armies says:
"Consider all this, and call for the
mourners.
Send for the women who mourn at
funerals.
18 Quick! Begin your weeping!
Let the tears flow from your eyes.
19 Hear the people of Jerusalem crying in
despair,
'We are ruined! We are completely
humiliated!
We must leave our land,
because our homes have been torn
down.' "
20 Listen, you women, to the words of the
LORD;
open your ears to what he has to say.
Teach your daughters to wail;
teach one another how to lament.
21 For death has crept in through our
windows
and has entered our mansions.
It has killed off the flower of our youth:
Children no longer play in the streets,
and young men no longer gather in
the squares.

22 This is what the LORD says:
"Bodies will be scattered across the
fields like clumps of manure,
like bundles of grain after the
harvest.
No one will be left to bury them."

23 This is what the LORD says:
"Don't let the wise boast in their [i]wisdom,
or the powerful boast in their power,
or the rich boast in their riches.
24 But those who wish to boast
should boast in this alone:
that they truly know me and understand
that I am the LORD
who demonstrates unfailing love
and who brings justice and
righteousness to the earth,
and that I delight in these things.
I, the LORD, have spoken!

25"A time is coming," says the LORD, "when
I will punish all those who are circumcised
in body but not in spirit—26the Egyptians,
Edomites, Ammonites, Moabites, the people who live in the desert in remote places,
and yes, even the people of Judah. And like
all these pagan nations, the people of Israel
also have uncircumcised hearts."

9:15-16 ***The LORD . . . the God of Israel*** then issued another decree. The Lord would provide ***bitterness*** and ***poison*** in the form of exile and widespread death in unknown countries.

9:17-26 This series of four short poems and a brief prose passage are messages from the Lord, presumably delivered to the people of Judah by Jeremiah. Three of the poems describe the effects of the Lord's judgment on the people; the fourth poem is an exhortation. The prose section predicts doom on Judah and her neighboring nations.

9:17 The Lord commanded the people to organize the professional ***mourners;*** these individuals commonly performed at ancient Near Eastern ***funerals*** (see Amos 5:16; Mark 5:38).

9:18-19 The mourners had to start their work immediately, mourning those who had already died and grieving for doomed Jerusalem. The mourners were to join the ***people of Jerusalem*** (Hebrew *of Zion*) who had no ***homes*** and were forced to flee as refugees.

9:20-21 Because of the many deaths in the city, not enough professional mourners were available. The ***women*** were urged to quickly ***teach*** their ***daughters*** to be skilled mourners.

9:23-24 This short poem discusses the nature of true wisdom.

9:23 Intellectuals might ***boast*** about the knowledge they have accumulated. The king and his royal court might flaunt their ***power*** with pomp and ceremony. Wealthy merchants might display ***their riches*** by wearing splendid clothes and constructing majestic buildings. All of these would be destroyed at the time of God's judgment.

9:24 The Lord would recognize just one kind of ***boast***—the testimony of persons who ***truly know*** and ***understand*** that ***the LORD*** is the one true God (1 Cor 1:31; 2 Cor 10:17). • ***unfailing love:*** This key covenant term (Hebrew *khesed*) carries the basic meaning of passionate loyalty. It is often undeserved, and the word may be translated as "mercy," "grace," "kindness," or *love.* It is the OT equivalent of the NT affirmation that "God is love" (1 Jn 4:8). • ***righteousness:*** God deals with his people on an ethical, moral level. He does what is right in every situation. • ***I delight in these things:*** God does not find joy in bringing vicious sinners to judgment and then punishing them. Rather, he actively seeks to redeem sinners.

9:25 Because arrogant sin ruled the nation, there would soon come a ***time*** when the Lord would decree a sentence of doom. • The rite of circumcision among the Hebrew people went back to Abraham (Gen 17:10-14). Through the centuries, this rite became so closely associated with being God's covenant people that the Israelites assumed that it guaranteed their nation a lasting relationship with the Lord. Being ***circumcised in body*** is not enough, however; a person must also be ***circumcised . . . in spirit.*** The inner life must be radically separated from idol worship and completely committed to placing ***the LORD*** at the center of life and practice (Rom 2:25-29).

9:26 The ***Egyptians*** lived to the southwest on both sides of the Nile River. The ***Edomites*** lived to the south and southeast of Judah. The ***Ammonites*** lived east of the Jordan River. The ***Moabites*** lived east of the Dead Sea. These nations practiced circumcision but had ***uncircumcised hearts*** because all of them worshiped many false deities. • ***in remote places:*** Or *and clip the corners of their hair.* The Hebrew can be interpreted either way.

Idolatry Brings Destruction

10 Hear the word that the LORD speaks
to you, O Israel! 2This is what the
LORD says:

"Do not act like the other nations,
who try to read their future in the
stars.
Do not be afraid of their predictions,
even though other nations are
terrified by them.
3 Their ways are futile and foolish.
They cut down a tree, and a craftsman
carves an idol.
4 They decorate it with gold and silver
and then fasten it securely with
hammer and nails
so it won't fall over.
5 Their gods are like
helpless scarecrows in a cucumber
field!
They cannot speak,
and they need to be carried because
they cannot walk.
Do not be afraid of such gods,
for they can neither harm you nor do
you any good."

6 LORD, there is no one like you!
For you are great, and your name is
full of power.
7 Who would not fear you, O King of
nations?
That title belongs to you alone!
Among all the wise people of the earth
and in all the kingdoms of the world,
there is no one like you.
8 People who worship idols are stupid and
foolish.
The things they worship are made of
wood!
9 They bring beaten sheets of silver from
Tarshish
and gold from Uphaz,
and they give these materials to skillful
craftsmen
who make their idols.
Then they dress these gods in royal blue
and purple robes
made by expert tailors.
10 But the LORD is the only true God.
He is the living God and the
everlasting King!
The whole earth trembles at his anger.
The nations cannot stand up to his
wrath.

11Say this to those who worship other
gods: "Your so-called gods, who did not make
the heavens and earth, will vanish from the
earth and from under the heavens."

10:2
Lev 18:3
Isa 47:12-14
10:4
Isa 40:19; 41:7
10:5
Ps 115:5
Isa 41:23-24; 46:1, 7
10:6
Deut 33:26
Ps 48:1; 96:4
Isa 12:6
Jer 10:16
10:7
Ps 22:28
Dan 2:27-28
1 Cor 1:19-20
10:8
Jer 4:22
10:9
Ps 72:10; 115:4
Isa 40:19
10:10
Ps 10:16; 29:10; 76:7
Isa 65:16
Jer 50:46
10:11
Ps 96:5
Isa 2:18
Zeph 2:11

10:1-25 This poetic passage has three parts. The first is a contrast between the Lord and pagan idols (10:1-16). The second is a two-part reflection on the destruction that lay ahead for the idol-worshipers (10:17-18, 19-22). The third part is a prayer for God to act with restraint in the coming judgment and not to allow the pagan nations to go unpunished (10:23-25).

10:1-16 This poetic passage severely criticizes idol worship and strongly affirms the unity and majesty of the one true God. It is neither a rational discussion of divinity in nature nor a carefully crafted statement about God's attributes; rather, it is a poem about the foolishness of worshiping idols that the worshipers themselves have made, along with vigorous affirmations of faith that boldly declare who God is.

10:1 As usual, Jeremiah identified the source of his message (see note at 2:2) and urged his audience not simply to *hear*, but to pay careful attention to the *word* of *the LORD*. In Hebrew thought, the person who does not respond has not truly heard.

10:2 The Lord commanded Israel (particularly Judah, because it was all that remained of Israel) to *act* differently from *other nations.* He warned them to reject certain people, such as astrologers who claim to *read their future in the stars.*

10:3 The stars are unable to predict anything—only the Lord knows the future. • A wooden *idol* was carved from *a tree;* a *craftsman* carved the wood until it looked something like a creature that lives on earth (Isa 40:18-20; 44:9-20).

10:4 The carved image possessed no beauty or value of its own. Humans had to apply *gold and silver* to make it look impressive (see 10:9). Similarly, the image had no strength to stand by itself. It had to be secured to a foundation *with hammer and nails.*

10:5 Just as *scarecrows* in a garden can do nothing more than scare ignorant birds, idols are feared only by ignorant people (see note at 8:4-7).

10:6 *there is no one like you!* See Isa 40:21-31; 44:5-8.

10:7 The *fear* of the Lord is not craven terror, but profound reverence and submission to his discipline (Job 28:28; Ps 34:11-14; Prov 1:7). It results in contentment (Prov 10:23). • *King of nations:* God is not limited to being the Lord of one small nation; his reign is worldwide. Jeremiah pointed out that no man-made deity could ever claim that title; not even *wise people* deserve such reverence.

10:9 The people who created idols had to send far away for metal. They had to purchase *silver from Tarshish* on the southern tip of Spain. They had to buy *gold from Uphaz* (or *Ophir*) in Arabia. The *skillful craftsmen* and *expert tailors* put their best efforts into changing an otherwise worthless piece of wood or stone into an attractive artifact (see 10:4-5 and notes).

10:10 Pagan deities are neither alive nor permanent. They can easily be destroyed or put in museums. Mythical stories about idols showed them engaging in all sorts of immoral conduct because the people who invented them wanted to justify their own immorality. The *true God* is holy and just and abhors immoral behavior.

10:11 The pagan deities were not present at the creation of the *heavens and earth*, nor are they everlasting. • The original text of this verse is in Aramaic, perhaps indicating that it was a quotation of an Aramaic saying and that this passage was addressed to the exiles in Babylon, where Aramaic was spoken.

10:12 Job 9:8; 38:4-7 Ps 78:69; 148:4-5 Isa 40:22; 45:18 Jer 51:15
10:13 Job 36:27-29 Ps 29:3-9; 135:7
10:14 //Jer 51:17
10:15 Isa 41:24 Jer 8:12; 14:22
10:16 Deut 32:9 Isa 45:7 Jer 10:12; 31:35; 32:18 //Jer 51:19
10:17 Ezek 12:3-12
10:18 1 Sam 25:29 Jer 14:17
10:19 Jer 4:31 Mic 7:9
10:20 Isa 51:18 Jer 4:20; 31:15 Lam 1:5; 2:4

12 But God made the earth by his power,
and he preserves it by his wisdom.
With his own understanding
he stretched out the heavens.
13 When he speaks in the thunder,
the heavens roar with rain.
He causes the clouds to rise over the earth.
He sends the lightning with the rain
and releases the wind from his storehouses.
14 The whole human race is foolish and has no knowledge!
The craftsmen are disgraced by the idols they make,
for their carefully shaped works are a fraud.
These idols have no breath or power.
15 Idols are worthless; they are ridiculous lies!
On the day of reckoning they will all be destroyed.
16 But the God of Israel is no idol!
He is the Creator of everything that exists,
including Israel, his own special possession.
The Lord of Heaven's Armies is his name!

The Coming Destruction

17 Pack your bags and prepare to leave;
the siege is about to begin.
18 For this is what the Lord says:
"Suddenly, I will fling out
all you who live in this land.
I will pour great troubles upon you,
and at last you will feel my anger."

19 My wound is severe,
and my grief is great.
My sickness is incurable,
but I must bear it.
20 My home is gone,
and no one is left to help me rebuild it.

God's Uniqueness (10:1-16)

Jer 14:22 Gen 1:1–2:4 Exod 15:11; 20:2-6 Deut 4:32-39; 33:26 Job 38:1–41:34 Ps 86:8; 115:4-7; 139:1-18 Isa 42:8; 44:9-20 Amos 4:13; 5:8-9 Rev 15:3-4

From the moment of his call to be the Lord's messenger, Jeremiah testified that the living God is the Creator of all things, including time and space. God is not part of nature; he creates and rules nature and therefore cannot be divided into an unlimited number of gods and goddesses.

Those who believed in many gods identified their deities with the natural world; as a result, they easily misunderstood the nature of the one true God. The nature deities and their images were false, lifeless, and immobile (10:1-5). They could not communicate with people or relate to individuals. They could not even move about by their own power, because they had none.

The Lord God is uniquely different from false gods. As Creator, God stands wholly apart from the things he has created. He has always existed as the living God, the intelligent Designer who decreed that the universe should function according to his laws. He gave life to the plants and animals found on the earth, and he endowed each with the power to reproduce and multiply. As God, he is present everywhere and knows all things. He is the living God of love, holiness, justice, and power.

As the one true living God, the Lord relates to his specially made humans on a personal basis, despite his otherness. He reaches into the lives of individuals and reveals his will so that each person can understand God's desires and respond to him. The Lord, who created all things, seeks an individual relationship with each of his people.

10:12-16 This stanza contains several strong affirmations of God's nature.

10:12 Jeremiah affirmed that the Lord's ***power, wisdom,*** and ***understanding*** are the attributes with which he creates and sustains creation.

10:13 This affirmation struck at the essence of Baal, the Canaanite god of storm and fertility. The Canaanites believed that Baal actually was the ***thunder*** and the ***rain,*** but the Lord claimed them as his creations (Ps 135:5-7) through which he can speak and even ***roar*** (Job 37:2-5).

10:16 ***the God of Israel:*** Literally ***the Portion of Jacob.*** The Hebrew idiom suggests that God himself is everything the people need. See also note on 5:20. The God of Israel is not to be compared to pagan deities. As ***the Creator,*** God selected the people of ***Israel,*** rescued them from Egypt, and brought them into Canaan; the Lord redeemed them from slavery to make them his chosen people.

10:17-22 An announcement of judgment (10:17-18) is followed by a lament over what that judgment would mean (10:19-22).

10:17-18 This short decree about the coming exile is probably related to the first invasion of Judah by the Babylonians in 605 BC (see note on Dan 1:1); however, it could also have applied to the invasions of 597, 586, or 581 BC, when some of the people of Judah were taken into exile (see notes on 52:28-30). • ***I will fling out all you:*** This expression might include the refugees who fled to nearby countries as well as the exiles taken to Babylon.

10:19 Jeremiah suffered personal loss along with his people; he spoke for the nation at large as well as for himself.

10:20 Jeremiah's beloved ***home*** community of Anathoth was destroyed; even the town's ***children*** were taken into exile. The same was true of the entire nation.

My children have been taken away,
and I will never see them again.
21 The shepherds of my people have lost
their senses.
They no longer seek wisdom from the
LORD.
Therefore, they fail completely,
and their flocks are scattered.
22 Listen! Hear the terrifying roar of great
armies
as they roll down from the north.
The towns of Judah will be destroyed
and become a haunt for jackals.

Jeremiah's Prayer

23 I know, LORD, that our lives are not our
own.
We are not able to plan our own course.
24 So correct me, LORD, but please be gentle.
Do not correct me in anger, for I
would die.
25 Pour out your wrath on the nations that
refuse to acknowledge you—
on the peoples that do not call upon
your name.
For they have devoured your people
Israel;
they have devoured and consumed
them,
making the land a desolate wilderness.

Judah's Broken Covenant

11 The LORD gave another message to
Jeremiah. He said, 2"Remind the
people of Judah and Jerusalem about the
terms of my covenant with them. 3Say to
them, 'This is what the LORD, the God of Israel, says: Cursed is anyone who does not
obey the terms of my covenant! 4For I said
to your ancestors when I brought them out
of the iron-smelting furnace of Egypt, "If
you obey me and do whatever I command
you, then you will be my people, and I will
be your God." 5I said this so I could keep my
promise to your ancestors to give you a land
flowing with milk and honey—the land you
live in today.' "

Then I replied, "[i]Amen, LORD! May it be so."

6Then the LORD said, "Broadcast this
message in the streets of Jerusalem. Go
from town to town throughout the land and
say, 'Remember the ancient covenant, and
do everything it requires. 7For I solemnly
warned your ancestors when I brought them
out of Egypt, "Obey me!" I have repeated
this warning over and over to this day, 8but
your ancestors did not listen or even pay attention. Instead, they stubbornly followed
their own evil desires. And because they refused to obey, I brought upon them all the
curses described in this covenant.' "

9Again the LORD spoke to me and said, "I
have discovered a conspiracy against me
among the people of Judah and Jerusalem.
10They have returned to the sins of their
forefathers. They have refused to listen to
me and are worshiping other gods. Israel
and Judah have both broken the covenant
I made with their ancestors. 11Therefore,
this is what the LORD says: I am going to
bring calamity upon them, and they will not

10:21 Jer 23:2; Ezek 34:2, 8
10:22 Jer 9:11; 49:33
10:23 Prov 19:21; 20:24; Isa 26:7
10:24 Ps 6:1
10:25 Ps 79:6; Jer 8:16; 50:7; Zeph 1:6; 3:8
11:3 Deut 27:26; Gal 3:10
11:4 Exod 19:5; 24:3, 7; Deut 4:20; 1 Kgs 8:51; Jer 31:32; Zech 8:8
11:5 Exod 13:5; Deut 7:12; Jer 32:22; [i]*amen* (0543) ‣Num 5:22
11:6 Jer 3:12; 7:2
11:7 Exod 15:26; 2 Chr 36:15; Jer 7:25; 11:4
11:8 Lev 26:14-43; Jer 7:24; 9:14; 35:15; Ezek 20:8
11:9 Ezek 22:25
11:10 Deut 9:7; Judg 2:11-13; Jer 3:6-9; 13:10; Ezek 16:59
11:11 Jer 6:19; 25:35

10:21 The *shepherds* (priests and prophets; see 5:29-31) had turned their backs on the *wisdom from the LORD* that had been preserved in priestly memory and in the prophetic messages, both verbal and written. The divine decree predicted the utter failure of these leaders, as well the resultant scattering of the people.

10:22 The invading *armies* would reduce every town to rubble, and *jackals* (wild dogs) would make their dens in the tumbled ruins.

10:23-25 Jeremiah wanted the Lord to *pour out* his *wrath*, not simply on Judah, but on *the nations* who *devoured your people Israel* (literally *devoured Jacob;* see note on 5:20); cp. Isa 26:9-11; Hab 1:17. These other kingdoms had gone so far in their brutality that the countryside was a *desolate wilderness*. Verse 25 is a quotation from Ps 79:6-7.

11:1-17 The Lord reminded Jeremiah of several messages (Exod 19:5) that had been the basis for the relationship between the Lord and Israel over many centuries. Because the kingdom of Judah was the only remaining portion of the nation of Israel, its people were the defendants in their upcoming trial before the Lord. This event probably occurred during the reign of Jehoiakim.

11:1-3 The Lord authorized *Jeremiah* to present the legal charges against *the people of Judah and Jerusalem*. With the power of the divine name behind the spoken words, the Lord brought forward the *terms* of the *covenant* pertaining to the curses that would come upon those who did not *obey* (see Deut 27:15-26; 28:15-68).

11:4 The Egyptians knew how to smelt iron, but the *iron-smelting furnace of Egypt* was also a metaphor for the Israelites' slavery in that land from which the Lord had rescued them. God had also promised to be uniquely theirs if they would be uniquely his (Exod 6:7).

11:5 The Lord wanted to give Israel prosperity and blessing. *Milk* implies cattle, sheep, and goats. *Honey*, the product of bees, implies the presence of many different flowering and fruit-bearing plants. • The word *Amen* is a Hebrew word that can be translated *may it be so*. The NLT includes both the Hebrew word and its translation.

11:6-7 Jeremiah was to use every available means to *broadcast* the Lord's *message* to as many people as he could. As he visited every *town* and walked *the streets of Jerusalem*, he reminded the people to *remember* and *obey* the requirements of *the ancient covenant*.

11:8 The OT books of Numbers, Judges, Samuel, and Kings describe how the people of Israel repeatedly violated the *covenant* right up to Jeremiah's time.

11:9-10 *conspiracy:* The word connotes "betrayal" or "treason" (cp. 2 Kgs 11:14). • *Judah and Jerusalem* would no longer worship the Redeemer God, but would give themselves to *worshiping other gods*. Both *Israel* (probably referring here to the ten northern tribes) *and Judah* had *broken the covenant*.

11:11 The Lord warned Jeremiah ahead of time about the decree that he would

11:12 Deut 32:37; Jer 44:17
11:13 Jer 2:28; 7:9-10
11:14 Ps 66:18; Jer 7:16; 14:11; Hos 5:6
11:15 Jer 13:27
11:16 Ps 52:8; 83:2; Isa 27:11; Jer 21:14
11:17 Jer 2:21; 32:29
11:18 1 Sam 23:11-12; 2 Kgs 6:9-10
11:19 Ps 83:4; 109:13; Isa 53:7; Jer 18:18
11:20 Ps 7:9; Jer 17:10; 20:12; [k]*shapat* (8199) ‣Mic 7:3
11:21 Jer 1:1; 12:5-6; 20:10; 26:8; 38:4
11:22 Jer 18:21; 21:14
11:23 Jer 6:9; 23:12; Hos 9:7; Mic 7:4
12:1 Ezra 9:15; Job 13:3; Jer 5:27-28; 11:20; Hab 1:4

escape. Though they beg for mercy, I will
not listen to their cries. 12 Then the people
of Judah and Jerusalem will pray to their
idols and burn incense before them. But
the idols will not save them when disaster
strikes! 13 Look now, people of Judah; you
have as many gods as you have towns. You
have as many altars of shame—altars for
burning incense to your god Baal—as there
are streets in Jerusalem.

14 "Pray no more for these people, Jeremiah. Do not weep or pray for them, for I
will not listen to them when they cry out to
me in distress.

15 "What right do my beloved people have
to come to my Temple,
when they have done so many
immoral things?
Can their vows and sacrifices prevent
their destruction?
They actually rejoice in doing evil!
16 I, the LORD, once called them a thriving
olive tree,
beautiful to see and full of good fruit.
But now I have sent the fury of their
enemies
to burn them with fire,
leaving them charred and broken.

17 "I, the LORD of Heaven's Armies, who
planted this olive tree, have ordered it destroyed. For the people of Israel and Judah
have done evil, arousing my anger by burning incense to Baal."

A Plot against Jeremiah

18 Then the LORD told me about the plots my
enemies were making against me. 19 I was
like a lamb being led to the slaughter. I had
no idea that they were planning to kill me!
"Let's destroy this man and all his words,"
they said. "Let's cut him down, so his name
will be forgotten forever."

20 O LORD of Heaven's Armies,
you make righteous [k]judgments,
and you examine the deepest
thoughts and secrets.
Let me see your vengeance against them,
for I have committed my cause to you.

21 This is what the LORD says about the
men of Anathoth who wanted me dead.
They had said, "We will kill you if you do not
stop prophesying in the LORD's name." 22 So
this is what the LORD of Heaven's Armies
says about them: "I will punish them! Their
young men will die in battle, and their boys
and girls will starve to death. 23 Not one of
these plotters from Anathoth will survive,
for I will bring disaster upon them when
their time of punishment comes."

Jeremiah Questions the LORD's Justice

12 1 LORD, you always give me justice
when I bring a case before you.
So let me bring you this complaint:
Why are the wicked so prosperous?
Why are evil people so happy?

issue against the people. ***Calamity*** was approaching, and no prayers could prevent it. The time for God's ***mercy*** had passed.

11:12 The ***people of Judah and Jerusalem*** prayed and worshiped in their time of trouble, but not to the Lord; instead, they prayed ***to their idols.*** They were bonded to unreal and powerless images of wood and stone instead of to the one true God (see note on 10:9).

11:13 Idolatry was so rampant in Judah that not a town or street could be found without an idol present.

11:14 The Lord told Jeremiah not to ***weep or pray*** for the people of Jerusalem (see 7:16); the Lord had shut his ears to any prayers they might direct to him. Because the people were committed to worshiping Baal, any prayer they offered would be a charade.

11:15 The people's worship included the words and ceremonies the Lord required, but their worship was insincere; they did not love God or their neighbors.

11:16-17 At the time of the Exodus, the Lord regarded Israel as ***a thriving olive tree.*** King David likened himself to an olive tree (Ps 52:8), and the apostle Paul used this image when discussing how Gentiles could partake of the blessings of salvation (Rom 11:16-21).

11:18-23 The Lord warned Jeremiah of the ***plot*** against him. Jeremiah prayed, and the Lord promised to rescue him.

11:18-19 The Lord had warned Jeremiah at the time of his commissioning (1:19) that opposition would threaten his life. Jeremiah saw himself as ***a lamb being led to the slaughter,*** with no power to resist the betrayal of the shepherd he trusted (Ps 23:1). This opposition occurred before Jeremiah's trial in the Temple courtyard, early in the reign of Jehoiakim (between 608 and 605 BC; see ch 26). Some scholars believe that this verse prefigures the death of Christ, as does the suffering servant of Isa 53:7.

11:20 Jeremiah wanted the Lord to punish his enemies since the Lord knew their ***deepest thoughts and secrets.*** As events unfolded, Jeremiah discovered that the Lord had his own way of dealing with his foes.

11:21-23 Jeremiah's enemies even included family and relatives in his hometown of ***Anathoth,*** over whose fate he grieved (10:20). They demanded that he should ***stop prophesying in the LORD's name.*** In line with the Lord's promise to take care of him (1:19), the Lord told Jeremiah that even the families of his foes, including ***their boys and girls,*** would lose their lives ***when their time of punishment*** came. Jeremiah would have been deeply hurt by this pronouncement.

12:1-4 Jeremiah wondered why a just God did not immediately punish the wicked. Jeremiah could not stand the continued wickedness, yet he also grieved for the terrible human suffering that he saw coming (10:19-25).

12:1 Jeremiah affirmed the Lord's ***justice*** when dealing with him in the past. However, since he was obedient, he could not understand why his life was being threatened. By contrast, those who were ***wicked*** and ***evil*** seemed to be ***prosperous*** and ***happy.***

2 You have planted them,
and they have taken root and prospered.
Your name is on their lips,
but you are far from their hearts.
3 But as for me, LORD, you know my heart.
You see me and test my thoughts.
Drag these people away like sheep to be butchered!
Set them aside to be slaughtered!
4 How long must this land mourn?
Even the grass in the fields has withered.
The wild animals and birds have disappeared
because of the evil in the land.
For the people have said,
"The LORD doesn't see what's ahead for us!"

The LORD's Reply to Jeremiah

5 "If racing against mere men makes you tired,
how will you race against horses?
If you stumble and fall on open ground,
what will you do in the thickets near the Jordan?
6 Even your brothers, members of your own family,
have turned against you.
They plot and raise complaints against you.
Do not trust them,
no matter how pleasantly they speak.

7 "I have abandoned my people, my special possession.
I have surrendered my dearest ones to their enemies.
8 My chosen people have roared at me like a lion of the forest,
so I have treated them with contempt.
9 My chosen people act like speckled vultures,
but they themselves are surrounded by vultures.
Bring on the wild animals to pick their corpses clean!
10 "Many rulers have ravaged my vineyard,
trampling down the vines
and turning all its beauty into a barren wilderness.
11 They have made it an empty wasteland;
I hear its mournful cry.
The whole land is desolate,
and no one even cares.
12 On all the bare hilltops,
destroying armies can be seen.
The sword of the LORD devours people
from one end of the nation to the other.
No one will escape!
13 My people have planted wheat
but are harvesting thorns.
They have worn themselves out,
but it has done them no good.
They will harvest a crop of shame
because of the fierce anger of the LORD."

12:2 Isa 29:13; Ezek 17:5-10; 33:31; Titus 1:16
12:3 Ps 7:9; 139:1-4; Jer 11:20
12:4 Jer 5:31; Hos 4:3; Joel 1:10-17
12:5 Jer 50:44
12:6 Gen 37:4-11; Ps 69:8; Prov 26:25
12:7 Jer 7:29; 11:15; Hos 11:1-4
12:8 Hos 9:15; Amos 6:8
12:9 2 Kgs 24:2; Isa 56:9; Jer 7:33; 15:3; 34:20
12:10 Ps 80:8-16; Isa 5:1-7; Lam 1:10
12:11 Jer 4:20, 27; 25:11
12:12 Isa 34:6; Jer 47:6; Amos 9:4
12:13 Lev 26:16; Deut 28:38; Isa 55:2; Jer 4:26; 17:10; 25:37-38

12:2 Jeremiah was irked that the Lord allowed evil people to become established and enjoy prosperity and happiness.

12:3 Although Jeremiah's words seem self-righteous, he was submissive to the Lord's personal searching of his *heart.* Jeremiah was also angry enough to demand that his enemies suffer the fate they had intended for him. He hoped they would be ***butchered*** or ***slaughtered*** like helpless *sheep.* Jeremiah did not seem to desire their forgiveness or their return to the Lord.

12:4 Jeremiah expressed feelings of helplessness; the Lord's decree of desolation for the land seemed excessive. Jeremiah did recognize the *evil* of the people's sneering claim that the *LORD* could not *see* the future (cp. Isa 46:10).

12:5-13 The Lord rebuked his messenger and answered his question with several other questions.

12:5 Jeremiah's *racing against mere men* was the conflict he experienced with his family and friends. It could not be compared to the *race against horses* that would take place when the foreign army arrived. The coming war would be as severe as finding one's way through the *thickets near the Jordan.*

12:6 Jeremiah's *family* was a microcosm of Judah; they would *plot . . . against* Jeremiah behind his back (11:9) while speaking *pleasantly* to his face. They wanted to convince him that the Lord would not let the Babylonians harm the people of Judah and Jerusalem, and they hoped to stop him from bringing shame on the family (cp. Mark 3:21).

12:7-13 God called the people of Judah his ***special possession,*** his ***dearest ones,*** his ***chosen people,*** and his *vineyard.* However, they had become hostile to him, so they had to be ***surrendered*** to ***their enemies.*** Perhaps the most severe justice they could face was for the Lord to step back and let the people suffer the consequences of their evil ways.

12:9 The people of Judah would become prey to huge flocks of *speckled vultures* (or *speckled hyenas*). The people would soon be *corpses* that *wild animals* would *pick . . . clean.*

12:10-13 The corrupt *rulers* of Judah had already desolated the land by leading the people into sin (e.g., 2 Kgs 16:8-19; 21:16; 23:33-35); the invading army would simply complete the task.

12:10 A *vineyard* is a frequent metaphor for God's people (e.g., Isa 5:1-10; Matt 21:33-45; John 15:1-8).

12:11 Sorrow gripped the Lord as he saw the *empty wasteland.* He had ordered the invasion according to the terms of the Sinai Covenant, but the act gave him no satisfaction. Sadly, *no one* other than God even cared.

12:12 The invading *armies* were the *sword* that *the LORD* sent to destroy the land through murder, looting, vandalism, and rape.

12:13 The Lord found no joy in seeing his people's crops eaten by invaders, who left only *thorns.* However, the apostasy of the people of Judah merited *the fierce anger of the LORD* (cp. Ezek 16:36-39), resulting in *shame.*

12:14
Isa 11:11-16
Jer 2:3; 49:1; 50:11-12
Zeph 2:8-10
Zech 2:8

12:15
Jer 49:6, 39

12:16
Josh 23:7
Isa 49:6
Jer 3:17; 4:2; 5:7; 16:19

12:17
Ps 2:8-12
Isa 60:12

13:1
Jer 13:11

A Message for Israel's Neighbors

14Now this is what the LORD says: "I will
uproot from their land all the evil nations
reaching out for the possession I gave my
people Israel. And I will uproot Judah from
among them. 15But afterward I will return
and have compassion on all of them. I will
bring them home to their own lands again,
each nation to its own possession. 16And if
these nations truly learn the ways of my people, and if they learn to swear by my name,
saying, 'As surely as the LORD lives' (just as
they taught my people to swear by the name
of Baal), then they will be given a place
among my people. 17But any nation who
refuses to obey me will be uprooted and destroyed. I, the LORD, have spoken!"

Jeremiah's Linen Loincloth

13 This is what the LORD said to me:
"Go and buy a linen loincloth and
put it on, but do not wash it." 2So I bought

God Protects His Servant (11:18-23)

Jer 1:18-19; 20:1-2, 7-13; 26:24; 36:19-20, 26; 39:11-14
Gen 20:3-7; 31:24
Num 14:10-35
2 Kgs 6:14-20
Job 1:9-11
Ps 91:1-16
Matt 2:13-22; 10:28-31
John 15:20
Acts 12:1-11
2 Cor 6:4-5
2 Tim 2:10-13; 3:11-13
Heb 11:4-37
Jas 1:12
1 Pet 1:6; 3:14-17; 4:12-19
Rev 14:12

When God called Jeremiah as his messenger, he promised to protect him. One aspect of this protection was spiritual, as the Lord gave Jeremiah the inner strength of a fortified city (1:18). God's protection was also physical: "They will fight you, but they will fail" (1:19).

During Josiah's reign (640–609 BC), Jeremiah did not encounter much personal danger, but the situation changed dramatically when Jehoiakim came to power (609–598 BC). Hostility from the king and his family toward the prophet surfaced early in Jehoiakim's reign. Jeremiah suddenly found his life in danger, but the Lord reassured him of divine protection (11:18-23). That promise seemed to be contradicted when Pashhur arrested Jeremiah, had him whipped, and placed him in stocks (20:1-2). Jeremiah rebuked the Lord for seemingly misleading him, but he soon regained his trust in the Lord (20:7-13).

Also, early in Jehoiakim's reign, Jeremiah was arrested and placed on trial (ch 26). The Lord fulfilled his promise to strengthen Jeremiah inwardly, which allowed the prophet to remain calm. The outer protection came from some elders in the community who had served under King Josiah. They reminded the group of Hezekiah's response to danger a century before, and Ahikam saved Jeremiah's life (26:24). Jeremiah then went into hiding when Jehoiakim's officers sought to kill him (36:19-20, 26). The Lord provided a silent wall of friends who refused to reveal Jeremiah's hiding place until after Jehoiakim's death.

The new king, Zedekiah, was kinder to Jeremiah, but Jeremiah's life was in danger several times during the siege of Jerusalem. At one point, the king's officials cast him into a muddy cistern. God protected Jeremiah by prompting a foreigner, Ebed-melech, to rescue the prophet. Zedekiah then placed Jeremiah in protective custody (ch 38).

Jeremiah survived the fall of Jerusalem, though he was almost taken captive to Babylon. God prompted the Babylonian general to release Jeremiah from bondage and to give him a choice between going to Babylon as a free man and staying with Gedaliah, the newly appointed governor of Judah (39:11-14; 40:1-6). God also protected Jeremiah from Johanan and his companions, who took Jeremiah and Baruch to Egypt against their will (43:1-7).

God faithfully kept his promises to Jeremiah, as he still faithfully keeps his promises to all of his people. He does not always promise to protect those who serve him (see 2 Cor 6:4-5; 2 Tim 2:10-13; 3:11-13; 1 Pet 2:21-23; 3:14-17; Rev 14:12), but he does promise eternal salvation to those who trust in him (Jas 1:12; 1 Pet 1:6; 4:12-19).

12:14-17 The Lord explained an important aspect of Jeremiah's commission (see 1:10).

12:14 No ***evil nations*** would receive protection from God's punishment, not even those nations that God used to punish Judah. He would ***uproot*** them. • The Lord would also ***uproot Judah,*** but this is a positive reference to deliverance from exile.

12:15 ***I will . . . have compassion on all of them:*** Even other nations, as wicked as they were, could be restored after experiencing disaster.

12:16 To experience God's compassion (12:15), the people of other ***nations*** needed to convert from idolatry and ***learn the ways of*** God's ***people.*** This conversion would require a public submission to the terms of the Sinai covenant that included the words, ***as surely as the LORD lives.*** In addition, they would need to reject any oaths made in ***the name of Baal,*** by which they had persuaded Israelites to worship foreign idols.

12:17 If these nations refused to ***obey*** the Lord, they would be ***uprooted and destroyed*** (1:10). • ***I, the LORD, have spoken:*** This statement gave God's declaration the force of a divine decree.

13:1-14 The Lord told Jeremiah to act out a parable (see also chs 18, 19, 27; see "Prophetic Sign Acts" at Ezek 4:1-17, p. 1319). The parable joined action with words to reinforce and illustrate special aspects of the Lord's response to Judah's rebellion. Jeremiah seemed unable to fully grasp the evil consequences of rejecting the Lord's demand that the people worship him as the one true God. The direct relationship between Jeremiah and the Lord was the framework for this event.

13:1-2 God instructed Jeremiah to leave a ***linen loincloth*** unwashed to

the loincloth as the LORD directed me, and
I put it on.
3Then the LORD gave me another message: 4"Take the linen loincloth you are
wearing, and go to the Euphrates River. Hide
it there in a hole in the rocks." 5So I went
and hid it by the Euphrates as the LORD had
instructed me.
6A long time afterward the LORD said to
me, "Go back to the Euphrates and get the
loincloth I told you to hide there." 7So I went
to the Euphrates and dug it out of the hole
where I had hidden it. But now it was rotting and falling apart. The loincloth was
good for nothing.
8Then I received this message from the
LORD: 9"This is what the LORD says: This
shows how I will rot away the pride of Judah and Jerusalem. 10These wicked people
refuse to listen to me. They stubbornly follow their own desires and worship other
gods. Therefore, they will become like this
loincloth—good for nothing! 11As a loincloth clings to a man's waist, so I created
Judah and Israel to cling to me, says the
LORD. They were to be my people, my pride,
my glory—an honor to my name. But they
would not listen to me.
12"So tell them, 'This is what the LORD, the
God of Israel, says: May all your jars be filled
with wine.' And they will reply, 'Of course!
Jars are made to be filled with wine!'
13"Then tell them, 'No, this is what the
LORD means: I will fill everyone in this land
with drunkenness—from the king sitting on
David's throne to the priests and the prophets, right down to the common people of
Jerusalem. 14I will smash them against each
other, even parents against children, says
the LORD. I will not let my pity or mercy
or compassion keep me from destroying
them.'"

A Warning against Pride

15 Listen and pay attention!
Do not be arrogant, for the LORD has
spoken.
16 Give glory to the LORD your God
before it is too late.
Acknowledge him before he brings
darkness upon you,
causing you to stumble and fall on the
darkening mountains.
For then, when you look for light,
you will find only terrible darkness
and gloom.
17 And if you still refuse to listen,
I will weep alone because of your
pride.
My eyes will overflow with tears,
because the LORD's flock will be led
away into exile.

18 Say to the king and his mother,
"Come down from your thrones
and sit in the dust,
for your glorious crowns
will soon be snatched from your heads."
19 The towns of the Negev will close their
gates,
and no one will be able to open them.
The people of Judah will be taken away
as captives.
All will be carried into exile.
20 Open up your eyes and see
the armies marching down from the
north!

13:2 Isa 20:2
13:4 Jer 51:63
13:5 Exod 39:42-43; 40:16
13:9 Lev 26:19
13:10 Jer 13:15-17
13:11 Exod 19:5-6; Deut 32:10-11; Ps 81:11; Isa 43:21; Jer 7:24; 33:9
13:13 Ps 60:3; 75:8; Jer 25:27
13:14 Isa 27:11; Jer 6:21; 16:5; 19:9-11
13:15 Prov 16:5
13:16 Ps 96:8; Isa 5:30; 59:9; Amos 5:18
13:17 Jer 9:1; 23:1-2; Mal 2:2; Luke 19:41-42
13:18 2 Kgs 24:12, 15; 2 Chr 33:12, 19
13:20 Jer 1:15; 6:22; 13:17; 23:2

symbolize Judah's unrighteousness (cp. Isa 64:5; Rev 19:8). This piece of clothing is comparable to modern-day underwear.

13:3-5 The *Euphrates River* (Hebrew *Perath;* also in 13:5, 6, 7) is 300 miles north of Jerusalem. Jeremiah probably joined a merchant caravan for protection as he walked or rode a donkey for the 600-mile round trip. Jeremiah did not know the purpose of the trip, but he obeyed God's instructions.

13:6-7 The safest time to travel was during the dry season, from June to September. The most likely time for cloth to rot was during the wet season, October to May. • *A long time afterward* was probably between six and ten months.

13:8-9 The parable was the Lord's way of expressing how disgusting *the pride of Judah and Jerusalem* had become and how he was allowing the consequences of sin to take their course.

13:10-11 The rotten *loincloth* represented the people of *Judah and Israel,* whose *wicked* rebellion had corrupted them and made them worthless. • *clings:* The same Hebrew word can be translated "joins" and is used to describe marital faithfulness (Gen 2:24). • *my people . . . an honor to my name:* See also Exod 19:5, 6; Deut 32:10-12; Eph 2:7; 3:10.

13:12-14 *Of course!* The people assumed that the Lord would continue to bless them as he had in the past (Ps 104:15; Prov 9:2-5). However, the *wine* was not a symbol of blessing; in this case, *drunkenness* symbolized God's wrath (cp. Rev 14:10).

13:15-16 Jeremiah pled with the people to *listen* and *not be arrogant,* but to change their attitude. If they refused to *acknowledge* the Lord as the one true God of Israel, a *terrible darkness* would fall upon the nation.

13:17 Jeremiah had learned that if the people did not acknowledge the Lord, they would *be led away into exile.* The thought of it filled him with grief.

13:18-19 The *king* was probably Jehoiakim's son Jehoiachin, who was crowned in 597 BC after the death of his father; *his mother* was Nehushta (see 2 Kgs 24:1-9). Jehoiachin was eighteen years old and reigned for just three months; this message was probably delivered during his short reign. His *glorious crowns* would soon be taken from him by the Babylonians (see 2 Kgs 24:11-16). The treasures of the Temple and palace would be given to the Babylonians, and the royalty and elite of *Judah* would be *carried into exile.* At the same time, Judah's southern neighbors would take over the *towns of the Negev,* the desert area from the city of Beersheba to the Gulf of Aqaba.

13:20-22 King Jehoiachin did not seem concerned about the well-being of his

13:21
Isa 13:8
Jer 4:31; 38:22
13:22
Jer 2:17-19; 9:2-9
13:23
Prov 27:22
Jer 4:22
13:24
Lev 26:33
Jer 9:16; 18:17
Ezek 5:2, 12
13:25
Ps 78:11-12; 106:7
Jer 2:32; 3:21
13:26
Lam 1:8
Hos 2:10
13:27
Prov 1:22
Jer 2:20; 5:7-8; 11:15
14:2
Isa 3:26
Jer 11:11
Zech 7:13
14:3
2 Sam 15:30
1 Kgs 18:5
2 Kgs 18:31
14:4
Joel 1:11, 19-20
14:5
Isa 15:6
14:6
Job 39:5-6
Joel 1:18
14:7
Isa 59:12
Hos 5:5
14:8
Ps 9:9
Isa 43:3; 63:8
Jer 17:13
14:9
Num 11:23
Ps 46:5
Isa 50:2; 63:19
Jer 8:19; 15:16
14:10
Ps 119:101
Jer 2:25; 6:20; 44:21-23
Hos 8:13

Where is your flock—
your beautiful flock—
that he gave you to care for?
21 What will you say when the LORD takes
the allies you have cultivated
and appoints them as your rulers?
Pangs of anguish will grip you,
like those of a woman in labor!
22 You may ask yourself,
"Why is all this happening to me?"
It is because of your many sins!
That is why you have been stripped
and raped by invading armies.
23 Can an Ethiopian change the color of his
skin?
Can a leopard take away its spots?
Neither can you start doing good,
for you have always done evil.

24 "I will scatter you like chaff
that is blown away by the desert winds.
25 This is your allotment,
the portion I have assigned to you,"
says the LORD,
"for you have forgotten me,
putting your trust in false gods.
26 I myself will strip you
and expose you to shame.
27 I have seen your adultery and lust,
and your disgusting idol worship out
in the fields and on the hills.
What sorrow awaits you, Jerusalem!
How long before you are pure?"

Judah's Terrible Drought

14 This message came to Jeremiah from the LORD, explaining why he was holding back the rain:

2 "Judah wilts;
commerce at the city gates grinds to
a halt.
All the people sit on the ground in
mourning,
and a great cry rises from Jerusalem.
3 The nobles send servants to get water,
but all the wells are dry.
The servants return with empty pitchers,
confused and desperate,
covering their heads in grief.
4 The ground is parched
and cracked for lack of rain.
The farmers are deeply troubled;
they, too, cover their heads.
5 Even the doe abandons her newborn
fawn
because there is no grass in the field.
6 The wild donkeys stand on the bare hills
panting like thirsty jackals.
They strain their eyes looking for grass,
but there is none to be found."
7 The people say, "Our wickedness has
caught up with us, LORD,
but help us for the sake of your own
reputation.
We have turned away from you
and sinned against you again and again.
8 O Hope of Israel, our Savior in times of
trouble,
why are you like a stranger to us?
Why are you like a traveler passing
through the land,
stopping only for the night?
9 Are you also confused?
Is our champion helpless to save us?
You are right here among us, LORD.
We are known as your people.
Please don't abandon us now!"

10 So this is what the LORD says to his
people:
"You love to wander far from me
and do not restrain yourselves.

beautiful flock, the people of Judah. Judah suffered abuse at the hands of its supposed ***allies*** as a result of the king's ***many sins***.

13:23 *an Ethiopian* (Hebrew *a Cushite*): People have no choice about the ***color*** of their ***skin***, just as ***a leopard*** has no choice about being spotted. In the same way, God's people were born trapped by ***evil***. They had no ability to change on their own, and they refused to allow the Lord to change them.

13:24-27 The divine Judge decreed condemnation.

13:24 ***I will scatter you like chaff:*** This word-picture represented the Exile of the people of Judah. Cp. Ps 1:4-5.

13:25 The people of Judah could not escape their ***assigned*** punishment. They had ***forgotten*** God and had turned to ***false gods***.

13:26 God allowed the Babylonians to ***strip*** Judah of all its treasures and take the people captive.

13:27 Judah's ***idol worship*** included ritual sex acts ***in the fields and on the hills***. The Lord wanted his people to be spiritually and sexually ***pure*** in relation to him.

14:1-22 This chapter is a three-way conversation among the Lord, Jeremiah, and the people. It was sparked by a serious drought that affected the land.

14:2-3 During a drought, no crops were sold in the markets at the Jerusalem ***gates***. Previous harvests could not be stored long, so starvation threatened the people. Cisterns constructed to collect water dried up, and with no rain, no water was available for drinking or for cooking meals. As a result, ***a great cry*** went up from ***Jerusalem***.

14:4-6 Both people and animals were helpless in the drought. • The ***farmers*** would ***cover their heads*** with coarse burlap to express shame, humiliation, and mourning.

14:7-9 Although the people confessed their sins, they did not turn from their ***wickedness***. They tried to manipulate God into helping them by questioning his love, wisdom, and power, while still claiming the special privilege of being his people.

14:10 The Lord's answer to their self-serving prayer cut to the heart of the issue. Their status as God's ***people*** had

Therefore, I will no longer accept you as
my people.
Now I will remember all your
wickedness
and will punish you for your sins."

The Lord Forbids Jeremiah to Intercede

11 Then the LORD said to me, "Do not pray for
these people anymore. 12 When they fast, I
will pay no attention. When they present
their burnt offerings and grain offerings to
me, I will not accept them. Instead, I will devour them with war, famine, and disease."
13 Then I said, "O Sovereign LORD, their
prophets are telling them, 'All is well—no
war or famine will come. The LORD will
surely send you peace.'"
14 Then the LORD said, "These prophets
are telling lies in my name. I did not send
them or tell them to speak. I did not give
them any messages. They prophesy of [a]vi-
sions and revelations they have never seen
or heard. They speak foolishness made up
in their own lying hearts. 15 Therefore, this
is what the LORD says: I will punish these
lying prophets, for they have spoken in my
name even though I never sent them. They
say that no war or famine will come, but
they themselves will die by war and famine!
16 As for the people to whom they prophesy—
their bodies will be thrown out into the
streets of Jerusalem, victims of famine and
war. There will be no one left to bury them.
Husbands, wives, sons, and daughters—all
will be gone. For I will pour out their own
wickedness on them. 17 Now, Jeremiah, say
this to them:

"Night and day my eyes overflow with tears.
I cannot stop weeping,
for my virgin daughter—my precious
people—
has been struck down
and lies mortally wounded.
18 If I go out into the fields,
I see the bodies of people slaughtered
by the enemy.
If I walk the city streets,
I see people who have died of
starvation.
The prophets and priests continue with
their work,
but they don't know what they're
doing."

A Prayer for Healing

19 LORD, have you completely rejected
Judah?
Do you really hate Jerusalem?
Why have you wounded us past all hope
of healing?
We hoped for peace, but no peace
came.
We hoped for a time of healing, but
found only terror.
20 LORD, we confess our wickedness
and that of our ancestors, too.
We all have sinned against you.
21 For the sake of your reputation, LORD, do
not abandon us.
Do not disgrace your own glorious
throne.
Please remember us,
and do not break your covenant
with us.
22 Can any of the worthless foreign gods
send us rain?
Does it fall from the sky by itself?
No, you are the one, O LORD our God!
Only you can do such things.
So we will wait for you to help us.

Judah's Inevitable Doom

15 Then the LORD said to me, "Even if
Moses and Samuel stood before me
pleading for these people, I wouldn't help
them. Away with them! Get them out of my

14:11 Jer 7:16; 11:14
14:12 Isa 1:15; Jer 8:13
14:13 Jer 5:12; 6:14; 8:11; 23:17
14:14 Jer 5:31; 23:16, 25-26; 27:9-10; [a]*khazon* (2377) ›Dan 1:17
14:15 Ezek 14:10
14:16 Ps 79:2-3; Prov 1:31; Jer 7:33; 8:1-2; 13:22-25; 15:2-3
14:17 Jer 8:21; 9:1; Lam 2:13
14:18 Jer 6:25; Lam 1:20; Ezek 7:15
14:19 Job 30:26; Jer 8:15; 30:13; 1 Thes 5:3
14:20 Ps 32:5; Jer 3:25
14:21 Ps 25:11; Jer 3:17; 14:7; 17:12
14:22 1 Kgs 17:1; Isa 41:29; Jer 5:24; 10:3; Lam 3:26
15:1 Exod 32:11-14; 1 Sam 7:9; Ps 99:6; 106:23; Ezek 14:14, 20

been destroyed by their ***wickedness***, so their prayer was absurd and God's judgment would proceed.

14:11-12 For the third time (see 7:16; 11:14), God told Jeremiah not to pray for the people of Judah and Jerusalem. It would be pointless for the people to ***fast***, since the Lord had decided to ***pay no attention***. The priest's presentation of ***burnt offerings and grain offerings***, which the Lord had given Moses as a way of worshiping him (see Lev 1–2), would be wasted effort, because the Lord would ***not accept them***. Instead, the Lord would respond with ***war, famine, and disease***.

14:13-16 ***their prophets:*** The government of Judah supported a corps of prophets who promoted the religious views of the king and his advisers. The Lord often condemned them, along with the officials and the priests. Here, the Lord exposed them as impostors and described what would happen to them and to the people to whom they prophesied.

14:17-18 As he surveyed Judah's condition, God vividly expressed his grief through a short poem. The Lord takes no pleasure in the death of the wicked (Ezek 18:23; 33:11).

14:19-22 Despite the Lord's command to the contrary (14:11), Jeremiah prayed for God to mitigate the disaster that was occurring and the greater disaster that would befall them.

14:19 ***Jerusalem:*** Hebrew *Zion*. (See "Mount Zion, the City of God" at Ps 48, p. 947.)

14:22 Worship of other ***gods*** is useless. Only the Creator of the universe has the power to make nature do his bidding.

15:1-9 The Lord's reply to Jeremiah's prayer (14:19-22) was that Judah's destruction was inevitable.

15:1 ***Moses and Samuel*** were noted for their intercessory prayer. Several times, when they prayed for the rebellious Israelites, the Lord withdrew his threatened punishment (see Exod 32:11-14;

15:2
Jer 14:12; 24:10; 43:11
Ezek 5:2, 12
15:3
Lev 26:16, 22, 25
Deut 28:26
Isa 18:6
Ezek 14:21
15:4
2 Kgs 23:26-27; 24:3-4
Jer 24:9; 29:18
15:5
Ps 69:20
Jer 13:14
15:6
Jer 6:11, 19; 7:16, 24
Zeph 1:4
15:7
Jer 18:21; 51:2
Hos 9:12-16
15:8
Isa 3:25-26; 4:1
15:9
1 Sam 2:5
Isa 47:9
Amos 8:9
15:10
Deut 23:19
Job 3:3
Jer 1:18-19; 20:7-8, 14
15:11
Isa 41:10
15:12
Jer 28:14
15:13
Jer 17:3
15:14
Deut 28:64
Jer 16:13; 17:4

sight!
2 And if they say to you, 'But where can we go?' tell them, 'This is what the LORD says:

" 'Those who are destined for death, to death;
those who are destined for war, to war;
those who are destined for famine, to famine;
those who are destined for captivity, to captivity.'

3 "I will send four kinds of destroyers against them," says the LORD. "I will send the sword to kill, the dogs to drag away, the vultures to devour, and the wild animals to finish up what is left.
4 Because of the wicked things Manasseh son of Hezekiah, king of Judah, did in Jerusalem, I will make my people an object of horror to all the kingdoms of the earth.

5 "Who will feel sorry for you, Jerusalem?
Who will weep for you?
Who will even bother to ask how you are?
6 You have abandoned me
and turned your back on me,"
says the LORD.
"Therefore, I will raise my fist to destroy you.
I am tired of always giving you another chance.
7 I will winnow you like grain at the gates of your cities
and take away the children you hold dear.
I will destroy my own people,
because they refuse to change their evil ways.
8 There will be more widows
than the grains of sand on the seashore.
At noontime I will bring a destroyer
against the mothers of young men.
I will cause anguish and terror
to come upon them suddenly.
9 The mother of seven grows faint and gasps for breath;
her sun has gone down while it is still day.
She sits childless now,
disgraced and humiliated.
And I will hand over those who are left
to be killed by the enemy.
I, the LORD, have spoken!"

Jeremiah's Complaint

10 Then I said,
"What sorrow is mine, my mother.
Oh, that I had died at birth!
I am hated everywhere I go.
I am neither a lender who threatens to foreclose
nor a borrower who refuses to pay—
yet they all curse me."

11 The LORD replied,
"I will take care of you, Jeremiah.
Your enemies will ask you to plead on their behalf
in times of trouble and distress.
12 Can a man break a bar of iron from the north,
or a bar of bronze?
13 At no cost to them,
I will hand over your wealth and treasures
as plunder to your enemies,
for sin runs rampant in your land.
14 I will tell your enemies to take you
as captives to a foreign land.
For my anger blazes like a fire
that will burn forever."

Num 14:13-20; 1 Sam 7:8-10). But now, even their intervention would have been ineffective.

15:2 The people had no place to *go* to escape *death . . . war . . . famine,* and *captivity.*

15:4 Judah's apostasy could be traced back to *Manasseh son of Hezekiah,* the king who reigned 697–642 BC (see 2 Kgs 21:1-18; 2 Chr 33:1-20).

15:5 These three questions are rhetorical—the answer is, "No one!"

15:6-7 The people had heard the charge that they had *abandoned* God and *turned* their *back on* him before (2:13), but they had not taken it seriously. Though the Lord had often given them *another chance* to repent, their sin provoked him to carry out the curses of the Sinai covenant (Deut 27:15-26).

15:8-9 Both the old and the *young men* would die.

15:10-21 Jeremiah bared his heart to God over the unjust treatment he was receiving because he was delivering the Lord's message. In response, the Lord promised to protect and care for his prophet.

15:10 Feelings of grief gripped Jeremiah when people *hated* and cursed him for no reason.

15:11-14 The Lord replied to Jeremiah's lament with reassurance and then explained what would be happening soon.

15:11 When *trouble and distress* fell upon the people, they would ask *Jeremiah* to *plead on their behalf.*

15:12 *Iron* and *bronze* are metaphors for the strong resolve that the Lord would give to Jeremiah (1:18).

15:13-14 It is not clear whether the Lord was speaking of Jeremiah's or of Judah's future. If Jeremiah's, this prediction was fulfilled after the fall of Jerusalem (586 BC), when Jeremiah and Baruch were taken to Egypt against their will (see chs 41–44). If it refers to Judah's future, the prediction was fulfilled in the fall of Jerusalem and the Exile. • ***will burn forever:*** As in some Hebrew manuscripts (see also 17:4); most Hebrew manuscripts read ***will burn against you.***

15 Then I said,

"LORD, you [b]know what's happening to me.
Please step in and help me. Punish my
persecutors!
Please give me time; don't let me die young.
It's for your sake that I am suffering.
16 When I discovered your words, I
devoured them.
They are my joy and my heart's delight,
for I bear your name,
O LORD God of Heaven's Armies.
17 I never joined the people in their merry
feasts.
I sat alone because your hand was
on me.
I was filled with indignation at their
sins.
18 Why then does my suffering continue?
Why is my wound so incurable?
Your help seems as uncertain as a
seasonal brook,
like a spring that has gone dry."

19 This is how the LORD responds:

"If you [c]return to me, I will [c]restore you
so you can continue to serve me.
If you speak good words rather than
worthless ones,
you will be my spokesman.
You must [c]influence them;
do not let them [c]influence you!
20 They will fight against you like an
attacking army,
but I will make you as secure as a
fortified wall of bronze.
They will not conquer you,
for I am with you to protect and
rescue you.
I, the LORD, have spoken!
21 Yes, I will certainly keep you safe from
these wicked men.
I will rescue you from their cruel
hands."

Jeremiah Forbidden to Marry

16 The LORD gave me another message.
He said, 2 "Do not get married or have
children in this place. 3 For this is what the
LORD says about the children born here in
this city and about their mothers and fathers: 4 They will die from terrible diseases.
No one will mourn for them or bury them,
and they will lie scattered on the ground
like manure. They will die from war and
famine, and their bodies will be food for the
vultures and wild animals."

Judah's Coming Punishment

5 This is what the LORD says: "Do not go to
funerals to mourn and show sympathy for
these people, for I have removed my protection and peace from them. I have taken
away my unfailing love and my mercy. 6 Both
the great and the lowly will die in this land.
No one will bury them or mourn for them.
Their friends will not cut themselves in sorrow or shave their heads in sadness. 7 No
one will offer a meal to comfort those who
mourn for the dead—not even at the death
of a mother or father. No one will send a
cup of wine to console them.
8 "And do not go to their feasts and parties.
Do not eat and drink with them at all. 9 For
this is what the LORD of Heaven's Armies,
the God of Israel, says: In your own lifetime,
before your very eyes, I will put an end to
the happy singing and laughter in this land.
The joyful voices of bridegrooms and brides
will no longer be heard.

15:15
Ps 69:7-9
Jer 20:8
[b]*zakar* (2142)
‣Gen 8:1

15:16
Job 23:12
Ps 119:103

15:17
Ps 102:7
2 Cor 6:17

15:18
Jer 30:15

15:19
Ezek 3:17; 44:23
[c]*shub* (7725)
‣Ezek 14:6

15:20
Ps 46:7
Isa 41:10
Jer 1:8, 18-19
Ezek 3:9

15:21
Ps 37:40
Isa 49:26
Jer 39:11-12

16:3-4
Ps 79:2; 83:10
Isa 18:6
Jer 15:2-3; 34:20

16:5
Ps 25:6
Isa 27:11
Jer 12:12; 13:14
Ezek 24:16-23

16:6
Deut 14:1
Ezek 9:6

16:7
Ezek 24:17

16:8
Eccl 7:2-4
Isa 22:12-14
Jer 15:17

16:9
Jer 7:34; 25:10
Hos 2:11

16:10
Deut 29:24-25
1 Kgs 9:8-9
Jer 5:19; 13:22

16:11
Neh 9:26-29
Ps 106:35-41
1 Pet 4:3

15:15-18 Jeremiah's prayer sheds light on a crucial moment in his relationship with the Lord, when persecution had shattered his strength. It is possible that Jeremiah had begun to let his thinking be influenced by the rebellious people of Judah.

15:16-17 Jeremiah was glad to declare God's word, even though it meant that he could not participate in the *merry feasts* of his sinful people. He protested the apparent injustice he had suffered (15:18).

15:18 Jeremiah posed two rhetorical questions that seem to presuppose that he should not have to suffer.

15:19 The Lord confronted Jeremiah with the need to make a decision. If Jeremiah decided to *return* to a disposition of service and submission, the Lord would *restore* him to further usefulness. If Jeremiah took care to utter *good words* of submission, faith, and obedience, and reject *worthless ones* (such as those that the false prophets spoke, 14:14-16), Jeremiah could continue to be the Lord's *spokesman.*

15:20-21 The Lord reaffirmed the promises he had made to Jeremiah when he called him to be a prophet (see 1:18-19).

16:1-18 Jeremiah's life was to be a sign or a parable (see note on 13:1-14), as the Lord instructed him not to marry (16:1-4) and not to go to funerals (16:5-7) or celebrations (16:8-9).

16:1-2 In Hebrew society, bachelors were rare and males were expected to *get married* in their early twenties. However, the severe crisis of the time apparently required Jeremiah to be a divine messenger without family obligations. He needed to depend entirely on the Lord (cp. 1 Cor 7:26-35).

16:3-4 Jeremiah's lack of children was the basis for a lesson about the future. The time would soon come when so many *children* and parents would die that no one would remain to *mourn for them or bury them.*

16:5-7 The ban on *funerals* and mourning was a parable with a message to the people of Judah. Destruction would be so great and widespread that *no one* would *mourn* properly or *comfort* others.

16:8-9 The ban on attending *feasts and parties* isolated Jeremiah from meaningful social contact, but the Lord gave it special importance. The entire nation and its social interaction would soon cease to exist.

16:12 Jer 3:10; 7:24; 9:14 Mark 7:21
16:13 Deut 4:26-27; 28:36 Jer 5:19; 15:14
16:14-15 Deut 15:15 Isa 11:11-16; 43:18-19 Jer 23:7-8
16:16 Isa 2:21 Amos 4:2; 9:1-3 Hab 1:14-15
16:17 Ps 90:8 Jer 23:24; 32:19 Luke 12:2 1 Cor 4:5 Heb 4:13
16:18 Num 35:34 Jer 2:7; 3:9 Rev 18:6
16:19 Ps 18:1-2 Isa 25:4 Jer 3:17; 4:2 Nah 1:7
16:20 Ps 115:4-8 Jer 5:7 Hos 8:4-6 Gal 4:8
16:21 Ps 83:18 Isa 43:3 Amos 5:8
17:1 Job 19:24 Prov 3:3; 7:3 2 Cor 3:3
17:2 Exod 34:13 Jer 3:6
17:3 Isa 39:4-6 Jer 15:13; 20:5

10"When you tell the people all these
things, they will ask, 'Why has the LORD decreed such terrible things against us? What
have we done to deserve such treatment?
What is our sin against the LORD our God?'
11"Then you will give them the LORD's
reply: 'It is because your ancestors were unfaithful to me. They worshiped other gods
and served them. They abandoned me and
did not obey my word. 12And you are even
worse than your ancestors! You stubbornly
follow your own evil desires and refuse to
listen to me. 13So I will throw you out of
this land and send you into a foreign land
where you and your ancestors have never
been. There you can worship idols day and
night—and I will grant you no favors!'

Hope despite the Disaster

14"But the time is coming," says the LORD,
"when people who are taking an oath will
no longer say, 'As surely as the LORD lives,
who rescued the people of Israel from the
land of Egypt.' 15Instead, they will say, 'As
surely as the LORD lives, who brought the
people of Israel back to their own land
from the land of the north and from all the
countries to which he had exiled them.' For
I will bring them back to this land that I
gave their ancestors.
16"But now I am sending for many fishermen who will catch them," says the LORD. "I
am sending for hunters who will hunt them
down in the mountains, hills, and caves. 17I
am watching them closely, and I see every
sin. They cannot hope to hide from me. 18I
will double their punishment for all their
sins, because they have defiled my land
with lifeless images of their detestable
gods and have filled my territory with their
evil deeds."

Jeremiah's Prayer of Confidence

19 LORD, you are my strength and fortress,
my refuge in the day of trouble!
Nations from around the world
will come to you and say,
"Our ancestors left us a foolish heritage,
for they worshiped worthless idols.
20 Can people make their own gods?
These are not real gods at all!"
21 The LORD says,
"Now I will show them my power;
now I will show them my might.
At last they will know and understand
that I am the LORD.

Judah's Sin and Punishment

17 1 "The sin of Judah
is inscribed with an iron chisel—
engraved with a diamond point on their
stony hearts
and on the corners of their altars.
2 Even their children go to worship
at their pagan altars and Asherah poles,
beneath every green tree
and on every high hill.
3 So I will hand over my holy mountain—
along with all your wealth and treasures
and your pagan shrines—
as plunder to your enemies,
for sin runs rampant in your land.

16:10 The Lord told Jeremiah to expect questions from the people that would express their self-righteousness and their belief that the Lord should never harm them.

16:11-13 Jeremiah's reply was the message he received when he was commissioned: The people had *abandoned* the Lord for idols (ch 2), so the Lord would abandon them.

16:14-18 Jeremiah's message was two-pronged: Judgment does not erase eventual hope (16:14-15), but neither does hope cancel out the certainty of judgment (16:16-18).

16:14-15 The Lord planned to bring his people back from exile to the Promised Land, an event that would be on par with the exodus from Egypt (see Ezra 1–6). The Exodus was the primary event in Israel's history that had demonstrated the reality and power of the one true God.

16:16 The ***fishermen*** and ***hunters*** were the Babylonian soldiers God used to mete out his judgment (cp. Hab 1:14-16).

16:18 The ***punishment*** was ***double***—slaughter and exile—because the people of Judah had violated the two most important commandments. They did not love God (Deut 6:4-5), and they did not love their neighbors (Lev 19:18; see also Matt 22:37-40).

16:19-20 Jeremiah responded by worshiping the Lord for his protection in times of ***trouble*** and his provision of salvation for people ***from around the world.***

16:21 The Lord will require all people to know his ***power*** and ***might*** and to ***understand*** that he is ***the LORD*** (cp. Exod 6:7; 8:22).

17:1-4 The families of Judah were committed to Baal worship; once again, the Lord listed the sins that justified their judgment.

17:1 A stone mason used ***an iron chisel*** or ***a diamond point*** to permanently inscribe images and texts on stones. Idol worship had so hardened the thoughts, emotions, and will of the people that it seemed impossible for them to change. • In OT times, ***the corners of . . . altars*** had projections called "horns" (e.g., Exod 27:1-2). According to covenant rules, when an animal sacrifice was offered, blood was applied to these horns. How Baal worshipers treated them is unknown.

17:2 ***Asherah poles*** were cut from trees and erected near altars dedicated to Baal, the Canaanite storm god. ***Asherah*** was the Canaanite goddess who symbolized the fertility of moist ground that could produce crops. Ritual sex was performed near these altars to cause rain to fall, seeds to sprout, and plants to grow. A ***tree*** growing near an altar could also represent this fertility goddess. The people of Judah were so depraved that parents encouraged their ***children*** to join them in these rituals.

17:3 The Lord's ***holy mountain*** was the Temple Mount in Jerusalem; ***wealth and treasures*** were stored there.

4 The wonderful possession I have
reserved for you
will slip from your hands.
I will tell your enemies to take you
as captives to a foreign land.
For my anger blazes like a fire
that will burn forever."

Wisdom from the Lord

5 This is what the Lord says:
"Cursed are those who put their trust in
mere humans,
who rely on human strength
and turn their hearts away from the
Lord.
6 They are like stunted shrubs in the
desert,
with no hope for the future.
They will live in the barren wilderness,
in an uninhabited salty land.

7 "But blessed are those who trust in the
Lord
and have made the Lord their hope
and confidence.
8 They are like trees planted along a
riverbank,
with roots that reach deep into the
water.
Such trees are not bothered by the heat
or worried by long months of drought.
Their leaves stay green,
and they never stop producing fruit.

9 "The human [d]heart is the most deceitful
of all things,
and desperately wicked.
Who really knows how bad it is?
10 But I, the Lord, search all hearts
and examine secret motives.
I give all people their due rewards,
according to what their actions deserve."

Jeremiah's Trust in the Lord

11 Like a partridge that hatches eggs she
has not laid,
so are those who get their wealth by
unjust means.
At midlife they will lose their riches;
in the end, they will become poor old
fools.
12 But we worship at your throne—
eternal, high, and glorious!
13 O Lord, the hope of Israel,
all who turn away from you will be
disgraced.
They will be buried in the dust of the
earth,
for they have abandoned the Lord,
the fountain of living water.

14 O Lord, if you heal me, I will be truly
healed;
if you [e]save me, I will be truly [e]saved.
My praises are for you alone!
15 People scoff at me and say,
"What is this 'message from the Lord'
you talk about?
Why don't your predictions come true?"

16 Lord, I have not abandoned my job
as a shepherd for your people.
I have not urged you to send disaster.
You have heard everything I've said.
17 Lord, don't terrorize me!
You alone are my hope in the day of
disaster.
18 Bring shame and dismay on all who
persecute me,
but don't let me experience shame
and dismay.
Bring a day of terror on them.
Yes, bring double destruction upon
them!

17:4 Deut 28:48; Isa 5:25; Jer 7:20; 12:7; 15:14
17:5 2 Chr 32:8; Ps 146:3; Isa 30:1; 31:3; Ezek 29:6-7
17:6 Deut 29:23; Jer 48:6
17:7 Ps 34:8; 40:4; 84:12; Prov 16:20
17:8 Ps 1:3; 92:12-14; Jer 14:1-6
17:9 Matt 13:15; Mark 2:17; 7:21-22; Rom 1:21; 7:11; Eph 4:22; [d]*leb* (3820) ▸Dan 11:28
17:10 1 Sam 16:7; Jer 11:20; Rom 8:27
17:12 Jer 14:21
17:13 Jer 14:8
17:14 Deut 10:21; Ps 54:1; Jer 33:6; [e]*yasha'* (3467) ▸Ezek 37:23
17:15 Isa 5:19; Amos 5:18
17:16 Jer 12:3
17:17 Jer 16:19; Nah 1:7
17:18 Ps 35:4, 26; Jer 20:11
17:20 Jer 19:3-4
17:21 Num 15:32-36; Neh 13:15-21; Mark 3:1-5; John 5:9-12

17:4 ***The wonderful possession,*** the Promised Land, would ***slip from*** Judah's ***hands*** when the people were taken ***as captives to*** Babylon.

17:5-10 This meditation on the folly of trusting in humans is contrasted with the wisdom of trusting in the Lord.

17:5 ***Trust*** is the disposition of the heart that results in obedience (cp. 11:4; Deut 27:15-26).

17:6 The people of Judah would be utterly helpless in the time of calamity because they had switched their trust from the Lord to human capabilities. The people of Judah would be just like ***shrubs in the desert*** that are ***stunted*** because they lack water.

17:7-8 ***Those who trust in the Lord,*** like ***trees planted along a riverbank,*** will have abundant resources and be well prepared to meet the vicissitudes of life. • ***Water*** represents the law of the Lord (cp. Ps 1; Ezek 47:1-12; Rev 2:1-2).

17:9-10 By nature, the ***heart*** of all ***human*** beings is ***deceitful*** and ***desperately wicked.*** Only the Lord ***really knows how bad it is.***

17:11-18 Jeremiah affirmed that he had learned this lesson and did indeed trust in the Lord.

17:11-13 Jeremiah commended the Lord's faithfulness to his people, in contrast to the fate awaiting those who turned away from the Lord.

17:11 Jeremiah cited a general principle (cp. Ps 73) that was not necessarily universal (Job 21:27-33): Those who have gained ***wealth by unjust means*** eventually lose those riches.

17:12 God's faithful people ***worship*** the sovereign Lord, not money.

17:14-18 Jeremiah asked that since he had been faithful to the Lord, the Lord would rescue him from his persecutors and give him healing, salvation, and vindication.

17:14 Only the Lord can ***heal*** and ***save,*** so ***praises*** are due to him ***alone.***

17:15 Jeremiah's predictions had not yet come true, so the people treated him with scorn; they might have even called him a false prophet (cp. Deut 18:21-22).

17:16 Because he was faithful, Jeremiah appealed to the Lord for vindication.

17:17 Jeremiah had a natural fear of the coming national ***disaster,*** so he turned to the Lord for protection.

17:18 Jeremiah wanted his persecutors to experience the ***shame and dismay*** they deserved, the very feelings that he was experiencing (17:15).

[f]*shabbath* (7676)
‣ Ezek 20:20

17:22
Exod 20:8; 31:13
Ezek 20:12

17:23
Jer 7:26; 19:15

17:24
Exod 15:26; 20:8-11
Deut 11:13
Ezek 20:20

17:25
2 Sam 7:16
Ps 132:13-14
Jer 22:4
Luke 1:32
Heb 12:2

17:26
Ps 107:22
Jer 33:11

17:27
Jer 39:8
Ezek 20:47
Amos 2:5

18:2
Jer 19:1-2

18:6
Isa 45:9; 64:8
Matt 20:15
Rom 9:20-21

18:7
Jer 1:10

18:8
Jer 7:3-7
Ezek 18:21
Jon 3:10

18:9
Jer 31:28
Amos 9:11-15

18:10
1 Sam 2:30
Jer 7:24-28
Ezek 33:18

18:11
2 Kgs 17:13
Isa 1:16-19
Jer 4:6; 11:11
Acts 26:20

18:12
Deut 29:19
Jer 2:25; 16:12

Observing the Sabbath

19This is what the LORD said to me: "Go and
stand in the gates of Jerusalem, first in the
gate where the king goes in and out, and
then in each of the other gates. 20Say to all
the people, 'Listen to this message from the
LORD, you kings of Judah and all you people
of Judah and everyone living in Jerusalem.
21This is what the LORD says: Listen to my
warning! Stop carrying on your trade at Jerusalem's gates on the [f]Sabbath day. 22Do
not do your work on the Sabbath, but make
it a holy day. I gave this command to your
ancestors, 23but they did not listen or obey.
They stubbornly refused to pay attention or
accept my discipline.

24" 'But if you obey me, says the LORD, and
do not carry on your trade at the gates or
work on the Sabbath day, and if you keep it
holy, 25then kings and their officials will go
in and out of these gates forever. There will
always be a descendant of David sitting on
the throne here in Jerusalem. Kings and their
officials will always ride in and out among
the people of Judah in chariots and on horses,
and this city will remain forever. 26And from
all around Jerusalem, from the towns of
Judah and Benjamin, from the western foothills and the hill country and the Negev, the
people will come with their burnt offerings
and sacrifices. They will bring their grain
offerings, frankincense, and thanksgiving
offerings to the LORD's Temple.

27" 'But if you do not listen to me and refuse to keep the Sabbath holy, and if on the
Sabbath day you bring loads of merchandise through the gates of Jerusalem just as
on other days, then I will set fire to these
gates. The fire will spread to the palaces,
and no one will be able to put out the roaring flames.' "

The Potter and the Clay

18 The LORD gave another message to
Jeremiah. He said, 2"Go down to the
potter's shop, and I will speak to you there."
3So I did as he told me and found the potter working at his wheel. 4But the jar he was
making did not turn out as he had hoped, so
he crushed it into a lump of clay again and
started over.

5Then the LORD gave me this message:
6"O Israel, can I not do to you as this potter
has done to his clay? As the clay is in the
potter's hand, so are you in my hand. 7If I
announce that a certain nation or kingdom
is to be uprooted, torn down, and destroyed,
8but then that nation renounces its evil ways,
I will not destroy it as I had planned. 9And if
I announce that I will plant and build up a
certain nation or kingdom, 10but then that
nation turns to evil and refuses to obey me,
I will not bless it as I said I would.

11"Therefore, Jeremiah, go and warn all
Judah and Jerusalem. Say to them, 'This is
what the LORD says: I am planning disaster
for you instead of good. So turn from your
evil ways, each of you, and do what is right.' "

12But the people replied, "Don't waste
your breath. We will continue to live as we
want to, stubbornly following our own evil
desires."

17:19-27 Motivated by greed, the people of ***Jerusalem*** were violating the sanctity of the ***Sabbath day*** (see Exod 20:8-11; Deut 5:12-15). If they observed the Sabbath, they would lose income from trade. The Lord spelled out the reasons why they should keep the Sabbath ***holy.***

17:19-20 The Lord instructed Jeremiah to go from gate to gate where business was transacted and confront the offenders face to face, beginning with ***the king.***

17:21-22 Trading on ***the Sabbath*** was wrong and had to be stopped. The Sabbath was not a time to buy and sell, but was established in the Sinai covenant as ***a holy day*** (Exod 29:8-11; 31:12-17) when the people of Israel were to rest and honor the Lord.

17:23 ***they did not listen or obey:*** The people probably considered the Sabbath too costly to observe, so they ignored it or overlooked its violations.

17:24-25 The Lord was willing to give the people a chance to change their ways. By choosing to ***obey*** God, the people could enjoy unending peace and the continuation of the kingdom and the city of ***Jerusalem*** possible. • The promise of ***chariots*** and ***horses*** represented the Lord's blessing.

17:26 If the people repented, the Lord's blessings would extend to the ***towns of Judah and Benjamin.*** • ***The western foothills*** (Hebrew *the Shephelah*) stretched north and south between the coastal plain of the Mediterranean Sea and the ***hill country,*** where Jerusalem rested. • The ***Negev*** was the desert that stretched from Beersheba southward to the Gulf of Aqaba. People from all these areas would come with their offerings to worship the Lord in his ***Temple.***

17:27 ***I will set fire to these gates:*** This event occurred in 586 BC (2 Kgs 25:9).

18:1-11 The Lord had Jeremiah take part in an object lesson. What Jeremiah observed at ***the potter's shop*** became a picture of what the Lord was about to do with Judah.

18:1-4 Jeremiah watched as the potter formed an earthen jar, then crushed it and started over.

18:5-6 The Lord likened himself to ***this potter.*** He could set standards of perfection and choose to destroy or reshape his work.

18:7-10 If a ***nation or kingdom*** rejected the one true God, then God could decree that it ***be uprooted, torn down, and destroyed*** (cp. 1:10). If the nation changed ***its evil ways,*** the Lord's anger would relent and he would ***not destroy*** it.

18:11 The Lord planned to deal with ***Judah and Jerusalem*** as the potter dealt with the clay (18:4). However, they could still escape ***disaster*** if they would reject their ***evil ways*** and ***do what is right.***

18:12 Instead of heeding the Lord's message, ***the people*** of Judah ridiculed it, refused to change, and made a brazen commitment to pursue their ***own evil desires.***

13So this is what the LORD says:
"Has anyone ever heard of such a thing,
even among the pagan nations?
My virgin daughter Israel
has done something terrible!
14 Does the snow ever disappear from the
mountaintops of Lebanon?
Do the cold streams flowing from
those distant mountains ever run
dry?
15 But my people are not so reliable, for
they have deserted me;
they burn incense to worthless idols.
They have stumbled off the ancient
highways
and walk in muddy paths.
16 Therefore, their land will become desolate,
a monument to their stupidity.
All who pass by will be astonished
and will shake their heads in
amazement.
17 I will scatter my people before their
enemies
as the east wind scatters dust.
And in all their trouble I will turn my
back on them
and refuse to notice their distress."

A Plot against Jeremiah

18Then the people said, "Come on, let's plot a way to stop Jeremiah. We have plenty of priests and wise men and prophets. We don't need him to teach the word and give us advice and prophecies. Let's spread rumors about him and ignore what he says."

19 LORD, hear me and help me!
Listen to what my enemies are saying.
20 Should they repay evil for good?
They have dug a pit to kill me,
though I pleaded for them
and tried to protect them from your
anger.
21 So let their children starve!
Let them die by the sword!
Let their wives become childless widows.
Let their old men die in a plague,
and let their young men be killed in
battle!
22 Let screaming be heard from their
homes
as warriors come suddenly upon
them.
For they have dug a pit for me
and have hidden traps along my path.
23 LORD, you know all about their
murderous plots against me.
Don't forgive their crimes and blot out
their sins.
Let them die before you.
Deal with them in your anger.

Jeremiah's Shattered Jar

19 This is what the LORD said to me: "Go
and buy a clay jar. Then ask some of
the leaders of the people and of the priests
to follow you. 2Go out through the Gate of
Broken Pots to the garbage dump in the
valley of Ben-Hinnom, and give them this
message. 3Say to them, 'Listen to this message from the LORD, you kings of Judah
and citizens of Jerusalem! This is what the
LORD of Heaven's Armies, the God of Israel,
says: I will bring a terrible disaster on this
place, and the ears of those who hear about
it will ring!
4" 'For Israel has forsaken me and
turned this valley into a place of wickedness. The people burn incense to foreign
gods—idols never before acknowledged by

18:13 Jer 2:10-11; 23:14; Hos 6:10
18:15 Isa 62:10; 65:7; Jer 2:32; 6:16; 7:9; 44:17
18:16 Jer 25:9; 50:13; Ezek 33:28-29
18:17 Jer 13:24
18:18 Ps 52:2; Jer 2:8; 5:13; 8:8; 11:19; 20:10; Mal 2:7
18:20 Ps 35:7; 57:6; 106:23; Jer 5:26
18:21 Ps 109:9-20; Jer 9:21; 11:22; 14:16
18:22 Ps 140:5; Jer 6:26
18:23 Jer 6:15; 7:20; 17:4
19:1 Num 11:16
19:2 Josh 15:8; Jer 7:31
19:3 1 Sam 3:11
19:4 Deut 28:20; 2 Kgs 21:6, 16; Isa 65:11; Jer 2:34; 7:6, 9; 11:13; 17:13; Dan 11:31

18:13-17 The Lord answered that he would scatter his people who had deserted him.

18:13 ***Has anyone ever heard of such a thing?*** In other ***nations***, people did not turn their backs on their national deities (2:11-13), but ***Israel*** blatantly mocked the one true God.

18:14-15 The answer to these two rhetorical questions was "No." The snow and the streams of ***the mountaintops of Lebanon*** were perennially reliable. By contrast, the Lord's people were ***not so reliable.*** • ***The ancient highways*** represented a life of faithfulness to the covenant (6:16), while the ***muddy paths*** symbolized a life of self-serving paganism.

18:16-17 The Lord pronounced sentence on Judah and Jerusalem. • ***their land will become desolate . . . I will scatter my people:*** In 605–586 BC, Judah and Jerusalem were progressively emptied of residents. • ***as the east wind scatters dust:*** During the summer, a strong hot wind from the east can blow sand and dust from the desert into Judah. • ***I will turn my back on them:*** The people would no longer experience a covenant relationship with the Lord.

18:18-23 Jeremiah made an impassioned plea for vengeance on those who were trying to subvert his ministry.

18:18 The people hated ***Jeremiah*** because his authoritative messages challenged the messages of their leaders, so they plotted ***to stop*** him.

18:19-20 Jeremiah reminded the Lord of the injustice of his enemies' opposition.

18:21-23 In his prayer for vengeance, Jeremiah asked God to fulfill his promised curses against those who violated his covenant (cp. Deut 27:11-26; 28:15-68; see also "Prayers for Vengeance" at Ps 137, p. 1017).

19:1-15 Jeremiah acted out another parable (see note at 13:1-14) that demonstrated to the leaders of Judah that the Lord would utterly destroy their idolatrous and murderous nation.

19:2 ***the valley of Ben-Hinnom:*** See note on 7:30-34.

19:4-5 ***The people burn incense:*** According to the Sinai Covenant, offering incense while worshiping the Lord was to be an act of the priests (Exod 30:8). Offering incense to idols was a terrible affront to the Lord. • ***the blood of innocent children:*** Child sacrifice was practiced in Baal worship, and sometimes by ***the kings of Judah*** (2 Kgs 17:17; Ps 106:37-38).

19:5 Lev 18:21; 2 Kgs 17:17; Ps 106:37-38; Jer 32:35
19:6 //Jer 7:32
19:7 Ps 33:10-11; 79:2-3; Isa 28:17-18
19:8 1 Kgs 9:8; 2 Chr 7:21; Jer 18:16
19:9 Deut 28:53, 55; Lam 4:10; Ezek 5:10
19:10 Jer 19:1
19:11 Ps 2:9; Isa 30:14; Jer 7:32; Rev 2:27
19:13 Deut 4:19; 2 Kgs 17:16; Jer 7:18; 8:2; 32:29; 52:13; Ezek 20:28; Zeph 1:5
19:14 Jer 26:2
19:15 Neh 9:17, 29; Ps 58:4; Jer 7:26; 17:23
20:1 1 Chr 24:14; Ezra 2:37-38

this generation, by their ancestors, or by the kings of Judah. And they have filled this place with the blood of innocent children. [5]They have built pagan shrines to Baal, and there they burn their sons as sacrifices to Baal. I have never commanded such a horrible deed; it never even crossed my mind to command such a thing! [6]So beware, for the time is coming, says the LORD, when this garbage dump will no longer be called Topheth or the valley of Ben-Hinnom, but the Valley of Slaughter.

[7]" 'For I will upset the careful plans of Judah and Jerusalem. I will allow the people to be slaughtered by invading armies, and I will leave their dead bodies as food for the vultures and wild animals. [8]I will reduce Jerusalem to ruins, making it a monument to their stupidity. All who pass by will be astonished and will gasp at the destruction they see there. [9]I will see to it that your enemies lay siege to the city until all the food is gone. Then those trapped inside will eat their own sons and daughters and friends. They will be driven to utter despair.'

[10]"As these men watch you, Jeremiah, smash the jar you brought. [11]Then say to them, 'This is what the LORD of Heaven's Armies says: As this jar lies shattered, so I will shatter the people of Judah and Jerusalem beyond all hope of repair. They will bury the bodies here in Topheth, the garbage dump, until there is no more room for them. [12]This is what I will do to this place and its people, says the LORD. I will cause this city to become defiled like Topheth. [13]Yes, all the houses in Jerusalem, including the palace of Judah's kings, will become like Topheth—all the houses where you burned incense on the rooftops to your star gods, and where liquid offerings were poured out to your idols.' "

[14]Then Jeremiah returned from Topheth, the garbage dump where he had delivered this message, and he stopped in front of the Temple of the LORD. He said to the people there, [15]"This is what the LORD of Heaven's Armies, the God of Israel, says: 'I will bring disaster upon this city and its surrounding towns as I promised, because you have stubbornly refused to listen to me.' "

Jeremiah and Pashhur

20 Now Pashhur son of Immer, the priest in charge of the Temple of the LORD, heard what Jeremiah was prophesying.

The Lord of Nations (18:5-11)

Jer 25:15-29; 46:1–51:64; Exod 8:20-22; 9:29; 2 Kgs 19:22-37; Dan 2:19-21; 4:34-37; Hag 2:7; Matt 28:18-20; Acts 12:21-23; Rom 13:1-7

Both the OT and the NT claim that the Lord is the one true God and that God is supreme over all nations and all peoples in all ages. The Scriptures affirm this supremacy as true even when rulers in those nations do not believe in or acknowledge the one true God. Kings and emperors might believe that they control all events in their realms, but they are wrong. The Lord God is always in control.

The OT prophets, including Jeremiah, declared that the Lord God of Israel decided who would become king or emperor of each nation. These rulers were held accountable before God concerning the morality of their policies and how they were carried out. This claim is apparent in Jer 18, 25, 46–51.

As the Lord deals with the nations, his goal has always been to bring these nations and their people to himself. God wants all nations to obey him and his laws, as expressed in the Sinai Covenant. If these nations fail to recognize the reality of the one true God, they will suffer severe judgment. To selected nations, God did soften judgment by promising that a remnant would remain to continue their history (see Jer 46–51).

The Lord desires the conversion of every nation on earth to sincere devotion and commitment to himself. He has always wanted all people to live righteous lives and to experience the joy of truly worshiping him.

19:6 ***Valley of Slaughter:*** Cp. 7:32.

19:9 The ***siege*** of Jerusalem lasted for two and a half years, resulting in severe famine and ***despair*** (see 2 Kgs 25:1-4). • ***their own sons and daughters:*** Cp. Deut 28:53-57.

19:10-13 ***Judah,*** the nation that these leaders represented, would be utterly ***shattered*** and broken ***beyond all hope of repair.*** Never again would Judah be a sovereign nation with a Davidic king (see 33:17-18 and notes), and the city of Jerusalem would be ***defiled like Topheth,*** the unclean valley (see note on 7:30-34).

19:14-15 Jeremiah concluded his message at ***the Temple of the LORD,*** where the common people could hear him.

20:1-6 The persecution suffered by ***Jeremiah*** moved from words to action. Jeremiah was ***whipped*** and placed ***in stocks*** overnight on the charge that he had blasphemed ***the Temple.*** When he was released, Jeremiah gave his jailer a message of personal condemnation from the Lord.

20:1-2 ***Pashhur,*** the head of the police who kept order in ***the Temple*** area, ranked second to the high priest in authority. Evidently, he had heard ***Jeremiah*** proclaim the Lord's decree about

2So he arrested Jeremiah the prophet and
had him whipped and put in stocks at the
Benjamin Gate of the LORD's Temple.
3The next day, when Pashhur finally released him, Jeremiah said, "Pashhur, the
LORD has changed your name. From now on
you are to be called 'The Man Who Lives in
Terror.' 4For this is what the LORD says: 'I will
send terror upon you and all your friends,
and you will watch as they are slaughtered
by the swords of the enemy. I will hand the
people of Judah over to the king of Babylon.
He will take them captive to Babylon or run
them through with the sword. 5And I will
let your enemies plunder Jerusalem. All the
famed treasures of the city—the precious
jewels and gold and silver of your kings—
will be carried off to Babylon. 6As for you,
Pashhur, you and all your household will
go as captives to Babylon. There you will
die and be buried, you and all your friends
to whom you prophesied that everything
would be all right.'"

Jeremiah's Complaint

7 O LORD, you misled me,
and I allowed myself to be misled.
You are stronger than I am,
and you overpowered me.
Now I am mocked every day;
everyone laughs at me.
8 When I speak, the words burst out.
"Violence and destruction!" I shout.
So these messages from the LORD
have made me a household joke.
9 But if I say I'll never mention the LORD
or speak in his name,
his word burns in my heart like a fire.
It's like a fire in my bones!
I am worn out trying to hold it in!
I can't do it!
10 I have heard the many rumors about me.
They call me "The Man Who Lives in
Terror."
They threaten, "If you say anything, we
will report it."
Even my old friends are watching me,
waiting for a fatal slip.
"He will trap himself," they say,
"and then we will get our revenge on
him."
11 But the LORD stands beside me like a
great warrior.
Before him my persecutors will
stumble.
They cannot defeat me.
They will fail and be thoroughly
humiliated.
Their dishonor will never be forgotten.
12 O LORD of Heaven's Armies,
you test those who are righteous,
and you examine the deepest
thoughts and secrets.
Let me see your vengeance against them,
for I have committed my cause to you.
13 Sing to the LORD!
[g]Praise the LORD!
For though I was poor and needy,
he rescued me from my oppressors.

14 Yet I curse the day I was born!
May no one celebrate the day of my
birth.
15 I curse the messenger who told my
father,
"Good news—you have a son!"
16 Let him be destroyed like the cities of
old
that the LORD overthrew without
mercy.
Terrify him all day long with battle
shouts,

20:2
1 Kgs 22:27
2 Chr 16:10; 24:21
Job 13:27
Jer 1:19; 37:13; 38:7
Zech 14:10

20:4
Jer 29:21; 39:6-7
Ezek 26:21

20:5
2 Kgs 20:17
2 Chr 36:10
Jer 15:13; 17:3;
27:21-22

20:6
Jer 14:14-15
Lam 2:14

20:7
Ps 22:7
Lam 3:14
Ezek 3:14
Mic 3:8

20:8
2 Chr 36:16
Jer 6:10

20:9
Job 32:18-20
Ps 39:3
Jer 4:19
Acts 4:20

20:10
1 Kgs 19:2
Neh 6:6-13
Ps 31:13; 41:9
Jer 18:18

20:11
Deut 32:35-36
Jer 1:8; 15:20

20:12
Ps 7:9; 17:3; 59:10;
62:8; 139:23
Jer 11:20; 17:10

20:13
Ps 34:6; 69:33
Jer 15:21; 31:7
[g]*halal* (1984)
‣ Judg 16:24

20:14
Job 3:3-6

20:15
Gen 21:6-7

---

the destruction of Jerusalem, including the Temple. He regarded it as such blasphemy that he thought Jeremiah should be punished.

20:3 ***The Man Who Lives in Terror:*** Hebrew *Magor-missabib,* which means "surrounded by terror"; also in 20:10. Cp. 46:5; Ps 31:13.

20:4-5 This is the first instance in which ***Babylon*** is named as the country whose armies would invade ***Judah*** and take the people into exile. The invaders would take the ***precious jewels and gold and silver,*** leaving Judah without resources.

20:6 ***Pashhur*** would be confronted with the proof that he had been a false prophet.

20:7 ***you misled me:*** Jeremiah spoke of his calling from the Lord (1:5-10) using the same Hebrew word that elsewhere refers to sexual seduction (Exod 22:16).

20:8-9 Jeremiah found it impossible not to speak ***the words*** of God's judgment, even though his ***messages*** turned him into ***a household joke*** (cp. Job 32:18-20; Ps 39:1-3; Acts 4:18-20).

20:10 The people sarcastically threw back on Jeremiah the name that he had given to Pashhur, ***The Man Who Lives in Terror*** (20:3). Even Jeremiah's ***old friends*** looked for ways to twist his words and trip him up.

20:11 Jeremiah realized that God was ***like a great warrior*** standing at his side. Jeremiah's ***persecutors*** were at a real disadvantage and would completely ***fail.***

20:12 Jeremiah placed his complete trust in the ***LORD of Heaven's Armies*** (see 5:14), who alone could carry out the ***vengeance*** due to the prophet's enemies.

20:13 Suddenly, relief and joy came to Jeremiah's soul; he recalled that even when he was ***poor and needy,*** the Lord had ***rescued*** him from his ***oppressors.***

20:14-18 Jeremiah's hope of deliverance did not negate the reality of his circumstances. Shocked by his persecution, Jeremiah wished that he were already dead or that he had never been born (cp. 16:3-4; Job 3).

20:16 The ***cities of old*** were probably Sodom and Gomorrah (Gen 19:24-29).

20:17
Job 3:10-11, 16; 10:18-19
20:18
Job 3:20; 14:1
Ps 102:3
Jer 15:10
1 Cor 4:9-13
21:1
2 Kgs 25:18-21
1 Chr 9:12
Jer 29:25, 29; 37:3
21:2
2 Kgs 25:1-2
Ps 44:1-4
21:4
Zech 14:2
21:5
Isa 5:25; 63:10
Jer 6:12
21:6
Jer 14:12; 32:24
21:7
2 Chr 36:17
Jer 13:14
Ezek 7:9
Hab 1:6-10
21:8
Deut 30:15, 19
21:9
Jer 38:2; 39:18

17 because he did not kill me at birth.
Oh, that I had died in my mother's
womb,
that her body had been my grave!
18 Why was I ever born?
My entire life has been filled
with trouble, sorrow, and shame.

4. MESSAGES OF JUDGMENT (21:1–28:17)

Messages about the Kings of Judah (21:1–23:8)

No Deliverance from Babylon

21 The LORD spoke through Jeremiah
when King Zedekiah sent Pashhur
son of Malkijah and Zephaniah son of Maaseiah, the priest, to speak with him. They
begged Jeremiah, 2 "Please speak to the LORD
for us and ask him to help us. King Nebuchadnezzar of Babylon is attacking Judah.
Perhaps the LORD will be gracious and do a
mighty miracle as he has done in the past.
Perhaps he will force Nebuchadnezzar to
withdraw his armies."

3 Jeremiah replied, "Go back to King Zedekiah and tell him, 4 'This is what the LORD,
the God of Israel, says: I will make your
weapons useless against the king of Babylon and the Babylonians who are outside
your walls attacking you. In fact, I will bring
your enemies right into the heart of this city.
5 I myself will fight against you with a strong
hand and a powerful arm, for I am very angry. You have made me furious! 6 I will send
a terrible plague upon this city, and both
people and animals will die. 7 And after all
that, says the LORD, I will hand over King
Zedekiah, his staff, and everyone else in
the city who survives the disease, war, and
famine. I will hand them over to King Nebuchadnezzar of Babylon and to their other
enemies. He will slaughter them and show
them no mercy, pity, or compassion.'

8 "Tell all the people, 'This is what the
LORD says: Take your choice of life or death!
9 Everyone who stays in Jerusalem will die
from war, famine, or disease, but those who

The Choice of Life or Death (21:8-9)

Jer 3:12-15; 4:3-4; 7:5-7; 18:7-11; 21:8-9; 23:22; 26:13; 27:12-18; 35:15; 36:3-7; 44:5
Deut 11:26-29; 30:15-20
Prov 9:1-18; 11:19; 18:21
Isa 1:19-20
Ezek 18:23-24
Rom 6:23; 8:6
Rev 2:10

Jeremiah put it bluntly: "Take your choice of life or death" (21:8). The prophet warned King Zedekiah and his people to submit to the Lord's instruction. If they did, they would live; if not, they would die.

The Lord had offered such a choice before. Earlier in Jeremiah's ministry, the Lord confronted the people of Judah with an opportunity to change, such as when God appealed to the people to come home to him (3:12–4:4). If they rejected idol worship, admitted their guilt, and confessed that they were rebels, God would cleanse their minds and hearts, and they could live peacefully in the land. However, the people scornfully rejected this offer again and again (7:5-7; 18:8-11; 23:22; 26:13; 27:12-13; 29:32; 35:15; 36:3-7; 44:5). The Lord warned them that if they rejected the path of life, they would experience judgment (25:28). This note sounds all through God's covenant dealings with his people: Obey the covenant—life as God designed it—and live, or refuse to obey the Creator's design and die (8:3; Lev 18:5; Deut 30:19).

In Jeremiah's day, only a few chose life; the majority rebelled and experienced death. In the end, the people led by Zedekiah ignored the Lord, defied the Babylonian army, and suffered judgment. They intentionally rejected the gift of life.

20:17-18 Jeremiah saw no meaning to his *life.*

21:1–28:17 From this point forward in the book of Jeremiah, there is specific information about the last several kings of Judah, particularly Jehoiakim and Zedekiah. The narratives are mostly written in prose and are not always in exact chronological sequence.

21:1-10 This section moves to the beginning of the Babylonian siege of Jerusalem in 588 BC (cp. 52:1-23; 2 Kgs 24:18–25:21; 2 Chr 36:11-21). The Lord communicated with Judah through his messenger Jeremiah.

21:1 The reign of ***King Zedekiah*** spanned 597–586 BC. • The ***Pashhur*** mentioned here is not the one mentioned in 20:1-6 because they had different fathers. He and ***Zephaniah*** bore the full authority of the king, yet when they met the prophet, ***they begged Jeremiah*** for the Lord's help. Clearly, they regarded Jeremiah as a man of great authority. Zedekiah recognized Jeremiah's prophetic authority, but he lacked the courage or the moral integrity to do what Jeremiah directed him to do in the Lord's name.

21:2 ***Nebuchadnezzar . . . is attacking Judah:*** This event probably occurred around the beginning of the siege of Jerusalem in 588 BC (2 Kgs 25:1). • Zedekiah did not pray to the Lord as his ancestor Hezekiah had done (2 Kgs 19:14-20, 29-37; 2 Chr 32:20-22; Isa 37:1-7, 14-20). However, the king expected Jeremiah to perform the miracle of turning away the Lord's anger. • ***Nebuchadnezzar:*** Hebrew *Nebuchadrezzar,* a variant spelling of Nebuchadnezzar; also in 21:7.

21:3-7 The Lord answered King Zedekiah's messengers with a judicial decree (see note on 2:2). Resisting the Babylonians would be ***useless*** because the Lord was fighting against Jerusalem. • ***Babylonians:*** Or *Chaldeans;* also in 21:9.

21:8-10 Although the Lord had decided to destroy the city of ***Jerusalem*** regardless, individual ***people*** still had a ***choice*** between ***life,*** probably as slaves in Babylon, ***or death*** by Babylonian swords (cp. Deut 20:10-13).

go out and surrender to the Babylonians
will live. Their reward will be life! 10For I
have decided to bring disaster and not
good upon this city, says the LORD. It will be
handed over to the king of Babylon, and he
will reduce it to ashes.'

Judgment on Judah's Kings

11"Say to the royal family of Judah, 'Listen to
this message from the LORD! 12This is what
the LORD says to the dynasty of David:

" 'Give justice each morning to the people
you judge!
Help those who have been robbed;
rescue them from their oppressors.
Otherwise, my anger will burn like an
unquenchable fire
because of all your sins.
13 I will personally fight against the people
in Jerusalem,
that mighty fortress—
the people who boast, "No one can touch
us here.
No one can break in here."
14 And I myself will punish you for your
sinfulness,
says the LORD.
I will light a fire in your forests
that will burn up everything around
you.' "

A Message for Judah's Kings

22 This is what the LORD said to me:
"Go over and speak directly to the
king of Judah. Say to him, 2'Listen to this
message from the LORD, you king of Judah,
sitting on David's throne. Let your attendants and your people listen, too. 3This is
what the LORD says: Be fair-minded and
just. Do what is right! Help those who
have been robbed; rescue them from their
oppressors. Quit your evil deeds! Do not
mistreat foreigners, orphans, and widows.
Stop murdering the innocent! 4If you obey
me, there will always be a descendant of David sitting on the throne here in Jerusalem.
The king will ride through the palace gates
in chariots and on horses, with his parade of
attendants and subjects. 5But if you refuse
to pay attention to this warning, I swear by
my own name, says the LORD, that this palace will become a pile of rubble.' "

A Message about the Palace

6Now this is what the LORD says concerning
Judah's royal palace:

"I love you as much as fruitful Gilead
and the green forests of Lebanon.
But I will turn you into a desert,
with no one living within your walls.
7 I will call for wreckers,
who will bring out their tools to
dismantle you.
They will tear out all your fine cedar
beams
and throw them on the fire.

8"People from many nations will pass by
the ruins of this city and say to one another,
'Why did the LORD destroy such a great
city?' 9And the answer will be, 'Because
they violated their covenant with the LORD
their God by worshiping other gods.' "

A Message about Jehoahaz

10 Do not weep for the dead king or mourn
his loss.
Instead, weep for the captive king
being led away!
For he will never return to see his
native land again.

21:10 2 Chr 36:19; Jer 32:28-29; 39:8; 44:11, 27; 52:13
21:11 Jer 17:20
21:12 Isa 1:17; Jer 7:5, 20; 17:4; 22:3; Nah 1:6; Zech 7:9-10
21:13 2 Sam 5:6-7; Ps 125:2; Jer 49:4; Lam 4:12; Ezek 13:8; Obad 1:3-4
21:14 2 Chr 36:19; Jer 52:13
22:2 Isa 9:7; Jer 17:25; 22:4; Luke 1:32
22:3 Exod 22:21-24; Ps 72:4; Jer 7:6; 19:4; 21:12; 22:17
22:4 Jer 17:25
22:5 Amos 6:8; Heb 6:13
22:6 Isa 6:11; Jer 7:34
22:7 Isa 10:3-6, 33-34; Jer 4:6-7
22:8 Deut 29:24-26; 1 Kgs 9:8-9; 2 Chr 7:20, 22; Jer 16:10
22:9 2 Chr 34:25; Jer 11:3
22:10 Jer 16:7; 44:14

21:11-14 Far from performing a miracle for the *dynasty of David*, God was going to hold them accountable for their sins.

21:11-12 The Lord gave the *royal family of Judah* the choice of treating *the people* with *justice* or facing the Lord's *anger*.

21:13-14 The *people in Jerusalem* had put their complete faith in the *mighty fortress* of the city, believing it could not be conquered (see 2 Kgs 18:35-37; 2 Chr 32:20-23; Isa 37:36-38). The Lord had protected the city in the past, but now the Lord was fighting against it. • *light a fire in your forests:* See Isa 6:13.

22:1–23:8 This collection of messages to the last Davidic kings of Judah culminates in the promise that God would one day place a true descendant of David over his people.

22:1-5 Jeremiah delivered a statement, drawn from the Sinai covenant, that summarized the duties of a king of Judah. Fulfillment of these duties would ensure the continuation of the dynasty of David in Jerusalem; refusal would bring the unimaginable disappearance of the palace and the kingdom.

22:3 The *evil deeds* of Judah's leaders included not being *right* or *fair-minded and just*. They had also refused to *help those* who had been *robbed* or to *rescue* the oppressed, and they mistreated *foreigners, orphans, and widows* (see Isa 58:6-7; Mic 6:8; Zech 7:9-10; 8:16-17; Matt 23:23).

22:6-9 After the Temple, *Judah's royal palace* was the nation's most important building. It was an expensive building produced by the best craftsmen (1 Kgs 7:1-12), and it was the king's home and the center of his government. Although the Lord loved the palace, it would not escape the destruction he decreed for Jerusalem.

22:6-7 Valuable crops were raised in the valleys and on the slopes of *Gilead*, the highlands rising eastward from the Jordan Valley. • *Lebanon* was the area north of Israel along the seacoast, including the high mountain ridge on the country's eastern side. It was famous for its stately *cedar* trees.

22:8-9 The ruin of Jerusalem would proclaim to other *nations* the consequences of Judah's violation of *their covenant with the LORD their God*.

22:10-30 This section contains a series of severe indictments against the descendants of Josiah.

22:10-12 The *dead king* was Josiah, who was killed by the Egyptians at

ring on my right hand, I would pull you off.
25 I will hand you over to those who seek to
kill you, those you so desperately fear—to
King Nebuchadnezzar of Babylon and the
mighty Babylonian army. 26 I will expel you
and your mother from this land, and you
will die in a foreign country, not in your native land. 27 You will never again return to
the land you yearn for.

28 "Why is this man Jehoiachin like a
discarded, broken jar?
Why are he and his children to be
exiled to a foreign land?
29 O earth, earth, earth!
Listen to this message from the LORD!
30 This is what the LORD says:
'Let the record show that this man
Jehoiachin was childless.
He is a failure,
for none of his children will succeed
him on the throne of David
to rule over Judah.'

The Righteous Descendant

23 "What sorrow awaits the leaders
of my people—the shepherds of my
sheep—for they have destroyed and scattered the very ones they were expected to
care for," says the LORD.
2 Therefore, this is what the LORD, the
God of Israel, says to these shepherds: "Instead of caring for my flock and leading
them to safety, you have deserted them and
driven them to destruction. Now I will pour
out judgment on you for the evil you have
done to them. 3 But I will gather together
the remnant of my flock from the countries
where I have driven them. I will bring them
back to their own sheepfold, and they will
be fruitful and increase in number. 4 Then
I will appoint responsible shepherds who
will care for them, and they will never be
afraid again. Not a single one will be lost or
missing. I, the LORD, have spoken!

5 "For the time is coming,"
says the LORD,
"when I will raise up a righteous [h]descendant
from King David's line.
He will be a King who rules with wisdom.
He will do what is just and right
throughout the land.
6 And this will be his name:
'The LORD Is Our Righteousness.'
In that day Judah will be saved,
and Israel will live in safety.

7 "In that day," says the LORD, "when people are taking an oath, they will no longer
say, 'As surely as the LORD lives, who rescued the people of Israel from the land of
Egypt.' 8 Instead, they will say, 'As surely as
the LORD lives, who brought the people of
Israel back to their own land from the land
of the north and from all the countries to
which he had exiled them.' Then they will
live in their own land."

Messages for Judah (23:9–26:24)
Judgment on False Prophets

9 My heart is broken because of the false
prophets,
and my bones tremble.

22:25 2 Kgs 24:15-16; Jer 34:20
22:28 Hos 8:8
22:29 Jer 6:19; Mic 1:2
22:30 Matt 1:12
23:1 Isa 56:9-12; Jer 10:21; 50:6; Ezek 13:3; 34:1-2; Zech 11:17
23:2 Exod 32:34; Jer 44:22
23:3 Isa 11:11-16; Jer 31:7-8; 32:37
23:4 Jer 3:15; 31:10; John 6:39; 10:14-15, 28; 1 Pet 1:5
23:5 Isa 9:6-7; 11:1-5; 53:2; Jer 33:15-16; Zech 3:8; 6:12-13
[h]*tsemakh* (6780) ‣Jer 33:15
23:6 Matt 1:21-23; Rom 3:21-22; 1 Cor 1:30
23:7-8 Isa 43:18-19; Jer 16:14-15
23:9 Hab 3:16

22:28), the ***son of Jehoiakim,*** came to the throne at the age of eighteen in 597 BC. The Babylonians attacked Jerusalem because of his father's rebellion against ***Nebuchadnezzar.*** After only three months on the throne, Jehoiachin had sense enough to surrender, and he was taken captive to ***Babylon*** (2 Kgs 24:8-14), along with most of the royal family.

22:25-27 Young king Jehoiachin was ***desperately*** afraid that the Babylonians would kill him, but instead they took him into exile.

22:25 ***Nebuchadnezzar:*** Hebrew *Nebuchadrezzar,* a variant spelling of Nebuchadnezzar. • ***Babylonian:*** Or *Chaldean.*

22:28-30 This poem, a taunt directed at Jehoiachin, included two rhetorical questions with the expected answer, "I don't know." However, Jehoiachin's sins and those of his forefathers were the reasons for his fate. Still, the people of Jerusalem seemed unwilling to accept the justice of his exile.

22:29 ***O earth:*** Faithful nature is called as a witness in God's case against his faithless people (see also 6:19; Deut 30:19; Isa 1:2).

22:30 Although ***Jehoiachin*** had seven sons (see 1 Chr 3:17), he was called ***childless*** because none of them ever sat on the ***throne*** of ***Judah.*** His uncle Zedekiah later reigned as king of Judah, but many Israelites regarded Jehoiachin as the last legitimate king of David's dynasty (see note on Ezek 1:2).

23:1-8 The Lord rebuked the three kings (ch 22) and contrasted them with the righteous leader he would place over his people after the Exile.

23:1 Kings in the ancient Near East were often referred to as ***shepherds.*** Good shepherds would protect and ***care for*** their people, but Judah's kings ***scattered*** their people instead.

23:3 As a good shepherd, the Lord would gather the exiles and place them in ***their own sheepfold,*** the land of Judah. There, they would be ***fruitful and increase in number*** (cp. Gen 1:28; 17:6-8).

23:4 Once the people were back in Judah (23:3), the Lord would ***appoint responsible shepherds.*** As good leaders, they would ***care for*** the people.

23:5 ***A righteous descendant*** (literally *a righteous branch*) of ***King David's line,*** whose ruling power had temporarily come to an end, would ***be a King.*** In stark contrast to the three kings the Lord had just rebuked (ch 22), this King would have ***wisdom*** and act in a way that ***is just and right*** (33:15; Isa 11:1-5; 53:2; Zech 3:8; Luke 1:32-33).

23:6 This ruler would have the name ***The LORD Is Our Righteousness*** (Hebrew *Yahweh Tsidqenu*), an interesting reversal of Zedekiah's Hebrew name (*Tsidqiyyahu*), which means "Righteous is the LORD." Zedekiah's character and the chaos of his reign were the opposite of the future King's character and the salvation and ***safety*** that his reign would offer.

23:7-8 Cp. 16:14.

23:9-32 These short poems and interjections appear to be excerpts from

22:11-12
2 Kgs 23:30-34
22:13
Jer 17:11
Hab 2:9
Jas 5:4
22:14
Isa 5:8-9
Hab 1:4
22:15
2 Kgs 23:25
Jer 21:12; 42:6
22:16
Ps 72:1-4, 12-13
Jer 9:24
22:17
Jer 6:13; 8:10
Luke 12:15-20
22:18
1 Kgs 13:30
22:19
Jer 36:30
22:20
Deut 32:49
22:21
Jer 3:24-25; 13:10; 19:15; 32:30
22:22
Jer 30:14
22:23
Jer 4:31
22:24
Hag 2:23

11 For this is what the LORD says about Jehoahaz, who succeeded his father, King Josiah,
and was taken away as a captive: "He will
never return. 12 He will die in a distant land
and will never again see his own country."

A Message about Jehoiakim

13 And the LORD says, "What sorrow awaits
Jehoiakim,
who builds his palace with forced
labor.
He builds injustice into its walls,
for he makes his neighbors work for
nothing.
He does not pay them for their labor.
14 He says, 'I will build a magnificent palace
with huge rooms and many windows.
I will panel it throughout with fragrant
cedar
and paint it a lovely red.'
15 But a beautiful cedar palace does not
make a great king!
Your father, Josiah, also had plenty to
eat and drink.
But he was just and right in all his
dealings.
That is why God blessed him.
16 He gave justice and help to the poor and
needy,
and everything went well for him.
Isn't that what it means to know me?"
says the LORD.
17 "But you! You have eyes only for greed
and dishonesty!
You murder the innocent,
oppress the poor, and reign ruthlessly."

18 Therefore, this is what the LORD says
about Jehoiakim, son of King Josiah:

"The people will not mourn for him,
crying to one another,
'Alas, my brother! Alas, my sister!'
His subjects will not mourn for him,
crying,
'Alas, our master is dead! Alas, his
splendor is gone!'
19 He will be buried like a dead donkey—
dragged out of Jerusalem and
dumped outside the gates!
20 Weep for your allies in Lebanon.
Shout for them in Bashan.
Search for them in the regions east of
the river.
See, they are all destroyed.
Not one is left to help you.
21 I warned you when you were prosperous,
but you replied, 'Don't bother me.'
You have been that way since childhood—
you simply will not obey me!
22 And now the wind will blow away your
allies.
All your friends will be taken away as
captives.
Surely then you will see your
wickedness and be ashamed.
23 It may be nice to live in a beautiful
palace
paneled with wood from the cedars of
Lebanon,
but soon you will groan with pangs of
anguish—
anguish like that of a woman in labor.

A Message for Jehoiachin

24 "As surely as I live," says the LORD, "I will
abandon you, Jehoiachin son of Jehoiakim,
king of Judah. Even if you were the signet

the Battle of Megiddo in 609 BC. The people of Judah were not to ***weep*** or ***mourn*** his death. Their sorrow should center on Josiah's son, whom they had chosen as the new king. After three months, King ***Jehoahaz*** (Hebrew *Shallum*, another name for Jehoahaz) was taken into exile in Egypt, where he spent the rest of his life (2 Kgs 23:1-33; 2 Chr 36:1-8).

22:13-23 Egypt placed another of Josiah's sons, Eliakim, on the throne in Jerusalem. His name was changed to ***Jehoiakim***. Most of the material in chs 7–20 was probably written during Jehoiakim's reign (609–598 BC). The Lord indicted him because of his faithlessness and greed, brought him to trial, declared him guilty, and pronounced the death penalty against him.

22:13 Because ***Jehoiakim*** forced poor men to work as slaves with no pay, his building projects had ***injustice*** built into their ***walls***. • ***with forced labor:*** Literally *by unrighteousness*.

22:14 ***a magnificent palace:*** Archaeologists have unearthed the foundations of what is believed to be this palace three miles south of Jerusalem. The foundations indicate that the building had ***huge rooms***.

22:15-16 If Jehoiakim wanted ***plenty to eat and drink***, he did not have to resort to corruption and oppression. Compared with his prosperous ***father, Josiah***, Jehoiakim was not ***a great king***. Josiah, by contrast, had been ***just and right in all his dealings***, a servant of God and his people. Because he had lived up to the requirements of the ancient covenant, ***God blessed him***.

22:17 Unlike his father, Josiah, Jehoiakim practiced ***greed and dishonesty*** and ignored the requirements of the covenant.

22:18-23 God delivered his verdict against Jehoiakim's terrible sins. Neither his family nor ***his subjects*** would ***mourn for him***.

22:19 Jehoiakim died in disgrace (see note on 2 Kgs 24:6).

22:20 Jehoiakim might have believed that the nation's close neighbors, including ***Lebanon*** and ***Bashan***, would support him in a time of crisis. They could not, because the Babylonians had already ***destroyed*** them. • ***Bashan*** was ***in the regions east of the*** Jordan ***river*** (or *in Abarim*).

22:22 The days of prosperity were gone, and chaos enveloped Judah. Like a ***wind*** sweeping through the land, the Babylonians would defeat Judah's allies and take many ***captives***. • ***Surely then you will see:*** Royal self-delusions would be swept aside and the consequences of ***wickedness*** would cause the king to be ***ashamed***.

22:24-30 ***Jehoiachin*** (Hebrew *Coniah*, a variant spelling of Jehoiachin; also in

23:10 Ps 107:34
Jer 5:7-8; 9:10; 12:4
Hos 4:2-3
23:11 Jer 6:13; 7:9-10; 8:10
23:12 Ps 35:6
Isa 8:22
Jer 13:16
John 12:35
23:13 1 Kgs 18:18-21
Jer 2:8
23:14 Isa 1:9-10
Jer 5:30-31; 29:23
Ezek 13:22-23
Matt 11:24
23:15 Deut 29:18
Jer 8:14; 9:15
23:16 Jer 14:14
Ezek 13:2-3, 6
Matt 7:15
2 Cor 11:13-15
Gal 1:8-9
1 Jn 4:1
23:17 Jer 5:12; 8:11
Amos 9:10
Mic 2:11; 3:11
23:18 Job 15:8; 33:13-14
23:19 //Jer 30:23
Amos 1:14
23:20 Isa 55:11
Jer 30:24
Zech 1:5-6

I stagger like a drunkard,
like someone overcome by wine,
because of the holy words
the LORD has spoken against them.
10 For the land is full of adultery,
and it lies under a curse.
The land itself is in mourning—
its wilderness pastures are dried up.
For they all do evil
and abuse what power they have.

11 "Even the priests and prophets
are ungodly, wicked men.
I have seen their despicable acts
right here in my own Temple,"
says the LORD.
12 "Therefore, the paths they take
will become slippery.
They will be chased through the dark,
and there they will fall.
For I will bring disaster upon them
at the time fixed for their punishment.
I, the LORD, have spoken!

13 "I saw that the prophets of Samaria were
terribly evil,
for they prophesied in the name of
Baal
and led my people of Israel into sin.
14 But now I see that the prophets of
Jerusalem are even worse!
They commit adultery and love
dishonesty.
They encourage those who are doing evil
so that no one turns away from their
sins.
These prophets are as wicked
as the people of Sodom and
Gomorrah once were."

15 Therefore, this is what the LORD of Heaven's Armies says concerning the prophets:

"I will feed them with bitterness
and give them poison to drink.
For it is because of Jerusalem's prophets
that wickedness has filled this land."

16 This is what the LORD of Heaven's Armies says to his people:

"Do not listen to these prophets when
they prophesy to you,
filling you with futile hopes.
They are making up everything they say.
They do not speak for the LORD!
17 They keep saying to those who despise
my word,
'Don't worry! The LORD says you will
have peace!'
And to those who stubbornly follow their
own desires,
they say, 'No harm will come your
way!'

18 "Have any of these prophets been in the
LORD's presence
to hear what he is really saying?
Has even one of them cared enough
to listen?
19 Look! The LORD's anger bursts out like a
storm,
a whirlwind that swirls down on the
heads of the wicked.
20 The anger of the LORD will not diminish
until it has finished all he has planned.
In the days to come
you will understand all this very
clearly.

a session in which the Lord prepared Jeremiah to prosecute the false prophets of Jerusalem. Because these leaders had misused the Lord's name, they incurred his wrath (Exod 20:7).

23:9-10 Jeremiah stood in the Lord's presence, shocked by the severity of the Lord's decrees of doom on the religious leaders.

23:10 People everywhere engaged in ***adultery***. They thought that the ritual sex of Baal worship would guarantee good crops, but instead it brought the ***curse*** of a crop-destroying drought upon the people of Judah.

23:11 Judah's religious leaders had committed ***despicable acts***, not just in their private lives and in the hills and fields where pagan worship occurred, but even in the ***Temple***, in the presence of the Lord.

23:12 As a result of their wickedness, these priests and prophets would have no stability in their lives; every moment would be filled with danger.

23:13-14 ***Samaria***, the capital of the northern kingdom of ***Israel***, had been dominated by ***Baal*** worship supported by the government ***prophets*** (1 Kgs 18:19; see also Jer 16:12). The religious leaders of Judah were ***even worse***.
• ***Sodom and Gomorrah*** represented the worst of this kind of wickedness (Gen 18:20).

23:15 Although the people needed to be held responsible for their own sins, ***the prophets*** bore the blame for Jerusalem's spiritual apostasy.

23:16-32 The Lord appealed to the ***people*** to reject ***these prophets*** and listen instead to his ***word***.

23:16 The false prophets gave the people ***futile hopes;*** they had not been commissioned to ***speak for the LORD***, and their ideas came from their own imaginations.

23:17 These prophets lied to the people, assuring them that ***peace*** would soon come to those ***who*** would ***despise*** the Lord's ***word***. However, the Lord had already decreed destruction.

23:18-19 These prophets invented their messages (23:16); they had never ***been in the LORD's presence***, and none of them ***cared enough to listen*** to God's instruction.

23:19-20 Contrary to the lies of the false prophets, the world was facing the ***storm*** of ***the LORD's anger***. The political situation was ***a whirlwind*** that would soon strike ***the wicked***. The Lord had planned this punishment and would ensure that it took place. After the war, the survivors would look back and see that Jeremiah had prophesied correctly.

21 "I have not sent these prophets,
yet they run around claiming to speak
for me.
I have given them no message,
yet they go on prophesying.
22 If they had stood before me and listened
to me,
they would have spoken my words,
and they would have turned my people
from their evil ways and deeds.
23 Am I a God who is only close at hand?"
says the LORD.
"No, I am far away at the same time.
24 Can anyone hide from me in a secret
place?
Am I not everywhere in all the
[i]heavens and earth?"
says the LORD.

25"I have heard these prophets say, 'Listen
to the dream I had from God last night.' And
then they proceed to tell lies in my name.
26How long will this go on? If they are prophets, they are prophets of deceit, inventing
everything they say. 27By telling these false
dreams, they are trying to get my people to
forget me, just as their ancestors did by worshiping the idols of Baal.

28 "Let these false prophets tell their
dreams,
but let my true messengers faithfully
proclaim my every word.
There is a difference between straw
and grain!
29 Does not my word burn like fire?"
says the LORD.
"Is it not like a mighty hammer
that smashes a rock to pieces?

30"Therefore," says the LORD, "I am against
these prophets who steal messages from
each other and claim they are from me. 31I
am against these smooth-tongued prophets
who say, 'This prophecy is from the LORD!'
32I am against these false prophets. Their
imaginary dreams are flagrant lies that lead
my people into sin. I did not send or appoint
them, and they have no message at all for my
people. I, the LORD, have spoken!

False Prophecies and False Prophets

33"Suppose one of the people or one of the
prophets or priests asks you, 'What prophecy has the LORD burdened you with now?'
You must reply, 'You are the burden! The
LORD says he will abandon you!'
34"If any prophet, priest, or anyone else
says, 'I have a prophecy from the LORD,'
I will punish that person along with his
entire family. 35You should keep asking
each other, 'What is the LORD's answer?' or
'What is the LORD saying?' 36But stop using
this phrase, 'prophecy from the LORD.' For
people are using it to give authority to their
own ideas, turning upside down the words
of our God, the living God, the LORD of Heav-
en's Armies.
37"This is what you should say to the
prophets: 'What is the LORD's answer?' or
'What is the LORD saying?' 38But suppose
they respond, 'This is a prophecy from the
LORD!' Then you should say, 'This is what
the LORD says: Because you have used this

23:21
Jer 14:14
23:22
Jer 35:15
Zech 1:4
1 Thes 1:9-10
23:23
Ps 139:1-10
23:24
Job 22:13-14
Ps 139:7-12
Isa 29:15-16
[i]*shamayim* (8064)
‣ Mal 3:10
23:25
Jer 8:6; 29:8
23:26
1 Tim 4:1-2
23:27
Deut 13:1-3
Judg 3:7; 8:33-34
23:28
1 Cor 3:12-13
23:29
Jer 5:14; 20:9
2 Cor 10:4-5
23:30
Ezek 13:8
23:32
Lam 2:14
23:33
Isa 13:1
Jer 12:7
Nah 1:1
Hab 1:1
Zech 9:1
23:34
Lam 2:14
Zech 13:3
23:35
Jer 33:3; 42:4
23:36
Jer 10:10
2 Pet 3:16
23:39
Jer 7:14-15
Ezek 8:18

23:21-24 In this stanza, the Lord expressed his keen disappointment and disgust toward the false *prophets.*

23:22 The messages of the false prophets would have been quite different if they had actually come from the Lord. God wanted the people to reject *their evil ways* (such as Baal worship) and turn to the one true God.

23:23-24 The Lord revealed the difference between himself and the Canaanite nature deities. The pagan deities were *close at hand,* as part of nature. The Lord was close at hand because he created all nature, but he was also *far away* in his distinction from it. His essence is different from nature, yet he is present *in all the heavens and earth.*

23:25-27 The false prophets placed a high value on *dreams.* The claim to have had a *dream* supposedly gave authority to the prophet's message. However, *these prophets* were *inventing everything they* said in order to lead the people away from the Lord.

23:28 The Lord temporarily allowed the ***false prophets*** to ***tell their dreams.*** At the same time, the Lord had his ***true messengers,*** such as Jeremiah, to ***proclaim*** his ***every word.*** This allowed the people to see the difference between the useless dreams of the false prophets (***straw***) and the nourishing words of the Lord's messengers (***grain***); cp. Ps 1:3-4.

23:29 The Lord's ***word*** has power, ***like fire,*** to destroy false prophecies. It would smash the seemingly impregnable fortress of Jerusalem ***like a mighty hammer.***

23:30-32 The Lord rebuked and opposed the ***prophets*** who spoke lies in his name.

23:33-40 The Lord presented a hypothetical conversation to show Jeremiah how to handle the false prophets.

23:33 These false ***prophets*** might taunt Jeremiah by asking for the latest message the Lord had ***burdened*** him with. • ***You are the burden!*** As in Greek version and Latin Vulgate; Hebrew reads ***What burden?*** This is a wordplay—it was common for a prophetic message to be called "a burden." The false prophets were a heavy load that the Lord would throw off and ***abandon.***

23:34-35 Someone might falsely brag that he had heard ***a prophecy from the LORD.*** However, such a ***person*** and his ***entire family*** would be punished (cp. Num 16:27-32; Josh 7:24-25).

23:36 The Lord warned that no one should claim to have a ***prophecy from the LORD*** in order to exert ***authority*** over other people. Doing so would be contrary to God's ***words*** and constitute a misuse of his name (Exod 20:7; see also Matt 20:25-28).

23:37-40 ***What is the LORD saying?*** The Lord had decreed that he would punish the people of Judah and ***expel*** false prophets. Any prophecy that stated otherwise was not ***a prophecy from the LORD.***

23:40
Jer 20:11
Ezek 5:14-15

24:1
2 Kgs 24:10-16
2 Chr 36:10
Jer 27:19-21; 29:1-2

24:2
Jer 29:17

24:3
Jer 1:11, 13

24:5
Zech 13:9

24:6
Jer 29:10; 31:4; 32:37, 41; 33:7
Ezek 11:17

phrase, "prophecy from the LORD," even
though I warned you not to use it, 39I will
forget you completely. I will expel you from
my presence, along with this city that I gave
to you and your ancestors. 40And I will make
you an object of ridicule, and your name will
be infamous throughout the ages.' "

Good and Bad Figs

24 After King Nebuchadnezzar of
Babylon exiled Jehoiachin son of
Jehoiakim, king of Judah, to Babylon along
with the officials of Judah and all the craftsmen and artisans, the LORD gave me this
vision. I saw two baskets of figs placed in
front of the LORD's Temple in Jerusalem.
2One basket was filled with fresh, ripe figs,
while the other was filled with bad figs that
were too rotten to eat.
3Then the LORD said to me, "What do you
see, Jeremiah?"
I replied, "Figs, some very good and some
very bad, too rotten to eat."
4Then the LORD gave me this message:
5"This is what the LORD, the God of Israel,
says: The good figs represent the exiles I
sent from Judah to the land of the Babylonians. 6I will watch over and care for them,

Cultural Collapse (24:1-10)

Jer 7:4-15; 19:1-7; 28:10-17
Josh 1:1-9; 11:16-23
1 Sam 4:1-22
2 Kgs 17:6-18; 23:1–25:30
Dan 7:1–8:27

Suddenly and completely, impressive cultures full of creative and skilled people fall apart. While digging, archaeologists often find a layer of ash between strata of remarkable artifacts; the ash indicates the destruction of the culture. This is one of the most disturbing aspects of human history.

Israel's history is replete with cycles of courage and success followed by disaster. Men of God led Israel into new periods of power (Joshua, Samuel, David, Solomon), but the nation repeatedly fell into worshiping many deities instead of the one true God. Repeatedly, God's people fell under judgment as their culture disintegrated and their political independence was replaced with servitude and oppression.

The northern kingdom of Israel was especially captivated by the idol-worship of Baal and Asherah. As a result, the Lord turned the northern kingdom over to the Assyrians, who demolished it in 722 BC.

In Jeremiah's time, the same spiritual and political collapse was occurring in the southern kingdom of Judah. Some of the nation's kings, including Josiah, faithfully followed the covenant ban on idol worship and led the people of Judah back to the Lord. However, Josiah's sons did not carry on the reforms begun by their father. Jehoiakim had no interest in continuing his father's revival of devotion to the Lord, seeing that as an impediment to his own political power. He was so hardened toward the Lord that he did his best to kill Jeremiah, the Lord's messenger. Zedekiah was more fearful than hardened, but he also refused to return to the Lord.

The Lord's messages through Jeremiah contain strong indictments of Judah's devotion to Baal (2:8; 7:9; 11:13, 17; 12:16; 19:5; 23:13, 27; 32:29, 35) and condemn the immorality that accompanied this sin. Judah's moral and spiritual rottenness—exemplified by its greed, hate, and violence—were exposed for all to see.

Despite their stubborn refusal to turn away from idol worship and back to worship of the one true God, the people of Judah hoped that the Lord would work a miracle by defeating the Babylonian army and sending it back home. They thought that the Temple would magically protect them, not understanding that God's disgust over what they were doing there would speed their destruction (7:4-15). They were totally unprepared to face the horror of defeat in war and the destruction of their nation, their capital, and their Temple. They were unaware that their spiritual and moral collapse had already made their doom certain.

23:39 ***I will forget you completely:*** Some Hebrew manuscripts and Greek version read *I will surely lift you up.*

23:40 The false prophets would be ***an object of ridicule.*** Their predictions would be proved false when Jerusalem was destroyed and the people of the city were taken into exile.

24:1-10 This section is a discussion of the meaning of the exile of 597 BC. Some were saying that it had been God's way of getting the rotten figs out of the barrel (Jerusalem) so that the good figs would survive. Jeremiah said that the exact opposite was the case. The good figs had been taken out of the barrel (into exile) so that the rotten figs would not destroy them.

24:1 Babylon's ***King Nebuchadnezzar*** (Hebrew *Nebuchadrezzar,* a variant spelling of Nebuchadnezzar) had taken ***Jehoiachin*** (Hebrew *Jeconiah,* a variant spelling of Jehoiachin) into captivity to ***Babylon*** in 597 BC. Jehoiachin's surrender had spared Jerusalem, but its treasures and 10,000 of its elite citizens had gone into exile (2 Kgs 24:8-16). • Typically, ***baskets of figs*** would be displayed in a market rather than in the Temple area.

24:4-7 The people exiled from Jerusalem had a better future than those who remained in the land, because the Lord would ***plant*** the exiles as a new community of reformed people (see 1:10).

24:5 ***Babylonians:*** Or *Chaldeans.*

and I will bring them back here again. I will
build them up and not tear them down.
I will plant them and not uproot them.
7I will give them hearts that recognize me
as the LORD. They will be my people, and
I will be their God, for they will return to
me wholeheartedly.
8"But the bad figs," the LORD said, "represent King Zedekiah of Judah, his officials,
all the people left in Jerusalem, and those
who live in Egypt. I will treat them like bad
figs, too rotten to eat. 9I will make them
an object of horror and a symbol of evil
to every nation on earth. They will be disgraced and mocked, taunted and cursed,
wherever I scatter them. 10And I will send
war, famine, and disease until they have vanished from the land of Israel, which I gave
to them and their ancestors."

Seventy Years of Captivity

25 This message for all the people of
Judah came to Jeremiah from the
LORD during the fourth year of Jehoiakim's
reign over Judah. This was the year when
King Nebuchadnezzar of Babylon began
his reign.
2Jeremiah the prophet said to all the people in Judah and Jerusalem, 3"For the past
twenty-three years—from the thirteenth
year of the reign of Josiah son of Amon,
king of Judah, until now—the LORD has
been giving me his messages. I have faithfully passed them on to you, but you have
not listened.
4"Again and again the LORD has sent you
his servants, the prophets, but you have
not listened or even paid attention. 5Each
time the message was this: 'Turn from the
evil road you are traveling and from the
evil things you are doing. Only then will I
let you live in this land that the LORD gave
to you and your ancestors forever. 6Do not
provoke my anger by worshiping idols you
made with your own hands. Then I will not
harm you.'
7"But you would not listen to me," says
the LORD. "You made me furious by worshiping idols you made with your own
hands, bringing on yourselves all the disasters you now suffer. 8And now the LORD of
Heaven's Armies says: Because you have
not listened to me, 9I will gather together
all the armies of the north under King
Nebuchadnezzar of Babylon, whom I have
appointed as my deputy. I will bring them
all against this land and its people and
against the surrounding nations. I will completely destroy you and make you an object
of horror and contempt and a ruin forever.
10I will take away your happy singing and
laughter. The joyful voices of bridegrooms
and brides will no longer be heard. Your
millstones will fall silent, and the lights in
your homes will go out. 11This entire land
will become a desolate wasteland. Israel
and her neighboring lands will serve the
king of Babylon for seventy years.
12"Then, after the seventy years of captivity are over, I will punish the king of Babylon

24:7 Jer 29:13; 31:33; 32:40; Zech 8:8; Heb 8:10
24:8 Jer 29:17; 39:5; 44:26-30; Ezek 12:13
24:9 1 Kgs 9:7; Ps 44:13-14; Isa 65:15; Jer 15:4; 29:18; 34:17
24:10 Isa 51:19; Jer 21:9; 27:8; Ezek 5:12-17
25:2 Jer 1:2; 7:25-26; 11:7-8; 26:5; 36:2-3
25:3 2 Kgs 24:1-2; Jer 36:1; 46:2
25:5 Gen 17:8-10; Isa 55:6-7; Jer 4:1; 7:7; 35:15
25:6 Deut 6:14; 8:19; 2 Kgs 17:35
25:7 2 Kgs 17:17; 21:15; Jer 7:19; 32:30-33
25:10 Eccl 12:3-4; Isa 24:8-11; Jer 16:9; Ezek 26:13
25:11 Dan 9:2; Zech 7:5
25:12 Ezra 1:1; Isa 13:14; Jer 29:10; 50:1–51:64

24:7 The Lord would do a marvelous work in the ***hearts*** of the exiles, helping them to ***recognize*** (literally *know*) ***the LORD*** as a personal God (1 Chr 28:9; Ps 9:10; 36:10; Isa 19:21; 52:6; Dan 11:32; Hos 2:20; Titus 1:16; 1 Jn 4:6-8). • ***They will be my people, and I will be their God:*** God's covenant with Israel would become a personal reality to them (Exod 6:7; 19:5; Deut 29:13; Rev 21:7). • ***wholeheartedly:*** The exiles would not mix religious loyalties; they would be completely committed to the one true God.

24:8-10 The ***bad figs*** were those ***left in Jerusalem***, and the Lord would ***scatter them*** because of their rottenness. Those included in this group ranged from the remainder of the royal family to the common people. In 586 BC, Zedekiah's reign ended exactly as predicted here.

25:1-14 The Lord had long been patient with Jerusalem's rebellion and refusal to listen, but now the time for judgment was at hand.

25:1 ***The fourth year of Jehoiakim's reign*** and the accession year of Nebuchadnezzar's reign was 605 BC. One of the first acts of Babylon's king ***Nebuchadnezzar*** (Hebrew *Nebuchadrezzar*, a variant spelling of Nebuchadnezzar; also in 25:9) was to force Judah's king Jehoiakim to confess loyalty to him.

25:3 ***The thirteenth year of the reign of Josiah*** was 627 BC; Jeremiah's ministry began that same year.

25:4 For many generations, God had sent ***prophets*** to the people, but they had not ***paid attention*** to the Lord's warnings.

25:5-6 The Lord appealed to his people to ***turn from . . . the evil things*** they were ***doing*** that provoked his ***anger***. Then he would ***not harm*** them, but instead pour out his covenant blessings.

25:7-9 The people had ***not listened*** to the Lord's decrees to turn from their evil ways; instead, they kept ***worshiping idols***. So the Lord would ***completely destroy*** them. The Hebrew term used here refers to the complete consecration of things or people to the Lord, either by destroying them or by giving them as an offering.

25:10 All forms of festivity, even simple pleasures such as ***singing and laughter***, would cease. • ***millstones . . . lights:*** After the destruction of Judah, no one would remain to do the work or to enjoy its fruits.

25:11 ***seventy years:*** This is the first instance of a specific time period assigned to the Exile. The prediction was fulfilled either from 605 BC (the first exile to Babylon) to around 538 BC (when Cyrus allowed the exiles to return to Judea), or from 586 BC (the destruction of the Temple) to 515 BC (the dedication of the Second Temple). Or, the number can be seen as symbolic: God's judgment on Jerusalem would last a perfect lifetime, and for the exact length of time that God had determined.

25:12-14 Although the Lord used them to carry out judgment on Judah, the ***Babylonians*** (or ***Chaldeans***) would be held accountable ***for their sins***, for their brutality, and for their abuse of those they defeated. In 539 BC, Babylon was conquered by Cyrus the Persian, and the people were taken into captivity.

25:13 Jer 36:4, 29, 32
25:14 Jer 27:7; 50:9
25:15 Jer 51:7
25:17 Jer 1:10
25:18 Isa 51:17
25:19 Jer 46:2-28
25:20 Job 1:1; Jer 47:1-7
25:21 Jer 48:1-47; 49:1-22; Amos 1:13-15; 2:1-3
25:22 Jer 47:4; Zech 9:2-4
25:23 Jer 49:7-8
25:25 Jer 49:34
25:26 Jer 50:9; 51:41
25:27 Ezek 21:4-5; Hab 2:17
25:29 Prov 11:31; 1 Pet 4:17
25:30 Joel 2:11; 3:13; Amos 1:2
25:31 Isa 66:16; Hos 4:1

and his people for their sins," says the LORD.
"I will make the country of the Babylonians
a wasteland forever. 13I will bring upon
them all the terrors I have promised in this
book—all the penalties announced by Jeremiah against the nations. 14Many nations
and great kings will enslave the Babylonians, just as they enslaved my people. I will
punish them in proportion to the suffering
they cause my people."

The Cup of the LORD's Anger

15This is what the LORD, the God of Israel,
said to me: "Take from my hand this cup
filled to the brim with my anger, and make
all the nations to whom I send you drink
from it. 16When they drink from it, they
will stagger, crazed by the warfare I will
send against them."

17So I took the cup of anger from the
LORD and made all the nations drink from
it—every nation to which the LORD sent me.
18I went to Jerusalem and the other towns
of Judah, and their kings and officials drank
from the cup. From that day until this, they
have been a desolate ruin, an object of horror, contempt, and cursing. 19I gave the cup
to Pharaoh, king of Egypt, his attendants,
his officials, and all his people, 20along
with all the foreigners living in that land.
I also gave it to all the kings of the land of
Uz and the kings of the Philistine cities of
Ashkelon, Gaza, Ekron, and what remains
of Ashdod. 21Then I gave the cup to the nations of Edom, Moab, and Ammon, 22and
the kings of Tyre and Sidon, and the kings of
the regions across the sea. 23I gave it to Dedan, Tema, and Buz, and to the people who
live in distant places. 24I gave it to the kings
of Arabia, the kings of the nomadic tribes of
the desert, 25and to the kings of Zimri, Elam,
and Media. 26And I gave it to the kings of
the northern countries, far and near, one after the other—all the kingdoms of the world.
And finally, the king of Babylon himself
drank from the cup of the LORD's anger.

27Then the LORD said to me, "Now tell
them, 'This is what the LORD of Heaven's
Armies, the God of Israel, says: Drink from
this cup of my anger. Get drunk and vomit;
fall to rise no more, for I am sending terrible wars against you.' 28And if they refuse to
accept the cup, tell them, 'The LORD of Heav-
en's Armies says: You have no choice but to
drink from it. 29I have begun to punish Jerusalem, the city that bears my name. Now
should I let you go unpunished? No, you
will not escape disaster. I will call for war
against all the nations of the earth. I, the
LORD of Heaven's Armies, have spoken!'

30"Now prophesy all these things, and say
to them,

" 'The LORD will roar against his own land
from his holy dwelling in heaven.
He will shout like those who tread grapes;
he will shout against everyone on earth.
31 His cry of judgment will reach the ends
of the earth,
for the LORD will bring his case
against all the nations.

For centuries, ***many nations and great kings*** reduced the Babylonians to slavery, and the territory did not become independent again until 1932, as modern Iraq.

25:15-38 The Lord is the sovereign king of ***all the nations***, and their rebellion was about to result in judgment. • ***to whom I send you:*** Jeremiah did not physically travel to each nation. The message he delivered from the Lord spread mostly through written material, much of it in the book of Jeremiah, which has been read throughout the world.

25:15 The messages of wrath that the Lord gave to Jeremiah were represented as a ***cup*** full of the wine of the Lord's ***anger*** (Rev 14:10). Jeremiah was to make the nations ***drink from it;*** God wanted them to hear the messages of condemnation and to experience the promised judgment.

25:16 Upon drinking from the cup (25:15), the nations would ***stagger*** as though drunken. They would be ***crazed by the warfare*** and would thus be unable to protect themselves. They would feel hopeless and helpless, and in their confusion, they would panic.

25:17 ***So I . . . made all the nations drink from it:*** Jeremiah accomplished this by announcing God's judgment.

25:18 Everyone ***drank from the cup***, meaning that the leaders heard the words of judgment. • ***From that day until this:*** Jeremiah probably delivered the Lord's messages at the time of the siege and fall of Jerusalem (588–586 BC).

25:19-20 The ***foreigners*** who heard the prophet's message included many refugees who fled from Judah and neighboring countries to ***Egypt*** when the Babylonians invaded. • ***Uz*** was a region on the northern border of Arabia; ***Ashkelon, Gaza, Ekron,*** and ***Ashdod*** were ***Philistine cities*** near the Mediterranean Sea.

25:21-22 The small nations of ***Edom, Moab, and Ammon*** were east and southeast of the Dead Sea. The Phoenician cities of ***Tyre and Sidon*** were to the northwest, along the Mediterranean Sea. The ***regions across the sea*** were probably the islands of Cyprus and Crete.

25:23-26 ***Dedan, Tema, . . . Buz,*** and ***Zimri*** were located in the desert area east of the Jordan Valley, north of ***Arabia. Elam*** and ***Media***, located in the highlands to the east of ***Babylon***, made up the core of the Persian empire, which conquered Babylon in 539 BC.

25:23 ***who live in distant places:*** Or ***who clip the corners of their hair.*** The Hebrew can be interpreted either way.

25:26 ***Babylon:*** Hebrew ***Sheshach***, a code name for Babylon.

25:27-29 These kingdoms had to ***drink from this cup of*** the Lord's ***anger*** (see note on 25:15). They would be unable to escape the disaster that would overwhelm them. ***Jerusalem*** experienced God's judgment, and so would the surrounding nations.

25:30-31 First, the Lord spoke through Jeremiah ***against his own land***, Judah; then Jeremiah delivered the messages of God's judgment ***against everyone on earth.***

He will judge all the people of the earth,
slaughtering the wicked with the sword.
I, the LORD, have spoken!' "

32 This is what the LORD of Heaven's Armies says:
"Look! Disaster will fall upon nation after nation!
A great whirlwind of fury is rising
from the most distant corners of the earth!"

33In that day those the LORD has slaughtered will fill the earth from one end to the other. No one will mourn for them or gather up their bodies to bury them. They will be scattered on the ground like manure.

34 Weep and moan, you evil shepherds!
Roll in the dust, you leaders of the flock!
The time of your slaughter has arrived;
you will fall and shatter like a fragile vase.
35 You will find no place to hide;
there will be no way to escape.
36 Listen to the frantic cries of the shepherds.
The leaders of the flock are wailing in despair,
for the LORD is ruining their pastures.
37 Peaceful meadows will be turned into a wasteland
by the LORD's fierce anger.
38 He has left his den like a strong lion seeking its prey,
and their land will be made desolate
by the sword of the enemy
and the LORD's fierce anger.

Jeremiah's Escape from Death

26 This message came to Jeremiah from
the LORD early in the reign of Jehoiakim son of Josiah, king of Judah. 2"This is
what the LORD says: Stand in the courtyard
in front of the Temple of the LORD, and make
an announcement to the people who have
come there to worship from all over Judah.
Give them my entire message; include every
word. 3Perhaps they will listen and turn
from their evil ways. Then I will change my
mind about the disaster I am ready to pour
out on them because of their sins.
4"Say to them, 'This is what the LORD
says: If you will not listen to me and obey
my word I have given you, 5and if you will
not listen to my servants, the prophets—for
I sent them again and again to warn you, but
you would not listen to them—6then I will
destroy this Temple as I destroyed Shiloh,
the place where the Tabernacle was located.
And I will make Jerusalem an object of cursing in every nation on earth.' "
7The priests, the prophets, and all the
people listened to Jeremiah as he spoke in
front of the LORD's Temple. 8But when Jeremiah had finished his message, saying
everything the LORD had told him to say,
the priests and prophets and all the people at the Temple mobbed him. "Kill him!"
they shouted. 9"What right do you have to
prophesy in the LORD's name that this Temple will be destroyed like Shiloh? What do
you mean, saying that Jerusalem will be destroyed and left with no inhabitants?" And
all the people threatened him as he stood in
front of the Temple.
10When the officials of Judah heard what

25:32 Isa 30:30; 34:2-3
25:33 Isa 5:25; Jer 16:4; Ezek 39:4, 7
25:34 Isa 34:7; Jer 50:27
25:35 Jer 11:11
25:37 Isa 27:11
25:38 Jer 4:7; 5:6; Hos 5:14; 13:7-8
26:2 Deut 4:2; Jer 7:2; 19:14; 42:4; Acts 20:20, 27
26:3 Isa 1:16-19; Jer 36:3-7
26:4 Lev 26:14; 1 Kgs 9:6; Isa 1:20; Jer 17:27; 22:5; 44:10, 23
26:5 Ezra 9:11; Jer 25:4
26:6 Ps 78:60-61; Jer 7:12, 14
26:7 Jer 5:31; Mic 3:11
26:8 Jer 11:19
26:10 Acts 21:31-32

25:32-33 ***Disaster . . . great whirlwind of fury:*** These words emphasize the awful nature of the wars that tore many nations apart during the 500s BC.

25:34-35 The earth's ***evil shepherds*** were vicious tyrants who ruled the nations. • ***Roll in the dust:*** A sign of distress.

25:36 ***ruining their pastures:*** The nations led by evil ***shepherds*** (25:34) would be destroyed because the Lord would enforce his sentence.

25:37-38 The Lord's judgment would be so terrifying that it would be ***like a strong lion seeking its prey.*** As the object of ***the LORD's fierce anger,*** the nations would be helpless.

25:38 Following this verse, the Greek translation of the OT (the Septuagint) attaches chs 46–51, which deal primarily with the nations listed in ch 25.

26:1-24 Jeremiah was put on trial in the presence of the priests and prophets. The sanctity of the Temple was an issue, for Jeremiah declared that the Lord would destroy the Temple as well as Jerusalem.

26:1 ***early in the reign of Jehoiakim:*** The first year of Jehoiakim's reign was 608 BC.

26:2 Jeremiah stood ***in the courtyard*** of ***the Temple*** because ***the people*** of ***Judah*** gathered there during the scheduled annual festivals.

26:3 The Lord gave the people a choice about what would happen to them in the future. If they would ***turn from their evil ways,*** the Lord would ***change*** his ***mind.*** The standard of judgment was his covenant with Israel (see Deut 5:1-21; 27:1–28:68). When Israel obeyed the terms of the covenant, the Lord blessed the people. When Israel persistently and stubbornly disobeyed, the Lord eventually punished them.

26:4-6 The people's ancestors had chosen the way of disobedience; as a result, their sanctuary at ***Shiloh,*** north of Jerusalem, had been ***destroyed*** (7:12-15; 1 Sam 1–4). Similarly, continued disobedience of the covenant commands by the people in Jeremiah's day would result in the destruction of the ***Temple*** and ***Jerusalem.***

26:7-9 The crowd ***at the Temple*** wanted to ***kill*** Jeremiah for blasphemy because he had spoken against the Temple. This charge carried the death penalty (Lev 24:16). The prophet's opponents argued that the Lord's holy Temple could not possibly be destroyed. The priests and prophets had accepted the pagan idea that temples were indestructible because deities dwelt within them.

26:10-15 Court trials were customarily held at a gateway to the city. City gateways at this time were covered and multi-chambered. In this location,

26:11
Jer 18:23; 38:4
Matt 26:66
Acts 6:11-14

26:13
Jer 7:3, 5; 18:11

26:15
Num 35:33
Prov 6:16-17
Matt 23:34-38

26:16
Jer 36:19, 25; 38:7, 13
Acts 5:34-39; 23:9, 29; 25:25; 26:31

26:18
Mic 1:1; 3:12

26:19
2 Chr 29:6-11; 32:26
Isa 37:1, 15-20

26:20
Josh 9:17
1 Sam 6:21

26:21
1 Kgs 19:2-4
2 Chr 16:10
Jer 36:26
Matt 10:23, 28

26:22
Jer 36:12

26:23
Jer 2:30

26:24
2 Kgs 22:12-14
Jer 1:18-19; 39:14; 40:5-6

27:2
Jer 28:10, 13; 30:8

27:3
Jer 25:21-22

27:5
Deut 9:29
Ps 115:15-16; 146:5-6
Jer 10:12; 32:17; 51:15
Acts 17:26

was happening, they rushed over from the palace and sat down at the New Gate of the Temple to hold court. 11The priests and prophets presented their accusations to the officials and the people. "This man should die!" they said. "You have heard with your own ears what a traitor he is, for he has prophesied against this city."

12Then Jeremiah spoke to the officials and the people in his own defense. "The LORD sent me to prophesy against this Temple and this city," he said. "The LORD gave me every word that I have spoken. 13But if you stop your sinning and begin to obey the LORD your God, he will change his mind about this disaster that he has announced against you. 14As for me, I am in your hands—do with me as you think best. 15But if you kill me, rest assured that you will be killing an innocent man! The responsibility for such a deed will lie on you, on this city, and on every person living in it. For it is absolutely true that the LORD sent me to speak every word you have heard."

16Then the officials and the people said to the priests and prophets, "This man does not deserve the death sentence, for he has spoken to us in the name of the LORD our God."

17Then some of the wise old men stood and spoke to all the people assembled there. 18They said, "Remember when Micah of Moresheth prophesied during the reign of King Hezekiah of Judah. He told the people of Judah,

'This is what the LORD of Heaven's
Armies says:
Mount Zion will be plowed like an open
field;
Jerusalem will be reduced to ruins!
A thicket will grow on the heights
where the Temple now stands.'

19But did King Hezekiah and the people kill him for saying this? No, they turned from their sins and worshiped the LORD. They begged him for mercy. Then the LORD changed his mind about the terrible disaster he had pronounced against them. So we are about to do ourselves great harm."

20At this time Uriah son of Shemaiah from Kiriath-jearim was also prophesying for the LORD. And he predicted the same terrible disaster against the city and nation as Jeremiah did. 21When King Jehoiakim and the army officers and officials heard what he was saying, the king sent someone to kill him. But Uriah heard about the plan and escaped in fear to Egypt. 22Then King Jehoiakim sent Elnathan son of Acbor to Egypt along with several other men to capture Uriah. 23They took him prisoner and brought him back to King Jehoiakim. The king then killed Uriah with a sword and had him buried in an unmarked grave.

24Nevertheless, Ahikam son of Shaphan stood up for Jeremiah and persuaded the court not to turn him over to the mob to be killed.

The Yoke of Babylon (27:1–28:17)
Jeremiah Wears an Ox Yoke

27 This message came to Jeremiah from the LORD early in the reign of Zedekiah son of Josiah, king of Judah.

2This is what the LORD said to me: "Make a yoke, and fasten it on your neck with leather straps. 3Then send messages to the kings of Edom, Moab, Ammon, Tyre, and Sidon through their ambassadors who have come to see King Zedekiah in Jerusalem. 4Give them this message for their masters: 'This is what the LORD of Heaven's Armies, the God of Israel, says: 5With my great strength and powerful arm I made the earth and all

---

where the commerce of the city went in and out, the elders of the city would congregate where they could be called upon to apply their wisdom to legal conflicts. In this case, the *officials* were fair; they gave each party an opportunity to present its side of the quarrel.

26:12-13 ***Jeremiah*** argued that ***the LORD*** had ***sent*** him to speak against the ***city*** and the ***Temple;*** he added that the impending disaster would not occur if the people of Jerusalem chose to ***obey the LORD.***

26:14-15 Jeremiah submitted calmly to authority and placed his life in the officials' ***hands;*** however, he warned them that they would bear the ***responsibility*** for their decision if they killed ***an innocent man.***

26:16 Jeremiah was successful in his defense; he convinced the ***officials and the people*** that he was innocent because he spoke for ***the LORD.***

26:17-19 Societies in the ancient Near East greatly revered ***wise old men.*** Few people survived to old age, and those who did had a valuable store of memory. • ***Micah of Moresheth*** had lived during ***the reign of King Hezekiah*** (728–686 BC), more than 100 years earlier. Micah had written a small collection of his prophecies, from which the elders quoted a verse (Mic 3:12) that predicted the destruction of ***Mount Zion*** and ***Jerusalem.*** These elders counseled the people to do as Hezekiah had done when he ***turned from*** his ***sins*** and ***worshiped the LORD.*** Although the people of Judah relinquished their plan to harm Jeremiah, they did not heed the second part of the old men's counsel.

26:24 ***Ahikam*** had served under King Josiah (2 Kgs 22:12-14).

27:1-22 The Lord ordered Jeremiah to send messages to the ambassadors from nearby countries to announce the Lord's judgment upon them. He was to illustrate his message by wearing a wooden yoke. This event took place in 594–593 BC (see 28:1).

27:1 ***Zedekiah:*** As in some Hebrew manuscripts and Syriac version (see also 27:3, 12); most Hebrew manuscripts read ***Jehoiakim.***

27:4-5 The entire weight of the divine name was behind this message (see

its people and every animal. I can give these things of mine to anyone I choose. [6]Now I will give your countries to King Nebuchadnezzar of Babylon, who is my servant. I have put everything, even the wild animals, under his control. [7]All the nations will serve him, his son, and his grandson until his time is up. Then many nations and great kings will conquer and rule over Babylon. [8]So you must submit to Babylon's king and serve him; put your neck under Babylon's yoke! I will punish any nation that refuses to be his slave, says the LORD. I will send war, famine, and disease upon that nation until Babylon has conquered it.

[9]" 'Do not listen to your false prophets, fortune-tellers, interpreters of dreams, mediums, and sorcerers who say, "The king of Babylon will not conquer you." [10]They are all liars, and their lies will lead to your being driven out of your land. I will drive you out and send you far away to die. [11]But the people of any nation that submits to the king of Babylon will be allowed to stay in their own country to farm the land as usual. I, the LORD, have spoken!' "

[12]Then I repeated this same message to King Zedekiah of Judah. "If you want to live, submit to the yoke of the king of Babylon and his people. [13]Why do you insist on dying—you and your people? Why should you choose war, famine, and disease, which the LORD will bring against every nation that refuses to submit to Babylon's king? [14]Do not listen to the false prophets who keep telling you, 'The king of Babylon will not conquer you.' They are liars. [15]This is what the LORD says: 'I have not sent these prophets! They are telling you lies in my name, so I will drive you from this land. You will all die—you and all these prophets, too.' "

[16]Then I spoke to the priests and the people and said, "This is what the LORD says: 'Do not listen to your prophets who claim that soon the gold articles taken from my Temple will be returned from Babylon. It is all a lie! [17]Do not listen to them. Surrender to the king of Babylon, and you will live. Why should this whole city be destroyed? [18]If they really are prophets and speak the LORD's messages, let them pray to the LORD of Heaven's Armies. Let them pray that the articles remaining in the LORD's Temple and in the king's palace and in the palaces of Jerusalem will not be carried away to Babylon!'

[19]"For the LORD of Heaven's Armies has spoken about the pillars in front of the Temple, the great bronze basin called the Sea, the water carts, and all the other ceremonial articles. [20]King Nebuchadnezzar of Babylon left them here when he exiled Jehoiachin son of Jehoiakim, king of Judah, to Babylon, along with all the other nobles of Judah and Jerusalem. [21]Yes, this is what the LORD of Heaven's Armies, the God of Israel, says about the precious things still in the Temple and in the palace of Judah's king: [22]'They will all be carried away to Babylon and will stay there until I send for them,' says the LORD. 'Then I will bring them back to Jerusalem again.' "

Jeremiah Condemns Hananiah

28 One day in late summer of that same year—the fourth year of the reign of Zedekiah, king of Judah—Hananiah son of Azzur, a prophet from Gibeon, addressed me publicly in the Temple while

27:6 Jer 21:7; 22:25; 28:14; 43:10; Ezek 29:18-20
27:7 Isa 14:4-6; Jer 25:12; 44:30
27:8 Jer 24:10; 29:17; 42:15-16; Ezek 14:21; 17:19-21
27:9 Exod 22:18; Deut 18:10; Isa 8:19; Mal 3:5
27:10 Jer 23:25
27:11 Jer 21:9; 38:2; 40:9-12; 42:10-11
27:13 Jer 38:23; Ezek 18:31
27:14 Ezek 13:22
27:15 2 Chr 25:16; Jer 23:21, 25; 29:9
27:16 2 Kgs 24:13; 2 Chr 36:7, 10; Dan 1:2
27:18 1 Sam 7:8; 12:19, 23; 1 Kgs 18:24
27:19 1 Kgs 7:15; 2 Kgs 25:13, 17; Jer 52:17-23
27:20 2 Kgs 24:14-16
27:22 Ezra 5:13-15; 7:9; Jer 29:10; 32:5; 34:2-3
28:1 Jer 27:12

note on 2:2). The Lord's authority over everything was a direct challenge to the false nature deities worshiped by each of the nations addressed.

27:6-8 God had given ***Nebuchadnezzar*** authority over the whole region, so resistance to him was futile. ***All the nations*** would ***serve him*** and his descendants. The fall of ***Babylon*** at the hand of Cyrus took place in 539 BC during the reign of Belshazzar, a ***grandson*** of Nebuchadnezzar.

27:8 ***Babylon's yoke:*** Cp. 21:8-10; 27:2-3.

27:9-10 Jeremiah warned against those who delivered messages contrary to those of the Lord. ***False prophets*** made predictions that supported idol worship; ***fortune-tellers*** claimed to have special abilities to predict future events by reading the stars, staring into crystal balls, and analyzing animal livers; ***interpreters of dreams*** predicted the future by analyzing people's dreams and explaining what would happen; ***mediums*** claimed to converse with dead people; ***sorcerers*** specialized in casting spells to hurt or bless people by saying certain words or phrases that would concentrate evil or blessing on someone. • ***The king of Babylon will not conquer you:*** This prediction was false; Nebuchadnezzar conquered the entire region beginning in 605 BC.

27:12-15 The terms of God's decree (27:4-11) applied to Judah as much as to the surrounding nations.

27:16 The ***gold articles*** and other treasures had been taken ***from*** the ***Temple*** in 597 BC.

27:18-19 Even the false ***prophets*** were called upon to repent and ***pray to the LORD.***

27:20-22 When Judah's king ***Jehoiachin*** (Hebrew *Jeconiah,* a variant spelling of *Jehoiachin*) was taken prisoner, ***King Nebuchadnezzar*** of ***Babylon*** left the large, valuable furniture in the ***Temple,*** all of which he ***carried away*** in 586 BC.

27:22 When Cyrus of Persia allowed the exiles to return in 538 BC, they also brought the Temple furnishings ***back to Jerusalem*** with them (Ezra 1:7-11; 5:13-15).

28:1-17 Soon after the events of ch 27, a false prophet named ***Hananiah*** publicly confronted Jeremiah in the Temple courtyard. Each prophet gave what he claimed was a message from the Lord, but only Jeremiah's prediction came true.

28:1 ***One day in late summer:*** Literally *In the fifth month* of the ancient Hebrew lunar calendar. The fifth month in the fourth year of Zedekiah's reign occurred within the months of August

28:3 2 Chr 36:10; Jer 27:16; Dan 1:2
28:4 2 Kgs 25:27; Jer 22:10; 27:8
28:6 Jer 11:5
28:7 1 Kgs 22:28
28:8 1 Kgs 14:15; 17:1; 22:17; Isa 5:5-7; Joel 1:20; Amos 1:2; Nah 1:2
28:9 Deut 18:22
28:10 Jer 27:2
28:11 Jer 14:14-15; 27:10
28:12 Jer 1:2
28:13 Ps 107:16
28:14 Deut 28:48; Jer 25:11; 27:6, 8
28:15 Jer 29:31; Lam 2:14; Ezek 13:2-3, 22; 22:28
28:16 Deut 6:15; 13:5; 1 Kgs 13:34; Jer 20:6; 29:32
29:2 2 Kgs 24:12; Jer 22:24-28; 24:1
29:4 Jer 24:5

all the priests and people listened. He said,
2"This is what the LORD of Heaven's Armies, the God of Israel, says: 'I will remove
the yoke of the king of Babylon from your
necks. 3Within two years I will bring back
all the Temple treasures that King Nebuchadnezzar carried off to Babylon. 4And I
will bring back Jehoiachin son of Jehoiakim,
king of Judah, and all the other captives that
were taken to Babylon. I will surely break
the yoke that the king of Babylon has put on
your necks. I, the LORD, have spoken!' "

5Jeremiah responded to Hananiah as they
stood in front of all the priests and people
at the Temple. 6He said, "Amen! May your
prophecies come true! I hope the LORD does
everything you say. I hope he does bring
back from Babylon the treasures of this
Temple and all the captives. 7But listen now
to the solemn words I speak to you in the
presence of all these people. 8The ancient
prophets who preceded you and me spoke
against many nations, always warning of
war, disaster, and disease. 9So a prophet
who predicts peace must show he is right.
Only when his predictions come true can
we know that he is really from the LORD."

10Then Hananiah the prophet took the
yoke off Jeremiah's neck and broke it in
pieces. 11And Hananiah said again to the
crowd that had gathered, "This is what the
LORD says: 'Just as this yoke has been broken, within two years I will break the yoke
of oppression from all the nations now subject to King Nebuchadnezzar of Babylon.' "
With that, Jeremiah left the Temple area.

12Soon after this confrontation with
Hananiah, the LORD gave this message to Jeremiah: 13"Go and tell Hananiah, 'This is what
the LORD says: You have broken a wooden
yoke, but you have replaced it with a yoke
of iron. 14The LORD of Heaven's Armies, the
God of Israel, says: I have put a yoke of iron
on the necks of all these nations, forcing
them into slavery under King Nebuchadnezzar of Babylon. I have put everything, even
the wild animals, under his control.' "

15Then Jeremiah the prophet said to Hananiah, "Listen, Hananiah! The LORD has not
sent you, but the people believe your lies.
16Therefore, this is what the LORD says: 'You
must die. Your life will end this very year because you have rebelled against the LORD.' "

17Two months later the prophet Hananiah died.

5. MESSAGES TO THE EXILES IN BABYLON (29:1-32)

A Letter to the Exiles

29 Jeremiah wrote a letter from Jerusalem to the elders, priests, prophets,
and all the people who had been exiled to
Babylon by King Nebuchadnezzar. 2This
was after King Jehoiachin, the queen mother,
the court officials, the other officials of Judah, and all the craftsmen and artisans had
been deported from Jerusalem. 3He sent
the letter with Elasah son of Shaphan and
Gemariah son of Hilkiah when they went to
Babylon as King Zedekiah's ambassadors to
Nebuchadnezzar. This is what Jeremiah's
letter said:

4This is what the LORD of Heaven's
Armies, the God of Israel, says to all
the captives he has exiled to Babylon
from Jerusalem: 5"Build homes, and
plan to stay. Plant gardens, and eat the

---

and September 593 BC. Also see note on 1:3.) • The ***people*** were ***in the Temple,*** so it was probably the occasion of one of the annual fall festivals, either the Day of Atonement (Lev 23:26-32) or the Festival of Shelters (Lev 23:33-36).

28:2-3 Hananiah's message was the approved propaganda, but he used strong terms (see notes on 2:2, 9) to claim the Lord's authority. • Judah had been under the ***yoke of the king of Babylon*** since 597 BC.

28:4 The false prophet's message claimed that ***Jehoiachin*** (Hebrew *Jeconiah,* a variant spelling of Jehoiachin) would return, which implied that Zedekiah held a lower status as ruler over the kingdom of Judah (see note on Ezek 1:2). • ***I, the LORD, have spoken:*** Hananiah closed with the same strong appeal to divine authority that Jeremiah often used.

28:5-6 *Amen!* (literally *So be it!*): Jeremiah would have been happy to see this prediction fulfilled.

28:7-9 Only when a prophet's ***predictions come true*** can people be certain that he has spoken the Lord's word (Deut 18:20-22).

28:10-11 The false prophet Hananiah ***broke*** the yoke that Jeremiah was wearing (27:2) as a sign of what the Lord would do. • ***Jeremiah left*** the confrontation without replying, probably because he had not yet received the Lord's response.

28:12-14 Jeremiah received and delivered the Lord's response to the false prophecy. The ***wooden yoke*** that ***Hananiah*** broke was replaced by a metaphorical ***yoke of iron.*** Subjection to ***Babylon*** was an absolute certainty, for the Lord had decreed it.

28:15-17 ***You must die:*** The Lord's decree for ***Hananiah*** was the lawful penalty for false prophets (Deut 13:1-5). The Lord carried out the decree that ***very year;*** Jeremiah's prophecy was validated when it was fulfilled ***two months later*** (literally *In the seventh month of that same year;* see 28:1 and the note there). In contrast, Hananiah's prediction that the Temple treasures would be returned in two years was not fulfilled. The Lord demonstrated that he was still in control.

29:1-23 Jeremiah contacted the Hebrew exiles in Babylon by letter. To reach all the scattered Israelites, his letter would be read repeatedly from settlement to settlement.

29:2 ***Jehoiachin:*** Hebrew *Jeconiah,* a variant spelling of Jehoiachin. • ***had been deported from Jerusalem:*** This refers to the exile of 597 BC.

food they produce. 6 Marry and have
children. Then find spouses for them so
that you may have many grandchildren.
Multiply! Do not dwindle away! 7 And
work for the peace and prosperity of
the city where I sent you into exile. Pray
to the LORD for it, for its welfare will
determine your welfare."
8 This is what the LORD of Heaven's
Armies, the God of Israel, says: "Do not let
your prophets and fortune-tellers who are
with you in the land of Babylon trick you.
Do not listen to their dreams, 9 because
they are telling you lies in my name. I
have not sent them," says the LORD.
10 This is what the LORD says: "You will
be in Babylon for seventy years. But then
I will come and do for you all the good
things I have promised, and I will bring
you home again. 11 For I know the plans
I have for you," says the LORD. "They are
plans for good and not for disaster, to give
you a future and a hope. 12 In those days
when you pray, I will listen. 13 If you look
for me wholeheartedly, you will find me.
14 I will be found by you," says the LORD. "I
will end your captivity and restore your
fortunes. I will gather you out of the
nations where I sent you and will bring
you home again to your own land."
15 You claim that the LORD has raised
up prophets for you in Babylon. 16 But
this is what the LORD says about the
king who sits on David's throne and all
those still living here in Jerusalem—your
relatives who were not exiled to Babylon.
17 This is what the LORD of Heaven's
Armies says: "I will send war, famine,
and disease upon them and make them
like bad figs, too rotten to eat. 18 Yes, I
will pursue them with war, famine, and
disease, and I will scatter them around
the world. In every nation where I
send them, I will make them an object
of damnation, horror, contempt, and
mockery. 19 For they refuse to listen
to me, though I have spoken to them
repeatedly through the prophets I
sent. And you who are in exile have not
listened either," says the LORD.
20 Therefore, listen to this message
from the LORD, all you captives there
in Babylon. 21 This is what the LORD
of Heaven's Armies, the God of Israel,
says about your prophets—Ahab son of
Kolaiah and Zedekiah son of Maaseiah—
who are telling you lies in my name: "I
will turn them over to Nebuchadnezzar
for execution before your eyes. 22 Their
terrible fate will become proverbial,
so that the Judean exiles will curse
someone by saying, 'May the LORD make
you like Zedekiah and Ahab, whom the
king of Babylon burned alive!' 23 For
these men have done terrible things
among my people. They have committed
adultery with their neighbors' wives and
have lied in my name, saying things I did
not command. I am a witness to this. I,
the LORD, have spoken."

A Message for Shemaiah

24 The LORD sent this message to Shemaiah
the Nehelamite in Babylon: 25 "This is what
the LORD of Heaven's Armies, the God of
Israel, says: You wrote a letter on your own
authority to Zephaniah son of Maaseiah,
the priest, and you sent copies to the other
priests and people in Jerusalem. You wrote
to Zephaniah,

29:6 Jer 16:1-4
29:7 Ezra 6:10; Dan 4:27; 1 Tim 2:1-2
29:8 Jer 14:14; 23:21, 25, 27
29:9 Jer 27:15; 29:31
29:10 2 Chr 36:21-23; Jer 24:6-7; Dan 9:2; Zeph 2:7; Zech 7:5
29:11 Ps 40:5; Isa 40:9-11; Jer 23:5-6; 30:9-10, 18-22
29:12 Ps 145:19; Jer 33:3
29:13 Deut 4:29; 1 Chr 22:19; 2 Chr 22:9; Jer 24:7
29:14 Deut 30:1-10; Isa 43:5-6; Jer 12:15; 16:14-15; 30:3
29:16 Jer 38:2-3
29:17 Jer 24:3
29:18 Isa 65:15; Jer 25:9; 42:18; Lam 2:15-16
29:19 Jer 6:19; 26:5
29:20 Jer 24:5; Ezek 11:9
29:21 Jer 14:14-15; Lam 2:14
29:22 Isa 65:15
29:23 2 Sam 13:12; Prov 5:21; Jer 5:8; 7:11
29:25 2 Kgs 25:18; Jer 21:1; 37:3

29:5-7 Jeremiah urged the exiled people to ***plan to stay*** in Babylon for a long time. God wanted them to become productive citizens, concerned and praying ***to the LORD*** for the ***welfare*** of the Babylonian communities in which they lived, so their population could grow. They should not listen to false prophecies such as Hananiah's, promising that they would be coming home shortly.

29:8-9 The next divine command warned against false ***prophets and fortune-tellers.***

29:10 The exiled people of Judah would ***be in Babylon for seventy years;*** this was not new information (see 25:11 and note), but Jeremiah's audiences in Jerusalem had not believed him. Now that those people were in exile, they needed to accept reality.

29:11 The Lord's ***plans for good,*** to prosper the exiled people and to return them to the land of Judah, gave them ***a future and a hope.*** This promise was specific to the exiles in Babylon, but it has given hope to millions of God's people in various difficult circumstances.

29:12-13 Through Jeremiah, the Lord reminded the exiled people that if they would ***look for*** him ***wholeheartedly,*** they would ***find*** him. The Exile taught the Israelites to reject false gods and give their wholehearted devotion to the Lord (Deut 6:4-6). It also gave them a new commitment to the revealed word of God.

29:15 False ***prophets*** could still be found among the exiles; they held out hope for the survival of Jerusalem and a quick end to the Exile.

29:16-18 To keep the exiles in ***Babylon*** from thinking that they were worse off than those left behind, the Lord reiterated his decree of disaster for the ***bad figs*** still in Jerusalem (see 24:6-10); their time of horror was yet to come.

29:20-22 Although Jeremiah was in Jerusalem, God was able to tell him what was happening in Babylon, just as he was able to tell Ezekiel in Babylon what was happening in Jerusalem (Ezek 8). • The Lord named two prophets who were ***telling . . . lies*** in his ***name,*** and sentenced them to death (Deut 18:20-22; cp. Jer 26:14-15; 28:16-17).

29:21 ***Nebuchadnezzar:*** Hebrew *Nebuchadrezzar,* a variant spelling of Nebuchadnezzar.

29:24-32 A prophet in Babylon named ***Shemaiah*** took issue with Jeremiah's written advice that the exiles should

29:26 Deut 13:1-5; Jer 20:1-2; Hos 9:7; Zech 13:1-5; John 10:20; Acts 16:24; 26:24-25; 2 Cor 5:13
29:27 Jer 1:1
29:31 Jer 14:14-15; 28:15; Ezek 13:8, 16, 22-23
29:32 Deut 13:5; 1 Sam 2:30-34; Jer 22:30; 28:16; 36:31
30:2 Jer 25:13; 36:4, 28, 32; Hab 2:2
30:3 Ps 53:6; Jer 3:18; 16:15; 23:7-8; 29:10; 30:18; Ezek 20:42; 36:24; Zeph 3:20
30:5 Isa 5:30; Jer 6:25; Amos 5:16-18
30:6 Jer 4:31; 6:24; 22:23
30:7 Isa 2:12; Jer 2:27; 50:19; Lam 1:12; Dan 9:12; Joel 2:11
30:8 Isa 9:4; Ezek 34:27
30:9 Ezek 34:23-24; 37:24; Hos 3:5; Luke 1:69; Acts 2:30; 13:23-24
30:10 Isa 35:9; 43:5; 44:2; Jer 23:3; 29:14; 46:27-28; Mic 4:4

26“The LORD has appointed you to
replace Jehoiada as the priest in charge
of the house of the LORD. You are
responsible to put into stocks and neck
irons any crazy man who claims to
be a prophet. 27So why have you done
nothing to stop Jeremiah from Anathoth,
who pretends to be a prophet among
you? 28Jeremiah sent a letter here to
Babylon, predicting that our captivity
will be a long one. He said, ‘Build homes,
and plan to stay. Plant gardens, and eat
the food they produce.’ ”

29But when Zephaniah the priest received
Shemaiah’s letter, he took it to Jeremiah and
read it to him. 30Then the LORD gave this
message to Jeremiah: 31“Send an open letter
to all the exiles in Babylon. Tell them, ‘This
is what the LORD says concerning Shemaiah
the Nehelamite: Since he has prophesied
to you when I did not send him and has
tricked you into believing his lies, 32I will
punish him and his family. None of his descendants will see the good things I will do
for my people, for he has incited you to rebel
against me. I, the LORD, have spoken!’ ”

6. MESSAGES OF HOPE (30:1–33:26)

Promises of Deliverance

30 The LORD gave another message to
Jeremiah. He said, 2“This is what the
LORD, the God of Israel, says: Write down
for the record everything I have said to you,
Jeremiah. 3For the time is coming when I
will restore the fortunes of my people of Israel and Judah. I will bring them home to
this land that I gave to their ancestors, and
they will possess it again. I, the LORD, have
spoken!”

4This is the message the LORD gave concerning Israel and Judah. 5This is what the
LORD says:

“I hear cries of fear;
there is terror and no peace.
6 Now let me ask you a question:
Do men give birth to babies?
Then why do they stand there,
ashen-faced,
hands pressed against their sides
like a woman in labor?
7 In all history there has never been such a
time of terror.
It will be a time of trouble for my
people Israel.
Yet in the end they will be saved!
8 For in that day,”
says the LORD of Heaven’s Armies,
“I will break the yoke from their necks
and snap their chains.
Foreigners will no longer be their masters.
9 For my people will serve the LORD
their God
and their king descended from David—
the king I will raise up for them.

10 “So do not be afraid, Jacob, my servant;
do not be dismayed, Israel,”
says the LORD.
“For I will bring you home again from
distant lands,
and your children will return from
their exile.
Israel will return to a life of peace and
quiet,
and no one will terrorize them.

---

accept a long exile (29:4-23). Shemaiah sent a letter to a leading priest in Jerusalem, urging him to take action against Jeremiah; Jeremiah responded with a letter to the exiles that condemned Shemaiah.

29:29 ***Zephaniah*** had enough good sense to show ***Jeremiah*** the letter from Shemaiah.

29:30-32 Since Shemaiah had no commission from the Lord, he was a liar; he tried to persuade the exiles to believe in a brief exile. With a threefold invocation of the Lord’s authority (see note on 2:2), Shemaiah was charged, convicted, and sentenced to execution.

30:1–33:26 These four chapters are often called “The Book of Consolation,” a high point in OT revelation. In contrast to the many messages of judgment that Jeremiah delivered to his people, these messages are filled with hope and point to a marvelous future restoration.

30:1-24 This series of messages is mainly positive, with only two verses carrying a tone of judgment (30:23-24). They speak of the beneficial effects of the destruction of Jerusalem and of the Exile.

30:3 The new messages expand on the theme of 29:10-14 (see 3:18; 16:15; 24:6). The fall of Jerusalem and the Exile did not mark the end of the Lord’s relationship with Israel. The Lord had a wonderful future for the remnant of his ***people.*** Descendants of people from the northern kingdom of ***Israel*** who were taken into exile by the Assyrians in 722 BC would be restored. Likewise, descendants of the people of ***Judah*** who were taken into Babylonian exile in 597 and 586 BC would return to the Promised Land. • ***I will bring them home:*** The first major return from exile occurred in 538 BC (Ezra 1–6), the second in 458 BC (Ezra 7–10), and the third in 445 BC (Neh 1–13).

30:7 The ***time of trouble*** was the Babylonian capture and the final destruction of Judah in 586 BC. • ***Israel:*** Literally *Jacob;* also in 30:10b, 18; see note on 5:20.

30:8 Although the return of the exiles began in 538 BC, ***foreigners*** were still ***their masters*** for most of Israel’s history from the Exile through the Roman period. However, Israel experienced a measure of freedom during that time.

30:9 After the Exile, the Israelites cast aside their persistent worship of idols and truly served ***the LORD their God.*** • The Lord would provide a ***king,*** also a descendant of ***David,*** who would be called the Messiah (Isa 55:3-4; Ezek 34:23; 37:24; Hos 3:5; Luke 1:69; Acts 2:30; 13:22-23).

30:10 The gathering of exiles would include those held in Babylon and also those who were scattered in ***distant lands.*** The Lord’s promised gifts would include ***peace and quiet*** without fearsome enemies.

11 For I am with you and will save you,"
says the LORD.
"I will completely destroy the nations
where I have scattered you,
but I will not completely destroy you.
I will discipline you, but with justice;
I cannot let you go unpunished."

12 This is what the LORD says:
"Your injury is incurable—
a terrible wound.
13 There is no one to help you
or to bind up your injury.
No medicine can heal you.
14 All your lovers—your allies—have left you
and do not care about you anymore.
I have wounded you cruelly,
as though I were your enemy.
For your sins are many,
and your guilt is great.
15 Why do you protest your punishment—
this wound that has no cure?
I have had to punish you
because your sins are many
and your guilt is great.

16 "But all who devour you will be devoured,
and all your enemies will be sent into exile.
All who plunder you will be plundered,
and all who attack you will be attacked.
17 I will give you back your health
and heal your wounds," says the LORD.
"For you are called an outcast—
'Jerusalem for whom no one cares.'"

18 This is what the LORD says:
"When I bring Israel home again from captivity
and restore their fortunes,
Jerusalem will be rebuilt on its ruins,
and the palace reconstructed as before.
19 There will be joy and songs of thanksgiving,
and I will multiply my people, not diminish them;
I will honor them, not despise them.
20 Their children will prosper as they did long ago.
I will establish them as a nation before me,
and I will punish anyone who hurts them.
21 They will have their own ruler again,
and he will come from their own people.
I will invite him to approach me," says the LORD,
"for who would dare to come unless invited?
22 You will be my people,
and I will be your God."
23 Look! The LORD's anger bursts out like a storm,
a driving wind that swirls down on the heads of the wicked.
24 The fierce anger of the LORD will not diminish
until it has finished all he has planned.
In the days to come
you will understand all this.

Hope for Restoration

31 "In that day," says the LORD, "I will be the God of all the families of Israel, and they will be my people. 2This is what the LORD says:

30:11 Jer 1:8, 19; 4:27; 5:10, 18; 10:24; 46:28
30:12 Jer 15:18
30:13 Jer 14:19; 46:11
30:14 Jer 22:20, 22; Lam 1:2; 2:4-5
30:16 Isa 14:2; Jer 2:3; 10:25
30:17 Ps 107:20; Isa 56:8; Jer 8:22; 33:6
30:18 1 Chr 29:1, 19; Ps 48:3; 122:7; Jer 31:38-40
30:19 Isa 12:1; 51:3; 55:5; 60:9; Jer 17:26; 33:11; *todah* (8426) ‣Jer 33:11
30:20 Isa 54:14
30:21 Exod 3:5; Num 16:5
30:22 Exod 6:7; Jer 32:38; Hos 2:23; Zech 13:9
30:23-24 //Jer 23:19-20
30:24 Jer 4:8
31:1 Gen 17:7-8; Jer 30:22; Rom 11:26-28
31:2 Exod 33:14; Josh 1:13

30:11 The Lord could make these promises because he was *with* his people and had the power to *save* them. He promised to destroy vicious *nations* and preserve his people. Still, the Lord would *discipline* his people if they sinned.

30:12-14 The exiles suffered *injury—a terrible wound*—because of their many *sins.* • *lovers . . . allies:* The Lord used these terms to refer to nations, especially Egypt, that had been Judah's trusted friends (see 4:30 and note; see also Ezek 16:15-63).

30:15 The Israelites had no right to *protest* their *punishment;* they deserved their exile, and God's justice demanded that they be punished.

30:16 *all who devour you will be devoured:* See 25:11-12.

30:17 *I will . . . heal your wounds:* The people would return from exile and their sins would be removed. • *Jerusalem:* Hebrew *Zion*.

30:18 The walls of *Jerusalem* were *rebuilt* in 445 BC under Nehemiah's leadership (Neh 12:22-43).

30:19-21 The rebuilt Jerusalem would be the center of a healthy and growing nation. Its growing population would experience *joy* and sing *songs of thanksgiving.* The city would be honored by its neighbors, and its streets would be filled with *children* who would grow up and *prosper.* The nation would have its *own ruler again.*

30:22 The Lord wanted to establish a nation whose *people* were totally committed to worshiping him as the one true *God* (Exod 6:7; Ezek 36:38).

30:23 The reestablished nation was still held accountable for rebellion. The Lord reserved the authority to express his stormy *anger* against *the wicked.*

30:24 Punishment remained an important aspect of what the Lord had *planned.* The Israelites, including Jeremiah, found it difficult to reconcile divine promises with divine *anger.* Looking back on events at a later time would help the people to *understand* this paradox.

31:1 *In that day:* This phrase refers to the return from exile that began in 538 BC. • *all the families of Israel:* The coming restoration included all twelve tribes of Israel.

31:2 The Lord directed his message to those who would *survive the coming destruction* at the fall of Jerusalem in 586 BC.

31:3 Deut 4:37; 7:8; Ps 25:6
31:4 Isa 30:32; Jer 24:6; 33:7
31:5 Ps 107:37; Isa 65:21; Ezek 28:26
31:6 Isa 2:3; Mic 4:2
31:7 Ps 14:7; 28:9; Isa 37:31; 61:9; Jer 20:13; 23:3
31:8 Deut 30:4; Isa 40:11; 43:6; Ezek 34:16; Mic 4:6
31:9 Isa 49:10; 63:13

"Those who survive the coming
destruction
will find blessings even in the barren
land,
for I will give rest to the people of
Israel."

3 Long ago the LORD said to Israel:
"I have loved you, my people, with an
everlasting love.
With unfailing love I have drawn you
to myself.
4 I will rebuild you, my virgin Israel.
You will again be happy
and dance merrily with your
tambourines.
5 Again you will plant your vineyards on
the mountains of Samaria
and eat from your own gardens there.
6 The day will come when watchmen will
shout
from the hill country of Ephraim,
'Come, let us go up to Jerusalem
to worship the LORD our God.' "

7 Now this is what the LORD says:
"Sing with joy for Israel.
Shout for the greatest of nations!
Shout out with praise and joy:
'Save your people, O LORD,
the remnant of Israel!'
8 For I will bring them from the
north
and from the distant corners of the
earth.
I will not forget the blind and lame,
the expectant mothers and women
in labor.
A great company will return!
9 Tears of joy will stream down their
faces,
and I will lead them home with great
care.
They will walk beside quiet streams
and on smooth paths where they will
not stumble.
For I am Israel's father,
and Ephraim is my oldest child.

Future Hope (30:1–33:26)

Jer 3:11–4:2; 16:14-15; 23:3-8; 29:10-14; 46:27
Isa 2:3-4; 4:2; 11:1-16; 35:1-10; 52:11-12
Hos 3:4-5
Amos 9:11-15
Heb 9:13-15; 12:22-24

The book of Jeremiah contains many messages of judgment and doom, but flashes of hope occasionally shine through.

The first ray of hope in Jeremiah is found in the Lord's appeal to Israel to turn from idolatry back to the Lord God and the Sinai Covenant (3:11–4:2). A positive response would open a bright future for the people. They could know the salvation that heals hearts (3:22-23), and Israel would become a blessing to all nations. The nation would not be destroyed if the people repented, which would bring God's anger to an end (4:1-2). Even in times of crisis before the fall of Jerusalem, promises of a wonderful future offered hope for the nation (see 16:15; 23:3-8; 29:10-14; 30:1–33:26).

After the fall of Jerusalem, the Lord again offered hope to the exiles in Babylon. After seventy years, the exiles who turned to the Lord would return to the Promised Land to rebuild the Temple and the city of Jerusalem. A functioning community would know peace and prosperity (see 46:27-28; chs 50–51). Babylon would be destroyed as the capital of a great empire, and the exiles would return to Judah. These events occurred in 539–538 BC.

In addition to Jeremiah, the Lord specifically offered hope to two individuals. Baruch (Jeremiah's scribe) and Ebed-melech (the royal servant who saved Jeremiah from the cistern) both received the divine promise that they would survive the coming fall of Jerusalem (39:16-18; 45:1-5).

Hope for the new nation extended well into the future, as the Lord promised a righteous descendant of King David who would rule over the Lord's people (23:5; 33:15). Jesus Christ is that righteous descendant; through his death on the cross, he became the mediator of a new covenant (Heb 9:13-15; 12:22-24).

31:3 *Long ago,* the Lord had revealed himself during the Exodus (see Exod 15:13; 20:6; 34:6-7; Num 14:18-19; Deut 5:10; 7:7, 10, 12-13; 10:15, 18).

31:4 In their homeland, the Israelites had been guilty of "adultery" with false gods. The restored community would be like a ***virgin,*** as though the people had never forsaken the Lord. The happiness and joy of their celebrations would manifest this transformation.

31:5 *Samaria* was located in north central Israel.

31:6 In the fully restored nation, the kingdom would no longer be divided (1 Kgs 12:16-29; Ezek 37:16-22). • *Jerusalem:* Hebrew *Zion;* also in 31:12.

31:7 *Israel:* Literally *Jacob;* also in 31:11; see note on 5:20. • The ***remnant*** refers to those who were living in exile.

31:8 The Lord promised to gather the surviving exiles from wherever they were scattered without overlooking the weak and helpless. • The ***great company*** of exiles who returned in 538–536 BC numbered 49,697 (Ezra 2:64).

31:9 Those returning to their homeland would cry for *joy,* knowing the Lord as their shepherd (Ps 23:1-3) and feeling secure (see Isa 35:10) with God as their ***father.***

10 "Listen to this message from the LORD,
you nations of the world;
proclaim it in distant coastlands:
The LORD, who scattered his people,
will gather them and watch over them
as a shepherd does his flock.
11 For the LORD has [k]redeemed Israel
from those too strong for them.
12 They will come home and sing songs of
joy on the heights of Jerusalem.
They will be radiant because of the
LORD's good gifts—
the abundant crops of grain, new wine,
and olive oil,
and the healthy flocks and herds.
Their life will be like a watered garden,
and all their sorrows will be gone.
13 The young women will dance for joy,
and the men—old and young—will
join in the celebration.
I will turn their mourning into joy.
I will comfort them and exchange
their sorrow for rejoicing.
14 The priests will enjoy abundance,
and my people will feast on my good
gifts.
I, the LORD, have spoken!"

Rachel's Sadness Turns to Joy

15 This is what the LORD says:

"A cry is heard in Ramah—
deep anguish and bitter weeping.
Rachel weeps for her children,
refusing to be comforted—
for her children are gone."

16 But now this is what the LORD says:
"Do not weep any longer,
for I will reward you," says the LORD.
"Your children will come back to you
from the distant land of the enemy.
17 There is hope for your future," says the
LORD.
"Your children will come again to their
own land.
18 I have heard Israel saying,
'You disciplined me severely,
like a calf that needs training for the
yoke.
Turn me again to you and restore me,
for you alone are the LORD my God.
19 I turned away from God,
but then I was sorry.
I kicked myself for my stupidity!
I was thoroughly ashamed of all I did
in my younger days.'
20 "Is not Israel still my son,
my darling child?" says the LORD.
"I often have to punish him,
but I still love him.
That's why I long for him
and surely will have mercy on him.
21 Set up road signs;
put up guideposts.
Mark well the path
by which you came.
Come back again, my virgin Israel;
return to your towns here.
22 How long will you wander,
my wayward daughter?
For the LORD will cause something new
to happen—
Israel will embrace her God."

23 This is what the LORD of Heaven's Armies, the God of Israel, says: "When I bring
them back from captivity, the people of Judah and its towns will again say, 'The LORD

31:10 Isa 40:11; 66:19
31:11 Isa 44:23; 48:20
[k]ga'al (1350)
‣ Lam 3:58
31:12 Isa 2:2; 35:10; 58:11; 60:20; 65:19
Hos 2:22
Joel 3:18
Mic 4:1
John 16:22
31:13 Ps 30:11
Isa 51:11; 61:3
Zech 8:4-5
31:14 Jer 50:19
31:15 Ps 77:2
Jer 10:20
*Matt 2:17-18
31:16 Isa 25:8; 30:19
Jer 30:3
Ezek 11:17
31:17 Jer 29:11
31:18 Job 5:17
Ps 80:3, 7, 19; 94:12
Jer 17:14
Hos 4:16
31:19 Ezek 36:31
Luke 18:13
31:20 Isa 55:7
Hos 11:8; 14:4
31:21 Isa 48:20; 52:11
31:23 Ps 48:1; 87:1
Isa 1:26
31:24 Ezek 36:10
Zech 8:4-8
31:25 Ps 107:9
John 4:14
31:26 Prov 3:24
Zech 4:1

31:10 *you nations of the world:* Jeremiah was referring to countries with people exiled from Israel. ***The LORD*** promised to ***gather*** his people and be their ***shepherd*** in place of the wicked shepherds who had led Israel and Judah astray.

31:11 The Lord alone could accomplish the people's release from exile.

31:12 The restored community would enjoy ***the LORD's good gifts.*** The people could expect ***abundant crops*** to spring forth in the fields with no appeal to Baal. The ***sorrows*** of their exile would be cast off, and the returnees could expect to be fruitful, ***like a watered garden.***

31:13 The Lord would replace ***mourning,*** a daily experience in exile, with his ***comfort*** and a continual outpouring of ***rejoicing*** (see Isa 40:1-3; 61:3).

31:14 The ***priests*** and the ***people*** would ***enjoy abundance*** because the people would pay their tithes rather than robbing God (Mal 3:8-12).

31:15-40 The Lord expanded on his future project of rebuilding a new nation out of a people who had suffered greatly during their lengthy captivity.

31:15 ***Rachel,*** Jacob's favorite wife, was the mother of Joseph (father of the tribes of Ephraim and Manasseh in the northern kingdom) and Benjamin (whose descendants were in the southern kingdom). She represented the mothers in all Israel whose children were taken into exile. • Matthew 2:18 quotes this verse in relation to the slaughter of the young boys in Bethlehem.

31:16-17 Rachel should not ***weep,*** because the Lord promised to bring her exiled ***children*** out of captivity and back ***to their own land.***

31:18-19 ***Israel*** (literally *Ephraim,* referring to the northern kingdom of *Israel;* also in 31:20) was now repenting of its sins and humbly asking for restoration; the people realized that they had no power to redeem themselves. They were turning away from idols and affirming that God ***alone*** is ***the LORD.***

31:19 When the exiles realized the ***stupidity*** of their sins, they were ***ashamed.***

31:20 The exiled people had been in the Lord's memory all along. God responded to his people's repentance with a father's love for his wayward children (cp. Luke 15:11-24).

31:21 ***road signs . . . guideposts:*** The Lord guided his people physically back to the land of Israel and spiritually back to their covenant relationship with the Lord.

31:22 ***Israel will embrace her God:*** Literally *a woman will surround a man.*

31:27
Ezek 36:9-11
Hos 2:23
31:28
Jer 1:10
Dan 9:14
31:29
Lam 5:7
Ezek 18:2
31:30
Deut 24:16
Ezek 18:4, 20
31:31-34
*Heb 8:8-12
31:31
Jer 32:40
Ezek 37:26
Luke 22:20
1 Cor 11:25
[a]*berith* (1285)
‣Jer 33:21
31:32
Deut 1:31; 5:2-3
Isa 63:12

bless you, O righteous home, O holy mountain!' 24Townspeople and farmers and
shepherds alike will live together in peace
and happiness. 25For I have given rest to the
weary and joy to the sorrowing."
26At this, I woke up and looked around.
My sleep had been very sweet.
27"The day is coming," says the LORD,
"when I will greatly increase the human population and the number of animals here in
Israel and Judah. 28In the past I deliberately
uprooted and tore down this nation. I overthrew it, destroyed it, and brought disaster
upon it. But in the future I will just as deliberately plant it and build it up. I, the LORD,
have spoken!
29"The people will no longer quote this
proverb:

'The parents have eaten sour grapes,
but their children's mouths pucker at
the taste.'

30All people will die for their own sins—
those who eat the sour grapes will be the
ones whose mouths will pucker.
31"The day is coming," says the LORD,
"when I will make a new [a]covenant with the
people of Israel and Judah. 32This covenant
will not be like the one I made with their
ancestors when I took them by the hand
and brought them out of the land of Egypt.
They broke that covenant, though I loved

The New Covenant (31:31-34)

Isa 11:1-9; 54:13-15
Ezek 37:24-28
Matt 26:27-28
Luke 22:20
Rom 11:25-36
1 Cor 11:23-26
2 Cor 3:6-18
Heb 8:8–9:28

One section in the book of Jeremiah (chs 30–33) stands above other passages in the OT in its optimistic view of Israel's future. The high point (31:31-34) is the announcement that the Lord God will form a new covenant with his people. It points toward Jesus of Nazareth, whose death would seal this new covenant.

One sentence in particular gives a new context to the key affirmation of the Sinai covenant: "I will be their God, and they will be my people" (31:33; see also Exod 6:7). The relationship between God and his people envisioned in the Sinai Covenant was surrounded by laws chiseled in stone and a priestly class in charge of all religious institutions and activities. The new covenant would differ from the old in one primary way: It would no longer be external to the worshipers, but would now be written on their hearts (31:33). The great defect of the old covenant was that it lacked the power to enable people to do what it commanded (Rom 8:3). The new covenant would be internalized through the power of the Holy Spirit, whose indwelling would be made possible through the sacrifice of Christ (Ezek 36:24-27). Thus, it would become possible for people everywhere (not just a select few) to fulfill God's covenant plan for life as summed up in the two "Great Commandments" (Matt 22:35-40): "You must love the LORD your God" (Deut 6:5) and "Love your neighbor as yourself" (Lev 19:18).

In the new covenant, God's role as Creator goes beyond making all material things. The new covenant would achieve the goal that the old one pointed to, but could not reach: creating new persons and a new community. The goal is a deep transformation of sinners, beginning with forgiveness of sins and culminating in a holiness exemplified by good works (Eph 1:4; 2:8-10). According to the NT, all believers in Jesus Christ will know him directly by the activity of the Holy Spirit. They will know him personally and experience him powerfully, as only a few did in OT times.

Jesus applied the new covenant to himself when he instituted the communion ritual (Matt 26:28; Mark 14:24; Luke 22:20; see also 1 Cor 11:25; 2 Cor 3:6). Jesus' death inaugurated the new covenant, and Christians commemorate that reality each time they take communion.

Hebrews 8:8-12 quotes Jer 31:31-34, and Heb 9 contrasts the old and new covenants. The writer clearly states that Jesus' death brought the new covenant into existence and made him the mediator of the covenant for whoever believes in him.

31:26 Evidently, either Jeremiah or his scribe had fallen asleep and was awakened with a start. His *sleep* was *very sweet*, like the rest and joy promised by the Lord (31:25).

31:27 A clear indication of the Lord's care for ***Israel and Judah*** would be their ***population*** growth and ***the number of animals*** grazing in their pastures.

31:28 *The future* refers to the return of the exiled people to the Promised Land, which the Lord had promised to ***plant*** and ***build*** (see 1:10).

31:29-30 Some seemed to think that this ***proverb*** (apparently a misinterpretation of Exod 20:5; 34:7; Num 14:18) meant that innocent children were dying because of their parents' sins. The Lord made it clear that each individual is punished for his or her own sins (see Lam 5:7; Ezek 18:2-32; 33:10-20).

31:31 *The day* of the ***new covenant*** was realized when Jesus Christ accomplished his redemptive mission on earth (see Heb 8:8-12).

31:32-34 The key difference between the *new covenant* and the *one* God ***made with their ancestors*** is that the Lord

them as a husband loves his wife," says the
LORD.
33 "But this is the new covenant I will
make with the people of Israel on that day,"
says the LORD. "I will put my instructions
deep within them, and I will write them on
their hearts. I will be their God, and they
will be my people. 34 And they will not need
to teach their neighbors, nor will they need
to teach their relatives, saying, 'You should
know the LORD.' For everyone, from the
least to the greatest, will know me already,"
says the LORD. "And I will forgive their wickedness, and I will never again remember
their sins."

35 It is the LORD who provides the sun to
light the day
and the moon and stars to light the
night,
and who stirs the sea into roaring
waves.
His name is the LORD of Heaven's
Armies,
and this is what he says:
36 "I am as likely to reject my people Israel
as I am to abolish the laws of nature!"
37 This is what the LORD says:
"Just as the heavens cannot be measured
and the foundations of the earth
cannot be explored,
so I will not consider casting them away
for the evil they have done.
I, the LORD, have spoken!

38 "The day is coming," says the LORD,
"when all Jerusalem will be rebuilt for me,
from the Tower of Hananel to the Corner
Gate. 39 A measuring line will be stretched
out over the hill of Gareb and across to
Goah. 40 And the entire area—including the
graveyard and ash dump in the valley, and
all the fields out to the Kidron Valley on the
east as far as the Horse Gate—will be holy to
the LORD. The city will never again be captured or destroyed."

Jeremiah's Land Purchase

32 The following message came to Jeremiah from the LORD in the tenth
year of the reign of Zedekiah, king of Judah.
This was also the eighteenth year of the
reign of King Nebuchadnezzar. 2 Jerusalem
was then under siege from the Babylonian
army, and Jeremiah was imprisoned in the
courtyard of the guard in the royal palace.
3 King Zedekiah had put him there, asking
why he kept giving this prophecy: "This is
what the LORD says: 'I am about to hand this
city over to the king of Babylon, and he will
take it. 4 King Zedekiah will be captured by
the Babylonians and taken to meet the king
of Babylon face to face. 5 He will take Zedekiah to Babylon, and I will deal with him
there,' says the LORD. 'If you fight against
the Babylonians, you will never succeed.' "
6 At that time the LORD sent me a message.
He said, 7 "Your cousin Hanamel son of Shallum will come and say to you, 'Buy my field
at Anathoth. By law you have the right to
buy it before it is offered to anyone else.' "
8 Then, just as the LORD had said he would,
my cousin Hanamel came and visited me in
the prison. He said, "Please buy my field at
Anathoth in the land of Benjamin. By law
you have the right to buy it before it is offered to anyone else, so buy it for yourself."
Then I knew that the message I had heard
was from the LORD.

31:33 *Heb 10:16
31:34 Isa 11:9; 43:25 Jer 50:20 Mic 7:18 Rom 11:27 1 Thes 4:9 *Heb 10:17 1 Jn 2:27
31:35 Gen 1:14-18
31:36 Isa 54:9-10 Amos 9:8-9
31:37 Isa 40:12 Jer 33:22, 24-26 Rom 11:2-5, 26-27
31:38 2 Chr 26:9 Neh 3:1; 12:39 Zech 14:10
31:40 2 Kgs 23:6 Neh 3:28 Joel 3:17 Zech 14:20
32:1 2 Kgs 25:1-2 Jer 39:1-2
32:2 Neh 3:25
32:3 Jer 21:4-7; 26:8-9; 34:2-3
32:4 2 Kgs 25:4-7 Jer 37:17; 39:4-7
32:5 Ezek 12:12-13; 17:9-10, 15
32:7 Lev 25:25 Ruth 4:3-4
32:8 1 Sam 9:16-17; 10:3-7
32:9 Gen 23:16 Matt 27:9-10
32:10 Ruth 4:1, 9 Isa 8:1-2

would ***write*** his ***instructions deep within*** his people's ***hearts*** (see Heb 11:16). The old covenant was external and legal, whereas the new covenant would be a vital, person-to-person relationship. The new covenant would emphasize the redeeming, transforming change of an individual's spiritual nature.

31:34 The old covenant had to be taught (see Deut 6:4-9), but the heart of the new covenant would be an inner, personal relationship with the Lord. • ***I will forgive:*** Each repentant believer would experience God's forgiveness. • ***I will never again remember:*** When sins are forgiven, they can never bring divine judgment (see Heb 11:17). • Jesus' death inaugurated the new covenant (see Matt 26:28; Mark 14:24; Luke 22:20; 1 Cor 11:25; 2 Cor 3:6; Heb 8:1-13; 9:15; 12:22-24).

31:35-37 The Lord compared his promise of the new covenant to his faithfulness in maintaining ***the laws of nature.***

31:38 The Lord revealed his plan for ***Jerusalem*** to ***be rebuilt.*** The ***Tower of Hananel*** stood at the northeast corner of the old city, while the ***Corner Gate*** had been at the northwest corner (2 Kgs 14:13; 2 Chr 26:9).

31:39 ***Gareb*** and ***Goah*** do not appear elsewhere in Scripture, but they were probably on the west side of the city.

31:40 Jerusalem will be an eternal ***holy . . . city,*** present in the heavenly realm and on the new earth (Rev 21–22). • The ***graveyard and ash dump*** were in the valley of Ben-Hinnom (see note on 7:30-34) on the south side of the city and the ***Kidron Valley on the east*** (2 Kgs 23:4-6). • The exact location of the ***Horse Gate*** on the eastern wall is unknown.

32:1 ***The tenth year of the reign of Zedekiah*** and ***the eighteenth year of the reign of King Nebuchadnezzar*** was 587 BC, just before the fall of Jerusalem. • ***Nebuchadnezzar:*** Hebrew *Nebuchadrezzar,* a variant spelling of Nebuchadnezzar; also in 32:28.

32:2 ***Jerusalem*** had been ***under siege*** since January 588 BC (2 Kgs 25:1). • ***Jeremiah*** favored surrender to the Babylonians, but the thought angered many who believed that they could successfully defy the foreign army. To protect Jeremiah, Zedekiah ***imprisoned*** him in ***the courtyard of the guard*** (37:21).

32:4-5 Continuing to resist ***the Babylonians*** (or ***Chaldeans;*** also in 32:5, 24, 25, 28, 29, 43) was hopeless; it would result in disaster for the city and for ***Zedekiah.***

32:6-8 ***Anathoth*** was Jeremiah's hometown (1:1). • ***By law you have the right:*** Hebrew custom required Jeremiah's cousin to offer the land first to his nearest relative (see Lev 25:25, 32; Ruth 4:1-4).

32:15
Jer 30:18; 31:5, 12
Amos 9:14-15

32:16
Gen 32:9-12
Jer 12:1
Phil 4:6-7
[b]*palal* (6419)
‣Jon 2:1

32:17
Gen 18:14
2 Kgs 19:15
Ps 102:25
Isa 40:26-29
Jer 27:5

32:18
Exod 34:6-7
Deut 7:9-10
1 Kgs 16:1-3
Ps 50:1; 145:3
Jer 10:16; 20:11; 31:35
Matt 23:32-36

32:19
Job 34:21; Ps 62:12;
Jer 17:10; 23:24;
John 5:29

32:20
Ps 78:43; 105:27
Isa 63:12, 14
Dan 9:15

32:21
Deut 4:34; 26:8
1 Chr 17:21

32:22
Exod 13:5
Deut 1:8
Ps 105:9-11
Jer 11:5

32:23
Ezra 9:7
Jer 2:7
Dan 9:11-12

32:24
Josh 23:15-16

9So I bought the field at Anathoth, paying
Hanamel seventeen pieces of silver for it. 10I
signed and sealed the deed of purchase before witnesses, weighed out the silver, and
paid him. 11Then I took the sealed deed
and an unsealed copy of the deed, which
contained the terms and conditions of the
purchase, 12and I handed them to Baruch
son of Neriah and grandson of Mahseiah.
I did all this in the presence of my cousin
Hanamel, the witnesses who had signed the
deed, and all the men of Judah who were
there in the courtyard of the guardhouse.

13Then I said to Baruch as they all listened, 14"This is what the LORD of Heaven's
Armies, the God of Israel, says: 'Take both
this sealed deed and the unsealed copy,
and put them into a pottery jar to preserve
them for a long time.' 15For this is what the
LORD of Heaven's Armies, the God of Israel,
says: 'Someday people will again own property here in this land and will buy and sell
houses and vineyards and fields.' "

Jeremiah's Prayer

16Then after I had given the papers to Baruch, I [b]prayed to the LORD:

17"O Sovereign LORD! You made the
heavens and earth by your strong hand
and powerful arm. Nothing is too hard
for you! 18You show unfailing love
to thousands, but you also bring the
consequences of one generation's sin
upon the next. You are the great and
powerful God, the LORD of Heaven's
Armies. 19You have all wisdom and do
great and mighty miracles. You see the
conduct of all people, and you give them
what they deserve. 20You performed
miraculous signs and wonders in the
land of Egypt—things still remembered
to this day! And you have continued to
do great miracles in Israel and all around
the world. You have made your name
famous to this day.

21"You brought Israel out of Egypt
with mighty signs and wonders, with
a strong hand and powerful arm, and
with overwhelming terror. 22You gave
the people of Israel this land that you
had promised their ancestors long
before—a land flowing with milk and
honey. 23Our ancestors came and
conquered it and lived in it, but they
refused to obey you or follow your
word. They have not done anything you
commanded. That is why you have sent
this terrible disaster upon them.

24"See how the siege ramps have been
built against the city walls! Through

32:9-12 Many people might have thought that Jeremiah did a foolish thing when he agreed to buy the land. After the fall of Jerusalem and the exile of many people, the value of the land would drop to almost nothing. Still, Jeremiah immediately ***bought the field***. • ***seventeen pieces:*** Hebrew *17 shekels*, about 7 ounces or 194 grams in weight. • Matt 27:9-10 refers to the "prophecy of Jeremiah," which might be an allusion to this event.

32:10 Jeremiah carefully followed the proper legal procedures for buying property. The ***deed of purchase*** was a sheet of papyrus that listed the terms of the purchase in Hebrew. Jeremiah ***signed and sealed the deed*** and paid the purchase price in the presence of ***witnesses*** (Gen 23:3-18; 2 Sam 24:20-24).

32:11-12 According to custom, a copy of the ***deed*** was made. The two documents were entrusted to the care of Jeremiah's secretary, ***Baruch***. This was done publicly, ***in the courtyard of the guardhouse***.

32:13-14 According to custom, the two copies of the ***deed*** were placed in a ***pottery jar*** so that they would be preserved ***for a long time***.

32:15 Jeremiah explained the reason for his purchase: He was making an investment in the future that God had promised. ***Someday*** exiled survivors of the destruction of Judah would return, and worthless land would again become productive and valuable. Jeremiah had already predicted that the exile would last for seventy years (25:11-12; 29:10). Jeremiah's purchase was a declaration of faith in the Lord's plan for restoring his people.

32:16-25 This prayer of Jeremiah differed from his previous prayers, which expressed strong emotions of anguish and despair and even sharp criticism of the Lord's treatment of the people of Judah. This prayer was calm, affirming, and worshipful.

32:16 Jeremiah ***prayed*** in response to his purchase of land.

32:17 As the all-powerful Creator of all things, the ***Sovereign LORD*** could do what he had promised for his people.

32:18 The Lord consistently showed his ***unfailing love***, but he also held generations accountable for their sins, and their children harvested the consequences. Through his mercy and his judgment, ***the LORD*** demonstrated his unlimited power. Jeremiah was confident that the Lord would show his love to his people as he had promised.

32:19 The Lord knows what each person does, and he holds each one accountable as he judges their sins fairly.

32:20 The Lord had done ***great miracles*** throughout the history of ***Israel***, but he had also been active ***all around the world***. As a result, everyone knew about Israel's God.

32:21 The first great miracle in Israel's history was the exodus from ***Egypt***, an act filled with ***mighty signs and wonders***. These divine acts caused ***terror*** in Egypt and among the desert tribes.

32:22 God also gave the productive Promised Land to Israel. • ***milk and honey:*** See note on 11:5.

32:23 After Israel entered the Promised Land, they quickly turned from faithfully obeying the Lord. Generation after generation up to Jeremiah's day was guilty of rebellion. This long history of sin was the cause of the present ***terrible disaster***. Previously, Jeremiah had trouble accepting that this act of God was just, but now he saw that the Lord's ***word*** was true.

32:24 Jeremiah was amazed at the skill of the attacking Babylonians. They used ***ramps*** to lay siege to the walled ***city***. Within Jerusalem, he saw the horrors of ***war, famine, and disease***. It was

war, famine, and disease, the city will be
handed over to the Babylonians, who will
conquer it. Everything has happened
just as you said. 25And yet, O Sovereign
LORD, you have told me to buy the field—
paying good money for it before these
witnesses—even though the city will
soon be handed over to the Babylonians."

A Prediction of Jerusalem's Fall

26Then this message came to Jeremiah
from the LORD: 27"I am the LORD, the God of
all the peoples of the world. Is anything too
hard for me? 28Therefore, this is what the
LORD says: I will hand this city over to the
Babylonians and to Nebuchadnezzar, king
of Babylon, and he will capture it. 29The
Babylonians outside the walls will come in
and set fire to the city. They will burn down
all these houses where the people provoked
my anger by burning incense to Baal on the
rooftops and by pouring out liquid offerings to other gods. 30Israel and Judah have
done nothing but wrong since their earliest
days. They have infuriated me with all their
evil deeds," says the LORD. 31"From the time
this city was built until now, it has done
nothing but anger me, so I am determined
to get rid of it.

32"The sins of Israel and Judah—the sins
of the people of Jerusalem, the kings, the officials, the priests, and the prophets—have
stirred up my anger. 33My people have
turned their backs on me and have refused
to return. Even though I diligently taught
them, they would not receive instruction
or obey. 34They have set up their abominable idols right in my own Temple, defiling
it. 35They have built pagan shrines to Baal
in the valley of Ben-Hinnom, and there they
sacrifice their sons and daughters to Molech.
I have never commanded such a horrible
deed; it never even crossed my mind to command such a thing. What an incredible evil,
causing Judah to sin so greatly!

A Promise of Restoration

36"Now I want to say something more about
this city. You have been saying, 'It will fall
to the king of Babylon through war, famine,
and disease.' But this is what the LORD, the
God of Israel, says: 37I will certainly bring
my people back again from all the countries
where I will scatter them in my fury. I will
bring them back to this very city and let
them live in peace and safety. 38They will be
my people, and I will be their God. 39And I
will give them one heart and one purpose:

32:27
Num 16:22; 27:16
Matt 19:26

32:28
Jer 19:7-12; 34:2-3

32:29
2 Chr 36:19
Jer 19:13; 21:10; 39:8; 44:17-19, 25; 52:13

32:31
1 Kgs 11:7-8
2 Kgs 21:4-7, 15; 23:27; 24:3-4
Jer 5:9-11; 6:6-7
Matt 23:37

32:32
Ezra 9:7
Isa 1:23
Jer 2:26; 44:17, 21

32:33
2 Chr 36:15-16
Jer 25:3; 26:5; 35:15

32:34
Jer 7:30
Ezek 8:5

32:35
Lev 18:21; 20:2-5
2 Chr 28:2-3; 33:6
Acts 7:43

32:37
Deut 30:3
Isa 11:11-16
Jer 23:6
Ezek 11:17; 34:25, 28
Hos 1:11
Amos 9:14-15
Zech 14:11

32:38
*2 Cor 6:16

32:39
Deut 11:18-21
Ezek 37:25
John 17:21
Acts 4:32

---

obvious that the ***Babylonians*** would ***conquer*** the city. A sense of awe swept through Jeremiah as he realized that he was seeing the fulfillment of ***everything*** the Lord had ***said***.

32:25 Jeremiah was still puzzled about the Lord's command ***to buy the field*** (32:8). That field would be under the control of the Babylonian army, and the purchase price drew on Jeremiah's ***good money***, his savings. Because the Lord had decreed that ***the city*** would be destroyed, the purchase appeared futile from a human perspective. Also see note on 32:44.

32:26-41 The Lord responded to Jeremiah's concern (32:25) with several affirmations. The Lord had decided on his course of action, the events of the immediate and long-range future had been established, and real doom was hanging over Jerusalem.

32:26-27 The Lord affirmed that he is the sovereign ***God of all the peoples of the world.*** • Using a rhetorical question, the Lord also affirmed that nothing is ***too hard*** for him.

32:28-29 The Lord affirmed that the army of ***Nebuchadnezzar*** would soon crash through the walls, Jerusalem would be captured, and ***fire*** would consume everything that could ***burn***. • ***Baal*** worship was both a family affair and a national commitment (see note on 7:17-18). All the places used for idol worship, including individual ***houses***, would be destroyed.

32:30-35 The Lord continued to affirm his plans, recounting that ***Israel and Judah*** had done ***evil***, had turned their backs on the Lord, and had ***stirred up*** his ***anger*** against their sin.

32:30 The people of ***Israel*** (the northern tribes) and ***Judah*** (the southern tribes) had worshiped idols for centuries, ***since their earliest days***, contrary to God's ancient covenant with them. The Lord was ***infuriated*** by these ***evil deeds***.

32:31 ***The time this city was built*** was during the reigns of David and Solomon, when Jerusalem became the capital city of Israel. During the history of the northern kingdom of Israel, every king promoted worship of false gods. In the kingdom of Judah, only a few kings encouraged worship of the Lord, usually without lasting success (e.g., 2 Chr 14:3; 17:6; 29:5; 33:15-16; 34:3, 31-32). The northern kingdom had already been destroyed (2 Kgs 17:5-12), and now the Lord had decided ***to get rid*** of the southern kingdom of Judah (see Deut 8:19-20).

32:34-35 The people had sinned by defiling God's ***own Temple*** with ***abominable idols*** (Ezek 8:3). The leaders of Judah were also known to ***sacrifice*** their own children to an Ammonite deity named ***Molech*** (see note at 7:30-34).

32:36-44 The Lord affirmed (see note on 32:26-41) that the destruction of Jerusalem would not bring an end to his plans. Beyond the immediate doom, the Lord planned a future of salvation and restoration for his people.

32:36-37 Jeremiah was responsible for repeating whatever the Lord told him, even if the messages seemed contradictory on the surface. Jeremiah had been saying for years that God was going to destroy the city. Now he was saying that God would rebuild the city. Cp. Isa 38:1-6.

32:37 God would ***certainly bring*** his ***people back again*** to Jerusalem, where they would ***live in peace and safety***.

32:38-40 The new covenant (31:31-34) would take root deep within the spiritual being of the people, both as individuals and in the community. • ***They will be my people, and I will be their God:*** A deep relationship between God and his people would finally be realized, as had been the intent of the ***covenant*** all along (7:23; Lev 26:12; Ezek 11:20; 37:23; Zech 8:8).

32:39 Under the new covenant, the people would ***worship*** the one true God rather than idols.

32:40 Isa 55:3
32:41 Deut 30:9; Isa 65:19; Jer 31:28; Amos 9:15
32:42 Jer 31:28; Zech 8:14-15
32:43 Jer 32:15, 25; Ezek 37:11-14
33:2 Exod 3:15; 15:3
33:3 Ps 50:15; Isa 48:6; 55:6-7
33:4 Isa 32:13-14
33:5 Jer 21:10
33:6 Isa 66:12; Jer 17:14
33:7 Ps 85:1; Jer 30:18; 32:44; Amos 9:14-15
33:8 Ps 51:2; Jer 50:20; Heb 9:11-14
33:9 Ps 40:3; Isa 62:2, 4; Jer 16:19; 24:6; Hos 3:5
33:10-11 Isa 35:10
33:11 [c]*todah* (8426) ‣Jon 2:9
33:12 Ezek 34:12-14; Zeph 2:6-7

to worship me forever, for their own good
and for the good of all their descendants.
[40]And I will make an everlasting covenant
with them: I will never stop doing good for
them. I will put a desire in their hearts to
worship me, and they will never leave me.
[41]I will find joy doing good for them and
will faithfully and wholeheartedly replant
them in this land.
[42]"This is what the LORD says: Just as I
have brought all these calamities on them,
so I will do all the good I have promised
them. [43]Fields will again be bought and sold
in this land about which you now say, 'It has
been ravaged by the Babylonians, a desolate
land where people and animals have all disappeared.' [44]Yes, fields will once again be
bought and sold—deeds signed and sealed
and witnessed—in the land of Benjamin
and here in Jerusalem, in the towns of Judah and in the hill country, in the foothills
of Judah and in the Negev, too. For someday
I will restore prosperity to them. I, the LORD,
have spoken!"

Promises of Peace and Prosperity

33 While Jeremiah was still confined
in the courtyard of the guard, the
LORD gave him this second message: [2]"This
is what the LORD says—the LORD who made
the earth, who formed and established it,
whose name is the LORD: [3]Ask me and I will
tell you remarkable secrets you do not know
about things to come. [4]For this is what the
LORD, the God of Israel, says: You have torn
down the houses of this city and even the
king's palace to get materials to strengthen
the walls against the siege ramps and
swords of the enemy. [5]You expect to fight
the Babylonians, but the men of this city
are already as good as dead, for I have determined to destroy them in my terrible anger.
I have abandoned them because of all their
wickedness.
[6]"Nevertheless, the time will come when
I will heal Jerusalem's wounds and give it
prosperity and true peace. [7]I will restore
the fortunes of Judah and Israel and rebuild
their towns. [8]I will cleanse them of their
sins against me and forgive all their sins of
rebellion. [9]Then this city will bring me joy,
glory, and honor before all the nations of
the earth! The people of the world will see
all the good I do for my people, and they will
tremble with awe at the peace and prosperity I provide for them.
[10]"This is what the LORD says: You have
said, 'This is a desolate land where people
and animals have all disappeared.' Yet in
the empty streets of Jerusalem and Judah's
other towns, there will be heard once more
[11]the sounds of joy and laughter. The joyful
voices of bridegrooms and brides will be
heard again, along with the joyous songs of
people bringing [c]thanksgiving offerings to
the LORD. They will sing,

'Give thanks to the LORD of Heaven's
Armies,
for the LORD is good.
His faithful love endures forever!'

For I will restore the prosperity of this land
to what it was in the past, says the LORD.
[12]"This is what the LORD of Heaven's
Armies says: This land—though it is now desolate and has no people and animals—will

32:41 ***find joy:*** The Lord's anger at seeing his people worship sex-idols and his grief in punishing them for breaching the old covenant would be gone. No longer would he uproot them (1:10); instead, it would be his delight to ***replant*** them.

32:42-43 God's promises for good were just as certain as the judgments that were being carried out as the Babylonians laid siege to Jerusalem.

32:44 ***fields will once again be bought and sold:*** The Lord directly answered Jeremiah's query (32:25). Jeremiah had ***signed and sealed and witnessed*** a deed for his inherited property (32:9-11), and people would do the same throughout the land of Judah. • ***the foothills of Judah:*** Hebrew *the Shephelah.*

33:1-26 As the city of Jerusalem and the king of Judah were falling to invaders, God gave Jeremiah a greater understanding of his long-range plan. The promises could only come true after the promised destruction. The hope of the nation was not to be found in escape from destruction but in the purification that destruction would bring. • ***Jeremiah was . . . confined in the courtyard of the guard*** in the royal palace from the latter part of 587 BC, when the siege was underway, until the fall of Jerusalem in August 586 BC (see 32:2).

33:2 The Lord grounded this message in his power as the Creator of all things, and in the power of his ***name.***

33:4 Zedekiah and his men had ***torn down*** some structures to defend the city's walls against the Babylonians' ***siege ramps and swords.***

33:5 ***Babylonians:*** Or *Chaldeans.* • The ***men*** were ***already as good as dead*** because the Lord had decreed the destruction of the city.

33:8 The Lord promised to ***cleanse*** and ***forgive all their sins of rebellion;*** this was the foundation upon which the new, everlasting covenant would rest (31:34; 32:38-41).

33:9 Once the new covenant was established, ***all the nations of the earth*** would see the Lord's blessing on Jerusalem.

33:10-11 Although seventy years of exile would come first, the Lord's curse (7:34) would be reversed (25:10-12). Singing would be a hallmark of the restored worship (Ps 136:1). This prediction was fulfilled in 538–536 BC when worship in Jerusalem was restored and the foundations of the Second Temple were laid (Ezra 3).

33:11 ***bridegrooms and brides:*** Contrast the earlier prophecies in 7:34 and 25:10.

33:12 The ***land*** was ***desolate*** as a result of the Babylonian invasion.

once more have pastures where shepherds
can lead their flocks. 13Once again shepherds will count their flocks in the towns of
the hill country, the foothills of Judah, the
Negev, the land of Benjamin, the vicinity of
Jerusalem, and all the towns of Judah. I, the
LORD, have spoken!
14"The day will come, says the LORD,
when I will do for Israel and Judah all the
good things I have promised them.

15 "In those days and at that time
I will raise up a righteous [d]descendant
from King David's line.
He will do what is just and right
throughout the land.
16 In that day Judah will be saved,
and Jerusalem will live in safety.
And this will be its name:
'The LORD Is Our Righteousness.'

17For this is what the LORD says: David will
have a descendant sitting on the throne of
Israel forever. 18And there will always be Levitical [e]priests to offer burnt offerings and
grain offerings and sacrifices to me."
19Then this message came to Jeremiah
from the LORD: 20"This is what the LORD
says: If you can break my covenant with
the day and the night so that one does not
follow the other, 21only then will my [f]cov-
enant with my servant David be broken.
Only then will he no longer have a descendant to reign on his throne. The same is
true for my covenant with the Levitical
priests who minister before me. 22And as
the stars of the sky cannot be counted and
the sand on the seashore cannot be measured, so I will multiply the descendants
of my servant David and the Levites who
[g]minister before me."
23The LORD gave another message to Jeremiah. He said, 24"Have you noticed what
people are saying?—'The LORD chose Judah
and Israel and then abandoned them!' They
are sneering and saying that Israel is not
worthy to be counted as a nation. 25But this
is what the LORD says: I would no more reject my people than I would change my laws
that govern night and day, earth and sky. 26I
will never abandon the [h]descendants of
Jacob or David, my servant, or change the
plan that David's [h]descendants will rule the
[h]descendants of Abraham, Isaac, and Jacob.
Instead, I will restore them to their land and
have mercy on them."

7. JERUSALEM'S DESTRUCTION (34:1–39:18)

A Warning for Zedekiah

34 King Nebuchadnezzar of Babylon
came with all the armies from the
kingdoms he ruled, and he fought against
Jerusalem and the towns of Judah. At that
time this message came to Jeremiah from
the LORD: 2"Go to King Zedekiah of Judah,
and tell him, 'This is what the LORD, the God
of Israel, says: I am about to hand this city
over to the king of Babylon, and he will burn
it down. 3You will not escape his grasp but
will be captured and taken to meet the king
of Babylon face to face. Then you will be exiled to Babylon.
4" 'But listen to this promise from the
LORD, O Zedekiah, king of Judah. This is
what the LORD says: You will not be killed
in war 5but will die peacefully. People will
burn incense in your memory, just as they

33:13 Lev 27:32; Jer 17:26; Luke 15:4
33:14 Hag 2:6-9
33:15 Ps 72:1-5; Isa 11:1-5; [d]*tsemakh* (6780) ‣Zech 3:8
33:16 1 Cor 1:30; 2 Cor 5:21; Phil 3:9
33:17 1 Kgs 2:4; Ps 89:29-37
33:18 Deut 18:1; Ezek 44:15; Heb 13:15; [e]*kohen* (3548) ‣Joel 2:17
33:20-21 2 Sam 23:5; 2 Chr 21:7; Ps 104:19-23; Isa 54:9
33:21 [f]*berith* (1285) ‣Ezek 37:26
33:22 Gen 22:17; [g]*sharath* (8334) ‣Exod 24:13
33:24 Neh 4:2-4; Ps 44:13-14; Isa 11:13; Jer 3:7-8, 10, 18; Ezek 36:2
33:25 Ps 74:16-17
33:26 Hos 2:23; [h]*zera'* (2233) ‣Gen 3:15
34:1 2 Kgs 25:1; Jer 1:15; Dan 2:37-38
34:2 2 Chr 36:11-12; Jer 37:1-4
34:3 2 Kgs 25:4-7; Jer 21:7

33:13 *the foothills of Judah:* Hebrew *the Shephelah.*

33:14-18 Picking up on the discussion of flaws in Zedekiah and the other kings of David's dynasty (23:1-5), the Lord revealed the glories of the new ruler of the future.

33:14-15 *The day will come . . . In those days:* These phrases point beyond the exiles' return to a more distant event mentioned previously by the Lord's prophets (Isa 32:1-2). They indicate the NT fulfillment of God's plan in Jesus Christ, the Good Shepherd (John 10:11) and the *righteous descendant* (literally *a righteous branch;* Isa 4:2; 11:1; Zech 3:8; 6:12, 13). • *He:* An individual, not a remnant, would be a fair judge and bring justice with his pronouncements.

33:16 *The LORD Is Our Righteousness:* Hebrew *Yahweh Tsidqenu;* see 23:5-6, where this title is given to the Messiah. This name was a reversal of Zedekiah's name (*Tsidqiyyahu,* "Righteous is the LORD"). Zedekiah did not live up to his name, but the Messiah would do so.

33:17 Though Zedekiah was the last *descendant* of *David* to rule over the kingdom of Judah (see 19:10-13 and note), the Messiah, a future descendant of David, would be Israel's king *forever.*

33:18 After the exiles returned to Jerusalem, *Levitical priests* conducted worship in the new Temple (Ezra 6:13-22).

33:19-22 Jeremiah delivered God's promise that the new covenant of the Lord with the descendant of *David* and with the *Levitical priests* would be as sure as the sequence of day and night.

33:23-26 The Lord had rejected individuals, cities, and kingdoms, but he would *never abandon* his people, who stretched across many generations.

34:1–39:18 This section begins with the prediction of Jerusalem's fall and Zedekiah's captivity (34:1-7); the fulfillment of that prediction comes toward the end (39:1-10). These messages underline the truth that the old covenant had been irreparably broken, especially by those kings descended from David who should have been most committed to maintaining it.

34:1-7 The Lord encouraged Zedekiah, even though he was a weak leader who lacked courage. The message contains judgment and a promise.

34:2 No matter what *King Zedekiah* did, Jerusalem would fall. The Lord would not rescue the *city.*

34:4-5 Even though the Babylonians would defeat *Judah,* the Lord promised to protect *Zedekiah* during the war; the king would *die peacefully* and be honored by the survivors of the siege. But see 39:5-7 for a description of Zedekiah's being captured and tortured and then taken away to Babylon.

34:5 2 Chr 16:14; 21:19
34:7 Josh 10:3, 10; 2 Kgs 14:19; 2 Chr 11:5-10
34:8 Lev 25:39-46; Neh 5:1-13
34:11 Hos 6:4
34:13 Deut 5:2-3, 27; Jer 31:32
34:14 Exod 21:2; 1 Kgs 9:22; 2 Kgs 17:13-14
34:15 Neh 10:29
34:16 Exod 20:7; 1 Sam 15:11; Ezek 18:24
34:17 Lev 26:34-35; Deut 28:25, 64; Matt 7:2
34:18 Gen 15:10; Hos 6:7; Mic 7:1-5
34:20 1 Sam 17:46; Jer 19:7
34:21 2 Kgs 25:18-21; Ezek 17:16
34:22 Jer 44:22
35:1 2 Kgs 23:34-36; Dan 1:1
35:2 1 Kgs 6:5-6, 8; 1 Chr 2:55

did for your ancestors, the kings who preceded you. They will mourn for you, crying,
"Alas, our master is dead!" This I have decreed, says the LORD.'"
6So Jeremiah the prophet delivered the
message to King Zedekiah of Judah. 7At this
time the Babylonian army was besieging Jerusalem, Lachish, and Azekah—the only
fortified cities of Judah not yet captured.

Freedom for Hebrew Slaves

8This message came to Jeremiah from the
LORD after King Zedekiah made a covenant
with the people, proclaiming freedom for
the slaves. 9He had ordered all the people
to free their Hebrew slaves—both men and
women. No one was to keep a fellow Judean
in bondage. 10The officials and all the people had obeyed the king's command, 11but
later they changed their minds. They took
back the men and women they had freed,
forcing them to be slaves again.
12So the LORD gave them this message
through Jeremiah: 13"This is what the LORD,
the God of Israel, says: I made a covenant
with your ancestors long ago when I rescued them from their slavery in Egypt. 14I
told them that every Hebrew slave must be
freed after serving six years. But your ancestors paid no attention to me. 15Recently you
repented and did what was right, following
my command. You freed your slaves and
made a solemn covenant with me in the
Temple that bears my name. 16But now you
have shrugged off your oath and defiled my
name by taking back the men and women
you had freed, forcing them to be slaves
once again.
17"Therefore, this is what the LORD says:
Since you have not obeyed me by setting
your countrymen free, I will set you free to
be destroyed by war, disease, and famine.
You will be an object of horror to all the
nations of the earth. 18Because you have
broken the terms of our covenant, I will
cut you apart just as you cut apart the calf
when you walked between its halves to solemnize your vows. 19Yes, I will cut you apart,
whether you are officials of Judah or Jerusalem, court officials, priests, or common
people—for you have broken your oath. 20I
will give you to your enemies, and they will
kill you. Your bodies will be food for the vultures and wild animals.
21"I will hand over King Zedekiah of Judah and his officials to the army of the king
of Babylon. And although Babylon's king
has left Jerusalem for a while, 22I will call
the Babylonian armies back again. They
will fight against this city and will capture
it and burn it down. I will see to it that all
the towns of Judah are destroyed, with no
one living there."

The Faithful Recabites

35 This is the message the LORD gave
Jeremiah when Jehoiakim son of
Josiah was king of Judah: 2"Go to the settlement where the families of the Recabites
live, and invite them to the LORD's Temple.
Take them into one of the inner rooms, and
offer them some wine."

34:6-7 King Rehoboam had made ***Lachish*** and ***Azekah*** into forts (2 Chr 11:5-10). Located on low hills southwest of Jerusalem, these towns guarded the key roads leading up from the great highway on the coast into the heartland of Judah. Military messages written on pieces of pottery have been found in the gateway of Lachish, reporting the progress of the Babylonians as they moved toward it.

34:8–35:19 Here are faithless (34:8-22) and faithful (35:1-19) examples of covenant-keeping.

34:8-22 ***Zedekiah*** ordered the ***people to free*** their ***slaves;*** he was apparently trying to curry favor with God by enforcing the covenant requirements regarding the Hebrew ownership of slaves (Exod 21:2-4) that had been neglected since Moses' time. However, the order was worse than useless because the people soon went back on this new affirmation of the ***covenant***, just as they had broken their treaty with Nebuchadnezzar (see Ezek 21:23-24) and their original covenant with the Lord. The Lord would punish them as their treachery deserved.

34:15-16 The slaveholders had done ***what was right*** in releasing their slaves; they had obeyed God's ***command.*** But their ***covenant*** had been made ***in the Temple***, and when they broke their covenant, they ***defiled*** God's ***name*** and treated it with contempt (in violation of Deut 5:11).

34:17-20 Because of their sin in breaking ***the terms of*** their ***covenant***, the Lord would ***cut*** them ***apart*** and separate them from his protective care. This expression relates to the covenant ceremony of killing and cutting a ***calf*** sacrifice into two parts from head to tail. Those making a covenant walked between the laid-out portions to indicate their willingness to be similarly ***cut apart*** if they violated the covenant (see Gen 15:9-18). All classes of people in Judah had ***broken*** their ***oath***, so they would all receive the punishment to which they had agreed.

34:21-22 Pharaoh Hophra had a treaty with Zedekiah to help him if he were attacked (Isa 30:1-3; 31:1-3). The Babylonians ***left Jerusalem*** to fight against Pharaoh Hophra (37:5-7), but their departure was temporary.

35:1–36:32 These two chapters look back two decades to the time when Jehoiakim was on the throne.

35:1-19 The Recabites' obedience to their ancestor contrasted sharply with the Israelites' rebellion against the Lord their God.

35:1 This incident took place during Jehoiakim's reign, when the Babylonian army first attacked Jerusalem (605 BC; see 35:11).

35:2 The ***Recabites*** were descendants of Jehonadab son of Recab, a Kenite who had served under Jehu, king of Israel (2 Kgs 10:15, 23; 1 Chr 2:55). Jeremiah probably knew that the Recabites did not drink ***wine***, but he obeyed the Lord's command.

3So I went to see Jaazaniah son of Jeremiah and grandson of Habazziniah and all
his brothers and sons—representing all the
Recabite families. 4I took them to the Temple, and we went into the room assigned to
the sons of Hanan son of Igdaliah, a man of
God. This room was located next to the one
used by the Temple officials, directly above
the room of Maaseiah son of Shallum, the
Temple gatekeeper.
5I set cups and jugs of wine before them
and invited them to have a drink, 6but they
refused. "No," they said, "we don't drink
wine, because our ancestor Jehonadab son
of Recab gave us this command: 'You and
your descendants must never drink wine.
7And do not build houses or plant crops or
vineyards, but always live in tents. If you
follow these commands, you will live long,
good lives in the land.' 8So we have obeyed
him in all these things. We have never had a
drink of wine to this day, nor have our wives,
our sons, or our daughters. 9We haven't
built houses or owned vineyards or farms
or planted crops. 10We have lived in tents
and have fully obeyed all the commands of
Jehonadab, our ancestor. 11But when King
Nebuchadnezzar of Babylon attacked this
country, we were afraid of the Babylonian
and Syrian armies. So we decided to move
to Jerusalem. That is why we are here."
12Then the LORD gave this message to
Jeremiah: 13"This is what the LORD of Heav-
en's Armies, the God of Israel, says: Go and
say to the people in Judah and Jerusalem,
'Come and learn a lesson about how to obey
me. 14The Recabites do not drink wine to
this day because their ancestor Jehonadab
told them not to. But I have spoken to you
again and again, and you refuse to obey me.
15Time after time I sent you prophets, who
told you, "Turn from your wicked ways, and
start doing things right. Stop worshiping
other gods so that you might live in peace
here in the land I have given to you and
your ancestors." But you would not listen
to me or obey me. 16The descendants of
Jehonadab son of Recab have obeyed their
ancestor completely, but you have refused
to listen to me.'
17"Therefore, this is what the LORD God of
Heaven's Armies, the God of Israel, says: 'Because you refuse to listen or answer when I
call, I will send upon Judah and Jerusalem
all the disasters I have threatened.' "
18Then Jeremiah turned to the Recabites
and said, "This is what the LORD of Heav-
en's Armies, the God of Israel, says: 'You
have obeyed your ancestor Jehonadab in
every respect, following all his instructions.' 19Therefore, this is what the LORD
of Heaven's Armies, the God of Israel, says:
'Jehonadab son of Recab will always have descendants who serve me.' "

Baruch Reads the LORD's Messages

36 During the fourth year that Jehoiakim son of Josiah was king in Judah,
the LORD gave this message to Jeremiah:
2"Get a scroll, and write down all my messages against Israel, Judah, and the other
nations. Begin with the first message back
in the days of Josiah, and write down every
message, right up to the present time. 3Per-
haps the people of Judah will repent when
they hear again all the terrible things I have
planned for them. Then I will be able to forgive their sins and wrongdoings."

35:4 1 Kgs 12:22; 1 Chr 9:18
35:5 Amos 2:12
35:6 Lev 10:9; 2 Kgs 10:15, 23; 1 Chr 2:55; Luke 1:15
35:7 Exod 20:12; Heb 11:9
35:8 Prov 4:1-2, 10; 6:20; Col 3:20
35:9 Ps 37:16; 1 Tim 6:6
35:11 2 Kgs 24:1-2; Dan 1:1-2
35:13 Isa 28:9-12
35:14 2 Chr 36:15; Isa 30:9
35:15 Deut 6:14; Jer 29:19; Ezek 18:30-32; Acts 26:20
35:16 Mal 1:6
35:17 Prov 1:24-25; Mic 3:12; Luke 13:34-35; Rom 10:21
35:18 Exod 20:12; Eph 6:1-3
35:19 Jer 15:19
36:1 Jer 25:1-3; 45:1
36:2 Jer 1:2-3, 5, 9-10; 25:9-29; Zech 5:1-2
36:3 Isa 55:7; Jer 18:8, 11; 26:3; Mark 4:12; Acts 3:19

35:3 The *Jeremiah* mentioned here was not the prophet; he and the others represented the *Recabite* community.

35:4 Jeremiah the prophet carefully described the location of the room in the Temple, taking note that *Hanan*, the man in charge, was ***a man of God***. During this idolatrous time in Judah's history, the prophet had some friends in high places who remained believers in the one true God.

35:6-10 ***Jehonadab*** (Hebrew *Jonadab*, a variant spelling of Jehonadab; also in 35:10, 14, 16, 18, 19; see 2 Kgs 10:15) had bound his descendants to a nomadic lifestyle free of the trappings of sedentary life, and the Recabites had been obedient.

35:11 ***Nebuchadnezzar:*** Hebrew *Nebuchadrezzar*, a variant spelling of Nebuchadnezzar. • ***Babylonian and Syrian:*** Or *Chaldean and Aramean.*

35:12-19 The Lord applied the Recabites' example in stark contrast to the people of Judah. The Recabites had been deprived of many good things in life, yet they remained obedient.

35:14-16 The Recabites never drank ***wine***, simply because their human ***ancestor*** had told them not to. The people of Israel should have been even more willing to listen and obey when the Lord told them to ***turn from*** their ***wicked ways*** and live according to his laws.

35:17-19 The Lord pronounced punishment on Judah's sin.

35:19 One of the ***descendants*** of ***Jehonadab son of Recab*** apparently returned from Babylon after the Exile and helped to rebuild the wall of Jerusalem (see Neh 3:14).

36:1-32 This description of Jehoiakim's cynical response to God's attempt to call him to repentance and covenant obedience (36:3, 7) graphically underscores the hopelessness of the situation. • Nowhere else does the OT provide this much detail about the process of preserving spoken messages in written form.

36:1-2 The ***fourth year*** of Jehoiakim's reign was 605 BC. This was the year Nebuchadnezzar first attacked Jerusalem (see note on Dan 1:1). • In those days, a ***scroll*** was a roll of papyrus or leather strips joined edge to edge and rolled up.

36:3 The Lord gave ***the people of Judah*** every opportunity to ***repent.*** God wanted the messages of judgment not just to alarm his people, but to awaken them to the judgment they would face if they did not turn from idol-worship. If they heeded the alarm, repented, and sincerely worshiped the one true God, he would ***forgive their sins and wrongdoings.***

36:4 Jer 32:12 Ezek 2:9
36:5 Jer 32:2
36:6 Zech 8:19
36:7 1 Kgs 8:33 2 Kgs 22:13 Jer 26:3 [i]*tekhinnah* (8467) ‣Dan 9:20
36:10 Jer 26:10

4 So Jeremiah sent for Baruch son of
Neriah, and as Jeremiah dictated all the
prophecies that the LORD had given him,
Baruch wrote them on a scroll. 5 Then Jeremiah said to Baruch, "I am a prisoner here
and unable to go to the Temple. 6 So you go
to the Temple on the next day of fasting,
and read the messages from the LORD that
I have had you write on this scroll. Read
them so the people who are there from all
over Judah will hear them. 7 Perhaps even
yet they will turn from their evil ways and
[i]ask the LORD's forgiveness before it is too
late. For the LORD has threatened them with
his terrible anger."
8 Baruch did as Jeremiah told him and
read these messages from the LORD to the
people at the Temple. 9 He did this on a day
of sacred fasting held in late autumn, during the fifth year of the reign of Jehoiakim
son of Josiah. People from all over Judah
had come to Jerusalem to attend the services at the Temple on that day. 10 Baruch
read Jeremiah's words on the scroll to all

Jer 30:2-3; 45:1; 51:60-64
Exod 17:14; 31:18; 34:27-28
Deut 31:9-13
Isa 30:8
Ezek 43:11
Dan 7:1
Luke 1:1-4
John 5:46-47; 20:30-31; 21:24-25
Acts 1:1-2
Rom 15:4
1 Cor 10:11
Phlm 1:21
2 Tim 3:16-17
Heb 13:22
1 Pet 5:12
2 Pet 1:20-21
1 Jn 1:4; 2:12-24; 5:13
Rev 1:11; 10:4; 21:5; 22:18-19

Writing Prophecy (36:1-32)

When Jeremiah's ministry was in crisis during his public trial in the Temple grounds (ch 26), friends saved his life, but he was banned from speaking. King Jehoiakim expressed his anger by having the prophet Uriah killed and by sending officers to arrest Jeremiah. Would this signal the end of Jeremiah's public ministry? Was oral delivery of the Lord's messages the only way to get the divine word to the leaders and people of Judah?

Killing and silencing prophets did not stop divine messages from the Lord—the Lord's word could be broadcast effectively in writing. The Lord told the prophet to write down all the messages he had ever delivered (ch 36). Jeremiah had a helper, Baruch, who was skilled in writing messages on papyrus (an ancient form of paper) and making as many copies as were needed. While Jeremiah and Baruch were in hiding, they purchased a scroll (a roll of papyrus) and prepared it to receive the written messages. When the writing was finished, the scroll was read in the Temple courtyard and in the presence of King Jehoiakim. The king cut up the scroll and burned it, but Jeremiah wrote the messages again on a new scroll, adding new material. Throughout the remainder of Jeremiah's ministry, he had his messages written on papyrus and sent to the leaders of various countries, as well as to the exiles in Babylon.

The earliest example of writing the word of God appears in Exodus, where Moses was commanded to write down the words of the covenant (Exod 24:4, but see also Exod 17:14). It is specifically stated that Moses wrote the entire book of Deuteronomy (Deut 31:9, 24). The existence of the written book of the Law probably stimulated a tradition of writing down certain elements of what God was revealing (Josh 24:26; 1 Sam 10:25; 1 Chr 29:29; 2 Chr 9:29; Isa 8:16-17; 30:8). Many of Israel's historical writings are said to have been kept by prophets (see 2 Chr 12:15; 13:22).

These written documents, especially those written on leather scrolls, were kept in communities for a long time, and many copies were made from one document. These copies were so valuable that they were carefully preserved for centuries. The copies were also translated into any number of languages. The book of Jeremiah and the writings of other prophets, wise men, and teachers have been preserved, collected, and handed down to us as the Old and New Testaments, giving us a written record of God's messages to his people long ago (see 2 Tim 3:16-17; 2 Pet 1:20-21).

36:4 Evidently, Jeremiah was not skilled in writing, so he enlisted the services of a scribe named ***Baruch***. As they sat in their private quarters, ***Jeremiah*** repeated message after message from memory. It is not known whether Baruch had a role in composition or arrangement, or whether he simply recorded exactly what Jeremiah dictated.

36:5 ***Jeremiah*** was either ***a prisoner*** under house arrest, or he had been banished from ***the Temple*** grounds.

36:6 The ***next day of fasting*** was a national festival, but it is not clear which one (none of the annual festivals occurred in the ninth month; see note on 36:8-9). Reading the written scroll to the multitude gathered in the ***Temple*** would have placed Baruch in danger of arrest or assault.

36:7 Jeremiah repeated the purpose for writing the scroll (36:3) and reading it in public. • ***Perhaps . . . turn from their evil ways:*** The people could still receive the Lord's ***forgiveness*** and avert his ***anger***.

36:8-9 Baruch filled the columns of the scroll with Jeremiah's messages from the Lord. Finally, a day of fasting was announced toward the end of 604 BC. Baruch faithfully obeyed Jeremiah's order to read the scroll in the ***Temple***, where many people crowded the courtyard. • ***in late autumn:*** Literally ***in the ninth month*** of the ancient Hebrew lunar calendar (also in 36:22). The ninth month in the fifth year of Jehoiakim's reign occurred within the months of November and December 604 BC. See also note on 1:3. Israel had no traditional recurring festival during the ninth month, so apparently another ***day of sacred fasting*** had been scheduled.

36:10 ***Baruch . . . stood in front of the Temple room of Gemariah:*** That is,

the people. He stood in front of the Temple room of Gemariah, son of Shaphan the
secretary. This room was just off the upper
courtyard of the Temple, near the New Gate
entrance.
11When Micaiah son of Gemariah and
grandson of Shaphan heard the messages
from the LORD, 12he went down to the
secretary's room in the palace where the
administrative officials were meeting. Elishama the secretary was there, along with
Delaiah son of Shemaiah, Elnathan son of
Acbor, Gemariah son of Shaphan, Zedekiah
son of Hananiah, and all the other officials.
13When Micaiah told them about the messages Baruch was reading to the people,
14the officials sent Jehudi son of Nethaniah,
grandson of Shelemiah and great-grandson
of Cushi, to ask Baruch to come and read
the messages to them, too. So Baruch took
the scroll and went to them. 15"Sit down
and read the scroll to us," the officials said,
and Baruch did as they requested.
16When they heard all the messages, they
looked at one another in alarm. "We must
tell the king what we have heard," they said
to Baruch. 17"But first, tell us how you got
these messages. Did they come directly
from Jeremiah?"
18So Baruch explained, "Jeremiah dictated them, and I wrote them down in ink,
word for word, on this scroll."
19"You and Jeremiah should both hide,"
the officials told Baruch. "Don't tell anyone
where you are!" 20Then the officials left the
scroll for safekeeping in the room of Elishama the secretary and went to tell the king
what had happened.

King Jehoiakim Burns the Scroll

21The king sent Jehudi to get the scroll. Jehudi brought it from Elishama's room and
read it to the king as all his officials stood
by. 22It was late autumn, and the king was
in a winterized part of the palace, sitting in
front of a fire to keep warm. 23Each time
Jehudi finished reading three or four columns, the king took a knife and cut off that
section of the scroll. He then threw it into
the fire, section by section, until the whole
scroll was burned up. 24Neither the king
nor his attendants showed any signs of fear
or repentance at what they heard. 25Even
when Elnathan, Delaiah, and Gemariah
begged the king not to burn the scroll, he
wouldn't listen.
26Then the king commanded his son
Jerahmeel, Seraiah son of Azriel, and Shelemiah son of Abdeel to arrest Baruch and
Jeremiah. But the LORD had hidden them.

Jeremiah Rewrites the Scroll

27After the king had burned the scroll
on which Baruch had written Jeremiah's
words, the LORD gave Jeremiah another
message. He said, 28"Get another scroll, and
write everything again just as you did on
the scroll King Jehoiakim burned. 29Then
say to the king, 'This is what the LORD says:
You burned the scroll because it said the
king of Babylon would destroy this land
and empty it of people and animals. 30Now
this is what the LORD says about King Jehoiakim of Judah: He will have no heirs to sit
on the throne of David. His dead body will
be thrown out to lie unburied—exposed to
the heat of the day and the frost of the night.
31I will punish him and his family and his

36:12 Jer 26:22
36:13-15 2 Kgs 22:9-10
36:16 Amos 7:10-11; Acts 24:25
36:18 Jer 36:4
36:19 1 Kgs 17:3; 18:4; Jer 26:20-24
36:21 2 Kgs 22:9-10; 2 Chr 34:18; Ezek 2:4-5
36:22 Amos 3:15
36:23 Prov 1:29-30; Isa 5:18-19; 28:14, 22
36:24 2 Kgs 19:1-2; Ps 36:1; Acts 5:34-39
36:26 1 Kgs 19:1-3, 10, 14; Jer 15:20-21
36:28 Jer 28:13-14; Zech 1:5-6
36:29 Deut 29:19; Isa 30:10-11; 45:9; Jer 25:8-11; 26:9
36:30 2 Kgs 24:12-15; Jer 22:30
36:31 Deut 28:15-19; Prov 29:1; Jer 19:15

Baruch obtained permission from this high official to read to the public. This elevated location ***near the New Gate entrance*** was close to where Jeremiah's public trial had taken place a few years earlier (26:10). • ***Gemariah*** had a godly heritage. His father, ***Shaphan,*** had participated in Josiah's reading of the scrolls found in the Temple (2 Kgs 22:8-10).

36:11-13 ***Micaiah*** realized the importance of ***the messages from the LORD*** that Baruch was reading, so he made sure that the ***administrative officials*** of the palace knew what was being said.

36:14-16 The palace ***officials*** acted quickly. When they heard ***Baruch*** reading Jeremiah's messages, they were terrified and decided to report the situation to the king.

36:17-18 The officials wanted to know the source of the ***scroll*** and its ***messages.***

36:19-20 The officials showed their respect for Jeremiah and Baruch by advising that they ***should both hide;*** they showed their respect for the Lord's messages by placing the scroll in ***safekeeping*** while they went to inform the king.

36:21 ***Jehudi*** was well educated, and was perhaps a scribe. Only the elite were trained to read and write.

36:23-24 Jehoiakim was so antagonistic and hardened that after ***three or four columns*** of the scroll were read, he cut off the ***section*** with a sharp ***knife*** and ***threw it into the fire.*** Jehoiakim's father, Josiah, had responded very differently when the newly discovered Book of the Law was read to him (2 Kgs 22:11).

36:25 The three officials who ***begged the king*** not to destroy ***the scroll*** probably held positions of great power, because Jehoiakim did not punish them for trying to preserve Jeremiah's scroll.

36:26 Once ***the LORD had hidden them,*** no one betrayed Jeremiah and Baruch. The Lord can protect his servants.

36:27-32 While in hiding, Jeremiah and Baruch rewrote all the messages that had been recorded on the destroyed scroll onto a new roll of papyrus. No human king can destroy God's words. Instead, Jehoiakim was brought before God's court and sentenced to death.

36:29-31 To die without ***heirs*** or a decent burial was to suffer the worst imaginable fate (see 22:19 and note; Eccl 6:3). Jehoiakim's son Jehoiachin ruled for just three months. Unlike his father, Jehoiachin took Jeremiah's warning seriously and surrendered to the Babylonians, who took him and others to Babylon as captives (22:24-30; 2 Kgs 24:8-16).

attendants for their sins. I will pour out on them and on all the people of Jerusalem and Judah all the disasters I promised, for they would not listen to my warnings.' "

32So Jeremiah took another scroll and dictated again to his secretary, Baruch. He wrote everything that had been on the scroll King Jehoiakim had burned in the fire. Only this time he added much more!

Zedekiah Calls for Jeremiah

37 Zedekiah son of Josiah succeeded Jehoiachin son of Jehoiakim as the king of Judah. He was appointed by King Nebuchadnezzar of Babylon. 2But neither King Zedekiah nor his attendants nor the people who were left in the land listened to what the LORD said through Jeremiah.

3Nevertheless, King Zedekiah sent Jehucal son of Shelemiah, and Zephaniah the priest, son of Maaseiah, to ask Jeremiah, "Please pray to the LORD our God for us." 4Jeremiah had not yet been imprisoned, so he could come and go among the people as he pleased.

5At this time the army of Pharaoh Hophra of Egypt appeared at the southern border of Judah. When the Babylonian army heard about it, they withdrew from their siege of Jerusalem.

6Then the LORD gave this message to Jeremiah: 7"This is what the LORD, the God of Israel, says: The king of Judah sent you to ask me what is going to happen. Tell him, 'Pharaoh's army is about to return to Egypt, though he came here to help you. 8Then the Babylonians will come back and capture this city and burn it to the ground.'

9"This is what the LORD says: Do not fool yourselves into thinking that the Babylonians are gone for good. They aren't! 10Even if you were to destroy the entire Babylonian army, leaving only a handful of wounded survivors, they would still stagger from their tents and burn this city to the ground!"

Jeremiah Is Imprisoned

11When the Babylonian army left Jerusalem because of Pharaoh's approaching army, 12Jeremiah started to leave the city on his way to the territory of Benjamin, to claim his share of the property among his relatives there. 13But as he was walking through the Benjamin Gate, a sentry arrested him and said, "You are defecting to the Babylonians!" The sentry making the arrest was Irijah son of Shelemiah, grandson of Hananiah.

14"That's not true!" Jeremiah protested. "I had no intention of doing any such thing." But Irijah wouldn't listen, and he took Jeremiah before the officials. 15They were furious with Jeremiah and had him flogged and imprisoned in the house of Jonathan the secretary. Jonathan's house had been converted into a prison. 16Jeremiah was put into a dungeon cell, where he remained for many days.

17Later King Zedekiah secretly requested that Jeremiah come to the palace, where the king asked him, "Do you have any messages from the LORD?"

"Yes, I do!" said Jeremiah. "You will be defeated by the king of Babylon."

18Then Jeremiah asked the king, "What crime have I committed? What have I done against you, your attendants, or the people that I should be imprisoned like this? 19Where are your prophets now who told

36:32 Exod 34:1
37:1 2 Kgs 24:17; 1 Chr 3:15-16; 2 Chr 36:9-10; Jer 22:24, 28; Ezek 17:12-21
37:2 2 Kgs 24:18-20; 2 Chr 36:12; Prov 29:12
37:3 Jer 2:26-27; 21:1-2; 52:24
37:5 Ezek 17:15-16
37:7 Isa 30:1-3; 31:1-3; Jer 21:1-2; Ezek 17:17
37:8 Jer 34:22
37:9 Jer 29:8; Obad 1:3; Eph 5:6
37:10 Lev 26:36-38; Isa 30:17; Joel 2:11
37:12 Jer 32:8
37:13 Jer 18:18; 20:10; Zech 14:10; Acts 24:5-9, 13
37:14 Ps 27:12; Jer 40:4-6; Matt 5:11-12
37:15 Jer 18:23; 38:6; Matt 21:35; Acts 5:18; Heb 11:36
37:17 Jer 21:7; 38:14-16, 24-27; Ezek 12:12-13; 17:19-21
37:18 1 Sam 24:9; 26:18; John 10:32; Acts 25:8, 10-11
37:19 Deut 32:37-38

37:1–38:28 The focus now returns to Zedekiah, who succeeded his nephew Jehoiachin as king of Judah. These chapters record encounters between Zedekiah and Jeremiah that make plain Zedekiah's inability to commit himself wholeheartedly to God's word (cp. Deut 10:12-13). Zedekiah is a classic example of a "person with divided loyalty" (Jas 1:6-8).

37:1-2 These verses summarize Zedekiah's reign and his entire response to the Lord's messages through Jeremiah.

37:1 ***Jehoiachin:*** Hebrew *Coniah,* a variant spelling of Jehoiachin. • ***Nebuchadnezzar:*** Hebrew *Nebuchadrezzar,* a variant spelling of Nebuchadnezzar.

37:3-4 In asking for prayer, ***Zedekiah*** apparently hoped that Jeremiah's petitions would magically defeat the enemy (see 14:7-9 and note).

37:5 The Babylonians began their ***siege of Jerusalem*** in 588 BC (see note on 52:4). But they left Jerusalem because ***the army of Pharaoh Hophra*** (literally *the army of Pharaoh;* see 44:30) was coming to help ***Judah.*** The Babylonians hoped to block and defeat the Egyptians, which they did. • ***Babylonian:*** Or *Chaldean;* also in 37:10, 11.

37:6-10 The Lord answered Jeremiah's prayer (37:3) with a warning for Zedekiah. The Egyptians would provide no lasting help, and the Babylonians would return to destroy Jerusalem—a prophecy that was fulfilled in 586 BC.

37:8 ***Babylonians:*** Or *Chaldeans;* also in 37:9, 13.

37:11-12 When the Babylonians went to face the Egyptians, Jeremiah decided to walk three miles north to his hometown, Anathoth, ***to claim his share of the property among his relatives there*** (literally *to separate from there in the midst of the people*). He wanted to see his newly purchased property (32:1-25).

37:13-16 ***The sentry*** and other ***officials*** of Judah misinterpreted Jeremiah's action as desertion.

37:17 By asking Jeremiah about other ***messages from the LORD,*** the king indicated that he was fearful of the future and still hoped that the Lord would defeat the Babylonians. Jeremiah answered quickly and emphatically that there was no hope for the kind of divine intervention that had destroyed the Assyrian army during Hezekiah's reign (2 Kgs 19:8-37).

37:18-20 Jeremiah evidently assumed that Zedekiah was involved in his arrest and imprisonment. The prophet would have been in poor physical condition after being flogged and confined without medical treatment and with little food.

you the king of Babylon would not attack
you or this land? 20Listen, my lord the king,
I beg you. Don't send me back to the dungeon in the house of Jonathan the secretary,
for I will die there."
21So King Zedekiah commanded that
Jeremiah not be returned to the dungeon.
Instead, he was imprisoned in the courtyard of the guard in the royal palace. The
king also commanded that Jeremiah be
given a loaf of fresh bread every day as long
as there was any left in the city. So Jeremiah
was put in the palace prison.

Jeremiah in a Cistern

38 Now Shephatiah son of Mattan, Gedaliah son of Pashhur, Jehucal son of
Shelemiah, and Pashhur son of Malkijah
heard what Jeremiah had been telling the
people. He had been saying, 2"This is what
the LORD says: 'Everyone who stays in Jerusalem will die from war, famine, or disease,
but those who surrender to the Babylonians
will live. Their reward will be life. They will
live!' 3The LORD also says: 'The city of Jerusalem will certainly be handed over to the
army of the king of Babylon, who will capture it.' "
4So these officials went to the king and
said, "Sir, this man must die! That kind of
talk will undermine the morale of the few
fighting men we have left, as well as that of
all the people. This man is a traitor!"
5King Zedekiah agreed. "All right," he
said. "Do as you like. I can't stop you."
6So the officials took Jeremiah from his
cell and lowered him by ropes into an empty
cistern in the prison yard. It belonged to
Malkijah, a member of the royal family.
There was no water in the cistern, but there
was a thick layer of mud at the bottom, and
Jeremiah sank down into it.
7But Ebed-melech the Ethiopian, an important court official, heard that Jeremiah
was in the cistern. At that time the king
was holding court at the Benjamin Gate,
8so Ebed-melech rushed from the palace
to speak with him. 9"My lord the king," he
said, "these men have done a very evil thing
in putting Jeremiah the prophet into the cistern. He will soon die of hunger, for almost
all the bread in the city is gone."
10So the king told Ebed-melech, "Take
thirty of my men with you, and pull Jeremiah out of the cistern before he dies."
11So Ebed-melech took the men with him
and went to a room in the palace beneath
the treasury, where he found some old rags
and discarded clothing. He carried these to
the cistern and lowered them to Jeremiah
on a rope. 12Ebed-melech called down to Jeremiah, "Put these rags under your armpits
to protect you from the ropes." Then when
Jeremiah was ready, 13they pulled him out.
So Jeremiah was returned to the courtyard
of the guard—the palace prison—where he
remained.

Zedekiah Questions Jeremiah

14One day King Zedekiah sent for Jeremiah
and had him brought to the third entrance
of the LORD's Temple. "I want to ask you
something," the king said. "And don't try to
hide the truth."
15Jeremiah said, "If I tell you the truth,
you will kill me. And if I give you advice, you
won't listen to me anyway."

37:20 Jer 38:26
37:21 Job 5:20; Ps 33:18-19; Isa 33:16; Jer 52:6
38:1 Jer 21:8
38:2 Jer 21:9; 42:17
38:3 Jer 21:10; 32:3-5
38:4 1 Kgs 18:17-18; Jer 26:11; Amos 7:10; Acts 16:20-21
38:5 2 Sam 3:39
38:6 Ps 40:2; 69:1-2, 14; Jer 37:15-16; Zech 9:11; Acts 16:24
38:9 Jer 37:21; 52:6
38:13 Jer 37:21; 39:14-15
38:14 1 Kgs 22:16; Jer 21:1-2; 37:17
38:15 Luke 22:67-68

37:21 The king defied his officials and ordered the guards to keep Jeremiah ***in the courtyard of the guard in the royal palace*** under protective custody. Considering the scarcity of food during the long siege, ***a loaf of fresh bread every day*** was a generous ration.

38:1-13 Jeremiah was free to talk to people while he was in the prison courtyard. He repeated the Lord's decrees of judgment, but this stirred fierce anger among some of the government officials. Zedekiah showed his cowardice by letting these men put Jeremiah in a muddy cistern; the king also had a courageous moment when he permitted a palace servant to rescue Jeremiah and return him to the palace prison.

38:1 The ***Gedaliah*** mentioned here had a different father than the Gedaliah in 40:6. • The first ***Pashhur*** might have been the man in 20:1. The second ***Pashhur*** had a different father. • ***Jehucal:*** Hebrew *Jucal,* a variant spelling of Jehucal; see 37:3.

38:2 ***Babylonians:*** Or *Chaldeans;* also in 38:18, 19, 23.

38:4 The ***officials*** apparently believed that the ***morale*** of the ***men*** resisting the Babylonian army outside the walls of the city would be harmed if Jeremiah continued to prophesy, so they put him on trial for treason.

38:5 When the officials angrily confronted ***King Zedekiah*** and made their demands, he was weak and cowardly.

38:6 In the presence of everyone in the palace courtyard, Jeremiah was thrown into ***an empty cistern.*** At the bottom was ***a thick layer of mud*** that slowly enveloped Jeremiah's body.

38:7-8 ***the Ethiopian*** (Hebrew *the Cushite;* cp. Luke 17:18; Acts 28:28): Jeremiah's rescuer was not from Judah; he was a foreigner who dared to defy the other officials. He ran to the ***Benjamin Gate,*** where Jeremiah was first arrested (37:11-13), and rushed into the king's presence without ceremony.

38:10 The rescue party included ***thirty . . . men,*** perhaps indicating that Zedekiah felt the need to keep his officials from attacking it.

38:11-12 ***Ebed-melech,*** the Ethiopian rescuer (38:7), was a caring person who wanted to protect Jeremiah's weakened body as much as possible.

38:14-16 Zedekiah so desperately wanted a miracle to save his kingdom from the attacking Babylonian armies that he arranged a secret meeting with Jeremiah.

38:14 The location of ***the third entrance of the LORD's Temple*** is not known. The gates of the Temple had small rooms nearby, so the private meeting probably took place in one of them.

38:16 Isa 42:5; Jer 37:17
38:17 2 Kgs 25:27-30; Ps 80:7, 14; Jer 21:8-10; 27:12, 17
38:18 2 Kgs 25:4-10; Jer 27:8; 37:8
38:19 Isa 51:12-13; 57:11; Jer 39:9; John 12:42
38:20 Isa 55:3; Jer 7:23; 11:4, 8; 26:13
38:22 Jer 6:12; 8:10; 43:6
38:23 2 Kgs 25:7; Jer 39:6; 41:10
38:26 Jer 37:15-16, 20
38:27 1 Sam 10:15-16; 16:2-5
38:28 Ps 23:4; Jer 37:20-21; 39:13-14
39:1-7 //Jer 52:4-11
39:1 2 Kgs 25:1-12
39:2 2 Kgs 25:4; Jer 52:7
39:3 Jer 21:3-4
39:4 2 Kgs 25:4; Isa 30:15-16; Jer 52:7; Amos 2:14

16So King Zedekiah secretly promised
him, "As surely as the LORD our Creator
lives, I will not kill you or hand you over to
the men who want you dead."
17Then Jeremiah said to Zedekiah, "This
is what the LORD God of Heaven's Armies,
the God of Israel, says: 'If you surrender to
the Babylonian officers, you and your family will live, and the city will not be burned
down. 18But if you refuse to surrender, you
will not escape! This city will be handed
over to the Babylonians, and they will burn
it to the ground.' "
19"But I am afraid to surrender," the king
said, "for the Babylonians may hand me over
to the Judeans who have defected to them.
And who knows what they will do to me!"
20Jeremiah replied, "You won't be handed
over to them if you choose to obey the LORD.
Your life will be spared, and all will go well
for you. 21But if you refuse to surrender,
this is what the LORD has revealed to me:
22All the women left in your palace will
be brought out and given to the officers of
the Babylonian army. Then the women will
taunt you, saying,

'What fine friends you have!
  They have betrayed and misled you.
When your feet sank in the mud,
  they left you to your fate!'

23All your wives and children will be led out
to the Babylonians, and you will not escape.
You will be seized by the king of Babylon,
and this city will be burned down."
24Then Zedekiah said to Jeremiah, "Don't
tell anyone you told me this, or you will die!
25My officials may hear that I spoke to you,
and they may say, 'Tell us what you and the
king were talking about. If you don't tell us,
we will kill you.' 26If this happens, just tell
them you begged me not to send you back
to Jonathan's dungeon, for fear you would
die there."
27Sure enough, it wasn't long before the
king's officials came to Jeremiah and asked
him why the king had called for him. But Jeremiah followed the king's instructions, and
they left without finding out the truth. No
one had overheard the conversation between
Jeremiah and the king. 28And Jeremiah remained a prisoner in the courtyard of the
guard until the day Jerusalem was captured.

The Fall of Jerusalem
Jer 39:1-10 // Jer 52:3b-16 // 2 Kgs 24:20b–25:12

39 In January of the ninth year of
King Zedekiah's reign, King Nebuchadnezzar came with his army to besiege
Jerusalem. 2Two and a half years later, on
July 18 in the eleventh year of Zedekiah's
reign, the Babylonians broke through the
wall, and the city fell. 3All the officers of
the Babylonian army came in and sat in triumph at the Middle Gate: Nergal-sharezer
of Samgar, and Nebo-sarsekim, a chief officer, and Nergal-sharezer, the king's adviser,
and all the other officers.
4When King Zedekiah and all the soldiers
saw that the Babylonians had broken into
the city, they fled. They waited for nightfall
and then slipped through the gate between
the two walls behind the king's garden and
headed toward the Jordan Valley.

38:17-18 Jeremiah laid out the Lord's decree. Zedekiah could save the city by surrendering or he could watch as it was destroyed by the invaders.

38:19 Zedekiah still feared his fellow countrymen—this time, those who had *defected*—more than he feared the Lord or the *Babylonians*, so he rejected Jeremiah's advice. This was Jeremiah's last message to the king.

38:20-22 Jeremiah reassured Zedekiah that everything would *go well* if Zedekiah chose *to obey the LORD.* If he refused, even his *friends* would abandon him.

38:24-28 When Zedekiah's fear of his *officials* surfaced again, he demanded that Jeremiah keep secret what he had told the king. • The officials might have suspected that Zedekiah was about to surrender to the enemy. Jeremiah obeyed the king's order to keep quiet, and he spent the final days of the siege in the palace prison under the king's protection.

39:1-10 Just as Jeremiah had predicted (34:1-7), the Lord's judgment fell on Zedekiah and the kingdom of Judah. For other accounts of this event, see 52:4-16; 2 Kgs 25:1-21; 2 Chr 36:11-21; Ezek 24:1-14.

39:1 ***In January:*** Literally *in the tenth month* of the ancient Hebrew lunar calendar. A number of events in Jeremiah can be cross-checked with dates in surviving Babylonian records and related accurately to our modern calendar. This event occurred on January 15, 588 BC; see 52:4 and note. • ***Nebuchadnezzar:*** Hebrew *Nebuchadrezzar,* a variant spelling of Nebuchadnezzar; also in 39:11.

39:2 The Babylonian siege took a long time because the stone walls of Jerusalem were thick and their resistance was strong. • ***Two and a half years later, on July 18:*** Literally *On the ninth day of the fourth month.* This day was July 18, 586 BC; also see note on 39:1.

39:3 High ranking *officers* came into the city to oversee its destruction and *sat in triumph at the Middle Gate,* showing how important this victory was to the Babylonians. According to custom, victorious officials positioned themselves at one of the gates, since judicial and administrative matters were controlled at gateways. • ***Nergal-sharezer of Samgar, and Nebo-sarsekim:*** Or *Nergal-sharezer, Samgar-nebo, Sarsekim.*

39:4 The steep slopes of the Kidron Valley on the east side and the Ben-Hinnom Valley on the west and south sides of Jerusalem forced the Babylonian army to concentrate their men to the north. This made it possible for Zedekiah, his family, and his officials to slip out of the south end of the city, cross the Kidron Valley, and travel up and over the Mount of Olives. Although they made this move after *nightfall,* the noise of their departure alerted Babylonian sentries, and soldiers were soon chasing them. • ***the Jordan Valley:*** Hebrew *the Arabah.*

5But the Babylonian troops chased the
king and caught him on the plains of Jericho.
They took him to King Nebuchadnezzar of
Babylon, who was at Riblah in the land of Hamath. There the king of Babylon pronounced
judgment upon Zedekiah. 6He made Zedekiah watch as they slaughtered his sons and
all the nobles of Judah. 7Then they gouged
out Zedekiah's eyes, bound him in bronze
chains, and led him away to Babylon.
8Meanwhile, the Babylonians burned Jerusalem, including the palace, and tore down
the walls of the city. 9Then Nebuzaradan,
the captain of the guard, sent to Babylon the
rest of the people who remained in the city
as well as those who had defected to him.
10But Nebuzaradan left a few of the poorest
people in Judah, and he assigned them vineyards and fields to care for.

Jeremiah Remains in Judah

11King Nebuchadnezzar had told Nebuzaradan, the captain of the guard, to find
Jeremiah. 12"See that he isn't hurt," he said.
"Look after him well, and give him anything
he wants." 13So Nebuzaradan, the captain
of the guard; Nebushazban, a chief officer;
Nergal-sharezer, the king's adviser; and the
other officers of Babylon's king 14sent messengers to bring Jeremiah out of the prison.
They put him under the care of Gedaliah
son of Ahikam and grandson of Shaphan,
who took him back to his home. So Jeremiah
stayed in Judah among his own people.

A Message for Ebed-melech

15The LORD had given the following message to Jeremiah while he was still in
prison: 16"Say to Ebed-melech the Ethiopian, 'This is what the LORD of Heaven's
Armies, the God of Israel, says: I will do
to this city everything I have threatened. I
will send disaster, not prosperity. You will
see its destruction, 17but I will rescue you
from those you fear so much. 18Because
you trusted me, I will give you your life as a
reward. I will rescue you and keep you safe.
I, the LORD, have spoken!' "

8. AFTER THE DESTRUCTION OF JERUSALEM (40:1–44:30)

A Message for Jeremiah

40 The LORD gave a message to Jeremiah after Nebuzaradan, the captain
of the guard, had released him at Ramah. He
had found Jeremiah bound in chains among
all the other captives of Jerusalem and Judah
who were being sent to exile in Babylon.
2The captain of the guard called for Jeremiah and said, "The LORD your God has
brought this disaster on this land, 3just as he
said he would. For these people have sinned
against the LORD and disobeyed him. That
is why it happened. 4But I am going to take
off your chains and let you go. If you want to
come with me to Babylon, you are welcome.
I will see that you are well cared for. But if
you don't want to come, you may stay here.
The whole land is before you—go wherever
you like. 5If you decide to stay, then return
to Gedaliah son of Ahikam and grandson of
Shaphan. He has been appointed governor
of Judah by the king of Babylon. Stay there
with the people he rules. But it's up to you;
go wherever you like."
Then Nebuzaradan, the captain of the
guard, gave Jeremiah some food and money and let him go. 6So Jeremiah returned to
Gedaliah son of Ahikam at Mizpah, and he
lived in Judah with the few who were still
left in the land.

Gedaliah Governs in Judah

Jer 40:7-9 // 2 Kgs 25:22-24

7The leaders of the Judean guerrilla bands
in the countryside heard that the king of

39:5 Jer 32:4-5; 52:8-9 Lam 4:20
39:6 Jer 24:8-10; 34:18-21; 52:10
39:7 2 Kgs 25:7 Jer 52:11 Ezek 12:13
39:8 2 Kgs 25:9-10 Neh 1:3
39:9 2 Kgs 25:11, 20 Jer 52:12-16, 26
39:10 2 Kgs 25:12
39:11 Job 5:15-16 Jer 1:8; 15:20-21
39:12 1 Pet 3:13
39:14 2 Kgs 22:12, 14 Jer 26:24; 40:1-6
39:16 Jer 21:10 Zech 1:6
39:17 Ps 41:1-2; 50:14-15
39:18 Ps 34:22 Jer 17:7-8 Rom 10:11
40:1 Eph 6:20
40:2 Deut 29:24-28 Jer 22:8-9; 50:7
40:3 Dan 9:11
40:4 Gen 20:15 Jer 39:11-12
40:5 2 Kgs 25:23
40:6 Jer 39:14
40:7 2 Kgs 25:23-24 Jer 39:10; 52:16

39:5 Zedekiah and his royal party fled on foot, so it was not difficult for strong and healthy soldiers to capture the group near ***Jericho.*** The enemy troops then forced their captives to walk (see note on 39:9) more than 200 miles north to ***Riblah***, where ***King Nebuchadnezzar*** had his field headquarters. • ***Babylonian:*** Or *Chaldean;* similarly in 39:8.

39:6 Zedekiah's last sight was the slaughter of ***his sons and all the nobles of Judah.*** Their slaughter ensured that Zedekiah's rule could never continue.

39:7 After the soldiers ***gouged out Zedekiah's eyes,*** he had to walk 400 miles to ***Babylon,*** blinded, in great pain, and with his arms ***in bronze chains.***

39:9 ***sent to Babylon the rest of the people:*** The usual practice in that time was to tie a person's hands together, and then tie him or her to the person in front, making a long line of grief-stricken captives.

39:11–44:30 These chapters describe the events that followed the destruction of Jerusalem, especially as they affected Jeremiah.

39:11-14 It is not fully known how Jeremiah and his urging the king to surrender to Babylon came to Nebuchadnezzar's attention. Perhaps it was through the messages that Jeremiah sent to the exiles (ch 29; see 40:2-3).

39:15-17 ***Ebed-melech*** had saved Jeremiah from death in the muddy cistern (38:7-13). This promise was a solemn decree (see note on 2:2).

39:16 ***the Ethiopian:*** Hebrew *the Cushite.*

40:1-6 This passage provides some details about what happened to Jeremiah immediately after the fall of Jerusalem.

40:2-3 ***The captain of the guard*** quoted the prediction of ***the LORD*** through Jeremiah that had now been fulfilled.

40:6 Gedaliah's new headquarters were in ***Mizpah***, eight miles north of the ruined Jerusalem.

40:7-12 The new government was organized under Gedaliah, who belonged to a family of high rank. His grandfather Shaphan had taken King

40:8 Jer 41:1
40:9 2 Kgs 25:24; Jer 27:11
40:10 Jer 35:19; 39:10
40:11 1 Sam 11:1; Isa 11:14; 16:4-5
40:12 Jer 43:5
40:13 2 Kgs 25:23; Jer 41:10
40:15 1 Sam 26:8; 2 Sam 21:17; Jer 42:1-2
40:16 Matt 10:16
41:1 2 Kgs 25:25; Jer 39:14; 40:5-8, 13-14
41:2 2 Sam 3:27; 20:8-10; Ps 41:9; 109:5; John 13:18
41:5 Deut 14:1; Josh 18:1; 1 Kgs 16:24; Ps 78:60; Jer 16:6

Babylon had appointed Gedaliah son of Ahikam as governor over the poor people who were left behind in Judah—the men, women, and children who hadn't been exiled to Babylon. 8So they went to see Gedaliah at Mizpah. These included: Ishmael son of Nethaniah, Johanan and Jonathan sons of Kareah, Seraiah son of Tanhumeth, the sons of Ephai the Netophathite, Jezaniah son of the Maacathite, and all their men.

9Gedaliah vowed to them that the Babylonians meant them no harm. "Don't be afraid to serve them. Live in the land and serve the king of Babylon, and all will go well for you," he promised. 10"As for me, I will stay at Mizpah to represent you before the Babylonians who come to meet with us. Settle in the towns you have taken, and live off the land. Harvest the grapes and summer fruits and olives, and store them away."

11When the Judeans in Moab, Ammon, Edom, and the other nearby countries heard that the king of Babylon had left a few people in Judah and that Gedaliah was the governor, 12they began to return to Judah from the places to which they had fled. They stopped at Mizpah to meet with Gedaliah and then went into the Judean countryside to gather a great harvest of grapes and other crops.

A Plot against Gedaliah

13Soon after this, Johanan son of Kareah and the other guerrilla leaders came to Gedaliah at Mizpah. 14They said to him, "Did you know that Baalis, king of Ammon, has sent Ishmael son of Nethaniah to assassinate you?" But Gedaliah refused to believe them.

15Later Johanan had a private conference with Gedaliah and volunteered to kill Ishmael secretly. "Why should we let him come and murder you?" Johanan asked. "What will happen then to the Judeans who have returned? Why should the few of us who are still left be scattered and lost?"

16But Gedaliah said to Johanan, "I forbid you to do any such thing, for you are lying about Ishmael."

The Murder of Gedaliah

Jer 41:1-3, 17-18 // 2 Kgs 25:25-26

41 But in midautumn, Ishmael son of Nethaniah and grandson of Elishama, who was a member of the royal family and had been one of the king's high officials, went to Mizpah with ten men to meet Gedaliah. While they were eating together, 2Ishmael and his ten men suddenly jumped up, drew their swords, and killed Gedaliah, whom the king of Babylon had appointed governor. 3Ishmael also killed all the Judeans and the Babylonian soldiers who were with Gedaliah at Mizpah.

4The next day, before anyone had heard about Gedaliah's murder, 5eighty men arrived from Shechem, Shiloh, and Samaria

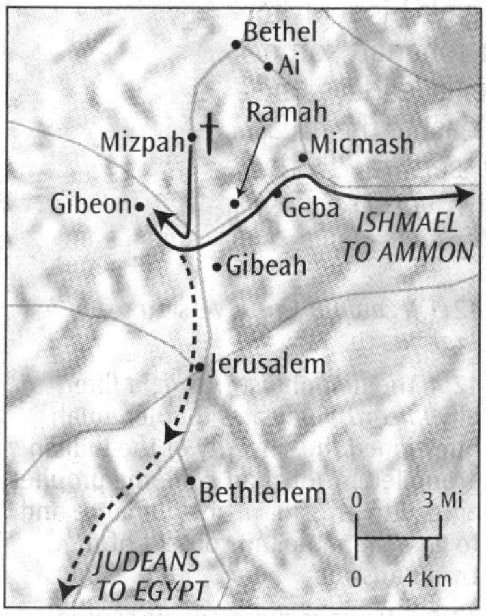

Gedaliah Is Assassinated, 586 BC (Jer 40:7–41:18; see also 2 Kgs 25:22-26). After the destruction of JERUSALEM, Gedaliah made MIZPAH his headquarters. Here Ishmael murdered him (†) and many others, including those on a pilgrimage from the north (41:5-8). Ishmael and his company (solid lines) took their prisoners toward GIBEON, then fled eastward TO AMMON. The people of Judah, fearing the Babylonians, exiled themselves TO EGYPT (dotted line).

Josiah the scroll of the law that sparked reformation (2 Kgs 22:10). Gedaliah's father, Ahikam, had held a high post in Jehoiakim's close circle of officials, and he had saved Jeremiah's life (26:24).

40:7-8 News spread swiftly among the ***Judean guerrilla bands*** and the ***poor people who were left behind*** about Gedaliah's appointment as governor. A small group of guerrilla leaders arranged to meet with Gedaliah in order to gain a better understanding of the new governor's plans.

40:9-10 Gedaliah did his best to assure the Judean guerrillas that peaceful settlement under the rule of the ***Babylonians*** (or *Chaldeans;* also in 40:10) would bring prosperity.

40:11-12 The new governor's promises encouraged people of Judah who had ***fled*** to neighboring countries to move back to their land. The mention of a ***great harvest*** indicates that the Babylonians had not destroyed the crops when they laid siege to Jerusalem.

40:14 ***Ammon*** was a small highland nation east of the Jordan Valley. • ***Ishmael son of Nethaniah*** had royal blood in his veins (2 Kgs 25:25).

40:16 Gedaliah's response betrayed his naiveté and the lack of trust in advisers that infected the whole chaotic situation.

41:1-2 ***in midautumn:*** Literally *in the seventh month* of the ancient Hebrew lunar calendar. This month occurred within the months of October and November 586 BC; also see note on 39:1. These events took place three months after the fall of Jerusalem. • ***While they were eating together:*** It was common practice that no evil deed should be done while eating at a host's table. With this attack, Ishmael viciously violated Gedaliah's hospitality.

41:3 ***Babylonian:*** Or *Chaldean.*

41:4-5 The murderers kept their deed secret until the ***next day***, when men from ***Shechem, Shiloh, and Samaria*** to the north arrived on their way south to the ruins of Jerusalem. Their appearance and the offerings they carried indicated that they were on their way to plead for mercy from the Lord (Lev 2:1; 14:2-9).The annual Festival of Shelters

to worship at the Temple of the LORD.
They had shaved off their beards, torn
their clothes, and cut themselves, and had
brought along grain offerings and frankincense. 6Ishmael left Mizpah to meet them,
weeping as he went. When he reached
them, he said, "Oh, come and see what has
happened to Gedaliah!"
7But as soon as they were all inside the
town, Ishmael and his men killed all but
ten of them and threw their bodies into a
cistern. 8The other ten had talked Ishmael
into letting them go by promising to bring
him their stores of wheat, barley, olive oil,
and honey that they had hidden away. 9The
cistern where Ishmael dumped the bodies
of the men he murdered was the large one
dug by King Asa when he fortified Mizpah
to protect himself against King Baasha of
Israel. Ishmael son of Nethaniah filled it
with corpses.
10Then Ishmael made captives of the
king's daughters and the other people who
had been left under Gedaliah's care in Mizpah by Nebuzaradan, the captain of the
guard. Taking them with him, he started
back toward the land of Ammon.
11But when Johanan son of Kareah and
the other guerrilla leaders heard about Ishmael's crimes, 12they took all their men and
set out to stop him. They caught up with him
at the large pool near Gibeon. 13The people
Ishmael had captured shouted for joy when
they saw Johanan and the other guerrilla
leaders. 14And all the captives from Mizpah
escaped and began to help Johanan. 15Mean-
while, Ishmael and eight of his men escaped
from Johanan into the land of Ammon.
16Then Johanan son of Kareah and the
other guerrilla leaders took all the people
they had rescued in Gibeon—the soldiers,
women, children, and court officials whom
Ishmael had captured after he killed Gedaliah. 17They took them all to the village of
Geruth-kimham near Bethlehem, where
they prepared to leave for Egypt. 18They
were afraid of what the Babylonians would
do when they heard that Ishmael had killed
Gedaliah, the governor appointed by the
Babylonian king.

Warning to Stay in Judah

42 Then all the guerrilla leaders, including Johanan son of Kareah
and Jezaniah son of Hoshaiah, and all the
people, from the least to the greatest, approached 2Jeremiah the prophet. They said,
"Please pray to the LORD your God for us. As
you can see, we are only a tiny remnant compared to what we were before. 3Pray that
the LORD your God will show us what to do
and where to go."
4"All right," Jeremiah replied. "I will pray
to the LORD your God, as you have asked,
and I will tell you everything he says. I will
hide nothing from you."
5Then they said to Jeremiah, "May
the LORD your God be a faithful witness
against us if we refuse to obey whatever
he tells us to do! 6Whether we like it or
not, we will obey the LORD our God to
whom we are sending you with our plea.
For if we obey him, everything will turn
out well for us."
7Ten days later the LORD gave his reply to
Jeremiah. 8So he called for Johanan son of
Kareah and the other guerrilla leaders, and
for all the people, from the least to the greatest. 9He said to them, "You sent me to the
LORD, the God of Israel, with your request,

41:6 Jer 50:4
41:7 Isa 59:7; Ezek 22:27; 33:24, 26
41:9 1 Sam 13:6; 1 Kgs 15:17-22; 2 Chr 16:1-6; Heb 11:37-38
41:10 Jer 40:11-12; 43:6
41:11 Jer 40:7-8, 13-16
41:12 2 Sam 2:13
41:16 Jer 42:8, 14; 43:4-7
41:17 2 Sam 19:37-38
41:18 Isa 57:11; Luke 12:4-5
42:1 Jer 40:8, 12-13
42:2 Deut 28:62; Isa 1:9; Acts 8:24
42:3 Ps 86:11; Prov 3:6; Mic 4:2
42:4 Ps 40:10; Jer 23:28
42:5 Jer 43:4; Mic 1:2
42:6 Exod 24:7; Deut 5:29; Jer 7:23
42:7 Ps 27:14
42:9 2 Kgs 22:15

was held at this time of year at the Temple (Lev 23:33-36), and the *eighty* worshipers were probably unarmed.

41:8 The surviving ***ten*** men had quick wits and saved their lives by promising to provide what Ishmael's men needed most: ***wheat, barley, olive oil, and honey.***

41:9 *dug by King Asa when he fortified Mizpah:* See 2 Chr 16:1-6. That passage does not refer to cisterns, but the need for water and grain storage would have required such structures, and several cisterns have been found in the ruins of the city.

41:10 Some of ***the king's daughters*** somehow escaped being killed or taken into exile.

41:11-12 *Johanan* and his companions learned of Gedaliah's death in time to attack Ishmael's party at the ***pool near Gibeon,*** which was only a few miles south of Mizpah.

41:16 *Johanan* had with him a variety of important people, including ***soldiers, women, children, and court officials*** (or *eunuchs*).

41:17-18 The group led by Johanan headed south, past the ruins of Jerusalem to ***Geruth-kimham,*** a small village ***near Bethlehem.*** During this trip, the leaders decided that they would be safe from Babylonian reprisals if they fled to ***Egypt.*** The ***Babylonians*** (or ***Chaldeans***) were cruel, and no one trusted them to seek out the true culprit in Gedaliah's death.

42:1-3 The party of Judean guerrillas and the people they had rescued (41:16) came to Jeremiah with what sounded like a sincere request for guidance.

42:1 *Jezaniah:* Greek version reads *Azariah;* cp. 43:2.

42:4 The first phrase, ***All right*** (literally *I heard*), indicates that Jeremiah questioned the sincerity of the Judean group led by Johanan. Still, the prophet agreed to ***pray*** for divine guidance and to give them the full content of the Lord's answer.

42:5-6 Perhaps these people sensed that Jeremiah doubted their sincerity. They responded by making a solemn oath: They committed to obey the Lord's instructions and to submit to punishment if they failed to keep the oath. They were confident that the Lord's answer would be what they wanted to hear.

42:10-12 The Lord replied that he wanted the people to stay in Judea and settle down, and he would plant them

42:10 Jer 31:28; Hos 11:8; Joel 2:13; Jon 3:10; 4:2
42:11 Ps 46:7, 11; Isa 43:5; Jer 41:18; Rom 8:31
42:12 Ps 106:45-46; Prov 16:7
42:14 Jer 41:17
42:15 Jer 44:12
42:16 Jer 44:13, 27
42:17 Jer 44:13-14, 28
42:18 2 Chr 36:16-19; Jer 29:18-19; 39:1-9
42:19 Deut 17:16; Ezek 2:5
42:20 Ezek 14:3
42:21 Deut 11:26; Ezek 2:7
42:22 Jer 43:11; Hos 9:6
43:2 2 Chr 36:13; Jer 5:12-13; 38:4; 42:5
43:3 Jer 36:4, 10, 32
43:4 Jer 42:5-6, 10-12
43:5 Jer 40:11-12
43:6 Jer 40:7
43:8 Jer 44:1; 46:14; Ezek 30:18
43:10 Jer 25:8-9, 11; 27:6; 46:13
43:11 Isa 19:1-25; Ezek 29:19-20
43:12 Jer 46:25; Ezek 30:13

and this is his reply: 10'Stay here in this land.
If you do, I will build you up and not tear you
down; I will plant you and not uproot you.
For I am sorry about all the punishment I
have had to bring upon you. 11Do not fear
the king of Babylon anymore,' says the LORD.
'For I am with you and will save you and rescue you from his power. 12I will be merciful
to you by making him kind, so he will let you
stay here in your land.'
13"But if you refuse to obey the LORD your
God, and if you say, 'We will not stay here;
14instead, we will go to Egypt where we will
be free from war, the call to arms, and hunger,' 15then hear the LORD's message to the
remnant of Judah. This is what the LORD of
Heaven's Armies, the God of Israel, says: 'If
you are determined to go to Egypt and live
there, 16the very war and famine you fear
will catch up to you, and you will die there.
17That is the fate awaiting every one of you
who insists on going to live in Egypt. Yes,
you will die from war, famine, and disease.
None of you will escape the disaster I will
bring upon you there.'
18"This is what the LORD of Heaven's
Armies, the God of Israel, says: 'Just as my
anger and fury have been poured out on the
people of Jerusalem, so they will be poured
out on you when you enter Egypt. You will
be an object of damnation, horror, cursing,
and mockery. And you will never see your
homeland again.'
19"Listen, you remnant of Judah. The
LORD has told you: 'Do not go to Egypt!'
Don't forget this warning I have given you
today. 20For you were not being honest
when you sent me to pray to the LORD your
God for you. You said, 'Just tell us what the
LORD our God says, and we will do it!' 21And
today I have told you exactly what he said,
but you will not obey the LORD your God any
better now than you have in the past. 22So
you can be sure that you will die from war,
famine, and disease in Egypt, where you insist on going."

Jeremiah Taken to Egypt

43 When Jeremiah had finished giving
this message from the LORD their
God to all the people, 2Azariah son of Hoshaiah and Johanan son of Kareah and all
the other proud men said to Jeremiah, "You
lie! The LORD our God hasn't forbidden us
to go to Egypt! 3Baruch son of Neriah has
convinced you to say this, because he wants
us to stay here and be killed by the Babylonians or be carried off into exile."
4So Johanan and the other guerrilla leaders
and all the people refused to obey the LORD's
command to stay in Judah. 5Johanan and the
other leaders took with them all the people
who had returned from the nearby countries
to which they had fled. 6In the crowd were
men, women, and children, the king's daughters, and all those whom Nebuzaradan, the
captain of the guard, had left with Gedaliah.
The prophet Jeremiah and Baruch were also
included. 7The people refused to obey the
voice of the LORD and went to Egypt, going as
far as the city of Tahpanhes.
8Then at Tahpanhes, the LORD gave another message to Jeremiah. He said, 9"While
the people of Judah are watching, take some
large rocks and bury them under the pavement stones at the entrance of Pharaoh's
palace here in Tahpanhes. 10Then say to
the people of Judah, 'This is what the LORD
of Heaven's Armies, the God of Israel, says:
I will certainly bring my servant Nebuchadnezzar, king of Babylon, here to Egypt. I will
set his throne over these stones that I have
hidden. He will spread his royal canopy over
them. 11And when he comes, he will destroy
the land of Egypt. He will bring death to
those destined for death, captivity to those
destined for captivity, and war to those destined for war. 12He will set fire to the temples
of Egypt's gods; he will burn the temples
and carry the idols away as plunder. He will
pick clean the land of Egypt as a shepherd
picks fleas from his cloak. And he himself
will leave unharmed. 13He will break down
the sacred pillars standing in the temple of

---

in the land (see 1:10). Judea's time of judgment was over. • ***For I am with you and will save you:*** The Lord was calling the remnant of Judea to trust him for protection against ***the king of Babylon.***

42:13-22 Jeremiah had already prophesied Egypt's destiny; it would be destroyed by the Babylonians (46:2-26). This ***remnant of Judah*** would walk into the path of the Lord's judgment if they continued on ***to Egypt.***

42:21 Like their ancestors, this group of people from Judah trusted in the Egyptians to protect them, rather than in the Lord.

43:1-7 Johanan and the rest of the people betrayed their oath (42:20) when they chose not to trust in the Lord's answer through Jeremiah.

43:3 It is not known why *Baruch* was blamed. • ***Babylonians:*** Or *Chaldeans.*

43:7 The ***city of Tahpanhes*** (2:16; Ezek 30:18), now known as Tell Dafneh, guarded the road entering Egypt at its northeast corner.

43:10 ***Nebuchadnezzar:*** Hebrew *Nebuchadrezzar,* a variant spelling of Nebuchadnezzar. Cp. 42:2-22; Ezek 29:19-20. According to an Akkadian inscription, Nebuchadnezzar invaded Egypt in 568–567 BC, less than twenty years after Jeremiah's message.

43:12-13 In the ancient Near East, ***temples*** and ***idols*** were regarded as power centers, so successful invaders usually destroyed them.

43:13 The ***sacred pillars*** were highly prized by the ancient Egyptians. • ***in the***

the sun in Egypt, and he will burn down the
temples of Egypt's gods.' "

Judgment for Idolatry

44 This is the message Jeremiah received concerning the Judeans
living in northern Egypt in the cities of
Migdol, Tahpanhes, and Memphis, and in
southern Egypt as well: 2"This is what the
LORD of Heaven's Armies, the God of Israel,
says: You saw the calamity I brought on Jerusalem and all the towns of Judah. They now
lie deserted and in ruins. 3They provoked
my anger with all their wickedness. They
burned incense and worshiped other gods—
gods that neither they nor you nor any of
your ancestors had ever even known.
4"Again and again I sent my servants, the
prophets, to plead with them, 'Don't do these
horrible things that I hate so much.' 5But my
people would not listen or turn back from
their wicked ways. They kept on burning incense to these gods. 6And so my fury boiled
over and fell like fire on the towns of Judah
and into the streets of Jerusalem, and they
are still a desolate ruin today.
7"And now the LORD God of Heaven's Armies, the God of Israel, asks you: Why are
you destroying yourselves? For not one
of you will survive—not a man, woman, or
child among you who has come here from
Judah, not even the babies in your arms.
8Why provoke my anger by burning incense
to the idols you have made here in Egypt?
You will only destroy yourselves and make
yourselves an object of cursing and mockery for all the nations of the earth. 9Have
you forgotten the sins of your ancestors, the
sins of the kings and queens of Judah, and
the sins you and your wives committed in
Judah and Jerusalem? 10To this very hour
you have shown no remorse or reverence.
No one has chosen to follow my word and
the decrees I gave to you and your ancestors
before you.
11"Therefore, this is what the LORD of
Heaven's Armies, the God of Israel, says: I
am determined to destroy every one of you!
12I will take this remnant of Judah—those
who were determined to come here and live
in Egypt—and I will consume them. They
will fall here in Egypt, killed by war and
famine. All will die, from the least to the
greatest. They will be an object of damnation, horror, cursing, and mockery. 13I will
punish them in Egypt just as I punished
them in Jerusalem, by war, famine, and disease. 14Of that remnant who fled to Egypt,
hoping someday to return to Judah, there
will be no survivors. Even though they long
to return home, only a handful will do so."
15Then all the women present and all the
men who knew that their wives had burned
incense to idols—a great crowd of all the
Judeans living in northern Egypt and southern Egypt—answered Jeremiah, 16"We will
not listen to your messages from the LORD!
17We will do whatever we want. We will
burn incense and pour out liquid offerings
to the Queen of Heaven just as much as we
like—just as we, and our ancestors, and our
kings and officials have always done in the
towns of Judah and in the streets of Jerusalem. For in those days we had plenty to eat,
and we were well off and had no troubles!
18But ever since we quit burning incense to

44:1 Isa 19:13; Jer 43:7; 46:14
44:2 Isa 6:11; Mic 3:12
44:3 Deut 13:6; 32:17; Jer 32:30-32
44:4 Jer 32:34-35; 35:15; Ezek 8:10; Zech 7:7
44:6 Isa 51:17-20; Jer 7:17, 34
44:7 Jer 9:21; Ezek 33:11
44:8 1 Kgs 9:7-8; 2 Kgs 17:15-17; 2 Chr 7:19-20; Jer 11:12, 17; 1 Cor 10:21-22
44:9 Jer 7:9-10, 17-18
44:10 Jer 6:15; 8:12
44:11 Lev 26:17; Jer 21:10; Amos 9:4
44:12 Isa 65:15; Jer 42:15-18, 22
44:13 Jer 24:10
44:14 Isa 10:20; Rom 9:27
44:15 Jer 5:1-5
44:16 Jer 8:6; 13:10
44:17 Exod 16:3; 2 Kgs 17:16; Jer 7:18; Hos 2:5-9; Phil 3:19
44:18 Num 11:5-6; Mal 3:13-15

temple of the sun: Or *in Heliopolis.* The sun was the supreme deity of the Egyptian religion. The ruins of this city are about six miles northeast of modern Cairo.

44:1 After their arrival in Egypt, the refugees of Judah scattered throughout the country. ***Migdol*** was a fortress near ***Tahpanhes*** (see note on 43:7) in the northeastern corner of ***Egypt. Memphis*** (Hebrew *Noph*) was the original capital of Egypt. It became the religious center of northern Egypt, and its ruins are located on the west side of the Nile River, about thirteen miles southwest of Cairo. Some refugees had already moved to ***southern Egypt*** (Hebrew *Pathros*), following the Nile River upstream.

44:2 Jeremiah's message appealed to the common knowledge he and his audience shared about the ***calamity*** that had wiped out ***Judah*** and ***Jerusalem.***

44:3 Since the Exodus, worship of false ***gods*** had been forbidden in Israel.

44:9 These Judean refugees had learned nothing; they had already forgotten their former sins and how God had judged them.

44:11 The Lord pronounced a death sentence, backed by the authority of his own name.

44:12 Unlike those exiled to Babylon, to whom the Lord had given hope (see 33:7-18; Ezek 34:12-15; 36:24-31), this ***remnant of Judah*** had no future.

44:15-19 The people did not accept Jeremiah's pronouncement of judgment; they had abandoned even the pretense of serving the Lord (42:1-3) and were completely committed to idolatry.

44:15 This group of Judeans had probably gathered to observe a pagan festival. • ***in northern Egypt and southern Egypt:*** Hebrew *in Egypt, in Pathros.*

44:17 The Judean refugees imagined that they had freedom. They apparently believed that obedience to the Lord entailed bondage and that their pagan worship was the way to fulfillment. • The ***Queen of Heaven*** was worshiped under a variety of names throughout the ancient Near East. In Assyria and Babylon she was called "Ishtar," and the Canaanites called her "Astarte." In the OT, she is usually called "Asherah" and associated with Baal. Manasseh gave her official status in Judah (2 Kgs 21:7), but Josiah prohibited worship of her (2 Kgs 23:1-19). She was associated with the planet Venus and with all types of reproduction among plants and animals, so she was a popular idol among farmers and herdsmen. Offerings of incense, food, and liquids were regarded as magical triggers that would induce reproduction and prosperity.

44:18 These Judeans believed that worshiping the ***Queen of Heaven*** provided prosperity and that ceasing to worship

44:19 Num 30:6-7
44:21 Jer 11:13; 14:10 Ezek 8:10-11; 16:24 Hos 7:2
44:22 Isa 7:13 Jer 4:4; 25:11, 18, 38; 30:14
44:23 1 Kgs 9:9 Jer 7:13-15; 40:3 Dan 9:11-12
44:24 Jer 43:7
44:25 Ezek 20:39 Jas 1:13-15
44:26 Gen 22:16 Deut 32:40 Ps 50:16-17 Heb 6:13, 18
44:27 Jer 1:10
44:28 Isa 14:27; 46:9-10 Zech 1:5-6
44:29 Isa 40:8 Matt 24:15-16, 32
44:30 2 Kgs 25:4-7 Jer 46:25 Ezek 29:3
45:1 Jer 25:1; 36:4, 18, 32
45:3 Ps 6:6 2 Cor 4:1, 16 Gal 6:9
45:4 Jer 18:7-10
45:5 Isa 66:16 Matt 6:25, 31-32 Rom 12:16

the Queen of Heaven and stopped worshiping her with liquid offerings, we have been
in great trouble and have been dying from
war and famine."
19"Besides," the women added, "do you
suppose that we were burning incense and
pouring out liquid offerings to the Queen
of Heaven, and making cakes marked with
her image, without our husbands knowing
it and helping us? Of course not!"
20Then Jeremiah said to all of them, men
and women alike, who had given him that
answer, 21"Do you think the LORD did not
know that you and your ancestors, your
kings and officials, and all the people were
burning incense to idols in the towns of Judah and in the streets of Jerusalem? 22It was
because the LORD could no longer bear all
the disgusting things you were doing that
he made your land an object of cursing—a
desolate ruin without inhabitants—as it is
today. 23All these terrible things happened
to you because you have burned incense to
idols and sinned against the LORD. You have
refused to obey him and have not followed
his instructions, his decrees, and his laws."
24Then Jeremiah said to them all, including the women, "Listen to this message
from the LORD, all you citizens of Judah
who live in Egypt. 25This is what the LORD
of Heaven's Armies, the God of Israel, says:
'You and your wives have said, "We will keep
our promises to burn incense and pour out
liquid offerings to the Queen of Heaven,"
and you have proved by your actions that
you meant it. So go ahead and carry out your
promises and vows to her!'
26"But listen to this message from the
LORD, all you Judeans now living in Egypt:
'I have sworn by my great name,' says the
LORD, 'that my name will no longer be spoken by any of the Judeans in the land of
Egypt. None of you may invoke my name
or use this oath: "As surely as the Sovereign
LORD lives." 27For I will watch over you to
bring you disaster and not good. Everyone
from Judah who is now living in Egypt will
suffer war and famine until all of you are
dead. 28Only a small number will escape
death and return to Judah from Egypt.
Then all those who came to Egypt will find
out whose words are true—mine or theirs!
29" 'And this is the proof I give you,' says
the LORD, 'that all I have threatened will
happen to you and that I will punish you
here.' 30This is what the LORD says: 'I will
turn Pharaoh Hophra, king of Egypt, over to
his enemies who want to kill him, just as I
turned King Zedekiah of Judah over to King
Nebuchadnezzar of Babylon.' "

9. A MESSAGE FOR BARUCH (45:1-5)

45 The prophet Jeremiah gave a message to Baruch son of Neriah in the
fourth year of the reign of Jehoiakim son
of Josiah, after Baruch had written down
everything Jeremiah had dictated to him.
He said, 2"This is what the LORD, the God of
Israel, says to you, Baruch: 3You have said,
'I am overwhelmed with trouble! Haven't
I had enough pain already? And now the
LORD has added more! I am worn out from
sighing and can find no rest.'
4"Baruch, this is what the LORD says: 'I
will destroy this nation that I built. I will uproot what I planted. 5Are you seeking great
things for yourself? Don't do it! I will bring
great disaster upon all these people; but I
will give you your life as a reward wherever
you go. I, the LORD, have spoken!' "

her would cause *war and famine* (cp. Hos 2:8). Their mindset was completely pagan.

44:20-30 This group of Judeans in Egypt had severed themselves from all meaningful relationship with the one true God of Israel; they were condemned to death.

44:20-23 The destruction of Judah and Jerusalem had not been due to the Lord's inability to provide prosperity; rather, he *could no longer bear all the disgusting things* the people *were doing*.

44:24-25 The Lord released the people to serve the Queen of Heaven; they would bear the consequences of their decision (cp. Rom 1:24, 28).

44:26-28 The *Judeans* in *Egypt* were now forever free of covenant obligations to the Lord. They were also banned from covenant protection. They chose to sever their relationship with the one true God of Israel, so they retained no privileges—they could not pray or make oaths in God's name. Still, the Lord would not be absent from their lives, because he would see to it that *disaster* plagued them. Those who individually turned to the Lord in repentance would enjoy salvation and blessings. Even in Egypt, a small remnant of people trusted in the Lord (e.g., Jeremiah and Baruch).

44:30 *Pharaoh Hophra* was killed by *his enemies* in Egypt in 570 BC. • *Nebuchadnezzar:* Hebrew *Nebuchadrezzar,* a variant spelling of Nebuchadnezzar. • This verse concludes the record of Jeremiah's forty-year ministry. Nothing is known about where, when, or how Jeremiah died.

45:1-5 This chapter is dated 605 BC, more than two decades prior to the preceding chapters. Jeremiah's secretary, Baruch, was *overwhelmed with trouble*, and the Lord promised him safety.

45:1 The *fourth year of the reign of Jehoiakim* was 605 BC. This event occurred during the same year that Baruch spent long hours in a hiding place, where he wrote down the messages the Lord had given to Jeremiah (36:1-4).

45:3 Jehoiakim had threatened to kill both Jeremiah and Baruch, which forced the prophet and the scribe into hiding. Baruch was physically exhausted, and he felt sorry for himself.

45:5 Baruch could depend on divine protection, no matter what trouble came his way. The several chapters preceding this one show that the Lord fulfilled this promise. Baruch was with Jeremiah when they were taken to Egypt.

10. MESSAGES FOR THE NATIONS (46:1–51:64)

46 The following messages were given to Jeremiah the prophet from the LORD concerning foreign nations.

Messages about Egypt (46:2-28)

2 This message concerning Egypt was given in the fourth year of the reign of Jehoiakim son of Josiah, the king of Judah, on the occasion of the battle of Carchemish when Pharaoh Neco, king of Egypt, and his army were defeated beside the Euphrates River by King Nebuchadnezzar of Babylon.

3 “Prepare your shields,
and advance into battle!
4 Harness the horses,
and mount the stallions.
Take your positions.
Put on your helmets.
Sharpen your spears,
and prepare your armor.
5 But what do I see?
The Egyptian army flees in terror.
The bravest of its fighting men run
without a backward glance.
They are terrorized at every turn,”
says the LORD.
6 “The swiftest runners cannot flee;
the mightiest warriors cannot escape.
By the Euphrates River to the north,
they stumble and fall.
7 “Who is this, rising like the Nile at
floodtime,
overflowing all the land?
8 It is the Egyptian army,
overflowing all the land,
boasting that it will cover the earth like
a flood,
destroying cities and their people.
9 Charge, you horses and chariots;
attack, you mighty warriors of Egypt!
Come, all you allies from Ethiopia, Libya,
and Lydia
who are skilled with the shield and bow!
10 For this is the day of the Lord, the LORD
of Heaven’s Armies,
a day of vengeance on his enemies.
The sword will devour until it is satisfied,
yes, until it is drunk with your blood!
The Lord, the LORD of Heaven’s Armies,
will receive a sacrifice today
in the north country beside the
Euphrates River.

11 “Go up to Gilead to get medicine,
O virgin daughter of Egypt!
But your many treatments
will bring you no healing.
12 The nations have heard of your shame.
The earth is filled with your cries of
despair.
Your mightiest warriors will run into
each other
and fall down together.”

13 Then the LORD gave the prophet Jeremiah this message about King Nebuchadnezzar’s plans to attack Egypt.

14 “Shout it out in Egypt!
Publish it in the cities of Migdol,
Memphis, and Tahpanhes!
Mobilize for battle,
for the sword will devour everyone
around you.

46:1 Jer 1:10; Ezek 29-32
46:2 2 Kgs 23:29; 2 Chr 35:20
46:3 Joel 3:9
46:4 Ezek 21:9-11
46:5 Isa 42:17; Jer 6:25; 49:29; Ezek 39:18
46:6 Isa 30:16; Dan 11:18
46:7 Jer 47:2
46:8 Isa 10:13; 37:24
46:9 Nah 2:4; 3:9
46:10 Isa 31:8; 34:6; Zeph 1:7
46:11 Jer 8:22; 30:13; Ezek 30:21-26; Nah 3:19
46:12 Jer 2:36; Nah 3:8-10
46:13 Isa 19:1; Jer 43:10-11
46:14 Jer 44:1; Nah 2:13

46:1–51:64 This series of messages is directed toward foreign nations (see 1:5, 10, and similar messages in Isa 13–23; Ezek 25–32; Amos 1:3–2:3; see map, p. 679). Through Nebuchadnezzar, the Lord was going to judge all the nations from the Euphrates River to Egypt for their rebellion and sins against him (cp. Lev 18:24-25). Ultimately, Babylon would also come under God’s judgment (50:1–51:64). These chapters were probably written while Jeremiah and Baruch were in hiding (36:27-32). Among the pronouncements of doom on the foreign nations for their sins are a few statements of hope for salvation. Collections of oracles against the nations are also found in Isaiah (Isa 13–23) and Ezekiel (Ezek 25–32). Although God used surrounding nations to punish his rebellious people, those nations were also held accountable for their actions. The Lord is not only the God of Israel; he is the God of the entire world.

46:2-12 Jeremiah used the results of a battle known to Jehoiakim to warn him and the people of Jerusalem that Egypt could not protect them from Babylon. ***Pharaoh Neco*** had thought that the time was ripe to become the dominant power in the ancient Near East, so he moved north in 609 BC. After Neco spent several years trying to help fragments of the Assyrian army stop the westward movements of the Babylonian army, he was soundly defeated at ***Carchemish*** on the ***Euphrates River*** in 605 BC. Soon after that, the Babylonian army surrounded Jerusalem and forced Jehoiakim to become a vassal of Babylon.

46:2 ***battle of Carchemish:*** This event occurred in 605 BC, during the fourth year of Jehoiakim’s reign (according to the calendar system in which the new year begins in the spring; see “Chronology: Israel’s Monarchy,” p. 562). • ***Nebuchadnezzar:*** Hebrew *Nebuchadrezzar,* a variant spelling of Nebuchadnezzar; also in 46:13, 26.

46:3-4 Military commands such as these would have been issued when the soldiers were excited, well armed, and ready to fight.

46:7-8 In spite of Pharaoh Neco’s ***boasting*** and the imposing presence of his soldiers, his tactics did not confuse the enemy or win the battle (cp. 1 Kgs 20:11).

46:9-10 The Lord had decreed that ***Egypt*** would lose the battle, so allies would be of little help. The battle of Carchemish was pivotal to the rise of Babylon as the great empire of the area. • ***from Ethiopia, Libya, and Lydia:*** Hebrew *from Cush, Put, and Lud.*

46:11 ***Gilead*** was known as a source of healing plants (see note on 8:22).

46:13-24 The defeat at Carchemish created chaos in Egypt and among its armies. The Lord was executing judgment on Egypt.

46:14 ***Memphis:*** Hebrew *Noph;* also in 46:19.

46:15 Ps 18:39; 68:1-2
46:16 Lev 26:36-37; Jer 51:9
46:17 1 Kgs 20:10-11; Isa 19:11-16
46:18 1 Kgs 18:42; Ps 89:12; Jer 48:15
46:19 Isa 20:4; Ezek 30:13

15 Why have your warriors fallen?
They cannot stand, for the LORD has knocked them down.
16 They stumble and fall over each other
and say among themselves,
'Come, let's go back to our people,
to the land of our birth.
Let's get away from the sword of the enemy!'
17 There they will say,
'Pharaoh, the king of Egypt, is a loudmouth
who missed his opportunity!'

18 "As surely as I live," says the King,
whose name is the LORD of Heaven's Armies,
"one is coming against Egypt
who is as tall as Mount Tabor,
or as Mount Carmel by the sea!
19 Pack up! Get ready to leave for exile,
you citizens of Egypt!
The city of Memphis will be destroyed,
without a single inhabitant.
20 Egypt is as sleek as a beautiful young cow,
but a horsefly from the north is on its way!

BARUCH THE SCRIBE (45:1-5)

Jer 32:9-15; 36:1-21; 36:26-32; 43:1-7

Baruch the son of Neriah was a royal scribe in Jerusalem who served as secretary for Jeremiah the prophet. His brother Seraiah was a "staff officer" in Zedekiah's administration (51:59-64). Baruch's family evidently ranked highly in the administration of Judah.

In the fourth year of King Jehoiakim of Judah (605 BC), Jeremiah prophesied God's judgment against Judah (36:1-3). Jeremiah sent for Baruch, who wrote the prophecy down (36:4) and read the words of the prophecy to the people (36:8-19). When the message reached Jehoiakim, he destroyed the scroll and called for Baruch's and Jeremiah's arrest (36:21-26). But they had gone into hiding, where Jeremiah repeated the prophecy and Baruch again wrote it down (36:27-32).

At about that time, God gave Baruch a personal message through Jeremiah (Jer 45:1-5). Baruch might have been troubled about the loss of career prospects or personal comfort resulting from his association with Jeremiah. God comforted Baruch with an assurance of protection and instructed him not to seek "great things" for himself, because the promise of Judah's destruction was certain.

When Jerusalem was destroyed in 586 BC, Baruch remained with Jeremiah and the others who remained in the land. Apparently Baruch was viewed as influential: The rebel leaders wanted to go to Egypt and Jeremiah warned them against it (42:1-22), so they accused Baruch of persuading Jeremiah. They did not listen, but took Baruch and Jeremiah with them to Egypt (43:1-7). We do not know how, when, or where Baruch died. One tradition records that he was taken to Babylon when Nebuchadnezzar invaded Egypt. It is also possible that Baruch died in Egypt.

Although God warned Baruch not to pursue great things, and he seemed to die without honors, his legacy might in fact be the book of Jeremiah, which he clearly had a hand in producing—a book that warns of judgment and eloquently expresses the hope for the new covenant (31:31-34).

In 1975, a clay impression (*bulla*) formed from a scribe's seal was found with the words "[Belonging to] Berechiahu, son of Neriahu, the scribe" (*Berechiahu* is the long form of the name *Baruch*). Each scribe, and each government official, had a unique seal bearing his name, with which he would seal documents to verify their authenticity—it was the ancient equivalent of a signature. The seal would be pressed into soft clay to form an impression (*bulla*), which was affixed to the signed document. The *bulla* of Baruch dates from the time of Jeremiah and Baruch; the other *bullae* found include the names of several other individuals in Jeremiah (e.g., "Gemariah the son of Shaphan," 36:10-12, 25; Ishmael, 40:7–41:10). Most scholars have concluded that the Baruch *bulla* was in fact formed by the seal of Baruch, Jeremiah's scribe. These *bullae*, seemingly insignificant artifacts of an ancient civilization, provide independent historical verification of some of the details of Jeremiah's account.

46:15-17 The Lord filled the Egyptian soldiers with fear, and no one could keep them in military order as they fled from Carchemish through Canaan to their Egyptian homes. Back in *Egypt*, they would become strong critics of *Pharaoh* Neco and say that he was *a loudmouth.*

46:18 *Mount Tabor* towers over the eastern part of the Jezreel Valley. *Mount Carmel* rises above the coastline of the Mediterranean Sea.

46:19 *Memphis will be destroyed:* This happened in 568–567 BC, when Nebuchadnezzar invaded Egypt (see note on 43:10).

21 Egypt's mercenaries have become like
fattened calves.
They, too, will turn and run,
for it is a day of great disaster for Egypt,
a time of great punishment.
22 Egypt flees, silent as a serpent gliding
away.
The invading army marches in;
they come against her with axes like
woodsmen.
23 They will cut down her people like trees,"
says the LORD,
"for they are more numerous than
locusts.
24 Egypt will be humiliated;
she will be handed over to people
from the north."

25The LORD of Heaven's Armies, the God
of Israel, says: "I will punish Amon, the god
of Thebes, and all the other gods of Egypt. I
will punish its rulers and Pharaoh, too, and
all who trust in him. 26I will hand them over
to those who want them killed—to King Nebuchadnezzar of Babylon and his army. But
afterward the land will recover from the ravages of war. I, the LORD, have spoken!

27 "But do not be afraid, Jacob, my servant;
do not be dismayed, Israel.
For I will bring you home again from
distant lands,
and your children will return from
their exile.
Israel will return to a life of peace and
quiet,
and no one will terrorize them.
28 Do not be afraid, Jacob, my servant,
for I am with you," says the LORD.
"I will completely destroy the nations to
which I have exiled you,
but I will not completely destroy you.
I will discipline you, but with justice;
I cannot let you go unpunished."

A Message about Philistia (47:1-7)

47 This is the LORD's message to the
prophet Jeremiah concerning the
Philistines of Gaza, before it was captured
by the Egyptian army. 2This is what the
LORD says:

"A flood is coming from the north
to overflow the land.
It will destroy the land and everything
in it—
cities and people alike.
People will scream in terror,
and everyone in the land will wail.
3 Hear the clatter of stallions' hooves
and the rumble of wheels as the
chariots rush by.
Terrified fathers run madly,
without a backward glance at their
helpless children.
4 "The time has come for the Philistines to
be destroyed,
along with their allies from Tyre and
Sidon.
Yes, the LORD is destroying the remnant
of the Philistines,
those colonists from the island of Crete.
5 Gaza will be humiliated, its head shaved
bald;
Ashkelon will lie silent.
You remnant from the Mediterranean
coast,
how long will you lament and mourn?
6 "Now, O sword of the LORD,
when will you be at rest again?

46:25 Isa 20:5-6; Jer 43:12-13; Ezek 30:13-16
46:26 Jer 44:30; Ezek 29:8-14; 32:11
46:27 Isa 41:13-14; Jer 23:3-4; 30:10-11; 50:19
46:28 Ps 46:7; Isa 43:2; Jer 10:24; Amos 9:8-9
47:1 Jer 25:17, 20; Amos 1:6; Zeph 2:4
47:2 Isa 14:31
47:3 Jer 8:16
47:4 Gen 10:13-14; Isa 14:31; 23:5; Amos 9:7
47:5 Jer 25:19-20; Amos 1:7-8; Zeph 2:4, 7; Zech 9:5
47:6 Jer 12:12

46:21 Egypt depended on hired *mercenaries* from other countries who had no interest in dying for *Egypt*. Under threat, they would *turn and run*.

46:22-23 The picture of ***a serpent gliding away*** illustrates the panic that gripped Egypt. The invaders would chop the people to pieces ***like woodsmen*** after swarming into the country like *locusts*.

46:25-26 ***Amon*** was a fertility god worshiped in ***Thebes*** (Hebrew *No*), the capital of Southern Egypt. Amon's idol, in the form of a ram, represented the sun. The Egyptians thought that this god was very powerful, but like all the other deities of Egypt, it would be destroyed by the all-powerful God of Israel. The ***Pharaoh***, who claimed to be the son of the sun-god, would suffer the same fate. • ***the land will recover:*** In 601 BC, Nebuchadnezzar attacked Egypt, did great damage, and then withdrew. He invaded the land again in 568–567 BC (43:8-13; Ezek 29:19).

46:27 ***Israel:*** Literally *Jacob;* see note on 5:20. • ***I will bring you home again:*** The exiles began returning to Judea in 538 BC. Israel was disciplined but not destroyed.

47:1-7 This message from the Lord was directed against the Philistine cities along the southeastern coast of the Mediterranean Sea and their allies farther north. The Lord had determined that these cities would be destroyed in connection with the Babylonian invasion of the area.

47:2 ***A flood:*** This metaphor depicts the movement of the Babylonian armies into the coastal area, beginning in 609 BC and peaking in 605 BC (cp. 1:11-14).

47:4 ***The time has come . . . the LORD is destroying:*** The Lord controlled what would happen, as well as when events would occur. • The ***Philistines*** had come into the southeastern coastal areas ***from the island of Crete*** (Hebrew *from Caphtor*) between 1200 and 1100 BC. The northern cities, ***Tyre and Sidon***, were colonized at about the same time by distant cousins of the Philistines who mixed with the native Canaanites.

47:5 ***Gaza*** was a major Philistine city. • ***head shaved bald:*** The city's people expressed their grief by following this ritual (cp. Isa 15:2; Mic 1:16). • ***Ashkelon***, another Philistine city a few miles north on the coast, would be emptied. • ***the Mediterranean coast:*** Literally *the plain.*

47:6 ***O sword of the LORD:*** God used the Babylonians to enact his justice. This

47:7 Ezek 14:17 Mic 6:9
48:1 Num 32:37-38 Jer 48:22-23 Ezek 25:9-10
48:2 Isa 15:4-5; 16:13-14
48:5 Isa 15:5
48:7 Num 21:29 Jer 9:23
48:8 Josh 13:10, 17, 21
48:9 Isa 16:2
48:10 1 Kgs 20:42 Jer 47:6-7
48:11 Zeph 1:12 Zech 1:15

Go back into your sheath;
rest and be still.

7 "But how can it be still
when the LORD has sent it on a mission?
For the city of Ashkelon
and the people living along the sea
must be destroyed."

A Message about Moab (48:1-47)

48 This message was given concerning Moab. This is what the LORD of Heaven's Armies, the God of Israel, says:

"What sorrow awaits the city of Nebo;
it will soon lie in ruins.
The city of Kiriathaim will be humiliated
and captured;
the fortress will be humiliated and
broken down.
2 No one will ever brag about Moab again,
for in Heshbon there is a plot to
destroy her.
'Come,' they say, 'we will cut her off from
being a nation.'
The town of Madmen, too, will be
silenced;
the sword will follow you there.
3 Listen to the cries from Horonaim,
cries of devastation and great
destruction.
4 All Moab is destroyed.
Her little ones will cry out.
5 Her refugees weep bitterly,
climbing the slope to Luhith.
They cry out in terror,
descending the slope to Horonaim.
6 Flee for your lives!
Hide in the wilderness!
7 Because you have trusted in your wealth
and skill,
you will be taken captive.
Your god Chemosh, with his priests and
officials,
will be hauled off to distant lands!

8 "All the towns will be destroyed,
and no one will escape—
either on the plateaus or in the valleys,
for the LORD has spoken.
9 Oh, that Moab had wings
so she could fly away,
for her towns will be left empty,
with no one living in them.
10 Cursed are those who refuse to do the
LORD's work,
who hold back their swords from
shedding blood!

11 "From his earliest history, Moab has
lived in peace,
never going into exile.
He is like wine that has been allowed to
settle.
He has not been poured from flask to
flask,
and he is now fragrant and smooth.
12 But the time is coming soon," says the
LORD,
"when I will send men to pour him
from his jar.

---

request might have come from the Philistine cities being attacked by the Babylonians. The people were eager for the attacks against them to stop.

47:7 The punishment would not end soon, because the judge had declared his judgment and his ***mission*** had to be accomplished: ***Ashkelon . . . must be destroyed.***

48:1–49:6 The Lord decreed the destruction and future restoration of Moab and Ammon, the two nations descended from Lot, Abraham's nephew (Gen 19:36-38).

48:1-47 Moab, one of two nations descended from Abraham's nephew Lot (Gen 19:36-38), was the next nation brought to trial in the Lord's courtroom (cp. Isa 15:1–16:14). Moab's territory lay between the Arnon River and the Zered Brook east of the Dead Sea. At the time, the Moabites felt self-assured because they were relatively free from the military reach of the Babylonians. However, the Lord found the Moabites to be greedy and cruel, and their worship was vicious and sensuous.

48:1 The powerful Judge, ***the God of Israel*** (see note on 2:2), introduced the indictments and decrees against Moab. • The ***city of Nebo*** was on the side of Mount Nebo (Num 32:3, 38), several miles east of the north end of the Dead Sea. • The ***city of Kiriathaim*** was built by the tribe of Reuben (Josh 13:19) in the highlands east of the Dead Sea.

48:2 ***Heshbon*** was located between the Jabbok and Arnon rivers, east of the Dead Sea. • ***Madmen*** was apparently another name for Dibon, a town near Heshbon; it would also be destroyed. *Madmen* sounds like a Hebrew word meaning "silence"; it should not be confused with the English word *madmen.*

48:3-4 Little is known about the village of ***Horonaim*** (see Isa 15:5); it was probably situated near the southeastern shore of the Dead Sea. • ***Her little ones will cry out:*** Greek version reads *Her cries are heard as far away as Zoar.*

48:5-6 ***Luhith*** was another small village near Horonaim. The sorrows of oppression would reach into the smallest places. • ***Hide in the wilderness:*** Or ***Hide like a wild donkey;*** or ***Hide like a juniper shrub;*** or ***Be like*** [the town of] ***Aroer.*** The meaning of the Hebrew is uncertain.

48:7 The people of Moab bragged about their ***wealth and skill,*** but their most serious sin was devotion to a deity named ***Chemosh;*** this false god represented the magical power of reproduction, but it would become clear that Chemosh was powerless.

48:8-10 The Lord sentenced all the ***towns*** of ***Moab*** to destruction, and he warned the agents of his judgment to faithfully carry out his decree.

48:9 ***Oh, that Moab had wings so she could fly away:*** Or ***Put salt on Moab, / for she will be laid waste.*** The Hebrew can be interpreted either way.

48:11-12 ***Moab*** had a long history of relative ***peace*** and a culture that its people highly valued. Vineyards were plentiful in Moab. After the juice was squeezed from the grapes, the ***wine*** was stored in clay flasks until it became ***fragrant and smooth.***

They will pour him out,
then shatter the jar!
13 At last Moab will be ashamed of his idol Chemosh,
as the people of Israel were ashamed of their gold calf at Bethel.

14 "You used to boast, 'We are heroes, mighty men of war.'
15 But now Moab and his towns will be destroyed.
His most promising youth are doomed to slaughter,"
says the King, whose name is the LORD of Heaven's Armies.
16 "Destruction is coming fast for Moab;
calamity threatens ominously.
17 You friends of Moab,
weep for him and cry!
See how the strong scepter is broken,
how the beautiful staff is shattered!

18 "Come down from your glory
and sit in the dust, you people of Dibon,
for those who destroy Moab will shatter Dibon, too.
They will tear down all your towers.
19 You people of Aroer,
stand beside the road and watch.
Shout to those who flee from Moab,
'What has happened there?'

20 "And the reply comes back,
'Moab lies in ruins, disgraced;
weep and wail!
Tell it by the banks of the Arnon River:
Moab has been destroyed!'
21 Judgment has been poured out on the towns of the plateau—
on Holon and Jahaz and Mephaath,
22 on Dibon and Nebo and Beth-diblathaim,
23 on Kiriathaim and Beth-gamul and Beth-meon,
24 on Kerioth and Bozrah—
all the towns of Moab, far and near.
25 "The strength of Moab has ended.
His arm has been broken," says the LORD.

26 "Let him stagger and fall like a drunkard,
for he has rebelled against the LORD.
Moab will wallow in his own vomit,
ridiculed by all.
27 Did you not ridicule the people of Israel?
Were they caught in the company of thieves
that you should despise them as you do?

28 "You people of Moab,
flee from your towns and live in the caves.
Hide like doves that nest
in the clefts of the rocks.
29 We have all heard of the pride of Moab,
for his pride is very great.
We know of his lofty pride,
his arrogance, and his haughty heart.
30 I know about his insolence,"
says the LORD,
"but his boasts are empty—
as empty as his deeds.
31 So now I wail for Moab;
yes, I will mourn for Moab.
My heart is broken for the men of Kir-hareseth.

32 "You people of Sibmah, rich in vineyards,
I will weep for you even more than I did for Jazer.
Your spreading vines once reached as far as the Dead Sea,
but the destroyer has stripped you bare!
He has harvested your grapes and summer fruits.
33 Joy and gladness are gone from fruitful Moab.
The presses yield no wine.
No one treads the grapes with shouts of joy.
There is shouting, yes, but not of joy.

34 "Instead, their awful cries of terror
can be heard from Heshbon clear across to
Elealeh and Jahaz; from Zoar all the way to
Horonaim and Eglath-shelishiyah. Even the
waters of Nimrim are dried up now.

48:13 1 Kgs 12:29; Isa 45:16; Hos 10:6
48:14 Ps 33:16-17; Isa 10:13-16
48:15 Jer 46:18; 50:27
48:16 Isa 13:22
48:17 Isa 14:5
48:18 Josh 13:9, 17; Isa 47:1
48:19 Josh 12:2
48:20 Num 21:13; Isa 16:7
48:21 Josh 13:18; Isa 15:4
48:23 Josh 13:19
48:24 Amos 2:2
48:25 Ps 10:15; 75:10; Zech 1:19-21
48:26 Jer 25:15, 27
48:27 Lam 2:15-17; Zeph 2:8
48:28 Ps 55:6; Song 2:14; Isa 2:19
48:29 Ps 138:6; Isa 16:6; Zeph 2:8
48:31 Isa 15:5; 16:7, 11
48:32 Isa 16:8-9
48:33 Isa 16:10
48:34 Gen 13:10; Isa 15:4-6

48:13 The Lord's judgment would make the Moabites *ashamed* that *Chemosh* was unable to protect them from harm, just as the Israelites of the northern kingdom were ashamed that the false gods they worshiped in apostasy were not able to protect them from the Assyrians (1 Kgs 12:28-29; 13:33-34; Hos 8:5-6). • ***ashamed of their gold calf at Bethel:*** Literally *ashamed when they trusted in Bethel.* See 1 Kgs 12:28-30.

48:18-19 ***Dibon*** and nearby ***Aroer*** were key Moabite cities.

48:20 When the news spread that ***Moab*** lay ***in ruins, disgraced*** and ***destroyed***, panic would rapidly increase in the ***Arnon*** Valley.

48:21-25 Eleven Moabite villages would soon hear that ***the strength*** of Moab's ***arm*** was ***broken.*** This meant that the villages had no one to defend them against the advancing enemy.

48:21 ***Jahaz:*** Hebrew *Jahzah*, a variant spelling of Jahaz.

48:26-27 Moab's hatred for Israel was ultimately ***against the LORD.***

48:31 The Lord had to punish ***Moab*** and other nations that sinned, but it caused him to ***mourn.*** • ***Kir-hareseth*** (Hebrew *Kir-heres*, a variant spelling of Kir-hareseth; also in 48:36) was Moab's capital city.

48:32 ***Sibmah*** and ***Jazer*** were conquered and rebuilt by the tribe of Reuben (Num 32:3, 38; Josh 13:19), who transformed the high plateau east of ***the Dead Sea*** (Hebrew *the sea of Jazer*) into vineyards.

48:34-39 These verses describe the effects of the Lord's judgment on the Moabite people. • The Moabite towns

48:35 Isa 15:2
48:36 Isa 16:11
48:37 Isa 15:2-3
48:38 Jer 25:34
48:40 Jer 49:22
48:41 Jer 30:6; 49:22
48:42 Ps 83:4; Jer 48:26
48:43 Isa 24:17; Lam 3:47
48:44 1 Kgs 19:17; Amos 5:19
48:45 Num 21:28-29; Ps 135:10-11
48:46 Num 21:29
48:47 Jer 12:17; 49:39
49:1 Ezek 25:2; Amos 1:13
49:2 2 Sam 11:1; Isa 14:2; Ezek 21:28
49:3 Josh 7:2-5; 8:1-29; Jer 48:2, 7
49:4 Ps 62:10-11; Ezek 28:4-5; 1 Tim 6:17

35 “I will put an end to Moab,” says the
LORD, “for the people offer sacrifices at the
pagan shrines and burn incense to their
false gods. 36 My heart moans like a flute for
Moab and Kir-hareseth, for all their wealth
has disappeared. 37 The people shave their
heads and beards in mourning. They slash
their hands and put on clothes made of burlap. 38 There is crying and sorrow in every
Moabite home and on every street. For I
have smashed Moab like an old, unwanted
jar. 39 How it is shattered! Hear the wailing!
See the shame of Moab! It has become an
object of ridicule, an example of ruin to all
its neighbors.”
40 This is what the LORD says:

“Look! The enemy swoops down like an eagle,
spreading his wings over Moab.
41 Its cities will fall,
and its strongholds will be seized.
Even the mightiest warriors will be in anguish
like a woman in labor.
42 Moab will no longer be a nation,
for it has boasted against the LORD.
43 “Terror and traps and snares will be your lot,
O Moab,” says the LORD.
44 “Those who flee in terror will fall into a trap,
and those who escape the trap will step into a snare.
I will see to it that you do not get away,
for the time of your judgment has come,”
says the LORD.
45 “The people flee as far as Heshbon
but are unable to go on.
For a fire comes from Heshbon,
King Sihon’s ancient home,
to devour the entire land
with all its rebellious people.
46 “O Moab, they weep for you!
The people of the god Chemosh are destroyed!
Your sons and your daughters
have been taken away as captives.
47 But I will restore the fortunes of Moab
in days to come.
I, the LORD, have spoken!”

This is the end of Jeremiah’s prophecy concerning Moab.

A Message about Ammon (49:1-6)

49 This message was given concerning
the Ammonites. This is what the
LORD says:

“Are there no descendants of Israel
to inherit the land of Gad?
Why are you, who worship Molech,
living in its towns?
2 In the days to come,” says the LORD,
“I will sound the battle cry against
your city of Rabbah.
It will become a desolate heap of ruins,
and the neighboring towns will be burned.
Then Israel will take back the land
you took from her,” says the LORD.
3 “Cry out, O Heshbon,
for the town of Ai is destroyed.
Weep, O people of Rabbah!
Put on your clothes of mourning.
Weep and wail, hiding in the hedges,
for your god Molech, with his priests and officials,
will be hauled off to distant lands.
4 You are proud of your fertile valleys,
but they will soon be ruined.
You trusted in your wealth,
you rebellious daughter,
and thought no one could ever harm you.

listed here were located along the small rivers that flow from the east into the Dead Sea.

48:35-37 The Moabites expressed their sorrow and grief with customary actions; they shaved their ***heads and beards***, cut their ***hands***, and used ***burlap*** for clothing (41:5; Job 1:20).

48:39 The Lord’s judgment of ***Moab*** would cause nearby countries to realize that the same kind of ruin might be their punishment.

48:40 The ***eagle*** represents speed and surprise; its victim is caught and carried off before it is able to react.

48:43-45 Between the ***terror*** (Hebrew *pakhad*), the ***traps*** (Hebrew *pakhath*), and a ***snare*** (Hebrew *pakh*), there would be no escape for the people of Moab.

48:45 If the Moabites fled north, they would be met by their enemies at Heshbon. • ***a fire comes from Heshbon:*** Cp. Num 21:28.

48:47 The Lord would have mercy on Moab; he promised that the people would prosper at some time in the future.

49:1-6 Ammon was the next nation brought to trial in the Lord’s courtroom. Ammon was the second of Lot’s descendants (see note on 48:1-47); its territory was north of Moab and east of Israel. The destruction of Ammon occurred shortly after the fall of Jerusalem.

49:1 After the fall of the northern kingdom of ***Israel*** in 722 BC, the Ammonites moved into territory that had been vacated by the tribe of ***Gad***. • The Ammonites worshiped a fertility god named ***Molech*** (“ruler”), who was a lot like Baal (“master”). • ***Molech:*** Hebrew *Malcam*, a variant spelling of Molech; also in 49:3.

49:2 ***Rabbah***, the capital of Ammon, was destroyed in 582 BC.

49:3 The Ammonites might have thought that their deity, ***Molech***, was powerful. However, the coming invader would take this idol into exile ***with his priests and officials;*** their ritual magic would be exposed as a fraud.

49:4-6 The Ammonites ***trusted in*** their ***wealth***, but it could not provide security. The Lord ensured their judgment and their future restoration.

5 But look! I will bring terror upon you,"
says the Lord, the LORD of Heaven's Armies.
"Your neighbors will chase you from your land,
and no one will help your exiles as they flee.
6 But I will restore the fortunes of the Ammonites
in days to come.
I, the LORD, have spoken."

Messages about Edom (49:7-22)

7This message was given concerning Edom.
This is what the LORD of Heaven's Armies
says:

"Is there no wisdom in Teman?
Is no one left to give wise counsel?
8 Turn and flee!
Hide in deep caves, you people of Dedan!
For when I bring disaster on Edom,
I will punish you, too!
9 Those who harvest grapes
always leave a few for the poor.
If thieves came at night,
they would not take everything.
10 But I will strip bare the land of Edom,
and there will be no place left to hide.
Its children, its brothers, and its neighbors
will all be destroyed,
and Edom itself will be no more.
11 But I will protect the orphans who remain among you.
Your widows, too, can depend on me for help."

12And this is what the LORD says: "If the
innocent must suffer, how much more must
you! You will not go unpunished! You must
drink this cup of judgment! 13For I have
sworn by my own name," says the LORD,
"that Bozrah will become an object of horror and a heap of ruins; it will be mocked and cursed. All its towns and villages will be desolate forever."

14 I have heard a message from the LORD
that an ambassador was sent to the nations to say,
"Form a coalition against Edom,
and prepare for battle!"
15 The LORD says to Edom,
"I will cut you down to size among the nations.
You will be despised by all.
16 You have been deceived
by the fear you inspire in others
and by your own [j]pride.
You live in a rock fortress
and control the mountain heights.
But even if you make your nest among the peaks with the eagles,
I will bring you crashing down,"
says the LORD.

17 "Edom will be an object of horror.
All who pass by will be appalled
and will gasp at the destruction they see there.
18 It will be like the destruction of Sodom and Gomorrah
and their neighboring towns," says the LORD.
"No one will live there;
no [k]one will inhabit it.
19 I will come like a lion from the thickets of the Jordan,
leaping on the sheep in the pasture.
I will chase Edom from its land,
and I will appoint the leader of my choice.

49:5 Jer 16:16; Lam 4:15
49:6 Jer 48:47; 49:39
49:7 Gen 36:11, 15; Isa 34:5-6; Amos 1:12
49:8 Isa 21:13; Jer 25:23
49:9 Obad 1:5
49:11 Ps 68:5; Zech 7:10
49:12 Jer 25:15, 28-29; 1 Pet 4:17
49:13 Isa 34:6, 9-15
49:14 Jer 50:14
49:15 Obad 1:1-4; Luke 1:51
49:16 Isa 14:13-15; Amos 9:2; [j]*zadon* (2087) ›Jer 50:31
49:17 Jer 51:37; Ezek 35:7
49:18 Gen 19:24-25; Deut 29:23; Amos 4:11; [k]*ben 'adam* (1121, 0120) ›Ezek 2:1
49:19 Isa 46:9; Jer 50:44

49:7-22 The people of *Edom* were descendants of Esau, Jacob's brother (Gen 32:3). The land of Edom lay south of Moab, in the highlands rising east of the Arabah Valley. The divine Judge exercised his right to hold every nation accountable.

49:7-8 ***Is there no wisdom:*** Edom was famous for its wise men, but they would suddenly appear foolish because they were unaware of the coming doom. • ***Teman*** and ***Dedan*** were cities of Edom.

49:8 *Edom:* Literally *Esau;* also in 49:10.

49:9-11 Harvesters customarily left some of the crop for the poor (Lev 19:9-10); ***thieves*** would take only those ***grapes*** they could get quickly and easily. The invaders would take their time and mercilessly ***strip*** Edom ***bare,*** leaving only ruin behind them. However, the Lord promised to be merciful to the defeated nation's ***orphans*** and ***widows.***

49:12-22 The ***cup of judgment*** symbolized the fulfillment of the Lord's decrees (see 25:15-17). This section vividly depicts the aftermath of a nation's drinking from that cup.

49:12 The ***innocent*** included victims of child sacrifice and social injustice. The wicked needed to suffer in a greater way when the divine Judge carried out justice.

49:13 ***Bozrah*** was a fortress built on top of a high rock with steep sides, but no place in Edom would be safe.

49:14 The ***ambassador*** might have been an angel sent by God (cp. 1 Kgs 22:20-22).

49:15-16 The leaders of Edom thought themselves powerful because they stirred ***fear*** in those who passed through their land on the Kings' Highway (see map, p. 285). • Edom had a ***rock fortress,*** now called Petra; it was hard to find and could only be approached through a deep, narrow gorge. Even this remote place could not secure the Edomites against the Lord's judgment.

49:18 As had occurred with ***the destruction of Sodom and Gomorrah,*** Edom would become uninhabited.

49:19 In divine judgment, the Lord would use the Babylonians to ***come like a lion . . . leaping on the sheep*** as they chased Edom's leaders out of the land. • The Lord's rhetorical questions implied the answer, "No one ***can challenge*** the Lord; he is the only Almighty ***ruler.***"

49:20 Isa 14:24, 27; Jer 50:45; Mal 1:4-5
49:21 Jer 50:46; Ezek 26:15, 18
49:22 Isa 13:8; Jer 48:40-41
49:23 Exod 15:15; Isa 10:9; 57:20; Jer 39:5; Amos 6:2; Nah 2:10
49:25 Jer 51:41
49:26 Jer 50:30
49:27 1 Kgs 15:18-20; Amos 1:3-5
49:28 Isa 21:16-17
49:29 Jer 46:5
49:30 Jer 25:8-9, 24; 27:6
49:31 Judg 18:7; Isa 47:8
49:32 Jer 9:25-26; 25:23; Ezek 12:14-15
49:33 Isa 13:20-22; Zeph 2:9, 13-15
49:34 Gen 10:22; 2 Kgs 24:17-18; Isa 11:11; Dan 8:2
49:35 Isa 22:6; Jer 51:56

For who is like me, and who can
challenge me?
What ruler can oppose my will?"

20 Listen to the LORD's plans against Edom
and the people of Teman.
Even the little children will be dragged
off like sheep,
and their homes will be destroyed.
21 The earth will shake with the noise of
Edom's fall,
and its cry of despair will be heard all
the way to the Red Sea.
22 Look! The enemy swoops down like an
eagle,
spreading his wings over Bozrah.
Even the mightiest warriors will be in
anguish
like a woman in labor.

A Message about Damascus (49:23-27)

23 This message was given concerning Damascus. This is what the LORD says:

"The towns of Hamath and Arpad are
struck with fear,
for they have heard the news of their
destruction.
Their hearts are troubled
like a wild sea in a raging storm.
24 Damascus has become feeble,
and all her people turn to flee.
Fear, anguish, and pain have gripped her
as they grip a woman in labor.
25 That famous city, a city of joy,
will be forsaken!
26 Her young men will fall in the streets
and die.
Her soldiers will all be killed,"
says the LORD of Heaven's Armies.
27 "And I will set fire to the walls of
Damascus
that will burn up the palaces of Benhadad."

A Message about Kedar and Hazor (49:28-33)

28 This message was given concerning Kedar and the kingdoms of Hazor, which were attacked by King Nebuchadnezzar of Babylon. This is what the LORD says:

"Advance against Kedar!
Destroy the warriors from the East!
29 Their flocks and tents will be captured,
and their household goods and
camels will be taken away.
Everywhere shouts of panic will be heard:
'We are terrorized at every turn!'
30 Run for your lives," says the LORD.
"Hide yourselves in deep caves, you
people of Hazor,
for King Nebuchadnezzar of Babylon
has plotted against you
and is preparing to destroy you.

31 "Go up and attack that complacent nation,"
says the LORD.
"Its people live alone in the desert
without walls or gates.
32 Their camels and other livestock will all
be yours.
I will scatter to the winds these people
who live in remote places.
I will bring calamity upon them
from every direction," says the LORD.
33 "Hazor will be inhabited by jackals,
and it will be desolate forever.
No one will live there;
no one will inhabit it."

A Message about Elam (49:34-39)

34 This message concerning Elam came to the prophet Jeremiah from the LORD at the beginning of the reign of King Zedekiah of Judah. 35 This is what the LORD of Heaven's Armies says:

"I will destroy the archers of Elam—
the best of their forces.

49:21 *Red Sea:* Literally *sea of reeds.*

49:22 The *eagle,* a common bird in the rugged mountains of Edom, is a metaphor for the rapid penetration of the region by the Babylonians (see note on 48:40).

49:23-27 *Damascus,* the capital of Aram (ancient Syria), and the Aramean cities of *Hamath and Arpad,* indicate Aram as the next object of the Lord's judgment.

49:25 Damascus had a long history of power and glory at the hub of major trade routes. Its people enjoyed prosperity and *joy,* but they would lose these pleasures when they were *forsaken* by the Lord.

49:27 The city's *walls* and *palaces* were probably built with timbers from the slopes of Mount Hermon. • *Ben-hadad* (literally *son of the mighty one*) was the royal title given to a long line of Aramean kings.

49:28-33 The nomads of *Kedar* roamed freely in the upper Arabian Desert east of Palestine. They were a belligerent people (Ps 120:5-7; Isa 21:13-16) who raised flocks and herds for lucrative trade with Tyre (Ezek 27:21). • *Hazor* was a region east of Damascus inhabited by nomads. • The poem urges *King Nebuchadnezzar* to attack, and it describes the impact of the battles.

49:28-29 The Babylonians wanted to defeat *the warriors* of *Kedar* so they could capture their rich *household goods and camels.* • *Nebuchadnezzar:* Hebrew *Nebuchadrezzar,* a variant spelling of Nebuchadnezzar; also in 49:30.

49:30 The Lord exhorted the *people of Hazor* to *run* and hide, even though it would do them no good. *Nebuchadnezzar,* the Babylonian king, had them on his agenda for conquest.

49:32 *who live in remote places:* Or *who clip the corners of their hair.* The Hebrew can be interpreted either way.

49:34-39 The final poetic message of this series was addressed to *Elam.* This nation, known for its ferocity, was located in the Zagros Mountains, far to the east beyond Babylon (Ezek 32:24).

49:35 The Elamite warriors were expert *archers,* but their skills could not save *Elam.*

36 I will bring enemies from all directions,
and I will scatter the people of Elam
to the four winds.
They will be exiled to countries
around the world.
37 I myself will go with Elam's enemies to
shatter it.
In my fierce anger, I will bring great
disaster
upon the people of Elam," says the
LORD.
"Their enemies will chase them with the
sword
until I have destroyed them
completely.
38 I will set my throne in Elam," says the
LORD,
"and I will destroy its king and
officials.
39 But I will restore the fortunes of Elam
in days to come.
I, the LORD, have spoken!"

Messages about Babylon (50:1–51:64)

A Message about Babylon

50 The LORD gave Jeremiah the prophet
this message concerning Babylon
and the land of the Babylonians. 2This is
what the LORD says:

"Tell the whole world,
and keep nothing back.
Raise a signal flag
to tell everyone that Babylon will fall!
Her images and idols will be shattered.
Her gods Bel and Marduk will be
utterly disgraced.
3 For a nation will attack her from the
north
and bring such destruction that no
one will live there again.
Everything will be gone;
both people and animals will flee.

Hope for Israel and Judah

4 "In those coming days,"
says the LORD,
"the people of Israel will return home
together with the people of Judah.
They will come weeping
and seeking the LORD their God.
5 They will ask the way to Jerusalem
and will start back home again.
They will bind themselves to the LORD
with an eternal covenant that will
never be forgotten.
6 "My people have been lost sheep.
Their shepherds have led them astray
and turned them loose in the
mountains.
They have lost their way
and can't remember how to get back
to the sheepfold.
7 All who found them devoured them.
Their enemies said,
'We did nothing wrong in attacking
them,
for they sinned against the LORD,
their true place of rest,
and the hope of their ancestors.'

49:36 Ezek 5:10; Rev 7:1
49:37 Jer 6:19; 30:24
49:39 Jer 48:47
50:1 Isa 13:1; Rev 14:8
50:2 Isa 46:1; Jer 51:31
50:3 Zeph 1:3
50:4 Ezra 3:12-13; Isa 11:12-13; Jer 31:9; Hos 1:11
50:5 Isa 55:3; Jer 6:16; 32:40
50:6 Isa 53:6; Jer 13:16; Ezek 34:15-16; Matt 9:36
50:7 Jer 17:13

49:36 The common aftermath of a successful invasion was for the victors to *scatter* the refugees far and wide.

49:37 The Lord would express his ***fierce anger*** through the ***great disaster*** to come upon ***Elam***. No specific charge is mentioned here, but like other nations, Elam served false gods and was cruel in its wars against its neighbors.

49:38 ***I will set my throne in Elam:*** The Lord would express his supreme authority by destroying Elam's ***king and officials***.

49:39 The Lord's decree of judgment was balanced by his promise to ***restore the fortunes of Elam***. In 539 BC, a native of Elam named Cyrus conquered Babylon and founded the Persian empire. Susa, the former capital of Elam, then became the capital of the Persian empire (Esth 1:2). Cyrus would be God's anointed instrument to set the Judeans free (Isa 44:28–45:1).

50:1–51:64 This message of judgment on Babylon is the longest for any nation except Judah, and threats against Babylon are interwoven with promises for Judah's restoration. Babylon was the Lord's agent for destroying the other civilizations of the Near East, but it was also guilty of its own sins. The Lord would judge Babylon by doing to her what she had done to others (50:15).

50:1 ***Babylonians:*** Or *Chaldeans;* also in 50:8, 25, 35, 45.

50:2 Raising ***a signal flag*** was a favored method for warning that an enemy was approaching a city (cp. Isa 13:2). • The people of Babylon would be under divine judgment because they worshiped the ***gods Bel*** (the Babylonian name for *Baal*) and ***Marduk*** (the Babylonian deity of wind, storm, and fertility). • ***idols:*** The Hebrew term (literally *round things*) probably alludes to dung.

50:3 The ***nation . . . from the north*** was the Persian nation led by Cyrus in 539 BC. Persia was east of Babylon, but it first struck Babylonia in the north and then moved south. The attack destroyed the powerful Babylonian empire.

50:4-10 This poetic interlude was a message of hope for the Israelite exiles in Babylon in contrast to the judgment and oppression they had been experiencing. The divine Judge is also the divine Savior.

50:4 ***In those coming days:*** In 538, 458, and 445 BC, some exiles of Israel moved back to their homeland. • The people of ***Israel*** and ***Judah*** would ***come weeping*** with joy and repentance, choosing to worship ***the LORD their God*** instead of worshiping idols.

50:5 ***Jerusalem:*** Hebrew *Zion;* also in 50:28. • ***an eternal covenant:*** See 31:23-34.

50:6 The ***shepherds*** of Israel and Judah, such as Jeroboam I and Manasseh (see 1 Kgs 12:25–13:34; 2 Kgs 21:1-18), had led the people away from the Lord. • The ***mountains*** were both literal and metaphorical—Baal worship tended to take place at high elevations.

50:7 This verse continues the metaphor of lost sheep (50:6), connecting Israel's vulnerability to attack with

50:8 Jer 51:6 Rev 18:4
50:10 Jer 51:24, 35
50:11 Jer 12:14; 46:20
50:12 Jer 22:6
50:13 Jer 18:16
50:14 Hab 2:8, 17
50:15 Ps 137:8
50:16 Jer 46:16
50:17 2 Kgs 18:9-13; 24:1, 10-12 Jer 4:7
50:18 Isa 10:12 Nah 3:7, 18-19
50:19 Jer 31:10

8 "But now, flee from Babylon!
Leave the land of the Babylonians.
Like male goats at the head of the flock,
lead my people home again.
9 For I am raising up an army
of great nations from the north.
They will join forces to attack Babylon,
and she will be captured.
The enemies' arrows will go straight to
the mark;
they will not miss!
10 Babylonia will be looted
until the attackers are glutted with loot.
I, the LORD, have spoken!

Babylon's Sure Fall

11 "You rejoice and are glad,
you who plundered my chosen people.
You frisk about like a calf in a meadow
and neigh like a stallion.
12 But your homeland will be overwhelmed
with shame and disgrace.
You will become the least of nations—
a wilderness, a dry and desolate land.
13 Because of the LORD's anger,
Babylon will become a deserted
wasteland.
All who pass by will be horrified
and will gasp at the destruction they
see there.

14 "Yes, prepare to attack Babylon,
all you surrounding nations.
Let your archers shoot at her; spare no
arrows.
For she has sinned against the LORD.
15 Shout war cries against her from every
side.
Look! She surrenders!
Her walls have fallen.
It is the LORD's vengeance,
so take vengeance on her.
Do to her as she has done to others!
16 Take from Babylon all those who plant
crops;
send all the harvesters away.
Because of the sword of the enemy,
everyone will run away and rush back
to their own lands.

Hope for God's People

17 "The Israelites are like sheep
that have been scattered by
lions.
First the king of Assyria ate them up.
Then King Nebuchadnezzar of
Babylon cracked their bones."
18 Therefore, this is what the LORD of
Heaven's Armies,
the God of Israel, says:
"Now I will punish the king of Babylon
and his land,
just as I punished the king of
Assyria.
19 And I will bring Israel home again to its
own land,
to feed in the fields of Carmel and
Bashan,
and to be satisfied once more
in the hill country of Ephraim and
Gilead.

their apostasy in turning away from the Lord. ***Their enemies*** rationalized their mistreatment of Israel by saying that the Israelites had ***sinned against the LORD.*** These enemies understood that the Israelites' ***true place of rest*** and ***hope*** was in the Lord.

50:8-9 The Lord urged the Israelites to leave when he ordered ***an army of great nations*** (Persia and its allies) to ***attack Babylon*** in 539 BC.

50:10 ***Babylonia:*** Or *Chaldea.*

50:11-16 These verses describe in vivid detail the defeat of Babylon by the Persian invasion (see ch 51; Isa 13:14; 21:1-10; 44:28; 47:1-5; Dan 5). Babylon was never an important kingdom again. The city of Babylon was leveled in 485 BC. Archaeological excavation of Babylon began in 1899, and the remains of Babylon were brought to light over several decades.

50:11 ***rejoice . . . frisk about:*** The Babylonians had been light-hearted and carefree because they had ***plundered*** the Lord's ***people*** in Jerusalem. They gave no thought to the well-being of those they conquered.

50:12 ***your homeland:*** Literally *your mother.* • The divine Judge rendered his verdict, describing the ***disgrace*** of a defeated Babylon.

50:14 The Lord ordered armies ***to attack Babylon*** with a multitude of ***arrows,*** the artillery of that age. • ***she has sinned against the LORD:*** The primary charge leveled against other nations was also directed toward ***Babylon.***

50:15 The Lord's judgment was fulfilled when Babylon surrendered and her ***walls*** fell. ***The LORD's vengeance*** carried out justice by doing to Babylon what ***she*** had ***done to others*** (cp. Deut 19:21; Luke 6:38).

50:16 As Babylon fell, farmers fled and left their ***crops*** behind. The slaughter on the battlefield caused the people to ***run away.***

50:17-20 Another poetic interlude laments Israel's sufferings and promises future restoration.

50:17 ***Assyria*** conquered the northern kingdom of Israel in 734–722 BC, and ***Nebuchadnezzar*** (Hebrew *Nebuchadrezzar,* a variant spelling of Nebuchadnezzar) conquered the southern kingdom of Judah in 605–586 BC.

50:18 ***Therefore:*** This word introduces two divine decrees. The first decree condemned ***Babylon*** to complete annihilation, like the punishment the Lord gave Assyria (Nah 3). Assyria fell in 612 BC; Babylon fell in 539 BC.

50:19 ***I will bring Israel home:*** The second divine decree (see note on 50:18) promises restoration for Israel, specifically the people of the northern tribes, whose land was defined by the indicated landmarks. • ***Carmel*** is a mountain range close to the Mediterranean Sea in the northwestern corner of Israel. • ***Bashan*** was a region in the highlands rising east of the Sea of Galilee. • The tribe of ***Ephraim*** occupied the ***hill country*** in the central part of Israel west of the Jordan River. • ***Gilead*** was a highland area that rose on the east side of the Jordan River, opposite Ephraim.

20 In those days," says the LORD,
"no sin will be found in Israel or in Judah,
for I will forgive the remnant I preserve.

The LORD's Judgment on Babylon

21 "Go up, my warriors, against the land of Merathaim
and against the people of Pekod.
Pursue, kill, and completely destroy them,
as I have commanded you," says the LORD.
22 "Let the battle cry be heard in the land,
a shout of great destruction.
23 Babylon, the mightiest hammer in all the earth,
lies broken and shattered.
Babylon is desolate among the nations!
24 Listen, Babylon, for I have set a trap for you.
You are caught, for you have fought against the LORD.
25 The LORD has opened his armory
and brought out weapons to vent his fury.
The terror that falls upon the Babylonians
will be the work of the Sovereign LORD of Heaven's Armies.
26 Yes, come against her from distant lands.
Break open her granaries.
Crush her walls and houses into heaps of rubble.
Destroy her completely, and leave nothing!
27 Destroy even her young bulls—
it will be terrible for them, too!
Slaughter them all!
For Babylon's day of reckoning has come.
28 Listen to the people who have escaped from Babylon,
as they tell in Jerusalem
how the LORD our God has taken vengeance
against those who destroyed his Temple.
29 "Send out a call for archers to come to Babylon.
Surround the city so none can escape.
Do to her as she has done to others,
for she has defied the LORD, the Holy One of Israel.
30 Her young men will fall in the streets and die.
Her soldiers will all be killed,"
says the LORD.
31 "See, I am your enemy, you [a]arrogant people,"
says the Lord, the LORD of Heaven's Armies.
"Your day of reckoning has arrived—
the day when I will punish you.
32 O land of [b]arrogance, you will stumble and fall,
and no one will raise you up.
For I will light a fire in the cities of Babylon
that will burn up everything around them."
33 This is what the LORD of Heaven's Armies says:
"The people of Israel and Judah have been wronged.
Their captors hold them and refuse to let them go.
34 But the one who [c]redeems them is strong.
His name is the LORD of Heaven's Armies.
He will defend them
and give them rest again in Israel.
But for the people of Babylon
there will be no rest!

50:20 Jer 31:34; Mic 7:19
50:21 Ezek 23:23
50:22 Jer 4:19-21
50:23 Jer 51:20-24
50:24 Job 9:4; 40:2, 9; Jer 48:43
50:25 Isa 13:4-5
50:26 Isa 14:23
50:27 Ps 37:13; Ezek 7:7
50:28 Ps 149:6-9; Isa 48:20; Lam 1:10
50:29 Exod 10:3; Ps 137:8
50:30 Jer 18:21
50:31 Nah 2:13; [a]*zadon* (2087) ‣Jer 50:32
50:32 Isa 10:12-15; Jer 21:14; [b]*zadon* (2087) ‣Ezek 7:10
50:33 Isa 14:17; 58:6
50:34 Isa 14:3-7; 43:14; Mic 7:9; [c]*go'el* (1350) ‣Ruth 2:20

50:20 The Lord would ***forgive the remnant*** of people from ***Israel*** and ***Judah;*** they would seek the Lord as they returned to their homeland (50:4-5; see chs 31; 33).

50:21 The judgments against Babylon continue. The divine Judge is also portrayed as the divine commander of the armies. The Persians were the Lord's ***warriors*** against Babylon, just as Babylon had been his warriors against Judah (25:9). • ***Merathaim*** (literally *double rebellion*) refers to the southern part of the Tigris and Euphrates river valley. ***Pekod*** (literally *punishment*) designates a people living on the eastern side of the same valley. These people were Babylonian. • ***completely destroy:*** The Hebrew term used here refers to the complete consecration of things or people to the Lord, either by destroying them or by giving them as an offering; see Lev 27:28-29; Josh 6:21; 1 Sam 15:3.

50:28 The exiles returning to Jerusalem would be able to encourage those left behind that the enemy had been punished as God had promised and that his promised restoration of Israel was beginning.

50:29-30 Skilled ***archers*** would kill the Babylonian ***soldiers*** even as those soldiers had ***killed*** their victims in battle (see note at 50:15). This was the Lord's way of judging the ruthless empire builders who had ***defied*** the one true God by worshiping other deities (50:38).

50:31-32 Because of the Lord's decree, the ***arrogant*** Babylonian empire would never rise again as a mighty power in the world.

50:33-34 ***The people of Israel and Judah*** had suffered greatly. The Lord's act of redemption would ***defend them*** and ***give them rest again in Israel.*** God is ***strong,*** and he is as able to redeem as he is to punish.

50:35 Jer 47:6; Dan 5:1-2, 7-8
50:36 Isa 44:25
50:37 Ps 20:7-8; Jer 25:19-20; 48:41
50:39 Isa 13:20
50:40 Gen 19:24-25; Luke 17:28-30; 2 Pet 2:6; Jude 1:7
50:41 Isa 13:2-5
50:42 Isa 13:17-18; Hab 1:8
50:43 Jer 30:6
50:44 Num 16:5; Job 41:10; Isa 46:9
50:46 Jer 10:10; Ezek 26:18
51:1 Jer 4:11-12
51:2 Jer 15:7; Matt 3:12
51:3 Jer 46:4
51:5 Isa 54:7-8; Jer 33:24-26

35 "The sword of destruction will strike the
Babylonians,"
says the LORD.
"It will strike the people of Babylon—
her officials and wise men, too.
36 The sword will strike her wise
counselors,
and they will become fools.
The sword will strike her mightiest
warriors,
and panic will seize them.
37 The sword will strike her horses and
chariots
and her allies from other lands,
and they will all become like women.
The sword will strike her treasures,
and they all will be plundered.
38 The sword will even strike her water
supply,
causing it to dry up.
And why? Because the whole land is
filled with idols,
and the people are madly in love with
them.

39 "Soon Babylon will be inhabited by
desert animals and hyenas.
It will be a home for owls.
Never again will people live there;
it will lie desolate forever.
40 I will destroy it as I destroyed Sodom
and Gomorrah
and their neighboring towns," says
the LORD.
"No one will live there;
no one will inhabit it.

41 "Look! A great army is coming from the
north.
A great nation and many kings
are rising against you from far-off
lands.
42 They are armed with bows and
spears.
They are cruel and show no mercy.
As they ride forward on horses,
they sound like a roaring sea.
They are coming in battle formation,
planning to destroy you, Babylon.
43 The king of Babylon has heard reports
about the enemy,
and he is weak with fright.
Pangs of anguish have gripped him,
like those of a woman in labor.

44 "I will come like a lion from the thickets
of the Jordan,
leaping on the sheep in the pasture.
I will chase Babylon from its land,
and I will appoint the leader of my
choice.
For who is like me, and who can
challenge me?
What ruler can oppose my will?"

45 Listen to the LORD's plans against
Babylon
and the land of the Babylonians.
Even the little children will be dragged
off like sheep,
and their homes will be destroyed.
46 The earth will shake with the shout,
"Babylon has been taken!"
and its cry of despair will be heard
around the world.

51

1 This is what the LORD says:
"I will stir up a destroyer against
Babylon
and the people of Babylonia.
2 Foreigners will come and winnow her,
blowing her away as chaff.
They will come from every side
to rise against her in her day of
trouble.
3 Don't let the archers put on their armor
or draw their bows.
Don't spare even her best soldiers!
Let her army be completely destroyed.
4 They will fall dead in the land of the
Babylonians,
slashed to death in her streets.
5 For the LORD of Heaven's Armies
has not abandoned Israel and Judah.

50:35-38 Babylon would experience exactly the kind of violence it had meted out. The same charges were brought against ***Babylon*** as were brought against Israel, Judah, Egypt, and their neighbors. All of them worshiped ***idols*** instead of the one true God. • ***The sword of destruction*** refers to the Persian army.

50:38 The Euphrates River ran through the city of Babylon, providing its ***water supply.*** The Persians were reputed to have diverted the river during the siege by digging a canal around the city walls and then attacking through the riverbed.

50:39-40 The doom of ***Babylon*** would be like the utter desolation of ***Sodom and Gomorrah*** (Gen 19:24-25).

50:40 ***as I:*** Literally *as God.*

50:43 The Babylonians would experience the same terror their own victims had felt (cp. 6:22-23).

50:44-46 These verses essentially repeat 49:19-21, with ***Babylon*** in place of Edom.

51:1-2 The ***destroyer*** selected by the Lord was Persia, led by Cyrus, who came ***against Babylon*** in 539 BC. • ***Babylonia:*** Hebrew *Leb-kamai,* a code name for Babylonia.

51:3-4 God took the role of commander and ordered the destroyer to wipe out ***the Babylonians.*** • ***completely destroyed:*** The Hebrew term used here refers to the complete consecration of things or people to the LORD, either by destroying them or by giving them as an offering; see Lev 27:28-29; 1 Sam 15:3. • ***Babylonians:*** Or *Chaldeans;* also in 51:54.

51:5 Although the Israelites had committed many sins ***against the Holy One,***

He is still their God,
even though their land was filled with sin
against the Holy One of Israel."

6 Flee from Babylon! Save yourselves!
Don't get trapped in her punishment!
It is the LORD's time for vengeance;
he will repay her in full.
7 Babylon has been a gold cup in the LORD's hands,
a cup that made the whole earth drunk.
The nations drank Babylon's wine,
and it drove them all mad.
8 But suddenly Babylon, too, has fallen.
Weep for her.
Give her medicine.
Perhaps she can yet be healed.
9 We would have helped her if we could,
but nothing can save her now.
Let her go; abandon her.
Return now to your own land.
For her punishment reaches to the heavens;
it is so great it cannot be measured.
10 The LORD has vindicated us.
Come, let us announce in Jerusalem
everything the LORD our God has done.

11 Sharpen the arrows!
Lift up the shields!
For the LORD has inspired the kings of the Medes
to march against Babylon and destroy her.
This is his vengeance against those
who desecrated his Temple.
12 Raise the battle flag against Babylon!
Reinforce the guard and station the watchmen.
Prepare an ambush,
for the LORD will fulfill all his plans against Babylon.
13 You are a city by a great river,
a great center of commerce,
but your end has come.
The thread of your life is cut.
14 The LORD of Heaven's Armies has taken this vow
and has sworn to it by his own name:
"Your cities will be filled with enemies,
like fields swarming with locusts,
and they will shout in triumph over you."

A Hymn of Praise to the LORD

15 The LORD made the earth by his power,
and he preserves it by his wisdom.
With his own understanding
he stretched out the heavens.
16 When he speaks in the thunder,
the heavens are filled with water.
He causes the clouds to rise over the earth.
He sends the lightning with the rain
and releases the wind from his storehouses.

17 The whole human race is foolish and has no knowledge!
The craftsmen are disgraced by the idols they make,
for their carefully shaped works are a fraud.
These idols have no breath or power.
18 Idols are worthless; they are ridiculous lies!
On the day of reckoning they will all be destroyed.
19 But the God of Israel is no idol!
He is the Creator of everything that exists,
including his people, his own special possession.
The LORD of Heaven's Armies is his name!

Babylon's Great Punishment

20 "You are my battle-ax and sword,"
says the LORD.
"With you I will shatter nations
and destroy many kingdoms.

51:6 Num 16:26; Rev 18:4
51:7 Jer 25:15; Rev 14:8-10; 18:3
51:9 Jer 46:16
51:10 Isa 40:2; Mic 7:9
51:11 Joel 3:9-10
51:12 Jer 4:28
51:13 Hab 2:9-11
51:14 Nah 3:15
51:15 Ps 146:5-6; Jer 10:12-16; Rom 1:20
51:16 Job 37:2-5; Ps 18:13; 135:7; Jon 1:4
51:17 Isa 44:18-20; Hab 2:18-19
51:19 //Jer 10:16
51:20 Mic 4:12-13

he was *still their God,* and he planned to save them.

51:6 The Israelites were urged to ***flee from Babylon*** at the appropriate ***time*** to avoid being caught up in the Lord's ***vengeance*** against Babylon (cp. 50:8).

51:7 ***Babylon*** had been ***a gold cup,*** a vessel of unusual power and wealth that the Lord had used for a time to rule every nation in the ancient Near East. • ***The nations drank Babylon's wine:*** All those nations had suffered greatly under Babylon's heavy hand.

51:8 Jeremiah foresaw the collapse of the Babylonian empire. Although the Lord was carrying out justice, the event called for mourning.

51:9-10 ***Nothing*** could ***save*** Babylon; ***her punishment*** could not ***be measured.*** After Babylon collapsed, it would be time for the exiles to ***return*** home, where they could tell others of God's wonderful acts on their behalf. • ***Jerusalem:*** Hebrew *Zion;* also in 51:24.

51:11-12 ***Lift up the shields!*** Greek version reads *Fill up the quivers.* • The ***kings of the Medes*** included Cyrus, who marched against Babylon and overthrew it in 539 BC.

51:15-19 This anthem of praise affirms the Lord's uniqueness and majesty. It contrasts the reality of the one true God with the emptiness of idols.

51:15-16 As the Creator and preserver of all things, God, not Baal, controls the storm with its ***thunder, lightning, rain,*** and ***wind.*** The Lord can use these forces whenever he desires.

51:19 ***the God of Israel:*** Literally *the Portion of Jacob.* See note on 10:16.

51:20 ***You:*** Possibly Cyrus, whom God used to conquer Babylon. Cp. Isa 44:28; 45:1. The Lord had chosen and empowered King Cyrus of Persia to turn the Babylonian empire to dust.

51:21 Exod 15:1
51:22 Isa 13:15-16, 18
51:25 Rev 8:8
51:26 Isa 13:19-22
51:27 Gen 8:4; 10:3; 2 Kgs 19:37; Isa 13:2-5
51:29 Jer 10:10; Amos 8:8
51:30 Ps 76:5; Isa 13:7-8; 45:1
51:33 Isa 21:10; Joel 3:13
51:34 Job 20:15; Ps 137:8; Isa 24:1-3
51:35 Ps 137:8
51:36 Ps 140:12; Rom 12:19

21 With you I will shatter armies—
destroying the horse and rider,
the chariot and charioteer.
22 With you I will shatter men and women,
old people and children,
young men and maidens.
23 With you I will shatter shepherds and flocks,
farmers and oxen,
captains and officers.

24 "I will repay Babylon
and the people of Babylonia
for all the wrong they have done
to my people in Jerusalem," says the LORD.

25 "Look, O mighty mountain, destroyer of the earth!
I am your enemy," says the LORD.
"I will raise my fist against you,
to knock you down from the heights.
When I am finished,
you will be nothing but a heap of burnt rubble.
26 You will be desolate forever.
Even your stones will never again be used for building.
You will be completely wiped out,"
says the LORD.
27 Raise a signal flag to the nations.
Sound the battle cry!
Mobilize them all against Babylon.
Prepare them to fight against her!
Bring out the armies of Ararat, Minni, and Ashkenaz.
Appoint a commander,
and bring a multitude of horses like swarming locusts!
28 Bring against her the armies of the nations—
led by the kings of the Medes
and all their captains and officers.

29 The earth trembles and writhes in pain,
for everything the LORD has planned
against Babylon stands unchanged.
Babylon will be left desolate without a single inhabitant.
30 Her mightiest warriors no longer fight.
They stay in their barracks, their courage gone.
They have become like women.
The invaders have burned the houses
and broken down the city gates.
31 The news is passed from one runner to the next
as the messengers hurry to tell the king
that his city has been captured.
32 All the escape routes are blocked.
The marshes have been set aflame,
and the army is in a panic.

33 This is what the LORD of Heaven's Armies,
the God of Israel, says:
"Babylon is like wheat on a threshing floor,
about to be trampled.
In just a little while
her harvest will begin."

34 "King Nebuchadnezzar of Babylon has eaten and crushed us
and drained us of strength.
He has swallowed us like a great monster
and filled his belly with our riches.
He has thrown us out of our own country.
35 Make Babylon suffer as she made us suffer,"
say the people of Zion.
"Make the people of Babylonia pay for spilling our blood,"
says Jerusalem.

The LORD's Vengeance on Babylon

36 This is what the LORD says to Jerusalem:

"I will be your lawyer to plead your case,
and I will avenge you.
I will dry up her river,
as well as her springs,
37 and Babylon will become a heap of ruins,
haunted by jackals.
She will be an object of horror and contempt,
a place where no one lives.

51:24 *Babylonia:* Or *Chaldea;* also in 51:35.

51:27-28 ***Ararat*** was the mountainous region north of ***Babylon.*** • ***Ashkenaz*** was Noah's great-grandson through Japheth and Gomer (Gen 10:2-3); his descendants probably lived in Ararat, as did the people of ***Minni,*** who are otherwise unknown. • ***signal flag:*** See note on 50:2.

51:29-30 The terrible fall of ***Babylon*** happened just as the Lord had planned. The Babylonian soldiers lost all desire to ***fight,*** and the Persian invaders quickly penetrated its city walls.

51:31 This ***king*** was Nabonidus; at the time, he was at Borsippa, north of Babylon. His son Belshazzar was regent in Babylon. See Dan 5:1-30.

51:33 The wealth of the city was likened to ***wheat on a threshing floor;*** the looting of Babylon was like a ***harvest.***

51:34 ***Nebuchadnezzar:*** Hebrew *Nebuchadrezzar,* a variant spelling of Nebuchadnezzar.

51:35 ***Make Babylon suffer as she made us suffer:*** See "Prayers for Vengeance" at Ps 137, p. 1017.

51:36 ***I will be your lawyer:*** In response to the people's request (51:35), the Lord would prosecute Babylon for its brutal sins.

51:37 The looting of the city and the damage to its structures would inspire ***contempt*** rather than awe in its visitors.

38 Her people will roar together like strong
lions.
They will growl like lion cubs.
39 And while they lie inflamed with all their
wine,
I will prepare a different kind of feast
for them.
I will make them drink until they fall
asleep,
and they will never wake up again,"
says the LORD.
40 "I will bring them down
like lambs to the slaughter,
like rams and goats to be sacrificed.

41 "How Babylon is fallen—
great Babylon, praised throughout the
earth!
Now she has become an object of horror
among the nations.
42 The sea has risen over Babylon;
she is covered by its crashing waves.
43 Her cities now lie in ruins;
she is a dry wasteland
where no one lives or even passes by.
44 And I will punish Bel, the god of Babylon,
and make him vomit up all he has
eaten.
The nations will no longer come and
worship him.
The wall of Babylon has fallen!

A Message for the Exiles

45 "Come out, my people, flee from
Babylon.
Save yourselves! Run from the LORD's
fierce anger.
46 But do not panic; don't be afraid
when you hear the first rumor of
approaching forces.
For rumors will keep coming year by
year.
Violence will erupt in the land
as the leaders fight against each
other.
47 For the time is surely coming
when I will punish this great city and
all her idols.
Her whole land will be disgraced,
and her dead will lie in the streets.
48 Then the heavens and earth will rejoice,
for out of the north will come
destroying armies
against Babylon," says the LORD.
49 "Just as Babylon killed the people of
Israel
and others throughout the world,
so must her people be killed.
50 Get out, all you who have escaped the
sword!
Do not stand and watch—flee while
you can!
Remember the LORD, though you are in a
far-off land,
and think about your home in
Jerusalem."

51 "We are ashamed," the people say.
"We are insulted and disgraced
because the LORD's Temple
has been defiled by foreigners."
52 "Yes," says the LORD, "but the time is
coming
when I will destroy Babylon's idols.
The groans of her wounded people
will be heard throughout the land.
53 Though Babylon reaches as high as the
heavens
and makes her fortifications
incredibly strong,
I will still send enemies to plunder her.
I, the LORD, have spoken!

51:39 Ps 76:5; Jer 25:27
51:42 Dan 9:26
51:43 Isa 13:20
51:44 Ezra 1:7; Isa 25:12
51:45 Gen 19:12-16; Isa 48:20; Acts 2:40
51:46 Isa 19:2
51:47 Isa 21:9; 46:1-2
51:48 Isa 44:23; Rev 18:20
51:51 Lam 1:10
51:53 Job 20:6-7

51:38-40 The Lord proclaimed that he would use ***wine*** to turn the ***lion*** that once terrorized and destroyed nations (5:6; 25:38; 49:19) into an easily-subdued lamb. Wine as an instrument of wrath was usually figurative (25:15-29), but here it was literal (see Dan 5).

51:41 ***Babylon:*** Hebrew *Sheshach*, a code name for Babylon.

51:42 ***The sea*** represents the armies that overwhelmed ***Babylon***. The ***crashing waves*** symbolize the assault against the city.

51:44 The defeat of its chief deity, ***Bel***, was the ultimate disaster for ***Babylon***. This idol's lavish adornments would be taken away, and its supposed power would be exposed as a monumental fraud.

51:45-53 The Lord was concerned about the spiritual and physical well-being of the Jewish exiles in Babylon, where their political situation was perilous. The Lord pointed to the future, when the exiles would be redeemed from disgrace and return with great joy to live in their own land.

51:45-46 As the Lord described the terrors of his angry judgment against ***Babylon***, he pointed his people to their homeland to assure them of their safety. As an enemy army headed toward Babylon, the leaders inside the city were blaming ***each other***. Vicious in-fighting was tearing Babylon apart.

51:47-48 The Lord's punishment of ***Babylon*** would cause the ***heavens and earth*** to ***rejoice*** at this display of God's justice.

51:49-50 Babylon's penalty would match the brutality it had poured out on the Israelites and other nations.

51:51 The exiled people carried a heavy load of shame and disgrace for their past sins. The ***LORD's Temple*** was ***defiled*** when the Babylonians destroyed it in 586 BC.

51:52 ***Yes:*** The Lord agreed with his people that their past was shameful, but he gave them hope for the future when Babylon's power would be broken.

51:53 Babylon's ***fortifications*** could not protect it; the city would certainly be plundered, for ***the LORD*** had ***spoken*** and decreed their punishment.

51:55 Ps 69:2
51:56 Ps 76:3; 94:1-2
51:57 Ps 76:5-6
51:58 Hab 2:13
51:62 Isa 13:19-22; Ezek 35:9
51:63 Rev 18:21
51:64 Nah 1:8-9
52:1 2 Kgs 8:22; 24:18-20
52:2 Jer 36:30-31
52:3 2 Chr 36:13
52:4 2 Kgs 25:1-7; Jer 39:1

Babylon's Complete Destruction

54 "Listen! Hear the cry of Babylon,
the sound of great destruction from
the land of the Babylonians.
55 For the LORD is destroying Babylon.
He will silence her loud voice.
Waves of enemies pound against her;
the noise of battle rings through the
city.
56 Destroying armies come against Babylon.
Her mighty men are captured,
and their weapons break in their
hands.
For the LORD is a God who gives just
punishment;
he always repays in full.
57 I will make her officials and wise men
drunk,
along with her captains, officers, and
warriors.
They will fall asleep
and never wake up again!"
says the King, whose name is
the LORD of Heaven's Armies.

58 This is what the LORD of Heaven's
Armies says:
"The thick walls of Babylon will be
leveled to the ground,
and her massive gates will be burned.
The builders from many lands have
worked in vain,
for their work will be destroyed by fire!"

Jeremiah's Message Sent to Babylon

59 The prophet Jeremiah gave this message
to Seraiah son of Neriah and grandson
of Mahseiah, a staff officer, when Seraiah
went to Babylon with King Zedekiah of Judah. This was during the fourth year of
Zedekiah's reign. 60 Jeremiah had recorded
on a scroll all the terrible disasters that
would soon come upon Babylon—all the
words written here. 61 He said to Seraiah,
"When you get to Babylon, read aloud everything on this scroll. 62 Then say, 'LORD, you
have said that you will destroy Babylon so
that neither people nor animals will remain
here. She will lie empty and abandoned forever.' 63 When you have finished reading the
scroll, tie it to a stone and throw it into the
Euphrates River. 64 Then say, 'In this same
way Babylon and her people will sink, never
again to rise, because of the disasters I will
bring upon her.' "

This is the end of Jeremiah's messages.

11. HISTORICAL APPENDIX: JUDGMENT ON JERUSALEM (52:1-34)

The Fall of Jerusalem

Jer 52:1-3a // 2 Kgs 24:18-20a // 2 Chr 36:11-12
Jer 52:3b-11 // 2 Kgs 24:20b–25:7 // Jer 39:1-7

52 Zedekiah was twenty-one years
old when he became king, and
he reigned in Jerusalem eleven years. His
mother was Hamutal, the daughter of Jeremiah from Libnah. 2 But Zedekiah did what
was evil in the LORD's sight, just as Jehoiakim had done. 3 These things happened
because of the LORD's anger against the people of Jerusalem and Judah, until he finally
banished them from his presence and sent
them into exile.

Zedekiah rebelled against the king
of Babylon. 4 So on January 15, during
the ninth year of Zedekiah's reign, King
Nebuchadnezzar of Babylon led his entire
army against Jerusalem. They surrounded
the city and built siege ramps against its
walls. 5 Jerusalem was kept under siege until
the eleventh year of King Zedekiah's reign.

51:54 As ***Babylon*** was destroyed, the din of battle would be overwhelming. People would scream and yell, soldiers would shout their battle cries, and boulders would crash against each other as walls were torn down.

51:55-56 The destruction of ***Babylon*** was not a historical accident—***the LORD*** was in control and would bring it to pass. • The ***noise*** (51:54) would dissolve into the ***silence*** of death. The invading army would kill or capture the Babylonian soldiers, and the population would flee into the countryside.

51:57 Belshazzar, the ruler of the city, and his ***officers*** had a feast at which drunkenness was dominant; it ended in their death (Dan 5).

51:59-64 Just as Babylon had destroyed Jerusalem, this great kingdom would itself be destroyed. This passage contains a message sent to Babylon seven years before the fall of Jerusalem.

51:59 ***King Zedekiah*** made a trip ***to Babylon*** to build trust between himself and Nebuchadnezzar. It was probably during this visit that Zedekiah swore an oath of loyalty to the Babylonian king (2 Chr 36:13). ***The fourth year of Zedekiah's reign*** was 593 BC.

51:63-64 Throwing ***the scroll . . . into the Euphrates River*** signaled the permanent destruction of ***Babylon.***

52:1-34 This chapter repeats the narrative of 2 Kgs 24:18–25:30, which recounts the final month of Jerusalem's existence with a few added details and changes. The repetition of this passage emphasizes Jeremiah's integrity as a true prophet of Almighty God. Everything Jeremiah had predicted about the destruction of the holy city and the end of the kingdom of Judah came true. Likewise, everything that he predicted about the Exile, the sufferings of the exiled survivors in Babylon, and their return from exile, came true.

52:4 ***on January 15:*** Literally *on the tenth day of the tenth month* of the ancient Hebrew lunar calendar. A number of events in Jeremiah can be cross-checked with dates in surviving Babylonian records and related accurately to our modern calendar. This day was January 15, 588 BC. • ***Nebuchadnezzar:*** Hebrew *Nebuchadrezzar,* a variant spelling of Nebuchadnezzar; also in 52:12, 28, 29, 30.

[6]By July 18 in the eleventh year of Zedekiah's reign, the famine in the city had become very severe, and the last of the food was entirely gone. [7]Then a section of the city wall was broken down, and all the soldiers fled. Since the city was surrounded by the Babylonians, they waited for nightfall. Then they slipped through the gate between the two walls behind the king's garden and headed toward the Jordan Valley.

[8]But the Babylonian troops chased King Zedekiah and caught him on the plains of Jericho, for his men had all deserted him and scattered. [9]They took him to the king of Babylon at Riblah in the land of Hamath. There the king of Babylon pronounced judgment upon Zedekiah. [10]He made Zedekiah watch as they slaughtered his sons and all the other officials of Judah. [11]Then they gouged out Zedekiah's eyes, bound him in bronze chains, and led him away to Babylon. Zedekiah remained there in prison until the day of his death.

The Temple Destroyed

Jer 52:12-16 // 2 Kgs 25:8-12 // Jer 39:8-10
Jer 52:17-27 // 2 Kgs 25:13-21

[12]On August 17 of that year, which was the nineteenth year of King Nebuchadnezzar's reign, Nebuzaradan, the captain of the guard and an official of the Babylonian king, arrived in Jerusalem. [13]He burned down the Temple of the LORD, the royal palace, and all the houses of Jerusalem. He destroyed all the important buildings in the city. [14]Then he supervised the entire Babylonian army as they tore down the walls of Jerusalem on every side. [15]Nebuzaradan, the captain of the guard, then took as exiles some of the poorest of the people, the rest of the people who remained in the city, the defectors who had declared their allegiance to the king of Babylon, and the rest of the craftsmen. [16]But Nebuzaradan allowed some of the poorest people to stay behind in Judah to care for the vineyards and fields.

[17]The Babylonians broke up the bronze pillars in front of the LORD's Temple, the bronze water carts, and the great bronze basin called the Sea, and they carried all the bronze away to Babylon. [18]They also took all the ash buckets, shovels, lamp snuffers, basins, dishes, and all the other bronze articles used for making sacrifices at the Temple. [19]Nebuzaradan, the captain of the guard, also took the small bowls, incense burners, basins, pots, lampstands, dishes, bowls used for liquid offerings, and all the other articles made of pure gold or silver.

[20]The weight of the bronze from the two pillars, the Sea with the twelve bronze oxen beneath it, and the water carts was too great to be measured. These things had been made for the LORD's Temple in the days of King Solomon. [21]Each of the pillars was 27 feet tall and 18 feet in circumference. They were hollow, with walls 3 inches thick. [22]The bronze capital on top of each pillar was 7½ feet high and was decorated with a network of bronze pomegranates all the way around. [23]There were 96 pomegranates on the sides, and a total of 100 on the network around the top.

52:6 Jer 38:9
52:7 Jer 39:2, 4-7
52:8 Jer 21:7; 38:23
52:9 2 Kgs 25:6; Jer 39:5
52:10 Jer 39:6
52:11 Ezek 12:13
52:12 2 Kgs 25:8-21
52:13 2 Chr 36:19; Ps 74:6-8; Jer 39:8
52:14 2 Kgs 25:10
52:17 1 Kgs 7:15-36
52:18 1 Kgs 7:45
52:19 1 Kgs 7:50
52:20 1 Kgs 7:47
52:22 1 Kgs 7:20, 42

52:6 ***By July 18 in the eleventh year of Zedekiah's reign:*** Literally *By the ninth day of the fourth month* [in the eleventh year of Zedekiah's reign]. This day was July 18, 586 BC; also see note on 52:4.

52:7 ***the Babylonians:*** Or *the Chaldeans;* similarly in 52:8, 17. • ***the Jordan Valley:*** Hebrew *the Arabah.*

52:9 ***Riblah,*** which Jeremiah recorded as being ***in the land of Hamath*** (see 39:5), was several hundred miles north of Jerusalem.

52:10 ***and all the other officials of Judah:*** This phrase is an addition to the narrative in 2 Kgs 25:7. Though the soldiers deserted ***Zedekiah*** as they fled to Jericho (52:8), the officials did not do so.

52:11 The last sentence of the verse is an addition to the 2 Kgs 25 text (see note on 52:1-34).

52:12-21 This section adds some details not found in 2 Kgs 25 (see note on 52:1-34). The Babylonians gained vast wealth by looting all the precious metals in the Temple before it was burned. • The Babylonian looters had to break large metal items into pieces in order to get them on wagons and carry them away. • ***18 feet in circumference. They were hollow, with walls 3 inches thick:*** These words are an addition to the 2 Kgs 25 text (see note on 52:1-34).

52:12 ***On August 17 of that year:*** Literally *On the tenth day of the fifth month* of the ancient Hebrew lunar calendar. This day was August 17, 586 BC; also see note on 52:4. This date is three days later than the one recorded in 2 Kgs 25:8; the reason for the discrepancy is not known.

52:13 ***He burned down the Temple:*** Although the Temple was constructed mostly of stone, beams of cedar were laid among the stones. Cedar panels covered the walls, and cypress planks were used for the floors. Wood was also used for window frames and for doors (see 1 Kgs 6). All of this wood burned. • ***destroyed all the important buildings:*** Or *destroyed the houses of all the important people.*

52:14 ***Babylonian:*** Or *Chaldean.*

52:15 ***some of the poorest of the people:*** Jeremiah added this phrase (cp. 2 Kgs 25:11) and changed "population" to ***craftsmen.***

52:17-23 This section includes a more detailed list of Temple furnishings than in 1 Kgs 6:1-38.

52:21 ***27 feet tall and 18 feet in circumference:*** Hebrew *18 cubits* [8.1 meters] *tall and 12 cubits* [5.4 meters] *in circumference.* • ***3 inches thick:*** Hebrew *4 fingers thick* [8 centimeters]. • Jeremiah added "and 18 feet in circumference" and the last sentence (cp. 2 Kgs 25:17).

52:22 ***7½ feet:*** Hebrew *5 cubits* [2.3 meters].

52:23 Jeremiah added this verse, which is not in 2 Kgs 25 (see note on 52:1-34).

52:24
2 Kgs 25:18
Ezra 7:1

52:27
Jer 13:19
Mic 4:10

52:28
2 Kgs 24:2-3, 12-16

52:31
2 Kgs 25:27-30
Ps 3:3

52:33
2 Sam 9:7, 13

24Nebuzaradan, the captain of the guard,
took with him as prisoners Seraiah the
high priest, Zephaniah the priest of the second rank, and the three chief gatekeepers.
25And from among the people still hiding in the city, he took an officer who had
been in charge of the Judean army; seven
of the king's personal advisers; the army
commander's chief secretary, who was in
charge of recruitment; and sixty other citizens. 26Nebuzaradan, the captain of the
guard, took them all to the king of Babylon
at Riblah. 27And there at Riblah, in the land
of Hamath, the king of Babylon had them
all put to death. So the people of Judah were
sent into exile from their land.

28The number of captives taken to
Babylon in the seventh year of Nebuchadnezzar's reign was 3,023. 29Then in
Nebuchadnezzar's eighteenth year he took
832 more. 30In Nebuchadnezzar's twenty-
third year he sent Nebuzaradan, the captain
of the guard, who took 745 more—a total of
4,600 captives in all.

Hope for Israel's Royal Line
Jer 52:31-34 // 2 Kgs 25:27-30

31In the thirty-seventh year of the exile of
King Jehoiachin of Judah, Evil-merodach
ascended to the Babylonian throne. He
was kind to Jehoiachin and released him
from prison on March 31 of that year. 32He
spoke kindly to Jehoiachin and gave him a
higher place than all the other exiled kings
in Babylon. 33He supplied Jehoiachin with
new clothes to replace his prison garb and
allowed him to dine in the king's presence
for the rest of his life. 34So the Babylonian
king gave him a regular food allowance as
long as he lived. This continued until the
day of his death.

52:25 ***seven:*** The parallel in 2 Kgs 25:18 reads "five."

52:28-30 The numbers in these verses amplify the data given in 2 Kgs 24:14-16 regarding the deportation of exiles in 597 BC. The deportation in 52:30 is not mentioned elsewhere in Scripture; it was probably a Babylonian reprisal for Gedaliah's murder (41:1-3). This suggests that the person(s) responsible for making this adaptation lived after 581 BC, probably in Babylon, and knew the content of Jeremiah's account of the fall of Jerusalem.

52:28 This exile ***in the seventh year of Nebuchadnezzar's reign*** occurred in 597 BC. The account in 2 Kgs 24:12-14 states that this event occurred in Nebuchadnezzar's eighth year. This difference reflects two ancient Near Eastern methods of calculating the beginning of a king's reign. In 2 Kings, the year in which Nebuchadnezzar ascended the throne is treated as the first year of his reign. Jeremiah apparently started counting the first *full* year as Nebuchadnezzar's first year (see "Chronology: Israel's Monarchy," p. 562).

52:29 This exile in the ***eighteenth year*** of Nebuchadnezzar's reign occurred in 586 BC, when Jerusalem was destroyed.

52:30 This exile in the ***twenty-third year*** of Nebuchadnezzar's reign occurred in 581 BC. See note on 52:28-30.

52:31-34 This paragraph repeats 2 Kgs 25:27-30. This part of the narrative supplies the fulfillment of Jeremiah's prediction of Jehoiachin's future (see 22:24-30). • ***Evil-merodach*** reigned in Babylon 561–560 BC. Several inscriptions found in a basement near Babylon's Ishtar Gate tell of rations of food provided to Jehoiachin and his family.

52:31 ***He was kind to:*** Literally *He raised the head of.* • ***on March 31 of that year:*** Literally *on the twenty-fifth day of the twelfth month* of the ancient Hebrew lunar calendar. This day was March 31, 561 BC; also see note on 52:4.

THE BOOK OF

LAMENTATIONS

Most of us have been observers, not participants, in wars. Most of us have not experienced the death of our nation, and we know little of the agony of utter despair; but others in our world have experienced total devastation as their cities or nations have been destroyed by wars, earthquakes, tsunamis, or hurricanes. Reading the book of Lamentations can give us a point of entry into their experience. It can help us to face the darkest aspects of human existence.

SETTING

A catastrophe had wiped out the kingdom of Judah, its capital (Jerusalem), its Temple, and most of its people. After a long siege, the Babylonian army breached Jerusalem's defenses and took control. They deported many of the people of Judah to exile in Babylon, and they destroyed the city of Jerusalem, including the Temple of God. Only a few survivors were left in the land, including Jeremiah the prophet. Nothing else was left, and the hopes of God's people were nearly dead.

SUMMARY

The book of Lamentations is a collection of five highly structured and emotionally powerful poems that lament Jerusalem's destruction. The first four poems are acrostics based on the twenty-two letters of the Hebrew alphabet, with each successive stanza beginning with the next letter (a feature that is lost in translation). Chapter 5 has twenty-two verses but is not an acrostic.

Chapter 1 describes Jerusalem's ruins. Jerusalem is personified as a woman who was once a famous princess but is now a wounded slave, lamenting the contrast between her past and present with intense agony and shame. The woman acknowledges that she has earned her distress, and she prays that the Lord will relieve her miserable condition.

Chapter 2 summarizes the shameful situation of the false prophets, city leaders, and young women. The author agonizes as he watches starving children and weeping mothers, lying prophets and mocking enemies. It happened because God withdrew his mercy and kept his promise to judge his people when they sinned against him.

Chapter 3 is an eyewitness account of God's wrath. The author is sickened by the carnage; he is abused, without hope, and crushed by shame. Then hope suddenly floods his soul in the realization that God's anger will not last forever. God's faithfulness, love, kindness, and goodness are the ultimate, saving reality. The battered believer sings. Yet the hurt remains, and his tears flow abundantly as he pours out his repentant prayer.

Chapter 4 is a gloomy description of the devastation before and after the walls of Jerusalem were breached, in contrast to the city's years of glory. God was justly punishing the vicious sins of his people, and they could not escape his judgment.

There is no attempt to hide the horror of the destruction that the people experienced. The reader is invited to ground zero of the devastation, there to stand dumbfounded by the enormity of the collapse of this once glorious city.

DIANNE BERGANT
Lamentations

The prayer in chapter 5 asks God to carefully consider the people's plight; it ends with a plea for salvation, if salvation is still available.

In all five poems, pain and distress are paired with faith and hope. The suffering of the present seems more real than the possibility of redemption in the future, but God's love and faithfulness remain.

AUTHORSHIP

The book of Lamentations does not identify its author. The poems take place within the context of the situation immediately before and after the fall of Jerusalem in 586 BC, so the prophet Jeremiah has long been identified as the author. It was probably written with the help of Baruch, his assistant and scribe. Jeremiah also wrote laments at the time of King Josiah's death (2 Chr 35:25). The five poems of Lamentations are thematically unified by the desolation of Jerusalem, and Jeremiah was in Jerusalem through all of its disasters, from its first defeat in 605 BC through its final destruction in 586 BC. The author of Lamentations freely pours out his emotions, as does Jeremiah in the book that bears his name. Both books are about the future of the nation.

There are a number of other parallels between the books of Jeremiah and Lamentations. Compare the treatment of the following themes: troubled widows (1:1; 5:3; cp. Jer 15:8; 18:21); weeping people (1:2, 16; 2:18; 3:48-49; cp. Jer 4:8; 6:26; 9:1; 13:17; 14:17; 25:34); sins (1:5, 10, 18, 22; 3:42; 4:13-14; 5:7; cp. Jer 2:34; 4:17; 14:20; 30:14-16; 31:29; 51:51); punishment (2:2-22; 3:39; 5:14-16; cp. Jer 6:11, 25; 7:14; 16:2-4; 18:21; 51:30, 34; 52:14); false prophets (2:14; cp. Jer 23:25-29; 29:8-9); bitterness (3:19; cp. Jer 9:15); pits (3:53, 55; cp. Jer 37:16; 38:6-13); and clay pots (4:2; cp. Jer 19:11). Such parallels support Jeremiah's authorship. However, some OT scholars ascribe Lamentations to a much later author.

OUTLINE

1:1–22
Sorrow in Jerusalem

2:1–22
God's Anger at Sin

3:1–66
Hope in the Lord's Faithfulness

4:1–22
God's Anger Satisfied

5:1–22
Prayer for Restoration

MEANING AND MESSAGE

What positive meaning can be gained from staring at blackened stones hour after hour, or from walking among starving children and wailing mothers, or from remembering false prophets who promised rescue from the Babylonian army encamped around Jerusalem? What significance is there in watching priests, who had been confident that the sacrifices they offered would provide victory and success, wander the city searching for food? How can one believe in God's goodness when corpses lie everywhere?

But the author did find meaning in the calamity. The false worship and immoral behavior of the leaders and the people had brought disaster upon them. God was angry because his people rejected his sovereignty and

TIMELINE

640–609 BC
Josiah as king of Judah

about 627~580 BC
Jeremiah as prophet

609 BC
Jehoahaz as king of Judah, taken prisoner to Egypt

609–598 BC
Jehoiakim as king of Judah

605–562 BC
Nebuchadnezzar II as king of Babylon

605 BC
Nebuchadnezzar invades Judah, first deportation

597 BC
Jehoiachin as king of Judah

Apr 597 BC
Nebuchadnezzar captures Jerusalem, plunders Temple, second deportation, takes Jehoiachin to Babylon

597–586 BC
Zedekiah as king of Judah

about 593~570 BC
Ezekiel as prophet in Babylon

586 BC
Nebuchadnezzar captures and destroys Jerusalem, takes people of Judah into exile, end of the southern kingdom of Judah

about 586 BC
Obadiah as prophet

538 BC
Cyrus's decree allows exiles to return to Judea

Apr–May 536 BC
Temple rebuilding begins

515 BC
Temple rebuilding is completed

ignored his reality as the one, true God. They had violated their covenant with the Lord, and the Lord had judged them, as he had promised to do (cp. Lam 1:3, 5 with Deut 28:32-33; Lam 1:9 with Deut 28:43; Lam 1:16 with Deut 28:41; Lam 2:20; 4:10 with Deut 28:53; Lam 3:14, 45 with Deut 28:37; and Lam 4:16 with Deut 28:48-50). God's punishment was righteous and just (1:18); he does not tolerate human rebellion.

But what about the future? Those in anguish can plead before God (1:20-22). They can understand that in catastrophe, God fulfills justice (2:17; see Lev 26:14-17). In the midst of utter sorrow, they can experience the Lord's mercy. Those who truly seek God have hope. God is great in his faithfulness (3:21-26). Misery threatens to overwhelm the soul, but moments of hope bring light (3:29-33). God is eternal, and his throne forever dominates the universe. Though doubts and fears continue to assault the human spirit, God remains dependable. God's anger, which has a just foundation, is temporary. God's anger ceases when confession and repentance begin, and it becomes possible to sing of God's great faithfulness. The ultimate goal is that each person, and each community, will experience God's forgiveness and restoration.

FURTHER READING

H. L. ELLISON
Lamentations in *Expositor's Bible Commentary,* vol. 6 (1986)

DUANE GARRETT AND PAUL R. HOUSE
Song of Songs / Lamentations (2004)

R. K. HARRISON
Jeremiah & Lamentations (1973)

ELMER A. MARTENS
Lamentations in *Cornerstone Biblical Commentary,* vol. 8 (2005)

1. SORROW IN JERUSALEM (1:1-22)

1 Jerusalem, once so full of people,
is now deserted.
She who was once great among the nations
now sits alone like a widow.
Once the queen of all the earth,
she is now a slave.

2 She sobs through the night;
tears stream down her cheeks.
Among all her lovers,
there is no one left to comfort her.
All her friends have betrayed her
and become her enemies.

3 Judah has been led away into captivity,
oppressed with cruel slavery.
She lives among foreign nations
and has no place of rest.
Her enemies have chased her down,
and she has nowhere to turn.

4 The roads to Jerusalem are in mourning,
for crowds no longer come to
celebrate the festivals.
The city gates are silent,
her priests groan,
her young women are crying—
how bitter is her fate!

5 Her oppressors have become her
masters,
and her enemies prosper,
for the LORD has punished Jerusalem
for her many sins.
Her children have been captured
and taken away to distant lands.

6 All the majesty of beautiful Jerusalem
has been stripped away.
Her princes are like starving deer
searching for pasture.
They are too weak to run
from the pursuing enemy.

1:1 Isa 22:2; Jer 40:9
1:2 Job 19:13-14; Ps 6:6; 77:2-6; Jer 2:25; 22:20-22; Mic 7:5
1:3 Lev 26:39; Deut 28:64-67; 2 Kgs 25:4-5
1:4 Jer 9:11; 10:22; Lam 2:6-7; Joel 1:8-13
1:5 Ps 90:7-8; Ezek 8:17-18; 9:9-10
1:6 Jer 13:18

1:1-22 Each of the first four chapters of this book is an acrostic, laid out in the order of the Hebrew alphabet. The first word of each verse begins with a successive Hebrew letter. Chapters 1, 2, and 4 have one verse for each of the twenty-two Hebrew letters. Chapter 3 contains twenty-two stanzas of three verses each. • Chapter 1 mourns the destruction and desolation of Jerusalem, recognizing that this was God's well-deserved judgment on Israel's sins.

1:2 The *lovers* were the fertility deities, Baal and Asherah, who were worshiped by most people in Judah. Her *friends* were her military allies, notably Egypt, who was no match for Babylon (Jer 37:5-11).

1:3 The woman of 1:1 is the nation of *Judah.* • *led away into captivity:* This happened four times:
605 BC (Dan 1:3-4)
597 BC (2 Kgs 24:12-16; Ezek 1:2-3; Jer 52:28)
586 BC (2 Kgs 25:5-7, 18-21; Jer 39:5-10, 52:29)
581 BC (Jer 52:30).

1:4 *Jerusalem* (Hebrew *Zion;* also in 1:17): In the Psalms and in the prophetic books, Zion represents the city of Jerusalem. In Lamentations, Zion is a poetic name for the city, even in ruins. Hebrews 12:22-24 speaks of the heavenly Zion (see also Rev 14:1-5). • The annual *festivals* in Jerusalem were the Passover, Unleavened Bread, First Harvest, Harvest (Pentecost), Trumpets, the Day of Atonement, and Shelters (Tabernacles). See Lev 23:1-44 and chart on p. 235. • The main duties of the *priests* were carried out in the Temple and its surrounding area. Since the Temple was in ruins, they had no jobs and hence no future.

1:5 *for her many sins:* Judah's sins before the Babylonian invasion are outlined in 2 Kgs 21:1-9, 16; 24:3-4 (cp. 2 Chr 33:1-10, 22-23 and 2 Chr 36:11-16). Similarly, a list of Israel's sins before Assyria destroyed it is found in 2 Kgs 17:14-23.

1:6 *of beautiful Jerusalem:* Literally *of the daughter of Zion.*

1:7
Jer 37:7; 48:27
Lam 4:17

1:8
Isa 59:2-13

1:9
Ps 74:23
Eccl 4:1
Isa 3:8
Jer 13:17-18
Ezek 24:13

1:10
Ps 74:4-8
Isa 64:10-11
Jer 51:51

1:11
1 Sam 30:12

1:12
Isa 13:13
Jer 4:8; 18:16; 48:27

1:13
Job 19:6; 30:30
Ps 22:14
Jer 44:6
Hab 3:16

1:14
Prov 5:22
Isa 47:6
Jer 28:13-14; 32:3, 5
Ezek 25:4, 7

1:15
Isa 41:2
Jer 13:24; 37:10

1:16
Ps 69:20
Eccl 4:1
Lam 1:2

1:17
2 Kgs 24:2-4
Isa 1:15
Jer 4:31

1:18
Deut 28:32, 41
1 Sam 12:14-15
Ps 119:75
Jer 12:1

1:19
Job 19:13-19
Jer 14:15
Lam 1:2; 2:20

7 In the midst of her sadness and
wandering,
Jerusalem remembers her ancient
splendor.
But now she has fallen to her enemy,
and there is no one to help her.
Her enemy struck her down
and laughed as she fell.

8 Jerusalem has sinned greatly,
so she has been tossed away like a
filthy rag.
All who once honored her now despise
her,
for they have seen her stripped naked
and humiliated.
All she can do is groan
and hide her face.

9 She defiled herself with immorality
and gave no thought to her future.
Now she lies in the gutter
with no one to lift her out.
"LORD, see my misery," she cries.
"The enemy has triumphed."

10 The enemy has plundered her
completely,
taking every precious thing she
owns.
She has seen foreigners violate her
sacred Temple,
the place the LORD had forbidden
them to enter.

11 Her people groan as they search for
bread.
They have sold their treasures for
food to stay alive.
"O LORD, look," she mourns,
"and see how I am despised.

12 "Does it mean nothing to you, all you
who pass by?
Look around and see if there is any
suffering like mine,
which the LORD brought on me
when he erupted in fierce anger.

13 "He has sent fire from heaven that burns
in my bones.
He has placed a trap in my path and
turned me back.
He has left me devastated,
racked with sickness all day long.

14 "He wove my sins into ropes
to hitch me to a yoke of captivity.
The Lord sapped my strength and
turned me over to my enemies;
I am helpless in their hands.

15 "The Lord has treated my mighty men
with contempt.
At his command a great army has come
to crush my young warriors.
The Lord has trampled his beloved city
like grapes are trampled in a winepress.

16 "For all these things I weep;
tears flow down my cheeks.
No one is here to comfort me;
any who might encourage me are far
away.
My children have no future,
for the enemy has conquered us."

17 Jerusalem reaches out for help,
but no one comforts her.
Regarding his people Israel,
the LORD has said,
"Let their neighbors be their enemies!
Let them be thrown away like a filthy
rag!"

18 "The LORD is right," Jerusalem says,
"for I rebelled against him.
Listen, people everywhere;
look upon my anguish and despair,
for my sons and daughters
have been taken captive to distant lands.

19 "I begged my allies for help,
but they betrayed me.
My priests and leaders
starved to death in the city,
even as they searched for food
to save their lives.

1:7 ***laughed as she fell:*** See also Jer 24:9; Ezek 22:5; 36:4.

1:8-9 ***Jerusalem*** was ***stripped*** of everything of physical and spiritual value that the people cherished.

1:10 For historical accounts of these events, see 2 Kgs 25:8-17; 2 Chr 36:13-21; Jer 52:4-30.

1:13 The destruction of Jerusalem at the hands of the Babylonians was like ***fire from heaven.***

1:14 For their ***sins,*** the people of Judah were tied to one another with ***ropes*** and taken as captives into exile.

1:15 ***his beloved city*** (literally *the virgin daughter of Judah*): God had given special care to Jerusalem, like a father protecting his daughter. But her sins had been persistent, and her punishment was horrible. • ***like grapes . . . trampled in a winepress:*** This common procedure for extracting juice from grapes is used vividly in Isa 63:3 to show the horrors of punishment. In Rev 14:18-20; 19:15, the image graphically represents universal judgment.

1:17 ***Israel:*** Literally *Jacob.* The names "Jacob" and "Israel" are often interchanged throughout the Old Testament, referring sometimes to the individual patriarch and sometimes to the nation.

1:19 ***I begged my allies:*** Egypt had a great deal of interest in Judah because Judah controlled the only good route to the north. However, Egypt turned her back on Judah when Babylon attacked Jerusalem (Jer 37:5-11). • When there was little rain in the fall and spring in Palestine, a summer without rain could destroy crops and cause a food shortage. The food supply also ran out under the prolonged siege of a city (Jan 588–July 586 BC), and many people ***starved to death*** (2 Kgs 25:2-3; cp. Jer 37:21).

20 "LORD, see my anguish!
My heart is broken
and my soul despairs,
for I have rebelled against you.
In the streets the sword kills,
and at home there is only death.

21 "Others heard my groans,
but no one turned to comfort me.
When my enemies heard about my troubles,
they were happy to see what you had done.
Oh, bring the day you promised,
when they will suffer as I have suffered.

22 "Look at all their evil deeds, LORD.
Punish them,
as you have punished me
for all my sins.
My groans are many,
and I am sick at heart."

2. GOD'S ANGER AT SIN (2:1-22)

2 The Lord in his anger
has cast a dark shadow over
beautiful Jerusalem.
The fairest of Israel's cities lies in the dust,
thrown down from the heights of heaven.
In his day of great anger,
the Lord has shown no mercy even to his Temple.

2 Without mercy the Lord has destroyed
every home in Israel.
In his anger he has broken down
the fortress walls of beautiful Jerusalem.
He has brought them to the ground,
dishonoring the kingdom and its rulers.

3 All the strength of Israel
vanishes beneath his fierce anger.
The Lord has withdrawn his protection
as the enemy attacks.
He consumes the whole land of Israel
like a raging fire.

4 He bends his bow against his people,
as though he were their enemy.
His strength is used against them
to kill their finest youth.
His fury is poured out like fire
on beautiful Jerusalem.

5 Yes, the Lord has vanquished Israel
like an enemy.
He has destroyed her palaces
and demolished her fortresses.
He has brought unending sorrow and tears
upon beautiful Jerusalem.

6 He has broken down his Temple
as though it were merely a garden shelter.
The LORD has blotted out all memory
of the holy festivals and Sabbath days.
Kings and priests fall together
before his fierce anger.

7 The Lord has rejected his own altar;
he despises his own sanctuary.
He has given Jerusalem's palaces
to her enemies.
They shout in the LORD's Temple
as though it were a day of celebration.

8 The LORD was determined
to destroy the walls of beautiful Jerusalem.
He made careful plans for their destruction,
then did what he had planned.
Therefore, the ramparts and walls
have fallen down before him.

1:20 Isa 16:11; Jer 4:19
1:21 Ps 35:15; Isa 14:5-6; 47:6; Jer 30:16
1:22 Neh 4:4-5; Ps 137:7-8
2:1 Ps 99:5; 132:7; Isa 64:11; Ezek 28:14-16
2:2 Ps 21:9; 89:39-40; Lam 3:43
2:3 Ps 75:5, 10; Isa 42:25; Jer 21:14
2:4 Job 6:4; 16:13; Jer 7:20; Lam 3:12-13
2:5 Jer 52:13; Lam 2:2
2:6 Lam 1:4; Zeph 3:18
2:7 Ps 74:3-8; Isa 64:11; Ezek 7:20-22
2:8 2 Kgs 21:13; Isa 34:11; Amos 7:7-9

1:20 The leaders and people of Judah had *rebelled* (Jer 2:17; 5:6, 23) by rejecting the one true God and his commandments and by resisting the invaders God had sent (2 Kgs 24:1, 20; 2 Chr 36:13).

1:21 *the day you promised:* The poet's spirit was heartened by the belief that God would set up a day when everyone—oppressors and victims—would be judged justly (see Isa 13:6, 9; Jer 46:10-12, 27-28; Amos 5:18-20; Obad 1:15; 1 Thes 5:2-3; 2 Thes 2:2).

1:22 See "Prayers for Vengeance" at Ps 137, p. 1017.

2:1-22 This chapter is an acrostic poem; each verse begins with a successive Hebrew letter (see note on 1:1-22). It graphically portrays the Lord as Jerusalem's destroyer.

2:1 ***beautiful Jerusalem:*** Literally *the daughter of Zion;* also in 2:8, 10, 18. See note on 1:4. • ***the heights of heaven:*** Jerusalem's buildings were splendid, adorned with precious metals and jewels. Jerusalem had the reputation of being the sacred city of the Lord. • ***his Temple*** (literally *his footstool*): Cp. 1 Chr 28:2; Ps 99:5; 132:7.

2:2 ***Israel:*** Literally *Jacob;* also in 2:3b. See note on 1:17. • ***beautiful Jerusalem:*** Literally *the daughter of Judah;* also in 2:5.

2:3-4 ***bends his bow:*** In the past, the Lord had been a mighty warrior on Israel's behalf (see Exod 14:13–15:21; Josh 23:9-11; Judg 7:1-25; 2 Kgs 19:32-35); now he waged war against Jerusalem (see Isa 63:10; Ezek 24:25). • ***on beautiful Jerusalem:*** Literally *on the tent of the daughter of Zion.*

2:6 A ***garden shelter*** was a temporary structure that harvesters put up to provide shade. God had promised to take care of ***his Temple*** forever (1 Kgs 9:3), but now it seemed that he had abandoned it.

2:7 The Temple was destroyed because the sins that the priests and the people had committed within its walls had defiled its holiness (cp. Jer 7:3-15; 26:3-6, 12-13; Ezek 24:21).

2:8 ***Ramparts*** were stone walls or mounds of earth built around a city to protect it from assault by an enemy army.

2:9
Neh 1:3
Jer 14:14; 23:16
2:10
Job 2:13
Isa 3:26
Amos 8:3
Jon 3:6-8
2:11
Jer 4:19
Lam 2:19
2:12
Job 30:16
Ps 42:4
2:13
Lam 1:12
2:14
Ezek 22:25, 28; 23:36
Mic 3:8
2:15
Job 27:23
Ps 48:2; 50:2
Jer 18:16
2:16
Ps 22:13; 56:2
Lam 3:46
Obad 1:12-15
2:17
Deut 28:43-44
Ps 89:42
Lam 1:5
2:18
Ps 119:145
Lam 2:8
Hos 7:14
Hab 2:11
2:19
1 Sam 1:15
Ps 42:3-4
Isa 51:20
2:20
Exod 32:11
Deut 9:26
Ps 78:64
Jer 23:11-12
Lam 4:13, 16

9 Jerusalem's gates have sunk into the ground.
He has smashed their locks and bars.
Her kings and princes have been exiled to distant lands;
her law has ceased to exist.
Her prophets receive
no more visions from the LORD.

10 The leaders of beautiful Jerusalem
sit on the ground in silence.
They are clothed in burlap
and throw dust on their heads.
The young women of Jerusalem
hang their heads in shame.

11 I have cried until the tears no longer come;
my heart is broken.
My spirit is poured out in agony
as I see the desperate plight of my people.
Little children and tiny babies
are fainting and dying in the streets.

12 They cry out to their mothers,
"We need food and drink!"
Their lives ebb away in the streets
like the life of a warrior wounded in battle.
They gasp for life
as they collapse in their mothers' arms.

13 What can I say about you?
Who has ever seen such sorrow?
O daughter of Jerusalem,
to what can I compare your anguish?
O virgin daughter of Zion,
how can I comfort you?
For your wound is as deep as the sea.
Who can heal you?

14 Your prophets have said
so many foolish things, false to the core.
They did not save you from exile
by pointing out your sins.
Instead, they painted false pictures,
filling you with false hope.

15 All who pass by jeer at you.
They scoff and insult beautiful Jerusalem, saying,
"Is this the city called 'Most Beautiful in All the World'
and 'Joy of All the Earth'?"

16 All your enemies mock you.
They scoff and snarl and say,
"We have destroyed her at last!
We have long waited for this day,
and it is finally here!"

17 But it is the LORD who did just as he planned.
He has fulfilled the promises of disaster
he made long ago.
He has destroyed Jerusalem without mercy.
He has caused her enemies to gloat over her
and has given them power over her.

18 Cry aloud before the Lord,
O walls of beautiful Jerusalem!
Let your tears flow like a river
day and night.
Give yourselves no rest;
give your eyes no relief.

19 Rise during the night and cry out.
Pour out your hearts like water to the Lord.
Lift up your hands to him in prayer,
pleading for your children,
for in every street
they are faint with hunger.

20 "O LORD, think about this!
Should you treat your own people this way?
Should mothers eat their own children,
those they once bounced on their knees?

2:9 ***no more visions:*** Daniel and Ezekiel were ***prophets*** of the Lord who had visions while they lived among the exiles far from the land of Judah (Ezek 1:1; Dan 7:1). This verse refers to prophets in Jerusalem who claimed to have visions that proved to be false.

2:10 ***Burlap*** (or ***sackcloth***) was made of goat or camel hair and was often used for grain sacks or for items to be carried on pack animals. Poor people wore it as clothing because it was inexpensive, and people in mourning wore it as a sign of their deep sorrow (its dark color matched their mood, and its roughness matched their discomfort). • Throwing ***dust on their heads*** and clothing was a sign to neighbors that a family member had died.

2:13 ***Who can heal you?*** Reputed healers and prophets were all liars and frauds (Jer 6:13-14).

2:15 ***beautiful Jerusalem:*** Literally *the daughter of Jerusalem.*

2:16 Their ***enemies*** were glad that Jerusalem was defeated.

2:17 ***promises . . . made long ago:*** God's promises of blessing were always contingent upon Israel's obedience to the law (Deut 8). He had promised to destroy them if they disobeyed it (Lev 26).

2:18-19 Repentance and ***prayer*** are the proper responses when facing the devastation of God's judgment.

2:18 ***Cry aloud:*** Literally *Their heart cried.*

2:20 Jeremiah had predicted that the same cannibalism that occurred during a siege of Samaria (2 Kgs 6:28-29) would happen in Jerusalem (Jer 19:9; see also Lam 4:10; Ezek 5:10; cp. Deut 28:53-57).

Should priests and prophets be killed
within the Lord's Temple?

21 "See them lying in the streets—
young and old,
boys and girls,
killed by the swords of the enemy.
You have killed them in your anger,
slaughtering them without mercy.

22 "You have invited terrors from all around,
as though you were calling them to a
day of feasting.
In the day of the LORD's anger,
no one has escaped or survived.
The enemy has killed all the children
whom I carried and raised."

3. HOPE IN THE LORD'S FAITHFULNESS (3:1-66)

3 I am the one who has seen the
afflictions
that come from the rod of the LORD's
anger.
2 He has led me into darkness,
shutting out all light.
3 He has turned his hand against me
again and again, all day long.
4 He has made my skin and flesh grow old.
He has broken my bones.
5 He has besieged and surrounded me
with anguish and distress.
6 He has buried me in a dark place,
like those long dead.
7 He has walled me in, and I cannot escape.
He has bound me in heavy chains.
8 And though I cry and shout,
he has shut out my prayers.
9 He has blocked my way with a high stone
wall;
he has made my road crooked.
10 He has hidden like a bear or a lion,
waiting to attack me.
11 He has dragged me off the path and torn
me in pieces,
leaving me helpless and devastated.
12 He has drawn his bow
and made me the target for his arrows.
13 He shot his arrows
deep into my heart.
14 My own people laugh at me.
All day long they sing their mocking
songs.
15 He has filled me with bitterness
and given me a bitter cup of sorrow
to drink.

16 He has made me chew on gravel.
He has rolled me in the dust.
17 Peace has been stripped away,
and I have forgotten what prosperity is.
18 I cry out, "My splendor is gone!
Everything I had hoped for from the
LORD is lost!"

19 The thought of my suffering and
homelessness
is bitter beyond words.
20 I will never forget this awful time,
as I grieve over my loss.
21 Yet I still dare to [a]hope
when I remember this:

22 The faithful [b]love of the LORD never
ends!
His mercies never cease.
23 Great is his faithfulness;
his mercies begin afresh each
morning.
24 I say to myself, "The LORD is my
inheritance;
therefore, I will hope in him!"

2:21 2 Chr 36:17
2:22 Isa 24:17-18; Jer 16:2-4
3:3-4 Ps 38:2-8
3:5 Job 19:8
3:6 Ps 88:5-6; 143:3
3:8 Job 30:20; Ps 22:2
3:9 Isa 63:17; Hos 2:6
3:10 Job 10:16
3:11 Job 16:12-13; Hos 6:1
3:12 Ps 7:12-13
3:14 Ps 22:6-7; Lam 3:63
3:15 Jer 9:15
3:16 Ps 3:7; Prov 20:17
3:17 Jer 12:12
3:18 Job 17:15; Ezek 37:11
3:19 Lam 3:5, 15
3:20 Ps 42:5-6, 11; 43:5
3:21 Ps 130:7; [a]*yakhal* (3176) ‣Mic 7:7
3:22 Ps 78:38; Jer 3:12; Mal 3:6; [b]*khesed* (2617) ‣Zech 7:9
3:24 Ps 73:26

2:22 *calling them to a day of feasting:* The poet compares Jerusalem's destruction to an invitation to a banquet at which war, famine, wild animals, and sickness would feast on the wicked in Jerusalem (Deut 28:15-68; cp. Rev 19:17-21).

3:1-66 This chapter is an acrostic poem, the verses in each stanza beginning with a successive letter of the Hebrew alphabet (see note on 1:1-22). In it, the author laments what has happened (3:1-20, 48-54), remembers the faithful love of the Lord (3:21-25), describes how God's people should respond (3:26-47), and calls upon the Lord in prayer (3:55-66).

3:1-24 The author speaks of the suffering of Judah and Jerusalem as his own.

3:6-9 Some understand these verses as a poetic reference to Jeremiah's confinement in a muddy cistern before the destruction of Jerusalem (Jer 38:6-13).

3:9 *blocked my way . . . made my road crooked:* Sin causes confusion and cuts a person or a community off from a happy future. Innocent people know the future as a straight path that is easy to follow (Prov 21:8). Isaiah imagined God's activities as a parade on a straight road that his worshipers would prepare (Isa 40:3).

3:12 Cp. Job 6:4.

3:19 *is bitter beyond words* (or *is wormwood and gall*): Wormwood is a plant with a bitter taste; here it represents the emotional intensity of inner agony (Prov 5:4; Rev 8:11). Gall is a poisonous plant that causes severe physical pain if eaten; it is a powerful symbol for extremely stressful emotions (Deut 29:18; Ps 69:21). The survivor seems to be at a dead end from which he cannot escape.

3:22-33 God's love and faithfulness *never cease.* Just as God had been faithful in bringing judgment on Jerusalem for their sins, he would be faithful in bringing restoration to those who returned to him.

3:22 The *faithful love of the LORD* is the basis for the poet's recovery from deep depression. As with Jeremiah in the cistern (Jer 38:6-13) and Jonah in the stomach of the great fish (Jon 2:2-10), the Lord provided salvation from death. • *The faithful love of the LORD never ends:* As in Syriac version; Hebrew reads *The faithful love of the LORD keeps us from destruction.*

3:23 God's *faithfulness* speaks of his absolute reliability, which is evident in his daily *mercies.* He continually provides a habitable world in which we can live.

3:24 *The LORD is my inheritance:* The land of Canaan had been regarded as Israel's inheritance since the time of Moses (Exod 15:17; Josh 21:19; 1 Chr

3:25 Isa 25:9; 26:9
3:26 Ps 37:7
3:28 Jer 15:17
3:29 Job 16:15; 40:4
3:30 Isa 50:6; Matt 5:39
3:31 Ps 94:14; Isa 54:7-10
3:32 Ps 78:38; 106:43-45; c*rakham* (7355) ‣Hos 2:23
3:36 Hab 1:13
3:38 Jer 32:42; d*ʿelyon* (5945) ‣Gen 14:20
3:39 Mic 7:9; Heb 12:5-6; e*khet'* (2399) ‣Dan 9:5
3:40 2 Cor 13:5
3:42 Jer 14:20
3:47 Isa 24:17-18; Jer 48:43-44
3:49 Ps 77:2
3:50 Isa 63:15
3:52 1 Sam 26:20; Ps 11:1; 35:7
3:53 Jer 37:16
3:54 Ps 69:2; Jon 2:3-5
3:56 Job 34:28; Ps 55:1; 116:12
3:57 Isa 41:10-14
3:58 Ps 34:22; Jer 50:34; 51:36; f*ga'al* (1350) ‣Hos 13:14
3:59 Ps 26:1; 43:1

25 The LORD is good to those who depend
on him,
to those who search for him.
26 So it is good to wait quietly
for salvation from the LORD.
27 And it is good for people to submit at an
early age
to the yoke of his discipline:

28 Let them sit alone in silence
beneath the LORD's demands.
29 Let them lie face down in the dust,
for there may be hope at last.
30 Let them turn the other cheek to those
who strike them
and accept the insults of their enemies.

31 For no one is abandoned
by the Lord forever.
32 Though he brings grief, he also shows
[c]compassion
because of the greatness of his
unfailing love.
33 For he does not enjoy hurting people
or causing them sorrow.

34 If people crush underfoot
all the prisoners of the land,
35 if they deprive others of their rights
in defiance of the Most High,
36 if they twist justice in the courts—
doesn't the Lord see all these things?

37 Who can command things to happen
without the Lord's permission?
38 Does not the [d]Most High
send both calamity and good?
39 Then why should we, mere humans,
complain
when we are punished for our [e]sins?

40 Instead, let us test and examine our ways.
Let us turn back to the LORD.
41 Let us lift our hearts and hands
to God in heaven and say,
42 "We have sinned and rebelled,
and you have not forgiven us.

43 "You have engulfed us with your anger,
chased us down,
and slaughtered us without mercy.
44 You have hidden yourself in a cloud
so our prayers cannot reach you.
45 You have discarded us as refuse and
garbage
among the nations.

46 "All our enemies
have spoken out against us.
47 We are filled with fear,
for we are trapped, devastated, and
ruined."
48 Tears stream from my eyes
because of the destruction of my
people!

49 My tears flow endlessly;
they will not stop
50 until the LORD looks down
from heaven and sees.
51 My heart is breaking
over the fate of all the women of
Jerusalem.

52 My enemies, whom I have never harmed,
hunted me down like a bird.
53 They threw me into a pit
and dropped stones on me.
54 The water rose over my head,
and I cried out, "This is the end!"

55 But I called on your name, LORD,
from deep within the pit.
56 You heard me when I cried, "Listen to my
pleading!
Hear my cry for help!"
57 Yes, you came when I called;
you told me, "Do not fear."

58 Lord, you are my lawyer! Plead my case!
For you have [f]redeemed my life.
59 You have seen the wrong they have done
to me, LORD.
Be my judge, and prove me right.
60 You have seen the vengeful plots
my enemies have laid against me.

28:8; Ps 47:4), but the true inheritance of God's people is really God himself (see Ps 16:5-6; Eph 1:11; Heb 9:15; 1 Pet 1:3-4).

3:26 Those who are confident of God's plan can ***wait quietly*** for him to grant ***salvation***.

3:28 ***sit alone in silence:*** Humble submission stops the tongue and quiets the heart.

3:29 In the ancient Near East, lying ***face down in the dust*** expressed submission (Gen 17:1-3; Lev 9:24; Josh 7:6; 1 Sam 5:4; 1 Kgs 18:39; 1 Chr 21:16; Matt 17:5-6).

3:30 To ***turn the other cheek*** also expresses submission. Jesus evidently had this verse in mind when he taught his disciples to submit to persecution (Matt 5:39). This response sees all suffering as coming from the Lord's hand.

3:31 Cp. Ps 103:8-11.

3:34-36 The people of Judah were doing such things before Jerusalem was destroyed (see Jer 5:26-31; 21:11-14; 23:10-14; Mic 3:1-12).

3:37-39 Some calamities have natural causes (Luke 13:1-5), and bad things happen to the righteous as well as to the wicked (Matt 5:45); whatever happens, we should give thanks (1 Thes 5:18) and not ***complain***.

3:40-42 Repentance is the key to receiving salvation (Isa 1:27; Jer 3:22; Ezek 3:21).

3:48-66 The author focuses on the viciousness of the enemies and cries out to the Lord.

3:52-57 This passage might refer to Jeremiah's experience in the cistern (Jer 37:11-15; 38:1-13).

3:58-66 Jerusalem deserved punishment, but the ***enemies*** carried it out with undeserved cruelty. The writer calls upon God to punish them.

61 LORD, you have heard the vile names
they call me.
You know all about the plans they
have made.
62 My enemies whisper and mutter
as they plot against me all day long.
63 Look at them! Whether they sit or stand,
I am the object of their mocking songs.

64 Pay them back, LORD,
for all the evil they have done.
65 Give them hard and stubborn hearts,
and then let your curse fall on them!
66 Chase them down in your anger,
destroying them beneath the LORD's
heavens.

4. GOD'S ANGER SATISFIED (4:1-22)

4 How the gold has lost its luster!
Even the finest gold has become
dull.
The sacred gemstones
lie scattered in the streets!

2 See how the precious children of
Jerusalem,
worth their weight in fine gold,
are now treated like pots of clay
made by a common potter.

3 Even the jackals feed their young,
but not my people Israel.
They ignore their children's cries,
like ostriches in the desert.

4 The parched tongues of their little ones
stick to the roofs of their mouths in
thirst.
The children cry for bread,
but no one has any to give them.

5 The people who once ate the richest foods
now beg in the streets for anything
they can get.
Those who once wore the finest clothes
now search the garbage dumps for food.

6 The guilt of my people
is greater than that of Sodom,
where utter disaster struck in a moment
and no hand offered help.

7 Our princes once glowed with health—
brighter than snow, whiter than milk.
Their faces were as ruddy as rubies,
their appearance like fine jewels.

8 But now their faces are blacker than soot.
No one recognizes them in the streets.
Their skin sticks to their bones;
it is as dry and hard as wood.

9 Those killed by the sword are better off
than those who die of hunger.
Starving, they waste away
for lack of food from the fields.

10 Tenderhearted women
have cooked their own children.
They have eaten them
to survive the siege.

11 But now the anger of the LORD is satisfied.
His fierce anger has been poured out.
He started a fire in Jerusalem
that burned the city to its foundations.

12 Not a king in all the earth—
no one in all the world—
would have believed that an enemy
could march through the gates of
Jerusalem.

13 Yet it happened because of the sins of
her prophets
and the sins of her priests,
who defiled the city
by shedding innocent blood.

14 They wandered blindly
through the streets,
so defiled by blood
that no one dared touch them.

15 "Get away!" the people shouted at them.
"You're defiled! Don't touch us!"
So they fled to distant lands
and wandered among foreign nations,
but none would let them stay.

16 The LORD himself has scattered them,
and he no longer helps them.
People show no respect for the priests
and no longer honor the leaders.

3:61 Lam 5:1
3:62 Ps 59:7; 140:3
Ezek 36:3
3:63 Lam 3:14
3:64 Ps 28:4
Jer 51:24
3:65 Deut 2:30
Isa 6:10
4:1 2 Kgs 25:9-10
4:2 Isa 30:14
Jer 19:1, 11
4:3 Job 39:14-16
Lam 2:12
4:4 Jer 14:3
4:5 Jer 6:2
Amos 6:3-7
4:6 Gen 19:25
Jer 20:16
Ezek 16:48
4:7 Ps 51:7
4:8 Ps 102:5
Lam 5:10
4:9 Lev 26:39
4:10 Deut 28:53-55
2 Kgs 6:26-30
Lam 2:20
4:11 Deut 32:22
4:12 Jer 21:13
4:13 Jer 2:30; 26:8-9
Ezek 22:26
4:14 Deut 28:28-29
Isa 29:10; 56:10;
59:9-10
4:15 Lev 13:45-46
Jer 45:5
4:16 Isa 9:14-16
Jer 52:24-27
4:17 Jer 37:7
Lam 1:7
Ezek 29:16
4:18 Jer 5:31; 16:16
Amos 8:2

3:64-66 This prayer for vengeance is similar to several psalms (see "Prayers for Vengeance" at Ps 137, p. 1017).

4:1-22 This chapter is an acrostic poem; each verse begins with a successive letter of the Hebrew alphabet (see note on 1:1-22). Although God's people still experience his judgment, they will soon experience restoration.

4:2 ***precious children of Jerusalem:*** Literally *precious sons of Zion.* See note on 1:4.

4:3 ***like ostriches:*** See also Job 39:16.

4:6 ***guilt:*** Or *punishment.*

4:7 ***like fine jewels:*** (literally *like lapis lazuli*): Lapis lazuli is a beautiful blue stone that is soft enough to carve. It is often used in decorations and mosaics.

4:8 ***Skin*** sticking to ***bones*** is symptomatic of the final stages of starvation, just before death.

4:9 Long sieges result in a serious ***lack of food***. Even if people could get to the fields, they would find the crops destroyed or harvested to feed the soldiers.

4:11 ***in Jerusalem:*** Hebrew *in Zion.*

4:12 ***Not a king . . . could march through the gates of Jerusalem:*** Since God had delivered Jerusalem from Sennacherib of Assyria more than a century earlier (2 Kgs 19:36-37), Judeans had strongly believed that not even the mightiest king, Nebuchadnezzar of Babylon, could defeat the city.

4:15 It appears that these leaders ***fled*** from Jerusalem as refugees to other ***lands***.

4:19 Deut 28:49; Isa 5:26-28; Jer 4:13; Hab 1:8
4:20 Jer 39:5; Ezek 12:12-13
4:21 Isa 34:7; Amos 1:11; Obad 1:16
4:22 Isa 40:2; Jer 49:10
5:1 Ps 44:13-16
5:2 Isa 1:7; Hos 8:7-8; Zeph 1:13
5:3 Exod 22:24; Jer 15:8; 18:21
5:4 Isa 3:1
5:6 Hos 9:3
5:7 Jer 14:20; 16:12
5:9 Jer 40:9-12
5:10 Job 30:30; Lam 4:8
5:11 Isa 13:16; Zech 14:2
5:12 Isa 47:6; Lam 4:16
5:13 Jer 7:18
5:14 Isa 24:8; Jer 7:34
5:15 Jer 25:10; Amos 8:10
5:16 Job 19:9; Ps 89:39
5:19 Ps 45:6; 102:12
5:21 Ps 80:3; [g]*khadash* (2318) ‣1 Sam 11:14
5:22 Isa 64:9

17 We looked in vain for our allies
to come and save us,
but we were looking to nations
that could not help us.

18 We couldn't go into the streets
without danger to our lives.
Our end was near; our days were numbered.
We were doomed!

19 Our enemies were swifter than eagles in flight.
If we fled to the mountains, they found us.
If we hid in the wilderness,
they were waiting for us there.

20 Our king—the LORD's anointed, the very life of our nation—
was caught in their snares.
We had thought that his shadow
would protect us against any nation on earth!

21 Are you rejoicing in the land of Uz,
O people of Edom?
But you, too, must drink from the cup of the LORD's anger.
You, too, will be stripped naked in your drunkenness.

22 O beautiful Jerusalem, your punishment will end;
you will soon return from exile.
But Edom, your punishment is just beginning;
soon your many sins will be exposed.

5. PRAYER FOR RESTORATION (5:1-22)

5 LORD, remember what has happened to us.
See how we have been disgraced!
2 Our inheritance has been turned over to strangers,
our homes to foreigners.
3 We are orphaned and fatherless.
Our mothers are widowed.
4 We have to pay for water to drink,
and even firewood is expensive.
5 Those who pursue us are at our heels;
we are exhausted but are given no rest.
6 We submitted to Egypt and Assyria
to get enough food to survive.
7 Our ancestors sinned, but they have died—
and we are suffering the punishment they deserved!

8 Slaves have now become our masters;
there is no one left to rescue us.
9 We hunt for food at the risk of our lives,
for violence rules the countryside.
10 The famine has blackened our skin
as though baked in an oven.
11 Our enemies rape the women in Jerusalem
and the young girls in all the towns of Judah.
12 Our princes are being hanged by their thumbs,
and our elders are treated with contempt.
13 Young men are led away to work at millstones,
and boys stagger under heavy loads of wood.
14 The elders no longer sit in the city gates;
the young men no longer dance and sing.
15 Joy has left our hearts;
our dancing has turned to mourning.
16 The garlands have fallen from our heads.
Weep for us because we have sinned.
17 Our hearts are sick and weary,
and our eyes grow dim with tears.
18 For Jerusalem is empty and desolate,
a place haunted by jackals.

19 But LORD, you remain the same forever!
Your throne continues from generation to generation.
20 Why do you continue to forget us?
Why have you abandoned us for so long?
21 Restore us, O LORD, and bring us back to you again!
[g]Give us back the joys we once had!
22 Or have you utterly rejected us?
Are you angry with us still?

4:20 ***Our king . . . was caught:*** A reference to Zedekiah, who tried to flee but was caught and treated cruelly by Nebuchadnezzar (2 Kgs 25:4-7; Jer 39:4-7; 52:9-11).

4:21-22 The people of *Edom* were feeling secure and gloating over Jerusalem's misfortune, but they, too, would experience ***punishment*** for their *sins* (see Obad 1:1-21; Jer 49:7-22).

4:21 *Uz* was an area east of the Jordan River that extended south to Edom. It was Job's home (Job 1:1).

4:22 ***O beautiful Jerusalem:*** Literally *O daughter of Zion.* See note on 1:4. • The first ***return from exile*** occurred in 538 BC, after Cyrus of Persia defeated Babylon (2 Chr 36:22-23; Ezra 1:1-4).

5:1-22 Unlike the previous chapters, this chapter is not an alphabetic acrostic (see note on 1:1-22). It is a heartfelt prayer for restoration (cp. Dan 9:4-19).

5:10 There was a ***famine*** in the city during the siege (2 Kgs 25:3; Jer 37:21; 38:9; 52:6). See note on 4:8.

5:11 ***in Jerusalem:*** Hebrew *in Zion.*

5:12-17 These terrible things happened ***because*** the people had ***sinned*** (see Isa 24:7-12; Jer 7:24; 13:18; 25:10-11; Amos 8:10).

5:16 ***The garlands have:*** Or *The crown has.*

5:18 ***Jerusalem:*** Hebrew *Mount Zion.* • ***haunted by jackals:*** Cp. Isa 13:22; 34:13; Jer 9:11; 10:22; Mal 1:3.

5:22 ***have you utterly rejected us?*** The tragedy of the Exile raised the question of whether God would forgive sin and restore his people. God answered clearly through the prophets (Isa 40:27-31; 41:8-20) and by sending Christ (Matt 9:2-6; 26:28; Luke 24:47).

THE BOOK OF

EZEKIEL

The prophet Ezekiel's book contains strange visions, images, and messages that seem far removed from contemporary life. It is not easy reading, yet its message remains very relevant: God will purify his people and live among them forever. Even during the darkest days, God insisted that he would restore his people. This message offers hope and inspiration not just to the exiled people of Judah, but to all who put their trust in him.

SETTING

The book of Ezekiel was written during the difficult days of Judah's exile in Babylon (605–538 BC). As the Assyrian empire's power waned, the Babylonians gradually became more powerful. They captured the Assyrian capital of Nineveh (612 BC), and Babylonian domination was made complete with the defeat of the last resisting Assyrians at the decisive battle of Carchemish (605 BC). In the same year, the Babylonians raided Judah and took hostages from the upper classes back to Babylon, including Daniel and his three friends (Dan 1:1-5).

In 601 BC, King Jehoiakim of Judah rebelled against the Babylonians, and he died during the ensuing siege (598 BC). His son, Jehoiachin,

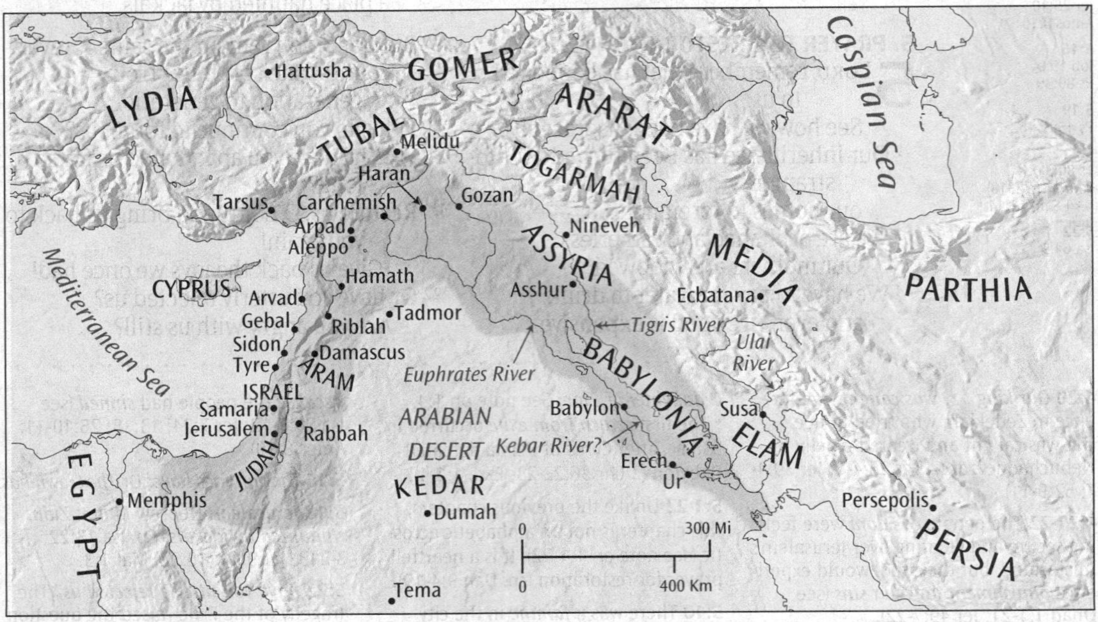

▲ **The Near East, about 593 BC.** When Ezekiel first received visions by the KEBAR RIVER, the Babylonians had gained control of the Near East and were in the process of subjugating and destroying the kingdom of JUDAH and asserting their power over EGYPT.

BABYLON 1:1, 3; 17:12-20; 21:19-23; 23:23; 24:1-2; 30:10, 24-25
EGYPT 29:1–32:32
LYDIA 27:10; 30:5
PERSIA 27:10; 38:5
RABBAH 21:20-21; 25:5
SIDON 28:20-24
ARAM (Syria) 27:16
TOGARMAH 27:14; 38:6
TUBAL 27:13; 32:26; 38:2; 39:1
TYRE 26:1–28:19; 29:18-20

reigned for only a brief period before he surrendered and was taken to Babylon in 597 BC. The Babylonians also took the prophet Ezekiel and other prominent people into exile and plundered many treasures from the Temple in Jerusalem.

While Ezekiel was in Babylon, the Babylonians placed Jehoiachin's uncle Zedekiah on the throne of Judah. When Zedekiah rebelled against Babylon, the Babylonians ravaged Judah and besieged Jerusalem in January 588 BC. The city was finally breached and destroyed in August 586 BC. The Babylonians forced Zedekiah to watch as they put his sons to death; then he was blinded and taken to Babylon with the other citizens of Judah who had skills useful to their overlords. These exiles remained in Babylon for a generation until the fortunes of the empire changed again (see Ezra).

Ezekiel's first visions took place in Babylon in 593 BC, when he was thirty years old (1:1-2).

OUTLINE

1:1–3:27
Ezekiel's Call and Commissioning

4:1–24:27
Oracles of Doom

25:1–32:32
Oracles against the Nations

33:1–48:35
Oracles of Good News

SUMMARY

Ezekiel's visions span the years leading up to and following the fall of Jerusalem in 586 BC. Before Jerusalem's fall, Ezekiel delivered the woeful message that judgment would come upon the people of Judah. After Jerusalem fell, however, Ezekiel conveyed a new vision of hope: Israel would emerge from the ashes of her past. Although the prophet mourned what had been lost, he dreamed of a bright future when the people would repent of the sins that brought their destruction and the Lord would establish the nation in holiness.

Ezekiel 1–3 tells of Ezekiel's call and commissioning as a prophet. His opening vision tells of the Lord's glory, ominously on the move (1:4-28). With images of motion and judgment, the vision depicts the Lord as the divine warrior in his heavenly chariot, coming to judge his people. During Ezekiel's call (2:1–3:15), the Spirit told him that the stubborn and rebellious people of Judah would not listen to his message. However, the Lord wanted him to be equally stubborn in faithfully delivering his message. Like a watchman (3:16-27), he should sound the alarm clearly and distinctly. God would hold the prophet accountable for delivering the message, not for the people's response.

In chs 4–24, Ezekiel delivers a litany of doom against Judah and Jerusalem. The prophet receives instructions to perform a series of sign acts depicting the coming siege and destruction of Jerusalem (see "Prophetic Sign Acts" at 4:1-17, p. 1319). Ezekiel 8–11 depicts Jerusalem's sins in four scenes of increasing abomination that clearly illustrate the reason for the coming destruction. God's glory departs from the sanctuary, and the Temple is completely destroyed. The poems, oracles, and visions throughout this section cumulatively establish the inevitability and justice of

TIMELINE

640–609 BC
Josiah as king of Judah

about 627~580 BC
Jeremiah as prophet

609–598 BC
Jehoiakim as king of Judah

605–562 BC
Nebuchadnezzar II as king of Babylon

605 BC
Battle of Carchemish; Nebuchadnezzar II defeats Pharaoh Neco II Nebuchadnezzar invades Judah, first deportation of captives

about 605~535 BC
Daniel in Babylon

597 BC
Jehoiachin as king of Judah

Apr 597 BC
Nebuchadnezzar captures Jerusalem, plunders Temple, takes Jehoiachin to Babylon; second deportation of captives

597–586 BC
Zedekiah as king of Judah

July 31, 593 BC
Ezekiel begins to prophesy (1:1)

586 BC
Nebuchadnezzar destroys Jerusalem, takes people of Judah into exile; end of the southern kingdom of Judah

Apr 26, 571 BC
Ezekiel's last recorded prophecy (29:17)

Apr 2, 561 BC
Jehoiachin is released from prison

Oct 539 BC
Cyrus II conquers Babylon

538 BC
Cyrus's decree allows exiles to return to Judea

Jerusalem's fall, culminating with the announcement of Nebuchadnezzar's siege of Jerusalem and a final message of the certainty of judgment (ch 24).

Ezekiel then turns toward hope, beginning with seven messages (chs 25–32) that indict the surrounding nations for having assisted the Babylonians and for delighting in Jerusalem's fall. These messages show that the promise God made to Abraham remained intact: "I will . . . curse those who treat you with contempt" (Gen 12:3). God's judgment was to come on all who took pleasure in the downfall of his people and who profited from their demise.

Ezekiel 33–48 completes the movement from judgment to hope, beginning with the decisive moment when the exiles finally hear the news of Jerusalem's fall (33:21). The Lord again commissions the prophet to minister as a watchman, proclaiming judgment on those who refuse to repent and promising life for those who do. Messages of hope promise a new shepherd with a renewed covenant and land where the people will dwell together in unity (chs 34–37).

The dark clouds of war threaten this picture of blessing (chs 38–39), but the Lord simply demonstrates the certainty of the new state of affairs. The Lord gathers the forces of Gog and his allies, not to judge his peacefully settled people, but to smash their enemies once and for all.

After God defeats Gog and his allies, he can reveal the final Temple and the reoriented land (chs 40–48). With architectural, ritual, and geographic imagery, Ezekiel's final vision depicts the same message as the rest of the book: God will raise his people to a new level of holiness so that he can once again dwell in their midst. Those who were faithful in the past receive renewed access to God's presence, while those who were less faithful remain on the margins. A river of life flows out from the final Temple; as it flows, it grows and transforms death into life. God's final words to his people do not warn of abandonment and destruction; rather, they promise fellowship and life.

Exile. It is not simply being homeless. Rather, it is knowing that you do have a home, but that your home has been taken over by enemies. Exile. It is not being without roots. On the contrary, it is having deep roots which have now been plucked up, and there you are, with roots dangling, writhing in pain, exposed to a cold and jeering world, longing to be restored to native and nurturing soil. Exile is knowing precisely where you belong, but knowing that you can't go back, not yet.

TAMARA ESKENAZI
"Exile and Dreams of Return," Currents in Theology and Mission 18 (1990)

AUTHORSHIP AND DATE

In the opening verses of the book, the prophet Ezekiel claims that he is the author (1:3), and there is little reason to doubt his claim. The book shows all the interests expected from a priest such as Ezekiel, and the central event of Jerusalem's destruction dominates the book's structure. The prophet most likely wrote the book during the period in which his visions and messages were given (593–570 BC), with the completed composition probably dating shortly after the final message.

MEANING AND MESSAGE

Before 586 BC, both the exiles in Babylon and the people remaining in Judah were convinced that Jerusalem could not fall. They believed that the presence of the Temple and its prescribed rituals would guarantee the city's survival. Ezekiel had to tell them that they were completely wrong. Because the Temple and its rituals were corrupt and the hearts and lives of the people were thoroughly pagan, Jerusalem had to fall.

While all the OT prophets condemned sin and idolatry, perhaps none used quite such sweeping terms as Ezekiel. From their time in Egypt onward, the disobedience of God's people infected every branch of society and encompassed every form of offense against God. God could not ignore or condone such sin and would surely

judge his people soon. Nothing could save God's city or its people from his judgment.

Following the destruction of Jerusalem, the prophet addressed his people, who were in grave danger of disillusionment and despair. They felt spiritually dead, abandoned by God and cut off from his presence. They said, "Our sins are heavy upon us; we are wasting away! How can we survive?" (33:10). Babylonian deities, who seemed to have triumphed over the Lord, surrounded the people. No one had ever returned home from captivity. Their hopes dashed, they believed they had no choice but to settle in the pagan land of Babylon and become part of its culture.

To these disillusioned people, the prophet delivered a message of God's sovereignty and glory, depicting God as majestic, transcendent, and powerful. The Babylonian gods had certainly not defeated God; rather, the Lord had temporarily abandoned his land and dwelling place because of his people's sin. Although he left the defiled city of Jerusalem, this glorious God did not abandon his people. Instead, he went to the remnant of his people in exile (11:16), where Ezekiel himself first saw the Lord's glory (1:1). God was still controlling all things, even the Babylonian king Nebuchadnezzar's attempts to consult his own gods through divination (21:21-23; cp. Dan 2–4). The Lord had decreed the destruction of Jerusalem for its sins; Nebuchadnezzar simply acted as God's agent.

Destruction did not mark the end of the story for God's people. God had promised to bless Abraham's descendants, making them into a mighty nation and blessing all nations through them. The oracles against the nations surrounding Judah (chs 25–32) demonstrated that God had not forgotten his ancient promise that those who rejoiced at Israel's downfall would themselves be severely judged. God would not forever abandon his people. One day he would return to be their shepherd (34:11); he would transform the land and the people from death into life. God's glory would once again return to the Temple, which would never again be defiled. Further, God would gather his scattered people into his presence and replace the old ways of doing things with new laws and higher standards of holiness. When filled with God's Spirit, the hearts of the people would no longer defile the land with their sins.

Ezekiel points toward a greater revelation of hope fulfilled in Jesus Christ. Through him, God's glory fully dwells in our midst as light in the darkness of our exile (11:16; 43:1-5; John 1:14). The Good Shepherd restores justice for his sheep (34:1-24; John 10:11). He fills us with his Spirit and makes us new creatures in him (36:26-28; 37:1-14; 2 Cor 5:17). Those who have allied themselves with Christ have even greater access to God's presence than Ezekiel's visions anticipated. They are able to approach the throne of grace freely and drink from the life-giving water that flows from the throne (47:1-11; Rev 22:1-5). Everything that Ezekiel anticipated—and more—is ours in Christ.

FURTHER READING

DANIEL BLOCK
The Book of Ezekiel 1–24; 25–48 (1997, 1998)

IAIN DUGUID
Ezekiel (1999)

DEREK THOMAS
God Strengthens; Ezekiel Simply Explained (1993)

CHRISTOPHER J. H. WRIGHT
The Message of Ezekiel (2001)

1. EZEKIEL'S CALL AND COMMISSIONING (1:1–3:27)

Introduction (1:1-3)

1 On July 31 of my thirtieth year, while I
was with the Judean exiles beside the
Kebar River in Babylon, the heavens were
opened and I saw visions of God. 2This
happened during the fifth year of King
Jehoiachin's captivity. 3(The LORD gave this
message to Ezekiel son of Buzi, a priest,
beside the Kebar River in the land of the
Babylonians, and he felt the hand of the
LORD take hold of him.)

A Vision of Living Beings (1:4-28)

4As I looked, I saw a great storm coming
from the north, driving before it a huge
cloud that flashed with lightning and
shone with brilliant light. There was fire
inside the cloud, and in the middle of the
fire glowed something like gleaming amber.
5From the center of the cloud came four living beings that looked human, 6except that
each had four faces and four wings. 7Their
legs were straight, and their feet had hooves
like those of a calf and shone like burnished
bronze. 8Under each of their four wings
I could see human hands. So each of the
four beings had four faces and four wings.
9The wings of each living being touched
the wings of the beings beside it. Each one
moved straight forward in any direction
without turning around.

10Each had a human face in the front, the
face of a lion on the right side, the face of
an ox on the left side, and the face of an
eagle at the back. 11Each had two pairs of
outstretched wings—one pair stretched out
to touch the wings of the living beings on

1:1 Num 12:6; Isa 1:1; Dan 8:1-2; Acts 7:56; Rev 4:1; 19:11
1:2 2 Kgs 24:12
1:3 2 Kgs 3:15
1:4 Jer 23:19
1:5 Rev 4:6-8
1:6 Ezek 1:10; 10:14, 21
1:7 Dan 10:6; Rev 1:15; 2:18
1:8 Ezek 10:8, 21
1:9 Ezek 10:22
1:10 Ezek 10:14; Rev 4:7

1:1–3:27 OT prophetic books often begin with a "call narrative" that gives details of the prophet's commissioning to his office (e.g., Jer 1:4-19). The prophetic call narrative demonstrated that the prophet's words were legitimate, showing that he spoke as the Lord's ambassador. It often introduced themes that his prophecy would address in greater detail, just as the overture to a symphony introduces the musical motifs that form the basis for the composition that follows. The focus of Ezekiel's call narrative is the Lord's impending judgment of his people.

1:1-3 The opening verses locate the prophet's ministry among the exiles from Judah who had been carried off to Babylon.

1:1 ***On July 31:*** Literally *On the fifth day of the fourth month* of the ancient Hebrew lunar calendar. A number of dates in Ezekiel can be cross-checked with dates in surviving Babylonian records and related accurately to our modern calendar. This event occurred on July 31, 593 BC. • ***of my thirtieth year*** (or *in the thirtieth year*): Priests began to minister in the Jerusalem Temple when they were thirty years old. Ezekiel was a priest (see 1:3), but he was ***with the Judean exiles . . . in Babylon*** and was therefore unable to serve in the usual ways. Ezekiel's identity as a priest in exile is significant to the message that follows. The exiles felt cut off from God and from conventional ways of appealing to him in the Temple. In the ancient world, most gods were closely tied to particular lands, so it was easy for those who were removed from the Promised Land to assume that the Lord was no longer interested in them. That God's word had come to a prophet among the exiles in Babylon showed that God had not forgotten them and still had a future for them. • The ***Kebar River*** was probably a large irrigation canal in the Nippur region southeast of Babylon. The Babylonians had deported the previous occupants because of their Assyrian sympathies and replaced them with exiles from elsewhere in their empire, including Judah. The Babylonians generally resettled peoples by ethnic groups and allowed them to retain their identity, unlike the Assyrians, whose policy of exile was to disperse and scatter populations. This difference later made it possible for the remnant of the exiles of Judah to return to their homeland. Those who had been exiled from the northern kingdom by the Assyrians were not able to return in the same way.

1:2 ***This happened during the fifth year of King Jehoiachin's captivity:*** The word of the Lord first came to Ezekiel in 593 BC, while Judah was still a semi-independent state (see Ezekiel Introduction, "Setting," p. 1310). Judah had been subjugated by the Babylonians in 597 BC, and King Jehoiachin had been carried into exile in Babylon at that time. Jehoiachin's uncle, Zedekiah, ruled Judah as a Babylonian vassal (597–586 BC). Ezekiel dates his prophecy with reference to Jehoiachin's captivity rather than to Zedekiah's reign because he seems to have viewed Zedekiah as a stand-in for the lawful king, Jehoiachin. Zedekiah later rebelled against Nebuchadnezzar (2 Kgs 24:20), who besieged the city of Jerusalem (588 BC), destroyed it, and burned the Temple (586 BC).

1:3 Ezekiel was a ***priest*** by descent and a prophet because ***the hand of the LORD*** was upon him. Priests offered sacrifices in the Temple and explained God's law. Prophets delivered God's words of blessing or curse to the people and interceded with God for them. Ezekiel's ministry included aspects of both priestly and prophetic mediation between God and the Israelites. • ***Babylonians:*** Or *Chaldeans.*

1:4-28 The language of this opening vision is that of *theophany,* a physical manifestation of God (see note on Deut 1:33). It was difficult for Ezekiel to describe what he saw, as is evident from his frequent use of "looked like," "something like," and "seemed." The overall effect is nonetheless clear and menacing; verbs of motion are combined with symbols of judgment to warn that God's judgment will inevitably fall upon rebellious Jerusalem.

1:4 ***I saw a great storm:*** This language speaks of theophany (see note on 1:4-28) as God appears in judgment. That this fiery presence is ***coming from the north,*** the direction from which Israel's enemies had traditionally come, compounds the perception of danger. God was coming as a mighty warrior, not to rescue his people but to bring judgment against them. • ***like gleaming amber:*** Or *like burnished metal;* also in 1:27.

1:5-9 At ***the center*** of the fiery cloud were ***four living beings,*** each having ***four faces and four wings.*** Four is a number of completeness; these composite creatures summed up the created order.

1:10 Each had ***the face of a lion,*** the greatest of the wild animals; ***the face of an ox,*** the greatest of domestic animals; ***the face of an eagle,*** the greatest of the birds; and ***a human face,*** representing the pinnacle of creation. The guardians of Mesopotamian palaces also combined features of these same four creatures (though not the four faces).

1:11-14 These fiery creatures had both *wings* and legs, enabling them to move ***like . . . lightning*** in any ***direction.*** No

1:11 Isa 6:2; Ezek 10:16, 19
1:12 Ezek 1:9, 20
1:13 Ps 104:4; Rev 4:5
1:14 Matt 24:27
1:16 Ezek 10:9-13
1:17 Ezek 1:12
1:18 Ezek 10:9-13; Rev 4:6, 8
1:19 Ezek 10:16-17, 19
1:21 Ezek 10:17
1:22 Ezek 10:1

either side of it, and the other pair covered
its body. [12]They went in whatever direction
the spirit chose, and they moved straight
forward in any direction without turning
around.
[13]The living beings looked like bright
coals of fire or brilliant torches, and lightning seemed to flash back and forth among
them. [14]And the living beings darted to and
fro like flashes of lightning.
[15]As I looked at these beings, I saw four
wheels touching the ground beside them,
one wheel belonging to each. [16]The wheels
sparkled as if made of beryl. All four wheels
looked alike and were made the same; each
wheel had a second wheel turning crosswise within it. [17]The beings could move in
any of the four directions they faced, without turning as they moved. [18]The rims of
the four wheels were tall and frightening,
and they were covered with eyes all around.
[19]When the living beings moved, the
wheels moved with them. When they flew
upward, the wheels went up, too. [20]The spirit
of the living beings was in the wheels. So
wherever the spirit went, the wheels and the
living beings also went. [21]When the beings
moved, the wheels moved. When the beings
stopped, the wheels stopped. When the beings flew upward, the wheels rose up, for the
spirit of the living beings was in the wheels.
[22]Spread out above them was a surface
like the sky, glittering like crystal. [23]Beneath
this surface the wings of each living being

God's Glory with His People (1:1-28)

Ezek 11:16; 37:26; 43:1-5; 44:4; Exod 15:11; 33:18–34:8; 40:34; Ps 19:1-11; Isa 4:5-6; 6:3; 40:5; 42:8; 43:7; 58:8; 60:1-2; Hab 2:14; Matt 17:2; 28:20; Luke 2:32; John 1:14; 2 Cor 4:4-6; Heb 1:3; Rev 21:10-11, 23

The presence and absence of God's glory is a central theme in Ezekiel. The opening vision depicts God's glory as powerful and majestic. In earlier times, this visible glory was the sign of God's presence among his people (see Exod 40:34; 1 Kgs 8:10-11). Now God's glory appears to the prophet Ezekiel while he is exiled in Babylon.

The reason for that shift becomes clear in Ezekiel's vision of chs 8–11, in which he sees the abominations that had polluted the Temple in Jerusalem and forced God's glory to depart. Without God's presence, the Temple had become an empty shell awaiting destruction. God was not evicted by the superior might of the Babylonian army; he departed because his people were defiled. Their sin drove him away from the land he had promised to Abraham, Isaac, and Jacob. For a time, the Lord went from Jerusalem to Babylon to become a sanctuary for the exiles there (see 11:16).

God would not abandon his people forever. After pouring out his wrath in full measure on their sin, he would restore a remnant to their land and sanctify them by his Spirit so that he could once again dwell in their midst in a new sanctuary (37:26). God's glory, dwelling among his people forever (43:1-5), is at the heart of Ezekiel's vision of their restoration. Never again would God abandon them.

The glory of God has come to us fully in the person of Jesus Christ. As John testifies, "We have seen his glory, the glory of the Father's one and only Son" (John 1:14). The aged Simeon saw the baby Jesus brought to the Temple and described him as "a light to reveal God to the nations, and . . . the glory of your people Israel" (Luke 2:32). Jesus' glory was veiled while he was on earth, though for a moment on the Mount of Transfiguration his radiance was revealed to his closest disciples (Matt 17:2). He experienced his own abandonment by God as he hung on the cross, bearing the curse for our sin (Matt 27:46). Now, as the exalted and glorified Lord, he sits at God's right hand (Eph 1:20). By his Spirit, he has promised never to abandon us, but to be with us to the end of time (Matt 28:20).

one could run away from such fearsome beasts. In the similar vision of ch 10, they are identified as cherubim, agents of divine judgment.

1:15 The living creatures were not the only cause for fear—in their midst, Ezekiel saw ***four wheels*** that were part of a divine war chariot. Chariots were among the most feared weapons of war in the ancient world.

1:16-17 It would be impossible to build a physical chariot in which ***each wheel had a second wheel turning crosswise within it.*** This picture depicts a chariot that could travel equally well in any direction, symbolizing God's freedom of movement in judgment.

1:18 The wheels were ***tall and frightening, and they were covered with eyes*** (cp. 10:12). There was no more hope of hiding from this chariot than of running from it.

1:19-21 The chariot was infused with ***the spirit of the living beings,*** and the whole assembly moved as a single entity.

1:22-25 The ***surface like the sky, glittering like crystal*** separated the realm of God's presence (heaven) from the realm of humanity (earth). References to the sky, the cherubim (see note on 1:11-14), and the rainbow (1:28) remind us of the opening chapters of Genesis and suggest that the narrative about to unfold concerns the destruction of what God had created, followed by its re-creation. Just as God destroyed the world he had made with a flood and then restored it through Noah, Ezekiel's world was also being unmade and restored.

stretched out to touch the others' wings,
and each had two wings covering its body.
24As they flew, their wings sounded to me
like waves crashing against the shore or like
the voice of the Almighty or like the shouting of a mighty army. When they stopped,
they let down their wings. 25As they stood
with wings lowered, a voice spoke from beyond the crystal surface above them.

26Above this surface was something that
looked like a [a]throne made of blue lapis lazuli. And on this [a]throne high above was a
figure whose appearance resembled a man.
27From what appeared to be his waist up, he
looked like gleaming amber, flickering like
a fire. And from his waist down, he looked
like a burning flame, shining with splendor. 28All around him was a glowing halo,
like a rainbow shining in the clouds on a
rainy day. This is what the glory of the LORD
looked like to me. When I saw it, I fell face
down on the ground, and I heard someone's
voice speaking to me.

Ezekiel's Call (2:1–3:15)

2 "Stand up, [b]son of man," said the voice.
"I want to speak with you." 2The Spirit
came into me as he spoke, and he set me
on my feet. I listened carefully to his words.
3"Son of man," he said, "I am sending you
to the nation of Israel, a rebellious nation
that has rebelled against me. They and their
ancestors have been rebelling against me
to this very day. 4They are a stubborn and
hard-hearted people. But I am sending you
to say to them, 'This is what the [c]Sovereign
LORD says!' 5And whether they listen or
refuse to listen—for remember, they are
rebels—at least they will know they have
had a prophet among them.

6"Son of man, do not fear them or their
words. Don't be afraid even though their
threats surround you like nettles and briers
and stinging scorpions. Do not be dismayed
by their dark scowls, even though they are
rebels. 7You must give them my messages
whether they listen or not. But they won't
listen, for they are completely rebellious!
8Son of man, listen to what I say to you. Do
not join them in their rebellion. Open your
mouth, and eat what I give you."

9Then I looked and saw a hand reaching out to me. It held a scroll, 10which he
unrolled. And I saw that both sides were
covered with funeral songs, words of sorrow, and pronouncements of doom.

1:24 Ezek 43:2; Rev 19:6
1:26 Exod 24:10; Isa 6:1; 54:11; Ezek 10:1; Rev 1:13; [a]*kisse'* (3678) ‣Zech 6:13
1:27 Ezek 3:23
1:28 Rev 1:17; 4:3; 10:1
2:1 [b]*ben 'adam* (1121, 0120) ‣Dan 7:13
2:2 Dan 8:18
2:3 1 Sam 8:7-8; Dan 9:5-13
2:4 Isa 48:4; Jer 5:3; [c]*'adonay Yahweh* (0136, 3068) ‣Amos 3:7
2:6 Jer 1:8
2:7 Jer 1:7, 17
2:8 Jer 15:16; Rev 10:9
2:9 Rev 5:1-5; 10:8-11

1:24 *the Almighty:* Hebrew *Shaddai.*

1:26-27 On the *throne* of God was ***a figure whose appearance resembled a man.*** Ezekiel's ability to describe the scene was overwhelmed by the magnificence of the sight. This human form revealed the Lord's overpoweringly radiant glory that had once filled the Tabernacle and the Temple as a visible manifestation of God's presence (cp. Dan 7:9-10; Rev 1:12-17). While God's awesome presence in human form comforts his faithful people, it signifies inevitable judgment for those who are disobeying him. This vision presages God's coming to earth as a man in Jesus Christ.

1:28 ***rainbow shining in the clouds:*** This image combines the prospect of judgment with a note of mercy. The storm clouds were going to drop a full load of judgment on God's sinful people, but a rainbow, the sign of hope that God established after the flood (Gen 9:12-17), would appear also. Although the destruction of Jerusalem and the exile of its people to Babylon would be a severe catastrophe in which many would die, God would not forget his promise to keep a remnant alive. Judgment would not be God's final word. • When Ezekiel saw ***the glory of the LORD,*** he ***fell face down on the ground*** as though dead—a common human response to God's glory (cp. Lev 9:23-24; Num 22:31; 1 Kgs 18:38-39; 1 Chr 21:16; 2 Chr 7:1-3; Matt 17:5-6).

2:1-10 Being a prophet was neither a career choice nor an occupation passed down from father to son like the priesthood. God called prophets to their task, and the story of their call is often included in their writings (see, e.g., Isa 6:1-13; Jer 1:4-19; Jon 1:1-2).

2:1-2 *Stand up:* God empowered Ezekiel by the ***Spirit*** so that he was able to obey this command as God ***set*** him ***on*** his ***feet.*** What God would later do for the people as a whole (cp. 37:4-10), he did first for the prophet.

2:3 The Lord addressed Ezekiel regularly as ***son of man*** (Hebrew *ben-'adam,* "son of Adam"). This phrase reminded Ezekiel that he was profoundly different from the heavenly beings before whom he stood. In contrast to them, he was a child of the dust, a mere mortal. It also marked him out from ***the nation of Israel*** (literally *the sons of Israel*). They were ***a rebellious nation,*** true descendants of Jacob, whose defining characteristic was striving with God and man (Gen 32:28). As a son of Adam, Ezekiel represented a new community of faith, empowered by the Spirit to form a life of radical obedience. He was a sign of hope to the exiles. Jesus is the ultimate *son of man* who combines in himself the human aspect of the title with the exalted heavenly aspect (Dan 7:13-14; Rev 1:13-20). By obeying where Adam failed, Jesus became the first member of God's new community of faith. All other children of Adam find hope in him.

2:4-5 Israel was ***stubborn and hard-hearted***—they would not heed Ezekiel, whose message would bear little immediate fruit. However, they would ***know*** that they ***had a prophet among them*** who was speaking God's word.

2:6 Ezekiel's ministry would be as painful as traversing a thicket of ***nettles and briers and stinging scorpions.***

2:7 Ezekiel would not be accountable for the people's response to the message, only for his own faithful delivery of God's word.

2:8 Ezekiel must not resemble the disobedient and rebellious people around him. The first Adam disobeyed God's command not to ***eat*** the apparently desirable fruit of knowledge (Gen 2:17); Ezekiel was to obey by eating the apparently undesirable words of God.

2:9–3:1 There was so much judgment on the ***scroll*** that ***both sides were covered*** with writing. Ezekiel had to declare the curses for covenant breaking (Deut 28:15-68) to a rebellious people (cp. Zech 5:2-4). The scroll covered with messages of judgment is an apt image of the content of chs 1–24.

3:1 Ezek 2:9
3:2 Jer 25:17
3:3 Jer 15:16; Rev 10:9-10
3:8 Jer 1:18
3:10 Job 22:22; Ezek 2:8
3:11 Ezek 2:5, 7
3:12 Ezek 8:3; Acts 2:2; 8:39
3:13 2 Sam 5:24; Ezek 1:15, 24; 10:5, 16-17
3:14 Ezek 8:1
3:15 Job 2:13

3 The voice said to me, "Son of man, eat
what I am giving you—eat this scroll!
Then go and give its message to the people
of Israel." 2So I opened my mouth, and he
fed me the scroll. 3"Fill your stomach with
this," he said. And when I ate it, it tasted as
sweet as honey in my mouth.
4Then he said, "Son of man, go to the people of Israel and give them my messages.
5I am not sending you to a foreign people
whose language you cannot understand. 6No,
I am not sending you to people with strange
and difficult speech. If I did, they would
listen! 7But the people of Israel won't listen
to you any more than they listen to me! For
the whole lot of them are hard-hearted and
stubborn. 8But look, I have made you as obstinate and hard-hearted as they are. 9I have
made your forehead as hard as the hardest
rock! So don't be afraid of them or fear their
angry looks, even though they are rebels."
10Then he added, "Son of man, let all my
words sink deep into your own heart first.
Listen to them carefully for yourself. 11Then
go to your people in exile and say to them,
'This is what the Sovereign LORD says!' Do
this whether they listen to you or not."
12Then the Spirit lifted me up, and I
heard a loud rumbling sound behind me.
(May the glory of the LORD be praised in
his place!) 13It was the sound of the wings
of the living beings as they brushed against
each other and the rumbling of their
wheels beneath them.
14The Spirit lifted me up and took me away.
I went in bitterness and turmoil, but the
LORD's hold on me was strong. 15Then I came
to the colony of Judean exiles in Tel-abib,

EZEKIEL THE PROPHET (2:1-10; 24:15-27)

Ezekiel, a priest and prophet (1:3), was born around 623 BC, was probably raised in Jerusalem, and was married (24:16-18). He went into exile in Babylon with Jehoiachin in 597 BC, where he lived by the Kebar River. He was called to be a prophet in Babylon on July 31, 593 BC (1:1). All we know of his personal life is from the book named after him.

Among the prophets, Ezekiel's speech and actions are perhaps the most surprising. Ezekiel often reinforced his prophetic words with strange actions, such as illustrating his message about the dire lack of food in the final siege of Jerusalem by eating food cooked over dung (4:12). Another time, he lay motionless for 430 days, one day for each year of Israel's and Judah's sin (4:4-7). When Ezekiel's wife died suddenly during the Exile, he was forbidden to mourn her in public (24:16-18). Her death was a solemn warning of what would happen in Judah (24:15-27). Ezekiel's strange actions were designed to grab people's attention.

At first, Ezekiel's messages were rejected, but his prophecies were later vindicated as they began to come true and the nation was purged of idolatry. His teaching emphasized holiness, purity, resurrection, and the ritual law. His message of hope encouraged the exiles to remain faithful during the dark hours of their captivity, and after their return it kept them looking toward a greater fulfillment.

The circumstances of Ezekiel's death are unknown, and he is not mentioned elsewhere in the OT. The NT has over 60 references to Ezekiel's prophecies, mostly in the book of Revelation. Ezekiel's prophetic vision extended beyond his immediate future to the final judgment and the great hope of heaven.

3:2-3 Although the scroll looked bitter, Ezekiel found it ***as sweet as honey*** when he ate it. Adam's disobedience turned bitter, but Ezekiel's obedience became pleasant and satisfying. Psalm 119:103 also describes God's words as "sweeter than honey."

3:4-7 Ezekiel was sent to God's people, ***the people of Israel,*** whom one would expect to be eager to listen to the Lord. However, it would have been easier for the prophet if he had been sent to ***people with strange and difficult speech*** who could not understand him. This ***hard-hearted*** community refused to obey the Lord.

3:8-9 God would make Ezekiel as thoroughly persistent in presenting God's message as the people were in rejecting it.

3:10 Ezekiel ***first*** had to internalize God's messages himself before delivering them to the exiles among whom he lived.

3:11 ***whether they listen to you or not:*** The Lord's message was not subject to debate, negotiation, or rejection; things would happen as he said.

3:12 ***May the glory of the LORD be praised in his place!*** In the Hebrew text, this exclamation of praise is odd in both placement and grammar. With the emendation of a single Hebrew letter, a possible reading is *as the glory of the LORD rose from its place.*

3:14-15 ***The Spirit lifted me up:*** Ezekiel was brought back from his visionary experience to the ordinary world of the exiles. Ezekiel regularly experienced the powerful impact of the Spirit's transporting him to another location (see also 8:3; 11:1, 24; 40:1-3; 43:5). • After the Spirit departed from him, Ezekiel experienced the conflicting emotions associated with his commission. As a prophet who spoke for God, he began to feel the ***bitterness and turmoil*** of God's anger against the sins of his people.

3:15 The exact location of ***Tel-abib*** in Babylonia has not been determined. • As one of the exiles, Ezekiel was ***overwhelmed*** by the prospect of this fearsome judgment. As with Job's

beside the Kebar River. I was overwhelmed
and sat among them for seven days.

Ezekiel's Commission as Watchman (3:16-27)

16After seven days the LORD gave me a
message. He said, 17"Son of man, I have
appointed you as a watchman for Israel.
Whenever you receive a message from me,
warn people immediately. 18If I warn the
wicked, saying, 'You are under the penalty
of death,' but you fail to deliver the warning,
they will die in their sins. And I will hold
you responsible for their deaths. 19If you
warn them and they refuse to repent and
keep on sinning, they will die in their sins.
But you will have saved yourself because
you obeyed me.
20"If righteous people turn away from
their righteous behavior and ignore the obstacles I put in their way, they will die. And if
you do not warn them, they will die in their
sins. None of their righteous acts will be remembered, and I will hold you responsible
for their deaths. 21But if you warn righteous
people not to sin and they listen to you and
do not sin, they will live, and you will have
saved yourself, too."
22Then the LORD took hold of me and said,
"Get up and go out into the valley, and I will
speak to you there." 23So I got up and went,
and there I saw the glory of the LORD, just
as I had seen in my first vision by the Kebar
River. And I fell face down on the ground.
24Then the Spirit came into me and set
me on my feet. He spoke to me and said, "Go
to your house and shut yourself in. 25There,
son of man, you will be tied with ropes so
you cannot go out among the people. 26And
I will make your tongue stick to the roof of
your mouth so that you will be speechless
and unable to rebuke them, for they are rebels. 27But when I give you a message, I will
loosen your tongue and let you speak. Then
you will say to them, 'This is what the Sovereign LORD says!' Those who choose to listen
will listen, but those who refuse will refuse,
for they are rebels.

2. ORACLES OF DOOM (4:1–24:27)

Prophecies against Jerusalem and the Land (4:1–7:27)

Sign Act 1: The Besieged Brick

4 "And now, son of man, take a large clay
brick and set it down in front of you.
Then draw a map of the city of Jerusalem on
it. 2Show the city under siege. Build a wall
around it so no one can escape. Set up the
enemy camp, and surround the city with
siege ramps and battering rams. 3Then take
an iron griddle and place it between you
and the city. Turn toward the city and demonstrate how harsh the siege will be against

3:17 Isa 52:8; 58:1; 62:6; Jer 6:17; Ezek 33:7-9
3:18 Ezek 33:6, 8
3:19 2 Kgs 17:13-14; Ezek 33:3, 9; Acts 18:6
3:20 Jer 6:21; Ezek 18:24; 33:18; Zeph 1:6
3:21 Acts 20:31
3:22 Acts 9:6
3:23 Ezek 1:1, 28; Acts 7:55
3:24 Ezek 2:2
3:25 Ezek 4:8
3:26 Luke 1:20, 22
3:27 Ezek 33:22
4:1 Isa 20:2; Jer 13:1; 19:1
4:2 Ezek 21:22
4:3 Isa 8:18; 20:3; Jer 39:1-2; Ezek 5:2; 12:6, 11; 24:24-27

---

counselors, no words were possible at first, and he sat silently *for seven days* (see Job 2:13).

3:16-19 Ezekiel was called to be a *watchman*, a familiar image for OT prophets (see Isa 56:10; Jer 6:17; Hos 9:8). The watchman was a lookout for the community. He was responsible for providing advance warning of approaching enemies so that the people could take refuge in time. In this case, the enemy they had to fear was not a human invader but God. As difficult as his task was, the blood of those he failed to warn would be on his head if he remained silent.

3:20-21 The prophet spoke to two classes of people, the *righteous* and the wicked. Ezekiel was to address his message indiscriminately, for both the righteous and the wicked would be judged on the basis of their response to his words (cp. Matt 13:3-9, 18-23). Those who heeded him would receive life; those who rejected his message would receive death, even if they had previously been righteous. Faith in the Lord's word through his prophet was the sole criterion that divided those who would live from those who would die.

3:22-23 The Lord summoned Ezekiel *out into the valley*, into a wilderness that was away from other people. • Although this was the second time he had seen *the glory of the LORD*, it was not something to which Ezekiel had grown accustomed. Its awesome magnificence prostrated him.

3:24-25 Ezekiel was God's prisoner, *shut . . . in* his house and *tied with ropes*. It is not clear whether these were literal ropes used to express the hostility of his fellow exiles toward the prophet, or a vivid image of their opposition and his restricted mobility among them. His complete captivity was striking, including the limitation placed on his speech (3:26-27); it would be a sign to the people.

3:26-27 Even Ezekiel's *tongue* was under arrest, bound to the *roof* of his *mouth* except when God freed it to speak his words of judgment. He was not physiologically incapable of speaking, but his communication was so restricted by God that he could only deliver the message of disaster that God gave him; all other speech was prohibited. This made Ezekiel's role more limited than that of most prophets, who were free to intercede for and mediate between God and his people. Ezekiel could not speak on their behalf because the time for dialogue between God and his people had passed. No further appeal was possible against the coming judgment. Ezekiel's speech would be restricted until the news of Jerusalem's fall arrived (24:27). At that point, with the completion of God's judgment on his people, the prophet's tongue would be freed to intercede for them again.

4:1–24:27 In words and in mimed actions, the prophet Ezekiel declared the certainty of impending judgment on Jerusalem. God's people, having broken the terms of the Lord's covenant with them at Mount Sinai, now faced the curses of death and destruction that were attached to that covenant. Only after these curses had taken effect could there be any hope for the future.

4:1–7:27 These chapters focus on words and actions that proclaim doom to the city of Jerusalem (chs 4–5) and to the surrounding land of Judah (chs 6–7).

4:1-2 The first of Ezekiel's sign acts (see "Prophetic Sign Acts" at 4:1-17, facing page) was to create a detailed tableau depicting *Jerusalem . . . under siege*.

4:3 The prophet was to take on the role of God in this dramatic scene. The *iron griddle* set up between him and the city showed that Jerusalem had cut itself off from God. Meanwhile, the prophet was

4:4 Lev 10:17; Num 18:1
4:5 Num 14:34
4:6 Dan 9:24-26; Rev 11:2-3
4:7 Ezek 21:2
4:8 Ezek 3:25
4:9 Exod 9:32; Isa 28:25
4:10 Ezek 45:12
4:12 Isa 36:12
4:13 Dan 1:8; Hos 9:3

Jerusalem. This will be a warning to the people of Israel.

Sign Act 2: The Prone Prophet

4"Now lie on your left side and place the sins of Israel on yourself. You are to bear their sins for the number of days you lie there on your side. 5I am requiring you to bear Israel's sins for 390 days—one day for each year of their sin. 6After that, turn over and lie on your right side for 40 days—one day for each year of Judah's sin.

7"Meanwhile, keep staring at the siege of Jerusalem. Lie there with your arm bared and prophesy her destruction. 8I will tie you up with ropes so you won't be able to turn from side to side until the days of your siege have been completed.

Sign Act 3: The Defiled Bread

9"Now go and get some wheat, barley, beans, lentils, millet, and emmer wheat, and mix them together in a storage jar. Use them to make bread for yourself during the 390 days you will be lying on your side. 10Ration this out to yourself, eight ounces of food for each day, and eat it at set times. 11Then measure out a jar of water for each day, and drink it at set times. 12Prepare and eat this food as you would barley cakes. While all the people are watching, bake it over a fire using dried human dung as fuel and then eat the bread." 13Then the LORD said, "This is how Israel will eat defiled bread in the Gentile lands to which I will banish them!"

Prophetic Sign Acts (4:1-17)

Ezek 2:6–3:3; 3:4-9; 5:1–6:14; 12:1-28; 21:19-23; 24:1-14, 16-27; 37:15-28; Jer 13:1-11; 19:1-15; 25:15; Hos 1:2-9; 3:1-3; Matt 26:26-28; 27:45-54; Mark 6:11; 11:12-21; Luke 22:17-20; Rom 6:3-5; 1 Cor 10:16-17; 11:23-32

Ezekiel frequently behaved in unusual, even outlandish, ways. His actions were strange even in ancient Israel, not just from a modern perspective. Unlike modern readers, however, who might think that the prophet was psychologically disturbed, ancient observers understood these *sign acts* as a regular part of a prophet's communication style. Sign acts were dramatic visual aids performed in public to increase the impact of the message and help people *feel* the truth as much as *hear* it. Their purpose was to drive the message unforgettably into people's hearts.

Other prophets of Israel and Judah also performed sign acts (see Isa 20:2-6; Jer 13:1-11), but Ezekiel was required to act out his message more frequently than any other (see 4:1-8, 9-17; 5:1-4; 6:11-12; 12:3-16, 17-20; 21:19-22; 24:15-27; 37:16-26), perhaps because he was communicating to a particularly hardened audience (2:6). The sign acts reinforced the content of his message and underlined the depth of his personal commitment to it. For example, after he swallowed the word of God (2:8–3:3), Ezekiel embodied it for the exiles (3:4-9) in a series of judgment scenes (chs 4–6). This dramatic form of communication is difficult for even a hostile audience to ignore or forget.

The ultimate sign act is the cross of Jesus Christ (see Matt 27:32-54). There God visibly depicted his wrath against sin in the darkness, the earthquake, and the agony of the sinless one who was apparently abandoned by his Father. God also depicted his profound love for the world in that he would rather die than let his people go. The cross is a confrontational message of God's love and wrath that is hard to ignore or forget.

to ***turn*** his face aggressively toward the city, showing that God's attention had not flagged but that he was implacably determined to destroy Jerusalem in the coming siege.

4:4-8 The prophet's second sign act was related to the first, but this time he was to act the roles of both God and victims of the ***siege***. As a siege victim, he was tied up ***with ropes*** (4:8) and confined to a single position. Possibly Ezekiel was not confined continually during this 14-month period, but performed this sign on a daily basis. As Ezekiel represented Israel, he was ***to bear Israel's sins*** symbolically by lying on one side, without bringing atonement and forgiveness to Israel.

4:4-5 ***Israel*** indicates the whole covenant community, not just the northern kingdom. The number ***390*** has been interpreted in various ways. A likely explanation is that 390 represents years, perhaps from early in Solomon's reign (971–931 BC) to the destruction of Jerusalem (586 BC; see 2 Kgs 25:3-7).

4:6 Judah was the community of those in exile, whose sojourn outside the land was represented by the symbolic figure of ***40*** years. They were a lost generation, just like the generation that spent 40 years in the wilderness for their sin (Num 14:34). • The 430 days of Ezekiel's confinement (cp. 4:5) parallel the 430 years that Israel spent in Egypt (Exod 12:40), hinting that there would be a new exodus at the end of the Exile.

4:7 Throughout the depiction, Ezekiel continued to represent God. With his ***arm bared***, he stared at the ***siege of Jerusalem*** and prophesied ***her destruction***.

4:9-17 The near-starvation diet of ***eight ounces*** (Hebrew ***20 shekels*** [228 grams]) ***of food*** and ***a jar*** (Hebrew ***⅙ of a hin*** [about 1 pint or 0.6 liters]) ***of water for each day*** represent siege rations and reflect a desperate situation in which there was not enough of any one kind of grain to make a whole loaf.

4:12-13 Cooking over ***human dung*** would render the bread ceremonially unclean, thus defiling Ezekiel when he ate it. The Israelites had to eat ***defiled bread*** in exile, when it was extremely difficult to observe kosher dietary laws. They would be unclean and cut off from the cleansing presence of the Lord.

[14]Then I said, "O Sovereign LORD, must I
be defiled by using human dung? For I have
never been defiled before. From the time I
was a child until now I have never eaten any
animal that died of sickness or was killed by
other animals. I have never eaten any meat
forbidden by the law."
[15]"All right," the LORD said. "You may
bake your bread with cow dung instead
of human dung." [16]Then he told me, "Son
of man, I will make food very scarce in Jerusalem. It will be weighed out with great
care and eaten fearfully. The water will be
rationed out drop by drop, and the people
will drink it with dismay. [17]Lacking food
and water, people will look at one another in
terror, and they will waste away under their
punishment.

Sign Act 4: The Shaved Prophet

5 "Son of man, take a sharp sword and
use it as a razor to shave your head
and beard. Use a scale to weigh the hair
into three equal parts. [2]Place a third of it at
the center of your map of Jerusalem. After
acting out the siege, burn it there. Scatter
another third across your map and chop it
with a sword. Scatter the last third to the
wind, for I will scatter my people with the
sword. [3]Keep just a bit of the hair and tie it
up in your robe. [4]Then take some of these
hairs out and throw them into the fire, burning them up. A fire will then spread from
this remnant and destroy all of Israel.

The Sign Acts Interpreted

[5]"This is what the Sovereign LORD says:
This is an illustration of what will happen to
Jerusalem. I placed her at the center of the
nations, [6]but she has rebelled against my
regulations and decrees and has been even
more wicked than the surrounding nations.
She has refused to obey the regulations and
decrees I gave her to follow.
[7]"Therefore, this is what the Sovereign
LORD says: You people have behaved worse
than your neighbors and have refused to
obey my decrees and regulations. You have
not even lived up to the standards of the nations around you. [8]Therefore, I myself, the
Sovereign LORD, am now your enemy. I will
punish you publicly while all the nations
watch. [9]Because of your detestable idols, I
will punish you like I have never punished
anyone before or ever will again. [10]Parents
will eat their own children, and children
will eat their parents. I will punish you and
scatter to the winds the few who survive.
[11]"As surely as I live, says the Sovereign
LORD, I will cut you off completely. I will
show you no pity at all because you have defiled my Temple with your vile images and
detestable sins. [12]A third of your people
will die in the city from disease and famine.
A third of them will be slaughtered by the
enemy outside the city walls. And I will scatter a third to the winds, chasing them with
my sword. [13]Then at last my anger will be
spent, and I will be satisfied. And when my
fury against them has subsided, all Israel
will know that I, the LORD, have spoken to
them in my jealous anger.
[14]"So I will turn you into a ruin, a mockery in the eyes of the surrounding nations
and to all who pass by. [15]You will become
an object of mockery and taunting and horror. You will be a warning to all the nations
around you. They will see what happens
when the LORD punishes a nation in anger
and rebukes it, says the LORD.
[16]"I will shower you with the deadly arrows of famine to destroy you. The famine
will become more and more severe until

4:14 Lev 17:15; 22:8 Deut 14:3-5 Isa 65:4; 66:17 Ezek 9:8; 20:49 Acts 10:14
4:16 Lev 26:26 Isa 3:1 Lam 5:4 Ezek 5:16; 12:18-19
4:17 Lev 26:39 Ezek 24:23; 33:10
5:1 Lev 21:5 Isa 7:20 Ezek 44:20 Dan 5:27
5:2 Lev 26:33 Jer 39:1-2 Ezek 4:1-8
5:3 Jer 39:10
5:4 Jer 41:12
5:5 Jer 6:6 Lam 1:1 Ezek 4:1
5:6 Ezek 16:47
5:8 Jer 24:9 Ezek 5:15; 15:7 Zech 14:2
5:9 Dan 9:12 Matt 24:21
5:10 Lev 26:29 Ps 44:11 Jer 19:9 Amos 9:9 Zech 2:6; 7:14
5:11 Jer 7:9-11 Ezek 8:5-6, 16, 18
5:12 Jer 15:2; 44:27 Ezek 6:11-12; 12:14 Amos 9:9 Zech 2:6
5:13 Isa 1:24; 59:17 Lam 4:11 Ezek 36:6; 38:19
5:14 Ps 74:3-10; 79:1-4 Ezek 22:4

4:14-15 The prophet protested that he had never eaten anything unclean. The Lord relented, allowing Ezekiel to cook his food over ***cow dung*** and to follow the law regarding disposal of human excrement (see Deut 23:12-14).

5:1-4 The prophet was required to perform two further sign acts. First, he used ***a sharp sword . . . as a razor*** to ***shave*** his ***head and beard,*** tangibly demonstrating the destruction described in ch 4 (cp. Isa 7:20). Shaving off a man's hair implied the loss of his manhood and was a gesture of dishonor (see 2 Sam 10:4-5). Second, Ezekiel weighed ***the hair*** he had shaved off ***into three equal parts*** to show that God's measured judgment would take three different forms.

5:2 Ezekiel was to ***burn*** one third of the hair to represent those who would die of famine during the siege. He was to ***chop*** another third of the hair ***with a sword*** to represent those who would die violent deaths. He was to ***scatter*** the final third ***to the wind*** to represent those who would be sent into exile.

5:3-4 Ezekiel was to tie ***just a bit of the hair*** in his ***robe*** to show that a ***remnant*** would be safe, but even ***some*** of them would die in ***the fire*** of exile. Few would survive the multiple catastrophes about to befall God's people.

5:5-6 The reason for God's judgment on his people is made abundantly clear: Israel had broken its covenant relationship with God.

5:7-13 The covenant between God and his people underlies Ezekiel's messages (see "The Purpose of God's Covenant" at Exod 19:3-6, p. 157). In stating the charges against his fellow Israelites, Ezekiel explicitly draws from the language of the covenant that was made on Mount Sinai and renewed in Deuteronomy. Israel's refusal ***to obey*** God's ***decrees and regulations,*** especially in their worship of ***detestable idols*** that ***defiled*** the Lord's ***Temple,*** contravened God's requirements (cp. Lev 26:1-2, 14-15). Consequently, the curses for disobeying the Lord (Lev 26:16-43; Deut 28:15-68) would now come into effect.

5:10 ***Parents will eat their own children:*** This horrific prospect was an anticipated consequence of famine (see 2 Kgs 6:26-30), and one of the curses of disobedience (see Lev 26:29).

5:15 Isa 66:15-16 Jer 22:8-9 Ezek 25:17 1 Cor 10:11
5:16 Deut 32:23-24
5:17 Ezek 14:21
6:2 Ezek 36:1
6:3 Ezek 36:4
6:4 Lev 26:30 2 Chr 14:5 Isa 27:9 Ezek 6:6
6:6 Zech 13:2
6:8 Isa 6:13 Jer 44:14, 28 Ezek 7:16; 14:22
6:9 Deut 30:2 Job 42:6 Ps 78:40 Isa 7:13; 43:24 Ezek 20:43 Hos 11:8
6:11 Ezek 5:12; 7:15; 9:4; 25:6
6:12 Lam 4:11-12 Ezek 5:13 Dan 9:7
6:13 1 Kgs 14:23 2 Kgs 16:4 Isa 57:5-7 Ezek 20:27-28 Hos 4:13
6:14 Isa 5:25 Ezek 14:13
7:2 Ezek 11:13 Amos 8:2, 10

every crumb of food is gone. 17 And along
with the famine, wild animals will attack
you and rob you of your children. Disease
and war will stalk your land, and I will bring
the sword of the enemy against you. I, the
LORD, have spoken!"

Judgment against Israel's Mountains

6 Again a message came to me from the
LORD: 2 "Son of man, turn and face the
mountains of Israel and prophesy against
them. 3 Proclaim this message from the Sovereign LORD against the mountains of Israel.
This is what the Sovereign LORD says to the
mountains and hills and to the ravines and
valleys: I am about to bring war upon you,
and I will smash your pagan shrines. 4 All
your altars will be demolished, and your
places of worship will be destroyed. I will
kill your people in front of your idols. 5 I
will lay your corpses in front of your idols
and scatter your bones around your altars.
6 Wherever you live there will be desolation,
and I will destroy your pagan shrines. Your
altars will be demolished, your idols will
be smashed, your places of worship will be
torn down, and all the religious objects you
have made will be destroyed. 7 The place
will be littered with corpses, and you will
know that I alone am the LORD.
8 "But I will let a few of my people escape
destruction, and they will be scattered
among the nations of the world. 9 Then when
they are exiled among the nations, they will
remember me. They will recognize how
hurt I am by their unfaithful hearts and lustful eyes that long for their idols. Then at last
they will hate themselves for all their detestable sins. 10 They will know that I alone am
the LORD and that I was serious when I said
I would bring this calamity on them.
11 "This is what the Sovereign LORD says:
Clap your hands in horror, and stamp your
feet. Cry out because of all the detestable
sins the people of Israel have committed.
Now they are going to die from war and
famine and disease. 12 Disease will strike
down those who are far away in exile. War
will destroy those who are nearby. And
anyone who survives will be killed by famine. So at last I will spend my fury on them.
13 They will know that I am the LORD when
their dead lie scattered among their idols
and altars on every hill and mountain and
under every green tree and every great
shade tree—the places where they offered
sacrifices to their idols. 14 I will crush them
and make their cities desolate from the wilderness in the south to Riblah in the north.
Then they will know that I am the LORD."

The Coming of the End

7 Then this message came to me from the
LORD: 2 "Son of man, this is what the Sovereign LORD says to Israel:

"The end is here!
Wherever you look—

6:1-14 The two oracles of judgment in this chapter (6:2-10 and 6:11-14) present two alternatives—a positive future through repentance, or continued rebellion and a dark future of total annihilation. Either way, the Lord's power and holiness would be manifested.

6:1-3 The circle of judgment broadened out from Jerusalem to include ***the mountains of Israel,*** which were Israel's political heartland. This territory had belonged to Israel continuously since the time of Joshua, and it had been infected by idolatry. The hill country had become home to many ***pagan shrines*** (literally *high places*)—raised stone platforms that often housed idols or became the location for sacrifices and pagan festivities. Most predated Israel's entry into the land, and God had commanded Israel to destroy them (Deut 12:2-3). However, in many cases, the Israelites had permitted them to remain in place, and the political and religious leaders had ignored or even encouraged those who worshiped there.

6:4-7 The *corpses* and *bones* of the dead worshipers scattered around an altar would defile the altar and make it unfit for use. • ***idols:*** The Hebrew term (literally *round things*) probably alludes to dung; also in 6:5, 6, 9, 13. This word occurs forty-eight times in the OT, and thirty-nine of the occurrences are found in Ezekiel—all of them in reference to idols. When used in this way, it is a term of strong derision.

6:8-10 A remnant would be ***scattered among the nations of the world*** to bear witness to God's faithfulness to his covenant. They would recognize the reality of their own ***unfaithful hearts*** and ***hate themselves for all their detestable sins,*** and ***they will know*** that God's threat of ***calamity*** on covenant breakers was absolutely serious. Some of those who ***know that I alone am the LORD*** might even experience the other side of God's faithfulness: his swiftness to forgive those who repent. In the book of Exodus, Israel came to know that God is the Lord through his mighty acts of rescue (see Exod 6:7). Unfortunately, their behavior showed that they had forgotten. They would come again to that knowledge through God's acts of judgment.

6:11 Ezekiel's message did not end on the encouraging thought of possible repentance. He returned to the theme of judgment with its three-fold calamity of ***war and famine and disease.***

6:12 ***anyone who survives:*** See 5:3-4.

6:13-14 ***Riblah:*** As in some Hebrew manuscripts; most Hebrew manuscripts read *Diblah.* The symbols for "r" and "d" are easily confused in Hebrew; Riblah was located on the northern border of Israel and is well known from other biblical books. At Riblah, Nebuchadnezzar set up his tribunal and executed the sons of Zedekiah and many other leading citizens of Judah (2 Kgs 25:6, 21).

7:1-27 Chapter 7 contains three messages of doom (7:3-4, 5-9, 10-27). They reminded Judah that their forthcoming destruction was not a random twist of fate but an act of the Lord's judgment.

7:1-2 As the prophet unfolded his message, the scope of the threatened judgment kept increasing, like ripples spreading outward from a stone dropped into a pond. Now the judgment he announced was not just for ***Israel,*** as in ch 6, but against the whole

east, west, north, or south—
your land is finished.
3 No hope remains,
for I will unleash my anger against
you.
I will call you to account
for all your detestable sins.
4 I will turn my eyes away and show no pity.
I will repay you for all your detestable
sins.
Then you will know that I am the LORD.

5 "This is what the Sovereign LORD says:
Disaster after disaster
is coming your way!
6 The end has come.
It has finally arrived.
Your final doom is waiting!
7 O people of Israel, the day of your
destruction is dawning.
The time has come; the day of trouble
is near.
Shouts of anguish will be heard on the
mountains,
not shouts of joy.
8 Soon I will pour out my fury on you
and unleash my anger against you.
I will call you to account
for all your detestable sins.
9 I will turn my eyes away and show no pity.
I will repay you for all your detestable
sins.
Then you will know that it is I, the LORD,
who is striking the blow.

10 "The day of judgment is here;
your destruction awaits!
The people's wickedness and [d]pride
have blossomed to full flower.
11 Their violence has grown into a rod
that will beat them for their
wickedness.
None of these proud and wicked people
will survive.
All their wealth and prestige will be
swept away.
12 Yes, the time has come;
the day is here!
Buyers should not rejoice over bargains,
nor sellers grieve over losses,
for all of them will fall
under my terrible anger.
13 Even if the merchants survive,
they will never return to their business.
For what God has said applies to
everyone—
it will not be changed!
Not one person whose life is twisted by
sin
will ever recover.

14 "The trumpet calls Israel's army to
mobilize,
but no one listens,
for my fury is against them all.
15 There is war outside the city
and disease and famine within.
Those outside the city walls
will be killed by enemy swords.
Those inside the city
will die of famine and disease.
16 The survivors who escape to the
mountains
will moan like doves, weeping for their
sins.
17 Their hands will hang limp,
their knees will be weak as water.
18 They will dress themselves in burlap;
horror and shame will cover them.
They will shave their heads
in sorrow and remorse.

19 "They will throw their money in the
streets,
tossing it out like worthless trash.

7:4 Ezek 6:7; 11:21; 22:31; Hos 9:7
7:5 2 Kgs 21:12-13; Nah 1:9
7:7 Isa 22:5; Ezek 12:23-25, 28
7:8 Isa 42:25; Ezek 9:8; 14:19; 33:20; 36:19; Nah 1:6
7:10 Ps 89:32; Isa 10:5; [d]*zadon* (2087) ›Obad 1:3
7:12 Isa 5:13-14; Ezek 6:11-12; 1 Cor 7:29-31; Jas 5:8-9
7:14 Num 10:9; Jer 4:5
7:15 Jer 14:18; Ezek 6:11-12; 12:16
7:16 Isa 38:14; 59:11; Ezek 6:8; 14:22; Nah 2:7
7:17 Job 21:6; Isa 13:7; Ezek 21:7; 22:14; Heb 12:12
7:18 Isa 15:3; Ezek 27:31; Amos 8:10
7:19 Prov 11:4; Isa 2:20

land, ***east, west, north, or south.*** This global judgment upon God's people would be tantamount to the end of the world. Judgment was no longer imminent, as in the previous oracles; it had arrived.

7:3-4 There was ***no hope*** that God would change his mind. • ***Then you will know that I am the LORD:*** When they received exactly what they deserved, the people would recognize the Lord's power and holiness.

7:5-9 A second message reiterates the personal nature of the coming judgment. The people would not simply know that God is the Lord, as in 7:4. The Lord, who once showed himself to his people as "the Lord who heals you" (Exod 15:26), had now become "the Lord who strikes you." The day of the Lord had come (Joel 1:15; Amos 5:18-20).

7:10 ***blossomed to full flower:*** In their ***wickedness and pride,*** the people of Israel were ripe to be plucked (cp. Amos 8:1-2).

7:11 ***Their violence has grown into a rod that will beat them:*** God would use their own violence to punish them by giving them over to internal strife and conflict (cp. Prov 6:27). ***Wealth and prestige*** could not save them against the coming torrent of destruction.

7:12-27 Comprehensive judgment is depicted in two parallel panels, 7:12-18 and 7:19-27. Each begins with the futility of material gain in view of this impending judgment and moves through the arrival of war and its associated horrors to a declaration of universal ineffectiveness, terror, and mourning.

7:12-13 Commercial transactions would lose their meaning. There would be no such thing as a good deal or a bad deal; ***buyers*** and ***sellers*** alike would face God's ***terrible anger.***

7:14 When Israel sounded the ***trumpet*** in holy war, the troops would not rally and the enemy would not be terrified, as in the past (see Num 10:9; Josh 6:4-20; Judg 6:34; 7:16-22; Neh 4:18-20).

7:19 Even ***silver and gold,*** the traditional last resorts in times of crisis, would be unable to ***save*** or ***satisfy*** their owners. They would dispose of them ***like worthless trash*** (literally *impurity*), something hateful and disgusting that they could not wait to be rid of.

7:20
Isa 30:22
7:21
2 Kgs 24:13
Ps 74:2-8
7:22
Jer 18:17
Ezek 39:23-24
7:23
Jer 27:2
Ezek 8:17; 9:9
Hos 4:2
7:24
2 Chr 7:20
Ezek 21:31; 28:7; 33:28
7:25
Ezek 13:10, 16
7:26
Ps 74:9
Isa 47:11
Jer 4:20; 18:18; 37:17
Ezek 21:7; 22:26
Mic 3:6
7:27
Ps 35:26
Ezek 26:16
8:2
Ezek 1:4, 27-28
8:3
Ezek 3:12; 11:1
Dan 5:5

Their silver and gold won't save them
on that day of the LORD's anger.
It will neither satisfy nor feed them,
for their greed can only trip them up.
20 They were proud of their beautiful
jewelry
and used it to make detestable idols
and vile images.
Therefore, I will make all their wealth
disgusting to them.
21 I will give it as plunder to foreigners,
to the most wicked of nations,
and they will defile it.
22 I will turn my eyes from them
as these robbers invade and defile my
treasured land.

23 "Prepare chains for my people,
for the land is bloodied by terrible
crimes.
Jerusalem is filled with violence.
24 I will bring the most ruthless of nations
to occupy their homes.
I will break down their proud fortresses
and defile their sanctuaries.
25 Terror and trembling will overcome my
people.
They will look for peace but not find it.
26 Calamity will follow calamity;
rumor will follow rumor.
They will look in vain
for a vision from the prophets.
They will receive no teaching from the
priests
and no counsel from the leaders.
27 The king and the prince will stand
helpless,
weeping in despair,
and the people's hands
will tremble with fear.
I will bring on them
the evil they have done to others,
and they will receive the punishment
they so richly deserve.
Then they will know that I am the LORD."

The Temple Vision (8:1–11:25)
Idolatry in the Temple: Four Abominations

8 Then on September 17, during the
sixth year of King Jehoiachin's captivity, while the leaders of Judah were in my
home, the Sovereign LORD took hold of me.
2 I saw a figure that appeared to be a man.
From what appeared to be his waist down,
he looked like a burning flame. From the
waist up he looked like gleaming amber. 3 He
reached out what seemed to be a hand and
took me by the hair. Then the Spirit lifted
me up into the sky and transported me to
Jerusalem in a vision from God. I was taken

7:20-22 Their formerly precious objects were contaminated and contaminating because they were used *to make detestable idols and vile images.* • God would hand over his *treasured land,* the home of his sanctuary (Deut 12:5, 11), to brutal and ruthless pagans. Since Israel had repeatedly failed to distinguish between true and false places of worship, continued in pagan worship at the high places, and even brought idols into the Temple (8:1-18), God would destroy the pagan centers of worship in the land and even in the Temple in Jerusalem. In the past God had defended Jerusalem against overwhelming odds (see 2 Kgs 18–19), but now he would abandon her to her well-deserved fate.

7:23-27 Neither religious authorities (*prophets* and *priests*) nor civil *leaders* (*king* or *prince*) could bring the *peace* the people were looking for. High-born and low-born alike would be helpless in facing their judgment. In the complete absence of guidance and direction, no hope would be left for the people.

8:1–11:25 This section depicts the defilement of the Jerusalem Temple (ch 8), which led to its being abandoned by the Lord and its subsequent destruction (9:1–11:13). This abandonment was actually good news for those already in exile, for the Lord was coming to dwell with them, identifying them as the ones who bore hope for the future of God's people.

8:1-18 In visionary form, the prophet Ezekiel was shown four ways in which the people were engaged in practices that defiled their land. This vision explains why the presence of the Lord left his sanctuary.

8:1 *on September 17:* Literally *on the fifth day of the sixth month* of the ancient Hebrew lunar calendar. This event occurred on Sept 17, 592 BC; see also note on 1:1. • We are in the *sixth year of King Jehoiachin's captivity* (see note on 1:2), and fourteen months have elapsed since the opening vision of the book. During most of the intervening time, the prophet had been performing the sign acts of ch 4. Ezekiel 8–9 depicts in visions the same defilement and consequent judgment of Jerusalem that ch 7 lays out in oracles. In this case, the prophet directed the message to *the leaders* (literally *elders*) *of Judah,* who had gathered at Ezekiel's *home.* They were probably seeking a word of encouragement and comfort from the Lord (see also 14:1; 20:1), but what they received was a denunciation of the sins of the communities they represented.

8:2-3 While the leaders were gathered, Ezekiel saw in a vision what *appeared to be a man.* The description is similar to the description in 1:26-27. This time, however, Ezekiel was *lifted . . . up into the sky and transported . . . to Jerusalem.* • *appeared to be . . . looked like . . . seemed to be:* What Ezekiel saw defied human description (see note on 1:4-28).

8:2 *like gleaming amber:* Or *like burnished metal.*

8:3-16 God showed Ezekiel four scenes of increasing abomination from the false worship that the people of Israel were performing in the Lord's Temple. The comprehensiveness of Jerusalem's defilement may be seen from the varied locations of their acts of idolatry, the kinds of people involved, the deities worshiped, and the varied cultures from which these deities had been imported. It was the ultimate eclectic worship service, with abomination piled upon abomination.

8:3-6 In the first abomination, the *large idol* was probably an image of the Canaanite goddess Asherah that had been placed at this gate to guard the city from attack. Most of Jerusalem's historic enemies came against her from the north, which would explain the idol's location at the *north gate.* This idol had *made the LORD very jealous* because the Lord deserved all honor and worship as Israel's protector

to the north gate of the inner courtyard of
the Temple, where there is a large idol that
has made the LORD very jealous. 4Suddenly,
the glory of the God of Israel was there, just
as I had seen it before in the valley.
5Then the LORD said to me, "Son of man,
look toward the north." So I looked, and
there to the north, beside the entrance to
the gate near the altar, stood the idol that
had made the LORD so jealous.
6"Son of man," he said, "do you see what
they are doing? Do you see the detestable
sins the people of Israel are committing to
drive me from my Temple? But come, and
you will see even more detestable sins than
these!" 7Then he brought me to the door of
the Temple courtyard, where I could see a
hole in the wall. 8He said to me, "Now, son of
man, dig into the wall." So I dug into the wall
and found a hidden doorway.
9"Go in," he said, "and see the wicked
and detestable sins they are committing in
there!" 10So I went in and saw the walls engraved with all kinds of crawling animals
and detestable creatures. I also saw the various idols worshiped by the people of Israel.
11Seventy leaders of Israel were standing
there with Jaazaniah son of Shaphan in
the center. Each of them held an incense
burner, from which a cloud of incense rose
above their heads.
12Then the LORD said to me, "Son of man,
have you seen what the leaders of Israel are
doing with their idols in dark rooms? They
are saying, 'The LORD doesn't see us; he has
deserted our land!'" 13Then the LORD added,
"Come, and I will show you even more detestable sins than these!"
14He brought me to the north gate of the
LORD's Temple, and some women were sitting there, weeping for the god Tammuz.
15"Have you seen this?" he asked. "But I will
show you even more detestable sins than
these!"
16Then he brought me into the inner
courtyard of the LORD's Temple. At the
entrance to the sanctuary, between the entry room and the bronze altar, there were
about twenty-five men with their backs to
the sanctuary of the LORD. They were facing
east, bowing low to the ground, worshiping
the sun!
17"Have you seen this, son of man?" he
asked. "Is it nothing to the people of Judah
that they commit these detestable sins, leading the whole nation into violence, thumbing
their noses at me, and provoking my anger?
18Therefore, I will respond in fury. I will neither pity nor spare them. And though they
cry for mercy, I will not listen."

The Slaughter of Idolaters

9 Then the LORD thundered, "Bring on
the men appointed to punish the city!
Tell them to bring their weapons with
them!" 2Six men soon appeared from the
upper gate that faces north, each carrying
a deadly weapon in his hand. With them
was a man dressed in linen, who carried a
writer's case at his side. They all went into

8:4 Ezek 1:27-28
8:5 Ps 78:58; Jer 3:2; 7:30; 32:34; Ezek 8:3; Zech 5:5
8:6 2 Kgs 23:4-5; Ezek 5:11; 8:9, 17
8:8 Ezek 12:5
8:10 Exod 20:4
8:11 Num 11:16, 25; 16:17, 35; Jer 19:1; Luke 10:1
8:12 Ezek 9:9
8:14 Ezek 44:4; 46:9
8:16 Deut 4:19; 17:3; 2 Chr 29:6; Job 31:26-28; Jer 2:27; 44:17; Ezek 23:39
8:17 Jer 7:18-19; Ezek 7:10-11, 23; 9:9; 16:26; Amos 3:10; Mic 2:2
8:18 Isa 1:15; Jer 11:11; Mic 3:4; Zech 7:13
9:2 Ezek 10:2
9:3 Ezek 10:4; 11:22-23

(Ps 121:1-4). The Lord was offended by this idol that purported to protect the Lord's chosen city.

8:7-8 The first abomination was very public, and the second was very private. In order to witness it in his vision, the prophet had to ***dig into the wall*** to access a ***hidden doorway***.

8:10 The practice of worshiping deities shaped like ***crawling animals and detestable creatures*** most likely came from Egypt. • ***idols:*** The Hebrew term (literally *round things*) probably alludes to dung. See note on 6:4-7.

8:11 These ***seventy leaders*** are a shocking contrast to the seventy leaders of Moses' day who were given the unique privilege of seeing God (Exod 24:1-11) and were given the same Spirit as Moses (Num 11:16-30). ***Jaazaniah***, the leader of this group, was, ironically, the ***son of Shaphan***, a godly leader who was prominently involved in Josiah's reforms (2 Kgs 22:3-14). • The ***incense***, intended to ward off dangers from demonic spirits, helped instead to bring God's judgment upon the land.

8:12-13 The Lord could ***see*** what ***the leaders of Israel*** were doing, and he revealed these things to his prophet (cp. Luke 12:3). See note on 10:12.

8:14-15 The third abomination was that ***women were . . . weeping for the god Tammuz*** at ***the north gate of the LORD's Temple***. This Babylonian ritual marked the death and descent into the underworld of the god Dumuzi (Tammuz). Every year, this deity was thought to lose his power and then regain it in a cycle that paralleled the annual rhythms of nature. Ritual mourning for Tammuz was intended to hasten the return of fertility to the natural order. Ritual lamentation for a false, dead god had thus been substituted for praise and worship of the true and living God.

8:16 The fourth and crowning act of idolatry took place in the very heart of the Temple complex, in ***the inner courtyard of the LORD's Temple***, as close as anyone could approach to the Temple building without actually entering it. • The ***twenty-five men . . . worshiping the sun*** were possibly priests, as none but priests should have had access to this area, though they might have been non-priests flaunting the rules of access. Though physically closer than anyone else to the Lord's presence, they had turned ***their backs to the sanctuary*** of their Creator. Instead of worshiping him, they worshiped what he had created (cp. Rom 1:25).

8:17-18 The abominations that the Israelites were committing in the Temple complex were tantamount to ***thumbing*** (literally *putting the twig* [or *branch*] *to*) ***their noses*** at the Lord. This gesture was at least defiant, and possibly vulgar.

9:1-2 The prophet did not have to wait long for judgment to come. The Lord summoned his angelic warriors ***to punish the city***, and seven men appeared in response. ***Six men*** each carried ***a deadly weapon***, while the seventh was ***dressed in linen*** and ***carried a writer's case***. They stood ready for action in the ***Temple courtyard***, next to the ***bronze altar*** where sacrifices were normally offered.

9:4 Exod 12:7, 13; Ps 119:53, 136; Jer 13:17; 2 Cor 1:22; 2 Tim 2:19; Rev 7:2-3
9:6 2 Chr 36:17; Ezek 5:11; 8:11-12; Rev 9:4
9:7 Ezek 7:20-22
9:8 1 Chr 21:16; Ezek 11:13; Amos 7:2-6
9:9 2 Kgs 21:16; Ps 10:11; 94:7; Isa 29:15; Ezek 7:23; 8:12; 22:2-3, 29; Mic 3:1-3; 7:3; [e]*'azab* (5800) ‣Dan 11:30
9:10 Isa 65:6; Ezek 7:4; 8:18; 11:21; 24:14; Hos 9:7
10:1 Exod 24:10; Ezek 1:22, 26; Rev 4:2-3
10:2 Ps 18:10-13; Isa 6:6; Ezek 1:15-21; 10:13; Rev 8:5
10:3 Ezek 8:3, 16
10:4 Exod 40:34-35; Isa 6:1-4; Ezek 1:27-28; 9:3; 11:22-23
10:5 Job 40:9; Ezek 1:24; Rev 10:3; [f]*kerub* (3742) ‣Ezek 10:15

the Temple courtyard and stood beside the bronze altar.

3Then the glory of the God of Israel rose up from between the cherubim, where it had rested, and moved to the entrance of the Temple. And the LORD called to the man dressed in linen who was carrying the writer's case. 4He said to him, "Walk through the streets of Jerusalem and put a mark on the foreheads of all who weep and sigh because of the detestable sins being committed in their city."

5Then I heard the LORD say to the other men, "Follow him through the city and kill everyone whose forehead is not marked. Show no mercy; have no pity! 6Kill them all—old and young, girls and women and little children. But do not touch anyone with the mark. Begin right here at the Temple." So they began by killing the seventy leaders.

7"Defile the Temple!" the LORD commanded. "Fill its courtyards with corpses. Go!" So they went and began killing throughout the city.

8While they were out killing, I was all alone. I fell face down on the ground and cried out, "O Sovereign LORD! Will your fury against Jerusalem wipe out everyone left in Israel?"

9Then he said to me, "The sins of the people of Israel and Judah are very, very great. The entire land is full of murder; the city is filled with injustice. They are saying, 'The LORD doesn't see it! The LORD has [e]abandoned the land!' 10So I will not spare them or have any pity on them. I will fully repay them for all they have done."

11Then the man in linen clothing, who carried the writer's case, reported back and said, "I have done as you commanded."

The LORD's Glory Leaves the Temple

10 In my vision I saw what appeared to be a throne of blue lapis lazuli above the crystal surface over the heads of the cherubim. 2Then the LORD spoke to the man in linen clothing and said, "Go between the whirling wheels beneath the cherubim, and take a handful of burning coals and scatter them over the city." He did this as I watched.

3The cherubim were standing at the south end of the Temple when the man went in, and the cloud of glory filled the inner courtyard. 4Then the glory of the LORD rose up from above the cherubim and went over to the door of the Temple. The Temple was filled with this cloud of glory, and the courtyard glowed brightly with the glory of the LORD. 5The moving wings of the [f]cherubim sounded like the voice of God Almighty and could be heard even in the outer courtyard.

6The LORD said to the man in linen clothing, "Go between the cherubim and take some burning coals from between the wheels." So the man went in and stood beside one of the wheels. 7Then one of the

9:3 ***The glory of the God of Israel,*** the visible manifestation of his presence, now began to depart from the defiled Temple. First, it ***rose up from between the cherubim,*** that is, from above the Ark in the Most Holy Place, where it normally rested. From there, it ***moved to the entrance to the Temple,*** ready to leave its former throne.

9:4-6 Just as the man dressed in linen (9:2-3) reenacted the marking of those kept safe at the first Passover (Exod 12:7-13), the angels of destruction reenacted comprehensive judgment (Exod 12:28-30), this time on ***old and young, girls and women and little children.*** Not just the firstborn males, as in Egypt, but everyone who did not have ***the mark*** that identified them as those who mourned over the sins of the city (cp. Rev 7:1-8) were destroyed.

9:7 ***Defile the Temple!*** Unlike Queen Athaliah, who was dragged out of the Temple before she was executed so that her blood would not defile the holy site (2 Kgs 11:15-16), these idolaters were to be killed in the Temple, which was already so defiled by their idolatry that nothing sacred was left there. Without God's holy presence, concern for the sanctity of the building was an empty gesture.

9:8 Ezekiel feared that he might be the only person ***left*** after the Lord expressed his ***fury.***

9:9-10 The Lord replied that he would fully repay Israel's sins (but see 9:3-4, 11).

9:11 ***I have done as you commanded:*** The remnant had been successfully marked to save them from the wrath to come (9:3-4).

10:1-22 The Temple provided an earthly residence where the Lord's glory could dwell among his people. This central blessing of the covenant could only be maintained if the people were holy. In the face of their defilement, the Lord abandoned his house, leaving it and the surrounding city vulnerable to the impending assault of the Babylonians.

10:1-2 Almost the same vision of fearsome glory that Ezekiel had seen earlier in Babylonia (ch 1) now appeared to him in the Jerusalem Temple. In a building filled with heavenly symbols, Ezekiel clearly perceived that the living creatures he had seen earlier were ***cherubim,*** the enforcers of divine judgment (Gen 3:24). • The ***burning coals*** that the priestly figure was instructed to gather showed that the defiled Jerusalem was to be burned by fire, as the city of Sodom had been (see 16:46-50). The implication of the Lord's abandoning his city was later worked out in history: Several years after this vision, Nebuchadnezzar burned the city of Jerusalem and filled it with corpses.

10:3-22 As if reluctant to leave, the ***glory of the LORD*** (10:4) moved slowly and haltingly, by stages. ***From above the cherubim*** in the Most Holy Place, it moved to ***the door of the Temple,*** paused, then ***hovered above the cherubim*** (10:18) and moved to the ***east gate*** of the courtyard (10:19), where it again paused. The glory of the Lord later left the city altogether (11:23; see note on 11:22-23).

10:5 ***God Almighty:*** Hebrew *El-Shaddai.*

cherubim reached out his hand and took some live coals from the fire burning among them. He put the coals into the hands of the man in linen clothing, and the man took them and went out. 8(All the cherubim had what looked like human hands under their wings.)

9I looked, and each of the four cherubim had a wheel beside him, and the wheels sparkled like beryl. 10All four wheels looked alike and were made the same; each wheel had a second wheel turning crosswise within it. 11The cherubim could move in any of the four directions they faced, without turning as they moved. They went straight in the direction they faced, never turning aside. 12Both the cherubim and the wheels were covered with eyes. The cherubim had eyes all over their bodies, including their hands, their backs, and their wings. 13I heard someone refer to the wheels as "the whirling wheels." 14Each of the four cherubim had four faces: the first was the face of an ox, the second was a human face, the third was the face of a lion, and the fourth was the face of an eagle.

15Then the [g]cherubim rose upward. These were the same living beings I had seen beside the Kebar River. 16When the cherubim moved, the wheels moved with them. When they lifted their wings to fly, the wheels stayed beside them. 17When the cherubim stopped, the wheels stopped. When they flew upward, the wheels rose up, for the spirit of the living beings was in the wheels.

18Then the [h]glory of the LORD moved out from the door of the Temple and hovered above the cherubim. 19And as I watched, the cherubim flew with their wheels to the east gate of the LORD's Temple. And the glory of the God of Israel hovered above them.

20These were the same living beings I had seen beneath the God of Israel when I was by the Kebar River. I knew they were cherubim, 21for each had four faces and four wings and what looked like human hands under their wings. 22And their faces were just like the faces of the beings I had seen at the Kebar, and they traveled straight ahead, just as the others had.

Judgment on Israel's Leaders

11 Then the Spirit lifted me and brought me to the east gateway of the LORD's Temple, where I saw twenty-five prominent men of the city. Among them were Jaazaniah son of Azzur and Pelatiah son of Benaiah, who were leaders among the people.

2The Spirit said to me, "Son of man, these are the men who are planning evil and giving wicked counsel in this city. 3They say to the people, 'Is it not a good time to build houses? This city is like an iron pot. We are safe inside it like meat in a pot.' 4Therefore, son of man, prophesy against them loudly and clearly."

5Then the Spirit of the LORD came upon me, and he told me to say, "This is what the LORD says to the people of Israel: I know what you are saying, for I know every thought that comes into your minds. 6You have murdered many in this city and filled its streets with the dead.

7"Therefore, this is what the Sovereign LORD says: This city is an iron pot all right, but the pieces of meat are the victims of your injustice. As for you, I will soon drag you from this pot. 8I will bring on you the sword of war you so greatly fear, says the Sovereign LORD. 9I will drive you out of Jerusalem and hand you over to foreigners, who will carry out my judgments against you. 10You will be slaughtered all the way to the borders of Israel. I will execute judgment on you, and you will know that I am the LORD. 11No, this city will not be an iron pot for you, and you will not be like meat safe inside it. I will judge you even to the borders of Israel, 12and you will know that I am the LORD. For you have refused to obey my decrees and regulations; instead, you have copied the standards of the nations around you."

13While I was still prophesying, Pelatiah son of Benaiah suddenly died. Then I fell

10:9 Ezek 1:16-17
10:11 Ezek 1:17
10:12 Ezek 1:18; Rev 4:6, 8
10:14 1 Kgs 7:27-30, 36; Ezek 1:6, 10; 10:21; Rev 4:7
10:15 Ezek 1:3-6, 19-21; [g]*kerub* (3742) ▸Ezek 28:14
10:17 Ezek 1:12
10:18 Ps 18:10; [h]*kabod* (3519) ▸Mal 2:2
10:19 Ezek 1:22
10:20 Ezek 1:5, 26; 10:15
10:21 Ezek 1:6, 8; 10:14; 41:18-20
10:22 Ezek 1:10, 12
11:1 Ezek 8:3; 43:5
11:2 Isa 30:1; Mic 2:1
11:3 Jer 1:13; Ezek 24:3, 6; 2 Pet 3:4
11:4 Ezek 3:4, 17
11:5 Jer 11:20; 17:10
11:6 Isa 1:15; Ezek 7:23; 22:2-6, 9, 12, 27; Matt 23:35
11:7 2 Kgs 25:18-22; Jer 52:24-27
11:9 Deut 28:36, 49-50; Ps 106:41
11:10 Num 34:8-9; Josh 13:5
11:12 Ezek 8:10, 14, 16; 18:8-9
11:13 Ezek 9:8

10:12 *covered with eyes:* The elders' earlier statement that "the LORD doesn't see us" (8:12) was foolish and false.

10:14 *the face of an ox:* Hebrew reads *the face of a cherub;* cp. 1:10.

10:19-22 From this point on, the city was doomed; God, whose threatening judgment appeared in such fearsome majesty in the opening chapter of Ezekiel, had abandoned it.

11:1-11 Having given Ezekiel a glimpse of the divine perspective on Jerusalem, the Spirit brought him back to overhear the words of the city's inhabitants. The ***wicked*** counselors asserted that though the assault by the Babylonians (the fire) was troublesome (hot), the defenses of the city (the ***iron pot***) were sufficient to protect them (the ***meat***). These counselors were telling people to ***build houses***—on stolen land (see 11:15, 17 and notes)—in which they could live safely. God, however, was determined to judge the wicked.

11:3 *We are safe inside it like meat in a pot:* Literally *This city is the pot, and we are the meat.*

11:8-10 God had once rescued his people from foreigners in Egypt, but now he would ***hand*** them ***over to foreigners*** for judgment.

11:12 *decrees and regulations:* See note on 5:7-13.

11:13 The judgment that the Lord pronounced occurred immediately.
• ***O Sovereign LORD, are you going to kill everyone in Israel?*** If those who still

face down on the ground and cried out, "O Sovereign LORD, are you going to kill everyone in Israel?"

Hope for Exiled Israel

14Then this message came to me from the LORD: 15"Son of man, the people still left in Jerusalem are talking about you and your relatives and all the people of Israel who are in exile. They are saying, 'Those people are far away from the LORD, so now he has given their land to us!'

16"Therefore, tell the exiles, 'This is what the Sovereign LORD says: Although I have scattered you in the countries of the world, I will be a sanctuary to you during your time in exile. 17I, the Sovereign LORD, will gather you back from the nations where you have been scattered, and I will give you the land of Israel once again.'

18"When the people return to their homeland, they will remove every trace of their vile images and detestable idols. 19And I will give them singleness of heart and put a new spirit within them. I will take away their stony, stubborn heart and give them a tender, responsive heart, 20so they will obey my decrees and regulations. Then they will truly be my people, and I will be their God. 21But as for those who long for vile images and detestable idols, I will repay them fully for their sins. I, the Sovereign LORD, have spoken!"

The LORD's Glory Leaves Jerusalem

22Then the cherubim lifted their wings and rose into the air with their wheels beside them, and the glory of the God of Israel hovered above them. 23Then the glory of the LORD went up from the city and stopped above the mountain to the east.

24Afterward the Spirit of God carried me back again to Babylonia, to the people in exile there. And so ended the vision of my visit to Jerusalem. 25And I told the exiles everything the LORD had shown me.

More Oracles of Judgment (12:1–24:27)

Signs of the Coming Exile

12 Again a message came to me from the LORD: 2"Son of man, you live among rebels who have eyes but refuse to see. They have ears but refuse to hear. For they are a rebellious people.

3"So now, son of man, pretend you are being sent into exile. Pack the few items an exile could carry, and leave your home to go somewhere else. Do this right in front of the people so they can see you. For perhaps they will pay attention to this, even though they are such rebels. 4Bring your baggage outside during the day so they can watch you. Then in the evening, as they are watching, leave your house as captives do when they begin a long march to distant lands. 5Dig a hole through the wall while they are

11:15 Ezek 33:24
11:16 Jer 29:7, 11
11:17 Isa 11:11-16; Jer 24:5-6
11:18 Ezek 5:11; 37:23
11:19 Jer 24:7; 32:39; Ezek 36:26; Zech 7:12; 2 Cor 3:3
11:20 Ezek 36:27
11:21 Jer 16:18
11:22 Ezek 10:19
11:23 Ezek 8:4; Zech 14:4
11:24 Ezek 8:3; 37:1
11:25 Ezek 2:7
12:2 Isa 6:9-10; Jer 5:21; Ezek 2:6-8; Matt 13:13-14; John 9:39-41
12:3 Jer 26:3; 36:3, 7; Luke 20:13; 2 Tim 2:25
12:4 2 Kgs 25:4; Jer 39:4; 52:7

remained in the land were destined for such comprehensive destruction, who would be God's people?

11:15-16 Those who remained in the land regarded the exiles as ***far away from the LORD,*** with no one to protect their interests in their family land holdings. ***Relatives*** (literally *men of your redemption*) would normally have redeemed Ezekiel's family property if he fell into debt or other trouble. Since the exiles had been transported as family groups, there was no one left in Judah to guard their inherited properties.
• ***he has given their land to us!*** Those remaining in the land considered the exiles to be under God's judgment and their ancestral lands to have been forfeited. The very opposite was true. The future of Israel lay with the far-off exiles, as the Lord had gone into exile with them and would ***be a sanctuary*** to them during their ***time in exile*** (see 11:22-23).

11:17 The exile in Babylon would last only until God had exercised his judgment. After this, there would be a new exodus of God's people from ***the nations where*** they had been ***scattered*** back to ***the land of Israel.*** Their land, which was currently being stolen from them by those who remained in Judah, would be restored to them.

11:19 The external change in the fortunes of God's people would be matched by an internal change; their ***singleness of heart*** would mark undivided loyalty to the Lord and replace their wayward affections of the past. A ***tender, responsive heart*** (literally *a heart of flesh*) would replace their ***stony, stubborn heart*** (literally *the heart of stone*), and in place of the old idolatrous spirit they would receive ***a new spirit*** (see 36:26-27).

11:20 Their changed hearts and spirits would enable the Lord's people to ***obey*** his ***decrees and regulations*** so that the goal of the covenant relationship—***people*** living with ***their God*** in their midst—might at last be achieved. The new heart and new spirit promised here to God's people has become a reality (Heb 8:8-13). Through the outpouring of the Spirit at Pentecost, God's people have become a new creation (2 Cor 5:17).

11:21 Those who remained in the land would reap what they had sown. God would ***repay them fully for their sins,*** especially those involving ***vile images and detestable idols.***

11:22-23 Ezekiel's vision of the Temple (chs 8–11) concludes with the chariot bearing the ***glory of . . . God*** away from the Temple. The ***glory of the LORD*** would depart from defiled Jerusalem, go east to Babylon with the exiles, and identify with their suffering (11:16). God's glory halted temporarily above ***the mountain to the east*** of Jerusalem, the Mount of Olives, as if waiting to see the judgment descend upon the rebellious city. Having departed to the east, it would also return from the east to the renewed Temple (ch 43).

11:24 *Babylonia:* Or *Chaldea.*

12:1–24:27 This section collects diverse prophecies and sign acts that are united in their condemnation of Jerusalem and its leaders.

12:1-2 The inhabitants of Judah were not the only ones who had stony, stubborn hearts that were reluctant to hear the prophet's message (11:19). The exiles among whom Ezekiel lived were also ***rebellious people*** who would ***refuse to see*** that their ways were evil and decline to ***hear*** his message, just like those left behind in Judah.

12:5-7 Ezekiel was to ***dig a hole through the wall*** as though sneaking out of a

watching and go out through it. 6As they
watch, lift your pack to your shoulders and
walk away into the night. Cover your face
so you cannot see the land you are leaving.
For I have made you a sign for the people
of Israel."
7So I did as I was told. In broad daylight
I brought my pack outside, filled with the
things I might carry into exile. Then in the
evening while the people looked on, I dug
through the wall with my hands and went
out into the night with my pack on my
shoulder.
8The next morning this message came
to me from the LORD: 9"Son of man, these
rebels, the people of Israel, have asked you
what all this means. 10Say to them, 'This
is what the Sovereign LORD says: These actions contain a message for King Zedekiah
in Jerusalem and for all the people of Israel.'
11Explain that your actions are a sign to
show what will soon happen to them, for
they will be driven into exile as captives.
12"Even Zedekiah will leave Jerusalem at
night through a hole in the wall, taking only
what he can carry with him. He will cover
his face, and his eyes will not see the land he
is leaving. 13Then I will throw my net over
him and capture him in my snare. I will
bring him to Babylon, the land of the Babylonians, though he will never see it, and he
will die there. 14I will scatter his servants
and warriors to the four winds and send
the sword after them. 15And when I scatter
them among the nations, they will know
that I am the LORD. 16But I will spare a few of
them from death by war, famine, or disease,
so they can confess all their detestable sins
to their captors. Then they will know that I
am the LORD."
17Then this message came to me from
the LORD: 18"Son of man, tremble as you
eat your food. Shake with fear as you
drink your water. 19Tell the people, 'This is
what the Sovereign LORD says concerning
those living in Israel and Jerusalem: They
will eat their food with trembling and sip
their water in despair, for their land will
be stripped bare because of their violence.
20The cities will be destroyed and the
farmland made desolate. Then you will
know that I am the LORD.' "

A New Proverb: No Further Delay

21Again a message came to me from the
LORD: 22"Son of man, you've heard that
proverb they quote in Israel: 'Time passes,
and prophecies come to nothing.' 23Tell the
people, 'This is what the Sovereign LORD
says: I will put an end to this proverb, and
you will soon stop quoting it.' Now give
them this new proverb to replace the old
one: 'The time has come for every prophecy to be fulfilled!'
24"There will be no more false visions
and flattering predictions in Israel. 25For
I am the LORD! If I say it, it will happen.
There will be no more delays, you rebels of
Israel. I will fulfill my threat of destruction
in your own lifetime. I, the Sovereign LORD,
have spoken!"
26Then this message came to me from the
LORD: 27"Son of man, the people of Israel
are saying, 'He's talking about the distant future. His visions won't come true for a long,
long time.' 28Therefore, tell them, 'This is
what the Sovereign LORD says: No more
delay! I will now do everything I have threatened. I, the Sovereign LORD, have spoken!' "

Judgment against False Prophets

13 Then this message came to me from
the LORD: 2"Son of man, prophesy
against the false prophets of Israel who

12:6 Isa 8:18; Ezek 4:3; 24:24
12:7 Ezek 24:18
12:9 Ezek 2:5-8; 17:12; 24:19
12:10 2 Kgs 9:25; Isa 13:1; Mal 1:1
12:11 Jer 15:2; 52:15, 28-30
12:12 2 Kgs 25:4; Jer 39:4; 52:7
12:13 Isa 24:17; Jer 39:7; 52:11; Hos 7:12
12:14 Ezek 5:2; 17:21
12:16 Jer 22:8-9
12:18 Ezek 4:16
12:19 Isa 6:11; Zech 7:14
12:20 Isa 7:23-24; Jer 25:9; Ezek 5:14; 36:3; Dan 9:17
12:22 Jer 5:12; Amos 6:3; 2 Pet 3:3-4
12:23 Joel 2:11; Zeph 1:14
12:24 Jer 14:13-16; Zech 13:2-4
12:25 Num 14:28-34; Hab 1:5
12:27 Dan 10:14
13:2 Isa 9:15; 56:9-12; Jer 37:19

besieged city without being noticed, as Zedekiah later attempted to do (2 Kgs 25:4).

12:10 ***King Zedekiah in Jerusalem:*** Literally *the prince in Jerusalem;* similarly in 12:12.

12:12-13 King Zedekiah was unable to see the coming judgment, so he would be unable to see either ***the land he is leaving*** or ***the land of the Babylonians*** (or *Chaldeans*). This prophecy was fulfilled when the Babylonians captured Zedekiah as he fled from besieged Jerusalem. After making him watch while his sons were tortured to death, the Babylonians gouged out his eyes (2 Kgs 25:1-7). This terrible fate for Judah's last king was not simply due to the Babylonians' imperial expansionist ambitions. More fundamentally, the Lord wanted to ***capture him*** in his ***snare.***

12:16 The unhappy ***few*** survivors would ***confess all their detestable sins to their captors,*** not necessarily in repentance, but in recognition that the Lord had acted justly in judgment against them.

12:17-20 For Ezekiel to ***tremble*** and ***shake*** while eating and drinking was a sign act that reflected the terrible anxiety of the inhabitants of Jerusalem and Judah as they saw their inevitable doom approaching. When the exiles learned that their former homeland had been destroyed, they would realize that they were not cast-offs from God's plan, but rather the fortunate ones who had escaped his comprehensive judgment (see Jer 24:1-8).

12:21–14:11 The messages in this section address the issue of true and false prophecy.

12:22 Ezekiel's hearers were so reluctant to open their ears to the message of the prophets that they had coined a ***proverb*** to express their skepticism.

12:23-25 In response to the people's unbelief (12:22), the Lord framed a ***new proverb*** for the people, using similar words but with an opposite meaning.

12:26-28 The people responded with a second proverb, and again the Lord refuted them. What the Lord had ***threatened,*** he would do.

13:1-3 The fundamental difference between true and false prophets was that false prophets were ***inventing their own***

13:3
Jer 23:28-32
Lam 2:14

13:5
Ps 106:23
Isa 58:12

13:6
Jer 28:15; 29:8

13:8
Nah 2:13

13:9
Ezra 2:59-63
Ps 69:28
Jer 20:3-6
Dan 12:1

13:10
Jer 8:11; 50:6

13:13
Exod 9:24-25
Ps 18:12-13
Rev 11:19; 16:21

13:14
Mic 1:6

are inventing their own prophecies. Say to them, 'Listen to the word of the LORD. 3This is what the Sovereign LORD says: What sorrow awaits the false prophets who are following their own imaginations and have seen nothing at all!'

4"O people of Israel, these prophets of yours are like jackals digging in the ruins. 5They have done nothing to repair the breaks in the walls around the nation. They have not helped it to stand firm in battle on the day of the LORD. 6Instead, they have told lies and made false predictions. They say, 'This message is from the LORD,' even though the LORD never sent them. And yet they expect him to fulfill their prophecies! 7Can your visions be anything but false if you claim, 'This message is from the LORD,' when I have not even spoken to you?

8"Therefore, this is what the Sovereign LORD says: Because what you say is false and your visions are a lie, I will stand against you, says the Sovereign LORD. 9I will raise my fist against all the prophets who see false visions and make lying predictions, and they will be banished from the community of Israel. I will blot their names from Israel's record books, and they will never again set foot in their own land. Then you will know that I am the Sovereign LORD.

10"This will happen because these evil prophets deceive my people by saying, 'All is peaceful' when there is no peace at all! It's as if the people have built a flimsy wall, and these prophets are trying to reinforce it by covering it with whitewash! 11Tell these whitewashers that their wall will soon fall down. A heavy rainstorm will undermine it; great hailstones and mighty winds will knock it down. 12And when the wall falls, the people will cry out, 'What happened to your whitewash?'

13"Therefore, this is what the Sovereign LORD says: I will sweep away your whitewashed wall with a storm of indignation, with a great flood of anger, and with hailstones of fury. 14I will break down your wall right to its foundation, and when it falls, it will crush you. Then you will know that I am the LORD. 15At last my anger against the

False Prophets (13:1-23)

Ezek 22:28
Deut 13:1-5; 18:22
1 Kgs 22:8-28
Jer 6:13-15; 14:13-16; 20:1-6; 28:1-17; 29:21-32; 50:6
Mic 3:5
2 Cor 11:13-15
2 Tim 4:3-4
2 Pet 2:1-3

Alongside the true prophets of the Lord, the Bible tells of many individuals who set themselves up as prophets on their own authority. They had no true calling from God, but nonetheless claimed to speak for him. Often it was hard for people to discern the difference, especially since false prophets usually told them what they wanted to hear (see, e.g., 1 Kgs 22:11-12; Jer 28:1-4).

Because of this difficulty, and the Lord's merciful delay in bringing judgment upon his rebellious people, many people doubted that God's word through the prophets would ever be fulfilled (Isa 5:19). Others denied that anything would happen within their lifetimes. Might not the punishment that had so often been delayed be delayed a little longer?

Ezekiel prophesied that in the coming judgment upon Jerusalem, false prophets would be cut off so that people would no longer be confused about who the true prophets were (13:8-9). There would also be no more delay to God's judgment—the Lord was coming very soon to fulfill the words he had spoken (13:11). Everyone would see which words God had really spoken and which words the false prophets had conjured out of their own imaginations.

prophecies, while true prophets spoke ***the word of the LORD.*** Now these false prophets would receive a word from the Lord about their own destruction. ***Sorrow*** awaited these deceived and deceiving messengers.

13:4-5 The false prophets are compared to ***jackals digging in the ruins*** to prey on the small animals living there. The false prophets did not ***repair the breaks in the walls*** by calling the people who were suffering at the hands of the Babylonians to repent, live holy lives, and fight evil. Instead, they gained prestige—and perhaps money—by telling lies that encouraged the people to continue to rebel. Like jackals, these false prophets were actually breaking the walls down, not building them up (cp. Neh 4:3).

13:6-7 Although the false prophets knew that their words were ***lies*** and ***false predictions,*** they confidently expected God to ***fulfill their prophecies.*** These false hopes gave God's people a false sense of security that would prove empty and destructive on the coming day of judgment (cp. Jer 6:14).

13:8-9 The false prophets' desire for personal safety would be counterproductive. They would be ***banished from the community*** and would ***never again set foot in their own land.***

13:10-16 The people's "righteousness" was a ***flimsy wall*** in danger of collapse. Rather than doing the hard work of constructing ***their wall*** properly by calling the people to repentance, the false prophets were content to give it a coat of ***whitewash*** by telling the people that ***peace would come to Jerusalem.*** This external touch-up made the wall appear more solid than it was. Its true weakness would be exposed by ***a heavy rainstorm.*** Water would flow into the unsealed cracks, wash away the mortar, and allow the stones to fall away. In this case, the storm would be the ***great flood of*** God's ***anger,*** which would destroy the people's pretense to righteousness and the false prophets who had encouraged it. Meanwhile, they would have ***no peace.***

wall and those who covered it with whitewash will be satisfied. Then I will say to you:
'The wall and those who whitewashed it are
both gone. 16They were lying prophets who
claimed peace would come to Jerusalem
when there was no peace. I, the Sovereign
LORD, have spoken!'

Judgment against False Women Prophets

17"Now, son of man, speak out against the
women who prophesy from their own
imaginations. 18This is what the Sovereign LORD says: What sorrow awaits you
women who are ensnaring the souls of my
people, young and old alike. You tie magic
charms on their wrists and furnish them
with magic veils. Do you think you can
trap others without bringing destruction
on yourselves? 19You bring shame on me
among my people for a few handfuls of
barley or a piece of bread. By lying to my
people who love to listen to lies, you kill
those who should not die, and you promise
life to those who should not live.
20"This is what the Sovereign LORD says:
I am against all your magic charms, which
you use to ensnare my people like birds. I
will tear them from your arms, setting my
people free like birds set free from a cage.
21I will tear off the magic veils and save my
people from your grasp. They will no longer
be your victims. Then you will know that I
am the LORD. 22You have discouraged the
righteous with your lies, but I didn't want
them to be sad. And you have encouraged
the wicked by promising them life, even
though they continue in their sins. 23Be-
cause of all this, you will no longer talk of
seeing visions that you never saw, nor will
you make predictions. For I will rescue
my people from your grasp. Then you will
know that I am the LORD."

The Idolatry of Divided Hearts

14 Then some of the leaders of Israel visited me, and while they were sitting
with me, 2this message came to me from
the LORD: 3"Son of man, these leaders have
set up idols in their hearts. They have embraced things that will make them fall into
sin. Why should I listen to their requests?
4Tell them, 'This is what the Sovereign LORD
says: The people of Israel have set up idols
in their hearts and fallen into sin, and then
they go to a prophet asking for a message.
So I, the LORD, will give them the kind of answer their great idolatry deserves. 5I will do
this to capture the minds and hearts of all
my people who have turned from me to worship their detestable idols.'
6"Therefore, tell the people of Israel, 'This
is what the Sovereign LORD says: [i]Repent
and [i]turn away from your idols, and stop
all your detestable sins. 7I, the LORD, will
answer all those, both Israelites and foreigners, who reject me and set up idols in their
hearts and so fall into sin, and who then
come to a prophet asking for my advice. 8I
will turn against such people and make a
terrible example of them, eliminating them
from among my people. Then you will know
that I am the LORD.
9" 'And if a prophet is deceived into giving
a message, it is because I, the LORD, have deceived that prophet. I will lift my fist against
such prophets and cut them off from the
community of Israel. 10False prophets and
those who seek their guidance will all be

13:16 Isa 57:21
13:17 Judg 4:4; 2 Kgs 22:14; Luke 2:36; Acts 21:9; Rev 2:20
13:18 2 Pet 2:14
13:19 Prov 28:21; Jer 23:14, 17; Mic 3:5
13:21 Ps 91:3; 124:7
13:22 Amos 5:12; 2 Pet 2:18-19
13:23 Mic 3:6; Zech 13:3
14:1 2 Kgs 6:32
14:3 Isa 1:15
14:4 1 Kgs 21:20-24; 2 Kgs 1:16; Isa 66:4
14:5 Jer 2:11; Hos 10:2; Zech 7:12
14:6 1 Sam 7:3; Neh 1:9; Isa 30:22; 55:6-7; [i]*shub* (7725) ›Ezek 18:30
14:7 Exod 12:48; 20:10
14:8 Isa 65:15
14:9 Jer 6:14-15

13:17-19 Like the false male prophets (13:1-16), some women prophets proclaimed words that came only from ***their own imaginations***. The false male prophets had been using conventional forms of prophecy, but the women used magical techniques involving ***charms*** and ***veils***. Motivated by personal gain (***a few handfuls of barley or a piece of bread***), they promised life and death (cp. 3:17-21; 33:1-9), but to the wrong people.

13:20-23 The false women prophets did not define who qualified for life or death in the way that God did, so their ministry ***discouraged the righteous*** by making them feel that their obedience was in vain. It also ***encouraged the wicked*** to believe that they could ***continue in their sins*** without penalty. The result of this misdirection was to ***ensnare*** both the righteous and the wicked, giving both groups false ideas about God.

14:1-3 The ***leaders*** of the exiled community ***of Israel*** came to visit Ezekiel again, probably seeking encouragement (see note on 8:1). The people were tainted with the same kinds of sin, such as idolatry, that affected the people in Judah (cp. 8:10-12).

14:3 ***idols:*** The Hebrew term (literally *round things*) probably alludes to dung; also in 14:4, 5, 6, 7. See note on 6:4-7.

14:4-5 Though the exiles were going through the motions of seeking the Lord, their hearts had ***turned from*** the Lord ***to worship their detestable idols***. It was tempting for the exiles to think that the Babylonians' many military successes demonstrated that true power lay with the Babylonian gods rather than with the Lord.

14:6-7 When ***asking for*** God's ***advice***, rebels should only expect the response to be, ***Repent***.

14:8 Instead of answering these people through a false prophet with a word of divine guidance, the Lord would answer them directly with a terrible act of judgment, thus ***eliminating them*** from among his people. Whether this indicates death or excommunication, these half-hearted leaders would be removed from the covenant community, the only place where true life is to be found.

14:9-10 False prophets, who sought to counteract God's will by prophesying what God had not spoken, would do God's will unwittingly—they and other rebels would be deceived and confirmed in their rebellion. False prophets and rebellious people alike were thus ***punished for their sins*** (see also Deut 13; 1 Kgs 22:6-23).

14:11 Ezek 11:20; 44:10, 15
14:13 Ezek 15:8; 20:27
14:14 Gen 6:8; Job 1:1, 5; Dan 10:11; Heb 11:7
14:16 Gen 19:29
14:17 Ezek 5:12; 21:3-4; 25:13; Zeph 1:3
14:19 Jer 14:12; Ezek 5:12
14:21 Amos 4:6-10; Rev 6:4-8

punished for their sins. [11]In this way, the
people of Israel will learn not to stray from
me, polluting themselves with sin. They will
be my people, and I will be their God. I, the
Sovereign LORD, have spoken!' "

The Certainty of the LORD's Judgment

[12]Then this message came to me from the
LORD: [13]"Son of man, suppose the people of
a country were to sin against me, and I lifted
my fist to crush them, cutting off their food
supply and sending a famine to destroy
both people and animals. [14]Even if Noah,
Daniel, and Job were there, their righteousness would save no one but themselves, says
the Sovereign LORD.

[15]"Or suppose I were to send wild animals to invade the country, kill the people,
and make the land too desolate and dangerous to pass through. [16]As surely as I
live, says the Sovereign LORD, even if those
three men were there, they wouldn't be able
to save their own sons or daughters. They
alone would be saved, but the land would be
made desolate.

[17]"Or suppose I were to bring war against
the land, and I sent enemy armies to destroy
both people and animals. [18]As surely as I
live, says the Sovereign LORD, even if those
three men were there, they wouldn't be able
to save their own sons or daughters. They
alone would be saved.

[19]"Or suppose I were to pour out my fury
by sending an epidemic into the land, and
the disease killed people and animals alike.
[20]As surely as I live, says the Sovereign LORD,
even if Noah, Daniel, and Job were there,
they wouldn't be able to save their own sons
or daughters. They alone would be saved by
their righteousness.

[21]"Now this is what the Sovereign LORD
says: How terrible it will be when all four

Divine Sovereignty and Human Responsibility (14:9-11)

Ezek 17:24; 36:25-26; 1 Sam 2:6-7; 1 Kgs 22:19-22; 2 Chr 20:6; Job 1:8-12; 2:2-6; Ps 115:3; 135:6-14; Isa 45:6-7; Lam 3:37-40; Dan 2:20-22; Amos 3:6; 4:6-11; Rom 1:18-25; 9:8-33; 12:2; Eph 4:20-24; 2 Thess 2:11-12; Jas 1:13-14; 4:12-16; Heb 13:20-21

How can God deceive a prophet and still hold him accountable for his actions? Ezekiel 14 raises this question in many people's minds. How can we reconcile God's sovereign control over all things with the personal choices and decisions for which we will be called to account?

The Bible traces all things back to God's sovereignty. That the rain falls on the just and unjust alike is part of God's sovereign plan (Matt 5:45). Even a false prophet could give a prophecy that led people astray only with the Lord's permission or direction.

At the same time, God is in no way responsible for our sin; it is our responsibility because it comes from our own sinful desires. In giving deceitful messages to false prophets, God was simply giving them and their hearers exactly what they wanted (cp. 2 Thes 2:11). Unless God restrained them from their sin, they would naturally choose lies instead of the truth and worship creation in place of the Creator (Rom 1:18-25). God simply gave them permission to enact their hearts' sinful desires.

The remarkable fact is not that God allows some sinners to persist in their chosen delusions, but that he saves sinners, changes our natures, and gives us the desire to do good for the glory of God (see 36:25-26; Rom 8:1-11; Eph 2:10).

14:11 The goal of God's judgment was not the total destruction of the exiles but their salvation, so that ***the people of Israel*** would ***learn not to stray*** from the Lord.

14:12-20 Israel had not been unjustly singled out for judgment. If any ***country were to sin against*** the Lord, the result would be the same. It is clear that Israel is in view here, however, because the language used to describe their sin is used elsewhere to describe a breach in Israel's covenant relationship with the Lord. The covenant was broken, so the nation would inevitably and justly experience the covenant curses that they had ratified at the time the covenant was first made (Lev 26). • The covenant curses are itemized in four test cases. Each case envisions one of the curses listed in Lev 26: ***famine*** (14:13-14; see Lev 26:26), ***wild animals*** (14:15-16; see Lev 26:22), ***war*** (14:17-18; see Lev 26:25), and ***disease*** (14:19-20; see Lev 26:25).

14:14, 20 ***Noah, Daniel, and Job:*** Each of these men was famous for standing firm in the midst of a wicked generation. If anyone could merit a stay of judgment from God, they could. However, even if a land contained these three outstanding men of God, their righteousness would not suffice to save even their closest relatives from the coming disaster (14:20). How much less would it save a rebellious country! • Since the Hebrew spelling of the name ***Daniel*** (Hebrew *Dani'el*; also in 28:3) is slightly different from that of the biblical prophet Daniel (Hebrew *Daniyye'l*), who was Ezekiel's younger contemporary in Babylon, some have proposed that Ezekiel was referring to a legendary pagan hero named Danel. However, minor variations in the spelling of names are common in the Hebrew OT. Ezekiel and his hearers would certainly have known of the biblical prophet Daniel as a model of righteousness and wisdom. It is unlikely that a prophet as radically outspoken against idolatry as Ezekiel would have picked a pagan figure like Danel to represent unparalleled righteousness and wisdom. So Ezekiel is most likely referring to the prophet Daniel.

14:21 ***Jerusalem*** was worse off than the hypothetical country of 14:12-20 in two

of these dreadful punishments fall upon Jerusalem—war, famine, wild animals, and disease—destroying all her people and animals. 22Yet there will be survivors, and they will come here to join you as exiles in Babylon. You will see with your own eyes how wicked they are, and then you will feel better about what I have done to Jerusalem. 23When you meet them and see their behavior, you will understand that these things are not being done to Israel without cause. I, the Sovereign LORD, have spoken!"

The Parable of the Worthless Vine

15 Then this message came to me from the LORD: 2"Son of man, how does a grapevine compare to a tree? Is a vine's wood as useful as the wood of a tree? 3Can its wood be used for making things, like pegs to hang up pots and pans? 4No, it can only be used for fuel, and even as fuel, it burns too quickly. 5Vines are useless both before and after being put into the fire!

6"And this is what the Sovereign LORD says: The people of Jerusalem are like grapevines growing among the trees of the forest. Since they are useless, I have thrown them on the fire to be burned. 7And I will see to it that if they escape from one fire, they will fall into another. When I turn against them, you will know that I am the LORD. 8And I will make the land desolate because my people have been unfaithful to me. I, the Sovereign LORD, have spoken!"

The Parable of the Unfaithful Wife

16 Then another message came to me from the LORD: 2"Son of man, confront Jerusalem with her detestable sins. 3Give her this message from the Sovereign LORD: You are nothing but a Canaanite! Your father was an Amorite and your mother a Hittite. 4On the day you were born, no one cared about you. Your umbilical cord was not cut, and you were never washed, rubbed with salt, and wrapped in cloth. 5No one had the slightest interest in you; no one pitied you or cared for you. On the day you were born, you were unwanted, dumped in a field and left to die.

6"But I came by and saw you there, helplessly kicking about in your own blood. As you lay there, I said, 'Live!' 7And I helped you to thrive like a plant in the field. You grew up and became a beautiful jewel. Your breasts became full, and your body hair grew, but

14:22 Ezek 36:20
14:23 Jer 22:8-9
15:2 Ps 80:8-16; Isa 5:1-7; Hos 10:1; John 15:1-6
15:4 Isa 27:11; Heb 6:8
15:7 Lev 26:17; 1 Kgs 19:17; Isa 24:18; Amos 5:19; 9:1-4
16:2 Isa 58:1; Hos 8:1
16:4 Hos 2:3
16:5 Deut 32:10
16:7 Exod 1:7

---

respects. First, Jerusalem did not have Noah, Daniel, and Job; instead, the city was filled with unrighteous people. Second, it would not be hit with one single judgment plague but with ***all four of these dreadful punishments*** at once. It is therefore not surprising that ***all her people and animals*** would be destroyed.

14:22-23 Some ***survivors*** would emerge from the devastating judgment (14:21) and join those already in exile. They would not survive because of their righteousness or that of their relatives, but simply as an object lesson for those in exile. As the exiles saw the depravity of this remnant, they would ***feel better about what*** God had ***done to Jerusalem.*** The exiles would know that God had not acted ***without cause*** but had acted with justice in his judgment upon Jerusalem.

15:1–24:14 This section contains a series of eight metaphors, each reiterating from a different angle the certainty of Jerusalem's forthcoming judgment. The images are of a worthless vine (ch 15); a faithless wife (ch 16); a vine and two eagles (ch 17); sour grapes (ch 18); a lion and her cubs (ch 19); a sword (ch 21); two degenerate sisters (ch 23); and a cooking pot (ch 24).

15:1-5 The ***wood of a tree*** can be used to make all kinds of useful objects, ***pegs*** being the simplest and most basic. ***A vine's wood,*** however, has no strength, size, or beauty, so it is useless for pegs and it is not even good ***as fuel*** because ***it burns too quickly.*** It is completely ***useless.***

15:6 ***The people of Jerusalem are like grapevines:*** Cp. Ps 80:8-9; Isa 5:1-7; Jer 2:21; John 15:1-6. • If grapevines grow ***among the trees of the forest,*** they do not bear fruit because they lack sufficient sunlight.

15:7 Anyone who escaped from ***one fire*** of God's judgment (probably a reference to the defeat of Judah by Nebuchadnezzar in 597 BC; 2 Kgs 21:1-4) would simply ***fall into another*** (the destruction of Jerusalem in 586 BC).

15:8 ***unfaithful:*** See 6:9; 16:17; Hos 2. Jerusalem had gone after idols instead of faithfully serving the true God. Such behavior broke the covenant between the Lord and his people, with the inevitable result that the ***land*** would become ***desolate.***

16:1-63 Jerusalem is exposed as a wanton prostitute. Even in the relatively mild form of the English translation, ch 16 is hard to read, and it was at least as shocking in the ancient context. Ezekiel was graphically communicating the full ugliness and offensiveness of Judah's sin. He refused to be polite when discussing his people's depravity. In fact, his refusal to tone down the offensiveness of Jerusalem's sin is precisely the point of the passage. The offensive nature of the portrayal was critical to its effectiveness because Ezekiel's hearers could understand that God's awful judgment upon them was justified only if they first understood the magnitude of their sin in his sight. A less graphic presentation would not have adequately communicated this message.

16:1-3 Ezekiel begins with Jerusalem's unpromising origins; it came from ***Canaanite*** roots and was the offspring of ***an Amorite and . . . a Hittite.*** The city of Jerusalem predated the conquest under Joshua and was never captured during that campaign. Instead, it retained its native Canaanite population even after David conquered it.

16:4-5 Jerusalem's parents were heartless and did not perform the usual obstetrical practices. Ordinarily, someone cut the ***umbilical cord, washed*** the infant, smeared ***salt*** and oil over her body, and swaddled her tightly ***in cloth.*** Instead, as was common with baby girls in the ancient world, Jerusalem was abandoned: ***dumped in a field and left to die.***

16:6-7 While Jerusalem was in a helpless and hopeless condition, the Lord intervened with his life-giving word. Without that, she would certainly have died. The Lord had no obligation to rescue this abandoned child, for she would simply have been one among

16:8
Gen 22:16-18
Exod 19:5; 24:7-8
Ruth 3:9
Jer 2:2
Hos 2:18-20
[j]*dod* (1730)
‣Ezek 23:17

16:11
Gen 24:22, 47
Isa 3:18-19

16:12
Jer 13:18

16:13
Deut 32:13-14
Ps 45:13-14

16:14
1 Kgs 10:1, 24
Ps 50:2
Lam 2:15

16:15
Isa 57:8
Jer 2:20
Ezek 27:3

16:19
Hos 2:8

16:20
Exod 13:2, 12
Ps 106:37-38
Jer 7:31

16:21
2 Kgs 17:17
Jer 19:5

16:24
Ps 78:58
Isa 57:5-7

16:25
Prov 9:14

16:26
Jer 7:18-19

16:27
Isa 9:12

16:28
2 Kgs 16:7-18
2 Chr 28:16-23

16:30
Prov 9:13
Isa 3:9
Rev 17:1-6

16:31
Isa 52:3

you were still naked. 8And when I passed
by again, I saw that you were old enough for
[j]love. So I wrapped my cloak around you to
cover your nakedness and declared my marriage vows. I made a covenant with you, says
the Sovereign LORD, and you became mine.
9"Then I bathed you and washed off your
blood, and I rubbed fragrant oils into your
skin. 10I gave you expensive clothing of fine
linen and silk, beautifully embroidered, and
sandals made of fine goatskin leather. 11I
gave you lovely jewelry, bracelets, beautiful
necklaces, 12a ring for your nose, earrings
for your ears, and a lovely crown for your
head. 13And so you were adorned with gold
and silver. Your clothes were made of fine
linen and were beautifully embroidered.
You ate the finest foods—choice flour, honey,
and olive oil—and became more beautiful
than ever. You looked like a queen, and so
you were! 14Your fame soon spread throughout the world because of your beauty. I
dressed you in my splendor and perfected
your beauty, says the Sovereign LORD.
15"But you thought your fame and beauty
were your own. So you gave yourself as a
prostitute to every man who came along.
Your beauty was theirs for the asking. 16You
used the lovely things I gave you to make
shrines for idols, where you played the
prostitute. Unbelievable! How could such
a thing ever happen? 17You took the very
jewels and gold and silver ornaments I had
given you and made statues of men and worshiped them. This is adultery against me!
18You used the beautifully embroidered
clothes I gave you to dress your idols. Then
you used my special oil and my incense to
worship them. 19Imagine it! You set before
them as a sacrifice the choice flour, olive oil,
and honey I had given you, says the Sovereign LORD.
20"Then you took your sons and daughters—the children you had borne to
me—and sacrificed them to your gods. Was
your prostitution not enough? 21Must you
also slaughter my children by sacrificing
them to idols? 22In all your years of adultery and detestable sin, you have not once
remembered the days long ago when you
lay naked in a field, kicking about in your
own blood.
23"What sorrow awaits you, says the Sovereign LORD. In addition to all your other
wickedness, 24you built a pagan shrine and
put altars to idols in every town square.
25On every street corner you defiled your
beauty, offering your body to every passerby in an endless stream of prostitution.
26Then you added lustful Egypt to your
lovers, provoking my anger with your increasing promiscuity. 27That is why I struck
you with my fist and reduced your boundaries. I handed you over to your enemies,
the Philistines, and even they were shocked
by your lewd conduct. 28You have prostituted yourself with the Assyrians, too. It
seems you can never find enough new lovers! And after your prostitution there, you
still were not satisfied. 29You added to your
lovers by embracing Babylonia, the land of
merchants, but you still weren't satisfied.
30"What a sick heart you have, says the
Sovereign LORD, to do such things as these,
acting like a shameless prostitute. 31You
build your pagan shrines on every street

many facing such a fate. Yet out of his grace and mercy, the Lord enabled her not merely to survive but to *thrive.* Instead of dying in the field, she *grew up* like *a plant* into maturity and beauty. The city of Jerusalem prospered before becoming an Israelite city, and it was the Lord's doing.

16:8 At this time, the Lord *wrapped* his *cloak around* her, an act that represented a commitment to marriage (cp. Ruth 3:9). The Lord *made a covenant* with Jerusalem, and in the terms of the metaphor, he married her. When the Lord entered into a covenant with David and his descendants, he also chose Jerusalem as the place for his name to be honored (see 1 Kgs 9:3-4; Ps 132).

16:9-10 The Lord did for Jerusalem what her parents had never done: he *washed,* anointed, and clothed her, thus reversing the circumstances of her birth. • The Lord provided Jerusalem with adornments fit for a queen, including materials elsewhere associated with the Tabernacle (see Exod 25:3-5; 26:1-14). This reminded her people that she was chosen as the home of God's sanctuary and the king's palace.

16:11-14 She was adorned with *jewelry* and fed with the very *finest foods.* She was known throughout the world for her *beauty* and *splendor*—both gifts from the Lord.

16:15-19 Instead of appreciating the good things God had given her, Jerusalem prostituted her *fame and beauty* to false gods and offered to idols the clothes, jewels, food, and oil that the Lord had given her.

16:20-22 Jerusalem even gave her *sons and daughters* as sacrifices to false gods. Child sacrifice was practiced among the nations around Israel as a sign of total commitment to a deity, especially in the worship of the gods Molech and Chemosh (see Deut 12:31; 2 Kgs 3:27). Israel sometimes participated in this *detestable sin.*

16:23-25 Prophets commonly described idolatry in terms of adultery (see Hos 2), but Ezekiel goes into much more detail than any other prophet. He depicts Jerusalem as not just foolish or misguided, but rotten to the core. Her adultery had taken place *on every street corner*, and she had an inexhaustible appetite for increasingly depraved entertainments.

16:26-29 Jerusalem actively promoted *promiscuity* in pursuing *Egypt*, the *Assyrians*, and *Babylonia* (or *Chaldea*) in alliances that were financially costly and that rarely delivered the expected benefits. These alliances would have been just as reprehensible if they [illegible] delivered tangible political be[illegible] cause they demonstrated [illegible] the Lord. Inevitably [illegible] into worship of [illegible]

corner and your altars to idols in every square. In fact, you have been worse than a prostitute, so eager for sin that you have not even demanded payment. 32Yes, you are an adulterous wife who takes in strangers instead of her own husband. 33Prostitutes charge for their services—but not you! You give gifts to your lovers, bribing them to come and have sex with you. 34So you are the opposite of other prostitutes. You pay your lovers instead of their paying you!

Judgment Against the Unfaithful Wife

35"Therefore, you prostitute, listen to this message from the LORD! 36This is what the Sovereign LORD says: Because you have poured out your lust and exposed yourself in prostitution to all your lovers, and because you have worshiped detestable idols, and because you have slaughtered your children as sacrifices to your gods, 37this is what I am going to do. I will gather together all your allies—the lovers with whom you have sinned, both those you loved and those you hated—and I will strip you naked in front of them so they can stare at you. 38I will punish you for your murder and adultery. I will cover you with blood in my jealous fury. 39Then I will give you to these many nations who are your lovers, and they will destroy you. They will knock down your pagan shrines and the altars to your idols. They will strip you and take your beautiful jewels, leaving you stark naked. 40They will band together in a mob to stone you and cut you up with swords. 41They will burn your homes and punish you in front of many women. I will stop your prostitution and end your payments to your many lovers.

42"Then at last my fury against you will be spent, and my jealous anger will subside. I will be calm and will not be angry with you anymore. 43But first, because you have not remembered your youth but have angered me by doing all these evil things, I will fully repay you for all of your sins, says the Sovereign LORD. For you have added lewd acts to all your detestable sins. 44Everyone who makes up proverbs will say of you, 'Like mother, like daughter.' 45For your mother loathed her husband and her children, and so do you. And you are exactly like your sisters, for they despised their husbands and their children. Truly your mother was a Hittite and your father an Amorite.

46"Your older sister was Samaria, who lived with her daughters in the north. Your younger sister was Sodom, who lived with her daughters in the south. 47But you have not merely sinned as they did. You quickly surpassed them in corruption. 48As surely as I live, says the Sovereign LORD, Sodom and her daughters were never as wicked as you and your daughters. 49Sodom's sins were pride, gluttony, and laziness, while the poor and needy suffered outside her door. 50She was proud and committed detestable sins, so I wiped her out, as you have seen.

51"Even Samaria did not commit half your sins. You have done far more detestable things than your sisters ever did. They seem righteous compared to you. 52Shame on you! Your sins are so terrible that you make your sisters seem righteous, even virtuous.

53"But someday I will restore the fortunes of Sodom and Samaria, and I will restore you, too. 54Then you will be truly ashamed of everything you have done, for your sins make them feel good in comparison. 55Yes, your sisters, Sodom and Samaria, and all their people will be restored, and at that time you also will be restored. 56In your proud days you held Sodom in contempt. 57But now your greater wickedness has been exposed to all the world, and you

16:33 Hos 8:9-10; Joel 3:3; Luke 15:30
16:36 Jer 19:5; Ezek 20:31; 23:37
16:37 Isa 47:3; Nah 3:5-6
16:38 Ps 79:3, 5; Jer 18:21; Zeph 1:17; Rev 16:6
16:41 2 Kgs 25:9
16:42 2 Sam 24:25; Isa 40:1-2; 54:9-10
16:43 Ps 78:42; Isa 63:10
16:45 Isa 1:4
16:46 Gen 13:11-13; Jer 3:8-11
16:47 1 Kgs 16:31; 2 Kgs 21:9; Ezek 5:6-7
16:48 Matt 11:23-24
16:49 Gen 13:10; Ps 138:6; Isa 22:13; Luke 12:16-20
16:50 Gen 19:24-25
16:51 Jer 3:8-11; Matt 12:41-42
16:53 Isa 19:24-25
16:54 Jer 2:26
16:57 2 Kgs 16:5-7; 2 Chr 28:5-6, 18-23; Hos 2:10; 7:1

16:35-38 Since Jerusalem behaved like an adulteress, it was fitting that she should face an adulteress's death sentence. God would ***strip*** her ***naked*** in a symbolic act of divorce, thus reversing the clothin[illegible]aphor of marriage (see 16:8; H[illegible]hen the people would st[illegible]; Deut 22:22). Since [illegible]naked body ***with*** [illegible] the world just as [illegible]taphor was ful[illegible]ns destroyed [illegible] (literally [illegible]o dung. The Lord's fury would not be requited until the city had paid for all its former ***sins.***

16:44-45 Jerusalem's "parents" were ***a Hittite*** and ***an Amorite.*** Hittites and Amorites were previous occupants of Canaan who were cut off from the land because of their sins (cp. Gen 15:16). The pagan city of Jerusalem was captured and incorporated into Israel in David's time (2 Sam 5:6-10). Jerusalem's subsequent behavior was in keeping with her heredity.

16:46-50 ***Samaria***, Jerusalem's ***older*** (or ***larger***) ***sister***, had practiced deviant worship ever since Jeroboam introduced golden calves into his national shrines at Dan and Bethel (1 Kgs 12:28-33). • ***Sodom***, Jerusalem's ***younger*** (or ***smaller***) ***sister***, was a byword for sexual sin (Gen 19:4-9) and for ***pride, gluttony, laziness***, and neglect of the ***poor and needy***.

16:50 ***as you have seen:*** As in a few Hebrew manuscripts and Greek version; Masoretic Text reads ***as I have seen.***

16:51-52 In comparison to Jerusalem, ***Samaria*** and Sodom seemed virtuous. If God had justly destroyed both of Jerusalem's ***sisters*** for their sins, how would Jerusalem escape God's coming wrath?

16:53-54 The power of God's grace, even more than his judgment, would make Jerusalem feel ***ashamed*** of her association with such "parents" and "sisters" (16:44-52).

16:57 ***Edom:*** As in many Hebrew manuscripts and Syriac version; Masoretic Text reads ***Aram.***

16:58 Ezek 23:49
16:59 Isa 24:5
16:60 Jer 32:40
16:62 Jer 24:7
16:63 Ps 39:9; Dan 9:7-8; Rom 3:19
17:2 Ezek 20:49; 24:3
17:3 Jer 22:23; 48:40; Dan 4:22
17:5 Deut 8:7-9; Isa 44:4
17:7 Ezek 31:4
17:10 Ezek 19:12-14; Hos 13:15
17:13 2 Kgs 24:15-17; 2 Chr 36:13

are the one who is scorned—by Edom and
all her neighbors and by Philistia. 58 This is
your punishment for all your lewdness and
detestable sins, says the LORD.

59 "Now this is what the Sovereign LORD
says: I will give you what you deserve, for
you have taken your solemn vows lightly by
breaking your covenant. 60 Yet I will remember the covenant I made with you when
you were young, and I will establish an everlasting covenant with you. 61 Then you will
remember with shame all the evil you have
done. I will make your sisters, Samaria and
Sodom, to be your daughters, even though
they are not part of our covenant. 62 And I
will reaffirm my covenant with you, and you
will know that I am the LORD. 63 You will remember your sins and cover your mouth in
silent shame when I forgive you of all that
you have done. I, the Sovereign LORD, have
spoken!"

The Parable of the Vine and Two Eagles

17 Then this message came to me from
the LORD: 2 "Son of man, give this riddle, and tell this story to the people of Israel.
3 Give them this message from the Sovereign LORD:

"A great eagle with broad wings and long
feathers,
covered with many-colored
plumage,
came to Lebanon.
He seized the top of a cedar tree
4 and plucked off its highest branch.
He carried it away to a city filled with
merchants.
He planted it in a city of traders.
5 He also took a seedling from the land
and planted it in fertile soil.
He placed it beside a broad river,
where it could grow like a willow tree.
6 It took root there and
grew into a low, spreading vine.
Its branches turned up toward the eagle,
and its roots grew down into the
ground.
It produced strong branches
and put out shoots.
7 But then another great eagle came
with broad wings and full plumage.
So the vine now sent its roots and
branches
toward him for water,
8 even though it was already planted in
good soil
and had plenty of water
so it could grow into a splendid vine
and produce rich leaves and luscious
fruit.

9 "So now the Sovereign LORD asks:
Will this vine grow and prosper?
No! I will pull it up, roots and all!
I will cut off its fruit
and let its leaves wither and die.
I will pull it up easily
without a strong arm or a large army.
10 But when the vine is transplanted,
will it thrive?
No, it will wither away
when the east wind blows against it.
It will die in the same good soil
where it had grown so well."

The Parable Explained

11 Then this message came to me from the
LORD: 12 "Say to these rebels of Israel: Don't
you understand the meaning of this riddle
of the eagles? The king of Babylon came to
Jerusalem, took away her king and princes,
and brought them to Babylon. 13 He made

16:59-63 Jerusalem's sins were serious and had to be judged, but judgment was not God's last word on Jerusalem. She had been comprehensively ***breaking*** God's ***covenant*** and deserved the consequence of death, but God would ***remember*** the ***covenant*** he had made with her in the beginning. God's purposes for his people cannot be derailed even by their sin, for his covenant commitment is everlasting (Ps 136). God's forgiveness of her sins would finally bring Jerusalem to repentance.

17:1-24 This chapter uses a ***riddle***, a form of metaphorical speech that both conceals and reveals. It is also a fable, a story that communicates a moral message about humans by transposing it into the world of plants and animals. The imaginative context creates a distance between the story and the reality and thus disarms the hearer's defenses against an unpalatable message.

17:3-6 Babylonia was the ***city filled with merchants*** (see 16:29).

17:7-9 There was a second ***great eagle*** like the first, although not quite so glorious. • The fate of the vine was predictable. In seeking to gain more, it would lose what it already had. The second eagle would not do anything for it, and the anger of the first eagle would be justly aroused.

17:10 In Judah, the ***east wind*** blows from the desert and is therefore hot and dry.

17:11-18 The first eagle was Nebuchadnezzar, king of Babylon. The cedar sprig was Jehoiachin, who was carried off to Babylon by Nebuchadnezzar. The replacement that grew into a low vine was Zedekiah, and the second eagle was Egypt, from whom Zedekiah was seeking help in his bid to break free of the Babylonians. The hot east wind of judgment blew from Babylon, uprooting and withering Jerusalem. • The image of the eagle that spared no effort in providing for the vine seems to describe God's care for Israel more than Nebuchadnezzar's concern for Zedekiah. These connections point us to a fundamental analogy between Zedekiah's rebellion against his overlord, Nebuchadnezzar, and Israel's rebellion against the Lord. Zedekiah's rebellion against the might of the Babylonians was foolish to the point of being suicidal. Even more foolish was Israel's rebellion against the Lord, the God of heaven and earth.

a treaty with a member of the royal family and forced him to take an oath of loyalty. He also exiled Israel's most influential leaders, 14so Israel would not become strong again and revolt. Only by keeping her treaty with Babylon could Israel survive.

15"Nevertheless, this man of Israel's royal family rebelled against Babylon, sending ambassadors to Egypt to request a great army and many horses. Can Israel break her sworn treaties like that and get away with it? 16No! For as surely as I live, says the Sovereign LORD, the king of Israel will die in Babylon, the land of the king who put him in power and whose treaty he disregarded and broke. 17Pharaoh and all his mighty army will fail to help Israel when the king of Babylon lays siege to Jerusalem again and destroys many lives. 18For the king of Israel disregarded his treaty and broke it after swearing to obey; therefore, he will not escape.

19"So this is what the Sovereign LORD says: As surely as I live, I will punish him for breaking my covenant and disregarding the solemn oath he made in my name. 20I will throw my net over him and capture him in my snare. I will bring him to Babylon and put him on trial for this treason against me. 21And all his best warriors will be killed in battle, and those who survive will be scattered to the four winds. Then you will know that I, the LORD, have spoken.

22"This is what the Sovereign LORD says: I will take a branch from the top of a tall cedar, and I will plant it on the top of Israel's highest mountain. 23It will become a majestic cedar, sending forth its branches and producing seed. Birds of every sort will nest in it, finding shelter in the shade of its branches. 24And all the trees will know that it is I, the LORD, who cuts the tall tree down and makes the short tree grow tall. It is I who makes the green tree wither and gives the dead tree new life. I, the LORD, have spoken, and I will do what I said!"

The Proverb of Sour Grapes

18 Then another message came to me from the LORD: 2"Why do you quote this proverb concerning the land of Israel: 'The parents have eaten sour grapes, but their children's mouths pucker at the taste'? 3As surely as I live, says the Sovereign LORD, you will not quote this proverb anymore in Israel. 4For all people are mine to judge—both parents and children alike. And this is my rule: The person who sins is the one who will die.

5"Suppose a certain man is righteous and does what is just and right. 6He does not feast in the mountains before Israel's idols or worship them. He does not commit adultery or have intercourse with a woman during her menstrual period. 7He is a merciful creditor, not keeping the items given as security by poor debtors. He does not rob the poor but instead gives food to the hungry and provides clothes for the needy. 8He grants loans without interest, stays away

17:14 Jer 27:12-17; 38:17
17:15 2 Kgs 24:20; 2 Chr 36:13
17:16 Jer 52:11
17:17 Isa 36:6; Jer 37:7
17:18 1 Chr 29:24
17:20 Ezek 12:13; 20:36; 32:3
17:21 2 Kgs 25:5, 11; Amos 9:1-10
17:22 Ps 72:16; 80:15; Ezek 20:40; Zech 3:8; 4:12-14
17:24 Ps 96:12; Isa 55:12; Amos 9:11
18:2 Jer 31:29; Lam 5:7
18:4 Num 16:22; 27:16; Isa 42:5; 57:16; Zech 12:1; Rom 6:23
18:6 Deut 4:19
18:7 Lev 19:13; Matt 25:35-40; Luke 3:11
18:8 Exod 22:25; Lev 25:36; Deut 23:19; Zech 8:16

17:19-21 God would punish Israel's king for ***breaking*** his ***covenant*** with ***treason*** against the Lord who had planted him in the land of promise. • ***I will bring him to Babylon and put him on trial:*** See 2 Kgs 25:5-7.

17:21 ***his best warriors:*** Or *his fleeing warriors.* The meaning of the Hebrew is uncertain.

17:22-24 The last part of the chapter turns the fable around. Now the Lord would take ***a branch from the . . . cedar*** tree and ***plant it on . . . Israel's highest mountain.*** As elsewhere in the OT, tree imagery stands for the royal line, with a new shoot representing a fresh start (cp. Isa 11:1). The judgment upon the vine would not end the monarchy after all. God would plant a fresh branch that would grow into a more ***majestic cedar*** than the first cedar had ever been. Although the present dynasty of kings had reached a dead end in Zedekiah, a new beginning was not only possible but inevitable in God's time (see Hag 2:21-23; Matt 1:11-16; 2:1-11). • God ***cuts the tall tree down, makes the short tree grow tall,*** and ***gives the dead tree new life,*** enabling ***birds of every sort*** (representing the nations) to find shelter and shade under its branches. God's promise of an eternal throne for David would not ultimately be thwarted by the failures of David's descendants, the kings of Judah. One day, the dynasty of David—in the person of Jesus—would once again be raised up as the source of blessing for all nations.

18:1-2 The people had been quoting an aphorism, ***The parents have eaten sour grapes, but their children's mouths pucker at the taste,*** meaning that innocent children sometimes suffer because of their parents' actions. In Ezekiel's context, people were using this proverb to imply that the sins that had brought about the Exile had been committed by their forefathers, while they were paying the price (cp. Lam 5:7).

18:3-4 The Lord's response to the proverb of 18:1-2 was to categorically deny that it fit the situation. To the contrary, the Lord consistently punishes only those who are guilty (Deut 24:16). God is unswervingly just.

18:5-9 God's justice is worked out in a case study by following three hypothetical generations. In the first generation, a ***righteous . . . man*** was faithful in worshiping the Lord, sexually pure, and fair in dealing with others. A person who lives like that has no need to fear God's judgment.

18:6 ***idols:*** The Hebrew term (literally *round things*) probably alludes to dung; also in 18:12, 15. See note on 6:4-7. • ***does not . . . have intercourse with a woman during her menstrual period:*** See note on 36:17; see also Lev 15.

18:7 Borrowers might be required to give objects as security to ensure that the loan would be repaid. However, if the object was an outer garment (which might be a poor man's only valuable possession), it had to be returned before nightfall so that he could remain warm at night (see Exod 22:26-27).

18:8 Lending money with interest to those in need was outlawed because of the temptation it presented to abuse the borrower (see Exod 22:25).

18:9 Hab 2:4; Rom 1:17
18:12 2 Kgs 21:11; Isa 59:6-7; Amos 4:1
18:13 Ezek 33:4-5
18:14 2 Chr 29:6-10; 34:21
18:16 Job 31:16; Ps 41:1
18:19 Exod 20:5; Zech 1:3-6
18:20 Deut 24:16; Matt 16:27; Rom 2:6-9
18:21 Ezek 33:12, 19
18:22 Ps 18:20-24; Ezek 33:16; Mic 7:19
18:23 Ps 147:11; Ezek 33:11; 2 Pet 3:9
18:24 1 Sam 15:11; Prov 21:16; Ezek 33:18; Gal 3:3-4
18:25 Gen 18:25; Deut 32:4; Ezek 33:17, 20; Zeph 3:5; Mal 3:13-15
18:30 Ezek 14:6; 33:11; Hos 12:6; [k]*shub* (7725) ‣Ezek 18:32
18:31 Ps 51:10; Isa 1:16-17; 55:7; Acts 3:19
18:32 [a]*shub* (7725) ‣Zech 1:6
19:1 2 Kgs 25:5-7

from injustice, is honest and fair when judging others, 9and faithfully obeys my decrees and regulations. Anyone who does these things is just and will surely live, says the Sovereign LORD.

10"But suppose that man has a son who grows up to be a robber or murderer and refuses to do what is right. 11And that son does all the evil things his father would never do—he worships idols on the mountains, commits adultery, 12oppresses the poor and helpless, steals from debtors by refusing to let them redeem their security, worships idols, commits detestable sins, 13and lends money at excessive interest. Should such a sinful person live? No! He must die and must take full blame.

14"But suppose that sinful son, in turn, has a son who sees his father's wickedness and decides against that kind of life. 15This son refuses to worship idols on the mountains and does not commit adultery. 16He does not exploit the poor, but instead is fair to debtors and does not rob them. He gives food to the hungry and provides clothes for the needy. 17He helps the poor, does not lend money at interest, and obeys all my regulations and decrees. Such a person will not die because of his father's sins; he will surely live. 18But the father will die for his many sins—for being cruel, robbing people, and doing what was clearly wrong among his people.

19" 'What?' you ask. 'Doesn't the child pay for the parent's sins?' No! For if the child does what is just and right and keeps my decrees, that child will surely live. 20The person who sins is the one who will die. The child will not be punished for the parent's sins, and the parent will not be punished for the child's sins. Righteous people will be rewarded for their own righteous behavior, and wicked people will be punished for their own wickedness. 21But if wicked people turn away from all their sins and begin to obey my decrees and do what is just and right, they will surely live and not die. 22All their past sins will be forgotten, and they will live because of the righteous things they have done.

23"Do you think that I like to see wicked people die? says the Sovereign LORD. Of course not! I want them to turn from their wicked ways and live. 24However, if righteous people turn from their righteous behavior and start doing sinful things and act like other sinners, should they be allowed to live? No, of course not! All their righteous acts will be forgotten, and they will die for their sins.

25"Yet you say, 'The Lord isn't doing what's right!' Listen to me, O people of Israel. Am I the one not doing what's right, or is it you? 26When righteous people turn from their righteous behavior and start doing sinful things, they will die for it. Yes, they will die because of their sinful deeds. 27And if wicked people turn from their wickedness, obey the law, and do what is just and right, they will save their lives. 28They will live because they thought it over and decided to turn from their sins. Such people will not die. 29And yet the people of Israel keep saying, 'The Lord isn't doing what's right!' O people of Israel, it is you who are not doing what's right, not I.

30"Therefore, I will judge each of you, O people of Israel, according to your actions, says the Sovereign LORD. [k]Repent, and [k]turn from your sins. Don't let them destroy you! 31Put all your rebellion behind you, and find yourselves a new heart and a new spirit. For why should you die, O people of Israel? 32I don't want you to die, says the Sovereign LORD. [a]Turn back and live!

A Funeral Song for Israel's Kings

19 "Sing this funeral song for the princes of Israel:

2 "What is your mother?
A lioness among lions!

18:10-13 If the son of a righteous man does not walk in the ways of God or of his father, and his life is the opposite of everything the father stood for, he will be responsible for his own guilt and suffer God's judgment.

18:14-18 The righteous son of an evil man *will surely live.* God will judge each person individually.

18:17 ***He helps the poor:*** Greek version reads *He refuses to do evil.*

18:21-24 Ezekiel introduces two more case studies. Wicked people who turn away from their sins can experience God's forgiveness, and righteous people who begin sinning will be judged.

18:23-24 God does not *like to see wicked people die*, so he appointed Ezekiel as a watchman, whose role was to turn the wicked toward godly life while warning the righteous against falling away (3:16-19; 33:1-9).

18:25-29 Israel's problem was not that *the Lord* wasn't *doing what's right* but that they were persistently doing what was wrong. They thoroughly deserved God's judgment.

18:30-32 This chapter concludes with a passionate appeal to the ***people of Israel*** to ***turn back and live.*** It was not too late for them to repent, ***turn from*** their *sins,* and be forgiven. God promised ***a new heart and a new spirit*** (11:19; 36:26) to all who would turn from their ***rebellion*** and humbly come to him.

19:1-14 An ancient Near Eastern ***funeral song*** had a distinctive rhythm and style and usually extolled the virtues of the person who had died, contrasting past glory with the current loss. In this case, those being lamented were

She lay down among the young lions
and reared her cubs.
3 She raised one of her cubs
to become a strong young lion.
He learned to hunt and devour prey,
and he became a man-eater.
4 Then the nations heard about him,
and he was trapped in their pit.
They led him away with hooks
to the land of Egypt.

5 "When the lioness saw
that her hopes for him were gone,
she took another of her cubs
and taught him to be a strong young lion.
6 He prowled among the other lions
and stood out among them in his strength.
He learned to hunt and devour prey,
and he, too, became a man-eater.
7 He demolished fortresses
and destroyed their towns and cities.
Their farms were desolated,
and their crops were destroyed.
The land and its people trembled in fear
when they heard him roar.
8 Then the armies of the nations attacked him,
surrounding him from every direction.
They threw a net over him
and captured him in their pit.
9 With hooks, they dragged him into a cage
and brought him before the king of Babylon.
They held him in captivity,
so his voice could never again be heard
on the mountains of Israel.

10 "Your mother was like a vine
planted by the water's edge.
It had lush, green foliage
because of the abundant water.
11 Its branches became strong—
strong enough to be a ruler's scepter.
It grew very tall,
towering above all others.
It stood out because of its height
and its many lush branches.
12 But the vine was uprooted in fury
and thrown down to the ground.
The desert wind dried up its fruit
and tore off its strong branches,
so that it withered
and was destroyed by fire.
13 Now the vine is transplanted to the wilderness,
where the ground is hard and dry.
14 A fire has burst out from its branches
and devoured its fruit.
Its remaining limbs are not
strong enough to be a ruler's scepter.
"This is a funeral song, and it will be used in a funeral."

Israel's Past Rebellion

20 On August 14, during the seventh
year of King Jehoiachin's captivity,
some of the leaders of Israel came to request a message from the LORD. They sat
down in front of me to wait for his reply.
2Then this message came to me from the

19:3 2 Kgs 23:31
19:4 2 Kgs 23:33-34; 2 Chr 36:4
19:6 2 Kgs 24:9
19:9 2 Kgs 24:15; 2 Chr 36:6
19:10 Ps 80:8-11
19:12 Jer 31:28; Ezek 17:10; 28:17; Hos 13:15; John 15:6
19:13 2 Kgs 24:12-16; Hos 2:3
20:1 Ezek 8:1, 11-12

not yet dead, and the dirge contained a catalogue of their faults. This dirge profoundly communicated the certainty of their fate and the reasons for it. • The lion (19:2-9) and the vine (19:10-14) were familiar images for ***the princes of Israel***, the royal dynasty of Judah.

19:2-4 The first picture is of a ***lioness*** and ***one of her cubs***, whom she chose as the leader of her pack. This cub represented Jehoahaz, who reigned for a mere three months before being carried to Egypt by Pharaoh Neco (2 Kgs 23:33-34). • ***hunt . . . devour prey . . . man-eater:*** The prophet characterizes Jehoahaz's brief reign in entirely negative terms. • Lions were traditionally hunted with a net and a ***pit***, here a metaphor for the violent way that Jehoahaz would be carried ***away*** to ***Egypt***.

19:5-7 The behavior of the second cub was similar to that of the first but even more violent, as he ***destroyed their towns and cities***. This cub could represent Jehoiakim, Jehoiachin, or Zedekiah. It is not clear which towns and cities the king of Judah destroyed—the prophet might have been thinking of the negative effect that foolish foreign policy had on the cities and towns of Judah.

19:7 ***He demolished fortresses:*** As in Greek version; Hebrew reads *He knew widows.*

19:8-9 Jehoiakim (see note on 19:5-7) was captured and killed by the Babylonians in Judah. Jehoiachin was exiled to Babylon along with Ezekiel. Zedekiah's reign ended with the destruction of Jerusalem in 586 BC.

19:10 The ***vine*** is evidently Judah, whom the Lord had ***planted*** under optimum conditions.

19:11-12 Judah's pride led to its downfall as the Lord ***uprooted*** it in his wrath (cp. 17:1-10). He then replanted Judah in the ***desert*** of exile.

19:13-14 The ***fire*** (probably Zedekiah) that came from the vine's own ***branches*** consumed the ***fruit*** (the land and people). After this destruction, there was no branch left that was strong enough to be ***a ruler's scepter.*** Zedekiah would have no immediate successor.

20:1-3 ***On August 14:*** Literally *In the fifth month, on the tenth day* of the ancient Hebrew lunar calendar. This day was August 14, 591 BC; see also note on 1:1. Five more years would pass before the destruction of Jerusalem. • The ***leaders*** (literally *elders*) ***of Israel***—the leaders of the community in exile—came to Ezekiel once again, looking for a word from the Lord (see note on 8:1). Normally, seeking ***a message from the LORD*** is a good thing. But these leaders had already been condemned for their mixed motives (see ch 14), and the Lord would not receive their request. The question they asked Ezekiel is not recorded—perhaps they never had the opportunity to ask it.

20:3 Ezek 14:3
20:4 Ezek 16:2; 22:2
20:5 Exod 6:2-3, 7 Deut 7:6; 14:2 Ezek 6:2-9
20:6 Exod 33:3 Ps 48:2 Jer 33:24
20:7 Exod 20:2 Deut 29:16-18
20:8 Isa 63:10
20:9 Exod 32:11-14 Num 14:13
20:11 Exod 20:1-23 Lev 18:5
20:12 Exod 31:13, 17 Ezek 20:20
20:13 Num 14:11, 22 Isa 56:6
20:15 Ps 95:11
20:16 Ezek 11:21; 14:3-7
20:17 Jer 4:27; 5:18
20:18 Deut 4:3-4
20:19 Exod 6:7; 20:2 Deut 5:32
20:20 [b]*shabbath* (7676) ‣ Exod 16:23
20:21 Num 25:1-3
20:22 Job 13:21 Ps 78:38 Isa 48:9-11
20:23 Deut 28:64-68 Jer 15:4
20:24 Ezek 6:9
20:25 Ps 81:12 Rom 1:21-25, 28 2 Thes 2:9-11
20:26 Ezek 6:7; 20:30 Rom 11:8

LORD: 3“Son of man, tell the leaders of Israel,
‘This is what the Sovereign LORD says: How
dare you come to ask me for a message? As
surely as I live, says the Sovereign LORD, I
will tell you nothing!’
4“Son of man, bring charges against them
and condemn them. Make them realize
how detestable the sins of their ancestors
really were. 5Give them this message from
the Sovereign LORD: When I chose Israel—
when I revealed myself to the descendants
of Jacob in Egypt—I took a solemn oath
that I, the LORD, would be their God. 6I took
a solemn oath that day that I would bring
them out of Egypt to a land I had discovered
and explored for them—a good land, a land
flowing with milk and honey, the best of all
lands anywhere. 7Then I said to them, ‘Each
of you, get rid of the vile images you are
so obsessed with. Do not defile yourselves
with the idols of Egypt, for I am the LORD
your God.’
8“But they rebelled against me and would
not listen. They did not get rid of the vile
images they were obsessed with, or forsake the idols of Egypt. Then I threatened
to pour out my fury on them to satisfy my
anger while they were still in Egypt. 9But I
didn’t do it, for I acted to protect the honor
of my name. I would not allow shame to be
brought on my name among the surrounding nations who saw me reveal myself by
bringing the Israelites out of Egypt. 10So
I brought them out of Egypt and led them
into the wilderness. 11There I gave them my
decrees and regulations so they could find
life by keeping them. 12And I gave them my
Sabbath days of rest as a sign between them
and me. It was to remind them that I am the
LORD, who had set them apart to be holy.
13“But the people of Israel rebelled
against me, and they refused to obey my decrees there in the wilderness. They wouldn’t
obey my regulations even though obedience would have given them life. They also
violated my Sabbath days. So I threatened to
pour out my fury on them, and I made plans
to utterly consume them in the wilderness.
14But again I held back in order to protect the
honor of my name before the nations who
had seen my power in bringing Israel out
of Egypt. 15But I took a solemn oath against
them in the wilderness. I swore I would not
bring them into the land I had given them, a
land flowing with milk and honey, the most
beautiful place on earth. 16For they had
rejected my regulations, refused to follow
my decrees, and violated my Sabbath days.
Their hearts were given to their idols. 17Nev-
ertheless, I took pity on them and held back
from destroying them in the wilderness.
18“Then I warned their children not to
follow in their parents’ footsteps, defiling
themselves with their idols. 19‘I am the LORD
your God,’ I told them. ‘Follow my decrees,
pay attention to my regulations, 20and keep
my [b]Sabbath days holy, for they are a sign to
remind you that I am the LORD your God.’
21“But their children, too, rebelled against
me. They refused to keep my decrees and
follow my regulations, even though obedience would have given them life. And they
also violated my Sabbath days. So again
I threatened to pour out my fury on them
in the wilderness. 22Nevertheless, I withdrew my judgment against them to protect
the honor of my name before the nations
that had seen my power in bringing them
out of Egypt. 23But I took a solemn oath
against them in the wilderness. I swore I
would scatter them among all the nations
24because they did not obey my regulations.
They scorned my decrees by violating my
Sabbath days and longing for the idols of
their ancestors. 25I gave them over to worthless decrees and regulations that would not
lead to life. 26I let them pollute themselves
with the very gifts I had given them, and I allowed them to give their firstborn children
as offerings to their gods—so I might devastate them and remind them that I alone
am the LORD.

20:4-26 That the Lord would not answer their inquiry did not mean that he had nothing to say to them. Ezekiel would parade the ***detestable*** character of ***their ancestors*** before their eyes.

20:7 ***idols:*** The Hebrew term (literally *round things*) probably alludes to dung; also in 20:8, 16, 18, 24, 31, 39. See note on 6:4-7.

20:8-21 Each generation of Israelites rebelled against the Lord and refused to obey the commandments he gave them (20:8, 13, 21). Each time, the Lord ***threatened to pour out*** his ***fury*** upon them (20:8, 13, 21), but he relented for ***the honor of*** his ***name***, lest the nations around them should think the Lord’s power insufficient to bring his people into the Promised Land.

20:23 Because of their history of refusing to keep the Lord’s decrees or obey his regulations, God determined to ***scatter them among all the nations.***

20:25-26 ***I gave them over to worthless decrees and regulations . . . I let them pollute themselves:*** Or *I gave them worthless decrees and regulations. . . . I polluted them.* The Lord allowed the people of Israel to exercise their depravity in the complex and corrupting rituals of paganism and to suffer all of its terrible consequences (see Rom 1:18-25).

20:26 The Israelites even gave their ***firstborn children*** as offerings to the god Molech. This exactly reversed the Exodus, which freed the Israelites, the Lord’s “firstborn son” (Exod 4:22), to offer pure worship in the Promised Land.

Judgment and Restoration

27"Therefore, son of man, give the people of Israel this message from the Sovereign LORD: Your ancestors continued to blaspheme and betray me, 28for when I brought them into the land I had promised them, they offered sacrifices on every high hill and under every green tree they saw! They roused my fury as they offered up sacrifices to their gods. They brought their perfumes and incense and poured out their liquid offerings to them. 29I said to them, 'What is this high place where you are going?' (This kind of pagan shrine has been called Bamah—'high place'—ever since.)

30"Therefore, give the people of Israel this message from the Sovereign LORD: Do you plan to pollute yourselves just as your ancestors did? Do you intend to keep prostituting yourselves by worshiping vile images? 31For when you offer gifts to them and give your little children to be burned as sacrifices, you continue to pollute yourselves with idols to this day. Should I allow you to ask for a message from me, O people of Israel? As surely as I live, says the Sovereign LORD, I will tell you nothing.

32"You say, 'We want to be like the nations all around us, who serve idols of wood and stone.' But what you have in mind will never happen. 33As surely as I live, says the Sovereign LORD, I will rule over you with an iron fist in great anger and with awesome power. 34And in anger I will reach out with my strong hand and powerful arm, and I will bring you back from the lands where you are scattered. 35I will bring you into the wilderness of the nations, and there I will judge you face to face. 36I will judge you there just as I did your ancestors in the wilderness after bringing them out of Egypt, says the Sovereign LORD. 37I will examine you carefully and hold you to the terms of the covenant. 38I will purge you of all those who rebel and revolt against me. I will bring them out of the countries where they are in exile, but they will never enter the land of Israel. Then you will know that I am the LORD.

39"As for you, O people of Israel, this is what the Sovereign LORD says: Go right ahead and worship your idols, but sooner or later you will obey me and will stop bringing shame on my holy name by worshiping idols. 40For on my holy mountain, the great mountain of Israel, says the Sovereign LORD, the people of Israel will someday worship me, and I will accept them. There I will require that you bring me all your offerings and choice gifts and sacrifices. 41When I bring you home from exile, you will be like a pleasing sacrifice to me. And I will display my holiness through you as all the nations watch. 42Then when I have brought you home to the land I promised with a solemn oath to give to your ancestors, you will know that I am the LORD. 43You will look back on all the ways you defiled yourselves and will hate yourselves because of the evil you have done. 44You will know that I am the LORD, O people of Israel, when I have honored my name by treating you mercifully in spite of your wickedness. I, the Sovereign LORD, have spoken!"

Judgment against the Negev

45Then this message came to me from the LORD: 46"Son of man, turn and face the south and speak out against it; prophesy against the brushlands of the Negev. 47Tell the southern wilderness, 'This is what the

20:30 Judg 2:19
20:31 Ps 106:37-39 Jer 7:31 Ezek 16:20
20:32 Jer 2:25; 44:17
20:34 Jer 42:18; 44:6 Lam 2:4 *2 Cor 6:17
20:36 Deut 32:10 1 Cor 10:5-10
20:38 Ps 95:11 Ezek 34:17-22 Amos 9:9-10 Heb 4:3
20:39 Isa 1:12-15 Jer 44:25-26 Ezek 23:38-39
20:40 Isa 56:7; 60:7 Ezek 43:12, 27
20:41 Isa 27:12-13
20:43 Zech 12:10-14
20:46 Jer 13:19

20:27-31 Once in the Promised Land, Israel ***continued to blaspheme and betray*** the Lord. Their idolatry and wickedness continued to Ezekiel's day. Such apostate people would receive no answer from the Lord.

20:31 *and give your little children to be burned as sacrifices:* Or *and make your little children pass through the fire.*

20:32-38 As in the past, Israel's current rebellion had led to God's limited judgment, so that they were once again scattered among the nations. Earlier history made it clear that judgment would not be the end of the story, as the honor of God's name required that he fulfill his promises despite his people's sin. • Israel could never be ***like the nations all around . . . who serve idols of wood and stone*** (20:32). God had chosen them to be his and he would bring them back into the ***wilderness*** in a new exodus. It was not unmitigated good news, for a whole generation died in the wilderness after the first Exodus because of their sin. God would also ***judge*** and ***purge*** this generation in the wilderness, and those who were rebels, refusing to obey the Lord, would ***never enter the land of Israel***. The wilderness of the nations would be their final resting place.

20:34 *I will bring you back:* Greek version reads *I will welcome you.* Cp. 2 Cor 6:17.

20:39-44 The ***people of Israel*** might continue to ***worship . . . idols,*** but in the end, they would worship God in spirit and in truth on his ***holy mountain*** (see chs 40–48, in which the purified worship of God is restored in the Temple; cp. John 4:21-24). God's purpose in choosing Israel to be a holy nation would ultimately stand. The people would be ***a pleasing sacrifice*** to him and would ***display*** God's ***holiness***. The result of this new exodus would be pure worship, offered by a purified people who were saved by sovereign grace.

20:45-49 Verses 20:45-49 are numbered 21:1-5 in Hebrew text. • Like a parable, this prophecy both reveals and conceals its message, leading the people to complain that the prophet ***only talks in riddles*** (see Matt 13:10-17). It reveals the coming of an all-consuming judgment (a ***fire*** that will burn up ***every tree***), but conceals who is being judged.

20:46 *turn and face the south* (literally *turn toward Teman*): Teman was a town in Edom, southeast of Judah. • The ***Negev*** was southwest of the Dead Sea.

20:47 Isa 9:18
20:48 Jer 7:20; 17:27
20:49 Matt 13:12-13; John 16:25
21:2 Ezek 20:46
21:3 Isa 57:1; Jer 21:13; Ezek 5:8; Nah 2:13; 3:5
21:4 Jer 12:12; Ezek 7:2; 20:47
21:5 1 Sam 3:12; Nah 1:9
21:7 Isa 13:7; Ezek 7:26
21:9 Deut 32:41
21:10 Isa 34:5-6
21:12 Joel 1:13
21:14 Lev 26:21, 24
21:15 Josh 2:11; 2 Sam 17:10; Jer 17:27
21:17 Ezek 5:13

Sovereign LORD says: Hear the word of the
LORD! I will set you on fire, and every tree,
both green and dry, will be burned. The
terrible flames will not be quenched and
will scorch everything from south to north.
48 And everyone in the world will see that
I, the LORD, have set this fire. It will not be
put out.' "

49 Then I said, "O Sovereign LORD, they
are saying of me, 'He only talks in riddles!' "

The Song of the LORD's Sword

21 Then this message came to me from
the LORD: 2 "Son of man, turn and
face Jerusalem and prophesy against Israel
and her sanctuaries. 3 Tell her, 'This is what
the LORD says: I am your enemy, O Israel,
and I am about to unsheath my sword to
destroy your people—the righteous and the
wicked alike. 4 Yes, I will cut off both the
righteous and the wicked! I will draw my
sword against everyone in the land from
south to north. 5 Everyone in the world will
know that I am the LORD. My sword is in my
hand, and it will not return to its sheath until its work is finished.'

6 "Son of man, groan before the people!
Groan before them with bitter anguish and
a broken heart. 7 When they ask why you
are groaning, tell them, 'I groan because of
the terrifying news I have heard. When it
comes true, the boldest heart will melt with
fear; all strength will disappear. Every spirit
will faint; strong knees will become as weak
as water. And the Sovereign LORD says: It is
coming! It's on its way!' "

8 Then the LORD said to me, 9 "Son of man,
give the people this message from the Lord:

"A sword, a sword
  is being sharpened and polished.
10 It is sharpened for terrible slaughter
  and polished to flash like lightning!
Now will you laugh?
  Those far stronger than you have
    fallen beneath its power!
11 Yes, the sword is now being sharpened
  and polished;
  it is being prepared for the
    executioner.

12 "Son of man, cry out and wail;
  pound your thighs in anguish,
for that sword will slaughter my people
  and their leaders—
  everyone will die!
13 It will put them all to the test.
  What chance do they have?
  says the Sovereign LORD.

14 "Son of man, prophesy to them
  and clap your hands.
Then take the sword and brandish it
    twice,
  even three times,
to symbolize the great massacre,
  the great massacre facing them on
    every side.
15 Let their hearts melt with terror,
  for the sword glitters at every gate.
It flashes like lightning
  and is polished for slaughter!
16 O sword, slash to the right,
  then slash to the left,
wherever you will,
  wherever you want.
17 I, too, will clap my hands,
  and I will satisfy my fury.
  I, the LORD, have spoken!"

Omens for Babylon's King

18 Then this message came to me from the
LORD: 19 "Son of man, make a map and trace

20:47 A *green* tree does not normally burn easily, whereas a *dry* tree provides easy kindling. This fire of judgment would be so intense that it would burn all kinds of trees.

21:1-32 Verses 21:1-32 are numbered 21:6-37 in Hebrew text. • This chapter is unified by references to a *sword* (21:3-5, 9, 11-12, 14-16, 19, 28-30), which in each case depicts God's judgment.

21:3-5 The Lord was the fundamental *enemy* whom Israel had to fear, for he was about to unleash an all-encompassing judgment against it. • One would expect *the righteous* to avoid judgment and *the wicked* to receive it. This pairing parallels the green tree and the dry tree of the parable (20:47-48). The judgment of sin would be like a very hot fire burning all it touched.

21:6-7 Ezekiel's *groaning* showed that in the coming judgment, *the boldest heart* would *melt* and the *strong knees* would *become . . . weak*. The judgment that had previously been announced had now become a bitter reality (cp. 7:1-4).

21:8-11 *a sword is being sharpened and polished:* These processes prepared a weapon for deadly effectiveness; once it was prepared, it would be handed over to *the executioner*, who would use it against God's people.

21:10 *Now will you laugh? Those far stronger than you have fallen beneath its power!* The meaning of the Hebrew is uncertain.

21:12 *cry out and wail:* Ezekiel would represent the people's response to the judgment.

21:13 The meaning of the Hebrew in the first two lines is uncertain.

21:14-17 As the representative of the Lord, Ezekiel was to *clap* his *hands* in a threatening gesture and *take the sword and brandish it . . . three times* to represent the completeness of the coming *massacre*. There would be nowhere to run and nowhere to hide from the slashing sword of judgment when the Lord was ready to *satisfy* his *fury* by destroying his people. Their *hearts* would *melt with terror* at the awful massacre.

21:18-20 The sword of the Lord was not an abstract metaphor; it would take shape as *the sword of Babylon's king*. Nebuchadnezzar's preparation for this campaign was depicted when Ezekiel drew a map showing Nebuchadnezzar's two possible campaign objectives—

two routes on it for the sword of Babylon's
king to follow. Put a signpost on the road
that comes out of Babylon where the road
forks into two—20one road going to Ammon
and its capital, Rabbah, and the other to Judah and fortified Jerusalem. 21The king of
Babylon now stands at the fork, uncertain
whether to attack Jerusalem or Rabbah. He
calls his magicians to look for omens. They
cast lots by shaking arrows from the quiver.
They inspect the livers of animal sacrifices.
22The omen in his right hand says, 'Jerusalem!' With battering rams his soldiers will
go against the gates, shouting for the kill.
They will put up siege towers and build
ramps against the walls. 23The people of
Jerusalem will think it is a false omen, because of their treaty with the Babylonians.
But the king of Babylon will remind the people of their rebellion. Then he will attack
and capture them.
24"Therefore, this is what the Sovereign
Lord says: Again and again you remind me
of your sin and your guilt. You don't even
try to hide it! In everything you do, your sins
are obvious for all to see. So now the time of
your punishment has come!
25"O you corrupt and wicked prince of
Israel, your final day of reckoning is here!
26This is what the Sovereign Lord says:

"Take off your jeweled crown,
for the old order changes.
Now the lowly will be exalted,
and the mighty will be brought down.
27 Destruction! Destruction!
I will surely destroy the kingdom.
And it will not be restored until the one
appears
who has the right to judge it.
Then I will hand it over to him.

A Message for the Ammonites

28"And now, son of man, prophesy concerning the Ammonites and their mockery. Give
them this message from the Sovereign
Lord:

"A sword, a sword
is drawn for your slaughter.
It is polished to destroy,
flashing like lightning!
29 Your prophets have given false visions,
and your fortune-tellers have told lies.
The sword will fall on the necks of the
wicked
for whom the day of final reckoning
has come.
30 "Now return the sword to its sheath,
for in your own country,
the land of your birth,
I will pass judgment upon you.
31 I will pour out my fury on you
and blow on you with the fire of my
anger.
I will hand you over to cruel men
who are skilled in destruction.
32 You will be fuel for the fire,
and your blood will be spilled in your
own land.
You will be utterly wiped out,
your memory lost to history,
for I, the Lord, have spoken!"

The Charges against Jerusalem

22 Now this message came to me
from the Lord: 2"Son of man, are
you ready to judge Jerusalem? Are you

21:20 Deut 3:11; Jer 49:2; Ezek 25:5; Amos 1:14
21:21 Num 23:23; Prov 16:33
21:22 Ezek 4:2; 26:9
21:23 Ezek 17:16-18; 29:16
21:25 Ps 37:13; Ezek 7:2-7
21:26 Ps 75:7; Jer 13:18; Ezek 16:12; 17:24
21:27 Ps 2:6; Jer 23:5-6; Ezek 34:24; 37:24; Hag 2:21-22
21:28 Isa 31:8; Jer 12:12; Zeph 2:8-10
21:29 Jer 27:9; Ezek 13:6-9
21:30 Jer 47:6-7; Ezek 25:5
21:31 Ps 18:15; Nah 1:6; Hab 1:6, 10
21:32 Ezek 25:10; Mal 4:1

Rabbah, the capital of Ammon, and ***Jerusalem***, the capital of Judah.

21:21 ***Omens*** were supposedly signs from the gods that were obtained through divination. • ***cast lots by shaking arrows . . . inspect the livers:*** These were common methods of seeking omens from the gods.

21:23-24 A ***treaty with the Babylonians*** would not save ***the people of Jerusalem*** because they had been unfaithful to the terms of that treaty. The ***king of Babylon*** would ***remind the people of their rebellion*** by publicly demonstrating that rebellion against a covenant overlord had consequences. If this was true of rebellion against their Babylonian master, how much more when they rebelled against the Lord?

21:25-27 This judgment would extend against Zedekiah, the ***corrupt and wicked prince of Israel***, as well as against the people. Ezekiel identifies Zedekiah by title rather than by name, indicating that his office was also under judgment. He would be stripped of the emblems of royalty and brought low, while the Lord ***exalted*** the ***lowly***. The old order would experience ***destruction***. • ***the one appears who has the right to judge it:*** This coming judge is often understood to be the Messiah (cp. Gen 49:10). In this context, however, the Lord was handing Judah over to the Babylonians for judgment (see 23:24). Ezekiel was probably reshaping the traditional messianic oracle of Gen 49:10 into a message of imminent judgment by the hand of Nebuchadnezzar, acting as an agent of God. God temporarily took away the scepter from Judah because Israel's rulers had sinned, but he would eventually give it back.

21:28-29 ***The Ammonites*** had no cause to rejoice in the reprieve that came when Nebuchadnezzar went toward Jerusalem rather than Rabbah (21:18-20)—they, too, were among ***the wicked for whom the day of final reckoning*** had come.

21:30-32 The ***sword*** would ***return . . . to its sheath***, not to rest there, but to accomplish the Lord's judgment against its own country, Babylon. God would also ***pour out . . . fury*** and the ***fire of*** his ***anger*** on Babylon. It had no special protection simply because God had used it as his tool in judging others. Judgment may have begun with God's household (1 Pet 4:17), but it did not end there. God's judgment included the pagan nations around Judah.

22:1-31 Jerusalem, the holy city where God had placed his name, was the spiritual heart of Judah. It had been corrupted and defiled; instead of being filled with God, Jerusalem was filled with bloodshed. As a result, God's wrath would certainly fall on the city.

22:3 Ezek 23:37, 45; Zeph 3:3
22:4 2 Kgs 21:16; Ps 44:13-14; Ezek 5:14-15
22:6 Isa 1:23
22:7 Exod 22:22; 23:9; Prov 22:22-23
22:8 Ezek 23:38-39
22:9 Hos 4:2, 10, 14
22:10 Lev 18:8, 19
22:11 Lev 18:15; 2 Sam 13:14
22:12 Lev 19:13; 25:36; Deut 27:25; Ps 106:21; Mic 7:2-3
22:13 Prov 28:8; Isa 33:15; Amos 2:6-8
22:15 Deut 4:27; Zech 7:14
22:16 Ezek 6:4-7
22:18 Ps 119:119; Prov 17:3; Isa 1:22; 48:10; Jer 6:28
22:22 Ezek 20:8, 33; Hos 5:10
22:24 Ezek 24:13
22:25 Jer 2:30, 34; 15:8; Hos 6:9
22:26 Lev 10:10; 1 Sam 2:12-17; Ezek 44:23; Hag 2:11-14

ready to judge this city of murderers? Publicly denounce her detestable sins, 3and
give her this message from the Sovereign
LORD: O city of murderers, doomed and
damned—city of idols, filthy and foul—
4you are guilty because of the blood you
have shed. You are defiled because of the
idols you have made. Your day of destruction has come! You have reached the end
of your years. I will make you an object of
mockery throughout the world. 5O infamous city, filled with confusion, you will
be mocked by people far and near.

6"Every leader in Israel who lives within
your walls is bent on murder. 7Fathers and
mothers are treated with contempt. Foreigners are forced to pay for protection.
Orphans and widows are wronged and oppressed among you. 8You despise my holy
things and violate my Sabbath days of rest.
9People accuse others falsely and send them
to their death. You are filled with idol worshipers and people who do obscene things.
10Men sleep with their fathers' wives and
have intercourse with women who are
menstruating. 11Within your walls live men
who commit adultery with their neighbors'
wives, who defile their daughters-in-law,
or who rape their own sisters. 12There are
hired murderers, loan racketeers, and ex-
tortioners everywhere. They never even
think of me and my commands, says the
Sovereign LORD.

13"But now I clap my hands in indignation
over your dishonest gain and bloodshed.
14How strong and courageous will you be in
my day of reckoning? I, the LORD, have spoken, and I will do what I said. 15I will scatter
you among the nations and purge you of
your wickedness. 16And when I have been
dishonored among the nations because of
you, you will know that I am the LORD."

The LORD's Refining Furnace

17Then this message came to me from the
LORD: 18"Son of man, the people of Israel
are the worthless slag that remains after
silver is smelted. They are the dross that is
left over—a useless mixture of copper, tin,
iron, and lead. 19So tell them, 'This is what
the Sovereign LORD says: Because you are
all worthless slag, I will bring you to my
crucible in Jerusalem. 20Just as copper, iron,
lead, and tin are melted down in a furnace,
I will melt you down in the heat of my fury.
21I will gather you together and blow the
fire of my anger upon you, 22and you will
melt like silver in fierce heat. Then you will
know that I, the LORD, have poured out my
fury on you.' "

The Sins of Israel's Leaders

23Again a message came to me from the
LORD: 24"Son of man, give the people of
Israel this message: In the day of my indignation, you will be like a polluted land, a
land without rain. 25Your princes plot con-
spiracies just as lions stalk their prey. They
devour innocent people, seizing treasures
and extorting wealth. They make many widows in the land. 26Your priests have violated
my instructions and defiled my holy things.
They make no distinction between what is
holy and what is not. And they do not teach
my people the difference between what

22:1-5 Now Ezekiel was called upon to act as a prosecutor by detailing the indictment against Jerusalem that would bring about its judgment. The city was guilty of sins against fellow human beings, including ***the blood*** they had ***shed*** (see Gen 9:5-6), and of sins against God, such as making ***idols*** (see Exod 20:4-6). These two classes of sin ***defiled*** the city and made it ***guilty***, liable to judgment and unfit to appear in the presence of the holy God. As a result, Jerusalem faced guaranteed destruction and scorn. • ***idols:*** The Hebrew term (literally *round things*) probably alludes to dung; also in 22:4. See note on 6:4-7.

22:6-12 These charges against the people of Judah and their leaders were all drawn from God's law, especially from Lev 18–20, 25. Israel's many sins represented a wider failure to honor and trust the Lord and his commands. Such unfaithfulness to their covenant with the Lord could have only one result: The people of Israel would experience the covenant curses (Deut 8:19-20; 28:15-68).

22:7 ***Foreigners are forced to pay for protection:*** Cp. Exod 22:21; 23:9; Lev 19:33-34; Deut 10:18-19.

22:10 ***fathers' wives:*** See Lev 18:7-8. • ***have intercourse with women who are menstruating:*** See Lev 15:19-24.

22:13-16 God expressed his wrath first in the angry gesture of clapping his hands and then by pouring out judgment. The first judgment was that God would ***scatter*** the people of Judah among the nations to ***purge*** them of their ***wickedness.***

22:16 ***when I have been dishonored among the nations because of you:*** Or *when you have been dishonored among the nations.* Having his people scattered among the nations instead of dwelling in the land of promise inevitably dishonored the Lord, since it appeared that he was unable to give them what he had promised. However, the Lord was willing to endure that dishonor so that his forgetful people could learn to remember him.

22:17-22 Scattering was not the only aspect of judgment. God would also ***gather*** Judah into Jerusalem for judgment as metal is gathered into a smelter's furnace. This refining fire would not yield a purified remnant. Since only ***worthless slag*** would go in, only worthless molten slag would come out. The judgment would not cleanse the people but would destroy everything in its path.

22:23-24 The previous judgments on Jerusalem had not had a cleansing effect; Jerusalem remained ***polluted.***

22:25-29 This list of Jerusalem's sins focuses on the sins of the leaders in Judah (cp. Zeph 3:3-4). • ***princes*** (as in Greek version; Hebrew reads *prophets*): The princes and other leaders had abused their power by killing innocent people

is ceremonially clean and unclean. They disregard my Sabbath days so that I am dishonored among them. [27]Your leaders are like wolves who tear apart their victims. They actually destroy people's lives for money! [28]And your prophets cover up for them by announcing false visions and making lying predictions. They say, 'My message is from the Sovereign LORD,' when the LORD hasn't spoken a single word to them. [29]Even common people oppress the poor, rob the needy, and deprive foreigners of justice.

[30]"I looked for someone who might rebuild the wall of righteousness that guards the land. I searched for someone to stand in the gap in the wall so I wouldn't have to destroy the land, but I found no one. [31]So now I will pour out my fury on them, consuming them with the fire of my anger. I will heap on their heads the full penalty for all their sins. I, the Sovereign LORD, have spoken!"

The Parable of Two Degenerate Sisters

23 This message came to me from the LORD: [2]"Son of man, once there were two sisters who were daughters of the same mother. [3]They became prostitutes in Egypt. Even as young girls, they allowed men to fondle their breasts. [4]The older girl was named Oholah, and her sister was Oholibah. I married them, and they bore me sons and daughters. I am speaking of Samaria and Jerusalem, for Oholah is Samaria and Oholibah is Jerusalem.

[5]"Then Oholah lusted after other lovers instead of me, and she gave her love to the Assyrian officers. [6]They were all attractive young men, captains and commanders dressed in handsome blue, charioteers driving their horses. [7]And so she prostituted herself with the most desirable men of Assyria, worshiping their idols and defiling herself. [8]For when she left Egypt, she did not leave her spirit of prostitution behind. She was still as lewd as in her youth, when the Egyptians slept with her, fondled her breasts, and used her as a prostitute.

[9]"And so I handed her over to her Assyrian lovers, whom she desired so much. [10]They stripped her, took away her children as their slaves, and then killed her. After she received her punishment, her reputation was known to every woman in the land.

[11]"Yet even though Oholibah saw what had happened to Oholah, her sister, she followed right in her footsteps. And she was even more depraved, abandoning herself to her lust and prostitution. [12]She fawned over all the Assyrian officers—those captains and commanders in handsome uniforms, those charioteers driving their horses—all of them attractive young men. [13]I saw the way she was going, defiling herself just like her older sister.

[14]"Then she carried her prostitution even further. She fell in love with pictures that were painted on a wall—pictures of Babylonian military officers, outfitted in striking red uniforms. [15]Handsome belts encircled their waists, and flowing turbans crowned their heads. They were dressed like chariot officers from the land of Babylonia. [16]When she saw these paintings, she longed to give herself to them, so she sent

22:28 Jer 23:25-32; Ezek 13:6
22:29 Exod 23:9; Isa 5:7; Amos 3:10; Jas 5:4
22:30 Ps 106:23; Jer 5:1; Ezek 13:5
22:31 Isa 10:5; Ezek 7:3-9; 16:43; Rom 2:8-9
23:2 Jer 3:7-10; Ezek 16:46
23:5 Ezek 16:28; Hos 8:9-10
23:6 Ezek 23:12, 23
23:7 Hos 5:3; 6:10
23:8 Exod 32:4; 1 Kgs 12:28; 2 Kgs 17:16
23:9-10 Ezek 16:37
23:11 Jer 3:8-11
23:12 2 Kgs 16:7
23:14 Ezek 8:10; 16:29
23:16 Matt 5:28

---

and seizing their wealth. The ***priests*** had sinned by not teaching people the law so that they could distinguish between holy and profane, clean and unclean. The ***prophets*** announced false visions instead of a true word from God. As a result, the people went astray for lack of guidance.

22:30-31 In response to the sins of these former community leaders, the Lord sought someone who would ***rebuild the wall*** and ***stand in the gap*** as a true prophet (see 13:5), someone who would intercede for the people, as Moses did after the people sinned with the gold calf (Exod 32). The Lord ***found no one*** to deflect his wrath, so his ***fury*** would now be poured out upon them in full measure (cp. 11:21).

23:1-49 This chapter, like ch 16, gives the history of the northern and southern kingdoms of Israel and Judah in the form of an extended metaphor. It graphically depicts ***Samaria*** and ***Jerusalem***, the capital cities, as two immoral women. The metaphor emphasizes that their judgment was inevitable and well-deserved.

23:2 *sisters . . . daughters of the same mother:* They were descendants of the same nation, and their lives were essentially parallel. Even their names, Oholah and Oholibah, sound similar.

23:3 They ***became prostitutes*** by worshiping false gods.

23:4 Marriage is commonly used in the Bible as a symbol for the covenant relationship between God and his people (e.g., Isa 54:1-8; Eph 5:22-33). Adultery symbolizes Israel's spiritual unfaithfulness (e.g., Hos 1–3). God makes his covenants in spite of, not because of, his people's character (Rom 5:6-11).

23:5-8 *Oholah:* The northern kingdom, far from being converted by God's covenant of grace, was fascinated with the power and prestige of ***Assyria***. Alliances with Assyria were part of Israel's political strategy from the 800s BC, but in the end, such alliances did not keep Israel safe.

23:7 *idols:* The Hebrew term (literally *round things*) probably alludes to dung; also in 23:30, 37, 39, 49. See note on 6:4-7.

23:9-10 The northern kingdom was overrun by the ***Assyrian*** army in 722 BC, and its people were dispersed throughout the Assyrian empire.

23:11-18 Samaria's reputation and punishment were known to everyone in Ezekiel's time. Her sister, ***Oholibah*** (Jerusalem), followed the same pattern of life and was even worse than her sister. What a succession of Judah's kings regarded as wise political maneuvering—seeking alliances with Babylon as well as with Assyria—the prophet presents as a pattern of consistent, ever-deepening spiritual adultery.

23:14-16 *Babylonian . . . Babylonia:* Or *Chaldean . . . Chaldea.*

messengers to Babylonia to invite them to
come to her. 17So they came and committed
adultery with her, defiling her in the bed of
[c]love. After being defiled, however, she rejected them in disgust.

18"In the same way, I became disgusted
with Oholibah and rejected her, just as
I had rejected her sister, because she
flaunted herself before them and gave herself to satisfy their lusts. 19Yet she turned
to even greater prostitution, remembering
her youth when she was a prostitute in
Egypt. 20She lusted after lovers with genitals as large as a donkey's and emissions
like those of a horse. 21And so, Oholibah,
you relived your former days as a young
girl in Egypt, when you first allowed your
breasts to be fondled.

The LORD's Judgment on Oholibah

22"Therefore, Oholibah, this is what the
Sovereign LORD says: I will send your lovers
against you from every direction—those
very nations from which you turned away
in disgust. 23For the Babylonians will come
with all the Chaldeans from Pekod and
Shoa and Koa. And all the Assyrians will
come with them—handsome young captains, commanders, chariot officers, and
other high-ranking officers, all riding their
horses. 24They will all come against you
from the north with chariots, wagons, and
a great army prepared for attack. They will
take up positions on every side, surrounding you with men armed with [d]shields and
helmets. And I will hand you over to them
for punishment so they can do with you as
they please. 25I will turn my jealous anger
against you, and they will deal harshly with
you. They will cut off your nose and ears,
and any survivors will then be slaughtered
by the sword. Your children will be taken
away as captives, and everything that is left
will be burned. 26They will strip you of your
beautiful clothes and jewels. 27In this way, I
will put a stop to the lewdness and prostitution you brought from Egypt. You will never
again cast longing eyes on those things or
fondly remember your time in Egypt.

28"For this is what the Sovereign LORD
says: I will surely hand you over to your enemies, to those you loathe, those you rejected.
29They will treat you with hatred and rob
you of all you own, leaving you stark naked.
The shame of your prostitution will be exposed to all the world. 30You brought all this
on yourself by prostituting yourself to other
nations, defiling yourself with all their idols.
31Because you have followed in your sister's
footsteps, I will force you to drink the same
cup of terror she drank.

32"Yes, this is what the Sovereign LORD
says:

"You will drink from your sister's cup of
terror,
a cup that is large and deep.
It is filled to the brim
with scorn and derision.
33 Drunkenness and anguish will fill you,
for your cup is filled to the brim with
distress and desolation,
the same cup your sister Samaria
drank.
34 You will drain that cup of terror
to the very bottom.
Then you will smash it to pieces
and beat your breast in anguish.
I, the Sovereign LORD, have spoken!

35"And because you have forgotten me
and turned your back on me, this is what
the Sovereign LORD says: You must bear the
consequences of all your lewdness and prostitution."

The LORD's Judgment on Both Sisters

36The LORD said to me, "Son of man, you
must accuse Oholah and Oholibah of all
their detestable sins. 37They have committed both adultery and murder—adultery by
worshiping idols and murder by burning
as sacrifices the children they bore to me.
38Furthermore, they have defiled my Temple and violated my Sabbath day! 39On the

23:17 [c]*dod* (1730) ‣Prov 7:18
23:20 Ezek 17:15
23:21 Jer 3:9
23:23 2 Kgs 20:14-17; 24:2 Job 1:17 Jer 50:21 Ezek 21:19
23:24 Jer 39:5-6 [d]*magen* (4043) ‣Gen 15:1
23:25 Ezek 8:17-18; 23:47 Zeph 1:18
23:26 Ezek 16:39
23:27 Ezek 16:41
23:28 Jer 21:7-10
23:29 Deut 28:48 Ezek 16:37
23:30 Ezek 6:9
23:31 2 Kgs 21:13
23:32 Ps 60:3 Ezek 5:14-15
23:33 Jer 25:15
23:34 Ps 75:8 Isa 51:17
23:35 1 Kgs 14:9 Neh 9:26 Hos 13:6
23:36 Isa 58:1 Jer 1:10
23:38 2 Kgs 21:4, 7 Jer 17:27
23:39 Jer 7:9-11

23:19-20 When the people of Jerusalem thought of ***Egypt***, they did not remember the Lord's deliverance through the Exodus, but the forbidden pleasures they had enjoyed there.

23:22-24 Jerusalem's depravity made God's judgment inevitable. The very nations that she courted as her lovers would abuse her. Babylon would bring its allies, ***Pekod***, ***Shoa***, and ***Koa***. The names of these obscure tribes rhyme and sound like Hebrew words meaning "Punishment," "War cry," and "Shriek." Judah's sins were greater than her sister's, and her judgment would also be worse.

23:24 *from the north:* As in the Greek version; the meaning of the Hebrew is uncertain.

23:25-29 Stripping an adulterous wife naked—to expose in public what she had done in private—was a punishment for adultery (see note on 16:35-38). The Babylonians similarly stripped Jerusalem and Judah of everything valuable and exposed them to their own shame.

23:31-34 *your sister's cup of terror:* Jerusalem would have to drink from this bitter cup of judgment, as Samaria had. The pain of that judgment would cause her to ***beat*** (or *tear at*) her ***breast in anguish***.

23:36-43 The prophet again adopted the role of prosecuting attorney, whose task was to confront Jerusalem with her sins (described in detail in ch 22). Far from being holy cities, Jerusalem and Samaria had become ***worn-out prostitutes*** whose only attractiveness was in their availability.

very day that they sacrificed their children
to their idols, they boldly came into my Temple to worship! They came in and defiled
my house.
40"You sisters sent messengers to distant
lands to get men. Then when they arrived,
you bathed yourselves, painted your eyelids, and put on your finest jewels for them.
41You sat with them on a beautifully embroidered couch and put my incense and
my special oil on a table that was spread
before you. 42From your room came the
sound of many men carousing. They were
lustful men and drunkards from the wilderness, who put bracelets on your wrists and
beautiful crowns on your heads. 43Then I
said, 'If they really want to have sex with old
worn-out prostitutes like these, let them!'
44And that is what they did. They had sex
with Oholah and Oholibah, these shameless prostitutes. 45But righteous people will
judge these sister cities for what they really
are—adulterers and murderers.
46"Now this is what the Sovereign LORD
says: Bring an army against them and hand
them over to be terrorized and plundered.
47For their enemies will stone them and kill
them with swords. They will butcher their
sons and daughters and burn their homes.
48In this way, I will put an end to lewdness
and idolatry in the land, and my judgment
will be a warning to others not to follow
their wicked example. 49You will be fully
repaid for all your prostitution—your worship of idols. Yes, you will suffer the full
penalty. Then you will know that I am the
Sovereign LORD."

The Parable of the Cooking Pot

24 On January 15, during the ninth year
of King Jehoiachin's captivity, this
message came to me from the LORD: 2"Son
of man, write down today's date, because
on this very day the king of Babylon is beginning his attack against Jerusalem. 3Then
give these rebels an ᵉillustration with this
message from the Sovereign LORD:

"Put a pot on the fire,
and pour in some water.
4 Fill it with choice pieces of meat—
the rump and the shoulder
and all the most tender cuts.
5 Use only the best sheep from the flock,
and heap fuel on the fire beneath the pot.
Bring the pot to a boil,
and cook the bones along with the meat.
6 "Now this is what the Sovereign LORD says:
What sorrow awaits Jerusalem,
the city of murderers!
She is a cooking pot
whose corruption can't be cleaned out.
Take the meat out in random order,
for no piece is better than another.
7 For the blood of her murders
is splashed on the rocks.
It isn't even spilled on the ground,
where the dust could cover it!
8 So I will splash her blood on a rock
for all to see,
an expression of my anger
and vengeance against her.

9 "This is what the Sovereign LORD says:
What sorrow awaits Jerusalem,
the city of murderers!
I myself will pile up the fuel beneath her.
10 Yes, heap on the wood!
Let the fire roar to make the pot boil.
Cook the meat with many spices,
and afterward burn the bones.

23:40 2 Kgs 9:30; Ezek 16:13-16
23:41 Esth 1:6; Jer 44:17
23:42 Gen 24:30; Jer 51:7; Ezek 16:11-12, 49; Amos 6:3-6
23:45 Ezek 16:38
23:46 Jer 15:4; 24:9; 29:18; Ezek 16:38
23:47 Jer 39:8
23:49 Isa 59:18; Ezek 9:10
24:2 2 Kgs 25:1; Jer 39:1; 52:4
24:3 Jer 1:13-14; ᵉ*mashal* (4912) ‣1 Sam 10:12
24:4 Mic 3:2-3
24:5 Jer 52:10, 24-27
24:6 2 Kgs 24:3-4; Nah 3:1
24:7 Lev 17:13; Deut 12:16
24:8 Isa 26:21
24:9 Hab 2:12

23:42 ***drunkards:*** An alternate reading in the Masoretic Text reads *Sabeans.*

23:44-49 The sisters' enemies would ***stone them*** like adulteresses and ***kill them with swords*** as an invading army would do. In the typical pattern of invasion, not only the prostitutes but also ***their sons and daughters*** would die, and the enemy would ***burn their homes.*** Those who rebelled against the Lord and pursued idolatry would ***suffer the full penalty***, which is nothing short of death.

24:1-14 At first sight, the picture of a cooking ***pot*** is positive, conjuring expectations of good food and fellowship. Various choice pieces of a sacrificial animal had been gathered, a ***fire*** was kindled underneath the pot, and the contents were brought to a simmer. However, as in many parables, there is a sting in the tail of the story. What ought to have been a tasty meal had become a foul, profane mess. The ***choice pieces of meat*** that had gone in were uniformly corrupt when they came out. The pot represented ***Jerusalem*** (24:9); its contents would be burned and destroyed.

24:1 ***On January 15:*** Literally *On the tenth day of the tenth month* of the ancient Hebrew lunar calendar. This event occurred on Jan 15, 588 BC; see also note on 1:1. Ezekiel had been warning the people of this event, and it had now finally arrived (see also 2 Kgs 25:1-2).

24:2 ***is beginning his attack against*** (literally *is leaning on*): The same terminology was used when a worshiper pressed his hands on the animal he had brought to be sacrificed (Lev 1:4; 3:2). Jerusalem was thus identified as the sacrificial lamb to be slaughtered to the glory of God.

24:3 The people of Jerusalem were ***rebels*** against their treaty with Babylon and against their covenant with the Lord.

24:6-8 The ***cooking pot*** was beyond cleansing. Jerusalem was full of blood that she had shed and left exposed. The OT required that the blood of animals shed for meat be covered with earth (Lev 17:13). By leaving the blood of her innocent victims exposed, Jerusalem was doubly guilty. Her own blood would justly be ***splashed on the rocks*** (cp. Ps 137:8-9).

24:9-12 God declared that he would now make the cooking pot, ***Jerusalem***,

24:11 Mal 4:1
24:13 Ezek 8:18
24:14 Ps 33:9; Isa 55:11
24:16 Job 23:2; Song 7:10; Jer 13:17; 16:5; 22:10
24:17 Lev 21:10-12; 2 Sam 15:30; Jer 16:7
24:21 Ps 27:4; Jer 16:11; Ezek 23:47
24:23 Job 27:15; Ps 78:64
24:24 Ezek 4:3; Luke 11:29-30
24:25 Ps 48:2; 122:1-9; Jer 7:4; 11:22
24:26 1 Sam 4:12; Job 1:15-19; Ezek 33:21-22
24:27 Ezek 3:26; 33:22
25:2 Amos 1:13; Zeph 2:9

11 Now set the empty pot on the coals.
Heat it red hot!
Burn away the filth and corruption.
12 But it's hopeless;
the corruption can't be cleaned out.
So throw it into the fire.
13 Your impurity is your lewdness
and the corruption of your idolatry.
I tried to cleanse you,
but you refused.
So now you will remain in your filth
until my fury against you has been
satisfied.

14"I, the LORD, have spoken! The time
has come, and I won't hold back. I will not
change my mind, and I will have no pity
on you. You will be judged on the basis of
all your wicked actions, says the Sovereign
LORD."

The Death of Ezekiel's Wife

15Then this message came to me from the
LORD: 16"Son of man, with one blow I will
take away your dearest treasure. Yet you
must not show any sorrow at her death. Do
not weep; let there be no tears. 17Groan
silently, but let there be no wailing at her
grave. Do not uncover your head or take off
your sandals. Do not perform the usual rituals of mourning or accept any food brought
to you by consoling friends."
18So I proclaimed this to the people the
next morning, and in the evening my wife
died. The next morning I did everything
I had been told to do. 19Then the people
asked, "What does all this mean? What are
you trying to tell us?"
20So I said to them, "A message came to
me from the LORD, 21and I was told to give
this message to the people of Israel. This is
what the Sovereign LORD says: I will defile
my Temple, the source of your security and
pride, the place your heart delights in. Your
sons and daughters whom you left behind
in Judah will be slaughtered by the sword.
22Then you will do as Ezekiel has done. You
will not mourn in public or console yourselves by eating the food brought by friends.
23Your heads will remain covered, and your
sandals will not be taken off. You will not
mourn or weep, but you will waste away because of your sins. You will mourn privately
for all the evil you have done. 24Ezekiel is an
example for you; you will do just as he has
done. And when that time comes, you will
know that I am the Sovereign LORD."
25Then the LORD said to me, "Son of man,
on the day I take away their stronghold—
their joy and glory, their heart's desire, their
dearest treasure—I will also take away their
sons and daughters. 26And on that day a
survivor from Jerusalem will come to you
in Babylon and tell you what has happened.
27And when he arrives, your voice will suddenly return so you can talk to him, and you
will be a symbol for these people. Then they
will know that I am the LORD."

3. ORACLES AGAINST THE NATIONS (25:1–32:32)

A Message against Ammon (25:1-7)

25 Then this message came to me
from the LORD: 2"Son of man, turn
and face the land of Ammon and prophesy

as ***red hot*** as if it were in a refiner's furnace. Even this fire would not purge its corruption, however, for Jerusalem's impurity was indelible.

24:13-14 All that remained for Jerusalem was judgment without pity because of her wicked deeds and her refusal to turn back to the Lord.

24:15-17 Nowhere is a prophet's total involvement in his message demonstrated more vividly than when God took the life of Ezekiel's wife, and Ezekiel was not allowed to mourn his ***dearest treasure*** openly. Ezekiel was a priest (1:3), and all priests had restrictions placed on their mourning. The public rituals of torn clothes and an unkempt appearance would make one unclean, and priests were not permitted to make themselves unclean for any but the closest blood relatives (Lev 21:1-4). Ezekiel's lack of mourning was also a sign act that showed what was about to happen to Israel (24:20-24; see "Prophetic Sign Acts" at 4:1-17, p. 1319).

24:20-24 Ezekiel's lack of mourning (24:15-17) was a sign to Israel of what lay ahead for them. The Lord was about to take away ***the place your heart delights in***—the Temple of Jerusalem. God was going to desecrate it and destroy the sons and daughters they had left behind in Jerusalem. On that day, the people would behave as Ezekiel had done; they would not ***mourn in public*** or carry out the associated rituals. Though they would feel the loss deeply in their hearts, the scale of the devastation would be so overwhelming that there would be no opportunity for normal mourning rites. In the context of such terrible and complete desolation, only internal grief could be observed.

24:25-27 In the midst of this deep gloom and woe, on the very day when a survivor would arrive to confirm the fall of Jerusalem, there would also be a sign of hope for the people. On that day, Ezekiel's ***voice*** would ***suddenly return*** (see 3:26), and he would once again be able to pray to God for the people and intercede on their behalf. The final destruction of Jerusalem would complete the full outpouring of God's wrath and fury. On that day, Ezekiel would finally be able to speak words of hope to the shattered remnant of the exiles, so that they might know the Lord.

25:1–32:32 This section contains a series of oracles against surrounding nations. There are six shorter oracles against Judah's immediate neighbors, in clockwise geographical order, followed by a climactic seventh oracle against Egypt (chs 30–32). Through their experience of God's judgment, the nations would recognize God's sovereignty over all things. The nations might be used to bring about God's judgment of his people, but that would not exempt them from judgment. • One of the key purposes of these oracles against the nations was to affirm that the negative side of God's covenant with Abraham ("I will . . . curse those who treat you with

against its people. 3Give the Ammonites this message from the Sovereign LORD: Hear the word of the Sovereign LORD! Because you cheered when my Temple was defiled, mocked Israel in her desolation, and laughed at Judah as she went away into exile, 4I will allow nomads from the eastern deserts to overrun your country. They will set up their camps among you and pitch their tents on your land. They will harvest all your fruit and drink the milk from your livestock. 5And I will turn the city of Rabbah into a pasture for camels, and all the land of the Ammonites into a resting place for sheep and goats. Then you will know that I am the LORD.

6"This is what the Sovereign LORD says: Because you clapped and danced and cheered with glee at the destruction of my people, 7I will raise my fist of judgment against you. I will give you as plunder to many nations. I will cut you off from being a nation and destroy you completely. Then you will know that I am the LORD.

A Message against Moab (25:8-11)

8"This is what the Sovereign LORD says: Because the people of Moab have said that Judah is just like all the other nations, 9I will open up their eastern flank and wipe out their glorious frontier towns—Beth-jeshimoth, Baal-meon, and Kiriathaim. 10And I will hand Moab over to nomads from the eastern deserts, just as I handed over Ammon. Yes, the Ammonites will no longer be counted among the nations. 11In the same way, I will bring my judgment down on the Moabites. Then they will know that I am the LORD.

A Message against Edom (25:12-14)

12"This is what the Sovereign LORD says: The people of Edom have sinned greatly by avenging themselves against the people of Judah. 13Therefore, says the Sovereign LORD, I will raise my fist of judgment against Edom. I will wipe out its people and animals with the sword. I will make a wasteland of everything from Teman to Dedan. 14I will accomplish this by the hand of my people of Israel. They will carry out my vengeance with anger, and Edom will know that this vengeance is from me. I, the Sovereign LORD, have spoken!

A Message against Philistia (25:15-17)

15"This is what the Sovereign LORD says: The people of Philistia have acted against Judah out of bitter revenge and long-standing contempt. 16Therefore, this is what the Sovereign LORD says: I will raise my fist of judgment against the land of the Philistines. I will wipe out the Kerethites and utterly destroy the people who live by the sea. 17I will execute terrible vengeance against them to punish them for what they have done. And when I have inflicted my revenge, they will know that I am the LORD."

A Message against Tyre (26:1–28:19)

26 On February 3, during the twelfth year of King Jehoiachin's captivity, this message came to me from the LORD:

Coming Judgment: A Barren Rock

2"Son of man, Tyre has rejoiced over the fall of Jerusalem, saying, 'Ha! She who was the gateway to the rich trade routes to the east has been broken, and I am the heir! Because

25:3
Ps 70:2-3
Ezek 21:28; 26:2; 36:2

25:4
Deut 28:33, 51
Judg 6:3, 33
Isa 1:7

25:5
2 Sam 12:26
Jer 49:2
Ezek 21:20
Zeph 2:14-15

25:6
Job 27:23
Obad 1:12
Zeph 2:8, 10

25:7
Amos 1:14-15

25:8
Isa 15:1
Jer 48:1
Amos 2:1

25:9
Num 32:37-38; 33:49
Josh 13:17-20
1 Chr 5:8
Jer 48:23

25:13
Gen 36:34
Jer 49:7
Mal 1:3-4

25:14
Ezek 34:11
Nah 1:2-4
Heb 10:30-31

25:15
Isa 14:29-31
Joel 3:4
Amos 1:6-8
Zeph 2:4-7
Zech 9:5-8

25:16
1 Sam 30:14
Jer 47:4
Zeph 2:5

25:17
Ps 9:16

26:2
2 Sam 5:11
Isa 23:1
Jer 25:22

---

contempt," Gen 12:3) was in force. No one can assault God's people and escape unscathed, even when God's people are themselves under his judgment.

25:3-7 Because the *Ammonites* rejoiced over Judah's downfall and celebrated the destruction of Israel's Temple, they would experience invasion and destruction, as the prophet had already warned (21:28-32). Others would eat the Ammonites' produce and their people would be exterminated, just as had happened to Judah. The Ammonites' gods would be unable to save them from the Lord's wrath, and they would know that the Lord is the true God.

25:8-11 The ***people of Moab*** thought that they could attack ***Judah*** with impunity, as though it were ***just like all the other nations.*** This was not true—even though Judah had been acting as though it were (see 20:32)—because Judah had a covenant with God, and God would not ultimately reject Judah. Instead, like ***Ammon,*** Moab would be removed from the register of the nations and left perpetually desolate.

25:12-14 Ammon and Moab gloated at Judah's downfall, but ***Edom*** actively participated in it (see 35:5; Obad 1:1-21). • ***avenging:*** The people of Edom cut down fugitives and handed over survivors in aid of the Babylonians (Obad 1:11-14). They were opportunists, settling old scores that dated back to the ancient conflict between Jacob and Esau (Gen 27:41); they gained what they could for themselves out of Judah's difficulties. In return, the Lord would desolate their land.

25:15-17 The Philistines also had a ***long-standing contempt*** for Judah. Their crimes are not specified, but they did not escape the Lord's notice, and he would return ***vengeance*** for vengeance. Then they, too, would recognize the Lord's sovereign power. • The ***Kerethites*** were a Philistine tribe (see 1 Sam 30:14).

26:1–28:19 The message against ***Tyre,*** Israel's northwestern neighbor, is much more substantial than the short oracles preceding it. It takes the form of three nearly parallel panels (26:2-21; 27:1-36; and 28:1-19), each presenting a variation on the same message—that Tyre would ***come to a horrible end*** and ***exist no more*** (27:36).

26:1 ***On February 3, during the twelfth year of King Jehoiachin's captivity:*** Literally *In the eleventh year, on the first day of the month* of the ancient Hebrew lunar calendar year. Since an element is missing in the date formula here, scholars have reconstructed this probable reading: *In the eleventh [month of the twelfth] year, on the first day of the month.* This reading would put this message on February 3, 585 BC—about seven months after the fall of Jerusalem. Also see note on 1:1.

26:2 Like its neighbors, Tyre ***rejoiced over the fall of Jerusalem,*** which

26:3 Jer 50:42; 51:42
26:4 Isa 23:11; Amos 1:10
26:7 Dan 2:37, 47; Nah 2:3-4
26:8 Jer 6:6; 32:24; 52:4
26:10 Jer 39:3
26:11 Isa 5:28; 26:5; Hab 1:8
26:12 2 Chr 32:27; Isa 23:8, 18; Amos 5:11
26:13 Isa 24:8-9; Amos 6:5; Rev 18:22-23

she has been made desolate, I will become
wealthy!'
3"Therefore, this is what the Sovereign
LORD says: I am your enemy, O Tyre, and
I will bring many nations against you, like
the waves of the sea crashing against your
shoreline. 4They will destroy the walls of
Tyre and tear down its towers. I will scrape
away its soil and make it a bare rock! 5It will
be just a rock in the sea, a place for fishermen to spread their nets, for I have spoken,
says the Sovereign LORD. Tyre will become
the prey of many nations, 6and its mainland
villages will be destroyed by the sword.
Then they will know that I am the LORD.
7"This is what the Sovereign LORD says:
From the north I will bring King Nebuchadnezzar of Babylon against Tyre. He is king of
kings and brings his horses, chariots, charioteers, and great army. 8First he will destroy
your mainland villages. Then he will attack
you by building a siege wall, constructing a
ramp, and raising a roof of shields against
you. 9He will pound your walls with battering rams and demolish your towers with
sledgehammers. 10The hooves of his horses
will choke the city with dust, and the noise
of the charioteers and chariot wheels will
shake your walls as they storm through your
broken gates. 11His horsemen will trample
through every street in the city. They will
butcher your people, and your strong pillars
will topple.
12"They will plunder all your riches and
merchandise and break down your walls.
They will destroy your lovely homes and
dump your stones and timbers and even
your dust into the sea. 13I will stop the music

Messages against the Nations (25:1–32:32)

Ezek 9:6; 36:23; 39:7
Gen 12:3
Deut 23:3-6
Isa 13:1–23:18
Jer 25:29; 46:1–51:64
Dan 4:17
Amos 1:1–2:3; 3:2
Obad 1:1-16
John 15:18-24
Acts 3:25-26
Rom 2:9-10; 11:1-27
Eph 1:3-14
1 Pet 4:17
Rev 18:1-24

Why would a prophet from Judah address a prolonged discourse, such as chs 25–32, to nations that he had probably never visited and who would in all likelihood never hear the messages uttered against them? Why was he concerned about what these nations thought and did? It was because the real audience was the people of Judah.

These messages reminded God's people that God does not operate on a double standard, judging the sins of his own people while the nations around them were free to act as they wished. In many cases, God had used these wicked nations to punish his people. Though judgment begins with God's own household (1 Pet 4:17), it certainly does not end there. God will judge all, both inside and outside Israel, who rebel against him and his reign. All must come to acknowledge the Lord as the one true and sovereign God. The people of Judah had also been inclined to trust some of these nations (such as Egypt) to rescue them from God's judgment. The prophets reminded the people that no nation on earth can be trusted in place of God. In the end, all of them will bow before him.

The messages against the foreign nations also reminded the covenant community that in spite of God's judgment on them because of their sin, they were still his precious people. The foreign nations were not accused of sin in general or of crimes against humanity in general. They had all persecuted or insulted God's chosen people and had thereby affronted God. The negative side of God's covenant with Abraham was still in force: "I will . . . curse those who treat you with contempt" (Gen 12:3).

God's consistent purpose in history was to bring glory to himself. He did this by exiling his sinful people and by judging their arrogant oppressors. In this way, all would recognize God's power and holiness. Because God was still acting according to this consistent purpose, and the negative side of the covenant with Abraham was still in effect, there was still hope for the positive side of the covenant: "All the families on earth will be blessed through you" (Gen 12:3). God's purposes for his people were not exhausted; he would ultimately bring glory to himself by bringing them back from the distant lands to which they had been scattered (cp. Rom 11:1-27).

eliminated a rival trading center and potentially opened up new *trade routes* and markets for Tyre.

26:3-6 The *many nations* with which Tyre wanted to trade would instead come against her equipped for war, and like Jerusalem, she would become plunder for their armies. • *waves of the sea crashing against your shoreline:* This is a particularly apt metaphor for an assault on Tyre, which lay on a small coastal island.

26:7-11 Tyre's projected destruction is described in great detail, conveying certainty as to the conflict's outcome.

26:7 *Nebuchadnezzar:* Hebrew *Nebuchadrezzar,* a variant spelling of *Nebuchadnezzar.*

26:12-14 The end result was exactly as the prophet had described earlier in metaphorical language. Tyre would become *a bare rock,* a desolate haunt for local *fishermen to spread their nets* to dry, instead of a bustling center for long-distance trading vessels and caravans from the east (26:2). According to Josephus, Tyre was subsequently besieged by Nebuchadnezzar for thirteen years, although it was not finally destroyed until the time of Alexander the Great (332 BC).

of your songs. No more will the sound of
harps be heard among your people. [14]I will
make your island a bare rock, a place for
fishermen to spread their nets. You will
never be rebuilt, for I, the LORD, have spoken. Yes, the Sovereign LORD has spoken!

Mourning for Tyre: An Uninhabitable Ruin

[15]"This is what the Sovereign LORD says to
Tyre: The whole coastline will tremble at
the sound of your fall, as the screams of the
wounded echo in the continuing slaughter.
[16]All the seaport rulers will step down from
their thrones and take off their royal robes
and beautiful clothing. They will sit on
the ground trembling with horror at your
destruction. [17]Then they will wail for you,
singing this funeral song:

"O famous island city,
once ruler of the sea,
how you have been destroyed!
Your people, with their naval power,
once spread fear around the world.
[18] Now the coastlands tremble at your
fall.
The islands are dismayed as you
disappear.

[19]"This is what the Sovereign LORD says:
I will make Tyre an uninhabited ruin, like
many others. I will bury you beneath the
terrible waves of enemy attack. Great seas
will swallow you. [20]I will send you to the pit
to join those who descended there long ago.
Your city will lie in ruins, buried beneath
the earth, like those in the pit who have entered the world of the dead. You will have
no place of respect here in the land of the living. [21]I will bring you to a terrible end, and
you will exist no more. You will be looked
for, but you will never again be found. I, the
Sovereign LORD, have spoken!"

Tyre's Former Glory: An Elegy

27 Then this message came to me
from the LORD: [2]"Son of man, sing a
funeral song for Tyre, [3]that mighty gateway
to the sea, the trading center of the world.
Give Tyre this message from the Sovereign
LORD:

"You boasted, O Tyre,
'My beauty is perfect!'
[4] You extended your boundaries into the
sea.
Your builders made your beauty perfect.
[5] You were like a great ship
built of the finest cypress from Senir.
They took a cedar from Lebanon
to make a mast for you.
[6] They carved your oars
from the oaks of Bashan.
Your deck of pine from the coasts of
Cyprus
was inlaid with ivory.
[7] Your sails were made of Egypt's finest
linen,
and they flew as a banner above you.
You stood beneath blue and purple
awnings
made bright with dyes from the
coasts of Elishah.
[8] Your oarsmen came from Sidon and
Arvad;
your helmsmen were skilled men
from Tyre itself.
[9] Wise old craftsmen from Gebal did the
caulking.
Ships from every land came with
goods to barter for your trade.

[10]"Men from distant Persia, Lydia, and
Libya served in your great army. They hung
their shields and helmets on your walls, giving you great honor. [11]Men from Arvad and
Helech stood on your walls. Your towers
were manned by men from Gammad. Their

26:14 Deut 13:16; Job 12:14; Isa 14:27; Mal 1:4
26:15 Jer 49:21
26:16 Ps 35:26; Jon 3:6
26:17 Isa 14:12; Jer 48:39; 50:23
26:18 Isa 23:5-7, 10-15
26:19 Isa 8:7-8
26:20 Ps 88:6; Jon 2:2, 6; Zech 2:8
26:21 Ezek 27:36
27:2 Jer 7:20; 9:10, 17-20
27:5 Deut 3:9; Song 4:8
27:6 Num 21:33; Jer 22:20; Zech 11:2
27:7 Exod 25:4; Prov 7:16; Jer 10:9
27:8 Gen 10:18; 1 Kgs 9:27; 1 Chr 1:16
27:9 1 Kgs 5:18
27:10 Ezek 38:5

26:15-16 The economic impact of Tyre's fall would spread out to her trading partners along ***the whole coastline,*** causing their ***rulers*** to abdicate.

26:17-18 The *funeral song* (see note on 19:1-14) for Tyre would be taken up and repeated from place to place. • ***naval power . . . spread fear:*** Tyre's trading practices were apparently based on conquest, subjugation, and exploitation (see 28:16, 18).

26:19-21 God would demonstrate his sovereign power by utterly destroying Tyre. It would be as though that great city had sunk into the depths of the chaotic ocean ***waves,*** with its inhabitants condemned to the ***pit*** where the unrighteous ***dead*** reside, never to return.

27:1-36 The second panel of the prophet's address to Tyre (see note on 26:1–28:19) is a ***funeral song*** that contrasts past glory with present loss. It is connected with the previous chapter by being addressed to Tyre, by its imagery of a gateway and a trading center (see 26:1-2), and by the common conclusion ***you have come to a horrible end and will exist no more*** (cp. 26:21).

27:4-7 Tyre's past greatness is described in great detail under the metaphor of a mighty sailing ship created out of the very best resources from the surrounding nations.

27:5 ***Senir:*** Or *Hermon.*

27:6 ***Cyprus:*** Hebrew *Kittim.*

27:7 ***Elishah*** is the name for another part of Cyprus.

27:8-11 The ship of Tyre was manned by a crew gathered from the most famously ***skilled men*** in the world. • The locations described in this account cover most of the known world at the time. Tyre's influence was vast.

27:8-9 ***Sidon, Arvad,*** and ***Gebal*** were Mediterranean coastal towns.

27:10 ***Persia, Lydia, and Libya:*** Hebrew *Paras, Lud, and Put.* Persia was far to the east over land, while Lydia was northwest in what is now Turkey. Libya was southwest on the shore of the Mediterranean.

27:11 ***Helech*** is Cilicia, the area around

27:13 Gen 10:2-3; Isa 66:19; Ezek 38:2; Joel 3:3; Rev 18:13
27:15 Rev 18:12
27:16 Ezek 16:13, 18
27:17 Judg 11:33
27:18 Gen 14:15; Ezek 47:16-18
27:21 Isa 21:13; 60:7
27:22 Gen 10:7; 43:11; 1 Kgs 10:2; Isa 60:6; Ezek 38:13
27:23 2 Kgs 19:12; Isa 37:12; Amos 1:5; 6:2
27:26 Ps 48:7
27:29 Rev 18:17-19
27:30 1 Sam 4:12; 2 Sam 1:2; Jon 3:6; Rev 18:19
27:31 Isa 16:9; 22:12; Ezek 7:18; 29:18
27:32 Rev 18:18

shields hung on your walls, completing your
beauty.
12 "Tarshish sent merchants to buy your
wares in exchange for silver, iron, tin, and
lead. 13 Merchants from Greece, Tubal, and
Meshech brought slaves and articles of
bronze to trade with you.
14 "From Beth-togarmah came riding
horses, chariot horses, and mules, all in exchange for your goods. 15 Merchants came
to you from Dedan. Numerous coastlands
were your captive markets; they brought
payment in ivory tusks and ebony wood.
16 "Syria sent merchants to buy your rich
variety of goods. They traded turquoise,
purple dyes, embroidery, fine linen, and jewelry of coral and rubies. 17 Judah and Israel
traded for your wares, offering wheat from
Minnith, figs, honey, olive oil, and balm.
18 "Damascus sent merchants to buy
your rich variety of goods, bringing wine
from Helbon and white wool from Zahar.
19 Greeks from Uzal came to trade for your
merchandise. Wrought iron, cassia, and
fragrant calamus were bartered for your
wares.
20 "Dedan sent merchants to trade their
expensive saddle blankets with you. 21 The
Arabians and the princes of Kedar sent merchants to trade lambs and rams and male
goats in exchange for your goods. 22 The
merchants of Sheba and Raamah came
with all kinds of spices, jewels, and gold in
exchange for your wares.
23 "Haran, Canneh, Eden, Sheba, Asshur,
and Kilmad came with their merchandise, too. 24 They brought choice fabrics to
trade—blue cloth, embroidery, and multicolored carpets rolled up and bound with
cords. 25 The ships of Tarshish were your
ocean caravans. Your island warehouse was
filled to the brim!

The End of Tyre's Glory: The Sunken Ship

26 "But look! Your oarsmen
have taken you into stormy seas!
A mighty eastern gale
has wrecked you in the heart of the sea!
27 Everything is lost—
your riches and wares,
your sailors and pilots,
your ship builders, merchants, and warriors.
On the day of your ruin,
everyone on board sinks into the depths of the sea.
28 Your cities by the sea tremble
as your pilots cry out in terror.
29 All the oarsmen abandon their ships;
the sailors and pilots on shore come to stand on the beach.
30 They cry aloud over you
and weep bitterly.
They throw dust on their heads
and roll in ashes.
31 They shave their heads in grief for you
and dress themselves in burlap.
They weep for you with bitter anguish
and deep mourning.
32 As they wail and mourn over you,
they sing this sad funeral song:
'Was there ever such a city as Tyre,
now silent at the bottom of the sea?
33 The merchandise you traded
satisfied the desires of many nations.
Kings at the ends of the earth
were enriched by your trade.

Tarsus on the northeast shore of the Mediterranean. • The location of ***Gammad*** is less certain, but it may have been in northern Syria.

27:12-25 The vast system of transport was all at the service of Tyre's insatiable appetite for trade. The list of Tyre's trading partners goes on and on; Tyre was the source of a wide variety of commodities from slaves to horses, saddle blankets to silver, dyes to figs (cp. Rev 18:11-13). The cargo list for the ship is organized according to the different geographic regions with which she conducted trade, covering all points of the compass and including every trading center, major and minor. Virtually every precious object that could be bought or sold found a place somewhere on the list of Tyre's goods.

27:12 ***Tarshish*** was in the distant west, possibly in Spain.

27:13-14 ***Greece:*** Hebrew *Javan.* • ***Tubal, Meshech,*** and neighboring ***Beth-togarmah*** were regions in Anatolia (modern Turkey).

27:15 ***Dedan*** was a central Arabian oasis (see also 27:20), but it might also refer to a coastal region north of Tyre. Greek version reads *Rhodes,* an island southwest of modern Turkey.

27:16 ***Syria:*** Hebrew *Aram;* some manuscripts read *Edom.*

27:17 ***Minnith,*** located in Transjordan (the area east of the Jordan River), was a well-known source of wheat. • ***figs:*** The meaning of the Hebrew is uncertain.

27:18 ***Helbon*** was a town ten miles north of Damascus. ***Zahar*** may have been nearby, although its exact location is unknown.

27:19 ***Greeks from Uzal:*** Hebrew *Vedan and Javan from Uzal.* The meaning of the Hebrew is uncertain. Uzal may have been a town in the foothills of Anatolia. • ***Cassia*** and ***calamus*** were expensive perfumes.

27:20-21 ***Dedan:*** See note on 27:15. • ***Kedar*** was a region of Arabia named for a son of Ishmael (Gen 25:13).

27:22 ***Sheba*** was a kingdom in southwest Arabia. The location of ***Raamah*** is uncertain, but it was always associated with Sheba.

27:23 ***Haran, Canneh, Eden,*** and ***Asshur*** were all located in Mesopotamia (modern Iraq). ***Kilmad*** is otherwise unattested in ancient sources and may be a scribal error for "all Media" (the region northeast of Mesopotamia).

27:26 Though apparently unsinkable, this rich and heavily laden merchant ship was no match for the ***mighty eastern gale,*** the army of Babylon.

34 Now you are a wrecked ship,
broken at the bottom of the sea.
All your merchandise and crew
have gone down with you.
35 All who live along the coastlands
are appalled at your terrible fate.
Their kings are filled with horror
and look on with twisted faces.
36 The merchants among the nations
shake their heads at the sight of you,
for you have come to a horrible end
and will exist no more.' "

A Message for Tyre's King: The Fallen Angel

28 Then this message came to me from the LORD: 2"Son of man, give the prince of Tyre this message from the Sovereign LORD:

"In your great pride you claim, 'I am a god!
I sit on a divine throne in the heart of
the sea.'
But you are only a man and not a god,
though you boast that you are a god.
3 You regard yourself as wiser than Daniel
and think no secret is hidden from
you.
4 With your wisdom and understanding
you have amassed great wealth—
gold and silver for your treasuries.
5 Yes, your wisdom has made you very rich,
and your riches have made you very
proud.

6 "Therefore, this is what the Sovereign
LORD says:
Because you think you are as wise as a
god,
7 I will now bring against you a foreign
army,
the terror of the nations.
They will draw their swords against your
marvelous wisdom
and defile your splendor!
8 They will bring you down to the pit,
and you will die in the heart of the sea,
pierced with many wounds.
9 Will you then boast, 'I am a god!'
to those who kill you?
To them you will be no god
but merely a man!
10 You will die like an outcast
at the hands of foreigners.
I, the Sovereign LORD, have spoken!"

11Then this further message came to me from the LORD: 12"Son of man, sing this funeral song for the king of Tyre. Give him this message from the Sovereign LORD:

"You were the model of perfection,
full of wisdom and exquisite in
beauty.
13 You were in Eden,
the garden of God.
Your clothing was adorned with every
precious stone—
red carnelian, pale-green peridot,
white moonstone,
blue-green beryl, onyx, green jasper,
blue lapis lazuli, turquoise, and
emerald—
all beautifully crafted for you
and set in the finest gold.
They were given to you
on the day you were created.

27:34 Zech 9:3-4
27:36 Ps 37:10, 36; Jer 49:17; Zeph 2:15
28:2 Ps 82:6-7; 2 Thes 2:4
28:3 Dan 1:20
28:4 Zech 9:2-4
28:5 Job 31:24-25; Ps 52:7; Hos 12:7-8; 13:6
28:6 Exod 9:17
28:7 Dan 7:7; Hab 1:6-8
28:8 Ezek 27:26-27, 34
28:10 1 Sam 17:26, 36; Ezek 31:18
28:12 Ezek 27:2
28:13 Gen 2:8; Exod 28:17-20; 39:10-21; Isa 51:3; 54:11-12

27:36 ***shake their heads at the sight of you:*** Literally *hiss at you.* • Tyre's former occupants and her former trading partners join the lament for her lost way of life. This panel, like the previous one, ends with the statement that Tyre has ***come to a horrible end and will exist no more*** (cp. 26:21).

28:1-19 The third panel against Tyre (see note on 26:1–28:19) addresses and condemns its ruler, ***the prince of Tyre,*** for his pride. He personifies the city of Tyre, so his fate represents Tyre's fate. In his arrogance, the prince of Tyre laid claim to divinity and the power that goes with it, asserting that he sat on ***a divine throne,*** ruling the chaotic, untamable seas. The reality, however, was otherwise; he was ***only a man.*** • This chapter and Isa 14 (about the king of Babylon) have often been interpreted as referring to the heavenly conflict between God and Satan, "the prince of demons" (Matt 12:24). However, this view ignores the historical nature of both passages. Tyre and Babylon were real places and their kings were real men whose great power was matched by ***great pride.*** The king of Tyre's claim to be ***a god*** proved hollow. The political powers that oppose God and his people may be agents of Satan in his struggle against God. The sure demise of such human rulers foreshadows God's ultimate triumph over all the forces of darkness. Every power that sets itself up against the living God will be brought to destruction.

28:3-5 The prince of Tyre's claim to divine status was based on his wisdom and his wealth. His wisdom had made him ***very rich,*** and those ***riches*** had ***made*** him inordinately ***proud.***

28:6-7 The prince of Tyre's pride was the precursor to his fall (Prov 16:18). His claim to wisdom and power would be empty when the Lord brought the Babylonian ***army*** against him; ***they*** would ***draw their swords*** and cut him down to size.

28:8 The clearest demonstration that the prince of Tyre was a mortal man and not a divine being came when he was put to death by the Babylonians. His final resting place would not be in the heights with the gods, but in the ***pit,*** the residence of the dead. Like the city of Tyre, the prince of Tyre would die ***in the heart of the sea*** (cp. 27:26-27).

28:10 ***will die like an outcast:*** Literally *will die the death of the uncircumcised.* He would perish apart from a covenant relationship with God (cp. Gen 17:10-14).

28:12-19 This eulogy at first appears to take the prince of Tyre's aspirations to divinity seriously. He was the very ***model of perfection,*** full of ***wisdom and . . . beauty.*** It turns out to be a sarcastic lament.

28:12 ***funeral song:*** see note on 19:1-14.

28:13-14 Mocking Tyre's claim to antiquity and pre-eminence, Ezekiel describes its king as being present ***in Eden*** at the beginning of the world, as

28:14 Exod 25:17-20; Ezek 20:40; [f]*kerub* (3742) ›Gen 3:24
28:15 Isa 14:12
28:16 Ezek 8:17; Hab 2:8, 17
28:17 Isa 19:11
28:18 Amos 1:9-10; Mal 4:3
28:19 Jer 51:64
28:21 Gen 10:15-19; Isa 23:2-4, 12
28:23 Jer 51:52; Ezek 38:22
28:24 Num 33:55; Josh 23:13; Isa 55:13
28:25 Ps 106:47; Isa 11:12-13; Jer 23:8
28:26 Jer 32:15, 43-44; Amos 9:13-14

14 I ordained and anointed you
as the mighty [f]angelic guardian.
You had access to the holy mountain of God
and walked among the stones of fire.
15 "You were blameless in all you did
from the day you were created
until the day evil was found in you.
16 Your rich commerce led you to violence,
and you sinned.
So I banished you in disgrace
from the mountain of God.
I expelled you, O mighty guardian,
from your place among the stones of fire.
17 Your heart was filled with pride
because of all your beauty.
Your wisdom was corrupted
by your love of splendor.
So I threw you to the ground
and exposed you to the curious gaze of kings.
18 You defiled your sanctuaries
with your many sins and your dishonest trade.
So I brought fire out from within you,
and it consumed you.
I reduced you to ashes on the ground
in the sight of all who were watching.
19 All who knew you are appalled at your fate.
You have come to a terrible end,
and you will exist no more."

A Message against Sidon (28:20-24)

20Then another message came to me from
the LORD: 21"Son of man, turn and face the
city of Sidon and prophesy against it. 22Give
the people of Sidon this message from the
Sovereign LORD:

"I am your enemy, O Sidon,
and I will reveal my glory by what I do to you.
When I bring judgment against you
and reveal my holiness among you,
everyone watching will know
that I am the LORD.
23 I will send a plague against you,
and blood will be spilled in your streets.
The attack will come from every direction,
and your people will lie slaughtered within your walls.
Then everyone will know
that I am the LORD.
24 No longer will Israel's scornful neighbors
prick and tear at her like briers and thorns.
For then they will know
that I am the Sovereign LORD.

Restoration for Israel (28:25-26)

25"This is what the Sovereign LORD says: The
people of Israel will again live in their own
land, the land I gave my servant Jacob. For
I will gather them from the distant lands
where I have scattered them. I will reveal to
the nations of the world my holiness among
my people. 26They will live safely in Israel
and build homes and plant vineyards. And
when I punish the neighboring nations that
treated them with contempt, they will know
that I am the LORD their God."

the mighty angelic guardian—that is, as one of the heavenly beings that carried the Lord's throne in ch 1 and guarded the Garden in Gen 3. There in Eden, he had access to the ***holy mountain of God*** (mountains are often associated with God's presence in the Bible). • ***every precious stone:*** The identification of some of these gemstones is uncertain. The ***stones of fire*** may be an obscure reference to a hedge of sparkling gemstones around the Garden of Eden. The list of jewels that the prince of Tyre supposedly wore in his original glory adds to this image of his divine election since it includes nine of the twelve jewels found on the high priest's breastplate in Exod 28. This description satirizes the prince of Tyre's claim to a place among the divine beings, even higher than Adam's (see note on 28:12-19). • ***mighty angelic guardian:*** Literally *guardian cherub;* similarly in 28:16.

28:15-18 This sarcastic description of the prince of Tyre's greatness and pride sets him up for his coming fall, which is cast in terms reminiscent of the fall of humanity (Gen 3). As with Adam, the king of Tyre's supposedly ***blameless*** condition was not permanent, but came to an abrupt end when ***evil was found*** in him. His ***rich commerce*** and ***dishonest trade*** led him ***to violence*** (see note on 26:17-18). One who claimed to be greater than Adam could experience a fall from favor similar to Adam's and be ***banished . . . from the mountain of God,*** the place of God's favor. The prince of Tyre's God-given ***beauty*** and ***wisdom*** were corrupted by his pride, which inevitably led to disaster and exposed his true nature.

28:18-19 Far from being a deity who could sanctify a piece of ground by his presence, the prince of Tyre had the opposite effect. He ***defiled*** the holy ground of his ***sanctuaries.*** Judgment was pronounced on his city in the previous two panels, and it was the prince of Tyre's fate to ***come to a terrible end, and . . . exist no more*** (cp. 26:21; 27:36). The exalted captain would go down with his glorious ship and be brought to nothing by the Lord's act. • ***dishonest trade:*** See note on 26:17-18.

28:20-24 No specific charges are made against ***Sidon,*** Tyre's close neighbor to the north, though presumably it was guilty of similar offenses. Its rejoicing at Judah's destruction would not last.

28:22-23 The Lord planned to ***reveal*** his ***glory*** and ***holiness*** by bringing upon Sidon the threefold judgment of ***plague, blood,*** and ***attack*** (or *the sword*) on every side.

28:25-26 The Lord would not reveal his ***holiness*** simply by judging ***the nations*** for their pride, arrogance, and enmity toward his chosen people. He would also ***gather*** his people back to the land of Israel. There they would ***live safely*** and be able to ***build homes and plant vineyards,*** which were typical signs of covenantal blessing in the OT (see

A Message against Egypt (29:1–32:32)
Egypt, the Captured Sea Monster

29 On January 7, during the tenth year
of King Jehoiachin's captivity, this
message came to me from the LORD: 2"Son
of man, turn and face Egypt and prophesy
against Pharaoh the king and all the people
of Egypt. 3Give them this message from the
Sovereign LORD:

"I am your enemy, O Pharaoh, king of
Egypt—
you great monster, lurking in the
streams of the Nile.
For you have said, 'The Nile River is mine;
I made it for myself.'
4 I will put hooks in your jaws
and drag you out on the land
with fish sticking to your scales.
5 I will leave you and all your fish
stranded in the wilderness to die.
You will lie unburied on the open ground,
for I have given you as food to the wild
animals and birds.
6 All the people of Egypt will know that I
am the LORD,
for to Israel you were just a staff made
of reeds.
7 When Israel leaned on you,
you splintered and broke
and stabbed her in the armpit.
When she put her weight on you, you
gave way,
and her back was thrown out of joint.

8"Therefore, this is what the Sovereign
LORD says: I will bring an army against
you, O Egypt, and destroy both people and
animals. 9The land of Egypt will become a
desolate wasteland, and the Egyptians will
know that I am the LORD.

"Because you said, 'The Nile River is mine;
I made it,' 10I am now the enemy of both you
and your river. I will make the land of Egypt
a totally desolate wasteland, from Migdol
to Aswan, as far south as the border of Ethiopia. 11For forty years not a soul will pass
that way, neither people nor animals. It will
be completely uninhabited. 12I will make
Egypt desolate, and it will be surrounded
by other desolate nations. Its cities will
be empty and desolate for forty years, surrounded by other ruined cities. I will scatter
the Egyptians to distant lands.

13"But this is what the Sovereign LORD
also says: At the end of the forty years I will
bring the Egyptians home again from the
nations to which they have been scattered.
14I will restore the prosperity of Egypt and
bring its people back to the land of Pathros
in southern Egypt from which they came.
But Egypt will remain an unimportant,

29:2 Isa 19:1-17; Jer 46:2-25
29:3 Isa 27:1
29:4 2 Kgs 19:28; Isa 37:29; Ezek 38:4
29:5 Jer 7:33; 34:20
29:6 Isa 36:6
29:7 Jer 37:5-11; Ezek 17:15-17
29:9 Prov 18:12; 29:23
29:11 Jer 43:11-12
29:12 Jer 25:15-19; 27:6-11
29:13 Isa 19:22; Jer 46:26
29:14 Isa 11:11; Jer 44:1

Mic 4:4; Zech 3:10). After God acted to ***punish the neighboring nations*** and restore his people, they would be at rest. The nations would know that God is ***the Sovereign LORD*** through his powerful acts of judgment, and Israel would know that he was ***the LORD their God***, a title that speaks of God's covenant relationship of worship and fellowship with them.

29:1–32:32 The climactic seventh oracle against the nations is against Egypt, Israel's old enemy and ally. This is the longest of the oracles and, like the oracle against Tyre, addresses both the land of Egypt and its ruler. • Egypt played a central role through the centuries in tempting Israel and Judah away from their allegiance to the Lord. Israel had no sooner departed from Egypt than Egypt's idolatry became a snare for them. Egypt caused Judah to trust in chariots and horses instead of in the Lord, but Egypt proved unreliable when the moment of truth arrived. The Lord judged Egypt because it tempted Judah away from loyalty to him (cp. Luke 17:1-2).

29:1 ***On January 7:*** Literally *On the twelfth day of the tenth month* of the ancient Hebrew lunar calendar. This event occurred on January 7, 587 BC; see also note on 1:1. • This day in the ***tenth year*** since the exile of ***Jehoiachin*** was approximately one year after the beginning of the siege of Jerusalem (see note on 24:1).

29:3-16 The opening section of the oracle is a word of judgment against ***Pharaoh***, who is addressed as a great sea ***monster***. These creatures were a familiar part of ancient Near Eastern mythology as a manifestation of chaos that had to be tamed by the gods. Strikingly, these same sea monsters appear in demythologized form as part of God's good creation (Gen 1:21). In this chapter, however, the mythical image blends with the image of Pharaoh as a great crocodile, resting comfortably ***in the streams*** that laced the delta of ***the Nile***.

29:4-5 The picture of the mighty crocodile anticipates the arrival of the Lord as a great hunter. As with Tyre, a watery fortress would once again prove vulnerable to assault. The outwardly fearsome king of Egypt would be captured like any ordinary crocodile and brought out into ***the wilderness***, the place of judgment, along with his allies, the ***fish***. There he would die, and his body would be left dishonorably exposed for the wild animals and birds to eat.

29:6-7 Egypt's sin is once again associated with ***Israel***. Egypt was a ***staff made of reeds*** that repeatedly pretended to support Israel, while lacking the will and the substance to deliver the promised aid. Egypt constantly incited rebellion in Israel against Assyria and Babylonia without ever really providing help (cp. 2 Kgs 18:21). Although trusting in this cracked staff was Israel's sin, Egypt was also guilty and would face God's wrath for raising false hopes.

29:8-13 God's solution was to devastate the land of Egypt, making it into ***a desolate wasteland***. The threatened destruction would stretch from ***Migdol*** in the northeast down to ***Aswan*** in the south, leaving the whole of Egypt uninhabited for an entire generation of ***forty years*** (cp. 4:6). Egypt's fate would be like Judah's, as God would first ***scatter the Egyptians to distant lands*** and then ***bring the Egyptians home***. The Babylonians seem to have invaded Egypt successfully in 568 or 567 BC and carried off Egyptian prisoners of war who remained in exile until the time of Cyrus, a generation later.

29:10 ***from Migdol to Aswan, as far south as the border of Ethiopia:*** Hebrew *from Migdol to Syene as far as the border of Cush.*

29:14-16 Judah would ultimately be fully restored, but Egypt would ***remain***

29:15 Dan 11:42-43; Nah 3:8-9; Zech 10:11
29:16 Isa 30:1-3; 64:9; Hos 5:13; 8:13; 9:9
29:17 Ezek 24:1; 30:20
29:18 Jer 25:9; 27:6; Ezek 26:7-12
29:19 Jer 43:10-13; Ezek 30:10-12
29:20 Isa 10:6-7; 45:1-3
29:21 1 Sam 2:10; Ps 92:10; 132:17; Amos 3:7-8; Luke 21:15
30:2 Isa 13:6; 65:14; Joel 1:5, 11, 13, 15
30:5 Jer 25:20, 24
30:6 Isa 20:3-6

minor kingdom. 15It will be the lowliest of
all the nations, never again great enough to
rise above its neighbors.

16"Then Israel will no longer be tempted
to trust in Egypt for help. Egypt's shattered
condition will remind Israel of how sinful
she was to trust Egypt in earlier days. Then
Israel will know that I am the Sovereign
LORD."

Babylon's Reward: To Conquer Egypt

17On April 26, the first day of the new year,
during the twenty-seventh year of King
Jehoiachin's captivity, this message came to
me from the LORD: 18"Son of man, the army
of King Nebuchadnezzar of Babylon fought
so hard against Tyre that the warriors' heads
were rubbed bare and their shoulders were
raw and blistered. Yet Nebuchadnezzar
and his army won no plunder to compensate them for all their work. 19Therefore,
this is what the Sovereign LORD says: I will
give the land of Egypt to Nebuchadnezzar,
king of Babylon. He will carry off its wealth,
plundering everything it has so he can pay
his army. 20Yes, I have given him the land of
Egypt as a reward for his work, says the Sovereign LORD, because he was working for
me when he destroyed Tyre.

21"And the day will come when I will
cause the ancient glory of Israel to revive,
and then, Ezekiel, your words will be respected. Then they will know that I am the
LORD."

The Lament for Egypt

30 This is another message that came
to me from the LORD: 2"Son of man,
prophesy and give this message from the
Sovereign LORD:

"Weep and wail
for that day,
3 for the terrible day is almost here—
the day of the LORD!
It is a day of clouds and gloom,
a day of despair for the nations.
4 A sword will come against Egypt,
and those who are slaughtered will
cover the ground.
Its wealth will be carried away
and its foundations destroyed.
The land of Ethiopia will be ravished.
5 Ethiopia, Libya, Lydia, all Arabia,
and all their other allies
will be destroyed in that war.

6 "For this is what the LORD says:
All of Egypt's allies will fall,
and the pride of her power will
end.

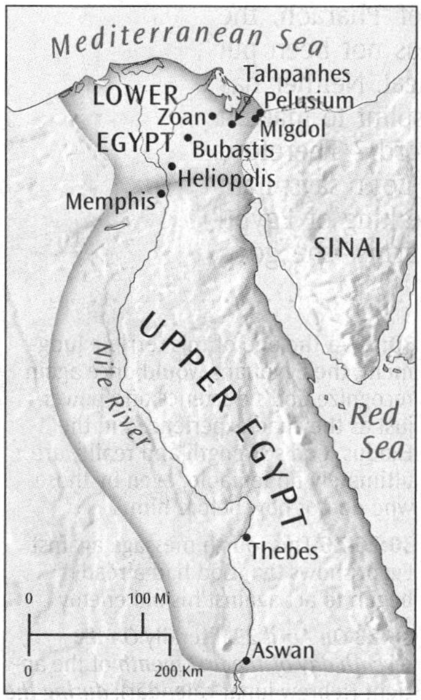

◀ **Egypt's Coming Destruction,** 587–567 BC (29:1–32:32). Ezekiel's messages concerning Egypt's destruction were given between 587 and 571 BC. The Babylonians invaded Egypt, brought destruction, and exiled some of its people in 568–567 BC, but did not retain lasting control.

an unimportant . . . kingdom. Israel would never again be tempted to call on ***Egypt for help*** instead of calling on the Lord. Egypt's restored but reduced position would make it a constant reminder of Israel's past folly in trusting it.

29:17-21 ***on April 26, the first day of the new year:*** Literally *on the first day of the first month* of the ancient Hebrew lunar calendar. This event occurred on April 26, 571 BC; see also note on 1:1. This message, delivered in ***the twenty-seventh year of Jehoiachin's captivity,*** has the latest recorded date of any of Ezekiel's messages, later even than his vision of the Temple in chs 40–48.

29:18-20 Nebuchadnezzar's campaign against Tyre (chs 26–28) had required a great deal of effort on the Babylonians' part for very little return in plunder. But the Lord considers his workers worthy of their hire, so ***to compensate them for all their work,*** he would reward them with ***the land of Egypt.***

29:18 ***Nebuchadnezzar:*** Hebrew *Nebuchadrezzar,* a variant spelling of Nebuchadnezzar; also in 29:19.

29:21 Even in these oracles against the nations, God's primary interest was in his own people. He would match the downward turn in Egypt's fortunes by commensurately reviving Israel. • ***I will cause the ancient glory of Israel to revive:*** Literally *I will cause a horn to sprout for the house of Israel.* A horn was a common symbol of strength and dignity (see Ps 132:17, where "power" represents the same Hebrew word; cp. Dan 7:7-8; 8:3). This restoration of Israel's glory would in turn validate Ezekiel's status as a true prophet, and he would be ***respected*** as he deserved. As a prophet, Ezekiel had fought a hard campaign in the Lord's service and had seen little public reward or recognition from his hearers. In the end, people would see that Ezekiel was indeed a true prophet, something that Nebuchadnezzar's failure to conquer Tyre may have called into question.

30:1-19 This third message against Egypt, using the form of a lament, essentially repeats the content of the first message (29:1-16). Judgment was to be poured out on Egypt and her allies.

30:4 ***Ethiopia:*** Hebrew *Cush;* similarly in 30:9.

30:5 ***Ethiopia, Libya, Lydia, all Arabia:*** Hebrew *Cush, Put, Lud, all Arabia, Cub. Cub* is otherwise unknown and may be another spelling for *Lub* (Libya).

From Migdol to Aswan
they will be slaughtered by the sword,
says the Sovereign LORD.
7 Egypt will be desolate,
surrounded by desolate nations,
and its cities will be in ruins,
surrounded by other ruined cities.
8 And the people of Egypt will know that I
am the LORD
when I have set Egypt on fire
and destroyed all their allies.
9 At that time I will send swift messengers
in ships
to terrify the complacent Ethiopians.
Great panic will come upon them
on that day of Egypt's certain
destruction.
Watch for it!
It is sure to come!

10 "For this is what the Sovereign LORD
says:
By the power of King Nebuchadnezzar
of Babylon,
I will destroy the hordes of Egypt.
11 He and his armies—the most ruthless of
all—
will be sent to demolish the land.
They will make war against Egypt
until slaughtered Egyptians cover the
ground.
12 I will dry up the Nile River
and sell the land to wicked men.
I will destroy the land of Egypt and
everything in it
by the hands of foreigners.
I, the LORD, have spoken!

13 "This is what the Sovereign LORD says:
I will smash the idols of Egypt
and the images at Memphis.
There will be no rulers left in Egypt;
terror will sweep the land.
14 I will destroy southern Egypt,
set fire to Zoan,
and bring judgment against Thebes.
15 I will pour out my fury on Pelusium,
the strongest fortress of Egypt,
and I will stamp out
the hordes of Thebes.
16 Yes, I will set fire to all Egypt!
Pelusium will be racked with pain;
Thebes will be torn apart;
Memphis will live in constant terror.
17 The young men of Heliopolis and
Bubastis will die in battle,
and the women will be taken away as
slaves.
18 When I come to break the proud
strength of Egypt,
it will be a dark day for Tahpanhes,
too.
A dark cloud will cover Tahpanhes,
and its daughters will be led away as
captives.
19 And so I will greatly punish Egypt,
and they will know that I am the
LORD."

The Broken Arms of Pharaoh

20On April 29, during the eleventh year of
King Jehoiachin's captivity, this message
came to me from the LORD: 21"Son of man,
I have broken the arm of Pharaoh, the
king of Egypt. His arm has not been put
in a cast so that it may heal. Neither has
it been bound up with a splint to make it
strong enough to hold a sword. 22Therefore,
this is what the Sovereign LORD says: I am
the enemy of Pharaoh, the king of Egypt!
I will break both of his arms—the good

30:8 Ps 58:11; Amos 1:4, 7, 10-14
30:9 Isa 18:1-2; Ezek 32:9-10; 38:11
30:12 Ezek 29:3, 9
30:13 Isa 2:18; Jer 44:1; 46:14
30:14 Ps 78:12, 43; Isa 19:11, 13
30:17 Gen 41:45
30:18 Lev 26:13; Jer 43:8-13
30:19 Ps 9:16; Ezek 5:8, 15
30:20 Ezek 26:1
30:21 Ps 10:15; 37:17; Jer 30:13; 46:11
30:22 2 Kgs 24:7; Jer 37:7; 46:1-12, 21-25

30:6-7 ***from Migdol to Aswan*** (Hebrew *to Syene*): This means "from north to south." See note on 29:8-13.

30:10 ***Nebuchadnezzar:*** Hebrew *Nebuchadrezzar,* a variant spelling of Nebuchadnezzar.

30:12 ***I will dry up the Nile River:*** Egypt was completely dependent on the Nile for its prosperity, so having the Nile dry up would threaten the Egyptians' livelihoods.

30:13-14 ***idols:*** The Hebrew term (literally *round things*) probably alludes to dung. See note on 6:4-7. • From ***Memphis*** (Hebrew *Noph;* also in 30:16), the most important city in the north, to ***Thebes,*** the most important city in the south, all of the cities of Egypt would be destroyed.

30:14 ***southern Egypt:*** Hebrew *Pathros.* • The location of ***Zoan*** is modern Tanis in the eastern part of the Nile delta, near where the Israelites had once worked as Pharoah's slaves. • ***Thebes*** (Hebrew *No;* also in 30:15, 16) was the sacred city of the god Amon and the capital of Upper Egypt in the south (so called because it was up the Nile River).

30:15 ***Pelusium*** (Hebrew *Sin;* also in 30:16) was a fortress town on the northeastern frontier of Egypt.

30:17 ***of Heliopolis and Bubastis*** (Hebrew *of Awen and Pi-beseth*): These cities were located in the Nile delta. • ***and the women:*** Or *and her cities.*

30:18 ***Tahpanhes*** was a fortress town on the northeastern frontier of Egypt. • ***dark day:*** Egypt would see its light turned to darkness when God came to judge it, as in the Exodus plague (Exod 10:21-23).

30:19 At the end of this terrible judgment, the Egyptians would once again recognize God's existence and power, just as they had experienced in the Exodus. God's strength and reality are ultimately undeniable, even by those who do not bow before him.

30:20-26 This fourth message against Egypt shows that God had already begun to act against his old enemy.

30:20 ***On April 29*** (literally *On the seventh day of the first month* of the ancient Hebrew lunar calendar), ***during the eleventh year of King Jehoiachin's captivity:*** This message was given on Apr 29, 587 BC; see also note on 1:1. Jerusalem was under siege by the Babylonians, but this message rules out even the faintest hope of assistance from the Egyptians.

30:21-23 ***broken the arm of Pharaoh:*** The Lord had already shattered the Egyp-

30:24 Isa 45:1, 5; Zeph 2:12; Zech 10:12
30:25 Josh 8:18; 1 Chr 21:16; Isa 5:25
31:2 Nah 3:8-9
31:4 Ezek 17:5, 8; Rev 17:1, 15
31:5 Ps 1:3
31:6 Ezek 17:23; Dan 4:12, 21; Matt 13:32
31:8 Gen 2:8-9; 13:10; Ps 80:10; Isa 51:3
31:10 2 Chr 32:25; Isa 14:13-14; Dan 5:20
31:11 Deut 18:12; Dan 5:18-19; Nah 3:18
31:12 Dan 4:14

arm along with the broken one—and I will
make his sword clatter to the ground. 23 I
will scatter the Egyptians to many lands
throughout the world. 24 I will strengthen
the arms of Babylon's king and put my
sword in his hand. But I will break the arms
of Pharaoh, king of Egypt, and he will lie
there mortally wounded, groaning in pain.
25 I will strengthen the arms of the king of
Babylon, while the arms of Pharaoh fall useless to his sides. And when I put my sword
in the hand of Babylon's king and he brings
it against the land of Egypt, Egypt will know
that I am the LORD. 26 I will scatter the Egyptians among the nations, dispersing them
throughout the earth. Then they will know
that I am the LORD."

The Fallen Tree: Egypt Compared to Assyria

31 On June 21, during the eleventh year
of King Jehoiachin's captivity, this
message came to me from the LORD: 2 "Son
of man, give this message to Pharaoh, king
of Egypt, and all his hordes:

"To whom would you compare your
greatness?
3 You are like mighty Assyria,
which was once like a cedar of
Lebanon,
with beautiful branches that cast deep
forest shade
and with its top high among the
clouds.
4 Deep springs watered it
and helped it to grow tall and
luxuriant.
The water flowed around it like a river,
streaming to all the trees nearby.
5 This great tree towered high,
higher than all the other trees
around it.
It prospered and grew long thick branches
because of all the water at its roots.
6 The birds nested in its branches,
and in its shade all the wild animals
gave birth.
All the great nations of the world
lived in its shadow.
7 It was strong and beautiful,
with wide-spreading branches,
for its roots went deep
into abundant water.
8 No other cedar in the garden of God
could rival it.
No cypress had branches to equal it;
no plane tree had boughs to compare.
No tree in the garden of God
came close to it in beauty.
9 Because I made this tree so beautiful,
and gave it such magnificent foliage,
it was the envy of all the other trees of
Eden,
the garden of God.

10 "Therefore, this is what the Sovereign
LORD says: Because Egypt became proud
and arrogant, and because it set itself so
high above the others, with its top reaching
to the clouds, 11 I will hand it over to a mighty
nation that will destroy it as its wickedness
deserves. I have already discarded it. 12 A foreign army—the terror of the nations—has
cut it down and left it fallen on the ground.
Its branches are scattered across the mountains and valleys and ravines of the land.
All those who lived in its shadow have gone
away and left it lying there.

tians' strength in the defeat of Pharaoh Hophra by Nebuchadnezzar (see Jer 37:5-11). Had Hophra succeeded in his mission, the pressure on Jerusalem would have been relieved, at least temporarily; now all hope of help from Egypt was gone. There was no prospect that the broken arm would *heal* or even be temporarily *bound up* so that Pharaoh could protect Jerusalem. Egypt would be totally helpless, unable even *to hold a sword* as it awaited the final death thrust.

30:24-26 While disabling Pharaoh (30:22), the Lord would *strengthen the arms of Babylon's king*, increasing the already uneven nature of the contest. The fate of the forthcoming battle of the superpowers rested entirely in the Lord's hands, and he had already determined its outcome. Nebuchadnezzar clashed with the Egyptians on a number of occasions, ending with victory in 567 BC.

31:1-18 Ezekiel called on the Egyptians to compare themselves to Assyria, which was like a great tree in Eden (31:9). If that tree was felled and sent down to the underworld, how did Egypt, whose glory could never compare to Assyria's, think it could stand?

31:1 ***On June 21:*** Literally *On the first day of the third month* of the ancient Hebrew lunar calendar. This event occurred on June 21, 587 BC; see also note on 1:1.

31:2-4 The ***cedar of Lebanon*** is a tree that was known for its visual splendor and commercial and military value. • Like a tree whose crown was ***among the clouds***, Assyria's military had once been strong beyond comparison to any other army.

31:6 Like a great tree, Assyria provided shelter for all of the ***birds*** and ***wild animals*** of the earth. This tree was more splendid than all the trees in the garden of God (that is, the garden of Eden), with a God-given beauty and stature reminiscent of the prince of Tyre in ch 28. Assyria's power was once so great that ***all the great nations of the world lived in its shadow***. Egypt's power was comparable.

31:10-11 ***Egypt*** (literally *you*) forgot that God had created her beauty, and she ***became proud and arrogant***. As with Tyre, such pride would inevitably lead to a fall. The God who set Egypt in such an exalted position would send a divine lumberjack, ***a mighty nation that*** would ***destroy it as its wickedness*** deserved. • ***I have already discarded it:*** The human agent would simply be carrying out God's decree.

31:12-14 Egypt's fate would teach the other nations that however high they set themselves, eventually they were all ***doomed to die*** and go down to ***the pit*** (see note on 26:17-18).

13 "The birds roost on its fallen trunk,
and the wild animals lie among its
branches.
14 Let the tree of no other nation
proudly exult in its own prosperity,
though it be higher than the clouds
and it be watered from the depths.
For all are doomed to die,
to go down to the depths of the earth.
They will land in the pit
along with everyone else on earth.

15 "This is what the Sovereign LORD says:
When Assyria went down to the grave, I
made the deep springs mourn. I stopped
its rivers and dried up its abundant water.
I clothed Lebanon in black and caused
the trees of the field to wilt. 16 I made the
nations shake with fear at the sound of its
fall, for I sent it down to the grave with all
the others who descend to the pit. And all
the other proud trees of Eden, the most
beautiful and the best of Lebanon, the ones
whose roots went deep into the water, took
comfort to find it there with them in the
depths of the earth. 17 Its allies, too, were all
destroyed and had passed away. They had
gone down to the grave—all those nations
that had lived in its shade.

18 "O Egypt, to which of the trees of Eden
will you compare your strength and glory?
You, too, will be brought down to the depths
with all these other nations. You will lie
there among the outcasts who have died by
the sword. This will be the fate of Pharaoh
and all his hordes. I, the Sovereign LORD,
have spoken!"

The Hunted Lion: A Warning for Pharaoh

32 On March 3, during the twelfth year
of King Jehoiachin's captivity, this
message came to me from the LORD: 2 "Son
of man, mourn for Pharaoh, king of Egypt,
and give him this message:

"You think of yourself as a strong young
lion among the nations,
but you are really just a sea monster,
heaving around in your own rivers,
stirring up mud with your feet.
3 Therefore, this is what the Sovereign
LORD says:
I will send many people
to catch you in my net
and haul you out of the water.
4 I will leave you stranded on the land to
die.
All the birds of the heavens will land
on you,
and the wild animals of the whole earth
will gorge themselves on you.
5 I will scatter your flesh on the hills
and fill the valleys with your bones.
6 I will drench the earth with your
gushing blood
all the way to the mountains,
filling the ravines to the brim.
7 When I blot you out,
I will veil the heavens and darken the
stars.
I will cover the sun with a cloud,
and the moon will not give you its
light.
8 I will darken the bright stars overhead
and cover your land in darkness.
I, the Sovereign LORD, have spoken!

9 "I will disturb many hearts when I bring
news of your downfall to distant nations
you have never seen. 10 Yes, I will shock
many lands, and their kings will be terrified
at your fate. They will shudder in fear for
their lives as I brandish my sword before
them on the day of your fall. 11 For this is
what the Sovereign LORD says:

31:13 Isa 18:6; Rev 19:17-18
31:14 Num 16:30-33; Ps 63:9; Jon 2:2, 6; Eph 4:9
31:15 Nah 2:8-10
31:16 Isa 14:8; Hag 2:7
31:17 Ps 9:17; Dan 4:11-12
31:18 Ps 52:7; Jer 9:25-26; Matt 13:19
32:2 Jer 46:7-8; Nah 2:11-13
32:3 Ezek 12:13
32:4 Jer 8:2
32:6 Exod 7:17; Isa 34:3, 7; Rev 14:20
32:7 Prov 13:9; Amos 8:9
32:8 Gen 1:14
32:9 Exod 15:14-16; Rev 18:10-15
32:10 Ezek 26:16; 27:35
32:11 Jer 46:26

31:15 The mourning over the great tree, *Assyria*, matched its great size. • The tallest cedar trees of the ancient world were found in ***Lebanon***. • To be ***clothed . . . in black*** meant wearing garments of mourning. • ***to the grave:*** Hebrew *to Sheol;* also in 31:16-17.

31:16-17 ***The nations*** all shook ***with fear*** at the shock waves created by Assyria's ***fall***. The great nations that had preceded it on the road to destruction and death were gratified to find it joining them in their disgrace, while its allies followed in its dangerous course.

31:18 The point of this extended analogy finally emerges. Although Egypt's ***strength and glory*** were unparalleled, it would be destroyed just as Assyria had been, and it would be disgraced along with the other nations that trusted in themselves and in their own greatness. • ***among the outcasts:*** Literally *among the uncircumcised* (see note on 28:10).

32:1 ***On March 3:*** Literally *On the first day of the twelfth month* of the ancient Hebrew lunar calendar. This event occurred on March 3, 585 BC; see also note on 1:1. This date was two months after the exiles in Babylon received word of Jerusalem's fall (see 33:21).

32:2-3 Ezekiel returns to the image of Pharaoh as a mighty beast (29:3). • Egypt's pharaohs used the ***lion*** and the ***sea monster*** (or ***crocodile***) as images of strength, yet both creatures could be hunted and killed, and that is what would happen to Pharaoh. God, through his agents (32:11-12), would hunt Pharaoh, ***catch*** him, and ***haul*** him in.

32:4-6 ***hills . . . valleys . . . mountains . . . ravines:*** In Hebrew, this literary device (*merism*) indicates both the boundaries and everything within them; here, it portrays the totality of God's judgment. The carnage is described using ***hyperbole*** to communicate the complete destruction of Egypt.

32:7-8 As in the previous chapter, Pharaoh's downfall would be accompanied by global ***darkness*** and widespread mourning. These images were commonly associated with the day of the Lord (cp. Joel 2:30). In this case, the darkness would also remind the Egyptians of the plague on Egypt at the time of the Exodus (Exod 10:21-22).

32:9-10 The surrounding ***nations*** and ***their kings*** would all be ***terrified*** at Egypt's downfall, fearing for their own future.

32:12 Ezek 28:7
32:15 Exod 7:5; 14:4, 18 Ps 83:17-18
32:16 2 Sam 3:33-34 2 Chr 35:25 Jer 9:17
32:18 Jer 1:10 Hos 6:5
32:19 Jer 9:25-26
32:20 Ps 28:3
32:21 Isa 14:9-12 Luke 16:23-24
32:23 Isa 14:15
32:24 Gen 10:22 Job 28:13 Ps 52:5 Jer 49:34-39
32:25 Ps 139:8
32:26 Gen 10:2 Isa 66:19
32:27 Prov 14:32

"The sword of the king of Babylon
 will come against you.
12 I will destroy your hordes with the
 swords of mighty warriors—
 the terror of the nations.
They will shatter the pride of Egypt,
 and all its hordes will be destroyed.
13 I will destroy all your flocks and herds
 that graze beside the streams.
Never again will people or animals
 muddy those waters with their feet.
14 Then I will let the waters of Egypt
 become calm again,
 and they will flow as smoothly as olive
 oil,
 says the Sovereign LORD.
15 And when I destroy Egypt
 and strip you of everything you own
and strike down all your people,
 then you will know that I am the LORD.
16 Yes, this is the funeral song
 they will sing for Egypt.
Let all the nations mourn.
 Let them mourn for Egypt and its
 hordes.
 I, the Sovereign LORD, have spoken!"

Egypt Falls into the Pit

17 On March 17, during the twelfth year, another message came to me from the LORD:
18 "Son of man, weep for the hordes of Egypt
and for the other mighty nations. For I will
send them down to the world below in company with those who descend to the pit.
19 Say to them,

'O Egypt, are you lovelier than the other
 nations?
 No! So go down to the pit and lie there
 among the outcasts.'

20 The Egyptians will fall with the many who
have died by the sword, for the sword is
drawn against them. Egypt and its hordes will
be dragged away to their judgment. 21 Down
in the grave mighty leaders will mockingly
welcome Egypt and its allies, saying, 'They
have come down; they lie among the outcasts, hordes slaughtered by the sword.'

22 "Assyria lies there surrounded by the
graves of its army, those who were slaughtered by the sword. 23 Their graves are in the
depths of the pit, and they are surrounded
by their allies. They struck terror in the
hearts of people everywhere, but now they
have been slaughtered by the sword.

24 "Elam lies there surrounded by the
graves of all its hordes, those who were
slaughtered by the sword. They struck terror in the hearts of people everywhere, but
now they have descended as outcasts to the
world below. Now they lie in the pit and
share the shame of those who have gone
before them. 25 They have a resting place
among the slaughtered, surrounded by the
graves of all their hordes. Yes, they terrorized the nations while they lived, but now
they lie in shame with others in the pit, all of
them outcasts, slaughtered by the sword.

26 "Meshech and Tubal are there, surrounded by the graves of all their hordes.
They once struck terror in the hearts of
people everywhere. But now they are outcasts, all slaughtered by the sword. 27 They
are not buried in honor like their fallen heroes, who went down to the grave with their
weapons—their shields covering their bodies and their swords beneath their heads.
Their guilt rests upon them because they
brought terror to everyone while they were
still alive.

32:11-12 The human agent of God's wrath, the ***sword of the king of Babylon,*** was coming to shatter the power of Egypt once and for all. This would be an even greater destruction than at the time of the first Passover, when only the firstborn humans and animals of Egypt died (Exod 12:29).

32:14 The great sea monster (32:2) would no longer thrash around in the stream, stirring up mud like an irate crocodile. After Pharaoh's demise, the ***waters of Egypt*** would flow again ***as smoothly as olive oil,*** with the untroubled serenity of death.

32:15-16 This total and final devastation of Egypt would result in their recognizing the power of the Lord, just as they did at the time of the Exodus.

32:17-32 This last, climactic message against Egypt sums up the whole series of messages against all of the nations.

32:17 ***On March 17:*** Literally *On the fifteenth day of the month* presumably in the twelfth month of the ancient Hebrew lunar calendar (see 32:1). This would put this message at the end of King Jehoiachin's twelfth year of captivity, on Mar 17, 585 BC; see also note on 1:1. Greek version reads *On the fifteenth day of the first month,* which would put this message on Apr 27, 586 BC, at the beginning of Jehoiachin's twelfth year.

32:18-20 In an earlier message (31:17-18), God had declared that Egypt would go down to join the other nations in the underworld. Here that idea is expanded. Egypt's destination was with the ***outcasts*** (literally *the uncircumcised;* also in 32:21, 24-26, 28-30, 32; see note on 28:10), along with those who fell ***by the sword.*** This place of horror, the ***pit*** (see note on 26:19-21), was already peopled by many nations that once wielded power but had now gone down to destruction (cp. Isa 14:9-11).

32:18 ***for the other mighty nations:*** The meaning of the Hebrew is uncertain.

32:21-30 ***Assyria . . . Elam . . . Meshech and Tubal . . . Edom . . . the princes of the north and the Sidonians:*** These nations that once ***struck terror in the hearts of people everywhere*** were now shadowy figures, spent forces in a world without meaning or joy. Assyria had been conquered by the Babylonians and Medes between 627 and 609 BC and had been removed from its previous status as a superpower.

32:21 ***in the grave:*** Hebrew *in Sheol.*

32:27 ***to the grave:*** Hebrew *to Sheol.* • ***their shields covering their bodies:*** The meaning of the Hebrew is uncertain.

28"You too, Egypt, will lie crushed and broken among the outcasts, all slaughtered by the sword.

29"Edom is there with its kings and princes. Mighty as they were, they also lie among those slaughtered by the sword, with the outcasts who have gone down to the pit.

30"All the princes of the north and the Sidonians are there with others who have died. Once a terror, they have been put to shame. They lie there as outcasts with others who were slaughtered by the sword. They share the shame of all who have descended to the pit.

31"When Pharaoh and his entire army arrive, he will take comfort that he is not alone in having his hordes killed, says the Sovereign LORD. 32Although I have caused his terror to fall upon all the living, Pharaoh and his hordes will lie there among the outcasts who were slaughtered by the sword. I, the Sovereign LORD, have spoken!"

4. ORACLES OF GOOD NEWS (33:1–48:35)

The Turning Point (33:1-33)

Ezekiel as Israel's Watchman

33 Once again a message came to me from the LORD: 2"Son of man, give your people this message: 'When I bring an army against a country, the people of that land choose one of their own to be a watchman. 3When the watchman sees the enemy coming, he sounds the alarm to warn the people. 4Then if those who hear the alarm refuse to take action, it is their own fault if they [g]die. 5They heard the alarm but ignored it, so the responsibility is theirs. If they had listened to the warning, they could have saved their lives. 6But if the watchman sees the enemy coming and doesn't sound the alarm to warn the people, he is responsible for their captivity. They will die in their sins, but I will hold the watchman responsible for their deaths.'

7"Now, son of man, I am making you a watchman for the people of Israel. Therefore, listen to what I say and warn them for me. 8If I announce that some wicked people are sure to die and you fail to tell them to change their ways, then they will die in their sins, and I will hold you responsible for their deaths. 9But if you warn them to repent and they don't repent, they will die in their sins, but you will have saved yourself.

The Watchman's Message

10"Son of man, give the people of Israel this message: You are saying, 'Our sins are heavy upon us; we are wasting away! How can we survive?' 11As surely as I live, says the Sovereign LORD, I take no pleasure in the death of wicked people. I only want them to turn from their wicked ways so they can live. Turn! Turn from your wickedness, O people of Israel! Why should you die?

12"Son of man, give your people this message: The righteous behavior of righteous people will not save them if they turn to sin, nor will the wicked behavior of wicked people destroy them if they repent and turn from their sins. 13When I tell righteous people that they will live, but then they sin, expecting their past righteousness to save them, then none of their righteous acts will be remembered. I will destroy them for their sins. 14And suppose I tell some wicked people that they will surely die, but then they turn from their sins and do what is just and right. 15For instance, they might give back a debtor's security, return what they have

32:29 Isa 34:5-15; Jer 49:7-22; Ezek 25:13
33:3 Neh 4:18-20; Hos 8:1; Joel 2:1
33:4 Jer 6:17; Ezek 18:13; Zech 1:4; Acts 18:6
[g]*dam* (1818) ›Gen 9:4
33:5 Exod 9:19-21, 25; Ps 95:7; Heb 11:7
33:6 Isa 56:10; Ezek 3:18, 20; 34:10
33:7 Isa 62:6-7; Jer 26:2; Acts 5:20
33:8 Ezek 18:4, 13, 18-20
33:9 Ezek 3:19, 21; Acts 13:40-46
33:10 Lev 26:39; Isa 49:14; Ezek 24:23
33:11 Ezek 18:23, 30-32; Hos 11:8; Acts 3:19; 1 Tim 2:4; 2 Pet 3:9
33:12 2 Chr 7:14; Ezek 3:20
33:13 Ezek 18:26; Heb 10:38; 2 Pet 2:20-21
33:14 Isa 55:7; Ezek 18:27; Hos 14:1, 4; Mic 6:8
33:15 Lev 6:4-5; Num 5:6-8; Luke 19:8

32:31-32 Pharaoh and all the power of Egypt will share a similar fate. For the time appointed by God, Pharaoh ***caused his terror to fall upon all the living***, yet when God decided to act, Egypt's power would be broken once and for all.

33:1–48:35 After the oracles of judgment in chs 1–24 and the oracles against the nations in chs 25–32, Ezekiel here describes the future renewal of the land, the covenant, the people, and the unity of Israel and Judah under new leadership.

33:2-4 ***watchman:*** See note on 3:16-19. Here the message about the watchman is part of Ezekiel's public proclamation, not a private commission. It puts more emphasis on the people who hear the watchman's message; they are responsible to ***take action*** in response to it. Just as the people before the destruction of Jerusalem were unwilling to hear the message of destruction, so the people after the Exile could not believe the message of hope. In both cases, in having to face the rejection of what he was saying, Ezekiel was tempted to keep quiet. God warned him again that he could not.

33:5-9 Ezekiel's message encouraged ***the people of Israel*** even now to ***repent*** so that they might live and not ***die***. The Lord had said that he would bring an army against their country, and this was evidently what was now happening. Ezekiel had been faithful to his calling as a watchman; no one who had heard his prophecy thus far could say that he did not ***warn the people*** of the coming judgment. However, the people had not heeded the warning; without a change of heart ***they*** would ***die in their sins***.

33:10-11 ***Our sins are heavy upon us! . . . How can we survive?*** Now that the people of Israel were finally taking the prophet's warnings seriously, there was danger of despair rather than a response of repentance and faith. Unlike deterministic fate, God's judgment leaves room for forgiveness. The sovereign Lord takes ***no pleasure in the death of wicked people***. Even ***wicked people . . . can live*** if they repent and ***turn from*** their ***wickedness.***

33:12-16 The principle stated in 33:10-11 is worked out in two case studies. The first involves ***righteous people*** who trust in their ***past righteousness*** to save them, even though they ***turn to sin***. God will ***destroy*** these people in ***their sins,*** notwithstanding their earlier ***righteous behavior.*** The second case study involves ***wicked people*** who ***repent***

33:16 Isa 1:18; 43:25 Ezek 18:22
33:17 Ezek 18:24-29
33:21 Jer 39:1-2 Ezek 24:1-2, 26
33:22 Ezek 3:26-27; 24:27 Luke 1:64
33:24 Isa 51:1-2 Jer 39:10 Acts 7:5 Rom 4:12-13
33:25 Lev 17:10-14 Deut 12:16, 23 Jer 7:9-10
33:26 Mic 2:1-2 Zeph 3:3
33:27 Isa 2:19 Jer 15:2-4 Ezek 5:12-14
33:28 Jer 44:22 Ezek 6:14; 36:34
33:29 Isa 29:13; 58:2 Ezek 23:33, 35
33:30 Ezek 14:3
33:31 Ps 78:36-37 Isa 29:13 Matt 13:22 Luke 12:15 1 Jn 3:18
33:32 Mark 6:20
33:33 Ezek 2:5; 33:29

stolen, and obey my life-giving laws, no longer doing what is evil. If they do this, then
they will surely live and not die. 16 None of
their past sins will be brought up again, for
they have done what is just and right, and
they will surely live.
17 "Your people are saying, 'The Lord isn't
doing what's right,' but it is they who are not
doing what's right. 18 For again I say, when
righteous people turn away from their righteous behavior and turn to evil, they will die.
19 But if wicked people turn from their wickedness and do what is just and right, they
will live. 20 O people of Israel, you are saying, 'The Lord isn't doing what's right.' But I
judge each of you according to your deeds."

Explanation of Jerusalem's Fall

21 On January 8, during the twelfth year of
our captivity, a survivor from Jerusalem
came to me and said, "The city has fallen!"
22 The previous evening the LORD had taken
hold of me and given me back my voice. So I
was able to speak when this man arrived the
next morning.
23 Then this message came to me from
the LORD: 24 "Son of man, the scattered
remnants of Judah living among the ruined
cities keep saying, 'Abraham was only one
man, yet he gained possession of the entire
land. We are many; surely the land has been
given to us as a possession.' 25 So tell these
people, 'This is what the Sovereign LORD
says: You eat meat with blood in it, you worship idols, and you murder the innocent. Do
you really think the land should be yours?
26 Murderers! Idolaters! Adulterers! Should
the land belong to you?'
27 "Say to them, 'This is what the Sovereign
LORD says: As surely as I live, those living in
the ruins will die by the sword. And I will
send wild animals to eat those living in the
open fields. Those hiding in the forts and
caves will die of disease. 28 I will completely
destroy the land and demolish her pride.
Her arrogant power will come to an end.
The mountains of Israel will be so desolate
that no one will even travel through them.
29 When I have completely destroyed the
land because of their detestable sins, then
they will know that I am the LORD.'
30 "Son of man, your people talk about you
in their houses and whisper about you at the
doors. They say to each other, 'Come on, let's
go hear the prophet tell us what the LORD is
saying!' 31 So my people come pretending to
be sincere and sit before you. They listen to
your words, but they have no intention of
doing what you say. Their mouths are full
of lustful words, and their hearts seek only
after money. 32 You are very entertaining to
them, like someone who sings love songs
with a beautiful voice or plays fine music
on an instrument. They hear what you say,
but they don't act on it! 33 But when all these
terrible things happen to them—as they certainly will—then they will know a prophet
has been among them."

---

of wickedness. Complete forgiveness is available from the Lord. Whatever their past, those who ***turn from their sins and do what is just and right*** will ***live.*** As with the word concerning the watchman, what had been said earlier is revisited. In ch 18, the people said that they were being punished for their parents' sins. Here they were apparently saying that their parents' sins had put the nation under an endless curse, so repentance was useless.

33:17-20 ***The Lord isn't doing what's right:*** The perception was that God's bringing Babylon to destroy Jerusalem was inappropriate. The Lord immediately refuted this argument (33:18). • ***they . . . are not doing what's right:*** The people's fault was in refusing to repent and in accusing God of injustice. • ***I judge each of you according to your deeds:*** The Lord's judgment upon his people is never arbitrary but is a fitting response to their sins. If they repent, trust the Lord for salvation, and ***do what is just and right,*** they have hope for the future (cp. Eph 2:8-10).

33:21 ***On January 8:*** Literally *On the fifth day of the tenth month* of the ancient Hebrew lunar calendar. This event occurred on Jan 8, 585 BC; see also note on 1:1. • A ***survivor*** arrived ***from Jerusalem,*** bringing eyewitness testimony of the city's fall. This news took more than five months to reach the exiles.

33:22 The news of Jerusalem's fall was a turning point for Ezekiel. His ***voice*** returned (see 3:26; 24:25-27), and he was finally able to speak freely. There was new hope for God's people.

33:23-33 Both those in Judah (33:23-29) and those in exile (33:30-33) continued to act as they had before Jerusalem fell.

33:23-26 Those who remained in ***the ruined cities*** of Judah hoped to turn the disaster of the Exile into an opportunity for personal profit rather than repentance. Claiming to be the sole remaining heirs of the promise to ***Abraham,*** they sought ***possession of the entire land.*** By their behavior, they proved that they were not really Abraham's children. They did not follow the laws prohibiting eating meat still containing ***blood*** (see Deut 12:23), they worshiped ***idols*** (the Hebrew term [literally *round things*] probably alludes to dung; see note on 6:4-7), and they murdered ***the innocent.*** The lives of such people were a denial of Abraham's faith, and they would not inherit the promise given him.

33:27-29 The rebels in Jerusalem would continue to inherit the curses of the Mosaic covenant—***the sword, wild animals,*** and ***disease*** (see Lev 26:22-25)—until the ***mountains of Israel*** were ***desolate*** and these sinners were utterly destroyed.

33:30-33 The situation was not significantly better among the exiles in Babylon. Ezekiel's presentations were now the topic of widespread discussion among the exiles, yet their hearts remained as untouched as the hearts of those in Judah. They would ***sit before*** Ezekiel ***pretending to be sincere,*** but with ***no intention of doing what*** the Lord told them. They found his messages entertaining, but the Lord warned them that time would demonstrate the power behind the words of a true ***prophet.***

Oracles of Restoration (34:1–37:28)

The Shepherds of Israel

34 Then this message came to me from the LORD: 2"Son of man, prophesy against the [h]shepherds, the leaders of Israel. Give them this message from the Sovereign LORD: What sorrow awaits you [h]shepherds who feed yourselves instead of your flocks. Shouldn't [h]shepherds feed their sheep? 3You drink the milk, wear the wool, and butcher the best animals, but you let your flocks starve. 4You have not taken care of the weak. You have not tended the sick or bound up the injured. You have not gone looking for those who have wandered away and are lost. Instead, you have ruled them with harshness and cruelty. 5So my sheep have been scattered without a shepherd, and they are easy prey for any wild animal. 6They have wandered through all the mountains and all the hills, across the face of the earth, yet no one has gone to search for them.

7"Therefore, you shepherds, hear the word of the LORD: 8As surely as I live, says the Sovereign LORD, you abandoned my flock and left them to be attacked by every wild animal. And though you were my shepherds, you didn't search for my sheep when they were lost. You took care of yourselves and left the sheep to starve. 9Therefore, you shepherds, hear the word of the LORD. 10This is what the Sovereign LORD says: I now consider these shepherds my enemies, and I will hold them responsible for what has happened to my flock. I will take away their right to feed the flock, and I will stop them from feeding themselves. I will rescue my flock from their mouths; the sheep will no longer be their prey.

The Good Shepherd

11"For this is what the Sovereign LORD says: I myself will search and find my sheep. 12I will be like a shepherd looking for his scattered flock. I will find my sheep and rescue them from all the places where they were scattered on that dark and cloudy day. 13I will bring them back home to their own land of Israel from among the peoples and nations. I will feed them on the mountains of Israel and by the rivers and in all the places where people live. 14Yes, I will give them good pastureland on the high hills of Israel. There they will lie down in pleasant places and feed in the lush pastures of the hills. 15I myself will tend my sheep and give them a place to lie down in peace, says the Sovereign LORD. 16I will search for my lost ones who strayed away, and I will bring them safely home again. I will bandage the injured and strengthen the weak. But I will destroy those who are fat and powerful. I will feed them, yes—feed them justice!

17"And as for you, my flock, this is what the Sovereign LORD says to his people: I will judge between one animal of the flock and another, separating the sheep from the goats. 18Isn't it enough for you to keep the best of the pastures for yourselves? Must you also trample down the rest? Isn't it enough for you to drink clear water for yourselves? Must you also muddy the rest with your feet? 19Why must my flock eat what you have trampled down and drink water you have fouled?

34:2 Jer 10:21; 23:1 / John 10:11; 21:15-17 / [h]*ro'eh* (7462) ‣ Amos 3:12
34:3 Isa 56:11 / Zech 11:5, 16
34:4 Zech 11:15-16 / 1 Pet 5:3
34:5 Jer 10:21; 23:2
34:6 1 Pet 2:25
34:8 Acts 20:29
34:11 John 10:16
34:12 Jer 23:3; 31:10 / Luke 19:10
34:14 Ps 23:2 / John 10:9
34:16 Isa 10:16; 49:26
34:17 Ezek 20:38 / Zech 10:3 / Mal 4:1 / Matt 25:32
34:18 Num 16:9, 13 / 2 Sam 7:19
34:21 Deut 33:17 / Dan 8:4 / Luke 13:14-16
34:22 Ps 72:12-14 / Jer 23:2-3 / Zech 11:7-9
34:23 Isa 40:11 / Jer 23:4-6; 30:9 / John 10:11 / Heb 13:20
34:24 Jer 30:9 / Ezek 37:24-25

34:1–37:28 These chapters show us the blessings that will flow from the Lord's return to his people. He will be their shepherd and provide them with better leadership (ch 34); he will restore the fruitfulness of the land and thus vindicate his own honor (chs 35–36); he will restore his people to life and unity (ch 37).

34:1-24 This chapter contains declarations of judgment and salvation. There will be judgment on the *shepherds* (the former kings of Judah) because they failed to care for their *flocks* (the people of Judah). The Lord will also judge the *fat sheep,* but he will intervene as a good shepherd to feed the remainder of the flock. The image of the *shepherd* perfectly conveys the toughness and tenderness of God's dealings with his people. The shepherd was also a common metaphor for a king in the ancient Near East. The earthly king was understood to represent the divine shepherd who had set him over his people. Shepherds had to protect their flocks against beasts, including lions and bears, while also knowing their sheep by name and tenderly leading them to good pasture and quiet waters. They had to endure cold, heat, wind, rain, and snow out on the hills with their charges. Good kings who led their people strongly and wisely resembled shepherds. The same image is used in the NT to describe pastors and elders, who are to oversee the flock assigned to their care without lording it over them (1 Pet 5:2-4). Jesus perfectly combines toughness and tenderness as the "great Shepherd of the sheep" (Heb 13:20).

34:2-6 ***What sorrow awaits you shepherds:*** Israel's leaders had not ***taken care of the weak*** or gone ***looking for those who*** had ***wandered away and*** were ***lost.*** They had pursued their own interests, feeding themselves at their flock's expense. They ruled the sheep ***with harshness and cruelty,*** recalling how the Egyptians treated the Israelites in Moses' time (Exod 1:13-14). The neglect and abuse of these cruel shepherds had ***scattered*** the Lord's flock ***across the face of the earth.***

34:7-11 The Lord vowed to ***hold*** the self-serving shepherds ***responsible*** for the consequences of their actions. He would remove them from their pastoral office and ***rescue*** his ***flock*** from their clutches so that they were no longer ***their prey.*** The Lord would go looking for his scattered flock (34:12) and bring them home.

34:12-16 The ***dark and cloudy day,*** the day of judgment (cp. note on 32:7-8), was completed. Now God would bring his people back to ***the mountains of Israel,*** the center of the land promised to the Patriarchs, and ***tend*** his ***sheep*** (see Ps 23).

34:17-19 The ***goats*** were the powerful, unrighteous members of the community.

34:25 Isa 11:6-9; Hos 2:18
34:26 Gen 12:2; Deut 28:12; Isa 32:15; 44:3; Zech 8:13; [i]*berakah* (1293) ‣ Mal 3:10
34:27 Lev 26:13; Ps 85:12; Isa 52:2-3
34:28 Jer 30:10; Ezek 39:26
34:29 Isa 60:21; Ezek 36:6, 15, 29
34:30 Ps 46:7, 11; Ezek 36:28; 37:27
34:31 Mic 7:14; John 10:11
35:2 Gen 36:6-8; Ezek 25:12
35:3 Jer 49:13, 17-18; Ezek 25:13
35:4 Ezek 6:6; Mal 1:2-4
35:5 Ezek 7:2; 21:25, 29; 25:12; Obad 1:10
35:6 Ezek 32:6
35:7 Ezek 25:13
35:8 Isa 34:5-6; Ezek 31:12; 32:4-5
35:9 Jer 49:13; Ezek 25:13
35:10 Ps 48:1-3; Ezek 36:2, 5

20“Therefore, this is what the Sovereign LORD says: I will surely judge between the fat sheep and the scrawny sheep. 21For you fat sheep pushed and butted and crowded my sick and hungry flock until you scattered them to distant lands. 22So I will rescue my flock, and they will no longer be abused. I will judge between one animal of the flock and another. 23And I will set over them one shepherd, my servant David. He will feed them and be a shepherd to them. 24And I, the LORD, will be their God, and my servant David will be a prince among my people. I, the LORD, have spoken!

The LORD's Covenant of Peace

25“I will make a covenant of peace with my people and drive away the dangerous animals from the land. Then they will be able to camp safely in the wildest places and sleep in the woods without fear. 26I will [i]bless my people and their homes around my holy hill. And in the proper season I will send the showers they need. There will be showers of [i]blessing. 27The orchards and fields of my people will yield bumper crops, and everyone will live in safety. When I have broken their chains of slavery and rescued them from those who enslaved them, then they will know that I am the LORD. 28They will no longer be prey for other nations, and wild animals will no longer devour them. They will live in safety, and no one will frighten them.

29“And I will make their land famous for its crops, so my people will never again suffer from famines or the insults of foreign nations. 30In this way, they will know that I, the LORD their God, am with them. And they will know that they, the people of Israel, are my people, says the Sovereign LORD. 31You are my flock, the sheep of my pasture. You are my people, and I am your God. I, the Sovereign LORD, have spoken!”

A Message against Edom

35 Again a message came to me from the LORD: 2“Son of man, turn and face Mount Seir, and prophesy against its people. 3Give them this message from the Sovereign LORD:

“I am your enemy, O Mount Seir,
and I will raise my fist against you
to destroy you completely.
4 I will demolish your cities
and make you desolate.
Then you will know that I am the LORD.

5“Your eternal hatred for the people of Israel led you to butcher them when they were helpless, when I had already punished them for all their sins. 6As surely as I live, says the Sovereign LORD, since you show no distaste for blood, I will give you a bloodbath of your own. Your turn has come! 7I will make Mount Seir utterly desolate, killing off all who try to escape and any who return. 8I will fill your mountains with the dead. Your hills, your valleys, and your ravines will be filled with people slaughtered by the sword. 9I will make you desolate forever. Your cities will never be rebuilt. Then you will know that I am the LORD.

10“For you said, ‘The lands of Israel and

34:20-22 ***the fat sheep and the scrawny sheep:*** Those with power and influence in society had taken all the good things for themselves and had left others without resources. God would ***judge between*** them and set things right.

34:23-24 ***one shepherd, my servant David:*** God planned to raise up David's offspring to succeed him (2 Sam 7:12-16). This “new David,” like the first one, would be the Lord's servant, a man after God's own heart, and a good shepherd of his people.

34:25-26 God planned to provide his people with a new and better ruler and to ***make a covenant of peace*** with them. Their present experience of ***dangerous animals***, drought, famine, and sword was the outworking of the curses of the covenant made at Sinai (see Lev 26:14-35). From now on, they would ***camp safely***, experiencing the blessings of that covenant; God would ***send the showers*** they needed for fruitfulness and peace (see Lev 26:4-13).

34:27-31 In this covenant of peace, God's people experience the blessings that flow from wholeness of relationship with God. This covenant was not essentially different from the original covenant concluded at Sinai. It offered the experience of genuine, lasting peace that the Sinai covenant offered but never delivered because of the sin of God's people. In place of the failed kings of the past, they would receive a new and perfect king. In place of the relationship with God that had been repeatedly broken by sin, they would once again be God's ***people, the sheep of*** his ***pasture***. Then they would achieve the goal of the covenant in that ***the Sovereign LORD*** would be their God and once again dwell in their midst.

35:1-15 This oracle is addressed to Edom, Israel's neighbor to the southeast, here personified by its central mountain, ***Mount Seir***. Edom was emblematic of all Israel's enemies (e.g., in their rejoicing at Israel's fall, 36:2; see also 25:12-14). The demise of Judah at the hands of the Babylonians might have given Edom room to thrive, but the Lord declared that this prosperity would be short-lived.

35:5-10 The ***eternal*** [or *ancient*] ***hatred*** of Edom for Israel went all the way back to their respective ancestors, Esau and Jacob (see Gen 25:19-34; 27:1-46; Num 20:14-21; 24:18; 2 Sam 8:13-14; 1 Kgs 11:14). Because of that enmity, the Edomites took advantage of the Babylonian destruction to ***butcher*** the Israelites ***when they were helpless***. They wanted to wipe out the descendants of Jacob and seize ***the lands of Israel and Judah***. The ***bloodbath*** they delighted to inflict on Israel would return on their own heads, as their people would be ***slaughtered by the sword***. Their everlasting hatred would be punished: Their land would become ***desolate forever***. This prophecy was fulfilled when the Edomites were displaced by a coalition of Arab tribes sometime during the 400s BC.

Judah will be ours. We will take possession of them. What do we care that the LORD is there!' [11]Therefore, as surely as I live, says the Sovereign LORD, I will pay back your angry deeds with my own. I will punish you for all your acts of anger, envy, and hatred. And I will make myself known to Israel by what I do to you. [12]Then you will know that I, the LORD, have heard every contemptuous word you spoke against the mountains of Israel. For you said, 'They are desolate; they have been given to us as food to eat!' [13]In saying that, you boasted proudly against me, and I have heard it all!

[14]"This is what the Sovereign LORD says: The whole world will rejoice when I make you desolate. [15]You rejoiced at the desolation of Israel's territory. Now I will rejoice at yours! You will be wiped out, you people of Mount Seir and all who live in Edom! Then you will know that I am the LORD.

Restoration for Israel: A Renewed Land

36 "Son of man, prophesy to Israel's mountains. Give them this message: O mountains of Israel, hear the word of the LORD! [2]This is what the Sovereign LORD says: Your enemies have taunted you, saying, 'Aha! Now the ancient heights belong to us!' [3]Therefore, son of man, give the mountains of Israel this message from the Sovereign LORD: Your enemies have attacked you from all directions, making you the property of many nations and the object of much mocking and slander. [4]Therefore, O mountains of Israel, hear the word of the Sovereign LORD. He speaks to the hills and mountains, ravines and valleys, and to ruined wastes and long-deserted cities that have been destroyed and mocked by the surrounding nations. [5]This is what the Sovereign LORD says: My jealous anger burns against these nations, especially Edom, because they have shown utter contempt for me by gleefully taking my land for themselves as plunder.

[6]"Therefore, prophesy to the hills and mountains, the ravines and valleys of Israel. This is what the Sovereign LORD says: I am furious that you have suffered shame before the surrounding nations. [7]Therefore, this is what the Sovereign LORD says: I have taken a solemn oath that those nations will soon have their own shame to endure.

[8]"But the mountains of Israel will produce heavy crops of fruit for my people—for they will be coming home again soon! [9]See, I care about you, and I will pay attention to you. Your ground will be plowed and your crops planted. [10]I will greatly increase the population of Israel, and the ruined cities will be rebuilt and filled with people. [11]I will increase not only the people, but also your animals. O mountains of Israel, I will bring people to live on you once again. I will make you even more prosperous than you were before. Then you will know that I am the LORD. [12]I will cause my people to walk on you once again, and you will be their territory. You will never again rob them of their children.

[13]"This is what the Sovereign LORD says: The other nations taunt you, saying, 'Israel is a land that devours its own people and robs them of their children!' [14]But you will never again devour your people or rob them of their children, says the Sovereign LORD. [15]I will not let you hear those other nations insult you, and you will no longer be mocked by them. You will not be a land that causes its nation to fall, says the Sovereign LORD."

Restoration for Israel: A Renewed Covenant

[16]Then this further message came to me from the LORD: [17]"Son of man, when the people of Israel were living in their own

35:11 Ps 9:16; 137:7; Ezek 25:14; Amos 1:11
35:12 Jer 50:7; Ezek 36:2
35:13 Isa 10:13-14; Ezek 36:3; Dan 11:36
35:14 Isa 44:23; 49:13; Jer 51:48
35:15 Isa 34:5-6; Lam 4:21; Obad 1:12, 15
36:1 Ezek 6:2-3
36:2 Deut 32:13; Ps 78:69; Isa 58:14; Ezek 35:10; Hab 3:19
36:3 Jer 2:15; 51:34; Ezek 35:13
36:4 Deut 11:11; Ps 79:4; Jer 48:27; Ezek 34:28
36:5 Isa 66:15-16; Jer 50:11; Mic 7:8
36:6 Ps 123:4; Ezek 34:29
36:8 Isa 27:6; Ezek 17:22-23; 34:26-29
36:9 Lev 26:9
36:10 Isa 27:6; 49:17-22; Jer 31:27-28
36:11 Jer 30:18; Ezek 16:55
36:12 Ezek 34:13-14; 47:14
36:13 Num 13:32
36:15 Isa 54:4
36:17 Jer 2:7
36:18 2 Chr 34:21, 25

35:11 ***to Israel:*** Literally *to them;* Greek version reads *to you.*

35:13-15 The Edomites mistakenly assumed that God's judgment of his people and his abandonment of the Temple meant that his covenant with Israel was no longer in effect. The Edomites had boasted and elevated themselves against both Israel and the Lord. The God of Israel would not tolerate such boasting, for he is the sovereign Lord of all. His choice of Israel and his giving them the land would not be revoked.

36:1-15 The destruction of Edom (ch 35) would prepare the way for the restoration of ***the mountains of Israel,*** reversing the devastation threatened in ch 6.

36:2 The ***ancient heights*** of Israel could not be stolen by their ***enemies*** because the Lord had given them to his people.

36:6-7 The period of enduring the ***shame*** of mockery and plundering would now be over for Israel, and Israel's enemies would soon endure ***their own shame*** by being mocked and plundered.

36:8-11 When God's ***people*** returned, ***Israel*** would experience an ***increase*** in ***population*** and fruitfulness, fulfilling the creation mandate of Gen 1:28.

36:12-13 God had intended for the land to provide abundantly for his people and their offspring; instead, it had robbed ***them of their children*** and devoured ***its own people.*** This was the direct result of Israel's failure to keep the terms of the covenant, which led to the Lord's judgment being imposed upon them with catastrophic results for them and their children (see 5:17). Now that the people were being transformed, they would receive the covenant blessing of a fruitful land.

36:16-38 Ezekiel reminded his hearers of their guilt and their need for God to change their hearts. In the future, God planned to cleanse his people. • Objects and people are divided in the OT into

36:19
Deut 28:64
36:20
Isa 52:5
Jer 33:24
*Rom 2:24
36:21
Ps 74:18
36:22
Deut 9:5-7
Ps 106:8
36:23
Ps 126:2
Ezek 20:41; 39:7
36:24
Isa 43:5-6
Ezek 34:13; 37:21
36:25
Zech 13:1
Heb 10:22
36:26
Ezek 11:19
2 Cor 5:17
36:27
Isa 59:21
Ezek 37:14
36:28
Jer 30:22
Ezek 14:11; 37:23, 27
36:29
Ezek 34:27-29
Hos 2:21-23
36:30
Lev 26:4
36:32
Deut 9:5

land, they defiled it by the evil way they lived. To me their conduct was as unclean as a woman's menstrual cloth. [18]They polluted the land with murder and the worship of idols, so I poured out my fury on them. [19]I scattered them to many lands to punish them for the evil way they had lived. [20]But when they were scattered among the nations, they brought shame on my holy name. For the nations said, 'These are the people of the LORD, but he couldn't keep them safe in his own land!' [21]Then I was concerned for my holy name, on which my people brought shame among the nations.

[22]"Therefore, give the people of Israel this message from the Sovereign LORD: I am bringing you back, but not because you deserve it. I am doing it to protect my holy name, on which you brought shame while you were scattered among the nations. [23]I will show how holy my great name is—the name on which you brought shame among the nations. And when I reveal my holiness through you before their very eyes, says the Sovereign LORD, then the nations will know that I am the LORD. [24]For I will gather you up from all the nations and bring you home again to your land.

[25]"Then I will sprinkle clean water on you, and you will be clean. Your filth will be washed away, and you will no longer worship idols. [26]And I will give you a new heart, and I will put a new spirit in you. I will take out your stony, stubborn heart and give you a tender, responsive heart. [27]And I will put my Spirit in you so that you will follow my decrees and be careful to obey my regulations.

[28]"And you will live in Israel, the land I gave your ancestors long ago. You will be my people, and I will be your God. [29]I will cleanse you of your filthy behavior. I will give you good crops of grain, and I will send no more famines on the land. [30]I will give you great harvests from your fruit trees and fields, and never again will the surrounding nations be able to scoff at your land for its famines. [31]Then you will remember your past sins and despise yourselves for all the detestable things you did. [32]But remember, says the Sovereign LORD, I am not doing this because you deserve it. O my people of

the categories of "clean" and "unclean," "sacred" and "profane" (see "Clean and Unclean" at Lev 11:1–15:33, p. 213). God had made Israel clean, while the Gentile nations had remained unclean. Then Israel as a nation became unclean because of their bloodshed and idolatry, which defiled the land. Because they behaved like the unclean nations, Israel's punishment of being scattered among the nations was fitting. In the future, God would make them clean so that he could dwell among them again. The other nations, seeing his holiness in his people, would once again know that he is the Holy One. In the NT, God's redemption through Christ redraws the lines between clean and unclean (see Acts 10:15). The Gentiles are no longer outside of God's grace; they too can receive the Holy Spirit and become clean. Jews and Gentiles together now make up the one people of God in Christ. Those who are in Christ Jesus are not only clean, but also holy by virtue of his priesthood. Therefore, they are able to come boldly into God's presence and experience his grace (Heb 12:18-29).

36:17 Covenant curses had come to Israel because God's people had ***defiled . . . their own land*** by their sinful behavior. • A ***menstrual cloth*** became polluted by contact with a woman's monthly flow of blood. This natural process was not sinful, but it was defiling in the same way that any loss of bodily life-fluids such as blood, sweat (see note on 44:17-19), or semen made people ceremonially unclean (see Lev 15).

36:18 Israel had made ***the land*** unfit for God's presence through ***murder and the worship of idols.*** As a result of their covenant breaking, they were expelled from the land and scattered among the nations (see Deut 29:22-28). • ***idols:*** The Hebrew term (literally *round things*) probably alludes to dung; also in 36:25. See note on 6:4-7.

36:20 This scattering also ***brought shame*** on the Lord's ***holy name.*** It was not so much the behavior of the exiles that robbed the Lord of his glory, but the very fact that they were in exile, insofar as it made the surrounding ***nations*** conclude that Israel's God had been unable to ***keep them safe in his own land.***

36:21-24 Out of concern for his own holiness, God sent Israel into exile. Concern for the honor of his ***holy name*** would lead him to ***gather*** them again to the land. Israel did not ***deserve*** this return from exile; it was simply a manifestation of the Lord's holiness and power in the sight of the nations. Israel could not remain forever outside the land that God had sworn to give to Abraham and his descendants.

36:25 It was not enough to bring Israel back to the land; they would also become a new, transformed Israel. God would ***sprinkle*** them with ***clean water*** to cleanse them from all of the impurities that had defiled the land. Such sprinkling with water was a routine part of Jewish purification ceremonies (see Num 19); it symbolized a fresh start, with their old sins washed away.

36:26 The Lord's renewal of his people was not merely an outward cleansing; the Lord would ***give*** Israel ***a new heart*** and ***a new spirit*** (11:19; 18:31). The heart and spirit are the sources of the thoughts and will that underlie action. Their ***stony, stubborn heart*** would now become ***a tender, responsive heart*** (literally *a heart of flesh*), ready to serve the Lord. The spirit of rebellion would be replaced with a spirit of obedience.

36:27-28 The ***Spirit*** of God would create life and light out of darkness and chaos (cp. Gen 1:2), producing an entirely new ability to follow God's ***decrees and . . . regulations.*** In the past, the Spirit of God had empowered people for specific tasks of service to the Lord (see Judg 3:10; 1 Sam 16:13). In the future, a more widespread empowerment by God's Spirit would enable his people to lead holy lives (see Joel 2:28-29). This renewed people would again ***live in Israel*** and make it fit for God's presence to dwell among them once again.

36:29-32 This transformation would bring the blessings of the covenant made with Moses, not its curses, and a new glory among the surrounding nations. This blessing would cause God's people to be profoundly ***ashamed*** of their past and to appreciate both their lack of merit and God's overwhelming grace.

Israel, you should be utterly ashamed of all
you have done!
33“This is what the Sovereign LORD says:
When I cleanse you from your sins, I will
repopulate your cities, and the ruins will be
rebuilt. 34The fields that used to lie empty
and desolate in plain view of everyone will
again be farmed. 35And when I bring you
back, people will say, ‘This former wasteland
is now like the Garden of Eden! The abandoned and ruined cities now have strong
walls and are filled with people!’ 36Then the
surrounding nations that survive will know
that I, the LORD, have rebuilt the ruins and
replanted the wasteland. For I, the LORD,
have spoken, and I will do what I say.
37“This is what the Sovereign LORD says:
I am ready to hear Israel’s prayers and to
increase their numbers like a flock. 38They
will be as numerous as the sacred flocks
that fill Jerusalem’s streets at the time of her
festivals. The ruined cities will be crowded
with people once more, and everyone will
know that I am the LORD.”

A Valley of Dry Bones: A Renewed People

37 The LORD took hold of me, and I
was carried away by the Spirit of
the LORD to a valley filled with bones. 2He
led me all around among the bones that covered the valley floor. They were scattered
everywhere across the ground and were
completely dried out. 3Then he asked me,
“Son of man, can these bones become living
people again?”
“O Sovereign LORD,” I replied, “you alone
know the answer to that.”
4Then he said to me, “Speak a prophetic
message to these bones and say, ‘Dry bones,
listen to the word of the LORD! 5This is what
the Sovereign LORD says: Look! I am going
to put breath into you and make you live
again! 6I will put flesh and muscles on you
and cover you with skin. I will put breath
into you, and you will come to life. Then you
will know that I am the LORD.’ ”
7So I spoke this message, just as he told
me. Suddenly as I spoke, there was a rat-
tling noise all across the valley. The bones
of each body came together and attached
themselves as complete skeletons. 8Then as
I watched, muscles and flesh formed over
the bones. Then skin formed to cover their
bodies, but they still had no breath in them.
9Then he said to me, “Speak a prophetic
message to the winds, son of man. Speak a
prophetic message and say, ‘This is what the
Sovereign LORD says: Come, O breath, from
the four winds! Breathe into these dead bodies so they may live again.’ ”
10So I spoke the message as he commanded me, and breath came into their
bodies. They all came to life and stood up
on their feet—a great army.
11Then he said to me, “Son of man, these
bones represent the people of Israel. They
are saying, ‘We have become old, dry
bones—all hope is gone. Our nation is finished.’ 12Therefore, prophesy to them and
say, ‘This is what the Sovereign LORD says:
O my people, I will open your graves of exile and cause you to rise again. Then I will
bring you back to the land of Israel. 13When
this happens, O my people, you will know
that I am the LORD. 14I will put my Spirit in
you, and you will live again and return home
to your own land. Then you will know that
I, the LORD, have spoken, and I have done
what I said. Yes, the LORD has spoken!’ ”

36:33 Isa 58:12; Zech 8:7-8
36:35 Isa 51:3
36:36 Hos 14:4-7
36:38 1 Kgs 8:63; 2 Chr 35:7-9
37:1 Jer 7:32–8:2; Ezek 33:22; 40:1; Acts 8:39
37:3 Deut 32:29; 1 Sam 2:6; Isa 26:19
37:4 Isa 42:18
37:5 Ps 104:29-30; John 20:22; Eph 2:5; Rev 11:11
37:6 Joel 2:27; 3:17
37:7 Jer 13:5-7
37:9 Ps 104:30; Hos 13:14
37:10 Jer 30:19; Rev 11:11
37:11 Ps 141:7; Isa 49:14
37:12 Deut 32:39; Isa 26:19; Ezek 36:24; Hos 13:14; Amos 9:14-15
37:14 Ezek 11:19; 36:27; Joel 2:28-29

36:35-38 The restored land would become ***like the Garden of Eden,*** the ultimate symbol of fertility and fruitfulness. The original garden would be enhanced by restored ***cities,*** overflowing with renewed humanity like ***Jerusalem's streets at the time of her festivals.*** The greatest blessing, however, would be God's willingness to ***hear Israel's prayers*** once more. He had once refused to listen to his rebellious people (14:3; 20:3), but now the Lord would turn his face toward them and hear their cries. The proof of this would be the number of people in the rebuilt cities who would acknowledge that the Lord is God.

37:1-14 From the promise of a vibrant city overflowing with life (36:38), the prophet was transported into a valley of death, surrounded on all sides by ***bones.*** It was a symbolic restatement of the promises that the Spirit of the Lord gives life (36:16-38).

37:2 This death scene seemed hopeless; these were not recently expired corpses but miscellaneous bones, ***scattered everywhere across the ground and . . . completely dried out.*** This scene symbolized the attitude of the people. Their hopes for themselves were not merely dead; they were dismembered and desiccated.

37:3 ***Son of man, can these bones become living people again?*** The expected answer was no, but Ezekiel knew that God's power is unlimited, so he turned the question back to God. The real issue was not whether the Lord was able to make these bones live, but whether it was his will to do so.

37:4-6 It was God's will that these bones should live. His will was mediated through the ***prophetic message*** that Ezekiel was to ***speak . . . to these bones,*** declaring that they should be restored into living, breathing bodies again, complete with ***flesh and muscles*** and ***breath.*** • The word translated ***breath*** can also be translated "spirit" or "wind," a play on words that continues throughout this chapter.

37:7-8 Ezekiel obediently fulfilled his commission to prophesy to the bones, and in response, they came together into whole bodies. Yet a body of ***bones, muscles and flesh,*** and ***skin*** is still a corpse. These people still had to be filled with ***breath*** if they were to live (as in Gen 2:7).

37:9-10 When Ezekiel prophesied to ***the four winds, . . . breath*** came into the re-formed bodies and they ***stood up on their feet*** as ***a great army*** prepared for

37:16
1 Kgs 12:16-20
2 Chr 10:17-19

37:17
Isa 11:13
Jer 50:4
Hos 1:11

37:18
Ezek 20:49; 24:19

37:21
Isa 43:5-6
Ezek 39:27

37:22
Isa 11:13
Jer 50:4
Ezek 34:13-14
Hos 1:11
[j]melek (4428)
‣Exod 1:8

37:23
Ezek 11:18
[k]yasha‘ (3467)
‣Zech 8:7

Reunion of Israel and Judah: A Renewed Unity
15Again a message came to me from the LORD:
16"Son of man, take a piece of wood and carve
on it these words: 'This represents Judah and
its allied tribes.' Then take another piece
and carve these words on it: 'This represents
Ephraim and the northern tribes of Israel.'
17Now hold them together in your hand as if
they were one piece of wood. 18When your
people ask you what your actions mean, 19say
to them, 'This is what the Sovereign LORD
says: I will take Ephraim and the northern
tribes and join them to Judah. I will make
them one piece of wood in my hand.'
20"Then hold out the pieces of wood
you have inscribed, so the people can see
them. 21And give them this message from
the Sovereign LORD: I will gather the people of Israel from among the nations. I will
bring them home to their own land from
the places where they have been scattered.
22I will unify them into one nation on the
mountains of Israel. One [j]king will [j]rule
them all; no longer will they be divided into
two nations or into two kingdoms. 23They
will never again pollute themselves with
their idols and vile images and rebellion, for
I will [k]save them from their sinful backsliding. I will cleanse them. Then they will truly
be my people, and I will be their God.

The Promise of New Life (37:1-28)

Ezek 18:31; 39:29
1 Kgs 17:17-24
2 Kgs 4:31-37; 13:20-21
Ps 16:10
Matt 22:31-32
Rom 8:11
2 Cor 5:17

Ezekiel 37 might at first appear to teach that all people will be resurrected from the dead, living again in new bodies after their present bodies die. However, Ezekiel's description here is not the universal resurrection of all flesh. He is not dealing with the general question, "Can human bones return to life?" Ezekiel and his audience were already familiar, from the miracles of Elijah and Elisha, with the possibility of dead people being raised to life (1 Kgs 17:17-24; 2 Kgs 4:31-37; 13:20-21). Instead, Ezekiel is addressing the particular question, "Can *these* bones live?"—that is, could a denuded, dismembered, and desiccated Judah be restored?

At that time, the Babylonians had devastated Judea in 586 BC, the Temple had been destroyed, and most of the people had been exiled to Babylon. The people still in Judah were a mere remnant, only the poorest of the poor (see 2 Kgs 25:8-12). Many concluded that there was no future for God's people. They said, "We have become old, dry bones—all hope is gone. Our nation is finished" (37:11). The question was not whether God *could* raise them to new life, but whether he *would* perform such a miracle for the dry bones that represented Israel.

The prophet answered this question with a resounding *Yes!* God would return his people to life through an outpouring of his Spirit in response to the prophet's word. Their death because of their sins was real, but God would not leave them in the grave (cp. Ps 16:10). Rather, he promised that in the future he would give his people life by his Spirit and would transform them into a new creation, a new Spirit-filled Israel. This new people of God would be raised to their feet as a mighty army that would serve the Lord.

God is capable of raising to life those who are physically dead, and he can restore to life a destroyed community. Similarly, he chooses to give the miracle of new birth to undeserving sinners (see John 3:5-7; Eph 2:1-7). He makes those whom the world would write off as irredeemable acceptable to himself in Christ (1 Cor 6:9-11), and he equips them for fruitful work in his service (Eph 4:12-13; 6:11-18).

action. This breath, emblematic of being filled with the Spirit, gave them life and empowered them for action, precisely as had happened to the prophet on two earlier occasions (1:28–2:2 and 3:23-24).

37:11-14 The oracle that follows explains this vision. The people in exile felt that they were as dead as ***old, dry bones.*** As a result, they felt that ***all hope*** was ***gone,*** but the Lord could and would restore them to life. God would once again call them ***my people,*** and he promised that he would ***open*** their ***graves of exile*** and ***bring*** them ***back to the land of Israel.***

37:14 As well as breath, the Lord would put his life-giving ***Spirit*** within his people. If the sovereign Lord had determined to raise them, no dryness on their part would hold him back.

37:15-28 The prophet then performed a sign act (see "Prophetic Sign Acts" at 4:1-17, p. 1319) that demonstrated the future reunification of God's people and the healing of the schism between the northern and southern tribes (see 1 Kgs 12).

37:16 ***This represents Ephraim and the northern tribes of Israel:*** Literally *This is Ephraim's wood, representing Joseph and all the house of Israel.*

37:19 The sovereign Lord would accomplish the reunification of Israel by his own hand.

37:20-25 When the kingdoms were reunited, the problems that had led to the schism would also be resolved. In place of the abusive and unfaithful leadership of Rehoboam that had split the nation in two (1 Kgs 12), God would supply a single servant leader, a shepherd king. Like ***David,*** he would unite the tribes. This restored people would also be renewed and cleansed from their ***idols and vile images*** so that the Lord might once again ***be their God.*** Thus purified, they would ***keep*** the Lord's ***decrees*** and ***live there forever.***

37:23 ***idols:*** The Hebrew term (literally *round things*) probably alludes to dung. See note on 6:4-7.

24“My servant David will be their king,
and they will have only one shepherd. They
will obey my regulations and be careful to
keep my decrees. 25They will live in the
land I gave my servant Jacob, the land where
their ancestors lived. They and their children and their grandchildren after them
will live there forever, generation after generation. And my servant David will be their
prince forever. 26And I will make a [a]cov-
enant of peace with them, an everlasting
[a]covenant. I will give them their land and
increase their numbers, and I will put my
Temple among them forever. 27I will make
my home among them. I will be their God,
and they will be my people. 28And when my
Temple is among them forever, the nations
will know that I am the LORD, who makes
Israel holy.”

The Final Test (38:1–39:29)
A Message against Gog

38 This is another message that came
to me from the LORD: 2“Son of man,
turn and face Gog of the land of Magog,
the prince who rules over the nations of
Meshech and Tubal, and prophesy against
him. 3Give him this message from the Sovereign LORD: Gog, I am your enemy! 4I will
turn you around and put hooks in your jaws
to lead you out with your whole army—your
horses and charioteers in full armor and a
great horde armed with shields and swords.
5Persia, Ethiopia, and Libya will join you,
too, with all their weapons. 6Gomer and all
its armies will also join you, along with the
armies of Beth-togarmah from the distant
north, and many others.

7“Get ready; be prepared! Keep all the
armies around you mobilized, and take
command of them. 8A long time from
now you will be called into action. In the
distant future you will swoop down on the
land of Israel, which will be enjoying peace
after recovering from war and after its
people have returned from many lands to
the mountains of Israel. 9You and all your
allies—a vast and awesome army—will roll
down on them like a storm and cover the
land like a cloud.

37:24 Jer 30:21; Hos 3:5
37:25 Isa 11:1
37:26 Jer 30:19; Heb 13:20; [a]*berith* (1285) ‣Hos 2:18
37:27 Lev 26:11; *2 Cor 6:16
37:28 Exod 31:13; Zeph 3:15
38:2 Ezek 39:1; Rev 20:8-9
38:4 Isa 43:17; Ezek 39:2; Dan 11:40
38:5 Gen 10:6-7; Ezek 27:10; 30:4-5
38:6 Gen 10:2-3; Ezek 27:14
38:8 Isa 11:11; Ezek 34:13
38:9 Isa 5:28; Jer 4:13; Joel 2:2

37:25-28 The *covenant of peace,* which is the blessing of covenant obedience, will be *everlasting.* The people’s earlier defilement had led to the Lord’s destruction of the Temple; now, their new purity would be matched by a renewed sanctuary, a *Temple* in which God could dwell in their midst forever. This final Temple will be the culmination of the success of God’s sanctifying program and demonstrate that the Lord is the one *who makes Israel holy.* Cp. chs 40–48; see “Temple Architecture as Theology” at 40:1–43:27, p. 1373.

37:26 ***I will give them their land and increase their numbers:*** Hebrew reads *I will give them and increase their numbers;* Greek version lacks the entire phrase.

38:1–39:29 The idyllic scene in ch 37 of the reunited nation living at peace in its own land gives way to gathering storm clouds in chs 38–39, a two-panel depiction of the assault, defeat, and disposal of the last enemy, *Gog.* Readers have long sought to identify Gog, who has sometimes been identified with Gyges, king of Lydia (about 680~644 BC). The biblical Gog, however, transcends historical categories; the text is less concerned with Gog’s identity than with the universal threat caused by the nations of the world. Yet even such an overwhelming force would be no serious threat to the restored people of God, for God was now dwelling in their midst. The symbolism of these chapters has much in common with psalms of Zion’s security (see, e.g., Pss 2, 46). If even a fearsome foe such as Gog could not separate God’s people from his protection, then surely nothing in all creation could do so. • Ezekiel’s account of Gog belongs to the genre of *apocalyptic* literature (see also Daniel Introduction, “Daniel as Apocalyptic Literature,” p. 1391; Zechariah Introduction, “Literary Genre,” p. 1526). Apocalyptic is different in style and focus from other types of prophetic literature. For the prophetic oracle, the words are the central focus, while for apocalyptic literature the vision is the key. Whereas the prophet delivering an oracle is like the prosecuting counsel, the writer of apocalyptic is acting as a witness, describing the heavenly realities that he has seen. Prophecy frequently looks toward salvation or judgment within the boundaries of this present world. Apocalyptic, by contrast, looks for a fulfillment that transcends space and time. The good news of apocalyptic is that in spite of present depressing appearances, the decisive battle has already taken place in heaven, and the forces of light have won—God reigns, and his kingdom will ultimately triumph. This news comforts the faithful during the present times of suffering and difficulty, but also exhorts them to continue being faithful, no matter what the opposition. Whatever the cost in terms of suffering, obedience is the only way to live while we look forward with hope to our final vindication when God acts decisively to bring in his new age of salvation.

38:1-6 Gog would lead a coalition of seven nations from the four corners of the world. The numbers seven and four both symbolize completeness (see note on 1:5-9); here, they indicate an invincible alliance coming from far and near in all directions, from which there would be no escape. ***Magog, Meshech and Tubal, Gomer,*** and ***Beth-togarmah*** were located in the north, in Anatolia and the region beyond the Black Sea. ***Persia*** was to the east, ***Ethiopia*** to the south, and ***Libya*** to the west.

38:4 Gog’s rebellion would be under God’s complete control. Though they would regard themselves as free-willed aggressors, they would actually be prisoners with ***hooks*** in their ***jaws*** (cp. 29:4).

38:5 ***Persia, Ethiopia, and Libya:*** Hebrew *Paras, Cush, and Put.*

38:8 ***A long time from now*** (literally *after many days*) . . . ***In the distant future*** (literally *in the end of the years*): This encounter is described as a climactic final battle that will precede a final state of peace. There are a variety of views as to whether this final battle is a literal event at the end of history or a literary depiction of the Lord’s protection of his permanently embattled people. Either way, the point remains that when the Lord’s favor rests upon his people, no one and nothing can separate them from that protection, even the most all-out assault of evil.

38:9 ***roll down on them like a storm:*** This is reminiscent of the threatening imagery of ch 1, when God was Israel’s enemy. At that time, Israel looked to the surrounding rebellious nations for protection; this time, Israel would look to God for protection from the nations.

38:10 Ps 36:4; Mic 2:1
38:11 Isa 37:24-25; Zech 2:4-5
38:12 Isa 10:6; Ezek 29:19
38:13 Isa 10:5-7
38:14 Jer 23:5-6; Zech 2:5, 8
38:16 Ezek 36:23
38:17 Isa 5:26-30; 34:1-6
38:18 Ps 18:7-8
38:19 Ezek 36:5-6; Joel 3:16; Hag 2:6-7; Heb 12:26-29
38:20 Jer 4:24; Nah 1:5-6; Zech 14:4-5
38:21 Judg 7:22; 2 Chr 20:23; Hag 2:22
38:22 Ps 11:6; Zech 14:12-15; Rev 16:21
38:23 Ps 9:16; Ezek 36:23
39:1 Ezek 38:2-4
39:2 Ezek 38:15
39:3 Ps 46:9; 76:3; Jer 21:4-5; Ezek 30:21-24; Hos 1:5
39:4 Isa 14:24-25; Ezek 29:5; 32:4-5
39:6 Jer 25:22; Ezek 30:8, 16; 38:22; Amos 1:4-7; Nah 1:6

10“This is what the Sovereign Lord says: At that time evil thoughts will come to your mind, and you will devise a wicked scheme. 11You will say, ‘Israel is an unprotected land filled with unwalled villages! I will march against her and destroy these people who live in such confidence! 12I will go to those formerly desolate cities that are now filled with people who have returned from exile in many nations. I will capture vast amounts of plunder, for the people are rich with livestock and other possessions now. They think the whole world revolves around them!’ 13But Sheba and Dedan and the merchants of Tarshish will ask, ‘Do you really think the armies you have gathered can rob them of silver and gold? Do you think you can drive away their livestock and seize their goods and carry off plunder?’

14“Therefore, son of man, prophesy against Gog. Give him this message from the Sovereign Lord: When my people are living in peace in their land, then you will rouse yourself. 15You will come from your homeland in the distant north with your vast cavalry and your mighty army, 16and you will attack my people Israel, covering their land like a cloud. At that time in the distant future, I will bring you against my land as everyone watches, and my holiness will be displayed by what happens to you, Gog. Then all the nations will know that I am the Lord.

17“This is what the Sovereign Lord asks: Are you the one I was talking about long ago, when I announced through Israel’s prophets that in the future I would bring you against my people? 18But this is what the Sovereign Lord says: When Gog invades the land of Israel, my fury will boil over! 19In my jealousy and blazing anger, I promise a mighty shaking in the land of Israel on that day. 20All living things—the fish in the sea, the birds of the sky, the animals of the field, the small animals that scurry along the ground, and all the people on earth—will quake in terror at my presence. Mountains will be thrown down; cliffs will crumble; walls will fall to the earth. 21I will summon the sword against you on all the hills of Israel, says the Sovereign Lord. Your men will turn their swords against each other. 22I will punish you and your armies with disease and bloodshed; I will send torrential rain, hailstones, fire, and burning sulfur! 23In this way, I will show my greatness and holiness, and I will make myself known to all the nations of the world. Then they will know that I am the Lord.

The Slaughter of Gog’s Hordes

39 “Son of man, prophesy against Gog. Give him this message from the Sovereign Lord: I am your enemy, O Gog, ruler of the nations of Meshech and Tubal. 2I will turn you around and drive you toward the mountains of Israel, bringing you from the distant north. 3I will knock the bow from your left hand and the arrows from your right hand, and I will leave you helpless. 4You and your army and your allies will all die on the mountains. I will feed you to the vultures and wild animals. 5You will fall in the open fields, for I have spoken, says the Sovereign Lord. 6And I will rain down fire on Magog and on all your allies who live safely on the coasts. Then they will know that I am the Lord.

38:10 The Lord’s “hook” in Gog’s “jaw” (38:4) would consist of Gog’s own ***wicked scheme*** to destroy the defenseless and unsuspecting Israelites and capture their plunder (cp. Ps 76:10).

38:13 The merchant nations of the world, from ***Sheba*** and ***Dedan*** in the east to ***Tarshish*** in the west, would line up to market the booty from the apparently sure victory of Gog and his allies.

38:14-16 Israel would be rich, ***living in peace*** and experiencing the fruit of obedient trust in the Lord. However, such obedience does not eliminate the possibility of threatening circumstances (cp. John 16:33). The odds might have seemed stacked against Israel, but Gog had failed to reckon with ***the Lord***. The Lord would use Gog and his allies as a tool for displaying his ***holiness*** in the sight of ***all the nations***.

38:14 ***then you will rouse yourself:*** As in Greek version; Hebrew reads *then you will know.*

38:17 Gog was not the prophesied “enemy from the north” of Jer 4–6 that God ***was talking about long ago***. Those prophecies had already found their fulfillment in the devastation that King Nebuchadnezzar of Babylon had wreaked on Judah.

38:18-20 Instead of being the agent of divine wrath, Gog would be subject to it. The Lord would vent on Gog the ***jealousy and blazing anger*** he had earlier visited on Israel. The scene would be so frightening that even innocent bystanders would ***quake in terror***. The earth would also tremble, destroying ***mountains, cliffs,*** and ***walls***.

38:21-23 ***The sword . . . disease and bloodshed . . . torrential rain, hailstones, fire, and burning sulfur!*** Israel had experienced similar punishments before (see 13:13); now they were executed on Israel’s enemies. The Divine Warrior was once again defending his people.

39:2 ***I will turn you around and drive you:*** The Lord would be ***bringing*** Gog against Israel in order to break him (see note on 38:4). • ***distant north:*** See note on 1:4.

39:3-4 This fearsome foe, Gog, would be left ***helpless;*** his corpse would be food for ***the vultures and wild animals***, like another Goliath (cp. 1 Sam 17:44-46).

39:5-6 Gog’s homeland would be devastated, and the destruction they had planned for the people who ***live safely*** would return upon their own heads.

7“In this way, I will make known my holy name among my people of Israel. I will not let anyone bring shame on it. And the nations, too, will know that I am the LORD, the Holy One of Israel. 8That day of judgment will come, says the Sovereign LORD. Everything will happen just as I have declared it.

9“Then the people in the towns of Israel will go out and pick up your small and large shields, bows and arrows, javelins and spears, and they will use them for fuel. There will be enough to last them seven years! 10They won’t need to cut wood from the fields or forests, for these weapons will give them all the fuel they need. They will plunder those who planned to plunder them, and they will rob those who planned to rob them, says the Sovereign LORD.

11“And I will make a vast graveyard for Gog and his hordes in the Valley of the Travelers, east of the Dead Sea. It will block the way of those who travel there, and they will change the name of the place to the Valley of Gog’s Hordes. 12It will take seven months for the people of Israel to bury the bodies and cleanse the land. 13Everyone in Israel will help, for it will be a glorious victory for Israel when I demonstrate my glory on that day, says the Sovereign LORD.

14“After seven months, teams of men will be appointed to search the land for skeletons to bury, so the land will be made clean again. 15Whenever bones are found, a marker will be set up so the burial crews will take them to be buried in the Valley of Gog’s Hordes. 16(There will be a town there named Hamonah, which means ‘horde.’) And so the land will finally be cleansed.

17“And now, son of man, this is what the Sovereign LORD says: Call all the birds and wild animals. Say to them: Gather together for my great sacrificial feast. Come from far and near to the mountains of Israel, and there eat flesh and drink blood! 18Eat the flesh of mighty men and drink the blood of princes as though they were rams, lambs, goats, and bulls—all fattened animals from Bashan! 19Gorge yourselves with flesh until you are glutted; drink blood until you are drunk. This is the sacrificial feast I have prepared for you. 20Feast at my banquet table—feast on horses and charioteers, on mighty men and all kinds of valiant warriors, says the Sovereign LORD.

21“In this way, I will demonstrate my glory to the nations. Everyone will see the punishment I have inflicted on them and the power of my fist when I strike. 22And from that time on the people of Israel will know that I am the LORD their God. 23The nations will then know why Israel was sent away to exile—it was punishment for sin, for they were unfaithful to their God. Therefore, I turned away from them and let their enemies destroy them. 24I turned my face away and punished them because of their defilement and their sins.

Restoration for God’s People

25“So now, this is what the Sovereign LORD says: I will end the captivity of my people; I will have mercy on all Israel, for I jealously guard my holy reputation! 26They will

39:7
Exod 20:7
Ezek 20:39

39:9
Ps 46:9

39:10
Isa 14:2
Mic 5:8
Hab 2:8

39:13
Jer 33:9
Ezek 28:22
Zeph 3:19-20

39:17
Isa 34:6-7
Jer 46:10
Zeph 1:7
Rev 19:17-18

39:18
Deut 32:14
Ps 22:12
Jer 51:40
Amos 4:1

39:20
Ps 76:5-6
Ezek 38:4
Hag 2:22
Rev 19:18

39:21
Exod 9:16
Ezek 38:16, 23

39:23
Isa 59:2
Ezek 36:18-19; 39:29

39:24
2 Kgs 17:7
Jer 2:17, 19; 4:18
Ezek 36:19

39:25
Jer 33:7
Ezek 34:13; 36:10
Hos 1:11

39:26
Ezek 34:25-28
Mic 4:4

39:7-8 God’s judgment on Gog would ***make known*** his ***holy name.*** Just as he once judged his own people for their sins for the sake of his reputation (36:16-20), now he would defend his restored people and judge their enemies.

39:9-10 Israel would be called upon to act only after Gog had been completely defeated and destroyed. As in some of their great battles in the past, Israel would be able to watch the Lord act and then pick up the spoils (e.g., 2 Kgs 6–7; 2 Chr 20). Ironically, the only items to survive the fire from heaven that destroyed Gog’s army would be wooden weaponry that would now be ***fuel*** for Israel’s fires for ***seven years,*** a number that often represents completeness in the OT. Those who came to plunder would become plunder. Their weapons would be unnecessary now that Israel’s last enemy had been destroyed.

39:11 The people would need to gather the plunder and bury the bodies of the slain soldiers. These corpses would otherwise defile the holy land, for contact with a corpse made a person ritually unclean. There were so many of these corpses that a ***vast graveyard*** would be required, big enough to fill an entire valley that would now be known as ***the Valley of Gog’s Hordes.* • *the Dead Sea:*** Literally *the sea.*

39:12-16 The body count would be so large that ***everyone in Israel*** would be involved in the clean-up process for ***seven months.*** Even after that initial period, there would be a continuing need for teams of professional morticians to go through the land, tagging remains so that they could be properly disposed of.

39:17 God would also provide his own disposal team of birds and wild animals, which he would ***gather*** for his ***great sacrificial feast.***

39:18-20 In most sacrificial feasts, humans dined on slaughtered animals. This feast would allow animals to dine on slaughtered humans ***as though they were rams, lambs, goats, and bulls.*** This reversal of the great messianic banquet (Isa 25:6) features the enemies of God as the menu rather than as the invited guests.

39:21-24 The Lord ***will demonstrate*** his ***glory*** in all of history. He did so through the ***punishment*** of Israel during their exile ***because of their defilement and their sins.***

39:25-29 God would also demonstrate his glory through his people’s return ***home*** from exile in ***the lands of their enemies.*** Once God had exhausted his wrath upon them for their sins, he would bring them ***home again*** and ***leave none of*** them ***behind.*** He would ***pour out*** his ***Spirit upon the people of Israel,*** transforming them in order to prevent a recurrence of their former situation. He would never again turn his face from them. His future favor on his people was assured (cp. Rom 8:31-39).

39:25 ***of my people:*** Literally *of Jacob.*

39:26 ***They will accept responsibility for:*** A few Hebrew manuscripts read *They will forget.*

39:27 Ezek 28:25-26; 37:21
39:29 Isa 32:15; Ezek 36:27; 37:14; Joel 2:28-29; Acts 2:17
40:1 2 Kgs 25:1-7; Jer 39:1-9
40:2 Ps 48:2; Ezek 20:40; Mic 4:1; Rev 21:10
40:3 Dan 10:5-6; Zech 2:1-2; Rev 11:1; 21:15
40:4 Jer 26:2; Ezek 43:10; 44:5; Acts 20:27
40:5 Ezek 42:20
40:6 Ezek 8:16; 11:1; 43:1
40:7 1 Kgs 6:5-10; 2 Chr 31:11; Jer 35:4; Ezek 40:29, 33, 36

accept responsibility for their past shame
and unfaithfulness after they come home
to live in peace in their own land, with no
one to bother them. 27When I bring them
home from the lands of their enemies, I
will display my holiness among them for
all the nations to see. 28Then my people
will know that I am the LORD their God, because I sent them away to exile and brought
them home again. I will leave none of my
people behind. 29And I will never again
turn my face from them, for I will pour out
my Spirit upon the people of Israel. I, the
Sovereign LORD, have spoken!"

The Renewed Temple and Land (40:1–48:35)

The New Temple Area

40 On April 28, during the twenty-
fifth year of our captivity—fourteen
years after the fall of Jerusalem—the LORD
took hold of me. 2In a vision from God he
took me to the land of Israel and set me
down on a very high mountain. From there
I could see toward the south what appeared
to be a city. 3As he brought me nearer, I
saw a man whose face shone like bronze
standing beside a gateway entrance. He was
holding in his hand a linen measuring cord
and a measuring rod.
4He said to me, "Son of man, watch and
listen. Pay close attention to everything I
show you. You have been brought here so
I can show you many things. Then you will
return to the people of Israel and tell them
everything you have seen."

The East Gateway

5I could see a wall completely surrounding
the Temple area. The man took a measuring
rod that was 10½ feet long and measured
the wall, and the wall was 10½ feet thick
and 10½ feet high.
6Then he went over to the eastern gateway. He climbed the steps and measured
the threshold of the gateway; it was 10½ feet
front to back. 7There were guard alcoves on
each side built into the gateway passage.
Each of these alcoves was 10½ feet square,
with a distance between them of 8¾ feet
along the passage wall. The gateway's inner
threshold, which led to the entry room at the
inner end of the gateway passage, was 10½
feet front to back. 8He also measured the
entry room of the gateway. 9It was 14 feet
across, with supporting columns 3½ feet

40:1–48:35 The final section of Ezekiel focuses on the new Temple (40:1–47:12; see "Temple Architecture as Theology" at 40:1–43:27, p. 1373; "Temple Legislation as Theology" at 44:1–46:18, p. 1379) and on reallotment of the land (47:13–48:35; see "Israel's Geography as Theology" at 47:13–48:35, p. 1386). The Temple at the center of the land was the capstone of God's program of restoring and sanctifying his people so that he could once again dwell in their midst (see 37:28). This Temple, which Ezekiel saw in a vision, was never actually constructed.

40:1–46:24 The prophet's tour of the new Temple proceeded from the outside of the Temple into its center. From the inside, he then returned outwards, ending up at the kitchens in the corners of the outer courtyard (46:19-24).

40:1 ***On April 28:*** Literally *At the beginning of the year, on the tenth day of the month* of the ancient Hebrew lunar calendar. This event occurred on April 28, 573 BC; see also note on 1:1. • ***twenty-fifth year:*** On the tenth day of the seventh month in a Jubilee year (the fiftieth year), trumpets were sounded to announce liberty throughout the land (Lev 25:8-13). This vision of a liberated future therefore took place halfway to the Jubilee, a natural time for looking ahead to the release already announced by the Lord through his prophet.

40:2 ***a very high mountain:*** Revelations from God often took place on mountaintops in the OT. Moses received God's law and the design for the Tabernacle at Mount Sinai (Exod 19–40), and he viewed the Promised Land that he would never enter from Pisgah Peak (Deut 34:1-4). So also on this mountaintop, Ezekiel met with God and saw the wonderful future that God had prepared for his people, even though he would not live to experience it.

40:3 ***a man whose face shone like bronze:*** An angelic guide would host Ezekiel's tour of the Temple. The bronze color is reminiscent of the heavenly creatures described in the opening vision (see 1:7). Unlike the guide for his previous visionary tour of the earthly Temple in chs 8–11, this guide was armed only with ***a linen measuring cord and a measuring rod,*** implements of construction rather than destruction. Measurement is a key theme in the chapters that follow, enabling the prophet to highlight the importance of certain parts of the Temple by making them larger and more precisely determined than other parts.

40:5-16 The exact architectural details of the Temple are difficult to translate, but the overall impression of these gates was unmistakable. They were fortress-like constructions, designed to keep out unauthorized intruders. The ***eastern gateway*** is described first since it was the most important. It lay on the sacred east–west axis of the Temple along which the entire construction was oriented, and it was the gate through which the glory of the Lord would finally return (43:1-5).

40:5 ***a wall completely surrounding the Temple area:*** Walls regulate and define space, marking an "inside" and an "outside." This wall was substantial; its function was to separate the "profane" area outside the Temple from the holy area inside so that this crucial distinction would never again be blurred (see 22:26). • ***10½ feet:*** Hebrew *6 long cubits* [3.2 meters], *each being a cubit* [18 inches or 45 centimeters] *and a handbreadth* [3 inches or 8 centimeters] *in length.* • ***10½ feet:*** Hebrew *1 rod* [3.2 meters]; also in 40:7.

40:6 ***10½ feet front to back:*** As in Greek version, which reads *1 rod* [3.2 meters] *deep;* Hebrew reads *1 rod deep, and 1 threshold, 1 rod deep.*

40:7 Six ***guard alcoves*** lined the inside of the gates, three on each side, confirming their defensive significance. These gates were similar in layout to those excavated at Hazor, Megiddo, and Gezer, but substantially larger in size. • ***8¾ feet:*** Hebrew *5 cubits* [2.7 meters]; also in 40:48.

40:8-9 At the end of 40:8, many Hebrew manuscripts add *which faced inward toward the Temple; it was 1 rod* [10.5 feet or 3.2 meters] *deep.* 9*Then he measured the entry room of the gateway.*

40:9 ***14 feet:*** Hebrew *8 cubits* [4.2 meters]. • ***3½ feet:*** Hebrew *2 cubits* [1.1 meters].

thick. This entry room was at the inner end of the gateway structure, facing toward the Temple.

10There were three guard alcoves on each side of the gateway passage. Each had the same measurements, and the dividing walls separating them were also identical. 11The man measured the gateway entrance, which was 17½ feet wide at the opening and 22¾ feet wide in the gateway passage. 12In front of each of the guard alcoves was a 21-inch curb. The alcoves themselves were 10½ feet on each side.

13Then he measured the entire width of the gateway, measuring the distance between the back walls of facing guard alcoves; this distance was 43¾ feet. 14He measured the dividing walls all along the inside of the gateway up to the entry room of the gateway; this distance was 105 feet. 15The full length of the gateway passage was 87½ feet from one end to the other. 16There were recessed windows that narrowed inward through the walls of the guard alcoves and their dividing walls. There were also windows in the entry room. The surfaces of the dividing walls were decorated with carved palm trees.

The Outer Courtyard

17Then the man brought me through the gateway into the outer courtyard of the Temple. A stone pavement ran along the walls of the courtyard, and thirty rooms were built against the walls, opening onto the pavement. 18This pavement flanked the gates and extended out from the walls into the courtyard the same distance as the gateway entrance. This was the lower pavement. 19Then the man measured across the Temple's outer courtyard between the outer and inner gateways; the distance was 175 feet.

The North Gateway

20The man measured the gateway on the north just like the one on the east. 21Here, too, there were three guard alcoves on each side, with dividing walls and an entry room. All the measurements matched those of the east gateway. The gateway passage was 87½ feet long and 43¾ feet wide between the back walls of facing guard alcoves. 22The windows, the entry room, and the palm tree decorations were identical to those in the east gateway. There were seven steps leading up to the gateway entrance, and the entry room was at the inner end of the gateway passage. 23Here on the north side, just as on the east, there was another gateway leading to the Temple's inner courtyard directly opposite this outer gateway. The distance between the two gateways was 175 feet.

The South Gateway

24Then the man took me around to the south gateway and measured its various parts, and they were exactly the same as in the others. 25It had windows along the walls as the others did, and there was an entry room where the gateway passage opened into the outer courtyard. And like the others, the gateway passage was 87½ feet long and 43¾ feet wide between the back walls of facing guard alcoves. 26This gateway also had a stairway of seven steps leading up to it, and an entry room at the inner end, and palm tree decorations along the dividing walls. 27And here again, directly opposite the outer gateway, was another gateway that led into the inner courtyard. The distance between the two gateways was 175 feet.

Gateways to the Inner Courtyard

28Then the man took me to the south gateway leading into the inner courtyard. He

40:14
Exod 27:9
1 Chr 28:6
Ps 100:4
Isa 62:9
Ezek 42:1

40:16
1 Kgs 6:4
Ezek 41:26

40:17
1 Chr 9:26
2 Chr 31:11
Ezek 46:21
Rev 11:2

40:22
1 Kgs 6:29-35; 7:36
2 Chr 3:5
Rev 7:9

40:23
Exod 27:9-18; 38:9-12

40:24
Ezek 46:9

40:11 *17½ feet:* Hebrew *10 cubits* [5.3 meters]. • *22¾ feet:* Hebrew *13 cubits* [6.9 meters].

40:12 *21-inch:* Hebrew *1-cubit* [53-centimeter]. • *10½ feet:* Hebrew *6 cubits* [3.2 meters].

40:13 *43¾ feet:* Hebrew *25 cubits* [13.3 meters]; also in 40:21, 25, 29, 30, 33, 36.

40:14 *105 feet:* Hebrew *60 cubits* [31.8 meters]. Greek version reads *20 cubits* [35 feet or 10.6 meters]. The meaning of the Hebrew in this verse is uncertain.

40:15 *87½ feet:* Hebrew *50 cubits* [26.5 meters]; also in 40:21, 25, 29, 33, 36.

40:16 The ***carved palm trees*** recall the rich fertility of the Garden of Eden (see also 1 Kgs 6:29).

40:17-19 The ***outer courtyard*** provided a buffer zone around the holy things in the inner courtyard, and ***thirty rooms*** were built around the walls. The purpose of these rooms is not stated, nor are their dimensions precisely given, which heightens the contrast between the relatively less significant outer area of the Temple and the crucially important central holy space. These rooms were most likely to be used by the Levites for a variety of activities.

40:19 *175 feet:* Hebrew *100 cubits* [53 meters]; also in 40:23, 27, 47.

40:20-27 The ***gateway on the north*** and the ***south gateway*** are described in similar terms, though in less detail than the east gateway. They were also a formidable defensive barrier against the intrusion of any defilement. There is no west gateway to the outer or the inner court because the area behind the Temple proper was blocked off to prevent access from the rear.

40:22 The ***steps*** that led up to each gate heightened the sense of their inaccessibility. The inner, more sacred areas of the Temple were significantly higher in elevation than the outer parts, which provided another dimension of separation.

40:28-34 The ***inner courtyard*** was separated from the outer courtyard by another series of substantial ***gateways***, similar in scale and function to the gateways of the outer courtyard. These gateways had entry rooms facing out-

40:35
Ezek 44:4; 47:2

40:38
1 Kgs 6:8
1 Chr 28:12
2 Chr 4:6
Neh 13:5, 9
Ezek 41:10; 42:13

measured it, and it had the same measurements as the other gateways.
29Its guard alcoves, dividing walls, and entry room were the same size as those in the others. It also had windows along its walls and in the entry room. And like the others, the gateway passage was 87½ feet long and 43¾ feet wide.
30(The entry rooms of the gateways leading into the inner courtyard were 14 feet across and 43¾ feet wide.)
31The entry room to the south gateway faced into the outer courtyard. It had palm tree decorations on its columns, and there were eight steps leading to its entrance.

32Then he took me to the east gateway leading to the inner courtyard. He measured it, and it had the same measurements as the other gateways.
33Its guard alcoves, dividing walls, and entry room were the same size as those of the others, and there were windows along the walls and in the entry room. The gateway passage measured 87½ feet long and 43¾ feet wide.
34Its entry room faced into the outer courtyard. It had palm tree decorations on its columns, and there were eight steps leading to its entrance.

35Then he took me around to the north gateway leading to the inner courtyard. He measured it, and it had the same measurements as the other gateways.
36The guard alcoves, dividing walls, and entry room of this gateway had the same measurements as in the others and the same window arrangements. The gateway passage measured 87½ feet long and 43¾ feet wide.
37Its entry room faced into the outer courtyard, and it had palm tree decorations on the columns. There were eight steps leading to its entrance.

Rooms for Preparing Sacrifices

38A door led from the entry room of one of the inner gateways into a side room, where

Temple Architecture as Theology (40:1–43:27)

Ezek 22:26
Exod 25:10–40:33
Lev 10:9-11
John 2:19
1 Cor 6:15-20
Heb 9:22–10:19
1 Pet 1:13-16
Rev 21:1-27

The Temple plan given in this passage does not seem physically buildable, nor was it intended to be. The details given in the plan are not sufficient to guide construction, as may be seen from varying diagrams created by scholars. The materials to be used are not specified, as they were in great detail for the Tabernacle (Exod 25:10–40:33). Neither is there evidence that any attempt was later made to build the Second Temple according to this plan. Ezekiel's plan for the Temple is evidently not a blueprint for future construction.

Instead, Ezekiel's Temple vision is a theological statement in the form of an architectural plan. Its message is intended to shame Ezekiel's generation for their past and motivate them to be faithful in the future (43:10-11). The vision describes a new world in which boundaries between the holy and the unholy are established and standards are raised, so that God may return to his Temple to dwell among his people once again (see 10:3-4, 18; 11:22-23). Access to the realm of the holy is considerably restricted. Those who were faithful in the past are granted renewed access, while those who had been unfaithful are marginalized. There is a deepened interest in the sacrifices of atonement and purification for the people.

This new Temple finds its fulfillment in Jesus, in whom God's glory is revealed. His body was the temple that was to be torn down in a final cataclysmic cleansing (John 2:19), and then he was raised from the dead. In Jesus, the light of God's holiness shone out clearly in the darkness, and the darkness was not able to extinguish it (John 1:5). His body was the perfect, once-for-all sacrifice that purified his people (Heb 10:12). Those who are in Christ now have the privilege of access through him to the heavenly Most Holy Place, the new Jerusalem. Its doors stand permanently open to those who have washed their robes and made them clean in the blood of the Lamb (see Rev 21).

Since we have been united to Christ and have become part of his body, the new temple, how can we live any longer as we once did? The Holy Spirit dwells in us, and our bodies no longer belong to ourselves but to him as parts of his new temple (1 Cor 6:15-20). A holy life is the mark of God's children (1 Pet 1:13-16).

ward toward the outer courtyard, rather than inward as at the outer gates.

40:30 *14 feet:* As in 40:9, which reads *8 cubits* [14 feet or 4.2 meters]; here the Hebrew reads *5 cubits* [8¾ feet or 2.7 meters]. Some Hebrew manuscripts and the Greek version lack this entire verse.

40:35-37 There is no mention of a wall around the inner courtyard, perhaps because it was elevated from the outer court by another ***eight steps***, perhaps a total of eight feet. If there were no wall around the inner court, there would be a freestanding archway that provided a clear view of activities in the inner area without any likelihood of accidental trespass into the realm of the sacred. Alternatively, reference to a wall around the inner court may simply have been omitted.

40:38-43 The ***sacrificial animals*** were ***slaughtered*** and ***prepared*** in rooms

the meat for sacrifices was washed. 39On each side of this entry room were two tables, where the sacrificial animals were slaughtered for the burnt offerings, sin offerings, and guilt offerings. 40Outside the entry room, on each side of the stairs going up to the north entrance, were two more tables. 41So there were eight tables in all—four inside and four outside—where the sacrifices were cut up and prepared. 42There were also four tables of finished stone for preparation of the burnt offerings, each 31½ inches square and 21 inches high. On these tables were placed the butchering knives and other implements for slaughtering the sacrificial animals. 43There were hooks, each 3 inches long, fastened to the foyer walls. The sacrificial meat was laid on the tables.

Rooms for the Priests

44Inside the inner courtyard were two rooms, one beside the north gateway, facing south, and the other beside the south gateway, facing north. 45And the man said to me, "The room beside the north inner gate is for the priests who supervise the Temple maintenance. 46The room beside the south inner gate is for the priests in charge of the altar—the descendants of Zadok—for they alone of all the Levites may approach the LORD to minister to him."

The Inner Courtyard and Temple

47Then the man measured the inner courtyard, and it was a square, 175 feet wide and 175 feet across. The altar stood in the courtyard in front of the Temple. 48Then he brought me to the entry room of the Temple. He measured the walls on either side of the opening to the entry room, and they were 8¾ feet thick. The entrance itself was 24½ feet wide, and the walls on each side of the entrance were an additional 5¼ feet long. 49The entry room was 35 feet wide and 21 feet deep. There were ten steps leading up to it, with a column on each side.

41 After that, the man brought me into the sanctuary of the Temple. He measured the walls on either side of its doorway, and they were 10½ feet thick. 2The doorway was 17½ feet wide, and the walls on each side of it were 8¾ feet long. The sanctuary itself was 70 feet long and 35 feet wide.

3Then he went beyond the sanctuary into the inner room. He measured the walls on either side of its entrance, and they were 3½ feet thick. The entrance was 10½ feet

40:39 Lev 1:2-17; 4:2-3; 5:6; 6:6; 7:1-2; Ezek 46:2
40:42 Exod 20:25
40:44 1 Chr 6:31-32; 16:41-43; 25:1-7
40:45 Lev 8:35; 1 Chr 9:23
40:46 1 Kgs 2:35; Ezek 43:19; 48:11
40:48 1 Kgs 6:3
40:49 Jer 52:17-23; Rev 3:12
41:1 Ezek 40:2-3, 17
41:2 1 Kgs 6:2, 17; 2 Chr 3:3

---

beside the gateways into the inner courtyards. This detail highlights the primary function of this new Temple as a place of sacrifice. The animals had to be washed and cut into pieces before they could be offered on the altar. • This new Temple in Ezekiel's vision was radically focused on sacrifices that atoned for sin. By contrast, the Temple in Jerusalem was both a center for sacrifice and a house for prayer (see 1 Kgs 8:27-30, 52-53; Isa 56:6-8; Matt 21:13).

40:42 ***31½ inches square and 21 inches high:*** Hebrew *1½ cubits* [80 centimeters] *long and 1½ cubits wide and 1 cubit* [53 centimeters] *high.*

40:43 The ***hooks*** might be used to store the knives and implements mentioned in 40:42. • ***3 inches:*** Hebrew *a handbreadth* [8 centimeters].

40:44 ***rooms:*** As in Greek version; Hebrew reads *rooms for singers.* • ***south:*** As in Greek version; Hebrew reads *east.*

40:46 The Lord at last rewarded the loyalty of ***Zadok*** (see 44:15) by decreeing that his ***descendants*** were the only ones permitted to ***approach the LORD to minister to him.*** Access to God in this Temple was restricted to those whom the Lord had chosen and who were fit to enter the holy space.

40:47 The themes of sacrifice and restricted access coalesce in the summary of the dimensions of the ***inner courtyard.*** It was a perfect ***square,*** the shape of holy spaces throughout the OT (see Exod 26:1-35; 1 Kgs 6:20). ***175 feet*** (100 cubits; see note on 40:19) on each side. Meanwhile, at its geometric center stood the ***altar*** of sacrifice, the only piece of furniture located in that space (the position of the altar is implied by the positions of the other items). Holy sacrifices had to be offered without threat of defilement to ensure the continuing presence of the Lord once he returned to fill the Temple with his glory.

40:48–41:3 ***The Temple*** was at the protected center of the Temple complex, adjacent to the inner court. It was located at the highest point of the complex, a further ***ten steps*** up from the inner court, which was itself eight steps above the outer court. Like Solomon's Temple before it, the Temple was made up of three areas: the ***entry room, the sanctuary,*** and the ***Most Holy Place.***

40:48 ***The entrance itself . . . 5¼ feet long:*** As in Greek version, which reads *The entrance was 14 cubits* [7.4 meters] *wide, and the walls of the entrance were 3 cubits* [1.6 meters] *on each side;* Hebrew lacks *14 cubits wide, and the walls of the entrance were.*

40:49 Outside the entry room were square (see 41:21) columns of unspecified function, just as in Solomon's Temple (1 Kgs 7:15-22). • ***35 feet:*** Hebrew *20 cubits* [10.6 meters]. • ***21 feet:*** As in Greek version, which reads *12 cubits* [21 feet or 6.4 meters]; Hebrew reads *11 cubits* [19¼ feet or 5.8 meters].

41:1-2 The Temple ***walls*** were ***10½ feet thick,*** but here the gates could be replaced by a ***doorway*** because only the priests would have access to the surrounding inner court. The sanctuary was the most important space in the new Temple, so it is described in the most detail and with the most precise measurements. • ***10½ feet:*** Hebrew *6 cubits* [3.2 meters]; also in 41:3, 5.

41:2 ***17½ feet:*** Hebrew *10 cubits* [5.3 meters]. • ***8¾ feet:*** Hebrew *5 cubits* [2.7 meters]; also in 41:9, 11. • ***70 feet long and 35 feet wide:*** Hebrew *40 cubits* [21.2 meters] *long and 20 cubits* [10.6 meters] *wide.*

41:3-4 The ***inner room*** was the ***Most Holy Place,*** the only square space within the Temple. It was reached by passing through three openings of decreasing width—access was increasingly restricted as one approached God. The entrance to the entry room was 24½ feet wide (40:48), and the doorway into the sanctuary was 17½ feet wide (41:2), but the entrance to the Most Holy Place was only 10½ feet wide. Ezekiel did not enter the Most Holy Place, but waited

41:4 Exod 26:33-34; 1 Kgs 6:20; 2 Chr 3:8; Heb 9:3-8
41:5 1 Kgs 6:5
41:6 1 Kgs 6:6, 10
41:7 1 Kgs 6:8
41:8 Ezek 40:5
41:10 Ezek 40:17
41:12 Ezek 42:1; Rev 21:27; 22:14-15
41:13 Ezek 40:47
41:15 Ezek 42:1, 10, 13
41:16 1 Kgs 6:4, 15
41:18 1 Kgs 6:29; 7:36; 2 Chr 3:5; Ezek 10:18
41:19 Ezek 1:10; 10:14
41:22 Exod 30:1-3, 8; Ezek 44:16; Mal 1:7, 12; Rev 8:3
41:23 1 Kgs 6:31-35
41:24 1 Kgs 6:34
41:26 Ezek 40:7-12

wide, and the walls on each side of the
entrance were 12¼ feet long. 4The inner
room of the sanctuary was 35 feet long and
35 feet wide. "This," he told me, "is the Most
Holy Place."

5Then he measured the wall of the Temple,
and it was 10½ feet thick. There was a row of
rooms along the outside wall; each room was
7 feet wide. 6These side rooms were built in
three levels, one above the other, with thirty
rooms on each level. The supports for these
side rooms rested on exterior ledges on the
Temple wall; they did not extend into the
wall. 7Each level was wider than the one below it, corresponding to the narrowing of
the Temple wall as it rose higher. A stairway
led up from the bottom level through the
middle level to the top level.

8I saw that the Temple was built on a terrace, which provided a foundation for the
side rooms. This terrace was 10½ feet high.
9The outer wall of the Temple's side rooms
was 8¾ feet thick. This left an open area
between these side rooms 10and the row
of rooms along the outer wall of the inner
courtyard. This open area was 35 feet wide,
and it went all the way around the Temple.
11Two doors opened from the side rooms
into the terrace yard, which was 8¾ feet
wide. One door faced north and the other
south.

12A large building stood on the west, facing the Temple courtyard. It was 122½ feet
wide and 157½ feet long, and its walls were
8¾ feet thick. 13Then the man measured
the Temple, and it was 175 feet long. The
courtyard around the building, including
its walls, was an additional 175 feet in
length. 14The inner courtyard to the east of
the Temple was also 175 feet wide. 15The
building to the west, including its two walls,
was also 175 feet wide.

The sanctuary, the inner room, and the
entry room of the Temple 16were all paneled with wood, as were the frames of the
recessed windows. The inner walls of the
Temple were paneled with wood above
and below the windows. 17The space above
the door leading into the inner room, and
its walls inside and out, were also paneled.
18All the walls were decorated with carvings of cherubim, each with two faces, and
there was a carving of a palm tree between
each of the cherubim. 19One face—that of a
man—looked toward the palm tree on one
side. The other face—that of a young lion—
looked toward the palm tree on the other
side. The figures were carved all along the
inside of the Temple, 20from the floor to the
top of the walls, including the outer wall of
the sanctuary.

21There were square columns at the entrance to the sanctuary, and the ones at the
entrance of the Most Holy Place were similar.
22There was an altar made of wood, 5¼ feet
high and 3½ feet across. Its corners, base,
and sides were all made of wood. "This," the
man told me, "is the table that stands in the
LORD's presence."

23Both the sanctuary and the Most Holy
Place had double doorways, 24each with
two swinging doors. 25The doors leading
into the sanctuary were decorated with
carved cherubim and palm trees, just as on
the walls. And there was a wooden roof at
the front of the entry room to the Temple.
26On both sides of the entry room were
recessed windows decorated with carved
palm trees. The side rooms along the outside wall also had roofs.

---

outside while the angel went in alone and measured it.

41:3 ***3½ feet:*** Hebrew *2 cubits* [1.1 meters]. • ***12¼ feet:*** Hebrew *7 cubits* [3.7 meters].

41:4 ***35 feet:*** Hebrew *20 cubits* [10.6 meters]; also in 41:4b, 10.

41:5-26 Around the Temple building were ninety ***side rooms*** on three levels. To the rear was a ***large building*** of unspecified purpose that might have protected the back of the Temple from unauthorized access. No one was permitted to approach God's presence from behind. The side rooms might have been designed to store priestly clothing and equipment.

41:5 ***7 feet:*** Hebrew *4 cubits* [2.1 meters].

41:8 ***10½ feet:*** Hebrew *1 rod, 6 cubits* [3.2 meters].

41:12 ***122½ feet wide and 157½ feet long . . . 8¾ feet thick:*** Hebrew *70 cubits* [37.1 meters] *wide and 90 cubits* [47.7 meters] *long, and its walls were 5 cubits* [2.7 meters] *thick.*

41:13 ***175 feet:*** Hebrew *100 cubits* [53 meters]; also in 41:13b, 14, 15.

41:15-20 The Temple building was ***all paneled with wood*** and decorated with palm trees and ***cherubim.*** The cherubim were like those described in Ezekiel's earlier visions of judgment (see 1:5-12; 10:2-14). But where those real-life cherubim had four faces, the carved two-dimensional models are depicted with only two faces—that of a lion, the highest of the wild animals, and a human, the pinnacle of the created order. Cherubim also adorned Solomon's Temple (1 Kgs 6:32); they were traditional symbols of judgment that complemented the palm trees, traditional symbols of blessing.

41:22 The only piece of furniture was an ***altar made of wood, the table that stands in the LORD's presence.*** This is presumably where the bread of the presence was daily laid out by the priests before the Lord (Exod 25:30). The description of this table as an altar highlights the focus on sacrifice in Ezekiel's Temple (see note on 40:38-43). • ***5¼ feet high and 3½ feet across:*** Hebrew *3 cubits* [1.6 meters] *high and 2 cubits* [1.1 meters] *across.*

Rooms for the Priests

42 Then the man led me out of the Temple courtyard by way of the north
gateway. We entered the outer courtyard
and came to a group of rooms against the
north wall of the inner courtyard. 2This
structure, whose entrance opened toward
the north, was 175 feet long and 87½ feet
wide. 3One block of rooms overlooked the
35-foot width of the inner courtyard. Another block of rooms looked out onto the
pavement of the outer courtyard. The two
blocks were built three levels high and
stood across from each other. 4Between
the two blocks of rooms ran a walkway 17½
feet wide. It extended the entire 175 feet of
the complex, and all the doors faced north.
5Each of the two upper levels of rooms was
narrower than the one beneath it because
the upper levels had to allow space for walk-
ways in front of them. 6Since there were
three levels and they did not have supporting columns as in the courtyards, each of
the upper levels was set back from the level
beneath it. 7There was an outer wall that separated the rooms from the outer courtyard;
it was 87½ feet long. 8This wall added length
to the outer block of rooms, which extended
for only 87½ feet, while the inner block—the
rooms toward the Temple—extended for
175 feet. 9There was an eastern entrance
from the outer courtyard to these rooms.
10On the south side of the Temple there
were two blocks of rooms just south of the
inner courtyard between the Temple and
the outer courtyard. These rooms were
arranged just like the rooms on the north.
11There was a walkway between the two
blocks of rooms just like the complex on
the north side of the Temple. This complex
of rooms was the same length and width as
the other one, and it had the same entrances
and doors. The dimensions of each were
identical. 12So there was an entrance in the
wall facing the doors of the inner block of
rooms, and another on the east at the end of
the interior walkway.
13Then the man told me, "These rooms
that overlook the Temple from the north
and south are holy. Here the priests who offer sacrifices to the LORD will eat the most
holy offerings. And because these rooms
are holy, they will be used to store the sacred offerings—the grain offerings, sin
offerings, and guilt offerings. 14When the
priests leave the sanctuary, they must not go
directly to the outer courtyard. They must
first take off the clothes they wore while
ministering, because these clothes are holy.
They must put on other clothes before entering the parts of the building complex open
to the public."
15When the man had finished measuring
the inside of the Temple area, he led me out
through the east gateway to measure the entire perimeter. 16He measured the east side
with his measuring rod, and it was 875 feet
long. 17Then he measured the north side,
and it was also 875 feet. 18The south side
was also 875 feet, 19and the west side was
also 875 feet. 20So the area was 875 feet on
each side with a wall all around it to separate what was holy from what was common.

The LORD's Glory Returns

43 After this, the man brought me
back around to the east gateway.
2Suddenly, the glory of the God of Israel
appeared from the east. The sound of his
coming was like the roar of rushing waters,

42:1 Ezek 40:2-3, 17; 41:9, 12-15
42:2 Ezek 41:13
42:3 Ezek 40:17; 41:10
42:4 Ezek 46:19
42:6 Ezek 41:6
42:7 Ezek 41:13-14
42:9 Ezek 44:5; 46:19
42:13 Lev 6:25, 29; 7:6; 10:13-17; Num 18:9-10
42:14 Exod 29:4-9; Isa 61:10; Zech 3:4-5
42:15 Ezek 43:1
42:16 Ezek 40:3, 5
43:1 Ezek 10:19; 40:6; 44:1; 46:1
43:2 Isa 6:3; Ezek 10:4, 18-19; 11:23; Rev 1:15; 18:1

42:1 Having reached the center of the Temple complex, Ezekiel began traveling outward again.

42:2 *175 feet:* Hebrew *100 cubits* [53 meters]; also in 42:8. • *87½ feet:* Hebrew *50 cubits* [26.5 meters]; also in 42:7, 8.

42:3-12 The rooms for the priests at the sides of the building to the rear of the sanctuary were ***three levels high*** so that the priests could enter at the top from the inner court (42:12) and emerge at the bottom in the outer court (42:9). These rooms were boundary spaces for activities that the priests had to perform on the way into and out of the inner court.

42:3 *35-foot:* Hebrew *20-cubit* [10.6-meter].

42:4 *17½ feet:* Hebrew *10 cubits* [5.3 meters]. • ***It extended the entire 175 feet of the complex:*** As in Greek and Syriac versions, which read *Its length was 100 cubits* [53 meters]; Hebrew reads *and a passage 1 cubit* [18 inches or 53 centimeters] *wide.*

42:10 *south:* As in Greek version; Hebrew reads *east.*

42:13-14 The priests would ***store the sacred offerings*** and ***eat the most holy offerings*** in these rooms. The ***clothes*** that the priests wore while ministering in the Lord's presence would be stored there, and the priests would ***put on other clothes . . . because these clothes were holy.*** All of these regulations represent a significant increase in the care taken to separate the holy from the profane, as compared to the similar laws in Leviticus (cp. Lev 6).

42:16-20 Having finished his tour of the inner courtyard, Ezekiel was shown the overall dimensions of the area. The whole complex was square, which denoted holiness (see note on 40:47) and differentiated it from the less regular design of Solomon's Temple and the Tabernacle before it, in which only the Most Holy Place was square. • The description of the Temple finished where it began, with a mention of ***a wall all around it*** (see 40:5); Ezekiel reminds us again that the purpose of that wall was ***to separate what was holy from what was common.***

42:16 *875 feet long:* As in 45:2 and in Greek version at 42:17, which reads *500 cubits* [265 meters]; Hebrew reads *500 rods* [5,250 feet or 1,590 meters]; similarly in 42:17, 18, 19, 20.

43:1-4 The sacred spaces described in the previous chapter were of no value

43:3
Jer 1:10
Ezek 3:23
43:4
Ezek 44:2
43:5
1 Kgs 8:10-11
2 Cor 12:2-4
43:6
Ezek 1:26; 40:3
43:7
Lev 26:30
Ps 47:8
Jer 16:18
Ezek 6:5; 37:26-28
43:8
Ezek 8:3
43:9
Ezek 18:30, 31
43:10
Ezek 40:4
43:11
Ezek 11:20; 12:3; 36:27; 44:5
43:12
Ezek 40:2
43:13
Exod 27:1-8
2 Chr 4:1
43:14
Ezek 45:19
43:15
Exod 27:2
Lev 9:9
1 Kgs 1:49-50
Ps 118:27
43:16
Exod 27:1
43:17
Exod 20:26
Ezek 40:6

and the whole landscape shone with his
glory. 3This vision was just like the others I
had seen, first by the Kebar River and then
when he came to destroy Jerusalem. I fell
face down on the ground. 4And the glory of
the LORD came into the Temple through the
east gateway.
5Then the Spirit took me up and brought
me into the inner courtyard, and the glory
of the LORD filled the Temple. 6And I heard
someone speaking to me from within the
Temple, while the man who had been measuring stood beside me. 7The LORD said
to me, "Son of man, this is the place of my
throne and the place where I will rest my
feet. I will live here forever among the people of Israel. They and their kings will not
defile my holy name any longer by their
adulterous worship of other gods or by
honoring the relics of their kings who have
died. 8They put their idol altars right next
to mine with only a wall between them and
me. They defiled my holy name by such
detestable sin, so I consumed them in my
anger. 9Now let them stop worshiping other
gods and honoring the relics of their kings,
and I will live among them forever.
10"Son of man, describe to the people of
Israel the Temple I have shown you, so they
will be ashamed of all their sins. Let them
study its plan, 11and they will be ashamed
of what they have done. Describe to them
all the specifications of the Temple—including its entrances and exits—and everything
else about it. Tell them about its decrees and
laws. Write down all these specifications
and decrees as they watch so they will be
sure to remember and follow them. 12And
this is the basic law of the Temple: absolute
holiness! The entire top of the mountain
where the Temple is built is holy. Yes, this is
the basic law of the Temple.

The Altar

13"These are the measurements of the altar: There is a gutter all around the altar
21 inches deep and 21 inches wide, with a
curb 9 inches wide around its edge. And this
is the height of the altar: 14From the gutter
the altar rises 3½ feet to a lower ledge that
surrounds the altar and is 21 inches wide.
From the lower ledge the altar rises 7 feet
to the upper ledge that is also 21 inches
wide. 15The top of the altar, the hearth, rises
another 7 feet higher, with a horn rising up
from each of the four corners. 16The top
of the altar is square, measuring 21 feet
by 21 feet. 17The upper ledge also forms

as long as they were empty (cp. 37:7-8). To be effective, the Temple must be occupied by ***the glory of the God of Israel,*** which had departed from it in ch 10. Now the glory would return in the same direction from which it had left, ***from the east.*** Unlike its slow, almost reluctant, departure, its return would be sudden, accompanied by the terrifying ***roar of rushing waters*** (see 1:24; Rev 1:15). As always, the prophet ***fell face down on the ground*** in response to this glory.

43:5-7a ***The Spirit*** then carried Ezekiel ***into the inner courtyard*** so that he could hear the Lord declare that the restored Temple was the palace in which his ***throne*** and his footstool were located, and that he would ***live . . . forever among the people of Israel.*** The identification of the Temple as God's dwelling and the seat of his sovereignty was not new (see, e.g., 1 Sam 4:4). The Temple would now be God's throne ***forever;*** never again would the sins of his people drive him away from his sanctuary.

43:7b-9 If God were to remain with his people, standards would have to be raised and regulations enforced that would guard against the repetition of past abuses. Israel ***and their kings*** would ***not defile*** God's ***holy name*** by their spiritual adultery with other gods or with ***relics of their kings who had died***—memorial markers to dead kings—within the grounds of the Temple of the living God. There was no place for honoring human kings in the palace of the divine King. In the future, the proper hierarchy would be reestablished by removing the residence of the earthly ruler to a greater distance from the spiritual center of the land (see 45:7). Putting the earthly ruler in his proper place was a necessary precondition for God's dwelling perpetually in his rightful place.

43:10-11 At this point, the prophet was given the rationale for the whole ***Temple*** vision. He was not the first person to receive the blueprint for a sanctuary from God (see Exod 25–40). This vision was not intended to spark a building project some time in the future when God would return his people to their land, but to convey a message to the people of Ezekiel's generation. As they would ***study its plan,*** Ezekiel's hearers should be convicted of their sins and ***be ashamed of what they have done.*** The conviction of sin should be induced as they studied ***its entrances and exits, its decrees and laws,*** and the overall ***plan.***

43:11 ***and they will be ashamed:*** As in Greek version; Hebrew reads *if they are ashamed.*

43:12 ***Absolute holiness*** on Israel's part was required if a holy God were to dwell in their midst forever.

43:13-16 The holiness of the Temple area would be maintained by keeping sinners out and by the sacrificial system. The importance of this aspect of Temple life is made clear by the detailed description of the ***altar*** of the inner court, which was located at the geometric center of the entire Temple complex. The altar shown to Ezekiel was almost three times as long and wide as the altar in front of the Tabernacle (see Exod 27:1-8).

43:13 ***measurements of the altar:*** Hebrew *measurements of the altar in long cubits, each being a cubit* [18 inches or 45 centimeters] *and a handbreadth* [3 inches or 8 centimeters] *in length.* • ***21 inches deep and 21 inches wide:*** Hebrew *a cubit* [53 centimeters] *deep and a cubit wide.* • ***9 inches:*** Hebrew *1 span* [23 centimeters]. • ***height:*** As in Greek version; Hebrew reads *base.*

43:14 ***3½ feet:*** Hebrew *2 cubits* [1.1 meters]. • ***21 inches:*** Hebrew *1 cubit* [53 centimeters]; also in 43:14d. • ***7 feet:*** Hebrew *4 cubits* [2.1 meters]; also in 43:15.

43:16 ***21 feet by 21 feet:*** Hebrew *12 cubits* [6.4 meters] *long and 12 cubits wide.*

a square, measuring 24½ feet by 24½ feet, with a 21-inch gutter and a 10½-inch curb all around the edge. There are steps going up the east side of the altar."

18Then he said to me, "Son of man, this is what the Sovereign LORD says: These will be the regulations for the burning of offerings and the sprinkling of blood when the altar is built. 19At that time, the Levitical priests of the family of Zadok, who minister before me, are to be given a young bull for a sin offering, says the Sovereign LORD. 20You will take some of its blood and smear it on the four horns of the altar, the four corners of the upper ledge, and the curb that runs around that ledge. This will cleanse and make atonement for the altar. 21Then take the young bull for the sin offering and burn it at the appointed place outside the Temple area.

22"On the second day, sacrifice as a sin offering a young male goat that has no physical defects. Then cleanse and make atonement for the altar again, just as you did with the young bull. 23When you have finished the cleansing ceremony, offer another young bull that has no defects and a perfect ram from the flock. 24You are to present them to the LORD, and the priests are to sprinkle salt on them and offer them as a burnt offering to the LORD.

25"Every day for seven days a male goat, a young bull, and a ram from the flock will be sacrificed as a sin offering. None of these animals may have physical defects of any kind. 26Do this each day for seven days to cleanse and make atonement for the altar, thus setting it apart for holy use. 27On the eighth day, and on each day afterward, the priests will sacrifice on the altar the burnt offerings and peace offerings of the people. Then I will accept you. I, the Sovereign LORD, have spoken!"

The Prince, Levites, and Priests

44 Then the man brought me back to the east gateway in the outer wall of the Temple area, but it was closed. 2And the LORD said to me, "This gate must remain closed; it will never again be opened. No one will ever open it and pass through, for the LORD, the God of Israel, has entered here. Therefore, it must always remain shut. 3Only the prince himself may sit inside this gateway to feast in the LORD's presence. But he may come and go only through the entry room of the gateway."

4Then the man brought me through the north gateway to the front of the Temple. I looked and saw that the glory of the LORD filled the Temple of the LORD, and I fell face down on the ground.

5And the LORD said to me, "Son of man, take careful notice. Use your eyes and ears, and listen to everything I tell you about the regulations concerning the LORD's Temple. Take careful note of the procedures for using the Temple's entrances and exits. 6And give these rebels, the people of Israel, this message from the Sovereign LORD: O people of Israel, enough of your detestable sins! 7You have brought uncircumcised foreigners into my sanctuary—people who have no heart for God. In this way, you defiled my Temple even as you offered me my food, the fat and blood of sacrifices. In addition to all your other detestable sins, you have broken my covenant. 8Instead of safeguarding my sacred rituals, you have hired foreigners to take charge of my sanctuary.

43:18 Exod 40:29; Lev 1:5, 11; Ezek 2:1; Heb 9:21-22
43:19 1 Kgs 2:35; Ezek 40:46; 44:15; Heb 7:27
43:20 Lev 8:15; 9:9
43:21 Exod 29:14; Lev 4:11-12; Heb 13:11
43:23 Exod 29:1
43:23 Exod 29:1
43:24 Lev 2:13; Num 18:19; Mark 9:49-50; Col 4:6
43:25 Exod 29:35-37; Lev 8:33, 35
43:27 Lev 3:1; 9:1; 17:5; Ezek 20:40
44:1 Ezek 40:6
44:2 Ezek 43:4
44:3 Gen 31:54; Exod 24:9-11; Ezek 37:25; 46:2, 8; Zech 6:12-13
44:4 Ezek 1:28; 3:23
44:5 Deut 12:32; 32:46; Ezek 40:4; 43:10-11
44:6 Ezek 2:5-7; 3:9; 1 Pet 4:3
44:7 Gen 17:14; Exod 12:43-49; Lev 22:25; 26:41; Jer 4:4; 9:26
44:8 Num 18:7
44:9 Joel 3:17; Zech 14:21

43:17 This altar was approached by ***steps going up the east side,*** as was Moses' altar. This reversal of the normal ancient Near Eastern practice of having the steps approach from the west was possibly to avoid any hint of sun worship (see 8:16). • ***24½ feet by 24½ feet:*** Hebrew *14 cubits* [7.4 meters] *long and 14 cubits wide.* • ***21-inch gutter and a 10½-inch curb:*** Hebrew *a gutter of 1 cubit* [53 centimeters] *and a curb of ½ a cubit* [27 centimeters].

43:18-21 The new altar had to be consecrated before it was used. • On the first day, the blood of ***a young bull*** was to be applied to the extremities of the altar, the ***horns*** and ***corners,*** as a sin offering. The body of the sin offering was then burnt ***outside*** the sacred ***area,*** as with the Tabernacle (cp. Lev 4:11-12).

43:25 The procedure for the second day was repeated for seven more days to complete the eight-day purification cycle. A similar procedure was followed when Solomon's Temple was consecrated (2 Chr 7:8-9).

43:26-27 These sin offerings properly set the Temple ***apart for holy use,*** so that the priests could once again ***sacrifice . . . the burnt offerings and peace offerings of the people.*** These offerings were necessary if the Lord were to ***accept*** his people.

44:1-31 Now that the glory of the Lord had returned to the Temple, questions of access were critical. Who could approach this holy God? Like ch 43, this chapter is concerned with the Temple's entrances and exits, as well as the duties and procedures associated with its use.

44:2 The outer east ***gate must remain*** perpetually ***closed*** because the Lord had now returned to his Temple and would never again leave it. He had also sanctified this gate by going through it, and no one else was ever to use it.

44:3 Though ***the prince*** had the significant privilege of being the only one allowed ***to feast in the LORD's presence*** inside the east outer ***gateway,*** he was restricted to entering and leaving the portico from the outer court. He was not to enter from outside the Temple complex by going through the gate, as the Lord had; the earthly ruler is a man, not God, and he must submit to God. The prince must also never forget that the Temple is God's palace, not his own private chapel.

44:6-8 The ***people of Israel*** were called ***rebels*** because they had failed to control access to the sanctuary in the past; they had hired ***uncircumcised foreigners***

44:10
Num 18:23
2 Kgs 23:8-9
Ezek 22:26
44:11
Num 3:5-37; 4:1-33;
16:8-9; 18:2, 6
1 Chr 26:1
2 Chr 29:34
44:12
2 Kgs 16:10-16
Ezek 14:3-4
Hos 4:6; 5:1
44:13
Num 18:3
2 Kgs 23:9
44:14
Num 18:4, 6
1 Chr 23:28, 32
44:15
Num 18:7
Jer 33:18-22
Ezek 48:11

9"So this is what the Sovereign LORD
says: No foreigners, including those who
live among the people of Israel, will enter my sanctuary if they have not been
circumcised and have not surrendered
themselves to the LORD. 10And the men of
the tribe of Levi who abandoned me when
Israel strayed away from me to worship
idols must bear the consequences of their
unfaithfulness. 11They may still be Temple guards and gatekeepers, and they may
slaughter the animals brought for burnt offerings and be present to help the people.
12But they encouraged my people to worship idols, causing Israel to fall into deep
sin. So I have taken a solemn oath that they
must bear the consequences for their sins,
says the Sovereign LORD. 13They may not approach me to minister as priests. They may
not touch any of my holy things or the holy
offerings, for they must bear the shame of
all the detestable sins they have committed.
14They are to serve as the Temple caretakers,
taking charge of the maintenance work and
performing general duties.
15"However, the Levitical priests of the
family of Zadok continued to minister faithfully in the Temple when Israel abandoned
me for idols. These men will serve as my
ministers. They will stand in my presence
and offer the fat and blood of the sacrifices,
says the Sovereign LORD. 16They alone will

Temple Legislation as Theology (44:1–46:18)

Ezek 8:1–11:25;
40:1–43:27
Isa 56:7

The rabbis of Judaism spent a great deal of time seeking to harmonize the laws of chs 44–48 with the laws of the Torah. They were unsuccessful, because the legislation in these chapters was no more intended to match that of Moses than the vision of the Temple building (chs 40–43) was designed to match the design of the Tabernacle or the Temple of Solomon. The description of the Temple regulations conveys a theological message of change, as did the earlier description of the Temple architecture (see "Temple Architecture as Theology" at 40:1–43:27, p. 1373).

These regulations highlighted the need for proper separation between the Temple and the palace, with the prince clearly in subordination to the Lord. The sacrificial rituals would also become more numerous and more focused on purification. Holy offerings would once again be made by holy people to the holy God. The new world was completely devoted to the separation of the holy from the unholy and to the cleansing of God's people. Since defilement of the Temple and idolatrous worship had driven the Lord out of his house (chs 8–11), an entirely new situation was necessary if God was to dwell once more among his people. The function of this legislation was to convict the prophet's hearers of their past abuses that had broken down the wall of separation between the holy and the unholy and to reassure them that God would restore his people's worship to its proper state.

The legislation puts the prince, the king descended from David, in a proper place of submission to the Lord. It finds its fulfillment with the coming of Christ. Jesus comes as a servant King who delights to do the Father's will (Matt 4:1-11; 20:25-28). He offered the perfect purification offering, cleansing the heavenly sanctuary once for all time (Heb 9:11-12, 23) and ensuring that God can dwell in the midst of his people forever. His blood cleanses us of all sin and enables sinners boldly to enter the heavenly Most Holy Place without fear of rejection.

to come ***into*** the ***sanctuary*** and probably employed them as Temple guards and gatekeepers. This task should not have been delegated to foreigners; it should have been performed by the Levites whom the Lord would assign to perform it (44:10).

44:9 ***No foreigners:*** This was not a blanket prohibition against non-Israelite access to the sanctuary. It only affected those who had ***not been circumcised and have not surrendered themselves to the LORD***. Genuine converts could be part of the new Israel (see 47:22-23).

44:10 ***when Israel strayed away from me to worship idols:*** The people had a long history of failing to follow God's plan for worship, including the specific sin of employing foreigners as temple guards (44:8). • ***idols:*** The Hebrew term (literally *round things*) probably alludes to dung; also in 44:12. See note on 6:4-7.

44:12-14 The Levites had ***encouraged . . . Israel to fall into deep sin*** by abandoning the Lord and worshiping idols. One of the ***consequences*** of that sin was that they could no longer enter the inner court of the Temple like the priests. However, by God's grace, they would still have a significant ministry in serving the people and slaughtering their sacrifices. • The people as a whole were placed at a greater distance from God because of their idolatry. Prior to the Exile they would have slaughtered their own sacrifices (see Lev 1:5, 11); now they must hand them over to the Levites to be slaughtered on their behalf.

44:15-16 In contrast to the Levites and the people who abandoned the Lord for idols, the ***Levitical priests of the family of Zadok*** remained faithful to the Lord. Zadok was the high priest of Solomon's day. His family's reward was renewed access to the inner courtyard, where they were to perform the crucial sacrificial rituals nearer to the presence of God. A repeated theme in these chapters is that those who were faithful in the past would be rewarded with closer access to God and greater privilege in his presence, while those who were unfaithful would be kept at a greater distance.

enter my sanctuary and approach my table
to serve me. They will fulfill all my requirements.
17"When they enter the gateway to the
inner courtyard, they must wear only linen
clothing. They must wear no wool while on
duty in the inner courtyard or in the Temple
itself. 18They must wear linen turbans and
linen undergarments. They must not wear
anything that would cause them to perspire.
19When they return to the outer courtyard
where the people are, they must take off the
clothes they wear while ministering to me.
They must leave them in the sacred rooms
and put on other clothes so they do not endanger anyone by transmitting holiness to
them through this clothing.
20"They must neither shave their heads
nor let their hair grow too long. Instead,
they must trim it regularly. 21The priests
must not drink wine before entering the
inner courtyard. 22They may choose their
wives only from among the virgins of Israel
or the widows of the priests. They may not
marry other widows or [b]divorced women.
23They will teach my people the difference
between what is holy and what is common,
what is ceremonially clean and unclean.
24"They will serve as judges to resolve any
disagreements among my people. Their decisions must be based on my regulations.
And the priests themselves must obey my
instructions and decrees at all the sacred
festivals, and see to it that the Sabbaths are
set apart as holy days.
25"A priest must not defile himself by being in the presence of a dead person unless
it is his father, mother, child, brother, or unmarried sister. In such cases it is permitted.
26Even then, he can return to his Temple duties only after being ceremonially cleansed
and then waiting for seven days. 27The first
day he returns to work and enters the inner
courtyard and the sanctuary, he must offer
a sin offering for himself, says the Sovereign LORD.
28"The priests will not have any property
or possession of land, for I alone am their
special possession. 29Their food will come
from the gifts and sacrifices brought to the
Temple by the people—the grain offerings,
the sin offerings, and the guilt offerings.
Whatever anyone sets apart for the LORD
will belong to the priests. 30The first of
the ripe fruits and all the gifts brought to
the LORD will go to the priests. The first
samples of each grain harvest and the first
of your flour must also be given to the
priests so the LORD will bless your homes.
31The priests may not eat meat from any
bird or animal that dies a natural death or
that dies after being attacked by another
animal.

Division of the Land

45 "When you divide the land among
the tribes of Israel, you must set
aside a section for the LORD as his holy portion. This piece of land will be 8⅓ miles long
and 6⅔ miles wide. The entire area will be

44:17 Exod 39:27-29
44:18 Exod 28:40, 42
44:19 Lev 16:23-24; Ezek 42:14; 46:20
44:20 Lev 21:5; Num 6:5
44:21 Lev 10:8-9
44:22 Lev 21:7, 13-15; [b]*garash* (1644) ‣ Lev 21:7
44:23 Lev 10:10; Deut 33:10; Ezek 22:26; Hos 4:6; Mal 2:6
44:24 Deut 17:8-9; 21:5; 2 Chr 19:8-10; Ezek 20:12, 20
44:25 Lev 21:1-3
44:26 Num 19:13-19
44:27 Num 6:9-11
44:28 Num 18:20; Deut 10:9; Josh 13:33
44:29 Lev 27:21, 28; Num 18:9, 14-15; Josh 13:14
44:30 Num 15:20; 18:12; 2 Chr 31:4-6, 10; Neh 10:35-37; Mal 3:10
44:31 Lev 22:8; Deut 14:21; Ezek 4:14

44:17-19 The privileged access of the priests carried heightened responsibilities for holiness. Their behavior was far more restricted than that of the people in general. They had to wear ***linen*** rather than ***wool*** so that their bodies would not be defiled by sweat (see note on 36:17), and they were to maintain a separate wardrobe of sacred garments. • ***endanger . . . by transmitting holiness to them:*** Holiness was a contagious quality that could be conveyed to anything with which it came into contact. The problem with this is that if a sacred object transmitted holiness to a profane object or person, there could be fatal consequences (cp. Lev 10:1-3; 1 Sam 6:19; 2 Sam 6:6-7).

44:20-27 The priests were to avoid contact with death, either through ***being in the presence of a dead person*** or through the ritual mourning practices in which they would ***shave their heads*** or ***let their hair grow*** completely free. They ***must not drink wine before entering the inner courtyard*** to avoid the risk of potentially fatal alcohol-induced errors (see Lev 10:9). Since only the descendants of Zadok could serve as priests, they were restricted in marriage to ***virgins of Israel*** or to ***widows of the priests*** to ensure the continuing purity of the priestly line. In all of these ways, the priests were to model the radical distinction between ***holy*** and ***common*** and between the ***ceremonially clean and unclean*** for the people.

44:28-30 Because the priests belonged to the Lord and were provided for through a share of the sacrificial ***offerings*** of the Temple, they would ***not have any property or possession of land.*** The Lord was their inheritance, and their temporal needs were to be supplied by the firstfruits of the people's harvests and the various offerings made at the Temple.

44:29 ***sets apart:*** The Hebrew term used here refers to the complete consecration of things or people to the LORD, either by destroying them or by giving them as an offering.

44:31 In their radical separation from the realm of death, they could not eat ***any bird or animal that*** died ***a natural death*** or was ***attacked by another animal.***

45:1-8 The division of the restored Promised Land among the tribes is described in detail in chs 47–48, but the central sacred section is described here because it included the area set aside for the priests to live in. Regaining a share in the land was a pressing concern for the exiles at a time when they had none. Ezekiel's interest, however, was not simply in promising that the land would be divided among them in a fair way. He wanted to remind them of what the Promised Land was about in the first place. It was a land in which God would dwell among his people. At the outset, therefore, the central part of the land would be assigned to the Lord as ***his holy portion.*** The main purpose of this was to provide a zone of holiness and protection around the Temple.

45:1 ***8⅓ miles long and 6⅔ miles wide:*** As in Greek version, which reads ***25,000 cubits*** [13.3 kilometers] ***long and 20,000 cubits*** [10.6 kilometers] ***wide;*** Hebrew reads ***25,000 cubits long and 10,000 cubits*** [3⅓ miles or 5.3 kilometers] ***wide.*** Cp. 45:3, 5; 48:9.

45:1 Josh 13:7; 14:2 Ps 16:5-6 Ezek 47:21; 48:8-9
45:2 Ezek 42:16-20
45:3 Ezek 48:10
45:4 Num 16:5 Ezek 40:45; 44:13-14; 48:10-11
45:5 Ezek 48:12-14
45:6 Ezek 48:15-16
45:7 Ezek 46:16-18; 48:21-22
45:8 Josh 11:23 Isa 11:3-5 Jer 23:5-6 Ezek 22:27; 46:18
45:9 Neh 5:1-5 Jer 6:7; 22:3 Zech 8:16
45:10 Lev 19:35-36 Deut 25:13-15 Prov 11:1; 16:11 Mic 6:10-11
45:12 Exod 30:13 Lev 27:25 Num 3:47

holy. 2A section of this land, measuring
875 feet by 875 feet, will be set aside for
the Temple. An additional strip of land
87½ feet wide is to be left empty all around
it. 3Within the larger sacred area, measure
out a portion of land 8⅓ miles long and
3⅓ miles wide. Within it the sanctuary of
the Most Holy Place will be located. 4This
area will be holy, set aside for the priests
who minister to the LORD in the sanctuary.
They will use it for their homes, and my
Temple will be located within it. 5The strip
of sacred land next to it, also 8⅓ miles long
and 3⅓ miles wide, will be a living area for
the Levites who work at the Temple. It will
be their possession and a place for their
towns.

6"Adjacent to the larger sacred area will
be a section of land 8⅓ miles long and 1⅔
miles wide. This will be set aside for a city
where anyone in Israel can live.

7"Two special sections of land will be
set apart for the prince. One section will
share a border with the east side of the sacred lands and city, and the second section
will share a border on the west side. Then
the far eastern and western borders of the
prince's lands will line up with the eastern
and western boundaries of the tribal areas.
8These sections of land will be the prince's
allotment. Then my princes will no longer
oppress and rob my people; they will assign
the rest of the land to the people, giving an
allotment to each tribe.

Rules for the Princes

9"For this is what the Sovereign LORD says:
Enough, you princes of Israel! Stop your violence and oppression and do what is just
and right. Quit robbing and cheating my
people out of their land. Stop expelling
them from their homes, says the Sovereign LORD. 10Use only honest weights and
scales and honest measures, both dry and
liquid. 11The homer will be your standard
unit for measuring volume. The ephah and
the bath will each measure one-tenth of a
homer. 12The standard unit for weight will
be the silver shekel. One shekel will consist
of twenty gerahs, and sixty shekels will be
equal to one mina.

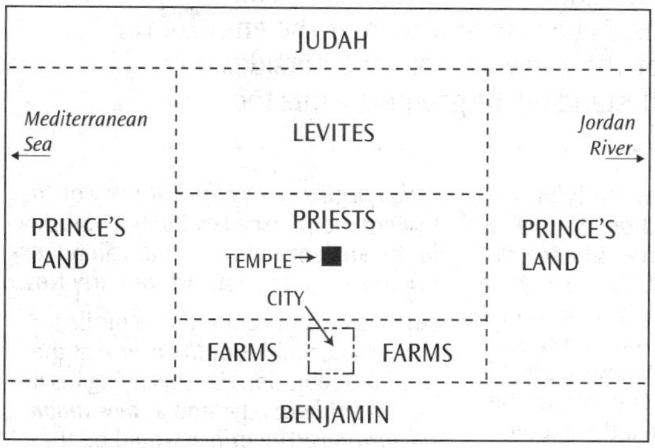

◀ **The Sacred Precinct (45:1-8; 48:8-22).** The Promised Land was meant to be a place where the holy God could live among his people. Ezekiel's vision makes God's presence the central fact of Israel's existence (see "Israel's Geography as Theology" at 47:13–48:35, p. 1386).

45:2 ***875 feet by 875 feet:*** Hebrew *500 cubits* [265 meters] *by 500 cubits, a square.* • ***87½ feet:*** Hebrew *50 cubits* [26.5 meters].

45:3-4 Within this holy portion, the Temple complex would form the Most Holy Place at the heart of a sacred square. Just as the Most Holy Place in the Temple was protected by an inner court that only the priests could enter, the Temple complex was surrounded by a section reserved only for ***priests.***

45:3 ***8⅓ miles long and 3⅓ miles wide:*** Hebrew *25,000 cubits* [13.3 kilometers] *long and 10,000 cubits* [5.3 kilometers] *wide;* also in 45:5.

45:5-6 To the north of this priestly strip was an area reserved for the ***Levites;*** to the south (48:15), the ***city*** was located on a half-size strip. The result was a square that was 8⅓ miles (25,000 cubits) on a side.

45:5 ***It will be their possession and a place for their towns:*** As in Greek version; Hebrew reads *They will have as their possession 20 rooms.*

45:6 ***8⅓ miles long and 1⅔ miles wide:*** Hebrew *25,000 cubits* [13.3 kilometers] *long and 5,000 cubits* [2.65 kilometers] *wide.*

45:7 On both sides of the larger sacred area (45:1-6), the remainder of the holy portion was assigned to the ***prince.*** The same principle of graded access that operated in the Temple was applied more broadly to the surrounding land. The Temple would be the geographical and spiritual heart of the new Israel. The land would be divided into strips running east to west, orienting the whole nation along the sacred east–west axis of the Temple. The city and the prince would still be important in the new economy, but they would no longer be at the center. The Lord was Israel's King, and his dwelling place would be the hub of their existence.

45:8-9 One tangible expression of the Lord's kingly rule was that he distributed the land to the prince as well as to the people. The prince was assigned a large enough piece of his own land to meet his needs and to allow him to support the ministry of the Temple without having to ***oppress*** and ***rob*** the ***people.***

45:10-12 When the prince gathered the offerings of the people for the Temple (see 45:13-17), he was not to adjust the scales so that he profited from the difference between what he took in from the people and what he gave out for the ministry of the Temple.

45:10 This verse can be translated literally *Use honest scales, an honest ephah, and an honest bath.*

45:11 The ***homer*** measures about 40 gallons or 182 liters. • The ***ephah*** is a dry measure; the ***bath*** is a liquid measure.

45:12 The ***shekel*** weighs about 0.4 ounces or 11 grams. • Elsewhere the ***mina*** is equated to 50 shekels.

Special Offerings and Celebrations

13"You must give this tax to the prince: one bushel of wheat or barley for every 60 you harvest, 14one percent of your olive oil, 15and one sheep or goat for every 200 in your flocks in Israel. These will be the grain offerings, burnt offerings, and peace offerings that will make atonement for the people who bring them, says the Sovereign LORD. 16All the people of Israel must join in bringing these offerings to the prince. 17The prince will be required to provide offerings that are given at the religious festivals, the new moon celebrations, the Sabbath days, and all other similar occasions. He will provide the sin offerings, burnt offerings, grain offerings, liquid offerings, and peace offerings to purify the people of Israel, making them right with the LORD.

18"This is what the Sovereign LORD says: In early spring, on the first day of each new year, sacrifice a young bull with no defects to purify the Temple. 19The priest will take blood from this sin offering and put it on the doorposts of the Temple, the four corners of the upper ledge of the altar, and the gateposts at the entrance to the inner courtyard. 20Do this also on the seventh day of the new year for anyone who has sinned through error or ignorance. In this way, you will purify the Temple.

21"On the fourteenth day of the first month, you must celebrate the [c]Passover. This festival will last for seven days. The bread you eat during that time must be made without yeast. 22On the day of Passover the prince will provide a young bull as a sin offering for himself and the people of Israel. 23On each of the seven days of the feast he will prepare a burnt offering to the LORD, consisting of seven young bulls and seven rams without defects. A male goat will also be given each day for a sin offering. 24The prince will provide a basket of flour as a grain offering and a gallon of olive oil with each young bull and ram.

25"During the seven days of the Festival of Shelters, which occurs every year in early autumn, the prince will provide these same sacrifices for the sin offering, the burnt offering, and the grain offering, along with the required olive oil.

46 "This is what the Sovereign LORD says: The east gateway of the inner courtyard will be closed during the six workdays each week, but it will be open on Sabbath days and the days of new moon celebrations. 2The prince will enter the entry room of the gateway from the outside. Then he will stand by the gatepost while the

45:15 Lev 1:4; 6:30
45:17 Lev 23:1-44; 1 Kgs 8:62-64; 2 Chr 31:3; Ezek 46:4-12
45:18 Exod 12:2; Lev 16:16, 20; 22:20; Heb 9:14
45:19 Lev 16:18-20; Ezek 43:20
45:20 Lev 4:27; Ps 19:12
45:21 Exod 12:18; Lev 23:5-8; Num 9:2-3; 28:16-17; [c]*pesakh* (6453) ‣ Exod 12:11
45:22 Lev 4:14
45:23 Lev 23:8; Num 28:16-25; Job 42:8
45:24 Num 28:12-15; Ezek 46:5-7
45:25 Lev 23:33-36; Num 29:12-38
46:1 Exod 20:9-10; Isa 66:23; Ezek 44:1-2
46:2 Ezek 44:3

45:13-17 The people were to provide for the regular daily ***offerings that will make atonement*** at the new Temple by means of a ***tax*** paid to ***the prince***. The prince was to provide all of the offerings for special occasions, such as ***the religious festivals, the new moon celebrations***, and ***the Sabbath days***. Both the regular daily offerings and the special festival offerings functioned ***to purify the people of Israel, making them right with the LORD***.

45:13 ***one bushel of wheat or barley for every 60:*** Hebrew *⅙ of an ephah from each homer of wheat and ⅙ of an ephah from each homer of barley*.

45:14 ***one percent of your olive oil:*** Hebrew *the portion of oil, measured by the bath, is ⅒ of a bath from each cor, which consists of 10 baths or 1 homer, for 10 baths are equivalent to a homer*.

45:17 ***to purify the people of Israel, making them right with the LORD:*** Or *to make atonement for the people of Israel*.

45:18 ***In early spring, on the first day of each new year:*** Literally *On the first day of the first month* of the Hebrew calendar. This day in the ancient Hebrew lunar calendar occurred in March or April.

45:20 ***will purify:*** Or *will make atonement for*.

45:21-25 The annual festivals in the new Temple had a similar purifying purpose. Instead of the three distinctive festivals of the Mosaic order (the feasts of Passover, Harvest, and Shelters), there were now only two virtually identical festivals, Passover and Shelters, spaced six months apart. The ***Passover*** feast still took place on the fourteenth day of the first month and resembled the earlier festival in many ways, though the number of sacrificial offerings was significantly higher than those prescribed in Num 28. The ***Festival of Shelters***, however, is not even explicitly named in the Hebrew text and has lost anything distinctive about its celebration except for the provision that ***the prince will provide*** the ***same sacrifices*** as for the Passover. It still occurs in the seventh month. The land's constant purification from sin emerges as a central theme.

45:21 ***the fourteenth day of the first month:*** This day in the ancient Hebrew lunar calendar occurred in late Mar, Apr, or early May.

45:24 ***a basket of flour as a grain offering and a gallon of olive oil:*** Hebrew *an ephah* [20 quarts or 22 liters] *of flour . . . and a hin* [3.8 liters] *of olive oil*.

45:25 ***the seven days of the Festival of Shelters, which occurs every year in early autumn:*** Literally *the festival which begins on the fifteenth day of the seventh month* (see Lev 23:34). This day in the ancient Hebrew lunar calendar occurred in late Sept, Oct, or early Nov.

46:1-15 Ezekiel continued to outline the responsibilities of ***the prince*** at the special celebrations by specifying his duties on ***Sabbath days*** and at ***new moon celebrations***. The prince would be the representative worshiper on behalf of the people. He would pass through the Temple in procession with them, and he would also be uniquely able to approach the realm of the sacred on their behalf.

46:1 The ***east gateway*** between the inner and outer courtyards would open once a week for the ***Sabbath***, once a month for ***new moon celebrations***, and when the prince offered voluntary burnt offerings or peace offerings (46:12). The east gate between the outer courtyard and the outside world was never to be opened again (44:2-3).

46:2 The prince would have the unique privilege of going through the eastern ***gateway*** to the inner courtyard as far as the ***entry room*** to ***worship***. This symbolized that God regarded him as more significant than the common people, but that he was still not fit to stand in God's presence apart from mediation by the priests.

46:3 Luke 1:10
46:4 Ezek 45:17
46:5 Ezek 45:24
46:7 Deut 16:17
46:8 Ezek 44:1-3
46:9 Ps 84:7
46:10 2 Chr 6:3; 7:4 Ps 42:4
46:11 Ezek 45:17
46:12 Lev 23:38 2 Chr 29:31 Ezek 44:3; 45:17
46:13 Exod 29:38 Num 28:3-4 Isa 50:4
46:14 Exod 29:42 Num 28:5-6
46:15 Exod 29:42 Num 28:6
46:16 2 Chr 21:3
46:17 Lev 25:10
46:18 1 Kgs 21:1-16 Ezek 45:8 Mic 2:1-2

priest offers his burnt offering and peace
offering. He will bow down in worship inside the gateway passage and then go back
out the way he came. The gateway will not
be closed until evening. 3The common people will bow down and worship the LORD in
front of this gateway on Sabbath days and
the days of new moon celebrations.

4"Each Sabbath day the prince will present to the LORD a burnt offering of six
lambs and one ram, all with no defects. 5He
will present a grain offering of a basket of
choice flour to go with the ram and whatever amount of flour he chooses to go with
each lamb, and he is to offer one gallon of olive oil for each basket of flour. 6At the new
moon celebrations, he will bring one young
bull, six lambs, and one ram, all with no defects. 7With the young bull he must bring a
basket of choice flour for a grain offering.
With the ram he must bring another basket
of flour. And with each lamb he is to bring
whatever amount of flour he chooses to
give. With each basket of flour he must offer one gallon of olive oil.

8"The prince must enter the gateway
through the entry room, and he must leave
the same way. 9But when the people come
in through the north gateway to worship
the LORD during the religious festivals, they
must leave by the south gateway. And those
who entered through the south gateway
must leave by the north gateway. They must
never leave by the same gateway they came
in, but must always use the opposite gateway. 10The prince will enter and leave with
the people on these occasions.

11"So at the special feasts and sacred festivals, the grain offering will be a basket of
choice flour with each young bull, another
basket of flour with each ram, and as much
flour as the prince chooses to give with
each lamb. Give one gallon of olive oil with
each basket of flour. 12When the prince
offers a voluntary burnt offering or peace
offering to the LORD, the east gateway to
the inner courtyard will be opened for him,
and he will offer his sacrifices as he does on
Sabbath days. Then he will leave, and the
gateway will be shut behind him.

13"Each morning you must sacrifice a
one-year-old lamb with no defects as a
burnt offering to the LORD. 14With the
lamb, a grain offering must also be given to
the LORD—about three quarts of flour with
a third of a gallon of olive oil to moisten the
choice flour. This will be a permanent law
for you. 15The lamb, the grain offering, and
the olive oil must be given as a daily sacrifice every morning without fail.

16"This is what the Sovereign LORD says:
If the prince gives a gift of land to one of his
sons as his inheritance, it will belong to him
and his descendants forever. 17But if the
prince gives a gift of land from his inheritance to one of his servants, the servant may
keep it only until the Year of Jubilee, which
comes every fiftieth year. At that time the
land will return to the prince. But when the
prince gives gifts to his sons, those gifts will
be permanent. 18And the prince may never
take anyone's property by force. If he gives
property to his sons, it must be from his
own land, for I do not want any of my people unjustly evicted from their property."

The Temple Kitchens

19In my vision, the man brought me through
the entrance beside the gateway and led me
to the sacred rooms assigned to the priests,
which faced toward the north. He showed
me a place at the extreme west end of these

46:3 The ordinary Israelites, the ***common people***, would be allowed to climb the stairs to the threshold to offer their worship when the gate was open on the ***Sabbath*** and the first day of the month; only then would they be able to see into the inner court. Otherwise, they were kept away from it.

46:5 ***a basket of choice flour . . . one gallon of olive oil:*** Hebrew *an ephah* [20 quarts or 22 liters] *of choice flour . . . a hin* [3.8 liters] *of olive oil;* similarly in 46:7, 11.

46:9-10 During ***religious festivals***, the people were to present themselves before the Lord by proceeding through the Temple from north to south or vice versa, with ***the prince*** in their midst. Their motion was to follow the profane north–south axis rather than the sacred east–west axis along which the priest's activities took place.

46:12 The ***voluntary burnt offering or peace offering*** was in addition to the regular daily offerings of meat, grain, and oil that symbolized the regular table fellowship and communion that had now been restored between God and his people.

46:14 ***about three quarts of flour with a third of a gallon of olive oil:*** Hebrew *1/6 of an ephah* [3.7 liters] *of flour with 1/3 of a hin* [1.3 liters] *of olive oil.*

46:16-18 Because the ***land*** assigned to ***the prince*** was the Lord's gift to him and to his family, he could not give it permanently to ***one of his servants.*** Each ***Year of Jubilee***, the fiftieth year when all land in Israel reverted to its original family owners, this land would revert to the crown. This provision was intended to remove the temptation for the king to acquire more and more land with which to reward his faithful servants, resulting in less land for the ordinary people. The land belonged to the Lord, and he divided it among his people. No one, not even the king, was permitted to tamper with the people's inheritance.

46:17 ***until the Year of Jubilee, which comes every fiftieth year:*** Literally *until the Year of Release;* see Lev 25:8-17.

46:19-24 The vision of the Temple proper (chs 40–46) concludes with a return to the point at which the tour began. The prophet began his tour in the outer court, and having traveled to the center and back out again twice, he completed it at the edges of the outer court, in ***the kitchens*** where the various ***sacrifices***

rooms. 20He explained, "This is where the
priests will cook the meat from the guilt
offerings and sin offerings and bake the
flour from the grain offerings into bread.
They will do it here to avoid carrying the
sacrifices through the outer courtyard and
endangering the people by transmitting holiness to them."
21Then he brought me back to the outer
courtyard and led me to each of its four
corners. In each corner I saw an enclosure.
22Each of these enclosures was 70 feet
long and 52½ feet wide, surrounded by
walls. 23Along the inside of these walls was
a ledge of stone with fireplaces under the
ledge all the way around. 24The man said to
me, "These are the kitchens to be used by
the Temple assistants to boil the sacrifices
offered by the people."

The Life-Giving River of Healing

47 In my vision, the man brought me
back to the entrance of the Temple.
There I saw a stream flowing east from beneath the door of the Temple and passing to
the right of the altar on its south side. 2The
man brought me outside the wall through
the north gateway and led me around to the
eastern entrance. There I could see the water flowing out through the south side of
the east gateway.
3Measuring as he went, he took me along
the stream for 1,750 feet and then led me
across. The water was up to my ankles. 4He
measured off another 1,750 feet and led
me across again. This time the water was
up to my knees. After another 1,750 feet, it
was up to my waist. 5Then he measured another 1,750 feet, and the river was too deep
to walk across. It was deep enough to swim
in, but too deep to walk through.
6He asked me, "Have you been watching,
son of man?" Then he led me back along
the riverbank. 7When I returned, I was surprised by the sight of many trees growing
on both sides of the river. 8Then he said to
me, "This river flows east through the desert
into the valley of the Dead Sea. The waters
of this stream will make the salty waters of
the Dead Sea fresh and pure. 9There will be
swarms of living things wherever the water
of this river flows. Fish will abound in the
Dead Sea, for its waters will become fresh.
Life will flourish wherever this water flows.
10Fishermen will stand along the shores
of the Dead Sea. All the way from En-gedi
to En-eglaim, the shores will be covered
with nets drying in the sun. Fish of every
kind will fill the Dead Sea, just as they fill
the Mediterranean. 11But the marshes and
swamps will not be purified; they will still
be salty. 12Fruit trees of all kinds will grow
along both sides of the river. The leaves
of these trees will never turn brown and
fall, and there will always be fruit on their
branches. There will be a new crop every
month, for they are watered by the river
flowing from the Temple. The fruit will be
for food and the leaves for healing."

Boundaries for the Land

13This is what the Sovereign LORD says: "Divide the land in this way for the twelve tribes
of Israel: The descendants of Joseph will be

46:20 Lev 2:4-7; 2 Chr 35:13
47:1 Ps 46:4; Joel 3:18; Zech 13:1; Rev 22:1, 17
47:2 Ezek 44:1-4
47:3 Ezek 40:3
47:5 Isa 11:9; Hab 2:14
47:6 Ezek 40:4; 44:5
47:7 Isa 60:21; 61:3; Rev 22:2
47:8 Deut 3:17; Isa 35:6-7; 41:17-19; 44:3
47:9 Isa 12:3; John 4:14; 7:37-38; Rev 21:6
47:10 Num 34:6; 2 Chr 20:2; Ps 104:25; Ezek 26:5; 48:28; Matt 13:47; Luke 5:5-9
47:12 Gen 2:9; Ps 1:3; Jer 17:8; Rev 22:2
47:13 Gen 48:5; Num 34:1-13; 1 Chr 5:1; Ezek 48:4-5

---

offered by the people were to be cooked. Some sacrifices were burned whole on the altar, while others were only partially burned, with portions being returned so that the worshiper could feast with his family in the Lord's presence.

46:22 ***70 feet long and 52½ feet wide:*** Hebrew *40 cubits* [21.2 meters] *long and 30 cubits* [15.9 meters] *wide.*

47:1-12 Once the Temple was restored to its central place among God's people, its beneficial influence, pictured here as a river, would spread outward, transforming death to life.

47:1 The source of the ***stream*** was within the Temple. • ***to the right of the altar on its south side:*** This location in Solomon's Temple was occupied by the Sea, a massive bronze pool that provided the water needed for cleansing (1 Kgs 7:23, 39). It also symbolized the subjugation of the forces of chaos (often represented by the sea) in the ordered cosmos of the Temple. In Ezekiel's vision, the static Sea had been transformed into a dynamic, life-giving river (cp. Gen 2:10-14; Ps 46).

47:3-5 At first, the stream was a mere trickle coming out from the gate of the Temple, but as it flowed out it became deeper and deeper until it was ***too deep to walk through.*** God's power and presence grows more and more impressive as its progression is observed throughout the land.

47:3 ***1,750 feet:*** Hebrew *1,000 cubits* [530 meters]; also in 47:4, 5.

47:6-9 The ***river*** grew as it went, bringing life to everything it touched, even the ***salty waters of the Dead Sea.***

47:8 ***the Dead Sea:*** Literally *the sea.*

47:10 From ***En-gedi,*** a town on the west side of the Dead Sea, to ***En-eglaim,*** a town on the east side, the Dead Sea would be brought from death to life. This water, so full of salt and other minerals that it is devoid of life, would teem with enough ***fish*** to support a major fishing industry. • ***the Mediterranean:*** Literally *the Great Sea;* also in 47:15, 17, 19, 20.

47:11 The useful salt deposits previously gathered from the Dead Sea area would not be lost—***the marshes and swamps*** would ***still be salty.***

47:12 Alongside this river of life, ***fruit trees of all kinds will grow.*** Like the righteous of Ps 1, their leaves will not wither, and they will bear their fruit in season. They will be so full of life that they will bear ***a new crop every month,*** and the leaves will be medicinal. The river's fertility brings concrete blessings to all of God's people. Wherever the waters of this river flow, there will be life.

47:13–48:35 The book of Ezekiel's final section charts the boundaries and the distribution of the land. Theology is expressed here through geography; issues of space, access, and position relative to the Temple are of crucial significance.

47:13 ***The descendants of Joseph will be given two shares of land:*** It was

47:14 Gen 12:7; Deut 1:8; Ezek 20:5-6
47:15 Num 34:7-9; Ezek 48:1
47:16 Num 13:21; 1 Kgs 8:65
47:17 Num 34:9; Ezek 48:1
47:18 Gen 13:10-11; Num 34:10-12
47:19 Num 34:3-5; Deut 32:51; Isa 27:12
47:20 Num 34:6
47:22 Isa 14:1; 56:6-7; Acts 11:18; Rom 10:12; Eph 2:12-14; Col 3:11
48:1 Exod 1:1; Josh 19:40-48
48:2 Gen 30:12-13; Josh 19:24-31
48:3 Gen 30:7-8; Josh 19:32-39
48:4 Gen 30:22-24; 41:51; 48:5, 14-20; Josh 13:29-31; 17:1-11
48:5 Josh 16:5-10; 17:8-10, 14-18
48:6 Josh 13:15-21
48:7 Josh 15:1-63
48:8 Ezek 45:1-6; Rev 21:3, 22

given two shares of land. 14 Otherwise each tribe will receive an equal share. I took a solemn oath and swore that I would give this land to your ancestors, and it will now come to you as your possession.

15 "These are the boundaries of the land:
The northern border will run from
the Mediterranean toward Hethlon,
then on through Lebo-hamath to
Zedad; 16 then it will run to Berothah
and Sibraim, which are on the border
between Damascus and Hamath, and
finally to Hazer-hatticon, on the border
of Hauran. 17 So the northern border
will run from the Mediterranean to
Hazar-enan, on the border between
Hamath to the north and Damascus to
the south.

18 "The eastern border starts at a point
between Hauran and Damascus and runs
south along the Jordan River between
Israel and Gilead, past the Dead Sea and
as far south as Tamar. This will be the
eastern border.

19 "The southern border will go west
from Tamar to the waters of Meribah
at Kadesh and then follow the course of
the Brook of Egypt to the Mediterranean.
This will be the southern border.

20 "On the west side, the
Mediterranean itself will be your border
from the southern border to the point
where the northern border begins,
opposite Lebo-hamath.

21 "Divide the land within these boundaries among the tribes of Israel. 22 Distribute the land as an allotment for yourselves and for the foreigners who have joined you and are raising their families among you. They will be like native-born Israelites to you and will receive an allotment among the tribes. 23 These foreigners are to be given land within the territory of the tribe with whom they now live. I, the Sovereign LORD, have spoken!

Allocation of the Land

48 "Here is the list of the tribes of Israel and the territory each is to receive. The territory of Dan is in the extreme north. Its boundary line follows the Hethlon road to Lebo-hamath and then runs on to Hazar-enan on the border of Damascus, with Hamath to the north. Dan's territory extends all the way across the land of Israel from east to west.

2 "Asher's territory lies south of Dan's and also extends from east to west. 3 Naphtali's land lies south of Asher's, also extending from east to west. 4 Then comes Manasseh south of Naphtali, and its territory also extends from east to west. 5 South of Manasseh is Ephraim, 6 and then Reuben, 7 and then Judah, all of whose boundaries extend from east to west.

8 "South of Judah is the land set aside for a special purpose. It will be 8⅓ miles wide and will extend as far east and west as the tribal territories, with the Temple at the center.

9 "The area set aside for the LORD's Temple will be 8⅓ miles long and 6⅔ miles

important to retain twelve portions of land. Since Levi had no portion, the descendants of Joseph's sons, Ephraim and Manasseh, received land as two tribes.

47:15-20 ***The boundaries*** of the new Promised Land were approximately those assigned in Num 34:1-12, from ***Lebo-hamath*** in the north to the ***Brook of Egypt*** in the south, and from the ***Mediterranean*** in the west to the ***Jordan River*** in the east. This promised land would now be possessed by the people, something they had never before done. Absent from this land was Transjordan, the area east of the Jordan River, which was the historic home of Reuben, Gad, and half of the tribe of Manasseh. It lay outside the boundaries promised to Moses and was therefore not part of the original promise, although historically many Israelites had lived there.

47:18 ***the Dead Sea:*** Literally *the eastern sea.* • ***Tamar:*** As in the Greek version; Hebrew reads *you will measure.*

47:19 ***waters of Meribah at Kadesh:*** Hebrew *waters of Meribath-kadesh.*

47:21-23 ***The land within these boundaries*** was to be divided ***among the tribes of Israel.*** Instead of the divided preexilic kingdoms, the future would see a single kingdom formed from the diverse unity of the twelve tribes and incorporating even resident ***foreigners*** and their families, provided that they had ***joined*** Israel as converts. These people were to ***receive an allotment,*** just like the ***native-born Israelites,*** and they could pass this inheritance on to their children. In view of the significance of the land to Ezekiel, this was a high privilege.

48:1-8 The land assigned to the tribes was arranged in strips running east to west through the land, rather than piecemeal as it was before the Exile. This was more than simply a way of ensuring that each tribe received equal access to the various resources of the land. It aligned the land with the sacred east–west axis that was so prominent in the Temple. As in the Temple, the size and shape of the central areas were clearly defined, while those on the margins were less closely determined (see note on 40:17-19). The four tribes most distant from the central sacred section (Dan, Asher, Naphtali, and Gad), and therefore in the least privileged position, were descended from the four sons of Jacob by Zilpah and Bilhah, the maidservants of his wives, Leah and Rachel. The eight sons from Leah and Rachel would receive the strips immediately north and south of the holy portion that contained the Temple. Immediately next to the holy portion were the tribes of Benjamin and ***Judah,*** which historically surrounded Jerusalem. Judah received the strip immediately to the north of the holy portion, as if to stress that whereas in the past the land had been divided into north and south—Israel and Judah—now Judah would be in the north.

48:8 ***8⅓ miles:*** Hebrew *25,000 cubits* [13.3 kilometers].

48:9-14 The holy portion was not quite

wide. [10]For the priests there will be a
strip of land measuring 8⅓ miles long by
3⅓ miles wide, with the LORD's Temple at
the center. [11]This area is set aside for the
ordained priests, the descendants of Zadok who served me faithfully and did not
go astray with the people of Israel and the
rest of the Levites. [12]It will be their special
portion when the land is distributed, the
most sacred land of all. Next to the priests'
territory will lie the land where the other
Levites will live.
[13]"The land allotted to the Levites will be
the same size and shape as that belonging
to the priests—8⅓ miles long and 3⅓ miles
wide. Together these portions of land will
measure 8⅓ miles long by 6⅔ miles wide.
[14]None of this special land may ever be sold
or traded or used by others, for it belongs to
the LORD; it is set apart as holy.
[15]"An additional strip of land 8⅓ miles
long by 1⅔ miles wide, south of the sacred
Temple area, will be allotted for public
use—homes, pasturelands, and common
lands, with a city at the center. [16]The city
will measure 1½ miles on each side—north,
south, east, and west. [17]Open lands will
surround the city for 150 yards in every
direction. [18]Outside the city there will be a
farming area that stretches 3⅓ miles to the
east and 3⅓ miles to the west along the border of the sacred area. This farmland will
produce food for the people working in the
city. [19]Those who come from the various
tribes to work in the city may farm it. [20]This
entire area—including the sacred lands and

48:10 Ezek 44:28; 45:4
48:11 Ezek 44:10-15
48:14 Lev 25:32-34
48:15 Ezek 42:20; 45:6
48:16 Rev 21:16

Israel's Geography as Theology (47:13–48:35)

Ezek 40:1–46:24
Rev 22:1-2

The prophet Ezekiel saw a future with strong links to the past, for the land of Israel was still the Promised Land that had been promised to the patriarchs. The division of the land in 47:13–48:35 combines spiritual ideals with a practical message that reinforces themes from earlier sections of the vision (chs 40–46).

The map in this vision does not resemble the earlier tribal patchwork established in Joshua's time (see map on p. 397). Here, each tribe was to receive an equal portion of the land, arranged in east-to-west strips that oriented the whole land on the same axis as the Temple at its center. These strips of land bear no connection to the actual geographic features of the land. The point seems to be that the old tribal jealousies and hatreds will be gone, as each tribe is on exactly the same footing as the others.

The monarchy is not abolished in this vision, but it is reformed, transformed, and given a place among the twelve tribes. The defiled city that was destroyed in the earlier chapters of Ezekiel gives way to a new holy city of unity and harmony for the tribes. The transforming river does its work of life-giving restoration, bringing the blessing that flows from God's Temple to bear on every aspect of the people's lives.

The whole vision of chs 40–48 encourages Ezekiel's hearers to repent of their past sins, to be faithful in the often-difficult present, and to hope for a brighter future through God's power and grace. The closing chapters of the book of Revelation present the same message as fulfilled in Christ (Rev 21–22). Jesus inaugurated the spiritual reality that Ezekiel described—the heavenly city "designed and built by God" (Heb 11:10).

at the exact center of the land; there were seven tribal strips to the north and only five to the south of it. While it was still not exactly central geographically, the spiritual center had apparently moved a significant distance north from where it used to be in Jerusalem.
• The importance of the holy portion *set aside for the LORD's Temple* is underlined by the detailed description of its dimensions and makeup, in contrast with the brevity of the descriptions of the tribal allocations. This *special portion* was devoted to God and was never to be *sold or traded or used by others.* It was made up of strips that ran from east to west and were allocated to the Levites, the priests, and the city. The area *for the ordained priests* immediately surrounded the Temple and protected it from anything unholy. It was flanked by an area to the north for *the Levites.*

48:9 ***8⅓ miles long and 6⅔ miles wide:*** As in one Greek manuscript and the Greek reading in 45:1: *25,000 cubits* [13.3 kilometers] *long and 20,000 cubits* [10.6 kilometers] *wide;* Hebrew reads *25,000 cubits long and 10,000 cubits* [3⅓ miles or 5.3 kilometers] *wide.* Similarly in 48:13. Cp. 45:1-5; 48:10-13.

48:10 ***8⅓ miles long by 3⅓ miles wide:*** Hebrew *25,000 cubits* [13.3 kilometers] *long by 10,000 cubits* [5.3 kilometers] *wide;* also in 48:13.

48:13 ***8⅓ miles long by 3⅓ miles wide . . . 8⅓ miles long and 6⅔ miles wide:*** See notes on 48:9, 10.

48:15-20 To the south was a narrower strip *for public use* where *the city* was located. The overall shape of the central area was thus a square. The city was a visible symbol and focus of unity for the twelve tribes, and home to residents *from the various tribes.*

48:15 ***8⅓ miles long by 1⅔ miles wide:*** Hebrew *25,000 cubits* [13.3 kilometers] *long by 5,000 cubits* [2.65 kilometers] *wide.*

48:16 ***1½ miles:*** Hebrew *4,500 cubits* [2.4 kilometers]; also in 48:30, 32, 33, 34.

48:17 ***150 yards:*** Hebrew *250 cubits* [133 meters].

48:18 ***3⅓ miles to the east and 3⅓ miles to the west:*** Hebrew *10,000 cubits* [5.3 kilometers] *to the east and 10,000 cubits to the west.*

48:21 Ezek 34:24; 45:7
48:23 Gen 35:16-19 Josh 18:21-28
48:24 Gen 29:33; 49:5-7 Josh 19:1-9
48:25 Gen 30:14-18 Josh 19:17-23
48:26 Gen 30:19-20 Josh 19:10-16
48:27 Gen 30:10-11 Josh 13:24-28 Ezek 47:19-20
48:28 Num 34:6
48:29 Ezek 47:13-23
48:31 Rev 21:12-13
48:35 Isa 12:6; 24:23 Jer 3:17; 23:6; 33:16 Joel 3:21 Zech 2:10 Rev 21:3; 22:3

the city—is a square that measures 8⅓ miles on each side.

21“The areas that remain, to the east and to the west of the sacred lands and the city, will belong to the prince. Each of these areas will be 8⅓ miles wide, extending in opposite directions to the eastern and western borders of Israel, with the sacred lands and the sanctuary of the Temple in the center. 22So the prince's land will include everything between the territories allotted to Judah and Benjamin, except for the areas set aside for the sacred lands and the city.

23“These are the territories allotted to the rest of the tribes. Benjamin's territory lies just south of the prince's lands, and it extends across the entire land of Israel from east to west. 24South of Benjamin's territory lies that of Simeon, also extending across the land from east to west. 25Next is the territory of Issachar with the same eastern and western boundaries.

26“Then comes the territory of Zebulun, which also extends across the land from east to west. 27The territory of Gad is just south of Zebulun with the same borders to the east and west. 28The southern border of Gad runs from Tamar to the waters of Meribah at Kadesh and then follows the Brook of Egypt to the Mediterranean.

29“These are the allotments that will be set aside for each tribe's exclusive possession. I, the Sovereign LORD, have spoken!

The Gates of the City

30“These will be the exits to the city: On the north wall, which is 1½ miles long, 31there will be three gates, each one named after a tribe of Israel. The first will be named for Reuben, the second for Judah, and the third for Levi. 32On the east wall, also 1½ miles long, the gates will be named for Joseph, Benjamin, and Dan. 33The south wall, also 1½ miles long, will have gates named for Simeon, Issachar, and Zebulun. 34And on the west wall, also 1½ miles long, the gates will be named for Gad, Asher, and Naphtali.

35“The distance around the entire city will be 6 miles. And from that day the name of the city will be ‘The LORD Is There.’ ”

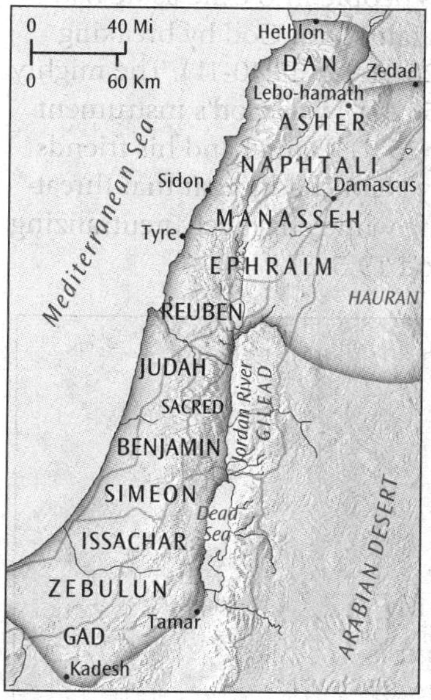

◀ **Ezekiel's Vision of Israel's New Boundaries (47:13–48:29).** The boundaries of Israel in Ezekiel's vision correspond to the ideal boundaries that Moses gave in Num 34:1-10; Ezekiel's boundaries thus encompass the ideal Israel and communicate a promise to Israel in exile that God would fully restore his people. Ezekiel's vision, in keeping with its theological character, does not give specific boundaries for each tribe, only the order of tribes from north to south (48:1-7, 23-29) and a notation that "each tribe will receive an equal share" (47:14).

48:20 *8⅓ miles:* Hebrew *25,000 cubits* [13.3 kilometers]; also in 48:21.

48:21-29 The area filling out the rest of the central portion to the east and west of the holy square was assigned to *the prince*. The prince was more important than the rest of the laity, but he was below the priests and Levites. The same message was delivered by the architecture of the Temple complex.

48:28 *waters of Meribah at Kadesh:* Hebrew *waters of Meribath-kadesh.* • *the Mediterranean:* Literally *the Great Sea.*

48:30-31 At the end of the book, Ezekiel focuses attention on the *exits to the city,* highlighting once again the theme of access that runs throughout chs 40–48. Like the Temple, the city was a measured square with twelve gates, one for each of the tribes, which established a focus of tribal unity. Unusually, the three most important gates, named for *Reuben* (the oldest of the sons of Israel), *Judah* (the royal tribe), and *Levi* (the priestly tribe), faced north rather than east. This is because the most important direction was northward toward the Temple, the center of the renewed land. South was the second most important side because it was on the axis that pointed toward the Temple.

48:32-34 The east-facing gates were assigned to the children of Rachel—*Joseph, Benjamin, and* (through her maidservant) *Dan.* The *south . . . gates* were assigned to *Simeon, Issachar, and Zebulun,* Leah's sons, whose lands would be south of the holy square. The least favored *west . . . gates* were assigned to the descendants of the concubines, *Gad, Asher, and Naphtali.*

48:35 *6 miles:* Hebrew *18,000 cubits* [9.6 kilometers]. • To cap off the whole vision, the city was given a new name, *The LORD Is There* (Hebrew *Yahweh Shammah*). Although the Lord had once departed from Jerusalem and ordered its destruction because of its gross idolatry and bloodshed, the new city was so much a part of the new order of things that it could receive that name. This also implied that the bloody city condemned in earlier chapters had now been replaced by a holy city, fit for God to dwell in among representatives of all twelve of Israel's tribes (cp. Isa 4:2-6; Zech 14:20-21). Thus the prophecy of 37:26-27 finally reached its conclusion and its fulfillment, as God established his sanctuary in the midst of his people forever, just as he promised.

THE BOOK OF
DANIEL

When Daniel came of age in Babylon, Jerusalem, the holy city, lay in ruins. Babylon was flourishing, but it would also soon wither and die. God's people, the children of Israel, were living as exiles in Babylonia. Could they hope to enjoy life as the Lord's chosen nation again? Through Daniel's experiences as a captive and as a government official, and through special messages, God revealed his power and his plan for history to Daniel, showing that he would rescue his people from exile and even from death (12:1-3).

SETTING

In 605 BC, Nebuchadnezzar attacked Jerusalem and captured some Israelites, including some of the young men of Judah's royal family (1:1-4). In this historical event, God began sending his people into exile as he had warned long ago. The Israelites had broken faith with God by breaking his covenant (Deut 28:36, 64; Jer 11:1-17; 25:11-12; 29:10-11). The mighty king Nebuchadnezzar II of Babylon (605–562 BC) was God's instrument and servant to punish his people Israel (Jer 25:9). Daniel and his friends began a process of enculturation ordered by Nebuchadnezzar that threatened to absorb them into a pagan way of life while effectively neutralizing their identity as the Lord's holy people (Exod 19:5-6).

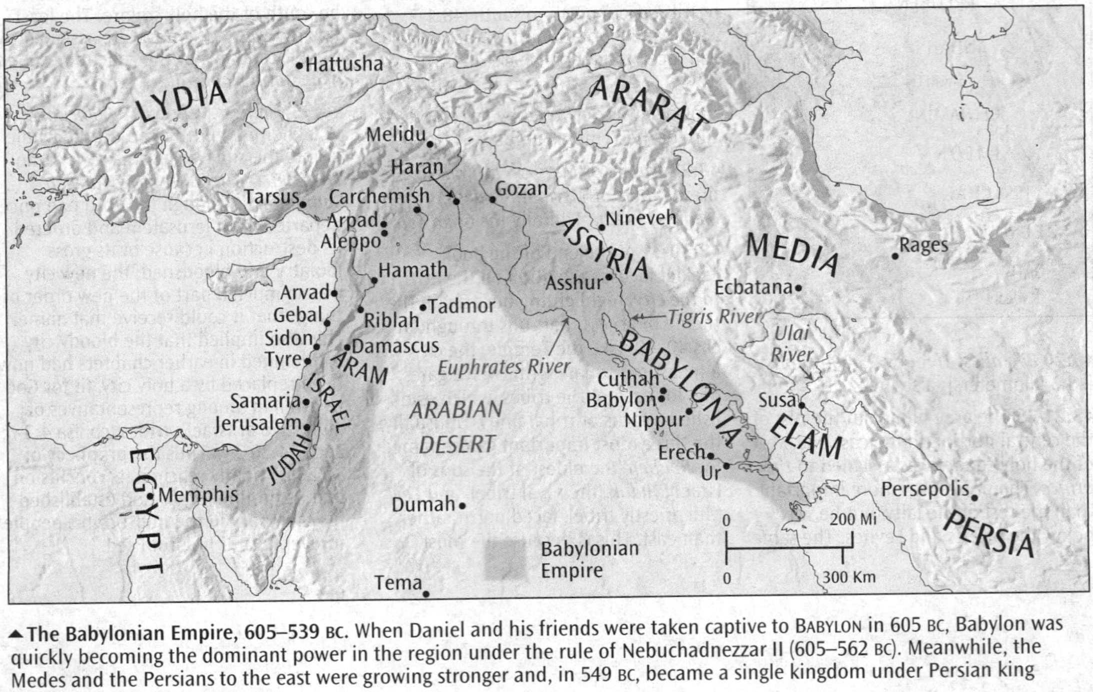

▲**The Babylonian Empire, 605–539 BC.** When Daniel and his friends were taken captive to BABYLON in 605 BC, Babylon was quickly becoming the dominant power in the region under the rule of Nebuchadnezzar II (605–562 BC). Meanwhile, the Medes and the Persians to the east were growing stronger and, in 549 BC, became a single kingdom under Persian king Cyrus II (559–530 BC).

Meanwhile, the Babylonians continued to devastate Judah and Jerusalem. In 597 BC, more Israelites were taken to Babylon, and in 586 BC, Jerusalem was destroyed and additional captives were taken. After 586 BC, Israel was no longer a nation and God's people were totally helpless and hopeless. At this low point in their existence, God's people became the tail of the nations, not their head (see Deut 28:13, 44). It seemed that they might simply be absorbed into Babylon and disappear from the stage of history.

OUTLINE

1:1–6:28
Daniel and His Friends

7:1–12:13
Daniel's Visions for the Present and Future

The promises that Abraham's descendants would be a blessing to all nations seemed hopelessly in default (Gen 12:1-3). The great Gentile superpowers of the ancient Near East, first Assyria and then Babylon, ruled the world. What would happen to Israel in exile? What would become of God's promises to Abraham, Isaac, Jacob, Moses (Exod 19–20), and David (2 Sam 7)? Would God act on the basis of his words of hope through his prophets (e.g., Gen 12:1-3; Exod 19:5-6; Isa 43:18-21; 44:28; 45:1, 13; Amos 9:11-15)? How would God rescue his people from exile?

Daniel went into exile in 605 BC. He maintained his integrity, honored his people, and glorified his God through the reigns of several Babylonian kings to the end of the Babylonian exile. During that time of shame and oppression, God showed Daniel visions of God's future kingdom, when its King would receive power and reign forever. As Daniel endured the "death of exile" (Ezek 37), he prayed faithfully and earnestly, and God answered his prayer.

In 539 BC, Cyrus of Persia shocked the world by invading Babylon, gaining entrance into the capital city, and subduing it and its blasphemous ruler, Belshazzar, just as the prophet Isaiah had predicted he would (Isa 44:26–45:7). Daniel witnessed the decree of the Persian king Cyrus II the Great that the captive peoples could return to their homes (Ezra 1:2-4). This fulfilled Jeremiah's prophecy that after seventy years of servitude to Babylon, God would restore his people (see Jer 25:11-12; 29:10-11).

The Lord brought his holy people back from exile, and he gave them encouragement for the future through Daniel by painting the canvas of history with visions and dreams. The holy people needed help in the new circumstances of the Exile and the return, and God spoke to give his people new hope as they faced a threatening future.

SUMMARY

The book of Daniel covers the period from about 605 to about 535 BC. Chapters 1–6 feature events and stories that demonstrate God's faithfulness to Daniel and his friends as they remained faithful to God and his law. These stories are in roughly chronological order. Three times, the Hebrew captives were faced with royal decrees that went against God's law (chs 1, 3, 6); all three times, they exhibited wisdom while obeying God, and he saved them from harm. Three times, God spoke through Daniel to interpret

TIMELINE

about 627~580 BC
Jeremiah as prophet

605–562 BC
Nebuchadnezzar II as king of Babylon

605 BC
Nebuchadnezzar invades Judah, first deportation

about 605~535 BC
▸ **Daniel in Babylon**

603 BC
Nebuchadnezzar's first dream

559–530 BC
Cyrus II as king of Persia

556–539 BC
Nabonidus as king of Babylon

553?–539 BC
Belshazzar as regent of Babylon (for Nabonidus)

Oct 539 BC
Cyrus II conquers Babylon

538 BC
Cyrus's decree allows exiles to return to Judea

536 BC
Temple rebuilding begins and is halted

Sept 21, 520 BC
Temple rebuilding resumes

515 BC
Temple rebuilding is completed

486–465 BC
Xerxes I (Ahasuerus) as king of Persia

about 480 BC
Esther becomes Queen of Persia

465–424 BC
Artaxerxes I as king of Persia

458 BC
Ezra travels to Jerusalem

445–433 BC
Nehemiah as governor of Judea

424–405 BC
Darius II (Nothus) as king of Persia

336–330 BC
Darius III (Codomanus) as king of Persia

336–323 BC
Alexander III (the Great) as king of Macedon

331 BC
End of the Persian empire

320–198 BC
The Ptolemies of Egypt rule Judea

198–63 BC
The Seleucids of Syria rule Judea

175–163 BC
Antiochus IV (Epiphanes)

167 BC
Antiochus defiles the Temple in Jerusalem

164 BC
Judas Maccabeus cleanses the Temple, origin of the Festival of Dedication (Hanukkah)

revelations he had given to pagan kings (chs 2, 4, 5). Daniel's words and subsequent events showed that God wields ultimate power and authority on earth.

In chs 7–12, the focus shifts to God's sovereignty over the course of history. As in chs 1–6, the visions of these chapters are in roughly chronological order. Chapter 7 uses animal symbolism to tell the same story found in ch 2: World history will culminate in the establishment of God's kingdom, but first there will be fierce opposition to God and his purposes. Chapter 8 highlights the roles of Persia and Greece, culminating in the acts of a wicked ruler who opposes God's people. Chapter 9 features Daniel's marvelous prayer that is inspired by Jeremiah's prophecy of seventy years of servitude (9:1-2). The prayer touched God's heart and helped to end the Exile. As a result of the prayer, the angel Gabriel is sent to Daniel to reveal the coming seventy sets of seven, an overview of God's plan to establish his people and deal with their oppressors (see "The Seventy Sets of Seven" at 9:24-27, p. 1413). In chs 10–12, the book concludes with a final vision that portrays history from the third year of Cyrus (536 BC), to the time of Greece and Rome, and on to the time of the resurrection (see "Resurrection" at 12:1-3, 13, p. 1421). Daniel was faithful to his calling, and he will be raised in the end.

AUTHOR AND DATE

Scholars have endlessly debated the date at which the book of Daniel was put into its final form. Most conservative scholars argue that Daniel wrote the book in the late 500s BC. The book claims to be predictive prophecy (2:29-31; 4:24; 7:1–12:13), and the author places Daniel in the 500s (2:1; 5:1; 10:1). The book displays excellent knowledge of Babylonian history, although some historical issues need to be resolved.

Other scholars argue for dating the book around 164 BC, primarily because Daniel describes events through about that time—the predictions in 11:1-35 are thought to be much too detailed about events that occurred between 190 and 164 BC to have been given 300 years beforehand. There are problems with assigning a late date to the book, however. Above all, the book in its present form is clearly attributed to Daniel alone. One of the major claims of Daniel is that God can predict the future (2:27-29; 10:21). If Daniel himself did not write the predictive prophecies, then the book's claims lack the integrity demanded of one of God's inspired prophets. Without denying the remarkable details, the question of prediction is not conclusive: Who is to say with what detail God may reveal the future to his prophets? Daniel's visions also have characteristics of *apocalyptic literature* (see facing page), and are models for many later apocalypses. Apocalyptic literature was especially popular among Jewish writings of the intertestamental period (after 400 BC), so it has been said that the book could not have been written prior to that time. However, recent studies have argued that apocalyptic thinking is present in biblical books from the exilic period as well. Therefore it is possible to think of Daniel as serving as a model for the later apocalypses. Viewing the book of Daniel as having been written in the 500s BC by Daniel is less problematic than dating it later to avoid the implication that it contains detailed predictive prophecy.

The God of Daniel is always there when you least expect him—in a stone, in a crematorium oven, on a whitewashed wall, in a pit of ferocious beasts.

JOHN E. GOLDINGAY, *Daniel*, p. 330

DANIEL AS LITERATURE

Daniel contains history, but it contains much more. It teaches the theological lessons of history by going behind earthly events to pull out and demonstrate their true meaning and significance. It is concerned mainly to show God's hand and plan by the way it reports its events.

Daniel as Wisdom Literature. Daniel is a book of wisdom intended to make God's people wise in God's ways. The wise person is purified through suffering, seeks the path of righteousness, and leads others into that way (11:33-35; 12:3). The wise person knows that God Most High is the God of gods, that he holds the future in his hands, and that he can rescue his people from any danger (3:16-18; 6:21-22; 12:1-3).

Daniel as Apocalyptic Literature. Certain parts of Daniel belong to a literary genre called *apocalyptic* ("revelation, unveiling what is hidden"). This genre pulls back the curtain of earthly history and reveals the activity of God, angels, and other spiritual powers behind the scenes. These activities affect historical events on the earth. Apocalyptic literature reveals reality, often by using rich symbolic language so that statues, animals, or horns can represent such things as kings, kingdoms, and persons.

It is important to interpret apocalyptic literature according to what its imagery intends. What is the reality and truth behind the imagery? The literary context and the historical background of a passage must be examined in order to properly interpret its symbolism. Sometimes the insights needed to interpret the imagery are found within the text (7:1-14, 16-17, 23-25). In other cases, a study of the social, political, military, or cultural milieu will yield helpful insights. For instance, studying the history of Babylon can be helpful in understanding why a certain image for Babylon (a golden head or a lion) is fitting. By going behind earthly events to demonstrate their true meaning, the book of Daniel teaches theological lessons.

The ancient Greek version of Daniel and the Latin Vulgate include three passages not found in the Hebrew manuscripts. These passages are included in Roman Catholic and Orthodox editions of the Bible, but not in Protestant editions.

The fortunes of kings and the affairs of men are subject to God's decrees. . . . he is able to accomplish his will despite the most determined opposition of the mightiest potentates on earth.

GLEASON L. ARCHER, JR., *Daniel* in *Expositor's Bible Commentary,* vol. 7, p. 8

MEANING AND MESSAGE

Daniel's major theological theme is that God's sovereignty is expressed in God's final purpose for humanity and in all of creation. History is on an inexorable march toward the Kingdom of God, in which God's sovereignty will be fully realized. God judges and rescues his people, controls history as he pleases on a universal scale, and raises up or brings down pagan kingdoms and kings. He decided when to conclude the Exile (9:18-19), and he defeats and controls the powers of evil (4:30, 32; 7:8, 20-21; 10:13; 11:28, 30-32). Heavenly powers bow to him (3:28; 4:23, 35; 5:5; 6:21; 8:16; 9:21; 10:5, 13; 12:1), and he has the power to raise the dead (12:1-3). His wisdom controls all things (3:18; 11:35). He is sovereign to choose and approve of those who are beloved and highly esteemed in his eyes (9:23; 10:11, 19). God establishes his kingdom over all the earth forever, and his people will rule over it with their King, the Son of Man (7:13, 22; Ps 110:1; Matt 24:27-44; 25:31; 26:2, 64; Mark 14:62; Rev 1:7).

FURTHER READING

R. A. ANDERSON
Daniel (1984)

JOYCE BALDWIN
Daniel: An Introduction and Commentary (1978)

JOHN E. GOLDINGAY
Daniel (1989)

TREMPER LONGMAN III
Daniel (1999)

STEPHEN R. MILLER
Daniel (1994)

E. J. YOUNG
The Prophecy of Daniel (1949)

1. DANIEL AND HIS FRIENDS (1:1–6:28)

Daniel in Nebuchadnezzar's Court (1:1-21)

Nebuchadnezzar's Victory over Jehoiakim

1 During the third year of King Jehoiakim's
reign in Judah, King Nebuchadnezzar of
Babylon came to Jerusalem and besieged it.
2 The Lord gave him victory over King Jehoiakim of Judah and permitted him to take
some of the sacred objects from the Temple of God. So Nebuchadnezzar took them
back to the land of Babylonia and placed
them in the treasure-house of his god.

Nebuchadnezzar Educates Young Hebrew Men

3 Then the king ordered Ashpenaz, his chief
of staff, to bring to the palace some of the
young men of Judah's royal family and other
noble families, who had been brought to Babylon as captives. 4 "Select only strong, healthy,
and good-looking young men," he said. "Make
sure they are well versed in every branch
of learning, are gifted with knowledge and
good judgment, and are suited to serve in
the royal palace. Train these young men
in the language and literature of Babylon."
5 The king assigned them a daily ration of
food and wine from his own kitchens. They
were to be trained for three years, and then
they would enter the royal service.
6 Daniel, Hananiah, Mishael, and Azariah
were four of the young men chosen, all from
the tribe of Judah. 7 The chief of staff renamed them with these Babylonian names:

Daniel was called Belteshazzar.
Hananiah was called Shadrach.
Mishael was called Meshach.
Azariah was called Abednego.

God's Blessing:
Appointment at the King's Palace

8 But Daniel was determined not to defile
himself by eating the food and wine given
to them by the king. He asked the chief
of staff for permission not to eat these

1:1 2 Kgs 24:1; 2 Chr 36:6
1:2 Isa 11:11; Jer 27:19-20; Zech 5:5-11
1:3 Isa 39:7
1:5 Dan 1:8, 19
1:6 Ezek 14:14, 20; 28:3; Matt 24:15
1:7 Dan 2:49; 3:12-30; 4:8; 5:12
1:8 Lev 11:47; Deut 32:38; Ezek 4:13-14; Hos 9:3

1:1–6:28 The first half of Daniel, in describing the experiences and wisdom of Daniel and his three Hebrew friends, demonstrates that God is the ruler of the world and that God's people need to be faithful and live and act wisely in every situation in which they find themselves.

1:1-21 God fulfilled his prophetic word by sending his rebellious people into exile (see Jer 25:11-12; 29:10). God also extended his grace to a remnant in exile, and he protected and prospered Daniel and three other young Hebrew captives. These young men received the best training of the time in the Babylonian king's court, and were thus well equipped to be God's witnesses in Babylon. They made the God of Israel known even in exile.

1:1-2 These verses explain how it was that Daniel and his friends were in Babylon and succinctly give the setting in which Daniel lived during the years of exile.

1:1 This event occurred in 605 BC, ***during the third year of King Jehoiakim's reign*** (see timeline, p. 677). Prior to this Jehoiakim (609–598 BC) had been a vassal of Egypt; his reign in Judah was exceedingly wicked (Jer 25:1-38; 2 Kgs 23:36–24:6; 2 Chr 36:5-8). The exile and captivity of Daniel and his friends in 605 BC prefigure the exile of the rest of the nation in 597 and 586 BC (see 2 Kgs 24:1–25:21). The Lord employed ***King Nebuchadnezzar of Babylon*** as his unwitting servant to accomplish his ends (cp. Jer 25:9; 27:6).

1:2 The ***Lord,*** who is sovereign over history, ***gave*** the ***victory*** to Nebuchadnezzar; it was not accomplished by the king's might or the power of his god Marduk, the high god of the Babylonian pantheon. The Lord used the Exile to judge and discipline his people, as had been threatened in the Law (e.g., Deut 28:64) and by the prophets (e.g., Jer 25:8-14). • The ***sacred objects*** had been dedicated and set aside for use in ***the Temple of God*** built by Solomon. After spending nearly seventy years in the ***treasure-house*** of Marduk, these vessels were further defiled by Belshazzar in 539 BC (5:1-4); they were later returned to the rebuilt Temple in Ezra's time (Ezra 1:7-11; 5:13-16). • ***the land of Babylonia*** (Hebrew ***the land of Shinar***): Israel's rebellion led them back to where rebellious humanity had constructed the Tower of Babel (Gen 11:2).

1:3-7 The Lord fulfilled his threat to make sons of the ***royal family*** serve in Babylon (Isa 39:7) despite their being heirs to the promises of Davidic kingship. Nebuchadnezzar made a powerful attempt to proselytize them by education, social and religious pressure, and name changes. Instead, their impact upon their pagan surroundings became the outstanding feature of their stay at the king's palace and court.

1:3 ***staff:*** Though often translated "eunuchs" (cp. Isa 39:7), in this case the Hebrew term (*saris*) likely means that ***Ashpenaz*** and those under his authority were high government officials (see 2 Kgs 8:6).

1:4 ***strong, healthy:*** They had no defect or blemish that would disqualify them; the Lord had the same requirements for Israel's priests (Lev 21:16-24; 22:17-25). These youths had the wisdom, knowledge, understanding, and character needed to function at the highest levels of government. • The ***literature of Babylon*** (or ***of the Chaldeans***) was immense and included wisdom and esoteric literature, creation stories, magic incantations, theogonies (origins and genealogies of the gods), legal corpora, ancient histories, letters, dream journals, vision manuals, and mathematical and astrological materials. The education of these ***young men***—all in a foreign ***language***—rivaled that of Moses under Pharaoh and Alexander under Aristotle.

1:5 The king attempted to create a bond of dependence, gratitude, and loyalty by giving them ***food and wine from his own kitchens.***

1:6-7 Their new Babylonian names were to help enculturate the Hebrews into the pagan Babylonian society. ***Daniel*** ("God is my Judge" or "God has judged") became ***Belteshazzar*** ("Bel [a Babylonian god] protects his life"). ***Hananiah*** ("the LORD is grace") became ***Shadrach*** (possibly meaning "command of Aku," another Babylonian god). ***Mishael*** ("who is God?") became ***Meshach*** ("who is Aku?"). ***Azariah*** ("the LORD helps") became ***Abednego*** ("servant of Nego/Nebo," another Babylonian god).

1:8-14 Daniel determined not to defile himself with the king's food and wine or to yield his religious and moral independence to the king. He gave God the opportunity to demonstrate his loving kindness and care toward his trustworthy servants. This strong reliance upon God by Daniel and his friends is a significant motif throughout the book (see also 2:16-23; 3:16-18; 6:16).

1:8 ***Daniel was determined not to defile himself:*** The meat and wine from

1:9 Ps 106:46; Prov 16:7
1:12 Dan 1:16
1:15 Exod 23:25; Prov 10:22
1:16 Dan 1:12

unacceptable foods. 9Now God had given
the chief of staff both respect and affection
for Daniel. 10But he responded, "I am afraid
of my lord the king, who has ordered that
you eat this food and wine. If you become
pale and thin compared to the other youths
your age, I am afraid the king will have me
beheaded."
11Daniel spoke with the attendant who
had been appointed by the chief of staff to
look after Daniel, Hananiah, Mishael, and
Azariah. 12"Please test us for ten days on a
diet of vegetables and water," Daniel said.
13"At the end of the ten days, see how we
look compared to the other young men who
are eating the king's food. Then make your
decision in light of what you see." 14The attendant agreed to Daniel's suggestion and
tested them for ten days.
15At the end of the ten days, Daniel and
his three friends looked healthier and better nourished than the young men who had
been eating the food assigned by the king.
16So after that, the attendant fed them only

DANIEL (1:1–12:13)

Ezek 14:14, 20; 28:3; Matt 24:15

Daniel is a stirring example of faith, wisdom, and endurance under difficulty and oppression. His life and prophecies affirm that God is in control and will have the final victory despite apparently dominant evil forces.

Daniel was a young man of Judah's royal family when the Babylonian army first attacked Jerusalem in 605 BC (1:3). Daniel was deported to Babylon with Azariah, Hananiah, and Mishael. King Nebuchadnezzar trained these young men to serve his growing empire. Daniel and his friends were the brightest and healthiest of the students, so they assumed important positions in Nebuchadnezzar's court.

Daniel's court career lasted nearly seventy years (cp. 1:21). He quickly established a reputation for intelligence and absolute fidelity to God. When Nebuchadnezzar had a troubling dream (ch 2), God revealed its meaning to Daniel, who explained it to the king. Later, Daniel interpreted a second dream about the king's pride (ch 4). Daniel urged Nebuchadnezzar to repent, but he did not. As a result, Nebuchadnezzar became temporarily deranged (4:28-34).

Daniel always treated the Babylonian king respectfully, and Nebuchadnezzar had high regard for Daniel, whose character and behavior led him to worship the Lord (though not exclusively). Daniel's faithfulness and prudence encourage later readers in similarly hostile cultures.

Later, Belshazzar, vice-regent of Babylon, profaned the sacred vessels from the Jerusalem Temple during a banquet (539 BC). A disembodied hand suddenly wrote the words "MENE, MENE, TEKEL, and PARSIN" on the palace wall, which Daniel interpreted as forecasting Babylon's imminent end. That same night, Belshazzar was killed by Persians who captured the capital (5:30).

Under Darius the Mede (539 BC), Daniel became an administrator of the realm (6:2). Daniel's capable management infuriated political enemies, who persuaded Darius to pass a decree forbidding worship of anyone but the king, under penalty of being cast into a lions' den. To preserve his religious integrity, Daniel violated the law, but he was miraculously unscathed by the lions. Thereafter he was restored to his office (6:17-28). Daniel's latest visions date from about this time (10:1, 4).

Daniel's prophecies are difficult to understand in detail, but their message is clear: Evil forces are now in power, but God is in control and will save his people. Jesus and NT authors cited Daniel, often using his imagery when speaking of the end times (e.g., cp. Dan 7:1-9 and Rev 13:1-10; Dan 7:13 and Rev 1:7; Dan 9:27 and Matt 24:15). Daniel had no doubts that God Most High would be victorious.

Nebuchadnezzar's table were probably unclean by Jewish standards. The Babylonians used unclean meats such as pork (see Lev 11:1-23; Deut 14:1-21), and their meat and wine had probably been dedicated to Babylonian gods. The other young Hebrews agreed with Daniel (1:12-16). They trusted God and obeyed his commands, and God blessed them (cp. Deut 28:1-14).

1:9 ***God*** worked on Daniel's behalf by influencing Ashpenaz's attitude (cp. Exod 11:3).

1:10 Ashpenaz was understandably ***afraid of*** the king.

1:11-13 Daniel found a wise solution that would protect his spiritual integrity and Ashpenaz's head.

1:12 ***vegetables and water:*** Such a diet would steer clear of offensive foods (1:8) and, as a kind of fast, would demonstrate mourning over their exile in a foreign land.

1:13-14 ***make your decision:*** Daniel's exemplary wisdom, prudence, and courtesy are seen in his respectful stance toward his ***attendant,*** who responded favorably.

1:15-21 In their training, Daniel and his friends completed a tough curriculum in the context of the most threatening pagan culture, yet they remained faithful to the Lord. As they mastered language, literature, and science, they pursued excellence and honored God, who added many gifts to their skills and learning.

vegetables instead of the food and wine provided for the others.
17God gave these four young men an unusual aptitude for understanding every
aspect of literature and wisdom. And God
gave Daniel the special ability to interpret
the meanings of [a]visions and dreams.
18When the training period ordered by
the king was completed, the chief of staff
brought all the young men to King Nebuchadnezzar. 19The king talked with them,
and no one impressed him as much as Daniel, Hananiah, Mishael, and Azariah. So they
entered the royal service. 20Whenever the
king consulted them in any matter requiring wisdom and balanced judgment, he
found them ten times more capable than
any of the magicians and enchanters in his
entire kingdom.
21Daniel remained in the royal service until the first year of the reign of King Cyrus.

Nebuchadnezzar's Dream (2:1-49)
A Dream Troubles Nebuchadnezzar

2 One night during the second year of his
reign, Nebuchadnezzar had such disturbing dreams that he couldn't sleep. 2He
called in his magicians, enchanters, sorcerers, and astrologers, and he demanded that
they tell him what he had dreamed. As they
stood before the king, 3he said, "I have had
a dream that deeply troubles me, and I must
know what it means."
4Then the astrologers answered the king
in Aramaic, "Long live the king! Tell us the
dream, and we will tell you what it means."
5But the king said to the astrologers, "I am
serious about this. If you don't tell me what
my dream was and what it means, you will
be torn limb from limb, and your houses
will be turned into heaps of rubble! 6But if
you tell me what I dreamed and what the
dream means, I will give you many wonderful gifts and honors. Just tell me the dream
and what it means!"
7They said again, "Please, Your Majesty.
Tell us the dream, and we will tell you what
it means."
8The king replied, "I know what you are
doing! You're stalling for time because you
know I am serious when I say, 9'If you don't
tell me the dream, you are doomed.' So you
have conspired to tell me lies, hoping I will

1:17 1 Kgs 3:12, 28; Job 32:8; Dan 1:20; 2:19; 7:1; 8:1; [a]*khazon* (2377) ‣ Dan 8:1
1:19 Gen 41:46; Dan 1:5
1:20 Num 14:22; Isa 19:3; Dan 1:17; 2:2, 27-28; 4:18; 5:7
1:21 Dan 6:28; 10:1
2:1 Gen 40:5-8; 41:1, 8; Esth 6:1; Job 33:15-17; Dan 6:18
2:3 Dan 4:5
2:4 Ezra 4:7; Isa 36:11; Dan 3:9; 5:10
2:5 Ezra 6:11; Dan 2:12; 3:29
2:6 Dan 2:48; 5:7, 16, 29
2:9 Esth 4:11; Isa 41:22-24
2:10 Dan 2:27

1:17 All *four young men* were outstanding students. *God gave Daniel the special ability to interpret . . . visions and dreams,* which were often prophetic (cp. Joseph, Gen 37:5-11).

1:19 *The king talked with* all the young men who were trained, not just Daniel and his three friends. This was a thorough oral examination and discussion of things that were most important to the king. God arranged for the four young men to be his witnesses among the nations, and they were greatly honored by being appointed to positions of power, responsibility, and opportunity (cp. Gen 41:37-40; 45:5; Exod 2:1-10).

1:20 The *magicians* were a class of soothsayer priests who could also interpret dreams (cp. Gen 44:1-15) and do wonders (cp. Exod 7:11). The term *enchanters* (Hebrew *'ashap*), found only in Daniel, comes from an Akkadian term for people who uttered spells.

1:21 *the first year of the reign of King Cyrus:* Cyrus the Great ruled over Persia (559–530 BC), Media (from 549 BC), and Babylon (from 539 BC). He thus created the Persian empire (539–331 BC; see notes on 5:30, 31; cp. Isa 45:1-2).

2:1–6:28 This section contains stories and dreams from the experiences of Daniel and his friends in Babylon. Daniel exercised his special gift of understanding the meaning of dreams and his mastery of literature and science (1:17). Chapter 2 gives a broad schematic view of all history until the appearance of God's kingdom (2:44-49). Chapters 3–6 portray the demise of Babylon and the rise of Persia. History moves toward its inexorable goal—the everlasting Kingdom of God (2:44; 4:2-3, 34; 6:26).

Chapter 2	Chapter 7	Kingdom
Head of Gold	Lion	Babylon
Chest and Arms of Silver	Bear	Media–Persia
Belly and Thighs of Bronze	Leopard	Greece
Legs of Iron	Fourth Beast	Rome

▲ **Four World Empires.** The empires of ch 2 and ch 7 have traditionally been identified as shown.

2:1-49 God gave a dream that encompassed the flow of world history over the centuries, and Daniel interpreted the enigmatic imagery of this revelation. This dream and its interpretation reflect a key theme of the book—the assured final establishment of the Kingdom of God as the ultimate goal of history (2:44-45; 7:9-14, 26-27). These verses also demonstrate the inability of paganism to discern the activity and plans of Israel's God.

2:1-3 Nebuchadnezzar's dream disturbed him so much that he called on his specially trained advisers to help him.

2:1 The *second year* of Nebuchadnezzar's *reign* was 603 BC (see timeline, p. 1389). If the three-year training period for Daniel and his friends is understood as having occurred in parts of three calendar years, it could have been completed by this time (cp. 2:48).

2:2 *magicians, enchanters:* See note on 1:20. • *Sorcerers* were incantation priests or ritual technicians. • *Astrologers* (or *Chaldeans;* also in 2:4, 5, 10) studied the heavenly bodies to discern the times and seasons of major events.

2:3 *a dream that deeply troubles me:* The king had reason to fear that his throne might be in danger from other groups.

2:4 *in Aramaic:* The original text from this point through chapter 7 is in Aramaic. This change to Aramaic is also found in the Dead Sea Scrolls. Aramaic had been established by the Assyrians as the lingua franca of international communication. The practice was continued by the Babylonians. • *Tell us the dream:* The Babylonian wise men needed to know the contents of the dream in order to look them up in reference books. They did not depend on divine revelation.

2:9 Only someone with supernatural insight could tell Nebuchadnezzar the contents of his dream (cp. Mark 2:9-12).

2:10-11 The Babylonian wise men

2:11
Gen 41:39
Exod 29:45
Isa 57:15
Dan 5:11

2:12
Ps 76:10
Dan 2:5; 3:13

2:13
Dan 1:19-20

2:14
Dan 2:24

2:18
Gen 18:28
Isa 37:4
Jer 33:3
Ezek 36:27
Dan 2:23

2:19
Num 12:6
2 Kgs 6:8-12
Job 33:15-16
Dan 7:2, 7

2:20
1 Chr 29:11-12
Job 12:13
Ps 103:1-2; 113:2
Dan 2:21-23

change my mind. But tell me the dream, and
then I'll know that you can tell me what it
means."
10The astrologers replied to the king, "No
one on earth can tell the king his dream!
And no king, however great and powerful,
has ever asked such a thing of any magician,
enchanter, or astrologer! 11The king's demand is impossible. No one except the gods
can tell you your dream, and they do not live
here among people."

The King's Lethal Decree

12The king was furious when he heard this,
and he ordered that all the wise men of
Babylon be executed. 13And because of the
king's decree, men were sent to find and kill
Daniel and his friends.
14When Arioch, the commander of the
king's guard, came to kill them, Daniel
handled the situation with wisdom and discretion. 15He asked Arioch, "Why has the
king issued such a harsh decree?" So Arioch
told him all that had happened. 16Daniel went
at once to see the king and requested more
time to tell the king what the dream meant.

Prayer and Praise for Divine Help

17Then Daniel went home and told his
friends Hananiah, Mishael, and Azariah
what had happened. 18He urged them to ask
the God of heaven to show them his mercy
by telling them the secret, so they would
not be executed along with the other wise
men of Babylon. 19That night the secret was
revealed to Daniel in a vision. Then Daniel
praised the God of heaven. 20He said,

"Praise the name of God forever and ever,
for he has all wisdom and power.

Four World Empires (2:1-45; 7:1-28)

Two panoramic visions in Daniel present God's sovereignty over history. Nebuchadnezzar had the first vision (ch 2), and Daniel had another like it (ch 7). In each of these visions, four of the kingdoms of the world are presented.

There have always been questions about the identities of the four empires, but historically there has also been consensus. Hippolytus (AD 170–236), one of the early church fathers, identified the four kingdoms as Babylonia, Media-Persia, Greece, and Rome. The church father and historian Eusebius of Caesarea (AD 260–340) initially identified the first kingdom as Assyria (which once also controlled Babylon), but he later agreed with Hippolytus, as did most of the church fathers. Later, Jerome and Augustine accepted this same understanding, and conservative interpreters largely still agree.

In antiquity and in our era, some interpreters have argued that Greece is the fourth empire, and they treat the Medes as a separate kingdom. This interpretation is due in part to denying the possibility of prediction and assuming that the book was written about 164 BC, when the Roman empire had not yet arisen. But Media and Persia are usually regarded as one empire, and the Median kingdom had been mostly assimilated by the Persians by the time Cyrus II conquered Babylon in 539 BC.

Rome is then seen as the fourth kingdom, but the bestial, demonic, and inhumane characteristics of the vision extend beyond the historical Rome. The visions represent a panorama of the whole world and its governments; all will be destroyed and replaced by the Kingdom of God, the "rock cut from a mountain" (2:34). The metals of the statue become progressively less valuable in ch 2, while the animal imagery of ch 7 becomes more menacingly fierce, violent, and inhumane. These features represent a deterioration of human civilization across the centuries, even as the Kingdom of God grows in power and stature (2:35).

could possibly interpret dreams, but they could not retell them without being told, and they recognized that ***such a thing*** was only possible for divinity (cp. 2:17-23, 27-28).

2:12 ***The king was furious*** because contradicting or refusing the king's command was an offense punishable by death. The king was supposed to be treated as divine, so they were violating protocol in saying that he was not. The king's sages were also supposed to have a connection with the divine, but they admitted that they did not. The offense to the king was so severe that ***he ordered that all the wise men of Babylon be executed***. The king's rage foreshadows 11:11-35.

2:16 The fact that Daniel could go ***at once to see the king*** shows his authority and influence. Daniel demonstrated his wisdom and excellent protocol at the royal court by using gentle words to turn away anger (cp. Prov 15:1).

2:17-23 With faith and wisdom, Daniel prayed for God's intervention (cp. Phil 4:6). When God answered his prayer, Daniel praised God for giving him wisdom and knowledge (2:20-21). The God of heaven produced the dream and its meaning, demonstrating his supremacy over all other gods, including the gods of Babylon.

2:18 Daniel appealed to God's ***mercy*** (see Exod 34:6-7). God was not obligated to answer Daniel's prayer, but doing so would accord with his character.

2:20-23 Daniel acknowledged and praised Israel's God (***God of my ancestors***, 2:23) as the source of the dream and its interpretation.

21 He controls the course of world events;
he removes kings and sets up other
kings.
He gives wisdom to the wise
and knowledge to the scholars.
22 He reveals deep and mysterious things
and knows what lies hidden in darkness,
though he is surrounded by light.
23 I thank and praise you, God of my
ancestors,
for you have given me wisdom and
strength.
You have told me what we asked of you
and revealed to us what the king
demanded."

Daniel Interprets the Dream

24 Then Daniel went in to see Arioch, whom
the king had ordered to execute the wise
men of Babylon. Daniel said to him, "Don't
kill the wise men. Take me to the king, and I
will tell him the meaning of his dream."
25 Arioch quickly took Daniel to the king
and said, "I have found one of the captives
from Judah who will tell the king the meaning of his dream!"
26 The king said to Daniel (also known as
Belteshazzar), "Is this true? Can you tell me
what my dream was and what it means?"
27 Daniel replied, "There are no wise men,
enchanters, magicians, or fortune-tellers
who can reveal the king's secret.
28 But there
is a God in heaven who reveals secrets, and
he has shown King Nebuchadnezzar what
will happen in the future. Now I will tell you
your dream and the visions you saw as you
lay on your bed.
29 "While Your Majesty was sleeping, you
dreamed about coming events. He who reveals secrets has shown you what is going to
happen.
30 And it is not because I am wiser
than anyone else that I know the secret of
your dream, but because God wants you to
understand what was in your heart.
31 "In your vision, Your Majesty, you saw
standing before you a huge, shining statue
of a man. It was a frightening sight.
32 The
head of the statue was made of fine gold.
Its chest and arms were silver, its belly and
thighs were bronze,
33 its legs were iron,
and its feet were a combination of iron and
baked clay.
34 As you watched, a rock was
cut from a mountain, but not by human
hands. It struck the feet of iron and clay,
smashing them to bits.
35 The whole statue
was crushed into small pieces of iron, clay,
bronze, silver, and gold. Then the wind blew
them away without a trace, like chaff on a
threshing floor. But the rock that knocked
the statue down became a great mountain
that covered the whole earth.
36 "That was the dream. Now we will tell
the king what it means.
37 Your Majesty, you
are the greatest of kings. The God of heaven
has given you sovereignty, power, strength,
and honor.
38 He has made you the ruler over
all the inhabited world and has put even the
wild animals and birds under your control.
You are the head of gold.
39 "But after your kingdom comes to an
end, another kingdom, inferior to yours, will
rise to take your place. After that kingdom
has fallen, yet a third kingdom, represented
by bronze, will rise to rule the world.

2:21 1 Kgs 3:9-10; 4:29; Job 12:18-19; Ps 75:6-7; Dan 7:25; Jas 1:5
2:22 Job 12:22; 26:6; Ps 139:12; Isa 45:7; Jer 23:24; Dan 2:19, 28; Jas 1:17; 1 Jn 1:5
2:23 Gen 31:42; Dan 2:21
2:24 Dan 2:12-13; Acts 27:24
2:25 Gen 41:14; Dan 1:6; 5:13; 6:13
2:27 Dan 2:2, 10-11; 5:7-8
2:28 Gen 40:8; 41:16; Dan 2:22, 45
2:30 Gen 41:16; Ps 139:2; Isa 45:3; Dan 1:17
2:34 Dan 8:25; Zech 4:6
2:35 Ps 1:4; 37:10; Isa 17:13; Hos 13:3
2:37 Isa 10:8; 47:5; Jer 27:6-7; Ezek 26:7; Hos 8:10
2:38 Ps 50:10

2:21 The dream revealed the Lord as the sovereign king of history (see 2:29-45).

2:24 Daniel's influence with *Arioch* indicates Daniel's wisdom and stature in the royal service.

2:25 There were *captives* in Babylon from other nations besides *Judah*. • Daniel, one of Abraham's offspring, brought the blessing of God's revelation to the Babylonian king (see Gen 12:3).

2:26 *Is this true?* Nebuchadnezzar was surprised that a non-Babylonian could have this ability since the Babylonian religion and culture strongly emphasized their own wise men as "purveyors of the heavens."

2:27-28 Daniel made it clear that no human could do what was required (cp. 2:10-11; see also Gen 41:16).

2:28 *a God in heaven:* Daniel proclaimed one true God who rules all things (2:20-21), not a limited local deity such as the ones the Babylonians worshiped. The God of Daniel's ancestors (2:23) is the *God in heaven who reveals secrets.* The Babylonian gods could not do this. • *what will happen:* In the ancient world, dreams were often understood as revealing *the future.*

2:29-30 God had shown the king the long march of future history. Nebuchadnezzar was keenly interested in history, pursuing knowledge of the past and seeking to make a place for himself as history went forward. *God* wanted Nebuchadnezzar *to understand* the course of history, perhaps to impress upon him that Israel's God, the God of heaven, is the God of all history.

2:31-33 The progression downward is one of value: from the most valuable, *gold* (2:32), to the least valuable, *iron and baked clay* (2:33).

2:32 There were gradations of gold; *fine gold* was the highest quality. • *thighs:* Above the knees.

2:33 *legs:* Below the knees.

2:34 The phrase *from a mountain* is implied (cp. 2:35) but is not in the Aramaic text.

2:35 *covered* (literally *filled*) *the whole earth:* Cp. Gen 1:28; Exod 1:7; Matt 28:18-20. This new kingdom would replace all other kingdoms.

2:36-38 *you are the greatest of kings* (literally *king of kings*): Nebuchadnezzar had attained kingship over all other empires and their kings. He was the appointed ruler for that time in history (Jer 25:8-9).

2:39 *inferior to yours:* Silver was inferior in value to gold, as the chest is lower than the head. Nebuchadnezzar was an enormously stable ruler who held the Neo-Babylonian empire together. Persia, by contrast, was often threatened with internal divisions and instability around the periphery.

2:40
Dan 7:7, 23
2:44
Ps 2:9; 145:13
Isa 9:6-7; 60:12
Ezek 37:25
Mic 4:7
2:45
Gen 41:28, 32
Dan 2:29
Rev 22:6
2:46
Lev 26:31
Dan 3:5, 7
Acts 10:25; 14:13
Rev 19:10; 22:8
2:47
Deut 10:17
2 Sam 7:22
Dan 3:15; 4:25
Amos 3:7
2:48
Gen 41:39-43
Dan 2:6; 3:1, 12, 30; 5:16
2:49
Esth 2:19, 21
Dan 3:12-30
Amos 5:15
3:1
Isa 46:6
Jer 16:20
Dan 2:31
Hab 2:19
3:2
Dan 3:3, 27; 6:1-7
3:4
Isa 40:9; 58:1
Dan 3:7; 4:1; 6:25
Rev 14:6
3:5
Dan 3:7, 10

40Following that kingdom, there will be a
fourth one, as strong as iron. That kingdom
will smash and crush all previous empires,
just as iron smashes and crushes everything it strikes. 41The feet and toes you saw
were a combination of iron and baked clay,
showing that this kingdom will be divided.
Like iron mixed with clay, it will have some
of the strength of iron. 42But while some
parts of it will be as strong as iron, other
parts will be as weak as clay. 43This mixture
of iron and clay also shows that these kingdoms will try to strengthen themselves by
forming alliances with each other through
intermarriage. But they will not hold together, just as iron and clay do not mix.
44"During the reigns of those kings, the
God of heaven will set up a kingdom that
will never be destroyed or conquered. It
will crush all these kingdoms into nothingness, and it will stand forever. 45That is the
meaning of the rock cut from the mountain,
though not by human hands, that crushed
to pieces the statue of iron, bronze, clay, silver, and gold. The great God was showing
the king what will happen in the future. The
dream is true, and its meaning is certain."

Nebuchadnezzar Rewards Daniel

46Then King Nebuchadnezzar threw himself down before Daniel and worshiped
him, and he commanded his people to offer
sacrifices and burn sweet incense before
him. 47The king said to Daniel, "Truly, your
God is the greatest of gods, the Lord over
kings, a revealer of mysteries, for you have
been able to reveal this secret."
48Then the king appointed Daniel to a
high position and gave him many valuable
gifts. He made Daniel ruler over the whole
province of Babylon, as well as chief over all
his wise men. 49At Daniel's request, the king
appointed Shadrach, Meshach, and Abednego to be in charge of all the affairs of the
province of Babylon, while Daniel remained
in the king's court.

Rescue from a Furious King (3:1-30)

Nebuchadnezzar Demands Worship

3 King Nebuchadnezzar made a gold
statue ninety feet tall and nine feet wide
and set it up on the plain of Dura in the province of Babylon. 2Then he sent messages to
the high officers, officials, governors, advisers, treasurers, judges, magistrates, and all
the provincial officials to come to the dedication of the statue he had set up. 3So all
these officials came and stood before the
statue King Nebuchadnezzar had set up.
4Then a herald shouted out, "People of all
races and nations and languages, listen to the
king's command! 5When you hear the sound
of the horn, flute, zither, lyre, harp, pipes,
and other musical instruments, bow to the
ground to worship King Nebuchadnezzar's

2:41-42 *as weak as clay:* Feet are crucial to stability; the feet were brittle and illustrate how precarious the whole image—that is, earthly kingdoms and their power—would be.

2:43 ***Just as iron and clay do not mix, . . . intermarriage*** among different people groups could weaken political alliances rather than produce real or lasting unity. This empire would be fragmented.

2:44 ***Those kings*** were probably kings that arose within the fourth kingdom and attempted to strengthen themselves by alliances of intermarriage. However, the phrase might refer to all the kings of the statue as God's kingdom persistently breaks into the flow of history. • ***it will stand forever:*** Only a kingdom whose authority and power are from God (see John 18:36) can ***never be destroyed,*** for all earthly kingdoms crumble.

2:45 The Babylonians often pictured the earth as a mountain (or *ziggurat*); hence, ***the rock*** would cover or replace the entire earth. • ***The dream is true:*** The dream, clearly explained by divine revelation, was truth from God. • ***its meaning is certain:*** God guaranteed that what the dream communicated would certainly take place.

2:46 The Aramaic word translated ***worshiped*** could also be translated "paid him homage or honor," but not necessarily so. Nebuchadnezzar was a pagan; his religion had many gods, and he thought that the spirit of the gods was in Daniel (4:8; cp. 5:11). Nevertheless, he was recognizing that what Daniel had done was not the result of the ordinary human spirit (cp. Gen 41:38).

2:47 ***greatest of gods . . . Lord over kings:*** Nebuchadnezzar repaid the compliment (2:37-38), acknowledging by his words and actions (2:46) that God is supreme over all, even over Nebuchadnezzar himself.

2:48 ***Daniel*** was made ***ruler*** over ***Babylon*** as the king's deputy (cp. Gen 41:37-46).

2:49 Daniel delegated the administration of the province to his three friends so that he could remain ***in the king's court*** as his counselor.

3:1-30 Nebuchadnezzar's megalomania, perhaps encouraged by the vision of ch 2, inspired him to construct a gilded statue and demand that everyone in his empire worship it. He had not learned the lesson that God cannot be captured in any created thing. The three young Hebrews refused to worship it as a god. They were faithful to the Lord, and the Lord rescued them from the king's wrath.

3:1 ***ninety feet tall and nine feet wide:*** Aramaic *60 cubits* [27 meters] *tall and 6 cubits* [2.7 meters] *wide.* • The ***plain of Dura*** might be the plain adjacent to the city of Babylon, or the Aramaic term might refer to the magnificent outer wall of Babylon described by the Greek historian Herodotus. • ***statue:*** Literally *image.*

3:2 The various classes of people were all governmental ***officials.***

3:3 ***all these officials:*** Literally *the high officers, officials, governors, advisers, treasurers, judges, magistrates, and all the provincial officials.*

3:5 The identification of some of these ***musical instruments*** is uncertain. ***Pipes*** could be rendered "drums," or possibly this was a word of musical direction that indicated being "in harmony" with the ***other*** instruments.

gold statue. 6Anyone who refuses to obey will immediately be thrown into a blazing furnace."

7So at the sound of the musical instruments, all the people, whatever their race or nation or language, bowed to the ground and worshiped the gold statue that King Nebuchadnezzar had set up.

8But some of the astrologers went to the king and informed on the Jews. 9They said to King Nebuchadnezzar, "Long live the king! 10You issued a decree requiring all the people to bow down and worship the gold statue when they hear the sound of the horn, flute, zither, lyre, harp, pipes, and other musical instruments. 11That decree also states that those who refuse to obey must be thrown into a blazing furnace. 12But there are some Jews—Shadrach, Meshach, and Abednego—whom you have put in charge of the province of Babylon. They pay no attention to you, Your Majesty. They refuse to serve your gods and do not worship the gold statue you have set up."

13Then Nebuchadnezzar flew into a rage and ordered that Shadrach, Meshach, and Abednego be brought before him. When they were brought in, 14Nebuchadnezzar said to them, "Is it true, Shadrach, Meshach, and Abednego, that you refuse to serve my gods or to worship the gold statue I have set up? 15I will give you one more chance to bow down and worship the statue I have made when you hear the sound of the musical instruments. But if you refuse, you will be thrown immediately into the blazing furnace. And then what god will be able to rescue you from my power?"

16Shadrach, Meshach, and Abednego replied, "O Nebuchadnezzar, we do not need to defend ourselves before you. 17If we are thrown into the blazing furnace, the God whom we serve is able to save us. He will rescue us from your power, Your Majesty. 18But even if he doesn't, we want to make it clear to you, Your Majesty, that we will never serve your gods or worship the gold statue you have set up."

The Blazing Furnace

19Nebuchadnezzar was so furious with Shadrach, Meshach, and Abednego that his face became distorted with rage. He commanded that the furnace be heated seven times hotter than usual. 20Then he ordered some of the strongest men of his army to bind Shadrach, Meshach, and Abednego and throw them into the blazing furnace. 21So they tied them up and threw them into the furnace, fully dressed in their pants, turbans, robes, and other garments. 22And because the king, in his anger, had demanded such a hot fire in the furnace, the flames killed the soldiers as they threw the three men in. 23So Shadrach, Meshach, and Abednego, securely tied, fell into the roaring flames.

24But suddenly, Nebuchadnezzar jumped up in amazement and exclaimed to his advisers, "Didn't we tie up three men and throw them into the furnace?"

"Yes, Your Majesty, we certainly did," they replied.

25"Look!" Nebuchadnezzar shouted. "I see four men, unbound, walking around in the fire unharmed! And the fourth looks like a god!"

26Then Nebuchadnezzar came as close as he could to the door of the flaming furnace and shouted: "Shadrach, Meshach, and Abednego, servants of the Most High God, come out! Come here!"

So Shadrach, Meshach, and Abednego stepped out of the fire. 27Then the high officers, officials, governors, and advisers crowded around them and saw that the fire had not touched them. Not a hair on

3:6
Jer 29:22
Dan 3:11, 15, 21; 6:7
Matt 13:42
Rev 9:2; 14:11

3:8
Ezra 4:12-16
Esth 3:8-9

3:10
Dan 6:12

3:13
Dan 2:12; 3:19

3:14
Isa 46:1
Dan 3:1; 4:8

3:15
Exod 5:2
Isa 36:18-20
Jer 50:2
Dan 2:47

3:16
Dan 1:7; 3:12

3:17
1 Sam 17:37
Ps 27:1-2
Isa 26:3-4
Jer 1:8

3:18
Josh 24:15
1 Kgs 19:14
Dan 3:28

3:19
Lev 26:18-28

3:22
Dan 2:15

3:25
Ps 91:3-9
Isa 43:2
Jer 1:8, 19

3:26
Deut 4:20
1 Kgs 8:51
Dan 3:17; 4:2

3:27
Isa 43:2
Dan 3:2
Heb 11:34

3:7 ***the musical instruments:*** Literally *the horn, flute, zither, lyre, harp, and other musical instruments.* • ***all the people:*** Outside of Israel, idol worship was normal, so ***all the*** non-Jewish ***people*** obeyed the king's command.

3:11 In some situations, the Lord's people must ***refuse to obey*** the established authorities in order to remain faithful to the Lord (cp. Acts 4:19; 5:29; Rom 13:1-7).

3:12 These ***Jews*** had defied his ***Majesty*** the king, specifically by refusing to worship his statue. Defying the king was an act of high treason (cp. 2:10-13).

3:13 Nebuchadnezzar was capable of deadly ***rage*** against even his most honored officials (cp. 2:12, 48-49).

3:14 ***Is it true?*** The Aramaic word is used only here in the OT. The king may have been asking, "Are your actions deliberate?"

3:15 ***I will give you one more chance:*** The three men's earlier relationship to the king may have helped them get a second chance. • ***the musical instruments:*** Literally *the horn, flute, zither, lyre, harp, pipes, and other musical instruments.*

3:16-18 The three men declared their faithfulness to God above all. They were entrusting themselves to the God who had rescued the entire nation of Israel ***from*** the ***power*** of Pharaoh (Exod 18:10). God later revealed that even after this life, those who are faithful unto death will be delivered (12:1-3).

3:23 In the Greek version and the Latin Vulgate, *The Prayer of Azariah* and *The Song of the Three Jews* are inserted after 3:23 (see "Author and Date," p. 1390).

3:25 ***walking around:*** The same word is used in Gen 3:8-9. • ***like a god*** (literally *like a son of the gods*): The king understood the being as the Lord's angel (3:28).

3:26 The title ***Most High*** is often used to refer to ***God*** (e.g., 4:2, 24-25; 7:25; Gen 14:18; Num 24:16; Deut 32:8-9; Ps 73:11; Isa 14:14). In Canaanite religion, it often referred to Baal.

3:28
Ps 34:7-8
Isa 37:36
Dan 3:25; 6:22
Acts 5:19; 12:7
3:29
Ezra 6:11
Dan 3:12, 15
3:30
Dan 2:49; 3:12
4:1
Dan 6:25
4:2
Dan 3:26; 4:17, 24-25, 34
4:3
Deut 4:34
Ps 77:19
Isa 25:1
Dan 2:44; 4:34; 6:26
4:4
Ps 30:6
Isa 47:7-8
4:5
Dan 4:10, 13
4:6
Gen 41:8
Dan 2:2

their heads was singed, and their clothing
was not scorched. They didn't even smell of
smoke!

Nebuchadnezzar Praises God

28Then Nebuchadnezzar said, "Praise
to the God of Shadrach, Meshach, and
Abednego! He sent his angel to rescue his
servants who trusted in him. They defied
the king's command and were willing to
die rather than serve or worship any god
except their own God. 29Therefore, I make
this decree: If any people, whatever their
race or nation or language, speak a word
against the God of Shadrach, Meshach, and
Abednego, they will be torn limb from limb,
and their houses will be turned into heaps
of rubble. There is no other god who can
rescue like this!"

30Then the king promoted Shadrach,
Meshach, and Abednego to even higher positions in the province of Babylon.

Nebuchadnezzar's Exile and Restoration (4:1-37)

Nebuchadnezzar's Dream about a Tree

4 King Nebuchadnezzar sent this message to the people of every race and
nation and language throughout the world:

"Peace and prosperity to you!

2"I want you all to know about the
miraculous signs and wonders the Most
High God has performed for me.

3 How great are his signs,
how powerful his wonders!
His kingdom will last forever,
his rule through all generations.

4"I, Nebuchadnezzar, was living in my
palace in comfort and prosperity. 5But
one night I had a dream that frightened
me; I saw visions that terrified me as
I lay in my bed. 6So I issued an order
calling in all the wise men of Babylon, so
they could tell me what my dream meant.

NEBUCHADNEZZAR II (1:1–4:37)

2 Kgs 24:1–25:30
2 Chr 36:6-21
Jer 21:1-10; 22:24-27; 24:1; 25:1-14; 27:4-8; 28:14; 29:1-23; 32:1-5, 26-31; 34:1-3; 37:1; 39:1-14; 43:10-13; 46:2, 13-26; 49:28-33; 50:17; 51:34; 52:4-16, 28-30
Ezek 26:7; 29:18-20; 30:10-11

King Nebuchadnezzar II reigned over Babylon from 605 to 562 BC. He extended and secured the empire of his father, Nabopolassar (626–605 BC). Beyond the scriptural record, many ancient Babylonian documents report Nebuchadnezzar's accomplishments.

In 626 BC, Babylon, like Judah, was under the domination of Assyria, but in that year Nabopolassar began a revolt that would change the world. In 612 BC, the Babylonians captured Nineveh, Assyria's capital, and again defeated the Assyrians at Haran in 609 BC. By the time of this battle, Nabopolassar's son Nebuchadnezzar played a leading role in the army. In 605 BC, Nebuchadnezzar defeated the remnant of the Assyrian army at Carchemish; this victory also pushed the Egyptians back within their borders. In the same year, Nabopolassar died and his son became king.

Following his victory at Carchemish in 605 BC, Nebuchadnezzar conquered Syria and surrounding areas, including Judah. In that year, Nebuchadnezzar besieged Jerusalem for the first time (1:1-2; 2 Kgs 24:1). He took away a number of the Temple vessels and some of the leading young citizens of Judah, including Daniel and his three friends. Nebuchadnezzar captured Jerusalem again in 597 BC (2 Kgs 24:10-17). He later besieged Jerusalem in 588 BC and destroyed the city and Temple in 586 BC, exiling most of the remaining people (2 Kgs 25:1-21).

The most detailed and interesting description of Nebuchadnezzar is found in Daniel. He brought Daniel and his friends to Babylon in order to educate them in the ways of Babylonia, but God used Daniel to teach Nebuchadnezzar about himself. Nebuchadnezzar recognized the Lord's great power and wisdom, though he probably never worshiped the true God exclusively. After being humbled for his great pride (4:28-33), Nebuchadnezzar acknowledged the Lord's exclusive sovereignty and power (4:34-37).

3:28 The king was surprised that God could ***rescue*** his people, but the three Hebrew men knew that their God could deliver them (3:17).

3:30 ***promoted:*** A related word is used in Gen 39:2. The men were rewarded for their righteousness and their faithfulness to the Lord.

4:1-37 In his pride, King Nebuchadnezzar convinced himself that he had built Babylon (4:30; cp. Gen 11:1-9). He disregarded the warning of the Most High God (4:24-27). He had still not learned the lesson God was teaching him through these experiences, that the God of Daniel stands outside the world of time and space, and no human is equal to him. So God's decree of judgment fell upon Nebuchadnezzar (4:17, 25-26; see Prov 16:18).

4:1-3 Verses 4:1-3 are numbered 3:31-33 in the Aramaic text.

4:4-37 Verses 4:4-37 are numbered 4:1-34 in the Aramaic text.

4:4 God did not allow the king to remain in the ***comfort and prosperity*** of his ***palace;*** injustice and oppression were in the city (4:27), and the king was full of pride (4:30).

4:5 Nebuchadnezzar's ***dream*** disrupted the false peace and serenity of the king's misguided life.

7When all the magicians, enchanters,
astrologers, and fortune-tellers came
in, I told them the dream, but they could
not tell me what it meant. 8At last Daniel
came in before me, and I told him the
dream. (He was named Belteshazzar
after my god, and the spirit of the holy
gods is in him.)
9"I said to him, 'Belteshazzar, chief
of the magicians, I know that the spirit
of the holy gods is in you and that no
mystery is too great for you to solve. Now
tell me what my dream means.
10" 'While I was lying in my bed, this
is what I dreamed. I saw a large tree in
the middle of the earth. 11The tree grew
very tall and strong, reaching high into
the heavens for all the world to see. 12It
had fresh green leaves, and it was loaded
with fruit for all to eat. Wild animals
lived in its shade, and birds nested in its
branches. All the world was fed from
this tree.
13" 'Then as I lay there dreaming, I saw
a messenger, a holy one, coming down
from heaven. 14The messenger shouted,

"Cut down the tree and lop off its
branches!
Shake off its leaves and scatter its
fruit!
Chase the wild animals from its shade
and the birds from its branches.
15 But leave the stump and the roots in
the ground,
bound with a band of iron and
bronze
and surrounded by tender grass.
Now let him be drenched with the
dew of heaven,
and let him live with the wild
animals among the plants of the
field.
16 For seven periods of time,
let him have the mind of a wild
animal
instead of the mind of a human.
17 For this has been decreed by the
messengers;
it is commanded by the holy ones,
so that everyone may know
that the Most High rules over the
kingdoms of the world.
He gives them to anyone he chooses—
even to the lowliest of people."

18" 'Belteshazzar, that was the dream
that I, King Nebuchadnezzar, had. Now
tell me what it means, for none of the
wise men of my kingdom can do so. But
you can tell me because the spirit of the
holy gods is in you.'

Daniel Explains the Dream

19"Upon hearing this, Daniel (also known
as Belteshazzar) was overcome for a time,
frightened by the meaning of the dream.
Then the king said to him, 'Belteshazzar,
don't be alarmed by the dream and what
it means.'
"Belteshazzar replied, 'I wish the
events foreshadowed in this dream
would happen to your enemies, my lord,
and not to you! 20The tree you saw was
growing very tall and strong, reaching
high into the heavens for all the world
to see. 21It had fresh green leaves and
was loaded with fruit for all to eat. Wild
animals lived in its shade, and birds
nested in its branches. 22That tree, Your
Majesty, is you. For you have grown
strong and great; your greatness reaches
up to heaven, and your rule to the ends
of the earth.
23" 'Then you saw a messenger, a holy
one, coming down from heaven and

4:7 Isa 44:25; Jer 27:9-10; Dan 2:7
4:8 Dan 1:7; 4:9, 18
4:9 Gen 41:38; Ezek 28:3; Dan 1:20; 2:4-5, 47-48; 4:8; 5:11
4:10 Ezek 31:3-4
4:12 Jer 27:6-7; Ezek 31:7; Matt 13:32; Luke 13:19
4:13 Deut 33:2; Ps 89:7; Dan 8:13
4:14 Jer 51:5-6; Ezek 31:10-14; Matt 3:10; 7:19; Rev 10:3; 18:2
4:15 Job 14:7-9
4:16 Dan 5:21
4:17 1 Sam 2:8; Ps 9:16; Dan 4:25; 11:21; Rom 13:1
4:18 Gen 41:8; 1 Kgs 14:2-3; Dan 4:7; 5:8
4:19 1 Sam 3:17; 2 Sam 18:32; Dan 7:15, 28; 8:27
4:22 2 Sam 12:7; Jer 27:6-7; Dan 2:37-38

4:7 The professionals could not interpret the dream even though it was told to them this time (cp. 2:1-11). Their dream manuals failed them (see note on 2:4). • For the list of state advisers see also note on 2:2. There was some overlap in these vocations. • ***astrologers:*** Or *Chaldeans* (see also 2:5, 10; 3:8; 5:7, 11, 30).

4:8-9 ***At last:*** Nebuchadnezzar appealed first to his Babylonian advisers; in spite of his high position, Daniel, an exiled Jew, was a last resort. • ***spirit of the holy gods is in him:*** See 2:47; cp. 5:11. Despite his previous experience of the Most High God, Nebuchadnezzar still believed in many gods. In Egypt, Pharaoh had asserted the same thing of Joseph (Gen 41:37-38). It was the Most High God who assisted Daniel (4:24). Nevertheless, for the great king to say that Daniel had the spirit of the holy gods in him showed great respect and helps to explain Daniel's immunity from harassment (see ch 3).

4:11 ***The tree . . . reaching high into the heavens*** possibly alludes to the Tower of Babel (Gen 11:1-9).

4:13 ***a messenger:*** Literally *a watcher;* also in 4:23. • ***a holy one:*** The term "holy" is not widely used in the Semitic languages outside of the Bible. It simply refers to that which is out of the ordinary or non-human. Nebuchadnezzar was most probably using it that way here.

4:14-17 ***The messenger*** had full authority as the representative of the Most High to announce God's decrees and demand that they be fulfilled.

4:16 ***Seven periods of time*** may refer to a seven-year period (cp. 7:25; 9:24-25). • ***mind of a wild animal:*** See 4:31-33.

4:17 ***the messengers:*** Literally *the watchers.* • ***the Most High rules:*** God distributes kingship and kingdoms to whomever he will, ***even to the lowliest*** (e.g., Joseph, Gen 41:41-57; David, 1 Sam 16—2 Sam 5).

4:22 The ***tree*** is a haven of sustenance, rest, and safety for the world (cp. Gen 2:15-17; Rev 22:14). • ***your greatness reaches up to heaven:*** Cp. Gen 11:1-9.

4:23 ***Cut down the tree:*** The tree must be cut down because of Nebuchadnezzar's pride (4:27-30).

4:25
Job 40:11-12
Ps 75:7; 107:40
Jer 27:5
Dan 4:17, 33; 5:21

4:26
Dan 4:31

4:27
Gen 41:33-37
1 Kgs 21:29
Ps 41:1-3
Prov 28:13
Isa 55:6-7
Ezek 18:21-22
Jon 3:9

4:28
Num 23:19
Zech 1:6

4:29
2 Pet 3:9

4:30
Hab 2:4

4:33
Dan 4:25; 5:21

4:34
Ps 102:24
Jer 10:10
Dan 4:2; 5:18, 21
Rev 4:10; 10:6

4:35
Job 42:2
Ps 135:6
Isa 40:17; 43:13; 45:9
Dan 6:27
Rom 9:20

4:36
2 Chr 33:12-13
Prov 22:4

4:37
Exod 18:11
Ps 33:4-5
Matt 23:12

saying, "Cut down the tree and destroy it.
But leave the stump and the roots in the
ground, bound with a band of iron and
bronze and surrounded by tender grass.
Let him be drenched with the dew of
heaven. Let him live with the animals of
the field for seven periods of time."
24" 'This is what the dream means,
Your Majesty, and what the Most High
has declared will happen to my lord the
king. 25You will be driven from human
society, and you will live in the fields
with the wild animals. You will eat grass
like a cow, and you will be drenched
with the dew of heaven. Seven periods
of time will pass while you live this way,
until you learn that the Most High rules
over the kingdoms of the world and
gives them to anyone he chooses. 26But
the stump and roots of the tree were left
in the ground. This means that you will
receive your kingdom back again when
you have learned that heaven rules.
27" 'King Nebuchadnezzar, please
accept my advice. Stop sinning and do
what is right. Break from your wicked
past and be merciful to the poor. Perhaps
then you will continue to prosper.'

The Dream's Fulfillment

28"But all these things did happen to
King Nebuchadnezzar. 29Twelve months
later he was taking a walk on the flat
roof of the royal palace in Babylon. 30As
he looked out across the city, he said,
'Look at this great city of Babylon! By
my own mighty power, I have built this
beautiful city as my royal residence to
display my majestic splendor.'
31"While these words were still in his
mouth, a voice called down from heaven,
'O King Nebuchadnezzar, this message
is for you! You are no longer ruler of this
kingdom. 32You will be driven from
human society. You will live in the fields
with the wild animals, and you will eat
grass like a cow. Seven periods of time
will pass while you live this way, until
you learn that the Most High rules over
the kingdoms of the world and gives
them to anyone he chooses.'
33"That same hour the judgment was
fulfilled, and Nebuchadnezzar was
driven from human society. He ate grass
like a cow, and he was drenched with the
dew of heaven. He lived this way until
his hair was as long as eagles' feathers
and his nails were like birds' claws.

Nebuchadnezzar Praises God

34"After this time had passed, I,
Nebuchadnezzar, looked up to heaven.
My sanity returned, and I praised and
worshiped the Most High and honored
the one who lives forever.

His rule is everlasting,
  and his kingdom is eternal.
35 All the people of the earth
  are nothing compared to him.
He does as he pleases
  among the angels of heaven
  and among the people of the earth.
No one can stop him or say to him,
  'What do you mean by doing these
    things?'

36"When my sanity returned to me, so
did my honor and glory and kingdom. My
advisers and nobles sought me out, and
I was restored as head of my kingdom,
with even greater honor than before.
37"Now I, Nebuchadnezzar, praise and
glorify and honor the King of heaven. All
his acts are just and true, and he is able
to humble the proud."

4:25-26 ***until you learn that the Most High rules:*** God's goal was proper recognition of God's rule.

4:27 ***Stop sinning and do what is right:*** Righteousness and justice exalt a nation and extend the reign of a king; the lack of it dooms a people. Daniel humbly pled with the king to change his ways. • ***be merciful to the poor:*** This was a requirement of God's law (Exod 23:6-11; Deut 15:10-11; Prov 29:14; 31:9) as well as Babylon's. A former great king of Babylon, Hammurabi (about 1792–1750 BC), claimed to have been charged by his god Marduk to shepherd and protect the orphaned, the widowed, and the oppressed. • ***Perhaps then:*** Daniel recognized that God was free to act or not act (cp. 3:16-18); because he is a merciful God, he might take pity on the condemned king (cp. Exod 32:30; 1 Sam 14:6; 2 Sam 12:22; Joel 2:14; Amos 5:15; Zeph 2:3; 2 Tim 2:25).

4:28-33 Because Daniel's warning went unheeded, the dream became reality.

4:30 The ***city of Babylon*** had magnificent walls covered with royal blue ceramic tile and gold-colored lions and dragons. The Hanging Gardens of Babylon were also part of the city's ***splendor,*** as was the dazzling Ishtar Gate. The king recognized all this as a reflection of his own glory and power, not as a gift of the Most High God.

4:32 The king who took Israel into exile for seventy years experienced his own exile for ***seven periods of time*** until he was purified of his pride.

4:33 This disease, called boanthropy, causes a person to behave like an ox. Several ancient sources lend support to this account, and the king's annals are notably empty from 582 to 575 BC.

4:34-37 Nebuchadnezzar now acknowledged and submitted to the higher authority of the ***Most High,*** the ***King of heaven*** (see note on 4:25-26).

4:35 ***He does as he pleases:*** God has absolute power in ***heaven*** and on ***earth.***

4:37 The Most High God is the ***King of heaven*** as well as of earth. Human pride has no place before him, even that of the greatest of human kings.

Demise of the Head of Gold (5:1-30)

Belshazzar's Sacrilegious Debauchery

5 Many years later King Belshazzar gave a great feast for 1,000 of his nobles, and he drank wine with them. 2While Belshazzar was drinking the wine, he gave orders to bring in the gold and silver cups that his predecessor, Nebuchadnezzar, had taken from the Temple in Jerusalem. He wanted to drink from them with his nobles, his wives, and his concubines. 3So they brought these gold cups taken from the Temple, the house of God in Jerusalem, and the king and his nobles, his wives, and his concubines drank from them. 4While they drank from them they praised their idols made of gold, silver, bronze, iron, wood, and stone.

The Writing on the Wall

5Suddenly, they saw the fingers of a human hand writing on the plaster wall of the king's palace, near the lampstand. The king himself saw the hand as it wrote, 6and his face turned pale with fright. His knees knocked together in fear and his legs gave way beneath him.

7The king shouted for the enchanters, astrologers, and fortune-tellers to be brought before him. He said to these wise men of Babylon, "Whoever can read this writing and tell me what it means will be dressed in purple robes of royal honor and will have a gold chain placed around his neck. He will become the third highest ruler in the kingdom!"

8But when all the king's wise men had come in, none of them could read the writing or tell him what it meant. 9So the king grew even more alarmed, and his face turned pale. His nobles, too, were shaken.

10But when the queen mother heard what was happening, she hurried to the banquet hall. She said to Belshazzar, "Long live the king! Don't be so pale and frightened. 11There is a man in your kingdom who has within him the spirit of the holy gods. During Nebuchadnezzar's reign, this man was found to have insight, understanding, and wisdom like that of the gods. Your predecessor, the king—your predecessor King Nebuchadnezzar—made him chief over all the magicians, enchanters, astrologers, and fortune-tellers of Babylon. 12This man Daniel, whom the king named Belteshazzar, has exceptional ability and is filled with divine knowledge and understanding. He can interpret dreams, explain riddles, and solve difficult problems. Call for Daniel, and he will tell you what the writing means."

Daniel Explains the Writing

13So Daniel was brought in before the king. The king asked him, "Are you Daniel, one of the exiles brought from Judah by my predecessor, King Nebuchadnezzar? 14I have heard that you have the spirit of the gods within you and that you are filled with insight, understanding, and wisdom. 15My wise men and enchanters have tried to read the words on the wall and tell me their

5:1 Esth 1:3; Isa 22:12-14
5:2 2 Kgs 24:13; Ezra 1:7-11; Dan 1:2
5:4 Rev 9:20
5:6 Ps 69:23; Ezek 7:17; 21:7; Dan 7:28; Nah 2:10
5:7 Gen 41:42-44; Isa 44:25; 47:13; Ezek 16:11; Dan 5:11, 16, 29; 6:2-3
5:9 Job 18:11-14; Isa 21:2-4; Jer 6:24; Dan 5:6
5:10 Dan 3:9; 6:6
5:11 Gen 41:11-15; Dan 2:47; 4:8-9; 5:14
5:12 Dan 4:18
5:13 Dan 1:1; 2:25
5:15 Isa 47:12; Dan 5:8

5:1-30 Earthly kingdoms all pass away. As Nebuchadnezzar's dream implied, Babylon would pass away and a new sovereign kingdom would take its place (2:39). After Nebuchadnezzar's death in 562 BC, violence and debauchery increased in the palaces of Babylon until, during Belshazzar's feast in 539 BC, even God's holy vessels were polluted and defiled. God's judgment came with lightning swiftness that night (5:30), and the next kingdom took over (see 2:32, 39; 5:31).

5:1 *Many years later:* This chapter opens in October 539 BC (see note on 5:30). • The name ***Belshazzar*** means "Bel Protects [the King]" (Bel was a Babylonian god). Nabonidus (556–539 BC) placed his son Belshazzar on the Babylonian throne around 553 BC as ruler in his stead. Then, taking the idols of Babylon with him, Nabonidus moved to Teima in northwest Arabia, where he stayed for ten years. He returned to Babylon only in the unsuccessful attempt to oppose the Persians.

5:2-4 The ***gold and silver cups*** from the Temple in Jerusalem had been taken into captivity along with the people (1:2), but previous Babylonian kings had not defiled them. They were eventually returned to Jerusalem (Ezra 1:7-11). • ***predecessor*** (literally *father;* also in 5:11, 13, 18): Belshazzar was the oldest son of Nabonidus; his relationship with Nebuchadnezzar is uncertain. • ***While they drank from them they praised their idols:*** If Belshazzar had ever known of the honor Nebuchadnezzar had shown toward the Most High God decades earlier (4:34-37), he had long forgotten it. Two ancient Greek historians, Herodotus and Xenophon, record the all-night festivities, dancing, and excessive drinking that took place as the city was taken by Persia.

5:5-6 The supernatural ***hand*** shocked and terrified the carousers. Yet Belshazzar remained unrepentant (5:29; cp. Jer 38:19-24; Acts 24:25).

5:7 ***astrologers:*** Or *Chaldeans;* also in 5:11. • ***Purple robes*** and a ***gold chain*** are associated with royalty and power. • ***third highest:*** After Nabonidus and Belshazzar himself (see note on 5:1). For many years the existence of Nabonidus was unknown from non-biblical sources, and scholars puzzled over why Belshazzar did not offer Daniel the second highest position. This provides further evidence of Daniel's historical authenticity.

5:8 As before, the Babylonian ***wise men*** were unable to interpret the omen (cp. 2:4-11; 4:7; 5:15).

5:10 ***the queen mother*** (literally *the queen*): She was probably Belshazzar's mother, not his wife. • ***Long live the king!*** was the standard greeting (also in 2:4); ironically, Belshazzar would die that night (5:30). • ***Don't be so pale and frightened:*** Cp. 1 Sam 28:20-25.

5:11-12 The queen mother reasoned that someone who had ***the spirit of the holy gods*** and could ***interpret dreams*** (see 1:17) should also be able to interpret ***the writing.***

5:15 None of the Babylonian wise men could break the heavenly code

5:16
Gen 40:8
5:17
2 Kgs 5:16
5:18
Jer 27:5-7
Dan 2:37; 4:2, 17; 5:21
5:19
Prov 16:14
Dan 2:12; 3:6; 11:3
5:20
Exod 9:17
Isa 14:13-15
Jer 13:18
Dan 4:30
Luke 18:14
5:21
Exod 9:14-16
Ps 83:17-18
Ezek 17:24
5:22
Exod 10:3
2 Chr 33:23; 36:12
5:23
2 Kgs 14:10
Job 3:14; 12:10
Jer 10:23; 50:29
Dan 5:3-4
Hab 2:18-19

meaning, but they cannot do it. 16I am told
that you can give interpretations and solve
difficult problems. If you can read these
words and tell me their meaning, you will be
clothed in purple robes of royal honor, and
you will have a gold chain placed around
your neck. You will become the third highest ruler in the kingdom."
17Daniel answered the king, "Keep your
gifts or give them to someone else, but I will
tell you what the writing means. 18Your Majesty, the Most High God gave sovereignty,
majesty, glory, and honor to your predecessor, Nebuchadnezzar. 19He made him so
great that people of all races and nations
and languages trembled before him in fear.
He killed those he wanted to kill and spared
those he wanted to spare. He honored those
he wanted to honor and disgraced those he
wanted to disgrace. 20But when his heart
and mind were puffed up with arrogance,
he was brought down from his royal throne
and stripped of his glory. 21He was driven
from human society. He was given the mind
of a wild animal, and he lived among the
wild donkeys. He ate grass like a cow, and
he was drenched with the dew of heaven,
until he learned that the Most High God
rules over the kingdoms of the world and appoints anyone he desires to rule over them.
22"You are his successor, O Belshazzar,
and you knew all this, yet you have not humbled yourself. 23For you have proudly defied
the Lord of heaven and have had these cups
from his Temple brought before you. You
and your nobles and your wives and concubines have been drinking wine from them
while praising gods of silver, gold, bronze,
iron, wood, and stone—gods that neither
see nor hear nor know anything at all. But
you have not honored the God who gives
you the breath of life and controls your destiny! 24So God has sent this hand to write
this message.

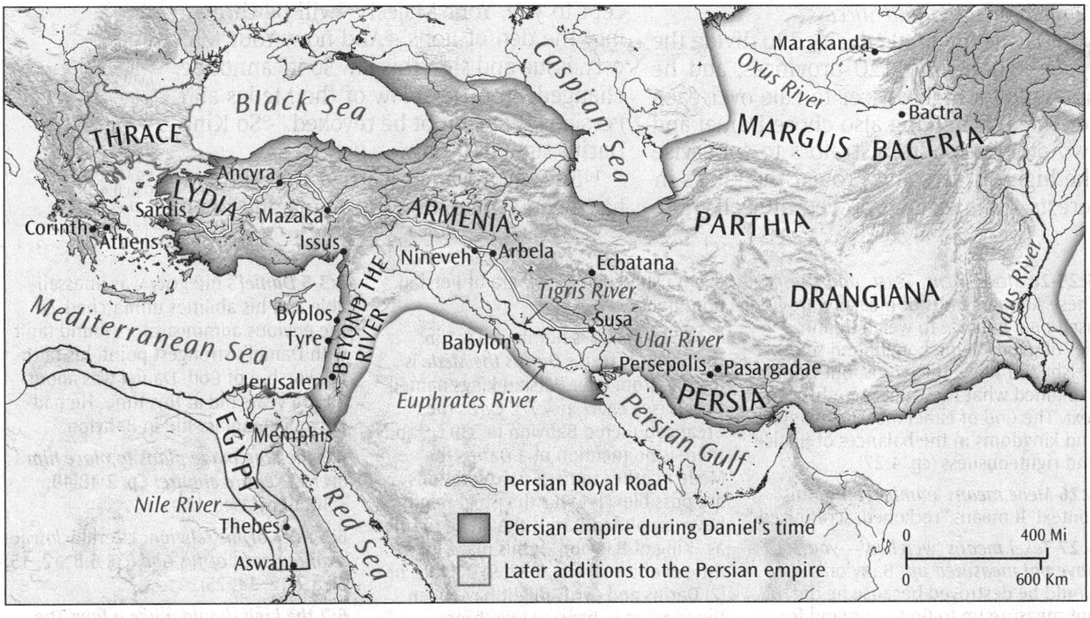

▲**The Persian Empire, 539–331 BC (5:30–6:1; 8:3-4).** Cyrus II seized BABYLON and annexed the Babylonian empire in 539 BC, creating the greatest empire history had ever seen (see 1 Chr 36:23; Ezra 1:2). Areas brought into the empire after the time of Daniel include THRACE and EGYPT. The Persian empire lasted, though not in its full extent, until Alexander defeated the Persian army in 331 BC. • During the Persian period, Israel was called the land BEYOND THE RIVER (see notes on Ezra 4:10; Neh 2:7).

(cp. 2:27; 4:7). Only true wise men or prophets can interpret God's messages. Daniel knew that it was the Spirit of God who enabled him to do so (cp. 2:28; 5:24).

5:17 Daniel interpreted the writing, but required no pay from the wicked king (cp. Gen 14:21-24; 2 Kgs 5:15-16).

5:18-21 Daniel presented Nebuchadnezzar as an object lesson that should have guided his successors. Instead, Belshazzar had made the same mistake of exalting himself and dishonoring the *Most High God*.

5:20 A rebel against God characteristically has a ***heart and mind*** that are ***puffed up*** (or *hardened*) ***with arrogance*** (see Exod 7:13; Josh 11:20; Isa 14:3-5). Nebuchadnezzar was ***brought down*** when he became puffed up with arrogance, and Belshazzar would be as well.

5:21 ***the Most High God rules . . . and appoints anyone he desires:*** God had taught Nebuchadnezzar this lesson, and it was the heart of God's message to Belshazzar. God would appoint a new ruler that very night (5:30-31).

5:22 ***successor*** (literally *son*): See note on 5:2-4.

25“This is the message that was written:
MENE, MENE, TEKEL, and PARSIN. 26This is
what these words mean:

Mene means ‘numbered’—God has
numbered the days of your reign and
has brought it to an end.
27 *Tekel* means ‘weighed’—you have been
weighed on the balances and have not
measured up.
28 *Parsin* means ‘divided’—your kingdom
has been divided and given to the
Medes and Persians.”

29Then at Belshazzar’s command, Daniel
was dressed in purple robes, a gold chain
was hung around his neck, and he was
proclaimed the third highest ruler in the
kingdom.
30That very night Belshazzar, the Babylonian king, was killed.
31And Darius the Mede took over the
kingdom at the age of sixty-two.

Daniel in the Lions’ Den (6:1-28)
Daniel’s Integrity and Success

6 Darius the Mede decided to divide the
kingdom into 120 provinces, and he
appointed a high officer to rule over each
province. 2The king also chose Daniel and
two others as administrators to supervise
the high officers and protect the king’s interests. 3Daniel soon proved himself more
capable than all the other administrators
and high officers. Because of Daniel’s great
ability, the king made plans to place him
over the entire empire.
4Then the other administrators and high
officers began searching for some fault in
the way Daniel was handling government
affairs, but they couldn’t find anything
to criticize or condemn. He was faithful,
always responsible, and completely trustworthy. 5So they concluded, “Our only
chance of finding grounds for accusing
Daniel will be in connection with the rules
of his religion.”

The King Falls into a Trap
6So the administrators and high officers
went to the king and said, “Long live King
Darius! 7We are all in agreement—we administrators, officials, high officers, advisers,
and governors—that the king should make
a law that will be strictly enforced. Give orders that for the next thirty days any person
who prays to anyone, divine or human—except to you, Your Majesty—will be thrown
into the den of lions. 8And now, Your Majesty, issue and sign this law so it cannot be
changed, an official law of the Medes and
Persians that cannot be revoked.” 9So King
Darius signed the law.
10But when Daniel learned that the law
had been signed, he went home and knelt

5:26 Isa 13:6, 17; Jer 50:41-43
5:27 Job 31:6; Ps 62:9
5:28 Isa 21:2; 45:1-2; Dan 5:31; 6:28
5:30 Isa 21:4-9; Jer 51:11, 31, 39, 57
5:31 Dan 6:1; 9:1
6:1 Esth 1:1
6:2 Ezra 4:22; Esth 7:4; Dan 2:48-49; 5:16, 29
6:3 Gen 41:40; Dan 5:12
6:4 Gen 43:18; Luke 23:14-15; Phil 2:15
6:5 Acts 24:13-16
6:6 Neh 2:3
6:7 Ps 59:3; 62:4; 64:2-6; Dan 6:16; Matt 12:14
6:8 Esth 1:19; 3:12; Isa 10:1; Dan 6:12-13; Matt 24:35
6:9 Ps 118:9; 146:3
6:10 1 Kgs 8:48-49; Ps 34:1; 95:6; Dan 9:4-19; 1 Thes 5:17-18

5:25-28 ***MENE, MENE, TEKEL, and PARSIN:*** These Aramaic units of measure are used on a balance to weigh quantities of goods being bought and sold. Belshazzar knew the words, but Daniel explained what they meant in this context. The God of Israel measures kings and kingdoms in the balances of justice and righteousness (cp. 4:27).

5:26 ***Mene means ‘numbered’:*** In this context, it means “reckoned, scrutinized.”

5:27 ***Tekel means ‘weighed’—you . . . have not measured up:*** Babylon’s king would be destroyed because he did not measure up to God’s demand for righteousness and mercy (see 4:27; 5:22-24).

5:28 ***Parsin*** (Aramaic *Peres,* the singular of *Parsin*) ***means ‘divided’*** (or *halved*): The Babylonian empire would be divided and given to two peoples, the Medes and the Persians.

5:29 Instead of responding to the message, Belshazzar honored Daniel. • ***proclaimed the third highest ruler:*** Daniel did not desire the honor, and in a few hours it would be meaningless. God would reward Daniel in due time (12:13).

5:30 ***Babylonian:*** Or *Chaldean.* • ***was killed:*** The Persians and Medes conquered Babylon in October 539 BC. The event ushered in a new era of Persian dominance.

5:31 Verse 5:31 is numbered 6:1 in the Aramaic text. • ***Darius the Mede*** is distinct from later Persian kings named Darius (see chart, p. 797). Cyrus the Great conquered Babylon in 539 BC, and there is no mention of a Darius the Mede in other sources. Two solutions are possible: (1) Cyrus the Great might have appointed Darius the Mede to rule as “King of Babylon” in his place for a little over a year (cp. 6:28; 9:1; 11:1); or (2) Darius and Cyrus might have been the same man bearing two throne names—one name from the Medes, the other from the Persians (see also note on 6:28). The portrayal of Darius in ch 6 suggests that he was in fact Cyrus, the ruler of all Media, Persia, and Babylonia.

6:1-28 God rescued and delivered his faithful servant Daniel (5:23; 6:20), whereas Belshazzar’s dead gods could not save him. • Verses 6:1-28 are numbered 6:2-29 in the Aramaic text.

6:2 The three ***administrators*** placed over the whole territory reported directly to the king. • ***and protect the king’s interests:*** Rebels could bring down the empire, so these administrators had to be absolutely trustworthy.

6:3-5 ***Daniel’s*** integrity was unassailable and his abilities unmatched, so the envious administrators found fault with Daniel’s strongest point, his faithful worship of God. Daniel was about 80~85 years old at this time. He had led an exemplary life in Babylon.

6:3 ***the king made plans to place him over the entire empire:*** Cp. 2:48-49; 3:30; Gen 41:40-43.

6:5 ***rules of his religion:*** Literally *law* [or *requirements*] *of his God* (cp. 6:8, 12, 15; Ezra 7:12, 14, 25).

6:7 ***the king should make a law:*** The request was couched as an appeal to truth and justice, but it was really an appeal to the king’s pride, with ulterior motives (6:4-5). • We already know that Daniel would not break God’s law to obey a human order (cp. 1:5-8; 3:4-12).

6:8 ***cannot be changed . . . cannot be revoked:*** Cp. Esth 1:19. Human laws all pass away, but God’s law lasts forever (Ps 93:5; 119:152). This devotion to established laws was one of the special features of the Persian empire. Finally, the profusion of laws so swamped them in bureaucracy that they could not function efficiently.

6:10-11 ***as usual:*** Daniel’s regular prayer time established him in the daily

6:11 Ps 37:32-33; Dan 6:6
6:12 Esth 1:19; Dan 3:8-12; 6:8; Acts 16:19-21
6:13 Esth 3:8; Dan 3:12; Acts 5:29
6:14 Mark 6:26
6:15 Esth 8:8; Ps 94:20-21; Dan 6:8, 12
6:16 Job 5:19; Ps 37:39-40; Jer 38:5
6:17 Lam 3:53; Matt 27:66
6:18 2 Sam 12:16-17; Esth 6:1; Rev 18:22
6:20 Jer 32:17; Dan 3:17; Hos 12:6
6:22 Ps 91:11-13; Acts 12:11; 2 Tim 4:17; Heb 11:33
6:23 Ps 118:8; Isa 26:3; Dan 3:17, 28
6:24 Deut 19:18-19; 2 Kgs 14:6
6:25 Ezra 1:1-2; Esth 3:12; 8:9; Hos 1:10; 1 Pet 1:2
6:26 Ps 93:1-2
6:27 Dan 4:3

down as usual in his upstairs room, with
its windows open toward Jerusalem. He
prayed three times a day, just as he had always done, giving thanks to his God. 11 Then
the officials went together to Daniel's house
and found him praying and asking for God's
help. 12 So they went straight to the king and
reminded him about his law. "Did you not
sign a law that for the next thirty days any
person who prays to anyone, divine or human—except to you, Your Majesty—will be
thrown into the den of lions?"

"Yes," the king replied, "that decision
stands; it is an official law of the Medes and
Persians that cannot be revoked."

13 Then they told the king, "That man
Daniel, one of the captives from Judah, is ig-
noring you and your law. He still prays to his
God three times a day."

God Rescues Daniel

14 Hearing this, the king was deeply troubled,
and he tried to think of a way to save Daniel.
He spent the rest of the day looking for a
way to get Daniel out of this predicament.

15 In the evening the men went together to
the king and said, "Your Majesty, you know
that according to the law of the Medes and
the Persians, no law that the king signs can
be changed."

16 So at last the king gave orders for Daniel to be arrested and thrown into the den of
lions. The king said to him, "May your God,
whom you serve so faithfully, rescue you."

17 A stone was brought and placed over
the mouth of the den. The king sealed the
stone with his own royal seal and the seals
of his nobles, so that no one could rescue
Daniel. 18 Then the king returned to his palace and spent the night fasting. He refused
his usual entertainment and couldn't sleep
at all that night.

19 Very early the next morning, the king got
up and hurried out to the lions' den. 20 When
he got there, he called out in anguish, "Daniel, servant of the living God! Was your God,
whom you serve so faithfully, able to rescue
you from the lions?"

21 Daniel answered, "Long live the king!
22 My God sent his angel to shut the lions'
mouths so that they would not hurt me, for I
have been found innocent in his sight. And I
have not wronged you, Your Majesty."

23 The king was overjoyed and ordered
that Daniel be lifted from the den. Not
a scratch was found on him, for he had
trusted in his God.

24 Then the king gave orders to arrest the
men who had maliciously accused Daniel.
He had them thrown into the lions' den,
along with their wives and children. The
lions leaped on them and tore them apart
before they even hit the floor of the den.

Darius Praises God

25 Then King Darius sent this message to
the people of every race and nation and language throughout the world:

"Peace and prosperity to you!

26 "I decree that everyone throughout
my kingdom should tremble with fear
before the God of Daniel.

For he is the living God,
and he will endure forever.
His kingdom will never be destroyed,
and his rule will never end.
27 He rescues and saves his people;
he performs miraculous signs and
wonders
in the heavens and on earth.
He has rescued Daniel
from the power of the lions."

---

worship of God. • ***Jerusalem*** was God's chosen city (1 Kgs 11:36). Though the Temple was gone, it was unthinkable to forget Jerusalem (Ps 137:5-6). Some day, the Temple would be rebuilt (Isa 2:2-4; 44:28).

6:14 The king had not thought through all the consequences of signing the law. • ***deeply troubled:*** Or *very angry* for being tricked. He did not want to execute his best servant.

6:16 Caught in the officials' trap, the king had to carry out the law, but he respected Daniel's integrity in worshiping his God (cp. 3:15; 6:20).

6:17 ***his own royal seal and the seals of his nobles:*** The multiple sealing of the lions' den made a covert rescue impossible. Neither the king nor the officials could open the den without breaking the other seals so that the other parties would know about it.

6:18 The king ***spent the night fasting*** because he mourned over what he had done and hoped that Daniel's God would rescue him. The king ***couldn't sleep at all*** because he knew that Daniel was an innocent and noble man.

6:19 ***Very early:*** Literally *at dawn*, the earliest possible hour.

6:20 ***Was your God . . . able?*** There was no question about whether Daniel had served God ***faithfully***, so if God didn't rescue him it would have told the king that God was not able to do so. • ***living God:*** The king probably knew what Daniel's God had done during the reigns of Nebuchadnezzar and Belshazzar. The term *living God* is particularly used in the Bible to contrast the Lord with lifeless idols (see, e.g., Deut 5:26; Josh 3:10; Isa 37:17-18).

6:21-22 ***My God sent his angel:*** The law of the Medes and Persians proved impotent. God has the power to defend his faithful servant and his own reputation.

6:25-27 ***King Darius sent this message:*** As Nebuchadnezzar had done previously (cp. 3:28-29; 4:34-37), the current ruler of the civilized world testified to all his subjects that ***the God of Daniel*** is the ***living God*** with real power and a kingdom that ***will never be destroyed.***

6:27 ***He rescues and saves. . . . He has rescued Daniel:*** This proclamation moves from the general to the specific. Daniel was a specific example of God's rescuing power. God continues to act on behalf of his people, just as he has always done.

28So Daniel prospered during the reign of
Darius and the reign of Cyrus the Persian.

2. DANIEL'S VISIONS FOR THE PRESENT AND FUTURE (7:1–12:13)

Israel and the Nations (7:1-28)

Daniel's Vision of Four Beasts

7 Earlier, during the first year of King Belshazzar's reign in Babylon, Daniel had a
dream and saw visions as he lay in his bed.
He wrote down the dream, and this is what
he saw.
2In my vision that night, I, Daniel, saw a
great storm churning the surface of a great
sea, with strong winds blowing from every direction. 3Then four huge beasts came up out
of the water, each different from the others.
4The first beast was like a lion with eagles' wings. As I watched, its wings were
pulled off, and it was left standing with its
two hind feet on the ground, like a human
being. And it was given a human mind.
5Then I saw a second beast, and it looked
like a bear. It was rearing up on one side,
and it had three ribs in its mouth between
its teeth. And I heard a voice saying to it,
"Get up! Devour the flesh of many people!"
6Then the third of these strange beasts
appeared, and it looked like a leopard. It
had four bird's wings on its back, and it had
four heads. Great authority was given to
this beast.
7Then in my vision that night, I saw a
fourth beast—terrifying, dreadful, and very
strong. It devoured and crushed its victims
with huge iron teeth and trampled their
remains beneath its feet. It was different
from any of the other beasts, and it had ten
horns.
8As I was looking at the horns, suddenly
another small horn appeared among them.
Three of the first horns were torn out by the
roots to make room for it. This little horn
had eyes like human eyes and a mouth that
was boasting arrogantly.

9 I watched as thrones were put in place
  and the Ancient One sat down to
    judge.
His clothing was as white as snow,
  his hair like purest wool.
He sat on a fiery throne
  with wheels of blazing fire,
10 and a river of fire was pouring out,
  flowing from his presence.
Millions of angels ministered to him;
  many millions stood to attend him.

7:1 Job 33:14-16; Jer 36:4; Dan 2:1, 26-28; 4:5-9; Joel 2:28
7:2 Rev 7:1
7:3 Rev 13:1
7:7 Rev 12:3; 13:1
7:9 Ezek 1:13; 10:2, 6; Mark 9:3; Rev 1:14
7:10 Ps 50:3; 97:3; Isa 30:27; Dan 7:22, 26; 12:1; Rev 5:11; 20:11-15
7:11 Rev 19:20; 20:10
7:13 *Matt 26:64; *Mark 13:26; *Luke 21:27; Rev 1:13; 14:14

6:28 ***the reign of Darius and the reign of Cyrus the Persian:*** Or *the reign of Darius, that is, the reign of Cyrus the Persian.* Such usage of "and" is common in Aramaic; many believe that Cyrus and Darius were one man (see note on 5:31).

7:1–12:13 The second half of the book features visions given to Daniel. These visions showed Daniel and his people, both those in exile and those who had returned to Judea, that the future is securely in God's hands. All empires will ultimately fall before the Kingdom of Heaven. Daniel's people will be rescued from all their troubles (12:1-3), and God will resurrect and judge all humankind (12:13). Daniel interpreted these visions with help from divine messengers (7:10; 8:15; 9:22; 10:14; 12:7).

7:1-28 This chapter contains a terrifying vision (7:2-14) and its interpretation (7:17-27). The sequence of kingdoms recalls Nebuchadnezzar's dream some forty-five years earlier (2:1-45).

7:1 *Earlier:* This vision occurred before the events in ch 6; ***the first year of King Belshazzar's reign*** was 556 BC (or perhaps as late as 553 BC). Belshazzar was co-regent with his father, Nabonidus. • Daniel *wrote down* this vision.

7:2 The *sea* is also an image of evil or chaos in the OT (see Ps 89:10; Isa 5:30; 57:20), as it was throughout the ancient Near East.

7:3-7 The kingdoms of the world are represented as *four huge beasts* (7:17; cp. Rev 13:1-2).

7:4 The *lion* and eagle are dignified rulers in their realms. Lions featured prominently in ancient art and architecture. Nebuchadnezzar and Babylon are represented as a lion and an eagle attacking Edom (Jer 49:19, 22). • This beast became like ***a human being*** and ***was given a human mind:*** Nebuchadnezzar had taken on the mind of a beast (4:16, 32, 33), but then was restored and learned to acknowledge the Most High God (4:34-37).

7:5 The *second beast* probably represents Persia (2:34-40; 6:9, 12, 15; 8:20). • The ***bear*** was known for its vicious attacks (Prov 28:15). ***Three ribs*** may refer to Babylon, Media, and Lydia, all of whom Cyrus conquered. • ***many people:*** God called Cyrus and Persia to conquer many nations (Isa 41:2-3; 44:28; 45:1, 13; 46:11).

7:6 The *leopard* was known for its speed and agility (Hab 1:8). ***Four bird's wings*** and ***four heads*** indicate the worldwide lightning thrusts of this fierce nation. Greece conformed to this symbolism well, especially under Alexander the Great, whose kingdom was divided into four parts following his death (about 323 BC).

7:7 The fourth beast was *different* in kind, not just degree. It was made of non-living metal. It was hardly animal; it was impersonal, utterly violent, and merciless, and even its *iron teeth* were a perfect killing machine. Most commentators, both ancient and modern, find this fourth beast best embodied in the Roman empire and its kings. • ***ten horns:*** In this kind of apocalyptic literature, horns can stand for kings, power, and strength.

7:8 Many believe that the fourth kingdom was only partially and preliminarily represented in Rome. Another more brutal kingdom beyond Rome, but like it, would come through the dominion of a final *little horn*, a human being with great power and arrogance (cp. 8:9-12, 23-25; 9:25-27; 11:36-45; 12:1-7).

7:9-10 The kingdoms of the world are represented by fierce animals; the Kingdom of God is represented by a divine-human figure (also in 7:13-14) and by holy people. • ***the Ancient One*** (literally *an Ancient of Days;* also in 7:13, 22): This name is a circumlocution for God, whose existence preceded all the nations and peoples of the earth. • ***White . . . hair*** and ***clothing*** represent wisdom and purity. The ***river of fire*** speaks of God's purifying *presence.*

7:10 Taken together, the ***millions*** and ***many millions*** indicate numbers beyond calculation. • ***the books:*** God keeps records and uses them as the basis for his judgment (cp. 10:21; 12:1;

[b]*bar 'anash* (1247, 0606)
‣Dan 8:17

7:14
Ps 2:6-8; 72:17; 102:22
Dan 7:27
Eph 1:20-22
Heb 12:28
Rev 1:6

7:15
Dan 4:19; 7:28

7:16
Dan 8:13-16; 10:5-6, 11-12
Zech 1:8-11
Rev 5:5; 7:13-14

Then the court began its session,
and the books were opened.

11I continued to watch because I could
hear the little horn's boastful speech. I kept
watching until the fourth beast was killed
and its body was destroyed by fire. 12The
other three beasts had their authority taken
from them, but they were allowed to live a
while longer.

13As my vision continued that night, I saw
someone like a [b]son of man coming with
the clouds of heaven. He approached the
Ancient One and was led into his presence.
14He was given authority, honor, and sovereignty over all the nations of the world, so
that people of every race and nation and
language would obey him. His rule is eternal—it will never end. His kingdom will
never be destroyed.

The Vision Is Explained

15I, Daniel, was troubled by all I had seen,
and my visions terrified me. 16So I approached one of those standing beside the
throne and asked him what it all meant. He
explained it to me like this: 17"These four
huge beasts represent four kingdoms that

The Little Horn (7:8, 11, 20-21, 24-26)

Dan 8:9-12; 9:26-27
Mark 13:14
2 Thes 2:5-12
2 Jn 1:7
Rev 13:1-10; 20:10

The little horn in Daniel's vision stands for a king, and it has personal features such as human eyes and a mouth. This imagery is characteristic of apocalyptic literature (see Daniel Introduction, "Daniel as Literature," p. 1391). The little horn captures Daniel's attention because of its "boastful speech" and its violent actions against other kings, God's people, and the Most High.

What or who is the little horn? The little horn of 7:8 is closely tied to the figures of evil in 9:27 and 11:40-45. Antiochus IV Epiphanes (8:9-14, 23-25; 11:21-39) has characteristics similar to the little horn of 7:8, but they do not appear to be identical. Ancient and modern interpreters have held that the little horn is the antichrist to come. Some maintain that certain historical persons of the Greek and Roman empires have preliminarily fulfilled the vision (e.g., Antiochus IV Epiphanes, Nero, Caligula, Domitian). According to this view, this being yet to come will be a man, not a demon or Satan.

It is also helpful to see the little horn as representing the embodiment of evil that is directed against God and his people. Some interpreters believe that no single man will fulfill this vision, but that the vision represents the evil forces at work in the world. Others hold that the antichrist has already come. The little horn and the idea of the antichrist do have an ultimate fulfillment, but that is better revealed in the NT (cp. Matt 24:15; Mark 13:14; 2 Thes 2:5-12; 1 John 2:18-22; 4:3; 2 Jn 1:7; Rev 13:1, 5; 16:13-14; 17:11; 19:20-21; 20:10).

This little horn reminds God's people that evil is embodied in an arrogant king and a royal system that violently oppose God and his people. This king usurps the kingdoms of this world (7:8), but his demonic system will not prevail because evil will be destroyed. God's people can take comfort in knowing that this final onslaught and manifestation of evil will be short lived (Rev 12:12) and the works of this hellish kingdom will be demolished (7:11-12). God's chosen leader, the Son of Man installed by the Ancient One (7:9-10, 13-14), will rule by God's divine approval and power, and his reign will prevail in an indestructible kingdom. God's people are encouraged to endure and be faithful. They live in hope of a righteous kingdom in which God will live among his people (Exod 19:5-6; 25:8; Rev 21:3). "The passionate commitment of the LORD of Heaven's Armies will make this happen!" (Isa 9:7).

Exod 32:32; Ps 69:28; 139:16; Mal 3:16; Phil 4:3; Rev 20:12, 15; 21:27).

7:11 God's judgment brought about the destruction of ***the fourth beast . . . by fire***.

7:12 ***a while longer*** (literally *for a season and a time*): God, the Judge of the nations, can extend the lives of nations and individuals (cp. 4:27). Defeated nations who have lost their political and military hegemony can continue to live on culturally and ethnically, and can retain their national identities. This happened with the Assyrians, the Babylonians, the Persians, and the Greeks.

7:13-14 This being ***like a son of man***, unlike the arrogant little horn, did not boast and was not violent. He did not violently overthrow other kings, and he received God's favor and blessing. He ***was led*** into God's presence and was presented to him. God gave him kingship and a kingdom. This figure is the Messiah, God's chosen and anointed King.

7:13 ***like a son of man*** (or *like a Son of Man*): He was like a human being (cp. 3:25 and note). • His ***coming with the clouds of heaven*** suggests that he was a divine being (cp. Ps 68:4; 97:2; Matt 24:30; 26:64; Mark 13:26; 14:62; Luke 21:27; Rev 1:7; 1 Thes 4:17).

7:14 Unlike the rulers and kingdoms of the earth which pass away, his ***rule is eternal*** and ***will never be destroyed. His kingdom*** is given to the holy people of the Most High (7:27), and it "fills" the earth (2:35, 44-45).

7:15-16 Daniel dared to approach the beings ***standing beside the throne*** of God, and he was helped, not harmed.

7:17 ***beasts represent . . . kingdoms:*** God gave Daniel a vision of the course of history, a feat no human could accomplish. These kingdoms ***from the earth*** (cp. 7:2) are not heavenly kingdoms but human kingdoms of this world.

will arise from the earth. 18But in the end,
the holy people of the Most High will be
given the kingdom, and they will rule forever and ever."
19Then I wanted to know the true meaning of the fourth beast, the one so different
from the others and so terrifying. It had
devoured and crushed its victims with iron
teeth and bronze claws, trampling their remains beneath its feet. 20I also asked about
the ten horns on the fourth beast's head
and the little horn that came up afterward
and destroyed three of the other horns.
This horn had seemed greater than the others, and it had human eyes and a mouth that
was boasting arrogantly. 21As I watched,
this horn was waging war against God's
holy people and was defeating them, 22un-
til the Ancient One—the Most High—came
and judged in favor of his holy people. Then
the time arrived for the holy people to take
over the kingdom.
23Then he said to me, "This fourth beast
is the fourth world power that will rule
the earth. It will be different from all the
others. It will devour the whole world, trampling and crushing everything in its path.
24Its ten horns are ten kings who will rule
that empire. Then another king will arise,
different from the other ten, who will
subdue three of them. 25He will defy the
Most High and oppress the holy people of
the Most High. He will try to change their
sacred festivals and laws, and they will be
placed under his control for a time, times,
and half a time.
26"But then the court will pass judgment, and all his power will be taken away
and completely destroyed. 27Then the sovereignty, power, and greatness of all the

7:18 Isa 60:12-14; Dan 7:22, 25, 27; Rev 2:26-27; 20:4
7:21 Rev 13:7
7:22 Dan 7:10; 1 Cor 6:2-3
7:24 Rev 17:12
7:25 Dan 4:2; 11:36; 12:7; Rev 12:14; 13:6-7; 18:24
7:26 Rev 17:14; 19:2
7:27 Ps 2:6-12; 22:27; 86:9; 145:13; Isa 60:12; Dan 2:44; 4:34; 7:14, 18, 22; Luke 1:33; Rev 11:1, 5; 20:4

The Son of Man (7:13-14)

Matt 24:30; 26:24; Mark 13:26; Luke 21:27; John 12:34; Rev 1:13; 14:14

The Hebrew and Aramaic idiom "son of man" means "human being." The majestic yet humble figure in 7:13-14 is "like a son of man," meaning that he looked like a man, but he also appears to be more than merely human. His exact identity is not specified, but his role is clear: The Most High has appointed him to rule an eternal, universal kingdom that will be over all other nations. He also represents his own people, the holy people of the Most High. They will also share in this son of man's kingdom over all peoples and nations (7:22).

The scene surrounding this son of man indicates his divine characteristics. That he comes "with the clouds of heaven" (7:13) indicates his heavenly origin (cp. Ps 68:4; 97:2; Nah 1:3). The Lord God covered himself with a cloud in the book of Exodus (Exod 13:21-22; 19:9). God's people will be caught up into the clouds (1 Thes 4:17) at the resurrection as Jesus was received into a cloud at his ascension (Acts 1:9). This son of man receives his kingdom with humility and holiness without arrogantly grasping after it. He is opposite in character to the "little horn" (7:8).

Jesus identifies himself with this Son of Man (Matt 24:30; 25:11; 26:24; Mark 13:26; Luke 21:27; John 12:34; see also Acts 7:56; Heb 2:6; Rev 1:13; 14:14). Revelation 1:7 likewise yokes this figure with Jesus Christ, the one who was pierced for our sins. God the Father has given Jesus all authority and power to rule over all things (7:14; Matt 28:18) and to win people from all the nations and kingdoms of the world (Matt 28:19-20). God's purpose in calling Abraham was to make a great nation through his people (Gen 12:1-3; cp. Dan 2:44-45), and Jesus fulfilled it.

7:18 ***The holy people*** (also in 7:21, 22, 25, 27) are people who belong exclusively to God and share his character. In Daniel's era it referred to the people of Israel. • Only the ***Most High*** God can declare what the end of history will be. Other ancient writers spoke of the ages or eras of earthly history, but none knew how it would all end.

7:19-28 Daniel requested and received more information about ***the fourth beast,*** the ***ten horns,*** and the ***little horn.***

7:21 The object of the little horn's hatred and arrogance was ***God's holy people.*** In this, the little horn was like Pharaoh and Haman (see Exod 1:22; Esth 3:8-9; cp. Dan 11:36-40).

7:22 ***The Ancient One*** turned the tide of the battle when he ***judged in favor of his holy people.*** In God's ***time,*** his people would ***take over the kingdom*** with their King (7:13-14).

7:24-25 ***Its ten horns are ten kings:*** This number might refer to ten specific individuals, or it might be a symbolic number meaning that this kingdom lasted through the reigns of many kings (cp. Rev 13:1). • ***Then another king,*** who corresponds to the "little horn" (7:21), ***will defy the Most High and oppress the holy people*** by blaspheming the Lord, trying to interfere with worship of the Lord, trying to make the holy people follow his religion, and subjecting them to constant threats. • ***a time, times, and half a time:*** The text is not explicit as to the length of time. Nonetheless, the period of oppression for the holy people would be limited and would end suddenly and unexpectedly.

7:26 God's ***court*** has the authority to ***pass judgment*** and the power to remove and destroy this arrogant king.

7:27 When this arrogant king has been destroyed, God's ***kingdom*** will be established ***forever*** over ***all the kingdoms under heaven*** (cp. Ps 2; Isa 9:6-7). ***The holy people of the Most High*** will be officers of God's kingdom (cp. Luke 22:29-30; 1 Cor 6:2-3; Rev 3:21; 20:4).

8:1
[c]*khazon* (2377)
‣Dan 9:24

8:2
Gen 10:22; 14:1
Esth 1:2
Isa 11:11
Jer 25:25

8:3
Dan 8:20

8:4
Deut 33:17
1 Kgs 22:11
Ezek 34:21

8:5
Dan 8:8, 21; 11:3

8:8
2 Chr 26:16
Dan 5:20; 7:2; 8:22
Rev 7:1

kingdoms under heaven will be given to the
holy people of the Most High. His kingdom
will last forever, and all rulers will serve and
obey him."
28That was the end of the vision. I, Daniel,
was terrified by my thoughts and my face
was pale with fear, but I kept these things
to myself.

Israel's Rescue from a Furious King (8:1-27)
Daniel's Vision of a Ram, a Goat, and a Small Horn

8 During the third year of King Belshazzar's reign, I, Daniel, saw another
[c]vision, following the one that had already
appeared to me. 2In this vision I was at the
fortress of Susa, in the province of Elam,
standing beside the Ulai River.
3As I looked up, I saw a ram with two
long horns standing beside the river. One of
the horns was longer than the other, even
though it had grown later than the other
one. 4The ram butted everything out of
his way to the west, to the north, and to the
south, and no one could stand against him
or help his victims. He did as he pleased
and became very great.
5While I was watching, suddenly a male
goat appeared from the west, crossing the
land so swiftly that he didn't even touch the
ground. This goat, which had one very large
horn between its eyes, 6headed toward the
two-horned ram that I had seen standing beside the river, rushing at him in a rage. 7The
goat charged furiously at the ram and struck
him, breaking off both his horns. Now the
ram was helpless, and the goat knocked
him down and trampled him. No one could
rescue the ram from the goat's power.
8The goat became very powerful. But at

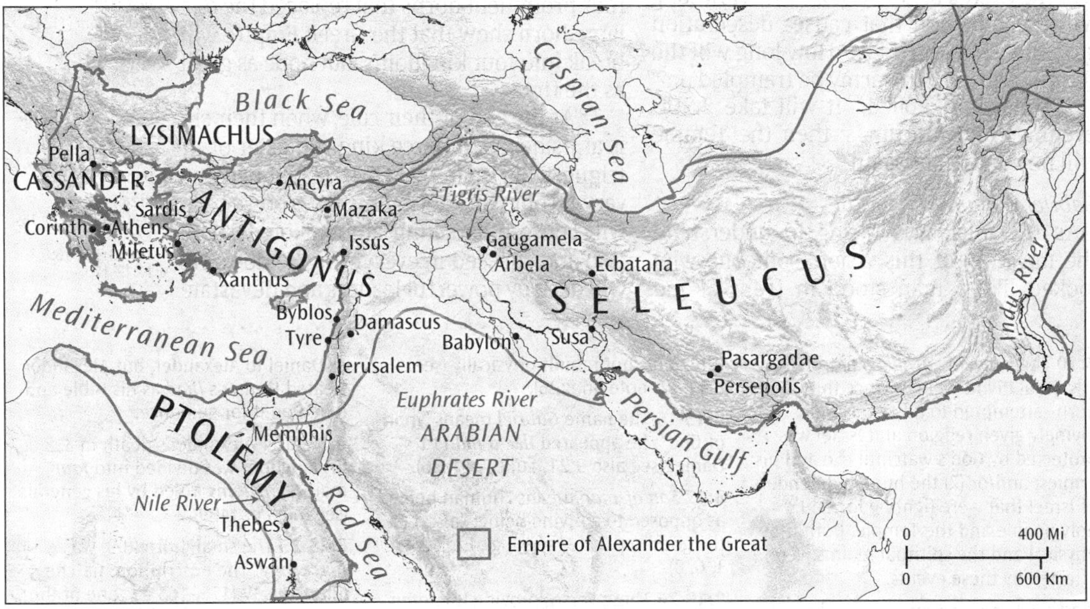

▲**The Greek Empire, 331–323 BC (8:5-8).** Alexander the Great ruled Macedonia beginning in 336 BC. He defeated the Persian army at ISSUS in 333 BC and at GAUGAMELA in 331 BC, and annexed the area controlled by the Persian Empire. Following Alexander's death in 323 BC, his empire was divided among his generals, among whom were CASSANDER in Macedonia, LYSIMACHUS near the Black Sea, ANTIGONUS in Asia and Syria, PTOLEMY in Egypt, and SELEUCUS in Babylonia and Persia. The successors of Antigonus gained control of Macedonia, bringing the number of major kingdoms from five to four. These generals and their descendants, particularly the Ptolemies and the Seleucids, were the key powers surrounding Judea from 323 BC down to the Roman period.

8:1-27 This vision expands the vision of ch 7, developing additional symbolism regarding the second and third beasts (7:5-6). Its report about a small horn that arises from the goat has similarities with the "little horn" of 7:8, 20-25; the "ruler" of 9:26-27; and the "despicable man" of 11:21-45.

8:1 The original text from this point through ch 12 is in Hebrew. See note on 2:4. The author probably changes back to Hebrew because he now focuses again (as with 1:1–2:4a) on the holy people, Israel, and their vicissitudes to the end. • ***The third year of King Belshazzar's reign*** was around 554~551 BC. It was about two years after the vision of ch 7 and over a decade before the fall of Babylon in 539 BC (5:31).

8:2 ***Susa,*** located in the lowlands of the Zagros Mountains, was one of Persia's capital cities (cp. Ezra 4:9; Neh 1:1; Esth 1:2). It was a fortified capital whose architecture was decorated with glazed griffins, winged bulls, and lions. • The ***Ulai River*** (or *Ulai Gate;* also in 8:16) was probably a man-made canal.

8:3-4 ***the river:*** Or *the gate;* also in 8:6. • ***Two long horns*** implies that there were two major nations in this kingdom represented by a ram (see 8:20-21). • God allowed the nation to do ***as it pleased;*** God was still in control (cp. Isa 45:1-4).

8:5-12 The symbolism is explained in 8:21-25.

the height of his power, his large horn was
broken off. In the large horn's place grew
four prominent horns pointing in the four
directions of the earth. [9]Then from one of
the prominent horns came a small horn
whose power grew very great. It extended toward the south and the east and toward the
glorious land of Israel. [10]Its power reached
to the heavens, where it attacked the heavenly army, throwing some of the heavenly
beings and some of the stars to the ground
and trampling them. [11]It even challenged
the Commander of heaven's army by canceling the daily sacrifices offered to him
and by destroying his Temple. [12]The army
of heaven was restrained from responding
to this rebellion. So the daily sacrifice was
halted, and truth was overthrown. The horn
succeeded in everything it did.
[13]Then I heard two holy ones talking to
each other. One of them asked, "How long
will the events of this vision last? How long
will the rebellion that causes desecration
stop the daily sacrifices? How long will the
Temple and heaven's army be trampled on?"
[14]The other replied, "It will take 2,300
evenings and mornings; then the Temple
will be made right again."

Gabriel Explains the Vision

[15]As I, Daniel, was trying to understand
the meaning of this vision, someone who
looked like a man stood in front of me.
[16]And I heard a human voice calling out
from the Ulai River, "Gabriel, tell this man
the meaning of his vision."
[17]As Gabriel approached the place where
I was standing, I became so terrified that
I fell with my face to the ground. "[d]Son of
man," he said, "you must understand that
the events you have seen in your vision relate to the time of the end."
[18]While he was speaking, I fainted and
lay there with my face to the ground. But
Gabriel roused me with a touch and helped
me to my feet.
[19]Then he said, "I am here to tell you
what will happen later in the time of wrath.
What you have seen pertains to the very end
of time. [20]The two-horned ram represents
the kings of Media and Persia. [21]The shaggy
male goat represents the king of Greece, and
the large horn between his eyes represents
the first king of the Greek Empire. [22]The
four prominent horns that replaced the one
large horn show that the Greek Empire will
break into four kingdoms, but none as great
as the first.
[23]"At the end of their rule, when their sin
is at its height, a fierce king, a master of intrigue, will rise to power. [24]He will become
very strong, but not by his own power. He
will cause a shocking amount of destruction and succeed in everything he does. He
will destroy powerful leaders and devastate

8:9 Dan 8:23; 11:16, 41
8:10 Jer 48:26, 42; Dan 7:7; 8:7; 11:31; Rev 12:4
8:11 Ezek 46:14; Dan 11:31, 36-37; 12:11
8:12 Isa 59:14
8:13 Ps 74:10; 79:5; Dan 4:13, 23; 12:6, 8; Luke 21:24; Heb 10:29; Rev 6:10; 11:2
8:14 Dan 7:25; 12:7, 11; Rev 11:2-3; 12:14; 13:5
8:15 Dan 7:13; 10:16, 18
8:16 Dan 9:21; Luke 1:19, 26
8:17 Ezek 1:28; 6:2; 44:4; Dan 2:46; 8:19; 11:35, 40; Rev 1:17
[d]*ben 'adam* (1121, 0120) ‣Num 23:19
8:18 Ezek 2:2; Dan 10:9-10, 16, 18; Luke 9:32
8:19 Dan 8:15-17
8:24 Dan 8:11-13; 11:36; 12:7; Rev 13:3-9; 16:6; 17:12-17

8:10 The *heavenly army* could refer to (1) actual divine beings, since the "small horn" attempted to destroy Israel's divinely given religion and Israel was protected by God's watchful eye and his armies; and/or (2) the human defenders of Israel that were fighting for God's holy people and the Temple. Both the physical and the spiritual realms were affected by these events.

8:11-12 The meaning of the Hebrew for these verses is uncertain.

8:11 God is the ***Commander of heaven's army*** (cp. Josh 5:13-15; 1 Sam 4:4; 1 Kgs 22:19) to whom ***the daily sacrifices*** were offered in ***his Temple***, where God's name resided and Israel worshiped its King (Isa 18:7; Ezek 43:6-7). • ***destroying*** (literally *casting down*): The religious function of the Temple was disabled.

8:12 God ***restrained*** the heavenly army for reasons known only to him. • The ***truth*** of God's law, embodied in true worship, was also ***overthrown*** (literally *cast down;* see note on 8:11).

8:13-14 ***How long:*** God's people were called en masse to endure this period to the end. • The ***Temple*** would then be ***made right*** for its proper religious functions, not rebuilt physically (see 8:11-12; note on 8:26).

8:15-16 The name ***Gabriel*** means "man of God"; he appeared ***like a man*** to Daniel (see also 9:21; Luke 1:19, 26).

8:17 ***Son of man*** means "human being," as opposed to a divine being, "a son of the gods" (cp. 7:13; see, e.g., Ezek 2:1, 3, 6, 8).

8:19-26 These verses provide the interpretation of the vision of 8:3-14.

8:19 ***the very end of time:*** There is an appointed time for the end of history.

8:20 The smaller horn represents ***Media***, which began as an independent kingdom in 670 BC. The larger horn represents ***Persia***, which dominated Media during Cyrus's reign (see 7:5).

8:21 ***of Greece:*** Hebrew *of Javan.* • ***The large horn*** represents Alexander the Great, the mighty ***first king*** who forged ***the Greek Empire.*** Two centuries after Daniel, Alexander would swiftly conquer the world (8:5); he overcame Persia in 331 BC. Alexander died in 323 BC at the age of thirty-three, but not before he arrogantly allowed himself to be called a god. • Josephus records that some Jewish priests showed the book of Daniel to Alexander, but Alexander treated Homer's *Iliad* as his Bible and relied on it for guidance.

8:22 After Alexander's death in 323 BC, his kingdom was divided into ***four*** major ***kingdoms***, ruled by his generals (see map, p. 1409).

8:23-25 The small horn (8:9) was ***a fierce king***. The description matches Antiochus IV (175–163 BC), one of the Seleucids (cp. 11:21-45). He bore the name "Epiphanes" ("The Manifest Presence [of God]"), but many, including Jews, mockingly called him "Epimanes" ("Mad Man"). By desolating the Temple and Jewish worship (8:11-12), Antiochus tried to destroy Judaism and unify his kingdom under the cult of Hellenistic culture. Some Jews were swept up in the program of Hellenism and adopted Greek ways.

8:24 ***not by his own power:*** Secretive and deceptive spiritual maneuvers and seemingly fortuitous events of history—all under God's sovereign control—brought Antiochus IV to power. • ***a shocking amount of destruction:*** See *1 Maccabees* 1:10-63, which describes many of the evils that Antiochus IV instigated.

8:25
Job 34:20
Dan 2:34, 45

8:27
Dan 7:28; 8:17
Hab 3:16

9:1
Dan 5:31; 11:1

9:2
2 Chr 36:21
Ezra 1:1
Jer 25:11; 29:10
Zech 7:5

9:4
Deut 7:9, 21
Neh 9:32
[e]*yadah* (3034)
‣ Lev 16:21

9:5
Ps 106:6; 119:176
Isa 53:6
Lam 1:18, 20
Dan 9:11
[f]*khata'* (2398)
‣ Hos 4:7

9:6
2 Chr 36:16
Jer 44:4-5, 21

9:7
Ezra 9:6-7
Ps 44:15
Jer 2:26-27; 3:25; 23:6; 33:16
Dan 9:18

the holy people. 25He will be a master of deception and will become arrogant; he will destroy many without warning. He will even take on the Prince of princes in battle, but he will be broken, though not by human power.

26"This vision about the 2,300 evenings and mornings is true. But none of these things will happen for a long time, so keep this vision a secret."

27Then I, Daniel, was overcome and lay sick for several days. Afterward I got up and performed my duties for the king, but I was greatly troubled by the vision and could not understand it.

Daniel's Prayer, Gabriel's Response (9:1-27)

Daniel's Prayer for His People

9 It was the first year of the reign of Darius the Mede, the son of Ahasuerus, who became king of the Babylonians. 2During the first year of his reign, I, Daniel, learned from reading the word of the LORD, as revealed to Jeremiah the prophet, that Jerusalem must lie desolate for seventy years. 3So I turned to the Lord God and pleaded with him in prayer and fasting. I also wore rough burlap and sprinkled myself with ashes.

4I prayed to the LORD my God and [e]confessed:

"O Lord, you are a great and awesome God! You always fulfill your covenant and keep your promises of unfailing love to those who love you and obey your commands. 5But we have [f]sinned and done wrong. We have rebelled against you and scorned your commands and regulations. 6We have refused to listen to your servants the prophets, who spoke on your authority to our kings and princes and ancestors and to all the people of the land.

7"Lord, you are in the right; but as you see, our faces are covered with shame. This is true of all of us, including the people of Judah and Jerusalem and all

---

8:25 The *Prince of princes* is the King of Israel, the ruler of heaven and earth (7:9-10, 13-14). Antiochus, at the time of his death, exalted himself as God and intended to destroy Jerusalem. • ***he will be broken:*** Just as Antiochus IV came to power by supernatural means (8:24), so he was destroyed by God's hand rather than ***by human power.*** His end was to be eaten by worms (*1 Maccabees* 6:7-16 and *2 Maccabees* 9:4-28; cp. Herod Agrippa, Acts 12:20-23).

8:26 ***about the 2,300 evenings and mornings*** (literally *about the evenings and mornings;* cp. 8:14): This could refer to a period of 1,150 days (1,150 evenings + 1,150 mornings, about 3½ years) or 2,300 days (about 7 years). Antiochus IV deposed high priest Onias III in 171 BC. He desecrated the Temple in December 167 BC and offered unclean sacrifices. The Temple and the altar were cleansed and used again in December 164 BC, seven years after Onias was deposed and just over three years after the Temple was desecrated (see *1 Maccabees* 1:54; 4:52-53; *2 Maccabees* 10:5). • ***keep this vision a secret:*** It would have been unwise for Daniel to share this vision at that time during Belshazzar's reign, when it would have smelled of insurrection or treason.

9:1-19 Daniel prayed for his people, realizing that Jerusalem's seventy years of desolation were due to end. His prayer is comparable to prayers of Solomon (1 Kgs 8:14-61), Ezra (Ezra 9), and Nehemiah (Neh 9). God answered Daniel's prayer very quickly (see notes on 9:1, 19; see also 9:20-27).

9:1 ***Darius the Mede:*** See note on 5:31. • ***Ahasuerus*** is the Hebrew rendering of a Persian word taken into Greek as "Xerxes." The father of Darius the Mede must have been a different Xerxes from the later Xerxes I, who reigned from 486 to 465 BC (see Esth 1:1); the time of this vision was 539 BC. It has been argued that the name Xerxes/Ahasuerus is an ancient throne name for Persian kings. • ***of the Babylonians:*** Or *of the Chaldeans.*

9:2 ***reading . . . Jeremiah:*** Daniel apparently had a copy of Jeremiah's prophecies. • ***Jerusalem must lie desolate for seventy years:*** See Jer 25:11-12; 29:10. Jerusalem was destroyed in 586 BC (see 2 Kgs 25:8), and the first return occurred in 538 BC—about 48 years later. The rebuilding of the city began almost at once (see Ezra 3; Isa 44:28), and the rebuilt Temple was completed in 515 BC—about seventy-one years after it was destroyed (Ezra 6:15). Daniel might have thought of Jerusalem's "destruction" as having begun with his own exile in 605 BC (see Jer 25:11-12), with sixty-seven years between 605 and 538 BC.

9:3 Daniel realized that the seventy years were nearly at an end, so he ***turned to the Lord God*** seeking restoration for his people and the city of Jerusalem. • People in mourning often wore ***burlap*** and ***ashes*** (cp. Neh 9:1; Esth 4:1; Lam 2:10; Luke 10:13). • Focused prayer was often accompanied by ***fasting*** to put spiritual concerns ahead of physical needs.

9:4-11a God's faithfulness contrasted sharply with his people's unfaithfulness and rebellion. When Daniel confessed the sins of his people, he included himself among them (9:5), though he had lived a laudatory life (see "Community Identity" at Lev 4:3, 13-21, p. 199). Daniel prayed the equivalent of a high priestly prayer on behalf of his people, using many quotations from and allusions to the Torah, prophets, and psalms.

9:4 ***the LORD*** (Hebrew *Yahweh*): The covenant name of God (Exod 6:2-3; 20:2) is found in Daniel only in this chapter. • God is faithful to his ***covenant*** with his people ***who love . . . and obey*** him (cp. Exod 34:6-7; Deut 7:9; Rom 8:28). God's ***unfailing love*** (Hebrew *khesed,* elsewhere translated "grace," "mercy," "kindness") is his fundamental nature that is the cause of faith, hope, and worship throughout the Bible (see Num 14:18; Neh 9:17; Ps 108:4; 136:1-26; Jon 2:4; 1 Jn 4:7-8).

9:5 Daniel used four different words meaning sin: The people had ***sinned*** (literally *missed the mark*), ***done wrong*** (i.e., committed a bent or twisted act), ***rebelled*** against the covenant, and ***scorned*** (literally *turned away from*) the Lord's instructions.

9:6 God's ***servants the prophets*** were his specially called and inspired spokesmen (9:10; Deut 18:15-22; 2 Kgs 17:23; 21:10-15; Jer 7:25; 25:4).

9:7-14 ***Lord, you are in the right:*** God orchestrated the Exile as a judgment on unfaithful Israel (9:11b-14). God had given ample warning that it would happen (see Deut 28:36-37, 49-68).

Israel, scattered near and far, wherever
you have driven us because of our
disloyalty to you. 8O LORD, we and our
kings, princes, and ancestors are covered
with shame because we have sinned
against you. 9But the Lord our God is
merciful and forgiving, even though we
have rebelled against him. 10We have not
[g]obeyed the LORD our God, for we have
not followed the instructions he gave us
through his servants the prophets. 11All
Israel has disobeyed your instruction
and turned away, refusing to listen to
your voice.

"So now the solemn curses and
judgments written in the Law of Moses,
the servant of God, have been poured
down on us because of our sin. 12You
have kept your word and done to us
and our rulers exactly as you warned.
Never has there been such a disaster as
happened in Jerusalem. 13Every curse
written against us in the Law of Moses
has come true. Yet we have refused to
seek mercy from the LORD our God by
turning from our sins and recognizing
his truth. 14Therefore, the LORD
has brought upon us the disaster he
prepared. The LORD our God was right
to do all of these things, for we did not
obey him.

15"O Lord our God, you brought lasting
honor to your name by rescuing your
people from Egypt in a great display of
power. But we have sinned and are full of
wickedness. 16In view of all your faithful
mercies, Lord, please turn your furious
anger away from your city Jerusalem,
your holy mountain. All the neighboring
nations mock Jerusalem and your people
because of our sins and the sins of our
ancestors.

17"O our God, hear your servant's
prayer! Listen as I plead. For your own
sake, Lord, smile again on your desolate
sanctuary.

18"O my God, lean down and listen to
me. Open your eyes and see our despair.
See how your city—the city that bears
your name—lies in ruins. We make this
plea, not because we deserve help, but
because of your mercy.

19"O Lord, hear. O Lord, forgive.
O Lord, listen and act! For your own sake,
do not delay, O my God, for your people
and your city bear your name."

Gabriel's Message about the Anointed One

20I went on praying and confessing my sin
and the sin of my people, [h]pleading with the
LORD my God for Jerusalem, his holy mountain. 21As I was praying, Gabriel, whom I
had seen in the earlier vision, came swiftly
to me at the time of the evening sacrifice.
22He explained to me, "Daniel, I have come
here to give you insight and understanding.
23The moment you began praying, a command was given. And now I am here to tell
you what it was, for you are very precious to

9:9 Neh 9:17-21
9:10 2 Kgs 17:13-15; 18:12
[g]*shama'* (8085) ‣Zech 6:15
9:11 Isa 1:2-4; Jer 8:5-10
9:12 Jer 44:2-6; Zech 1:6
9:13 Deut 28:15-68; Jer 2:30; 5:3
9:14 Jer 31:28; 44:27
9:15 Deut 5:15; Neh 9:10; Jer 32:20
9:16 Ps 87:1-3; Ezek 5:14
9:17 Num 6:24-26; Ps 80:3, 7, 19; Lam 5:18
9:18 Ps 80:14; Isa 37:17; Jer 7:12
9:19 Ps 44:23; 74:10-11
9:20 Ps 145:18; Isa 6:5; 58:9; Zech 1:14
[h]*tekhinnah* (8467) ‣1 Kgs 8:28
9:21 Exod 29:39; 1 Kgs 18:36; Ezra 9:4; Dan 8:16
9:22 Dan 8:16; 10:21; Zech 1:9
9:23 Matt 24:15

9:12 God's act of driving Israel into exile for breaking his covenant was unique in all of history. Israel's exodus from Egypt, their exile, and their return from Babylon are still unequaled (see also Isa 23:14-21; Jer 29:10).

9:13 ***Every curse written against us in the Law of Moses*** is summarized in Lev 26 and Deut 27–28. When the people entered into the covenant they swore to be obedient, calling down curses on themselves if they failed (see Exod 24:7-8; Josh 8:34-35).

9:15-19 Daniel cried out for God to rescue his people and end the Exile, relying on God's mercy and God's desire to honor his own name. Daniel's prayer is among the great intercessory prayers of God's OT people (see also Exod 32:11-14; Ezra 9:1-15; Neh 9:1-37).

9:15 God could bring *lasting honor* to his *name by rescuing* his *people* from exile in Babylonia, just as he did when he rescued them *from Egypt* (cp. Ezek 36:19-24).

9:16 ***mock Jerusalem and your people:*** God's name was dishonored when his chosen city and his chosen people were ridiculed because of their helplessness before their enemies, making it appear that their God was helpless (9:19; cp. Ezek 36:19-20).

9:17 ***For your own sake:*** That is, for God's own honor (9:19).

9:18 ***because of your mercy:*** God's compassionate and merciful character gave Daniel hope (cp. Exod 34:6; Jon 4:1-3; Mic 6:8).

9:19 ***listen and act! . . . do not delay:*** Daniel prayed this prayer in 539 BC (see 9:1). Shortly thereafter (in 538 BC), King Cyrus gave his decree allowing the Jewish people to return to Judea (Ezra 1:1-4). The new Temple in Jerusalem was completed in 515 BC (Ezra 6:15). God returned the Israelites from exile in response to their prayers and repentance, just as the Exile had been his response to his people's sins and rebellion. • ***your people and your city bear your name:*** God's reputation was associated with Jerusalem (Neh 1:9) and his people, Israel (Exod 5:22–6:1).

9:20-27 God's immediate answer to Daniel's prayer was to send his messenger Gabriel to explain Daniel's vision (see note on 9:23). Gabriel's explanation covered the near and distant future of Daniel's people.

9:20 ***my sin and the sin of my people:*** See note on 9:4-11a.

9:21 ***Gabriel . . . earlier vision:*** See 8:15-16. • ***evening sacrifice:*** Before the destruction of the Temple, Israel had offered two sacrificial lambs daily, one in the morning and one in the evening (Exod 29:41). Daniel apparently observed these times daily with prayer (6:10, 13; cp. Ps 55:17).

9:22 In the book of Daniel, *insight and understanding* are key words that often refer to the meaning of God's revelation (cp. 1:4; 9:13, 25; 11:33, 35). God did not promise Daniel the answers to all of his questions, but rather, a basic grasp of the issues. God is in charge of history.

9:23 ***a command was given*** (literally *a word went forth*): This command might have been God's decree to end the Exile and return his people to Jerusalem and Judea, or it might have been the

The Seventy Sets of Seven (9:24-27)

"I shall simply repeat the view of each . . . and leave it to the reader's judgment as to whose explanation ought to be followed." Jerome, *Commentary on Daniel*

The seventy sevens (or *weeks*) of Dan 9:24-27 have always puzzled students of the Bible. The two main interpretations are as follows.

Dan 7:8, 11, 20-21, 24-27; 8:9-14; 11:29-31, 40-45; 12:7, 11

SCENARIO A: THE REIGN OF ANTIOCHUS IV (175–163 BC). The seventy sets of seven refer to history from Cyrus II of Persia (539 BC; see 9:25; Ezra 1:2-4) to Antiochus IV (175–163 BC; see 8:23-25; 11:21-39). In this scenario, the "Anointed One" was high priest Onias III (see note on 9:26), and the "ruler" (9:26-27) was Antiochus IV, whose treaty with the people of Judea in 174 BC was supposed to allow them to practice their faith peacefully. But in 170 BC, Antiochus attacked Jerusalem, killed many, and looted the Temple. Then in 167 BC he put an end to the sacrifices and offerings, forced the Jews to stop practicing their faith on pain of death, and desecrated the Temple with a "sacrilegious object": He placed a statue of Zeus on the altar of burnt offering, where he sacrificed pigs and other unclean animals (cp. 11:21-35). Antiochus was struck with a painful disease, and he died in 163 BC—"the fate decreed for this defiler" was "finally poured out on him" (9:27; see 8:25; cp. *1 Maccabees* 1:10-64; 6:7-16; *2 Maccabees* 9:4-28). In Scenario A, when Jesus spoke of the "sacrilegious object that causes desecration," he was referring to the Jews' experience in the time of Antiochus as a paradigm of the things that would happen in the future (see note on 9:27; Matt 24:15; cp. Luke 21:20; 2 Thes 2:3-4).

SCENARIO B: THE DEATH OF CHRIST (AD 30 or 33). The seventy weeks are a prophecy concerning Jesus Christ, the Anointed Messiah. In this scenario, the "seventy sets of seven" began either with the decree of Cyrus (538 BC; Ezra 1:1-4) or with one of the decrees of Artaxerxes (458 or 445 BC; Ezra 7:8-26; Neh 2:1-10). The death of Christ then occurred either at the end of sixty-nine sets of seven (seven plus sixty-two, 9:25-26), or at the midpoint of the seventieth (9:27). These two options have implications for how the seventy sets of seven are brought to completion. In the first option, the seventieth set of seven is seen as a future time not yet fulfilled. In the second option, the seventieth set of seven is seen as having been completed when the Romans destroyed Jerusalem and the Temple in AD 70. If the decree of Cyrus is seen as the starting point, the 490 years are symbolic. However, if the decree given to Nehemiah to rebuild the city (445 BC; Neh 2:1) is taken as the starting point (9:25), then there were very nearly 483 years (69 x 7 years) between that date and the death of Christ in AD 30 or 33.

Option 1: The Seventieth Set of Seven Remains to Be Fulfilled in the Future. Many interpreters have argued that Christ's death occurred at the end of the sixty-ninth set of seven, and the seventieth set of seven is yet to be fulfilled. In that case, there is now a long gap from the sixty-ninth set of seven to the seventieth. The seventieth still lies in the future and corresponds to the reign of the antichrist during the Tribulation at the end of history (cp. 2 Thes 2:5-12; 1 Jn 2:18-22; 4:3; 2 Jn 1:7; Rev 13:1, 5; 16:13-14; 17:11; 19:20-21; 20:10).

Option 2: The Seventieth Set of Seven Was Completed When Rome Destroyed Jerusalem and the Temple in AD 70. Other interpreters have held that the seventy weeks were fulfilled with the coming of Christ, his death and resurrection, and the destruction of Jerusalem and its Temple in AD 70. In this case, Christ began his ministry at the end of the sixty-ninth set of seven, about AD 28. He ministered for approximately three and one-half years, then was killed in the middle of the seventieth seven. The remaining half-seven ended when the "ruler"—one or more of the Roman rulers—destroyed Jerusalem and its Temple in AD 70. The war and its miseries now continue between God's people and the kingdom of this world to the very end, when Christ will return, judge the wicked, and establish his kingdom.

Although difficult to assign to a definite period of history, the seventy sets of seven are significant: They demonstrate God's sovereignty over history and emphasize his ability to bring his plans for his people to completion. The number seventy (seven times ten) represents completeness. God's seventy years of exile for his people (9:2) were enough to chastise them; those years are more than matched by the time period to reclaim them (see note on 9:24).

God. Listen carefully so that you can understand the meaning of your vision.
24“A period of seventy sets of seven has
been decreed for your people and your holy
city to finish their rebellion, to put an end
to their sin, to [i]atone for their guilt, to bring
in everlasting righteousness, to confirm the
prophetic [j]vision, and to anoint the Most
Holy Place. 25Now listen and understand!
Seven sets of seven plus sixty-two sets of
seven will pass from the time the command
is given to rebuild Jerusalem until a ruler—
the Anointed One—comes. Jerusalem will
be rebuilt with streets and strong defenses,
despite the perilous times.
26“After this period of sixty-two sets
of seven, the Anointed One will be killed,
appearing to have accomplished nothing,
and a ruler will arise whose armies will destroy the city and the Temple. The end will
come with a flood, and war and its miseries are decreed from that time to the very
end. 27The ruler will make a treaty with the
people for a period of one set of seven, but
after half this time, he will put an end to the
sacrifices and offerings. And as a climax to

9:24
Lev 25:8
Num 14:34
[i]*kapar* (3722)
›Exod 32:30
[j]*khazon* (2377)
›Hos 12:10

9:26
Isa 53:8
Nah 1:8
Matt 24:2
Mark 9:12; 13:2
Luke 19:43-44; 24:26

9:27
Isa 10:23; 28:22
Dan 11:31
*Matt 24:15
*Mark 13:14
*Luke 21:20

---

command to explain the future to Daniel (9:24-27). • ***you are very precious to God:*** Also in 10:11, 19. • It is unclear what ***your vision*** refers to: It could be the restoration of Jerusalem and God’s people that Daniel read about in Jeremiah and envisioned in his prayer (9:2-20), or one of the earlier visions (e.g., ch 8; cp. 8:27).

9:24-27 Gabriel further explained the meaning of Daniel’s vision (9:22-23). Because the vision of ch 8 culminated with Antiochus IV (see 8:23-25; cp. 11:21-39), many interpreters understand this explanation as also pointing to Antiochus. Others understand it as culminating in the death of Christ, followed by the destruction of Jerusalem in AD 70 and the coming of the antichrist.

9:24 Many understand the ***period of seventy sets of seven*** (literally *seventy sevens,* or *seventy weeks*) as seventy “weeks of years”—i.e., 490 years. However, they are not called “years” in the Hebrew text, and it has proven difficult to assign this period to an actual historical period of 490 years. Therefore, many interpreters believe that the numbers are not intended as calendar years but as symbolic periods of time to fulfill the visions. Just as Jerusalem suffered a lifetime of desolation (9:2; see note on Jer 25:11), the city would experience many lifetimes of restoration. • The period of time was ***for your people*** (the Jews) ***and your holy city*** (Jerusalem). The six purposes listed here appear to refer to the restoration of the Jews and the city of Jerusalem. Other interpreters see these six purposes as representing God’s universal work of redemption in the world. • God would ***finish*** the ***rebellion*** of the Israelites, and he would also finish the rebellions of human rulers who defy the Lord and attack the holy people (7:8, 22, 25-26; 8:13-14; 11:29-45). • To ***confirm the prophetic vision*** means to fulfill the content of the visionary answer to Daniel’s prayer. • ***the Most Holy Place*** (Or *the Most Holy One;* literally *a most holy*): Some interpreters see this as referring to the restored Most Holy Place in the Temple in 164 BC. Others see it as referring to the anointing of Christ and his church as God’s own temple (Matt 12:6; Eph 2:19-22).

9:25 ***Seven sets of seven plus sixty-two sets of seven:*** Literally *Seven sevens plus sixty-two sevens.* • The ***command . . . to rebuild Jerusalem*** and its Temple marks the beginning of the seventy sets of seven. The event that best fits this description is the decree of Cyrus the Great in 538 BC that allowed the Jews to return to Jerusalem and begin rebuilding (see 5:31; 9:1; Ezra 1:2-4). Less likely are the decrees of Artaxerxes I in 458 BC (see Ezra 7:12-26) and 445 BC (see Neh 2:5-8). • ***a ruler—the Anointed One:*** Or *an anointed one, a prince;* similarly in 9:26. Literally *a messiah, a prince.* Many interpreters see Christ as fulfilling this prophecy, so they understand this passage as describing history from the time of Daniel to the time of Christ. However, an “anointed one” can refer to any of Israel’s kings or priests, who were ordained by anointing with oil. If the passage was fulfilled in the time of Antiochus IV, then the anointed one was probably the high priest at the time, Onias III (cp. 11:22). • ***and strong defenses*** (Or *and a moat,* or *and trenches*): The vision refers to ***Jerusalem*** as being physically ***rebuilt.*** The rebuilding of the Temple was completed in 515 BC (Ezra 3–6); in 445 BC, Nehemiah completed the wall of Jerusalem (Neh 2–6). • The ***perilous times*** can refer to the history of Jerusalem and its Temple from the time the decree was published until the end of the seventy sets of seven (see 11:2-45).

9:26 ***After this period of sixty-two sets of seven:*** Literally *After sixty-two sevens.* • ***the Anointed One*** (literally *an anointed*): Those who see the fulfillment of this passage in the time of Antiochus IV point to the murder of the high priest Onias III in 171 BC as the fulfillment of this prophecy (see note on 11:22). Those who see the fulfillment of this passage in the time of Christ will refer this prophecy to the crucifixion of the Messiah in AD 30 or 33. • The ***ruler*** who ***will arise*** could refer to Antiochus IV, who attempted to ***destroy*** the Jewish people and their worship in the Temple between 171 and 164 BC (see *1 Maccabees* 1:20-40). Many believe, however, that the destruction of ***the city and the Temple*** refers to the destruction of Jerusalem by the Romans in AD 66–70. • ***The end*** refers to the completion of the seventy sets of seven. The text implies that ***the very end*** is a later time, and that the ***war*** would continue into the future (cp. Matt 24:4-8; Mark 13:5-8). • The image of a ***flood*** often represents an invading army (cp. 11:10, 22, 40; Nah 1:8) or devastating destruction.

9:27 ***The ruler*** (literally *he*): Most interpreters understand this pronoun as referring to the ruler of 9:26. Some think that it refers back to the anointed one of 9:25-26 and is thus a prophecy about Christ, meaning that Christ caused a covenant to prevail and removed the need for sacrifices and offerings by his death. However, the word behind ***make a treaty*** has the sense of imposing a covenant, evidently by the use of force or intimidation. Antiochus IV imposed a covenant with the people of Judea following the beginning of his rule in 175 BC (cp. 11:23; see *1 Maccabees* 1:10-15). Other interpreters believe that this prophecy was fulfilled in the events of AD 66–70. For still others, it refers to a future ruler. • ***for a period of one set of seven:*** Literally *for one seven.* • The phrase ***put an end*** refers to a destructive action, not an act of God’s salvation such as the Messiah would accomplish by his death. In 167 BC, Antiochus IV ordered the people of Judea to cease all practice of Jewish worship in the Temple and instead practice pagan worship, on pain of death (see *1 Maccabees* 1:41-63). Similarly, the Roman general Titus put an end ***to the sacrifices and offerings*** in the Temple when he destroyed it in AD 70. • ***And as a climax to all his terrible deeds:*** Literally *And on the wing of abominations;* the meaning of the Hebrew is uncertain. • ***a sacrilegious object that causes desecration*** (literally *an abomination of desolation*): Cp. 8:13; 11:31; 12:11. This term (Hebrew *shiqqutsim meshomem*) is

10:1 Dan 1:17, 21; 2:21; 6:28
10:2 Ezra 9:4-5; Neh 1:4; *k'abal* (0056) ‣Amos 9:5
10:4 Ezek 1:3; Dan 8:2
10:5 Dan 12:6-7; Rev 1:13
10:6 Rev 1:14-15; 2:18
10:7 Acts 9:7
10:8 Dan 7:28; 8:27; Hab 3:16
10:9 Gen 15:12; Dan 8:18
10:10 Jer 1:9
10:11 Job 4:14-15; Ezek 2:1; Dan 8:16-17
10:12 Dan 9:20-23; 10:2-3, 19
10:13 Dan 10:21; 12:1; Jude 1:9; Rev 12:7
10:14 Dan 2:28; 8:26; 12:4, 9

all his terrible deeds, he will set up a sacrilegious object that causes desecration, until the fate decreed for this defiler is finally poured out on him."

Israel's Rescue from Destruction (10:1–12:7)
Daniel's Vision of a Messenger

10 In the third year of the reign of King Cyrus of Persia, Daniel (also known as Belteshazzar) had another vision. He understood that the vision concerned events certain to happen in the future—times of war and great hardship.
2 When this vision came to me, I, Daniel, had been in [k]mourning for three whole
weeks. 3 All that time I had eaten no rich food. No meat or wine crossed my lips, and I used no fragrant lotions until those three weeks had passed.
4 On April 23, as I was standing on the
bank of the great Tigris River, 5 I looked up
and saw a man dressed in linen clothing, with a belt of pure gold around his waist.
6 His body looked like a precious gem. His face flashed like lightning, and his eyes flamed like torches. His arms and feet shone like polished bronze, and his voice roared like a vast multitude of people.
7 Only I, Daniel, saw this vision. The men with me saw nothing, but they were suddenly terrified and ran away to hide. 8 So I
was left there all alone to see this amazing vision. My strength left me, my face grew deathly pale, and I felt very weak. 9 Then I
heard the man speak, and when I heard the sound of his voice, I fainted and lay there with my face to the ground.
10 Just then a hand touched me and lifted me, still trembling, to my hands and knees.
11 And the man said to me, "Daniel, you are very precious to God, so listen carefully to what I have to say to you. Stand up, for I have been sent to you." When he said this to me, I stood up, still trembling.
12 Then he said, "Don't be afraid, Daniel. Since the first day you began to pray for understanding and to humble yourself before your God, your request has been heard in heaven. I have come in answer to your
prayer. 13 But for twenty-one days the spirit prince of the kingdom of Persia blocked my way. Then Michael, one of the archangels, came to help me, and I left him there with the spirit prince of the kingdom of Persia.
14 Now I am here to explain what will happen to your people in the future, for this vision concerns a time yet to come."

---

possibly a mocking play on the Semitic name for Zeus (*Ba'al Shamayim*, "Lord of the Heavens"). Idol-gods are often referred to as *shiqquts*, "abomination," "desolation," elsewhere in the Bible (see Deut 29:17; 2 Chr 15:8; Isa 66:3; Jer 32:34; Ezek 20:7), and the similarity between the sounds of *shomem*, "devastation, destruction, desolation" and *shamayim* is clear. In December 167 BC, Antiochus IV erected an image of Zeus atop the altar of burnt offering in the Temple court and sacrificed unclean animals there. The same phrase (*abomination of desolation*) is used in *1 Maccabees* 1:54 to describe that altar and its sacrifices. Jesus and other NT authors anticipated a desolating sacrilege in the future (Matt 24:15; Mark 13:14; Luke 21:20; 2 Thes 2:3-4). After Titus destroyed the Temple in Jerusalem in AD 70, the Romans set up their idols in the Temple precinct and made sacrifices to their gods (see Josephus, *War* 6.6.1). The apostle John later observed that many antichrists had appeared (1 Jn 2:18-23) and that the spirit of the antichrist was at work in the world (1 Jn 4:3). • The time of destruction is under God's control, and the ***fate decreed for this defiler*** is certain to come (cp. 7:11; 8:25; 11:45). So it is with every ruler who exalts himself against God and seeks to destroy God's people.

10:1–12:13 This final vision reaches historically from 536 BC to a distant future when Daniel would be raised from the dead and receive his inheritance. All earthly kingdoms would be destroyed, the eternal kingdom of the Son of Man would arise, God's people would finally be rescued, and death—the ultimate enemy—would be defeated.

10:1 ***The third year of the reign of King Cyrus*** was 536 BC, not long after Cyrus issued his decree for the peoples and nations to return to their ancestral homes (2 Chr 36:22-23; Ezra 1:1-2). Daniel's prayer (9:4-19) had been answered—the Exile had ended. • ***Belteshazzar:*** See 1:7.

10:2-3 ***Daniel*** was apparently ***in mourning*** because of his previous visions (10:14, 16).

10:4 ***On April 23:*** Literally *On the twenty-fourth day of the first month* of the ancient Hebrew lunar calendar. This date in the book of Daniel can be cross-checked with dates in surviving Persian records and can be related accurately to our modern calendar. This event occurred on April 23, 536 BC.

10:5-6 The ***man dressed in linen clothing*** is an unidentified messenger of the Lord (cp. 10:16, 18; 12:6-7; see also Ezek 9:3).

10:7-9 Daniel's response was typical for humans in the presence of heavenly beings (cp. Josh 5:14; Isa 6:5; Acts 9:7-9; Rev 1:17).

10:11 ***very precious to God:*** See also 9:23; 10:19.

10:13 ***the spirit prince:*** Literally *the prince;* also in 10:20. • The spiritual forces behind the various nations, such as the spirit prince of Persia or the spirit prince of Greece, ***blocked*** the ***way*** of God's messenger who responded to the prayers of God's people (see 10:20–11:1). • ***one of the archangels*** (literally *one of the chief princes*): An archangel was a chief among God's heavenly messengers. • ***and I left him there with the spirit prince of the kingdom of Persia:*** As in one Greek version; Hebrew reads *and I was left there with the kings of Persia.* The meaning of the Hebrew is uncertain. • Daniel's world, and ours, is populated by more than meets the human eye. Daniel is shown the great events of history enacted against a background of a real spiritual world where spiritual beings support or hinder God's people, where the conflicts of the ages are also carried out. Behind all of this, the Ancient of Days sovereignly guides all things and sits in judgment upon the process and its conclusion. God's covenant with his people, and their relationship with him through prayer, are central to this process—the world is not ultimately governed by angels and spirit princes, but by the Ancient of Days, who hears the prayers of his people.

15While he was speaking to me, I looked
down at the ground, unable to say a word.
16Then the one who looked like a man
touched my lips, and I opened my mouth
and began to speak. I said to the one standing in front of me, "I am filled with anguish
because of the vision I have seen, my lord,
and I am very weak. 17How can someone like
me, your servant, talk to you, my lord? My
strength is gone, and I can hardly breathe."
18Then the one who looked like a man
touched me again, and I felt my strength
returning. 19"Don't be afraid," he said, "for
you are very precious to God. Peace! Be encouraged! Be strong!"
As he spoke these words to me, I suddenly
felt stronger and said to him, "Please speak to
me, my lord, for you have strengthened me."
20He replied, "Do you know why I have
come? Soon I must return to fight against
the spirit prince of the kingdom of Persia,
and after that the spirit prince of the kingdom of Greece will come. 21Meanwhile, I
will tell you what is written in the Book of
[a]Truth. (No one helps me against these spirit
princes except Michael, your spirit prince.
11:1I have been standing beside Michael to
support and strengthen him since the first
year of the reign of Darius the Mede.)

Kings of the South and North

11 2"Now then, I will reveal the truth to
you. Three more Persian kings will
reign, to be succeeded by a fourth, far richer

10:15 Ezek 24:27; Luke 1:20
10:16 Jer 1:9; Dan 7:15; 8:15
10:17 Exod 24:10-11; Isa 6:1-5
10:18 Isa 35:3-4
10:19 Josh 1:6-9; Judg 6:23; Isa 35:4; 43:1; Dan 10:12
10:20 Dan 8:21; 11:2
10:21 Dan 12:1, 4
[a]*'emeth* (0571) ‣Exod 34:6
11:1 Dan 5:31; 9:1

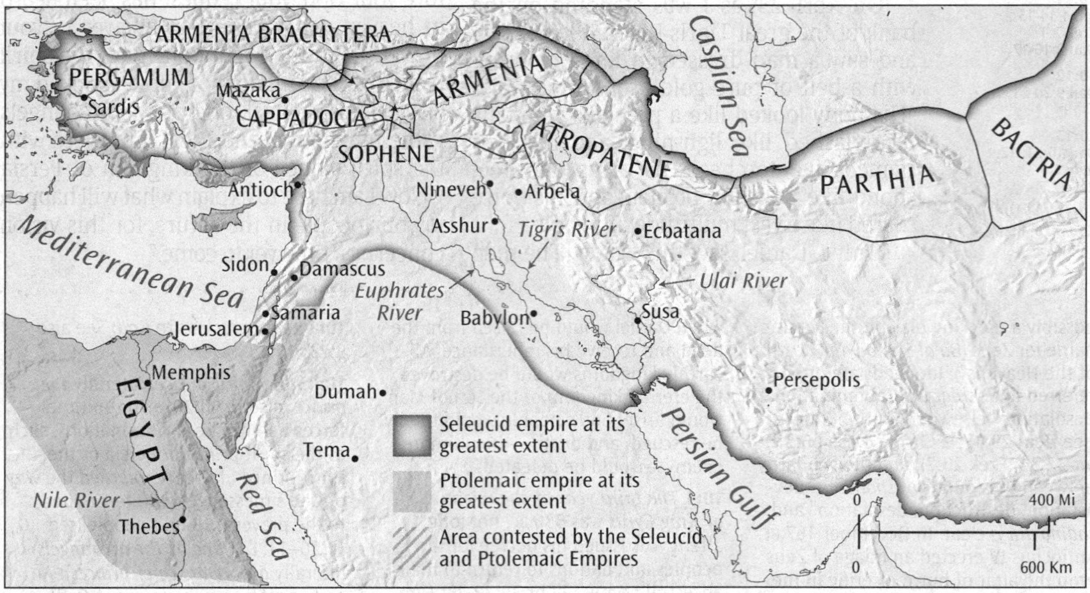

▲**The Ptolemies and the Seleucids, 323–198 BC (11:4-12).** While the Ptolemies ruled in EGYPT, the Seleucids gained control of most of the area previously held by the Persian Empire. Control over Israel and southern Syria was contested (11:4-12). The struggles of the great powers became a source of persecution and hardship for the Jews living in Judea. In 198 BC, Antiochus III (223–187 BC) secured control of Israel and southern Syria.

10:16 ***Then the one who looked like a man:*** As in most manuscripts of the Masoretic Text; one manuscript of the Masoretic Text and one Greek version read *Then something that looked like a human hand.* • ***touched my lips:*** Cp. Exod 4:11-12; Isa 6:5-7.

10:19 God's word gives strength to his servants (cp. Ps 29:11; 68:35).

10:20 The messenger described empires in terms of the ***spirit prince*** representing each of them. The Persian empire had just begun and would later be replaced by the Greek empire (cp. 8:3-7, 19-21). • ***of Greece:*** Hebrew *of Javan.*

10:21 ***Book of Truth*** (literally *writing of truth*): The messenger was not speaking of himself, but from what was written in God's Book of Truth. Compare God's book in 7:9-10; Exod 32:32-33. See also 12:1; Ps 139:16. The Book of Truth contains what is revealed in 11:2–12:7. • ***against these spirit princes except Michael, your spirit prince*** (literally *against these except Michael, your prince*): God divided up the nations, partitioning out the nations and their princes (Deut 32:8). God was over Israel, and Michael was Israel's spirit prince.

11:1 ***beside Michael:*** Literally *beside him.* • ***Darius the Mede:*** See note on 5:31; ***the first year*** was probably 539 BC.

11:2–12:7 The messenger provided a grand sweep of history, from the time of Persia, through the break-up of Greece, the rise and defeat of a wicked king or series of kings (11:21-45), and the final resurrection and triumph of God's people.

11:2 ***Three more Persian kings:*** These Persian kings who followed Cyrus II were most likely Cambyses (530–522 BC), Gaumata (522 BC, a usurper), and Darius I (521–486 BC). The ***fourth*** was probably Xerxes I (486–465 BC; see note on Esth 1:1), whose riches were legendary, as were his army of 1,700,000 soldiers and his huge navy (see Herodotus, *Histories* 7.6), which he used ***to fight against the kingdom of Greece*** (Hebrew *of Javan*). He was unsuccessful, as the Persians failed to defeat the growing power of Greece. God's sovereign hand

11:2 Dan 8:21, 26; 10:1, 20-21
11:3 Dan 5:19; 8:4-5, 21; 11:16, 36
11:4 Jer 49:36; Ezek 37:9; Dan 7:2; 8:8; Zech 2:6; Rev 7:1
11:5 Dan 11:9, 11, 14, 25, 40
11:6 Dan 11:7, 13, 15, 40
11:7 Dan 11:19, 38-39

than the others. He will use his wealth to stir
up everyone to fight against the kingdom of
Greece.
3“Then a mighty king will rise to power
who will rule with great authority and accomplish everything he sets out to do. 4But
at the height of his power, his kingdom
will be broken apart and divided into four
parts. It will not be ruled by the king’s descendants, nor will the kingdom hold the
authority it once had. For his empire will be
uprooted and given to others.
5“The king of the south will increase in
power, but one of his own officials will become more powerful than he and will rule
his kingdom with great strength.
6“Some years later an alliance will be
formed between the king of the north and
the king of the south. The daughter of the
king of the south will be given in marriage
to the king of the north to secure the alliance, but she will lose her influence over
him, and so will her father. She will be
abandoned along with her supporters. 7But
when one of her relatives becomes king of
the south, he will raise an army and enter

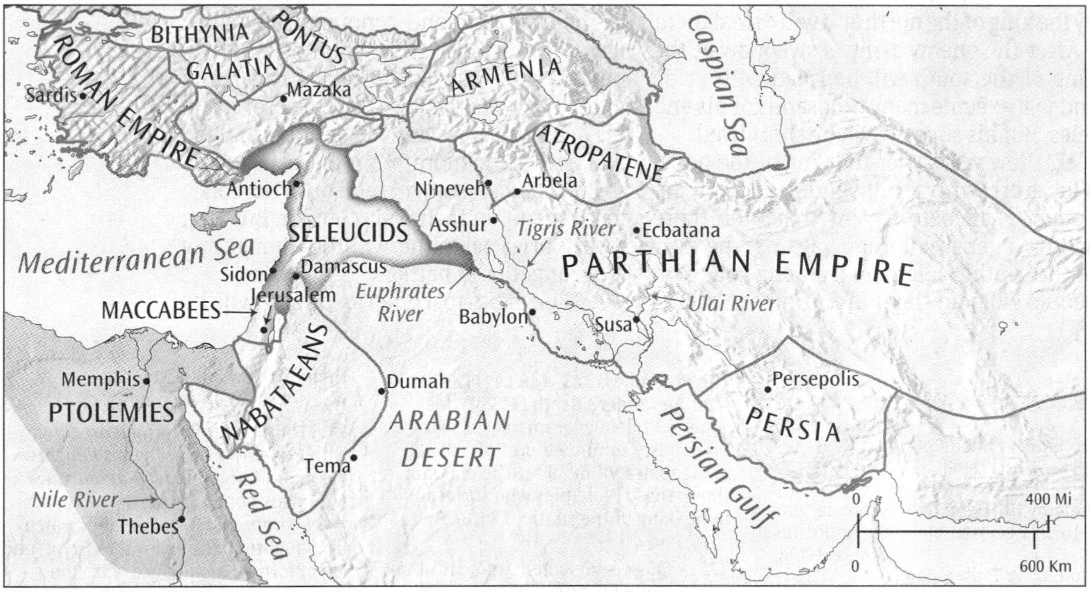

▲**The Ptolemies and the Seleucids, 198–139 BC (11:13-45).** The SELEUCIDS maintained control of Israel from 198 to 143 BC; the events of this period are described in 11:13-39. Seleucid domination of Judea reached its climax under Antiochus IV Epiphanes (175–163 BC), who attempted to stamp out the Jewish religion, and in 167 BC desecrated the Temple with offerings of swine and a statue of Zeus. Judas Maccabeus then led a revolt; Maccabean resistance to the Seleucid kings continued until 143 BC. Then, in 142 BC, Judea officially gained independence under the MACCABEES through the leadership of Simon Maccabeus, Judas’s brother. The Seleucids were overcome by the PARTHIANS in 139 BC. Meanwhile the ROMAN EMPIRE was growing in the west. Judea remained independent until 63 BC, when Jerusalem surrendered to the Roman army.

was at work behind the historical events of this chapter.

11:3 The ***mighty king*** was Alexander the Great (see note on 8:21, 336–323 BC), who conquered much of the known world in thirteen years, from Greece to India and from far into the north to Egypt in the south. His tutor had been Aristotle.

11:4 Alexander died on June 10, 323 BC in Babylon at the age of thirty-three. He was ***at the height of his power*** and willing to be worshiped as a god. • Alexander’s ***descendants*** were not capable of governing, and his brother Philip was incompetent. • ***For his empire will be . . . given to others:*** Several of Alexander’s generals divided his empire; by 301 BC, their conflicts had resulted in ***four parts*** (see 7:4-7; 8:8-12 and notes). God orchestrates history, and its end belongs to him.

11:5-45 Throughout this passage, ***the king of the south*** describes Alexander’s general Ptolemy and his descendants, who ruled Egypt; ***the king of the north*** describes Alexander’s general Seleucus and his descendants, who ruled Syria and Mesopotamia. In the period following Alexander’s death, the kings of Egypt and Syria vied for control of the strategically located land of Palestine. The holy city and the holy people lay between these two powers. These battles continued until their appointed end (11:27, 35, 40, 45; 12:1, 7). These events are described historically in *1, 2,* and *3 Maccabees* and by Herodotus, Livy, Polybius, Porphyry, and Josephus.

11:5 The first ***king of the south*** was Ptolemy I Soter (323–285 BC). One of his ***own officials*** was Seleucus I Nicator (321–281 BC), who took over the rule of Syria. Both men were military commanders under Alexander the Great. Initially (320–198 BC), Palestine was under the control of the Ptolemies.

11:6 An ***alliance*** was formed between Antiochus II Theos, the ***king of the north*** (261–246 BC), and Ptolemy II Philadelphus, the ***king of the south*** (284–246 BC). Antiochus married Ptolemy’s ***daughter*** Berenice Syra in 250 BC, then ***abandoned*** her in 246 BC. She and Antiochus were then murdered.

11:7-8 ***one of her relatives*** (literally *a branch from her roots*): Berenice’s brother, Ptolemy III Euergetes, became ***king of the south*** (246–221 BC), invaded Syria with his ***army,*** defeated ***the king***

the fortress of the king of the north and
defeat him. 8When he returns to Egypt, he
will carry back their idols with him, along
with priceless articles of gold and silver. For
some years afterward he will leave the king
of the north alone.
9"Later the king of the north will invade
the realm of the king of the south but will
soon return to his own land. 10However, the
sons of the king of the north will assemble
a mighty army that will advance like a flood
and carry the battle as far as the enemy's
fortress.
11"Then, in a rage, the king of the south
will rally against the vast forces assembled
by the king of the north and will defeat them.
12After the enemy army is swept away, the
king of the south will be filled with pride
and will execute many thousands of his enemies. But his success will be short lived.
13"A few years later the king of the north
will return with a fully equipped army far
greater than before. 14At that time there
will be a general uprising against the king
of the south. Violent men among your own
people will join them in fulfillment of this
vision, but they will not succeed. 15Then the
king of the north will come and lay siege
to a fortified city and capture it. The best
troops of the south will not be able to stand
in the face of the onslaught.
16"The king of the north will march onward unopposed; none will be able to stop
him. He will pause in the glorious land of Israel, intent on destroying it. 17He will make
plans to come with the might of his entire
kingdom and will form an alliance with the
king of the south. He will give him a daughter in marriage in order to overthrow the
kingdom from within, but his plan will fail.
18"After this, he will turn his attention
to the coastland and conquer many cities.
But a commander from another land will
put an end to his insolence and cause him
to retreat in shame. 19He will take refuge in
his own fortresses but will stumble and fall
and be seen no more.
20"His successor will send out a tax collector to maintain the royal splendor. But after
a very brief reign, he will die, though not
from anger or in battle.
21"The next to come to power will be

11:8 Isa 37:19; 46:1-2; Jer 43:12-13
11:10 Isa 8:8; Jer 46:7-8; 51:42; Dan 11:26, 40
11:13 Dan 12:7
11:15 Jer 6:6; Ezek 4:2; 17:17
11:16 Josh 1:5; Dan 5:19; 8:9; 11:3, 36, 41
11:17 2 Kgs 12:17; Ezek 4:3, 7
11:18 Gen 10:5; Isa 66:19; Zeph 2:11
11:19 Ps 27:2; 37:36; Jer 46:6; Ezek 26:21
11:20 Isa 60:17

Ptolemy I Soter (323–285 BC) [11:5]
Ptolemy II Philadelphus (284–246 BC) [11:6]
Ptolemy III Euergetes (246–221 BC) [11:7-9] — Berenice Syra (m. Antiochus II) (250 BC) [11:6]
Ptolemy IV Philopator (221–203 BC) [11:10-12]
Ptolemy V Epiphanes (203–181 BC) [11:14-17]
Ptolemy VI Philometor (181–146 BC) [11:25-28]

The Ptolemies, 323–146 BC (11:5-28) After Alexander's death (323 BC), his general Ptolemy became Egypt's king; his dynasty continued until the death of Cleopatra VII in 30 BC. The diagram shows those Ptolemies who correspond to the king of the south in 11:5-28.

of the north (Seleucus II Callinicus, 246–226 BC), occupied *the fortress* cities of Antioch and Seleucia, and built the Ptolemaic kingdom to its greatest extent. When he returned *to Egypt,* he took *their idols* with him, but left Seleucus II on the throne.

11:9 Seleucus II, still *the king of the north,* tried to *invade* Egypt in 242 BC but was defeated by Ptolemy III.

11:10-12 The *sons* of Seleucus II were Seleucus III Ceraunus (226–223 BC) and Antiochus III the Great (223–187 BC). • *a mighty army that will advance like a flood:* Antiochus III aggressively sought to regain lost territory, including Palestine. • *as far as the enemy's fortress:* Antiochus III advanced to Raphia on the border of Egypt in 217 BC. In the ensuing battle, *the king of the south*—Ptolemy IV Philopater (221–203 BC)—defeated Antiochus III and retained control of Palestine.

11:12-13 Ptolemy IV's *success* was *short lived.* In 198 BC, *the king of the north*—Antiochus III—returned. • Antiochus III had been conquering lands to the north and east, from which he raised *a fully equipped army far greater than before* (cp. *3 Maccabees* 1:1-5).

11:14 *A general uprising* of Jews and rebel Egyptians who favored Antiochus III arose. The *king of the south* was Ptolemy V Epiphanes (203–181 BC). • *they will not succeed:* The Egyptian commander, Scopas, quelled the rebellion (200 BC).

11:15 At Paneas in 198 BC, *the king of the north* (Antiochus III) defeated the Egyptian general Scopas, besieged and captured Sidon, *a fortified city,* and took control of Palestine.

11:16 *the glorious land of Israel:* Literally *the glorious land;* cp. 8:9. • *intent on destroying it:* Antiochus III sought to hellenize the Jews and destroy their ancient customs, but he was flattered by Jews who received him well, and he granted them special privileges. They were allowed to live according to their own laws. His son Antiochus IV was not so accommodating (11:21-39).

11:17 Antiochus III formed *an alliance* with Ptolemy V by giving his *daughter,* Cleopatra I, to Ptolemy V *in marriage.* Antiochus hoped *to overthrow* Egypt *from within, but his plan* failed when his daughter became loyal to Egypt, and Egypt formed an alliance with Rome.

11:18 Antiochus III extended his holdings into *the coastland*—including Anatolia, Macedonia, and Greece—but he was defeated by the Romans in 191 and 190 BC. The *commander from another land* was the famous Roman general Scipio, who put a stop to Antiochus III's expansionist policies and caused *him to retreat in shame* from his western acquisitions.

11:19 Antiochus III thereafter remained within his *own fortresses,* where he was assassinated in 187 BC.

11:20 Antiochus III's *successor* was his son Seleucus IV Philopater (187–175 BC), who was known for his infamous act of sending Heliodorus, *a tax collector,* to exact large sums of money *to maintain the royal splendor* (but also to pay the ruinous tribute imposed on the Seleucids by Rome). Heliodorus attempted to plunder the Temple in Jerusalem but was divinely thwarted (see *2 Maccabees* 3:1-40). Seleucus was murdered by Heliodorus *after a very brief reign* of seven years.

11:21-39 *The next to come to power* was Antiochus IV Epiphanes (175–163 BC;

11:24
Num 13:20
Neh 9:25
Ezek 34:14

11:27
Ps 52:1; 64:6
Jer 9:3-5
Dan 11:35, 40
Hab 2:3
Acts 17:31

11:28
[b]*lebab* (3824)
‣Gen 42:28

11:30
Gen 10:4
Num 24:24
Jer 2:10
[c]*'azab* (5800)
‣Josh 1:5

11:31
Dan 8:11-13; 9:27; 12:11
Matt 24:15
Mark 13:14

11:32
Dan 11:21, 34
Mic 5:7-9
Zech 9:13-16; 10:3-6

a despicable man who is not in line for
royal succession. He will slip in when least
expected and take over the kingdom by
flattery and intrigue. 22Before him great
armies will be swept away, including a covenant prince. 23With deceitful promises, he
will make various alliances. He will become
strong despite having only a handful of followers. 24Without warning he will enter
the richest areas of the land. Then he will
distribute among his followers the plunder
and wealth of the rich—something his predecessors had never done. He will plot the
overthrow of strongholds, but this will last
for only a short while.
25"Then he will stir up his courage and
raise a great army against the king of the
south. The king of the south will go to battle with a mighty army, but to no avail, for
there will be plots against him. 26His own
household will cause his downfall. His army
will be swept away, and many will be killed.
27Seeking nothing but each other's harm,
these kings will plot against each other at
the conference table, attempting to deceive
each other. But it will make no difference,
for the end will come at the appointed time.
28"The king of the north will then return
home with great riches. On the way he will
set [b]himself against the people of the holy
covenant, doing much damage before continuing his journey.
29"Then at the appointed time he will
once again invade the south, but this time
the result will be different. 30For warships
from western coastlands will scare him off,
and he will withdraw and return home. But
he will vent his anger against the people of
the holy covenant and reward those who
[c]forsake the covenant.
31"His army will take over the Temple
fortress, pollute the sanctuary, put a stop to
the daily sacrifices, and set up the sacrilegious object that causes desecration. 32He
will flatter and win over those who have
violated the covenant. But the people who

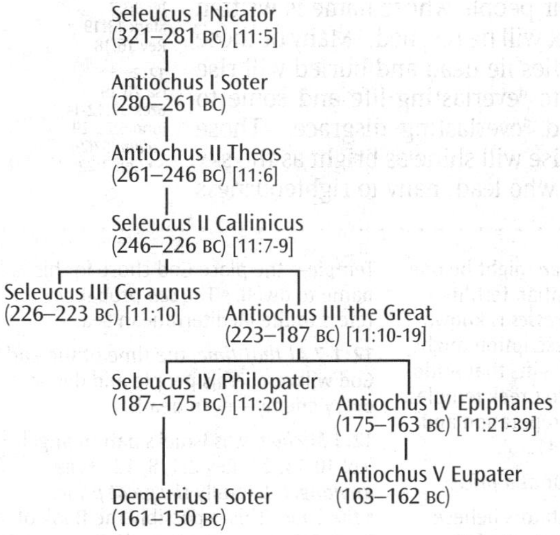

◂ **The Seleucids, 321–150 BC (11:5-39)** Seleucus I, a Macedonian commander in Alexander's army, took control of the province of Babylon in 321 BC; his dynasty ruled until 60 BC. The diagram includes those Seleucids who correspond to the king of the north in 11:5-39.

see note at 8:23-25). He is also the "small horn" of 8:9-14, 23-26. He is described vividly in *1 Maccabees* 1:7–6:16; *2 Maccabees* 1:1–10:5; *4 Maccabees* 4:15–18:5. Antiochus was ***despicable*** both because he had usurped the kingship and for his deeds as king. He was ***not in line for royal succession***, but usurped the throne from his brother's son.

11:22 The ***covenant prince*** was Onias III, the high priest (cp. notes on 9:25-26). He was removed by Antiochus IV in 175 BC and replaced by his brother Jason (*2 Maccabees* 4:7-10). In 171 BC, Onias was murdered by Menelaus, who then became high priest (171–162 BC). Menelaus supported Antiochus IV's program of hellenization (see notes on 9:26-27).

11:23 ***deceitful promises:*** Antiochus IV introduced Greek religion into Judea, helped by lawless ***followers*** who supported his policies (see *1 Maccabees* 1:11-15).

11:24 ***richest areas of the land:*** Antiochus IV seized the riches of the Temple, took large tributes from Jerusalem, and stationed troops there (*1 Maccabees* 1:29-40).

11:25-27 The ***king of the south*** was Ptolemy VI Philometor (181–146 BC). Antiochus IV attacked Egypt twice between 170 and 168 BC (*1 Maccabees* 1:17-19).

11:28 Antiochus IV plundered Jerusalem and the Temple in 170 BC, killing thousands and enslaving others (*1 Maccabees* 1:20-42; *2 Maccabees* 5:1-23). His arrogance was unbounded (*1 Maccabees* 1:24-25; cp. Dan 7:28; 8:9).

11:29-35 Antiochus IV invaded ***the south*** [Egypt]. . . ***once again*** (see Polybius, *Histories* 29.1). • The ***warships from western coastlands*** (Hebrew *from Kittim*) refers to the Romans. The Roman general Popilius Laenas drew a circle in the sand, forced Antiochus to stand inside it, and made him decide whether to return home or prepare for war with Rome before exiting the circle. Fearing the Roman fleet, Antiochus chose to ***withdraw and return home***. He then vented ***his anger*** and humiliation against the Jews, ***the people of the holy covenant***. He took Jerusalem in 167 BC and rewarded those who would come over to him. He polluted the altar (see 8:9-14, 23-26), stopped the sacrifices, set up a statue of the Greek god Zeus in the Temple, and harassed and killed whoever refused to ***forsake the covenant*** (cp. 9:27; see *1 Maccabees* 1:62-64; cp. Matt 24:15).

11:31 ***the sacrilegious object that causes desecration:*** Literally *the abomination of desolation*. See note on 9:27.

11:32-35 The ***wise*** are those who ***know their God*** and his laws and follow them, even in a hostile and deceptive environment. Many were martyred for their faithfulness to God and his laws during this time (*1 Maccabees* 1:11; 7:19; *2 Maccabees* 6–7).

know their God will be strong and will resist him.

33“Wise leaders will give instruction to many, but these teachers will die by fire and sword, or they will be jailed and robbed. 34During these persecutions, little help will arrive, and many who join them will not be sincere. 35And some of the wise will fall victim to persecution. In this way, they will be refined and cleansed and made pure until the time of the end, for the appointed time is still to come.

36“The king will do as he pleases, exalting himself and claiming to be greater than every god, even blaspheming the God of gods. He will succeed, but only until the time of wrath is completed. For what has been determined will surely take place. 37He will have no respect for the gods of his ancestors, or for the god loved by women, or for any other god, for he will boast that he is greater than them all. 38Instead of these, he will worship the god of fortresses—a god his ancestors never knew—and lavish on him gold, silver, precious stones, and expensive gifts. 39Claiming this foreign god’s help, he will attack the strongest fortresses. He will honor those who submit to him, appointing them to positions of authority and dividing the land among them as their reward.

40“Then at the time of the end, the king of the south will attack the king of the north. The king of the north will storm out with chariots, charioteers, and a vast navy. He will invade various lands and sweep through them like a flood. 41He will enter the glorious land of Israel, and many nations will fall, but Moab, Edom, and the best part of Ammon will escape. 42He will conquer many countries, and even Egypt will not escape. 43He will gain control over the gold, silver, and treasures of Egypt, and the Libyans and Ethiopians will be his servants.

44“But then news from the east and the north will alarm him, and he will set out in great anger to destroy and obliterate many. 45He will stop between the glorious holy mountain and the sea and will pitch his royal tents. But while he is there, his time will suddenly run out, and no one will help him.

The Time of the End

12 “At that time Michael, the archangel who stands guard over your nation, will arise. Then there will be a time of anguish greater than any since nations first came into existence. But at that time every one of your people whose name is written in the book will be rescued. 2Many of those whose bodies lie dead and buried will rise up, some to [d]everlasting life and some to shame and [d]everlasting disgrace. 3Those who are wise will shine as bright as the sky, and those who lead many to righteousness

11:33 Matt 24:9; John 16:2; Heb 11:36-38
11:34 Dan 11:21, 32; Matt 7:15; Rom 16:18
11:35 Deut 8:16; Prov 17:3; Dan 12:10; Zech 13:9; John 15:2
11:36 Deut 10:17; Ps 136:2; Isa 10:25; 14:13; 26:20; Dan 2:47; 5:20; 7:8, 11; 8:11; 9:27; 11:3; 2 Thes 2:4; Rev 13:5-6
11:40 Isa 5:28; Jer 4:13; Dan 11:27, 35; 12:4, 9
11:41 Jer 48:47; 49:6
11:43 2 Chr 12:3; Ezek 30:4-5; Nah 3:9
11:45 Isa 65:25; 66:20; Dan 9:16, 20
12:1 Jer 30:7; Mark 13:19; Rev 16:18
12:2 Isa 26:19; Ezek 37:12-14; John 5:28-29; [d]*‘olam* (5769) ›Gen 3:22

11:34 A *little help* came when the family of Mattathias and those around them, who were called Maccabees, instigated a national revolt which Antiochus, occupied elsewhere, could not put down. In 164 BC, three years after the Temple had been desecrated, the Maccabees recaptured Jerusalem, removed the sacrilegious object (the statue of Zeus), cleansed the altar, and restored the daily sacrifices (8:11-14, 26; *1 Maccabees* 1:59). This event is commemorated in *Hanukkah* (see John 10:22).

11:36-40 Some interpreters see these verses as a transition from the earthly Antiochus IV to a character larger than history (7:8).

11:36 Antiochus IV thought himself equal to God (*2 Maccabees* 9:1–10:12), but God would hem him in ***until the time of wrath*** was ***completed***. • ***what has been determined will surely take place:*** Antiochus suddenly contracted a painful disease and died in 163 BC in the mountains of Persia (see 8:25; *1 Maccabees* 4:52-53; 6:16; *2 Maccabees* 9:4, 28; 10:5).

11:37-38 ***no respect for the gods of his ancestors:*** Antiochus IV forsook the Syrian gods in order to worship Greek gods. • ***The god loved by women*** might be one of the Canaanite or Egyptian fertility deities. • No ***god of fortresses*** is known from history, but this description might be fulfilled by the ***lavish*** gifts that Antiochus gave to cities and to Greek temples, perhaps to increase his reputation and power (see Livy, *History* 41.20).

11:39 ***as their reward:*** Or *at a price.*

11:40-45 Most commentators believe these verses describe ***the time of the end*** of history (cp. Mark 13:14; 2 Thes 2:3-12; Rev 19:19-21). These verses echo the career of Antiochus IV, but we have no historical record of the events described here. Antiochus was a paradigm for future rulers who set themselves against the God of gods.

11:40 No known ***king of the south*** or ***king of the north*** did these things.

11:41 ***the glorious land of Israel*** (literally *the glorious land*): Israel (cp. 8:9; 11:16) is again the center of attack by an evil king. • ***Moab, Edom,*** and ***Ammon*** were nations surrounding ancient Israel and Judea.

11:43 ***Ethiopians:*** Hebrew *Cushites.*

11:45 The ***glorious holy mountain*** includes Zion, Jerusalem, and the Temple—the place God chose for his name to dwell. • The ***sea*** probably refers to the Mediterranean Sea.

12:1-7 ***At that time,*** the time of the end, God will rescue his people and defeat every enemy—even death.

12:1 ***Michael*** was Israel’s patron angel (cp. 10:13, 21; Rev 2:1, 8, 12). • ***the archangel:*** Literally *the great prince.* • ***the book:*** This is possibly the Book of Truth (10:21; cp. 7:10). • ***will be rescued:*** All previous “rescues” of God’s people in Daniel (e.g., 3:28; 6:27) had foreshadowed, and now culminated in, the resurrection from the dead (12:2-3).

12:2 ***Everlasting life*** is completely without ***shame*** or ***disgrace*** (cp. Gen 2:25; 3:7).

12:3 ***Those who are wise*** know their God (cp. 1:4, 17; 8:25; 9:22, 25; 11:32-35; 12:10). • To ***shine*** is a familiar metaphor for life, purity, righteousness, and glory.

12:4 Daniel was to ***keep*** the ***prophecy a secret*** (cp. 7:28; 8:26); it would be unveiled at God’s proper time, ***the time of the end***.

12:5 The ***river*** was the Tigris River (10:4). • The ***two others*** witnessed to God’s promises (see Num 35:30; Deut 19:15).

12:3 Isa 53:11
12:4 Isa 8:16; Rev 22:10
12:6 Zech 1:12-13; Mark 13:4
12:7 Luke 21:24; Rev 10:5-7; 12:14
12:10 Rev 22:11
12:11 Dan 9:27; 11:31; Matt 24:15; Mark 13:14
12:12 Isa 30:18
12:13 Ps 16:5; Rev 14:13

will shine like the stars forever. [4]But you,
Daniel, keep this prophecy a secret; seal up
the book until the time of the end, when
many will rush here and there, and knowledge will increase."
[5]Then I, Daniel, looked and saw two
others standing on opposite banks of the
river. [6]One of them asked the man dressed
in linen, who was now standing above the
river, "How long will it be until these shocking events are over?"
[7]The man dressed in linen, who was
standing above the river, raised both his
hands toward heaven and took a solemn
oath by the One who lives forever, saying, "It
will go on for a time, times, and half a time.
When the shattering of the holy people has
finally come to an end, all these things will
have happened."
[8]I heard what he said, but I did not understand what he meant. So I asked, "How will
all this finally end, my lord?"
[9]But he said, "Go now, Daniel, for what
I have said is kept secret and sealed until
the time of the end. [10]Many will be purified, cleansed, and refined by these trials.
But the wicked will continue in their wickedness, and none of them will understand.
Only those who are wise will know what it
means.
[11]"From the time the daily sacrifice is
stopped and the sacrilegious object that
causes desecration is set up to be worshiped,
there will be 1,290 days. [12]And blessed are
those who wait and remain until the end of
the 1,335 days!
[13]"As for you, go your way until the end.
You will rest, and then at the end of the days,
you will rise again to receive the inheritance
set aside for you."

Resurrection (12:1-3, 13)

Job 19:25-27; Matt 27:50-53; 28:1-20; 1 Cor 15:1-58; Rev 20:1-15

Daniel 12:1-3 clearly teaches that the dead will be resurrected, as Daniel was told that he would be raised in this resurrection (12:13).

The resurrection will not be the same for all people. Two distinct groups of people will be raised: (1) those resurrected to experience new life, and (2) those resurrected to experience shame. These two groups are distinguished by moral, ethical, and spiritual characteristics. The resurrection will unveil the true nature of a person, and there will be an ethical and spiritual accounting to God Most High.

The first group will experience a new existence called "everlasting life." The expression is found only here in the OT. Everlasting life refers more to the quality of life than to its length. Those who are truly wise know, relate to, and experience God, and they teach others this righteousness and wisdom (11:33). They are refined, cleansed, and made pure before their God. The moral and ethical glory of those resurrected in Daniel's first group is indicated by the metaphors "shine as bright as the sky" and "shine like stars forever."

The second group experiences everlasting shame and disgrace instead of everlasting life because they are not morally, ethically, or spiritually renewed. The NT book of Revelation expands upon these two groups of Daniel's vision (see Rev 20:4-6, 11-15).

God's people will finally be rescued from death, not just from human kings, fire, or lions. Everlasting life destroys death. Those who are raised have had their names inscribed in the Book of Truth (cp. 10:21; Rev 20:12), and the Judge—the Ancient of Days—approves of them (7:9-10, 26-27; cp. Rev 20:6).

12:7 ***time, times, and half a time:*** God appoints times for all things as he rules the flow of earthly and heavenly events (see note on 7:24-25). • ***The shattering of the holy people*** was part of God's purpose to purify them (12:10).

12:8-10 God withheld exactly *how* and when ***all this*** would ***finally end***. Daniel would not see the end (12:13); his job was to finish out his life in faith. • ***purified, cleansed, and refined:*** God would use violent and terrifying times to improve the moral and religious character of his people (cp. 11:35). • Being ***wise*** includes having insight into God's ways and walking accordingly. ***The wicked*** will not ***understand*** or change ***their wickedness*** even if the vision is explained to them.

12:11-12 ***the sacrilegious object that causes desecration:*** Literally *the abomination of desolation.* See 8:13-14, 23-26; 11:29-35. See note on 9:27. • God's people must ***wait and remain*** faithful when the events of the end come. • ***1,290 days . . . 1,335 days:*** Some interpreters see these numbers as relating to specific events in the reign of Antiochus IV Epiphanes. Others see them as purely symbolic. The number ***1,290*** equals 43 lunar months of 30 days each, which is approximately 3½ years in the solar calendar. This might represent the final half of the final "set of seven" (9:27). The number ***1,335*** might represent simply an extra 45 days of waiting ***until the end.*** Those who endure the whole time, and then some, will see God act on behalf of his people (12:11).

12:13 Daniel died before the final end, but he knew that he would rise again! Here, ***the end*** refers to that time when even the dead will rise (12:1-3) and the everlasting Kingdom of God Most High is established.

THE BOOK OF

HOSEA

Hosea the prophet experienced betrayal and anguish because of his wife's adultery. Yet the book of Hosea has more to do with divine brokenness than with a broken human relationship. Hosea's experiences reveal God's agony over his people's sins. God's justice requires judgment, but in his love, God promises to redeem his chosen people. Hosea opens a window for us into the very heart of God.

SETTING

Throughout the history of ancient Israel, few eras were more confused or turbulent than the mid-700s BC, when Hosea prophesied.

Hosea began his ministry toward the end of the long and stable reign of Jeroboam II (793–753 BC). Despite being an evil king (2 Kgs 14:24), Jeroboam was a strong and capable leader who expanded the boundaries of Israel to an extent not seen since the glorious days of David and Solomon (2 Kgs 14:25-28). Jeroboam's territorial expansion brought great wealth to some Israelites, but left many others poor and destitute. Hosea's predecessor, Amos, repeatedly denounced the social injustices that produced such a gap between rich and poor in Israel.

Jeroboam II died early in Hosea's ministry, and with his death the comfortable, prosperous world of the Israelites changed forever. Three decades later, in 722 BC, the northern kingdom of Israel was destroyed by the relentless onslaught of the Assyrian empire. During this time, six different kings sat on Israel's throne. Only one died a natural death—usurpers assassinated four of these kings, and Hoshea, the final king, died in Assyrian captivity.

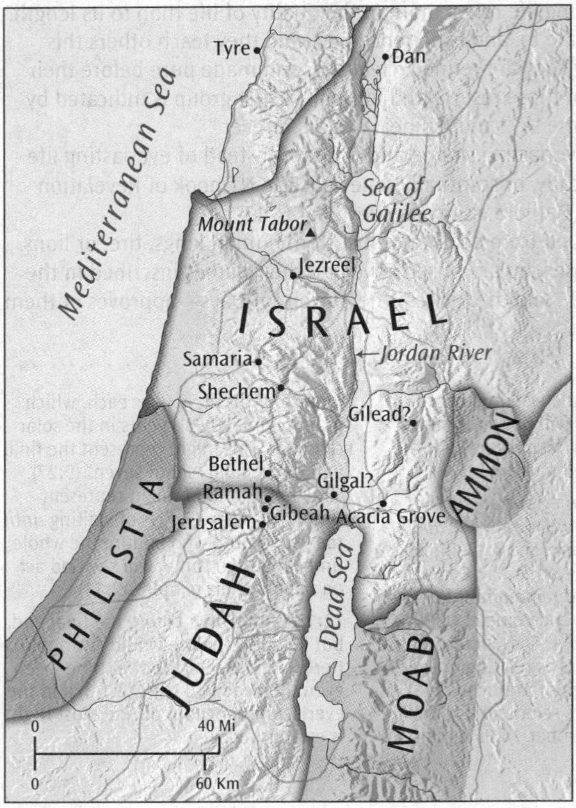

◀ **Israel and Judah in Hosea's Early Ministry, about 760~750 BC.** When Hosea began his ministry, Jeroboam II was king of ISRAEL. His long reign (793–753 BC) brought to the northern kingdom a period of great prosperity, stability, and peace. However, Hosea warned that judgment was soon to come, as it did following Jeroboam's death.

ACACIA GROVE 5:2
BETHEL 10:15; 12:4
GIBEAH, RAMAH 5:8; 9:9; 10:9
GILEAD 6:8; 12:11
GILGAL 4:15; 9:15; 12:11
JEZREEL 1:4-5; 1:11; 2:22
MOUNT TABOR 5:1
SAMARIA 7:1-7; 8:5-6; 10:5-8; 13:16
SHECHEM 6:9
TYRE 9:13

From its founding, the northern kingdom had worshiped pagan gods. Now they turned even more fully to these deities. In their desperate political situation, the Israelites grasped at any straw that might save them from the coming destruction, but they refused to turn to the Lord.

Hosea was God's messenger to this confused, frantic nation in its final days. The prophet proclaimed God's coming judgment, but he also offered the Israelites a message of hope, imploring them to return to the Lord their God, who alone could heal and restore them.

OUTLINE

1:1
Superscription: Introducing the Prophet

1:2–3:5
The Unfaithful Wife

4:1–14:9
Hosea's Messages of Warning

SUMMARY

Hosea 1–3 describes a small segment of the prophet's life, focusing on his unhappy marriage to an unfaithful wife. The purpose of this section is not to present a biography but to illuminate God's painful relationship with Israel, his chosen people. Just as Hosea's wife, Gomer, was unfaithful, Israel acted like a prostitute by worshiping Canaanite gods. Hosea proclaimed God's judgment, but he also announced God's desire to reclaim his wayward bride and restore her relationship with him.

Hosea 4–14 contains a diverse collection of Hosea's prophecies, from early in his ministry until just before the destruction of Israel in 722 BC. They are presented in roughly chronological order, from the reign of Jeroboam through the reign of Hoshea. In these chapters, the prophet Hosea presents God's charges against the people of Israel and especially against their leaders. The consequences for their sin will be severe—the nation will be destroyed. However, God would not give up his chosen people, and the book concludes with a divine promise of future restoration.

AUTHOR AND DATE

We know nothing about the prophet Hosea apart from this book. We know his father's name (1:1), that he was married to a woman named Gomer, and that he had children with her.

Hosea prophesied to the northern kingdom of Israel from around 760 BC until just before the fall of Israel in 722 BC (see 1:1). Hosea would have memorized his oral prophecies, and eventually he or his followers would have written them down in several collections that were later gathered into a single anthology. This work might have been done in the southern kingdom of Judah sometime after the fall of Israel in 722 BC.

LITERARY CHARACTERISTICS

Hosea was very literate and intimately acquainted with Israel's history and faith. His prophecies rely on figurative language and other literary devices such as proverbs and folk sayings. These literary and rhetorical techniques made God's message more intelligible and compelling to the Israelites.

TIMELINE

793–753 BC
Jeroboam II as king of Israel

792–740 BC
Uzziah (Azariah) as king of Judah

about 760~750 BC
Amos as prophet

about 760~722 BC
Hosea as prophet

about 755~750 BC
Jonah as prophet

753–752 BC
Zechariah as king of Israel

752 BC
Shallum as king of Israel (1 month)

752–742 BC
Menahem as king of Israel

752–740 BC
Pekah as king in Gilead?

744–727 BC
Tiglath-pileser III as king of Assyria

742–740 BC
Pekahiah as king of Israel

740–732 BC
Pekah as king of Israel

about 740~685 BC
Isaiah as prophet

about 735~725 BC
Micah as prophet

732–722 BC
Hoshea as king of Israel

726–722 BC
Shalmaneser V as king of Assyria

722 BC
Samaria is destroyed by Assyria, end of the northern kingdom of Israel

MEANING AND MESSAGE

God's covenant with Israel stands at the center of Hosea's prophecy. When God entered into covenant with Israel at Mount Sinai, he offered the Israelites the incredible opportunity of living in intimate relationship with the Creator and sustainer of the universe. The covenant promised spiritual and material blessings to his people, while obligating them to live rightly before him. He had faithfully kept his covenant with the Israelites and they had enjoyed his blessings, but they had chosen to rebel against him and disregard his plan and purpose.

Marriage is the most powerful and memorable symbol of the covenant relationship between the Lord and Israel. As Israel's loving husband, the Lord provided her with everything she needed: land, food, drink, clothing, and security. Yet like an adulterous spouse, Israel sought fulfillment through the idolatrous worship of the Canaanite gods. These deities became Israel's lovers, and she attributed all of God's blessings to them. The personal life of the prophet Hosea with his wife Gomer played out in miniature this same drama of the wife's unfaithfulness and the husband's anguish over his wayward bride.

Through idolatry, Israel rejected her covenant with the Lord. In response, Hosea proclaimed God's judgment on sinful Israel. Judgment is the inevitable consequence of sin under the covenant. Yet even as the covenant was the foundation for divine judgment, it was also the basis for God's mercy. God did not judge Israel simply to punish her; his desire was to redeem her. Divine judgment was intended to turn Israel back to God, her true husband, so that in his mercy, he might restore her and reestablish his covenant with her.

God's mercy is not in opposition to his judgment. Hosea shows that God's mercy is extended to Israel *through* judgment, not *instead* of judgment; the Lord's promises of hope always follow his judgment. God has done the same thing for us through the cross of Christ.

FURTHER READING

DAVID HUBBARD
Hosea (1990)

RICHARD PATTERSON
Hosea in *Cornerstone Biblical Commentary*, vol. 10 (2008)

GARY V. SMITH
Hosea/Micah/Amos (2001)

DOUGLAS STUART
Hosea—Jonah (1987)

1. SUPERSCRIPTION: INTRODUCING THE PROPHET (1:1)

1 The LORD gave this message to Hosea
son of Beeri during the years when Uzziah, Jotham, Ahaz, and Hezekiah were
kings of Judah, and Jeroboam son of Jehoash was king of Israel.

2. THE UNFAITHFUL WIFE (1:2–3:5)

Hosea's Wife and Children

2When the LORD first began speaking to
Israel through Hosea, he said to him, "Go
and marry a prostitute, so that some of her
children will be conceived in prostitution.
This will illustrate how Israel has acted like
a prostitute by turning against the LORD
and worshiping other gods."
3So Hosea married Gomer, the daughter of Diblaim, and she became pregnant
and gave Hosea a son. 4And the LORD said,
"Name the child Jezreel, for I am about to
punish King Jehu's dynasty to avenge the

1:1
2 Kgs 15:32-38; 16:2-20; 18:1-8
2 Chr 26:1-23; 27:1-9; 28:1-27; 29:1-32
Mic 1:1

1:2
Jer 3:1
Hos 2:5; 3:1

1:4
2 Kgs 10:1-36

1:1 ***The LORD gave this message:*** The book of Hosea begins by declaring that these are not merely human words but a message from the only true God (cp. Joel 1:1; Mic 1:1; Zeph 1:1). • ***Hosea son of Beeri:*** Several other important people in the OT are also named Hosea (or Hoshea; both are spelled the same in Hebrew; Num 13:8; 2 Kgs 17:1). Hosea means "the Lord saves," an appropriate name for this prophet. • ***Jeroboam . . . king of Israel:*** Hosea prophesied to the northern kingdom of Israel during the reigns of its last seven kings, though only one of them, Jeroboam II, is listed here (see the Introduction and Timeline for details). • Hebrew *Joash*, a variant spelling of Jehoash.

1:2–3:5 This section describes a small segment of the prophet's life, focusing on his unhappy marriage and illuminating God's painful relationship with Israel, his chosen people.

1:2-3 ***a prostitute*** (Or *a promiscuous woman*): Some have found it impossible to believe that God would command a prophet to marry a prostitute. As a result, there is a long tradition of interpreting this passage symbolically. Many in the early church believed that the marriage did not actually take place. They thought that this passage was an allegory in which Hosea represented the Lord and Gomer represented Israel. Today, most interpreters regard the marriage as a real one, but they differ in their ideas about Gomer's occupation prior to the marriage. Some suggest that Gomer was an ordinary prostitute, while others suggest that she was one of the sacred prostitutes involved in Canaanite fertility worship. Another possibility is that Gomer was a young woman who had not previously participated in illicit sexual activity, but whom God knew to be predisposed toward adultery and prostitution.

1:4 *Jezreel* is a fertile valley in north

1:7
Ps 44:3-7
Isa 30:18

1:9
*1 Pet 2:10

1:10
Gen 22:17; 32:12
Isa 63:16; 64:8
Jer 33:22
*Rom 9:26
[a]*ben 'el* (1121, 0410)
‣Gen 6:2

1:11
Isa 11:12
Jer 30:21
Ezek 37:21-24
Hos 3:5

2:2
Isa 50:1
Hos 4:5

2:3
Isa 20:2-3; 32:13-14
Jer 14:3
Ezek 16:7, 22
Hos 13:15

2:5
Jer 2:25; 3:1-2
Ezek 23:16-17, 40-45

murders he committed at Jezreel. In fact, I
will bring an end to Israel's independence.
5I will break its military power in the Jezreel
Valley."
6Soon Gomer became pregnant again
and gave birth to a daughter. And the LORD
said to Hosea, "Name your daughter Lo-
ruhamah—'Not loved'—for I will no longer
show love to the people of Israel or forgive
them. 7But I will show love to the people of
Judah. I will free them from their enemies—
not with weapons and armies or horses and
charioteers, but by my power as the LORD
their God."
8After Gomer had weaned Lo-ruhamah,
she again became pregnant and gave birth
to a second son. 9And the LORD said, "Name
him Lo-ammi—'Not my people'—for Israel
is not my people, and I am not their God.
10"Yet the time will come when Israel's
people will be like the sands of the seashore—too many to count! Then, at the
place where they were told, 'You are not my
people,' it will be said, 'You are [a]children
of the living God.' 11Then the people of Judah and Israel will unite together. They will
choose one leader for themselves, and they
will return from exile together. What a day
that will be—the day of Jezreel—when God
will again plant his people in his land.
2:1"In that day you will call your brothers
Ammi—'My people.' And you will call your
sisters Ruhamah—'The ones I love.'

Charges against an Unfaithful Wife

2 2 "But now bring charges against
Israel—your mother—
for she is no longer my wife,
and I am no longer her husband.
Tell her to remove the prostitute's
makeup from her face
and the clothing that exposes her
breasts.
3 Otherwise, I will strip her as naked
as she was on the day she was born.
I will leave her to die of thirst,
as in a dry and barren wilderness.
4 And I will not love her children,
for they were conceived in
prostitution.
5 Their mother is a shameless prostitute
and became pregnant in a shameful
way.
She said, 'I'll run after other lovers

central Israel. • ***The murders*** Jehu ***committed at Jezreel*** are described in 2 Kgs 9–10.

1:5 King Tiglath-pileser III of Assyria fulfilled this prophecy in 733 BC when he defeated Israelite forces and captured the Valley of Jezreel.

1:6 ***Lo-ruhamah:*** The names of Hosea's children were part of his prophetic message (cp. Isa 7:10–8:8).

1:7 For many years, the kingdom of Israel had depended upon its ***armies*** and ***horses and charioteers*** for security, but its confidence was completely misplaced. Safety and security are only to be found in God's ***power as the LORD.***

1:9 The name ***Lo-ammi*** carries the harshest judgment of all, because it seems to announce the end of Israel's covenant relationship with the Lord. The cherished title ***my people***—bestowed upon Israel when they lived obediently in covenant with the Lord their God (Lev 26:12; see also Exod 6:7)—was now withdrawn due to their blatant unfaithfulness. • ***I am not their God:*** The Hebrew behind this declaration can be translated *I am not 'I AM' for you* (cp. Exod 3:14). The third child's name prophetically announces that the Israelites stand outside the covenant and are no longer privileged to call upon the *I AM.*

1:10-11 Verses 1:10-11 are numbered 2:1-2 in the Hebrew text, and they mark an abrupt shift in Hosea's prophecy from judgment to hope. In the next three verses, Hosea transforms the names of Gomer's three children from names of divine punishment on Israel into names of blessing and hope. This dramatically demonstrates God's sovereign power of reversal from darkness to light, judgment to hope, and even death to life.

1:10 ***sands of the seashore:*** This promise of future population growth for God's people echoes the promise given to the patriarchs Abraham and Jacob (Gen 22:17; 32:12). • ***You are children of the living God:*** This expression is found nowhere else in the OT, but Paul quoted this verse (Rom 9:26) to establish that God had also called the Gentiles to salvation.

1:11 ***Judah and Israel will unite together:*** For almost 200 years, Israel and Judah had been divided into separate kingdoms by political rivalry. When God restores his people, he will reunite the divided kingdoms under a single leader as in the time of David, and he will reverse the curse of exile (see also Ezek 37:15-28). • ***The day of Jezreel*** (*Jezreel* means "God plants"): Hosea announced that in a coming time, God would restore the original meaning of Jezreel. It would signify blessing and growth rather than judgment.

2:1-23 Verses 2:1-23 are numbered 2:3-25 in the Hebrew text.

2:1 ***Ammi—'My people':*** God will also restore the name of the third child to its covenantal meaning. • ***Ruhamah—'The ones I love':*** Israel will once again be the object of God's love and compassion.

2:2-23 ***bring charges against Israel:*** At first glance, the Lord, as the aggrieved husband, appears to be issuing a bill of divorce against his unfaithful spouse, Israel (see Deut 24:1). As the passage continues, however, it becomes clear that God's purpose in this lawsuit is not divorce, but reconciliation (2:14-23). God's case against Israel is intended to awaken Israel to her sin and offer her a chance to return to her true husband. The Lord's desire for reconciliation with Israel is all the more surprising inasmuch as the law stipulated the death penalty for an adulterous spouse (Deut 22:22; see also Gen 38:24; Lev 21:9).

2:3 The Lord warns unfaithful Israel that unless she repents and returns to her covenant partner, he will ***strip her . . . naked*** (see also 2:10). Ezekiel also employs this image of judgment and shame (Ezek 16:36-37).

2:5 The only evidence needed to prove Israel's unfaithfulness comes from her own words: ***I'll run after other lovers.*** Israel's lovers were the Canaanite fertility deities, especially the baals (local representations of Baal). The Israelites worshiped them because they believed that these gods controlled the reproductive forces in nature. The Israelites attributed to them the basic necessities of life, ***food and water,*** their ***clothing of wool and linen,*** and ***oil,*** used for both sacred and secular purposes.

and sell myself to them for food and
water,
for clothing of wool and linen,
and for olive oil and drinks.'
6 "For this reason I will fence her in with
thornbushes.
I will block her path with a wall
to make her lose her way.
7 When she runs after her lovers,
she won't be able to catch them.
She will search for them
but not find them.
Then she will think,
'I might as well return to my
husband,
for I was better off with him than
I am now.'
8 She doesn't realize it was I who gave her
everything she has—
the grain, the new wine, the olive oil;
I even gave her silver and gold.
But she gave all my gifts to [b]Baal.
9 "But now I will take back the ripened
grain and new wine
I generously provided each harvest
season.
I will take away the wool and linen
clothing
I gave her to cover her nakedness.
10 I will strip her naked in public,
while all her lovers look on.
No one will be able
to rescue her from my hands.
11 I will put an end to her annual festivals,
her new moon celebrations, and her
Sabbath days—
all her appointed festivals.
12 I will destroy her grapevines and fig trees,
things she claims her lovers gave her.
I will let them grow into tangled thickets,
where only wild animals will eat the
fruit.
13 I will punish her for all those times
when she burned incense to her
images of [c]Baal,
when she put on her earrings and jewels
and went out to look for her lovers
but forgot all about me,"
says the LORD.

The LORD's Love for Unfaithful Israel

14 "But then I will win her back once again.
I will lead her into the desert
and speak tenderly to her there.
15 I will return her vineyards to her
and transform the Valley of Trouble
into a gateway of hope.
She will give herself to me there,
as she did long ago when she was
young,
when I freed her from her captivity
in Egypt.
16 When that day comes," says the LORD,
"you will call me 'my husband'
instead of 'my [d]master.'
17 O Israel, I will wipe the many names of
Baal from your lips,
and you will never mention them again.

2:6 Job 19:8
2:7 Jer 2:2; 3:1; Ezek 23:4; Hos 5:13
2:8 Ezek 16:18; Hos 8:4; [b]*ba'al* (1168) ‣ Hos 2:13
2:9 Hos 8:7
2:10 Ezek 16:37
2:11 Isa 1:13-14; Jer 7:34; 16:9
2:12 Jer 5:17; 8:13
2:13 Jer 7:9; Ezek 23:40-42; Hos 4:13; 11:2; [c]*ba'al* (1168) ‣ Hos 2:16
2:14 Ezek 20:33-38
2:15 Josh 7:26; Jer 2:1-3; Ezek 16:8, 22
2:16 Isa 54:5; Hos 2:7; [d]*ba'al* (1168) ‣ 1 Kgs 16:31

2:6-7 *For this reason* (literally *Therefore*): The initial Hebrew word of 2:6 (also of 2:9 and 2:14) introduces God's judgment on Israel. Because of her idolatry, the Lord would restrict Israel's access to the Canaanite fertility gods. Like an aggressive prostitute, she will pursue ***her lovers***; but she will ***not find them***. In the end, Israel will conclude that it is ***better*** to ***return to*** her rightful ***husband***.

2:8 *She doesn't realize* (literally *she doesn't know*): Israel needs to know God personally and experientially (see "Knowing God" at 6:3, 6, p. 1431). Had the Israelites known the Lord in this way, they would have realized that every good thing in their lives came from him, not from the baals.

2:9-13 God's first judgment (2:6-7) was to restrict the Israelites; this second judgment would be to remove and destroy what he alone had given them.

2:11 From the context (2:13, 16-17), as well as from similar passages in Isa 1:12-17 and Amos 5:21-24, it seems clear that the Israelites had defiled the legitimate ***festivals, new moon celebrations***, and ***Sabbath days*** by combining worship of the Lord with worship of the Canaanite fertility god, Baal. God rejects such *syncretism* (mixing of different faiths) and declared that he would remove these unholy days from Israel's calendar.

2:13 While the Israelites were worshiping Canaanite gods, they ***forgot*** the Lord. For Hosea, ***to forget*** is not a lapse of memory, but the opposite of *knowing* the Lord (see 8:14; 13:6; Job 8:12-13; see also "Knowing God" at 6:3, 6, p. 1431). Had Israel truly known the Lord, they would never have indulged in Baal worship.

2:14-15 The third judgment (see note on 2:6-7) is completely unexpected. The Lord, who had innocently suffered Israel's repeated unfaithfulness, announces that he will take the initiative in wooing Israel in order to ***win her back once again***. He will ***lead her into the desert*** where he first entered into covenant with her, away from the seductive influences of Canaanite religion. • The ***Valley of Trouble*** (Hebrew *valley of Achor*) was the scene of Israel's first act of disobedience after they entered the Promised Land (Josh 7:24-26). The Lord had both the will and the power to grant Israel a new beginning after their sin and trouble (Josh 8:1-22), so Israel would again be offered a ***gateway of hope***.

2:16 *that day:* This seemingly unremarkable phrase is actually quite important in the prophets. It refers to the coming day of the Lord (see Joel 1:15; 2:1; Amos 5:18), when the Lord will act decisively in human history on behalf of his people. • ***'my husband' instead of 'my master'*** (Hebrew *'my baal'*): In this coming day, Israel will enter into a new relationship with her God. No longer will Israel call God "master" (Hebrew *ba'al*), which connotes subservience and was also the name of the chief Canaanite fertility god. Instead, she will address the Lord as "husband," implying partnership and companionship (Gen 2:23-24).

2:17 To avoid any possible syncretism (see note on 2:11) between the Lord and Baal, God would ***wipe the many names of Baal from*** Israel's ***lips***.

2:18
Lev 26:5-6
Job 5:23
Isa 2:4
Ezek 34:25; 39:1-10
[e]*berith* (1285)
‣Mal 2:4

2:20
Jer 31:34
Hos 6:6; 13:4

2:21
Zech 8:12

2:22
Jer 31:27-28
Joel 2:19

2:23
Hos 1:6, 9
*Rom 9:25
*1 Pet 2:10
[f]*rakham* (7355)
‣Zech 10:6

3:2
Ruth 4:10

3:4
Judg 17:6

3:5
Jer 50:4-5
Ezek 34:24

4:1
Isa 59:4
Jer 7:28
Hos 12:2
Mic 6:2

18 On that day I will make a [e]covenant
with all the wild animals and the birds
of the sky
and the animals that scurry along the
ground
so they will not harm you.
I will remove all weapons of war from
the land,
all swords and bows,
so you can live unafraid
in peace and safety.
19 I will make you my wife forever,
showing you righteousness and justice,
unfailing love and compassion.
20 I will be faithful to you and make you mine,
and you will finally know me as the
LORD.

21 "In that day, I will answer,"
says the LORD.
"I will answer the sky as it pleads for
clouds.
And the sky will answer the earth
with rain.
22 Then the earth will answer the thirsty
cries
of the grain, the grapevines, and the
olive trees.
And they in turn will answer,
'Jezreel'—'God plants!'
23 At that time I will plant a crop of Israelites
and raise them for myself.
I will show [f]love
to those I called 'Not [f]loved.'
And to those I called 'Not my people,'
I will say, 'Now you are my people.'
And they will reply, 'You are our
God!' "

Hosea's Wife Is Redeemed

3 Then the LORD said to me, "Go and love your wife again, even though she commits adultery with another lover. This will illustrate that the LORD still loves Israel, even though the people have turned to other gods and love to worship them."

2 So I bought her back for fifteen pieces of silver and five bushels of barley and a measure of wine. 3 Then I said to her, "You must live in my house for many days and stop your prostitution. During this time, you will not have sexual relations with anyone, not even with me."

4 This shows that Israel will go a long time without a king or prince, and without sacrifices, sacred pillars, priests, or even idols! 5 But afterward the people will return and devote themselves to the LORD their God and to David's descendant, their king. In the last days, they will tremble in awe of the LORD and of his goodness.

3. HOSEA'S MESSAGES OF WARNING (4:1–14:9)

The LORD's Case against Israel

4 Hear the word of the LORD, O people
of Israel!

2:18 ***On that day*** the Lord would make a ***covenant*** with his creation and his people, a covenant of ***peace and safety.***

2:19-20 ***I will make you my wife:*** This Hebrew verb, used three times in these verses, can be translated with our seldom-used word *betroth.* In the ancient world, betrothal entailed all the legal steps of a marriage, including the payment of a bride price by the groom. The only thing missing was the marriage ceremony and sexual consummation. The Lord vowed to betroth Israel to himself ***forever.*** To ensure the eternal nature of this new marriage, God provided a bride price that included five priceless qualities: ***righteousness and justice, unfailing love and compassion,*** and faithfulness. As a result, the Lord said, Israel ***will finally know me*** (cp. 2:13).

2:21-22 Unfaithful Israel thought her food and clothing were gifts from her lovers, the baals (2:5), but ***in that day*** they will know that the Lord alone is the source of all fertility and blessing. He will ***answer the sky,*** the ***clouds,*** and ***the earth,*** initiating the true cycle of fertility for the land. When the Lord is recognized as the only source of life, then the name ***Jezreel*** will regain its true meaning: ***God plants!***

2:23 As God has promised (2:1), on the coming day of the Lord he will reverse the names of Gomer's children. He ***will show love*** to ***'Not loved'*** (Hebrew *Lo-ruhamah;* see 1:6). To ***'Not my people'*** (Hebrew *Lo-ammi;* see 1:9), he will say, ***'Now you are my people.'*** The only fitting response from God's people is ***"You are our God!"***

3:1 ***Go and love your wife again, even though she*** (Or *Go and love a woman who*): The Lord commanded Hosea to restore his marriage as testimony that the Lord had promised to restore wayward Israel. • ***love to worship them:*** Literally *love their raisin cakes.* The worship of Asherah, a Canaanite fertility goddess, often included offerings of *raisin cakes.*

3:2 ***So I bought her back:*** The biblical text does not indicate why the prophet needed to purchase his wife. Most interpreters have assumed that the unfaithful Gomer had fallen into debt and become a slave. The meager price Hosea paid for her may indicate that Gomer was considered a slave of little value (see Exod 21:32; Lev 27:4). • ***fifteen pieces of silver:*** Hebrew *15 shekels of silver,* about 6 ounces or 171 grams in weight. • ***five bushels of barley and a measure of wine:*** As in Greek version, which reads *a homer of barley and a wineskin full of wine;* Hebrew reads *a homer* [5 bushels or 182 liters] *of barley and a lethech* [2.5 bushels or 91 liters] *of barley.*

3:3-4 Just as Hosea's wife was required to live ***many days*** without ***sexual relations,*** Israel would be deprived of the institutions (***king or prince***), practices (***sacrifices***), and objects (***sacred pillars . . . or even idols***) that had been foundational to its life and worship.

3:3 ***not even with me:*** Or *and I will live with you.*

3:4 ***priests:*** Hebrew *ephod,* the vest worn by the priest.

3:5 The Lord's purpose for depriving the Israelites of these things was to get them to ***return*** to him in reverential ***awe*** and recognize him alone as the source of all ***goodness.*** • ***David's descendant, their king:*** Literally *to David their king.*

4:1–14:9 This diverse collection of Hosea's prophecies is presented in

The LORD has brought charges against
you, saying:
"There is no faithfulness, no kindness,
no knowledge of God in your land.
2 You make vows and break them;
you kill and steal and commit
adultery.
There is violence everywhere—
one murder after another.
3 That is why your land is in mourning,
and everyone is wasting away.
Even the wild animals, the birds of the
sky,
and the fish of the sea are
disappearing.
4 "Don't point your finger at someone else
and try to pass the blame!
My complaint, you priests,
is with you.
5 So you will stumble in broad daylight,
and your false prophets will fall with
you in the night.
And I will destroy Israel, your mother.
6 My people are being destroyed
because they don't know me.
Since you priests refuse to know me,
I refuse to recognize you as my priests.
Since you have forgotten the laws of your
God,
I will forget to bless your children.
7 The more priests there are,
the more they [g]sin against me.
They have exchanged the glory of God
for the shame of idols.
8 "When the people bring their sin
offerings, the priests get fed.
So the priests are glad when the
people sin!
9 'And what the priests do, the people
also do.'
So now I will punish both priests and
people
for their wicked deeds.
10 They will eat and still be hungry.
They will play the prostitute and gain
nothing from it,
for they have deserted the LORD
11 to worship other gods.

"Wine has robbed my people
of their understanding.
12 They ask a piece of wood for advice!
They think a stick can tell them the
future!
Longing after idols
has made them foolish.
They have played the prostitute,
serving other gods and deserting their
God.
13 They offer sacrifices to idols on the
mountaintops.
They go up into the hills to burn
incense
in the pleasant shade of oaks, poplars,
and terebinth trees.

4:2 Hos 6:8-9; 7:1-4; 10:4
4:3 Isa 24:4; 33:9; Zeph 1:3
4:4 Deut 17:12; Ezek 3:26; Amos 5:10, 13
4:5 Ezek 14:3, 7; Hos 5:5
4:6 Hos 4:14; Zech 11:8-9, 15-17; Mal 2:7-8
4:7 Hos 10:1; 13:6; Hab 2:16; Rom 1:23; [g]*khata'* (2398) ▸Gen 39:9
4:9 Isa 24:2; Jer 5:31
4:11 Isa 5:12; 28:7
4:12 Isa 44:19; Jer 2:27
4:13 Jer 2:20; 3:6; Ezek 6:13; Hos 2:13; 11:2

roughly chronological order, from early in his ministry during the reign of Jeroboam II until just before the destruction of Israel in 722 BC. Hosea presents God's charges against Israel, tells them of the severe consequences for their sin, and concludes with a divine promise of future restoration.

4:1 ***The LORD has brought charges against you:*** Hosea issued a divine indictment against Israel for breaking their covenant with the Lord (see also Isa 3:13; Mic 6:2). The charges first focus on sins of omission, the qualities that should characterize the people of Israel but were absent. In Israel ***there is no faithfulness, no kindness, no knowledge of God***. These theologically rich words describe the inward trust and devotion from which godly lives should spring.

4:2 The prophet also charged the Israelites for their sins of commission. The crimes listed here are all prohibited in the Ten Commandments (Exod 20:3-17; Deut 5:7-21), the fundamental list of covenant responsibilities. Because the Israelites did not know the Lord, they did not practice even the most basic standards of covenant life.

4:3 God's judgment inevitably falls upon sinful people. Because of the Israelites' sin, their ***land*** and all of nature would suffer.

4:4-5 When we are accused of a crime, our human inclination is to ***blame*** someone else, but God makes it clear that the blame for Israel's apostasy lay with her religious leaders, ***priests***, and ***false prophets***. • God's judgment on the priests and prophets was that they would ***stumble*** and ***fall*** (the same word in Hebrew), both professionally and personally.

4:4 ***My complaint, you priests, is with you:*** Literally *Your people are like those with a complaint against the priests.*

4:6 Because the ***priests*** refused ***to know*** the Lord, neither did the people know their God. As a result, the people were ***being destroyed***. • A primary function of the priests of Israel was to know, practice, and teach ***the laws of . . . God***. Ironically, these guardians of the law had ***forgotten*** it.

4:7 The last sentence is translated from the Syriac version and an ancient Hebrew tradition; Masoretic Text reads *I will turn their glory into shame.*

4:9 The people followed the evil example of their religious leaders; as a result, God would ***punish both priests and people for their wicked deeds***.

4:10 God's judgment matches the punishment to the crime. The Israelites worshiped Canaanite fertility deities with the expectation of bountiful crops and herds, but God's judgment was that they would ***still be hungry*** and their religious prostitution would ***gain*** them ***nothing***.

4:12 ***They ask a piece of wood for advice!*** For millennia, people have worshiped natural objects such as wood and stones that they believed embodied spirits and gods (Jer 2:27). Biblical religion completely rejects such practices and beliefs (Exod 20:4-5; Isa 44:19).

4:13 Many Canaanite religious rites were practiced ***on the mountaintops*** and ***hills***. On these pagan "high places," sacred trees were usually used in fertility worship (1 Kgs 14:23; Jer 2:20). • Israelite ***daughters*** and brides also committed sexual acts in the worship of Baal; they were possibly forced to do so by their fathers and husbands.

4:14 Deut 23:17 Rom 1:31
4:16 Isa 5:17; 7:25
4:17 Ps 81:12
4:19 Hos 12:1; 13:15
5:3 Amos 5:12
5:4 Hos 4:6, 14
5:5 2 Kgs 17:19-20 Ezek 23:31-35
5:6 Isa 1:15 Ezek 8:6 Mic 6:6-7
5:7 Hos 2:4

"That is why your daughters turn to
prostitution,
and your daughters-in-law commit
adultery.
14 But why should I punish them
for their prostitution and adultery?
For your men are doing the same thing,
sinning with whores and shrine
prostitutes.
O foolish people! You refuse to
understand,
so you will be destroyed.

15 "Though you, Israel, are a prostitute,
may Judah avoid such guilt.
Do not join the false worship at Gilgal or
Beth-aven,
even though they take oaths there in
the LORD's name.
16 Israel is stubborn,
like a stubborn heifer.
So should the LORD feed her
like a lamb in a lush pasture?
17 Leave Israel alone,
because she is married to idolatry.
18 When the rulers of Israel finish their
drinking,
off they go to find some prostitutes.
They love shame more than honor.
19 So a mighty wind will sweep them away.
Their sacrifices to idols will bring
them shame.

The Failure of Israel's Leaders

5 "Hear this, you priests.
Pay attention, you leaders of Israel.
Listen, you members of the royal family.
Judgment has been handed down
against you.
For you have led the people into a snare
by worshiping the idols at Mizpah and
Tabor.
2 You have dug a deep pit to trap them at
Acacia Grove.
But I will settle with you for what you
have done.
3 I know what you are like, O Ephraim.
You cannot hide yourself from me,
O Israel.
You have left me as a prostitute leaves
her husband;
you are utterly defiled.
4 Your deeds won't let you return to your
God.
You are a prostitute through and
through,
and you do not know the LORD.

5 "The arrogance of Israel testifies against
her;
Israel and Ephraim will stumble under
their load of guilt.
Judah, too, will fall with them.
6 When they come with their flocks and
herds
to offer sacrifices to the LORD,
they will not find him,
because he has withdrawn from them.
7 They have betrayed the honor of the
LORD,
bearing children that are not his.
Now their false religion will devour
them
along with their wealth.

8 "Sound the alarm in Gibeah!
Blow the trumpet in Ramah!
Raise the battle cry in Beth-aven!

4:14 God declared that he would not single out the young women for their prostitution. This declaration contrasts with double standards that were common in ancient cultures. • ***shrine prostitutes:*** The Hebrew word refers to female prostitutes who were dedicated to the service of Baal and Asherah in the temples of Baal (Deut 23:18).

4:15 ***Beth-aven*** means "house of wickedness"; it is being used as another name for Bethel, which means "house of God" (see also 5:8; 10:5). Bethel was the most important worship center in the northern kingdom of Israel (see Amos 7:13).

4:17 ***Israel:*** Hebrew *Ephraim,* referring to the northern kingdom of *Israel.*

4:18 The last sentence is translated from the Greek version; the meaning of the Hebrew is uncertain.

5:1 Hosea again condemns the religious and political ***leaders of Israel.*** They ***have led the people into*** idolatry as hunters trap wild animals in ***a snare.*** • The specific sins at ***Mizpah and Tabor*** are not known.

5:2 ***at Acacia Grove:*** Hebrew *at Shittim.* The meaning of the Hebrew for this sentence is uncertain. • ***I will settle with you:*** God's judgment (Hebrew *musar,* "discipline") would inevitably fall upon Israel's leaders. God did not judge Israel simply to punish them, but to correct them so that his people would return to him.

5:3 ***you are utterly defiled:*** The word translated *defiled* is used frequently in the Pentateuch to describe ritual uncleanness, a physical condition that disqualified a person from worshiping God in the Temple (Lev 11–15). The prophets used the concept as a metaphor for Israel's moral uncleanness as the result of her idolatry (Isa 6:5; Mic 2:10).

5:4 Israel's idolatrous practices were so ingrained that they were apparently powerless to ***return*** to the Lord. • ***You are a prostitute through and through*** (literally *the spirit of prostitution is within them*): Israel's sin was not simply a behavior; it was the nation's essential nature. They instinctively preferred the corrupt to the pure. Only through God's work of salvation could Israel escape.

5:6-7 The people might think that they could win God's favor with their ***sacrifices,*** but Hosea warned them that ***they*** would ***not find him;*** God had left them to the consequences of their sin.

5:7 ***their false religion . . . their wealth:*** The meaning of this sentence in Hebrew is uncertain.

5:8-9 Hosea sounded the ***alarm*** to warn the Israelites of God's coming judgment. Because of their sins, the Lord had become Israel's enemy and would punish them. • ***Gibeah, Ramah,*** and ***Beth-aven*** (Beth-aven means "house of

Lead on into battle, O warriors of
Benjamin!
9 One thing is certain, Israel:
On your day of punishment,
you will become a heap of
rubble.
10 "The leaders of Judah have become like
thieves.
So I will pour my anger on them like a
waterfall.
11 The people of Israel will be crushed and
broken by my judgment
because they are determined to
worship idols.
12 I will destroy Israel as a moth consumes
wool.
I will make Judah as weak as rotten
wood.
13 "When Israel and Judah saw how sick
they were,
Israel turned to Assyria—
to the great king there—
but he could neither help nor cure
them.
14 I will be like a lion to Israel,
like a strong young lion to Judah.
I will tear them to pieces!
I will carry them off,
and no one will be left to rescue
them.
15 Then I will return to my place
until they admit their guilt and turn
to me.
For as soon as trouble comes,
they will earnestly search for me."

A Call to Repentance

6 "Come, let us return to the LORD.
He has torn us to pieces;
now he will heal us.
He has injured us;
now he will bandage our wounds.
2 In just a short time he will restore us,
so that we may live in his presence.
3 Oh, that we might know the LORD!
Let us press on to know him.
He will respond to us as surely as the
arrival of dawn
or the coming of rains in early spring."
4 "O Israel and Judah,
what should I do with you?" asks the
LORD.
"For your love vanishes like the morning
mist
and disappears like dew in the sunlight.
5 I sent my prophets to cut you to pieces—
to slaughter you with my words,
with judgments as inescapable as light.
6 I want you to show love,
not offer [h]sacrifices.
I want you to know me
more than I want burnt offerings.
7 But like Adam, you broke my covenant
and betrayed my trust.
8 "Gilead is a city of sinners,
tracked with footprints of blood.

5:9 Isa 28:1-4; 37:3; Hos 9:11-17
5:10 Deut 27:17; Ps 32:6; 93:3-4; Ezek 7:8
5:12 Ps 39:11; Isa 51:8
5:13 Jer 30:12
5:14 Ps 7:2; 50:22; Hos 13:7
5:15 Isa 64:7-9; Jer 2:27
6:1 2 Chr 7:14; Isa 30:26; Jer 50:4; Hos 14:4; Zeph 2:1-3
6:2 Ps 30:5
6:3 Isa 2:3; Joel 2:23; Mic 4:2
6:4 Ps 78:34-37; Hos 13:3
6:5 Heb 4:12
6:6 Ps 40:6-8; Mic 6:6-8; *Matt 9:13; 12:7
[h]*zebakh* (2077) ‣Hos 13:2

wickedness"; it is being used as another name for Bethel, which means "house of God") are all cities in the tribal territory of *Benjamin*.

5:9 ***Israel:*** Hebrew *Ephraim,* referring to the northern kingdom of *Israel;* also in 5:11, 12, 13, 14.

5:10 ***thieves*** (literally *those who move a boundary marker*): The Lord was the owner of the land, which he entrusted to the tribes following the conquest (see Josh 13:8–19:51). To move a boundary marker and change God's allotted boundaries was to steal from God (Deut 19:14). Such an act rightly invoked divine punishment (Deut 27:17).

5:11 ***determined to worship idols:*** Or *determined to follow human commands.* The meaning of the Hebrew is uncertain.

5:12 ***as a moth . . . rotten wood:*** Sin can destroy the very fabric and foundation of a people while leaving them unaware that the destruction has taken place.

5:13 In a final effort to avoid complete destruction, the Israelites overthrew King Pekah and placed a new king, Hoshea, on the throne. Hoshea then appealed to the Assyrian king Shalmaneser for peace (2 Kgs 15:29-30; 17:3), but these diplomatic maneuvers could ***neither help nor cure*** Israel—they would soon be destroyed by Assyria.

5:15 Hosea again reminded Israel that divine judgment was not merely punitive. God's purpose was to convince Israel to ***admit their guilt*** and return to the Lord (see 2:2, 14).

6:1-3 In response to God's acts of judgment on Israel, the religious leaders called the people to ***return to the LORD*** in repentance and urged everyone to ***know the LORD.*** • The ***rains in early spring*** were essential to the agricultural cycle of the land.

6:4 The response of ***Israel*** (Hebrew *Ephraim,* referring to the northern kingdom of Israel) was inadequate; God lamented that their ***love*** disappeared like ***morning mist*** and ***dew***.

6:6 In one of Hosea's key verses, God names the most important qualities that should characterize the Israelites' covenant lives with him. First, the Lord wants his people ***to show love*** (Greek version translates this Hebrew term as *to show mercy;* cp. Matt 9:13; 12:7) more than he wants ***sacrifices.*** Love (Hebrew *khesed*) includes faithfulness (see 4:1; 6:4; see also "God's Covenant Love" at Deut 33:3, p. 365). God is always faithful (Ps 136), and he requires the same of his people. Second, the Lord wants Israel ***to know*** him (literally *to know God*) more than he wants ***burnt offerings.*** Knowing God is much more than simply knowing facts about God (see "Knowing God," facing page). An intimate personal relationship with God is characterized by complete trust and integrity. Sacrifice still had a proper place in Israelite religion, but only when it was offered by a people who truly knew and loved God (see Isa 1:10-17; Amos 5:21-24; Mic 6:6-8).

6:7-11 Hosea traces the way that human rebellion against God began with Adam and spread through the cities of Israel to the land of Judah.

6:7 ***But like Adam:*** Or *But at Adam.*

6:9 Jer 7:9; Ezek 22:9; Hos 4:2
6:11 Jer 51:33; Joel 3:13
7:1 Ezek 24:13; Hos 7:13
7:2 Jer 2:19; Hos 8:13
7:3 Hos 7:5; Mic 7:3
7:4 Jer 9:2; 23:10
7:5 Isa 28:1
7:7 Isa 64:7

9 Priests form bands of robbers,
waiting in ambush for their victims.
They murder travelers along the road to Shechem
and practice every kind of sin.
10 Yes, I have seen something horrible in Ephraim and Israel:
My people are defiled by prostituting themselves with other gods!

11 "O Judah, a harvest of punishment is also waiting for you,
though I wanted to restore the fortunes of my people.

Israel's Love for Wickedness

7 "I want to heal Israel, but its sins are too great.
Samaria is filled with liars.
Thieves are on the inside
and bandits on the outside!
2 Its people don't realize
that I am watching them.
Their sinful deeds are all around them,
and I see them all.
3 "The people entertain the king with their wickedness,
and the princes laugh at their lies.
4 They are all adulterers,
always aflame with lust.
They are like an oven that is kept hot
while the baker is kneading the dough.
5 On royal holidays, the princes get drunk with wine,
carousing with those who mock them.
6 Their hearts are like an oven
blazing with intrigue.
Their plot smolders through the night,
and in the morning it breaks out like a raging fire.
7 Burning like an oven,
they consume their leaders.
They kill their kings one after another,
and no one cries to me for help.

8 "The people of Israel mingle with godless foreigners,
making themselves as worthless as a half-baked cake!

Knowing God (6:3, 6)

Hos 2:20; 4:1, 6; Gen 6:9; 18:17-33; Exod 33:8-11; Num 12:6-8; Isa 5:13; 11:9; 43:10; Jer 9:24; 31:33-34; John 10:14-15; 17:3; Gal 4:9; Phil 3:10; Col 1:10; 1 Thes 4:3-5; 2 Thes 1:7-8; Titus 1:16; Heb 8:10-13; 1 Jn 2:4; 4:6, 8; 3 Jn 1:11

More than any other prophet, Hosea emphasizes the importance of knowing God. Israel would ultimately be destroyed (4:6) because they did not know God (4:1).

For us, knowledge means information, facts, and concepts. But in biblical times, knowledge was centered in personal relationships. To know someone is to enter into a close relationship with that person. Knowing God involves much more than simply mastering facts and information about him. It even transcends discussions about the nature and character of God, as important as those are. Knowing God means entering into an intimate relationship with him. It means identifying with God and learning to view everything as God does. Knowing God will transform our thoughts and actions, our priorities and values, and our relationships with fellow human beings. It is far more important than religious rites, sacrifices and burnt offerings, or any other religious activities (see Jer 9:23-24; 31:34).

6:9 ***Priests form bands of robbers:*** Hosea again condemns the religious leaders for their crimes (see 4:4-8).

6:10 ***something horrible:*** The prophet uses this rare word (also in Jer 18:13) to describe the depth of Israel's sin in breaking God's covenant and betraying his trust.

7:1-2 ***I want to heal Israel*** (Hebrew *Ephraim*, referring to the northern kingdom of Israel; also in 7:8, 11): God's overwhelming desire was to heal Israel's harlotry (see 14:4) and restore her to right relationship with him, but she was ***filled with liars, thieves, and bandits.*** • The Israelites might have thought that the Lord was unaware of their sins, but he was ***watching them,*** and he saw everything they did.

7:3-7 The northern kingdom of Israel saw a succession of seven different ***kings*** during the final twenty-five years of its existence, four of whom were assassinated by usurpers. This passage refers to the vicious and bloody political ***intrigue*** that characterized these years.

7:3 The prophet did not record the name of this ***king,*** but many believe he was Hoshea, the northern kingdom's last monarch.

7:4 ***adulterers:*** Hosea used this term earlier to describe spiritual apostasy (3:1); it refers here to those who were disloyal to the king.

7:6 A simile aptly compares the plots and political intrigue during this turbulent time to a red-hot ***oven*** that ***breaks out*** to ignite the entire land. • ***Their plot smolders:*** Literally *Their baker sleeps.*

7:7 ***They kill their kings:*** The people of Israel assassinated one king after another as they desperately attempted to save their nation and their lives from the invading Assyrian army. Throughout these last years, they relied upon their own plans and plots and never thought to cry out to the Lord, their only true source of help.

7:8-12 Israel ignored the Lord in their international politics as well as in their domestic policies. ***Like silly, witless doves,*** they had flown in a frenzy between Assyria and Egypt, the major powers of their day, vainly trying to make treaties and alliances that would save their land.

7:8 ***The people of Israel mingle with godless foreigners:*** By relying upon foreign nations rather than God for security, the Israelites were no longer a pure, holy nation, set apart for the Lord. • Flatbread must be turned over at the proper time to ensure that it is baked on both sides rather than burned on one side and raw on the other. Israel was ***a half-baked cake*** and was therefore ***worthless.***

9 Worshiping foreign gods has sapped
their strength,
but they don't even know it.
Their hair is gray,
but they don't realize they're old and
weak.
10 Their arrogance testifies against them,
yet they don't return to the LORD their
God
or even try to find him.

11 "The people of Israel have become like
silly, witless doves,
first calling to Egypt, then flying to
Assyria for help.
12 But as they fly about,
I will throw my net over them
and bring them down like a bird from
the sky.
I will punish them for all the evil
they do.

13 "What sorrow awaits those who have
deserted me!
Let them die, for they have rebelled
against me.
I wanted to redeem them,
but they have told lies about me.
14 They do not cry out to me with sincere
hearts.
Instead, they sit on their couches and
wail.
They cut themselves, begging foreign
gods for grain and new wine,
and they turn away from me.
15 I trained them and made them strong,
yet now they plot evil against me.
16 They look everywhere except to the
Most High.
They are as useless as a crooked bow.
Their leaders will be killed by their
enemies
because of their insolence
toward me.
Then the people of Egypt
will laugh at them.

Israel Harvests the Whirlwind

8 "Sound the alarm!
The enemy descends like an eagle
on the people of the LORD,
for they have broken my covenant
and revolted against my law.
2 Now Israel pleads with me,
'Help us, for you are our God!'
3 But it is too late.
The people of Israel have rejected what
is good,
and now their enemies will chase
after them.
4 The people have appointed kings
without my consent,
and princes without my knowledge.
By making idols for themselves from
their silver and gold,
they have brought about their own
destruction.

5 "O Samaria, I reject this calf—
this idol you have made.
My fury burns against you.
How long will you be incapable of
innocence?

7:9 Isa 1:7
7:10 Hos 5:5
7:11 Hos 12:1
7:12 Ezek 12:13
7:13 Matt 23:37
7:14 Amos 2:8
7:15 Nah 1:9
7:16 Ps 78:57; Ezek 23:32; Hos 9:3, 6
8:1 Hab 1:8
8:4 Hos 2:8; 13:10
8:5 Jer 13:27

7:9 *foreign gods* (literally *foreigners*): Israel's political involvement with foreign nations had harmed their spiritual well-being.

7:11 When invaded by *Assyria*, Israel turned to *Egypt* for help. When Egypt proved powerless, Israel tried to appease Assyria by becoming its *vassal* (a subservient kingdom).

7:12 Like a fowler hunting birds, the Lord would ***throw*** his ***net over*** silly, witless Israel to punish them. • ***I will punish them for all the evil they do:*** Literally *I will punish them because of what was reported against them in the assembly.*

7:13 ***What sorrow:*** This word (Hebrew *'oy*) was used at funerals to mourn the dead. In God's eyes, Israel was as good as dead because ***they*** had ***rebelled against*** him. Rebellion against a human king was a capital crime; how much more serious it was for God's people to rebel against their heavenly king. • ***I wanted to redeem them:*** This Hebrew word means paying a fee to repatriate someone who has been enslaved. It is often associated with the exodus from Egypt. The Lord desired to do for the Israelites what he did when he brought their ancestors out of their slavery to pagan gods, ***but they . . . told lies about*** him.

7:14 ***They cut themselves*** (As in Greek version; Hebrew reads *They gather together*): Self-mutilation was characteristic of Canaanite worship (see 1 Kgs 18:28); it was prohibited in Israel (Deut 14:1).

7:16 ***A crooked*** (literally *loose*) ***bow*** cannot propel its arrow to the target; it depicts Israel's futility apart from God (see 7:8, 11).

8:1 ***Sound the alarm:*** The ram's horn trumpet (*shofar*) called the people to worship (Ps 98:6); it was also (as here) the signal for battle (2 Sam 20:1). God was sending an ***enemy***, the Assyrians, to execute his judgment on Israel. • ***revolted against my law:*** God's law (Hebrew *torah*) is much more than the sum of the individual laws in the Pentateuch. It represents the totality of God's instruction to his people through his words and his deeds. Loving fulfillment of the Torah was Israel's part of the covenant. They had broken God's commandments, and they had turned aside from their covenant relationship with the Lord.

8:3 Jesus tells us that God alone is ***good*** (Mark 10:18). God is the source of every good thing, yet Israel ***rejected*** him.

8:4 ***appointed kings without my consent:*** The Israelites quickly disposed of one king and appointed another if they thought it might save their nation (see 7:7). They did all of this without consulting their true king, the Lord.

8:5-6 ***this calf:*** When Jeroboam I (931–910 BC), the first king of the northern kingdom of Israel, ascended the throne, he established places of worship in the cities of Dan and Bethel so that the people would not travel to the Temple in Jerusalem, the capital of the southern kingdom. At each site, he erected a gold calf for the people to worship (1 Kgs 12:26-30).

8:6
Hos 13:2
8:7
Isa 66:15
Nah 1:3
8:8
Jer 51:34
8:9
Jer 2:24
Ezek 16:33
8:10
Ezek 16:37
Hos 10:10
8:13
Hos 7:2
1 Cor 4:5
8:14
Jer 17:27
Hos 2:13; 4:6; 13:6
9:1
Isa 22:12-13
9:2
Hos 2:9
9:3
Ezek 4:13
9:4
Exod 29:40
Hag 2:14
9:5
Hos 2:11
Joel 1:13

6 This calf you worship, O Israel,
was crafted by your own hands!
It is not God!
Therefore, it must be smashed to bits.

7 "They have planted the wind
and will harvest the whirlwind.
The stalks of grain wither
and produce nothing to eat.
And even if there is any grain,
foreigners will eat it.
8 The people of Israel have been
swallowed up;
they lie among the nations like an old
discarded pot.
9 Like a wild donkey looking for a mate,
they have gone up to Assyria.
The people of Israel have sold
themselves—
sold themselves to many lovers.
10 But though they have sold themselves to
many allies,
I will now gather them together for
judgment.
Then they will writhe
under the burden of the great king.

11 "Israel has built many altars to take away
sin,
but these very altars became places
for sinning!
12 Even though I gave them all my laws,
they act as if those laws don't apply
to them.
13 The people of Israel love their rituals of
sacrifice,
but to me their sacrifices are all
meaningless.
I will hold my people accountable for
their sins,
and I will punish them.
They will return to Egypt.
14 Israel has forgotten its Maker and built
great palaces,
and Judah has fortified its cities.
Therefore, I will send down fire on their
cities
and will burn up their fortresses."

Hosea Announces Israel's Punishment

9 O people of Israel,
do not rejoice as other nations do.
For you have been unfaithful to your
God,
hiring yourselves out like prostitutes,
worshiping other gods on every
threshing floor.
2 So now your harvests will be too small to
feed you.
There will be no grapes for making
new wine.
3 You may no longer stay here in the
LORD's land.
Instead, you will return to Egypt,
and in Assyria you will eat food
that is ceremonially unclean.
4 There you will make no offerings of
wine to the LORD.
None of your sacrifices there will
please him.
They will be unclean, like food touched
by a person in mourning.
All who present such sacrifices will be
defiled.
They may eat this food themselves,
but they may not offer it to the LORD.
5 What then will you do on festival days?
How will you observe the LORD's
festivals?

8:7 When Hosea proclaimed divine judgment, the punishment fit the crime (see note on 4:10). Through their idolatry and political intrigue, the Israelites had ***planted*** the seeds of their own destruction (see Gal 6:7).

8:9 ***Like a wild donkey:*** Hosea compared Israel's worship of the Canaanite fertility gods to an animal in heat that was desperate to mate (see Jer 2:23-24). • ***Israel:*** (Hebrew *Ephraim*, referring to the northern kingdom of *Israel;* also in 8:11.)

8:10 ***I will now gather them together:*** Although God sometimes promises to gather his people for deliverance (Zech 10:8-10), here the Lord would gather them ***for judgment*** (Joel 3:11).

8:11 ***Israel has built many altars:*** As Israel's idolatry increased, her religious activities increased in an attempt ***to take away sin;*** instead, these rites only increased her sin.

8:13 ***their sacrifices are all meaningless:*** See 6:6; Isa 1:10-17; Amos 5:21-24; Mic 6:6-8. • ***They will return to Egypt,*** the place of slavery (Deut 28:68). God's dealings with Israel did not end with judgment. The divine purpose of judgment was to restore Israel to the status they had when they came out of Egypt, so that they could experience a new beginning (see 2:14-15).

8:14 ***Israel has forgotten its Maker:*** See 2:13. • God's judgment is often described as ***fire*** sent upon the royal ***palaces*** and ***fortresses*** (see Amos 1:4, 7).

9:1 ***do not rejoice:*** This is probably a reference to the Festival of Shelters, when Israel celebrated the final harvest of the year. This festival was ordained by God (Deut 16:13-15), but the Israelites had turned it into a wild pagan festival, just ***as other nations*** had. • ***hiring yourselves out like prostitutes*** (literally *you have loved a prostitute's pay*): The Israelites ignorantly believed that their grain and wine were payment for their worship of the Canaanite fertility god.

9:2 As punishment for their prostitution, the Lord would so reduce the Israelites' ***harvests*** that they would go hungry (cp. Hag 1:3-11).

9:3 God would exile the Israelites to Assyria in 722 BC. There, in an unclean land, they would eat ***ceremonially unclean*** food, further separating themselves from their covenant with the Lord.

9:4 In exile, the Israelites could not offer legitimate sacrifices because any sacrifice in a foreign land was ***unclean*** and ***defiled.***

6 Even if you escape destruction from
Assyria,
Egypt will conquer you, and Memphis
will bury you.
Nettles will take over your treasures of
silver;
thistles will invade your ruined homes.

7 The time of Israel's punishment has come;
the day of payment is here.
Soon Israel will know this all too well.
Because of your great sin and hostility,
you say, "The prophets are crazy
and the inspired men are fools!"
8 The prophet is a watchman over Israel
for my God,
yet traps are laid for him wherever he
goes.
He faces hostility even in the house
of God.
9 The things my people do are as depraved
as what they did in Gibeah long ago.
God will not forget.
He will surely punish them for their
sins.

10 The LORD says, "O Israel, when I first
found you,
it was like finding fresh grapes in the
desert.
When I saw your ancestors,
it was like seeing the first ripe figs of
the season.
But then they deserted me for Baal-peor,
giving themselves to that shameful
idol.
Soon they became vile,
as vile as the god they worshiped.
11 The glory of Israel will fly away like a bird,
for your children will not be born
or grow in the womb
or even be conceived.
12 Even if you do have children who grow up,
I will take them from you.
It will be a terrible day when I turn away
and leave you alone.
13 I have watched Israel become as
beautiful as Tyre.
But now Israel will bring out her
children for slaughter."

14 O LORD, what should I request for your
people?
I will ask for wombs that don't give
birth
and breasts that give no milk.

15 The LORD says, "All their wickedness
began at Gilgal;
there I began to hate them.
I will drive them from my land
because of their evil actions.
I will love them no more
because all their leaders are rebels.
16 The people of Israel are struck down.
Their roots are dried up,
and they will bear no more fruit.
And if they give birth,
I will slaughter their beloved children."

17 My God will reject the people of Israel
because they will not listen or obey.
They will be wanderers,
homeless among the nations.

The LORD's Judgment against Israel

10 How prosperous Israel is—
a luxuriant vine loaded with fruit.
But the richer the people get,
the more pagan altars they build.

9:6 Isa 5:6; 7:23; Hos 10:8
9:7 Isa 10:3; Jer 10:15; 29:26; Lam 2:14; Ezek 7:2-7; 13:3, 10; *nabi'* (5030) ›Amos 7:14
9:9 Isa 31:6; Hos 7:2; 8:13
9:10 Num 25:1-9; 2 Kgs 17:15
9:11 Hos 4:7
9:12 Hos 7:13
9:15 Isa 1:23; Hos 7:2; 12:2; Amos 4:4; 5:5
9:16 Ezek 24:21
10:1 1 Kgs 14:23; Isa 5:1-7; Ezek 15:1-5; Hos 8:11; 12:11

9:6 *Even if* some Israelites were to *escape* Assyrian exile by fleeing to *Egypt*, God's relentless judgment would reach them there. • *Memphis* was the capital of northern Egypt.

9:7 Apostate Israelites refused to believe God's words of judgment as delivered by the prophets and mockingly cried that *the prophets* were *crazy*.

9:8 The *watchman* stood guard on the wall of the city to warn of any threat (1 Sam 14:16). In the same way, a *prophet* was God's watchman, stationed to warn Israel of her sin and of the judgment that sin would inevitably bring (see Jer 6:17; Ezek 3:17). Despite his service to the people, all the prophet received was *hostility*. • *Israel:* Hebrew *Ephraim*, referring to the northern kingdom of Israel; also in 9:11, 13, 16.

9:9 *what they did in Gibeah long ago:* See Judg 19–21.

9:10 *when I first found you:* Hosea, like Ezekiel (Ezek 16), speaks of the Lord's finding and adopting chaste, innocent Israel *in the desert*. But Israel soon *deserted* God for idols at *Baal-peor* (Num 25:1-4). Participation in idolatry had made the Israelites *vile*. This strong word can also be translated "detestable" (Deut 29:17) or "abominable" (Jer 7:30). They inevitably resembled what they worshiped.

9:11 Israel worshiped the baals to ensure that they would have many children, but God would punish them by preventing birth, pregnancy, and even conception.

9:13 *for slaughter:* Rather than gaining them more children, the Israelites' idolatry would backfire, resulting in their children's deaths.

9:15 *All their wickedness began at Gilgal:* Gilgal was the base camp for Joshua's army (Josh 5:10; 10:6, 43) and the place where Saul was made king (1 Sam 11:15). Saul also disobeyed God and was rejected as king at Gilgal (1 Sam 13:8-15; 15:10-23). Israel's leaders, including its first king, had led the nation away from their true king, the Lord. • *I will love them no more:* Although a different Hebrew word is used here, the prophetic judgment reflects the name of Hosea's daughter (1:6).

9:17 *wanderers:* God's judgment on the Israelites would cut them off from the land, leaving them with no home.

10:1 Although Israel was God's *luxuriant*, fruitful vine (see Isa 5:1-7; Jer 2:21; Ezek 17:6), she falsely attributed her prosperity to the Canaanite fertility gods, rather than to the Lord, and she spent the riches God had given her to enhance her worship of idols. • *sacred pillars:* Stone pillars could be

10:2
1 Kgs 18:21
Hos 10:8
Mic 5:13
Zeph 1:5

10:4
Ps 12:4
Hos 4:2

10:5
Hos 8:5

10:6
Hos 10:5

10:8
Hos 5:8; 9:6; 10:5
*Luke 23:30
Rev 6:16

10:10
Ezek 5:13

10:11
Jer 28:14

The more bountiful their harvests,
the more beautiful their sacred pillars.
2 The hearts of the people are fickle;
they are guilty and must be punished.
The LORD will break down their altars
and smash their sacred pillars.
3 Then they will say, "We have no king
because we didn't fear the LORD.
But even if we had a king,
what could he do for us anyway?"
4 They spout empty words
and make covenants they don't intend
to keep.
So injustice springs up among them
like poisonous weeds in a farmer's
field.

5 The people of Samaria tremble in fear
for what might happen to their calf
idol at Beth-aven.
The people mourn and the priests wail,
because its glory will be stripped away.
6 This idol will be carted away to Assyria,
a gift to the great king there.
Ephraim will be ridiculed and Israel will
be shamed,
because its people have trusted in
this idol.
7 Samaria and its king will be cut off;
they will float away like driftwood on
an ocean wave.
8 And the pagan shrines of Aven, the place
of Israel's sin, will crumble.
Thorns and thistles will grow up
around their altars.
They will beg the mountains, "Bury us!"
and plead with the hills, "Fall on us!"

9 The LORD says, "O Israel, ever since Gibeah,
there has been only sin and more sin!
You have made no progress whatsoever.
Was it not right that the wicked men
of Gibeah were attacked?
10 Now whenever it fits my plan,
I will attack you, too.
I will call out the armies of the nations
to punish you for your multiplied sins.

11 "Israel is like a trained heifer treading
out the grain—
an easy job she loves.
But I will put a heavy yoke on her
tender neck.

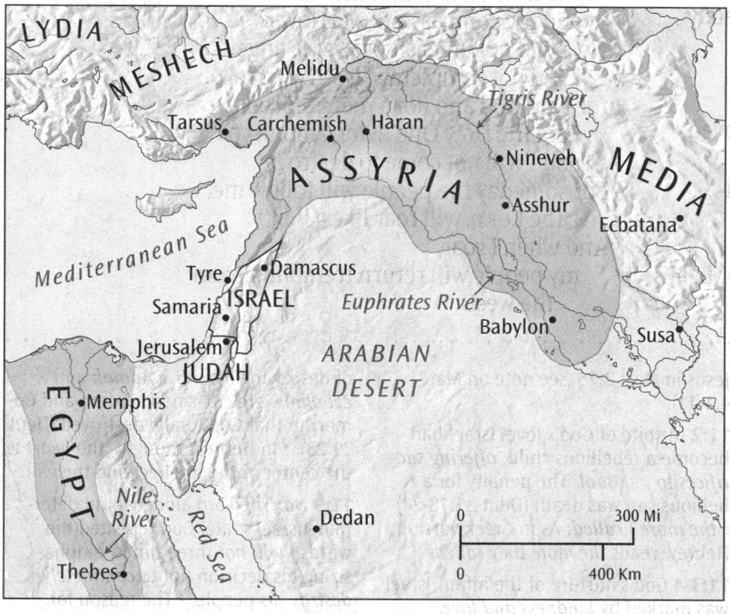

◀ **The Near East in Hosea's Time (9:1-17).** At the beginning of Hosea's ministry, ISRAEL and JUDAH were independent kingdoms, but the powers of ASSYRIA and EGYPT were a concern (9:6). After Jeroboam II died in 753 BC, the kingdom of Israel lost its security and independence and was finally destroyed by the Assyrians in 722 BC.

acceptable memorials (Gen 35:20; Josh 24:26-27), but God prohibited the Israelites from using them in worship as the Canaanites did (Exod 23:24; Deut 16:22).

10:3 ***We have no king:*** Some interpreters see these words as an acknowledgement, after the destruction of Israel, that they had been punished and the monarchy had come to an end because they ***didn't fear the LORD*** (see "Fear of the LORD" at Prov 1:7, p. 1030). Others regard this as the Israelites' arrogant rejection of the Lord's kingship.

10:4 The perversion of justice is like bitter, ***poisonous weeds*** (Amos 6:12).

10:5-6 Israel's gold ***calf idol*** (see 8:5-6) would become a prize of war for the invading Assyrians. • ***Beth-aven*** means "house of wickedness"; it is being used as another name for Bethel, which means "house of God." • ***will be stripped away:*** Or *will be taken away into exile.*

10:8 *Aven* is a reference to Beth-aven; see 10:5a and the note there. • The only response of Israelites who survived the coming catastrophe would be to implore the mountains and hills, ***"Bury us! . . . Fall on us!"*** See Luke 23:30.

10:9-10 The horrible events at ***Gibeah*** (Judg 19–21) set the pattern of sin for the people of the northern kingdom of Israel (see 9:9). God's punishment was that they would be overwhelmingly defeated in war, just as in the time of the Judges (see Judg 2:10-15).

10:11 Because ***Israel*** (Hebrew *Ephraim,* referring to the northern kingdom of Israel) was not faithful to the covenant, the Lord placed on her ***a heavy yoke***—the divine correction required to bring her back to him. • ***and Israel:*** Literally *and Jacob.* The names "Jacob" and "Israel" are often interchanged throughout the Old Testament, referring sometimes to the individual patriarch and sometimes to the nation.

I will force Judah to pull the plow
and Israel to break up the hard ground.
12 I said, 'Plant the good seeds of righteousness,
and you will harvest a crop of love.
Plow up the hard ground of your hearts,
for now is the time to seek the LORD,
that he may come
and shower righteousness upon you.'
13 "But you have cultivated wickedness
and harvested a thriving crop of sins.
You have eaten the fruit of lies—
trusting in your military might,
believing that great armies
could make your nation safe.
14 Now the terrors of war
will rise among your people.
All your fortifications will fall,
just as when Shalman destroyed Beth-arbel.
Even mothers and children
were dashed to death there.
15 You will share that fate, Bethel,
because of your great wickedness.
When the day of judgment dawns,
the king of Israel will be completely destroyed.

The LORD's Love for Israel

11 "When Israel was a child, I loved him,
and I called my son out of Egypt.
2 But the more I called to him,
the farther he moved from me,
offering sacrifices to the images of Baal
and burning incense to idols.
3 I myself taught Israel how to walk,
leading him along by the hand.
But he doesn't know or even care
that it was I who took care of him.
4 I led Israel along
with my ropes of kindness and love.
I lifted the yoke from his neck,
and I myself stooped to feed him.

5 "But since my people refuse to return to me,
they will return to Egypt
and will be forced to serve Assyria.
6 War will swirl through their cities;
their enemies will crash through their gates.
They will destroy them,
trapping them in their own evil plans.
7 For my people are determined to desert me.
They call me the Most High,
but they don't truly honor me.

8 "Oh, how can I give you up, Israel?
How can I let you go?
How can I destroy you like Admah
or demolish you like Zeboiim?
My heart is torn within me,
and my compassion overflows.
9 No, I will not unleash my fierce anger.
I will not completely destroy Israel,
for I am God and not a mere mortal.
I am the Holy One living among you,
and I will not come to destroy.
10 For someday the people will follow me.
I, the LORD, will roar like a lion.
And when I roar,
my people will return trembling from the west.

10:12 Prov 11:18; Isa 45:8
10:13 Ps 33:16; Gal 6:7-8
10:14 2 Kgs 17:3
11:1 Exod 4:22; Hos 2:15; 12:9, 13; 13:4; *Matt 2:15
11:2 Judg 10:6; 2 Kgs 17:13-15; Isa 65:7; Jer 18:15; Hos 2:13; 13:1-2
11:3 Deut 1:31; Jer 30:17
11:4 Exod 16:32; Ps 78:25; Jer 31:2-3
11:6 Hos 13:16
11:7 Jer 8:5
11:8 Gen 14:8; Deut 29:23; Hos 6:4; 7:1; Matt 23:37
11:9 Deut 13:17; Isa 5:24; 12:6; 41:14; Jer 26:3
11:10 Isa 31:4; 66:2, 5; Hos 3:5; 6:1-3; Joel 3:16; Amos 1:2; 3:4

10:12 Using metaphors from agriculture, God set forth his requirements for his people and a promise of blessing if they did what he commanded (see 6:6; 8:7). Even as Hosea announced God's judgment, he offered Israel the chance to repent and receive God's blessing.

10:14 ***When Shalman destroyed Beth-arbel:*** This event is not mentioned elsewhere in the Bible or in other available sources, but it was evidently well known to Hosea's audience.

11:1-11 God agonized over Israel's unfaithfulness. Despite all he had done, Israel had become a rebel. Justice required severe punishment, but the final sentence for Israel would be determined by God's tender compassion for his people, not by an abstract principle.

11:1 ***my son:*** The Lord adopted Israel when he delivered him ***out of Egypt.*** This verse is quoted in reference to Jesus in Matt 2:15 (see note on Matt 4:1-11).

11:2 In spite of God's love, Israel had become a rebellious child, ***offering sacrifices to . . . Baal.*** The penalty for a rebellious son was death (Deut 21:18-21). • ***the more I called:*** As in Greek version; Hebrew reads *the more they called.*

11:3-4 God's nurture of the infant Israel was marked by ***kindness and love.***

11:3 ***Israel:*** Hebrew *Ephraim,* referring to the northern kingdom of Israel; also in 11:8, 9, 12.

11:5-7 Because the Israelites had refused to return to the Lord, ***they*** would ***return to Egypt and . . . serve Assyria.*** Their past bondage in Egypt was a symbol for their coming exile in Assyria.

11:8 Though justice demanded Israel's death, the Lord recoiled at the thought of giving Israel up, of letting them go, of destroying his son. • ***Admah*** and ***Zeboiim*** were cities near Sodom and Gomorrah that God totally destroyed (Deut 29:23). • In Hebrew thought, the ***heart*** is the center of the intellect and the will.

11:9 ***No:*** The Lord alone would determine Israel's fate. God repeated the words ***I will not*** three times, emphasizing his decision not to ***completely destroy*** his people. • The reason for the divine decision is, ***I am the Holy One living among you.*** God's holiness distinguishes him from every created thing (see "God's Absolute Holiness" at Lev 10:3, p. 210). An offended ***mortal*** might very well destroy a rebel out of pique and spite. The Holy One does not operate out of those motives.

11:10-11 Israel's sin would not have the final word; God, in his holy love, would ***roar like a lion*** (see Amos 1:2; 3:8) to call his people ***home*** from exile.

11:11
Isa 11:11; 60:8
Ezek 28:25-26
Hos 7:11

12:1
Gen 41:6
Jer 22:22
Ezek 17:10

12:2
Hos 4:1
Mic 6:2

12:3
Gen 25:22-26

12:4
Gen 28:13-19; 32:24-30; 35:9-15

12:5
Exod 3:15

12:6
Mic 7:7

12:7
Prov 11:1
Amos 8:5
Mic 6:11

12:8
Hos 13:6
Rev 3:17

12:9
Lev 23:42

12:10
2 Kgs 17:13
Ezek 17:2; 20:49
Heb 1:1
[j]*khazon* (2377)
‣Hab 2:2

12:12
Gen 28:5; 29:20

12:13
Exod 14:19-22
Isa 63:11-12

11 Like a flock of birds, they will come
from Egypt.
Trembling like doves, they will return
from Assyria.
And I will bring them home again,"
says the LORD.

Charges against Israel and Judah

12 Israel surrounds me with lies and
deceit,
but Judah still obeys God
and is faithful to the Holy One.

12 The people of Israel feed on the
wind;
they chase after the east wind all day
long.
They pile up lies and violence;
they are making an alliance with
Assyria
while sending olive oil to buy support
from Egypt.
2 Now the LORD is bringing charges
against Judah.
He is about to punish Jacob for all his
deceitful ways,
and pay him back for all he has done.
3 Even in the womb,
Jacob struggled with his brother;
when he became a man,
he even fought with God.
4 Yes, he wrestled with the angel and
won.
He wept and pleaded for a blessing
from him.
There at Bethel he met God face to
face,
and God spoke to him—
5 the LORD God of Heaven's Armies,
the LORD is his name!
6 So now, come back to your God.
Act with love and justice,
and always depend on him.

7 But no, the people are like crafty
merchants
selling from dishonest scales—
they love to cheat.
8 Israel boasts, "I am rich!
I've made a fortune all by myself!
No one has caught me cheating!
My record is spotless!"

9 "But I am the LORD your God,
who rescued you from slavery in
Egypt.
And I will make you live in tents again,
as you do each year at the Festival of
Shelters.
10 I sent my prophets to warn you
with many [j]visions and parables."
11 But the people of Gilead are
worthless
because of their idol worship.
And in Gilgal, too, they sacrifice bulls;
their altars are lined up like the heaps
of stone
along the edges of a plowed field.
12 Jacob fled to the land of Aram,
and there he earned a wife by tending
sheep.
13 Then by a prophet
the LORD brought Jacob's descendants
out of Egypt;
and by that prophet
they were protected.

11:12–12:14 Israel had perpetrated *lies and deceit* since the time of Jacob.

11:12 Verse 11:12 is numbered 12:1 in Hebrew text. • ***but Judah still obeys God and is faithful to the Holy One:*** Or *and Judah is unruly against God, the faithful Holy One.* The meaning of the Hebrew is uncertain.

12:1-14 Verses 12:1-14 are numbered 12:2-15 in Hebrew text.

12:1 ***Israel:*** Hebrew *Ephraim,* referring to the northern kingdom of Israel; also in 12:8, 14. • ***alliance with Assyria:*** In order to save his land, Hoshea became a vassal of King Shalmaneser of Assyria (2 Kgs 17:3). Hoshea soon rebelled against Shalmaneser by withholding tribute and turned to King So of ***Egypt*** for ***support*** (2 Kgs 17:4). • ***east wind:*** See note on Job 38:24-27.

12:2 ***Jacob*** sounds like the Hebrew word for "deceiver."

12:3 ***Jacob struggled with his brother*** (literally *he supplanted his brother*): This verb (Hebrew *'aqab*) forms the root of Jacob's name. Even before he was born, Jacob acted out the meaning of his name by supplanting his brother Esau (Gen 25:26). • As an adult, Jacob ***even fought with God*** (see Gen 32:22-30) and was renamed "Israel," meaning "God fights."

12:4 ***at Bethel he met God:*** See Gen 28:11-22. • ***to him:*** As in Greek and Syriac versions; Hebrew reads *to us.*

12:6 The Lord admonished Israel to live no longer as Jacob did, but to return to God and ***act with love and justice.***

12:7-8 During the reign of Jeroboam II (793–753 BC), Israelite ***merchants*** became fabulously wealthy, often by using deceitful business practices like ***dishonest scales*** (see Amos 8:5-6). • The Hebrew term translated ***merchants*** is *kena'an* ("Canaan"). Canaanite traders were notorious in the ancient world for their crafty dealings. The Israelites had imitated their pagan neighbors not only in religion, but also in commerce.

12:9 ***I will make you live in tents again:*** God's judgment on the wealthy Israelite merchants was for them to return to the humble dwellings of the Exodus. There is also a word of hope here: God's plan of salvation for Israel would begin anew in the wilderness (see 2:14-15). • ***as you do each year at the Festival of Shelters:*** Literally *as in the days of your appointed feast.*

12:11 ***Gilead*** and ***Gilgal*** were Israelite cities in which Baal was worshiped instead of the Lord (see 4:15; 6:8; 9:15).

12:12 ***he:*** Literally *Israel.* See note on 10:11.

12:13 ***by a prophet:*** Moses' faithful obedience to God contrasts with Israel's disobedience. • ***brought Jacob's descendants:*** Literally *brought Israel.* See note on 10:11.

14 But the people of Israel
have bitterly provoked the LORD,
so their Lord will now sentence them to death
in payment for their sins.

The LORD's Anger against Israel

13 When the tribe of Ephraim spoke,
the people shook with fear,
for that tribe was important in Israel.
But the people of Ephraim sinned by worshiping Baal
and thus sealed their destruction.
2 Now they continue to sin by making silver idols,
images shaped skillfully with human hands.
"[k]Sacrifice to these," they cry,
"and kiss the calf idols!"
3 Therefore, they will disappear like the morning mist,
like dew in the morning sun,
like chaff blown by the wind,
like smoke from a chimney.

4 "I have been the LORD your God
ever since I brought you out of Egypt.
You must acknowledge no God but me,
for there is no other savior.
5 I took care of you in the wilderness,
in that dry and thirsty land.
6 But when you had eaten and were satisfied,
you became proud and forgot me.
7 So now I will attack you like a lion,
like a leopard that lurks along the road.
8 Like a bear whose cubs have been taken away,
I will tear out your heart.
I will devour you like a hungry lioness
and mangle you like a wild animal.

9 "You are about to be destroyed, O Israel—
yes, by me, your only helper.
10 Now where is your king?
Let him save you!
Where are all the leaders of the land,
the king and the officials you demanded of me?
11 In my anger I gave you kings,
and in my fury I took them away.

12 "Ephraim's guilt has been collected,
and his sin has been stored up for punishment.
13 Pain has come to the people
like the pain of childbirth,
but they are like a child
who resists being born.
The moment of birth has arrived,
but they stay in the womb!
14 "Should I ransom them from the [a]grave?
Should I [b]redeem them from death?
O death, bring on your terrors!
O [a]grave, bring on your plagues!
For I will not take pity on them.
15 Ephraim was the most fruitful of all his brothers,
but the east wind—a blast from the LORD—
will arise in the desert.
All their flowing springs will run dry,
and all their wells will disappear.
Every precious thing they own
will be plundered and carried away.

12:14 2 Kgs 17:7-18; Ezek 18:10-13
13:1 Hos 2:8-17
13:2 Isa 44:17-20; 46:6; Jer 10:2-5; Hos 8:6; [k]*zabakh* (2076) ‣Mal 1:8
13:3 Ps 68:2; Isa 17:13; Dan 2:35; Hos 6:4
13:4 Exod 20:2-3; Isa 43:11; 45:21-22
13:5 Deut 2:7; 8:15; 32:10
13:6 Hos 2:13; 4:6; 8:14
13:8 Ps 50:22
13:10 2 Kgs 17:4; Hos 8:4
13:11 1 Sam 8:7; 1 Kgs 14:7-10; Hos 10:7
13:12 Deut 32:34-35; Rom 2:5
13:13 Mic 4:9-10
13:14 Isa 25:8; Ezek 37:12-13; 1 Cor 15:55; Phil 3:21; [a]*she'ol* (7585) ‣Jon 2:2; [b]*ga'al* (1350) ‣Mic 4:10

13:1 At the height of its power, ***the tribe of Ephraim*** evoked terror among other Israelites (see Isa 7:2). • ***and thus sealed their destruction*** (literally *and he* [Ephraim] *died*): Because of their idolatry, they had cut themselves off from the Lord, the only true source of life.

13:2 The Hebrew word translated *idols* is the same one used of the gold calf (Exod 32:4, 8; see also 10:5-6; Amos 5:5-6). • ***kiss the calf idols:*** The Canaanite religious rituals included kissing images of Baal (1 Kgs 19:18).

13:3 God's judgment on idolatrous Ephraim was that *they* would ***disappear*** (cp. note on 6:4). • ***Mist . . . dew . . . chaff*** and ***smoke*** signify impermanence.

13:4-5 ***there is no other savior:*** The Lord had proved this to Israel during the Exodus and the wilderness wandering.

13:6 ***you became proud and forgot me:*** They did not rely on the Lord for security, but on their kings, armies, and economic prosperity (see 2:13).

13:7-8 God had executed judgment on Israel through the Assyrian army, his instrument of punishment. The description of God's ***attack*** speaks of the Assyrians' cruelty to those they conquered.

13:9 ***me, your only helper:*** See Ps 70:5; 115:9; 121:2; 124:8. Israel's sin had turned their helper into their destroyer.

13:10 ***where is*** (as in Greek and Syriac versions and Latin Vulgate; Hebrew reads *I will be*) ***your king?*** When Hoshea's alliance with Egypt failed (see 12:1), he tried to make peace with Assyria, but he was captured and imprisoned (2 Kgs 17:4). The Israelites had relied on their armies and kings to save them rather than on the Lord, and now there was no one to save them.

13:11 Israel had crowned her kings without consulting the Lord, so now he would take them away in ***fury***.

13:12 God had carefully ***stored up*** the record of Israel's ***sin*** and ***guilt***. She could not escape her ***punishment***.

13:13 Israel was like a child in the womb ***who resists being born*** (literally *an unwise son*). Incredibly, Israel would rather ***stay in the womb*** than receive life from the Lord.

13:14 The term here translated ***the grave*** (Hebrew *Sheol*) refers to the realm of the dead (see Job 3:11-19; note on Job 7:9). The Lord is sovereign even over Sheol, and he could ***redeem*** Israel if he chose to. But he ***will not take pity*** on the Israelites, and he calls upon ***death*** to punish them. • Greek version of this couplet reads *O death, where is your punishment? / O grave* [Hades], *where is your sting?* Cp. 1 Cor 15:55.

13:15
Jer 51:36
Hos 10:1
13:16
2 Kgs 15:16
14:2
Mic 7:18-19
Heb 13:15
‘nasa’ (5375)
‣ Mic 7:18
14:3
Ps 10:14; 68:5
Mic 5:10
14:4
Isa 57:18
Zeph 3:17
14:5
Song 2:1
Matt 6:28
14:6
Ps 52:8
Jer 11:16
14:7
Ps 91:1-4
14:8
Isa 41:19
Hos 14:3
14:9
Ps 107:43
Isa 1:28; 26:7
Jer 9:12

16 The people of Samaria
must bear the consequences of their guilt
because they rebelled against their God.
They will be killed by an invading army,
their little ones dashed to death
against the ground,
their pregnant women ripped open by swords.”

Healing for the Repentant

14 Return, O Israel, to the LORD your God,
for your sins have brought you down.
2 Bring your confessions, and return to the LORD.
Say to him,
“Forgive all our sins and graciously receive us,
so that we may offer you our praises.
3 Assyria cannot save us,
nor can our warhorses.
Never again will we say to the idols we have made,
‘You are our gods.’
No, in you alone
do the orphans find mercy.”

4 The LORD says,
“Then I will heal you of your faithlessness;
my love will know no bounds,
for my anger will be gone forever.
5 I will be to Israel
like a refreshing dew from heaven.
Israel will blossom like the lily;
it will send roots deep into the soil
like the cedars in Lebanon.
6 Its branches will spread out like beautiful olive trees,
as fragrant as the cedars of Lebanon.
7 My people will again live under my shade.
They will flourish like grain and blossom like grapevines.
They will be as fragrant as the wines of Lebanon.

8 “O Israel, stay away from idols!
I am the one who answers your prayers and cares for you.
I am like a tree that is always green;
all your fruit comes from me.”

9 Let those who are wise understand these things.
Let those with discernment listen carefully.
The paths of the LORD are true and right,
and righteous people live by walking in them.
But in those paths sinners stumble and fall.

13:16 In 722 BC, Assyria captured *Samaria*, the capital of the northern kingdom (2 Kgs 17:5-6). Thousands died during the three-year siege, and thousands more were sent into exile. This was ***because they rebelled against their God.*** • The horrible practice of killing ***pregnant women*** is also mentioned in Amos 1:13 and 2 Kgs 15:16. • This verse is numbered 14:1 in the Hebrew text.

14:1-9 Destruction was not God’s last word to his covenant people. Although judgment must come, God’s healing, restoring grace is always more powerful than human sin. • These verses are numbered 14:2-10 in the Hebrew text.

14:2-3 Hosea composed a model prayer of confession to help his people return to the Lord. God’s prophets not only identified with God in his outrage over Israel’s rebellion; they also identified with the people in their broken condition (see also Dan 9:4-19). • ***Forgive all our sins:*** The Israelites should throw themselves upon God’s mercy and grace, freely acknowledging their many sins. • ***so that we may offer you our praises*** (as in Greek and Syriac versions, which read *may repay the fruit of our lips;* Hebrew reads *may repay the bulls of our lips*): Israel’s inclination was to offer animal sacrifices for sin, but the Lord had made it clear that sacrifices were not the solution (see 6:6). Israel should offer God genuine repentance.

14:3 The Israelites must renounce their dependence upon ***idols***, foreign alliances, and their own military strength. Although they were God’s own children (11:1), they made themselves ***orphans*** through their rebellion. When they sincerely and completely repented, they could again ***find mercy.***

14:4 ***Then I will heal you:*** Healing by God is the only solution for the disease of sin. The Lord heals all our diseases, both physical and spiritual (Ps 103:3).

14:5-7 Hosea describes the effect of God’s healing love on repentant Israel. God promises to provide the fertility that Israel had sought from the baals.

14:5 ***like a refreshing dew:*** In the semi-desert climate of Israel, dew was an important source of life-giving moisture (Gen 27:28; Deut 33:28). • ***it will send roots deep:*** When Israel lived in faithfulness to their covenant with the Lord, they would be solid and stable like the majestic ***cedars in Lebanon*** (Ps 92:12).

14:7 ***under my shade:*** A place of safety and relief (Ps 91:1; Isa 25:4).

14:8 Hosea exhorts ***Israel*** (Hebrew *Ephraim,* referring to the northern kingdom of Israel) one final time to ***stay away from idols.*** Their life comes only from the Lord; he is an evergreen ***tree*** that always bears ***fruit.***

14:9 This final verse commends Hosea’s words to ***wise*** and discerning believers of all generations.

THE BOOK OF

JOEL

When disaster strikes, we usually respond in one of two ways. We either turn to God and enter a new relationship with him shaped by a fuller understanding of his nature and character, or we turn away from God and blame him or others for our troubles. Some even deny God's existence. The people of ancient Israel experienced disaster and were faced with this same decision. Would they turn away from God in their time of trouble or turn to him and seek his blessings?

SETTING

Joel prophesied to the people of Judah and Jerusalem in the midst of a catastrophe that threatened their very existence. A locust plague of unprecedented proportions had struck the land. Millions of voracious insects arrived in wave after wave to consume every green plant—vegetable gardens, grain crops, grapevines, fruit trees, and even the grass upon which their sheep and goats grazed. In the face of such a disaster, all human and animal life was at risk. In the ancient world, there were no insecticides to kill the locusts, no stocks of non-perishable food for emergencies, and no relief agencies to bring in food supplies. Such a plague brought with it the specter of death for thousands upon thousands, especially the very young and the very old.

During such a perilous time, it was only natural that the people of Judah and Jerusalem would ask hard questions about the justice and mercy of God. *Is God truly in charge of heaven and earth? Is he sovereign? Is he good?* They also looked inward at their own sin and moral responsibility for the plague. *Has God sent the locust plague to punish us for our failure to live in right relationship with him? Will God be merciful to us? Do we have a future?* In response to such questions, the prophet Joel delivered the word of the Lord to his people.

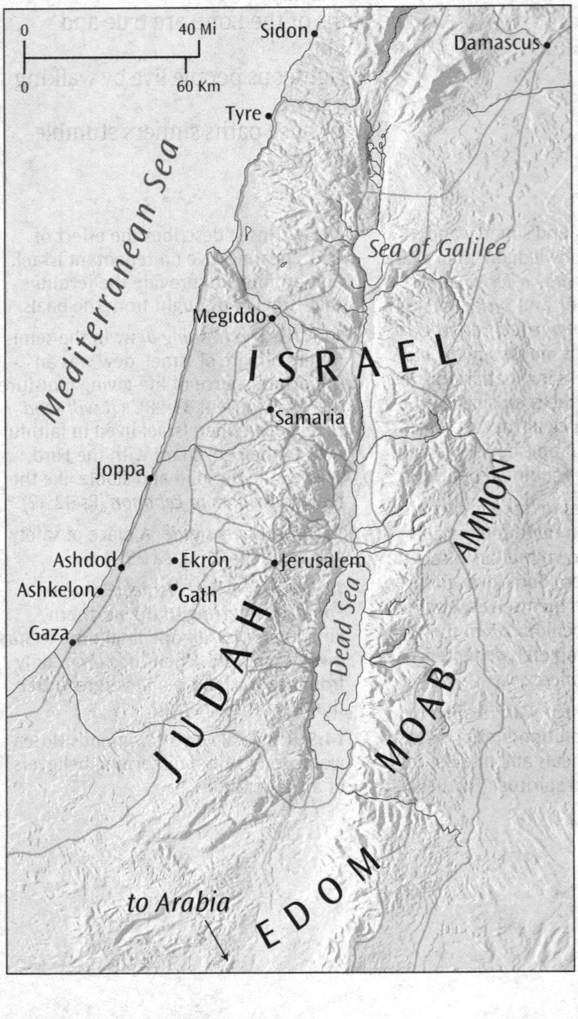

Setting of Joel. Joel might have prophesied during the reign of Jeroboam II (793–753 BC) or following the Exile (after 538 BC). The area around JUDAH is shown, along with places mentioned in 3:4-8.

SUMMARY

The book of Joel consists of two nearly equal parts. In the first section (1:1–2:17), the prophet describes the devastating locust plague that afflicted Judah and Jerusalem. The plague was so severe that it laid waste the entire land, destroying grains, vines, and trees. The effects of the plague were further compounded by a drought that left the land parched and burned. As a result, both humans and animals groaned with hunger, and the people had nothing left to bring to the Temple as an offering to the Lord. Therefore, in 2:12-17, Joel calls on the people to repent and throw themselves on the mercy of their compassionate God. (Other commentators have understood this passage as an apocalyptic description of the coming day of the Lord, using the language of a locust plague to describe an invading human army.)

In the second part of the book (2:18–3:21), the Lord promises to take pity on his people and restore their land following the locust plague. In 2:18-27, Joel describes how God will restore their material lives in the immediate future, replenishing their fields, orchards, vineyards, and flocks. In 2:28–3:21, Joel turns his attention to the more distant future when God will restore their spiritual lives. At that time, God will pour out his Spirit on all people who respond to him in faith. God will also render judgment on the peoples and nations that refuse to acknowledge his lordship.

OUTLINE

1:1
Superscription: Introducing the Prophet

1:1–2:17
A Devastating Locust Plague

2:18–3:21
Future Restoration and Hope

DATE OF WRITING

Not to know the time of Hosea would be to readers a great loss, for there are many parts which would not be explained without a knowledge of history; but as to Joel there is . . . less need of this; for the importance of his doctrine is evident, though his time be obscure and uncertain.

JOHN CALVIN, *Joel, Amos & Obadiah: A Commentary on the Minor Prophets*, vol. 2, p. xv

We do not know when the prophet Joel lived and prophesied. Unlike most of the prophetic books, his book does not list the kings under whom he ministered (see, e.g., Amos 1:1; Mic 1:1), nor does it provide any other clear historical information. For this reason, scholars have proposed many different dates for Joel.

In the Hebrew and English Bibles, Joel is placed between Hosea and Amos, who prophesied during the 700s BC. This has led some to propose that Joel was an early prophet who may have lived even before Amos and Hosea. Because the book makes no mention of a king and regards the priesthood favorably, these interpreters believe that Joel prophesied while Joash (835–796 BC) was still a child, when the kingdom was under the oversight of Jehoiada the priest (see 2:17; 2 Kgs 12).

On the other hand, when these considerations are coupled with others,

TIMELINE

835–796 BC
Joash (Jehoash) as king of Judah

about 760~750 BC
Amos as prophet

about 760~722 BC
Hosea as prophet

about 740~685 BC
Isaiah as prophet

722 BC
Assyria destroys Samaria, end of the northern kingdom of Israel

about 627~580 BC
Jeremiah as prophet

586 BC
Nebuchadnezzar destroys Jerusalem, takes people of Judah into exile, end of the southern kingdom of Judah

586~538 BC
Exile in Babylon

538 BC
Cyrus's decree allows exiles to return to Judea

Aug 29–Dec 18, 520 BC
Haggai as prophet

Nov 520–Dec 7, 518 BC
Zechariah as prophet

515 BC
Temple rebuilding is completed

458 BC
Ezra travels to Jerusalem

445–433 BC
Nehemiah as governor of Judea

about 400 BC
1–2 Chronicles is written

The two great themes of Joel encompass the two major poles of the gospel. First, Joel announces God's very real judgment on human sin, a judgment that concerns the whole world of nature and nations. Second, however, Joel proclaims the merciful grace of God, who will not give over his covenant people and his creation to final destruction. In proclaiming this message, the prophecies of Joel are never out-of-date.

ELIZABETH ACHTEMEIER
Minor Prophets I

they seem to point to a much later date for Joel. Joel never refers to the northern kingdom of Israel or to its capital city, Samaria, suggesting that the prophet lived after their destruction in 722 BC. Likewise, Joel never mentions Assyria or Babylon, Israel's great enemies from the 700s to 500s BC, leading many to argue that these two empires were already long past for Joel. Because the monarchy ended with the Exile in 586 BC, many scholars see this as an indication that Joel lived after the Jewish people began returning to their own land in 538 BC.

Finally, there are numerous passages in which Joel could be seen as drawing upon or directly quoting the words and ideas of prophets such as Amos, Zephaniah, Obadiah, and Ezekiel. Although it is possible that Joel ministered before these prophets and that they were the ones who borrowed from him (see notes on Amos 1:2; 9:13), it is also possible that Joel adapted the earlier prophetic words to speak God's word to people who faced an entirely new situation.

These observations do not prove that Joel lived and prophesied after the Exile, but they are convincing enough that the majority of biblical scholars accept a postexilic date. Fortunately, knowing the exact time in history that Joel prophesied is less important in his case than it is for other prophets. Joel's message concerns issues that are relevant to every age.

MEANING AND MESSAGE

Throughout the book of Joel, we clearly see God's sovereignty over all creation. He is Lord of both the natural world and human civilization. The locust plague was not merely a natural event; the army of insects came at God's command (2:11). The Lord controls rain and drought, fertility and famine, blessing and destruction. All peoples, both Israelites and non-Israelites, are subject to his sovereign judgment, but divine sovereignty does not negate human responsibility. Because human sin has so negatively affected the natural world, Joel calls the people of Judah and Jerusalem to repentance.

Joel can offer the Israelites the opportunity to repent because he knows that God is merciful and compassionate. It is God's nature to forgive those who repent rather than to judge them, to restore rather than to destroy. Quoting an ancient text (Exod 34:6-7), Joel extends God's gracious invitation to the Israelites: "Return to the LORD your God, for he is merciful and compassionate, slow to get angry and filled with unfailing love" (2:13).

For Joel, the proper way to express repentance was through the official Temple worship presided over by the priests. This may seem surprising because several earlier prophets had denounced the official worship because of widespread corruption among the priests and leaders (see Amos 5:21-24; Isa 1:10-18), but Joel recognized the value in worship when it is performed with a sincere heart that is fully open to God (an attitude characteristic of postexilic prophets—see Haggai, Zechariah, and Malachi). In worship, invisible eternal realities are represented by physical objects and actions. However, the prophet reminds the Israelites that religion is much more than outward display; true worship is founded on inward transformation (2:13). The solution to corrupt worship is not to abandon worship, but to worship God in spirit and in truth (John 4:23-24).

FURTHER READING

ELIZABETH ACHTEMEIER
Minor Prophets I (1996)

LESLIE C. ALLEN
The Books of Joel, Obadiah, Jonah and Micah (1976)

DAVID W. BAKER
Joel, Obadiah, Malachi (2006)

To a people who faced disaster, Joel brought the message that their God was fully in control of the future. He assured them that on the day of the Lord (1:15; 2:1; see "The Day of the LORD" at 2:1-32, p. 1445), God would intervene in the world to judge the wicked and to establish peace and justice. Then he will pour out his Spirit on every class, gender, and age, making it possible for his people to live in accord with his law. The wrongs that all too often dominate our fallen world will only be righted when God fully and finally comes into his creation (2:28–3:21; see Matt 16:27; Acts 2:16-40; Col 2:13-22; Rev 21:1–22:21).

JAMES L. CRENSHAW
Joel (1995)

DAVID A. HUBBARD
Joel and Amos (1989)

DOUGLAS STUART
Hosea—Jonah (1987)

RICHARD PATTERSON
Joel in *Cornerstone Biblical Commentary*, vol. 10 (2008)

1:1 Jer 1:2; Acts 2:16
1:2 Jer 30:7; Joel 2:2, 16
1:3 Exod 10:2
1:4 Deut 28:38-39; Isa 33:4; Joel 2:25; Nah 3:15-16; a'arbeh (0697) ›Joel 2:25
1:5 Joel 3:3
1:6 Joel 2:2, 11; Rev 9:8
1:7 Isa 5:6; Amos 4:9
1:9 Joel 1:13; 2:14
1:10 Isa 24:4, 7
1:11 Amos 5:16

1. SUPERSCRIPTION: INTRODUCING THE PROPHET (1:1)

1 The LORD gave this message to Joel son of Pethuel.

2. A DEVASTATING LOCUST PLAGUE (1:2–2:17)

Mourning over the Locust Plague

2 Hear this, you leaders of the people.
Listen, all who live in the land.
In all your history,
has anything like this happened before?
3 Tell your children about it in the years to come,
and let your children tell their children.
Pass the story down from generation to generation.
4 After the cutting locusts finished eating the crops,
the swarming [a]locusts took what was left!
After [a]them came the hopping locusts,
and then the stripping locusts, too!
5 Wake up, you drunkards, and weep!
Wail, all you wine-drinkers!
All the grapes are ruined,
and all your sweet wine is gone.
6 A vast army of locusts has invaded my land,
a terrible army too numerous to count.
Its teeth are like lions' teeth,
its fangs like those of a lioness.
7 It has destroyed my grapevines
and ruined my fig trees,
stripping their bark and destroying it,
leaving the branches white and bare.
8 Weep like a bride dressed in black,
mourning the death of her husband.
9 For there is no grain or wine
to offer at the Temple of the LORD.
So the priests are in mourning.
The ministers of the LORD are weeping.
10 The fields are ruined,
the land is stripped bare.
The grain is destroyed,
the grapes have shriveled,
and the olive oil is gone.
11 Despair, all you farmers!
Wail, all you vine growers!
Weep, because the wheat and barley—
all the crops of the field—are ruined.

1:1–2:17 Joel describes the devastating locust plague that afflicted Judah and Jerusalem.

1:1 ***The LORD gave this message*** (literally *The word of the LORD came*): The LORD, not the human prophet, was the ultimate source of these words. • The name ***Joel*** means "the LORD [Yahweh] is God." Joel's father, ***Pethuel***, is unknown apart from this verse.

1:2 ***Hear this:*** Joel summoned the inhabitants of the land to pay close attention to the prophetic word. • ***Leaders*** (literally *elders*): The prophet asked the community elders, ***has anything like this happened before?*** It hadn't—this disaster was unique in the history of God's people.

1:3 God's people would ***tell*** future generations about what was taking place so that their descendants would benefit from the lessons they had learned (cp. Deut 4:9; 6:20-25).

1:4 The disaster that had befallen Judah was a catastrophic plague of ***locusts***. The precise identification of the four kinds of *locusts* mentioned here is uncertain. Some commentators have understood the words to represent four ancient empires that conquered Israel. Others have suggested that the words indicate four stages in the development of locusts. Most likely, the prophet was using multiple terms to emphasize the extent of the destruction wrought by wave after wave of the voracious insects.

1:5 ***Wake up . . . Wail:*** The prophet sought to arouse the people and alert them to the gravity of the locust plague.

1:6 ***A vast army of locusts:*** Literally *A nation.*

1:7 The destructive power of locusts is well documented in both ancient and modern times. The insatiable insects consume annual crops such as grains and vegetables, and they destroy perennial fruit-bearing trees and vines, ***leaving the branches white and bare.***

1:8 ***Weep like a bride*** (literally *a virgin*): Judah is compared to a young betrothed woman whose marriage is never consummated due to ***the death of her husband.***

1:9 The locust plague threatened the people of Judah with starvation and brought the regular daily animal sacrifices and offerings of ***grain*** and ***wine*** at ***the Temple*** in Jerusalem to a halt (cp. Exod 29:38-41; Num 28:2-8).

1:10 The locusts destroyed the three essential staple crops of ancient Israel: ***grain, grapes,*** and ***olive oil.***

12 The grapevines have dried up,
and the fig trees have withered.
The pomegranate trees, palm trees, and
apple trees—
all the fruit trees—have dried up.
And the people's joy has dried up with
them.
13 Dress yourselves in burlap and weep, you
priests!
Wail, you who serve before the altar!
Come, spend the night in burlap,
you ministers of my God.
For there is no grain or wine
to offer at the Temple of your God.
14 Announce a time of fasting;
call the people together for a solemn
meeting.
Bring the leaders
and all the people of the land
into the Temple of the LORD your God,
and cry out to him there.
15 The day of the LORD is near,
the day when destruction comes from
the [b]Almighty.
How terrible that day will be!
16 Our food disappears before our very
eyes.
No joyful celebrations are held in the
house of our God.
17 The seeds die in the parched ground,
and the grain crops fail.
The barns stand empty,
and granaries are abandoned.
18 How the animals moan with hunger!
The herds of cattle wander about
confused,
because they have no pasture.
The flocks of sheep and goats bleat in
misery.
19 LORD, help us!
The fire has consumed the wilderness
pastures,
and flames have burned up all the
trees.
20 Even the wild animals cry out to you
because the streams have dried up,
and fire has consumed the wilderness
pastures.

Locusts Invade like an Army

2 1 Sound the alarm in Jerusalem!
Raise the battle cry on my holy
mountain!
Let everyone tremble in fear
because the day of the LORD is upon us.
2 It is a day of darkness and gloom,
a day of thick clouds and deep
blackness.
Suddenly, like dawn spreading across
the mountains,
a great and mighty army appears.
Nothing like it has been seen before
or will ever be seen again.
3 Fire burns in front of them,
and flames follow after them.
Ahead of them the land lies
as beautiful as the Garden of Eden.

1:12 Song 2:3; Hab 3:17-18; Hag 2:19
1:13 1 Kgs 21:27; Jer 4:8
1:14 Jon 3:8
1:15 Isa 13:9; Jer 30:7; Ezek 7:2-13; Joel 2:1; [b]*shadday* (7706) ›Gen 17:1
1:16 Isa 3:7; Amos 4:6-7
1:17 Isa 17:10-11
1:19 Ps 50:15; 91:15; Mic 7:7
1:20 1 Kgs 17:7; 18:5; Ps 104:21; Joel 1:18
2:1 Joel 1:15; 2:11, 15, 31; 3:14; Zeph 1:16
2:2 Dan 9:12; Joel 1:2, 6; 2:5, 10-11, 31
2:3 Gen 2:8; Ps 105:34-35; Isa 51:3

1:12 Drought had intensified the devastation of the locust plague; everything had *withered* and *dried up* (see also 1:19-20). Spiritually, *the people's joy* had *dried up* along with *the fruit trees.*

1:13-14 The *priests* were to lead *all the people* in public rites of mourning at *the Temple*. Their outward actions must be matched by authentic inward change (see 2:13).

1:15 The locust plague was not simply a natural event, but a sign that *the day of the LORD* was near. Beginning with Amos in the 700s BC (Amos 5:18), the prophets had spoken of a future time when God would intervene in human history to judge the wicked and vindicate the righteous. • *destruction . . . from the Almighty:* The Hebrew text highlights the similar sounds of the word *destruction* (*shod*) and the title *the Almighty* (*shadday*).

1:17 Plague and drought had so reduced the food supply that *the barns* stood *empty*.

1:18 The inhabitants of Judah were hard pressed by the famine; even *sheep and goats*, animals that can live on very meager forage, *bleat in misery* for lack of food.

1:19 *LORD, help us!* (literally *to you, LORD, I cry*): Joel responded to the plague with an earnest prayer. The people's only recourse was to turn to the sovereign Lord of heaven and earth and appeal to his goodness; he alone could reverse their desperate situation.

1:20 All creation suffers because of human sin (Gen 3:17-18; 9:2; Rom 8:20-21)—*even the wild animals cry out* to God. The Hebrew word translated "cry out" is the same word used in Ps 42:1 of the deer that "longs" for streams of water. The beasts, urgently requiring their food and drink, set an example of how the people of Judah and Jerusalem should seek their Lord (cp. Isa 1:3).

2:1-11 Some regard this section as a second account of the locust plague described in ch 1, but in ch 1, the plague is in the past, whereas in this section, the verb tenses seem to depict it as a future event. Thus, others see it as a warning of yet another locust plague. Still other commentators have understood this passage as an apocalyptic description of the coming *day of the LORD,* using the language of a locust plague to describe an invading human army.

2:1 When an ancient city was attacked, the watchmen on the city wall would *sound the alarm* by blowing on a ram's horn, the *shofar* (see also 2:15), to call all the defenders to repel the enemy. • *Jerusalem:* Hebrew *Zion;* also in 2:15, 23.

2:2 Some religious leaders had taught the people of Jerusalem and Judah that the day of the Lord would be a time of blessing for God's people. Echoing the prophet Zephaniah (Zeph 1:15), Joel proclaimed that it would instead be *a day of darkness and gloom* (see also Amos 5:18-20).

2:3 The destruction wrought by the invading army would be like a raging wildfire. Before the attack, the land looked like *the Garden of Eden*, but afterwards, it would be *nothing but desolation* (a reversal of Isa 51:3 and Ezek 36:35).

2:4 Rev 9:7
2:5 Isa 5:24; 30:30 Rev 9:9
2:6 Isa 13:8 Jer 30:6
2:7 Isa 5:26-29
2:9 Exod 10:6 Jer 9:21 John 10:1
2:10 Ps 18:7 Isa 13:10 Joel 2:31; 3:15 Nah 1:5 Matt 24:29; 27:51 *Mark 13:24-25
2:11 Ps 46:6 Joel 2:1; 3:16
2:12 Deut 4:29-30

Behind them is nothing but desolation;
not one thing escapes.
4 They look like horses;
they charge forward like warhorses.
5 Look at them as they leap along the
mountaintops.
Listen to the noise they make—like
the rumbling of chariots,
like the roar of fire sweeping across a
field of stubble,
or like a mighty army moving into battle.

6 Fear grips all the people;
every face grows pale with terror.
7 The attackers march like warriors
and scale city walls like soldiers.
Straight forward they march,
never breaking rank.
8 They never jostle each other;
each moves in exactly the right position.
They break through defenses
without missing a step.
9 They swarm over the city
and run along its walls.
They enter all the houses,
climbing like thieves through the
windows.
10 The earth quakes as they advance,
and the heavens tremble.
The sun and moon grow dark,
and the stars no longer shine.
11 The LORD is at the head of the column.
He leads them with a shout.
This is his mighty army,
and they follow his orders.
The day of the LORD is an awesome,
terrible thing.
Who can possibly survive?

A Call to Repentance

12 That is why the LORD says,
"Turn to me now, while there is time.
Give me your hearts.

The Day of the LORD (2:1-32)

Joel 1:15; 3:14-16
Isa 13:6-13
Jer 46:10
Ezek 30:1-5
Amos 5:18-20
Zeph 1:14-18; 2:1-3
Zech 14:1-21
Mal 4:5-6
Acts 2:17-21
1 Thes 5:1-4
2 Pet 3:3-14

The day of the Lord is a central concept in the book of Joel. The term *day of the LORD* first appeared in the prophecy of Amos (Amos 5:18), but it did not originate with him. Amos was correcting a popular misunderstanding that the Israelites already held. They believed that the day of the Lord would be a joyous day of salvation when God would intervene in the world to judge Israel's enemies and reestablish Israelite rule over all of greater Canaan. Amos warned them that the day of the Lord would not be light for them, but darkness, for they were in rebellion against the Lord (e.g., Amos 5:10-12, 21-27). Self-confident Israelites assumed that God was always on their side, but their sins had, in fact, made them God's enemies, and they deserved his full punishment. A little over a century after Amos, Zephaniah said very similar things to the Judeans about the day of the Lord (e.g., Zeph 1:7-18). The theme became part of the standard vocabulary of the prophets, often being referred to simply as "that day" (Isa 2:11; 27:1; Jer 31:1; Hos 2:18; Mic 7:11; Zech 3:10).

Joel interpreted the locust plague much as Amos or Zephaniah would have done (see 1:7-9, 14-18). Joel saw the plague as a sign that the day of the Lord was near, and that God was judging the people of Judah and Jerusalem for their sins. Their only proper response was to gather in the Temple and repent. In the second half of the book, however, Joel foretold a day of the Lord yet to come. At that time, God would pour out his Spirit on Israel (2:28-32); he would restore his repentant people, vindicate them, and punish the nations that had oppressed them. In this way, Joel combines both understandings of the day of the Lord. It is a day of judgment for all who rebel against God, including sinful Israelites. But it is also a day of salvation for those who have listened to the words of the prophets and have turned to the Lord.

2:4-5 ***They look like horses:*** The resemblance between locusts and horses (see also Rev 9:7) heightens the image of the locusts as an army (see note on 2:1-11). • ***Listen to the noise they make:*** The noise made by a locust swarm can be deafening. • ***like warhorses:*** Or *like charioteers.*

2:6 ***Fear grips all the people:*** Anticipating the invasion prepared the people for the call to repentance in 2:12-14.

2:7-9 The locusts would invade urban as well as agricultural areas, advancing like a disciplined, well-trained army to ***scale city walls*** and ***swarm over the city.*** Finding every means of entrance, they would even climb ***like thieves through the windows.***

2:10 The quaking of the ***earth*** and the ***heavens*** is a typical sign of *theophany,* an appearance of God (see Exod 19:16-19; Isa 13:13; Nah 1:5-6). The darkening of ***the sun and moon*** symbolizes divine judgment (Isa 13:9-11).

2:11 ***The LORD is at the head of the column*** (literally *the LORD utters his voice before his army*): The coming destruction was not simply an act of nature or the result of human activity, but an act of God. • ***This is his mighty army:*** God executed this judgment. • ***Who can possibly survive?*** Apart from God's grace and mercy, no one can.

2:12-17 Joel calls on the people to repent and throw themselves on the mercy of their compassionate God.

2:12 This verse begins with the words ***the LORD says,*** a phrase that frequently accompanies divine speeches in the

Come with fasting, weeping, and
mourning.
13 Don't tear your clothing in your grief,
but tear your hearts instead."
Return to the LORD your God,
for he is merciful and
compassionate,
[c]slow to get angry and filled with
unfailing love.
He is eager to relent and not punish.
14 Who knows? Perhaps he will give you a
reprieve,
sending you a blessing instead of this
curse.
Perhaps you will be able to offer grain
and wine
to the LORD your God as before.

15 Blow the ram's horn in Jerusalem!
Announce a time of fasting;
call the people together
for a solemn meeting.
16 Gather all the [d]people—
the elders, the children, and even the
babies.
Call the bridegroom from his quarters
and the bride from her private room.
17 Let the [e]priests, who minister in the
LORD's presence,
stand and weep between the entry
room to the Temple and the altar.
Let them pray, "Spare your people,
LORD!
Don't let your special possession
become an object of mockery.
Don't let them become a joke for
unbelieving foreigners who say,
'Has the God of Israel left them?' "

3. FUTURE RESTORATION AND HOPE (2:18–3:21)

The LORD's Promise of Restoration

18 Then the LORD will pity his people
and [f]jealously guard the honor of his
land.
19 The LORD will reply,
"Look! I am sending you grain and new
wine and olive oil,
enough to satisfy your needs.
You will no longer be an object of
mockery
among the surrounding nations.
20 I will drive away these armies from the
north.
I will send them into the parched
wastelands.
Those in the front will be driven into the
Dead Sea,
and those at the rear into the
Mediterranean.
The stench of their rotting bodies will
rise over the land."

Surely the LORD has done great things!
21 Don't be afraid, my people.
Be glad now and rejoice,
for the LORD has done great things.
22 Don't be afraid, you animals of the field,
for the wilderness pastures will soon
be green.

2:13 Exod 34:6; Amos 7:2-6; [c]*'arek 'appayim* (0750, 0639) ‣Jon 4:2
2:14 Hag 2:19
2:15 Num 10:3; Joel 2:1
2:16 [d]*qahal* (6951) ‣Gen 28:3
2:17 Ps 44:13; 79:10; Isa 37:20; [e]*kohen* (3548) ‣Mic 3:11
2:18 Isa 60:10; Zech 1:14; [f]*qana'* (7065) ‣Zeph 1:18
2:19 Ezek 34:29; 36:15; Hos 2:21-22
2:20 Deut 11:24; Jer 1:14-15; Zech 14:8
2:22 Ps 65:12-13

prophets. This is the only time that it occurs in Joel ("says the LORD" in 3:1 is supplied by the translators), and it indicates that this gracious invitation came directly from God. • ***Turn to me now, while there is time:*** The Lord implored his people to repent because the day of judgment was near. There was still opportunity to avoid the coming destruction if they returned to the Lord their God with true repentance. • Unlike other prophets, Joel never catalogs the sins committed by the people of Judah and Jerusalem. Perhaps they were so obvious that he did not feel the need to list them.

2:13 One means of showing grief in the ancient world was to ***tear*** one's ***clothing*** (Gen 37:34; 2 Sam 3:31; 2 Kgs 19:1). • ***tear your hearts:*** In Hebrew, the heart is the center of thought, faith, and will. God's people were to go beyond external demonstrations of repentance to repent inwardly—to change their orientation, priorities, and attitudes. This could only happen if they would ***return to the LORD.*** • ***for he is merciful and compassionate . . . and filled with unfailing love:*** The people's only hope was in the merciful character of the Lord (see also Exod 34:6-7; Num 14:18; Neh 9:17; Ps 86:15; 103:8; 145:8; Jon 4:2). God's desire is not to punish, but to forgive and restore his people.

2:14 ***Who knows?*** Joel's simple question acknowledges God's absolute sovereignty (see also Jon 3:9). God is not obligated to restore us merely because we perform certain rituals. Forgiveness comes only through divine grace, but Joel knew that God was inclined to forgive (2:13).

2:15 Joel called for a ***time of fasting*** and ***a solemn meeting*** for the purpose of seeking God.

2:16 ***bridegroom . . . and the bride:*** Newlyweds were exempt from most civic duties in ancient Israel (Deut 24:5; Luke 14:20), but in this emergency, everyone would be summoned to the Temple to cry out to God.

2:17 ***Spare your people, LORD!*** Assembled at the Temple, the religious leaders and all the people were to do the only thing possible in their desperate situation: seek the mercy and compassion of God.

2:18–3:21 Up to this point, the book of Joel has focused on God's judgment upon Judah and Jerusalem, but from here on, it describes God's promise of restoration. If the people sincerely repent, God will respond graciously.

2:18-27 God promised to restore his people's material lives in the immediate future, replenishing their fields, orchards, vineyards, and flocks.

2:18 Since both ***people*** and ***land*** suffered from God's judgment, both would be the objects of his zealous compassion.

2:19-20 ***grain and new wine and olive oil:*** God would restore the fruits of the land. This would again make available the elements necessary for sacrifice and worship (see 1:10, 13). God would also eradicate the invading ***armies from the north.***

2:20 ***into the Dead Sea . . . into the Mediterranean:*** Literally *into the eastern sea, . . . into the western sea.*

2:21-22 ***Don't be afraid:*** God's great deliverance would be full and complete.

2:23 Ps 149:2; Hos 6:3; Zech 10:1
2:25 [g]'arbeh (0697) ›Nah 3:15
2:26 Ps 67:5-7; Isa 45:17
2:27 Lev 26:11-12; Isa 45:5-6, 18; Joel 3:17, 21
2:28-32 *Acts 2:17-21
2:29 1 Cor 12:13; Gal 3:28
2:30-31 Joel 2:1, 10; 3:15; Matt 24:29; Mark 13:24-25
2:32 Isa 4:2; *Rom 10:13
3:2 Isa 66:16, 18; Ezek 36:1-5; Joel 3:12, 14

The trees will again be filled with fruit;
fig trees and grapevines will be loaded down once more.
23 Rejoice, you people of Jerusalem!
Rejoice in the LORD your God!
For the rain he sends demonstrates his faithfulness.
Once more the autumn rains will come,
as well as the rains of spring.
24 The threshing floors will again be piled high with grain,
and the presses will overflow with new wine and olive oil.

25 The LORD says, "I will give you back what you lost
to the swarming [g]locusts, the hopping locusts,
the stripping locusts, and the cutting locusts.
It was I who sent this great destroying army against you.
26 Once again you will have all the food you want,
and you will praise the LORD your God,
who does these miracles for you.
Never again will my people be disgraced.
27 Then you will know that I am among my people Israel,
that I am the LORD your God, and there is no other.
Never again will my people be disgraced.

The LORD's Promise of His Spirit

28 "Then, after doing all those things,
I will pour out my Spirit upon all people.
Your sons and daughters will prophesy.
Your old men will dream dreams,
and your young men will see visions.
29 In those days I will pour out my Spirit
even on servants—men and women alike.
30 And I will cause wonders in the heavens and on the earth—
blood and fire and columns of smoke.
31 The sun will become dark,
and the moon will turn blood red
before that great and terrible day of the LORD arrives.
32 But everyone who calls on the name of the LORD
will be saved,
for some on Mount Zion in Jerusalem will escape,
just as the LORD has said.
These will be among the survivors
whom the LORD has called.

Judgment against Enemy Nations

3 1 "At the time of those events," says the LORD,
"when I restore the prosperity of Judah and Jerusalem,
2 I will gather the armies of the world
into the valley of Jehoshaphat.
There I will judge them
for harming my people, my special possession,

2:23 ***autumn rains . . . rains of spring:*** God would once again restore the regular pattern of rainfall, and the drought (1:12, 20) would be reversed.

2:25 The Lord promised restitution for the terrible damage done by the locusts (see 1:4, 10, and notes). • The precise identification of the four kinds of ***locusts*** mentioned here is uncertain.

2:26-27 ***and you will praise the LORD your God:*** God's promised restoration of their crops and food supply should lead the people of Judah and Jerusalem to praise and adoration, acknowledging that the Lord was in their midst and that he alone is God.

2:28–3:21 In the more distant future, God would restore his people's spiritual lives, pour out his Spirit on all people who respond to him in faith, and render judgment on the peoples and nations that refuse to acknowledge his lordship.

2:28-32 The prophet looked beyond his time to the future day of the Lord, when God would pour out his Spirit in ways never before seen and would perform signs and wonders for all humanity to see. The apostle Peter quoted this passage as being fulfilled on the day of Pentecost (Acts 2:16-21). • Verses 2:28-32 are numbered 3:1-5 in the Hebrew text.

2:28-29 ***I will pour out my Spirit upon all people:*** In Israel, the empowering gift of God's Spirit had previously been given only to select individuals such as judges (Judg 3:10; 15:14), priests (2 Chr 24:20), kings (1 Sam 10:10), and prophets (Isa 61:1). A time was coming when the Spirit would be given to every one of God's people, regardless of gender, age, or social position. In fulfillment of Moses' wish that every Israelite might be a prophet (Num 11:29), all would ***prophesy*** and ***see visions.*** In Acts 2, Peter expanded this promise to include people from all over the known world who were gathered in Jerusalem, regardless of their ethnicity (Acts 2:39; see also Gal 3:28).

2:30-31 The future outpouring of God's Spirit would be accompanied by signs and ***wonders. Blood and fire and . . . smoke,*** together with the darkening of the ***sun*** and the ***moon,*** are indications of God's coming in judgment (see 2:10; Mark 13:24; Rev 6:12).

2:31 ***terrible:*** Greek version reads *glorious.*

2:32 ***everyone who calls on the name of the LORD will be saved:*** Calling on the name of God should not be a final act of desperation; it accompanies a lifelong commitment of worship, service, and fellowship with the Lord (see Gen 12:8; Ps 105:1; Isa 12:4; Rom 10:13; 12:1-2). • Those ***whom the LORD has called*** are his chosen remnant, the ***survivors*** of judgment who worship him (see 2 Kgs 19:31; Ezra 9:8-15; Isa 10:20-22).

3:1-21 Verses 3:1-21 are numbered 4:1-21 in the Hebrew text.

3:1-16 Joel here foretold divine judgment on the nations, particularly those that had oppressed God's people.

3:2-3 The Lord would assemble the ***armies of the world*** (literally *all the*

for scattering my people among the
nations,
and for dividing up my land.
3 They threw dice to decide which of my
people
would be their slaves.
They traded boys to obtain prostitutes
and sold girls for enough wine to get
drunk.

4"What do you have against me, Tyre and
Sidon and you cities of Philistia? Are you trying to take revenge on me? If you are, then
watch out! I will strike swiftly and pay you
back for everything you have done. 5You
have taken my silver and gold and all my
precious treasures, and have carried them
off to your pagan temples. 6You have sold
the people of Judah and Jerusalem to the
Greeks, so they could take them far from
their homeland.
7"But I will bring them back from all the
places to which you sold them, and I will
pay you back for everything you have done.
8I will sell your sons and daughters to the
people of Judah, and they will sell them to
the people of Arabia, a nation far away. I,
the LORD, have spoken!"

9 Say to the nations far and wide:
"Get ready for war!
Call out your best warriors.
Let all your fighting men advance for
the attack.
10 Hammer your plowshares into swords
and your pruning hooks into spears.
Train even your weaklings to be
warriors.
11 Come quickly, all you nations everywhere.
Gather together in the valley."
And now, O LORD, call out your warriors!
12 "Let the nations be called to arms.
Let them march to the valley of
Jehoshaphat.
There I, the LORD, will sit
to pronounce judgment on them all.
13 Swing the sickle,
for the harvest is ripe.
Come, tread the grapes,
for the winepress is full.
The storage vats are overflowing
with the wickedness of these people."
14 Thousands upon thousands are waiting
in the valley of decision.
There the day of the LORD will soon
arrive.
15 The sun and moon will grow dark,
and the stars will no longer shine.
16 The LORD's voice will roar from Zion
and thunder from Jerusalem,
and the heavens and the earth will
shake.
But the LORD will be a refuge for his
people,
a strong fortress for the people of
Israel.

Blessings for God's People

17 "Then you will know that I, the LORD
your God,
live in Zion, my holy mountain.
Jerusalem will be holy forever,
and foreign armies will never conquer
her again.
18 In that day the mountains will drip with
sweet wine,
and the hills will flow with milk.
Water will fill the streambeds of Judah,

3:3 Obad 1:11; Nah 3:10
3:4 Ezek 25:15-17; 26:1-3
3:5 2 Kgs 12:18; 2 Chr 21:16-17
3:7 Isa 43:5-6; Jer 23:8
3:9 Isa 34:1; Jer 46:3; 51:27; Zech 14:2-3
3:10 Isa 2:4; Mic 4:3
3:12 Ps 76:8-9; Isa 3:13; Joel 3:2, 14
3:13 Hos 6:11; Matt 13:39; Mark 4:29; Rev 14:15-19
3:14 Isa 34:2-8; Joel 2:1; 3:2, 12
3:15 Joel 2:10, 31
3:16 Hos 11:10; Amos 1:2
3:17 Isa 11:9; Ezek 20:40
3:18 Exod 3:8; Amos 9:13

nations) in the *valley of Jehoshaphat* (*Jehoshaphat* means "the LORD judges"). This valley was not connected with King Jehoshaphat of Judah (1 Kgs 22:41); rather, the title identifies the site as the place where God would render his decision (see 3:14) regarding the fate of the nations. • *threw dice:* Literally *cast lots.* • The sins of the nations include exiling God's covenant people and victimizing helpless *boys* and *girls* in an inhuman slave trade (cp. Ezek 27:13; Rev 18:13).

3:4-6 The Phoenician cities of *Tyre and Sidon* and the *cities of Philistia* were guilty of looting the *precious treasures* of Jerusalem and selling its people as slaves *to the Greeks* (literally *to the peoples of Javan;* see Amos 1:6, 9).

3:7-8 The people of Tyre, Sidon, and Philistia had enslaved Israelites, so the Lord would punish them by selling their *sons and daughters* into slavery. • *to the people of Arabia:* Hebrew *to the Sabeans.*

3:9 The *nations* are mockingly called to a futile *war* against the Lord that will end in their destruction and judgment.

3:10 *Hammer your plowshares into swords:* Deliberately reversing an image from Isa 2:4 and Mic 4:3, Joel ordered the nations to mobilize every resource for the forthcoming battle. Even those unfit for war, the *weaklings,* must become soldiers.

3:12 The battle would take place in the *valley of Jehoshaphat* (see note on 3:2-3), where the Lord would *pronounce judgment on them all.*

3:13 God would defeat the nations like a *sickle* that mows down stalks of grain and like workers who tread *grapes* in the *winepress* (see Isa 63:2-3; Rev 14:14-20). • *for the harvest is ripe:* Greek version reads *for the harvest time has come.* Cp. Mark 4:29.

3:14 *Thousands upon thousands* (literally *roaring, roaring;* or *crowds, crowds*): The repetition of the Hebrew word captures the chaotic noise made by an immense crowd. • *valley of decision:* The name of the valley is changed (cp. 3:2-3, 12) because now the Lord's judgment had been decided.

3:16 *The LORD's voice,* like that of a lion, would *roar from Zion,* shaking heaven and earth and terrifying sinners (see Amos 1:2). Yet this same ferocious lion is also a *refuge for his people.*

3:17 *Then you will know:* God's ultimate purpose is that his people should know him and share his *holy* character. They must learn that he alone is God and that he reigns over all creation from *Zion,* his *holy mountain* (see also 2:27). The only true security in the present, and the only hope for the future, comes from God's presence.

3:19
Amos 1:11
Obad 1:10

3:20
Ezek 37:25
Amos 9:15

3:21
Isa 4:4
Ezek 36:25, 29
Rev 22:3

and a fountain will burst forth from
the LORD's Temple,
watering the arid valley of acacias.
19 But Egypt will become a wasteland
and Edom will become a wilderness,
because they attacked the people of Judah
and killed innocent people in their
land.

20 "But Judah will be filled with people
forever,
and Jerusalem will endure through all
generations.
21 I will pardon my people's crimes,
which I have not yet pardoned;
and I, the LORD, will make my home
in Jerusalem with my people."

3:18 Blessings will flow from the Lord's sovereign presence in Zion (see also Ezek 47:1-12; Amos 9:13). There will be a superabundance of ***sweet wine*** and ***milk***. The Temple, God's own dwelling on earth, will be the source of a spring that will forever water the ***arid*** landscape (see Zech 14:8; Rev 22:1-2). • ***valley of acacias:*** Hebrew *valley of Shittim.*

3:19 Even as Judah is restored, her ancient enemies ***Egypt*** and ***Edom*** will experience God's judgment for their crimes against his people.

3:20-21 The conclusion of Joel's prophecy is the antithesis of its beginning. In ch 1, Judah's future seemed in grave doubt. Plague and drought, the signs of divine judgment, threatened Judah's existence. Now Joel ends with the divine assurance that ***Judah . . . and Jerusalem*** (Hebrew *Zion*) ***will endure through all generations.*** God's people in every generation rest secure in the hope that his kingdom will reign over heaven and earth (see also Isa 9:6-7; Dan 2:44; 7:13-14).

THE BOOK OF AMOS

"Prepare to meet your God," Amos proclaimed to those who worshiped idols (4:12). Let there be "a mighty flood of justice," Amos admonished the rich who oppressed the poor (5:24). What brought this shepherd from Tekoa to Bethel to pronounce such powerful judgments? Amos did not make his living as a professional prophet (7:14); the "roar" of God (1:2; 3:8) had moved him to make the journey. His message calls for righteousness—right worship that yields right social ethics. God's people still need the prophet's help to make that connection.

SETTING

In 931 BC, the kingdom of Israel split into two lesser kingdoms: the northern kingdom (Israel) and the southern kingdom (Judah). The king of the north, Jeroboam I, did not want his subjects to go to Jerusalem (in the south) to worship, so he established shrines at Dan and Bethel. Drawing on an earlier precedent (Exod 32), Jeroboam used images of young bulls to represent the Lord (1 Kgs 12:25-33). This move typified the northern kingdom's rejection of God's revelation in defining both their worship and their ethics. Because pagan religions focused on acquiring power, paganized Israel became an abuser of the powerless.

The calf shrines that Jeroboam I established at Dan and Bethel (1 Kgs 12:29), together with the presence of the baals (local representations of the Canaanite storm-god), reduced the worship of Yahweh (the LORD) in the northern kingdom to a pagan religion like that of Israel's neighbors. The purpose of this worship was only to receive some desired benefit. When Elijah challenged the priests of Baal on Mount Carmel, it was because the people wanted to worship both Yahweh and Baal. However, Elijah left them without that alternative (1 Kgs 18:21, 24). The message of Amos was similar.

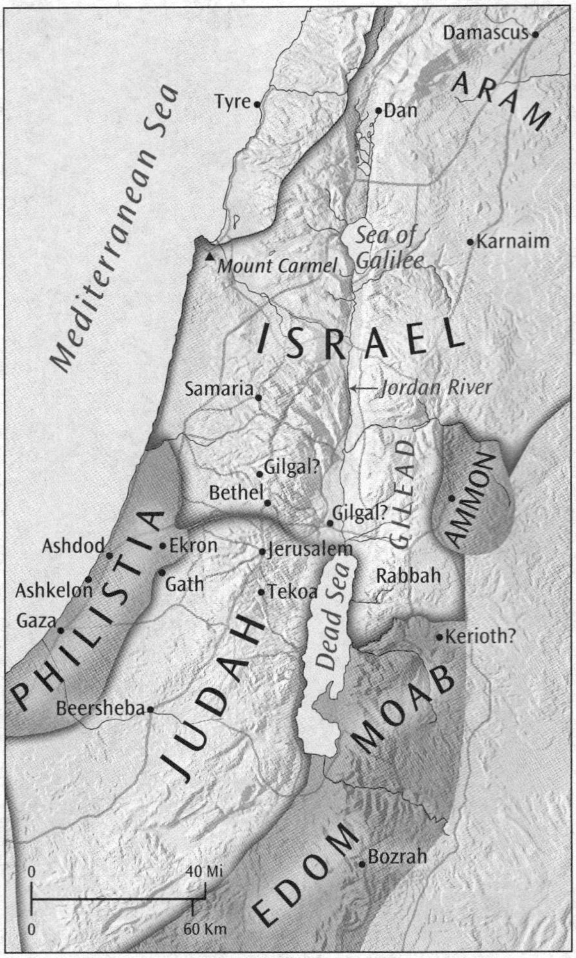

Israel and Judah, around 753 BC. At the time of Amos's ministry, Israel under King Jeroboam II (793–753 BC) was prosperous and proud, but judgment was soon to come.

When Amos arrived in Israel (shortly before 753 BC), the rich were getting richer and the poor were getting poorer. Egypt was also in decline. Around 801 BC, the Assyrians had captured Damascus but were forced to withdraw due to problems elsewhere. In the resulting power vacuum, both Israel (2 Kgs 14:23-29) and Judah (2 Kgs 15:1-7; 2 Chr 26) flourished, recovering some of the territory they had lost to Aram. The two kingdoms increased in prosperity, but the greater prosperity merely increased the power of those who already had it. Those who had no power were even more oppressed.

In response to this situation, Amos traveled from Tekoa (in Judah) to the northern shrine at Bethel, where he called Israel to account for its apostasy and inhumanity.

OUTLINE

1:1-2
Superscription: Introducing the Prophet

1:3–2:16
Eight Judgments on Israel and Its Neighbors

3:1–5:17
Three Messages of Judgment against Israel

5:18–6:14
Two Prophetic "Woes" against Israel

7:1–9:10
Five Visions: The Sentence on Israel

9:11-15
Promise: The LORD Will Restore Israel

SUMMARY

Amos delivered his prophetic messages at the Bethel shrine. He confronted Israel with the message that lip service is not enough in worship of the Lord.

After a brief introduction (1:1-2), the first section of Amos (1:3–2:16) is a series of eight indictments. The prophet directs the first seven charges against surrounding nations, with the eighth against Israel itself. By first charging Israel's enemies with war crimes and theological aberrations, Amos wins the sympathy and agreement of his hearers. Then he says, "The people of Israel, too, have sinned."

What follows (3:1–5:17) is framed by three prophetic messages. The first (3:1-2) accuses Israel of abusing its privileged status as God's chosen people. The second (4:1-3) is an indictment of Israel's party crowd. The third (5:1-2) is a funeral song for the predicted death of the nation. Between the prophetic messages Amos includes rhetorical questions (3:3-6), metaphors from his life as a shepherd (3:8, 12), sarcastic irony (4:4-5), historical recitation (4:6-11), hymn fragments (4:13; 5:8-9), puns (5:5), pleas for repentance, and predictions of the doom that awaits the unrepentant.

The third section of Amos (5:18–6:14) contains two prophetic messages of woe: the first is a warning to those who proclaim the day of the Lord as a time when God will reestablish Israel as a leading nation (5:18-27); the second admonishes those who trust in their wealth, houses, or fortifications to save them (6:1-14).

The fourth section (7:1–9:10) contains five prophetic oracles based on visions. Amos first wins over his hearers with visions of two judgments that would be averted (7:1-6), but then drives home his message with two judgments that would not be turned aside (7:7-9; 8:1-3). These visions are interrupted by a brief biographical vignette (7:10-17). The final vision is of the complete destruction of Israel and its religious system (9:1-10).

TIMELINE

931 BC
The kingdom is divided
Jeroboam I of Israel builds calf shrines

931–910 BC
Jeroboam I as king of Israel

793–753 BC
Jeroboam II as king of Israel

792–767 BC
Uzziah's (Azariah's) co-reign with Amaziah

about 781 BC
Jeroboam II reclaims Israel's territory from Syria

767 BC
King Amaziah of Judah dies

767–740 BC
Uzziah (Azariah) as sole regent of Judah

about 760~750 BC
Amos as prophet

753 BC
Jeroboam II of Israel dies

722 BC
Samaria is destroyed by Assyria, end of the northern kingdom of Israel

The dark days in which [Amos] lived called for a man of sturdy moral fiber and fearlessness. Such was Amos. His character, molded in the harsh terrain of the wilderness of Tekoa, enabled him to stand before the priest and the people, proclaiming the word God had given him.

THOMAS E. MCCOMISKEY, *Amos*

Finally (9:11-15), Amos promises better days to come, a time of healing and restoration when Jerusalem would be rebuilt, the dynasty of David would be reestablished in the land, and people would live in the peace of God's kingdom.

DATE AND LOCATION

Amos's ministry was brief, perhaps limited to a single year. Its setting was the royal shrine at Bethel in the northern kingdom (7:13), a short time before the death of Jeroboam II in 753 BC (1:1).

RECIPIENTS

Amos directed his message to all the Israelite people, but especially to the rich, powerful, and self-indulgent (see especially 5:18–6:8). While Amos clearly considered Israel's split from Judah and the Jerusalem sanctuary as the primary cause of its moral and spiritual decline, he was aware that Judah was also slipping away from a pure worship of the Lord (2:4-5). Thus, the book includes condemnation of those "who lounge in luxury in Jerusalem," as well as indictment of the smugly secure in Samaria (see 6:1).

THE PROPHET AMOS

All that is known about the life of Amos comes from the book bearing his name. According to the superscription, he was a shepherd (*noqed*) from Tekoa (modern *Teku'a*), a small, fortified town about five miles south of Bethlehem in Judah.

Earlier scholars often characterized the prophet as a poor sheepherder who represented the marginalized classes in Judah and who was unjustly oppressed by wealthy landowners. More recent studies, however, have taken a different direction. The Hebrew word commonly used for a shepherd is *ro'eh* (as in Ps 23:1), not *noqed*. In its only occurrence as a noun outside the book of Amos, the word describes Mesha, king of Moab, as one who regularly delivered a substantial tribute of wool and sheep to Israel (2 Kgs 3:4). The term *noqed* probably designates someone who owned sheep rather than a shepherd who worked for someone else. A second insight comes from Amos 7:14. Here Amos uses a different word for *shepherd* (*boqer;* literally *herder*), perhaps indicating that he owned cattle, a sign of considerable wealth. Amos further describes himself as one who tends sycamore-fig trees (7:14), the fruit of which was used for animal fodder. The word that is used (*boles*) does not occur elsewhere, but in the context of *boqer*, it may mean someone who raised sycamore-figs, rather than a worker who tended the orchards of others.

The emerging picture, then, is not one of a simple herder who tended the sheep and trees of others, but of an owner and manager of livestock and trees. This newer perspective on Amos harmonizes well with the contents of his prophecy. The book is written in excellent Judean Hebrew and shows a keen awareness of Israel's heritage as well as its contemporary political and economic circumstances.

"Let Justice roll down like waters in a mighty stream," said the Prophet Amos. He was seeking not consensus but the cleansing action of revolutionary change.

MARTIN LUTHER KING, JR., *"Let Justice Roll Down"*

MEANING AND MESSAGE

Moses uniquely depicted God as ethical and as caring deeply for the powerless (see, e.g., Deut 24:10-22). But Israel's apostasy and moral corruption permitted oppression of the poor and powerless. Material

prosperity erroneously came to be seen as a sign of God's favor, and the people prized appearances over substance. This violated God's requirements for a holy people.

Proper worship of the true God yields ethical behavior toward others. But corrupt worship and theology will corrupt human relationships. Theology yields morality, right worship yields good works, and faith yields practical change. It is not enough to give lip service to God. Morality cannot be defined simply as personal purity or integrity; it also includes social obligations born of the conviction that all human life is God's creation and bears his image (Gen 1:26-27). Service to God is expressed through service to his creatures.

Because this cry for humane treatment of the downtrodden applies to all people in every generation, Amos has inspired great social reformers. For example, Dr. Martin Luther King, Jr., used these denunciations and exhortations in his own preaching as a stimulus for the American civil rights movement of the 1950s and 1960s.

FURTHER READING

JAMES MONTGOMERY BOICE
The Minor Prophets (2002)

ANDREW HILL
Amos in *Cornerstone Biblical Commentary,* vol. 10 (2008)

DAVID ALLAN HUBBARD
Joel & Amos (1989)

DOUGLAS STUART
Hosea—Jonah (1987)

1:1
2 Sam 14:2
2 Kgs 14:23-29
Zech 14:5

1:2
Isa 42:13
Jer 12:4; 14:2; 25:30
Joel 1:18-19; 3:16

1:3
Isa 8:4
Amos 2:1, 4, 6

1:4
1 Kgs 20:1
2 Kgs 6:24

1. SUPERSCRIPTION: INTRODUCING THE PROPHET (1:1-2)

1 This message was given to Amos, a shepherd from the town of Tekoa in Judah. He received this message in visions two years before the earthquake, when Uzziah was king of Judah and Jeroboam II, the son of Jehoash, was king of Israel.

2 This is what he saw and heard:

"The LORD's voice will roar from Zion
and thunder from Jerusalem!
The lush pastures of the shepherds will dry up;
the grass on Mount Carmel will wither and die."

2. EIGHT JUDGMENTS ON ISRAEL AND ITS NEIGHBORS (1:3–2:16)

Judgment on Aram

3 This is what the LORD says:

"The people of Damascus have sinned again and again,
and I will not let them go unpunished!
They beat down my people in Gilead
as grain is threshed with iron sledges.
4 So I will send down fire on King Hazael's palace,
and the fortresses of King Ben-hadad will be destroyed.
5 I will break down the gates of Damascus

1:1 *message* (literally *words*): This standard way of introducing a prophetic message (Jer 1:1; see also Hag 1:12) emphasizes its form and content. • *shepherd* (Hebrew *noqed*): This word is used just one other time in the OT, to describe the king of Moab as a "sheep breeder" (2 Kgs 3:4). Amos describes his vocation in 7:14 using a different Hebrew word (*boqer,* which means "herder"; see Amos Introduction, "The Prophet Amos," facing page). Amos was not a professional prophet serving the court or the Temple. • Amos *received this message in visions*—that is, by divine revelation (see Isa 1:1). • Amos depicts *the earthquake* that occurred during the reign of Uzziah (Zech 14:5) as an act of God's judgment (3:14-15; 6:11, 14; 8:8; 9:1, 9). • *Uzziah*, also called Azariah (792–740 BC), was the most powerful king of Judah after the division of the kingdom. • *Jeroboam II* (793–753 BC), who descended from the dynasty of Jehu, took advantage of a power vacuum in the region and recovered territory earlier lost to the Arameans. • *Jehoash:* Hebrew *Joash,* a variant spelling of Jehoash.

1:2 This quote from Joel 3:16 speaks of judgment at the day of the Lord (see also note on 9:13). • Mount *Zion* (the Temple in Jerusalem) was the logical source of a message from *the LORD*. • *Mount Carmel* rises from the Mediterranean Sea and is well watered even in time of drought. If all *the grass on Mount Carmel* withered, it would be the sign of a catastrophic drought.

1:3–2:16 The eight judgments of this prophecy proceed from the most obvious enemy, Damascus, to the least obvious, Israel itself. The sequence would have engaged Israel's attention as they heard God's judgment against their enemies, but Amos eventually confronted the people with God's judgment on them.

1:3-5 *Damascus*, the capital of *Aram,* was brutal in its treatment of the people of *Gilead,* Israel's territory east of the Jordan. By the time Ahab died (853 BC), Damascus had captured Ramoth in Gilead (1 Kgs 22:3). Around 801 BC, Assyria captured Damascus, and the city never again held the power it had wielded in its prime.

1:3 *have sinned again and again:* Literally *have committed three sins, even four* (also in 1:6, 9, 11, 13). This expression is used for a repeated act of rebellion against the natural order established by God. The Hebrew phrase does not denote a strict count but a pattern of repeated violations. • *beat down my people:* Threshing *grain* involved separating the heads of the grain from their hulls by pulling wooden *sledges* with sharp teeth over the cut grain (Isa 41:15; see Mic 4:13). This description provides a graphic picture of the brutality of the people of Damascus.

1:4 *I will send down fire:* In ancient times conquered cities were burned by invading armies (see also 1:7, 10, 12, 14; 2:2, 5). The conquest of Damascus would be God's judgment on them. • *Hazael* reigned as king of Damascus (about 843–802 BC) after he seized the throne by assassination. *Ben-hadad* was Hazael's son and successor (about 802–792 BC).

1:5 *Aven* and *Beth-eden* were both connected with Aram and Damascus. *Aven* (meaning *evil, wickedness*) refers to the valley between the Lebanon and

and slaughter the people in the valley
of Aven.
I will destroy the ruler in Beth-eden,
and the people of Aram will go as
captives to Kir,"
says the LORD.

Judgment on Philistia

6This is what the LORD says:

"The people of Gaza have sinned again
and again,
and I will not let them go unpunished!
They sent whole villages into exile,
selling them as slaves to Edom.
7 So I will send down fire on the walls of
Gaza,
and all its fortresses will be
destroyed.
8 I will slaughter the people of Ashdod
and destroy the king of Ashkelon.
Then I will turn to attack Ekron,
and the few Philistines still left will
be killed,"
says the Sovereign LORD.

Judgment on Tyre

9This is what the LORD says:

"The people of Tyre have sinned again
and again,
and I will not let them go unpunished!
They broke their treaty of brotherhood
with Israel,
selling whole villages as slaves to
Edom.
10 So I will send down fire on the walls of
Tyre,
and all its fortresses will be
destroyed."

Judgment on Edom

11This is what the LORD says:

"The people of Edom have sinned again
and again,
and I will not let them go unpunished!
They chased down their relatives, the
Israelites, with swords,
showing them no mercy.
In their rage, they slashed them continually
and were unrelenting in their anger.
12 So I will send down fire on Teman,
and the fortresses of Bozrah will be
destroyed."

Judgment on Ammon

13This is what the LORD says:

"The people of Ammon have sinned
again and again,
and I will not let them go unpunished!
When they attacked Gilead to extend
their borders,
they ripped open pregnant women
with their swords.
14 So I will send down fire on the walls of
Rabbah,
and all its fortresses will be destroyed.
The battle will come upon them with
shouts,
like a whirlwind in a mighty storm.

1:6 1 Sam 6:17; Jer 47:1, 5; Ezek 35:5; Amos 1:9, 11; Obad 1:11
1:8 Isa 14:29-31; Jer 47:1-7; Ezek 25:16; Zeph 2:4-7; Zech 9:6
1:9 1 Kgs 5:1; 9:11-14; Isa 23:1-18
1:11 Num 20:14-21; Isa 34:5-6; 63:1-3; Jer 49:7-22; Ezek 25:12-14; Obad 1:10-12; Mic 7:18
1:12 Jer 49:7, 20; Obad 1:9
1:13 2 Kgs 15:16; Jer 49:1-6; Ezek 25:2-7; Hos 13:16
1:14 Jer 49:2; Amos 2:2

Anti-Lebanon mountains or the plain of Damascus. The city-state ***Beth-eden*** was north of Aram, elsewhere simply called *Eden* (2 Kgs 19:12; Ezek 27:23). • The Arameans originally came from ***Kir*** (9:7), probably in southern Babylonia; Kir was where Assyria deported them when Damascus fell (2 Kgs 16:9). Just as Egypt was a symbol of captivity for Israel (see Deut 28:68), Kir represented captivity for Aram.

1:6 The Philistine city of ***Gaza***, on the seacoast at the southwest edge of Palestine, was the gateway for traffic between Africa and Asia. Its sin was slave trading; Philistia had raided Israel or Judah and sold ***whole villages*** into slavery ***to Edom***.

1:7 ***I will send down fire:*** Uzziah conquered Philistia (2 Chr 26:6); in 701 BC, the Assyrian invasion ended the distinct identity of the Philistines.

1:8 The Philistine cities of ***Ashdod*** and ***Ashkelon*** were on or near the seacoast, while ***Ekron*** lay inland. Gath is not mentioned here, as it had been conquered earlier by Hazael (2 Kgs 12:17) and then Uzziah (2 Chr 26:6). • ***the few Philistines still left:*** The Philistines maintained their ethnic identity through the Assyrian period, but this distinction faded by the time of the Persians (Zech 9:5-7).

1:9 ***Tyre*** and Sidon were the principal seaports of Phoenicia. • Tyre's crime, like Philistia's (1:6-8), was ***selling whole villages*** of Israelite captives to the Edomites ***as slaves***, a captivity made more bitter by a sense of betrayal (see 2 Sam 5:11; 1 Kgs 5:1, 11; 16:30-31). Tyre's reputation was "anything is for sale"; Isaiah portrayed the city as a prostitute peddling her wares (Isa 23:15-17).

1:10 ***fire on the walls:*** The main part of Tyre was built on an island, making it almost impossible to capture (see Ezek 26:1–28:19).

1:11 ***Edom*** was another betrayer (see 1:9; Gen 36; see also Gen 25:23-30; 27:39-40). • The NLT adds ***the Israelites*** to make explicit what ***relatives*** (literally *brother*) means (see Gen 25:25-30). "Brothers" can also refer to parties to a treaty (see 1:9). Apparently Edom exerted constant pressure on the borders of Israel and Judah, raiding and plundering at moments of weakness (Obad 1:1-9; Jer 49:7-22).

1:12 With the destruction of the major cities of ***Teman*** and ***Bozrah***, Edom lost its capacity for continual warfare. Babylon destroyed Edom shortly after Judah in 553 BC (see Jer 27:1-22; 49:7-22; note on Obad 1:18).

1:13 Israel regarded the people of ***Ammon*** as kin who also betrayed them. The Ammonites (like the Moabites, 2:1) were descendants of Lot, Abraham's nephew (Gen 19:37-38). Ammon had been a constant threat to Gilead (see Judg 10:7-9). • In ancient times, conquering armies commonly ***ripped open pregnant women*** (2 Kgs 8:12; 15:16; Hos 13:16); they also raped the women and slaughtered the children of the towns they seized (Isa 13:16, 18; Lam 5:11; Hos 10:14; 13:16; Nah 3:10; Zech 14:2).

1:14 ***Rabbah*** was the chief city of the Ammonites (2 Sam 12:26). • Ammon (1:13) was crushed by the Assyrians in the 800s BC, then attacked and depopulated by the Babylonians in the 700s.

1:15
Jer 49:3
2:1
Isa 15:1-9; 16:1-14
Jer 48:1-7
Zech 2:8-9
2:2
Jer 48:24, 41, 45
2:3
Isa 40:23
2:4
Judg 2:17-20
2 Kgs 17:19
Amos 3:2
2:5
Jer 17:27
Hos 8:14
2:6
2 Kgs 18:12
Joel 3:3, 6
Amos 5:11; 8:4-6

15 And their king and his princes will go
into exile together,"
says the LORD.

Judgment on Moab

2 This is what the LORD says:
"The people of Moab have sinned again
and again,
and I will not let them go unpunished!
They desecrated the bones of Edom's king,
burning them to ashes.
2 So I will send down fire on the land of
Moab,
and all the fortresses in Kerioth will
be destroyed.
The people will fall in the noise of battle,
as the warriors shout and the ram's
horn sounds.
3 And I will destroy their king
and slaughter all their princes,"
says the LORD.

God's Judgment on Judah

4 This is what the LORD says:
"The people of Judah have sinned again
and again,
and I will not let them go unpunished!
They have rejected the instruction of the
LORD,
refusing to obey his decrees.
They have been led astray by the same
lies
that deceived their ancestors.
5 So I will send down fire on Judah,
and all the fortresses of Jerusalem
will be destroyed."

Judgment on Israel

6 This is what the LORD says:
"The people of Israel have sinned again
and again,
and I will not let them go unpunished!

Social Justice (2:6-8)

Amos 5:7-17, 23-24
Exod 23:1-12
Lev 19:9-18
Deut 10:17-20; 16:18-20; 24:10-22
1 Kgs 21:1-24
2 Chr 19:4-11
Ps 94:20-23; 146:3-9
Prov 22:8-9; 31:8-9
Eccl 5:8-9
Isa 1:17; 5:7; 9:6-7; 10:1-2; 42:1-4; 58:4-12
Mal 3:5
Matt 12:15-21; 23:23
Luke 10:25-37
Heb 1:8-9

In the OT, prophets often confronted evil in society and articulated a demand for social justice. An early example of this is found in Elijah's response to the murder of Naboth, followed by his rebuke of Ahab (1 Kgs 21:16-24, 800s BC). The social aspect of the prophetic message became even more prominent among the prophets of the 700s BC (Hosea and Amos in Israel, Micah and Isaiah in Judah), with Amos as the most articulate spokesman on this issue.

Amos was appalled by Israel's abuse of the powerless (2:6-8; 3:10). Unlike the surrounding nations, Israel had known God in a uniquely personal and intimate manner and then turned away from him (2:9-12; 3:1-2). The people of Israel had refused to worship God appropriately and had oppressed the powerless, so God would meet them in judgment (4:12), not mercy. Because God created the whole world (4:13; 5:8), there was no escape (2:14), no place to hide (9:2-4). God's judgment would seek them out wherever they were.

The theme of God's universal judgment continues in the NT (see Luke 12:48; Heb 9:27). God wants justice to flow like a mighty river (5:24). Those who oppose it will be swept away.

1:15 ***their king:*** Hebrew *malkam*, possibly referring to their god Molech; see also Jer 49:1-3. In ancient times, people believed that a conquered nation's god or gods went ***into exile together*** with them (see 5:26-27; 1 Sam 5:1-2; Isa 46:1).

2:1 ***have sinned again and again:*** Literally *have committed three sins, even four* (also in 2:4, 6); see note on 1:3. • ***desecrated the bones:*** In some past skirmish, the Moabites had captured ***Edom's king.*** Cremation was considered a form of desecration; if the ***ashes*** (literally *lime*) of the king were used in plaster, the insult would be compounded.

2:2-3 ***Kerioth,*** a major town (Jer 48:20-24), is mentioned on the Moabite Stone as a shrine to Chemosh, Moab's god. Perhaps the Moabites burned the remains of Edom's king or offered him as a human sacrifice at this site. Because of the desecration of the Edomite king's corpse, God would destroy the ***king*** of Moab and his officers. This fate probably came upon them through an invasion by Sargon II of Assyria (715/713 BC; cp. Isa 15:1–16:14). Josephus (*Antiquities* 10.9.7) implies a further destruction in 582 BC (see also Jer 48; Ezek 25:8-11; Zeph 2:8-11).

2:4-5 The southern kingdom of ***Judah*** was closest to the northern kingdom of Israel in blood ties and geography, but bitterness existed between the nations. The north regarded the descendants of David in the south as abusive kings who had caused the schism by their forced labor and heavy taxes.

2:4 ***rejected the instruction*** (Hebrew *torah*) ***of the LORD:*** The pagan nations listed to this point had committed atrocities that violated a general sense of human decency, but Judah had gone further; they held the word of God and yet had rejected its teachings (see Hos 4:6; 8:1). God holds people responsible in proportion to the privilege they have received (see 3:2). • ***led astray by the same lies:*** Having discarded God's true instruction, Judah turned to a substitute found in pagan *syncretism* (the combining of elements from different belief systems) and idolatry (see 1 Kgs 14:22-24).

2:5 Judah's paganism brought the same punishment as the sins of its pagan neighbors: *fire* (1:4, 7, 10, 12, 14; 2:2) that would destroy Jerusalem. The Babylonians burned Jerusalem when they captured it in 586 BC (see 2 Kgs 25:9; Neh 2:17; 4:2).

2:6-16 ***Israel:*** After leading the people through a litany of sins committed by Israel's neighbors, Amos arrived at his real point: The Israelites would suffer a similar fate (cp. Nathan's use of prophetic rhetoric to induce self-indictment, 2 Sam 12:1-13).

2:6 ***Honorable people*** are the "righteous," those who enjoyed a right

They sell honorable people for silver
and poor people for a pair of sandals.
7 They trample helpless people in the dust
and shove the oppressed out of the way.
Both father and son sleep with the same woman,
corrupting my holy name.
8 At their religious festivals,
they lounge in clothing their debtors put up as security.
In the house of their gods,
they drink wine bought with unjust fines.

9 "But as my people watched,
I destroyed the Amorites,
though they were as tall as cedars
and as strong as oaks.
I destroyed the fruit on their branches
and dug out their roots.
10 It was I who rescued you from Egypt
and led you through the desert for forty years,
so you could possess the land of the Amorites.
11 I chose some of your sons to be prophets
and others to be Nazirites.
Can you deny this, my people of Israel?"
asks the LORD.
12 "But you caused the Nazirites to sin by making them drink wine,
and you commanded the prophets, 'Shut up!'

13 "So I will make you groan
like a wagon loaded down with sheaves of grain.
14 Your fastest runners will not get away.
The strongest among you will become weak.
Even mighty warriors will be unable to save themselves.
15 The archers will not stand their ground.
The swiftest runners won't be fast enough to escape.
Even those riding horses won't be able to save themselves.
16 On that day the most courageous of your fighting men
will drop their weapons and run for their lives,"
says the LORD.

3. THREE MESSAGES OF JUDGMENT AGAINST ISRAEL (3:1–5:17)

Punishment for a Chosen People

3 Listen to this message that the LORD has spoken against you, O people of Israel and Judah—against the entire family I rescued from Egypt:

2 "From among all the families on the earth,
I have been intimate with you alone.

2:7 Hos 4:14; Amos 5:12; 8:4
2:8 Exod 22:26; Amos 4:1; 6:6
2:9 Ezek 17:9; Mal 4:1
2:10 Exod 3:8; 12:51; Deut 2:7; 8:2-4
2:11 Num 6:2-3; Jer 7:25
2:12 Isa 30:10; Jer 11:21; Amos 7:13, 16
2:14 Ps 33:16; Isa 30:16-17; Jer 9:23
2:15 Isa 31:3; Jer 51:56; Ezek 39:3
2:16 Judg 4:15-16
3:1 Jer 8:3; 13:11
3:2 Exod 19:5-6; Deut 7:6; Ezek 20:36-38; Rom 2:9

relationship with God and other people. The parallel with ***poor people*** creates the idea of the "righteous needy." The law of Moses urged those who had much to help those in need by lending freely (Deut 15:7-11). As a last resort, those too poor to pay their debts could become bond servants to repay their debts through labor (Lev 25:39-43). These righteous needy were being sold into bond servitude for ***a pair of sandals,*** a hyperbole for the pittance they owed (see 8:6). The sandals were a pledge given for the debt or a token used to seal a bargain (see Ruth 4:7).

2:7 To ***trample . . . people*** was to treat them ruthlessly (see also 8:4). • The ***helpless*** and ***oppressed*** were people exploited by a socio-economic system that denied them the justice guaranteed by law (Exod 23:6-8). • That ***father and son sleep with the same woman*** demonstrated the moral destitution of the Israelites; the law of Moses prohibited this practice (Lev 18:7-8, 15; 20:11-12). • ***corrupting my holy name:*** In worshiping various fertility gods, Israel and surrounding nations engaged in "sacred prostitution" (see Hos 4:10-14). Sexual relations with a shrine prostitute were thought to ensure plentiful crops and thriving herds of livestock. This verse suggests that these acts were performed in the name of the Lord. When performed as religious rituals, these corrupt actions treat God's name as worthless.

2:8 The irony is that the oppressors of the poor flaunted their sins at ***religious festivals.*** • The Torah allowed a lender to take a poor man's cloak as ***security*** for a debt, but it was not to be kept overnight, because the nights were cold (Exod 22:26-27; Deut 24:12-13). A widow's ***clothing*** was never to be taken as security for a debt (Deut 24:17). • ***their gods:*** Or ***their God.*** • ***unjust fines:*** The wealthy bribed judges and used their influence to keep the poor, who could not defend themselves, from obtaining a fair hearing (5:12).

2:9 ***Amorites*** is used here as a general term to denote the inhabitants of Canaan (see Gen 15:16; Judg 6:10).

2:11-12 In addition to priests, God provided ***prophets*** to speak his word and will (Deut 18:15-19) and holy men called ***Nazirites,*** who were dedicated to the Lord by vows that included abstention from fermented drinks (Num 6:1-21). Israel showed its disregard for God by telling both the Nazirites and the prophets to ignore and violate God's calling (see 7:12-13).

2:14-16 The chapter concludes with a description of the battle in which Israel would be defeated and would flee (see Ps 33:16-17).

2:15 ***The archers*** stood in the last ranks. If they fled, it meant the forward ranks had collapsed.

2:16 Amos later calls ***that day*** the "day of the LORD" (5:18); both terms indicate the time of judgment on Israel (see also 8:3).

3:1–5:17 Amos directs the three prophetic messages in this section against Israel, indicting them for a false understanding of their status as God's chosen people. The messages show a progression toward judgment.

3:1-2 The first ***message*** from ***the LORD*** warns Israel that its status as God's elect will not excuse them from God's judgment. Instead, they will be held to a higher standard than the surrounding nations.

3:1 Amos begins with a reference to God's goodness to Israel when he ***rescued*** them ***from Egypt*** (see 2:10).

3:2 The word translated ***been intimate*** indicates personal and experiential knowledge that often extends beyond

3:3
Gen 5:22; 6:9
Lev 26:23-24

3:4
Ps 104:21
Hos 11:10

3:6
Isa 14:24-27
Jer 6:1
Hos 5:8

3:7
Gen 18:17
Dan 9:22-27
John 15:15
[a]*'adonay Yahweh*
(0136, 3068)
‣Hab 3:19

3:8
Jer 20:9
Acts 4:20

3:9
Amos 8:6

3:10
Ps 14:4
Jer 4:22
Amos 5:7; 6:12
Hab 2:8-11
Zeph 1:9
Zech 5:3-4

3:11
Amos 6:14

3:12
1 Sam 17:34-37
[b]*ro'eh* (7462)
‣Zech 13:7

3:13
Ezek 2:7

3:14
Amos 4:4; 5:5-6;
7:10, 13

That is why I must punish you
for all your sins."
3 Can two people walk together
without agreeing on the direction?
4 Does a lion ever roar in a thicket
without first finding a victim?
Does a young lion growl in its den
without first catching its prey?
5 Does a bird ever get caught in a trap
that has no bait?
Does a trap spring shut
when there's nothing to catch?
6 When the ram's horn blows a warning,
shouldn't the people be alarmed?
Does disaster come to a city
unless the LORD has planned it?
7 Indeed, the [a]Sovereign LORD never does anything
until he reveals his plans to his servants the prophets.
8 The lion has roared—
so who isn't frightened?
The Sovereign LORD has spoken—
so who can refuse to proclaim his message?
9 Announce this to the leaders of Philistia
and to the great ones of Egypt:
"Take your seats now on the hills around Samaria,
and witness the chaos and oppression in Israel."
10 "My people have forgotten how to do right,"
says the LORD.
"Their fortresses are filled with wealth
taken by theft and violence.
11 Therefore," says the Sovereign LORD,
"an enemy is coming!
He will surround them and shatter their defenses.
Then he will plunder all their fortresses."
12 This is what the LORD says:

"A [b]shepherd who tries to rescue a sheep
from a lion's mouth
will recover only two legs or a piece of an ear.
So it will be for the Israelites in Samaria
lying on luxurious beds,
and for the people of Damascus
reclining on couches.

13 "Now listen to this, and announce it throughout all Israel," says the Lord, the LORD God of Heaven's Armies.

14 "On the very day I punish Israel for its sins,
I will destroy the pagan altars at Bethel.

mere intellectual awareness. It can indicate formal recognition and acknowledgement (Exod 1:8; 5:2), personal experience (Gen 2:17), or sexual relations (Gen 4:1). This word is frequently used of God's relationship with Israel (Hos 5:3) and of Israel's ideal relationship with God (Hos 2:20). Because of Israel's privileged status, God would hold them accountable for all their sins, not just some of them. God holds people accountable in terms of what has been given them (Luke 12:47-48).

3:3-6 Amos explains his call to prophesy with a series of rhetorical questions that must be answered in the negative. But the metaphorical language carries deeper meaning than is implied in the questions themselves.

3:3 Amos's *walk* with God was evidence that his message was in accord with ***the direction*** of God's plans for Israel's judgment.

3:4 Amos's messages have God behind them: what he says will, in fact, happen to Israel. God is the *lion* who roars, and he has already found his *victim*—the people of Israel who are ready for judgment.

3:5 The ***trap*** pictures the consequences of Israel's sin. Israel fully deserved the judgment that Amos proclaimed.

3:6 ***disaster . . . the LORD has planned:*** God sends both the good and pleasant, and the harmful and painful (Isa 45:7; Lam 3:38; see Deut 28; Job 2:10).

3:8 God, ***the lion, has roared*** from Mount Zion (1:2) and compelled Amos to prophesy (see 7:14-16).

3:9 The prophet now turns to two of Israel's enemies, ***Philistia*** (Hebrew *Ashdod,* one of the key cities of Philistia) and ***Egypt***. He invites them to surround ***Samaria*** (the capital of the kingdom of Israel) to see its ***chaos and oppression***. Israel appeared strong from the outside, but it was rotten within, rife with class struggles. The enemies would take advantage of Israel's internal weakness (see 3:11).

3:10 Israel's rich people acquired their ***wealth*** through their neglect and brutal treatment of the poor and helpless (see 2:6-8).

3:11 The real ***enemy*** was not Egypt or Philistia, but Assyria, the only superpower in the region.

3:12 ***A shepherd who tries to rescue:*** The people of both Israel and Judah believed that, because of their chosen status, God would intervene to rescue them and never let them perish. The prophet's words are ironic: their rescue would be like a shepherd who arrives too late to save the sheep, and who can pull ***only two legs or a piece of an ear*** from the mouth of the lion. • ***So it will be . . . reclining on couches:*** The meaning of the Hebrew in this sentence is uncertain. Some have interpreted this statement to mean that only the fabric of a few couches would survive the Assyrian siege of Samaria. Accordingly, the last two lines of this verse could be translated *So it will be when the Israelites in Samaria are rescued / with only a broken bed and a tattered pillow.*

3:13 The Lord's message is to go to ***all Israel*** (literally *the house of Jacob*). The names "Jacob" and "Israel" are often interchanged in the OT, referring sometimes to the individual patriarch and sometimes to the nation. Jacob was the ancestor of both Israel and Judah (see 3:1). • The witnesses who are told to ***listen*** could be the nations summoned in 3:9, the inhabitants of Samaria, or bands of prophets. • ***LORD God of Heaven's Armies:*** This title, traditionally "LORD God of Hosts" (also in 4:13; 5:14-16, 27; 6:8), portrays God as commander of the heavenly armies; this is the true God of the universe, not a local deity (see also Exod 15:3).

3:14 ***pagan altars at Bethel:*** The shrine at Bethel, built by Jeroboam I shortly after his inauguration (1 Kgs 12:26-33),

The horns of the altar will be cut off
and fall to the ground.
15 And I will destroy the beautiful homes of the wealthy—
their winter mansions and their summer houses, too—
all their palaces filled with ivory,"
says the LORD.

Punishment for an Abusive People

4 1 Listen to me, you fat cows
living in Samaria,
you women who oppress the poor
and crush the needy,
and who are always calling to your husbands,
"Bring us another drink!"
2 The Sovereign LORD has sworn this by his holiness:
"The time will come when you will be led away
with hooks in your noses.
Every last one of you will be dragged away
like a fish on a hook!
3 You will be led out through the ruins of the wall;
you will be thrown from your fortresses,"
says the LORD.

4 "Go ahead and offer sacrifices to the idols at Bethel.
Keep on disobeying at Gilgal.
Offer sacrifices each morning,
and bring your tithes every three days.
5 Present your bread made with yeast
as an offering of thanksgiving.
Then give your extra voluntary offerings
so you can brag about it everywhere!
This is the kind of thing you Israelites love to do,"
says the Sovereign LORD.

6 "I brought hunger to every city
and famine to every town.
But still you would not return to me,"
says the LORD.

7 "I kept the rain from falling
when your crops needed it the most.
I sent rain on one town
but withheld it from another.
Rain fell on one field,
while another field withered away.
8 People staggered from town to town
looking for water,
but there was never enough.
But still you would not return to me,"
says the LORD.

9 "I struck your farms and vineyards with blight and mildew.

3:15 Judg 3:20; 1 Kgs 22:39; Jer 36:22
4:1 Ps 22:12; Amos 2:8; 3:9; 5:11; 6:11
4:2 Isa 37:29; Jer 16:16; Ezek 29:4; 38:4
4:3 Ezek 12:5, 12
4:5 Lev 7:13; 22:18-21; Hos 9:1, 10
4:6 Isa 3:1; Jer 14:18; Hag 2:17
4:7 1 Kgs 8:35-36; Zech 14:17
4:8 1 Kgs 18:5; Jer 14:3-4; Ezek 4:16; Mic 6:14; Hag 1:6
4:9 Deut 28:22; Joel 2:25

continued through the dynasty of Jehu (2 Kgs 10:29), from whom Jeroboam II descended. This shrine merged worship of Yahweh (the LORD) with the pagan symbol of a bull. When the altars were destroyed, the Bethel shrine, the king's official sanctuary (7:13), and the northern kingdom would also be ruined.

3:15 ***Ivory*** represents the immense, ill-gotten wealth of the rich. Archaeologists have found some of these ivory inlays in the ruins of Samaria.

4:1-3 In this message Amos holds Samaria's wives accountable for urging their husbands to perform ruthless acts in order to provide them with money for their parties.

4:1 ***you fat cows*** (literally *you cows of Bashan*): Bashan was famous for its fierce, fat bulls (Ps 22:12; Ezek 39:18). Amos uses the feminine form (cows) to paint a picture of Israel's upper class wives, who cared little for the poor. Their only concern was to extract enough wealth from the needy to support their own consumption.

4:2 ***has sworn this by his holiness:*** Holiness speaks of God as existing outside of and independent of creation; his nature is wholly other than what he has created. The oath is similar to 6:8; 8:7. • ***hooks:*** The Assyrians were known for their inhumane treatment of war captives (see 2 Chr 33:11; cp. 2 Kgs 19:28). A *stela* (stone pillar with an inscription) discovered in northern Syria shows the Assyrian king Esarhaddon holding cords that pass through the lips of two war captives. A recent scholar has suggested that *hooks* referred to the rings inserted into the noses of cattle to manage them.

4:3 ***The wall*** of Samaria that these women trusted for security could not protect them. • ***thrown from your fortresses:*** Or *thrown out toward Harmon*, possibly a reference to Mount Hermon. The meaning of the Hebrew is uncertain.

4:4-5 The prophet's sarcasm shows how far Israel had strayed from God's ways. Israel had plenty of religion but no reverence for God.

4:4 Amos lampoons the Israelites' worthless piety. • ***Bethel,*** site of Jacob's famous vision of the ladder with angels descending and ascending (Gen 28:11-22), was the southern seat of the religion established by Jeroboam I (see 3:14; 1 Kgs 12:28-29). ***Gilgal,*** Israel's campsite after they crossed the Jordan (Josh 4:19–5:9), had become a popular shrine by the time of Amos and Hosea (Hos 4:15; 9:15; 12:11). • ***sacrifices each morning . . . tithes every three days:*** Israelite males were to appear before the Lord at the sanctuary three times each year (Exod 23:14-19; 34:23; Deut 16:16-17). Tithes were typically paid annually (Deut 14:22-29), with a special tithe paid every three years (see Deut 14:28; 26:12). Amos is making the point that the Israelites were religious to the point of absurdity, but they balked at being godly (5:15; Hos 6:6; Mic 6:8; see Luke 11:42).

4:5 Leavened ***bread*** (that is, sourdough fermented by wild ***yeast***) was for daily consumption. The more primitive unleavened bread (made without yeast) became a sacred symbol, commemorating Israel's affliction as slaves in Egypt (Deut 16:3), the Passover (Exod 12:17-20), and their hasty departure from that land (Exod 12:34, 39). Unleavened bread thus became altar bread (Lev 6:17; 7:12). However, ***bread made with yeast*** could accompany a peace ***offering of thanksgiving*** (Lev 7:13).

4:6-11 God sent natural disasters to bring his people to repentance, but each time they failed to respond in any sincere manner. Amos ends the account of each disaster with the refrain, ***"But still you would not return to me," says the LORD.***

4:10
Exod 9:3-6
Lev 26:25
Isa 9:13
Jer 11:22; 18:21
Amos 8:3

4:11
Gen 19:24-25
Jer 23:14

4:13
Job 38:4-11
Ps 135:7; 139:2
Dan 2:28, 30
Amos 5:8; 8:9
'tsaba' (6635)
›Amos 9:5

5:1
Jer 9:10
Ezek 19:1, 14

5:2
Isa 51:18
Jer 14:17; 50:32
Amos 8:14

5:4
Deut 4:29; 32:46-47

Locusts devoured all your fig and
olive trees.
But still you would not return to me,"
says the LORD.

10 "I sent plagues on you
like the plagues I sent on Egypt long ago.
I killed your young men in war
and led all your horses away.
The stench of death filled the air!
But still you would not return to me,"
says the LORD.

11 "I destroyed some of your cities,
as I destroyed Sodom and Gomorrah.
Those of you who survived
were like charred sticks pulled from
a fire.
But still you would not return to me,"
says the LORD.

12 "Therefore, I will bring upon you all the
disasters I have announced.
Prepare to meet your God in
judgment, you people of Israel!"

13 For the LORD is the one who shaped the
mountains,
stirs up the winds, and reveals his
thoughts to mankind.
He turns the light of dawn into darkness
and treads on the heights of the earth.
The LORD God of Heaven's ‹Armies is
his name!

A Call to Repentance before Punishment

5 Listen, you people of Israel! Listen to
this funeral song I am singing:

2 "The virgin Israel has fallen,
never to rise again!
She lies abandoned on the ground,
with no one to help her up."

3The Sovereign LORD says:

"When a city sends a thousand men to
battle,
only a hundred will return.
When a town sends a hundred,
only ten will come back alive."

4Now this is what the LORD says to the family of Israel:

"Come back to me and live!

Worship in Jerusalem (5:4-5)

Deut 12:5
1 Kgs 11:36
2 Chr 6:6
Neh 1:9; 11:1
Isa 2:3; 52:1; 56:7
Joel 3:17
Zech 8:20-22
Matt 4:5
Luke 19:46
John 2:16; 4:21-24
Heb 12:18-29
Rev 21:2, 10; 22:19

The OT prophets realized that genuine worship depends on a proper understanding of God and his requirements. God's authorized worship took place at the Temple in Jerusalem. The Lord roared from Zion and thundered from Jerusalem (1:2). Because the Lord is not part of this world and cannot be manipulated by it, he alone determines how people may come to him. It was unacceptable for the Israelites to worship God in any place other than his sanctioned Temple in Jerusalem. But sacrifice and ritual are not substitutes for genuine piety (4:4; 5:25). The shrines at Bethel, Gilgal, and Beersheba did not suffice; no matter how many sacrifices or how elaborate the rituals (5:4-5), these were not the places for worship God had chosen.

In the NT, worship is no longer tied to a particular location; worship may occur wherever believers choose to gather (Matt 18:20). But it must be conducted as God directs: "in spirit and in truth" (John 4:23-24). Jesus wholeheartedly agreed with the requirement that worship be authentic, not merely formal.

4:10 God had used ***plagues*** to convince ***Egypt*** to let Israel go (Exod 9:2-3; 7:14–12:30; Ps 91:6; Hab 3:5); he promised to bring the plagues of Egypt on Israel if they continued to turn away from him to worship pagan gods (Deut 28:27, 60). • ***and led all your horses away:*** Or *and slaughtered your captured horses.*

4:11 As with the plagues on Egypt (4:10), the plagues on Israel increased in magnitude and intensity (cp. 4:12). • ***as I destroyed*** (literally *as when God destroyed*): The thought that God would treat his own people in the same way as he had treated ***Sodom and Gomorrah*** (Gen 19:24-25) was shocking to their theology (see "God's Sovereignty over All Nations" at 9:7, p. 1465).

4:12 This is one of the two great thematic verses in Amos (the second is 5:24). Since Israel would not repent, it must ***meet . . . God in judgment.***

4:13 This verse appears to be a hymn fragment, possibly sung by the worshipers at Bethel (for other hymn fragments, see 5:8-9; 9:5-6). Israel had been treating God as a *baal*—a local god with limited power. But the God they professed to worship and whom they would face in judgment is all powerful.

5:1-3 The charges against Israel had been filed (3:1-2; 4:1-3); now it was time for judgment. Amos made this point clear by singing a funeral song for Israel, as though the nation were already dead.

5:1 ***funeral song:*** The Hebrew word (*qinah*) describes a special rhythm (3+2 beats) used for funeral dirges (most of the book of Lamentations is written in *qinah*). The ominous significance was clear: Israel had already died and now awaited burial.

5:2 When used to describe political powers, ***virgin*** refers to a state of being unconquered by a foreign power (e.g., Babylon, Isa 47:1; Jerusalem, Lam 2:13; cp. Lam 1:1).

5:3 This verse is a reversal of the promises made in Lev 26:8.

5:4 ***Come back to me and live*** implies a condition: In order to live, Israel should seek the Lord (also in 5:6). Otherwise, the funeral song (5:1-2) would become Israel's death sentence.

5 Don't worship at the pagan altars at
Bethel;
don't go to the shrines at Gilgal or
Beersheba.
For the people of Gilgal will be dragged
off into exile,
and the people of Bethel will be
reduced to nothing."
6 Come back to the LORD and live!
Otherwise, he will roar through Israel
like a fire,
devouring you completely.
Your gods in Bethel
won't be able to quench the flames.
7 You twist justice, making it a bitter pill
for the oppressed.
You treat the righteous like dirt.
8 It is the LORD who created the stars,
the Pleiades and Orion.
He turns darkness into morning
and day into night.
He draws up water from the oceans
and pours it down as rain on the
land.
The LORD is his name!
9 With blinding speed and power he
destroys the strong,
crushing all their defenses.

10 How you hate honest judges!
How you despise people who tell the
truth!
11 You trample the poor,
stealing their grain through taxes and
unfair rent.
Therefore, though you build beautiful
stone houses,
you will never live in them.
Though you plant lush vineyards,
you will never drink wine from them.
12 For I know the vast number of your [d]sins
and the depth of your rebellions.
You oppress good people by taking
bribes
and deprive the poor of justice in the
courts.
13 So those who are smart keep their
mouths shut,
for it is an evil time.

14 Do what is good and run from evil
so that you may live!
Then the LORD God of Heaven's Armies
will be your helper,
just as you have claimed.
15 Hate evil and love what is good;
turn your courts into true halls of
justice.
Perhaps even yet the LORD God of
Heaven's Armies
will have mercy on the remnant of his
people.

16 Therefore, this is what the Lord, the LORD
God of Heaven's Armies, says:

"There will be crying in all the public
squares
and mourning in every street.
Call for the farmers to weep with you,
and summon professional mourners
to wail.
17 There will be wailing in every vineyard,
for I will destroy them all,"
says the LORD.

4. TWO PROPHETIC "WOES" AGAINST ISRAEL (5:18–6:14)

Woe to Those Who Desire the Day of the LORD

18 What sorrow awaits you who say,
"If only the day of the LORD were here!"

5:6 Deut 4:24
5:7 Amos 5:12; 6:12
5:8 Job 9:9; 12:22; 37:13; 38:31-34; Amos 9:6
5:9 Amos 2:14; Mic 5:11
5:10 Amos 5:15
5:11 Isa 59:15; Mic 6:15
5:12 Isa 1:23; Amos 2:6; [d]*pesha'* (6588) ›Gen 50:17
5:14 Mic 3:11
5:15 Ps 97:10; Joel 2:14; Rom 12:9
5:16 Joel 1:8, 11; Amos 8:3, 10
5:17 Isa 16:10
5:18 Isa 5:30; Jer 30:7; Joel 1:15; 2:1, 31

5:5 ***Beersheba*** was another site (see note on 4:4) with ties to the patriarchal era (e.g., Abraham, Gen 21:33; 22:19) that had been made into a shrine. • ***Gilgal . . . exile:*** A wordplay using alliteration (Hebrew *hagilgal galoh yigleh*).

5:6 The northern kingdom of ***Israel*** (literally *the house of Joseph*) was dominated by the tribes of Joseph's sons, Ephraim and Manasseh (see note on 5:15; see Hos 5:3, 5).

5:8-9 Amos quotes a second hymn fragment (see 4:13; 9:5-6). Once again, the prophet emphasizes the contrast between the cosmic God and the local gods. • ***Stars,*** celestial bodies, and constellations such as ***Pleiades*** and ***Orion*** were regarded as deities in the ancient world. Not so, says Amos; the Lord made them and placed them in the sky. • ***water:*** The ancients had observed a process that they did not understand (evaporation and condensation). However, the Lord understands and controls natural processes that seem mysterious to humans.

5:10 Amos resumes the thought begun in 5:7. Israel's courts, controlled by the wealthy, depended on corrupt judges and hired witnesses. They had no use for what was true, but only for what was expedient to their own cause (5:12).

5:11 ***stone houses:*** Again, Amos targets the rich. The houses of peasants were built of mud brick. Cut stone, the result of laborious handwork, was very expensive.

5:13 Witnesses pleaded that they saw and heard nothing. Truthfulness had become a liability (5:10) and might endanger the one who spoke it.

5:14 Amos makes his earlier hints (5:4, 6) more explicit: Israel must ***do what is good*** and right in order to survive.

5:15 ***the remnant of his people:*** The Hebrew text uses *the remnant of Joseph* to refer to the northern kingdom, who were still God's people despite their rebellion and idolatry.

5:16-17 ***crying . . . mourning . . . wailing:*** Grief would result from the widespread and certain destruction that lay ahead (5:1-2).

5:16 ***farmers . . . professional mourners:*** This expression is a graphic way of describing that everyone would grieve.

5:18–6:14 The pronouncements of ***sorrow*** in this section develop two themes: (1) Israel's apostasy would make the "day of the LORD" a day of judgment, not salvation; and (2) Judah's spiritual complacency would also bring judgment.

5:19 Job 20:24
5:20 Isa 13:10
5:21 Lev 26:31; Isa 1:11-16; Jer 14:12; Hos 5:6
5:22 Isa 66:3
5:24 Jer 22:3; Mic 6:8
6:1 Exod 19:5; Isa 32:9-11
6:2 Gen 10:10; 1 Sam 17:23; 2 Kgs 18:34; 2 Chr 26:6; Isa 10:9
6:3 Amos 9:10
6:4 Ezek 34:2-3

You have no idea what you are wishing
for.
That day will bring darkness, not light.
19 In that day you will be like a man who
runs from a lion—
only to meet a bear.
Escaping from the bear, he leans his
hand against a wall in his house—
and he's bitten by a snake.
20 Yes, the day of the LORD will be dark and
hopeless,
without a ray of joy or hope.

21 "I hate all your show and pretense—
the hypocrisy of your religious
festivals and solemn assemblies.
22 I will not accept your burnt offerings
and grain offerings.
I won't even notice all your choice
peace offerings.
23 Away with your noisy hymns of praise!
I will not listen to the music of your
harps.
24 Instead, I want to see a mighty flood of
justice,
an endless river of righteous living.

25 "Was it to me you were bringing sacrifices and offerings during the forty years
in the wilderness, Israel? 26 No, you served
your pagan gods—Sakkuth your king god
and Kaiwan your star god—the images you
made for yourselves. 27 So I will send you
into exile, to a land east of Damascus," says
the LORD, whose name is the God of Heav-
en's Armies.

Woe to the People of Judah and Israel

6 1 What sorrow awaits you who lounge
in luxury in Jerusalem,
and you who feel secure in Samaria!
You are famous and popular in Israel,
and people go to you for help.
2 But go over to Calneh
and see what happened there.
Then go to the great city of Hamath
and down to the Philistine city of Gath.
You are no better than they were,
and look at how they were destroyed.
3 You push away every thought of coming
disaster,
but your actions only bring the day of
judgment closer.
4 How terrible for you who sprawl on ivory
beds
and lounge on your couches,
eating the meat of tender lambs from
the flock
and of choice calves fattened in the
stall.

5:18 Amos again confronts the Israelites' distorted view of their chosen status (see 3:2). • The phrase ***What sorrow awaits you*** denotes despair brought on by a great tragedy. • The ***day of the LORD*** in the OT (see Isa 13:6, 9) was a time when God would intervene in the world to set right those things that had gone wrong. God's intervention would mean vindication for the righteous, but judgment for the wicked. Israel thought that on ***that day*** (see also 8:3, 9, 13; 9:11) God would save them. However, because the Israelites had been wicked, the day of the Lord would ***bring darkness, not light***. Assyria conquered the northern kingdom in 722 BC (2 Kgs 17:7-23), fulfilling this prophecy.

5:21-27 Amos again confronts the religious hypocrisy and spiritual unfaithfulness of the Israelites (see 4:4-5; Isa 1:10-20).

5:22 God would not accept the ***offerings*** (see Lev 1–6) of the Israelites because they were attempts to manipulate him magically rather than signs of true repentance and faith.

5:24 This is the second of the great thematic verses in Amos (see 4:12). • ***endless river:*** The streams or gullies (wadis) in Israel's dry areas contained water only temporarily during rainy seasons. However, God wanted continual, not just seasonal, justice.

5:25-26 Although the people of Israel claimed that God had to bless them because of the Sinai Covenant, Amos demonstrated that they had been fundamentally pagan from the very earliest days of the covenant.

5:25 Israel's relationship with God was based on true devotion that yielded obedience (1 Sam 15:22-23). ***Sacrifices*** representing repentance and faith could repair a breach made by sin, but it was not a substitute for a life lived in accordance with God's word. • ***Forty years in the wilderness*** was the duration of Israel's wandering after the rebellion at Kadesh-barnea (see Num 14:32-35).

5:26-27 The names that appear in 5:26 have given rise to several conjectures, but many interpreters consider them to be names of unidentified pagan gods. The ***king god*** may well be Molech, god of the Ammonites (see 1:15). The word translated ***you served*** may mean *you will lift up*, in which case the prophet is making a contrast between Israel or Judah, who carried their idols, and God, who carries his people (see Isa 46:1-7). The Greek version of these verses reads *No, you carried your pagan gods—the shrine of Molech, the star of your god Rephan, and the images you made for yourselves. So I will send you into exile, to a land east of Damascus.* Cp. Acts 7:43.

6:1 ***Jerusalem . . . Samaria:*** A message including Jerusalem is unexpected, but it shows that God plays no favorites; whoever rebels against God will experience ***sorrow***. The Hebrew text uses the terms *Zion . . . Mount Samaria*, indicating the citadels of the two cities. The people of both Judea and Israel were smug and self-important, believing that the fortresses of the cities of Jerusalem and Samaria were impregnable (see also 4:3). Relying on physical power instead of on God is sin.

6:2 ***Calneh*** and ***Hamath*** were Aramean city-states under Israelite influence (see 2 Kgs 14:28). Calneh fell to Assyria in 738 BC, and Hamath was forced to pay tribute shortly thereafter. Uzziah had broken down the wall of ***Gath*** (2 Chr 26:6), but it also fell to Assyria in 711 BC. • ***You are no better:*** Israel itself fell in 722 BC (see note on 5:18).

6:3 ***day of judgment*** (literally *seat of violence*): By this term, Amos either meant that Israel's behavior hastened the violence of the Assyrian conquest, or that the people encouraged everyday violence against the poor by pushing the ***thought of coming disaster*** from their minds.

6:4 ***Meat*** was typically used to honor distinguished guests. The common food was bread, fruit, vegetables, and dairy products. The everyday use of meat shows the opulence of the wealthy classes.

5 You sing trivial songs to the sound of the harp
and fancy yourselves to be great musicians like David.
6 You drink wine by the bowlful
and perfume yourselves with fragrant lotions.
You care nothing about the ruin of your nation.
7 Therefore, you will be the first to be led away as captives.
Suddenly, all your parties will end.

The Lord Swears by His Own Name

8The Sovereign LORD has sworn by his own name, and this is what he, the LORD God of Heaven's Armies, says:

"I despise the arrogance of Israel,
and I hate their fortresses.
I will give this city
and everything in it to their enemies."

9(If there are ten men left in one house, they will all die. 10And when a relative who is responsible to dispose of the dead goes into the house to carry out the bodies, he will ask the last survivor, "Is anyone else with you?" When the person begins to swear, "No, by . . . ," he will interrupt and say, "Stop! Don't even mention the name of the LORD.")

11 When the LORD gives the command,
homes both great and small will be smashed to pieces.
12 Can horses gallop over boulders?
Can oxen be used to plow them?
But that's how foolish you are when you turn justice into poison
and the sweet fruit of righteousness into bitterness.
13 And you brag about your conquest of Lo-debar.
You boast, "Didn't we take Karnaim by our own strength?"
14 "O people of Israel, I am about to bring an enemy nation against you,"
says the LORD God of Heaven's Armies.
"They will oppress you throughout your land—
from Lebo-hamath in the north
to the Arabah Valley in the south."

5. FIVE VISIONS: THE SENTENCE ON ISRAEL (7:1–9:10)

Vision 1: A Locust Swarm

7 The Sovereign LORD showed me a vision. I saw him preparing to send a vast swarm of locusts over the land. This was after the king's share had been harvested from the fields and as the main crop was

6:5 1 Chr 15:16; 23:5; Isa 5:12
6:8 Lev 26:30
6:9 Amos 5:3
6:10 1 Sam 31:12; Amos 5:13; 8:3
6:11 Amos 3:15
6:12 Hos 10:4; Amos 5:7, 11-12
6:14 Num 34:7-8; 2 Kgs 14:25; Jer 5:15
7:1 Exod 10:12-16; Nah 3:15-17

6:5-6 These verses provide a picture of drunken revelry.

6:6 ***wine by the bowlful:*** The word translated *bowl* (Hebrew *mizraq*) is related to a verb meaning *sprinkle* or *splash* (Hebrew *zaraq;* see Exod 24:6); the same word identified the basins used for sprinkling blood or water in religious ceremonies (see 2 Kgs 12:13; 25:15), adding a sense of sacrilege to this description of their drunkenness. • ***of your nation:*** The Hebrew text reads *of Joseph,* referring to the northern kingdom of Israel; see notes on 5:6, 15.

6:8 The most solemn oath the Lord could pronounce was ***by his own name*** (see also Gen 22:16; Jer 51:14; cp. Amos 4:2; Ps 110:4; Heb 6:13-14). • ***arrogance of Israel*** (literally *pride of Jacob;* see note on 3:13; 8:7): *Jacob* can mean *cheat* (Gen 27:36), whereas *Israel* means *he struggles with God* (Gen 32:28). Amos uses *Jacob* to express the obstinate arrogance that so often characterized the people of Israel.

6:9-10 These verses graphically picture the wholesale slaughter by military conquest promised in 6:8.

6:10 ***to dispose of the dead:*** Or *to burn the dead.* The meaning of the Hebrew is uncertain. Cremation was very uncommon in the ancient Near East (see note on 2:1), so some interpret this phrase to mean *burn a memorial fire* (see Jer 34:5). Others take it to mean *dispose of the remains,* rather than perform a cremation. Yet the context—the need to dispose of multiple bodies to avoid putrefaction and disease (6:9; see 8:3)—supports the idea that it means cremation.

6:12 It would be foolish to run ***horses . . . over boulders,*** because unshod horses cannot run on rocks without serious damage to their hooves. It is also obvious that ***oxen*** cannot ***plow*** rocks. A slight adjustment to the word division of the Hebrew text yields *plow the sea with oxen,* an equally absurd suggestion. • ***that's how foolish you are:*** The point of the comparisons now becomes obvious, as Israel's own absurdity surfaces in the moral realm. • ***you turn justice into poison:*** The people perverted what is just and right, turning it into something toxic and bitter (see also 5:7).

6:13 ***Lo-debar*** and ***Karnaim*** were part of the territory regained from the Arameans by Jeroboam II (2 Kgs 14:25-28). Amos makes puns on their names: *Lo-debar* means *nothing* and *Karnaim* means *horns,* a term that symbolizes *strength.*

6:14 ***Lebo-hamath*** marked the northern border of Solomon's influence (1 Kgs 8:65) and of the land recovered by Jeroboam II. The Dead Sea (called the sea of ***the Arabah;*** see note on 2 Kgs 14:25) marked the southern border of Jeroboam's recovered territory. The irony was clear: all of this recovered land would be oppressed by the ***enemy nation*** (Assyria).

7:1–9:10 This section contains five visions. It is helpful to compare the progression of these five visions with the judgments listed in 4:6-11 (famine, drought, crop devastation, plagues, destruction).

7:1-6 The first two visions set up a mood of hopeful expectancy. God calls for judgment, but then revokes it at the prophet's intercession.

7:1 ***Locusts*** (see 4:9) were one of the plagues brought upon Egypt (Exod 10:4). Great swarms of locusts periodically invaded these lands, typically in times of drought. • ***king's share:*** The first harvest went to the king as taxes, whereas the later harvest of the ***main crop*** fed the farmer and his family. However, if locusts devoured this crop, starvation would follow.

7:2
Exod 10:15
Isa 37:4
Jer 14:7; 42:2
Ezek 9:8; 11:13

7:3
Deut 32:36
Jer 26:19
Hos 11:8

7:4
Isa 66:15-16
Amos 2:5

7:6
Amos 7:3

7:8
Isa 28:17; 34:11
Amos 8:2

7:9
2 Kgs 15:8-10

7:10
1 Kgs 12:31-32
2 Kgs 14:23-24

7:12
1 Sam 9:9

7:13
1 Kgs 12:29, 32; 13:1
Amos 2:12
Acts 4:17-18

7:14
1 Kgs 20:35
2 Kgs 2:3-7; 4:38
[e]*nabi'* (5030)
‣Mal 4:5

7:15
Jer 1:7
Ezek 2:3-4

7:16
Amos 7:13
Mic 2:6

7:17
Jer 14:16; 20:6
Hos 4:13-14

coming up. [2]In my vision the locusts ate every green plant in sight. Then I said, "O Sovereign LORD, please forgive us or we will not survive, for Israel is so small."

[3]So the LORD relented from this plan. "I will not do it," he said.

Vision 2: A Fiery Drought

[4]Then the Sovereign LORD showed me another vision. I saw him preparing to punish his people with a great fire. The fire had burned up the depths of the sea and was devouring the entire land. [5]Then I said, "O Sovereign LORD, please stop or we will not survive, for Israel is so small."

[6]Then the LORD relented from this plan, too. "I will not do that either," said the Sovereign LORD.

Vision 3: A Plumb Line

[7]Then he showed me another vision. I saw the Lord standing beside a wall that had been built using a plumb line. He was using a plumb line to see if it was still straight. [8]And the LORD said to me, "Amos, what do you see?"

I answered, "A plumb line."

And the Lord replied, "I will test my people with this plumb line. I will no longer ignore all their sins. [9]The pagan shrines of your ancestors will be ruined, and the temples of Israel will be destroyed; I will bring the dynasty of King Jeroboam to a sudden end."

Interlude: Challenge and Response

[10]Then Amaziah, the priest of Bethel, sent a message to Jeroboam, king of Israel: "Amos is hatching a plot against you right here on your very doorstep! What he is saying is intolerable. [11]He is saying, 'Jeroboam will soon be killed, and the people of Israel will be sent away into exile.' "

[12]Then Amaziah sent orders to Amos: "Get out of here, you prophet! Go on back to the land of Judah, and earn your living by prophesying there! [13]Don't bother us with your prophecies here in Bethel. This is the king's sanctuary and the national place of worship!"

[14]But Amos replied, "I'm not a professional [e]prophet, and I was never trained to be [e]one. I'm just a shepherd, and I take care of sycamore-fig trees. [15]But the LORD called me away from my flock and told me, 'Go and prophesy to my people in Israel.' [16]Now then, listen to this message from the LORD:

"You say,
'Don't prophesy against Israel.
Stop preaching against my people.'
[17] But this is what the LORD says:
'Your wife will become a prostitute in
this city,
and your sons and daughters will be
killed.
Your land will be divided up,
and you yourself will die in a foreign
land.

7:2 ***Israel is so small:*** The population base of the kingdom was not large enough to ***survive*** such radical depletion. • ***Israel:*** Literally *Jacob;* also in 7:5; see note on 3:13.

7:3-6 ***The LORD relented*** twice in response to Amos's intercession.

7:4 This ***fire*** symbolizes oppressive heat and drought. • ***depths of the sea:*** Although the Hebrew word properly indicates the sea, Amos probably did not suppose that the Mediterranean would disappear. More likely, this is a poetic reference to large bodies of fresh water (such as the Kinnereth Sea/Sea of Galilee) that Israel could use to irrigate its fields.

7:7-9 This vision begins like the previous two (7:2-3, 4-6), but this time the Lord allows no intercession. The abrupt shift in outcome contributed to the power of Amos's message.

7:8 The Hebrew word translated ***plumb line*** (Hebrew *'anak*) is similar to the word for groaning (*'anakhah*, see Isa 35:10; Lam 1:22), alluding to great suffering when God would hold them accountable.

7:9 ***pagan shrines . . . temples:*** Every vestige of the apostate Israelite religion, from the common high places to the royal shrine at Bethel, would be destroyed. • ***of your ancestors*** (literally *of Isaac*): Isaac stands for Israel's ancestors, the fathers of the nation. • ***dynasty of King Jeroboam:*** Jeroboam II died of natural causes (2 Kgs 14:29), but the murder of his son and successor, Zechariah, after a reign of less than a year (2 Kgs 15:8-10; see 10:28-31), initiated instability in Israel's government that it never overcame (2 Kgs 15:10-31).

7:10-17 This section graphically depicts the corruption of the priesthood, reinforcing the point of the visions on either side of it, that judgment is inescapable.

7:11 Amaziah misinterpreted Amos's words as a threat on Jeroboam's life. Amos was calling the people to repentance, not sedition.

7:12 ***Go on back to . . . Judah, and earn your living by prophesying:*** Amaziah assumed that the supposedly backward Judeans would appreciate Amos's words, and that Amos was looking to be paid for his preaching.

7:13 ***king's sanctuary:*** According to Amaziah, the urbane and sophisticated Israelites did not appreciate the prophet. Amaziah's loyalties were clearly to the throne; he wanted to keep the king happy in order to keep his job.

7:14 Amos was not a ***professional prophet*** or even a disciple in training (literally *I'm not a prophet nor the son of a prophet*). He had no financial incentive to leave his livelihood in order to prophesy. • ***shepherd:*** The Hebrew word here is not the same as in 1:1, and is not found elsewhere in the OT. It is related to a word for cattle, suggesting that Amos may have raised cattle as a breeder or herder (see Amos Introduction, "The Prophet Amos," p. 1452). • The ***sycamore-fig*** was gathered for cattle feed.

7:15 Amos was not motivated by financial gain. Instead, the Lord's voice (see 1:2; 3:8) moved Amos to ***prophesy***.

7:16 ***against my people*** (literally *against the house of Isaac*): Isaac represents all Israel (see also note on 7:9; cp. 5:6, 15; 6:6).

7:17 Because Amaziah had tried to silence Amos (7:12-13), the Lord confronted Amaziah with a grim prophecy of what his life would be like after the Assyrian siege.

And the people of Israel will certainly
become captives in exile,
far from their homeland.' "

Vision 4: A Basket of Ripe Fruit

8 Then the Sovereign LORD showed me
another vision. In it I saw a basket
filled with ripe fruit. 2"What do you see,
Amos?" he asked.
I replied, "A basket full of ripe fruit."
Then the LORD said, "Like this fruit, Israel
is ripe for punishment! I will not delay their
punishment again. 3In that day the singing
in the Temple will turn to wailing. Dead bodies will be scattered everywhere. They will
be carried out of the city in silence. I, the
Sovereign LORD, have spoken!"

Interlude: Indictments on Israel

4 Listen to this, you who rob the poor
and trample down the needy!
5 You can't wait for the Sabbath day to be
over
and the religious festivals to end
so you can get back to cheating the
helpless.
You measure out grain with dishonest
measures
and cheat the buyer with dishonest
scales.
6 And you mix the grain you sell
with chaff swept from the floor.
Then you enslave poor people
for one piece of silver or a pair of
sandals.

7 Now the LORD has sworn this oath
by his own name, the Pride of Israel:
"I will never forget
the wicked things you have done!
8 The earth will tremble for your deeds,
and everyone will mourn.
The ground will rise like the Nile River at
floodtime;
it will heave up, then sink again.

9 "In that day," says the Sovereign LORD,
"I will make the sun go down at noon
and darken the earth while it is still
day.
10 I will turn your [f]celebrations into times
of mourning
and your singing into weeping.
You will wear funeral clothes
and shave your heads to show your
sorrow—
as if your only son had died.
How very bitter that day will be!

11 "The time is surely coming," says the
Sovereign LORD,
"when I will send a famine on the
land—
not a famine of bread or water
but of hearing the words of the LORD.
12 People will stagger from sea to sea
and wander from border to border
searching for the word of the LORD,
but they will not find it.
13 Beautiful girls and strong young men
will grow faint in that day,
thirsting for the LORD's word.
14 And those who swear by the shameful
idols of Samaria—
who take oaths in the name of the god
of Dan

8:2 Jer 24:1-3; Amos 7:8
8:3 Hos 10:5-6; Amos 5:23
8:4 Amos 2:6-7; 5:11
8:5 Neh 13:15-21; Hos 12:7
8:7 Deut 33:26-29; Ps 10:11; 47:4; 68:34; Hos 7:2; 8:13
8:8 Ps 18:7; 114:3-7; Jer 46:8; Amos 9:5
8:9 Amos 4:13; 5:8; Mic 3:6; Matt 27:45; Mark 15:33; Luke 23:44-45
8:10 Isa 15:2-3; Ezek 7:18; Amos 5:23; 6:4-7
[f]*khag* (2282) ▸Exod 23:15
8:12 Ezek 20:3, 31
8:13 Isa 41:17; Lam 1:18; 2:21; Hos 2:3
8:14 1 Kgs 12:28-29

8:1 This vision resumes the prophetic sermon begun in 7:1 and interrupted by the dialogue with Amaziah.

8:2 *ripe for punishment* (literally *the end has come*): Amos makes a play on words between ***ripe fruit*** (Hebrew *qayits*) and *the end has come* (Hebrew *ba' haqqets*). The end had come for God's people, Israel, because they were ripe fruit, ready to be harvested in judgment.

8:4-14 This section expands the indictments and judgments listed earlier (read with 2:6–6:14).

8:5 Work was explicitly forbidden on the ***Sabbath day*** (Exod 20:9-10); Amos implies that shops were closed during pagan new-moon ***religious festivals*** as well. • ***You measure out . . . with dishonest scales:*** Literally *You make the ephah small and the shekel great, and you deal falsely by using deceitful balances.* The ***ephah*** was a unit for measuring grain, and the ***shekel*** was a unit of weight. In this way merchants were ***cheating the helpless:*** They cheated their customers by measuring grain with small ephahs, and they cheated their suppliers by using heavy shekels on the scales. This practice was forbidden by God's law (Lev 19:35-36; Deut 25:13-16; see Prov 11:1; 16:11; 20:10, 23).

8:7 ***the Pride of Israel*** (literally *the pride of Jacob;* see note on 3:13): The same phrase alludes in 6:8 to Israel's arrogance. Here, the phrase is probably a name for God, who is the legitimate object of Israel's pride. Elsewhere (Ps 47:4; Nah 2:2), this phrase refers to the Promised Land under a king from David's line (cp. Jer 13:9; Ezek 32:12). If the phrase here means the land, it would spotlight Israel's perverse pride in its national and geographic identity.

8:9 The day of the Lord would invert the cosmos. Jeremiah used similar imagery to describe the desecration of Judah as the Babylonian armies approached (Jer 4:23; see also Isa 13:10; 34:4; 50:3; Ezek 32:7-8; Joel 2:10, 31; Mic 3:6).

8:11-14 ***famine . . . of hearing the words of the LORD:*** God sent prophets to Israel to speak his words directly to them, but Israel commanded the prophets not to prophesy (2:11-12). Now they had what they wanted, but it was a silence more terrible than his roar and thunder: God became distant (see Ezek 7:26; 20:3; Mic 3:4, 7). The time for speaking was over; the time of judgment had come.

8:12 ***from border to border*** (literally *from north to east*): The natural boundaries of Israel were ***from sea to sea:*** the Mediterranean Sea on the west and the Dead Sea on the south. The other borders are simply called the *north* and the *east.*

8:14 The ***god of Dan*** refers to the northern shrine of the gold calf established by Jeroboam I (see 1 Kgs 12:28-29; 2 Kgs 10:29). • ***the god of Beersheba*** (literally *the way of Beersheba*): Evidently Beersheba had become a center of worship in the southern kingdom. Archaeologists have found the remains of

9:1 Zeph 2:14
9:2 Ps 139:7-10
9:3 Job 34:22; Ps 139:9-11; Isa 27:1; Jer 16:16
9:4 Lev 26:33; Jer 44:11
9:5 Ps 46:2, 6; Isa 64:1; [g]*tsaba'* (6635) ‣Deut 4:19; [h]*'abal* (0056) ‣Gen 37:34
9:6 Ps 104:3, 6, 13

and make vows in the name of the god
of Beersheba—
they will all fall down,
never to rise again."

Vision 5: God Stands at the Altar

9 Then I saw a vision of the Lord standing beside the altar. He said,

"Strike the tops of the Temple columns,
so that the foundation will shake.
Bring down the roof
on the heads of the people below.
I will kill with the sword those who
survive.
No one will escape!

2 "Even if they dig down to the place of
the dead,
I will reach down and pull them up.
Even if they climb up into the heavens,
I will bring them down.
3 Even if they hide at the very top of
Mount Carmel,
I will search them out and capture them.
Even if they hide at the bottom of the
ocean,
I will send the sea serpent after them
to bite them.
4 Even if their enemies drive them into
exile,
I will command the sword to kill them
there.
I am determined to bring disaster upon
them
and not to help them."

5 The Lord, the LORD of Heaven's [g]Armies,
touches the land and it melts,
and all its people [h]mourn.
The ground rises like the Nile River at
floodtime,
and then it sinks again.
6 The LORD's home reaches up to the
heavens,
while its foundation is on the earth.
He draws up water from the oceans
and pours it down as rain on the land.
The LORD is his name!

God's Sovereignty over All Nations (9:7)

Exod 15:18; Deut 32:8; 1 Chr 29:11-12; 2 Chr 20:6; Ps 2:1-12; 7:6-8; 10:16; 22:28; 47:2; 72:11; 83:18; 93:1-5; 103:19; Dan 2:20-21, 47; 4:34-37; Matt 28:18-20; Acts 17:24-26; 1 Tim 1:17; 6:15; Rev 15:3-4; 17:14; 19:16

In the ancient world, nations often considered religion in terms of a national god or gods. The king of Aram, for example, believed Israel's "gods" were tied to the hills and would not be able to act elsewhere (1 Kgs 20:23). Jephthah demonstrated a pagan heritage (see Judg 11:1-3) by saying that the god Chemosh had given the Ammonites their land (Judg 11:24). The prophet Amos, by contrast, knew that God alone had brought the Philistines from Crete and the Arameans from Kir (9:7). God had created the entire cosmos, not just Israel (4:13; 5:8), so he was perfectly justified in requiring that nations conduct their affairs with justice and mercy (1:3–2:3).

One heresy prevalent among the people of Judah and Israel was that, in spite of their sinfulness, God would eventually vindicate them because of his covenant with them (Jer 7:4; cp. Amos 3:1-2; 9:10). They developed a false theology of the day of the Lord: They thought that God's intervention in history meant deliverance for them and destruction for their enemies. Amos directly confronted this false notion of privilege (9:7; see also 5:18-20). The day of the Lord would not absolve sinful Israel; rather, God would use it to punish them.

Israel's position of privilege among the nations made them more responsible, not less. While the surrounding nations would be punished for their particularly grievous sins, Israel would be punished for all their sins (3:2). The NT further develops the theme of the greater responsibility of God's people: Those who receive much are responsible for much (Luke 12:48; Jas 3:1).

a horned altar (cp. illustrations, pp. 91, 173, 176) in the ruins of Beersheba.

9:1 ***I saw . . . the LORD*** (see 7:1): God ceased to reveal how or why he would punish Israel; he was now poised to act. • ***beside the altar:*** Judgment must begin with the center of worship (cp. 1 Pet 4:17). This altar probably refers to the Bethel shrine, although it could refer to the *Temple* in Jerusalem.

9:2-4 God is inescapable (cp. Ps 139:7-12). When people trust, believe, and obey God, his inescapability is a great blessing. But because Israel rejected God's revelation, his presence would mean judgment, not comfort.

9:2 ***to the place of the dead*** (literally *to Sheol*): In the OT, Sheol is a place beneath the earth where the dead have their abode.

9:3 Though *Mount Carmel* is not the highest mountain in the region, its lofty grandeur often represents the beauty and richness of the land. • ***sea serpent:*** In the ancient Near East, the sea was a symbol of chaos, often pitted against the national god (cp. Ps 74:14; 89:10; 104:26). However, the biblical text does not grant divine status to the sea monster ("Leviathan," also called "Rahab"; Ps 89:9-10), but sees it as subject to the Lord's command and judgment (Isa 27:1). Here, Amos portrays God's sovereign power to summon the sea serpent to his service.

9:5-6 Amos uses a third hymn fragment (also 4:13; 5:8-9) to remind Israel that God's domain is universal.

7 "Are you Israelites more important
to me
than the Ethiopians?" asks the LORD.
"I brought Israel out of Egypt,
but I also brought the Philistines from
Crete
and led the Arameans out of Kir.

8 "I, the Sovereign LORD,
am watching this sinful nation of
Israel.
I will destroy it
from the face of the earth.
But I will never completely destroy the
family of Israel,"
says the LORD.
9 "For I will give the command
and will shake Israel along with the
other nations
as grain is shaken in a sieve,
yet not one true kernel will be lost.
10 But all the sinners will die by the
sword—
all those who say, 'Nothing bad will
happen to us.'

6. PROMISE: THE LORD WILL RESTORE ISRAEL (9:11-15)

Restoration of David's Kingdom

11 "In that day I will restore the fallen
house of David.
I will repair its damaged walls.
From the ruins I will rebuild it
and restore its former glory.
12 And Israel will possess what is left of
Edom
and all the nations I have called to be
mine."
The LORD has spoken,
and he will do these things.

Restoration of the People and the Land

13 "The time will come," says the LORD,
"when the grain and grapes will grow
faster
than they can be harvested.
Then the terraced vineyards on the hills
of Israel
will drip with sweet wine!
14 I will bring my exiled people of Israel
back from distant lands,

9:7
2 Chr 14:9, 12
Isa 20:4-5; 43:3

9:8
Jer 5:10
Joel 2:32
Amos 7:17

9:9
Isa 30:28

9:11
Isa 16:5; 63:11

9:13
Lev 26:5
Joel 3:18, 20

9:14
Isa 61:4
Jer 30:18; 31:28

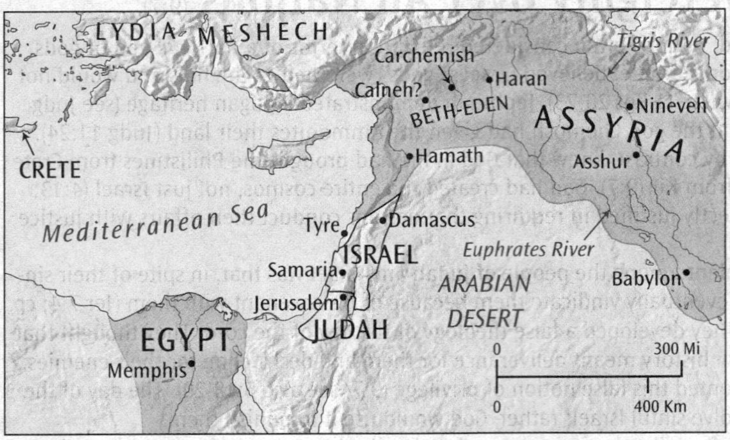

◀ **Lands Beyond Israel and Judah** (9:7). The Lord had raised up other peoples of the world just as he had raised up the people of Israel. So they should not be so proud as to think that they would escape punishment just because they were Israelites.

9:7 ***the Ethiopians*** (literally *the Cushites*): *Cush* (see Gen 10:6-7) was south of the Second Cataract of the Nile (cp. Isa 18:1) and was often linked with *Egypt*, its neighbor to the north. • Israel's exodus ***out of Egypt*** is compared to two other ancient migrations: the ***Philistines from Crete*** (literally *from Caphtor;* see also Jer 47:4) and the ***Arameans out of Kir*** (cp. 1:5; 2 Kgs 16:9).

9:8 Although God would severely punish Israel by uprooting and scattering them, he would ***never completely destroy*** them. A remnant would always exist. • ***the family of Israel:*** Literally *the house of Jacob*; see note on 3:13.

9:9-10 Even the Lord's most severe judgment is just. Only ***the sinners*** are destroyed, but ***not one true kernel will be lost***; God will save the righteous, who are faithful to him.

9:11-15 As the prophets often did, Amos closes his litany of judgments with a message of hope and restoration. Though Jerusalem and its Temple would be destroyed, David's line of kings cut off (Ps 89:38-51), and its people taken into captivity, God would restore a remnant of Israel (see also Isa 2:2-4; 4:2; 11:1-5).

9:11-12 ***house of David*** (or *kingdom of David;* literally *tent of David*): Amos portrays true worship of God as built around the Jerusalem Temple, with a descendant of David ruling over a united kingdom including both Israel and Judah (cp. Isa 9:6-7; 11:1-5). • ***and restore its former glory . . . all the nations I have called to be mine:*** The Greek version reads *and restore its former glory, / so that the rest of humanity, including the Gentiles— / all those I have called to be mine—might seek me.* Cp. Acts 15:16-17.

9:12 ***Edom*** (see 1:11) represents the enemies of God and of Israel (see Isa 34:5-6, 11; 63:1). In the time of restoration, God's enemies are to be subject to his people and to God himself. • ***the nations I have called:*** God promised Abraham that he would be a blessing to all the people of the earth (Gen 12:2-3). God's kingdom would embrace the outcasts and foreigners previously excluded (Isa 56; see Acts 8:27-39).

9:13-15 The coming age would restore the natural harmony lost in Eden (Gen 3) and would bring a new era of prosperity.

9:13 ***the hills . . . will drip with sweet wine:*** Amos began (1:2) with a quote from Joel 3:16. He now closes with an allusion to Joel 3:18, pointing poetically to a future time when humans will

9:15
Ezek 34:28

and they will rebuild their ruined cities
and live in them again.
They will plant vineyards and gardens;
they will eat their crops and drink
their wine.

15 I will firmly plant them there
in their own land.
They will never again be uprooted
from the land I have given them,"
says the LORD your God.

once again live in harmony with God's creation.

9:14-15 God promised not to completely destroy his people (9:8) but to bring the surviving remnant back to the land (see Hos 2:23).

THE BOOK OF OBADIAH

"Am I my brother's keeper?" This ancient question, posed by Cain when the Lord inquired about his missing brother Abel, has become a metaphor for sidestepping responsibility. But Cain was in fact guilty of murdering his brother. Even to stand aloof when innocent people are violated is to share in the crime. Edom, a neighbor and relative of Judah, watched in delight and participated as Babylon destroyed Jerusalem. Now the prophet Obadiah would hold Edom accountable. God's retribution always follows such injustice.

SETTING

Obadiah is a prophecy against Edom, a people that descended from Jacob's brother, Esau (see Gen 25:30), and inhabited the highlands east of the Jordan and south of the Dead Sea. The country of Edom was also known as Seir (Gen 32:3; 36:20-21, 30).

Edom existed throughout most of Israel's monarchy (about 1050–586 BC) and was often a vassal to the southern kingdom of Judah (2 Sam 8:14; 1 Kgs 11:14-16; 2 Kgs 8:20-22; cp. 2 Kgs 3:9-14). Edom was probably infiltrated and supplanted by Arab kingdoms in 600~400 BC. In postexilic and NT times, Edom resurfaced in southern Judah under the Greek name *Idumea,* whose most infamous citizen was Herod the Great, the self-styled "King of the Jews."

As a nation, Edom replayed Esau's original animosity toward Jacob. Edom was, for example, one of the nations that opposed Israel's exodus from Egypt (Num 20:14-21; 21:4). Much later, when the kingdom of Judah was attacked and taken into exile by the Babylonians, Edom not only rejoiced in the event, but also sided with the Babylonians against Israel, seeking to

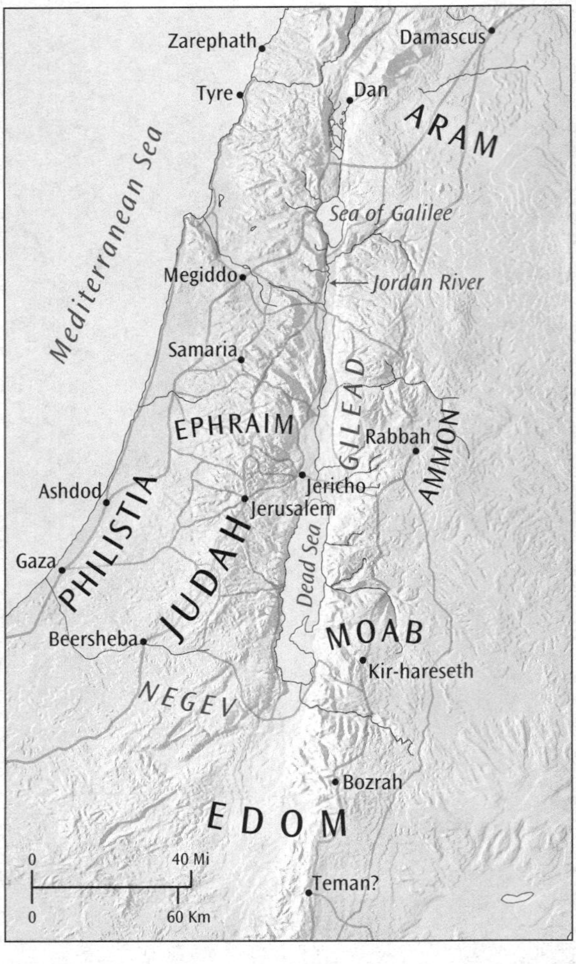

◄ **Key Places in Obadiah, about 586 BC.** The Babylonians destroyed JERUSALEM in 586 BC and took most of the people of JUDAH into exile. The surrounding peoples helped the Babylonians and rejoiced over Judah's destruction. None helped or rejoiced more than the people of EDOM, so Obadiah announced their judgment by God. • EDOM was noted for its rocky strongholds (v 3), its pride and self-sufficiency (vv 2-4), and its wisdom tradition (v 8).

enrich themselves. This infidelity toward their "brother" Israel (see note on v 10) prompted Obadiah's prophecy.

SUMMARY

Obadiah is built around two related themes: the destruction of Edom, and the vindication and restoration of Judah. In Obadiah's introduction (vv 1-9), a messenger is sent to call the nations to battle against Edom (v 1), and the forthcoming reality of Edom's judgment is announced (vv 2-9). The overthrow of Edom would completely destroy the pride of this nation that was secure in its physical location and its intellectual achievements.

The second section (vv 10-14) gives the reasons for Edom's humiliation in a series of taunts. The errant nation had a duty to its brother Jacob (v 10) that they not only ignored but actively repudiated.

In the third and final section (vv 15-21), Obadiah envisions a coming day of the Lord (v 15) that will culminate in a universal Kingdom belonging to the Lord (v 21). Those who do evil will suffer evil consequences (vv 15-16), and those who have suffered unjustly will be restored (vv 17-21). The people of Jerusalem will repossess the land inherited from their forefathers and will spill over their borders in every direction. Their nemesis, Edom, will be subjugated as an example of what happens to those who oppose the Lord's rule, and the whole world will recognize the Lord as King.

OUTLINE

v 1
The Message from the LORD

vv 2-9
Edom's Judgment Announced

vv 10-14
Reasons for Edom's Punishment

vv 15-21
Edom Destroyed, Israel Restored

AUTHOR AND DATE

Obadiah's name means "servant of the LORD." He is known only from his prophecy and from clues that the text provides as to his time and place. Several individuals in OT Israel were named Obadiah, including King Ahab's palace supervisor at an earlier time (1 Kgs 18:3-16).

Obadiah's prophecy was motivated by the invasion and at least partial destruction of the kingdom of Judah, which had its capital in Jerusalem. In 586 BC, the Babylonian king Nebuchadnezzar terminated Judah's independence and exiled its last king, Zedekiah (2 Kgs 25). Outside of the book of Obadiah, there is little reference to Edom's specific response to this event (see also Isa 34:5-10). Obadiah probably wrote his prophecy shortly after Jerusalem was destroyed in 586 BC.

LITERARY FEATURES

Beginning with a standard prophetic message form, the prophecy divides into three sections that set forth the contrasting fates of Edom, Israel, and the nations in light of the retributive justice and coming triumph of the Kingdom of the Lord.

TIMELINE

640–609 BC
Josiah as king of Judah

about 627~580 BC
Jeremiah as prophet

612 BC
Nineveh is conquered by Babylon

609–598 BC
Jehoiakim as king of Judah

605–562 BC
Nebuchadnezzar II as king of Babylon

586 BC
Nebuchadnezzar destroys Jerusalem

around 586 BC
▸ Obadiah as prophet

556–539 BC
Nabonidus as king of Babylon

553 BC
Nabonidus burns cities of Edom

600~400 BC
Edom infiltrated and displaced by Arab tribes

after 400s BC
Edom reemerges as Idumea in southern Judah

Were God's great promises to his people doomed never to come true? Was Edom to get away with its perfidy scot-free, and the other nations too?

LESLIE C. ALLEN
The Books of Joel, Obadiah, Jonah, and Micah, p. 137

Obadiah's message about Edom echoes many of the classical prophets, and parts of it closely follow Jer 49:9, 14-16. It should probably be read in conjunction with other prophecies regarding Edom's future role, and may even function as an expansion of such passages as Joel 3:19 and Amos 9:12.

MEANING AND MESSAGE

On first reading, it is easy to regard Obadiah's prophecy as little more than a prophetic tirade in which the Lord's wrath is directed toward Israel's enemies. The Lord's wrath is real, and evil does not go unpunished, but the book has far more to say than this.

Nations, like individuals, should attend carefully to what they plant, because the time of harvest will quickly come. God is offended by wrongdoing, and he brings justice for the oppressed. What Edom did to Judah, whether actively or passively, would rebound on them (vv 2-9) according to the ancient law of retribution (*lex talionis*), which states, "As you have done . . . so it will be done to you" (v 15).

In the concluding section (vv 15-21), the day of the Lord breaks in on the world, bringing full justice to the oppressed, punishment to the oppressors, and the onset of a universal kingdom in which the Lord rules over all nations. On a local and historical level, this meant that Israel would be restored to her land and given sovereignty over the lands of Edom. On a universal level, Edom's submission was part of a larger historical movement. Not just Edom, but "all . . . nations" (v 16) will drink the cup of the Lord's wrath. When the Lord returns as King to a restored Jerusalem, Mount Zion will be at the very center of the new order.

This picture of God dominates Obadiah's theology and forces modern readers to face an unpopular decision. Whom will we serve—a god who is indifferent to evil, or the God of justice that we find in Obadiah? Those who share the contemporary disposition to be offended by a "God who would condemn anyone to hell" may shrink from Obadiah's unambiguous condemnation of Edom's perfidy. But only a God who judges can reassure us that evil will not ultimately triumph.

Obadiah looks forward at the conclusion of his prophecy (v 21) to that new day when "the LORD himself will be king." This hope of Israel becomes the hope of the whole world in Christ's announcement that "the Kingdom of God is near" (Mark 1:15; Luke 10:9-12; 21:31-33).

FURTHER READING

LESLIE C. ALLEN
The Books of Joel, Obadiah, Jonah, and Micah (1976)

DAVID W. BAKER
Joel, Obadiah, Malachi (2006)

FRANK E. GAEBELEIN
Four Minor Prophets: Their Message for Today (1970)

RICHARD PATTERSON
Obadiah in *Cornerstone Biblical Commentary*, vol. 10 (2008)

1:1 Ps 137:7; Isa 34:5-15; 63:1-6; Jer 49:7-22; Ezek 25:12-14; Joel 3:19; Amos 1:11-12
1:2 Num 24:15-19
1:3 Isa 16:6; Jer 49:15-16; Rev 18:7; [a]*zadon* (2087) ›Deut 17:12
1:4 Job 39:26-30; Isa 14:12-15
1:5-6 Jer 49:9-10
1:7 Isa 19:11-14; Jer 30:14
1:8 Job 5:12-14; Isa 19:3, 13-14; 29:14
1:9 Jer 49:20-22; Amos 1:12
1:10 Ezek 25:12-14

The Message from the LORD (v 1)

1 This is the vision that the Sovereign LORD revealed to Obadiah concerning the land of Edom.

We have heard a message from the LORD
that an ambassador was sent to the nations to say,
"Get ready, everyone!
Let's assemble our armies and attack Edom!"

Edom's Judgment Announced (vv 2-9)

2 The LORD says to Edom,
"I will cut you down to size among the nations;
you will be greatly despised.
3 You have been deceived by your own [a]pride
because you live in a rock fortress
and make your home high in the mountains.
'Who can ever reach us way up here?'
you ask boastfully.
4 But even if you soar as high as eagles
and build your nest among the stars,
I will bring you crashing down,"
says the LORD.
5 "If thieves came at night and robbed you
(what a disaster awaits you!),
they would not take everything.
Those who harvest grapes
always leave a few for the poor.
But your enemies will wipe you out completely!
6 Every nook and cranny of Edom
will be searched and looted.
Every treasure will be found and taken.
7 "All your allies will turn against you.
They will help to chase you from your land.
They will promise you peace
while plotting to deceive and destroy you.
Your trusted friends will set traps for you,
and you won't even know about it.
8 At that time not a single wise person
will be left in the whole land of Edom,"
says the LORD.
"For on the mountains of Edom
I will destroy everyone who has understanding.
9 The mightiest warriors of Teman
will be terrified,
and everyone on the mountains of Edom
will be cut down in the slaughter.

Reasons for Edom's Punishment (vv 10-14)

10 "Because of the violence you did
to your close relatives in Israel,

---

v 1 The word *vision* introduces a prophetic book (Isa 1:1; Nah 1:1); it also defines what a prophet saw or sensed as a divine word (Ezek 12:26-27; Dan 8:1). A vision that did not come from the Lord was false (Jer 14:14; 23:16), the ultimate proof being its lack of fulfillment (Ezek 12:22-24). By contrast, true visions of near or distant events do come to fruition (Ezek 12:25; Hab 2:3). Prophetic visions came in various forms (dreams, extrasensory experiences; e.g., Dan 8:2). The absence of visions is a mark of divine abandonment (Lam 2:9; Ezek 7:26; Mic 3:6). • ***Sovereign LORD*** is one of several names for the God of Israel. • ***Obadiah*** was a common Hebrew name that meant "servant of the LORD." The prophet Obadiah is unknown apart from this book. • ***an ambassador was sent to the nations:*** In ancient warfare, allies would be contacted about joining a military coalition to punish an enemy or defend against attack. Here the Sovereign Lord calls ***the nations*** to redress Edom's evil pride. • ***Let's assemble:*** This is a willing coalition, though ironically, they will be punished later for their own evil deeds (vv 15-16).

vv 2-4 ***I will cut you down:*** Several messages of judgment rehearse Edom's specific sins against Israel (vv 10-14; Ezek 25:12-14; 36:5; Jer 49:7-22). Edom frequently appears among the nations that opposed Israel and the Lord (Isa 34; Ezek 35–36; Amos 9). • ***down to size among the nations . . . your own pride:*** Edom's rocky topography mimicked Edom's pride. The height of the mountain fortress that provided their security only emphasizes the height from which Edom would fall. Edomite princes were among the arrogant rulers of the nations (Ezek 32:29; cp. Gen 36; 1 Chr 1:43-54).

vv 5-7 The Babylonians completely destroyed Jerusalem. By sharing in the plunder, Edom deserved equal retribution (see note on vv 15-18).

v 5 Edom's destroyers would take everything, unlike thieves and harvesters. ***Thieves*** would leave anything that would hinder an immediate, successful escape; harvesters would ***always leave*** gleanings ***for the poor*** (Deut 24:19, cp. Ruth 2; Matt 12:1).

v 6 ***Edom*** (Hebrew *Esau;* also in vv 8-9, 18-19, 21): The Hebrew text uses the name of Esau, Jacob's brother, indicating Edom's violation of a fraternal relationship (vv 10-14).

v 7 ***allies*** (literally *men of the covenant*): Edom should have been the ally of its brother Israel, but instead, Edom had made a covenant with Babylon. • ***promise you peace*** (literally *men of peace*, paralleling *men of the covenant*): It was poetic justice that Edom's treachery with Babylon was rewarded by Babylon's treachery against Edom.

v 8 ***At that time*** (literally *in that day*): The Hebrew word *yom,* "*day,*" occurs twelve times in vv 8-15, often translated "when" or "at that time." The time referred to in v 8 is the beginning of the end, when God steps in to reverse the fortunes of his people. • ***wise person . . . everyone who has understanding:*** Edom took pride in its wisdom tradition (cp. Jer 49:7). For example, the book of Job is set in Edomite territory.

vv 10-14 ***Because of the violence you did . . . in Israel:*** The basis for Esau's condemnation is stated in v 10 (cp. Isa 34; Jer 49:7-22; Joel 3:19; Amos 1:11-12) and amplified in vv 11-14, where Edom's treachery is described. In legal terms, the evidence of these verses supports the charge of covenant breaking.

v 10 ***your close relatives in Israel:*** Literally *your brother Jacob.* The names "Jacob" and "Israel" are often interchanged throughout the OT, referring sometimes to the individual patriarch and sometimes to the nation.

you will be filled with shame
and destroyed forever.
11 When they were invaded,
you stood aloof, refusing to help them.
Foreign invaders carried off their
wealth
and cast lots to divide up Jerusalem,
but you acted like one of Israel's
enemies.
12 "You should not have gloated
when they exiled your relatives to
distant lands.
You should not have rejoiced
when the people of Judah suffered
such misfortune.
You should not have spoken arrogantly
in that terrible time of trouble.
13 You should not have plundered the land
of Israel
when they were suffering such
calamity.
You should not have gloated over their
destruction
when they were suffering such
calamity.
You should not have seized their wealth
when they were suffering such
calamity.
14 You should not have stood at the
crossroads,
killing those who tried to escape.
You should not have captured the
survivors
and handed them over in their
terrible time of trouble.

Edom Destroyed, Israel Restored (vv 15-21)

15 "The day is near when I, the LORD,
will judge all godless nations!
As you have done to Israel,
so it will be done to you.
All your evil deeds
will fall back on your own heads.
16 Just as you swallowed up my people
on my holy mountain,
so you and the surrounding nations
will swallow the punishment I pour
out on you.
Yes, all you nations will drink and
stagger
and disappear from history.
17 "But Jerusalem will become a refuge for
those who escape;
it will be a holy place.
And the people of Israel will come back
to reclaim their inheritance.
18 The people of Israel will be a raging fire,
and Edom a field of dry stubble.
The descendants of Joseph will be a
flame
roaring across the field, devouring
everything.
There will be no survivors in Edom.
I, the LORD, have spoken!
19 "Then my people living in the Negev
will occupy the mountains of Edom.

1:11 Ps 137:7; Joel 3:3; Nah 3:10
1:12 Ezek 35:15; Mic 4:11
1:13 Ezek 35:5
1:15 Jer 50:29; Ezek 30:3; Joel 1:15; Hab 2:8
1:16 Jer 25:15; 49:12
1:17 Isa 14:1-3; Amos 9:11-15
1:18 Zech 12:6
1:19 Jer 31:5; 32:44

v 11 Outside of this book, nothing specific is known of Edom's role during the various Babylonian invasions of Judah (in 605, 597, and 586 BC). Responsibility toward one's neighbor is a specific requirement of God's law (e.g., Deut 22:1-4; cp. Matt 25:41-46), especially when there is either a specific "treaty of brotherhood" (Amos 1:9) or a historical relationship that is regarded as fraternal (see notes on vv 6, 10, 12).

vv 12-14 All societies are held accountable for sins such as those of Edom (see, e.g., the oracles against Israel's neighbors in Amos 1:3–2:3). Among the sins that the Edomites committed against Judah were sharing with the Babylonians in plundering the land (v 13) and either killing or repatriating Judean fugitives (v 14).

v 12 The tribes of Israel were Edom's ***relatives*** (literally *brother;* see notes on vv 6, 10; cp. Num 20:14). • Edom and other local nations had apparently deceived themselves into thinking that rapprochement with Nebuchadnezzar in 586 BC would bring them respite. Their time of judgment would come.

vv 15-18 The law of retribution (*lex talionis*) is that we harvest what we plant. Edom's treachery, compounded by her pride, is more than returned when the cup of vengeance comes around to her lips. Justice would bring deliverance for Israel and punishment for Edom (see also Jer 49:7-22; Ezek 32:29; Mal 1:2-5).

v 15 ***The day is near when I, the LORD, will judge*** (literally *the day of the LORD is near*): Although the day of the Lord was sometimes a temporal event (e.g., the forthcoming destruction of Edom; Joel's locust plague, Joel 1:15), in its final form that day encompasses God's final retribution on ***all godless nations.*** • ***As you have done:*** For those who experience judgment, their ***evil deeds*** will shape their punishment.

v 17 ***Jerusalem*** (literally *Mount Zion*) would become ***a refuge for those who escape.*** A remnant of Judah remained in Jerusalem (see Jer 40:11-12). The Lord's mountain of refuge sharply contrasts with Edom's failed cliff fortresses. • ***their inheritance:*** The land God gave to Abraham (Gen 12:1-7) would be returned to his descendants in perpetuity. • ***the people of Israel:*** Literally *house of Jacob;* also in v 18. See note on v 10. This promise of a return for the Judeans but not for the Edomites is picked up by the prophet Malachi (Mal 1:4-5).

v 18 The principle of retribution is expressed in the vivid image of ***a raging fire*** burning Edom to extinction. Edomite cities were burned by Babylonian king Nabonidus in 553 BC.

vv 19-21 History yields to the day when the entire world will belong to the Lord as his kingdom. This message encourages God's people and warns the nations that forget God.

vv 19-20 God's people living in ***the Negev, the foothills of Judah,*** and ***Benjamin*** (three regions of Judah) would ***possess*** territories of their neighbors (***Edom, the Philistine plains, Gilead***). Restored Israel would recover ***Ephraim and Samaria*** (territory lost in 722–721 BC to Assyria) and expand its borders to those lands promised in the conquest (***the Philistine plains, the land of Gilead, the Phoenician coast***). See also Ezek 47:13-23.

v 19 ***the foothills of Judah:*** Hebrew *the Shephelah;* see map on p. 372.

1:20
1 Kgs 17:9
1:21
Ps 22:28
Zech 14:9
Rev 11:15; 19:6

Those living in the foothills of Judah
will possess the Philistine plains
and take over the fields of Ephraim
and Samaria.
And the people of Benjamin
will occupy the land of Gilead.
20 The exiles of Israel will return to their land
and occupy the Phoenician coast as
far north as Zarephath.
The captives from Jerusalem exiled in
the north
will return home and resettle the
towns of the Negev.
21 Those who have been rescued will go up
to Mount Zion in Jerusalem
to rule over the mountains of
Edom.
And the LORD himself will be king!"

v 20 ***in the north:*** Hebrew *in Sepharad,* probably a colony of Jewish exiles in Asia Minor who would return to the Negev. The scene corresponds with some actual events but looks beyond any single movement of refugees to the end times.

v 21 ***Those who have been rescued:*** As in Greek and Syriac versions; Hebrew reads *Rescuers.* • ***to Mount Zion:*** Or *from Mount Zion.* God's people ascend his holy mountain ***to rule over*** (or *to judge*) the mountains of their ancient foe Edom as a precursor to the coming universal Kingdom.

THE BOOK OF JONAH

Jonah is well-known and loved for the amazing and ironic events it recounts. Although Jonah is the main character, the book's main purpose is not to teach us about him but to teach us about God. Through Jonah's experience, God, the all-powerful Creator, reveals that though he is a God who will pour out his wrath on the wicked, he is also one who eagerly pours out his mercy on those who repent—including those we would too quickly deem to be beyond mercy.

SETTING

Jonah was a prophet in the northern kingdom of Israel during the politically prosperous but spiritually dark reign of Jeroboam II (793–753 BC). Despite Jeroboam's spiritual failures (see 2 Kgs 14:23-24), God allowed him to continue the expansion of territory begun under his father, King Jehoash. This expansion, predicted by God through Jonah (2 Kgs 14:25, 28), eventually brought Israel's territory back to approximately what it had been in the glory days of David and Solomon (see 1 Kgs 8:65). When Jonah prophesied, nationalistic zeal was running high.

The book of Jonah records the prophet's visit to Nineveh, a key city in the Assyrian empire. Assyria's power had swelled in previous decades. During that time, Shalmaneser III of Assyria (858–824 BC) extended the influence of the empire well into Palestine. Assyrian annals from that period record Shalmaneser confronting the Israelite king Ahab (1 Kgs 17–22), among others, at the famous battle of Qarqar (853 BC). But during the reigns of Jehoash (798–782 BC) and Jeroboam II (793–753 BC) in Israel, Assyria's dominance in the region waned because of failed leadership and continued resistance on the frontiers. Jonah preached in Nineveh when the Assyrian empire was at this low point, probably around 755 BC.

Some years following Jonah's visit to Nineveh, Assyria began reasserting itself throughout the Near East during the reign of Tiglath-pileser III (744–727 BC). In 722 BC, a few decades after Jonah, Assyria

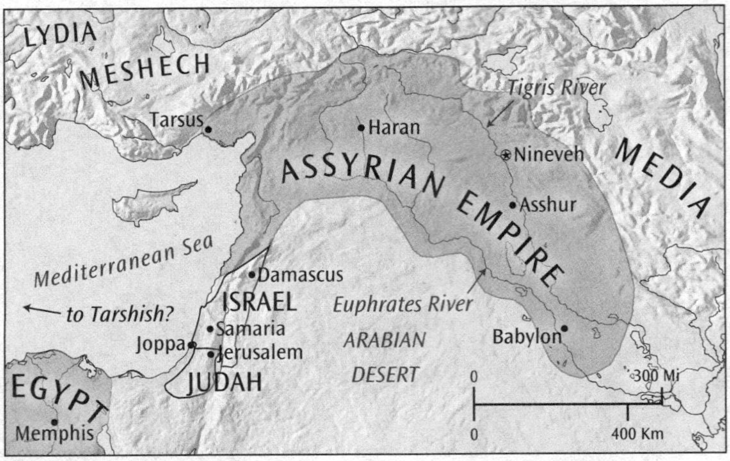

◂ **Setting of Jonah, about 755 BC.** When God called Jonah to prophesy judgment in NINEVEH, ASSYRIAN power was at a low point, but the Assyrians had already proven to be brutal enemies. When God's call came, Jonah fled the other direction—he took a ship from JOPPA toward TARSHISH, which was probably located at the far end of the MEDITERRANEAN SEA. Jonah later obeyed God's call and preached to the people of NINEVEH. Assyria thus incurred no judgment in the time of Jonah.

sacked Samaria and brought the northern kingdom of Israel to an end. A century later, the prophet Nahum of Judah announced the imminent destruction of Nineveh and the Assyrian empire for its pervasive wickedness. Nineveh was destroyed by the Babylonians in 612 BC. The repentance brought about through Jonah's preaching evidently took no lasting root.

SUMMARY

The book of Jonah falls naturally into two parts. Chapters 1–2 recount Jonah's initial rejection of the Lord's commission to warn Nineveh of the judgment it had incurred because of its wickedness. Instead of heading for Nineveh, Jonah set out by ship in the opposite direction (1:3). The Lord sent a raging storm to chasten the prophet. After a frantic attempt by the pagan sailors to appease whatever god had been offended, Jonah was "discovered" and was cast overboard. God showed his power by calming the storm, and in a twist of irony, the pagan sailors worshiped God while his prophet presumably plunged to a shameful death. But God had other plans and showed his power to save Jonah. Jonah was swallowed by a "great fish," within which he apparently repented (ch 2). After three days and nights, the fish spit Jonah out onto dry land.

In chs 3–4, God renews his commission of the prophet to preach to Nineveh. This time Jonah obeys, leading to yet another irony. Nineveh repented en masse upon hearing Jonah's warnings (ch 3), and God refrained from executing the judgment that Jonah had warned was coming (3:10). Jonah, not able to accept God's outpouring of mercy toward Israel's pagan enemies, moved from selfish anger to suicidal despair (ch 4). God once more deployed his power over nature to chasten Jonah, this time through the rapid growth and demise of a plant that shaded the pouting prophet from the sun. The book ends rather abruptly, leaving Jonah and the reader pondering God's final question to the prophet: Should God (and his people) not desire sinners to receive God's mercy rather than his wrath?

OUTLINE

1:1–2:10
Jonah's Disobedience, Discipline, and Deliverance

3:1–4:11
Jonah's Obedience, Anger, and Admonishment

AUTHOR AND DATE

The book of Jonah does not identify its author. The title derives from the name of the main character. Jonah may have written the book, though whether he wrote it or not does not affect its integrity as Scripture. If someone other than Jonah wrote the book, it was probably a prophetic associate of his.

GENRE

Unlike other prophetic books, Jonah is almost entirely narrative rather than a collection of prophetic messages. But is it a *historical* narrative? Many have insisted that the book is fictional because it describes miraculous events, and diverse attempts have been made to classify the book according to

TIMELINE

853 BC
Battle of Qarqar

798–782 BC
Jehoash as king of Israel

793–753 BC
Jeroboam II as king of Israel

about 760~750 BC
Amos as prophet

about 760~722 BC
Hosea as prophet

about 755~750 BC
▸ **Jonah as prophet**

744–727 BC
Tiglath-pileser III as king of Assyria

722 BC
Samaria is destroyed by Assyria, end of the northern kingdom of Israel

701 BC
Sennacherib invades Judah

about 645~615 BC
Nahum as prophet

612 BC
Nineveh is conquered by Babylon

This is alone true wisdom, to submit ourselves wholly to the will of God.

JOHN CALVIN
Commentary on Jonah, s.v. 4:3

some non-historical literary genre, the most popular choices being parable and "didactic story." Although the author of Jonah did utilize certain literary devices to make his point (the use of poetry, irony, and language common to parables is clear), the book presents itself as a historical account (see 1:1), and it is best understood as a historical narrative whose purpose includes communicating the theological and moral significance of the events that occurred.

MEANING AND MESSAGE

Jonah is unique among the prophetic books. It narrates God's sending of a prophet to Assyria, an enemy of Israel, and the widespread repentance that resulted. The lesson Jonah learned was evidently one that the entire nation of Israel needed. That lesson may be summed up in the last line of Jonah's psalm-prayer, "my salvation comes from the LORD alone" (2:9, literally *salvation belongs to the LORD*). Salvation is the Lord's to give to whomever he pleases, and those who have received God's mercy must not try to restrict the flow of God's mercy to others, even their enemies (see 4:1-11).

Salvation, then, whether from the threat of physical harm or from judgment, is directly related to God's sovereignty. The sailors were saved after God calmed the storm. Jonah was saved from drowning when God sent the fish to swallow him. There is no domain, even in the depths of the ocean, from which God cannot deliver and protect human life. Likewise, there is no nation that God cannot judge (3:4, 9) or save from judgment (3:10; see Jer 18:7-10).

The book of Jonah reveals that even in the OT God was eager to bring salvation beyond the borders of Israel. Israel was his covenant people, and from the beginning his desire was to bless the nations through Israel (see Gen 12:3). Jonah fled because he was well aware of God's desire to see wicked Gentiles repent and be saved from judgment (4:2; cp. Exod 34:6-7). Jonah did not have God's heart for the nations, or he would have eagerly desired that they turn from idols to know the God of heaven, who created the world (1:9; see 2 Pet 3:9).

FURTHER READING

DESMOND ALEXANDER
Jonah in *Obadiah, Jonah, Micah* (1988)

LESLIE C. ALLEN
The Books of Joel, Obadiah, Jonah and Micah (1976)

JAMES BRUCKNER
Jonah, Nahum, Habakkuk, Zephaniah (2004)

RICHARD PATTERSON
Jonah in *Cornerstone Biblical Commentary*, vol. 10 (2008)

DOUGLAS STUART
Hosea–Jonah (1987)

1. JONAH'S DISOBEDIENCE, DISCIPLINE, AND DELIVERANCE (1:1–2:10)

Jonah Runs from the LORD

1 The LORD gave this message to Jonah
son of Amittai: 2 "Get up and go to the
great city of Nineveh. Announce my judgment against it because I have seen how
wicked its people are."
3 But Jonah got up and went in the opposite
direction to get away from the LORD. He
went down to the port of Joppa, where he
found a ship leaving for Tarshish. He bought
a ticket and went on board, hoping to escape
from the LORD by sailing to Tarshish.
4 But the LORD hurled a powerful wind
over the sea, causing a violent storm that

1:1
2 Kgs 14:25
Matt 12:39-41; 16:4
Luke 11:29-30, 32

1:2
2 Kgs 19:36
Ezra 9:6
Isa 58:1
Jer 1:7-10
Hos 7:2
Jon 3:3

1:1–2:10 Jonah initially rejected the Lord's commission to warn Nineveh of the judgment it had incurred because of its wickedness.

1:1 ***Jonah son of Amittai*** was from Gath-hepher, a town located on the border of the tribal areas of Naphtali and Zebulun. He ministered to the northern kingdom of Israel during the reign of Jeroboam II (793–753 BC; see 2 Kgs 14:25).

1:2 By Jonah's day, ***Nineveh*** already had quite a long history (see Gen 10:12). It was a key city in the Assyrian empire until its destruction in 612 BC (see Nah 1–3). Nineveh's ruins are located across the Tigris River from the modern city of Mosul, Iraq. • ***great city:*** See note on 3:3.

1:3 Jonah's attempt to ***get away from the LORD*** was futile. One cannot ***escape*** God (Ps 139:7-10) or disobey his will without consequence (Deut 8:5). Jonah's reluctance to go to Nineveh is understandable, however. Assyria was an enemy of Israel known for its violence (3:8; see also Nah 3:1-4). Jonah did not want these non-Israelites to have the opportunity to repent and be saved (4:2). • ***Joppa*** was a key port city on the Mediterranean coast (2 Chr 2:16; Ezra 3:7); it is now a suburb of modern Tel-Aviv. • ***Tarshish*** was possibly the port city of Tartessos in Spain, in which case Jonah was attempting to flee as far as imaginable in the opposite direction from Nineveh. Tarsus in Asia Minor is another possibility. Some think *Tarshish* is a general reference to the sea or to any destination accessible by sea.

1:4 God's power over nature is a prominent theme throughout Jonah (see 1:4, 9, 13-16, 17; 2:3, 10; 4:6-7; see note on 1:16).

threatened to break the ship apart. 5Fearing
for their lives, the desperate sailors shouted
to their gods for help and threw the cargo
overboard to lighten the ship.
But all this time Jonah was sound asleep
down in the hold. 6So the captain went
down after him. "How can you sleep at a
time like this?" he shouted. "Get up and
pray to your god! Maybe he will pay attention to us and spare our lives."

Sailors Throw Jonah into the Sea

7Then the crew cast lots to see which of
them had offended the gods and caused the
terrible storm. When they did this, the lots
identified Jonah as the culprit. 8"Why has
this awful storm come down on us?" they
demanded. "Who are you? What is your
line of work? What country are you from?
What is your nationality?"
9Jonah answered, "I am a Hebrew, and I
[a]worship the LORD, the God of heaven, who
made the sea and the land."
10The sailors were terrified when they
heard this, for he had already told them he
was running away from the LORD. "Oh, why
did you do it?" they groaned. 11And since
the storm was getting worse all the time,
they asked him, "What should we do to you
to stop this storm?"
12"Throw me into the sea," Jonah said,
"and it will become calm again. I know that
this terrible storm is all my fault."
13Instead, the sailors rowed even harder
to get the ship to the land. But the stormy sea
was too violent for them, and they couldn't
make it. 14Then they cried out to the LORD,
Jonah's God. "O LORD," they pleaded, "don't
make us die for this man's sin. And don't
hold us responsible for his death. O LORD,
you have sent this storm upon him for your
own good reasons."
15Then the sailors picked Jonah up and
threw him into the raging sea, and the
storm stopped at once! 16The sailors were
awestruck by the LORD's great power, and
they offered him a sacrifice and vowed to
serve him.
17Now the LORD had arranged for a great
fish to swallow Jonah. And Jonah was inside
the fish for three days and three nights.

Jonah's Prayer and Deliverance

2 Then Jonah [b]prayed to the LORD his God
from inside the fish. 2He said,

"I cried out to the LORD in my great
trouble,
and he answered me.

1:3 Gen 3:8; 4:16; 2 Chr 2:16; 9:21; Ps 139:7; Isa 23:6; Acts 9:36
1:5 1 Kgs 18:26; Acts 27:18-19, 38
1:6 Ps 107:28-29; Jon 3:8-9
1:7 Josh 7:14, 18-19; 1 Sam 14:41-42
1:8 Gen 47:3
1:9 Gen 1:9; Ezra 1:2; 5:11; Neh 1:4; 9:6; [a]*yare'* (3372) ‣ Exod 1:17
1:12 John 11:50
1:15 Ps 89:9; Mark 4:41
1:16 Ps 66:13-14
1:17 Matt 12:40; 16:4
2:1 Ps 130:1; [b]*palal* (6419) ‣ Gen 20:17
2:2 Ps 18:4-6; 22:24

1:5-6 Jonah's ongoing *sleep* was perhaps induced by God to advance the crisis to a point where it was clear that the sailors' *gods* could not help (1:6).

1:7-8 Use of *lots* was permitted by God for certain purposes (see Lev 16:8; Josh 18:6; 1 Chr 26:12-16; Acts 1:26); however, divination in general, as practiced in the wider ancient world, was displeasing to the Lord (Deut 18:9-13). • ***to see who had offended the gods:*** It was fairly common in the ancient Near East to assume that bad fortune was the result of a god's taking offense.

1:9 *a Hebrew:* See also Gen 41:12; Exod 1:15; 2:11. • Jonah worshiped ***the LORD,*** who in contrast to the sailors' false gods ***made the sea and the land,*** and thus controlled them. Many gods were believed to have jurisdiction over specific realms and functions. The designation ***God of heaven*** likely conveyed the superiority of that deity over all others, as heaven is the highest realm. The OT consistently proclaims that the Lord alone is the one true God (see, e.g., Deut 6:4), while at times adopting language that reflects his superiority to the false gods that occupied the imaginations of pagan peoples (see Ps 95:3-5).

1:12 *Throw me:* Jonah's calmness in giving this direction is surprising. But he was willing to face death with equanimity rather than give the hated Assyrians a chance to repent.

1:13-14 *Instead, the sailors rowed even harder:* It was now clear that Jonah was the one who had offended the Lord, but the sailors were apparently concerned that ***the LORD*** would be more offended if they killed one of his prophets.

1:16 *awestruck:* God's display of power over the storm-tossed sea moved ***the sailors*** to worship. Although sacrifices and vows were aspects of Israelite worship (e.g., Ps 116:17-18), it is unlikely that the sailors were completely converted from the worship of false gods; they probably added Israel's god to their list. It is ironic that pagan sailors honored ***the LORD*** while the Lord's prophet, having dishonored him, apparently plunged to his death (see also note on 2:8-9).

1:17 Verse 1:17 is numbered 2:1 in the Hebrew text. • Some critics consider it impossible that Jonah could be delivered from death in the belly of ***a great fish.*** In making this judgment, they oppose themselves to one of the book's main theological themes—that God is supremely sovereign over nature (see note on 1:4). If God exists, and he created and controls nature (1:9, 16; see also Gen 1:21), a miraculous event of this magnitude is not unfathomable. The book presents the fish episode as a historical event. • No indication is given as to the species of the fish, nor is identifying a species crucial to validating the significance of the account. Granted God's creative power, the fish that swallowed Jonah might well have been specially formed and appointed by the Lord for this particular event. If God exists and can work miracles, Jonah's need for oxygen and protection from digestive processes poses no problem (cp. Dan 3:14-27). On the other hand, certain species are large enough to have served the purpose (e.g., the whale shark), and similar incidents have been recorded in modern times. • Jesus later referred to Jonah's stay in the belly of the fish ***for three days and three nights*** in predicting the duration of his time in the grave (Matt 12:39-41). • ***Arranged for*** is the first of four occurrences of the same Hebrew word in the book (see 4:6, 7, 8). All four occurrences speak of God's effortless control over all the forces of nature.

2:1-10 Verses 2:1-10 are numbered 2:2-11 in the Hebrew text.

2:1-9 Realizing that the Lord had graciously delivered him by sending the fish, Jonah composed this psalm-like prayer. Its careful structure, conforming to the pattern of an individual song of thanksgiving, suggests that it may have been composed after the event, as Jonah recalled his emotions and concerns.

2:2 Jonah's psalm-prayer opens by

I called to you from the land of the [c]dead,
and LORD, you heard me!
3 You threw me into the ocean depths,
and I sank down to the heart of the sea.
The mighty waters engulfed me;
I was buried beneath your wild and stormy waves.
4 Then I said, 'O LORD, you have driven me
from your presence.
Yet I will look once more toward your
holy Temple.'

5 "I sank beneath the waves,
and the waters closed over me.
Seaweed wrapped itself around my head.
6 I sank down to the very roots of the mountains.
I was imprisoned in the earth,
whose gates lock shut forever.
But you, O LORD my God,
snatched me from the jaws of death!
7 As my life was slipping away,
I remembered the LORD.
And my earnest prayer went out to you
in your holy Temple.
8 Those who worship [d]false gods
turn their backs on all God's mercies.
9 But I will offer sacrifices to you with
songs of [e]praise,
and I will fulfill all my vows.
For my salvation comes from the
LORD alone."

10 Then the LORD ordered the fish to spit
Jonah out onto the beach.

2. JONAH'S OBEDIENCE, ANGER, AND ADMONISHMENT (3:1–4:11)

Jonah Goes to Nineveh and Preaches

3 Then the LORD spoke to Jonah a second
time: 2 "Get up and go to the great city
of Nineveh, and deliver the message I have
given you."
3 This time Jonah obeyed the LORD's command and went to Nineveh, a city so large
that it took three days to see it all. 4 On the
day Jonah entered the city, he shouted to the
crowds: "Forty days from now Nineveh will
be destroyed!" 5 The people of Nineveh [f]be-
lieved God's message, and from the greatest
to the least, they declared a fast and put on
burlap to show their sorrow.

The People of Nineveh Repent

6 When the king of Nineveh heard what
Jonah was saying, he stepped down from

[c]*she'ol* (7585) ▸Gen 37:35
2:3 Ps 42:7
2:4 1 Kgs 8:38; Ps 5:7; 31:22
2:5 Ps 69:1; Lam 3:54
2:6 Ps 16:10; 30:3; Isa 38:17; 40:12
2:7 2 Chr 30:27; Ps 18:6; 77:10-11; 142:3
2:8 [d]*hebel* (1892) ▸Ps 39:5
2:9 Ps 3:8; 50:14; 68:20; Hos 14:2; [e]*todah* (8426) ▸Lev 7:15
3:2 Jer 1:17; Ezek 2:7
3:3 Jon 1:2; 4:11
3:4 Matt 12:41; Luke 11:32
3:5 [f]*'aman* (0539) ▸Gen 15:6

recalling a previous prayer that was not so polished yet was all the more fervent—his cry for help while on the verge of drowning. • ***from the land of the dead*** (literally *from the belly of Sheol*): Sheol was thought to be the abode of the dead (see Isa 14:15; Ezek 31:15-17). The belly metaphor for Sheol is found nowhere else in the OT; it pictures Jonah's experience of being delivered from Sheol through the *belly* of a fish.

2:4 On the brink of drowning, Jonah called out for help, for life, and for God's renewed presence. It is ironic that Jonah spoke of God as driving Jonah from his ***presence***, for that was Jonah's own aim in fleeing to Tarshish (1:3). • ***I will once more:*** Either Jonah was confident that he would be rescued and thus worship again in the Temple in Jerusalem, or he was calling to the Lord in his Temple from the sea (cp. 2:7).

2:6 Jonah's metaphors (***roots of the mountains; imprisoned in the earth***) reflect ancient concepts of the underworld, with the dead being deep within the earth (see also 2:2). At one point Jonah felt hopelessly doomed to death's prison. • ***But:*** The transition is powerful. Jonah, though certain of his own death, was not beyond God's gracious reach. • ***the jaws of death*** (literally *the pit*): The Hebrew term normally denotes the habitat of the dead. Jonah's language again makes it clear that at this point he considered himself as good as dead.

2:7 *I remembered the LORD:* In this context, Jonah's statement means "I turned my thoughts to the Lord in prayer." • ***earnest prayer . . . holy Temple:*** The Temple was God's special dwelling place in Israel's worship, even though God is present everywhere at all times (Ps 139:7-10; Jer 23:23-24).

2:8-9 The conclusion to Jonah's psalm-prayer bears similarity to 1:16: The sailors also responded to the Lord's power to save and acts of mercy with ***sacrifices*** and ***vows***.

3:1–4:11 God again commands Jonah to preach to Nineveh. This time Jonah obeys, leading to an irony: The city repents, as Jonah had feared, and he is angry at God.

3:1-2 The second part of the book opens as the first part did (see 1:1-2).

3:3 *a city so large that it took three days to see it all:* Literally *a great city to God, of three days' journey.* God desired to save rather than destroy such a vast city, one teeming with human and natural resources (4:11). This desire on God's part was precisely what Jonah fought against (see 4:2, 10-11). • The city's circumference was roughly three miles, and it would not have taken three days to walk around it. This description possibly indicates how long it took Jonah to spread his message throughout the city. It might also include the surrounding villages along with the city.

3:4 *Forty days from now Nineveh will be destroyed!* Jonah's message apparently did not include a contingency clause—e.g., "But if you repent, God will not destroy you" (note the king's uncertainty in 3:9). Jonah knew, however, of God's desire for people to repent rather than be destroyed (3:10; 4:2).

3:5-6 For the second time in this short book, pagans respond favorably to the Lord (cp. 1:16). • In ancient Israel, fasting would often accompany prayer and repentance in times of distress (see 2 Sam 1:12; Neh 1:4). Wearing ***burlap*** and sitting on ***a heap of ashes*** would often accompany mourning and sorrowful repentance (see Gen 37:34; Job 16:15; Lam 2:10). The Assyrians apparently had similar customs. These activities allowed the participants to express their grief in a tangible way for all, including God, to see. • The repentance of the Ninevites was an indictment against the hard-hearted in Jesus' day (Matt 12:41).

3:6 The ***king of Nineveh*** was either an unknown governor of the city or perhaps the king of Assyria, who might have used Nineveh as a regular seat of government (cp. 2 Kgs 19:9-13).

3:7-8 By extending the fast and the

3:7
2 Chr 20:3
3:8
Ps 130:1-2
Jon 1:6, 14
3:9
Joel 2:14
3:10
Jer 18:8
Amos 7:3, 6
4:2
Exod 34:6
Ps 86:5
Joel 2:13
[g]*'arek 'appayim* (0750, 0639)
‣Nah 1:3
4:3
1 Kgs 19:4
Job 6:8-9
4:7
Joel 1:12
4:8
Isa 49:10
Ezek 19:12
Hos 13:15
4:11
Jon 1:2; 3:2; 3:10

his throne and took off his royal robes. He
dressed himself in burlap and sat on a heap
of ashes. 7Then the king and his nobles sent
this decree throughout the city:

> "No one, not even the animals from your
> herds and flocks, may eat or drink any-
> thing at all. 8People and animals alike
> must wear garments of mourning, and
> everyone must pray earnestly to God.
> They must turn from their evil ways
> and stop all their violence. 9Who can
> tell? Perhaps even yet God will change
> his mind and hold back his fierce anger
> from destroying us."

10When God saw what they had done and
how they had put a stop to their evil ways,
he changed his mind and did not carry out
the destruction he had threatened.

Jonah's Anger at the Lord's Mercy

4 This change of plans greatly upset Jonah, and he became very angry. 2So he
complained to the LORD about it: "Didn't I
say before I left home that you would do
this, LORD? That is why I ran away to Tarshish! I knew that you are a merciful and
compassionate God, [g]slow to get angry and
filled with unfailing love. You are eager to
turn back from destroying people. 3Just kill
me now, LORD! I'd rather be dead than alive
if what I predicted will not happen."

4The LORD replied, "Is it right for you to
be angry about this?"

An Object Lesson in God's Mercy

5Then Jonah went out to the east side of the
city and made a shelter to sit under as he
waited to see what would happen to the city.
6And the LORD God arranged for a leafy
plant to grow there, and soon it spread its
broad leaves over Jonah's head, shading him
from the sun. This eased his discomfort,
and Jonah was very grateful for the plant.

7But God also arranged for a worm! The
next morning at dawn the worm ate through
the stem of the plant so that it withered
away. 8And as the sun grew hot, God arranged for a scorching east wind to blow on
Jonah. The sun beat down on his head until
he grew faint and wished to die. "Death is
certainly better than living like this!" he exclaimed.

9Then God said to Jonah, "Is it right for
you to be angry because the plant died?"

"Yes," Jonah retorted, "even angry enough
to die!"

10Then the LORD said, "You feel sorry
about the plant, though you did nothing
to put it there. It came quickly and died
quickly. 11But Nineveh has more than
120,000 people living in spiritual darkness,
not to mention all the animals. Shouldn't I
feel sorry for such a great city?"

---

mourning rituals to animals, the king communicated that this dire emergency required all normal operations to cease so that everyone might pray earnestly and repent of ***their evil ways***. The ***violence*** that had come to permeate their society topped the list.

3:10 ***he changed his mind:*** Had the people of Nineveh not repented, God would have destroyed them (3:4). But God was ready to meet their repentance with mercy (see 4:2, 11). In God's mind, the change did not reverse his original intention, because his disposition always included the possibility of mercy. Nor does this change in God's mind say anything about God's foreknowledge. Historically, the church has believed that God knows the future fully (see Ps 139:4; Isa 46:10; Dan 2:28-29; Matt 24:36). Nothing in this account contradicts that belief.

4:1-7 The account takes an unexpected turn. Jonah, himself a recipient of God's mercy, complains about the mercy that the Lord has dispensed to the Assyrians. The prophet's insolence only magnifies God's grace (see 4:8-11 for God's response).

4:1 ***This change of plans*** (literally *It*): See note on 3:10.

4:2 Jonah expresses his motive in originally fleeing from the Lord (1:3): He knew that the Lord would not destroy the wicked Ninevites if they repented. • ***I knew:*** Jonah practically quotes Exod 34:6-7, a passage set in the context of Israel's covenant relationship with the Lord. Even in the OT, God was concerned to spread salvation to the nations (cp. Matt 28:18-20).

4:3-5 Jonah's desire to die rather than embrace God's will (see also 4:8-9), and his willingness to wait in hope that the city would be destroyed (4:5), are signs of his hard-heartedness and his hatred for the Assyrians.

4:4 The Lord's reply is a rhetorical question. The implied answer is "No, of course not!" The object lesson that follows (4:6-11) reveals why Jonah ought not to be angry.

4:6 ***The LORD*** is God's covenant name in relation to Israel (see, e.g., Ps 72:18). ***God*** did these things to show his covenant love toward Jonah and to those in Israel who had the same attitude. • ***arranged for:*** see note on 1:17.

4:11 ***people living in spiritual darkness*** (literally *people who don't know their right hand from their left*): God graciously sent the light of his prophetic word into a wicked city. Not all who encounter God's light respond favorably (cp. John 3:19-21), but God is eager to save those who receive his word in genuine repentance and faith. • The book closes abruptly, leaving the reader to ponder God's final question to Jonah. God would rather save than destroy. Those who have received his mercy must be glad for that same mercy to be shown to others, even to their enemies.

THE BOOK OF

MICAH

Micah announced devastation for both Jerusalem and Samaria. God's judgment was coming against false prophets, against Israel's wayward leaders, and against the rich who oppressed the poor. God's indictment against his people resulted in their ruin, but after ruin would come restoration. Through Micah, God's Spirit provided a strong word of hope for Israel's future. The Lord promised to rescue the remnant of Israel—they would return to their land as God's renewed people. God promised to subdue their enemies and send his ruler from Bethlehem. Micah exclaims simply but powerfully that there is no God like the Lord.

SETTING

Micah delivered his prophecies during the reigns of the southern kings Jotham (750–732 BC), Ahaz (743–715 BC), and Hezekiah (728–686 BC), all of whom had relatively long reigns. At that time, both Israel and Judah were characterized by moral and religious corruption, social oppression, political intrigue, economic injustice, personal vice, deception, and treachery.

Jotham was a moderately good king, but he did not remove the high places where illicit worship of idols competed with proper worship of God at the Temple in Jerusalem. Since the Lord was not entirely pleased with Jotham's reign, he raised up King Rezin of Aram (whose capital was Damascus) and King Pekah of Israel to oppress Judah (2 Kgs 15:32-38).

Ahaz, Jotham's son, followed the evil ways of the northern kings of Israel. He engaged in forbidden practices, including child sacrifice, pagan incense burning, and fertility worship (2 Kgs 16:1-4). When the Edomites moved into the areas of southwest Palestine conquered by Rezin and Pekah (2 Kgs 16:5-6), Ahaz made an alliance with Assyrian

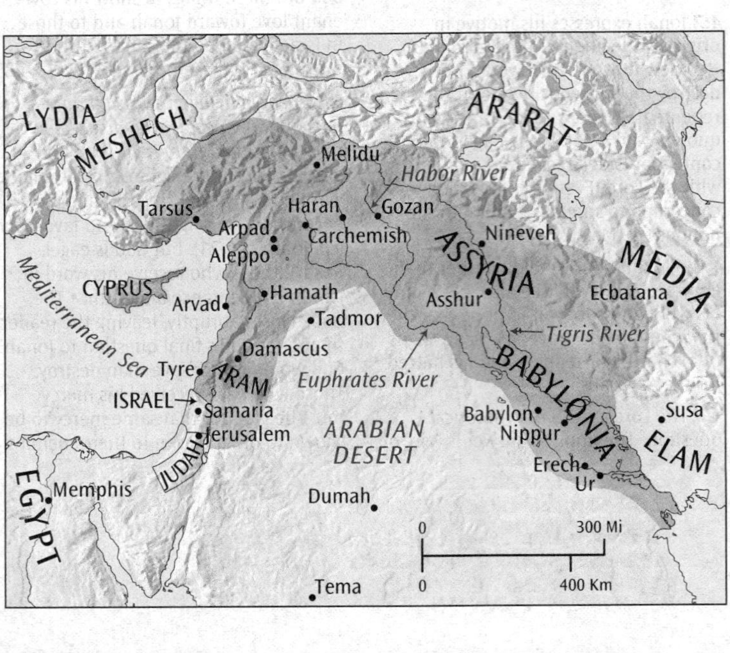

◂ **The Near East in the Time of Micah, about 735~725 BC.** Micah warned that SAMARIA and the kingdom of ISRAEL would be destroyed (1:2-7), and so it happened in 722 BC at the hands of the Assyrians. Micah also prophesied the destruction of Jerusalem and the kingdom of Judah (1:9, 12; 3:10-12; 4:10–5:1); it finally happened at the hands of the Babylonians much later, in 605–586 BC.

king Tiglath-pileser III (744–727 BC) by paying gold from the Temple and the royal treasuries as tribute money to the Assyrians (2 Kgs 16:7-9). Ahaz corrupted Judah's worship by bringing pagan altars into Jerusalem (2 Kgs 16:10-13), and he inhibited worship of the Lord (2 Kgs 16:14-20).

In contrast to his father Ahaz, Hezekiah was an outstanding king. Hezekiah witnessed the fall of Samaria (722 BC) to the Assyrians under Shalmaneser V (726–722 BC) and Sargon II (721–705 BC). During his reign, in 701 BC, God delivered Jerusalem from destruction at the hands of King Sennacherib of Assyria (704–681 BC), but Sennacherib still devastated some forty-six cities in Israel and Judah (2 Kgs 18:1–19:37). God also healed Hezekiah from a serious disease. But then Hezekiah arrogantly received envoys from the Babylonian king Merodach-baladan, who sought an alliance with Hezekiah against Assyria (2 Kgs 20:12-21).

During the early years of this period, before the destruction of Samaria, the northern kings of Israel were Pekah (752–732 BC) and Hoshea (732–722 BC). Under both kings, Israel strayed further in the ways of Jereboam I, who had caused Israel to turn from God (2 Kgs 15:28). During Pekah's reign, parts of northern Israel were taken into captivity (2 Kgs 15:29). Pekah was assassinated by Hoshea, who reigned until the fall of Samaria in 722 BC (2 Kgs 15:30-31; 17:6).

As Micah had warned, the northern kingdom of Israel was destroyed and its people were taken into exile. Hoshea had revolted against Assyria and had appealed to Egypt for help, but when Shalmaneser V heard of Hoshea's treachery, he besieged Samaria, captured it, and destroyed it in 722 BC after a three-year siege. Hoshea was imprisoned, the Israelites were dispersed among Assyrian provinces and vassal kingdoms (2 Kgs 17:5-6), and people from various nations were brought into the devastated land of Israel to live (2 Kgs 17:24-41). Israel's false worship led to its destruction and rejection by the Lord.

OUTLINE

1:1
Superscription: Introducing the Prophet

1:2–2:13
Warning and Hope

3:1–5:15
Judgment and Restoration

6:1–7:20
Indictment and Renewal

SUMMARY

Following the superscription (1:1), each of three sections begins by calling Israel to "listen" (1:2–2:13; 3:1–5:15; 6:1–7:6). Judgment poured from the Lord through Micah's prophecies against Samaria, Jerusalem, the wealthy, the corrupt, the false prophets, the oppressive leaders, and other nations. The people of Israel failed to follow God's ways and did not respond to the benefits he had given them. The Lord's indictment was ironclad: Israel would be ruined and go into exile.

Micah's message of judgment is interspersed with words of hope, however (see 2:12-13; 4:1-8, 13; 5:2-15; 7:7-20). In the end, judgment would be replaced by the Lord's grace, unfailing love, faithfulness, forgiveness,

TIMELINE

753–752 BC
Zechariah as king of Israel

752 BC
Shallum as king of Israel (1 month)

752–742 BC
Menahem as king of Israel

750–740 BC
Jotham's co-reign with Uzziah

750–732 BC
Jotham as king of Judah

744–727 BC
Tiglath-pileser III as king of Assyria

743–735 BC
Ahaz as vice-regent under Jotham

743–715 BC
Ahaz as king of Judah

742–740 BC
Pekahiah as king of Israel

740–732 BC
Pekah as king of Israel

about 740~685 BC
Isaiah as prophet

735–732 BC
Ahaz's co-reign with Jotham

about 735~725 BC
Micah as prophet

732–722 BC
Hoshea as king of Israel

728–715 BC
Hezekiah's co-reign with Ahaz

728–686 BC
Hezekiah as king of Judah

727–722 BC
Shalmaneser V as king of Assyria

722 BC
Fall of Samaria, end of the northern kingdom of Israel

721–705 BC
Sargon II as king of Assyria

With passionate forthrightness, [Micah] attacks the social evils of his day. His stubborn refusal to float on the tide of his social environment, and his courageous stand for his convictions of God's truth, must commend Micah to . . . every age.

LESLIE C. ALLEN
Joel, Obadiah, Jonah, and Micah, p. 241

pardon, and compassion. Israel would be restored and renewed, and God would fulfill his promises to Abraham and Isaac.

AUTHORSHIP AND DATE

Micah was the primary author and editor of this book. He was a native of Moresheth, a town about twenty-one miles (thirty-five kilometers) southwest of Jerusalem. Passages such as 4:6-8 and 7:8-20 suggest to some that a later editor completed the present form of the book in the early postexilic era (538–458 BC). This conclusion is not necessary, however. The prophet Micah is not the only preexilic prophet to prophesy a return (e.g., Isa 52:4-12; Hos 11:10-11; Amos 9:11-15).

Micah used figurative language to describe events. This makes it hard to determine the exact circumstances taking place when Micah prophesied and wrote. Some of Micah's prophecies were probably given before the destruction of Samaria in 722 BC (see 1:1, 6; 6:16). Later, the Assyrian march into Israel and Judah in 701 BC is reflected in 1:10-15. Micah's prediction concerning the fall of Jerusalem (3:12) was given in the reign of Hezekiah (728–686 BC) and is referred to much later by Jeremiah (Jer 26:16-19). Micah's ministry thus seems to have coincided almost exactly with that of Isaiah; the similarity of Isa 2:2-5 and Mic 4:1-4 supports this conclusion.

MEANING AND MESSAGE

Micah's message is clear in 4:1-5; 5:1-4; and 7:20: God's plans for his people will prevail, and the nations will come to know God through his people Israel and his chosen ruler (5:2). The Lord's faithful promises to Abraham and Jacob would be realized.

Much like Isaiah, Micah insisted that Israel's hope would not be in escaping judgment, but it would be mediated to them *through* judgment. The people had become so corrupt that their only hope for an extended future was through the fires of judgment. That was a very hard concept for the people of Israel to grasp.

God's goal is to have a special people (7:14) of unparalleled moral and spiritual integrity and excellence. God will accept nothing less, but only his actions on behalf of his remnant people can create righteousness in them (see 2 Pet 3:13). God's word stands forever. His prophetic word through Micah, empowered by his Spirit (3:8), will be fulfilled, because the words of the true prophet always come to pass (cp. Deut 18; Jer 26:17-18).

FURTHER READING

LESLIE ALLEN
The Books of Joel, Obadiah, Jonah and Micah (1976)

ANDREW HILL
Micah in *Cornerstone Biblical Commentary*, vol. 10 (2008)

THOMAS E. MCCOMISKY
Micah in *Expositor's Bible Commentary*, vol. 7 (1985)

RALPH P. SMITH
Micah–Malachi (1984)

BRUCE WALTKE
Micah (1988)

1. SUPERSCRIPTION: INTRODUCING THE PROPHET (1:1)

1 The LORD gave this message to Micah of Moresheth during the years when Jotham, Ahaz, and Hezekiah were kings of Judah. The visions he saw concerned both Samaria and Jerusalem.

2. WARNING AND HOPE (1:2–2:13)

Warnings against Samaria and Jerusalem

2 Attention! Let all the people of the world
listen!
Let the earth and everything in it hear.
The Sovereign LORD is making
accusations against you;

1:1
1 Chr 3:12-13
Jer 26:18

1:2
Ps 50:7
Jer 6:19

1:1 *Micah* is presumably a short form of Micaiah, which means "Who is like the Lord?" • ***Moresheth*** was a fortress city located a short distance southeast of Gath in the low-lying hills of southwestern Judah. • ***Jotham, Ahaz, and Hezekiah*** (see Micah Introduction, "Setting," p. 1480): The reigns of these three kings covered about 65 years total (about 750–686 BC). • God's ***message*** came to Micah in ***visions.*** • ***Samaria and Jerusalem*** were the capitals of northern Israel and Judah. Sometimes these city names refer to their entire countries.

1:2–2:13 This message of judgment introduces some of the major concerns of Micah's prophecies and asserts God's determination to judge his people and put them into exile (1:16; 2:4-5), but it concludes with the Lord's assurance that he will rescue a

1:3 Isa 26:21; Amos 4:13
1:4 Ps 97:5; Isa 64:1-2; Nah 1:5
1:5 2 Chr 34:3-4; Amos 8:14
1:6 Jer 31:5; Ezek 13:14
1:7 Deut 9:21; 23:18; 2 Chr 34:7
1:8 Isa 13:21-22; 20:2-4
1:9 Jer 30:11-15; Mic 1:12
1:11 Ezek 23:29
1:12 Job 30:26; Isa 59:9-11; Jer 8:15; 14:19

the Lord speaks from his holy
Temple.
3 Look! The LORD is coming!
He leaves his throne in heaven
and tramples the heights of the earth.
4 The mountains melt beneath his feet
and flow into the valleys
like wax in a fire,
like water pouring down a hill.
5 And why is this happening?
Because of the rebellion of Israel—
yes, the sins of the whole nation.
Who is to blame for Israel's rebellion?
Samaria, its capital city!
Where is the center of idolatry in Judah?
In Jerusalem, its capital!

6 "So I, the LORD, will make the city of
Samaria
a heap of ruins.
Her streets will be plowed up
for planting vineyards.
I will roll the stones of her walls into the
valley below,
exposing her foundations.
7 All her carved images will be smashed.
All her sacred treasures will be
burned.
These things were bought with the money
earned by her prostitution,
and they will now be carried away
to pay prostitutes elsewhere."

The Prophet Mourns His People

8 Therefore, I will mourn and lament.
I will walk around barefoot and naked.
I will howl like a jackal
and moan like an owl.
9 For my people's wound
is too deep to heal.
It has reached into Judah,
even to the gates of Jerusalem.

10 Don't tell our enemies in Gath;
don't weep at all.
You people in Beth-leaphrah,
roll in the dust to show your despair.
11 You people in Shaphir,
go as captives into exile—naked and
ashamed.
The people of Zaanan
dare not come outside their walls.
The people of Beth-ezel mourn,
for their house has no support.
12 The people of Maroth anxiously wait for
relief,
but only bitterness awaits them

---

remnant from exile (2:12-13).

1:2-7 This oracle concerns Samaria prior to 722 BC, when Samaria was destroyed and its people were deported. ***The Sovereign LORD*** was coming to judge his people.

1:2 ***Attention!*** translates the same word that introduces the *Shema* ("Listen!") in Deut 6:4. • The ***holy Temple*** is the Lord's heavenly abode, not the corrupt Temple in Jerusalem (1:2-3).

1:3 ***Tramples the heights*** implies a theophany, an appearance of the God who is behind the historical convulsions about to afflict Samaria (cp. Deut 33:29; Ps 108:13; Amos 4:13). God is sovereign over nations and nature. The Canaanite god Baal was also thought to be active in this manner—descriptions of God like this one emphasize that the Lord, not Baal, is truly sovereign.

1:4 The strong and apparently immovable ***mountains*** will ***melt*** at the Lord's presence (see Ps 97:5). Nothing can stand against him.

1:5 ***Rebellion*** is parallel to ***sins;*** these two key words describe Israel's failure in the OT. • ***Israel:*** Literally ***Jacob***. The names "Jacob" and "Israel" are often interchanged throughout the OT, referring sometimes to the individual patriarch and sometimes to the nation. • ***Who? . . . Where?*** The capital cities of God's people should have been holy places, but they were sources of corruption instead. ***Samaria***, capital of the northern kingdom of Israel, was built by Omri (885–874 BC) as a political, military, and economic crossroads of the ancient Near East. Omri was an evil king, and so his city was evil (cp. 6:16). • ***Jerusalem:*** The prophet would not allow the people of Judah to be smug about the northern kingdom's imminent destruction. Judah's beautiful Temple was no different from a Canaanite ***center of idolatry*** (literally *high place*).

1:6-7 ***a heap of ruins:*** The Lord threatened to devastate his treasured cities. Assyria virtually annihilated ***Samaria*** in 724–722 BC in a horrendous three-year siege. • Samaria, like most cities, was built on a hill. Here, ***the stones of her walls*** crash ***into the valley below*** as they are violently dismantled. Ancient armies would systematically shatter city walls down to their foundation stones. • Samaria and Jerusalem were filled with ***carved images*** and ***sacred treasures*** put there by worshipers or taken as war booty. • ***Prostitution*** pictures Israel's persistent spiritual and physical waywardness. This metaphor was regularly used by the Israelite prophets to express Israel's abandonment of the Lord, her true husband, in order to obtain the blessings promised by the pagan gods. In addition, the worship of those gods often in fact involved sexual activity. • ***Elsewhere*** refers to the exile of Samaria into Assyria and its various provinces and conquered vassal states (722 BC). The same outcome was forecast for Jerusalem (3:12; Jer 26:18).

1:8-16 In response to the Lord's predicted judgment, Micah walked around ***barefoot and naked*** to express mourning (cp. Lam 2:10; Isa 20:2; Ezek 24:17), vividly depicting what would happen to Samaria (Israel) and Jerusalem (Judah). They would be stripped of their wealth, power, and population. • A ***jackal*** and an ***owl*** make forlorn sounds and live in forsaken wilderness areas (Isa 34:13; Jer 50:39).

1:9 ***into Judah . . . Jerusalem:*** The corruption now permeated the entire nation, north to south.

1:10-15 The cities listed were in the lowlands of southwestern Judah's coastal areas. The sequence may represent the Assyrian army's march down the coastal plain and from there into Judah's heartland in 703–701 BC.

1:10 ***Gath*** sounds like the Hebrew term for "tell." • ***Beth-leaphrah*** means "house of dust."

1:11 ***Shaphir*** means "pleasant." • ***Exile*** was the ultimate, most devastating curse (Deut 4:29; 28:37, 48; Jer 25:7-11). • ***Zaanan*** sounds like the Hebrew term for "come out." • ***Beth-ezel*** means "adjoining house."

1:12 ***Maroth*** sounds like the Hebrew term for "bitter." • ***even to . . . Jerusalem:*** God's judgment reaches wherever corruption has taken hold (cp. 1:9).

as the LORD's judgment reaches
even to the gates of Jerusalem.
13 Harness your chariot horses and flee,
you people of Lachish.
You were the first city in Judah
to follow Israel in her rebellion,
and you led Jerusalem into sin.
14 Send farewell gifts to Moresheth-gath;
there is no hope of saving it.
The town of Aczib
has deceived the kings of Israel.
15 O people of Mareshah,
I will bring a conqueror to capture
your town.
And the leaders of Israel
will go to Adullam.
16 Oh, people of Judah, shave your heads in
sorrow,
for the children you love will be
snatched away.
Make yourselves as bald as a vulture,
for your little ones will be exiled to
distant lands.

Judgment against Wealthy Oppressors

2 1 What sorrow awaits you who lie
awake at night,
thinking up evil plans.
You rise at dawn and hurry to carry them
out,
simply because you have the power
to do so.
2 When you want a piece of land,
you find a way to seize it.
When you want someone's house,
you take it by fraud and violence.
You cheat a man of his property,
stealing his family's inheritance.
3 But this is what the LORD says:
"I will reward your evil with evil;
you won't be able to pull your neck out
of the noose.
You will no longer walk around proudly,
for it will be a terrible time."
4 In that day your enemies will make fun
of you
by singing this song of despair about
you:
"We are finished,
completely ruined!
God has confiscated our land,
taking it from us.
He has given our fields
to those who betrayed us."
5 Others will set your boundaries then,
and the LORD's people will have no say
in how the land is divided.

True and False Prophets

6 "Don't say such things,"
the people respond.
"Don't prophesy like that.
Such disasters will never come our
way!"
7 Should you talk that way, O family of
Israel?
Will the LORD's [a]Spirit have patience
with such behavior?

1:13 Josh 10:3
1:14 Josh 15:44
1:15 Josh 12:15; 15:35, 44
1:16 Isa 22:12
2:1 Prov 3:29-30; Isa 32:7; Hos 7:6-7
2:2 1 Kgs 21:1-16; Isa 5:8
2:3 Isa 2:11-12; Jer 18:11
2:4 Jer 6:12; 8:10; Hab 2:6
2:5 Deut 32:8; Josh 18:4, 10
2:6 Isa 30:10; Amos 2:12
2:7 Ps 15:1-2; 84:11; Jer 15:16
[a]*ruakh* (7307) ›Zech 4:6

1:13 ***Lachish*** sounds like the Hebrew term for "team of horses." Lachish was the second most important city in Judah, after Jerusalem, and was Judah's main center of defense against their enemies. Even today, a massive *tell* over 150 feet (46 meters) high remains. Lachish fell in 701 BC, having been besieged, terrified, starved, and demolished by Sennacherib's war engines. Sennacherib celebrated its fall as one of his greatest victories and featured the event in monumental carvings on his palace walls. • ***Jerusalem:*** Literally *the daughter of Zion.*

1:14 ***Farewell gifts*** said good-bye to the doomed people of ***Moresheth-gath*** as that city also became Assyrian property. • ***Moresheth*** sounds like the Hebrew term for "gift" or "dowry." • ***Aczib*** means "deception."

1:15 ***Mareshah*** sounds like the Hebrew term for "conqueror." • ***the leaders*** (literally *the glory*): The leaders of Israel should have been Israel's "glory" by setting examples of moral excellence and wise, caring leadership. Instead, God's shepherds corrupted their nation (Ezek 11:34). • ***Adullam*** was destroyed by Assyria in 701 BC.

1:16 The people of Judah, including Jerusalem, were ***exiled*** and deported ***to distant lands*** in Babylonia in 605, 597, and 586 BC. Babylon was some 1,000 miles (1,700 kilometers) from Jerusalem. • ***shave your heads:*** This act of mourning and despair (see also Jer 41:5) could also signify purification (Lev 14:7-10; Num 6:10-11).

2:1-2 ***Power*** had corrupted the wealthy, who should have been ready to help their fellow Israelites (cp. Gen 4:9; Josh 1:14). • ***Thinking up evil plans . . . because you have the power to do so*** indicates a corrupt heart, mind, and character (Gen 6:5). • ***When you want:*** They possessed the ***property*** of others in a way that amounted to stealing, and broke God's law that forbids coveting (Exod 20:17). A ***family's inheritance*** was a sacred gift from the Lord, intended as a permanent possession (Lev 25:8-55; cp. 1 Kgs 21; Isa 5:8). God looked for righteousness among his people, but instead he found oppression (1 Kgs 10:9; Isa 5:7; 2 Pet 2:13).

2:3-5 The Lord, the Judge, reads out the sentence. He would pay back his people's ***evil*** hearts and actions ***with evil*** in kind. The prophet was engaging in wordplay here. The Hebrew word translated "evil" has a wide range of meaning. It can connote moral evil, as in the first instance; it can also connote calamity or disaster as in the second instance. The Lord would bring calamity on them in response to their wickedness.

2:4 The power brokers would be ***ruined*** financially as their enemies confiscated their property. The land that they had seized unjustly from fellow Israelites would be violently taken from them (2:5). • ***those who betrayed us:*** Or *those who took us captive.*

2:6 There was a pathetic attempt to stifle the words of a true prophet. • ***the people respond:*** Or *the prophets respond;* Hebrew reads *they prophesy.* They thought that exile and other ***such disasters*** could not happen to them, but they were wrong.

2:7-10 The maltreatment of their fellow Israelites was tantamount to an attack

2:8
Jer 12:8
Mic 3:2-3; 7:2-3
2:9
Jer 10:20
2:10
Lev 18:24-28
Deut 12:9
Ps 106:38
2:11
Jer 5:31
Mic 3:5, 11
2:12
Isa 11:11
Mic 4:7; 5:7; 7:18
3:1
Jer 5:5
[b]*mishpat* (4941)
‣ Mic 6:8
3:2
Ezek 22:27
3:3
Ps 14:4
Ezek 11:7
Zeph 3:3

If you would do what is right,
you would find my words comforting.
8 Yet to this very hour
my people rise against me like an enemy!
You steal the shirts right off the backs
of those who trusted you,
making them as ragged as men
returning from battle.
9 You have evicted women from their pleasant homes
and forever stripped their children of all that God would give them.
10 Up! Begone!
This is no longer your land and home,
for you have filled it with sin
and ruined it completely.

11 Suppose a prophet full of lies would say to you,
"I'll preach to you the joys of wine and alcohol!"
That's just the kind of prophet you would like!

A Word of Hope for Restoration
12 "Someday, O Israel, I will gather you;
I will gather the remnant who are left.
I will bring you together again like sheep in a pen,
like a flock in its pasture.
Yes, your land will again
be filled with noisy crowds!
13 Your leader will break out
and lead you out of exile,
out through the gates of the enemy cities,
back to your own land.
Your king will lead you;
the LORD himself will guide you."

3. JUDGMENT AND RESTORATION (3:1–5:15)

Judgment against Israel's Leaders

3 1 I said, "Listen, you leaders of Israel!
You are supposed to know [b]right from wrong,
2 but you are the very ones
who hate good and love evil.
You skin my people alive
and tear the flesh from their bones.
3 Yes, you eat my people's flesh,
strip off their skin,
and break their bones.
You chop them up
like meat for the cooking pot.

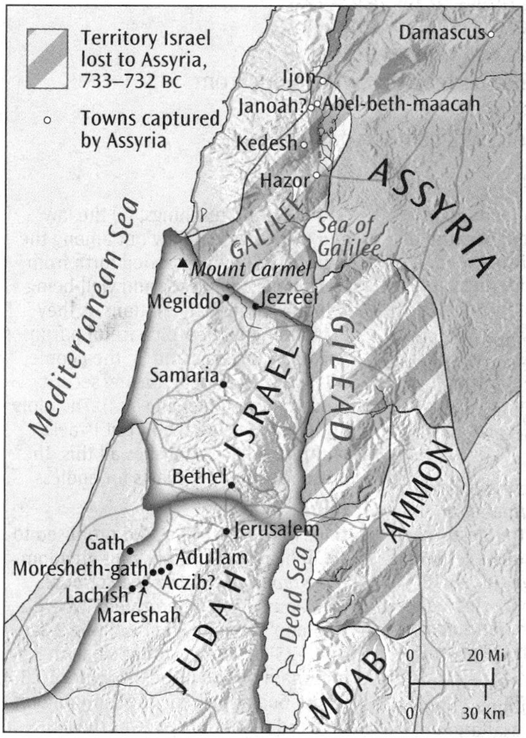

◂ **The Assyrian Invasion, 733–732 BC (1:10-15).** The Assyrian army invaded the kingdom of ISRAEL in 733–732 BC and conquered many of the northern and eastern areas of the nation, as shown (see 2 Kgs 15:29). The promised judgment of Israel thus began; it was completed in 722 BC when ASSYRIA invaded once again, destroyed SAMARIA, and exiled the people of Israel.

against the Lord and his prophet. The fault lay with the people, not with Micah's inspired and righteous message. • ***O family of Israel:*** Literally *O house of Jacob?* See note on 1:5.

2:11 ***a prophet full of lies:*** These evil people loved to hear deceptions from their favorite good-time prophets (cp. Jer 28:8-9). False prophets proclaimed assurance that Israel and Judah could escape from judgment. When judgment came, they had no comfort to give.

2:12-13 God showed his love and care for his rebellious people by giving them a promise of hope even as he spoke of exile and despair. Israel would be scattered, but they would be brought back (cp. Deut 4:26-29; 30:1-6).

2:13 ***The LORD*** did lead Israel ***out of exile,*** foreshadowing the even greater freedom from slavery that the Messiah, Jesus Christ, would later bring.

3:1–5:15 This message indicts the evil leaders who were destroying God's people and contrasts them with a glorious vision of God's kingdom and the reign of a righteous king. After suffering judgment and exile, a purified people of Israel would return and experience God's blessings.

3:1-4 Micah relentlessly indicted the ***leaders of Israel*** because they were responsible for the peoples' well-being. The horrors here depict the terrors of a people under siege (cp. 2 Kgs 6:29; Deut 28:53).

3:1 The leaders, who were ***supposed to know*** true judgment and justice (6:8; Deut 10:12-13), were morally responsible for Israel's guilt.

3:2-3 The leaders, like wild animals, destroyed their own people.

4 Then you beg the LORD for help in times
of trouble!
Do you really expect him to answer?
After all the evil you have done,
he won't even look at you!"

5 This is what the LORD says:
"You false prophets are leading my
people astray!
You promise peace for those who give
you food,
but you declare war on those who
refuse to feed you.
6 Now the night will close around you,
cutting off all your visions.
Darkness will cover you,
putting an end to your predictions.
The sun will set for you prophets,
and your day will come to an end.
7 Then you seers will be put to shame,
and you fortune-tellers will be
disgraced.
And you will cover your faces
because there is no answer from God."
8 But as for me, I am filled with power—
with the Spirit of the LORD.
I am filled with justice and strength
to boldly declare Israel's sin and
rebellion.
9 Listen to me, you leaders of Israel!
You hate justice and twist all that is
right.
10 You are building Jerusalem
on a foundation of murder and
corruption.
11 You rulers make decisions based on bribes;
you ᶜpriests teach God's laws only for
a price;
you prophets won't prophesy unless you
are paid.
Yet all of you claim to depend on the
LORD.
"No harm can come to us," you say,
"for the LORD is here among us."
12 Because of you, Mount Zion will be
plowed like an open field;
Jerusalem will be reduced to ruins!
A thicket will grow on the heights
where the Temple now stands.

The LORD's Future Reign in Zion
Mic 4:1-3 // Isa 2:2-4

4 1 In the last days, the mountain of the
LORD's house
will be the highest of all—
the most important place on earth.
It will be raised above the other hills,
and people from all over the world
will stream there to worship.
2 People from many nations will come and
say,
"Come, let us go up to the mountain of
the LORD,
to the house of Jacob's God.
There he will teach us his ways,
and we will walk in his paths."
For the LORD's teaching will go out from
Zion;
his word will go out from Jerusalem.

3:4 Deut 31:17; Ps 18:41; Prov 1:28; Isa 1:15; 59:2; Mic 7:13
3:5 Jer 6:14; 14:14-15
3:6 Isa 8:20-22; 29:10; 59:10; Amos 8:9-10
3:7 Isa 44:25; Zech 13:4
3:8 Isa 58:1; 61:1-2
3:9 Isa 1:23
3:10 Jer 22:13-17; Ezek 22:25-28; Hab 2:9-12
3:11 Isa 48:2; Hos 4:18; ᶜ*kohen* (3548) ‣Zech 6:13
3:12 Jer 9:11; 26:18
4:1-3 //Isa 2:2-4
4:1 Ps 22:27; 86:9; Jer 3:17
4:2 Ps 25:8-12; Isa 2:3; 4:3; 42:1-4; Jer 31:6; Zech 14:8-9

3:4 *Then:* Even after oppressing the Lord's people, the leaders would selfishly ***beg*** for ***help*** from ***the LORD***.

3:5 The ***false prophets*** were among the spiritual leaders of Israel, so they fell under Micah's accusations. Prophets were supposed to call Israel to the true way, not to send them astray (see Deut 13, 18). These prophets used their gifts to benefit themselves.

3:6-7 Micah announced God's judgment on the false prophets. Without God's special communications, these seers and fortune tellers were like the pagan court prophets of such nations as Babylon, Mari, and especially Assyria, who were expected to toe the party line but who had no real revelation from the Lord (cp. 1 Sam 28:6; Amos 8:11-12).

3:8 There was a strong contrast between the true prophet and the false prophets (3:5-7). Truth, ***justice,*** and ***power*** come from God's ***Spirit,*** who gave Micah the moral and ethical ***strength*** to declare his true message about the ***sin and rebellion*** of his people.

3:9-12 The ***leaders of Israel*** were ***building Jerusalem*** on a ***foundation of murder and corruption.*** Because of this, the city would be dismantled; it would be reduced to wilderness and ruins (3:12).

3:11 ***the LORD is here among us:*** This expression indicates the Lord's approval (see Exod 3:12, 14; 25:8; Hag 2:5; Zech 2:11) and his dwelling among his people. The false prophets wrongly claimed God's presence.

3:12 ***Mount Zion,*** where the Lord once lived, would become ***a thicket,*** an uninhabitable wilderness. Utter destruction awaited the fallen ***Jerusalem.*** Jeremiah later quoted this passage (Jer 26:18). • Just as a ***field*** needs to be cleared to prepare it for cultivation, ***Jerusalem*** had to be ***reduced to ruins*** in judgment.

4:1-5 Micah's prophecy moves from utter despair to an eruption of hope as he expresses the future exaltation of Mount Zion in Jerusalem. God's plan to bless all nations (Gen 12:3) through Abraham's descendants will be realized when the nations and the Lord's people ***stream*** to ***the LORD's house . . . to worship.*** There (1) they will learn to follow God's law and teachings; (2) the law and teachings will flow out among the nations as they are carried forth from God's house; (3) peace and well-being will grow among the nations as they turn their energies to peaceful purposes and abandon war; and (4) the people will live without fear, having security, prosperity, and blessing (4:4). The idols of the nations fail them, but Israel's faithful God accomplishes all this; the prosperity he brings lasts for endless ages (4:5).

4:1-2 ***In the last days:*** God promised to act in history to establish his kingdom. • The ***mountain of the LORD's house*** was Mount Zion in Jerusalem, where Solomon's Temple was built (see 2 Sam 24:18-25). It recalls Mount Sinai, the mountain of God (Exod 3:1; Num 10:33), where God appeared. The mountain of the Lord has significance as the place where God makes his identity known and his fellowship available. • ***teach us his ways . . . his paths:*** The wisdom of God's laws and the knowledge of his ways will give the nations life (Deut 4:6; 32:47).

4:3
Isa 11:3-5
4:4
Lev 26:6
Isa 40:5
4:5
2 Kgs 17:29, 34
Zech 10:12
4:6
Zeph 3:19
4:7
Isa 9:6-7; 24:23
4:8
Ps 48:12
Isa 1:26
Zech 9:10
4:9
Jer 8:19
4:10
2 Kgs 20:18
Isa 48:20
Hos 2:14
Mic 7:8-12
[d]*ga'al* (1350)
‣ Lev 25:25
4:11
Isa 5:25-30
4:12
Ps 147:19-20
Isa 55:8

3 The LORD will mediate between peoples
and will settle disputes between
strong nations far away.
They will hammer their swords into
plowshares
and their spears into pruning hooks.
Nation will no longer fight against
nation,
nor train for war anymore.
4 Everyone will live in peace and
prosperity,
enjoying their own grapevines and
fig trees,
for there will be nothing to fear.
The LORD of Heaven's Armies
has made this promise!
5 Though the nations around us follow
their idols,
we will follow the LORD our God
forever and ever.

Israel's Return from Exile

6 "In that coming day," says the LORD,
"I will gather together those who are
lame,
those who have been exiles,
and those whom I have filled with
grief.
7 Those who are weak will survive as a
remnant;
those who were exiles will become a
strong nation.
Then I, the LORD, will rule from
Jerusalem
as their king forever."
8 As for you, Jerusalem,
the citadel of God's people,
your royal might and power
will come back to you again.
The kingship will be restored
to my precious Jerusalem.

9 But why are you now screaming in
terror?
Have you no king to lead you?
Have your wise people all died?
Pain has gripped you like a woman in
childbirth.
10 Writhe and groan like a woman in labor,
you people of Jerusalem,
for now you must leave this city
to live in the open country.
You will soon be sent in exile
to distant Babylon.
But the LORD will rescue you there;
he will [d]redeem you from the grip of
your enemies.

11 Now many nations have gathered against
you.
"Let her be desecrated," they say.
"Let us see the destruction of
Jerusalem."
12 But they do not know the LORD's
thoughts
or understand his plan.
These nations don't know
that he is gathering them together
to be beaten and trampled
like sheaves of grain on a threshing
floor.

4:3 The *shalom* ("well-being, peace") of the Lord will cover the earth, and instruments of destruction will be used for peaceful pursuits. From its earliest records, ancient history is an account of war, of one people's subjugation of other peoples and nations. Warfare and violence reached a frenzied peak in the Assyrian and Babylonian kingdoms. • ***swords into plowshares:*** Implements of war will become tools for production. Alternatively, some scholars believe that this phrase means reducing "swords into metal shards," which would render them useless.

4:4 ***Everyone*** will be free of enemies as in Solomon's time (1 Kgs 4:25; cp. Isa 36:16; Zech 3:10). • The prophets frequently described God as the ***LORD of Heaven's Armies***. This military title expresses his control of the universe and his unlimited power. The warrior kings of the ancient Near East were no match for the Lord.

4:6-7 Usually the remnants of destroyed cities in the ancient Near East were lost or assimilated. When Israel's ***remnant*** was rescued, it would be the foundation of the Lord's new people (Deut 4:26-31; 30:1-5; 2 Kgs 19:31; Isa 10:21; Jer 29:10-14; Ezra 9:8; Neh 1:2).

4:7 ***Jerusalem:*** Literally *Mount Zion.*

4:8 ***As for you, Jerusalem, the citadel of God's people:*** Literally *As for you, Migdal-eder, / the Ophel of the daughter of Zion.* Jerusalem was a fortified royal capital city with a watchtower for the defense and security of its people. • ***The kingship will be restored:*** Cp. Amos 9:11-15; see 2 Sam 7:11-16.

4:9 Israel's ***king*** and ***wise people*** were supposed to provide leadership and embody the Lord's instructions and covenant in their lives (Deut 17:18-20). Now, however, the people would be without godly leadership (cp. Judg 17:6; 18:1; 21:25).

4:10 ***you people of Jerusalem:*** Literally *O daughter of Zion.* • ***Distant Babylon*** lay about 1,000 miles (1,700 kilometers) from Jerusalem; it could not be reached by cutting across the barren eastern desert. • The Lord's ***rescue*** of his people from sure death in Babylon would surpass his bringing them out of Egypt. They were formed in the womb of suffering and awaited a promising rebirth (Isa 43:1-5; cp. Ezek 37). • For Micah, Babylon represented the concept of exile. In Micah's time (the late 700s and early 600s BC), there was not even the whisper of a Babylonian empire replacing the Assyrians. But Micah was speaking for God, who knows the future.

4:11-13 ***gathered against you:*** While closely tied to the historical assault of Babylon against Jerusalem in 588–586 BC, this oracle also bears on a future in which the idealized and restored ***Jerusalem*** of 4:1-5 will be attacked (cp. Rev 20:7-9).

4:11 ***of Jerusalem:*** Literally *of Zion.*

4:12 God reveals his plans to his servants (Amos 3:7; Dan 2:19-23), but the ***nations don't know***—they are not privy to God's great plans or to his behind-the-scenes activity on his people's behalf. The hopes and plans of the nations around Israel were in vain—the Lord's plans for his unique people will

13 "Rise up and crush the nations,
O Jerusalem!"
says the LORD.
"For I will give you iron horns and bronze
hooves,
so you can trample many nations to
pieces.
You will present their stolen riches to
the LORD,
their wealth to the LORD of all the
earth."

A Ruler from Bethlehem

5 1 Mobilize! Marshal your troops!
The enemy is laying siege to
Jerusalem.
They will strike Israel's leader
in the face with a rod.

2 But you, O Bethlehem Ephrathah,
are only a small village among all the
people of Judah.
Yet a ruler of Israel will come from you,
one whose origins are from the
distant past.
3 The people of Israel will be abandoned
to their enemies
until the woman in labor gives birth.
Then at last his fellow countrymen
will return from exile to their own
land.
4 And he will stand to lead his flock with
the LORD's strength,
in the majesty of the name of the
LORD his God.
Then his people will live there
undisturbed,
for he will be highly honored around
the world.
5 And he will be the source of peace.

When the Assyrians invade our land
and break through our defenses,
we will appoint seven rulers to watch
over us,
eight princes to lead us.
6 They will rule Assyria with drawn
swords
and enter the gates of the land of
Nimrod.
He will rescue us from the Assyrians
when they pour over the borders to
invade our land.

The Remnant Purified

7 Then the remnant left in Israel
will take their place among the
nations.
They will be like dew sent by the LORD
or like rain falling on the grass,
which no one can hold back
and no one can restrain.

4:13 Isa 41:15-16; 60:9
5:1 Job 16:10; Lam 3:30
5:2 Ps 102:25; Jer 30:21; Zech 9:9; *Matt 2:6; John 1:1-2; 7:42
5:3 Isa 10:20-22; Hos 11:8; Mic 4:10; 5:7-8; 7:13
5:4 Isa 9:6; 52:10; Mic 7:14
5:5 Isa 8:7-8
5:6 Gen 10:8-11; Isa 37:36-37; Nah 2:11-13
5:7 Deut 32:2; Ps 72:6

---

prevail, and he will rule the nations (Gen 12:1-3; 15:12-21; Exod 19:4-6; Isa 45:23; 66:23). • At the ***threshing floor, grain*** was ***beaten and trampled*** to separate it from the chaff. So, too, the nations will be crushed (4:13).

4:13 *"Rise up and crush the nations, O Jerusalem!"* Literally *"Rise up and thresh, O daughter of Zion."* • The ***horns*** and ***hooves*** of bulls and horses represent strength, as do both ***iron*** and ***bronze.*** Metal shoes may have been used on the feet of animals who trod out the grain. God will strengthen his peoples to defeat their enemies. • ***stolen riches:*** Many nations had accumulated wealth by unjust means (war, plunder, oppressive tributes, forced labor, and conscription). The ***LORD of all the earth*** owned all of this wealth to begin with (Exod 19:5). • ***You will present:*** The Hebrew term (*kharam,* "dedicate") refers to military spoils of war that were dedicated, or set aside, as holy to the Lord (see Lev 27:28-29).

5:1-15 This section calls Israel to prepare for the vicious onslaught of Israel's enemy, Assyria (5:5b-6). This siege of terror, death, and destruction will not annihilate Israel, for God will bring forth a ruler (5:2-5a) to lead his people back from exile. God's preservation and purification of the remnant (5:7-14) will complete their restoration as God's victorious people.

5:1 Verse 5:1 is numbered 4:14 in the Hebrew text. • ***Israel's leader*** was defeated by the Assyrians (cp. 6:9). Striking a person ***with a rod*** expressed contempt (cp. 1 Kgs 22:24).

5:2-15 Verses 5:2-15 are numbered 5:1-14 in the Hebrew text.

5:2 *Ephrathah* was the ancient name of ***Bethlehem*** (Gen 35:16; Ruth 4:11), David's birth place. In the future, an even more significant ***ruler*** than David would arise from there (Matt 2:5-6; John 7:42). The future king's activities would stretch from the ***distant past*** (Hebrew *qedem*; cp. Deut 33:27; Isa 37:26; Prov 8:22-23) into a still future time, suggesting a divine-human being.

5:4-5 Following the Exile, Prince Zerubbabel, a descendant of David, was among the returned exiles and became the focus of Israel's hopes (see Hag 2:20-23), but he mysteriously disappeared. A greater ruler than Zerubbabel was needed. The leader from Bethlehem would be a ***source of peace***; Isaiah called him the Prince of Peace (Isa 9:6). Only Jesus fits this description.

5:5 The ***Assyrians*** destroyed northern Israel in 722 BC. Sennacherib shut up King Hezekiah of Jerusalem "like a bird in a cage" (Sennacherib's own words) in 701 BC and devastated over forty-six cities in Judah. The hoped-for deliverer-king did not appear in those days. The Assyrians represent all of Israel's enemies. • ***seven rulers . . . eight princes:*** This literary expression indicates that an abundance of leaders will be supplied as needed to lead Israel.

5:6 *the land of Nimrod:* Nimrod laid the foundations of the ancient Assyrian and Babylonian civilizations (Gen 10:8-11).

5:7-15 God's purpose was not to create another nation like all the other nations (Exod 19:4-6; Num 23:9; Jer 7:23), but to have his own people who would walk in his ways and be holy as he is holy (Lev 11:45). In that day (5:10), God will rule a redeemed and purified people, healed of violence and the ravages of war.

5:7 *in Israel:* Literally *in Jacob;* also in 5:8. See note on 1:5. • ***The remnant*** are those whom God's grace preserved to be the foundation of his new people (Ezra 9:8-15; Neh 1:2). • ***Dew*** and ***rain*** are gifts from the Lord; no person can prevent his sending them.

5:8 Gen 49:9; Ps 50:22; Zech 10:5
5:9 Ps 10:12
5:10 Hos 14:3; Zech 9:10
5:11 Isa 2:12-17; Hos 10:14; Amos 5:9
5:12 Deut 18:10-12
5:13 Isa 2:8, 18-19
5:14 Exod 34:13
5:15 Ps 149:7; Isa 1:24; 65:12
6:2 Hos 4:1; 12:2
6:3 Jer 2:5, 31
6:4 Exod 20:1-2; Ps 77:20
6:5 Num 22:5-6; 25:1; Josh 5:9-10
6:6 Ps 40:6-8; 51:16-17
6:7 Lev 18:21; 20:1-5; Ps 50:9; Isa 40:16

8 The remnant left in Israel
will take their place among the nations.
They will be like a lion among the
animals of the forest,
like a strong young lion among flocks
of sheep and goats,
pouncing and tearing as they go
with no rescuer in sight.
9 The people of Israel will stand up to their
foes,
and all their enemies will be wiped out.

10 "In that day," says the LORD,
"I will slaughter your horses
and destroy your chariots.
11 I will tear down your walls
and demolish your defenses.
12 I will put an end to all witchcraft,
and there will be no more fortune-
tellers.
13 I will destroy all your idols and sacred
pillars,
so you will never again worship the
work of your own hands.
14 I will abolish your idol shrines with their
Asherah poles
and destroy your pagan cities.
15 I will pour out my vengeance
on all the nations that refuse to
obey me."

4. INDICTMENT AND RENEWAL (6:1–7:20)

The LORD Defines What Is Good!

6 Listen to what the LORD is saying:
"Stand up and state your case
against me.
Let the mountains and hills be called
to witness your complaints.
2 And now, O mountains,
listen to the LORD's complaint!
He has a case against his people.
He will bring charges against Israel.

3 "O my people, what have I done to you?
What have I done to make you tired
of me?
Answer me!
4 For I brought you out of Egypt
and redeemed you from slavery.
I sent Moses, Aaron, and Miriam to
help you.
5 Don't you remember, my people,
how King Balak of Moab tried to have
you cursed
and how Balaam son of Beor blessed
you instead?
And remember your journey from
Acacia Grove to Gilgal,
when I, the LORD, did everything I
could
to teach you about my faithfulness."
6 What can we bring to the LORD?
What kind of offerings should we give
him?
Should we bow before God
with offerings of yearling calves?
7 Should we offer him thousands of rams
and ten thousand rivers of olive oil?
Should we sacrifice our firstborn
children
to pay for our sins?

5:8-9 God's people will have a unique ***place among the nations*** of the world (Gen 12:3; Exod 19:4-6). They will be the head and not the tail (Deut 28:13), and invincible as ***a lion*** (cp. Esth 6:13) as God gives them hegemony over the nations. • The Lord will judge ***their foes*** (see 5:15) if they continue to rebel against him. The Lord's desire, however, is ultimately to bless the nations, not to curse or destroy them (Gen 12:3; Jon 4:11; John 3:16).

5:10-14 The Lord's actions for and against his people purify them. The Lord removed several abominable things imported from the pagan cultures of Mesopotamia and Canaan.

5:13-14 ***sacred pillars . . . Asherah poles:*** Stones were set up as places or objects of worship; they could represent pagan deities. The Asherah poles were green poles or trees that represented the goddess Asherah and her powers of fertility. Both the stones and the trees may have had sexual implications—one male, the other female. Asherah was seen as the mother of gods and El's (or Baal's) consort.

6:1-16 The Lord presented, argued, and decided the case against his rebellious people, Israel. This section is formally presented as a legal court case (cp. Isa 1:2-4; Jer 2:4-9; Hos 4:1-19). Using the scenario of the courtroom, the Lord challenged his people to state their case against him, for he had a case against them (6:1-5)—they had not fulfilled his requirements (6:6-8), so they were guilty (6:9-12). The guilty verdict is followed by Israel's sentencing (6:13-16).

6:1-2 ***mountains and hills:*** All creation is ***called*** as a ***witness*** (cp. Josh 24:27); in other ancient Near Eastern treaties, the gods of the respective countries were called as witnesses.

6:3 ***tired of me:*** The Lord asks rhetorically if he has done something to turn Israel away from him. But their contempt for God arose from their own ingratitude (6:4-5).

6:4-5 The Lord had ***brought*** Israel ***out of Egypt*** and had preserved them and blessed them throughout their journey to the Promised Land. God encouraged and warned Israel always to ***remember*** what he had done for them from Sinai onward (Exod 3:15; Deut 5:15; Ps 77:11; 111:4; see also Pss 78, 136). • ***Balak . . . Balaam:*** (see Num 22–24). • ***Acacia Grove*** (Hebrew *Shittim*), located on the east of the Jordan River, was Israel's base camp before entering the Promised Land (see Num 25:1; Josh 2:1; 3:1). The trip from there to ***Gilgal*** (west of the Jordan River) bears witness to God's covenant ***faithfulness***. God's saving acts brought the Israelites into the Promised Land.

6:6-7 Israel's case was hopeless, but they queried the Lord as to how they could placate or please him. The proffered items are listed in a crescendo of significance, from ***calves*** to ***rams*** and ***olive oil*** to ***firstborn children***. None of this was sufficient or acceptable to God, who judges the heart (1 Sam 15:22; 16:7; Jer 17:9).

8 No, O people, the LORD has told you what
is good,
and this is what he requires of you:
to do what is [e]right, to love mercy,
and to walk humbly with your God.

Israel's Guilt and Punishment

9 Fear the LORD if you are wise!
His voice calls to everyone in
Jerusalem:
"The armies of destruction are coming;
the LORD is sending them.
10 What shall I say about the homes of the
wicked
filled with treasures gained by
cheating?
What about the disgusting practice
of measuring out grain with dishonest
measures?
11 How can I tolerate your merchants
who use dishonest scales and weights?
12 The rich among you have become
wealthy
through extortion and violence.
Your citizens are so used to lying
that their tongues can no longer tell
the truth.
13 "Therefore, I will wound you!
I will bring you to ruin for all your
sins.
14 You will eat but never have enough.
Your hunger pangs and emptiness will
remain.
And though you try to save your money,
it will come to nothing in the end.
You will save a little,
but I will give it to those who conquer
you.
15 You will plant crops
but not harvest them.
You will press your olives
but not get enough oil to anoint
yourselves.
You will trample the grapes
but get no juice to make your wine.
16 You keep only the laws of evil King
Omri;
you follow only the example of wicked
King Ahab!
Therefore, I will make an example of you,
bringing you to complete ruin.
You will be treated with contempt,
mocked by all who see you."

The Prophet's Misery Turned to Hope

7 1 How miserable I am!
I feel like the fruit picker after the
harvest
who can find nothing to eat.
Not a cluster of grapes or a single early
fig
can be found to satisfy my hunger.

6:8 Deut 10:12-13; Isa 57:15; [e]*mishpat* (4941) ›Hab 1:4
6:10 Jer 5:26-27; Amos 3:10; 8:5
6:12 Isa 3:8
6:13 Isa 1:5-7; 6:11
6:14 Lev 26:26; Isa 9:20; 30:6
6:15 Deut 28:38-40; Jer 12:13; Amos 5:11; Zeph 1:13
6:16 1 Kgs 16:25, 29-33; Jer 7:24; 18:15-16; 25:9
7:1 Isa 28:4; Hos 9:10

6:8 *Good* means what is right in God's eyes; God is the source of all goodness (Gen 1; Exod 33:19; 34:6-7; Deut 12:28). • *what is right* (Hebrew *mishpat,* often translated "justice"): God's order in the world requires treatment of others in fair, non-manipulative, non-oppressive ways. • *mercy* (Hebrew *khesed*): This passionate, undeserved loyalty is the defining quality in God's holy character (see Ps 136). Those who know God will act in the same way toward others (see Gen 21:22-24; Josh 2:12-14; Matt 5:43-48). • *walk humbly:* Humility must characterize God's people. They must not live in a spirit of arrogance or special privilege. They must be humble and reverently fear God. *Mishpat* and *khesed* are incompatible with human arrogance. God desires us to be in an on-going intimate relationship with him (a "walk"; cp. Deut 28:9; Josh 22:5) that transforms the way we relate to other people.

6:9-16 People in Jerusalem were here invited to learn the lesson from Samaria: If you oppress others in order to have an abundance for yourself (6:10-12), you will never have enough however much you get (6:13-15), and eventually you will lose even that (6:16). It is fitting for such people to become an object of scorn, not to receive honor and adulation (6:16).

6:9 Those who are wise *fear the LORD;* God's *voice calls to everyone in Jerusalem* to learn wisdom (cp. Prov 1:7, 20, 28). • *The armies of destruction . . . sending them:* Literally *Listen to the rod. / Who appointed it?* Assyria would carry out the Lord's plan to destroy Samaria, while Babylon would be the instrument of destruction for Jerusalem (4:10).

6:10-12 The Lord had specific accusations against his people. They had become a community of deceit that was ripe for rejection and destruction. Falsely acquired wealth, unethical business practices, threats, and violence characterized this supposed people of God (see 2 Kgs 6:25; Amos 8:5-6; Hos 12:7-8). They could not change, because lying was their way of life (cp. Prov 6:16-19). Israel was completely corrupt.

6:10 *of measuring out grain with dishonest measures?* Literally *of using the short ephah?* The ephah was a unit for measuring grain.

6:13-16 *I will wound you!* This phrase introduces all of the curses that God had promised to bring upon the disobedient and rebellious people of Israel (see Deut 28:15-68).

6:16 *evil King Omri . . . wicked King Ahab:* These kings began perhaps the most rebellious dynasty to reign in northern Israel (885–841 BC; 1 Kgs 16:23—2 Kgs 10:17), and Elijah condemned them to annihilation (2 Kgs 10:17). No northern kings of Israel followed the laws of Moses (cp. 1:5-6). Omri and his son Ahab were the epitome of evil kings (e.g., 1 Kgs 18:4; 21:1-26). Omri's dynasty was destroyed in 841 BC (2 Kgs 9:14–10:17), and the people of Israel who followed their evil example would similarly be destroyed.

7:1-20 Hopeless deception and corruption permeated God's people (7:1-6); God's mercy, however, would triumph and Israel would be restored (7:11-13). God's mercy, compassion, and unfailing love would prevail (7:14-20). Micah mourned his people's condition and looked to the Lord for help (7:7-10).

7:1 *The fruit picker after the harvest:* After the second crop of figs and fruit in August–September, no further yield was produced for several months (cp. Isa 16:9; Jer 48:32). No one could be found to *satisfy* Micah's *hunger* for righteousness (7:2-6).

7:2
Isa 57:1; 59:7
Jer 5:26
Hos 5:1

7:3
Prov 4:16-17
Mic 3:11
[f]*shapat* (8199)
‣Gen 18:25

7:4
Isa 10:3; 22:5
Ezek 2:6
Nah 1:10

7:5
Jer 9:4-5

7:6
*Matt 10:35-36
*Luke 12:53

7:7
Ps 4:3; 130:5
[g]*yakhal* (3176)
‣Job 13:15

7:8
Prov 24:15-16
Isa 9:2
Amos 9:11

7:9
Ps 37:6
Jer 50:34

2 The godly people have all disappeared;
not one honest person is left on the earth.
They are all murderers,
setting traps even for their own brothers.
3 Both their hands are equally skilled at doing evil!
Officials and [f]judges alike demand bribes.
The people with influence get what they want,
and together they scheme to twist justice.
4 Even the best of them is like a brier;
the most honest is as dangerous as a hedge of thorns.
But your judgment day is coming swiftly now.
Your time of punishment is here, a time of confusion.
5 Don't trust anyone—
not your best friend or even your wife!
6 For the son despises his father.
The daughter defies her mother.
The daughter-in-law defies her mother-in-law.
Your enemies are right in your own household!

7 As for me, I look to the LORD for help.
I [g]wait confidently for God to save me,
and my God will certainly hear me.
8 Do not gloat over me, my enemies!
For though I fall, I will rise again.
Though I sit in darkness,
the LORD will be my light.
9 I will be patient as the LORD punishes me,
for I have sinned against him.

What Is Good (6:8)

Exod 33:19; 34:6-7
Deut 8:3; 16:19-20
1 Kgs 3:11
Ezra 7:25
Neh 9:31
Isa 2:9; 5:15; 30:18; 38:15
Dan 9:18
Hos 6:6
Amos 5:12, 15
Mal 2:17; 3:15

Micah 6:8, a well-known and oft-memorized verse, answers a series of questions put forth by a confused people who had lost their moral and spiritual bearings.

The people of Israel wanted to know what they could do to be acceptable to the Lord. In an oppressive and deceitful society, they had lost a sense of what the Lord regards as good. God gave them a concrete answer: He is not seeking mechanical, ritualistic worship (6:5-6), but that his people do what is right in relationship with him and in their relationships with each other. As they are motivated by love, their actions will be tempered by justice, mercy, and humility (see 7:18-20). God's people are not to oppress others, but to do what is just, righteous, and honest toward one another.

Micah 6:8 summarizes what God had already made known in the past to Israel: Humility, faith, and obedience are pleasing to him. God declared this message to Abraham (Gen 15:6; 17:1, 9), to Moses at Sinai (Exod 20–23), through his prophets (e.g., Deut 6:1-8; Hos 6:6), and through Israel's wise men (Prov 1:7).

It pleases God when his people walk humbly in faith before him, as exemplified by Moses (Num 12:3), Habakkuk (Hab 3:17-19), Daniel (Dan 9:1-19), and Ezra (Ezra 9:5-15). Real spirituality and devotion is in doing good, seeking justice, relieving oppression, defending orphans, and aiding widows (see Exod 22:21-24; 23:2-12; Deut 15:4-11; 24:12-15; Neh 5:1-13; Jer 22:16; Amos 5:7-24; Dan 4:27; Jas 1:27). These acts are marks of God's own character (Ps 146:9; Matt 11:5).

7:2-6 The people of Israel were without law, justice, or righteousness. Everyone took advantage of others for self-aggrandizement; they had created a society in which all forms of oppression were the norm.

7:2 ***not one honest person is left:*** This complaint is frequent in the prophets (see Isa 59:16; Jer 5:1; Ezek 22:30). • In the ancient Near East, people fished and hunted by *setting traps* and using nets (cp. Ps 10:9; Prov 1:17; Isa 51:20). • ***their own brothers:*** All fellow Israelites were regarded as brothers.

7:3 ***Both their hands:*** That is, they had perfected the skills for doing evil. • ***Officials and judges alike demand bribes:*** Rulers and judges were forbidden to *twist justice* (Exod 18:19-22; Deut 16:18-20). Israel's judicial system was completely corrupt.

7:4 ***your judgment day is coming:*** The people of Israel would soon be conquered by the Assyrians, the people of Judah would soon face destruction at the hands of the Babylonians, and all the people of the earth will soon face God in judgment.

7:5-6 ***Don't trust anyone:*** Bitterness, corruption, and treachery had poisoned the community of the Lord's people (cp. Matt 10:34-36; Luke 12:52-53).

7:7-10 In the midst of despair, Micah prays with a psalm of hope and confidence in the Lord (cp. Hab 2:4; 3:16-18).

7:8 ***Though I sit in darkness:*** The prophet confidently trusts in God to be his *light* (cp. Ps 27:1) even in deep difficulty, knowing that his enemies would not overcome him (cp. Ps 23:4-5). God's Spirit gave him the power and confidence to perform his prophetic task (3:8).

7:9 ***I have sinned:*** The prophet and other godly people recognize their own failure and culpability, yet trust in the Lord for redemption. • The Lord's *righteousness* brings salvation and rescue for his people.

But after that, he will take up my case
and give me justice for all I have
suffered from my enemies.
The LORD will bring me into the light,
and I will see his righteousness.
10 Then my enemies will see that the LORD
is on my side.
They will be ashamed that they
taunted me, saying,
"So where is the LORD—
that God of yours?"
With my own eyes I will see their
downfall;
they will be trampled like mud in the
streets.
11 In that day, Israel, your cities will be
rebuilt,
and your borders will be extended.
12 People from many lands will come and
honor you—
from Assyria all the way to the towns
of Egypt,
from Egypt all the way to the Euphrates
River,
and from distant seas and
mountains.
13 But the land will become empty and
desolate
because of the wickedness of those
who live there.

The LORD's Compassion on Israel

14 O LORD, protect your people with your
shepherd's staff;
lead your flock, your special
possession.
Though they live alone in a thicket
on the heights of Mount Carmel,
let them graze in the fertile pastures of
Bashan and Gilead
as they did long ago.

15 "Yes," says the LORD,
"I will do mighty miracles for you,
like those I did when I rescued you
from slavery in Egypt."

16 All the nations of the world will stand
amazed
at what the LORD will do for you.
They will be embarrassed
at their feeble power.
They will cover their mouths in silent
awe,
deaf to everything around them.
17 Like snakes crawling from their
holes,
they will come out to meet the LORD
our God.
They will fear him greatly,
trembling in terror at his presence.
18 Where is another God like you,
who [h]pardons the guilt of the
remnant,
overlooking the sins of his special
people?
You will not stay angry with your people
forever,

7:10 Isa 51:23; Zech 10:5
7:11 Amos 9:11
7:12 Isa 11:16; 19:23-25
7:13 Isa 3:10-11; Mic 6:13
7:14 Amos 9:11
7:15 Exod 3:20
7:16 Mic 3:7
7:17 Gen 3:14; Ps 9:20; 72:9
7:18 Exod 34:9; Num 14:18-19; Jer 4:2; 32:41
[h]*nasa'* (5375) ‣Gen 50:17

7:10 ***where is the Lord?*** This taunt rebuked God and those who trusted him. God had promised always to be with his people and their leaders (Gen 46:3-4; Exod 3:12). God was dishonored by these taunts, and he would act to clear his name (cp. Ezek 20:9; 36:19-26).

7:11-12 ***That day*** includes (1) 538 BC, when Israel began to return from exile in Babylon (see Ezra 1–2); and (2) the final restoration of God's people (see Amos 9:11-15). As the nations flow to a renewed Israel, God's purposes through Abraham will be fulfilled (Gen 12:3).

7:12 ***the Euphrates River:*** Literally *the river.*

7:13 ***land:*** Or *earth.* • Before their restoration, Israel must be disciplined (Deut 4:29; 28:37, 48, 63; 30:1-6). • ***empty and desolate:*** The people's intransigent ***wickedness*** brought on God's judgments.

7:14-20 The Lord promised to completely renew Israel, his special possession (see Exod 19:5; Mal 3:17). Judgment would not mean the destruction of hope, but a cleansing so that true hope could prevail. The restoration would be God's work alone as he restored the remnant of his special people and removed their guilt by his love, compassion, and faithfulness (see Exod 32:12-14).

7:14 • With a ***shepherd's staff,*** an ancient Near Eastern shepherd could defend his sheep from wild beasts. Likewise, the prophet prayed that God would protect his people from hostile Gentile nations (cp. Exod 4:1-5). • ***special possession:*** Cp. Exod 19:5; Deut 7:6; 14:2; 26:18; Mal 3:17; 1 Pet 2:9. • ***on the heights of Mount Carmel:*** Or *surrounded by a fruitful land.* • ***Bashan and Gilead,*** east of the Jordan River, were part of the Lord's earliest gifts to the Israelite tribes of Reuben, Gad, and Manasseh (Josh 13:15-31). Assyria annexed these territories and took these tribes away in the 700s BC. Israel's ownership would be restored and expanded.

7:15 Israel's enslavement to sin and to other nations called for ***mighty miracles*** such as those that brought Israel out of ***Egypt.***

7:16 The promise that ***all the nations*** would be blessed by the descendants of Abraham (Gen 12:3) would be fulfilled in this restoration of God's special people.

7:17 ***Like snakes,*** the nations had struck at the heel of Israel (cp. Gen 3:14-15). The prophets regularly depicted foreign nations as poisonous, deceitful serpents (Isa 14:29; Jer 8:17; Ezek 29:1-3). Now these nations would be humbled (cp. Ps 72:9). ***Crawling*** and "eating dust" were metaphors for defeat and humiliation.

7:18-20 These verses provide a fine brief summary of OT theology. God is unique; there is no one and nothing else like him. Because of his ***unfailing love*** (Hebrew *khesed*), he does not destroy his people whom he judges, but instead restores them (see Exod 36:6-7). His ***faithfulness*** means that he can be trusted to do good regardless of the cost to himself (see Ps 89:1-2). • ***Where is another God like you:*** This question probably plays off of Micah's name ("Who is like the Lord?"). God's character is unequaled among the gods of the nations. His actions and words spring from his character (Exod 34:6-7). God

7:19
Isa 43:25
Jer 50:20
7:20
Gen 24:27; 32:9-10
Deut 7:8, 12
Luke 1:72

because you delight in showing
unfailing love.
19 Once again you will have compassion
on us.
You will trample our sins under your
feet
and throw them into the depths of the
ocean!
20 You will show us your faithfulness and
unfailing love
as you promised to our ancestors
Abraham and Jacob long ago.

pardons, shows compassion, triumphs over his peoples' ***sins***, and seals those sins away. The Lord's ***unfailing love*** moved him to choose Israel from the beginning (Deut 7:8), consistent with his covenant faithfulness to Israel's ***ancestors*** (Deut 7:20; 9:1–10:22). By his unfailing love, God continues to offer hope to those who trust in him.

THE BOOK OF NAHUM

No one likes being in the path of imminent disaster, nor is the menacing threat of enemy invasion a pleasant thought. Can God protect in such circumstances? Will God judge wicked aggressors? Nahum's reply is a clear yes. Nahum's prophecy assures us that God still controls earth's history. His messages are a warning to oppressors and a comfort to the oppressed.

SETTING

In Nahum's time, the kingdom of Judah was in danger of being swallowed by a great superpower, the Assyrian empire. From Nineveh, the capital, the great king Ashurbanipal (668–626 BC) brought Assyrian might to its zenith. Its military power and cultural influence spanned the length and breadth of the ancient Near East. Even the age-old city of Thebes had felt the conqueror's heel (3:8-10).

The times were less than encouraging for Nahum and the people of Judah. Israel, their sister kingdom to the north, had already fallen to the Assyrians in 722 BC, and Judah now faced the same imperial enemy. To make matters worse, Ashurbanipal had recently captured Judah's king, the wicked Manasseh (697–642 BC), and taken him to Babylon (2 Chr 33:10-11). Following his release from captivity, a repentant Manasseh (2 Chr 33:12-17) attempted to undo his former wickedness (2 Kgs 21:1-18; 2 Chr 33:1-9). Despite his efforts, his prior evil influence still permeated the land. This, coupled with the long shadow of Assyrian supremacy, cast a cloud of doom over God's people. Thus, Nahum's prophetic messages of Nineveh's fall and of hope for Judah's future were timely.

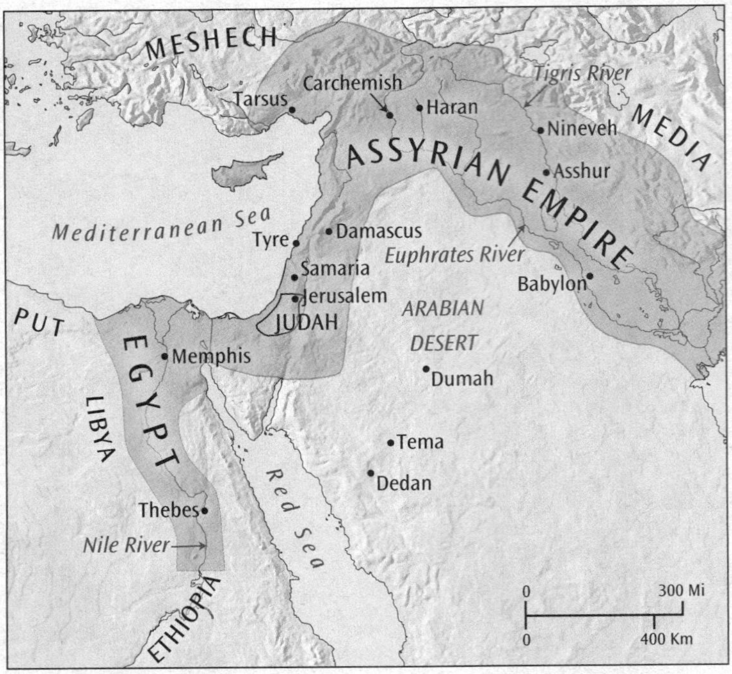

The Near East during Nahum's Time (about 645~615 BC). The Assyrian empire under King Ashurbanipal (668–626 BC) reached its peak and threatened to engulf Judah. Yet Nahum brought hope and the promise that the Assyrian empire would be destroyed. After Ashurbanipal's death, Assyria quickly lost its strength, and its capital Nineveh was sacked by the Babylonians in 612 BC, marking the end of Assyrian dominance.
ASSYRIA 1:12-14; 3:18
JUDAH 1:15; 2:2
THEBES, EGYPT, LIBYA, PUT, ETHIOPIA 3:8-10

The seeds of Assyria's fall were already being sown in Nahum's day. After King Ashurbanipal repelled a strong coalition of enemies to the west and resisted his brother's challenge to the throne, he busied himself with literary and artistic pursuits. Affairs of state languished, and Assyria grew increasingly weak. After Ashurbanipal's death (626 BC), one after another of the great cities of Assyria began falling to foreign invaders. Then the unthinkable happened—Nineveh itself fell in 612 BC, as Nahum had predicted.

SUMMARY

Nahum opens his prophecy with a consideration of God (1:1-11). The prophet depicts God's power in two striking poetic passages, 1:2-6 and 1:7-11. God is sovereign over all people and over the natural world. Nahum's poems portray God's judgment against wickedness and his goodness toward those who put their trust in him. The opening verses give assurance that God will administer his justice fairly.

Nahum then explains what God's sovereign justice means in the flow of history (1:12-15). No nation is so great that it will not pay for its evil, and God is aware of the plight of those who are oppressed. The prophet assures the people of Judah that they will soon know changed circumstances. Peace and stability will return, and God's people will be able to enjoy the uninterrupted worship of God.

After predicting the siege of Nineveh and the return of normal conditions in Judah (2:1-2), Nahum describes the fall of the Assyrian capital in two vivid portrayals (2:3-10; 3:1-7). Between the two accounts, Nahum contemplates Nineveh's destruction in a brief, taunting song. With biting satire, he declares God's intention of bringing an end to proud Nineveh's greed (2:11-13).

Nahum builds upon his second description of Nineveh's fall through another satire of the city. Nineveh would be no more defensible than Egypt's capital, Thebes (3:8-13), which Assyria had destroyed. He closes his prophecy with yet another piece of satire (3:14-19). Sensing the hopelessness of Nineveh's plight, he taunts the city's citizens by urging them to call upon all their resources in order to defend themselves. Of course, that would do no good. Nineveh would lie fatally wounded with no one to help or even mourn her passing.

AUTHOR

Beyond the little that can be gleaned from his writings, nothing is known of Nahum, the author of this short prophecy. In the Hebrew text, he is identified as "Nahum the Elkoshite" (1:1). Elkosh could be his clan name, but more likely it was his hometown, which was probably located in southwest

OUTLINE

1:1
Superscription: Introducing the Prophet

1:1-15
The LORD's Anger against Nineveh

2:1-13
The Fall of Nineveh

3:1-19
The LORD's Judgment against Nineveh

TIMELINE

728–686 BC
Hezekiah as king of Judah

701 BC
Jerusalem rescued from Sennacherib's assault

697–642 BC
Manasseh as king of Judah

680–669 BC
Esarhaddon as king of Assyria

668–626 BC
Ashurbanipal as king of Assyria

663 BC
Thebes is destroyed by Assyria

about 645~615 BC
Nahum as prophet

648 BC
Manasseh rebels against Assyria

645 BC
Manasseh's exile, repentance, and return

642–640 BC
Amon as king of Judah

640–609 BC
Josiah as king of Judah

626 BC
Death of Ashurbanipal

612 BC
Nineveh is conquered by Babylon

Nahum's message is essential and timeless: the Lord reigns and will have the final word against evil.

KENNETH L. BARKER AND WAYLON BAILEY
Micah, Nahum, Habakkuk, Zephaniah

FURTHER READING

O. PALMER ROBERTSON
The Books of Nahum, Habakkuk, and Zephaniah (1990)

KENNETH L. BARKER AND WAYLON BAILEY
Micah, Nahum, Habakkuk, Zephaniah (1990)

RICHARD PATTERSON
Nahum in *Cornerstone Biblical Commentary*, vol. 10 (2008)

Judah. The details of the book show that he was well acquainted with the city of Nineveh.

DATE

Nahum mentions the fall of Thebes (663 BC; 3:10), and predicts the fall of Nineveh, which occurred in 612 BC. Therefore, Nahum spoke these prophecies sometime between 663 and 612 BC. Exactly when he did so within this span of years is debatable. It may have been some time late in the reign of Manasseh (about 648~645 BC), perhaps during his attempted reforms after being released from Assyrian captivity (2 Chr 33:12-16); or, it may have been later, during the early or middle part of righteous King Josiah's reign (640–609 BC).

MEANING AND MESSAGE

No empire, however great, is beyond God's scrutiny. Sooner or later, all must give an account of their actions to the Lord. The reality of the sovereign God's righteous justice lies beneath the predicted judgment of Nineveh and Assyria. He is in control of everyone and everything on earth. This assures us of God's concern for all who suffer, whether from the horrors and atrocities of war or from any other oppression. A burdened humankind can be confident that divine justice will ultimately prevail.

God is long-suffering (1:3), and his people must be patient. The assurance that this good and caring Lord (1:7) has a distinct purpose for his people (2:2) encourages them to a life of faith and trust. Beyond the book's menacing tone lies the good news of hope (1:15). The prophet predicts a coming day when God's people will once again worship him in wondrous peace and joy. They will at last be free of those who would take away their freedom. It is no wonder that subsequent writers of Scripture found in Nahum's good news a promise of the gospel message (Rom 10:15; see also Isa 52:7). Jesus Christ provides the opportunity for personal deliverance from sin. Knowing that the unbeliever faces an even greater doom than that of fallen Nineveh motivates a missionary effort to carry the good news of the gospel to a dying world.

1:1
Isa 13:1
Zeph 2:13

1:2
Exod 20:5
Deut 4:24; 32:35
Ps 94:1

1:3
Exod 34:5-7
Ps 50:3; 104:3
[a]*'arek 'appayim* (0750, 0639)
‣Exod 34:6

1:4
Isa 33:9
Matt 8:26

1:5
Exod 19:19
2 Sam 22:8-9
Mic 1:4

1:6
1 Kgs 19:11
Jer 10:10
Mal 3:2

1:7
1 Chr 16:34
Ps 25:8; 100:5

1:8
Isa 8:7

1:9
Ps 2:1-4; 21:11

1:10
Isa 9:18
Mal 4:1

1. SUPERSCRIPTION: INTRODUCING THE PROPHET (1:1)

1 This message concerning Nineveh came as a vision to Nahum, who lived in Elkosh.

2. THE LORD'S ANGER AGAINST NINEVEH (1:2-15)

God's Sovereignty

2 The LORD is a jealous God,
filled with vengeance and rage.
He takes revenge on all who oppose him
and continues to rage against his enemies!
3 The LORD is [a]slow to get angry, but his power is great,
and he never lets the guilty go unpunished.
He displays his power in the whirlwind and the storm.
The billowing clouds are the dust beneath his feet.
4 At his command the oceans dry up,
and the rivers disappear.
The lush pastures of Bashan and Carmel fade,
and the green forests of Lebanon wither.
5 In his presence the mountains quake,
and the hills melt away;
the earth trembles,
and its people are destroyed.
6 Who can stand before his fierce anger?
Who can survive his burning fury?
His rage blazes forth like fire,
and the mountains crumble to dust in his presence.

God's Irresistible Justice

7 The LORD is good,
a strong refuge when trouble comes.
He is close to those who trust in him.
8 But he will sweep away his enemies
in an overwhelming flood.
He will pursue his foes
into the darkness of night.
9 Why are you scheming against the LORD?
He will destroy you with one blow;
he won't need to strike twice!
10 His enemies, tangled like thornbushes
and staggering like drunks,
will be burned up like dry stubble in a field.
11 Who is this wicked counselor of yours
who plots evil against the LORD?

1:1 *message . . . vision:* This opening, similar to that of other prophetic books (cp. Obad 1:1; Hab 1:1; Mal 1:1), identifies Nahum as a prophet, one who uttered messages from God. • *Nineveh* became the capital of the Assyrian empire sometime shortly after 705 BC and remained so until its destruction in 612 BC. • The name *Nahum* means "comfort" or "encouragement." An important theme of his prophecy is that God will bring encouragement to his people through Nineveh's downfall (1:12-15; see Isa 40:1).

1:2-11 This short, two-stanza hymn (1:2-6, 7-11) tells of God's sovereign power.

1:2-6 The hymn's first stanza draws from biblical texts commemorating Israel's exodus from Egypt. The message is that everything in all creation is subject to God's sovereign power, and God will ensure the punishment of those *who oppose him*.

1:2 *jealous* (or *zealous*): God zealously guards the welfare of his people and zealously desires their faithfulness (see Exod 20:4-5; Deut 4:23-24; 6:4; Jer 2:1–3:5). • God's *vengeance and rage* cannot be confused with the human attitude of "getting even." God's actions emerge from his holiness (Jer 50:28-29), justice (Isa 63:1-9), and faithfulness to the covenant with his people (Lev 26:23-25; Isa 1:24-26). His vengeance is never arbitrary.

1:3 *slow to get angry:* God's patience with disobedience is linked to his faithful love (Exod 34:6; Num 14:18; Ps 103:8; Joel 2:13). This trait had disappointed Jonah, who wanted Nineveh destroyed immediately (Jon 4:2). Because God is patient, he sometimes delays the deserved punishment of sinners (Neh 9:29-30; Rom 2:4; 2 Pet 3:9), but those *guilty* of persisting in sin will ultimately face God's judgment (Exod 34:7; Rom 14:10; 2 Cor 5:10; Rev 14:6-7). • *the whirlwind and the storm:* This imagery describes the fury of God's judgment against the wicked (see also Isa 29:6).

1:4 Like clouds (1:3) and mountains (1:5), *oceans* and *rivers* are under God's sovereign control. The OT prophets often recall God's actions against the seas and rivers during the Exodus (Exod 15:8-10; 2 Sam 22:16; Ps 66:6; 77:16; Hab 3:15). God's power over the waters repudiated the mythology of the ancient Canaanites, who believed that the oceans and the rivers were under the control of the sea-god, Yam. • *Bashan,* situated east of the Sea of Galilee, was known for its rich pastureland, ideal for raising cattle (cp. Mic 7:14). • *Carmel,* on the Mediterranean coast in central Canaan, was noted for its beauty and fruitfulness (Song 7:5; Jer 50:19). • *Lebanon* was famed for its great cedars (1 Kgs 5:6-18). Nahum lists these areas to demonstrate that even the most fertile and productive places on earth cannot withstand the power of God's judgment.

1:5 OT poetry often mentions the shaking of *the earth* to commemorate the Exodus period (e.g., Ps 18:7; Hab 3:6; see Exod 19:18).

1:6 The Hebrew word translated *rage* is repeated from 1:2. Its repetition brackets 1:2-6 as a single poetic unit.

1:7-11 This second stanza (see note on 1:2-11) concentrates on God's sovereignty, righteousness, and justice in dealing with all people.

1:7 *The LORD is good:* God acts equitably when he judges the wicked. He also provides *refuge* for *those who trust in him*. He accepts them and protects them in the midst of life's trials (Ps 18:2; 62:5-7). God's rich goodness can lead individuals to repentance (Rom 2:2-4).

1:8 *overwhelming flood:* A metaphor for the powerful nature of God's judgment (see 2:6).

1:9 *Why are you scheming:* No scheme or human plot against God can succeed. Human plans are worthless if they do not match God's plans (Ps 2; Isa 14:26-27; 23:9).

1:11 The *wicked counselor* is the Assyrian king. God had also dealt with the arrogant conceit of an Assyrian king in Hezekiah's time (about 701 BC; see 2 Kgs 19:35-36). Assyria's *wicked counselor* contrasts with the coming Messiah, the King who is a "Wonderful Counselor" (Isa 9:6).

Good News for Judah, Bad News for Nineveh

12 This is what the LORD says:
"Though the Assyrians have many allies,
they will be destroyed and disappear.
O my people, I have punished you
before,
but I will not punish you again.
13 Now I will break the yoke of bondage
from your neck
and tear off the chains of Assyrian
oppression."

14 And this is what the LORD says
concerning the Assyrians in
Nineveh:
"You will have no more children to carry
on your name.
I will destroy all the idols in the
temples of your gods.
I am preparing a grave for you
because you are despicable!"

15 Look! A messenger is coming over the
mountains with good news!
He is bringing a message of peace.
Celebrate your festivals, O people of
Judah,
and fulfill all your vows,
for your wicked enemies will never
invade your land again.
They will be completely destroyed!

3. THE FALL OF NINEVEH (2:1-13)

Warning to Nineveh

2 1 Your enemy is coming to crush you,
Nineveh.
Man the ramparts! Watch the roads!
Prepare your defenses! Call out your
forces!

2 Even though the destroyer has destroyed
Judah,
the LORD will restore its honor.
Israel's vine has been stripped of
branches,
but he will restore its splendor.

3 Shields flash red in the sunlight!
See the scarlet uniforms of the valiant
troops!
Watch as their glittering chariots move
into position,
with a forest of spears waving above
them.
4 The chariots race recklessly along the
streets
and rush wildly through the squares.
They flash like firelight
and move as swiftly as lightning.
5 The king shouts to his officers;
they stumble in their haste,
rushing to the walls to set up their
defenses.

1:13 Isa 9:4; Jer 2:20
1:14 Nah 3:4-6
1:15 Isa 29:7-8; 40:9; 52:7; Rom 10:15
2:2 Isa 60:15; Ezek 37:21-23
2:3 Ezek 23:14-15
2:4 Jer 4:13; Nah 3:2
2:5 Jer 46:12

1:12 The Assyrians' ***allies*** were vassal or subordinate kingdoms, including once-powerful Egypt. Ironically, a coalition of former allies gradually brought down the great Neo-Assyrian empire between 625 and 605 BC. • ***O my people*** refers to Judah, whom God had ***punished*** earlier when the Assyrian king Sennacherib (704–681 BC) launched a campaign (701 BC) against the western states of the Near East. While Sennacherib failed to take Jerusalem (2 Kgs 19:32-36), he boasted in his annals of carrying away Jerusalem's tribute and an enormous amount of booty from forty-six cities in Judah. Although Judah was now reduced to vassalage and faced the constant possibility of Assyrian aggression, Assyria did not defeat the southern kingdom. Babylon did so, however, in 586 BC. Sadly, neither Israel nor Judah heeded God's repeated warnings that failure to repent would result in judgment (Hos 11:5; Joel 2:1-27).

1:14 ***no more children:*** Nineveh would be completely annihilated. Cutting off a person's ***name*** and leaving him without a descendant meant utterly destroying him (1 Sam 24:21; Job 18:17; Isa 14:22). • None of Assyria's venerated ***gods*** could deliver Nineveh from God's death sentence. • God was already ***preparing a grave*** for Nineveh and directing Assyria's enemies to destroy the city. Assyria's proud cities fell one by one to the combined attacks of the Chaldeans, the Medes, and the Ummanmanda. Nineveh itself fell in 612 BC.

1:15 Verse 1:15 is numbered 2:1 in the Hebrew text. • Nahum supplements his prophecy of Judah's release from bondage (1:13) with a prediction of the arrival of a ***messenger*** bringing the ***good news*** of restored peace (see also Isa 52:7). The ***message of peace*** was that Assyria's hold on Judah would be broken and God's people would be free of its burden. This took place during the reign of Josiah (640–609 BC), after the death of the Assyrian king Ashurbanipal in 626 BC. This political message is a foretaste of God's final triumph over evil, when his people will be released from bondage to sin through the saving work of the Messiah and be given eternal peace (Zeph 3:13; Luke 2:10-14; Acts 10:34-43; Rom 10:15; Eph 2:14-18).

2:1-13 Verses 2:1-13 are numbered 2:2-14 in the Hebrew text.

2:1 Although Nineveh's defenders might fully prepare to protect the city with ***ramparts . . . roads . . . defenses***, and ***forces***, their efforts were doomed to failure (1:1-14).

2:2 The ***vine*** symbolizes God's blessing his people (Isa 27:2-6), while the ***stripped*** vine reflects God's previous chastisement of them (Isa 5:1-7). The children of Israel were in a sad state compared to the days of the great kings David and Solomon, but God promised to ***restore*** the ***splendor*** of his people.

2:3 ***with a forest of spears waving above them:*** This phrase follows the Hebrew text; the Greek and Syriac versions read *the horses whipped into a frenzy*.

2:4 ***Chariots*** were virtually unstoppable in battle because of their maneuverability and power.

2:5 The Assyrian king overcomes the initial shock of Nineveh's being attacked and ***shouts to his officers***. He and the city have been caught off guard and they rush ***to the walls*** to thwart the siege. • ***to set up their defenses*** (literally *the covering is prepared*): The meaning of the Hebrew term here is uncertain. *Covering* probably refers to something the attackers or the defenders used to protect themselves from armaments hurled through the air.

2:7 Isa 32:12; 59:11
2:8 Jer 46:5
2:10 Josh 2:11
2:11 Isa 5:29
2:13 Ps 46:8-9
3:1 Ezek 24:6-9

6 The river gates have been torn open!
The palace is about to collapse!
7 Nineveh's exile has been decreed,
and all the servant girls mourn its capture.
They moan like doves
and beat their breasts in sorrow.
8 Nineveh is like a leaking water reservoir!
The people are slipping away.
"Stop, stop!" someone shouts,
but no one even looks back.
9 Loot the silver!
Plunder the gold!
There's no end to Nineveh's treasures—
its vast, uncounted wealth.
10 Soon the city is plundered, empty, and ruined.
Hearts melt and knees shake.
The people stand aghast,
their faces pale and trembling.

Nahum Ridicules Nineveh's Greatness

11 Where now is that great Nineveh,
that den filled with young lions?
It was a place where people—like lions
and their cubs—
walked freely and without fear.
12 The lion tore up meat for his cubs
and strangled prey for his mate.
He filled his den with prey,
his caverns with his plunder.

13 "I am your enemy!"
says the LORD of Heaven's Armies.
"Your chariots will soon go up in smoke.
Your young men will be killed in battle.
Never again will you plunder conquered nations.
The voices of your proud messengers
will be heard no more."

4. THE LORD'S JUDGMENT AGAINST NINEVEH (3:1-19)

Woe to Nineveh

3 1 What sorrow awaits Nineveh,
the city of murder and lies!
She is crammed with wealth
and is never without victims.

The God Who Gives Justice (3:4)

Nah 1:3-10
Exod 34:6-7
Ps 9:7-8; 67:4
Isa 1:24-28; 11:1-9; 40:22-24
Jer 46:27-28
Joel 3:1-2
Jon 3:1–4:11
Acts 10:34-43; 17:30-31
Rev 20:11-15

Nahum concentrates on Nineveh's judgment because God's justice demands it (1:14; 2:13; 3:4). God is just (Ps 9:7-8); he detests sin and rewards people and nations justly in accord with what they do (Ps 67:4; Isa 1:27; Jer 46:28; Joel 3:1-8; Acts 17:31). God is in sovereign control of the natural world (1:4-6, 8) and of all nations (1:3, 6-10, 15). The world and its inhabitants stand helpless when opposing him (Job 41:10-11; Isa 40:22-24).

God's justice sometimes may seem slow in coming (1:3). If God seems to delay judgment, it is because he is patient and merciful toward people (Jon 3–4; 2 Pet 3:9-15). God does not execute justice with rigid disinterest; he gives justice with love and seeks to bring those who deserve only judgment into a family relationship (see Exod 34:6-7).

Nahum's "good news" (1:15) was that all who trust in God will one day enjoy the peace and well-being that come with the final defeat of evil (see also Isa 11:1-9; Zeph 3:13). The ultimate fulfillment of this promise began in the life, death, and resurrection of Jesus Christ (Acts 10:34-43; Rom 10:9-15). Those who believe in the Lord Jesus experience the blessings of salvation in part now as they await God's final judgment of evil and the coming of his kingdom in its fullness (see Rev 20:7–22:5).

2:6 The rush to defend (2:5) comes too late; the defenses are already breached. • Nineveh was served by a reservoir formed by a double dam on the Khosr River, a tributary of the Tigris that flowed through the city. The reservoir was augmented by a series of flood *gates*. The Greek historian Diodorus reported that during this time torrential rains had already swelled the city's river system. By first closing, then opening the flood gates, Nineveh's attackers released the pent-up water as a battering ram against the city walls.

2:7 Because *Nineveh's exile* had *been decreed* by God, it would certainly happen. • To *beat their breasts* was a common sign of mourning (see, e.g., Luke 18:13).

2:8 The people will run away as fast as water flows from a breached *reservoir* (see note on 2:6).

2:9 The *vast, uncounted wealth* of other nations poured into the Assyrian capital as trade, tribute, and booty, but it was gone in an instant. Ruthless aggression and wickedness may succeed temporarily, but ultimately they will be destroyed (Prov 13:22; Obad 1:15; Luke 12:16-20).

2:10 *plundered, empty, and ruined:* The Hebrew here is alliterated for effect: *buqah umbuqah umbullaqah*. The effect might be translated into English as "devastated, despoiled, and destroyed."

2:11-13 Following the description of Nineveh's fall (2:1-10), Nahum inserts the first of three taunt songs (see also 3:8-13, 14-19; this was a common form in the ancient Near East). In biting satire, he compares Nineveh to a lion's *den*. King Sennacherib and other Assyrian kings had compared themselves to *lions*, even decorating their palaces with artistic representations of lions and of themselves on lion hunts. However, with God as its enemy, Nineveh would no longer be the lair of an invincible predator.

2:13 *young men:* Literally *young lions.* • Examples of the *voices* of Assyria's *proud messengers* are found in 2 Kgs 18:19–19:13.

3:1 *city of murder:* The Assyrians' graphic cruelty is well documented. Their practices included cutting off

2 Hear the crack of whips,
the rumble of wheels!
Horses' hooves pound,
and chariots clatter wildly.
3 See the flashing swords and glittering spears
as the charioteers charge past!
There are countless casualties,
heaps of bodies—
so many bodies that
people stumble over them.
4 All this because Nineveh,
the beautiful and faithless city,
mistress of deadly charms,
enticed the nations with her beauty.
She taught them all her magic,
enchanting people everywhere.
5 "I am your enemy!"
says the LORD of Heaven's Armies.
"And now I will lift your skirts
and show all the earth your
nakedness and shame.
6 I will cover you with filth
and show the world how vile you
really are.
7 All who see you will shrink back
and say,
'Nineveh lies in ruins.
Where are the mourners?'
Does anyone regret your
destruction?"

Nahum Ridicules Nineveh's Strength

8 Are you any better than the city of
Thebes,
situated on the Nile River,
surrounded by water?
She was protected by the river on all
sides,
walled in by water.
9 Ethiopia and the land of Egypt
gave unlimited assistance.
The nations of Put and Libya
were among her allies.
10 Yet Thebes fell,
and her people were led away as
captives.
Her babies were dashed to death
against the stones of the streets.
Soldiers threw dice to get Egyptian
officers as servants.
All their leaders were bound in
chains.
11 And you, Nineveh, will also stagger like a
drunkard.
You will hide for fear of the attacking
enemy.
12 All your fortresses will fall.
They will be devoured like the ripe
figs
that fall into the mouths
of those who shake the trees.
13 Your troops will be as weak
and helpless as women.
The gates of your land will be opened
wide to the enemy
and set on fire and burned.

Nahum Ridicules Nineveh's Defenses

14 Get ready for the siege!
Store up water!
Strengthen the defenses!
Go into the pits to trample clay,
and pack it into molds,
making bricks to repair the walls.
15 But the fire will devour you;
the sword will cut you down.

3:2 Nah 2:3-4
3:3 Isa 34:13
3:4 Isa 47:9; Rev 17:1-6; 18:2-3
3:5 Isa 47:3
3:6 Job 9:31; Isa 14:16
3:7 Isa 51:19; Jer 15:5
3:8 Isa 19:6-8; Jer 46:25; Ezek 30:14-16
3:9 Isa 20:5-6; Jer 46:9
3:10 2 Kgs 8:12; Ps 137:9; Hos 13:16
3:11 Isa 49:26; Jer 25:15-27
3:13 Isa 19:16; Jer 50:37; 51:30
3:14 2 Chr 32:3-4; Nah 2:1
3:15 Isa 66:15-16; Joel 1:4

external body parts—such as noses, ears, hands, and feet—and execution by impalement on stakes. They heaped up severed heads before the gates of besieged cities. The eyes of victims might also be put out and their skin stripped from their bodies while they were still alive.

3:2-3 These short, staccato phrases dramatize the effects of seeing and hearing the battle. • Assyrian ***chariots*** and ***charioteers*** were feared far and wide.

3:4 ***mistress of deadly charms:*** The Assyrians charmed other nations with wealth and promises of safety and prosperity, but then victimized them through military might and economic exploitation. Therefore, their punishment was a just recompense for their deeds (see Prov 24:12; Joel 3:4-8; Rev 18:6; 20:12).

3:5 Twice God tells Nineveh, ***I am your enemy*** (also 2:13). Nineveh's judgment stands as a historical reminder that the Lord abhors sin and will deal with people and nations according to their deeds (Ps 9:7-8; 62:12; Jer 46:28; Acts 17:31). One day, God's justice will fall worldwide on those who have rebelled against him (Rev 17–19).

3:8 ***Thebes*** (Hebrew *No-amon;* also in 3:10), the historic capital of Egypt, was situated on both sides of the Nile in Upper Egypt. It achieved its greatest fame as the political, religious, and cultural center of Egypt's great New Kingdom (1550–1069 BC). Though no longer Egypt's capital in the 600s BC, the city was still a thriving metropolis.

3:9-10 ***Thebes fell*** to the Assyrians under King Ashurbanipal in 663 BC. Before Ashurbanipal's victory, Thebes had seemed to have unconquerable defenses, as well as the help of all Egypt and its allies: ***Ethiopia*** (Hebrew *Cush*), ***Put*** (perhaps the fabled land of Punt, located near what is now coastal Somalia), and ***Libya***. None of these, however, had effectively protected Thebes. • ***babies were dashed to death:*** Ancient conquerors had the heinous practice of exterminating the infants of their enemies in this way (2 Kgs 8:12; Ps 137:9; Isa 13:16, 18). • ***Soldiers threw dice*** (literally *They cast lots*) for the spoils of war, while the ***leaders*** of the conquered people ***were bound in chains*** (see 2 Kgs 25:7; Jer 40:1, 4; Joel 3:3; Obad 1:11).

3:12 ***ripe figs:*** Cp. Amos 8:1-2; Rev 6:13.

3:14 ***Get ready . . . Strengthen:*** Nahum used sarcasm to stress that no amount of preparation would make the Assyrians able to withstand God's wrath (note also the sarcastic tone of 2:11-13).

b'arbeh (0697)
‣ Exod 10:4

3:18
1 Kgs 22:17
Ps 76:5-6
Isa 56:10
Jer 50:18

3:19
Jer 30:13
Lam 2:15
Mic 1:9

The enemy will consume you like
locusts,
devouring everything they see.
There will be no escape,
even if you multiply like swarming
[b]locusts.
16 Your merchants have multiplied
until they outnumber the stars.
But like a swarm of locusts,
they strip the land and fly away.
17 Your guards and officials are also like
swarming locusts
that crowd together in the hedges on
a cold day.
But like locusts that fly away when the
sun comes up,
all of them will fly away and
disappear.

18 Your shepherds are asleep, O Assyrian
king;
your princes lie dead in the dust.
Your people are scattered across the
mountains
with no one to gather them
together.
19 There is no healing for your wound;
your injury is fatal.
All who hear of your destruction
will clap their hands for joy.
Where can anyone be found
who has not suffered from your
continual cruelty?

3:15 The OT often uses *locusts* as a metaphor for armies (see Joel 2:1-11).

3:16 Assyrian ***merchants*** had spread throughout the Near East like ***locusts***, filling Nineveh with untold wealth. But just as locusts desire only to satisfy their insatiable appetites and then fly off, the merchants will take their goods and go in the time of Nineveh's distress, leaving a needy populace behind.

3:17 *guards:* Or *princes.*

3:18 ***shepherds:*** With the leaders gone, Nineveh's ***people*** would be ***scattered*** like sheep. • ***lie dead*** (literally *sleep*; see John 11:11-14): Assyria's leaders, asleep during Nineveh's crisis, would sleep in death. By contrast, Israel's Shepherd does not slumber (Ps 121:3), and he will gather Israel's lost sheep (Jer 23:3; Ezek 36:35).

3:19 Nineveh deserved ***destruction*** rather than ***healing***. Although God had been patient with Nineveh in Jonah's day (Jon 3:10), the Assyrians had returned to ***cruelty*** and would reap the harvest of their own evil (see Prov 11:16-19; Isa 66:5-6; Hos 8:7). Those who had ***suffered*** under Assyria's ***cruelty*** would welcome this message with ***joy***.

THE BOOK OF HABAKKUK

"Why do you allow injustice?" Habakkuk asked God. "Why do you tolerate evil?" God did not answer Habakkuk's questions directly. Instead, much as he did with Job, God gave Habakkuk a vision of his deity. Whether or not the prophet understood God's ways, he could safely trust him. Habakkuk's questions echo in the hearts of all God-fearing people. The book of Habakkuk does not offer easy answers to the problem of evil in the world. Instead, it gives sound reasons to exercise faith in the sovereign, holy, and just God, who will ultimately bring justice to his world.

SETTING

Habakkuk lived during a time when Judah had long been under the power of Assyria. The Assyrian empire had engulfed most of the ancient Near East, from Mesopotamia to the Egyptian capital city of Thebes. But by Habakkuk's day (late 600s BC), Assyria was showing signs of the weakness that would ultimately spell its doom. After finishing military campaigns in the mid 640s BC, the Assyrian king Ashurbanipal became preoccupied with literary and artistic pursuits. His growing inattention to the administration of his empire brought weakness abroad and uprisings within.

At Ashurbanipal's death, Assyria was faced with a new threat. In Babylon, King Nabopolassar (626–605 BC) proclaimed his independence from Assyria and laid the foundation for a Neo-Babylonian empire that would last for nearly a century (626–539 BC). Nabopolassar conquered one after another of Assyria's principal cities. The capital city of Nineveh fell in 612 BC, and the remaining Assyrian forces were subsequently defeated at Haran (609 BC) and Carchemish (605 BC).

When Nabopolassar's son Nebuchadnezzar II

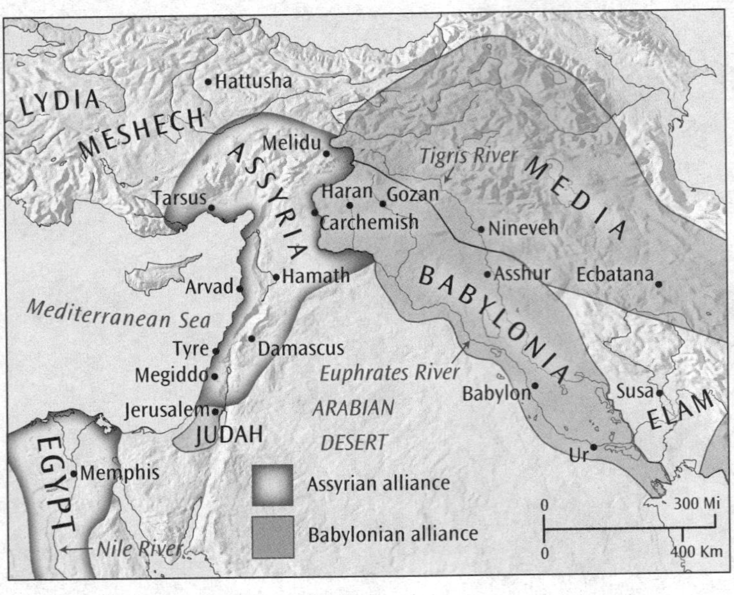

The Setting of Habakkuk, 609~605 BC. Habakkuk probably prophesied during the reign of Jehoiakim (609–598 BC), before the Babylonian invasion in 605 BC. When Habakkuk received his messages from the Lord, JUDAH had descended into wickedness. Between 612 and 605 BC, the Babylonians conquered the Assyrians and then, in 605 BC, swept unopposed into Judah. Thus began the process leading to the destruction of Judah and JERUSALEM in 605–586 BC.

(605–562 BC) succeeded him, his empire extended over vast portions of the ancient Near East. Nebuchadnezzar launched a series of campaigns against the kingdom of Judah, successfully attacking Jerusalem on three occasions and carrying many of its people into slavery. The last of these attacks (586 BC) resulted in the final overthrow of the kingdom of Judah.

Except for the final years of the godly king Josiah (640–609 BC), violence and injustice characterized Judean society from the evil reign of Manasseh (697–642 BC) to the fall of Jerusalem (586 BC). In many ways Manasseh was the opposite of his godly father, Hezekiah (see 2 Kgs 21:1-9; 2 Chr 33:2-9). Manasseh actively promoted pagan rites that pre-Israelite settlers of Canaan had practiced. This apostasy doomed Judah. Manasseh's later repentance and attempts to undo his earlier evils (2 Chr 33:15-19) did not result in lasting change. When his son Amon took the throne, he reintroduced all of the paganism practiced by his father (2 Kgs 21:21-22). The subsequent ministries of prophets such as Zephaniah, Jeremiah, and Ezekiel, and the reform efforts of Josiah (2 Chr 34:1–35:19) failed to produce lasting change. Even during Josiah's reforms, the people of Judah remained entrenched in their apostasy. As a result, Judah's later kings were all condemned for their wickedness (2 Kgs 23:32, 37; 24:19; Jer 22:1-30; 27:1-22; 36:30-31).

OUTLINE

1:1
Superscription: Introducing the Prophet

1:2–2:20
Habakkuk's Perplexity

3:1-19
Habakkuk's Prayer

Both externally and internally, the nation of Judah was in a precarious state. It was during this last, tragic period of Judah's history as an independent state that Habakkuk saw wickedness and injustice all around him (1:2-4).

SUMMARY

Habakkuk's prophecy is a dialogue between God and the prophet. In the opening verses, Habakkuk contemplates the violent society Judah had become. He cannot understand why God seems to ignore Judah's sin. Habakkuk feels that despite his repeated cries, God simply is not listening to him (1:2-4). God's first answer is that he is about to deal with Judah's violence by bringing an even more violent people, the Babylonians, to judge them (1:5-11).

This answer perplexes Habakkuk even more (1:12–2:1). Judah was indeed wicked, but why would God use people who were even more wicked to chastise his own people? God's answer to this question focuses on his justice in punishing both Judah and the Babylonians (2:2-5). Both failed to maintain God's high standards of faith and morality. Both merited God's judgment. In a series of five taunt songs (2:6-20), God lists his charges against all who are corrupt and do injustice. Undoubtedly, this included the Babylonians; even if God is using people to accomplish his purposes,

TIMELINE

697–642 BC
Manasseh as king of Judah

668–626 BC
Ashurbanipal as king of Assyria

about 645~615 BC
Nahum as prophet

642–640 BC
Amon as king of Judah

640–609 BC
Josiah as king of Judah

about 635~622 BC
Zephaniah as prophet

632 BC
Josiah begins to seek the Lord

about 630~605 BC
Habakkuk as prophet

628 BC
Josiah's first reform

about 627~580 BC
Jeremiah as prophet

626–605 BC
Nabopolassar as king of Babylon

612 BC
Nineveh is conquered by Babylon

609–598 BC
Jehoiakim as king of Judah

605–562 BC
Nebuchadnezzar II as king of Babylon

605 BC
Battle of Carchemish

586 BC
Nebuchadnezzar destroys Jerusalem, takes people of Judah into exile, end of the southern kingdom of Judah

538 BC
Cyrus's decree allows exiles to return to Judea

Habakkuk loved God, but he was prepared, as few others would be, to engage him in a probing dialogue about the rightness of his actions.

DAVID BAKER
Nahum, Habakkuk, Zephaniah, p. 43

FURTHER READING

O. PALMER ROBERTSON
The Books of Nahum, Habakkuk, and Zephaniah (1990)

KENNETH L. BARKER AND WAYLON BAILEY
Micah, Nahum, Habakkuk, Zephaniah (1990)

RICHARD PATTERSON
Habakkuk in *Cornerstone Biblical Commentary*, vol. 10 (2008)

they are still responsible for living according to God's moral standards. If they do not, they cannot escape punishment.

The final chapter opens with Habakkuk's prayer for God's mercy on Judah, even while he chastens them (3:1-2). Habakkuk then records a psalm of praise that reflects poetically on the account of God's redemption of his people during the Exodus (3:3-15). Habakkuk closes with a declaration of commitment and a note of praise (3:16-19).

AUTHOR

Nothing is known about Habakkuk except that he was a prophet of Judah. One manuscript of the later apocryphal book *Bel and the Dragon* identifies Habakkuk as a Levite. If accurate, this might help explain the musical notations in the third chapter (3:1, 3, 9, 13, 19), as the Temple music leaders were Levites (see 1 Chr 6:31-47; 25:1-31). Habakkuk's rich use of figurative language and his careful compositional structure indicate his high literary sensitivity. His hatred of the immorality and social breakdown that sin causes also demonstrates his deep spiritual concern that God's people live by God's standards.

DATE

The date of Habakkuk's prophecy is uncertain. The circumstances mentioned in the book fit best with a time late in the divided kingdom, but preceding Judah's exile to Babylon; therefore, the prophecy can be dated to 645–586 BC. Habakkuk's complaint about social injustice (1:2-4) and his attention to the Neo-Babylonian empire (1:5-11; 2:6-20) also favor a date during this time frame.

Regarding a more specific date, three general positions have been advanced. (1) Many date the book to the time of King Jehoiakim (609–598 BC), whose evil disposition and wicked actions (2 Kgs 24:1-3) brought both condemning prophecies (Jer 22:18-19; 26:3-6; 36:27-32) and the threat of Babylonian invasion (Jer 25). (2) Others argue for the early days of Josiah (640–609 BC), who, prior to the finding of the Book of the Law in 622 BC, dealt with rampant apostasy (2 Chr 34:1-7). (3) Still others defend the traditional Jewish view that Habakkuk lived during the time of the independent reign of Manasseh (686–642 BC), whose wickedness (2 Kgs 21:16-17) and reinstatement of Canaanite worship and pagan rites (2 Kgs 21:1-11; 2 Chr 33:1-9, 19-20) caused God's pronouncement of Judah's doom (2 Kgs 21:12-15).

MEANING AND MESSAGE

When violence and corruption abound and evil appears to rule, the faithful may be tempted to wonder whether God really cares or is really in control. Habakkuk's dialogue helps us to understand that God does not despise such questions when they are carried to him in prayer from an honest heart.

Habakkuk's prophecy reaffirms that God is in control of history and that his dealings are always just and right. Believers must be willing to accept God's answers and delight in his will, even if those are completely foreign to their own thinking. God does see and care deeply about what happens on earth. Although people may not perceive it, God's sovereign hand is at work, and he will ultimately bring matters to a proper and just conclusion (2:2-3, 14).

The Babylonians worshiped the raw power that brought them bounty. God's charges against the Babylonians remind readers to worship God alone (cp. 1 Jn 5:21).

God's message to Habakkuk emphasizes that the believer's holy life of faith and faithfulness must reproduce God's high moral and ethical qualities (1:12; 2:4). Those who trust and actively serve God will be able to rejoice in the Lord (3:18; Phil 4:4) and live triumphantly under any circumstances (2:20; 3:16-19). NT writers reinforce this message (Rom 1:16-17; Gal 3:11; Heb 10:35-39).

1. SUPERSCRIPTION: INTRODUCING THE PROPHET (1:1)

1 This is the message that the prophet Habakkuk received in a vision.

2. HABAKKUK'S PERPLEXITY (1:2–2:20)

Habakkuk Questions God's Inactivity

2 How long, O LORD, must I call for help?
But you do not listen!
"Violence is everywhere!" I cry,
but you do not come to save.
3 Must I forever see these evil deeds?
Why must I watch all this misery?
Wherever I look,
I see destruction and violence.
I am surrounded by people
who love to argue and fight.
4 The [a]law has become paralyzed,
and there is no [b]justice in the courts.
The wicked far outnumber the righteous,
so that [b]justice has become perverted.

What Lies Ahead for Judah

5 The LORD replied,
"Look around at the nations;
look and be amazed!
For I am doing something in your own day,
something you wouldn't believe
even if someone told you about it.
6 I am raising up the Babylonians,
a cruel and violent people.
They will march across the world
and conquer other lands.
7 They are notorious for their cruelty
and do whatever they like.
8 Their horses are swifter than
cheetahs
and fiercer than wolves at dusk.
Their charioteers charge from far away.
Like eagles, they swoop down to
devour their prey.
9 "On they come, all bent on violence.
Their hordes advance like a desert
wind,
sweeping captives ahead of them like
sand.
10 They scoff at kings and princes
and scorn all their fortresses.
They simply pile ramps of earth
against their walls and capture them!
11 They sweep past like the wind
and are gone.
But they are deeply guilty,
for their own strength is their god."

1:1 Isa 13:1; Nah 1:1
1:2 Ps 13:1-4; 22:1-2; Jer 14:9
1:3 Ps 55:9-11; Jer 20:8
1:4 Ps 22:12; 119:126; Isa 5:20; [a]*torah* (8451) ‣Exod 13:9; [b]*mishpat* (4941) ‣Gen 18:25
1:5 Isa 29:9; *Acts 13:41
1:6 Deut 28:49-50; 2 Kgs 24:2
1:7 Jer 39:5-9
1:8 Jer 4:13
1:10 2 Kgs 25:6-7; 2 Chr 36:6; Jer 32:24; 33:4-5; Ezek 26:7-11
1:11 Jer 4:11-12

1:1 The word *message* (or *oracle*) identifies the book as God's revelation through his prophet (cp. Nah 1:1; Mal 1:1).

1:2-4 To Habakkuk, God seemed indifferent to the *evil* permeating society in Judah (1:3-4) and unresponsive to his complaints about it (1:2).

1:2 ***call for help? . . . do not listen!*** The call/answer motif in Scripture often demonstrates the speaker's trust in God as a refuge or guide (see Ps 102:1-2) and indicates intimate communion between the believer and God (Ps 145:18; Isa 65:24).

1:3 In Habakkuk's day, ***destruction and violence*** permeated Judean society (see Habakkuk Introduction, "Setting," p. 1502).

1:4 Habakkuk expresses his concern about the injustice and unrighteousness he saw all around him (see 1:12-13; 2:4, 9), even ***in the courts,*** where the ***law*** was no longer effective in maintaining ***justice.***

1:5-11 God's answer to Habakkuk's question is startling. God would send a violent people—***the Babylonians***—to deal with the violence in Judah. The Babylonian army, well-trained and battle-hardened, was an unstoppable force.

1:5 ***Look . . . look:*** Two different Hebrew verbs, both of which are here translated *look*, are translated as *see* and *watch* in 1:3. This forms a literary link between Habakkuk's questions in 1:3 and God's reply in 1:5-11. • ***Look around at the nations; look and be amazed:*** Greek version reads *Look, you mockers; / look and be amazed and die.* Cp. Acts 13:41.

1:6 ***Babylonians:*** Or *Chaldeans.*

1:7 ***do whatever they like:*** No relief from injustice would come from the Babylonians. They were a law unto themselves, which added to the prophet's perplexity at God's decision to use them to punish Judah.

1:8 The vivid images of ***cheetahs*** (or *leopards*), ***wolves,*** and ***eagles*** depict the speed, ferocity, and predatory nature of the Babylonian attacks against Judah (see Jer 4:13; 48:40; 49:22).

1:9 The Babylonians indeed took many ***captives*** from Judah into exile between 605 and 586 BC (Dan 1:1-3).

1:10 The ancient battle tactic of building ***ramps of earth*** against the walls of cities under attack is widely attested in the ancient Near East (e.g., 2 Kgs 19:32; Nah 2:1).

1:11 ***their own strength is their god:*** The Babylonians worshiped many false gods. The arrogant confidence they placed on their military strength amounted to one more idol in the mix.

Habakkuk Questions God's Use of the Babylonians

12 O LORD my God, my Holy One, you who
are eternal—
surely you do not plan to wipe us out?
O LORD, our Rock, you have sent these
Babylonians to correct us,
to punish us for our many sins.
13 But you are pure and cannot stand the
sight of evil.
Will you wink at their treachery?
Should you be silent while the wicked
swallow up people more righteous
than they?
14 Are we only fish to be caught and killed?
Are we only sea creatures that have no
leader?
15 Must we be strung up on their hooks
and caught in their nets while they
rejoice and celebrate?
16 Then they will worship their nets
and burn incense in front of them.
"These nets are the gods who have made
us rich!"
they will claim.
17 Will you let them get away with this
forever?
Will they succeed forever in their
heartless conquests?

2 1 I will climb up to my watchtower
and stand at my guardpost.
There I will wait to see what the LORD
says
and how he will answer my complaint.

What Lies Ahead for the Babylonians

2 Then the LORD said to me,

"Write my ᶜanswer plainly on tablets,
so that a runner can carry the correct
message to others.
3 This vision is for a future time.
It describes the end, and it will be
fulfilled.
If it seems slow in coming, wait patiently,
for it will surely take place.
It will not be delayed.

4 "Look at the proud!
They trust in themselves, and their
lives are crooked.
But the righteous will live by their
faithfulness to God.
5 Wealth is treacherous,
and the arrogant are never at rest.
They open their mouths as wide as the
grave,
and like death, they are never
satisfied.
In their greed they have gathered up
many nations
and swallowed many peoples.

6 "But soon their captives will taunt them.
They will mock them, saying,

1:12 Deut 32:4, 30-31
1:13 Ps 50:21; 1 Pet 1:15-16
1:15 Jer 16:16
1:16 Jer 44:17-18
1:17 Isa 14:6
2:1 Ps 5:3; 85:8; Isa 21:8
2:2 Deut 27:8; Isa 8:1; Rev 1:19; ᶜ*khazon* (2377) ‣1 Sam 3:1
2:3 Dan 8:17-19; 9:24-27; 10:1, 14; *Heb 10:37
2:4 Ps 10:4; 49:16-20; Prov 3:6; 16:3; *Rom 1:17; *Gal 3:11; *Heb 10:38
2:6 Isa 14:4-5, 10; Jer 50:13, 34-35; Hab 2:9, 12, 15, 19

1:12–2:1 Habakkuk found it difficult to harmonize God's answer (1:5-11) with what he understood about God's character. How could a holy and just God chastise Judah by using a people more unrighteous than they were?

1:12 Despite his perplexity, Habakkuk did not renounce God. With the words ***my God, my Holy One,*** he reaffirmed his commitment to the Lord before asking serious questions about what God had revealed to him. • In light of God's character and covenant relationship with Israel, Habakkuk was certain that God would not ***wipe*** his people ***out.*** • ***to correct us:*** Cp. Heb 12:5-11. • ***our Rock:*** A common image of God's faithfulness and strength (see Deut 32:15; 1 Sam 2:2; Ps 18:2; 1 Cor 10:4; 1 Pet 2:6-8).

1:14-15 ***fish . . . hooks . . . nets:*** Habakkuk portrays the Babylonians as fishermen, drawing in conquered peoples.

1:16 See note on 1:11; cp. 1 Jn 5:21.

2:1 ***I will . . . stand at my guardpost:*** Like a sentinel on duty (see also 2 Sam 18:24-28; 2 Kgs 9:17-20; Ezek 33:2-6), Habakkuk waited expectantly to see how God would ***answer*** his ***complaint,*** even if that meant being reproved by the Lord. • ***he:*** As in Syriac version; Hebrew reads *I.*

2:2-20 God responds to Habakkuk's second complaint (1:12–2:1) without explaining why he chose to use the Babylonians. Rather, he assures Habakkuk that all violence and injustice will be punished.

2:2-5 Habakkuk's mission was to make it clear to people that even if God's justice ***seems slow in coming,*** it will come.

2:2 God instructs the prophet to ***write*** the ***message*** (literally *vision*) ***plainly*** so that it will be understood, preserved, and shared with others.

2:3-4 ***If it seems slow . . . faithfulness to God:*** Greek version reads *If the vision is delayed, wait patiently, / for it will surely come and not delay. / ⁴I will take no pleasure in anyone who turns away. / But the righteous person will live by my faith.* Cp. Rom 1:17; Gal 3:11; Heb 10:37-38.

2:3 ***will surely take place:*** In a set ***future time*** known only to the Lord, he will intervene in earth's history and bring it to a proper culmination, vindicating the righteous and judging the wicked. God's people must ***wait patiently,*** knowing that the divine plan is on schedule (see Heb 10:35-38).

2:4 God is aware of the self-centeredness of the ***proud.*** Their ***crooked*** lives demonstrate their unrighteousness; they refuse God's instruction and gratify their own desires (Prov 12:15; 21:8, 29; 29:27). In contrast, the ***righteous*** enjoy proper judicial standing before God. They make God's righteous standards their own and reproduce them in their lives. • ***faithfulness:*** Hebrew *'emunah.* In Genesis, the same Hebrew root (*'mn*) describes Abram's trust in God (Gen 15:6). God transforms the hearts of those who trust him so they can faithfully follow God's holy standards. See also Rom 1:16-17; Gal 3:11; Heb 10:37-39.

2:5 ***Wealth:*** As in Dead Sea Scroll 1QpHab; other Hebrew manuscripts read *Wine.* • ***the grave:*** Hebrew *Sheol.*

2:6-20 Five taunt songs (2:6-8, 9-11, 12-14, 15-17, 18-20) portray God's future judgment of the Babylonians (and others who, like the Babylonians, indulge in violence and injustice). God allows them to seal their own doom. Those who suffer will be able to repeat these taunts when the wicked come

2:7
Prov 29:1
2:8
Isa 33:1
Zech 2:8-9
2:9
Jer 22:13
2:11
Josh 24:27
Luke 19:40
2:12
Mic 3:10
Hab 2:9, 15, 19
2:13
Isa 50:11
2:14
Ps 22:27; 86:9
Isa 11:9
Zech 14:9
2:15
Hos 7:5
2:16
Jer 25:15-16

'What sorrow awaits you thieves!
Now you will get what you deserve!
You've become rich by extortion,
but how much longer can this go on?'
7 Suddenly, your debtors will take action.
They will turn on you and take all you have,
while you stand trembling and helpless.
8 Because you have plundered many nations,
now all the survivors will plunder you.
You committed murder throughout the countryside
and filled the towns with violence.
9 "What sorrow awaits you who build big houses
with money gained dishonestly!
You believe your wealth will buy security,
putting your family's nest beyond the reach of danger.
10 But by the murders you committed,
you have shamed your name and forfeited your lives.
11 The very stones in the walls cry out against you,
and the beams in the ceilings echo the complaint.
12 "What sorrow awaits you who build cities
with money gained through murder and corruption!
13 Has not the LORD of Heaven's Armies promised
that the wealth of nations will turn to ashes?
They work so hard,
but all in vain!
14 For as the waters fill the sea,
the earth will be filled with an awareness
of the glory of the LORD.
15 "What sorrow awaits you who make your neighbors drunk!
You force your cup on them
so you can gloat over their shameful nakedness.
16 But soon it will be your turn to be disgraced.
Come, drink and be exposed!
Drink from the cup of the LORD's judgment,

Human Perplexity and God's Purpose (2:2-20)

Hab 1:2-11; 3:2-19
Deut 29:29
Ps 47:9; 139:6; 145:3
Isa 55:8-9
Dan 4:25, 35
Rom 11:33-34; 13:1
Acts 17:24-26
Eph 1:3-10
Col 1:15-20
2 Pet 3:15

Habakkuk had a candid relationship with God: The prophet felt free to bring his honest concerns to the Lord, and God did not rebuke him for doing so. From Habakkuk's perspective, God seemed inactive in the face of the violence and social injustice plaguing Judah (1:2-4). God then revealed that he would take action: He was going to raise up the Babylonians—a nation even more wicked than Judah—to punish Judah (1:5-11). This perplexed Habakkuk, yet God's assurance that justice would be done and a vision of God's glory brought the prophet to settled faith (cp. 2:4) and praise (3:16-19).

Habakkuk's spiritual journey is similar to that of most believers. When times of doubt and discouragement come, believers need to approach the Lord and share their concerns with him. Like Habakkuk, we need to search God's word for a fresh glimpse of who God is and what he is like in order to renew our trust in the One who alone is truly God.

Habakkuk 2:2-20 reminds us that the Lord is not an absentee god; he acts sovereignly in all that comes to pass so that everything might work toward his purpose (2:3, 14; see also Ps 47:9; Acts 17:24-26; Col 1:15-20). The Lord is a holy and merciful God who acts in history to redeem his people (3:2-15; see also Eph 1:3-10; 2 Pet 3:15) so that all may ultimately see his glory (2:14).

to judgment (see 1:14-17). Each taunt contains a pronouncement of *sorrow*, a judgment, and the reason for God's judgment.

2:6-8 In the first of Habakkuk's taunt songs, he condemns the Babylonians for despoiling the nations. • ***thieves . . . extortion:*** The imagery compares Babylonians to creditors whose oppressive measures cause their ***debtors*** to rise up against them. Greed can easily mar an individual's or nation's spiritual fiber (Luke 12:15; Eph 5:3).

2:9-11 In the second taunt song, the Babylonians are condemned for their dishonest dealings. Since the Babylonians obtained the means to ***build big houses*** through deceit and ***dishonesty***, they ***forfeited*** their ***lives***.

2:12-14 In the third taunt song, the Babylonians are condemned for the ***murder and corruption*** of human life and society that brought wealth to ***build*** their ***cities***. God would make their apparent gain prove to be a total loss. • ***earth will be filled:*** The antithesis of violence and ill-gotten wealth is the ***awareness of the glory of the LORD***, which God promises to make as pervasive as water in the ocean (Isa 11:9).

2:15-17 In the fourth taunt song, the Babylonians are condemned for their disgraceful acts against people, ***animals***, and the environment. They are like a man who seems to be hospitable, but after getting his ***neighbors drunk***, strips them of everything. However, the Babylonians will be disgraced after drinking from ***the cup of the LORD's judgment*** (see Jer 25:15-17; cp. John 18:11).

2:16 ***be exposed:*** Dead Sea Scrolls and Greek and Syriac versions read *stagger*.

and all your glory will be turned to
shame.
17 You cut down the forests of Lebanon.
Now you will be cut down.
You destroyed the wild animals,
so now their terror will be yours.
You committed murder throughout the
countryside
and filled the towns with violence.

18 "What good is an idol carved by man,
or a cast image that deceives you?
How foolish to trust in your own creation—
a god that can't even talk!
19 What sorrow awaits you who say to
wooden idols,
'Wake up and save us!'
To speechless stone images you say,
'Rise up and teach us!'
Can an idol tell you what to do?
They may be overlaid with gold and silver,
but they are lifeless inside.
20 But the LORD is in his holy Temple.
Let all the earth be silent before him."

3. HABAKKUK'S PRAYER (3:1-19)

Plea for Mercy

3 This prayer was sung by the prophet Habakkuk:

2 I have heard all about you, LORD.
I am filled with awe by your amazing
works.
In this time of our deep need,
help us again as you did in years gone by.
And in your anger,
remember your mercy.

Praise for the Mighty God

3 I see God moving across the deserts
from Edom,
the Holy One coming from Mount
Paran.
His brilliant splendor fills the heavens,
and the earth is filled with his praise.
4 His coming is as brilliant as the sunrise.
Rays of light flash from his hands,
where his awesome power is hidden.
5 Pestilence marches before him;
plague follows close behind.
6 When he stops, the earth shakes.
When he looks, the nations tremble.
He shatters the everlasting mountains
and levels the eternal hills.
He is the Eternal One!
7 I see the people of Cushan in distress,
and the nation of Midian trembling
in terror.

8 Was it in [d]anger, LORD, that you struck
the rivers
and parted the sea?

2:17
Jer 51:35
2:18
Isa 42:17
Jer 2:27-28; 50:2
2:19
1 Kgs 18:26-29
Jer 10:4-5
2:20
Zeph 1:7
Zech 2:13
3:2
Ps 78:38-39; 85:6
Isa 54:8
Jer 10:7
3:3
Deut 5:24
Ps 48:10; 113:4; 148:13
3:4
Job 26:14
Ps 18:12; 104:1
3:5
Exod 12:29-30
Deut 32:24-25
3:7
Exod 15:14
3:8
Exod 7:19-20
[d]*'ap* (0639)
›Num 32:13

2:18-20 In the fifth taunt song, the Babylonians are condemned for their devotion to idolatry. Whether ***idols*** are ***carved*** or ***cast*** by the hand of ***man***, they can neither ***save*** nor ***teach*** their worshipers (Isa 42:17). Only ***the LORD*** truly deserves our worship (2:20; Exod 20:2-6; cp. Eccl 5:1-2).

2:20 The taunt songs close with a declaration: The one who is sovereign over all nations is not a Babylonian idol (2:18-20) but the Holy God. Unlike the lifeless Babylonian idols, the living God indwells his ***holy Temple***. God's presence fills his heavenly sanctuary (Isa 6:1-5)—and in Habakkuk's time, it filled the Temple in Jerusalem (1 Kgs 8:10-11). God controls ***all the earth*** and expects people to worship him in humble submission (Ps 63:1-4; Jer 10:1-10; Mic 7:16; Zech 2:13).

3:1-19 Habakkuk's prophecy concludes with a psalm-like ***prayer***.

3:1 Hebrew adds *according to shigionoth*, probably indicating the musical setting for the prayer.

3:2 Habakkuk stands in ***awe*** before the Sovereign One who sits enthroned in his holy Temple (2:20). • In light of God's message of Judah's coming chastisement, Habakkuk prays that God, who has miraculously intervened on Israel's behalf in the past, will once ***again*** make known his work of redemption (see also Ps 77).

3:3-15 The prophet praises God's power to save. These two praise stanzas (3:3-7 and 3:8-15) are a poetic reflection upon Israel's Exodus experience. Although Habakkuk's focus is upon God's redemption of his people, his imagery occasionally reflects ideas found in ancient Near Eastern tales concerning the gods (e.g., pestilence and plague, 3:5; river and sea, 3:8; sun and moon, 3:11). This imagery reminds Habakkuk's original readers that the Lord alone is the one true God who is sovereign over all these things.

3:3 ***Edom*** (Hebrew *Teman*): Teman was one of Edom's chief cities (see also Job 2:11; Jer 49:7); the term could refer to the entire region of Edom where the city was located (cp. Obad 1:9). Habakkuk's use of the term in conjunction with ***Mount Paran*** suggests that he had the broader region in mind. • ***Holy One*** is a prominent title for God, as holiness is his defining characteristic (1:12; see also Exod 15:11; 2 Kgs 19:22; Ps 77:13; Isa 6:3). • ***Mount Paran:*** The region of Paran included the mountain range west and south of Edom and northeast of Mount Sinai, as well as a broad desert area in the Sinai Peninsula. • Hebrew adds *selah;* also in 3:9, 13. The meaning of this Hebrew term is uncertain; it is probably a musical or literary term.

3:4 ***brilliant as the sunrise:*** The Lord, who once appeared on Mount Sinai and filled the southern land with his glory, fills the heavens with his splendor.

3:5-6 God is the divine warrior who intervenes on behalf of his own (see 3:8-15; see also Isa 63:1-6).

3:5 Habakkuk personifies ***pestilence*** (see Deut 32:24) and ***plague*** (see Exod 7–12; Amos 4:10) as soldiers in God's army, fulfilling his purposes.

3:7 ***Midian*** occupied the southern part of the region just east of the Jordan (see Gen 36:35); the nation was ***trembling in terror*** at the earth-shaking power of God's presence (3:6).

3:8-15 ***The LORD*** is a Divine Warrior for his people, moving in redemptive power on their behalf. The motif of God as Divine Warrior spans both OT and NT: It is seen in Israel's exodus from Egypt, their movement to Mount Sinai (Exod 15:1-18), their approach to the promised land from the south, and their triumphs in the early conquest period (e.g., Judg 5:4-5; Ps 18:8-16; 77:16-20; a key NT example is Rev 19:11-21).

3:8 ***struck the rivers . . . parted the sea:*** See Exod 7:19-20; 14:15-31. • ***chariots***

3:10
Ps 93:3

3:12
Isa 41:15

3:13
Ps 110:6

3:14
Judg 7:22
Dan 11:40

3:15
Hab 3:8

3:17
Jer 5:17
Joel 1:10-12
Amos 4:9

3:18
Ps 97:12
Isa 12:2
Luke 1:47
Phil 4:4

3:19
Ps 18:13; 46:1-5
[e]*Yahweh 'adonay* (3068, 0136)
‣Zeph 1:7

Were you displeased with them?
No, you were sending your chariots of salvation!
9 You brandished your bow
and your quiver of arrows.
You split open the earth with flowing rivers.
10 The mountains watched and trembled.
Onward swept the raging waters.
The mighty deep cried out,
lifting its hands to the LORD.
11 The sun and moon stood still in the sky
as your brilliant arrows flew
and your glittering spear flashed.

12 You marched across the land in anger
and trampled the nations in your fury.
13 You went out to rescue your chosen people,
to save your anointed ones.
You crushed the heads of the wicked
and stripped their bones from head to toe.
14 With his own weapons,
you destroyed the chief of those
who rushed out like a whirlwind,
thinking Israel would be easy prey.
15 You trampled the sea with your horses,
and the mighty waters piled high.

Pledge for the Future

16 I trembled inside when I heard this;
my lips quivered with fear.
My legs gave way beneath me,
and I shook in terror.
I will wait quietly for the coming day
when disaster will strike the people who invade us.
17 Even though the fig trees have no blossoms,
and there are no grapes on the vines;
even though the olive crop fails,
and the fields lie empty and barren;
even though the flocks die in the fields,
and the cattle barns are empty,
18 yet I will rejoice in the LORD!
I will be joyful in the God of my salvation!
19 The [e]Sovereign LORD is my strength!
He makes me as surefooted as a deer,
able to tread upon the heights.

(For the choir director: This prayer is to be accompanied by stringed instruments.)

of salvation: An ironic echo of the Egyptian chariots, which pursued the Israelites when God led them to escape through the Red Sea (Exod 14:9).

3:9-11 Only God controls the forces of the natural world.

3:10 ***waters:*** See note on 3:8; see also Exod 15:1-18.

3:11 ***sun and moon:*** See Josh 10:12-13.

3:15 ***sea . . . waters:*** The section ends as it began (3:8).

3:16 Although the full realization of God's mighty power sapped Habakkuk's strength to the point that he ***trembled***, he would ***wait quietly*** (see 2:3) for God's judgment to descend. • ***My legs gave way beneath me:*** Literally *Decay entered my bones.*

3:17-19 After recounting God's mighty acts of redemption (3:2-15), and pausing to consider them (3:16), Habakkuk now reaffirms his trust in God as he closes his prayer. • ***Even though . . . yet I will rejoice:*** Even if God never pours out material blessing on his people again, he is still worthy of all the trust and praise they can give. Come what may, the prophet could ***rejoice***, knowing that the ***LORD*** is not only Israel's Redeemer, but also the source of his own ***salvation***.

3:19 Habakkuk owed whatever ***strength*** he had to ***the Sovereign LORD***, his Savior (3:18). Habakkuk compared his spiritual climb to a ***deer*** swiftly ascending to the mountaintops and gracefully gliding over them (cp. Ps 18:32-33). • ***He makes me as surefooted as a deer:*** Or *He gives me the speed of a deer.*

THE BOOK OF ZEPHANIAH

"That terrible day of the LORD is near. . . . A day of ruin and desolation, a day of darkness and gloom" (1:14-15). Zephaniah's words send a chill through the soul. Will God's wrath spell the end to everything? Zephaniah's prophecy portrays the coming judgment, but it also presents God's promise that his faithful people will one day enjoy a world of everlasting righteousness and joy.

SETTING

Zephaniah, like Habakkuk, lived in changing times (see Habakkuk Introduction, "Setting," p. 1502). Toward the end of Assyrian king Ashurbanipal's last military campaigns, King Amon apparently led Judah to participate in the widespread anti-Assyrian uprising that took place in many of the western countries of the Near East. Since Ashurbanipal moved swiftly to quell defectors, Judah's leaders assassinated Amon (in about 640 BC) and replaced him with his son Josiah.

Josiah was only eight years old when he became king of Judah. He enjoyed a long reign (640–609 BC) as a righteous king. In the eighteenth year of his reign, while repairs were being made to the Temple, a scroll of the Book of the Law was found (2 Kgs 22:8; 2 Chr 34:14-15). After hearing the law read to him, King Josiah led his people in renewal and reform, reinstating biblical religious observances (2 Kgs 23:1-25; 2 Chr 34:29–35:19).

Before this pivotal event, the kingdom of Judah largely followed the idolatrous practices of Manasseh and Amon. Judah's people were so devoted to apostasy that it ultimately brought about their doom (2 Kgs 21:10-25; 2 Chr 33:17, 21-24).

Zephaniah prophesied early in Josiah's reign, after

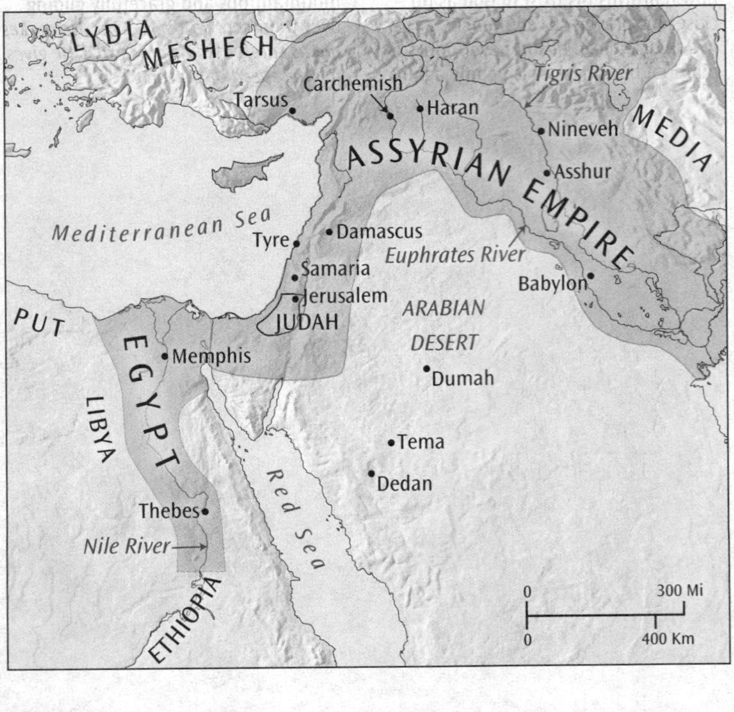

The Near East during Zephaniah's Time (about 635~622 BC). Zephaniah prophesied early in the reign of Josiah (640–609 BC), before Josiah began making reforms (2 Kgs 22:3–23:27). At that time, the ASSYRIAN EMPIRE was at the height of its power under King Ashurbanipal (668–626 BC).

ASSYRIA 2:13
ETHIOPIA 2:12; 3:10
JERUSALEM 1:4, 12; 3:1-20
JUDAH 1:1, 4, 8; 2:7
NINEVEH 2:13

the death of Amon and before the Book of the Law was rediscovered. The time was characterized by religious indifference, social injustice, and economic greed (1:4-13; 3:1-4, 7). A true prophet of God was needed, and Zephaniah was such a man; he may have helped prepare people's hearts for Josiah's sweeping reforms.

SUMMARY

Zephaniah begins his prophecy by announcing *the day of the Lord*. This term signified God's coming judgment on the whole sinful earth (1:2-3, 14-18), including his people in Judah and Jerusalem (1:4-13). Much like the people of Israel in the time of Amos some 125 years earlier, the people of Judah looked forward to "that day" as a time when God would vindicate them by destroying their enemies. Like Amos, however, Zephaniah had to tell his people that their covenant relationship with God did not make them immune to judgment. Because the day of the Lord would fall impartially on all wicked people, Zephaniah urged his fellow citizens to repent, to seek the Lord, and to live righteously in all humility (2:1-3). Perhaps then they might experience the Lord's protection in the coming time of wrath.

The implications of Zephaniah's prophecy are clear. The nations neighboring Judah would suffer terrible judgment because of their crimes against God's people, their arrogant pride, and their defiance of the Lord (2:4-15). However, Judah would not escape the Lord's chastening hand, because its spiritual and civil leaders had led society into total corruption despite knowing God's standards. In addition, the people of Judah had not taken proper notice of God's sovereign judgment on other nations for crimes like their own (3:1-7).

These impending judgments were just a precursor to a coming time of judgment that would engulf all nations on earth (3:8). However, judgment would not be the end: The day of judgment would come so that a day of salvation could follow (3:9-20). God promised restoration and blessing for a remnant from Israel and for all people (3:9).

Zephaniah records God's future plan to remove all proud and arrogant people from the earth; only those who "trust in the name of the Lord" will remain (3:12). God will gather his scattered people and restore them to their land, where they will live in righteousness and safety, worshiping the Lord (3:9-12). The "remnant of Israel" will enjoy the outpouring of God's blessings and rejoice in him forever (3:13-19). The judgment and salvation announced in Zephaniah foreshadow God's final act of bringing judgment and salvation at the return of Jesus Christ (see Rev 19:11–22:5).

OUTLINE

1:1
Superscription: Introducing the Prophet

1:2–2:3
Prophecies about the Day of the Lord

2:4–3:20
Results of the Day of the Lord

AUTHOR

Little is known of Zephaniah beyond the lineage in 1:1, which traces his ancestry to Hezekiah. Jewish and Christian expositors traditionally equate

TIMELINE

697–642 BC
Manasseh as king of Judah

about 645~615 BC
Nahum as prophet

642–640 BC
Amon as king of Judah

640–609 BC
Josiah as king of Judah

about 635~622 BC
Zephaniah as prophet

632 BC
Josiah begins to seek the Lord

about 630~605 BC
Habakkuk as prophet

628 BC
Josiah's first reform

about 627~580 BC
Jeremiah as prophet

622 BC
Josiah finds the Book of the Law

612 BC
Nineveh is conquered by Babylon

586 BC
Nebuchadnezzar destroys Jerusalem

538 BC
Cyrus's decree allows exiles to return to Judea

Zephaniah's prophecy . . . [embraces] both judgment and salvation in their totality, so as to form one complete picture . . . the establishment of divine righteousness in the earth.

C. F. KEIL
Zephaniah in *Biblical Commentary on the Old Testament*

this Hezekiah with the king of that name (see 2 Kgs 18:1–20:20), which would mean that Zephaniah was of royal descent and probably a positive influence in the life of young King Josiah. The unusual attention to four generations of family lineage indicates at the very least that Zephaniah came from a distinguished family.

Zephaniah lived in Jerusalem and was aware of conditions there (1:10-13). He was a man of keen spiritual sensitivity and moral perception who decried the apostasy and immorality of the people, especially of those in positions of leadership (1:4-6, 9, 17; 3:1-4, 7, 11). He denounced the materialism and greed that exploited the poor (1:8, 10-13, 18). He was aware of world conditions and announced God's judgment on the nations for their sins (2:4-15). Above all, this prophet had a deep concern for the Lord's reputation (1:6; 3:7) and for all who humbly trust in God (2:3; 3:9, 12-13).

DATE

Zephaniah himself recorded that his prophetic ministry was during the time of Josiah (640–609 BC; see 1:1). Several facts suggest that Zephaniah prophesied during the early days of Josiah's reign, before the discovery of the Book of the Law and the reforms that followed. Zephaniah reported that religious practices in Judah were still plagued with Canaanite syncretistic rites such as those that characterized the era of Manasseh (1:4-5, 9); many failed to worship the Lord at all (1:6); royalty were enamored of wearing the clothing of foreign merchants (1:8) who had extensive business enterprises in Jerusalem (1:10-11); and Judah's society was beset by socio-economic ills (1:12-13, 18) and political and religious corruption (3:1-4, 7, 11). Josiah's reforms corrected much of this (about 622 BC; 2 Kgs 23:4-14). Therefore, a date between 635 and 622 BC for Zephaniah's prophecy is likely.

MEANING AND MESSAGE

Like his contemporaries Nahum and Habakkuk, Zephaniah presents God as the sovereign Lord of earth's history. God, the judge of all (1:2-3, 7, 14-18; 3:8), punishes the wickedness of people (1:8-9, 17; 3:7, 11) and nations (2:4-15; 3:6). This sovereign Judge has determined a time when he will intervene in the world's history to subdue wickedness and bring in everlasting righteousness. That day (the *day of the* L*ORD*) will include all nations (1:2-4; 2:4-15; 3:8). God will pour out his wrath in judgment against humanity's sin and rebellion.

Zephaniah focuses on the basic problem of human pride (2:15), which engenders a spirit of inner wickedness (1:3-6, 17; 3:1, 4) and causes people to reason that God will not intervene in human affairs (1:12). They go on in their violence and deceit (1:9), and their greed oppresses those around them (1:10-11, 13, 18; 3:3). God may rescind the penalty that sinners deserve if they show true repentance (2:1-3), but such spiritual virtues as righteousness, humility, faith, and truth are necessary (3:12-13). God will regather and purify a humble and faithful remnant (3:9-10), restore them to their land (3:20), and give them victory over their enemies (2:7, 9). Jerusalem will be a blissful place (3:11, 18) because God will save and bless his people (3:14-20).

Zephaniah's message of personal accountability for sin is echoed in NT teachings (Rom 2:5-6; 2 Cor 5:10; Rev 6:17; 19:11-21). It remains true that God's rich grace is available to those of humble heart (1 Pet 5:5-6), so that they may find forgiveness of sin (Eph 1:7) and the sure hope of everlasting life and blessedness (Titus 3:4-7; Rev 21:1–22:5).

FURTHER READING

O. PALMER ROBERTSON
The Books of Nahum, Habakkuk, and Zephaniah (1990)

KENNETH L. BARKER AND WAYLON BAILEY
Micah, Nahum, Habakkuk, Zephaniah (1990)

RICHARD PATTERSON
Zephaniah in *Cornerstone Biblical Commentary*, vol. 10 (2008)

1:1
2 Kgs 22:1–23:28
2 Chr 34:1–35:26
1:2
Isa 6:11
1:3
Isa 6:11-12
Jer 4:25; 9:10
1:4
2 Kgs 23:4-7
1:5
1 Kgs 11:33
1:6
Isa 1:4; 9:13
1:7
Isa 34:6
Hab 2:20
Zech 2:13
[a]*'adonay Yahweh*
(0136, 3068)
›Gen 15:2
1:8
Isa 24:21-23
1:9
Amos 3:10
1:10
2 Chr 33:14
Neh 3:3; 12:39

1. SUPERSCRIPTION: INTRODUCING THE PROPHET (1:1)

1 The LORD gave this message to Zephaniah when Josiah son of Amon was
king of Judah. Zephaniah was the son of Cushi, son of Gedaliah, son of Amariah, son of
Hezekiah.

2. PROPHECIES ABOUT THE DAY OF THE LORD (1:2–2:3)

Judgment against the Whole Earth

2 "I will sweep away everything
from the face of the earth," says the
LORD.
3 "I will sweep away people and animals
alike.
I will sweep away the birds of the sky
and the fish in the sea.
I will reduce the wicked to heaps of
rubble,
and I will wipe humanity from the
face of the earth," says the LORD.

Judgment against Judah and Jerusalem

4 "I will crush Judah and Jerusalem with
my fist
and destroy every last trace of their
Baal worship.
I will put an end to all the idolatrous
priests,
so that even the memory of them will
disappear.
5 For they go up to their roofs
and bow down to the sun, moon, and
stars.
They claim to follow the LORD,
but then they worship Molech, too.
6 And I will destroy those who used to
worship me
but now no longer do.
They no longer ask for the LORD's
guidance
or seek my blessings."

The Day of the LORD for Jerusalem

7 Stand in silence in the presence of the
[a]Sovereign LORD,
for the awesome day of the LORD's
judgment is near.
The LORD has prepared his people for a
great slaughter
and has chosen their executioners.
8 "On that day of judgment,"
says the LORD,
"I will punish the leaders and princes of
Judah
and all those following pagan customs.
9 Yes, I will punish those who participate
in pagan worship ceremonies,
and those who fill their masters'
houses with violence and deceit.
10 "On that day," says the LORD,
"a cry of alarm will come from the
Fish Gate
and echo throughout the New Quarter
of the city.
And a great crash will sound from the
hills.
11 Wail in sorrow, all you who live in the
market area,
for all the merchants and traders will
be destroyed.

1:1–2:3 Zephaniah's message from the Lord warns about worldwide judgment (1:1-6) and exhorts his readers to repent (1:7-13) before the devastation overtakes them (1:14-18) and to seek the Lord and live righteously and humbly before him in the hope that they may be spared his judgment (2:1-3).

1:1 ***The LORD gave this message:*** Zephaniah was a prophet, God's spokesman. • ***Hezekiah*** probably indicates the king of that name (see 2 Kgs 18:1–20:20).

1:2-3 The list of the things that God will ***sweep away*** in his judgment is in reverse order to their creation (Gen 1:20-26): ***people and animals . . . birds . . . fish,*** because judgment is a reversal of creation. • ***I will reduce the wicked to heaps of rubble:*** The meaning of this line in Hebrew is uncertain.

1:4-6 Having pronounced judgment on the whole earth (1:2-3), Zephaniah now focuses attention on his own people, ***Judah and Jerusalem.***

1:4 When Zephaniah made this prophecy, before Josiah's reforms in 622 BC, ***idolatrous priests*** rampantly promoted ***Baal worship*** and other forms of paganism (2 Kgs 23:5).

1:5 Scripture denounced the practice of worshiping heavenly bodies such as the ***sun, moon, and stars*** (see Deut 4:15-19; 2 Kgs 21:3; 23:12). • ***Molech:*** Hebrew *Malcam,* a variant spelling of Molech; or it could possibly mean *their king.* Here it refers to the Canaanite god Baal, the Ammonite god Milcom, or the pagan deity Molech. Although the law explicitly prohibited Molech worship (Lev 20:1-5), it remained a constant temptation to Israel (2 Kgs 16:3; 21:6).

1:7-18 The entire passage must be seen as one vast event. Some aspects would be fulfilled at Jerusalem's fall in 586 BC; others would be repeated in various historical epochs (such as the destruction of Jerusalem in AD 70) until the whole prophecy is fulfilled at the end of time when God acts fully and finally to judge the world and renew creation (Rev 19:11–22:5).

1:7 ***has prepared his people for a great slaughter and has chosen their executioners:*** Literally *has prepared a sacrifice and sanctified his guests.* Foreigners will *slaughter* the wicked among the Lord's people.

1:8 The ***leaders and princes of Judah*** were the tribal chieftains of Israel (Num 1:4), court officials (1 Chr 22:17), district supervisors (1 Kgs 20:14-15), city officials (Judg 8:6), military leaders (1 Kgs 2:5; 2 Kgs 1:9-14; 25:23, 26), or even religious leaders (Ezra 8:24). Their influential role put them in a position of heightened responsibility before God (cp. Jas 3:1).

1:9 ***those who participate in pagan worship ceremonies*** (literally *those who leap over the threshold*): The people of Judah perpetuated the pagan custom of leaping over the threshold of a temple to avoid contact with it, in deference to that pagan god (see 1 Sam 5:1-5).

1:10 The ***Fish Gate*** was in the northern section of Jerusalem (Neh 12:39). • ***the New Quarter of the city:*** Or *the Second Quarter,* a newer section of Jerusalem. Hebrew reads *the Mishneh.*

12 "I will search with lanterns in
Jerusalem's darkest corners
to punish those who sit complacent in
their sins.
They think the LORD will do nothing to
them,
either good or bad.
13 So their property will be plundered,
their homes will be ransacked.
They will build new homes
but never live in them.
They will plant vineyards
but never drink wine from them.

The Day of the LORD for the Whole Earth

14 "That terrible day of the LORD is near.
Swiftly it comes—
a day of bitter tears,
a day when even strong men will cry
out.
15 It will be a day when the LORD's anger is
poured out—
a day of terrible distress and anguish,
a day of ruin and desolation,
a day of darkness and gloom,
a day of clouds and blackness,
16 a day of trumpet calls and battle cries.
Down go the walled cities
and the strongest battlements!
17 "Because you have sinned against the
LORD,
I will make you grope around like the
blind.
Your blood will be poured into the dust,
and your bodies will lie rotting on the
ground."
18 Your silver and gold will not save you
on that day of the LORD's anger.
For the whole land will be devoured
by the fire of his [b]jealousy.
He will make a terrifying end
of all the people on earth.

A Call to Repentance

2 1 Gather together—yes, gather together,
you shameless nation.
2 Gather before judgment begins,
before your time to repent is blown
away like chaff.
Act now, before the fierce fury of the
LORD falls
and the terrible day of the LORD's
anger begins.

1:12 Jer 16:16-17; Amos 6:1
1:13 Deut 28:30; Amos 5:11
1:14 Ezek 7:16-18
1:15 Isa 22:5; Joel 2:2
1:16 Isa 2:12-15; Jer 4:19
1:17 Deut 28:28-29; Ps 79:3; 83:10; Isa 59:10; Jer 8:2; 9:22
1:18 Zeph 3:8
[b]*qin'ah* (7068) ‣Zeph 3:8
2:1 2 Chr 20:4; Jer 3:3; 6:15; Joel 1:14
2:2 Zeph 1:18

The Day of the LORD (2:1-3)

Zeph 3:8-20
Isa 2:1-22; 13:6-9
Joel 1:15; 2:1-32
Amos 5:18-20; 9:11-15
1 Cor 5:5
1 Thes 5:2
2 Pet 3:10

Zephaniah paints a graphic word picture of the future day of God's judgment. That day will engulf all nations and cause terrible havoc on the earth. Accordingly, God's people must repent immediately in the hope of finding a place of refuge in that day (2:1-3).

The humble and trusting remnant must patiently await God's day of restoration (3:8). Following God's day of judgment, a purified people will worship and rejoice in the Lord's saving work and enjoy his presence forever (3:9-20). The horrifying spectacle of judgment leads to ultimate blessing.

Disaster beyond any yet seen is coming to the whole world. Zephaniah reveals that the day of the Lord forms a continuum from the time at hand to the distant future (see also Isa 2:1-22; Amos 5:18-20; 9:11-15). For the northern kingdom, the day of the Lord came when Assyria destroyed Samaria as God promised through Amos. The day of the Lord came for the southern kingdom with the invasions of Babylon in 605–586 BC and the destruction of Jerusalem. Zephaniah also speaks of the great and final day of the Lord, when all sin and opposition will be put away forever (3:9-13).

The day of the Lord's judgment can begin at any moment. All people in every age should trust in the Lord (3:12) and wait patiently (3:8) for God to fulfill his will and purposes. Believers must concern themselves with the coming judgment of the world, warning others of the seriousness of unbelief, while living faithfully in the hope of God's promised future.

1:13 God would send an invading force to plunder Jerusalem. The destruction would come so quickly that those with ill-gotten gain would not survive to enjoy their wealth.

1:14-18 The meaning of the ***day of the LORD*** broadens to include God's dealings with the whole ***earth***.

1:15 ***darkness and gloom:*** See also Isa 13:9-10; Joel 2:1-2; Amos 5:18-20.

1:17 ***grope around like the blind:*** An example of God's justice (see also Rom 1:21-32). Because God's people were blind ethically and spiritually (see Exod 23:8; Rom 2:19; 1 Jn 2:11) and had ***sinned against the LORD*** and his commandments, they would incur the just penalties specified in God's covenant with them (Deut 28:28-29).

1:18 ***the people on earth:*** Or *the people living in the land.*

2:1-3 In light of the horrifying spectacle he has described, Zephaniah calls on his ***nation*** to ***repent*** and ***humble*** themselves before God.

2:2 Farmers threshed grain on windy hilltops. When they tossed the mixed grain and ***chaff*** in the air, the wind blew the chaff away while the heavier grain fell back to the ground. The opportunity to ***repent*** was a fleeting one.

2:3
Ps 57:1
Amos 5:6, 14-15
[c]*'anaw* (6035)
‣Num 12:3
[d]*tsedeq* (6664)
‣Lev 19:15

2:4
Amos 1:6-8
Zech 9:5

2:5
Isa 14:29, 31

2:7
Isa 32:14
Zeph 3:20

2:8
Ezek 25:3, 8

2:9
Isa 11:14; 15:1-9

2:10
Isa 16:6-10
Jer 48:28-31
Zeph 2:8

2:11
Joel 2:11
Zeph 1:4; 3:4

2:12
Isa 20:3-4

3 Seek the LORD, all who are [c]humble,
and follow his commands.
Seek to do what is [d]right
and to live humbly.
Perhaps even yet the LORD will protect you—
protect you from his anger on that day
of destruction.

3. RESULTS OF THE DAY OF THE LORD (2:4–3:20)

Judgment against Philistia

4 Gaza and Ashkelon will be abandoned,
Ashdod and Ekron torn down.
5 And what sorrow awaits you Philistines
who live along the coast and in the
land of Canaan,
for this judgment is against you, too!
The LORD will destroy you
until not one of you is left.
6 The Philistine coast will become a
wilderness pasture,
a place of shepherd camps
and enclosures for sheep and goats.
7 The remnant of the tribe of Judah will
pasture there.
They will rest at night in the
abandoned houses in Ashkelon.
For the LORD their God will visit his
people in kindness
and restore their prosperity again.

Judgment against Moab and Ammon

8 "I have heard the taunts of the
Moabites
and the insults of the Ammonites,
mocking my people
and invading their borders.
9 Now, as surely as I live,"
says the LORD of Heaven's Armies, the
God of Israel,
"Moab and Ammon will be destroyed—
destroyed as completely as Sodom
and Gomorrah.
Their land will become a place of
stinging nettles,
salt pits, and eternal desolation.
The remnant of my people will plunder
them
and take their land."
10 They will receive the wages of their
pride,
for they have scoffed at the people of
the LORD of Heaven's Armies.
11 The LORD will terrify them
as he destroys all the gods in the land.
Then nations around the world will
worship the LORD,
each in their own land.

Judgment against Ethiopia and Assyria

12 "You Ethiopians will also be slaughtered
by my sword," says the LORD.

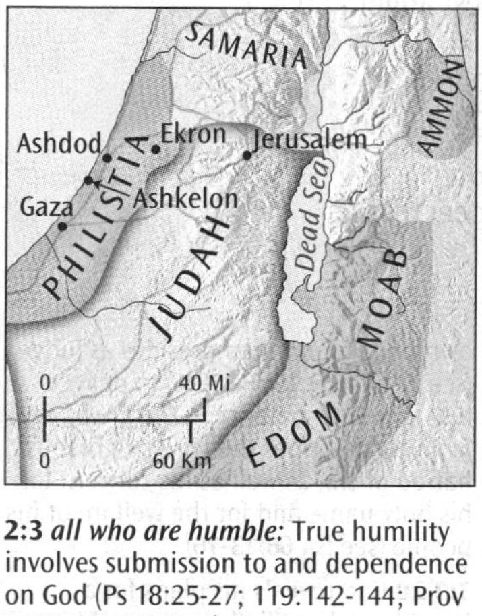

◂ **Judah's Doomed Neighbors** (2:4-11). Zephaniah announced God's judgment against both JUDAH and its long-time foes all around, including PHILISTIA, MOAB, and AMMON.

2:3 ***all who are humble:*** True humility involves submission to and dependence on God (Ps 18:25-27; 119:142-144; Prov 15:33; 18:12; 22:4).

2:4–3:20 Zephaniah turns his attention to the judgment of the foreign nations (2:4-15) before returning to the judgment of Judah and Jerusalem (3:1-8). He then outlines God's plans for his purified and obedient people (3:9-20).

2:4-15 Zephaniah began his pronouncements with the ***Philistines,*** whose kingdom lay on Judah's west (2:4-7). He moved on to ***Moab and Ammon*** in the east (2:8-11), and finally singled out Cush (Ethiopia) to the south (2:12) and ***Assyria*** to the ***north*** (2:13-15).

2:4 King Nebuchadnezzar of Babylon conquered the Philistine cities of ***Gaza and Ashkelon . . . Ashdod and Ekron.*** Gaza remained deserted, but the others recovered and continued into later times. Zephaniah does not mention Gath, the fifth major Philistine city (see 1 Sam 6:17), which had either disappeared or become unimportant by Zephaniah's time.

2:5 OT scholars believe the ***Philistines*** (Hebrew *Kerethites*) came from the island of Crete (cp. Ezek 25:16).

2:6 ***pasture . . . shepherd camps and enclosures for sheep:*** The destruction of cities and their return to a natural state represents a severe form of punishment from God. See also Isa 7:23-25; 13:19-21; 32:9-15; Ezek 35:9.

2:7 The Baal worshipers (1:4) and the Philistines would never be restored (2:4-6; see also Amos 1:8). By contrast, God promised to return the ***remnant*** of his people to their land, care for them, and ***restore*** them to ***prosperity*** (3:18-20; Isa 11:11-16; Jer 23:1-8; Ezek 34:11-16, 20-31).

2:8 The ***Moabites*** and ***Ammonites*** were Israel's traditional foes. The Israelites fought with them frequently (see 2 Kgs 3:1-27; 2 Chr 20:1-30) and they remained Israel's enemies to the end (2 Kgs 25:25; Jer 40:11-14). • ***mocking . . . invading:*** The Israelites not only suffered repeated attacks by the Moabites and Ammonites (see Amos 1:13) but also endured their insults over their successes.

2:9 The destruction of ***Sodom and Gomorrah*** serves as an example of God's severe judgment of sin, both in the OT (Deut 29:23; Isa 1:9; Jer 23:14; Amos 4:11) and in the NT (Luke 10:12; Rom 9:29; 2 Pet 2:6). • ***salt pits:*** A ruinous waste (Deut 29:23; Ps 107:34; Jer 17:6). Sowing the earth with salt was a mark of permanent judgment (see Judg 9:45) because it made the ground barren.

2:11 ***nations . . . will worship the LORD:*** At the end of history, all people in all places will worship God alone (3:9; Ps 66:4; Zech 14:16; Mic 4:1-2).

2:12 ***Ethiopians:*** Hebrew *Cushites.* While the Hebrew term can refer to any nation or peoples along the southern edge of the known world of that time, here it refers specifically to the Ethiopian dynasty that ruled Egypt.

13 And the LORD will strike the lands of the
north with his fist,
destroying the land of Assyria.
He will make its great capital, Nineveh, a
desolate wasteland,
parched like a desert.
14 The proud city will become a pasture for
flocks and herds,
and all sorts of wild animals will settle
there.
The desert owl and screech owl will
roost on its ruined columns,
their calls echoing through the gaping
windows.
Rubble will block all the doorways,
and the cedar paneling will be
exposed to the weather.
15 This is the boisterous city,
once so secure.
"I am the greatest!" it boasted.
"No other city can compare with me!"
But now, look how it has become an utter
ruin,
a haven for wild animals.
Everyone passing by will laugh in
derision
and shake a defiant fist.

Judgment against Jerusalem and the Whole World

3 1 What sorrow awaits rebellious,
polluted Jerusalem,
the city of violence and crime!
2 No one can tell it anything;
it refuses all correction.
It does not trust in the LORD
or draw near to its God.
3 Its leaders are like roaring lions
hunting for their victims.
Its judges are like ravenous wolves at
evening time,
who by dawn have left no trace of
their prey.
4 Its prophets are arrogant liars seeking
their own gain.
Its priests defile the Temple by
disobeying God's instructions.
5 But the LORD is still there in the city,
and he does no wrong.
Day by day he hands down justice,
and he does not fail.
But the wicked know no shame.
6 "I have wiped out many nations,
devastating their fortress walls and
towers.
Their streets are now deserted;
their cities lie in silent ruin.
There are no survivors—
none at all.
7 I thought, 'Surely they will have
reverence for me now!
Surely they will listen to my warnings.
Then I won't need to strike again,
destroying their homes.'
But no, they get up early
to continue their evil deeds.
8 Therefore, be patient," says the LORD.
"Soon I will stand and accuse these
evil nations.
For I have decided to gather the
kingdoms of the earth
and pour out my fiercest anger and
fury on them.
All the earth will be devoured
by the fire of my ᵉjealousy.

The LORD Will Deliver His People

9 "Then I will purify the speech of all
people,

2:13 Nah 3:7
2:14 Isa 34:11
2:15 1 Kgs 9:7-8; Isa 22:2-7; 32:14; 47:8
3:1 Jer 6:6
3:2 Ps 78:22; Jer 5:3
3:3 Ezek 22:6-12
3:4 Ezek 22:26; Mal 2:7-9
3:5 Jer 3:3
3:6 Zeph 2:5
3:7 Hos 9:9
3:8 Ps 27:14; Ezek 38:14-23; Zeph 1:18; ᵉ*qin'ah* (7068) ‣Zech 1:14
3:9 Ps 22:27

2:13 Zephaniah turns from the south (2:12) to the ***north***. Like Nahum before him, he announces the imminent demise of ***Assyria***.

2:14 To drive home his point about Nineveh's fate, Zephaniah invokes powerful imagery: ***Rubble*** would fill the ***doorways*** through which the wealthy and powerful of Nineveh had once walked. The eerie sounds of owls hooting in empty ***windows*** would punctuate the city's desolation.

2:15 ***utter ruin:*** The doom was so certain and irreversible (see Nah 1:14; 2:13; 3:19) that Zephaniah saw no future for Assyria or its capital. So complete was Nineveh's devastation that the Greek historian Xenophon once passed by its ruins unaware that it was there. • ***laugh . . . shake a defiant fist:*** Those who suffered under Assyria's cruel empire would be glad seeing its demise.

3:1-8 Zephaniah pronounces a message of sorrow for Judah and Jerusalem and admonishes them to wait patiently for the results of God's righteous judgment.

3:1 ***Polluted Jerusalem*** had wandered far from its call to be a holy city (Isa 52:1).

3:3-4 See also Ezek 22:23-29.

3:5 ***He does no wrong***, unlike those mentioned in 3:3-4.

3:7 ***get up early:*** Jerusalem's citizens couldn't wait to jump out of bed in the morning and do more ***evil deeds*** (Prov 1:16). They had moved far from the ways of their ancestor Abraham, who arose early to obey God's command (Gen 22:3).

3:8 ***be patient:*** See Hab 2:3. • ***stand and accuse:*** The prophet portrays a courtroom scene where God rises first as witness (see also Jer 29:23; Mal 3:5) on his own behalf, and then presides as judge (see also Job 9:15; Ps 50:6) to deliver his righteous sentence. • ***The fire of my jealousy*** describes the Lord's righteous hatred of sin, as well as his concern for his holy name and for the welfare of his people (see Isa 66:13-16).

3:9-20 God reveals his plans for a humble and purified remnant of his people (3:9-13) and encourages them to rejoice in the coming abundant blessings of their saving Lord (3:14-20).

3:9-13 The glorious future described in these verses provides further reason to wait patiently for the Lord (3:8). Like fellow prophets Isaiah, Nahum, and Habakkuk, Zephaniah uses judgment and hope as twin themes.

3:9 God intends for the blessings promised to the faithful remnant of 3:9-13 to reach people from every nation of

3:10 Ps 68:31 Isa 60:7
3:11 Isa 11:9
3:12 Nah 1:7
3:13 Hos 2:18 Mic 4:7 Rev 14:5
3:15 Isa 33:22 Ezek 37:26-28 Zech 8:3
3:16 Isa 35:3-4 Heb 12:12-13
3:17 Isa 62:5; 63:1
3:19 Isa 60:14 Ezek 34:16
3:20 Isa 56:5; 66:22 Ezek 37:12 Zeph 2:7

so that everyone can worship the
LORD together.
10 My scattered people who live beyond the
rivers of Ethiopia
will come to present their offerings.
11 On that day you will no longer need to be
ashamed,
for you will no longer be rebels
against me.
I will remove all proud and arrogant
people from among you.
There will be no more haughtiness on
my holy mountain.
12 Those who are left will be the lowly and
humble,
for it is they who trust in the name of
the LORD.
13 The remnant of Israel will do no wrong;
they will never tell lies or deceive one
another.
They will eat and sleep in safety,
and no one will make them afraid."

14 Sing, O daughter of Zion;
shout aloud, O Israel!
Be glad and rejoice with all your heart,
O daughter of Jerusalem!
15 For the LORD will remove his hand of
judgment
and will disperse the armies of your
enemy.
And the LORD himself, the King of
Israel,
will live among you!
At last your troubles will be over,
and you will never again fear disaster.
16 On that day the announcement to
Jerusalem will be,
"Cheer up, Zion! Don't be afraid!
17 For the LORD your God is living among
you.
He is a mighty savior.
He will take delight in you with gladness.
With his love, he will calm all your
fears.
He will rejoice over you with joyful
songs."

18 "I will gather you who mourn for the
appointed festivals;
you will be disgraced no more.
19 And I will deal severely with all who have
oppressed you.
I will save the weak and helpless ones;
I will bring together
those who were chased away.
I will give glory and fame to my former
exiles,
wherever they have been mocked and
shamed.
20 On that day I will gather you together
and bring you home again.
I will give you a good name, a name of
distinction,
among all the nations of the earth,
as I restore your fortunes before their
very eyes.
I, the LORD, have spoken!"

the world. Not just Israel, but *all people* would be transformed, call on the Lord (see Isa 55:5), and serve him (see Isa 59:19-21; Zech 14:16). The spread of the Good News to all nations furthered the fulfillment of this vision (Matt 28:19-20; Rom 10:9-13).

3:10 The *rivers of Ethiopia* (Hebrew *Cush*) are the distant headwaters of the Nile River. The ancient world considered the origin of the Nile a great mystery, so the expression speaks of the farthest reaches of the earth.

3:12 Jesus the Messiah perfectly expresses the ethical qualities predicted for the godly remnant of Israel (Isa 42:1-4; 53:3, 7-9; Zech 9:9; see Matt 11:28-30; 12:15-21; Phil 2:1-8; 1 Pet 2:23).

3:14 ***Sing . . . shout aloud . . . ! Be glad and rejoice:*** The cumulative effect of these commands emphasizes that God's people will one day experience unsurpassed joy.

3:15 The true *King of Israel* was always to be the Lord (Num 23:21; 1 Sam 8:7; Isa 44:6). • ***will live among you:*** See also Isa 54:4-8; 57:14-19; 62:10-12; Ezek 48:35; Joel 3:17, 21.

3:17 ***a mighty savior:*** God was Israel's Divine Warrior and Redeemer (see Ps 24:8-10; Isa 42:13; Hab 3:8-15). One of God's titles is "the Mighty God" (Isa 10:21). This title also applies to the Messiah (Isa 9:6). • ***With his love, he will calm all your fears:*** Or *He will be silent in his love.* Greek and Syriac versions read *He will renew you with his love.* • ***He will rejoice over you:*** Not only will Jerusalem and all Israel *rejoice* in God (3:14) but God will also rejoice over them as a purified and faithful people (see 3:12-13).

3:18-20 The repeated use of ***I will*** in these verses underscores God's further assurances to his people.

3:18 ***I will gather you . . . disgraced no more:*** The meaning of the Hebrew for this verse is uncertain. The Lord's assurance stands in stark contrast to the pronouncements at the beginning of the book, when God threatened to gather the nations to sweep the people of Judah from the face of the earth (1:2-4). Now he promises to gather up those who have been driven from Jerusalem and lead them safely home.

3:19 God will turn his people's former shame into *glory and fame* (see Deut 26:19; Isa 62:7; Mic 4:6-8; cp. 1 Pet 5:4).

3:20 ***On that day:*** After a time of terrible wrath and judgment, the day of the Lord culminates in everlasting blessings for all who trust in him (3:9, 12; see Ps 2:12; Isa 45:22; see also Rev 19:11–22:5). • ***I, the LORD, have spoken!*** Zephaniah's prophecy, entirely from God (see also 1:1-3, 10; 2:9; 3:8), is utterly trustworthy.

THE BOOK OF HAGGAI

The Jerusalem Temple still lay in ruins nearly twenty years after the Hebrews returned to Judah from exile in Babylon. Surely God's house deserved better! Yet the people of Judah were themselves living in comfortable homes. Haggai pointed out this discrepancy and successfully roused the people to rebuild the Lord's Temple. Haggai gave Israel a renewed vision of how their efforts would serve God's plan for his people.

SETTING

In 538 BC Cyrus the Great, king of Persia, issued a decree permitting conquered peoples who had been deported by the Babylonians to return to their homelands (see Ezra 1). The first emigrants to return to Jerusalem were led by Sheshbazzar, a prince of Judah and the first governor of the restored community (Ezra 1:5-11). In their enthusiasm, the returned exiles soon began to rebuild the altar and the Temple (Ezra 3), but local pagan residents threatened the Israelites and discouraged them from their God-given work (Ezra 4:4-24). The construction site lay neglected for nearly twenty years after their return.

The Hebrew people were gloomy during this period. Selfishness crippled community spirit, and apathy and disillusionment detracted from their worship. Only a small percentage of Hebrew exiles had actually returned to Judah, the city walls still lay in ruins, the Temple of God was a pile of rubble, and drought and blight ravaged the land. Judah languished as a Persian vassal state while the surrounding nations harassed the leadership in Jerusalem and thwarted their timid improvement efforts.

Haggai began preaching in 520 BC. The immediate occasion for Haggai's sermons was a severe drought affecting Judah (1:11). God sent him to motivate the Israelites to rebuild God's Temple and to encourage the spiritual renewal of the people of Jerusalem. In response, Judah resumed the rebuilding (1:14), and the project was completed in March 515 BC (see Ezra 6:15).

SUMMARY

Each of Haggai's four messages highlights a different theological concern. The first sermon

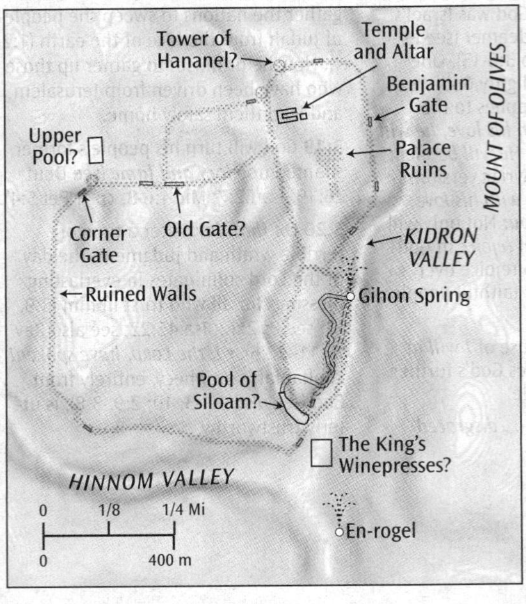

Jerusalem after the Exile, 520 BC. After many of the Jews returned from exile in 538 BC, they inhabited the land of Judea. The Judeans, however, were surrounded by hostile neighbors and had become discouraged by opposition and want. Haggai's preaching encouraged them to finish rebuilding the Temple in Jerusalem, the spiritual center of their nation.

(1:1-15) challenged the Judeans to stop giving their personal comfort first priority and to focus on restoring proper worship of God by rebuilding his Temple.

The second message (2:1-9) assured the community that God had not forgotten the promises of blessing and restoration made by the earlier prophets. The glory of the Lord would once again fill the Temple (2:7). These were not just empty words to bolster a beleaguered remnant, but the sure words of God's promise to his chosen people.

The third message (2:10-19) has ritual purity as its dominant theme. Haggai reminded his audience that the instructions of the law of Moses were still operative. God expects his people to be holy, even as he is holy (see Lev 11:44-45).

Haggai's final and perhaps most important message (2:20-23) reestablished the prominence of King David's descendants in Israel's religious and political life. David's dynasty was crucial to the restoration of the Hebrew people after the Babylonian exile (see Jer 23:5; 33:15; Ezek 37:24). Zerubbabel was a descendant of King David; his commission to serve as the Lord's "signet ring" marked the beginning of God's restoration of Israel (2:23; cp. Jer 22:24) and pointed to Jesus Christ, a descendant of David (Matt 1:1) who would rule in righteousness forever.

OUTLINE

1:1-15
A Call to Rebuild the Temple

2:1-23
A Message of Encouragement

AUTHOR

The book of Haggai is silent as to its authorship, but it is probable that Haggai wrote his own sermons (1:1, 3). The Bible records no biographic information about the prophet Haggai, but his ministry is attested by Ezra 6:14. Haggai probably wrote his book some time between delivering his sermons (520 BC) and the completion of the Temple (515 BC), an event that the prophecy does not mention.

DATE

Haggai's speeches occurred within a four-month period in the second year of the rule of Darius I, king of Persia (see notes on 1:1, 15; 2:1, 10). Haggai's ministry in postexilic Judah overlapped that of Zechariah, who began preaching in Jerusalem in November 520 BC (see Zech 1:1).

LITERARY GENRE

While not a magnum opus like the books of Isaiah or Jeremiah, Haggai does have literary polish. Haggai especially uses rhetorical questions to emphasize his thesis in three of the four messages (see 1:4; 2:3, 19). He repeats words or phrases to set the tone for his sermons (e.g., the repeated "look at what's happening," 1:5, 7; 2:15), and he engages in wordplay on occasion (e.g., Hebrew *khareb*, "ruins" [1:4] and *khoreb*, "drought" [1:11]).

Haggai's speeches are presumably third person prose summaries of more

TIMELINE

538 BC
Cyrus's decree allows exiles to return to Judea, Sheshbazzar leads first group of exiles to Jerusalem

538 / 537 BC
The altar is rebuilt

536 BC
Temple rebuilding begins and is halted

530–522 BC
Cambyses II as king of Persia

521–486 BC
Darius I Hystaspes as king of Persia

Aug 29—Dec 18, 520 BC
Haggai as prophet

Sept 21, 520 BC
Temple rebuilding resumes

Nov 520—Dec 7, 518 BC
Zechariah as prophet

Mar 12, 515 BC
Temple rebuilding is completed

[Haggai] has the unique place among the prophets of having been really listened to and his words obeyed.

ROBERT L. ALDEN
Expositor's Bible Commentary, vol. 7, p. 572

lengthy sermons. The messages are *oracles*—authoritative messages inspired by God. Oracles often include formula expressions that use stock words and phrases. Several of these formulas occur in Haggai: the "date" formula (e.g., "the second year of King Darius's reign," 1:1; 2:1, 10, 20), the "message" formula ("the LORD gave/sent a message," 1:1; 2:1, 10, 20), the "God-as-speaker" formula ("says the LORD," 1:7, 13; 2:4), and the "covenant relationship" formula ("I am with you," 2:4-5).

MEANING AND MESSAGE

Haggai's four brief sermons sounded a wake-up call to a community that was spiritually asleep. His message was to "get up and go to work" rebuilding the Jerusalem Temple.

Haggai correlated the community's lack of agricultural and economic success with their neglect of the Lord's Temple. He rebuked the people for their disinterest in worshiping God and called them to repentance and spiritual renewal. When the people responded positively and began the work of rebuilding, Haggai encouraged them with the promise of God's continuing presence and help.

Haggai called the people of Jerusalem to authentic worship, trust in God's word, personal holiness, and obedience to divinely appointed leadership. Haggai emphasizes the abiding presence of God's Spirit (1:13-14; 2:4-5), a theme shared with Zechariah (Zech 1:16; 8:23; see Ezek 37:27-28).

FURTHER READING

JOYCE G. BALDWIN
Haggai, Zechariah, Malachi (1972)

MARK J. BODA
Haggai, Zechariah (2004)

ANDREW HILL
Haggai in *Cornerstone Biblical Commentary*, vol. 10 (2008)

RALPH L. SMITH
Micah—Malachi (1984)

1. A CALL TO REBUILD THE TEMPLE (1:1-15)

Reflection on Recent Events

1 On August 29 of the second year of
King Darius's reign, the LORD gave a
message through the prophet Haggai to
Zerubbabel son of Shealtiel, governor of
Judah, and to Jeshua son of Jehozadak, the
high priest.
2"This is what the LORD of Heaven's Armies says: The people are saying, 'The time
has not yet come to rebuild the house of
the LORD.'"
3Then the LORD sent this message
through the prophet Haggai: 4"Why are
you living in luxurious houses while my
house lies in ruins? 5This is what the LORD
of Heaven's Armies says: Look at what's happening to you! 6You have planted much but

1:1 Ezra 2:2; 3:8; 5:1-2; 6:6-14; Zech 6:11
1:4 2 Sam 7:2; Hag 1:9
1:6 Hag 1:9; 2:16

1:1-15 The first *message* calls the people of Jerusalem to focus on restoring proper worship of God.

1:1 This introductory statement (*superscription*) identifies the author, the audience, the date, and the occasion prompting the prophecy. • ***On August 29:*** Literally *On the first day of the sixth month* of the ancient Hebrew lunar calendar. A number of dates in Haggai can be cross-checked with dates in surviving Persian records and related accurately to our modern calendar. This event occurred on August 29, 520 BC. • ***the second year:*** King Darius I (Hystaspes) ruled Persia 521–486 BC, early in the Persian empire (539–331 BC). The messages of Haggai are among the most precisely dated prophecies in the OT. • ***Prophet*** (Hebrew *nabi'*) designates ***Haggai*** as a representative of God who speaks with the authority of God who sent him. • ***Zerubbabel*** led one group of Hebrews back to Palestine after the Babylonian exile and was the Persian-appointed governor of Judah at the time of Haggai's ministry (see Ezra 2:1-2; 3:2; Neh 7:7). • ***Jeshua*** (Hebrew *Joshua*, a variant spelling of *Jeshua*; also in 1:12, 14.) was the high priest at that time. Under his supervision, the altar was rebuilt and the second Temple was dedicated (Ezra 3:2; 5:2; 6:15).

1:2 ***LORD of Heaven's Armies:*** Haggai's and Zechariah's favorite expression for God emphasizes the invincible power behind God's word. The Lord can call on infinite numbers of heavenly troops to carry out his will at a moment's notice (2 Kgs 6:17; Matt 26:53). This thought was intended to encourage the Judeans, who felt helpless and insignificant. • ***The time has not yet come:*** Poor crop yields from drought and pestilence had so weakened Judah's economy (1:6, 9-11) that the people thought they could not afford to rebuild the Temple. Haggai convinced them they could not afford to leave the Temple in ruins, for God would not bless and prosper them if they did not rebuild the Lord's house (1:4, 7-8).

1:4 *Why are you?* Rhetorical questions in prophetic literature call for agreement rather than a reply (see 2:3). The purpose of this question is to remove the listeners' opportunity to offer excuses in response to the message. • The ***luxurious*** (or *covered, paneled*) ***houses*** of the people contrasted with God's Temple, which was ***in ruins*** (or *desolate*) and thus unusable.

1:5 ***Look at what's happening to you*** (literally *Set your heart on these matters*): For the Hebrews, the *heart* is the place where thinking, feeling, and willing all occur. So this command (also 1:5, 7; 2:15, 18) calls upon the people to think carefully and draw the proper conclusions about the connection between what's happening to them (drought and poverty, 1:6) and their failure to restore proper worship of the Lord (1:8-9).

1:6 ***eat . . . drink . . . put on clothes:*** Each of these conveys continuous action (i.e., you keep filling your plates . . . you keep drinking and drinking . . . you put on layer after layer of clothes), heightening the sense of futility.

1:8 Ezra 3:7-13; Ps 132:13-14; Hag 2:7, 9
1:9 Isa 40:7; Hag 1:4
1:10 Deut 28:24; 1 Kgs 8:35-36; 17:1; Joel 1:18-20
1:11 Deut 28:22-24
1:12 Ps 112:1; Isa 50:10; Hag 1:1
1:13 Mal 2:7; 3:1
1:14-15 Ezra 5:2; Neh 4:6; Hag 1:1

harvest little. You eat but are not satisfied.
You drink but are still thirsty. You put on
clothes but cannot keep warm. Your wages
disappear as though you were putting them
in pockets filled with holes!

Exhortation to Begin Construction

[7]"This is what the LORD of Heaven's Armies says: Look at what's happening to
you! [8]Now go up into the hills, bring down
timber, and rebuild my house. Then I will
take pleasure in it and be honored, says
the LORD. [9]You hoped for rich harvests,
but they were poor. And when you brought
your harvest home, I blew it away. Why? Because my house lies in ruins, says the LORD
of Heaven's Armies, while all of you are
busy building your own fine houses. [10]It's
because of you that the heavens withhold
the dew and the earth produces no crops.
[11]I have called for a drought on your fields
and hills—a drought to wither the grain
and grapes and olive trees and all your
other crops, a drought to starve you and
your livestock and to ruin everything you
have worked so hard to get."

Obedience to God's Call

[12]Then Zerubbabel son of Shealtiel, and
Jeshua son of Jehozadak, the high priest,
and the whole remnant of God's people
began to obey the message from the LORD
their God. When they heard the words of
the prophet Haggai, whom the LORD their
God had sent, the people feared the LORD.
[13]Then Haggai, the LORD's messenger, gave
the people this message from the LORD: "I
am with you, says the LORD!"

[14]So the LORD sparked the enthusiasm
of Zerubbabel son of Shealtiel, governor of
Judah, and the enthusiasm of Jeshua son of
Jehozadak, the high priest, and the enthusi-
asm of the whole remnant of God's people.
They began to work on the house of their
God, the LORD of Heaven's Armies, [15]on
September 21 of the second year of King
Darius's reign.

2. A MESSAGE OF ENCOURAGEMENT (2:1-23)

The New Temple's Diminished Splendor

2 Then on October 17 of that same year,
the LORD sent another message through

Spiritual Renewal (1:7-15)

Deut 30:2-4; Ps 22:27; Isa 11:9–12:6; 44:22, 26-28; 61:6-7; Jer 24:4-7; Amos 4:6-12; Zech 9:9; 14:9; Mal 3:1

Haggai repeatedly charged his audience to reflect on how their current situation resulted from neglecting their relationship with God (1:5-7; 2:15-18). Haggai called the people to lay a spiritual foundation of reverence for God in their hearts before building the Lord's Temple. God's chastisement in a series of natural disasters called for repentance (2:17). Spiritual renewal had to accompany the physical reconstruction of the Temple (1:12).

The theme of spiritual renewal helps tie Haggai, Zechariah, and Malachi together. Israel's failure to obey God highlights the need for the appearance of the Lord's "servant" (2:23)—the righteous shepherd-king (Zech 9:9), who is Christ the Lord (Mal 3:1). Then God's presence among his people will return, creation will be restored, and worship of the Lord will be universal.

• ***pockets filled with holes*** (literally *a pierced bag*): The image depicts the loss of wages. Many families faced poverty despite their steady labors.

1:8 ***Now go up into the hills:*** The stands of trees around Jerusalem were insufficient to meet the demands of the Temple project. Such supplies would have been imported from Lebanon and Syria to the north. • The challenge to ***rebuild my house*** underscores the importance of worship in the life of the community and the need for a proper sanctuary so worship of the Lord might take place according to the law. The land would experience blessing and prosperity when the Lord's Temple—his dwelling place—was rebuilt (2:4).

1:9 ***I blew it away:*** The Lord destroyed the harvest because the people's priorities were wrong—they thought only of themselves rather than of God. • ***says the LORD of Heaven's Armies:*** The "God-as-speaker formula," which often closes a prophecy (1:13; 2:8, 17, 23), verified Haggai's message as the sure word of God.

1:11 ***I have called for a drought:*** The people failed to recognize their plight as a divine judgment on their misplaced priorities, so Haggai interpreted the situation in light of the curses attached to the covenant (Deut 28:15-68, especially vv 22-24, 38-40). • ***Drought*** (Hebrew *khoreb*) is a wordplay on "ruins" (1:4, 9; Hebrew *khareb*)— Judah's experiences corresponded with the condition in which they had left the Lord's Temple.

1:12 ***The whole remnant*** means the people who returned from Babylon. All of them were united in the rebuilding project. • ***the people feared the LORD:*** They responded with reverence and worship, and they reordered their priorities by placing spiritual values above their material prosperity.

1:13 Haggai's unusual title as ***the LORD's messenger*** (the same Hebrew phrase is often translated *angel of the LORD*) ascribes distinctive authority to Haggai as the Lord's agent. • ***I am with you:*** This affirmed God's covenant with them, his personal presence, and his support in the building project (2:4-5; see Gen 26:3; Exod 3:12; Isa 41:10; 43:5; Jer 30:11).

1:14 ***The LORD sparked the enthusiasm*** (literally *stirred the spirit*) of the people to accomplish his purposes (see Ezra 1:1; Isa 13:17; 41:25; Jer 51:1, 11). True worship of God prompts sacrificial service by God's people.

1:15 ***on September 21:*** Literally *on the twenty-fourth day of the sixth month* of the ancient Hebrew lunar calendar. This event occurred on September 21, 520 BC; see also note on 1:1.

2:1-9 Haggai's second message assures the community that God has not forgotten his promises, made by earlier prophets, to bless and restore them

the prophet Haggai. 2"Say this to Zerubbabel son of Shealtiel, governor of Judah, and
to Jeshua son of Jehozadak, the high priest,
and to the remnant of God's people there
in the land: 3'Does anyone remember this
house—this Temple—in its former splendor? How, in comparison, does it look to
you now? It must seem like nothing at all!
4But now the LORD says: Be strong, Zerubbabel. Be strong, Jeshua son of Jehozadak, the
high priest. Be strong, all you people still
left in the land. And now get to work, for I
am with you, says the LORD of Heaven's Armies. 5My Spirit remains among you, just as
I promised when you came out of Egypt. So
do not be afraid.'

The New Temple's Restored Splendor

6"For this is what the LORD of Heaven's Armies says: In just a little while I will again
shake the heavens and the earth, the oceans
and the dry land. 7I will shake all the nations, and the treasures of all the nations
will be brought to this Temple. I will fill this
place with glory, says the LORD of Heaven's
Armies. 8The silver is mine, and the gold
is mine, says the LORD of Heaven's Armies.
9The future glory of this Temple will be
greater than its past glory, says the LORD
of Heaven's Armies. And in this place I will
bring peace. I, the LORD of Heaven's Armies,
have spoken!"

Blessings Promised for Obedience

10On December 18 of the second year of
King Darius's reign, the LORD sent this message to the prophet Haggai: 11"This is what
the LORD of Heaven's Armies says. Ask the
priests this question about the law: 12'If one
of you is carrying some meat from a holy
sacrifice in his robes and his robe happens
to brush against some bread or stew, wine
or olive oil, or any other kind of food, will it
also become holy?' "

The priests replied, "No."

13Then Haggai asked, "If someone becomes ceremonially unclean by touching a
dead person and then touches any of these
foods, will the food be defiled?"

And the priests answered, "Yes."

2:3 Ezra 3:12
2:4 Deut 31:23; Acts 7:9; Eph 6:10-12
2:5 Exod 29:45-46; Neh 9:10; Isa 63:11, 14
2:6 Ezek 38:19; *Heb 12:26
2:7 1 Kgs 8:11; Isa 60:4-9
2:10 Hag 1:15
2:12 Exod 29:37; Ezek 44:19; Matt 23:19
2:13 Num 19:11-12, 22

(e.g., Isa 35:1-10; 40:1-11; 52:1-12; Jer 32:36-44; 33:6-26).

2:1 ***on October 17 of that same year:*** Literally *on the twenty-first day of the seventh month* of the ancient Hebrew lunar calendar. This event (in the second year of Darius's reign) occurred on October 17, 520 BC; see also note on 1:1. This was the last day of the Festival of Tabernacles, the celebration of the summer harvest (see Lev 23:34-43). Hundreds of years earlier, Solomon's Temple had been dedicated during this festival (1 Kgs 8:2). Haggai's message was timed to offer the people hope and encouragement in their present distress and discouragement.

2:2 ***Jeshua:*** Hebrew *Joshua*, a variant spelling of Jeshua; also in 2:4.

2:3 The ***former splendor*** belonged to Solomon's Temple (1 Kgs 6:38), which some of the older people of Judah had seen in their youth before going into exile in Babylon. They wept when they saw the new foundation laid (Ezra 3:12-13), because it seemed ***like nothing at all*** by comparison.

2:4 ***But now . . . be strong:*** This marks a shift from rebuke and challenge to encouragement and affirmation (cp. Josh 1:6-7).

2:5 ***My Spirit remains among you:*** See Exod 29:46; Isa 63:11; Ezek 36:26-27. • ***just as I promised*** (literally *the word I cut with you*): The phrase "cut a covenant" is the Hebrew idiom for making a covenant (see Gen 15:18; Exod 34:27). Haggai's phrase, "cut a word," is unique in the OT, using language that purposefully creates a connection between his prophecy and God's covenant relationship with his people. By making this connection, Haggai underscored the continuity of God's actions in rescuing his people, first from Egypt and then from Babylon (see Ezek 20:33-38).

2:6-7 God ***will again shake the heavens and the earth*** at the coming day of judgment (see Isa 2:19-21; 30:28). The previous shaking was the judgment on Egypt at the time of the Exodus (2:21-22; Exod 14:31). The NT relates ***in just a little while*** to the return of Jesus Christ (Heb 12:26-27). Haggai probably saw God's ultimate judgment foreshadowed in events to take place after his time (e.g., the fall of Persia to Greece, the fall of Greece to Rome; see Dan 2:39-45).

2:7 ***Treasures . . . will be brought*** to the Temple by all the nations as tribute and homage to the God of Israel.

2:9 ***future glory:*** Haggai might have in mind the Messiah's coming to his Temple (see Mal 3:1). Jesus was presented in the Lord's Temple as an infant (Luke 2:22), and he taught there as an adult (Luke 19:45-47). Jesus, the human Word of God, is greater than the Temple (Matt 12:6; see John 2:13-22). Although it was recognized by only a few, Jesus' presence in the Temple far outshone the glory in the Tabernacle at the time of Moses and in Solomon's Temple (cp. Luke 2:29-32). • ***in this place I will bring peace:*** The priestly benediction (Num 6:24-26) was pronounced as part of the Temple liturgy. In the last days, God would make a covenant of peace with Israel (Ezek 34:25; 37:26). The good result of rebuilding the Temple was a guarantee on that future *peace*.

2:10-19 The theme of the third message is the law's instructions about ritual purity. These instructions were still operative. God expects his people to be holy, even as he is holy (Lev 11:44-45).

2:10 ***On December 18:*** Literally *On the twenty-fourth day of the ninth month* of the ancient Hebrew lunar calendar (similarly in 2:18). This event occurred on December 18, 520 BC; see also note on 1:1.

2:11 ***Ask the priests:*** The priests' job was to teach and interpret ***the law*** (Deut 33:10; Mal 2:7-9), so the message about ceremonial purity was directed to them.

2:12 ***will it also become holy?*** This question refers to ***meat from a holy sacrifice*** and the way in which ceremonial purity and impurity could be transferred (see "Clean and Unclean" at Lev 11:1–15:33, p. 213). Carrying the holy sacrifice—the meat set aside and prepared for the offering—rendered one's robe holy (cp. Lev 6:18). This holiness, however, could not be transmitted to a third object.

2:13 Ceremonial uncleanness is transmitted much more easily than ceremonial purity. Anyone touching a corpse became defiled and thus unclean. Anything touched by a ***ceremonially unclean*** person was also rendered impure (see Num 19:11-13, 22). Haggai applies this in 2:14.

2:14 Prov 15:8; Isa 1:11-15
2:15 Ezra 3:10; 4:24; Hag 1:5
2:16 Hag 1:9
2:18 Hag 2:10
2:21 Hag 2:6; Heb 12:26
2:22 Mic 5:10

14Then Haggai responded, "That is
how it is with this people and this nation,
says the LORD. Everything they do and
everything they offer is defiled by their
sin. 15Look at what was happening to you
before you began to lay the foundation of
the LORD's Temple. 16When you hoped for
a twenty-bushel crop, you harvested only
ten. When you expected to draw fifty gallons from the winepress, you found only
twenty. 17I sent blight and mildew and hail
to destroy everything you worked so hard
to produce. Even so, you refused to return
to me, says the LORD.
18"Think about this eighteenth day of
December, the day when the foundation of
the LORD's Temple was laid. Think carefully.
19I am giving you a promise now while the
seed is still in the barn. You have not yet harvested your grain, and your grapevines, fig
trees, pomegranates, and olive trees have
not yet produced their crops. But from this
day onward I will bless you."

Promises for Zerubbabel

20On that same day, December 18, the LORD
sent this second message to Haggai: 21"Tell
Zerubbabel, the governor of Judah, that I am
about to shake the heavens and the earth.
22I will overthrow royal thrones and destroy
the power of foreign kingdoms. I will overturn their chariots and riders. The horses
will fall, and their riders will kill each other.
23"But when this happens, says the LORD
of Heaven's Armies, I will honor you, Zerubbabel son of Shealtiel, my servant. I will
make you like a signet ring on my finger,
says the LORD, for I have chosen you. I, the
LORD of Heaven's Armies, have spoken!"

2:14 ***That is how it is with this people:*** Simply returning from exile to the land God promised Israel did not make the people of Judah holy. They were still unclean, since they were not obeying the instructions of God's covenant with them. Their work and even their worship were contaminated by impurity; the ruins of the Lord's Temple had symbolized the people's disobedience. The rebuilding of the Temple was a tangible sign of changed hearts and renewed obedience to God's covenant.

2:15 *Look at what was happening* (see note on 1:5): Divine blessing, whether spiritual or material, is contingent upon the obedience of God's people (Deut 30:6-10). Haggai called the people to persist in the self-examination that leads to repentance and in the fear of the Lord that his first message initiated (see 1:7, 12).

2:17 *Return* often signifies repentance. • ***you refused:*** The Hebrew people were stubborn and rebellious from the time of Moses (Deut 31:27) to the time of Jesus (Matt 17:17). • ***blight and mildew:*** What happened was the result of disobedience to God's covenant (see Deut 28:22).

2:18 ***Think about this eighteenth day of December, the day:*** Or *On this eighteenth day of December, think about the day;* literally *Think about this day onward, this twenty-fourth day of the ninth month*, according to the ancient Hebrew lunar calendar. This date was December 18, 520 BC; see also note on 1:1. • Some believe that the phrase *the day* refers to the date of the initial clearing of rubble from the Temple site and the procuring of building materials (September 21, 520 BC; see 1:14-15).

2:19 ***I am giving you a promise now while the seed is still in the barn*** (literally *Is the seed yet in the barn?*): The promise of a bountiful crop calls attention to God's faithfulness to his covenant people. The Temple was not yet complete, but God was promising to extend its blessings at once. • ***But from this day onward I will bless you:*** God was gracious in responding immediately to his people's efforts toward spiritual renewal and obedience (see Ps 111:4-5).

2:20-23 Haggai's final message is perhaps the most important; it reestablishes the prominence of David's descendant in Israel's religious and political life. The dynasty of David was key to restoring the Hebrew people after the Babylonian exile (see Jer 23:5; Ezek 37:24). God had cursed David's descendant, King Jehoiachin, at the time of the Exile (Jer 22:24-30), but Haggai's last message overturns that curse and reinstates the covenant with David (see 2 Sam 7:4-17) as the means by which God will carry out his promises to bless and restore Israel.

2:20 ***On that same day, December 18:*** Literally *On the twenty-fourth day of the [ninth] month;* see notes on 2:10, 18.

2:21 ***Zerubbabel, the governor***, was a descendant of David through Jehoiachin (1 Chr 3:19). Haggai's affirmation thus overturns the curse on Jehoiachin (Jer 22:24-30). However, Zerubbabel abruptly disappears from the biblical record. He was possibly deposed as Judean governor or even executed by King Darius, who was attempting to control his newly acquired empire. The expectations here ascribed to Zerubbabel, and his status as a descendant of David, might have made him a political threat to Darius.

2:22 ***I will overturn their chariots and riders:*** The prophet's language would remind Israel of their deliverance from the Egyptian army (see Exod 15:1-21). The ambiguity of the threat of God's judgment makes it unclear whether Haggai is referring to events in the distant future or to something more immediate involving the Persian empire (e.g., the Greek-Persian wars during the reigns of Darius I and Xerxes or the later Peloponnesian War).

2:23 The ***signet ring*** was a symbol of kingship. An engraved stone set in a gold or silver finger ring was used to seal or endorse official documents. The image here emphasizes the divine authority invested in ***Zerubbabel*** and assures the people of God's continuing involvement in the political process (despite the failures of the Hebrew monarchs). The designation of Zerubbabel as the *signet* of the Lord no doubt rekindled expectations for the Messiah, since Zerubbabel was a descendant of King David. Yet the declaration ultimately points beyond Zerubbabel (see note on 2:21) to one of his descendants (see Matt 1:12; Luke 1:32-33; 3:27).

THE BOOK OF ZECHARIAH

The people of God who had returned to Judea from exile were being oppressed by neighboring nations. As a result, the people were discouraged and they let their Temple lie in ruins. Zechariah encouraged them with a vision of things to come. God continued to love Jerusalem and Judah, and his unwavering plan was to live there again with his people and establish his rule over all the earth. Zechariah warned Israel not to repeat the sins that had led to exile, and he called those who wavered between God's truth and human wisdom to return to God, obey the commands of God's covenant, and practice justice in the land.

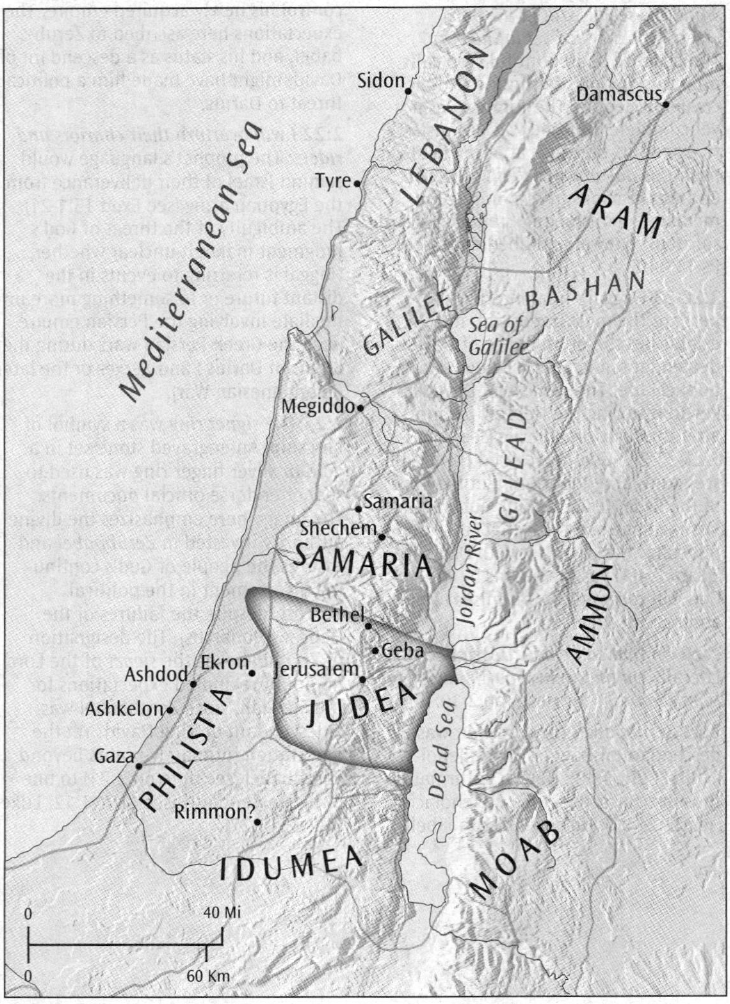

◄ **Key Places in Zechariah, 520 BC.** Zechariah's messages gave a vision of hope for God's people living in Judea, while promising judgment for the neighboring nations.

ARAM, DAMASCUS 9:1-2
ASHDOD, ASHKELON, EKRON, GAZA 9:5-7
BETHEL 7:2
GEBA 14:10
GILEAD, LEBANON, BASHAN 10:10; 11:1-2
MEGIDDO 12:11
RIMMON 14:10
SIDON, TYRE 9:2-5

SETTING

Cyrus, king of Persia, issued a decree in 538 BC permitting conquered peoples who had been deported by the Babylonians to return to their homelands (see Ezra 1). The first Jewish emigrants to return to Jerusalem were led by Sheshbazzar, the first governor of the restored community (Ezra 1:5-11). During his administration, the returning Jews laid the foundation for a new Temple (538~536 BC; see Ezra 5:16), but soon abandoned the project. The construction site lay neglected for nearly two decades as the people experienced economic

hardship, political oppression and harassment, and spiritual barrenness (see Haggai).

In response to their distress, God raised up two prophets to initiate the physical rebuilding and spiritual renewal of Jerusalem. The prophet Haggai, who preached for only four months in late 520 BC, challenged the Hebrew community to rebuild the Jerusalem Temple. The people responded favorably to Haggai's message and began to reconstruct the Lord's Temple that year (Hag 1:12-15). The prophet Zechariah complemented Haggai's message by calling for the spiritual renewal of God's people (1:3-6; 7:8-14). Zechariah's ministry in Jerusalem lasted for at least two years.

The rebuilding of the Temple was completed in March 515 BC during the reign of Persian king Darius I. It was rededicated to the Lord's worship at the Passover celebration that same year (Ezra 5:2; 6:13-22).

OUTLINE

1:1-6
Prelude: A Call to Return to the Lord

1:7–6:15
Zechariah's Visions

7:1–8:23
Zechariah's Sermons

9:1–14:21
Zechariah's Oracles

SUMMARY

Zechariah's task was to prepare the people for proper worship in the Temple once the building project was completed. He was commissioned to speak "kind and comforting words" from the Lord (1:13), and he did so by rebuking, exhorting, and encouraging God's people.

The people of Judah committed blatant social and moral sins; they were passively rebellious and spiritually apathetic. Zechariah called the people to return to God through genuine repentance (1:3-5). Only spiritual renewal could foster true worship and meaningful service in the Temple, which was under construction at the prompting of the prophet Haggai. Only obedience to the Lord would usher in the long-awaited blessing, prosperity, and righteousness of the messianic age (6:9-15; 8:13).

God's plan to do good to Jerusalem was contingent upon the community's adherence to God's laws, especially those governing their treatment of one another (7:8-12; 8:14-17). Before the nations would seek the Lord in Jerusalem, Israel must seek God's favor, act justly, and show kindness and mercy to widows, orphans, and foreigners (7:9-10; 14:16-21).

AUTHOR

The book of Zechariah is silent about its authorship, but Zechariah probably wrote down his own sermons. The superscription (1:1) identifies Zechariah as the son of Berekiah and the grandson of Iddo, as Ezra confirms (Ezra 5:1; 6:14). Nehemiah informs us that Iddo returned to Jerusalem from exile in Babylon with Zerubbabel and Jeshua (Neh 12:4). Nehemiah also lists Zechariah as the head of the family of priests descended from Iddo (Neh 12:1, 16). This suggests that Zechariah was both a priest and prophet in Jerusalem.

TIMELINE

538 BC
Cyrus's decree allows exiles to return to Judea, Sheshbazzar leads first group of exiles to Jerusalem, Zerubbabel as governor of Judea

530–522 BC
Cambyses II as king of Persia

536 BC
Temple rebuilding begins and is halted

521–486 BC
Darius I Hystaspes is king of Persia

Aug 29–Dec 18, 520 BC
Haggai as prophet

Sep 21, 520 BC
Temple rebuilding resumes

Nov 520–Dec 7, 518 BC
Zechariah as prophet

Oct~Nov 520 BC
Zechariah's first message (1:1-6)

Feb 15, 519 BC
Zechariah's second message (1:7–6:8)

Dec 7, 518 BC
Zechariah's third message (7:1–8:23)

515 BC
Temple rebuilding is completed

Zechariah occupies a position of singular importance towards the close of the prophetic period in virtue of its . . . more complete conception of the true character of the Deliverer.

F. KIRKPATRICK
The Doctrine of the Prophets, p. 435

DATE

Zechariah's ministry began just two months after Haggai's, in 520 BC. Zechariah's last dated message was delivered in 518 BC. The first portion of the book (chs 1–8) was probably written down between 520 and 515 BC, since Zechariah makes no reference to the completion and dedication of the Jerusalem Temple in 515 BC (see Ezra 6:13-22). Zechariah's undated messages (chs 9–14) perhaps indicate that his ministry continued well beyond the completion of the Temple.

Some biblical scholars assign chs 9–11 to a "Second Zechariah" and chs 12–14 to a "Third Zechariah." However, the vocabulary and grammar show remarkable literary continuity throughout the entire book, and archaeological discoveries and socio-political considerations support a unified composition. Zechariah probably composed chs 9–14 later in his life, perhaps between 500 and 470 BC.

RECIPIENTS

Zechariah's messages were intended for the people living in and around Jerusalem after their return from exile (1:3). Within Zechariah's sermons and visions are words specifically addressed to the governor Zerubbabel, the high priest Jeshua, and the rest of the priests (see 3:8-9; 4:6-7; 7:4).

LITERARY GENRE

Zechariah is prophetic literature containing messages that call God's people to repentance, to renew corporate worship, and to practice social justice.

In addition, Zechariah contains apocalyptic or vision literature. This genre of writing interprets current events and predicts future events by means of symbolic language, ciphers, and codes. Such writing is usually accompanied by an angelic mediator (see 1:9). The settings, characters, and events of apocalyptic literature tend to go beyond ordinary reality. The visions depict literal events, but the symbolic descriptions do not necessarily represent the events literally. Apocalyptic literature announces an end to the status quo and opens up alternative possibilities as a result of God's impending intervention in human affairs.

Later Jewish apocalyptic literature placed heavy emphasis on the future restoration of Israel in the day of the Lord. Zechariah's prophecy was more concerned with social justice in the present. Three types of messages are usually associated with apocalyptic literature in the Bible: (1) encouragement for the oppressed, (2) warnings to the oppressor, and (3) calls to faith for those wavering between God's truth and human wisdom.

MEANING AND MESSAGE

The book of Zechariah calls for repentance, spiritual renewal, and return to right relationship with God (1:1-6). Zechariah's duty was to comfort and strengthen a small, discouraged remnant of God's people (1:13; 8:6-15). Zechariah also reinforced Haggai's summons to rebuild the Jerusalem Temple (8:9, 13).

Zechariah's messages came to him as visions of the future that promised peace to Israel, judgment of the nations, restoration of Jerusalem, responsible government by God's appointed leadership, and righteousness among God's people (1:7–6:15). Zechariah emphasized that social justice was Israel's right response to God (7:8-12; 8:14-17).

FURTHER READING

JOYCE G. BALDWIN
Haggai, Zechariah, Malachi (1972)

MARK J. BODA
Haggai, Zechariah (2004)

ANDREW HILL
Zechariah in *Cornerstone Biblical Commentary,* vol. 10 (2008)

E. H. MERRILL
An Exegetical Commentary: Haggai, Zechariah, Malachi (1994)

Zechariah's last two messages instill hope in God by focusing on the future restoration of Israel (chs 9–14). The prophet forecasts the Lord's return to his Temple (9:8-10), Israel's rescue from her enemies (12:1-14), and the establishment of God's kingdom in Jerusalem (14:9-11). Zechariah presents the Messiah as a suffering shepherd (13:7) and as a righteous king (9:9) who will bring salvation to Israel and peace to the nations (9:10, 16).

1:1 Ezra 4:24; 5:1 Neh 12:4, 16
1:2 2 Chr 36:16
1:3 Isa 31:6 Mal 3:7
1:4 2 Chr 24:19; 29:6-10; 36:15 Jer 6:17; 11:6-8
1:5 John 8:52
1:6 Jer 12:16-17 Lam 2:17 [a]*shub* (7725) ‣Deut 30:10

1. PRELUDE: A CALL TO RETURN TO THE LORD (1:1-6)

1 In November of the second year of King Darius's reign, the LORD gave this message to the prophet Zechariah son of Berekiah and grandson of Iddo:

2"I, the LORD, was very angry with your ancestors. 3Therefore, say to the people, 'This is what the LORD of Heaven's Armies says: Return to me, and I will return to you, says the LORD of Heaven's Armies.' 4Don't be like your ancestors who would not listen or pay attention when the earlier prophets said to them, 'This is what the LORD of Heaven's Armies says: Turn from your evil ways, and stop all your evil practices.'

5"Where are your ancestors now? They and the prophets are long dead. 6But everything I said through my servants the prophets happened to your ancestors, just as I said. As a result, they [a]repented and said, 'We have received what we deserved from the LORD of Heaven's Armies. He has done what he said he would do.' "

2. ZECHARIAH'S VISIONS (1:7–6:15)

A Man among the Myrtle Trees

7Three months later, on February 15, the LORD sent another message to the prophet Zechariah son of Berekiah and grandson of Iddo.

Returning to the LORD (1:3)

Zech 7:9-14; 8:16-17
1 Sam 7:2-11
Isa 1:16-20; 55:7
Hos 6:1-3; 14:1-7
Hag 1:12
Mal 3:7
Matt 3:2-10; 22:34-40
Acts 17:24-31

Zechariah's message to those returning to Jerusalem from exile is found in his opening statement, "Return to me, and I will return to you, says the LORD of Heaven's Armies" (1:3). Zechariah's call to repentance was a call for the people of Israel to be in right relationship with God by renewing their commitment to God's covenant with them. Other OT prophets communicated the same message (see Isa 1:16-20; Hos 6:1-3; Hag 1:12; Mal 3:7). Zechariah warned his audience to learn from the past because violating the covenant had sent an earlier generation into exile (7:11-14).

Zechariah's interest in Israel's relationship with God extended to issues of social justice. Obedience to God's covenant leads naturally to the practice of justice, honesty, fairness, mercy, and kindness (7:9-10; 8:16-17). Zechariah's concern for right relationship with God and others in the covenant community anticipated Jesus' later teaching on the most important OT commandments: to love God above all, and to love one's neighbor as one's self (Matt 22:34-40).

1:1-6 The prelude identifies the book's themes as repentance and spiritual renewal, and establishes a tone of hope and encouragement.

1:1 This superscription, or introductory statement, classifies the book of Zechariah as an *oracle*, an authoritative message inspired by God. *The prophet Zechariah* was God's emissary, designated to speak with God's authority. • *King Darius's reign* (521–486 BC) was in the early years of the Persian empire (539–331 BC). • *In November:* Literally *In the eighth month.* A number of dates in Zechariah can be cross-checked with dates in surviving Persian records and related accurately to our modern calendar. This month of the ancient Hebrew lunar calendar occurred within the months of October and November 520 BC.

1:3 *the LORD of Heaven's Armies:* God has an infinite number of angelic troops ready to carry out his will (see 2 Kgs 6:17; Matt 26:53). The phrase was probably meant to be an encouragement to the Judeans. • *Return to me:* A person who repents makes a complete turnaround—a shift away from sin and self toward loyalty to God and his covenant (see Isa 44:22; Mal 3:7; see also Ps 80:3-14; 85:4-8).

1:4 Before the Exile, *earlier prophets* actively called Judah and Israel to repentance. Zechariah especially reflects the prophetic influence of Jeremiah and Ezekiel. • *ancestors who would not listen:* The people of Israel (2 Kgs 17:13-14) and Judah (2 Chr 36:15-16) were taken into exile because they stubbornly refused to heed the word of the Lord (cp. 2 Chr 30:7).

1:6 *everything . . . happened:* The covenant curses (Deut 28:15-68) had overtaken their *ancestors* who refused to obey God.

1:7–6:15 These eight visions addressed the Judeans' fears that prevented them from responding in faith to God's promises. These visions, which occurred two months after Haggai's final two messages (Hag 2:10-19, 20-23), suggest that Haggai's prophecies were being fulfilled.

1:7-17 Zechariah's first vision depicts God's concern for Jerusalem (1:7-15), followed by a response (1:16-17) that confirmed God's intentions to rebuild his Temple and restore the city's prosperity.

1:7 *Three months later, on February 15:* Literally *On the twenty-fourth day of the eleventh month, the month of Shebat, in the second year of Darius.* This event occurred on February 15, 519 BC; see also note on 1:1.

8In a vision during the night, I saw a man
sitting on a red horse that was standing
among some myrtle trees in a small valley.
Behind him were riders on red, brown, and
white horses. 9I asked the angel who was
talking with me, "My lord, what do these
horses mean?"
"I will show you," the angel replied.
10The rider standing among the myrtle
trees then explained, "They are the ones the
LORD has sent out to patrol the earth."
11Then the other riders reported to the
angel of the LORD, who was standing among
the myrtle trees, "We have been patrolling
the earth, and the whole earth is at peace."
12Upon hearing this, the angel of the
LORD prayed this prayer: "O LORD of Heav-
en's Armies, for seventy years now you have
been angry with Jerusalem and the towns
of Judah. How long until you again show
mercy to them?" 13And the LORD spoke
kind and comforting words to the angel
who talked with me.
14Then the angel said to me, "Shout this
message for all to hear: 'This is what the
LORD of Heaven's Armies says: My love for Jerusalem and Mount Zion is [b]passionate and
strong. 15But I am very angry with the other
nations that are now enjoying peace and
security. I was only a little angry with my people, but the nations inflicted harm on them
far beyond my intentions.
16" 'Therefore, this is what the LORD says:
I have returned to show mercy to Jerusalem.
My Temple will be rebuilt, says the LORD of
Heaven's Armies, and measurements will be
taken for the reconstruction of Jerusalem.'
17"Say this also: 'This is what the LORD of
Heaven's Armies says: The towns of Israel
will again overflow with prosperity, and the
LORD will again comfort Zion and choose Jerusalem as his own.' "

Four Horns and Four Blacksmiths

18Then I looked up and saw four animal
horns. 19"What are these?" I asked the angel who was talking with me.
He replied, "These horns represent the
nations that scattered Judah, Israel, and Jerusalem."
20Then the LORD showed me four blacksmiths. 21"What are these men coming to
do?" I asked.
The angel replied, "These four horns—
these nations—scattered and humbled
Judah. Now these blacksmiths have come to
terrify those nations and throw them down
and destroy them."

Future Prosperity of Jerusalem

2 When I looked again, I saw a man with
a measuring line in his hand. 2"Where
are you going?" I asked.
He replied, "I am going to measure Jerusalem, to see how wide and how long it is."

1:8 Neh 8:15; Isa 41:19; 55:13; Zech 6:2-3; Rev 6:4
1:9 Zech 2:3
1:11 Isa 14:7
1:12 Ps 74:10; Isa 64:9-12; Jer 25:11-12; Dan 9:2
1:13 Isa 40:1-2; Zech 4:1
1:14 Zech 1:17; 8:2; [b]*qana'* (7065) ›Gen 37:11
1:15 Ps 123:4; Amos 1:11
1:16 Ezra 6:14-15; Isa 54:8-10; Zech 2:10
1:17 Isa 44:26; 51:3
1:19 1 Kgs 22:11
1:20 Isa 44:12; 54:16
1:21 Ps 75:10; Zech 1:18-19
2:1 Ezek 40:3-5
2:2 Jer 31:39; Rev 21:15-17

1:8 The *vision during the night* follows a standard pattern: an introductory statement, a description of the vision, the prophet's request for an interpretation, and an angelic explanation. • The *myrtle trees* were probably in the wooded Kidron *valley* outside of Jerusalem. The Lord had symbolically returned to the city's outskirts but had not yet entered Jerusalem because the Temple was still under construction. • The colors of the *red, brown, and white horses* are not significant to this vision's meaning. These angelic *riders* patrolled the earth (1:10), showing God's continuing concern over Jerusalem.

1:10 *Patrol* suggests the angelic riders' ongoing scrutiny of *the earth*.

1:11 The man sitting on a red horse among the myrtle trees (1:8) is called the *angel of the LORD* (cp. Gen 16:7-13; Exod 23:23; 32:34; Judg 13:21-22).

1:14 ***My love . . . is passionate and strong:*** This phrase, sometimes translated as "I am very jealous," reflects intense, single-minded devotion that could produce hatred and envy or zeal and devotion. God is jealous—as the one true and living God, he has exclusive rights to his creatures' worship (see Exod 20:5; 34:14). • ***Jerusalem*** signifies the territories ruled by Judean kings; ***Mount Zion*** was the site of the Lord's Temple.

1:16 ***and measurements will be taken for the reconstruction of Jerusalem:*** Literally *and the measuring line will be stretched out over Jerusalem* (cp. Job 38:5; Jer 31:39).

1:17 The repetition of ***again*** (four times in Hebrew) emphasizes the certainty of God's intention to restore Jerusalem.

1:18-21 The second vision states God's plan to bring his judgment against the nations who destroyed Jerusalem and exiled Judah. The prophet leaves unspecified the identity of nations represented by the four horns; it is best to view the number four as symbolic of all those nations who will face divine judgment for scattering the people of God. • Verses 1:18-21 are numbered 2:1-4 in the Hebrew text.

1:18-19 ***Then I looked up*** suggests that the prophet was interrupted by another vision while still preoccupied with the previous one (also in 2:1; 5:1; 6:1). • ***Horns*** symbolized power and authority in the biblical world and might represent an individual ruler (see Dan 7:8; 8:8), a dynasty (see note on 1 Sam 2:10), or ***nations***.

1:20 The word translated ***blacksmiths*** could refer to any sort of craftsmen (mason, carpenter, smith). If the horns representing the nations were metal (see 1 Kgs 22:11), then blacksmiths were appropriate to the task of destroying them (see 2 Chr 24:12; Isa 44:12).

1:21 ***humbled Judah:*** They literally *lifted up their horns against Judah.* • The Lord would cut off those horns, ***throw them down*** to the ground, and bring an end to their authority. The Judeans did not need to fear the surrounding nations.

2:1-13 Verses 2:1-13 are numbered 2:5-17 in the Hebrew text.

2:1-5 The scope of the visions narrows from the cosmos (vision 1), to the nations (vision 2), to the city of Jerusalem. The vision itself (2:1-3) is followed by an explanation of its meaning (2:4-5).

2:2 ***how wide and how long it is*** (Or *how long and wide it is to be*): By taking this measurement, God showed that he was planning for Jerusalem's future.

2:5 Zech 2:10-11
2:6 Isa 48:20; Jer 3:18; 31:10
2:8 Deut 32:10; Isa 60:7-14
2:9 Isa 14:2
2:10 Zech 9:9
2:11 Mic 4:2
2:12 Deut 32:9; Zech 1:17
2:13 Ps 78:65-66; Hab 2:20; Zeph 1:7
3:1 Ezra 5:2; Job 1:6-12; Ps 109:6; Hag 1:1; Zech 6:11
[c]*mal'ak* (4397) ‣Zech 12:8
[d]*satan* (7854) ‣Zech 3:2

3 Then the angel who was with me went
to meet a second angel who was coming
toward him. 4 The other angel said, "Hurry,
and say to that young man, 'Jerusalem will
someday be so full of people and livestock
that there won't be room enough for everyone! Many will live outside the city walls.
5 Then I, myself, will be a protective wall of
fire around Jerusalem, says the LORD. And I
will be the glory inside the city!' "

The Exiles Are Called Home

6 The LORD says, "Come away! Flee from
Babylon in the land of the north, for I have
scattered you to the four winds. 7 Come
away, people of Zion, you who are exiled in
Babylon!"

8 After a period of glory, the LORD of Heav-
en's Armies sent me against the nations who
plundered you. For he said, "Anyone who
harms you harms my most precious possession. 9 I will raise my fist to crush them, and
their own slaves will plunder them." Then
you will know that the LORD of Heaven's Armies has sent me.

10 The LORD says, "Shout and rejoice,
O beautiful Jerusalem, for I am coming
to live among you. 11 Many nations will
join themselves to the LORD on that day,
and they, too, will be my people. I will live
among you, and you will know that the
LORD of Heaven's Armies sent me to you.
12 The land of Judah will be the LORD's special possession in the holy land, and he will
once again choose Jerusalem to be his own
city. 13 Be silent before the LORD, all humanity, for he is springing into action from his
holy dwelling."

Cleansing for the High Priest

3 Then the angel showed me Jeshua the
high priest standing before the [c]angel of
the LORD. The [d]Accuser, Satan, was there at
the angel's right hand, making accusations

God's Presence with His People (2:10-11)

Zech 1:16-17; 2:5; 4:6; 8:3, 23; 14:9; Gen 26:3; 31:3; Exod 3:12; Deut 31:23; Josh 1:5; Judg 6:16; Isa 7:14; 43:2; 52:8; Ezek 37:27; Joel 3:21; Hag 2:5; John 1:14

Zechariah was certain that God would once again live among his people and that the glory of the Lord would rest in Jerusalem (1:16; 2:5, 10-11; 8:3, 23). God's presence would return with the rebuilding of the Temple, and Israel would experience spiritual restoration and renewed agricultural bounty (1:17; 4:8-9; 6:15; Hag 2:19). In the future, God's presence would rescue Jerusalem and the people of Israel from enemy nations; the Lord would be enthroned as King over all the earth, and the whole earth would worship the one true God (9:16; 10:6; 12:9; 14:9). In both the present and the future, the return of the Lord's presence to Jerusalem was connected with the enabling work of God's Spirit (4:6; 12:10; Hag 2:5).

Zechariah's vision of the Lord's return to his people is the same message that was given by other OT prophets (see Isa 52:8; Joel 3:21). Zechariah's promise of the Lord's presence in Jerusalem anticipated the coming of Jesus the Messiah and the awesome mystery of the Word of God becoming human and living on earth among us (John 1:14).

2:5 The ***wall of fire*** represents divine protection (cp. 2 Kgs 6:17). • ***I, myself, will be:*** The emphatic construction of the verb "to be" might be a direct reference to God's name (Exod 3:14-15). • ***Fire*** and ***glory*** allude to the Exodus (see Exod 13:22, 14:20; 40:34).

2:6-13 God's call for the exiles' return from Babylon anticipated his people's restoration to the land of Israel (2:6-9) and the restoration of his presence to his people in Jerusalem (2:10-13).

2:6 ***Come away!*** The emphatic command carries the force of a promise that the Lord would lead his people out of exile and into a restored Jerusalem (cp. Isa 55:1). • ***the land of the north:*** It was necessary to travel north in order to move to the east, so Babylonia was thought of as lying in the north. • ***four winds:*** The Hebrew exiles would return to Judah and Jerusalem from all directions (see Ezek 12:14; 37:9).

2:8 ***After a period of glory, the LORD of Heaven's Armies sent me:*** The meaning of the Hebrew is uncertain. *Glory* possibly refers to God (see 2:5), who sent the prophet. • ***Anyone who harms you harms my most precious possession*** (literally *Anyone who touches you touches the pupil of his eye*): This might refer to Israel as God's elect; it might also mean that those who harmed Israel poked themselves in the eye by bringing God's judgment upon themselves.

2:9 ***their own slaves will plunder them:*** At the Exodus, the Egyptians paid the Israelites to leave their land (see Exod 11:2-3; 12:35-36).

2:10 ***O beautiful Jerusalem:*** Literally *O daughter of Zion.*

2:12 Israel is the Lord's inheritance or ***special possession***—the people of Israel belonged to the Lord (Deut 32:9-10). • The ***land*** was ***holy*** because of God's glorious presence in the Jerusalem Temple (see Ps 11:4; 15:1).

2:13 ***Be silent:*** The force of the Hebrew word (*has*) is similar to our English word "hush" (see Hab 2:20; Zeph 1:7).

3:1-10 The prophet's vision depicts a heavenly courtroom with the prosecuting attorney (Satan) accusing the defendant (Jeshua the high priest) of being unfit for his priestly duties.

3:1 ***Jeshua*** (Hebrew *Joshua,* a variant spelling of Jeshua; also in 3:3, 4, 6, 8, 9) was ***the high priest,*** the religious leader among those who returned to Judah from exile in Babylon (Ezra 2:2). Jeshua partnered with Zerubbabel, the governor of the restored community, in rebuilding the Jerusalem Temple (Ezra 5:2; Hag 2:1-5). • ***The Accuser, Satan*** (literally *The satan;* similarly in 3:2) designates a member of the heavenly court whose role is to accuse human beings of wrongdoing, to act

against Jeshua. 2And the LORD said to [e]Satan,
"I, the LORD, reject your accusations, [e]Satan.
Yes, the LORD, who has chosen Jerusalem, rebukes you. This man is like a burning stick
that has been snatched from the fire."
3Jeshua's clothing was filthy as he stood
there before the angel. 4So the angel said
to the others standing there, "Take off his
filthy clothes." And turning to Jeshua he said,
"See, I have taken away your sins, and now I
am giving you these fine new clothes."
5Then I said, "They should also place
a clean turban on his head." So they put
a clean priestly turban on his head and
dressed him in new clothes while the angel
of the LORD stood by.
6Then the angel of the LORD spoke very
solemnly to Jeshua and said, 7"This is what
the LORD of Heaven's Armies says: If you follow my ways and carefully serve me, then
you will be given authority over my Temple
and its courtyards. I will let you walk among
these others standing here.
8"Listen to me, O Jeshua the high priest,
and all you other priests. You are symbols
of things to come. Soon I am going to bring
my servant, the [f]Branch. 9Now look at the
jewel I have set before Jeshua, a single stone
with seven facets. I will engrave an inscription on it, says the LORD of Heaven's Armies,
and I will remove the sins of this land in a
single day.
10"And on that day, says the LORD of
Heaven's Armies, each of you will invite
your neighbor to sit with you peacefully under your own grapevine and fig tree."

A Lampstand and Two Olive Trees

4 Then the angel who had been talking
with me returned and woke me, as
though I had been asleep. 2"What do you see
now?" he asked.
I answered, "I see a solid gold lampstand
with a bowl of oil on top of it. Around the
bowl are seven lamps, each having seven
spouts with wicks. 3And I see two olive
trees, one on each side of the bowl." 4Then
I asked the angel, "What are these, my lord?
What do they mean?"
5"Don't you know?" the angel asked.
"No, my lord," I replied.
6Then he said to me, "This is what the
LORD says to Zerubbabel: It is not by force
nor by strength, but by my [g]Spirit, says
the LORD of Heaven's Armies. 7Nothing,
not even a mighty mountain, will stand in

3:2
[e]*satan* (7854)
‣1 Kgs 11:14
3:3
Ezra 9:15
3:4
Isa 43:25; 61:10
3:7
1 Kgs 3:14
Isa 62:9
3:8
Isa 4:2; 11:1; 53:2
Jer 33:15
Ezek 12:11
Zech 6:12
[f]*tsemakh* (6780)
‣Zech 6:12
3:9
Jer 31:34
Zech 4:10
3:10
1 Kgs 4:25
Mic 4:4
4:1
Zech 1:9
4:2
Exod 25:31, 37
Rev 4:5
4:3
Zech 4:11-12, 14
Rev 11:4
4:5
Zech 1:9
4:6
Isa 11:2-4
Hos 1:7
Hag 2:4-5
Eph 6:17
[g]*ruakh* (7307)
‣Gen 1:2

as prosecuting attorney (see Job 1:6). The adversarial role may be performed by either human or divine beings (see Num 22:22; 1 Sam 29:4; 1 Chr 21:1). By NT times, *Satan* was a personal name for the prince of demons (Mark 3:22; 2 Cor 4:4; Eph 6:11; Rev 20:2). • The Accuser's position of authority in the heavenly court is shown by his standing ***at the angel's right hand.***

3:2-3 *The LORD* is both defense attorney and judge; he censures the prosecution's arguments, dismisses the case, and declares Jeshua innocent because he has been chosen and cleansed by God. • ***Like a burning stick that has been snatched from the fire,*** Jeshua and other Hebrew exiles were plucked by God from near destruction in Babylon. • Jeshua's ***filthy clothes*** (3:3) symbolize the guilt and pollution of sin that prompted the divine judgment of exile. The ***accusations*** of ***Satan*** probably implied that just as a polluted priest was unfit for Temple service, the Hebrews were unfit to be God's chosen people.

3:4 *Take off his filthy clothes:* This action dramatizes the removal of sin and guilt from Jeshua and the Hebrew people, restoring them to their former position through God's cleansing.

3:5 The high priest's ***turban*** bore a gold medallion inscribed with the words "HOLY TO THE LORD" (Exod 28:36-38; see also note on 14:20). The ***clean turban*** was placed on Jeshua's head as an act of ordination that reinstated him as priest and mediator for the people.

3:6-7 Restoration was contingent upon obedience to God (see also Deut 30:19-20).

3:8 The high priest ***Jeshua*** and the ***other priests*** were ***symbols*** of greater realities. • ***Servant*** and ***Branch*** are both titles for the Messiah (Isa 42:1; 53:2; Jer 23:5; 33:15). As servant, the Messiah obeys God's will by becoming a sin offering so that many might be made righteous (Isa 53:11; see Acts 3:13; 4:27). The Branch is a metaphor for kingship that identifies the Messiah as David's descendant (Isa 11:1; Jer 23:5).

3:9 The ***single stone*** signifies authority. It might refer to the final stone of the Temple laid by Zerubbabel (4:7), the "foundation stone" of the restored Jerusalem (Isa 28:16), or the precious stones on the ephod of the high priests (Exod 25:7; 35:9). • The ***seven facets*** (literally *seven eyes*) of the stone imply perfection and completeness of knowledge and wisdom. They might relate to the seven lamps of the golden lampstand (4:2) or to God's "sevenfold Spirit" (Rev 1:4). • The ***inscription*** is reminiscent of the names of the tribes inscribed on the stones of the high priest's shoulder-pieces (Exod 39:6). • The removal of Israel's sin in a ***single day*** alludes to the Day of Atonement (Lev 16). It foreshadows Christ's crucifixion, when the Lamb of God would take away the sin of the world (John 1:29).

3:10 *That day* is shorthand for "the day of the Lord" (see 2:11; Isa 2:11; Joel 2:1; Zeph 1:14), the day of God's intervention in history when God will judge the wicked, deliver the righteous, and restore creation (see 12:8; 14:3-4).

4:1-14 This vision affirms that through his Spirit, God would enable Zerubbabel and Jeshua to rebuild the Temple.

4:1 *woke me:* The series of visions (1:7–6:8) came to Zechariah in a single night. The prophet slept briefly before this fifth vision.

4:2 *gold lampstand:* The golden menorah of the Tabernacle (Exod 25:31) was duplicated in the new Temple as a symbol of God's purity and holiness and the light of his revelation. • The ***two olive trees*** represent the offices of priest and king in Israel; they are emblems for Jeshua and Zerubbabel. The golden ***oil*** (see also 4:12-14) represents God's Holy Spirit.

4:6 Jeshua and Zerubbabel would have success in the rebuilding of the Jerusalem Temple, not by their own ***force*** or ***strength,*** but because of the presence of God's empowering ***Spirit*** (cp. Hag 2:4-5).

4:7 ***A mighty mountain . . . will become a level plain*** is a figure of speech in both OT (see Isa 40:4; 49:11) and NT

4:7 Ezra 3:11-13; Jer 51:25
4:9 Ezra 3:8-10; 5:16; Zech 6:12-15
4:10 Amos 7:2, 7-8; Hag 2:3; Zech 3:9; Rev 1:12
4:14 Zech 3:1-7; Rev 11:4
5:1 Jer 36:1-6; Ezek 2:9-10
5:3 Exod 20:15; Jer 26:6; Mal 3:8-9
5:4 Lev 14:34-45; Jer 2:26; Hos 4:2-3; Hab 2:9-11; Mal 3:5
5:5 Zech 1:9
5:6 Lev 19:36; Amos 8:5

Zerubbabel's way; it will become a level
plain before him! And when Zerubbabel
sets the final stone of the Temple in place,
the people will shout: 'May God bless it! May
God bless it!' "
8Then another message came to me from
the LORD: 9"Zerubbabel is the one who laid
the foundation of this Temple, and he will
complete it. Then you will know that the
LORD of Heaven's Armies has sent me. 10Do
not despise these small beginnings, for the
LORD rejoices to see the work begin, to see
the plumb line in Zerubbabel's hand."
(The seven lamps represent the eyes of
the LORD that search all around the world.)
11Then I asked the angel, "What are
these two olive trees on each side of the
lampstand, 12and what are the two olive
branches that pour out golden oil through
two gold tubes?"
13"Don't you know?" he asked.
"No, my lord," I replied.
14Then he said to me, "They represent the
two heavenly beings who stand in the court
of the Lord of all the earth."

A Flying Scroll

5 I looked up again and saw a scroll flying
through the air.
2"What do you see?" the angel asked.
"I see a flying scroll," I replied. "It appears
to be about 30 feet long and 15 feet wide."
3Then he said to me, "This scroll contains
the curse that is going out over the entire
land. One side of the scroll says that those
who steal will be banished from the land;
the other side says that those who swear
falsely will be banished from the land. 4And
this is what the LORD of Heaven's Armies
says: I am sending this curse into the house
of every thief and into the house of everyone who swears falsely using my name.
And my curse will remain in that house and
completely destroy it—even its timbers and
stones."

A Woman in a Basket

5Then the angel who was talking with me
came forward and said, "Look up and see
what's coming."
6"What is it?" I asked.

God's Commitment to His People (4:10)

Zech 2:13; 4:9; 14:3; 1 Sam 15:29; 2 Sam 7:28-29; 2 Chr 36:21; Isa 42:1-9; 49:15; John 14:1-4; 17:17; Acts 1:6-11; Titus 1:2; Rev 21:5

Zechariah told Zerubbabel not to "despise . . . small beginnings" (4:10). God had acted in the past for the ultimate good of his people, even in the Babylonian exile (7:12-14; see 14:3). God would accomplish his purposes for Israel's well-being in his own way and time. The people of Israel could take courage in the present and have hope for the future because God keeps his word and fulfills his promises (4:9).

All humanity should be silent before the Lord, "for he is springing into action from his holy dwelling" (2:13). God wants patience and faith from his people, not a strident voice. God kept his word and fulfilled the promises he made through Zechariah by sending Jesus the Messiah into the world to bring salvation for all people. Jesus' word, that he will one day return and fully establish his Kingdom, may also be trusted (Matt 24:27, 30; see Acts 1:6-11).

(see Matt 17:20; 1 Cor 13:2). Faith in God enables his servants to overcome seemingly impossible obstacles. • The capstone or headstone (*final stone*) completes a stone wall or building (see Ps 118:22). • *May God bless it!* (literally *'Grace, grace to it'*): This prayer seeks God's favor and blessing on the new Temple.

4:10 A *plumb line,* a cord with a tin or lead weight attached to one end, is used in construction to ensure that a wall is vertical. • *The seven lamps* (Or *The seven facets* [see 3:9]; literally *These seven*): *Seven* signifies completeness or perfection. God sees all that takes place on earth; he controls the fates of peoples and nations.

4:14 *two heavenly beings* (literally *two sons of [olive] oil,* who were anointed with oil as part of their commissioning): Under the leadership of Jeshua and Zerubbabel, the religious and civic leaders of Jerusalem after the return from exile (3:1, 7; 4:6-7; Hag 1:14; 2:2-3), the Temple of the Lord was rebuilt and worship was restored in Jerusalem.

5:1-4 Zechariah's vision of the flying scroll reminded the leaders and people of postexilic Judah that they were still obligated to follow God's commands. The blessings and curses of the law (Deut 28) were still in effect.

5:1 *looked up again:* This is the sixth of eight visions that Zechariah had in the same night. • A *scroll,* the equivalent of a book in biblical times, was usually made of rolled parchment or leather, but was sometimes of papyrus, tin, or copper. This scroll was *flying,* unfurled like a banner for all to see.

5:2 *30 feet long and 15 feet wide:* Hebrew *20 cubits* [9 meters] *long and 10 cubits* [4.5 meters] *wide.*

5:3 *curse* (or *oath*): A covenant included curses on violators of the agreement. (see Deut 29:12-21).

5:4 *This curse* is sent like a law officer to punish violations of God's covenant (see Ps 147:15; Isa 55:11).

5:5-11 The seventh vision continues the theme of cleansing that began with the acquittal of the high priest Jeshua (3:1-10). The removal of Wickedness, much like the removal of Jeshua's filthy garments (3:4), was a gracious act of pardon by the covenant-keeping God.

5:6 The *basket* (Hebrew *ephah*) was a standard unit of dry measure, approximately ½ bushel (20 quarts or 22 liters); also in 5:7. The OT prophets' condemnation of unjust ephahs creates a natural association between the ephah basket and evil (see Ezek 45:10; Mic 6:10). • *the sins:* As in Greek version; Hebrew reads *the appearance.*

He replied, "It is a basket for measuring grain, and it's filled with the sins of everyone throughout the land."

7Then the heavy lead cover was lifted off the basket, and there was a woman sitting inside it. 8The angel said, "The woman's name is Wickedness," and he pushed her back into the basket and closed the heavy lid again.

9Then I looked up and saw two women flying toward us, gliding on the wind. They had wings like a stork, and they picked up the basket and flew into the sky.

10"Where are they taking the basket?" I asked the angel.

11He replied, "To the land of Babylonia, where they will build a temple for the basket. And when the temple is ready, they will set the basket there on its pedestal."

Four Chariots

6 Then I looked up again and saw four chariots coming from between two bronze mountains. 2The first chariot was pulled by red horses, the second by black horses, 3the third by white horses, and the fourth by powerful dappled-gray horses. 4"And what are these, my lord?" I asked the angel who was talking with me.

5The angel replied, "These are the four spirits of heaven who stand before the Lord of all the earth. They are going out to do his work. 6The chariot with black horses is going north, the chariot with white horses is going west, and the chariot with dappled-gray horses is going south."

7The powerful horses were eager to set out to patrol the earth. And the LORD said, "Go and patrol the earth!" So they left at once on their patrol.

8Then the LORD summoned me and said, "Look, those who went north have vented the anger of my Spirit there in the land of the north."

The Crowning of Jeshua

9Then I received another message from the LORD: 10"Heldai, Tobijah, and Jedaiah will bring gifts of silver and gold from the Jews exiled in Babylon. As soon as they arrive, meet them at the home of Josiah son of Zephaniah. 11Accept their gifts, and make a crown from the silver and gold. Then put the crown on the head of Jeshua son of Jehozadak, the high priest. 12Tell him, 'This is what the LORD of Heaven's Armies says: Here is the man called the [h]Branch. He will branch out from where he is and build the

5:8 Hos 12:7; Mic 6:11
5:11 Gen 10:10; Isa 11:11; Dan 1:2
6:1 Zech 1:18; 6:5
6:2 Rev 6:4-5
6:3 Rev 6:2
6:5 Jer 49:36; Ezek 37:9; Dan 7:2; Rev 7:1
6:6 Ezek 1:4; Dan 11:5-6, 9, 40
6:8 Jer 1:14-15; Ezek 5:13; Zech 1:15
6:9 Zech 1:1; 7:1; 8:1
6:10 Ezra 7:14-16; 8:26-30
6:12 Isa 4:2-3; 11:1; Jer 23:5-6; Zech 3:8; 4:6-9; [h]*tsemakh* (6780) ›Isa 4:2
6:13 Ps 110:4; Isa 9:6; 11:10; *kisse'* (3678) ›2 Sam 7:13

5:7-8 The evil *woman* in a *basket* represents a seductive and dangerous force that is difficult to contain. The sin of idolatry had previously provoked God's judgment (2 Kgs 17:16-18; 2 Chr 36:14).

5:7 The ***heavy lead cover*** (literally *a talent* [seventy-five pounds] *of lead*) is not a natural cover for an ephah basket, but shows that extraordinary measures were needed to seal the basket's unholy contents.

5:8 *Wickedness* refers to evil generally; whether moral or ceremonial, it is opposed to righteousness (see Prov 13:6; Ezek 33:12). The word *wickedness* (Hebrew *rish'ah*) is similar in Hebrew to the name Asherah, the fertility goddess of the ancient Near East (see Deut 7:5; 16:21; Jer 44:17-25).

5:9 The depiction of divine or angelic winged creatures as women is unusual in the OT. If the *two women* are the Lord's servants, they are unique angels. If they are the attendants of Wickedness (a foreign goddess), their submission to God's command demonstrates his power over false gods.

5:11 Idolatry is potently and aggressively evil; it cannot be confined, but must be shipped back to its source (Babylonia) by God's decree. This symbolism indicates that God is able to purge his people of all the various forms of wickedness that separated them from him. • ***the land of Babylonia*** (Hebrew *the land of Shinar*) was the land of Hebrew captivity (Mic 4:10). The prophets condemn it as wicked and idolatrous (Isa 46–47; Jer 50–51). In the NT, Babylon represents the evil Roman empire (Rev 17:5; 18:2; see 1 Pet 5:13).

6:1-8 In Zechariah's first and last visions, God sends horses to patrol the earth. Both visions show God's sovereignty and his concern for the nations, a vital component of Zechariah's message of comfort and encouragement to postexilic Judah.

6:1 *Chariots* symbolize the swift and decisive power of God's intervention in human affairs. • The ***two bronze mountains*** are enhanced images of the two bronze pillars that once flanked the entrance to Solomon's Temple (1 Kgs 7:13-22). ***Bronze*** symbolizes the impregnable strength of God's dwelling.

6:2-3 *red . . . black . . . white . . . dappled-gray horses:* Zechariah attaches no particular significance to the colors of the horses in his vision (cp. Rev 6:1-8).

6:5 The ***four spirits*** (or ***the four winds***) ***of heaven*** are divine council members who report to God on their reconnaissance missions to the four compass points (see 2:6). The whole world is under God's dominion. The teams of chariot horses are agents of God's judgment.

6:6 *is going west:* Literally *is going after them.*

6:7 The teams of horses are portrayed as ***powerful*** and ***eager*** to do the Lord's work (6:5). They move only at the Lord's command (6:7).

6:8 *the LORD summoned me:* The series of visions closes with a direct word from the Lord to Zechariah. In bypassing the interpreting angel, God emphasizes the sure and effective implementation of his word to Israel. • ***have vented the anger of my Spirit*** (literally *have given my Spirit rest*): "Spirit" can mean "anger," as it does here (see Judg 8:3; Isa 33:11).

6:9-15 This authoritative message accompanies Zechariah's eighth vision (6:1-8). Jeshua's symbolic coronation as both king and priest was not an actual political arrangement for Judah; it probably symbolizes the coming of the Messiah, ***the Branch*** (6:12; cp. 3:8).

6:10 *Heldai, Tobijah, and Jedaiah* were apparently couriers designated by Jews in Babylon to carry donations to the Temple building fund.

6:11 This ***crown*** (as in Greek and Syriac versions; Hebrew reads *crowns*) was probably made of two bands of metal, one gold and one silver. Each band represented one of the offices (king and priest) to which ***Jeshua*** (Hebrew *Joshua,* a variant spelling of *Jeshua*) was appointed.

6:12-13 *The Branch* is a title for the Messiah (see 3:8), whom Jeshua

[i]*kohen* (3548)
‣Mal 2:7

6:15
Isa 56:6-8; 60:10
Zech 3:7
[k]*shama'* (8085)
‣Deut 4:30

7:2
Zech 8:21

7:3
Ezra 3:10-12

7:5
Isa 58:5
Zech 1:12
Matt 5:16; 6:2, 5, 16; 23:5

7:7
Jer 17:26; 22:21
Zech 1:4

7:9
Mic 6:8
Zech 8:16

Temple of the LORD. 13 Yes, he will build the Temple of the LORD. Then he will receive royal honor and will rule as king from his [i]throne. He will also serve as [j]priest from his [i]throne, and there will be perfect harmony between his two roles.'

14 "The crown will be a memorial in the Temple of the LORD to honor those who gave it—Heldai, Tobijah, Jedaiah, and Josiah son of Zephaniah."

15 People will come from distant lands to rebuild the Temple of the LORD. And when this happens, you will know that my messages have been from the LORD of Heaven's Armies. All this will happen if you [k]carefully [k]obey what the LORD your God says.

3. ZECHARIAH'S SERMONS (7:1–8:23)

A Call to Justice and Mercy

7 On December 7 of the fourth year of King Darius's reign, another message came to Zechariah from the LORD. 2 The people of Bethel had sent Sharezer and Regemmelech, along with their attendants, to seek the LORD's favor. 3 They were to ask this question of the prophets and the priests at the Temple of the LORD of Heaven's Armies: "Should we continue to mourn and fast each summer on the anniversary of the Temple's destruction, as we have done for so many years?"

4 The LORD of Heaven's Armies sent me this message in reply: 5 "Say to all your people and your priests, 'During these seventy years of exile, when you fasted and mourned in the summer and in early autumn, was it really for me that you were fasting? 6 And even now in your holy festivals, aren't you eating and drinking just to please yourselves? 7 Isn't this the same message the LORD proclaimed through the prophets in years past when Jerusalem and the towns of Judah were bustling with people, and the Negev and the foothills of Judah were well populated?' "

8 Then this message came to Zechariah from the LORD: 9 "This is what the LORD of Heaven's Armies says: Judge fairly, and show

---

represents. • ***he will build the Temple of the LORD:*** Just as Jeshua the high priest helped to build the Temple in Jerusalem (Ezra 3:1-2, 8-9; 5:2), Jesus the Messiah would build the eternal heavenly Temple through his death, burial, and resurrection (John 2:19-22; 4:23-24; Eph 2:19-22; Heb 8:1-2). • The Messiah would ***rule as king,*** a role associated with David and the tribe of Judah (2 Sam 7:12-16). • ***He will also serve as priest from his throne*** (or *There will be a priest by his throne*): The Messiah's priestly role is associated with Aaron and the tribe of Levi (Exod 29:44). • Jeshua's crown or crowns (see note on 6:11) represent his ***two roles.*** Melchizedek also fulfilled the double functions of priest and king (Gen 14:17-20), as does the Messiah (Ps 110:4; Heb 7:1-3, 15-17).

6:14 The symbolic ***crown*** that united kingship and priesthood was placed in the Temple as a ***memorial*** to the donors of gold and silver. It was also a permanent reminder of Jeshua's coronation as priest-king and a visual aid for priests in teaching this new development. • ***Heldai:*** As in Syriac version (compare 6:10); Hebrew reads *Helem.* • ***Josiah:*** As in Syriac version (compare 6:10); Hebrew reads *Hen.* Josiah was honored for his role as broker for the meeting between Zechariah and the three former exiles.

6:15 Exiled Jews in Babylon and other ***distant lands*** helped to rebuild the Temple; all Israel could identify with the structure.

7:1–8:23 These sermons provide a transition between the visions of the present (chs 1–6) and those of the near future (chs 9–11) and the more distant future (chs 12–14). Chapter 7 discusses fasting over past disasters; ch 8 focuses on feasting over future blessings.

7:1-14 Zechariah's sermons were prompted by delegates from Bethel who posed a practical question (7:2-3). Although Zechariah answered the question later (8:18-19), he responded first with rhetorical questions that focused on the people's self-centered motives (7:5-6). Zechariah then outlined God's expectations for Israel (7:8-10; see Jer 22:3) and recounted what had happened to those who disobeyed previously (7:11-14).

7:1 ***On December 7:*** Literally *On the fourth day of the ninth month, the month of Kislev,* of the ancient Hebrew lunar calendar. This event occurred on December 7, 518 BC; also see note on 1:1. • ***of the fourth year of King Darius's reign:*** The two sermons of chs 7–8 came almost two years after the visions of chs 1–6.

7:2 ***The people of Bethel had sent Sharezer and Regemmelech*** (Or *Bethel-sharezer had sent Regemmelech.* Or *The people had sent [a man named] Bethel-sharezer*): The exact meaning is uncertain. • ***to seek the LORD's favor*** (literally *to soften the face of the LORD*): They were asking God to grant a petition or to rule on a question. Their request was probably accompanied by a sacrifice or offering.

7:3 The delegation from Bethel posed a practical procedural ***question.*** • ***mourn and fast each summer on the anniversary of the Temple's destruction:*** Literally *mourn and fast in the fifth month.* The Temple had been destroyed in the fifth month of the ancient Hebrew lunar calendar (August 586 BC); see 2 Kgs 25:8.

7:4-7 Rather than answering the question right away, Zechariah first confronted his hearers with their selfish motives and hypocrisy. The most important issue was whether or not their heart's desire was really to please God and do his will; if not, it made no difference whether or not they kept a fast.

7:5 According to Jeremiah, ***seventy years of exile*** in Babylon (see Jer 25:11-12; 29:10) were to make up the Sabbath years of rest for the land that had gone unobserved for nearly 500 years (2 Chr 36:21; see Exod 23:10-11; Lev 26:34-35). • ***fasted and mourned in the summer and in early autumn:*** Literally *fasted and mourned in the fifth and seventh months.* The fifth month of the ancient Hebrew lunar calendar usually occurs within the months of July and August. The seventh month usually occurs within the months of September and October; both the Day of Atonement and the Festival of Shelters were celebrated in the seventh month. While the summer fast lamented the destruction of Solomon's Temple (7:3), the early autumn fast either commemorated the assassination of Gedaliah, governor of Judah (see 2 Kgs 25:22-25; Jer 41:1-3), or it was the Day of Atonement (Lev 23:26-32).

7:7 ***Isn't this the same message:*** E.g., see Isa 1:11-20; 58:3-7. • ***the foothills of Judah:*** Hebrew *the Shephelah.*

mercy and [a]kindness to one another. 10 Do
not oppress widows, orphans, foreigners,
and the poor. And do not scheme against
each other.
11 "Your ancestors refused to listen to
this message. They stubbornly turned away
and put their fingers in their ears to keep
from hearing. 12 They made their hearts as
hard as stone, so they could not hear the instructions or the messages that the LORD of
Heaven's Armies had sent them by his Spirit
through the earlier prophets. That is why
the LORD of Heaven's Armies was so angry
with them.
13 "Since they refused to listen when I
called to them, I would not listen when they
called to me, says the LORD of Heaven's Armies. 14 As with a whirlwind, I scattered
them among the distant nations, where
they lived as strangers. Their land became
so desolate that no one even traveled
through it. They turned their pleasant land
into a desert."

Promised Blessings for Jerusalem

8 Then another message came to me
from the LORD of Heaven's Armies:
2 "This is what the LORD of Heaven's Armies
says: My love for Mount Zion is passionate
and strong; I am consumed with passion for
Jerusalem!
3 "And now the LORD says: I am returning
to Mount Zion, and I will live in Jerusalem.
Then Jerusalem will be called the Faithful
City; the mountain of the LORD of Heaven's
Armies will be called the Holy Mountain.
4 "This is what the LORD of Heaven's
Armies says: Once again old men and
women will walk Jerusalem's streets with
their canes and will sit together in the city
squares. 5 And the streets of the city will be
filled with boys and girls at play.
6 "This is what the LORD of Heaven's Armies says: All this may seem impossible to
you now, a small remnant of God's people.
But is it impossible for me? says the LORD of
Heaven's Armies.
7 "This is what the LORD of Heaven's Armies says: You can be sure that I will [b]rescue
my people from the east and from the west.
8 I will bring them home again to live safely
in Jerusalem. They will be my people, and
I will be faithful and just toward them as
their God.
9 "This is what the LORD of Heaven's Armies says: Be strong and finish the task!
Ever since the laying of the foundation of
the Temple of the LORD of Heaven's Armies,

[a]*khesed* (2617) ‣ Exod 20:6

7:10 Exod 22:22; Deut 24:14-18; Prov 22:22-23; Zech 8:17

7:11 Ps 58:4-5; Jer 8:5; Acts 7:57

7:12 Neh 9:30; Jer 17:1; Ezek 3:9; Dan 9:11-12

7:13 Prov 1:24-28; Isa 1:15; Jer 11:10-14

7:14 Deut 28:64; Jer 12:10; 23:19; 44:6

8:3 Zech 2:10

8:4 Isa 65:20-22

8:5 Jer 30:19-20

8:6 Ps 118:23; Jer 32:17, 27

8:7 Ps 107:2-3; Isa 11:11; 43:5; Amos 9:14-15

[b]*yasha'* (3467) ‣ Exod 14:13

8:8 Ezek 37:28; Zech 2:11; 10:10

7:10 ***Widows, orphans, foreigners, and the poor*** often did not have access to the legal protection afforded the average citizen (cp. Deut 24:14, 17-18). Fasting and social justice should go hand in hand (see Isa 58:6-7).

7:11 ***Your ancestors refused to listen:*** They ignored God's commands (see Jer 11:10). • ***stubbornly turned away*** (or *set a defiant shoulder*): The idiom signifies haughty stubbornness (see Neh 9:29). • ***Put their fingers in their ears*** places full responsibility upon the people for their obstinacy (cp. Isa 6:10). The same expression is used of Pharaoh when he "became stubborn" (or "hardened his heart") against God and refused to release the Hebrews (Exod 8:32).

7:12 To make one's heart ***as hard as stone*** is to steel one's will against the will of God (see Jer 17:1; cp. Ezek 3:9). • ***Instructions*** (Hebrew *torah*) refer to God's laws and commands as taught and interpreted by the prophets.

7:14 ***As with a whirlwind, I scattered them:*** The scattering of the Hebrews among the nations was one of the curses for violating the Mosaic covenant (Deut 28:36-37, 64). • The ***pleasant land*** was the land of God's covenant promise (Ps 106:24; Jer 3:19). • ***Their land became . . . desolate*** through divine judgment on their covenant unfaithfulness and idolatry (Jer 12:10).

8:1-23 This section of Zechariah's sermons is connected to the previous one by the topics of fasting (questions posed in 7:2-7 are answered in 8:18-19) and the ethical demands of covenant relationship with the Lord (7:8-10; 8:16-17). The tone and message shift from admonition and judgment to exhortation and restoration. Fasting would change to feasting (8:19).

8:2 *Passion* (or *jealousy, zeal*) is a basic element of the OT concept of God (see also 1:14). God's passion identifies him as a personal deity, not an abstract natural force. God is passionate for his word and for the people of his covenant. His passion results in punishment for sin, restoration for repentance, and reward for the pursuit of righteousness.

8:3 ***I will live in Jerusalem:*** The great hope of the postexilic community was that the Lord would return to dwell among his people again (see 1:16-17; Hag 2:4-7; Ezek 48:35). • ***I am returning:*** God would return to Jerusalem not just because the Temple had been rebuilt but because the Hebrew community had been purified (ch 3). • Isaiah compared Jerusalem to a faithful woman who became a prostitute (Isa 1:21). Zechariah shared Isaiah's vision of Jerusalem's change into a ***Faithful City*** (or *city of truth*) again (Isa 1:26).

8:4-5 The images of ***old men and women*** walking and of ***boys and girls*** playing in the streets indicate repopulation and resumption of normal family life in the once decimated city of Jerusalem. The return of God's presence to his rebuilt Temple would bring peace and safety to the city's inhabitants (see Jer 33:10-11).

8:6 The OT portrays God as able to do the ***impossible*** and the miraculous—nothing is too hard for the God who made the heavens and the earth (Gen 18:14; Jer 32:17, 27; see also Matt 19:26).

8:7 ***from the east and from the west:*** This is an idiom meaning *from all the regions to which the Hebrews were dispersed* (compare Isa 43:5-6).

8:8 ***They will be my people, and I will be . . . their God:*** This adoption formula depicts the intimate bond between Israel and God in covenant relationship (see Exod 19:5-6; Jer 30:22; 31:33; Ezek 34:30-31; Hos 2:23).

8:9-13 This section highlights the reversal of Jerusalem's fortunes as the Temple was rebuilt (cp. 2 Chr 15:3-7). The exhortation to ***be strong*** (8:9, 13) is an *inclusio* (a set of rhetorical bookends) for the section.

8:9 ***Laying of the foundation*** refers to Zerubbabel's and Jeshua's initial work of rebuilding the Temple in 536 BC (Ezra

8:9 Ezra 5:1; 6:14; Hag 2:4
8:10 Isa 19:2; Amos 3:6; 9:4; Hag 1:6-11; 2:16-19
8:11 Isa 12:1
8:12 Gen 27:28
8:13 Ps 72:17; Jer 29:18; Dan 9:11; Zech 14:11
8:14 Jer 4:28; Ezek 24:14
8:15 Jer 29:11
8:16 *Eph 4:25
8:17 Zech 5:3-4; 7:10; Mal 3:5
8:19 Isa 12:1; Zech 7:3-5; 8:16; Luke 1:74-75; [c]*shalom* (7965) ‣Josh 9:15
8:20 Zech 2:11; 14:16

you have heard what the prophets have been
saying about completing the building. 10 Before the work on the Temple began, there
were no jobs and no money to hire people or
animals. No traveler was safe from the enemy, for there were enemies on all sides. I
had turned everyone against each other.
11 "But now I will not treat the remnant
of my people as I treated them before, says
the LORD of Heaven's Armies. 12 For I am
planting seeds of peace and prosperity
among you. The grapevines will be heavy
with fruit. The earth will produce its crops,
and the heavens will release the dew. Once
more I will cause the remnant in Judah and
Israel to inherit these blessings. 13 Among
the other nations, Judah and Israel became
symbols of a cursed nation. But no longer!
Now I will rescue you and make you both
a symbol and a source of blessing. So don't
be afraid. Be strong, and get on with rebuilding the Temple!
14 "For this is what the LORD of Heaven's
Armies says: I was determined to punish
you when your ancestors angered me, and
I did not change my mind, says the LORD
of Heaven's Armies. 15 But now I am determined to bless Jerusalem and the people of
Judah. So don't be afraid. 16 But this is what
you must do: Tell the truth to each other.
Render verdicts in your courts that are
just and that lead to peace. 17 Don't scheme
against each other. Stop your love of telling
lies that you swear are the truth. I hate all
these things, says the LORD."
18 Here is another message that came
to me from the LORD of Heaven's Armies.
19 "This is what the LORD of Heaven's Armies says: The traditional fasts and times
of mourning you have kept in early summer,
midsummer, autumn, and winter are now
ended. They will become festivals of joy
and celebration for the people of Judah. So
love truth and [c]peace.
20 "This is what the LORD of Heaven's
Armies says: People from nations and
cities around the world will travel to Jerusalem. 21 The people of one city will say to

God's Love for Jerusalem (1:14; 8:2)

Zech 8:15; 9:9; 11:6-12; 13:7, 9; 14:9, 16, 21; Deut 31:6-8; Isa 48:10-11; 52:5-10; Mal 3:3

Zechariah's emphasis on God's love for Jerusalem shows that God makes covenants and keeps them (1:14; 8:2, 15). God rules over the nations, and his love for the nation of Israel meant that he would save it and destroy its enemies (11:6-12). Our holy God will transform the created order and establish the long-awaited Kingdom of the Lord over all the earth (14:9). All the nations will worship the King, the Lord Almighty (14:9, 16, 21).

Zechariah presents the Messiah as a suffering shepherd (13:7) and a righteous king (9:9). The Messiah's ministry will redeem people who are loyal to God (13:9). This prediction was realized in the life of Jesus the Messiah, who announced that "the Kingdom of God has arrived among you" (Matt 12:28).

3:8-13). The Temple reconstruction project was quickly abandoned and was not resumed until *the prophets* Haggai and Zechariah prompted it sixteen years later (Ezra 5:1-2; Hag 1:1).

8:10 *enemies:* The neighboring peoples opposed the rebuilding of the Temple (Ezra 4). Later, enemies opposed Nehemiah's rebuilding of the wall around Jerusalem (Neh 4).

8:12 *Peace* (Hebrew *shalom*) is an important theme underlying Zechariah's message (8:10, 12, 16, 19). God's presence in the rebuilt Temple would bring peace to Judah (see Hag 2:6-9). Zechariah uses the agricultural cycle to represent God's blessing (see Hag 2:18-19), which would reverse the drought conditions that Haggai described (Hag 1:10). • The small community that returned to Judah from exile were called the *remnant* (see Hag 1:12, 14). Theologically, the remnant are a bridge between God's punishment and his promise of restoration (see Hag 1:12, 14).

8:14-15 *determined:* The repetition of this word emphasizes God's sovereignty in judging Israel's sin and then in blessing them.

8:16 God expects his people to act with integrity and justice (see Eph 4:25). • The *courts* (literally *the gates*): Legal proceedings were conducted at the gates of the city or Temple (see Deut 21:19; 25:7).

8:17 In Zechariah's time, the people of Judah were guilty of the same sins that brought about the Babylonian exile. Such behavior put God's plans for restoration in jeopardy (see 7:8-10; 8:16). • *I hate all these things:* God's hatred of evil (Ps 5:5; Prov 6:16-19) stems from his absolute holiness (Ps 5:4; 15:1; 24:3).

8:19 Here the Lord finally answers the question posed by the delegates from Bethel (7:2-3). • *in early summer, midsummer, autumn, and winter:* Literally *in the fourth, fifth, seventh, and tenth months.* The fourth month of the ancient Hebrew lunar calendar usually occurs within the months of June and July. The fifth month usually occurs within the months of July and August. The seventh month usually occurs within the months of September and October. The tenth month usually occurs within the months of December and January. The fast in early summer commemorated the breaching of Jerusalem's walls (2 Kgs 25:3-4; Jer 52:6-7). The midsummer fast lamented the burning of Solomon's Temple (2 Kgs 25:8-10; Jer 52:12-14). The fast in autumn marked the assassination of Gedaliah, governor of Jerusalem (2 Kgs 25:22-25; Jer 41:1-3) or the Day of Atonement (Lev 23:26-32). The fast in winter recalled the beginning of the siege of Jerusalem (2 Kgs 25:1; Jer 52:4). • The fasts will turn to feasts when God restores Israel and sets his glory among the nations (Isa 65:18-19).

the people of another, 'Come with us to Jerusalem to ask the LORD to bless us. Let's
worship the LORD of Heaven's Armies. I'm
determined to go.' 22 Many peoples and powerful nations will come to Jerusalem to seek
the LORD of Heaven's Armies and to ask for
his blessing.
23 "This is what the LORD of Heaven's
Armies says: In those days ten men from different nations and languages of the world
will clutch at the sleeve of one Jew. And they
will say, 'Please let us walk with you, for we
have heard that God is with you.'"

4. ZECHARIAH'S ORACLES (9:1–14:21)

First Oracle (9:1–11:17)

Judgment against Israel's Enemies

9 This is the message from the LORD against the land of Aram and the city of Damascus, for the eyes of humanity, including all the tribes of Israel, are on the LORD.

2 Doom is certain for Hamath,
near Damascus,
and for the cities of Tyre and Sidon,
though they are so clever.
3 Tyre has built a strong fortress
and has made silver and gold
as plentiful as dust in the streets!
4 But now the LORD will strip away Tyre's
possessions
and hurl its fortifications into the sea,
and it will be burned to the ground.
5 The city of Ashkelon will see Tyre fall
and will be filled with fear.
Gaza will shake with terror,
as will Ekron, for their hopes will be
dashed.
Gaza's king will be killed,
and Ashkelon will be deserted.
6 Foreigners will occupy the city of Ashdod.
I will destroy the pride of the Philistines.
7 I will grab the bloody meat from their
mouths
and snatch the detestable sacrifices
from their teeth.
Then the surviving Philistines will
worship our God
and become like a clan in Judah.
The Philistines of Ekron will join my
people,
as the ancient Jebusites once did.
8 I will guard my Temple
and protect it from invading armies.
I am watching closely to ensure
that no more foreign oppressors
overrun my people's land.

8:22 Isa 49:6, 22-23; 60:3-12
8:23 Isa 45:14; 60:14
9:1 Amos 1:1-5
9:2 Jer 49:23; Ezek 28:1-5
9:3 Josh 19:29
9:4 Isa 23:1-7; Ezek 27:32; 28:16, 18
9:8 Isa 52:1; 54:14

8:23 ***God is with you:*** God's presence restored the ideal of fellowship between God and human beings (Gen 3:8; Exod 24:9-11; 25:8; Isa 7:14; 57:15; Ezek 43:7; John 1:14).

9:1–14:21 The second part of Zechariah stands apart from the first in several ways. Zechariah 9–14 is distinctively apocalyptic, combining cryptic historical allusions with futuristic visions. The messages alternate between threats of judgment for other nations and promises of deliverance for Israel. The section contains no explicit references to Zechariah, but uses God's direct speech. The messages probably date from a later period in Zechariah's ministry.

9:1–11:17 ***This is the message:*** Literally *An Oracle: The message.* This is the *superscription* (introductory heading) for the entire section; it includes the technical term *message* (or *oracle, burden*), a prophetic pronouncement of judgment; the use of this word invests the message with divine authority. These messages can be related to events between Zechariah's time and the coming of Christ.

9:1-8 This encouraging message told the Judeans that they had nothing to fear from their three most prominent neighbors—Syria (*Aram*), the Phoenicians (*Tyre and Sidon*), and *the Philistines.* All three were rivals of Judah; they were always trying to take commercial and territorial advantage. God said that their efforts would be in vain.

9:1 The *land of Aram* (Hebrew *land of Hadrach*) was a city-state on the northern boundary of Israel, on the caravan route connecting Mesopotamia to the Mediterranean coast. Aram was sometimes an ally and sometimes an enemy to Israel and Judah. • ***Damascus***, the capital of Aram, was the northern boundary of the ideal Hebrew state (Ezek 47:16-18).

9:2 ***Hamath***, a fortress city on one of the southern trade routes from Asia Minor, was on the northern boundary of Israel (see Num 13:21; Josh 13:5). • The twin port cities of ***Tyre and Sidon*** were independent Phoenician kingdoms located on the Mediterranean coast north of Israel (modern-day Lebanon); they are often paired in biblical texts (e.g., Ezra 3:7; Joel 3:4; Luke 10:13-14). The cities were legendary for their maritime trade wealth, but OT prophets condemned their pride and oppressive policies and predicted their destruction (Isa 23; Ezek 26:3-14; Amos 1:9-10).

9:3-4 ***Strong fortress*** (Hebrew *matsor*) is a pun on the name of the city of Tyre (Hebrew *tsor*). This famed island fortress (Isa 23:4; Ezek 26:5) was captured and destroyed by Alexander the Great in 332 BC.

9:5-6 ***Ashkelon . . . Gaza . . . Ekron . . . Ashdod:*** These Philistine cities, located on the coastal plain of Israel, were defeated by David (2 Sam 5:17-25) but later regained some autonomy. The prophets Amos and Zephaniah pronounced similar judgments against the same four cities (Amos 1:6-8; Zeph 2:4-7).

9:6 ***foreigners:*** This Hebrew word occurs elsewhere only in Deut 23:2, where it refers to illegitimate children. Zechariah uses it to signify the Philistines' eventual loss of political and social identity.

9:7 ***bloody meat:*** The Philistines ate meat that had not been drained of blood and was therefore unclean (Gen 9:4; Lev 3:17; Acts 15:20). • ***Detestable sacrifices*** were despicable practices associated with idolatry. Here they suggest eating unclean foods (see Lev 11:2-23). • ***the surviving Philistines will worship our God:*** This anticipates Philip's ministry in the cities of the Philistine coastal plain (Acts 8:40). • ***like a clan in Judah:*** Literally *a leader in Judah.* • The ***Jebusites*** were a Canaanite group (see Gen 10:16; 1 Chr 1:14) living in and around Jerusalem. The city of Jebus (Jerusalem) was sacked and burned during the days of the judges (Judg 1:8); it was later recaptured by David, who made it the capital of his kingdom (2 Sam 5:6-10). The Jebusites were absorbed by the Israelites through intermarriage during David's reign (see 2 Sam 5:13).

9:9 Ps 97:6-8; Isa 9:6-7; 57:15; Jer 23:5-6; Zech 2:10; *Matt 21:5; *John 12:15
9:10 Ps 72:17; Isa 57:18-19; Mic 4:2-10; 5:4
9:11 Exod 24:8; Heb 10:29
9:12 Isa 61:7; Joel 3:16
9:13 Ps 45:3; Jer 51:20; Joel 3:6-8
9:14 Ps 18:14; Isa 27:13; 31:5
9:15 Zech 12:6
9:16 Isa 62:3

Zion's Coming King

9 Rejoice, O people of Zion!
Shout in triumph, O people of Jerusalem!
Look, your king is coming to you.
He is righteous and victorious,
yet he is humble, riding on a donkey—
riding on a donkey's colt.
10 I will remove the battle chariots from Israel
and the warhorses from Jerusalem.
I will destroy all the weapons used in battle,
and your king will bring peace to the nations.
His realm will stretch from sea to sea
and from the Euphrates River to the ends of the earth.
11 Because of the covenant I made with you,
sealed with blood,
I will free your prisoners
from death in a waterless dungeon.
12 Come back to the place of safety,
all you prisoners who still have hope!
I promise this very day
that I will repay two blessings for each of your troubles.
13 Judah is my bow,
and Israel is my arrow.
Jerusalem is my sword,
and like a warrior, I will brandish it
against the Greeks.
14 The LORD will appear above his people;
his arrows will fly like lightning!
The Sovereign LORD will sound the ram's horn
and attack like a whirlwind from the southern desert.
15 The LORD of Heaven's Armies will protect his people,
and they will defeat their enemies by hurling great stones.
They will shout in battle as though drunk with wine.
They will be filled with blood like a bowl,
drenched with blood like the corners of the altar.
16 On that day the LORD their God will rescue his people,
just as a shepherd rescues his sheep.
They will sparkle in his land
like jewels in a crown.
17 How wonderful and beautiful they will be!
The young men will thrive on abundant grain,
and the young women will flourish on new wine.

9:9-17 The second message of Zechariah's first oracle (chs 9–11) presents the juxtaposition of warfare and peace that has defined human history. Judah's coming deliverer-king will be victorious in battle, yet righteous and humble (9:9), and will bring peace to the nations in his universal reign (9:10).

9:9 ***O people of Zion!*** Literally *O daughter of Zion!* • ***Your king*** refers to a future king from David's line, described earlier as the Branch (3:8; 6:12-13). • ***and victorious:*** Literally *and is being vindicated.* • The ***donkey*** was a ***humble*** animal, and ***riding on a donkey*** signaled that its rider came in peace (see Matt 21:5; John 12:15).

9:10 As used here, ***Israel*** (literally *Ephraim,* referring to the northern kingdom of Israel; also in 9:13) stands in contrast to Judah, the southern kingdom. The pairing of ***Israel*** and ***Jerusalem*** signifies a reunited Israel and the regaining of the covenant land. • The kingdoms of Assyria, Babylonia, Persia, and Israel were established by military conquest. By contrast, the kingdom of the Messiah will dismantle the machinery of war and eradicate all arsenals of ***weapons*** (see Isa 2:4; 9:5; Mic 5:10-11; Joel 3:10). • The ***Euphrates River*** (literally *the river*) was the northern boundary of the Promised Land (Gen 15:18). • ***the ends of the earth*** (or *the end of the land*): The righteous king will establish universal peace.

9:11 The ***covenant . . . sealed with blood*** probably refers to the blood sacrifice that sealed the Mosaic covenant (Exod 24:8). • The ***prisoners*** were Jews still living as exiles in Mesopotamia after the Babylonian exile. The Jews who remained in Persia and Babylon were spiritual exiles because they lived outside the Promised Land of spiritual blessing and rest (see Deut 12:10). One of the Messiah's defining activities would be to free prisoners (Isa 61:1; Luke 4:17-22; Rom 7:6; Eph 4:8).

9:12 ***Come back to the place of safety:*** This is a call for the Jews still in Babylon to return to the land of Judah.

9:13 ***Jerusalem*** (Hebrew *Zion*): The Persians and ***the Greeks*** (literally *the sons of Javan*) were engaged in a power struggle in Zechariah's time. In the future, God would judge the Greeks (who could represent all Gentiles). Zechariah is possibly alluding to Daniel's vision (Dan 8:21-22).

9:14 ***appear above his people:*** Zechariah borrows the image of a winged sun disk that artists pictured as protectively hovering over the Persian king. The Lord will protect Israel, go before them in battle, and show them his power. • The ***ram's horn*** issues a summons (Num 10:2-3, 7-10; Isa 27:13) and declares God's presence and power (Exod 19:19; 20:18). • The ***whirlwind*** depicts God as a warrior of devastating power and unpredictable swiftness (Ps 77:18; Isa 21:1; 29:6; 66:15). References to ***lightning*** bring Mount Sinai to mind (Exod 19:16) and with it God's covenant promises to Israel.

9:15 In ancient battles, ***great stones*** (literally *sling-stones*) were hurled at defenders on city walls and catapulted onto the inhabitants inside. The Maccabees' triumph over the Hellenistic Greeks in the 100s BC might have partially fulfilled Zechariah's prophecy of Israel's defeat of the Greeks (see *1 Maccabees* 3:16-24; 4:6-16; 7:40-50). • ***They will be filled with blood . . . drenched with blood:*** When the Lord unleashes his armies against the Greeks, the amount of bloodshed will be vast. • ***like a bowl:*** Ceremonial sprinkling bowls filled with animal blood were used in the rituals of sacrifice. This image almost suggests that the vanquishing of the Lord's enemies is in some sense an offering to him (see Exod 24:6; Lev 1:5; 16:18).

9:16 ***On that day:*** See note on 3:10. • The OT prophets portrayed the Messiah as a king and as a faithful ***shepherd*** (see Ezek 34:12, 16, 23; 37:24; John 10:1; Heb 13:20; 1 Pet 5:4).

9:17 ***abundant grain . . . new wine:*** Agricultural prosperity was a tangible sign of God's blessing (see Joel 2:19; Amos 9:13; cp. Hag 1:11).

The Lord Will Restore His People

10 1 Ask the Lord for rain in the spring,
for he makes the storm clouds.
And he will send showers of rain
so every field becomes a lush
pasture.
2 Household gods give worthless advice,
fortune-tellers predict only lies,
and interpreters of dreams pronounce
falsehoods that give no comfort.
So my people are wandering like lost
sheep;
they are attacked because they have
no shepherd.
3 "My anger burns against your
shepherds,
and I will punish these leaders.
For the Lord of Heaven's Armies has
arrived
to look after Judah, his flock.
He will make them strong and glorious,
like a proud warhorse in battle.
4 From Judah will come the cornerstone,
the tent peg,
the bow for battle,
and all the rulers.
5 They will be like mighty warriors in
battle,
trampling their enemies in the mud
under their feet.
Since the Lord is with them as they
fight,
they will overthrow even the enemy's
horsemen.
6 "I will strengthen Judah and save Israel;
I will restore them because of my
[d]compassion.
It will be as though I had never rejected
them,
for I am the Lord their God, who will
hear their cries.
7 The people of Israel will become like
mighty warriors,
and their hearts will be made happy
as if by wine.
Their children, too, will see it and be
glad;
their hearts will rejoice in the Lord.
8 When I whistle to them, they will come
running,
for I have redeemed them.
From the few who are left,
they will grow as numerous as they
were before.
9 Though I have scattered them like seeds
among the nations,
they will still remember me in distant
lands.
They and their children will survive
and return again to Israel.
10 I will bring them back from Egypt
and gather them from Assyria.
I will resettle them in Gilead and
Lebanon
until there is no more room for them
all.
11 They will pass safely through the sea of
distress,

10:1 Jer 10:13; Hos 6:3; Joel 2:23-24
10:2 Ezek 34:5, 8; Mic 3:6-11; Matt 9:36; Mark 6:34
10:3 Ezek 34:2, 7, 12
10:5 2 Sam 22:43
10:6 Isa 54:8; [d]*rakham* (7355) ‣ Exod 33:19
10:8 Isa 5:26; 7:18-19; Jer 33:22; Ezek 36:11
10:9 1 Kgs 8:47-48; Ezek 6:9
10:10 Isa 11:11-16; 49:19-21
10:11 Isa 19:5-7; Ezek 30:13; Zeph 2:13

10:1–11:3 God will strengthen his people by his power and restore them because of his compassion (10:6, 12). With its references to shepherds (10:2-3; 11:3), the passage prepares for the following allegory of the good and evil shepherds (11:4-17).

10:1-3 This is a rebuke of false ***shepherds,*** human leaders who do not have their people's good at heart.

10:1 ***Rain*** was a sign of divine blessing (see Joel 2:23)—***the Lord*** was the source of the rain, but Israel's leaders had led the people to trust in false gods instead.

10:2 ***Household gods*** might refer to ancestor statues used in rituals of necromancy (conjuring up the spirits of the dead); consultation with the dead was a widespread practice in the ancient world, but God's law made it taboo for the Hebrews (see Lev 20:27; Deut 18:10-11).

10:3 ***My anger burns:*** Israel is often the object of this divine wrath, incited by disobedience to covenant stipulations or by lapses into idolatry (see Exod 22:22-24; Deut 6:14-15; Josh 7:1; Judg 2:20; Heb 10:31). • ***these leaders*** (or *these male goats*): This is a figure of speech for princes, since male goats typically lead goat herds.

10:4-12 A true shepherd is promised.

10:4 A ***cornerstone*** is the first-laid foundation stone upon which a building's superstructure rests (see Job 38:6; Ps 118:22; Isa 28:16; Eph 2:20). • Just as a ***tent peg*** anchors a tent to the ground, so Judah will provide the future leaders needed to stabilize the Hebrew nation. • Many understand cornerstone, tent peg, and ***bow for battle*** as titles for the Messiah (cp. Isa 22:20-23; Zech 9:13).

10:6 ***save:*** This Hebrew word is also used for the exodus from Egypt (see Exod 14:30). Salvation and victory come from God (Ps 3:8; Isa 63:1). • ***Israel:*** Literally *the house of Joseph.* • God saves and restores his people Israel because of his ***compassion*** (see Exod 33:19; Ps 103:13; 111:4; Lam 3:32).

10:7 ***of Israel:*** Literally *of Ephraim.*

10:8 ***When I whistle to them:*** Shepherds in biblical times herded their flocks by whistling or piping to them (see Judg 5:16). • ***Redeemed*** can also mean "ransomed"—buying slaves out of their servitude or indentured status (see Deut 15:15; 24:18). • ***numerous as . . . before:*** The proliferation of the Hebrew people was one of God's covenant promises to Abraham (Gen 12:1-3; 22:17; 32:12).

10:10 The Lord had previously whistled for the armies of ***Egypt*** and ***Assyria*** to come against King Ahaz of Judah because of his unbelief (Isa 7:18). The two nations were especially symbolic of the slavery and exile endured by the Hebrews. • ***Gilead*** is a fertile region east of the Jordan River and south of the Sea of Galilee that is suitable for grain growing and pasturing; it was settled by the tribes of Manasseh and Gad. • ***Lebanon*** sometimes defined the northern edge of the Promised Land (see Deut 11:24; Josh 1:4). God's restoration and resettlement of the Hebrews would be so complete that even the fringe areas of Israelite territory would teem with people.

10:11 ***the sea of distress*** (Or *the sea of Egypt,* referring to the Red Sea): When the Hebrews returned to the land of

10:12 Mic 4:5
11:3 Jer 2:15; 25:34-36; 50:44
11:5 Jer 50:7; Ezek 34:2-6; Hos 12:8; 1 Tim 6:9
11:6 Isa 9:19-21; Jer 13:14; Zech 8:10; 14:13
11:7 Ps 90:17; 133:1; Ezek 37:16-23
11:9 Ps 69:22-28; Jer 15:2-3
11:10 Jer 14:21

for the waves of the sea will be held
back,
and the waters of the Nile will dry up.
The pride of Assyria will be crushed,
and the rule of Egypt will end.
12 By my power I will make my people strong,
and by my authority they will go
wherever they wish.
I, the LORD, have spoken!"

11 1 Open your doors, Lebanon,
so that fire may devour your
cedar forests.
2 Weep, you cypress trees, for all the
ruined cedars;
the most majestic ones have fallen.
Weep, you oaks of Bashan,
for the thick forests have been cut
down.
3 Listen to the wailing of the shepherds,
for their rich pastures are destroyed.
Hear the young lions roaring,
for their thickets in the Jordan Valley
are ruined.

The Good and Evil Shepherds

4 This is what the LORD my God says: "Go
and care for the flock that is intended for
slaughter. 5 The buyers slaughter their sheep
without remorse. The sellers say, 'Praise the
LORD! Now I'm rich!' Even the shepherds
have no compassion for them. 6 Likewise,
I will no longer have pity on the people of
the land," says the LORD. "I will let them fall
into each other's hands and into the hands
of their king. They will turn the land into a
wilderness, and I will not rescue them."

7 So I cared for the flock intended for
slaughter—the flock that was oppressed.
Then I took two shepherd's staffs and
named one Favor and the other Union. 8 I
got rid of their three evil shepherds in a single month.

But I became impatient with these sheep,
and they hated me, too. 9 So I told them, "I
won't be your shepherd any longer. If you
die, you die. If you are killed, you are killed.
And let those who remain devour each
other!"

10 Then I took my staff called Favor and
cut it in two, showing that I had revoked the
covenant I had made with all the nations.
11 That was the end of my covenant with
them. The suffering flock was watching me,
and they knew that the LORD was speaking
through my actions.

Israel from exile in Babylon, they had to ford the Euphrates River; this is likened to a second exodus from Egypt (see Isa 43:2-6, 16-17), which would have included crossing ***the Nile*** River.

10:12 This verse repeats the earlier promise that God would strengthen his ***people*** (10:6; see Isa 41:8-10; cp. Ps 18:1; 22:19; 28:8; 29:11). • ***By my power:*** Literally *In the LORD.*

11:1-3 This taunt song against Lebanon and Bashan concludes the preceding message of deliverance and restoration for Israel (10:1-12); it could also introduce the following message about good and evil shepherds (11:4-17).

11:1 ***Lebanon,*** boasting snow-covered mountains and fruitful valleys, was a symbol of strength and fertility.

11:2 Like Lebanon, ***Bashan*** had superb stands of timber. Lebanon and Bashan are often paired (Isa 2:13; Jer 22:20-22; Ezek 27:5-6) in representing nations that God would judge when he would regather and restore the people of Israel (see 10:11).

11:3 ***Shepherds*** and ***lions*** figuratively represent the leaders of Lebanon and Bashan, lamenting the destruction of their forested slopes, their pride, and their livelihood (see 11:1-2).

11:4-17 The metaphor of the Hebrew leaders as shepherds binds together the last three messages (9:9–11:17) of Zechariah's first oracle (chs 9–11). This message combines allegory with symbolic action on Zechariah's part to dramatize the wickedness of Israel's shepherds. The prophet acts out a parable of a "good shepherd" called by God to lead and unite his people, but the people rejected this shepherd and with it the promise of protection from the nations (11:10) and unity between Judah and Israel (11:14). Zechariah's symbolic actions foreshadow the ministry of Jesus the Messiah as the Good Shepherd (see John 10:1-21).

11:4 The people of Israel are God's ***flock*** (see Isa 40:11; Mic 5:4). The relative helplessness of sheep places a premium on their careful shepherding. • ***intended for slaughter:*** Like sheep fattened for butchering, the people are being treated as disposable goods in a corrupt economy.

11:5 The sheep (the Hebrew people) were being sold as slaves to ***buyers***—occupying foreign powers, foreign allies, or domestic slave-traders (see Amos 2:6). • The ***sellers*** were the shepherds, leaders of the people who were more concerned with getting ***rich*** than with the well-being of the sheep.

11:7 ***Shepherd's staffs*** symbolize leadership and authority. • ***Favor:*** This staff symbolized God's choice of Israel as his people (see Gen 12:1-3) and the promise of a leader like King David (see 2 Sam 7:12-16). • ***Union:*** Ezekiel's staff (Ezek 37:16-17) represented the unity of the Hebrew tribes as a single nation during King David's reign (2 Sam 5:1-3).

11:8 The enigmatic historical reference to ***three evil shepherds*** has prompted more than forty different attempts to identify them. None of these explanations is effective. *Three* symbolizes completeness. God raises up good shepherds to remove evil shepherds for the well-being of his people.

11:9 ***devour each other!*** This might refer literally to the cannibalism that resulted from famine during the siege of Jerusalem in 588–586 BC (see Lam 4:10) and later in AD 70 (see Josephus, *War* 7.4.4). The expression may also be a metaphor for various forms of exploitation and oppression (see Mic 3:3; Gal 5:15).

11:10 Unlike Ezekiel, who dramatized the reunification of the Hebrew kingdoms (Ezek 37:15-19), Zechariah dramatized the division by cutting the staffs ***in two*** (see also 11:14). The cutting of the staffs indicated the broken covenant bond between God and his people (11:11) and the bond of unity between the kingdoms of Judah and Israel (11:14). • A ***covenant*** between the Lord and ***all the nations*** is otherwise unknown. Zechariah might actually have been proclaiming the dissolution of the covenant binding Israel to God as his people (see Hos 1:6-9).

12And I said to them, "If you like, give me
my wages, whatever I am worth; but only
if you want to." So they counted out for my
wages thirty pieces of silver.
13And the LORD said to me, "Throw it to
the potter"—this magnificent sum at which
they valued me! So I took the thirty coins
and threw them to the potter in the Temple
of the LORD.
14Then I took my other staff, Union,
and cut it in two, showing that the bond
of unity between Judah and Israel was broken.
15Then the LORD said to me, "Go again
and play the part of a worthless shepherd.
16This illustrates how I will give this nation
a shepherd who will not care for those
who are dying, nor look after the young,
nor heal the injured, nor feed the healthy.
Instead, this shepherd will eat the meat of
the fattest sheep and tear off their hooves.

17 "What sorrow awaits this worthless
shepherd
who abandons the flock!
The sword will cut his arm
and pierce his right eye.
His arm will become useless,
and his right eye completely
blind."

Second Oracle (12:1–14:21)

Future Deliverance for Jerusalem

12 This message concerning the fate
of Israel came from the LORD: "This
message is from the LORD, who stretched
out the heavens, laid the foundations of the
earth, and formed the human spirit. 2I will
make Jerusalem like an intoxicating drink
that makes the nearby nations stagger when
they send their armies to besiege Jerusalem
and Judah. 3On that day I will make Jerusalem an immovable rock. All the nations will
gather against it to try to move it, but they
will only hurt themselves.
4"On that day," says the LORD, "I will cause
every horse to panic and every rider to lose
his nerve. I will watch over the people of Judah, but I will blind all the horses of their
enemies. 5And the clans of Judah will say to
themselves, 'The people of Jerusalem have
found strength in the LORD of Heaven's Armies, their God.'
6"On that day I will make the clans of Judah like a flame that sets a woodpile ablaze
or like a burning torch among sheaves of
grain. They will burn up all the neighboring
nations right and left, while the people living in Jerusalem remain secure.
7"The LORD will give victory to the rest
of Judah first, before Jerusalem, so that the

11:12-13 *Matt 27:9-10; Acts 1:18-19
11:14 Zech 11:6
11:15 Zech 11:17
11:16 Jer 23:2, 22; Ezek 34:2-6
11:17 Zech 10:2; 11:15
12:1 Job 26:7; Jer 51:15; Heb 1:10-12
12:2 Ps 75:8; Isa 51:17, 22-23
12:3 Dan 2:34-35, 44-45; Matt 21:44
12:6 Isa 10:16-18; Obad 1:18
12:7 Amos 9:11

11:12 ***Thirty pieces of silver*** was the price of a slave (see Exod 21:32). In the allegory, the silver was severance pay for the shepherd (11:9). The Gospel writers find the fulfillment of this passage in the betrayal of Jesus for thirty silver coins by Judas (see Matt 26:15; 27:9-10).

11:13 ***to the potter*** (Syriac version reads *into the treasury;* cp. Matt 27:6-10): Some scholars speculate that a guild of potters might have been minor Temple officials due to the continual need for sacred vessels (see Lev 6:28). Others, noting the similarity between *potter* (Hebrew *yotser*) and *treasury* (*'otsar*), follow the Syriac version (see Matt 27:6, 10; Jer 32:6-9). The Greek OT translates this sentence as "throw it into the furnace," suggesting that the silver was melted down and recast into a silver vessel for use in Temple rituals. • ***Thirty coins*** (or *pieces of silver*) was a ***magnificent sum*** of money (nearly two years' wages for the average laborer).

11:15 The ***worthless shepherd*** represents corrupt leaders, in contrast with the good shepherd (cp. Ezek 34:7-16).

11:16 ***the young:*** Or *the scattered.* • ***Tear off their hooves*** is a Hebrew idiom for a wanton and ravenous search for the last morsel of edible meat on an animal carcass (see Mic 3:3).

11:17 This oracle of woe is a poetic curse against the worthless shepherd for abandoning the flock. The ***arm*** and ***right eye*** represent the physical and mental abilities of the shepherd. The maimed arm and blind eye make the worthless shepherd powerless and end his selfish, opportunistic rule.

12:1–14:21 The theme of Jerusalem versus the nations binds the four messages of Zechariah's second oracle together; the nations are gathered against Jerusalem at the beginning (12:1-9) and the end (14:1-15) of the oracle. Through the repetition of the phrase ***on that day***, the oracle looks to the future day of the Lord. The picture it presents mixes judgment with blessing for Jerusalem. The oracle's focal point is the cleansing of the people of Israel (13:1); it culminates with God's universal Kingdom (14:16-21). These visions of the future encouraged the Judeans of Zechariah's day to be faithful in spite of their seeming insignificance and helplessness.

12:1 ***This:*** Literally *An Oracle: This.*

12:2 ***intoxicating drink*** (literally *bowl of reeling* or *cup of staggering*): The cup of alcoholic drink is a metaphor for God's judgment (Isa 51:17; Jer 25:15; Hab 2:16; Matt 26:39, 42; Rev 14:10; 16:1). Jerusalem would be instrumental in God's judgment on ***the nearby nations.***

12:3 Jerusalem will be ***an immovable rock*** that cuts and gashes those who attempt to conquer and control it, because the city was founded by the Lord, who loves it more than any other city of Israel (Ps 87:1-2). In Zechariah, imagery involving a stone is associated with the Temple (3:9; 4:7; 10:4).

12:4 Madness, blindness, and ***panic*** were among the curses threatened against Israel for covenant disobedience (Deut 28:28). The day of the Lord will witness a reversal as these curses are turned against Israel's enemies (see 2 Kgs 7:6-7). • ***watch over*** (literally *open my eyes*): The open eyes of God represent divine provision for those in desperate need (see Gen 16:13-14; 21:19-21).

12:5 ***the LORD of Heaven's Armies:*** This title emphasizes God's irrepressible power (see the note on 1:3). The frequent repetition of this title in Zechariah's second oracle (chs 12–14) assured his audience that the divine promises concerning Judah's victory would certainly be fulfilled (12:7).

12:6 ***flame*** (literally *fire pan*): Bronze or gold fire pans were used to carry hot coals to and from the sacrificial altars of the Tabernacle and the Temple (Exod 27:3; 1 Kgs 7:50). God would set Israel among the nations like a burning firepan to destroy or purify them.

12:8 Exod 14:19; Lev 26:8; Ps 82:6; Mic 7:8; Zech 9:14-15; [e]*mal'ak* (4397) ‣Gen 16:7
12:10 Isa 53:5; Joel 2:28-29; John 19:34-37; Rev 1:7
12:11 Matt 24:30
13:1 Num 19:9-22; Ps 51:2, 7
13:2 Exod 23:13; 1 Kgs 22:22; Hos 2:17
13:3 Deut 13:6-11; Jer 23:25
13:4 2 Kgs 1:8; Mic 3:6-7; Matt 3:4

people of Jerusalem and the royal line of
David will not have greater honor than the
rest of Judah. 8On that day the LORD will defend the people of Jerusalem; the weakest
among them will be as mighty as King David! And the royal descendants will be like
God, like the [e]angel of the LORD who goes
before them! 9For on that day I will begin
to destroy all the nations that come against
Jerusalem.
10"Then I will pour out a spirit of grace
and prayer on the family of David and on
the people of Jerusalem. They will look on
me whom they have pierced and mourn
for him as for an only son. They will grieve
bitterly for him as for a firstborn son who
has died. 11The sorrow and mourning in
Jerusalem on that day will be like the great
mourning for Hadad-rimmon in the valley
of Megiddo.
12"All Israel will mourn, each clan by itself, and with the husbands separate from
their wives. The clan of David will mourn
alone, as will the clan of Nathan, 13the clan
of Levi, and the clan of Shimei. 14Each of
the surviving clans from Judah will mourn
separately, and with the husbands separate
from their wives.

A Fountain of Cleansing

13 "On that day a fountain will be opened
for the dynasty of David and for the
people of Jerusalem, a fountain to cleanse
them from all their sins and impurity.
2"And on that day," says the LORD of
Heaven's Armies, "I will erase idol worship
throughout the land, so that even the names
of the idols will be forgotten. I will remove
from the land both the false prophets and
the spirit of impurity that came with them.
3If anyone continues to prophesy, his own father and mother will tell him, 'You must die,
for you have prophesied lies in the name of
the LORD.' And as he prophesies, his own father and mother will stab him.
4"On that day people will be ashamed to
claim the prophetic gift. No one will pretend to be a prophet by wearing prophet's

---

12:8 ***The angel of the LORD*** is God, represented as a Divine Warrior, rescuer, and protector (see 1:11; 3:1; Exod 14:19; 15:3; Isa 59:15b-20; 63:1-6). By divine enabling, the weak will be imbued with God's power.

12:10 ***pour out:*** This word describes the outpouring of God's spirit of prophecy upon Israel and all people on the day of the Lord (cp. Joel 2:28-29; Ezek 39:28-29) and God's judgment upon the wicked (Lam 2:4; Hos 5:10; Zeph 3:8). • ***a spirit*** (Or *the Spirit*) ***of grace:*** God's unmerited and unsought favor persuades God's people to seek him in contrite and repentant ***prayer*** (see Ps 86:15-16). • ***me whom they have pierced:*** The NT understands the piercing of God as a reference to the piercing of the Messiah, Jesus of Nazareth (John 19:34-37; Rev 1:7).

12:11 The name ***Hadad-rimmon*** combines the names of two Syrian deities, the storm-god Hadad and the thunder-god Rimmon. The ***great mourning*** for these gods may be similar to the weeping for Tammuz, one of the rituals practiced in the Mesopotamian fertility cults. • Joshua captured ***Megiddo*** (Josh 12:21), a major city on the southwest edge of the Jezreel Valley; it was allotted to the tribe of Manasseh (Josh 17:11). Megiddo controlled a key pass on the great highway from Egypt to Mesopotamia, and so was of great strategic importance. It was a district capital during Solomon's reign (1 Kgs 4:12). King Josiah was mortally wounded in a battle against Pharaoh Neco and the Egyptians on the plain of Megiddo (2 Chr 35:22-23), and the mountain of Megiddo is the site of the great battle depicted in Rev 16:16.

12:12-14 ***The clan of David . . . Nathan . . . Levi, and . . . Shimei:*** Zechariah might be referring to the royal families (David and his son Nathan; see 1 Chr 14:4) and the priestly families (Levi and his grandson Shimei; see Num 3:16-18; 1 Chr 6:16-17). Alternatively, the four families might represent the four principal classes of leadership in OT times: the king (David, 1 Sam 16:1-13; the prophet (Nathan, 2 Sam 7:2), the priest (Levi, Deut 33:8-11), and the tribal leader (Shimei, 1 Kgs 1:8; 4:18). The first interpretation correlates with Zechariah's emphasis on the Branch that will be both king and priest (see 6:12-13). • ***each clan by itself:*** This separation depicts the depth and totality of Israel's mourning.

13:1-6 The second message (13:1-6) of the second oracle (chs 12–14) focuses on cleansing from sin.

13:1 A ***fountain*** is a spring of pure, flowing water for cleansing and purification (see 14:8; John 4:14; Rev 22:1-2). • God's cleansing of Israel will include leaders (represented by the ***dynasty of David***) and all the people of Judah and Israel (signified by ***the people of Jerusalem***, the spiritual center of the nation). • ***to cleanse them:*** This cleansing, symbolized in the ritual washings of OT worship (see Exod 30:17-21), was provided in the new covenant as promised by Jeremiah (Jer 31:34) and Ezekiel (Ezek 36:25; see Heb 10:1-22). • ***all their sins and impurity:*** The Hebrews would experience a complete moral and spiritual cleansing because of their sorrow over their sin (Zech 12:10-14).

13:2 By cleansing Israel, God would ***erase*** their former penchant for ***idol worship***, giving them a new heart and enabling them to worship God alone (Jer 31:33; 32:38-40; Ezek 36:25-28). • In the biblical world, one's name embodied one's existence. When ***the names of the idols*** are ***forgotten***, they cease to exist. • The ***false prophets*** misrepresented God by fabricating divine revelations or by speaking in the name of other gods (Deut 13:5-11; 18:17-22). They led Israel astray by encouraging idol worship (Jer 23:13, 25) and would continue to do so (see Neh 6:12-14; Mark 13:22; 2 Pet 2:1; 1 John 4:1-3) until ***that day***, the day of the Lord.

13:3 ***You must die:*** According to God's law, a false prophet must be executed (Deut 13:5, 10; 18:20). The Israelites had tolerated false prophets and killed the Lord's true prophets. In the future, the situation would be reversed.

13:4-6 God's total cleansing of his people from their impurities will strike such fear among the people that false prophets will deny or conceal their identity, even lying about the nature and purpose of their activities that might be associated with the prophets of idolatrous cults.

13:4 ***ashamed to claim the prophetic gift*** (literally *ashamed of his vision*): The OT prophet was sometimes identified as a visionary "seer" (see 1 Sam 9:9-19; 2 Kgs 17:13), since divine revelation often came to them in dreams or night

clothes. 5He will say, 'I'm no prophet; I'm
a farmer. I began working for a farmer as
a boy.' 6And if someone asks, 'Then what
about those wounds on your chest?' he will
say, 'I was wounded at my friends' house!'

The Scattering of the Sheep

7 "Awake, O sword, against my [f]shepherd,
the man who is my partner,"
says the LORD of Heaven's Armies.
"Strike down the [f]shepherd,
and the sheep will be scattered,
and I will turn against the lambs.
8 Two-thirds of the people in the land
will be cut off and die," says the LORD.
"But one-third will be left in the land.
9 I will bring that group through the fire
and make them pure.
I will refine them like silver
and purify them like gold.
They will call on my name,
and I will answer them.
I will say, 'These are my people,'
and they will say, 'The LORD is our
God.'"

The LORD Will Rule the Earth

14 Watch, for the day of the LORD is
coming when your possessions will
be plundered right in front of you! 2I will
gather all the nations to fight against Jerusalem. The city will be taken, the houses
looted, and the women raped. Half the population will be taken into captivity, and the
rest will be left among the ruins of the city.
3Then the LORD will go out to fight
against those nations, as he has fought in
times past. 4On that day his feet will stand
on the Mount of Olives, east of Jerusalem.
And the Mount of Olives will split apart,
making a wide valley running from east to
west. Half the mountain will move toward
the north and half toward the south. 5You
will flee through this valley, for it will reach
across to Azal. Yes, you will flee as you did
from the earthquake in the days of King Uzziah of Judah. Then the LORD my God will
come, and all his holy ones with him.
6On that day the sources of light will no
longer shine, 7yet there will be continuous

13:5 Amos 7:14
13:7 Isa 40:11; 53:4-5, 10; *Matt 26:31; *Mark 14:27; [f]*ro'eh* (7462) ›Gen 29:9
13:8 Zech 11:6-9
13:9 Isa 48:10; Hos 2:23; Zech 12:10
14:1 Mal 4:1
14:4 Ezek 11:23; Mic 1:3-4; Zech 4:7
14:5 Isa 29:6; Matt 16:27; 25:31; Jude 1:14
14:6 Acts 2:16, 20
14:7 Rev 21:23-25; 22:5

visions (e.g., Zech 1:7–6:15). • ***prophet's clothes:*** A coarse cloak of camel or goat hair distinctively garbed the OT Hebrew prophets (see 2 Kgs 1:8; Matt 3:4).

13:5 ***I'm a farmer:*** This might be a parody of Amos 7:14.

13:6 ***wounds on your chest?*** (literally *wounds between your hands?*): These wounds might be cuts or bruises that ecstatic prophets, especially in Canaanite religious circles, sometimes gave themselves (see 1 Kgs 18:28). False prophets would make excuses for themselves, such as, ***I was wounded at my friends' house!***

13:7-9 This message describes a coming day when God's appointed shepherd of Israel would be struck down, and the sheep (the people of Israel) would be scattered. A portion of the nation would be given over to divine judgment, while part of the nation would experience spiritual renewal, fulfilling Zechariah's vision of God once again among his people (see 1:16; 2:5, 10-11; 8:3, 23). The Gospel writers connect portions of this passage (13:7) to the scattering of Jesus' disciples as a result of the events surrounding his arrest, trial, and execution by the Romans (see Matt 26:31, 56).

13:7 The ***sword*** is personified as a warrior being called to ***awake*** in battle, heightening its image as God's servant, an instrument of death (see Isa 31:8; 34:6; 66:16). • ***My shepherd*** signifies the Messiah, the coming leader of Israel (see Ezek 34:23; 37:24). • ***My partner*** conveys the equality of the shepherd with God (see Matt 26:31; Mark 14:27).

13:8 ***Two-thirds . . . one-third:*** The divine judgment would be catastrophic, but God would preserve a remnant and forgive their sin (see Isa 65:9; Jer 50:20; Ezek 5:2-12; Rev 9:15-18).

13:9 ***Fire*** is a metaphor for God's judgment (see Isa 66:15; Jer 4:4; Ezek 36:5; Amos 5:6). God's ***fire*** may either destroy the wicked or, as here, test and purify the righteous. • ***refine them . . . like gold:*** God is the divine metallurgist, using fire to burn the dross out of metal (Isa 1:25; Mal 3:2-3). • ***These are my people . . . The LORD is our God:*** The declarations of loyalty by God and Israel restore their broken covenant relationship (11:10, 14; see Exod 19:5; Jer 30:22; 31:33; Hos 2:23).

14:1-21 Zechariah closes with visions of judgment, salvation, and God's universal kingdom. In the future, Israel would be besieged, teetering on the verge of total destruction, when the Lord himself would intervene and rescue his people (14:3-4) and punish their enemies with a terrible plague (14:12). Israel would be restored as God's people, and Jerusalem would be exalted as the center of civilization (14:16-17). God's rule would be established over all the earth (14:9), and the created order would be transformed (14:6-10). Fittingly, God's holiness would be the pervasive characteristic of his rule over all the earth (14:20-21). Zechariah's message stimulates the people of God to hope in the Sovereign King of Israel, who will bring justice and restoration.

14:1 ***The day of the LORD*** will bring judgment and deliverance and will reverse the fortunes of many (see Amos 5:18; cp. Matt 19:28-30; Luke 13:23-30).

14:2 ***The rest*** is the remnant of Israel that survived the sack of Jerusalem (see 13:8).

14:3 ***fought in times past:*** An example would be the exodus from Egypt (Exod 14–15; see Isa 42:13).

14:4 Jesus ascended into heaven from ***the Mount of Olives***, and the angels' message to Jesus' disciples (Acts 1:11-12) implied that he would return in a similar fashion. • Zechariah envisions an earthquake that will ***split apart*** the Mount of Olives and create a valley running east and west through the fissure. This valley will become an escape route for Hebrews fleeing Jerusalem during the assault by the nations (14:5). This event is probably connected to the return of Jesus at the end of the age (see Matt 24; Rev 6:12; 11:13; 16:18).

14:5 ***Azal:*** The meaning of the Hebrew is uncertain. Some identify Azal (Hebrew *'atsal*) as a district on the northeast side of Jerusalem inhabited by descendants of Azel (1 Chr 8:37-39; 9:43-44; see "Beth-ezel," Mic 1:11). Others emend the Hebrew to *'etsel*, "alongside or the side [of it]." • The date of ***the earthquake in the days of King Uzziah*** is unknown, but Amos began his ministry two years before it (Amos 1:1). • The ***holy ones*** are probably the multitude of angels that worship God and serve as his army (see Ps 89:5, 7). • ***with him:*** As in Greek version; Hebrew reads *with you.*

14:6 ***the sources of light will no longer shine:*** Literally *there will be no light, no cold or frost.* The meaning of the Hebrew is uncertain.

14:8
Ezek 47:1-12
John 7:37-38
Rev 22:1-2

14:9
Deut 6:4
Ps 47:7
Zech 9:9
Eph 4:5

14:10
2 Kgs 14:13

14:11
Ps 48:8
Rev 22:3

14:14
Zech 12:2

14:16
Isa 60:6-9; 66:18-21
[g]*khawah* (7812)
‣Gen 22:5

14:20
Exod 39:30
Ezek 46:20

14:21
Neh 8:10
Rom 14:6-7
1 Cor 10:31

day! Only the LORD knows how this could
happen. There will be no normal day and
night, for at evening time it will still be light.
[8]On that day life-giving waters will flow
out from Jerusalem, half toward the Dead
Sea and half toward the Mediterranean,
flowing continuously in both summer and
winter.
[9]And the LORD will be king over all the
earth. On that day there will be one LORD—
his name alone will be worshiped.
[10]All the land from Geba, north of Judah,
to Rimmon, south of Jerusalem, will become
one vast plain. But Jerusalem will be raised
up in its original place and will be inhabited
all the way from the Benjamin Gate over to
the site of the old gate, then to the Corner
Gate, and from the Tower of Hananel to the
king's winepresses. [11]And Jerusalem will be
filled, safe at last, never again to be cursed
and destroyed.
[12]And the LORD will send a plague on
all the nations that fought against Jerusalem. Their people will become like walking
corpses, their flesh rotting away. Their
eyes will rot in their sockets, and their
tongues will rot in their mouths. [13]On that
day they will be terrified, stricken by the
LORD with great panic. They will fight their
neighbors hand to hand. [14]Judah, too, will
be fighting at Jerusalem. The wealth of all
the neighboring nations will be captured—
great quantities of gold and silver and fine
clothing. [15]This same plague will strike the
horses, mules, camels, donkeys, and all the
other animals in the enemy camps.
[16]In the end, the enemies of Jerusalem
who survive the plague will go up to Jerusalem each year to [g]worship the King, the
LORD of Heaven's Armies, and to celebrate
the Festival of Shelters. [17]Any nation in the
world that refuses to come to Jerusalem to
worship the King, the LORD of Heaven's Armies, will have no rain. [18]If the people of
Egypt refuse to attend the festival, the LORD
will punish them with the same plague that
he sends on the other nations who refuse
to go. [19]Egypt and the other nations will all
be punished if they don't go to celebrate the
Festival of Shelters.
[20]On that day even the harness bells
of the horses will be inscribed with these
words: HOLY TO THE LORD. And the cooking pots in the Temple of the LORD will
be as sacred as the basins used beside the
altar. [21]In fact, every cooking pot in Jerusalem and Judah will be holy to the LORD of
Heaven's Armies. All who come to worship
will be free to use any of these pots to boil
their sacrifices. And on that day there will
no longer be traders in the Temple of the
LORD of Heaven's Armies.

14:7 ***continuous day:*** The day of the Lord will bring fundamental changes to the created order (see Isa 60:19-22; Rev 21:22-25). This promise emphasizes that the sun and moon are created by God and are not eternal deities—light does not originate with them.

14:8 The ***life-giving waters . . . from Jerusalem*** symbolize God's life-giving presence among his people (see Ezek 47:1-12; Joel 3:18; John 7:37-39; Rev 22:1-2). • ***half toward the Dead Sea and half toward the Mediterranean*** (literally *half toward the eastern sea and half toward the western sea*): Divine blessings will extend both east and west, ***flowing continuously:*** They will never stop bringing healing (see Isa 30:23-26).

14:9 ***the LORD will be king***: Zechariah envisions the ultimate fulfillment of many Psalms (see Pss 47–48, 93, 97–99). • ***there will be one LORD:*** This promise reaffirms Israel's creed (Deut 6:4), and signals a final end of all idolatry.

14:10 The towns ***Geba*** and ***Rimmon*** represent the north–south extent of the district including Jerusalem.

14:12 As divine Judge, God strikes those who rebel against him with a sudden and deadly ***plague*** (see Exod 9:14; Num 14:36-37; 2 Sam 24:10-25; Jer 14:11-12).

14:13 The day of the Lord will bring terror to God's enemies (12:4; see Isa 22:5).

14:14 The day of the Lord is characterized by reversal: The capture of the ***wealth*** of the ***nations*** overturns the looting of Jerusalem announced earlier (14:1). • ***great quantities of gold and silver:*** The Lord's Temple will receive "the treasures of all the nations" (Hag 2:7-8).

14:16 ***Enemies . . . will . . . worship the King:*** Another reversal will occur on the day of the Lord (cp. Phil 2:8-11). • The annual ***Festival of Shelters*** marked the beginning of the fall harvest season and commemorated Israel's wilderness experience after the exodus from Egypt (see Exod 23:14-19; Lev 23:33-43; Num 29:12-40; Deut 16:13-17). The festival gave the worshiping community an opportunity to thank God for his provision. It encouraged social concern for the disadvantaged and reliance on God as pilgrims in this world. Thanksgiving will characterize worship in the messianic era (see Isa 51:3; Jer 33:11).

14:17 ***come to Jerusalem to worship:*** Jerusalem, with God's Temple, is envisioned as the center of God's universal kingdom (8:20-22; see Isa 56:6-7; 66:19-23; Mic 4:1; Hag 2:7; Rev 21:1-2, 10-27). • ***no rain:*** This was one of the curses God pronounced against Israel for covenant disobedience (see Deut 28:22-24). That curse extended to all the nations, as God's rule extends over all peoples (cp. 10:1).

14:20 ***HOLY TO THE LORD:*** See note on 3:5. The priesthood was set apart for the Lord, as was the nation of Israel (Exod 19:6; Lev 11:44-45). That identity will be fulfilled in the messianic kingdom (Rom 11:16-17; Eph 1:4; 5:27; 1 Pet 1:15-16). The inscription on ***the harness bells*** and the ***cooking pots*** shows how pervasive holiness will be in that day.

14:21 ***every cooking pot:*** The holiness of God's kingdom will transform even mundane utensils into sacred vessels like those used in the sacrificial ritual of the Temple, eliminating all OT distinctions between the sacred and the profane. • ***traders*** (literally *Canaanites*): Commercial activity was associated with the Canaanites (see Hos 12:7; Zeph 1:11). The expression might be a euphemism for idolaters or another way of saying that under God's rule, traditional ethnic boundaries will be dissolved. The passage may anticipate the work of Jesus in cleansing the Jerusalem Temple as a prelude to the greater work of cleansing the heart of those who believe in him by the Holy Spirit (see John 2:13-16; 1 Cor 6:11; Titus 3:5).

THE BOOK OF

MALACHI

Malachi had a multifaceted ministry. As a sensitive pastor, Malachi offered God's love to a disheartened people. As a wise theologian, he instructed the people of Judah in basic doctrine that emphasized God's nature. As a stern prophet, Malachi rebuked corrupt priests and warned of God's judgment. As a spiritual mentor, he called his people to more sincere worship and challenged them to live by the ethical standards of God's covenant. Malachi conveys God's simple but vital word to Israel: "I have always loved you" (1:2).

SETTING

Malachi wrote to Jews in the Persian province of Judea, probably during the reign of King Darius I of Persia (521–486 BC). Jewish exiles returning from Babylon had recently resettled in Judah, joining others who had not been deported.

At the time when Malachi preached, the Temple had been rebuilt, but it paled in comparison to Solomon's Temple. The priests and the Levites were the power-brokers of Judah, yet Temple worship was in a sorry state. The apathetic priests actually led people into sin, not out of it. Worshipers offered inferior animals as sacrifices and neglected God's requirements for tithes and offerings. The hopes raised by Haggai and Zechariah for a revival of David's dynasty through Zerubbabel seemed to have disappeared.

Malachi confronted a people given to religious cynicism, political skepticism, and spiritual disillusionment. They expected prosperity (Hag 2:7, 18-19), a king from David's line (Ezek 34:13, 23-24), and the new covenant promised through Jeremiah (Jer 31:23, 31-34), but they saw none of these things. In the minds of many, God had failed his people.

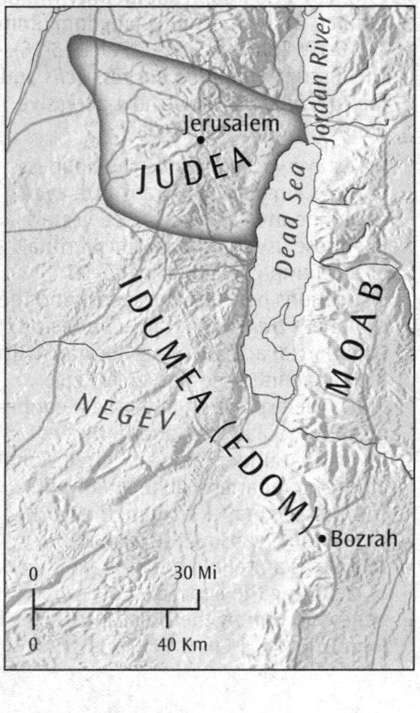

◂ **The Setting of Malachi, 400s BC.**
When God's people in Judea became discouraged and unfaithful in the decades following their return from exile, Malachi spoke words of encouragement and correction.
IDUMEA (EDOM) 1:3-5
JERUSALEM 2:11; 3:4

SUMMARY

Malachi is a brief theology of God intended to correct the wrong thinking of the people of Judah about their covenant relationship with the Lord. Malachi introduces his thesis—that God loves Israel (1:2)—in his first message (1:2-5). The prophet then debates this thesis with his audience in the five messages that follow. The second message (1:6–2:9), aimed specifically at the priests and Levites serving in the second Temple, affirms that God is the Lord and Father of all

Israel and deserves true worship. The third message (2:10-16) extends the implications of God's love to human relationships, especially marriage. The fourth message (2:17–3:5) highlights God's justice, appeals for honesty in speech and in business, and seeks genuine social concern. The fifth message (3:6-12) emphasizes God's faithfulness to his word and calls Israel to a similar faithfulness in worship, especially in the giving of tithes and offerings. The final message (3:13–4:3) reiterates God's desire for Israel to be honest and faithful in worship, in view of the coming day of the Lord.

Malachi's pastoral heart is evident in his preaching: he begins and ends with a message of encouragement (1:2; 4:2).

OUTLINE

1:1
Superscription: Introducing the Prophet

1:2-5
First Message: The Lord's Love for Israel

1:6–2:9
Second Message: Indictment of a Corrupt Priesthood

2:10-16
Third Message: A Call to Faithfulness

2:17–3:5
Fourth Message: The Coming Day of Judgment

3:6-12
Fifth Message: A Call to Repentance

3:13–4:3
Sixth Message: The Coming Day of Judgment

4:4-6
Epilogue: Looking to Moses and Elijah

AUTHOR

The book of Malachi is silent about its authorship, but it is assumed that the prophet Malachi wrote down his own sermons because of the statement in 1:1 ("the message that the LORD gave . . . through the prophet Malachi"). Malachi spoke for God; his title of *prophet* verifies his commission as a divine messenger.

DATE

Unlike the books of other prophets, Malachi contains no date formula that links the prophet's message to the reign of any particular king (e.g., Zeph 1:1; Hag 1:1; Zech 1:1). Nonetheless, the book may be dated between the completion of the second Temple (515 BC) and the reforms of Ezra the scribe (457 BC; see Ezra 7:8). Malachi's language is similar to that of Haggai and Zechariah, and it seems likely that Malachi was a slightly later contemporary of these two prophets. It is possible (though not certain) that the battle between the Persians and the Greeks at Marathon (about 490 BC) prompted Malachi's message (see Herodotus, *The Persian Wars* 6.102-117). The prophet may have interpreted the titanic struggle between East and West as a partial fulfillment of Haggai's prediction that God was about "to shake the heavens and earth" and "overthrow royal thrones" (Hag 2:21-22).

LITERARY GENRE

As with Haggai and Zechariah, Malachi's messages are authoritative proclamations inspired by God. The literary form of Malachi's prophecies is similar to legal procedures (or trial speeches) and disputations. A disputation pits the speaker against his audience in combative dialogue. In Malachi,

TIMELINE

521–486 BC
Darius I Hystaspes as king of Persia

Aug 29–Dec 18, 520 BC
Haggai as prophet

Nov 520–Dec 7, 518 BC
Zechariah as prophet

515 BC
Temple rebuilding is completed

400s BC
▶ **Malachi as prophet**

458 BC
Ezra travels to Jerusalem

445 BC
Nehemiah travels to Jerusalem

445–433 BC
Nehemiah as governor of Judea

[Malachi] delivers his message with an indignant earnestness, reproves the Pharisaic wickedness of the present, points forward to the glorious yet dreadful future, and disappears as suddenly as he came.

THOMAS V. MOORE
Haggai and Malachi, pp. 101–102

the disputation typically features (1) a declared truth claim by the prophet, (2) a rebuttal by the audience phrased as a question, (3) the prophet's answer to the audience's rebuttal by restatement of his initial premise, and (4) the presentation of additional supporting evidence. The desired outcome in a covenant lawsuit and in disputation is to leave the opponent speechless by removing all grounds for argument. This rhetorical question-and-argument format gave rise to the dialogue method of exposition peculiar to the later rabbinic schools of Judaism (see, for example, the teaching method of Jesus in Matt 5:21-22, 27-28: "You have heard. . . . But I say, . . .").

MEANING AND MESSAGE

Malachi seeks to motivate people to conform to God's plan. Malachi's preaching has an overarching concern with the covenant that established a relationship between God and Israel, with its attendant obligations and responsibilities.

Three of Malachi's messages deal with right relationships. The prophet's premise is that right knowledge is essential to maintaining right relationships. He addresses right relationships in marriage by decrying divorce and encouraging marital loyalty. He also addresses right relationships in the community at large by focusing on honesty and integrity in the light of God's character.

Malachi calls God's people back to a right understanding of God as Israel's Father, Master, and covenant God. Malachi urges a return to right worship through participation in the Temple sacrifices with integrity. Malachi also encourages appropriate giving to God, because God is gracious and generous in his response to those who are faithful.

FURTHER READING

JOYCE G. BALDWIN
Haggai, Zechariah, Malachi (1972)

ANDREW HILL
Malachi in *Cornerstone Biblical Commentary,* vol. 10 (2008)

PIETER A. VERHOEF
The Books of Haggai and Malachi (1987)

RALPH L. SMITH
Micah–Malachi (1984)

1. SUPERSCRIPTION: INTRODUCING THE PROPHET (1:1)

1 This is the message that the LORD gave
to Israel through the prophet Malachi.

2. FIRST MESSAGE: THE LORD'S LOVE FOR ISRAEL (1:2-5)

2"I have always loved you," says the LORD.
But you retort, "Really? How have you
loved us?"
And the LORD replies, "This is how I
showed my love for you: I loved your ances- 1:2-3 *Rom 9:13
tor Jacob, 3but I rejected his brother, Esau,
and devastated his hill country. I turned 1:4 Isa 9:10
Esau's inheritance into a desert for jackals."
4Esau's descendants in Edom may say, 1:5 Ps 35:27; 48:1
"We have been shattered, but we will rebuild the ruins."
But the LORD of Heaven's Armies replies,
"They may try to rebuild, but I will demolish
them again. Their country will be known as
'The Land of Wickedness,' and their people

1:1 ***This is the message*** (literally *An Oracle: The message*) ***that the LORD gave to Israel:*** This superscription classifies the book of Malachi as an authoritative message from God and identifies the author and audience, though not the date or occasion. The word *oracle* impregnates Malachi's message with authority and urgency. His audience was expected to pay attention and respond. • ***Malachi*** means "my messenger."

1:2-5 Malachi's sermons are literary *disputations*—a format that calls to mind the setting of a courtroom and establishes the tone of a trial for the prophet's message. This first disputation presents the truth that God loves Israel (1:2). The prophet then debates this thesis with his audience in the five messages that follow.

1:2 ***loved:*** In portraying a relationship between the Lord and Israel, love has covenant implications. The term may be equated with God's choice, or *election,* of Israel as his people. Malachi's message indicates that the other dimensions of God's unconditional covenant love for Israel (such as his patient mercy; see 3:6, 17) are also still operative. See also Rom 9:13.

1:3 ***rejected*** (literally *hated,* the antonym of *loved* in 1:2): Love and hate form a polar word pair in OT legal and prophetic texts (see Deut 7:9-10; Amos 5:15), often used to describe the alienation of a broken covenant relationship. Here, God says that he rejected Esau (and his descendants, the Edomites). Esau had despised and rejected covenant relationship with the Lord (see Gen 25:34; 26:34-35). • ***Esau*** was the ancestor of the Edomite nation, and his ***inheritance,*** the territory of Edom, was located on the southeastern rim of the Dead Sea. The mention of Jacob and Esau calls to mind the twin brothers' rivalry (Gen 25:23-26).

1:4 ***the LORD of Heaven's Armies*** (Hebrew *Yahweh tseba'oth*): This name for God is prominent in OT prophetic literature. *Heaven's Armies* are the angelic armies at God's command; the phrase emphasizes the invincible power of God. • ***The Land of Wickedness:*** Esau was selfish and contemptuous of the tokens of the Lord's covenant (see Gen 25:34). The nation of Edom came to personify the pride of self-centered

1:6 Exod 20:12; Deut 31:12; Isa 1:2; Matt 25:41-44
1:7 Lev 21:6-8
1:8 Lev 1:3; Deut 15:21
[a]*zabakh* (2076) ‣ Mal 1:14
1:9 Lev 23:33-44; Ps 51:17
1:10 Isa 1:13; Jer 14:12
1:11 Ps 113:3; Isa 60:6-7
1:13 Isa 43:22-24

will be called 'The People with Whom the LORD Is Forever Angry.' 5When you see the destruction for yourselves, you will say, 'Truly, the LORD's greatness reaches far beyond Israel's borders!' "

3. SECOND MESSAGE: INDICTMENT OF A CORRUPT PRIESTHOOD (1:6–2:9)

Unworthy Sacrifices

6The LORD of Heaven's Armies says to the priests: "A son honors his father, and a servant respects his master. If I am your father and master, where are the honor and respect I deserve? You have shown contempt for my name!

"But you ask, 'How have we ever shown contempt for your name?'

7"You have shown contempt by offering defiled sacrifices on my altar.

"Then you ask, 'How have we defiled the sacrifices?'

"You defile them by saying the altar of the LORD deserves no respect. 8When you give blind animals as [a]sacrifices, isn't that wrong? And isn't it wrong to offer animals that are crippled and diseased? Try giving gifts like that to your governor, and see how pleased he is!" says the LORD of Heaven's Armies.

9"Go ahead, beg God to be merciful to you! But when you bring that kind of offering, why should he show you any favor at all?" asks the LORD of Heaven's Armies.

10"How I wish one of you would shut the Temple doors so that these worthless sacrifices could not be offered! I am not pleased with you," says the LORD of Heaven's Armies, "and I will not accept your offerings. 11But my name is honored by people of other nations from morning till night. All around the world they offer sweet incense and pure offerings in honor of my name. For my name is great among the nations," says the LORD of Heaven's Armies.

12"But you dishonor my name with your actions. By bringing contemptible food, you are saying it's all right to defile the Lord's table. 13You say, 'It's too hard to serve the LORD,' and you turn up your noses at my commands," says the LORD of Heaven's Armies. "Think of it! Animals that are stolen and crippled and sick are being presented as offerings! Should I accept from you such offerings as these?" asks the LORD.

God's Love for Israel (1:2)

Exod 12:1–13:16; Ps 47:4; 78:2-4, 7, 12-13; 98:3; 105:26-27, 37; 106:7-8; Hos 3:1; 11:1; 1 Cor 5:7; 11:20-34; 15:1-4

Malachi's message, like those of many of his fellow prophets, was a variation on an old theme—God's covenant love for Israel (1:2). Malachi's call to examine the events of history for evidence of God's love and power connects his book to the larger story of salvation in the Bible. The psalmist, for instance, boldly proclaims the glorious deeds of the Lord to the next generation, so that each generation might "set its hope anew on God, . . . obeying his commands" (Ps 78:2-4, 7). The touchstone for God's activity in OT history was the exodus from Egypt, the redemptive event of the Old Testament (see Ps 78:12-13; 105:26-27, 37; 106:7-8). Israel commemorated that event annually in the Festival of Passover and included a catechism for instructing the next generation in the mighty deeds of God (Exod 12–13).

The touchstone for God's activity in all of history is the event of Christ—the birth, life, death, burial, and resurrection of Jesus the Messiah. These events in history form the Good News (1 Cor 15:1-4). Like the first covenant, it is commemorated with a feast—the Lord's Supper (1 Cor 11:20-34)—and the observance of this meal includes proclaiming that "Christ, our Passover Lamb, has been sacrificed" (see 1 Cor 5:7; 11:26).

existence (see Jer 49:16). The Edomites were also allies of Babylon in the destruction of Jerusalem (see Ps 137:7-9; Obad 1:10, 12).

1:6–2:9 Malachi's second message affirms the Lord's role as God and Father of Israel; he alone deserves true worship. The first part (1:6-14) shows how the Israelites had dishonored God in spite of his fatherly care and masterly power. The second part (2:1-9) warns the priests of Judah against sacrificing sick and defective animals and faults them for not teaching God's *instructions* (2:6-8).

1:6 ***shown contempt for my name:*** God's *name* is his reputation or character (cp. Ezek 36:19-24). The Judeans were showing how little they thought of God by giving him worthless offerings.

1:7 ***defiled the sacrifices?*** As in Greek version; Hebrew reads *defiled you?* Ritual uncleanness or contamination disqualified an object or person from being in the ceremonies of worship to the Lord. The defilement in this case resulted from ignoring the laws concerning acceptable animal sacrifices (Lev 22:17-25; Deut 15:21).

1:8 The ***governor*** was Persia's appointed overseer of the province of Judah. The juxtaposition of *my altar* (1:7) and *your governor* (1:8) reveals a confusion of loyalties among the Levitical priests.
• ***says the LORD of Heaven's Armies:*** This phrase is known as the messenger formula in prophetic speech and signifies that God's authority stands behind the prophet's message.

1:11 ***is honored:*** Or *will be honored.* • ***offer:*** Or *will offer.*

1:12 ***Dishonor*** was an ongoing state of affairs. Ironically, the guardians of Israel's covenant relationship with the Lord were habitually profaning his Temple with impure sacrifices.

14"Cursed is the cheat who promises
to give a fine ram from his flock but then
[b]sacrifices a defective one to the Lord. For I
am a great king," says the LORD of Heaven's
Armies, "and my name is feared among the
nations!

A Warning to the Priests

2 "Listen, you priests—this command is
for you! 2Listen to me and make up your
minds to [c]honor my name," says the LORD
of Heaven's Armies, "or I will bring a terrible curse against you. I will curse even the
blessings you receive. Indeed, I have already
cursed them, because you have not taken
my warning to heart. 3I will punish your descendants and splatter your faces with the
manure from your festival sacrifices, and I
will throw you on the manure pile. 4Then
at last you will know it was I who sent you
this warning so that my [d]covenant with
the Levites can continue," says the LORD of
Heaven's Armies.

5"The purpose of my covenant with the
Levites was to bring life and peace, and that
is what I gave them. This required reverence
from them, and they greatly revered me and
stood in awe of my name. 6They passed on
to the people the truth of the instructions
they received from me. They did not lie or
cheat; they walked with me, living good and
righteous lives, and they turned many from
lives of sin.

7"The words of a [e]priest's lips should preserve knowledge of God, and people should
go to him for instruction, for the priest is
the messenger of the LORD of Heaven's Armies. 8But you priests have left God's paths.
Your instructions have caused many to
stumble into sin. You have corrupted the
covenant I made with the Levites," says the
LORD of Heaven's Armies. 9"So I have made
you despised and humiliated in the eyes of
all the people. For you have not obeyed me
but have shown favoritism in the way you
carry out my instructions."

4. THIRD MESSAGE: A CALL TO FAITHFULNESS (2:10-16)

10Are we not all children of the same Father? Are we not all [f]created by the same
God? Then why do we betray each other, violating the covenant of our ancestors?

11Judah has been unfaithful, and a detestable thing has been done in Israel and in
Jerusalem. The men of Judah have defiled
the LORD's beloved sanctuary by marrying
women who worship idols. 12May the LORD
cut off from the nation of Israel every last
man who has done this and yet brings an offering to the LORD of Heaven's Armies.

1:14 Exod 12:5; Lev 22:18-21; Ps 72:8-11; [b]*zabakh* (2076) ‣Gen 46:1
2:2 [c]*kabod* (3519) ‣Gen 31:1
2:4 Num 3:12; [d]*berith* (1285) ‣Gen 9:9
2:5 Num 25:12
2:6 Deut 33:10
2:7 Lev 10:11; Num 27:21; Deut 17:8-11; [e]*kohen* (3548) ‣Gen 14:18
2:8 Neh 13:29; Isa 9:16; Ezek 44:10
2:9 Deut 1:17; 1 Sam 2:30
2:10 Exod 19:5; Josh 24:3; Jer 31:9; [f]*bara'* (1254) ‣Gen 1:1
2:11 Ezra 9:1-2; Jer 3:7-9

1:14 *Cursed:* To "bind with a curse" was to deliver an individual over to misfortune as punishment for a serious crime against the community (see Deut 27:15-26; Jer 48:10). Malachi spoke for the Lord, so the curse was a pronouncement of doom.

2:2 *make up your minds:* This was an issue of the will, not the emotions. • *terrible curse:* Malachi had in mind the utter destruction of those who violated God's covenant (see Deut 28:20).

2:4 *my covenant with the Levites:* If the Levites would give themselves to serving God and forsake their own glory, God would give them life and peace (2:5; cp. Num 8:5-26; 25:12-13). Their special responsibility was to teach God's instructions (2:7).

2:7 The priests had been entrusted with the sacred *knowledge of God* as revealed in the law of Moses. Through their role as teachers, they were guardians of God's covenant with Israel (Deut 33:9-10). • *messenger* (Hebrew *mal'ak*): This may be a wordplay on the name *Malachi* (*mal'aki*). Usually this title was reserved for Hebrew prophets in the OT, but Malachi ascribes prophetic duties to *the priest,* since the priests were to interpret God's word.

2:9 *shown favoritism* (literally *lifted up the face*): The expression is also found in 1:8 ("see how pleased he is"). The priests should have administered the law with kindness and fairness, but they had not done so. It was ridiculous for the priests to suppose that God would show them favor when they had shown partiality in discharging the prescribed duties of their office.

2:10-16 Malachi's third message shows that the failure to keep the covenant extended from the priests to the people as a whole. They did not keep covenant with the Lord or with their fellow countrymen when they married foreign women, and they broke their covenants with their wives when they divorced them. The prophet now speaks to his audience as to fellow citizens, with a striking change in style from adversarial indictment (2:8-9) to inclusive plea (2:10).

2:10 *children of the same Father . . . created by the same God* (or *by one God*): These divine titles underscore the Lord's uniqueness as Creator and his exclusive role as Israel's Father. *One God* echoes the *Shema,* Israel's creed of monotheism (Deut 6:4-5). • *betray:* The central thesis of this third message is that divorce is a betrayal. • *covenant of our ancestors:* The prophet alludes to the covenant formed at Mount Sinai, reminding the people that the law of Moses stipulated responsibility both to God and to one another.

2:11 *Judah has been unfaithful* (or *treacherous*), *and a destestable thing has been done in Israel and in Jerusalem:* Men were divorcing their wives for the economic advantage of intermarriage with non-Israelite *women who* worshiped *idols.* Through these marriages, Jewish men gained access to the merchant guilds and trading cartels already in place when the Israelites returned from Babylonia. Malachi equates this adultery with idolatry. Israelite history had shown that intermarriage with foreign women went hand in hand with worship of foreign gods. Loyalty was to be the hallmark of Israel's covenant relationships, whether with God or with a marriage partner. Divorce treats with contempt the oneness of the marriage covenant (2:15; see Gen 2:24).

2:12 *cut off:* The intent was to blot out or destroy evildoers, in contrast to social banishment or religious excommunication. • *from the nation of Israel:* Literally *from the tents of Jacob.* The names "Jacob" and "Israel" are often interchanged throughout the OT, referring sometimes to the individual patriarch and sometimes to the nation.

2:14
Prov 5:18
2:15
Gen 2:24
Matt 19:4-6
1 Cor 7:10, 14
2:16
Matt 5:31; 19:6-8
Mark 10:4-5
2:17
Isa 5:20; 43:22, 24
Zeph 1:12
3:1
*Matt 11:10
*Mark 1:2
*Luke 7:27
3:2
Ezek 22:14
Matt 3:10-12
Rev 6:16-17
3:3
Dan 12:10
3:4
2 Chr 7:1-3
Ps 51:19
3:5
Exod 22:22
Jer 7:9-10
Jas 5:4

13Here is another thing you do. You cover
the LORD's altar with tears, weeping and
groaning because he pays no attention to
your offerings and doesn't accept them
with pleasure. 14You cry out, "Why doesn't
the LORD accept my worship?" I'll tell you
why! Because the LORD witnessed the vows
you and your wife made when you were
young. But you have been unfaithful to her,
though she remained your faithful partner,
the wife of your marriage vows.
15Didn't the LORD make you one with
your wife? In body and spirit you are his.
And what does he want? Godly children
from your union. So guard your heart; remain loyal to the wife of your youth. 16"For
I hate divorce!" says the LORD, the God of Israel. "To divorce your wife is to overwhelm
her with cruelty," says the LORD of Heaven's
Armies. "So guard your heart; do not be unfaithful to your wife."

5. FOURTH MESSAGE: THE COMING DAY OF JUDGMENT (2:17–3:5)

17You have wearied the LORD with your
words.
"How have we wearied him?" you ask.
You have wearied him by saying that all
who do evil are good in the LORD's sight, and
he is pleased with them. You have wearied
him by asking, "Where is the God of justice?"

3 "Look! I am sending my messenger,
and he will prepare the way before me.
Then the Lord you are seeking will suddenly
come to his Temple. The messenger of the
covenant, whom you look for so eagerly, is
surely coming," says the LORD of Heaven's
Armies.
2"But who will be able to endure it when
he comes? Who will be able to stand and
face him when he appears? For he will be
like a blazing fire that refines metal, or like
a strong soap that bleaches clothes. 3He will
sit like a refiner of silver, burning away the
dross. He will purify the Levites, refining
them like gold and silver, so that they may
once again offer acceptable sacrifices to the
LORD. 4Then once more the LORD will accept
the offerings brought to him by the people of
Judah and Jerusalem, as he did in the past.
5"At that time I will put you on trial. I am
eager to witness against all sorcerers and
adulterers and liars. I will speak against
those who cheat employees of their wages,
who oppress widows and orphans, or who
deprive the foreigners living among you
of justice, for these people do not fear me,"
says the LORD of Heaven's Armies.

6. FIFTH MESSAGE: A CALL TO REPENTANCE (3:6-12)

6"I am the LORD, and I do not change. That
is why you descendants of Jacob are not

2:14 The expression *faithful partner* identifies a marriage companion (Greek OT *koinōnos*, "joint partner"). The Hebrew word, used for a seam or a joint in construction (e.g., Exod 26:6-11), suggests a permanent bond. • *marriage vows* (literally *covenant*): Marriage is a solemn covenant to which God is witness (see Prov 2:17).

2:15 *Didn't the LORD make you one with your wife? In body and spirit you are his:* Or *Didn't the one LORD make us and preserve our life and breath?* or *Didn't the one LORD make her, both flesh and spirit?* The Hebrew can be interpreted in various ways.

2:16 *hate:* God hates a broken covenant (see 1:3; Hos 9:15). This is appropriate because God's relationship with people is characterized by faithfulness, and he expected no less from Israel (Exod 34:6; Deut 7:9). • *To divorce* (literally *send away*) means to expel a marriage partner. Malachi wanted to correct the abuse of the divorce laws (see Deut 24:1-4). • *to overwhelm her with cruelty:* Literally *to cover one's garment with violence.* Cruelty entails acts of violence or wrongdoing. The estrangement of divorce is a violent and cruel social crime. To divorce one's wife is treachery against her and against the marriage covenant. It breaks the heart, destroys relationships, violates the integrity of the family, damages the children's well-being, and puts the future in jeopardy.

2:17–3:5 Malachi's fourth message concerns the disparity between God's justice and human justice (2:17). If the book of Malachi were a courtroom drama, the fourth message would be the formal indictment against Judah. Malachi indicts dutiful but heartless religiosity (see 3:14) that acts contrary to God's justice; he appeals for honesty and genuine social concern.

2:17 Malachi's audience had *wearied* God by questioning his justice.

3:1 *my messenger* (Hebrew *mal'aki*): This is a wordplay on Malachi's name. The messenger may be either an angel or a human being functioning as a divine courier. Jesus identified John the Baptist by pointing to this passage (see Matt 11:10; Mark 1:2; Luke 7:27). • Malachi's audience would probably have understood *the messenger of the covenant* to be a divine being (cp. Exod 23:20-23). The Christian church has understood Jesus Christ to be the messenger of the new covenant.

3:2 *blazing fire:* The dross of the people's wickedness must be burned away by the fires of divine testing and chastisement (Isa 1:25; Jer 6:29; Ezek 22:22). • *strong soap:* An alkaline detergent was made from plants (see Jer 2:22). The blazing fire and strong soap signify the testing (by smelting) and cleansing (by laundering) that would restore Israel's faithfulness to its covenant with the Lord.

3:5 The words *eager to witness* suggest a legal proceeding in which God is both prosecuting attorney (accuser) and key witness (provider of evidence) against postexilic Judah. • *Sorcerers* practiced witchcraft, black magic, or fortune-telling for personal gain. The coming day of God's judgment would either purify the sinful Judeans (3:3) or destroy them (4:1-2).

3:6-12 Malachi's fifth message echoes the first (1:2-5) by emphasizing God's faithfulness to his promises. He calls Israel to a similar faithfulness in worship, especially in giving their tithes and offerings. If Malachi is a courtroom drama, the fifth message is the judge's verdict. The real message is repentance—God wants honest and sincere worship from his people, of which tithing is a symbol.

already destroyed. [7]Ever since the days
of your ancestors, you have scorned my decrees and failed to obey them. Now return
to me, and I will return to you," says the
LORD of Heaven's Armies.
"But you ask, 'How can we return when we
have never gone away?'
[8]"Should people cheat God? Yet you have
cheated me!
"But you ask, 'What do you mean? When
did we ever cheat you?'
"You have cheated me of the [g]tithes and
offerings due to me. [9]You are under a curse,
for your whole nation has been cheating me.
[10]Bring all the [h]tithes into the storehouse
so there will be enough food in my Temple.
If you do," says the LORD of Heaven's Armies, "I will open the windows of [i]heaven
for you. I will pour out a [j]blessing so great
you won't have enough room to take it in!
Try it! Put me to the test! [11]Your crops will
be abundant, for I will guard them from insects and disease. Your grapes will not fall
from the vine before they are ripe," says
the LORD of Heaven's Armies. [12]"Then all
nations will call you blessed, for your land
will be such a delight," says the LORD of
Heaven's Armies.

7. SIXTH MESSAGE: THE COMING DAY OF JUDGMENT (3:13–4:3)

The People's Arrogance

[13]"You have said terrible things about me,"
says the LORD.
"But you say, 'What do you mean? What
have we said against you?'
[14]"You have said, 'What's the use of serving God? What have we gained by obeying
his commands or by trying to show the
LORD of Heaven's Armies that we are sorry
for our sins? [15]From now on we will call
the arrogant blessed. For those who do evil
get rich, and those who dare God to punish
them suffer no harm.'"

The LORD's Promise of Mercy

[16]Then those who feared the LORD spoke
with each other, and the LORD listened to
what they said. In his presence, a scroll of
remembrance was written to record the
names of those who feared him and always
thought about the honor of his name.
[17]"They will be my people," says the LORD
of Heaven's Armies. "On the day when I act
in judgment, they will be my own special
treasure. I will spare them as a father spares
an obedient child. [18]Then you will again see
the difference between the righteous and

3:7
Zech 1:3
3:8
Neh 13:11
[g]*ma'aser* (4643)
‣Mal 3:10
3:10
[h]*ma'aser* (4643)
‣Gen 14:20
[i]*shamayim* (8064)
‣Gen 1:1
[j]*berakah* (1293)
‣Gen 2:3
3:12
Deut 28:3-12
Isa 61:9; 62:4
3:14-15
Ps 73:13
3:16
Ps 56:8
3:17
Ps 103:13
1 Pet 2:9
3:18
Ps 58:11

3:7 In context of covenant relationship, ***return*** expresses a change of loyalty on the part of Israel or God. Typically, the term is understood as repentance, a complete change of direction back to God or a total reorientation toward the Lord. The imperative verb conveys urgency and demands an immediate response from the audience. The indictment of insincere worship builds on similar charges in the second disputation (see 1:6-14), just as God's promise to "open the windows of heaven" (3:10) affirms his power as "a great king" (see 1:14).

3:8-9 Malachi appeals to Judah for a comprehensive renewal of their practice of giving to the Lord. • ***Tithes,*** a tenth of the produce of the land, were required offerings (see Deut 12:6, 11, 17). ***Offerings*** were additional gifts or contributions made to the Lord or his sanctuary that included produce, material goods (such as construction materials or garments), or personal valuables (such as gold, silver, or precious stones). • Judah's recent experience resulted from God's *curse* (see Deut 28:20, 27). Malachi thus urgently called the community to repent, turn to the Lord, and do what the covenant required.

3:10 ***Put me to the test!*** The divine invitation to test the Lord offers the restoration community an opportunity to prove his faithfulness to his covenant promises.

3:11 ***from insects and disease:*** Literally *from the devourer.*

3:12 ***all nations will call you blessed:*** Abundant yields of produce would once again show the world the Lord's favor toward Israel.

3:13–4:3 Malachi's final message contains two distinct but related speeches, the first emphasizing service to the Lord (3:13-18) and the second contrasting the fate of the wicked with that of the righteous (4:1-3). Each speech concludes with the messenger formula (see note on 1:8). The prophet revisits themes from the fourth message (3:1-5) as he reiterates God's desire for honesty and faithfulness in worship in view of coming judgment on the day of the Lord. If Malachi is a courtroom drama, this last disputation is the sentencing. While wickedness seems to triumph over righteousness and God seems delinquent in judging sin in the community, the coming day of the Lord will vindicate God's justice as the wicked are separated from the righteous by the fire of God's judgment.

3:13 ***You have said terrible things about me:*** The people had accused God of favoring evildoers and had openly questioned his justice (see 2:17), but the Lord loves justice (Ps 9:16; 37:28).

3:14 ***What have we gained?*** The people assumed that righteous acts would result in material blessing (Deut 28). • ***sorry for our sins:*** The idea was to parade mournfully or walk in funeral garb to demonstrate penitence, as though such acts were righteous in themselves (see Matt 6:1-18).

3:15 To ***call the arrogant blessed*** was blasphemy against God's justice (see 3:13).

3:16-18 The prophet here serves as a recorder, reporting the audience's reaction to his final message and God's response to the discussion among ***those who feared the LORD.*** Although God listened to their deliberations (see 3:16), there is no evidence that Malachi's message effected any real change in the majority of his listeners.

3:16 ***A scroll of remembrance***—a Persian tradition—was a catalog of ***names*** with a record of events associated with those individuals. We are not told how many people signed the scroll. • ***Those who feared him*** were people who were loyal to the Lord as God, obedient to God's commands, and righteous in conduct and worship.

3:17 ***special treasure:*** Israel had a privileged status as God's people; they were his private property.

4:1 Isa 5:24 Mal 3:2
4:2 Isa 30:26; 35:6
4:3 Mic 7:10
4:4 Deut 4:1
4:5 Matt 11:14 Mark 9:11-13 Luke 1:17 John 1:21 [k]*nabi'* (5030) ‣Gen 20:7
4:6 Isa 11:4 Luke 1:17 Rev 19:15 [a]*kherem* (2764) ‣Exod 22:20

the wicked, between those who serve God
and those who do not."

The Coming Day of Judgment

4 The LORD of Heaven's Armies says,
"The day of judgment is coming, burning like a furnace. On that day the arrogant
and the wicked will be burned up like straw.
They will be consumed—roots, branches,
and all.

2"But for you who fear my name, the Sun
of Righteousness will rise with healing in
his wings. And you will go free, leaping with
joy like calves let out to pasture. 3On the day
when I act, you will tread upon the wicked
as if they were dust under your feet," says
the LORD of Heaven's Armies.

8. EPILOGUE: LOOKING TO MOSES AND ELIJAH (4:4-6)

4"Remember to obey the Law of Moses, my
servant—all the decrees and regulations
that I gave him on Mount Sinai for all Israel.
5"Look, I am sending you the [k]prophet
Elijah before the great and dreadful day
of the LORD arrives. 6His preaching will
turn the hearts of fathers to their children,
and the hearts of children to their fathers.
Otherwise I will come and strike the land
with a [a]curse."

Preaching to a Tough Crowd (3:16)

Mal 1:3, 7; 2:2, 16; 3:5, 14-18; 4:1
Gen 19:6-11
Exod 17:1-13
Judg 9:1-21
1 Kgs 22:8-28
Jer 28:1-17
John 10:24-39
Acts 22:30–23:10

Malachi's sermons were directed to a tough audience. Among those in his congregation were the disillusioned (1:3), the cynical (1:7; 2:2), the callous (2:16), the dishonest (3:5), the apathetic (3:14-15), the doubters and skeptics (3:16-18), and the truly wicked (4:1). What does a preacher say to this kind of crowd?

Malachi engaged his audience rhetorically through dialogue in a series of disputations. The prophet's strong rebuke and clever anticipation of his audience's rebuttals hit their mark. "Those who feared the LORD spoke with each other, and the LORD listened" (3:16). Malachi's rhetorical style was a wake-up call that said, "The day of judgment is coming" (4:1).

4:1-3 This message shifts away from the disputation format, directly warning the people that repentance is the only proper response to the Lord's message because God's judgment is inescapable.

4:1 Verses 4:1-6 are numbered 3:19-24 in the Hebrew text.

4:2 ***the Sun of Righteousness will rise with healing in his wings*** (Or *the sun of righteousness will rise with healing in its wings.*): The source for the title *Sun of Righteousness* might have been the winged sun disk that is ubiquitous in ancient Near Eastern iconography. Here it might be a title for the Messiah or a figurative description of a new era of righteousness in which God will overturn the curse of sin. Israel's spiritual restoration, or healing, would be based on God's cleansing the people and forgiving their sins (see Jer 33:6-8; cp. Jer 8:14-15). It would result from a collective confession of sin and their turning back to God (3:7; cp. Jer 14:19-20). • ***in his wings:*** Outstretched wings are a symbol of God's protection and rescue (see Exod 19:4; Deut 32:10-11; Ps 17:8; 18:10).

4:4-6 The book concludes with an epilogue containing appeals to Moses and Elijah, two ideal models of faith in the Lord and of the ideals of the Law and Prophets (see Matt 17:1-4). The two are upheld as examples for Malachi's audience to follow. In ancient Hebrew tradition, the two appeals may have served as postscripts for the scroll that contained the twelve Minor (shorter) Prophets. If so, the first postscript (4:4) connects the scroll to the Law of Moses. The second (4:5-6) ties the scroll of the Minor Prophets to the Major (longer) Prophets—Isaiah, Jeremiah, and Ezekiel.

4:4 The first postscript reminds Judah ***to obey the Law of Moses.*** Israel's identity was rooted in the Exodus and defined by the Sinai Covenant mediated by Moses (see Deut 34:10-12). • ***Sinai:*** Hebrew *Horeb,* another name for Sinai.

4:5-6 The second postscript warns that divine judgment of the wicked is indeed approaching, and promises divine deliverance and restoration of the righteous. • ***Elijah*** is a supreme example of a prophet of God who preached repentance with messages that were authenticated by signs and wonders (see Luke 1:17; Jas 5:17-18). Elijah was a forerunner of the ***day of the LORD*** (see 3:1). The NT identifies John the Baptist as the prophet who prepared the way for Jesus the Messiah (see Matt 11:11-15; Luke 1:17).

4:6 ***His preaching will turn the hearts of fathers to their children:*** Two key themes prominent in Malachi and the OT prophets in general are the turning of hearts and the ministry of reconciliation. ***Turn*** is the OT term for repentance and indicates a complete change of loyalties. Turning toward God results in reconciliation between generations (see 2 Cor 5:18-20). • ***strike the land with a curse:*** The word *curse* implies total destruction (see Deut 7:26; 1 Sam 15:18; Zech 14:11). The people of Israel who did not respond to God's prophet would face utter oblivion, as had been the fate of their Canaanite predecessors (e.g., Josh 6:17).

THE HISTORICAL BACKGROUND OF THE Intertestamental Period

The Old Testament ends with the Jewish people reestablished in their land. During the time from Malachi to Christ, the people of Israel lived under six different governments: the Persian empire, the Greek empire, the Ptolemies of Egypt, the Seleucids of Syria, self-rule under the Maccabees (Hasmoneans), and finally Roman rule.

THE INTER-TESTAMENTAL PERIOD

The Persian Empire (549–331 BC). Cyrus II (559–530 BC) inaugurated the Persian empire with his conquest of Media in 549 BC and Babylonia in 539 BC. Cyrus's policy was to allow peoples exiled by the Babylonians to return to their homelands, rebuild, and reinstitute their forms of worship. From 538 to 430 BC, many Jewish people returned to Judea, restored Jerusalem, rebuilt the Temple, and reestablished their lives in relative peace. Meanwhile, Jews who remained in Mesopotamia enjoyed prosperity. The last historical narratives of the OT recount this period (Ezra, Nehemiah, and Esther; see also Josephus, *Antiquities* 11).

Greek Rule (331–320 BC). When Alexander the Great of Macedonia (336–323 BC) conquered and annexed the Persian empire, very little changed for the people of Judea. Alexander's rule, though brief, was nevertheless formative for culture: (1) He extended the use of the Greek language around the Mediterranean world and the Near East; (2) he founded the city of Alexandria in Egypt, which became a Greek cultural center for several hundred years; and (3) during his reign, Alexander was recognized as a god, setting a precedent for later rulers. Following Alexander's death, his generals (the *Diadochoi*) struggled for dominance in their own realms. By 320 BC, the divisions were settled (see map, p. 1409). The two kingdoms that most impacted the Jewish people were Egypt, under the Ptolemies (323–30 BC), and Syria, under the Seleucids (321–64 BC).

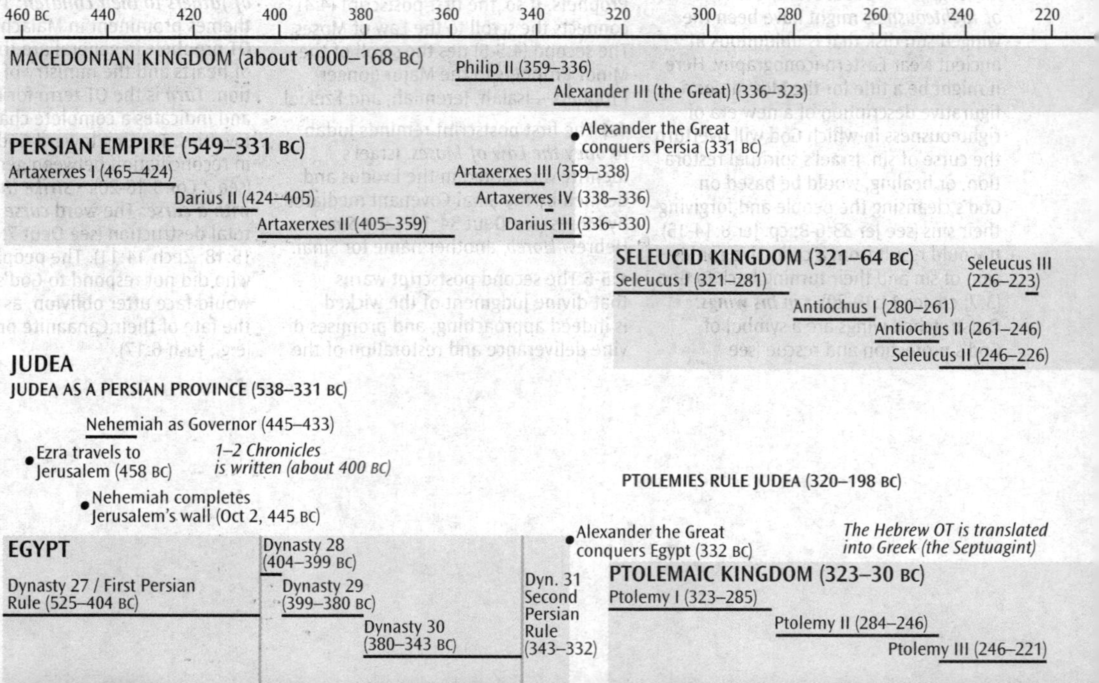

INTRODUCTION TO THE NEW TESTAMENT

The New Testament both fulfills (Matt 5:17-20) and completes (Rom 10:4) the Old Testament. What the prophets looked forward to and longed to see (1 Pet 1:10-12a), and what the angels intensely watched (1 Pet 1:12b), came in the person of Jesus, Israel's Messiah, God's Son, the God-man. The coming of the "unique one, who is himself God" (John 1:18) is the central point not only of human history but of eternity itself. The NT tells the story of his coming and its effects in the inaugural group of believers, the early church.

In the pages of the NT we encounter a holy God as he exhibits his justice and love, both judging sin, and forgiving and overcoming sin. We also encounter sinful mankind as some people repent and others resist God's offer of salvation. Every reader is asked to identify with the people whose stories are told and come to a decision regarding his or her own relationship with this holy God. In the Gospels, theology becomes drama as we see the story of salvation acted out in living events. In the letters, theology is presented as the writers address problems in the early church and give divinely inspired solutions.

The NT is the word of God, written under the inspiration of the Holy Spirit (2 Tim 3:16; 2 Pet 1:20-21) by people who were giving God's words to mankind. As such, it is the most important book ever written and the only possible guide for the Christian life. Believers must make its teaching the center of their life and conduct, and every nonbeliever must be given the opportunity to hear its truths.

SETTING AND BACKGROUND

The events of the NT take place in the central regions of the Roman empire, from the land of Palestine west to Rome. During the period 167–142 BC, Judea won its freedom from the Hellenistic Seleucids of Syria due to the rebellion instigated by Mattathias and his sons. Then Rome conquered the lands west of the Euphrates under Pompey. Beginning in 63 BC, Palestine was under Roman authority, and continued to be for the entire period of the NT.

Palestine was composed of three districts: Judea to the south, Samaria in the center, and Galilee to the north. From the time of the return from exile under Ezra and Nehemiah, Samaria had been the enemy of the other two. Those tensions were very real in the time of Jesus' ministry and early in the book of Acts.

The land of Judea had somewhat sparse vegetation, but Galilee was a rich agricultural land. As a result, Galilee was bought up by wealthy landowners who divided up their estates into tenant farms, with half the crops belonging to the owners and half to the farmers. Many of Jesus' parables reflect this reality. Moreover, Galilee had many Gentile cities and many Gentiles living in it, so it was not as conservative as Judea in the south and was looked down on by southern Jews. Most of the Pharisees came from Judea.

The Jordan River flowed from the Sea of Galilee (a lake 13 miles long by 7 miles wide [21 by 11 kilometers]) in the north down to the Dead Sea in the south and formed the eastern boundary of Palestine. On to the east and to the north lay Gentile lands, including the Decapolis, a group of ten Gentile towns east of the Jordan River and near the lake. Jesus deliberately ministered there on several occasions.

After Pentecost, the Good News moved out into the Gentile lands, beginning with Antioch, the capital of Syria. The church in Antioch became Paul's sponsoring church; from there he and Barnabas took their first missionary journey to the island of Cyprus west of Syria and to the province of Galatia (the western part of modern Turkey). It was a rugged, mountainous area, and we have little idea of the rigors of these travels. Then, on the next two missionary journeys, Paul traversed the rest of Asia Minor and went over to Greece. In Acts 18:18-23, Paul covered 1500 miles from the end of his second missionary journey to the beginning of his third.

Toward the end of his third missionary journey, Paul again traveled a great distance from Corinth, through Macedonia, and finally to Jerusalem. After being arrested in Jerusalem and held as a prisoner in Caesarea, Paul was taken to Rome, where a growing church was located. Paul's desire was to spend the rest of his life in the western part of the Roman empire (from Rome to Spain; see Rom 15:20-29), but God had other plans. When Paul was released, he went back to Greece and the province of Asia. Later, the province of Asia was the focus of the book of Revelation, written by the apostle John.

THE STORY OF THE NEW TESTAMENT

Like the OT, the NT begins by identifying the "beginning" (John 1:1). A new, spiritual creation begins with the appearance of the incarnate God, Jesus the Messiah. Matthew and Luke begin with Jesus' virgin birth and childhood, showing the way a sovereign God intervened in human history to bring his Son into an evil world. Born around 6 BC, Jesus began his ministry about AD 28 (the fifteenth year of Tiberius, Luke 3:1; the forty-sixth year of rebuilding the Temple, John 2:20). His ministry lasted until he was crucified in AD 30 or 33. During these years, Jesus confronted and challenged four main groups—the disciples (who believed but struggled),

the crowds (who were enamored but would not commit), the religious leaders (who rejected him and plotted to take his life), and the demons (who knew exactly who he was but were overpowered and bound by him). Jesus encountered each group with the reality that the Kingdom had come through him and all must repent and believe in him; in the cosmic war with the unclean spirits, he had absolute power and gave his authority over them to his disciples (Mark 3:15).

At the third of three Passovers (John 2:13; 6:4; 11:55), Jesus was arrested, brought up on false charges, and crucified. But he was not just an innocent victim—he died at the God-appointed time (John 7:30; 8:20; 12:23), and he went to the cross voluntarily and in full control. He knew that he was the suffering servant of Isaiah 53, whose death was a vicarious atonement: He was dying as a substitute for us (Mark 10:45; 14:24). His death and resurrection show him to be the glorified Messiah (John 3:17; 8:28; 12:32; 19:19-21). On the third day after his death, God raised him from the dead as the first of a great harvest of those who have died (1 Cor 15:20), guaranteeing the reality of resurrection and eternal life. He appeared many times over a forty-day period (Acts 1:3) both in Jerusalem and Galilee, proving to the disciples that he was alive, bringing to himself his brothers who formerly were unbelievers (1 Cor 15:7), and launching the church in its mission to all the world (Matt 28:19; Acts 1:8).

At first, the church did not understand the command to go to the nations, even after Pentecost, and so the Spirit led them step by step out of Jerusalem (Acts 8:1-3), into Samaria (Acts 8:4-25) and to the ends of the earth (the rest of Acts). He did so by leading Peter to Cornelius (Acts 10) and then by confronting Paul (an implacable enemy of Christianity until Jesus confronted him personally on the way to Damascus, Acts 9) and calling Paul to be the apostle to the Gentiles. Antioch of Syria, the third-largest city in the Roman world, became the hub of the mission, and all three of Paul's missionary journeys proceeded from there. Paul's pattern remained constant throughout his ministry (as noted in Rom 1:16): He would begin proclaiming the Good News in Jewish synagogues. All of his sermons to the Jews centered on Jesus' fulfillment of OT expectations and ended with Jesus' death and resurrection as the basis of salvation and a call for repentance. When the Jews rejected Paul (often violently), he would go to the Gentiles and proclaim Jesus as the fulfillment of their pagan hopes. The book of Acts proclaims the power of the Holy Spirit in bringing Jews and Gentiles to belief in Jesus and helping believers recapitulate the life and ministry of Jesus in their own lives and ministries.

When Paul was arrested, imprisoned, and sent to Rome, a new phase of persecution of Christians and proclamation of the Good News ensued. Paul's two years in prison (AD 60–62) saw a great deal of evangelistic fervor (cp. Phil 1:12-14, which might have been written during this time). Yet at the same time Jewish opposition increased. Jewish opponents denounced Christians to the Roman authorities, arguing that the new movement was not a Jewish sect and should be declared an illegal foreign religion. This strategy was successful, leading to increased Roman persecution—as seen in the terrible slaughter under Nero, when Paul and Peter were executed (AD 64~65). Yet throughout this time of rejection and death, the church responded with spiritual power and "rejoicing that God had counted them worthy to suffer disgrace for the name of Jesus" (Acts 5:41). Their numbers continued to grow throughout the first century.

At the same time, however, certain heresies began to develop. Some Jewish Christian teachers demanded that all Gentiles who wanted to be Christians needed to first become Jewish. Paul indicted them as false teachers because they replaced the cross with Judaism (Gal 1:6-8; 2 Cor 11:13-15; Phil 3:18-19). There were also those who combined Judaism with Hellenism (Greek religion; see Colossians, 1–2 Timothy). Finally, there was a brand of proto-Gnosticism that stressed salvation through *gnosis,* or knowledge, and allowed immorality (see 1 John, Rev 2). These kinds of heresies continued in the following centuries and prompted the early church to develop both a canon and a set of doctrines that defined true orthodoxy.

THE CANON OF THE NT

The term *canon* means "measuring rod" or "norm" and was originally used to identify the set of standard doctrines for the church. From the 300s AD, it has referred to those books of the OT and NT that are considered authentic Scripture. There is no evidence of a movement toward an official canon before the middle of the 100s AD, but there were three preliminary stages during the first century. First, the words of Jesus were treated as canonical from the beginning, as seen in Paul's use of Luke 10:7 alongside Deut 25:4 (1 Tim 5:18). Second, early Christian creeds and hymns (containing official summaries of orthodox truth) were used in the same way as OT passages to anchor important arguments (e.g., Rom 1:3-4; Col 1:15-20; Heb 1:3-4). Third, Paul's epistles were collected and recognized early (2 Pet 3:15-16). These steps did not constitute an official collection, but they were recognized as authoritative materials.

The church fathers of the 100s AD (Clement, Ignatius, Polycarp, the *Didache*) similarly recognized the authority of the writings now constituting the NT, but they did not call them Scripture.

In the 200s and 300s AD, a set of criteria for accepting works as genuine slowly emerged. An accepted book had to have been (1) written by an

1. Narrative	2. Paul's Letters	3. General Letters
Matthew Mark Luke John Acts	Romans 1 Corinthians 2 Corinthians Galatians Ephesians Philippians Colossians 1 Thessalonians 2 Thessalonians 1 Timothy 2 Timothy Titus Philemon	Hebrews James 1 Peter 2 Peter 1 John 2 John 3 John Jude Revelation

The NT Canon ▸

apostle or someone connected with an apostle (e.g., Mark in connection with Peter, Luke in connection with Paul); (2) accepted by a majority of the churches; and (3) understood as containing orthodox doctrine. The churches eventually came to a consensus, and the NT canon was formalized: In AD 367, Athanasius of Alexandria gave the first official list of the twenty-seven books that are accepted today. Of the official church councils, the council in Laodicea (AD 363) accepted all but Revelation, while councils in Hippo (AD 393) and Carthage (AD 397) accepted all twenty-seven.

Even though the process of officially recognizing the canon of the NT took over 300 years, all the books of the NT were quoted, alluded to, and accepted by a wide number of churches very early. The early church recognized those books that God had inspired through the apostles and their associates; the inspiration of those books was indicated by their apostolic authorship and their agreement with "the faith that God has entrusted once for all time to his holy people" (Jude 1:3). For more on the development of the NT canon, see "Introduction to the Time After the Apostles," p. 2201.

INTERPRETING THE NT

Many Christians take a subjective, individualistic stance toward the meaning of Scripture; we tend to think that, as long as my heart is touched, I have found the meaning. We also tend to think that if we read and memorize Scripture, its meaning will automatically become clear. It is not so.

All true interpretation seeks the meaning that the author intended to convey. For the Bible, the focus on the author's intent is even more important, for there is both the human author who penned the words and the divine Author who inspired the text. In order to perceive the true intent of the human author and the divine Author of Scripture, we must carefully study the context, culture, and background behind each book. The following instructions will help guide our study:

1. Consider the passage as part of a larger whole

Words and sentences have no meaning (only possible meanings) apart from the context in which they are embedded. No author ever writes sentences by themselves; they are always part of a developing message, and each part is chosen for what it adds to the whole communication. The student must study how the words fit together and which meaning the words have in a particular context (because each word might have many possible meanings). Consider the whole section and then the paragraph, asking what the words as well as the sentences add to the whole. How does the author develop the argument, and what does the author want the readers to do with it?

2. Consider the cultural background of the text

The NT was produced within the Jewish and Greco-Roman cultures of the first century. Those ways of life have been gone for nearly 2,000 years, and we have no access to them without serious study. Fortunately, the scholars who produced the study materials in the *NLT Study Bible* are experts in these areas, and they explain the cultural background behind each book and passage. For example, Jesus' parables (in the Gospels) and John's apocalyptic writing (in the book of Revelation) come alive with such background studies. So, too, it is important to know who the Pharisees were (see "The Pharisees" at Matt 3:7, p. 1581) and what a "talent" was (see Matt 25:15 and note) when trying to understand individual passages.

3. Identify the genre or type of literature for each passage

Recognizing the genre of each passage helps us to know how it was intended to be understood.

- The Gospels and Acts are theological narrative. We must study the point of view and flow from story to story, noting the theological message of each as well as the larger plot development of the whole.
- The Gospels also contain parables. We must recognize the background behind each parable (e.g., the commercial or agricultural metaphors at play) and distinguish those parts that carry theological meaning from those that are simply part of the story line (i.e., we must avoid allegorizing every element of the parables). Above all, we must ask what Jesus meant by the parable in its context, not what we can read into it.
- The letters of Paul and others are straightforward didactic letters, but we still need to see the cultural background behind each individual letter as well as the rhetorical flow of passages like Romans 7 or Hebrews 6.
- Many books contain apocalyptic sections (e.g., Mark 13; 2 Thes 2; 2 Pet 2; Revelation). The difficult symbols in these sections take their meaning from a common core of symbols inherited from the OT and intertestamental Jewish literature. While there will always be debates regarding the meaning of apocalyptic sections for today, the basic contours of meaning can be established with reference to the commonly understood symbolism. The study materials on these passages will help the reader to understand what is going on (see also Revelation Introduction, "Apocalyptic Writing," p. 2163).

There are many levels to understanding the text of Scripture. The deeper we go into the meaning of the biblical texts, the more treasures are waiting.

MEANING AND MESSAGE

The NT has several primary themes, but all flow from the OT concept of a holy God who is characterized by justice and love. Sin was brought into this world by Adam, so every person is controlled by sin and naturally rejects God's offer of salvation.

The overarching story of Scripture asks the question, how can a loving God be just and at the same time bring a people to himself as his chosen children? Both the OT and the NT answer this question. God is absolutely sovereign and Lord of all he created, yet he created this world in order to have fellowship with those made in his image.

1. The OT and the NT

The relationship between the testaments is one of promise and fulfillment. Both the OT and the NT describe a gracious, merciful God

who draws his people to himself. At the same time, he is a God of justice and judgment who must punish sin. The purpose of the law was to point out sin and to prepare for Christ (see Romans, Galatians). Thus Jesus fulfilled the law by summing it up in himself and in his teaching (Matt 5:17-20).

Most of the arguments in the NT letters are directly grounded in the OT. There are about three hundred quotations and thousands of allusions to the OT; Revelation has 400–600 allusions by itself. Since the OT is inspired Scripture (2 Tim 3:16), the writers wanted to build their arguments on it.

2. Jesus: Messiah, Lord of All, and Son of God

The central figure of the NT is Jesus Christ. Born of the virgin Mary (cp. Isa 7:14), he was the expected Messiah who inaugurated God's Kingdom. With him the last days have begun but are yet to be consummated. He did not come as the conquering king that people expected but as the suffering servant (Isa 52:13–53:12) who suffered and died. He came in order to die on the cross for us (Phil 2:6-8). He was not only human but was "the unique One, who is himself God" (John 1:18; cp. John 1:1; 8:58; 10:30) and took on human flesh (John 1:14). In his life he defeated the powers of evil and exercised authority over the natural forces he had created. In his death and resurrection he satisfied God's judgment against sin and conquered death for all who believe. As the glorified Lord he will come again to end human history, vindicate his holy people, and destroy evil once and for all (1 Thes 4:13–5:10; Rev 19).

3. Sin and Salvation

Jesus came to give himself on the cross as the sacrifice for sin in our place. Sin is an invading army that enters our realm, establishes a bridgehead in our life, defeats us, and then enslaves us (see Rom 5:12–7:8). There is only one answer: the salvation that God has made possible in Jesus Christ. His death atones for sin (i.e., satisfies the penalty it requires), provides the ransom payment that frees us from slavery to sin, and results in God's declaring all who believe in Jesus to be innocent and right with him (see Rom 3:24-25). Through faith in Jesus' work of atonement and resurrection, we are "born again" (John 3:3), adopted as God's children (Rom 8:14-17), and given the promise of eternal life (John 3:16).

4. Christian Responsibility

When God declares us righteous through Christ, he begins the process by which we are transformed and enabled to live rightly before him. This is called sanctification, the growth of the believer in holiness (separation from the world and for God). Good deeds do not save us (Eph 2:8-9), but good deeds are the necessary result of salvation and prove that one has indeed been saved (Eph 2:10; Jas 2:14-26). Jesus demands absolute surrender to himself and will not accept a halfhearted commitment (Mark 8:34-38; Luke 9:57-62). We have not truly heard God's word until we obey it (Jas 1:19-27).

5. Christian Community

Jesus established not so much a movement called Christianity or an institution called "the church," but a community of people who together make up the church. Believers are commanded to gather regularly, form communities, and share the Christian life together (Heb 10:24-25). Nearly all of the commands in the NT are in the plural, meaning they are to be obeyed by a community and not only by individuals. We must help one another follow the Lord and keep his word.

6. Final Judgment and the End of Evil

The NT is absolutely clear: This world will end and a new world will begin. Jesus will return, end this created order tainted by sin (Rom 8:18-22; 2 Pet 3:7, 10), and destroy evil once and for all. At that event all people, both believers and nonbelievers, both saved and unsaved, will stand before God and give account of their lives (Heb 13:17; Jas 3:1). Every person, both believers and nonbelievers, will be "judged by their works" (2 Cor 5:10; Rev 14:13; 18:6; 20:13; 22:12) by a just God who gives to all people as they deserve. God's people who trust in him will receive the crown of life, while God's enemies who rebel against him will receive eternal torment. (Those who claim that eternal punishment is unjust do not understand the wickedness of sin or the holiness of God, who abhors sin.) When God brings final justice, his people will rejoice at the destruction of evil and the coming of the eternal, holy kingdom of God (Rev 19:6-8).

FURTHER READING

F. F. BRUCE
The Canon of Scripture (1988)

D. A. CARSON AND DOUGLAS J. MOO
Introduction to the New Testament (2005)

WALTER A. ELWELL AND ROBERT YARBROUGH
Encountering the New Testament: A Historical and Theological Survey (2005)

ROBERT H. GUNDRY
Survey of the New Testament (2003)

SCOT MCKNIGHT AND GRANT R. OSBORNE
The Face of New Testament Studies: A Survey of Recent Research (2004)

INTRODUCTION TO THE
FOUR GOSPELS

How could an obscure Galilean peasant and carpenter with no academic training and no social status, one who died the most ignominious death imaginable, establish a movement that would conquer the Roman world and become a worldwide religious force? Moreover, how do we affirm the historical trustworthiness of such incredible stories about a man who controlled nature's forces, healed the sick, cast out demons, raised the dead, and was raised himself after being crucified?

The Gospels tell us the story of Jesus—his virgin birth and childhood; his inauguration to ministry; his impact on the people of Judea, Samaria, Galilee, and Phoenicia during his messianic ministry; and his death and resurrection. It is the most important story that history will ever tell, for it chronicles the life of the extraordinary Son of God who has come into this world.

SETTING

The setting for the Gospels includes both Jewish and Greco-Roman cultures (see also "The Historical Background of the Intertestamental Period," p. 1552). Jesus lived and died in the Jewish world of the first century, and Jesus and his disciples ministered primarily to the Jewish people. But Jesus was raised in Galilee and conducted his ministry mainly in "Galilee where so many Gentiles live" (Matt 4:15), so he also reached out to Gentiles, and his resurrection inaugurated the mission to Gentiles (Matt 28:19).

During the time of Jesus, Jewish territories were ruled by the descendants of Herod the Great and by Roman governors like Pontius Pilate who resided at Caesarea but came to Jerusalem for festivals. Jewish civic affairs were handled by the Sanhedrin, the Jewish high council that consisted mainly of Sadducees and Pharisees (see "The Pharisees" at Matt 3:7, p. 1581; "The Sadducees" at Matt 16:1-12, p. 1610).

THE FOUR GOSPELS

Each of the four Gospels presents Jesus' life in a different way with different themes, showing different nuances of Jesus the man and of the various groups who encountered him.

- Matthew's Gospel is the Jewish Gospel. It shows how Jesus fulfilled the Torah and provided the final understanding of it. It represents Jesus as the descendant of David who fulfills the OT promises for the Messiah, the King of Israel. In Matthew, Jesus gives the principles for living as citizens of God's Kingdom (e.g., Matt 5–7). Jesus leads the disciples to overcome their failures and find understanding, in spite of their "little faith."
- Mark centers on Jesus as Messiah and Son of God. Mark reports the disciples' difficulties: They misunderstand and fail as they try to follow Jesus. Mark shows the nature of true discipleship through characters who appear briefly, like the woman from Phoenicia, the father of the demon-possessed boy, and blind Bartimaeus.
- Luke has more on the subject of social concern than any other Gospel. Luke also highlights the importance of prayer, the Spirit, and worship. He shows how, through Jesus, God has worked out his salvation in human history and become Lord of all.
- In John, Jesus is the living revealer of God who encounters all people with the "light of the world" and the "bread of life" and with the need to believe. Jesus is "the unique One, who is himself God" and has entered this world and brought the glory of God's presence into the world and among his own people.

Each Gospel is meant to be studied on its own. Each has unique perspectives and theological messages that supplement the others and challenge readers in important ways. God chose to inspire four different writers because each perspective is important for the church.

SUMMARY

All four Gospels tell the story of Jesus' life, death, and resurrection. Two of the Gospels (Mark and John) contain prologues that describe Jesus as the Messiah, the Son of God, the "Word" or living voice of God, and God incarnate. The other two Gospels (Matthew and Luke) begin with accounts of Jesus' genealogy, birth, and childhood. Matthew relates how God supernaturally overcame Herod's evil attempt to thwart the divine plan of Jesus' coming into the world. Luke relates the births of the prophet John the Baptist and Jesus, the greater prophet.

Only John tells of the early months of Jesus' ministry, how he drew his first disciples from the group following John the Baptist and then traveled frequently from Galilee to Jerusalem for festivals (John 1–7). Matthew, Mark, and Luke—the "synoptic" Gospels that have the "same look"—focus on Jesus' ministry in Galilee.

None of the Gospel writers take a chronological approach to Jesus' life. Instead, the Gospels are more topical, organized to provide a theological portrait of Jesus' actions, teachings, and impact.

From the start Jesus combined miracles with teaching, so that the crowds were astounded with his words and deeds (Mark 1:21-28). He controlled every aspect of his creation: He could stop the forces of nature, heal the sick, raise the dead, and cast out demons (Mark 3:27), and he gave the same authority to his disciples (Mark 3:14-15). He chose twelve disciples, included them in his ministry, and frequently

sent them out on missions (Luke 9–10). The crowds were enamored with Jesus and flocked after him, but they were unwilling to commit themselves to him. In the end, they called for his death (Mark 15:8-15). The Jewish leaders, by contrast, utterly opposed him and plotted to kill him almost from the beginning (Mark 3:6).

The turning point in Jesus' ministry was at Caesarea Philippi, when Peter called him Messiah but refused to accept that it meant suffering and death (Mark 8:27-33). Shortly afterward Jesus was transfigured, his preexistent glory radiating through his humanity (Mark 9:1-8). Then Jesus "resolutely set out for Jerusalem" to fulfill his mission (Luke 9:51). His journey to his God-ordained destiny saw him gradually retreat from public ministry and focus on his disciples (Luke 9:51–19:27). He knew that he was destined to die as the substitute for our sins in order to ransom us from judgment (Mark 10:45).

Jesus arrived at Jerusalem one week before Passover, was anointed for burial, and then entered the city on a donkey. In doing this, he announced that he did not come as a conqueror but as the humble Messiah, the King who brings peace (John 12). Throughout the week leading up to Passover, when the people purified themselves for the festival, Jesus prepared the nation for judgment by cleansing the Temple, cursing the fig tree, and teaching on the Mount of Olives about the coming judgment. He also debated the Jewish leaders and showed himself to be the true interpreter of the law. He then concluded the preparation of his disciples at the Last Supper. There he prophesied his betrayal by Judas, his desertion by all of them, and the giving of his body and blood for the forgiveness of humanity. He had four "trials" that night—a meeting with Annas (John 18:13), then with the Sanhedrin, a trial before Pilate, and a meeting with Herod (Luke 23:7-12). Though Pilate knew that Jesus was innocent, he relented to the demands of the Jewish leaders and turned him over to be crucified.

Jesus was crucified at 9:00 a.m. It turned absolutely dark at noon, and he died at 3:00 p.m. He was given a royal burial in an unused tomb that Friday before dusk and was in the tomb until Sunday morning (three days and nights in Jewish reckoning). Jesus was then vindicated and exalted by rising as Messiah and Lord. He showed himself to his followers for forty days in three venues: in Jerusalem (Luke, John); in Galilee (Matthew, John); and finally at his ascension on the Mount of Olives (Luke, Acts). During this time Jesus also met his brothers who had never believed in him, and they became followers (see 1 Cor 15:7; James Introduction, p. 2110; Jude Introduction, p. 2156). Jesus also strengthened and commissioned his disciples to carry on his work (Matt 28:18-20; John 21:1-25).

AUTHORSHIP

The Gospels are anonymous; they do not explicitly name their authors. Thus it is common for critical scholars to assume the title of each Gospel does not reflect the author. Yet the Church Fathers were nearly unanimous in asserting the reliability of each Gospel's authorship. For example, Papias wrote early in the 100s AD that Matthew wrote in the Aramaic dialect, and affirmation of authorship by Matthew was widespread (e.g., Irenaeus, Clement of Alexandria, Eusebius, Origen). For more about authorship, see the introduction to each Gospel.

COMPOSITION AND SOURCES

Mark was most likely the first Gospel written. The synoptic Gospels—Matthew, Mark, and Luke—are related literarily. Many passages have nearly the same wording (e.g., Matt 19:13-15 // Mark 10:13-16 // Luke 18:15-17) or order of events (Matt 12:46–13:58 // Mark 3:31–6:6 // Luke 8:19-56). From the time of Augustine it was thought that the order of composition was Matthew, Mark, Luke. But in the last 200 years the majority of scholars have come to the conclusion that Mark was first and that Matthew and Luke used Mark as a source. Matthew tended to abbreviate Mark while adding his own emphases.

There are also 250 verses of Jesus' sayings that are shared by Matthew and Luke but not found in Mark, so most scholars believe that they both used a common source, perhaps oral, referred to as Q (from German *Quelle*, meaning "source").

John is separate from the others. Over 85% of his material is unique, and he follows a very different organization. John has long been thought of as the "spiritual Gospel," but scholars have been realizing that John actually has more on the historical and chronological aspects of Jesus' life than the others (although his organization is still not strictly chronological). He is the one who tells us that Jesus' ministry included three Passovers and several trips to Jerusalem. Some scholars think John was written by a group of John's disciples, but the book has a literary unity that belies that thesis, and there is nothing in it that could not have been written by the apostle John himself.

HISTORICAL RELIABILITY

There has been significant debate regarding the historicity of the Gospels. In the twentieth century, Rudolf Bultmann and his disciples (along with the more recent Jesus Seminar) argued that very little trustworthy material was to be found in the four canonical Gospels, that the sayings and stories about Jesus had been composed for the preaching needs of the early church. However, the 1970s and 1980s saw a reappraisal. More and more scholars began to assert that history and theology were not antithetical but complementary in the Gospels. A renewed "quest for the historical Jesus" began in the mid-1980s. Looking at the Jewish background, scholars like J. P. Meier, N. T. Wright, Craig Blomberg, and Darrell Bock have shown that the deeds and words of the Gospels can be affirmed as serious objects of historical study. Historical narrative can be differentiated from fictional narrative, and the Gospels are seen as combining narrative and historical interests. The historical narrative in the Gospels claims to portray real, eyewitness material (Luke 1:1-4; John 19:35, 21:24; 1 Cor 15:6; 2 Pet 1:16-18). These claims should be taken seriously.

INTERPRETATION

The word "Gospel" (Greek *euangelion*) means "Good News." In its verb form, it means "to proclaim Good News," so the Gospels are in a sense sermons about Jesus. They do not just tell the facts about Jesus' life;

they interpret his life. Each Gospel has as much theology as it does history. Therefore, the task of the reader is to catch the theological message as much as the historical story.

1. Study the context in which the passage is embedded

Each Gospel has its own structure, and sometimes stories or sayings are found in different contexts. The authors of the Gospels were not providing a day-by-day description of Jesus' ministry, but rather a topical or thematic presentation. Each Gospel's order has a theological purpose. For instance, Mark 4:35–5:43 collects four different types of miracles—controlling nature, casting out demons, healing the sick, raising the dead—into a single episode to emphasize the authority of Jesus. In light of this type of arrangement, it is important to study how the larger sections of the Gospels are organized and then how individual episodes are related to that arrangement. For example, Matt 8–9 has a careful outline: It consists of three blocks of three miracles each (8:1-17; 8:23–9:8; 9:18-34) divided by sections about discipleship (8:18-22; 9:9-13, 14-17).

2. Study the grammar and words of the passage

The words an author chooses are the key to the meaning of the sentence, and it is necessary to determine how they are being used. For instance, does the Greek word often translated "to save" mean, in a given context, to give a person spiritual salvation, or does it mean more generally to rescue that person from some danger? Does the Greek word translated "shameless persistence" in Luke 11:8 have that meaning in that context, or does it mean "avoiding shame"? Either meaning is possible, but it changes the meaning of the passage.

3. Study the cultural background behind the passage

Both the historical narrative and the parables assume cultural situations in the first-century Jewish world. Understanding that world helps greatly in understanding the Gospels. For instance, the man who wanted to go bury his father (Luke 9:59) could have meant it as an idiom for helping his father until he died, thus asking for an indefinite postponement, but it more likely refers to the sacred responsibility of a son's burial duties (Gen 25:9; 35:29). The background behind the parable of the shrewd manager (Luke 16:1-8) could be commercial, reflecting a loan of money, or a tenant farm situation where the farmers owed the owner half the crops. Understanding the background helps in determining what is happening in such situations.

4. Study the editorial differences in the texts

Each Gospel author tells the story of Jesus in a way that fits his theological purpose. There were far more events in Jesus' ministry and far more of his sayings than the Gospel writers could include, so they chose those details that fit their purpose. We can study the authors' editorial decisions by comparing the same story in, say, Mark and Matthew. For instance, in the story of walking on water in Mark 6:45-52, Mark ends at the point where the disciples failed to recognize Jesus, so Mark's account centers on their hardened hearts. Matthew tells the rest of the story, relating how Jesus allowed Peter to try walking on the water; he failed, but in the process they came to understand that Jesus really is "the Son of God" (Matt 14:33). Matthew and Mark tell the same story but highlight different messages from it.

MEANING AND MESSAGE

The Gospels teach about God the Father and Jesus Christ as his Son. Jesus has a unique relationship with his Father and ours—Jesus' every prayer except the one from the cross (Mark 15:34) begins with "Father." The coming of Jesus makes new intimacy with God available to those who put their trust in Jesus.

Jesus is the expected Messiah, the promised King of Israel. But he did not come to fulfill the Jewish expectations of a divine warrior who would defeat the Romans. He is the suffering servant who came to die for the sins of mankind. At the same time he is the Son of Man (the glorified figure of Dan 7:13-14 who will have dominion over all) and the "unique One, who is himself God" (John 1:1, 14, 18; 10:30).

Jesus brought God's Kingdom, God's reign, into this world. Jesus has achieved a new age of salvation through his atoning death on the cross, along with a new certainty about the afterlife through his resurrection. Through him the last days have begun, and those who trust in him have become God's people, citizens of his Kingdom. They have been given a new direction for living "righteous" lives through Jesus' teaching, and they have new authority as Jesus has constituted the church and given it the "keys of the kingdom" (Matt 16:18-19).

The disciples are the nucleus of the church, and they represent the church in their struggles to understand, in their failures, and in their triumphs due to the presence of Jesus. In contrast are the crowds and religious leaders. The crowds sought Jesus without being willing to commit. The leaders rejected Jesus at every turn and implacably opposed all that he stands for. Finally, the demons alone knew exactly who Jesus is and yet they are engaged in cosmic war against him. Above all this, Jesus is sovereign and reigns supreme. He went to the cross because it was his God-appointed destiny, and he knew he would be the substitute for our sin (Mark 10:45; 14:24).

Although Jesus has inaugurated the Kingdom age, the final consummation is still to come. God is the final Judge who will come with a final harvest to reward the righteous and doom the wicked to eternal suffering (Matt 13:40-43, 49-50; 24:29-31). Jesus will come again with his holy angels to bring about a final accounting with God.

FURTHER READING

CRAIG L. BLOMBERG
Jesus and the Gospels: An Introduction and Survey (1997)

DARRELL L. BOCK
Jesus According to Scripture: Restoring the Portrait from the Gospels (2007)

JOEL B. GREEN, SCOT MCKNIGHT, & I. HOWARD MARSHALL
Dictionary of Jesus and the Gospels (1992)

DAVID WENHAM & STEVE WALTON
Exploring the New Testament: A Guide to the Gospels and Acts (2005)

THE CHRONOLOGY OF THE Life of Jesus

Jesus' life is recorded in the four Gospels, which include quite a few details that help us to set Jesus' life chronologically into the flow of history. Nevertheless, some of the key dates in Jesus' life are uncertain. Three central issues are the date of his birth, the beginning of his ministry, and the date of his crucifixion and resurrection.

JESUS' BIRTH

The Reign of Herod the Great. When Jesus was born, Herod the Great was king of the Jews (Matt 2:1; Luke 1:5); Herod reigned from 37 to 4 BC and died in mid-March 4 BC. Jesus was a small child at the time, probably having been born at least several months before Herod died.

The Census Recorded in Luke. Jesus was born during a census of the Roman world commanded by Augustus Caesar, according to Luke (Luke 2:1-5). Roman historians, however, make no mention of a census around 4 BC. Yet we know that the Romans took their censuses throughout the empire, and we have documentation that censuses were taken in Egypt every fourteen years from AD 33/34 to AD 257/258. Furthermore, recent evidence has revealed that censuses were taken in Egypt in 11/10 BC, 4/3 BC, AD 4/5, and AD 11/12. It is reasonable to suppose that the census of Egypt in 4/3 BC also included Judea, or that a similar one was carried out there, in harmony with Luke 2:1.

Another difficulty is that Luke locates the census in the time when Quirinius served as governor of Syria. Josephus noted that Quirinius became governor after AD 6, and subsequently took a census (*Antiquities* 18.1.1; 20.5.2). Some scholars have argued, though, that according to ancient inscriptions, Quirinius also served in Syria as a special legate of Emperor Augustus before 6 BC. That could be the period to which Luke 2:2 refers. Another possibility is that Luke 2:2 could be translated as, "the previous census, before Quirinius was governor of Syria"; in this case, Luke would simply be noting Quirinius's term as governor and the census he

15 BC | 10 | 5 BC | AD 1 | 5 | 10 | 15

ROME

Octavian Augustus Caesar (27 BC—AD 14)

JEWISH TERRITORIES

Herod Antipas rules as tetrarch of Galilee and Perea (4 BC—AD 39)

Herod the Great as king of the Jews (37–4 BC)

Herod Archelaus rules Judea and Samaria (4 BC—AD 6)

Annas as high priest (AD 6–15)

6~4 BC Birth of Jesus in Bethlehem

Jesus in the Temple at age 12

conducted as a reference point to highlight the difficult time when Jews were first subjected to a Roman census and taxation, losing the last semblance of self-rule (see "The Historical Background of the Intertestamental Period," pp. 1552–1554).

Jesus was therefore born around 6~4 BC,[1] within about two years of the death of Herod.

JESUS' MINISTRY

John the Baptist. The beginning of Jesus' ministry can be dated after the beginning of John the Baptist's ministry. According to Luke 3:1-2, John the Baptist began preaching and baptizing in the fifteenth year of Tiberius Caesar (AD 14–37), so John's ministry began about AD 27. Although the length of time from the beginning of John's ministry to the baptism of Jesus is not stated in the NT, Jesus' ministry seems to have begun shortly after John's, perhaps in AD 28.

The Temple. When Jesus visited Jerusalem at Passover early in his ministry (John 2:13–3:21), he was told that the Temple had been under construction for forty-six years (John 2:20). Herod's work on the rebuilding of the Temple began in the eighteenth year of his reign (Josephus, *Antiquities* 15.11.1), which was 20/19 BC. So that occasion of Jesus' visit to the Temple occurred about AD 28.

Jesus' Age at the Beginning of His Ministry. According to Luke, Jesus began his ministry when he was "about thirty years old" (Luke 3:23). This description is approximate, giving a rough indication of time (cp. John 8:57). Luke, as a responsible historian, placed the public ministry of Jesus in relation both to world history (Luke 3:1-2) and to the national repentance movement spearheaded by John the Baptist. If Jesus' ministry began around AD 28, he was 32~34 years old.

The Length of Jesus' Ministry. Although the synoptic Gospels only mention one Passover festival during Jesus' ministry (Matt 26:17; Mark 14:1; Luke 22:1), the Gospel of John records three (John 2:13; 6:4; 11:55). Thus, different scholars have proposed that Jesus' ministry was as short as one year and as long as four. Most scholars see Jesus' ministry as lasting at least three years.

[1] Jesus' birth has a BC or "before Christ" date because Dionysius Exiguus in the sixth century made a mistake in calculations, and this mathematical error has remained in our calendar.

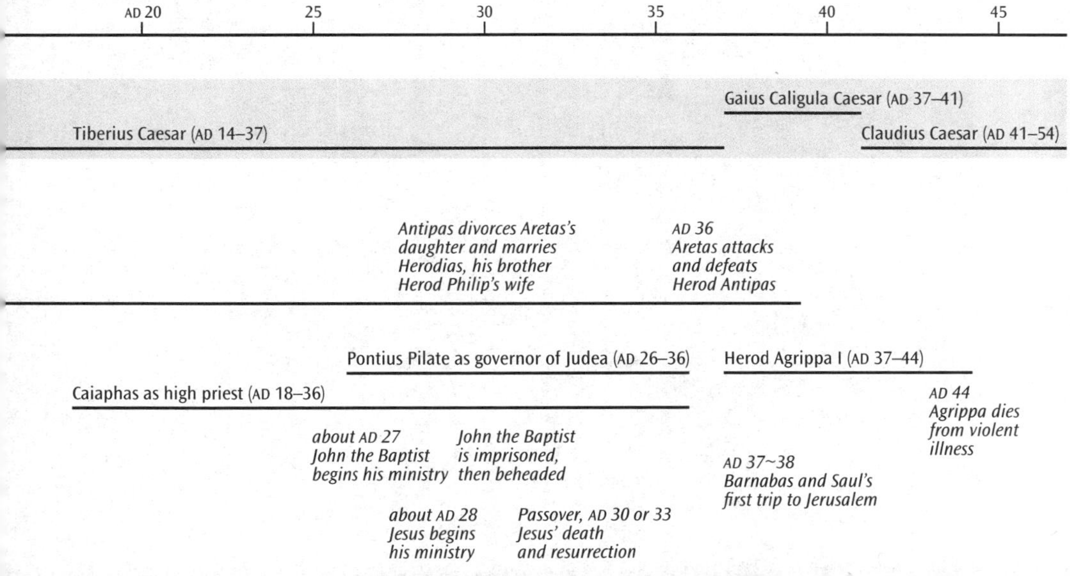

JESUS' DEATH

The Day of Jesus' Death. All four Gospels report that Jesus was crucified on a Friday, the day before the beginning of the Sabbath (Matt 27:62; Mark 15:42; Luke 23:54; John 19:31, 42). They all agree that Jesus was raised on Sunday, the third day according to Jewish reckoning.

Jesus' last supper with his disciples occurred in conjunction with the Passover celebration. According to the synoptic Gospels, the Last Supper was the Passover meal (Matt 26:17-35; Mark 14:12-25; Luke 22:7-38). In these three accounts the arrest, trial, and crucifixion of Jesus take place on the day following the Passover meal. John's account seems to suggest that the Last Supper took place one day before Passover, but a careful reading of John's description indicates that he is in harmony with the other Gospel writers (see note on John 19:14).

The Year of Jesus' Death. In the Jewish calendar, the Friday on which Jesus died was 14 Nisan, the first day of the Festival of Unleavened Bread (see charts, "Israel's Annual Calendar," p. 145, and "Israel's Festivals," p. 235). Therefore, Jesus' death occurred in a year in which 14 Nisan fell on a Friday. He must have died after AD 29 (even by the shortest calculation his ministry was at least a year) and before AD 36, the year that Caiaphas ended his high priesthood and Pontius Pilate ceased governing Judea. The two years that meet these criteria are AD 30 and 33. If his ministry was no longer than two or three years, he died in AD 30 at about 35 years old. If his ministry was longer, he died in AD 33 at about 38 years old.

CONCLUSION

The record of Jesus' life can be set into known historical facts without much difficulty, and the available evidence gives us confidence to believe that Jesus' life is historical and that the record of his life in the four Gospels is accurate. Yet there are many gaps in our historical knowledge of Jesus' life. As the apostle John later said about Jesus' ministry, "Jesus also did many other things. If they were all written down, I suppose the whole world could not contain the books that would be written" (John 21:25).

THE NLT HARMONY OF THE

Four Gospels

Ever since the time of Christ, many attempts have been made to harmonize the four Gospels, either into a single narrative or into a synopsis showing the relationships among the Gospel passages. Tatian's *Diatesseron* (about AD 170) is the earliest example of a single narrative made from the Gospels. Later, Eusebius of Caesarea (early 300s AD) developed a well-known synopsis and tables of cross-references for use in comparing the four Gospels. Many other similar works have since been done.

The *NLT Harmony of the Four Gospels* is a synopsis. Its primary purpose is to help readers understand the relationship among the Gospel passages, not to establish a strict chronology of Jesus' life. The authors of the Gospels themselves were more concerned with Jesus' message and the meaning of his life, death, and resurrection than with the details of historical chronology. By comparing and contrasting similar accounts in the different Gospels, readers can understand the message that each Gospel writer was emphasizing and their differences in perspective concerning the events of Jesus' life and his teachings (see "Introduction to the Four Gospels: Interpretation," p. 1562).

In addition to this synopsis, the *NLT Study Bible* includes parallel passage notations in the NLT text of the four Gospels. Those parallel notations are somewhat different from this synopsis, because they serve a different purpose. Whereas this synopsis provides an overview and includes every passage in the Gospels, the parallel passage notations provide much finer detail in comparing the different Gospel accounts. The reader is encouraged to use this synopsis for general overview and comparison, and then to use the parallel passage notations to compare the Gospel parallels more closely.

FURTHER READING

KURT ALAND, ED.
Synopsis of the Four Gospels (1987)

	Matthew	Mark	Luke	John
1. The Prologue to John's Gospel				1:1-18
2. The Preface to Luke's Gospel			1:1-4	
3. The Record of Jesus' Ancestors	1:1-17		3:23-38	
4. The Birth of John the Baptist Foretold			1:5-25	
5. The Birth of Jesus Foretold			1:26-38	
6. Mary Visits Elizabeth			1:39-45	
7. Mary's Song of Praise			1:46-56	
8. The Birth of John the Baptist			1:57-66	
9. Zechariah's Prophecy			1:67-79	
10. The Growth of John the Baptist			1:80	
11. The Birth of Jesus	1:18-25		2:1-7	
12. Shepherds Visit Jesus			2:8-20	
13. Jesus Is Circumcised			2:21	
14. Jesus Is Presented in the Temple			2:21-24	
15. The Prophecy of Simeon			2:25-35	
16. The Prophecy of Anna			2:36-38	
17. The Visit of the Wise Men	2:1-12			
18. The Escape to Egypt	2:13-18			
19. The Return to Nazareth	2:19-23		2:39	
20. The Growth of Jesus			2:40	

	Matthew	Mark	Luke	John
21. Jesus Speaks with the Teachers			2:41-50	
22. Jesus Grows in Wisdom and Stature			2:51-52	
23. John the Baptist Prepares the Way for Jesus	3:1-12	1:1-8	3:1-18	1:19-28
24. The Baptism of Jesus	3:13-17	1:9-11	3:21-22	
25. Satan Tempts Jesus in the Wilderness	4:1-11	1:12-13	4:1-13	
26. John the Baptist's Testimony about Jesus				1:29-34
27. The First Disciples				1:35-51
28. The Wedding at Cana				2:1-12
29. Jesus Clears the Temple (cp. #163)				2:13-22
30. Jesus Ministers in Jerusalem				2:23-25
31. Jesus and Nicodemus				3:1-21
32. John the Baptist Exalts Jesus				3:22-36
33. Jesus Leaves for Galilee after Herod Arrests John	4:12	1:14a	3:19-20	4:1-3
34. Jesus Passes through Samaria				4:4-38
35. Many Samaritans Believe				4:39-42
36. Jesus Preaches in Galilee	4:13-17	1:14b-15	4:14-15	4:43-45
37. Jesus Heals an Official's Son				4:46-54
38. Jesus Is Rejected at Nazareth (cp. #79)			4:16-30	
39. Fishermen Follow Jesus	4:18-22	1:16-20	5:1-11	
40. Jesus Exorcises a Demon and Teaches with Authority		1:21-28	4:31-37	
41. Jesus Heals Peter's Mother-in-Law and Others	8:14-17	1:29-34	4:38-41	
42. Jesus Preaches throughout Galilee	4:23-25	1:35-39	4:42-44	
43. Jesus Heals a Man with Leprosy	8:1-4	1:40-45	5:12-16	
44. Jesus Forgives and Heals a Paralyzed Man	9:1-8	2:1-12	5:17-26	
45. Jesus Calls Matthew and Dines at His House	9:9-13	2:13-17	5:27-32	
46. A Discussion about Fasting	9:14-17	2:18-22	5:33-39	
47. Jesus Heals a Lame Man				5:1-15
48. Jesus Claims to Be the Son of God				5:16-47
49. The Disciples Pick Wheat on the Sabbath	12:1-8	2:23-28	6:1-5	
50. Jesus Heals on the Sabbath	12:9-15a	3:1-6	6:6-11	
51. Large Crowds Follow Jesus	12:15b-21	3:7-12	6:17-19	
52. Jesus Selects the Twelve Disciples		3:13-19	6:12-16	
53. Jesus' Sermon	5:1–7:29		cp. 6:20-49	
54. The Faith of a Roman Officer	8:5-13		7:1-10	
55. Jesus Raises a Widow's Son from the Dead			7:11-17	
56. Jesus Eases John the Baptist's Doubts	11:1-19		7:18-35	
57. Judgment for the Unbelievers	11:20-24			
58. Jesus' Prayer of Thanksgiving	11:25-30			
59. A Sinful Woman Anoints Jesus			7:36-50	
60. The Women Who Traveled with Jesus			8:1-3	
61. Jesus Is Accused of Being Empowered by Satan	12:22-37	3:20-30	cp. 11:14-23	
62. The Sign of Jonah	12:38-45		cp. 11:24-32	
63. Jesus' True Family	12:46-50	3:31-35	8:19-21	
64. The Parable of the Farmer Scattering Seed	13:1-9	4:1-9	8:4-8	
65. Jesus Explains the Parable of the Farmer Scattering Seed	13:10-23	4:10-25	8:9-18	
66. The Parable of the Growing Seed		4:26-29		
67. The Parable of the Wheat and Weeds	13:24-30			
68. The Parable of the Mustard Seed	13:31-32	4:30-32	13:18-19	
69. The Parable of the Yeast	13:33		13:20-21	
70. Comment on Jesus' Use of Parables	13:34-35	4:33-34		
71. Jesus Explains the Parable of the Wheat and Weeds	13:36-43			

	Matthew	Mark	Luke	John
72. The Parable of the Hidden Treasure	13:44			
73. The Parable of the Pearl Merchant	13:45-46			
74. The Parable of the Fishing Net	13:47-52			
75. Jesus Calms the Storm	8:23-27	4:35-41	8:22-25	
76. Jesus Heals a Demon-Possessed Man	8:29-34	5:1-20	8:26-39	
77. Jesus Heals a Woman and Raises a Girl from the Dead	9:18-26	5:21-43	8:40-56	
78. Jesus Heals the Blind and Mute	9:27-34			
79. Jesus Is Rejected at Nazareth (cp. #38)	13:53-58	6:1-6a		
80. Prayer for More Workers	9:35-38			
81. Jesus Sends Out the Twelve Disciples	10:1-15	6:6b-13	9:1-6	
82. Jesus Warns the Disciples of Persecution	10:16-42			
83. Herod Mistakes Jesus for John the Baptist Back from the Dead	14:1-2	6:14-16		
84. Herod Executes John the Baptist	14:3-12	6:14-29	9:7-9	
85. Jesus Miraculously Feeds 5,000	14:13-21	6:30-44	9:10-17	6:1-15
86. Jesus Walks on Water	14:22-33	6:45-52		6:16-21
87. All Who Touch Jesus Are Healed	14:34-36	6:53-56		
88. Jesus Is the True Bread of Heaven				6:22-59
89. Many Disciples Desert Jesus				6:60-71
90. Jesus Argues with the Pharisees	15:1-20	7:1-23		
91. A Woman from Phoenicia Believes in Jesus	15:21-28	7:24-30		
92. Jesus Heals Many People	15:29-31	7:31-37		
93. Jesus Miraculously Feeds 4,000	15:32-39	8:1-10		
94. Religious Leaders Demand a Sign	16:1-4	8:11-13		
95. Jesus Warns the Disciples about Corrupt Teachings	16:5-12	8:14-21		
96. Jesus Heals a Blind Man		8:22-26		
97. Peter Declares Jesus Is the Christ	16:13-20	8:27-30	9:18-21	
98. Jesus Predicts His Death and Resurrection the First Time	16:21-28	8:31–9:1	9:22-27	
99. The Transfiguration of Jesus	17:1-13	9:2-13	9:28-36	
100. Jesus Heals a Demon-Possessed Boy	17:14-21	9:14-29	9:37-43a	
101. Jesus Predicts His Death and Resurrection the Second Time	17:22-23	9:30-32	9:43b-45	
102. Jesus Is Questioned about the Temple Tax	17:24-27			
103. Argument about Who Is the Greatest	18:1-5	9:33-37	9:46-48	
104. The Disciples Forbid Another Man from Using Jesus' Name		9:38-41	9:49-50	
105. Jesus Warns against Temptation	18:6-10	9:42-50		
106. Correcting Another Believer	18:15-20			
107. The Parable of the Unforgiving Debtor	18:21-35			
108. Jesus' Brothers Ridicule Him				7:1-9
109. The Mistaken Zeal of James and John			9:51-56	
110. The Cost of Following Jesus	8:18-22		9:57-62	
111. Jesus Teaches Openly at the Temple				7:10-39
112. Division and Unbelief				7:40-52
113. Jesus Forgives an Adulterous Woman				7:53–8:11
114. Jesus Is the Light of the World				8:12-20
115. Jesus Warns the Unbelieving				8:21-30
116. Jesus Identifies God's True Children and Claims Deity				8:31-59
117. Jesus Heals a Man Born Blind				9:1-34
118. Spiritual Blindness				9:35-41
119. Jesus Is the Good Shepherd				10:1-21
120. Jesus Sends Out Seventy-Two Disciples			10:1-24	
121. The Parable of the Good Samaritan			10:25-37	
122. Jesus Visits Mary and Martha			10:38-42	

	Matthew	Mark	Luke	John
123. Jesus Teaches about Prayer			11:1-13	
124. Jesus Is Accused of Being in League with Satan			11:14-28	
125. The Sign of Jonah			11:29-32	
126. The Light Within			11:33-36	
127. Jesus Criticizes the Religious Leaders			11:37–12:12	
128. Jesus Speaks about Worldliness and Spiritual Alertness			12:13-59	
129. Jesus Calls the People to Repent			13:1-9	
130. Jesus Heals a Crippled Woman			13:10-21	
131. Jesus Claims to Be God's Son				10:22-39
132. Jesus Departs Jerusalem				10:40-42
133. The Narrow Door into the Kingdom			13:22-30	
134. Jesus Grieves over Jerusalem	23:37-39		13:31-35	
135. Jesus Heals on the Sabbath			14:1-6	
136. Jesus Teaches about Humility			14:7-14	
137. The Parable of the Great Feast (cp. #169)			14:15-24	
138. The Cost of Being a Disciple			14:25-35	
139. The Parable of the Lost Sheep	18:12-14		15:1-7	
140. The Parable of the Lost Coin			15:8-10	
141. The Parable of the Lost Son			15:11-32	
142. The Parable of the Shrewd Manager			16:1-13	
143. Jesus Confronts Scoffing Pharisees			16:14-18	
144. The Parable of the Rich Man and Lazarus			16:19-31	
145. Jesus Teaches about Forgiveness and Faith			17:1-10	
146. Jesus Raises Lazarus from the Dead				11:1-44
147. The Religious Leaders Plot to Murder Jesus				11:45-57
148. Jesus Heals Ten Men with Leprosy			17:11-19	
149. The Coming of the Kingdom			17:20-37	
150. The Parable of the Persistent Widow			18:1-8	
151. The Parable of the Pharisee and Tax Collector			18:9-14	
152. Jesus Teaches about Marriage and Divorce	19:1-12	10:1-12		
153. Jesus Blesses the Children	19:13-15	10:13-16	18:15-17	
154. The Rich Young Ruler	19:16-30	10:17-31	18:18-30	
155. The Parable of the Vineyard Workers	20:1-16			
156. Jesus Predicts His Death and Resurrection the Third Time	20:17-19	10:32-34	18:31-34	
157. Jesus Teaches about Service	20:20-28	10:35-45		
158. Jesus Heals the Blind	20:29-34	10:46-52	18:35-43	
159. Jesus Brings Salvation to Zacchaeus			19:1-10	
160. The Parable of the Ten Servants			19:11-27	
161. A Woman Anoints Jesus	26:6-13	14:3-9		cp. 12:1-11
162. Jesus Rides Triumphantly into Jerusalem [Sunday]	21:1-11	11:1-11	19:28-44	12:12-19
163. Jesus Clears the Temple (cp. #29) [Tuesday]	21:12-17	11:15-19	19:45-48	
164. The Significance of Jesus' Approaching Death				12:20-50
165. A Lesson from the Fig Tree [Wednesday]	21:18-22	11:12-14, 20-25		
166. Religious Leaders Challenge Jesus' Authority	21:23-27	11:27-33	20:1-8	
167. The Parable of the Two Sons	21:28-32			
168. The Parable of the Evil Farmers	21:33-46	12:1-12	20:9-19	
169. The Parable of the Wedding Feast (cp. #137)	22:1-14			
170. Taxes for Caesar	22:15-22	12:13-17	20:20-26	
171. Discussion about the Resurrection	22:23-33	12:18-27	20:27-40	
172. Discussion about the Greatest Commandment	22:34-40	12:28-34		

	Matthew	Mark	Luke	John
173. A Question about the Messiah	22:41-46	12:35-37	20:41-44	
174. Jesus Denounces the Religious Leaders	23:1-36	12:38-40	20:45-47	
175. The Widow's Offering		12:41-44	21:1-4	
176. Jesus Foretells the Future	24:1-51	13:1-37	21:5-38	
177. The Parable of the Ten Bridesmaids	25:1-13			
178. The Parable of the Three Servants	25:14-30			
179. The Final Judgment	25:31-46			
180. The Religious Leaders Continue Their Plot to Murder Jesus	26:1-5	14:1-2	22:1-2	
181. Judas Agrees to Betray Jesus	26:14-16	14:10-11	22:3-6	
182. Preparation for the Passover [Thursday]	26:17-19	14:12-16	22:7-13	
183. Jesus Washes the Disciples' Feet				13:1-20
184. The Last Supper	26:20-30	14:17-26	22:14-30	13:21-30
185. Jesus Predicts Peter's Denial	26:31-35	14:27-31	22:31-38	13:31-38
186. Jesus' Farewell Discourse				14:1–16:33
187. Jesus' Intercessory Prayer				17:1-26
188. Jesus Agonizes in the Garden	26:36-46	14:32-42	22:39-46	
189. Jesus Is Betrayed and Arrested [Friday]	26:47-56	14:43-52	22:47-53	18:1-11
190. Annas Questions Jesus				18:12-23
191. Jesus Is Brought before Caiaphas	26:57-68	14:53-65	22:54a, 63-65	18:24
192. Peter Denies Knowing Jesus	26:69-75	14:66-72	22:54b-62	18:25-27
193. Religious Leaders Condemn Jesus	27:1-2	15:1	22:66-71	
194. Judas Hangs Himself	27:3-10			
195. Jesus' Trial before Pilate	27:11-14	15:2-5	23:1-7	18:28-37
196. Jesus' Trial before Herod			23:8-12	
197. Pilate Hands Jesus over to Be Crucified	27:15-26	15:6-15	23:13-25	18:38–19:16a
198. Roman Soldiers Mock Jesus	27:27-31	15:16-19		
199. Jesus Is Led Away to Be Crucified	27:32-34	15:20-23	23:26-32	19:16b-17
200. Jesus Is Crucified	27:35-56	15:24-41	23:33-49	19:18-37
201. Jesus Is Laid in the Tomb	27:57-61	15:42-47	23:50-56	19:38-42
202. Guards Are Posted Outside the Tomb [Saturday]	27:62-66			
203. Women Come to the Empty Tomb and Report This to the Disciples [Sunday]	28:1-8	16:1-8	24:1-11	20:1-2
204. Peter and John See the Empty Tomb and John Believes			24:12	20:3-10
205. Jesus Appears to Mary Magdalene and Another Mary	28:9-10	16:9		20:11-17
206. Mary Magdalene Tells the Disciples She Has Seen Jesus		16:10-11		20:18
207. The Guards Report to the Sanhedrin	28:11-15			
208. Jesus Appears to Cleopas and His Companion		16:12-13	24:13-35	
209. Jesus Appears to the Disciples in Jerusalem		16:14	24:36-49	20:19-23
210. Jesus Appears to the Disciples with Thomas				20:24-29
211. Jesus Appears to Seven Disciples				21:1-23
212. Jesus Gives the Great Commission	28:16-20	16:15-18		
213. Jesus Ascends into Heaven		16:19-20	24:50-53	
214. The Reason John Wrote His Gospel				20:30-31
215. The Epilogue of John's Gospel				21:24-25

THE GOSPEL ACCORDING TO MATTHEW

Matthew demonstrates that Jesus of Nazareth is the long-awaited Messiah, the king of Israel, who fulfills the Old Testament promises yet turns the expectation of his contemporaries on its head. The Gospel of Matthew shows how both Jewish and non-Jewish people fit together in God's unfolding Kingdom. It challenges the reader to live with total commitment to Jesus Christ as king.

SETTING

Matthew wrote his Gospel when the early Christian community was at a crossroads. Would it remain a sect of Judaism or separate itself from Judaism and become a separate faith? Matthew's Gospel derives from a Christian community near Jerusalem, surrounded by Jews who had not left their Jewish faith. This community, unlike the Christians of Paul's churches, had to answer socially to the stipulations of Jewish law on a daily basis.

The Christians reading Matthew's Gospel were challenged to live as Jewish Christians among Jews who were fully committed to the Torah. The letter from James similarly evokes a Christianity that is still firmly attached to the synagogue (Jas 2:1-13). It uses categories so typical of Judaism that one is unsure if it is Christianity or Judaism (Jas 1:26-27; 2:14-26) as it presents its own vision of Christianity in terms of wisdom and obedience (Jas 3:13-18; 4:1-12). Here is a Jewish Christianity that remains as firm in its commitment to the Jewish community as to its glorious Lord (cp. Acts 15).

Matthew's Gospel tells how the life of Jesus affected Jewish Christians who were struggling with ritual, legal, social, and political concerns. For those early Christians,

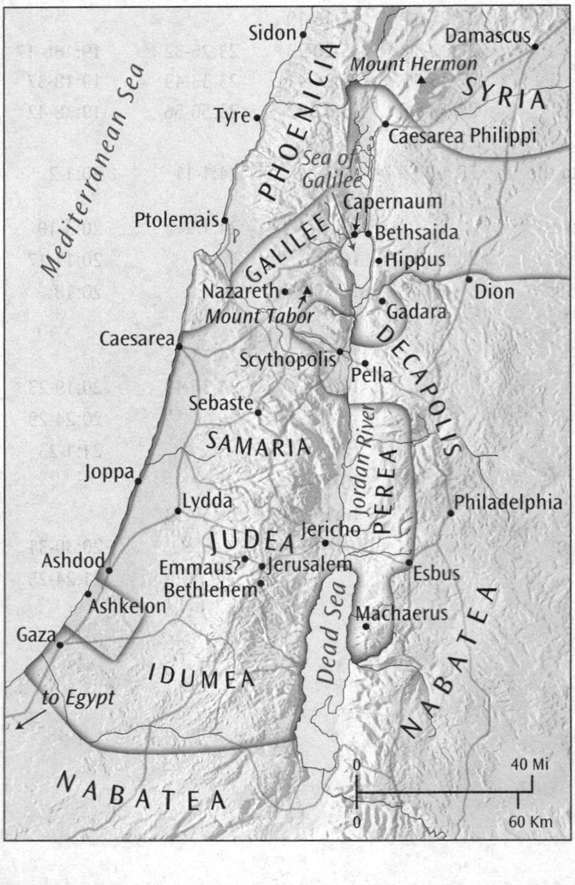

◄ **Key Places in the Gospel of Matthew.** Jesus was born in BETHLEHEM (1:18-25), grew up in NAZARETH (2:19-23), began his ministry in GALILEE (4:12-17), and died in JERUSALEM (26:36–27:66). At the time of Jesus' birth, Herod the Great ruled as king of GALILEE, SAMARIA, JUDEA, IDUMEA, PEREA, the part of DECAPOLIS encompassing HIPPUS and GADARA, and the regions NE of the SEA OF GALILEE (borders shown). Upon Herod's death in 4 BC, his kingdom was divided among his sons: Antipas became tetrarch of GALILEE and PEREA; Archelaus became ethnarch of Judea (see 2:22); and Philip became tetrarch of the regions NE of the Sea of Galilee. When Archelaus died in AD 6, Judea began to be ruled by Roman governors (*prefects*), including Pontius Pilate (AD 26–36), until the kingship of Herod Agrippa I (AD 37–44), who acquired all the territory that his grandfather Herod the Great had held.

Matthew answered the pressing question, "How are we to follow Jesus in our day, surrounded as we are by Judaism, while seeking to declare the Good News of the Kingdom to all?"

SUMMARY

Matthew's story follows Jesus from before his birth until after his death and resurrection. Jesus experiences a series of potential dangers as a child (2:1-23). As an adult, he embarks on a very short career, proclaiming God's righteousness (5:1–7:29) and performing astounding miracles (8:1–9:34); he broadens his reach by sending out twelve apostles (9:35–11:1). Most of Jesus' experience, however, is utter rejection at the hands of Galilean and Judean Jews (chs 11–17). He confronts the Jewish leaders in the Temple during his last week (chs 21–22), announces a final series of woes against authority figures who lead people astray (ch 23), and predicts that God will judge and destroy Jerusalem (chs 24–25). Jesus is arrested, tried, and executed by crucifixion (chs 26–27) for opposing the Jewish leaders and challenging the status quo. Then he is vindicated by his resurrection and gives the great commission to his disciples, to make disciples of all the nations (ch 28).

Matthew shapes his Gospel according to two structural principles. First, following an introduction (chs 1–4), Matthew alternates teaching material with narrative material. Thus, we have discourse and teaching in chs 5–7, 10, 13, 18, 23–25; and we have narrative in chs 8–9, 11–12, 14–17, 19–22, 26–28. Second, Matthew records Jesus' confrontation of Israel with God's message about the arrival of his Kingdom in the last days (4:12–11:1; see 4:17), followed by the responses this message evoked from various people (11:2–20:34). Matthew then tells of Jesus Christ's death and resurrection (21:1–28:20) for the salvation of humankind.

OUTLINE

1:1–2:23
Prologue—The Birth of Jesus

3:1–4:11
Introduction—Preparation for Jesus' Ministry

4:12–11:1
The Messiah Confronts Israel

11:2–20:34
The Responses to the Messiah

21:1–28:20
The Messiah Accomplishes Salvation

AUTHORSHIP

Matthew therefore composed the oracles in the Hebrew language [or, "in a Hebrew style"] and each interpreted them as he was able.

PAPIAS OF HIERAPOLIS, *Eusebius, Church History 3.39.15-16*

Matthew was a tax collector whom Jesus befriended and called to a life of justice and obedience (9:9). Matthew invited many friends to spend an evening with Jesus (9:10-13), and Matthew is named among the twelve apostles (10:2-4; see also Mark 3:16-19; Luke 6:14-16; Acts 1:13). Early church tradition reports that after he composed the first Gospel, Matthew

TIMELINE

about 6~4 BC
Birth of Jesus

about AD 28
Jesus' baptism by John

Passover, AD 30 or 33
Jesus' crucifixion and resurrection

AD 49~50
The council in Jerusalem

AD 65~80
Matthew writes the Gospel of Matthew

AD 66–70
War between Romans and Jews at Jerusalem

AD 70
Jerusalem and the Temple are destroyed

moved from Palestine in the AD 60s to evangelize India (Eusebius, *Church History* 3.24.6).

An important statement was made in the early AD 100s by Papias, Bishop of Hierapolis (see above). Papias's statement is traditionally understood to mean that the apostle Matthew wrote a Gospel in Hebrew or Aramaic, and that this Gospel was later translated into Greek, perhaps by someone who also knew the Gospel of Mark. Recent studies suggest that Papias was referring to Matthew's Jewish style, not to his language (Hebrew or Aramaic), because Matthew's Gospel does not appear to be "translation Greek" (i.e., the type of Greek that is often found in materials translated from other languages).

In the 1800s, scholars became convinced that Matthew had used Mark's Gospel as a source. These scholars argued that since an apostle would not have used another Gospel (and one written by a non-apostle at that!) to record Jesus' life, Matthew was not the author of the Gospel bearing his name. Early tradition connects the Gospel of Mark with the apostle Peter, a fact that makes Matthew's dependence on Mark more understandable. There is no conflict with one apostle (Matthew) using the accounts of another apostle (Peter) as a convenient source from which to shape his own report.

The Gospel according to Matthew is among the most influential books ever written. . . . It is wonderfully complete, linking Jesus with his Jewish origins and Old Testament background, pointing forward to the growth of the Gentile Christian mission, and embodying . . . the teaching, actions, parables, miracles, death, and resurrection of the central figure.

MICHAEL GREEN, *The Message of Matthew*, p. 11

OCCASION OF WRITING

Unlike the letters of Paul or the Revelation of John, the settings of the Gospels must be inferred from comments and emphases within the books themselves (see 24:15; 27:46; 28:15), since direct evidence is unavailable. Matthew appears to have been written at a time when Christians and Jews were fiercely debating such issues as how to obey the law (5:17-48; 15:1-20), who the Messiah is (1:1–2:23), who the true people of God are (Israel or the church; 21:33-46), who the rightful leaders of God's people are (4:18-22; 10:2-4; 21:43; 23:1-36; 28:16-20), and how Gentiles are related to the church and to Israel (2:1-12; 3:7-10; 4:12-16; 8:5-13; 15:21-28; 28:16-20).

There is serious debate as to whether Matthew's Gospel sprang from a community that was still within Judaism or one that was already outside Judaism. In other words, had Matthew's Christian community separated from Judaism, or was it still within Judaism's umbrella? Or, was Matthew written for a general audience rather than a specific community? Early Christianity was diverse; some Christian leaders, such as James, maintained a long-term relationship with the Jewish communities. In discussing this question, scholars examine the following passages: 2:1-12; 4:12-16; 8:5-13; 10:5-6; 15:21-28; 17:24-27; 19:28; 21:43; 22:7; 23:1-39.

DATE AND LOCATION

Matthew was probably written sometime between AD 65 and 80. Those who argue that Matthew used Mark's Gospel as a source usually date Matthew after AD 70; those who claim it is independent tend to date it earlier. Some have suggested that Matthew's Gospel was written in the AD 50s. Many today think that Matthew was first written at Antioch in Syria, which is more probable than any other proposed setting.

MEANING AND MESSAGE

Matthew argues the case that Jesus fulfills the ancient faith of Israel and the OT hope: In him the Messiah and the day of the Lord have come.

A few do follow Jesus. In following the instruction of Jesus, these disciples would evangelize the whole world and build a community (the church) that would include both Jews and Gentiles. In general, however, Israel refuses to follow its Messiah, and Jesus utters disastrous warnings that they will experience the judgment of God (chs 23–25) unless they repent.

Matthew's Gospel is distinctive in its presentation of Jesus as Messiah and Teacher, its emphasis on the Kingdom of Heaven, its strong call to discipleship, its constant pattern of OT fulfillment, its incisive criticism of the Jewish religious leaders, and its universal outlook that includes Gentiles in the Kingdom.

The Messiah (Christ). Matthew emphasizes Jesus as the Messiah (Christ) (1:1, 16-18; 11:2-3; 16:16, 20; 23:10). He focuses on Jesus as the fulfillment of OT expectations, though not in the manner his Jewish contemporaries expected. For Matthew, Jesus is clearly the Son of God, born of the Virgin Mary in order to bring salvation to his people (1:21). In short, Jesus is "Immanuel, God with us" (1:23; 28:20).

The Kingdom of Heaven. The expression "Kingdom of Heaven," used thirty times by Matthew, is a roundabout way for Jews to say "Kingdom of God." Matthew uses this term to evoke (1) the invisible but present rule of God on earth through the saving work of Jesus the Messiah; (2) the fulfillment of OT promises (4:17; 11:11-15); (3) the saving activity of God, often through quiet and humble means (11:25; 13:24-30, 36-43); (4) the power and strength of God's activity (11:2-6, 12-13; 12:28); (5) the coming of the Kingdom within a "generation" (10:23; 16:28; 24:34); (6) the final, climactic judgment of God (25:31-46); and (7) the final, perfect fellowship of all God's holy people with the Father (8:11-12; 13:43; 22:1-14; 26:29). The Kingdom of Heaven shows God's perfect reign through Jesus the Messiah among his people, beginning with the church and consummated in the eternal Kingdom of glory and fellowship.

Discipleship. Matthew's Gospel stresses Jesus' call to men and women to be baptized, to follow him as disciples, to obey his teachings (28:20), and to enjoy fellowship with him. Jesus summarizes the requirements of discipleship in his Sermon on the Mount (5:1–7:29), and this theme recurs throughout Matthew (e.g., 10:1-42; 16:24-26). Matthew shows the disciples overcoming their failures through Christ's help (see 14:28-33; 16:5-12).

Fulfillment of the OT. More than any other Gospel, Matthew stresses the deep correspondence between OT expectations and promises and their fulfillment in Jesus. In the style of a Jewish commentary, Matthew links OT texts to events in the life of Jesus that fulfill those texts and frequently draws out analogies between the OT and the NT. Matthew's procedure is anchored in the belief that what God has done once in Israel, he is doing again, finally and fully, in Jesus the Messiah.

Universal Outlook. In a book so strongly Jewish in orientation, it is surprising to find such an emphasis on the inclusion of Gentiles in the Messiah's saving work. More than any other, this Gospel emphasizes that the Good News is for all, including Gentiles. This stance put Matthew at odds with the Jewish community of his time on two

Matthew's story of Jesus . . . is a masterpiece. . . . More often than not we know the teaching of Jesus in . . . Matthew's formulations.

DONALD A. HAGNER,
Matthew 1–13, p. xi

FURTHER READING

CRAIG L. BLOMBERG
Matthew (1992)

D. A. CARSON
Matthew in *Expositor's Bible Commentary*, vol. 8 (1984)

R. T. FRANCE
Matthew: Evangelist and Teacher (1989)

MICHAEL GREEN
The Message of Matthew: The Kingdom of Heaven (2000)

CRAIG S. KEENER
A Commentary on the Gospel of Matthew (1999)

DAVID TURNER
Matthew in *Cornerstone Biblical Commentary*, vol. 11 (2005)

fundamental questions: Who are the people of God? What future is there for the nation of Israel? The birth narratives show that God saves Gentiles, and throughout the book Gentiles are portrayed positively. Since God is sovereign, his Messiah is King of all creation. Though God has worked especially in and through the nation of Israel (see 10:5-6; 15:24), the inauguration of the Kingdom of Heaven shares God's good favor with the nations as well (see 28:18-20).

1. PROLOGUE—THE BIRTH OF JESUS (1:1–2:23)

The Ancestors of Jesus the Messiah (1:1-17)

Matt 1:1-17; cp. Luke 3:23-38

1 This is a record of the ancestors of Jesus the Messiah, a descendant of David and of Abraham:

2 Abraham was the father of Isaac.
Isaac was the father of Jacob.
Jacob was the father of Judah and his brothers.
3 Judah was the father of Perez and Zerah (whose mother was Tamar).
Perez was the father of Hezron.
Hezron was the father of Ram.
4 Ram was the father of Amminadab.
Amminadab was the father of Nahshon.
Nahshon was the father of Salmon.
5 Salmon was the father of Boaz (whose mother was Rahab).
Boaz was the father of Obed (whose mother was Ruth).
Obed was the father of Jesse.
6 Jesse was the father of King David.
David was the father of Solomon (whose mother was Bathsheba, the widow of Uriah).
7 Solomon was the father of Rehoboam.
Rehoboam was the father of Abijah.
Abijah was the father of Asa.
8 Asa was the father of Jehoshaphat.
Jehoshaphat was the father of Jehoram.
Jehoram was the father of Uzziah.
9 Uzziah was the father of Jotham.
Jotham was the father of Ahaz.
Ahaz was the father of Hezekiah.
10 Hezekiah was the father of Manasseh.
Manasseh was the father of Amon.
Amon was the father of Josiah.
11 Josiah was the father of Jehoiachin and his brothers (born at the time of the exile to Babylon).
12 After the Babylonian exile:
Jehoiachin was the father of Shealtiel.
Shealtiel was the father of Zerubbabel.
13 Zerubbabel was the father of Abiud.
Abiud was the father of Eliakim.
Eliakim was the father of Azor.
14 Azor was the father of Zadok.
Zadok was the father of Akim.
Akim was the father of Eliud.
15 Eliud was the father of Eleazar.
Eleazar was the father of Matthan.
Matthan was the father of Jacob.
16 Jacob was the father of Joseph, the husband of Mary.
Mary gave birth to Jesus, who is called the Messiah.

1:1-17 //Luke 3:23-38
1:1 Gen 22:18; 2 Sam 7:12-14; 1 Chr 17:11; Ps 89:3-4; 132:11; Isa 9:6; 11:1; Matt 22:42; John 7:42; Rom 1:3; Gal 3:16; Rev 22:16
1:2 Gen 21:3, 12; 25:26; 29:35; 1 Chr 1:34
1:3 Gen 38:29-30; Ruth 4:12, 18-19; 1 Chr 2:4-5, 9
1:4-5 Ruth 4:13, 17-22; 1 Chr 2:10-12, 15; Heb 11:31
1:6 Ruth 4:17, 22; 2 Sam 12:24; 1 Chr 2:13-15
1:7-10 1 Chr 3:10-14
1:11 2 Kgs 24:14-16; 1 Chr 3:15-16; Jer 27:20; Dan 1:1-2
1:12 1 Chr 3:17, 19; Ezra 3:2
1:16 Matt 27:17, 22; Luke 2:11

1:1–2:23 This account demonstrates that Jesus' lineage and birth (ch 1), as well as the geography of his early years (ch 2), fulfilled OT expectations, and that attempts to thwart God's will do not succeed (2:1-15; see also 27:62-66).

1:1 The phrase ***a record of the ancestors*** introduces 1:1-17. A similar phrase is used in Genesis to introduce each section of that book (see Genesis Introduction, "Summary," p. 15). • ***Jesus the Messiah, a descendant of David*** (literally *Jesus the Messiah, son of David*): These names are repeated in reverse order in the genealogy, an example of a literary form known as *chiasm* (arrangement of elements in mirror-image). Being identified as a ***descendant of David*** introduces Jesus as Messiah (see 12:23; 22:42-45), while the connection to ***Abraham*** emphasizes God's covenant with Israel and the extension of that covenant to include all nations (see Gen 12:3; Matt 28:16-20).

1:3 ***Ram:*** Greek *Aram,* a variant spelling of Ram; also in 1:4. See 1 Chr 2:9-10.

1:5 ***Rahab*** was the Gentile prostitute who risked her life to harbor Joshua's two spies in Jericho (Josh 2:1-21). Her inclusion in the ancestry of the Messiah emphasizes the grace of God. Elsewhere she is commended for her faith in the God of Israel and for righteous deeds (Heb 11:31; Jas 2:25).

1:7 ***Asa*** (Greek *Asaph,* a variant spelling of Asa; also in 1:8. See 1 Chr 3:10): Probably the OT king (1 Kgs 15:9-24; 1 Chr 3:10) and not the psalmist (Asaph; 1 Chr 6:39; 25:1-2; Pss 50, 73–83). Matthew's focus is on the ancestral line from David to the Messiah.

1:8 ***Jehoram:*** Greek *Joram,* a variant spelling of Jehoram. See 1 Kgs 22:50 and note on 1 Chr 3:11. • ***father of*** (or *ancestor of;* also in 1:11): The term includes several generations here (2 Chr 21:1–26:1), as it does in the case of Josiah (1:11) and Shealtiel (1:12). The genealogy omits Ahaziah, Joash, and Amaziah (2 Kgs 8:24; 1 Chr 3:11; 2 Chr 22:1, 11; 24:27), perhaps because of their association with Ahab and Jezebel.

1:10 ***Amon:*** Greek *Amos,* a variant spelling of Amon. See 1 Chr 3:14.

1:11-12 ***father:*** Josiah was the grandfather of ***Jehoiachin*** (Greek *Jeconiah,* a variant spelling of Jehoiachin); see 2 Kgs 23:34; 24:6; note on 1 Chr 3:16.

1:12-16 Although the OT is clearly the source for 1:1-11, Matthew is probably also dependent upon royal archives and oral traditions for 1:12-16.

1:12 ***Shealtiel:*** See 1 Chr 3:17-19; Ezra 3:2.

1:16 This genealogy is traced through ***Joseph,*** who stands in David's line (see also notes on Luke 3:23-38).

1:18-25
//Luke 2:1-7
1:18
Luke 1:27, 35
Gal 4:4
1:19
Deut 24:1
1:20
Luke 1:35
1:21
Luke 1:31; 2:11, 21
Acts 5:31; 13:23
Heb 7:25

17 All those listed above include fourteen
generations from Abraham to David, fourteen from David to the Babylonian exile,
and fourteen from the Babylonian exile to
the Messiah.

OT Patterns Fulfilled (1:18–2:23)

The Birth of Jesus the Messiah

Matt 1:18-25; cp. Luke 2:1-7

18 This is how Jesus the Messiah was born.
His mother, Mary, was engaged to be married to Joseph. But before the marriage
took place, while she was still a virgin, she
became pregnant through the power of
the Holy Spirit. 19 Joseph, her fiancé, was a
good man and did not want to disgrace her
publicly, so he decided to break the engagement quietly.
20 As he considered this, an angel of the
Lord appeared to him in a dream. "Joseph,
son of David," the angel said, "do not be
afraid to take Mary as your wife. For the
child within her was conceived by the Holy
Spirit. 21 And she will have a son, and you
are to name him Jesus, for he will save his
people from their sins."

Genealogy of Jesus (1:1-17)

Gen 12:1-3
2 Sam 7:16
Luke 3:23-38

Both Matthew and Luke provide genealogies of Jesus (1:1-17; Luke 3:23-38). The two genealogies differ from David to Joseph, Jesus' legal father. Matthew follows the line of David's son Solomon, while Luke follows the line of Nathan, another of David's sons. One possible explanation is that Matthew records Joseph's genealogy while Luke records Mary's (see note on Luke 3:23).

Genealogies were kept quite accurately in Judaism, as Josephus confirms (Josephus, *Life* 1). Genealogies were important in the OT and in Judaism because land rights were apportioned to families in Israel and because certain offices, such as priest and king, were inherited from father to son. Genealogies sometimes ran a record from the past to the present to illustrate religious themes, family descent, or political ties, as well as simple chronology (1 Chr 1–9). Most such lists were representative rather than a complete list of every individual.

The purpose of Matthew's genealogy, unlike Luke's (Luke 3:23-38), is to show Jesus' heritage as running from Abraham through David. Jesus' genealogy confirms him as a legitimate heir to the throne of David. While Jesus' genealogy in Matthew goes back to Abraham, the father of the Jewish race, the genealogy in Luke goes all the way back to Adam. This is consistent with Luke's emphasis on Jesus as the Savior for all people everywhere.

The unusual mention of women with stained reputations (Tamar, Rahab, Ruth, and Bathsheba), several of them Gentiles, is noteworthy in Matthew's genealogy. Their mention here emphasizes God's gracious acts of redeeming even those deemed unworthy by others.

Jesus' genealogy does not prove that Jesus is the Messiah, but it does make him a possible candidate. His identity as the Messiah becomes evident in other ways (11:2-6). God had providentially guided the course of history to its climax in Jesus Christ. Jesus is presented as the anticipated Messiah of the OT, the Savior of his people, and the King descended from David assuming his throne (see 2 Sam 7:16). He is heir to Abraham and ultimately fulfills God's promises to Abraham (Gen 12:1-3).

1:17 Matthew states that each period has ***fourteen generations,*** but the first and third periods list only thirteen. A legitimate Jewish and OT approach would count David in both the first and second groupings and include Jesus in the third grouping. This further reinforces that Matthew is probably stressing the *gematria* (letters representing numbers): The letters in the Hebrew word *dawid* ("David") also add up to fourteen. Matthew is highlighting Jesus' credentials as the Messiah (1:1).

1:18 ***Jesus the Messiah*** (literally *Jesus the Christ*): Using *Messiah* in the translation accurately communicates that it is a title rather than a personal name ("Jesus Christ"). • ***engaged to be married:*** In Judaism, engagement (or betrothal) meant a permanent relationship (Mal 2:14) that could be broken only by legal process; thus, Mary was considered Joseph's wife and he her husband (see 1:20; Deut 22:23-24), even though they had not had sexual relations. Mary's status as a ***virgin*** at the time of Jesus' conception ***through the power of the Holy Spirit*** helps authenticate Jesus' divinity.

1:19 As a ***good man***—that is, as one who obeyed the law (see Luke 1:6)—Joseph could not take Mary as his wife since she was a suspected adulteress. He could exonerate himself by publicly exposing Mary to trial and having her put to death (Deut 22:23-27; Num 5:11-31), or pay a fine and ***break the engagement*** (literally *divorce her;* see also *Mishnah Sotah* 1:1-5). Joseph mercifully decided to do the latter ***quietly.***

1:20 The ***angel of the Lord*** declared to Joseph ***in a dream*** (see 2:12-13, 19, 22) that Mary had been neither seduced nor violated; instead, the baby ***was conceived by the Holy Spirit*** (Luke 1:34-35), who often has a creative and life-generating role (Gen 1:2; Ezek 37:1-14; John 3:5-8).

1:21 ***Jesus*** is the Greek form of the Hebrew name *Yeshua,* which means "The LORD saves." The name appropriately describes his role: ***he will save his people from their sins.*** • ***His people*** may refer either to Israel as a nation (2:6) or to the Messiah's people, the church, which is comprised of both Jews and Gentiles (4:15-16; 16:18; 28:18-20).

22 All of this occurred to fulfill the Lord's
message through his prophet:

23 "Look! The virgin will conceive a child!
She will give birth to a son,
and they will call him Immanuel,
which means 'God is with us.'"

24 When Joseph woke up, he did as the angel of the Lord commanded and took Mary
as his wife. 25 But he did not have sexual relations with her until her son was born. And
Joseph named him Jesus.

Visitors from the East

2 Jesus was born in Bethlehem in Judea,
during the reign of King Herod. About
that time some wise men from eastern
lands arrived in Jerusalem, asking, 2 "Where
is the newborn king of the Jews? We saw
his star as it rose, and we have come to worship him."

3 King Herod was deeply disturbed when
he heard this, as was everyone in Jerusalem. 4 He called a meeting of the leading
priests and teachers of religious law and
asked, "Where is the [a]Messiah supposed to
be born?"

5 "In Bethlehem in Judea," they said, "for
this is what the prophet wrote:

6 'And you, O Bethlehem in the land of
Judah,

1:23
*Isa 7:14; 8:8, 10
John 1:14
1 Tim 3:16
Rev 21:3

1:25
Luke 1:31

2:1
Luke 1:5; 2:4-7

2:2
Num 24:17
Jer 23:5
Matt 2:9
Rev 22:16

2:4
[a]*christos* (5547)
‣ Luke 2:11

2:5
John 7:42

2:6
*Mic 5:2

HEROD THE GREAT (2:1-20)

Luke 1:5

Herod the Great was the Roman-appointed king of Judea (37–4 BC) at the time of Jesus' birth (2:1; Luke 1:5). He was a strong military leader, a brilliant politician, and a cruel tyrant. Born into an Idumean (Edomite) family with links to the Romans, he rose to power by gaining Roman favor and retained it by cruelly suppressing his opponents. Herod was known for his large building projects, especially his magnificent reconstruction of the Jewish Temple in Jerusalem, begun 20~19 BC (Josephus, *Antiquities* 15.8.1). Herod earned the title "the Great" because of his reputation as a great builder. He was the one who built Caesarea and made it the Roman headquarters in Palestine.

Herod the Great was also known for his family troubles and his brutal treatment of those who opposed him or whom he considered threats. He murdered two of his wives and three of his own sons when he suspected them of plotting against him. Caesar Augustus once said that he would rather be Herod's *swine* than his *son* (a play on words in Greek since the two words sound alike—*hus, huios*). When Jesus was born toward the end of Herod's reign and Herod heard him referred to as a future "king," Herod attempted to have him killed also. Unable to locate the boy, Herod then ordered the massacre of all the boys less than two years old in the Bethlehem area (see 2:1-20)—an act typical of his ruthlessness and paranoia.

Though Herod gained the title "king of the Jews," the Jewish people never accepted him as a legitimate king because he was not from the line of David and because he was an Edomite (a descendant of Esau) rather than a Jew. His greatest accomplishment was the rebuilding and beautification of the Jerusalem Temple, making it one of the most magnificent buildings in the ancient world.

1:22-23 ***Look! . . . Immanuel:*** Isa 7:14; 8:8, 10 (Greek version). Jesus' birth from a ***virgin*** fulfills Isa 7:14. The Hebrew term *'almah* (*virgin* or *young maiden*) was translated *parthenos* ("virgin") in the Greek OT that Matthew quotes. Matthew understands the *'almah* of Isaiah as foreshadowing the Virgin Mary.

1:25 ***Until*** probably implies that Joseph had ***sexual relations*** with Mary after the birth of Jesus. • ***And Joseph named him Jesus,*** thus showing his acceptance of the child as his own.

2:1-2 Attentiveness to the ***star*** indicates that the ***wise men*** were astrologers; their awareness of the OT (perhaps Num 24:17) suggests that they were from Babylonia, where Jews were numerous. The men were Gentiles, which anticipates Gentile acceptance into the Kingdom of God (8:11-12; 15:21-28; 28:16-20). Throughout the entire Gospel, unlikely Gentiles worship the Jewish Messiah, while the Jewish leaders (Herod, high priests, teachers of religious law, Pharisees) oppose him.

2:1 ***Bethlehem*** (see note on 2:6) was David's hometown (1 Sam 16:1-13; John 7:42). • ***King Herod,*** or Herod the Great, had a meteoric career; he rose from being governor of Galilee to being king of Galilee, Judea, and Samaria (37–4 BC). His career was marked by unflinching loyalty to Rome, magnificent building enterprises (including a substantial renovation of the Temple in Jerusalem), family hostility, suspicion, and ruthless murder of his own family members (Josephus, *Antiquities* 15.7.1-5) and of innocent children (2:16-18). • ***wise men:*** Or *royal astrologers;* Greek reads *magi;* also in 2:7, 16.

2:2 ***star as it rose:*** Or *star in the east.* • Matthew regularly describes Jesus as receiving ***worship*** (2:2, 8, 11; 8:2; 9:18; 14:33; 15:25; 20:20; 28:9, 17), thus identifying Jesus as God.

2:3 ***Herod was deeply disturbed*** because he feared this child would rival him as king of the Jews.

2:4 ***The leading priests*** had political and religious clout and ministered predominantly in the Temple (see 21:23). Herod gathered the ***teachers of religious law*** because they were trained to know OT prophecies and were often influential Pharisees.

2:6 The quotation is from Mic 5:2-4; 2 Sam 5:2. • ***Bethlehem,*** a small village,

[b]*poimainō* (4165)
‣Matt 9:36
2:9
Matt 2:2
2:11
Ps 72:10
Isa 60:6
2:12
Matt 2:22
2:13
Matt 1:20; 2:19
2:15
*Hos 11:1
2:18
*Jer 31:15
2:19
Matt 1:20; 2:12

are not least among the ruling cities
of Judah,
for a ruler will come from you
who will be the [b]shepherd for my
people Israel.' "

7Then Herod called for a private meeting
with the wise men, and he learned from
them the time when the star first appeared.
8Then he told them, "Go to Bethlehem and
search carefully for the child. And when
you find him, come back and tell me so that
I can go and worship him, too!"
9After this interview the wise men went
their way. And the star they had seen in
the east guided them to Bethlehem. It went
ahead of them and stopped over the place
where the child was. 10When they saw the
star, they were filled with joy! 11They entered the house and saw the child with his
mother, Mary, and they bowed down and
worshiped him. Then they opened their
treasure chests and gave him gifts of gold,
frankincense, and myrrh.
12When it was time to leave, they returned
to their own country by another route, for
God had warned them in a dream not to return to Herod.

The Escape to Egypt
13After the wise men were gone, an angel
of the Lord appeared to Joseph in a dream.
"Get up! Flee to Egypt with the child and his
mother," the angel said. "Stay there until I
tell you to return, because Herod is going to
search for the child to kill him."
14That night Joseph left for Egypt with
the child and Mary, his mother, 15and they
stayed there until Herod's death. This fulfilled what the Lord had spoken through
the prophet: "I called my Son out of Egypt."
16Herod was furious when he realized
that the wise men had outwitted him. He
sent soldiers to kill all the boys in and
around Bethlehem who were two years old
and under, based on the wise men's report
of the star's first appearance. 17Herod's brutal action fulfilled what God had spoken
through the prophet Jeremiah:

18 "A cry was heard in Ramah—
weeping and great mourning.
Rachel weeps for her children,
refusing to be comforted,
for they are dead."

The Return to Nazareth
19When Herod died, an angel of the Lord
appeared in a dream to Joseph in Egypt.

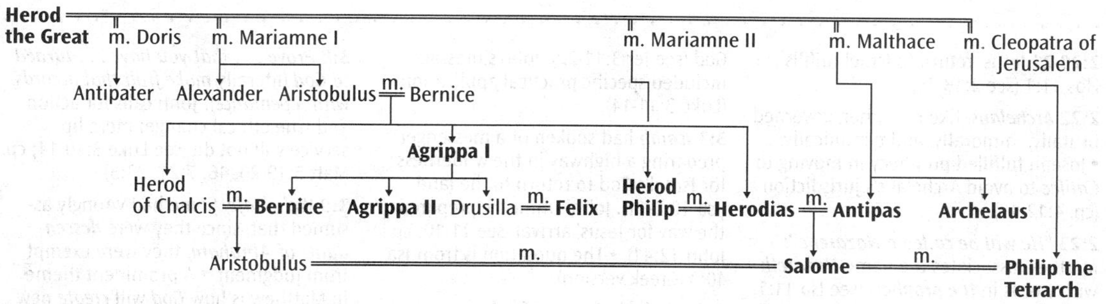

▲**The Herod Family (2:1-20).** Those whose names are in bold type appear in the NT. • HEROD THE GREAT: See profile, facing page. • HEROD PHILIP: See Mark 6:17. • ARCHELAUS: See 2:22. • HEROD ANTIPAS: See profile, p. 1659. • PHILIP THE TETRARCH: See Luke 3:1; notes on Mark 8:22-26, 27-28. • HEROD AGRIPPA I: See profile, p. 1851. • HERODIAS: See 14:3-11; Mark 6:17-29. • SALOME: See 14:6-8; Mark 6:22-28. • HEROD AGRIPPA II: See profile, p. 1879. • BERNICE: See Acts 25:13, 23; 26:30. • FELIX: See Acts 23:24–24:27. • For more about the Herod family, see Josephus, *Antiquities* 17–18.

had a privileged status as the birthplace of King David. The religious leaders knew from the prophets (1:22) that the Messiah would be born there. • ***the ruling cities:*** Literally *the rulers.* • King David had been a ***shepherd*** in his youth, and as king he became the shepherd of Israel (2 Sam 5:2). Micah 5:2-4 foresees the Messiah as a shepherd (cp. Ps 23:1).

2:8-10 The ***star*** was placed by God to guide the ***wise men*** to the Messiah (see Num 24:17); the details are unknown.

2:11 The wise men offered extravagant ***gifts of gold, frankincense, and myrrh*** to the King (see Ps 72:10-17; Isa 60:1-22). The tradition that there were three wise men originated from the number of gifts, but the text does not specify how many wise men there were.

2:13-15 ***Flee to Egypt . . . until I tell you to return:*** This fulfills Hos 11:1 (see note on 4:1-11; see also Gen 15:13-16; 46:1-5; Exod 15:1-21).

2:15 ***I called my Son out of Egypt:*** See Hos 11:1, which refers to the Exodus.

2:16 ***kill all the boys:*** Herod was notorious for his viciousness—he killed his own son to protect his throne, which led to the saying, "It is safer to be Herod's swine [Greek *hus*] than his son [Greek *huios*]," because Herod kept kosher. • ***two years old and under:*** Herod calculated the probable age of the child from the ***wise men's report.***

2:18 The quotation is from Jer 31:15. • ***Ramah***, a village near Bethlehem, is the place of ***Rachel***'s burial (Gen 35:18-20; Jer 31:15-17).

2:19 After ***Herod*** the Great ***died*** in 4 BC, Caesar split up his kingdom. Herod's son Archelaus (2:22) was appointed over Judea, Samaria, and Idumea, while Antipas (14:1-12; Luke 13:31-32) was appointed over Galilee and Perea.

20“Get up!” the angel said. “Take the child
and his mother back to the land of Israel,
because those who were trying to kill the
child are dead.”
21So Joseph got up and returned to the
land of Israel with Jesus and his mother.
22But when he learned that the new ruler
of Judea was Herod’s son Archelaus, he
was afraid to go there. Then, after being
warned in a dream, he left for the region of
Galilee. 23So the family went and lived in a
town called Nazareth. This fulfilled what
the prophets had said: “He will be called a
Nazarene.”

2. INTRODUCTION—PREPARATION FOR JESUS’ MINISTRY (3:1–4:11)

John the Baptist Prepares the Way for the Messiah

Matt 3:1-3 // Mark 1:2-3 // Luke 3:2b-6 // John 1:23
Matt 3:4-6 // Mark 1:4-6
Matt 3:7-10 // Luke 3:7-9
Matt 3:11-12 // Mark 1:7-8 // Luke 3:15-18 // John 1:24-28

3 In those days John the Baptist came
to the Judean wilderness and began
preaching. His message was, 2“Repent of
your sins and turn to God, for the Kingdom
of [c]Heaven is near.” 3The prophet Isaiah was
speaking about John when he said,

“He is a voice shouting in the wilderness,
‘Prepare the way for the [d]LORD’s coming!
Clear the road for him!’ ”

4John’s clothes were woven from coarse
camel hair, and he wore a leather belt
around his waist. For food he ate locusts
and wild honey. 5People from Jerusalem
and from all of Judea and all over the Jordan
Valley went out to see and hear John. 6And
when they confessed their sins, he baptized
them in the Jordan River.
7But when he saw many Pharisees and
Sadducees coming to watch him baptize,
he denounced them. “You brood of snakes!”
he exclaimed. “Who warned you to flee
God’s coming wrath? 8Prove by the way you
live that you have repented of your sins and
turned to God. 9Don’t just say to each other,
‘We’re safe, for we are descendants of Abraham.’ That means nothing, for I tell you, God
can create children of Abraham from these
very stones. 10Even now the ax of God’s judgment is poised, ready to sever the roots of
the trees. Yes, every tree that does not produce good fruit will be chopped down and
thrown into the fire.
11“I [e]baptize with water those who repent
of their sins and turn to God. But someone
is coming soon who is greater than I am—so
much greater that I’m not worthy even to
be his slave and carry his sandals. He will

2:20 Exod 4:19
2:22 Matt 2:12
2:23 Judg 13:5, 7; Luke 2:39
3:1-12 //Mark 1:1-8; //Luke 3:1-18; //John 1:19-28
3:2 Matt 4:17; 10:7; Mark 1:15; [c]*ouranos* (3772) ‣Matt 16:3
3:3 *Isa 40:3; Mal 3:1; Luke 1:76; [d]*kurios* (2962) ‣Matt 12:8
3:4 Lev 11:22; 2 Kgs 1:8
3:6 Mark 1:4
3:7 Matt 12:34; 23:33; John 8:44; Rom 5:9; Eph 5:6; Col 3:6
3:8 Acts 26:20
3:9 John 8:33, 37, 39; Acts 13:26; Rom 2:28-29; 4:12
3:10 Matt 7:19; Luke 13:7; John 15:6

2:20-21 Jesus’ return to Israel fulfills Hos 11:1 (see 2:13-15).

2:22 ***Archelaus,*** like his father, governed brutally, immorally, and tyrannically. • Joseph fulfilled prophecy in moving to ***Galilee*** to avoid Archelaus’s jurisdiction (cp. 4:12-16).

2:23 ***“He will be called a Nazarene”:*** Matthew associates the name ***Nazareth*** with words in ***the prophets*** (see Isa 11:1, where the Messiah is called a “Branch,” [Hebrew *netser*]; and Judg 13:5, where Samson is called a “Nazirite”).

3:1 ***John the Baptist*** announced Jesus’ coming (see Mark 1:1-11; Luke 3:1-22; John 1:6-8, 19-34) and prepared people to receive him (3:3). John attracted large crowds (3:5) and a group of disciples (9:14). This group continued for a short time as a movement, even as the Christian church emerged (see Acts 18:24-28). • John’s locale in ***the Judean wilderness*** had symbolic significance: The wilderness was associated with the giving of the law (see Exod 19:1) and with God’s final redemption of Israel at the end of history (see Isa 40:3).

3:2 ***is near*** (or *has come,* or *is coming soon*): The prophetic call to return to God in repentance (cp. Isa 1:16-20) involves total reorientation from pride and sin to humble obedience to God (see Jer 3:11-22). John’s message included specific practical application (Luke 3:11-14).

3:3 ***Isaiah*** had spoken of a messenger preparing a highway in the wilderness for Israel’s God to return to the land (Isa 40:1-11). John’s ministry prepared the way for Jesus’ arrival (see 11:10; cp. John 12:41). • The quotation is from Isa 40:3 (Greek version).

3:4 ***John’s clothes*** and ***food*** correspond to those of his prophetic predecessor, Elijah (2 Kgs 1:8; Mal 4:5; *Sirach* 48:10-11).

3:5-6 John’s ministry became so popular that many ***people from Jerusalem*** and ***Judea*** came to hear him. • ***they confessed their sins:*** Those who responded to John’s preaching and turned away from sin were prepared to receive Jesus’ ministry (Luke 7:27, 29). • ***he baptized them:*** John’s practice of baptism may have originated with the OT idea of purification (see Isa 1:16; 4:4; Ezek 36:25).

3:7 The ***Pharisees’*** name derives from the Hebrew term *perushim,* meaning either *separated ones* or *exact interpreters.* • The ***Sadducees,*** a priestly class, probably derive their name from Zadok the priest (2 Sam 15:24-29; Ezek 44:10-16). • ***coming to watch him baptize:*** Or *coming to be baptized.*

3:8 ***Prove . . . that you have . . . turned to God*** (literally *make fruit that accords with repentance*): John calls for action and true ethical change; mere lip service will not do (see Luke 3:10-14; cp. Matt 5:19-20, 46; 7:21; 23:3).

3:9 ***We’re safe:*** Some had wrongly assumed that, since they were ***descendants of Abraham,*** they were exempt from judgment. • A prominent theme in Matthew is how ***God*** will ***create*** new ***children of Abraham*** by bringing the Gentiles into God’s people and removing from his people Jews who reject the Messiah (see 8:11-12; 21:43; 22:1-14; 28:16-20; Rom 4:9-25; Gal 3:6-14, 29).

3:11 ***with water:*** Or *in water.* • ***who is greater than I am:*** Despite his popularity and growing following, John had a clear sense of his role as subordinate to the Messiah. • ***I’m not worthy even to be his slave:*** In Jewish culture, to remove and carry someone’s sandals, even those of a rabbi, was too lowly a task even for the rabbi’s disciple. It was a job reserved for slaves. • ***with the Holy Spirit and with fire*** (or *in the Holy Spirit and in fire*): This happened at Pentecost (see Joel 2:28-29; Acts 2); the ministry of Jesus, empowered by the Holy Spirit (see 12:28; Luke 4:14), may also be included. ***Fire*** may refer to purification (Zech 13:9) or judgment (Mal 4:1; see Isa 1:25; 4:4;

3:11 John 1:26-27, 31, 33 Acts 1:5; 2:3-4; 19:4 [e]*baptizō* (0907) ›Matt 28:19
3:12 Matt 13:30
3:13-17 //Mark 1:9-11 //Luke 3:21-22
3:16 Isa 11:2 John 1:31-34
3:17 Gen 22:2 Ps 2:7 Matt 17:5

[e]baptize you with the Holy Spirit and with
fire. 12He is ready to separate the chaff
from the wheat with his winnowing fork.
Then he will clean up the threshing area,
gathering the wheat into his barn but burning the chaff with never-ending fire."

The Baptism of Jesus: God Proclaims His Messiah
Matt 3:13-17 // Mark 1:9-11 // Luke 3:21-22 // John 1:29-34

13Then Jesus went from Galilee to the Jordan
River to be baptized by John. 14But John
tried to talk him out of it. "I am the one who needs to be baptized by you," he said, "so why are you coming to me?"

15But Jesus said, "It should be done, for
we must carry out all that God requires." So John agreed to baptize him.

16After his baptism, as Jesus came up out
of the water, the heavens were opened and he saw the Spirit of God descending like
a dove and settling on him. 17And a voice
from heaven said, "This is my dearly loved Son, who brings me great joy."

THE PHARISEES (3:7)

Matt 5:20; 9:10-14, 34; 12:1-14, 22-24, 38-40; 15:1-14; 16:1-12; 19:3; 21:45; 22:15, 34; 23:1-7, 13-31; 27:62-64 Mark 2:23-25; 3:1-6; 7:1-13; 8:11-12; 12:13-17 Luke 5:17-21, 29-32; 6:6-11; 7:28-30, 36-49; 11:37-54; 12:1-3; 13:31; 14:1-6; 15:1-2; 16:13-15; 17:20-21; 18:9-14; 19:38-40 John 1:24-25; 3:1; 7:31-32, 45-52; 8:3-10, 13; 9:13-34, 40; 11:46-57; 12:17-19, 42; 18:3 Acts 5:27-40; 15:5; 23:6-10; 26:4-5 Phil 3:5-7

The Pharisees were one of three major Jewish sects, along with the Sadducees and the Essenes. The Pharisees were a non-political lay movement within Judaism. They arose from the *hasidim* (pious ones), who opposed the syncretizing (combining together) of Greek culture and religion with Judaism in the 100s BC. They attempted, by rigorous examination of the details of the OT law, to make the law accessible and practical to people seeking to be obedient Jews. They taught strict adherence to the law, not only the written law of Moses (*torah*), but also the oral traditions which they claimed Moses had passed down to them. Their goal was to defend the written law against any possible infringement. They were God-fearing and law-abiding people. They were famous for passing their interpretations from generation to generation by word of mouth, establishing an oral tradition concerning legal matters. They made the law applicable by extracting from it specific guidelines for many possible situations. They argued that if the law were obeyed by all, the nation would be purged of sin and God would establish his Kingdom over all the nations. This gave their concern for obedience a goal in the future. Although the Pharisees were small in number, their influence on Israel was widespread (e.g., 15:12-14; see Josephus, *War* 2.8.14; *Antiquities* 13.10.5). The primary influence of the Pharisees was in the local synagogue communities, while the Sadducees were more influential in the Temple worship in Jerusalem and in the Sanhedrin, the Jewish high council. The traditions of the Pharisees developed into the rabbinic writings known as the *Mishnah* and the *Talmud*.

Unlike the Sadducees (see "The Sadducees" at 16:1-12, p. 1610), the Pharisees had a strong belief in the resurrection of the dead (see Acts 23:8). After the destruction of Jerusalem in AD 70, the Pharisees provided leadership and direction for the people of Israel.

Jesus often came into conflict with the Pharisees, accusing them of hypocrisy and of elevating human rules over God's righteous standards. Jesus opposed the Pharisees because they were leading people away from God's plan for redemption. In Matthew, the Pharisees oppose the work of God from the outset (3:7), mostly because of their meticulous observance of the law (23:23-26) and Jesus' shocking disregard of their traditions (15:1-20). They were the theological shepherds of Israel (12:38; cp. 9:36), but Jesus castigates them as hypocrites for their perversions of doctrine and practice (see ch 23).

Mal 3:2-3). It is a "Spirit-and-fire baptism"; the Messiah puts into effect what John could only prepare—thoroughgoing judgment and purification.

3:12 Farmers would use a ***winnowing fork*** to toss harvested grain into the air, allowing the useless husks (***chaff***) to blow away. The Messiah's ministry divides all humanity into two groups: (1) ***the wheat***, that is, those who respond, forming the new people of God; and (2) ***the chaff***, the unrepentant (see 3:8).

3:14 As John had already confessed (3:11-12), he was lesser than the Messiah, so he felt unfit to baptize him.

3:15 ***for we must carry out all that God requires:*** Or *for we must fulfill all righteousness.* This statement refers to accomplishing what the OT demanded or foreshadowed (e.g., Jer 31:31-34). "Righteousness" in Matthew refers to behavior that conforms to God's will (see 5:20; 6:1, 33; 21:32).

3:16 ***opened:*** Some manuscripts read *opened to him.* • The ***Spirit of God descending like a dove*** was anointing Jesus, through whom salvation would come. This event was like a king's being anointed with oil at his coronation. The Holy Spirit empowered Jesus to accomplish God's salvation and defeat Satan (see 12:18, 28). This same Spirit empowers Jesus' followers (10:20; Acts 1:8).

3:17 ***my dearly loved Son*** (see Ps 2:7): The title "Son of God" reveals and clarifies Jesus' nature and role (see 4:3, 6; 14:33; 16:16; 17:5; 26:63; 27:54; 28:19). In his unique relationship to the Father, Jesus accomplishes salvation as the trusting and obedient Son. • ***who brings me great joy:*** God the Father confirmed his Son's ministry with language from Isaiah (Isa 42:1) and so prepared Israel for his ministry.

The Temptation of Jesus: Satan Tests the Messiah
Matt 4:1-11 // Mark 1:12-13 // Luke 4:1-13

4 Then Jesus was led by the Spirit into
the wilderness to be tempted there by
the [f]devil. 2For forty days and forty nights
he fasted and became very hungry.
3During that time the devil came and said
to him, "If you are the Son of God, tell these
stones to become loaves of bread."
4But Jesus told him, "No! The Scriptures
say,

'People do not live by bread alone,
but by every word that comes from
the mouth of God.' "

5Then the devil took him to the holy city,
Jerusalem, to the highest point of the Temple, 6and said, "If you are the Son of God,
jump off! For the Scriptures say,

'He will order his angels to protect you.
And they will hold you up with their hands
so you won't even hurt your foot on a
stone.' "

7Jesus responded, "The Scriptures also
say, 'You must not test the LORD your God.' "
8Next the devil took him to the peak of
a very high mountain and showed him all
the kingdoms of the world and their glory.
9"I will give it all to you," he said, "if you will
kneel down and worship me."
10"Get out of here, [g]Satan," Jesus told him.
"For the Scriptures say,

'You must worship the LORD your God
and serve only him.' "

11Then the devil went away, and [h]angels
came and took care of Jesus.

3. THE MESSIAH CONFRONTS ISRAEL (4:12–11:1)

Narrative: Introduction to Jesus' Ministry (4:12-25)

The Ministry of Jesus Begins
Matt 4:12-17; cp. Mark 1:14-15; Luke 4:14-15

12When Jesus heard that John had been arrested, he left Judea and returned to Galilee.
13He went first to Nazareth, then left there
and moved to Capernaum, beside the Sea of
Galilee, in the region of Zebulun and Naphtali. 14This fulfilled what God said through
the prophet Isaiah:

4:1-11
//Mark 1:12-13
//Luke 4:1-13

4:1
Gen 3:1-7
1 Thes 3:5
[f]*diabolos* (1228)
‣ Matt 25:41

4:2
Exod 34:28
1 Kgs 19:8

4:4
*Deut 8:3

4:6
*Ps 91:11-12

4:7
*Deut 6:16

4:10
*Deut 6:13
[g]*satanas* (4567)
‣ Matt 16:23

4:11
1 Kgs 19:4-8
Luke 22:43
Heb 1:14
Jas 4:7
[h]*angelos* (0032)
‣ Matt 22:30

4:12-17
//Mark 1:14-15
//Luke 4:14-15

4:1-11 Parallels between Adam and Jesus are obvious in this account of Jesus' temptation. Jesus is the second Adam (see Rom 5:12-19) and the second Israel (2:15). In contrast to the ancient Israelites, he fulfilled Israel's history by successfully wandering through the desert without sinning. He proved himself the obedient Son of God by defeating Satan in spiritual combat. And because he underwent temptation himself as a human, Jesus is able to sympathize with the temptations we face (see Heb 2:14-18; 4:15) and help us overcome them as he did (1 Cor 10:13).

4:1 ***Jesus was led by the Spirit:*** The temptation was providentially arranged by God as a test of the Messiah's character (see Deut 8:2). • ***to be tempted there by the devil:*** This test of character, initiated by God (who tempts no one; see Jas 1:13-14), was accomplished through the devil's own desire to lure Jesus into sin.

4:2 ***forty days and forty nights*** (see Exod 24:18; 34:28; 1 Kgs 19:8): Israel was tested in the wilderness for forty years (Exod 16:35; Deut 1:3).

4:3-4 Jesus refused to use his supernatural power to obtain the food that he trusted God to provide. Unlike the people of Israel, who sorely tested God through complaint and unbelief (see Exod 16), Jesus refused to question God's faithfulness. Instead, he trusted God to provide for his true need, the sustenance of ***every word that comes from the mouth of God.***

4:3 ***the devil:*** Literally *the tempter.*

4:4 Jesus was quoting Deut 8:3.

4:5-7 Jesus refused to test God by presuming upon God's protection.

4:6 Now the devil quotes Ps 91:11-12.

4:7 ***The Scriptures also say:*** Countering the devil's appeal to Scripture, Jesus invoked a deeper scriptural principle of honoring God, which the devil ignored. See Deut 6:16.

4:8-10 Satan, called the ruler of this world (John 12:31), offered to hand over ***all the kingdoms of the world and their glory*** to Jesus to keep him from accomplishing the will of his Father. • ***Glory*** refers to political power and dominion (e.g., 6:29). Satan's strategy was to get Jesus to abuse his sonship, thus diverting him from the path of suffering and obedience that climaxed at the cross. • ***You must . . . only him:*** Deut 6:13.

4:11 ***Then the devil went away:*** Jesus' rebuff of Satan here foreshadows his victory over demons (12:28), Satan's defeat through the Cross (Col 2:14-15), and the final victory at the end of history (Rom 16:20; Rev 12:7-17; 20:2-3, 10). • ***Angels,*** who had already been involved in the Messiah's arrival and protection (1:20, 24; 2:13, 19), now ***came and took care of Jesus*** after his temptation, in fulfillment of the OT (4:6; see Ps 91:11-12).

4:12–11:1 Having been announced by John and the Father (3:13-17), and having obediently endured the testing in the wilderness (4:1-11), the Messiah was prepared for his ministry. He first confronted the Galilean Israelites with the message of the Kingdom.

4:12 ***John had been arrested*** by Herod Antipas (see 14:1-12). Antipas was tetrarch of Galilee and Perea, where John was probably working at the time. • ***When Jesus heard . . . he left Judea and returned to Galilee:*** As in Joseph's flight to Nazareth (2:22-23), an escape from danger can also be God's providential direction (4:14-16). Jesus withdrew to avoid martyrdom before finishing his work of revealing the Kingdom.

4:13 ***Capernaum*** was in Galilee, a district viewed negatively by the religious establishment in Judea and Jerusalem (see John 1:46; 7:41-42, 52). Many Judeans considered Galileans to be uncultured, with a lazy command of the language (cp. 26:73), a factor sometimes thought to affect the accuracy of their teachings. Galilee also had a proportionately larger Gentile population than Judea did.

4:14-16 ***through the prophet Isaiah:*** See Isa 9:1-2 (Greek version).

4:15-16
*Isa 9:1-2; 42:6-7
Luke 2:32
John 1:5
4:17
Matt 3:2; 10:7
4:18-22
//Mark 1:16-20
//Luke 5:1-11
4:19
Matt 16:17-18
John 1:43
4:20
Mark 10:28
Luke 18:28
4:23-25
Luke 6:17-19
4:23
Matt 9:35
Mark 1:39
Luke 4:15

15 "In the land of Zebulun and of Naphtali,
beside the sea, beyond the Jordan
River,
in Galilee where so many Gentiles
live,
16 the people who sat in darkness
have seen a great light.
And for those who lived in the land
where death casts its shadow,
a light has shined."

17 From then on Jesus began to preach,
"Repent of your sins and turn to God, for the
Kingdom of Heaven is near."

The First Disciples
Matt 4:18-22 // Mark 1:16-20

18 One day as Jesus was walking along the
shore of the Sea of Galilee, he saw two
brothers—Simon, also called Peter, and Andrew—throwing a net into the water, for
they fished for a living.
19 Jesus called out to
them, "Come, follow me, and I will show you
how to fish for people!"
20 And they left their
nets at once and followed him.
21 A little farther up the shore he saw two
other brothers, James and John, sitting in a
boat with their father, Zebedee, repairing
their nets. And he called them to come, too.
22 They immediately followed him, leaving
the boat and their father behind.

Crowds Follow Jesus

23 Jesus traveled throughout the region of
Galilee, teaching in the synagogues and
announcing the Good News about the Kingdom. And he healed every kind of disease
and illness.
24 News about him spread as far
as Syria, and people soon began bringing to
him all who were sick. And whatever their
sickness or disease, or if they were demon
possessed or epileptic or paralyzed—he
healed them all.
25 Large crowds followed
him wherever he went—people from Galilee, the Ten Towns, Jerusalem, from all over
Judea, and from east of the Jordan River.

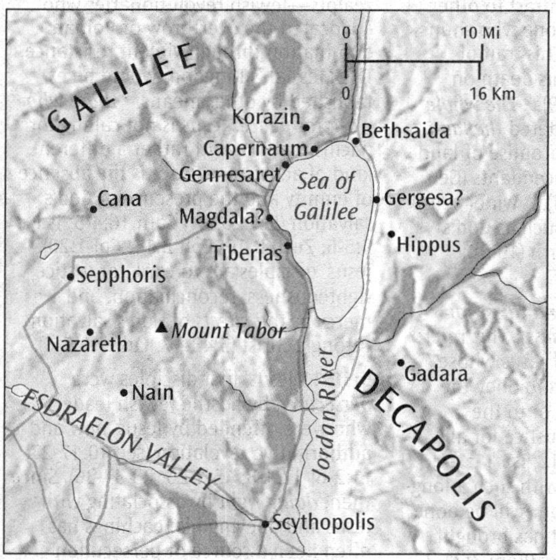

◄ **Jesus' Ministry in Galilee (Matt 4:12–15:20; see also 15:29–16:12; 17:22–18:1; Mark 1:14-21; Luke 4:14-31; John 4:43-54).** After Jesus learned that John the Baptist had been put in prison (4:12), he moved to the Galilean seaside town of CAPERNAUM and made it his base of operations for much of his ministry.
CAPERNAUM 4:13; 8:5; 11:23; 17:24
SEA OF GALILEE 4:13, 18; 15:29
NAZARETH 2:23; 4:13

4:17 Jesus' message centered on the imminent arrival of the ***Kingdom of Heaven*** and the repentance that it necessitates (see 3:2; 10:7). • ***is near:*** Or *has come,* or *is coming soon.*

4:18-22 The call of the first disciples illustrates one of the purposes of Jesus' ministry: to call people to follow him in self-denying obedience (cp. 4:17, 23-25).

4:18 ***Simon, also called Peter,*** became the leader of the apostles (see 14:28; 15:15; 16:16) and the representative disciple (14:29-30; 16:15-19, 22-23).

4:19 ***Come, follow me:*** This involved accepting the beliefs and lifestyle of a master as one's own (16:24; Deut 5:33; 1 Kgs 19:19-21). • ***fish for people:*** The disciples would participate in the saving and judging work of the Kingdom (see 10:5-15; 13:47-51; Ezek 29:4-5; Amos 4:2).

4:20-22 ***leaving the boat and their father:*** Following Jesus as his disciples involved both commitment and cost on the part of the brothers (see 8:18-22; 10:38; 16:24; 19:21).

4:23-25 This summary marks the central theme of the section (4:23–9:38): the ministry and message of the Messiah. In ancient writings, chapter divisions were unknown; authors would instead begin and end a section with the same expression (called an *inclusio;* see 9:35).

4:23 The Messiah's ministry has three main features: ***teaching, announcing . . . the Kingdom,*** and healing. • ***The synagogues*** were centers for prayer, study, and exposition of Scripture and tradition. They were the social centers of many Jewish villages. The hypocrisy and hostility of the Jewish leaders was evident at the synagogues (6:2, 5; 10:17; 12:9-14; 13:54; 23:6, 34). • ***Announcing the Good News*** means presenting the message ***about the Kingdom*** of Heaven (9:35; 24:14; 26:13; also Mark 1:1; Rom 1:16). Most often, the message evokes hostility (see 9:32-34; 10:27-28; 13:1-9, 18-23).

4:24-25 During Jesus' day, much of Palestine was in the Roman jurisdiction of Syria (a term that could refer to the entire eastern shore of the Mediterranean). Matthew mentions ***Syria*** to show how widespread the news of Jesus was. • The word translated ***epileptic*** refers to epilepsy or demonic oppression. In 17:15, one so described "falls into fire and water," that is, the boy was unable to control himself. • The ***Ten Towns*** (Greek *Decapolis*) was a federation of ten cities, east of the Jordan and mostly southeast of the Sea of Galilee (Damascus, Raphana, Hippos, Abila [or Canatha], Gadara, Scythopolis, Pella, Dion, Gerasa, and Philadelphia [Amman]). These cities were predominantly Gentile and Hellenistic in culture.

The Sermon on the Mount: Jesus' Call to Righteousness (5:1–7:29)

Introduction

5 One day as he saw the crowds gathering, Jesus went up on the mountainside and sat down. His disciples gathered around him, 2 and he began to teach them.

The Beatitudes

Matt 5:3-12 // Luke 6:20-23

3 "God [i]blesses those who are poor and
realize their need for him,
for the Kingdom of Heaven is theirs.
4 God blesses those who mourn,
for they will be comforted.
5 God blesses those who are humble,
for they will inherit the whole earth.
6 God blesses those who hunger and thirst
for justice,
for they will be satisfied.
7 God blesses those who are merciful,
for they will be shown mercy.
8 God blesses those whose [i]hearts are pure,
for they will see God.
9 God blesses those who work for peace,
for they will be called the children
of God.
10 God blesses those who are persecuted
for doing right,
for the Kingdom of Heaven is theirs.

11 "God blesses you when people mock you and persecute you and lie about you and say all sorts of evil things against you because you are my followers. 12 Be happy about it! Be very glad! For a great reward awaits you in heaven. And remember, the ancient prophets were persecuted in the same way.

Teaching about Salt and Light

Matt 5:13; cp. Mark 9:49-50; Luke 14:34-35
Matt 5:15 // Mark 4:21 // Luke 8:16; 11:33

13 "You are the salt of the earth. But what

5:1 Luke 6:12 John 6:3
5:3-12 //Luke 6:20-23
5:3 Isa 57:15 Matt 25:34 [i]*makarios* (3107) ‣ Luke 6:20
5:4 Isa 61:2-3
5:5 Ps 37:11 Rom 4:13
5:7 Jas 2:13
5:8 Ps 24:3-5 [i]*kardia* (2588) ‣ Matt 15:18
5:9 Heb 12:14 Jas 3:18
5:10 2 Tim 2:12
5:11 1 Pet 4:14

5:1–7:29 This is the first of five lengthy discourses in Matthew (see also 9:35–11:1; 13:1-53; 18:1–19:2; 23:1–26:1). The theme of the Sermon on the Mount is the Messiah's call to righteousness. Paul understood righteousness in terms of God's saving acts and of a person's standing before God. Jesus uses the term for moral behavior that conforms to God's will, as James does. Specifically, righteousness is doing the will of God as Jesus reveals it. This "revelation of righteousness" unifies the entire Sermon.

5:3 ***poor and realize their need for him*** (literally *poor in spirit*; cp. Luke 6:20, 24): In the OT, the poor are often depicted as especially pious because oppression by the wealthy leads them to trust in the Lord for salvation and deliverance rather than relying on the power of wealth (11:5; Ps 37:14-15; 40:17; 69:28-33; Isa 61:1; 66:2). In both Matthew's and Luke's accounts, the "poor" are indeed physically poor, but their trust in God, not their poverty, is what makes them blessed (Isa 57:15; 66:2).

5:4 ***Those who mourn*** were those who lamented the spiritual and national condition of Israel (see 23:37-39; Isa 61:2-3; Joel 1:8-13; 2:12-13, 18-19; Rom 9:1-5; 1 Cor 5:2; Jas 4:9). Personal grief, whether caused by sin or tragedy, may also be in view (Mark 16:10; Rev 18:11, 19). • ***will be comforted:*** The passive voice is used out of reverence for the holy name of God; the phrase could also be rendered *God will comfort them* (see also 5:6-7, 9). Comfort will accompany the fulfillment of all that God has promised (Isa 40:1-2; 61:2-3).

5:5 ***those who are humble:*** See Ps 37:11, which Jesus practically quotes here. Elsewhere, Jesus describes himself in similar terms—in contrast to other teachers (11:29) and as one who shuns pride (12:17-21; 21:5). This trait of Jesus is exemplified in his death on the cross (1 Pet 2:23; 3:9). • ***The whole earth*** could also be rendered *the land*, thus referring to God's promise of land to Abraham and his descendants (Gen 12:7; 17:8; see Isa 60:21). A wider sense may also be intended, such as God's reign over the entire earth (19:28; 28:18-20; Ps 115:16).

5:6 ***those who hunger and thirst for justice*** (or *for righteousness*): This refers either to the follower of Jesus whose driving purpose in life is to obey the Lord (cp. 3:15; 5:10, 20) or to the disciple's desire to see justice for all people (Ps 11:7; 85:10-12; Isa 11:1-4; Jer 23:5-6; 33:16). One with such a longing often prays, "May your will be done on earth" (6:10). • Christ has brought ***justice*** and righteousness (Rom 3:21-22; 5:1); the disciples ***will be satisfied*** with it (cp. Ps 42:1-2; 63:1-2).

5:7 Jesus made a cardinal virtue of being ***merciful,*** that is, showing kindness to those in distress (see 6:12, 14-15; 9:13; 12:7; 18:23-35; 23:23; 25:31-46). Those who are merciful now will find God's mercy in the final judgment.

5:8 ***Those whose hearts are pure*** (see Ps 24:3-5; 51:7; Isa 6:5) are contrasted with those who thought that they had satisfied God's will through ceremonial conformity to tradition (23:25-26). Jesus insisted on simple, true heart-righteousness (see 6:1-24; 15:1-20; 23:23-28; Deut 6:5). • ***They will see God*** and thereby attain even more than Moses did (see Exod 33:18-23; 34:5-7; see also Ps 73:1).

5:9 This beatitude probably targeted zealots—Jewish revolutionaries who advocated the overthrow of Roman domination through violent resistance. The Messiah's Kingdom would be established by other means. • ***those who work for peace:*** Jesus is not calling for pacifism per se, but rather a different kind of activism. • ***Peace*** is the absence of enmity and the presence of God's salvation (Lev 26:6; 1 Sam 16:4-5; Isa 9:5-6; Zech 8:16; Eph 2:14; Col 1:20). Jesus' disciples are to work for justice, righteousness, reconciliation, and mercy as the *effects* of God's salvation through Christ (5:43-47; Luke 10:5-6).

5:10-11 Jesus' first disciples were ***persecuted*** by hostile Jewish leaders who were offended by Jesus' new and authoritative revelation (see 10:17-23; 11:2-6; 12:1-8; 15:1-20; 23:34-36). Since then, ***doing right*** by associating with Jesus and obeying his teachings has often been a source of persecution (10:24-25; 2 Tim 3:12).

5:11 Some manuscripts do not include ***and lie about you.***

5:12 The ***great reward*** Jesus mentions is not something earned by suffering for doing right; it is God's blessing to those who have expressed his grace to others (see 10:41-42; 20:1-16). • The ***ancient prophets*** are closely connected with the NT apostles (see also 13:16-17; 23:29-36; Eph 2:20).

5:13-16 The disciples' good deeds will have profoundly positive effects on the world around them, to the glory of God. With this comes a warning from Jesus: Do nothing that might jeopardize that positive impact.

5:13 ***Salt*** was used for cleansing and preservation from decay (Ezek 16:4),

5:12
2 Chr 36:16
Acts 7:52
Jas 5:10
5:14
Phil 2:15
5:16
1 Pet 2:12
[k]*patēr* (3962)
‣Matt 6:9
5:17
Rom 3:31
5:18
Luke 16:17; 21:33
5:19
Jas 2:10
5:21
*Exod 20:13
*Deut 5:17
Rom 13:9
Jas 2:11
5:22
Eph 4:26
Jas 1:19-20

good is salt if it has lost its flavor? Can you
make it salty again? It will be thrown out
and trampled underfoot as worthless.
14“You are the light of the world—like a
city on a hilltop that cannot be hidden. 15No
one lights a lamp and then puts it under a
basket. Instead, a lamp is placed on a stand,
where it gives light to everyone in the house.
16In the same way, let your good deeds shine
out for all to see, so that everyone will praise
your heavenly [k]Father.

Teaching about the Law
Matt 5:17-20; cp. Luke 16:17

17“Don’t misunderstand why I have come.
I did not come to abolish the law of Moses
or the writings of the prophets. No, I came
to accomplish their purpose. 18I tell you the
truth, until heaven and earth disappear, not
even the smallest detail of God’s law will disappear until its purpose is achieved. 19So
if you ignore the least commandment and
teach others to do the same, you will be
called the least in the Kingdom of Heaven.
But anyone who obeys God’s laws and
teaches them will be called great in the
Kingdom of Heaven.
20“But I warn you—unless your righteousness is better than the righteousness of
the teachers of religious law and the Pharisees, you will never enter the Kingdom of
Heaven!

Teaching about Anger
Matt 5:25 // Luke 12:57-59

21“You have heard that our ancestors were
told, ‘You must not murder. If you commit
murder, you are subject to judgment.’ 22But I

The Blessings of Jesus (5:3-12)

Matt 11:6; 13:16; 16:17; 24:46; 25:34
Ps 1:1-3; 106:3; 112:1; 119:1-2
Isa 56:1-2
Luke 6:20-26

The blessings of Jesus are called Beatitudes because the Latin Vulgate translates the Greek word for *blessed* as *beati*. No single word can capture all that Jesus is communicating with this term here. He is describing the special favor of God toward his people, both physically and spiritually, and the consequences of living within that favor. Jesus calls men and women to follow him as he proclaims the message of the Kingdom to Israel (see also 11:6; 13:16; 16:17; 24:46). The Beatitudes describe the lifestyle and character of a follower of Jesus. Those who are blessed have repented in response to the proclamation of the Kingdom (4:17-22). The Beatitudes (5:3-12) are connected with Isa 61:1-3. The Spirit endows, leads to proclamation, and blesses the poor, the humble, and the righteous.

The NLT’s use of “God blesses” conveys the ideas of divine origin and approval (see 25:34), fulfillment (see 11:6; 13:16; 16:17), reversal (see Luke 1–2; 6:20-26), and the condition of obedience required in order to enjoy the blessings (see Ps 1:1, 3-6; 106:3; 112:1; 119:1-2; Prov 8:32; Isa 56:2). The blessings are inaugurated with the Messiah’s coming, with a confident hope that they will be enjoyed eternally and completely.

in forming covenants (Lev 2:13; Num 18:19; see note on 2 Chr 13:5), and as flavor (Job 6:6; Mark 9:50). • Salt that *lost its flavor* became useless, insipid, or dull (see Mark 9:50; Luke 14:34).

5:14 ***light of the world . . . city on a hilltop:*** The attractive quality of the disciples’ lives will draw other people to live similarly and to glorify God (see Isa 2:2-5; 42:6; 49:6; 51:4; 56:6-8; 60:1-3; Phil 2:15).

5:16 ***praise your heavenly Father:*** Religious hypocrites seek praise for themselves; Jesus’ disciples should seek praise for God (see 1 Pet 2:12).

5:17 ***Abolish*** would mean to eliminate and replace ***the law of Moses*** and ***the writings of the prophets*** (i.e., the whole OT) as the revelation of God’s will. • ***Accomplish their purpose*** might mean to obey perfectly, to complete the teaching of, or to bring about OT prophecies (see 1:22; 2:15, 17, 23). Jesus himself is the realization of all that both the Prophets and the Law taught and expected. Now that Christ, the fulfillment, has come, the OT must be understood in light of him (Luke 24:26, 44).

5:19 The realization of the law in Christ means that obedience to all of his commands (see 28:20) is the only acceptable response for his disciples. • ***Commandment*** refers to the OT commands (5:18) as now fulfilled in Christ’s teaching (see 5:21-48). • ***the least in the Kingdom of Heaven:*** Jesus may mean that such an individual will enter the Kingdom, but only barely and with low status; alternatively, some Jewish evidence suggests that he is referring to damnation (cp. 8:12, where “those for whom the Kingdom was prepared” are eternally excluded).

5:20 ***unless your righteousness is better:*** Jesus’ disciples must have the substantially new kind of righteousness that Jesus teaches and makes possible (illustrated in 5:21-47 and summed up in 5:48); it is both quantitatively and qualitatively distinct. Just as Jesus is greater than the Temple (12:6) and Jonah (12:41), so the righteousness of his followers far outstrips that of the ***teachers of religious law and the Pharisees*** (see 3:7-9).

5:21-47 ***You have heard. . . . But I say:*** Jesus contrasts his own teaching to six misinterpretations of the law. Each antithesis provides an example of the surpassing righteousness of Jesus. Jesus reveals the will of God as it contrasts with traditions.

5:21 ***our ancestors were told:*** The expression refers to the traditional interpretation of the teachers of religious law and Pharisees. Though their traditions prohibited ***murder,*** they did not prohibit hatred. The surpassing righteousness of Jesus demands reconciliation (5:23-24); merely refraining from committing murder is not sufficient (5:22). • ***‘You must not murder . . .’:*** Exod 20:13; Deut 5:17.

5:22 ***angry with someone:*** Some manuscripts add *without cause.*

say, if you are even angry with someone, you are subject to judgment! If you call someone an idiot, you are in danger of being brought before the court. And if you curse someone, you are in danger of the fires of [a]hell.

[23]"So if you are presenting a sacrifice at the altar in the Temple and you suddenly remember that someone has something against you, [24]leave your sacrifice there at the altar. Go and be reconciled to that person. Then come and offer your sacrifice to God.

[25]"When you are on the way to court with your adversary, settle your differences quickly. Otherwise, your accuser may hand you over to the judge, who will hand you over to an officer, and you will be thrown into prison. [26]And if that happens, you surely won't be free again until you have paid the last penny.

Teaching about Adultery

[27]"You have heard the commandment that says, 'You must not commit adultery.' [28]But I say, anyone who even looks at a woman with lust has already committed adultery with her in his heart. [29]So if your eye—even your good eye—[b]causes you to lust, gouge it out and throw it away. It is better for you to lose one part of your body than for your whole body to be thrown into [c]hell. [30]And if your hand—even your stronger hand—[b]causes you to sin, cut it off and throw it away. It is better for you to lose one part of your body than for your whole body to be thrown into [c]hell.

Teaching about Divorce

Matt 5:31-32; cp. Matt 19:9; Mark 10:11-12; Luke 16:18

[31]"You have heard the law that says, 'A man can divorce his wife by merely giving her a written notice of divorce.' [32]But I say that a man who divorces his wife, unless she has been unfaithful, causes her to commit adultery. And anyone who marries a divorced woman also commits adultery.

Teaching about Vows

[33]"You have also heard that our ancestors were told, 'You must not break your vows; you must carry out the vows you make to the LORD.' [34]But I say, do not make any vows! Do not say, 'By heaven!' because heaven is God's throne. [35]And do not say, 'By the earth!' because the earth is his footstool. And do not

[a]*geenna* (1067) ‣ Matt 5:29

5:25-26 Matt 18:34-35 Luke 12:58-59

5:27 *Exod 20:14 *Deut 5:18 Matt 19:18 Mark 10:19 Luke 18:20 Rom 13:9 Jas 2:11

5:29-30 Matt 18:8-9 Mark 9:43-47

[b]*skandalizō* (4624) ‣ Matt 16:23

[c]*geenna* (1067) ‣ Matt 11:23

5:31 *Deut 24:1 Matt 19:7 Mark 10:4

5:32 1 Cor 7:10-11

5:33 Lev 19:12 Num 30:2 Deut 23:21

5:34 Isa 66:1 Matt 23:22 Jas 5:12

5:35 Ps 48:2 Isa 66:1

5:37 Jas 5:12

• ***judgment . . . the court . . . hell:*** The second and third punishments are more severe than would have been typical in Jesus' day, emphasizing the surpassing righteousness of Jesus and his followers (see 5:20). They did not tolerate unreconciled relationships or any devaluation of others. • ***If you call someone an idiot:*** The Greek uses an Aramaic term of contempt: *If you say to your brother, "Reqa'."* The Aramaic term *reqa'* means something like "empty head," and the clause probably means the same as ***if you curse someone*** (literally *if you say, 'You fool'*; see Jas 2:20). Devaluation of people is a sin that manifests itself in various ways. • ***hell:*** Greek *Gehenna;* see note on 5:29.

5:23-26 Jesus gives two illustrations of reconciliation in community and society.

5:23 ***sacrifice:*** Literally *gift;* also in 5:24.

5:26 ***the last penny:*** Greek *the last kodrantes* (i.e., quadrans), the smallest Roman coin (cp. Luke 12:59).

5:27-30 Jesus' righteousness uncovers sin at a deeper level than the external; he reveals the true intent of the law.

5:27 ***You must not commit adultery:*** Exod 20:14; Deut 5:18.

5:29-30 ***good eye . . . gouge it out . . . stronger hand . . . cut it off:*** These graphic images call for radical separation from sin. But even self-mutilation, radical as it would be, cannot stop a lustful mind. Jesus is calling for the surpassing righteousness that only he can bring.

5:29 ***your eye—even your good eye:*** Literally *your right eye.* • ***hell*** (Greek *Gehenna*): Gehenna originally referred to a valley outside Jerusalem where some of the kings of Judah worshiped idols and performed human sacrifice by fire (2 Chr 28:3; 33:6; Jer 7:31; 32:35). The site was eventually destroyed by Josiah (2 Kgs 23:10). In the NT, Gehenna describes the place of punishment by God. Unless disciples have surpassing righteousness, they will not enter the Kingdom (5:20) but will be punished eternally (5:22; 23:33).

5:30 ***your hand—even your stronger hand:*** Literally *your right hand.*

5:31-32 Jesus challenges the misapplication of the OT provision for ***divorce*** (see Deut 24:1-4; cp. Matt 19:3-9): Following the rules does not make divorce acceptable. Jesus allows only one legitimate reason for divorce, sexual infidelity, and forbids casual divorce (see also 1 Cor 7:10-11).

5:31 ***A man can divorce his wife . . . notice of divorce:*** Deut 24:1. A notice of divorce is a document stating the legality of a divorce. Evidence suggests that such a document permitted remarriage. "The essential formula in the notice of divorce is, 'Lo, you are free to marry any man.' . . . The essential formula in a writ of emancipation is, 'Lo, you are a freedwoman: lo, you belong to yourself' " (*Mishnah Gittin* 9:3).

5:32 The exception clause permits but does not demand divorce when one partner has ***been unfaithful*** (see also 19:9). Notably, Jesus does not demand death for the guilty party (see Deut 22:21-22). • The implication seems to be that by divorcing his wife for illegitimate reasons, the man ***causes her to commit adultery*** by wrongly putting her in a situation where she remarries and so breaks the law. • ***anyone who marries a divorced woman:*** It is not clear whether Jesus is referring to any woman who is divorced, regardless of the reason, or only to a woman who is divorced without an acceptable reason (unfaithfulness). The underlying assumption in Jewish divorce law was simple: Legitimate divorces permitted remarriage.

5:33-37 Jesus here summarizes the OT teaching on oaths (Lev 19:12; Num 30:2-4; Deut 23:21-23; Ps 50:14; Zech 8:17). The Pharisees had degrees of commitment for oaths—for example, ones that did not mention God were not as binding. Jesus shows that because God is related to all things (***heaven, earth, Jerusalem, my head***; see also 23:16-22), breaking any oath breaks God's command (see Exod 20:7). The point is that one must be altogether truthful. Jesus' righteousness elevates the disciple's everyday yes and no to the level of binding oath. Oaths become superfluous to the honest person (Jas 5:12).

5:33 ***You must not break your vows . . . to the Lord:*** Num 30:2.

5:38 *Exod 21:24 *Lev 24:20 *Deut 19:21
5:39 Rom 12:17 1 Cor 6:7 1 Pet 3:9
5:40 1 Cor 6:7
5:42 Deut 15:7-11
5:43 *Lev 19:18 Rom 13:9 Gal 5:14 Jas 2:8
5:44 Exod 23:4-5 Prov 25:21 Luke 23:34 Acts 7:60 Rom 12:14, 20 1 Cor 4:12
5:45 Eph 5:1
5:48 Lev 19:2 Deut 18:13 1 Pet 1:16 [d]*teleios* (5046) ‣1 Cor 13:10
6:1-2 Matt 23:5
6:2 [e]*hupokritēs* (5273) ‣Matt 6:5
6:5 Luke 18:10-14 [f]*hupokritēs* (5273) ‣Matt 15:7
6:6 2 Kgs 4:33

say, 'By Jerusalem!' for Jerusalem is the city of the great King. 36Do not even say, 'By my head!' for you can't turn one hair white or black. 37Just say a simple, 'Yes, I will,' or 'No, I won't.' Anything beyond this is from the evil one.

Teaching about Revenge
Matt 5:38-42; cp. Luke 6:27-31

38"You have heard the law that says the punishment must match the injury: 'An eye for an eye, and a tooth for a tooth.' 39But I say, do not resist an evil person! If someone slaps you on the right cheek, offer the other cheek also. 40If you are sued in court and your shirt is taken from you, give your coat, too. 41If a soldier demands that you carry his gear for a mile, carry it two miles. 42Give to those who ask, and don't turn away from those who want to borrow.

Teaching about Love for Enemies
Matt 5:43-48; cp. Luke 6:32-36

43"You have heard the law that says, 'Love your neighbor' and hate your enemy. 44But I say, love your enemies! Pray for those who persecute you! 45In that way, you will be acting as true children of your Father in heaven. For he gives his sunlight to both the evil and the good, and he sends rain on the just and the unjust alike. 46If you love only those who love you, what reward is there for that? Even corrupt tax collectors do that much. 47If you are kind only to your friends, how are you different from anyone else? Even pagans do that. 48But you are to be [d]perfect, even as your Father in heaven is [d]perfect.

Teaching about Giving to the Needy

6 "Watch out! Don't do your good deeds publicly, to be admired by others, for you will lose the reward from your Father in heaven. 2When you give to someone in need, don't do as the [e]hypocrites do—blowing trumpets in the synagogues and streets to call attention to their acts of charity! I tell you the truth, they have received all the reward they will ever get. 3But when you give to someone in need, don't let your left hand know what your right hand is doing. 4Give your gifts in private, and your Father, who sees everything, will reward you.

Teaching about Prayer
Matt 6:9-13 // Luke 11:1-4

5"When you pray, don't be like the [f]hypocrites who love to pray publicly on street corners and in the synagogues where everyone can see them. I tell you the truth, that is all the reward they will ever get. 6But when you pray, go away by yourself, shut the

---

5:38-42 The OT permitted proportionate retribution (Exod 21:24-25; Deut 19:16-21), which was to prevent punishments from far exceeding the severity of the offense. Jesus, however, does not permit personal retaliation at all among his followers. Jesus' way is not to insist on justice but to find victory through suffering and the cross (1 Pet 2:23). Some have taken this passage as a guide for all of life (including politics). Others understand it merely as the willingness to forgo one's personal rights and to forgive as God has forgiven (see 5:48; 18:23-35). Like the servant in Isa 50:4-9 and 53:7 (see also Matt 12:15-21), Jesus' followers are to apply the same virtue to honor, possessions, time, or property. Righteousness does not insist on its own way.

5:38 ***the law that says the punishment must match the injury: 'An eye for an eye, and a tooth for a tooth'***: Literally *the law that says: 'An eye for an eye and a tooth for a tooth.'* Exod 21:24; Lev 24:20; Deut 19:21.

5:41 Forced labor was a humiliating fact of Roman occupation (see 27:32); Jesus turned it into an occasion for exuberant service to God. This saying shows Jesus' opposition to Jewish revolutionaries, who advocated violent resistance (see 5:9). • ***mile:*** Greek *milion* (4,854 feet or 1,478 meters).

5:42 See Deut 15:7-11.

5:43-47 ***Love your neighbor:*** Lev 19:18. • ***hate your enemy:*** Jesus is opposing not the OT, but a traditional, though mistaken (cp. Exod 23:4-5), interpretation of the OT. The "hate" clause is not in the OT (but see Ps 139:21-22).

5:44 ***love your enemies:*** Some manuscripts add *Bless those who curse you. Do good to those who hate you.* Cp. Luke 6:27-28.

5:45 By loving all people, Jesus' followers would not *become* children of God; they would show by their actions that they are indeed God's ***true children***, according to his nature and will (see Deut 10:18-19).

5:47 ***If you are kind only to your friends*** (literally, *If you greet only your brothers*): Jews were instructed to greet Gentiles for the sake of maintaining peaceful relations, but such greetings were not the same as those for "brothers"—i.e., fellow Jews.

5:48 This verse ties 5:20-48 together as a unit (see note on 4:23-25). • ***you are to be perfect:*** The term means maturity and wholeness in response to Jesus' proclamation of the Kingdom, and complete consecration to God (19:21; Eph 4:13; Phil 3:15; Col 1:28; 4:12; 1 Jn 4:18). Perfection has love at its core (see Luke 6:36).

6:1 This verse introduces the theme of 6:2-18, that righteousness should not be done for public recognition but as a service to God. • ***Good deeds*** are acts that conform to God's pattern for proper behavior: e.g., gift giving (6:2-4), prayer (6:5-15), and fasting (6:16-18). Jesus urges secrecy to counteract the human propensity to seek praise for oneself rather than for God (cp. 5:16).

6:2 ***the hypocrites:*** See note on 23:13. • The ***blowing*** of ***trumpets*** accompanied major rituals, including public fasts.

6:4 ***your Father . . . will reward you:*** Both now and at the final judgment at the end of history (25:31-46).

6:5 ***When you pray:*** Jews prayed regularly at 9 AM and 3 PM (see Acts 3:1) and had frequent times of public prayer. Hypocrites deliberately sought to be in public places at such times, to be seen by all. • ***the hypocrites:*** See note on 23:13.

6:6 ***go away by yourself:*** Jesus is not prohibiting corporate prayer (see 18:19-20; Luke 11:2-4), but is instructing his followers to avoid using prayer as a means of drawing attention to themselves.

door behind you, and pray to your Father in
private. Then your Father, who sees everything, will reward you.
7“When you pray, don't babble on and on
as people of other religions do. They think
their prayers are answered merely by repeating their words again and again. 8Don't
be like them, for your Father knows exactly
what you need even before you ask him!
9“Pray like this:

Our [g]Father in heaven,
may your name be kept holy.
10 May your Kingdom come soon.
May your will be done on earth,
as it is in heaven.
11 Give us today the food we need,
12 and forgive us our sins,
as we have forgiven those who sin
against us.
13 And don't let us yield to [h]temptation,
but rescue us from the evil one.

14“If you forgive those who sin against
you, your heavenly Father will forgive you.
15But if you refuse to forgive others, your Father will not forgive your sins.

Teaching about Fasting

16“And when you fast, don't make it obvious,
as the hypocrites do, for they try to look miserable and disheveled so people will admire
them for their fasting. I tell you the truth,
that is the only reward they will ever get.
17But when you fast, [i]comb your hair and
wash your face. 18Then no one will notice
that you are fasting, except your Father, who
knows what you do in private. And your Father, who sees everything, will reward you.

Teaching about Money and Possessions

Matt 6:19-21 // Luke 12:33-34
Matt 6:22-23 // Luke 11:34-36
Matt 6:24 // Luke 16:13

19“Don't store up treasures here on earth,
where moths eat them and rust destroys
them, and where thieves break in and steal.
20Store your treasures in heaven, where
moths and rust cannot destroy, and thieves
do not break in and steal. 21Wherever your
treasure is, there the desires of your heart
will also be.
22“Your eye is a lamp that provides light
for your body. When your eye is good, your
whole body is filled with light. 23But when
your eye is bad, your whole body is filled
with darkness. And if the light you think
you have is actually darkness, how deep that
darkness is!
24“No one can serve two masters. For you
will hate one and love the other; you will be
devoted to one and despise the other. You
cannot serve both God and money.

Teaching about Worry

Matt 6:25-34 // Luke 12:22-32

25“That is why I tell you not to worry about
everyday life—whether you have enough

6:7 Eccl 5:1-2
6:9-13 //Luke 11:2-4
6:9 [g]*patēr* (3962) ‣Matt 7:11
6:10 Matt 26:39, 42
6:11 Prov 30:8; John 6:32
6:13 Luke 22:40; 22:46; 2 Thes 3:3; [h]*peirasmos* (3986) ‣Mark 1:13
6:14 Mark 11:25; Col 3:13
6:15 Matt 18:21-35
6:16 Isa 58:4-14
6:17 [i]*aleiphō* (0218) ‣Mark 6:13
6:18 Matt 6:4, 6
6:19-21 //Luke 12:33-34
6:19 Prov 23:4; Jas 5:2-3
6:20 Matt 19:21; Mark 10:21; Luke 18:22; 1 Tim 6:19
6:22-23 //Luke 11:34-36
6:23 Matt 20:15; Mark 7:22

6:7-8 God cannot be coaxed by endless repetition. The Lord's Prayer (6:9-13) is a model of simplicity in contrast with pagan wordiness.

6:9-13 The Lord's Prayer is similar in form to a common Jewish prayer (the *qaddish*). Jesus gave this prayer to his followers as a succinct expression of their new faith.

6:9 ***Pray like this:*** In contrast to the vain repetition of pagan prayers (6:7-8), "the Lord's Prayer" is a model of simplicity. • Jews rarely addressed God as *Father*, but Jesus did so in every prayer but one (Mark 15:34). • ***may your name be kept holy:*** God's name is profaned by the sin of his people (Isa 29:22-24; Jer 34:15-16; Ezek 39:7; Amos 2:7).

6:10 In praying for God's *Kingdom* to *come soon*, Jesus' disciples pray for his justice, righteousness, peace, and mercy to be established. • Outside God's *will*, no person will be permitted into God's presence (7:21; 12:50; 21:28-32). • ***on earth, as it is in heaven:*** This probably refers to all of the first three petitions, not just the third.

6:11 ***Give us today the food we need*** (or *Give us today our food for the day;* or *Give us today our food for tomorrow*): The disciple, after confidently asking God to provide for daily needs, can go about Kingdom ministry relieved of care (6:25-34).

6:12 ***as we have forgiven*** (see also 6:14-15; 18:21-35): Forgiving others is a reflection of a repentant, regenerate heart, which makes our own forgiveness possible. Those who have experienced God's forgiveness will forgive. Jesus implies that those who are unwilling to forgive have not perceived God's mercy, and perhaps have never truly repented.

6:13 ***And don't let us yield to temptation*** (or *And keep us from being tested*): Just as Jesus was tested (4:1-11), temptation will test the disciple's character. Jesus urges prayer for God's enabling to stand the test (see 26:41; Ps 141:4). • ***from the evil one:*** Or *from evil.* The alternate reading refers to sin in general; the NLT reading refers to Satan, the tempter (see Jas 1:13). • Some manuscripts add *For yours is the kingdom and the power and the glory forever. Amen;* this doxology was added later (probably based on 1 Chr 29:11-13) to tailor the prayer to the liturgy.

6:16 Prayer and fasting are frequently connected (Lev 23:27-32; Neh 9:1-2; Zech 7:3-5; 8:19; Luke 18:12). The practice had been abused before Jesus' time (Isa 58:3-12). • ***the hypocrites:*** See note on 23:13.

6:20 ***treasures in heaven:*** This was a common image for Jews of Jesus' day; doing God's commands became virtually equivalent to accumulating treasures with God. The context (6:19; Luke 12:33) suggests that Jesus primarily had acts of charity in mind.

6:22 ***Your eye is a lamp:*** It gives ***light*** to the ***body*** and so enlightens the entire person. • ***Good*** means morally healthy, with simple, wholehearted devotion to God (6:24). Here it connotes generosity.

6:24 The term for ***money*** (traditionally *mammon*) is an Aramaic term for profits or material possessions. Since God tolerates no rivals, Jesus repeatedly warns of the danger of accumulating riches (13:22; 19:16-30; 26:14-16; 27:3-10; 28:11-15), which can be an idol (see Eph 5:5; Col 3:5). We must trust God to meet our needs (4:3-4; 6:8, 11, 25-34; 7:7-11; 10:9-14; 14:15-21; 15:32-38), and the community of disciples is to be mutually supportive (6:2-4; 10:40-42; 19:21; 23:23-24; 25:31-46; 26:6-13; 27:57-61).

6:25-34 Jesus taught an anxiety-free existence of simple trust in God for

6:24 //Luke 16:13
6:25-34 //Luke 12:22-31
6:25 Phil 4:6; 1 Tim 6:6, 8; 1 Pet 5:7
6:26 Job 38:41
6:29 1 Kgs 10:4-7
6:30 Matt 8:26; 14:31; 16:8
6:32 Matt 6:8; Luke 12:30
6:33 Ps 37:4, 25; Mark 10:29, 30
6:34 Exod 16:4
7:1-2 //Luke 6:37-42; Rom 2:1-3; 14:4; 1 Cor 4:5; 5:12; Jas 4:11-12
7:3-5 //Luke 6:37-38, 41-42

food and drink, or enough clothes to wear.
Isn't life more than food, and your body
more than clothing? [26]Look at the birds.
They don't plant or harvest or store food in
barns, for your heavenly Father feeds them.
And aren't you far more valuable to him
than they are? [27]Can all your worries add a
single moment to your life?
[28]"And why worry about your clothing?
Look at the lilies of the field and how they
grow. They don't work or make their clothing, [29]yet Solomon in all his glory was not
dressed as beautifully as they are. [30]And if
God cares so wonderfully for wildflowers
that are here today and thrown into the fire
tomorrow, he will certainly care for you.
Why do you have so little faith?
[31]"So don't worry about these things,
saying, 'What will we eat? What will we
drink? What will we wear?' [32]These things
dominate the thoughts of unbelievers, but
your heavenly Father already knows all your
needs. [33]Seek the Kingdom of God above
all else, and live righteously, and he will give
you everything you need.
[34]"So don't worry about tomorrow, for tomorrow will bring its own worries. Today's
trouble is enough for today.

Wisdom: Do Not Judge Others
Matt 7:1-5 // Luke 6:37-42

7 "Do not judge others, and you will not be
judged. [2]For you will be treated as you
treat others. The standard you use in judging
is the standard by which you will be judged.
[3]"And why worry about a speck in your
friend's eye when you have a log in your
own? [4]How can you think of saying to
your friend, 'Let me help you get rid of that
speck in your eye,' when you can't see past
the log in your own eye? [5]Hypocrite! First
get rid of the log in your own eye; then you
will see well enough to deal with the speck
in your friend's eye.

Little Faith (6:30)

Matt 7:21-28; 8:26; 13:58; 14:31; 16:8; 17:20; 22:34-40; Luke 12:28; Jas 1:6-7

The term "little faith" and related Greek terms are used five times in Matthew (6:30; 8:26; 14:31; 16:8; 17:20) and only once elsewhere (Luke 12:28; cp. Jas 1:6-7). The term refers to a specific event rather than to ongoing and permanent failure. In Matthew, this is due either to lack of knowledge on the part of Jesus' disciples (16:8) or to acting without faith in a particular incident. If someone always lacks faith, it would be described as "unbelief" (see 13:58). As examples of "little faith," the disciples in 6:30 do not understand their value or God's providential protection; in 8:26 and 14:31 they do not understand God's protection in the midst of physical danger; in 16:8 they do not understand Jesus' saying regarding yeast; and in 17:20 they are not able to exorcise a demon. These are instances of failure to be consistent with a calling rather than of having no faith whatsoever.

The term *faith* reflects at least two ideas: *trust* (personal reliance upon the Lord) and *belief* (affirmation of truths). Matthew's concern with "little faith" is about lack of trust by a follower of Jesus in a specific situation, rather than a failure to have basic belief in Jesus as Lord and Savior. Jesus wants his followers not only to believe in him, but also to trust, love, and obey him (see 7:21-28; 22:34-40).

provisions. Jesus' disciples had abandoned all (4:18-22; 9:9; 10:5-14); Jesus gave them comforting reassurance that God would provide for their needs.

6:26 Jesus' logic progresses from lesser to greater: If the Father tends to ***birds*** (the lesser), and the disciple is ***far more valuable to him*** (the greater), then he will certainly tend to the disciples' needs (see also 10:29-31).

6:30 ***Little faith*** results from the failure to understand one's value to God and the extent of God's providential protection.

6:32 ***unbelievers*** (literally *Gentiles*): Those who fail to know God and follow his will (see also 20:19). • ***your heavenly Father already knows:*** Prayer does not inform God about ***needs;*** it expresses trust in his provision.

6:33 Here Jesus gives the positive alternative to worrying. Single-minded commitment to God and seeking his reign through Christ (see 6:19-24) must be the primary concern of Jesus' disciples. • Some manuscripts do not include ***of God.***

7:1 Jesus calls for people to stop oppressively controlling others in the name of pastoral concern. Mercy is a dominant theme in Jesus' teaching and practice (9:9-13; 12:1-7), but not at the expense of clear opposition to sin (see 18:15-20; 23:13-33). The judgment Jesus prohibits often involves rigorous scrutiny of trivial matters (see 23:23-24). God alone has the right to judge (see Jas 4:11-12). • ***you will not be judged:*** This might refer to God's judgment at the end of history (see 5:7). God measures us by our treatment of others (see 6:12; 18:21-35).

7:2 ***For you will be treated as you treat others:*** Or *For God will judge you as you judge others.* • ***The standard you use in judging is the standard by which you will be judged:*** Or *The measure you give will be the measure you get back.*

7:3-5 Jesus exhorts his disciples to minister to others rather than condemning them. Reference to a ***speck*** (speck of dust, chip of wood) versus a ***log*** in the ***eye*** is hyperbolic imagery, intended to heighten the contrast (see 5:29; 23:23-24; Mic 6:6-8).

7:3 ***your friend's eye:*** Literally *your brother's eye;* also in 7:5.

7:4 ***your friend:*** Literally *your brother.*

Wisdom: Do Not Throw Pearls to Pigs

6“Don’t waste what is holy on people who are unholy. Don’t throw your pearls to pigs! They will trample the pearls, then turn and attack you.

Wisdom: Effective Prayer

Matt 7:7-11 // Luke 11:9-13

7“Keep on asking, and you will receive what you ask for. Keep on seeking, and you will find. Keep on knocking, and the door will be opened to you. 8For everyone who asks, receives. Everyone who seeks, finds. And to everyone who knocks, the door will be opened.

9“You parents—if your children ask for a loaf of bread, do you give them a stone instead? 10Or if they ask for a fish, do you give them a snake? Of course not! 11So if you sinful people know how to give good gifts to your children, how much more will your heavenly [j]Father give good gifts to those who ask him.

Wisdom: The Golden Rule

Matt 7:12 // Luke 6:31

12“Do to others whatever you would like them to do to you. This is the essence of all that is taught in the [k]law and the prophets.

Call to Decision: The Narrow Gate

Matt 7:13-14; cp. Luke 13:24

13“You can enter God’s Kingdom only through the narrow gate. The highway to hell is broad, and its gate is wide for the many who choose that way. 14But the gateway to life is very narrow and the road is difficult, and only a few ever find it.

The Tree and Its Fruit

Matt 7:15-20; cp. Matt 12:33-35 // Luke 6:43-45

15“Beware of false prophets who come disguised as harmless sheep but are really vicious wolves. 16You can identify them by their fruit, that is, by the way they act. Can you pick grapes from thornbushes, or figs from thistles? 17A good tree produces good fruit, and a bad tree produces bad fruit. 18A good tree can’t produce bad fruit, and a bad tree can’t produce good fruit. 19So every tree that does not produce good fruit is chopped down and thrown into the fire. 20Yes, just as you can identify a tree by its fruit, so you can identify people by their actions.

True Disciples

Matt 7:21-23; cp. Luke 13:25-27

21“Not everyone who calls out to me, ‘Lord! Lord!’ will enter the Kingdom of Heaven. Only those who actually do the will of my Father in heaven will enter. 22On judgment day many will say to me, ‘Lord! Lord! We prophesied in your name and cast out demons in your name and performed many miracles in your name.’ 23But I will reply,

7:7-11
//Luke 11:9-13

7:7
Matt 21:22
Mark 11:24
John 14:13-14; 15:7; 16:23-24
Jas 1:5-6
1 Jn 3:21-22; 5:14-15

7:11
Jas 1:17
[j]*patēr* (3962)
‣ Rom 4:11

7:12
Luke 6:31
Rom 13:8-10
Gal 5:14
[k]*nomos* (3551)
‣ Matt 23:23

7:13
//Luke 13:24

7:14
John 14:6
Acts 14:22

7:15
Jer 23:16
Matt 24:11, 24
Luke 6:26
Acts 20:29
Rom 16:17
2 Pet 2:1
1 Jn 4:1

7:16-20
Matt 12:33
//Luke 6:43-44

7:21-23
//Luke 13:25-27

7:21
Luke 6:46
Jas 1:22

7:22
Acts 19:13-15

7:6 Rabbis often referred to important ideas or Scripture verses as ***pearls***. The mysteries of the Kingdom (13:11) are ***holy*** (see Exod 29:33; Lev 2:3; 22:10-16; Num 18:8-10). • ***Don’t waste what is holy on people who are unholy:*** Literally *Don’t give the sacred to dogs.* Jews often referred to Gentiles as dogs (see 15:26; see Ps 22:16, 20) or ***pigs*** because those animals were unclean (Lev 11). Some interpreters understand this statement as warning that the message of the Kingdom would not be well received by many Gentiles. Others see it as a warning about offering the message of the Kingdom to the resistant Jewish leaders (see 5:20; 10:11-14; see also Heb 10:29) or to unbelievers in general (see 18:17; see also 1 Cor 2:13-16; 2 Pet 2:21-22).

7:7-8 This passage teaches persistence in prayer, but Jesus does not teach that God will grant extravagant desires. God’s people are to seek daily provision and spiritual blessing (6:10-11).

7:12 ***the law and the prophets:*** The teaching of Jesus in 5:21–7:6 is the goal and true expression of the law of Moses. Love is at the core of discipleship (see also Gal 5:13-14, 18).

7:13-27 The Sermon on the Mount closes with a call to decide about Jesus and his teaching (see 4:23; 9:35). Those who hear Jesus’ message regarding the Kingdom must follow him to obtain eternal life or disown him and experience God’s condemnation. There is no middle way (Deut 30:15-20; Ps 1; Prov 12:28; Jer 21:8).

7:13 Entering ***through the narrow gate*** refers to the decision to follow Jesus as the Messiah. The ***wide*** gate and ***broad*** highway refer to the decision not to follow Jesus and his teachings. • ***The highway to hell*** (literally *The road that leads to destruction*): The reference to hell means being thrown into the fire, not entering the Kingdom of Heaven, being banished from the presence of Jesus, and being ruined (7:19-23, 27).

7:14 ***Few*** people come to the light that is revealed in Christ (see 19:23; 20:16; 22:14; see also John 3:19; 6:66-71).

7:15-20 ***False prophets*** speak what people want to hear rather than calling people to live according to God’s will. Deuteronomy 13:1-5 and 18:21-22 set standards for evaluating a prophet’s truthfulness: His words must conform to God’s word, and his predictions must come true. Jesus unpacks the first requirement: A prophet’s actions must match his words in order to be believable; accordingly, a true prophet’s actions will also match God’s word. Just as the ***fruit*** indicates the nature of a ***tree***, so one’s life indicates either a regenerate or unregenerate heart. False prophets are expected at the end of the age (see 24:11, 24; Acts 20:28-35; Rev 13:11-18; 16:13; 19:20; 20:10). In order not to be deceived, Christians must be discerning (see 1 Cor 12:10; 14:29; 1 Thes 5:21; 1 Jn 4:1-3; Rev 2:20).

7:16-17 ***Good*** and ***bad fruit*** refers to moral behavior (see 3:8, 10; 12:33-37; 13:8; 21:43; Gal 5:19-23).

7:18 Spiritual rebirth is absolutely necessary if one is to ***produce*** the ***good fruit*** that Jesus demands. Good works flow from faith; good works and faith cannot be separated (see Jas 2:14-26).

7:21 ***The will of my Father*** is expressed in Jesus’ teachings (see also 12:50; 21:28-32; Rom 2:13; Jas 1:22-27).

7:22 ***judgment day:*** The OT concept is the “day of the Lord,” when God will come to rescue the faithful and judge the oppressors (Isa 13–14; Joel 2; Zeph 1:14-16). In Jesus’ teaching, this day is when all will be judged for their response to him (see 10:15; 11:20-24; 12:36; 24:19-50; 25:13, 31-46; Acts 17:31; Rom 2:16). • Neither charismatic gifts nor public accomplishments in Jesus’ ***name*** will necessarily bring God’s acceptance; the decisive issue is obedience (7:21).

7:23
Matt 25:12, 41
7:24-27
//Luke 6:47-49
7:24
2 Tim 2:19
Jas 1:22
[a]*petra* (4073)
‣ Matt 16:18
7:26
Jas 1:23-24
7:27
Ezek 13:10-12
7:28
Matt 13:54
Mark 1:22; 6:2
Luke 4:32
John 7:46
8:1-4
//Mark 1:40-44
//Luke 5:12-14
8:4
Lev 14:1-32
[b]*marturion* (3142)
‣ Luke 9:5
8:5-13
//Luke 7:1-10
8:5-7
John 4:43-54
8:8
Ps 107:20

'I never knew you. Get away from me, you
who break God's laws.'

Building on a Solid Foundation
Matt 7:24-27 // Luke 6:47-49

24"Anyone who listens to my teaching and
follows it is wise, like a person who builds
a house on solid [a]rock. 25Though the rain
comes in torrents and the floodwaters rise
and the winds beat against that house, it
won't collapse because it is built on bedrock. 26But anyone who hears my teaching
and doesn't obey it is foolish, like a person
who builds a house on sand. 27When the
rains and floods come and the winds beat
against that house, it will collapse with a
mighty crash."

Response to the Sermon
Matt 7:28-29; cp. Mark 1:21-22 // Luke 4:31-32

28When Jesus had finished saying these
things, the crowds were amazed at his
teaching, 29for he taught with real authority—
quite unlike their teachers of religious law.

Narrative: Jesus' Ministry (8:1–9:34)
Jesus Heals a Man with Leprosy
Matt 8:1-4 // Mark 1:40-45 // Luke 5:12-16

8 Large crowds followed Jesus as he came
down the mountainside. 2Suddenly,
a man with leprosy approached him and
knelt before him. "Lord," the man said, "if
you are willing, you can heal me and make
me clean."
3Jesus reached out and touched him. "I
am willing," he said. "Be healed!" And instantly the leprosy disappeared. 4Then
Jesus said to him, "Don't tell anyone about
this. Instead, go to the priest and let him examine you. Take along the offering required
in the law of Moses for those who have been
healed of leprosy. This will be a public [b]testi-
mony that you have been cleansed."

The Faith of a Roman Officer
Matt 8:5-13 // Luke 7:1-10

5When Jesus returned to Capernaum, a Roman officer came and pleaded with him,
6"Lord, my young servant lies in bed, paralyzed and in terrible pain."
7Jesus said, "I will come and heal him."
8But the officer said, "Lord, I am not worthy to have you come into my home. Just
say the word from where you are, and my
servant will be healed. 9I know this because
I am under the authority of my superior officers, and I have authority over my soldiers. I
only need to say, 'Go,' and they go, or 'Come,'
and they come. And if I say to my slaves, 'Do
this,' they do it."

7:23 ***I never knew you:*** These people were never converted, even though they did great things in God's name. They ***break God's laws*** through rejection of the Father's will as taught by Jesus. Having never known Christ, they never learned to do what he commanded.

7:24-27 The emphasis in this whole sermon (5:3–7:27) is on doing what Jesus teaches by walking in righteousness (5:20). To hear and not obey is to choose the wide gate and the broad highway that lead to destruction (Jas 1:22-25; 2:14-26). Decision is necessary in light of what has been revealed. See Lev 26; Deut 28; 30.

7:24 A ***wise . . . person*** perceives that Jesus is the fulfillment of OT promises, willingly submits to him, and walks the path that ultimately leads to blessing (5:3-12; 7:13-14). • Building ***a house*** directly on ***rock*** provides a much stronger foundation than would a dry, sandy riverbed or floodplain (7:26).

7:25-27 The storm is a metaphor for God's all-knowing judgment (see Jer 23:19; Ezek 1:4).

7:28-29 Jesus began teaching only his disciples (5:1), but ***crowds*** had followed up the mountainside as well. • Unlike the ***teachers of religious law,*** whose authority was derived from the Scriptures they quoted or from the teachings of previous scholars, Jesus taught ***with real***—that is, direct—***authority***. He quoted Scripture in the Sermon, but his teaching was based on his own authority as the Messiah.

8:1–9:34 Here the Kingdom of God is manifested with supernatural power (see 4:23-25; 11:2-6). It reaches people who had been excluded from the blessing of God: Gentiles, lepers, blind people, sick women, demoniacs, tax collectors, those with a chronic hemorrhage, and the dead. Jesus shows compassion, but the religious leaders are provoked to opposition. Jesus calls his followers to faith and discipleship.

8:2 ***Leprosy*** refers to various skin diseases. Lepers were ceremonially unclean; they were excluded from society unless they became symptom-free and a priest pronounced them ***clean*** (see 8:4; Lev 14:2-32). On some occasions, leprosy was a judgment from God (Num 12:9-15; 2 Kgs 5:27; 15:5).

8:3 ***Be healed:*** Jesus' healing of lepers was tangible evidence of the Kingdom in his person and ministry (11:2-6).

8:4 The leper's healing would be ***a public testimony***—either that the religious leaders were wrong not to trust in the Messiah (10:18) or that Jesus was not against the ***law of Moses*** (5:17). • ***the offering required in the law of Moses for those who have been healed of leprosy:*** See Lev 14:2-32.

8:5-13 Jesus once again ministered to the marginalized or ostracized. The centurion was a Gentile soldier, and ministry to him would have evoked strong resentment from both the nationalistic and the separatist wings of Jewish society.

8:5 ***Capernaum*** is located on the Sea of Galilee, about two and a half miles west of the Jordan River outlet. In Jesus' day, it was a prosperous fishing village. Standing at a crucial junction on the Great Trunk Road linking Mesopotamia and Egypt, it was an international village, and much of Jesus' Galilean ministry was based there (e.g., 4:13; 8:14-17). • ***a Roman officer*** (Greek *a centurion;* similarly in 8:8, 13): A centurion, one of sixty commanders in a legion, commanded 100 Roman soldiers (see also Mark 15:39; Acts 10:1; 27:1).

8:6 ***young servant:*** Or *child;* also in 8:13.

8:7 ***I will come*** (cp. Acts 10:9-35; Gal 2:11-14): Some have rendered this as a question: *Shall I* [a Jew] *come* [into the house of a Gentile, risking defilement] *and heal him?*

8:8-10 The centurion recognized Jesus' ***authority***. From his own experience, he knew that when he gave orders, they were quickly obeyed. He perceived that God had entrusted Jesus with authority to work miracles. The centurion's

10 When Jesus heard this, he was amazed.
Turning to those who were following him,
he said, "I tell you the truth, I haven't seen
faith like this in all Israel! 11 And I tell you
this, that many Gentiles will come from all
over the world—from east and west—and sit
down with Abraham, Isaac, and Jacob at the
feast in the Kingdom of Heaven. 12 But many
Israelites—those for whom the Kingdom
was prepared—will be thrown into outer
darkness, where there will be weeping and
gnashing of teeth."
13 Then Jesus said to the Roman officer,
"Go back home. Because you believed, it
has happened." And the young servant was
healed that same hour.

Jesus Heals Our Diseases

Matt 8:14-17 // Mark 1:29-34 // Luke 4:38-41

14 When Jesus arrived at Peter's house, Peter's mother-in-law was sick in bed with a
high fever. 15 But when Jesus touched her
hand, the fever left her. Then she got up and
prepared a meal for him.
16 That evening many demon-possessed
people were brought to Jesus. He cast out
the evil spirits with a simple command, and
he healed all the sick. 17 This fulfilled the
word of the Lord through the prophet Isaiah, who said,

"He took our sicknesses
and removed our diseases."

The Cost of Following Jesus

Matt 8:18-22 // Luke 9:57-62

18 When Jesus saw the crowd around him,
he instructed his disciples to cross to the
other side of the lake.
19 Then one of the teachers of religious
law said to him, "Teacher, I will follow you
wherever you go."
20 But Jesus replied, "Foxes have dens to
live in, and birds have nests, but the Son of
Man has no place even to lay his head."
21 Another of his disciples said, "Lord, first
let me return home and bury my father."
22 But Jesus told him, "Follow me now. Let
the spiritually dead bury their own dead."

Jesus Calms the Storm

Matt 8:23-27 // Mark 4:35-41 // Luke 8:22-25

23 Then Jesus got into the boat and started
across the lake with his disciples. 24 Suddenly, a fierce storm struck the lake, with
waves breaking into the boat. But Jesus was
sleeping. 25 The disciples went and woke
him up, shouting, "Lord, save us! We're going to drown!"
26 Jesus responded, "Why are you afraid?
You have so little faith!" Then he got up and
rebuked the wind and waves, and suddenly
there was a great calm.
27 The disciples were amazed. "Who is
this man?" they asked. "Even the winds and
waves obey him!"

Jesus Exercises Authority over Demons

Matt 8:28-34 // Mark 5:1-20 // Luke 8:26-39

28 When Jesus arrived on the other side of
the lake, in the region of the Gadarenes,
two men who were possessed by demons
met him. They lived in a cemetery and were

8:10-12
Ps 107:3
Matt 13:41-42; 21:43
//Luke 13:28-29
Acts 10:45; 11:18; 14:27
Eph 3:6

8:13
Matt 9:29; 15:28
John 4:50-51

8:14-16
//Mark 1:29-34
//Luke 4:38-41

8:17
*Isa 53:4

8:19-22
//Luke 9:57-62

8:22
Matt 9:9
Mark 2:14
John 1:43; 21:19

8:23-27
//Mark 4:36-41
//Luke 8:22-25

8:26
Ps 89:10; 107:25-32
Matt 6:30

8:28-34
//Mark 5:1-17
//Luke 8:26-37

---

faith shows that the Kingdom of God includes Gentiles (8:11).

8:11-12 The influx of ***Gentiles*** fulfills OT promises (Isa 2:2-3). God's promise to ***Abraham*** included being a blessing to many nations (Gen 18:18). Christ fulfills this promise (Gal 3:8, 16).

8:16-17 Jesus is the authoritative Lord over every disease and demon.

8:16 ***with a simple command:*** Jesus' authority extended beyond touch; his words brought healing and life.

8:17 ***He took our sicknesses and removed our diseases*** (Isa 53:4): When he took the sins of humanity, the Messiah also took our sickness. Sickness exists because sin is in the world, and one of the effects of Jesus' taking our sin on the cross is physical healing (1 Pet 2:24). Jesus' healings and exorcisms demonstrated, in fulfillment of Scripture, that he is the Messiah (see 11:2-6; 12:28; 1 Cor 11:29-30; Jas 5:13-16).

8:18-22 Jesus confronted two would-be followers with what it truly means to follow him.

8:19 The ***teachers of religious law*** had a prestigious vocation of preserving, learning, and interpreting the Scriptures for the good of society. The way to God was thought to be through them (15:13-14; 23:13).

8:20 Following Jesus is not easy; it involves more than intellectual mastery. Following Jesus entails being willing to forgo life's normal comforts. • ***Son of Man*** is a title Jesus used for himself.

8:21 ***Another of his disciples:*** This statement suggests that the teacher of 8:19 was a disciple as well. ***Lord*** suggests a stronger commitment to Jesus. • ***bury my father:*** This was one of the highest religious duties in Judaism, but Jesus requires total commitment to him.

8:22 ***Let the spiritually dead bury their own dead*** (literally *Let the dead bury their own dead*): Jesus' opponents would have misconstrued this instruction as blatant disregard for the fifth commandment to honor one's parents (Exod 20:12), but in essence it is a restatement of the first commandment (Exod 20:1-3). It was warranted by Jesus' messianic authority and the impact of the Kingdom upon normal human life, including family ties and commitments (see 10:34-39; 12:46-50; 19:29; Zech 13:3; Luke 14:26-27).

8:23-27 The episode at sea extends the theme of what true discipleship involves. The storm challenged the disciples to entrust their very lives to Jesus for protection and deliverance. Jesus even has authority over dangerous weather and the sea (see Job 38:8-11; Ps 29:1-11; 65:1-13; 89:9; 107:23-32).

8:24 ***a fierce storm struck the lake:*** Sudden squalls are common on the Sea of Galilee, which is among mountains.

8:27 ***Who is this man?*** Salvation requires a proper answer to this question and active faith in him. Jesus' disciples had still failed to understand.

8:28-34 This episode focuses on Jesus' authority as well as on the cost of following him; those who walk by faith will, like the Messiah, also experience opposition.

8:29
Mark 1:24
Luke 4:34
2 Pet 2:4

8:34
Acts 16:39

9:1-8
//Mark 2:3-12
//Luke 5:18-26

9:3
Matt 26:65
John 10:33

9:4
Matt 12:25
Luke 6:8; 9:47; 11:17

so violent that no one could go through that area.

29They began screaming at him, "Why are you interfering with us, Son of God? Have you come here to torture us before God's appointed time?"

30There happened to be a large herd of pigs feeding in the distance. 31So the demons begged, "If you cast us out, send us into that herd of pigs."

32"All right, go!" Jesus commanded them. So the demons came out of the men and entered the pigs, and the whole herd plunged down the steep hillside into the lake and drowned in the water.

33The herdsmen fled to the nearby town, telling everyone what happened to the demon-possessed men. 34Then the entire town came out to meet Jesus, but they begged him to go away and leave them alone.

Jesus Heals a Paralyzed Man
Matt 9:1-8 // Mark 2:1-12 // Luke 5:17-26

9 Jesus climbed into a boat and went back across the lake to his own town. 2Some people brought to him a paralyzed man on a mat. Seeing their faith, Jesus said to the paralyzed man, "Be encouraged, my child! Your sins are forgiven."

3But some of the teachers of religious law said to themselves, "That's blasphemy! Does he think he's God?"

4Jesus knew what they were thinking, so he asked them, "Why do you have such evil thoughts in your hearts? 5Is it easier to say

The Son of Man (8:18-22)

Matt 8:20; 9:6; 10:23; 11:19; 12:8, 32, 40; 13:37, 41; 16:13, 27-28; 17:9, 12, 22; 19:28; 20:18, 28; 24:27, 30, 37-39, 44; 25:31; 26:2, 24, 45, 64
Ezek 2:1-8; 3:1, 4, 10, 17, 25; 4:1
Dan 7:13-14; 8:17
Mark 2:10
John 1:51; 3:13-14; 5:27; 6:27, 53, 62; 8:28; 9:35; 12:23, 34; 13:31
Acts 7:56
Heb 2:6
Rev 1:13; 14:14

"Son of Man" was Jesus' favorite way to refer to himself. The phrase is just as odd in Greek as in English: It translates the Hebrew phrase *ben 'adam,* an idiom that means "human being" or "person" (see, e.g., Ezek 2:1-8). One reason Jesus preferred this name was because it was not an inflammatory title such as "Christ" or "Messiah." The term is used in three ways in the Gospels:

(1) The background to Jesus' use of the title is Dan 7:13-14, where an exalted messianic figure "like a son of man" (that is, having human form) comes with the clouds of heaven and is given great glory and power. Jesus understood himself as that one who would return to earth in the clouds of heaven (see Mark 8:38; 13:26; 14:62). Sometimes Jesus used "Son of Man" in this sense, to refer to his role as judge, deliverer, savior, and vindicator (10:23; 13:41; 16:27; 19:28; 24:27, 30, 37, 44; 25:31; 26:64).

(2) Often Jesus used "Son of Man" to describe himself as a suffering redeemer (12:40; 17:9, 12, 22; 20:18, 28; 26:2, 24, 45). This sense is rooted in Isa 52:13–53:12.

(3) At times, Jesus apparently used "Son of Man" to refer to himself as the representative of humans (8:20; 11:19; 12:8, 32; 13:37). The book of Ezekiel uses "son of man" in a similar sense (e.g., Ezek 2:1-8).

Jesus did not use "Son of Man" to distinguish his humanity from his deity ("Son of God"). By using this title, Jesus could define himself as Messiah on his own terms. He used "Son of Man" to describe his total identity and as a veiled suggestion that those who watched and heard him should pay attention to who he is.

8:28 ***Gadarenes:*** Other manuscripts read *Gerasenes;* still others read *Gergesenes.* Cp. Mark 5:1; Luke 8:26. • ***possessed by demons . . . so violent:*** Demon-possession was often accompanied by violence, revulsion at the presence of the Son of God (8:29), inability to speak (9:32; 12:22), blindness (12:22), seizures (17:15), and self-destructive behavior (17:15). With Jesus' exorcisms, the power of the Kingdom broke into human history (12:28).

8:29 Those controlled by Satan immediately recognized Jesus' true identity as the ***Son of God*** (see Mark 1:24) and answered the question asked by Jesus' disciples when he had calmed the storm (8:27). Elsewhere, Jesus' true nature and identity are acknowledged by the Father (3:17; 17:5), Satan (4:3, 6), humans (14:33; 16:16; 27:54), and Christ himself (11:27; 24:36; 28:19). • ***God's appointed time*** is the final, eternal damnation of all who oppose God (see Jude 1:6; Rev 20:10).

8:31 The ***demons*** were no match for Jesus' authority; they desperately ***begged*** to avoid imminent doom.

8:32 Jesus' word had sufficient authority to expel demons. • ***drowned:*** Jesus had begun to defeat the enemy (12:28; Luke 10:17-20; Rom 16:20; Col 2:15).

8:34 The tragedy of the incident is that those who witnessed the Son of God's power to give salvation feared having their world upset, so they rejected him.

9:1-17 Controversy ensued among Jesus' opponents, the teachers of religious law and Pharisees (9:1-13), and among the disciples of John the Baptist (9:14-17).

9:1 ***His own town*** was Capernaum (Mark 2:1), where he apparently relocated from Nazareth after being rejected there (4:13; Luke 4:16-31).

9:3 ***Does he think he's God?*** God alone could forgive sins (Ps 103:3; Isa 43:25; Jer 50:20). The ***teachers of religious law*** failed to comprehend Jesus' mission as God's incarnate Son (3:17; 11:25-27). As God's Messiah (1:1; 11:2-6), he was saving mankind (8:17; 26:26-28).

9:4 ***knew:*** Some manuscripts read *saw.*

9:5 It is ***easier*** for Jesus to pronounce

'Your sins are forgiven,' or 'Stand up and
walk'? 6 So I will prove to you that the Son
of Man has the authority on earth to forgive
sins." Then Jesus turned to the paralyzed
man and said, "Stand up, pick up your mat,
and go home!"
7 And the man jumped up and went home!
8 Fear swept through the crowd as they saw
this happen. And they praised God for sending a man with such great authority.

Jesus Calls Notorious Sinners
Matt 9:9-13 // Mark 2:13-17 // Luke 5:27-32

9 As Jesus was walking along, he saw a man
named Matthew sitting at his tax collector's booth. "Follow me and be my disciple,"
Jesus said to him. So Matthew got up and
followed him.
10 Later, Matthew invited Jesus and his disciples to his home as dinner guests, along
with many tax collectors and other disreputable sinners.
11 But when the Pharisees saw
this, they asked his disciples, "Why does
your teacher eat with such scum?"
12 When Jesus heard this, he said, "Healthy
people don't need a doctor—sick people do."
13 Then he added, "Now go and learn the
meaning of this Scripture: 'I want you to show
[c]mercy, not offer sacrifices.' For I have come
to call not those who think they are righteous,
but those who know they are sinners."

9:6-8
Matt 15:31
Luke 7:16
Acts 9:33-35

9:9-13
//Mark 2:14-17
//Luke 5:27-32

9:11
Matt 11:19
Luke 15:1-2; 19:7

9:13
*Hos 6:6
Mic 6:6-8
Matt 12:7
Luke 19:10
1 Tim 1:15
[c]*eleos* (1656)
‣ Matt 23:23

MATTHEW (LEVI) (9:9-10)

Matt 10:3
Mark 2:14-15; 3:18
Luke 5:27-29; 6:15
Acts 1:13

Matthew was a tax collector for the Romans and became one of Jesus' twelve apostles. According to early tradition, he was the author of the Gospel of Matthew.

Though he is called Matthew in all the lists of the apostles (10:3; Mark 3:18; Luke 6:15; Acts 1:13), he is referred to as Levi—his other name—in two of the accounts of his calling (Mark 2:14; Luke 5:27-29; cp. Matt 9:9-10). His father was named Alphaeus (Mark 2:14), but there is no certainty that he is the brother of James the son of Alphaeus (the two are not linked in the lists of the apostles, as the other pairs of brothers are).

Jews who collected taxes for the Romans were generally considered despicable sinners by their fellow Jews. They profited from working for the occupying forces and engaged in legalized extortion. Thus it is significant that Jesus called a tax collector to become one of his followers. When Jesus was criticized by the Pharisees for accepting Matthew's invitation to his home for dinner, and for eating with tax collectors and other disreputable sinners, Jesus used the occasion to teach the importance of compassion (9:13). He emphasized that it was precisely for such sinners—not those who considered themselves righteous—that he had come (9:9-13; Mark 2:14-17; Luke 5:27-32). Matthew responded immediately to Jesus' call, leaving everything behind to follow Jesus (Luke 5:28). The implication is that he never turned back to tax collecting or his former way of life.

Matthew's Gospel, written for his fellow Jews, gives us a Jewish perspective on the life and teachings of Jesus, and it includes topics of special interest for those from a Jewish background (see Matthew Introduction). His Gospel was the most popular Gospel in the early church—which is probably why it occurs first in the canonical sequence.

forgiveness, since that might have no verifiable effects; it is harder to enable a paralytic to *walk*. The miracle, visible to all, corroborates Jesus' authority to forgive sins and forces all who witness it to decide about Jesus.

9:6 ***So I will prove:*** Jesus performed the miracle to reveal his authority and identity as God's Messiah (see 11:2-6; 12:28). • ***Son of Man*** is a title Jesus used for himself as the redeemer and judge (Dan 7:13-14).

9:8 The mixture of *fear* and praise in the crowd's response corresponds to the awesome truth they perceived about Jesus. He is indeed the Son of God who has *authority* on earth to forgive sins (9:6). • ***for sending a man with such great authority:*** Literally *for giving such authority to human beings.*

9:9-13 Jesus, as Lord and Messiah, tore down the barriers that prevented righteous Jews from intermingling with those who were unclean or sinful.

9:9 ***Matthew*** was also called Levi (Mark 2:14). Matthew might have had two names, or he might have been given a new name by Jesus.

9:10 The Jewish people despised Jewish *tax collectors* (5:46-47; 18:15-20), who cooperated with Roman oppressors and were considered betrayers of the Israelite nation. Many also considered them unclean because of their frequent contact with Gentiles and because of the idolatrous images on Roman coins. Tax-collection was a private enterprise. In each district, Rome granted the right to collect taxes to the highest bidder (cp. Luke 19:1-10). Anything collected above the bid was profit for the collectors, who, driven by greed, often used extortion.

9:11 ***with such scum?*** Literally *with tax collectors and sinners?*

9:13 ***I want you to show mercy, not offer sacrifices*** (Hos 6:6 [Greek version]): God's desire is applied to the question of table fellowship with sinners; Jesus' *mercy* in eating with sinners contrasts with the Pharisees' separation from sinners (symbolized as *sacrifices*). • Jesus revealed the true spiritual condition of the Pharisees, ***who think they are righteous;*** they failed to recognize that they were in fact unrighteous and in need of the Messiah's salvation. See 7:1-5; 8:11-12; 19:30; 20:16; 21:43.

9:14-17 //Mark 2:18-22 //Luke 5:33-39
9:15 John 3:29
9:18-26 //Mark 5:22-43 //Luke 8:41-56
9:22 Matt 9:29 Mark 10:52 Luke 7:50; 17:19 Acts 3:16
9:23 2 Chr 35:25 Jer 9:17-18

A Discussion about Fasting

Matt 9:14-17 // Mark 2:18-22 // Luke 5:33-39

14 One day the disciples of John the Baptist
came to Jesus and asked him, "Why don't
your disciples fast like we do and the Pharisees do?"
15 Jesus replied, "Do wedding guests
mourn while celebrating with the groom?
Of course not. But someday the groom will
be taken away from them, and then they
will fast.
16 "Besides, who would patch old clothing
with new cloth? For the new patch would
shrink and rip away from the old cloth, leaving an even bigger tear than before.
17 "And no one puts new wine into old
wineskins. For the old skins would burst
from the pressure, spilling the wine and ruining the skins. New wine is stored in new
wineskins so that both are preserved."

Jesus Heals in Response to Faith

Matt 9:18-26 // Mark 5:21-43 // Luke 8:40-56

18 As Jesus was saying this, the leader of a
synagogue came and knelt before him. "My
daughter has just died," he said, "but you
can bring her back to life again if you just
come and lay your hand on her."
19 So Jesus and his disciples got up and
went with him.
20 Just then a woman who
had suffered for twelve years with constant bleeding came up behind him. She
touched the fringe of his robe,
21 for she
thought, "If I can just touch his robe, I will
be healed."
22 Jesus turned around, and when he saw
her he said, "Daughter, be encouraged! Your
faith has made you well." And the woman
was healed at that moment.
23 When Jesus arrived at the official's
home, he saw the noisy crowd and heard

Eating Together (9:10-13)

Matt 8:11-12; 9:10-13; 11:19; 26:26-29 Gen 18:1-8 Exod 24:9-11 2 Kgs 25:27-30 Luke 7:36-50; 15:1-2; 19:1-10; 22:14-21 Acts 2:46-47 1 Cor 11:20-34 Gal 2:11-16 Eph 2:14-18

Eating meals together was a religious matter among the Pharisees and other observant Jews. Righteous Jews enacted many regulations to prevent themselves from being ceremonially defiled at meals. It was not done so much to exclude others as to show commitment to the law.

Most Jews lived by the food laws most of the time. Jesus did so, too. But he regularly, purposefully, and offensively ate with those who were ritually unclean or whose commitment to the law was inferior. Sharing a meal with another indicated both covenantal and social equality (cp. 26:26-29; 2 Kgs 25:27-30). The Pharisees, believing that separation from such sinners was a necessity for righteousness, were offended by Jesus' sharing meals with such people (9:10; 11:19; 21:28-32; Luke 7:41-50; 15:1-2; 19:1-10).

Jesus' sharing meals with sinful people enacted God's grace—he extended God's love and forgiveness, welcoming open participation in a new society. This practice developed into the early Christian communion meals (Acts 2:46; 1 Cor 11:17-34). As is clear from the Last Supper, the meals Jesus shared with his followers anticipated the feast in the Kingdom of Heaven (26:29; see 8:11-12). The apostle Paul extended Jesus' practice to enable fellowship between Jews and Gentiles in the church (see Gal 2:11-21). Jesus tore down the barriers separating us from one another and from God (Eph 2:14-18) and calls us into fellowship with all his people.

9:14 ***fast*** (some manuscripts read *fast often*): Fasting expressed personal humility and repentance (2 Sam 12:16-23; Dan 9:3). It called attention to the national need for repentance (Lev 16:29-31; Neh 9:1) and probably sought to hasten the arrival of the Messiah through purification. The fact that ***Jesus*** and his ***disciples*** did not fast (11:18-19) subtly proclaimed that the Messiah had already arrived (see also 6:16).

9:15 ***wedding guests . . . groom:*** John the Baptist had also described the Messiah and his disciples in this way (John 3:29), drawing on OT imagery to reveal Jesus' status (see Isa 54:5-6; Matt 25:1-13). • ***taken away:*** This is Jesus' first prediction of his violent death (see 16:21; 17:12, 22-23; 20:18-19; 26:2, 26-35; Isa 53:8). • ***then they will fast:*** Jesus may be referring to the disciples' sorrow immediately after Jesus' crucifixion, or to the disciples' lifestyle after Jesus' death and resurrection (see Acts 9:9; 13:2-3; 14:23; 27:9, 33).

9:16-17 These riddle-like parables contrast the new covenant that Jesus has established (26:26-29) with the old covenant, especially in relation to such rituals as fasting. Jesus consummates, but does not abolish, the law (5:17-20; see Gal 2:21; 5:4). Yet the new covenant requires new practices.

9:18-34 Jesus is the Messiah whose power knows no boundaries. He calls people to have faith in him.

9:18 ***lay your hand on her:*** The laying-on of hands is a visible symbol of prayer for God's power to flow into someone, often resulting in new life or ministries (19:13; Num 27:18-23; Deut 34:9). • The man believed that Jesus had the power to raise the dead (cp. 1 Kgs 17:8-24; 2 Kgs 4:18-37).

9:20 The woman's ***constant bleeding*** rendered her always ceremonially unclean and made whoever she touched unclean as well (Lev 15:25-30). But instead of rendering Jesus unclean, her touching him made her clean, a stunning reversal that illustrates Jesus' power to redeem and sanctify (see 14:36; Mark 3:10). • ***fringe:*** The tassels at the bottom of a tunic (23:5; Num 15:37-41) reminded Jews to live in accord with God's law.

9:22 ***Your faith has made you well*** (literally *has saved you*): Physical healing demonstrated her spiritual salvation (see 8:17).

9:23 ***noisy crowd . . . funeral music:*** Sorrow over the death of a family member was publicly expressed, with

the funeral music. 24"Get out!" he told them.
"The girl isn't dead; she's only asleep." But
the crowd laughed at him. 25After the crowd
was put outside, however, Jesus went in and
took the girl by the hand, and she stood up!
26The report of this miracle swept through
the entire countryside.

Jesus Heals the Blind and Demon Possessed
Matt 9:27-31; cp. Matt 20:29-34 // Mark 10:46-52 // Luke 18:35-43
Matt 9:32-34 // Matt 12:22-24 // Luke 11:14-15; cp. Mark 3:22

27After Jesus left the girl's home, two blind
men followed along behind him, shouting,
"Son of David, have mercy on us!"
28They went right into the house where
he was staying, and Jesus asked them, "Do
you believe I can make you see?"
"Yes, Lord," they told him, "we do."
29Then he touched their eyes and said, "Because of your faith, it will happen." 30Then
their eyes were opened, and they could see!
Jesus sternly warned them, "Don't tell anyone about this." 31But instead, they went out
and spread his fame all over the region.
32When they left, a demon-possessed
man who couldn't speak was brought to
Jesus. 33So Jesus cast out the demon, and
then the man began to speak. The crowds
were amazed. "Nothing like this has ever
happened in Israel!" they exclaimed.
34But the Pharisees said, "He can cast out
demons because he is empowered by the
prince of demons."

Discourse: Jesus Extends His Ministry (9:35–11:1)

The Problem: The Need for Workers
Matt 9:37-38 // Luke 10:2

35Jesus traveled through all the towns and
villages of that area, teaching in the synagogues and announcing the Good News
about the Kingdom. And he healed every
kind of disease and illness. 36When he saw
the crowds, he had compassion on them
because they were confused and helpless,
like sheep without a [d]shepherd. 37He said to
his disciples, "The harvest is great, but the
workers are few. 38So pray to the Lord who
is in charge of the harvest; ask him to send
more workers into his fields."

The Solution: Jesus Chooses the Twelve Apostles
Matt 10:1-4 // Mark 3:13-19 // Luke 6:12-16

10 Jesus called his twelve disciples together and gave them authority to
cast out evil spirits and to heal every kind of
disease and illness. 2Here are the names of
the twelve [e]apostles:

first, Simon (also called Peter),
then Andrew (Peter's brother),
James (son of Zebedee),
John (James's brother),

9:24 Mark 9:26-27; John 11:11-13
9:25 Acts 9:40
9:27 Matt 20:29-31; Mark 10:47
9:30 Mark 7:36
9:31 Mark 7:36
9:32-33 Matt 12:22; Mark 7:32, 35; 9:17, 25; Luke 11:14
9:34 Matt 12:24; Mark 3:22; Luke 11:15
9:35 Matt 4:23
9:36 *Num 27:17; 1 Kgs 22:17; *2 Chr 18:16; Ezek 34:5; *Zech 10:2; Mark 6:34
[d]*poimēn* (4166) ‣ Matt 26:31
9:37-38 //Luke 10:2; John 4:35
10:2-4 //Mark 3:13-19; //Luke 6:12-16; John 1:40-49; Acts 1:13
10:2 [e]*apostolos* (0652) ‣ Acts 1:25
10:4 Matt 26:25; 27:3; Mark 14:44; John 6:64; 12:4; 13:2, 26-27

musical accompaniment and dirges by professional mourners. "Even the poorest in Israel should hire not less than two flutes and one wailing woman" (*Mishnah Ketubbot* 4:4).

9:24 Though she was physically dead, from Jesus' perspective ***the girl*** was just ***asleep***—she would soon be raised back to life (see Isa 26:19; John 11:11-14, 25; 1 Thes 4:14).

9:27 Eye diseases were common in the ancient world. Blindness was often considered to be divine punishment (see Exod 4:11; Deut 28:28; 2 Kgs 6:18; John 9:2-3). The OT predicts that the Messiah's coming would bring restoration of sight for the blind (11:4-5; Isa 29:18-19; 35:5-6). • ***Son of David*** is a messianic title particularly associated with miraculous healings (see 1:1; 12:23; 15:22; 20:30-31; 2 Sam 7:12-16).

9:28 Jesus intended his question to elicit confessions of faith from the two men.

9:32-34 The Messiah's acts invoke faith, astonishment, and derisive rejection.

9:32 Enabling the deaf to hear and the mute to speak is a sign of the Kingdom of God (11:4-5; Isa 35:5-6).

9:35–11:1 Jesus here extends his ministry (shown in 4:23–9:34) to others within Israel through his disciples (10:5-6). Jesus' instructions to his disciples (10:5-42) focus on missionary activity and its consequent opposition and hardship.

9:35 This verse connects with the section begun at 4:23. Matthew has presented Jesus to his readers as the Messiah who teaches, preaches, heals, casts out demons, and calls for a decisive response of faith.

9:36 ***like sheep without a shepherd:*** Jesus lamented the Pharisees' pastoral negligence (see 12:11-12; 18:12). Their attacks against Jesus were a clear indication of their hard-hearted rejection of God. The crowds languished due to pastoral neglect and mistreatment (10:5-6; 15:12-14; 23:4; Zech 11:16).

9:37-38 ***Harvest*** refers to the multitudes (see also 13:24-30, 36-43; Mark 4:26-29; John 4:35-38; Rev 14:15-20). • ***the Lord who is in charge of the harvest:*** All ministries are ultimately under God's call (see 23:8-10, 13), so Jesus urges his disciples to pray for God himself to call more ***workers.***

10:1 ***Jesus called his twelve disciples*** as workers in the harvest (9:37-38). The choice of twelve is not accidental—it recalls the twelve tribes of Israel. Jesus was appointing new leaders for the new people of God under his reign as Messiah (16:18-19; 18:18; 19:28; 21:43). • ***gave them authority*** (9:6-8; 28:18): Jesus enabled the Twelve to perform ministries that the Jewish leaders could not accomplish (9:32-34; 10:5-8). The authority ***to cast out evil*** (literally ***unclean***) ***spirits*** (8:28) and ***to heal*** are ascribed to Jesus (4:23; 8:1–9:35) in similar terms.

10:2-4 The four lists of the apostles (see also Mark 3:16-19; Luke 6:14-16; Acts 1:13) are all different, although the differences are minimal. The order within each list varies slightly, but only the names ***Thaddaeus*** (10:3; Mark 3:18) and Judas son of James (Luke 6:16; Acts 1:13) differ. They might be two names for the same man.

10:2 The ***apostles*** are ambassadors or messengers, authorized and sent by an authority to represent and accomplish prescribed tasks (see 10:1-8, 40; 28:16-20). The term is also used for Paul (Gal 1:1). • ***first, Simon (also called Peter):*** Peter had priority in time (4:18-22; 16:17-19) and position as the representative leader of the apostles (see 19:27; 26:33; Acts 2:14).

10:5-15
//Mark 6:7-13
//Luke 9:1-6

10:5
2 Kgs 17:24
John 4:9

10:6
Jer 50:6
Matt 15:24

10:7
Matt 3:2; 4:17

10:8
[f]*daimonion* (1140)
‣ Matt 12:24

10:9-10
1 Cor 9:14
1 Tim 5:18

10:12-13
//Luke 10:5-6

10:14-15
//Luke 10:10-12
Acts 13:51

3 Philip,
Bartholomew,
Thomas,
Matthew (the tax collector),
James (son of Alphaeus),
Thaddaeus,
4 Simon (the zealot),
Judas Iscariot (who later betrayed him).

Jesus Sends Out the Twelve Apostles

Matt 10:5-15 // Mark 6:6b-13 // Luke 9:1-6;

5 Jesus sent out the twelve apostles with
these instructions: "Don't go to the Gentiles
or the Samaritans, 6 but only to the people of
Israel—God's lost sheep. 7 Go and announce
to them that the Kingdom of Heaven is near.
8 Heal the sick, raise the dead, cure those
with leprosy, and cast out [f]demons. Give as
freely as you have received!
9 "Don't take any money in your money
belts—no gold, silver, or even copper coins.
10 Don't carry a traveler's bag with a change
of clothes and sandals or even a walking
stick. Don't hesitate to accept hospitality, because those who work deserve to be fed.
11 "Whenever you enter a city or village,
search for a worthy person and stay in his
home until you leave town. 12 When you enter the home, give it your blessing. 13 If it
turns out to be a worthy home, let your blessing stand; if it is not, take back the blessing.
14 If any household or town refuses to
welcome you or listen to your message,
shake its dust from your feet as you leave.

Compassionate Healer (9:36)

Matt 9:35-36; 14:14; 15:32; 18:23-30; 20:29-34
Deut 13:18; 30:3
1 Kgs 8:50-51
Prov 28:13
Isa 14:1; 49:10, 13; 54:7-10; 55:7; 60:10
Jer 12:14-15; 33:26
Ezek 39:25
Mic 7:18-20
Hab 3:2
Zech 1:16; 10:6
Luke 10:33-37; 15:20-32

Jesus is frequently described as one who "had compassion." This expression is used of Jesus in complex situations where (1) distress is expressed (18:23-26; 20:29-33) and Jesus remedies the distress (18:27; 20:34), (2) Jesus shows deep emotion (14:14; 15:32; 18:27; 20:34), or (3) there is a contrast with those who are not compassionate (9:34-36; 18:27-30; 20:31-34). The phrase "had compassion" refers only to Jesus, except when used in parables where it refers either to God the Father or to Jesus (18:27; Luke 10:33; 15:20).

In the OT, the term "compassion" is used for God's covenant love for Israel. God withdrew this compassion to judge Israel's obstinate unfaithfulness (Isa 13:18; 27:11; 63:15; Jer 6:2-3; 13:14). God restored his compassion when Israel repented (Deut 13:18; 30:3; 1 Kgs 8:50; Prov 28:13; Isa 55:7). The OT often describes the messianic age as a time of God's compassion (Isa 14:1; 49:10, 13; 54:8, 10; 60:10; Jer 12:15; 33:26; 42:12; Ezek 39:25; Mic 7:19; Hab 3:2; Zech 1:16; 10:6). The resurgence of this term in the Gospels reflects this, as the messianic age has dawned and God's covenant love is once again active in Israel.

10:3 *Matthew (the tax collector)* (see 9:9) is also called Levi (Mark 2:14). • ***Thaddaeus:*** Other manuscripts read *Lebbaeus;* still others read *Lebbaeus who is called Thaddaeus.*

10:4 ***the zealot:*** Greek *the Cananean,* an Aramaic term for Jewish nationalists. Zealots were militant Jews who thought violence and war were capable of accomplishing the will of God. As a Jewish nationalist, ***Simon*** was probably zealous for the law (Acts 22:3-5; Gal 1:14; Phil 3:6). Josephus blamed the Zealot party for the great war with Rome in AD 66–70. • ***Iscariot*** might refer to someone from Kerioth in southern Judea (Josh 15:25) or from Kerioth in Perea (Jer 48:24).

10:5 ***Don't go to the Gentiles:*** Jesus' mission was limited to Jews at this stage (15:24). Through the Jews, God would reach the Gentiles (Isa 2:2-4; 42:6-7; 49:6; 60:3). • Jews regarded ***Samaritans*** as impure Jews (Luke 17:18) because of their intermarriage with Gentiles during and after the Assyrian and Babylonian exiles (2 Kgs 17:24-41). Tension was provoked in 128 BC when the Jewish leader John Hyrcanus destroyed the Samaritan temple on Mount Gerizim (Josephus, *Antiquities* 13.9.1).

10:6 Being ***lost*** is the result of neglect by their shepherds (9:36; 15:24).

10:7-8 By doing these things in the name and authority of Jesus, the apostles demonstrated Jesus' status as Messiah (see 11:2-6).

10:7 ***is near:*** Or *has come,* or *is coming soon.*

10:8 ***Give as freely as you have received!*** While remuneration is not improper (1 Cor 9:3-19; Gal 6:6; 1 Tim 5:17), Jesus urged the apostles to avoid accusations of greed (see Acts 8:20; 20:33).

10:9-10 Jesus' disciples were to trust in God's provision (6:11, 25-34; 7:7-11), to avoid greed that would give others the opportunity to defame the Lord's name, and to encourage the newly formed communities to provide for their leaders' needs (see 1 Cor 9:3-19).

10:12 ***give it your blessing:*** Greetings were more significant than a simple hello. Often, a greeting would convey a blessing for those who received it (cp. Ruth 2:4).

10:13 ***A worthy home*** would embrace the message about Jesus and the Kingdom (10:37-38; 22:8). • The disciples' ***blessing*** was an offer of salvation; to ***take back the blessing*** was a sign of judgment as the offer was withdrawn.

10:14 ***shake its dust from your feet:*** This prophet-like gesture (see "Prophetic Sign Acts" at Ezek 4:1-17, p. 1319) is explained by the Israelite custom of expressing displeasure with ungodliness by shaking off Gentile dust whenever crossing the border into Israel. The gesture signifies the disciples' rejection of those who oppose God's work (see Acts 18:6). Pronouncing judgment on those who reject the message is part of proclaiming the Good News about the Kingdom (see 11:20-24; 13:10-15; 23:37-39; 24:1-36).

15 I tell you the truth, the wicked cities of Sodom and Gomorrah will be better off than such a town on the judgment day.

16 "Look, I am sending you out as sheep among wolves. So be as shrewd as snakes and harmless as doves. 17 But beware! For you will be handed over to the courts and will be flogged with whips in the synagogues. 18 You will stand trial before governors and kings because you are my followers. But this will be your opportunity to tell the rulers and other unbelievers about me. 19 When you are arrested, don't worry about how to respond or what to say. God will give you the right words at the right time. 20 For it is not you who will be speaking—it will be the Spirit of your Father speaking through you.

21 "A brother will betray his brother to death, a father will betray his own child, and children will rebel against their parents and cause them to be killed. 22 And all nations will hate you because you are my followers. But everyone who endures to the end will be saved. 23 When you are persecuted in one town, flee to the next. I tell you the truth, the Son of Man will return before you have reached all the towns of Israel.

24 "Students are not greater than their teacher, and slaves are not greater than their master. 25 Students are to be like their teacher, and slaves are to be like their master. And since I, the master of the household, have been called the [g]prince of demons, the members of my household will be called by even worse names!

Instruction Not to Fear Opposition

Matt 10:26-36 // Luke 12:2-9, 51-53
Matt 10:37-38 // Luke 14:25-27

26 "But don't be afraid of those who threaten you. For the time is coming when everything that is covered will be revealed, and all that is secret will be made known to all. 27 What I tell you now in the darkness, shout abroad when daybreak comes. What I whisper in your ear, shout from the housetops for all to hear!

28 "Don't be afraid of those who want to kill your body; they cannot touch your soul. Fear only God, who can destroy both soul and body in hell. 29 What is the price of two sparrows—one copper coin? But not a single sparrow can fall to the ground without your Father knowing it. 30 And the very hairs on your head are all numbered. 31 So don't be afraid; you are more valuable to God than a whole flock of sparrows.

32 "Everyone who acknowledges me publicly here on earth, I will also acknowledge before my Father in heaven. 33 But everyone who denies me here on earth, I will also deny before my Father in heaven.

10:15
Gen 18:20–19:29
Matt 11:23-24
2 Pet 2:6
Jude 1:7

10:16
Luke 10:3
Acts 20:29

10:17-22
//Mark 13:9-13
//Luke 21:12-19

10:17
Acts 5:40; 22:19; 26:11
Heb 11:36-38

10:18
Acts 25:24-26

10:19-20
Luke 12:11-12
Acts 4:8

10:21
Mic 7:6

10:22
John 15:21

10:24
John 13:16; 15:20

10:25
[g]*beelzeboul* (0954)
‣ Matt 12:24

10:26-33
//Luke 12:2-9

10:26
Mark 4:22

10:28
Isa 8:12-13
Heb 10:31

10:30
1 Sam 14:45
2 Sam 14:11
Luke 21:18
Acts 27:34

10:31
Matt 6:26; 12:12

10:15 God destroyed ***Sodom and Gomorrah*** for their wickedness (Gen 18:16–19:29). Now, with a more complete revelation in Jesus Christ, a town that rejected the disciples' preaching would receive a more complete judgment. • ***such a town:*** An entire village or city is culpable when a significant majority rejects the message (see Acts 13:45-47, 50-51; 14:1-7). However, individuals who respond in faith are saved (e.g., Lot; see Gen 19:1-29; 2 Pet 2:6-9).

10:16 False leaders who prey upon people's spiritual vulnerability rather than exercise appropriate pastoral care are often called ***wolves*** (Ezek 22:27; Zeph 3:3; cp. Prov 28:15). • ***be as shrewd as snakes and harmless as doves:*** The proverb calls for being astute but not deceitful.

10:18 ***But this will be your opportunity to tell the rulers and other unbelievers about me:*** Or *But this will be your testimony against the rulers and other unbelievers.*

10:19-20 As God gave Moses a spokesman in Aaron (Exod 4:10-17), so God would give Jesus' disciples the ***right words at the right time*** through ***the Spirit*** (John 14:26; Acts 4:8).

10:21-22 Jews regularly associated family strife with the last times (see 24:9-10). Jesus experienced such conflicts as well (12:46-50). • ***Everyone who endures to the end*** refers to those who remain faithful to Jesus, to the point of death or until his return (10:23). • ***will be saved:*** Though some have taken this phrase to mean temporal deliverance from persecution (such as release from prison), the idea here is eternal salvation for those who remain faithful.

10:22 ***because you are my followers:*** Literally *on account of my name.*

10:23 ***Son of Man*** is a title Jesus used for himself. • ***will return:*** Scholars are divided as to whether this refers to the second coming of Christ for his church or an earlier coming in judgment—namely, the destruction of Jerusalem in AD 70 (see 16:28). • ***before you have reached:*** Jesus meant either "before you have *fled* through all the towns" or "before you have *evangelized* all the towns." The focus on persecution in the context (see 10:17-39) favors the former, suggesting that the towns were like cities of refuge (Num 35:9-32). The emphasis is on how widespread the rejection of the message will be—i.e., "not until the whole nation has run you out of town."

10:24 ***Students:*** Or *Disciples.*

10:25 In Jesus' day, Satan was often called ***prince of demons.*** The Greek term is *Beelzeboul* (other manuscripts read *Beezeboul*), from the name of an OT pagan deity, Baal-zebul ("lord, the prince"). The Latin version reads *Beelzebub,* which is a transliteration of a Hebrew phrase ("lord of flies"), which was most likely a Jewish insult of Baal-zebul (see 2 Kgs 1:2).

10:28 Jesus' disciples are to ***fear only God*** by obeying him and testifying of him; in contrast to human authorities, God's authority and judgment are unlimited. • ***hell*** (Greek *Gehenna*): See note on 5:29.

10:29-31 Because God cares about every sparrow, and because Jesus' disciples are much more valuable, certainly the disciples need not fear—God will providentially care for them.

10:29 ***one copper coin:*** Greek *one assarion* (i.e., one "as," a Roman coin equal to 1⁄16 of a denarius).

10:32-33 God accepts the one ***who acknowledges*** Jesus ***publicly*** in the context of trial and persecution (10:16-25). These verses pertain to a person's pattern of life (see 7:13-27) and not to a single confession or a single denial. For example, Judas acknowledged Jesus in individual instances yet was damned

10:32 Rom 10:9
Rev 3:5
10:33 Mark 8:38
Luke 9:26
2 Tim 2:12
10:34-36 //Luke 12:51-53
10:34 [h]*eirēnē* (1515)
‣ Luke 2:14
10:35-36 *Mic 7:6
10:37 Luke 14:26
10:38 Matt 16:24
Mark 8:34
Luke 9:23; 14:27
10:39 Matt 16:25
Mark 8:35
Luke 9:24; 17:33
John 12:25
10:40 John 12:44; 13:20
10:41 1 Kgs 17:9-24
2 Kgs 4:8-37
11:2-19 //Luke 7:18-35
11:3 Mal 3:1
11:5 Isa 35:4-6; 42:7, 18; 61:1
Luke 4:18-19
11:6 Matt 13:57
11:7 Matt 3:5
11:9 Matt 14:5; 21:26
Luke 1:76
11:10 Exod 23:20
*Mal 3:1
Mark 1:2
Luke 7:27

34"Don't imagine that I came to bring [h]peace to the earth! I came not to bring [h]peace, but a sword.

35 'I have come to set a man against his father,
a daughter against her mother,
and a daughter-in-law against her
mother-in-law.
36 Your enemies will be right in your
own household!'

37"If you love your father or mother more than you love me, you are not worthy of being mine; or if you love your son or daughter more than me, you are not worthy of being mine. 38If you refuse to take up your cross and follow me, you are not worthy of being mine. 39If you cling to your life, you will lose it; but if you give up your life for me, you will find it.

40"Anyone who receives you receives me, and anyone who receives me receives the Father who sent me. 41If you receive a prophet as one who speaks for God, you will be given the same reward as a prophet. And if you receive righteous people because of their righteousness, you will be given a reward like theirs. 42And if you give even a cup of cold water to one of the least of my followers, you will surely be rewarded."

Conclusion

11 When Jesus had finished giving these instructions to his twelve disciples, he went out to teach and preach in towns throughout the region.

4. THE RESPONSES TO THE MESSIAH (11:2–20:34)

Narrative: Rejected by Leaders, Accepted by Disciples (11:2–12:50)

Jesus and John the Baptist
Matt 11:2-19 // Luke 7:18-35

2John the Baptist, who was in prison, heard about all the things the Messiah was doing. So he sent his disciples to ask Jesus, 3"Are you the Messiah we've been expecting, or should we keep looking for someone else?"

4Jesus told them, "Go back to John and tell him what you have heard and seen—5the blind see, the lame walk, the lepers are cured, the deaf hear, the dead are raised to life, and the Good News is being preached to the poor. 6And tell him, 'God blesses those who do not turn away because of me.'"

7As John's disciples were leaving, Jesus began talking about him to the crowds. "What kind of man did you go into the wilderness to see? Was he a weak reed, swayed by every breath of wind? 8Or were you expecting to see a man dressed in expensive clothes? No, people with expensive clothes live in palaces. 9Were you looking for a prophet? Yes, and he is more than a prophet. 10John is the man to whom the Scriptures refer when they say,

'Look, I am sending my messenger ahead
of you,
and he will prepare your way before
you.'

(26:23-24), whereas Peter denied Jesus (see 26:69-75) yet was saved.

10:34-39 Allegiance to Jesus has priority over allegiance to family.

10:34 Jesus did bring *peace* (John 14:27), but not of a social and political kind. Instead, Jesus calls humans to make a decision about him, which brings a *sword*—i.e., division (see 8:21-22; 12:46-50; Luke 12:51).

10:35-36 The quotation is from Mic 7:6.

10:37-39 The cross was a Roman instrument of torture and execution (27:27-55). To *take up your cross and follow* Jesus involves loving him above all other things and being willing to follow him regardless of the physical or social consequences.

10:41 *receive a prophet as one who speaks for God:* Literally *receive a prophet in the name of a prophet.* • *The same reward as a prophet* (literally *A prophet's reward)* means either the same reward a prophet would receive or the benefit of the prophet's ministry. • *Righteous people* are those who conform their behavior to God's law as taught by both John the Baptist (21:32) and Jesus (see 3:15), and therefore are approved by God (13:43, 49; 25:37-46).

10:42 *The least of my followers* probably refers to the low social standing of most of Jesus' followers (cp. 5:3; 18:1-5 and 6:5; 23:5-12).

11:2–20:34 This section highlights the two primary responses to Jesus: acceptance and rejection. The first section (11:2–12:50) features the rejection of Jesus by Jewish leaders while his disciples were learning to understand and accept him.

11:2-19 This section begins with John the Baptist's doubt, but it ends by exalting his faith and ministry (11:7-19). The people's rejection of John (11:16-19) foreshadows their later rejection of Jesus.

11:2 *John* was arrested (4:12) by Herod Antipas because he had denounced Herod's immoral relationship with Herodias, his half-brother's wife (14:1-12). • *the things the Messiah was doing:* These actions demonstrated that he is the Messiah (8:1–9:34).

11:3 *Are you the Messiah we've been expecting?* Literally *Are you the one who is coming?* See Ps 118:26.

11:5 Jesus' miracles of compassion inaugurated the Kingdom of God (12:28; see Isa 29:18-19; 35:5-6; 61:1). Jesus expected John to understand that he was fulfilling OT expectations.

11:6 *who do not turn away because of me* (or *who are not offended by me*): The works listed in 11:5 were intended to drive John and his disciples to a decision regarding Jesus. Jesus was aware, however, that certain unexpected elements of his ministry would cause some to reject him.

11:7 *a weak reed, swayed by every breath of wind:* An unstable person. The implied answer to Jesus' rhetorical question is no.

11:10 The quotation is from Mal 3:1.

11“I tell you the truth, of all who have ever
lived, none is greater than John the Baptist.
Yet even the least person in the Kingdom
of Heaven is greater than he is! 12And from
the time John the Baptist began preaching
until now, the Kingdom of Heaven has been
forcefully advancing, and violent people are
attacking it. 13For before John came, all the
prophets and the law of Moses looked forward to this present time. 14And if you are
willing to accept what I say, he is Elijah, the
one the prophets said would come. 15Any-
one with ears to hear should listen and
understand!

16“To what can I compare this generation?
It is like children playing a game in the public square. They complain to their friends,

17 ‘We played wedding songs,
and you didn’t dance,
so we played funeral songs,
and you didn’t mourn.’

18For John didn’t spend his time eating and
drinking, and you say, ‘He’s possessed by
a demon.’ 19The Son of Man, on the other
hand, feasts and drinks, and you say, ‘He’s a
glutton and a drunkard, and a friend of tax
collectors and other sinners!’ But wisdom is
shown to be right by its results.”

Judgment for the Unbelievers
Matt 11:20-24 // Luke 10:12-15

20Then Jesus began to denounce the towns
where he had done so many of his miracles,
because they hadn’t repented of their sins
and turned to God. 21“What sorrow awaits
you, Korazin and Bethsaida! For if the miracles I did in you had been done in wicked
Tyre and Sidon, their people would have
repented of their sins long ago, clothing
themselves in burlap and throwing ashes
on their heads to show their remorse. 22I
tell you, Tyre and Sidon will be better off on
judgment day than you.

23“And you people of Capernaum, will
you be honored in heaven? No, you will go
down to the ⁱplace of the dead. For if the
miracles I did for you had been done in
wicked Sodom, it would still be here today.
24I tell you, even Sodom will be better off on
judgment day than you.”

Jesus’ Prayer of Thanksgiving
Matt 11:25-27 // Luke 10:21-22

25At that time Jesus prayed this prayer:
“O Father, Lord of heaven and earth, thank
you for hiding these things from those who
think themselves wise and clever, and for revealing them to the childlike. 26Yes, Father,
it pleased you to do it this way!

27“My Father has entrusted everything to
me. No one truly knows the Son except the
Father, and no one truly knows the Father
except the Son and those to whom the Son
chooses to reveal him.”

28Then Jesus said, “Come to me, all of you
who are weary and carry heavy burdens,

11:12-13 Luke 16:16
11:14 Mal 4:5; Matt 17:10-13; Mark 9:11-13; Luke 1:17; John 1:21
11:15 Matt 13:9, 43; Mark 4:9, 23; Luke 8:8; 14:35; Rev 2:7
11:18 Matt 3:4; Luke 1:15
11:19 Matt 9:11, 14
11:20-24 //Luke 10:13-15
11:21-22 Isa 23:1-8; Ezek 26–28; Joel 3:4-8; Amos 1:9-10; Zech 9:2-4; Matt 10:15
11:23 *Isa 14:13, 15; ⁱ*hadēs* (0086) ‣Matt 16:18
11:25-27 //Luke 10:21-22; 1 Cor 1:26-29; Eph 1:17-18
11:27 Matt 28:18; John 3:35; 10:15; 17:2, 25-26

11:11 *John the Baptist* was the greatest person ever to have lived. Yet *the least* of Jesus’ followers are ***greater*** than John because they live in the new covenant of salvation through Christ (see 4:17).

11:12 ***the Kingdom of Heaven has been forcefully advancing:*** Or *the Kingdom of Heaven has suffered from violence.* These alternatives reflect either a positive or negative nuance of the Greek verb. In Luke 16:16, a different verb (“preached”) makes it a clearly positive statement. • ***violent people are attacking it:*** This phrase may also have a positive or negative sense. If negative, it might refer to those who imprisoned John (see 11:2; 14:1-12), and *attacking* might mean either that they were trying to attack the Kingdom but were unable to thwart God’s sovereign plans, or that they were attacking it by persecuting its members. In Luke 16:16 this statement has the positive sense that they were “eager to get in” and were forcefully laying claim to the kingdom through radical trust and obedience.

11:14-15 ***Elijah, the one the prophets said would come:*** See Mal 4:5. John is the fulfillment of OT expectations of Elijah’s return (17:10-13).

11:16-19 John’s prophetic message is represented by ***funeral songs***—he didn’t drink wine and he often fasted (11:18; see 3:4). Jesus’ message is seen in ***wedding songs*** and in ***feasts and drinks*** (see 9:9-17). In both cases, ***this generation*** responds to God’s messenger with indifference and rejection.

11:18-19 Here Jesus describes the specific ways in which *John* and Jesus offended the present generation. John, who stayed in the wilderness and ate locusts and honey (3:1, 4), was accused of being ***possessed by a demon;*** while Jesus, who ate and drank freely, was accused of being a rebellious son (see Deut 21:18-21).

11:19 *Son of Man* is a title Jesus used for himself.

11:20-24 The *miracles* Jesus performed confirmed him as Messiah (11:5-6) and demanded repentance (11:20). Rejecting the Messiah would result in terrible judgment because the evidence of Jesus’ identity was clear.

11:21-24 As Jesus moved through the villages of Galilee—from ***Korazin*** to ***Bethsaida*** to ***Capernaum***—he gave the people a greater revelation of himself, with a correspondingly more severe judgment when they refused to listen. The severity is indicated by comparison with the pagan cities of ***Tyre*** (Isa 23; Ezek 26:1–28:19), ***Sidon*** (Ezek 28:20-23), and ***Sodom*** (Gen 18:22–19:29).

11:23 ***the place of the dead:*** Greek *Hades,* which corresponds to the Hebrew term *Sheol* (see note on Ps 6:5).

11:25-30 This passage focuses on the remnant who, despite the present generation’s overall rejection of the Messiah, willingly embrace him and follow his teachings.

11:25 ***those who think themselves wise and clever:*** The Pharisees and teachers of religious law thought their access to God was guaranteed through their knowledge and practice of the law. Jesus’ disciples were more ***childlike*** (see 21:15-16).

11:27 Jesus was revealing his intimate relationship to the ***Father.*** Everything he said and did was rooted in this Father–Son unity (see John 10:14-15; 14:6-7; 15:23-24; 16:15; 17:25-26).

11:28 The ***heavy burdens*** were likely caused by the legal requirements of the teachers of religious law and Pharisees

11:29
*Jer 6:16
11:30
1 Jn 5:3
12:1-8
//Mark 2:23-28
//Luke 6:1-5
12:2
Exod 20:10
Deut 5:14
Luke 13:14; 14:3
John 5:10; 7:23; 9:16
12:3
1 Sam 21:1-6
12:4
Lev 24:5-9
12:5
Num 28:9-10
12:6
Matt 12:41-42
Luke 11:31-32
12:7
*Hos 6:6
Mic 6:6-8
Matt 9:13
12:8
[j]*kurios* (2962)
‣ Matt 27:63
12:9-14
//Mark 3:1-6
//Luke 6:6-11
12:10
Luke 13:14; 14:3
John 9:16
12:11
Luke 14:5
12:12
Matt 6:26; 10:31
12:15
//Mark 3:7-12
//Luke 6:17-19
12:18-21
*Isa 42:1-4
[k]*pneuma* (4151)
‣ Rom 8:10

and I will give you rest. 29Take my yoke upon you. Let me teach you, because I am humble and gentle at heart, and you will find rest for your souls. 30For my yoke is easy to bear, and the burden I give you is light."

A Discussion about the Sabbath
Matt 12:1-8 // Mark 2:23-28 // Luke 6:1-5

12 At about that time Jesus was walking through some grainfields on the Sabbath. His disciples were hungry, so they began breaking off some heads of grain and eating them. 2But some Pharisees saw them do it and protested, "Look, your disciples are breaking the law by harvesting grain on the Sabbath."

3Jesus said to them, "Haven't you read in the Scriptures what David did when he and his companions were hungry? 4He went into the house of God, and he and his companions broke the law by eating the sacred loaves of bread that only the priests are allowed to eat. 5And haven't you read in the law of Moses that the priests on duty in the Temple may work on the Sabbath? 6I tell you, there is one here who is even greater than the Temple! 7But you would not have condemned my innocent disciples if you knew the meaning of this Scripture: 'I want you to show mercy, not offer sacrifices.' 8For the Son of Man is [j]Lord, even over the Sabbath!"

Jesus Heals on the Sabbath
Matt 12:9-14 // Mark 3:1-6 // Luke 6:6-11

9Then Jesus went over to their synagogue, 10where he noticed a man with a deformed hand. The Pharisees asked Jesus, "Does the law permit a person to work by healing on the Sabbath?" (They were hoping he would say yes, so they could bring charges against him.)

11And he answered, "If you had a sheep that fell into a well on the Sabbath, wouldn't you work to pull it out? Of course you would. 12And how much more valuable is a person than a sheep! Yes, the law permits a person to do good on the Sabbath."

13Then he said to the man, "Hold out your hand." So the man held out his hand, and it was restored, just like the other one! 14Then the Pharisees called a meeting to plot how to kill Jesus.

Jesus, God's Chosen Servant

15But Jesus knew what they were planning. So he left that area, and many people followed him. He healed all the sick among them, 16but he warned them not to reveal who he was. 17This fulfilled the prophecy of Isaiah concerning him:

18 "Look at my Servant, whom I have
chosen.
He is my Beloved, who pleases me.
I will put my [k]Spirit upon him,

(see 23:4). • ***rest:*** Spiritual refreshment in either a present or a future sense (cp. 1:21; Heb 4:8-11).

11:29-30 A ***yoke***, which forms a harness between two animals, is a metaphor for the demands of discipleship. In contrast to the "yoke" of the religious leaders, Jesus' yoke is ***easy*** and ***light***, not because it is less demanding (see 7:13-14), but because the power of the Messiah (by the Holy Spirit) makes it possible (see Acts 15:10; 1 Jn 5:3). Jesus was most likely contrasting his yoke to the religious demands of Israel's spiritual leaders (23:4; Acts 15:10), which included 613 OT commands and their expansion through tradition. Jesus urged those who were suffering from the burdens of the Pharisees' stipulations to come to him (11:28) in order to find the salvation their hearts desired. It is a call to salvation involving a life of obedience to Jesus' new teachings. People are invited to enter a relationship with a ***humble and gentle*** teacher.

12:1-14 Matthew places Jesus' offer of rest (11:28-30) in close connection with a discussion of the Sabbath. Jesus' rest liberates people from human traditions concerning the Sabbath (cp. Heb 4:1-11). The Pharisees rejected Jesus because of their commitment to tradition.

12:1-8 This exchange highlights the Pharisees' lack of compassion as they imposed a burdensome yoke (11:29-30).

12:1 The ***Sabbath***, the seventh day of the week, was to be a day of complete rest according to OT laws (Gen 2:2-3; Exod 20:8-11). The Sabbath is fulfilled in Christ (cp. Heb 4:1-11).

12:3-7 The Pharisees did not understand that the Sabbath was designed to benefit people. Their view of the Sabbath placed onerous burdens on people.

12:3-4 Ritual laws were at times rightly suspended for particular people or circumstances (1 Sam 21:1-6).

12:5-6 Priests worked ***on the Sabbath*** (Lev 24:8-9; Num 28:9-10), and this was not offensive to Pharisees. If the priests' work for the ***Temple*** on the Sabbath is allowed, then certainly Jesus can do the same because he is ***greater than the Temple*** (see 4:23; 9:35; 11:2-6, 20-30).

12:7 ***I want you to show mercy, not offer sacrifices:*** Hos 6:6. The Pharisees' view of the Sabbath was unscriptural since it broke the deeper principle of mercy.

12:8 ***The Son of Man*** is a title Jesus used for himself. Jesus is superior to David, the priests, and the Temple. He reigns ***even over the Sabbath***.

12:9-14 This second Sabbath controversy castigates the Pharisees for elevating regulations over human needs (see 12:7, 11-12).

12:9 ***their synagogue:*** A disunion was developing between Jesus and Judaism (also 4:23).

12:10 ***Does the law permit:*** Rabbinic tradition permitted healing on the Sabbath only if life was in danger. Since life was not in jeopardy, the Pharisees thought healing was not permitted.

12:11-12 Their practice of rescuing animals but neglecting fellow humans was inconsistent.

12:15-21 This summary of Jesus' ministry clarifies Jesus' nature as the Messiah, the ***Servant*** of God who will bring salvation ***to the nations*** (see Isa 42:1-4).

12:18-21 These verses quote Isa 42:1-4 (Greek version for 42:4).

12:18 This quotation parallels Jesus' baptism (3:13-17). • ***Justice*** (or ***judgment***) can have positive or negative implications; the context here favors a positive meaning (12:20; cp. 23:23).

and he will proclaim justice to the
nations.
19 He will not fight or shout
or raise his voice in public.
20 He will not crush the weakest reed
or put out a flickering candle.
Finally he will cause justice to be
victorious.
21 And his name will be the hope
of all the world."

The Source of Jesus' Power

Matt 12:22-32 // Mark 3:22-30 // Luke 11:14-23
Matt 12:33-35 // Luke 6:43-45; cp. Matt 7:15-20

22Then a demon-possessed man, who was
blind and couldn't speak, was brought to
Jesus. He healed the man so that he could
both speak and see. 23The crowd was
amazed and asked, "Could it be that Jesus is
the Son of David, the Messiah?"
24But when the Pharisees heard about the
miracle, they said, "No wonder he can cast
out [a]demons. He gets his power from [b]Sa-
tan, the prince of [a]demons."
25Jesus knew their thoughts and replied, "Any kingdom divided by civil war
is doomed. A town or family splintered by
feuding will fall apart. 26And if Satan is
casting out Satan, he is divided and fighting
against himself. His own kingdom will not
survive. 27And if I am empowered by [c]Satan,
what about your own exorcists? They cast
out demons, too, so they will condemn you
for what you have said. 28But if I am casting out demons by the Spirit of God, then
the Kingdom of God has arrived among
you. 29For who is powerful enough to enter
the house of a strong man like Satan and
plunder his goods? Only someone even
stronger—someone who could tie him up
and then plunder his house.
30"Anyone who isn't with me opposes me,
and anyone who isn't working with me is actually working against me.
31"So I tell you, every sin and blasphemy
can be forgiven—except blasphemy against
the Holy Spirit, which will never be forgiven.
32Anyone who speaks against the Son of
Man can be forgiven, but anyone who
speaks against the Holy Spirit will never be
forgiven, either in this world or in the world
to come.
33"A tree is identified by its fruit. If a
tree is good, its fruit will be good. If a tree
is bad, its fruit will be bad. 34You brood of
snakes! How could evil men like you speak
what is good and right? For whatever is in
your heart determines what you say. 35A
good person produces good things from
the treasury of a good heart, and an evil
person produces evil things from the treasury of an evil heart. 36And I tell you this,
you must give an account on judgment day
for every idle word you speak. 37The words
you say will either acquit you or condemn
you."

The Sign of Jonah

Matt 12:38-42 // Luke 11:16, 29-32
Matt 12:43-45 // Luke 11:24-26

38One day some teachers of religious law
and Pharisees came to Jesus and said,
"Teacher, we want you to show us a miraculous [d]sign to prove your authority."

12:22-32
//Mark 3:20-30
//Luke 11:14-23

12:22-23
Matt 9:32-33

12:24
Matt 9:34
[a]*daimonion* (1140)
‣Mark 7:26
[b]*beelzeboul* (0954)
‣Matt 12:27

12:25
Matt 9:4

12:27
Matt 9:34
Acts 19:13
[c]*beelzeboul* (0954)
‣Mark 3:22

12:28
Acts 10:38

12:30
Mark 9:40
Luke 9:50

12:31-32
Mark 3:28-30
Luke 12:10

12:33
Matt 7:16-20
Luke 6:43-45

12:34
Matt 3:7; 23:33

12:38-42
Matt 16:4
//Luke 11:29-32

12:38
Matt 16:1
Mark 8:11-12
Luke 11:16
John 2:18; 6:30
1 Cor 1:22
[d]*sēmeion* (4592)
‣Matt 24:30

12:20 Instead of increasing people's spiritual burden, Jesus offers compassionate forgiveness and sustenance (see 11:28-30; 12:1-14).

12:22-45 The Messiah was rejected by the Pharisees, the teachers of religious law, and his own generation.

12:23 Amazement was a common response to Jesus' miracles (Mark 2:12; 6:51; Luke 2:47; 8:56; 24:22). • ***Could it be:*** The question expected a negative answer: Jesus did not fit their expectations for the Messiah, but his miracles did prompt the question.

12:24 ***Satan:*** Greek *Beelzeboul;* also in 12:27. Other manuscripts read *Beezeboul;* Latin version reads *Beelzebub.* See note on 10:25.

12:26 Jesus argued, in essence, "If I cast out demons under the influence of Satan, then Satan is dividing his camp, which obviously would be a foolish thing for Satan to do."

12:27 ***what about your own exorcists*** (literally *your sons*): Jesus forced them to think consistently. If demons are cast out under Satan's influence, then their disciples were equally guilty (see Acts 19:13-16).

12:28 The Pharisees were being confronted with and were rejecting the ***Kingdom of God*** itself (see Luke 17:20-21; 1 Jn 3:8). Jesus' miracles brought the power of the Kingdom into the present reality; its ultimate consummation awaits Christ's second coming.

12:29 This parable forced the Pharisees to answer a simple question: Can anyone cast out demons without first binding Satan's powers and thus opposing him (see Isa 49:24-26; 53:12)? • ***tie him up:*** Jesus overcame Satan first at his temptation (4:1-11), then throughout his ministry (see Luke 10:17-20), and ultimately on the Cross (see Col 2:14-15).

12:31 In the face of the Pharisees' accusations of Satanic influence, Jesus had just argued that he, the Messiah, cast out demons through the power of the Holy Spirit. In this context, ***blasphemy against the Holy Spirit*** can only mean attributing the ministry and exorcisms of Jesus to Satan's power.

12:32 One may stumble over Jesus' mysterious revelation of himself as ***Son of Man*** and be ***forgiven,*** but one cannot be forgiven for attributing the work of the Spirit to Satan. The present-day analogy is the outright rejection of the conviction of the ***Holy Spirit*** concerning Christ—that is, the ultimate rejection of the Good News by an unbeliever (cp. Heb 6:4-6; 1 Jn 5:16-21).

12:33-37 Jesus got to the heart of the matter: The Pharisees did not accept him or the divine origin of his ministry because they were wicked (see 7:15-27).

12:36-37 The ***idle word,*** in this context, was the accusation that Jesus had demonic inspiration. • What one says will ***acquit*** or ***condemn;*** one's words reflect the true condition of the heart.

12:38 ***a miraculous sign to prove:*** A popular expectation of the Messiah,

12:40
Jon 1:17

12:41
Jon 1:2; 3:5

12:42
1 Kgs 10:1-10
2 Chr 9:1-12
Matt 12:6

12:43-45
//Luke 11:24-26

12:45
2 Pet 2:20

12:46-50
//Mark 3:31-35
//Luke 8:19-21

12:46
Mark 6:3
John 2:12; 7:3-5
Acts 1:14

12:50
John 15:14

13:1-15
//Mark 4:1-12
//Luke 8:4-10

13:3
[e]*parabolē* (3850)
‣Matt 13:10

13:9
Matt 11:15; 13:43

[39]But Jesus replied, "Only an evil, adulterous generation would demand a miraculous sign; but the only sign I will give them is the sign of the prophet Jonah. [40]For as Jonah was in the belly of the great fish for three days and three nights, so will the Son of Man be in the heart of the earth for three days and three nights.

[41]"The people of Nineveh will stand up against this generation on judgment day and condemn it, for they repented of their sins at the preaching of Jonah. Now someone greater than Jonah is here—but you refuse to repent. [42]The queen of Sheba will also stand up against this generation on judgment day and condemn it, for she came from a distant land to hear the wisdom of Solomon. Now someone greater than Solomon is here—but you refuse to listen.

[43]"When an evil spirit leaves a person, it goes into the desert, seeking rest but finding none. [44]Then it says, 'I will return to the person I came from.' So it returns and finds its former home empty, swept, and in order. [45]Then the spirit finds seven other spirits more evil than itself, and they all enter the person and live there. And so that person is worse off than before. That will be the experience of this evil generation."

The True Family of Jesus
Matt 12:46-50 // Mark 3:31-35 // Luke 8:19-21

[46]As Jesus was speaking to the crowd, his mother and brothers stood outside, asking to speak to him. [47]Someone told Jesus, "Your mother and your brothers are outside, and they want to speak to you."

[48]Jesus asked, "Who is my mother? Who are my brothers?" [49]Then he pointed to his disciples and said, "Look, these are my mother and brothers. [50]Anyone who does the will of my Father in heaven is my brother and sister and mother!"

Discourse: Jesus Teaches through Parables (13:1-52)

Parable of the Farmer Scattering Seed
Matt 13:1-13 // Mark 4:1-12, 25 // Luke 8:4-10, 18
Matt 13:16-17 // Luke 10:23-24
Matt 13:18-23 // Mark 4:13-20 // Luke 8:11-15

13 Later that same day Jesus left the house and sat beside the lake. [2]A large crowd soon gathered around him, so he got into a boat. Then he sat there and taught as the people stood on the shore. [3]He told many stories in the form of [e]parables, such as this one:

"Listen! A farmer went out to plant some seeds. [4]As he scattered them across his field, some seeds fell on a footpath, and the birds came and ate them. [5]Other seeds fell on shallow soil with underlying rock. The seeds sprouted quickly because the soil was shallow. [6]But the plants soon wilted under the hot sun, and since they didn't have deep roots, they died. [7]Other seeds fell among thorns that grew up and choked out the tender plants. [8]Still other seeds fell on fertile soil, and they produced a crop that was thirty, sixty, and even a hundred times as much as had been planted! [9]Anyone with ears to hear should listen and understand."

---

probably fueled by biblical accounts about Moses (Exod 4:1-9; see also Isa 7:11, 14; 38:7-8), was that the Messiah would display spectacular miracles on command (see 16:1-4; Luke 23:8; John 2:18; 4:48; 6:30; 7:31; 9:16; 11:47; 1 Cor 1:22).

12:39-40 To ***demand*** a ***sign*** demonstrates a lack of faith. • The ***sign of the prophet Jonah*** consisted of Jonah's "resurrection" from the large fish after ***three days and three nights*** as well as his preaching (12:41; Luke 11:32); it was analogous to Jesus' burial and resurrection and his preaching. Jesus was drawing a parallel between Jonah's experience and what he himself would experience. He was not predicting an exact chronology of his death and resurrection. • ***Heart of the earth*** is a euphemism for the grave.

12:41-42 ***someone greater:*** Jesus is greater than the Temple (12:6), a prophet (***Jonah***), and a king (***Solomon***); therefore, rejection of him entails greater judgment on this "evil, adulterous generation" (12:39).

12:42 ***The queen of Sheba:*** Literally *The queen of the south.* See 1 Kgs 10:1-13.

12:43-45 The Messiah came in victory over demonic powers, but instead of repenting, the nation as a whole rejected the Messiah. Just as an exorcised demon will return if the house is not properly prepared against it, so judgment would come to ***this evil generation*** for rejecting the Messiah.

12:43 ***evil:*** Literally *unclean.* • Demons were thought to prefer the arid ***desert*** (see Rev 18:2; cp. Isa 13:21; 34:14).

12:47 Some manuscripts do not include v 47. Cp. Mark 3:32; Luke 8:20.

12:48-50 Those who are true members in Jesus' family do ***the will of*** the ***Father,*** as expressed in the commands of Jesus (see 7:21). Obedience does not earn entrance into this family, but one cannot be considered a member if he or she is not obedient (see 3:15; 5:17-48; 6:10, 12; 7:13-27; 21:31).

13:1-53 In the third major discourse recorded by Matthew (see note on 5:1–7:29), Jesus here recognized the separation of his followers from others (13:14, 16) and began to reveal the secrets of the Kingdom privately to them through parables.

13:3-9 This parable (interpreted in 13:18-23) addresses the mostly negative responses of the Jewish nation to Jesus and his message. • ***Parables*** (Greek *parabolē*) are stories that usually express an analogy between a common aspect of life and a spiritual truth. To understand a parable, it is necessary to locate the central analogy and understand it in its historical context and in the context of the Gospel text; then the central message can be understood. Speculative allegorical meanings that were not intended should not be found in every element of a parable.

10His disciples came and asked him,
"Why do you use [f]parables when you talk to
the people?"
11He replied, "You are permitted to understand the secrets of the Kingdom of Heaven,
but others are not. 12To those who listen to
my teaching, more understanding will be
given, and they will have an abundance of
knowledge. But for those who are not listening, even what little understanding they
have will be taken away from them. 13That
is why I use these parables,

For they look, but they don't really see.
They hear, but they don't really listen
or understand.

14This fulfills the prophecy of Isaiah that
says,

'When you hear what I say,
you will not understand.
When you see what I do,
you will not comprehend.
15 For the hearts of these people are hardened,
and their ears cannot hear,
and they have closed their eyes—
so their eyes cannot see,
and their ears cannot hear,
and their hearts cannot understand,
and they cannot turn to me
and let me heal them.'

16"But blessed are your eyes, because they
see; and your ears, because they hear. 17I tell
you the truth, many prophets and righteous
people longed to see what you see, but they
didn't see it. And they longed to hear what
you hear, but they didn't hear it.
18"Now listen to the explanation of the
parable about the farmer planting seeds:
19The seed that fell on the footpath represents those who hear the message about
the Kingdom and don't understand it. Then
the evil one comes and snatches away the
seed that was planted in their hearts. 20The
seed on the rocky soil represents those who
hear the message and immediately receive
it with joy. 21But since they don't have deep
roots, they don't last long. They fall away
as soon as they have problems or are persecuted for believing God's word. 22The seed
that fell among the thorns represents those
who hear God's word, but all too quickly
the message is crowded out by the worries
of this life and the lure of wealth, so no
fruit is produced. 23The seed that fell on
good soil represents those who truly hear
and understand God's word and produce a
harvest of thirty, sixty, or even a hundred
times as much as had been planted!"

Parable of the Wheat and Weeds

24Here is another story Jesus told: "The Kingdom of Heaven is like a farmer who planted
good seed in his field. 25But that night as the
workers slept, his enemy came and planted
weeds among the wheat, then slipped
away. 26When the crop began to grow and
produce grain, the weeds also grew.
27"The farmer's workers went to him and
said, 'Sir, the field where you planted that

13:10
[f]*parabolē* (3850)
›Mark 4:2

13:11
Matt 11:25; 16:17
1 Cor 2:10, 14
Col 1:27
1 Jn 2:20, 27

13:12
Matt 25:29
Mark 4:25
Luke 19:26

13:13
Jer 5:21

13:14-15
*Isa 6:9-10

13:16-17
//Luke 10:23-24

13:17
John 8:56
Heb 11:13
1 Pet 1:10-12

13:18-23
//Mark 4:13-20
//Luke 8:11-15

13:22
Matt 19:23
Luke 12:16-21
1 Tim 6:9-10, 17

13:24
Mark 4:26-29

13:10 From this point on, Jesus rarely taught the general public. Instead, he focused on teaching those who had committed themselves to him (13:1–20:34), though he would once again confront Israel (21:1–23:39). • ***The people*** were the unbelieving opponents mentioned again in 13:11 ("others") and 13:12 ("those who are not listening").

13:11-15 Jesus' answer to the disciples' question (13:10) was essentially that the people's stubborn unbelief and rejection of Jesus had brought God's condemnation.

13:11 ***You are permitted to understand:*** God had enabled the disciples to comprehend Jesus' significance and to respond to his message of the Kingdom in faith and obedience (see 13:19, 23). • ***the secrets*** (literally *the mysteries*) ***of the Kingdom of Heaven:*** Namely, that salvation is available to them in Jesus as the fulfillment of OT promises.

13:13 Jesus told *parables*, and those who believed understood while those who had rejected Jesus found that his parables intensified their unbelief. • ***they don't really see . . . listen or understand:*** They lacked the faith that perceives the truth (13:19, 23) and acts upon it (Mark 8:18; John 12:40; see also Jer 5:21).

13:14-15 The quotation is from Isa 6:9-10 (Greek version). Like that of *Isaiah*, Jesus' message has a dual effect: It judges people for unbelief and disobedience, and it creates a remnant of faithful ones who accomplish the Lord's will (21:43).

13:16-17 Jesus brought into reality what the *prophets* and OT saints desired to *see* and *hear*, that is, the fulfillment of OT promises (see Isa 52:15; John 8:56; 1 Pet 1:10).

13:19 ***don't understand it:*** Responding to the *message* of *the Kingdom* is directly related to discerning its significance.

13:20-21 ***don't have deep roots . . . don't last long:*** The problem is a lack of persevering faith and obedience (see 7:13-27; 10:22), particularly when persecution arises.

13:22 Jesus spoke of competing demands in life, (see also 8:18-22). ***The worries of this life*** can become so great that they divert one from the path of faithful obedience (see 6:19-34). ***The lure of wealth***, particularly in its ability to deceive, appears often in Matthew (e.g., 4:8-10; 6:24; 13:44-45). God does not desire that his people have wealth as much as that they have faith, obey him, and willingly help those in need (e.g., 19:21; 25:31-46).

13:23 ***produce a harvest:*** Probably a general reference to faithful obedience to Jesus' commands (e.g., 5:1–7:27; 28:20).

13:24-30 This *story* is explained in 13:36-43.

13:25 ***Weeds*** (or *tares*, bearded darnel) are almost indistinguishable from *wheat* and so were left until growth revealed their true nature. Malevolent contamination of crops in this manner was punishable by law.

13:30 Matt 3:12
13:31-32 //Mark 4:30-32 //Luke 13:18-19
13:32 Ps 104:12; Ezek 17:23; 31:6; Dan 4:12, 21
13:33 //Luke 13:20-21; 1 Cor 5:6; Gal 5:9; [g]*zumē* (2219) ‣Matt 16:6
13:34 John 16:25
13:35 *Ps 78:2
13:36 Matt 15:15
13:38 John 8:44; 1 Jn 3:10
13:39 Joel 3:13; Rev 14:15

good seed is full of weeds! Where did they
come from?’
28“ ‘An enemy has done this!’ the farmer
exclaimed.
“ ‘Should we pull out the weeds?’ they
asked.
29“ ‘No,’ he replied, ‘you’ll uproot the
wheat if you do. 30Let both grow together
until the harvest. Then I will tell the harvesters to sort out the weeds, tie them into
bundles, and burn them, and to put the
wheat in the barn.’ ”

Parable of the Mustard Seed
Matt 13:31-32 // Mark 4:30-32 // Luke 13:18-19

31Here is another illustration Jesus used:
“The Kingdom of Heaven is like a mustard
seed planted in a field. 32It is the smallest
of all seeds, but it becomes the largest of
garden plants; it grows into a tree, and birds
come and make nests in its branches.”

Parable of the Yeast
Matt 13:33 // Luke 13:20-21

33Jesus also used this illustration: “The
Kingdom of Heaven is like the [g]yeast a
woman used in making bread. Even though
she put only a little yeast in three measures
of flour, it permeated every part of the
dough.”

Parables Fulfill Prophecy
Matt 13:34-35; cp. Mark 4:33-34

34Jesus always used stories and illustrations
like these when speaking to the crowds. In
fact, he never spoke to them without using
such parables. 35This fulfilled what God
had spoken through the prophet:

“I will speak to you in parables.
I will explain things hidden since the
creation of the world.”

Parable of the Wheat and Weeds Explained

36Then, leaving the crowds outside, Jesus
went into the house. His disciples said,
“Please explain to us the story of the weeds
in the field.”
37Jesus replied, “The Son of Man is the
farmer who plants the good seed. 38The field
is the world, and the good seed represents
the people of the Kingdom. The weeds are
the people who belong to the evil one. 39The
enemy who planted the weeds among the
wheat is the devil. The harvest is the end of
the world, and the harvesters are the angels.

Jesus and Satan (13:19)

Matt 4:1-11; 12:24-29; 13:39; 16:23; 1 Chr 21:1; Job 1:6-12; 2:1-7; Zech 3:1-2; Luke 10:17-20; 13:16; 22:3, 31-32; John 12:31; 13:27; Acts 5:3; 26:17-18; Rom 16:20; 2 Cor 4:4; 11:13-14; 2 Thes 2:9; 1 Tim 2:14; 5:15; Rev 12:9; 20:2-7

Jesus was opposed by a personal agent of sin and evil (4:1-11). In Matthew, he is called “Satan” (meaning *Adversary;* 4:10; 16:23), the “devil” (4:1-11; 13:39), the “tempter” (see note on 4:3), the “prince of demons” (9:34), “Beelzeboul” (see note on 12:24), the “evil one” (6:13; 13:19), and “the enemy” (13:39). See also “Satan, the Adversary” at Job 1:6–2:7, p. 857.

Jesus’ mission of announcing and bringing in the Kingdom of God inevitably led to conflict with Satan’s forces, including exorcisms (see 8:16-17, 28-34; 9:32-34; 10:1, 7-8; 12:28). Matthew records that Satan has power over kingdoms (4:8-9; 12:26) and that he has angels at his command (see note on 25:41). Satan’s primary tool is temptation, and his goal is to generate disobedience to God (4:1-11; 6:13; 16:23). Since Christ is the agent of God for the salvation of human beings, Satan attacked Christ first (4:1-11). But Christ has defeated him and will eventually strip Satan of all his powers (25:41, 46).

13:28-30 Just as Jesus rebuked the sons of Zebedee for wanting to destroy unbelieving villages (Luke 9:54-55), he prohibited his followers from retaliating against enemies. Judgment is God’s work (see 7:1-5). Jesus urges his followers to wait patiently for God’s righteous judgment (*the harvest*; see Luke 13:6-9).

13:31-33 Jesus used surprising, evocative imagery in these parables, either to emphasize the inevitable growth of ***the Kingdom*** through proclamation of the gospel or, more probably, to emphasize the contrast between insignificant beginnings and glorious consummation, and to exhort the disciples to patience (see also 16:24–17:13).

13:33 Normally ***yeast*** refers to the influence of evil (e.g., 16:6; 1 Cor 5:6; Gal 5:9); here, however, it is positive, speaking of the all-pervasive influence of the ***Kingdom***.

13:34-35 Even Jesus’ manner of teaching fulfilled OT predictions. Psalm 78:2-3 speaks of passing down the history of God’s revelation to children of the next generation. Jesus’ revelation is the climax of that history (13:10-17; 1 Cor 2:7).

13:35 This verse quotes Ps 78:2. • Some manuscripts do not include ***of the world.***

13:36-43 These verses are the interpretation of the parable told in 13:24-30. The ***people of the Kingdom*** (***wheat***) coexist with nonmembers (***weeds***) in the world (***field***) until the end of history. The mystery of the Kingdom is that it is present in the world without weeding out the wicked in judgment; Jesus’ disciples must learn patience (see notes on 13:28-30, 31-33).

13:36 They ***went into the house*** (see 13:1). Jesus taught in parables publicly, but the interpretations were reserved for his ***disciples*** in private. • ***Please explain:*** Though the disciples were privileged to know the mysteries of the Kingdom (13:11-17), they did not understand the parables until Jesus explained them.

13:37 ***Son of Man*** is a title Jesus used for himself.

13:38 ***The field is the world:*** The Kingdom includes all nations (28:16-20). • The ***people of the Kingdom*** are those who follow Jesus (13:11-17, 23; 21:43).

13:39 ***the world:*** Or ***the age;*** also in 13:40, 49.

40“Just as the weeds are sorted out and
burned in the fire, so it will be at the end of
the world. 41The Son of Man will send his
angels, and they will remove from his Kingdom everything that causes sin and all who
do evil. 42And the angels will throw them
into the fiery furnace, where there will be
weeping and gnashing of teeth. 43Then the
righteous will shine like the sun in their Father’s Kingdom. Anyone with ears to hear
should listen and understand!

Parable of the Hidden Treasure

44“The Kingdom of Heaven is like a treasure
that a man discovered hidden in a field. In
his excitement, he hid it again and sold
everything he owned to get enough money
to buy the field.

Parable of the Pearl

45“Again, the Kingdom of Heaven is like a
merchant on the lookout for choice pearls.
46When he discovered a pearl of great value,
he sold everything he owned and bought it!

Parable of the Fishing Net

47“Again, the Kingdom of Heaven is like a
fishing net that was thrown into the water
and caught fish of every kind. 48When the
net was full, they dragged it up onto the
shore, sat down, and sorted the good fish
into crates, but threw the bad ones away.
49That is the way it will be at the end of the
world. The angels will come and separate the
wicked people from the righteous, 50throw-
ing the wicked into the fiery furnace, where
there will be weeping and gnashing of teeth.
51Do you understand all these things?”
“Yes,” they said, “we do.”

Teachers of Religious Law in the Kingdom

52Then he added, “Every teacher of religious
law who becomes a disciple in the Kingdom
of Heaven is like a homeowner who brings
from his storeroom new gems of truth as
well as old.”

Narrative: Jesus Leads the Disciples to Confession (13:53–16:20)

Jesus Rejected at Nazareth

Matt 13:53-58 // Mark 6:1-6 // Luke 4:16-24

53When Jesus had finished telling these
stories and illustrations, he left that part
of the country. 54He returned to Nazareth,
his hometown. When he taught there in the
synagogue, everyone was amazed and said,
“Where does he get this wisdom and the
power to do miracles?” 55Then they scoffed,
“He’s just the carpenter’s son, and we know
Mary, his mother, and his brothers—James,
Joseph, Simon, and Judas. 56All his sisters
live right here among us. Where did he
learn all these things?” 57And they were
deeply offended and refused to believe in
him.
Then Jesus told them, “A prophet is
honored everywhere except in his own
hometown and among his own family.”
58And so he did only a few miracles there
because of their unbelief.

Herod and the Death of John the Baptist

Matt 14:1-2 // Mark 6:14-16 // Luke 9:7-9
Matt 14:13-21 // Mark 6:32-44 // Luke 9:10b-17 // John 6:1-15
Matt 14:3-12 // Mark 6:17-29; cp. Luke 3:19-20

14 When Herod Antipas, the ruler of
Galilee, heard about Jesus, 2he said to
his advisers, “This must be John the Baptist

13:41 Matt 24:31 Mark 13:27
13:42 Matt 8:12; 13:50; 22:13; 24:51; 25:30 Luke 13:28
13:43 Dan 12:3
13:44 Phil 3:7-8
13:47 Matt 22:10
13:50 Matt 8:12; 13:42; 22:13; 24:51; 25:30 Luke 13:28
13:53-58 //Mark 6:1-6 //Luke 4:16-30
13:53 Matt 7:28
13:54 John 7:15
13:55 Matt 12:46 Luke 3:23 John 6:42
13:57 Luke 4:24 John 4:44
14:1-12 //Mark 6:14-29 //Luke 9:7-9

13:40-42 The harvest of judgment, which began with the first coming of *the Son of Man* (3:12), will be completed when he returns (Rev 14:14-16).

13:41 ***his Kingdom:*** Not until the “end of the world” (13:40) will the rule of the *Son of Man* be visible over all things.

13:43 ***The righteous*** do the will of God as revealed by Jesus, in contrast to those “who do evil” (13:41).

13:44-46 Another mystery of the Kingdom (13:11) is that its value exceeds all other treasures, and so everything should be forfeited to acquire it (see 19:21, 29; Phil 3:7).

13:44 ***treasure . . . hidden in a field:*** Treasures were buried for protection against thieves and military enemies (25:25). • ***In his excitement:*** Those who discover *the Kingdom* find greater joy in it than can be found in any temporal pleasure (see 1 Pet 1:8).

13:47-50 This parable refers to God’s judgment at the last day (25:31-46), which will eternally separate the wicked from the righteous. This note of warning reinforces the urgency of the previous two calls to decision.

13:49 The *wicked* are those who do not do the will of God as revealed in Jesus, and the *righteous* are those who do (see 5:21-48; 6:1, 33; 7:13-27; 12:33-37; 16:27).

13:51 The ability to ***understand*** the mysteries of the Kingdom is a gift from God (13:10-17, 23).

13:52 A ***teacher of religious law who becomes a disciple in the Kingdom*** has had his allegiance radically altered toward Jesus as the way of salvation. • ***new gems of truth as well as old:*** The sequence reflects the preeminence of the new covenant inaugurated in Jesus (5:17-20; 19:16-22) over the old covenant administered under Abraham and Moses.

13:54-58 That Jesus was rejected at home is part of the ongoing theme of the Messiah’s rejection by his own people (see 12:1-50; 15:1-20; 16:1-12).

13:55-56 ***carpenter’s son:*** A carpenter (literally *craftsman*) worked with his hands, whether in wood, metal, or stone. • ***Joseph:*** Other manuscripts read *Joses;* still others read *John.*

13:57 They were ***deeply offended.*** Dwelling on Jesus’ all-too-common heritage (John 6:42), they could not see his uncommon significance.

13:58 Faith is required both to understand Jesus’ message (13:10-17) and to experience his miracles.

14:1 ***Herod Antipas, the ruler of Galilee:*** Greek *Herod the tetrarch.* Herod Antipas was a son of King Herod the Great and was ruler over Galilee (see genealogy, p. 1579). Antipas’s official title was *tetrarch* (ruler of a fourth

14:3
Luke 3:19-20
14:4
Lev 18:16; 20:21
14:5
Matt 11:9; 21:26
14:10
Matt 17:12
14:12
Acts 8:2
14:13-21
//Mark 6:32-44
//Luke 9:10-17
//John 6:1-13
14:14
Matt 9:36
Mark 1:41
Heb 2:17-18; 4:15; 5:1-3
14:16-20
2 Kgs 4:42-44
14:19-22
Matt 15:35-39
Mark 8:6-10
14:22-33
//Mark 6:45-52
//John 6:15-21
14:23
Luke 9:28
14:26
Luke 24:37

raised from the dead! That is why he can do
such miracles."
3For Herod had arrested and imprisoned
John as a favor to his wife Herodias (the former wife of Herod's brother Philip). 4John
had been telling Herod, "It is against God's
law for you to marry her." 5Herod wanted to
kill John, but he was afraid of a riot, because
all the people believed John was a prophet.
6But at a birthday party for Herod, Herodias's daughter performed a dance that
greatly pleased him, 7so he promised with a
vow to give her anything she wanted. 8At her
mother's urging, the girl said, "I want the
head of John the Baptist on a tray!" 9Then
the king regretted what he had said; but because of the vow he had made in front of
his guests, he issued the necessary orders.
10So John was beheaded in the prison, 11and
his head was brought on a tray and given to
the girl, who took it to her mother. 12Later,
John's disciples came for his body and buried it. Then they went and told Jesus what
had happened.

Jesus Feeds Five Thousand

13As soon as Jesus heard the news, he left
in a boat to a remote area to be alone. But
the crowds heard where he was headed and
followed on foot from many towns. 14Jesus
saw the huge crowd as he stepped from the
boat, and he had compassion on them and
healed their sick.
15That evening the disciples came to him
and said, "This is a remote place, and it's
already getting late. Send the crowds away
so they can go to the villages and buy food
for themselves."
16But Jesus said, "That isn't necessary—
you feed them."
17"But we have only five loaves of bread
and two fish!" they answered.
18"Bring them here," he said. 19Then he
told the people to sit down on the grass.
Jesus took the five loaves and two fish,
looked up toward heaven, and blessed them.
Then, breaking the loaves into pieces, he
gave the bread to the disciples, who distributed it to the people. 20They all ate as much
as they wanted, and afterward, the disciples picked up twelve baskets of leftovers.
21About 5,000 men were fed that day, in addition to all the women and children!

Jesus Walks on Water

Matt 14:22-33 // Mark 6:45-52 // John 6:16-21

22Immediately after this, Jesus insisted that
his disciples get back into the boat and
cross to the other side of the lake, while he
sent the people home. 23After sending them
home, he went up into the hills by himself
to pray. Night fell while he was there alone.
24Meanwhile, the disciples were in trouble far away from land, for a strong wind
had risen, and they were fighting heavy
waves. 25About three o'clock in the morning Jesus came toward them, walking on
the water. 26When the disciples saw him
walking on the water, they were terrified. In
their fear, they cried out, "It's a ghost!"
27But Jesus spoke to them at once. "Don't
be afraid," he said. "Take courage. I am
here!"
28Then Peter called to him, "Lord, if it's
really you, tell me to come to you, walking
on the water."

---

part of a kingdom) of Galilee and Perea (4 BC—AD 39; see 2:19-22). Jesus referred to Antipas as "that fox" (Luke 13:32), and John the Baptist justly condemned him for adultery (14:3-12; Luke 3:19-20). See "Herod Antipas" at Mark 6:14-29, p. 1659.

14:2 There was a rumor that *John* had been resurrected (see 16:14).

14:3-12 The popular appeal of John's message posed a political threat (see Josephus, *Antiquities* 18.5.2). Years after John's execution, the Jews viewed Herod's military defeat at the hands of Aretas (AD 36) as a just recompense for putting an innocent man to death.

14:4 ***John*** had continually warned ***Herod*** of his sin (see Lev 18:6; 20:21).

14:6 ***Herodias's daughter*** was probably Salome, a daughter from Herodias's previous marriage to Philip. Sexually provocative dances such as this were a regular occurrence for depraved royalty.

14:7 Such an extravagant, foolish oath was consistent with Herod Antipas's character (see "Herod Antipas" at Mark 6:14-29, p. 1659).

14:8 The practice of bringing a ***head . . . on a tray*** was not unknown in the ancient world (see Josephus, *Antiquities* 13.4.8; 14.15.13; 18.5.1; 20.5.1).

14:13-21 Jesus' actions consistently fulfilled OT promises regarding the Kingdom and the Messiah (11:5-6; 12:28). Here Jesus evoked the memory of God's provision of manna for the Israelites (Exod 16; see John 6:32), demonstrating that he is the promised end-time prophet (see Deut 18:15-16).

14:21 ***5,000 men . . . in addition to all the women and children:*** The count was of families, denoted by heads of households, rather than individuals.

14:22-33 Jesus' power over nature presented the disciples with the opportunity to trust in him as the *Son of God* (14:33; see also 8:23-27; Ps 8:6; Heb 2:8-9).

14:22 After the miraculous feeding, the crowds sought to make Jesus king (John 6:15), prompting his withdrawal because it was not the appropriate time.

14:23 Jesus often sought solitude in order to ***pray***, particularly in conjunction with important events in his life and ministry (26:36-46; Mark 1:35; Luke 5:16; 6:12; 9:28).

14:25 ***About three o'clock in the morning:*** Literally *In the fourth watch of the night.* This was approximately 3:00–6:00 AM by Roman reckoning.
• The fact that ***Jesus came . . . walking on the water*** demonstrates God's sovereign reign over the stormy waters (see Job 9:8; Ps 77:19; Isa 43:16).

14:27 ***I am here:*** Or *The 'I AM' is here;* literally *I am.* See Exod 3:14. This declaration is associated with the appearance of God himself (see also John 8:24; 18:5-6).

29“Yes, come,” Jesus said.

So Peter went over the side of the boat and walked on the water toward Jesus. 30But when he saw the strong wind and the waves, he was terrified and began to sink. “Save me, Lord!” he shouted.

31Jesus immediately reached out and grabbed him. “You have so little faith,” Jesus said. “Why did you doubt me?”

32When they climbed back into the boat, the wind stopped. 33Then the disciples worshiped him. “You really are the Son of God!” they exclaimed.

Jesus Heals the Sick
Matt 14:34-36 // Mark 6:53-56; cp. John 6:22-25

34After they had crossed the lake, they landed at Gennesaret. 35When the people recognized Jesus, the news of his arrival spread quickly throughout the whole area, and soon people were bringing all their sick to be healed. 36They begged him to let the sick touch at least the fringe of his robe, and all who touched him were healed.

Jesus Teaches about Inner Purity
Matt 15:1-20 // Mark 7:1-23

15 Some Pharisees and teachers of religious law now arrived from Jerusalem to see Jesus. They asked him, 2“Why do your disciples disobey our age-old tradition? For they ignore our tradition of ceremonial hand washing before they eat.”

3Jesus replied, “And why do you, by your traditions, violate the direct commandments of God? 4For instance, God says, ‘Honor your father and mother,’ and ‘Anyone who speaks disrespectfully of father or mother must be put to death.’ 5But you say it is all right for people to say to their parents, ‘Sorry, I can’t help you. For I have vowed to give to God what I would have given to you.’ 6In this way, you say they don’t need to honor their parents. And so you cancel the word of God for the sake of your own tradition. 7You [h]hypocrites! Isaiah was right when he prophesied about you, for he wrote,

> 8 ‘These people honor me with their lips,
> but their hearts are far from me.
> 9 Their worship is a farce,
> for they teach man-made ideas as
> commands from God.’ ”

10Then Jesus called to the crowd to come and hear. “Listen,” he said, “and try to understand. 11It’s not what goes into your mouth that defiles you; you are defiled by the words that come out of your mouth.”

12Then the disciples came to him and asked, “Do you realize you offended the Pharisees by what you just said?”

13Jesus replied, “Every plant not planted by my heavenly Father will be uprooted, 14so ignore them. They are blind guides leading the blind, and if one blind person guides another, they will both fall into a ditch.”

15Then Peter said to Jesus, “Explain to us the parable that says people aren’t defiled by what they eat.”

16“Don’t you understand yet?” Jesus asked. 17“Anything you eat passes through the stomach and then goes into the sewer. 18But the words you speak come from the [i]heart—that’s what defiles you. 19For from the heart come evil thoughts, murder, adultery, all sexual immorality, theft, lying, and [j]slander. 20These are what defile you. Eating with unwashed hands will never defile you.”

14:31 Matt 6:30
14:33 Ps 2:7; Matt 16:16; 26:63; 27:54; Mark 1:1; Luke 22:70; John 1:49; 6:69; Rom 1:4
14:34-36 //Mark 6:53-56
14:36 Matt 9:20-21
15:1-20 //Mark 7:1-23
15:2 Luke 11:38
15:4 *Exod 20:12; 21:17; *Lev 20:9; *Deut 5:16; Matt 19:19; Mark 10:19; Luke 18:20; Eph 6:2
15:7 [h]*hupokritēs* (5273) ‣ Matt 22:18
15:8-9 *Isa 29:13
15:9 Col 2:20-22
15:11 Matt 12:34; Acts 10:14-15
15:13 Isa 60:21; 61:3; John 15:2; 1 Cor 3:9
15:14 Matt 23:16, 24; Luke 6:39; Rom 2:19
15:18 Matt 12:34; Jas 3:6; [i]*kardia* (2588) ‣ Mark 12:30
15:19 Rom 1:29-31; 1 Cor 5:10-11; 6:9-10; Gal 5:19-21; [j]*blasphēmia* (0988) ‣ Mark 2:7

14:30 Some manuscripts do not include *strong.*

14:34-36 On the purpose of Jesus’ miracles, see notes on 4:23; 11:5-6; 12:28.

15:1-20 Jesus indicted the Pharisees for disobeying God’s law in their zeal to preserve traditions.

15:1 ***Jerusalem*** was the location of the Temple and thus the seat of authority in Judaism; this gave the ambassadors greater leverage in their arguments with Jesus.

15:2 The Jewish teachers’ ***age-old tradition*** sought to apply the written Torah to common circumstances in the ordinary course of life. This ***tradition*** was memorized and passed on orally from teacher to student (cp. 1 Cor 11:23; 15:1-5). • To ***ignore*** the ***tradition of . . . hand washing*** (see Mark 7:2-4; Luke 11:38) was considered disobedient to the Torah and unfaithful to God’s will for Israel (cp. 23:25-26).

15:4 ***Honor your father and mother:*** Exod 20:12; Deut 5:16. • ***Anyone . . . death:*** Exod 21:17 (Greek version); Lev 20:9 (Greek version).

15:5 ***vowed to give to God:*** Such a gift was likely donated at the Temple (see Mark 7:11; see also Prov 28:24), but functioned as a way to dodge financial responsibility for one’s ***parents.***

15:6 ***cancel:*** Because of a greater commitment to their traditions, the Pharisees in effect rendered God’s law nonbinding, turning their piety into sinful disregard for the ***word of God.*** • ***their parents:*** Literally *their father;* other manuscripts read *their father or their mother.*

15:7 ***You hypocrites!*** See note on 23:13.

15:8-9 The quotation is from Isa 29:13 (Greek version).

15:11 ***what goes into your mouth:*** Jesus was speaking here either of foods that were not permitted (e.g., pork or shellfish) or of food contaminated by unclean hands (15:20). • That which ***defiles*** makes a person unfit for communion with God. Jesus pressed the matter beyond ceremonial purity to true inner purity (see 15:18-19; 23:25-26; Acts 10; 11:5-9; Rom 14:14). • One’s ***words*** are a measure of one’s character (see 15:18-20; Jas 3:1-12).

15:13 ***not planted by my heavenly Father:*** These Pharisees did not belong to the true people of God (see 3:9-12; Isa 5:1-7; Jer 45:4). They ***will be uprooted*** at the final judgment (see 3:10; 8:12).

SIMON PETER (14:28-31)

Matt 4:18-20; 8:14; 10:2; 15:15; 16:16-19, 22-23; 17:1-4, 24-27; 18:21; 19:27; 26:33-45, 58, 69-75
Mark 1:16-18, 29-30, 36-37; 3:16; 5:37; 8:29-33; 9:2-6; 10:28; 11:21; 13:3-4; 14:29-42, 54, 66-72; 16:7-8
Luke 4:38; 5:3-10; 6:14; 8:45, 51; 9:20, 28-33; 12:41; 18:28; 22:8, 31-34, 55-62; 24:12, 34
John 1:40-42, 44; 6:8, 68; 13:6-10, 24, 36-38; 18:10-11, 15-18, 25-27; 20:2-6; 21:2-21
Acts 1–12; 15:7-11
Gal 2:7-16
1–2 Peter

Simon Peter was the most prominent of the twelve apostles. After Jesus' death, he became the primary spokesman for the early Christians in Jerusalem and was the apostle primarily responsible for evangelizing the Jews (Gal 2:7-8).

The Hebrew name *Simeon* (transliterated in English as "Simon") was probably his original name. *Cephas* is the transliteration of an Aramaic name given him by Jesus, meaning "rock"—translated in Greek as *Petros* (English "Peter"; see 16:17-18; Luke 6:14; John 1:42).

Though Bethsaida was Peter's hometown (John 1:44), he later lived in Capernaum. He was a married man (1 Cor 9:5). At one point, when visiting Peter's home, Jesus healed Peter's mother-in-law (8:5, 14-15; Mark 1:21, 29-31; Luke 4:31, 38-39).

Originally fishermen, Peter and his brother Andrew were among the first to be called by Jesus to be disciples, together with James and John, their fishing partners (4:18-22; Mark 1:16-20; cp. Luke 5:1-11; John 1:35-51). They were ordinary, minimally educated working men (Acts 4:13).

Peter's name occurs first on every list of the twelve apostles (10:2; Mark 3:16; Luke 6:14; Acts 1:13). Together with the brothers James and John, Peter was part of an "inner circle" of disciples who were with Jesus on certain special occasions—the healing of Jairus's daughter (Mark 5:37; Luke 8:51), Jesus' transfiguration (17:1; Mark 9:2; Luke 9:28), and Jesus' prayer in the garden (26:37; Mark 14:33; cp. Mark 13:3).

Bold and impulsive (26:33; Mark 14:29; Luke 5:8; 22:33; John 13:37; 21:7), Peter was the first of the disciples to confess his belief in Jesus as the Messiah (16:15-16; Mark 8:29; Luke 9:20). He also reproved Jesus when Jesus spoke of his coming death—a notion that did not fit Peter's view of the Messiah—and was in turn rebuked by Jesus for it (16:22-23; Mark 8:32-33). However, Jesus spoke of Peter as a key person he would use to build the church (16:18-19).

Peter, together with John, surreptitiously entered the courtyard of the high priest when Jesus was taken there for interrogation. But when challenged by people who recognized him (partly because of his Galilean accent), he vigorously denied all knowledge of Jesus (26:69-75; Mark 14:66-72; Luke 22:54-62)—as Jesus had said he would, in spite of Peter's insistence that he would never do so (26:33-35; Mark 14:29-31; Luke 22:31-34). Peter immediately felt deep remorse.

After the news of Jesus' resurrection, Peter was one of the first to run to the tomb to see if it was true (John 20:3-6), and he appears to have been the first of the Twelve to whom the risen Jesus showed himself (Luke 24:34; 1 Cor 15:5). Much of Jesus' conversation recorded by John in his last chapter was with Peter, whom Jesus encouraged to "feed my sheep" (John 21:15-17).

Following the coming of the Holy Spirit on the Day of Pentecost (Acts 2:1-13), Peter quickly emerged as the primary spokesman for the early Christians. From that point on, as recorded in Acts 1–12, he played a crucial role in the spread of the gospel in Judea, boldly preaching to the crowds (Acts 2:14-41; 3:12-26; 5:21, 42), healing people (Acts 3:1-11; 5:12-16; 9:32-43), and—even under arrest—speaking fearlessly to the authorities (Acts 4:1-20; 5:26-32). Twice he miraculously escaped from prison (Acts 5:18-25; 12:6-11). He also assumed leadership in the administrative affairs of the quickly growing community of disciples (Acts 5:3-11).

Peter was the first to bring the Good News to Gentiles (Acts 10:1-48; see Matt 16:18). Later, he played a key role in the Jerusalem council concerning Gentile converts, arguing that Gentiles should not be compelled to observe the law of Moses but should be accepted on the basis of their faith in Christ alone (Acts 15:7-10). Later, however, he was rebuked by Paul for his inconsistency on this point when he visited Antioch (Gal 2:11-16).

Other than his taking his wife with him on at least some of his mission trips (1 Cor 9:5), few details are known about Peter's later life and missionary work (did he spend time at Corinth? cp. 1 Cor 1:12; 3:22). Widespread early tradition says that Peter was crucified—like his Lord, just as Jesus had predicted (John 21:18-19)—in Rome during Nero's persecution of Christians in AD 64–65. The reliability of the tradition that he was crucified upside-down is less certain.

Peter was likely the source of the material recorded by Mark in his Gospel, which Mark learned when he was assisting Peter in his evangelistic work in Italy near the end of his life. Peter is also traditionally understood to be the author of 1 Peter (written from Rome—"Babylon," 1 Pet 5:13) and 2 Peter.

In the New Testament, Peter stands as a reassuring example of Christ's forgiving grace for those who know they've failed him—and of the way Christ can graciously restore and use such people for his glory, in spite of their failings.

The Faith of a Gentile Woman
Matt 15:21-28 // Mark 7:24-30
21Then Jesus left Galilee and went north
to the region of Tyre and Sidon. 22A Gentile woman who lived there came to him,
pleading, "Have mercy on me, O Lord, Son
of David! For my daughter is possessed by a
demon that torments her severely."
23But Jesus gave her no reply, not even
a word. Then his disciples urged him to
send her away. "Tell her to go away," they
said. "She is bothering us with all her begging."
24Then Jesus said to the woman, "I was
sent only to help God's lost sheep—the people of Israel."
25But she came and worshiped him, pleading again, "Lord, help me!"
26Jesus responded, "It isn't right to take
food from the children and throw it to the
dogs."
27She replied, "That's true, Lord, but even
dogs are allowed to eat the scraps that fall
beneath their masters' table."
28"Dear woman," Jesus said to her, "your
faith is great. Your request is granted." And
her daughter was instantly healed.

Jesus Heals Many People
29Jesus returned to the Sea of Galilee and
climbed a hill and sat down. 30A vast crowd
brought to him people who were lame,
blind, crippled, those who couldn't speak,
and many others. They laid them before
Jesus, and he healed them all. 31The crowd
was amazed! Those who hadn't been able to
speak were talking, the crippled were made
well, the lame were walking, and the blind

15:21-28 //Mark 7:24-30
15:24 Matt 10:6; Rom 15:8
15:25 Matt 8:2
15:28 Matt 8:10
15:29-31 //Mark 7:31-37
15:30 Isa 35:5-6; Matt 4:23; 11:5; Luke 7:22

THE SADDUCEES (16:1-12)

Matt 3:7; 22:23-33; Mark 12:18-27; Luke 20:27-40; Acts 4:1-2; 5:17-18; 23:6-10

The Sadducees were made up of the priestly class (in contrast to the lay movement of the Pharisees). The Sadducees probably lived in the vicinity of Jerusalem and controlled the Temple system (Acts 4:1-2; 5:17). They were powerful aristocrats and mediators between Rome and Israel (see Josephus, *Antiquities* 13.10.6; *War* 2.10.5). They did not have great favor or influence with the people (Josephus, *Antiquities* 18.1.4). The term *Sadducee* probably derives from *Zadok*, the high priest during the reigns of David (2 Sam 8:17; 15:24; 1 Kgs 1:8) and Solomon (1 Kgs 1:26, 32-48; 1 Chr 12:26-28); both words have the same Hebrew root. The earliest historical reference to the Sadducees occurs during the reign of John Hyrcanus (135–104 BC), a descendant of the Maccabees (Josephus, *Antiquities* 13.10.6), but it is clear from this account that they had already existed for some time.

Their theological views are often contrasted with those of the Pharisees (Acts 23:8; see also Acts 4:1-2). The Pentateuch had primary authority for the Sadducees. They rejected the oral tradition so cherished by the Pharisees. Also in contrast with the Pharisees, the Sadducees did not believe in the resurrection of the dead (see 22:23-33) or angelic beings (see Acts 23:8). They rejected the sovereignty of God and the concept of final judgment. The Pharisees were so committed to belief in the resurrection that they sided with Paul against the Sadducees when he was on trial for disturbing the Temple (Acts 23:6-10).

Despite their differences, the Pharisees and Sadducees united with a single front against Jesus. If the Pharisees opposed Jesus because he made light of their oral traditions, the Sadducees opposed Jesus because he affirmed the supernatural world of angels and demons and appealed to a final judgment and resurrection.

With the destruction of the Temple in AD 70, the Sadducees disappeared from the scene. They left no written records. Since all our information about the Sadducees comes from their opponents, we have a limited idea of what they were really like.

15:21-28 This encounter highlights another controversial issue: Gentile participation in the Kingdom of the Messiah (see 8:11).

15:22 ***Gentile woman*** (literally *Canaanite woman*): Matthew uses this archaic OT expression to describe the woman as a pagan. • ***Lord, Son of David:*** The woman apparently perceived that Jesus was the Messiah (see 1:1; 9:27; 17:15; 20:30).

15:23 ***no reply:*** Jesus' silence was a test of the woman's faith (15:28; cp. 8:24; 14:16).

15:26 Jews often referred to pagans as *dogs*, which are ceremonially unclean (Lev 11:27). Jesus was speaking to the woman of her spiritual condition as a Gentile—as unclean and separated from God (cp. 7:6).

15:29-31 Jesus returned to a predominantly Gentile area and performed many miracles. Though Jesus was sent primarily for Israel's sake (15:21-28), the new era that he inaugurated is also the beginning of Gentile salvation (1:3, 5-6; 2:1-12; 4:12-16; 8:5-13; 15:21-28; 28:16-20). • Such healings are signs that the Kingdom has broken into history through Jesus' ministry (8:1–9:34; 11:5-6; 12:28). • ***the God of Israel:*** This phrase suggests that ***the crowd*** (15:30) was predominantly Gentile.

15:32-39 //Mark 8:1-10
15:32 Matt 9:36
15:33 Mark 6:37; John 6:5
15:34-37 Matt 14:17-20; Mark 6:38-43; Luke 9:13-17; John 6:9-13
15:37 Matt 16:10
15:38 Matt 14:21; Mark 6:44
16:1-12 //Mark 8:11-21
16:1 Matt 12:38; Luke 11:16; John 6:30; 1 Cor 1:22
16:2-3 Luke 12:54-56
16:3 [k]*ouranos* (3772) ‣Luke 23:43
16:4 Matt 12:39; Luke 11:29
16:6 Luke 12:1; [a]*zumē* (2219) ‣Matt 16:11
16:9 Matt 14:14-21; Mark 6:34-44; Luke 9:11-17; John 6:1-13

could see again! And they praised the God of Israel.

Jesus Feeds Four Thousand
Matt 15:32-39 // Mark 8:1-10

32 Then Jesus called his disciples and told them, "I feel sorry for these people. They have been here with me for three days, and they have nothing left to eat. I don't want to send them away hungry, or they will faint along the way."

33 The disciples replied, "Where would we get enough food here in the wilderness for such a huge crowd?"

34 Jesus asked, "How much bread do you have?"

They replied, "Seven loaves, and a few small fish."

35 So Jesus told all the people to sit down on the ground. 36 Then he took the seven loaves and the fish, thanked God for them, and broke them into pieces. He gave them to the disciples, who distributed the food to the crowd.

37 They all ate as much as they wanted. Afterward, the disciples picked up seven large baskets of leftover food. 38 There were 4,000 men who were fed that day, in addition to all the women and children. 39 Then Jesus sent the people home, and he got into a boat and crossed over to the region of Magadan.

Religious Leaders Demand a Miraculous Sign
Matt 16:1-4; cp. Mark 8:11-13; Luke 12:54-56

16 One day the Pharisees and Sadducees came to test Jesus, demanding that he show them a miraculous sign from heaven to prove his authority.

2 He replied, "You know the saying, 'Red sky at night means fair weather tomorrow; 3 red [k]sky in the morning means foul weather all day.' You know how to interpret the weather signs in the [k]sky, but you don't know how to interpret the signs of the times! 4 Only an evil, adulterous generation would demand a miraculous sign, but the only sign I will give them is the sign of the prophet Jonah." Then Jesus left them and went away.

Yeast of the Pharisees and Sadducees
Matt 16:5-12 // Mark 8:14-21; cp. Luke 12:1

5 Later, after they crossed to the other side of the lake, the disciples discovered they had forgotten to bring any bread. 6 "Watch out!" Jesus warned them. "Beware of the [a]yeast of the Pharisees and Sadducees."

7 At this they began to argue with each other because they hadn't brought any bread. 8 Jesus knew what they were saying, so he said, "You have so little faith! Why are you arguing with each other about having no bread? 9 Don't you understand even yet? Don't you remember the 5,000 I fed with

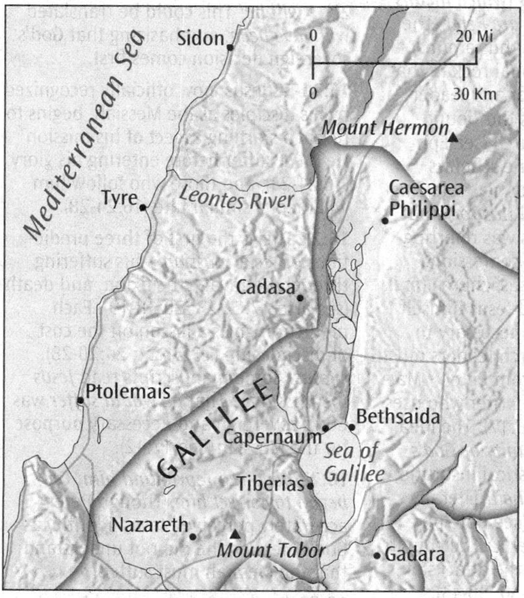

◂ **Jesus' Ministry outside Israel (Matt 15:21-28; see also 16:13-20; Mark 7:1–8:30; Luke 9:18-20).** The map shows the border between Jewish and Gentile territory. At least twice Jesus traveled outside of Jewish territories: In the region of TYRE and SIDON he released the daughter of a Gentile woman from demons (15:21-28), and at CAESAREA PHILIPPI Peter declared that Jesus is the Messiah (16:13-20).

15:32-39 The previous feeding miracle (see 14:13-21) was for Jews, whereas this one extended to Gentiles; it thus develops the theme of 15:27. Through this miracle Jesus demonstrated that he is the true bread of life (see 16:5-12; John 6).

15:39 ***Magadan*** is an unknown site, perhaps *Magdala* (as in some Greek manuscripts; see also Mark 8:10).

16:1-12 Having been warmly received in the Gentile world, Jesus returned to his fellow countrymen only to encounter further rejection.

16:2-3 Jesus made a deliberate play on their words when they sought a "sign from heaven" (16:1). They were able to read the ***weather*** in ***the sky*** (Greek *ouranos*, the same word translated "heaven"), but they failed to discern the Messiah despite the many signs already given (see 11:1-6). • Several manuscripts do not include any of the words in 16:2-3 after ***He replied.***

16:3 The ***signs of the times*** were Jesus himself (16:4) and the various miracles that he performed (cp. 11:2-6; 12:28).

16:4 ***the sign of the prophet Jonah:*** Literally *the sign of Jonah.*

16:9-10 Jesus had demonstrated to his disciples that he is the true bread of life (15:32-39; John 6:35, 48), whereas the Jewish leaders, particularly in their teachings, were like yeast in permeating everything they touched with their sinfulness (see next note).

five loaves, and the baskets of leftovers you
picked up? 10 Or the 4,000 I fed with seven
loaves, and the large baskets of leftovers
you picked up? 11 Why can't you understand
that I'm not talking about bread? So again I
say, 'Beware of the [b]yeast of the Pharisees
and Sadducees.'"
12 Then at last they understood that he
wasn't speaking about the yeast in bread,
but about the deceptive teaching of the
Pharisees and Sadducees.

Peter's Declaration of Faith, Jesus' Blessing
Matt 16:13-16, 20 // Mark 8:27-30 // Luke 9:18-21; cp. John 6:67-69

13 When Jesus came to the region of Caesarea Philippi, he asked his disciples, "Who
do people say that the Son of Man is?"
14 "Well," they replied, "some say John the
Baptist, some say Elijah, and others say Jeremiah or one of the other prophets."
15 Then he asked them, "But who do you
say I am?"
16 Simon Peter answered, "You are the
Messiah, the Son of the living God."
17 Jesus replied, "You are blessed, Simon
son of John, because my Father in heaven
has revealed this to you. You did not learn
this from any [c]human being. 18 Now I say to
you that you are [d]Peter (which means 'rock'),
and upon this [d]rock I will build my [e]church,
and all the powers of [f]hell will not conquer
it. 19 And I will give you the keys of the Kingdom of Heaven. Whatever you forbid on
earth will be forbidden in heaven, and whatever you permit on earth will be permitted
in heaven."
20 Then he sternly warned the disciples
not to tell anyone that he was the Messiah.

Narrative: Jesus Reveals His Suffering and Glory (16:21–17:27)

Jesus First Predicts His Death
Matt 16:21-23 // Mark 8:31-33 // Luke 9:22

21 From then on Jesus began to tell his disciples plainly that it was necessary for him to
go to Jerusalem, and that he would suffer
many terrible things at the hands of the elders, the leading priests, and the teachers of
religious law. He would be killed, but on the
third day he would be raised from the dead.
22 But Peter took him aside and began
to reprimand him for saying such things.
"Heaven forbid, Lord," he said. "This will
never happen to you!"
23 Jesus turned to Peter and said, "Get away
from me, [g]Satan! You are a [h]dangerous trap
to me. You are seeing things merely from a
human point of view, not from God's."

16:10 Mark 8:1-9
16:11 [b]*zumē* (2219) ‣Mark 8:15
16:13-20 //Mark 8:27-30 //Luke 9:18-21
16:14 Mark 6:14-15
16:16 John 1:34, 49; 6:69; 11:27; 20:31
16:17 Gal 1:16 [c]*sarx* (4561) ‣Matt 26:41
16:18 John 1:42; 1 Pet 2:4-5 [d]*petros* (4074) ‣Mark 15:46 [e]*ekklēsia* (1577) ‣Matt 18:17 [f]*hadēs* (0086) ‣Matt 18:9
16:19 Isa 22:22; John 20:23; Rev 1:18; 3:7
16:21-28 //Mark 8:31–9:1 //Luke 9:21-27
16:21 John 2:19; 1 Cor 15:3-4
16:23 [g]*satanas* (4567) ‣Luke 10:18 [h]*skandalon* (4625) ‣Matt 18:6

16:11-12 ***Yeast*** is often a symbol of sin and evil (see Exod 12:8, 15; Lev 6:16-17; Gal 5:9); here it indicates the permeating nature of the ***deceptive teaching***.

16:13 ***Caesarea Philippi***, located approximately twenty-five miles north of Capernaum, hosted many shrines to the Roman god of nature, Pan. • ***Son of Man*** is a title Jesus used for himself.

16:14 ***Some***, such as Herod Antipas (14:1-2), thought Jesus was ***John the Baptist*** resurrected. • ***Elijah*** was expected as a forerunner to the Messiah (11:14; 17:10-12; Mal 3:1; 4:5-6). • ***Jeremiah or one of the other prophets:*** Some Jews expected Jeremiah to be raised (see *2 Maccabees* 15:13-16). Jesus' strong stand on sensitive matters (5:17; 15:1-20) may have led some to think Jesus was Jeremiah. Jesus was not yet understood as God's Messiah.

16:16 Peter's acknowledgment of Jesus as ***the Messiah, the Son of the living God*** (3:17) shows that his eyes had been opened by faith (see 11:25-27; 14:33; 27:54). • ***the Messiah:*** Or *the Christ. Messiah* (a Hebrew term) and *Christ* (a Greek term) both mean "the anointed one."

16:17 God ***revealed*** to Peter his plan of salvation in Jesus, the Messiah. This moment of revelation was a high point in the unfolding of God's will for humanity (cp. Gal 1:16; 3:23; Eph 3:5). • ***Simon son of John:*** Greek *Simon bar-Jonah;* see John 1:42; 21:15-17.

16:18 ***that you are Peter (which means 'rock'):*** Literally *that you are Peter.* The phrase ***upon this rock*** is thus a pun: Peter was the foundational rock in that he was the first confessor and leader of the apostles—he was the "founding member" of the church (see Eph 2:20-22; Rev 21:14). Some scholars have suggested that Jesus was referring to himself when he said ***this rock***, but it seems clear that Jesus was referring either to Peter or to his confession. However, it is clearly Jesus' church (***my church***), not Peter's, and Jesus himself ***will build*** it. So it is not necessary to conclude that later church leaders must derive their authority from Peter. • Matthew is the only Gospel writer who uses the term ***church*** (also 18:17). The idea here is more *the community of God's people* than an ecclesiastical institution. • ***and all the powers of hell:*** Literally *and the gates of Hades* (see note on 11:23). • ***will not conquer it:*** The church will not be defeated by the attacks of Satan (see 11:12; 13:24-30, 36-43).

16:19 ***Keys*** are an image for access to privileged knowledge that gives one authority (see 13:16-17; 23:13; Isa 22:22; Rev 3:7). • ***forbid*** (or *bind*, or *lock*) . . . ***permit*** (or *loose*, or *open*): Jesus granted to Peter (and later to the rest of the Twelve, 18:18) the authority to teach the will of God as revealed in Jesus Christ (13:52; 18:15-20; 23:2-12; 28:16-20). • ***will be:*** This could be translated *will have been*, emphasizing that God's sovereign decision comes first.

16:21-28 Jesus, now officially recognized by his disciples as the Messiah, begins to reveal a startling aspect of his mission: He must suffer before entering his glory (16:21-23), and those who follow him will meet a similar fate (16:24-28).

16:21 This is the first of three predictions of Jesus' *passion*—his suffering through betrayal, crucifixion, and death (see also 17:22-23; 20:18-19). Each prediction gives a lesson on the cost of discipleship (16:24-27; 20:20-28). • ***Jesus:*** Some manuscripts read *Jesus the Messiah.* • That ***he would suffer*** was God's sovereign and necessary purpose for the Messiah (see 17:12).

16:22 ***began to reprimand him:*** Or *began to correct him.* Though Peter accurately perceived Jesus' identity as God's Messiah, he did not understand that the Messiah must suffer.

16:23 As when ***Satan*** tempted Jesus to assume royal privileges without first enduring the cross (see 4:8-10), so now Jesus perceived Peter's suggestion as incited by satanic forces. • ***dangerous trap:*** Literally *stumbling block*; see "Jesus, a Source of Stumbling" at 21:42-46, p. 1623.

18:1-5
//Mark 9:33-37
//Luke 9:46-48
18:3
Matt 19:14
Mark 10:15
Luke 18:17
1 Pet 2:2
18:4
Matt 20:26-27
Mark 10:43-44
Luke 22:26
18:5
Matt 10:40
Luke 10:16
John 13:20
18:6-9
//Mark 9:42-48
//Luke 17:1-2
1 Cor 8:12-13
18:6
[j]*skandalizō* (4624)
‣Rom 9:32
18:8-9
Matt 5:29-30
18:9
[k]*geenna* (1067)
‣Matt 23:33
18:10
Acts 12:15
Heb 1:14
18:12-14
//Luke 15:3-7

But before he had a chance to speak,
Jesus asked him, "What do you think, Peter?
Do kings tax their own people or the people
they have conquered?"
26"They tax the people they have conquered," Peter replied.
"Well, then," Jesus said, "the citizens are
free! 27However, we don't want to offend
them, so go down to the lake and throw in
a line. Open the mouth of the first fish you
catch, and you will find a large silver coin.
Take it and pay the tax for both of us."

Discourse: Jesus Teaches about Community Life (18:1-35)

The Greatest in the Kingdom

Matt 18:1-5 // Mark 9:33-37 // Luke 9:46-48

18 About that time the disciples came
to Jesus and asked, "Who is greatest
in the Kingdom of Heaven?"
2Jesus called a little child to him and put
the child among them. 3Then he said, "I tell
you the truth, unless you turn from your
sins and become like little children, you
will never get into the Kingdom of Heaven.
4So anyone who becomes as humble as this
little child is the greatest in the Kingdom
of Heaven. 5And anyone who welcomes a
little child like this on my behalf is welcoming me.

Warning against Causing Sin

Matt 18:6-9 // Mark 9:42-48 // Luke 17:1-3a

6"But if you cause one of these little ones
who trusts in me to [j]fall into sin, it would be
better for you to have a large millstone tied
around your neck and be drowned in the
depths of the sea.
7"What sorrow awaits the world, because
it tempts people to sin. Temptations are inevitable, but what sorrow awaits the person
who does the tempting. 8So if your hand or
foot causes you to sin, cut it off and throw
it away. It's better to enter eternal life with
only one hand or one foot than to be thrown
into eternal fire with both of your hands
and feet. 9And if your eye causes you to sin,
gouge it out and throw it away. It's better to
enter eternal life with only one eye than to
have two eyes and be thrown into the fire
of [k]hell.
10"Beware that you don't look down on
any of these little ones. For I tell you that in
heaven their angels are always in the presence of my heavenly Father.

Parable of the Lost Sheep

Matt 18:12-14 // Luke 15:3-7

12"If a man has a hundred sheep and one of
them wanders away, what will he do? Won't
he leave the ninety-nine others on the hills
and go out to search for the one that is lost?
13And if he finds it, I tell you the truth, he
will rejoice over it more than over the ninety-
nine that didn't wander away! 14In the same
way, it is not my heavenly Father's will that
even one of these little ones should perish.

17:25-26 As an obedient Jew, Jesus would have paid the tax annually, and he did pay it. Jesus' point was that as God's Son, he is greater than the Temple (12:5-6), and he makes a decisive break with it (see 16:18-19; 21:33-46).

17:25 *Peter?* Literally *Simon?* • ***their own people or the people they have conquered?*** Literally *their sons or others?*

17:27 ***a large silver coin:*** Greek *a stater,* a Greek coin equivalent to four drachmas. It was adequate to pay the tax for both of them (see note on 17:24).

18:1-35 This fourth major discourse in Matthew (see note on 5:1–7:29) focuses on responses to the Messiah—acceptance by the disciples and rejection by the Jewish leaders and most of the populace. In light of this growing polarization, Jesus began to instruct his followers on the nature of community life. For a community to live according to Jesus' standards, it must live with humility (18:1-5), sensitivity (18:6-9), compassion (18:10-14), discipline (18:15-18), and forgiveness (18:21-35). As with the other discourses, a concluding formula (19:1-2) bridges to the next section.

18:1 *About that time:* Matthew connects the disciples' questions with the previous discussion concerning the Temple. The disciples began to assume that their new freedom in relation to Jewish authority entitled them to authority of their own. In addition, talk of special revelations (11:25-27; 13:11-17) and roles of leadership (10:2-4; 19:28) probably gave rise to jealous comparisons and petty desires for power among the disciples, perhaps revolving around the apparent privilege of Peter (17:25) or Peter, James, and John (17:1-3).

18:3 ***Like little children*** means to be humble (18:4). The disciples had been intent on status and ambition.

18:5 Jesus moved the discussion toward solidarity within the community; to welcome a humble follower of Jesus is to welcome Jesus himself (see 10:40-42). • ***on my behalf:*** Literally *in my name.*

18:6 To ***cause one . . . to fall into sin*** is to lead believing children (or possibly believing adults who become "like children"; see 18:3) to reject Christ and abandon the faith. • The designation ***little ones*** emphasizes their humility (5:3-12; 18:4; 19:13-15). • Though the thought of being drowned with a ***large millstone*** around the neck is frightful, Jesus warned that causing another to fall away will bring far greater misery (18:7; 26:24; Rev 18:21; see Matt 22:13).

18:8-9 Concern shifts to the individual: Get rid of whatever ***causes you to sin*** (see 5:29-30; Col 3:5-17).

18:9 ***the fire of hell:*** Greek *the Gehenna of fire.* See note on 5:29.

18:10 ***Don't look down on*** them, either by refusing to receive them (18:5-6) or by refusing to give pastoral care when needed (18:12-14; see 19:13-15). • ***their angels:*** See 4:5-7; Heb 1:14. • Some manuscripts add verse 11, *And the Son of Man came to save those who are lost.* Cp. Luke 19:10.

18:12 Just as a shepherd will work to recover a lost ***sheep,*** the "little ones" (18:6) must not be despised or neglected.

18:14 The shepherd's joy is also the joy of the Father; the purpose of pastoral care is so God will not lose any of his sheep.

Correcting Another Believer

15"If another believer sins against you, go
privately and point out the offense. If the
other person listens and confesses it, you
have won that person back. 16But if you are
unsuccessful, take one or two others with
you and go back again, so that everything
you say may be confirmed by two or three
witnesses. 17If the person still refuses to listen, take your case to the [a]church. Then if he
or she won't accept the [a]church's decision,
treat that person as a pagan or a corrupt tax
collector.
18"I tell you the truth, whatever you forbid on earth will be forbidden in heaven,
and whatever you permit on earth will be
permitted in heaven.
19"I also tell you this: If two of you agree
here on earth concerning anything you ask,
my Father in heaven will do it for you. 20For
where two or three gather together as my
followers, I am there among them."

Parable of the Unforgiving Debtor

21Then Peter came to him and asked, "Lord,
how often should I forgive someone who
sins against me? Seven times?"
22"No, not seven times," Jesus replied,
"but seventy times seven!
23"Therefore, the Kingdom of Heaven
can be compared to a king who decided to
bring his accounts up to date with servants
who had borrowed money from him. 24In
the process, one of his debtors was brought
in who owed him millions of dollars. 25He
couldn't pay, so his master ordered that he
be sold—along with his wife, his children,
and everything he owned—to pay the debt.
26"But the man fell down before his master and begged him, 'Please, be patient with
me, and I will pay it all.' 27Then his master
was filled with pity for him, and he released
him and forgave his debt.
28"But when the man left the king, he
went to a fellow servant who owed him a
few thousand dollars. He grabbed him by
the throat and demanded instant payment.
29"His fellow servant fell down before
him and begged for a little more time. 'Be
patient with me, and I will pay it,' he pleaded.
30But his creditor wouldn't wait. He had the
man arrested and put in prison until the
debt could be paid in full.
31"When some of the other servants saw
this, they were very upset. They went to the
king and told him everything that had happened. 32Then the king called in the man
he had forgiven and said, 'You evil servant!
I forgave you that tremendous debt because
you pleaded with me. 33Shouldn't you have
mercy on your fellow servant, just as I had
mercy on you?' 34Then the angry king sent

18:15 Lev 19:17; Luke 17:3; Gal 6:1; Jas 5:19-20
18:16 *Deut 19:15; John 8:17; 2 Cor 13:1; 1 Tim 5:19
18:17 Rom 16:17; 1 Cor 6:1-6; [a]*ekklēsia* (1577) ‣Rom 16:5
18:18 Matt 16:19; John 20:23
18:19 Matt 7:7; 21:22; Mark 11:24; John 15:7; 16:23; Jas 1:5; 1 Jn 3:22; 5:14-15
18:20 Matt 28:20; John 14:23
18:21-22 Luke 17:3-4
18:23 Matt 25:19
18:25 Lev 25:39; 2 Kgs 4:1; Neh 5:5
18:27 Luke 7:42
18:34 Matt 5:25-26; Luke 12:58-59

18:15-35 The believing community must not be fractured into rival parties and unreconciled relationships. Its members are to pursue reconciliation (18:15-20) and forgive willingly (18:21-35). At times, however, stern discipline may be necessary (18:17).

18:15-20 Restoration begins privately and should be made public only as a last resort.

18:15 *If another believer* (literally *If your brother*) *sins,* brotherly love requires us to ***go privately and point out the offense*** (Lev 19:17; Luke 17:3; Gal 6:1; 1 Tim 5:20; Titus 3:10). • Some manuscripts do not include *against you.*

18:16 By requiring the presence of ***one or two others,*** Jesus prevented slanderous, unsubstantiated accusations from being presented to the congregation (see John 8:17; 2 Cor 13:1; 1 Tim 5:19; Heb 10:28).

18:17 ***The church*** is the local Christian community. • The unrepentant person is to be considered a ***pagan or a corrupt tax collector,*** a wicked transgressor of the law. Church discipline by exclusion (excommunication; see Acts 5:1-6; Rom 16:17; 1 Cor 5:1-13; 2 Cor 6:14-18; Gal 5:7-12; 2 Thes 3:14-15) is rooted in the conviction that God's people are to be holy and that sin corrupts fellowship, both between people and between the people and God. The goal is neither vindictive retribution nor a public display of power, but restoration of the wayward to holiness and fellowship (18:10-15; Gal 6:1; Jas 5:19-20).

18:18-20 These sayings provide the basis for a process of discipline and restoration in the community of disciples.

18:18 *forbid* (or *bind,* or *lock*) . . . *permit* (or *loose,* or *open;* see 16:19): The privilege and authority granted to Peter (16:19) are here granted to the church (or possibly to the twelve apostles, 18:1). The decisions of the community, when in accord with God's will, are eternally binding.

18:19 ***anything you ask:*** In the context of church discipline (18:15-17), this suggests that discipline must be done in prayer.

18:20 Christ is present in the process of discipline, so the process is a ratification of God's decision. • ***gather together as my followers:*** Literally *gather together in my name.*

18:21-35 Peter's suggestion of ***seven times*** was generous, so Jesus' answer was startling. The disciple's willingness to forgive should be like God's forgiving grace, limitless and free (see 18:10-14). Those who do not forgive in this way cannot themselves have experienced God's forgiveness (18:35; see 6:12).

18:21 ***someone:*** Literally *my brother.*

18:22 ***seventy times seven:*** Or *seventy-seven times;* either way, Jesus prescribes limitless readiness to forgive from the heart (18:35; cp. Gen 4:23-24).

18:24 ***millions of dollars*** (Greek *10,000 talents* [375 tons or 340 metric tons of silver]): The *talent* was the highest unit of currency, but its value fluctuated. The debt was clearly impossible to pay—this amount exceeded the tax revenue of all Galilee.

18:26 ***I will pay it all:*** The exaggerated debt and the slave's promise amplify the greatness of the king's mercy and the slave's unforgiving attitude (18:29-30).

18:28 ***a few thousand dollars*** (Greek *100 denarii;* a denarius was equivalent to a laborer's full day's wage): The first servant's debt was about one million times greater than this sum owed to him.

18:34 This is how God responds (18:35) to anyone unwilling to forgive. • ***until he had paid his entire debt:*** I.e., permanently, because he could never repay.

18:35
Matt 6:15
Mark 11:25
Eph 4:32
Col 3:13
19:1-9
//Mark 10:1-12
19:2
Matt 4:23
19:3
Matt 5:31
19:4
*Gen 1:27; 5:2
19:5
*Gen 2:24
1 Cor 6:16
Eph 5:31
19:7
*Deut 24:1
Matt 5:31
^b*biblion* (0975)
‣ Luke 4:17
19:9
Matt 5:32
Luke 16:18
1 Cor 7:10-11
19:11
1 Cor 7:7-9, 17
19:12
1 Cor 7:32, 34
19:13-15
//Mark 10:13-16
//Luke 18:15-17
19:14
Matt 18:2-3
19:16-30
//Mark 10:17-31
//Luke 18:18-30
19:16
Matt 19:29
Luke 10:25

the man to prison to be tortured until he had paid his entire debt.

35“That's what my heavenly Father will do to you if you refuse to forgive your brothers and sisters from your heart.”

Narrative: Jesus Instructs on the Way to Jerusalem (19:1–20:34)

Jesus Leaves Galilee
Matt 19:1-2 // Mark 10:1

19 When Jesus had finished saying these things, he left Galilee and went down to the region of Judea east of the Jordan River. 2Large crowds followed him there, and he healed their sick.

Jesus' Teaching about Divorce and Marriage
Matt 19:3-12 // Mark 10:2-12; cp. Matt 5:31-32; Luke 16:18

3Some Pharisees came and tried to trap him with this question: “Should a man be allowed to divorce his wife for just any reason?”

4“Haven't you read the Scriptures?” Jesus replied. “They record that from the beginning ‘God made them male and female.’” 5And he said, “‘This explains why a man leaves his father and mother and is joined to his wife, and the two are united into one.’ 6Since they are no longer two but one, let no one split apart what God has joined together.”

7“Then why did Moses say in the law that a man could give his wife a ^bwritten notice of divorce and send her away?” they asked.

8Jesus replied, “Moses permitted divorce only as a concession to your hard hearts, but it was not what God had originally intended. 9And I tell you this, whoever divorces his wife and marries someone else commits adultery—unless his wife has been unfaithful.”

10Jesus' disciples then said to him, “If this is the case, it is better not to marry!”

11“Not everyone can accept this statement,” Jesus said. “Only those whom God helps. 12Some are born as eunuchs, some have been made eunuchs by others, and some choose not to marry for the sake of the Kingdom of Heaven. Let anyone accept this who can.”

Jesus Blesses the Children
Matt 19:13-15 // Mark 10:13-16 // Luke 18:15-17

13One day some parents brought their children to Jesus so he could lay his hands on them and pray for them. But the disciples scolded the parents for bothering him.

14But Jesus said, “Let the children come to me. Don't stop them! For the Kingdom of Heaven belongs to those who are like these children.” 15And he placed his hands on their heads and blessed them before he left.

The Rich Man
Matt 19:16-22 // Mark 10:17-22 // Luke 18:18-23

16Someone came to Jesus with this question: “Teacher, what good deed must I do to have eternal life?”

18:35 ***That's what my heavenly Father will do to you:*** Prison and torture (18:34) is thus a metaphor for hell (see 5:22). • ***your brothers and sisters:*** Literally *your brother.*

19:1–20:34 Jesus was now on the move toward Jerusalem (19:1; 20:29; 21:1), with a further opportunity for instructing the disciples on various aspects of discipleship.

19:3 There were two divergent views on when one was ***allowed to divorce*** one's wife (see also note on Mark 10:4). One group of Pharisees, following Rabbi Shammai, argued that divorce was allowed only in the case of adultery or other grave sin, while the other group, following Rabbi Hillel, contended that a man could divorce his wife for ***any reason***, such as if she burned his dinner.

19:4-5 The Pharisees were not considering *all* of God's word. The Creator had made marriage as a permanent union. • ***God made them male and female:*** Gen 1:27; 5:2. • ***This explains why . . . the two are united into one:*** Gen 2:24. See also 1 Cor 6:16; 7:10-16.

19:6 Since God made marriage a union, humans do not have the right to break that union. Jesus affirmed the indissolubility of marriage.

19:7-8 ***why did Moses say*** (literally *command*): The Pharisees thought Jesus had contradicted a command of the law (see Deut 24:1-4), but Moses ***permitted divorce only as a concession*** to their ***hard hearts.*** Jesus introduced the revolutionary principle that God's permission is not necessarily his desire (see 1 Cor 6:12). Divorce is never God's desire (Mal 2:14-16); it is an expression of human sin.

19:9 Jesus permits only one legitimate reason for a man to divorce: if ***his wife has been unfaithful*** (see 5:32). In the face of those who thought divorce could be taken lightly, Jesus affirms God's created order: Marriage was designed to be permanent (see Mark 10:11-12). • ***commits adultery:*** This speaks only of the man who divorces his wife unlawfully. In such a case, his remarriage is adulterous. Jesus' motivation is to reestablish the permanency of marriage. • Some manuscripts add *And anyone who marries a divorced woman commits adultery.* Cp. 5:32.

19:11 ***This statement*** refers to the disciples' comment (19:10).

19:12 ***and some choose not to marry:*** Literally *and some make themselves eunuchs.* • ***Eunuchs*** are males castrated either by a birth defect or by a surgical operation. Jesus also uses the term metaphorically for those who decide to remain celibate (see Luke 14:26; 18:29; 1 Cor 7:7-8). • ***for the sake of the Kingdom:*** Jesus was not denigrating marriage; he was simply indicating that the unmarried often have greater potential for ministry (see 1 Cor 7:25-35).

19:13 Jesus would ***lay his hands*** on others to bless them (see Luke 4:40; 13:13; see also Gen 48:14-15; Acts 19:6). • ***The disciples,*** motivated to protect Jesus, ***scolded the parents,*** demonstrating a wrong attitude toward children (see 18:5-6, 10).

19:16 ***Teacher:*** Some manuscripts read *Good Teacher.*

17“Why ask me about what is good?” Jesus replied. “There is only One who is good. But to answer your question—if you want to receive eternal life, keep the commandments.”

18“Which ones?” the man asked.

And Jesus replied: “ ‘You must not murder. You must not commit adultery. You must not steal. You must not testify falsely.
19Honor your father and mother. Love your neighbor as yourself.’ ”

20“I’ve obeyed all these commandments,” the young man replied. “What else must I do?”

21Jesus told him, “If you want to be perfect, go and sell all your possessions and give the money to the poor, and you will have treasure in heaven. Then come, follow me.”

22But when the young man heard this, he went away sad, for he had many possessions.

Rewards of Discipleship
Matt 19:23-30 // Mark 10:23-31 // Luke 18:24-30

23Then Jesus said to his disciples, “I tell you the truth, it is very hard for a rich person to enter the Kingdom of Heaven.
24I’ll say it again—it is easier for a camel to go through the eye of a needle than for a rich person to enter the Kingdom of God!”

25The disciples were astounded. “Then who in the world can be saved?” they asked.

26Jesus looked at them intently and said, “Humanly speaking, it is impossible. But with God everything is possible.”

27Then Peter said to him, “We’ve given up everything to follow you. What will we get?”

28Jesus replied, “I assure you that when the world is made new and the Son of Man sits upon his glorious throne, you who have been my followers will also sit on twelve thrones, judging the twelve tribes of Israel.
29And everyone who has given up houses or brothers or sisters or father or mother or children or property, for my sake, will receive a hundred times as much in return and will inherit eternal life.
30But many who are the greatest now will be least important then, and those who seem least important now will be the greatest then.

Parable of the Vineyard Workers

20 “For the Kingdom of Heaven is like the landowner who went out early one morning to hire workers for his vineyard.
2He agreed to pay the normal daily wage and sent them out to work.

3“At nine o’clock in the morning he was passing through the marketplace and saw some people standing around doing nothing.
4So he hired them, telling them he would pay them whatever was right at the end of the day.
5So they went to work in the vineyard. At noon and again at three o’clock he did the same thing.

6“At five o’clock that afternoon he was in town again and saw some more people standing around. He asked them, ‘Why haven’t you been working today?’

19:17 Lev 18:5; Luke 10:28
19:18 *Exod 20:13-16; *Deut 5:17-21
19:19 Exod 20:12; *Lev 19:18; Deut 5:16; Matt 5:43-44; 22:39; Luke 10:27; Rom 13:9
19:21 Acts 2:45; 4:34-37
19:23 Matt 13:22; 1 Tim 6:9-10
19:26 Gen 18:14; Job 42:2; Jer 32:17; Zech 8:6
19:27 Matt 4:19
19:28 Luke 22:28-30; Rev 3:21
19:30 Matt 20:16; Mark 10:31; Luke 13:30
20:1 Matt 21:28, 33

19:17 *Why ask me?* The man, as a Jew, should have known that God’s standard of goodness is clearly reflected in his commandments. The man’s questions (also 19:20) show that he was not trusting in the adequacy of God’s revealed will. • ***only One . . . is good:*** The man may have believed he could act with perfect goodness on his own, whereas only God is truly *good* and thus the source of all goodness. • ***keep*** (some manuscripts read *continue to keep*) ***the commandments:*** Jesus has in mind either leading the man to see his sinfulness by asking him to do the impossible, or more probably, restating that good works are a telling gauge of the truthfulness of a person’s faith (see 7:13-27).

19:18-19 The quotation is from Exod 20:12-16; Deut 5:16-20; Lev 19:18.

19:21-22 By calling the man to *go and sell* and *come, follow me,* Jesus revealed that the man had not in fact kept the first of the ten commandments (Exod 20:3). His ***possessions***—his wealth and security—had become his god (see 6:20, 24; 13:44-46).

19:23 Jesus draws a lesson for discipleship from the rich man’s tragic denial. It is *hard* for the *rich* to humble themselves, admit their need, and trust in God (see 5:3; Luke 6:24; 1 Tim 6:9-10). • ***Kingdom of Heaven*** is equivalent here to *eternal life* (19:16-17, 29) or to *salvation* as the result of God’s regenerating work (19:25-26).

19:24 ***easier for a camel:*** This analogy reinforces the difficulty that wealthy people face in entering the Kingdom. A few manuscripts have a Greek word meaning *rope* (Greek *kamilos*) instead of *camel* (Greek *kamēlos*), a difference of only one letter. • ***to go through the eye of a needle:*** The image makes the wealthy entering the Kingdom an impossibility. The situation is not utterly hopeless, however (19:26-27). See also note on Mark 10:25.

19:26 God’s regenerating grace is absolutely essential before the wealthy are able to repent from their idolatry, abandon their possessions if called to do so, and follow Jesus (19:21).

19:28 ***when the world is made new:*** Or *in the regeneration.* • ***you . . . will also sit on twelve thrones:*** The disciples’ part in judging is a reversal—those who are wealthy and powerful now will be judged by those who are humble and poor (see 19:30). • ***Son of Man*** is a title Jesus used for himself. • ***Judging*** can mean both ruling and condemning (see Rev 20:4).

19:30 Literally *But many who are first will be last; and the last, first.*

20:1-16 This parable is similar to the parable of the Lost Son (Luke 15:11-32). In both, God’s grace is shown to two parties while one grumbles about unjust treatment.

20:2 ***the normal daily wage:*** Greek *a denarius,* the payment for a full day’s labor; similarly in 20:9, 10, 13.

20:8 Lev 19:13 Deut 24:15
20:15 Deut 15:9
20:16 Matt 19:30 Mark 10:31 Luke 13:30
20:17-19 //Mark 10:32-34 //Luke 18:31-34
20:18-19 Matt 16:21; 17:22-23 Luke 9:22 Acts 2:23
20:20-28 //Mark 10:35-45
20:21 Matt 19:28
20:22 Matt 26:39, 42 Mark 14:36 Luke 22:42 John 18:11
20:23 Acts 12:2 Rev 1:9
20:24-28 //Luke 22:24-27
20:26 Matt 23:11 Mark 9:35 Luke 9:48 [c]*diakonos* (1249) ‣Rom 16:1
20:27 [d]*doulos* (1401) ‣John 13:16
20:28 Isa 53:10 Phil 2:7 1 Tim 2:6 1 Pet 1:18-19 [e]*lutron* (3083) ‣Mark 10:45
20:29-34 //Mark 10:46-52 //Luke 18:35-43

7“They replied, ‘Because no one hired us.’
“The landowner told them, ‘Then go out
and join the others in my vineyard.’
8“That evening he told the foreman to
call the workers in and pay them, beginning with the last workers first. 9When
those hired at five o’clock were paid, each
received a full day’s wage. 10When those
hired first came to get their pay, they assumed they would receive more. But they,
too, were paid a day’s wage. 11When they
received their pay, they protested to the
owner, 12‘Those people worked only one
hour, and yet you’ve paid them just as much
as you paid us who worked all day in the
scorching heat.’
13“He answered one of them, ‘Friend, I
haven’t been unfair! Didn’t you agree to
work all day for the usual wage? 14Take
your money and go. I wanted to pay this
last worker the same as you. 15Is it against
the law for me to do what I want with my
money? Should you be jealous because I am
kind to others?’
16“So those who are last now will be first
then, and those who are first will be last.”

Jesus Predicts His Death and Resurrection
Matt 20:17-19 // Mark 10:32-34 // Luke 18:31-34

17As Jesus was going up to Jerusalem, he
took the twelve disciples aside privately and
told them what was going to happen to him.
18“Listen,” he said, “we’re going up to Jerusalem, where the Son of Man will be betrayed
to the leading priests and the teachers of
religious law. They will sentence him to
die. 19Then they will hand him over to the
Romans to be mocked, flogged with a whip,
and crucified. But on the third day he will
be raised from the dead.”

Jesus Teaches about Serving Others
Matt 20:20-28 // Mark 10:35-45; cp. Luke 22:24-27

20Then the mother of James and John, the
sons of Zebedee, came to Jesus with her
sons. She knelt respectfully to ask a favor.
21“What is your request?” he asked.
She replied, “In your Kingdom, please let
my two sons sit in places of honor next to
you, one on your right and the other on your
left.”
22But Jesus answered by saying to them,
“You don’t know what you are asking! Are
you able to drink from the bitter cup of suffering I am about to drink?”
“Oh yes,” they replied, “we are able!”
23Jesus told them, “You will indeed drink
from my bitter cup. But I have no right to
say who will sit on my right or my left. My Father has prepared those places for the ones
he has chosen.”
24When the ten other disciples heard
what James and John had asked, they were
indignant. 25But Jesus called them together
and said, “You know that the rulers in this
world lord it over their people, and officials
flaunt their authority over those under
them. 26But among you it will be different.
Whoever wants to be a leader among you
must be your [c]servant, 27and whoever wants
to be first among you must become your
[d]slave. 28For even the Son of Man came not
to be served but to serve others and to give
his life as a [e]ransom for many.”

Jesus Heals Two Blind Men
Matt 20:29-34 // Mark 10:46-52 // Luke 18:35-43; cp. Matt 9:27-31

29As Jesus and the disciples left the town
of Jericho, a large crowd followed behind. 30Two blind men were sitting beside
the road. When they heard that Jesus was

20:8 Payment followed the day’s work (Deut 24:14-15).

20:16 See 5:19; 8:11-12.

20:18 *Son of Man* is a title Jesus used for himself.

20:19 *the Romans:* Literally *the Gentiles.*

20:20-28 Each prediction of Jesus’ suffering in Matthew is connected to instruction on the nature of discipleship in light of that suffering (see 16:24-28; 17:24–18:5). This teaching called the Messiah’s disciples to follow his example of service and sacrifice.

20:20-21 This mother’s question appears to have been inspired by her sons, since Jesus responded to the sons rather than to the mother (cp. Mark 10:35-37).

20:21 The promise of sitting in positions of authority ***in*** God’s ***Kingdom*** had already been given (19:28); the brothers’ request seems to have been motivated out of selfish desire for prominence, with no regard for the suffering the Messiah would soon undergo (see 23:6; Luke 14:7-11).

20:22 The ***cup*** refers to Jesus’ duty, calling, and destiny (see 26:39; John 18:11; see also Ps 75:8; Isa 51:17, 22; Rev 16:19).

20:23 ***You will indeed:*** James was eventually martyred (Acts 12:2), and John suffered significant persecution (Acts 4:3; 5:40; Rev 1:9).

20:24 The ***other disciples . . . were indignant:*** Selfish ambition was apparently not unique to ***James and John*** (see also 21:15; 26:8; Luke 13:14).

20:25-28 The desire for power is characteristic of pagan ***rulers in this world.*** It ought not to be a trait of those who follow the ***Son of Man*** (18:1-5; 19:13-15; 23:1-12).

20:27 The word ***slave*** is a common metaphor for the submissive relationship of a disciple to his master (8:9; 10:24-25; 24:45-51; 25:14-30). Jesus’ disciples serve others, following Jesus’ example (e.g., John 13:1-17).

20:28 This expression, the ***Son of Man came,*** suggests Jesus’ preexistence (see Dan 7:13-14). • Jesus was describing his voluntary offering of himself as ***a ransom for many,*** to pay the debt all people owe (see 26:26-29; Isa 53:10-12; Rom 3:24), thereby buying them out of slavery (see Gal 5:1).

20:29-34 The blind men’s expression of faith in the ***Son of David*** was an acknowledgment of Jesus as the Messiah (see 21:9; 22:42; 2 Sam 7:12-16).

coming that way, they began shouting,
"Lord, Son of David, have mercy on us!"
31 "Be quiet!" the crowd yelled at them.
But they only shouted louder, "Lord, Son
of David, have mercy on us!"
32 When Jesus heard them, he stopped
and called, "What do you want me to do for
you?"
33 "Lord," they said, "we want to see!"
34 Jesus felt sorry for them and touched their
eyes. Instantly they could see! Then they followed him.

5. THE MESSIAH ACCOMPLISHES SALVATION (21:1–28:20)

Narrative: Jesus Confronts the Leaders in Jerusalem (21:1–22:46)

Jesus' Messianic Entry into Jerusalem

Matt 21:1-11 // Mark 11:1-11 // Luke 19:28-40 // John 12:12-19

21 As Jesus and the disciples approached Jerusalem, they came to
the town of Bethphage on the Mount of Olives. Jesus sent two of them on ahead. 2 "Go
into the village over there," he said. "As soon
as you enter it, you will see a donkey tied
there, with its colt beside it. Untie them and
bring them to me. 3 If anyone asks what you
are doing, just say, 'The Lord needs them,'
and he will immediately let you take them."
4 This took place to fulfill the prophecy
that said,

5 "Tell the people of Jerusalem,
'Look, your King is coming to you.
He is humble, riding on a donkey—
riding on a donkey's colt.'"

6 The two disciples did as Jesus commanded. 7 They brought the donkey and the
colt to him and threw their garments over
the colt, and he sat on it.
8 Most of the crowd spread their garments on the road ahead of him, and others
cut branches from the trees and spread
them on the road. 9 Jesus was in the center
of the procession, and the people all around
him were shouting,

"Praise God for the Son of David!
Blessings on the one who comes in the
name of the LORD!
Praise God in highest heaven!"

10 The entire city of Jerusalem was in an
uproar as he entered. "Who is this?" they
asked.
11 And the crowds replied, "It's Jesus, the
prophet from Nazareth in Galilee."

Jesus Clears the Temple

Matt 21:12-13 // Mark 11:15-17 // Luke 19:45-46; cp. John 2:13-16

12 Jesus entered the Temple and began to
drive out all the people buying and selling
animals for sacrifice. He knocked over
the tables of the money changers and the
chairs of those selling doves. 13 He said to
them, "The Scriptures declare, 'My Temple
will be called a house of prayer,' but you
have turned it into a den of thieves!"

Jesus Heals in the Temple

14 The blind and the lame came to him in the
Temple, and he healed them. 15 The leading
priests and the teachers of religious law
saw these wonderful miracles and heard
even the children in the Temple shouting,
"Praise God for the Son of David."
But the leaders were indignant. 16 They
asked Jesus, "Do you hear what these children are saying?"
"Yes," Jesus replied. "Haven't you ever
read the Scriptures? For they say, 'You have

21:1-9 //Mark 11:1-10 //Luke 19:28-38 //John 12:12-19
21:5 *Isa 62:11 *Zech 9:9
21:9 *Ps 118:25-26; 148:1 Luke 13:35
21:11 Luke 7:16, 39 John 1:21, 25; 6:14; 7:40; 9:17
21:12-17 //Mark 11:15-19 //Luke 19:45-48 //John 2:13-22
21:13 *Isa 56:7 *Jer 7:11
21:14 Isa 35:5-6
21:15 Matt 21:9
21:16 *Ps 8:2

21:1–28:20 Jesus' entry into Jerusalem initiates Matthew's account of how the Messiah's suffering and resurrection establish salvation.

21:1 *Bethphage* (a Hebrew name meaning *house of figs*) was probably located on the eastern slope of the ***Mount of Olives*** between Bethany and Jerusalem proper.

21:3 Jesus was revealing himself as ***the Lord*** who, as king of Israel, ascends to Mount Zion on a donkey (21:5; see Zech 9:9).

21:4-5 The OT fulfillment here emphasizes the Messiah's non-violent, ***humble,*** and saving work (see 11:28-30; Zech 9:9-10; Isa 62:11).

21:5 ***Tell the people of Jerusalem:*** Literally *Tell the daughter of Zion;* Isa 62:11. • ***donkey's colt:*** Zech 9:9.

21:7 ***over the colt, and he sat on it:*** Literally *over them, and he sat on them.*

21:9 This verse quotes Ps 118:25-26; 148:1. • ***Praise God:*** Greek *Hosanna,* a Hebrew exclamation of praise that literally means "save now"; also in 21:15.

21:11 The crowds with Jesus understood him to be a ***prophet,*** empowered by God to teach and to perform miracles. • The description ***from Nazareth in Galilee*** highlights Jesus' humble origins (see 2:23).

21:12-13 The close association of the Temple cleansing (see John 2:13-16) with the cursing of the fig tree (21:18-19) reveals Jesus as the Messiah who confronted Israel and warned that God judges those who reject the Messiah and his message.

21:12 ***Buying and selling*** took place within ***the Temple*** complex, in the Court of the Gentiles. • ***Money changers*** profited from the exchange of money from other currencies into official Jewish currency. Jesus criticized the commercialism that profaned the holiness of the Temple (see Mark 11:11-18).

21:13 Jesus' actions were justified, because God's glory was being desecrated through financial exploitation. • ***My Temple . . . a den of thieves:*** Isa 56:7; Jer 7:11.

21:15 The Jewish leaders' stubborn refusal to believe is contrasted with the exuberant faith and ***praise*** of little ***children*** (see 18:1-14; 19:13-15).

21:16 ***Haven't you ever read the Scriptures?*** Jesus put this penetrating question to opponents who did not perceive the fulfillment of messianic promises in his ministry. See also 12:3, 5; 19:4; 21:42; 22:31. • ***You have taught children and infants to give you praise:*** Ps 8:2 (Greek version).

21:17
Mark 11:1
John 11:1, 18; 12:1

21:18-22
//Mark 11:12-14, 20-24

21:21
Matt 17:20
Luke 17:6
1 Cor 13:2
Jas 1:6

21:22
Matt 7:7-11
John 14:13-14

21:23-27
//Mark 11:27-33
//Luke 20:1-8

21:23
Acts 4:7

21:26
Matt 11:9

21:28
Luke 15:11

21:32
Matt 3:1-12
Luke 3:12-13; 7:29-30

21:33-46
//Mark 12:1-12
//Luke 20:9-19

21:33
Isa 5:1-2

taught children and infants to give you praise.' " [17]Then he returned to Bethany, where he stayed overnight.

Jesus Curses the Fig Tree
Matt 21:18-19 // Mark 11:12-14
Matt 21:20-22 // Mark 11:20-25

[18]In the morning, as Jesus was returning to Jerusalem, he was hungry, [19]and he noticed a fig tree beside the road. He went over to see if there were any figs, but there were only leaves. Then he said to it, "May you never bear fruit again!" And immediately the fig tree withered up.

[20]The disciples were amazed when they saw this and asked, "How did the fig tree wither so quickly?"

[21]Then Jesus told them, "I tell you the truth, if you have faith and don't doubt, you can do things like this and much more. You can even say to this mountain, 'May you be lifted up and thrown into the sea,' and it will happen. [22]You can pray for anything, and if you have faith, you will receive it."

Jesus' Authority Is Challenged
Matt 21:23-27 // Mark 11:27-33 // Luke 20:1-8

[23]When Jesus returned to the Temple and began teaching, the leading priests and elders came up to him. They demanded, "By what authority are you doing all these things? Who gave you the right?"

[24]"I'll tell you by what authority I do these things if you answer one question," Jesus replied. [25]"Did John's authority to baptize come from heaven, or was it merely human?"

They talked it over among themselves. "If we say it was from heaven, he will ask us why we didn't believe John. [26]But if we say it was merely human, we'll be mobbed because the people believe John was a prophet." [27]So they finally replied, "We don't know."

And Jesus responded, "Then I won't tell you by what authority I do these things.

Parable of the Two Sons

[28]"But what do you think about this? A man with two sons told the older boy, 'Son, go out and work in the vineyard today.' [29]The son answered, 'No, I won't go,' but later he changed his mind and went anyway. [30]Then the father told the other son, 'You go,' and he said, 'Yes, sir, I will.' But he didn't go.

[31]"Which of the two obeyed his father?"

They replied, "The first."

Then Jesus explained his meaning: "I tell you the truth, corrupt tax collectors and prostitutes will get into the Kingdom of God before you do. [32]For John the Baptist came and showed you the right way to live, but you didn't believe him, while tax collectors and prostitutes did. And even when you saw this happening, you refused to believe him and repent of your sins.

Parable of the Evil Tenant Farmers
Matt 21:33-46 // Mark 12:1-12 // Luke 20:9-19

[33]"Now listen to another story. A certain landowner planted a vineyard, built a wall

---

21:19 ***there were only leaves:*** Mark observes that "it was too early in the season for fruit" (see Mark 11:13). It was spring (just before Passover); figs form in the spring but ripen in the fall. • ***immediately the fig tree withered:*** Matthew has apparently compressed the story (cp. 21:18-22; Mark 11:13-14, 20-23). The cursing of the fig tree is a symbolic gesture depicting God's judgment on Israel for rejecting the Messiah (see 3:9; 8:11-12). Like a fig tree that shows promise but no fruit, the Israelites (especially the hypocritical leaders) did not bear the fruit of receiving the Messiah (see 21:33-46).

21:22 Jesus was exhorting the disciples to trust in God and to pray accordingly. He was not offering God's unconditional endorsement of all that they might desire (1 Jn 5:14-15).

21:23–22:46 This section focuses on the Jewish leaders' attack on Jesus' authority. In each case, Jesus' wisdom revealed the leaders' spiritual blindness. These debates also revealed Jesus' status as Messiah and the consequences of rejecting him. Tragically, the leaders grew more resistant with each encounter and plotted to eliminate Jesus (21:23, 46; 22:15-17, 23, 34, 41).

21:23 ***Elders*** (literally *elders of the people*) were family heads from each tribe who were members of the Sanhedrin in Jerusalem (cp. Ezra 5:5; 6:14; 10:8).

21:24 Jesus propounded a riddle, the solution to which answered the leaders' question and forced them into a dilemma that revealed their hearts (21:25-26). Answering by counter-question was typical for such debates.

21:25 ***John's*** ministry, like Jesus' (see 3:1, 5-6), was controversial, especially after John's public denouncement of the sins of Herod Antipas (see 14:4). The leaders did not want to acknowledge that John's ministry was from God, since they had refused to ***believe John*** by repenting of their sins (3:2) and accepting Jesus as the Messiah (John 1:29-34).

21:27 The leaders lacked integrity and courage to confess what they believed about John. So Jesus' refusal to answer their original question was fair.

21:28–22:14 Three parables expose the guilt of those who had rejected the Messiah and forfeited their privilege as God's chosen people. The new people of God are only those who embrace the Messiah.

21:28-32 This parable continues the point about John's significance.

21:29-31 ***"The first":*** Other manuscripts read *"The second."* In still other manuscripts the first son says "Yes" but does nothing, the second son says "No" but then repents and goes, and the answer to Jesus' question is that the second son obeyed his father.

21:29 ***I won't go:*** This response must have offended Jews who were taught to show outward respect for the authority of a father (see 8:21-22).

21:32 ***The right way to live*** is in conformity to God's will (3:15; 5:20; see also Prov 8:20; 12:28).

21:33-46 In this ***story*** Jesus draws on Isa 5:1-7. The people of Israel who rejected God's Messiah forfeited the privilege of being God's people. The Christian community, comprised of both Jews and Gentiles, has now been called to be the people of God (cp. Rom 9:4-8; 11:1-12).

around it, dug a pit for pressing out the
grape juice, and built a lookout tower. Then
he leased the vineyard to tenant farmers and
moved to another country. 34At the time of
the grape harvest, he sent his servants to collect his share of the crop. 35But the farmers
grabbed his servants, beat one, killed one,
and stoned another. 36So the landowner
sent a larger group of his servants to collect
for him, but the results were the same.
37"Finally, the owner sent his son, thinking, 'Surely they will respect my son.'
38"But when the tenant farmers saw his
son coming, they said to one another, 'Here
comes the heir to this estate. Come on, let's
kill him and get the estate for ourselves!'
39So they grabbed him, dragged him out of
the vineyard, and murdered him.
40"When the owner of the vineyard returns," Jesus asked, "what do you think he
will do to those farmers?"
41The religious leaders replied, "He will
put the wicked men to a horrible death
and lease the vineyard to others who will
give him his share of the crop after each
harvest."
42Then Jesus asked them, "Didn't you ever
read this in the Scriptures?

'The stone that the builders rejected
has now become the cornerstone.
This is the LORD's doing,
and it is wonderful to see.'

43I tell you, the Kingdom of God will be
taken away from you and given to a nation
that will produce the proper fruit. 44Any-
one who stumbles over that stone will be
broken to pieces, and it will crush anyone
it falls on."
45When the leading priests and Pharisees
heard this parable, they realized he was telling the story against them—they were the
wicked farmers. 46They wanted to arrest
him, but they were afraid of the crowds,
who considered Jesus to be a prophet.

Parable of the Wedding Feast
Matt 22:1-14; cp. Luke 14:15-24

22 Jesus also told them other parables.
He said, 2"The Kingdom of Heaven
can be illustrated by the story of a king who
prepared a great wedding feast for his son.
3When the banquet was ready, he sent his
servants to notify those who were invited.
But they all refused to come!
4"So he sent other servants to tell them,
'The feast has been prepared. The bulls and
fattened cattle have been killed, and everything is ready. Come to the banquet!' 5But
the guests he had invited ignored them and
went their own way, one to his farm, another
to his business. 6Others seized his messengers and insulted them and killed them.
7"The king was furious, and he sent out
his army to destroy the murderers and burn
their town. 8And he said to his servants,
'The wedding feast is ready, and the guests I
invited aren't worthy of the honor. 9Now go
out to the street corners and invite everyone
you see.' 10So the servants brought in everyone they could find, good and bad alike, and
the banquet hall was filled with guests.

21:35
Matt 23:34, 37
21:41
Matt 8:11-12
Luke 21:24
Acts 13:46
21:42
*Ps 118:22-23
Isa 28:16
Acts 4:11
Eph 2:20
1 Pet 2:6-7
21:44
Isa 8:14-15
Dan 2:34-35, 44-45
21:46
Matt 21:26
22:1-10
//Luke 14:15-24
22:3
Matt 21:34
22:4
Matt 21:36
22:6
Matt 21:35
22:7
Luke 19:27
22:8
Acts 13:46
22:10
Matt 13:47-48

21:34-35 ***sent his servants:*** The prophets had spoken God's word to Israel. The tenant ***farmers*** represented the leaders of Israel, whom Jesus held responsible for the deaths of God's prophets (23:29-37)

21:37 ***Finally:*** God's revelation climaxed in Jesus (see 13:16-17; Heb 1:1-2).

21:40 ***When the owner of the vineyard returns*** refers to the Lord's coming in judgment (see 16:27; 24:1-36).

21:41 The Jewish ***religious leaders*** pronounced their own condemnation.

21:42 The ***cornerstone*** was either the first stone of the foundation or the capstone (as of an arch), the last to be laid. The very ***stone that the builders rejected*** as unworthy of use was, in fact, the most important. Jesus was referring to his own role in the Kingdom of God (21:43) and to the religious leaders' rejection of him. • The quotation is from Ps 118:22-23.

21:43 ***taken away from you:*** Either the privilege of being God's chosen nation no longer belonged to the Jews, or the religious leaders had lost the privilege of being leaders of God's people (see Rom 9–11). • The Christian community is ***a nation that will produce the proper fruit***—that is, a life of trust and obedience that demonstrates the inauguration of the Kingdom (see 3:8; 7:15-20; 12:33; 13:8, 26).

21:44 Though in a short while the Messiah's opponents would gain a brief victory, they would ultimately be ***broken*** and the ***stone*** would ***crush*** them because the cross became the gateway to Jesus' vindication and triumph (see also Dan 2:34-35, 44-45). • This verse is not included in some early manuscripts. Cp. Luke 20:18.

21:45 This explanation fits with Matthew's theme of God's judgment on the Jewish leaders who misled the people of Israel (see 23:13-15).

22:1-14 In this parable, Israel, having repeatedly rejected God's word in the past, rejects the Messiah and is judged as a result. In Israel's place, God raised up the church (16:17-19; 21:43), of which righteousness is also expected (Rom 11:11-24).

22:2 The ***king*** represents God, whose ***son*** is Jesus (Gal 4:4; Heb 1:1-2). • The ***feast*** represents the Kingdom of the Messiah.

22:3-5 ***Those who were invited*** refers to the nation of Israel, who ***ignored*** God's ***servants***, the prophets (see note on 21:33-46).

22:7 Jesus was alluding to the coming destruction of Jerusalem in AD 70 (see 23:37-39; 24:2).

22:8 Those who reject God's invitation ***aren't worthy*** to enter his Kingdom (cp. 3:8; 10:13, 37-38).

22:9 ***everyone you see:*** God's invitation is no longer restricted to the nation of Israel (see 28:16-20; cp. 10:5-6; 15:21-28).

22:10 ***good and bad alike:*** See 13:24-50.

22:12
Matt 20:13; 26:50
22:13
Matt 8:12; 25:30
22:14
2 Pet 1:10
Rev 17:14
[f]*klētos* (2822)
‣ Rom 1:6
22:15-22
//Mark 12:13-17
//Luke 20:20-26
22:17
Matt 17:25
22:18
[g]*hupokritēs* (5273)
‣ Matt 23:13
22:21
Rom 13:7
22:23-33
//Mark 12:18-27
//Luke 20:27-40
22:23
Acts 23:8
1 Cor 15:12

11"But when the king came in to meet the guests, he noticed a man who wasn't wearing the proper clothes for a wedding. 12'Friend,' he asked, 'how is it that you are here without wedding clothes?' But the man had no reply. 13Then the king said to his aides, 'Bind his hands and feet and throw him into the outer darkness, where there will be weeping and gnashing of teeth.'

14"For many are [f]called, but few are chosen."

Taxes for Caesar
Matt 22:15-22 // Mark 12:13-17 // Luke 20:20-26

15Then the Pharisees met together to plot how to trap Jesus into saying something for which he could be arrested. 16They sent some of their disciples, along with the supporters of Herod, to meet with him. "Teacher," they said, "we know how honest you are. You teach the way of God truthfully. You are impartial and don't play favorites. 17Now tell us what you think about this: Is it right to pay taxes to Caesar or not?"

18But Jesus knew their evil motives. "You [g]hypocrites!" he said. "Why are you trying to trap me? 19Here, show me the coin used for the tax." When they handed him a Roman coin, 20he asked, "Whose picture and title are stamped on it?"

21"Caesar's," they replied.

"Well, then," he said, "give to Caesar what belongs to Caesar, and give to God what belongs to God."

22His reply amazed them, and they went away.

Discussion about Life in the Resurrection
Matt 22:23-33 // Mark 12:18-27 // Luke 20:27-40

23That same day Jesus was approached by some Sadducees—religious leaders who say there is no resurrection from the dead.

Jesus, a Source of Stumbling (21:42-46)

Matt 11:5-6; 13:54-58; 15:10-12; 17:27
Lev 19:14
Prov 24:17-18
Isa 3:8; 8:14-15; 10:3-4; 28:12-13; 59:9-10
Jer 13:15-17; 18:15-17; 20:11-13; 31:7-9; 50:31-32
Hos 4:4-7; 5:5-7; 14:8-9
Mal 2:7-9
Mark 6:3
Luke 20:17-19
John 6:60-69
Rom 9:30-33; 11:7-12; 14:12-13, 20-21
1 Cor 1:21-23; 8:9-13; 10:31–11:1
2 Cor 6:3
Gal 5:11
1 Pet 2:5-8
1 Jn 2:10

Jesus continually offended the Jewish leaders and those who followed them (11:5-6). Though he was born in David's line, his mother's reputation was tainted (1:18-25; 13:53-58). Jesus himself was from Nazareth (2:23), a very unprestigious place. His ministry was in Galilee, a backwater distant from official Judaism (4:12-16). His closest associate was the inexplicable John, who baptized people and prophetically castigated the political leaders (11:2-19; 14:3-12). Jesus was evasive in his dialogues (e.g., 13:10-15; 17:24-27; 19:3-10; 21:23-27), he refused to produce signs proving his messianic claims (12:38-42; 16:1-4), and he was accompanied by outcasts of society (9:9-13; 11:16-19). He offended Jewish sensibilities, disregarded Jewish traditions (5:17-20; 9:14-17; 12:1-14; 15:1-20; 21:1-17), and purposefully avoided recognition (8:4; 12:15-21). His revelations were reserved for the unlikely (11:25-27; 13:16-17; 16:13-20), and he often spoke of his own humiliating death (16:21; 17:22-23; 20:18-19; 26:2). Jesus did not come with the flash and spark of someone in need of attention, nor did he make his status and calling glowingly obvious. Instead, he chose the path of humility, privacy, and revelation recognized by faith.

In the end, Jesus was vindicated: He won arguments (15:1-20), exorcized demons (8:28-34), healed wondrously (9:1-8), raised people from the dead (9:18-26), and ultimately rose from the dead himself (28:1-10). His quiet but effective ministry inaugurated God's Kingdom (11:2-6).

22:11 The term ***proper clothes*** corresponds to spiritual fruit that demonstrates real faith (see 7:13-27).

22:13 ***Weeping and gnashing of teeth*** express the intense pain and sorrow that result from condemnation for sin and unbelief (see 8:12; 13:42, 50; 24:51; 25:30). • ***Outer darkness*** is a metaphor for eternal punishment.

22:14 While many people are ***called***—they hear the invitation to the Kingdom—few are actually ***chosen*** by God and respond in faithful obedience to Jesus.

22:15-22 Roman taxation was a controversial issue in first-century Palestine (see also 17:24-27).

22:16 The Pharisees, strict nationalists who resented Roman rule, were normally at odds with the ***supporters of Herod.*** Here, the unlikely alliance arose from a mutual hatred of Jesus.

22:17 ***Is it right . . . or not?*** The question was designed to trap Jesus. If he answered no, he could be arrested for rebellion against Rome. If he answered yes, he could be accused of supporting Roman oppression.

22:18 ***You hypocrites!*** See note on 23:13.

22:19 ***a Roman coin:*** Greek *a denarius.*

22:20 The poll tax had to be paid using the denarius coin, which bore the ***picture and title*** of Caesar. OT prohibitions against images (Exod 20:4; Lev 26:1; Deut 4:15-24) made the use of this coin controversial among Jews (see Josephus, *War* 2.9.2-3). Some Roman procurators apparently produced coins without images for use in Palestine in order not to offend the Jewish conscience.

22:21 Jesus outwitted his opponents by affirming the honor due to ***Caesar,*** while clearly differentiating it from the supreme honor and allegiance due to ***God.*** Loyalty to God does not necessarily entail disloyalty to the governing authorities. Jesus was acknowledging two dominions, Caesar's and God's, the latter having priority (Acts 4:19).

22:23-33 The ***resurrection*** was an important issue of Jesus' day, but the question was raised only to trap Jesus.

22:23 The ***Sadducees*** (see 3:7) described a situation involving *levirate* marriage (see Gen 38:6-11; Deut 25:5-6), which they considered proof that ***resurrection from the dead*** is not possible.

They posed this question: 24“Teacher, Moses said, ‘If a man dies without children, his brother should marry the widow and have a child who will carry on the brother’s name.’ 25Well, suppose there were seven brothers. The oldest one married and then died without children, so his brother married the widow. 26But the second brother also died, and the third brother married her. This continued with all seven of them. 27Last of all, the woman also died. 28So tell us, whose wife will she be in the [h]resurrection? For all seven were married to her.”

29Jesus replied, “Your mistake is that you don’t know the Scriptures, and you don’t know the power of God. 30For when the dead rise, they will neither marry nor be given in marriage. In this respect they will be like the [i]angels in heaven.

31“But now, as to whether there will be a resurrection of the dead—haven’t you ever read about this in the Scriptures? Long after Abraham, Isaac, and Jacob had died, God said, 32‘I am the God of Abraham, the God of Isaac, and the God of Jacob.’ So he is the God of the living, not the dead.”

33When the crowds heard him, they were astounded at his teaching.

The Most Important Commandment
Matt 22:34-40 // Mark 12:28-31; cp. Luke 10:25-28

34But when the Pharisees heard that he had silenced the Sadducees with his reply, they met together to question him again. 35One of them, an expert in religious law, tried to trap him with this question: 36“Teacher, which is the most important commandment in the law of Moses?”

37Jesus replied, “ ‘You must love the LORD your God with all your heart, all your soul, and all your mind.’ 38This is the first and greatest commandment. 39A second is equally important: ‘Love your neighbor as yourself.’ 40The entire law and all the demands of the prophets are based on these two commandments.”

Whose Son Is the Messiah?
Matt 22:41-46 // Mark 12:35-37 // Luke 20:41-44

41Then, surrounded by the Pharisees, Jesus asked them a question: 42“What do you think about the Messiah? Whose son is he?”

They replied, “He is the son of David.”

43Jesus responded, “Then why does David, speaking under the inspiration of the Spirit, call the Messiah ‘my Lord’? For David said,

44 ‘The LORD said to my Lord,
Sit in the place of honor at my right hand
until I humble your enemies beneath
your feet.’

45Since David called the Messiah ‘my Lord,’ how can the Messiah be his son?”

46No one could answer him. And after that, no one dared to ask him any more questions.

Discourse: Jesus Predicts His Return (23:1–25:46)

Jesus Criticizes the Religious Leaders
Matt 23:1-14; cp. Mark 12:38-40 // Luke 20:45-47

23 Then Jesus said to the crowds and to his disciples, 2“The teachers

22:24 *Deut 25:5-6
22:28 [h]*anastasis* (0386) ‣Mark 12:18
22:29 John 20:9
22:30 [i]*angelos* (0032) ‣Matt 25:41
22:32 *Exod 3:6, 15-16 Acts 7:32
22:33 Matt 7:28; 13:54 Mark 11:18 Luke 2:47
22:34-40 //Mark 12:28-34 //Luke 10:25-28
22:35 Luke 10:25
22:37 *Deut 6:5
22:39 *Lev 19:18 Matt 5:43; 19:19 Mark 12:31 Luke 10:27 Rom 13:9 Gal 5:14 Jas 2:8
22:40 Matt 7:12 Luke 10:25-28 Rom 13:10
22:41-46 //Mark 12:35-37 //Luke 20:41-44
22:43 2 Sam 23:2 Acts 2:30 2 Pet 1:20-21
22:44 *Ps 110:1 Acts 2:34-35 Heb 1:13
22:46 Mark 12:34 Luke 20:40
23:1-36 //Mark 12:38-40 //Luke 11:37-52; 20:45-47

22:24 The quotation is from Deut 25:5-6.

22:29 The *power of God* most likely refers to God’s ability to raise the dead.

22:30 ***like the angels in heaven:*** Jesus was not teaching genderlessness (i.e., androgyny) nor disparaging the divine order of marriage and sexuality; rather, he was affirming that people will be transformed into a glorious new existence (see 1 Cor 15:35-49; 2 Cor 5:1-5) in which aspects of the present order, such as marriage, will not be present.

22:31-32 Since God spoke of being ***the God of Abraham*** in the present tense, this proves that Abraham still lives, and thus that there is a resurrection.

22:31 ***read about this in the Scriptures? Long after Abraham, Isaac, and Jacob had died, God said:*** Literally *read about this? God said to you.*

22:32 ***I am the God of Abraham, the God of Isaac, and the God of Jacob:*** Exod 3:6.

22:36 Since many strict Jews saw all commandments as equally binding, a careless response to this question could lead to the accusation of undermining the law of God.

22:37 Jesus answers from the Shema (Deut 6:4-9), one of the core statements of God’s covenant with Israel. (The first Hebrew word of Deut 6:4-9 is *shema‘*, “hear.”) • ***You must love the LORD your God with all your heart, all your soul, and all your mind:*** Deut 6:5.

22:39 ***Love your neighbor as yourself:*** Lev 19:18; see also Rom 13:9; Gal 5:6, 14; Jas 2:8.

22:40 ***are based on:*** Jesus’ statement affirmed the unity and coherence of God’s will, as recorded in Scripture.

22:41-46 Having successfully defended himself against his opponents’ traps (21:23–22:40), Jesus questioned them as to how the Messiah can be called both the son of David and, at the same time, the Lord of David (Ps 110:1).

22:42 ***the son of David:*** See note on 9:27; see also 2 Sam 7:12-14; Ps 2:7-9; 110; Isa 11:1, 10; Jer 23:5-6.

22:44 The quotation is from Ps 110:1, which is frequently cited by NT authors to describe Jesus (see Acts 2:34-35; 1 Cor 15:25; Heb 1:13; 2:8; 10:12-13; Rev 3:21).

22:45 ***how can the Messiah be his son?*** The answer is that Jesus is more than the son of David: He is the Son of God (14:33).

22:46 ***No one could answer him*** because they had never thought the Messiah would be God as a human being in the flesh (see John 1:1-14).

23:1–25:46 This final, extended discourse (see note on 5:1–7:29) centers on judgment for rejecting the Messiah.

23:1 The religious leaders had sought a reason to accuse Jesus publicly

23:2
Ezra 7:6, 25
Neh 8:1-4
23:4
Luke 11:46
Acts 15:20
Gal 6:13
23:5
Num 15:37-40
Deut 6:6-8
Matt 6:1-2
23:6
Luke 14:7
23:7
[j]*rhabbi* (4461)
‣ Matt 26:49
23:11
Matt 20:26-27
Mark 9:35; 10:43-45
Luke 9:48; 22:26
23:12
Prov 29:23
Ezek 21:26
Luke 14:11; 18:14
23:13
Luke 11:52
[k]*hupokritēs* (5273)
‣ Matt 24:51

of religious law and the Pharisees are the
official interpreters of the law of Moses.
3 So practice and obey whatever they tell
you, but don't follow their example. For they
don't practice what they teach. 4 They crush
people with unbearable religious demands
and never lift a finger to ease the burden.
5 "Everything they do is for show. On their
arms they wear extra wide prayer boxes
with Scripture verses inside, and they wear
robes with extra long tassels. 6 And they love
to sit at the head table at banquets and in
the seats of honor in the synagogues. 7 They
love to receive respectful greetings as they
walk in the marketplaces, and to be called
[j]'Rabbi.'
8 "Don't let anyone call you 'Rabbi,' for
you have only one teacher, and all of you are
equal as brothers and sisters. 9 And don't address anyone here on earth as 'Father,' for
only God in heaven is your spiritual Father.
10 And don't let anyone call you 'Teacher,'
for you have only one teacher, the Messiah.
11 The greatest among you must be a servant. 12 But those who exalt themselves will
be humbled, and those who humble themselves will be exalted.
13 "What sorrow awaits you teachers of religious law and you Pharisees. [k]Hypocrites!
For you shut the door of the Kingdom of
Heaven in people's faces. You won't go in
yourselves, and you don't let others enter
either.
15 "What sorrow awaits you teachers of religious law and you Pharisees. Hypocrites!
For you cross land and sea to make one
convert, and then you turn that person into
twice the child of hell you yourselves are!

(21:23–22:46), but found none. Jesus now turned ***to the crowds and to his disciples*** to openly indict the religious leaders for their numerous failures to conform to God's righteous standards.

23:2 ***the Pharisees are the official interpreters of the law of Moses:*** Literally *the Pharisees sit in the seat of Moses.* They transmitted the oral traditions that were associated with the law and thought to be from Moses, and they judged religious and social matters on the basis of these traditions (see 15:2).

23:3 ***practice and obey:*** This was not a blanket endorsement of all that the Pharisees ***teach*** (see 15:1-20; 16:5-12; 23:13-39). It might refer only to what was in accord with the law of Moses, or it might be bitter irony or sarcasm. Jesus might also have been counseling conformity to the Pharisees' teachings to avoid giving offense (17:24-27).

23:4 ***unbearable religious demands:*** There were 613 legal prohibitions and commands, according to the rabbis (see 11:28-30; Acts 15:10, 28). • ***never lift a finger:*** The religious leaders were unwilling to consider relaxing traditional legal statutes.

23:5 ***On their arms . . . extra long tassels*** (literally *They enlarge their phylacteries and lengthen their tassels*): Pious Jews wore, on the head and upper left arm, a small pouch or box (phylactery) containing written copies of important OT commands (see Deut 6:6-9; 11:18-19). • Wearing ***tassels*** was another custom associated with piety (see 9:20; see also Num 15:38-41). Lengthening the tassels called attention to their wearer's pious practices.

23:6 The ***seats of honor in the synagogues*** were near the scrolls of the Torah and facing the congregation (they were "on the platform").

23:7 ***Rabbi,*** from Aramaic, means "master" or "teacher." It was a title of authority and respect.

23:8-12 Jesus does not prohibit the use of titles (especially for one's own father), but rather the assumption of undue honor by those who transmit knowledge about God. The community of Jesus is a brotherhood of equals, each of whom knows God (see 12:46-50; 18:15-20). The terms ***Rabbi, Father,*** and ***Teacher*** are roughly equivalent.

23:8 ***Rabbi:*** These men functioned in Judaism as mediators for dispensing knowledge about God (see 23:7). The new covenant, by contrast, has ***only one teacher,*** Jesus himself as Messiah (see Jer 31:31-34). • ***brothers and sisters:*** Literally *brothers.*

23:9 Writings from later Judaism provide ample evidence of revering the teachers by calling them ***Father*** (for example, see *Mishnah Eduyyoth* 1:4). • ***God . . . is your spiritual Father:*** See 6:9; Mal 2:10; cp. 1 Cor 4:15.

23:10 ***Teacher:*** This title denotes the function and office of leading others into knowledge about God. Jesus, not the scribes and Pharisees, is the ***teacher*** of God's will (5:17).

23:11-12 Jesus' disciples should lead by serving, in stark contrast to Israel's religious leaders (who are described in 23:5-7).

23:13-36 Matthew collected seven statements of ***what sorrow awaits you*** (literally *woe to you*), drawing upon similar OT listings (Isa 5:8-23; Hab 2:6-20) and arranged them to climax in the murder of the prophets.

23:13 ***What sorrow awaits you:*** A stark warning of judgment from God. • ***Hypocrites!*** In English, hypocrisy describes a contradiction between reality and appearance. But in biblical usage, hypocrisy is misperceiving God's will, leading people astray, and thus incurring God's judgment. Coupled with this is often a desire for prestige and power (23:5-12), abuse of teaching authority, false teachings on doctrine or practice (23:13-22), and preoccupation with ethical minutiae (23:23-28). An accurate English term for this combination of factors is *heresy.* The Pharisees and teachers of religious law displayed all of these characteristics. As the Christian church began to grow, these characteristics continued to appear (e.g., 1 Tim 4:1-3; 2 Pet 2:1-22), so God's children always need to guard against them (Jas 4:7-10; 1 Pet 2:1-3). • ***shut the door of the Kingdom:*** By their false teaching and opposition to Jesus (see 9:32-34; 12:22-37; 15:12-14; 21:15; John 9:13-34), the ***teachers of religious law*** and ***Pharisees*** prevented others from hearing and believing the truth about the Messiah. • Some manuscripts add verse 14, *What sorrow awaits you teachers of religious law and you Pharisees. Hypocrites! You shamelessly cheat widows out of their property and then pretend to be pious by making long prayers in public. Because of this, you will be severely punished.* Cp. Mark 12:40; Luke 20:47.

23:15 A ***convert*** (proselyte) made a full conversion to Judaism, performing such observances as baptism, sacrifice, and circumcision (see Acts 13:43). A convert was thus distinct from a "God-fearer," who adopted certain Jewish beliefs, most notably monotheism, without fully converting to Judaism (see Luke 7:4-5; Acts 10:2). It is likely that ***to make one convert*** means to persuade God-fearers to become full converts to Judaism by undergoing circumcision (cp. Gal 2:3, 14; 5:2-12; 6:12-13). • ***of hell:*** Greek *of Gehenna;* also in 23:33. See note on 5:29.

16"Blind guides! What sorrow awaits you!
For you say that it means nothing to swear
'by God's Temple,' but that it is binding to
swear 'by the gold in the Temple.' 17Blind
fools! Which is more important—the gold
or the Temple that makes the gold sacred?
18And you say that to swear 'by the altar' is
not binding, but to swear 'by the gifts on the
altar' is binding. 19How blind! For which is
more important—the gift on the altar or the
altar that makes the gift sacred? 20When
you swear 'by the altar,' you are swearing by
it and by everything on it. 21And when you
swear 'by the Temple,' you are swearing by
it and by God, who lives in it. 22And when
you swear 'by heaven,' you are swearing by
the throne of God and by God, who sits on
the throne.

23"What sorrow awaits you teachers of religious law and you Pharisees. Hypocrites!
For you are careful to tithe even the tiniest
income from your herb gardens, but you
ignore the more important aspects of the
[a]law—justice, [b]mercy, and faith. You should
tithe, yes, but do not neglect the more important things. 24Blind guides! You strain
your water so you won't accidentally swallow a gnat, but you swallow a camel!

25"What sorrow awaits you teachers of religious law and you Pharisees. Hypocrites!
For you are so careful to clean the outside
of the cup and the dish, but inside you are
filthy—full of greed and self-indulgence!
26You blind Pharisee! First wash the inside
of the cup and the dish, and then the outside will become clean, too.

27"What sorrow awaits you teachers of religious law and you Pharisees. Hypocrites!
For you are like whitewashed tombs—beautiful on the outside but filled on the inside
with dead people's bones and all sorts of impurity. 28Outwardly you look like righteous
people, but inwardly your hearts are filled
with hypocrisy and lawlessness.

29"What sorrow awaits you teachers of religious law and you Pharisees. Hypocrites!
For you build tombs for the prophets your
ancestors killed, and you decorate the monuments of the godly people your ancestors
destroyed. 30Then you say, 'If we had lived
in the days of our ancestors, we would never
have joined them in killing the prophets.'

31"But in saying that, you testify against
yourselves that you are indeed the descendants of those who murdered the prophets.
32Go ahead and finish what your ancestors
started. 33Snakes! Sons of vipers! How will
you escape the judgment of [c]hell?

34"Therefore, I am sending you prophets
and wise men and teachers of religious law.
But you will kill some by crucifixion, and
you will flog others with whips in your synagogues, chasing them from city to city. 35As
a result, you will be held responsible for the
murder of all godly people of all time—from
the murder of righteous Abel to the murder
of Zechariah son of Berekiah, whom you
killed in the Temple between the sanctuary
and the altar. 36I tell you the truth, this judgment will fall on this very generation.

Jesus Grieves over Jerusalem
Matt 23:37-39 // Luke 13:34-35

37"O Jerusalem, Jerusalem, the city that kills
the prophets and stones God's messengers!
How often I have wanted to gather your children together as a hen protects her chicks
beneath her wings, but you wouldn't let me.

23:16 Isa 9:16; Matt 5:33-35; 15:14; Rom 2:19
23:19 Exod 29:37
23:21 1 Kgs 8:13; Ps 26:8
23:22 Ps 11:4; Isa 66:1; Matt 5:34; Acts 7:49
23:23 Lev 27:30; Hos 6:6; Mic 6:8; Zech 7:9; Luke 11:42
[a]*nomos* (3551) ‣Luke 16:17
[b]*eleos* (1656) ‣Luke 1:50
23:24 Matt 23:16
23:25 Mark 7:4
23:27 Luke 11:44; Acts 23:3
23:28 Luke 16:15
23:31 Luke 11:50-51; Acts 7:52
23:33 Matt 3:7; 12:34; Luke 3:7
[c]*geenna* (1067) ‣Mark 9:43
23:34 Matt 10:23; Acts 7:52; 22:19; 2 Cor 11:23-25; 1 Thes 2:15
23:35 Gen 4:8; 2 Chr 24:20-21; Zech 1:1; Heb 11:4
23:37-39 //Luke 13:34-35
23:38 1 Kgs 9:7-8; Jer 12:7; 22:5; Ezek 10:4, 18-19

23:16-22 The religious leaders declared certain oaths less binding in order to commit fraud. Jesus calls for honest fulfillment of commitments (see 5:33-37).

23:23-24 ***tithe even the tiniest income from your herb gardens*** (literally *tithe the mint, the dill, and the cumin*): The ***teachers of religious law*** and ***Pharisees*** thought that meticulous tithing demonstrated their zeal for the law. Without denying the validity of the ***tithe,*** Jesus revealed how they had utterly failed to attend to the ***more important aspects of the law*** (Isa 1:16-17; Jer 22:3; Hos 6:6; Mic 6:8; Zech 7:9).

23:24 ***gnat . . . camel:*** These words form a pun in Aramaic (*qalma . . . gamla*), the language Jesus probably spoke. See Lev 11:4, 23, where gnats and camels are both forbidden as food.

23:26 Internal purity will result in external righteousness, but the reverse is not true (6:19-34; 12:33-37; 15:15-20). • Some manuscripts do not include ***and the dish.***

23:27-28 It was a Jewish custom to coat limestone ***tombs*** (perhaps funerary urns or ossuaries) with a mixture of marble and lime to fill their porous surfaces, giving them a more pleasing appearance and helping visitors to Jerusalem to notice the graves and avoid touching them so as not to contaminate themselves. Jesus is not criticizing the adorning of tombs; rather, he points to the similarity between these ***whitewashed tombs*** and the ***teachers of religious law*** and ***Pharisees.*** Both may have looked good on the outside, but both were contaminated and impure within.

23:29 By building and decorating the ***tombs for the prophets,*** the ***teachers of religious law*** and ***Pharisees*** showed outward solidarity with the prophets, while inwardly they were of the same sinful character as their ***ancestors*** who had murdered the prophets.

23:32 ***finish what your ancestors started:*** By killing God's Messiah, they would bring to completion Israel's history of killing God's messengers (see 1 Thes 2:14-16).

23:35 The span from ***Abel*** (Gen 4:8-11) to ***Zechariah*** (2 Chr 24:15-22) follows the order of the Hebrew OT, in which 2 Chr is the last book. The implication is that this generation will be guilty of every murder of the righteous in the OT (cp. 27:25).

23:37 Despite the severe judgment Jesus had just leveled against Israel (23:29-36), he truly longed for them to repent and receive God's grace. • ***as a hen:*** An image of protective care (see

23:39
*Ps 118:26
Matt 21:9
Mark 11:10
Luke 19:38
24:1-35
//Mark 13:1-31
//Luke 21:5-36
24:2
Luke 19:44
24:3
Matt 13:39; 28:20
Luke 17:30
[d]*parousia* (3952)
‣ Matt 24:37
24:4
Mark 13:5
24:5
Matt 24:11, 23-24
John 5:43
1 Jn 2:18
24:6
Dan 2:28-29
24:7
Isa 19:2
24:9-14
Matt 10:17-22
24:9
John 16:2
24:11
Matt 24:5, 24
24:14
Matt 28:19
Rev 3:10; 14:6
24:15
Dan 9:27; 11:31; 12:11

38And now, look, your house is abandoned
and desolate. 39For I tell you this, you will
never see me again until you say, 'Blessings
on the one who comes in the name of the
LORD!'"

Jesus Predicts Future Events

Matt 24:1-8 // Mark 13:1-8 // Luke 21:5-11
Matt 24:9-14 // Mark 13:9-13 // Luke 21:12-19; cp. Matt 10:16-25
Matt 24:15-22 // Mark 13:14-20 // Luke 21:20-24

24 As Jesus was leaving the Temple
grounds, his disciples pointed out to
him the various Temple buildings. 2But he
responded, "Do you see all these buildings?
I tell you the truth, they will be completely
demolished. Not one stone will be left on
top of another!"
3Later, Jesus sat on the Mount of Olives.
His disciples came to him privately and said,
"Tell us, when will all this happen? What
sign will signal your [d]return and the end of
the world?"
4Jesus told them, "Don't let anyone mislead you, 5for many will come in my name,
claiming, 'I am the Messiah.' They will
deceive many. 6And you will hear of wars
and threats of wars, but don't panic. Yes,
these things must take place, but the end
won't follow immediately. 7Nation will go
to war against nation, and kingdom against
kingdom. There will be famines and earthquakes in many parts of the world. 8But all
this is only the first of the birth pains, with
more to come.
9"Then you will be arrested, persecuted,
and killed. You will be hated all over the
world because you are my followers. 10And
many will turn away from me and betray
and hate each other. 11And many false
prophets will appear and will deceive
many people. 12Sin will be rampant everywhere, and the love of many will grow cold.
13But the one who endures to the end will
be saved. 14And the Good News about the
Kingdom will be preached throughout the
whole world, so that all nations will hear it;
and then the end will come.
15"The day is coming when you will see
what Daniel the prophet spoke about—the
sacrilegious object that causes desecration

---

also Deut 32:11; Ruth 2:12; Ps 17:8; 36:7; 57:1; 61:4; 91:4).

23:38 ***your house is abandoned and desolate:*** God would withdraw his presence from the Temple (Ezek 10:18-19; 11:22-23; cp. Matt 1:23), and both the Temple and Jerusalem would be destroyed. • Some manuscripts do not include *and desolate.*

23:39 ***Blessings on the one who comes in the name of the LORD:*** Ps 118:26. This is possibly the prediction of an end-time conversion of the nation of Israel to the Messiah (see also Rom 11:12-32).

24:1-31 Some believe ch 24 pertains to the return of Christ at the end of history. Others view the chapter as a prediction of the events of AD 70, when Jerusalem and the Temple were destroyed by the Romans. Others believe it refers to both. See also notes on Mark 13.

24:1 The architecture of *the Temple* was a source of pride among Jews—see note on Mark 13:1.

24:2 ***Not one stone:*** The destruction of Jerusalem and the Temple was a sign of God's judgment (see 1 Kgs 9:7-9; Jer 7:8-15; 9:10-12; 26:6, 18; Mic 3:12; see also Isa 64:11; Luke 19:44; Acts 6:14).

24:3 The Greek term translated *return* is *parousia,* which can mean *coming* or *appearing.* • ***end of the world*** (or *end of the age*): This expression refers to the climax and end of an epoch in salvation history (see 13:39-40, 49; also Heb 9:26). Jesus' second coming will bring normal history to a close with decisive judgment. The disciples assumed that the destruction of the Temple and the end of history were closely connected.

24:4-8 Jesus warned the disciples not to be deceived by impostors or overwhelmed by catastrophes in hope of a premature end to history. Time must run its predestined course. The signs predicted in 24:4-8 are not necessarily at the end; rather, they are signs prior to the end.

24:5 ***claiming, 'I am the Messiah':*** A series of false prophets and miracle workers evoked messianic images and persuaded the masses to follow them in hope of deliverance during the period between AD 30 and 70 (Josephus, *Antiquities* 18.4.1; 20.5.1; 20.8.6; *War* 6.5.2). The earliest recorded instance of an outright claim to be the Messiah was Bar Kochba's claim in AD 132. It is not clear whether Jesus is referring only to impostors in the period prior to the destruction of the Temple or to false messiahs throughout the church age or perhaps during a future tribulation.

24:6 ***these things must take place:*** Tumultuous times are part of God's sovereign plan as he brings history to a close (see 24:7, 29-30; 2 Thes 2:8-12). • ***The end*** could refer to the close of an epoch (such as at AD 70) or the end of human history as we now know it (cp. 24:13-14; see also 10:22; 13:39-40, 49).

24:8 ***first of the birth pains:*** Intense anguish is expected just prior to Jesus' second coming (see also 24:29-31; Isa 13:8; 26:17; Jer 4:31; 6:24; Mic 4:9-10).

24:9 ***hated*** (see Acts 28:22): At the end of the first century, the Roman historian Tacitus described Christians as "the hated ones of mankind" (Tacitus, *Annales* 15.44). The affliction of the righteous sometimes has the purpose of inciting repentance and obedience (see Exod 4:31; Deut 4:30; Judg 10:6-16; Ps 34:19; 37:39; 50:15). • ***because you are my followers:*** Literally *on account of my name.*

24:10 Persecution will lead some to abandon loyalty to Jesus (10:25; 13:21; 16:24-28; 26:33).

24:12 ***the love of many will grow cold*** (see Rev 2:4): If the love within the community of Jesus' disciples diminishes to the point of extinction, then the community ceases to be what God has designed it to be.

24:13 The one who *endures* maintains faithful allegiance to Jesus despite persecution. Here, *the end* may refer to the end of one's own life, the judgment on Israel in AD 70, or the end of history.

24:14 ***throughout the whole world:*** This anticipates the expansive Gentile mission (see 21:43; 28:16-20). There will be a delay prior to *the end,* however short or long, during which the Good News will spread significantly throughout the nations. • ***all nations:*** Or *all peoples.* • ***The end*** will be signaled by a "sacrilegious object" (24:15), furious persecution (24:16-28), and finally the sign of the Son of Man (24:29-31).

24:15 ***Daniel . . . spoke about*** a profaning or desolating of the Temple (see

standing in the Holy Place.” (Reader, pay attention!) 16“Then those in Judea must flee to the hills. 17A person out on the deck of a roof must not go down into the house to pack. 18A person out in the field must not return even to get a coat. 19How terrible it will be for pregnant women and for nursing mothers in those days. 20And pray that your flight will not be in winter or on the Sabbath. 21For there will be greater anguish than at any time since the world began. And it will never be so great again. 22In fact, unless that time of calamity is shortened, not a single person will survive. But it will be shortened for the sake of God’s chosen ones.

False Messiahs

Matt 24:23-28 // Mark 13:21-23 // Luke 17:23-24, 37b

23“Then if anyone tells you, ‘Look, here is the Messiah,’ or ‘There he is,’ don’t believe it. 24For [e]false messiahs and false prophets will rise up and perform great signs and wonders so as to deceive, if possible, even God’s chosen ones. 25See, I have warned you about this ahead of time.

26“So if someone tells you, ‘Look, the Messiah is out in the desert,’ don’t bother to go and look. Or, ‘Look, he is hiding here,’ don’t believe it! 27For as the lightning flashes in the east and shines to the west, so it will be when the Son of Man comes. 28Just as the gathering of vultures shows there is a carcass nearby, so these signs indicate that the end is near.

The Coming of the Son of Man

Matt 24:29-36 // Mark 13:24-32 // Luke 21:25-33

29“Immediately after the anguish of those days,

the sun will be darkened,
  the moon will give no light,
the stars will fall from the sky,
  and the powers in the heavens will be
    shaken.

30And then at last, the [f]sign that the Son of Man is coming will appear in the heavens, and there will be deep mourning among all the peoples of the earth. And they will see the Son of Man coming on the clouds

24:17 Luke 17:31
24:21 Dan 12:1; Joel 2:2; Rev 3:10; 7:14
24:23-24 Luke 17:21-23; 2 Thes 2:9-10; 1 Jn 4:1-3; Rev 13:13-14
24:24 [e]*pseudochristos* (5580) ‣Mark 13:22
24:26-27 Luke 17:23-24
24:28 Luke 17:37; Rev 19:17
24:29 Isa 13:10; 34:4; Ezek 32:7; Joel 2:10, 31; 3:15; Rev 6:12-13
24:30 *Dan 7:13; Zech 12:10-14; Rev 1:7; [f]*sēmeion* (4592) ‣Mark 16:17

Dan 8:13; 9:27; 11:31; 12:11). • ***the sacrilegious object that causes desecration*** (literally *the abomination of desolation;* see Dan 9:27; 11:31; 12:11): Attempts to identify a specific fulfillment include: (1) a false priest assuming the priesthood (see Josephus, *War* 4.3.6-10); (2) the presence of unlawful images of God or humans, or certain humans themselves (such as Antiochus Epiphanes, Caligula, Vespasian, or Titus) who were not to be allowed within the Temple precincts (see Josephus, *War* 4.4.1–4.7.1); (3) the presence of the antichrist in the Temple (cp. *1 Maccabees* 1:54-64; *2 Maccabees* 8:17). • ***Reader, pay attention!*** This covert statement reflects a special bond between writer and reader, based on a shared understanding that the events being described fulfill the prophecies of Dan 9, 11, and 12.

24:20 Josephus records the ***winter*** swelling of the Jordan River, which made it more difficult to cross (see Josephus, *War* 4.7.5). Muddy roads also made travel difficult in winter. • Normally Jews did not travel ***on the Sabbath*** in order to rest as God had commanded (see Gen 2:1-3; Exod 20:8-11; 23:12; 31:12-17; Lev 23:3; Deut 5:12-15; Jer 17:19-27).

24:21 ***greater anguish:*** Similar language is found in Neh 9:37; Jer 11:16; Dan 12:1; Joel 2:1-17. The blatant savagery of the times has been documented by Josephus (see *War* 5.10.2-3).

24:22 ***God’s chosen ones*** endure (24:13) and remain faithful (24:37–25:46; see Isa 65:8-9; Rom 11:7).

24:24 ***false messiahs and false prophets*** (see 7:15; 24:4-8; also Acts 13:6; 2 Pet 2:1; 1 Jn 2:18; 4:1): Revelation describes a particular false prophet (see Rev 16:13). • ***signs and wonders:*** Not all miracles are proof of God’s approval (see Deut 13:1-4; Rev 13:13).

24:26-28 These verses are an expansion of 24:23. The place and manner of the Messiah’s appearing was disputed among Jews. The Messiah’s glorious appearance and vindication will be unmistakable.

24:26 Some Jewish prophets persuaded the masses to follow them into the ***desert*** to see signs of deliverance (cp. 24:4-8). • ***hiding here:*** This is perhaps a reference to secretive sects, such as those at Qumran, or to the small fellowship groups associated with the Pharisees.

24:27-28 ***Lightning*** may be an allusion to the astrological phenomena attending the Messiah’s coming (see 24:29-31; 1 Thes 4:13-18). It is not the suddenness of ***lightning*** that is in view but rather the magnitude of its visibility. Very possibly, Jesus gave these sayings to ward off premature excitement regarding ***the end*** (1 Thes 4:13–5:10; 2 Thes 2:1-12).

24:27 ***Son of Man*** is a title Jesus used for himself.

24:28 ***Just as . . . is near:*** Literally *Wherever the carcass is, the vultures gather.*

24:29-31 These sayings form the climax of the discourse and answer the second of the disciples’ initial questions (see 24:3). Some take 24:29-31 to refer to God’s judgment on the Jewish people in AD 70, using apocalyptic images and metaphors to describe it. Others see a reference to the second coming of Christ at the end of history.

24:29 ***the sun will be darkened . . . will be shaken:*** See Isa 13:10; 34:4; Joel 2:10. This phenomenon can be taken literally, as befitting the climactic self-disclosure of God’s Son, or metaphorically, as for a cosmically significant event (see Acts 2:17-21; Heb 12:26-27; 2 Pet 3:10; Rev 6:12-13). Similar apocalyptic language is used frequently in the OT for describing political disasters and the collapse of a government as cosmic judgments from God (e.g., Isa 13:9-16; Ezek 32:1-10; Joel 2:1-17; Amos 8:7-10).

24:30 ***the sign that the Son of Man is coming*** (literally *the sign of the Son of Man*): The ***sign*** is probably the ***Son of Man*** himself (see 12:38-42; 16:4). His ***coming*** expresses his vindication (see 26:64) and will bring ***deep mourning*** to those who experience God’s judgment. • ***All the peoples of the earth*** could be translated *all the tribes of the land.* The term used here is not the usual Greek term for Gentile nations (*ethnoi*), but a term used frequently of the tribes (*phulai*) of Israel (*the land*), suggesting that a national disaster in Israel might be in view (see 21:43; Zech 12:10-14). • ***the Son of Man coming on the clouds:*** See Dan 7:13. Many believe that this means a descent of the Son of Man from God’s presence to reside on earth

24:31
1 Cor 15:52
1 Thes 4:16
Rev 8:2; 11:15

24:33
Jas 5:9

24:34
Matt 16:28

24:35
Matt 5:18
Luke 16:17

24:36
Acts 1:7
1 Thes 5:1-2

24:37-39
Gen 6:9–7:24
//Luke 17:26-27

24:37
[g]*parousia* (3952)
‣1 Cor 15:23

24:40-41
Luke 17:34-35

24:42
Matt 25:13
Luke 12:40
1 Thes 5:6
Rev 3:3; 16:15

24:45-51
//Luke 12:41-48

24:51
Matt 8:12; 25:30
[h]*hupokritēs* (5273)
‣Mark 7:6

25:1
Luke 12:35-38

of heaven with power and great glory.
31 And he will send out his angels with the
mighty blast of a trumpet, and they will
gather his chosen ones from all over the
world—from the farthest ends of the earth
and heaven.

32 "Now learn a lesson from the fig tree.
When its branches bud and its leaves begin
to sprout, you know that summer is near.
33 In the same way, when you see all these
things, you can know his return is very near,
right at the door. 34 I tell you the truth, this
generation will not pass from the scene
until all these things take place. 35 Heaven
and earth will disappear, but my words will
never disappear.

36 "However, no one knows the day or hour
when these things will happen, not even the
angels in heaven or the Son himself. Only
the Father knows.

Jesus' Return Will Be Sudden
Matt 24:37-41; cp. Luke 17:26-27, 34-35

37 "When the Son of Man [g]returns, it will
be like it was in Noah's day. 38 In those days
before the flood, the people were enjoying
banquets and parties and weddings right
up to the time Noah entered his boat. 39 People didn't realize what was going to happen
until the flood came and swept them all
away. That is the way it will be when the Son
of Man comes.

40 "Two men will be working together in
the field; one will be taken, the other left.
41 Two women will be grinding flour at the
mill; one will be taken, the other left.

Be Ready for the Lord's Coming
Matt 24:42-51 // Luke 12:39-48

42 "So you, too, must keep watch! For you
don't know what day your Lord is coming.
43 Understand this: If a homeowner knew
exactly when a burglar was coming, he
would keep watch and not permit his house
to be broken into. 44 You also must be ready
all the time, for the Son of Man will come
when least expected.

45 "A faithful, sensible servant is one to
whom the master can give the responsibility
of managing his other household servants
and feeding them. 46 If the master returns
and finds that the servant has done a good
job, there will be a reward. 47 I tell you the
truth, the master will put that servant in
charge of all he owns. 48 But what if the servant is evil and thinks, 'My master won't be
back for a while,' 49 and he begins beating
the other servants, partying, and getting
drunk? 50 The master will return unannounced and unexpected, 51 and he will cut
the servant to pieces and assign him a place
with the [h]hypocrites. In that place there will
be weeping and gnashing of teeth.

Parable of the Ten Bridesmaids

25 "Then the Kingdom of Heaven
will be like ten bridesmaids who
took their lamps and went to meet the

as Judge and Deliverer—i.e., the second coming of Christ. Others have argued that this describes the Son of Man coming in judgment, but not necessarily the second coming of Christ (see 10:23; 16:27; 19:28; 25:31; 26:64; 28:18).

24:31 Many believe that the rapture of God's people through ***angels*** (13:41; 16:27; 25:31) is predicted here. Others believe that ***angels*** here are human messengers (11:10; Luke 7:24; 9:52; Jas 2:25) and that Jesus is describing the expansion of the Good News among Gentiles (see 21:33-46; 22:1-14; Deut 30:1-10; Isa 27:13; Zech 2:6-13). • ***from all over the world:*** Literally *from the four winds.*

24:33 ***all these things:*** This expression, used first at 23:36 ("this judgment"), refers to the events associated with the destruction of the Temple (see 24:2, 8). • ***his return*** (literally *he* or *it*): It could mean Jesus' return (see Jas 5:9; Rev 3:20), the destruction of the Temple, or the end of history (see Luke 21:31).

24:34 ***this generation:*** Or *this age,* or *this nation.* In Matthew, generation is used particularly for contemporary, unbelieving Jews, especially focusing on the leaders who have led people away from the Messiah (11:16; 12:39, 41-42, 45; 16:4; 23:36).

24:35 Jesus' words are as sure as God's own (see 5:18; Isa 40:8; 55:11; 59:21).

24:36 ***The day*** is the day of judgment. • ***or the Son:*** Jesus' limited knowledge is suggested also in Acts 1:7. Because the day is unknown, Jesus' hearers should be vigilant and faithful (see 24:37–25:46). This statement ought to deter those who attempt to calculate the date of our Lord's return. • Some manuscripts do not include ***or the Son himself.***

24:37–25:46 Jesus now applied his predictions (24:1-36) to his followers so they will be faithful and prepared for his second coming.

24:37-41 Jesus' second coming, like the flood (Gen 7), will come upon people unawares. The only adequate preparation is a life of consistent vigilance and obedience (cp. Luke 17:26-27, 34-35).

24:37 ***When the Son of Man returns:*** Jesus' second coming (see 24:3; cp. Luke 17:26). • ***in Noah's day*** (see Gen 6:9-22; 2 Pet 2:5; 3:5-6): The comparison here does not concern the magnitude of sins, but a lack of discernment about what God is doing, accompanied by a preoccupation with life's festivities (6:19-34).

24:40-41 The term ***taken*** most likely means taken in judgment, at AD 70 or at the end of history; ***left*** would then mean remaining to enter the new era of either the church (see 21:43; 22:1-14) or the Millennium.

24:42 To ***keep watch*** is to maintain active, energetic, single-minded obedience to the Lord (see 25:13; 26:38-41).

24:45-51 This parable and the three that follow (25:1-13, 14-30, 31-46) each dramatize the need for faithful obedience during the delay of Jesus' second coming.

24:45 ***servant:*** It is possible that Jesus' listeners would have thought of God's special servants, the prophets and lawgivers; however, Jesus so frequently used *servant* figuratively that it is more likely a description of every disciple's responsibility (see 10:24-25; 13:27-28; 18:23-35; 20:26).

25:1-13 This parable reinforces the need for individuals to be watchful

bridegroom. 2 Five of them were foolish, and five were wise. 3 The five who were foolish didn't take enough olive oil for their lamps, 4 but the other five were wise enough to take along extra oil. 5 When the bridegroom was delayed, they all became drowsy and fell asleep.

6 "At midnight they were roused by the shout, 'Look, the bridegroom is coming! Come out and meet him!'

7 "All the bridesmaids got up and prepared their lamps. 8 Then the five foolish ones asked the others, 'Please give us some of your oil because our lamps are going out.'

9 "But the others replied, 'We don't have enough for all of us. Go to a shop and buy some for yourselves.'

10 "But while they were gone to buy oil, the bridegroom came. Then those who were ready went in with him to the marriage feast, and the door was locked. 11 Later, when the other five bridesmaids returned, they stood outside, calling, 'Lord! Lord! Open the door for us!'

12 "But he called back, 'Believe me, I don't know you!'

13 "So you, too, must keep watch! For you do not know the day or hour of my return.

Parable of the Three Servants

Matt 25:14-30 // Luke 19:11-27

14 "Again, the Kingdom of Heaven can be illustrated by the story of a man going on a long trip. He called together his servants and entrusted his money to them while he was gone. 15 He gave five bags of silver to one, two bags of silver to another, and one bag of silver to the last—dividing it in proportion to their abilities. He then left on his trip.

16 "The servant who received the five bags of silver began to invest the money and earned five more. 17 The servant with two bags of silver also went to work and earned two more. 18 But the servant who received the one bag of silver dug a hole in the ground and hid the master's money.

19 "After a long time their master returned from his trip and called them to give an account of how they had used his money. 20 The servant to whom he had entrusted the five bags of silver came forward with five more and said, 'Master, you gave me five bags of silver to invest, and I have earned five more.'

21 "The master was full of praise. 'Well done, my good and faithful servant. You have been faithful in handling this small amount, so now I will give you many more responsibilities. Let's celebrate together!'

22 "The servant who had received the two bags of silver came forward and said, 'Master, you gave me two bags of silver to invest, and I have earned two more.'

23 "The master said, 'Well done, my good and faithful servant. You have been faithful in handling this small amount, so now I will give you many more responsibilities. Let's celebrate together!'

24 "Then the servant with the one bag of silver came and said, 'Master, I knew you were a harsh man, harvesting crops you didn't plant and gathering crops you didn't cultivate. 25 I was afraid I would lose your money, so I hid it in the earth. Look, here is your money back.'

26 "But the master replied, 'You wicked and lazy servant! If you knew I harvested crops I didn't plant and gathered crops I didn't cultivate, 27 why didn't you deposit

25:5 1 Thes 5:6
25:8 Luke 12:35-40
25:10 Luke 13:24-25; Rev 19:9
25:13 Matt 24:42, 44; Mark 13:35; Luke 12:40
25:14-30 //Luke 19:11-27
25:15 Matt 18:24-25; Rom 12:3, 6
25:19 Matt 18:23
25:21 Matt 24:45-46; Luke 16:10
25:29 Matt 13:12; Mark 4:25; Luke 8:18
25:30 Matt 8:12; Luke 13:28

and to prepare for the return of Christ (25:13; see also Luke 12:35-36).

25:1 ***To meet the bridegroom*** is an image for the coming of the Messiah (see Mark 2:19-20). • Details of wedding customs during the period are not known. Some think that the bride was led to the home of the bridegroom, who would stay away until the time appointed for the wedding feast. The ***bridesmaids*** (or *virgins;* also in 25:7, 11), who had already escorted the bride to the groom's home, would then wait for news of his arrival and escort him to the feast (25:10). Others think the groom may have come late in the night to the bride's home, where he was announced. Then, after celebrating with the bride's guests, the groom would take his bride under torches or lamps to his home.

25:3 While some have speculated that the *oil* symbolizes something specific (such as the Holy Spirit), it probably merely supports the point that proper preparation for the second coming of Christ is needed.

25:5 Both the prudent and the foolish bridesmaids sleep while waiting. The parable criticizes only the foolish bridesmaids' failure to bring enough oil.

25:6 The arrival of the ***bridegroom*** at ***midnight*** while the bridesmaids slept further highlights the fact that the second coming of Jesus will come suddenly, at a time that no one can anticipate (24:42-51).

25:14-30 This parable teaches that the Lord expects his servants to be faithful to the task given to them while waiting for his return. The delay of Christ's return will cause some to turn to evil deeds (24:48-49), some to inactivity (25:3), and some to fearful passivity (25:18).

25:15 ***bags of silver:*** Greek *talents;* also throughout the story. A talent is equal to 75 pounds or 34 kilograms.

25:19 ***After a long time:*** This highlights the long delay of Christ's return (24:45-51).

25:21 See 24:45-51; Luke 16:10. • ***Let's celebrate together*** (literally *Enter into the joy of your master* [or *your Lord*]; also in 25:23) is a metaphor for the Father's approval and perhaps for the messianic banquet (see 6:1, 4, 6, 18; 9:9-17).

25:24 ***I knew you were . . . harsh:*** A false understanding of his master becomes this servant's excuse for laziness.

25:31
Deut 33:2
Dan 7:13
Zech 14:5
Matt 19:28
Acts 1:11
1 Thes 4:16
2 Thes 1:7
Rev 20:11
25:32
Ezek 34:17, 20
Rev 20:12
25:33
Luke 12:32
25:34
Luke 22:30
1 Cor 15:50
Gal 5:21
25:35-36
Job 31:32
Isa 58:7
Heb 13:3
Jas 2:15-16
25:40
Prov 19:17
Matt 10:40, 42
25:41
Matt 7:23
Mark 9:48
2 Pet 2:4
Jude 1:7
Rev 20:10
[i]*diabolos* (1228)
‣John 8:44
[j]*angelos* (0032)
‣Matt 26:53

my money in the bank? At least I could have
gotten some interest on it.'
28"Then he ordered, 'Take the money
from this servant, and give it to the one with
the ten bags of silver. 29To those who use
well what they are given, even more will be
given, and they will have an abundance. But
from those who do nothing, even what little
they have will be taken away. 30Now throw
this useless servant into outer darkness,
where there will be weeping and gnashing
of teeth.'

The Final Judgment: The Sheep and the Goats

31"But when the Son of Man comes in his
glory, and all the angels with him, then he
will sit upon his glorious throne. 32All the
nations will be gathered in his presence,
and he will separate the people as a shepherd separates the sheep from the goats.
33He will place the sheep at his right hand
and the goats at his left.
34"Then the King will say to those on his
right, 'Come, you who are blessed by my Father, inherit the Kingdom prepared for you
from the creation of the world. 35For I was
hungry, and you fed me. I was thirsty, and
you gave me a drink. I was a stranger, and
you invited me into your home. 36I was naked, and you gave me clothing. I was sick,
and you cared for me. I was in prison, and
you visited me.'
37"Then these righteous ones will reply,
'Lord, when did we ever see you hungry
and feed you? Or thirsty and give you something to drink? 38Or a stranger and show
you hospitality? Or naked and give you
clothing? 39When did we ever see you sick
or in prison and visit you?'
40"And the King will say, 'I tell you the
truth, when you did it to one of the least of
these my brothers and sisters, you were doing it to me!'
41"Then the King will turn to those on
the left and say, 'Away with you, you cursed
ones, into the eternal fire prepared for the
[i]devil and his [j]demons. 42For I was hungry, and you didn't feed me. I was thirsty,
and you didn't give me a drink. 43I was a

Faith and Works (25:31-46)

Matt 3:2, 8-10; 4:17; 5:3-12, 20-48; 7:13-27; 10:32-33; 11:20-24; 12:33-42; 13:3-9, 18-23; 15:15-20; 16:27
Gal 5:6, 16-26
Eph 2:8-10; 5:3-9
Heb 2:1-4
Jas 2:14-26
1 Jn 1:5-10
Rev 21:6-8

The parable of the sheep and the goats is an example of the indissoluble link between faith and works. The connection between faith, works, and final approval is a consistent feature of Jesus' teachings (e.g., 7:13-27; 13:3-9, 18-23; 16:27). For Jesus, works are a sure indicator of faith, which begins with repentance (3:8-10)—a conversion of the heart and mind that involves turning away from sin to God (4:17; see also 3:2; 11:20-24; 12:38-42).

Jesus did not teach salvation by works—he taught the necessity of a conversion (an internal reorientation toward God by an act of God's grace), which results in a life of obedience. Good works are the natural consequence of a relationship with Jesus Christ (see, e.g., 7:15-20; 10:32-33; 12:33-37; 13:10-17; 15:15-20; 16:17).

Jesus promises blessing and reward to those who live in accord with God's will (5:3-12). Consequently, righteousness is required of those who want to enter the Kingdom (5:20-48; 7:21; 22:11-14; 23:3). Faith that does not result in works is not saving faith (Jas 2:14-26). A misapplication of the concept of salvation by grace alone has led to a dichotomy between faith and works. Salvation is not achieved by works, but neither is it without works (see Gal 5:6, 21; Eph 2:10; 5:5; Heb 2:1-4; 1 Jn 1:5-10; Rev 21:8).

25:29 God gives abundant grace to those who are faithful with what they have already been given (see 13:12).

25:31-46 This is a description of the final judgment of which Jesus had been warning (see 7:13-27; 8:10-12; 11:20-24; 12:38-42; 13:24-30, 36-43; 16:24-28; 24:37–25:30).

25:31 To *sit upon his glorious throne* is here a posture of judgment (see 19:28; 22:44; Dan 7:13-14). • *Son of Man* is a title Jesus used for himself.

25:32 *nations:* Or *peoples.*

25:33 The *right hand* is the place of honor (Gen 48:13-20; Ps 110:1).

25:34 *prepared for you from the creation of the world:* This might be a reference to God's choosing individuals for salvation in eternity past (see 13:10-17; Eph 1:4; Rev 17:8), or it might simply refer to the Kingdom itself as a place (cp. 25:41).

25:35-36 The deeds described here, often called "deeds of mercy," were acts of compassion shown to the helpless (see Isa 58:1-12; Ezek 18:7; Jas 1:26-27). These good deeds are not attempts to merit God's favor; rather, they arise from a love for Christ that results in compassion toward others (see 6:1-4).

25:37 *These righteous ones* (see 5:6, 20) are those who do God's will as taught by Jesus, expressed most clearly in deeds of love (7:12; 9:9-13; 22:34-40; 25:35-40).

25:40 *my brothers and sisters* (literally *my brothers*): This expresses either Jesus' solidarity with his disciples (see 10:42; 18:1-14; Gal 6:10) or Jesus' solidarity with humanity in general, irrespective of the faith of the one being helped (see 6:1-4; 25:43; Prov 19:17). The use of *brothers and sisters* points to the first interpretation (12:46-50; 18:15-35; 23:8; 28:10) but does not invalidate social responsibility for other people in general (see Luke 10:30-37).

25:41 *his demons:* Literally *his angels,* or *his messengers.*

stranger, and you didn't invite me into your home. I was naked, and you didn't give me clothing. I was sick and in prison, and you didn't visit me.'

44"Then they will reply, 'Lord, when did we ever see you hungry or thirsty or a stranger or naked or sick or in prison, and not help you?'

45"And he will answer, 'I tell you the truth, when you refused to help the least of these my brothers and sisters, you were refusing to help me.'

46"And they will go away into eternal punishment, but the righteous will go into eternal life."

Jesus' Arrest (26:1-56)

The Plot to Kill Jesus

Matt 26:1-5 // Mark 14:1-2 // Luke 22:1-2

26 When Jesus had finished saying all these things, he said to his disciples, 2"As you know, Passover begins in two days, and the Son of Man will be handed over to be crucified."

3At that same time the leading priests and elders were meeting at the residence of Caiaphas, the high priest, 4plotting how to capture Jesus secretly and kill him. 5"But not during the Passover celebration," they agreed, "or the people may riot."

Jesus Anointed at Bethany

Matt 26:6-13 // Mark 14:3-9; cp. Luke 7:36-50; John 12:1-11

6Meanwhile, Jesus was in Bethany at the home of Simon, a man who had previously had leprosy. 7While he was eating, a woman came in with a beautiful alabaster jar of expensive perfume and poured it over his head.

8The disciples were indignant when they saw this. "What a waste!" they said. 9"It could have been sold for a high price and the money given to the poor."

10But Jesus, aware of this, replied, "Why criticize this woman for doing such a good thing to me? 11You will always have the poor among you, but you will not always have me. 12She has poured this perfume on me to prepare my body for burial. 13I tell you the truth, wherever the Good News is preached throughout the world, this woman's deed will be remembered and discussed."

Judas Agrees to Betray Jesus

Matt 26:14-16 // Mark 14:10-11 // Luke 22:3-6

14Then Judas Iscariot, one of the twelve disciples, went to the leading priests 15and asked, "How much will you pay me to betray Jesus to you?" And they gave him thirty pieces of silver. 16From that time on, Judas began looking for an opportunity to betray Jesus.

25:45
Prov 14:31; 17:5

25:46
Dan 12:2
John 3:15, 36; 5:29
Acts 13:46-48
Rom 2:7-8
Gal 6:8

26:1-5
//Mark 14:1-2
//Luke 22:1-2
John 11:45-53

26:2
Exod 12:1-27
Matt 20:18-19; 27:26
Mark 15:15
Luke 24:7, 20
John 19:16

26:3
Ps 2:2
John 11:47-53
Acts 4:6

26:6-13
//Mark 14:3-9
//John 12:1-8

26:11
Deut 15:11

26:14-16
//Mark 14:10-11
//Luke 22:3-6
John 11:57

26:15
Exod 21:32
Zech 11:12

26:17-30
//Mark 14:12-26
//Luke 22:7-14, 22-23
//John 13:21-30

25:46 The Greek term translated *eternal* can mean either "lasting forever" or "lasting for an age," in this case "the age to come" (13:39-40, 49; 24:3; John 17:3; 2 Thes 1:9; Phlm 1:15; 1 Jn 5:11, 13). Some hold out hope that the punishment of the damned will, after "an age," be ended by annihilation or forgiveness. The parallel between *eternal life* and *eternal punishment* suggests strongly that it means "lasting forever," since eternal life does not end (see also Luke 16:19-31; Heb 6:2; Rev 20:10).

26:2 The irony is that the Son of Man, who is to judge the nations (25:31-46), must first be wrongly judged and condemned to death by evil people. Jesus' death was the ultimate Passover sacrifice (see John 19:31-37; 1 Cor 5:7). • *Son of Man* is a title Jesus used for himself.

26:3 ***The residence of Caiaphas, the high priest,*** was near the Temple in Jerusalem's Upper City. Since it was not the normal meeting place, this gathering was *ad hoc*, urgent, and probably secretive. The council chamber, the traditional meeting place for the Sanhedrin, was located either at the southern end of the Court of the Israelites in the Temple, or on the western edge of the Temple hill. • Joseph *Caiaphas,* son-in-law of Annas (see John 18:13), was high priest from AD 18 to 36 (John 11:49), the longest tenure of any high priest from the time of Herod's rule until AD 70. His father-in-law, Annas, had been deposed but continued to be called high priest as well (see Luke 3:2; John 18:13, 19-24).

26:5 Jerusalem was flooded with pilgrims at *Passover,* and the Jewish leaders worried about having their authority taken away if they caused or allowed anything that resembled revolt against Rome (see 21:8-11, 14-16).

26:6-13 A similar anointing took place earlier in Galilee (Luke 7:36-50). Matthew's insertion of the episode at this point (cp. John 12:1-8) sets the Jewish leaders' murderous plotting (26:3-5) and Judas's betrayal (26:14-16) in sharp contrast to the woman's praiseworthy actions.

26:6 ***Simon, a man who had previously had leprosy:*** Jesus' presence in the man's home exhibited the forgiving, healing love Jesus often showed toward outcasts (see 8:7; 9:10).

26:7 ***eating:*** Or *reclining.* • The ***jar of expensive perfume*** was a burial ointment (see Mark 16:1; Luke 23:56–24:1; John 12:1-7; 19:38-42) made of nard, which was harvested in India. The value of this jar of perfume was nearly a year's wages (John 12:5).

26:8 ***The disciples were indignant:*** John 12:4 indicates that Judas Iscariot incited this reaction.

26:12 ***to prepare my body for burial:*** It is not clear whether the woman fully understood the significance of her actions. In addition to preparation for burial, the anointing also speaks of Jesus as king (1 Sam 10:1; 2 Kgs 9:6) and priest (Exod 29:7).

26:14-16 Judas's betrayal was a part of God's sovereign plan (Acts 1:16-17). • ***Iscariot:*** See note on 10:4. Judas sold himself to the authorities (see also John 11:57), concealed it (26:25), and then took them to Jesus at the appropriate time so they could carry out their plans (26:47-56; see John 18:2). Later, Judas was overcome by guilt and committed suicide (27:3-10; see Acts 1:15-22). Judas was apparently known for his greed (26:14-15; John 12:4-6; 13:29). It is also possible that he was motivated by disappointment over the nature of Jesus' reign as Messiah, his own humiliation over the anointing of Jesus (see John 12:1-8), or resentment over the leadership of the Galilean apostles, Peter and John. See also "Judas Iscariot" at Mark 14, p. 1685.

26:18 ***My time:*** The Messiah would now

26:17
Exod 12:18-20
Deut 16:5-8

26:23
Ps 41:9

26:24
Ps 22:7-8, 16-18
Isa 53:8-9
Luke 24:25-27, 46
1 Pet 1:10-11

26:28
Exod 24:8
Jer 31:31
Zech 9:11
Heb 9:20
[k]*diathēkē* (1242)
‣ Mark 14:24
[a]*hamartia* (0266)
‣ Luke 1:77

26:29
Acts 10:41
[b]*ampelos* (0288)
‣ Mark 14:25

26:30
Ps 113–118

The Last Supper

Matt 26:17-19 // Mark 14:12-16 // Luke 22:7-13
Matt 26:20-25 // Mark 14:17-21 // Luke 22:21-23 // John 13:21-30
Matt 26:26-30 // Mark 14:22-26 // Luke 22:14-20

17On the first day of the Festival of Unleavened Bread, the disciples came to Jesus and
asked, "Where do you want us to prepare
the Passover meal for you?"
18"As you go into the city," he told them,
"you will see a certain man. Tell him, 'The
Teacher says: My time has come, and I will eat
the Passover meal with my disciples at your
house.'" 19So the disciples did as Jesus told
them and prepared the Passover meal there.
20When it was evening, Jesus sat down at
the table with the twelve disciples. 21While
they were eating, he said, "I tell you the
truth, one of you will betray me."
22Greatly distressed, each one asked in
turn, "Am I the one, Lord?"
23He replied, "One of you who has just
eaten from this bowl with me will betray
me. 24For the Son of Man must die, as the
Scriptures declared long ago. But how terrible it will be for the one who betrays him. It
would be far better for that man if he had
never been born!"
25Judas, the one who would betray him,
also asked, "Rabbi, am I the one?"
And Jesus told him, "You have said it."
26As they were eating, Jesus took some
bread and blessed it. Then he broke it in
pieces and gave it to the disciples, saying,
"Take this and eat it, for this is my body."
27And he took a cup of wine and gave
thanks to God for it. He gave it to them and
said, "Each of you drink from it, 28for this is
my blood, which confirms the [k]covenant between God and his people. It is poured out
as a sacrifice to forgive the [a]sins of many.
29Mark my words—I will not drink [b]wine
again until the day I drink it new with you
in my Father's Kingdom."
30Then they sang a hymn and went out to
the Mount of Olives.

---

complete the work for which he was commissioned, to die for the sins of the world.

26:20 ***Jesus sat down at the table:*** Or *Jesus reclined.* • ***the twelve disciples:*** Some manuscripts read *the Twelve.*

26:23 ***eaten from this bowl with me:*** It was the custom for everyone present to dip their food into a common bowl, which probably contained herbs and fruit puree. Sharing a meal was a sign of friendship and trust, making a betrayer's presence all the more startling (26:21; but see John 13:26).

26:24 ***as the Scriptures declared:*** Jesus might have been referring to Isa 53:7-9 or to the broad OT theme of a suffering Messiah. This verse combines God's sovereign will with human responsibility.

26:25 Judas referred to Jesus as *Rabbi,* while the other disciples call him "Lord" (26:22). • ***"You have said it":*** This enigmatic statement affirmed that Judas was the betrayer.

26:26-29 The Last Supper derives its significance in part from the Jewish Passover (see Exod 12). The phases of the Jewish liturgy for Passover are as follows: (1) Festal blessing; (2) first cup (see Luke 22:17-18); (3) eating bitter herbs (see 26:23 and note); (4) eating unleavened bread (26:26; Mark 14:22); (5) second cup is mixed; (6) the Passover *haggadah* (reading) is given (Exod 12); (7) first part of the *hallel* (Pss 113–114; see note on Pss 113–118); (8) second cup is taken; (9) blessing and eating of unleavened bread (26:26; Mark 14:22; Luke 22:19); (10) the Passover lamb is eaten; (11) third cup (26:27-28; Mark 14:23-24; Luke 22:20); (12) fourth cup (see 26:29[?]; Mark 14:25[?]); (13) time of fellowship; (14) second part of the *hallel* (Pss 115–118; see Matt 26:30). None of the NT accounts of the Last Supper includes every aspect of a typical Jewish Passover. However, the most important aspects of the Passover that gave meaning to the early Christian celebration of the Lord's Supper are included (see 1 Cor 11:23-25). Jesus, the Lamb of God, is the ultimate Passover lamb and the perfect sacrifice for sin. • ***this is my body . . . my blood:*** Ever since the Reformation, there have been three dominant interpretations of Jesus' statements concerning the bread and the wine: (1) that the bread and wine change into the actual body and blood of Jesus Christ (*transubstantiation*); (2) that Christ is mysteriously present in the sacrament either spiritually (*real presence*) or "in, with, and under" the bread and wine (*consubstantiation*); (3) that the bread and wine symbolize the body and blood of Christ, benefiting the recipient through the Spirit by faith (*symbolism*). See also note on Mark 14:22-25.

26:26 The unleavened *bread* of the Passover (Exod 12:18) is also described as the "bread of suffering" (Deut 16:3), referring to hardships in Egypt. • The customary blessing over the bread in the Passover meal was "Blessed are you, O Lord our God, King of the universe, who brings forth bread from the earth."

26:27 He *gave thanks.* The traditional blessing for the Passover cup was "Blessed are you, O Lord our God, King of the universe, who creates the fruit of the vine." An early Christian variant is, "We give thanks to you, our Father, for the Holy Vine of David, your child, whom you made known to us through Jesus your child; glory be to you forever" (*Didache* 9.2). • The four cups of the Passover meal correspond to the fourfold promise of Exod 6:6-7, with two for deliverance, one for redemption (see 26:27-28), and one for fellowship (see 26:29).

26:28 ***the covenant:*** Some manuscripts read *the new covenant.* Under God's covenant with Israel, the blood of sheep or goats (Exod 12:5, 13; 24:8) was shed and placed on the two doorposts and on the lintel at Passover (Exod 12:7). The blood of Jesus, the sinless Lamb of God, establishes a new covenant (see Jer 31:31). The idea of the *covenant* is God's unilateral commitment to establish salvation for mankind, fulfilling the promise to Abraham (see Gen 12; Gal 3:15-29; 4:12-31). • ***to forgive the sins of many:*** Jesus shed his *blood* as a sacrifice for sin (see Jer 31:31-34; Mark 14:24). Some have understood *many* to refer only to God's chosen people, while others have understood *many* to be an expression meaning "all" (cp. 20:28).

26:29 ***until the day:*** Though the ***Kingdom*** had been inaugurated in Jesus' ministry, it awaits final consummation (see 1 Cor 15:20-28; Rev 19–22). • ***until the day I drink it new:*** The final consummation of the Kingdom is pictured as a feast like the Passover, symbolizing an eternal fellowship of love and peace.

26:30 ***They sang a hymn:*** Some have suggested that the *Great Hallel* (Ps 136) was sung.

Jesus Predicts Peter's Denial
Matt 26:31-35 // Mark 14:27-31; cp. Luke 22:31-34;
cp. John 13:36-38
31On the way, Jesus told them, "Tonight all of
you will desert me. For the Scriptures say,

'God will strike the [c]Shepherd,
and the sheep of the flock will be
scattered.'

32But after I have been raised from the dead,
I will go ahead of you to Galilee and meet
you there."
33Peter declared, "Even if everyone else
deserts you, I will never desert you."
34Jesus replied, "I tell you the truth, Peter—this very night, before the rooster
crows, you will deny three times that you
even know me."
35"No!" Peter insisted. "Even if I have to
die with you, I will never deny you!" And all
the other disciples vowed the same.

Jesus Prays in Gethsemane
Matt 26:36-46 // Mark 14:32-42 // Luke 22:39-46
36Then Jesus went with them to the olive
grove called Gethsemane, and he said, "Sit
here while I go over there to pray." 37He
took Peter and Zebedee's two sons, James
and John, and he became anguished and distressed. 38He told them, "My soul is crushed
with grief to the point of death. Stay here
and keep watch with me."
39He went on a little farther and bowed
with his face to the ground, praying, "My
Father! If it is possible, let this cup of suffering be taken away from me. Yet I want your
will to be done, not mine."
40Then he returned to the disciples
and found them asleep. He said to Peter,
"Couldn't you watch with me even one hour?
41Keep watch and pray, so that you will not
give in to temptation. For the spirit is willing, but the [d]body is weak!"
42Then Jesus left them a second time
and prayed, "My Father! If this cup cannot
be taken away unless I drink it, your will be
done." 43When he returned to them again,
he found them sleeping, for they couldn't
keep their eyes open.
44So he went to pray a third time, saying
the same things again. 45Then he came to
the disciples and said, "Go ahead and sleep.
Have your rest. But look—the time has come.
The Son of Man is betrayed into the hands
of sinners. 46Up, let's be going. Look, my betrayer is here!"

Jesus Is Betrayed and Arrested
Matt 26:47-56 // Mark 14:43-52 // Luke 22:47-53 //
John 18:1-12
47And even as Jesus said this, Judas, one of
the twelve disciples, arrived with a crowd
of men armed with swords and clubs. They
had been sent by the leading priests and
elders of the people. 48The traitor, Judas,
had given them a prearranged signal: "You
will know which one to arrest when I greet
him with a kiss." 49So Judas came straight
to Jesus. "Greetings, [e]Rabbi!" he exclaimed
and gave him the kiss.
50Jesus said, "My friend, go ahead and do
what you have come for."
Then the others grabbed Jesus and arrested him. 51But one of the men with Jesus
pulled out his sword and struck the high
priest's slave, slashing off his ear.
52"Put away your sword," Jesus told him.
"Those who use the sword will die by the
sword. 53Don't you realize that I could ask
my Father for thousands of [f]angels to protect us, and he would send them instantly?
54But if I did, how would the Scriptures be

26:31-35 //Mark 14:27-31 //Luke 22:31-34 //John 13:36-38
26:31 *Zech 13:7; John 16:32; [c]*poimēn* (4166) ‣Mark 6:34
26:32 Matt 28:7
26:34 Matt 26:69-75; Mark 14:66-72; Luke 22:56-62; John 18:25-27
26:35 John 13:37
26:36-46 //Mark 14:32-42 //Luke 22:40-46
26:36 John 18:1
26:38 *Ps 42:6; 43:5; John 12:27
26:39 Matt 20:22; John 5:30; 6:38; Heb 5:7-8
26:41 Matt 6:13; [d]*sarx* (4561) ‣John 1:14
26:45 John 12:23-27; 13:1; 17:1
26:47-56 //Mark 14:43-50 //Luke 22:47-53 //John 18:3-11
26:49 [e]*rhabbi* (4461) ‣Mark 9:5
26:52 Gen 9:6; Rev 13:10
26:53 2 Kgs 6:16-17; Ps 91:11; Dan 7:10; [f]*angelos* (0032) ‣Matt 28:2
26:54 Ps 22:7-8, 16-18; Isa 53:8-9; Luke 24:25-27, 46; 1 Pet 1:10-11

26:31 *God will strike* (literally *I will strike*; Zech 13:7): In Zech 13:7-9, the *Shepherd*, God's partner, is struck down (understood by Jesus as a prediction of his own death), and out of the scattered *sheep* emerge a purged, purified remnant of faithful ones (Zech 13:8-9). In the short term, the disciples would soon *be scattered* and deny association with Jesus (26:34, 56, 69-75).

26:32 Jesus foresaw a time of restoration for the disciples despite their imminent abandonment of him (see ch 28; John 21).

26:35 While Peter's denial receives the most attention, *all the other disciples* denied or avoided association with Christ as well (see 26:56).

26:36-46 This scene reveals the depth of Jesus' awareness of the suffering that awaited him on the cross, as well as his utter commitment to God's will (see 20:28). Expressions in 26:41-42 echo the Lord's Prayer (6:9-13).

26:36 *Gethsemane* is the name of an olive orchard approximately 250 yards east of Jerusalem's Golden Gate, overlooking the Kidron Valley on the edge of the Mount of Olives. Jesus and his disciples apparently met there often (Luke 22:39-40; John 18:1-2).

26:37 *He took Peter . . . James and John:* These three, apparently the leaders of the apostles, received special revelation (17:1-13) and accompanied Jesus in this difficult hour. • Jesus *became anguished and distressed* from contemplating the Father's plan for him, to absorb God's wrath toward humans for their sin (see 27:45-46).

26:38 *crushed with grief:* See John 12:27; cp. Ps 42:5-6, 11; 43:5.

26:39 *If it is possible:* Jesus' heart's desire was for uninterrupted communion with the Father instead of coming under God's wrath. • *Yet I want your will to be done:* His resolution to do the Father's will was firm (4:1-11; 16:23; John 6:38).

26:42 *If this cup cannot be taken away:* Literally *If this cannot pass.*

26:49 *Judas . . . gave him the kiss:* Judas's use of a sign of affection to betray Jesus amplifies the heinousness of his betrayal.

26:51 *one of the men with Jesus:* This was Peter (John 18:26).

26:53 *thousands* (literally *twelve legions*): Jesus used Roman military language (a *legion* consisted of approximately 6,000 soldiers) to describe the aid he could receive from God. Jesus was not a helpless victim; he permitted his own arrest.

26:55
Mark 12:35
Luke 21:37
John 7:14, 28; 18:20
26:56
Isa 53:7
Zech 13:7
Matt 26:31
26:57-68
//Mark 14:53-65
//Luke 22:54-55, 63-71
//John 18:13-14, 19-24
26:58
Mark 14:66
Luke 22:55
John 18:15
26:60
Deut 19:15
Ps 27:12
26:61
Matt 27:40
John 2:19
Acts 6:14
26:63
Matt 16:16-18

fulfilled that describe what must happen now?"

55 Then Jesus said to the crowd, "Am I some dangerous revolutionary, that you come with swords and clubs to arrest me? Why didn't you arrest me in the Temple? I was there teaching every day. 56 But this is all happening to fulfill the words of the prophets as recorded in the Scriptures." At that point, all the disciples deserted him and fled.

Jesus' Trial (26:57–27:26)

Jesus' Trial before the Jewish High Council

Matt 26:57-68 // Mark 14:53-65 // Luke 22:63-71; cp. John 18:19-24

57 Then the people who had arrested Jesus led him to the home of Caiaphas, the high priest, where the teachers of religious law and the elders had gathered. 58 Meanwhile, Peter followed him at a distance and came to the high priest's courtyard. He went in and sat with the guards and waited to see how it would all end.

59 Inside, the leading priests and the entire high council were trying to find witnesses who would lie about Jesus, so they could put him to death. 60 But even though they found many who agreed to give false witness, they could not use anyone's testimony. Finally, two men came forward 61 who declared, "This man said, 'I am able to destroy the Temple of God and rebuild it in three days.'"

62 Then the high priest stood up and said to Jesus, "Well, aren't you going to answer these charges? What do you have to say for yourself?" 63 But Jesus remained silent. Then the high priest said to him, "I demand in the name of the living God—tell us if you are the Messiah, the Son of God."

THE JEWISH HIGH COUNCIL (26:59)

Matt 26:57-68
Mark 14:53-65; 15:1, 43
Luke 22:66-71; 23:50-54
John 11:47-53
Acts 5:21-41; 6:11–8:1; 22:30–23:10; 23:26-30

The high council of Jewish aristocrats in Jerusalem was endowed with considerable power in governing the Jewish people. It is traditionally called the Sanhedrin, a transliteration of the Greek word *sunedrion* ("council").

According to Jewish tradition, the Sanhedrin dates from Moses' choice of seventy elders (Num 11:16), but the earliest datable reference is found in Josephus (*Antiquities* 12.3.3) from the time of Antiochus the Great (223–187 BC). The Sanhedrin probably emerged from a self-governing body of leaders under the Persians (see Ezra 5:5-9; Neh 2:16). The high council was always controlled by the priestly class under the leadership of the high priest, though these priests were influenced to various degrees by Roman rulers and Pharisees. Herod the Great exercised a particularly heavy hand over the affairs of the Sanhedrin.

The Sanhedrin managed the internal legal and religious affairs of Judaism, including judicial decisions not resolved in lesser courts (called "local sanhedrins"), criminal justice and arrests, and official (though unenforceable) decisions regarding Jewish matters (e.g., Acts 9:1-2). Though the Sanhedrin could not of its own accord put tried criminals to death (e.g., John 18:31), apparently it could do so with the support of Roman officials.

The destruction of Jerusalem in AD 70 eliminated the high council as the ruling body of Judaism.

26:54 For Jesus to have resisted would have impeded the fulfillment of God's saving work (see 16:21-23).

26:55 The leaders' clandestine behavior was driven by fear of the masses who revered Jesus (see 21:26, 46; 26:3-5).

26:56 It is not clear which of *the Scriptures* Jesus was alluding to—perhaps Isa 53, or perhaps the OT theme of a suffering Messiah in general. • As Jesus had predicted earlier that evening, ***all the disciples deserted him*** (26:31-35).

26:57–27:26 The Gospels record Jesus as undergoing five hearings: (1) an informal hearing before Annas (John 18:13-24); (2) a night hearing before the Sanhedrin (26:59-66); (3) a morning hearing before the Sanhedrin (27:1-2); (4) a hearing before Herod Antipas (Luke 23:6-12); and (5) a two-stage trial before Pilate (27:11-31; see Luke 23:6-12). It all amounts to two trials, a Jewish trial and a Roman trial.

26:57-68 This hearing might have been little more than an unofficial preliminary hearing designed to establish consensus on the terms of the charges. The Jewish leaders were under considerable pressure to keep this incident secret, lest their actions cause a riot (see 21:26, 46; 26:5, 55; John 11:45-53).

26:58 ***the high priest's courtyard:*** This location suggests an *ad hoc* meeting of the Sanhedrin at the palace of the high priest (26:3).

26:59 ***were trying to find witnesses:*** The verb tense suggests an extended, perhaps desperate, attempt to find any testimony that could lead to a formal accusation (see Mark 14:55-56). • ***the entire high council:*** Greek *the Sanhedrin.*

26:60 ***could not use anyone's testimony:*** The evidence was too insubstantial or inconsistent to meet their goal of a death sentence until ***two men came forward*** (Deut 17:6; 19:15) with testimonies that did not conflict.

26:61 The charge is either a misunderstanding or a deliberate distortion of Jesus' prediction of his death and resurrection (see John 2:19-21).

26:63 ***if you are the Messiah:*** This question from ***the high priest*** was prompted by Zech 6:12, which had predicted that the Messiah would rebuild the Temple (cp. 26:61).

64 Jesus replied, "You have said it. And in the future you will see the Son of Man seated in the place of power at God's right hand and coming on the clouds of heaven."

65 Then the high priest tore his clothing to show his horror and said, "Blasphemy! Why do we need other witnesses? You have all heard his blasphemy. 66 What is your verdict?"

"Guilty!" they shouted. "He deserves to die!"

67 Then they began to spit in Jesus' face and beat him with their fists. And some slapped him, 68 jeering, "Prophesy to us, you Messiah! Who hit you that time?"

Peter Denies Jesus
Matt 26:69-75 // Mark 14:66-72 // Luke 22:54-62 // John 18:15-18, 25-27

69 Meanwhile, Peter was sitting outside in the courtyard. A servant girl came over and said to him, "You were one of those with Jesus the Galilean."

70 But Peter denied it in front of everyone. "I don't know what you're talking about," he said.

71 Later, out by the gate, another servant girl noticed him and said to those standing around, "This man was with Jesus of Nazareth."

72 Again Peter denied it, this time with an oath. "I don't even know the man," he said.

73 A little later some of the other bystanders came over to Peter and said, "You must be one of them; we can tell by your Galilean accent."

74 Peter swore, "A curse on me if I'm lying—I don't know the man!" And immediately the rooster crowed.

75 Suddenly, Jesus' words flashed through Peter's mind: "Before the rooster crows, you will deny three times that you even know me." And he went away, weeping bitterly.

Jesus Is Taken to the Roman Governor
Matt 27:1-2 // Mark 15:1 // Luke 23:1 // John 18:28

27 Very early in the morning the leading priests and the elders of the people met again to lay plans for putting Jesus to death. 2 Then they bound him, led him away, and took him to Pilate, the Roman governor.

Judas Hangs Himself
Matt 27:3-10; cp. Acts 1:18-19

3 When Judas, who had betrayed him, realized that Jesus had been condemned to die, he was filled with remorse. So he took the thirty pieces of silver back to the leading priests and the elders. 4 "I have sinned," he declared, "for I have betrayed an innocent man."

"What do we care?" they retorted. "That's your problem."

26:64
Ps 110:1
*Dan 7:13
Matt 24:30
Rev 1:7

26:65-66
Lev 24:16
John 19:7

26:67
Isa 50:6; 53:5

26:69-75
//Mark 14:66-72
//Luke 22:55-62
//John 18:16-18, 25-27

26:75
Matt 26:34
Mark 14:30
Luke 22:34
John 13:38

27:1-2
Mark 15:1
Luke 23:1-2
John 18:28

27:3
Matt 26:14-15

26:64 ***You have said it:*** This purposefully enigmatic response is essentially an affirmative answer (see 26:25; 27:11); Mark has "I AM" (Mark 14:62). • ***you will see:*** By quoting Dan 7:13, Jesus affirmed that he was the Son of Man who would be vindicated and exalted by God. • ***seated in the place of power at God's right hand*** (literally *seated at the right hand of the power;* see Ps 110:1): Jews were reluctant to name God directly (see note on 5:4). • The term ***coming on the clouds of heaven*** (see Dan 7:13) could refer either to the destruction of Jerusalem in AD 70 or to Jesus' second coming at the end of history.

26:65 ***Blasphemy!*** Caiaphas evidently understood Jesus' claim to be the exalted Son of Man as a blasphemy against God's majesty. The Son of Man (Dan 7:13-14) was closely associated with this majesty.

26:67-68 Such abuse fulfills Isa 50:6; 53:4-9 and Jesus' own predictions (16:21; 17:22-23; 20:18-19; 26:2; see also Mark 14:65).

26:69-75 Peter's denials fulfill Jesus' prediction (26:34).

26:71 ***Jesus of Nazareth:*** Or *Jesus the Nazarene.*

26:73 ***your Galilean accent:*** Jews from Galilee had a distinctive accent, compared with those from Judea (cp. 4:13 and note).

26:75 When the crowing of the ***rooster*** reminded Peter of Jesus' prediction (26:34), he was struck with sorrow.

27:1-2 The Jewish leaders were ready to level charges against Jesus before Pilate so that he would order Jesus' execution. Pilate, a Gentile, fulfills Jesus' prediction (20:19).

27:1 The charge of blasphemy (26:65-66), though sufficient for the death penalty among Jews, would not convince a Roman judge. Hence, ***the leading priests and the elders*** conspired together to prepare a more political charge consistent with capital offenses in Roman law (see 27:11-26; Luke 23:2).

27:2 Tiberius Caesar appointed ***Pilate*** to be the ***governor*** (or *prefect*) of Judea. Pilate ruled primarily from Caesarea, not Jerusalem, from AD 26 to AD 36. Though he had sovereign power in Judea, Pilate was ultimately responsible to the legate of Syria, the central authority in the eastern portion of the Roman empire. Josephus records several instances where Pilate's disregard for the sanctity of Jewish customs led to revolt.

27:3-10 There are two accounts of Judas's death—this one and Acts 1:18-19. There are differences between the two: (1) Matthew states that the priests bought the field (27:6-7), while Acts seems to suggest that Judas bought it (Acts 1:18); (2) Matthew reports that Judas committed suicide by hanging himself (27:5), while Acts enigmatically refers to a fall and an abdominal rupture (Acts 1:18); (3) Matthew implies that the field of blood was so named because it became a place of burial (27:7-8), while Acts suggests that it was because of Judas's violent death there (Acts 1:19). The two accounts are compatible if one takes the account in Acts as describing the effects of the actions described in Matthew.

27:3 Judas ***was filled with remorse*** (Greek *metamelomai*), but he did not repent (Greek *metanoeō*), which would have changed his heart and resulted in obedience and a relationship with God based on faith.

27:4 ***an innocent man:*** Jesus' innocence is a dominant theme in the narrative of his suffering (see 23:35; 26:55-56, 59-60; 27:18-19, 24; see also Luke 23:47).

27:5-10
Acts 1:18-19
27:9-10
*Jer 32:6-9
*Zech 11:12-13
27:11-14
//Mark 15:2-5
//Luke 23:3-5
//John 18:33-38
27:12
Isa 53:7
Matt 26:63
John 19:9
1 Pet 2:23
27:14
Mark 14:61
27:15-26
//Mark 15:6-15
//Luke 23:13-25
//John 18:39–19:16
27:19
Job 33:14-16
27:20
Acts 3:14
27:22
Matt 1:16
27:24
Deut 21:5-9
Ps 26:6
27:25
Acts 5:28

5 Then Judas threw the silver coins down
in the Temple and went out and hanged himself.
6 The leading priests picked up the coins.
"It wouldn't be right to put this money in the
Temple treasury," they said, "since it was payment for murder." 7 After some discussion
they finally decided to buy the potter's field,
and they made it into a cemetery for foreigners. 8 That is why the field is still called the
Field of Blood. 9 This fulfilled the prophecy
of Jeremiah that says,

"They took the thirty pieces of silver—
the price at which he was valued by
the people of Israel,
10 and purchased the potter's field,
as the LORD directed."

Jesus' Trial before Pilate
Matt 27:11-14 // Mark 15:2-5 // Luke 23:2-5 // John 18:29-38b

11 Now Jesus was standing before Pilate, the
Roman governor. "Are you the king of the
Jews?" the governor asked him.
Jesus replied, "You have said it."
12 But when the leading priests and the
elders made their accusations against him,
Jesus remained silent. 13 "Don't you hear
all these charges they are bringing against
you?" Pilate demanded. 14 But Jesus made
no response to any of the charges, much to
the governor's surprise.

Jesus Is Sentenced to Death
Matt 27:15-26 // Mark 15:6-15 // Luke 23:13-25 // John 18:38b–19:16

15 Now it was the governor's custom each
year during the Passover celebration to release one prisoner to the crowd—anyone
they wanted. 16 This year there was a notorious prisoner, a man named Barabbas. 17 As
the crowds gathered before Pilate's house
that morning, he asked them, "Which one
do you want me to release to you—Barabbas,
or Jesus who is called the Messiah?" 18 (He
knew very well that the religious leaders
had arrested Jesus out of envy.)
19 Just then, as Pilate was sitting on the
judgment seat, his wife sent him this message: "Leave that innocent man alone. I
suffered through a terrible nightmare
about him last night."
20 Meanwhile, the leading priests and the
elders persuaded the crowd to ask for Barabbas to be released and for Jesus to be put
to death. 21 So the governor asked again,
"Which of these two do you want me to release to you?"
The crowd shouted back, "Barabbas!"
22 Pilate responded, "Then what should I
do with Jesus who is called the Messiah?"
They shouted back, "Crucify him!"
23 "Why?" Pilate demanded. "What crime
has he committed?"
But the mob roared even louder, "Crucify
him!"
24 Pilate saw that he wasn't getting anywhere and that a riot was developing. So
he sent for a bowl of water and washed his
hands before the crowd, saying, "I am innocent of this man's blood. The responsibility
is yours!"
25 And all the people yelled back, "We will

27:5 ***hanged himself:*** Judas's suicide resulted from a guilt-stricken, unrepentant conscience. His death satisfied OT law regarding the punishment of a false witness (see Deut 19:16-21).

27:6 ***since it was payment for murder:*** Literally *since it is the price for blood.*

27:7 ***Foreigners*** were Gentiles who died in Jerusalem. An asset whose owner could not be traced was used for public charity. In this instance, unclean money was used to buy an unclean place for unclean people.

27:8 ***Field of Blood*** is a way of describing a cemetery (cp. Acts 1:18-19).

27:9-10 ***the prophecy of Jeremiah:*** The citation is from Zech 11:12-13. Matthew might merely have been conforming to the Jewish custom of citing books by referring to the first book in the particular scroll—the first book in the scroll containing Zechariah would have been Jeremiah. Or, Matthew might have thought of similar passages in Jeremiah (Jer 19:1-13; 18:2-6; 32:6-15) along with Zech 11:12-13. • Matthew sees a striking resemblance between Zechariah's actions and those of the leading priests. Both contexts deal with the rejection of God's messenger who was to be king of God's people. • ***They took:*** Or *I took.* The Greek can be interpreted either way. • ***as the LORD directed:*** Literally *as the LORD directed me.* Zech 11:12-13; Jer 32:6-9.

27:11-26 The Roman trial included an initial hearing before Pilate (27:11-14), one before Herod Antipas (Luke 23:6-16), and a second hearing before Pilate (27:15-26).

27:11 ***king of the Jews:*** The Sanhedrin's original charge of blasphemy (26:65-66; 27:1) held no interest to the Romans, who saw it as a Jewish religious question (cp. Acts 25:18-20). The charge was therefore changed to incriminate Jesus in Roman eyes as a political rebel (see Luke 23:2).

27:15 Pilate's *custom* seems out of character; he was not known for wanting to please his Jewish subjects. However, if Pilate's position with Caesar was precarious at this point (see note on John 19:12; see Philo, *On the Embassy to Gaius* 159–161), then this gesture may have been to keep the peace and thus avoid negative attention from Rome.

27:16 ***notorious prisoner . . . named Barabbas*** (some manuscripts read *Jesus Barabbas;* also in 27:17): Elsewhere he is called a "revolutionary" (Mark 15:7; John 18:40), a term that also denotes a robber or insurrectionist (see Luke 23:19). To the zealots, Barabbas was a hero.

27:19 ***through a terrible nightmare*** (cp. 1:20): It is ironic that a pagan recognizes and takes a stand for Jesus' innocence, while the Jewish crowd does not.

27:24 ***The responsibility is yours!*** The priests had said the same thing to Judas (27:4).

27:25 ***all the people*** (see 21:43): This does not mean every living Jew. Instead,

take responsibility for his death—we and our children!"

26So Pilate released Barabbas to them. He ordered Jesus flogged with a lead-tipped whip, then turned him over to the Roman soldiers to be crucified.

Jesus' Death and Burial (27:27-66)

The Soldiers Mock Jesus

Matt 27:27-31 // Mark 15:16-20 // John 19:1-3

27Some of the governor's soldiers took Jesus into their headquarters and called out the entire regiment. 28They stripped him and put a scarlet robe on him. 29They wove thorn branches into a crown and put it on his head, and they placed a reed stick in his right hand as a scepter. Then they knelt before him in mockery and taunted, "Hail! King of the Jews!" 30And they spit on him and grabbed the stick and struck him on the head with it. 31When they were finally tired of mocking him, they took off the robe and put his own clothes on him again. Then they led him away to be crucified.

The Crucifixion

Matt 27:32-44 // Mark 15:21-32 // Luke 23:26-43 // John 19:17-24

32Along the way, they came across a man named Simon, who was from Cyrene, and the soldiers forced him to carry Jesus' cross. 33And they went out to a place called Golgotha (which means "Place of the Skull"). 34The soldiers gave him wine mixed with bitter gall, but when he had tasted it, he refused to drink it.

35After they had nailed him to the cross, the soldiers gambled for his clothes by throwing dice. 36Then they sat around and kept guard as he hung there. 37A sign was fastened above Jesus' head, announcing the charge against him. It read: "This is Jesus, the King of the Jews." 38Two revolutionaries were crucified with him, one on his right and one on his left.

39The people passing by shouted abuse, shaking their heads in mockery. 40"Look at you now!" they yelled at him. "You said you were going to destroy the Temple and rebuild it in three days. Well then, if you are the Son of God, save yourself and come down from the cross!"

41The leading priests, the teachers of religious law, and the elders also mocked Jesus. 42"He saved others," they scoffed, "but he can't save himself! So he is the King of Israel, is he? Let him come down from the cross right now, and we will believe in him!

27:26 Isa 53:5; John 19:1
27:27-31 //Mark 15:16-20; John 18:28, 33; 19:2-3
27:29 Ps 22:8; Isa 53:3; John 19:2-3
27:30 Isa 50:6
27:31 Isa 53:7
27:32-44 //Mark 15:21-32; //Luke 23:26-43; //John 19:17-24
27:34 Ps 69:21
27:35 *Ps 22:18
27:38 Isa 53:12
27:39 Ps 22:7; 109:25; Lam 2:15
27:40 Matt 26:61; John 2:19-20

---

those urging Jesus' condemnation are representative of all of unbelieving Israel, whose actions bring consequences for the nation as a whole (e.g., the destruction of Jerusalem in AD 70). • ***We will take responsibility for his death—we and our children*** (literally ***His blood be on us and on our children;*** see 23:35; 2 Sam 1:16; 14:9; Jer 51:35; Acts 5:28; 18:6; 20:26): Christians have at times misunderstood and misused this verse in persecution of Jews, but it is not an indictment against Jews in general.

27:26 When a man was ***flogged,*** he was beaten with whips that had leather thongs at the end, some with sharp bone, ***lead,*** or rock fragments stuck to the ends of the thongs (see also Deut 25:1-3; 1 Kgs 12:11, 14; Acts 16:22; 22:25; 2 Cor 11:24-25).

27:27-31 In the Jewish trial Jesus was mocked as a prophet (26:67-68); here he is mocked as a king.

27:27 The ***governor's soldiers*** were auxiliary troops recruited from non-Jewish residents of Palestine. • ***Their headquarters*** (or *The Praetorium*) was located at the official residence of the governor in Jerusalem (the Antonia Fortress on the northwest corner of the Temple compound).

27:28-29 The ***scarlet robe*** was probably the cloak of a soldier meant to emulate royal garb solely for the purpose of ridiculing Jesus. • Weaving ***thorn branches into a crown*** was a mockery of Jesus as king.

27:32-44 Ironically, the taunts and ridicule of the crowd express the truth about Jesus: He is the Son of God and King of Israel, the Messiah.

27:32 Normally, the victim carried his own ***cross.*** Only the crossbeam was carried; the vertical pole would be waiting at the crucifixion site. ***Simon*** might have been ***forced*** because Jesus was weak from the effects of scourging. The act of enlisting Simon might also have been a further mockery. Jesus was treated as one who deserved a servant even though he was being marched to his death. • ***Cyrene*** was a city in northern Africa.

27:34 Giving Jesus ***wine mixed with bitter gall*** was probably intended for ridicule (see Ps 69:21). It was also a sedative—Jesus probably rejected it in order to suffer fully for our sins (see Isa 53:10). • ***Gall,*** otherwise known as wormwood, is a bitter narcotic made from the oil of Artemisia (cp. Mark 15:23).

27:35 ***they . . . nailed him to the cross:*** Crucifixion, though not generally practiced by Jews, was a widespread Roman punishment for military and political offenders, particularly slaves, rebels, and insurrectionists. The sheer cruelty and the public spectacle of crucifixion worked as a powerful social deterrent. Victims were flogged and then crucified naked, adding to the humiliation. It was seen as the most painful of all possible deaths; it involved intense suffering, exposure to weather and insects, suffocation, and often a final violent thrust of a spear to end life. Further, since crucifixion was a curse from God (Deut 21:22-23), the act was particularly heinous to Jewish sensibilities. Paradoxically, what was so despicable among humans has become the instrument of our salvation. Jesus previously had instructed his disciples to take up their crosses and follow him (16:24). • ***by throwing dice:*** Literally *by casting lots.* A few late manuscripts add ***This fulfilled the word of the prophet: "They divided my garments among themselves and cast lots for my robe."*** See Ps 22:18.

27:37 The official charge was ***fastened*** to the cross above the criminal's ***head;*** Jesus was crucified for political sedition.

27:38 Crucifying Jesus between ***two*** convicted ***revolutionaries*** (or ***criminals;*** also in 27:44) added further humiliation and guilt by association.

27:40 ***if you are the Son of God:*** This taunt recalls Jesus' temptation at the very beginning of his public ministry (4:1-11), in which the devil appealed to Jesus' privileged status in order to tempt him to avoid suffering (see also 16:21-23).

27:45-56
//Mark 15:33-41
//Luke 23:44-49
//John 19:28-37
27:45
Amos 8:9
27:46
*Ps 22:1
27:48
Ps 69:21
John 19:29-30
27:51
Exod 26:31-33
Heb 10:19-20
27:52
Ezek 37:12
27:55-56
Luke 8:2-3
27:57-61
//Mark 15:42-47
//Luke 23:50-56
//John 19:38-42
27:60
Matt 28:2
Mark 16:3-4
Luke 24:2
John 20:1
27:61
Matt 27:56; 28:1
Mark 15:40, 47; 16:1
Luke 24:10
John 19:25

43He trusted God, so let God rescue him
now if he wants him! For he said, 'I am the
Son of God.'" 44Even the revolutionaries
who were crucified with him ridiculed him
in the same way.

The Death of Jesus
Matt 27:45-56 // Mark 15:33-41 // Luke 23:44-49 // John 19:28-30

45At noon, darkness fell across the whole
land until three o'clock. 46At about three
o'clock, Jesus called out with a loud voice,
"Eli, Eli, lema sabachthani?" which means
"My God, my God, why have you abandoned
me?"
47Some of the bystanders misunderstood and thought he was calling for the
prophet Elijah. 48One of them ran and filled
a sponge with sour wine, holding it up to
him on a reed stick so he could drink. 49But
the rest said, "Wait! Let's see whether Elijah
comes to save him."
50Then Jesus shouted out again, and he
released his spirit. 51At that moment the curtain in the sanctuary of the Temple was torn
in two, from top to bottom. The earth shook,
rocks split apart, 52and tombs opened. The
bodies of many godly men and women who
had died were raised from the dead. 53They
left the cemetery after Jesus' resurrection,
went into the holy city of Jerusalem, and appeared to many people.
54The Roman officer and the other soldiers at the crucifixion were terrified by
the earthquake and all that had happened.
They said, "This man truly was the Son of
God!"
55And many women who had come from
Galilee with Jesus to care for him were
watching from a distance. 56Among them
were Mary Magdalene, Mary (the mother of
James and Joseph), and the mother of James
and John, the sons of Zebedee.

The Burial of Jesus
Matt 27:57-61 // Mark 15:42-47 // Luke 23:50-56 // John 19:38-42

57As evening approached, Joseph, a rich
man from Arimathea who had become a
follower of Jesus, 58went to Pilate and asked
for Jesus' body. And Pilate issued an order
to release it to him. 59Joseph took the body
and wrapped it in a long sheet of clean
linen cloth. 60He placed it in his own new
tomb, which had been carved out of the
rock. Then he rolled a great stone across
the entrance and left. 61Both Mary Magdalene and the other Mary were sitting across
from the tomb and watching.

27:45 ***Darkness*** symbolizes the judgment of God or, more specifically, the arrival of the day of the Lord (see Amos 8:9-10; 5:18, 20; also Jer 4:27-28; 13:16; 15:9).

27:46 ***Eli, Eli:*** Some manuscripts read *Eloi, Eloi.* This cry means *My God, my God,* but the similarity in sound accounts for the people's confusion (27:47). • ***My God, my God, why have you abandoned me?*** Ps 22:1. Jesus was experiencing God's wrath for the sins of humanity.

27:47 It was widely believed that ***Elijah*** would return before the day of the Lord (11:14-15; 17:10-13; Mal 4:5).

27:48 The ***sour wine*** was vinegar. The drink was probably designed to mock Jesus (cp. Ps 69:21 with Matt 27:34) by pretending to help assuage his thirst. Others have suggested that it was given as an act of genuine kindness.

27:49 Some manuscripts add *And another took a spear and pierced his side, and out flowed water and blood.* Cp. John 19:34.

27:50 Each of the four Gospels highlights different aspects of Jesus' last moments. • ***released his spirit:*** This emphasizes the sovereignty of Jesus in that he released himself to death (see also John 19:30). • ***shouted out again*** (see 27:46): This cry was Jesus' final prayer (see Luke 23:46).

27:51 The significance of the splitting of the ***curtain*** in ***the Temple*** is that the wall dividing people from God has been torn down by the death of Jesus Christ (see also Eph 2:11-22; Heb 6:19; 9:1–10:25). • ***The earth shook, rocks split apart:*** These are portents of the arrival of judgment (see Exod 19:18; Judg 5:4; Ps 18:7; Joel 3:14-17; Amos 8:8-10). Josephus records the appearance about AD 30 of a star resembling a sword and a spontaneous opening of the gates of the Temple (Josephus, *War* 6.5.3-4).

27:52-53 ***tombs opened:*** Jesus' climactic death inaugurated the Kingdom of God by breaking the powers of death and establishing the final resurrection (see Isa 26:19; Dan 12:2; 1 Cor 15; Col 1:18; Heb 2:14-15). • These ***godly*** ones either did not enter the city until ***after Jesus' resurrection*** or they were not ***raised*** until then, with Jesus as the firstfruits (see 1 Cor 15:20, 23; Col 1:18). If that is the case, Matthew has included this episode to form a more powerful commentary on the impact of Jesus' death.

27:54 The ***Roman officer*** (literally *centurion*) ***and the other soldiers*** were Gentiles. • ***the Son of God:*** This may be an unqualified affirmation that Jesus is the unique ***Son of God*** (see 14:33; 16:16) or possibly a more general affirmation of Jesus' innocence (see Luke 23:47). They are responding to ***the earthquake and all that had happened*** as evidence of divine interest in this occasion.

27:58 In Roman crucifixion, the bodies of criminals were often left to rot. Deut 21:22-23 prohibits a body from remaining on a cross or a gallows overnight. Joseph's action was in accordance with Jewish law, while his motivation was probably his loyalty to Jesus. • ***Pilate issued an order:*** Pilate was accommodating, probably because he did not believe Jesus was guilty of insurrection (see 27:24-26).

27:59-60 Burial customs were important in Judaism, especially in contrast to the Greeks and Romans, who cremated their dead. Leaving a corpse unburied was the severest form of judgment (Deut 21:22-23; 2 Kgs 9:37; Ps 79:3; Jer 16:4, 6; Ezek 29:5; Rev 11:9). Death was lamented and mourned (Mark 5:38-39); the body was washed (Acts 9:37), anointed (26:6-13; John 12:3, 7; 19:39), and wrapped in burial cloths (27:59; see Gen 50:2-3). The body was placed in a tomb (see 23:27) that had been tunneled into a rock or carved into the side of a cave wall (see illustration, p. 1813). The entrance to a tomb was often closed with a huge ***stone*** and sealed to prevent ceremonial uncleanness or robbery. There were also some cemeteries (see 27:7). • ***clean linen . . . new tomb:*** Both reflect ceremonial purity. Joseph had purchased the tomb for his own family, but it had not yet been used.

The Guards at the Tomb
62The next day, on the Sabbath, the leading
priests and Pharisees went to see Pilate.
63They told him, "[g]Sir, we remember what
that deceiver once said while he was still
alive: 'After three days I will rise from the
dead.' 64So we request that you seal the
tomb until the third day. This will prevent
his disciples from coming and stealing
his body and then telling everyone he was
raised from the dead! If that happens, we'll
be worse off than we were at first."
65Pilate replied, "Take guards and secure
it the best you can." 66So they [h]sealed the
tomb and posted guards to protect it.

Jesus' Resurrection and Commission (28:1-20)
Jesus Is Raised from the Dead
Matt 28:1-10 // Mark 16:1-11 // Luke 24:1-12 // John 20:1-18

28 Early on Sunday morning, as the
new day was dawning, Mary Magdalene and the other Mary went out to visit
the tomb.
2Suddenly there was a great earthquake!
For an [i]angel of the Lord came down from
heaven, rolled aside the stone, and sat on it.
3His face shone like lightning, and his clothing was as white as snow. 4The guards shook
with fear when they saw him, and they fell
into a dead faint.
5Then the angel spoke to the women.
"Don't be afraid!" he said. "I know you are
looking for Jesus, who was crucified. 6He
isn't here! He is risen from the dead, just as
he said would happen. Come, see where his
body was lying. 7And now, go quickly and
tell his disciples that he has risen from the
dead, and he is going ahead of you to Galilee. You will see him there. Remember what
I have told you."
8The women ran quickly from the tomb.
They were very frightened but also filled
with great joy, and they rushed to give the
disciples the angel's message. 9And as they
went, Jesus met them and greeted them.
And they ran to him, grasped his feet, and
worshiped him. 10Then Jesus said to them,
"Don't be afraid! Go tell my brothers to leave
for Galilee, and they will see me there."

The Report of the Guards
11As the women were on their way, some of
the guards went into the city and told the
leading priests what had happened. 12A
meeting with the elders was called, and

27:63 Matt 12:40; 16:21; 17:23; 20:19; Mark 8:31; 9:31; 10:34; Luke 9:22; 18:33
[g]*kurios* (2962) ‣Mark 12:9
27:64 Matt 28:13
27:66 Dan 6:17
[h]*sphragizō* (4972) ‣1 Cor 9:2
28:1-8 //Mark 16:1-11 //Luke 24:1-11 //John 20:1-10
28:2 [i]*angelos* (0032) ‣Mark 8:38
28:3 Dan 7:9; 10:5-6
28:6 Matt 12:40; 16:21; 17:23; 20:19; Mark 8:31; 9:31; 10:34; Luke 9:22; 18:33; 24:7
28:7 Matt 26:32; Mark 14:28; 16:7
28:10 John 20:17; Rom 8:29; Heb 2:11-13, 17
28:13 Matt 27:64

WOMEN NAMED MARY (27:55-56, 61)

Matt 28:1; Mark 15:40-41, 47; 16:1-9; Luke 8:2-3; 10:38-42; 24:1-10; John 11:1-6, 17-24; 12:3-8; 19:25; 20:1-2, 11-18; Acts 12:12

Four other Marys, apart from the mother of Jesus (see p. 1701), are mentioned in the Gospels:

(1) Mary Magdalene (probably from Magdala in Galilee) was freed from demon possession by Jesus (Mark 16:9) and became a faithful follower and financial supporter of Jesus and his disciples (Luke 8:2-3; cp. Matt 27:55-56; Mark 15:40-41). She was present when Jesus was crucified and buried (27:55-56, 61; Mark 15:40-41, 47; John 19:25; cp. Luke 23:49, 55-56), and she went to the tomb early on Sunday morning to embalm him. She was among the first to be told of his Resurrection (28:1-8; Mark 16:1-8; Luke 24:1-11, 22-24), and she was the first to see the resurrected Jesus (28:9-10; Mark 16:9-11; John 20:1-2, 11-18).

(2) Mary the mother of James the younger (not the same as James the apostle) and Joseph was also among the women who were present when Jesus was crucified and buried (27:55-56, 61—the "other Mary"; Mark 15:40-41, 47; cp. Luke 23:55). She first heard the news of his resurrection (28:1-8; Mark 16:1-8; Luke 24:1-11), and she first saw the risen Jesus (28:9-10; Mark 16:9-10).

(3) Mary of Bethany was the sister of Martha and Lazarus; their family was much loved by Jesus (John 11:5). Jesus commended Mary for her eagerness to learn from him (Luke 10:38-42). In grateful response to what Jesus did in raising her brother from the dead (John 11:32-45), Mary anointed Jesus' feet with very expensive perfume, an act defended by Jesus when others criticized it as extravagant (26:6-13; Mark 14:3-9; John 12:1-11).

(4) Mary the wife of Clopas was also among the women watching when Jesus was crucified (John 19:25). Her husband Clopas is not mentioned elsewhere in the NT.

27:62-66 This incident bolsters the truth of Jesus' resurrection—it is inconceivable that Matthew would fabricate such a story since witnesses abounded who could have countered the claims.

27:62 ***The next day, on the Sabbath:*** Or *On the next day, which is after the Preparation.*

28:1-10 The discovery of the empty tomb and the various resurrection appearances are presented with different emphases in each of the four Gospels. Matthew focuses on the reunion in Galilee, the attempt on the part of the Jewish leaders to discredit the resurrection, and the significance of the resurrection for the salvation of the world.

28:1 *Early on Sunday morning:* Literally *After the Sabbath, on the first day of the week.* • ***Mary Magdalene*** (see 27:56): The mention of two women as witnesses lends credibility to the historicity of the account—an inventor of tales would not have used women as witnesses, since a woman's testimony was considered less reliable than a man's.

28:16-20
//Luke 24:36-49
//John 20:19-23
28:16
Matt 26:32; 28:7-10
28:18
Dan 7:13-14
John 3:35; 13:3; 17:2
Eph 1:20-22
Phil 2:9-10
28:19
Luke 24:47
Acts 1:8; 2:38
[j]*baptizō* (0907)
‣ Mark 16:16
28:20
Matt 18:20
John 14:23

they decided to give the soldiers a large
bribe. 13They told the soldiers, "You must
say, 'Jesus' disciples came during the night
while we were sleeping, and they stole
his body.' 14If the governor hears about
it, we'll stand up for you so you won't get
in trouble." 15So the guards accepted the
bribe and said what they were told to say.
Their story spread widely among the Jews,
and they still tell it today.

The Messiah's Great Commission to His Disciples
Matt 28:16-20; cp. Mark 16:14-18

16Then the eleven disciples left for Galilee,
going to the mountain where Jesus had
told them to go. 17When they saw him,
they worshiped him—but some of them
doubted!

18Jesus came and told his disciples, "I
have been given all authority in heaven
and on earth. 19Therefore, go and make
disciples of all the nations, [j]baptizing them
in the name of the Father and the Son and
the Holy Spirit. 20Teach these new disciples
to obey all the commands I have given you.
And be sure of this: I am with you always,
even to the end of the age."

The Resurrection of Jesus (28:1-10)

Matt 16:21; 17:9, 23; 20:19; 26:32
Mark 14:28
Luke 9:22; 14:14
John 2:19-22; 5:21; 6:39-40; 11:1-44; 14:20; 21:14
Acts 1:21-22; 2:22-36; 3:15, 26; 4:2, 10, 33; 5:30; 10:39-40; 13:29-31; 17:18, 32; 23:6-10
Rom 1:4; 4:24-25; 6:4-5, 9; 7:4; 8:11, 34; 10:9
1 Cor 6:14; 15:4, 12-23, 35, 42-44, 52
2 Cor 1:9; 4:14; 5:15
Gal 1:1
Eph 1:19-20; 2:5-6
Phil 3:10-11
Col 2:12; 3:1
1 Thes 1:10; 4:14
2 Tim 2:8, 18
Heb 6:2; 11:35
1 Pet 1:21; 3:18, 21
Rev 20:4-8, 11-15

Scripture unanimously depicts the personal and bodily resurrection of Jesus from the dead by the power of God, but numerous other attempts to explain it have emerged: (1) Jesus never really died—instead, he lost consciousness and regained it after being laid in a cool tomb (the swoon theory); (2) the disciples of Jesus stole his body and then lied about a resurrection (28:12-15); (3) the disciples had hallucinations and dreams that they mistakenly confused with a physical resurrection; and (4) the resurrection is a personal experience in the heart of faith, not an event in history. Behind such suggestions lies a deep-seated skepticism toward the supernatural, or at least toward whether a miraculous event could have happened. Such suggestions fail to take into account the fact that for NT authors and their audiences, the term "resurrection" could only have meant the literal reanimation of a dead corpse (see 1 Cor 15).

The historicity of Jesus' resurrection and the historical reliability of the biblical accounts are supported by (1) the evidence of an empty tomb; (2) the presence of women as witnesses (no one would have made up a story with women as witnesses, since the testimony of a woman was considered to be less reliable than that of a man); (3) the varied but basically unified accounts of Jesus' post-resurrection appearances; (4) the transformation of the disciples from a fearful band into fearless followers; and (5) the disciples' ability to overcome the scandal of following a crucified man (Deut 21:23 indicates that one who dies such a death has fallen under God's curse). Judaism had no concept of a dying and rising Messiah that could conveniently be applied to Jesus. Inventing something no one would find conceivable would have made little sense. The most reasonable conclusion is that Jesus did, in fact, rise from the dead.

28:12 Such a ***bribe*** was contrary to the law (see Exod 20:16; 23:8). • ***elders:*** See note on 21:23.

28:13 ***stole his body:*** Tomb robbery was a common problem in the ancient world, so such an accusation would have been entirely believable.

28:15 ***still tell it today:*** Justin Martyr wrote to Jews of his day (about AD 165), "You have sent . . . men throughout all the world to proclaim, 'A godless and lawless heresy has sprung from one Jesus, a Galilean deceiver, whom we crucified, but his disciples stole him by night from the tomb . . . and now [the disciples] deceive men by asserting that he has risen from the dead and ascended into heaven' " (Justin Martyr, *Dialogue with Trypho* 108). This misinformation probably became widespread after the disciples began to proclaim Jesus' resurrection (see Acts 2:22-36).

28:17 ***some of them doubted:*** This might be a veiled reference to Thomas (John 20:24-29), but all eleven might have experienced a mixture of both worship and doubt (see also 14:31; Luke 24:10-11; John 20:24-29).

28:18 Jesus' ***authority*** is power delegated from the Father (see 7:29; 9:6-8; 21:23-27; 26:64; John 3:35).

28:19 ***go and:*** Literally *going*, a participle that supports the main imperative, ***make disciples***. Matthew probably intended ***go*** to be understood as a separate command (as it is translated) and not as a circumstantial modifier (i.e., *while you go;* cp. the same construction in 9:6; Acts 10:20). • ***make disciples:*** A disciple is one who repents of sin, trusts in Jesus for salvation, and obeys his teachings. • ***all the nations*** (or *all peoples*): The mission to the Gentile nations formally began here (see 10:5-6; 15:24; see also 1:1; 2:1-12; 8:5-13; 21:43; 24:14; 26:13). • Two aspects of making ***disciples*** are ***baptizing*** and teaching (28:20). Baptism indicates public identification with, and surrender to, Jesus and the work he has done for salvation (see 3:13-17; 10:32-33; 20:28; 26:28; Acts 2:38; Rom 6:1-11; 1 Pet 3:21). • ***In the name of*** means entrance into a relationship and its benefits, which come to those who truly believe. • ***Father . . . Son . . . Holy Spirit:*** This is a formulaic expression for the nature of God as a trinity (see also 1 Cor 12:4-6; 2 Cor 13:14; Eph 4:4-6; 2 Thes 2:13-14; 1 Pet 1:2; Rev 1:4-6).

28:20 ***Teach:*** The disciples' curriculum is comprised of ***all the commands*** of Jesus (e.g., the Sermon on the Mount, 5:1–7:29). The church is to be marked by its obedience to Jesus' commands (5:17-20; 7:13-27). Jesus' authority and presence are the basis for the disciples' mission (see also 1:23; 18:20).

THE GOSPEL ACCORDING TO MARK

In his opening verse, Mark provides readers with the main key to understanding his Gospel: Although we can learn much about the disciples and other characters from reading Mark, it is most important to understand what he is teaching about Jesus: It is about "Jesus the Messiah, the Son of God" (1:1).

SETTING

It is generally agreed that Mark was the first of the four canonical Gospels to be written. Before the writing of Mark, there were no Gospels as such. The gospel traditions were circulated or "delivered" orally under the supervision of the eyewitnesses and ministers of the word of God (Luke 1:2). As these eyewitnesses began to die, it became important to record the gospel traditions in writing. According to church tradition, after the martyrdom of Peter in the mid-60s AD, the church in Rome asked John Mark to put into writing the accounts of Jesus' life and teachings that Peter had delivered to them orally. As a result, Mark became the first to compose what we call a "Gospel," a written account of Jesus' life and teachings, from the oral materials about Jesus.

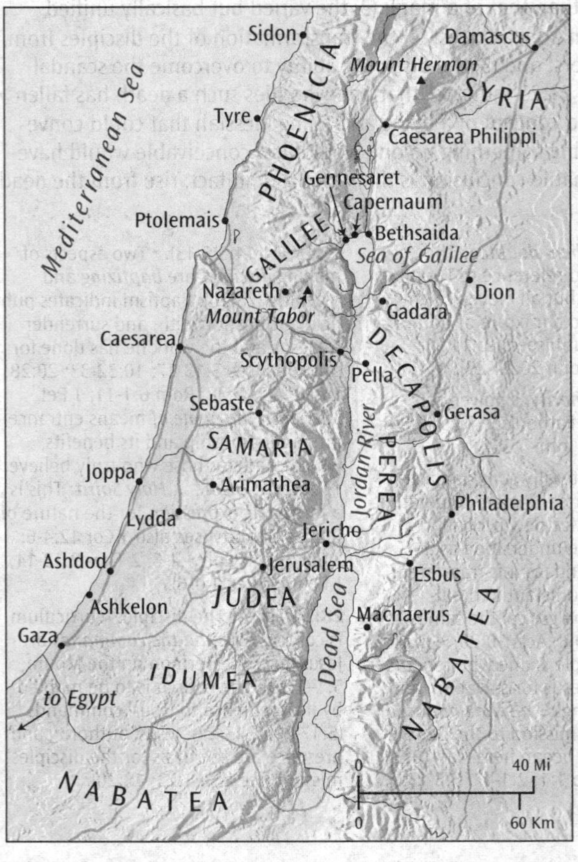

◀ **Key Places in the Gospel of Mark.** The book of Mark is organized geographically: After Jesus' baptism by John in the JORDAN RIVER (1:1-15), it describes Jesus' ministry in GALILEE (1:16–9:50), followed by his ministry in JUDEA including his death and resurrection (10:1–16:8).

SUMMARY

The overall structure of Mark is geographical. The first nine chapters narrate events of Jesus' ministry in Galilee and its environs. In chapter 10, Jesus and the disciples travel from Galilee to Jerusalem, and the last chapters of the book (chs 11–16) take place in and around Jerusalem. (Matthew and Luke, in their use of Mark, followed this geographical outline, but John organized his Gospel in a different way.)

Within the geographical outline, Mark has arranged much of his material topically. Thus we have collections of miracle stories (1:21-45; 4:35–5:43), controversy stories (2:1–3:6; 12:13-37), parables (4:1-34), and teachings about the end (13:5-37). Some of the materials include indicators of chronological sequence: Jesus' ministry began with

his baptism (1:2-11; see Acts 1:22; 10:37) and temptation (1:12-13); his suffering, death, and resurrection occurred at the end (11:1–16:8). A few individual accounts are tied together chronologically, such as Peter's confession at Caesarea Philippi (8:27-33) and Jesus' transfiguration (9:1-13; see also 1:29, 35).

The major turning point in Jesus' ministry is highlighted in 8:27-33, very near the center of the book. At Caesarea Philippi, the disciples for the first time confess their belief that Jesus is the Messiah (8:29). Upon this acknowledgment, Jesus "began to tell them" of his forthcoming death and resurrection (8:31; cp. Matt 16:21). Jesus' death and resurrection are the dominant theme of 8:31–16:8.

AUTHOR

Although all four Gospels are introduced by a title assigning them to a specific author ("The Gospel according to Mark"), these titles are not part of the original manuscripts. The earliest known reference to the authorship of Mark comes from Papias at the beginning of the second century. The early church historian Eusebius quotes Papias as having said, "Mark became Peter's interpreter and wrote accurately all that he remembered, not, indeed, in order, of the things said or done by the Lord. For he had not heard the Lord, nor had he followed him, but later on . . . followed Peter" (Eusebius, *Church History* 3.39.16).

The early church was unanimous in attributing this Gospel to John Mark. It is unlikely that Papias and others would have attributed this Gospel to a non-apostle with a tarnished reputation (see Acts 13:13; 15:36-41) unless Mark were in fact the author.

The author of this Gospel was bilingual, as the Aramaic phrases in its Greek text suggest (e.g., 5:41; 7:34; 15:34). He was also Jewish, in that he knew and explained various Jewish customs to his Gentile readers (e.g., 7:3-4; 14:12). This fits with the view that John Mark could be the author. John Mark was a Jew who was raised in Jerusalem (Acts 12:12). He thus knew Aramaic (the native language of the people of Judea) and was familiar with Jewish customs.

Some have objected that this Gospel does not clearly indicate a connection between Mark and Peter and that it looks more polished as a literary composition than one might expect from a direct record of Peter's eyewitness testimony. But if this Gospel was written near or after Peter's death (see "Date," p. 1644), Peter had been telling these stories for over thirty years. Through continual retelling, his gospel account would have become well polished. There are also references to Peter in this Gospel that might be due to Mark's personal connection with him (e.g., 1:16-20; 8:32-33; 9:5-6; 14:28-31, 66-72). It fits the evidence well to consider this Gospel as

OUTLINE

1:1-13
The Beginning of the Good News

1:14–5:43
Who Is This Jesus?

6:1–8:26
Jesus Is Misunderstood

8:27–10:52
Preparing for Jerusalem

11:1–13:37
Jesus' Ministry in Jerusalem

14:1–16:20
The Death and Resurrection of Jesus

TIMELINE

about 6~4 BC
Birth of Jesus

about AD 28
Jesus' baptism by John

Passover, AD 30 or 33
Jesus' crucifixion and resurrection

AD 49~50
The council in Jerusalem

AD 65~70
Mark writes the Gospel of Mark

AD 66–70
War between Romans and Jews at Jerusalem

AD 70
Jerusalem and the Temple are destroyed

having indeed been written by John Mark, Barnabas's cousin, based on Peter's gospel accounts (see "John Mark" at Acts 13:4-5, 13, p. 1852).

DATE

John Mark probably wrote down Peter's teaching about Jesus around the time of Peter's death. Peter died in Rome around AD 64 in the persecution that Nero waged against Christians (see "Simon Peter" at Matt 14:28-31, p. 1609). Mark probably wrote this Gospel in the late 60s, and various considerations support this hypothesis. (1) The emphasis on faithfulness in time of persecution (4:17; 8:34-38; 10:30; 13:9-13) suggests a time during or shortly after Nero's persecution in the mid-60s. (2) The lack of any clear allusion to the fall of Jerusalem suggests a time before AD 70. (3) However, the Jewish revolt (AD 66–73) had apparently already begun, and the destruction of Jerusalem was rapidly drawing near (see 13:1-37).

AUDIENCE

The Gospel of Mark was written for the church in Rome, according to tradition. It is clear that the original readers were Greek-speaking and that they were Gentiles, because the author explains Jewish customs (e.g., 7:3-4; 14:12) and distinguishes his readers from "the Jews" (7:3).

The original readers were Christians. They were familiar with the gospel traditions, for the author does not explain such things as who John the Baptist was (1:2-8), who Isaiah the prophet was (1:2), where Capernaum was located (1:21; 2:1), various OT references (2:25-26), who King Herod was (6:14-29), or who the Pharisees and teachers of religious law were (7:1).

It is also apparent that the readers were Romans, as indicated by the "Latinisms" in Mark. In 6:27, he uses a Latin word meaning "soldier"; in 12:42, he uses a Roman coin (the *quadran*) to explain the meaning of "two *lepta*" (Greek coins); and in 15:39, 44-45, he uses the Latin word "centurion" rather than the Greek word with the same meaning that Matthew and Luke use.

> *Mark is master of the unexpected. . . . The medium of irony is important for the Second Evangelist, who throughout the Gospel portrays Jesus as one who challenges, confounds, and sometimes breaks conventional stereotypes, whether religious, social, or political.*
>
> JAMES R. EDWARDS
> *The Gospel according to Mark*, p. 12

LITERARY FEATURES

Mark's own editorial work can be seen most clearly in his introductory statements (e.g., 1:21-22; 2:1; 4:1; 7:1), in his explanatory comments (e.g., 1:16; 2:15; 5:8, 28, 42; 6:14, 17, 20, 52; 7:3-4), and in his summaries (e.g., 1:14-15, 34, 39; 3:7-12; 6:53-56).

Mark repeats various terms and expressions to show progress, such as "suddenly," "at once," and "immediately" (e.g., 1:23; 3:6; 6:45). He uses the Greek present tense in the narrative to give a sense of immediacy (e.g., 1:12, 21, 38, 40, 44; 2:3; 3:13). Mark also often sandwiches one story within another (e.g., 3:22-30 into 3:20-21, 31-35; 5:25-34 into 5:21-24, 35-43; 11:15-19 into 11:12-14, 20-26); in the last example, this sandwiching indicates that the middle part (11:15-19, the cleansing of the Temple) is to be understood in light of the story surrounding it (11:12-14, 20-26, the cursing of the fig tree)—the cleansing of the Temple was a symbolic act of judgment (cp. 13:3-37). Thus, Mark's editorial work relates different events and shows meaningful connections.

MEANING AND MESSAGE

Mark's main purpose in writing his Gospel is stated in the opening verse of the Gospel: He wanted his readers to know that Jesus of Naza-

reth is "the Messiah, the Son of God." The title "Son of God" occurs frequently in Mark, and there are diverse witnesses to Jesus' status as God's son: the demons (1:34; 3:11; 5:7; cp. 1:24); God himself (1:11; 9:7); Mark, the author (1:1); a Roman centurion (15:39); and Jesus himself (12:6; 13:32; 14:61-62).

During his life, the Son of God needed to protect himself and his followers from the prevailing misconceptions in the minds of the people about what the term "Christ" (or "Messiah") meant (see "The Secret of the Messiah" at 3:11-12, p. 1653). Jesus' ultimate mission as the Son of God is explained through his death, in which he gave his life as a ransom for many. The call to Christian discipleship is a call to follow the Messiah, the Son of God, and receive the benefits of his life and death (see "Following Jesus" at 8:34-38, p. 1667). Jesus' ministry as Son of God during his life on earth also points forward to his return as the Son of God, ruling God's Kingdom (see "The Day is Coming" at 13:1-37, p. 1681).

The Person of Christ. Mark's major theological emphasis is the identity of Jesus of Nazareth. For Mark, Jesus is above all "the Messiah, the Son of God." Other titles for Jesus occur in Mark's Gospel, including Jesus' own favorite, "Son of Man" (e.g., 2:10). But in Mark's Gospel all of these titles, as well as his actions (e.g., 1:22; 4:41), point to his identity as the Christ (or Messiah), the Son of God.

The Death of Jesus. The Gospel of Mark has been called "a passion narrative with an extended introduction" because of Mark's focus on the account of Jesus' *passion*—his suffering, death, and resurrection. Throughout the Gospel we find numerous references to the death of Jesus (2:19-20; 3:6; 8:31; 9:9, 12, 31; 10:33-34, 45; 12:1-11; 14:1-11, 21, 24-25, 36; 14:64–15:47). Mark emphasizes that Jesus' death was part of God's plan for his life. His death was a divine necessity (8:31), for God had willed it (10:45; 14:36). The Scriptures of the OT also teach of the Messiah's death (9:12; 14:21, 27, 49). Jesus came to give his life as a ransom for many (10:45) and to pour out his blood sacrificially in order to establish a new covenant (14:24).

Christian Discipleship. Mark emphasizes the importance of following Jesus by denying one's self and taking up one's cross (see 8:34). Christian discipleship does not permit a half-hearted response but requires leaving everything to follow Jesus (1:18, 20; 10:21, 29). Christian discipleship might even bring persecution and martyrdom (13:9-13a), but Christians are promised that endurance in faith means salvation (13:13b) and eternal life (10:30).

The "Secret of the Messiah." Throughout Mark's Gospel, Jesus tells others not to broadcast his true identity. Yet the secret is not and cannot be kept (7:36). Jesus is too great. Jesus creates such wonder and amazement that he simply cannot be hidden. His identity breaks through, so that all recognize that he is indeed the Messiah, the Son of God, the Lord of all creation.

The Coming of God's Kingdom. The arrival of God's Kingdom is central to Jesus' message. People need to repent and believe the gospel because the Kingdom of God has arrived (1:14-15). Old Testament promises are being fulfilled. Life in the Kingdom is different from what it was during the time awaiting the Kingdom.

Mark's Gospel has been described as 'a passion-narrative with an extended introduction.' The reason that almost half of Mark's sixteen chapters describe the final period of Jesus' ministry is that it is in his suffering, death, and resurrection that the revelation of God in Christ is most clearly seen.

WILLIAM L. LANE
The Gospel of Mark, p. 2

FURTHER READING

DARRELL BOCK
Mark in *Cornerstone Biblical Commentary*, vol. 11 (2005)

R. ALAN COLE
Mark (1961)

CRAIG A. EVANS
Mark 8:27–16:20 (2000)

R. T. FRANCE
Mark (2002)

ROBERT GUELICH
Mark 1–8:26 (1989)

ROBERT H. STEIN
Mark (2008)

1. THE BEGINNING OF THE GOOD NEWS (1:1-13)

John the Baptist Prepares the Way

Mark 1:2-3 // Matt 3:1-3 // Luke 3:2b-6 // John 1:23
Mark 1:4-6 // Matt 3:4-6
Mark 1:7-8 // Matt 3:11-12 // Luke 3:15-18 // John 1:24-28

1 This is the [a]Good News about Jesus the
Messiah, the Son of God. It began 2 just
as the prophet Isaiah had written:

"Look, I am sending my messenger ahead
of you,
and he will prepare your way.
3 He is a voice shouting in the
wilderness,
'Prepare the way for the LORD's coming!
Clear the road for him!'"

4 This messenger was John the Baptist. He
was in the wilderness and preached that
people should be baptized to show that
they had [b]repented of their sins and turned
to God to be forgiven. 5 All of Judea, including all the people of Jerusalem, went out
to see and hear John. And when they confessed their sins, he baptized them in the
Jordan River. 6 His clothes were woven from
coarse camel hair, and he wore a leather belt
around his waist. For food he ate locusts
and wild honey.
7 John announced: "Someone is coming
soon who is greater than I am—so much
greater that I'm not even worthy to stoop
down like a slave and untie the straps of his
sandals. 8 I baptize you with water, but he
will baptize you with the Holy Spirit!"

The Baptism of Jesus

Mark 1:9-11 // Matt 3:13-17 // Luke 3:21-22 // John 1:29-34

9 One day Jesus came from Nazareth in Galilee, and John baptized him in the Jordan
River. 10 As Jesus came up out of the water,
he saw the heavens splitting apart and the
Holy Spirit descending on him like a dove.

1:1 [a]*euangelion* (2098) ›Mark 1:14
1:2-8 //Matt 3:1-11 //Luke 3:1-16 //John 1:19-28
1:2-3 *Isa 40:3 *Mal 3:1 Matt 17:10-12 John 1:23
1:4 Acts 13:24; 19:4 [b]*metanoia* (3341) ›Luke 3:8
1:6 Lev 11:22 2 Kgs 1:8 Zech 13:4
1:7 Acts 13:25
1:8 Joel 2:28 Acts 2:4; 10:45; 11:16
1:9-11 //Matt 3:13-17 //Luke 3:21-22
1:11 Gen 22:2 Ps 2:7 Mark 9:7 2 Pet 1:17

1:1 Mark opens with an introduction. This Gospel is ***about Jesus.*** With every account in Mark, one should ask, "What is Mark teaching about Jesus in this passage?" • ***Good News,*** a frequent term in Mark (see 1:14-15; 8:35; 10:29; 13:10; 14:9), is frequently translated *gospel*. See note on 1:15. • The Hebrew word ***Messiah*** (Greek *christos*) is often translated *Christ*. Both Messiah and Christ mean "anointed." In the OT, priests (Exod 28:41; Lev 16:32; 21:10), kings (2 Sam 1:14, 16; 19:21; Ps 2), and prophets (1 Kgs 19:16) were anointed with oil to indicate the Lord's presence, blessing, and authority for the tasks to which God called them. As time went on, Israelites increasingly looked forward to the coming of the Messiah, "the Anointed One," a descendant of David who would be Israel's king. The first-century political connotations of this title were such that Jesus avoided openly declaring that he was the Messiah (see "The Secret of the Messiah" at 3:11-12, p. 1653; see also 8:27-30; 14:61-63; 15:2, 26; John 4:25-26). • Some manuscripts do not include ***the Son of God;*** this title emphasizes Jesus' unique relationship with God the Father (1:11; 9:7; 12:4-6; 14:61-62).

1:2-8 This account is not primarily about John the Baptist, the messenger, but about the one he announces as "Jesus the Messiah, the Son of God" (1:1).

1:2-3 Mark includes OT prophecies to support his account of the Good News about Jesus Christ. John the Baptist's role as the prophetic messenger reveals that Jesus is the promised Lord—Christ, the Son of God. • ***Isaiah:*** Mark follows the Jewish practice of mentioning only the most prominent of the sources that make up the quotation (Mal 3:1; Isa 40:3).

1:2 This portion of the quotation is from Mal 3:1.

1:3 John the Baptist was the ***voice shouting in the wilderness*** for people to ***prepare the way for the LORD's coming*** (this portion of the quotation is from Isa 40:3, Greek version). In Isaiah, this prophecy refers to the coming of the Lord, the God of Israel. Here it refers to the Lord Jesus (see 12:35-37). The early church called itself "the Way," probably in reference to this promise (see Acts 9:2; 19:9, 23; 22:4; 24:14, 22; cp. Acts 2:28; 18:25-26; Rom 2:20; 2 Pet 2:2, 21).

1:4 ***John***'s mission as the Lord's ***messenger*** was to prepare people for the Messiah's coming (see Luke 1:76-77) by instructing them to confess ***their sins,*** turn to God for forgiveness, and ***be baptized.*** Those who did this were prepared to receive Jesus' message (see Luke 7:29-30). See "John the Baptist" at John 1:19-37, p. 1771. • That John ***was in the wilderness,*** probably the desert area around the Jordan River north of the Dead Sea, shows that he was the "voice" of whom Isaiah had spoken (1:3). • ***be baptized:*** The exact origin of John's baptism is unclear. The Qumran community had an initiatory "baptism" which was repeated regularly, but John's baptism was once for all. Jewish proselyte baptism has also been seen as a possible source, but it is more likely that such baptisms were not practiced until after John's ministry. See also "Baptism" at Acts 2:38, 41, p. 1828.

1:5 ***All of Judea:*** John the Baptist created a lot of interest. It was generally believed that there had been no prophet for over 400 years, so prophets were associated with Israel's past and with the future reign of the Messiah. John preached repentance like the ancient prophets, and he dressed like the great prophet Elijah (1:6), who was predicted to return in the last days (Mal 4:5).

1:6 ***camel hair . . . leather belt:*** Cp. Elijah (2 Kgs 1:8). • ***For food*** John ***ate*** what was available in the wilderness; ***locusts*** were allowed as food (cp. Lev 11:20-24).

1:7 ***Someone is coming:*** John knew that he was preparing for the Messiah's coming, but he did not yet know that Jesus was he (cp. Luke 7:18-23).

1:8 John's baptism prepared people for God's Kingdom by calling them to repentance. The baptism of Jesus brought the gift of the ***Holy Spirit,*** through whom sinful people become God's children (Rom 8:15-16; 1 Cor 12:13; Gal 4:6). • ***with:*** Or *in,* twice in this verse.

1:9 Jesus' home at this time was in ***Nazareth,*** a small town in lower ***Galilee*** (Matt 2:19-23; Luke 2:39). Jesus soon left Nazareth for Capernaum, a city on the Sea of Galilee (Matt 4:13). • ***John baptized him:*** Jesus' reason for receiving the baptism of repentance is explained in Matt 3:14-15.

1:10 The expression ***the heavens splitting apart*** indicates Jesus' unique access to God the Father; in 15:38, the same verb includes believers in that access through Jesus' death. • All four Gospels refer to the Spirit descending ***on him*** (or *toward him,* or *into him*) ***like a dove.*** The Spirit, who was involved in the first creation, acted with Jesus in bringing the new creation (Gen 1:2; Rom 8:15-17; 1 Cor 6:11; Eph 1:13-14; 2 Thes 2:13).

1:12-13
//Matt 4:1-11
//Luke 4:1-13

1:13
[c]*peirazō* (3985)
‣ Mark 14:38

1:14-15
//Matt 4:12-17
//Luke 4:14-15

11 And a voice from heaven said, "You are my
dearly loved Son, and you bring me great
joy."

The Temptation of Jesus
Mark 1:12-13 // Matt 4:1-11 // Luke 4:1-13

12 The Spirit then compelled Jesus to go into
the wilderness, 13 where he was [c]tempted
by Satan for forty days. He was out among
the wild animals, and angels took care of
him.

2. WHO IS THIS JESUS? (1:14–5:43)

Introduction to Jesus' Ministry (1:14-20)

A Summary of Jesus' Message
Mark 1:14-15; cp. Matt 4:12-17; Luke 4:14-15

14 Later on, after John was arrested, Jesus
went into Galilee, where he preached God's

The Coming of God's Kingdom (1:14-15)

Mark 4:11, 26-32; 8:31-38; 9:1, 47; 10:23-25, 29-31; 13:24-27, 32-37; 14:25, 62
Jer 31:31-34
Joel 2:28-32
Matt 4:23; 5:3; 6:10; 25:31-46
Luke 2:25-38; 4:18-19, 42-43; 6:20; 10:18-20; 11:20
Acts 1:6-8; 2:16-21
1 Cor 15:22-28
Titus 2:11-14

The arrival of God's Kingdom was central to Jesus' proclamation. People are to repent and believe the gospel because God's Kingdom has arrived in the person of Jesus (1:14-15; 4:11, 26, 30; 9:47; Matt 4:23; 5:3; 6:10; Luke 4:42-43; 6:20).

The arrival of God's Kingdom was eagerly awaited by the people of Israel, for it would fulfill the many promises of God that had not yet been realized:

- The Spirit would not only come again, as he had in the past, but he would come upon each individual believer in fulfillment of Joel 2:28-32 (cp. Acts 2:16-21).
- Satan would be defeated (3:27; Luke 10:18), as was already being demonstrated by Jesus' exorcisms (2:1-12; 3:11; 5:1-20).
- The new covenant promised in Jeremiah 31:31-34 would be established (14:24).
- The resurrection from the dead would produce its firstfruits (8:31; 9:9, 31; 10:33-34; 16:6; 1 Cor 15:20, 23).
- God's Anointed, the promised Son of David (Matt 2:1-12; Luke 2:25-38) would arrive.

These dimensions of God's Kingdom have already been fulfilled in the coming, death, resurrection, and ascension of Jesus.

Immediately prior to the arrival of Jesus and John the Baptist, Israel was oppressed by Rome and without true prophets or the active presence of God's Spirit. Instead of a king descended from David, a Roman governor ruled the land. In such a situation, fasting was appropriate. With the coming of Jesus came the coming of God's Kingdom, and things radically changed. The Spirit was once again active in the land, working through the prophet John the Baptist and in the ministry of Jesus. For those with eyes to see, the promised Messiah, or Christ, had appeared. Because God's Kingdom was with them in the person of Jesus, the disciples could not fast like the Pharisees and the disciples of John the Baptist (2:18-20). Fasting became inappropriate, for the OT promises were being fulfilled. It was time to celebrate and feast (2:19-20), because God's reign had begun (Luke 11:20). People were already entering into the Kingdom (10:23-25, 29-31) and experiencing its manifestations (9:1).

There is a future, not-yet-realized dimension of God's Kingdom that awaits Christ's return (14:25). The Jews' national hope for the arrival of God's Kingdom (see Acts 1:6) are mostly part of this "not yet" dimension (Acts 1:7-8). The ultimate judgment of evil, the final establishment of justice, and the eradication of disease, poverty, and even death will find their fulfillment when Jesus, the Son of Man, returns in glory, gathers his elect (13:24-27; Titus 2:11-14), judges the world (8:38; 13:26; 14:62; Matt 25:31-46; 2 Tim 4:1; Rev 14:14-20), and resurrects the dead (1 Thes 4:13–5:11; 1 Cor 15:12-57). Although the time of Christ's return is unknown (13:32), Christians are to be alert and watch for his coming (13:33, 35, 37) in anticipation of their "blessed hope" (Titus 2:13).

1:11 ***You are my dearly loved Son:*** See "The Son of God" at 4:35-41, p. 1655. By age twelve, Jesus was aware of his unique relationship with God the Father (Luke 2:49).

1:12-13 ***The Spirit then compelled Jesus*** (cp. Matt 4:1; Luke 4:1): Jesus was victorious over Satan and temptation from the beginning of his ministry; the later exorcisms (1:21-34; 3:11-12; 5:1-20; 9:14-27) are an outworking of that victory (see 3:27). • Jesus was tempted in ***the wilderness*** of Judea. ***Satan*** and ***wild animals*** (Isa 13:19-22; Ezek 34:25) give the wilderness an evil aura. The wild animals included dogs, wolves, leopards, jackals, and bears. • The period of ***forty days*** recalls Israel's forty years of testing in the wilderness. Israel failed, but Jesus was victorious—he was tempted without sinning (Heb 2:18; 4:15; cp. Jas 1:3, 12; 1 Pet 1:7; Rev 2:10).

1:14-15 This summary introduces 1:14–3:6. Such summaries (see also 3:7-12; 6:6) help hearers understand what follows; most of Mark's original audience would have heard the Gospel read aloud.

1:14 Jesus' ministry is described as beginning ***after John was arrested.*** There was some overlap (John 3:22-24; 4:1-2),

[d]Good News. 15“The time promised by God has come at last!” he announced. “The Kingdom of God is near! Repent of your sins and believe the [e]Good News!”

The First Disciples
Mark 1:16-20 // Matt 4:18-22

16One day as Jesus was walking along the shore of the Sea of Galilee, he saw Simon and his brother Andrew throwing a net into the water, for they fished for a living. 17Jesus called out to them, “Come, follow me, and I will show you how to fish for people!” 18And they left their nets at once and followed him.

19A little farther up the shore Jesus saw Zebedee’s sons, James and John, in a boat repairing their nets. 20He called them at once, and they also followed him, leaving their father, Zebedee, in the boat with the hired men.

Jesus’ Healing Miracles (1:21-45)

Jesus Casts Out an Evil Spirit
Mark 1:21-28 // Luke 4:31-37

21Jesus and his companions went to the town of Capernaum. When the Sabbath day came, he went into the synagogue and began to teach. 22The people were amazed at his teaching, for he taught with real authority—quite unlike the teachers of religious law.

23Suddenly, a man in the synagogue who was possessed by an evil spirit began shouting, 24“Why are you interfering with us, Jesus of Nazareth? Have you come to destroy us? I know who you are—the Holy One of God!”

25Jesus cut him short. “Be quiet! Come out of the man,” he ordered. 26At that, the evil spirit screamed, threw the man into a convulsion, and then came out of him.

27Amazement gripped the audience, and they began to discuss what had happened. “What sort of new teaching is this?” they asked excitedly. “It has such authority! Even evil spirits obey his orders!” 28The news about Jesus spread quickly throughout the entire region of Galilee.

Jesus Heals Many People
Mark 1:29-34 // Matt 8:14-17 // Luke 4:38-41

29After Jesus left the synagogue with James and John, they went to Simon and Andrew’s home. 30Now Simon’s mother-in-law was

1:14
[d]*euangelion* (2098)
‣Mark 1:15

1:15
Gal 4:4
Eph 1:10
[e]*euangelion* (2098)
‣Rom 1:1

1:16-20
//Matt 4:18-22
//Luke 5:1-11
John 1:35-42

1:19
Matt 10:2
Mark 3:17; 10:35
Luke 5:10

1:21-28
//Luke 4:31-41

1:22
Matt 7:28-29
Luke 2:45-47

1:24
Matt 8:29
John 6:69

1:26
Mark 9:20, 26

1:29-34
//Matt 8:14-17
//Luke 4:38-41

---

but most of Jesus’ ministry occurred after John’s. John also belongs primarily to the old order (Matt 11:7-14), while Jesus belongs primarily to the new. Both men fulfilled God’s plan through being arrested and executed (6:14-29; 9:31; 10:33). Jesus began preaching in ***Galilee*** at this time, but John 2:13–4:43 suggests that Jesus had had an earlier ministry in Judea. • ***God’s Good News:*** Some manuscripts read *the Good News of the Kingdom of God.*

1:15 Jesus’ preaching is summarized by his announcement that the Kingdom of God had come, and that people needed to repent and believe the Good News about the Messiah (1:1). • The ***Kingdom of God*** is not tied to a territory; it dynamically began in Jesus’ person and extended to his followers. • In response to the arrival of God’s Kingdom, people are called to ***repent*** (to turn from sin and yield to God), and to have faith in God’s ***Good News***. In Jesus’ time, the Good News was the arrival of God’s reign through the Messiah. For Mark’s later audience, it was the news of Jesus’ death, resurrection, ascension, and promised return (15:1–16:8). All people, Jews and Gentiles alike, need God’s forgiveness through repentance and faith in Jesus.

1:16-20 The call of the two pairs of brothers—Simon and Andrew, James and John—followed an earlier encounter with Jesus (John 1:35-42).

1:16 ***Simon*** is called “Peter” in 3:16 and thereafter.

1:17 Mark uses Jesus’ invitation—***Come, follow me*** (1:20; 8:34)—and the expression “to follow him” (1:18; 2:14-15; 3:7; 5:24) to indicate what it means to be a Christian (see “Following Jesus” at 8:34-38, p. 1667).

1:19-20 ***Zebedee’s sons . . . leaving their father:*** Jesus later taught that this is the kind of thing that his followers will do (8:34-35; Matt 10:37-39).

1:21-28 Jesus’ exorcisms reveal Jesus’ identity (see note on 1:23-24) and his power over Satan (see notes on 1:12-13 and 3:27; see also 1:34, 39; 3:11-12, 22; 5:1-20; 6:13; 7:24-30; 9:14-29).

1:21 Mark introduces his first account of an exorcism with ***Jesus and his companions*** going ***into the synagogue*** in Capernaum. Jesus’ teaching in the synagogue suggests that he already had a reputation as a teacher and was therefore invited to speak (cp. Acts 13:15).

1:22 ***The teachers of religious law*** were professional scribes—scholars who taught, copied, and interpreted Jewish law for the people. They were primarily associated with the Pharisees (see “The Pharisees” at Matt 3:7, p. 1581). The scribes’ authority was derived from quoting other scribes (cp. Matt 5:21-48). Jesus’ teaching caused amazement because he spoke and acted with ***real authority*** (see 1:27; 5:20; 6:2; 7:37; 10:24-32; 11:18; 15:5).

1:23-24 The demon spoke through the man ***who was possessed by an evil*** (literally *unclean*) ***spirit*** (1:24). Demons frequently cause disease (9:17, 27; Matt 17:15) and self-destructive behavior (Mark 1:26; 5:2-5; 9:17-18, 20-22). Demons know who Jesus is (1:34); they consistently testify that he is ***the Holy One of God*** (see 3:11; 5:7). • In saying ***us***, the evil spirit spoke on behalf of all demons. It recognized Jesus’ complete authority and understood that he had come to interfere with and ***destroy*** evil.

1:25 Jesus did not need to shout or utter magic words. He simply spoke with the authority of the Son of God (1:1), and the evil spirit obeyed. • ***Be quiet!*** Jesus commanded the evil spirit not to make him known. This is an instance of the “messianic secret,” an expression for passages in Mark in which Jesus commands demons or people not to reveal his identity (1:25, 34; 3:11-12; 8:30; 9:9; see “The Secret of the Messiah” at 3:11-12, p. 1653).

1:26 The screams and convulsions caused by the ***evil*** (literally *unclean*; also in 1:27) ***spirit*** were its parting cries of defeat (5:13; 9:26; cp. 15:37).

1:27-28 The ***amazement*** caused by this exorcism ***quickly*** spread the ***news about Jesus.*** • ***What sort of new teaching is this?*** Jesus’ healings and exorcisms were understood holistically as being part of his teaching (1:21-22, 27; cp. 1:38-39; 3:14-15; 6:2, 5, 12-13, 30).

1:29-30 ***Simon*** (Peter) was married (see 1 Cor 9:5).

1:34 Mark 3:12
1:35-39 //Luke 4:42-44
1:38 Isa 61:1
1:39 Matt 4:23; 9:35
1:40-45 //Matt 8:2-4 //Luke 5:12-16
1:44 Lev 14:1-32
2:1-12 //Matt 9:1-8 //Luke 5:18-26
2:2 Eph 2:17 Heb 2:3
2:5 Luke 7:48

sick in bed with a high fever. They told Jesus
about her right away. 31So he went to her
bedside, took her by the hand, and helped
her sit up. Then the fever left her, and she
prepared a meal for them.

32That evening after sunset, many sick
and demon-possessed people were brought
to Jesus. 33The whole town gathered at the
door to watch. 34So Jesus healed many people who were sick with various diseases,
and he cast out many demons. But because
the demons knew who he was, he did not allow them to speak.

Jesus Preaches in Galilee

35Before daybreak the next morning, Jesus
got up and went out to an isolated place to
pray. 36Later Simon and the others went out
to find him. 37When they found him, they
said, "Everyone is looking for you."

38But Jesus replied, "We must go on to
other towns as well, and I will preach to
them, too. That is why I came." 39So he
traveled throughout the region of Galilee,
preaching in the synagogues and casting
out demons.

Jesus Heals a Man with Leprosy

Mark 1:40-45 // Matt 8:1-4 // Luke 5:12-16

40A man with leprosy came and knelt in
front of Jesus, begging to be healed. "If you
are willing, you can heal me and make me
clean," he said.

41Moved with compassion, Jesus reached
out and touched him. "I am willing," he said.
"Be healed!" 42Instantly the leprosy disappeared, and the man was healed. 43Then
Jesus sent him on his way with a stern warning: 44"Don't tell anyone about this. Instead,
go to the priest and let him examine you.
Take along the offering required in the law
of Moses for those who have been healed of
leprosy. This will be a public testimony that
you have been cleansed."

45But the man went and spread the
word, proclaiming to everyone what had
happened. As a result, large crowds soon
surrounded Jesus, and he couldn't publicly
enter a town anywhere. He had to stay out
in the secluded places, but people from
everywhere kept coming to him.

Controversy Stories (2:1–3:6)

Jesus Heals a Paralyzed Man

Mark 2:1-12 // Matt 9:1-8 // Luke 5:17-26

2 When Jesus returned to Capernaum
several days later, the news spread
quickly that he was back home. 2Soon the
house where he was staying was so packed
with visitors that there was no more room,
even outside the door. While he was preaching God's word to them, 3four men arrived
carrying a paralyzed man on a mat. 4They
couldn't bring him to Jesus because of the
crowd, so they dug a hole through the roof
above his head. Then they lowered the man
on his mat, right down in front of Jesus. 5See-
ing their faith, Jesus said to the paralyzed
man, "My child, your sins are forgiven."

1:31 Jesus healed Simon's mother-in-law instantaneously (see also 1:40-45; 2:1-12; 3:1-6; 5:25-34; 7:31-37; 8:22-26; 10:46-52); her ***fever left***, and she got up and ***prepared a meal*** for her guests.

1:32-34 These public healings took place ***after sunset*** following the Sabbath (1:21, 29), and there were many witnesses (see also 1:39; 3:10-11; 6:5, 53-56).

1:33 Jesus' popularity among the crowds was growing (also in 1:37, 39, 45), as contrasted with the growing rejection by the leaders (2:1–3:6).

1:34 ***the demons knew who he was:*** See 1:23-25.

1:35 Despite Jesus' busy ministry, he sought time ***to pray*** (6:46; 14:32-39). Mark emphasizes the importance of prayer in Jesus' life (cp. Luke 3:21; 6:12; 9:18, 28-29; 11:1-4; 18:1; 22:32).

1:38-39 Prayer (1:35) equipped Jesus to ***preach***, teach, heal, and cast out demons. • Jesus' mission in ***Galilee*** centered on ***preaching in the synagogues***, where he took the opportunity to speak (1:21; Luke 4:16-30). Paul later used this same opportunity (Acts 13:5, 14-15; 14:1; 16:13; 17:1). • Jesus counted on Jewish hospitality when ***he traveled*** (cp. 6:10; Luke 10:7; Gen 18:1-8; 19:1-8; Heb 13:2; 3 Jn 1:5-8). • The ***region of Galilee*** was roughly forty miles north to south and twenty-five miles east to west (sixty-five by forty kilometers). In Jesus' day, Galilee was ruled by Herod Antipas (see "Herod Antipas" at 6:14-29, p. 1659).

1:40 ***Leprosy*** refers to a number of skin diseases (or even mildew in a building). An infected person was considered unclean and was ostracized from family and society (Lev 13:45-46; Num 12:9-12; 2 Chr 26:16-21; Luke 17:12).

1:41 Jesus' willingness to touch a ceremonially unclean leper reflects the new order of the Kingdom of God (1:15; 5:25-34; Luke 7:36-50; see Matt 10:8; 11:5). • ***Moved with compassion:*** Some manuscripts read *Moved with anger.*

1:43-45 Jesus told the man to ***go to the priest*** to certify his healing and to make the appropriate sacrificial offering (see Lev 14:2-32). This would be the ***public testimony*** of his healing. • Despite Jesus' ***stern warning, . . . the man went and spread the word***, so that Jesus was not able to go into ***town*** but had to preach in more ***secluded places***. Jesus' fame could not be confined as ***people from everywhere*** came to see him (3:7-8).

2:1–3:6 Five controversy stories (2:1-12, 13-17, 18-22, 23-28; 3:1-6), grouped by their common theme, reveal Jesus' great authority and the leaders' hostility toward him.

2:1-12 This controversy story is also a miracle story, which links it to the previous collection (1:21-45).

2:1 ***back home:*** See Matt 4:13. The crowd's size shows Jesus' popularity.

2:4 ***because of the crowd:*** See 2:1. • ***The roof*** would have been flat, constructed of mud, thatch, and branches. They literally ***dug a hole*** to make an opening.

2:5 Jesus saw the ***faith*** of the paralytic and the four men who brought him. • ***your sins are forgiven:*** Those listening understood Jesus' words as a claim to divine authority (2:6-10; Luke 7:48-49).

6But some of the teachers of religious
law who were sitting there thought to
themselves, 7"What is he saying? This is
[f]blasphemy! Only God can forgive sins!"
8Jesus knew immediately what they were
thinking, so he asked them, "Why do you
question this in your hearts? 9Is it easier to
say to the paralyzed man 'Your sins are forgiven,' or 'Stand up, pick up your mat, and
walk'? 10So I will prove to you that the Son
of Man has the authority on earth to forgive
sins." Then Jesus turned to the paralyzed
man and said, 11"Stand up, pick up your mat,
and go home!"
12And the man jumped up, grabbed his
mat, and walked out through the stunned
onlookers. They were all amazed and
praised God, exclaiming, "We've never seen
anything like this before!"

Jesus Calls Notorious Sinners

Mark 2:13-17 // Matt 9:9-13 // Luke 5:27-32

13Then Jesus went out to the lakeshore
again and taught the crowds that were
coming to him. 14As he walked along, he
saw Levi son of Alphaeus sitting at his tax
collector's booth. "Follow me and be my disciple," Jesus said to him. So Levi got up and
followed him.
15Later, Levi invited Jesus and his disciples to his home as dinner guests, along with
many tax collectors and other disreputable
sinners. (There were many people of this
kind among Jesus' followers.) 16But when
the teachers of religious law who were Pharisees saw him eating with tax collectors
and other sinners, they asked his disciples,
"Why does he eat with such scum?"
17When Jesus heard this, he told them,
"Healthy people don't need a doctor—sick
people do. I have come to call not those who
think they are righteous, but those who
know they are sinners."

A Discussion about Fasting

Mark 2:18-22 // Matt 9:14-17 // Luke 5:33-39

18Once when John's disciples and the Pharisees were fasting, some people came to
Jesus and asked, "Why don't your disciples
fast like John's disciples and the Pharisees
do?"
19Jesus replied, "Do wedding guests fast
while celebrating with the groom? Of course
not. They can't fast while the groom is with
them. 20But someday the groom will be taken
away from them, and then they will fast.
21"Besides, who would patch old clothing
with new cloth? For the new patch would
shrink and rip away from the old cloth, leaving an even bigger tear than before.
22"And no one puts new wine into old
wineskins. For the wine would burst the
wineskins, and the wine and the skins
would both be lost. New wine calls for new
wineskins."

A Discussion about the Sabbath

Mark 2:23-28 // Matt 12:1-8 // Luke 6:1-5

23One Sabbath day as Jesus was walking
through some grainfields, his disciples

2:7
Ps 130:3-4
Isa 43:25
[f]*blasphēmeō* (0987)
▸Mark 3:28

2:8
Matt 16:8

2:12
Matt 9:33

2:13-17
//Matt 9:9-13
//Luke 5:27-32

2:14
John 1:43

2:17
Luke 19:10
1 Tim 1:15

2:18-22
//Matt 9:14-17
//Luke 5:33-38

2:19
John 2:1-10; 3:29
Rev 19:7

2:20
Luke 17:22

2:22
Gal 3:1-3

2:23-28
//Matt 12:1-8
//Luke 6:1-5

2:23
Deut 23:25

2:6-7 *Only God can forgive sins,* yet Jesus had authority to do so (2:10).

2:9-11 It is *easier to say . . . your sins are forgiven* because this claim cannot be directly proved or disproved, while the claim to heal can be. Jesus showed his ability to heal in order to show his authority to forgive. • *Son of Man* is a title Jesus used for himself; see "The Son of Man" at Matt 8:18-20, p. 1593).

2:12 *We've never seen anything like this before!* Mark consistently records Jesus creating amazement (1:22, 27; 4:41; 6:50-51).

2:13-17 This controversy centers on Jesus' befriending *disreputable sinners* such as *tax collectors* and *eating with* them.

2:13-15 *Levi* was also called Matthew (cp. Matt 9:9-10). Certain people are known by two names in the NT (e.g., Simon=Peter; Saul=Paul; Judas son of James=Thaddaeus, see note on 3:18). • Tax collectors levied income and property taxes, while toll collectors took sales taxes, customs, and road tolls. Toll collectors and tax collectors were all hated by Jews because they often gouged the public (Luke 19:8), and as agents of the Romans, they were regarded as traitors. Jesus invited Levi, a toll collector, to follow him, joining Peter, Andrew, James, and John (1:16-20).

2:16 *The teachers of religious law who were Pharisees* (literally *the scribes of the Pharisees*) understood Jesus' act of eating with sinners as intentionally accepting them as friends (Luke 15:1-2; 19:5, 7; Acts 11:2-18; Gal 2:11-12). Jesus indicated that these *tax collectors* and *sinners* were invited to share in the Kingdom of God. In Jesus' ministry, even Gentiles were invited to share the Kingdom (5:1-20; 7:24-30; cp. Matt 8:5-13; Luke 7:1-10; John 4:43-54). • *Pharisees:* See "The Pharisees" at Matt 3:7, p. 1581. • *with such scum?* Literally *with tax collectors and sinners?*

2:17 Jesus answered his opponents with a well-known proverb, comparing himself to a *doctor* and *sinners* to *sick people.* Salvation is for those who *know they are sinners,* not those who *think they are righteous* (Luke 16:15; 18:9; Rom 3:23).

2:18-22 This controversy deals with *fasting,* which Jesus did not practice with his disciples. The Pharisees regularly fasted two days a week, on Mondays and Thursdays (Luke 18:12), and Jews often fasted when mourning or specially seeking the Lord's favor (Lev 16:29-31; 1 Sam 31:13; 2 Sam 1:12; 12:21-23; Ezra 8:23; Esth 4:3; Matt 6:16).

2:19-20 Jesus was like a groom at his wedding, so fasting was inappropriate. It was a time for celebration (Luke 15:23-25, 32). The disciples would fast when Jesus was *taken away* by death (see Acts 13:2-3; 14:23).

2:21-22 *Old* customs of the old covenant are incompatible with the *new* arrival of God's Kingdom. Common experience shows that an unshrunken *new patch* sewn on *old clothing* will tear the old cloth as it shrinks. Similarly, brittle *old wineskins* will burst when *new wine* ferments in them. Jesus' meaning was that the fasting of the old cannot mix with the feasting of the new (see also notes on Matt 9:15-17).

2:23-28 In this controversy, Jesus and his disciples are accused of breaking the

2:25-26
1 Sam 21:1-6

2:27
Exod 23:12
Deut 5:14
John 7:21-24

3:1-6
//Matt 12:9-14
//Luke 6:6-11

3:5
Mark 6:52; 8:17
[g]orgē (3709)
‣John 3:36

3:6
Matt 22:15-16
Mark 12:13

3:7-12
//Matt 12:15-16
//Luke 6:17-19

3:7-8
Matt 4:25

3:10
Mark 4:1

3:11-12
Mark 1:24-25, 34
Luke 4:41
Acts 16:16-17

3:13-19
//Matt 10:1-4
//Luke 6:12-16

3:14
Mark 6:30

began breaking off heads of grain to eat.
24But the Pharisees said to Jesus, "Look, why
are they breaking the law by harvesting
grain on the Sabbath?"

25Jesus said to them, "Haven't you ever
read in the Scriptures what David did when
he and his companions were hungry? 26He
went into the house of God (during the days
when Abiathar was high priest) and broke
the law by eating the sacred loaves of bread
that only the priests are allowed to eat. He
also gave some to his companions."

27Then Jesus said to them, "The Sabbath
was made to meet the needs of people, and
not people to meet the requirements of the
Sabbath. 28So the Son of Man is Lord, even
over the Sabbath!"

Jesus Heals on the Sabbath
Mark 3:1-6 // Matt 12:9-14 // Luke 6:6-11

3 Jesus went into the synagogue again
and noticed a man with a deformed
hand. 2Since it was the Sabbath, Jesus' enemies watched him closely. If he healed the
man's hand, they planned to accuse him of
working on the Sabbath.

3Jesus said to the man with the deformed
hand, "Come and stand in front of everyone." 4Then he turned to his critics and
asked, "Does the law permit good deeds on
the Sabbath, or is it a day for doing evil? Is
this a day to save life or to destroy it?" But
they wouldn't answer him.

5He looked around at them [g]angrily and
was deeply saddened by their hard hearts.
Then he said to the man, "Hold out your
hand." So the man held out his hand, and it
was restored! 6At once the Pharisees went
away and met with the supporters of Herod
to plot how to kill Jesus.

Expansion of Jesus' Ministry (3:7-19)
Crowds Follow Jesus
Mark 3:7-12 // Luke 6:17-19

7Jesus went out to the lake with his disciples,
and a large crowd followed him. They came
from all over Galilee, Judea, 8Jerusalem, Idumea, from east of the Jordan River, and
even from as far north as Tyre and Sidon.
The news about his miracles had spread far
and wide, and vast numbers of people came
to see him.

9Jesus instructed his disciples to have a
boat ready so the crowd would not crush
him. 10He had healed many people that day,
so all the sick people eagerly pushed forward to touch him. 11And whenever those
possessed by evil spirits caught sight of him,
the spirits would throw them to the ground
in front of him shrieking, "You are the Son
of God!" 12But Jesus sternly commanded
the spirits not to reveal who he was.

Jesus Chooses the Twelve Apostles
Mark 3:13-19 // Matt 10:1-4 // Luke 6:12-16

13Afterward Jesus went up on a mountain
and called out the ones he wanted to go
with him. And they came to him. 14Then
he appointed twelve of them and called
them his apostles. They were to accompany
him, and he would send them out to preach,

Sabbath (Exod 20:8-11). Picking ***grain*** by hand in another person's field was lawful (Deut 23:25). The charge was that by rubbing the chaff from the kernels, the disciples were working on ***the Sabbath,*** which was forbidden (Exod 34:21).

2:25-26 Jesus countered with reference to an incident in the life of King ***David*** (1 Sam 21). When David and his followers ate ***the sacred loaves***—the twelve loaves in the Tabernacle that only priests were allowed to eat—they ***broke the law*** (see Lev 24:5-9). But deeper principles were at work (2:27-28).

2:27-28 Since Jesus is the Lord of humanity (Phil 2:9-11; Eph 1:20-22; 1 Cor 15:25-28) and since the Sabbath was ***made to meet the needs of people*** (see notes on Matt 12:3-7), he is ***Lord . . . over the Sabbath.*** As with Jesus' authority to forgive sins (2:7), this was a claim to divine authority.

3:1-6 This account concludes the collection of controversy stories (2:1–3:6). As in the preceding story, Jesus is in conflict with the Pharisees over the Sabbath; as with the first story, the controversy involves a healing (2:1-12).

3:1-2 The scene ***again*** involves a ***synagogue,*** probably in Capernaum (1:21, 29). The presence of a crippled man on the Sabbath (3:1-2) created a situation that ***Jesus' enemies*** wished to exploit ***if he healed the man's hand,*** so they ***watched him closely.***

3:3-4 Jesus challenged his enemies' view that doing ***good deeds*** was forbidden on the Sabbath (cp. Luke 13:10-17). • ***To destroy . . . life*** may refer to an incident in which the Maccabees decided to fight if attacked on the Sabbath (*1 Maccabees* 2:32-41). These great Jewish heroes were willing to kill on the Sabbath, yet the Pharisees would not allow ***good deeds on the Sabbath.*** Jesus' question shamed them into silence but did not change their hearts (3:5).

3:5-6 Jesus' opponents' ***hard hearts*** would not listen to sound reason, so instead of having changed attitudes, they began ***to plot how to kill*** him (see also 11:18; 12:12; 14:1-2, 10-11).

3:7-12 Jesus' departure to ***the lake*** (the Sea of Galilee) sets the scene for 4:1–5:43. The multitude that came to see John the Baptist (1:7) was surpassed by the multitude that came to see Jesus. • ***Idumea*** was the NT name for ancient Edom (see map, p. 1642; cp. map, p. 626). • ***Tyre and Sidon*** were Phoenician cities on the Mediterranean coast that Jesus later visited (7:24, 31).

3:9 The ***boat*** probably belonged to Peter and Andrew or to James and John. The crowd's desire to see Jesus was so great that he needed to escape the ***crush*** of people (4:1; 5:24, 31).

3:10 Jesus ***healed many people that day;*** perhaps he healed ***all the sick*** (cp. Matt 12:15).

3:11-12 The ***evil*** (literally ***unclean***) ***spirits*** knew who Jesus was (1:34; see also 1:22; 5:7), but Jesus did not want his identity revealed (see "The Secret of the Messiah" at 3:11-12, p. 1653).

3:13-19 The scene now changes to a ***mountain,*** and Mark tells how Jesus called his disciples, which is reminiscent of God's call of OT prophets (Exod 3:14-22; 1 Sam 3:4-14; Jer 1:5-19).

15 giving them authority to cast out demons.
16 These are the twelve he chose:

Simon (whom he named Peter),
17 James and John (the sons of Zebedee,
but Jesus nicknamed them "Sons of
Thunder"),
18 Andrew,
Philip,
Bartholomew,
Matthew,
Thomas,
James (son of Alphaeus),
Thaddaeus,
Simon (the zealot),
19 Judas Iscariot (who later betrayed him).

Jesus, His Family, and Satan (3:20-35)

Jesus' Family Thinks He Is Crazy

20 One time Jesus entered a house, and the
crowds began to gather again. Soon he and
his disciples couldn't even find time to eat.
21 When his family heard what was happening, they tried to take him away. "He's out of
his mind," they said.

The Source of Jesus' Power

Mark 3:22-27 // Matt 12:22-30 // Luke 11:14-23; cp. Matt 9:32-34
Mark 3:28-30 // Matt 12:31-32 // Luke 12:10

22 But the teachers of religious law who
had arrived from Jerusalem said, "He's
possessed by [h]Satan, the prince of demons.
That's where he gets the power to cast out
demons."
23 Jesus called them over and responded
with an illustration. "How can Satan cast
out Satan?" he asked. 24 "A kingdom divided
by civil war will collapse. 25 Similarly, a
family splintered by feuding will fall apart.
26 And if Satan is divided and fights against
himself, how can he stand? He would never
survive. 27 Let me illustrate this further.
Who is powerful enough to enter the house
of a strong man like Satan and plunder his
goods? Only someone even stronger—someone who could tie him up and then plunder
his house.
28 "I tell you the truth, all sin and [i]blas-
phemy can be forgiven, 29 but anyone who
blasphemes the Holy Spirit will never be
forgiven. This is a sin with eternal consequences." 30 He told them this because they
were saying, "He's possessed by an evil
spirit."

The True Family of Jesus

Mark 3:31-35 // Matt 12:46-50 // Luke 8:19-21

31 Then Jesus' mother and brothers came to
see him. They stood outside and sent word

3:16 Matt 16:17-18; John 1:42
3:17 Luke 9:54
3:20-30 //Matt 12:22-32; //Luke 11:14-23
3:22 John 7:20; 8:48, 52; 10:20; [h]*beelzeboul* (0954) ‣Luke 11:15
3:27 Isa 49:24-25
3:28-30 //Matt 12:31-32; Luke 12:10; 1 Jn 5:16
3:28 [i]*blasphēmia* (0988) ‣Mark 7:22
3:31-35 //Matt 12:46-50; //Luke 8:19-21
3:31 Mark 6:3; John 7:3-5

3:14-15 Jesus ***appointed twelve*** to represent Israel's twelve tribes and to proclaim that the Kingdom of God had arrived. He called them ***apostles*** (Greek *apostoloi,* "emissaries"; some manuscripts do not include ***and called them his apostles***). He chose them ***to accompany him*** and to be sent out (Greek *apostellō*) ***to preach*** and ***to cast out demons.*** They represented Jesus and were endowed with his ***authority.***

3:16-18 ***Simon*** and ***Andrew*** were brothers, as were ***James and John*** (1:16-20). • ***Peter*** is the Greek equivalent of the Aramaic *kepa',* meaning "rock."

3:17 ***but Jesus nicknamed them "Sons of Thunder":*** Literally *whom he named Boanerges, which means Sons of Thunder,* a nickname that probably speaks of their character (cp. Luke 9:53-54).

3:18 ***Philip*** is fifth on all four lists of the twelve disciples (Matt 10:1-4; Luke 6:12-16; Acts 1:13); ***James*** the ***son of Alphaeus*** (not the son of Zebedee and brother of John) is always ninth. ***Bartholomew*** might be Nathanael (John 1:43-51), and ***Matthew*** is probably Levi, the tax collector (2:14; Matt 9:9). Although ***Thomas*** is referred to as "the twin" (John 11:16; 20:24; 21:2), nothing else is said in the NT about this. ***Thaddaeus*** (Matt 10:3) is missing from Luke's list; he might be Judas, the son of James (Luke 6:16; Acts 1:13). The second ***Simon*** is ***the zealot*** (literally *the Cananean,* an Aramaic term for Jewish nationalists). That a government official (Matthew) and an anti-government activist were among the twelve apostles testifies to Jesus' ability to change people's hearts and overcome natural antagonism.

3:19 Identifying ***Judas*** as ***Iscariot*** suggests that Mark wanted to avoid confusing him with another Judas (Luke 6:16; Acts 1:13). *Iscariot* probably comes from *'ish* ("man of") *qeriyoth* ("Kerioth," a town in Judea). • ***who later betrayed him:*** See 14:10-11, 43-46.

3:20-35 This story about Jesus and his family (3:20-21 and 31-35) brackets a controversy story about Jesus' exorcisms (3:22-30); this arrangement identifies Jesus' family with the religious leaders in opposing him.

3:20 That Jesus and the disciples can't ***find time to eat*** emphasizes Jesus' great popularity with ***the crowds*** (3:7-9).

3:21 ***He's out of his mind:*** Mark does not explain whether the attempt by Jesus' ***family*** to seize him was motivated by sincere but misguided concern, or by hostility. Jesus' brothers and sisters were not among his followers until after his resurrection (3:31-35; John 7:3-5; 1 Cor 15:7 mentions James, the brother of Jesus, who became a leader of the Jerusalem church, Acts 15:13-21).

3:22 ***The teachers of religious law*** (see note on 1:22) ***from Jerusalem*** attributed Jesus' apparent madness to his being ***possessed by Satan*** (Greek *Beelzeboul;* other manuscripts read *Beezeboul;* Latin version reads *Beelzebub;* see note on Matt 10:25). Jesus' opponents credited his miracle-working ability to Satan (as in the rabbinic work, *Sanhedrin* 3:43a, where miracle-working is ascribed to sorcery).

3:23-27 Jesus showed the absurdity of this charge by giving several analogies. ***Satan*** would not undo his own work.

3:27 Jesus provided a better explanation for his ability to cast out demons: Someone ***stronger*** than Satan had arrived (1:7) and was able to loot Satan's house. Jesus, the Messiah, the Son of God (1:1), was introducing God's Kingdom and rescuing people from Satan's power.

3:28-30 The phrase ***I tell you the truth*** introduces many of Jesus' sayings and gives emphasis to what follows (see also 8:12; 9:1, 41; 10:15, 29; 11:23; 12:43; 13:30; 14:9, 18, 25, 30). • ***All sin and blasphemy can be forgiven,*** but there is ***a sin with eternal consequences***—blasphemy against ***the Holy Spirit.*** To blaspheme the Holy Spirit is to attribute the work of God to ***an evil*** (literally *unclean*) ***spirit.*** Resisting and denouncing the work of God in this way prevents the convicting work of the Spirit that leads to repentance, saving faith in God, and pardon for sin (see also note on Matt 12:31; cp. Heb 6:4-6; 1 Jn 5:16-17).

3:34
John 20:17
Rom 8:29
Heb 2:11

3:35
Matt 7:21
[i]*thelēma* (2307)
‣Rom 12:2

4:1-9
//Matt 13:1-9
//Luke 8:4-8

4:2
Mark 4:33-34
[k]*parabolē* (3850)
‣Mark 4:33

for him to come out and talk with them.
32There was a crowd sitting around Jesus,
and someone said, "Your mother and your
brothers are outside asking for you."
33Jesus replied, "Who is my mother?
Who are my brothers?" 34Then he looked
at those around him and said, "Look, these
are my mother and brothers. 35Anyone who
does God's [i]will is my brother and sister and
mother."

Jesus Teaches in Parables (4:1-34)
Parable of the Farmer Scattering Seed
Mark 4:1-12 // Matt 13:1-13 // Luke 8:4-10

4 Once again Jesus began teaching by
the lakeshore. A very large crowd soon
gathered around him, so he got into a boat.
Then he sat in the boat while all the people
remained on the shore. 2He taught them by
telling many stories in the form of [k]parables,
such as this one:
3"Listen! A farmer went out to plant some
seed. 4As he scattered it across his field,
some of the seed fell on a footpath, and the
birds came and ate it. 5Other seed fell on
shallow soil with underlying rock. The seed
sprouted quickly because the soil was shallow. 6But the plant soon wilted under the
hot sun, and since it didn't have deep roots,
it died. 7Other seed fell among thorns that
grew up and choked out the tender plants
so they produced no grain. 8Still other seeds
fell on fertile soil, and they sprouted, grew,

The Secret of the Messiah (3:11-12)

Mark 1:34, 44; 5:43; 7:36; 8:29-30; 9:9, 30-31
Matt 8:4; 16:20
Luke 9:21

Throughout the Gospel of Mark, Jesus tells others—those he healed or raised from the dead, the disciples who recognized him as the Christ, and the demons who had a correct understanding of his true identity—not to reveal his identity (e.g., 1:34, 44; 3:11-12; 5:43; 7:36; 8:29-30; 9:9, 26, 30).

Why did Jesus command those he healed and those who knew his true identity to keep his healings and identity secret? The answer involves how the Roman authorities would have responded to an extremely popular preacher who proclaimed the arrival of God's Kingdom, performed marvelous healings, and openly allowed his followers to call him Israel's long-awaited Messiah and King. Roman authorities would not tolerate such a situation and would immediately seek to suppress such a movement. In the Roman empire, there was no room for another kingdom or for a messianic rescuer from Roman occupation.

Thus, though Jesus acknowledged to his disciples that he was the Messiah (8:26-30), he did not intend to overthrow Rome (see "The Coming of God's Kingdom" at 1:14-15, p. 1647). So it was expedient for Jesus to teach about God's Kingdom in parables (4:1-34, especially 4:10-12), to minimize the excitement created by his miracles (1:44; 5:43; 7:36; 8:26), to conceal his presence at times from the people (7:24; 9:30-31), to conceal his teaching from outsiders (4:10-13, 33-34; 7:17; 9:28), and to command those who knew his true identity not to reveal it (1:25, 34; 3:11-12; 8:29-30; 9:9). Jesus came "to give his life as a ransom for many" (10:45), not to lead the nation of Israel in rebellion against Rome.

Why does Mark emphasize this secrecy in his Gospel when Matthew only relates it twice (Matt 8:4; 16:20) and Luke only once (Luke 9:21)? In Mark, the secrecy motif shows Jesus' greatness. Jesus Christ, the Son of God (1:1), could not be hidden. The secret was not and cannot be kept (7:36), for Jesus is too great. Those who experienced and witnessed his healing touch could not help but proclaim what he had done. Jesus' identity broke through, and it became clear that he is indeed the Messiah, the Son of God, the Lord over nature, disease, and death.

3:31-35 Mark resumes from 3:20-21.
• *Your mother and your brothers* (some manuscripts add *and sisters*): Jesus' brothers are normally understood to have been children born to Joseph and Mary after Jesus' birth (see also 6:3; Matt 1:25; 12:46; John 19:26-27); some interpreters instead believe that they were either Joseph's children by an earlier marriage or Jesus' cousins, due to the Roman Catholic belief that Mary was perpetually a virgin.

3:33-34 In God's Kingdom, one's true relatives are determined not by blood but by a faith relationship (see also 10:29-30).

3:35 Doing *God's will* includes repentance from sin, faith in God, and following Jesus (1:15, 18, 20).

4:1-34 In this section Mark collects a number of Jesus' teaching parables.

4:1 Jesus again uses *a boat* to avoid the press of the *crowd* when he is *teaching* (3:9; Luke 5:2-3).

4:2 *Parables* are often stories (Luke 15:11-32; 18:1-8) but can also be proverbs (3:24-25; Luke 4:23), similes and metaphors (Matt 5:14; 10:16), riddles (7:15; 14:58), comparisons (Matt 13:33; Luke 15:3-7), examples (Luke 10:30-35; 12:16-21), or allegories (4:3-9; 12:1-12).

4:3-9 The collection begins with the longest parable and its interpretation (4:13-20), focusing on various types of soil as an analogy for various conditions of the human heart.

and produced a crop that was thirty, sixty,
and even a hundred times as much as had
been planted!" 9Then he said, "Anyone with
ears to hear should listen and understand."

Jesus' Purpose for Teaching in Parables

10Later, when Jesus was alone with the
twelve disciples and with the others who
were gathered around, they asked him what
the parables meant.

11He replied, "You are permitted to understand the [a]secret of the Kingdom of God.
But I use parables for everything I say to
outsiders, 12so that the Scriptures might be
fulfilled:

'When they see what I do,
they will learn nothing.
When they hear what I say,
they will not understand.
Otherwise, they will turn to me
and be forgiven.' "

Interpretation of the Parable of the Farmer Scattering Seed

Mark 4:13-20 // Matt 13:18-23 // Luke 8:11-15

13Then Jesus said to them, "If you can't understand the meaning of this parable, how
will you understand all the other parables?
14The farmer plants seed by taking God's
word to others. 15The seed that fell on the
footpath represents those who hear the
message, only to have Satan come at once
and take it away. 16The seed on the rocky
soil represents those who hear the message and immediately receive it with joy.
17But since they don't have deep roots, they
don't last long. They fall away as soon as
they have problems or are persecuted for
believing God's word. 18The seed that fell
among the thorns represents others who
hear God's word, 19but all too quickly the
message is crowded out by the worries of
this life, the lure of [b]wealth, and the desire
for other things, so no fruit is produced.
20And the seed that fell on good soil represents those who hear and accept God's word
and produce a harvest of thirty, sixty, or
even a hundred times as much as had been
planted!"

Parable of the Lamp

Mark 4:21-25 // Luke 8:16-18; cp. Matt 5:15; 13:12; Luke 11:33

21Then Jesus asked them, "Would anyone
light a lamp and then put it under a basket or
under a bed? Of course not! A lamp is placed
on a stand, where its light will shine. 22For
everything that is hidden will eventually be
brought into the open, and every secret will
be brought to light. 23Anyone with ears to
hear should listen and understand."

24Then he added, "Pay close attention to
what you hear. The closer you listen, the
more understanding you will be given—and
you will receive even more. 25To those who
listen to my teaching, more understanding
will be given. But for those who are not listening, even what little understanding they
have will be taken away from them."

Parable of the Growing Seed

26Jesus also said, "The Kingdom of God
is like a farmer who scatters seed on the

4:9
Matt 11:15
Mark 4:23
Rev 2:7

4:10-12
//Matt 13:10-17
//Luke 8:9-10

4:11
[a]*mustērion* (3466)
‣1 Cor 2:1

4:12
*Isa 6:9-10
John 12:39-40
Acts 28:26-27

4:13-20
//Matt 13:18-23
//Luke 8:11-15

4:14
Eph 3:8
Jas 1:18
1 Pet 1:23-25

4:15
2 Cor 4:4
1 Pet 5:8

4:19
1 Tim 6:9-10, 17
1 Jn 2:15-17
[b]*ploutos* (4149)
‣Rom 11:33

4:21-25
Matt 5:15
//Luke 8:16-18

4:22
Matt 10:26
Luke 12:2

4:23
Matt 11:15; 13:43

4:25
Matt 13:12; 25:29
Luke 19:26

4:26-27
1 Cor 3:6-7

4:10 The scene changes from Jesus' teaching a very large crowd from a boat to his being ***alone with the twelve disciples and . . . others.*** Their question concerns all the ***parables*** (4:33-34), not just this one.

4:11-12 Jesus' real followers were ***permitted to understand the secret*** (literally *mystery*) ***of the Kingdom of God***—namely, that the Kingdom of God had come (1:14-15) and that Christ, the Son of God, was in their midst (1:1). For outsiders, it all seemed like riddles.
• Jesus' reply to the disciples' question suggests that the parables were intended to prevent outsiders from understanding them, so that they would be unable to repent and be forgiven. The quotation from Isa 6:9-10 (Greek version) suggests that it was an intentional judgment on the hearers. Jesus' teaching in parables, and the resultant unbelief of outsiders, fulfilled what ***the Scriptures*** had predicted. The sensitive nature of Jesus' teaching about the Kingdom of God (a theme that would have made Roman authorities very uneasy) made teaching in parables useful in defusing this issue.

4:13 If Jesus' hearers could not ***understand*** the parable, they might lack the grace of citizenship in Christ's Kingdom. However, even the insiders required Jesus' explanation.

4:14-20 The interpretation of the parable of the four soils is allegorical. The ***farmer*** represents a preacher of ***God's word*** (4:14). The four types of soil that receive ***the seed*** represent different responses to the preaching of the word. The point of this parable and its interpretation is that hearers should be good soil and heed God's word (4:9). Only those who produce fruit and endure to the end will be saved (13:13; 8:35; Rev 2:10-11).

4:21-25 These sayings are connected with the exhortation ***to hear*** (4:9, 23-24) and with the distinction between insiders and outsiders (4:11-12, 24-25). They illustrate what citizens of the Kingdom will do.

4:21 A lamp is lighted to ***shine*** and give people light, not to remain hidden. Citizens of the Kingdom are responsible for putting the light of the Good News ***on a stand*** (4:17).

4:22-23 One day the lamp (i.e., Jesus; cp. John 8:12) will shine his ***light*** on ***everything that is hidden***, on every thought and secret action (13:26; 14:62; see Phil 2:10-11). The time to ***listen*** is before this occurs (4:9).

4:24 Those who listen and respond will be given ***more understanding***, but those outside (4:11-12) will have greater darkness (2 Cor 3:14-16). • ***The closer you listen, the more understanding you will be given:*** Or *The measure you give will be the measure you get back.*

4:26-34 Mark now gives additional seed parables (4:3-20). Their common theme is the secret of the Kingdom of God (4:11). The parables of the seed growing secretly (4:26-29) and of the mustard seed (4:30-32) describe different stages of the seed-growth process. The Kingdom of God is hidden (4:21), but growth is certain (4:26-29) and the result will be glorious (4:32).

4:28-29 Matt 9:37-38; Rev 14:15
4:30-32 //Matt 13:31-32; //Luke 13:18-19
4:32 Ezek 17:23; 31:6; Dan 4:12, 21
4:33 Matt 13:34-35; [c]parabolē (3850) ‣ Luke 5:36
4:34 John 16:25
4:35-41 //Matt 8:23-27; //Luke 8:22-25
4:37-38 Jon 1:4-6

ground. [27]Night and day, while he's asleep or awake, the seed sprouts and grows, but he does not understand how it happens. [28]The earth produces the crops on its own. First a leaf blade pushes through, then the heads of wheat are formed, and finally the grain ripens. [29]And as soon as the grain is ready, the farmer comes and harvests it with a sickle, for the harvest time has come."

Parable of the Mustard Seed
Mark 4:30-32 // Matt 13:31-32 // Luke 13:18-19

[30]Jesus said, "How can I describe the Kingdom of God? What story should I use to illustrate it? [31]It is like a mustard seed planted in the ground. It is the smallest of all seeds, [32]but it becomes the largest of all garden plants; it grows long branches, and birds can make nests in its shade."

A Summary of Jesus' Parable Ministry
Mark 4:33-34; cp. Matt 13:34-35

[33]Jesus used many similar [c]stories and illustrations to teach the people as much as they could understand. [34]In fact, in his public ministry he never taught without using parables; but afterward, when he was alone with his disciples, he explained everything to them.

Jesus Is Lord over All (4:35–5:43)
Jesus Calms the Storm
Mark 4:35-41 // Matt 8:23-27 // Luke 8:22-25

[35]As evening came, Jesus said to his disciples, "Let's cross to the other side of the lake." [36]So they took Jesus in the boat and started out, leaving the crowds behind (although other boats followed). [37]But soon a fierce storm came up. High waves were breaking into the boat, and it began to fill with water.

The Son of God (4:35-41)

Mark 1:1, 11, 24; 3:11; 4:41; 5:7; 7:37; 8:29-31; 9:7; 12:1-12; 13:32; 14:61-62; 15:2, 32-39
Gen 6:2
Exod 4:22
Deut 32:5-6
2 Sam 7:14
1 Chr 22:10; 28:6
Job 2:1; 38:7
Ps 2:7; 29:1; 82:6; 89:6, 26-27
Jer 3:19; 31:9, 20
Hos 11:1
Mal 2:10
Matt 26:63-68
Luke 1:32-35; 4:41
John 1:18; 3:16-17, 35-36; 5:19-26; 11:27; 14:13; 17:5, 24; 20:31
Acts 13:33
Rom 1:4; 5:10; 8:3, 32
2 Cor 1:19
Gal 2:20; 4:4-5
Eph 4:13
1 Thes 1:10
Heb 1:2-14; 3:6; 5:5
1 Jn 1:3; 2:22; 3:23; 4:9-10, 14; 5:20
2 Jn 1:3, 9
Rev 2:18

Time and again Jesus' healings, exorcisms, raising of the dead, and teachings created wonder, awe, amazement, and fear (e.g., 1:22, 27; 4:41; 5:15, 20, 33; 7:37; 9:15; 10:24, 26, 32; 12:17; 15:5, 44; 16:5-6, 8). This amazement emphasizes the miraculous nature of Jesus' ministry. Mark wanted his readers to ask themselves, "Who is this man, that even the wind and waves obey him?" (4:41). Mark has already given the answer: Jesus is "the Messiah, the Son of God" (1:1).

In the OT, the title "Son of God" is applied to the people of Israel (Exod 4:22; Deut 32:5-6, 18-19; Ps 82:6; Jer 3:19; 31:9, 20; Hos 11:1; Mal 2:10) and the angels (Gen 6:2; Job 1:6; 2:1; 38:7; Ps 29:1; 89:6). It is also applied to Israel's king in a special way—the anointed king was seen as God's "son" (2 Sam 7:14; 1 Chr 22:10; 28:6; Ps 2:7; 89:26-27). The coming Messiah (Israel's king, a descendant of David) was also called the Son of God in Jewish literature (the Apocrypha, the Mishnah, the Dead Sea Scrolls). Jews in the first century thus understood the Messiah as being the Son of God.

Immediately following Jesus' introduction in 1:1, his identity as "the Son of God" was affirmed by God at his baptism (1:11) and by demons at the start of his ministry (1:24; see also 1:34; 3:11; 5:7). Later, the disciples recognized Jesus as the Messiah (8:29) and Jesus began to teach them of his forthcoming death (8:31). Then, at Jesus' transfiguration, God affirmed the disciples' confession (9:7). As Jesus approached his death, he affirmed his unique identity as God's Son, both through his teaching (12:6; 13:32) and at his trial (14:61-62).

The climactic confession of Jesus' identity as God's Son took place at the crucifixion, where a Roman centurion was the first human in Mark's Gospel to recognize that Jesus is truly the Son of God (15:39). Jesus' identity as the Son of God is evidenced by his exorcisms and God's recognition. But his sacrificial death and the way he died (15:33-38) provide the supreme evidence that he is the Son of God.

4:26-29 This parable focuses on the seed and its inevitable growth. • Just as ***the earth produces the crops on its own***, the consummation of God's Kingdom does not depend on human action. • The ***leaf blade***, the ***heads of wheat***, and ripened ***grain*** describe normal stages in a seed's growth.

4:29 ***Harvest time*** is analogous to the final inauguration of God's Kingdom. A ***sickle*** is a frequent symbol of the final judgment (Jer 50:16; Joel 3:13; Rev 14:14-19).

4:30-32 Jesus contrasts a very small beginning with a large result. The ***mustard seed*** is proverbially small (see Matt 17:20).

4:33-34 Mark's summary of this section indicates that 4:3-32 is a collection of parables, not a chronological description of Jesus' teaching on a specific day. • Jesus' private explanation of the parables to the disciples shows that they were not outsiders, even though they sometimes lacked understanding (cp. 4:13).

4:35–5:43 The three miracle stories in this section are connected by a shared location (the Sea of Galilee), the presence of the disciples, the use of a boat, and a common theme, ***Who is this man?*** (4:41).

4:35-41 This passage focuses on the greatness of Jesus Christ, the Son of God. Jesus' authority over natural forces demonstrated his divinity. • ***the other side:*** The eastern side of the Sea of Galilee was the region of the Gerasenes (5:1). • The fact that ***other boats followed*** shows Jesus' fame.

38Jesus was sleeping at the back of the
boat with his head on a cushion. The disciples woke him up, shouting, "Teacher, don't
you care that we're going to drown?"
39When Jesus woke up, he rebuked the
wind and said to the waves, "Silence! Be still!"
Suddenly the wind stopped, and there was
a great calm. 40Then he asked them, "Why
are you afraid? Do you still have no faith?"
41The disciples were absolutely terrified.
"Who is this man?" they asked each other.
"Even the wind and waves obey him!"

Jesus Exercises Authority over Demons
Mark 5:1-20 // Matt 8:28-34 // Luke 8:26-39

5 So they arrived at the other side of the
lake, in the region of the Gerasenes.
2When Jesus climbed out of the boat, a man
possessed by an evil spirit came out from
a cemetery to meet him. 3This man lived
among the burial caves and could no longer
be restrained, even with a chain. 4Whenever
he was put into chains and shackles—as he
often was—he snapped the chains from his
wrists and smashed the shackles. No one
was strong enough to subdue him. 5Day and
night he wandered among the burial caves
and in the hills, howling and cutting himself with sharp stones.
6When Jesus was still some distance
away, the man saw him, ran to meet him,
and bowed low before him. 7With a shriek,
he screamed, "Why are you interfering with
me, Jesus, Son of the Most High God? In the
name of God, I beg you, don't torture me!"
8For Jesus had already said to the spirit,
"Come out of the man, you evil spirit."
9Then Jesus demanded, "What is your
name?"
And he replied, "My name is Legion, because there are many of us inside this man."
10Then the evil spirits begged him again
and again not to send them to some distant
place.
11There happened to be a large herd of
pigs feeding on the hillside nearby. 12"Send
us into those pigs," the spirits begged. "Let
us enter them."
13So Jesus gave them permission. The
evil spirits came out of the man and entered
the pigs, and the entire herd of about 2,000
pigs plunged down the steep hillside into
the lake and drowned in the water.
14The herdsmen fled to the nearby town
and the surrounding countryside, spreading the news as they ran. People rushed
out to see what had happened. 15A crowd
soon gathered around Jesus, and they saw
the man who had been possessed by the legion of demons. He was sitting there fully
clothed and perfectly sane, and they were
all afraid. 16Then those who had seen what
happened told the others about the demon-
possessed man and the pigs. 17And the
crowd began pleading with Jesus to go away
and leave them alone.
18As Jesus was getting into the boat, the
man who had been demon possessed

4:39 Ps 107:25-32
4:41 Ps 33:8-9
5:1-20 //Matt 8:28-34 //Luke 8:26-39
5:7-8 Acts 16:17
5:15 Matt 4:24
5:18 Ps 116:12

4:38 Jesus was probably asleep under the stern, using a bag of ballast sand as a pillow. In 1986, a boat dating from Jesus' time was discovered in the mud near the northwest shore of the Sea of Galilee. It is 26½ feet long, 7½ feet wide, and 4½ feet deep, with an elevated stern. It could hold up to fifteen people.

4:39-40 The disciples still lacked ***faith*** in Jesus (4:41), despite their numerous opportunities to experience his power and authority (1:21-34, 40-45; 2:1-12; 3:1-5).

4:41 The disciples were ***absolutely terrified***—a frequent response to Jesus in Mark (5:15, 33; 6:50; 9:32; 10:32; 11:18; 16:8). • ***Who is this man?*** Readers already know that Jesus is the Messiah, the Son of God (1:1, 11, 24; 3:11).

5:1-20 Jesus and the disciples ***arrived at the other side of the lake***, completing the journey begun in 4:35. As in 1:21-28 and 3:11, the demons truly recognized (1:34) that Jesus was the ***Son of the Most High God***. For the first time in the Gospel of Mark, a Gentile was the recipient of Jesus' healing ministry (see note on 5:10-13; cp. 7:24-30).

5:1 ***The region of the Gerasenes*** (other manuscripts read *Gadarenes;* still others read *Gergesenes;* see Matt 8:28; Luke 8:26): Textual and geographical problems make the exact location uncertain. Manuscript evidence supports Gerasa, a city in this region located thirty-seven miles southeast of the Sea of Galilee (5:13). Some manuscripts read "Gadarenes"; Gadara was five miles southeast of the Sea of Galilee. A few manuscripts read "Gergesenes"; the town of Gergesa was located on a steep bank on the Sea of Galilee's eastern shore.

5:2-5 Mark focuses on Jesus. The ***evil*** (literally *unclean;* also in 5:8, 13) ***spirit*** had great strength, but Jesus' authority was even greater (5:6-13).

5:6-8 Despite the man's horrible condition, Jesus' coming provided him a glimmer of hope; he ran and knelt before Jesus, seeking help. • ***Son of the Most High God:*** Evil spirits know Jesus' true identity (1:24, 34; 3:11). • There was no struggle; Jesus was in charge and the evil spirit obeyed the Master. ***Torture*** is the final judgment awaiting evil spirits (Matt 8:29; Luke 8:31).

5:9 A ***legion*** was a Roman military unit of 5,000–6,000 men. Here it describes the presence of ***many*** evil spirits.

5:10-13 The spirits' persistent begging shows Jesus' mastery over them. They were permitted to enter a ***herd of about 2,000 pigs***, whose presence marks this as Gentile territory (see note on 5:1). Some have focused on the economic loss of the pigs or have speculated about why Jesus let the demons destroy them, but Mark and his readers were interested in how Jesus saved the man.

5:15-16 The contrast between the former and present condition of ***the man who had been possessed*** was a testimony of Jesus' saving power.

5:17 The frightened people asked ***Jesus to go away.*** Fear and amazement are frequent responses to the mighty acts of Jesus (cp. 1:22, 27; 2:12; 4:41; 6:50-51). The response to Jesus' saving work varied (cp. 4:14-20).

5:18 Unlike his neighbors (5:17), the man experienced God's grace and wanted ***to go with him*** (literally ***to be with him***; see 3:14).

5:20
Ps 116:16
Isa 63:7
1 Tim 1:13-14

5:21-43
//Matt 9:18-26
//Luke 8:40-56

5:23
Matt 8:3
Mark 6:5; 7:32; 8:23, 25
Luke 4:40; 13:13
Acts 9:12, 17; 28:8

5:25
Lev 15:25-30

5:27
Mark 3:10
Acts 19:11-12

5:30
Luke 6:19

5:34
Mark 10:52
Luke 7:50; 17:19; 18:42
Acts 14:9

5:36
John 11:25-40

5:39
John 11:11

5:40
Acts 9:40

begged to go with him. 19But Jesus said,
"No, go home to your family, and tell them
everything the Lord has done for you and
how merciful he has been." 20So the man
started off to visit the Ten Towns of that region and began to proclaim the great things
Jesus had done for him; and everyone was
amazed at what he told them.

Jesus Heals in Response to Faith
Mark 5:21-43 // Matt 9:18-26 // Luke 8:40-56

21Jesus got into the boat again and went back
to the other side of the lake, where a large
crowd gathered around him on the shore.
22Then a leader of the local synagogue,
whose name was Jairus, arrived. When
he saw Jesus, he fell at his feet, 23pleading
fervently with him. "My little daughter is
dying," he said. "Please come and lay your
hands on her; heal her so she can live."
24Jesus went with him, and all the people
followed, crowding around him. 25A woman
in the crowd had suffered for twelve years
with constant bleeding. 26She had suffered
a great deal from many doctors, and over
the years she had spent everything she had
to pay them, but she had gotten no better. In
fact, she had gotten worse. 27She had heard
about Jesus, so she came up behind him
through the crowd and touched his robe.
28For she thought to herself, "If I can just
touch his robe, I will be healed." 29Immedi-
ately the bleeding stopped, and she could
feel in her body that she had been healed of
her terrible condition.
30Jesus realized at once that healing
power had gone out from him, so he turned
around in the crowd and asked, "Who
touched my robe?"
31His disciples said to him, "Look at this
crowd pressing around you. How can you
ask, 'Who touched me?' "
32But he kept on looking around to see
who had done it. 33Then the frightened
woman, trembling at the realization of what
had happened to her, came and fell to her
knees in front of him and told him what she
had done. 34And he said to her, "Daughter,
your faith has made you well. Go in peace.
Your suffering is over."
35While he was still speaking to her, messengers arrived from the home of Jairus,
the leader of the synagogue. They told him,
"Your daughter is dead. There's no use troubling the Teacher now."
36But Jesus overheard them and said to Jairus, "Don't be afraid. Just have faith."
37Then Jesus stopped the crowd and
wouldn't let anyone go with him except Peter, James, and John (the brother of James).
38When they came to the home of the synagogue leader, Jesus saw much commotion
and weeping and wailing. 39He went inside
and asked, "Why all this commotion and
weeping? The child isn't dead; she's only
asleep."
40The crowd laughed at him. But he made
them all leave, and he took the girl's father
and mother and his three disciples into the

5:19-20 Jesus' mission for the man was to tell others the great things *the Lord* had done for him. Mark thus identifies Jesus as the Lord. • ***tell them everything:*** Unlike other occasions, Jesus did not try to keep his identity secret (see "The Secret of the Messiah" at 3:11-12, p. 1653), perhaps because it was less dangerous in this Gentile area. • ***Ten Towns:*** Greek *Decapolis* (see note on Matt 4:24-25).

5:21-43 Two healing miracles are connected by the need for faith (5:34, 36). The story of Jairus's daughter brackets the story of the healing of the woman who had constant bleeding (5:25-34; see Mark Introduction, "Literary Features," p. 1644), during which Jairus's sick daughter died (5:35-43).

5:21-22 As Jesus arrived in Galilee on ***the other*** (i.e., west) ***side of the lake, . . . a leader of the local synagogue*** named ***Jairus*** approached him. Jairus organized the worship services at the synagogue (cp. Acts 13:15) and represented the Jewish community to the outside world.

5:23 The father wanted Jesus to ***heal her*** physically (literally *that she might be saved*; see 3:4; 5:28, 34; 6:56; 10:52; 15:30-31).

5:24-34 As Jesus goes to Jairus's home with a great crowd following, Mark introduces ***a woman in the crowd*** who suffered from ***constant bleeding***. This condition not only brought poor health, but made her ceremonially unclean and thus unable to participate in the normal life of the community (see Lev 15:25-27; "Clean and Unclean" at Lev 11:1–15:33, p. 213). She was a model of the kind of faith that Jairus should have.

5:27-29 The woman's ***faith*** (5:34) convinced her that just touching Jesus' clothing would bring healing; this took place ***immediately***.

5:33-34 The woman responded in fear—not from guilt, but from ***the realization*** that she had experienced a mighty miracle from God. Unlike the fear of the Gerasenes (5:15-17), her fear was positive and brought Jesus' blessing. She experienced God's grace and salvation.

5:35-43 Since Jairus had left home, his daughter had died. Jesus reassured Jairus that, despite the death of his daughter and the seeming hopelessness of the situation, Jairus should not be afraid but ***have faith*** in Jesus.

5:36 ***overheard:*** Or *ignored*. • ***Just have faith:*** As the woman had (5:28).

5:37 ***Peter, James, and John*** became Jesus' inner circle (see 3:16-17; 9:2; 14:33).

5:38 The ***commotion and weeping and wailing*** confirmed the report of the messengers and dramatized the hopelessness of the situation. Such outbursts of grief were typical of funerals in Jesus' day, where professional mourners were often hired (cp. Matt 9:23).

5:39 Sleep is a metaphor for death (John 11:11; 1 Thes 4:13-15). ***The child isn't dead*** because she will be resurrected—***she's only asleep***, and will shortly "wake up" and resume her life. The same Greek word translated here as "sleep" refers to death in Matt 27:52; Acts 7:60; 13:36; 1 Cor 15:6, 18, 20, 51; 1 Thes 4:13-15.

5:40 Because ***the crowd*** did not understand Jesus' words, they ***laughed at him***, knowing that the girl had died. ***He***

room where the girl was lying. 41Holding
her hand, he said to her, *"Talitha koum,"*
which means "Little girl, get up!" 42And the
girl, who was twelve years old, immediately
stood up and walked around! They were
overwhelmed and totally amazed. 43Jesus
gave them strict orders not to tell anyone
what had happened, and then he told them
to give her something to eat.

3. JESUS IS MISUNDERSTOOD (6:1–8:26)

Jesus Is Rejected at Nazareth

Mark 6:1-6a // Matt 13:53-58 // Luke 4:16-24

6 Jesus left that part of the country and
returned with his disciples to Nazareth, his hometown. 2The next Sabbath he
began teaching in the synagogue, and many
who heard him were amazed. They asked,
"Where did he get all this wisdom and the
power to perform such miracles?" 3Then
they scoffed, "He's just a carpenter, the son
of Mary and the brother of James, Joseph,
Judas, and Simon. And his sisters live right
here among us." They were deeply offended
and refused to believe in him.
4Then Jesus told them, "A prophet is
honored everywhere except in his own
hometown and among his relatives and his
own family." 5And because of their unbelief,
he couldn't do any miracles among them except to place his hands on a few sick people
and heal them. 6And he was amazed at their
unbelief.

Jesus Sends Out the Twelve Disciples

Mark 6:6b-13 // Matt 10:5-15 // Luke 9:1-6;
cp. Luke 10:1-11

Then Jesus went from village to village, teaching the people. 7And he called his twelve
disciples together and began sending them
out two by two, giving them authority to
cast out evil spirits. 8He told them to take
nothing for their journey except a walking
stick—no food, no traveler's bag, no money.
9He allowed them to wear sandals but not to
take a change of clothes.
10"Wherever you go," he said, "stay in the
same house until you leave town. 11But if
any place refuses to welcome you or listen
to you, shake its dust from your feet as you
leave to show that you have abandoned
those people to their fate."

5:41-42 Luke 7:14
5:43 Matt 8:4; Mark 1:44; 7:36
6:1-6 //Matt 13:53-58; //Luke 4:16-30
6:2 John 7:15
6:3 John 6:42
6:4 John 4:44
6:5 Matt 9:18
6:7-13 //Matt 10:1, 5-15; //Luke 9:1-6
6:7 Luke 10:1
6:8-9 Luke 10:4
6:10 Luke 10:7
6:11 Luke 10:11; Acts 13:51

made them all leave, probably to keep them from discouraging the parents any further.

5:41 Mark translates *Talitha koum* for his Greek-speaking readers as *Little girl, get up!* The Aramaic terms are not magical; they are simply the actual words Jesus spoke when he raised the little girl, since Aramaic was his native language. The Aramaic terms that Mark records probably come from learning the story in Aramaic in Jerusalem.

5:42 Jesus' authority over death was demonstrated when the little girl ***immediately stood up and walked around,*** with no need for recuperation. The transformation was instant and absolute.

5:43 The miracle is followed by a command not to tell anyone what had happened (see "The Secret of the Messiah," at 3:11-12, p. 1653). • ***give her something to eat:*** The Lord of nature, demons, illness, and death is also concerned with the daily needs of his creatures.

6:1-6a Nazareth's rejection of Jesus contrasts ironically with the faith displayed by others, and the miracles ***he couldn't do*** contrasts with the power displayed elsewhere.

6:1-2 The people's amazement at Jesus' teaching was due to the ***wisdom*** of his teaching and his ***power*** to heal and cast out demons.• ***Where did he get:*** His quiet years in Nazareth had not prepared them to accept him as an authoritative teacher and healer.

6:3-4 The residents of Nazareth thought of Jesus only as ***a carpenter*** (literally *craftsman*). • ***He's just a carpenter, the son of Mary:*** Some manuscripts read *He's just the son of the carpenter and of Mary.* One expects "son of Joseph"; this phrasing probably indicates that Joseph had died by this time. • ***brother . . . his sisters:*** See note on 3:31-35. • ***Joseph:*** Most manuscripts read *Joses;* see Matt 13:55. • ***They were deeply offended:*** They thought Jesus was claiming to be someone he could not possibly be.

6:5-6a Faith and healing are frequently connected in Mark (2:5; 5:34, 36; 9:23-24; 10:52). Jesus' miracles were not performances but the partial realization of God's Kingdom; entrance to that Kingdom and its benefits require repentance and faith (1:15). • ***A few sick people*** were healed, but the unbelief that Jesus encountered in his own village ***amazed*** him, a unique occurrence. • This section of Mark (3:7–6:6a) speaks of Jesus' rejection by his family (3:21, 31-35), the scribes (3:22), and the people of Gerasa (5:17); it ends with rejection by people in his hometown (6:1-6a). Along the way, a few people believed and were healed. This ending is similar to the ending of the previous section (1:14–3:6).

6:6b–8:21 Jesus' mission and the disciples' misunderstanding are prominent themes in this section.

6:6b This summary of Jesus' healing and preaching ministry introduces an account concerning the disciples. Jesus' teaching from ***village to village*** probably took place around the Sea of Galilee and perhaps Capernaum (see 2:1).

6:7-13 Jesus now sent the ***disciples*** out to preach and heal. During this mission, Jesus' memorable teachings were engraved in their minds by retelling, and it prepared them to remember and retell later what Jesus did and taught (Luke 1:2).

6:7 ***two by two:*** This practice fulfilled the OT requirement of two witnesses (Num 35:30; Deut 17:6; 19:15; see Matt 18:16) and provided for companionship and mutual help (Acts 13:1-3; 15:22, 39, 40). • ***giving them authority:*** Jesus can delegate his authority (see 1:27; 2:10) to others. • The disciples were to ***cast out evil*** (literally *unclean*) ***spirits*** and to preach and heal (6:12-13; see 6:30).

6:8-9 The instructions for the disciples' mission were about what they should leave behind (***food . . . bag . . . money . . . change of clothes***). They were to travel light, counting on Jewish hospitality for food and lodging (cp. Luke 22:35-37). • ***no money:*** Literally *no copper coins in their money belts.*

6:10 They were to ***stay in the same house*** and not abuse hospitality by seeking out better offers of food and lodging.

6:11 The shaking of ***dust*** from the ***feet*** is best interpreted as a symbolic act pronouncing God's judgment upon those who rejected the apostles' preaching (cp. Acts 18:6), which was really a rejection of Jesus and of God, who sent him (9:37).

6:12-13 The message ***to repent*** is an abbreviation of the fuller message of 1:15.

6:13 Luke 10:34; Jas 5:14; [d]aleiphō (0218) ‣ Luke 7:38
6:14-29 //Matt 14:1-12 //Luke 9:7-9
6:15 Matt 16:14
6:17-18 Lev 18:15-16; 20:21; Luke 3:19-20

12So the disciples went out, telling everyone they met to repent of their sins and turn to God. 13And they cast out many demons and healed many sick people, [d]anointing them with olive oil.

Herod and the Death of John the Baptist

Mark 6:14-16 // Matt 14:1-2 // Luke 9:7-9
Mark 6:17-29 // Matt 14:3-12; cp. Luke 3:19-20

14Herod Antipas, the king, soon heard about Jesus, because everyone was talking about him. Some were saying, "This must be John the Baptist raised from the dead. That is why he can do such miracles." 15Others said, "He's the prophet Elijah." Still others said, "He's a prophet like the other great prophets of the past."

16When Herod heard about Jesus, he said, "John, the man I beheaded, has come back from the dead."

17For Herod had sent soldiers to arrest and imprison John as a favor to Herodias. She had been his brother Philip's wife, but

HEROD ANTIPAS (6:14-29)

Mark 1:14; Matt 14:1-12; Luke 3:1, 19-20; 9:7-9; 13:31-33; 23:7-12, 15; Acts 4:27

Herod Antipas, sixth son of Herod the Great, was ruler of Galilee and Perea from 4 BC to AD 39, during the life of Jesus and in the region where Jesus Christ and John the Baptist concentrated their ministries.

Following the example of his father, Herod Antipas founded cities. Sepphoris, his first project, was the largest city in Galilee. It was Antipas's capital city until he built Tiberias, named in honor of the reigning emperor, Tiberius (AD 14–37). The city Tiberias was on the western shore of the Sea of Galilee. Antipas completed the city in AD 23 and made it his capital.

Herod Antipas offended many Jews by divorcing his wife and marrying Herodias, the wife of his half brother, Herod Philip (see diagram, p. 1579). Antipas's marriage to Herodias was in violation of the law of Moses (Lev 18:16; 20:21) because Herod's brother Philip was still alive. When John the Baptist spoke out strongly against this illegal marriage, Antipas imprisoned him (6:17-18); Herod was afraid John's denunciation would lead to a political revolt (Josephus, *Antiquities* 18.5.2). Herodias's daughter later danced for Herod, evoking a rash promise from him to give her anything she wanted (Matt 14:1-12). Herodias took the opportunity to have John beheaded.

It was obvious to Antipas that Jesus' ministry was even more remarkable than John's (see 6:14-16; Matt 14:1-2; Luke 9:7-9), but he was reluctant to use force to bring about a meeting, for fear of arousing the people against him. Jesus, for his part, was openly critical of Herod Antipas (8:15; Luke 13:31-33). Eventually, Jesus withdrew from Antipas's territories.

When Jesus was finally arrested, Pilate could find no fault in Jesus, so he sent him to Herod Antipas, who was in Jerusalem for Passover. Pilate may also have been attempting to reconcile himself to Antipas. Their relationship had been rather strained since the Galilean massacre (Luke 13:1), and because Pilate had brought votive shields that bore the image of Tiberius and were considered blasphemous by the Jews (Philo, *On the Embassy to Gaius* 299–304). When Jesus was brought before Antipas, Herod only mocked him and sent him back to Pilate (Luke 23:7-11). The main political accomplishment of the incident was that Herod and Pilate were reconciled (Luke 23:12).

Herod Antipas was later defeated in war by King Aretas, whose daughter he had divorced (Jews interpreted this defeat as an act of divine judgment). He was then deposed by Emperor Gaius in AD 39 and sent into exile, in response to accusations from Herod Agrippa I of Antipas's conspiracy against Rome (see "Herod Agrippa I" at Acts 12:1-4, p. 1851).

6:14-29 The account of John the Baptist's death, sandwiched between the sending out and the return of the disciples, continues the theme of Jesus' authority and power (see 6:7, 14). John's fate and the warning given to the disciples in their missionary charge (6:11) also foreshadowed Jesus' death. The one greater even than John (1:8) would soon be handed over to religious and political leaders and put to death (8:31; 9:31; 10:33).

6:14 ***Herod Antipas:*** See "Herod Antipas," above. • ***soon heard about Jesus:*** The successful mission in Galilee and Perea of six teams of disciples (6:12-13) spread Jesus' fame throughout the region. • ***Some were saying:*** Some manuscripts read *He was saying.* • ***This must be John the Baptist raised from the dead:*** Either Herod was thinking that the spirit of John the Baptist had come to rest upon Jesus at his death, as the spirit of Elijah came upon Elisha, or he was saying figuratively in exasperation, "This is John the Baptist all over again!"

6:15 The return of ***the prophet Elijah*** had been prophesied in Mal 3:1; 4:5-6 (cp. 9:11-13).

6:17 ***imprison John:*** The Jewish historian Josephus (*Antiquities* 18.5.2) says that John was imprisoned in the fortress of Macherus in Perea. • Josephus (*Antiquities* 18.5.4) states that ***Herodias*** was the wife of Herod Antipas's half brother, Herod ***Philip*** (see diagram, p. 1579; cp. Josephus, *Antiquities* 18.5.1).

Herod had married her. 18John had been telling Herod, "It is against God's law for you to marry your brother's wife." 19So Herodias bore a grudge against John and wanted to kill him. But without Herod's approval she was powerless, 20for Herod respected John; and knowing that he was a good and holy man, he protected him. Herod was greatly disturbed whenever he talked with John, but even so, he liked to listen to him.

21Herodias's chance finally came on Herod's birthday. He gave a party for his high government officials, army officers, and the leading citizens of Galilee. 22Then his daughter, also named Herodias, came in and performed a dance that greatly pleased Herod and his guests. "Ask me for anything you like," the king said to the girl, "and I will give it to you." 23He even vowed, "I will give you whatever you ask, up to half my kingdom!"

24She went out and asked her mother, "What should I ask for?"

Her mother told her, "Ask for the head of John the Baptist!"

25So the girl hurried back to the king and told him, "I want the head of John the Baptist, right now, on a tray!"

26Then the king deeply regretted what he had said; but because of the vows he had made in front of his guests, he couldn't refuse her. 27So he immediately sent an executioner to the prison to cut off John's head and bring it to him. The soldier beheaded John in the prison, 28brought his head on a tray, and gave it to the girl, who took it to her mother. 29When John's disciples heard what had happened, they came to get his body and buried it in a tomb.

Jesus Feeds Five Thousand

Mark 6:30-31 // Luke 9:10a
Mark 6:32-44 // Matt 14:13-21 // Luke 9:10b-17 // John 6:1-15

30The apostles returned to Jesus from their ministry tour and told him all they had done and taught. 31Then Jesus said, "Let's go off by ourselves to a quiet place and rest awhile." He said this because there were so many people coming and going that Jesus and his apostles didn't even have time to eat.

32So they left by boat for a quiet place, where they could be alone. 33But many people recognized them and saw them leaving, and people from many towns ran ahead along the shore and got there ahead of them. 34Jesus saw the huge crowd as he stepped from the boat, and he had compassion on them because they were like sheep without a [e]shepherd. So he began teaching them many things.

35Late in the afternoon his disciples came to him and said, "This is a remote place, and it's already getting late. 36Send the crowds away so they can go to the nearby farms and villages and buy something to eat."

37But Jesus said, "You feed them."

"With what?" they asked. "We'd have to work for months to earn enough money to buy food for all these people!"

38"How much bread do you have?" he asked. "Go and find out."

6:23
Esth 5:3-6; 7:2

6:30
Luke 9:10; 10:17

6:31
Mark 3:20

6:32-44
//Matt 14:13-21
//Luke 9:10-17
//John 6:5-13

6:34
*Num 27:17
*1 Kgs 22:17
*2 Chr 18:16
*Zech 10:2
Matt 9:36
[e]*poimēn* (4166)
‣Luke 2:8

6:37
2 Kgs 4:42-44
Matt 15:33
Mark 8:4

6:38
Matt 15:34
Mark 8:5

6:18 Mark gives the moral-religious reason for the imprisonment and execution of John the Baptist. Josephus refers to the political reason (fear that John's great popularity might start a revolution; Josephus, *Antiquities* 18.5.2). Similarly, the religious reasons for Jesus' condemnation (14:63-64) became political when he was brought before Pontius Pilate (15:2; Luke 23:2-3). • ***It is against God's law:*** Not only was the relationship adulterous (Lev 20:10), but it violated the further law against marrying a brother's wife (Lev 18:16; 20:21).

6:19-28 ***Herodias's*** role in the murder of John the Baptist recalls the story of Jezebel (1 Kgs 19:1-2). Herod succumbed to pressure (6:26-28), which foreshadows the later story of Pontius Pilate, who put Jesus to death against his better judgment (cp. 6:20, 25-28 with 15:6-15).

6:22 ***his daughter, also named Herodias:*** Some manuscripts read *the daughter of Herodias herself.* Herodias's daughter was also named Salome (Josephus, *Antiquities* 18.5.4).

6:29 This verse is similar to the description of Jesus' death and burial (see 15:43-46). Disciples of John existed after his death until at least the AD 200s (see Acts 18:24–19:7).

6:30-44 The disciples' mission concludes (6:6b-13, 30-34), followed by the account of the feeding of the 5,000 (6:35-44; see also Matt 14:13-21; Luke 9:10-17; John 6:1-15). The feeding of the 4,000 is sufficiently different to indicate that these were two separate occasions (see 8:1-10).

6:30 Mark calls Jesus' disciples ***apostles*** here to indicate their new status as those who had been sent out (see note on 3:14-15) and to avoid possible confusion between them and John the Baptist's disciples. • The apostles reported the success of what they had *done and taught.*

6:31-33 ***Let's go:*** Jesus and the disciples probably proceeded northward along the western shore of the Sea of Galilee toward Bethsaida (Luke 9:10), in sight of the crowds ***along the shore.*** • ***so many people:*** The great crowds demonstrate the success of the apostolic mission and the greatness of Jesus, whom the apostles represented.

6:34 ***they were like sheep without a shepherd:*** God's people need a shepherd (Num 27:16-17; 1 Kgs 22:17; 2 Chr 18:16; see Jer 13:10; Ezek 34:23). *Teaching* people God's word is compared to feeding sheep in Jewish literature (e.g., Ezek 34:1-24; *2 Baruch* 77:13-15).

6:35-36 The *place* where Jesus taught was ***remote,*** but it still had ***farms and villages . . . nearby*** where the people could ***buy something to eat.***

6:37 Just as the disciples were able to cast out demons and heal through his power (6:7, 13, 30), Jesus suggests that they should be able to *feed* the crowd. Their reply considered only what they themselves were capable of doing. They did not consider Jesus' power. • ***We'd have to work for months to earn enough money:*** Literally *It would take 200 denarii.* A denarius was equivalent to a laborer's full day's wage.

6:41 Matt 14:19
6:45-52 //Matt 14:22-33 //John 6:16-21
6:52 Mark 8:17-21
6:53-56 //Matt 14:34-36
6:56 Matt 9:20 Mark 5:27 Luke 8:44

They came back and reported, "We have five loaves of bread and two fish."

39Then Jesus told the disciples to have the people sit down in groups on the green grass. 40So they sat down in groups of fifty or a hundred.

41Jesus took the five loaves and two fish, looked up toward heaven, and blessed them. Then, breaking the loaves into pieces, he kept giving the bread to the disciples so they could distribute it to the people. He also divided the fish for everyone to share. 42They all ate as much as they wanted, 43and afterward, the disciples picked up twelve baskets of leftover bread and fish. 44A total of 5,000 men and their families were fed from those loaves!

Jesus Walks on Water
Mark 6:45-52 // Matt 14:22-33 // John 6:16-21

45Immediately after this, Jesus insisted that his disciples get back into the boat and head across the lake to Bethsaida, while he sent the people home. 46After telling everyone good-bye, he went up into the hills by himself to pray.

47Late that night, the disciples were in their boat in the middle of the lake, and Jesus was alone on land. 48He saw that they were in serious trouble, rowing hard and struggling against the wind and waves. About three o'clock in the morning Jesus came toward them, walking on the water. He intended to go past them, 49but when they saw him walking on the water, they cried out in terror, thinking he was a ghost. 50They were all terrified when they saw him.

But Jesus spoke to them at once. "Don't be afraid," he said. "Take courage! I am here!" 51Then he climbed into the boat, and the wind stopped. They were totally amazed, 52for they still didn't understand the significance of the miracle of the loaves. Their hearts were too hard to take it in.

Jesus Heals the Sick
Mark 6:53-56 // Matt 14:34-36; cp. John 6:22-25

53After they had crossed the lake, they landed at Gennesaret. They brought the boat to shore 54and climbed out. The people recognized Jesus at once, 55and they ran throughout the whole area, carrying sick people on mats to wherever they heard he was. 56Wherever he went—in villages, cities, or the countryside—they brought the sick

6:41 The words *took, blessed, breaking,* and *giving* echo Jesus' words at the Last Supper (14:22-25). Both events envision the final messianic banquet in which believers will eat and drink with Jesus in the Kingdom of God (14:25; Matt 5:6; 22:1-10; see Rev 2:7; 19:7-9; 22:1-2, 14, 17-19).

6:42-44 This miracle makes Elisha's great miracle of feeding of 100 people with twenty loaves (2 Kgs 4:42-44) seem trivial by comparison. Readers of the Gospel must ask themselves, "Who is this man who does such things?" (4:41). He is the Messiah, the Son of God (1:1).

6:45-52 This story is a manifestation of Jesus' glory to the disciples (6:48-50). It is also a rescue story (6:47-48, 51) and a story about the disciples' lack of understanding (6:51-52).

6:45-46 The disciples proceeded *to Bethsaida,* the home of Peter and Andrew (John 1:44), while Jesus dismissed the crowd and went apart *to pray*. Jesus was a man of prayer (1:35) and urged his disciples to pray (see 14:38).

6:48 It was *about three o'clock in the morning* (literally *about the fourth watch of the night,* which began at 3:00 AM): This was a Roman designation of time (Jews reckoned only three watches), which supports the view that Mark wrote for Christians in Rome. • Mark does not explain how Jesus *saw* his disciples' plight late at night in the middle of the lake (cp. John 6:19), as it is not important to the story. • *Jesus came toward them, walking on the water:* It appears that Jesus' purpose was to rescue the disciples from the storm. However, Mark then states that Jesus *intended to go past them*. Numerous attempts have been made to explain this, but the best explanation is that "to go past them" speaks of a divine manifestation (cp. Exod 33:18–34:6; 1 Kgs 19:11-13): Jesus apparently sought to show his divine glory to the disciples. This understanding is supported by the disciples' fear, a response often associated with theophany. • Many have tried to rationalize the miracle of Jesus' walking on the sea, but Mark, Matthew, and John clearly understood this as a miracle, beyond natural explanation. If Jesus is in fact the Son of God, there is no need to find another explanation.

6:49-50 The disciples' *terror* is understandable—humans cannot walk on water, so they concluded that they were seeing a ghost. As in many divine manifestations, the Lord gave a word of assurance: *Don't be afraid* and *Take courage!* The reason is, *I am here!* It was not a ghost but Jesus—their friend, Savior, and Lord. • *I am here!* (or *The 'I AM' is here;* Greek reads *I am*): Because Jesus' walking on the sea and stilling the storm were miraculous, Mark's original readers would have understood the exclamation *I am* as a parallel to God's self-description in the OT (Exod 3:14; Deut 32:39; Isa 41:4; 43:10-13) and thus as a reference to Jesus' divinity.

6:51 Jesus' entrance into the boat calmed the storm. • *totally amazed:* They were reverential and awed at the greatness of Jesus Christ, the Son of God (cp. 2:12; 5:24; Matt 14:33).

6:52 The account ends with a comment about the disciples' dullness. It was not from lack of opportunity to believe in Jesus—they had witnessed *the miracle of the loaves* and many other miracles—but because *their hearts were too hard*, usually a quality of Jesus' opponents (e.g., 3:5; see also 8:17, 21; 9:32). Later their hearts would be softened, and they would understand (Luke 24:44-49; John 12:16; 13:7).

6:53-56 This summary of Jesus' ministry in Galilee emphasizes his great popularity and healing ability.

6:53 *Gennesaret* refers to a fertile plain, 3.5 miles long by 0.5 miles wide (5.6 by 0.8 kilometers), between Tiberius and Capernaum on the northwest coast of the Sea of Galilee. The original journey was to Bethsaida (6:45), so perhaps the winds (6:48) blew the ship off course and they landed at Gennesaret. Alternatively, 6:45 might indicate the direction of the journey (i.e., northeast), and not the actual goal of the voyage.

out to the marketplaces. They begged him to let the sick touch at least the fringe of his robe, and all who touched him were healed.

Jesus Teaches about Inner Purity

Mark 7:1-23 // Matt 15:1-20

7 One day some Pharisees and teachers of religious law arrived from Jerusalem to see Jesus. 2They noticed that some of his disciples failed to follow the Jewish ritual of hand washing before eating. 3(The Jews, especially the Pharisees, do not eat until they have poured water over their cupped hands, as required by their ancient traditions. 4Similarly, they don't eat anything from the market until they immerse their hands in water. This is but one of many traditions they have clung to—such as their ceremonial washing of cups, pitchers, and kettles.)

5So the Pharisees and teachers of religious law asked him, "Why don't your disciples follow our age-old tradition? They eat without first performing the hand-washing ceremony."

6Jesus replied, "You [f]hypocrites! Isaiah was right when he prophesied about you, for he wrote,

'These people honor me with their lips,
but their hearts are far from me.
7Their worship is a farce,
for they teach man-made ideas as commands from God.'

8For you ignore God's law and substitute your own tradition."

9Then he said, "You skillfully sidestep God's law in order to hold on to your own tradition. 10For instance, Moses gave you this law from God: 'Honor your father and mother,' and 'Anyone who speaks disrespectfully of father or mother must be put to death.' 11But you say it is all right for people to say to their parents, 'Sorry, I can't help you. For I have vowed to give to God what I would have given to you.' 12In this way, you let them disregard their needy parents. 13And so you cancel the word of God in order to hand down your own tradition. And this is only one example among many others."

14Then Jesus called to the crowd to come and hear. "All of you listen," he said, "and try to understand. 15It's not what goes into your body that defiles you; you are defiled by what comes from your heart."

7:1-23
//Matt 15:1-20

7:2
Luke 11:38
Acts 10:14, 28

7:3
Gal 1:14
Col 2:8

7:4
Matt 23:25
Luke 11:39

7:6-7
*Isa 29:13
Col 2:22.

7:6
[f]*hupokritēs* (5273)
‣Luke 6:42

7:9
Isa 24:4-5

7:10
*Exod 20:12; 21:17
*Lev 20:9
*Deut 5:16
1 Tim 5:8

7:15
1 Cor 8:8
1 Tim 4:4

6:56 The *fringe* of a garment refers to the tassels worn by Jewish men on their robes (see Num 15:38-39; Deut 22:12). Just touching the fringe of the garment of Jesus the Messiah, the Son of God, brought healing to the sick (see also 3:10; 5:28).

7:1-23 This account has no direct connection with what precedes it. It assumes only a context such as "Once in the ministry of Jesus." After setting the scene (7:1-4), Mark introduces the Pharisees' question (7:5) followed by Jesus' response (7:6-23). The first part of Jesus' response (7:6-13) centers around two OT passages and a twofold attack on the Pharisees' traditions (7:6-8, 9-13). In the second part (7:14-23), Jesus teaches about what does and does not truly defile.

7:1 Readers already know that the ***Pharisees and teachers of religious law*** were hostile to Jesus (see 2:16, 24; 3:6, 22).

7:2-4 Mark explains the Pharisaic practices of ritual cleansing for his non-Jewish (Gentile) readers. The ***ancient traditions*** (literally *the traditions of the elders*) were as yet unwritten accounts that the Pharisees believed had been given to Moses on Mount Sinai along with the written law. They were written down around AD 200 in the Mishnah, one of the key sources for understanding ancient Judaism.

7:3 ***poured water over their cupped hands:*** Literally *washed with the fist.*

7:4 ***immerse their hands:*** Some manuscripts read *sprinkle themselves.* • ***cups, pitchers, and kettles:*** Some manuscripts add *and dining couches.*

7:5 Since ***the Pharisees*** believed that their oral traditions were given to Moses as part of God's divine revelation, they asked Jesus why his disciples did not keep them. After all, teachers were responsible for the behavior of their disciples (see 2:24).

7:6-8 Jesus first responds by quoting Isa 29:13 (Greek version), which deals with the ***farce*** of equating ***man-made ideas*** with God's commands. It describes well the situation in which the Pharisees had substituted their human ***tradition*** for ***God's law.***

7:9-13 Next, Jesus provides an ***instance*** where the Pharisees' traditions contradicted ***God's law*** and allowed them to ***sidestep*** its requirements. • ***'Honor your father and mother':*** See Exod 20:12; Deut 5:16. • ***'Anyone who speaks disrespectfully of father or mother must be put to death':*** See Exod 21:17 (Greek version); Lev 20:9 (Greek version).

7:11-12 ***But you say:*** The contrast with God's law is emphatic—their tradition repudiated God's command for people to honor their parents by providing for their needs. • ***'For I have vowed to give to God what I would have given to you':*** Literally *'What I would have given to you is Corban' (that is, a gift).* The tradition said that people could sidestep their obligation to support their parents by dedicating some of their resources to God, thus disregarding and dishonoring their ***needy parents.***

7:13 The result of such traditions was to ***cancel the word of God.*** • ***only one example among many others:*** It was not an isolated instance; see, e.g., Isa 1:10-20; 58:1-14.

7:14-23 Jesus' second argument against the Pharisees was a proverb that Jesus told ***the crowd.*** Later, in the privacy of a home, Jesus explained it to his disciples (7:17-23). It concerns moral distinctions about eating. Eating affects the digestive system, but moral issues involve the ***heart.*** The heart is a metaphor for the seat of moral decision making. How a person eats (with clean or unclean hands) or what a person eats (clean or unclean food) affects only the digestive tract, so it has no bearing on the moral issues of the soul. To help his later readers understand the implications of Jesus' teaching, Mark adds the interpretive comment ***By saying this, he declared that every kind of food is acceptable in God's eyes.*** In the apostolic church, Peter and Paul were instrumental in bringing this implication to light (see Acts 10:1–11:18; Rom 14:14; 1 Cor 8:8; Gal 2:11-21).

7:15 Some manuscripts add verse 16, *Anyone with ears to hear should listen and understand.* Cp. 4:9, 23.

7:17
Mark 9:28

7:19
Acts 10:15; 11:9
Rom 14:1-12
Col 2:16
1 Tim 4:3-5

7:21-22
Rom 1:29-31
Gal 5:19-21
Titus 1:15

7:22
[g]*blasphēmia* (0988)
‣ Luke 12:10

7:24-30
//Matt 15:21-28

7:26
[h]*daimonion* (1140)
‣ Mark 16:17

7:31-37
//Matt 15:29-31

7:33
Mark 8:23
John 9:6

7:34
Matt 14:19
Mark 6:41
John 11:41; 17:1

17 Then Jesus went into a house to get away from the crowd, and his disciples asked him what he meant by the parable he had just used. 18 "Don't you understand either?" he asked. "Can't you see that the food you put into your body cannot defile you? 19 Food doesn't go into your heart, but only passes through the stomach and then goes into the sewer." (By saying this, he declared that every kind of food is acceptable in God's eyes.)

20 And then he added, "It is what comes from inside that defiles you. 21 For from within, out of a person's heart, come evil thoughts, sexual immorality, theft, murder, 22 adultery, greed, wickedness, deceit, lustful desires, envy, [g]slander, pride, and foolishness. 23 All these vile things come from within; they are what defile you."

The Faith of a Gentile Woman

Mark 7:24-30 // Matt 15:21-28

24 Then Jesus left Galilee and went north to the region of Tyre. He didn't want anyone to know which house he was staying in, but he couldn't keep it a secret. 25 Right away a woman who had heard about him came and fell at his feet. Her little girl was possessed by an evil spirit, 26 and she begged him to cast out the [h]demon from her daughter.

Since she was a Gentile, born in Syrian Phoenicia, 27 Jesus told her, "First I should feed the children—my own family, the Jews. It isn't right to take food from the children and throw it to the dogs."

28 She replied, "That's true, Lord, but even the dogs under the table are allowed to eat the scraps from the children's plates."

29 "Good answer!" he said. "Now go home, for the demon has left your daughter." 30 And when she arrived home, she found her little girl lying quietly in bed, and the demon was gone.

Jesus Heals a Deaf Man

31 Jesus left Tyre and went up to Sidon before going back to the Sea of Galilee and the region of the Ten Towns. 32 A deaf man with a speech impediment was brought to him, and the people begged Jesus to lay his hands on the man to heal him.

33 Jesus led him away from the crowd so they could be alone. He put his fingers into the man's ears. Then, spitting on his own fingers, he touched the man's tongue. 34 Looking up to heaven, he sighed and said,

---

7:20-22 These verses summarize thirteen things that truly defile a person. These actions and vices all come from the heart.

7:24-30 The discussion of clean and unclean and of undefiled and defiled in 7:1-23 has prepared readers for the story of the Gentile woman's faith. For Jews, Gentiles were defiled by definition, because they did not keep the regulations of the OT (see Acts 10:1–11:18, especially 10:14-15; 11:2-3, 8-9).

7:24 The city of *Tyre* (some manuscripts add *and Sidon*) and its surrounding regions lie on the Mediterranean coast in modern-day Lebanon. Originally an island, Tyre became a peninsula when Alexander the Great constructed a half-mile ramp from the mainland in 332 BC. Tyre had one of the most important harbors on the eastern side of the Mediterranean Sea. People earlier had come from Tyre to hear Jesus and see him work miracles (3:7-8), which explains how the Tyrian woman knew of him. • There is much discussion about why Jesus *left Galilee* to visit this Gentile *region.* Mark provides no explanation, so any suggestion is pure speculation. Mark's Gentile readers, however, would have understood this journey by Jesus as foreshadowing the church's mission to the Gentile world that led to their own conversion (for more about the genesis of the church in Rome, see Romans Introduction, p. 1889).

7:25-26 The woman was from *Syrian Phoenicia* and therefore a Gentile. The urgency and intensity of the woman's petition is seen in her falling at Jesus' feet and begging.

7:25 *evil:* Literally *unclean.*

7:27-28 Jesus' reply to the woman seems like a harsh refusal, but their interaction indicates that he wanted to see her faith (cp. Matt 15:28). • ***First I should feed the children—my own family, the Jews:*** Literally *Let the children eat first.* Jesus' use of *first* did not exclude her as a Gentile from the grace of God, but indicated that his mission was first to the Jews (Acts 13:46; Rom 1:16). The woman responded to Jesus' words with humility and faith. She acknowledged the priority of the Jewish people but argued that there was more than enough food for the ***dogs*** as well. (In Jewish literature, Gentiles were frequently referred to as dogs, which were seen as filthy scavengers rather than as adorable pets; see also note on Rev 22:15.) The woman's persistence and acknowledgment of Jesus as ***Lord*** were rewarded.

7:29-30 For similar healings from a distance, see Matt 8:5-13 // Luke 7:1-10 and John 4:46-54.

7:31-37 This miracle is very similar in order and vocabulary to the healing of the blind man in 8:22-26. Healing miracles in the Gospels follow a similar pattern—the constant telling and retelling of similar stories probably standardized their form and wording. • This healing miracle includes a change of scene. Although some interpret the next miracle as occurring in the Gentile world (Sidon or Decapolis), it probably took place after Jesus returned to the Sea of Galilee (see note on Matt 4:13). The next incident takes place there (8:10) without a change of scene.

7:31 *Ten Towns:* Greek *Decapolis* (see note on Matt 4:24-25).

7:33 The healing was performed privately (7:33; see 5:40-45; 8:23) to prevent the spread of messianic fervor (see "The Secret of the Messiah" at 3:11-12, p. 1653; cp. John 6:15). • Jesus also used saliva in a healing at 8:23, where he spit on a man's eyes in curing his blindness. The medicinal use of saliva in ancient times is well documented.

7:34 Since Jesus was *looking up to heaven* when *he sighed*, his sigh is probably best understood as a prayerful gesture. • ***Ephphatha*** is an Aramaic term that Mark translates for his readers (see also 3:17; 5:41; 14:36; 15:34). These are not magical formulas or incantations; Mark is simply recounting some of the original words Jesus spoke. Matthew and Luke do not seem to have attributed any special significance to the Aramaic words of Jesus, since they did not include them in their Gospels.

"Ephphatha," which means, "Be opened!"
35 Instantly the man could hear perfectly,
and his tongue was freed so he could speak
plainly!
36 Jesus told the crowd not to tell anyone,
but the more he told them not to, the more
they spread the news. 37 They were completely amazed and said again and again,
"Everything he does is wonderful. He even
makes the deaf to hear and gives speech to
those who cannot speak."

Jesus Feeds Four Thousand
Mark 8:1-10 // Matt 15:32-39

8 About this time another large crowd
had gathered, and the people ran out
of food again. Jesus called his disciples and
told them, 2 "I feel sorry for these people.
They have been here with me for three days,
and they have nothing left to eat. 3 If I send
them home hungry, they will faint along the
way. For some of them have come a long
distance."
4 His disciples replied, "How are we supposed to find enough food to feed them out
here in the wilderness?"
5 Jesus asked, "How much bread do you
have?"
"Seven loaves," they replied.
6 So Jesus told all the people to sit down on
the ground. Then he took the seven loaves,
thanked God for them, and broke them into
pieces. He gave them to his disciples, who
distributed the bread to the crowd. 7 A few
small fish were found, too, so Jesus also
blessed these and told the disciples to distribute them.
8 They ate as much as they wanted. Afterward, the disciples picked up seven large
baskets of leftover food. 9 There were about
4,000 people in the crowd that day, and
Jesus sent them home after they had eaten.
10 Immediately after this, he got into a boat
with his disciples and crossed over to the region of Dalmanutha.

Pharisees Demand a Miraculous Sign
Mark 8:11-13; cp. Matt 12:38-39 // Luke 11:16, 29;
cp. Matt 16:1-4

11 When the Pharisees heard that Jesus had
arrived, they came and started to argue with
him. Testing him, they demanded that he
show them a miraculous sign from heaven
to prove his authority.
12 When he heard this, he sighed deeply
in his spirit and said, "Why do these people

7:36 Matt 8:4
7:37 Isa 35:5-6
8:1-10 //Matt 15:32-39 Mark 6:32-44
8:2 Matt 9:36
8:4 Num 11:21-22 2 Kgs 4:42-43
8:7 Matt 14:19
8:10 Matt 15:39
8:11-21 //Matt 16:1-12 Luke 11:16, 29 John 6:30

7:36-37 Despite his desire to avoid attention, Jesus' greatness shone too brightly—his person, his teaching, and his ability to heal inspired awe, and he could not be hidden (see "The Secret of the Messiah" at 3:11-12, p. 1653).

8:1-10 The stories about feeding the 4,000 and the 5,000 are similar. All four Gospels report the earlier feeding of the 5,000 (6:35-44; Matt 14:13-21; Luke 9:10-17; John 6:1-15), but only Mark and Matthew (Matt 15:32-39) also record the feeding of the 4,000 as a separate miracle (8:19-21; Matt 16:9-10). The details of the events are different.

8:1-3 The last reference to a ***large crowd*** was at the feeding of the 5,000 (6:34). Jesus showed compassion in 6:34 because the people "were like sheep without a shepherd." These stories reflect Jesus' concern for the total person—this time especially for the people's hunger. They were in the wilderness (8:4) and had no food (8:1). They had been with Jesus for three days and had nothing to eat (8:2), and they had come a long way and needed to eat before returning home (8:3).

8:4 The disciples' frustration at the situation reveals their dullness. They knew how God provided manna ***in the wilderness*** for his people in Moses' time (Exod 16). They were now in the presence of one far greater than Moses (see 9:5-7) and had recently seen him feed a greater number of people in a similar situation (6:30-44). However, they still did not understand (cp. 6:52). Even so, Jesus worked through them to bring physical and spiritual food to the hungry (8:6-8). What they could not do by themselves, the mighty Son of God would do through them.

8:5 ***Seven loaves:*** Numerous attempts have been made to allegorize the numbers in the two feeding miracles, but the lack of consensus among these interpretations, and the reference to "a few fish" in the present story, suggest that the numbers are not symbolic. None of the Gospel writers associate any clear significance with these numbers, and this should warn us against doing so. As with the feeding of the 5,000, the purpose of the numbers is to magnify the greatness of the miracle and of Jesus.

8:6-7 ***took, thanked God, distributed:*** These terms foreshadow the Last Supper (cp. 14:22-25).

8:8 ***They ate as much as they wanted:*** The superabundance of food shows the all-surpassing nature of God's Kingdom and of the one who brought it.

8:10-13 As in the earlier feeding miracle (6:30-44), the feeding of the 4,000 is followed by Jesus' crossing the Sea of Galilee by boat (cp. 6:45) and the Pharisees' initiating a dispute demanding that Jesus perform some miraculous sign (cp. 7:1-23). • The location of ***Dalmanutha*** is unknown. Matthew 15:39 has *Magadan* instead of *Dalmanutha*.

8:11 The antagonism of ***the Pharisees*** was persistent (2:16-18, 24; 3:6; 7:1-5; 10:2; 12:13, 15). The request for a sign is at times acceptable (Judg 6:36-40; 2 Kgs 20:8-11; Isa 7:10-12; see also John 2:18-19), but in this case it was obstinate testing of God. • The sought-after ***sign*** was not a healing, an exorcism, a raising from the dead, or a nature miracle, for there had been many of these already, and Jesus' ability to work such signs was well-known (1:32-34, 45; 3:7-12; 6:53-56) even to the Pharisees (3:22). What they sought was ***a miraculous sign from heaven***—that is, directly from God—that would demonstrate once for all that Jesus was the Christ. No sign, however, could ever convince them of this. For those whose hearts were open to the truth, the miracles that Jesus had already done (Luke 7:22) were clear and irrefutable signs that Jesus was the Messiah, the Son of God. For those outside (4:11-12), no sign could make them believe (cp. Luke 6:19-31).

8:12 ***he sighed deeply:*** See note on 7:34. • ***I tell you the truth:*** Jesus' response was as strong as an oath meaning, "[May God's judgment fall upon me] if I ***give this generation any such sign.***" Such oaths express an unbending

keep demanding a miraculous sign? I tell
you the truth, I will not give this generation
any such sign." 13So he got back into the
boat and left them, and he crossed to the
other side of the lake.

Yeast of the Pharisees and Sadducees
Mark 8:14-21 // Matt 16:5-12; cp. Luke 12:1

14But the disciples had forgotten to bring
any food. They had only one loaf of bread
with them in the boat. 15As they were crossing the lake, Jesus warned them, "Watch
out! Beware of the [i]yeast of the Pharisees
and of Herod."
16At this they began to argue with each
other because they hadn't brought any
bread. 17Jesus knew what they were saying,
so he said, "Why are you arguing about having no bread? Don't you know or understand
even yet? Are your hearts too hard to take it
in? 18'You have eyes—can't you see? You have
ears—can't you hear?' Don't you remember
anything at all? 19When I fed the 5,000 with
five loaves of bread, how many baskets of
leftovers did you pick up afterward?"
"Twelve," they said.
20"And when I fed the 4,000 with seven
loaves, how many large baskets of leftovers
did you pick up?"
"Seven," they said.
21"Don't you understand yet?" he asked
them.

Jesus Heals a Blind Man

22When they arrived at Bethsaida, some people brought a blind man to Jesus, and they
begged him to touch the man and heal him.
23Jesus took the blind man by the hand and
led him out of the village. Then, spitting on
the man's eyes, he laid his hands on him and
asked, "Can you see anything now?"
24The man looked around. "Yes," he said,
"I see people, but I can't see them very clearly.
They look like trees walking around."
25Then Jesus placed his hands on the
man's eyes again, and his eyes were opened.
His sight was completely restored, and he
could see everything clearly. 26Jesus sent
him away, saying, "Don't go back into the village on your way home."

4. PREPARING FOR JERUSALEM (8:27–10:52)

Ministry outside Galilee (8:27–9:50)

Peter's Declaration of Faith
Mark 8:27-30 // Matt 16:13-16, 20 // Luke 9:18-21; cp. John 6:67-69

27Jesus and his disciples left Galilee and
went up to the villages near Caesarea Philippi. As they were walking along, he asked
them, "Who do people say I am?"

8:15 Luke 12:1
[i]*zumē* (2219) ‣ Luke 12:1
8:17 Isa 6:9-10; Mark 6:52
8:18 *Jer 5:21; Ezek 12:2; Matt 13:13
8:19 Mark 6:41-44; Luke 9:17; John 6:13
8:20 Matt 15:37
8:23 Mark 7:33; John 9:6
8:26 Matt 8:4
8:27-30 //Matt 16:13-20; //Luke 9:18-21; John 6:67-71

commitment (see Gen 14:22-23; Num 32:10-11; Ruth 1:17; 1 Sam 3:17; 20:13; 2 Sam 3:35; 19:13). • Jesus elsewhere describes *this generation* as "adulterous and sinful" (8:38) and "faithless" (9:19).

8:14-21 This account of the journey across the Sea of Galilee reflects on Jesus' greatness, as manifested in the two feeding miracles, and emphasizes the dullness of the disciples, who do not ***see, hear,*** or ***understand*** because of their hardened hearts (see 4:9-20; 6:52).

8:14 The reference to having ***only one loaf of bread*** reminds readers of recent occasions when the disciples had not had enough bread and Jesus miraculously provided enough bread to feed thousands of people.

8:15 Matthew says that ***the yeast of the Pharisees*** refers to their false teaching (Matt 16:12). It could also refer to their unbelief and hardness of heart (8:10-13). The reference to ***Herod*** could refer to his unwillingness to accept what he knew to be true (6:14, 16, 20).

8:16 The disciples completely missed the point of Jesus' warning (8:15) and forgot that because Jesus was with them, their supply of ***bread*** was irrelevant.

8:17-20 Jesus asked eight questions that rebuked the disciples. They, of all people, should have been aware of the miraculous power of the Son of God. Although the disciples still remembered the feeding miracles, they never considered the implications for their immediate situation.

8:18 ***You have eyes . . . can't you hear?*** Jer 5:21.

8:19-20 Jesus' questions precisely recalled the feeding miracles (6:30-44; 8:1-10).

8:21 ***Don't you understand yet?*** This question implies a time when they would truly understand. Mark's readers knew that Jesus' resurrection would give the disciples understanding of Jesus' identity and power (see, e.g., Acts 4:23-31).

8:22-26 Earlier, Jesus and the disciples set out unsuccessfully for Bethsaida (6:45); here, they arrive, and Jesus heals a blind man. Only Mark has this two-part healing; it might connect with the opening of the disciples' spiritual eyes in the next account (8:27-38). • John 1:44 identifies ***Bethsaida*** as the home of Peter, Andrew, James, and John (see also John 12:21). This small fishing village, although technically part of Gaulanitis, was generally considered part of Galilee (John 12:21). It was relocated and given status as a city by Philip the Tetrarch (Josephus, *Antiquities* 18.2.1).

8:23 ***spitting on the man's eyes:*** See 7:33; cp. John 9:6-7. Attempts to diagnose the man's exact medical condition are speculative and unprofitable, diverting attention from the miracle.

8:24-25 The healing was not instantaneous—the man saw imperfectly at first. Jesus' second laying on of hands brought complete healing. Who is this man who stills the sea and heals the blind? Peter reveals this in the next account—he is the Messiah (8:29).

8:26 The story ends with Jesus telling the healed man to keep the event a secret (see "The Secret of the Messiah" at 3:11-12, p. 1653).

8:27–9:1 This section is the first cycle containing a prediction by Jesus of his suffering (8:31), an error by the disciples (8:32-33), and a collection of Jesus' sayings about discipleship (8:34–9:1). Cp. 9:30–10:31.

8:27-38 Peter's declaration of Jesus as Messiah and Jesus' first prediction of his death mark a turning point in Mark's Gospel and a new stage in Jesus' life. The question, "Who is this man?" raised by the disciples in 4:41, is now answered by Peter.

8:27-28 Philip the Tetrarch, son of Herod the Great, built ***Caesarea Philippi*** on the slopes of Mount Hermon about twenty-five miles (forty

28“Well,” they replied, “some say John the
Baptist, some say Elijah, and others say you
are one of the other prophets.”
29Then he asked them, “But who do you
say I am?”
Peter replied, “You are the Messiah.”
30But Jesus warned them not to tell anyone about him.

Jesus First Predicts His Death
Mark 8:31-33 // Matt 16:21-23 // Luke 9:22

31Then Jesus began to tell them that the Son
of Man must suffer many terrible things
and be rejected by the elders, the leading
priests, and the teachers of religious law.
He would be killed, but three days later he
would rise from the dead. 32As he talked
about this openly with his disciples, Peter
took him aside and began to reprimand him
for saying such things.
33Jesus turned around and looked at his
disciples, then reprimanded Peter. “Get
away from me, Satan!” he said. “You are seeing things merely from a human point of
view, not from God’s.”

Teachings about Discipleship
Mark 8:34–9:1 // Matt 16:24-28 // Luke 9:23-27

34Then, calling the crowd to join his disciples, he said, “If any of you wants to be my
follower, you must turn from your selfish
ways, take up your cross, and follow me. 35If
you try to hang on to your life, you will lose it.
But if you give up your life for my sake and
for the sake of the Good News, you will save
it. 36And what do you benefit if you gain the
whole world but lose your own soul? 37Is
anything worth more than your soul? 38If
anyone is ashamed of me and my message
in these adulterous and sinful days, the
Son of Man will be ashamed of that person
when he returns in the glory of his Father
with the holy ʲangels.”

9 Jesus went on to say, “I tell you the truth,
some standing here right now will not
die before they see the Kingdom of God arrive in great power!”

The Transfiguration
Mark 9:2-10 // Matt 17:1-9 // Luke 9:28-36

2Six days later Jesus took Peter, James, and

8:28
Matt 14:2

8:29
Matt 16:20
Luke 9:20
John 6:69; 11:27

8:31–9:1
//Matt 16:21-28
//Luke 9:21-27

8:34
Matt 10:38
Luke 14:27

8:35
Matt 10:39
Luke 17:33
John 12:25

8:38
Matt 10:33
Luke 12:9
2 Tim 2:12
ʲ*angelos* (0032)
‣Luke 16:22

9:2-10
//Matt 17:1-9
//Luke 9:28-36
2 Pet 1:17-18

kilometers) north of the Sea of Galilee. The more famous Caesarea on the coast had been built by Philip’s father. • ***Who do people say I am?*** As a good teacher, Jesus asked a question to elicit his disciples’ understanding. The response is similar to 6:14-16. • ***John the Baptist:*** See notes on 6:14-15. • ***one of the other prophets:*** Jesus was clearly considered a prophet (6:4; 14:65; Luke 7:16, 39; 13:33; 24:19).

8:29-30 ***But who do you say I am?*** In the Greek text, *you* is emphatic. Peter responded for the group, ***You are the Messiah*** (or *the Christ; Messiah* (a Hebrew term) and *Christ* (a Greek term) both mean “the anointed one.” Peter’s confession was correct, as the command ***not to tell anyone about him*** indicates (see “The Secret of the Messiah” at 3:11-12, p. 1653; see also 1:1; 14:61-62; Matt 16:17).

8:31-38 ***Then*** Jesus began to teach the disciples that he would ***suffer*** and ***be killed*** in Jerusalem and ***three days later . . . rise from the dead.*** Jesus now explicitly predicted what he had revealed in veiled form (2:19-20). In response, Peter objected, so Jesus taught him and the other disciples the nature of his mission and what it really means to follow him.

8:31 ***Son of Man*** is a title Jesus used for himself (see “The Son of Man” at Matt 8:18-20, p. 1593). • It was a divine necessity that Jesus ***must suffer*** (see also 9:11; 13:7, 10). The immediate cause for Jesus’ suffering was ***the elders, the leading priests, and the teachers of religious law*** (see 10:33; 11:18, 27; 14:1, 43, 53), but the ultimate cause was the will of God. • Jesus’ death would not be the end, for three days later he ***would rise from the dead.*** • ***Three days later*** is a synonym for *on the third day* (Matt 16:21; Luke 9:22) and *after three days and three nights* (Matt 12:40).

8:32 Peter understood what Jesus had said, but he did not accept it. Peter shared the popular idea that the Messiah was to be a victorious national ruler (See “Jesus the Messiah” at Matt 16:16, p. 1613), so he thought Jesus’ talk of suffering and death was nonsense. • ***began to reprimand him for saying such things:*** Or *began to correct him.*

8:33 Jesus ***looked at his disciples*** before he publicly rebuked Peter; he wanted them to understand that Peter was wrong. • ***Get away from me, Satan*** does not mean that Peter was demon-possessed. Peter spoke ***from a human point of view, not from God’s***, so he unwittingly spoke for Satan, the god of this world (2 Cor 4:4), and repeated Satan’s temptation (cp. Matt 4:8-10).

8:34-38 Jesus’ invitation to ***his disciples*** and ***the crowd*** lays out the cost of being his ***follower.*** • To ***turn from your selfish ways*** involves letting Jesus determine your goals and purposes in life. To ***take up your cross*** is metaphorical (cp. Luke 9:23); it indicates that faithfulness to Jesus must extend, if required, even to the point of death. To ***follow*** Jesus’ teaching and example is a continual commitment.

8:35 ***If you try to hang on*** to (literally *save*) ***your life*** by keeping it from Jesus, ***you will lose it*** in the next world. But if you lose it to Jesus and his cause (the spread of the ***Good News***), ***you will save it*** forever.

8:36-37 The implied answer to Jesus’ rhetorical question is that possessing the entire world has no value if you give up eternal life. “He is no fool who gives what he cannot keep to gain that which he cannot lose” (Jim Elliot). You need ***your soul*** (or ***your self***) to enjoy the benefits of the world to come. When you forfeit your life or soul, there is nothing you can give to purchase it back.

8:38 When Jesus, as ***the Son of Man***, returns in glory to judge the world, he will be ashamed of those who were ashamed to be identified with him and his message (cp. Matt 7:21-23; 10:32-33; Luke 12:8-9; 2 Tim 2:12).

9:1 The introductory ***I tell you the truth*** indicates that the promise in this verse is important, but the meaning of the promise is much debated. It might suggest that some of the disciples will (1) witness Jesus’ resurrection from the dead (ch 16); (2) experience the coming of the Spirit upon the church (Acts 2); (3) see the fall of Jerusalem in AD 70; or (4) witness Jesus’ transfiguration as a foretaste of God’s coming Kingdom. Mark’s placement of the promise right before the transfiguration account (9:2-8) indicates that he probably meant the transfiguration as the fulfillment (see 2 Pet 1:16-18).

9:2-8 This account is tied to 8:27–9:1 both chronologically (***six days later***) and

9:2
[k]*metamorphoō* (3339)
‣Rom 12:2

9:3
Dan 7:9
Matt 28:3

9:5
[a]*rhabbi* (4461)
‣Mark 10:51

9:7
Exod 40:34
Deut 18:15
Heb 1:2; 2:3; 12:25

9:11-13
//Matt 17:10-12

John, and led them up a high mountain to
be alone. As the men watched, Jesus' appearance was [k]transformed, 3and his clothes
became dazzling white, far whiter than
any earthly bleach could ever make them.
4Then Elijah and Moses appeared and began talking with Jesus.
5Peter exclaimed, "[a]Rabbi, it's wonderful
for us to be here! Let's make three shelters
as memorials—one for you, one for Moses,
and one for Elijah." 6He said this because he
didn't really know what else to say, for they
were all terrified.
7Then a cloud overshadowed them, and a
voice from the cloud said, "This is my dearly
loved Son. Listen to him." 8Suddenly, when
they looked around, Moses and Elijah were
gone, and they saw only Jesus with them.
9As they went back down the mountain,
he told them not to tell anyone what they
had seen until the Son of Man had risen
from the dead. 10So they kept it to themselves, but they often asked each other what
he meant by "rising from the dead."

Jesus Discusses Elijah
Mark 9:11-13 // Matt 17:10-13

11Then they asked him, "Why do the teachers

Following Jesus (8:34-38)

Mark 1:15-20; 2:14-15; 3:13-15; 5:18-20; 6:6-13, 30-32; 9:38-50; 10:17-31; 11:22-25; 13:9-13
Hos 6:3
Matt 10:37-39; 28:18-20
Luke 14:25-35; 24:47-49
John 8:12; 10:27; 12:26
Acts 1:8; 2:42-47; 4:16-20; 8:4; 9:19-30; 11:19-24; 13:1-3
Rom 1:1-16; 10:7-15
1 Cor 9:16
Eph 5:1
Col 1:23
2 Tim 4:2
1 Pet 2:21

One of the core purposes of Mark's Gospel is to help his readers understand and accept the call to take up their cross and follow Jesus. This call is addressed not only to those who would be Jesus' apostles (3:13-14; cp. 1:16-20; 6:1; 10:28) but to all who desired to follow him (8:34; cp. 2:14-15; 10:21, 52). For some, the call to discipleship is very hard (10:24), but God provides grace (10:27). Others find it easy to respond to Jesus' call (2:14-15; cp. Luke 7:36-50).

For everyone, following Jesus requires a total commitment to turn from selfish ways (8:34-35). Taking up one's cross is a metaphor for giving up one's life to follow Jesus even to death, as illustrated by Jesus' crucifixion. For example, Peter, Andrew, James, and John left their homes and their source of income to follow Jesus (1:16-20). For a rich man, turning from his selfish ways required selling all he had and giving the proceeds to the poor (10:21, 28). Following Jesus also means being identified with him without being ashamed, and being faithful to Jesus and his teachings (8:38; cp. Rom 10:9). It requires removing anything that would interfere with following Jesus, regardless of how painful doing so might be (9:43-48). It requires entrusting one's life entirely to Jesus (1:15; 5:34; 10:52) and repenting of sin (1:15; 6:12). It even requires putting loyalty to Jesus above loyalty to one's own father and mother (Matt 10:37; Luke 14:26). Jesus explicitly commanded his disciples to proclaim his message, as recorded elsewhere (Matt 28:18-20; Luke 24:47-49; Acts 1:8). Jesus and the apostles, through their teaching and example, call Jesus' followers to proclaim the Good News wherever they may be (see Acts 2:14-42; 3:12-26; 4:1-2, 20; 8:4; 9:20; 11:19-26; 13:1-3; Rom 1:1-16; 10:14-15; 15:18-21; 1 Cor 9:16; Col 1:23; 1 Thes 2:9; 2 Tim 4:2).

Alongside Jesus' demands for discipleship are the rewards of following Jesus. Those who follow Jesus are promised entrance into the Kingdom of God (9:43-47; 10:23-31; cp. 1:15). They receive his forgiveness for their sins (2:7, 10; 3:28; 11:25), and they become members of the family of God (10:30). They are saved from judgment (8:35; 10:26; 13:13) and obtain eternal life (9:43; 10:17, 23, 30).

thematically (9:7). • The presence of ***Peter, James, and John*** (see also 5:37; 13:3; 14:33) might be the fulfillment of 9:1 ("some standing here"). Some interpreters believe that the pre-incarnate glory of the Son of God broke through the veil of his humanity (John 1:14; 17:5) at the transfiguration. It is more likely that this event was an advance glimpse of the Son of Man's future glory (see Matt 16:28; 2 Pet 1:16-18; cp. Exod 34:28-35; 2 Cor 3:7-18).

9:4 The appearance of ***Elijah and Moses,*** might indicate the fulfillment of the law and the prophets in Jesus (see Matt 5:17; cp. Mal 4:4-5).

9:5-6 The suggestion to build ***three shelters as memorials*** (literally *three tabernacles;* see Lev 23:33-43; Num 29:12-34) places Moses, Elijah, and Jesus on the same footing. The suggestion ignores Peter's own earlier confession (8:29) and the fact that only Jesus had been transfigured (9:2-3).

9:7 ***a cloud:*** Cp. Exod 40:34-35. • The ***voice from the cloud*** issued a stern rebuke of Peter's suggestion: ***This is my dearly loved Son***—not an equal of Moses and Elijah. God's voice also confirmed Peter's earlier confession (8:29), and it indirectly rebuked Peter for rejecting Jesus' prediction of his suffering (8:32) by telling him and the other disciples to ***listen to him.***

9:8 ***Only Jesus*** remained, not Moses or Elijah. Jesus was clearly superior to Elijah and Moses.

9:9 Secrecy would no longer be necessary after ***the Son of Man had risen from the dead,*** because Jesus the Messiah would then be clearly understood as apolitical and non-militaristic, so he could be proclaimed openly to all (see Acts 2:36; 3:6). • ***Son of Man*** is a title Jesus used for himself.

9:10 Only after the fact did the three disciples understand what Jesus ***meant by "rising from the dead."***

9:11 The disciples wanted to understand the prediction ***that Elijah must return before the Messiah comes*** (literally

of religious law insist that Elijah must return before the Messiah comes?"

12Jesus responded, "Elijah is indeed coming first to get everything ready. Yet why do the Scriptures say that the Son of Man must suffer greatly and be treated with utter contempt? 13But I tell you, Elijah has already come, and they chose to abuse him, just as the Scriptures predicted."

Jesus Heals a Demon-Possessed Boy
Mark 9:14-29 // Matt 17:14-21 // Luke 9:37-43a

14When they returned to the other disciples, they saw a large crowd surrounding them, and some teachers of religious law were arguing with them. 15When the crowd saw Jesus, they were overwhelmed with awe, and they ran to greet him.

16"What is all this arguing about?" Jesus asked.

17One of the men in the crowd spoke up and said, "Teacher, I brought my son so you could heal him. He is possessed by an evil spirit that won't let him talk. 18And whenever this spirit seizes him, it throws him violently to the ground. Then he foams at the mouth and grinds his teeth and becomes rigid. So I asked your disciples to cast out the evil spirit, but they couldn't do it."

19Jesus said to them, "You faithless people! How long must I be with you? How long must I put up with you? Bring the boy to me."

20So they brought the boy. But when the evil spirit saw Jesus, it threw the child into a violent convulsion, and he fell to the ground, writhing and foaming at the mouth.

21"How long has this been happening?" Jesus asked the boy's father.

He replied, "Since he was a little boy. 22The spirit often throws him into the fire or into water, trying to kill him. Have mercy on us and help us, if you can."

23"What do you mean, 'If I can'?" Jesus asked. "Anything is possible if a person believes."

24The father instantly cried out, "I do believe, but help me overcome my unbelief!"

25When Jesus saw that the crowd of onlookers was growing, he rebuked the evil spirit. "Listen, you spirit that makes this boy unable to hear and speak," he said. "I command you to come out of this child and never enter him again!"

26Then the spirit screamed and threw the boy into another violent convulsion and left him. The boy appeared to be dead. A murmur ran through the crowd as people said, "He's dead." 27But Jesus took him by the hand and helped him to his feet, and he stood up.

28Afterward, when Jesus was alone in the house with his disciples, they asked him, "Why couldn't we cast out that evil spirit?"

9:13
Ps 22:6-7
Isa 50:6; 53:3
Matt 11:14

9:14-29
//Matt 17:14-20
//Luke 9:37-42

9:20
Mark 1:26

9:23
Matt 21:21
Mark 11:23-24
Luke 17:6
John 11:40
Acts 14:9

9:24
Luke 17:5

9:25
Acts 10:38

9:26
Mark 1:26

9:27
Matt 8:15

---

that Elijah must come first; see Mal 4:5-6). How did this prediction fit with Jesus' proclamation of God's Kingdom and his prediction of his own death, resurrection, and return (8:31, 38; 9:9)?

9:12 The teachers of the law were correct: ***Elijah*** must return before the consummation of God's Kingdom, but Scripture also said that the ***Son of Man*** would ***suffer greatly*** (e.g., Ps 22; Isa 52:13–53:12).

9:13 The teachers of the law erred by not realizing that Elijah had already come (see Matt 17:11-13; cp. Mal 4:5-6). As a result, they failed to recognize that the Kingdom of God had already come and that the Messiah's suffering and death that were predicted in Scripture were already taking place.

9:14-29 This is the fourth and last exorcism in Mark (1:21-28; 5:1-20; 7:24-30). The disciples were unable to perform the exorcism, so Jesus performed it, emphasizing the necessity of faith (cp. 2:5; 5:34; 10:52). This is another example of Jesus' great healing ability and of the disciples' failure (8:32-33; 9:5-7).

9:14 Jesus and the three disciples (Peter, James, and John) rejoined the other disciples, the crowd, and the teachers of the law. This account is similar to the story of Moses descending from Mount Sinai to rejoin the people of Israel (Exod 34:29-35).

9:15 Some have suggested that just as Moses reflected God's glory when he descended from the mountain, Jesus' glorious transfiguration was still evident, so the crowds responded ***with awe***. It is equally possible that Jesus' arrival after being absent was enough to elicit the awe of the crowd.

9:18 These symptoms are often associated with epilepsy (see Matt 17:15), but Mark emphasizes the demonic origin of the child's problem (9:17-18, 25-26, 28). The disciples' inability to heal the child magnifies the effect of Jesus' power (9:25-26). • ***becomes rigid:*** Or *becomes weak*.

9:19 ***Jesus said to them:*** Jesus might have been speaking to the disciples, the father (9:22-24), the crowd, or all present. • ***How long . . . ?*** Their lack of faith was obstinate and hard-hearted (cp. 3:5; 6:52; 8:17; 10:5).

9:20 The demon's reaction was nonverbal (contrast 1:24; 5:7, 9-10; see also 1:34b; 3:11-12) but violent, as the father had described (9:18).

9:21-22 The demon's activity had been taking place ***since he was a little boy***, and the demon had tried to kill the child in various ways. • ***if you can:*** The father's request indicates that his faith had been severely dampened (9:18).

9:23 Jesus challenged the man to believe in the power of God—***Anything is possible if a person believes*** (see 11:22-24), while lack of faith can hinder God's saving activity (see 6:5).

9:24 In desperation, the father cried out that he believed, though weakly.

9:25 The crowd was approaching, so Jesus quickly proceeded with the exorcism. • ***evil spirit:*** Literally *unclean spirit*. • The ***I*** in the ***command*** to the demon is emphatic, dramatizing Jesus' authority and power. • ***never enter him again!*** At times exorcisms could be temporary (see Matt 12:43-45; Luke 11:24-26).

9:26-27 The demon's violent reaction revealed its strength and showed Jesus' greatness (cp. 1:25-26; 5:15).

9:28-29 The account ends, surprisingly, by stressing the importance of prayer rather than of faith (cp. 11:22-24). • ***only by prayer:*** Some manuscripts read *only by prayer and fasting*.

29 Jesus replied, "This kind can be cast out
only by prayer."

Jesus Again Predicts His Death
Mark 9:30-32 // Matt 17:22-23 // Luke 9:43b-45

30 Leaving that region, they traveled through
Galilee. Jesus didn't want anyone to know he
was there, 31 for he wanted to spend more
time with his disciples and teach them. He
said to them, "The Son of Man is going to
be betrayed into the hands of his enemies.
He will be killed, but three days later he
will rise from the dead." 32 They didn't understand what he was saying, however, and
they were afraid to ask him what he meant.

The Greatest in the Kingdom
Mark 9:33-37 // Matt 18:1-5 // Luke 9:46-48

33 After they arrived at Capernaum and settled in a house, Jesus asked his disciples,
"What were you discussing out on the road?"
34 But they didn't answer, because they had
been arguing about which of them was the
greatest. 35 He sat down, called the twelve
disciples over to him, and said, "Whoever
wants to be first must take last place and be
the servant of everyone else."

36 Then he put a little child among them.
Taking the child in his arms, he said to them,
37 "Anyone who welcomes a little child like
this on my behalf welcomes me, and anyone
who welcomes me welcomes not only me
but also my Father who sent me."

Various Teachings of Jesus
Mark 9:38-40 // Luke 9:49-50
Mark 9:41; cp. Matt 10:42
Mark 9:42-48 // Matt 18:6-9 // Luke 17:1-3a
Mark 9:49-50; cp. Matt 5:13; Luke 14:34-35

38 John said to Jesus, "Teacher, we saw someone using your name to cast out demons,
but we told him to stop because he wasn't
in our group."

39 "Don't stop him!" Jesus said. "No one
who performs a miracle in my name will
soon be able to speak evil of me. 40 Anyone
who is not against us is for us. 41 If anyone
gives you even a cup of water because you
belong to the Messiah, I tell you the truth,
that person will surely be rewarded.

42 "But if you cause one of these little ones
who trusts in me to fall into sin, it would be
better for you to be thrown into the sea
with a large millstone hung around your
neck. 43 If your hand causes you to sin, cut it
off. It's better to enter eternal life with only
one hand than to go into the unquenchable
fires of [b]hell with two hands. 45 If your foot
causes you to sin, cut it off. It's better to enter eternal life with only one foot than to be
thrown into hell with two feet. 47 And if your
eye causes you to sin, gouge it out. It's better
to enter the Kingdom of God with only one
eye than to have two eyes and be thrown
into hell, 48 'where the maggots never die
and the fire never goes out.'

9:30-32
//Matt 17:22-23
//Luke 9:43-45

9:31
Matt 16:21
Mark 8:31
Luke 9:22
Acts 20:22-23

9:33-37
//Matt 18:1-5
//Luke 9:46-48

9:34
Luke 22:24

9:35
Matt 20:27

9:37
Matt 10:40; 25:40
Luke 10:16
John 13:20

9:38-41
Num 11:26-29
//Luke 9:49-50
Phil 1:15-18

9:39
1 Cor 12:3

9:40
Matt 12:30
Luke 11:23

9:41
Matt 10:42

9:42-48
//Matt 18:6-9
//Luke 17:1-2

9:43
Matt 5:30; 18:8
[b]*geenna* (1067)
‣ Luke 12:5

9:47
Matt 5:29

9:48
*Isa 66:24
2 Thes 1:9

9:30–10:31 This section is the second cycle (see note on 8:27–9:1) containing a prediction about Jesus' suffering (9:30-32), an error by the disciples (9:33-34), and teaching about discipleship (9:35–10:31).

9:31 Jesus continued to seek privacy (see 7:24) for teaching the disciples about his coming suffering. • ***The Son of Man is going to be betrayed:*** See 14:10-11, 41-45.

9:32 The disciples were still unable to accept Jesus' teaching concerning his death or to recognize how it fit into God's plan.

9:33-50 Because the disciples did not understand Jesus' prediction of his suffering, they were unable to see its implications for their own lives.

9:33-34 ***Capernaum*** was Jesus' home in Galilee (1:21; 2:1). • Jesus' disciples ***didn't answer*** his question because they knew that he would disapprove of their discussion. • ***about which of them was the greatest:*** This issue would come up again in 10:35-37.

9:35 Jesus ***sat down***, assuming the role of a teacher (see 4:1-2; 12:41; Matt 5:1; Luke 4:20; 5:3). True greatness in God's Kingdom involves being ***the servant of everyone else***, not the master, as Jesus would make clear by his own example in 10:45.

9:36-37 In Jesus' day, children were not romanticized as innocent and pure, but were considered to be weak and inferior. Children were to be received ***on my behalf*** (literally *in my name*). Welcoming a child is an example of humbly taking the last place and serving everyone else (9:35; cp. 10:13-16). Other sayings about receiving or rejecting Jesus also involve receiving or rejecting his followers (Matt 10:40; 25:31-46; Luke 10:16; John 13:20).

9:38-41 An unknown exorcist was casting out demons in Jesus' name though he was not one of the twelve disciples (9:38-40). John objected, but Jesus corrected him. • ***we told him to stop:*** Cp. 10:35-43; Luke 9:51-55. • The success of the unknown exorcist is contrasted with the failure of the disciples in the previous account (9:14-29).

9:40 The negative parallel to this proverb is found in Luke 11:23. These two proverbs should be understood as complementary, not contradictory, for Luke includes them both (Luke 9:50; 11:23). The exorcist casting out demons in Jesus' name was not against Jesus, but for him.

9:42-50 ***if you cause . . . sin:*** The consequences of causing sin ties these verses together (9:42-43, 45, 47). These sayings were not meant to be interpreted literally, for carrying them out would not prevent sin (see Matt 15:10-20). What Jesus conveys by these warnings is that no sin is worth going to hell for. It is better to repent—even if repenting is as painful as cutting off a hand, foot, or eye—than to suffer the punishment of hell.

9:43 ***hell:*** Greek *Gehenna;* also in 9:45, 47. Gehenna means "valley of Hinnom," which bordered Jerusalem on the southwest. It was a garbage dump for the city, and the continual burning of refuse there became a metaphor for the final place of judgment for the wicked.

9:43-45 Some manuscripts add vv 44 and 46, *'where the maggots never die and the fire never goes out.'* See 9:48. These two verses were almost certainly copied from 9:48 and were not in the original text of Mark. Most of the best manuscripts do not include these verses, but a few include them.

9:48 The eternality of hell is emphasized by the terms ***never die*** and ***never goes out*** (cp. 9:43). The horror of hell is emphasized by its portrayal as a place

49"For everyone will be tested with fire.
50Salt is good for seasoning. But if it loses its
flavor, how do you make it salty again? You
must have the qualities of salt among yourselves and live in peace with each other."

On the Way to Jerusalem (10:1-52)

Jesus Leaves Galilee

Mark 10:1 // Matt 19:1-2

10 Then Jesus left Capernaum and went
down to the region of Judea and into
the area east of the Jordan River. Once again
crowds gathered around him, and as usual
he was teaching them.

Jesus' Teaching about Divorce and Marriage

Mark 10:2-12 // Matt 19:3-12; cp. Matt 5:31-32; Luke 16:18

2Some Pharisees came and tried to trap
him with this question: "Should a man be
allowed to divorce his wife?"
3Jesus answered them with a question:
"What did Moses say in the law about divorce?"
4"Well, he permitted it," they replied. "He
said a man can give his wife a written notice
of divorce and send her away."
5But Jesus responded, "He wrote this
commandment only as a concession to your
hard hearts. 6But 'God made them male and
female' from the beginning of creation.
7'This explains why a man leaves his father
and mother and is joined to his wife, 8and
the two are united into one.' Since they are
no longer two but one, 9let no one split apart
what God has joined together."
10Later, when he was alone with his disciples in the house, they brought up the
subject again. 11He told them, "Whoever
divorces his wife and marries someone else
commits adultery against her. 12And if a
woman divorces her husband and marries
someone else, she commits adultery."

Jesus Blesses the Children

Mark 10:13-16 // Matt 19:13-15 // Luke 18:15-17

13One day some parents brought their children to Jesus so he could touch and bless
them. But the disciples scolded the parents
for bothering him.
14When Jesus saw what was happening,
he was angry with his disciples. He said to
them, "Let the children come to me. Don't
stop them! For the Kingdom of God belongs

9:50 Matt 5:13; Luke 14:34; Rom 12:18; Col 4:6
10:1-12 //Matt 19:1-12
10:4 *Deut 24:1-3
10:6 *Gen 1:27; 5:2
10:7-8 *Gen 2:24; 1 Cor 6:16; Eph 5:31
10:11 Matt 5:32; Luke 16:18; 1 Cor 7:10-11
10:13-16 //Matt 19:13-15; //Luke 18:15-17

of everlasting *fire*, and of decay and corruption where *maggots* eternally eat everything away (cp. Isa 66:24). The putrid smell of decay and the presence of maggots in the Valley of Hinnom may lie behind this imagery (see note on 9:43). This imagery is a powerful warning for people to repent in order to escape the punishment of hell.

9:49-50 ***tested with fire:*** Literally *salted with fire;* other manuscripts add *and every sacrifice will be salted with salt.* The fire of testing has a purifying effect, like salt (see also 1 Pet 1:7; 4:12; Rev 3:18). ***Salt*** also refers to Christian character. Genuine Christian character will have a genuinely purifying influence. • ***But if it loses its flavor:*** The salt mined from the Dead Sea often contained gypsum, so although it looked like perfectly good salt, it was useless. It did not taste salty, and it created a disposal problem.

10:1-2 The Pharisees' question about divorce was much debated in Judaism, but it had a hostile purpose as they ***tried to trap*** Jesus (see 2:16, 18, 24; 7:5; 8:11; 12:13). John the Baptist was beheaded over his teaching that Herod Antipas's divorce and remarriage was unlawful (6:18-19), and according to the Jewish historian Josephus, John was martyred close to Jesus' current location ***east of the Jordan River,*** at Herod Antipas's fortress at Macherus (see 6:28; Josephus, *Antiquities* 18.5.2). If Jesus answered in agreement with John the Baptist, the Pharisees could indict him before Herod. But if Jesus said that divorce was lawful, he would be contradicting a prophet.

10:3 Jesus answered the Pharisees' trick question with a counter-question (cp. Matt 22:20).

10:4 The Pharisees quoted what Moses ***permitted.*** There was much debate among rabbis as to what constituted the "something wrong" (see Deut 24:1) that made divorce permissible. Rabbi Shammai allowed divorce only on the basis of sexual immorality. Rabbi Hillel permitted divorce even if a woman burned her husband's dinner or was less attractive than someone else (*Mishnah Gittin* 9:10).

10:5-9 God permitted divorce as a concession to the ***hard hearts*** of the people. But God's will is more aptly expressed in the passages that Jesus quotes from the law of Moses (Gen 1:27; 2:23-24; see also Mal 2:16). Jesus shows that God delights in marriage, which is the creation of a new union in which two become one. No one should rebel against God's will by seeking to split apart what God has united.

10:6 ***God made them male and female:*** Gen 1:27; 5:2.

10:7-8 The quotation is from Gen 2:24. • Some manuscripts do not include ***and is joined to his wife.***

10:10 Jesus often explained his teaching to his disciples in the privacy of a ***house*** (see 7:17; 9:28, 33).

10:11-12 ***Whoever divorces . . . and marries someone else commits adultery:*** The parallel in Luke 16:18 agrees with Mark and mentions no exceptions to this prohibition of divorce, Matthew's parallel account allows an exception in cases of infidelity (Matt 19:9; see also Matt 5:32). Paul also allows an exception if an unbelieving partner deserts the marriage (1 Cor 7:15). Mark's account focuses on the core principles—God hates divorce (Mal 2:16), marriage is meant to be for life, and divorce betrays the divine purpose of marriage.

10:13-16 Jesus' love and concern for ***children*** has already been seen in 5:41-43; 9:36-37, 42. Jesus uses the incident to teach that ***the Kingdom of God belongs to those who are like these children.***

10:13 The ages of the ***children*** cannot be determined from this passage. The Greek word *paidia* can refer to a broad spectrum of ages, from a twelve-year-old child (5:41-42) down to an eight-day-old infant (Gen 17:12, Greek version). • ***the disciples scolded the parents:*** See note on Luke 18:15.

10:14-15 Mark does not explain what characteristics of children make them fit for ***the Kingdom of God;*** Matthew 18:4-5 suggests that the attributes in-

10:15 Matt 18:3
10:16 Mark 9:36
10:17-31 //Matt 19:16-30 //Luke 18:18-30
10:19 *Exod 20:12-16 *Deut 5:16-20 Rom 13:9
10:21 Matt 6:19-20 Luke 12:33 Acts 2:44-45
10:24 Matt 7:13-14 John 3:5
10:27 Gen 18:14 Job 42:2 Mark 14:36

to those who are like these children. 15 I tell you the truth, anyone who doesn't receive the Kingdom of God like a child will never enter it." 16 Then he took the children in his arms and placed his hands on their heads and blessed them.

The Rich Man
Mark 10:17-22 // Matt 19:16-22 // Luke 18:18-23

17 As Jesus was starting out on his way to Jerusalem, a man came running up to him, knelt down, and asked, "Good Teacher, what must I do to inherit eternal life?"

18 "Why do you call me good?" Jesus asked. "Only God is truly good. 19 But to answer your question, you know the commandments: 'You must not murder. You must not commit adultery. You must not steal. You must not testify falsely. You must not cheat anyone. Honor your father and mother.' "

20 "Teacher," the man replied, "I've obeyed all these commandments since I was young."

21 Looking at the man, Jesus felt genuine love for him. "There is still one thing you haven't done," he told him. "Go and sell all your possessions and give the money to the poor, and you will have treasure in heaven. Then come, follow me."

22 At this the man's face fell, and he went away sad, for he had many possessions.

The Rewards of Discipleship
Mark 10:23-31 // Matt 19:23-30 // Luke 18:24-30

23 Jesus looked around and said to his disciples, "How hard it is for the rich to enter the Kingdom of God!" 24 This amazed them. But Jesus said again, "Dear children, it is very hard to enter the Kingdom of God. 25 In fact, it is easier for a camel to go through the eye of a needle than for a rich person to enter the Kingdom of God!"

26 The disciples were astounded. "Then who in the world can be saved?" they asked.

27 Jesus looked at them intently and said,

---

clude humility and the ability to receive things simply.

10:17-31 The story of the rich man continues the themes of discipleship begun in 9:33 and the requirements for entering the Kingdom of God (10:13-16). The attitude of the rich man contrasts sharply with the childlike faith necessary for entering the Kingdom of God.

10:17 The rich man (10:22) was a young ruler (Matt 19:20; Luke 18:18) who showed respect toward Jesus by kneeling and calling Jesus ***Good Teacher***. ***Teacher*** is a frequent title for Jesus in Mark (see 4:38; 5:35; 9:17, 38; 10:20, 35; 12:14, 19, 32; 13:1; 14:14); the addition of *good* is unique.

10:18 Jesus' reply has troubled interpreters for centuries. Jesus was probably objecting to the man's loose application of the term *good* to any human being, since ultimate goodness and perfection belong to God alone. Without in any way denying his own goodness, Jesus wanted to focus the rich man's attention on ***God***. The rich man wanted to enter the Kingdom of God, and Jesus was contrasting God's goodness with the man's own human sinfulness (see note on 10:21).

10:19 Jesus' reply seems strange to Christians who are familiar with Paul's teaching on this subject (e.g., Rom 3:20; Gal 2:16). In naming five of the Ten Commandments Jesus was not implying that the man could earn eternal life by keeping them; he was telling him what God's standards are and allowing the man to evaluate his own performance. Truly loving God with all one's heart, soul, mind, and strength, and one's neighbor as one's self (12:30-31), requires trusting in God's grace, accepting Jesus' sacrificial death on our behalf (10:45; 14:24), and keeping his commands (John 15:10; 1 Jn 2:4; 3:22). • The commandments are quoted from Exod 20:12-16 // Deut 5:16-20.

10:20 The man's reply was naive (as to what it really means to keep these commands; see Matt 5:21-48), but it was not arrogant, as the lack of any rebuke (cp. 12:13-17; Matt 23:1-36) indicates.

10:21 Instead of having an extended discussion about what it means to truly keep the commandments, Jesus focused on the specific issue that revealed this man's problem. He still lacked ***one thing:*** He loved riches more than he loved God, thus breaking the first and most important commandment (12:29-30; Exod 20:3; Deut 6:5). Entering the Kingdom of God requires repentance (1:15; 6:12), and Jesus helped this man to understand exactly what repentance entailed for him. He did not need, as he might have thought, to attain a higher level of personal righteousness. He needed to enter God's Kingdom through repentance and wholehearted love for God, thereby obtaining eternal life. He must deny himself (8:34) and love God first and foremost by giving away his money. For other commands involving a negative [***sell all***] and a positive [***follow me***] element, see 1:15, 18, 20; 10:28; see also Acts 2:38; 20:21. • Jesus' command to the rich man was not a universal requirement for entering the Kingdom of God, but was addressed to his particular situation. It teaches anyone seeking eternal life that nothing else can come before God; repentance (1:15; 6:12) requires the removal of anything that we place above God.

10:22 Mark records the rich man's tragic choice. The man departed, still possessing his earthly riches (Matt 6:19), but lacking eternal treasure (Matt 13:44-46). His demeanor (***face fell . . . sad***) showed his awareness that his awful choice had brought him sorrow rather than joy.

10:23-27 Jesus astounded the disciples by reversing the idea, popular at that time, that riches were a sign of God's favor.

10:24 In response to the disciples' amazement, Jesus addressed them affectionately as ***dear children.*** • ***very hard:*** Some manuscripts read *very hard for those who trust in riches.*

10:25 Jesus was emphatically warning that riches are an obstacle to entering the Kingdom of God. The ***camel*** was the largest animal in Palestine, the ***eye of a needle*** the smallest hole. Some rich people are evidently able to overcome the problem created by riches and follow Jesus, but Jesus' followers came from among the poor more than from the rich. • Explanations about a gate in the Jerusalem wall called the "Eye of the Needle" are ill-conceived. There never was such a gate, and this explanation loses sight of Jesus' frequent use of hyperbole in his teaching (see also Matt 7:3-5; 23:24).

10:26 ***The disciples were astounded:*** It was generally believed that wealth was a sign of God's blessing that enabled the rich to do good deeds. Accordingly, it was assumed that the rich had an inside track on entering the Kingdom of God. The disciples' question was natural, given this understanding. God's assessment was the opposite of their conventional wisdom.

"Humanly speaking, it is impossible. But not
with God. Everything is possible with God."
28Then Peter began to speak up. "We've
given up everything to follow you," he
said.
29"Yes," Jesus replied, "and I assure you
that everyone who has given up house or
brothers or sisters or mother or father or
children or property, for my sake and for
the Good News, 30will receive now in return
a hundred times as many houses, brothers,
sisters, mothers, children, and property—
along with persecution. And in the world
to come that person will have eternal life.
31But many who are the greatest now will
be least important then, and those who
seem least important now will be the greatest then."

Jesus Predicts His Death and Resurrection
Mark 10:32-34 // Matt 20:17-19 // Luke 18:31-34
32They were now on the way up to Jerusalem,
and Jesus was walking ahead of them. The
disciples were filled with awe, and the people following behind were overwhelmed
with fear. Taking the twelve disciples aside,
Jesus once more began to describe everything that was about to happen to him.
33"Listen," he said, "we're going up to Jerusalem, where the Son of Man will be betrayed
to the leading priests and the teachers of
religious law. They will sentence him to die
and hand him over to the Romans. 34They
will mock him, spit on him, flog him with
a whip, and kill him, but after three days he
will rise again."

Jesus Teaches about Serving Others
Mark 10:35-45 // Matt 20:20-28; cp. Luke 22:24-27
35Then James and John, the sons of Zebedee,
came over and spoke to him. "Teacher," they
said, "we want you to do us a favor."
36"What is your request?" he asked.
37They replied, "When you sit on your
glorious throne, we want to sit in places of
honor next to you, one on your right and the
other on your left."
38But Jesus said to them, "You don't know
what you are asking! Are you able to drink
from the bitter cup of suffering I am about
to drink? Are you able to be baptized with
the baptism of suffering I must be baptized
with?"
39"Oh yes," they replied, "we are able!"
Then Jesus told them, "You will indeed
drink from my bitter cup and be baptized
with my baptism of suffering. 40But I have
no right to say who will sit on my right or my

10:28 Mark 1:18
10:30 2 Tim 3:12
10:31 Matt 20:16; Luke 13:30
10:32-34 //Matt 20:17-19 //Luke 18:31-34
10:33 Matt 16:21; 17:22-23; Mark 8:31; 9:31; Luke 24:7
10:34 Isa 50:6
10:35-45 //Matt 20:20-28
10:38 Luke 12:50; John 18:11
10:39 Acts 12:2; Rev 1:9

10:27 This verse tends to be interpreted in one of two ways: (1) Although salvation by one's own effort is impossible, by God's grace people can be saved through faith (Eph 2:8-10). (2) God can give an unusual grace that enables people to overcome their sinful love of riches and believe. Mark does not explain his understanding.

10:28 The disciples had done what Jesus told the rich man to do—they had ***given up everything to follow*** Jesus (1:16-20; 8:34-38).

10:29-30 Jesus assured his disciples that they would receive whatever they had given up for him many times over, including a new family in Christ (***brothers, sisters, mothers, children***) and Christian hospitality (***houses***). • ***a hundred times***: What is gained in following Jesus far outweighs any loss. ***And in the world to come*** they will inherit the ***eternal life*** that the rich man desired but did not receive.

10:31 ***But many . . . greatest then:*** Literally *But many who are first will be last; and the last, first.* The account ends with a proverb, contrasting the way that God understands life and how people generally understand it (for similar sayings, see Matt 20:16; Luke 13:30). For those with eyes to see and ears to hear (4:9-12; 8:18), the Kingdom of God has already come, and the overturning of this world's values has begun.

10:32-34 The disciples' ***awe*** and the people's ***fear*** cast a dark shadow over what lay ahead, given the hostility of the Jerusalem leaders toward Jesus (see 3:22-30; 7:1-13). Taking the disciples aside again, Jesus described the coming events in the greatest detail yet (see also 8:31; 9:31). He knew what was about to happen; what awaited him in Jerusalem was neither a tragedy nor fate, but God's will (see 8:31-33; Acts 4:27-28). As the Son of God, Jesus had unique knowledge of his upcoming unique death as the Savior of the world.

10:33 ***Son of Man*** is a title Jesus used for himself. • The ***leading priests*** and the ***teachers of religious law*** were the human agents who fulfilled God's purpose through their hatred of Jesus. • They did not have the right of capital punishment (John 18:31), so they had to hand Jesus over to ***the Romans*** (literally *the Gentiles*) to carry out the actual execution.

10:35-45 Following Jesus' third prediction of his suffering (10:32-33) comes another example of the disciples' failure (see 8:31-33; 9:31-34). The first part of the account involves the foolish request of James and John (10:35-37) and Jesus' reply to them (10:38-40). Then Jesus explains to the other disciples what greatness and leadership in the Kingdom of God mean (10:41-44). Jesus' own supreme example of servanthood (10:45) illustrates and concludes this account.

10:37 The brothers' request indicates that James and John correctly understood that Jesus was the Messiah (see 8:29; 9:2-8). However, they completely misunderstood what it meant to be a leader in God's Kingdom (10:41-45).

10:38 The two brothers didn't ***know*** what they were ***asking:*** To share in his glory, they must share in his suffering as servants. • ***to drink from the bitter cup:*** Drinking from a cup is often associated with suffering and death (Ps 75:8; Isa 51:17, 22; Jer 25:15; 49:12; Lam 4:21; see also Mark 14:24, 36). • The ***baptism of suffering*** recalls Jesus' total commitment to God's calling at his baptism, and it speaks of the believer's own baptism into Jesus' death, burial, and resurrection (Rom 6:3-5; Col 2:12).

10:39 James and John did ***indeed drink*** a ***bitter cup . . . of suffering*** for Jesus. James died for his faith (Acts 12:1-5). John died an old man, having experienced persecution (Tertullian, *The Soul* 50; Jerome, *Commentary on Galatians* 6, 10). Yet the death of James and John was not the same as that of Jesus—no believer can die Jesus' death as a vicarious sacrifice for the sins of the world (10:45) or experience the divine wrath as he did (15:34).

10:40 Whatever James and John would

10:42 Luke 22:25-27 1 Pet 5:3
10:43-44 Matt 23:11 Mark 9:35 Luke 22:26
10:45 Matt 20:28 John 13:14 Phil 2:7 1 Tim 2:5-6 Titus 2:14 [c]*lutron* (3083) ‣Luke 24:21
10:46-52 //Matt 20:29-34 //Luke 18:35-43
10:47 Isa 11:1 Jer 23:5-6 Matt 9:27; 15:22
10:51 [d]*rhabbouni* (4462) ‣John 1:38
10:52 Matt 9:22 Mark 5:34 Luke 7:50; 8:48; 17:19
11:1-10 //Matt 21:1-9 //Luke 19:28-38 //John 12:12-19

left. God has prepared those places for the ones he has chosen."

41When the ten other disciples heard what James and John had asked, they were indignant. 42So Jesus called them together and said, "You know that the rulers in this world lord it over their people, and officials flaunt their authority over those under them. 43But among you it will be different. Whoever wants to be a leader among you must be your servant, 44and whoever wants to be first among you must be the slave of everyone else. 45For even the Son of Man came not to be served but to serve others and to give his life as a [c]ransom for many."

Jesus Heals Bartimaeus, a Blind Beggar
Mark 10:46-52 // Matt 20:29-34 // Luke 18:35-43; cp. Matt 9:27-31

46Then they reached Jericho, and as Jesus and his disciples left town, a large crowd followed him. A blind beggar named Bartimaeus (son of Timaeus) was sitting beside the road. 47When Bartimaeus heard that Jesus of Nazareth was nearby, he began to shout, "Jesus, Son of David, have mercy on me!"

48"Be quiet!" many of the people yelled at him.

But he only shouted louder, "Son of David, have mercy on me!"

49When Jesus heard him, he stopped and said, "Tell him to come here."

So they called the blind man. "Cheer up," they said. "Come on, he's calling you!" 50Bartimaeus threw aside his coat, jumped up, and came to Jesus.

51"What do you want me to do for you?" Jesus asked.

"My [d]rabbi," the blind man said, "I want to see!"

52And Jesus said to him, "Go, for your faith has healed you." Instantly the man could see, and he followed Jesus down the road.

5. JESUS' MINISTRY IN JERUSALEM (11:1–13:37)

Jesus Confronts the Leaders in Jerusalem (11:1-25)

Jesus' Messianic Entry into Jerusalem
Mark 11:1-11 // Matt 21:1-11 // Luke 19:28-40 // John 12:12-19

11 As Jesus and his disciples approached Jerusalem, they came to the towns of Bethphage and Bethany on the Mount

---

experience, Jesus did not have the authority to grant their request. Only *God* the Father could (see also 13:32).

10:41 ***the ten other disciples . . . were indignant:*** Perhaps they wanted the special places requested by James and John for themselves. All of Jesus' disciples needed a new understanding of what leadership in God's Kingdom means (10:42-45).

10:42-44 The unbelieving world (***the rulers in this world***) thinks that leadership means lording it over others. Just as Jesus' role as Messiah and Son of God meant suffering and death (8:31; 9:31; 10:32-34, 45), being his follower involves serving others, not ruling over them (9:35; John 10:11).

10:45 Jesus offered his own example to demonstrate what leadership in God's Kingdom means. • Jesus understands his death ***as a ransom.*** A ransom was a payment made to free a slave or captive. • The expression ***for many*** is probably an allusion to Isa 53:12, where *many* means *all* (cp. Rom 5:15, 18-20). Jesus died as the substitute for all. Later, Jesus would speak of his blood as being poured out for many (14:24).

10:46-52 The healing of blind Bartimaeus is the last healing miracle recorded in Mark. This event and the healing of the blind man in 8:22-26 form bookends around this section (see Mark Introduction, "Literary Features," p. 1644). It is also a bridge to Jesus' entrance into Jerusalem as Israel's Messiah in 11:1-11. Bartimaeus's confession (***Jesus, Son of David***) prepares the reader for the confession of the people upon Jesus' arrival in Jerusalem (11:10).

10:46 ***they reached Jericho:*** The journey Jesus began in 10:1 was nearing its conclusion. Jericho was the last major city in the Jordan River valley before Jerusalem. It may be the oldest continually-occupied city in the world. In Jesus' day, it was no longer located on the much smaller site of OT times (Tell es-Sultan), but had been moved and greatly enlarged. The road from Jericho up to Jerusalem was steep, with a difference in elevation of about 3,000 feet (about 1,000 meters). • The ***large crowd*** following Jesus might have been fellow pilgrims traveling to Jerusalem for Passover, but they certainly show Jesus' great popularity and charisma. • ***A blind beggar . . . was sitting beside the road:*** This was a good location for collecting alms from religious pilgrims going to Jerusalem.

10:47-48 ***Bartimaeus heard:*** Jesus' great fame had spread to Jericho, even as it had spread to Gentile areas (3:8). • ***Jesus, Son of David:*** Mark does not explain how Bartimaeus knew of Jesus' Davidic ancestry. Perhaps he knew that Jesus was the Messiah. The blind man, however, did not associate this title with political or military goals as did the vast majority of people in his day. Instead, Bartimaeus believed that Jesus was concerned with bringing God's Kingdom to the poor, maimed, lame, and blind, and he requested mercy and healing (10:51)—which was in harmony with Jesus' own understanding (cp. Luke 4:18-19).

10:50 ***threw aside his coat:*** Bartimaeus's response is best understood as simply a spontaneous act of joy and anticipation rather than as a symbolic casting off of his old way of life or leaving all to follow Jesus.

10:51 When Jesus asked what Bartimaeus wanted, Bartimaeus addressed Jesus as ***My rabbi*** (Greek uses the Hebrew term *Rabboni,* found only here and in John 20:16). Bartimaeus's request, ***I want to see!*** revealed his faith, without which he might simply have asked for alms. The reports he had heard about Jesus enabled him to cry out for the miracle of sight.

10:52 The man's ***faith*** was rewarded, and he was ***healed*** (literally *saved*; see 5:23, 28, 34; 6:56; Matt 9:22; Luke 8:48). The healing was performed without touch, in contrast to the healing of the blind man in 8:22-26. Bartimaeus ***followed Jesus*** (see also 1:18; 2:14-15; 6:1; 8:34; 10:21, 28, 32) ***down the road*** (or *on the way;* cp. 1:2-3; 10:32).

11:1–13:37 This section centers on Jesus' relationship to the Jerusalem Temple. Mark's geographical arrangement places in 11:1–16:8 all his accounts of Jesus' teachings and events associated with Jerusalem. • The section

of Olives. Jesus sent two of them on ahead.
2“Go into that village over there,” he told
them. “As soon as you enter it, you will see
a young donkey tied there that no one has
ever ridden. Untie it and bring it here. 3If
anyone asks, ‘What are you doing?’ just say,
‘The Lord needs it and will return it soon.’ ”
4The two disciples left and found the colt
standing in the street, tied outside the front
door. 5As they were untying it, some bystanders demanded, “What are you doing,
untying that colt?” 6They said what Jesus
had told them to say, and they were permitted to take it. 7Then they brought the colt to
Jesus and threw their garments over it, and
he sat on it.
8Many in the crowd spread their garments on the road ahead of him, and others
spread leafy branches they had cut in the
fields. 9Jesus was in the center of the procession, and the people all around him were
shouting,

“Praise God!
Blessings on the one who comes in the
name of the LORD!
10 Blessings on the coming Kingdom of our
ancestor David!
Praise God in highest heaven!”

11So Jesus came to Jerusalem and went
into the Temple. After looking around carefully at everything, he left because it was
late in the afternoon. Then he returned to
Bethany with the twelve disciples.

Jesus Curses the Fig Tree—Part 1

Mark 11:12-14 // Matt 21:18-19
Mark 11:18-19 // Luke 19:47-48

12The next morning as they were leaving
Bethany, Jesus was hungry. 13He noticed
a fig tree in full leaf a little way off, so he
went over to see if he could find any figs.
But there were only leaves because it was
too early in the season for fruit. 14Then
Jesus said to the tree, “May no one ever eat
your fruit again!” And the disciples heard
him say it.

Jesus Clears the Temple

Mark 11:15-17 // Matt 21:12-13 // Luke 19:45-46

15When they arrived back in Jerusalem,
Jesus entered the Temple and began to drive

11:2 1 Sam 6:7; Zech 9:9
11:9-10 *Ps 118:26; 148:1
11:11 Matt 21:10, 17
11:12-14 //Matt 21:18-19
11:15-19 //Matt 21:12-17; //Luke 19:45-48; //John 2:13-22

concludes (13:1-37) with Jesus’ second extended teaching discourse (see 4:1-34), now focusing on the destruction of the Temple and the coming of the Son of Man. It is the climax for numerous statements within 11:1–13:37 concerning the divine judgment about to fall on Jerusalem and the Temple (see especially 11:12-25 and 12:1-12).

11:1 ***Jerusalem*** was Jesus’ goal. During the week before his crucifixion, Jesus apparently stayed in ***Bethany*** with his disciples (11:11-12; 14:3-9). • The ***Mount of Olives*** is frequently associated with the site of the final judgment (Zech 14:4) and the place where the Messiah will manifest himself (Ezek 11:23; 43:1-5; see also Josephus, *Antiquities* 20.8.6). • As he did at other times, ***Jesus sent two of them*** (see 6:7).

11:2-3 There have already been numerous examples of Jesus’ supernatural knowledge (2:8; 3:5; 5:30, 32; 8:17, 31), but the people’s acceptance of the reply that ***the Lord needs it*** (11:3, 6) suggests that Jesus had prearranged it (cp. 14:13-16). Jesus had intentionally planned to enter Jerusalem in fulfillment of Zech 9:9.

11:3 ***The Lord needs it and will return it soon:*** Mark’s readers have already seen the word *Lord* used to refer to Jesus (1:3; 2:28; 5:19; see also 12:36-37; 13:35), so they would understand it as referring to the Lord Jesus Christ, who needed the colt (Rom 10:9; Phil 2:11).

11:4-6 The disciples carried out Jesus’ instructions and found things as he had said.

11:7-8 ***the colt . . . he sat on it:*** Cp. Zech 9:9; some of the people undoubtedly understood that they were witnessing the arrival of the Messiah. • The disciples made a seat for Jesus with their outer garments and others spread ***garments*** and ***branches*** from nearby trees into an honorary pathway for ***Jesus*** to ride upon to Jerusalem (see 1 Kgs 1:38-48; 2 Kgs 9:13).

11:9-10 ***Praise God!*** (Greek *Hosanna,* an exclamation of praise that literally means “save now!”) ***Blessings on the one who comes in the name of the LORD!*** These exclamations come from Ps 118:25-26; 148:1. By the first century AD, *Hosanna* was no longer used literally as a cry for rescue from enemies, but had become an idiomatic expression of joy and jubilation (cp. “Praise the Lord!” as used today). For the people, it was the exuberant welcome (Luke 19:38-40) of a famous pilgrim, the prophet from Galilee (Matt 21:11). The miracle of raising Lazarus from the dead might have contributed to the excitement of the day (John 12:9-11), but even the disciples did not truly understand this event until later (John 12:16). For Jesus, though, it was a fulfillment of prophecy. Jesus prepared for the occasion carefully and offered himself to the people of Israel as God’s Anointed, the Messiah.

11:11 The account ends surprisingly: The exuberant crowd disappears and Jesus’ actual entrance into the Temple is anticlimactic in comparison to his approach. Apparently, in the minds of the people, nothing important had taken place. Jesus’ ***looking around*** prepares the reader for God’s judgment on the Temple (11:15-17).

11:12-25 In the synoptic Gospels, Jesus’ messianic entry into Jerusalem is intimately associated with the cleansing of the Temple (see 11:15-17; cp. Matt 21:1-17; Luke 19:28-48). In John, however, the account of the cleansing is recorded early in Jesus’ ministry (John 2:13-22). It is uncertain whether there were two separate cleansings of the Temple (an early event recorded in John and this later event recorded in Matthew, Mark, and Luke) or just one cleansing recorded at different places by John and the synoptic writers. • In Mark’s account, the cursing of the fig tree (11:12-14, 20-25) forms an *inclusio* (bookends) around the cleansing of the Temple (11:15-19). Mark thus indicates that Jesus’ cleansing of the Temple should be interpreted in light of his cursing of the fig tree—as an act of judgment rather than reformation.

11:13-14 ***it was too early in the season for fruit:*** Jesus did not curse the fig tree merely because it lacked fruit. Rather, he was performing a prophetic sign act like those of earlier prophets (Isa 20:1-6; Jer 13:1-11; 19:1-13; Ezek 4:1-17). Just as Jesus judged the fruitless fig tree, so too he judged the Temple and the worship of Israel, in which he found no fruit. This judgment was fulfilled in AD 70 with the destruction of Jerusalem and the Temple by the Romans.

11:17
*Isa 56:7
*Jer 7:11
11:18
Matt 21:46
Mark 12:12
Luke 20:19
11:20-25
//Matt 21:20-22
11:22
Matt 17:20
Luke 17:6
Jas 1:5-8
11:24
Matt 7:7
11:25
Matt 5:23; 6:12, 14; 18:23-25
11:27-33
//Matt 21:23-27
//Luke 20:1-8

out the people buying and selling animals
for sacrifices. He knocked over the tables of
the money changers and the chairs of those
selling doves, 16and he stopped everyone
from using the Temple as a marketplace.
17He said to them, "The Scriptures declare,
'My Temple will be called a house of prayer
for all nations,' but you have turned it into a
den of thieves."

18When the leading priests and teachers
of religious law heard what Jesus had done,
they began planning how to kill him. But
they were afraid of him because the people
were so amazed at his teaching.

19That evening Jesus and the disciples
left the city.

Jesus Curses the Fig Tree—Part 2
Mark 11:20-25 // Matt 21:20-22

20The next morning as they passed by the
fig tree he had cursed, the disciples noticed
it had withered from the roots up. 21Peter
remembered what Jesus had said to the tree
on the previous day and exclaimed, "Look,
Rabbi! The fig tree you cursed has withered
and died!"

22Then Jesus said to the disciples, "Have
faith in God. 23I tell you the truth, you can
say to this mountain, 'May you be lifted up
and thrown into the sea,' and it will happen.
But you must really believe it will happen
and have no doubt in your heart. 24I tell you,
you can pray for anything, and if you believe that you've received it, it will be yours.
25But when you are praying, first forgive
anyone you are holding a grudge against, so
that your Father in heaven will forgive your
sins, too."

Controversies in Jerusalem (11:27–12:44)
Jesus' Authority Is Challenged
Mark 11:27-33 // Matt 21:23-27 // Luke 20:1-8

27Again they entered Jerusalem. As Jesus
was walking through the Temple area, the

11:15-19 The largest part of ***the Temple*** in Jerusalem was the Court of the Gentiles, surrounded by covered porticoes (see illustrations, pp. 1753, 1786–1787). It was here that this selling probably took place.

11:15-16 ***When they arrived back:*** Upon entering the Temple, Jesus was intensely disturbed by the buying and selling of sacrificial animals and by the exchange of money. It was supervised by priests, who alone could certify that a potential sacrificial offering was acceptable. The practice of selling sacrificial animals was meant to ensure that only blemish-free animals were used in the service of the Temple. It was facilitated by setting up exchange tables in areas around Jerusalem, but exchange tables were set up within the Temple itself on the fifteenth of Adar, the month before Passover. Usually the exchange rate involved a 4- to 8-percent commission. Because of the large number of half-shekels (see Exod 30:11-16) and sacrifices involved, the money exchange and the sale of sacrificial animals was quite profitable. Jewish literature of the time was intensely critical of the priests for accumulating great wealth by robbing the poor. Jesus was not opposed to the Temple nor attacking the sacrificial system (1:44; Matt 5:17-19, 23; 17:24-27; Luke 17:14; Acts 6:7; 21:20-26), but he viewed this profiteering as theft and as desecrating the holy place. • Jesus' actions probably did not affect as large a number of people as is sometimes envisioned. These actions took place in one part of the large Court of the Gentiles and would not have been observed by most people in other parts of the Temple. The lack of interference by the Roman authorities suggests that they did not observe the event or did not regard it as a riot or as insurrection. Furthermore, at Jesus' trial, this action is never mentioned. It was not a massive attempt to stop all such activity, but a symbolic act foretelling the judgment soon to befall the Temple and the city.

11:16 ***from using the Temple as a marketplace:*** Or *from carrying merchandise through the Temple.* The Temple was also defiled by its use as a shortcut for carrying things from one part of the city to another. Other rabbis also forbade this practice (see *Mishnah Berakhot* 9.5; see Josephus, *Against Apion* 2.8).

11:17 Jesus quoted Isa 56:7 and Jer 7:11 in defense of his action. The first quotation emphasizes the importance of the Temple for Gentiles. God's house was intended by its very architecture (i.e., the Court of the Gentiles) to assist Gentiles in becoming children of Abraham. Jesus' act of judgment fell upon the leaders of Israel for hindering the Gentiles' access to the Temple. They were desecrating the Temple by taking part of the Temple specifically designated as ***a house of prayer for all nations*** and turning it into ***a den of thieves*** through the profiteering taking place (see note on 11:15-16).

11:18 ***The leading priests and teachers of religious law*** plotted to kill Jesus because they feared him. His great influence among the people, the amazement created by his actions, and the influence of his teaching threatened their position (see 3:6; 12:12; 14:1-2, 10-11). Their response shows that reform was not enough: God's judgment was necessary.

11:19 ***Jesus and the disciples left*** (literally *they left;* other manuscripts read *he left*): They presumably returned to Bethany (11:11; 14:3).

11:20-21 Jesus' miraculous power to judge the fig tree testified to his authority to bring about the judgment of Jerusalem that he had foretold. If Mark's original readers were hearing his Gospel read to them in the late AD 60s, they knew that Roman legions were already enacting this prophetic judgment against Jerusalem.

11:22-23 The importance of Jesus' words is emphasized by his emphatic ***I tell you the truth.*** • ***This mountain*** probably indicates the Temple Mount, not the Mount of Olives. The judgment of the Temple is the focus of 11:12-25; it will be referred to again in 12:9 and at great length in 13:1-37. Jesus' reference to destroying the Temple would later be raised at his trial (14:58) and crucifixion (15:29).

11:24-25 Two additional sayings on prayer are tied to 11:23 by the word ***believe.*** In the first (11:24), we are told that we will receive what we ask for (see Matt 7:7) if we pray with the faith described in 11:23. • Forgiveness is the second condition for answered prayer. Only when we forgive others can our most important prayer, that God forgive us, be answered (Matt 5:23-24; 6:12, 14-15; Luke 6:37; 11:4; cp. Luke 7:41-43, 47; Eph 4:32; Col 3:13). • Some manuscripts add v 26, *But if you refuse to forgive, your Father in heaven will not forgive your sins* (cp. Matt 6:15).

11:27-33 Following the cleansing of the Temple (11:15-17; Matt 21:12-22; Luke 19:45-46), Jesus' opponents question his authority to do so (see also Matt 21:23-27; Luke 20:1-8; cp. John 2:18-22).

leading priests, the teachers of religious law,
and the elders came up to him. 28They demanded, "By what authority are you doing
all these things? Who gave you the right to
do them?"
29"I'll tell you by what authority I do these
things if you answer one question," Jesus
replied. 30"Did John's authority to baptize
come from heaven, or was it merely human?
Answer me!"
31They talked it over among themselves.
"If we say it was from heaven, he will ask why
we didn't believe John. 32But do we dare say
it was merely human?" For they were afraid
of what the people would do, because everyone believed that John was a prophet. 33So
they finally replied, "We don't know."
And Jesus responded, "Then I won't tell
you by what authority I do these things."

Parable of the Evil Tenant Farmers

Mark 12:1-12 // Matt 21:33-46 // Luke 20:9-19

12 Then Jesus began teaching them
with stories: "A man planted a vineyard. He built a wall around it, dug a pit for
pressing out the grape juice, and built a
lookout tower. Then he leased the vineyard
to tenant farmers and moved to another
country. 2At the time of the grape harvest,
he sent one of his servants to collect his
share of the crop. 3But the farmers grabbed
the servant, beat him up, and sent him back
empty-handed. 4The owner then sent another servant, but they insulted him and
beat him over the head. 5The next servant
he sent was killed. Others he sent were either beaten or killed, 6until there was only
one left—his son whom he loved dearly. The
owner finally sent him, thinking, 'Surely
they will respect my son.'
7"But the tenant farmers said to one
another, 'Here comes the heir to this estate. Let's kill him and get the estate for
ourselves!' 8So they grabbed him and murdered him and threw his body out of the
vineyard.
9"What do you suppose the [e]owner of
the vineyard will do?" Jesus asked. "I'll tell

11:32 Matt 14:5; 21:46
12:1-12 //Matt 21:33-46 //Luke 20:9-19
12:1 Isa 5:1-2
12:5 2 Chr 24:21; 36:15-16 Neh 9:26 Matt 23:34-37 Acts 7:52 1 Thes 2:15
12:6 Rom 8:3 Gal 4:4
12:8 Heb 13:12
12:9 [e]*kurios* (2962) ‣Acts 16:31

11:27 Upon returning ***again*** to ***Jerusalem*** (see 11:1, 11, 15), Jesus and the disciples entered the Temple. The constant repetition of ***Jerusalem*** reminds readers of what would soon take place there (10:32-34; see 8:31; 9:31; 14:1–16:8). • In the Temple, Jesus encountered ***the leading priests, the teachers of religious law, and the elders***. These three groups made up the seventy-one–member high council (the ruling body of the nation). From earlier encounters with them (8:31; see also 14:43, 53; 15:1), we expect them to oppose Jesus.

11:28 Jesus' ***authority*** includes his divine authority to cast out demons (1:22, 27; 5:1-13), heal (1:29–2:12; 5:21-43), forgive sins (2:10), and now to cleanse the Temple. Jesus' authority clearly was from God, but the religious leaders were unwilling to accept it.

11:29-30 Jesus often replied to his opponents with counter questions (e.g., 2:8-9, 19, 25-26; 3:4, 23; 10:3, 38; see also 12:16), which is an effective way both to teach and to refute.

11:31-32 Jesus clearly placed his opponents in a bind, for either a "yes" or a "no" would damage their reputation and authority in the eyes of the people. Denying John's prophetic authority would probably anger the people. Affirming it would mean that they should have accepted what John said, including what he said about Jesus. This answer would also answer their own question (11:28).

11:33 In answering, ***"We don't know,"*** the religious leaders of the nation admitted that they could not answer a simple question that the people had no difficulty in answering: John was sent from God. They thus forfeited the religious leadership of the nation on this question. Their hardness of heart (3:5; 7:6), their unwillingness to see (4:12), and their deliberate refusal to accept the truth made further discussion fruitless. Their blindness and hostility toward God's servants John the Baptist and Jesus, their desecration of the Temple, and their plot to kill Jesus all revealed why God's judgment would come within that very generation (13:30).

12:1-12 The events of 11:27–12:44 all take place in the Temple (see 11:27; 13:1). This story (literally *parable*) is intimately tied to the previous question about Jesus' authority (11:27-33) by the introductory words, ***Then Jesus began teaching them***. This parable is an extended reply by Jesus to the religious leaders. • Jesus intended his audience to interpret this parable in light of Isa 5:1-7, a similar story of someone planting a vineyard, building a lookout tower, putting a fence around the vineyard, and digging a pit for a wine vat. A similar question is asked: ***What do you suppose the owner of the vineyard will do?*** (12:9; cp. Isa 5:4). Isaiah specifically identifies the vineyard as the people of Israel (Isa 5:7); Jesus' hearers and Mark's readers would similarly have understood the present story as an allegory about the Israelites. Other details in the story are also clearly meant to be interpreted allegorically: The tenants represent the leaders of Israel; the owner represents God; the servants represent the OT prophets; the beloved son represents Jesus, the Son of God; the murder of the son represents Jesus' crucifixion; and the giving of the vineyard to others represents the judgment coming upon Israel (11:15-17; 13:1-37). The interpretation would have been more clear to Mark's readers than to Jesus' original audience, but the religious leaders who were Jesus' contemporaries understood it clearly enough that they sought to kill him (12:12).

12:1 The antecedent to ***them*** is the religious leaders of 11:27 (also in 12:12). • The beginning description of the story comes from Isa 5:1-7. Jesus' audience knew the book of Isaiah well and would immediately have recalled this allegory of the vineyard.

12:2-5 ***The time of the grape harvest*** probably refers to the time, some four years after planting, when a new vineyard would produce its first harvest. The owner's ***share of the crop*** would have been a quantity of grapes or wine, given in payment for the lease of the vineyard. • In the OT, prophets are often referred to as ***servants*** (Jer 7:25-26; Amos 3:7; Zech 1:6); they were repeatedly mistreated and killed by Israelite leaders (1 Kgs 18:13; 19:10, 14; 2 Chr 24:20-27; 36:15-16; Jer 26:20-23; Neh 9:26; see Matt 23:34, 37; 1 Thes 2:15).

12:6 Mark's early readers would immediately have associated ***his son whom he loved dearly*** with Jesus (cp. 1:11; 9:7; see also 1:1; 3:11; 5:7).

12:7 The reasoning of the tenants is unclear to us, although it was apparently clear to the original hearers, requiring no further explanation (cp. Matt 21:38;

12:10-11
*Ps 118:22-23
Acts 4:11
Rom 9:33
Eph 2:20
1 Pet 2:5-7

12:12
Mark 11:18

12:13-17
//Matt 22:15-22
//Luke 20:20-26

12:17
Rom 13:7

12:18-27
//Matt 22:23-33
//Luke 20:27-38
Acts 23:8
1 Cor 15:12

12:18
[f]*anastasis* (0386)
‣John 5:29

12:19
*Gen 38:8
*Deut 25:5

you—he will come and kill those farmers and lease the vineyard to others. 10 Didn't you ever read this in the Scriptures?

'The stone that the builders rejected
has now become the cornerstone.
11 This is the LORD's doing,
and it is wonderful to see.' "

12 The religious leaders wanted to arrest Jesus because they realized he was telling the story against them—they were the wicked farmers. But they were afraid of the crowd, so they left him and went away.

Taxes for Caesar
Mark 12:13-17 // Matt 22:15-22 // Luke 20:20-26

13 Later the leaders sent some Pharisees and supporters of Herod to trap Jesus into saying something for which he could be arrested. 14 "Teacher," they said, "we know how honest you are. You are impartial and don't play favorites. You teach the way of God truthfully. Now tell us—is it right to pay taxes to Caesar or not? 15 Should we pay them, or shouldn't we?"

Jesus saw through their hypocrisy and said, "Why are you trying to trap me? Show me a Roman coin, and I'll tell you." 16 When they handed it to him, he asked, "Whose picture and title are stamped on it?"

"Caesar's," they replied.

17 "Well, then," Jesus said, "give to Caesar what belongs to Caesar, and give to God what belongs to God."

His reply completely amazed them.

Discussion about Life in the Resurrection
Mark 12:18-27 // Matt 22:23-33 // Luke 20:27-40

18 Then Jesus was approached by some Sadducees—religious leaders who say there is no [f]resurrection from the dead. They posed this question: 19 "Teacher, Moses gave us a law that if a man dies, leaving a wife without children, his brother should marry the

Luke 20:14). Perhaps with the son's coming, they assumed that the father had died, and that the murder of the son would leave the vineyard without a living claimant. Then ownership would fall to those who had been working the vineyard for years.

12:8 ***threw his body out of the vineyard:*** The tenants' disgraceful treatment of the son is heightened by their not even burying his body. Cp. Heb 13:12-13.

12:9 The parable concludes with two rhetorical questions (cp. 3:23, 33; 4:13; 7:18; 8:12). The first corresponds to what the "LORD of Heaven's Armies" says in the parable of the vineyard (Isa 5:5-7). Although some interpret Jesus' answer as meaning that God would replace the evil Jewish leaders (11:27; 12:12) with more faithful ones, Mark's readers likely would have understood the ***others*** to whom the vineyard would be given as the Gentile church (cp. Matt 21:43; Rom 9:25-33; 11:13-24). Thus, Jesus' parable connects with the coming destruction of Jerusalem (11:15-19; 13:1-37; 14:58; 15:29).

12:10-11 In his second rhetorical question, Jesus used a quotation from Ps 118:22-23. The rejected ***stone*** (the Son) had ***become the cornerstone*** of God's Kingdom (cp. Acts 4:11; 1 Pet 2:4, 6-7). The phrase is traditionally understood as the buried cornerstone that is part of the foundation, but it could be the capstone at the top of a building that marks its completion (cp. note on Matt 21:42). Whichever stone is meant, it was the most important one. Despite the evil intention of ***the builders***—the religious leaders—all they did was in accordance with God's will (Acts 4:28), which was ***wonderful to see.*** Those who put Jesus to death were God's instruments in his plan for the Son of Man to give his life as a ransom for many (10:45).

12:12 ***The religious leaders:*** Literally *They.* For the second time, the presence of ***the crowd*** thwarted their evil intentions (see 11:31-32; 14:1-2).

12:13-17 Having failed in questioning Jesus' authority, Jesus' enemies tried to alienate his audience. Readers are aware from the beginning that the flattery of the ***Pharisees and supporters of Herod*** (see 3:6) was insincere; they wanted only to ***trap Jesus into saying something for which he could be arrested.*** The question ***is it right to pay taxes to Caesar or not?*** had been carefully thought out by Jesus' opponents. It presented Jesus with a dilemma. To say yes would alienate the people, for they despised the Romans and hated paying them taxes. To say no would make him a revolutionary and force an immediate confrontation with the Roman authorities, resulting in his arrest.

12:14 ***taxes:*** The Greek word refers to a poll tax or head tax; see note on 2:13-15; see also Luke 2:1-2; Acts 5:37.

12:15 Jesus' surprising reply revealed his wisdom. • ***a Roman coin*** (Greek *a denarius*): Apparently the poll tax had to be paid in Roman coinage.

12:16 The ***picture and title*** on the coin was almost certainly that of Tiberius ***Caesar,*** who reigned from AD 14–37. The inscription read, "Tiberius Caesar Augustus, Son of [the] Divine Augustus" on one side and "High Priest" on the other.

12:17 ***give to Caesar what belongs to Caesar:*** Jesus' words cannot be taken as those of an anti-Roman zealot opposing Jewish taxation by Caesar. Jesus clearly indicates elsewhere that he was opposed to the zealot cause (see Matt 5:9, 39, 41; 26:52). However, Jesus' statement cannot be understood as pro-Roman, either, because service to God is fundamental, and God is ultimately over Caesar. Like the evil farmers in the previous parable, the religious leaders had not given God what belonged to him.

12:18-27 This is the third controversy story of the series begun in 11:27. As in most NT references to the ***Sadducees,*** the setting is the Temple (Matt 22:23-33 // Luke 20:27-40; Acts 4:1-3; 5:12, 17; 22:30–23:10; the exceptions are Matt 3:7; 16:1-12). • The Sadducees' question (12:19-23) was carefully crafted and based on a commandment of Moses (Deut 25:5-6; see Gen 38:6-11; Ruth 4). Since all seven men could not have the woman as wife in the resurrection, and since none of them had a special claim, the Sadducees thought that they had proven the absurdity of the doctrine of the resurrection and refuted the Pharisees and Jesus (cp. Matt 12:41-42; Luke 16:19-31; see also Mark 8:31; 9:31; 10:34).

12:18 This is the only place in Mark where the ***Sadducees*** are mentioned by name, although they are included in references to the leading priests (see 8:31; 10:33; 11:18, 27). Sadducees did not believe in the ***resurrection from the dead*** (see Acts 4:1-2; 23:8). See also "The Sadducees" at Matt 16:1, p. 1610.

12:19 ***a law:*** See Deut 25:5-6. The Sadducees based their views only on the books of Moses. • Like the Pharisees (12:14), they addressed Jesus as ***Teacher.*** The Sadducees were fond of debating with religious teachers (see Josephus, *Antiquities* 18.1.4).

widow and have a child who will carry on
the brother's name. 20Well, suppose there
were seven brothers. The oldest one married and then died without children. 21So
the second brother married the widow, but
he also died without children. Then the
third brother married her. 22This continued with all seven of them, and still there
were no children. Last of all, the woman
also died. 23So tell us, whose wife will she
be in the resurrection? For all seven were
married to her."

24Jesus replied, "Your mistake is that you
don't know the Scriptures, and you don't
know the power of God. 25For when the
dead rise, they will neither marry nor be
given in marriage. In this respect they will
be like the angels in heaven.

26"But now, as to whether the dead will
be raised—haven't you ever read about this
in the writings of Moses, in the story of the
burning bush? Long after Abraham, Isaac,
and Jacob had died, God said to Moses, 'I am
the God of Abraham, the God of Isaac, and
the God of Jacob.' 27So he is the God of the
living, not the dead. You have made a serious error."

The Most Important Commandment

Mark 12:28-31 // Matt 22:34-40; cp. Luke 10:25-28

28One of the teachers of religious law was
standing there listening to the debate. He
realized that Jesus had answered well, so he
asked, "Of all the commandments, which is
the most important?"

29Jesus replied, "The most important commandment is this: 'Listen, O Israel! The LORD
our God is the one and only LORD. 30And you
must love the LORD your God with all your
[g]heart, all your soul, all your mind, and all
your strength.' 31The second is equally important: 'Love your neighbor as yourself.'
No other commandment is greater than
these."

32The teacher of religious law replied,
"Well said, Teacher. You have spoken the
truth by saying that there is only one God
and no other. 33And I know it is important
to love him with all my heart and all my understanding and all my strength, and to love

12:25 1 Cor 15:42, 49, 52
12:26 *Exod 3:6
12:27 Matt 22:32; Luke 20:38
12:28-34 //Matt 22:34-40; //Luke 10:25-28
12:29-30 *Deut 6:4-5; *Josh 22:5; Luke 10:27
12:30 [g]*kardia* (2588) ›John 14:1
12:31 *Lev 19:18; Rom 13:9; Gal 5:14; Jas 2:8
12:32 *Deut 4:35, 39; 6:4; *Jos 22:5; *Isa 45:21; 1 Cor 8:4-6
12:33 *Lev 19:18; *1 Sam 15:22; *Hos 6:6; Mic 6:6-8

12:24-27 Jesus' response had two elements. First, he rebuked the Sadducees' ignorance of the ***Scriptures*** (i.e., the OT), where the resurrection of the dead is referred to most clearly in the Prophets (Isa 26:19; Ezek 37:1-14) and the Writings (Job 19:26; Ps 16:9-11; 49:15; 73:23-26; Dan 12:2; see "Introduction to the Old Testament: The Order of the Hebrew Bible," p. 4). However, the Sadducees accepted only the Torah (Genesis—Deuteronomy), so Jesus answered them from the Torah. The reference to God as ***the God of Abraham, the God of Isaac, and the God of Jacob*** (see Exod 3:6, 15-16) showed that God's covenant with the patriarchs could not be broken by death. They were still alive (Matt 8:11-12; 13:17; Luke 16:19-31; John 8:56), for God ***is the God of the living, not the dead***. God's covenant relationship with his people extends beyond their physical death, which means that the afterlife must be a reality. • Second, Jesus challenged the Sadducees' ignorance of God's ***power***. They thought that life in the resurrection would have to be an extension of mortal life. Instead, it is life raised to an entirely new level. In this new existence, there is no need for sexual reproduction because there is no more death. The intimacy of marriage is superseded by fellowship with a multitude of fellow believers and with God (10:29-30; Matt 19:28-29; Luke 18:29-30; Rev 21:1-4). It is in this respect that resurrected believers ***will be like the angels in heaven***. • Jesus' argument demonstrates his wisdom before his opponents and affirms the hope of the resurrection for his followers. Jesus is "the resurrection and the life" (John 11:25); he has conquered death and assured those who believe in him that they will "not perish but have eternal life" (John 3:16).

12:26 ***in the story . . . God said to Moses:*** Literally *in the story of the bush? God said to him.*

12:28-34 After the three hostile challenges of 11:27–12:27, the reader might expect the next question to Jesus to be hostile (see 11:28; 12:13, 15, 19-23), but this was not a hostile counter. Earlier references in Mark to the teachers of religious law have portrayed them as antagonistic (2:6-7, 16; 3:22; 7:1, 5; 8:31; 9:14; 10:33; 11:18, 27), and Jesus will warn the crowds against their hypocrisy (12:38-40), but this teacher was positively inclined toward Jesus (12:28, 32) and praised him (12:32-33). Jesus described the man's answer to his question as having understanding, and Jesus said that the man was not far from the Kingdom of God (12:34).

12:28 ***Of all the commandments:*** The Torah (Genesis—Deuteronomy) contains 613 separate commandments, and Jewish teachers frequently debated about which were more important than others. No command was considered unimportant, but some were recognized as more fundamental than others (see Matt 22:40). Rabbi Hillel's answer to this question was, "What is hateful to you, do not do to your neighbor" (*Babylonian Shabbat* 31a; see also *Tobit* 4:15). Other suggestions included Prov 3:6; Isa 33:15-16; 56:1; Amos 5:4; Mic 6:8; and Hab 2:4.

12:29-31 Jesus' reply combined two widely separated commands from the Torah. • The first, Deut 6:4-5, was probably the best known verse in the OT, for it was repeated twice daily by observant Jews. It is called the *Shema* because it begins with the word ***Listen*** (Hebrew *shema'*). The first command corresponds to the first part of the Ten Commandments (Exod 20:2-11), which deals with a person's relationship to God. • The oneness of God is foundational to Jewish and Christian monotheism and is the basis for the command to love God with all one's ***heart*** (thinking and affection), ***soul*** (desire and feeling), ***mind*** (understanding), and ***strength*** (energy and power). • The second command is from Lev 19:18. It corresponds to the second part of the Ten Commandments (Exod 20:12-17), which concerns a person's relationship with other people. The second command is based on the natural inclination of people to look after themselves. Its importance to the early church can be seen in its frequent repetition (Matt 5:43-44; 19:19; 25:31-46; Rom 13:8-10; Gal 5:14; Jas 2:8; *Didache* 1.2; 2.7). The two commands are not independent, but are intimately associated as one commandment. Their integration precludes religious mysticism that addresses only a person's relationship with God or humanism that addresses only human relationships.

12:32-33 The scribe's affirmation adds emphasis to the importance of these two commands for authentic devotion.

12:34
Matt 22:46
Luke 20:40

12:35-37
//Matt 22:41-46
//Luke 20:41-44

12:36
2 Sam 23:2
*Ps 110:1

12:37
Rom 1:3; 9:5
Rev 22:16

12:38-40
//Matt 23:1-36
//Luke 11:37-52;
20:45-47

12:39
Luke 11:43; 14:7-11

12:41-44
//Luke 21:1-4

12:41
2 Kgs 12:9
John 8:20

12:43-44
1 Kgs 17:8-16
2 Cor 8:12

my neighbor as myself. This is more important than to offer all of the burnt offerings
and sacrifices required in the law."
34Realizing how much the man understood, Jesus said to him, "You are not far
from the Kingdom of God." And after that,
no one dared to ask him any more questions.

Whose Son Is the Messiah?
Mark 12:35-37 // Matt 22:41-46 // Luke 20:41-44

35Later, as Jesus was teaching the people in
the Temple, he asked, "Why do the teachers of religious law claim that the Messiah
is the son of David? 36For David himself,
speaking under the inspiration of the Holy
Spirit, said,

'The Lord said to my Lord,
Sit in the place of honor at my right hand
until I humble your enemies beneath
your feet.'

37Since David himself called the Messiah
'my Lord,' how can the Messiah be his son?"
The large crowd listened to him with great
delight.

Jesus Criticizes the Teachers of Religious Law
Mark 12:38-40 // Luke 20:45-47; cp. Matt 23:1-36

38Jesus also taught: "Beware of these teachers of religious law! For they like to parade
around in flowing robes and receive respectful greetings as they walk in the
marketplaces. 39And how they love the
seats of honor in the synagogues and the
head table at banquets. 40Yet they shamelessly cheat widows out of their property
and then pretend to be pious by making
long prayers in public. Because of this, they
will be more severely punished."

The Widow's Offering
Mark 12:41-44 // Luke 21:1-4

41Jesus sat down near the collection box
in the Temple and watched as the crowds
dropped in their money. Many rich people
put in large amounts. 42Then a poor widow
came and dropped in two small coins.
43Jesus called his disciples to him and
said, "I tell you the truth, this poor widow
has given more than all the others who are
making contributions. 44For they gave a tiny
part of their surplus, but she, poor as she is,
has given everything she had to live on."

12:34 The account ends with Jesus' commending the teacher of religious law for recognizing that this twofold command was more important than burnt offerings and sacrifices (see Hos 6:6). We are left uncertain as to the fate of this man. He was ***not far from the Kingdom of God***, but did he enter it? Mark might have intentionally left this question unanswered so that each reader would wrestle with the question, *Have I entered the Kingdom of God?*

12:35-37 After having answered various questions, mostly from opponents, Jesus now asked a question (see 8:27; Matt 17:25; 21:31; Luke 10:36). The ***Messiah*** was considered ***the son of David*** because of such passages as Isa 9:2-7; 11:1-5; Jer 23:5-6; 33:15-16; Ezek 34:23-24; 37:24-28. Jesus' question did not deny that the Messiah was a descendant of David (10:47-48; 11:10; see Rom 1:3-4), but he demonstrated that this description, while correct, is inadequate. The Messiah is far more!

12:36 Psalm 110:1 is the OT verse most quoted in the NT. Since David authored the psalm, the statement "***The Lord*** [God] ***said to my*** [David's] ***Lord*** [the Messiah]" indicates that the Messiah is David's Lord. Thus, the Messiah could not simply be David's ***son.*** He is the Son of God who sits at God's right hand (14:62) and will come to judge the world (8:38; 13:24-27, 32-37).

12:38-39 ***teachers of religious law:*** See 1:22. The warning here is similar to the one against the Pharisees and Herod in 8:15. The scribes broke the two greatest commands (12:30-31). They broke the first command by failing to love God and failing to reserve for him alone the reverence and adoration they sought for themselves. • ***Flowing robes*** were probably the garments worn by religious men; ***respectful greetings*** perhaps meant being called "Rabbi" (see Matt 23:7). The ***seats of honor*** were in the front of the synagogue facing the congregation.

12:40 The teachers of religious law broke the second command by failing to love their neighbors, as was seen in their cheating widows ***of their property.*** They clearly were cheating the most vulnerable and needy people despite God's concern for ***widows*** (Deut 14:29; Ps 68:5; 146:9; Isa 1:17; Jer 7:6; 49:11) and his condemnation of those who mistreat them (Isa 1:23; Ezek 22:7; Zech 7:10; Mal 3:5). The scribes wore a hypocritical cloak of false piety (see Matt 6:5-6; Luke 18:11-12). • ***they will be more severely punished:*** In the final judgment (9:42-48; see Luke 14:11).

12:41-44 This account of a poor widow highlights the contrast between the falsely pious religious leaders (12:38-40) and those who truly love God. The emphasis of the passage falls on Jesus' pronouncement, ***I tell you the truth***, in which the widow is described as having given ***more than*** the rich.

12:41-42 The word translated ***collection box*** can refer to a building within the Temple compound in which Temple money was stored, but here it refers to one of thirteen money chests into which gifts were placed. As Jesus watched, many rich people put in large sums. Then he noticed a poor widow put in ***two small coins.*** (Greek ***two lepta, which is a kodrantes*** [i.e., a quadrans]. The use of the Roman term (*quadrans*) supports the view that Mark wrote his Gospel for the church in Rome; see Mark Introduction, "Audience," p. 1644.) These two coins were worth one sixty-fourth of a *denarius*, a normal day's pay (Matt 20:1-2).

12:43-44 ***Jesus called his disciples*** to hear his teaching (see 3:23; 6:7; 8:1; 10:42; see also 7:14; 8:34). Jesus' pronouncement in 12:43 revealed a radical difference between his thinking and that of the world. No one would have named a building after the widow for her gift of two small coins, but Jesus and his Father look at a person's heart (1 Sam 16:7). The widow was doing exactly what Jesus told the rich young ruler to do (10:21) and what he taught his disciples (1:18, 20; 8:34-37; 10:28-29). Like the woman of 14:3-9, the poor widow loved God with all her heart, soul, mind, and strength (12:30).

Jesus Teaches about the Future (13:1-37)

Jesus Predicts Future Events

Mark 13:1-8 // Matt 24:1-8 // Luke 21:5-11
Mark 13:9-13 // Matt 24:9-14 // Luke 21:12-19
Mark 13:14-20 // Matt 24:15-22 // Luke 21:20-24

13 As Jesus was leaving the Temple that
day, one of his disciples said, "Teacher,
look at these magnificent buildings! Look at
the impressive stones in the walls."
2Jesus replied, "Yes, look at these great
buildings. But they will be completely demolished. Not one stone will be left on top
of another!"
3Later, Jesus sat on the Mount of Olives
across the valley from the Temple. Peter,
James, John, and Andrew came to him privately and asked him, 4"Tell us, when will
all this happen? What sign will show us that
these things are about to be fulfilled?"
5Jesus replied, "Don't let anyone mislead you, 6for many will come in my name,
claiming, 'I am the Messiah.' They will deceive many. 7And you will hear of wars and
threats of wars, but don't panic. Yes, these
things must take place, but the end won't
follow immediately. 8Nation will go to war
against nation, and kingdom against kingdom. There will be earthquakes in many
parts of the world, as well as famines. But
this is only the first of the birth pains, with
more to come.
9"When these things begin to happen,
watch out! You will be handed over to the local councils and beaten in the synagogues.
You will stand trial before governors and
kings because you are my followers. But
this will be your opportunity to tell them

13:1-31
//Matt 24:1-35
//Luke 21:5-36
13:2
Luke 19:44
13:5
2 Thes 2:3, 10-12
1 Tim 4:1
2 Tim 3:13
1 Jn 4:6
13:6
John 5:43
13:8
2 Chr 15:6
Isa 19:2
13:9-12
//Matt 10:17-22
//Luke 21:12-16
13:10
Rom 10:18

13:1-37 Chapter 13 brings to a conclusion the section begun at 11:1. Israel's failure to produce fruit (11:12-26; 12:38-40) and its leaders' hostility toward God's anointed, the Messiah (11:1-11, 27-33; 12:13-17, 18-27), would result in judgment and the destruction of Jerusalem and the Temple.

13:1 *Leaving the Temple*, Jesus was heading to the Mount of Olives (13:3). • *look at these magnificent buildings!* The sight of the Temple would have been awe-inspiring (see note on 11:15-19). It was the largest temple complex in the world, with immense stones. One stone that has been uncovered in the western wall is estimated to weigh 600 tons. With its white stones, gold trim, and the gold-covered roof, the Temple complex looked like a snow-covered mountain; in the sun it was a blinding sight (Josephus, *War* 5.5.6). The Talmud says that "He who has not seen the temple in its full construction has never seen a glorious building in his life" (*Babylonian Sukkah* 51b).

13:2 Jesus' reply to the disciples was shocking. This glorious and massive Temple complex, a symbol of strength and permanence and God's favor for the Jews, would be totally, irrevocably destroyed. • *Not one stone will be left on top of another!* Jesus' prediction emphasized the total devastation that would result from the Roman army's systematic attack on the entire Temple complex (Josephus, *Antiquities* 6.9.1; 7.1.1.). To say that Jesus' prediction was not fulfilled because some of the foundation stones still stand is to misunderstand the language of prophecy. One does not expect a prophet to say that 97.9% of these stones will be removed! Anyone in the first century who visited Jerusalem after AD 70 would have acknowledged that Jesus' prediction had been fulfilled.

13:3-4 *Andrew* appeared here with the trio, *Peter, James,* and *John* (5:37; 9:2; 14:33), completing the two sets of brothers (1:16-20; 3:16-18). • Jesus' prediction elicited two questions from the disciples. Although some scholars argue that the second question goes beyond the first in looking to the coming of the Son of Man at the end of the age, it is best to interpret these two questions as focusing on the time and the sign associated with the destruction of Jerusalem and the Temple (cp. 13:29-30; Luke 21:7). These questions follow naturally from Jesus' prediction in 13:2. The desire to know the *sign* reflected the disciples' desire to be forewarned and prepared for *all . . . these things*.

13:5-23 This section is often divided into two parts, 13:5-13 and 13:14-23. The first part is often interpreted as describing the destruction of Jerusalem, which occurred in AD 70, while the second part is taken to describe the coming of the Son of Man in the future. It is best, however, to interpret all of 13:5-23 as describing events surrounding the destruction of Jerusalem in AD 70 because: (1) 13:5-23 is Jesus' answer to the two questions (13:4) that deal with the destruction of Jerusalem (13:2); (2) The commands to flee Judea (13:14-16), the woe announced upon pregnant and nursing women (13:17), and the prayer that it not take place in winter (13:18) make sense if they refer to the events of AD 70 but not if they refer to the future return of Christ; (3) Three warnings in this passage (13:5, 9, 23) tie this passage together and indicate that 13:5-23 should be understood as a unit. • The subdivisions of this section are arranged as a chiasm (X-pattern):

A: Deceivers claim to be the Messiah (13:5-6).
B: There are reports of fighting and natural disasters (13:7-8).
C: There is persecution of believers (13:9-13).
B′: The fighting in Judea and resulting tribulation begin (13:14-20).
A′: Deceivers claim to be the Messiah (13:21-23).

13:5-6 Jesus warned his followers not to be misled by the many false messiahs who would come *claiming, 'I am the Messiah'* (literally *claiming, 'I am'*) and would *deceive many* into following them. These false claimants would profess to be the long-awaited Jewish Messiah (not Jesus per se) or to speak on the Messiah's behalf. Such claimants included Theudas the Galilean (Acts 5:36), Simon the son of Gioras, and John of Gischala, who deceived many in the AD 60s.

13:7 The Greek word translated *must* is also used in 8:31. In both instances, God's sovereignty over events is emphasized. • *but the end won't follow immediately:* These things would occur, and just as birth pains are followed by childbirth, God's judgment on Jerusalem would follow. However, these events did not indicate that it was going to happen right away.

13:9 The second *watch out!* warns of persecution that was to come upon Christians (see 6:11; 8:34-38; 10:30; see 4:17). Jewish Christians would be brought before *local councils* of Jewish leaders, who had authority over Jewish communities. We read of such a council in Matt 10:17 and probably in Matt 5:22 (see also Acts 4:1-22). • *beaten in the synagogues:* Paul's beatings in 2 Cor 11:24-25 were probably inflicted in the local synagogue. • The followers of Jesus would also be susceptible to *trial before governors and kings* (see Acts 23:24; 24:10-27; 25:1–26:32). Such

13:11 Matt 10:19-20; Luke 12:11-12
13:12 Mic 7:6
13:13 Matt 10:22; John 15:18-21
13:14 *Dan 9:27; 11:31; 12:11; Matt 24:15; 2 Thes 2:3

about me. [10]For the Good News must first
be preached to all nations. [11]But when you
are arrested and stand trial, don't worry in
advance about what to say. Just say what
God tells you at that time, for it is not you
who will be speaking, but the Holy Spirit.
[12]"A brother will betray his brother to
death, a father will betray his own child,
and children will rebel against their parents and cause them to be killed. [13]And
everyone will hate you because you are my
followers. But the one who endures to the
end will be saved.
[14]"The day is coming when you will see
the sacrilegious object that causes desecration standing where he should not be."
(Reader, pay attention!) "Then those in Judea must flee to the hills. [15]A person out on

The Day Is Coming (13:1-37)

Mark 8:38; 14:25; Matt 5:8; 6:10; 13:41-42; 23:39; 24:3–25:46; Luke 6:24-26; 16:19-31; 19:41-44; 21:5-36; John 14:1-3; Acts 1:6-7; 10:42; Rom 8:22-23; 16:20; 1 Cor 1:7-8; 15:35-58; 2 Cor 1:14; Phil 1:6, 10; 2:16; 3:21; 1 Thes 4:13-18; 2 Thes 2:2-14; 2 Tim 4:1-8; Titus 2:11-13; Heb 9:28; 10:25, 37; 1 Pet 1:7, 13; 5:1-4; 2 Pet 3:7-13; 1 Jn 2:28; Rev 1:7; 6:15-17; 21:1–22:7, 12, 20

Jesus predicted three future events in the synoptic Gospels. One was his own death and resurrection (e.g., 8:31; 9:31; 10:33-34); this was a past event when the Gospels were written.

The second event that Jesus predicted was the destruction of Jerusalem in AD 70 (13:2-23, 28-31; 14:58; 15:29; Matt 24:3-28; Luke 19:41-44; 21:5-24; John 2:19; Acts 6:14). This event was probably about to happen when Mark wrote his Gospel (see "Date," p. 1644). It would not signify the very end, so the Christian community should not be troubled, but must live in faithful watchfulness for the Son of God's return in glory, which might be soon (13:34-37).

The third event that Jesus predicted was his own future return (8:38; 13:24-27, 32-37; 14:25; Matt 23:39; 24:3, 29-31; 24:36–26:46; Luke 21:25-36; John 14:1-3). References to Jesus' return can be found in every book of the NT except 3 John (see, e.g., 1 Cor 1:7-8; 3:13; 5:5; 2 Cor 1:14; Phil 1:6, 10; 2:16; 1 Thes 5:1-11; 2 Thes 2:2; 2 Tim 1:12, 18; 4:1, 8).

When Jesus returns, the promises about God's Kingdom will be completely fulfilled. Jesus will bring judgment and destruction for Satan and his angels (Rom 16:20; 2 Thes 2:3-12). Unbelievers will also experience eternal judgment (e.g., Matt 13:41-42; 25:31-46; Luke 6:24-26; 16:19-31; Acts 10:42; Eph 5:6; Col 3:6; Heb 10:25; 2 Pet 3:7; Jude 1:6; Rev 1:7; 6:14, 17). Meanwhile, the faithful (1 Thes 4:13-18), will be resurrected to experience the joy of eternal life. God will gather his chosen people (13:27) for salvation (Heb 1:14; 9:28), grace (1 Pet 1:13), and glory (1 Thes 2:12; 2 Thes 2:14; 1 Pet 1:7; 5:1, 4). He will give his people a priceless inheritance (1 Pet 1:4) and new eternal bodies (1 Cor 15:35-57; Phil 3:21; 1 Thes 4:13-18). All of creation will also be rescued from its curse (Gen 3:17-18) and be transformed (Rom 8:22-23; 2 Pet 3:12-13; Rev 21:1–22:5). Sorrow, tears, mourning, and death will no longer exist (Rev 21:4-5). Those who have had faith during this life will see God (Matt 5:8; Rev 22:4).

In light of these promises, believers in Jesus are to prayerfully await his return (Matt 6:10; Rev 22:20). We should not speculate dates for his coming (13:32; Acts 1:7), but should live in a way that is honorable (1 Jn 2:28) and be prepared (Matt 24:36–25:30; 1 Thes 5:1-11).

trials were due to their being followers of Jesus (13:9, 13), not on account of real wrongdoing (see 1 Pet 4:14-16). • ***But this will be your opportunity to tell them about me:*** Or *But this will be your testimony against them.* The Greek can be interpreted either way.

13:10 Such trials (13:9, 11) would be a means through which the ***Good News*** would ***be preached to all nations*** (or *all peoples*). This would all take place ***first***—i.e., before the destruction of Jerusalem. For Paul's understanding of how the Good News had already been preached to every nation in his day, see Rom 16:26; Col 1:6, 23 (see also Rom 1:5, 8; 10:18; 15:19, 23).

13:11 A word of encouragement follows the warning of 13:9. Jesus' followers need not fear what they should say in these circumstances. The early followers of Jesus were generally uneducated and without political influence (see Acts 4:10-17; 1 Cor 1:26), so this assurance would have comforted them. Believers are not prohibited from thinking about what they will say, but they need not ***worry*** about it.

13:12-13 There would be no single group, not even their own families, to whom persecuted Christians could automatically flee or turn for help (see Matt 10:35-36; Luke 12:53). They would be universally hated because of their allegiance to Jesus (***because you are my followers,*** literally *on account of my name*). Those who remain faithful to death (***to the end***) will be saved from eternal punishment (see also 8:35; Rev 2:7, 10, 17, 26-28; 3:5, 12, 21).

13:14-20 Jesus now gave the sign requested in 13:4 and instructed his followers how to respond when they saw it. In 13:5-13, they were told not to be alarmed, but they were told that ***those in Judea must flee to the hills.***

13:14 ***The day is coming when you will see the sacrilegious object that causes desecration*** (literally *the abomination of desolation;* see Dan 9:27; 11:31; 12:11): Mark did not explain what this object would be, but Jewish readers in the first century were familiar with the term. The prophet Daniel had foretold that such an object would stand in the Temple in Jerusalem (Dan 9:27; 11:31), and many Jews understood the events in Jerusalem in 167–164 BC, during the time of Antiochus Epiphanes IV, to be a fulfillment of that prophecy. (The deuterocanonical book of *1 Maccabees,* written about 100 BC, narrates Antiochus's reign and describes how Antiochus and his followers erected a "sacrilegious object causing desecration on top of the altar for burnt offerings," *1 Maccabees* 1:54, 59). • ***standing where he*** (or *it*) ***should not be:*** In light of the historical background and the reference to Jerusalem (13:2, 4) and Judea (13:14), this clause clearly refers to something inappropriate happening in

the deck of a roof must not go down into the
house to pack. 16 A person out in the field
must not return even to get a coat. 17 How
terrible it will be for pregnant women and
for nursing mothers in those days. 18 And
pray that your flight will not be in winter.
19 For there will be greater anguish in those
days than at any time since God created the
world. And it will never be so great again.
20 In fact, unless the Lord shortens that time
of calamity, not a single person will survive.
But for the sake of his chosen ones he has
shortened those days.

False Messiahs

Mark 13:21-23 // Matt 24:23-27 // Luke 17:23-24

21 "Then if anyone tells you, 'Look, here is
the Messiah,' or 'There he is,' don't believe
it. 22 For [h]false messiahs and false prophets
will rise up and perform signs and wonders
so as to deceive, if possible, even God's chosen ones. 23 Watch out! I have warned you
about this ahead of time!

13:17
Luke 23:29

13:19
Dan 9:26; 12:1
Joel 2:2
Rev 7:14

13:21
Luke 17:23

13:22
Deut 13:1-3
2 Thes 2:9-10
Rev 13:13
[h]*pseudochristos* (5580)
›1 Jn 2:18

13:23
2 Pet 3:17

---

the Temple in Jerusalem. • ***(Reader, pay attention!):*** Mark alerted his original readers to pay attention to his description of this sign, which indicates that the expression required careful thought and discernment. Mark's readers were to look for a sign that was similar to what had happened in the time of Antiochus Epiphanes. • Although the phrase *sacrilegious object that causes desecration* is grammatically neuter, the word *standing* is grammatically masculine, so it refers to a person and not a thing. Suggestions as to who it might have been include: (1) the emperor Caligula, who in AD 39–40 attempted to erect a statue of himself in the Temple (Josephus, *Antiquities* 12.8.2-3); (2) Pontius Pilate (AD 26–36), who attempted to have the Roman soldiers march into Judea displaying their standards, which were considered idolatrous by Jews (Josephus, *War* 2.9.2-3); (3) the Zealots in AD 69–70, when they committed atrocities in the Temple, appointed an unqualified person as the high priest of the nation, and "came into the sanctuary with polluted feet" (Josephus, *War* 4.3.4-8); (4) the Roman general Titus, who after conquering Jerusalem in AD 70 forced entry into the Temple as well (Josephus, *War* 6.4.7); (5) Titus's soldiers, who set up their standards in the Temple, sacrificed to them, and proclaimed Titus as emperor (Josephus, *War* 6.6.1); (6) the destruction of the Temple itself in AD 70; or (7) a future event involving the coming of the antichrist (see 2 Thes 2:3-4). The context and source of the expression eliminate several of these theories. In Daniel and *1 Maccabees,* the expression involves the Temple, its altar, and its sacrificial rituals. In Mark 13:14-20, it is a sign for people to flee Judea, and what it refers to must occur while there is still time to flee (i.e., before the Roman army had occupied Judea and besieged Jerusalem). Explanations 1 and 2 are too early to serve as a recognizable sign to flee Judea, they didn't actually defile the Temple, and the Christians did not flee Jerusalem. Explanations 4–6 occurred too late, for there would have been no opportunity to flee after Titus entered Jerusalem. Explanation 7 does not refer to the destruction of Jerusalem in AD 70, which is the subject of 13:14-20, and the coming of the antichrist would not be limited to Judea. Explanation 3, however, fits well: It occurred in AD 69–70, shortly before Titus besieged Jerusalem, which would have given Christians a brief opportunity to leave Jerusalem before it was besieged; and it involved actions that defiled the holy place in the Temple. This interpretation also helps to distinguish the sign of the coming disaster (the sacrilegious person) from the disaster itself (the destruction of Jerusalem and the Temple). • ***Then:*** At the appearance of the sacrilege, those in Judea were to ***flee to the hills.*** The early church historian Eusebius tells of a prophetic oracle given to the Jerusalem church that caused them to flee the city before its destruction (Eusebius, *Church History* 3.5.3).

13:15-16 A person relaxing on the *roof* of his Judean home should not even pack after seeing this sign, but come down and flee. Likewise, a ***person out in the field*** should not return home to retrieve his *coat.* Believers were to flee from the approaching Roman army as soon as they saw the sign of 13:14. The Roman army did not practice a swift "blitzkrieg" kind of warfare. Their movement tended to be cautious, methodical, and relentless. Jesus warned against playing a waiting game to see how things would develop.

13:17 The intensity of the coming disaster is illustrated by the suffering of the most vulnerable. In that day, the joy of motherhood (see Luke 1:25, 57-59) would be accompanied by ***terrible*** trouble.

13:18 ***In winter,*** the wadis (canyon-like riverbeds) are flooded, travel is more difficult, and survival is harder.

13:19 ***greater anguish in those days than at any time since God created the world:*** Such hyperbole is common in Semitic expression; it heightens the terror of that horrible time and should not be taken as an exact statistical analysis of how this suffering ranks alongside other disasters. • ***And it will never be so great again:*** The events of 13:14-23 would not bring history to an end; history would continue after the destruction of the Temple in AD 70.

13:20 God's shortening of his timetable for the ***days*** of ***calamity*** is referred to frequently in intertestamental Jewish literature (e.g., *2 Esdras* 2:13; *2 Baruch* 20:1). This statement emphasizes the horrors of this tribulation experienced by God's people, but also God's mercy in shortening this time. • ***not a single person will survive:*** The whole population of Judea might have been destroyed if the days of anguish had been longer. • ***chosen ones*** (literally *elect*): Followers of Jesus.

13:21-23 The larger section (13:5-23) concludes with another warning about messianic pretenders. Here the pretenders are associated with the events of AD 70, whereas in 13:5-6 they were associated with the normal course of events. Along with false messiahs, prophets would appear and perform miraculous signs and wonders (13:22), hoping to deceive not only the Jews of Judea and Jerusalem but even the Christians (***God's chosen ones***). Jesus ***warned*** his followers not to believe such reports. When the Messiah comes from heaven (13:26), everyone will see and know it (see Rev 1:7). • ***Watch out!*** This warning unifies the section (13:5-23) and brings it to a close (see note on 13:5-23). Jesus' teaching in this section was to warn his followers in Judea and Jerusalem not to be misled by false messianic hopes and claims. Many Jews succumbed to such claims in the late AD 60s, and Josephus (*Antiquities* 17.10.8) describes the great harm done by these pretenders, who encouraged the Jewish people to resist the Romans. Nothing should distract Christians from fleeing Judea and Jerusalem when they see the abomination of desolation taking place. • For Mark's readers in Rome, Jesus' message had a different application. Mark wanted his readers to watch out for those who promised timetables for prophecy to be fulfilled. They could not know the time (13:32), and a frenzy about the second coming of Christ was forbidden, but they were to be alert (13:33-37) and prepare themselves for persecution (13:9-13; see 8:34-38) according to Jesus' words of encouragement (13:11, 13).

13:24-25
*Isa 13:10; 34:4
Ezek 32:7-8
*Joel 2:10, 31; 3:15
Rev 6:12-14; 8:12

13:26
*Dan 7:13
Matt 16:27
Rev 1:7

13:27
Deut 30:4
Zech 2:6

13:31
Matt 5:18
Luke 16:17

13:32
Acts 1:7

The Coming of the Son of Man
Mark 13:24-33 // Matt 24:29-36 // Luke 21:25-33

24"At that time, after the anguish of those
days,

the sun will be darkened,
the moon will give no light,
25 the stars will fall from the sky,
and the powers in the heavens will be
shaken.

26Then everyone will see the Son of Man
coming on the clouds with great power and
glory. 27And he will send out his angels to
gather his chosen ones from all over the
world—from the farthest ends of the earth
and heaven.
28"Now learn a lesson from the fig tree.
When its branches bud and its leaves begin
to sprout, you know that summer is near.
29In the same way, when you see all these
things taking place, you can know that his
return is very near, right at the door. 30I tell
you the truth, this generation will not pass
from the scene before all these things take
place. 31Heaven and earth will disappear,
but my words will never disappear.
32"However, no one knows the day or
hour when these things will happen, not

13:24-27 *At that time, after the anguish of those days:* Many scholars argue that the cosmic signs of 13:24-25, the coming of the Son of Man in 13:26, and the gathering of the chosen ones from throughout the world in 13:27 are metaphorical ways of referring to the destruction of Jerusalem in AD 70 and to the vindication of the Son of Man by that event. The traditional interpretation, though, is that, whereas the former material refers to the destruction of Jerusalem, this passage refers to the coming of the Son of Man (the *parousia*) that will occur at the end of history. This interpretation fits better for several reasons: (1) *After* the anguish of those days means after the destruction of Jerusalem, not during it, and *at that time* (literally *in those days*) could occur at any time after the events of 13:5-23; (2) several words used in 13:26 are used elsewhere to describe the coming of the Son of Man: *glory* (8:38), *power* and *clouds* (14:62); and (3) in light of the early church's longing and praying for the return of the Lord Jesus (1 Cor 16:22; Rev 22:20), Mark's readers would have interpreted 13:26 as the second coming of Jesus, which will bring history as we know it to a close. The prophets, Jesus, and the Gospel writers described this event as though seen through a telescope, and the distance between events is unclear; no one knows the time for this event except God himself (13:32). The events of 13:5-23 and 13:24-27 are part of the same great, divine act that includes the coming of the Son of Man, his ministry, death, and resurrection, the judgment of Jerusalem in AD 70, and the Son of Man's final coming in glory.

13:24b-25 See Isa 13:10; 34:4; Joel 2:10. Some of the language used in the NT to describe Jesus' second coming, such as the "trumpet call of God" (1 Thes 4:16), appears to be metaphorical, and in the OT, cosmic language is frequently used to describe historical events metaphorically (see Isa 11:1-9; 13:9-11; Jer 4:23-28; Ezek 32:1-16). So it is possible that this imagery could refer to a past event, such as the destruction of Jerusalem, if that is the meaning of 13:24-27. However, the NT writers clearly understood the coming of the Son of Man to be the visible and personal return of Jesus in the future (see Acts 1:9-11).

13:26 *Son of Man* is a title Jesus used for himself. • *coming . . . glory:* See Dan 7:13.

13:27 The Son of Man, at his coming, will gather his chosen people—those who believe in him and follow him—*from all over the world* (literally *from the four winds*; Zech 2:6) and *from the farthest ends of the earth and heaven* (see Deut 13:7; 30:4; Isa 42:10; 62:11). This hope is expressed frequently in the OT (e.g., Ps 107:2-3; Isa 11:11-16; 27:12-13; 43:5-13; 49:12; 60:1-9; Jer 31:10). For Mark's readers, this passage would have provided encouragement to endure and remain faithful despite the persecutions foretold in 13:9-13. The Son of Man's coming will also bring judgment on the unrighteous (8:38; 13:32-37; Matt 13:41-43; 24:36-51; 25:1-12, 31-46).

13:28-31 This passage contains the *lesson* (literally *parable*) of *the fig tree* (13:28-30) and two sayings (13:30-31). It is closely tied to 13:4-23 by the words *all these things* (13:4) and the expression *when you see* (13:29; cp. 13:14).

13:29 *his return* (literally *he/it is near*): The Greek has no explicit subject, so the choice between "he is near" or "it is near" depends on whether 13:29-30 refers to 13:4-23 or to 13:24-27. The NLT text understands it as referring to the return of the Son of Man. Because words in 13:4 are echoed in 13:29 and 30 (see note on 13:28-31), others interpret it as referring to the destruction of Jerusalem. Just as the sprouting of the fig tree is a herald of summer, the desolating sacrilege (13:14) would be a harbinger of Jerusalem's destruction.

13:30 *This generation* (or *this age*, or *this nation*) was to witness the fulfillment of these events. That generation did witness the destruction of Jerusalem. Those, however, who hold that *all these things* refers to the coming of the Son of Man have to interpret this generation as meaning something other than "people alive at this time." It could refer to the continued existence of the Jewish people, the whole human race, the Christian community, or the last generation of the end time.

13:31 Jesus personally guaranteed what he had said. *My words* include specifically what Jesus said in the whole discourse of ch 13. Mark's readers would have understood this as guaranteeing the truth of all Jesus' teachings known to them (Luke 1:2). Like the OT Scriptures (see Isa 40:8), Jesus' words are eternal. His teachings are more abiding than the fundamental elements of creation. The basic elements of creation will pass away (see also Ps 102:25-26; Isa 40:6-8; 51:6; Matt 5:18; Luke 16:17; 2 Pet 3:7, 10; Rev 20:11), but Jesus' words *will never disappear*.

13:32-37 Just as 13:28-31 picks up the theme of 13:5-23 in speaking of the destruction of Jerusalem, 13:32-37 picks up the theme of 13:24-27 and speaks of the coming of the Son of Man. An introductory warning against speculations concerning the end time (13:32) is followed by a warning to be on guard because one cannot know the time of the end (13:33). A story illustrates the need to be ready for the Lord's return (13:34), and its application repeats the need to watch lest they be found unprepared (13:35-36); the concluding warning is also for watchfulness (13:37).

13:32 The statement *no one knows the day or hour* (cp. Acts 1:7) introduces the warning to be watchful (13:33-37) and discourages speculation. • Jesus refers to himself as *the Son*, higher than *the angels* in an ascending hierarchy that begins with *no one* and ends with *only the Father*. The authenticity of this saying is assured by the limitation it places on the Son's knowledge, something the early church would not likely have imagined—in the apocryphal gospels (about AD 150–300), the tendency is

even the angels in heaven or the Son himself. Only the Father knows. 33And since
you don't know when that time will come,
be on guard! Stay alert!

Watch for the Master's Return

34"The coming of the Son of Man can be illustrated by the story of a man going on a
long trip. When he left home, he gave each
of his slaves instructions about the work
they were to do, and he told the gatekeeper
to watch for his return. 35You, too, must
keep watch! For you don't know when the
master of the household will return—in the
evening, at midnight, before dawn, or at
daybreak. 36Don't let him find you sleeping
when he arrives without warning. 37I say to
you what I say to everyone: Watch for him!"

6. THE DEATH AND RESURRECTION OF JESUS (14:1–16:20)

The Plot to Kill Jesus

Mark 14:1-2 // Matt 26:1-5 // Luke 22:1-2

14 It was now two days before Passover and the Festival of Unleavened
Bread. The leading priests and the teachers
of religious law were still looking for an opportunity to capture Jesus secretly and kill
him. 2"But not during the Passover celebration," they agreed, "or the people may riot."

Jesus Anointed at Bethany

Mark 14:3-9 // Matt 26:6-13; cp. Luke 7:36-50; cp. John 12:1-11

3Meanwhile, Jesus was in Bethany at the
home of Simon, a man who had previously
had leprosy. While he was eating, a woman
came in with a beautiful alabaster jar of
expensive perfume made from essence of
nard. She broke open the jar and poured
the perfume over his head.
4Some of those at the table were indignant.
"Why waste such expensive perfume?" they
asked. 5"It could have been sold for a year's
wages and the money given to the poor!" So
they scolded her harshly.
6But Jesus replied, "Leave her alone. Why
criticize her for doing such a good thing to
me? 7You will always have the poor among
you, and you can help them whenever you
want to. But you will not always have me.
8She has done what she could and has
anointed my body for burial ahead of time.
9I tell you the truth, wherever the Good
News is preached throughout the world,
this woman's deed will be remembered and
discussed."

13:33-37 Matt 25:13-14; Luke 12:35-40; Rom 13:11; Eph 6:17-18; Col 4:2; 1 Thes 5:6
14:1-2 //Matt 26:1-5; //Luke 22:1-2; John 11:55-57
14:3-9 //Matt 26:6-13; //John 12:1-8
14:3 Luke 7:37-38
14:7 Deut 15:11
14:8 John 19:40

to exalt and magnify Jesus' divine attributes (e.g., see the *Infancy Gospel of Thomas*). In the miracle of the incarnation, Jesus experienced limitation (10:40; 13:32). If the Son himself did not know the day or hour, Christians should refrain from seeking such knowledge for themselves.

13:33-37 These verses contain four variations of the same basic warning: ***Be on guard! Stay alert!*** (some manuscripts add ***and pray;*** 13:33), and ***watch.*** The repetition emphasizes the need to be vigilant.

13:34-35 The point of the story is not that the return of the Lord is uncertain or unexpected (see Matt 24:45-51; 25:1-30; Luke 12:36-38; 19:12-27), but that there will be no sign or warning of his coming. The parable is allegorical in at least two respects, with the ***master*** (Greek *kurios*) understood as the Lord [*kurios*] Jesus Christ and the ***slaves*** or household servants as the Christian community. But to allegorize ***the gatekeeper*** as the apostles or Peter was a post-NT development. • ***in the evening, at midnight, before dawn*** (literally *the cock's crowing*), ***or at daybreak:*** The four periods of the night correspond to the Roman division of the night into four watches of three hours each and simply mean that the master can return at any time during the night.

13:37 The passage, originally addressed to the disciples (*you*, see also 13:5), is also directed to all readers of Mark's Gospel (*everyone*). • ***Watch for him!*** Although 13:32-37 warns about being ready, the early church experienced this vigilance as a joyous anticipation of "that wonderful day when the glory of our great God and Savior, Jesus Christ, will be revealed" (Titus 2:13). Even Greek Christians in the first century repeated the Aramaic prayer, *Marana tha* ("Come, Lord," see 1 Cor 16:22; Rev 22:20) and today, we still "eagerly look forward to his appearing" (2 Tim 4:8).

14:1–16:8 The final section of Mark is the narrative of Jesus' suffering, death, and resurrection—the last few days of his life.

14:1-2 The plot by the ***leading priests*** and ***teachers of religious law*** to kill Jesus (see 3:6; 11:18; 12:12) now comes to a climax.

14:3-9 The story of Jesus' being anointed by a woman in Bethany (14:3-9) sets the scene for events to follow. Luke's account (Luke 7:36-50) is significantly different and might be a different event. This incident took place in ***Bethany***, two miles east of Jerusalem on the lower, eastern slope of the Mount of Olives, where Jesus apparently stayed when he was in Judea (11:1, 11-12). The home belonged to ***Simon***, a former leper (lepers were isolated from society; perhaps he had been healed by Jesus; see 1:40-45). • ***eating:*** Or *reclining*. The meal was a banquet, as indicated by their reclining. A woman (see John 12:3) broke the neck of a sealed, ***alabaster jar*** containing ***expensive perfume*** (pure ***nard***) and poured it all on Jesus' head (see Exod 29:4-7; 2 Kgs 9:1-6).

14:4-5 ***Some*** (cp. Matt 26:8; John 12:4-5) were indignant over what they considered a ***waste*** of the expensive perfume, said to have been worth ***a year's wages*** (Greek *300 denarii*) for the average worker. A denarius was equivalent to a laborer's full day's wage. This large amount of money could have been ***given to the poor***, and it was obligatory to remember the poor during Passover.

14:6-8 Jesus defended the woman's action. That the disciples would ***always have the poor*** among them did not minimize Jesus' concern for the poor. The opportunity to minister directly to Jesus was limited. Only hours remained! She chose the best thing she could do with her perfume.

14:8 Jesus interprets the woman's action. She had ***anointed*** his ***body*** in preparation for his ***burial***. Whether the woman was consciously motivated by Jesus' imminent death is unclear; her loving act served the purpose Jesus assigned it.

14:9 Although Mark does not give the woman's name, her ***deed*** (14:6) is indeed remembered as the story of Jesus is told ***throughout the world***.

14:10-11 In sharp contrast to the

14:10-11
//Matt 26:14-16
//Luke 22:3-6

14:12-26
//Matt 26:17-25
//Luke 22:7-14, 21-23
//John 13:21-30

14:12
Exod 12:14-21
Deut 16:1-4
1 Cor 5:7-8

14:14
Exod 12:8
Lev 23:5

14:18
*Ps 41:9

Judas Agrees to Betray Jesus
Mark 14:10-11 // Matt 26:14-16 // Luke 22:3-6
10Then Judas Iscariot, one of the twelve disciples, went to the leading priests to arrange to
betray Jesus to them. 11They were delighted
when they heard why he had come, and they
promised to give him money. So he began
looking for an opportunity to betray Jesus.

The Last Supper
Mark 14:12-16 // Matt 26:17-19// Luke 22:7-13
Mark 14:17-21 // Matt 26:20-25 // Luke 22:21-23 //
John 13:21-30
Mark 14:22-26 // Matt 26:26-30 // Luke 22:14-20
12On the first day of the Festival of Unleavened Bread, when the Passover lamb
is sacrificed, Jesus' disciples asked him,
"Where do you want us to go to prepare the
Passover meal for you?"
13So Jesus sent two of them into Jerusalem
with these instructions: "As you go into the
city, a man carrying a pitcher of water will
meet you. Follow him. 14At the house he
enters, say to the owner, 'The Teacher asks:
Where is the guest room where I can eat
the Passover meal with my disciples?' 15He
will take you upstairs to a large room that is
already set up. That is where you should prepare our meal." 16So the two disciples went
into the city and found everything just as
Jesus had said, and they prepared the Passover meal there.
17In the evening Jesus arrived with the
twelve disciples. 18As they were at the table eating, Jesus said, "I tell you the truth,
one of you eating with me here will betray
me."

JUDAS ISCARIOT (14:10-11, 18-21, 43-45)

Mark 3:19
Matt 10:4; 26:14-16, 23-25, 46-50; 27:3-10
Luke 6:16; 22:3-6, 22, 47-48
John 6:70-71; 12:4-6; 13:2, 18, 21-30; 17:12; 18:2-5
Acts 1:16-26

Judas Iscariot is infamous for betraying Jesus to the authorities (3:19; Matt 10:4; Luke 6:16).

The meaning of the name "Iscariot" (John 6:71; 13:26) is uncertain; it might refer to a village named Kerioth. He is not the same as Judas son of James (Luke 6:16; Acts 1:13).

Among the apostles, Judas Iscariot came to be known as greedy; he carried the money bag and had the reputation of stealing from it (John 12:6). The money offered him as a bribe by the leading priests later convinced him to betray Jesus (14:10-11; Matt 26:14-16; Luke 22:3-6).

Jesus called Judas himself a devil (John 6:70) and predicted the betrayal (14:18-21). The devil put the idea of betrayal into Judas's mind, and Satan "entered" him at the time of the betrayal (Luke 22:3; John 13:2, 27). Judas led a group of soldiers and officers to the garden of Gethsemane in the middle of the night, where he found Jesus and betrayed him with the prearranged signal, a kiss of greeting (14:43-52). Later, Judas was apparently overcome by remorse for betraying an innocent man, and he hanged himself (Matt 27:3-10; Acts 1:18-19).

Jesus clearly understood Judas's betrayal as part of God's plan for redemption: It brought about the death of the Messiah as the ultimate sacrifice for sin (14:21; Matt 26:24; Luke 22:22; cp. Matt 26:54). Even though Judas served God's plan, his tragic end was clearly deserved (Acts 1:25). It would have been better for Judas if he had never been born (14:21; Matt 26:24; cp. Luke 22:22; John 17:12). Judas's fate soberly warns those who are apparently followers of Jesus but have never committed themselves to him personally (cp. Heb 6:4-6).

woman, Judas Iscariot, one of the twelve disciples, offered ***to betray Jesus*** for ***money*** (Matt 26:15; 27:3, 9).

14:12-32 The preparation for the Passover meal (14:12-16) introduces the story of the Last Supper (14:22-25). • The Last Supper is associated with the Passover meal (14:12, 14, 16; Matt 26:17-19; Luke 22:7-8, 11, 13, 15; cp. John 18:28; 19:14). Many pilgrims celebrated Passover in Jerusalem, where God's Temple was located (see Deut 16:2).

14:12 The time ***when the Passover lamb is sacrificed*** was twilight on the 14th of Nisan (Exod 12:6). This date falls in March or April each year.

14:13-15 Jesus' instructions to the disciples are similar to those of 11:2-6, suggesting that Jesus had prearranged a place for eating the Passover and Last Supper with his disciples. Jesus' careful preparations for this meal emphasize its importance. The two disciples were to ***prepare*** the ***Passover meal***, which included the lamb (which had to be slaughtered, skinned, cleaned, and roasted over an open fire), unleavened bread, a bowl of salt water, bitter herbs, and a bowl of a fruit puree, or *kharosheth*. Enough wine mixed with water was needed so that Jesus and the disciples could each drink four cups to celebrate God's fourfold blessing (Exod 6:6-7).

14:17 With the coming of ***evening, Jesus arrived with the twelve disciples*** (literally *the Twelve*) at the upstairs guest room. "The Twelve" refers to Jesus' disciples as a group; ten arrived with Jesus, since two of them were already there (14:13).

14:18 ***As they were at the table:*** Or *As they reclined.* The Passover was eaten in a reclining position, as were other banquet meals. During the Passover meal, someone (usually the youngest son) would ask the host, "Why is this night different from other nights?" The father or host would then recount the stories of the Passover and the Exodus (Deut 26:5-9). The elements of the Passover meal were symbolic. The Passover lamb served as a reminder of the blood of the sacrificial lambs that protected Israelite homes from the angel of death, which visited the firstborn in Egypt (Exod 12:28-30). Unleavened bread recalled the rapid exodus of God's people (Exod 12:31-34, 39). The salt water represented the tears of their bondage and the crossing of the Red Sea, and the bitter herbs their slavery. The four cups of wine acknowledged God's fourfold promise in Exod 6:6-7 (see notes

19 Greatly distressed, each one asked in
turn, "Am I the one?"
20 He replied, "It is one of you twelve who
is eating from this bowl with me. 21 For the
Son of Man must die, as the Scriptures declared long ago. But how terrible it will be
for the one who betrays him. It would be
far better for that man if he had never been
born!"
22 As they were eating, Jesus took some
bread and blessed it. Then he broke it in
pieces and gave it to the disciples, saying,
"Take it, for this is my body."
23 And he took a cup of wine and gave
thanks to God for it. He gave it to them,
and they all drank from it. 24 And he said to
them, "This is my blood, which confirms the
[i]covenant between God and his people. It is
poured out as a sacrifice for many. 25 I tell you
the truth, I will not drink [j]wine again until the
day I drink it new in the Kingdom of God."
26 Then they sang a hymn and went out to
the Mount of Olives.

Jesus Predicts Peter's Denial
Mark 14:27-31 // Matt 26:31-35; cp. Luke 22:31-34;
John 13:36-38
27 On the way, Jesus told them, "All of you
will desert me. For the Scriptures say,
'God will strike the Shepherd,
and the sheep will be scattered.'
28 But after I am raised from the dead, I will
go ahead of you to Galilee and meet you
there."
29 Peter said to him, "Even if everyone else
deserts you, I never will."
30 Jesus replied, "I tell you the truth, Peter—
this very night, before the rooster crows
twice, you will deny three times that you
even know me."
31 "No!" Peter declared emphatically.
"Even if I have to die with you, I will never
deny you!" And all the others vowed the
same.

Jesus Prays in Gethsemane
Mark 14:32-42 // Matt 26:36-46 // Luke 22:39-46
32 They went to the olive grove called Gethsemane, and Jesus said, "Sit here while I go
and pray." 33 He took Peter, James, and John
with him, and he became deeply troubled
and distressed. 34 He told them, "My soul
is crushed with grief to the point of death.
Stay here and keep watch with me."
35 He went on a little farther and fell to
the ground. He prayed that, if it were possible, the awful hour awaiting him might
pass him by. 36 "[k]Abba, Father," he cried out,
"everything is possible for you. Please take

14:21
Ps 22:1-21
Isa 53:3-8

14:22-25
//Matt 26:26-29
//Luke 22:15-20
//1 Cor 11:23-25

14:23
1 Cor 10:16

14:24
[i]*diathēkē* (1242)
‣Luke 22:20

14:25
[j]*ampelos* (0288)
‣Luke 22:18

14:27-31
//Matt 26:31-35
//Luke 22:31-34
//John 13:36-38

14:27
*Zech 13:7

14:28
Matt 28:7
Mark 16:7

14:32-42
//Matt 26:36-46
//Luke 22:39-46
John 18:1

14:33
Matt 17:1
Mark 9:2
Luke 9:28

14:34
*Ps 42:6; 43:5
Isa 53:10
John 12:27

14:36
Matt 20:22
John 5:30; 6:38; 18:11
Rom 8:15
Gal 4:6
[k]*abba patēr* (0005, 3962)
‣Rom 8:15

---

on Matt 26:26-29). • The terrible deed of betraying Jesus was more heinous in that the betrayer was ***one of*** those ***eating with*** him (see Ps 41:9; 55:12-14).

14:19 The disciples were shocked and saddened, asking, ***Am I the one?*** This is the first they had heard that Jesus would be betrayed (though the reader has known it since 3:19). Jesus maintained his betrayer's anonymity.

14:21 ***Son of Man*** is a title Jesus used for himself. • ***must die, as the Scriptures declared:*** See, e.g., Isa 52:13–53:12. Jesus foreknew this betrayal as part of the divine plan (cp. 8:31-33), but his betrayer was condemned. Jesus and the Gospel writers do not explain how God's sovereignty and Judas's human responsibility can coexist, but both are stated without compromise (see John 19:11).

14:22-25 The Lord's Supper began with a blessing. In modern practice, Christians ask God to bless the food; Jews in Jesus' day blessed God for providing the food with the words, "Blessed are you, O Lord our God, King of the universe, who brings forth bread from the earth." • ***this is my body. . . . This is my blood:*** Some understand these words to mean that the bread and wine are transformed into the very body and blood of Jesus (*transubstantiation*); others, that the bread and wine remain bread and wine but that the real presence of Jesus is found in them (*consubstantiation*). In these two views, when one participates in the Lord's Supper, one actually eats and drinks the body and blood of Jesus. A third view is that in eating the bread and wine, Christians spiritually feed on Jesus. A fourth view is that the meal is primarily a memorial, and the elements are symbolic of Jesus' sacrifice on our behalf. See also John 6:53-63 and notes.

14:24 The cup of wine represented Jesus' blood, ***poured out as a sacrifice*** (10:45; Isa 53:12). It initiated ***the covenant*** (some manuscripts read *the new covenant*) that God has made with his people (Luke 22:20; 1 Cor 11:25; see Exod 24:8; Zech 9:11; Heb 9:18-20; 10:26-29). The term ***many*** refers to all people (see 10:45; Rom 5:15-19).

14:25 ***the day I drink it new:*** Jesus will have a great banquet for his followers when he returns and fully establishes ***the Kingdom of God.***

14:26-27 ***Then they sang a hymn:*** It was customary to end the Passover by singing the last part of the *hallel* psalms (Pss 114–118). • The singing of hymns brought the Passover meal and Last Supper to a conclusion, and Jesus and the disciples departed for ***the Mount of Olives*** to spend the night. As they proceeded, Jesus told his disciples that they would all ***desert*** him, which had to happen because the Scriptures foretold it. • ***God will strike:*** Literally *I will strike.* See Zech 13:7. As a result, ***the sheep*** (the disciples) would be scattered.

14:28 Despite predictions of their failure, the account included encouragement and hope. After Jesus was ***raised from the dead,*** he met the disciples in ***Galilee*** (see 16:7), where they were forgiven and restored (see John 21:1-23).

14:29-31 Peter's protests and Jesus' rebuke recall 8:32-33. Despite Peter's protests, his denial took place within a few hours.

14:32 ***Gethsemane*** (Aramaic, "oil press") remains an olive grove to this day. It is called a garden in John 18:1, and Luke 22:39 indicates that it was a favorite place for Jesus and his disciples.

14:33-34 Jesus went ahead with ***Peter, James, and John*** (5:37-43; 9:2-9; see also 13:3) and asked them to ***watch*** with him, meaning to agonize with and for him in prayer.

14:35-36 Jesus ***fell to the ground*** to pray because of his deep distress (see Gen 17:1-3; Lev 9:24; Num 14:5; 16:4). Since it was normal to pray out loud, Jesus' prayer was probably overheard by the three disciples, who would not have fallen asleep immediately. • Jesus

14:38
Rom 7:22-23
[a]*peirasmos* (3986)
‣ Luke 4:2

14:43-50
//Matt 26:47-56
//Luke 22:47-53
//John 18:3-12

14:47
John 18:10

14:49
Isa 53:7-9
Luke 24:44

14:50
Ps 88:8
John 16:32

this cup of suffering away from me. Yet I want your will to be done, not mine."

37 Then he returned and found the disciples asleep. He said to Peter, "Simon, are you asleep? Couldn't you watch with me even one hour? 38 Keep watch and pray, so that you will not give in to [a]temptation. For the spirit is willing, but the body is weak."

39 Then Jesus left them again and prayed the same prayer as before. 40 When he returned to them again, he found them sleeping, for they couldn't keep their eyes open. And they didn't know what to say.

41 When he returned to them the third time, he said, "Go ahead and sleep. Have your rest. But no—the time has come. The Son of Man is betrayed into the hands of sinners. 42 Up, let's be going. Look, my betrayer is here!"

Jesus Is Betrayed and Arrested

Mark 14:43-52 // Matt 26:47-56 // Luke 22:47-53 // John 18:1-12

43 And immediately, even as Jesus said this, Judas, one of the twelve disciples, arrived with a crowd of men armed with swords and clubs. They had been sent by the leading priests, the teachers of religious law, and the elders. 44 The traitor, Judas, had given them a prearranged signal: "You will know which one to arrest when I greet him with a kiss. Then you can take him away under guard." 45 As soon as they arrived, Judas walked up to Jesus. "Rabbi!" he exclaimed, and gave him the kiss.

46 Then the others grabbed Jesus and arrested him. 47 But one of the men with Jesus pulled out his sword and struck the high priest's slave, slashing off his ear.

48 Jesus asked them, "Am I some dangerous revolutionary, that you come with swords and clubs to arrest me? 49 Why didn't you arrest me in the Temple? I was there among you teaching every day. But these things are happening to fulfill what the Scriptures say about me."

50 Then all his disciples deserted him and ran away. 51 One young man following behind was clothed only in a long linen shirt. When the mob tried to grab him, 52 he slipped out of his shirt and ran away naked.

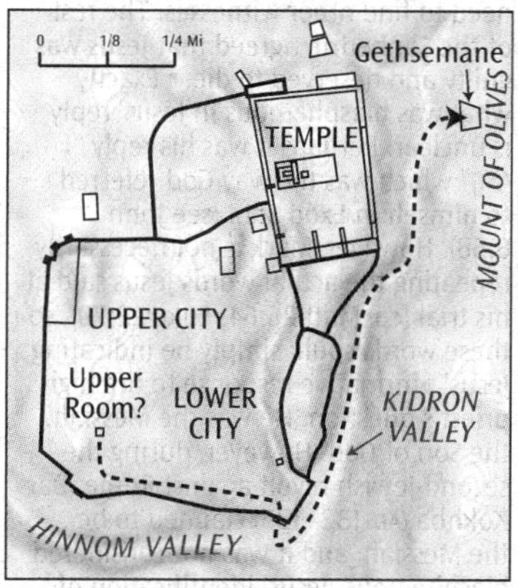

◂ **The Last Supper and Gethsemane (Mark 14:12-42; Matt 26:17-56; Luke 22:7-46; John 13:1-38; 18:1-11).** Knowing the time for his death was drawing near, Jesus shared a final Passover meal with his disciples in an Upper Room in Jerusalem (14:12-25). After the meal, Jesus and his disciples went out to the Garden of Gethsemane on the Mount of Olives, where Judas betrayed him (14:26-52).

addressed God as *Abba,* which is an Aramaic term for *Father* and indicates their intimate relationship (see Rom 8:15; Gal 4:6). • ***Please take this cup . . . from me:*** In faith, Jesus expressed his own feelings and desires to the Father. It was not only the physical agony of crucifixion that terrified him, but also the unique death that he would experience. He who knew no sin would experience the wrath of God against sin (15:34; 2 Cor 5:21; Gal 3:13). • ***Yet I want your will to be done, not mine:*** Jesus' submission to the Father's will is a model for his followers.

14:37-38 ***are you asleep?*** The question was a rebuke, for Jesus knew that Peter had been sleeping. • Though ***the spirit is willing*** to avoid ***temptation*** (see Rom 7:18, 22-23), ***the body*** (literally *the flesh,* which denotes the general weakness and vulnerability of humanity) ***is weak.***

14:41-42 The content of Jesus' prayer was probably the same as before (see 14:35-36, 39). The ***third*** failure of Peter, James, and John to watch and pray recalls Jesus' prediction that Peter would deny him three times (14:30, 66-72). • The words ***sleep*** and ***have your rest*** can be interpreted as a command, as in the NLT. Others take it as an exclamation ("You are sleeping and resting!"). Still others take it as a rhetorical question ("Are you sleeping and resting?"). • ***the time*** (literally *hour*) ***has come:*** The passion of Jesus had begun, the hour for pouring out the blood of the sacrificial lamb (14:24). This statement coincided with the arrival of Judas and the armed crowd seeking to seize Jesus. Jesus was ***betrayed into the hands of sinners*** for whom he willingly went to the cross (2:17; 10:45; 14:21). • ***Up, let's be going:*** Jesus accepted the cup God had given him. He went out to defeat his enemies by dying for them.

14:43 ***Judas***'s treachery in Jesus' arrest is heightened by the reference to him as ***one of the twelve disciples.*** Having agreed with the leading priests to betray Jesus at the right time and place (14:10-11), he led an armed group to seize Jesus secretly at night apart from the people (14:1-2). Although they wanted to avoid a conflict, the ***crowd*** was large enough to quell any resistance by Jesus or his followers (cp. Luke 22:52; John 18:3).

14:44-45 Gethsemane was dark, and Jesus was personally unknown to most of the crowd sent to seize him (see John 18:7-8), so Judas had given a sign by which he would identify Jesus. Judas addressed Jesus as ***Rabbi*** and greeted him ***with a kiss,*** a common form of greeting (1 Sam 10:1; 2 Sam 19:39; Luke 7:45).

14:47 ***One of the men with Jesus*** (Peter, see John 18:10) attempted a hurried defense by ***slashing off*** the ***ear*** of ***the high priest's slave*** (see Luke 22:50-51).

14:49 ***But*** everything was taking place ***to fulfill what the Scriptures say about*** Jesus. Mark thus reassured his readers that these events were part of God's divine plan. See Isa 53:7-9.

14:50 As Jesus had predicted just hours before (14:27-31), ***all his disciples deserted him.***

14:51-52 The account of Jesus' arrest ends with this comment about an unnamed ***young man.*** There does not seem to be any theological reason for Mark to record this incident. The older explanation, that it is an autobiographical detail about Mark, is as good as any.

Jesus' Trial before the Jewish High Council
Mark 14:53-65 // Matt 26:57-68 // Luke 22:63-71;
cp. John 18:19-24

53They took Jesus to the high priest's home
where the leading priests, the elders, and
the teachers of religious law had gathered.
54Meanwhile, Peter followed him at a distance and went right into the high priest's
courtyard. There he sat with the guards,
warming himself by the fire.

55Inside, the leading priests and the
entire high council were trying to find evidence against Jesus, so they could put him
to death. But they couldn't find any. 56Many
false witnesses spoke against him, but they
contradicted each other. 57Finally, some
men stood up and gave this false testimony:
58"We heard him say, 'I will destroy this
Temple made with human hands, and in
three days I will build another, made without human hands.' " 59But even then they
didn't get their stories straight!

60Then the high priest stood up before
the others and asked Jesus, "Well, aren't you
going to answer these charges? What do
you have to say for yourself?" 61But Jesus
was silent and made no reply. Then the high
priest asked him, "Are you the Messiah, the
Son of the Blessed One?"

62Jesus said, "I AM. And you will see the
Son of Man seated in the place of power at
God's right hand and coming on the clouds
of heaven."

63Then the high priest tore his clothing
to show his horror and said, "Why do we
need other witnesses? 64You have all heard
his blasphemy. What is your verdict?"

"Guilty!" they all cried. "He deserves to
die!"

65Then some of them began to spit at
him, and they blindfolded him and beat
him with their fists. "Prophesy to us," they
jeered. And the guards slapped him as they
took him away.

14:53-65
//Matt 26:57-68
//Luke 22:54-55, 63-71
//John 18:12-14, 19-24
14:54
Matt 26:3
John 18:18
14:56
Ps 35:11
Prov 6:16-19; 19:5
14:58
Mark 15:29
John 2:19
14:61
Isa 53:7
1 Pet 2:23
14:62
*Ps 110:1
*Dan 7:13
Matt 16:27; 24:30
Mark 8:38; 13:26
Acts 1:11
1 Thes 4:16
2 Thes 1:7
Rev 1:7; 22:20
14:63
Lev 10:6; 21:10
Num 14:6
14:64
Lev 24:16
John 19:7

14:53-65 The story of Jesus' trial follows immediately upon his arrest. Objections have been raised as to the historicity of the various accounts of Jesus' trial, because of differences of detail from the rules found in the Mishnah tractate *Mishnah Sanhedrin.* However, (1) the Mishnah was written around AD 200, whereas the Gospel of Mark was written in the late 60s, over 130 years earlier; (2) the rules found in *Mishnah Sanhedrin* idealize what later rabbis thought should take place in such trials and do not necessarily describe what did in fact take place; (3) it is questionable whether the Sadducees leading the Sanhedrin would have followed the Pharisaic rules found in *Mishnah Sanhedrin* (see Acts 23:6-10); (4) the rules found in *Mishnah Sanhedrin* sometimes conflict with what the Jewish historian Josephus wrote; (5) existing laws of conduct were not necessarily followed—Jesus was being tried by a kangaroo court, in which the sentence was predetermined and only the charge for carrying it out was sought (14:55); (6) if we must choose between the trial accounts found in the Gospels and *Mishnah Sanhedrin,* there is no reason to choose the reliability of *Mishnah Sanhedrin* over that of the Gospels.

14:53-54 ***The leading priests, the elders, and the teachers of religious law*** were not synonymous with the "entire high council" (14:55; 15:1), or Sanhedrin, but they made up a large part of it. Peter followed Jesus ***into the high priest's courtyard,*** where the Sanhedrin was meeting. The stage is set for Peter's denial (14:66-72).

14:55-59 The trial took place before ***the entire high council*** (Greek *the Sanhedrin*), which had seventy members and was led by the high priest. The Gospels portray a formal trial: There was a search for witnesses (14:55), eyewitness testimony (14:56-59), Jesus being placed under oath (Matt 26:63), Jesus being allowed to defend himself (14:60), the high priest tearing his robe (14:63), and the concluding verdict by the Sanhedrin (14:64). This does not mean that it was a fair trial—the decision to put Jesus to death had already been made. Evidence was not sought to determine the truth, but to obtain a guilty verdict and death sentence. • ***False witnesses*** giving ***false testimony*** misrepresented what Jesus said about the destruction and rebuilding of the Temple (see 15:29; John 2:19; Acts 6:14). Because the false witnesses ***contradicted each other,*** their testimony was unacceptable (Num 35:30; Deut 17:6; 19:15).

14:60-61 Since the false witnesses failed to agree (14:56), the high priest sought incriminating testimony from Jesus.

14:62 ***I AM:*** Or *The 'I AM' is here;* or *I am the LORD.* See Exod 3:14; cp. note on 6:49-50. The reader has known from the beginning that Jesus was the Messiah, the Son of God (1:1). This was acknowledged by demons (1:24; 3:11; 5:7), by God (1:11; 9:7), and by the disciples (8:29-30), but this is the first time that Jesus openly and publicly acknowledged that he was the Messiah. • The second part of Jesus' reply was that he would sit ***in the place of power at God's right hand*** (literally *at the right hand of the power;* see Ps 110:1), which foretold his resurrection and ascension (Luke 24:50-51; Acts 1:9-11; see Phil 2:9; Heb 1:3) and his triumphal ***coming on the clouds of heaven*** (see Dan 7:13) to judge the world. At Jesus' return, roles will be reversed, and those judging the Son of Man will be judged by him.

14:63-64 ***The high priest tore his clothing*** at Jesus' response. This was a judicial act that indicated a guilty verdict and signified that there was no need to find other witnesses. The rest of the Sanhedrin agreed that Jesus was guilty and deserved to die. • Exactly what was blasphemous in Jesus' reply is unclear. Perhaps it was his reply "I AM," which was the way God referred to himself in Exod 3:14 (see John 8:58). However, Mark is not necessarily repeating the actual words Jesus said at his trial (cp. Matt 26:64; Luke 22:70), so these words could simply be indicating Jesus' affirmative response to the high priest's question. He was the Messiah, the Son of God. However, during the second Jewish revolt against Rome, Bar Kokhba (AD 132–135) claimed to be the Messiah, and it was not considered blasphemous. Jesus' identification of himself as the Son of Man cannot have been considered blasphemous, for we have over fifty instances before Jesus' trial in which he used this title, and the charge of blasphemy was never raised. Yet it was too much for the high priest and the Sanhedrin when Jesus clearly claimed to be the Son of Man of Dan 7:13 coming in God's name to judge the world. Not to mention that during his ministry, Jesus forgave sins (2:5-7; Luke 7:48-50), claimed to be the Son of God (12:6), pronounced judgment upon the Temple (14:58), and claimed to be Lord of the Sabbath (2:28). Already convinced that Jesus should be put to death, the religious leaders now pronounced the predetermined guilty verdict (14:55).

14:65 ***spit:*** See 10:34. • ***Prophesy:*** See 6:4, 15; 8:28; 14:58. • Similar abuse would follow his trial before Pontius Pilate (15:16-20).

14:65
Isa 50:6; 53:5

14:66-72
//Matt 26:69-75
//Luke 22:56-62
//John 18:15-18, 25-27

14:70
Mark 1:16-18
Acts 2:7

14:72
Mark 14:30

15:1
Matt 27:1
Luke 23:1
John 18:28

15:2-15
//Matt 27:11-14
//Luke 23:2-3, 18-25
//John 18:29–19:16

15:5
Isa 53:7
Mark 14:60-61
Luke 23:9

15:11
Acts 3:14

Peter Denies Jesus

Mark 14:66-72 // Matt 26:69-75 // Luke 22:54-62 // John 18:15-18, 25-27

66 Meanwhile, Peter was in the courtyard below. One of the servant girls who worked for the high priest came by 67 and noticed Peter warming himself at the fire. She looked at him closely and said, "You were one of those with Jesus of Nazareth."

68 But Peter denied it. "I don't know what you're talking about," he said, and he went out into the entryway. Just then, a rooster crowed.

69 When the servant girl saw him standing there, she began telling the others, "This man is definitely one of them!" 70 But Peter denied it again.

A little later some of the other bystanders confronted Peter and said, "You must be one of them, because you are a Galilean."

71 Peter swore, "A curse on me if I'm lying—I don't know this man you're talking about!" 72 And immediately the rooster crowed the second time.

Suddenly, Jesus' words flashed through Peter's mind: "Before the rooster crows twice, you will deny three times that you even know me." And he broke down and wept.

Jesus' Trial before Pilate

Mark 15:1-5 // Matt 27:1-2, 11-14 // Luke 23:1-5 // John 18:28-38a

15 Very early in the morning the leading priests, the elders, and the teachers of religious law—the entire high council—met to discuss their next step. They bound Jesus, led him away, and took him to Pilate, the Roman governor.

2 Pilate asked Jesus, "Are you the king of the Jews?"

Jesus replied, "You have said it."

3 Then the leading priests kept accusing him of many crimes, 4 and Pilate asked him, "Aren't you going to answer them? What about all these charges they are bringing against you?" 5 But Jesus said nothing, much to Pilate's surprise.

Jesus Is Sentenced to Death

Mark 15:6-15 // Matt 27:15-26 // Luke 23:13-25 // John 18:38b–19:16

6 Now it was the governor's custom each year during the Passover celebration to release one prisoner—anyone the people requested. 7 One of the prisoners at that time was Barabbas, a revolutionary who had committed murder in an uprising. 8 The crowd went to Pilate and asked him to release a prisoner as usual.

9 "Would you like me to release to you this 'King of the Jews'?" Pilate asked. 10 (For he realized by now that the leading priests had arrested Jesus out of envy.) 11 But at this point the leading priests stirred up the crowd to demand the release of Barabbas instead of Jesus. 12 Pilate asked them, "Then what should I do with this man you call the king of the Jews?"

13 They shouted back, "Crucify him!"

14 "Why?" Pilate demanded. "What crime has he committed?"

But the mob roared even louder, "Crucify him!"

14:66-72 Peter's predicted denials (see 14:30), occurred during Jesus' trial.

14:67 The title ***Jesus of Nazareth*** (or *Jesus the Nazarene*) might have been contemptuous, for Judeans held a low view of Galileans (John 1:46; 7:41, 52).

14:68 ***Peter denied*** that he knew Jesus. To escape further questions, he left the courtyard and went to ***the entryway.*** • Some manuscripts do not include ***Just then, a rooster crowed;*** it might be a later scribal addition to the text of Mark.

14:69-70 The ***servant girl*** repeated her accusation to ***other bystanders.*** The others thought Peter was Jesus' follower because he was ***a Galilean*** (see Matt 26:73; cp. Acts 2:7).

14:71 ***Peter swore:*** He took an oath that his denial was true.

14:72 Upon Peter's third denial, ***the rooster crowed the second time*** and Jesus' prediction was fulfilled (14:30). While Jesus stood boldly before the Sanhedrin, Peter quailed before those with little power, cursed Jesus, and swore that he did not know him. Recalling Jesus' words, Peter ***wept.***

15:1-15 Following the story of Peter's denial, Mark turns back to Jesus and what happened at his trial. Pilate's wavering under pressure fits what is known of him from other sources.

15:1 ***Very early in the morning:*** Roman trials usually began at dawn. It is not clear whether this was a second meeting of ***the entire high council*** (Greek *the Sanhedrin*), or whether the account refers back to the decision of the council in 14:63-64 and resumes at this point. • Since the high council lacked authority to institute capital punishment (John 18:31), they had to take Jesus to ***Pilate, the Roman governor*** of Judea from AD 26–36. Pilate's normal residence was on the coast at Caesarea, but he stayed in Jerusalem during Passover, when Israel's celebration of the Exodus raised hopes of deliverance from Roman rule.

15:2 The term ***king of the Jews*** is the Gentile equivalent of the Jewish title, "King of Israel" (15:32). • ***You have said it:*** Jesus' reply to Pilate's question is found in all four Gospels; Jesus clearly understood himself to be a king (10:37-38; 11:9-10; 12:35-37), and Pilate eventually crucified him on this charge (15:26), although Pilate understood that Jesus was not a political threat (John 18:33-39).

15:3-5 Pilate sought a self-defense from Jesus concerning the charges.

15:6-8 The ***custom*** described in 15:6-8 is not known outside of the Gospels, but all four Gospels refer to it (Matt 27:15-21; Luke 23:18-25; John 18:37-40); in many instances prisoners in the ancient world were released on special holidays. • ***Barabbas:*** See also Matt 27:16-17; Luke 23:19. • ***who had committed murder in an uprising:*** Pilate's willingness to release Barabbas (15:15) probably indicates that he had not killed Roman citizens or soldiers.

15:9-14 Pilate apparently hoped to release Jesus, but the crowd was ***stirred up*** beyond discussion.

15 So to pacify the crowd, Pilate released
Barabbas to them. He ordered Jesus flogged
with a lead-tipped whip, then turned him
over to the Roman soldiers to be crucified.

The Soldiers Mock Jesus
Mark 15:16-20 // Matt 27:27-31 // John 19:1-3

16 The soldiers took Jesus into the courtyard
of the governor's headquarters (called the
Praetorium) and called out the entire regiment. 17 They dressed him in a purple robe,
and they wove thorn branches into a crown
and put it on his head. 18 Then they saluted
him and taunted, "Hail! King of the Jews!"
19 And they struck him on the head with a
reed stick, spit on him, and dropped to their
knees in mock worship. 20 When they were
finally tired of mocking him, they took off
the purple robe and put his own clothes on
him again. Then they led him away to be
crucified.

The Crucifixion
Mark 15:21-28 // Matt 27:32-38 // Luke 23:26-34 // John 19:17-24
Mark 15:29-32 // Matt 27:39-44 // Luke 23:35-43

21 A passerby named Simon, who was from
Cyrene, was coming in from the countryside just then, and the soldiers forced him
to carry Jesus' cross. (Simon was the father of Alexander and Rufus.) 22 And they
brought Jesus to a place called Golgotha
(which means "Place of the Skull"). 23 They
offered him wine drugged with myrrh, but
he refused it.
24 Then the soldiers nailed him to the cross.
They divided his clothes and threw dice to
decide who would get each piece. 25 It was
nine o'clock in the morning when they crucified him. 26 A sign announced the charge
against him. It read, "The King of the Jews."
27 Two revolutionaries were crucified with
him, one on his right and one on his left.
29 The people passing by shouted abuse,
shaking their heads in mockery. "Ha! Look
at you now!" they yelled at him. "You said
you were going to destroy the Temple and
rebuild it in three days. 30 Well then, save
yourself and come down from the cross!"
31 The leading priests and teachers of religious law also mocked Jesus. "He saved
others," they scoffed, "but he can't save himself! 32 Let this Messiah, this King of Israel,
come down from the cross so we can see it

15:15 Isa 53:5-6
15:16-20 //Matt 27:27-31 //John 19:2-3
15:19 Isa 50:6
15:21-32 //Matt 27:32-44 //Luke 23:26-43 //John 19:17-27
15:23 Ps 69:21
15:24 *Ps 22:18
15:25 John 19:14
15:29 Ps 22:7; 109:2 Mark 14:58 John 2:19
15:32 Zeph 3:15

15:15 ***to pacify the crowd:*** To protect his job, Pilate ordered a completely innocent man to be crucified. • ***He ordered Jesus flogged:*** Flogging was preliminary to crucifixion. It was done with leather thongs tipped with metal, stone, or bone. This laceration of the flesh could itself bring death. Jesus' prediction in 10:34 was now being fulfilled.

15:16-41 The crucifixion account is one of the most historically certain accounts of ancient history. Only the most naive would credit the early church with creating a story in which the object of their faith was crucified, for this story was and still is an offense to Jews and absurd nonsense to Gentiles (1 Cor 1:23).

15:16 The ***entire regiment*** (literally *cohort,* one-tenth of a legion) was about 600 men. Those called out were probably all the soldiers currently on duty in the ***Praetorium***.

15:17 ***a purple robe:*** Purple cloth, made with an expensive dye, was worn by royalty and other wealthy individuals (Luke 16:19; *1 Maccabees* 10:20, 62; 11:58). This robe may have been a centurion's out-of-service robe.

15:18 ***King of the Jews:*** The formal charge (15:2) Jesus' conviction (15:26).

15:21-22 After they left the walled city of Jerusalem, Jesus' strength apparently failed. The Roman soldiers forced ***Simon . . . from Cyrene*** in northern Africa ***to carry Jesus' cross*** (cp. Matt 5:41). Normally, a crucifixion victim was forced to carry the horizontal crossbeam (the *patibulum*) of his own cross to the place of execution. The vertical post (the *staticulum*) was sometimes left permanently in the ground as a warning and deterrent (like a hangman's scaffold in a public square). • Simon was ***the father of Alexander and Rufus,*** who were probably known to Mark's readers (cp. Rom 16:13). • ***Golgotha*** is Aramaic, meaning ***Place of the Skull***. In the Latin Vulgate, "skull" is *calvariae* ("Calvary"). In Jesus' day, Golgotha lay outside the walled city of Jerusalem (John 19:20; see Matt 27:32; Heb 13:12). When Herod Antipas later enlarged the city with the "third wall," Golgotha was enclosed.

15:23 Whether Jesus was ***offered*** a drink of ***wine drugged with myrrh*** in kindness (Prov 31:6) or in mockery is uncertain. Jesus ***refused*** the drink, for he had committed himself to drinking the cup that God had given him (10:38-39; 14:36). • Myrrh has been used since before Jesus' time to treat wounds and infections and for digestive ailments.

15:24 Crucifixion goes back to the Medes and Persians in the 600s BC. It spread to the eastern Mediterranean world in the 300s BC through Alexander the Great and became the dominant form of capital punishment in the Roman empire until AD 337, when it was banned by Constantine. It was slow, shameful, and torturous. The victim sometimes lived for days, and crows and dogs would feed on the victims even before they died. A person could be fixed to the cross by ropes or, as with Jesus (Luke 24:39; John 20:25, 27; see Col 2:14), by nails between the bones of the victim's wrists. To prevent premature death by asphyxiation, a footrest or a seat was often placed on the vertical beam. • All four Gospels report that the soldiers ***divided his clothes*** among themselves. • ***threw dice:*** Literally *cast lots.* See Ps 22:18.

15:25 Mark records Jesus' crucifixion as occurring at the third hour, or ***nine o'clock in the morning***. John 19:14 gives the time as around the sixth hour, or noon. These are rough estimates of time, and events in the later morning were typically described as occurring around either the third (Matt 20:3; Acts 2:15) or sixth hour (15:33; Matt 20:5; 27:45; Luke 23:44; John 4:6; 19:14; Acts 10:9).

15:26 Although the title ***King of the Jews*** was intended to mock Jesus, it was accurate and meaningful for Mark.

15:27 ***Two revolutionaries:*** Or *Two criminals.* Jesus, the most important victim, was placed in the center. • Some manuscripts add v 28, *And the Scripture was fulfilled that said, "He was counted among those who were rebels."* See Isa 53:12; also cp. Luke 22:37.

15:29-32 Jesus was being mocked and abused by the people passing by, the religious leaders, and the revolutionaries. • ***The people passing by shouted abuse*** (literally *blasphemed*), wagged their heads in contempt (see Lam 2:15),

15:33-41
//Matt 27:45-56
//Luke 23:44-49
//John 19:28-30
15:34
*Ps 22:1
15:36
Ps 69:21

and believe him!" Even the men who were
crucified with Jesus ridiculed him.

The Death of Jesus
Mark 15:33-41 // Matt 27:45-56 // Luke 23:44-49 //
John 19:28-30

33 At noon, darkness fell across the whole
land until three o'clock. 34 Then at three
o'clock Jesus called out with a loud voice,
"Eloi, Eloi, lema sabachthani?" which means
"My God, my God, why have you abandoned
me?"
35 Some of the bystanders misunderstood
and thought he was calling for the prophet Elijah. 36 One of them ran and filled a
sponge with sour wine, holding it up to him
on a reed stick so he could drink. "Wait!" he
said. "Let's see whether Elijah comes to take
him down!"
37 Then Jesus uttered another loud cry

PONTIUS PILATE (15:1-15, 43-45)

Matt 27:2, 11-26, 57-58, 62-65
Luke 3:1; 13:1; 23:1-25, 52
John 18:28–19:16, 19-22, 31, 38
Acts 3:13; 4:27; 13:28
1 Tim 6:13

Pontius Pilate was the Roman governor of Judea from AD 26 to 36, including the time of Jesus' death in AD 30 or 33. Pilate gave the official order for Jesus to be crucified.

As the governor of Judea, Pilate was in control of all the Roman occupation forces, he appointed the Jewish high priests, and was in control of the Temple and its funds. He was the only one who had the authority to execute criminals (see John 18:31), so the Jewish authorities were compelled to bring charges before Pilate in order to see Jesus executed (15:1).

Pilate was sometimes abusive as governor. He appropriated Temple funds to construct a thirty-five-mile aqueduct for Jerusalem, and provoked a major protest. In response, Pilate had soldiers infiltrate the crowds in disguise and beat the offenders to death with clubs (Josephus, *War* 2.9.4; *Antiquities* 18.3.2). Another time, Pilate murdered some Galileans "as they were offering sacrifices at the Temple" (Luke 13:1); this incident might have estranged him from Herod Antipas (see "Herod Antipas" at 6:14-29, p. 1659). Pilate also tried to bring images of Caesar into Jerusalem for worship. Later (AD 36), Pilate slaughtered pilgrims who followed a Samaritan false prophet, an event that led to his dismissal by Tiberius in the same year.

Each Gospel records Pilate's role in the death of Jesus (15:1; Matt 27:2; Luke 23:1; John 18:29; see also Acts 3:13; 4:27; 13:28; 1 Tim 6:13). After interrogating Jesus, he was convinced that Jesus had done nothing deserving of death, so he tried to return the case to the Jewish authorities. When they resisted, he tried to pass Jesus to Herod Antipas for judgment—but he, too, refused the case. Pilate finally tried appealing to a traditional Roman custom of freeing a prisoner on Passover. Meanwhile, his wife had been deeply troubled by a dream about "that innocent man" (Matt 27:19). But the clamor of the crowd became threatening, and the Jewish leaders began insinuating that Pilate was not taking Jesus' threat to Rome seriously. Pilate yielded to Jewish pressure. He ordered that Jesus be whipped and then crucified, with the title "King of the Jews" posted on a sign over his head—but only after strenuously objecting and declaring himself to be innocent of the guilt of such an unjust death (15:2-15; Matt 27:11-26; Luke 23:2-25; John 18:29–19:22). Pilate's sympathy for Jesus stands as a testimony that Jesus posed no threat to the Roman government but only to the Jewish leadership.

Shortly after Jesus' death, Pilate gave special permission to Joseph of Arimathea to take the body of Jesus from the cross and bury it (15:42-46; Matt 27:57-61; Luke 23:50-53; John 19:38-42). He also gave permission to the Jewish authorities to seal the tomb, to make sure no one would steal the body or make false claims about Jesus coming back to life (Matt 27:62-65).

Little is known of Pilate after his dismissal in AD 36; Eusebius reports that Pilate committed suicide during the reign of Caligula, AD 37–41 (Eusebius, *Church History* 2.7).

and ridiculed his claim that he would destroy the Temple (see 14:58).

15:32 The two ***men who were crucified with Jesus*** also mocked him. One might expect compassion from those suffering a similar cruel fate (cp. Luke 23:39-43).

15:33 ***At noon*** (literally *the sixth hour*) darkness came over the whole land ***until three o'clock*** (literally *the ninth hour*). The ***whole land*** probably means all of Judah. The ***darkness*** was both literal and symbolic—it revealed the sinister nature of what was happening and was a taste of the judgment that Jesus predicted would come upon Israel (see 13:1-31; 14:58; 15:29).

15:34 ***Eloi, Eloi . . . why have you abandoned me:*** Jesus' loud cry is reported in its original Aramaic and then translated for Greek readers. • ***"My God, my God, why have you abandoned me?"*** Jesus quotes Ps 22:1. This saying is best interpreted in light of 14:27; Ps 22:1-31; Isa 53:10; 2 Cor 5:21; and Gal 3:13. Jesus' divine purpose in becoming a ransom for many (10:45) was now being realized.

15:35-36 The Aramaic term *Eloi* and its Hebrew equivalent *Eli* (Matt 27:46) sound sufficiently close to "Elijah" that some bystanders thought that Jesus was calling out for ***the prophet Elijah*** to rescue him (see Mal 4:5).

15:37 The death of Jesus, like the crucifixion, is told with stark simplicity.

and breathed his last. 38And the curtain in
the sanctuary of the Temple was torn in two,
from top to bottom.
39When the Roman officer who stood facing him saw how he had died, he exclaimed,
"This man truly was the Son of God!"
40Some women were there, watching from
a distance, including Mary Magdalene, Mary
(the mother of James the younger and of
Joseph), and Salome. 41They had been followers of Jesus and had cared for him while he
was in Galilee. Many other women who had
come with him to Jerusalem were also there.

The Burial of Jesus
Mark 15:42-47 // Matt 27:57-61 // Luke 23:50-56 // John 19:38-42

42This all happened on Friday, the day of
preparation, the day before the Sabbath. As
evening approached, 43Joseph of Arimathea
took a risk and went to Pilate and asked for
Jesus' body. (Joseph was an honored member of the high council, and he was waiting
for the Kingdom of God to come.) 44Pilate
couldn't believe that Jesus was already dead,
so he called for the Roman officer and asked
if he had died yet. 45The officer confirmed
that Jesus was dead, so Pilate told Joseph
he could have the body. 46Joseph bought
a long sheet of linen cloth. Then he took
Jesus' body down from the cross, wrapped
it in the cloth, and laid it in a tomb that had
been carved out of the [b]rock. Then he rolled
a stone in front of the entrance. 47Mary Magdalene and Mary the mother of Joseph saw
where Jesus' body was laid.

Jesus Is Raised from the Dead
Mark 16:1-8 // Matt 28:1-8a // Luke 24:1-12 // John 20:1-10

16 Saturday evening, when the Sabbath ended, Mary Magdalene, Mary
the mother of James, and Salome went out
and purchased burial spices so they could
anoint Jesus' body. 2Very early on Sunday
morning, just at sunrise, they went to the
tomb. 3On the way they were asking each
other, "Who will roll away the stone for us
from the entrance to the tomb?" 4But as
they arrived, they looked up and saw that
the stone, which was very large, had already
been rolled aside.
5When they entered the tomb, they saw
a young man clothed in a white robe sitting
on the right side. The women were shocked,
6but the angel said, "Don't be alarmed. You
are looking for Jesus of Nazareth, who was
crucified. He isn't here! He is risen from the
dead! Look, this is where they laid his body.
7Now go and tell his disciples, including
Peter, that Jesus is going ahead of you to Galilee. You will see him there, just as he told
you before he died."

15:38
Exod 26:31-33
Heb 10:19-20

15:40-41
Luke 8:2-3

15:42-47
//Matt 27:57-61
//Luke 23:50-56
//John 19:38-42

15:43
Luke 2:25, 38

15:46
Acts 13:29
[b]*petra* (4073)
‣ Luke 6:48

16:1-8
//Matt 28:1-8
//Luke 24:1-10
//John 20:1-8

16:1
Luke 23:56
John 19:39-40

16:3
Mark 15:46

16:5
John 20:12
Acts 1:10; 10:30

16:6
Acts 2:23-32
Rom 1:3-4
1 Cor 15:4-12, 20
Rev 1:18

16:7
Matt 26:32
Mark 14:28
John 21:1

15:38 ***The curtain*** that ***was torn in two*** might have been the one that separated the sanctuary from the courtyard (a magnificent tapestry eighty feet tall) or the one that separated the Most Holy Place from the rest of the sanctuary. If it was the former, the tearing (like the darkness, 15:33) was visible to people; it would indicate that Jesus' prediction of the sanctuary's destruction (14:58; 15:29) was being fulfilled spiritually (see Rom 9–11) but awaited physical fulfillment in AD 70. If it was the interior curtain that tore, it was probably a sign that, just as the heavens were split for Jesus to reveal his direct access to God (see note on 1:10), his death now extended this access to his followers (see Heb 6:19-20; 9:3-14; 10:19-20).

15:39 ***the Roman officer:*** Literally *the centurion;* similarly in 15:44-45. The Latin word *centurion* refers to an officer in charge of 100 men. • ***who stood facing him:*** Some manuscripts add *heard his cry and.* • Jesus as ***the Son of God*** was announced by God (1:11; 9:7), by demons (1:24, 34; 3:11; 5:7), by Mark (1:1), by Jesus himself (12:6; 13:32; 14:61-62), and now by a Gentile officer.

15:40-41 These ***women*** had supplied some of Jesus' economic needs (see Luke 8:2-3). They were also present at the burial (15:47) and the empty tomb (16:1-8) and would be the first witnesses of Jesus' resurrection. • ***Mary Magdalene,*** from the village of Magdala near the shore of the Sea of Galilee, was a key figure in the resurrection accounts (16:1, 9; Matt 28:1; Luke 24:10; John 20:1, 11-18). • ***Mary (the mother of James the younger):*** This James might have been James the son of Alphaeus (3:18). See "Women Named Mary" at Matt 27:55-56, p. 1640. • ***Salome*** is mentioned only here and in 16:1. • ***Joseph:*** Greek *Joses;* also in 15:47. See Matt 27:56.

15:42 ***This all happened on Friday, the day of preparation:*** Literally *It was the day of preparation.*

15:43-45 ***Joseph of Arimathea*** (possibly from the village of Ramathaim, twenty miles northwest of Jerusalem) was ***an honored member of the high council*** (Greek *the Sanhedrin*) and a secret disciple of Jesus who ***was waiting for the Kingdom of God to come*** (see Matt 27:57; Luke 23:50-51; John 19:38). He courageously requested the body of Jesus from Pilate for burial. Since he was a member of the high council and was not known to be Jesus' disciple, it served Rome's purposes to grant his request: It would satisfy Jewish concerns about leaving the dead exposed after sunset (Deut 21:22-23), and Jesus' disciples would not receive the body.

15:46 ***Joseph*** prepared ***Jesus' body*** for burial and laid it in his own ***tomb*** (see Matt 27:60; see illustration, p. 1813).

16:1 At the end of the Sabbath at sunset, the shops reopened and the women were able to buy ***burial spices*** to anoint Jesus' body (16:1). Their purpose was not to embalm the body, but to alleviate the stench that a decaying body would create. • The women were clearly not anticipating Jesus' resurrection. Even the empty tomb would fail to convince them that Jesus had been raised from the dead (John 20:2, 11-15).

16:2 ***on Sunday morning:*** Literally *on the first day of the week;* also in 16:9.

16:3-4 The women wondered how the large ***stone*** sealing ***the tomb*** could be removed (see illustration, p. 1813). God had ***already*** rolled the stone away to let the women and disciples in.

16:6 ***Jesus of Nazareth:*** Or *Jesus the Nazarene.*

16:7 The angel's message for the disciples repeated Jesus' prediction and promise (14:28). The disciples' desertion and denial would be forgiven and their apostolic commission restored.

16:9-11
Matt 28:1-10
John 20:11-18

16:12-13
Luke 24:13-35

16:14-18
Matt 28:16-20
Luke 24:36-49
John 20:19-23
Acts 1:6-8

16:15
Col 1:23

16:16
Acts 2:38; 16:31, 33
[c]*baptizō* (0907)
‣ Acts 2:38

16:17
Acts 2:4, 11; 8:7; 10:46; 16:18; 19:6
[d]*sēmeion* (4592)
‣ Acts 4:16
[e]*daimonion* (1140)
‣ Luke 4:33
[f]*glōssa* (1100)
‣ Acts 2:4

16:18
Luke 10:19
Acts 28:3-6

16:19-20
Luke 24:50-53
Acts 1:9-11

16:19
Ps 110:1
Rom 8:34
Col 3:1
Heb 1:3

8The women fled from the tomb, trembling and bewildered, and they said
nothing to anyone because they were too
frightened.

[*Shorter Ending of Mark*]

Then they briefly reported all this to Peter and his companions. Afterward Jesus himself sent them out from east to west with the sacred and unfailing message of salvation that gives eternal life. Amen.

[*Longer Ending of Mark*]

Mark 16:9-11; cp. Matt 28:8-10; John 20:11-18
Mark 16:12-13; cp. Luke 24:13-34
Mark 16:14-18; cp. Matt 28:16-20

9After Jesus rose from the dead early on
Sunday morning, the first person who saw
him was Mary Magdalene, the woman from
whom he had cast out seven demons. 10She
went to the disciples, who were grieving
and weeping, and told them what had happened. 11But when she told them that Jesus
was alive and she had seen him, they didn't
believe her.
12Afterward he appeared in a different
form to two of his followers who were walking from Jerusalem into the country. 13They
rushed back to tell the others, but no one
believed them.
14Still later he appeared to the eleven disciples as they were eating together. He rebuked
them for their stubborn unbelief because
they refused to believe those who had seen
him after he had been raised from the dead.
15And then he told them, "Go into all
the world and preach the Good News to
everyone. 16Anyone who believes and is
[c]baptized will be saved. But anyone who refuses to believe will be condemned. 17These
miraculous [d]signs will accompany those
who believe: They will cast out [e]demons in
my name, and they will speak in new [f]lan-
guages. 18They will be able to handle snakes
with safety, and if they drink anything poisonous, it won't hurt them. They will be able
to place their hands on the sick, and they
will be healed."

Mark 16:19-20 // Luke 24:50-53 // Acts 1:6-11

19When the Lord Jesus had finished talking with them, he was taken up into heaven
and sat down in the place of honor at God's
right hand. 20And the disciples went everywhere and preached, and the Lord worked
through them, confirming what they said
by many miraculous signs.

16:8 The account ends with the women fleeing the tomb in bewilderment. • ***said nothing to anyone:*** This can be understood positively (they were not distracted from their commission to tell the disciples, 16:7; cp. Luke 10:4; 2 Kgs 4:29) or negatively (they failed to deliver the message). Cp. Luke 24:5-11; John 20:1-2, 18. • The most reliable early manuscripts of the Gospel of Mark end at v 8. Other manuscripts include various endings to the Gospel. A few include both the "shorter ending" and the "longer ending." The majority of manuscripts include the "longer ending" immediately after v 8.

16:9-20 Nearly all scholars agree that Mark did not write the "shorter" and "longer" endings. There are clear differences in their style, vocabulary, and theology. Also, the best two available Greek manuscripts (*Codex Sinaiticus* and *Codex Vaticanus*) lack these endings. However, there is reason to doubt that Mark intended to end his Gospel at 16:8: (1) Mark emphasizes the fulfillment of Jesus' predictions throughout his Gospel, and if the Gospel ended with 16:8, there would be no reference to the resurrection appearance(s) of Jesus; (2) all the other Gospels contain accounts of Jesus' appearances to the women and the disciples; (3) early readers of Mark evidently did not think the book could have ended with 16:8, because they wrote these endings; (4) there is no convincing explanation as to why Mark would have wanted to end his Gospel at 16:8 (all such explanations sound like modern existential literary interpretations that revel in paradox, very unlike the way a first-century Christian author would have thought); (5) it is strange for a Gospel to begin with a bold proclamation that Jesus is the Messiah (1:1) and end with the women's fear; (6) it would be unique for an ancient Greek book to end with *gar* ("because") as the last word—no other example of this has been found; and (7) 16:7 raises the expectation that the disciples will meet Jesus in Galilee—if 16:8 was the original ending of Mark, it is the only unfulfilled prediction in the Gospel. Many scholars conclude that the original ending was accidentally torn off and lost, or was never finished.

16:14 One early manuscript adds: *And they excused themselves, saying, "This age of lawlessness and unbelief is under Satan, who does not permit God's truth and power to conquer the evil [unclean] spirits. Therefore, reveal your justice now." This is what they said to Christ. And Christ replied to them, "The period of years of Satan's power has been fulfilled, but other dreadful things will happen soon. And I was handed over to death for those who have sinned, so that they may return to the truth and sin no more, and so they may inherit the spiritual, incorruptible, and righteous glory in heaven."*

16:17 Or *new tongues;* some manuscripts do not include *new.*

THE GOSPEL ACCORDING TO

LUKE

Luke describes the coming of Jesus as good news for the entire world—for people of every race, age, gender, ethnic group, and social position. With John the Baptist as his prophetic forerunner, Jesus came as the Son of God and as the Messiah, the King descended from David who defeats Satan and brings salvation and healing. As Jesus served and taught the people and proclaimed good news, the religious leaders opposed him. Jesus went to Jerusalem as the suffering servant, proclaimed judgment on the nation before being executed as a criminal, then rose from the dead to fulfill God's plan and launch his Spirit-driven mission to all the world. The risen Jesus, the Jewish Messiah, is the Savior of the whole world.

SETTING

Luke was written in the context of the growing conflict between the church and the synagogue in the mid-to-late first century AD. The early church did not view itself as a new religion, but as the fulfillment and completion of Judaism. The promises made to the Jews in the Hebrew Scriptures (the OT) were fulfilled through the life, death, and resurrection of Jesus Christ, and continued to be fulfilled through the missionary movement of the early church. During this time, more and more Gentiles (non-Jews) came into the church, while many Jews rejected the Good News. Division grew between those who believed that Jesus was the Messiah and those that denied this claim.

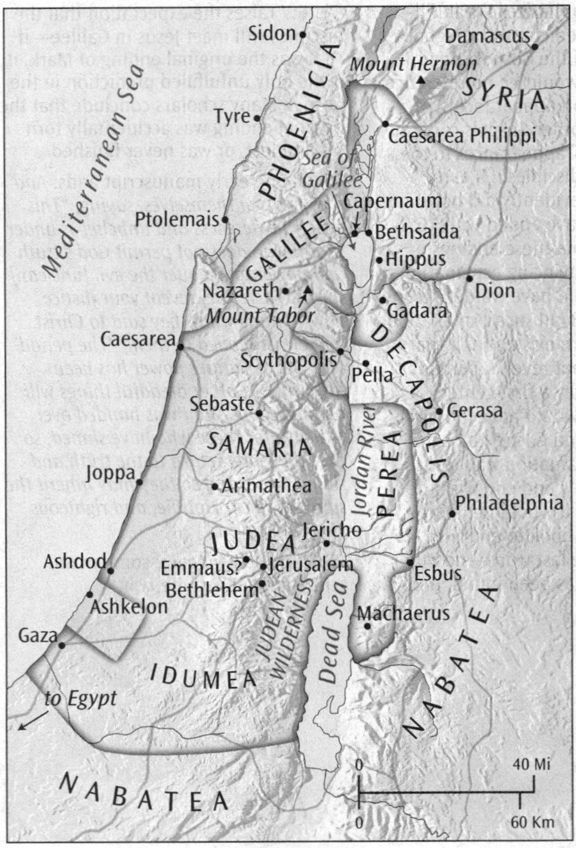

◀ **Key Places in the Gospel of Luke.** Luke begins with an account of John the Baptist's birth in the hill country of JUDEA (1:5-25, 39-66) and of Jesus' birth in BETHLEHEM (1:26-38; 2:1-40). Then, the narrative describes John's ministry in the wilderness of Judea and around the JORDAN RIVER (3:1-20), Jesus' baptism and temptation in the same region (3:21–4:13), his ministry in GALILEE (4:14–9:50), his journey to JERUSALEM (9:51–19:44; see map, p. 1747), the climax of Jesus' ministry in Judea (19:45–22:38), and his death and resurrection in Jerusalem (22:39–24:34). • The border on the map shows the extent of Herod the Great's kingdom, which was divided at his death in AD 4 (see map caption, p. 1572).

The pressing question in this conflict became, Who are the true people of God? Are they the church, made up of Jews and Gentiles who believe that Jesus is the Messiah? Or are they the Jews who reject Jesus as a false messiah? Luke addresses this question and demonstrates that Jesus is indeed the Messiah who calls all people, Jew and Gentile, to put their faith in him.

OUTLINE

1:1-4
Introduction

1:5–2:52
The Birth of the Savior

3:1–4:13
Preparation for the Savior's Ministry

4:14–9:50
The Ministry of the Savior in Galilee

9:51–19:27
The Savior on the Way to Jerusalem

19:28–24:53
The Climax of the Savior's Mission in Jerusalem

SUMMARY

Luke's Gospel begins with a formal prologue, written in the style of the fine Greco-Roman writers of Luke's day (1:1-4). This prologue demonstrates the author's literary skills and sets out the purpose of his work: to write a reliable historical account of the life of Jesus that would confirm the truth of the Christian message.

After this formal literary introduction, the writing style changes dramatically. Luke describes Jesus' birth (1:5–2:51) in a Jewish manner reminiscent of the Greek OT. This birth narrative clearly shows the Jewish roots of the gospel message and introduces themes that are developed in the rest of Luke and Acts.

In common with Matthew and Mark, Luke introduces Jesus' public ministry with accounts of John the Baptist (3:1-20), Jesus' baptism (3:21-22), Jesus' temptation (4:1-13), and descriptions of his ministry in and around Galilee (4:14–9:50). Jesus proclaimed the Kingdom of God, taught with authority, healed the sick, and cast out demons, demonstrating the authority of the Kingdom in his words and actions. As in Matthew and Mark, the high point of Jesus' Galilean ministry was Peter's confession that Jesus is the Messiah, followed by Jesus' explanation that the Messiah must suffer and die in Jerusalem (9:18-22). Jesus then headed toward Jerusalem to fulfill this mission (9:51–19:44). In this travel narrative—the most distinctive structural feature of Luke's Gospel—the author recounts many of Jesus' beloved stories and parables: the Good Samaritan, the Prodigal Son, the Rich Man and Lazarus, the story of Mary and Martha, and the Zacchaeus episode. The central theme of this section is God's love for the lost and Jesus' ministry to sinners, poor people, and outcasts. The theme of the entire Gospel is stated at the end of the Zacchaeus episode: "The Son of Man came to seek and save those who are lost" (19:10).

The climax of the narrative is Jesus' arrest, trial, and crucifixion (22:1–23:56). The central theme of the crucifixion is Jesus' innocence. Jesus is portrayed as the righteous suffering servant of the Lord (see Isa 52:13–53:12). At Jesus' death, the Roman officer at the foot of the cross cried out, "Surely this man was innocent" (23:47).

The narrative resolves with Jesus' resurrection (24:1-12). Luke's most

TIMELINE

37–4 BC
Herod the Great as king of Judea

about 6~4 BC
Birth of Jesus Christ

AD 18~36
Caiaphas as high priest

AD 26–36
Pontius Pilate as governor of Judea

about AD 27
John the Baptist begins his ministry

about AD 28
Jesus begins his ministry

Passover, AD 30 or 33
Jesus' crucifixion and resurrection

Pentecost, AD 30 or 33
The birth of the church in Jerusalem

AD 65~80
▸ **Luke writes the Gospel of Luke**

distinctive contribution here is the account of the disciples on the road to Emmaus (24:13-35). As he walked with two discouraged disciples who did not recognize him, Jesus taught them that his death was not a failure, but a fulfillment of OT promises. All of Scripture anticipated this great salvation event (24:25-27). The narrative ends with a brief account of the ascension (24:50-53), which is described more fully in the book of Acts (Acts 1:1-11).

Structurally, Luke follows Mark's basic outline, with a Galilean ministry followed by a journey to Jerusalem and the climax of Jesus' ministry there. The main differences are: (1) Like Matthew, Luke begins with a birth narrative, which serves as a thematic introduction to the work (chs 1–2); (2) Luke omits one major section of Mark's account of the Galilean ministry, sometime called his "great omission" (Mark 6:45–8:26); and (3) Luke expands Mark's account of the journey to Jerusalem from a single chapter (Mark 10) to ten chapters (9:51–19:44) and includes here a great deal of Jesus' teaching and his ministry to outcasts in Israel.

LUKE AS LITERATURE

Luke's Gospel must be read and interpreted alongside its companion volume, the book of Acts. Luke and Acts are two volumes of a single work written by the same author (Luke). The two are a literary and theological unity—when Luke wrote his Gospel, he already had the writing of Acts in mind. Themes introduced in the Gospel, such as the salvation of the Gentiles, reach their narrative completion in the book of Acts. Scholars refer to this single two-volume work as "Luke–Acts."

Luke's purpose in writing gives his Gospel, like the other three Gospels, a unique perspective and emphasis that can best be understood by reading Luke's Gospel as a distinct account of Christ's life. However, it can also be beneficial to compare the accounts in the different Gospels. See also the harmony of the Gospels, p. 1567.

AUTHORSHIP

Though all of the Gospels are, strictly speaking, anonymous (their authors do not name themselves), the author of Luke–Acts was Luke, a physician and sometime companion of the apostle Paul. In several first-person plural passages in Acts (the "we" sections), the author describes himself as a participant in Paul's missionary activities (Acts 16:10-17, 20:5-17, 21:1-18, 27:1–28:16). Luke was a Gentile (Col 4:11-14), and one of his central themes is that God's salvation is for Gentiles as well as for Jews.

Luke evidently came to faith in Christ through the ministry of the apostle Paul (see "Luke" at Acts 16:10, p. 1861). Even though he was not present during the earthly ministry of Jesus, he was a careful and astute historian. He drew on eyewitness accounts and on written and oral sources as he thoroughly investigated the events he reported. His purpose was to write so that "you can be certain of the truth of everything you were taught" (1:4).

OCCASION AND PLACE OF WRITING

The specific place of writing is uncertain, but Rome, Ephesus, Caesarea, and Achaia (southern Greece) have all been suggested. The date is also uncertain. The two most common theories are an earlier date,

AD 59–63, and a later date, AD 70–90. The earlier date is suggested by the ending of Acts, with Paul alive and in prison in Rome for two years (beginning about AD 60). If the Gospel was written before Acts, a date shortly before or during this imprisonment is likely (AD 59–63). A later date, after AD 70, has been proposed by those who believe that Luke used Mark's Gospel as a source and that Mark was written in the late 60s, just before the Jewish war of AD 66–70 (see Mark 13:14).

RECIPIENTS

Luke addressed his work to a man named Theophilus ("one who loves God"), most likely a patron who sponsored the expensive task of researching and writing a book of this length. Theophilus might have been a questioning unbeliever, but more likely he was a believer who desired more instruction concerning the origin of the Christian faith. The individual address is like a dedication. Luke–Acts is also intended for a larger Christian audience, one made up primarily of Gentile Christians, but with some Jewish Christians as well. These believers were seeking confirmation and assurance that God's plan of salvation was continuing, despite the rejection of Jesus by many of the Jews. Luke was affirming that the church, made up of both Jews and Gentiles who have accepted Jesus as the Messiah, represents the true people of God in the present age.

MEANING AND MESSAGE

The narrative of Luke–Acts positively affirms (1) that Jesus is the Messiah promised in the OT Scriptures; (2) that his death on the cross did not negate this claim, because the Messiah's death and resurrection were predicted in Scripture all along (24:26, 46); (3) that the mission to the Gentiles was initiated by the Spirit of God, was predicted in Scripture, and was part of God's purpose of bringing salvation to the whole world in the last days; and (4) that the Jews and Gentiles who make up the church are the people of God. The central theme of Luke's Gospel is that God's salvation, promised in the Scriptures, was fulfilled in the life, death, and resurrection of Jesus Christ.

A Historical Message. More than any other Gospel writer, Luke affirms that the story of Jesus is historical, and he assures his readers that the gospel message is authentic. He emphasizes that his account is based on reliable eyewitness testimony (1:1-4) and meticulously dates Jesus' ministry with reference to the rulers of his day (3:1-2).

Portrait of Jesus. Luke's portrait of Jesus reflects a theme of promise and fulfillment. Jesus is introduced as the promised Savior, the Messiah descended from King David. He was born in Bethlehem, the city of David, and will reign forever on David's throne (1:32-33; 2:4, 11). Jesus did not accomplish salvation through military power and conquest, but by suffering the fate of the prophets. He died as the servant of the Lord, fulfilling the promises of the OT. Through his death and resurrection, Jesus became the Savior of the world (2:11; Acts 2:36; 10:36). His servants now take this message of salvation to the ends of the earth.

Salvation for Outsiders. Luke emphasizes salvation for all who believe, especially with reference to the outsiders of Israel: the poor, sinners, despised Samaritans, women, and Gentiles.

Somehow of all the gospel writers one would have liked to meet Luke best of all, for this Gentile doctor who had the tremendous vision of the infinite sweep of the love of God must have been a lovely soul.

WILLIAM BARCLAY
The Gospel of Luke, p. 7

(1) *The poor.* The Kingdom of God brings a great reversal of fortunes. God exalts the poor and the humble, and he will humble the rich and the arrogant (1:51-55; 16:19-31). The gospel is good news for the poor and oppressed (4:18) because they most recognize their need of God (6:20-21). It is impossible for the rich to enter the Kingdom when they trust in their riches instead of in God (12:13-21; 18:18-30).

(2) *Sinners.* God's love for the lost is revealed most clearly in Jesus' association with sinners and tax collectors. He called a despised tax collector, Levi, to be his disciple. As the great physician, Jesus came to heal the "sick" (sinners), not the "healthy" (the self-righteous; 5:27-32). He commended an immoral woman who anointed his feet because she recognized God's forgiveness and loved greatly in response (7:36-50). He rebuked the Pharisees and teachers of religious law for their self-righteousness, hypocrisy, and lack of compassion. The repentant tax collector in the Temple received forgiveness, while the self-righteous Pharisee gained nothing (18:9-14). Even the chief tax collector Zacchaeus was forgiven when he repented and turned to God (19:1-10). Jesus forgave and offered a place in paradise to the repentant criminal on the cross (23:39-43). Jesus' parables express this same theme—for example, the father forgave his prodigal son when he returned to him (15:11-32). The message throughout is that the coming of God's Kingdom brings forgiveness to all who repent and believe.

(3) *Samaritans.* The Samaritans were despised outsiders, but in Luke, Jesus commends a Samaritan for his gratitude to God when he was healed of leprosy (17:11-19), and Jesus told the parable of the Good Samaritan, in which a despised Samaritan was the only true neighbor to a wounded Jew (10:29-37). God's salvation does not depend on ethnic identity or social status, but on a repentant heart and a life of love for God and others.

(4) *Women.* In first-century culture, women were viewed as inferiors, but Jesus elevated women to a position of dignity in the Kingdom of God. Luke's Gospel gives special prominence to women, and mentions thirteen of them who are not found in the other Gospels. The birth narrative is told from the perspective of women (Mary and Elizabeth). Luke alone mentions the women who financially supported Jesus (8:1-3). In his story of Mary and Martha, Mary is commended for learning as a disciple at Jesus' feet (10:38-42).

(5) *Gentiles.* The ultimate outsiders were the Gentiles, and Luke emphasizes that God's salvation extends even to them. Though arising within Israel, Jesus would be "a light to reveal God to the nations" (2:32), and "all people will see the salvation sent from God" (3:4-6; Isa 40:5). While Matthew's genealogy (Matt 1:1-17) emphasizes Jesus' Jewish ancestry by beginning with Abraham, the father of the Israelites, Luke's genealogy goes all the way back to Adam, the father of the entire human race (3:23-38). In his sermon at Nazareth, Jesus declared that God had always demonstrated grace toward the Gentiles (4:24-27). Luke's message is that God loves all people everywhere and desires that all who are lost should be found (15:1-32; 19:10).

Rejection by Many in Israel. The dark side of this inclusion of the Gentiles and other outsiders is that Jesus' message was rejected by many in Israel. At Nazareth, when he announced that God had blessed Gentiles in the past, the people rose up in anger to kill him (4:28-30).

FURTHER READING

DARRELL L. BOCK
Luke (1996)

JOEL B. GREEN
The Gospel of Luke (1997)

I. HOWARD MARSHALL
Luke: Historian and Theologian (1998)

MARK L. STRAUSS
Luke (2007)

ALLISON A. TRITES
Luke in *Cornerstone Biblical Commentary,* vol. 12 (2006)

This episode initiated the rejection of Jesus by his own people and anticipated the Jewish opposition to the church (as recounted in Acts). Jerusalem rejected its Messiah and so stood under God's judgment (13:33-35; 19:41-44), and this pattern continues in Acts. While many in Israel believed the gospel, still more rejected it. Israel was divided, and the gospel went out to the Gentiles. Luke emphasizes that this did not negate the gospel message; Israel's rejection of the gospel was predicted in the OT Scriptures and was a continuation of Israel's history of stubbornness and hard-heartedness (11:29-32, 47-51; 13:34-35; 19:41-44; 23:27-31; Acts 13:46; 28:25-28; see also Rom 9–11).

1:1-2 John 15:27; Acts 1:21-22; Heb 2:3; 2 Pet 1:16; 1 Jn 1:1-4
1:3 Acts 1:1
1:5 1 Chr 24:10; 2 Chr 31:2; Matt 2:1
1:8 1 Chr 24:19; 2 Chr 8:14
1:9 Exod 30:7

1. INTRODUCTION (1:1-4)

1 Many people have set out to write accounts about the events that have been fulfilled among us. 2They used the eyewitness reports circulating among us from the early disciples. 3Having carefully investigated everything from the beginning, I also have decided to write a careful account for you, most honorable Theophilus, 4so you can be certain of the truth of everything you were taught.

2. THE BIRTH OF THE SAVIOR (1:5–2:52)

Anticipating the Births of Jesus and John (1:5-56)

The Birth of John the Baptist Foretold

5When Herod was king of Judea, there was a Jewish priest named Zechariah. He was a member of the priestly order of Abijah, and his wife, Elizabeth, was also from the priestly line of Aaron. 6Zechariah and Elizabeth were righteous in God's eyes, careful to obey all of the Lord's commandments and regulations. 7They had no children because Elizabeth was unable to conceive, and they were both very old.

8One day Zechariah was serving God in the Temple, for his order was on duty that week. 9As was the custom of the priests, he was chosen by lot to enter the sanctuary of the Lord and burn incense. 10While the incense was being burned, a great crowd stood outside, praying.

11While Zechariah was in the sanctuary, an angel of the Lord appeared to him, standing to the right of the incense altar.

1:1-4 Luke begins his Gospel with a formal preface in the style of the best Greek writers of his day. These four verses are some of the finest literary Greek in the NT.

1:1 ***Many people have set out to write accounts:*** Luke was not the first to put the history of Jesus into written form. Most scholars believe that Luke used Mark's Gospel and other written and oral sources in his writing. • ***fulfilled:*** This word can simply mean "accomplished," but Luke is thinking of Jesus' fulfillment of OT promises (4:21; 24:44).

1:2 ***from the early disciples:*** Literally *from those who from the beginning were servants of the word.*

1:3 As a good historian, Luke ***carefully investigated everything*** in the history of Jesus ***from the beginning*** in order to present a reliable historical account. • ***a careful account:*** Some versions translate this phrase "in consecutive order," but it refers to an orderly or carefully written account, not to chronological sequence. • The name ***Theophilus*** means "loved by God" or "one who loves God"; it is probably a personal name, not a descriptive name. Different theories identify him as (1) an influential unbeliever, (2) a new convert needing instruction, (3) the judge overseeing Paul's trial (the book of Acts ends with Paul imprisoned in Rome, awaiting trial), or (4) the patron who sponsored Luke's writing project. The last possibility is the most likely, as it was common to dedicate a literary work to a financial patron and the Greek word translated ***most honorable*** indicates someone of high social status.

1:5–2:52 Luke's first two chapters give an account of Jesus' birth and introduce key themes that will appear later in Luke–Acts. The announcements and birth stories for Jesus and John the Baptist run side by side, showing their parallel roles in bringing God's salvation. At each point, Jesus is shown to be greater. John is the forerunner announcing Jesus' coming; Jesus is the Savior.

1:5 ***Herod was king of Judea:*** See "Herod the Great" at Matt 2:1-20, p. 1578. • ***a Jewish priest named Zechariah:*** The priests were descendants of Aaron, Moses' brother (Exod 28:1). • ***the priestly order of Abijah:*** See note on 1:8-9; see also 1 Chr 24:10. • ***Elizabeth was also from the priestly line of Aaron:*** It was considered especially pious for a priest to marry a woman from a priestly family.

1:7 ***Elizabeth was unable to conceive:*** Childbearing was viewed as the highest calling for a woman, and infertility brought social stigma and shame. God miraculously intervened in the lives of various OT women so they could bear children (Gen 18:10-12; 25:21; 30:22-23; Judg 13; 1 Sam 1).

1:8-9 ***his order was on duty that week . . . he was chosen by lot:*** It was common in OT times to cast lots (similar to throwing dice) to determine God's will (Prov 16:33; 1 Chr 26:13-16; Neh 11:1; Jon 1:7). There were twenty-four orders of priests (1 Chr 24:1-19) that took turns in the Temple, and lots were cast to determine which priest would serve in the sanctuary. There were a large number of priests, so this privilege might come only once in a priest's lifetime. The angel appeared at the most sacred moment of Zechariah's life. • ***to enter the sanctuary of the Lord and burn incense:*** See "Herod's Temple" at John 8:20, p. 1787. Luke uses the word here translated ***sanctuary*** (Greek *naos*) for the Temple building, not the whole Temple grounds, which he calls *hieron* (2:27). The Temple building included the Holy Place and the Most Holy Place (see Heb 9:1-5; see also illustration, p. 583). The priests burned incense twice a day in the Holy Place.

12 Zechariah was shaken and overwhelmed with fear when he saw him. 13 But the angel said, "Don't be afraid, Zechariah! God has heard your prayer. Your wife, Elizabeth, will give you a son, and you are to name him John. 14 You will have great joy and gladness, and many will rejoice at his birth, 15 for he will be great in the eyes of the Lord. He must never touch wine or other alcoholic drinks. He will be filled with the Holy Spirit, even before his birth. 16 And he will turn many Israelites to the Lord their God. 17 He will be a man with the spirit and power of Elijah. He will prepare the people for the coming of the Lord. He will turn the hearts of the fathers to their children, and he will cause those who are rebellious to accept the wisdom of the godly."

18 Zechariah said to the angel, "How can I be sure this will happen? I'm an old man now, and my wife is also well along in years."

19 Then the angel said, "I am Gabriel! I stand in the very presence of God. It was he who sent me to bring you this good news! 20 But now, since you didn't believe what I said, you will be silent and unable to speak until the child is born. For my words will certainly be fulfilled at the proper time."

21 Meanwhile, the people were waiting for Zechariah to come out of the sanctuary, wondering why he was taking so long. 22 When he finally did come out, he couldn't speak to them. Then they realized from his gestures and his silence that he must have seen a vision in the sanctuary.

23 When Zechariah's week of [a]service in the Temple was over, he returned home. 24 Soon afterward his wife, Elizabeth, became pregnant and went into seclusion for five months. 25 "How kind the Lord is!" she exclaimed. "He has taken away my disgrace of having no children."

The Birth of Jesus Foretold

26 In the sixth month of Elizabeth's pregnancy, God sent the angel Gabriel to Nazareth, a village in Galilee, 27 to a virgin named Mary. She was engaged to be married to a man named Joseph, a descendant of King David. 28 Gabriel appeared to her and said, "Greetings, favored woman! The Lord is with you!"

29 Confused and disturbed, Mary tried to think what the angel could mean. 30 "Don't be afraid, Mary," the angel told her, "for you have found favor with God! 31 You will conceive and give birth to a son, and you will name him Jesus. 32 He will be very great and will be called the Son of the Most High. The Lord God will give him the throne of his ancestor David. 33 And he will reign over Israel forever; his Kingdom will never end!"

34 Mary asked the angel, "But how can this happen? I am a virgin."

35 The angel replied, "The Holy Spirit will come upon you, and the power of the Most High will overshadow you. So the baby to be born will be holy, and he will be called the

1:13 Luke 1:30, 60
1:15 Num 6:3; Judg 13:4; Jer 1:5; Matt 11:11
1:16 Mal 4:5-6
1:17 Mal 4:5; Matt 17:11-13
1:18 Gen 18:11; Matt 18:10
1:19 Dan 8:16; 9:21
1:20 Ezek 3:26
1:23 [a]*leitourgia* (3009) ‣Rom 13:6
1:25 Gen 30:23; Isa 4:1
1:26 Matt 2:23
1:27 Matt 1:16, 18; Luke 2:5
1:31 Isa 7:14; Matt 1:21-23
1:32 2 Sam 7:12-16; Isa 9:6-7; 16:5; Jer 23:5; Phil 2:10; 1 Tim 6:15
1:33 Ps 89:3-4; Isa 9:7; Jer 33:17; Dan 2:44; 7:14, 27; Heb 1:8
1:35 Matt 1:20; Mark 1:1; John 1:34; 20:31; Rom 1:4

1:12-13 ***Zechariah was shaken and overwhelmed with fear:*** Fear and awe are common reactions when someone sees an ***angel*** or experiences the presence of God (Judg 6:22-23; 13:22; Isa 6:5). The person is often reassured by a saying such as ***Don't be afraid.*** • ***you are to name him John:*** John means "the Lord has shown favor." This favor came to Elizabeth and Zechariah through their son and to the Israelite nation through the Messiah, whose coming John would announce.

1:15 ***He must never touch wine or other alcoholic drinks:*** In the OT, abstaining from alcohol was part of the Nazirite vow of special dedication to God (see Num 6:1-21). This vow was usually temporary (see Acts 18:18; 21:23, 26); for some individuals such as Samson (Judg 13:4-7), Samuel (cp. 1 Sam 1:11), and John the Baptist, it was a lifelong commitment. • ***filled with the Holy Spirit, even before his birth*** (or ***even from birth***): See 1:41, 44.

1:17 ***He will be a man with the spirit and power of Elijah:*** The prophet Malachi predicted that God would send Elijah before the time of God's salvation (see Mal 3:1; 4:5-6). John fulfilled this role by preparing the way for the Lord's coming. The salvation that John announced and Jesus accomplished can reconcile broken families.

1:19 ***I am Gabriel!*** Two angels are named in Scripture: Gabriel (Dan 8:16; 9:21) and Michael (Dan 10:13; 12:1; Jude 1:9; Rev 12:7).

1:20 ***now . . . you will be silent and unable to speak:*** This discipline for Zechariah's lack of faith was also a sign that confirmed the prophecy. The Greek word translated *silent* in 1:22 can also mean "deaf" (7:22; cp. 1:62). • Zechariah is contrasted with Mary, who responded with faith (1:38).

1:24 ***went into seclusion for five months:*** The reason for this seclusion is unknown and does not seem related to any OT custom or command. Perhaps it was a spiritual retreat to honor God for answered prayer.

1:26 ***Nazareth, a village in Galilee,*** was an insignificant, disreputable little village southwest of the Sea of Galilee (see John 1:46).

1:27 ***engaged to be married:*** In Jewish culture, marriages were arranged, and engagement was a formal legal contract between two families. Girls were normally married by their mid-teens. • ***Joseph, a descendant of King David:*** See Matt 1:1-16. Joseph's ancestry is significant because the Messiah was to be a descendant of King David (2 Sam 7:11-16; Isa 9:7).

1:28 Some manuscripts add *Blessed are you among women* at the end of this verse.

1:31 ***you will name him Jesus:*** Jesus means "the Lord saves."

1:32-33 These verses echo God's covenant with David (2 Sam 7:11-16), the foundational promise of the coming Messiah (see also Isa 9:6-7; 11:1-5; Jer 23:5-6; 33:15-16; Ezek 37:24-25). • ***over Israel:*** Literally *over the house of Jacob.*

1:35 ***The Holy Spirit will come upon you:*** Jesus' conception was miraculous, by ***the power of the Most High.*** No further detail is provided as to how this happened.

1:37
Gen 18:14
1:41
Gen 25:22
Luke 1:15
1:42
Judg 5:24
1:43
Luke 2:11
1:46-55
1 Sam 2:1-10
Ps 34:2-3
1:47
1 Tim 1:1; 2:3
Titus 1:3; 2:10; 3:4
[b]*sōtēr* (4990)
‣ Luke 2:11

Son of God. 36What's more, your relative
Elizabeth has become pregnant in her old
age! People used to say she was barren, but
she has conceived a son and is now in her
sixth month. 37For nothing is impossible
with God."
38Mary responded, "I am the Lord's servant. May everything you have said about
me come true." And then the angel left her.

Mary Visits Elizabeth

39A few days later Mary hurried to the
hill country of Judea, to the town 40where
Zechariah lived. She entered the house and
greeted Elizabeth. 41At the sound of Mary's
greeting, Elizabeth's child leaped within
her, and Elizabeth was filled with the Holy
Spirit.
42Elizabeth gave a glad cry and exclaimed
to Mary, "God has blessed you above all
women, and your child is blessed. 43Why
am I so honored, that the mother of my
Lord should visit me? 44When I heard your
greeting, the baby in my womb jumped for
joy. 45You are blessed because you believed
that the Lord would do what he said."

The Magnificat: Mary's Song of Praise

46Mary responded,

"Oh, how my soul praises the Lord.
47 How my spirit rejoices in God my
[b]Savior!

MARY, MOTHER OF JESUS (Luke 1:26–2:51)

Matt 1:16, 18-25; 2:11, 13-23
Acts 1:14

Mary, the wife of Joseph, was the virgin mother of Jesus. Luke tells us that Mary, a young girl in Nazareth, was betrothed to Joseph, a local carpenter. Before the marriage took place, an angel announced to her that she would become pregnant by the power of God's Spirit and give birth to the Son of God (1:26-33). Mary responded to this extraordinary message in simple faith, humbly submitting herself to God's will (1:38, 46-55). Shortly thereafter, the message was confirmed by her relative Elizabeth, who spoke of Mary as the most blessed of all women (1:39-45). Mary's miraculous bearing of the Son of God was viewed as a fulfillment of prophecy (Isa 7:14).

Jesus' birth took place in unusual circumstances, when Joseph took Mary to Bethlehem to register for an official Roman census. The child was born in a stable because no other lodging was available (2:1-7). Some time later, Mary and Joseph fled to Egypt to save the child from Herod's massacre of young boys in the Bethlehem area (Matt 2:13-18). When they returned, they resettled in Nazareth to raise their family (2:39; Matt 2:19-23). After Jesus' birth, Mary apparently gave birth to several other sons and daughters (Matt 13:55-56; Mark 6:3). It is likely that Mary herself told Luke the details of Jesus' birth and the unusual events associated with it (2:51).

When Jesus was twelve years old, he stayed in the Temple during a family trip to Jerusalem. Mary and Joseph rebuked him for staying behind when they departed, but they did not understand Jesus' response (2:41-51). Early in Jesus' public ministry, Mary encouraged him to do a miracle at a wedding in Cana (John 2:1-11). Later, when she and Jesus' brothers went to see Jesus, he said that his disciples were his "real family" (8:19-21; Matt 12:46-50; Mark 3:31-35).

When Jesus was crucified, Mary was among the women looking on (cp. Mark 15:40, 47; John 19:25). As Jesus was dying, he asked John, the "disciple he loved," to take care of Mary as his own mother (John 19:26-27). After Jesus' death and resurrection, Mary was apparently a member of the believing community; she is listed among those who were praying together when the Spirit came on the Day of Pentecost (Acts 1:14).

God chose Mary to bring his Son, the Savior, into the world. For all Christians, she is a model of humble and obedient submission to God's will.

1:36 ***your relative Elizabeth:*** The KJV identifies Elizabeth as Mary's cousin, but the Greek term is more general.

1:37 ***nothing is impossible with God*** (some manuscripts read *For the word of God will never fail*): This verse echoes Gen 18:14.

1:39 ***The hill country of Judea*** was 80–100 miles away from Nazareth, at least a four-day journey.

1:41 ***Elizabeth's child leaped within her:*** See 1:15. John was already announcing the Messiah's coming. • ***Elizabeth was filled with the Holy Spirit:*** In the OT, being filled with the Spirit was often associated with a prophetic gift. The Spirit of prophecy was again appearing in Israel (see 1:67; 2:25, 27).

1:46-55 Mary's song is the first of three songs of praise in the birth narrative. It is called the *Magnificat* ("magnifies"), from the first word in the Latin translation. The song has many parallels to Hannah's prayer in 1 Sam 2:1-10. The fact that God cares for the oppressed and reverses their fortunes is a common theme throughout Luke's Gospel. The coming of God's Kingdom brings salvation to rejected and outcast people.

48 For he took notice of his lowly servant
girl,
and from now on all generations will
call me blessed.
49 For the Mighty One is holy,
and he has done great things for me.
50 He shows [c]mercy from generation to
generation
to all who fear him.
51 His mighty arm has done tremendous
things!
He has scattered the proud and
haughty ones.
52 He has brought down princes from their
thrones
and exalted the humble.
53 He has filled the hungry with good
things
and sent the rich away with empty
hands.
54 He has helped his servant Israel
and remembered to be merciful.
55 For he made this promise to our
ancestors,
to Abraham and his children forever."

56 Mary stayed with Elizabeth about three
months and then went back to her own
home.

The Births of John and Jesus (1:57–2:20)

The Birth of John the Baptist

57 When it was time for Elizabeth's baby to
be born, she gave birth to a son. 58 And when
her neighbors and relatives heard that the
Lord had been very merciful to her, everyone rejoiced with her.

59 When the baby was eight days old, they
all came for the circumcision ceremony.
They wanted to name him Zechariah, after
his father. 60 But Elizabeth said, "No! His
name is John!"

61 "What?" they exclaimed. "There is no
one in all your family by that name." 62 So
they used gestures to ask the baby's father
what he wanted to name him. 63 He motioned for a writing tablet, and to everyone's
surprise he wrote, "His name is John." 64 Instantly Zechariah could speak again, and he
began praising God.

65 Awe fell upon the whole neighborhood, and the news of what had happened
spread throughout the Judean hills. 66 Everyone who heard about it reflected on these
events and asked, "What will this child turn
out to be?" For the hand of the Lord was
surely upon him in a special way.

The Benedictus: Zechariah's Prophecy

67 Then his father, Zechariah, was filled with
the Holy Spirit and gave this prophecy:

68 "Praise the Lord, the God of Israel,
because he has visited and redeemed
his people.
69 He has sent us a mighty Savior
from the royal line of his servant
David,
70 just as he promised
through his holy prophets long ago.
71 Now we will be saved from our enemies
and from all who hate us.
72 He has been merciful to our ancestors
by remembering his sacred covenant—
73 the covenant he swore with an oath
to our ancestor Abraham.
74 We have been rescued from our enemies
so we can serve God without fear,
75 in holiness and righteousness
for as long as we live.

76 "And you, my little son,
will be called the prophet of the Most
High,

1:49 Ps 111:9; 126:3
1:50 Ps 103:13, 17
[c]eleos (1656)
› Luke 10:37
1:51 2 Sam 22:28
Ps 89:10
1:52 Job 5:12; 12:19
1:53 1 Sam 2:5
Ps 107:9
1:54 Ps 98:3
Isa 41:8
1:55 Gen 17:7; 22:17
1:59 Gen 17:12
Lev 12:3
Luke 2:21
Phil 3:5
1:66 Luke 2:19
Acts 11:21
1:67 Joel 2:28
1:68 Ps 41:13; 72:18; 106:48; 111:9
1:69 1 Sam 2:1-10
Ps 18:2; 132:17
Ezek 29:21
1:70 Jer 23:5
Acts 3:21
Rom 1:2-4
1:71 Ps 106:10
1:72-73 Ps 105:8-9; 106:45-46
1:73-74 Gen 22:16-18
1:75 Eph 4:24
1:76 Isa 40:3
Mal 3:1

1:48 ***all generations will call me blessed:*** In Middle Eastern culture, honor and shame were extremely important, and one's legacy to future generations was highly cherished.

1:51 ***His mighty arm*** personifies God's mighty power (see Ps 98:1; Isa 40:10).

1:54-55 Gabriel's words in 1:32-33 recalled God's covenant with David; here Mary alluded to God's covenant with ***Abraham*** (Gen 12:1-3; 17:3-8). • The coming of Jesus brought glory to Israel and salvation to the Gentiles (see 2:32).

1:59 God commanded every Israelite male to be circumcised when ***eight days old*** (Gen 17:9-14; Lev 12:3). ***Circumcision*** signified the child's incorporation into the covenant community of Israel. • ***They wanted to name him Zechariah:*** It was common to name a child after a relative. The family and friends were surprised because John was not the name of any of his relatives.

1:62-63 ***they used gestures:*** Zechariah was mute and deaf (see note on 1:20). Zechariah's obedience in naming the child ***John*** confirmed his faith, and his voice and hearing were restored.

1:66 ***the hand of the Lord:*** This *anthropomorphism* (describing God with human characteristics, cp. 1:51) meant that God was at work in John's life.

1:67-79 This second hymn of the birth narrative is called the *Benedictus* ("Blessed" or "Praise") from the first word of the Latin translation. The hymn expects God's Messiah to deliver the Israelites from their enemies. Salvation entails physical deliverance and forgiveness of sins (1:77).

1:68 ***he has visited and redeemed his people:*** This recalls the exodus from Egypt, when God rescued his people from Pharaoh (Exod 3:7-10, 17-20).

1:69 ***He has sent us a mighty Savior*** (literally ***has raised up a horn of salvation for us***): A "horn of salvation" was the horn of a powerful animal such as a ram or an ox. To "raise up a horn" invoked strength and power (see also Ps 89:24; 132:17). • ***from the royal line of his servant David:*** See note on 1:32-33.

1:71 ***saved from our enemies:*** The people of Israel hoped for rescue from their physical enemies, the Romans; Jesus brought salvation from sin, Satan, and death.

1:76-77 ***And you, my little son:*** Zechariah turned from speaking about the coming Messiah to address his newborn

1:77
Jer 31:34
[d]*hamartia* (0266)
‣Luke 3:3

1:78
Mal 4:2

1:79
Isa 9:2; 58:8; 60:1-2
Matt 4:16

1:80
Luke 2:40, 52

2:1-7
//Matt 1:18-25

2:5
Luke 1:27

2:6
Matt 1:25
Gal 4:4

2:7
Phil 2:7
[e]*prōtotokos* (4416)
‣Rom 8:29

2:8
[f]*poimēn* (4166)
‣John 10:11

because you will prepare the way for
the Lord.
77 You will tell his people how to find
salvation
through forgiveness of their [d]sins.
78 Because of God's tender mercy,
the morning light from heaven is
about to break upon us,
79 to give light to those who sit in darkness
and in the shadow of death,
and to guide us to the path of peace."

80 John grew up and became strong in
spirit. And he lived in the wilderness until
he began his public ministry to Israel.

The Birth of Jesus
Luke 2:1-7; cp. Matt 1:18-25

2 At that time the Roman emperor, Augustus, decreed that a census should
be taken throughout the Roman Empire.
2 (This was the first census taken when Quirinius was governor of Syria.) 3 All returned
to their own ancestral towns to register for
this census. 4 And because Joseph was a
descendant of King David, he had to go to
Bethlehem in Judea, David's ancient home.
He traveled there from the village of Nazareth in Galilee. 5 He took with him Mary, his
fiancée, who was now obviously pregnant.
6 And while they were there, the time
came for her baby to be born. 7 She gave
birth to her [e]first child, a son. She wrapped
him snugly in strips of cloth and laid him
in a manger, because there was no lodging
available for them.

The Shepherds and Angels
8 That night there were [f]shepherds staying
in the fields nearby, guarding their flocks

Praise and Rejoicing (1:44, 46-47, 64, 68)

Luke 2:13-14, 38; 5:25-26; 7:16; 13:13; 17:15-18; 18:43; 19:37-40; 24:51-53
Acts 2:47; 3:8-9; 4:21; 11:18; 13:48; 21:20
Isa 55:12

Praise and rejoicing are prominent in Luke's Gospel and in Acts. Throughout Luke's Gospel, the recipients of God's grace praise him for his wonderful deeds (1:44, 46, 64, 68; 2:13, 38; 5:25-26; 7:16; 13:13; 17:15-18; 18:43; 19:37; 24:53). In Acts, praise accompanies healings (Acts 2:47; 3:8-9; 4:21) and the salvation of the Gentiles (Acts 11:18; 13:48; 21:20).

This motif of praise is closely linked to a key theme in Luke, that the fulfillment of God's promise in the coming of Jesus the Messiah is a cause for joy and rejoicing. The OT prophets had predicted that nature itself would break forth in songs of praise when God's salvation arrived (see Isa 55:12). When Jesus entered Jerusalem at the end of his ministry, his disciples shouted and sang, "praising God for all the wonderful miracles they had seen" (19:37). The Pharisees called on Jesus to rebuke his disciples, but he responded, "If they kept quiet, the stones along the road would burst into cheers!" (19:37-40). At the end of the Gospel, the disciples "returned to Jerusalem filled with great joy. And they spent all of their time in the Temple, praising God" (24:52-53). The arrival of God's marvelous salvation is a cause for rejoicing and praise.

son, John, who would prepare the Messiah's way. • ***called the prophet of the Most High:*** John was the last and greatest in the line of OT prophets (see 7:28). • ***prepare the way for the Lord:*** See Isa 40:3; see note on 1:17.

1:78 ***the morning light from heaven is about to break upon us*** (or *the Morning Light from Heaven is about to visit us*): The Messiah is identified in the OT as a light shining in darkness (Isa 9:2; 42:6-7; 49:6; Mal 4:2).

1:80 ***John grew up and became strong in spirit:*** Cp. 2:40, 52; 1 Sam 2:21, 26; 3:19. • John probably ***lived in the wilderness*** west of the Jordan River and southeast of Jerusalem. It was a place of testing (Deut 8:2; Pss 78; 95; 107) as well as spiritual retreat and preparation (Exod 3; 1 Kgs 19:4-6, 11-18; Isa 40:3).

2:1-7 Having described John's birth, Luke gives a parallel account of Jesus' birth, with emphasis on its lowliness. Although he was the glorious Messiah, Jesus entered the world in humble circumstances.

2:1 Caesar ***Augustus,*** whose given name was Octavian, ruled the ***Roman Empire*** from 27 BC to AD 14. Prior to his time, Rome was a republic ruled by a senate. The Roman senate gave Augustus supreme authority as ***emperor*** and the republic became an empire. Augustus secured the empire's borders and established the *Pax Romana* ("Roman Peace"), a period of unprecedented stability and prosperity in the Mediterranean world. • ***A census*** registered the people for tax purposes.

2:2 ***Quirinius was governor of Syria:*** Quirinius held this post AD 6–9. In 6–4 BC, Quirinius also had authority over Judea, possibly through some kind of joint rule. He may have begun the census. Historical accounts mention three other censuses at that time (in Syria, Gaul, and Spain), and there was no reason not to have one in Judea, though it is not mentioned in secular records. Jesus was born around 6–4 BC, before Herod the Great died in 4 BC (see Matt 2:1-19).

2:3-4 Since ***Joseph was a descendant of King David,*** he returned to David's hometown of ***Bethlehem*** (1 Sam 17:12, 58; 20:6), a tiny village ***in Judea*** five miles south of Jerusalem, where Micah 5:2 predicted that the Messiah would be born.

2:5 ***Mary, his fiancée:*** See note on 1:27.

2:7 ***wrapped him snugly in strips of cloth:*** This common practice showed motherly love and care (see Ezek 16:4). • ***A manger*** was a feeding trough for animals. • ***no lodging available for them:*** This is a more accurate translation than the traditional "no room in the inn." The word translated *lodging* does not mean an inn (there were no inns in tiny Bethlehem), but either a guest room in a private house or a public shelter for travelers. Since there was no normal lodging, Joseph and Mary moved to an area reserved for animals.

2:8 ***Shepherds*** were sometimes portrayed in Judaism as drifters and dishonest troublemakers. This stereotype

of sheep. 9Suddenly, an angel of the Lord
appeared among them, and the radiance
of the Lord's glory surrounded them. They
were terrified, 10but the angel reassured
them. "Don't be afraid!" he said. "I bring
you good news that will bring great joy to
all people. 11The [g]Savior—yes, the [h]Messiah,
the Lord—has been born today in Bethlehem, the city of David! 12And you will
recognize him by this sign: You will find a
baby wrapped snugly in strips of cloth, lying in a manger."
13Suddenly, the angel was joined by a vast
host of others—the armies of heaven—praising God and saying,

14 "[i]Glory to God in highest heaven,
and [j]peace on earth to those with
whom God is pleased."

15When the angels had returned to
heaven, the shepherds said to each other,
"Let's go to Bethlehem! Let's see this thing
that has happened, which the Lord has told
us about."
16They hurried to the village and found
Mary and Joseph. And there was the baby,
lying in the manger. 17After seeing him,
the shepherds told everyone what had
happened and what the angel had said to
them about this child. 18All who heard the
shepherds' story were astonished, 19but
Mary kept all these things in her heart and
thought about them often. 20The shepherds
went back to their flocks, glorifying and
praising God for all they had heard and
seen. It was just as the angel had told them.

The Presentation of Jesus (2:21-38)

Jesus Is Presented in the Temple

21Eight days later, when the baby was circumcised, he was named Jesus, the name
given him by the angel even before he was
conceived.
22Then it was time for their purification
offering, as required by the law of Moses after the birth of a child; so his parents took
him to Jerusalem to present him to the Lord.
23The law of the Lord says, "If a woman's
first child is a boy, he must be dedicated to
the LORD." 24So they offered the sacrifice required in the law of the Lord—"either a pair
of turtledoves or two young pigeons."

The Prophecy of Simeon

25At that time there was a man in Jerusalem named Simeon. He was righteous and
devout and was eagerly waiting for the

2:9 Acts 5:19
2:11 Mic 5:2; John 4:42; 20:31; [g]*sōtēr* (4990) ‣John 4:42; [h]*christos* (5547) ‣John 1:17
2:13 Ps 103:20; Heb 1:6; Rev 5:11
2:14 Isa 57:19; Luke 19:38; [i]*doxa* (1391) ‣Luke 4:6; [j]*eirēnē* (1515) ‣John 14:27
2:17 Luke 2:10-12
2:19 Luke 2:51
2:21 Gen 17:12; Lev 12:3; Matt 1:21
2:22 Lev 12:2-6
2:23 *Exod 13:2, 12, 15
2:24 *Lev 5:11; 12:8
2:25 Isa 40:1; 49:13

was not universal, however; in the OT, shepherds are usually viewed positively (e.g., Ps 23:1). Jesus came to common people such as these poor and humble peasants. • ***staying in the fields:*** This suggests warmer months of the year, perhaps March through November, though some shepherds stayed out year-round. The actual month of Jesus' birth is unknown. • They were ***guarding their flocks*** against thieves and wild animals.

2:9-10 ***terrified:*** As with Zechariah and Mary, the angelic presence was glorious and frightening. The angel told the shepherds, ***"Don't be afraid"*** (cp. 1:11-13, 28-30). • ***I bring you good news:*** This verb (Greek *euangelizō*, "I evangelize") is from the same root as the word for "Good News" (Greek *euangelion*, sometimes translated *gospel;* e.g., Gal 2:5, 7, 14). Isaiah's prophecies describe God's salvation as good news (see, e.g., Isa 52:7; 61:1). • ***to all people*** (literally *to all the people*): In Luke's writings, "the people" (grammatical singular) always refers to the people of Israel. The shepherds were being told that Israel's salvation had arrived and would ultimately go to all nations.

2:11 ***The Messiah*** (Greek *Christos*, a translation of Hebrew *mashiakh*) means "Anointed One" and refers to the coming savior from David's line (see note on 1:32-33; see "The Messianic Hope" at 3:15, p. 1707). As the Good News moved from a Jewish context to the Gentile world, Christians began to use *Christos* less as a title and more as a name.

2:12 ***this sign:*** Shepherds would appreciate the paradox and incongruity between the security of ***strips of cloth*** and the lowly circumstances of ***lying in a manger.*** Seeing a baby in such a setting was very unusual—a fitting sign that God was at work.

2:13 ***The armies of heaven*** reveal God's sovereign power and authority (2 Kgs 6:17; Ps 148:2). "Lord of Heaven's Armies" is a common OT name for God (e.g., 1 Sam 1:11; 17:45; 2 Sam 7:8; Isa 5:16; Rom 9:29; Jas 5:4).

2:14 ***Glory to God in highest heaven:*** This short hymn is known as the *Gloria in excelsis Deo* from the first line of the Latin translation. The Messiah's coming brings glory to God in the heavens and peace to humans on earth. • ***peace on earth to those with whom God is pleased:*** Peace indicates total well-being, not just the absence of hostility. The traditional translation, "on earth peace, good will toward men" (KJV), is based on the reading of some late manuscripts. The NLT text follows more reliable early manuscripts. Peace comes to the recipients of God's grace.

2:19 ***Mary kept all these things in her heart:*** Perhaps Mary reflected on the significance of these events and wondered about Jesus' destiny. It is also possible that Luke says this because Mary was his source of information on these events.

2:20 ***Glorifying and praising God*** are major themes throughout Luke's Gospel (e.g., 1:64; 2:13, 28; 5:25-26; 7:16; 13:13; 17:15, 18; 18:43; 19:37; 23:47; 24:53).

2:21 ***Eight days later . . . circumcised:*** See note on 1:59.

2:22 ***Time for their purification offering:*** The law of Moses prescribed a forty-day period of ritual purification for women following childbirth (Lev 12:1-8), after which an offering was made (2:24). • ***to present him to the Lord:*** Every firstborn, whether human or animal, was to be offered to the Lord; humans were bought back with a redemption price (see Exod 13:1-2, 15; 34:19-20; Num 3:11-13; 18:15-16; Neh 10:35-36).

2:23 ***he must be dedicated to the LORD:*** This is quoted from Exod 13:2.

2:24 ***a pair of turtle doves or two young pigeons:*** This quote from Lev 12:8 pertains to the purification ceremony after childbirth (see note on 2:22); Joseph and Mary offered the sacrifice prescribed for the poor.

2:25 ***Simeon*** was ***righteous and devout,*** like Zechariah and Elizabeth (1:6). They represent the righteous remnant of Israel that awaited God's salvation (Isa 10:20-22). Some have assumed that Simeon was a priest; the text says only that he was a devout ***man in Jerusalem.***

2:26 Ps 89:48 John 8:51 Heb 11:5
2:30-31 Isa 40:5; 52:10 Acts 4:12
2:32 Isa 42:6-7; 46:13; 49:6 [k]*apokalupsis* (0602) ‣Rom 16:25
2:34 Isa 8:14 1 Cor 1:23 1 Pet 2:7-8
2:37 1 Tim 5:5
2:38 Isa 52:9 Luke 1:68; 24:21
2:39 Matt 2:23
2:40 Luke 1:80 [a]*charis* (5485) ‣Rom 3:24
2:41 Exod 12:24-27 Deut 16:1-8

Messiah to come and rescue Israel. The
Holy Spirit was upon him 26and had revealed to him that he would not die until he
had seen the Lord's Messiah. 27That day the
Spirit led him to the Temple. So when Mary
and Joseph came to present the baby Jesus
to the Lord as the law required, 28Simeon
was there. He took the child in his arms and
praised God, saying,

29 "Sovereign Lord, now let your servant
die in peace,
as you have promised.
30 I have seen your salvation,
31 which you have prepared for all
people.
32 He is a light to [k]reveal God to the nations,
and he is the glory of your people
Israel!"

33Jesus' parents were amazed at what
was being said about him. 34Then Simeon
blessed them, and he said to Mary, the baby's mother, "This child is destined to cause
many in Israel to fall, but he will be a joy
to many others. He has been sent as a sign
from God, but many will oppose him. 35As a
result, the deepest thoughts of many hearts
will be revealed. And a sword will pierce
your very soul."

The Prophecy of Anna
36Anna, a prophet, was also there in the
Temple. She was the daughter of Phanuel
from the tribe of Asher, and she was very
old. Her husband died when they had been
married only seven years. 37Then she lived
as a widow to the age of eighty-four. She
never left the Temple but stayed there day
and night, worshiping God with fasting and
prayer. 38She came along just as Simeon
was talking with Mary and Joseph, and she
began praising God. She talked about the
child to everyone who had been waiting expectantly for God to rescue Jerusalem.

Jesus' Early Years (2:39-52)
The Childhood of Jesus in Nazareth
39When Jesus' parents had fulfilled all the
requirements of the law of the Lord, they returned home to Nazareth in Galilee. 40There
the child grew up healthy and strong. He
was filled with wisdom, and God's [a]favor
was on him.

Jesus Speaks with the Teachers
41Every year Jesus' parents went to Jerusalem for the Passover festival. 42When Jesus
was twelve years old, they attended the festival as usual. 43After the celebration was
over, they started home to Nazareth, but

• ***eagerly waiting for the Messiah to come and rescue Israel*** (literally *awaiting Israel's consolation)*: This is an allusion to Isa 40:1, which promised comfort to Israel after returning from exile. • ***The Holy Spirit was upon him:*** See note on 1:41.

2:26 ***the Lord's Messiah*** (or *the Lord's Anointed*): This title, often used of David, came to refer to the Messiah, who would come from David's line.

2:27 ***to the Temple:*** This was the Temple compound, not the sanctuary. See note on 1:8-9.

2:29-32 This third great hymn of the birth narrative is called the *Nunc dimittis* ("now dismiss"), from the first words of the Latin translation. The hymn praises God for allowing Simeon to see God's salvation.

2:30 ***I have seen your salvation:*** The phrase echoes Isa 52:12.

2:31 The grammatical plural of ***people*** means all people, Jews and Gentiles (cp. note on 2:10).

2:32 The prophet Isaiah predicted that the coming Kingdom of God would bring salvation to all ***the nations*** (Isa 42:6-7; 49:6). • ***the glory of your people Israel!*** This quote from Isa 46:13 says that God's salvation will bring glory to Israel. Israel's role in the OT was to bring glory to God by revealing God's light to the nations.

2:34 ***to cause many in Israel to fall:*** Many Israelites rejected Jesus as the Messiah (see Isa 8:14-15). • ***a sign from God:*** See 11:29-30; cp. Isa 8:18.

2:35 ***the deepest thoughts of many hearts:*** Israel's true heart—whether for God or against him—would be revealed through their response to Jesus. • ***a sword will pierce your very soul:*** Mary would experience great pain at seeing her son rejected and dying on the cross.

2:36-38 ***Anna*** is the Greek equivalent of the Hebrew name Hannah, Samuel's mother (1 Sam 1–2; see note on 1:46-55). Jewish tradition identified seven OT women as prophets: Sarah, Miriam, Deborah, Hannah, Abigail, Huldah, and Esther. Anna was another prophetic witness to Jesus' identity as the Messiah. • ***The tribe of Asher***, one of the ten northern tribes of Israel, was named after Jacob's eighth son (Gen 30:12-13). Most of those who returned from Babylonian exile were from the tribe of Judah; other Israelites also knew their tribal ancestry in Jesus' day. The apostle Paul was from the tribe of Benjamin (Phil 3:5).

2:37 ***she lived as a widow to the age of eighty-four*** (Or *She had been a widow for eighty-four years*): In the ancient world, great age was associated with wisdom and honor. • ***She never left the Temple:*** This is probably hyperbole; we might say, "She was there all the time," reflecting her total dedication to God.

2:40 ***filled with wisdom, and God's favor was on him*** (cp. 1:80; 2:52): The twin statements about Jesus' wisdom (2:40, 52) frame the story that follows about Jesus' extraordinary wisdom at an early age.

2:41-51 Jesus' visit to Jerusalem when he was twelve is the only account from Jesus' childhood recorded in the Gospels. Its main theme is Jesus' early spiritual insight, including both his growing awareness of his unique father-son relationship with God and his unique mission.

2:41 ***Every year . . . the Passover festival:*** Passover, celebrating Israel's deliverance from slavery in Egypt, was one of three great annual festivals that Jewish men were expected to attend (Exod 23:14-17; Deut 16:16). Jesus' family was devout and observant.

2:42 ***Jesus was twelve years old:*** A Jewish boy entered into his covenant responsibilities at age thirteen (the *bar mitzvah* ceremony developed later to express this custom). With this visit, Jesus' parents were preparing him to fulfill his role in the covenant community.

Jesus stayed behind in Jerusalem. His parents didn't miss him at first, 44 because they
assumed he was among the other travelers.
But when he didn't show up that evening,
they started looking for him among their
relatives and friends.
45 When they couldn't find him, they
went back to Jerusalem to search for him
there. 46 Three days later they finally discovered him in the Temple, sitting among
the religious teachers, listening to them
and asking questions. 47 All who heard him
were amazed at his understanding and his
answers.
48 His parents didn't know what to think.
"Son," his mother said to him, "why have
you done this to us? Your father and I
have been frantic, searching for you everywhere."
49 "But why did you need to search?" he
asked. "Didn't you know that I must be in
my Father's house?" 50 But they didn't understand what he meant.
51 Then he returned to Nazareth with
them and was obedient to them. And his
mother stored all these things in her heart.
52 Jesus grew in wisdom and in stature
and in favor with God and all the people.

3. PREPARATION FOR THE SAVIOR'S MINISTRY (3:1–4:13)

John the Baptist Prepares the Way (3:1-20)

Introduction to John the Baptist's Ministry
Luke 3:2b-6 // Matt 3:1-3 // Mark 1:2-3 // John 1:23
Luke 3:7-9 // Matt 3:7-10

3 It was now the fifteenth year of the reign
of Tiberius, the Roman emperor. Pontius Pilate was governor over Judea; Herod
Antipas was ruler over Galilee; his brother
Philip was ruler over Iturea and Traconitis;
Lysanias was ruler over Abilene. 2 Annas
and Caiaphas were the [b]high priests. At this
time a message from God came to John son
of Zechariah, who was living in the wilderness. 3 Then John went from place to place
on both sides of the Jordan River, preaching
that people should be baptized to show that
they had repented of their [c]sins and turned
to God to be forgiven. 4 Isaiah had spoken of
John when he said,

"He is a voice shouting in the wilderness,
'Prepare the way for the LORD's coming!
Clear the road for him!
5 The valleys will be filled,
and the mountains and hills made level.
The curves will be straightened,
and the rough places made smooth.

2:47 Matt 7:28; John 7:15
2:48 Luke 3:23; 4:22
2:49 John 2:16
2:50 Mark 9:32
2:51 Luke 2:19
2:52 1 Sam 2:26; Prov 3:4; Luke 1:80
3:1-16 //Matt 3:1-12; //Mark 1:2-8; //John 1:19-28
3:2 Luke 1:80; [b]*archiereus* (0749) ‣John 18:19
3:3 Acts 13:24; 19:4; [c]*hamartia* (0266) ‣Rom 3:9
3:4-6 *Isa 40:3-5

2:44 ***they assumed he was among the other travelers:*** Joseph and Mary were probably traveling with a large caravan of relatives and friends from Galilee. Jesus probably spent a lot of time with his friends and relatives, so his parents were not worried at first.

2:46 The ***three days*** probably included one day traveling from Jerusalem, one day traveling back, and one day searching. • ***in the Temple:*** He was in the Temple compound, not the sanctuary. • ***listening to them and asking questions:*** Jesus was in the role of a student. In rabbinic instruction, a teacher responded to a student's question with a series of counter-questions. Jesus' insightful questions and answers amazed the teachers.

2:47 ***amazed at his understanding and his answers:*** Jesus fulfilled Isa 11:2.

2:49 ***Didn't you know that I must be in my Father's house?*** Or *"Didn't you realize that I should be involved with my Father's affairs?"* Jesus was aware that his greatest loyalty belonged to his Father in heaven.

2:51 Although Jesus recognized his relationship to his heavenly Father, he ***was obedient to*** his earthly parents. • ***his mother stored all these things in her heart:*** See note on 2:19.

2:52 ***Jesus grew in wisdom:*** See note on 2:40.

3:1–4:13 After the birth narrative, Luke sets the stage for Jesus' public ministry. He tells about the ministry of John the Baptist as forerunner of the Messiah and Jesus' baptism, genealogy, and temptation.

3:1 ***the fifteenth year of the reign of Tiberius:*** Tiberius Caesar became co-emperor with his stepfather Caesar Augustus in AD 11 and full emperor in AD 14, reigning until AD 37. Depending on which date Luke is referring to, John's public ministry began around AD 26/27 or AD 29/30; Jesus began his own ministry shortly thereafter. • ***Pilate:*** Pontius Pilate was governor of Judea from AD 26–36 (see "Pontius Pilate" at Mark 15:1-15, 43-45, p. 1691). • ***Herod Antipas was ruler:*** Literally *Herod was tetrarch.* Herod Antipas was a son of King Herod (see "Herod Antipas" at Mark 6:14-29, p. 1659). • Antipas's half ***brother Philip,*** another son of Herod the Great, was ***ruler*** (literally *tetrarch*) of the region northeast of Galilee from 4 BC until his death in AD 34. *Tetrarch* means "the ruler of a fourth of a kingdom"; the term came to mean any minor ruler. Philip the Tetrarch was another half-brother of both Antipas and Herod Philip (Matt 14:3; Mark 6:17; see diagram, p. 1579).

3:2 ***Annas and Caiaphas were the high priests:*** Annas was high priest AD 6–15 and was deposed by the Romans; his son-in-law Caiaphas was the current high priest (AD 18–36). Luke lists both names because Annas still wielded significant power behind the scenes (see John 18:13-14, 24; Acts 4:6). • ***a message from God came to John:*** John's calling as a prophet was similar to that of the OT prophets (see, e.g., Isa 6:1-13; Jer 1:1-19).

3:3 ***people should be baptized to show that they had repented of their sins and turned to God:*** John seems to have adapted the practice of baptism from Jewish rites using water to cleanse, or set apart, people and objects for God's service (cp. Lev 8:6). John called people to repent of their sins and prepare spiritually for the Messiah's coming. Their baptism publicly demonstrated their repentance and spiritual cleansing.

3:4-6 The quotation is from Isa 40:3-5 (Greek version); it speaks of God's delivering the Jews from exile in Babylon. After the Jews had returned from exile (Ezra 1–2), the passage became associated with God's end-time salvation. John shouted ***in the wilderness*** to prepare God's people for the Lord's coming. God's salvation is portrayed as a new exodus, bringing deliverance like the first exodus from Egypt. • ***Clear the road for him! . . . the rough places made smooth:*** The image reflects the Middle Eastern practice of preparing a road at the approach of a king, something like "rolling out the red carpet" (cp. 19:36-38).

3:6 Luke 2:30-31; Acts 28:28; Titus 2:11
3:7 Matt 12:34; 23:33
3:8 John 8:33, 37, 39; Acts 3:25; [d]*metanoia* (3341) ‣Luke 5:32
3:9 Matt 7:19; John 15:6
3:11 Jas 2:15; 1 Jn 3:17
3:12 Luke 7:29
3:13 Luke 19:8
3:14 Exod 23:1; Lev 19:11; 1 Tim 6:6

6 And then all people will see
the salvation sent from God.' "

7When the crowds came to John for baptism, he said, "You brood of snakes! Who warned you to flee God's coming wrath?
8Prove by the way you live that you have [d]repented of your sins and turned to God. Don't just say to each other, 'We're safe, for we are descendants of Abraham.' That means nothing, for I tell you, God can create children of Abraham from these very stones.
9Even now the ax of God's judgment is poised, ready to sever the roots of the trees. Yes, every tree that does not produce good fruit will be chopped down and thrown into the fire."

John Replies to Questions

10The crowds asked, "What should we do?"
11John replied, "If you have two shirts, give one to the poor. If you have food, share it with those who are hungry."
12Even corrupt tax collectors came to be baptized and asked, "Teacher, what should we do?"
13He replied, "Collect no more taxes than the government requires."
14"What should we do?" asked some soldiers.

John replied, "Don't extort money or make false accusations. And be content with your pay."

John Preaches about the Messiah

Luke 3:15-18 // Matt 3:11-12 // Mark 1:7-8 // John 1:24-28

15Everyone was expecting the Messiah to come soon, and they were eager to know whether John might be the Messiah.
16John

The Messianic Hope (3:15)

Luke 2:25-32; 2 Sam 7:11-16; Isa 9:6-7; 11:1-5; Jer 23:5-6; 33:15-16; Ezek 37:24-25

In the first century, many Jews eagerly looked for the coming of the Messiah, a deliverer who would defeat Israel's enemies and usher in an era of peace and prosperity for God's people.

The Hebrew word "Messiah," the equivalent of the Greek "Christ," means "Anointed One." The term comes from the practice of anointing kings in Israel with oil at their enthronement to confirm their appointment to rule the nation as God's representative.

There was widespread hope that a king from David's line would reestablish David's dynasty and reign in righteousness and justice on David's throne in Jerusalem. This hope had its foundation in 2 Sam 7:11-16, where God promised King David that he would raise up descendants after him and establish his throne forever. With the decline and subsequent collapse of Israel as a kingdom, the OT prophets predicted the coming of the Messiah (Isa 9:6-7; 11:1-5; Jer 23:5-6; 33:15-16; Ezek 37:24-25), the king who would deliver God's people and reign forever on David's throne.

Luke takes a special interest in showing that Jesus is truly the promised Messiah (1:32-33, 69-70; 3:15-16), but that he has fulfilled the messianic promises in a surprising way. After Peter confessed that Jesus is "the Messiah sent from God" (9:20), Jesus immediately began teaching about the Messiah's suffering. As Jesus approached Jerusalem for the last time, he was recognized as the King coming in the name of the Lord (18:38; 19:38), but then he was rejected (22:66-71) and crucified, mocked as "king of the Jews" (23:1-3) and "God's Messiah" (23:35).

On the third day, however, Jesus rose victorious from the dead, just as he predicted. During his appearances to the disciples he revealed that the Scriptures predicted all along that "the Messiah would have to suffer all these things before entering his glory" (24:26). Jesus' death and resurrection confirm that he is truly the Messiah and that his death brings restoration and forgiveness of sins (24:47).

3:7 *God's coming wrath* is the judgment for all who reject the gospel. Israel as a nation would experience this wrath in the destruction of Jerusalem in AD 70 (see 21:20-23).

3:8 *we are descendants of Abraham:* See note on 1:54-55. Some Jews believed that their descent from Abraham guaranteed their salvation (see John 8:33-39; Acts 7:2; Rom 4:1). • *That means nothing:* God had selected the Israelites as his people, and he could reject them and *create children of Abraham from these very stones* if he chose (cp. Hos 1:3-9; Rom 9:6-8, 27-28; 11:17-21).

3:9 *every tree that does not produce good fruit:* Israel would be judged as an unfruitful vineyard (see Isa 5:1-7; cp. Luke 13:7-9; 20:9-19).

3:11 *two shirts:* The Greek word refers to a long shirt worn next to the skin. Even the smallest surplus should be shared with others in need.

3:12 *corrupt tax collectors:* The word for "corrupt" is not literally in the Greek, but it accurately expresses the connotation that "tax collector" had for first-century readers. They despised tax collectors, who were notoriously corrupt and worked for the hated Roman authorities.

3:14 These *soldiers* were probably not Roman, but local Jewish troops under the authority of Herod Antipas. They might have been assigned to protect the tax collectors. John does not condemn either tax collectors or soldiers, but calls them to honesty and integrity.

answered their questions by saying, "I baptize you with water; but someone is coming
soon who is greater than I am—so much
greater that I'm not even worthy to be his
slave and untie the straps of his sandals.
He will baptize you with the Holy Spirit
and with fire. 17He is ready to separate the
chaff from the wheat with his winnowing
fork. Then he will clean up the threshing
area, gathering the wheat into his barn but
burning the chaff with never-ending fire."
18John used many such warnings as he announced the Good News to the people.

The Imprisonment of John
Luke 3:19-20; cp. Matt 14:3-12 // Mark 6:17-29

19John also publicly criticized Herod Antipas, the ruler of Galilee, for marrying
Herodias, his brother's wife, and for many
other wrongs he had done. 20So Herod put
John in prison, adding this sin to his many
others.

The Baptism of Jesus (3:21-22)
Luke 3:21-22 // Matt 3:13-17 // Mark 1:9-11 // John 1:29-34

21One day when the crowds were being
baptized, Jesus himself was baptized. As
he was praying, the heavens opened, 22and
the Holy Spirit, in bodily form, descended
on him like a dove. And a voice from heaven
said, "You are my dearly loved Son, and you
bring me great joy."

The Ancestors of Jesus (3:23-38)
Luke 3:23-38; cp. Matt 1:1-17

23Jesus was about thirty years old when he
began his public ministry.
Jesus was known as the son of Joseph.
Joseph was the son of Heli.
24 Heli was the son of Matthat.
Matthat was the son of Levi.
Levi was the son of Melki.
Melki was the son of Jannai.
Jannai was the son of Joseph.
25 Joseph was the son of Mattathias.
Mattathias was the son of Amos.
Amos was the son of Nahum.
Nahum was the son of Esli.
Esli was the son of Naggai.
26 Naggai was the son of Maath.
Maath was the son of Mattathias.
Mattathias was the son of Semein.
Semein was the son of Josech.
Josech was the son of Joda.
27 Joda was the son of Joanan.
Joanan was the son of Rhesa.
Rhesa was the son of Zerubbabel.
Zerubbabel was the son of Shealtiel.
Shealtiel was the son of Neri.
28 Neri was the son of Melki.
Melki was the son of Addi.
Addi was the son of Cosam.
Cosam was the son of Elmadam.
Elmadam was the son of Er.

3:16
Mark 1:4
John 1:26-27, 33
Acts 1:5; 2:3; 11:16; 13:25; 19:4

3:17
Matt 13:30

3:19-20
Matt 14:3
Mark 6:17

3:21-22
//Matt 3:13-17
//Mark 1:9-11
John 1:29-34

3:22
Gen 22:2
Ps 2:7
Isa 42:1
Matt 12:18; 17:5
Mark 9:7
Luke 9:35
2 Pet 1:17

3:23-38
//Matt 1:1-17

3:23
Luke 4:22
John 6:42

3:27
1 Chr 3:17
Ezra 3:2

3:16 *with water:* Or *in water.* • ***I'm not even worthy to be his slave and untie the straps of his sandals:*** The untying of sandals was done only by slaves (to make this connection clear, the NLT adds *be his slave and*). John thus greatly honored the Messiah. • ***baptize you with the Holy Spirit and with fire*** (or *in the Holy Spirit and in fire*): The OT prophets predicted that in the last days, God would pour out his Spirit on his people (Joel 2:28; Ezek 36:28-29; Isa 32:15). This prophecy was at least partially fulfilled on the Day of Pentecost (Acts 2). Fire is an image of judgment (see 3:9); it also has the power to cleanse and refine God's people (see 1 Cor 3:10-15; cp. Isa 4:4; Mal 3:2).

3:17 After being harvested, the kernels of ***wheat*** would be beaten off the stalks and then tossed in the air with a winnowing fork ***to separate*** them from ***the chaff.*** The heavy grain would fall to the ground as the lighter chaff blew away. This is an image of separation for judgment. • ***never-ending fire:*** See Isa 66:24.

3:19-20 ***Herod Antipas, the ruler of Galilee*** (literally *Herod the tetrarch*) divorced his first wife and married ***Herodias,*** the wife of his half ***brother*** Herod Philip. When John ***publicly criticized*** Herod for this sin, Herod imprisoned and later executed him (cp. 9:9; Mark 6:16-29). Herod's execution of John is also recorded by the Jewish historian Josephus (*Antiquities* 18.5.2).

3:21-22 Jesus' baptism marked the beginning of his public ministry and his anointing as the Messiah (the "Anointed One"). The voice of God from heaven confirmed Jesus' identity and mission.

3:21 ***As he was praying:*** Luke emphasizes Jesus' trust and reliance on God in prayer (5:16; 6:12; 9:18, 28; 11:1; 22:32, 41, 44; 23:34, 46). • ***the heavens opened:*** This image was a sign of God's presence (Isa 64:1), divine revelation (Ezek 1:1; John 1:51), and the end of an age (Rev 4:1; 15:5; 19:11).

3:22 The Spirit might have looked ***like a dove,*** or perhaps it ***descended*** in a dove-like manner. • ***You are my dearly loved Son, and you bring me great joy*** (some manuscripts read *my Son, and today I have become your Father*): This statement resonates with Ps 2:7 and Isa 42:1. The former identifies Jesus as the Messiah from David's line; the latter indicates his role as servant of the Lord. Jesus' identity was again declared from heaven at his transfiguration (9:35).

3:23-38 This genealogy reverses Matthew's order (Matt 1:1-17). Luke lists Jesus' lineage back to Adam, possibly to show Jesus' connection with all humanity as the Son of God (3:38). Matthew's genealogy descends from Abraham to Joseph, highlighting Jesus' status as the rightful heir of David's throne and the recipient of God's promises to Abraham. The great differences between the two genealogies have led some to propose that Luke's genealogy is that of Mary (see note on 3:23), who was probably among Luke's primary sources.

3:23 ***Jesus was about thirty years old:*** This is the only reference in the NT to Jesus' age during his public ministry, and it is an approximation. Jesus was born 6~4 BC (see note on 2:2) and began his ministry AD 27~29 (see note on 3:1), so Jesus was evidently 31~35 years old ***when he began his public ministry.*** • ***known as the son of Joseph:*** Jesus was the legal but not the biological son of Joseph. • ***Joseph was the son of Heli:*** If this is actually Mary's genealogy (see note on 3:23-38), then Joseph was Heli's son-in-law, a possible understanding of the Greek sentence.

3:27 ***Zerubbabel*** was the governor of Judea appointed by the Persians when the Jews returned from Babylonian exile. He supervised the rebuilding of the Temple (Ezra 3:2, 8).

3:31-33
Ruth 4:18-22
1 Sam 16:1, 13
2 Sam 5:14
1 Chr 2:9-12; 3:5

3:34-36
Gen 11:10-26
1 Chr 1:24-27

3:36-38
Gen 4:25–5:32
1 Chr 1:1-4

3:38
Gen 1:26-27; 2:7; 5:1-2

4:1-13
//Matt 4:1-11
//Mark 1:12-13
John 3:34

4:1
Isa 11:2; 61:1

4:2
Exod 34:28
1 Kgs 19:8
Heb 4:15
[e]*peirazō* (3985)
‣1 Cor 7:5

4:4
*Deut 8:3

4:6
Matt 28:18
John 12:31; 14:30
1 Jn 5:19
Rev 13:2
[f]*doxa* (1391)
‣Luke 9:32

4:8
*Deut 6:13; 10:20

29 Er was the son of Joshua.
Joshua was the son of Eliezer.
Eliezer was the son of Jorim.
Jorim was the son of Matthat.
Matthat was the son of Levi.
30 Levi was the son of Simeon.
Simeon was the son of Judah.
Judah was the son of Joseph.
Joseph was the son of Jonam.
Jonam was the son of Eliakim.
31 Eliakim was the son of Melea.
Melea was the son of Menna.
Menna was the son of Mattatha.
Mattatha was the son of Nathan.
Nathan was the son of David.
32 David was the son of Jesse.
Jesse was the son of Obed.
Obed was the son of Boaz.
Boaz was the son of Salmon.
Salmon was the son of Nahshon.
33 Nahshon was the son of Amminadab.
Amminadab was the son of Admin.
Admin was the son of Arni.
Arni was the son of Hezron.
Hezron was the son of Perez.
Perez was the son of Judah.
34 Judah was the son of Jacob.
Jacob was the son of Isaac.
Isaac was the son of Abraham.
Abraham was the son of Terah.
Terah was the son of Nahor.
35 Nahor was the son of Serug.
Serug was the son of Reu.
Reu was the son of Peleg.
Peleg was the son of Eber.
Eber was the son of Shelah.
36 Shelah was the son of Cainan.
Cainan was the son of Arphaxad.
Arphaxad was the son of Shem.
Shem was the son of Noah.
Noah was the son of Lamech.
37 Lamech was the son of Methuselah.
Methuselah was the son of Enoch.
Enoch was the son of Jared.
Jared was the son of Mahalalel.
Mahalalel was the son of Kenan.
38 Kenan was the son of Enosh.
Enosh was the son of Seth.
Seth was the son of Adam.
Adam was the son of God.

The Temptation of Jesus (4:1-13)
Luke 4:1-13 // Matt 4:1-11 // Mark 1:12-13

4 Then Jesus, full of the Holy Spirit, returned from the Jordan River. He was
led by the Spirit in the wilderness, 2 where
he was [e]tempted by the devil for forty days.
Jesus ate nothing all that time and became
very hungry.
3 Then the devil said to him, "If you are
the Son of God, tell this stone to become a
loaf of bread."
4 But Jesus told him, "No! The Scriptures
say, 'People do not live by bread alone.' "
5 Then the devil took him up and revealed
to him all the kingdoms of the world in a moment of time. 6 "I will give you the [f]glory of
these kingdoms and authority over them,"
the devil said, "because they are mine to
give to anyone I please. 7 I will give it all to
you if you will worship me."
8 Jesus replied, "The Scriptures say,

'You must worship the LORD your God
and serve only him.' "

9 Then the devil took him to Jerusalem, to
the highest point of the Temple, and said, "If

3:31 *Nathan* was David's third son, born to him in Jerusalem (2 Sam 5:14); he is not to be confused with Nathan the prophet (2 Sam 7:2).

3:32 *Boaz* was the husband of Ruth the Moabite (see Ruth 2–4). • ***Salmon:*** Greek *Sala,* a variant spelling of Salmon. See Ruth 4:20.

3:33 ***Amminadab was the son of Admin. Admin was the son of Arni:*** Some manuscripts read *Amminadab was the son of Aram. Arni* and *Aram* are alternate spellings of Ram. See 1 Chr 2:9-10.

3:38 ***Enosh:*** Greek *Enos,* a variant spelling of Enosh. See Gen 5:6. • ***Seth*** was the third son of Adam and Eve, born after Cain murdered Abel and God banished him (Gen 4:25-26). • ***Adam was the son of God:*** Adam had no earthly father since God created him. In the temptation that follows, Satan repeatedly says to Jesus, "If you are the Son of God. . . ." Adam, the first son of God, failed when tested, but Jesus, the Son of God in the fullest sense, successfully resisted temptation.

4:1-13 Satan tempted Jesus to bypass his Father's plan of salvation by taking power and glory for himself. The forty-day temptation in the wilderness parallels Israel's forty years of testing in the wilderness. Israel failed when tested, but Jesus was victorious.

4:1 ***in the wilderness:*** Some manuscripts read *into the wilderness.*

4:2 ***tempted by the devil:*** The term *diabolos* is a Greek translation of the Hebrew *satan,* meaning "accuser" or "adversary" (1 Chr 21:1; Job 1–2; Zech 3:1-2). Luke uses both terms ("devil," 4:3, 6, 13; 8:12; "Satan," 10:18; 11:18; 13:16; 22:3, 31). Adam and Eve were tested by Satan and failed; Jesus, the second Adam, resisted temptation and thus reversed the judgment against Adam and Eve.

4:3 ***If you are the Son of God:*** Both Israel and Adam are identified as God's sons (3:38; Exod 4:22-23; Hos 11:1). Jesus, the Son of God in the fullest sense, succeeded where Adam and Israel failed.

4:4 ***People do not live by bread alone*** (Deut 8:3): Israel complained constantly about hunger in the wilderness, but Jesus depended on God's strength to sustain him.

4:6 ***they are mine to give:*** The NT elsewhere describes Satan's limited rule over the present world order (John 12:31; 14:30; 16:11; Eph 2:2; 1 Jn 5:19).

4:8 ***You must worship the LORD your God and serve only him*** (Deut 6:13): Israel turned to idolatry when suffering hardship in the wilderness (Deut 9:12). Jesus refused to worship Satan.

you are the Son of God, jump off! 10 For the
Scriptures say,

'He will order his angels to protect and
guard you.
11 And they will hold you up with their
hands
so you won't even hurt your foot on a
stone.'"

12 Jesus responded, "The Scriptures also
say, 'You must not test the LORD your God.'"
13 When the devil had finished tempting
Jesus, he left him until the next opportunity
came.

4. THE MINISTRY OF THE SAVIOR IN GALILEE (4:14–9:50)

Beginning of the Galilean Ministry (4:14–5:16)

Return to Galilee

Luke 4:14-15; cp. Matt 4:12-17; Mark 1:14-15

14 Then Jesus returned to Galilee, filled with
the Holy Spirit's power. Reports about him
spread quickly through the whole region.
15 He taught regularly in their synagogues
and was praised by everyone.

Jesus Is Rejected at Nazareth

Luke 4:16-24 // Matt 13:53-58 // Mark 6:1-6a

16 When he came to the village of Nazareth,
his boyhood home, he went as usual to the
synagogue on the Sabbath and stood up to
read the Scriptures. 17 The [g]scroll of Isaiah
the prophet was handed to him. He unrolled
the [g]scroll and found the place where this
was written:

18 "The Spirit of the LORD is upon me,
for he has anointed me to bring Good
News to the poor.
He has sent me to proclaim that captives
will be released,
that the blind will see,
that the oppressed will be set free,
19 and that the time of the LORD's favor
has come."

20 He rolled up the scroll, handed it back
to the attendant, and sat down. All eyes
in the synagogue looked at him intently.
21 Then he began to speak to them. "The
Scripture you've just heard has been fulfilled this very day!"
22 Everyone spoke well of him and was
amazed by the gracious words that came
from his lips. "How can this be?" they asked.
"Isn't this Joseph's son?"
23 Then he said, "You will undoubtedly
quote me this proverb: 'Physician, heal
yourself'—meaning, 'Do miracles here in
your hometown like those you did in Capernaum.' 24 But I tell you the truth, no prophet
is accepted in his own hometown.
25 "Certainly there were many needy
widows in Israel in Elijah's time, when the
heavens were closed for three and a half
years, and a severe famine devastated the
land. 26 Yet Elijah was not sent to any of
them. He was sent instead to a foreigner—a
widow of Zarephath in the land of Sidon.
27 And there were many lepers in Israel in
the time of the prophet Elisha, but the only
one healed was Naaman, a Syrian."
28 When they heard this, the people in the
synagogue were furious. 29 Jumping up, they
mobbed him and forced him to the edge of
the hill on which the town was built. They
intended to push him over the cliff, 30 but he
passed right through the crowd and went
on his way.

4:10-11 *Ps 91:11-12
4:12 *Deut 6:16
4:13 Heb 4:15
4:14-15 //Matt 4:12-17 //Mark 1:14-15 John 4:43-45
4:16-30 //Matt 13:53-58 //Mark 6:1-6
4:17 [g]*biblion* (0975) ›John 20:30
4:18-19 *Isa 61:1-2
4:19 Lev 25:8-10 2 Cor 6:2
4:22 Luke 2:47 John 6:42; 7:15
4:23 Matt 4:13; 11:23 Mark 1:21-28; 2:1-12
4:24 Matt 13:57 Mark 6:4 John 4:44
4:25-26 1 Kgs 17:1-9; 18:1 Jas 5:17
4:27 2 Kgs 5:1-14
4:29 Num 15:35 Acts 7:58 Heb 13:12
4:30 John 8:59

4:10-11 The quotation is from Ps 91:11-12. Having been repulsed twice by Scripture, the devil now quoted Scripture to Jesus, citing a passage that assures God's people of his protection.

4:12 ***You must not test the LORD your God*** (Deut 6:16): In the wilderness, Israel constantly tested God's faithfulness, but Jesus responded with complete trust in God.

4:13 ***The next opportunity*** might have been Judas's betrayal (22:3-6, 21-22, 47-48); the supreme test came at Gethsemane (22:39-46).

4:14 ***Jesus returned to Galilee:*** The story of Jesus' ministry in Galilee begins here, and continues through 9:50. • ***filled with the Holy Spirit's power:*** At his baptism, Jesus was anointed and empowered to accomplish his role as the Messiah (see 3:22; 4:1, 14, 18).

4:16-30 Jesus' sermon in Nazareth previewed his whole public ministry. Jesus returned to his hometown synagogue to announce the good news that God's salvation had now arrived. The people were pleased until Jesus reminded them that God reaches out to Gentiles as well as to Jews. The infuriated crowd then attempted to kill him.

4:18-19 ***and that the time of the LORD's favor has come:*** Or *and to proclaim the acceptable year of the LORD.* The quotation is from Isa 61:1-2 (Greek version); 58:6. The "time of the LORD's favor" refers to the Year of Jubilee (Lev 25:8-55), when debts were erased, slaves were freed, and land was returned to its original owners. In Isa 61, the Year of Jubilee is a metaphor for God's salvation.

4:21 ***has been fulfilled:*** Jesus announced that because he was present, the new age of salvation had arrived. • ***this very day!*** Literally *today;* cp. 2:11; 5:26; 19:9; 23:43.

4:23 ***Physician, heal yourself*** was a common proverb in the ancient world. Here it might mean "prove your healing powers," or "help your own people, not just others." • ***like those you did in Capernaum:*** See 4:31-44.

4:25-26 ***widow of Zarephath:*** See 1 Kgs 17–18.

4:27 ***Naaman, a Syrian:*** See 2 Kgs 5.

4:28 ***The people in the synagogue were furious*** that Jesus pointed out the favor God had shown to Gentiles. The Jews viewed themselves as sole recipients of God's favor, and they were oppressed by Gentile overlords.

4:30 ***he passed right through the crowd:*** The main emphasis is on the sovereign majesty of Jesus. His time had not yet come (cp. John 7:30, 44; 8:20, 59). This attempt to kill Jesus anticipated his crucifixion, so his escape foreshadows his resurrection.

4:31-37 //Mark 1:23-28
4:31 Matt 4:13-16 John 2:12
4:32 Matt 7:28-29 John 7:46
4:33 ʰ*daimonion* (1140) ‣Luke 8:2
4:34 Luke 4:41 John 6:69
4:35 Luke 4:39-41
4:38-41 //Matt 8:14-17 //Mark 1:29-34
4:40-41 Matt 8:16-17 Mark 1:32-34
4:41 Mark 3:11
4:42-44 Matt 4:23 //Mark 1:35-39

Jesus Casts Out a Demon

Luke 4:31-37 // Mark 1:21-28

31Then Jesus went to Capernaum, a town in Galilee, and taught there in the synagogue every Sabbath day. 32There, too, the people were amazed at his teaching, for he spoke with authority.

33Once when he was in the synagogue, a man possessed by a ʰdemon—an evil spirit—began shouting at Jesus, 34"Go away! Why are you interfering with us, Jesus of Nazareth? Have you come to destroy us? I know who you are—the Holy One of God!"

35Jesus cut him short. "Be quiet! Come out of the man," he ordered. At that, the demon threw the man to the floor as the crowd watched; then it came out of him without hurting him further.

36Amazed, the people exclaimed, "What authority and power this man's words possess! Even evil spirits obey him, and they flee at his command!" 37The news about Jesus spread through every village in the entire region.

Jesus Heals Many People

Luke 4:38-41 // Matt 8:14-17 //Mark 1:29-34

38After leaving the synagogue that day, Jesus went to Simon's home, where he found Simon's mother-in-law very sick with a high fever. "Please heal her," everyone begged. 39Standing at her bedside, he rebuked the fever, and it left her. And she got up at once and prepared a meal for them.

40As the sun went down that evening, people throughout the village brought sick family members to Jesus. No matter what their diseases were, the touch of his hand healed every one. 41Many were possessed by demons; and the demons came out at his command, shouting, "You are the Son of God!" But because they knew he was the Messiah, he rebuked them and refused to let them speak.

Jesus Continues to Preach in Galilee

42Early the next morning Jesus went out to an isolated place. The crowds searched everywhere for him, and when they finally

The Suffering Prophet (4:22-24)

Luke 6:23, 26; 7:16; 11:47-52; 13:33-34; 24:17-21
Deut 18:15
Matt 5:12; 23:34-37
Acts 3:22-23; 7:37, 52

Jesus is described by many titles in the Gospels, including Messiah, Son of David, Son of Man, Son of God, and Lord. In Luke, a key title is "Prophet." Jesus was the prophet that Moses predicted in Deut 18:15.

As a prophet, Jesus preached God's word and performed miracles like those of the great OT prophets. When Jesus raised the widow's son, the people cried out, "A mighty prophet has risen among us" (7:16). The disciples on the Emmaus road identified him as "a prophet who did powerful miracles, and he was a mighty teacher" (24:19).

Like other prophets, Jesus suffered for his testimony (cp. 1 Kgs 19:3-18; Jer 11:18-19; 18:18; 20:1-2, 7-18; 26:7-11, 20-23; 38:1-6). While the people linked Jesus' prophetic office to his miracles and teaching, Jesus connected it especially to his suffering. At Nazareth, he affirmed that "no prophet is accepted in his own hometown" (4:24), and he later accused Israel of murdering its prophets (11:47-52). As he journeyed to Jerusalem, he exclaimed, "It wouldn't do for a prophet of God to be killed except in Jerusalem!" (13:33).

In the OT, when Israel did not heed God's prophets, divine judgment followed. Similarly, God's people had to listen to Jesus or face judgment (see Acts 3:22-23; 7:37).

Just as the revelation that Jesus is the Messiah confirms that he is the Savior for all people, so his role as prophet confirms that his message comes from God, and his words are the authentic word of God, which must be heard and obeyed.

4:31 Jesus moved from Nazareth to make ***Capernaum*** his base of operations during his Galilean ministry (see Mark 2:1).

4:33 ***an evil*** (literally *unclean;* also in 4:36) ***spirit: Unclean*** means "defiled" or "wicked"; hence, the NLT translation "evil spirit."

4:34 ***Have you come to destroy us?*** Though there was only one demon present, the plural *us* suggests that all of Satan's forces were aware and fearful of Jesus' coming. • ***I know who you are:*** A common ancient belief held that naming a spiritual power gave a person authority over it. The demon might have been attempting to gain power over Jesus.

4:36 ***What authority and power this man's words possess!*** Magicians and exorcists often used elaborate rituals and incantations. The people were amazed that Jesus merely spoke a word on his own authority and cast out the demon.

4:38 ***Simon's home:*** Simon was from Bethsaida (John 1:44), but his present home and fishing business were in Capernaum. • ***Simon's mother-in-law:*** Peter was married (see 1 Cor 9:5), but his wife is not named.

4:39 ***he rebuked the fever:*** The same Greek word was used when Jesus rebuked the demon (4:36). Jesus has full authority over physical and spiritual forces.

4:41 ***You are the Son of God!*** This was a title for the Messiah (see 2 Sam 7:14; Ps 2:7; 89:26-27). Luke often links the titles "Christ" and "Son of God" (9:35, 22:66-71; Acts 9:20, 22). • ***he . . . refused to let them speak:*** Jesus often showed his authority over demons by silencing them. He wanted to reveal his identity in his own way, not through their announcement.

found him, they begged him not to leave
them. 43But he replied, "I must preach the
Good News of the Kingdom of God in other
towns, too, because that is why I was sent."
44So he continued to travel around, preaching in synagogues throughout Judea.

The First Disciples: A Miraculous Catch of Fish

5 One day as Jesus was preaching on the
shore of the Sea of Galilee, great crowds
pressed in on him to listen to the word of
God. 2He noticed two empty boats at the water's edge, for the fishermen had left them
and were washing their nets. 3Stepping
into one of the boats, Jesus asked Simon, its
owner, to push it out into the water. So he
sat in the boat and taught the crowds from
there.
4When he had finished speaking, he said
to Simon, "Now go out where it is deeper,
and let down your nets to catch some fish."
5"Master," Simon replied, "we worked
hard all last night and didn't catch a thing.
But if you say so, I'll let the nets down again."
6And this time their nets were so full of fish
they began to tear! 7A shout for help brought
their partners in the other boat, and soon
both boats were filled with fish and on the
verge of sinking.
8When Simon Peter realized what had
happened, he fell to his knees before Jesus
and said, "Oh, Lord, please leave me—I'm
too much of a sinner to be around you." 9For
he was awestruck by the number of fish
they had caught, as were the others with
him. 10His partners, James and John, the
sons of Zebedee, were also amazed.
Jesus replied to Simon, "Don't be afraid!
From now on you'll be fishing for people!"
11And as soon as they landed, they left everything and followed Jesus.

Jesus Heals a Man with Leprosy

Luke 5:12-16 // Matt 8:1-4 // Mark 1:40-45

12In one of the villages, Jesus met a man
with an advanced case of leprosy. When
the man saw Jesus, he bowed with his face
to the ground, begging to be healed. "Lord,"
he said, "if you are willing, you can heal me
and make me clean."
13Jesus reached out and touched him. "I
am willing," he said. "Be healed!" And instantly the leprosy disappeared. 14Then
Jesus instructed him not to tell anyone
what had happened. He said, "Go to the
priest and let him examine you. Take along
the offering required in the law of Moses
for those who have been healed of leprosy.
This will be a public testimony that you have
been cleansed."
15But despite Jesus' instructions, the report of his power spread even faster, and

4:43 Luke 8:1
4:44 Matt 4:23; Mark 1:39
5:1-11 //Matt 4:18-22; //Mark 1:16-20
5:4 John 21:6
5:5 John 21:3
5:6 John 21:11
5:8 Gen 18:27; Job 42:5-6
5:11 Matt 19:27
5:12-14 //Matt 8:2-4; //Mark 1:40-44
5:14 Lev 14:2-32
5:15 Matt 9:26

4:43 The Greek verb translated *preach the Good News* corresponds to the noun often translated "gospel" ("Good News"; see note on 2:9-10; see also 1:19; 7:22; Matt 4:23; 24:14; Mark 1:1, 15; 16:15; Acts 8:4, 12; Rom 1:1-6, 15-17; 10:15-17; Gal 1:6-9; Eph 2:14-18; 3:6-7). • ***The Kingdom of God*** was Jesus' central concern (see Mark 1:15), and God's sovereign reign was established through Jesus' words and deeds.

4:44 ***Judea*** (some manuscripts read *Galilee*): Luke probably used *Judea* in the general sense of "the land of the Jews," since Jesus' ministry was then in Galilee in the north (see 5:1), not south in Judea.

5:1-11 This is the first call of disciples recorded in Luke; Matthew and Mark recount a (presumably earlier) call of the four fishermen brothers (Matt 4:18-22; Mark 1:16-20). Jesus demonstrated extraordinary authority in the miraculous catch of fish and in his call of Simon Peter.

5:1 ***the Sea of Galilee:*** Greek *the Lake of Gennesaret*, another name for the Sea of Galilee.

5:3 ***Simon*** is called "Peter" in 6:14 and thereafter. • ***So he sat in the boat and taught the crowds:*** By sitting in the boat slightly offshore, Jesus had a platform from which to address the people without being mobbed.

5:4 ***let down your nets to catch some fish:*** Peter was naturally skeptical when a rabbi told fishermen how to catch fish. Jesus' command was odd for three reasons: (1) When the sun came up, the fish moved to the bottom of the lake (which is why they fished at night); (2) they fished with a heavy dragnet hung over the side of the boat by two men (or between two boats) and could not go deep with it; (3) they had just fished all night with no results, and the prospects were now much more unlikely.

5:7 ***Their partners in the other boat*** were James and John, who with their father Zebedee were business partners with Peter (see 5:10; Mark 1:19-20) and Andrew (see Mark 1:16). • ***both boats were filled with fish:*** This dramatic miracle confirmed Jesus' authority over the forces of nature.

5:8 ***I'm too much of a sinner to be around you:*** Cp. Isa 6:5.

5:10 Jesus drew a spiritual analogy between *fishing* and seeking *people* for the Kingdom of God.

5:11 ***they left everything:*** Their sacrifice was remarkable in a culture that so highly valued loyalty to family and clan.

5:12 ***an advanced case of leprosy:*** "Leprosy" does not refer specifically to the modern disease known as leprosy (Hansen's disease), but to a variety of skin disorders. To avoid contagion, lepers were outcasts in the ancient world, required to live on the margins of society. The law of Moses set guidelines for the diagnosis and quarantine of leprosy (Lev 13–14; see note on Lev 13:1-46).

5:13 ***Jesus reached out and touched him:*** Most people feared catching the disease through physical contact, but Jesus showed compassion. Jesus was not contaminated by disease or evil, but brought healing and salvation. • ***Be healed:*** Literally *Be cleansed.* This act had spiritual and physical significance, since leprosy separated Israelites from social contact and religious practice.

5:14 Jesus often told those he healed ***not to tell anyone what had happened*** to avoid celebrity status. Nonetheless, news of these events spreads like wildfire (see 5:15-16; see "The Secret of the Messiah" at Mark 3:11-12, p. 1653). • ***Go to the priest and let him examine you. . . . the offering:*** Those healed of leprosy had to be declared clean by a priest, and a sacrifice was offered on their behalf (see Lev 14:2-32).

5:17-26
//Matt 9:1-8
//Mark 2:1-12
5:20
Luke 7:48
5:21
Isa 43:25; 55:7
Luke 7:49
5:22
Ps 139:1
Luke 6:8; 9:47
5:24-25
John 5:8-9
5:27-32
//Matt 9:9-13
//Mark 2:13-17
5:29-30
Luke 15:1-2; 19:1-9
5:32
ᶦ*metanoia* (3341)
‣Luke 24:47
5:33-39
//Matt 9:14-17
//Mark 2:18-22

vast crowds came to hear him preach and to
be healed of their diseases. 16But Jesus often
withdrew to the wilderness for prayer.

Controversies Begin (5:17–6:11)

Jesus Heals a Paralyzed Man
Luke 5:17-26 // Matt 9:1-8 // Mark 2:1-12

17One day while Jesus was teaching, some
Pharisees and teachers of religious law
were sitting nearby. (It seemed that these
men showed up from every village in all Galilee and Judea, as well as from Jerusalem.)
And the Lord's healing power was strongly
with Jesus.
18Some men came carrying a paralyzed
man on a sleeping mat. They tried to take
him inside to Jesus, 19but they couldn't
reach him because of the crowd. So they
went up to the roof and took off some tiles.
Then they lowered the sick man on his mat
down into the crowd, right in front of Jesus.
20Seeing their faith, Jesus said to the man,
"Young man, your sins are forgiven."
21But the Pharisees and teachers of religious law said to themselves, "Who does
he think he is? That's blasphemy! Only God
can forgive sins!"
22Jesus knew what they were thinking, so
he asked them, "Why do you question this
in your hearts? 23Is it easier to say 'Your sins
are forgiven,' or 'Stand up and walk'? 24So
I will prove to you that the Son of Man has
the authority on earth to forgive sins." Then
Jesus turned to the paralyzed man and said,
"Stand up, pick up your mat, and go home!"
25And immediately, as everyone watched,
the man jumped up, picked up his mat, and
went home praising God. 26Everyone was
gripped with great wonder and awe, and
they praised God, exclaiming, "We have
seen amazing things today!"

Jesus Calls Notorious Sinners
Luke 5:27-32 // Matt 9:9-13 // Mark 2:13-17

27Later, as Jesus left the town, he saw a tax
collector named Levi sitting at his tax collector's booth. "Follow me and be my disciple,"
Jesus said to him. 28So Levi got up, left everything, and followed him.
29Later, Levi held a banquet in his home
with Jesus as the guest of honor. Many of
Levi's fellow tax collectors and other guests
also ate with them. 30But the Pharisees and
their teachers of religious law complained
bitterly to Jesus' disciples, "Why do you eat
and drink with such scum?"
31Jesus answered them, "Healthy people
don't need a doctor—sick people do. 32I
have come to call not those who think they
are righteous, but those who know they are
sinners and need to ᶦrepent."

A Discussion about Fasting
Luke 5:33-39 // Matt 9:14-17 // Mark 2:18-22

33One day some people said to Jesus,
"John the Baptist's disciples fast and pray
regularly, and so do the disciples of the Pharisees. Why are your disciples always eating
and drinking?"

5:17-26 The healing of the paralyzed man initiated the conflicts Jesus had with religious leaders throughout his public ministry until he was crucified in Jerusalem.

5:17 ***Pharisees:*** See "The Pharisees" at Matt 3:7, p. 1581. • ***Teachers of religious law,*** also called "scribes" and "lawyers," were experts in interpreting the law of Moses. Most of the scribes were Pharisees, though some were Sadducees.

5:19 ***took off some tiles:*** Palestinian roofs were normally made of wooden beams covered with reeds and mud or clay. Either this roof had tiles, or else Luke was interpreting the episode for his Greek readers (cp. Mark 2:4, which speaks of *digging through* the roof).

5:22 ***Jesus knew what they were thinking:*** While the Pharisees were accusing Jesus of blasphemy, he was reading their minds—something only God can do.

5:23-24 Jesus showed his authority to forgive sins by healing the man.

5:24 ***Son of Man*** is a title Jesus used for himself (see "The Son of Man" at Matt 8:18-20, p. 1593).

5:25 ***praising God:*** See note on 2:20.

5:27-32 The call of Levi led to Jesus' second conflict with the religious leaders, and it introduced the idea that Jesus had come to save sinners.

5:27 ***tax collector:*** See note on 3:12. • Levi's ***tax collector's booth*** was probably a toll booth for goods in transit. • ***Levi*** was also called Matthew (Matt 9:9; see "Matthew (Levi)" at Matt 9:9-10, p. 1594).

5:29 ***with Jesus as the guest of honor:*** Matthew introduced Jesus to his friends and colleagues to honor Jesus for calling him as a disciple. It was common in the ancient world to repay honor with honor.

5:30 ***with such scum?*** Literally *with tax collectors and sinners?* Meals were rituals of social status in the ancient world, and eating with someone meant social acceptance of that person. The Pharisees refused to eat with tax collectors and other sinners, or to enter their homes, believing that this would defile them. They expected Jesus, as a rabbi, to do the same. Jesus shattered social norms by dining with sinners and allowing sinful people to touch him (5:29; 7:39; 15:1). The religious leaders severely criticized him for this and derisively called him "a friend of tax collectors and other sinners" (7:34).

5:31-32 Jesus responded that, like ***a doctor,*** his mission was to work with ***sick people,*** not the healthy. Jesus was not called to minister to self-righteous people, but those who recognized their spiritual need for God's grace and healing.

5:33 ***John the Baptist's disciples:*** Most rabbis had students who learned from them and served them (see also Acts 19:1-7). • ***fast and pray regularly:*** Many pious Jews fasted two days a week (18:12). Fasting was associated with spiritual preparation (Esth 4:16) and repentance (2 Sam 12:22; Joel 1:14; Jon 3:5). Fasting is not a means of righteousness (Isa 58:4-5; Jer 14:12), but a spiritual discipline for cultivating intimacy with God. Fasting is often linked with prayer and spiritual retreat. • ***Why are your disciples always eating and drinking?*** The point was that they did not fast regularly.

34Jesus responded, "Do wedding guests
fast while celebrating with the groom? Of
course not. 35But someday the groom will
be taken away from them, and then they
will fast."
36Then Jesus gave them this [j]illustration:
"No one tears a piece of cloth from a new garment and uses it to patch an old garment.
For then the new garment would be ruined,
and the new patch wouldn't even match the
old garment.
37"And no one puts new wine into old
wineskins. For the new wine would burst
the wineskins, spilling the wine and ruining the skins. 38New wine must be stored
in new wineskins. 39But no one who drinks
the old wine seems to want the new wine.
'The old is just fine,' they say."

A Discussion about the Sabbath

Luke 6:1-5 // Matt 12:1-8 // Mark 2:23-28

6 One Sabbath day as Jesus was walking
through some grainfields, his disciples
broke off heads of grain, rubbed off the
husks in their hands, and ate the grain.
2But some Pharisees said, "Why are you
breaking the law by harvesting grain on the
Sabbath?"
3Jesus replied, "Haven't you read in the
Scriptures what David did when he and his
companions were hungry? 4He went into
the house of God and broke the law by eating the sacred loaves of bread that only the
priests can eat. He also gave some to his
companions." 5And Jesus added, "The Son
of Man is Lord, even over the Sabbath."

Jesus Heals on the Sabbath

Luke 6:6-11 // Matt 12:9-14 // Mark 3:1-6

6On another Sabbath day, a man with a deformed right hand was in the synagogue
while Jesus was teaching. 7The teachers of
religious law and the Pharisees watched
Jesus closely. If he healed the man's hand,
they planned to accuse him of working on
the Sabbath.
8But Jesus knew their thoughts. He said
to the man with the deformed hand, "Come
and stand in front of everyone." So the man
came forward. 9Then Jesus said to his critics, "I have a question for you. Does the law
permit good deeds on the Sabbath, or is it a
day for doing evil? Is this a day to save life
or to destroy it?"
10He looked around at them one by one
and then said to the man, "Hold out your
hand." So the man held out his hand, and it
was restored! 11At this, the enemies of Jesus
were wild with rage and began to discuss
what to do with him.

Jesus Chooses the Twelve Apostles

Luke 6:12-16 // Matt 10:1-4 // Mark 3:13-19

12One day soon afterward Jesus went up on
a mountain to pray, and he prayed to God all

5:34 John 3:29
5:35 Luke 9:22; 17:22
5:36 [j]*parabolē* (3850) ‣Luke 12:41
6:1-5 //Matt 12:1-8 //Mark 2:23-28
6:1 Deut 23:25
6:2 John 5:10
6:3-4 1 Sam 21:6
6:4 Lev 24:5-9
6:6-11 //Matt 12:9-14 //Mark 3:1-6
6:7 Luke 14:1
6:8 Luke 5:22; 9:47
6:12-16 //Matt 10:2-4 //Mark 3:13-19

5:34-35 *Do wedding guests fast?* Just as it would be inappropriate for anyone to fast at a wedding celebration, it was inappropriate for people to fast while the Messiah was with them. God's final salvation is a great wedding feast that God prepares for his people (Isa 25:6-8; see "The Messianic Banquet" at 14:1-24, p. 1737).

5:36-38 ***a new garment . . . new wine:*** New cloth shrinks when washed and so tears the old; new wine expands with fermentation and breaks brittle old wineskins. In either case, both old and new are ruined. Both illustrations make the point that the old is incompatible with the new. Jesus did not come to patch up the old covenant, but to establish a new one. The Kingdom of God brings a whole new orientation to thinking and living.

5:39 *The old is just fine:* The religious leaders were resistant to change.

6:1-11 Jesus' conflicts with the religious leaders continued with two controversies over the Sabbath. The law of Moses required Jews to rest on the Sabbath (Exod 20:8-11; Deut 5:13-14), but the Pharisees had forgotten that the real reason for the Sabbath was to benefit human beings.

6:1 ***his disciples broke off heads of grain:*** The law allowed this kind of grazing while walking through someone else's field (Deut 23:24-25).

6:2 ***by harvesting grain:*** The disciples were not accused of stealing grain, but of working on the Sabbath. They were breaking rules established by oral tradition.

6:3 While fleeing from Saul (1 Sam 21), ***David . . . and his companions*** took refuge at the sanctuary of Nob. The priest Ahimelech gave them the consecrated Bread of the Presence that only priests were lawfully allowed to eat (Exod 25:30; Lev 24:9). Jesus' point was that a technical violation of the law is superseded by the higher law of meeting human needs. There might also be a comparison between David and Jesus as God's chosen and anointed kings of Israel.

6:5 *Son of Man* is a title Jesus used for himself (see "The Son of Man" at Matt 8:18-20, p. 1593). • ***Lord, even over the Sabbath:*** The saying is a play on words with a double meaning. First, *son of man* often means "human being," so Jesus affirmed that the Sabbath was made to serve human beings. *Son of Man* was also a title for the Messiah (see Dan 7:13-14). Jesus is Lord of the Sabbath because he created it.

6:6-7 ***watched Jesus closely:*** Jesus now had a reputation for placing human needs above the Sabbath commands, so the religious leaders hoped to catch him working on the Sabbath. • ***If he healed the man's hand:*** The rabbis of Jesus' day debated whether offering medical help was justified on the Sabbath; it was generally allowed only in extreme emergencies. The deformed hand was clearly not an emergency.

6:8 *Come and stand in front of everyone:* Jesus did not shy away from controversy, but was willing to confront the Pharisees' hypocrisy head on.

6:9 ***Is this a day to save life or to destroy it?*** Jesus' question penetrated the religious leaders' motives. They were plotting against Jesus (an evil act) because he was going to heal someone (a good act).

6:12 ***he prayed to God all night:*** See note on 3:21. Jesus prayed before important events and decisions such as choosing the Twelve, who would carry on his ministry after him.

6:13
John 6:70
6:14-15
Acts 1:13
6:17-19
//Matt 4:23-25
6:19
Matt 9:20
Mark 5:30
6:20-23
//Matt 5:1-12
6:20
[k]*makarios* (3107)
‣Luke 11:28
6:21
Eccl 3:4
Isa 55:1; 61:3
Rev 7:16-17
6:22
John 15:19; 16:2
1 Pet 4:14
6:23
2 Chr 36:16
Acts 5:41; 7:52
Jas 1:2
6:24
Jas 5:1
6:25
Isa 5:22; 65:13
6:26
Jas 4:4
6:27-35
//Matt 5:38-48
6:27
Prov 25:21
Rom 12:20
6:28
Rom 12:14

night. 13 At daybreak he called together all
of his disciples and chose twelve of them to
be apostles. Here are their names:

14 Simon (whom he named Peter),
Andrew (Peter's brother),
James,
John,
Philip,
Bartholomew,
15 Matthew,
Thomas,
James (son of Alphaeus),
Simon (who was called the zealot),
16 Judas (son of James),
Judas Iscariot (who later betrayed him).

Jesus Teaches His Disciples: The Great Sermon (6:17-49)

Crowds Follow Jesus
Luke 6:17-19 // Mark 3:7-12

17 When they came down from the mountain, the disciples stood with Jesus on a
large, level area, surrounded by many of his
followers and by the crowds. There were
people from all over Judea and from Jerusalem and from as far north as the seacoasts
of Tyre and Sidon. 18 They had come to hear
him and to be healed of their diseases; and
those troubled by evil spirits were healed.
19 Everyone tried to touch him, because
healing power went out from him, and he
healed everyone.

Beatitudes and Sorrows
Luke 6:20-23 // Matt 5:3-12

20 Then Jesus turned to his disciples and
said,

"God [k]blesses you who are poor,
for the Kingdom of God is yours.
21 God blesses you who are hungry now,
for you will be satisfied.
God blesses you who weep now,
for in due time you will laugh.

22 What blessings await you when people
hate you and exclude you and mock you
and curse you as evil because you follow
the Son of Man. 23 When that happens, be
happy! Yes, leap for joy! For a great reward
awaits you in heaven. And remember, their
ancestors treated the ancient prophets that
same way.

24 "What sorrow awaits you who are rich,
for you have your only happiness
now.
25 What sorrow awaits you who are fat and
prosperous now,
for a time of awful hunger awaits you.
What sorrow awaits you who laugh now,
for your laughing will turn to
mourning and sorrow.
26 What sorrow awaits you who are praised
by the crowds,
for their ancestors also praised false
prophets.

Love for Enemies
Luke 6:27-36; cp. Matt 5:38-48; Matt 7:12

27 "But to you who are willing to listen, I say,
love your enemies! Do good to those who
hate you. 28 Bless those who curse you. Pray
for those who hurt you. 29 If someone slaps
you on one cheek, offer the other cheek
also. If someone demands your coat, offer

6:13 *Disciples* were students and followers; *apostles* were specially commissioned representatives. • The number *twelve* symbolically represents the twelve tribes of Israel. The apostles represented the restored people of God.

6:14 *Simon (whom he named Peter):* Peter means "rock" or "stone" (see Matt 16:18).

6:15 *Matthew* was the tax collector also called Levi (see 5:27; Matt 9:9; 10:3). • *Simon (who was called the zealot): Zealot* probably meant that he had joined the Zealot movement, a group of Jews actively seeking to overthrow the Roman government. The diversity of Jesus' apostles is striking.

6:16 *Judas (son of James)* was probably also called Thaddaeus (Matt 10:3; Mark 3:18). He was a different man than Judas Iscariot or Jude the half brother of Jesus (who wrote the NT book of Jude). • *Judas Iscariot: Iscariot* probably means "from Kerioth," a village twelve miles south of Hebron.

6:17-49 The central theme of Jesus' great sermon is that an authentic life of righteousness accompanies repentance and acceptance into God's Kingdom.

6:17 *all over Judea . . . Tyre and Sidon:* Tyre and Sidon were coastal cities on the Mediterranean Sea northwest of Galilee. Jesus was gaining wide popularity.

6:18 *evil:* Literally *unclean.*

6:20-23 *God blesses* those who acknowledge their inadequacy and weakness and turn to God for strength. The value system of God's Kingdom is radically different from the world's value system, in which power and strength represent success.

6:20-21 *poor . . . hungry:* Cp. Matt 5:3, 6. Luke had physical and spiritual poverty in mind. Poverty and suffering tend to make us more dependent on God. The OT includes many promises that God will feed and comfort his people (Ps 22:26; 107:36-41; 126:1-6; Isa 49:10-13; 51:3; 65:13).

6:23 *treated the ancient prophets that same way:* See "The Suffering Prophet" at 4:22-24, p. 1711.

6:24-26 Promises of blessing for the poor and oppressed are balanced in Luke with predictions of *sorrow* for the rich and powerful. Those who trust in themselves will be humbled, while those who depend on God will be blessed. The OT prophets often pronounced woes against nations and rulers who oppressed God's people and rejected his sovereignty (e.g., Isa 3:11; 5:8; Jer 50:27; Zech 11:17).

6:27 *love your enemies!* People were commonly taught in the ancient world to love their family and friends and hate their enemies. Jesus announced a radical new ethic of loving even one's enemies and overcoming evil through self-sacrificial love for others, not through violence and hatred (cp. Rom 12:14-21).

your shirt also. 30Give to anyone who asks; and when things are taken away from you, don't try to get them back. 31Do to others as you would like them to do to you.

32"If you love only those who love you, why should you get credit for that? Even sinners love those who love them! 33And if you do good only to those who do good to you, why should you get credit? Even sinners do that much! 34And if you lend money only to those who can repay you, why should you get credit? Even sinners will lend to other sinners for a full return.

35"Love your enemies! Do good to them. Lend to them without expecting to be repaid. Then your reward from heaven will be very great, and you will truly be acting as children of the Most High, for he is kind to those who are unthankful and wicked. 36You must be compassionate, just as your Father is compassionate.

Do Not Judge Others
Luke 6:37-42 // Matt 7:1-5

37"Do not judge others, and you will not be judged. Do not condemn others, or it will all come back against you. Forgive others, and you will be forgiven. 38Give, and you will receive. Your gift will return to you in full—pressed down, shaken together to make room for more, running over, and poured into your lap. The amount you give will determine the amount you get back."

39Then Jesus gave the following illustration: "Can one blind person lead another? Won't they both fall into a ditch? 40Students are not greater than their teacher. But the student who is fully trained will become like the teacher.

41"And why worry about a speck in your friend's eye when you have a log in your own? 42How can you think of saying, 'Friend, let me help you get rid of that speck in your eye,' when you can't see past the log in your own eye? [a]Hypocrite! First get rid of the log in your own eye; then you will see well enough to deal with the speck in your friend's eye.

The Tree and Its Fruit
Luke 6:43-45 // Matt 12:33-35; cp. Matt 7:15-20

43"A good tree can't produce bad fruit, and a bad tree can't produce good fruit. 44A tree is identified by its fruit. Figs are never gathered from thornbushes, and grapes are not picked from bramble bushes. 45A good person produces good things from the treasury of a good heart, and an evil person produces evil things from the treasury of an evil heart. What you say flows from what is in your heart.

Building on a Solid Foundation
Luke 6:47-49 // Matt 7:24-27

46"So why do you keep calling me 'Lord, Lord!' when you don't do what I say? 47I will show you what it's like when someone comes to me, listens to my teaching, and then follows it. 48It is like a person building a house who digs deep and lays the foundation on solid [b]rock. When the floodwaters rise and break against that house, it stands firm because it is well built. 49But anyone who hears and doesn't obey is like a person who builds a house without a foundation. When the floods sweep down against that house, it will collapse into a heap of ruins."

6:30 Deut 15:7-8, 10
6:31 Matt 7:12
6:33-35 Lev 25:35-36
6:36 Matt 5:48
6:37-42 //Matt 7:1-5
6:38 Ps 79:12; Mark 4:24
6:39 Matt 15:14
6:40 Matt 10:24-25; John 13:16; 15:20
6:42 [a]*hupokritēs* (5273) ‣Luke 13:15
6:43-45 //Matt 7:17-20; 12:34-35
6:44 Matt 12:33
6:46 Mal 1:6; Matt 7:21
6:47-49 //Matt 7:24-27
6:48 [b]*petra* (4073) ‣John 1:42

6:30 ***when things are taken away from you, don't try to get them back:*** Jesus' point is that the cycle of hatred and violence that characterizes human nature can only be broken by responding with good, not evil (Rom 12:17). We win the world through self-sacrificial love. Jesus was not promoting injustice, as though believers should let criminals take advantage of the weak. God established governments to punish evildoers (Rom 13:1-5).

6:31 ***Do to others as you would like them to do to you:*** While the golden rule appears in some form in various religious and philosophical traditions, only in Jesus' teaching is love for all people, including enemies, the fundamental ethic that governs all behavior.

6:34-36 The law of Moses prohibited charging interest on loans to other Israelites in order to prevent exploitation of the poor (Exod 22:25; Lev 25:35-37; Deut 23:20). Jesus further instructed his followers to ***lend . . . without expecting to be repaid.*** By doing good even to those who do evil, we act ***as children of the Most High*** and imitate our ***Father*** in heaven, who ***is kind*** to all people (cp. Rom 5:8).

6:37-42 ***Do not judge others:*** Jesus condemned hypocritical judgment that denigrated another person. Those who condemn others will be judged by that same standard. God requires his people to love others by warning them of the dangers of sin (Gal 6:1; Heb 3:13). Exhortation is an act of love; judgment is an act of pride.

6:38 ***pressed down, shaken together:*** A generous grain merchant would top off the buyer's container, press it down, shake it to make more room, and then pour until the grain overflowed into the buyer's ***lap.*** • ***The amount you give will determine the amount you get back:*** Or *The measure you give will be the measure you get back.*

6:40 ***Students:*** Or *Disciples.*

6:41 ***your friend's eye:*** Literally *your brother's eye;* also in 6:42. • ***a log in your own:*** Jesus did not say that the speck in our friend's eye is not our business, but that we must first correct our own faults so that we can see clearly enough to remove the speck. Jesus condemned hypocritical judgment; lovingly holding one another accountable regarding sin is desirable.

6:42 ***Friend:*** Literally *Brother.*

6:45 What people take in and treasure determines what will emerge in their lives.

6:49 ***anyone who hears and doesn't obey:*** See Ezek 33:31-33.

7:1-10
//Matt 8:5-13
//John 4:43-54

7:2
John 4:47

7:5
Acts 10:2

7:7
Ps 107:20

7:11-16
1 Kgs 17:17-24
2 Kgs 4:32-37
Mark 5:21-24, 35-43
John 11:1-44

7:12
Luke 8:42; 9:38
[c]*monogenēs* (3439)
‣Luke 8:42

7:13
Luke 8:52

7:14
Luke 8:54
John 11:43
Acts 9:40

7:16
Luke 1:65-68

7:17
Matt 9:26

7:18-35
//Matt 11:2-19

7:19
Mal 3:1-3

Jesus' Compassionate Ministry (7:1-50)

The Faith of a Roman Officer

Luke 7:1-10 // Matt 8:5-13

7 When Jesus had finished saying all this to the people, he returned to Capernaum. 2At that time the highly valued slave of a Roman officer was sick and near death. 3When the officer heard about Jesus, he sent some respected Jewish elders to ask him to come and heal his slave. 4So they earnestly begged Jesus to help the man. "If anyone deserves your help, he does," they said, 5"for he loves the Jewish people and even built a synagogue for us."

6So Jesus went with them. But just before they arrived at the house, the officer sent some friends to say, "Lord, don't trouble yourself by coming to my home, for I am not worthy of such an honor. 7I am not even worthy to come and meet you. Just say the word from where you are, and my servant will be healed. 8I know this because I am under the authority of my superior officers, and I have authority over my soldiers. I only need to say, 'Go,' and they go, or 'Come,' and they come. And if I say to my slaves, 'Do this,' they do it."

9When Jesus heard this, he was amazed. Turning to the crowd that was following him, he said, "I tell you, I haven't seen faith like this in all Israel!" 10And when the officer's friends returned to his house, they found the slave completely healed.

Jesus Raises a Widow's Son

11Soon afterward Jesus went with his disciples to the village of Nain, and a large crowd followed him. 12A funeral procession was coming out as he approached the village gate. The young man who had died was a widow's [c]only son, and a large crowd from the village was with her. 13When the Lord saw her, his heart overflowed with compassion. "Don't cry!" he said. 14Then he walked over to the coffin and touched it, and the bearers stopped. "Young man," he said, "I tell you, get up." 15Then the dead boy sat up and began to talk! And Jesus gave him back to his mother.

16Great fear swept the crowd, and they praised God, saying, "A mighty prophet has risen among us," and "God has visited his people today." 17And the news about Jesus spread throughout Judea and the surrounding countryside.

Jesus and John the Baptist

Luke 7:18-35 // Matt 11:2-19

18The disciples of John the Baptist told John about everything Jesus was doing. So John called for two of his disciples, 19and he sent them to the Lord to ask him, "Are you the Messiah we've been expecting, or should we keep looking for someone else?"

20John's two disciples found Jesus and said to him, "John the Baptist sent us to ask, 'Are you the Messiah we've been expecting,

---

7:1-10 This episode shows God's message of salvation is for Gentiles as well as Jews.

7:2 ***a Roman officer*** (literally *centurion;* similarly in 7:6): A centurion was in charge of a "century," approximately 100 soldiers. There were 60 centuries, or 6,000 soldiers, in a Roman legion.

7:3 ***Jewish elders*** were leaders in the Jewish community. With his tendency to abbreviate accounts, Matthew has the centurion approaching Jesus (Matt 8:5-13). Luke tells the full story in which Jewish elders, and later the centurion's friends, act as intermediaries.

7:5 ***he loves the Jewish people and even built a synagogue for us:*** Such patronage by wealthy Gentiles was common in Jewish communities throughout the Roman empire. It suggests that the centurion might have been a "God-fearer" like Cornelius (Acts 10:2), a Gentile who worshiped the God of Israel but had not fully converted to Judaism.

7:6 ***I am not worthy of such an honor:*** The man was probably showing sensitivity to Jewish concerns; pious Jews would not enter the home of a Gentile, since it would make them ceremonially unclean (see Acts 10:28; 11:12). The centurion might also have been acknowledging Jesus' superior status.

7:8 ***the authority of my superior officers:*** The Roman army was renowned for its organization and discipline. The centurion recognized authority when he saw it in Jesus' words and actions.

7:9 ***I haven't seen faith like this in all Israel!*** While many in Israel were unresponsive to the Good News of salvation, some Gentiles believed and found salvation.

7:11-17 Jesus raised three people from the dead; the others were Jairus's daughter (8:40-56) and Lazarus (John 11:38-44). Jesus has authority over life and death (cp. 1 Kgs 17:17-24; 2 Kgs 4:18-37).

7:11 The location of ***the village of Nain*** is uncertain; it might be the modern town of Nein, six miles southeast of Nazareth.

7:12 ***A funeral procession:*** In Judaism, ***a large crowd*** of mourners and intense wailing signified great love for the deceased. Mourners were hired in some cases. • Widows were the most vulnerable members of society, and God had special concern for them (Exod 22:22; Deut 10:18; 27:19). This ***widow's only son*** was her means of support and hope for the future; his death was a terrible loss (see Jer 6:26; Amos 8:10; Zech 12:10).

7:13-14 The word translated ***coffin*** may refer to a casket or a funeral bier. A Jew was rendered unclean by touching a dead body or the coffin or bier (Lev 21:1, 11-12). As when he touched the man with leprosy (5:13), however, Jesus was not defiled. He replaced disease and death with cleansing and life.

7:16 ***A mighty prophet:*** Jesus was like Elijah and Elisha. • ***God has visited his people today:*** See note on 1:68.

7:18-23 ***The disciples of John the Baptist:*** See note on 5:33. John was now in prison (3:19-20), wondering whether Jesus was truly the Messiah, since he did not act like a powerful warrior–king who would overthrow the Romans. In response, Jesus defined his messianic role.

7:19 ***Are you the Messiah we've been expecting:*** Literally *Are you the one who is coming?* Also in 7:20.

or should we keep looking for someone
else?' "
21 At that very time, Jesus cured many
people of their diseases, illnesses, and evil
spirits, and he restored sight to many who
were blind. 22 Then he told John's disciples,
"Go back to John and tell him what you have
seen and heard—the blind see, the lame
walk, the lepers are cured, the deaf hear,
the dead are raised to life, and the Good
News is being preached to the poor. 23 And
tell him, 'God blesses those who do not turn
away because of me.' "
24 After John's disciples left, Jesus began
talking about him to the crowds. "What
kind of man did you go into the wilderness
to see? Was he a weak reed, swayed by every
breath of wind? 25 Or were you expecting to
see a man dressed in expensive clothes? No,
people who wear beautiful clothes and live
in luxury are found in palaces. 26 Were you
looking for a prophet? Yes, and he is more
than a prophet. 27 John is the man to whom
the Scriptures refer when they say,

'Look, I am sending my messenger ahead
of you,
and he will prepare your way before
you.'

28 I tell you, of all who have ever lived, none
is greater than John. Yet even the least person in the Kingdom of God is greater than
he is!"

29 When they heard this, all the people—
even the tax collectors—agreed that God's
way was right, for they had been baptized
by John. 30 But the Pharisees and experts in
religious law rejected God's plan for them,
for they had refused John's baptism.
31 "To what can I compare the people of
this generation?" Jesus asked. "How can I
describe them? 32 They are like children
playing a game in the public square. They
complain to their friends,

'We played wedding songs,
and you didn't dance,
so we played funeral songs,
and you didn't weep.'

33 For John the Baptist didn't spend his time
eating bread or drinking wine, and you say,
'He's possessed by a demon.' 34 The Son of
Man, on the other hand, feasts and drinks,
and you say, 'He's a glutton and a drunkard,
and a friend of tax collectors and other sinners!' 35 But wisdom is shown to be right by
the lives of those who follow it."

Jesus Is Anointed by a Sinful Woman

Luke 7:36-50; cp. Matt 26:6-13 // Mark 14:3-9;
cp. John 12:1-11

36 One of the Pharisees asked Jesus to have
dinner with him, so Jesus went to his home
and sat down to eat. 37 When a certain
immoral woman from that city heard he
was eating there, she brought a beautiful

7:22 *Isa 29:18-19; 35:5-6; 42:18; 61:1; Luke 4:18
7:26 Luke 1:76
7:27 *Exod 23:20; *Mal 3:1
7:28 Luke 1:15
7:29-30 Matt 21:32; Luke 3:7, 12
7:33 Luke 1:15
7:35 1 Cor 1:24
7:36-50 Matt 26:6-13; Mark 14:3-9; John 12:1-8

7:22 ***the blind see, the lame walk:*** A series of allusions to Isaiah (Isa 26:19; 29:18-19; 35:5-6; 61:1-2) defines God's salvation as the restoration of fallen creation. Jesus did not come to overthrow Roman rule over Judea, but for the greater purpose of reversing the effects of sin and death.

7:23 ***God blesses those who do not turn away because of me*** (or *who are not offended by me*): The blessing is for those who are able to put aside their personal agendas and preconceived ideas about the Messiah and accept Jesus' path of suffering.

7:27 The quotation is from Mal 3:1. In Mal 4:5-6, this messenger is identified with the prophet Elijah. Though John denied that he was Elijah (John 1:21-23), he came in the spirit and power of Elijah (1:17) to prepare the way for the Messiah (see notes on 1:17; 3:4-6).

7:28 Jesus praised John as the greatest person who ever lived under the old covenant. But even the least person in the ***Kingdom of God*** is greater than John. The blessings of the new covenant—free and complete forgiveness of sins, the indwelling presence of the Holy Spirit, and intimate knowledge of God—give believers in Jesus a new and greater position than even John enjoyed.

7:29 ***agreed that God's way was right:*** Or *praised God for his justice.* The Greek can be interpreted either way.

7:31-35 ***To what can I compare the people of this generation?*** Jesus compares Israel to fickle children in the marketplace who play games of make-believe. They called John the Baptist to dance (a wedding game), but the solemn prophet refused calling them instead to mourning and repentance for their sins. Then they called on Jesus to mourn (a funeral game), but he was the bridegroom who announced the joyful celebration banquet of the Kingdom of God, so it would not have been fitting for him to mourn (cp. Mark 2:19-20).

7:33 ***John the Baptist didn't spend his time eating bread or drinking wine:*** John lived an ascetic's life of self-denial, appropriate to his prophetic role of announcing God's Kingdom, the coming judgment, and the need for repentance and cleansing.

7:34 ***Son of Man*** is a title Jesus used for himself.

7:35 ***But wisdom is shown to be right by the lives of those who follow it*** (or *But wisdom is justified by all her children*): In Proverbs, Wisdom is personified as a woman who calls God's people to a life of godliness and obedience to God's commands (Prov 1:20-33; 8:1–9:6). Wisdom's children are those who live righteously, as God's word instructs.

7:36-50 Jesus' comment in 7:35 is now illustrated by one of "wisdom's children" (see note on 7:35), a repentant sinner who shows gratitude for the forgiveness she has received.

7:36 ***One of the Pharisees asked Jesus to have dinner with him*** (see "The Pharisees" at Matt 3:7, p. 1581): Jesus has more positive contact with the Pharisees in Luke than in the other Gospels. He was a respected teacher and healer, so it is not surprising that this Pharisee invited him to dinner. Not all Pharisees were antagonistic—some were interested in his teaching or merely curious. • ***and sat down to eat:*** Or *and reclined.*

7:37 ***a certain immoral woman:*** The implication is that she was a prostitute. • ***Alabaster*** is a soft marble—white,

7:38
[d]*aleiphō* (0218)
‣Luke 7:46
7:39
Matt 21:11
7:42
Matt 18:27
Col 2:13
7:44
Gen 18:4
1 Tim 5:10
7:45
Rom 16:16
1 Cor 16:20
2 Cor 13:12
1 Thes 5:26
1 Pet 5:14
7:46
2 Sam 12:20
Ps 23:5
[e]*aleiphō* (0218)
‣John 12:3
7:48-49
Luke 5:20-21
7:50
Matt 9:22
8:1
Matt 4:23
8:2
Matt 27:55-56
Mark 15:40-41
Luke 23:49
[f]*daimonion* (1140)
‣Luke 8:30
8:3
Matt 14:1
8:4-15
//Matt 13:1-23
//Mark 4:1-20

alabaster jar filled with expensive perfume.
38 Then she knelt behind him at his feet,
weeping. Her tears fell on his feet, and she
wiped them off with her hair. Then she
kept kissing his feet and [d]putting perfume
on them.

39 When the Pharisee who had invited
him saw this, he said to himself, "If this man
were a prophet, he would know what kind of
woman is touching him. She's a sinner!"

40 Then Jesus answered his thoughts.
"Simon," he said to the Pharisee, "I have
something to say to you."

"Go ahead, Teacher," Simon replied.

41 Then Jesus told him this story: "A man
loaned money to two people—500 pieces
of silver to one and 50 pieces to the other.
42 But neither of them could repay him, so
he kindly forgave them both, canceling
their debts. Who do you suppose loved him
more after that?"

43 Simon answered, "I suppose the one for
whom he canceled the larger debt."

"That's right," Jesus said. 44 Then he
turned to the woman and said to Simon,
"Look at this woman kneeling here. When
I entered your home, you didn't offer me water to wash the dust from my feet, but she
has washed them with her tears and wiped
them with her hair. 45 You didn't greet me
with a kiss, but from the time I first came in,
she has not stopped kissing my feet. 46 You
neglected the courtesy of olive oil to [e]anoint
my head, but she has [e]anointed my feet with
rare perfume.

47 "I tell you, her sins—and they are many—
have been forgiven, so she has shown me
much love. But a person who is forgiven little shows only little love." 48 Then Jesus said
to the woman, "Your sins are forgiven."

49 The men at the table said among themselves, "Who is this man, that he goes
around forgiving sins?"

50 And Jesus said to the woman, "Your
faith has saved you; go in peace."

The Good News of the Kingdom of God (8:1–9:17)

Women Who Followed Jesus

8 Soon afterward Jesus began a tour of
the nearby towns and villages, preaching and announcing the Good News about
the Kingdom of God. He took his twelve disciples with him, 2 along with some women
who had been cured of evil spirits and diseases. Among them were Mary Magdalene,
from whom he had cast out seven [f]demons;
3 Joanna, the wife of Chuza, Herod's business manager; Susanna; and many others
who were contributing from their own resources to support Jesus and his disciples.

Parable of the Farmer Scattering Seed

Luke 8:4-15 // Matt 13:1-13, 18-23 // Mark 4:1-20

4 One day Jesus told a story in the form of a
parable to a large crowd that had gathered
from many towns to hear him: 5 "A farmer
went out to plant his seed. As he scattered
it across his field, some seed fell on a footpath, where it was stepped on, and the birds
ate it. 6 Other seed fell among rocks. It began

---

yellow, or red—that was often used to make expensive containers like this ***beautiful . . . jar.***

7:38 ***she knelt behind him at his feet:*** At a banquet, guests reclined around a low table with their feet extended outward. The woman could not reach Jesus' head to anoint him, so she poured the perfume on his feet. • ***wiped them off with her hair:*** Letting down her hair in public was scandalous, and could have constituted grounds for her husband to divorce her; kissing his feet connoted reverence. She discarded propriety due to her gratitude.

7:40 ***Then Jesus answered his thoughts:*** See note on 5:22.

7:41 ***500 pieces of silver:*** Greek *500 denarii;* a denarius was equivalent to a laborer's full day's wage, so 500 denarii was almost two years' wages for a day laborer. The poor were often heavily indebted to the wealthy in first-century Galilee.

7:43 ***the one for whom he canceled the larger debt:*** Those who had been forgiven the most responded with greater gratitude and love. The woman made her extraordinary act of sacrificial love because Jesus had forgiven her sins.

7:44-46 Simon had neglected to show Jesus the common courtesies of hospitality. Since roads were dusty, a servant would ***wash the dust from*** a guest's ***feet.*** Greeting a guest ***with a kiss*** on both cheeks is normal in the Middle East even today. Anointing the ***head*** with ***olive oil*** was a way to honor a respected guest.

7:47 ***so she has shown me much love:*** This is a better translation than the traditional "because she loved much." It was not that her great love for Jesus caused him to forgive her, but that the forgiveness she had already received from Jesus prompted her love.

8:2-3 ***along with some women:*** Rabbis of Jesus' day did not have women disciples, so this was unusual. Some of these women, like Joanna, were from wealthy families and contributed financially to Jesus' ministry (see note on 7:5).

8:2 ***Magdalene*** means "from Magdala," a village north of Tiberias on the western side of the Sea of Galilee. ***Mary*** figures prominently in the burial and resurrection accounts (24:10; Mark 15:40, 47; John 19:25; 20:1, 18). Some have said that Mary Magdalene was the woman of 7:36-38, leading to the belief that she was a former prostitute. There is no basis for this speculation.

8:4-15 The ***parable*** of the farmer scattering seed depicts people's varied responses to Jesus' ministry of proclaiming God's Kingdom.

8:5 The custom in planting was first to scatter seed and then to plow it into the soil. • The seed that ***fell on a footpath*** running through the fields would not be plowed in, so it was ***stepped on*** and eaten by birds.

8:6 ***fell among rocks:*** Often there was a limestone layer nine to twelve inches under the soil, so that the rain was trapped and seed sprouted quickly in the moist soil. But when the rain stopped, the sun evaporated the trapped moisture and the plant died.

to grow, but the plant soon wilted and died
for lack of moisture. 7Other seed fell among
thorns that grew up with it and choked out
the tender plants. 8Still other seed fell on
fertile soil. This seed grew and produced a
crop that was a hundred times as much as
had been planted!" When he had said this,
he called out, "Anyone with ears to hear
should listen and understand."

9His disciples asked him what this parable meant. 10He replied, "You are permitted
to understand the secrets of the Kingdom of
God. But I use parables to teach the others
so that the Scriptures might be fulfilled:

'When they look, they won't really see.
When they hear, they won't
understand.'

11"This is the meaning of the parable: The
seed is God's word. 12The seeds that fell on
the footpath represent those who hear the
message, only to have the devil come and
take it away from their hearts and prevent
them from believing and being saved. 13The
seeds on the rocky soil represent those who
hear the message and receive it with joy. But
since they don't have deep roots, they believe for a while, then they fall away when
they face temptation. 14The seeds that fell
among the thorns represent those who hear
the message, but all too quickly the message
is crowded out by the cares and riches and
pleasures of this life. And so they never
grow into maturity. 15And the seeds that
fell on the good soil represent honest, good-
hearted people who hear God's word, cling
to it, and patiently produce a huge harvest.

Parable of the Lamp

Luke 8:16-18 // Mark 4:21-25; cp. Matt 5:15; 13:12; Luke 11:33

16"No one lights a lamp and then covers it
with a bowl or hides it under a bed. A lamp
is placed on a stand, where its light can be
seen by all who enter the house. 17For all
that is secret will eventually be brought
into the open, and everything that is concealed will be brought to light and made
known to all.

18"So pay attention to how you hear. To
those who listen to my teaching, more understanding will be given. But for those
who are not listening, even what they think
they understand will be taken away from
them."

The True Family of Jesus

Luke 8:19-21 // Matt 12:46-50 // Mark 3:31-35

19Then Jesus' mother and brothers came
to see him, but they couldn't get to him because of the crowd. 20Someone told Jesus,
"Your mother and your brothers are outside,
and they want to see you."

21Jesus replied, "My mother and my brothers are all those who hear God's word and
obey it."

Jesus Calms the Storm

Luke 8:22-25 // Matt 8:23-27 // Mark 4:35-41

22One day Jesus said to his disciples, "Let's
cross to the other side of the lake." So they
got into a boat and started out. 23As they
sailed across, Jesus settled down for a nap.
But soon a fierce storm came down on the
lake. The boat was filling with water, and
they were in real danger.

24The disciples went and woke him up,

8:10 *Isa 6:9-10
8:11 Jas 1:21; 1 Pet 1:23
8:12 1 Cor 1:21
8:14 Matt 19:23; 1 Tim 6:9, 10; 2 Tim 4:10
8:16-18 //Mark 4:21-25
8:16 Matt 5:15; Luke 11:33; Phil 2:15-16
8:17 Matt 10:26; Luke 12:2
8:18 Matt 25:29; Luke 19:26
8:19-21 //Matt 12:46-50; //Mark 3:31-35
8:22-25 //Matt 8:23-27; //Mark 4:35-41
8:23 Jon 1:4-5

8:7 ***fell among thorns:*** One type of weed looked very much like wheat as it grew, but it had larger roots and took away the moisture and nutrients that the wheat needed.

8:8 ***Anyone with ears to hear*** meant everyone who was willing to listen.

8:10 ***the secrets*** (literally *mysteries*) ***of the Kingdom of God:*** What was hidden in the past about God's reign was now revealed through Jesus' words and actions. • ***When they look . . . they won't understand:*** This quote is from Isa 6:9 (Greek version), a passage repeatedly used in the NT to explain Israel's rejection of the gospel (see also Matt 13:14-15; Mark 4:12; John 12:40; Acts 28:26-27). In its original context, the passage refers to God's certain judgment of Israel at the hands of the Assyrians. Israel's sin and rebelliousness had taken them beyond the point of no return, so God blinded them in preparation for judgment. Those who rejected Jesus' message were blind to the truth.

8:11 ***The seed is God's word:*** This refers to Jesus' preaching of the Good News of the Kingdom.

8:12 ***to have the devil come and take it away:*** See note on 4:2. Satan seeks to prevent unbelievers from seeing the truth.

8:13 ***Deep roots*** indicate spiritual depth and maturity. The Greek word translated ***temptation*** can also mean "testing" or "trials."

8:16-17 A small clay ***lamp*** was filled with olive oil and set in a wall alcove. Jesus' message provides light for those who listen, and it reveals their heart attitudes.

8:18 ***those who listen:*** Cp. Prov 9:9. • ***those who are not listening:*** See note on 8:10.

8:19-20 ***Jesus*** had four ***brothers***—James, Joseph, Judas, and Simon—and an unknown number of sisters (Mark 6:3; Matt 13:55). These children were probably born to Joseph and Mary after Jesus' virginal conception and birth. (On the other hand, some believe that Mary remained a lifelong virgin and that Joseph was therefore a widower with children from a previous marriage when he married Mary.)

8:21 ***those who hear God's word and obey it:*** Jesus was not rejecting his family, but announcing that spiritual relationships—being part of God's family—supersede family ties.

8:22-25 Jesus' calming of the storm demonstrated his authority over nature and strongly indicated his deity, since God is master of the seas (see Ps 65:7; 89:9; 104:6-7; 107:23-32).

8:23 ***a fierce storm came down on the lake:*** Severe storms are common on the Sea of Galilee, which lies in a valley surrounded by high hills.

8:26-39 //Matt 8:28-34 //Mark 5:1-20
8:28 Matt 8:29 Mark 1:23-24
8:30 [g]*daimonion* (1140) ‣Luke 9:1
8:31 Rev 9:1-2, 11; 20:3
8:37 Acts 16:39
8:40-56 //Matt 9:18-26 //Mark 5:21-43

shouting, "Master, Master, we're going to
drown!"
When Jesus woke up, he rebuked the
wind and the raging waves. Suddenly the
storm stopped and all was calm. 25Then he
asked them, "Where is your faith?"
The disciples were terrified and amazed.
"Who is this man?" they asked each other.
"When he gives a command, even the wind
and waves obey him!"

Jesus Exercises Authority over Demons
Luke 8:26-39 // Matt 8:28-34 // Mark 5:1-20

26So they arrived in the region of the Gerasenes, across the lake from Galilee. 27As
Jesus was climbing out of the boat, a man
who was possessed by demons came out
to meet him. For a long time he had been
homeless and naked, living in a cemetery
outside the town.
28As soon as he saw Jesus, he shrieked
and fell down in front of him. Then he
screamed, "Why are you interfering with
me, Jesus, Son of the Most High God?
Please, I beg you, don't torture me!" 29For
Jesus had already commanded the evil spirit
to come out of him. This spirit had often
taken control of the man. Even when he
was placed under guard and put in chains
and shackles, he simply broke them and
rushed out into the wilderness, completely
under the demon's power.
30Jesus demanded, "What is your name?"
"Legion," he replied, for he was filled
with many [g]demons. 31The demons kept
begging Jesus not to send them into the
bottomless pit.
32There happened to be a large herd of
pigs feeding on the hillside nearby, and the
demons begged him to let them enter into
the pigs.
So Jesus gave them permission. 33Then
the demons came out of the man and entered the pigs, and the entire herd plunged
down the steep hillside into the lake and
drowned.
34When the herdsmen saw it, they fled
to the nearby town and the surrounding
countryside, spreading the news as they
ran. 35People rushed out to see what had
happened. A crowd soon gathered around
Jesus, and they saw the man who had been
freed from the demons. He was sitting at
Jesus' feet, fully clothed and perfectly sane,
and they were all afraid. 36Then those who
had seen what happened told the others
how the demon-possessed man had been
healed. 37And all the people in the region of
the Gerasenes begged Jesus to go away and
leave them alone, for a great wave of fear
swept over them.
So Jesus returned to the boat and left,
crossing back to the other side of the lake.
38The man who had been freed from the
demons begged to go with him. But Jesus
sent him home, saying, 39"No, go back to
your family, and tell them everything God
has done for you." So he went all through
the town proclaiming the great things Jesus
had done for him.

Jesus Heals in Response to Faith
Luke 8:40-56 // Matt 9:18-26 // Mark 5:21-43

40On the other side of the lake the crowds
welcomed Jesus, because they had been
waiting for him. 41Then a man named Jairus, a leader of the local synagogue, came

---

8:24 ***he rebuked the wind and the raging waves:*** As Jesus rebuked demons (4:41) and diseases (4:39), so now he revealed his authority by rebuking the sea (cp. 2 Sam 22:16; Ps 18:15; 104:7; 106:9; Isa 50:2; Nah 1:4).

8:26-39 This exorcism demonstrated Jesus' authority over spiritual forces. It also contrasted the faith and devotion of the freed man with the fear and rejection of the townspeople.

8:26 ***the region of the Gerasenes*** (other manuscripts read *Gadarenes;* still others read *Gergesenes;* also in 8:37; see Matt 8:28; Mark 5:1): Gerasa was a city of the Decapolis, thirty miles southeast of the Sea of Galilee. Jesus deliberately went to a Gentile region and ministered there.

8:27 ***living in a cemetery outside the town:*** Touching a tomb or a dead body rendered a Jew unclean, or ceremonially defiled. Jesus willingly entered this unclean place to rescue a person enslaved by Satan.

8:28 ***Jesus, Son of the Most High God:*** See notes on 4:34, 41.

8:29 ***evil*** (literally *unclean*) ***spirit***: Unclean things are unfit for God's presence (see also the note on 4:33).

8:30 A Roman ***legion*** had about 6,000 soldiers, so this man had a great ***many demons***.

8:31 ***the bottomless pit*** (Or *the abyss,* or *the underworld*): The Greek word *abussos* means "bottomless" and often refers to the underworld prison of evil spirits or fallen angels (Rev 9:1-2, 11; 11:7; 17:8; 20:1, 3; cp. 2 Pet 2:4). The metaphor is taken from the apparently bottomless depth of the ocean (the ancients had no means for sounding the ocean depths, so to them it was bottomless).

8:32 ***a large herd of pigs:*** Pigs were unclean animals for Jews, which shows that the people of this region were Gentiles. The unclean demons were fit only for pigs.

8:35 ***sitting at Jesus' feet:*** The man sat in the position of a disciple, indicating his willingness to follow Jesus (see 8:37).

8:37 ***begged Jesus to go away:*** Jesus' power over spiritual forces frightened the townspeople, and their loss of property (the pigs) angered them. Their rejection contrasts with the faith of the healed man.

8:39 ***go back to your family:*** The role of disciples is to proclaim to the world what Jesus has done for them.

8:40-56 These two accounts of healing demonstrate Jesus' authority over disease and death, and illustrate the power of faith.

8:41 The ***leader of the local synagogue*** was the officer who maintained the local synagogue and organized services (see also 8:49; 13:14; Acts 13:15; 18:8, 17).

and fell at Jesus' feet, pleading with him to come home with him. 42His [h]only daughter, who was about twelve years old, was dying.

As Jesus went with him, he was surrounded by the crowds. 43A woman in the crowd had suffered for twelve years with constant bleeding, and she could find no cure. 44Coming up behind Jesus, she touched the fringe of his robe. Immediately, the bleeding stopped.

45"Who touched me?" Jesus asked.

Everyone denied it, and Peter said, "Master, this whole crowd is pressing up against you."

46But Jesus said, "Someone deliberately touched me, for I felt healing power go out from me." 47When the woman realized that she could not stay hidden, she began to tremble and fell to her knees in front of him. The whole crowd heard her explain why she had touched him and that she had been immediately healed. 48"Daughter," he said to her, "your faith has made you well. Go in peace."

49While he was still speaking to her, a messenger arrived from the home of Jairus, the leader of the synagogue. He told him, "Your daughter is dead. There's no use troubling the Teacher now."

50But when Jesus heard what had happened, he said to Jairus, "Don't be afraid. Just have faith, and she will be healed."

51When they arrived at the house, Jesus wouldn't let anyone go in with him except Peter, John, James, and the little girl's father and mother. 52The house was filled with people weeping and wailing, but he said, "Stop the weeping! She isn't dead; she's only asleep."

53But the crowd laughed at him because they all knew she had died. 54Then Jesus took her by the hand and said in a loud voice, "My child, get up!" 55And at that moment her life returned, and she immediately stood up! Then Jesus told them to give her something to eat. 56Her parents were overwhelmed, but Jesus insisted that they not tell anyone what had happened.

Jesus Sends Out the Twelve Disciples

Luke 9:1-6 // Matt 10:5-15 // Mark 6:6b-13; cp. Luke 10:1-11

9 One day Jesus called together his twelve disciples and gave them power and authority to cast out all [i]demons and to heal all diseases. 2Then he sent them out to tell everyone about the Kingdom of God and to heal the sick. 3"Take nothing for your journey," he instructed them. "Don't take a walking stick, a traveler's bag, food, money, or even a change of clothes. 4Wherever you go, stay in the same house until you leave town. 5And if a town refuses to welcome you, shake its dust from your feet as you leave to [j]show that you have abandoned those people to their fate."

6So they began their circuit of the villages, preaching the Good News and healing the sick.

Herod's Confusion

Luke 9:7-9 // Matt 14:1-2 // Mark 6:14-16

7When Herod Antipas, the ruler of Galilee, heard about everything Jesus was doing, he was puzzled. Some were saying that John

8:42
[h]*monogenēs* (3439)
‣Luke 9:38

8:43
Lev 15:25-30

8:46
Luke 5:17; 6:19

8:48
Matt 9:22
Mark 5:34
Luke 7:50; 17:19; 18:42

8:52
Luke 7:13

8:54
Luke 7:14

8:56
Matt 8:4
Mark 7:36
Luke 5:14

9:1-6
//Matt 10:5-15
//Mark 6:7-13

9:1
[i]*daimonion* (1140)
‣1 Cor 10:20

9:3
Luke 10:4; 22:35

9:4
Luke 10:5-7

9:5
Luke 10:10-11
Acts 13:51
[j]*marturion* (3142)
‣Acts 4:33

9:7-9
//Matt 14:1-12
//Mark 6:14-29

8:42 *His only daughter:* Or *His only child, a daughter.*

8:43 ***with constant bleeding:*** Some manuscripts add *having spent everything she had on doctors.* Perhaps it was a menstrual disorder. The tragedy was both physical and spiritual, for such bleeding rendered the woman ceremonially unclean and thereby precluded her participation in community worship (Lev 15:25-30).

8:44 ***The fringe of his robe*** probably refers to the tassels that pious Jews wore on the edges of their robes (see Num 15:38-39; Deut 22:12).

8:45 ***Who touched me?*** Jesus recognized the touch of faith by a needy person.

8:48 ***your faith has made you well*** (literally *your faith has saved you*). ***Go in peace:*** Jesus said the same thing to the woman who had anointed his feet (7:50). The Greek word for "save" can indicate either spiritual or physical healing. *Peace* (cp. Hebrew *shalom*) is spiritual wholeness, not just lack of conflict (see 1:79; 2:14, 29; 7:50; 19:38, 42; 24:36).

8:51 ***Peter, John,*** and ***James*** became the inner circle of Jesus' disciples (see 5:1-11; 9:28; Mark 14:32-33).

8:52 ***The house was filled with people weeping and wailing:*** See note on 7:12. • ***she's only asleep:*** Jesus emphasized the temporary nature of the girl's state. For believers, death is only temporary "sleep" (cp. John 11:11; the same term is translated as "dead/died" in Acts 7:60; 13:36; 1 Cor 11:30; 15:6, 18, 20, 51; 1 Thes 4:14-15; 5:10).

8:55 ***her life*** (or *her spirit*) ***returned:*** Like the raising of the widow's son (7:15), the girl's normal mortal life was restored. At the final resurrection, believers will receive immortal, glorified bodies (see note on 24:39).

8:56 ***not tell anyone:*** See note on 5:14.

9:1-6 Jesus now sent ***his twelve disciples*** (literally *the Twelve;* other manuscripts read *the twelve apostles*) to announce the Kingdom of God and demonstrate its authority by casting out demons and healing the sick. Jesus was training them to carry on his work after he was gone.

9:3 ***Take nothing for your journey:*** They were to live in dependence on God and on the charity of those to whom they ministered. • ***money:*** Or *silver coins.*

9:4 ***stay in the same house:*** They were to develop lasting relationships and be content without seeking better lodging or provisions.

9:5 ***shake its dust from your feet:*** Using a symbol of rejection, they were to leave such a town to the judgment it deserved.

9:7 ***Herod Antipas, the ruler of Galilee:*** Literally *Herod the tetrarch.* Herod Antipas was a son of King Herod and was ruler over Galilee. See notes on 3:1, 19-20.

9:8 Matt 11:14
9:9 Luke 23:8
9:10-17 //Matt 14:13-21 //Mark 6:30-44 //John 6:1-14
9:17 2 Kgs 4:44
9:18-20 //Matt 16:13-20 //Mark 8:27-30
9:19 Luke 9:7-8
9:20 John 6:68-69
9:21-27 //Matt 16:21-28 //Mark 8:31–9:1

the Baptist had been raised from the dead.
8Others thought Jesus was Elijah or one of
the other prophets risen from the dead.
9"I beheaded John," Herod said, "so who
is this man about whom I hear such stories?"
And he kept trying to see him.

Jesus Feeds Five Thousand
Luke 9:10a // Mark 6:30-31
Luke 9:10b-17 // Matt 14:13-21 // Mark 6:32-44 // John 6:1-15

10When the apostles returned, they told
Jesus everything they had done. Then he
slipped quietly away with them toward the
town of Bethsaida. 11But the crowds found
out where he was going, and they followed
him. He welcomed them and taught them
about the Kingdom of God, and he healed
those who were sick.
12Late in the afternoon the twelve disciples came to him and said, "Send the
crowds away to the nearby villages and
farms, so they can find food and lodging
for the night. There is nothing to eat here in
this remote place."
13But Jesus said, "You feed them."
"But we have only five loaves of bread
and two fish," they answered. "Or are you
expecting us to go and buy enough food for
this whole crowd?" 14For there were about
5,000 men there.
Jesus replied, "Tell them to sit down in
groups of about fifty each." 15So the people
all sat down. 16Jesus took the five loaves
and two fish, looked up toward heaven, and
blessed them. Then, breaking the loaves
into pieces, he kept giving the bread and
fish to the disciples so they could distribute
it to the people. 17They all ate as much as
they wanted, and afterward, the disciples
picked up twelve baskets of leftovers!

Climax of the Galilean Ministry (9:18-50)

Peter's Declaration of Faith
Luke 9:18-21 // Matt 16:13-20 // Mark 8:27-30; cp. John 6:67-69

18One day Jesus left the crowds to pray
alone. Only his disciples were with him, and
he asked them, "Who do people say I am?"
19"Well," they replied, "some say John the
Baptist, some say Elijah, and others say you
are one of the other ancient prophets risen
from the dead."
20Then he asked them, "But who do you
say I am?"
Peter replied, "You are the Messiah sent
from God!"

Jesus First Predicts His Death
Luke 9:22 // Matt 16:21-23 // Mark 8:31-33

21Jesus warned his disciples not to tell anyone who he was. 22"The Son of Man must
suffer many terrible things," he said. "He
will be rejected by the elders, the leading
priests, and the teachers of religious law. He
will be killed, but on the third day he will be
raised from the dead."

9:8 Jews expected that ***Elijah*** would come prior to God's final judgment (see notes on 1:17; 3:4-6). Some Jews expected that a prophet like Moses would come (Deut 18:15).

9:9 ***I beheaded John:*** See note on 3:19-20; see also Mark 6:14-29.

9:10-17 The feeding of the 5,000 recalls God's miraculous feeding of Israel with manna in the wilderness (Exod 16; see also 2 Kgs 4:42-44). It points forward to God's final salvation as a great feast for all nations (Isa 25:6-8; 65:13-14; see "The Messianic Banquet" at 14:1-24, p. 1737).

9:10 ***he slipped quietly away:*** Jesus knew that the disciples needed a time of spiritual retreat. • The ***town of Bethsaida*** was located on the northern shore of the Sea of Galilee, east of the Jordan River. It was the hometown of Peter, Andrew (John 1:44), and Philip (John 12:21).

9:11 ***He welcomed them:*** Although Jesus wished to retreat with his disciples, he had compassion on the crowds and ministered to them.

9:13 ***You feed them:*** After their ministry of healing the sick and casting out demons, Jesus wanted the disciples to demonstrate faith in God's ability to feed the crowds.

9:17 ***twelve baskets of leftovers:*** God abundantly provides for his people.

9:18-27 Peter's confession that Jesus was the Messiah marked a turning point, as Jesus moved from demonstrating his messianic authority through miracles to explaining the unexpected suffering of the Messiah. Jesus accepted the confession but clarified that his being the Messiah would involve suffering and death. He called his disciples to follow him regardless of the cost.

9:19 ***some say Elijah:*** See note on 9:8.

9:20 ***the Messiah:*** Or *the Christ. Messiah* (a Hebrew term) and *Christ* (a Greek term) both mean "the Anointed One." The phrase could be translated "the Lord's Anointed," a designation for the king of Israel (1 Sam 24:6, 10; 2 Sam 19:21; Ps 2:2). David was the Lord's anointed, as was the Messiah.

9:21-22 ***not to tell anyone who he was:*** Jesus did not want to encourage a popular uprising; his calling was not to overthrow Rome, but to suffer and die.

9:22 ***Son of Man*** is a title Jesus used for himself. • ***must suffer many terrible things:*** This was the first of Jesus' prophecies concerning his coming death in Jerusalem (see 9:44; 17:25; see also note on 18:31-34). Jesus would fulfill Isa 52:13–53:12, in which the servant of the Lord (the Messiah) became a saving sacrifice for God's people. These events were part of God's purpose and plan. Despite opposition from human beings and from the spiritual forces of Satan, God works through the actions of human beings to accomplish his purposes. Though wicked men plotted against Jesus and put him to death, God accomplished salvation by raising Jesus from the dead (24:7, 26-27, 44-47; Acts 2:23-24; 3:18; 4:28). • ***elders:*** See note on 7:3. • ***the teachers of religious law:*** See note on 5:17. • ***leading priests:*** Though Israel had only one high priest, the upper-class priests were the aristocracy; they served on the Sanhedrin and held positions of power in Jerusalem.

Teachings about Discipleship
Luke 9:23-27 // Matt 16:24-28 // Mark 8:34–9:1
23Then he said to the crowd, "If any of you
wants to be my follower, you must turn
from your selfish ways, take up your cross
daily, and follow me. 24If you try to hang on
to your life, you will lose it. But if you give up
your life for my sake, you will save it. 25And
what do you benefit if you gain the whole
world but are yourself lost or destroyed?
26If anyone is ashamed of me and my message, the Son of Man will be ashamed of
that person when he returns in his glory
and in the glory of the Father and the holy
angels. 27I tell you the truth, some standing
here right now will not die before they see
the Kingdom of God."

The Transfiguration
Luke 9:28-36 // Matt 17:1-9 // Mark 9:2-10
28About eight days later Jesus took Peter,
John, and James up on a mountain to pray.
29And as he was praying, the appearance of
his face was transformed, and his clothes
became dazzling white. 30Suddenly, two
men, Moses and Elijah, appeared and began
talking with Jesus. 31They were glorious to
see. And they were speaking about his exodus from this world, which was about to be
fulfilled in Jerusalem.
32Peter and the others had fallen asleep.
When they woke up, they saw Jesus' [k]glory
and the two men standing with him. 33As
Moses and Elijah were starting to leave, Peter, not even knowing what he was saying,
blurted out, "Master, it's wonderful for us
to be here! Let's make three shelters as memorials—one for you, one for Moses, and
one for Elijah." 34But even as he was saying
this, a cloud overshadowed them, and terror
gripped them as the cloud covered them.
35Then a voice from the cloud said, "This
is my Son, my Chosen One. Listen to him."
36When the voice finished, Jesus was there
alone. They didn't tell anyone at that time
what they had seen.

Jesus Heals a Demon-Possessed Boy
Luke 9:37-43a // Matt 17:14-21 // Mark 9:14-29
37The next day, after they had come down
the mountain, a large crowd met Jesus. 38A
man in the crowd called out to him, "Teacher,
I beg you to look at my son, my [a]only child.
39An evil spirit keeps seizing him, making
him scream. It throws him into convulsions
so that he foams at the mouth. It batters
him and hardly ever leaves him alone. 40I
begged your disciples to cast out the spirit,
but they couldn't do it."
41Jesus said, "You faithless and corrupt
people! How long must I be with you and
put up with you?" Then he said to the man,
"Bring your son here."

9:23
Matt 10:38
Luke 14:27

9:24
Matt 10:39
Luke 17:33
John 12:25

9:26
Matt 10:33
Luke 12:9
2 Tim 2:12

9:28-36
//Matt 17:1-13
//Mark 9:2-10

9:31-32
2 Pet 1:15-16

9:32
[k]*doxa* (1391)
‣Luke 12:27

9:35
Deut 18:15
Ps 2:7
Isa 42:1
Matt 3:17
2 Pet 1:17

9:37-43a
//Matt 17:14-20
//Mark 9:14-29

9:38
Luke 7:12
[a]*monogenēs* (3439)
‣John 1:14

9:23-27 ***If any of you wants to be my follower:*** After predicting his own suffering and death, Jesus taught that all who follow him must also experience death to self.

9:23 ***take up your cross daily:*** This did not simply mean carrying a heavy burden, but suffering a violent death by crucifixion. Believers must be completely willing to die to themselves and to live for God, even at the cost of their lives.

9:24 ***hang on to your life:*** Placing oneself on the throne denies Jesus. The result is to *lose* one's life, mainly at the last judgment (9:26; John 12:25).

9:26 ***the Son of Man . . . when he returns in his glory:*** See Dan 7:13-14; "The Son of Man" at Matt 8:18-20, p. 1593.

9:27 This difficult verse has been interpreted as referring to: (1) the second coming of Christ; (2) the destruction of Jerusalem in AD 70; (3) the resurrection of Jesus; and (4) the transfiguration, which follows in 9:28-36. The last possibility is the most likely.

9:28-36 At the transfiguration, Jesus' true glory was unveiled for three disciples to witness, confirming Peter's confession that Jesus was the Christ. Moses and Elijah confirmed that Jesus fulfilled the OT prophecies concerning the Messiah.

9:28 ***About eight days later:*** Mark says "after six days," referring to full days, while Luke includes parts of days. • ***Peter, John, and James*** were the inner circle of Jesus' disciples (see also 8:51; Mark 14:32-33). • ***a mountain:*** The site of the transfiguration is traditionally regarded as Mount Tabor in southern Galilee. Some have suggested Mount Hermon, which is closer to Caesarea Philippi, where Peter's confession (9:18-27) took place.

9:29 ***as he was praying:*** See note on 3:21. • ***his clothing became dazzling white*** (literally *became bright as a flash of lightning*): Jesus' pre-existent glory shone through his human body (cp. Ezek 1:4; Dan 7:9; see also Exod 34:29).

9:31 ***his exodus from this world:*** The Greek word *exodos* means "departure." As the exodus from Egypt was God's great act of deliverance in the OT, so Jesus' exodus from this world—his death, resurrection, and ascension—was God's great act of deliverance in the NT. Jesus would accomplish a new and greater exodus.

9:33 ***Let's make three shelters as memorials*** (literally *three tabernacles*): The Greek word translated *shelter* (*skēnē*) is the same word used in the Greek OT to refer to the Tabernacle, Israel's portable temple in the wilderness, and for the portable shelters Jews lived in during the Festival of Shelters (Lev 23:42; Neh 8:14-17). Peter might have wanted to prolong the event by giving Jesus, Moses, and Elijah a place to stay.

9:34 ***a cloud overshadowed them:*** Clouds often veil the presence of God (Exod 16:10; 19:9; 24:16).

9:35 The ***voice from the cloud*** recalls God's voice at Jesus' baptism (3:22). • ***This is my Son, my Chosen One*** (some manuscripts read *This is my dearly loved Son*): *My Chosen One* alludes to Isa 42:1, identifying Jesus as the suffering servant of the Lord. • ***Listen to him*** is from Deut 18:15, identifying Jesus as "the prophet like Moses" (see Acts 3:22; 7:37).

9:38 ***my only child:*** The loss of an only son was especially tragic, since this left no one to carry on the family name (see note on 7:12; see Gen 22:16; 1 Kgs 17:17-24; Jer 6:26; Amos 8:10; Zech 12:10).

9:39 ***An evil spirit keeps seizing him:*** Demons sometimes inflict physical illnesses such as lameness (13:11) and muteness (11:14).

9:41 ***You faithless and corrupt people:*** It is unclear whether Jesus was speaking to the disciples or to the people as a whole.

9:43b-45
//Matt 17:22-23
//Mark 9:30-32
2 Pet 1:16

9:44
Luke 18:32

9:45
Mark 9:32
Luke 18:34

9:46-48
//Matt 18:1-5
//Mark 9:33-37

9:47
Matt 9:4

9:48
Matt 10:40; 25:40
Luke 10:16

9:49-50
//Mark 9:38-40

9:50
Matt 12:30
Luke 11:23

42As the boy came forward, the demon
knocked him to the ground and threw him
into a violent convulsion. But Jesus rebuked
the evil spirit and healed the boy. Then he
gave him back to his father. 43Awe gripped
the people as they saw this majestic display
of God's power.

Jesus Again Predicts His Death

Luke 9:43b-45 // Matt 17:22-23 // Mark 9:30-32

While everyone was marveling at everything
he was doing, Jesus said to his disciples,
44"Listen to me and remember what I say.
The Son of Man is going to be betrayed into
the hands of his enemies." 45But they didn't
know what he meant. Its significance was
hidden from them, so they couldn't understand it, and they were afraid to ask him
about it.

The Greatest in the Kingdom

Luke 9:46-48 // Matt 18:1-5 // Mark 9:33-37

46Then his disciples began arguing about
which of them was the greatest. 47But Jesus
knew their thoughts, so he brought a little
child to his side. 48Then he said to them,
"Anyone who welcomes a little child like
this on my behalf welcomes me, and anyone
who welcomes me also welcomes my Father
who sent me. Whoever is the least among
you is the greatest."

Using the Name of Jesus

Luke 9:49-50 // Mark 9:38-40

49John said to Jesus, "Master, we saw someone using your name to cast out demons,
but we told him to stop because he isn't in
our group."
50But Jesus said, "Don't stop him! Anyone
who is not against you is for you."

JAMES, SON OF ZEBEDEE (Luke 9:28, 54)

Luke 5:10; 6:14; 8:51
Matt 4:21-22; 10:2; 17:1; 20:20-24; 26:37-46
Mark 1:19-20, 29; 3:17; 5:37; 9:2; 10:35-41; 13:3-4; 14:33-42
John 21:2
Acts 1:13; 12:2

James, son of Zebedee and brother of John, was one of the twelve apostles, and he was among the first to be killed as a follower of Jesus. His mother, Salome, was possibly the sister of Mary, the mother of Jesus, which would make him Jesus' cousin (cp. Matt 27:56; Mark 15:40; 16:1; John 19:25). His name usually occurs before that of John, which may suggest that James was the older of the two. He should not be confused with James, the son of Alphaeus (see 6:15) or James, the brother of Jesus (see p. 1858).

Originally fishermen like their father (Matt 4:21; Mark 1:19), James and John fished with Peter and Andrew, another pair of brothers who became disciples (5:10). They were among the first that Jesus called to be his disciples, and they left everything, including their father, to follow him (5:11; Matt 4:22; Mark 1:20). Jesus called them "Sons of Thunder" (Mark 3:17), which might imply that they had vehement personalities (9:54), but the exact connotation is unclear.

James and his brother John were among those closest to Jesus. With Peter, they formed an inner circle of trusted disciples who accompanied Jesus on special occasions, as when he healed Jairus's daughter (8:51; Mark 5:37), conversed with Elijah and Moses on the mountain (9:28; Matt 17:1-3; Mark 9:2), and agonized in prayer in the garden (Matt 26:37; Mark 14:33). At one point, the two brothers evoked the indignation of the other disciples by asking for special positions of privilege in the coming Kingdom (Matt 20:20-28; Mark 10:35-45; cp. Luke 22:24-27).

Perhaps because of James's prominence among the disciples, Herod Agrippa had him killed soon after Jesus' death, which pleased the Jewish leaders (Acts 12:2-3) and fulfilled Jesus' prediction about his drinking the bitter cup that Jesus drank (Matt 20:23; Mark 10:39).

James was an ordinary working person whom Jesus called to be his disciple. His willingness to leave everything he knew—work, family, and home—to follow Jesus in simple trust, and eventually to die for him, makes him a model of committed discipleship.

9:42 *evil:* Literally *unclean.*

9:44 See note on 9:22.

9:45 ***Its significance was hidden from them:*** The disciples were often slow to understand, partly because their eyes were blinded to the truth until after the resurrection (see note on Mark 6:52).

9:46-50 The disciples' failure to apprehend Jesus' impending death was now illustrated by their pride and selfishness.

9:46 Jesus had just predicted his own suffering and death, so the disciples' ***arguing about which of them was the greatest*** showed astonishing pride and insensitivity.

9:47 ***Jesus knew their thoughts:*** See 5:22; 7:40.

9:48 ***Anyone who welcomes a little child:*** To welcome means to bestow honor and to treat as a social equal. The statement is shocking, since children in Jesus' day had no social status in the community and were viewed as their parents' property. Jesus took the lowest and most vulnerable members of society and announced that welcoming them was equivalent to welcoming Jesus. • ***on my behalf*** (literally *in my name*): This means "as my representative." • ***Whoever is the least among you is the greatest:*** True leadership in Jesus' Kingdom is achieved through sacrificial service, not the exercise of power (see also Mark 10:42-45).

9:50 ***Anyone who is not against you is for you:*** Though not one of the Twelve, the man who was casting out demons was not to be discouraged since he, too, was proclaiming the message of the Kingdom. The statement was proverbial, however, and not an absolute truth, as Jesus made the inverse statement in 11:23. Wisdom is needed to apply a proverb properly in a given situation (see Proverbs Introduction, "Meaning and Message," p. 1028).

5. THE SAVIOR ON THE WAY TO JERUSALEM (9:51–19:27)

Discipleship along the Way (9:51–11:13)

Opposition from Samaritans

[51]As the time drew near for him to ascend
to heaven, Jesus resolutely set out for Jerusalem. [52]He sent messengers ahead to a
Samaritan village to prepare for his arrival.
[53]But the people of the village did not welcome Jesus because he was on his way to
Jerusalem. [54]When James and John saw
this, they said to Jesus, "Lord, should we call
down fire from heaven to burn them up?"
[55]But Jesus turned and rebuked them. [56]So
they went on to another village.

The Cost of Following Jesus

Luke 9:57-62 // Matt 8:18-22

[57]As they were walking along, someone said
to Jesus, "I will follow you wherever you go."
[58]But Jesus replied, "Foxes have dens to
live in, and birds have nests, but the Son of
Man has no place even to lay his head."
[59]He said to another person, "Come, follow me."
The man agreed, but he said, "Lord, first
let me return home and bury my father."
[60]But Jesus told him, "Let the spiritually
dead bury their own dead! Your duty is to
go and preach about the Kingdom of God."
[61]Another said, "Yes, Lord, I will follow
you, but first let me say good-bye to my
family."
[62]But Jesus told him, "Anyone who puts a
hand to the plow and then looks back is not
fit for the Kingdom of God."

Jesus Sends Out His Disciples

Luke 10:1-11; cp. 9:1-6; Matt 10:5-15; Mark 6:6b-13
Luke 10:2 // Matt 9:37-38
Luke 10:12-15 // Matt 11:20-24

10 The Lord now chose seventy-two
other disciples and sent them ahead
in pairs to all the towns and places he
planned to visit. [2]These were his instructions to them: "The harvest is great, but
the workers are few. So pray to the Lord
who is in charge of the harvest; ask him to
send more workers into his fields. [3]Now go,
and remember that I am sending you out
as lambs among wolves. [4]Don't take any
money with you, nor a traveler's bag, nor
an extra pair of sandals. And don't stop to
greet anyone on the road.
[5]"Whenever you enter someone's home,
first say, 'May God's peace be on this house.'
[6]If those who live there are peaceful, the
blessing will stand; if they are not, the
blessing will return to you. [7]Don't move

9:51 Mark 16:19; Luke 13:22; 17:11; 18:31; 19:28
9:54 2 Kgs 1:10, 12; Markk 3:17
9:57-62 //Matt 8:19-22
9:60 Matt 3:2
9:61 1 Kgs 19:20
9:62 Num 11:4-5; Phil 3:13
10:1 Mark 6:7
10:2 Matt 9:37-38; John 4:35
10:3 Matt 10:16
10:4 2 Kgs 4:29; Luke 9:3
10:7 1 Cor 9:6-14; 1 Tim 5:18

9:51–19:44 Jesus' journey to Jerusalem was a new phase in the suffering mission of the Messiah. In this section, Jesus prepared his disciples for what was to come, while the opposition from the Jewish leaders increased.

9:51 ***Jesus resolutely set out for Jerusalem:*** Though the route was indirect, Jerusalem was Jesus' ultimate destination.

9:52-53 ***a Samaritan village:*** Jews and Samaritans had a history of conflict and racial prejudice; they hated each other (see note on 10:33). The Samaritans, who worshiped on Mount Gerizim, probably assumed that Jesus was traveling to Jerusalem to worship there.

9:54 ***call down fire from heaven to burn them up:*** Some manuscripts add *as Elijah did.* Three times, Elijah called down fire from heaven against the enemies of God (1 Kgs 18:38; 2 Kgs 1:1-17). In their zeal, James and John wanted to do the same.

9:55-56 Some manuscripts add an expanded conclusion to verse 55 and an additional sentence in verse 56: *And he said, "You don't realize what your hearts are like. [56]For the Son of Man has not come to destroy people's lives, but to save them."*

9:57-62 As he traveled toward Jerusalem to suffer and die, Jesus explained the cost to those who wished to follow him.

9:58 ***no place even to lay his head:*** Any disciple of Jesus must be ready to go anywhere and to give up home and security.

9:59 ***let me . . . bury my father:*** Respect for parents was a very important value in first-century Israel. Among other things, this meant providing them with an honorable burial. Jesus called for a commitment that took precedence over all human relationships.

9:60 ***Let the spiritually dead bury their own dead!*** Literally *Let the dead bury their own dead.* The word "spiritually" accurately reflects Jesus' meaning, which is a play on the meaning of the word *dead.*

9:61-62 ***let me say good-bye to my family:*** The statement echoes Elisha's request of Elijah (1 Kgs 19:19-20). Jesus required an even more complete commitment from his disciples. • ***puts a hand to the plow and looks back:*** The ancient farmer guided a light plow with his left hand and his oxen with the right. Looking away would turn the plow out of its path. For a believer, looking back meant placing earthly concerns ahead of God.

10:1-20 ***The Lord now chose seventy-two*** (some manuscripts read *seventy;* also in 10:17): The mission of the Twelve (9:1-6) represented Jesus' ministry to Israel; this mission represented his outreach to the Gentiles. The numbers 72 or 70 represent the nations of the world. Genesis 10 lists 70 nations in the Hebrew text, but the Septuagint—the Greek OT—lists 72. Luke, who used the Septuagint, probably wrote 72, and then a later scribe "corrected" the text to agree with the Hebrew. The point is that the Good News is for both Jews and Gentiles.

10:2 ***The harvest*** refers to people who need to hear the Good News and be gathered to God's presence (cp. Isa 27:12). There was urgency to the task, just as crops have to be brought in at the exact time when they are ripe. ***More workers*** were needed.

10:3 ***lambs among wolves:*** Jesus' followers are not to dominate others, but to sacrifice themselves for the benefit of others. This makes them vulnerable (see Jer 5:6; Ezek 22:27; Hab 1:8; Zeph 3:3), but the Good Shepherd (Ps 23:1) protects them from the wolves.

10:4 ***Don't take any money with you:*** Cp. 9:3. Jesus' disciples were to depend on God and on the help of those whom they served. • ***don't stop to greet anyone on the road:*** This did not mean being antisocial, but staying focused on the task Jesus had given them.

10:5 ***God's peace*** means spiritual blessings and wholeness, the *shalom* of God (see note on 8:48).

10:9
Matt 3:2
10:12
Gen 19:24-25
Matt 10:15
10:13-16
//Matt 11:20-24
10:14
Isa 23
Ezek 26–28
10:15
*Isa 14:13, 15
10:16
Matt 10:40
John 5:23
1 Thes 4:8
10:18
Isa 14:12-15
John 12:31
Rev 12:8-9
[b]*satanas* (4567)
‣John 13:27
10:19
Acts 28:3-5
10:20
Exod 32:32
Isa 4:3
Phil 4:3
Rev 3:5
10:21-24
//Matt 11:25-27
10:22
Matt 28:18
John 1:18; 3:35
10:23-24
//Matt 13:16-17
10:24
1 Pet 1:10-14
10:25-28
//Matt 22:34-40
//Mark 12:28-31

around from home to home. Stay in one
place, eating and drinking what they provide. Don't hesitate to accept hospitality,
because those who work deserve their pay.
8"If you enter a town and it welcomes you,
eat whatever is set before you. 9Heal the
sick, and tell them, 'The Kingdom of God
is near you now.' 10But if a town refuses to
welcome you, go out into its streets and say,
11'We wipe even the dust of your town from
our feet to show that we have abandoned
you to your fate. And know this—the Kingdom of God is near!' 12I assure you, even
wicked Sodom will be better off than such
a town on judgment day.
13"What sorrow awaits you, Korazin and
Bethsaida! For if the miracles I did in you
had been done in wicked Tyre and Sidon,
their people would have repented of their
sins long ago, clothing themselves in burlap
and throwing ashes on their heads to show
their remorse. 14Yes, Tyre and Sidon will be
better off on judgment day than you. 15And
you people of Capernaum, will you be honored in heaven? No, you will go down to the
place of the dead."
16Then he said to the disciples, "Anyone
who accepts your message is also accepting
me. And anyone who rejects you is rejecting
me. And anyone who rejects me is rejecting
God, who sent me."
17When the seventy-two disciples returned, they joyfully reported to him, "Lord,
even the demons obey us when we use your
name!"
18"Yes," he told them, "I saw [b]Satan fall
from heaven like lightning! 19Look, I have
given you authority over all the power of
the enemy, and you can walk among snakes
and scorpions and crush them. Nothing
will injure you. 20But don't rejoice because
evil spirits obey you; rejoice because your
names are registered in heaven."

Jesus' Prayer of Thanksgiving
Luke 10:21-22 // Matt 11:25-27
Luke 10:23-24 // Matt 13:16-17

21At that same time Jesus was filled with
the joy of the Holy Spirit, and he said, "O Father, Lord of heaven and earth, thank you
for hiding these things from those who
think themselves wise and clever, and for revealing them to the childlike. Yes, Father, it
pleased you to do it this way.
22"My Father has entrusted everything to
me. No one truly knows the Son except the
Father, and no one truly knows the Father
except the Son and those to whom the Son
chooses to reveal him."
23Then when they were alone, he turned
to the disciples and said, "Blessed are the
eyes that see what you have seen. 24I tell
you, many prophets and kings longed to
see what you see, but they didn't see it. And
they longed to hear what you hear, but they
didn't hear it."

The Most Important Commandment
Luke 10:25-28; cp. Matt 22:34-40 // Mark 12:28-31

25One day an expert in religious law stood
up to test Jesus by asking him this question:
"Teacher, what should I do to inherit eternal
life?"
26Jesus replied, "What does the law of
Moses say? How do you read it?"

10:7 ***Don't move around from home to home:*** See note on 9:4. • ***because those who work deserve their pay:*** Those who minister for Jesus should receive compensation from those they serve (see also 1 Cor 9:14; 1 Tim 5:18).

10:9 The same mission was given to the Twelve (see 9:1). • ***Heal the sick:*** Healing was a sign of salvation (Isa 29:18-19; 35:5); it was physical evidence that the ***Kingdom of God*** was present (see note on 7:22).

10:11 See note on 9:5.

10:12 God destroyed ***Sodom*** and Gomorrah because of their wickedness (Gen 18:16–19:29).

10:13 ***Korazin and Bethsaida,*** two of the towns in which Jesus ministered, were located on the northern shore of the Sea of Galilee (see note on 9:10). • ***Tyre and Sidon*** were Gentile cities in Phoenicia, on the Mediterranean coast north of Galilee. The prophets had pronounced messages of judgment against their wickedness (Isa 23; Ezek 28).

10:15 ***Capernaum*** was Jesus' base of operations during his Galilean ministry; this town saw many of his miracles (see 4:31-41). • ***to the place of the dead*** (Greek *to Hades*): Though Capernaum was blessed by the Messiah's presence, it would be judged for its pride and rejection of Jesus.

10:18 ***I saw Satan fall from heaven like lightning!*** See Rev 12:7-12.

10:19 ***Snakes and scorpions*** were symbols of danger and evil (see Deut 8:15; Num 21:6-9; 1 Kgs 12:14; Isa 11:8; Ezek 2:6). Satan is the ancient serpent who tempted Eve (Gen 3:15; Rom 16:20; Rev 12:9; 20:2), and demonic forces are described as scorpions (Rev 9:3-4). • ***Nothing will injure you:*** This didn't mean that Jesus' followers should take dangerous chances. The point is that God protects his servants (e.g., Acts 28:3-6).

10:20 Disciples should not *rejoice* in their spiritual power, but in the greatness of God who freely gives them salvation. • ***your names are registered in heaven:*** For the record of salvation in heaven's books, see Exod 32:32-33; Ps 69:28; Isa 4:3; Dan 12:1; Mal 3:16-17; Phil 4:3; Heb 12:23; Rev 3:5; 13:8; 17:8; 20:12, 15; 21:27.

10:21 ***hiding these things:*** God uses simple things that a child can understand to shame ***those who think themselves wise*** but are foolish in God's eyes (see Isa 29:14; 1 Cor 1:18-31).

10:22 The ***Father*** and the ***Son*** share an intimate relationship. Jesus came to earth to ***reveal*** the Father to a lost world (see John 1:1-18).

10:23 ***that see what you have seen:*** The disciples witnessed the arrival of God's promised salvation, the inauguration of the Kingdom of God.

10:25 ***an expert in religious law:*** See note on 5:17.

27"The man answered, " 'You must love the
LORD your God with all your heart, all your
soul, all your strength, and all your mind.'
And, 'Love your neighbor as yourself.' "
28"Right!" Jesus told him. "Do this and
you will live!"

Parable of the Good Samaritan
29The man wanted to justify his actions, so
he asked Jesus, "And who is my neighbor?"
30Jesus replied with a story: "A Jewish
man was traveling from Jerusalem down
to Jericho, and he was attacked by bandits.
They stripped him of his clothes, beat him
up, and left him half dead beside the road.
31"By chance a priest came along. But
when he saw the man lying there, he crossed
to the other side of the road and passed him
by. 32A Temple assistant walked over and
looked at him lying there, but he also passed
by on the other side.
33"Then a despised Samaritan came
along, and when he saw the man, he felt
compassion for him. 34Going over to him,
the Samaritan soothed his wounds with olive oil and wine and bandaged them. Then
he put the man on his own donkey and took
him to an inn, where he took care of him.
35The next day he handed the innkeeper
two silver coins, telling him, 'Take care of

10:27 *Lev 19:18 *Deut 6:5
10:28 Lev 18:5 Rom 10:5
10:29 Luke 16:15
10:31 Lev 21:1-3

MARTHA, MARY, AND LAZARUS (10:38-42)

Matt 26:6-13
Mark 14:3-9
John 11:1-44; 12:1-11, 17

The sisters Martha and Mary lived with their brother Lazarus in Bethany, near Jerusalem; Jesus loved and visited this family. They are mentioned only in the Gospels of Luke and John (this Lazarus is not Lazarus the beggar from Luke 16:19-31).

Luke's account (10:38-42) focuses on the contrast between Martha and Mary. When Jesus visited their home, Martha was busy in the kitchen and became upset with her sister for not helping her prepare the meal. Jesus defended Mary's desire to simply sit and learn from him as the most important thing.

John's stories focus on Jesus' act of raising Lazarus from the dead (John 11:1-44; cp. Matt 26:6-13; Mark 14:3-9). When Jesus arrived in Bethany, four days after Lazarus had died, the sisters expressed their dismay that Jesus had not come in time to heal their sick brother. Jesus, deeply moved by the weeping of Lazarus' friends, went to the tomb and ordered Lazarus to come out. To everyone's astonishment, he did so, bound in the cloths he had been buried in. This amazing miracle exemplifies Jesus as the giver of eternal life (John 11:25-26). Ironically, this act of restoring Lazarus's life also galvanized the Jewish leaders to bring about Jesus' death because so many people were responding to Jesus' miracles (John 11:47-53; 12:10-11).

Soon thereafter, when the family invited Jesus for a celebration meal, Mary poured a bottle of extremely expensive perfume on Jesus as an expression of her gratitude. When people criticized her for what they considered an extravagant waste, Jesus defended her action, saying that it anticipated his coming death (John 12:1-8).

10:27 ***You must love the LORD your God:*** Jesus identified Deut 6:5 and Lev 19:18 as the two greatest commandments (Mark 12:28-34). Deuteronomy 6:5 is part of the prayer known as the *Shema,* which every Jew was to repeat daily.

10:28 ***Do this and you will live!*** Jesus was not suggesting that people would be saved by their works; rather, such love expresses genuine faith and devotion to the Lord.

10:29 ***who is my neighbor?*** A neighbor, in this context, was normally identified as a fellow Israelite.

10:30-37 Jesus' parable shows that true neighbors love even their enemies (10:29). Authentic spirituality is not based on ethnic identity or religious associations, but on love for God and for others.

10:30 The road ***from Jerusalem down to Jericho*** dropped 3,300 feet (1,000 meters) through rugged terrain where robbers often lay in wait for travelers.

10:31 ***a priest:*** Priests were descendants of Aaron from the tribe of Levi (Exod 28:1-3). They served in the Temple and offered sacrifices to God. • ***passed him by:*** A priest or a Levite became unclean and unable to serve in the Temple if he touched a dead body. This priest was unwilling to risk ritual impurity by helping a person in desperate trouble.

10:32 ***A Temple assistant*** (literally *a Levite*): Levites were members of the tribe of Levi. They were not given a tribal homeland in Israel, but were dedicated to God (Num 3:41, 45; 8:18; 35:2-3; Deut 18:1; Josh 14:3) as assistants to the priests in the service of the Temple.

10:33 ***a despised Samaritan:*** This reversal in the story must have left the listeners aghast. Jews and Samaritans hated each other (see 9:52-53; 17:16; John 4:4-42). After the Assyrians conquered the northern kingdom of Israel, Assyrian colonists intermarried with Israelites left in Samaria; these inhabitants became known as Samaritans. After the Judeans returned from Babylon, conflict arose between the Jews and the Samaritans (Ezra 4), who built a rival temple on Mount Gerizim and used their own version of the Pentateuch (Genesis—Deuteronomy) as their Scripture. Hatred between the two increased dramatically when the Jewish king John Hyrcanus attacked the Samaritans and destroyed the temple on Mount Gerizim (about 128 BC). In this context of mutual animosity, no first-century Jew would expect a despised Samaritan to help a wounded Jew. But in God's Kingdom, a despised foreigner becomes a helping neighbor!

10:34 *Oil* soothed the wound; *wine* was a disinfectant.

10:35 ***two silver coins:*** Greek *two*

10:37
[c]*eleos* (1656)
‣ Eph 2:4
10:38
John 11:1; 12:2-3
10:41
Matt 6:25-34
Luke 12:11, 22
10:42
Ps 27:4
Phil 3:13-14
11:1
Luke 3:21
11:2-4
//Matt 6:9-13
11:4
Matt 18:23-35
Mark 11:25
1 Cor 10:13
11:7
Gal 6:17
11:8
Luke 18:1-6

this man. If his bill runs higher than this, I'll pay you the next time I'm here.'

36 "Now which of these three would you say was a neighbor to the man who was attacked by bandits?" Jesus asked.

37 The man replied, "The one who showed him [c]mercy."

Then Jesus said, "Yes, now go and do the same."

Jesus Visits Martha and Mary

38 As Jesus and the disciples continued on their way to Jerusalem, they came to a certain village where a woman named Martha welcomed him into her home. 39 Her sister, Mary, sat at the Lord's feet, listening to what he taught. 40 But Martha was distracted by the big dinner she was preparing. She came to Jesus and said, "Lord, doesn't it seem unfair to you that my sister just sits here while I do all the work? Tell her to come and help me."

41 But the Lord said to her, "My dear Martha, you are worried and upset over all these details! 42 There is only one thing worth being concerned about. Mary has discovered it, and it will not be taken away from her."

Teaching about Prayer
Luke 11:1-4 // Matt 6:9-13
Luke 11:9-13 // Matt 7:7-11

11 Once Jesus was in a certain place praying. As he finished, one of his disciples came to him and said, "Lord, teach us to pray, just as John taught his disciples."

2 Jesus said, "This is how you should pray:

"Father, may your name be kept holy.
May your Kingdom come soon.
3 Give us each day the food we need,
4 and forgive us our sins,
as we forgive those who sin
against us.
And don't let us yield to temptation."

5 Then, teaching them more about prayer, he used this story: "Suppose you went to a friend's house at midnight, wanting to borrow three loaves of bread. You say to him, 6 'A friend of mine has just arrived for a visit, and I have nothing for him to eat.' 7 And suppose he calls out from his bedroom, 'Don't bother me. The door is locked for the night, and my family and I are all in bed. I can't help you.' 8 But I tell you this—though he won't do it for friendship's sake, if you keep knocking long enough, he will get up and

Jesus' Prayers (11:1-13)

Luke 3:21; 6:12; 9:28; 11:1-13; 18:1-8; 22:32, 39-46; 23:34, 46

In Luke's Gospel, Jesus prayed at critical events in his life: his baptism (3:21), before calling the Twelve (6:12), at the transfiguration (9:28), for Peter before his denial (22:32), and for his murderers from the cross (23:34). He also taught the disciples to pray (11:1-4) and told parables about the need for persistent prayer (11:5-13; 18:1-8).

Jesus' prayers are part of Luke's emphasis on the intimacy between the Father and the Son. Jesus lived in communion with the Father, followed the Father's purpose, and remained faithful to the Father's will. In Gethsemane, Jesus agonized over the suffering that lay ahead, but he prayed, "I want your will to be done, not mine" (22:42). On the cross, he expressed total dependence on the Father, uttering as his last words, "Father, I entrust my spirit into your hands!" (23:46). Jesus modeled for us a life of trust and dependence on our heavenly Father.

denarii. A denarius was equivalent to a laborer's full day's wage.

10:38-42 ***Martha . . . Mary*** and their brother Lazarus were good friends of Jesus who lived in Bethany, east of Jerusalem (see John 11:1).

10:39 ***Mary . . . sat at the Lord's feet*** in the position of a disciple (cp. Acts 22:3). Rabbis did not usually have female disciples.

10:40 ***Martha was distracted by the big dinner she was preparing:*** Hospitality was valued highly, and Martha was fulfilling the expected role of a woman. She was frustrated that Mary was not.

10:42 ***There is only one thing worth being concerned about. Mary has discovered it:*** Jesus' words were shocking. Women were expected to serve domestically and were forbidden to learn as disciples from a rabbi. Jesus validated Mary's desire to be Jesus' disciple.

11:1 ***praying:*** See note on 3:21.

11:2-4 ***This is how you should pray:*** The "Lord's Prayer" was a model for Jesus' disciples to follow.

11:2 Some manuscripts add additional phrases from the Lord's Prayer as it is presented in Matt 6:9-13.

11:3 ***Give us each day the food we need:*** Or *Give us each day our food for the day;* or *Give us each day our food for tomorrow.* The Greek can be interpreted in various ways.

11:4 ***And don't let us yield to temptation*** (or *And keep us from being tested*): This is a difficult phrase in the Greek. God does not tempt his people (Jas 1:13), but since testing is a growth-producing part of our Christian life (Jas 1:2-4), should believers pray to avoid it? The phrase probably means "protect us during temptation."

11:6 ***A friend of mine has just arrived for a visit:*** Standards of hospitality in first-century Jewish culture required a host to find adequate provisions for a visitor.

11:8 ***because of your shameless persistence*** (or *in order to avoid shame,* or *so his reputation won't be damaged*): Shame would also lie on the man who didn't want to get up, since hospitality was a community requirement. God protects his good name by providing for his people.

give you whatever you need because of your shameless persistence.

9"And so I tell you, keep on asking, and you will receive what you ask for. Keep on seeking, and you will find. Keep on knocking, and the door will be opened to you. 10For everyone who asks, receives. Everyone who seeks, finds. And to everyone who knocks, the door will be opened.

11"You fathers—if your children ask for a fish, do you give them a snake instead? 12Or if they ask for an egg, do you give them a scorpion? Of course not! 13So if you sinful people know how to give good gifts to your children, how much more will your heavenly Father give the Holy Spirit to those who ask him."

Growing Opposition along the Way (11:14-54)

The Source of Jesus' Power

Luke 11:14-23 // Matt 12:22-30 // Mark 3:22-27; cp. Matt 9:32-34
Luke 11:24-26 // Matt 12:43-45

14One day Jesus cast out a demon from a man who couldn't speak, and when the demon was gone, the man began to speak. The crowds were amazed, 15but some of them said, "No wonder he can cast out demons. He gets his power from [d]Satan, the prince of demons." 16Others, trying to test Jesus, demanded that he show them a miraculous sign from heaven to prove his authority.

17He knew their thoughts, so he said, "Any kingdom divided by civil war is doomed. A family splintered by feuding will fall apart. 18You say I am empowered by [e]Satan. But if Satan is divided and fighting against himself, how can his kingdom survive? 19And if I am empowered by [f]Satan, what about your own exorcists? They cast out demons, too, so they will condemn you for what you have said. 20But if I am casting out demons by the power of God, then the Kingdom of God has arrived among you. 21For when a strong man like Satan is fully armed and guards his palace, his possessions are safe—22until someone even stronger attacks and overpowers him, strips him of his weapons, and carries off his belongings.

23"Anyone who isn't with me opposes me, and anyone who isn't working with me is actually working against me.

24"When an evil spirit leaves a person, it goes into the desert, searching for rest. But when it finds none, it says, 'I will return to the person I came from.' 25So it returns and finds that its former home is all swept and in order. 26Then the spirit finds seven other spirits more evil than itself, and they all enter the person and live there. And so that person is worse off than before."

27As he was speaking, a woman in the crowd called out, "God bless your mother—the womb from which you came, and the breasts that nursed you!"

28Jesus replied, "But even more [g]blessed are all who hear the word of God and put it into practice."

The Sign of Jonah

Luke 11:29-32 // Matt 12:39-42

29As the crowd pressed in on Jesus, he said, "This evil generation keeps asking me to

11:9-13 //Matt 7:7-11
11:9 Matt 6:33
11:13 Jas 1:17
11:14-23 //Matt 12:22-32 //Mark 3:20-30
11:15 Matt 9:34 [d]*beelzeboul* (0954) ‣Luke 11:18
11:16 Matt 12:38; 16:1
11:17 Matt 9:4
11:18 [e]*beelzeboul* (0954) ‣Luke 11:19
11:19 [f]*beelzeboul* (0954) ‣Matt 10:25
11:20 Exod 8:19
11:22 Isa 49:24; 53:12
11:24-26 //Matt 12:43-45
11:27 Luke 1:28, 42, 48
11:28 Luke 6:47; 8:21 Jas 1:22 [g]*makarios* (3107) ‣John 20:29
11:29-32 //Matt 12:38-42 1 Cor 1:22

11:11-12 *if your children ask:* Some manuscripts add *for bread, do you give them a stone? Or [if they ask].* • ***A fish*** and ***an egg*** were common foods. ***A scorpion*** resembles an egg when it curls into a ball to lure its prey. Giving ***a snake*** or a scorpion would be a cruel practical joke, substituting something deadly for a good meal. No loving father would do such a thing.

11:13 ***give the Holy Spirit:*** Matthew's parallel (Matt 7:11) reads "give good gifts." The Holy Spirit is the greatest gift for believers, providing guidance, power, and the seal of salvation. Luke gives special prominence to the work of the Holy Spirit in Luke and Acts.

11:14-32 Jesus faced two challenges. He answered the first, an accusation that he was casting out demons by Satan's power (11:15), in 11:17-26. The second was a demand for miraculous signs (11:16), which he answered in 11:29-32.

11:14 ***a demon from a man who couldn't speak:*** Demons sometimes inflict physical disease or disability.

11:15 ***Satan:*** Greek *Beelzeboul;* also in 11:18-19; other manuscripts read *Beezeboul;* Latin version reads *Beelzebub. Beelzeboul* ("Baal, the prince") was the name of a Canaanite god that later came to be used as a name for Satan. The Jews mocked the name, calling him *Beelzebub* ("lord of the flies").

11:17 ***He knew their thoughts:*** See 5:22; 7:40; 9:47. • ***Any kingdom divided by civil war:*** Jesus' first response to the accusation was that he could not be working for Satan; he was tearing down Satan's kingdom by casting out demons.

11:20 ***by the power of God*** (literally *by the finger of God*): See Exod 8:19. • ***the Kingdom of God has arrived among you:*** Jesus' exorcisms were evidence that the Kingdom of God was present.

11:21-22 The ***strong man*** is ***Satan;*** the ***stronger*** man is Jesus. Jesus' exorcisms demonstrated that he was defeating and plundering Satan's property—those people held in bondage by him (cp. Isa 49:24-26).

11:23 ***Anyone who isn't with me opposes me:*** See note on 9:50.

11:24 ***evil*** (literally *unclean*) ***spirit:*** See note on 4:33.

11:26 ***seven other spirits:*** Seven may indicate completeness, meaning that the man was completely under their power, or it could simply indicate an overwhelming force.

11:28 ***even more blessed:*** Jesus again affirmed that our spiritual life and our relationship with God are more important than physical ancestry and family relationships (see note on 8:21).

11:29-30 ***The sign of Jonah*** could refer to the resurrection; Jonah's time in the fish was a sign to the Ninevites that God had sent him, like Jesus' time in the grave (see Matt 12:40). It could

11:30
Jon 1:17; 2:10

11:31
1 Kgs 10:1-10
2 Chr 9:1-12

11:32
Jon 3:5, 8, 10

11:33
Matt 5:15
Luke 8:16

11:34-36
//Matt 6:22-23

11:37-54
Matt 23:1-36
Mark 12:38-40
Luke 20:45-47

11:38
Mark 7:3-4

11:39
Matt 23:25
Mark 7:20-23

11:41
Luke 12:33

11:42
Lev 27:30
Matt 23:23

11:43
Matt 23:6-7
Mark 12:38-39

11:44
Matt 23:27-28

11:46
Matt 23:4

show them a miraculous sign. But the only
sign I will give them is the sign of Jonah.
30 What happened to him was a sign to the
people of Nineveh that God had sent him.
What happens to the Son of Man will be
a sign to these people that he was sent by
God.

31 "The queen of Sheba will stand up
against this generation on judgment day
and condemn it, for she came from a distant
land to hear the wisdom of Solomon. Now
someone greater than Solomon is here—but
you refuse to listen. 32 The people of Nineveh
will also stand up against this generation
on judgment day and condemn it, for they
repented of their sins at the preaching of
Jonah. Now someone greater than Jonah is
here—but you refuse to repent.

Receiving the Light
Luke 11:33 // Matt 5:15 // Mark 4:21 // Luke 8:16
Luke 11:34-36 // Matt 6:22-23

33 "No one lights a lamp and then hides it
or puts it under a basket. Instead, a lamp
is placed on a stand, where its light can be
seen by all who enter the house.

34 "Your eye is a lamp that provides light
for your body. When your eye is good, your
whole body is filled with light. But when
it is bad, your body is filled with darkness.
35 Make sure that the light you think you
have is not actually darkness. 36 If you are
filled with light, with no dark corners, then
your whole life will be radiant, as though a
floodlight were filling you with light."

Jesus Criticizes the Religious Leaders
Luke 11:37-52; cp. Matt 23:23-36

37 As Jesus was speaking, one of the Pharisees invited him home for a meal. So he
went in and took his place at the table. 38 His
host was amazed to see that he sat down to
eat without first performing the hand-washing ceremony required by Jewish custom.
39 Then the Lord said to him, "You Pharisees
are so careful to clean the outside of the cup
and the dish, but inside you are filthy—full
of greed and wickedness! 40 Fools! Didn't
God make the inside as well as the outside?
41 So clean the inside by giving gifts to the
poor, and you will be clean all over.

42 "What sorrow awaits you Pharisees!
For you are careful to tithe even the tiniest
income from your herb gardens, but you ignore justice and the love of God. You should
tithe, yes, but do not neglect the more important things.

43 "What sorrow awaits you Pharisees! For
you love to sit in the seats of honor in the
synagogues and receive respectful greetings as you walk in the marketplaces. 44 Yes,
what sorrow awaits you! For you are like hidden graves in a field. People walk over them
without knowing the corruption they are
stepping on."

45 "Teacher," said an expert in religious
law, "you have insulted us, too, in what you
just said."

46 "Yes," said Jesus, "what sorrow also
awaits you experts in religious law! For you
crush people with unbearable religious

simply mean that Jonah and Jesus both preached God's warning to repent (see 11:32). • *Son of Man* is a title Jesus used for himself.

11:31 ***The queen of Sheba*** (literally *The queen of the south*): Sheba was a kingdom in southern Arabia. The queen traveled a great distance to hear Solomon's wisdom (1 Kgs 10:1-13; 2 Chr 9:1-12).

11:33 ***No one lights a lamp and then hides it:*** See note on 8:16-17. • Some manuscripts do not include ***or puts it under a basket.***

11:35-36 ***Light*** and ***darkness*** are metaphors for good and evil (John 1:5; 3:19; 8:12; 12:35; Acts 26:18; Rom 13:12; 2 Cor 4:6; 6:14; Eph 5:8; 1 Thes 5:5; 1 Pet 2:9; 1 Jn 1:5; 2:8-9).

11:37 ***one of the Pharisees invited him home for a meal:*** See notes on 7:36 and 14:1. • ***and took his place at the table:*** Or *and reclined.*

11:38 ***the hand-washing ceremony required by Jewish custom:*** The Pharisees had developed elaborate washing rituals to ensure ceremonial purity (see Mark 7:1-5).

11:39 The ***Pharisees*** had meticulous rules for ceremonially cleaning cups and utensils for religious purity. Jesus accused them of cleaning only the ***outside of the cup*** (following external rules) but leaving the ***inside . . . filthy*** (keeping unrighteousness in their hearts).

11:41 ***by giving gifts to the poor:*** Acts of love reveal internal righteousness.

11:42-52 ***What sorrow awaits you Pharisees!*** Woes are the opposite of blessings (see note on 6:24-26). Jesus pronounced six woes, three against the Pharisees (11:42, 43, 44) and three against the teachers of religious law (11:46, 47, 52).

11:42 ***tithe even the tiniest income from your herb gardens*** (literally *tithe the mint, the rue, and every herb*): Tithing was required by the law (Deut 14:22-29; Lev 27:30-33; Num 18:21-32; 2 Chr 31:5-12). The Pharisees were meticulous in making sure that everything was properly tithed, but they ignored the ***more important*** issues—***justice and the love of God.***

11:43 The elders of the ***synagogues*** had special ***seats of honor.*** • The ***respectful greetings*** were honorable ways of addressing social and religious superiors (like addressing a judge as "your honor").

11:44 ***hidden graves in a field:*** Touching a grave or a dead body rendered a Jew ceremonially unclean (see note on 7:13-14). Jesus accused the religious leaders of being a defiling influence rather than a purifying one. This was a strongly offensive accusation (11:45).

11:45 ***an expert in religious law:*** The experts in religious law were closely aligned with the Pharisees and shared the same zeal for keeping the law of Moses.

11:46 ***unbearable religious demands:*** This refers to the oral tradition with all its intricate details on living according to *torah* (God's instruction in the books of Moses). The oral tradition placed a great burden upon the Jewish people.

demands, and you never lift a finger to ease
the burden. 47What sorrow awaits you! For
you build monuments for the prophets your
own ancestors killed long ago. 48But in fact,
you stand as witnesses who agree with what
your ancestors did. They killed the prophets, and you join in their crime by building
the monuments! 49This is what God in his
wisdom said about you: 'I will send prophets and apostles to them, but they will kill
some and persecute the others.'
50"As a result, this generation will be
held responsible for the murder of all God's
prophets from the creation of the world—
51from the murder of Abel to the murder of
Zechariah, who was killed between the altar
and the sanctuary. Yes, it will certainly be
charged against this generation.
52"What sorrow awaits you experts in
religious law! For you remove the key to
knowledge from the people. You don't enter
the Kingdom yourselves, and you prevent
others from entering."
53As Jesus was leaving, the teachers of religious law and the Pharisees became hostile
and tried to provoke him with many questions. 54They wanted to trap him into saying
something they could use against him.

Teaching and Preparation for Crisis along the Way (12:1–13:35)

A Warning against Hypocrisy

Luke 12:2-9 // Matt 10:26-33
Luke 12:10; cp. Matt 12:31-32 // Mark 3:28-30

12 Meanwhile, the crowds grew until
thousands were milling about and
stepping on each other. Jesus turned first to
his disciples and warned them, "Beware of
the [h]yeast of the Pharisees—their hypocrisy.
2The time is coming when everything that
is covered up will be revealed, and all that
is secret will be made known to all. 3What-
ever you have said in the dark will be heard
in the light, and what you have whispered
behind closed doors will be shouted from
the housetops for all to hear!
4"Dear friends, don't be afraid of those
who want to kill your body; they cannot do
any more to you after that. 5But I'll tell you
whom to fear. Fear God, who has the power
to kill you and then throw you into [i]hell. Yes,
he's the one to fear.
6"What is the price of five sparrows—two
copper coins? Yet God does not forget a single one of them. 7And the very hairs on your
head are all numbered. So don't be afraid;
you are more valuable to God than a whole
flock of sparrows.
8"I tell you the truth, everyone who acknowledges me publicly here on earth, the
Son of Man will also acknowledge in the
presence of God's angels. 9But anyone who
denies me here on earth will be denied before God's angels. 10Anyone who speaks
against the Son of Man can be forgiven, but
anyone who [j]blasphemes the Holy Spirit
will not be forgiven.
11"And when you are brought to trial in
the synagogues and before rulers and authorities, don't worry about how to defend
yourself or what to say, 12for the Holy Spirit
will teach you at that time what needs to be
said."

Parable of the Rich Fool

13Then someone called from the crowd,
"Teacher, please tell my brother to divide our
father's estate with me."

11:47 Matt 23:29-32
11:48 Acts 7:51-53; 8:1
11:49-51 Matt 23:34-36; 1 Cor 1:24, 30
11:51 Gen 4:8; 2 Chr 24:20-21
11:52 Matt 23:13
11:54 Luke 20:20
12:1 Matt 16:6, 11-12; [h]*zumē* (2219) ‣Luke 13:21
12:2-9 //Matt 10:26-33
12:2 Mark 4:22
12:4 John 15:14-15
12:5 Heb 10:31; [i]*geenna* (1067) ‣Luke 16:23
12:8 Luke 15:10; Rev 3:5
12:9 Mark 8:38; Luke 9:26; 2 Tim 2:12
12:10 Matt 12:31-32; Mark 3:28-29; 1 Jn 5:16; [j]*blasphēmeō* (0987) ‣John 10:33
12:11-12 Matt 10:19-20; Mark 13:11; Luke 21:12-15

11:48 *They killed the prophets:* See 1 Kgs 19:10, 14; Neh 9:26; Jer 2:30; 26:20-24. Luke portrays Jesus as "The Suffering Prophet" (4:22-24, p. 1711).

11:49 *This is what God in his wisdom said about you:* Literally *Therefore, the wisdom of God said.* In Proverbs, Wisdom is personified as a woman who imparts God's wisdom to human beings (Prov 1:20-33; 8:1–9:6). • The quotation is not explicitly from the OT.

11:51 *from the murder of Abel to the murder of Zechariah:* Abel's murder by his brother Cain was the first murder recorded in the OT (Gen 4:8). The stoning of Zechariah, son of Jehoiada (2 Chr 24:20-22) was the last, since Chronicles is the last book in the Hebrew OT (see Old Testament Introduction, "The Canon of the Old Testament," p. 4).

11:52 *the key to knowledge:* See Matt 16:19; 23:13.

12:1 *Yeast* permeates dough until it is entirely leavened. Leaven became a symbol for the permeating power of sin (Exod 12:14-20; 1 Cor 5:6). Like yeast, the hypocrisy *of the Pharisees* would spread until it affected all the people.

12:2-3 These verses are a warning against hypocrisy. All thoughts will be revealed by God, who knows all things and will judge every human being (Job 10:4-7; 11:11; Ps 11:4; 33:15; 139:12; Prov 15:3).

12:5 *hell* (Greek *Gehenna*): The Valley of Hinnom was a ravine along the southwestern side of Jerusalem. It became a metaphor for hell because Israelites had offered their children as sacrifices there (Jer 32:35) and later used it as a place to burn garbage (Jer 19:2, 10-13). Jesus' disciples should never be afraid of enemies who can only take away their life on earth. Instead, they should *fear God,* who can give eternal punishment.

12:6 *two copper coins* (Greek *two assaria* [Roman coins equal to 1⁄16 of a denarius]): The coin was worth about half an hour's work for a day laborer.

12:8 *Son of Man* is a title Jesus used for himself (see "The Son of Man" at Matt 8:18-20, p. 1593). • *will also acknowledge:* At the final judgment (see Dan 7:7-14).

12:10 The Holy Spirit draws people to God. One who *blasphemes the Holy Spirit* rejects his testimony about Jesus and so rejects God. This is the unpardonable sin (see notes on Matt 12:31-32).

12:11-12 *brought to trial:* Jesus predicted persecution from Jews *in the synagogues* and from Gentile *rulers and authorities.* Paul and other apostles faced both kinds of persecution throughout Acts.

12:13-21 This parable shows the danger of trusting in riches instead of in God.

12:13 *tell my brother to divide our*

12:14 Exod 2:14; Acts 7:27, 35
12:15 Job 20:20; 31:24; Ps 62:10; Eccl 5:10; 1 Tim 6:9-10
12:19 Prov 27:1; 1 Cor 15:32; Jas 5:1-5
12:20 Job 27:8; Ps 39:6-7; Eccl 2:18-20
12:22-31 //Matt 6:25-34
12:24 Job 38:41; Ps 147:9
12:27 1 Kgs 10:1-10; [k]*doxa* (1391) ▸John 1:14
12:30 Matt 6:8
12:32 Luke 22:29
12:33 Matt 19:21; Acts 2:45
12:35-36 Matt 25:1-13; Mark 13:33-37
12:35 *Exod 12:11

14Jesus replied, "Friend, who made me
a judge over you to decide such things
as that?" 15Then he said, "Beware! Guard
against every kind of greed. Life is not measured by how much you own."

16Then he told them a story: "A rich man
had a fertile farm that produced fine crops.
17He said to himself, 'What should I do? I
don't have room for all my crops.' 18Then
he said, 'I know! I'll tear down my barns
and build bigger ones. Then I'll have room
enough to store all my wheat and other
goods. 19And I'll sit back and say to myself,
"My friend, you have enough stored away for years to come. Now take it easy! Eat, drink, and be merry!"'

20"But God said to him, 'You fool! You will die this very night. Then who will get everything you worked for?'

21"Yes, a person is a fool to store up earthly wealth but not have a rich relationship with God."

Teaching about Money and Possessions
Luke 12:22-32 // Matt 6:25-34
Luke 12:33-34 // Matt 6:19-21

22Then, turning to his disciples, Jesus said,
"That is why I tell you not to worry about everyday life—whether you have enough food to eat or enough clothes to wear. 23For
life is more than food, and your body more
than clothing. 24Look at the ravens. They
don't plant or harvest or store food in barns, for God feeds them. And you are far more
valuable to him than any birds! 25Can all
your worries add a single moment to your
life? 26And if worry can't accomplish a little
thing like that, what's the use of worrying over bigger things?

27"Look at the lilies and how they grow.
They don't work or make their clothing, yet Solomon in all his [k]glory was not dressed as
beautifully as they are. 28And if God cares
so wonderfully for flowers that are here today and thrown into the fire tomorrow, he will certainly care for you. Why do you have so little faith?

29"And don't be concerned about what to eat and what to drink. Don't worry about
such things. 30These things dominate the thoughts of unbelievers all over the world, but your Father already knows your needs.
31Seek the Kingdom of God above all else, and he will give you everything you need.

32"So don't be afraid, little flock. For it gives your Father great happiness to give you the Kingdom.

33"Sell your possessions and give to those in need. This will store up treasure for you in heaven! And the purses of heaven never get old or develop holes. Your treasure will be safe; no thief can steal it and no moth
can destroy it. 34Wherever your treasure is,
there the desires of your heart will also be.

Be Ready for the Lord's Coming
Luke 12:39-48 // Matt 24:42-51

35"Be dressed for service and keep your
lamps burning, 36as though you were

---

father's estate: In Judaism, the oldest son received a double portion of the inheritance (Deut 21:17) and was responsible for dividing up the rest after his father's death. This younger brother wanted his share of the estate (cp. 15:11-32).

12:15 ***Guard against every kind of greed:*** See Exod 20:17; Deut 5:21; Job 31:24-25; Ps 49; Eccl 2:1-11.

12:16-20 On the surface, the *rich man* had a perfectly prudent plan, but the constant focus was on himself (cp. Eccl 5:10); he never considered giving crops to the needy. He assumed that his riches would last and only wanted a place to store them, without bringing God into the equation at all (Jas 4:13-17). His judgment was just.

12:19-20 ***My friend:*** Literally *Soul.* The man was speaking to himself. • ***You fool!*** In Scripture, a fool is not someone with a low intelligence, but one who dishonors and disobeys God (Ps 14:1-5). • ***You will die*** (literally *Your soul will be demanded from you*): The man was satisfied with his soul, but God was not.

12:22-34 Jesus' warning against greed (12:13-21) is followed by teaching about living in dependence on God. Jesus' disciples were to focus on God's Kingdom and his purpose in this world rather than being obsessed with possessions.

12:24 ***Look at the ravens:*** Ravens were unclean (Lev 11:15; Deut 14:14), yet God cared even for them (Ps 147:9).

12:25 ***add a single moment to your life*** (literally *add a single cubit to his length*): Worry cannot add even one step on the road of life.

12:27 ***Solomon*** was among the richest kings of the world in his day (see 2 Chr 9:13-22).

12:30 ***unbelievers:*** Greek *ethnē,* sometimes translated "the nations" or "the Gentiles." To a Jewish audience, it meant all who were not God's people.

12:31 ***Seek the Kingdom of God:*** See note on 4:43. Adopt God's value system, pursue his purpose in the world, and submit to his authority.

12:32 ***little flock:*** God is the shepherd of his people (Ps 23; Jer 13:17; Ezek 34; Zech 10:3). Israel's leaders were also identified as shepherds and were criticized for harming or neglecting their sheep (Ezek 34; Zech 10:3).

12:33 ***Sell your possessions and give to those in need:*** This is not a command to liquidate all personal possessions, since elsewhere in the Bible it is assumed that believers will own property. It means recognizing that everything we have is God's and should be used to serve him and his people (see note on 11:41; see also Acts 2:44-45; 4:32-34). Believers are responsible for meeting the needs of the poor, especially in the church (Gal 6:10). • ***treasure for you in heaven:*** See 16:1-13; Matt 6:19-21. When God gives wealth, he also gives a ministry to help the unfortunate.

12:35-48 Jesus compared his faithful followers to servants in a master's household who were always prepared for his return and faithfully managed the resources he had left with them.

12:35 ***keep your lamps burning:*** This is a picture of readiness and vigilance (Exod 27:20-21; Lev 24:2; Ps 18:28; Matt 25:1-13).

waiting for your master to return from the
wedding feast. Then you will be ready to
open the door and let him in the moment
he arrives and knocks. 37The servants who
are ready and waiting for his return will be
rewarded. I tell you the truth, he himself
will seat them, put on an apron, and serve
them as they sit and eat! 38He may come in
the middle of the night or just before dawn.
But whenever he comes, he will reward the
servants who are ready.

39"Understand this: If a homeowner
knew exactly when a burglar was coming,
he would not permit his house to be broken
into. 40You also must be ready all the time,
for the Son of Man will come when least expected."

41Peter asked, "Lord, is that [a]illustration
just for us or for everyone?"

42And the Lord replied, "A faithful, sensible servant is one to whom the master
can give the responsibility of managing
his other household servants and feeding
them. 43If the master returns and finds that
the servant has done a good job, there will
be a reward. 44I tell you the truth, the master will put that servant in charge of all he
owns. 45But what if the servant thinks, 'My
master won't be back for a while,' and he
begins beating the other servants, partying, and getting drunk? 46The master will
return unannounced and unexpected, and
he will cut the servant in pieces and banish
him with the unfaithful.

47"And a servant who knows what the
master wants, but isn't prepared and
doesn't carry out those instructions, will
be severely punished. 48But someone who
does not know, and then does something
wrong, will be punished only lightly. When
someone has been given much, much will
be required in return; and when someone
has been entrusted with much, even more
will be required.

Jesus Causes Division
Luke 12:51-53 // Matt 10:34-36

49"I have come to set the world on fire, and
I wish it were already burning! 50I have a
terrible baptism of suffering ahead of me,
and I am under a heavy burden until it is accomplished. 51Do you think I have come to
bring peace to the earth? No, I have come
to divide people against each other! 52From
now on families will be split apart, three in
favor of me, and two against—or two in favor and three against.

53 'Father will be divided against son
and son against father;
mother against daughter
and daughter against mother;
and mother-in-law against daughter-in-law
and daughter-in-law against
mother-in-law.' "

Interpreting the Times
Luke 12:54-56 // Matt 16:2-3
Luke 12:57-59 // Matt 5:25-26

54Then Jesus turned to the crowd and said,
"When you see clouds beginning to form
in the west, you say, 'Here comes a shower.'

12:37 Luke 17:7-8; John 13:4
12:39-46 //Matt 24:43-51
12:39 1 Thes 5:2; Rev 16:15
12:40 Mark 13:33
12:41 [a]*parabolē* (3850) ‣Luke 15:3
12:47 Deut 25:2; Jas 4:17
12:48 Lev 5:17; Num 15:27-30
12:50 Mark 10:38-39; Acts 20:22-23
12:51-53 //Matt 10:34-36
12:53 *Mic 7:6
12:54-56 1 Kgs 18:44; Matt 16:2-3

12:36 The *master* could *return from the wedding feast* at any time of day or night. Jesus' followers must always be faithful and prepared for his return.

12:37 ***he himself will seat them:*** In Middle Eastern culture, the master would never serve his servants! Jesus redefined the role of the master by serving his disciples, giving himself for them, and meeting all their needs (see 22:24-27). • ***An apron*** was typical garb for a servant.

12:38 ***in the middle of the night or just before dawn:*** Literally *in the second or third watch.*

12:40 ***the Son of Man will come:*** See "The Son of Man" at Matt 8:18-20, p. 1593.

12:42 The *faithful, sensible servant* was a household manager. Wealthy homeowners appointed gifted and educated slaves as chief executive officers over their affairs.

12:44 ***in charge of all he owns:*** Although servants in the Roman world were slaves (the master's property), they could rise to very high social status, owning property, managing the entire household, and acting with the master's authority.

12:46 ***he will cut the servant in pieces:*** Such brutal judgment was common in the ancient world. It is uncertain whether Jesus was talking about temporal punishment or eternal damnation. • ***and banish him with the unfaithful:*** This could either mean "treat him as an unbeliever" (a temporal judgment) or "send him to hell" (an eternal judgment), depending on whether Jesus was referring to discipline for a believer or condemnation of an unbeliever. The point is that an unfaithful servant faces stringent judgment.

12:47-48 ***who knows . . . who does not know:*** Sins of ignorance receive less punishment than intentional sins (Num 15:22-26; Ps 19:13; cp. Luke 23:34). • ***When someone has been given much:*** Believers will be held responsible for the knowledge and resources they have been given (see Jas 3:1). A sin in ignorance is still a sin.

12:49 ***I have come to set the world on fire:*** Jesus' ministry radically changed the status quo, bringing judgment on the wicked and purifying the righteous (see 3:16-17; 9:54; 17:29; Deut 4:24; Amos 5:6; Heb 12:29).

12:50 ***a terrible baptism of suffering:*** God's judgment is often pictured as an overwhelming flood (Ps 18:4; 42:7; 69:1-2; Isa 8:7-8; 30:27-28; Jon 2:5; see notes on Mark 10:38).

12:51-53 ***I have come to divide people:*** Jesus' ministry demands a decision for or against God that divides even family members.

12:53 Jesus quotes Mic 7:6, which was interpreted by the rabbis as the crisis and persecution that would lead to the Messiah's coming.

12:54 ***Clouds beginning to form in the west*** brought rain from the Mediterranean Sea.

12:58-59
Matt 5:25-26
13:2
John 9:2-3
13:3
Ps 7:12
13:4
John 9:7, 11
13:5
Ps 7:12
13:6
Isa 5:2
Matt 21:19
Mark 11:12-14
13:7
Hab 3:17
Matt 3:10
13:8
2 Pet 3:9, 15
13:10
Matt 4:23
13:13
Mark 5:23
13:14
Exod 20:9-10
Deut 5:13-14
Matt 12:10
Mark 3:2
Luke 6:7
John 5:16
13:15
Luke 14:5
[b]*hupokritēs* (5273)
‣ Matt 6:2

And you are right. [55]When the south wind
blows, you say, 'Today will be a scorcher.'
And it is. [56]You fools! You know how to interpret the weather signs of the earth and
sky, but you don't know how to interpret the
present times.
[57]"Why can't you decide for yourselves
what is right? [58]When you are on the way
to court with your accuser, try to settle the
matter before you get there. Otherwise,
your accuser may drag you before the judge,
who will hand you over to an officer, who
will throw you into prison. [59]And if that happens, you won't be free again until you have
paid the very last penny."

A Call to Repentance

13 About this time Jesus was informed
that Pilate had murdered some
people from Galilee as they were offering
sacrifices at the Temple. [2]"Do you think
those Galileans were worse sinners than all
the other people from Galilee?" Jesus asked.
"Is that why they suffered? [3]Not at all! And
you will perish, too, unless you repent of
your sins and turn to God. [4]And what about
the eighteen people who died when the
tower in Siloam fell on them? Were they the
worst sinners in Jerusalem? [5]No, and I tell
you again that unless you repent, you will
perish, too."

Parable of the Barren Fig Tree

[6]Then Jesus told this story: "A man planted
a fig tree in his garden and came again
and again to see if there was any fruit on
it, but he was always disappointed. [7]Finally,
he said to his gardener, 'I've waited three
years, and there hasn't been a single fig!
Cut it down. It's just taking up space in the
garden.'
[8]"The gardener answered, 'Sir, give it one
more chance. Leave it another year, and I'll
give it special attention and plenty of fer-
tilizer. [9]If we get figs next year, fine. If not,
then you can cut it down.' "

Jesus Heals on the Sabbath

[10]One Sabbath day as Jesus was teaching in a
synagogue, [11]he saw a woman who had been
crippled by an evil spirit. She had been bent
double for eighteen years and was unable
to stand up straight. [12]When Jesus saw her,
he called her over and said, "Dear woman,
you are healed of your sickness!" [13]Then he
touched her, and instantly she could stand
straight. How she praised God!
[14]But the leader in charge of the synagogue was indignant that Jesus had healed
her on the Sabbath day. "There are six days
of the week for working," he said to the
crowd. "Come on those days to be healed,
not on the Sabbath."
[15]But the Lord replied, "You [b]hypo-
crites! Each of you works on the Sabbath
day! Don't you untie your ox or your donkey from its stall on the Sabbath and lead
it out for water? [16]This dear woman, a

12:55 The hot *south wind* blows into Israel from the Arabian Desert to the south and east (Job 37:17; Jer 4:11).

12:58 *on the way to court:* This lawsuit over an unpaid debt would result in debtor's prison. The *officer* is the bailiff of the court or the warden of the prison. It is advisable to negotiate accounts *with your accuser,* if possible, before reaching the courtroom. It is also best to reckon with God before the final day of judgment.

12:59 *last penny:* Greek *last lepton* [the smallest Jewish coin].

13:1-4 Jesus was responding to a popular claim that bad things only happen to bad people. Sin has negative consequences, but not every bad thing is a result of sin. Jesus then clarified that all people are sinners who need to repent (13:3, 5; see Job 4:7; 8:4, 20; 22:5; see also Ps 34:21; 75:10; Prov 3:33; 10:3, 6-7, 16, 24-25; John 9:2-3).

13:1 *Pilate had murdered some people from Galilee:* This particular incident is not known from other sources, but Pilate was a ruthless governor who, on several occasions, violently suppressed revolts (see Josephus, *War* 2.9.2-4; *Antiquities* 18.3.1-2).

13:4 *when the tower in Siloam fell:* This incident is also unknown apart from this reference. The pool of Siloam was a reservoir in the southeastern corner of Jerusalem, so the tower might have been part of the southern wall of Jerusalem.

13:6-9 The parable of the barren fig tree illustrated Jesus' ministry to Israel. Unless the nation produced the fruit of repentance, it would face judgment. The parable is open-ended—Israel was being offered the chance to respond. Cp. Matt 21:18-19 // Mark 11:12-14.

13:6 *a fig tree:* Israel was sometimes portrayed as an unfruitful fig tree or a vineyard that God would judge (Isa 5:1-7; Mic 7:1-2; see Jer 8:13; 24:1-10; Hos 9:10).

13:9 *cut it down:* A stump or fallen tree was an image of judgment or destruction (see note on 3:9; see Isa 6:13; 10:34; 11:1; Jer 46:22; Dan 4:23; Matt 3:10; 7:19).

13:10 *as Jesus was teaching in a synagogue* (see 4:14-30): In the synagogue, visiting rabbis were often asked to teach after the Law and the Prophets were read.

13:11 *crippled by an evil spirit:* See note on 11:14.

13:14 *the leader in charge of the synagogue:* See note on 8:41. • *not on the Sabbath:* Rabbis debated whether to give medical help on the Sabbath and decided it was acceptable only in cases of extreme emergency (see note on 6:6-7).

13:15-16 *You hypocrites!* The religious leaders would take care of their own animals on the Sabbath (to protect their investment) but then refuse to meet the needs of a fellow human being. In an ironic wordplay, the same word is translated *untie* (13:15) and *released* (13:16). The religious leaders would free their animals but not a *daughter of Abraham*—one of God's chosen people and a recipient of his favor. • *in bondage by Satan:* Jesus' exorcisms and healings manifested the Kingdom of God and the defeat of Satan (see 11:20).

daughter of Abraham, has been held in
bondage by Satan for eighteen years. Isn't
it right that she be released, even on the
Sabbath?"
[17]This shamed his enemies, but all the
people rejoiced at the wonderful things he
did.

Parable of the Mustard Seed
Luke 13:18-19 // Matt 13:31-32 // Mark 4:30-32

[18]Then Jesus said, "What is the Kingdom of
God like? How can I illustrate it? [19]It is like
a tiny mustard seed that a man planted in
a garden; it grows and becomes a tree, and
the birds make nests in its branches."

Parable of the Yeast
Luke 13:20-21 // Matt 13:33

[20]He also asked, "What else is the Kingdom
of God like? [21]It is like the [c]yeast a woman
used in making bread. Even though she put
only a little yeast in three measures of flour,
it permeated every part of the dough."

The Narrow Door
Luke 13:25-27; cp. Matt 7:21-23
Luke 13:28-30; cp. Matt 8:11-12; Matt 19:30 // Mark 10:31

[22]Jesus went through the towns and villages,
teaching as he went, always pressing on
toward Jerusalem. [23]Someone asked him,
"Lord, will only a few be saved?"
He replied, [24]"Work hard to enter the narrow door to God's Kingdom, for many will
try to enter but will fail. [25]When the master
of the house has locked the door, it will be
too late. You will stand outside knocking
and pleading, 'Lord, open the door for us!'
But he will reply, 'I don't know you or where
you come from.' [26]Then you will say, 'But we
ate and drank with you, and you taught in
our streets.' [27]And he will reply, 'I tell you,
I don't know you or where you come from.
Get away from me, all you who do evil.'
[28]"There will be weeping and gnashing
of teeth, for you will see Abraham, Isaac, Jacob, and all the prophets in the Kingdom of
God, but you will be thrown out. [29]And people will come from all over the world—from
east and west, north and south—to take
their places in the Kingdom of God. [30]And
note this: Some who seem least important
now will be the greatest then, and some
who are the greatest now will be least important then."

Jesus Grieves over Jerusalem
Luke 13:34-35 // Matt 23:37-39

[31]At that time some Pharisees said to him,
"Get away from here if you want to live!
Herod Antipas wants to kill you!"
[32]Jesus replied, "Go tell that fox that I will
keep on casting out demons and healing
people today and tomorrow; and the third
day I will accomplish my purpose. [33]Yes,
today, tomorrow, and the next day I must
proceed on my way. For it wouldn't do for
a prophet of God to be killed except in Jerusalem!
[34]"O Jerusalem, Jerusalem, the city that
kills the prophets and stones God's messengers! How often I have wanted to gather
your children together as a hen protects her
chicks beneath her wings, but you wouldn't

13:16 Luke 4:18; 19:9
13:18-21 //Matt 13:31-33 //Mark 4:30-32
13:21 [c]*zumē* (2219) ›1 Cor 5:6
13:24 //Matt 7:13 Mark 10:25 1 Tim 6:12
13:25 //Matt 7:21-23 Matt 25:10-11
13:27 *Ps 6:8 Matt 25:12
13:28-29 //Matt 8:10-11
13:29 Ps 107:3 Isa 43:5; 49:12; 59:19 Rev 14:15; 21:13
13:30 Matt 19:30; 20:16 Mark 10:31
13:33 Matt 16:21
13:34-35 //Matt 23:37-39 Luke 19:41-44

13:17 Jesus' skillful argument ***shamed*** and silenced ***his enemies.*** Honor and shame were among the most important values in Jewish society.

13:18-21 The parables of the ***mustard seed*** and the ***yeast*** reveal the nature of the Kingdom of God. Like a mustard seed, it grows from a tiny size until it becomes enormous; like yeast leavening dough, it permeates the entire world.

13:18 ***the Kingdom of God:*** See note on 4:43.

13:19 ***the birds make nests:*** The birds represent people who find the Kingdom to be a place of protection and security.

13:21 ***It is like the yeast:*** Leaven can represent evil (see 12:1; 1 Cor 5:6; Gal 5:9), but here it is a positive image of the permeating, transforming power of the Kingdom.

13:23 ***will only a few be saved?*** Some believed that only a small number would be saved. Others thought that all Jews would be saved because they were descendants of Abraham (see note on 3:8).

13:25 ***When the master of the house has locked the door:*** At a banquet, the master of the household locked the door after the invited guests had arrived. • ***I don't know you:*** In Scripture, *knowing* often means being chosen by God for a special relationship (Isa 63:16; Jer 1:5; Amos 3:2). The people of Israel were God's chosen people who had descended from Abraham (***where you come from***), but those who failed to respond to the invitation did not have a relationship with God. The same can be said of all who fail to respond to the Good News of the Kingdom.

13:28 The expression ***weeping and gnashing of teeth*** portrays rejection and suffering. • ***Abraham, Isaac,*** and ***Jacob*** were the three great founding patriarchs of the nation of Israel.

13:29 While many of God's chosen people, the Israelites, have rejected the gospel, other ***people . . . from all over the world*** will respond to God's offer of salvation and attend the messianic banquet (see 14:15; 17:20; Isa 2:2; 25:6-8; 51:4; 52:10; 55:5; 56:7; 59:19; Mic 4:1-2; Zech 2:13; Mal 1:11).

13:30 The pithy aphorism is literally *Some are last who will be first, and some are first who will be last.*

13:31 ***Herod Antipas:*** See notes on 3:1, 19-20.

13:32 ***Go tell that fox:*** Among first-century Jews, foxes were viewed as destructive and worthless pests. • ***casting out demons and healing people:*** Jesus' exorcisms and healings were evidence that God's Kingdom was present; his resurrection on ***the third day*** would vindicate him and prove that he inaugurated God's Kingdom.

13:33 ***a prophet of God to be killed:*** See "The Suffering Prophet" at 4:22-24, p. 1711.

13:34 ***O Jerusalem, Jerusalem:*** See "The City of Jerusalem" at 20:21-24, p. 1752. • ***as a hen protects her chicks:*** Cp. Deut 32:11; Ruth 2:12; Ps 17:8; 36:7; 57:1; 61:4; 63:7; 91:4.

13:35
*Ps 118:26
Jer 12:7; 22:5
Luke 19:38
14:1
Luke 7:36; 11:37
14:3
Luke 6:9
14:5
Matt 12:11
14:7
Matt 23:6
14:8-11
Prov 25:6-7
Jas 4:10
14:11
Matt 23:12
Luke 18:14

let me. 35 And now, look, your house is abandoned. And you will never see me again
until you say, 'Blessings on the one who
comes in the name of the LORD!' "

Further Teaching along the Way (14:1–17:10)

Jesus Heals on the Sabbath

14 One Sabbath day Jesus went to eat
dinner in the home of a leader of
the Pharisees, and the people were watching him closely. 2 There was a man there
whose arms and legs were swollen. 3 Jesus
asked the Pharisees and experts in religious law, "Is it permitted in the law to heal
people on the Sabbath day, or not?" 4 When
they refused to answer, Jesus touched the
sick man and healed him and sent him
away. 5 Then he turned to them and said,
"Which of you doesn't work on the Sabbath? If your son or your cow falls into a
pit, don't you rush to get him out?" 6 Again
they could not answer.

Jesus Teaches about Humility

7 When Jesus noticed that all who had come
to the dinner were trying to sit in the seats
of honor near the head of the table, he gave
them this advice: 8 "When you are invited
to a wedding feast, don't sit in the seat of
honor. What if someone who is more distinguished than you has also been invited?
9 The host will come and say, 'Give this
person your seat.' Then you will be embarrassed, and you will have to take whatever
seat is left at the foot of the table!
10 "Instead, take the lowest place at the
foot of the table. Then when your host sees
you, he will come and say, 'Friend, we have a
better place for you!' Then you will be honored in front of all the other guests. 11 For
those who exalt themselves will be humbled, and those who humble themselves
will be exalted."
12 Then he turned to his host. "When you
put on a luncheon or a banquet," he said,
"don't invite your friends, brothers, relatives,

The Messianic Banquet (14:1-24)

Luke 5:29-35; 6:21; 7:36-50; 9:10-17; 11:37-41; 12:35-40; 13:24-30; 17:8; 22:30
Isa 25:6; 65:13-14

Through his teaching and miracles, Jesus announced that God's messianic banquet was about to be served. All may come and feast at the table of salvation in God's Kingdom.

Jesus described his ministry as a wedding feast, with himself as the groom (5:33-35) and the Kingdom of God as a great banquet. All were invited, but some refused to come (14:15-21). Jesus is often portrayed as eating with diverse people, from despised tax collectors to pious Pharisees (5:29-33; 7:36-50; 11:37-41; 14:1-6). Jesus also used imagery of feasting and banquets in his teaching and parables (5:33-35; 6:21; 12:35-40; 13:24-30; 14:7-14, 15-24; 17:8; 22:30). He fed vast multitudes with a few loaves and fishes (9:10-17).

The OT background to this feasting imagery is Isa 25:6, where God's final salvation is described as a great feast for all people: "The LORD of Heaven's Armies will spread a wonderful feast for all the people of the world. It will be a delicious banquet, with clear, well-aged wine and choice meat" (see also Isa 65:13-14).

Jesus' public ministry marked the invitation to the banquet and its inauguration. Through his death and resurrection, he achieved salvation. All people can now come to God's banquet table and receive the spiritual blessings of the Kingdom. At the same time, this banquet awaits its final consummation in the future Kingdom, when Jesus' disciples will "eat and drink at my table in my Kingdom" and "will sit on thrones, judging the twelve tribes of Israel" (22:30).

13:35 *your house is abandoned:* Jesus predicted the destruction of Jerusalem that took place in AD 70. • *Blessings on the one who comes in the name of the LORD!* This refers to Ps 118:26. Psalm 118 was one of the psalms sung by pilgrims going up to Jerusalem for the annual festivals. Here Jesus referred to his second coming.

14:1 *in the home of a leader of the Pharisees:* In the Gospel of Luke, Jesus is frequently seen dining. See also "The Pharisees" at Matt 3:7, p. 1581.

14:2 *whose arms and legs were swollen* (or *who had dropsy*): Dropsy, medically known as edema, is an accumulation of fluid in tissues or a body cavity that causes swelling. It is usually a symptom of a more serious illness.

14:3 *Is it permitted in the law to heal people on the Sabbath day?* This question was debated by the rabbis (see note on 6:6-7).

14:5 Jesus pointed out the Pharisees' hypocrisy. They would rescue an animal on the Sabbath to protect their investment, but would not help a human being. • *son:* Some manuscripts read *donkey.*

14:7 *the seats of honor:* Meals in the ancient world were rituals of social status. The place given to someone at the table was determined by their place in the social pecking order. The quality of the food served to each guest also depended on their status. These guests were jockeying for the places of highest honor.

14:8 Jesus' response was a commentary on Prov 25:6-7.

14:9 *Then you will be embarrassed:* Shame and honor were among the most important values in first century Jewish culture. This kind of humiliation would have been almost worse than death.

14:12-13 *don't invite your friends:* Jesus challenged the prevailing use of banquets to flaunt and elevate one's status

and rich neighbors. For they will invite you
back, and that will be your only reward. [13]In-
stead, invite the poor, the crippled, the lame,
and the blind. [14]Then at the resurrection of
the righteous, God will reward you for inviting those who could not repay you."

Parable of the Great Feast

Luke 14:15-24; cp. Matt 22:1-14

[15]Hearing this, a man sitting at the table
with Jesus exclaimed, "What a blessing it
will be to attend a banquet in the Kingdom
of God!"
[16]Jesus replied with this story: "A man
prepared a great feast and sent out many invitations. [17]When the banquet was ready, he
sent his servant to tell the guests, 'Come, the
banquet is ready.' [18]But they all began making excuses. One said, 'I have just bought a
field and must inspect it. Please excuse me.'
[19]Another said, 'I have just bought five pairs
of oxen, and I want to try them out. Please
excuse me.' [20]Another said, 'I now have a
wife, so I can't come.'
[21]"The servant returned and told his
master what they had said. His master
was furious and said, 'Go quickly into the
streets and alleys of the town and invite
the poor, the crippled, the blind, and the
lame.' [22]After the servant had done this,
he reported, 'There is still room for more.'
[23]So his master said, 'Go out into the country lanes and behind the hedges and urge
anyone you find to come, so that the house
will be full. [24]For none of those I first invited will get even the smallest taste of my
banquet.'"

The Cost of Being a Disciple

Luke 14:26-27 // Matt 10:37-38

Luke 14:34-35; cp. Matt 5:13; Mark 9:49-50

[25]A large crowd was following Jesus. He
turned around and said to them, [26]"If you
want to be my disciple, you must hate everyone else by comparison—your father and
mother, wife and children, brothers and
sisters—yes, even your own life. Otherwise,
you cannot be my disciple. [27]And if you do
not carry your own cross and follow me, you
cannot be my disciple.
[28]"But don't begin until you count the cost.
For who would begin construction of a building without first calculating the cost to see if
there is enough money to finish it? [29]Other-
wise, you might complete only the foundation before running out of money, and then
everyone would laugh at you. [30]They would
say, 'There's the person who started that
building and couldn't afford to finish it!'
[31]"Or what king would go to war against
another king without first sitting down
with his counselors to discuss whether his
army of 10,000 could defeat the 20,000
soldiers marching against him? [32]And if he
can't, he will send a delegation to discuss
terms of peace while the enemy is still far
away. [33]So you cannot become my disciple
without giving up everything you own.
[34]"Salt is good for seasoning. But if it
loses its flavor, how do you make it salty

14:14
Acts 24:15
14:16-24
//Matt 22:1-10
14:20
Deut 24:5
1 Cor 7:33
14:24
Matt 21:43
Acts 13:46
14:26-27
//Matt 10:37-38
14:26
Deut 33:9
Matt 16:24
Mark 8:34
Luke 9:23; 18:29
John 12:25
14:27
Matt 10:38; 16:24
Mark 8:34
Luke 9:23
14:33
Phil 3:7-8
14:34
Matt 5:13
Mark 9:50

in the community. The host would invite friends of equal status and a few who were higher. These honored guests would then be expected to reciprocate, raising the first host's social position and reputation. Jesus turned this hierarchy upside down by instructing his followers to invite those who had no social status and could not reciprocate. God invites sinful human beings to dine at his banquet table of salvation (see "The Messianic Banquet" at Luke 14:1-24, p. 1737).

14:14 ***the resurrection of the righteous:*** see Dan 12:2.

14:15-24 This parable portrays what was happening in Jesus' ministry. The rich, powerful, and elite rejected Jesus' invitation to God's salvation banquet and would be shut out. Meanwhile, poor people and outcasts responded to the invitation (see also 1:52-53; 6:21, 25; 10:15; 18:14).

14:15 ***to attend a banquet:*** Literally *to eat bread.*

14:17 ***Come, the banquet is ready:*** The invitations would have been sent much earlier; the guests were summoned when the meal was ready.

14:18 ***they all began making excuses:*** All such excuses would have been a great affront to the host, who had made a great investment in this important social event. These guests had previously accepted the invitation, and all of their excuses were weak. Clearly, they just didn't want to attend the banquet. • ***I have just bought a field and must inspect it:*** No one would buy a field without first inspecting it.

14:19 ***oxen, and I want to try them out:*** This is another weak excuse—no one would buy oxen without having seen them plow.

14:20 ***I now have a wife:*** Some see this as a legitimate excuse since the OT exempted men from military service in their first year of marriage (Deut 20:7; 24:5), but this feast was a local community event, not a distant war. Furthermore, in an Israelite village, a marriage and a banquet would never be planned at the same time, so there was no real conflict.

14:21 The ***poor, the crippled, the blind, and the lame*** were the outcasts of Israel, to whom Jesus ministered.

14:23 ***Go out into the country lanes:*** These invitees might be a reference to the Gentiles to whom the Good News eventually went (cp. Acts 9:15; 13:46-48; 18:4-6; Rom 11:11-12).

14:25-35 ***A large crowd was following Jesus:*** Jesus' popularity was high, but he was about to teach that the cost of following him was also very high.

14:26 ***you must hate everyone else:*** Following Jesus requires complete dedication. The phrase *by comparison* does not appear in the Greek, but it accurately represents Jesus' meaning. Love for family and one's *own life* must not compete with devotion to Christ.

14:27 To ***carry your own cross*** is a picture of dying to self. The horizontal beam of the cross was carried by the condemned criminal headed for crucifixion (see note on 23:26).

14:34 ***Salt . . . if it loses its flavor:*** Sodium chloride cannot actually lose

14:35 Matt 11:15
15:1 Matt 9:11; Luke 5:29; Gal 2:12
15:2 Luke 5:30
15:3 [d]*parabolē* (3850) ‣Luke 18:1
15:4-7 //Matt 18:12-14; Luke 19:10
15:12 Deut 21:17
15:18 Ps 51:4
15:20 Gen 45:14-15; 46:29

again? [35]Flavorless salt is good neither for
the soil nor for the manure pile. It is thrown
away. Anyone with ears to hear should listen and understand!"

Parable of the Lost Sheep
Luke 15:3-7 // Matt 18:12-14

15 Tax collectors and other notorious
sinners often came to listen to Jesus
teach. [2]This made the Pharisees and teachers of religious law complain that he was
associating with such sinful people—even
eating with them!

[3]So Jesus told them this [d]story: [4]"If a man
has a hundred sheep and one of them gets
lost, what will he do? Won't he leave the
ninety-nine others in the wilderness and
go to search for the one that is lost until
he finds it? [5]And when he has found it, he
will joyfully carry it home on his shoulders.
[6]When he arrives, he will call together his
friends and neighbors, saying, 'Rejoice with
me because I have found my lost sheep.' [7]In
the same way, there is more joy in heaven
over one lost sinner who repents and returns to God than over ninety-nine others
who are righteous and haven't strayed
away!

Parable of the Lost Coin
[8]"Or suppose a woman has ten silver coins
and loses one. Won't she light a lamp and
sweep the entire house and search carefully until she finds it? [9]And when she finds
it, she will call in her friends and neighbors
and say, 'Rejoice with me because I have
found my lost coin.' [10]In the same way, there
is joy in the presence of God's angels when
even one sinner repents."

Parable of the Lost Son
[11]To illustrate the point further, Jesus told
them this story: "A man had two sons. [12]The
younger son told his father, 'I want my share
of your estate now before you die.' So his
father agreed to divide his wealth between
his sons.

[13]"A few days later this younger son
packed all his belongings and moved to
a distant land, and there he wasted all his
money in wild living. [14]About the time his
money ran out, a great famine swept over
the land, and he began to starve. [15]He persuaded a local farmer to hire him, and the
man sent him into his fields to feed the
pigs. [16]The young man became so hungry
that even the pods he was feeding the pigs
looked good to him. But no one gave him
anything.

[17]"When he finally came to his senses, he
said to himself, 'At home even the hired servants have food enough to spare, and here I
am dying of hunger! [18]I will go home to my
father and say, "Father, I have sinned against
both heaven and you, [19]and I am no longer
worthy of being called your son. Please take
me on as a hired servant."'

[20]"So he returned home to his father.
And while he was still a long way off, his father saw him coming. Filled with love and

---

its saltiness. Jesus might be speaking hypothetically (if salt were to lose), or he might be referring to a combination of minerals that included salt. The salt around the Dead Sea was a mixture of sodium chloride and other minerals. When the sodium chloride was removed, what was left behind was "salt" without saltiness.

14:35 ***good neither for the soil nor for the manure pile:*** Salt had various uses in the ancient world, including flavoring (14:34), preserving, and weed-killing. The sludge left after removing the sodium chloride was useless.

15:1-32 Chapter 15 contains three related parables of things lost and found: a sheep (15:1-7), a coin (15:8-10), and a son (15:11-32). The loss of something loved causes deep sorrow, whereas finding it brings great joy and rejoicing. There is great rejoicing in heaven when lost sinners return to their heavenly Father.

15:1 *Tax collectors* were despised because they worked for the hated Roman authorities and were ***notorious*** for their corruption (see note on 3:12).

15:2 In their self-righteous hard-heartedness, ***the Pharisees and teachers of religious law*** did not care about lost people. Jesus embodied the heart of God, who longs for his wayward children to return.

15:4 A flock of ***a hundred sheep*** was of average size for a shepherd of modest means. God's people are often identified as the Lord's flock (Ps 23; Isa 53:6; Jer 13:17; Ezek 34; Zech 10:3). • ***leave the ninety-nine others:*** Other shepherds could watch the ninety-nine, so those left behind were not in danger. The shepherd would do anything to find the one that was lost.

15:8 ***ten silver coins*** (Greek *ten drachmas;* a drachma was the equivalent of a full day's wage): These coins might have been part of the woman's dowry. • ***light a lamp and sweep the entire house:*** Palestinian homes were poorly lit and normally had dirt or stone floors. Finding a small coin could be difficult.

15:11-32 Like the previous two parables (15:3-7, 8-10), the parable of the lost son demonstrates God's love for the lost and the joy he experiences when they return. It also allegorizes Jesus' ministry. The father represents God, the younger brother represents the tax collectors and sinners to whom Jesus ministered, and the older brother represents the religious leaders.

15:12 ***I want my share of your estate now:*** This appalling request essentially says, "To me, you are dead." There could be no greater insult to a father.

15:13 ***he wasted all his money in wild living:*** Jews considered the loss of family property to Gentiles in ***a distant land*** to be particularly disgraceful and grounds for excommunication (see also Deut 21:18-21).

15:15 ***Pigs*** were unclean animals (Lev 11:7; Deut 14:8), making this the most degrading job imaginable for a Jew.

15:20 ***his father saw him coming:*** His father was apparently watching the road, longing for his son's return. • ***he ran to his son:*** Running was considered undignified for the family patriarch, but the father was full of unbridled joy at his son's return.

compassion, he ran to his son, embraced him, and kissed him. 21His son said to him, 'Father, I have sinned against both heaven and you, and I am no longer worthy of being called your son.'

22"But his father said to the servants, 'Quick! Bring the finest robe in the house and put it on him. Get a ring for his finger and sandals for his feet. 23And kill the calf we have been fattening. We must celebrate with a feast, 24for this son of mine was dead and has now returned to life. He was lost, but now he is found.' So the party began.

25"Meanwhile, the older son was in the fields working. When he returned home, he heard music and dancing in the house, 26and he asked one of the servants what was going on. 27'Your brother is back,' he was told, 'and your father has killed the fattened calf. We are celebrating because of his safe return.'

28"The older brother was angry and wouldn't go in. His father came out and begged him, 29but he replied, 'All these years I've slaved for you and never once refused to do a single thing you told me to. And in all that time you never gave me even one young goat for a feast with my friends. 30Yet when this son of yours comes back after squandering your money on prostitutes, you celebrate by killing the fattened calf!'

31"His father said to him, 'Look, dear son, you have always stayed by me, and everything I have is yours. 32We had to celebrate this happy day. For your brother was dead and has come back to life! He was lost, but now he is found!' "

Parable of the Shrewd Manager

Luke 16:13 // Matt 6:24

16 Jesus told this story to his disciples: "There was a certain rich man who had a [e]manager handling his affairs. One day a report came that the manager was wasting his employer's money. 2So the employer called him in and said, 'What's this I hear about you? Get your [f]report in order, because you are going to be fired.'

3"The manager thought to himself, 'Now what? My boss has fired me. I don't have the strength to dig ditches, and I'm too proud to beg. 4Ah, I know how to ensure that I'll have plenty of friends who will give me a home when I am fired.'

5"So he invited each person who owed money to his employer to come and discuss the situation. He asked the first one, 'How much do you owe him?' 6The man replied, 'I owe him 800 gallons of olive oil.' So the manager told him, 'Take the bill and quickly change it to 400 gallons.'

7" 'And how much do you owe my employer?' he asked the next man. 'I owe him 1,000 bushels of wheat,' was the reply. 'Here,' the manager said, 'take the bill and change it to 800 bushels.'

8"The rich man had to admire the dishonest rascal for being so shrewd. And it is true that the children of this world are more shrewd in dealing with the world around them than are the children of the light. 9Here's the lesson: Use your worldly resources to benefit others and make friends. Then, when your earthly possessions are gone, they will welcome you to an eternal home.

15:22
Gen 41:42
Zech 3:4
Rev 6:11

15:24
Eph 2:1, 5; 5:14

15:31
Prov 29:3
John 17:10, 24

16:1
Luke 15:13, 30
[e]*oikonomos* (3623)
‣1 Cor 4:1

16:2
[f]*logos* (3056)
‣Luke 21:33

16:8
John 12:36
Eph 5:8
1 Thes 5:5

15:21 The son gave his rehearsed speech. Some manuscripts add *Please take me on as a hired servant.* The lack of this sentence in the better manuscripts suggests that his father didn't give him a chance to finish.

15:22 *The finest robe* belonged to the father; it affirmed the son's role as an heir and a cherished member of the household. • *Get a ring for his finger:* A ring was a symbol of authority. Like the robe, it indicated his status as son and heir.

15:23 The father would have been *fattening* a *calf* for a banquet. The son was welcomed as a visiting dignitary.

15:28 *The older brother was angry* that his father would forgive such a sinner when he, the faithful son, had worked hard to achieve his position. Like the religious leaders, he refused to rejoice when his brother was found.

15:30 *this son of yours:* He refused to acknowledge his own relationship to his brother.

15:31 *you have always stayed by me:* The parable is open-ended: it does not record the older brother's response. The religious leaders still had a chance to respond to Jesus' offer of the Kingdom.

16:1 *a certain rich man who had a manager:* Wealthy landowners commonly put managers over their estates.

16:2 *Get your report in order:* This financial statement was probably for the benefit of the manager's successor.

16:3 *I'm too proud to beg:* The Jewish wisdom writer Sirach said, "It is better to die than to beg" (*Sirach* 40:28), a reflection of Jewish attitudes.

16:5-7 The manager called in his master's debtors and reduced their debts, thus making friends who would help him during his unemployment.

16:6 *800 gallons . . . 400 gallons:* Greek *100 baths . . . 50 [baths].* The size of the bath—a standard liquid measure—is not known with certainty.

16:7 *1,000 bushels . . . 800 bushels:* Greek *100 korous . . . 80 [korous].* The size of the cor—a standard dry measure—is not known with certainty.

16:8-9 Jesus seems to commend the manager's dishonesty, but Jesus' point is that believers need to use resources shrewdly in preparation for eternity.

16:8 The ways of the world are the opposite of God's ways. *The children of this world* use all their resources to get ahead in this world. God's people do just the opposite (16:9). • *The children of the light* are the people of God (see John 12:36; 1 Thes 5:5).

16:9 *worldly resources:* This is a better translation than the traditional "mammon of unrighteousness" (KJV). Believers are to use their resources wisely for spiritual benefit. • *they will welcome you to an eternal home* (or *you will be welcomed into eternal homes*): *They* are probably the *friends.* Just as the manager's friends would give him security,

16:10-12
Matt 25:20-30
Luke 19:17-26
16:13
Matt 6:24
16:14
Luke 23:35
1 Tim 3:3
16:15
Prov 24:12
Matt 23:28
16:16
Matt 11:12-13
16:17
Matt 5:18
[g]*nomos* (3551)
‣Luke 24:44
16:18
Matt 5:32; 19:9
Mark 10:11-12
1 Cor 7:10-11
16:22
Matt 8:11
[h]*angelos* (0032)
‣Luke 24:23
16:23
[i]*hadēs* (0086)
‣Acts 2:27
16:24
Luke 3:8
16:25
Luke 6:24

10“If you are faithful in little things, you
will be faithful in large ones. But if you are
dishonest in little things, you won’t be honest with greater responsibilities. 11And if
you are untrustworthy about worldly wealth,
who will trust you with the true riches of
heaven? 12And if you are not faithful with
other people’s things, why should you be
trusted with things of your own?
13“No one can serve two masters. For you
will hate one and love the other; you will be
devoted to one and despise the other. You
cannot serve both God and money.”

The Pharisees and the Law
Luke 16:17; cp. Matt 5:18
Luke 16:18; cp. Matt 5:31-32; 19:9; Mark 10:11-12

14The Pharisees, who dearly loved their
money, heard all this and scoffed at him.
15Then he said to them, “You like to appear
righteous in public, but God knows your
hearts. What this world honors is detestable in the sight of God.
16“Until John the Baptist, the law of Moses
and the messages of the prophets were your
guides. But now the Good News of the Kingdom of God is preached, and everyone is
eager to get in. 17But that doesn’t mean
that the law has lost its force. It is easier
for heaven and earth to disappear than for
the smallest point of God’s [g]law to be overturned.
18“For example, a man who divorces his
wife and marries someone else commits
adultery. And anyone who marries a woman
divorced from her husband commits adultery.”

Parable of the Rich Man and Lazarus

19Jesus said, “There was a certain rich man
who was splendidly clothed in purple and
fine linen and who lived each day in luxury.
20At his gate lay a poor man named Lazarus
who was covered with sores. 21As Lazarus
lay there longing for scraps from the rich
man’s table, the dogs would come and lick
his open sores.
22“Finally, the poor man died and was
carried by the [h]angels to be with Abraham.
The rich man also died and was buried,
23and his soul went to the [i]place of the dead.
There, in torment, he saw Abraham in the
far distance with Lazarus at his side.
24“The rich man shouted, ‘Father Abraham, have some pity! Send Lazarus over here
to dip the tip of his finger in water and cool
my tongue. I am in anguish in these flames.’
25“But Abraham said to him, ‘Son, remember that during your lifetime you had
everything you wanted, and Lazarus had
nothing. So now he is here being comforted,
and you are in anguish. 26And besides, there
is a great chasm separating us. No one can
cross over to you from here, and no one can
cross over to us from there.’

---

the friends we win to the Kingdom will warmly welcome us for eternity.

16:13 ***No one can serve two masters:*** Complete love and devotion can be given only to one master.

16:14 ***The Pharisees . . . heard all this and scoffed:*** Wealth was commonly believed to be a reward from God, so the Pharisees derided Jesus’ warning against riches.

16:16 ***John the Baptist*** was a transitional figure—the last in the line of OT prophets and the herald of the age of salvation (see 1:5-25, 57-80; 3:1-20; 7:18-35). • ***everyone is eager to get in*** (or *everyone is urged to enter in*): The verb normally means “to suffer violence” and may have the negative sense of violent force into or against the Kingdom (see Matt 11:12). More likely, it carries here a positive sense of urgency to enter the Kingdom.

16:17 ***that doesn’t mean that the law has lost its force:*** Although the new covenant fulfilled the OT law and prophets, the law has not passed away (however, cp. Acts 15:23-29). • ***Heaven and earth*** will be destroyed and replaced by a new heaven and earth at the end of the age (Rev 21:1), but God’s word endures forever (Ps 119:89, 160; Isa 40:8; 55:10-11).

16:18 This ***example*** fit the context by showing that Jesus’ authoritative words interpreted and fulfilled the OT law. • ***a man who divorces his wife and marries someone else commits adultery:*** The OT allowed for divorce but did not sanction it (Deut 24:1-4), and the rabbis of Jesus’ day debated what constituted legitimate grounds. The school of Shammai allowed a man to divorce his wife only because of unfaithfulness, while the school of Hillel allowed divorce for almost any reason. Against such a casual attitude, Jesus said that breaking the marriage vow by divorce and marrying *someone else* was equivalent to adultery. Elsewhere (Matt 5:32; 19:9), Jesus provided a clear exception for cases of unfaithfulness.

16:19-31 This parable reiterates the theme of the danger of riches introduced in 16:13-15 and returns to the idea that the coming of God’s Kingdom will mean the reversal of fortunes. The rich, proud, and powerful will be humbled and brought low, while the poor, humble, and oppressed will be exalted.

16:19 ***Purple*** was the color of royalty; Phoenician purple was an expensive dye made from mollusks.

16:21 ***the dogs would come and lick his open sores:*** This is an image of misery and poverty. In Jewish culture, dogs were detestable, unclean scavengers.

16:22 ***carried by the angels to be with Abraham*** (literally *into Abraham’s bosom*): The Greek suggests a banquet at which guests reclined around a low table (see John 13:23). Lazarus was taken to the messianic banquet in the Kingdom of God (see “The Messianic Banquet” at 14:1-24, p. 1737).

16:23 ***The place of the dead*** (Greek *Hades*) can refer to the grave (death) generally, or to the place where the wicked go after death, as here.

16:24 ***I am in anguish in these flames:*** See note on 12:5; see also Matt 25:41; Rev 20:10, 14-15. • ***Send Lazarus:*** Ironically, the man was still treating Lazarus as a lowly servant.

16:26 ***No one can cross over to you from here:*** A person’s state after death is permanent.

27“Then the rich man said, ‘Please, Father Abraham, at least send him to my father’s home. 28For I have five brothers, and I want him to warn them so they don’t end up in this place of torment.’

29“But Abraham said, ‘Moses and the prophets have warned them. Your brothers can read what they wrote.’

30“The rich man replied, ‘No, Father Abraham! But if someone is sent to them from the dead, then they will repent of their sins and turn to God.’

31“But Abraham said, ‘If they won’t listen to Moses and the prophets, they won’t listen even if someone rises from the dead.’ ”

Teachings about Forgiveness and Faith
Luke 17:1-3a // Matt 18:6-9 // Mark 9:42-48
Luke 17:5-6; cp. Matt 17:20

17 One day Jesus said to his disciples, “There will always be temptations to sin, but what sorrow awaits the person who does the tempting! 2It would be better to be thrown into the sea with a millstone hung around your neck than to cause one of these little ones to fall into sin. 3So watch yourselves!

“If another believer sins, rebuke that person; then if there is repentance, forgive. 4Even if that person wrongs you seven times a day and each time turns again and asks forgiveness, you must forgive.”

5The apostles said to the Lord, “Show us how to increase our faith.”

6The Lord answered, “If you had faith even as small as a mustard seed, you could say to this mulberry tree, ‘May you be uprooted and thrown into the sea,’ and it would obey you!

7“When a servant comes in from plowing or taking care of sheep, does his master say, ‘Come in and eat with me’? 8No, he says, ‘Prepare my meal, put on your apron, and serve me while I eat. Then you can eat later.’ 9And does the master thank the servant for doing what he was told to do? Of course not. 10In the same way, when you obey me you should say, ‘We are unworthy servants who have simply done our duty.’ ”

Responses to the Kingdom along the Way (17:11–19:27)

Ten Healed of Leprosy

11As Jesus continued on toward Jerusalem, he reached the border between Galilee and Samaria. 12As he entered a village there, ten lepers stood at a distance, 13crying out, “Jesus, Master, have mercy on us!”

14He looked at them and said, “Go show yourselves to the priests.” And as they went, they were cleansed of their leprosy.

15One of them, when he saw that he was healed, came back to Jesus, shouting, “Praise God!” 16He fell to the ground at Jesus’ feet, thanking him for what he had done. This man was a Samaritan.

17Jesus asked, “Didn’t I heal ten men? Where are the other nine? 18Has no one returned to give glory to God except this foreigner?” 19And Jesus said to the man, “Stand up and go. Your faith has healed you.”

The Coming of the Kingdom

20One day the Pharisees asked Jesus, “When will the Kingdom of God come?”

16:29 Luke 24:27, 44; John 1:45; 5:45-47; Acts 15:21
16:31 John 11:44-48
17:1-3 //Matt 18:7; //Mark 9:42
17:3 Matt 18:15
17:5 Mark 9:24
17:6 Matt 17:20; 21:21
17:10 1 Cor 9:16
17:11 Luke 9:51-52; 13:22
17:12 Lev 13:46
17:14 Lev 14:2-3; Luke 5:14
17:16 Matt 10:5
17:19 Matt 9:22; Luke 7:50; 18:42
17:20 John 3:3; 18:36

16:31 ***they won’t listen even if someone rises from the dead:*** Wicked people refuse to repent even when faced with overwhelming evidence of the truth.

17:1 ***what sorrow awaits:*** Traditionally rendered *woe!* (see notes on 6:24-26; 11:42-52). • ***the person who does the tempting:*** Leaders bear a greater responsibility because they are accountable not only for themselves, but for those they lead (see Jas 3:1).

17:2 A ***millstone*** is a large round stone with a hole in its center, used to grind grain in a mill. A millstone could weigh hundreds of pounds.

17:3 ***another believer:*** Literally *your brother*, meaning a fellow member of God’s family.

17:4 ***Even if that person wrongs you seven times a day:*** Seven is not an exact number, but means “many times” (see Ps 119:164). See Matt 18:21-22.

17:6 ***A mustard seed*** was proverbial for something very small (see 13:19). • ***you could say to this mulberry tree, ‘May you be uprooted’:*** Black mulberry trees can live for hundreds of years and have a vast root system, making them very difficult to uproot. • ***it would obey you:*** This is not a call to use faith for arbitrary miracles. God has unlimited power, and those who trust in him will see him use it.

17:7-10 In Greco-Roman culture, servants existed to serve their masters faithfully. Faith (17:5-6) entails obedient submission to Christ and his commands.

17:11-19 This healing reveals Jesus’ compassion and power; in Luke, the blessings of salvation are joyfully received by many outside Israel.

17:11 ***As Jesus continued on toward Jerusalem:*** See note on 9:51–19:44.

17:12 ***ten lepers stood at a distance:*** See note on 5:12. Lepers were required to keep their distance and cry out, “Unclean!” (Lev 13:45-46).

17:14 ***Go show yourselves to the priests:*** Leviticus 14:2-32 sets out guidelines for priests to use in diagnosing leprosy and pronouncing a leper clean (see notes on 5:12, 14). • ***as they went:*** To leave without yet being healed required faith, which Jesus was testing (cp. 2 Kgs 5:9-14).

17:16 The one man who returned to thank Jesus ***was a Samaritan,*** a hated foreigner in the eyes of most Jews (see note on 10:33).

17:19 ***Your faith has healed you*** (or *Your faith has saved you*): The Greek verb can refer to either physical or spiritual healing. Jesus’ physical healings illustrate the salvation that his Kingdom brings.

17:20-37 This is the first of two discourses in Luke’s Gospel on the coming of the Kingdom and the return of the Son of Man (see also ch 21).

17:23
Mark 13:21
Luke 17:21; 21:8
17:24
1 Tim 6:15
17:25
Matt 16:21
Mark 8:31
Luke 9:22
17:26-27
//Matt 24:37-39
17:28
Gen 19:1-28
17:30
2 Thes 1:7
17:31
//Matt 24:17-18
//Mark 13:15-16
17:33
Matt 10:39; 16:25
Mark 8:35
Luke 9:24
John 12:25
17:35
//Matt 24:41
17:37
//Matt 24:28
18:1
Rom 12:12
Col 4:2
1 Thes 5:17
ʲ*parabolē* (3850)
‣ Luke 21:29

Jesus replied, "The Kingdom of God can't
be detected by visible signs. 21You won't be
able to say, 'Here it is!' or 'It's over there!' For
the Kingdom of God is already among you."

The Return of the Son of Man
Luke 17:23-24 // Matt 24:23-27 // Mark 13:21-23
Luke 17:26-27; cp. Matt 24:37-39
Luke 17:31; cp. Matt 24:17-18; Mark 13:15-16

22Then he said to his disciples, "The time
is coming when you will long to see the day
when the Son of Man returns, but you won't
see it. 23People will tell you, 'Look, there is
the Son of Man,' or 'Here he is,' but don't go
out and follow them. 24For as the lightning
flashes and lights up the sky from one end
to the other, so it will be on the day when
the Son of Man comes. 25But first the Son of
Man must suffer terribly and be rejected by
this generation.

26"When the Son of Man returns, it will
be like it was in Noah's day. 27In those days,
the people enjoyed banquets and parties
and weddings right up to the time Noah
entered his boat and the flood came and destroyed them all.

28"And the world will be as it was in the
days of Lot. People went about their daily
business—eating and drinking, buying
and selling, farming and building—29until
the morning Lot left Sodom. Then fire and
burning sulfur rained down from heaven
and destroyed them all. 30Yes, it will be
'business as usual' right up to the day when
the Son of Man is revealed. 31On that day a
person out on the deck of a roof must not
go down into the house to pack. A person
out in the field must not return home. 32Re-
member what happened to Lot's wife! 33If
you cling to your life, you will lose it, and if
you let your life go, you will save it. 34That
night two people will be asleep in one bed;
one will be taken, the other left. 35Two
women will be grinding flour together at
the mill; one will be taken, the other left."

37"Where will this happen, Lord?" the disciples asked.

Jesus replied, "Just as the gathering of vultures shows there is a carcass nearby, so these signs indicate that the end is near."

Parable of the Persistent Widow

18 One day Jesus told his disciples a
ʲstory to show that they should always pray and never give up. 2"There was
a judge in a certain city," he said, "who neither feared God nor cared about people. 3A
widow of that city came to him repeatedly,

17:20-21 ***When will the Kingdom of God come?*** The common understanding among Jews was that the Messiah would establish God's Kingdom in Jerusalem; he would defeat Israel's enemies and bring in a period of peace, prosperity, justice, and righteousness (see "The Messianic Hope" at 3:15, p. 1707; cp. Acts 1:6). The Pharisees were apparently challenging Jesus' claim to be the Messiah because he was not defeating the Romans or establishing his Kingdom physically on earth. Jesus did not reject this future manifestation of the Kingdom (see 21:27; Matt 24:30-31), but pointed out that the Kingdom of God was being revealed to them through his ministry, though they were missing it. • ***The Kingdom of God can't be detected by visible signs*** (or *by your speculations*): Jewish apocalyptic literature of Jesus' day looked for visible signs in the heavens to signal the coming of the Messiah's kingdom. Jesus elsewhere affirmed that such signs would appear (see 17:24; 21:25; Acts 2:19-20), but the Pharisees were missing the manifestation of the Kingdom in Jesus' immediate ministry (see note on 7:22). • ***the Kingdom of God is already among you*** (or *is within you*, or *is in your grasp*): The Kingdom of God was already being revealed through Jesus' words and actions. It is unlikely that Jesus would say, "The Kingdom of God is *within you*," to those who were rejecting his message.

17:22 ***you will long to see the day when the Son of Man returns*** (or *you will long for even one day with the Son of Man*): The Greek says simply, *you will long to see the days of the Son of Man*, which may refer to his time on earth with his disciples or to the time of his second coming. "Son of Man" is a title Jesus used for himself.

17:23-24 ***People will tell you, 'Look, there is the Son of Man':*** False Messiahs have arisen throughout history, but expectations for the Messiah were particularly high in the first century, as a variety of figures claimed to be God's agents of deliverance (see Acts 5:36-37; 21:38). Jesus warned his disciples not to follow these imposters. • ***For as the lightning flashes:*** When Jesus suddenly returns, it will be evident to everyone.

17:25 ***suffer terribly*** (or *suffer many things*): Jesus would soon suffer crucifixion (see note on 9:22).

17:26-29 ***in Noah's day . . . in the days of Lot:*** See Gen 6–9 for Noah and Gen 18:16–19:29 for Lot; both are stories of God's cataclysmic judgment against human wickedness.

17:32-33 ***Lot's wife*** turned into a pillar of salt when she looked longingly back at Sodom (Gen 19:26). She exemplifies those who *cling to . . . life*.

17:34-35 ***one will be taken, the other left:*** Some consider this separation to refer to the Rapture of the church, but the parallels drawn to God's judgment in the Flood and against Sodom (17:26-29), as well as the reference to vultures and a dead body (17:37), suggest that it occurs at the final judgment (see Mal 3:18; Matt 25:32). • Some manuscripts add verse 36, *Two men will be working in the field; one will be taken, the other left.* Cp. Matt 24:40.

17:37 ***Where will this happen, Lord?*** Literally *"Where, Lord?"* • ***Just as . . . the end is near:*** Literally *"Wherever the carcass is, the vultures gather."* • ***so these signs indicate that the end is near:*** This clause, which does not appear explicitly in the Greek, explains the significance of the cryptic saying about the vulture.

18:1-8 The parable of the persistent widow follows naturally from Jesus' teaching about coming troubles (17:20-37). Believers can face trials and persevere through persistent prayer.

18:2 ***a judge . . . who neither feared God nor cared about people:*** The two most important attributes for a good judge are regard for justice (fear of God), and compassion for people (see 2 Chr 19:6-7). This judge had neither.

18:3 ***A widow:*** God is concerned for widows, orphans, and foreigners—the most vulnerable members of ancient society—and has promised judgment against those who oppress them (Exod 22:22; Deut 10:18; 24:17; 27:19;

saying, 'Give me justice in this dispute with
my enemy.' 4The judge ignored her for a
while, but finally he said to himself, 'I don't
fear God or care about people, 5but this
woman is driving me crazy. I'm going to see
that she gets justice, because she is wearing
me out with her constant requests!'"
6Then the Lord said, "Learn a lesson from
this unjust judge. 7Even he rendered a just
decision in the end. So don't you think God
will surely give justice to his chosen people
who cry out to him day and night? Will he
keep putting them off? 8I tell you, he will
grant justice to them quickly! But when the
Son of Man returns, how many will he find
on the earth who have faith?"

Parable of the Pharisee and Tax Collector

9Then Jesus told this story to some who had
great confidence in their own righteousness and scorned everyone else: 10"Two
men went to the Temple to pray. One was a
Pharisee, and the other was a despised tax
collector. 11The Pharisee stood by himself
and prayed this prayer: 'I thank you, God,
that I am not a sinner like everyone else. For
I don't cheat, I don't sin, and I don't commit
adultery. I'm certainly not like that tax collector! 12I fast twice a week, and I give you a
tenth of my income.'
13"But the tax collector stood at a distance
and dared not even lift his eyes to heaven as
he prayed. Instead, he beat his chest in sorrow, saying, 'O God, be [k]merciful to me, for I
am a sinner.' 14I tell you, this sinner, not the
Pharisee, returned home justified before
God. For those who exalt themselves will
be humbled, and those who humble themselves will be exalted."

Jesus Blesses the Children

Luke 18:15-17 // Matt 19:13-15 // Mark 10:13-16

15One day some parents brought their little children to Jesus so he could touch and
bless them. But when the disciples saw this,
they scolded the parents for bothering him.
16Then Jesus called for the children and
said to the disciples, "Let the children come
to me. Don't stop them! For the Kingdom
of God belongs to those who are like these
children. 17I tell you the truth, anyone who
doesn't receive the Kingdom of God like a
child will never enter it."

The Rich Man

Luke 18:18-23 // Matt 19:16-22 // Mark 10:17-22

18Once a religious leader asked Jesus this
question: "Good Teacher, what should I do
to inherit eternal life?"
19"Why do you call me good?" Jesus
asked him. "Only God is truly good. 20But
to answer your question, you know the
commandments: 'You must not commit
adultery. You must not murder. You must
not steal. You must not testify falsely. Honor
your father and mother.'"
21The man replied, "I've obeyed all these
commandments since I was young."

18:5 Luke 11:7-8
18:7 Rev 6:10
18:8 1 Tim 4:1
18:11 Matt 6:5
18:12 Matt 23:23
18:13 [k]*hilaskomai* (2433) ›Rom 3:25
18:14 Prov 27:2; Matt 23:12; Luke 14:11
18:15-17 //Matt 19:13-15; //Mark 10:13-16
18:17 Matt 18:3
18:18-30 //Matt 19:16-30; //Mark 10:17-31
18:20 *Exod 20:12-16; *Deut 5:16-20

Ps 68:5; Isa 1:23; 10:2; Jer 22:3; Ezek 22:7; Amos 5:10-13; Zech 7:10; Mal 3:5). • ***Give me justice:*** The woman was in the right in this dispute—she was not asking for special favors.

18:5 *driving me crazy:* This colorful Greek expression means literally "striking the eye" or "giving me a black eye," as in boxing. The sense is of wearing someone down through persistence.

18:7 *God will surely give justice:* If persistence resulted in justice from this unjust judge, how much more will God, who loves both people and justice, answer our prayers.

18:8 *Son of Man* is a title Jesus used for himself (see "The Son of Man" at Matt 8:18-20, p. 1593). • ***when the Son of Man returns:*** This is an allusion to Dan 7:13-14. • ***how many will he find on the earth who have faith?*** The question is whether believers will remain faithful through the trials that will precede the coming of the Son of Man (see Matt 24:10-12; 2 Thes 2:3; 1 Tim 4:1).

18:9-14 The topic of prayer (18:1-8) leads into this parable about the right attitude for approaching God.

18:10 *a despised tax collector:* See notes on 3:12; 15:1.

18:11 *stood by himself and prayed this prayer:* Some manuscripts read *stood and prayed this prayer to himself.*

18:12 *I fast twice a week, and I give you a tenth of my income:* Fasting and tithing were signs of piety in Judaism. The law required fasting only once a year (Lev 16:29-31), but pious Jews in Jesus' day fasted twice a week (see also 5:33; 11:41-42).

18:13 *he beat his chest in sorrow:* This action indicated deep mourning and repentance.

18:14 Jesus' conclusion that only the tax collector went home justified before God would have shocked Jesus' audience, who regarded Pharisees as righteous and tax collectors as wicked. • ***those who exalt themselves will be humbled:*** See 1:52-53; 6:21, 25; 10:15; 14:11; 16:19-31.

18:15-17 This incident illustrates 18:14. • ***they scolded the parents:*** In this cultural context, children had no social status (see note on 9:48), so the disciples viewed them as an interruption to Jesus' important ministry.

18:17 *receive the Kingdom of God like a child:* Entrance into the Kingdom of God requires childlike faith and dependence on God.

18:18-30 The story of the rich ***religious leader*** warns against trusting in riches rather than pledging complete allegiance to God.

18:18 The man was probably ***a religious leader*** (traditionally *ruler*), not a political ruler. • ***what should I do to inherit eternal life?*** This question was commonly discussed by the rabbis of Jesus' day (see 10:27).

18:19 *Why do you call me good?* The man was calling Jesus "good" as a general compliment, but ***only God is truly good.*** Jesus was challenging the man's understanding of goodness—true goodness requires moral perfection.

18:20 *you know the commandments:* Jesus cites the fifth through ninth of the Ten Commandments (Exod 20:12-16; Deut 5:16-20), which pertain to relationships between human beings.

18:21 *I've obeyed all these commandments:* The man's claim to have kept all the commandments shows that he misunderstood the nature of true goodness.

18:22 Matt 6:20
18:28 Matt 4:19-20
18:31-34 //Matt 20:17-19 //Mark 10:32-34
18:31 Ps 22 Isa 53 Luke 9:51; 24:25-27, 44
18:32 Matt 16:21; 27:29-30 Luke 9:22, 44

22When Jesus heard his answer, he said,
"There is still one thing you haven't done.
Sell all your possessions and give the money
to the poor, and you will have treasure in
heaven. Then come, follow me."
23But when the man heard this he became very sad, for he was very rich.

The Rewards of Discipleship
Luke 18:24-30 // Matt 19:23-30 // Mark 10:23-31

24When Jesus saw this, he said, "How hard
it is for the rich to enter the Kingdom of
God! 25In fact, it is easier for a camel to go
through the eye of a needle than for a rich
person to enter the Kingdom of God!"
26Those who heard this said, "Then who
in the world can be saved?"
27He replied, "What is impossible for people is possible with God."
28Peter said, "We've left our homes to follow you."
29"Yes," Jesus replied, "and I assure you
that everyone who has given up house or
wife or brothers or parents or children, for
the sake of the Kingdom of God, 30will be
repaid many times over in this life, and will
have eternal life in the world to come."

Jesus Predicts His Death and Resurrection
Luke 18:31-34 // Matt 20:17-19 // Mark 10:32-34

31Taking the twelve disciples aside, Jesus said,
"Listen, we're going up to Jerusalem, where all
the predictions of the prophets concerning
the Son of Man will come true. 32He will be
handed over to the Romans, and he will be
mocked, treated shamefully, and spit upon.
33They will flog him with a whip and kill him,
but on the third day he will rise again."
34But they didn't understand any of this.
The significance of his words was hidden
from them, and they failed to grasp what he
was talking about.

Rich and Poor (18:18-30)

Luke 1:52-53; 4:18; 6:20-25; 12:13-34; 14:12-23; 16:19-31 Matt 5:3

Throughout Luke's Gospel, a reversal of worldly fortunes characterizes entrance into, or exclusion from, the Kingdom of God. Mary announced that God would lift up the poor and humble and bring down the rich and powerful (1:52-53). Jesus announced at Nazareth that the gospel is "Good News for the poor" (4:18). He pronounced blessings on the poor and hungry and woes against the rich and satisfied (6:20-25). This was a reversal of conventional wisdom, which held that God had blessed the rich and cursed the poor.

A number of Jesus' parables severely warn against the danger of riches. "The Parable of the Rich Fool" (12:13-21) reveals the consequence of storing up treasures on earth instead of having a rich relationship with God. "The Parable of the Rich Man and Lazarus" (16:19-31) shows the eternal cost of ignoring the poor and helpless while enjoying the good things in life. The rich man who asked Jesus the way to eternal life was devastated when Jesus said he must sell all that he had and give to the poor (18:18-30).

Who are the poor in Luke's Gospel? Are they the physically poor or those that are poor in spirit (cp. Matt 5:3)? Almost certainly it is both. The physically poor, who have very little, are naturally dependent on God for their needs. The rich and powerful are likely to be self-sufficient, forgetting their need for God. It is impossible for rich people to enter God's Kingdom as long as they trust in their riches to get them there (16:25-26). God accepts those who put their faith in him alone.

18:22 The man's love of his riches revealed that he had not perfectly obeyed God; he did not love God or others in the way that God requires (10:25-28). Love of riches is a form of idolatry (Eph 5:5; Col 3:5).

18:24 *When Jesus saw this:* Some manuscripts read *When Jesus saw how sad the man was.* • ***How hard it is for the rich to enter the Kingdom of God!*** Though Scripture sometimes speaks of riches as a blessing from God (2 Chr 1:11-12; Ps 112:3; 128:2; Prov 8:18; Isa 61:6), many passages warn against the danger of trusting riches instead of God (Ps 62:10; Prov 11:28; Jer 9:23-24; 49:4-5). • ***the eye of a needle:*** See note on Mark 10:25. This is not merely difficult, but impossible. No one can be saved while trusting in riches. Salvation comes only by dependence on God (18:27).

18:27 The point of the whole episode is that salvation is impossible by human effort, but possible by the grace of God.

18:28-30 ***We've left our homes to follow you:*** In contrast to the rich ruler, Peter and the other disciples had given up everything to follow Jesus. Jesus affirmed that they would receive back far more than they had given up.

18:30 ***repaid many times over in this life:*** Their reward would not necessarily be physical, but they would enjoy the blessings that come from spiritual wholeness and a right relationship with God.

18:31-34 This was Jesus' last prediction of his suffering and death before entering Jerusalem for his final week of ministry (see also 9:22, 44-45; 17:25).

18:31 Jesus' death was in fulfillment of ***all the predictions of the prophets;*** it was God's plan (24:25-26, 46; Acts 2:23; 3:18; 4:28). The primary prophecy about the suffering Messiah is Isa 52:13–53:12. Luke also refers to Ps 2 (Acts 4:25-26), Ps 16 (Acts 2:25-28), Ps 118:22 (Luke 20:17), and Isa 50:4-9 (18:32-33).

18:32-33 ***the Romans:*** Literally *the Gentiles.* • ***mocked. . . . They will flog him:*** See Isa 50:6.

18:34 ***The significance of his words was hidden from them:*** Not until after the resurrection did the disciples grasp the saving significance of Jesus' death (see 9:45; 24:13-34).

Jesus Heals a Blind Beggar
Luke 18:35-43 // Matt 20:29-34 // Mark 10:46-52;
cp. Matt 9:27-31

35As Jesus approached Jericho, a blind beggar was sitting beside the road. 36When
he heard the noise of a crowd going past,
he asked what was happening. 37They told
him that Jesus the Nazarene was going by.
38So he began shouting, "Jesus, Son of David, have mercy on me!"

39"Be quiet!" the people in front yelled at
him.

But he only shouted louder, "Son of David,
have mercy on me!"

40When Jesus heard him, he stopped and
ordered that the man be brought to him.
As the man came near, Jesus asked him,
41"What do you want me to do for you?"

"Lord," he said, "I want to see!"

42And Jesus said, "All right, receive your
sight! Your faith has healed you." 43Instantly
the man could see, and he followed Jesus,
praising God. And all who saw it praised
God, too.

Jesus and Zacchaeus

19 Jesus entered Jericho and made his
way through the town. 2There was
a man there named Zacchaeus. He was the
chief tax collector in the region, and he had
become very rich. 3He tried to get a look at
Jesus, but he was too short to see over the
crowd. 4So he ran ahead and climbed a sycamore-fig tree beside the road, for Jesus was
going to pass that way.

5When Jesus came by, he looked up at
Zacchaeus and called him by name. "Zacchaeus!" he said. "Quick, come down! I must
be a guest in your home today."

6Zacchaeus quickly climbed down and
took Jesus to his house in great excitement
and joy. 7But the people were displeased.
"He has gone to be the guest of a notorious
sinner," they grumbled.

8Meanwhile, Zacchaeus stood before the
Lord and said, "I will give half my wealth to
the poor, Lord, and if I have cheated people
on their taxes, I will give them back four
times as much!"

9Jesus responded, "Salvation has come
to this home today, for this man has shown
himself to be a true son of Abraham. 10For
the Son of Man came to seek and save those
who are lost."

Parable of the Ten Servants
Luke 19:11-27 // Matt 25:14-30

11The crowd was listening to everything
Jesus said. And because he was nearing Jerusalem, he told them a story to correct the
impression that the Kingdom of God would
begin right away. 12He said, "A nobleman
was called away to a distant empire to be

18:35-43 //Matt 20:29-34 //Mark 10:46-52
18:38 Matt 9:27
18:41 Mark 10:36
18:42 Matt 9:22 Luke 7:50; 17:19
18:43 Luke 19:37
19:1 Luke 18:35
19:4 1 Kgs 10:27 1 Chr 27:28
19:7 Matt 9:11 Luke 5:30; 15:2
19:8 Exod 22:1 Num 5:7 Luke 3:12-13
19:9 Matt 9:13 Acts 16:31-34 Rom 2:29 1 Tim 1:15
19:10 Ezek 34:12, 16 John 3:17
19:11-27 //Matt 25:14-30
19:11 Acts 1:6
19:12 Mark 13:34

18:35-43 This account again demonstrates Jesus' care for the poor and marginalized in Israel. It reminds the reader that Jesus is the Son of David, the Messiah (18:38), shortly before he enters Jerusalem as the king (19:28-44).

18:35 *Jericho* was located in an oasis in the Judean wilderness, eighteen miles (thirty kilometers) northeast of Jerusalem. At 820 feet (250 meters) below sea level, Jericho is the world's lowest city and one of the oldest.

18:37 *Jesus the Nazarene:* Or *Jesus of Nazareth.*

18:38 *Son of David* is a title for the Messiah, a descendant of David who would reign on David's throne forever (see "The Messianic Hope" at 3:15, p. 1707; see also 1:32-33; 2 Sam 7:11-16; Isa 9:6-7; 11:1-5; Jer 23:5-6; 33:15-16; Ezek 37:24-25).

19:1-10 The story of Zacchaeus is a fitting climax to Jesus' ministry to the outcasts of Israel on his journey to Jerusalem (9:51–19:44). The final verse of the episode (19:10) is often viewed as the theme verse of Luke's Gospel.

19:2 *The chief tax collector* for a particular region leased from the Romans the right to collect taxes, and then oversaw subordinate tax collectors from whom he collected a commission. This situation allowed Zacchaeus to get very rich, and chief tax collectors were hated even more than their subordinates (see notes on 3:12; 15:1; 18:10).

19:4 *climbed a sycamore-fig tree:* This act was very undignified for a man of Zacchaeus' power and wealth; it shows his genuine spiritual interest in Jesus.

19:5 *Zacchaeus! . . . I must be a guest:* Jesus knew Zacchaeus' name and invited himself to Zacchaeus' home, emphasizing his divine authority and that this appointment was made by God.

19:7 *the guest of a notorious sinner:* As with Levi earlier (5:27-32), Jesus' willingness to associate with sinners drew criticism (see note on 5:30).

19:8 *I will give them back four times:* Normal restitution for a wrong committed was to add twenty percent to the value of the goods lost (Lev 5:16; Num 5:7), though the penalty for theft of an animal was four or five times its value (Exod 22:1). Zacchaeus apparently regarded his financial gains as theft and promised the required restitution.

19:9 *this man has shown himself to be a true son of Abraham:* Zacchaeus was a child of Abraham by descent (a Jew); now he demonstrated faith like Abraham's (see Rom 4:11-12).

19:10 *Son of Man* is a title Jesus used for himself. • *to seek and save those who are lost:* The Lord is a shepherd who seeks lost sheep (see notes on 12:32; 15:4; see Ps 23:1; Isa 53:6; Jer 13:17; Ezek 34; Zech 10:3; 13:7).

19:11-27 This parable has two main purposes: (1) to teach stewardship, the need to manage gifts and resources well while the king (Jesus) is away (cp. Matt 25:14-30); and (2) to correct the impression that the *Kingdom of God would begin right away* upon Jesus' entrance into Jerusalem. Most Jews of Jesus' day expected that when the Messiah came, God's Kingdom would be established physically on earth, with Jerusalem at its center (see Isa 2:2-4; 35:1-10; 65:17-25; Jer 30-31; Ezek 37; 40–48; Mic 4:1-5).

19:12 *A nobleman was called away to a distant empire to be crowned king:* The account fits the situation of Judea as a client kingdom of the Roman empire. After the death of a king, claimants to the throne would go to Rome to try to gain support (see note on 19:14). Like the nobleman, Jesus would first depart (to heaven) to receive his royal

19:17 Luke 16:10
19:22 Job 15:6; Matt 12:37
19:26 Matt 13:12; Mark 4:25; Luke 8:18
19:27 Luke 19:14
19:28-38 //Matt 21:1-11; //Mark 11:1-11; //John 12:12-19

crowned king and then return. 13 Before he
left, he called together ten of his servants
and divided among them ten pounds of silver, saying, 'Invest this for me while I am
gone.' 14 But his people hated him and sent a
delegation after him to say, 'We do not want
him to be our king.'
15 "After he was crowned king, he returned and called in the servants to whom
he had given the money. He wanted to find
out what their profits were. 16 The first
servant reported, 'Master, I invested your
money and made ten times the original
amount!'
17 " 'Well done!' the king exclaimed. 'You
are a good servant. You have been faithful
with the little I entrusted to you, so you will
be governor of ten cities as your reward.'
18 "The next servant reported, 'Master, I
invested your money and made five times
the original amount.'
19 " 'Well done!' the king said. 'You will be
governor over five cities.'
20 "But the third servant brought back
only the original amount of money and said,
'Master, I hid your money and kept it safe.
21 I was afraid because you are a hard man
to deal with, taking what isn't yours and harvesting crops you didn't plant.'
22 " 'You wicked servant!' the king roared.
'Your own words condemn you. If you knew
that I'm a hard man who takes what isn't
mine and harvests crops I didn't plant,
23 why didn't you deposit my money in the
bank? At least I could have gotten some interest on it.'
24 "Then, turning to the others standing
nearby, the king ordered, 'Take the money
from this servant, and give it to the one who
has ten pounds.'
25 " 'But, master,' they said, 'he already has
ten pounds!'
26 " 'Yes,' the king replied, 'and to those
who use well what they are given, even more
will be given. But from those who do nothing, even what little they have will be taken
away. 27 And as for these enemies of mine
who didn't want me to be their king—bring
them in and execute them right here in
front of me.' "

6. THE CLIMAX OF THE SAVIOR'S MISSION IN JERUSALEM (19:28–24:53)

The Savior Arrives (19:28-44)

Jesus' Messianic Entry into Jerusalem

Luke 19:28-40 // Matt 21:1-11 // Mark 11:1-11 // John 12:12-19

28 After telling this story, Jesus went on
toward Jerusalem, walking ahead of his
disciples. 29 As he came to the towns of Bethphage and Bethany on the Mount of Olives,
he sent two disciples ahead. 30 "Go into that
village over there," he told them. "As you enter it, you will see a young donkey tied there
that no one has ever ridden. Untie it and

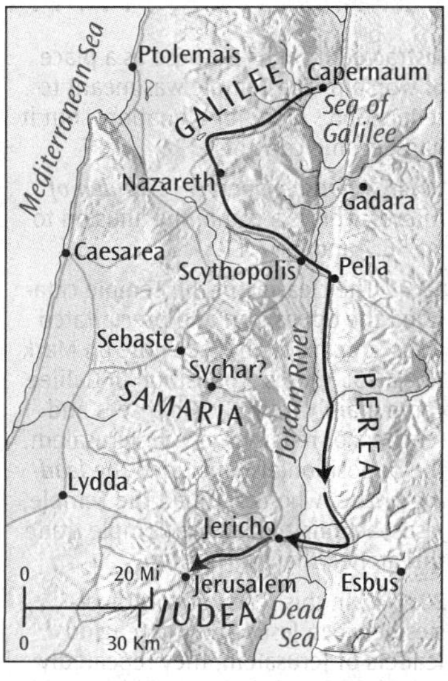

◄ **Jesus' Final Journey to Jerusalem (Luke 9:51–19:48; see also Matt 19:1; 20:17-19; 20:29–21:2; Mark 10:1-52).** When the time came, Jesus embarked on his final trip to JERUSALEM to face his impending death (9:51). From CAPERNAUM he traveled first to PEREA at the edge of JUDEA, then to JERICHO (18:35–19:27), to Bethany and Bethphage on the Mount of Olives, which is just outside Jerusalem (19:28-35; see illustration, p. 1753), and finally to Jerusalem itself (19:36-48).

authority; he will later return to rule God's people and judge those who have opposed him (see 19:14, 27).

19:13 ***ten pounds of silver:*** Greek *ten minas;* one mina was worth about three months' wages.

19:14 ***his people hated him and sent a delegation:*** This happened to Archelaus, the son of Herod the Great, who violently put down protests after the death of his father. In response, the Jews sent a delegation to plead against his kingship before the Roman emperor.

19:17 ***you will be governor of ten cities as your reward:*** Because of the servant's faithfulness, the king gave him a major position in his kingdom. Similarly, those who are faithful to Jesus in this life will receive greater responsibility here and great rewards in heaven.

19:23 ***deposit my money in the bank:*** Literally *put the money on the table,* which means to give it to moneylenders who would loan it out at interest.

19:26 ***even more will be given:*** Those who are faithful with a little will be entrusted with more (cp. 8:18).

19:27 ***as for these enemies of mine:*** Those who reject Jesus' reign as king will suffer his judgment. This part of the parable was directed against the religious leaders. • ***bring them in and execute them:*** A new king would often execute his opponents (see 1 Kgs 2:13-46; cp. Ps 2).

19:28-40 Jesus' triumphant entry into Jerusalem fulfilled Zech 9:9-10 and symbolically announced that he was the Messiah, the King of Israel.

19:29 ***Bethany*** was on the eastern slope of the Mount of Olives, two miles east of Jerusalem; it was the home of Lazarus and his sisters, Mary and Martha (John 11:1, 18; 12:1; see Luke 10:38). The location of ***Bethphage*** is uncertain, but it was probably near Bethany on the same road from Jericho. • ***The Mount of Olives*** overlooks Jerusalem from the east and has significance at the return of Christ (see Acts 1:11; Zech 14:4).

19:30 ***you will see a young donkey:*** It is unclear whether Jesus had arranged for the donkey ahead of time, or whether he used divine insight. Either way, Jesus'

bring it here. 31 If anyone asks, 'Why are
you untying that colt?' just say, 'The Lord
needs it.' "
32 So they went and found the colt, just as
Jesus had said. 33 And sure enough, as they
were untying it, the owners asked them,
"Why are you untying that colt?"
34 And the disciples simply replied, "The
Lord needs it." 35 So they brought the colt to
Jesus and threw their garments over it for
him to ride on.
36 As he rode along, the crowds spread out
their garments on the road ahead of him.
37 When he reached the place where the
road started down the Mount of Olives, all
of his followers began to shout and sing as
they walked along, praising God for all the
wonderful miracles they had seen.

38 "Blessings on the King who comes in the
name of the LORD!
Peace in heaven, and glory in highest
heaven!"

39 But some of the Pharisees among the
crowd said, "Teacher, rebuke your followers
for saying things like that!"
40 He replied, "If they kept quiet, the
stones along the road would burst into
cheers!"

Jesus Weeps over Jerusalem

41 But as he came closer to Jerusalem and saw
the city ahead, he began to weep. 42 "How
I wish today that you of all people would
understand the way to peace. But now it is
too late, and peace is hidden from your eyes.
43 Before long your enemies will build ramparts against your walls and encircle you
and close in on you from every side. 44 They
will crush you into the ground, and your children with you. Your enemies will not leave
a single stone in place, because you did not
accept your opportunity for salvation."

Teaching in the Temple Area (19:45–21:38)

Jesus Clears the Temple

Luke 19:45-46 // Matt 21:12-13 // Mark 11:15-17; cp. John 2:13-16
Luke 19:47-48 // Mark 11:18-19

45 Then Jesus entered the Temple and began
to drive out the people selling animals for
sacrifices. 46 He said to them, "The Scriptures declare, 'My Temple will be a house of
prayer,' but you have turned it into a den of
thieves."
47 After that, he taught daily in the Temple, but the leading priests, the teachers
of religious law, and the other leaders of
the people began planning how to kill him.
48 But they could think of nothing, because
all the people hung on every word he said.

Jesus' Authority Is Challenged

Luke 20:1-8 // Matt 21:23-27 // Mark 11:27-33

20 One day as Jesus was teaching the
people and preaching the Good
News in the Temple, the leading priests,
the teachers of religious law, and the elders
came up to him. 2 They demanded, "By what

19:36 2 Kgs 9:13
19:38 *Ps 118:26; 148:1 Luke 2:14; 13:35
19:40 Hab 2:11
19:41 Luke 13:34-35 John 11:35
19:43 Isa 29:3 Jer 6:6 Ezek 4:2 Luke 21:20
19:44 Ps 137:9 Luke 21:6
19:45-48 //Matt 21:12-17 //Mark 11:15-19 //John 2:13-22
19:46 *Isa 56:7 *Jer 7:11
19:47 Matt 26:55 Luke 21:37; 22:53 John 18:20
20:1-8 //Matt 21:23-27 //Mark 11:27-33

entrance into Jerusalem was a symbolic action. He rode a humble *donkey* rather than a war horse to confirm that he was fulfilling the role of the Messiah by bringing reconciliation and peace (Zech 9:9-10).

19:31 *The Lord needs it:* Subjects of a king were expected to make resources available for his use (see 1 Sam 8:16). The donkey's *colt* had never been ridden, so it was pure and suitable for a king.

19:36 ***The crowds spread out their garments*** to show honor and homage to this royal figure (see 2 Kgs 9:13).

19:38 ***Blessings on the King . . . glory in highest heaven!*** See Ps 118:26; 148:1. Psalm 118 was one of the psalms sung by pilgrims traveling to Jerusalem for one of the festivals (Pss 113–118). • Jesus brought *peace in heaven*—reconciliation between God and human beings—but peace on earth awaits the future (cp. 2:14; see 12:51-53; 19:41-44).

19:40 Compare Isa 55:12, in which nature is said to rejoice at the coming of God's salvation, and Hab 2:11, in which the stones of the walls cry out against Babylon.

19:42 *now it is too late:* Israel's rejection of Jesus was irrevocable.

19:43-44 Jesus foretold the siege and destruction of Jerusalem by the Romans in AD 70. The Jewish historian Josephus describes the horrific suffering of the inhabitants of Jerusalem during the Roman siege (*War* 5.1.1–7.1.1). • ***will not leave a single stone in place:*** This is an image of total devastation.

19:45-48 Having just entered Jerusalem as the Messiah, Jesus performed a messianic action (cp. Mal 3:1) by driving money changers and merchants selling animals for sacrifices out of the Temple. This cleansing was to restore true worship to the Temple. It was also symbolic of the judgment that Jesus had just pronounced against Israel (19:41-44).

19:45 Pilgrims coming to worship at the ***Temple*** would purchase ***animals for sacrifices*** in the Temple courts. Jesus also drove out the money changers who provided the correct currency for the Temple tax (Matt 21:12; Mark 11:15; see Exod 30:13-16; Neh 10:32-33). While these were necessary services, Jesus objected to the exploitation of the Temple for illicit commercial gain that distracted from its purpose as a place of worship. The Temple was meant to reflect God's glory for all nations, but it had become corrupt.

19:46 ***a house of prayer . . . a den of thieves:*** This is a combined allusion to Isa 56:7 and Jer 7:11.

19:47 The clearing of the Temple catalyzed the opposition and precipitated Jesus' crucifixion (but see note on Mark 11:12-25). • Jesus' opposition in Galilee came mainly from the Pharisees and teachers of religious law; in Jerusalem, the opposition also included the *leading priests,* who controlled the Temple. Jesus' actions against the Temple trade threatened their authority.

20:1-47 In this series of controversies between Jesus and the religious leaders of Jerusalem, they repeatedly questioned and challenged him, and he repeatedly outmatched them with his spiritual wisdom, insight, and authority.

20:1 ***the leading priests, the teachers of religious law, and the elders:*** The most influential Jewish leaders in Jerusalem converged against Jesus, who threatened their authority.

20:2 John 2:18; Acts 4:7; 7:27
20:4 Mark 1:4
20:6 Luke 7:29
20:9-19 Isa 5:1-7; //Matt 21:33-46; //Mark 12:1-12
20:10-12 2 Chr 36:15-16
20:14 Heb 1:2
20:17 *Ps 118:22; Acts 4:11
20:18 Isa 8:14-15; Dan 2:34-35
20:20-26 //Matt 22:15-22; //Mark 12:13-17

authority are you doing all these things?
Who gave you the right?"
3"Let me ask you a question first," he replied. 4"Did John's authority to baptize come
from heaven, or was it merely human?"
5They talked it over among themselves.
"If we say it was from heaven, he will ask
why we didn't believe John. 6But if we say
it was merely human, the people will stone
us because they are convinced John was a
prophet." 7So they finally replied that they
didn't know.
8And Jesus responded, "Then I won't tell
you by what authority I do these things."

Parable of the Evil Tenant Farmers
Luke 20:9-19 // Matt 21:33-46 // Mark 12:1-12

9Now Jesus turned to the people again and
told them this story: "A man planted a vineyard, leased it to tenant farmers, and moved
to another country to live for several years.
10At the time of the grape harvest, he sent
one of his servants to collect his share
of the crop. But the farmers attacked the
servant, beat him up, and sent him back
empty-handed. 11So the owner sent another
servant, but they also insulted him, beat
him up, and sent him away empty-handed.
12A third man was sent, and they wounded
him and chased him away.
13" 'What will I do?' the owner asked himself. 'I know! I'll send my cherished son.
Surely they will respect him.'
14"But when the tenant farmers saw his
son, they said to each other, 'Here comes
the heir to this estate. Let's kill him and get
the estate for ourselves!' 15So they dragged
him out of the vineyard and murdered
him.
"What do you suppose the owner of the
vineyard will do to them?" Jesus asked.
16"I'll tell you—he will come and kill those
farmers and lease the vineyard to others."
"How terrible that such a thing should
ever happen," his listeners protested.
17Jesus looked at them and said, "Then
what does this Scripture mean?

'The stone that the builders rejected
has now become the cornerstone.'

18Everyone who stumbles over that stone
will be broken to pieces, and it will crush
anyone it falls on."
19The teachers of religious law and the
leading priests wanted to arrest Jesus immediately because they realized he was
telling the story against them—they were
the wicked farmers. But they were afraid of
the people's reaction.

Taxes for Caesar
Luke 20:20-26 // Matt 22:15-22 // Mark 12:13-17

20Watching for their opportunity, the leaders sent spies pretending to be honest men.
They tried to get Jesus to say something that
could be reported to the Roman governor

20:2 ***By what authority are you doing all these things?*** Since these groups were the recognized Jewish authorities in Jerusalem, they wanted to know how Jesus could claim authority to enter Jerusalem as a king and drive the merchants from the Temple.

20:4-6 Jesus' question put the religious leaders in a double bind (see 20:5-6), as either answer would indict them.

20:6 ***the people will stone us:*** Stoning was the penalty for blasphemy (Lev 24:14-15), idolatry (Lev 20:2; Deut 13:10), and other sins of defiance against God. The people might have regarded rejection of an authentic prophet as blasphemy deserving of stoning.

20:7-8 The Jewish authorities refused to answer Jesus' question, so Jesus had no obligation to answer their question. Both their question and their refusal were guided by self-interest rather than integrity.

20:9-19 ***This story*** adapts Isaiah's Song of the Fruitful Vineyard (Isa 5:1-7) to allegorize Jesus' rejection by Israel's leaders. In Isaiah's allegory, the vineyard owner is God and Israel is the unfruitful vineyard that will be judged. Jesus added new characters—the tenant farmers were Israel's unrighteous leaders, the servants were the OT prophets (repeatedly rejected by Israel), and the son was Jesus. God would judge Israel's leaders for rejecting and murdering his Son.

20:9 ***leased it to tenant farmers:*** This was a common practice in first-century Palestine, especially in Galilee, where peasants would lease the right to raise crops from wealthy landowners.

20:10 ***the farmers attacked the servant:*** God's prophets were often mistreated and opposed (1 Kgs 19:10, 14; 2 Chr 24:21; 36:16; Neh 9:26; Jer 2:30; 26:20-24; 37:15; see "The Suffering Prophet" at 4:22-24, p. 1711).

20:13 ***my cherished son:*** The Messiah was predicted to have a unique father-son relationship with God (see note on 1:32-33; see 2 Sam 7:14; Ps 2:7; 89:26-29).

20:14 ***Let's kill him and get the estate for ourselves!*** They believed that killing the heir would give them power over the estate. They foolishly failed to realize that the owner was still alive and would demand justice. Similarly, the religious leaders thought that they could keep their authority over the people of Israel by killing Jesus.

20:17 ***The stone . . . cornerstone:*** Jesus cited Ps 118:22 to predict his rejection and restoration. The cornerstone was the key part of a building, used to support and align adjoining walls. Jesus was ***rejected*** by ***the builders*** (the religious leaders), but he would become the foundation of a new building (the church).

20:18 Jesus expanded the stone metaphor (20:17) with allusions to Isa 8:14-15 and Dan 2:34, 44-45. Although Israel rejected him, Jesus was the foundation for the new people of God, and he inaugurated a Kingdom that would last forever.

20:19 ***they realized he was telling the story against them:*** The story provoked the religious leaders to act it out by arresting and killing Jesus.

20:20-26 The religious leaders' question was meant to trap Jesus, but he once again outwitted them.

so he would arrest Jesus. 21“Teacher,” they
said, “we know that you speak and teach
what is right and are not influenced by what
others think. You teach the way of God
truthfully. 22Now tell us—is it right for us to
pay taxes to Caesar or not?”

23He saw through their trickery and said,
24“Show me a Roman coin. Whose picture
and title are stamped on it?”

“Caesar’s,” they replied.

25“Well then,” he said, “give to Caesar
what belongs to Caesar, and give to God
what belongs to God.”

26So they failed to trap him by what he
said in front of the people. Instead, they
were amazed by his answer, and they became silent.

Discussion about Life in the Resurrection
Luke 20:27-40 // Matt 22:23-33 // Mark 12:18-27

27Then Jesus was approached by some Sadducees—religious leaders who say there
is no resurrection from the dead. 28They
posed this question: “Teacher, Moses gave
us a law that if a man dies, leaving a wife but
no children, his brother should marry the
widow and have a child who will carry on
the brother’s name. 29Well, suppose there
were seven brothers. The oldest one married and then died without children. 30So
the second brother married the widow, but
he also died. 31Then the third brother married her. This continued with all seven of
them, who died without children. 32Finally,
the woman also died. 33So tell us, whose
wife will she be in the resurrection? For all
seven were married to her!”

34Jesus replied, “Marriage is for people
here on earth. 35But in the age to come,
those worthy of being raised from the dead
will neither marry nor be given in marriage.
36And they will never die again. In this
respect they will be like angels. They are
children of God and children of the resurrection.

37“But now, as to whether the dead will
be raised—even Moses proved this when
he wrote about the burning bush. Long after Abraham, Isaac, and Jacob had died, he
referred to the Lord as ‘the God of Abraham,
the God of Isaac, and the God of Jacob.’ 38So
he is the God of the living, not the dead, for
they are all alive to him.”

39“Well said, Teacher!” remarked some
of the teachers of religious law who were
standing there. 40And then no one dared to
ask him any more questions.

Whose Son Is the Messiah?
Luke 20:41-44 // Matt 22:41-46 // Mark 12:35-37

41Then Jesus presented them with a question. “Why is it,” he asked, “that the Messiah
is said to be the son of David? 42For David
himself wrote in the book of Psalms:

20:25 Luke 23:2; Rom 13:6-7
20:27-40 //Matt 22:23-33; //Mark 12:18-27
20:27 Acts 23:8
20:28 *Deut 25:5
20:36 John 1:12; Gal 4:5-7; 1 Jn 3:1-2
20:37 *Exod 3:6
20:41-44 //Matt 22:41-46; //Mark 12:35-37
20:42-43 *Ps 110:1

20:21 ***we know that you speak and teach what is right:*** This flattery was meant to throw Jesus off guard (see Ps 5:9; 12:2-3; 78:36; Prov 26:28; 28:23; 29:5; Ezek 12:24).

20:22 ***is it right for us to pay taxes to Caesar or not?*** If Jesus said yes, he would make the people angry, because they hated the burden of Roman taxation. If he said no, he would be accused of rebellion against the Roman authorities.

20:24 ***a Roman coin*** (Greek *a denarius*): This coin had the ***picture and title*** of the emperor Tiberius Caesar (see 3:1) ***stamped on it***.

20:25 ***give to Caesar what belongs to Caesar:*** Jesus’ brilliant answer could be taken in two ways. On the face of it, he said that this was Caesar’s money that should properly be paid to Caesar. Jesus’ Jewish listeners also knew that *what belongs to Caesar* was actually nothing, since everything in the universe belongs to God.

20:27 ***Sadducees . . . who say there is no resurrection from the dead:*** See “The Sadducees” at Matt 16:1, p. 1610.

20:28 ***Moses gave us a law:*** A dead man’s brother would marry the widow to produce children who would maintain the dead man’s name and property (Deut 25:5-6; see also Gen 38:8-10; Ruth 4:1-12).

20:29-33 ***Well, suppose there were seven brothers:*** A similar story of a woman married to seven husbands appears in the OT Apocrypha (*Tobit* 3:7-17; 6:10–8:18).

20:33 ***whose wife will she be in the resurrection?*** The Sadducees used this hypothetical situation in an attempt to show that the idea of resurrection was absurd. This was probably a stock polemic that the Sadducees used in debating the Pharisees.

20:35 ***will neither marry nor be given in marriage:*** Jesus emphasized that marriage is an institution for this life, not for the resurrection.

20:36 ***In this respect they will be like angels:*** Angels are not married and they are immortal. The Bible never teaches that people become angels (cp. Heb 1:5–2:18), but that we will be like them.

20:37 Having refuted the Sadducees’ argument about marriage, Jesus turned to the larger question concerning the resurrection. • ***even Moses proved this:*** Jesus used the books of Moses (Genesis—Deuteronomy)—the only Scripture the Sadducees recognized as authoritative—to prove the resurrection. • ***when he wrote . . . he referred to the Lord:*** Literally *when he wrote about the bush. He referred to the Lord.* • ***the God of Abraham . . . Jacob:*** Exod 3:6. God identified himself as the God of Abraham, Isaac, and Jacob long after these patriarchs had died. Since he was still their God, they must have had a continuing existence after death.

20:39 ***Well said, Teacher!*** Most ***teachers of religious law*** were Pharisees, so they agreed with Jesus on the resurrection and were pleased that he refuted the Sadducees.

20:40 Jesus’ wise answers confounded his opponents, thwarting their attempts to trap him.

20:41-44 Having silenced his opponents, Jesus took the offensive in challenging the religious leaders’ concept of the Messiah.

20:41 The OT predicted that ***the Messiah*** would be a descendant ***of David*** (see notes on 1:32-33; 18:38).

20:42-43 Jesus quotes Ps 110:1, which indicates that the Messiah is David’s Lord.

20:45-47
//Matt 23:1-36
//Mark 12:38-40
//Luke 11:37-54

21:1-4
//Mark 12:41-44

21:5-36
//Matt 24:1-35
//Mark 13:1-31

21:6
Luke 19:44

21:8
Luke 17:23

21:10
2 Chr 15:6
Isa 19:2

'The LORD said to my Lord,
Sit in the place of honor at my right
hand
43 until I humble your enemies,
making them a footstool under your
feet.'

44 Since David called the Messiah 'Lord,' how
can the Messiah be his son?"

Jesus Criticizes the Teachers of Religious Law
Luke 20:45-47 // Mark 12:38-40; cp. Matt 23:1-14

45 Then, with the crowds listening, he turned
to his disciples and said, 46 "Beware of these
teachers of religious law! For they like to
parade around in flowing robes and love
to receive respectful greetings as they walk
in the marketplaces. And how they love the
seats of honor in the synagogues and the
head table at banquets. 47 Yet they shamelessly cheat widows out of their property
and then pretend to be pious by making
long prayers in public. Because of this, they
will be severely punished."

The Widow's Offering
Luke 21:1-4 // Mark 12:41-44

21 While Jesus was in the Temple, he
watched the rich people dropping
their gifts in the collection box. 2 Then a
poor widow came by and dropped in two
small coins.
3 "I tell you the truth," Jesus said, "this
poor widow has given more than all the rest
of them. 4 For they have given a tiny part of
their surplus, but she, poor as she is, has
given everything she has."

Jesus Predicts Future Events
Luke 21:5-11 // Matt 24:1-8 // Mark 13:1-8
Luke 21:12-19 // Matt 24:9-14 // Mark 13:9-13; cp.
Matt 10:17-25
Luke 21:20-24 // Matt 24:15-22 // Mark 13:14-20

5 Some of his disciples began talking about
the majestic stonework of the Temple and
the memorial decorations on the walls.
But Jesus said, 6 "The time is coming when
all these things will be completely demolished. Not one stone will be left on top of
another!"
7 "Teacher," they asked, "when will all this
happen? What sign will show us that these
things are about to take place?"
8 He replied, "Don't let anyone mislead
you, for many will come in my name, claiming, 'I am the Messiah,' and saying, 'The
time has come!' But don't believe them.
9 And when you hear of wars and insurrec-
tions, don't panic. Yes, these things must
take place first, but the end won't follow
immediately." 10 Then he added, "Nation
will go to war against nation, and kingdom
against kingdom. 11 There will be great
earthquakes, and there will be famines

20:44 Jesus asked why David addressed ***his son*** (i.e., his descendant) as his ***Lord***. The implied answer was that the Messiah was more than just a human king descended from David. He is Lord of all (see 2:11; Acts 10:36). Psalm 110:1 became an important text for the apostles, confirming Jesus' identity as the Son of God (see Mark 14:62; Acts 2:34; 7:56; Rom 8:34; 1 Cor 15:25; Eph 1:20; Col 3:1; Heb 1:3, 13; 8:1; 10:12-13; 1 Pet 3:22; Rev 3:21).

20:46-47 Jesus continued on the offensive, warning against the hypocrisy and exploitation of the ***teachers of religious law***. • ***respectful greetings . . . seats of honor:*** See note on 11:43. • ***head table at banquets:*** See notes on 5:30; 14:7.

20:47 ***Yet they shamelessly cheat widows:*** This might mean exploiting widows' property over which they were appointed guardians; it could also mean coercing widows to give money beyond their means. Widows were the most vulnerable members of society, and God had special concern for them. He would judge those who exploited them (Exod 22:22; Deut 10:18; 27:19).

21:1-4 Jesus set the sacrificial offering of the ***poor widow*** in contrast to the greed and hypocrisy of ***the rich people***, including the teachers of religious law (20:45-47).

21:1 The Greek term translated ***collection box*** probably refers to the chests with trumpet-shaped openings used to collect offerings.

21:2 ***two small coins:*** Greek *two lepta*, the smallest of Jewish coins, together worth only about 1⁄64 of a denarius (the standard day's wage for a laborer).

21:4 The amount given counts for less than the heart attitude of the giver.

21:5-38 When Jesus predicted the destruction of the Temple of Jerusalem (21:6), his disciples questioned when it would take place and what signs would accompany it (21:7). Jesus responded by describing the events surrounding the destruction of the Temple and the return of the Son of Man (21:8-36). This sermon is known as the Olivet Discourse because the Mount of Olives was the site of Jesus' teaching (see Matt 24:3; Mark 13:3).

21:5 ***majestic stonework:*** Herod the Great rebuilt and restored the Jerusalem Temple, producing one of the great structures of the ancient world (see "Herod the Great" at Matt 2:1-20, p. 1578). According to Josephus, the massive white stones reflected the sun with such brilliance that from a distance the Temple looked like snow-covered mountains (*War* 5.5.6). • The ***memorial decorations*** were probably funded by offerings given by worshipers to fulfill vows.

21:6 ***Not one stone will be left on top of another:*** See note on 19:43-44.

21:8-11 Jesus foretold events that are often misinterpreted as signs of the end, such as the appearance of false messiahs, wars, earthquakes, famines, and severe persecution, but Jesus said that ***the end won't follow immediately***.

21:8 ***claiming, 'I am the Messiah'*** (literally *claiming, 'I am'*): See note on Mark 13:5-6.

21:11 Cataclysmic events such as these are often associated with the judgment of God (1 Sam 14:15; Ps 18:7-8; Isa 2:19, 21; 5:25; 13:13; 24:18; 29:5-6; Jer 14:12; 21:6-7; Ezek 14:21; Amos 1:1) and the end of the age (Isa 24:18; 29:5-6; Ezek 38:19; Joel 2:10; Hag 2:6, 21; Zech 14:4; cp. Rev 6:12; 8:5; 11:13, 19; 16:18). • ***great miraculous signs from heaven:*** See note on 21:25.

and plagues in many lands, and there will
be terrifying things and great miraculous
signs from heaven.
12"But before all this occurs, there will
be a time of great persecution. You will be
dragged into synagogues and prisons, and
you will stand trial before kings and governors because you are my followers. 13But
this will be your opportunity to tell them
about me. 14So don't worry in advance about
how to answer the charges against you, 15for
I will give you the right words and such wisdom that none of your opponents will be
able to reply or refute you! 16Even those closest to you—your parents, brothers, relatives,
and friends—will betray you. They will even
kill some of you. 17And everyone will hate
you because you are my followers. 18But not
a hair of your head will perish! 19By standing firm, you will win your souls.
20"And when you see Jerusalem surrounded by armies, then you will know
that the time of its destruction has arrived.
21Then those in Judea must flee to the hills.
Those in Jerusalem must get out, and those
out in the country should not return to
the city. 22For those will be days of God's
vengeance, and the prophetic words of the
Scriptures will be fulfilled. 23How terrible
it will be for pregnant women and for nursing mothers in those days. For there will be
disaster in the land and great anger against
this people. 24They will be killed by the
sword or sent away as captives to all the nations of the world. And Jerusalem will be
trampled down by the Gentiles until the period of the Gentiles comes to an end.

The Coming of the Son of Man
Luke 21:25-33 // Matt 24:29-36 // Mark 13:24-32

25"And there will be strange signs in the sun,
moon, and stars. And here on earth the nations will be in turmoil, perplexed by the
roaring seas and strange tides. 26People will
be terrified at what they see coming upon

21:12 Acts 12:4
21:13 Phil 1:12
21:14 Luke 12:11-12
21:15 Acts 6:10
21:18 Matt 10:30
21:22 Deut 32:35; Dan 9:24-27; Hos 9:7
21:23 Luke 23:29; 1 Cor 7:26, 28
21:24 Isa 5:5; 63:18; Dan 8:13; 2 Pet 3:10, 12; Rev 11:2
21:26 *Isa 34:4

The City of Jerusalem (21:20-24)

Luke 13:33-35; 19:41-44

The city of Jerusalem plays a crucial but ambivalent role throughout Luke and Acts. On the one hand, Jerusalem was the city of God, the great King—his presence dwelt there in his Temple. God would accomplish salvation in Jerusalem and the Good News would go out from there (as recorded in Acts). At the same time, Jerusalem symbolically represented God's rebellious people Israel, who had persecuted God's prophets in the past and were now rejecting his Son, the Messiah. This rejection would result in judgment against Jerusalem and its utter destruction by the Romans in AD 70 (13:33-35; 19:41-44; 21:20).

Jerusalem plays a key geographical role in the structure of Luke–Acts. The Gospel narrative begins in the Temple at the heart of Jerusalem, the most sacred place in the world, and Jesus' ministry culminated with his death and resurrection in Jerusalem. All this confirms that salvation emerged from Israel, fulfilling the promises made to Israel in the OT. The church then moved outward, taking the message of salvation from Jerusalem to the ends of the earth (Acts 1:8).

21:12-19 ***a time of great persecution:*** Jesus described the persecution that his followers would experience (see also Matt 10:17-22; Mark 13:9). The Jewish literature of Jesus' day similarly described a time of great tribulation prior to the arrival of God's final salvation.

21:12 ***dragged into synagogues:*** Jesus and his early followers were Jewish, and the earliest conflicts were with fellow Jews who did not accept Jesus as the Messiah. Jesus' followers were sometimes tried in the synagogue before a Jewish tribunal (cp. 2 Cor 11:24).

21:13 ***But this will be your opportunity to tell them about me:*** Or *This will be your testimony against them.* The Greek can be interpreted either way.

21:15 ***I will give you the right words:*** God often assured his prophets that he would give them the words to say (Exod 4:12, 15; Deut 18:18; Isa 50:4; 51:16; Jer 1:9). Jesus' disciples were to prepare themselves to be clear witnesses (see Col 4:5-6; 2 Tim 2:21; 1 Pet 3:15), knowing that the Spirit would help them to respond as powerfully as Jesus had done (20:20-44).

21:16 Families in Jewish and Gentile communities have often been divided as some members follow Jesus and some reject him.

21:17 ***because you are my followers:*** Literally *on account of my name.*

21:18-19 ***But not a hair of your head will perish!*** This idiom signifies full protection (1 Sam 14:45; 2 Sam 14:11; 1 Kgs 1:52; Dan 3:27). It refers here to the disciples' *souls,* because some would be martyred for their faith (21:16).

21:20-24 Jesus was describing the siege and destruction of Jerusalem that would take place in AD 70 (see note on 19:43-44).

21:21 ***Those in Jerusalem must get out:*** Because of this prophecy, Christians in Judea fled to the town of Pella in Decapolis before the destruction of Jerusalem in AD 70 (Eusebius, *Church History* 3.5).

21:22 ***For those will be days of God's vengeance:*** The destruction of Jerusalem was part of God's judgment for Israel's rejection of the Messiah.

21:24 ***until the period of the Gentiles comes to an end:*** Daniel predicted a period of successive Gentile empires before the coming of God's Kingdom (Dan 2:44; 7:27).

21:25 The prophets predicted that heavenly *signs* would precede the judgment of God at the end of the age (Isa 13:9-10; 34:4; Jer 4:23, 28; Ezek 32:7-8; Joel 2:10, 30-31; cp. Rev 6:13-14; 8:10; 9:1; 12:1, 3; 15:1).

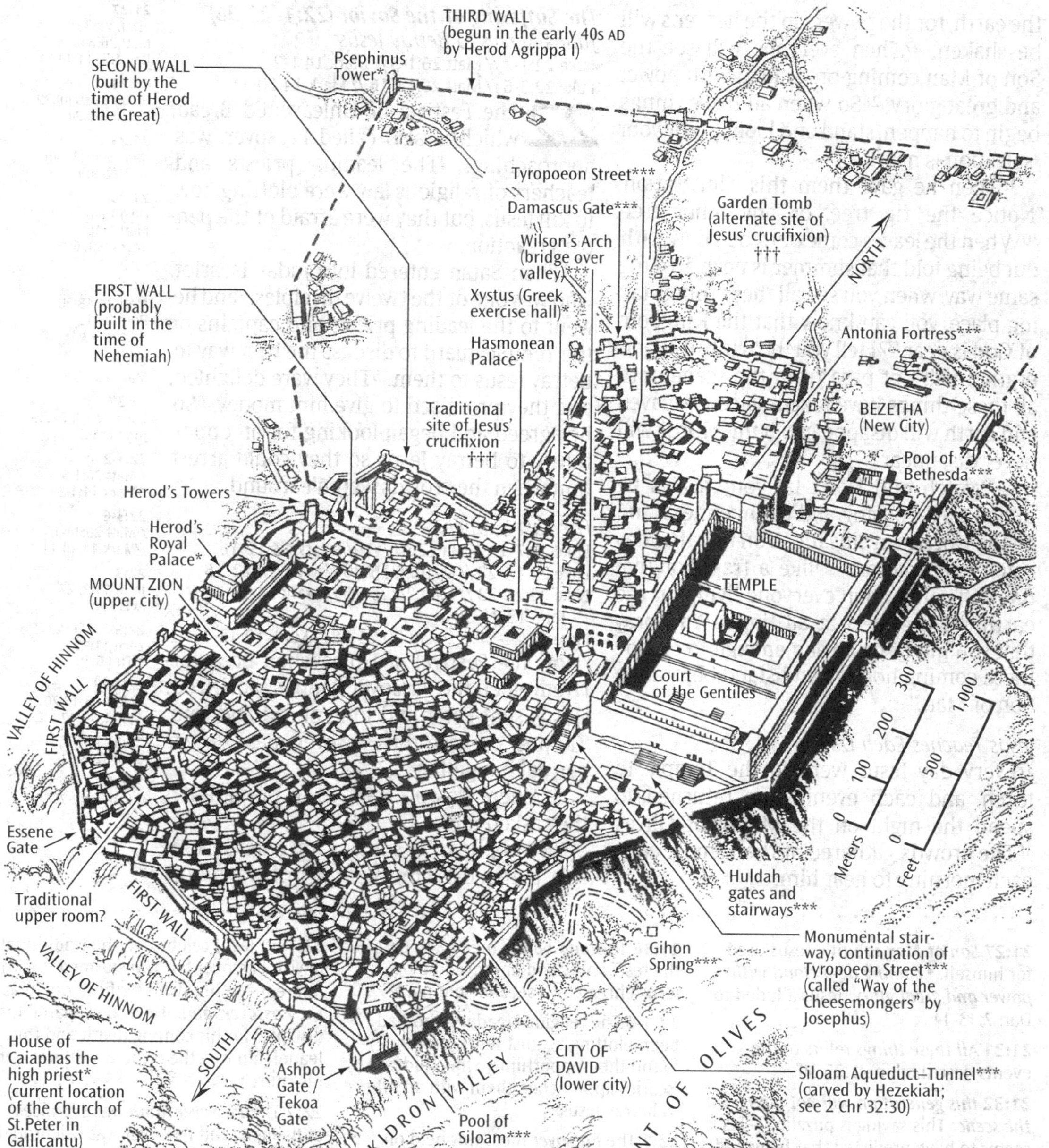

▲**First-Century Jerusalem (Luke 19:28–21:37).** At the time of Jesus and the apostles, Jerusalem was glorious and strong. Herod the Great (37–4 BC) had built extensively; his most prominent project was rebuilding the Temple (see illustration, p. 1787). Many events in the lives of Jesus and the apostles took place in Jerusalem. • Josephus described Jerusalem's three walls at the time of the Jewish rebellion (AD 66–70; see Josephus, *War* 5.4.1-4), with the "First Wall" being the oldest, and the "Third Wall" never reaching completion. Jerusalem was destroyed in AD 70 by the Roman general Titus. Later, Emperor Hadrian razed it completely in AD 135. • Buildings, streets, and roads are artist's concept only, unless otherwise named and located.

KEY: * Location generally known, architectural style unknown—artist's concept, Roman architecture assumed.
** Location and architecture unknown; known to exist from written history, shown here for illustrative purposes.
*** Physical evidence or remains used to determine location and/or appearance.

the earth, for the powers in the heavens will
be shaken. 27Then everyone will see the
Son of Man coming on a cloud with power
and great glory. 28So when all these things
begin to happen, stand and look up, for your
[a]salvation is near!"
29Then he gave them this [b]illustration:
"Notice the fig tree, or any other tree.
30When the leaves come out, you know without being told that summer is near. 31In the
same way, when you see all these things taking place, you can know that the Kingdom
of God is near. 32I tell you the truth, this generation will not pass from the scene until
all these things have taken place. 33Heaven
and earth will disappear, but my [c]words will
never disappear.
34"Watch out! Don't let your hearts be
dulled by carousing and drunkenness, and
by the worries of this life. Don't let that day
catch you unaware, 35like a trap. For that
day will come upon everyone living on the
earth. 36Keep alert at all times. And pray
that you might be strong enough to escape
these coming horrors and stand before the
Son of Man."

Jesus Teaches Each Day

37Every day Jesus went to the Temple to
teach, and each evening he returned to
spend the night on the Mount of Olives.
38The crowds gathered at the Temple early
each morning to hear him.

The Suffering of the Savior (22:1–23:56)

Judas Agrees to Betray Jesus

Luke 22:1-2 // Matt 26:1-5 // Mark 14:1-2
Luke 22:3-6 // Matt 26:14-16 // Mark 14:10-11

22 The Festival of Unleavened Bread,
which is also called Passover, was
approaching. 2The leading priests and
teachers of religious law were plotting how
to kill Jesus, but they were afraid of the people's reaction.
3Then Satan entered into Judas Iscariot,
who was one of the twelve disciples, 4and he
went to the leading priests and captains of
the Temple guard to discuss the best way to
betray Jesus to them. 5They were delighted,
and they promised to give him money. 6So
he agreed and began looking for an opportunity to betray Jesus so they could arrest
him when the crowds weren't around.

The Last Supper

Luke 22:7-13 // Matt 26:17-19// Mark 14:12-16
Luke 22:14-20 // Matt 26:26-30 // Mark 14:22-26
Luke 22:21-23 // Matt 26:20-25 // Mark 14:18-21 // John 13:21-30
Luke 22:24-27; cp. Matt 20:25-28 // Mark 10:42-45

7Now the Festival of Unleavened Bread arrived, when the Passover lamb is sacrificed.
8Jesus sent Peter and John ahead and said,
"Go and prepare the Passover meal, so we
can eat it together."
9"Where do you want us to prepare it?"
they asked him.
10He replied, "As soon as you enter Jerusalem, a man carrying a pitcher of water will

21:27 *Dan 7:13; Matt 26:64; Rev 1:7; 14:14
21:28 [a]*apolutrōsis* (0629) ‣ Rom 3:24
21:29 [b]*parabolē* (3850) ‣ Heb 9:9
21:33 Isa 40:6-8; Matt 5:18; [c]*logos* (3056) ‣ John 1:1
21:34 Matt 24:48-50; Rom 13:13; 1 Thes 5:3
21:36 Mark 13:33
21:37 Luke 19:47; 22:39; John 8:1-2
22:1-2 //Matt 26:1-5; //Mark 14:1-2
22:3-6 //Matt 26:14-16; //Mark 14:10-11
22:3 John 13:2, 27; Acts 1:17
22:5 Zech 11:12; 1 Tim 6:10
22:7-13 //Matt 26:17-20; //Mark 14:12-16
22:8 Exod 12:8-11
22:10 1 Sam 10:2-7

21:27 *Son of Man* is a title Jesus used for himself. • *coming on a cloud with power and great glory:* Jesus alluded to Dan 7:13-14.

21:31 *All these things* refers to the events described in 21:25-30.

21:32 *this generation will not pass from the scene:* This saying is puzzling—Jesus seems to have predicted that he would come again before the first generation of his disciples died out. There are three main interpretations: (1) the reference is to the destruction of Jerusalem in AD 70 when Jesus "came" in judgment against the nation of Israel; (2) "this generation" is not Jesus' contemporaries, but a future generation alive when these signs begin coming to fulfillment; (3) the term *generation* could be translated "race," referring to the Jewish race that will not disappear before Christ returns.

21:33 *Heaven and earth will disappear:* See note on 16:17.

21:34 The central theme of the discourse is *Watch out!* Believers are always to be alert and ready for Christ's return.

21:36 To *stand before* means "to pass the test" and stand approved before Jesus Christ at his second coming.

22:1-6 The religious leaders who had been plotting against Jesus (see 19:47) found their opportunity when Judas Iscariot approached them with an offer to betray Jesus.

22:1 The *Passover* meal was held on the 15th of Nisan (March~April) in the Jewish calendar and was immediately followed by the seven-day *Festival of Unleavened Bread* (Exod 12:1-20; 23:15; 34:18; Deut 16:1-8), sometimes also called Passover.

22:3 *Satan entered into Judas Iscariot:* See John 13:2; Acts 5:3. Satan had previously tempted Jesus (4:2), and had been waiting for this opportunity (4:13).

22:4 *captains of the Temple guard:* The Temple had its own police force.

22:5 Judas wanted the *money*. John tells us that he was a thief who stole from the disciples' common fund (John 12:6).

22:6 *when the crowds weren't around:* This was because of Jesus' popularity among the people.

22:7-30 Jesus celebrated the traditional Jewish Passover but transformed it with reference to his own sacrificial death as *the Passover lamb.* He also prepared his disciples for his coming death and the leadership role they would assume over his church.

22:7 The *Passover lamb* was *sacrificed* at twilight, and Passover was celebrated in the evening (see Exod 12:6-8).

22:8 *Go and prepare the Passover meal:* The lamb was roasted and eaten with bitter herbs and unleavened bread at the Passover meal (Exod 12:8; Num 9:11-12; Deut 16:3). The bitter herbs represented the bitterness of the Israelites' slavery in Egypt, and the unleavened bread recalled their haste in leaving Egypt.

22:10 *A man carrying a pitcher of water* would have been an unusual sight, because women normally carried the water.

22:11-12 The text does not say whether Jesus exhibited supernatural foreknowledge or whether he had made arrangements for this room ahead of time (see also 19:30-34).

22:15-20
//Matt 26:26-29
//Mark 14:22-25
//1 Cor 11:23-26
22:16
Luke 14:15
22:18
[d]*ampelos* (0288)
‣John 15:1
22:19
Luke 24:30
Acts 27:35
22:20
Exod 24:8
Jer 31:31-34
Heb 9:15-18
[e]*diathēkē* (1242)
‣1 Cor 11:25
22:21-23
//Matt 26:21-25
//Mark 14:18-21
//John 13:21-26
22:21
Ps 41:9
John 13:21
22:22
Acts 2:23; 4:28
22:24-27
//Matt 20:24-28
22:26
Matt 23:11
Mark 9:35
1 Pet 5:5
22:27
John 13:4-16
22:28-30
//Matt 19:28
22:31-34
//Matt 26:31-35
//Mark 14:27-31
//John 13:36-38
22:31
Job 1:6-12
Amos 9:9

meet you. Follow him. At the house he enters, 11say to the owner, 'The Teacher asks:
Where is the guest room where I can eat
the Passover meal with my disciples?' 12He
will take you upstairs to a large room that
is already set up. That is where you should
prepare our meal." 13They went off to the
city and found everything just as Jesus had
said, and they prepared the Passover meal
there.

14When the time came, Jesus and the
apostles sat down together at the table.
15Jesus said, "I have been very eager to eat
this Passover meal with you before my suffering begins. 16For I tell you now that I
won't eat this meal again until its meaning
is fulfilled in the Kingdom of God."

17Then he took a cup of wine and gave
thanks to God for it. Then he said, "Take
this and share it among yourselves. 18For
I will not drink [d]wine again until the Kingdom of God has come."

19He took some bread and gave thanks to
God for it. Then he broke it in pieces and
gave it to the disciples, saying, "This is my
body, which is given for you. Do this to remember me."

20After supper he took another cup of
wine and said, "This cup is the new [e]cov-
enant between God and his people—an
agreement confirmed with my blood, which
is poured out as a sacrifice for you.

21"But here at this table, sitting among us
as a friend, is the man who will betray me.
22For it has been determined that the Son of
Man must die. But what sorrow awaits the
one who betrays him." 23The disciples began to ask each other which of them would
ever do such a thing.

24Then they began to argue among themselves about who would be the greatest
among them. 25Jesus told them, "In this
world the kings and great men lord it over
their people, yet they are called 'friends of
the people.' 26But among you it will be different. Those who are the greatest among
you should take the lowest rank, and the
leader should be like a servant. 27Who is
more important, the one who sits at the table or the one who serves? The one who sits
at the table, of course. But not here! For I am
among you as one who serves.

28"You have stayed with me in my time
of trial. 29And just as my Father has granted
me a Kingdom, I now grant you the right
30to eat and drink at my table in my Kingdom. And you will sit on thrones, judging
the twelve tribes of Israel.

Jesus Predicts Peter's Denial
Luke 22:31-34; cp. Matt 26:31-35 // Mark 14:27-31; cp. John 13:36-38

31"Simon, Simon, Satan has asked to sift
each of you like wheat. 32But I have pleaded
in prayer for you, Simon, that your faith

22:14 *sat down together at the table* (or *reclined together*): The Jewish people followed Hellenistic practice at banquets by reclining on couches (see note on John 13:23).

22:15 Jesus ate the ***Passover meal*** with his disciples and followed the ritual order of the Passover celebration (see note on Matt 26:26-29).

22:16 ***until its meaning is fulfilled in the Kingdom of God:*** This celebration had as its goal the messianic banquet. Jesus' death as the true Passover lamb (1 Cor 5:7) inaugurated the Kingdom of God that will be completed at Jesus' second coming.

22:17 ***he took a cup of wine:*** The traditional Passover celebration used four cups of wine—at the opening benediction, after the Passover explanation, after the meal, and after a concluding psalm. This was probably the first cup that introduced the ceremony.

22:19-20 Using the bread and cup as symbols of his body and blood, Jesus instituted the communion service that the disciples were to practice in remembrance of his death. • ***This is my body, which is given for you:*** The unleavened bread of the Passover symbolized Jesus' death as the Passover lamb. His death would pay for the sins of the world (cp. 1 Cor 11:24-25). • Some manuscripts do not include 22:19b-20, *which is given for you . . . which is poured out as a sacrifice for you.*

22:20 God's covenants in the OT were ***confirmed*** with the ***blood*** of a sacrifice (Gen 15:9-10; Exod 24:8). Jesus' death established the ***new covenant*** that God had promised his people (Jer 31:31-34).

22:21-22 ***it has been determined:*** Though wicked men betrayed and killed Jesus, it was part of God's sovereign plan to accomplish salvation (see Acts 2:23).

22:22 ***Son of Man*** is a title Jesus used for himself. • ***what sorrow awaits the one who betrays him:*** Judas suffered guilt, condemnation, and a gruesome death for betraying Jesus (Matt 27:5; Acts 1:18).

22:24 ***who would be the greatest among them:*** See also Mark 9:33-37; 10:35-45.

22:25 ***friends of the people:*** This translates a Greek word that refers to the practice of rulers bestowing gifts and favors on their subjects to gain loyalty and honor. Jesus contrasted the world's leadership style—military power, coercion, and bribery—with his own servant leadership in sacrificing himself for others.

22:27 ***For I am among you as one who serves:*** Jesus defined true leadership as service—meeting the needs of others and empowering them to be all that God has called them to be (see Mark 10:45). This statement was striking in a culture for which status and power were central.

22:29-30 ***I now grant you the right to eat and drink at my table:*** See "The Messianic Banquet" at 14:1-24, p. 1737.

22:30 ***you will sit on thrones, judging the twelve tribes of Israel:*** This could be a figurative reference to the apostles' leadership in the church, or it could indicate their special role in the future when the Kingdom would be consummated on earth (cp. Eph 2:20; Rev 3:21; 20:4).

22:31 Regarding ***Satan***, see 4:2; 10:18; 11:15. Satan is the accuser of God's people (see Job 1:7; 2:2); he would test Simon Peter and the rest of the apostles. • ***asked to sift:*** Wheat was sifted through

should not fail. So when you have repented
and turned to me again, strengthen your
brothers."
33 Peter said, "Lord, I am ready to go to
prison with you, and even to die with you."
34 But Jesus said, "Peter, let me tell you
something. Before the rooster crows tomorrow morning, you will deny three times that
you even know me."
35 Then Jesus asked them, "When I sent
you out to preach the Good News and you
did not have money, a traveler's bag, or an extra pair of sandals, did you need anything?"
"No," they replied.
36 "But now," he said, "take your money
and a traveler's bag. And if you don't have
a sword, sell your cloak and buy one! 37 For
the time has come for this prophecy about
me to be fulfilled: 'He was counted among
the rebels.' Yes, everything written about
me by the prophets will come true."
38 "Look, Lord," they replied, "we have two
swords among us."
"That's enough," he said.

Jesus Prays on the Mount of Olives
Luke 22:39-46 // Matt 26:36-46 // Mark 14:32-42

39 Then, accompanied by the disciples, Jesus
left the upstairs room and went as usual to
the Mount of Olives. 40 There he told them,
"Pray that you will not give in to temptation."
41 He walked away, about a stone's throw,
and knelt down and prayed, 42 "Father, if
you are willing, please take this cup of suffering away from me. Yet I want your will
to be done, not mine." 43 Then an angel from
heaven appeared and strengthened him.
44 He prayed more fervently, and he was in
such agony of spirit that his sweat fell to the
ground like great drops of blood.
45 At last he stood up again and returned
to the disciples, only to find them asleep,
exhausted from grief. 46 "Why are you sleeping?" he asked them. "Get up and pray, so
that you will not give in to temptation."

Jesus Is Betrayed and Arrested
Luke 22:47-53 // Matt 26:47-56 // Mark 14:43-52 // John 18:1-12

47 But even as Jesus said this, a crowd approached, led by Judas, one of the twelve
disciples. Judas walked over to Jesus to
greet him with a kiss. 48 But Jesus said, "Judas, would you betray the Son of Man with
a kiss?"
49 When the other disciples saw what was
about to happen, they exclaimed, "Lord,
should we fight? We brought the swords!"
50 And one of them struck at the high
priest's slave, slashing off his right ear.
51 But Jesus said, "No more of this." And
he touched the man's ear and healed him.
52 Then Jesus spoke to the leading priests,

22:32 John 17:9, 15; 21:15
22:33 John 11:16
22:35 Matt 10:9-10; Luke 9:3
22:37 *Isa 53:12; Mark 15:27
22:39-46 //Matt 26:36-46 //Mark 14:32-42
22:40 Matt 6:13
22:47-53 //Matt 26:47-56 //Mark 14:43-49 //John 18:3-11

a sieve to separate the grain from the chaff. It is an image of extreme testing (see Isa 30:28; Amos 9:9). • The NLT's *each of you* is precise, because the Greek *you* is plural, referring to all the disciples. Jesus foresaw Peter's denial and the trials of the other disciples.

22:32 ***So when you have repented:*** This *you* is singular; it refers to Peter's restoration after his denial of Jesus.

22:33 See Acts 4:3; 5:18; 12:1-9, where Peter suffered trials and was repeatedly jailed. Church tradition relates that Peter was crucified in Rome, but his declaration of loyalty here was premature.

22:34 On Thursday evening, Jesus said that Peter would deny him ***before the rooster crows tomorrow morning*** (literally *before the rooster crows today*): This does not contradict Mark's "this very night, before the rooster crows twice" (Mark 14:30); Luke and Matthew are simply more general, and in Jewish reckoning, sunset was the beginning of the next day.

22:36 ***take your money and a traveler's bag:*** For their missions to Israel's villages, the apostles had traveled without provisions and depended on others' support (9:3; 10:3-4). In the dangerous days to come, they would have to plan more carefully. Jesus prepared his disciples for his suffering and death, and also for the establishing of the church and the worldwide proclamation of the Good News. • ***a sword:*** Jesus was probably not telling his followers to take up arms, but speaking metaphorically (see note on 22:38)—they must prepare themselves for a violent crisis.

22:37 ***He was counted among the rebels:*** Isa 53:12.

22:38 ***That's enough:*** The disciples' *two swords* were probably not enough to defend the whole group, and Jesus elsewhere rejected violence (22:49-51 // Matt 26:52). Jesus might have meant that two swords were sufficient to fulfill Isa 53:12. Or perhaps he meant, "Enough of this foolish talk—you are misunderstanding me."

22:39 ***Mount of Olives:*** See note on 19:29, where Jesus went to the Garden of Gethsemane (Mark 14:32; Matt 26:36).

22:42 ***please take this cup of suffering away:*** A cup is a metaphor for experiencing either judgment or blessing (see, e.g., Ps 23:5; 75:8; 116:13; Isa 51:17). Jesus felt all the emotions of his humanity, including fear and anxiety.

22:43-44 These verses are not included in many ancient manuscripts.

22:43 ***an angel from heaven:*** Angels often help and encourage human beings (see Heb 1:14; cp. 1 Kgs 19:5-8; Ps 91:11-12; Dan 3:28; 10:16-19).

22:44 ***his sweat fell to the ground like great drops of blood:*** The text does not say that Jesus sweated blood, as is often supposed, but that his sweat fell like blood pouring to the ground, which probably means that in his *agony* he sweated profusely.

22:45-46 Jesus' agonized prayer contrasted with the disciples' failure to be vigilant against *temptation*.

22:47 A *kiss* was a common greeting between friends. Judas's kiss highlighted his treachery.

22:51 ***he touched the man's ear and healed him:*** John tells us that the man's name was Malchus and that Peter was the one who cut off his ear (John 18:10). Peter probably thought that he was precipitating the final war and that the heavenly host was about to appear and destroy the Romans. When Jesus refused to fight, the terror-stricken disciples fled (Matt 26:56 // Mark 14:50).

22:53
Luke 19:47
John 7:30

22:54-62
//Matt 26:57-58, 69-75
//Mark 14:53-54, 66-72
//John 18:12-18, 25-27

22:61
Luke 7:13

22:63-65
//Matt 26:67-68
//Mark 14:65

22:66-71
//Matt 26:63-66; 27:1
//Mark 14:61-64; 15:1
//John 18:19-24

22:69
Ps 110:1
Dan 7:13
Acts 7:56

22:70
Matt 4:3

23:1-5
//Matt 27:1-2, 11-14
//Mark 15:2-5
//John 18:29-38

the captains of the Temple guard, and the
elders who had come for him. "Am I some
dangerous revolutionary," he asked, "that
you come with swords and clubs to arrest
me? 53Why didn't you arrest me in the Temple? I was there every day. But this is your
moment, the time when the power of darkness reigns."

Peter Denies Jesus

Luke 22:54-62 // Matt 26:69-75 // Mark 14:66-72 // John 18:15-18, 25-27

54So they arrested him and led him to the
high priest's home. And Peter followed at a
distance. 55The guards lit a fire in the middle of the courtyard and sat around it, and
Peter joined them there. 56A servant girl noticed him in the firelight and began staring
at him. Finally she said, "This man was one
of Jesus' followers!"
57But Peter denied it. "Woman," he said,
"I don't even know him!"
58After a while someone else looked at
him and said, "You must be one of them!"
"No, man, I'm not!" Peter retorted.
59About an hour later someone else insisted, "This must be one of them, because
he is a Galilean, too."
60But Peter said, "Man, I don't know what
you are talking about." And immediately,
while he was still speaking, the rooster
crowed.
61At that moment the Lord turned and
looked at Peter. Suddenly, the Lord's words
flashed through Peter's mind: "Before the
rooster crows tomorrow morning, you will
deny three times that you even know me."
62And Peter left the courtyard, weeping
bitterly.

Jesus Is Mocked and Beaten

Luke 22:63-65; cp. Matt 26:67-68 // Mark 14:65

63The guards in charge of Jesus began mocking and beating him. 64They blindfolded
him and said, "Prophesy to us! Who hit you
that time?" 65And they hurled all sorts of terrible insults at him.

Jesus' Trial before the Jewish High Council

Luke 22:66-71 // Matt 26:57-68 // Mark 14:53-65; cp. John 18:19-24

66At daybreak all the elders of the people
assembled, including the leading priests
and the teachers of religious law. Jesus was
led before this high council, 67and they said,
"Tell us, are you the Messiah?"
But he replied, "If I tell you, you won't believe me. 68And if I ask you a question, you
won't answer. 69But from now on the Son of
Man will be seated in the place of power at
God's right hand."
70They all shouted, "So, are you claiming
to be the Son of God?"
And he replied, "You say that I am."
71"Why do we need other witnesses?"
they said. "We ourselves heard him say it."

Jesus' Trial before Pilate

Luke 23:1-5 // Matt 27:1-2, 11-14 // Mark 15:1-5 // John 18:28-38a

23 Then the entire council took Jesus
to Pilate, the Roman governor.

22:52 The Greek word translated ***revolutionary*** normally means "thief," but the Romans used this term for violent revolutionaries who opposed Roman authority (such as Barabbas, 23:18-19). To patriotic Jews, they were freedom fighters; to the Romans, they were common thugs.

22:54 ***The high priest's home*** might have been the home of Caiaphas, the current high priest, or Annas, his father-in-law and the previous high priest (see note on 3:2; John 18:12-14).

22:59 ***because he is a Galilean:*** Peter's Galilean accent gave him away (cp. Judg 12:5-6).

22:61 ***the Lord turned and looked at Peter:*** Jesus was in the house being questioned and must have looked through a window or vestibule. When their eyes met and the rooster crowed, Peter remembered Jesus' prediction (22:34).

22:63 ***mocking and beating him:*** See 18:32; Isa 50:6; 53:3-5.

22:64 ***Prophesy to us! Who hit you that time?*** Jesus had a reputation as a prophet (4:24; 7:16, 39; 13:33; 24:19), so the soldiers mocked this claim.

22:66 ***At daybreak:*** It was Friday morning (see note on 22:34). • ***all the elders of the people assembled:*** The Jewish ***high council*** (Greek *their Sanhedrin*) was originally made up of the Jerusalem nobility, both civil leaders and priests, with the high priest as its head. In Jesus' time, the Sadducees still controlled the Sanhedrin (Acts 5:17), though leading Pharisees had also gained a prominent place on the council (Acts 23:7).

22:67-68 ***If I tell you, you won't believe me:*** Jesus pointed out the hypocrisy of the question. They had already made up their minds that he was not the Messiah, so it would do no good to answer.

22:69 Jesus referred to Ps 110:1 (see note on 20:42-43). Though he would be crucified, Jesus would be vindicated through his resurrection and exalted to ***God's right hand*** (see Acts 2:33-36; cp. Dan 7:13-14). Furthermore, he would ***be seated in the place of power*** as Judge. Jesus would soon sit in judgment over those who were trying him.

22:70 The significance of Jesus' statement (22:69) was not lost on the council members. The Messiah was expected to be ***the Son of God*** and have a special father–son relationship with God (see notes on 1:32-33; 4:41; cp. 2 Sam 7:14; Ps 2:7; 89:26). The Sanhedrin accused Jesus of claiming to be the Messiah (see notes on Mark 14:62, 63-64). • ***You say that I am:*** This is a qualified affirmation. Jesus probably meant, "What you say is true, but you do not understand what 'Messiah' means." They understood it as a confirmation (22:71).

22:71 ***Why do we need other witnesses?*** The high council regarded Jesus' confirmation that he was both the Messiah and the Son of God as a blasphemous claim and thus as confirmation of his guilt.

23:1 The ***council*** did not have the right to administer capital punishment (John 18:31), so they had to take Jesus before the ***Roman governor*** (see "Pontius Pilate" at Mark 15:1-15, p. 1691), who was in Jerusalem to maintain order during the potentially turbulent Passover festival.

2They began to state their case: "This man
has been leading our people astray by
telling them not to pay their taxes to the Roman government and by claiming he is the
Messiah, a king."
3So Pilate asked him, "Are you the king of
the Jews?"
Jesus replied, "You have said it."
4Pilate turned to the leading priests and
to the crowd and said, "I find nothing wrong
with this man!"
5Then they became insistent. "But he is
causing riots by his teaching wherever he
goes—all over Judea, from Galilee to Jerusalem!"

Jesus Is Sent to Herod Antipas

6"Oh, is he a Galilean?" Pilate asked. 7When
they said that he was, Pilate sent him to
Herod Antipas, because Galilee was under
Herod's jurisdiction, and Herod happened
to be in Jerusalem at the time.
8Herod was delighted at the opportunity
to see Jesus, because he had heard about
him and had been hoping for a long time to
see him perform a miracle. 9He asked Jesus
question after question, but Jesus refused
to answer. 10Meanwhile, the leading priests
and the teachers of religious law stood
there shouting their accusations. 11Then
Herod and his soldiers began mocking and
ridiculing Jesus. Finally, they put a royal
robe on him and sent him back to Pilate.
12(Herod and Pilate, who had been enemies
before, became friends that day.)

Jesus Is Sentenced to Death

Luke 23:13-25 // Matt 27:15-26 // Mark 15:6-15 //
John 18:38b–19:16

13Then Pilate called together the leading
priests and other religious leaders, along
with the people, 14and he announced his
verdict. "You brought this man to me, accusing him of leading a revolt. I have examined
him thoroughly on this point in your presence and find him innocent. 15Herod came
to the same conclusion and sent him back to
us. Nothing this man has done calls for the
death penalty. 16So I will have him flogged,
and then I will release him."
18Then a mighty roar rose from the crowd,
and with one voice they shouted, "Kill him,
and release Barabbas to us!" 19(Barabbas was
in prison for taking part in an insurrection
in Jerusalem against the government, and
for murder.) 20Pilate argued with them, because he wanted to release Jesus. 21But they
kept shouting, "Crucify him! Crucify him!"
22For the third time he demanded, "Why?
What crime has he committed? I have
found no reason to sentence him to death.
So I will have him flogged, and then I will
release him."
23But the mob shouted louder and louder,
demanding that Jesus be crucified, and
their voices prevailed. 24So Pilate sentenced
Jesus to die as they demanded. 25As they

23:2 Luke 20:25; John 19:12
23:4 1 Tim 6:13
23:8 Luke 9:9
23:9 John 19:9
23:12 Acts 4:27
23:13-25 //Matt 27:15-26 //Mark 15:6-15 //John 18:39–19:16
23:16 John 19:1; Acts 16:37
23:18 Acts 3:13-14

23:2 The religious charges against Jesus were now replaced by political ones in order to gain a Roman conviction. Pilate was only interested in what concerned Rome. The Jewish charge of blasphemy would not be sufficient, so the council had to show that Jesus was a danger to Rome. They accused Jesus of inciting insurrection against Roman taxation and claiming to be ***a king***. All but the last charge were false.

23:3 ***You have said it:*** This is the same vague answer that Jesus gave to the high council (22:70), emphasizing Jesus' acceptance of the title "king of the Jews," but suggesting that Pilate's understanding of the title was different from his own.

23:4 ***I find nothing wrong with this man!*** To Pilate, Jesus did not seem to be a political threat.

23:5 ***he is causing riots:*** This accusation was also false, but the religious leaders knew that Pilate feared civil unrest and revolt against Rome.

23:6-7 Realizing that Jesus was ***a Galilean*** and thus under the jurisdiction of ***Herod Antipas*** (see "Herod Antipas" at Mark 6:14-29, p. 1659), Pilate saw an opportunity to get out of this sticky situation without condemning an innocent man or angering the religious leaders.

23:8 ***Herod was delighted:*** He was curious about Jesus' power as a miracle worker and religious teacher, just as he had been curious about John the Baptist (9:7, 9; Mark 6:20).

23:9 ***Jesus refused to answer:*** See Isa 53:7.

23:12 ***Herod and Pilate, who had been enemies before:*** There was a history of bad blood between Herod Antipas and Pilate. Herod and three of his brothers had previously brought charges against Pilate before Tiberius Caesar when Pilate set up idolatrous golden shields in Jerusalem, and Tiberius had ordered Pilate to remove the shields. Pilate was also governing Judea, which Antipas's father, Herod the Great, had once ruled, and which Antipas hoped one day to claim as his own.

23:14-15 Pilate and Herod repeatedly declared Jesus ***innocent*** (23:4, 22)—Jesus was the righteous and innocent suffering servant of the Lord (see also 23:41, 47; Isa 53:11).

23:16-18 ***I will have him flogged*** (or *I will teach him a lesson!*): The Greek word can mean "instruct," "punish," or "discipline"; it refers to a relatively mild whipping given for lesser offenses. It was different from the severe flogging that Romans gave in preparation for crucifixion (see Matt 27:26; Mark 15:15). • Some manuscripts add v 17, *Now it was necessary for him to release one prisoner to them during the Passover celebration.* Cp. Matt 27:15; Mark 15:6; John 18:39. Because of this custom, the crowd demanded that Pilate ***release Barabbas*** to them.

23:19 Palestine was a breeding ground for insurrection in the decades leading up to the Jewish revolt of AD 66–74. The Jewish historian Josephus describes a series of first-century revolutionaries, such as Judas of Galilee, who opposed Roman rule and taxation.

23:24 ***So Pilate sentenced Jesus to die:*** Pilate, always the ruthless pragmatist, felt that it was worth a miscarriage of justice to avoid antagonizing the religious leaders and crowds and jeopardizing his political career (see John 19:12 and note).

23:26
Matt 27:32
Mark 15:21
John 19:17
23:29
Luke 21:23
23:30
Isa 2:19
*Hos 10:8
Rev 6:16
23:32
Isa 53:12
Matt 27:38
Mark 15:27
John 19:18
23:33-43
//Matt 27:33-44
//Mark 15:22-32
//John 19:17-24
23:34
*Ps 22:18
Acts 7:60
23:35
Ps 22:17
23:36
Ps 22:7; 69:21
Matt 27:48
23:43
2 Cor 12:3-4
Rev 2:7
[f]*paradeisos* (3857)
‣1 Cor 15:47
23:44-49
//Matt 27:45-56
//Mark 15:33-41
//John 19:28-30

had requested, he released Barabbas, the
man in prison for insurrection and murder.
But he turned Jesus over to them to do as
they wished.

The Crucifixion
Luke 23:26-34 // Matt 27:32-38 // Mark 15:21-27 //
John 19:17-24
Luke 23:35-43 // Mark 15:29-32 // Matt 27:39-44

26As they led Jesus away, a man named Simon, who was from Cyrene, happened to
be coming in from the countryside. The soldiers seized him and put the cross on him
and made him carry it behind Jesus. 27A
large crowd trailed behind, including many
grief-stricken women. 28But Jesus turned
and said to them, "Daughters of Jerusalem,
don't weep for me, but weep for yourselves
and for your children. 29For the days are
coming when they will say, 'Fortunate indeed are the women who are childless, the
wombs that have not borne a child and the
breasts that have never nursed.' 30People
will beg the mountains, 'Fall on us,' and
plead with the hills, 'Bury us.' 31For if these
things are done when the tree is green, what
will happen when it is dry?"
32Two others, both criminals, were led out
to be executed with him. 33When they came
to a place called The Skull, they nailed him
to the cross. And the criminals were also crucified—one on his right and one on his left.
34Jesus said, "Father, forgive them, for
they don't know what they are doing." And
the soldiers gambled for his clothes by
throwing dice.
35The crowd watched and the leaders
scoffed. "He saved others," they said, "let
him save himself if he is really God's Messiah, the Chosen One." 36The soldiers
mocked him, too, by offering him a drink
of sour wine. 37They called out to him, "If
you are the King of the Jews, save yourself!"
38A sign was fastened above him with these
words: "This is the King of the Jews."
39One of the criminals hanging beside
him scoffed, "So you're the Messiah, are
you? Prove it by saving yourself—and us, too,
while you're at it!"
40But the other criminal protested, "Don't
you fear God even when you have been sentenced to die? 41We deserve to die for our
crimes, but this man hasn't done anything
wrong." 42Then he said, "Jesus, remember
me when you come into your Kingdom."
43And Jesus replied, "I assure you, today
you will be with me in [f]paradise."

The Death of Jesus
Luke 23:44-49 // Matt 27:45-56 // Mark 15:33-41 //
John 19:28-30

44By this time it was about noon, and darkness fell across the whole land until three

23:26 ***Cyrene*** was a city in northern Africa. ***Simon*** might have been a Jewish pilgrim visiting Jerusalem for Passover (see note on Mark 15:21-22). • ***put the cross on him:*** Prisoners bound for crucifixion were normally forced to carry the crossbeam to the place of execution. It was fastened to the upright beam at the crucifixion site.

23:28 ***Jesus*** warned of the horrors that would come to ***Jerusalem*** during its siege and destruction in AD 70.

23:29 ***Fortunate indeed are the women who are childless:*** Childlessness was normally a cause of great shame (see note on 1:7), but during this catastrophe, those who didn't have to see their children starve to death would be the fortunate ones.

23:30 ***People will beg the mountains, 'Fall on us':*** Jesus was quoting Hos 10:8. Death would be better than the extended agony and suffering that Jerusalem would experience.

23:31 This verse could also be rendered, *If these things are done to me, the living tree, what will happen to you, the dry tree?* If the Romans crucified an innocent man ***when the tree*** was ***green*** (i.e., during a period of relative peace), what more horrible things would they do ***when it*** was ***dry*** (i.e., when the land had become a tinderbox of revolution)? During the siege of Jerusalem (AD 66–70), the Romans crucified thousands of Jews outside the city of Jerusalem.

23:33 ***The Skull:*** The Greek word *kranion* ("skull") is sometimes rendered *Calvary*, which comes from the Latin word for "skull." The Aramaic term is *Golgotha* (Mark 15:22; Matt 27:33). The location is uncertain, but it has traditionally been associated with the present Church of the Holy Sepulchre. A less likely location is Gordon's Calvary, a rock outcrop near the Garden Tomb (see illustration, p. 1753). • ***they nailed him to the cross:*** Victims were often tied to the cross or nailed through the wrists and ankles to hasten death—here, the bodies had to be buried before sunset due to the Sabbath.

23:34 ***Jesus said, "Father, forgive them, for they don't know what they are doing":*** This sentence is not included in many ancient manuscripts. • ***by throwing dice*** (literally *by casting lots;* see Ps 22:18; John 19:23-24): The prisoner's possessions were treated as spoils of war and divided among the soldiers.

23:35 ***The crowd watched and the leaders scoffed*** (see Ps 22:7-8): Psalm 22 speaks of David, a righteous sufferer, crying out to God for protection. Jesus, David's descendant, was the ultimate righteous sufferer who fulfilled Ps 22.

23:36 ***Sour wine*** (cp. Ps 69:21) was a popular ***drink*** of the lower classes, especially among soldiers.

23:38 The ***sign*** confirmed that Jesus was crucified on the charge of claiming to be ***the King of the Jews*** (cp. John 19:19-22).

23:42 ***remember me when you come into your Kingdom:*** The criminal was perhaps thinking of the resurrection at the end of time, when Jesus would be raised up and vindicated by God.

23:43 Jesus corrected the man by assuring him that ***today*** he would be vindicated in God's presence (see also 2:11; 4:21; 5:26; 19:9). • The word translated ***paradise*** comes from a Persian word that means "garden"; it was used in Jewish literature for the Garden of Eden and also for heaven, the place of eternal bliss for God's people (see 2 Cor 12:4; Rev 2:7; cp. Luke 16:22-23; 2 Cor 5:8).

23:44 ***Darkness*** symbolizes sorrow as well as God's judgment (Ps 23:4; Isa 8:22; 9:1-2).

o'clock. 45The light from the sun was gone. And suddenly, the curtain in the sanctuary of the Temple was torn down the middle. 46Then Jesus shouted, "Father, I entrust my spirit into your hands!" And with those words he breathed his last.

47When the Roman officer overseeing the execution saw what had happened, he worshiped God and said, "Surely this man was innocent." 48And when all the crowd that came to see the crucifixion saw what had happened, they went home in deep sorrow. 49But Jesus' friends, including the women who had followed him from Galilee, stood at a distance watching.

The Burial of Jesus

Luke 23:50-56 // Matt 27:57-61 // Mark 15:42-47 // John 19:38-42

50Now there was a good and righteous man named Joseph. He was a member of the Jewish high council, 51but he had not agreed with the decision and actions of the other religious leaders. He was from the town of Arimathea in Judea, and he was waiting for the Kingdom of God to come. 52He went to Pilate and asked for Jesus' body. 53Then he took the body down from the cross and wrapped it in a long sheet of linen cloth and laid it in a new tomb that had been carved out of rock. 54This was done late on Friday afternoon, the day of preparation, as the Sabbath was about to begin.

55As his body was taken away, the women from Galilee followed and saw the tomb where his body was placed. 56Then they went home and prepared spices and ointments to anoint his body. But by the time they were finished the Sabbath had begun, so they rested as required by the law.

The Resurrection and Ascension of the Savior (24:1-53)

Jesus Is Raised from the Dead

Luke 24:1-12 // Matt 28:1-10 // Mark 16:1-11 // John 20:1-18

24 But very early on Sunday morning the women went to the tomb, taking the spices they had prepared. 2They found that the stone had been rolled away from the entrance. 3So they went in, but they didn't find the body of the Lord Jesus. 4As they stood there puzzled, two men suddenly appeared to them, clothed in dazzling robes.

5The women were terrified and bowed with their faces to the ground. Then the men asked, "Why are you looking among

23:45 Exod 26:31-33; Heb 9:3, 8; 10:19-20
23:46 *Ps 31:5
23:48 Luke 18:13
23:49 Ps 38:11
23:50-56 //Matt 27:57-61; //Mark 15:42-47; //John 19:38-42
23:53 Luke 19:30
23:55 Luke 8:2; 23:49
23:56 Exod 12:16; 20:10; Lev 23:8
24:1-10 //Matt 28:1-8; //Mark 16:1-11; //John 20:1-8
24:1 John 20:19; 1 Cor 16:2
24:3 Mark 16:19; Acts 4:33
24:4 Acts 1:10

23:45 ***the curtain in the sanctuary of the Temple:*** One curtain separated the Temple courtyard from the Holy Place, and another separated the Holy Place from the Most Holy Place. Luke does not say which ***was torn down the middle,*** but it was probably the latter—Jesus' death put an end to the sacrificial system of the Temple and opened a new and permanent way into the presence of God (see Heb 10:19-20).

23:46 ***Father, I entrust my spirit into your hands!*** See Ps 31:5; Ps 31 is another psalm about a righteous sufferer (see note on 23:35).

23:47 ***the Roman officer:*** Literally *the centurion.* • ***innocent*** (or *righteous;* cp. Mark 15:39): See note on 23:14-15. The innocent and righteous servant of the Lord died as a sacrifice for the sins of his people (Isa 53:11).

23:48 ***went home in deep sorrow*** (literally *went home beating their breasts*): Beating the breast was a sign of sorrow and mourning.

23:50-51 Not all the religious leaders opposed Jesus—***Joseph*** had opposed the actions of the council. • The location of ***Arimathea in Judea*** is uncertain; it might be Ramathaim (= Ramah), twenty miles (thirty-two kilometers) northwest of Jerusalem.

23:52 ***He went to Pilate and asked for Jesus' body:*** The Romans used crucifixion as a public warning against revolt, so they did not generally allow a victim to be buried. Instead, they left the body exposed or rotting on the cross. An exception was made in this case, probably because Pilate knew that Jesus was innocent and because of Joseph's position of prestige on the Jewish high council.

23:53 The ***new tomb*** had probably been purchased by Joseph as a family tomb.

23:54 ***This was done late on Friday afternoon, the day of preparation*** (literally *It was the day of preparation*): The Greek text does not explicitly refer to Friday, but simply to the day of preparation for the Sabbath of Passover week; the Sabbath began Friday evening. • ***as the Sabbath was about to begin:*** The body had to be buried quickly, because the Jews could not work during the Sabbath, which began at sunset.

23:55-56 ***The women*** took special note of the tomb's location because they would return with ***spices and ointments to anoint his body.*** The spices were to mask the stench of a rotting corpse. A body would be ***placed*** on a stone bench in the side of ***the tomb*** until the flesh decomposed. The bones would then be collected and placed in a small ossuary, or bone box, and placed on a shelf in the tomb (see illustration, p. 1813). In this way, a tomb could be used for many family members over an extended period of time.

24:1-12 Women were the first to find the tomb empty and to hear the announcement of the resurrection. This is strong evidence for the historicity of the resurrection accounts. In first-century Judaism, women were not regarded as reliable witnesses, so the church would never have created stories in which women discovered the empty tomb.

24:1 ***But very early on Sunday morning*** (literally *But on the first day of the week, very early in the morning*): The early church worshiped on the first day of the week (Sunday) instead of the seventh (Saturday, the Sabbath) because Jesus rose on a Sunday morning (cp. Acts 20:7; Rev 1:10).

24:2 ***The stone*** was probably a large round stone that was ***rolled*** down a track to cover the tomb's ***entrance*** (see illustration, p. 1813).

24:4 ***two men suddenly appeared:*** Angels often appear as young men in Scripture (Gen 18:2; 19:1, 10; Josh 5:13; Judg 13:6-11; Heb 13:2). ***Dazzling*** white ***robes*** symbolize purity and holiness (Dan 10:5-6; Acts 1:10; Rev 4:4; 19:14).

24:5-7 Jesus had ***told*** his followers many times that he would rise from the dead (see 9:22, 44; 17:25; 18:31-34). Jesus' resurrection is a key tenet of the Christian faith (see 1 Cor 15:3-7, 12-57).

24:6 Matt 16:21; Luke 9:22
24:8 John 2:22
24:10 Matt 27:56; Luke 8:1-3
24:11 Mark 16:11
24:12 John 20:3-7
24:13-15 Mark 16:12-13
24:15 Matt 18:20
24:16 John 20:14; 21:4
24:18 John 19:25
24:20 Luke 23:13
24:21 Luke 1:68; Acts 1:6; [g]*lutroō* (3084) ‣1 Tim 2:6
24:22-23 Matt 28:1-8; Mark 16:1-8
24:23 [h]*angelos* (0032) ‣Acts 5:19

the dead for someone who is alive? 6He isn't here! He is risen from the dead! Remember what he told you back in Galilee, 7that the Son of Man must be betrayed into the hands of sinful men and be crucified, and that he would rise again on the third day."

8Then they remembered that he had said this. 9So they rushed back from the tomb to tell his eleven disciples—and everyone else—what had happened. 10It was Mary Magdalene, Joanna, Mary the mother of James, and several other women who told the apostles what had happened. 11But the story sounded like nonsense to the men, so they didn't believe it. 12However, Peter jumped up and ran to the tomb to look. Stooping, he peered in and saw the empty linen wrappings; then he went home again, wondering what had happened.

The Walk to Emmaus
Luke 24:13-34; cp. Mark 16:12-13

13That same day two of Jesus' followers were walking to the village of Emmaus, seven miles from Jerusalem. 14As they walked along they were talking about everything that had happened. 15As they talked and discussed these things, Jesus himself suddenly came and began walking with them. 16But God kept them from recognizing him.

17He asked them, "What are you discussing so intently as you walk along?"

They stopped short, sadness written across their faces. 18Then one of them, Cleopas, replied, "You must be the only person in Jerusalem who hasn't heard about all the things that have happened there the last few days."

19"What things?" Jesus asked.

"The things that happened to Jesus, the man from Nazareth," they said. "He was a prophet who did powerful miracles, and he was a mighty teacher in the eyes of God and all the people. 20But our leading priests and other religious leaders handed him over to be condemned to death, and they crucified him. 21We had hoped he was the Messiah who had come to [g]rescue Israel. This all happened three days ago.

22"Then some women from our group of his followers were at his tomb early this morning, and they came back with an amazing report. 23They said his body was missing, and they had seen [h]angels who told them Jesus is alive! 24Some of our men ran out to see, and sure enough, his body was gone, just as the women had said."

25Then Jesus said to them, "You foolish people! You find it so hard to believe all

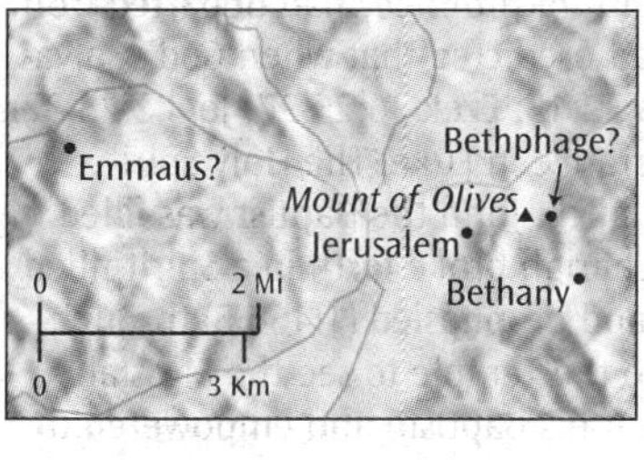

◂ **Jesus' Appearances after His Resurrection (Luke 24:13-52; see also Mark 16:12-13; John 20:19-25).** After Jesus' resurrection, he appears to several women at the tomb outside JERUSALEM (24:1-12; Matt 28:1-10; Mark 16:1-8; John 20:1-18). Later that day he appeared to two disciples on their way to EMMAUS (24:13-34) and then to most of the disciples in JERUSALEM (24:35-49; John 20:19-39). Later Jesus appeared in Galilee (Matt 28:16-17; John 21:1-23). Finally Jesus led his disciples to the MOUNT OF OLIVES, where he ascended to heaven (24:50-51; Acts 1:6-12).

24:7 *Son of Man* is a title Jesus used for himself. • Jesus rose ***on the third day***, counting Friday as the first day and Sunday as the third.

24:9 *His eleven disciples* were the Twelve minus Judas.

24:10 *Mary Magdalene* and ***Joanna*** are mentioned in 8:2-3. ***Mary the mother of James*** is not the mother of James and John (see Matt 27:56), but might be the mother of James, the son of Alphaeus (6:15). See "Women Named Mary" at Matt 27:55-56, p. 1640.

24:12 ***Peter . . . ran to the tomb to look:*** John also accompanied Peter (John 20:2-9).

24:13-34 This account is Luke's most important contribution to the resurrection narratives. Jesus corrected these disciples' misunderstanding by showing from Scripture that it was necessary for the Messiah to suffer. He then opened their eyes to the truth of his resurrection.

24:13 *two of Jesus' followers:* Jesus had many disciples in addition to the Twelve (see 10:1, 17). Nothing else is known of Cleopas (24:18) or the other disciple (who may have been his wife). They were probably returning from celebrating the Passover in Jerusalem. • ***seven miles:*** Greek *60 stadia* [11.1 kilometers].

24:16 ***God kept them from recognizing him:*** The Greek uses a passive construction (*they were kept from recognizing him*) known as a "divine passive," with God as the implied subject. God intentionally blinded their eyes until the moment of revelation, when Jesus broke bread with them (24:30-31; cp. 2 Kgs 6:17).

24:18 ***the only person in Jerusalem who hasn't heard about all the things:*** The Romans conducted crucifixions at major public crossroads to make an example of the victims and warn others against revolt. It was unthinkable to these disciples that a Passover pilgrim would not have heard of Jesus' crucifixion.

24:19 Jesus is often portrayed as a ***prophet*** in Luke's Gospel (see 7:16; cp. the description of Moses in Acts 7:22).

24:21 ***We had hoped he was the Messiah:*** Literally *we had hoped he was the one who would deliver Israel.* This is a reference to the Messiah—the crucifixion had dashed their hopes.

24:22 ***an amazing report:*** See 24:10-11.

24:25-26 ***the prophets wrote . . . that the Messiah would have to suffer:*** The crucifixion did not negate Jesus' identity as the Messiah but confirmed it, because the death of the Messiah was predicted in Scripture. Jesus rebuked the two for not recognizing from Scripture that the Messiah had to suffer (see Isa 50:4-9; 52:13–53:12; Pss 2; 16; 22; 118; cp. Luke 18:32; 20:17; 23:37; Acts 2:25-28; 4:25-26).

that the prophets wrote in the Scriptures. [26]Wasn't it clearly predicted that the Messiah would have to suffer all these things before entering his glory?" [27]Then Jesus took them through the writings of Moses and all the prophets, explaining from all the Scriptures the things concerning himself.

[28]By this time they were nearing Emmaus and the end of their journey. Jesus acted as if he were going on, [29]but they begged him, "Stay the night with us, since it is getting late." So he went home with them. [30]As they sat down to eat, he took the bread and blessed it. Then he broke it and gave it to them. [31]Suddenly, their eyes were opened, and they recognized him. And at that moment he disappeared!

[32]They said to each other, "Didn't our hearts burn within us as he talked with us on the road and explained the Scriptures to us?" [33]And within the hour they were on their way back to Jerusalem. There they found the eleven disciples and the others who had gathered with them, [34]who said, "The Lord has really risen! He appeared to Peter."

Jesus Appears to His Disciples

Luke 24:35-49 // John 20:19-23

[35]Then the two from Emmaus told their story of how Jesus had appeared to them as they were walking along the road, and how they had recognized him as he was breaking the bread. [36]And just as they were telling about it, Jesus himself was suddenly standing there among them. "Peace be with you," he said. [37]But the whole group was startled and frightened, thinking they were seeing a ghost!

[38]"Why are you frightened?" he asked. "Why are your hearts filled with doubt? [39]Look at my hands. Look at my feet. You can see that it's really me. Touch me and make sure that I am not a ghost, because ghosts don't have bodies, as you see that I do." [40]As he spoke, he showed them his hands and his feet.

[41]Still they stood there in disbelief, filled with joy and wonder. Then he asked them, "Do you have anything here to eat?" [42]They gave him a piece of broiled fish, [43]and he ate it as they watched.

24:26
Matt 26:24
Luke 24:7, 44
John 12:23-24; 13:31-32
Acts 17:3
Heb 2:10; 5:5

24:27
Gen 3:15
Num 21:8-9; 24:17
Deut 18:15, 18
Isa 4:2; 7:14; 9:1-2, 6-7
Ezek 34:23-24; 37:24-25

24:34
1 Cor 15:5

24:36-49
//Matt 28:16-20
//John 20:19-23

The Coming of the Spirit of God (24:49)

Luke 1:15, 35, 41, 67; 2:24-27; 3:22; 4:1, 18
Acts 2:4, 17-18
Num 24:2
Judg 3:10
1 Sam 10:10; 16:13
Isa 32:15
Ezek 11:5; 36:26-27
Joel 2:28-32

In the OT, the Spirit of God occasionally came upon individuals to empower them for God's service and for prophecy (Num 24:2; Judg 3:10; 1 Sam 10:10; 16:13; Ezek 11:5). In the Judaism of Jesus' day, there was a widespread belief that the Spirit of prophecy had departed from Israel with the last of the OT prophets. But the prophets had predicted that when God's salvation arrived, he would pour out his Spirit on all people (Isa 32:15; Ezek 36:26-27; Joel 2:28-32).

This prophecy finds its initial fulfillment in the birth narrative in Luke. The Holy Spirit inspired prophetic witness and guided the events of Jesus' birth. John the Baptist was filled with the Spirit even before he was born (1:15, 41), and Zechariah broke forth in a Spirit-filled hymn of praise to God (1:67). Mary conceived Jesus (1:35) and prophesied (1:46-55) through the power of the Spirit, and Simeon was led by the Spirit to the Temple to see the Messiah (2:24-27). Later in his life, Jesus was anointed by the Spirit at his baptism and empowered to accomplish his role as the Messiah (3:22; 4:1, 18).

Following his ascension, Jesus fulfilled the OT prophecies by pouring out his Spirit on his disciples on the Day of Pentecost, empowering them to take the Good News of salvation to the ends of the earth (24:49; Acts 1:8; 2:4, 17-18). Throughout Acts, the church accomplished its mission through the guidance, power, and direction of the Holy Spirit. For Luke, the coming of the Spirit marks the beginning of God's salvation—God's presence and power now reside with his people.

24:27 ***All the Scriptures,*** meaning all of the OT, point forward to the coming of Jesus the Messiah and the salvation that he would bring.

24:29 ***they begged him, "Stay the night with us":*** Middle Eastern hospitality demanded that they offer food and lodging to this stranger (Gen 18:3; 19:2; Judg 19:5-9).

24:30 ***As they sat down to eat*** (or *As they reclined*): The meal is a symbol of the messianic banquet and of the salvation that God is accomplishing (Isa 25:6-8; see "The Messianic Banquet" at 14:1-24, p. 1737). • ***Then he broke it and gave it to them:*** This action recalls the feeding of the 5,000 (9:16) and the institution of the Lord's Supper (22:19).

24:31 ***their eyes were opened:*** This is another example of the "divine passive" (see note on 24:16); God opened their eyes at the breaking of the bread. • ***at that moment he disappeared!*** In his resurrected and transformed body, Jesus had abilities not realized before the resurrection (see 24:36; 1 Cor 15:20-23, 35-57).

24:34 ***Peter*** (Greek *Simon*): This appearance to Simon Peter is not narrated in the Gospels, but Paul independently confirms it in 1 Cor 15:5.

24:39 ***ghosts don't have bodies, as you see that I do:*** In his resurrected state, Jesus was not an immaterial spirit, but had a real immortal and imperishable body. Believers will receive similar bodies at the final resurrection (1 Cor 15:35-57).

24:44
Luke 24:27
[i]*nomos* (3551)
‣Acts 15:5

24:47
Acts 2:38; 10:43;
13:38; 26:18
[i]*metanoia* (3341)
‣Acts 11:18

24:48
John 15:27

24:49
Acts 1:4-5; 2:1-4

24:50-53
Mark 16:19
Acts 1:4-14

24:53
Acts 2:46; 3:1; 5:42

44 Then he said, "When I was with you
before, I told you that everything written
about me in the [i]law of Moses and the
prophets and in the Psalms must be fulfilled." 45 Then he opened their minds to
understand the Scriptures. 46 And he said,
"Yes, it was written long ago that the Messiah would suffer and die and rise from the
dead on the third day. 47 It was also written
that this message would be proclaimed in
the authority of his name to all the nations,
beginning in Jerusalem: 'There is forgiveness of sins for all who [i]repent.' 48 You are
witnesses of all these things.

49 "And now I will send the Holy Spirit,
just as my Father promised. But stay here in
the city until the Holy Spirit comes and fills
you with power from heaven."

The Ascension

Luke 24:50-53 // Mark 16:19-20 // Acts 1:6-11

50 Then Jesus led them to Bethany, and lifting his hands to heaven, he blessed them.
51 While he was blessing them, he left them
and was taken up to heaven. 52 So they worshiped him and then returned to Jerusalem
filled with great joy. 53 And they spent all of
their time in the Temple, praising God.

24:44 ***the law of Moses and the prophets and in the Psalms:*** Jesus referred to the three sections of the Hebrew Scriptures: the Law, the Prophets, and the Writings (see Old Testament Introduction, "The Canon of the Old Testament," p. 4). The entire OT points to God's salvation through Christ.

24:46 ***that the Messiah would suffer and die:*** See note on 24:25-26.

24:47 The OT was the universal proclamation of the Gospel to ***all the nations*** (or *all peoples*): See Isa 42:6; 49:6; Joel 2:28-32; Amos 9:11-12; Acts 2:17-21; 13:47; 15:16-18.

24:48 The primary role of the apostles in the book of Acts was to be ***witnesses*** to the fulfillment of Scripture in the life, death, and resurrection of Jesus (see Acts 1:8).

24:49 ***I will send the Holy Spirit:*** The OT predicted that God would pour out his Spirit on all people (Isa 32:15; Jer 31:33; Ezek 36:26-27; Joel 2:28-32). This prediction was fulfilled on the Day of Pentecost (Acts 2:14-21).

24:50-53 Luke also narrates Jesus' ascension in Acts 1:1-11. For Luke, Jesus' ascension confirmed his vindication, exaltation, and enthronement at God's right hand as Messiah and Lord (Acts 2:24-36). From his position of glory and authority in heaven, Jesus guides and directs his church.

24:50 ***Bethany:*** See notes on 19:28-29; see also Acts 1:11-12; cp. Zech 14:4.

24:51 Cp. 2 Kgs 2:11. Jesus' ascension was his exaltation to a position of authority over all creation (see Acts 2:32-36; 5:31; Eph 1:19-23; Phil 2:9-11; Heb 1:13).

24:53 ***The Temple*** was a place of worship as well as of sacrifice. The apostles continued in their Jewish manner of worship because their goal was not to create a new religion but to announce the fulfillment of Scripture's promises of salvation through Jesus the Messiah.

THE GOSPEL ACCORDING TO JOHN

John wrote his Gospel to inspire faith. John knew Jesus intimately, and John's Gospel provides an intimate portrait of the Lord. John referred to himself as "the disciple Jesus loved." His Gospel has become the "beloved Gospel" of the church. Here we meet Nicodemus, doubting Thomas, Lazarus, and the Samaritan woman at the well. John records for us Jesus' most memorable sayings, his longest sermons, and his most profound miracles. Here we meet God face to face.

SETTING

A small community of Christians lived in ancient Ephesus during the late first century AD. They had learned the remarkable story of Jesus from the apostles Paul and John. This early church became strong in faith under the leadership of these men. While many stories circulated about Jesus, the apostle John had his own recollections and insights. In the later years of his life, John wrote these stories down, providing his followers—and us—with the fourth Gospel.

As an evangelist, pastor, and theologian, John's desire above all was for his followers to believe that Jesus Christ is the Son of God (20:31). He realized that they had not had the privilege of seeing Jesus' many signs and miracles as he had (20:29). John's authority and deep experience with Jesus ring out from every story he told. As a valued eyewitness to Jesus' life (19:35), John was the source of many stories from faraway Galilee and Judea. John had heard, seen, and touched the Word of life (see 1 Jn 1:1-4). He told about Nicodemus and rebirth, described Jesus' miracle at Cana, and recorded many other episodes.

As the Christians of Ephesus told their fellow citizens about Jesus, they quickly found themselves debating about Jesus with rabbis in the local synagogues. Was Jesus truly the Son of God? How could he

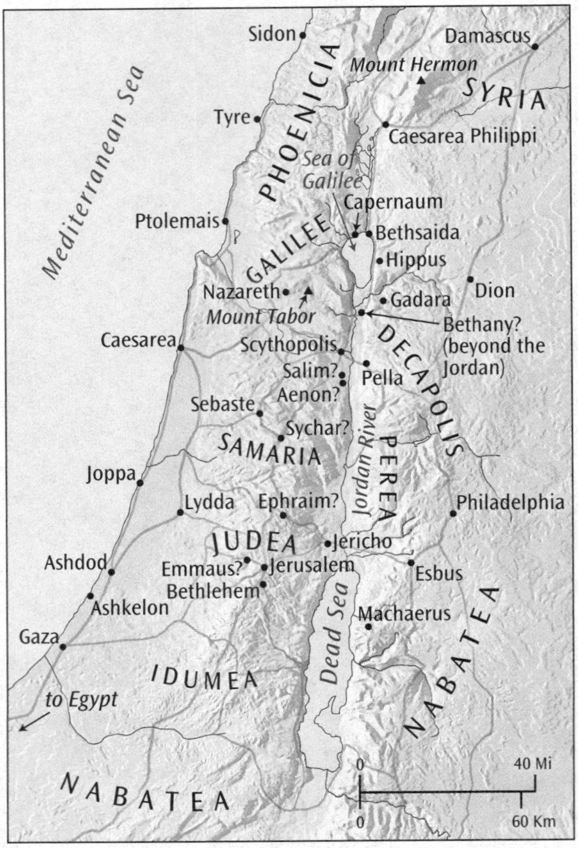

Key Places in the Gospel of John. The book of John describes Jesus' ministry in GALILEE (2:1-12; 4:43-54; 6:1–7:9), JERUSALEM (2:13–3:21; 5:1-47; 7:10-10:42; 12:12-50), JUDEA (3:22; 11:1-44; 12:1-11), and SAMARIA (4:4-42). The book includes a full account Jesus' death and resurrection in JERUSALEM (13:1–20:31) and his post-resurrection appearance to his disciples beside the SEA OF GALILEE (21:1-23).

be the Messiah? Can Christians legitimately claim to be "children of Abraham"? Could anyone prove that Jesus' claim of being sent from God was true? Guided by the Holy Spirit in his teaching and writing, John brilliantly led his Christian readers through these debates.

Tensions grew. As more Jews converted, small churches grew up alongside synagogues and began converting their members. Opposition to the Christian believers was inevitable. However, John stood by the church during terrible persecution and conflict. When it seemed that the fledgling church's struggle with the prestigious synagogue community would overwhelm them, John courageously gave witness to the ministry of Jesus Christ. When false teachers later brought internal controversy and conflict to the church, John again gave the community strength. Writing letters to encourage and exhort (see 1, 2, and 3 John), John became the heroic pastor–theologian of Asia Minor.

John's writing is as beloved today as it was in the earliest years of the church. Few books of the Bible have influenced Christian life and thought like John's profound and dynamic Gospel. By combining intimacy of expression with penetrating insight, John provides a deeply satisfying portrait of Christ.

OUTLINE

1:1-18
Prologue: Christ, the Eternal Word

1:19–12:50
The Book of Signs: The Word Displays His Glory

13:1–20:31
The Book of Glory: The Word Is Glorified

21:1-25
Epilogue: The Word Commissions His Followers

TIMELINE

about 6~4 BC
Birth of Jesus

AD 18~36
Caiaphas as high priest

AD 26–36
Pontius Pilate as governor of Judea

AD 28~29
Jesus clears the Temple

Passover, AD 30 or 33
Jesus' crucifixion and resurrection

AD 65~70
Mark writes the Gospel of Mark

AD 65~80
Matthew writes the Gospel of Matthew, Luke writes the Gospel of Luke

before AD 90
John writes the Gospel of John
John writes 1–3 John

AD 60s or 90s
John writes Revelation

SUMMARY

John divided his Gospel into two main sections: chs 1–12 and chs 13–21. The first section, which has been called "The Book of Signs," tells about Jesus' public ministry of revealing himself to the Jewish world. The second section, sometimes called "The Book of Glory," records Jesus' private words to his disciples and tells of his death and resurrection.

Chapters 1–12. The Gospel prologue (1:1-18) artfully summarizes the entrance of God's Word into the world. Jesus was baptized and called his earliest followers (1:19-51). Then a series of remarkable events (chs 2–4) highlights Jesus' revelation of himself to the Jews. At a wedding in Cana, Jesus turned water into wine. In Jerusalem, he used a whip to drive corruption and money-dealing out of the Temple. He debated the meaning of spiritual rebirth with a rabbi named Nicodemus. At a well in Samaria, he met a woman with a checkered marital history and offered her "living water," which no well can ever duplicate. In each of these events, Jesus unveiled his identity.

In the following section (chs 5–10), Jesus appears at a number of Jewish festivals, using ancient OT symbols and practices to reveal himself to God's people. On the Sabbath, Jesus worked by healing a lame man. On Passover, Jesus provided bread for 5,000. In the symbolic light of the Festival of Shelters, Jesus healed a blind man, reinforcing his own identity as the light

of the world. John's clear message is that Jesus came to fulfill what Judaism had promised since OT times.

Then Jesus began to prepare for his death and resurrection. John describes Jesus' arrival in Bethany, a town just east of Jerusalem (ch 11). His friend Lazarus had died, and Jesus raised him to life. Following this event (ch 12), Jesus made his final public appeal to the world to believe in him and his mission.

Chapters 13–21. John turns to Jesus' death and resurrection, reminding readers that the cross is not a sign of despair but a picture of glory and wonder. Jesus was returning to the Father and needed to prepare his disciples for his departure. At his final Passover meal (chs 13–17), Jesus disclosed to his disciples the things nearest to his heart. He told them candidly about his death and departure to the Father. He reassured them that he would not abandon them, but that he would return and turn their sorrow into joy. He promised them the gift of the Holy Spirit. Finally, Jesus prayed for them.

Following this Passover meal, Jesus led his followers east of the city and across a valley to an olive grove called Gethsemane (ch 18). Judas soon appeared with a large contingent of Roman soldiers and Temple guards. Following his arrest, Jesus stood before the Jewish high council to be interrogated, first by Annas and then by Caiaphas, the reigning high priest. By morning, the Jewish leaders took Jesus to the Roman governor, Pontius Pilate, who asked probing questions about Jesus' identity. Pilate, coaxed by the Jewish leaders, decided to crucify Jesus (ch 19).

The climax of John's Gospel is Jesus' resurrection from the dead (ch 20). This event begins a series of dramatic stories in which Jesus appeared to his followers and encouraged them. He gave them the Holy Spirit and commissioned them to represent him to the world. Jesus then gave his disciples their marching orders (ch 21). He reminded them of his power (21:1-14), reinstated Peter (21:15-17), and instructed him to follow him in his mission (21:18-23).

AUTHOR AND DATE

As with the other Gospels, John provides no explicit evidence as to its author, although the enigmatic figure of the "beloved disciple" provides clear clues (see 13:23; 19:26-27; 20:2-10; 21:7, 20-24). The Gospel of John must be connected with this person, for he is identified as the eyewitness source of this record of Jesus' life (19:35; 21:24).

Who was this beloved disciple? Leaders in the early church, beginning in AD 125, wrote that it was the apostle John, the son of Zebedee (see, e.g., Eusebius, *Church History* 3.23). This traditional view is sound and fully defensible. John was one of the Twelve and, along with James (his brother) and Peter, formed an inner circle around Jesus (Mark 3:17; Acts 1:13). The Gospel reflects this close perspective as it highlights Peter and John. Most scholars believe that John completed writing his Gospel by AD 90.

The truth which this Gospel enshrines—the truth that Jesus Christ is the very Word Incarnate—[is] the one study which alone can fitly prepare us for a joyful immortality hereafter.

J. B. LIGHTFOOT, *Biblical Essays*

RECIPIENTS

John most likely wrote his Gospel for Jewish Christians living abroad in the Mediterranean world; with their grasp of Hebrew slipping, these believers were caught between the Jewish and Greek cultures.

John's knowledge of Palestine and Judaism is reflected throughout his Gospel.

John assumed that his audience was unfamiliar with some particulars of Jesus' world. For example, he explained that *rabbi* is a Hebrew word meaning "teacher" (1:38), and he gave an alternate name for the Sea of Galilee (6:1). At the same time, John assumed that his readers were familiar with Jewish traditions, concepts, and festivals. They probably were also familiar with the basic story presented in Mark's Gospel. For example, John refers to John the Baptist's imprisonment (3:24) without ever telling the complete story.

I like the comparison of John's Gospel to a pool in which a child may wade and an elephant can swim. It is both simple and profound. It is for the beginner in the faith and for the mature Christian. Its appeal is immediate and never failing.

LEON MORRIS,
The Gospel according to John

MEANING AND MESSAGE

Revelation and Redemption. "The light shines in the darkness, and the darkness can never extinguish it" (1:5). The light of God has inhabited the world: Christ reveals the Father (14:9). In Christ we see the glory of God in a human being. Even though Jesus was persecuted, tried, and crucified, the light cannot be extinguished. Jesus' purpose in revealing God is to redeem people: "The Word gave life to everything that was created, and his life brought light to everyone" (1:4). Those who embrace Christ's revelation and redemption with faith will gain eternal life.

Worship and the Spirit. Worship must take place "in spirit and in truth" (4:24), energized and formed by the Spirit of God. Nicodemus had to be born of "water and Spirit" to enter the Kingdom of God (3:5). In Galilee, after feeding the 5,000, Jesus told the crowd that living bread is available in his body, which was to be sacrificed. He instructed them to consume his body and blood, symbolic of the Lord's Supper (6:51-59). Yet worship focusing only on the individual elements and not accompanied by the Spirit of God is worth nothing (6:63).

Jesus Christ. John recorded Jesus' descriptions about his nature, origin, and relationship to the Father. Jesus affirmed his oneness with the Father (10:30; 14:9-10) and their unity of purpose (5:17; 8:42), as well as their personal distinctiveness (14:28; 17:1-5). Jesus even used the very title ("I AM") that God used for himself in the OT, thus affirming his own deity (8:58; 18:5; Exod 3:14).

The Holy Spirit. John's Gospel underscores the Holy Spirit as a central feature of Jesus' human experience (chs 4, 7) and of our lives (ch 3). The transforming power of God's Spirit is a hallmark of true discipleship.

The Mission of the Church. God sent Jesus into the world (8:18) to proclaim his glory and to testify to the Good News of redemption. In his departure, the Son passed this mission on to the Spirit (16:5-11), who in turn would fill the church and empower believers to fulfill the mission of Jesus in the world (20:20-23; Matt 28:18-20; Acts 1:7-8).

The End Times. Early Christians anticipated the return of Christ, and John affirms this anticipation. Yet in the meantime, believers can experience Jesus' longed-for presence in the Holy Spirit. Jesus' announcement of the Spirit's coming echoes the language of his own second coming (see 14:15-23). In a vital way, Jesus is already with us in the Spirit as we continue to look forward to Christ's personal return at the end of history.

FURTHER READING

CRAIG L. BLOMBERG
The Historical Reliability of John's Gospel: Issues and Commentary (2001)

F. F. BRUCE
The Gospel of John: Introduction, Exposition and Notes (1983)

GARY M. BURGE
John (2000)

PHILIP W. COMFORT
I Am the Way: A Spiritual Journey through the Gospel of John (2001)

PHILIP W. COMFORT AND WENDELL C. HAWLEY
Opening John's Gospel and Epistles (2009)

GRANT OSBORNE
John in *Cornerstone Biblical Commentary*, vol. 13 (2007)

RODNEY A. WHITACRE
John (1999)

1. PROLOGUE: CHRIST, THE ETERNAL WORD (1:1-18)

1 1 In the beginning the [a]Word already
existed.
The [a]Word was with God,
and the [a]Word was God.
2 He existed in the beginning with God.
3 God created everything through him,
and nothing was created except
through him.
4 The Word gave life to everything that
was created,
and his life brought light to everyone.
5 The light shines in the darkness,
and the darkness can never
extinguish it.

6 God sent a man, John the Baptist, 7 to
tell about the light so that everyone might
believe because of his testimony. 8 John
himself was not the light; he was simply a
witness to tell about the light. 9 The one who
is the true light, who gives light to everyone,
was coming into the world.
10 He came into the very world he created,
but the world didn't recognize him. 11 He
came to his own people, and even they rejected him. 12 But to all who believed him and
accepted him, he gave the right to become
children of God. 13 They are reborn—not
with a physical birth resulting from human
passion or plan, but a birth that comes from
God.
14 So the [b]Word became [c]human and
made his home among us. He was full of unfailing love and faithfulness. And we have
seen his [d]glory, the [d]glory of the Father's
[e]one and only Son.
15 John testified about him when he
shouted to the crowds, "This is the one I
was talking about when I said, 'Someone is
coming after me who is far greater than I
am, for he existed long before me.' "
16 From his abundance we have all received one gracious blessing after another.

1:1 Gen 1:1; Col 1:15; [a]*logos* (3056) ‣John 1:14
1:3 1 Cor 8:6; Col 1:16-17; Heb 1:2
1:4 John 8:12; 11:25; 14:6; 1 Jn 5:12, 20
1:5 John 3:19; 9:5
1:9 1 Jn 2:8
1:12 Rom 8:15-16, 29
1:14 Rom 8:3; Gal 4:4-7; Phil 2:6-8; 1 Tim 3:16; 1 Jn 1:1; 4:2-3; [b]*logos* (3056) ‣Acts 6:2; [c]*sarx* (4561) ‣John 3:6; [d]*doxa* (1391) ‣Rom 3:23; [e]*monogenēs* (3439) ‣John 1:18

1:1-18 The beginning of this prologue (1:1-5) might be a poem or hymn sung by the earliest Christians. The prologue's themes—the coming of the light into the world, the rejection of the light, and its gift of new life to believers—prepares readers for the story that follows.

1:1 Echoing Gen 1:1, John's Gospel introduces Jesus Christ, through whom God created everything (1:3); Jesus also creates new life in those who believe (1:12-13). The Gospel opens with its central affirmation, that Jesus Christ, ***the Word*** (Greek *logos*), not only revealed God but ***was God***. In Greek thought, the *logos* was the rational principle guiding the universe and making life coherent. For Jewish people, the *logos* was the word of the Lord, an expression of God's wisdom and creative power. By Jesus' time, the *logos* was viewed as coming from God and having his personality (see Ps 33:6, 9; Prov 8:22-31); John affirmed this understanding (1:14).

1:3-4 ***and nothing was created except through him. The Word gave life to everything that was created:*** Or *and nothing that was created was created except through him. The Word gave life to everything.* The Greek grammar allows either possibility.

1:3 God is the *logos* (1:1-2); all that God does, the *logos* likewise does. Throughout his Gospel, John rightly viewed Jesus' actions as divine activity.

1:4-5 God created ***light*** and dispelled the ***darkness*** (Gen 1:2-5). The darkness resists God (3:19-21; 12:35; Matt 6:23; Acts 26:17-18; Eph 4:17-19; 5:7-14; 2 Pet 1:19; 1 Jn 1:5-7; 2:9-11).

1:4 ***The Word gave life:*** Life was God's original gift to his creatures (Gen 1:20-28; 2:7). Now the *logos* would give these creatures the possibility of new life through rebirth (1:13). • As one of his first creative acts, God ***brought light*** (Gen 1:3). Now, in the re-creation of humanity through Jesus Christ, God offered light and life anew. Light is a key theme in John's Gospel.

1:5 ***the darkness can never extinguish it:*** Or *the darkness has not understood it;* literally *the darkness cannot grasp it.* The Greek word *katalambanō* ("grasp") can mean either "understand" or "be hostile"; in John's Gospel, it means hostility. The darkness would try to destroy Jesus (the light), but it would fail. The light would successfully bring salvation to the world.

1:6-9 ***God sent a man, John the Baptist*** (literally *a man named John*) to herald Jesus' coming and to prepare God's people to receive Jesus as God's Son and Messiah (see 1:19-37; Luke 1:5-25, 57-80; 3:1-22; see also Isa 40:3; Mal 4:5-6).

1:8 Some Jews speculated that John the Baptist was the Messiah; some of his followers were even reluctant to follow Jesus (3:22-30). However, John the Baptist ***was not the light;*** his role was to announce Jesus (1:19-34).

1:10 ***The world*** cannot ***recognize*** the true light even when it encounters its Creator. The world lives in rebellion, loving darkness more than light (3:19; see "The World" at 17:5-26, p. 1807).

1:12 Only through divine renewal can people follow the light and enter God's family (3:1-17). • Individuals must believe in Christ ***to become children of God*** (12:35-36).

1:13 ***a birth that comes from God:*** People can escape the darkness only by God's grace (8:12; 12:35-36, 44-46).

1:14 The idea that ***the Word became human*** (literally *became flesh*) stunned both Greeks and Jews. Greeks separated the sphere of God from the mundane world of humanity, which they called *flesh* (Greek *sarx*). John wrote that God himself became *flesh* in Christ (cp. 1:1). Jesus' humanity and divinity were complete, not partial. The two ideas—Jesus as 100-percent divine and 100-percent human—form the bedrock of a Christian understanding of Christ. • ***the Word . . . made his home*** (Greek *skēnoō*, "pitched his tent") ***among us:*** This Greek word is related to the word used for the OT Tabernacle (Greek *skēnē*, "tent, tabernacle"), the tent in the wilderness where the Lord's glory resided and where Israel came to worship (Exod 25:8-9). The Father's glory in the Tabernacle (Exod 40:34-38) was now present in Jesus Christ (2:11; 12:23-28, 41; 17:1-5). • Jesus offered God's ***unfailing love and faithfulness*** (or *grace and truth*). Despite the world's hostile darkness, Jesus entered the world to save it (3:15-17).

1:15 ***he existed long before me:*** In a society where age was respected and honored (Lev 19:32; contrast Isa 3:5), John the Baptist emphasized Jesus' honor by pointing to his existence even before creation (1:1-3).

1:16 ***received one gracious blessing after another:*** Or *received the grace of Christ rather than the grace of the law;* a literal translation is *received grace upon grace.*

1:17
Exod 31:18; 34:28
[f]*christos* (5547)
›John 1:41

1:18
Col 1:15
[g]*monogenēs* (3439)
›John 3:16

1:19-28
Matt 3:1-12
Mark 1:2-8
Luke 3:1-16

1:20
Luke 3:15
John 3:28

1:21
Deut 18:15
Mal 4:5
Matt 11:14

1:23
*Isa 40:3
Mal 3:1

1:26
Matt 3:11
Mark 1:8
Luke 3:16

17For the law was given through Moses, but
God's unfailing love and faithfulness came
through Jesus [f]Christ. 18No one has ever
seen God. But the [g]unique One, who is himself God, is near to the Father's heart. He
has revealed God to us.

2. THE BOOK OF SIGNS: THE WORD DISPLAYS HIS GLORY (1:19–12:50)

Jesus and John the Baptist (1:19-51)

The Testimony of John the Baptist

John 1:23 // Matt 3:1-3 // Mark 1:2-3 // Luke 3:2b-6
John 1:24-28 // Matt 3:11-12 // Mark 1:7-8 // Luke 3:15-18

19This was John's testimony when the
Jewish leaders sent priests and Temple assistants from Jerusalem to ask John, "Who
are you?" 20He came right out and said, "I
am not the Messiah."
21"Well then, who are you?" they asked.
"Are you Elijah?"
"No," he replied.
"Are you the Prophet we are expecting?"
"No."
22"Then who are you? We need an answer
for those who sent us. What do you have to
say about yourself?"
23John replied in the words of the prophet
Isaiah:

"I am a voice shouting in the wilderness,
'Clear the way for the LORD's coming!'"

24Then the Pharisees who had been sent
25asked him, "If you aren't the Messiah or
Elijah or the Prophet, what right do you
have to baptize?"
26John told them, "I baptize with water,
but right here in the crowd is someone you

The Word (1:1-18)

Gen 1:3-28
Ps 33:6, 9
Prov 8:22-31
Isa 40:8
1 Jn 1:1
Rev 19:13

John raises the curtain on his Gospel with a stunning description of Jesus Christ as "the Word" (Greek *logos,* 1:1). Both Greek and Jewish listeners in the first century would immediately recognize the profound meaning of this title. Greeks would have thought of the seminal forces that sustain the universe. Jewish minds would have thought back to God creating the world with his word (Gen 1:3-28). In Jesus' day, the word of God took on creative personal attributes (Ps 33:6, 9). Jews viewed God's word as personifying divine wisdom. Through Wisdom, God extended himself into the cosmos, creating the world (Prov 8:22-31).

In John's drama, Jesus shares the same essence as God; the Son existed before time, and he was the agent of all creation. John anchors the divinity of Jesus in this ancient Jewish concept of Wisdom. The divine Wisdom that has existed from before time with God can now be known in Jesus Christ. In perhaps the most outrageous verse penned by an apostle, John writes that this Logos, this Wisdom, became flesh and lived among us as a human (1:14). What God is, the Logos is. The Logos is Jesus Christ.

1:17 *the law:* That is, the Torah, the first five books of the Bible (Genesis through Deuteronomy). • Although ***God's unfailing love and faithfulness*** (or *grace and truth*) are in the Torah, these qualities are fully revealed in Christ (3:16; 13:1).

1:18 Moses was denied his desire to see God directly (Exod 33:18-20). Only Jesus has seen the Father, so he alone completely knows him and can tell us about him (3:32-35; 14:9-10). • ***But the unique One, who is himself God*** (some manuscripts read *But the one and only Son*): The Son, who sees the Father, *is himself God*—not simply a messenger who knows something about God. John explicitly affirms Christ's deity. Jesus shares the substance of God's being.

1:19–12:50 Jesus reveals himself to the world through his miraculous signs and sermons. Audiences were divided: Some wanted to believe in him; others opposed him. This division intensifies as the book unfolds. Jesus ended his public ministry with a final appeal for people to believe in him (12:44-50).

1:19-51 John's Gospel gives limited attention to John the Baptist compared to the synoptic Gospels (Matt 3:1-6; Mark 1:2-6; Luke 1:1-24, 57-80; 3:1-13). Yet the apostle John wants us to see that John the Baptist correctly identified and exalted Jesus. John the Baptist's disciples leave him and follow Jesus; Jesus took over the ministry John began, increasing as John decreased (3:30).

1:19 ***Jewish leaders:*** See "The Jewish Leaders" at 5:9-18, p. 1779. • ***and Temple assistants:*** Literally *and Levites.*

1:20 The Jews expected the ***Messiah*** (the Hebrew form of the Greek word *Christ*) to bring spiritual leadership and political redemption to Israel (see Deut 18:15; see also the Jewish intertestamental book *Psalms of Solomon*).

1:21 ***Elijah*** was to be the Messiah's forerunner (Mal 4:5). John the Baptist fulfilled the forerunner's role, though he denied being the prophet Elijah (see Matt 11:14; Luke 1:17). • ***Are you the Prophet we are expecting?*** Literally *Are you the Prophet?* See Deut 18:15, 18; Mal 4:5-6; see also John 6:14; 7:40-41.

1:22-23 ***Then who are you?*** John the Baptist simply wanted to be known as ***a voice shouting in the wilderness*** (see Isa 40:3).

1:24 The ***Pharisees*** were deeply devoted to the Scriptures and earnestly desired a righteous life (see "Pharisees" at Matt 3:7, p. 1581). They also believed in the coming Messiah, which explains their inquiries here. Some Pharisees became believers in Jesus (Acts 15:5), including the apostle Paul (Acts 26:5; Phil 3:5).

1:25-26 Jewish baptisms were ritual washings for becoming ceremonially pure following contact with impurity (Lev 8:6; Num 19:7). • John's announcement of the Messiah's arrival required that participants confess their sins and be baptized (Matt 3:6). Baptism later became the symbol of membership in Jesus' kingdom (Acts 2:38; see also John 4:1-2). • ***with:*** Or *in;* also in 1:31, 33.

do not recognize. [27]Though his ministry follows mine, I'm not even worthy to be his slave and untie the straps of his sandal."

[28]This encounter took place in Bethany, an area east of the Jordan River, where John was baptizing.

Jesus, the Lamb of God
John 1:29-34 // Matt 3:13-17 // Mark 1:9-11 // Luke 3:21-22

[29]The next day John saw Jesus coming toward him and said, "Look! The [h]Lamb of God who takes away the sin of the world! [30]He is the one I was talking about when I said, 'A man is coming after me who is far greater than I am, for he existed long before me.' [31]I did not recognize him as the Messiah, but I have been baptizing with water so that he might be revealed to Israel."

[32]Then John testified, "I saw the Holy Spirit descending like a dove from heaven and resting upon him. [33]I didn't know he was the one, but when God sent me to baptize with water, he told me, 'The one on whom you see the Spirit descend and rest is the one who will baptize with the Holy Spirit.' [34]I saw this happen to Jesus, so I testify that he is the Chosen One of God."

The First Disciples

[35]The following day John was again standing with two of his disciples. [36]As Jesus walked by, John looked at him and declared, "Look! There is the [i]Lamb of God!" [37]When John's two disciples heard this, they followed Jesus.

[38]Jesus looked around and saw them following. "What do you want?" he asked them.

They replied, "[j]Rabbi" (which means "Teacher"), "where are you staying?"

[39]"Come and see," he said. It was about four o'clock in the afternoon when they went with him to the place where he was staying, and they remained with him the rest of the day.

[40]Andrew, Simon Peter's brother, was one of these men who heard what John said and then followed Jesus. [41]Andrew went to find his brother, Simon, and told him, "We have found the [k]Messiah" (which means "Christ").

[42]Then Andrew brought Simon to meet Jesus. Looking intently at Simon, Jesus said, "Your name is Simon, son of John—but you will be called Cephas" (which means "[a]Peter").

[43]The next day Jesus decided to go to Galilee. He found Philip and said to him, "Come, follow me." [44]Philip was from Bethsaida, Andrew and Peter's hometown.

[45]Philip went to look for Nathanael and told him, "We have found the very person Moses and the prophets wrote about! His name is Jesus, the son of Joseph from Nazareth."

[46]"Nazareth!" exclaimed Nathanael. "Can anything good come from Nazareth?"

"Come and see for yourself," Philip replied.

[47]As they approached, Jesus said, "Now here is a genuine son of Israel—a man of complete integrity."

[48]"How do you know about me?" Nathanael asked.

Jesus replied, "I could see you under the fig tree before Philip found you."

1:27
Mark 1:7
John 1:15
Acts 13:25

1:28
John 3:26; 10:40

1:29
Isa 53:7
1 Cor 5:7
1 Pet 1:19
[h]*amnos* (0286)
▸John 1:36

1:30
John 1:15, 27

1:32
Matt 3:16
Mark 1:10
Luke 3:22

1:33
Luke 3:16
Acts 1:5

1:34
John 1:49; 10:36; 11:27; 20:30-31

1:36
[i]*amnos* (0286)
▸Acts 8:32

1:38
[j]*rhabbi* (4461)
▸John 1:49

1:40
Matt 4:18-22
Mark 1:16
Luke 5:2-11

1:41
Ps 2:2
John 4:25
[k]*messias* (3323)
▸John 4:25

1:42
Matt 16:18
1 Cor 15:5
1 Pet 2:5
[a]*petros* (4074)
▸1 Cor 10:4

1:43
John 6:5-6; 12:20-22

1:45
Luke 24:25-27

1:27 A menial task such as removing a ***sandal*** was reserved for a ***slave;*** these tasks were never performed by a disciple.

1:29 The phrase ***Lamb of God*** might refer to the Passover sacrifice of a lamb (see "The Cross and Passover" at 19:17-36, p. 1812) or to the daily sacrifice in the Temple (Exod 29:38-46; Heb 10). See also Rev 5.

1:32 John the Baptist's second testimony (see 1:19-23) told what happened when Jesus was baptized. • In the OT, kings and prophets were anointed with ***the Holy Spirit***, but these anointings were temporary and tied to a particular office or occasion. By contrast, with the Spirit's ***resting*** on him, Jesus' anointing was permanent (see 3:34).

1:34 ***the Chosen One of God:*** Some manuscripts read *the Son of God.* See also Isa 42:1.

1:35-51 This section introduces the template for discipleship in John's Gospel. Disciples desired to ***come and see*** Jesus (1:39), and when they encountered him, they ***remained*** with him (see "Disciples of Jesus" at 9:1-41, p. 1789).

1:40-42 Simon is well known in the Gospels, not for his courage and faith, but for his failings (see 18:15-18, 25-27). Jesus named him ***Cephas*** ("the rock"; see 1:42 and note), referring to the great church leader he would later become (see Acts 1–5, 8–12, 15).

1:41 ***Messiah*** (a Hebrew term) and ***Christ*** (a Greek term) both mean "the Anointed One."

1:42 The names ***Cephas*** (from Aramaic) and ***Peter*** (from Greek) both mean "rock."

1:43-44 ***Galilee*** was the region of northern Israel around the Sea of Galilee. • ***Bethsaida*** ("house of fishing") was a village on Galilee's north shore and the home of Peter, Andrew, Nathanael, and Philip. Later, Peter and Andrew moved to Capernaum, a village west of Bethsaida (Mark 1:21, 29).

1:45 ***Philip***, a Greek name, and ***Nathanael***, a Hebrew name, represent the mix of cultures in Galilee. Jesus' message there addressed both audiences. When Greeks wanted to see Jesus in Jerusalem, they approached Philip (12:20-22). • ***Moses:*** Literally *Moses in the law.* • Jesus grew up in ***Nazareth***, a mountain village southwest of the Sea of Galilee.

1:46 ***Can anything good come from Nazareth?*** This village was not considered famous enough to be the hometown for a great leader (cp. Matt 13:53-58).

1:47 Jesus referred to Nathanael as ***a man of complete integrity***, contrasting him with Jacob, the scheming, deceitful patriarch whom God renamed ***Israel*** (see Gen 25:27-34; 27:1-36; 32:22-32). It is as though Nathanael embodied God's ideal for Israel.

1:48-49 Jesus captured Nathanael's attention by knowing his character (1:47), then he captured his worship by supernaturally knowing his previous actions. Nathanael witnessed a miracle and took a remarkable step of faith.

1:49
2 Sam 7:14
Ps 2:2
John 1:34; 20:31
b*rhabbi* (4461)
John 3:2
1:51
Gen 28:12

49Then Nathanael exclaimed, "bRabbi,
you are the Son of God—the King of Israel!"
50Jesus asked him, "Do you believe this
just because I told you I had seen you under
the fig tree? You will see greater things than
this." 51Then he said, "I tell you the truth,
you will all see heaven open and the angels
of God going up and down on the Son of
Man, the one who is the stairway between
heaven and earth."

Jesus and Jewish Institutions (2:1–4:54)

The Wedding at Cana: Purification Water Turned to Wine

2 The next day there was a wedding celebration in the village of Cana in Galilee.
Jesus' mother was there, 2and Jesus and his
disciples were also invited to the celebration. 3The wine supply ran out during the
festivities, so Jesus' mother told him, "They
have no more wine."

JOHN THE BAPTIST (1:19-37)

John 3:23-36; 4:1-3; 10:40-42
Matt 3:1-15; 4:12; 9:14; 11:2-19; 14:1-12; 16:14; 17:10-13; 21:24-27, 31-32
Mark 1:1-9, 14; 2:18; 6:14-29; 8:28; 9:11-13; 11:29-33
Luke 1:13-17, 36, 39-43, 57-66, 76-80; 3:1-21; 5:33; 7:18-35; 9:7-9, 19; 11:1; 16:16; 20:3-8
Acts 1:5; 10:37; 11:16; 18:25-26; 19:1-7

John the Baptist was a fiery open-air preacher who called people to repent and be baptized, to prepare for the coming of the Messiah. John acted in the role of Elijah, to prepare people for "the great and dreadful day of the LORD" (Mal 4:4-5; see Matt 11:14; 17:12; Mark 9:13).

John's birth, like that of Jesus, was miraculous. His parents had been unable to have children and were elderly (Luke 1:5-25). His mother, Elizabeth, was a relative of Mary, the mother of Jesus (Luke 1:36), so John was related to Jesus. The two miraculous births near the same time signaled the beginning of God's redeeming work.

John was filled with the Holy Spirit from birth and devoted his life to preparing people for the coming of the Lord (Luke 1:15-17). Living in the desert (Luke 1:80), he began preaching when he was about thirty years old. Dressed like a prophet and subsisting on desert food (locusts and wild honey, Matt 3:4; Mark 1:6), he called everyone to repent and be baptized (Matt 3:1-2; Mark 1:4; Luke 3:1-3). He even castigated the religious leaders who came to hear him (Matt 3:7).

Though John reluctantly baptized Jesus (Matt 3:13-17; Luke 3:21), he considered Jesus his superior, the one who would "baptize with the Holy Spirit and with fire" (1:33; Matt 3:11; Mark 1:7-8; Luke 3:16; cp. 3:23-30). He encouraged his followers to become Jesus' disciples—and many did, including Andrew and possibly John (1:35-40), as well as Apollos (Acts 18:24-26) and the twelve disciples at Ephesus (Acts 19:1-7).

Herod Antipas received harsh judgment from John because of Herod's unlawful marriage to Herodias, his brother Philip's wife. To please Herodias, Herod imprisoned John and then beheaded him (Matt 14:3-12; Mark 6:17-29; Luke 3:19-20). John's imprisonment marked the beginning of Jesus' public preaching (Matt 4:12; Mark 1:14).

Shortly before his death, John seemed to be confused about Jesus and sent messengers from prison to ask him if he really was the Messiah. Jesus did not do what most people anticipated the Messiah to do. Rather than bringing judgment and a visible kingdom, he brought forgiveness, healing, and a spiritual kingdom. To reassure John, Jesus spoke of the miraculous things God was doing through him (Luke 7:18-23).

John remained faithful to his calling throughout his life, consistently preaching repentance and the judgment of God, even to people who had no desire to hear it. Jesus referred to John as one of the greatest servants of God who had ever lived (Matt 11:2-19; Luke 7:18-35), the end of a long line of prophets anticipating the coming of the Kingdom of God (Luke 16:16). John stood on the threshold of the new age, proclaiming its coming to all who would hear.

1:51 *I tell you the truth* (Greek *amēn amēn*): Jesus often used this expression to emphasize what he was about to say. In John's Gospel, the Greek word *amēn* is always doubled. • ***you will all see heaven open:*** Jesus made the comparison with Jacob explicit (see note on 1:47; see Gen 28:10-22). Like Jacob, Nathanael would see God at work. Jesus himself is the new Bethel ("house of God," Gen 28:19), the place where God lives. • ***going up and down on the Son of Man, the one who is the stairway between heaven and earth:*** Literally *going up and down on the Son of Man;* see Gen 28:10-17. "Son of Man" is a title Jesus used for himself (see note on 9:35; see also Dan 7:13-14; Mark 8:31). • John the apostle used several names for Jesus (Son of God, Son of Man, Messiah). Knowing Jesus' true identity is necessary to fully understanding and following him.

2:1–10:42 Jesus illustrated his identity and work through the institutions and festivals of Judaism (see 2:1; 5:1).

2:1-25 Jesus appeared at two symbolic Jewish ceremonies. At a wedding in Cana (2:1-12), he replaced the ritual cleansing water with his own superior wine. Later he cleansed the Temple (2:13-25).

2:1 *The next day:* Literally *On the third day;* see 1:35, 43. • The ceremonies surrounding ***a wedding celebration*** could last as long as a week; weddings often included dramatic processions in which the groom would bring the bride to his home for the festivities (Matt 25:1-13).

2:3 When ***the wine supply ran out,*** the host's family would face embarrassment for failure to plan properly. Perhaps Jesus arrived unexpectedly (cp. Matt 25:1-13), bringing his circle of

4“Dear woman, that’s not our problem,”
Jesus replied. “My time has not yet come.”
5But his mother told the servants, “Do
whatever he tells you.”
6Standing nearby were six stone water
jars, used for Jewish ceremonial washing.
Each could hold twenty to thirty gallons.
7Jesus told the servants, “Fill the jars with
water.” When the jars had been filled, 8he
said, “Now dip some out, and take it to the
master of ceremonies.” So the servants followed his instructions.
9When the master of ceremonies tasted
the water that was now wine, not knowing
where it had come from (though, of course,
the servants knew), he called the bridegroom over. 10“A host always serves the best
wine first,” he said. “Then, when everyone
has had a lot to drink, he brings out the less
expensive wine. But you have kept the best
until now!”
11This miraculous sign at Cana in Galilee
was the first time Jesus revealed his glory.
And his disciples believed in him.
12After the wedding he went to Capernaum for a few days with his mother, his
brothers, and his disciples.

The Jerusalem Temple Is Cleansed
John 2:13-16; cp. Matt 21:12-13 // Mark 11:15-17 // Luke 19:45-46

13It was nearly time for the Jewish Passover
celebration, so Jesus went to Jerusalem.
14In the Temple area he saw merchants selling cattle, sheep, and doves for sacrifices;
he also saw dealers at tables exchanging
foreign money. 15Jesus made a whip from
some ropes and chased them all out of the
Temple. He drove out the sheep and cattle,

2:4 John 7:30; 8:20
2:6 Mark 7:3-4; John 3:25
2:9 John 4:46
2:11 John 2:23; 3:2; 4:54; 6:14; 11:47; 12:37
2:12 Matt 12:46-50
2:13-22 //Matt 21:12-17 //Mark 11:15-19 //Luke 19:45-48
2:13 Deut 16:1-6; John 6:4; 11:55

Miraculous Signs (2:1-11)

John 2:18, 23; 3:2; 4:48, 54; 6:2, 14, 26, 30; 7:31; 9:16; 10:41; 11:47; 12:18, 37; 15:24; 20:30
Exod 4:8-31; 7:3
Num 14:11, 22
Deut 4:34
Ps 74:9; 78:43
Matt 12:38-39
Acts 2:43; 4:16, 22, 30; 5:12; 8:6; 14:3; 15:12
Rom 15:19

The Gospels use three words to describe Jesus’ miraculous works. In Matthew, Mark, and Luke, the Greek word *dunamis* (“power”) describes an act of raw force that amazes observers and leads to the inevitable conclusion that God must be at work in Jesus (see Mark 6:2).

In John, however, this response of amazement is absent. John does not use the popular term *dunamis.* Instead, he labels each of Jesus’ miracles as a “sign” (Greek *sēmeion*), an event that has a deeper meaning. John also describes Jesus’ miracles as “works” (Greek *erga*, see 10:25; see 7:3, “miracles”; 9:3, “power”). Christ’s miracles were part of the work that God gave him to do (17:4), revealing the Father to the world.

John selectively records seven miraculous signs that occurred during Jesus’ ministry: (1) changing water to wine (2:1-11); (2) healing the official’s son (4:46-54); (3) healing a paralyzed man (5:1-17); (4) feeding 5,000 (6:1-15); (5) walking on water (6:16-21); (6) healing a blind man (9:1-41); and (7) raising Lazarus from the dead (11:38-44). John also records the miraculous catch of fish after Jesus’ resurrection (21:4-14). Most of the seven signs were met with belief (2:11; 4:48, 53; 11:45-48). However, the sign itself was not Jesus’ purpose. Instead, the message behind the sign is always in view, so the signs are usually matched to a discourse by Jesus. Jesus fed the 5,000, for example, not just to meet their needs, but so that people would see him as the bread of life (6:35), given for them when he died on the cross (6:51).

disciples, which might explain why his *mother* brought the problem to him. • A wedding banquet was a primary celebration in Jewish village life, and this episode also symbolized the joy of the Messiah’s arrival.

2:4 Jesus initially distanced himself from the *problem.* His mission and its timing could not be set by a human agenda. • Jesus’ *time* (literally *hour*) would come in the future when he was glorified as he was lifted up on the cross (12:23; 17:1).

2:6 Carved from solid rock, the *stone water jars* were used for religious washing ceremonies (see Mark 7:1-4). Jesus was about to fill Jewish ceremony with new content. • *twenty to thirty gallons:* Greek *2 or 3 measures* [75 to 113 liters].

2:9-10 The *master of ceremonies* cited a proverb. The *best wine* was always served *first* when palates were most sensitive; yet this miraculous wine, served last, was the very best imaginable. Good wine symbolized God’s blessing (Amos 9:13-14). The Messiah, God’s greatest blessing, had arrived at last.

2:11 Jesus had offered his first *miraculous sign* (see “Miraculous Signs” at 2:1-11, above). In it, he revealed the glory of God (see also 1:14; 11:4, 40).

2:13 *Passover,* an annual spring festival, commemorated Israel’s rescue from slavery in Egypt (Exod 12). Jews traveled to *Jerusalem* to participate in the festival (Deut 16:1-16). Because John refers to three Passover Festivals (2:13; 6:4; 11:55), many experts conclude that Jesus had a three-year public ministry.

2:14-17 Those who came for Passover needed to have approved sacrifices for worship. From this need grew a considerable industry for selling animals and exchanging money, but this business was being conducted in the Temple. Jesus, like a prophet, demanded that God’s house be returned to its intended uses—worship, prayer, instruction, and sacrifice. This put Jesus at odds with the Temple leadership. • The synoptic Gospels place the clearing of the Temple near the end of Jesus’ ministry (Matt 21:12-13; Mark 11:15-17; Luke 19:45-46). John might have placed his account of the event here to emphasize a connection with the miracle that transformed the water in purification jars into wine (2:1-11). The Temple and the stone jars were both instruments of purification in Judaism. Stone jars filled with water for ritual washing

2:16 Luke 2:49
2:17 *Ps 69:9
2:19 Matt 26:61; 27:40; Mark 14:58; Acts 6:14
2:21 John 10:38; 14:2, 10; 17:21; 1 Cor 3:16; 6:19
2:22 Luke 24:6-8; John 12:16; 14:26
2:23 John 7:31; 11:47-48
3:1-2 John 7:50; 19:39
3:2 Matt 22:16; Acts 2:22; 10:38; [c]*rhabbi* (4461) ›John 11:8
3:3 John 1:13; [d]*anōthen gennaō* (0509, 1080) ›John 3:7

scattered the money changers' coins over
the floor, and turned over their tables.
16Then, going over to the people who sold
doves, he told them, "Get these things out of
here. Stop turning my Father's house into a
marketplace!"
17Then his disciples remembered this
prophecy from the Scriptures: "Passion for
God's house will consume me."
18But the Jewish leaders demanded,
"What are you doing? If God gave you authority to do this, show us a miraculous sign
to prove it."
19"All right," Jesus replied. "Destroy this
temple, and in three days I will raise it up."
20"What!" they exclaimed. "It has taken
forty-six years to build this Temple, and you
can rebuild it in three days?" 21But when
Jesus said "this temple," he meant his own
body. 22After he was raised from the dead,
his disciples remembered he had said this,
and they believed both the Scriptures and
what Jesus had said.

Nicodemus: A Religious Leader Visits Jesus
23Because of the miraculous signs Jesus did
in Jerusalem at the Passover celebration,
many began to trust in him. 24But Jesus
didn't trust them, because he knew human
nature. 25No one needed to tell him what
mankind is really like.

3 There was a man named Nicodemus, a
Jewish religious leader who was a Pharisee. 2After dark one evening, he came to
speak with Jesus. "[c]Rabbi," he said, "we all
know that God has sent you to teach us.
Your miraculous signs are evidence that
God is with you."
3Jesus replied, "I tell you the truth, unless you are [d]born again, you cannot see the
Kingdom of God."

NICODEMUS (3:1-9)

John 7:50; 19:39-42

Nicodemus was a highly respected Jewish Pharisee (3:1), one of the prominent members of the high council, who appears to have become a convert of Jesus. He is mentioned only in the Gospel of John.

Intrigued by the authority of Jesus and the miracles he was doing, Nicodemus went to see him secretly, at night, in a serious attempt to discover who he really was. Jesus challenged him with the need to be born again, if he wished to be in the Kingdom of God (3:1-8). The Gospel does not give us Nicodemus's response.

Later, however, in opposition to his colleagues on the Jewish high council, he strongly argued that Jesus should be given a fair trial (7:50). After Jesus was crucified, he bought seventy-five pounds of expensive perfumed ointment for his burial, took it to the tomb, and assisted Joseph of Arimathea in burying him (19:39-42). Thus, Nicodemus appears to be an example of a Jewish Pharisee who came to believe in Jesus and was willing to express that commitment publicly after his death.

now contained Jesus' wine, and a stone Temple dedicated to sacrificial purification would be replaced by Christ himself (2:19-21). Another view is that Jesus cleared the Temple at the beginning and again at the end of his ministry.

2:17 ***Passion for God's house will consume me:*** Or *"Concern for God's house will be my undoing."* See Ps 69:9.

2:19 ***Destroy this temple:*** Herod the Great began reconstructing the Temple's magnificent structure in 20 BC, and work on it continued until AD 64. This explains why Jesus' audience was amazed when he claimed he could destroy and rebuild it in a few days. However, Jesus spoke figuratively of his body as the temple where God was present (see 1:14; 1:51)—his body was destroyed and restored in three days through the resurrection, rendering the Jerusalem Temple and its services obsolete. Later, at his trial, Jesus' symbolic reference to destroying the Temple was used as evidence of blasphemy (Mark 14:58).

2:22 ***they believed:*** Witnessing a miracle from God can inspire belief, but it is not the deepest faith possible (20:29).

2:24 ***Jesus didn't trust them:*** John uses a play on words here. Because of his signs, many people trusted in Jesus (2:23), but Jesus ***didn't trust them***. This did not refer to specific people Jesus met in Jerusalem, but to his knowledge of all humanity.

3:1 John links 2:25 and 3:1 by referring to humanity as a whole ("mankind," 2:25) and then to one specific ***man*** using the same Greek word (*anthrōpos*) in both verses.• ***Nicodemus*** was saturated in religious knowledge and had witnessed Jesus' work (2:13-24), but he had not experienced spiritual rebirth. • ***a Pharisee:*** See note on 1:24. He was elite, proud of his spiritual purity, and well educated in Jewish law.

3:2 ***After dark:*** Nicodemus might have feared public association with Jesus. Night also symbolizes the realm of evil, untruth, and unbelief (9:4; 11:10; 13:30).

3:3 ***born again:*** Or *born from above;* also in 3:7. John's expression "from above" (3:31; 19:11) means "from God." To experience spiritual rebirth, a person must be completely renewed through God's power. • Nicodemus interpreted Jesus' words physically; he demonstrated that those in darkness, who do not have spiritual rebirth, cannot understand Jesus or other "heavenly things" (3:12). Jesus sometimes used ironic misunderstanding as a teaching strategy (see "Misunderstanding" at 7:32-36, p. 1785).

4"What do you mean?" exclaimed Nicodemus. "How can an old man go back into his
mother's womb and be born again?"
5Jesus replied, "I assure you, no one can
enter the Kingdom of God without being
born of water and the Spirit. 6[e]Humans can
reproduce only [e]human life, but the Holy
Spirit gives birth to spiritual life. 7So don't
be surprised when I say, 'You must be [f]born
again.' 8The wind blows wherever it wants.
Just as you can hear the wind but can't tell
where it comes from or where it is going, so
you can't explain how people are born of
the Spirit."
9"How are these things possible?" Nicodemus asked.
10Jesus replied, "You are a respected Jewish teacher, and yet you don't understand
these things? 11I assure you, we tell you what
we know and have seen, and yet you won't
believe our testimony. 12But if you don't
believe me when I tell you about earthly
things, how can you possibly believe if I tell
you about heavenly things? 13No one has
ever gone to heaven and returned. But the
Son of Man has come down from heaven.
14And as Moses lifted up the bronze snake
on a pole in the wilderness, so the Son of
Man must be lifted up, 15so that everyone
who believes in him will have eternal life.
16"For God loved the world so much that
he gave his [g]one and only Son, so that everyone who believes in him will not perish but
have eternal life. 17God sent his Son into the
world not to judge the world, but to save the
world through him.
18"There is no judgment against anyone
who believes in him. But anyone who does
not believe in him has already been judged
for not believing in God's [h]one and only
Son. 19And the judgment is based on this
fact: God's light came into the world, but
people loved the darkness more than the
light, for their actions were evil. 20All who
do evil hate the light and refuse to go near
it for fear their sins will be exposed. 21But
those who do what is right come to the light
so others can see that they are doing what
God wants."

John the Baptist Exalts Jesus

22Then Jesus and his disciples left Jerusalem and went into the Judean countryside.
Jesus spent some time with them there, baptizing people.
23At this time John the Baptist was baptizing at Aenon, near Salim, because there was
plenty of water there; and people kept coming to him for baptism. 24(This was before
John was thrown into prison.) 25A debate
broke out between John's disciples and a
certain Jew over ceremonial cleansing. 26So
John's disciples came to him and said, "Rabbi,
the man you met on the other side of the
Jordan River, the one you identified as the

3:5 Ezek 36:26-27; Titus 3:5; 2 Pet 1:11
3:6 John 1:13; Rom 8:15-16; 1 Cor 15:50; Gal 4:6; [e]*sarx* (4561) ‣Rom 8:4
3:7 [f]*anōthen gennaō* (0509, 1080) ‣John 3:31
3:8 Eccl 11:5
3:13 John 6:38, 42; Eph 4:8-10
3:14 Num 21:8-9; John 8:28; 12:34
3:15 John 20:31; 1 Jn 5:11-12
3:16 Rom 5:8; 8:32; 1 Jn 4:9-10; 5:13; [g]*monogenēs* (3439) ‣John 3:18
3:17 John 12:47
3:18 John 5:24; [h]*monogenēs* (3439) ‣Heb 11:17
3:19 John 1:5, 9; 8:12; 9:5; 12:46
3:20 Eph 5:11-13
3:21 1 Jn 1:6
3:22 John 3:26; 4:1-2

3:5 ***water and the Spirit*** (or *and spirit;* the Greek word *Spirit* can also be translated *wind;* see note on 3:8): John the Baptist baptized with water; Jesus baptizes with the Spirit (1:33).

3:6 ***the Holy Spirit gives birth to spiritual life:*** Literally *what is born of the Spirit is spirit.*

3:7 The Greek word translated *You* is plural; also in 3:12.

3:8 ***Wind*** translates the same word in Greek as *spirit* (Greek *pneuma*). The wind is an apt image for ***the Spirit,*** who is sent from heaven and cannot be contained or controlled.

3:13 There is great distance between this world and ***heaven*** (see 1:51; 3:31; 6:38, 42). Jesus bridged that distance, validating his divine status by defeating death and returning to heaven (16:5-11). • ***Son of Man:*** Some manuscripts add *who lives in heaven.* "Son of Man" is a title Jesus used for himself.

3:14-15 Jesus was ***lifted up*** on the cross so that all people could understand the way of salvation, look to him in faith, and ***have eternal life.***

3:15 ***everyone who believes in him will have eternal life:*** Or *everyone who believes will have eternal life in him.* The Greek syntax allows for either interpretation.

3:16-21 Because there are no quotation marks around Jesus' speech in Greek, translators debate where Jesus' speech ends and John's commentary begins; 3:16-21 might be John's commentary.

3:16 The truth that ***God loved the world*** is basic to Christian understanding (1 Jn 4:9-10). God's love extends beyond the limits of race and nation, even to those who oppose him (see "The World" at 17:5-26, p. 1807). • The ***Son*** came to save—not condemn (3:17)—men and women who habitually embrace the darkness (3:19-21).

3:18 As light penetrates and exposes the world's darkness, God's ***judgment*** on the world ***has already*** begun. Those who see this light and recognize the tragedy of their own situation have the responsibility of ***believing in God's . . . Son*** (3:16-17).

3:19-20 When ***people*** live in spiritual ***darkness,*** they do not desire to be enlightened by Jesus, "the light of the world" (8:12; 9:5). Evil and darkness do not ignore the light; they wage war against it, trying to bring it down. But the darkness cannot extinguish the light (1:5). Those who refuse to believe live in darkness (cp. 13:30) and stumble because they cannot see (11:10). In the end, however, ***their sins will be exposed*** (5:28-30; Rev 20:11-15).

3:21 ***can see that they are doing what God wants:*** Or *can see God at work in what he is doing.* The Greek syntax allows for either interpretation.

3:22-36 John the Baptist identifies Jesus as the one who is truly from above (3:31); this requires John's followers to shift their allegiance to Jesus.

3:22 ***Jesus spent some time . . . baptizing:*** See 4:2, which clarifies that Jesus' disciples did the baptizing.

3:24 ***Before John was thrown into prison*** (see Matt 14:1-12; Mark 1:14; 6:14-29; Luke 3:19-20), he and Jesus worked together at the Jordan River. Once John was arrested, Jesus moved north into Galilee (Mark 1:14).

3:25 ***a certain Jew:*** Some manuscripts read *some Jews.*

3:26 ***everybody is going to him:*** Jesus' popularity made some of John's followers envious.

3:24
Matt 4:12
3:26
John 1:7, 34
3:27
John 19:11
1 Cor 4:7
Heb 5:4
3:28
Mal 3:1
John 1:20, 23
3:29
Matt 9:15
2 Cor 11:2
Rev 21:9
3:31
1 Jn 4:5
[i]*anōthen* (0509)
‣1 Pet 1:3
3:33
1 Jn 5:10
3:34
Luke 4:18
3:35
Matt 28:18
3:36
1 Jn 5:12-13
[j]*orgē* (3709)
‣Rom 1:18
4:5-6
Gen 33:19
Josh 24:32

Messiah, is also baptizing people. And everybody is going to him instead of coming to us."
27John replied, "No one can receive anything unless God gives it from heaven. 28You
yourselves know how plainly I told you, 'I
am not the Messiah. I am only here to prepare the way for him.' 29It is the bridegroom
who marries the bride, and the best man is
simply glad to stand with him and hear his
vows. Therefore, I am filled with joy at his
success. 30He must become greater and
greater, and I must become less and less.
31"He has come from [i]above and is greater
than anyone else. We are of the earth, and
we speak of earthly things, but he has come
from heaven and is greater than anyone
else. 32He testifies about what he has seen
and heard, but how few believe what he tells
them! 33Anyone who accepts his testimony
can affirm that God is true. 34For he is sent
by God. He speaks God's words, for God
gives him the Spirit without limit. 35The
Father loves his Son and has put everything
into his hands. 36And anyone who believes
in God's Son has eternal life. Anyone who
doesn't obey the Son will never experience
eternal life but remains under God's [j]angry
judgment."

The Samaritan Woman at the Well

4 Jesus knew the Pharisees had heard
that he was baptizing and making more
disciples than John 2(though Jesus himself
didn't baptize them—his disciples did). 3So
he left Judea and returned to Galilee.
4He had to go through Samaria on the
way. 5Eventually he came to the Samaritan
village of Sychar, near the field that Jacob
gave to his son Joseph. 6Jacob's well was
there; and Jesus, tired from the long walk,
sat wearily beside the well about noontime.
7Soon a Samaritan woman came to draw water, and Jesus said to her, "Please give me a
drink." 8He was alone at the time because
his disciples had gone into the village to buy
some food.

Believing (3:10-18)

John 1:12-13; 3:36; 4:39, 42; 5:24; 6:35-36; 7:38-39; 9:35-38; 11:25-27; 12:37; 20:25-31
Gen 15:6
2 Kgs 17:14
Isa 28:16
Mark 1:15; 9:23-24
Acts 10:43; 13:39
Rom 1:5, 16-17; 3:25; 10:9-10
Gal 3:5-7
Heb 4:3
1 Jn 3:23; 5:10, 13

Believing occupies a central place in John's Gospel. John does not use the noun *faith* that appears frequently elsewhere in the NT (e.g., see Matt 8:8-10; Mark 11:22-24; Acts 20:21; Rom 1:17; 3:27-31; 4:3-5; Heb 11:1-39; Jas 2:14-24; 1 Pet 1:5-7). John prefers the verb *believe* to underscore that faith is not static like a doctrine or a dogma, but dynamic, requiring action. In John's Gospel, "believing" in Jesus is the trait of all true disciples.

In the Gospel of John, the verb translated "believe" is often followed by the Greek preposition *eis* ("into"). No parallel exists for this in ancient Greek usage. For John, faith is not a status, but an investment in the person of Jesus. Faith means accepting who Jesus is and what he claims to be. Faith constitutes a commitment to let his call change the way we live. Faith is the work God wants from us (6:29) as we abide in Jesus' word, as we love him, and as we obey his commands (8:31; 15:1-17; see 1 Jn 5:10).

3:27-35 John the Baptist's speech was inspired by two issues: (1) Some had questioned the legitimacy of his baptism (see 1:26); and (2) his disciples were concerned that people were beginning to follow Jesus instead of John (3:26).

3:29 John the Baptist saw Jesus as the ***bridegroom*** and himself as ***the best man.*** His response deflected glory from himself and elevated Jesus' stature.

3:31 Jesus had ***come from above,*** so he was uniquely able to reveal the Father (1:18; 3:13). • Some manuscripts do not include ***and is greater than anyone else.***

3:34-35 The Father ***gives*** the Son ***the Spirit without limit*** as a sign of his profound love (3:35). It also illustrates Jesus' divinity. John presents the one God as three persons (cp. 1 Jn 5:5-12).

3:36 God gave the gift of ***eternal life,*** promising new life and intimacy in a present experience with God. • Those who reject the Son will not see life. The world in its darkness stands under ***God's angry judgment*** (Rom 1–3).

4:1-42 At a historic well in Samaria, Jesus offered himself as living water. Jesus engaged and confronted people with the revelation of God, and they either followed or fell away. • The ***Samaritan woman*** contrasted with Nicodemus at every turn: a woman (not a man), a Samaritan (not a Jew), a sinner (not righteous), and an outcast (not one of Israel's rabbis). While Nicodemus fell silent and never responded to Jesus' challenges (3:1-21), this woman acknowledged Jesus as Lord, remained in the light, and exhibited signs of discipleship (see 1:35-51).

4:1 ***Jesus:*** Some manuscripts read *The Lord.*

4:2 ***Jesus himself didn't baptize*** anyone, but left water baptism to ***his disciples.*** After his glorification on the cross (7:37-39), Jesus baptized in the Holy Spirit (1:33; Acts 2:4).

4:3 After John the Baptist had been imprisoned (see Mark 6:14-29), Jesus ***left Judea*** (cp. Mark 1:14).

4:4-6 In going north to Galilee, Jesus took the less-preferred route through ***Samaria.*** Samaria had a long history of tension with Judea (see 2 Kgs 17:24-41; Ezra 4:1-5; Neh 4:1-23; 6:1-19). In Jesus' day, harsh racial and cultural conflict existed between Jews and Samaritans. Jews normally avoided Samaria by first going east to Jericho, then following the Jordan Valley north. • ***Sychar*** was probably in the region of Shechem. Jesus had come to ***Jacob's well;*** Jacob had owned land near Shechem (Gen 33:18-19).

4:7 Due to the heat, it was customary for the women to ***draw water*** in early morning or evening. However, this woman lived in isolation, separated from her community. Jesus was compassionate toward outcasts.

9 The woman was surprised, for Jews
refuse to have anything to do with Samaritans. She said to Jesus, "You are a Jew, and
I am a Samaritan woman. Why are you asking me for a drink?"
10 Jesus replied, "If you only knew the gift
God has for you and who you are speaking
to, you would ask me, and I would give you
living water."
11 "But sir, you don't have a rope or a
bucket," she said, "and this well is very deep.
Where would you get this living water?
12 And besides, do you think you're greater
than our ancestor Jacob, who gave us this
well? How can you offer better water than
he and his sons and his animals enjoyed?"
13 Jesus replied, "Anyone who drinks
this water will soon become thirsty again.
14 But those who drink the water I give will
never be thirsty again. It becomes a fresh,
bubbling spring within them, giving them
eternal life."
15 "Please, sir," the woman said, "give me
this water! Then I'll never be thirsty again,
and I won't have to come here to get water."
16 "Go and get your husband," Jesus told
her.
17 "I don't have a husband," the woman
replied.
Jesus said, "You're right! You don't have a
husband—18 for you have had five husbands,
and you aren't even married to the man
you're living with now. You certainly spoke
the truth!"
19 "Sir," the woman said, "you must be a
prophet. 20 So tell me, why is it that you Jews
insist that Jerusalem is the only place of worship, while we Samaritans claim it is here at
Mount Gerizim, where our ancestors worshiped?"
21 Jesus replied, "Believe me, dear woman,
the time is coming when it will no longer
matter whether you worship the Father
on this mountain or in Jerusalem. 22 You
Samaritans know very little about the one
you worship, while we Jews know all about
him, for salvation comes through the Jews.
23 But the time is coming—indeed it's here
now—when true worshipers will worship
the Father in spirit and in truth. The Father
is looking for those who will worship him
that way. 24 For God is Spirit, so those who
worship him must worship in spirit and in
truth."
25 The woman said, "I know the [k]Messiah
is coming—the one who is called Christ.
When he comes, he will explain everything
to us."
26 Then Jesus told her, "I AM the Messiah!"
27 Just then his disciples came back.
They were shocked to find him talking to a
woman, but none of them had the nerve to
ask, "What do you want with her?" or "Why
are you talking to her?" 28 The woman left

4:9
Ezra 4:1-3; 9–10
Matt 10:5
Luke 9:52-53
John 8:48
Acts 10:45
1 Cor 12:13

4:10
Isa 12:3; 44:3
Jer 2:13; 17:13
John 7:37-39
Rev 7:17; 21:6; 22:17

4:14
John 6:35; 7:38

4:15
John 6:34

4:19
Matt 21:46
John 7:40; 9:17

4:20
Deut 11:29; 12:5-14
Josh 8:33

4:21
Mal 1:11
1 Tim 2:8

4:22
2 Kgs 17:28-41
Isa 2:3
Rom 3:1-2; 9:4-5

4:23-24
2 Cor 3:17-18
Phil 3:3

4:25
Deut 18:15
[k]*messias* (3323)
‣Acts 2:31

4:26
Mark 14:61-62
John 9:37

4:9 ***The woman was surprised*** because social taboos would keep a Jewish teacher like Jesus from speaking to her (4:18). However, Jesus did not let social taboos constrain him from giving her what she truly needed. • Some manuscripts do not include the first sentence of this verse.

4:10 Shechem had no rivers and thus no *living water* (see "Living Water," facing page). However, Jesus was speaking symbolically: This gift from God was the Holy Spirit (7:37-39).

4:11 Jacob's *well* was more than 100 feet (30 meters) deep, and required a long *rope* for drawing water. The woman misunderstood Jesus' words because she was still in darkness (see "Misunderstanding" at 7:32-36, p. 1785).

4:12 ***our ancestor Jacob:*** The Samaritan woman appealed with reverence to the sacred traditions attached to the well rather than to the presence of God before her.

4:14 The notion of ***a fresh, bubbling spring*** was a powerful image in the dry climate of Israel. Those who come to God will neither hunger nor thirst (see Isa 49:10; 55:1-3; Jer 2:13).

4:15 The woman asked Jesus for *this water*, but she did not grasp the spiritual implications of his words. To overcome the spiritual barrier, Jesus addressed her sin (4:16-18).

4:16-18 Immorality blocked the woman's understanding. Her marital affairs, including having *five husbands*, underscored her sinful life.

4:19-20 The woman dodged Jesus' moral probing and brought up the historical ethnic division between Jews and Samaritans.

4:19 ***a prophet:*** Jesus revealed knowledge about the woman (4:16-18) that was inaccessible to the average person (cp. 1:48). • As the woman's understanding of Jesus unfolded, her names for him became increasingly well informed. Earlier she recognized him as *a Jew* (4:9) and called him *sir* (4:11, 15, 19). Later she thought he might be *the Messiah* (4:29). Finally, the people of the village recognized him as *Savior of the world* (4:42). Her growing understanding of Jesus' identity is a testimony to John's readers (see 20:31).

4:20 The Samaritans worshiped ***at Mount Gerizim*** (literally *on this mountain*), which towered above Shechem. Both were important OT locations (see Gen 12:6-7; 33:19; Deut 11:29; Josh 8:33; 24:1, 25, 32).

4:21-22 Jesus affirmed that the ***Jews*** had preserved the right understanding of ***the one you worship.*** • ***salvation comes through the Jews:*** God gave the Jews a special relationship with him, and the Messiah was to be a Jew (see also Rom 9:4-5).

4:24 ***in spirit and in truth:*** One Greek preposition governs both words (literally *in spirit and truth*) and makes them a single concept. True worship occurs as God's Spirit reveals God's truth and reality to the worshiper. Jesus Christ is the Truth (14:6; cp. 14:17; 15:26).

4:26 ***I AM the Messiah*** (or *"The 'I AM' is here"*; or *"I am the LORD"*; Greek reads *"I am, the one speaking to you"*; see Exod 3:14): Jesus' phrase was unusual and emphatic, and it suggests identity with God (see 8:58; Exod 3:14).

4:27-30 ***The woman*** was tentative about Jesus' identity (4:29), yet she ran to ***the village*** and told ***everyone*** to ***come and see.*** Testifying to others is a mark of discipleship (see 1:39, 46).

4:29
John 7:26
4:34
John 5:30, 36; 6:38; 17:4
4:35
Matt 9:37
Luke 10:2
4:37
Job 31:8
Mic 6:15
1 Cor 3:6
4:42
Luke 2:11
1 Jn 4:14
[a]*sōtēr* (4990)
‣Acts 5:31
4:43-54
//Matt 8:5-13
//Luke 7:1-10
4:44
Matt 13:57
Luke 4:24
4:45
John 2:23
4:46
John 2:1-11

her water jar beside the well and ran back to the village, telling everyone, 29"Come and see a man who told me everything I ever did! Could he possibly be the Messiah?" 30So the people came streaming from the village to see him.

31Meanwhile, the disciples were urging Jesus, "Rabbi, eat something."

32But Jesus replied, "I have a kind of food you know nothing about."

33"Did someone bring him food while we were gone?" the disciples asked each other.

34Then Jesus explained: "My nourishment comes from doing the will of God, who sent me, and from finishing his work. 35You know the saying, 'Four months between planting and harvest.' But I say, wake up and look around. The fields are already ripe for harvest. 36The harvesters are paid good wages, and the fruit they harvest is people brought to eternal life. What joy awaits both the planter and the harvester alike! 37You know the saying, 'One plants and another harvests.' And it's true. 38I sent you to harvest where you didn't plant; others had already done the work, and now you will get to gather the harvest."

Many Samaritans Believe

39Many Samaritans from the village believed in Jesus because the woman had said, "He told me everything I ever did!" 40When they came out to see him, they begged him to stay in their village. So he stayed for two days, 41long enough for many more to hear his message and believe. 42Then they said to the woman, "Now we believe, not just because of what you told us, but because we have heard him ourselves. Now we know that he is indeed the [a]Savior of the world."

Jesus Heals a Government Official's Son

43At the end of the two days, Jesus went on to Galilee. 44He himself had said that a prophet is not honored in his own hometown. 45Yet the Galileans welcomed him, for they had been in Jerusalem at the Passover celebration and had seen everything he did there.

46As he traveled through Galilee, he came to Cana, where he had turned the water into wine. There was a government official in nearby Capernaum whose son was very sick. 47When he heard that Jesus had come from Judea to Galilee, he went and begged

Living Water (4:10-14)

John 7:38-39
Lev 14:5-6, 50-51; 15:13
Num 19:17-19
Song 4:15
Jer 2:13; 17:13
Jas 3:11-12

In Israel, a land that frequently experienced drought, people were keenly aware of water sources and water quality. Springs and rivers that ran all year were few, so the land relied on cisterns to catch and store the winter rains and wells to tap underground water tables. In Jewish culture, "dead water" referred to standing and stored water. "Living water" referred to moving water, as in rivers, springs, and rainfall. Such water was precious because it was fresh. Because it came directly from God, it was used for ritual washings (see Lev 14:5-6, 50-51; 15:13; Num 19:17-19).

The distinction between "dead" and "living" water explains why the woman of Samaria was so perplexed when Jesus offered her living water (4:12). Samaria has no river. If Jacob had to dig a well there, how could Jesus offer superior water?

Jesus mentioned living water again in Jerusalem at the autumn Festival of Shelters (7:37-39). The festival, which fell during a dry time of year, included an emphasis on water. In this setting, Jesus stepped forward and made an extravagant claim: Anyone looking for living water should come to him and drink. Jesus is the source of living water; he came directly from God and brought divine renewal.

4:32-34 While Jesus spoke to the Samaritan woman, the disciples were gone buying food (4:8); now they urged Jesus to eat. Jesus continued to speak symbolically, but they did not understand him (4:33). Later, when the disciples received the Spirit, they understood (2:22). Jesus received his nourishment from doing what his Father told him to do (see 5:30; 6:38; 7:18; 8:50; 9:4; 10:37-38; 12:49-50).

4:35 ***Four months between planting and harvest:*** Jesus cited a local parable to contrast the natural harvest with his own. It was harvest time in Samaria, and the fields were *ripe* (literally *white*). Jesus, however, had planted seed at the well and now was ***already*** reaping the ***harvest*** of belief among the Samaritans (4:39-42).

4:38 ***others:*** Jesus might have meant John the Baptist, or he might have been referring to the work he had just done with the Samaritan woman.

4:39-40 ***Many Samaritans:*** The religiously sophisticated "chosen people" in Jerusalem did not respond to Jesus with faith (ch 3). By contrast, many ***believed in Jesus*** because of the testimony of this outcast woman.

4:42 The Samaritans had experienced for themselves that Jesus was true. Their name for Jesus, ***Savior of the world*** (also used in 1 Jn 4:14), demonstrated that the Samaritans were keenly aware of their distance from Judaism. Jesus' ministry was not simply for Jews, but for all people (1:4-12; cp. 12:20-26).

4:44-45 Unlike Jesus' fellow Jews, ***the Galileans welcomed him,*** but their welcome was based on awe of Jesus' miracles (cp. 2:23-25), not true faith.

Jesus to come to Capernaum to heal his son, who was about to die.

48 Jesus asked, "Will you never believe in me unless you see miraculous signs and wonders?"

49 The official pleaded, "Lord, please come now before my little boy dies."

50 Then Jesus told him, "Go back home. Your son will live!" And the man believed what Jesus said and started home.

51 While the man was on his way, some of his servants met him with the news that his son was alive and well. 52 He asked them when the boy had begun to get better, and they replied, "Yesterday afternoon at one o'clock his fever suddenly disappeared!" 53 Then the father realized that that was the very time Jesus had told him, "Your son will live." And he and his entire household believed in Jesus. 54 This was the second miraculous sign Jesus did in Galilee after coming from Judea.

Jesus and the Sabbath (5:1-47)

Jesus Heals a Man on the Sabbath

5 Afterward Jesus returned to Jerusalem for one of the Jewish holy days. 2 Inside the city, near the Sheep Gate, was the pool of Bethesda, with five covered porches. 3 Crowds of sick people—blind, lame, or paralyzed—lay on the porches. 5 One of the men lying there had been sick for thirty-eight years. 6 When Jesus saw him and knew he had been ill for a long time, he asked him, "Would you like to get well?"

7 "I can't, sir," the sick man said, "for I have no one to put me into the pool when the water bubbles up. Someone else always gets there ahead of me."

8 Jesus told him, "Stand up, pick up your mat, and walk!"

9 Instantly, the man was healed! He rolled up his sleeping mat and began walking! But this miracle happened on the Sabbath, 10 so the Jewish leaders objected. They said to the man who was cured, "You can't work on the Sabbath! The law doesn't allow you to carry that sleeping mat!"

11 But he replied, "The man who healed me told me, 'Pick up your mat and walk.' "

12 "Who said such a thing as that?" they demanded.

13 The man didn't know, for Jesus had disappeared into the crowd. 14 But afterward Jesus found him in the Temple and told him, "Now you are well; so stop sinning, or something even worse may happen to you." 15 Then the man went and told the Jewish leaders that it was Jesus who had healed him.

Jesus Claims to Be the Son of God

16 So the Jewish leaders began harassing Jesus for breaking the Sabbath rules. 17 But

4:48 1 Cor 1:22
4:50 Matt 8:13; Mark 7:29
4:53 Acts 11:14; 16:14-15
4:54 John 2:11
5:1 Lev 23:1-2; Deut 16:1; John 2:13
5:2 Neh 3:1; 12:39
5:8 Matt 9:6; Mark 2:11; Luke 5:24
5:10 Neh 13:15-20; Jer 17:21; Matt 12:2
5:14 John 8:11
5:17 John 9:4; 14:10
5:18 John 1:1, 18; 10:30, 33; 20:28; Phil 2:6; Titus 2:13; 2 Pet 1:1; 1 Jn 5:21

4:48 Jesus sharply criticized the Galileans who desired ***miraculous signs and wonders*** before they would believe (see "Miraculous Signs" at 2:1-11, p. 1772; see also 6:30).

4:50 ***Your son will live!*** Jesus also healed the centurion's slave (Matt 8:5-13) and the Phoenician woman's daughter (Matt 15:21-28) from a distance.

4:53 Just like many others (2:23; 4:39), the official and his ***household believed in Jesus*** because of the miracle.

4:54 ***second miraculous sign . . . in Galilee:*** Two miracles at Cana (2:11; 4:46) frame this section of John's Gospel.

5:1–10:42 In this section Jesus appears at a series of Jewish festivals and uses their imagery to reveal more profound truths about himself. He appears at Sabbath (ch 5), Passover (ch 6), the Festival of Shelters (chs 7–9), and Hanukkah (ch 10). In each case, Jesus himself replaces some vital element in the ceremonies of the festival.

5:1-40 This chapter reads like a courtroom drama, with a description of the crime (5:1-15), followed by a decision to prosecute (5:16), a description of the charges (5:18), and Jesus' defense (5:17, 19-40).

5:1 ***one of the Jewish holy days:*** Because Jesus ***returned to Jerusalem*** for the celebration, it was probably one of the three pilgrimage festivals of Judaism (see Exod 23:14-17; Deut 16:16). These festivals lasted one week.

5:2 Greek copyists who had never been to Jerusalem had difficulty interpreting and spelling the name *Bethesda:* Other manuscripts read *Beth-zatha;* still others read *Bethsaida*. The best choice is *Beth-esda* ("house of flowing").

5:3 The pool of Bethesda had become a healing sanctuary for ***crowds of sick people*** who believed miraculous cures were possible. • Some manuscripts add an expanded conclusion to verse 3 and all of verse 4: *waiting for a certain movement of the water, 4 for an angel of the Lord came from time to time and stirred up the water. And the first person to step in after the water was stirred was healed of whatever disease he had.* Most scholars believe this was not part of John's original text, but it represents an ancient tradition that provided helpful background information.

5:5 No social program helped this man, who had been ill for ***thirty-eight years.*** Hygiene and mobility were impossible, and he likely begged for a living from people who came to use the pool (see 5:7). His situation seemed hopeless.

5:8-9 Jesus healed the sick man ***instantly***, only asking for his obedience. As proof of healing, Jesus told him to ***pick up*** his ***mat and walk.*** • Jesus worked this miracle ***on the Sabbath***, a weekly day of rest on which all work was prohibited (based on Gen 2:2; Exod 20:8). Jewish tradition outlined thirty-nine categories of work that were not allowed (*Mishnah Shabbat* 7:2). Carrying something such as a ***sleeping mat*** from one place to another was banned (5:10). Therefore, the healed man broke the tradition by obeying Jesus' command.

5:12 ***Who said such a thing?*** The story ominously turns from a miraculous wonder to a Sabbath crime requiring the identity of the healer who breached tradition.

5:14 ***stop sinning:*** Though the man had been healed physically, he still needed to learn obedience to the Lord. The man's next action (5:15) might indicate that he didn't listen.

5:16 ***harassing:*** Or *persecuting.*

5:19
John 8:28; 12:49; 14:10

5:21
John 11:25
[b]*zōopoieō* (2227)
‣John 6:63

5:22
John 3:17; 5:27

5:23
1 Jn 2:23

5:24
John 3:15; 20:30-31
1 Jn 3:14; 5:13

5:25
John 4:21; 6:63, 68

5:26
John 1:4; 6:57
1 Jn 5:11-12

5:27
John 9:39
Acts 10:42; 17:31

5:29
Dan 12:2
Matt 25:46
Acts 24:15
[c]*anastasis* (0386)
‣John 11:24

5:30
John 5:19; 6:38

5:31
John 8:13-14

5:32
John 8:18

Jesus replied, "My Father is always working, and so am I." 18So the Jewish leaders tried all the harder to find a way to kill him. For he not only broke the Sabbath, he called God his Father, thereby making himself equal with God.

19So Jesus explained, "I tell you the truth, the Son can do nothing by himself. He does only what he sees the Father doing. Whatever the Father does, the Son also does. 20For the Father loves the Son and shows him everything he is doing. In fact, the Father will show him how to do even greater works than healing this man. Then you will truly be astonished. 21For just as the Father [b]gives life to those he raises from the dead, so the Son [b]gives life to anyone he wants. 22In addition, the Father judges no one. Instead, he has given the Son absolute authority to judge, 23so that everyone will honor the Son, just as they honor the Father. Anyone who does not honor the Son is certainly not honoring the Father who sent him.

24"I tell you the truth, those who listen to my message and believe in God who sent me have eternal life. They will never be condemned for their sins, but they have already passed from death into life.

25"And I assure you that the time is coming, indeed it's here now, when the dead will hear my voice—the voice of the Son of God. And those who listen will live. 26The Father has life in himself, and he has granted that same life-giving power to his Son. 27And he has given him authority to judge everyone because he is the Son of Man. 28Don't be so surprised! Indeed, the time is coming when all the dead in their graves will hear the voice of God's Son, 29and they will rise again. Those who have done good will [c]rise to experience eternal life, and those who have continued in evil will [c]rise to experience judgment. 30I can do nothing on my own. I judge as God tells me. Therefore, my judgment is just, because I carry out the will of the one who sent me, not my own will.

Witnesses to Jesus

31"If I were to testify on my own behalf, my testimony would not be valid. 32But someone else is also testifying about me, and I assure you that everything he says about me is true. 33In fact, you sent investigators

The Jewish Leaders (5:9-18)

John 1:19-24; 2:18-20; 7:1, 10-13, 35-36; 9:13-34; 11:45-54; 12:41-43; 18:28-36; 19:6-8, 12-16, 31, 38; 20:19
Acts 6:10-12; 7:54-58; 12:11; 21:11; 25:1-3, 7; 26:1-11; 28:17-24
2 Cor 11:24

Jesus experienced numerous conflicts with Jewish leaders throughout his public ministry. These opponents viewed themselves as defending the Temple and its sacrifices or the synagogue and its teachings. In Jesus' final week in Jerusalem, these debates intensified (Matt 23) and contributed to the case against him.

When John wrote his Gospel, Christians were being persecuted by local Jewish synagogues, and the language of their debate spilled over into John's Gospel (see Acts 14:19; 1 Thes 2:14; cp. Gal 1:13-14). The Greek term translated "the Jewish leaders" could be literally translated "the Jews." This word took on a technical meaning: It refers to the Temple leadership who confronted Jesus, judged him, and orchestrated his crucifixion (see 1:19; 2:18; 5:9-18; 9:18-22).

This is important because the NT—and particularly John's Gospel—has often been seen as anti-Semitic. But the truth is that Jesus, who was himself a Jew, did not wrestle with "Jews" in general. His antagonists were the "Jewish leaders"—the brokers of religious power in first-century Jerusalem.

5:17 ***My Father is always working, and so am I:*** Although work was prohibited on the Sabbath, even rabbis agreed that God worked on the Sabbath in giving life (births) and in taking life (deaths). The heart of Jesus' defense was to compare himself to God; the Jewish leaders objected to this claim of divine privilege.

5:19-30 Jesus claimed that his work on the Sabbath was the same as God's work on the Sabbath. Jesus claimed to be equal with God, doing the things God does. Yet he submitted to God's will, doing ***only what . . . the Father*** willed.

5:21 Most Jews firmly believed in resurrection but viewed it as something God alone could accomplish. Jesus claimed that he ***gives life.***

5:22 In addition to giving life, Jesus claimed the ***absolute authority to judge,*** which belongs to God alone.

5:23 ***the Father . . . sent him:*** In the ancient world, a person could send an authorized representative to seal a contract or make an authoritative decision. Jesus claimed to be God's representative, so obeying him is the same as obeying God, and dishonoring Jesus is dishonoring God.

5:24 Jesus is the giver of ***life*** as well as the judge (see 5:21-22), but he never works independently of the Father.

5:27 ***Son of Man*** is a title Jesus used for himself.

5:31-40 God's law requires more than one witness in a trial (Deut 17:6), so Jesus acknowledged that his own testimony was admissible only when confirmed by other witnesses. Thus, he introduced a series of witnesses for his defense.

5:32 The first witness for Jesus' defense was God himself. Jesus might have had in mind God's voice at his baptism (Mark 1:11) or the presence of God that enabled Jesus to perform miracles.

to listen to John the Baptist, and his testimony about me was true. 34Of course, I have no need of human witnesses, but I say these things so you might be saved. 35John was like a burning and shining lamp, and you were excited for a while about his message. 36But I have a greater witness than John—my teachings and my miracles. The Father gave me these works to accomplish, and they prove that he sent me. 37And the Father who sent me has testified about me himself. You have never heard his voice or seen him face to face, 38and you do not have his message in your hearts, because you do not believe me—the one he sent to you.

39"You search the Scriptures because you think they give you eternal life. But the Scriptures point to me! 40Yet you refuse to come to me to receive this life.

41"Your approval means nothing to me, 42because I know you don't have God's [d]love within you. 43For I have come to you in my Father's name, and you have rejected me. Yet if others come in their own name, you gladly welcome them. 44No wonder you can't believe! For you gladly honor each other, but you don't care about the honor that comes from the one who alone is God.

45"Yet it isn't I who will accuse you before the Father. Moses will accuse you! Yes, Moses, in whom you put your hopes. 46If you really believed Moses, you would believe me, because he wrote about me. 47But since you don't believe what he wrote, how will you believe what I say?"

Jesus and Passover (6:1-71)

Jesus Feeds Five Thousand

John 6:1-15 // Matt 14:13-21 // Mark 6:32-44 // Luke 9:10b-17

6 After this, Jesus crossed over to the far side of the Sea of Galilee, also known as the Sea of Tiberias. 2A huge crowd kept following him wherever he went, because they saw his miraculous signs as he healed the sick. 3Then Jesus climbed a hill and sat down with his disciples around him. 4(It was nearly time for the Jewish Passover celebration.) 5Jesus soon saw a huge crowd of people coming to look for him. Turning to Philip, he asked, "Where can we buy bread to feed all these people?" 6He was testing Philip, for he already knew what he was going to do.

7Philip replied, "Even if we worked for months, we wouldn't have enough money to feed them!"

8Then Andrew, Simon Peter's brother, spoke up. 9"There's a young boy here with five barley loaves and two fish. But what good is that with this huge crowd?"

10"Tell everyone to sit down," Jesus said. So they all sat down on the grassy slopes. (The men alone numbered about 5,000.) 11Then Jesus took the loaves, gave thanks to God, and distributed them to the people. Afterward he did the same with the fish. And they all ate as much as they wanted. 12After everyone was full, Jesus told his disciples, "Now gather the leftovers, so that nothing is wasted." 13So they picked up the pieces and filled twelve baskets with scraps left by the

5:36 John 10:25, 38; 14:11; 15:24; 1 Jn 5:9
5:37 Deut 4:12; John 1:18; 8:18; 1 Tim 1:17
5:38 1 Jn 2:14
5:39 Luke 24:27, 44; Acts 13:27; Rom 2:17-20
5:41 John 12:43
5:42 [d]*agapē* (0026) ›John 15:9
5:45 John 9:28; Rom 2:17
5:46 Gen 3:15; Deut 18:15, 18; Luke 24:27, 44; Acts 26:22-23
5:47 Luke 16:31
6:1-13 //Matt 14:13-21; //Mark 6:32-44; //Luke 9:10-17
6:4 John 11:55
6:5 John 1:43
6:8 John 1:40
6:9 2 Kgs 4:43; John 21:9, 13

5:33-35 Jesus' second witness was ***John the Baptist,*** who pointed to Jesus as Messiah (1:29-34).

5:36 Jesus' third witness, his ***teachings*** and ***miracles,*** were signs that unveiled his true identity and pointed to the Father who sent him.

5:39-40 Jesus' fourth witness was ***the Scriptures.*** The OT pointed to the Messiah, and Jesus fulfilled its prophecies (see Luke 24:25-27).

5:41-47 Jewish trials sought to discover the truth. Falsely accused defendants could not only prove their innocence but also prosecute their accusers, which Jesus did here.

5:42 Jesus charged that the Jewish leaders did not ***have God's love within*** them. Without God's love, it was impossible for them to understand the things he was doing.

5:44 The Jewish leaders pursued ***honor*** and prestige from ***each other.*** They loved religious life, but they had forgotten to love God. This hypocrisy made them liable to judgment (5:45-46). • ***from the one who alone is God:*** Some manuscripts read *from the only One.*

5:45-46 Jesus' fifth and final witness was ***Moses,*** the founding father of Judaism. John had already compared Jesus with Moses (1:17; see also 6:14-15). The Jewish leaders were ignoring Moses' clear words about the Messiah (e.g., Deut 18:15).

6:1-71 Each story in this chapter uses the setting of the Passover Festival (6:4) to communicate a deeper meaning.

6:1-15 Jesus' feeding the 5,000 recalls the great OT miracle of bread when Israel was in the wilderness (Exod 16:1-36). The rabbis of Jesus' day expected the coming Messiah to "rain down food from heaven" once again (Exod 16:4), and he did.

6:5 ***Where can we buy bread:*** When the Israelites left Egypt following the first Passover and entered the desert, finding food and water was also their first concern (Exod 15:22–16:3).

6:7 ***Even if we worked for months, we wouldn't have enough money:*** Literally *200 denarii would not be enough.* A denarius was equivalent to a laborer's full day's wage.

6:9 ***Barley*** was the grain of the poor. The ***loaves*** were similar to pita bread. The ***two fish*** would have been salted, and with the ***five*** loaves of bread would make one meal.

6:10 The headcount of ***about 5,000*** reflected the ***men alone*** (Matt 14:21), as social custom dictated. With women and children included, the total number was far greater.

6:11 The modest meal provided the crowd with ***as much as they wanted,*** echoing the miraculous provision of manna in the wilderness (Exod 16:35). Moses had first supplied Israel with heavenly bread; Jesus was the new supplier (see note on 6:1-15).

6:14
Deut 18:15, 18
Acts 3:22; 7:37

6:16-23
//Matt 14:23-33
//Mark 6:47-51

6:19
Job 9:8

6:20
Matt 14:27

6:23
John 6:11

6:27
Matt 3:17; 17:5
Mark 1:11; 9:7
Luke 3:22
John 1:33; 4:14; 6:50-51, 54, 58
Acts 2:22
Rom 6:23

6:29
1 Jn 3:23

6:31
Exod 16:15
Num 11:7-9
Neh 9:15
*Ps 78:24; 105:40

6:33
John 6:41, 50

6:35
John 4:14; 6:48; 7:37-38

people who had eaten from the five barley loaves.

[14]When the people saw him do this miraculous sign, they exclaimed, "Surely, he is the Prophet we have been expecting!" [15]When Jesus saw that they were ready to force him to be their king, he slipped away into the hills by himself.

Jesus Walks on Water
John 6:16-21 // Matt 14:22-33 // Mark 6:45-52

[16]That evening Jesus' disciples went down to the shore to wait for him. [17]But as darkness fell and Jesus still hadn't come back, they got into the boat and headed across the lake toward Capernaum. [18]Soon a gale swept down upon them, and the sea grew very rough. [19]They had rowed three or four miles when suddenly they saw Jesus walking on the water toward the boat. They were terrified, [20]but he called out to them, "Don't be afraid. I am here!" [21]Then they were eager to let him in the boat, and immediately they arrived at their destination!

Jesus, the Bread of Life

[22]The next day the crowd that had stayed on the far shore saw that the disciples had taken the only boat, and they realized Jesus had not gone with them. [23]Several boats from Tiberias landed near the place where the Lord had blessed the bread and the people had eaten. [24]So when the crowd saw that neither Jesus nor his disciples were there, they got into the boats and went across to Capernaum to look for him. [25]They found him on the other side of the lake and asked, "Rabbi, when did you get here?"

[26]Jesus replied, "I tell you the truth, you want to be with me because I fed you, not because you understood the miraculous signs. [27]But don't be so concerned about perishable things like food. Spend your energy seeking the eternal life that the Son of Man can give you. For God the Father has given me the seal of his approval."

[28]They replied, "We want to perform God's works, too. What should we do?"

[29]Jesus told them, "This is the only work God wants from you: Believe in the one he has sent."

[30]They answered, "Show us a miraculous sign if you want us to believe in you. What can you do? [31]After all, our ancestors ate manna while they journeyed through the wilderness! The Scriptures say, 'Moses gave them bread from heaven to eat.' "

[32]Jesus said, "I tell you the truth, Moses didn't give you bread from heaven. My Father did. And now he offers you the true bread from heaven. [33]The true bread of God is the one who comes down from heaven and gives life to the world."

[34]"Sir," they said, "give us that bread every day."

[35]Jesus replied, "I am the bread of life. Whoever comes to me will never be hungry again. Whoever believes in me will never be thirsty. [36]But you haven't believed in me

---

6:14 *him:* Some manuscripts read *Jesus.* • ***he is the Prophet we have been expecting!*** The crowd understood the miracle as a fulfillment of OT promises (see Deut 18:15, 18; Mal 4:5-6).

6:15 The people ***were ready to force*** Jesus to become ***their king.*** To avoid this role, Jesus fled the crowd and commanded his disciples to go back across the lake (Mark 6:45-46).

6:18 East-west winds blowing down over the eastern cliffs of the Sea of Galilee late in the day commonly caused ***very rough*** waters and turbulent storms.

6:19 ***three or four miles:*** Greek *25 or 30 stadia* [4.6 or 5.5 kilometers]. • The disciples' fear of the storm was now surpassed by their fear of ***Jesus,*** who came ***walking on the water*** to help them. This act recalled Moses, who led Israel through the water (Exod 14; see Ps 77:19-20).

6:20 ***I am here*** (or *The 'I AM' is here;* Greek reads *I am;* see Exod 3:14): Jesus identified himself by the name God had revealed to Moses on Mount Sinai (see also 4:26; 6:35).

6:21 ***immediately they arrived at their destination:*** The immediacy was yet another of Jesus' miracles.

6:24 The ***crowd*** sailed north to ***Capernaum*** to search for Jesus because he had made Capernaum his home in Galilee (Mark 2:1).

6:26-59 This dialogue took place in the synagogue at Capernaum (6:59) shortly before Passover (6:4), when Jews read the account of the exodus from Egypt (see Exod 1–15).

6:26 The crowd, which had concluded that Jesus was a prophet and wanted to take advantage of him politically (see note on 6:15), failed to see the meaning of the miracle, which Jesus then explained (6:27-59).

6:27 Jesus' most profound gift was not physical bread, but eternal life, which the Father authorized him to give. Physical bread is ***perishable;*** the gift of Jesus, who is himself the bread of life (6:35), will last forever. • ***Son of Man*** is a title Jesus used for himself.

6:30 The crowd demanded ***a miraculous sign*** to demonstrate Jesus' status as Messiah. Jews believed that when the Messiah appeared, he would duplicate the great miracle of Moses. Manna would once again fall, and everyone would consider it a second exodus.

6:31 ***Moses gave them bread from heaven to eat:*** Exod 16:4; Ps 78:24.

6:32-33 Jesus corrected the people's argument: God, not Moses, fed Israel in the wilderness. The most important quest is to find and consume ***the true bread of God,*** who gives eternal life.

6:34 ***Sir, . . . give us that bread:*** This request parallels the request of the Samaritan woman (4:15). Spiritual awakening begins with a request for God's gift.

6:35 Jesus' ***I am*** statements in John depict Jesus' identity and ministry (see also 4:26; 8:12; 9:5; 10:7-9, 11-14; 11:25; 14:6; 15:1-5). Jesus purposefully used a phrase that would make his listeners think of the OT name for God (Exod 3:14). • ***I am the bread of life:*** Jesus is the true manna that descended from God (6:38). He satisfies the spiritual hunger of those who believe in him (cp. 4:10-13).

even though you have seen me. 37However, those the Father has given me will come to me, and I will never reject them. 38For I have come down from heaven to do the will of God who sent me, not to do my own will. 39And this is the will of God, that I should not lose even one of all those he has given me, but that I should raise them up at the last day. 40For it is my Father's will that all who see his Son and believe in him should have eternal life. I will raise them up at the last day."

41Then the people began to murmur in disagreement because he had said, "I am the bread that came down from heaven." 42They said, "Isn't this Jesus, the son of Joseph? We know his father and mother. How can he say, 'I came down from heaven'?"

43But Jesus replied, "Stop complaining about what I said. 44For no one can come to me unless the Father who sent me draws them to me, and at the last day I will raise them up. 45As it is written in the Scriptures, 'They will all be taught by God.' Everyone who listens to the Father and learns from him comes to me. 46(Not that anyone has ever seen the Father; only I, who was sent from God, have seen him.)

47"I tell you the truth, anyone who believes has eternal life. 48Yes, I am the bread of life! 49Your ancestors ate manna in the wilderness, but they all died. 50Anyone who eats the bread from heaven, however, will never die. 51I am the living bread that came down from heaven. Anyone who eats this bread will live forever; and this bread, which I will offer so the world may live, is my flesh."

52Then the people began arguing with each other about what he meant. "How can this man give us his flesh to eat?" they asked.

53So Jesus said again, "I tell you the truth, unless you eat the flesh of the Son of Man and drink his blood, you cannot have eternal life within you. 54But anyone who eats my flesh and drinks my blood has eternal life, and I will raise that person at the last day. 55For my flesh is true food, and my blood is true drink. 56Anyone who eats my flesh and drinks my blood remains in me, and I in him. 57I live because of the living Father who sent me; in the same way, anyone who feeds on me will live because of me. 58I am the true bread that came down from heaven. Anyone who eats this bread will not die as your ancestors did (even though they ate the manna) but will live forever."

59He said these things while he was teaching in the synagogue in Capernaum.

Many Disciples Desert Jesus

60Many of his disciples said, "This is very hard to understand. How can anyone accept it?"

61Jesus was aware that his disciples were complaining, so he said to them, "Does this offend you? 62Then what will you think if you see the Son of Man ascend to heaven again? 63The Spirit alone [e]gives eternal life. Human effort accomplishes nothing. And the very words I have spoken to you are spirit and life. 64But some of you do not believe me." (For Jesus knew from the beginning which ones didn't believe, and he knew who would betray him.) 65Then he said, "That is why I said that people can't come to me unless the Father gives them to me."

6:37 John 10:28-29; 17:2, 24
6:38 John 4:34; 5:30
6:39 John 10:28-29; 17:12; 18:9
6:40 John 12:45
6:41 John 6:33, 35, 51, 58
6:42 Luke 4:22; John 7:27-28
6:44 Jer 31:3; John 6:65; 12:32
6:45 *Isa 54:13; Jer 31:33-34; 1 Thes 4:9; Heb 8:10-11
6:46 John 1:18; 5:37; 7:29
6:47 John 3:15-16, 36
6:48 John 6:35, 41, 51, 58
6:51 John 10:10-11; Heb 10:10
6:54 John 6:39-40, 44
6:56 John 14:20; 15:4-7; 17:21-23; 1 Jn 2:24; 3:24
6:57 John 5:26
6:58 John 6:31
6:62 John 3:13; 17:5; Acts 1:9-11; Eph 4:8
6:63 John 3:34; Rom 8:2; 1 Cor 15:45; 2 Cor 3:6; 1 Pet 3:18
[e]*zōopoieō* (2227) ›Rom 4:17
6:64 Matt 26:23; John 13:11

6:37-40 Jesus' mission in the world is sure to succeed. God sent Jesus (6:38) and calls people to follow him (6:37, 44). Those who come to him are secure in Jesus' promise that he will not reject them or lose them (6:39).

6:37 ***those the Father has given:*** God moves in people's hearts, bringing them to Jesus.

6:41-42 When Jesus identified himself as the true ***bread . . . from heaven,*** the crowd faced a decision. • ***people:*** Literally *Jewish people;* also in 6:52. • ***Isn't this . . . the son of Joseph?*** They stumbled because their familiarity with Jesus made his claims seem outlandish.

6:43-51 ***Stop complaining:*** Rather than defending himself against their complaint (6:42), Jesus turns to the problem of their spiritual receptivity. Those who love the Father and listen to him will believe in Jesus.

6:45 ***in the Scriptures:*** Literally *in the prophets.* Isa 54:13.

6:49-50 Jesus connected the ***manna*** of the Exodus with himself, then pointed out a major difference: The Israelites remained mortal and ***they all died,*** whereas ***the bread from heaven*** (Jesus himself) provides eternal life (6:47, 51, 58).

6:51 ***this bread . . . is my flesh:*** The gift that brings life is now unveiled. On the cross, Jesus offered his flesh for the life of the world.

6:53-58 ***eat the flesh . . . drink his blood:*** Jesus answered the question the people asked (6:52). His words hinted at the Lord's Supper yet to come (see Luke 22:19). Since "flesh and blood" was a Jewish idiom for the whole person, Jesus might have been calling people to consume him fully by completely believing in him. Some Christian traditions see the bread as Christ's literal flesh broken for us and the wine as his literal blood poured out for us. Receiving communion means no less than embracing Jesus' life-giving sacrifice.

6:60-61 Jesus' language (6:53-58) was shocking, offensive (see Gen 9:4-5), and ***hard to understand*** for his disciples, just as it was to the crowd. Were they to take him literally? How would they eat his flesh? Jesus' answer is in 6:63.

6:63 The essence of Jesus' gift is found in the Holy ***Spirit alone,*** not in ***human effort*** (literally *the flesh*). Life and understanding come through the gift of the Spirit (see 14:15-20; 20:21-22). True life can be found only when the Holy Spirit infuses human life. To "eat the flesh of the Son of Man and drink his blood" (6:53) involves a spiritual rather than a physical act (see note on 6:53-58).

6:65 ***people can't come to me unless the Father gives them to me*** (see 6:44): Only

6:65 John 6:44
6:68 John 6:63
6:69 Matt 16:16; Mark 1:24; 8:29; Luke 9:20; 1 Jn 2:20
6:70-71 Matt 10:4; 26:14; John 13:27
7:1 John 5:18; 7:19; 8:37, 40
7:2 Lev 23:34; Deut 16:16
7:3 Matt 12:46
7:6 John 2:4; 7:30; 8:20
7:7 John 15:18
7:11 John 11:56
7:12 John 7:40-43
7:13 John 9:22-23
7:15 Matt 13:54; Luke 2:47; Acts 4:13
7:16 John 8:28; 12:49; 14:10
7:18 John 5:41, 44; 8:50, 54
7:19 John 1:17; 7:1, 25; 8:37-40
7:20 John 8:48, 52; 10:20
7:21-22 Gen 17:10-13; Lev 12:3
7:23 John 5:8-10, 16; Acts 7:8

66At this point many of his disciples
turned away and deserted him. 67Then
Jesus turned to the Twelve and asked, "Are
you also going to leave?"

68Simon Peter replied, "Lord, to whom
would we go? You have the words that give
eternal life. 69We believe, and we know you
are the Holy One of God."

70Then Jesus said, "I chose the twelve of
you, but one is a devil." 71He was speaking
of Judas, son of Simon Iscariot, one of the
Twelve, who would later betray him.

Jesus and the Festival of Shelters (7:1–8:59)

Jesus and His Brothers

7 After this, Jesus traveled around Galilee.
He wanted to stay out of Judea, where
the Jewish leaders were plotting his death.
2But soon it was time for the Jewish Festival of Shelters, 3and Jesus' brothers said to
him, "Leave here and go to Judea, where
your followers can see your miracles! 4You
can't become famous if you hide like this!
If you can do such wonderful things, show
yourself to the world!" 5For even his brothers didn't believe in him.

6Jesus replied, "Now is not the right time
for me to go, but you can go anytime. 7The
world can't hate you, but it does hate me because I accuse it of doing evil. 8You go on.
I'm not going to this festival, because my
time has not yet come." 9After saying these
things, Jesus remained in Galilee.

Jesus Teaches Openly at the Temple

10But after his brothers left for the festival,
Jesus also went, though secretly, staying out
of public view. 11The Jewish leaders tried
to find him at the festival and kept asking
if anyone had seen him. 12There was a lot
of grumbling about him among the crowds.
Some argued, "He's a good man," but others
said, "He's nothing but a fraud who deceives
the people." 13But no one had the courage
to speak favorably about him in public, for
they were afraid of getting in trouble with
the Jewish leaders.

14Then, midway through the festival,
Jesus went up to the Temple and began to
teach. 15The people were surprised when
they heard him. "How does he know so
much when he hasn't been trained?" they
asked.

16So Jesus told them, "My message is not
my own; it comes from God who sent me.
17Anyone who wants to do the will of God
will know whether my teaching is from God
or is merely my own. 18Those who speak for
themselves want glory only for themselves,
but a person who seeks to honor the one
who sent him speaks truth, not lies. 19Moses
gave you the law, but none of you obeys it! In
fact, you are trying to kill me."

20The crowd replied, "You're demon possessed! Who's trying to kill you?"

21Jesus replied, "I did one miracle on the
Sabbath, and you were amazed. 22But you
work on the Sabbath, too, when you obey
Moses' law of circumcision. (Actually, this
tradition of circumcision began with the patriarchs, long before the law of Moses.) 23For
if the correct time for circumcising your
son falls on the Sabbath, you go ahead and
do it so as not to break the law of Moses. So
why should you be angry with me for healing

God's light can penetrate the profound darkness of the world.

6:68-69 ***Simon Peter*** often served as spokesman for the Twelve (see also Matt 14:28-29; 16:16; 17:4; 18:21; 19:27; 26:33-35). • ***you are the Holy One of God:*** Other manuscripts read *you are the Christ, the Holy One of God;* still others read *you are the Christ, the Son of God;* and still others read *you are the Christ, the Son of the living God.* See Mark 1:24.

6:70-71 Once again Jesus demonstrated supernatural knowledge (see 1:47-49; 4:16-19). ***Judas*** would work for evil and ***betray*** Jesus to the authorities (12:4; 13:2; Matt 26:14-16). • ***Iscariot*** means "man from Kerioth," the home village of Judas's family.

7:1-52 This chapter is another account of Jesus during a Jewish festival, the Festival of Shelters. Jesus used elements of the festival to reveal his true identity to his Jewish compatriots and to show that he had fulfilled the festival's essential meaning (see 7:37-39; 8:12).

7:2 Jewish men were required to come to the Temple for the ***Festival of Shelters*** (Exod 23:14-17; Deut 16:16), an annual seven-day autumn harvest festival in Jerusalem six months after Passover (6:4). People lived in temporary shelters for the seven days as a reminder of the tents Israel used for forty years in the wilderness.

7:3-5 ***Jesus' brothers*** (see also Mark 3:31) reminded him of his religious obligation to celebrate the festival. Their words were cynical because at this time they didn't ***believe in him*** (7:5).

7:6-8 Jesus said that it was ***not the right time*** for him to go publicly to Jerusalem, although he later went secretly (12:1-19; see note on 12:23).

7:8 ***not going:*** Some manuscripts read *not yet going.*

7:15 ***people:*** Literally *Jewish people.* • The leaders wanted Jesus to show his credentials. Jesus had not ***been trained*** under a rabbi but was taught by his heavenly Father (cp. Peter and John, Acts 4:13; contrast Paul, Acts 22:3).

7:17 Those who truly want ***to do the will of God*** receive and accept Jesus and his ***teaching*** (see also 5:42-47). Those who focus on the world, by contrast, are not receptive to Christ.

7:19 ***Moses gave you the law, but none of you obeys it!*** The Jewish leaders were proud of the law of Moses, but ironically, in ***trying to kill*** Jesus, they were breaking the law (Exod 20:13).

7:20 ***You're demon possessed!*** See also 8:48-52; 10:20-21.

7:22 The law required ***circumcision*** on the eighth day (Lev 12:3) and permitted a boy to be circumcised even if that day fell on ***the Sabbath.*** Jesus argued as a rabbi would, from "the lesser to the greater," using circumcision as a precedent for healing, both of which are religious works.

a man on the Sabbath? 24Look beneath the surface so you can judge correctly."

Is Jesus the Messiah?

25Some of the people who lived in Jerusalem started to ask each other, "Isn't this the man they are trying to kill? 26But here he is, speaking in public, and they say nothing to him. Could our leaders possibly believe that he is the Messiah? 27But how could he be? For we know where this man comes from. When the Messiah comes, he will simply appear; no one will know where he comes from."

28While Jesus was teaching in the Temple, he called out, "Yes, you know me, and you know where I come from. But I'm not here on my own. The one who sent me is true, and you don't know him. 29But I know him because I come from him, and he sent me to you." 30Then the leaders tried to arrest him; but no one laid a hand on him, because his time had not yet come.

31Many among the crowds at the Temple believed in him. "After all," they said, "would you expect the Messiah to do more miraculous signs than this man has done?"

32When the Pharisees heard that the crowds were whispering such things, they and the leading priests sent Temple guards to arrest Jesus. 33But Jesus told them, "I will be with you only a little longer. Then I will return to the one who sent me. 34You will search for me but not find me. And you cannot go where I am going."

35The Jewish leaders were puzzled by this statement. "Where is he planning to go?" they asked. "Is he thinking of leaving the country and going to the Jews in other lands? Maybe he will even teach the Greeks! 36What does he mean when he says, 'You will search for me but not find me,' and 'You cannot go where I am going'?"

Jesus Promises Living Water

37On the last day, the climax of the festival, Jesus stood and shouted to the crowds, "Anyone who is thirsty may come to me! 38Anyone who believes in me may come and drink! For the Scriptures declare, 'Rivers of living water will flow from his heart.'" 39(When he said "living water," he was speaking of the Spirit, who would be given to everyone believing in him. But the Spirit had not yet been given, because Jesus had not yet entered into his glory.)

40When the crowds heard him say this, some of them declared, "Surely this man is the Prophet we've been expecting." 41Others said, "He is the Messiah." Still others said, "But he can't be! Will the Messiah come from Galilee? 42For the Scriptures clearly state that the Messiah will be born of the royal line of David, in Bethlehem, the village where King David was born." 43So the crowd was divided about him. 44Some even wanted him arrested, but no one laid a hand on him.

45When the Temple guards returned without having arrested Jesus, the leading

7:24 Isa 11:3-4; John 8:15
7:27 John 9:29
7:28-29 John 8:26, 55; 17:25
7:30 John 8:20
7:31 John 2:23; 8:30; 10:42; 11:45; 12:11, 42
7:33 John 13:33; 16:5, 10, 16-18
7:34 John 8:21; 13:33
7:37 Isa 55:1; John 4:10, 14; 6:35; Rev 22:17
7:38 Prov 18:4; Isa 58:11; Ezek 47:1-10; Joel 3:18
7:39 John 14:17-18; 16:7; 20:22; Rom 8:9; 1 Cor 15:45; 2 Cor 3:17
7:40 Deut 18:15; John 6:14
7:41 John 1:46
7:42 2 Sam 7:12; Ps 89:3-4; Mic 5:2; Matt 1:1; 2:5-10; Luke 2:4; John 7:52
7:43 John 9:16; 10:19
7:44 John 7:30

7:27 Some of the crowd thought that since they could trace Jesus' earthly origins, he could not be the Messiah. They believed that the Messiah would ***simply appear.***

7:29 ***I come from him:*** Jesus sidestepped the speculation (7:27, 40-44) about his earthly origins and focused on his heavenly origins. His astounding claim provoked the religious leaders to try to arrest him for blasphemy (7:30; cp. 10:30-33).

7:30 Jesus' opponents failed to arrest him because in God's sovereign plan, ***his time*** (literally *his hour*), when he would be glorified on the cross, ***had not yet come*** (see note on 12:23; see also 10:17-18; 18:6-8). All four arrest scenes in chs 7–8 stress that Jesus was in control, not the Jewish leaders.

7:32-36 Jesus announced his ***return to the one who sent*** him, the Father in heaven (17:1-7). However, the Pharisees misunderstood, thinking he was leaving Judea to go among Gentiles (whom Pharisees would never visit). • The leaders would ***not find*** Jesus after his ascension. • ***you cannot go where I am going:*** These Pharisees, still in darkness, could not enter heaven, so Jesus would be beyond their reach there.

7:35 ***the Jews in other lands?*** Or *the Jews who live among the Greeks?*

7:37-38 ***living water:*** See "Living Water" at 4:10-14, p. 1777. A water ceremony was held each day during the Festival of Shelters, with prayer for God to send rain in the late autumn. The final day, called "the great day," was ***the climax of the festival,*** when the ceremony was repeated seven times. Water was poured over the altar as Levites sang Isa 12:3 (see Zech 14:8; see also *Mishnah Sukkah* ch 4). • ***Anyone who is thirsty may come to me!*** Jesus fulfilled an essential element in the Festival of Shelters. He himself is the source of living water, available to ***anyone who believes.*** • *Anyone who is thirsty may come to me! 38Anyone who believes in me may come and drink! For the Scriptures declare, 'Rivers of living water will flow from his heart':* Or *"Let anyone who is thirsty come to me and drink. 38For the Scriptures declare, 'Rivers of living water will flow from the heart of anyone who believes in me.' "* The syntax of the Greek allows for either interpretation.

7:39 In Jesus' crucifixion and resurrection, his life and ***the Spirit*** were poured out (see 19:34; 20:22). • ***But the Spirit had not yet been given:*** Some manuscripts read *But as yet there was no Spirit.* Still others read *But as yet there was no Holy Spirit.*

7:40 ***Surely this man is the Prophet we've been expecting:*** See Deut 18:15, 18; Mal 4:5-6.

7:41-42 These Jews, different from the crowd (7:25-27) who thought ***the Messiah*** would appear mysteriously, believed the prophecy that the Messiah would be from ***Bethlehem*** of Judea (see Mic 5:2). However, they stumbled over the fact that Jesus seemed to be from ***Galilee,*** where he grew up.

7:45-52 The story concludes with the Jewish leaders frustrated and the world divided over Jesus (cp. 7:25-27, 31-32). • ***guards returned:*** See 7:32.

7:46 Matt 7:28
7:48 John 12:42
7:50 John 3:1-2; 19:39
7:51 Deut 1:16
7:52 Isa 9:1-2; Matt 4:14-16; John 1:46
8:2 Matt 26:55
8:5 Lev 20:10; Deut 22:22-24; Job 31:11
8:6 Matt 22:15
8:7 Deut 17:7
8:11 John 5:14

priests and Pharisees demanded, "Why didn't you bring him in?"

46"We have never heard anyone speak like this!" the guards responded.

47"Have you been led astray, too?" the Pharisees mocked. 48"Is there a single one of us rulers or Pharisees who believes in him? 49This foolish crowd follows him, but they are ignorant of the law. God's curse is on them!"

50Then Nicodemus, the leader who had met with Jesus earlier, spoke up. 51"Is it legal to convict a man before he is given a hearing?" he asked.

52They replied, "Are you from Galilee, too? Search the Scriptures and see for yourself—no prophet ever comes from Galilee!"

[*The most ancient Greek manuscripts do not include John 7:53–8:11.*]

53Then the meeting broke up, and everybody went home.

A Woman Caught in Adultery

8 Jesus returned to the Mount of Olives, 2but early the next morning he was back again at the Temple. A crowd soon gathered, and he sat down and taught them. 3As he was speaking, the teachers of religious law and the Pharisees brought a woman who had been caught in the act of adultery. They put her in front of the crowd.

4"Teacher," they said to Jesus, "this woman was caught in the act of adultery. 5The law of Moses says to stone her. What do you say?"

6They were trying to trap him into saying something they could use against him, but Jesus stooped down and wrote in the dust with his finger. 7They kept demanding an answer, so he stood up again and said, "All right, but let the one who has never sinned throw the first stone!" 8Then he stooped down again and wrote in the dust.

9When the accusers heard this, they slipped away one by one, beginning with the oldest, until only Jesus was left in the middle of the crowd with the woman. 10Then Jesus stood up again and said to the woman, "Where are your accusers? Didn't even one of them condemn you?"

11"No, Lord," she said.

And Jesus said, "Neither do I. Go and sin no more."

Misunderstanding (7:32-36)

John 1:10-11; 3:19-20; 9:40-41; 12:40
Isa 6:8-13; 56:10-11
Matt 13:11-17
Acts 26:18; 28:26-27
Rom 1:21
2 Cor 3:13-18; 4:3-4
Eph 4:17-19
Heb 5:2
2 Pet 2:12
1 Jn 2:9-11
Jude 1:10
Rev 3:17

Throughout John's Gospel, people encountering Jesus misunderstood him (see 3:4; 4:11, 33; 7:35; 11:12, 50). Jesus' hearers were divided over the question of Jesus' identity. When they perceived what he was really saying, some wanted to arrest him while others wanted to become his followers (7:43-44). Only later, when Jesus' disciples had received the Spirit (16:12-13), did they really understand his significance.

The world still lives in darkness and it cannot understand the realities of life or of God (1:5). Divine revelation is inaccessible to the world. In fact, when the light of God penetrates the darkness, exposing the ugliness of the world's life, many people flee deeper into the darkness because they prefer it to the light (3:19-20). Only the transforming power of God's Spirit can provide understanding and help people see clearly as children of God (3:21; 8:12; 12:35-36, 46).

7:49-51 *Nicodemus* (ch 3) was probably in the process of coming to faith (see 19:39). Contrary to the implication of 7:48, some of the Pharisees—not just the *ignorant* crowd—believed in Jesus.

7:52 *no prophet ever comes* (some manuscripts read *the prophet does not come*) *from Galilee!* The Jewish leaders were apparently unaware that Jesus had been born in Bethlehem of Judea, not in Galilee (see Matt 2:1; Luke 2:1-7).

7:53–8:11 This story, a later addition to the Gospel of John, does not appear in the earliest Greek manuscripts. However, it is likely an authentic story from Jesus' life.

8:3 The *teachers of religious law* were Jewish scholars who specialized in knowing the OT law and the oral traditions that interpreted the law.

8:4 The form of the Greek sentence emphasizes the legal claim against the woman. She had been caught while committing the sin *of adultery.* The law required two witnesses and carefully outlined what evidence was needed.

8:5 The requirement of the *law . . . to stone her* indicates that the woman was engaged or married (Lev 20:10; Deut 22:23-24). The law also stated that her lover should be killed with her, but these religious leaders apparently ignored their obligation to that part of the statute. • These men could have dealt with the woman privately and kept her from public shame, but Jesus was their real target as they demanded, *What do you say?* Would he neglect the law since he had a reputation for mercy? Or would he ignore the woman's tragedy?

8:6 It is impossible to know what *Jesus . . . wrote in the dust.* It has been suggested that he wrote the sins of the accusers.

8:7 Jesus' answer did not mean that an accuser had to be morally perfect to make legal accusations. His reference to *the one who has never sinned* points to the motives of the accusers.

8:9 The jury crumbled as *they slipped away.* One accuser departed, followed by another, and then a succession of bystanders.

8:11 *Neither do I:* Jesus' words of assurance did not suggest that the woman was innocent. Jesus views sin and judgment seriously, yet he looks graciously and forgivingly on those caught in sin's grip.

Jesus, the Light of the World

12 Jesus spoke to the people once more and
said, "I am the light of the world. If you follow me, you won't have to walk in darkness,
because you will have the light that leads to
life."
13 The Pharisees replied, "You are making
those claims about yourself! Such testimony
is not valid."
14 Jesus told them, "These claims are valid
even though I make them about myself.
For I know where I came from and where
I am going, but you don't know this about
me. 15 You judge me by human standards,
but I do not judge anyone. 16 And if I did, my
judgment would be correct in every respect
because I am not alone. The Father who
sent me is with me. 17 Your own law says
that if two people agree about something,
their witness is accepted as fact. 18 I am one
witness, and my Father who sent me is the
other."
19 "Where is your father?" they asked.
Jesus answered, "Since you don't know
who I am, you don't know who my Father
is. If you knew me, you would also know
my Father." 20 Jesus made these statements
while he was teaching in the section of the
Temple known as the Treasury. But he was
not arrested, because his time had not yet
come.

The Unbelieving People Warned

21 Later Jesus said to them again, "I am going
away. You will search for me but will die in
your sin. You cannot come where I am going."
22 The people asked, "Is he planning to
commit suicide? What does he mean, 'You
cannot come where I am going'?"
23 Jesus continued, "You are from below; I
am from above. You belong to this world; I
do not. 24 That is why I said that you will die
in your sins; for unless you believe that I AM
who I claim to be, you will die in your sins."
25 "Who are you?" they demanded.
Jesus replied, "The one I have always
claimed to be. 26 I have much to say about
you and much to condemn, but I won't. For
I say only what I have heard from the one
who sent me, and he is completely truthful."
27 But they still didn't understand that he
was talking about his Father.
28 So Jesus said, "When you have lifted up
the Son of Man on the cross, then you will
understand that I AM he. I do nothing on my

8:12 Isa 9:1-2; John 1:4-5, 9; 3:19; 9:5; 12:35-36, 46; 2 Cor 4:6
8:14 John 7:28; 9:29
8:16 John 5:30
8:17-18 Deut 17:6; 19:15; John 5:37; 1 Jn 5:7-9
8:19 John 14:7, 9
8:20 Mark 12:41; John 7:30
8:21 John 7:34, 36; 13:33
8:22 John 7:35
8:23 John 3:31; 17:14
8:24 Exod 3:14-15; John 4:26; 8:28, 58; 13:19
8:26 John 3:32-34; 12:49
8:28 John 3:14; 5:19; 8:24; 12:32

8:12-59 The debate about whether or not Jesus is the Messiah continues from 7:52. Jesus was still at the Festival of Shelters in Jerusalem. During the festival, the conflicts Jesus had endured in ch 7 continued and intensified.

8:12 During the Festival of Shelters, sixteen gold bowls in the inner courts of the Temple were filled with oil and lighted. Jesus stood beneath these lights in the Temple (8:20) and said that he was now the source of *the light.* Jesus' light brings salvation not only to Israel but to *the world,* regardless of race or locale.

8:13 The Pharisees charged that Jesus' *claims* were *not valid* because Jewish law (Deut 19:15) requires more than one witness (cp. 5:31-32; see 8:17).

8:14-15 Jesus answered the Pharisees' charges, saying that he could make such *claims* about himself because he knew both his origin (heaven) and his destination (heaven). He then pointed to the most vital witness for his case, his Father who sent him (8:16).

8:16 *The Father:* Some manuscripts read *The One.*

8:17 *if two people agree about something, their witness is accepted as fact:* See Deut 19:15.

8:19 Throughout the festival, Jesus' audience proved they were in the darkness as they misunderstood him (see "Misunderstanding" at 7:32-36, p. 1785). They wanted to meet Jesus' *father,* who is God. Since they did not truly know God, they were unable to understand Jesus.

8:20 The *Treasury* was located in the section of the Temple called the Court of the Women. Jesus often taught there so that both men and women could hear him (Mark 12:41). • *his time:* Literally *his hour.* See notes on 2:4; 12:23.

8:21 In the earlier debate at the festival, Jesus' origins were at issue (7:27). Here, Jesus mentioned *going away* to the place he came from, meaning heaven. However, once again, his words were misunderstood.

8:22 *people:* Literally *Jewish people;* also in 8:31, 48, 52, 57.

8:23 Jesus' listeners were *from below;* they could not comprehend Jesus' meaning because he was *from above* (3:31; see note on 3:3).

8:24 *unless you believe that I AM who I claim to be:* Literally *unless you believe that I am.* Jesus used God's divine name (see 4:26; Exod 3:14), but the listeners missed the nuance (8:25). • *die in your sins:* Jesus' presence in the world, as the light penetrating the darkness, is the world's only chance for salvation.

8:25 *Who are you?* Later they understood and tried to stone Jesus for blasphemy (8:59). • *The one I have always claimed to be:* Or *Why do I speak to you at all?* The Greek text can be interpreted either way.

8:28 *When you have lifted up the Son of Man on the cross, then you will understand that I AM he:* Literally *When you have lifted up the Son of Man, then you will know that I am.* "Son of Man" is a title Jesus used for himself. See note

▸ **Herod's Temple (John 8:20).** Herod the Great, king of Judea at the time of Jesus' birth (37–4 BC), rebuilt the Temple in Jerusalem. The new structure replaced and expanded on the Second Temple that had been built during the time of Haggai, after the Jews returned from exile in Babylon (see Ezra 1–6). Herod's massive project began in 20 BC, and the core of the new structure was finished in a decade, but the work was not fully completed until AD 64. This Temple was destroyed in AD 70, just six years after its completion. Many events of Jesus' life and ministry took place within the Temple compound (see also 1:19; 2:14-15, 19-21; 5:14; 7:14, 28-32; 8:2, 59; 10:23; 11:56; Matt 4:5; 21:12-15, 23; 24:1-2; 27:5-6, 51; Mark 11:11, 15-17, 27; 12:35, 41; 13:1-2; 15:38; Luke 1:8, 23; 2:27, 36-37, 46; 4:9; 10:32; 19:45-47; 20:1; 21:1, 5, 37-38; 23:45; 24:53; Acts 2:46; 3:1-8; 4:1; 5:12, 20-26, 42; 21:23-30).

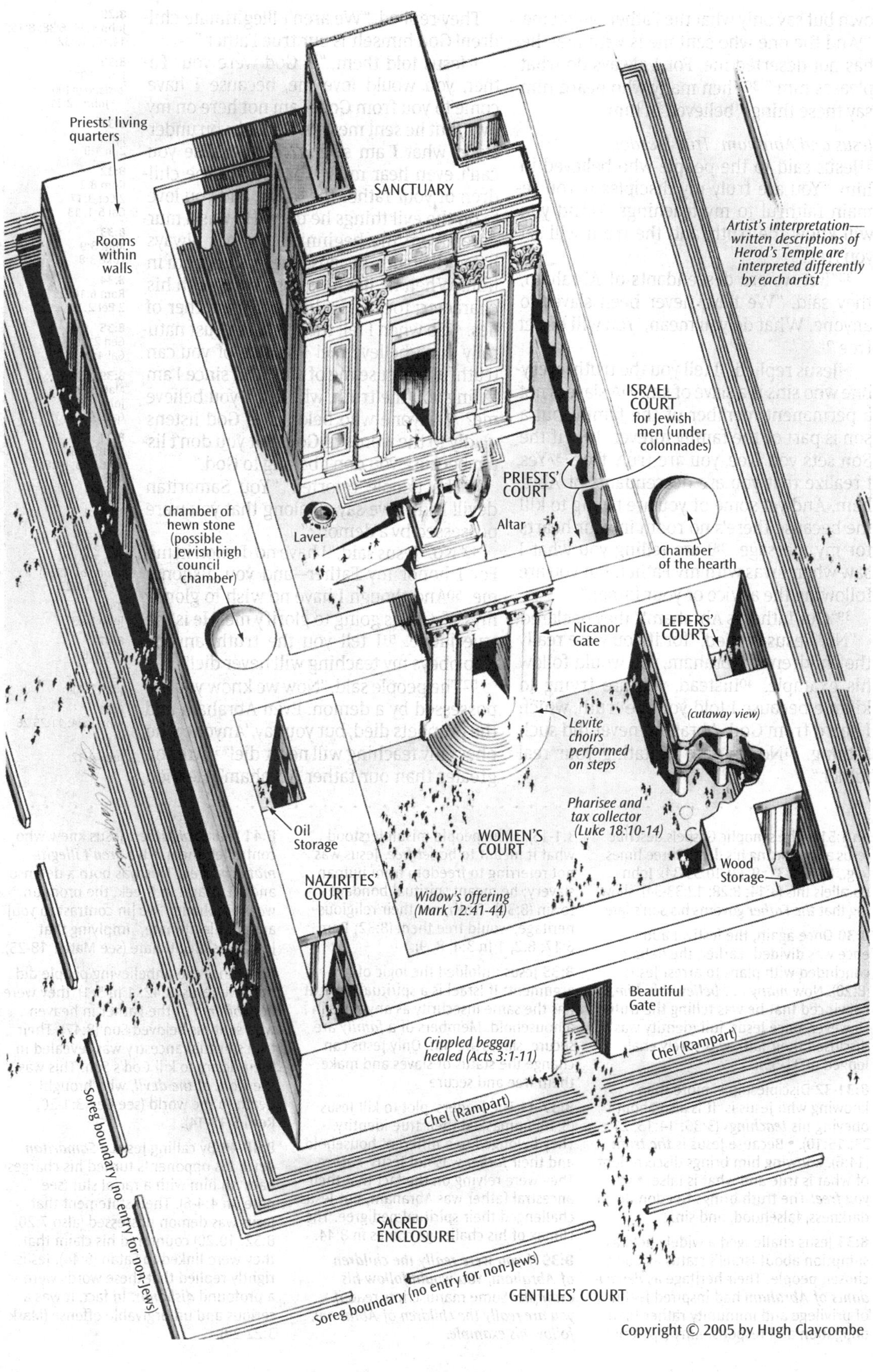
Priests' living quarters
SANCTUARY
Rooms within walls
Artist's interpretation—written descriptions of Herod's Temple are interpreted differently by each artist
ISRAEL COURT for Jewish men (under colonnades)
PRIESTS' COURT
Chamber of hewn stone (possible Jewish high council chamber)
Laver
Altar
Chamber of the hearth
Nicanor Gate
LEPERS' COURT
(cutaway view)
Levite choirs performed on steps
Pharisee and tax collector (Luke 18:10-14)
Oil Storage
WOMEN'S COURT
Wood Storage
NAZIRITES' COURT
Widow's offering (Mark 12:41-44)
Beautiful Gate
Crippled beggar healed (Acts 3:1-11)
Chel (Rampart)
Chel (Rampart)
Soreg boundary (no entry for non-Jews)
SACRED ENCLOSURE
GENTILES' COURT
Soreg boundary (no entry for non-Jews)

own but say only what the Father taught me.
29And the one who sent me is with me—he
has not deserted me. For I always do what
pleases him." 30Then many who heard him
say these things [f]believed in him.

Jesus and Abraham: True Freedom

31Jesus said to the people who believed in
him, "You are truly my disciples if you remain faithful to my teachings. 32And you
will know the truth, and the truth will set
you free."

33"But we are descendants of Abraham,"
they said. "We have never been slaves to
anyone. What do you mean, 'You will be set
free'?"

34Jesus replied, "I tell you the truth, everyone who sins is a slave of sin. 35A slave is not
a permanent member of the family, but a
son is part of the family forever. 36So if the
Son sets you free, you are truly free. 37Yes,
I realize that you are descendants of Abraham. And yet some of you are trying to kill
me because there's no room in your hearts
for my message. 38I am telling you what I
saw when I was with my Father. But you are
following the advice of your father."

39"Our father is Abraham!" they declared.
"No," Jesus replied, "for if you were really
the children of Abraham, you would follow
his example. 40Instead, you are trying to
kill me because I told you the truth, which
I heard from God. Abraham never did such
a thing. 41No, you are imitating your real
father."

They replied, "We aren't illegitimate children! God himself is our true Father."

42Jesus told them, "If God were your Father, you would love me, because I have
come to you from God. I am not here on my
own, but he sent me. 43Why can't you understand what I am saying? It's because you
can't even hear me! 44For you are the children of your father the [g]devil, and you love
to do the evil things he does. He was a murderer from the beginning. He has always
hated the truth, because there is no truth in
him. When he lies, it is consistent with his
character; for he is a liar and the father of
lies. 45So when I tell the truth, you just naturally don't believe me! 46Which of you can
truthfully accuse me of sin? And since I am
telling you the truth, why don't you believe
me? 47Anyone who belongs to God listens
gladly to the words of God. But you don't listen because you don't belong to God."

48The people retorted, "You Samaritan
devil! Didn't we say all along that you were
possessed by a demon?"

49"No," Jesus said, "I have no demon in me.
For I honor my Father—and you dishonor
me. 50And though I have no wish to glorify
myself, God is going to glorify me. He is the
true judge. 51I tell you the truth, anyone
who obeys my teaching will never die!"

52The people said, "Now we know you are
possessed by a demon. Even Abraham and
the prophets died, but you say, 'Anyone who
obeys my teaching will never die!' 53Are you
greater than our father Abraham? He died,

8:29 John 4:34; 6:38; 8:16; 14:10; 16:32
8:30 John 7:31
[f]*pisteuō* (4100) ‣John 12:11
8:31 John 15:7; 2 Jn 1:9
8:32 Rom 8:2; 2 Cor 3:17; Gal 5:1, 13
8:33 Matt 3:9; Luke 3:8
8:34 Rom 6:16, 20; 2 Pet 2:19
8:35 Gen 21:10; Gal 4:30
8:39 Matt 3:9; John 8:33; Gal 3:7, 14, 29
8:41 Deut 32:6; Isa 63:16; 64:8; Mal 1:6
8:42 1 Jn 5:1
8:44 Gen 3:4; 4:9; 1 Jn 3:8
[g]*diabolos* (1228) ‣Eph 4:27
8:45 John 18:37
8:47 1 Jn 4:6
8:50 John 5:41
8:51 John 5:24; 11:25-26
8:53 John 4:12

on 1:51. • The synoptic Gospels describe Jesus as predicting his death three times (e.g., Mark 8:31; 9:31; 10:33-34). John parallels this (3:14; 8:28; 12:33-34), showing that ***the Father*** governs his Son's fate.

8:30 Once again, the festival audience was divided. Earlier, the debate concluded with plans to arrest Jesus (8:20). Now ***many . . . believed in him,*** convinced that he was telling the truth. However, once Jesus' full identity was disclosed their faith was sorely challenged (8:31-59).

8:31-32 Discipleship is more than knowing who Jesus is. It is also about obeying his ***teachings*** (3:36; 14:15, 21, 23; 15:10). • Because Jesus is ***the truth*** (14:6), knowing him brings discernment of what is true and what is false. • ***set you free:*** The truth brings freedom from darkness, falsehood, and sin.

8:33 Jesus challenged a widely held assumption about Israel's status as God's chosen people. Their heritage as ***descendants of Abraham*** had inspired feelings of privilege and immunity rather than obligation and responsibility (cp. Amos 3:1-15). • The people misunderstood what it meant to be ***set free.*** Jesus was not referring to freedom from human slavery; he meant spiritual bondage to sin (8:34). Truth, not their religious heritage, would free them (8:32; Rom 6:17; 8:2; 1 Jn 3:4, 8, 9).

8:35 Jesus unfolded the logic of his argument: If Israel is a spiritual ***slave,*** it has the same insecurity as any slave in a household. Members of a ***family*** are secure, slaves are not. Only Jesus can change the status of slaves and make them free and secure.

8:37-41 The leaders' plot to kill Jesus (5:18) unmasked their true identity. They belonged to a different household, and their ***father*** was not Jesus' ***Father.*** They were relying on the fact that their ancestral father was Abraham, but Jesus challenged their spiritual pedigree. The climax of his challenge comes in 8:44.

8:39 ***if you were really the children of Abraham, you would follow his example:*** Some manuscripts read *if you are really the children of Abraham, follow his example.*

8:41 ***your real father:*** Jesus knew who controlled them. • ***We aren't illegitimate children!*** This was both a defense and an attack. In Greek, the pronoun *we* is emphatic: "*We* [in contrast to *you*] are not illegitimate," implying that Jesus was illegitimate (see Matt 1:18-25).

8:44 Since the unbelieving people did not love Jesus (8:42; 1 Jn 5:1), they were not ***children*** of the Father in heaven who sent his beloved Son (8:47). Their true spiritual ancestry was revealed in their desire to kill God's Son. This was the work of ***the devil,*** who brought death to the world (see Gen 3:1-20; Rom 5:12-14).

8:48-49 By calling Jesus a ***Samaritan devil,*** his opponents turned his charges back on him with a racial slur (see note on 4:4-6). Their statement that Jesus was demon possessed (also 7:20; 8:52; 10:20) countered his claim that they were linked to Satan (8:44). Jesus rightly replied that these words were a profound ***dishonor.*** In fact, it was a serious and unforgivable offense (Mark 3:22-29).

8:54 John 16:14; 17:5
8:55 John 7:28-29; 15:10
8:56 Gen 18:18; 22:17-18; Matt 13:17; Heb 11:13
8:58 Exod 3:14; Isa 43:10, 13; John 1:1; 8:24, 28
9:2 Exod 20:5; Ezek 18:20; Luke 13:2; John 9:34
9:3 John 11:4
9:4 John 5:17; 11:9; 12:35
9:5 Isa 49:6; John 1:4-5, 9; 8:12; 12:46
9:6 Mark 8:23
9:7 2 Kgs 5:10; Isa 35:5
9:8 Acts 3:10

and so did the prophets. Who do you think
you are?"
[54]Jesus answered, "If I want glory for myself, it doesn't count. But it is my Father who
will glorify me. You say, 'He is our God,' [55]but
you don't even know him. I know him. If I
said otherwise, I would be as great a liar as
you! But I do know him and obey him. [56]Your
father Abraham rejoiced as he looked forward to my coming. He saw it and was glad."
[57]The people said, "You aren't even fifty
years old. How can you say you have seen
Abraham?"
[58]Jesus answered, "I tell you the truth,
before Abraham was even born, I AM!" [59]At
that point they picked up stones to throw at
him. But Jesus was hidden from them and
left the Temple.

Jesus Brings Light to the Blind

9 As Jesus was walking along, he saw a
man who had been blind from birth.
[2]"Rabbi," his disciples asked him, "why was
this man born blind? Was it because of his
own sins or his parents' sins?"
[3]"It was not because of his sins or his parents' sins," Jesus answered. "This happened
so the power of God could be seen in him.
[4]We must quickly carry out the tasks assigned us by the one who sent us. The night
is coming, and then no one can work. [5]But
while I am here in the world, I am the light
of the world."
[6]Then he spit on the ground, made mud
with the saliva, and spread the mud over the
blind man's eyes. [7]He told him, "Go wash
yourself in the pool of Siloam" (Siloam
means "sent"). So the man went and washed
and came back seeing!
[8]His neighbors and others who knew
him as a blind beggar asked each other,
"Isn't this the man who used to sit and beg?"
[9]Some said he was, and others said, "No, he
just looks like him!"

Disciples of Jesus (9:1-41)

John 8:31-32; 12:25-26; 13:35; 18:36; Matt 5:11; 9:9-10; 10:16-22; 13:52; 16:24-28; 24:9; 27:57-58; Mark 15:40-41; Luke 14:26-33; Acts 9:2; Rom 15:5; 1 Cor 3:4-11; Eph 1:1

In the first half of John's Gospel, he introduces a variety of people who model true discipleship (see 1:19-51; 4:1-42; 9:1-41). Taken together, John provides a profile of the mature follower, or "disciple," of Christ.

What is this profile of a disciple? (1) *Disciples know who Jesus is.* In each story, titles for Jesus identify him correctly (see, e.g., 1:25, 34, 36, 38, 41; 4:19, 25, 31; 9:2, 17, 22). (2) *Disciples believe in Jesus.* They see Jesus' mighty works, listen to his profound words, and believe (see 1:50; 4:39-41; 9:35-38; see also 20:8, 25-31). (3) *Jesus' disciples understand that they must follow him if their discipleship is to be successful* (1:37-43; 8:12; 10:4-5, 27; 12:26; 21:19-22). Following implies genuine devotion, leaving what we have to embrace the journey with Jesus.

8:53 ***Who do you think you are?*** This question was antagonistic and aggressive. However, if Jesus is immortal, ruling over life and death, then he is greater than ***Abraham, the prophets,*** or any of the greatest people in Israel's history (8:58).

8:54 ***our God:*** Some manuscripts read *You say he is your God.*

8:56 Like his opponents, Jesus appealed to ***Abraham.*** Rabbis taught that God had given Abraham prophetic insight, teaching him about the coming age of the Messiah.

8:57 ***How can you say you have seen Abraham?*** (Some manuscripts read *How can you say Abraham has seen you?*): The Jewish leaders misunderstood Jesus: He was talking about his divine pre-existence, not his physical age.

8:58 ***before Abraham was even born, I AM!*** (Or *before Abraham was even born, I have always been alive;* Greek reads *before Abraham was, I am.*) Jesus' life spans the past from before creation (1:1-2) and sweeps beyond the present into eternity. • ***I AM:*** This title is reminiscent of God's name given on Mount Sinai (Exod 3:14; cp. John 4:26; Isa 43:11-13; 48:12).

8:59 Jesus' audience finally understood his claim to divinity (8:58), and they were furious. They believed they had heard blasphemy and ***picked up stones to throw at him,*** which was the proper legal response (Lev 24:16). • ***Jesus was hidden from them*** because God had appointed a different time for his death (see note on 12:23; see also 7:30, 44; Luke 4:29-30).

9:1-41 At the Festival of Shelters (chs 7–8), Jesus claimed to be the light of the world (8:12). Now John tells about Jesus giving light, both physically and spiritually, to a blind man who lived in darkness (see 9:5). The story ends with a splendid reversal of roles: The blind man who was assumed to be in spiritual darkness could see God's light, whereas the Pharisees, who could see physically and were thought to be enlightened, were shown to be spiritually blind.

9:2 The ***disciples*** assumed that someone's sin—the man's or ***his parents'***—had caused him to be ***born blind.*** Jesus corrected this common belief (9:3).

9:4 ***We must quickly carry out the tasks assigned us by the one who sent us:*** Other manuscripts read *I must quickly carry out the tasks assigned me by the one who sent me;* still others read *We must quickly carry out the tasks assigned us by the one who sent me.*

9:5 ***I am the light of the world:*** See note on 8:12.

9:6 During the NT era, ***saliva*** was used for medical purposes (see Mark 7:32-35; 8:22-25).

9:7 ***Siloam,*** a pool at the south end of the city of Jerusalem, was the source of water for the ceremonies at the Festival of Shelters. • ***Siloam means "sent":*** This phrase contained a double meaning: Jesus, who has been sent by God (4:34; 5:23, 37; 7:28; 8:26; 12:44; 14:24), told the blind man to wash in the pool called "sent."

But the beggar kept saying, "Yes, I am the same one!"

10They asked, "Who healed you? What happened?"

11He told them, "The man they call Jesus made mud and spread it over my eyes and told me, 'Go to the pool of Siloam and wash yourself.' So I went and washed, and now I can see!"

12"Where is he now?" they asked.

"I don't know," he replied.

13Then they took the man who had been blind to the Pharisees, 14because it was on the Sabbath that Jesus had made the mud and healed him. 15The Pharisees asked the man all about it. So he told them, "He put the mud over my eyes, and when I washed it away, I could see!"

16Some of the Pharisees said, "This man Jesus is not from God, for he is working on the Sabbath." Others said, "But how could an ordinary sinner do such miraculous signs?" So there was a deep division of opinion among them.

17Then the Pharisees again questioned the man who had been blind and demanded, "What's your opinion about this man who healed you?"

The man replied, "I think he must be a prophet."

18The Jewish leaders still refused to believe the man had been blind and could now see, so they called in his parents. 19They asked them, "Is this your son? Was he born blind? If so, how can he now see?"

20His parents replied, "We know this is our son and that he was born blind, 21but we don't know how he can see or who healed him. Ask him. He is old enough to speak for himself." 22His parents said this because they were afraid of the Jewish leaders, who had announced that anyone saying Jesus was the Messiah would be expelled from the synagogue. 23That's why they said, "He is old enough. Ask him."

24So for the second time they called in the man who had been blind and told him, "God should get the glory for this, because we know this man Jesus is a sinner."

25"I don't know whether he is a sinner," the man replied. "But I know this: I was blind, and now I can see!"

26"But what did he do?" they asked. "How did he heal you?"

27"Look!" the man exclaimed. "I told you once. Didn't you listen? Why do you want to hear it again? Do you want to become his disciples, too?"

28Then they cursed him and said, "You are his disciple, but we are disciples of Moses! 29We know God spoke to Moses, but we don't even know where this man comes from."

30"Why, that's very strange!" the man replied. "He healed my eyes, and yet you don't know where he comes from? 31We know that God doesn't listen to sinners, but he is ready to hear those who worship him and do his will. 32Ever since the world began, no one has been able to open the eyes of someone born blind. 33If this man were not from God, he couldn't have done it."

34"You were born a total sinner!" they answered. "Are you trying to teach us?" And they threw him out of the synagogue.

Spiritual Blindness

35When Jesus heard what had happened, he found the man and asked, "Do you believe in the Son of Man?"

9:14 Luke 13:14; John 5:9
9:16 John 3:2; 7:43
9:17 Matt 21:11
9:22 Luke 6:22; John 7:13; 12:42; 16:2; 19:38; Acts 5:13
9:24 Josh 7:19
9:28 John 5:45
9:29 John 8:14
9:31 Job 27:8-9; Ps 34:15; 66:18; 145:19; Prov 15:29; Isa 1:15; Jer 11:11; 14:12; Mic 3:4; Zech 7:13
9:33 John 3:2
9:34 John 9:2
9:37 John 4:26
9:39 Luke 4:18
9:40 Rom 2:19

9:11 The blind man identified ***Jesus*** and testified strongly about him. The man was healed of his physical infirmity, gained increasing spiritual insight (9:17, 33), and became Jesus' disciple (9:38; cp. 5:11-15).

9:13 The ***Pharisees*** (see 1:24) were arbiters of legal interpretation, so the community looked to them to explain this miracle. Rather than celebrate the healing, these religious leaders interrogated the man because Jesus had performed the miracle on the Sabbath (see 5:16-18).

9:17 The man had already identified his healer (9:11, 16). Now he made his own spiritual judgment, calling Jesus ***a prophet.***

9:18 The Pharisees wanted to discount the miracle and hoped the man's ***parents*** would deny the healing.

9:20-22 ***His parents*** confirmed that their son had been ***born blind,*** but they hesitated to judge how he could see because they were ***afraid*** of the social consequences.

9:24 ***God should get the glory for this:*** Or *Give glory to God, not to Jesus;* Greek reads *Give glory to God.* Cp. Josh 7:19.

9:28-29 The Pharisees could not defeat the logic of the miraculous sign (9:24-25, 30-33), so they turned from reason and ***cursed him*** (see 9:34). • The harsh division between Jesus and the religious leaders was clear. They considered those who followed Jesus to have rejected ***Moses*** and Judaism.

9:30 The Jewish leaders did not ***know where*** Jesus came from. The man's astonishment was understandable—a healing like this was unprecedented. Jesus' works confirmed his origin as from God. Once his true identity was known, belief and discipleship should have followed, but the Jewish leaders were willfully blind.

9:32-33 Only God could do something such as ***open the eyes of someone born blind.*** By healing the man, Jesus offered the Jewish leaders an unquestionable sign that he was ***from God*** and was the Messiah (cp. Ps 146:8; Isa 35:5; 42:7).

9:34 Discipline such as being thrown ***out of the synagogue*** was not uncommon. It brought social isolation that might require the man's departure from the village. Such serious persecution was precisely what Jesus predicted for his followers (15:18-27; 16:2).

9:35-38 Jesus pressed the man who had been blind to understand the miracle and the identity of his healer. Immediately, the man expressed faith and gave

9:41
John 15:22
10:2
Acts 20:28
10:4
Ps 80:1
John 10:27
10:6
John 16:25
10:7
John 14:6
10:8
Jer 23:1-2
Ezek 34:2-3
10:9
Ps 118:20
John 14:6
10:10
John 5:40
Acts 20:29
2 Pet 2:1
10:11
Isa 40:11
Ezek 34:11-16, 23
Heb 13:20
1 Pet 2:25
1 Jn 3:16
Rev 7:17
hpoimēn (4166)
›John 10:12

36The man answered, "Who is he, sir? I
want to believe in him."
37"You have seen him," Jesus said, "and he
is speaking to you!"
38"Yes, Lord, I believe!" the man said. And
he worshiped Jesus.
39Then Jesus told him, "I entered this
world to render judgment—to give sight to
the blind and to show those who think they
see that they are blind."
40Some Pharisees who were standing
nearby heard him and asked, "Are you saying we're blind?"
41"If you were blind, you wouldn't be
guilty," Jesus replied. "But you remain guilty
because you claim you can see.

Jesus and the Festival of Dedication (10:1-42)
The Good Shepherd and His Sheep

10 "I tell you the truth, anyone who
sneaks over the wall of a sheepfold,
rather than going through the gate, must
surely be a thief and a robber! 2But the one
who enters through the gate is the shepherd
of the sheep. 3The gatekeeper opens the
gate for him, and the sheep recognize his
voice and come to him. He calls his own
sheep by name and leads them out. 4After
he has gathered his own flock, he walks
ahead of them, and they follow him because
they know his voice. 5They won't follow a
stranger; they will run from him because
they don't know his voice."
6Those who heard Jesus use this illustration didn't understand what he meant, 7so
he explained it to them: "I tell you the truth,
I am the gate for the sheep. 8All who came
before me were thieves and robbers. But
the true sheep did not listen to them. 9Yes,
I am the gate. Those who come in through
me will be saved. They will come and go
freely and will find good pastures. 10The
thief's purpose is to steal and kill and destroy. My purpose is to give them a rich and
satisfying life.
11"I am the good hshepherd. The good
hshepherd sacrifices his life for the sheep.
12A hired hand will run when he sees a wolf

Jesus reverence due only to God (9:38; cp. 20:28).

9:35 *Son of Man:* Some manuscripts read *the Son of God.* "Son of Man" is a title Jesus used for himself (1:51; 3:13, 14; 5:27; 6:27, 53, 62; 8:28). The Greek translates a Hebrew and Aramaic phrase meaning "human being." People were not completely sure what Jesus meant by it (see 12:34). However, it signifies Jesus' identity as both human and as the Messiah (cp. Dan 7:13-14).

9:38-39 Some manuscripts do not include ***"Yes, Lord, I believe!" the man said. And he worshiped Jesus. Then Jesus told him.***

9:39 ***those who think they see:*** Literally *those who see.*

9:40-41 ***Are you saying we're blind?*** Jesus answered that those who claim to hold all religious truth will discover that they are ***blind,*** while those who recognize their spiritual poverty will find true sight. In the story, the blind man and his family frequently confessed that they did not know, while the Pharisees repeatedly stated their confidence and remained ***guilty*** because of their religious pride. If they had confessed their ignorance and admitted their spiritual blindness, they would be guiltless. Instead, their conscious and willful rejection of Jesus established their guilt.

10:1-42 Chapter 10 continues the series of festival sermons (see note on 5:1–10:42). Jesus now moves to Hanukkah (the Festival of Dedication), the timing of which is crucial to understanding the story (see note on 10:22).

10:1-21 This illustration of a shepherd and his sheep assumes a Middle Eastern understanding of shepherding and draws on OT tradition deeply embedded in first-century Jewish culture. God was the shepherd of Israel (Gen 49:24; Ps 23; 78:52-53; Isa 40:10-11). Spiritual and political leaders of Israel were also shepherds of God's people, the flock of God (Isa 56:9-12; Jer 23:1-4; Ezek 34). Jesus' sermon builds on the occasion of Hanukkah (see 10:22) to address the theme of shepherds, using this festival as an opportunity to reflect on Israel's leaders ("shepherds") in light of Ezek 34. Jesus presents himself as the only good shepherd (10:11-14).

10:1 A wilderness shepherd would build ***a sheepfold,*** a pen with low stone walls topped by thorny branches to hold his sheep at night and protect them from danger. • The pen had one ***gate*** (or opening in the wall) that was closed with branches. Any invasion of the pen was a threat to the flock. • A bad shepherd was like ***a thief and a robber.*** He exploited the sheep for his own interests and did not care for or nurture them. Bad shepherds took the sheep's milk and wool for themselves and butchered the sheep without providing for the animal's safety (Ezek 34:3; see Isa 56:11; Jer 23:1-4). This was Jesus' most stinging indictment of the Jewish leaders.

10:3 ***the sheep recognize his voice:*** The Middle Eastern shepherd is well known for having intimate knowledge of the sheep. Sheep are led with flute tunes, songs, or verbal commands.

10:4 A good shepherd always leads his sheep; he never drives them. When they recognize his voice, they trust his leadership and ***follow him.***

10:7 ***I am:*** See note on 6:35. A good shepherd is known for guarding the sheep at ***the gate*** as a sentry.

10:8 Some manuscripts do not include ***before me.***

10:9 ***will be saved*** (or ***will find safety***): As gatekeeper, Jesus keeps away those who might harm his sheep, keeping his sheep inside the pen where they are safe.

10:10 Jesus' followers must be wary of bad shepherds who desire ***to steal and kill and destroy.*** As the Hanukkah story was told to the Jewish people (see note on 10:22), they were reminded about false religious leaders whose failures had led to the loss of God's Temple in Jerusalem.

10:11-14 ***I am:*** See note on 6:35. The ***good shepherd*** leads his sheep, finds food and water, and locates paths in the wilderness (see Ps 23). The good shepherd stands between his sheep and danger (10:11) and fights to protect them. The OT describes God as Israel's shepherd (Ps 23; 80:1; Isa 40:10-11). The leaders of God's people should shepherd their flock as God does (Ezek 34:23). However, the leaders of Israel in Jesus' time were bad shepherds.

10:11-13 Small villages often created communal flocks and employed a ***hired hand*** to tend the sheep. However, an employee lacked the commitment of a true shepherd. The wilderness of Judea

coming. He will abandon the sheep because they don't belong to him and he isn't their [i]shepherd. And so the wolf attacks them and scatters the flock. 13The hired hand runs away because he's working only for the money and doesn't really care about the sheep.

14"I am the good shepherd; I know my own sheep, and they know me, 15just as my Father knows me and I know the Father. So I sacrifice my life for the sheep. 16I have other sheep, too, that are not in this sheepfold. I must bring them also. They will listen to my voice, and there will be one flock with one shepherd.

17"The Father loves me because I sacrifice my life so I may take it back again. 18No one can take my life from me. I sacrifice it voluntarily. For I have the authority to lay it down when I want to and also to take it up again. For this is what my Father has commanded."

19When he said these things, the people were again divided in their opinions about him. 20Some said, "He's demon possessed and out of his mind. Why listen to a man like that?" 21Others said, "This doesn't sound like a man possessed by a demon! Can a demon open the eyes of the blind?"

Jesus at Hanukkah

22It was now winter, and Jesus was in Jerusalem at the time of Hanukkah, the Festival of Dedication. 23He was in the Temple, walking through the section known as Solomon's Colonnade. 24The people surrounded him and asked, "How long are you going to keep us in suspense? If you are the Messiah, tell us plainly."

25Jesus replied, "I have already told you, and you don't believe me. The proof is the work I do in my Father's name. 26But you don't believe me because you are not my sheep. 27My sheep listen to my voice; I know them, and they follow me. 28I give them eternal life, and they will never perish. No one can snatch them away from me, 29for my Father has given them to me, and he is more powerful than anyone else. No one can snatch them from the Father's hand. 30The Father and I are one."

31Once again the people picked up

10:12
[i]*poimēn* (4166)
‣John 21:16
10:14
2 Tim 2:19
10:15
Matt 11:27
10:16
Isa 56:8
Ezek 37:24
John 11:52
Eph 2:14-18
10:17-18
Phil 2:8-9
Heb 5:8; 7:16
10:23
Acts 3:11; 5:12
10:24
Luke 22:67
10:25
John 5:36; 10:38; 14:11
10:26
John 8:47
10:28
John 6:37, 39; 17:12
10:29
John 14:28
17:2, 6, 24
10:30
John 1:1; 10:38; 14:8-11; 17:21-24

had many predators. When *a wolf* or other predators attacked, the hired hand would run rather than defend the sheep. Jesus will never do this; he will always stand between his sheep and danger.

10:14-17 ***I sacrifice my life for the sheep:*** Jesus was alluding to his crucifixion (ch 19).

10:15 The ***Father*** and the Son share a profound intimacy, which Jesus shares with his ***sheep*** through the Holy Spirit (14:23-31; 15:1-11).

10:16 ***other sheep:*** Believers outside Judaism would one day join Jesus' ***sheepfold*** (see 11:52). In Jesus' vision for his people, Jewish and Gentile believers from diverse cultures would become ***one flock with one shepherd*** (17:20-23).

10:18 ***No one can take my life from me:*** The Son's death was voluntary. Jesus was not a martyr or a victim. His decision to die was freely given in obedience and intimate relationship with his Father (see Acts 2:23-24). • Jesus' resurrection was not an afterthought in which God rescued his Son from tragedy. God could not be contained by a tomb, and since Jesus and the Father are one, Jesus possessed ***the authority*** to rise from death.

10:19-21 Jesus ***divided*** his audience yet again (see also 6:66-69; 7:43; 9:16), inspiring either opposition or faith. • ***He's demon possessed:*** Cp. 7:20; 8:48-49, 52. • ***people:*** Literally *Jewish people;* also in 10:24, 31.

10:22 ***Hanukkah*** was a ***winter*** festival that commemorated the rededication of the Temple after it had been defiled by Antiochus IV (175–163 BC). Two hundred years before Christ, Greek soldiers captured and pillaged the Jerusalem Temple, took its treasures and artifacts, and made it unusable for worship. In the winter of 165–164 BC, a Jewish army led by Judas Maccabeus reclaimed the Temple and rededicated it to the Lord. The Festival of Hanukkah ("dedication") marked this dedication (see *1 Maccabees* 3–4; *2 Maccabees* 8:1–10:8). During the festival, priests examined their commitment to service, using Ezek 34 as their principal text for reflection (also Jer 23:1-4; 25:32-38; Zech 11). At this Hanukkah celebration, Jesus used the shepherd theme from Ezek 34 to distinguish between himself as the good shepherd (10:11) and Israel's current religious leaders as bad shepherds (10:10, 12-13).

10:23 Massive covered colonnades surrounded the four sides of the central courtyard of the Temple. ***Solomon's Colonnade,*** on the east, provided shelter from winter weather.

10:24 The people who ***surrounded*** Jesus might have been seeking clarity, or they might have been hostile. In Luke 21:20 and Heb 11:30, the same word describes how Jerusalem and Jericho were surrounded before being destroyed; in Acts 14:20 it refers to Paul's disciples rallying around him after he was injured.

10:25-42 In Jesus' final public presentation of evidence about himself in this Gospel, he gives an exhaustive statement of his identity (10:30).

10:25 Jesus had already provided the Jewish people and their religious leaders with sufficient ***proof*** that he is the Son of God. The problem was not lack of information, but their unwillingness to ***believe*** him.

10:27-29 As the good shepherd, Jesus would die for his sheep and secure them from all predators and thieves (10:1, 8, 11; cp. Ezek 34:22-23). • The power of the ***Father,*** appearing in Christ, keeps his sheep safe. Believers cannot be taken from Jesus because no one is ***more powerful*** than he is. Their security is not sustained by their own efforts, but by Christ. • The word ***snatch*** implies violence (as in 6:15).

10:29 ***for my Father has given them to me, and he is more powerful than anyone else:*** Other manuscripts read *for what my Father has given me is more powerful than anything;* still others read *for regarding that which my Father has given me, he is greater than all.*

10:30 ***The Father*** and the Son are two separate persons with ***one*** purpose and nature (1:1, 14; 14:9; 20:28). This is the basis of Jesus' power to protect God's flock (10:28-29) and a stunning expression of Jesus' divinity.

10:31-33 The ***people*** realized Jesus' meaning (see 10:33) and wanted ***to***

10:33
Lev 24:16
Matt 26:63-66
John 1:1, 18; 5:18; 20:28
Rom 9:5
Phil 2:6
Titus 2:13
2 Pet 1:1
1 Jn 5:20
[j]*blasphēmia* (0988)
‣Eph 4:31

10:34
*Ps 82:6

10:36
John 5:17-20

10:42
John 2:23; 7:31; 8:30; 11:45; 12:11, 42

11:1
Matt 21:17
Luke 10:38

11:2
John 12:3

11:4
John 9:3

11:8
John 8:59; 10:31
[k]*rhabbi* (4461)
‣John 20:16

11:9
John 9:4

11:10
John 12:35

11:11
Dan 12:2
Matt 9:24; 27:52
Mark 5:39
Luke 8:52

stones to kill him. 32 Jesus said, "At my Father's direction I have done many good works. For which one are you going to stone me?"

33 They replied, "We're stoning you not for any good work, but for [j]blasphemy! You, a mere man, claim to be God."

34 Jesus replied, "It is written in your own Scriptures that God said to certain leaders of the people, 'I say, you are gods!' 35 And you know that the Scriptures cannot be altered. So if those people who received God's message were called 'gods,' 36 why do you call it blasphemy when I say, 'I am the Son of God'? After all, the Father set me apart and sent me into the world. 37 Don't believe me unless I carry out my Father's work. 38 But if I do his work, believe in the evidence of the miraculous works I have done, even if you don't believe me. Then you will know and understand that the Father is in me, and I am in the Father."

39 Once again they tried to arrest him, but he got away and left them. 40 He went beyond the Jordan River near the place where John was first baptizing and stayed there awhile. 41 And many followed him. "John didn't perform miraculous signs," they remarked to one another, "but everything he said about this man has come true." 42 And many who were there believed in Jesus.

Foreshadowing Jesus' Death and Resurrection (11:1–12:50)

Lazarus: A Model of Jesus' Resurrection

11 A man named Lazarus was sick. He lived in Bethany with his sisters, Mary and Martha. 2 This is the Mary who later poured the expensive perfume on the Lord's feet and wiped them with her hair. Her brother, Lazarus, was sick. 3 So the two sisters sent a message to Jesus telling him, "Lord, your dear friend is very sick."

4 But when Jesus heard about it he said, "Lazarus's sickness will not end in death. No, it happened for the glory of God so that the Son of God will receive glory from this." 5 So although Jesus loved Martha, Mary, and Lazarus, 6 he stayed where he was for the next two days. 7 Finally, he said to his disciples, "Let's go back to Judea."

8 But his disciples objected. "[k]Rabbi," they said, "only a few days ago the people in Judea were trying to stone you. Are you going there again?"

9 Jesus replied, "There are twelve hours of daylight every day. During the day people can walk safely. They can see because they have the light of this world. 10 But at night there is danger of stumbling because they have no light." 11 Then he said, "Our friend Lazarus has fallen asleep, but now I will go and wake him up."

---

kill him. The problem was not Jesus' *good works,* but his claim to divinity (see 6:42, 60; 7:29-30). Committing *blasphemy* was punishable by stoning (Lev 24:23; see John 8:59).

10:34-36 ***your own Scriptures:*** Literally *your own law.* See Ps 82:6. • ***I say, you are gods!*** If the word *god* could be applied to people other than the Lord, then Jesus was not breaking the law by referring to himself in this way. Yet Jesus is not just any son of God; he is the *Son of God* who was *sent . . . into the world.*

10:38 Jesus' ***miraculous works*** should help true believers ***know and understand*** that the full reality of God dwells in Jesus.

10:40 His revelation to the Jewish leaders now complete, Jesus retired to the region ***beyond the Jordan River*** where John the Baptist had once worked and where Jesus was baptized.

10:41 ***everything he said about this man has come true:*** See 1:19-51; 3:22-36. The fulfillment of John the Baptist's predictions confirms both that he was a prophet and that what he said about Jesus was true.

10:42 This is a note of irony. While Jesus found little faith among the religious leaders in the holy city of Jerusalem, in the desert he found ***many who . . . believed.***

11:1-57 The raising of Lazarus foreshadows Jesus' own coming death and resurrection. Even the description of Lazarus' grave (11:38, 44) prefigures Jesus' grave (20:1, 7). Shortly after this event, Jesus was anointed for burial (12:3) and the hour of his glorification began (12:23).

11:1 In Hebrew, ***Lazarus*** is a shortened form of *Eleazar* ("God helps"). Among Jews in the first century, it was the fourth-most-common name for a man (see also Luke 16:19-31). • ***Bethany*** was a small village east of Jerusalem just over the Mount of Olives (11:18), where Jesus often stayed when he was in Jerusalem. Jesus would have traveled through Bethany on the way to Jerusalem because most Jews used a route going east from Jerusalem, down to Jericho, and north to Galilee. • ***Mary and Martha*** were sisters (Luke 10:38-42). Martha was probably older; she was the host in Luke's story and here represented the family. Mary later anointed Jesus with perfume (12:1-8).

11:2 ***Mary who later poured the expensive perfume on the Lord's feet and wiped them with her hair:*** This incident is recorded in ch 12.

11:3 The ***two sisters*** had a dilemma. They knew Jesus' power as a healer, but they also realized that his return to Judea would entail personal risk (11:8).

11:4 Jesus' response paralleled his words about the man born blind (9:1-5). Jesus already knew that Lazarus was dead (11:14); he was talking about Lazarus' resurrection (11:43), which would bring ***glory*** to ***God.***

11:6 The trip from where Jesus was staying (see 10:40) to Jerusalem would have taken only one day, but Jesus followed his own sense of timing (2:4; 7:5-9) and would not be compelled by others.

11:8 The disciples were rightly worried about the risk (7:25; 8:37, 44, 59; 10:31, 39). • ***people:*** Literally *Jewish people;* also in 11:19, 31, 33, 36, 45, 54.

[12]The disciples said, "Lord, if he is sleeping, he will soon get better!" [13]They thought
Jesus meant Lazarus was simply sleeping,
but Jesus meant Lazarus had died.
[14]So he told them plainly, "Lazarus is
dead. [15]And for your sakes, I'm glad I wasn't
there, for now you will really believe. Come,
let's go see him."
[16]Thomas, nicknamed the Twin, said to
his fellow disciples, "Let's go, too—and die
with Jesus."
[17]When Jesus arrived at Bethany, he was
told that Lazarus had already been in his
grave for four days. [18]Bethany was only a
few miles down the road from Jerusalem,
[19]and many of the people had come to console Martha and Mary in their loss. [20]When
Martha got word that Jesus was coming, she
went to meet him. But Mary stayed in the
house. [21]Martha said to Jesus, "Lord, if only
you had been here, my brother would not
have died. [22]But even now I know that God
will give you whatever you ask."
[23]Jesus told her, "Your brother will rise
again."
[24]"Yes," Martha said, "he will rise when
everyone else [a]rises, at the last day."
[25]Jesus told her, "I am the resurrection
and the life. Anyone who believes in me will
live, even after dying. [26]Everyone who lives
in me and believes in me will never ever die.
Do you believe this, Martha?"
[27]"Yes, Lord," she told him. "I have always
believed you are the Messiah, the Son of
God, the one who has come into the world
from God." [28]Then she returned to Mary.
She called Mary aside from the mourners and told her, "The Teacher is here and
wants to see you." [29]So Mary immediately
went to him.
[30]Jesus had stayed outside the village, at
the place where Martha met him. [31]When
the people who were at the house consoling
Mary saw her leave so hastily, they assumed
she was going to Lazarus's grave to weep.
So they followed her there. [32]When Mary
arrived and saw Jesus, she fell at his feet and
said, "Lord, if only you had been here, my
brother would not have died."
[33]When Jesus saw her weeping and saw
the other people wailing with her, a deep anger welled up within him, and he was deeply
troubled. [34]"Where have you put him?" he
asked them.
They told him, "Lord, come and see."
[35]Then Jesus wept. [36]The people who were
standing nearby said, "See how much he
loved him!" [37]But some said, "This man
healed a blind man. Couldn't he have kept
Lazarus from dying?"
[38]Jesus was still angry as he arrived at the
tomb, a cave with a stone rolled across its
entrance. [39]"Roll the stone aside," Jesus told
them.
But Martha, the dead man's sister, protested, "Lord, he has been dead for four
days. The smell will be terrible."

11:16 Matt 10:3; John 14:5; 20:24-28; 21:2; Acts 1:13
11:17 John 11:39
11:20 Luke 10:38-42
11:22 John 16:30
11:23-24 Dan 12:2; John 5:28-29; Acts 24:15; Phil 3:21; 1 Thes 4:14
11:24 [a]*anastasis* (0386) ‣ Acts 1:22
11:25 John 1:4; 3:36; 5:21; 6:39-40; 14:6; Col 1:18; 3:4; 1 Jn 1:1-2; 5:10-11; Rev 1:17-18
11:26 John 8:51
11:27 Matt 16:16; John 6:14
11:35 Luke 19:41
11:37 John 9:6-7
11:39 John 11:17

11:16 ***Thomas, nicknamed the Twin*** (literally *Thomas, who was called Didymus*): See also 14:5; 20:24; 21:2; Mark 3:18. • ***Let's go, too—and die:*** Thomas knew that previous visits to Judea had been dangerous (5:18; 10:31, 39). Traveling to Jerusalem now would probably mean death for Jesus (cp. 11:49-50).

11:17 People were buried on the same day as their death. John noted that Lazarus had ***been in his grave for four days,*** so the miracle could not be construed as resuscitation.

11:18 ***was only a few miles:*** Greek *was about 15 stadia* [about 2.8 kilometers].

11:19 Life in NT times was lived publicly. Lazarus's large extended family, as well as the villagers, had arrived for a seven-day mourning period. To ***console*** the sisters ***in their loss,*** there was great wailing and crying (see 11:33 and note).

11:21 ***Lord, if only you had been here:*** Mary later repeated Martha's words (11:32), because both sisters knew Jesus' reputation as a healer. They concluded that Jesus would have healed Lazarus, but they did not imagine that Jesus would restore him from death.

11:22 ***whatever you ask:*** Martha thought that Jesus could still intervene in some way. Despite this, she objected when Jesus wanted to open the tomb (11:39); she wasn't thinking that Jesus would raise her brother from the dead.

11:24 ***when everyone else rises, at the last day:*** Martha misunderstood (cp. 11:11-13), thinking that Jesus was referring to the general resurrection of the dead at the end of time.

11:25 Jesus helped Martha to believe in him not simply as a healer, but as one who vanquishes death. • ***I am the resurrection and the life*** (some manuscripts do not include *and the life*): Victory over death is an aspect of living in association with Jesus. Although his followers are still mortal, they will enjoy eternal life after death. Regarding Jesus' *I am* statements, see the note on 6:35.

11:26-27 ***Do you believe this?*** Jesus was not asking if Martha believed he could bring Lazarus from the grave. Rather, did she believe that life itself is linked to Jesus? • ***"Yes, Lord":*** Even though the full implications were beyond her comprehension, she acknowledged that Jesus was indeed ***the Messiah.*** Yet she was surprised at the power he held.

11:28-32 Mary now joined the scene on the edge of the village, repeating her sister's plaintive cry. She fell at Jesus' feet, not in worship but in desperate grief.

11:33 The loud ***weeping*** and ***wailing*** typified public displays of grief in this culture (Mark 5:38), as did beating one's chest (Luke 18:13). • ***a deep anger welled up within him*** (or *he was angry in his spirit*), ***and he was deeply troubled:*** The Greek word expresses human outrage, fury, and anger. Jesus was furious, not at Martha or Mary, but at the futility of this scene and the people's unbelief in light of the reality of the resurrection.

11:39 Lazarus was buried in a tomb cut from the rocky hillside; such tombs were common. The tomb was closed and opened for further burials with a rolling ***stone*** that covered the entrance. A central door led to a cave room where burial benches were carved in stone along the inner wall. Horizontal burial chambers were cut along the top edge of the benches. See the illustration on p. 1813.

11:41 Matt 11:25
11:42 John 12:30
11:43 Luke 7:14
11:47 Matt 26:3-5
11:49 Matt 26:3
11:50 John 18:13-14
11:51 Exod 28:30; Num 27:21
11:52 Isa 49:6; Luke 2:32; John 10:16; 1 Jn 2:2
11:53 Matt 26:4
11:55 Exod 12:13; 2 Chr 30:17-19; Matt 26:1-2; Mark 14:1

[40]Jesus responded, "Didn't I tell you that you would see God's glory if you believe?" [41]So they rolled the stone aside. Then Jesus looked up to heaven and said, "Father, thank you for hearing me. [42]You always hear me, but I said it out loud for the sake of all these people standing here, so that they will believe you sent me." [43]Then Jesus shouted, "Lazarus, come out!" [44]And the dead man came out, his hands and feet bound in graveclothes, his face wrapped in a headcloth. Jesus told them, "Unwrap him and let him go!"

The Plot to Kill Jesus

[45]Many of the people who were with Mary believed in Jesus when they saw this happen. [46]But some went to the Pharisees and told them what Jesus had done. [47]Then the leading priests and Pharisees called the high council together. "What are we going to do?" they asked each other. "This man certainly performs many miraculous signs. [48]If we allow him to go on like this, soon everyone will believe in him. Then the Roman army will come and destroy both our Temple and our nation."

[49]Caiaphas, who was high priest at that time, said, "You don't know what you're talking about! [50]You don't realize that it's better for you that one man should die for the people than for the whole nation to be destroyed."

[51]He did not say this on his own; as high priest at that time he was led to prophesy that Jesus would die for the entire nation. [52]And not only for that nation, but to bring together and unite all the children of God scattered around the world.

[53]So from that time on, the Jewish leaders began to plot Jesus' death. [54]As a result, Jesus stopped his public ministry among the people and left Jerusalem. He went to a place near the wilderness, to the village of Ephraim, and stayed there with his disciples.

[55]It was now almost time for the Jewish Passover celebration, and many people from all over the country arrived in Jerusalem several days early so they could go through the purification ceremony before Passover began. [56]They kept looking for Jesus, but as they stood around in the

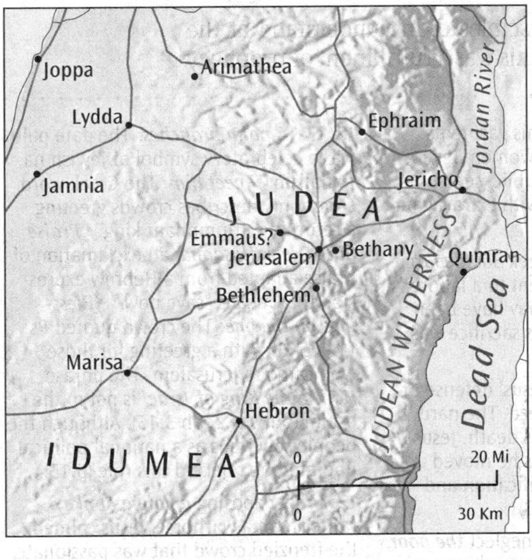

◀ Jesus' Ministry in Judea (11:1–12:19). Judea was a Roman prefecture under Pontius Pilate (see profile, p. 1691). John records much of Jesus' ministry in JERUSALEM (2:13–3:21; 5:1-47; 7:10–10:42; 12:12-50) and JUDEA (3:22; 11:1-44; 12:1-11). When the time came for Jesus' death, Jesus embarked on his final trip from Galilee to Jerusalem (see map, p. 1747). The events of 11:1–20:31 took place during Jesus' final period in and around Jerusalem.

11:45-46 As news of the miracle spread rapidly into the city of Jerusalem (12:9, 17), public opinion was again divided (6:66-69; 7:43; 9:16; 10:19; 11:37). Jesus' reputation as a healer and as one who could raise the dead was known in Galilee (see Matt 9:24-26; 10:8; 11:5). Now he had brought this power to Judea.

11:47 ***the high council:*** Greek *the Sanhedrin.*

11:48 The council's deliberations unveiled their fears that *everyone* would ***believe in him.*** If people believed that the Messiah had come, the political implications would be threatening. The Romans viewed Jewish messiahs with suspicion, and the movement surrounding Jesus might inspire them to invade and destroy Jerusalem and its Temple. • ***our Temple:*** Or *our position;* Greek reads *our place.*

11:49 ***Caiaphas*** was the ruler of the high council from AD 18–36. He worked for ten years alongside Pontius Pilate, governor of Judea (AD 26–36; see 18:29), keeping the peace with Rome. • ***at that time:*** Literally *that year;* also in 11:51.

11:50-51 ***it's better . . . that one man should die:*** Caiaphas's words were ironic. He meant that it was better for a revolutionary to die than to have the Romans crush the entire Jewish ***nation.*** But Caiaphas was correct in a way that he could not perceive. The salvation that Judaism needed had little to do with Rome; it would come through the cross of Christ. John notes that Caiaphas's inspiration was not ***his own,*** but came from God.

11:52 Christ's death was not for Israel only, but for all, including people of other cultures ***scattered around the world*** (10:16; 12:32).

11:53-54 When ***the Jewish leaders began to plot Jesus' death,*** Jesus made a judicious political move in response (11:54). • ***Ephraim*** was a village about twelve miles north of Jerusalem, where Jesus was safe from the Sanhedrin but close enough to walk to the upcoming Passover festival (11:55).

11:55-57 As crowds arrived in Jerusalem on pilgrimage for ***Passover*** (see 2:13), the city was buzzing with talk about Jesus and his miracle of raising Lazarus from the dead. People wondered if Jesus would be obedient to the law and come to the city to celebrate or play it safe in the countryside. The ***priests and Pharisees*** knew that Jesus was faithful to the law and would attend the festival, so they tried to make the city a trap for him.

Temple, they said to each other, "What do
you think? He won't come for Passover, will
he?" 57Meanwhile, the leading priests and
Pharisees had publicly ordered that anyone
seeing Jesus must report it immediately so
they could arrest him.

Jesus Anointed at Bethany
John 12:1-11; cp. Matt 26:6-13 // Mark 14:3-9; cp. Luke 7:36-50

12 Six days before the Passover celebration began, Jesus arrived in Bethany,
the home of Lazarus—the man he had
raised from the dead. 2A dinner was prepared in Jesus' honor. Martha served, and
Lazarus was among those who ate with
him. 3Then Mary took a twelve-ounce jar
of expensive perfume made from essence
of nard, and she [b]anointed Jesus' feet with
it, wiping his feet with her hair. The house
was filled with the fragrance.
4But Judas Iscariot, the disciple who
would soon betray him, said, 5"That perfume was worth a year's wages. It should
have been sold and the money given to the
poor." 6Not that he cared for the poor—he
was a thief, and since he was in charge of
the disciples' money, he often stole some
for himself.
7Jesus replied, "Leave her alone. She did
this in preparation for my burial. 8You will
always have the poor among you, but you
will not always have me."
9When all the people heard of Jesus' arrival, they flocked to see him and also to see
Lazarus, the man Jesus had raised from the
dead. 10Then the leading priests decided to
kill Lazarus, too, 11for it was because of him
that many of the people had deserted them
and [c]believed in Jesus.

Jesus' Messianic Entry into Jerusalem
John 12:12-19 // Matt 21:1-11 // Mark 11:1-11 // Luke 19:28-40

12The next day, the news that Jesus was on
the way to Jerusalem swept through the city.
A large crowd of Passover visitors 13took
palm branches and went down the road to
meet him. They shouted,

"Praise God!
Blessings on the one who comes in the
name of the LORD!
Hail to the King of Israel!"

14Jesus found a young donkey and rode on it,
fulfilling the prophecy that said:

15 "Don't be afraid, people of Jerusalem.
Look, your King is coming,
riding on a donkey's colt."

16His disciples didn't understand at the
time that this was a fulfillment of prophecy.

12:1-8 //Matt 26:6-13 //Mark 14:3-9
12:1 John 11:1
12:2 Luke 10:38-42
12:3 Luke 7:37-38 [b]*aleiphō* (0218) ‣Jas 5:14
12:4 John 6:71
12:6 John 13:29
12:7 John 19:40
12:8 Deut 15:11
12:10 Luke 16:31
12:11 [c]*pisteuō* (4100) ‣Acts 5:14
12:12-19 //Matt 21:1-11 //Mark 11:1-11 //Luke 19:28-38
12:13 Lev 23:40 *Ps 118:25-26 Zeph 3:15
12:15 Isa 35:4 *Zech 9:9
12:16 John 2:22; 7:39

12:1-50 Two stories build simultaneously. A growing number of people are praising Jesus (this climaxes in 12:12), and the authorities are increasingly determined to arrest him and put him to death. • John records three events that occurred just days prior to Passover (12:1-11, 12-19, 20-36). Then he explains why most of the people refused to believe and details Jesus' final public appeal (12:37-50).

12:1 Pilgrims from throughout Israel began arriving in Jerusalem the week *before the Passover.* The festival was on Thursday that year; Jesus arrived late the preceding Friday, just before the Sabbath.

12:2 *who ate:* Or *who reclined.* The typical posture for eating was to recline at a low table.

12:3 ***Mary . . . anointed Jesus' feet:*** Doing so was not awkward, because Jews reclined at formal meals, but it was certainly a dramatic gesture (cp. Matt 26:6-16; Mark 14:3-9). • ***a twelve-ounce jar:*** Greek *1 litra* [327 grams]. • ***Nard,*** a precious spice imported from North India, was sweet, red, and smelled like gladiola perfume. Twelve ounces of nard cost a year's wages (12:5). According to Mark, Mary also anointed Jesus' head (Mark 14:3), and the perfume ran down and scented his garments (Mark 14:8). • ***her hair:*** Women never unveiled their hair in public (see Luke 7:38). Mary was acting with extravagant abandon and devotion.

12:5 ***a year's wages:*** Greek *300 denarii.* A denarius was equivalent to a laborer's full day's wage. Judas may have been exaggerating, but Mary's sacrifice was certainly very costly.

12:7 ***Leave her alone:*** Jesus' defense of Mary interpreted her deed. The nard was a ***burial*** spice for his death. Jesus was readied for burial as he moved toward the hour of glorification and death (see note on 12:23).

12:8 Jesus would never neglect ***the poor,*** but this opportunity to serve him was unparalleled.

12:9 ***people:*** Literally *Jewish people;* also in 12:11.

12:11 ***had deserted them:*** Or *had deserted their traditions;* literally *had deserted.*

12:12 ***The next day*** was Sunday (see 12:1). • ***A large crowd*** of pilgrims (many from Galilee) camped in this region. As Jesus followed the road to Jerusalem, they cheered him. This triumphal entry appears in all four Gospels (Matt 21:1-11; Mark 11:1-11; Luke 19:29-38).

12:13-14 ***palm branches:*** The date palm was a celebratory symbol of Jewish nationalism. • ***meet him:*** The Greek word commonly describes crowds greeting a returning, triumphant king. • ***Praise God:*** Greek *Hosanna,* an exclamation of praise adapted from a Hebrew expression that means "save now." • ***Blessings on the one:*** The crowd quoted Ps 118:25-26, with a greeting for those who came to Jerusalem. The phrase ***Hail to the King of Israel*** is not in the psalm (but see Zeph 3:15). Although the people saw Jesus as a national political liberator, he rejected this role (6:15).

12:14 By choosing ***a young donkey*** rather than a warhorse, Jesus calmed the frenzied crowd that was passionate for his kingship. He also fulfilled OT predictions regarding the Messiah (see Zech 9:9) and showed that his kingship was not that of a warrior. His gift is life, not conquest.

12:15 This verse is a quotation of Zech 9:9 • ***people of Jerusalem:*** Literally *daughter of Zion.*

12:16 The crowds and even the ***disciples didn't understand*** Jesus' true significance. When the disciples received the Holy Spirit following Jesus' glorification, they fully comprehended who Jesus was (see 2:22).

12:17 John 11:43-44
12:18 John 12:11; 19:37
12:21 John 1:43-44
12:23 John 13:32; 17:1
12:24 1 Cor 15:36
12:25 Matt 10:39; Luke 9:24; 17:33
12:26 John 14:3; 17:24
12:27 Ps 6:3; Matt 26:38; Mark 14:34
12:28 Matt 3:17; 17:5; Mark 1:11; 9:7; Luke 3:22; 9:35; 2 Pet 1:17-18
12:31 John 14:30; 16:11; Eph 2:2
12:32 John 3:14; 6:44
12:34 Ps 89:4, 36; 110:4; Isa 9:7; Ezek 37:25; Dan 7:14

But after Jesus entered into his glory, they
remembered what had happened and realized that these things had been written
about him.
17Many in the crowd had seen Jesus call
Lazarus from the tomb, raising him from
the dead, and they were telling others about
it. 18That was the reason so many went out
to meet him—because they had heard about
this miraculous sign. 19Then the Pharisees
said to each other, "There's nothing we can
do. Look, everyone has gone after him!"

Jesus Predicts His Death

20Some Greeks who had come to Jerusalem
for the Passover celebration 21paid a visit
to Philip, who was from Bethsaida in Galilee. They said, "Sir, we want to meet Jesus."
22Philip told Andrew about it, and they went
together to ask Jesus.
23Jesus replied, "Now the time has come
for the Son of Man to enter into his glory. 24I
tell you the truth, unless a kernel of wheat
is planted in the soil and dies, it remains
alone. But its death will produce many new
kernels—a plentiful harvest of new lives.
25Those who love their life in this world will
lose it. Those who care nothing for their
life in this world will keep it for eternity.
26Anyone who wants to be my disciple must
follow me, because my servants must be
where I am. And the Father will honor anyone who serves me.
27"Now my soul is deeply troubled.
Should I pray, 'Father, save me from this
hour'? But this is the very reason I came!
28Father, bring glory to your name."
Then a voice spoke from heaven, saying,
"I have already brought glory to my name,
and I will do so again." 29When the crowd
heard the voice, some thought it was thunder, while others declared an angel had
spoken to him.
30Then Jesus told them, "The voice was for
your benefit, not mine. 31The time for judging this world has come, when Satan, the
ruler of this world, will be cast out. 32And
when I am lifted up from the earth, I will
draw everyone to myself." 33He said this to
indicate how he was going to die.
34The crowd responded, "We understood
from Scripture that the Messiah would live
forever. How can you say the Son of Man

12:17-19 This scene describes the apex of Jesus' popularity.

12:17 *were telling others:* Literally *were testifying.*

12:19 *everyone:* Literally *the world.* The Pharisees' words were more significant than they realized. Jesus came to reach the world (3:17), and the Pharisees said that Jesus had accomplished his task.

12:20 Among the people drawn to Jesus (12:19) were ***some Greeks,*** God-fearing Gentiles who had come to Passover to worship. Jesus' mission was not simply to Israel but encompassed the entire world (10:16; 11:52). Following Jesus' resurrection, the church's mission was to go beyond Judea to Samaria, and ultimately to the ends of the earth (Matt 28:19; Acts 1:8).

12:21 The Greeks approached ***Philip*** because he had a Greek name and was no doubt Greek.

12:23 Jesus often said that ***the time*** (literally *the hour*) had not yet ***come*** (2:4; 7:30; 8:20), but now it had. The coming of the Greeks also marked the beginning of the key moment in Jesus' ministry—the time of his glorification. This occurred when Jesus' sacrificial work on the cross was completed (19:30), he rose from the dead (ch 20), he gave the Spirit (20:22), and he returned to his place of glory in heaven (17:5, 11). The connection with the Greeks who had come to Jerusalem (12:20) was significant: Jesus' ministry among the Jews alone was finished and he now belonged to the wider world. • ***Son of Man*** is a title Jesus used for himself.

12:24 The central event of Jesus' glorification (12:23) was the cross. As with a ***kernel . . . planted in the soil,*** Jesus' ***death*** would bring abundant life.

12:25 For disciples, sacrifice and self-effacement are means of gaining the fullness of life provided by Jesus' sacrifice. Those who renounce the ***world*** will join Jesus in ***eternity*** and be honored by God just as Jesus is.

12:27 ***my soul is deeply troubled:*** John used the same term (Greek *tarassō*) to describe Jesus' strong emotion of agony before Lazarus' tomb (11:33; also 13:21). When Jesus stood before death, he could not be impassive. Jesus experienced genuine anguish, yet he remained strong in obedience to the Father's will (5:19-23; 6:37; 8:29, 38; 14:31).

12:28 ***a voice spoke from heaven:*** Cp. Matt 3:17; 17:5; Mark 1:11; 9:7; Luke 3:22; 9:35. • God had already ***brought glory*** to himself when Christ entered the world (1:14) and through Jesus' work, which showed God's power to the world. • ***I will do so again:*** The final display of glory would come at the cross (see 12:23; 17:1). In John, the cross is an event of ***glory*** as Christ was "lifted up" (12:32) and glorified there. Jesus was prepared for crucifixion like a king coming to his coronation; the cross was like a throne (see 19:19-22), and he was buried like royalty. Jesus' time of glorification included the entire sequence from arrest through resurrection.

12:29 It was impossible for people to comprehend what was happening with Jesus, and many of his signs led to confusion and division in ***the crowd.*** Only later did his disciples understand (2:22; 12:16), when Jesus was glorified and the Spirit was given. Still, God's voice symbolized his validation of his Son before the world.

12:31-33 ***The time for judging*** does not occur only on Judgment Day; it began when the light penetrated the darkness and unmasked it (3:19; 5:24; 9:39). • ***Satan, the ruler of this world,*** is the architect of darkness, corrupter of the world, and promoter of death. Although Satan's final demise lies in the future, the work of Christ unraveled Satan's domain (see Luke 10:17-18; Mark 3:27). Christ is now enthroned as ruler in heaven (Acts 7:55-56; Eph 1:19-22).

12:32-34 ***when I am lifted up from the earth*** (see 3:14; 8:28): The crowd did not understand what Jesus meant. The Greek verb refers to being exalted (Matt 23:12) or honored (Luke 10:15). In John, the cross was not a place of shame and disgrace for Jesus, but the place where Jesus' true glory was shown.

12:34 ***from Scripture:*** Literally *from the law.* • Popular Judaism believed that ***the Messiah would live forever*** and triumph over his foes. Jesus' point of view seemed incomprehensible.

will die? Just who is this Son of Man, anyway?"

35Jesus replied, "My light will shine for you just a little longer. Walk in the light while you can, so the darkness will not overtake you. Those who walk in the darkness cannot see where they are going. 36Put your trust in the light while there is still time; then you will become children of the light."

After saying these things, Jesus went away and was hidden from them.

The Unbelief of the People

37But despite all the miraculous signs Jesus had done, most of the people still did not believe in him. 38This is exactly what Isaiah the prophet had predicted:

"Lord, who has believed our message?
 To whom has the Lord revealed his
  powerful arm?"

39But the people couldn't believe, for as Isaiah also said,

40"The Lord has blinded their eyes
 and hardened their hearts—
so that their eyes cannot see,
 and their hearts cannot understand,
and they cannot turn to me
 and have me heal them."

41Isaiah was referring to Jesus when he said this, because he saw the future and spoke of the Messiah's glory. 42Many people did believe in him, however, including some of the Jewish leaders. But they wouldn't admit it for fear that the Pharisees would expel them from the synagogue. 43For they loved human praise more than the praise of God.

44Jesus shouted to the crowds, "If you trust me, you are trusting not only me, but also God who sent me. 45For when you see me, you are seeing the one who sent me. 46I have come as a light to shine in this dark world, so that all who put their trust in me will no longer remain in the dark. 47I will not judge those who hear me but don't obey me, for I have come to save the world and not to judge it. 48But all who reject me and my message will be judged on the day of judgment by the truth I have spoken. 49I don't speak on my own authority. The Father who sent me has commanded me what to say and how to say it. 50And I know his commands lead to eternal life; so I say whatever the Father tells me to say."

3. THE BOOK OF GLORY: THE WORD IS GLORIFIED (13:1–20:31)

The Passover Meal (13:1-30)

Jesus Washes His Disciples' Feet

13 Before the Passover celebration, Jesus knew that his hour had come to leave this world and return to his Father. He had loved his disciples during his ministry on earth, and now he loved them to the very end. 2It was time for supper, and the devil had already prompted Judas, son of Simon Iscariot, to betray Jesus. 3Jesus knew that the Father had given him authority over everything and that he had come from

12:35 John 8:12; 9:4; 12:46
12:36 John 8:59; Eph 5:8; 1 Thes 5:5
12:38 *Isa 53:1; Rom 10:16
12:40 *Isa 6:10; Matt 13:14
12:41 Isa 6:1
12:42 John 7:13, 48; 9:22-23; 12:11
12:43 John 5:44
12:45 John 14:9
12:46 John 1:4; 3:19; 8:12; 9:5
12:47 John 3:17; 8:15
13:1 John 16:28; 17:1
13:2 Luke 22:3; John 6:70-71

• ***who is this Son of Man, anyway?*** The Jews did not understand what sort of Messiah planned to die.

12:36 Jesus was ***the light*** (1:4, 7-9; 3:19-21; 8:12), and he urged the crowd to quickly make the choice to believe in him before it was too late. • They had the choice of becoming ***children of the light*** by rebirth through the power of God (1:12-13). • ***Jesus . . . was hidden from them:*** Jesus withdrew first from Judea (11:54) and then from this audience (12:36), and soon he would withdraw from the world (17:11).

12:37-38 Jesus' work was finished, yet ***most of the people . . . did not believe in him.*** His sermons before the world were complete and the signs had been displayed, but he was rejected (1:11). • The quotation is from Isa 53:1.

12:39-40 ***The people couldn't believe:*** John quotes Isa 6:10 to explain Israel's unbelief (see Matt 13:13-15; Mark 4:12; Luke 8:10; Acts 28:26-27). When revelation comes, we must believe. If we refuse, the light disappears (12:35-36). When God's light departs from the world, the darkness closes over unbelieving hearts.

12:41 ***Isaiah*** had glimpsed ***the Messiah's glory*** and how the world would respond (see Isa 6:10).

12:42-43 ***Many people did believe in him,*** but they ***wouldn't admit it.*** However, to follow Jesus involves telling others about him despite the social consequences (1:35-51; 4:1-42).

12:44-50 Jesus makes a final appeal for belief. These verses summarize chs 1–12. Jesus was sent by the Father, the sole source of his ministry. Jesus is the light shining in darkness to bring salvation and eternal life to all who believe in him.

12:49-50 The greatest error is for people to see the light and reject it, thinking it has no connection with the ***Father who sent*** the light.

13:1–20:31 This section focuses on the sign of the cross, the great climax of Jesus' life, as well as the time Jesus spent preparing his disciples for it (chs 13–17). Jesus is glorified through each event of these momentous days. Jesus' arrest, trial, crucifixion, and resurrection all evoke responses of awe. On the cross, Jesus is elevated in glory before the world (12:32).

13:1-38 The setting is Jesus' final Passover meal on Thursday evening, when Judas Iscariot betrays Jesus. John does not record the meal itself as the synoptic Gospels do (Matt 26:17-29; Mark 14:12-25; Luke 22:7-20; see also 1 Cor 11:23-26). John emphasizes other activities at the event, such as the foot washing (13:1-17), Judas's betrayal (13:18-30), and the prediction of Peter's denials (13:31-38).

13:1 ***he loved them to the very end:*** Or *he showed them the full extent of his love.*

13:2 ***Judas . . . Iscariot,*** who had refused to believe, was engulfed by darkness and had become Satan's pawn (see note on 12:39-40). • ***the devil had already prompted Judas:*** Or *the devil had already intended for Judas.*

13:4 Luke 12:37; 22:27
13:5 Luke 7:44; John 12:3
13:8 Ezek 36:25; 1 Cor 6:11; Eph 5:26; Titus 3:5
13:10 John 15:3
13:11 John 6:64, 70-71; 13:2
13:13 1 Cor 12:3
13:14 Luke 22:27; 1 Tim 5:10; 1 Pet 5:5
13:15 Phil 2:5-7; 1 Pet 5:3-5; 1 Jn 2:6; 3:16
13:16 [d]*doulos* (1401) ‣John 15:15
13:17 Jas 1:25
13:18 *Ps 41:9
13:20 Matt 10:40; Luke 10:16
13:21-30 //Matt 26:21-25; //Mark 14:18-21; //Luke 22:21-23
13:23 John 19:26
13:25 John 21:20

God and would return to God. 4So he got up
from the table, took off his robe, wrapped a
towel around his waist, 5and poured water
into a basin. Then he began to wash the disciples' feet, drying them with the towel he
had around him.
6When Jesus came to Simon Peter, Peter
said to him, "Lord, are you going to wash my
feet?"
7Jesus replied, "You don't understand now
what I am doing, but someday you will."
8"No," Peter protested, "you will never
ever wash my feet!"
Jesus replied, "Unless I wash you, you
won't belong to me."
9Simon Peter exclaimed, "Then wash my
hands and head as well, Lord, not just my
feet!"
10Jesus replied, "A person who has bathed
all over does not need to wash, except for
the feet, to be entirely clean. And you disciples are clean, but not all of you." 11For Jesus
knew who would betray him. That is what
he meant when he said, "Not all of you are
clean."
12After washing their feet, he put on his
robe again and sat down and asked, "Do
you understand what I was doing? 13You
call me 'Teacher' and 'Lord,' and you are
right, because that's what I am. 14And since
I, your Lord and Teacher, have washed your
feet, you ought to wash each other's feet. 15I
have given you an example to follow. Do
as I have done to you. 16I tell you the truth,
[d]slaves are not greater than their master.
Nor is the messenger more important than
the one who sends the message. 17Now that
you know these things, God will bless you
for doing them.
18"I am not saying these things to all of
you; I know the ones I have chosen. But this
fulfills the Scripture that says, 'The one
who eats my food has turned against me.'
19I tell you this beforehand, so that when
it happens you will believe that I Am the
Messiah. 20I tell you the truth, anyone who
welcomes my messenger is welcoming me,
and anyone who welcomes me is welcoming
the Father who sent me."

Jesus Predicts Judas's Betrayal

John 13:21-30 // Matt 26:20-25 // Mark 14:17-21 // Luke 22:21-23

21Now Jesus was deeply troubled, and he exclaimed, "I tell you the truth, one of you will
betray me!"
22The disciples looked at each other, wondering whom he could mean. 23The disciple
Jesus loved was sitting next to Jesus at the
table. 24Simon Peter motioned to him to ask,
"Who's he talking about?" 25So that disciple

13:4-5 Foot washing, common in the Hellenistic and Jewish cultures as a daily routine and as a gesture of hospitality (see Luke 7:36-50), was a lowly, menial task reserved for servants. When Jesus ***began to wash the disciples' feet***, he took the posture of a slave.

13:8 Based on the depth of his devotion to Jesus, it is understandable that ***Peter protested.*** But Jesus was not simply giving Peter a model of service; this was a symbolic pre-enactment of his greater act of sacrifice on the cross (13:7). Receiving Jesus' spiritual cleansing is a condition for discipleship, so if Peter could not accept this act, he could not be Jesus' disciple at all.

13:9 ***wash my hands and head as well:*** Peter misunderstood Jesus (cp. 2:19-20; 3:3-4). Peter thought that to have more water was to have more of Jesus. Only when Peter received the Spirit did everything become clear (e.g., see Acts 2:14-36).

13:10 Jesus referred to an ultimate cleansing through his sacrifice which makes ***a person*** clean ***all over.*** • Some manuscripts do not include *except for the feet.*

13:14-15 Jesus' acts of service, such as washing feet and dying on the cross, provided ***an example*** of personal sacrifice ***to follow.*** • ***wash each other's feet:*** Foot washing was so commonplace that Jesus might have intended a literal repetition of his act, or he might have seen it as symbolic. Either way, Jesus wants similar servanthood and sacrifice to characterize his followers.

13:16 ***slaves are not greater than their master:*** This proverb was popular and appears in many places (see also 15:20; Matt 10:24; Luke 6:40). Here, Jesus meant that the sacrifice modeled by the master should be seen in the life of the servant.

13:18 ***I am not saying these things to all of you:*** The subject of Judas's betrayal enters the story for the third time (13:2, 11). The matter weighed heavily on Jesus (13:21). • ***I know the ones I have chosen:*** The statement does not imply that Jesus chose only the eleven and that Judas was an outcast. Jesus chose Judas and gave him every opportunity to believe. He realized that Judas had embraced the darkness rather than the light (6:70). • ***The one who eats my food has turned against me*** (literally *has lifted his heel against me*): See Ps 41:9. Eating together was a cultural symbol of personal intimacy, which made Judas's betrayal all the more treacherous.

13:19 Judas's betrayal did not take Jesus unaware, and it should not shock his disciples ***when it happens.*** • ***that I Am the Messiah:*** Or *that the 'I Am' has come;* or *that I am the Lord;* literally *that I am.* By using the phrase "I am," Jesus clearly equated himself with the God of the OT. See Exod 3:14.

13:21 For the third time, ***Jesus was deeply troubled*** (literally *was troubled in his spirit;* Greek *tarassō;* see 11:33; 12:27). The personal betrayal of Judas brought Jesus profound grief.

13:23 ***The disciple Jesus loved*** appears at the cross (19:26-27), at the tomb (20:2-9), and at the resurrection (21:1, 20-23). He is the author of this Gospel (21:24-25). Some scholars believe that Lazarus was in fact the disciple whom Jesus loved (see 11:3, 5, 36), but the person referred to here was among the twelve apostles, usually identified as the apostle John. • ***was sitting next to Jesus at the table:*** Literally *was reclining on Jesus' bosom.* They were probably reclining at a *triclinium,* a U-shaped table with couches. Guests reclined on the couches, while the center provided access to servers. The diners supported their bodies by their left elbows while using their right hands for eating. Feet were extended away from the table (cp. Luke 7:38).

13:25 Peter told "the disciple Jesus loved" (13:23), who was sitting next to

leaned over to Jesus and asked, "Lord, who
is it?"
26Jesus responded, "It is the one to whom
I give the bread I dip in the bowl." And when
he had dipped it, he gave it to Judas, son of
Simon Iscariot. 27When Judas had eaten
the bread, [e]Satan entered into him. Then
Jesus told him, "Hurry and do what you're
going to do." 28None of the others at the table knew what Jesus meant. 29Since Judas
was their treasurer, some thought Jesus was
telling him to go and pay for the food or to
give some money to the poor. 30So Judas left
at once, going out into the night.

Jesus' Final Farewell (13:31–17:26)

Jesus Predicts Peter's Denial

John 13:36-38; cp. Matt 26:31-35 // Mark 14:27-31; cp. Luke 22:31-34

31As soon as Judas left the room, Jesus said,
"The time has come for the Son of Man to enter into his glory, and God will be glorified
because of him. 32And since God receives
glory because of the Son, he will soon give
glory to the Son. 33Dear children, I will be
with you only a little longer. And as I told
the Jewish leaders, you will search for me,
but you can't come where I am going. 34So
now I am giving you a new commandment:
Love each other. Just as I have loved you, you
should love each other. 35Your love for one
another will prove to the world that you are
my disciples."
36Simon Peter asked, "Lord, where are
you going?"
And Jesus replied, "You can't go with me
now, but you will follow me later."
37"But why can't I come now, Lord?" he
asked. "I'm ready to die for you."
38Jesus answered, "Die for me? I tell you
the truth, Peter—before the rooster crows
tomorrow morning, you will deny three
times that you even know me.

Jesus, the Way to the Father

14 "Don't let your [f]hearts be troubled.
Trust in God, and trust also in me.
2There is more than enough room in my
Father's home. If this were not so, would I
have told you that I am going to prepare a

13:27 Luke 22:3; John 13:2; [e]*satanas* (4567) ‣Acts 5:3
13:29 John 12:6
13:30 Luke 22:53
13:31-32 John 12:23; 17:1, 5
13:33 John 7:33-34; 8:21
13:34 Lev 19:18; Eph 5:2; 1 Thes 4:9; 1 Pet 1:22; 1 Jn 2:8; 3:23; 4:10-11
13:35 1 Jn 3:14; 4:20
13:36-38 //Matt 26:33-35; //Mark 14:29-31; //Luke 22:33-34
13:36 John 21:18; 2 Pet 1:14
14:1 [f]*kardia* (2588) ‣Acts 15:9
14:2 Ps 90:1; John 2:16, 19-21; 14:6

Jesus, to ask the betrayer's identity. As he reclined next to Jesus, he ***leaned over to Jesus*** and spoke privately.

13:26 Meals were eaten with flat ***bread***, which diners would ***dip*** into a common ***bowl***. When Jesus gave a morsel to Judas (cp. Ruth 2:14), the disciples might have thought Jesus was honoring him. They did not understand what was occurring. They even thought that Judas's departure (13:29) fulfilled an official duty for the feast! But Jesus was signaling to Judas that he understood Judas's plan and was not taken by surprise. Jesus' knowledge is profound and complete (see 1:48; 2:25).

13:27 When ***Satan entered into*** Judas (see Luke 22:3), he became an example of what happens to those who are consumed by the darkness. Satan uses such people as pawns in a wider struggle against the light. • ***Hurry and do what you're going to do:*** In issuing this command, Jesus once again showed that he was in control, not human beings or Satan (see note on 7:30).

13:28-29 ***None of the others*** suspected that something odd was happening. Passover evening was one of the only nights when the city gates were left open. The night was spent in prayer and meditation, ***money*** was given ***to the poor***, and provisions were always needed for this complex meal.

13:30 ***out into the night:*** Judas's departure was emblematic: The darkness had swallowed him completely (see note on 13:2; cp. 3:19). Jesus, the light of the world, is the antithesis of the night.

13:31–17:26 The OT and later Jewish literature include numerous examples of farewells in which a dying person offers last words to intimate friends (see Gen 49:1-27; Deut 31–34; Josh 23–24; 1 Sam 12; 1 Chr 28–29). Such farewells used a standard form. The dying person, surrounded by his loved ones, comforted them and exhorted them to obey the law. He prayed and blessed them and often left behind some writings. In some cases, the departing person passed on his "spirit" to his followers or his successor (see Num 27:18; Deut 34:9; 2 Kgs 2:9-14). Each of these elements is present in Jesus' farewell. • This section is often called the Upper Room Discourse, since the meal was taken in an "upstairs room" (Luke 22:39).

13:31 ***The time has come:*** Judas's departure into the night marks a solemn divide in the plot of the Gospel. Jesus was left with his intimate friends as the hour of glory was dawning. This time was launched by Judas's betrayal, and it culminated in the resurrection. • ***Son of Man*** is a title Jesus used for himself.

13:32 Some manuscripts do not include ***And since God receives glory because of the Son.***

13:33 Jesus addressed the apostles as his ***children***, marking the start of his farewell address.

13:34-35 That the disciples were to love one another was not ***a new commandment*** (see Lev 19:18). However, that they were to love each other with the sort of love modeled by Jesus was dramatic. Jesus' love for God was expressed in perfect obedience (14:31); now this kind of love was his command—that disciples express their love for Jesus in committed obedience.

13:37 Peter claimed to be ***ready to die*** for Jesus, yet his denials are well known in the synoptic Gospels (Matt 26:32-34; Mark 14:27-30; Luke 22:31-34). Although Peter's verve and devotion failed, he was restored (21:15-19).

14:1-31 Jesus provided answers to his disciples' many spoken and unspoken concerns.

14:1 Jesus had himself been ***troubled*** (Greek *tarassō*) on three occasions (11:33; 12:27; 13:21). His confidence in God's power made it possible for him to face these crises. Faced with the upsetting words of 13:33, the disciples confronted similar feelings. • ***Trust*** (or *believe*, or *have faith*) ***in God:*** Only trusting God would help them through his hour of death.

14:2 ***There is more than enough room in my Father's home*** (or *There are many rooms in my Father's house*): God's house is the dwelling place where he resides (Rev 21:9–22:5). The word translated "room" is related to the Greek verb meaning "remain, abide, dwell." Jesus promises that his followers will have a place to "dwell" alongside him, wherever he is. Later, this "dwelling" becomes a place of "indwelling" as Jesus makes his home in his followers' hearts through the Spirit (14:23). • ***If this were not so, would I have told you that I am going to prepare a place for***

14:3
John 14:10-11, 18-20;
16:16-22; 17:21-24
14:6
John 1:4, 14, 16; 8:32;
10:10; 11:25
Rom 5:2
Eph 2:18
Heb 10:20
1 Jn 5:20
14:7
John 6:46; 8:19
1 Jn 2:13
14:9
John 1:14, 18; 12:45
2 Cor 4:4
Col 1:15
Heb 1:3
14:10
John 5:19; 10:38;
17:11, 21-24

place for you? [3]When everything is ready,
I will come and get you, so that you will
always be with me where I am. [4]And you
know the way to where I am going."
[5]"No, we don't know, Lord," Thomas said.
"We have no idea where you are going, so
how can we know the way?"
[6]Jesus told him, "I am the way, the truth,
and the life. No one can come to the Father except through me. [7]If you had really
known me, you would know who my Father
is. From now on, you do know him and have
seen him!"
[8]Philip said, "Lord, show us the Father,
and we will be satisfied."
[9]Jesus replied, "Have I been with you
all this time, Philip, and yet you still don't
know who I am? Anyone who has seen me
has seen the Father! So why are you asking
me to show him to you? [10]Don't you believe
that I am in the Father and the Father is in
me? The words I speak are not my own, but
my Father who lives in me does his work
through me. [11]Just believe that I am in the
Father and the Father is in me. Or at least
believe because of the work you have seen
me do.
[12]"I tell you the truth, anyone who believes in me will do the same works I have
done, and even greater works, because I am

JOHN THE APOSTLE, SON OF ZEBEDEE (13:23-25)

John 18:15-16; 19:26-27; 20:2-10; 21:2, 7, 20-24
Matt 4:21-22; 10:2; 17:1; 20:20-24; 26:37-46
Mark 1:19-20, 29; 3:17; 5:37; 9:2, 38; 10:35-41; 13:3-4; 14:33-42
Luke 5:10; 6:14; 8:51; 9:28, 49, 54
Acts 1:13; 3:1-11; 4:1-22; 5:17-42; 8:14-25
Gal 2:9

John, brother of James and son of Zebedee, was one of the twelve apostles. Early tradition identifies him as the author of the Gospel of John, the Letters of John, and the book of Revelation.

John and his brother James were among those closest to Jesus (Mark 5:37; 9:2; 13:3; 14:33). His mother, Salome, might have been a sister of Mary, the mother of Jesus (cp. 19:25; Matt 27:56; Mark 15:40; 16:1). John's name usually occurs after James's, which suggests that John was younger. James and John were fishermen like their father (Matt 4:21; Mark 1:19). They fished with Peter and Andrew, another pair of brothers who became disciples (Luke 5:10). They were among the first whom Jesus called as disciples, and they left everything to follow him (Matt 4:22; Mark 1:20; Luke 5:11; cp. John 1:35-40). Jesus named them "Sons of Thunder" (Mark 3:17), which might imply that they were loud or short-tempered (cp. Luke 9:54). At one point, the two brothers evoked the indignation of the other disciples when they asked for special positions of privilege in the coming kingdom (Matt 20:20-28; Mark 10:35-45; cp. Luke 22:24-27).

Early tradition links John to five NT books: the Gospel of John, three Letters of John, and the book of Revelation. John is understood to be the unnamed "disciple Jesus loved" and "another disciple" (13:23-25; 18:15-16; 19:26-27; 20:2-10; 21:20-24). He was possibly the unnamed disciple of John the Baptist, who, together with Andrew, became an early follower of Jesus (1:35-40).

John's name occurs three times in Acts; each time he was working with Peter (Acts 3:1-11; 4:1-23; 8:14-25). Paul referred to him as one of the "pillars" of the church in Jerusalem (Gal 2:9).

The most widespread tradition about John's later life is that he moved to Ephesus, where he eventually became the bishop of Asia Minor, lived to an old age, and died peacefully in the company of friends. His Gospel provides the most profound portrait that we have of Jesus, and his letters provide one of the finest depictions of the Christian life (1 John).

you? Or *If this were not so, I would have told you that I am going to prepare a place for you.* Some manuscripts read *If this were not so, I would have told you. I am going to prepare a place for you.*

14:3 Some scholars believe that Jesus meant he would *come and get* his followers after the resurrection (14:18). Others think these words refer to Jesus' second coming. For the disciples, the more important coming was Jesus' return from the grave (ch 16).

14:6 ***I am:*** See note on 6:35. Access to the Father's presence is only through Jesus, who is ***the way, the truth, and the life.*** • The ***way*** to ***the Father*** is only through Jesus. Other religions and philosophies propose different avenues to God, but Jesus asserted that he is the one exclusive path to God. • Jesus is the ***truth*** because God is truth. • God is the source of eternal ***life.*** At Lazarus's tomb, Jesus showed his divine power over life and death (11:25).

14:7 ***If you had really known me, you would know who my Father is:*** Some manuscripts read *If you have really known me, you will know who my Father is.*

14:8 ***Philip*** did not yet understand that in Jesus he was seeing the full embodiment of God (14:9).

14:9 ***Anyone who has seen me has seen the Father!*** Cp. 1:1-2. Jesus Christ is God-in-the-flesh (1:14), which explains his capacity to accomplish divine works. Jesus did not simply teach about God; in him God can be found. Jesus' remarkable statement echoed what he had said at Hanukkah: "The Father and I are one" (10:30). This claim is at the root of the world's opposition to Christ (5:18).

14:10 Jesus' claims were astonishing (10:30, 37-38). Yet true faith recognizes Jesus' union with God ***the Father.***

14:12 Jesus promised that ***anyone who believes*** in him would perform great miracles and experience answers to

going to be with the Father. 13You can ask
for anything in my name, and I will do it, so
that the Son can bring glory to the Father.
14Yes, ask me for anything in my name, and
I will do it!

Jesus Promises the Holy Spirit
15"If you love me, obey my commandments.
16And I will ask the Father, and he will give
you another [g]Advocate, who will never leave
you. 17He is the Holy Spirit, who leads into
all truth. The world cannot receive him, because it isn't looking for him and doesn't
recognize him. But you know him, because
he lives with you now and later will be in you.
18No, I will not abandon you as orphans—I
will come to you. 19Soon the world will no
longer see me, but you will see me. Since I
live, you also will live. 20When I am raised
to life again, you will know that I am in my
Father, and you are in me, and I am in you.
21Those who accept my commandments
and obey them are the ones who love me.
And because they love me, my Father will
love them. And I will love them and reveal
myself to each of them."
22Judas (not Judas Iscariot, but the other
disciple with that name) said to him, "Lord,
why are you going to reveal yourself only to
us and not to the world at large?"
23Jesus replied, "All who love me will do
what I say. My Father will love them, and we
will come and make our home with each of
them. 24Anyone who doesn't love me will
not obey me. And remember, my words
are not my own. What I am telling you is
from the Father who sent me. 25I am telling

14:16 John 14:26; 15:26; Acts 1:4-5; [g]*paraklētos* (3875) › John 14:26
14:17 Rom 8:15-16; 1 Jn 3:24
14:18 Rom 8:23; 9:4; 2 Cor 4:9
14:20 John 10:38; 15:4-5; 16:16; 17:21-24
14:21 John 15:10; 16:27; 1 Jn 2:5; 2 Jn 1:6
14:22 Luke 6:16; Acts 10:41
14:23 Ps 91:1; Prov 8:17; John 15:10; Eph 3:17; 1 Jn 4:16; 5:3; Rev 3:20; 21:3

Our Advocate (14:1–16:15)

1 Sam 2:25; 24:15; 2 Sam 15:12; 1 Kgs 12:6-14; 1 Chr 27:32; Job 16:18-22; Isa 1:26; 9:6; Gal 3:19-20; 6:13; 1 Tim 2:5; Heb 8:6; 9:15; 12:24; 1 Jn 2:1

On four occasions, Jesus used an unusual word (Greek *paraklētos,* "called alongside," "advocate") to describe the Holy Spirit (14:16, 26; 15:26; 16:7). The same term occurs in Greek literature, where it refers to a legal advocate—someone who speaks in a person's defense and provides legal counsel. "Counselor" is a popular translation of this term, but the therapeutic connotations of this word in contemporary English are misleading; the older legal meaning of a lawyer providing advice or counsel is closer to the mark. "Comforter" is another popular translation, but this is also misleading; the older English meaning of someone who strengthens (an "encourager") is more accurate to the NT concept of *paraklētos.*

Jesus described the Spirit as *another* Advocate (14:16). Jesus, who is the first advocate (see 1 Jn 2:1), sent a second Advocate, the Holy Spirit. Every task of the Spirit in John 14–16 is a task Jesus undertook elsewhere in the Gospel. Jesus promised that the Holy Spirit would come to encourage, instruct, and strengthen his followers. In fact, the Spirit would sustain Jesus' own presence among his disciples. Five promises of the Spirit each indicate a different work that the Spirit does (14:16-17, 26; 15:26; 16:7, 13).

The Spirit became available to Jesus' disciples after his death (see 7:39; 20:22). The Spirit now continues the work of Jesus and his presence in the life of believers (14:16-24).

their prayers (see 1 Jn 5:14). These things would become possible when Jesus went to *the Father*, because he would send the Holy Spirit to empower the works (14:16). • The ***greater works*** will not outdo Jesus' work, but regular people empowered by the Spirit will be doing them. In the era of the Spirit, God promised to bring his Kingdom and power into the world in a way not seen before.

14:15 *If you love me:* Because Jesus loves the Father, he is obedient to what God directs him to say and do (12:49). If we love him, we will obey him, too (14:21, 23; 15:10, 14; see 1 Jn 2:3-4; 5:2). • *obey:* Other manuscripts read *you will obey;* still others read *you should obey.*

14:16 *another Advocate* (or *Comforter,* or *Encourager,* or *Counselor;* Greek reads *Paraclete;* also in 14:26): See "Our Advocate" at 14:1–16:15, above. The Spirit continues Jesus' work by advising, defending, and protecting believers.

14:17 The ***Holy Spirit, who leads into all truth*** (literally *the Spirit of truth;* see also 15:26; 16:13), communicates the truth about God. The Spirit maintains Jesus' presence in the world, duplicating and sustaining Jesus' work. • ***and later will be in you:*** Some manuscripts read *and is in you.*

14:18 Jesus had already assured his followers that they would not be spiritual ***orphans*** and that he would return to them (14:1-4). While he is away, they will be filled with the Spirit, who will sustain them with his presence (14:12-17).

14:20 Jesus' resurrection (14:19) inaugurated his spiritual union with his disciples, which is parallel to the union he enjoys with the ***Father*** (see 15:4-5; 1 Jn 1:3).

14:22 Several men are named ***Judas*** in the NT. Judas, the brother of Jesus, (Mark 6:3) wrote the epistle of Jude. Judas, the son of James, whom John is referring to here, is listed as an apostle in Luke 6:16; he is elsewhere identified as Thaddaeus (Matt 10:3; Mark 3:18). • ***Lord, why?*** Judas posed an important question. If Jesus planned to return mightily from death, why not use the opportunity to ***reveal*** himself definitively to the ***world*** and validate his power and identity?

14:23-24 Jesus answered Judas's question, explaining that his coming would be a profound spiritual revelation beyond the world's grasp. • Jesus' coming would occur in three experiences: his resurrection, the coming of the Spirit, and his second coming. When he comes in the Spirit, he and the Father will reside within believers, making a ***home with each of them*** (see note on 14:2).

14:24 John 7:16; 14:10
14:26 John 1:33; 15:26; 16:7; 20:22; 1 Jn 2:20, 27; [h]*paraklētos* (3875) ‣John 15:26
14:27 John 16:33; 20:19; Phil 4:7; Col 3:15; [i]*eirēnē* (1515) ‣Acts 10:36
14:29 John 13:19
14:30 John 12:31
14:31 John 10:18; 12:49
15:1 Ps 80:8-11; Isa 5:1-7; [j]*ampelos* (0288) ‣John 15:5
15:5 [k]*ampelos* (0288) ‣Jas 3:12
15:6 Matt 3:10
15:8 Gal 5:22-23

you these things now while I am still with you. 26But when the Father sends the [h]Advocate as my representative—that is, the Holy Spirit—he will teach you everything and will remind you of everything I have told you.

27"I am leaving you with a gift—[i]peace of mind and heart. And the [i]peace I give is a gift the world cannot give. So don't be troubled or afraid. 28Remember what I told you: I am going away, but I will come back to you again. If you really loved me, you would be happy that I am going to the Father, who is greater than I am. 29I have told you these things before they happen so that when they do happen, you will believe.

30"I don't have much more time to talk to you, because the ruler of this world approaches. He has no power over me, 31but I will do what the Father requires of me, so that the world will know that I love the Father. Come, let's be going.

Jesus, the True Vine of Israel

15 "I am the true [j]grapevine, and my Father is the gardener. 2He cuts off every branch of mine that doesn't produce fruit, and he prunes the branches that do bear fruit so they will produce even more. 3You have already been pruned and purified by the message I have given you. 4Remain in me, and I will remain in you. For a branch cannot produce fruit if it is severed from the vine, and you cannot be fruitful unless you remain in me.

5"Yes, I am the [k]vine; you are the branches. Those who remain in me, and I in them, will produce much fruit. For apart from me you can do nothing. 6Anyone who does not remain in me is thrown away like a useless branch and withers. Such branches are gathered into a pile to be burned. 7But if you remain in me and my words remain in you, you may ask for anything you want, and it will be granted! 8When you produce

Remaining in Christ (15:1-17)

John 6:56; 8:31; Exod 33:11; 34:28; Lev 8:35; Josh 7:11-12; 1 Sam 16:22; 2 Kgs 11:8; 2 Chr 15:2; Ps 22:11, 19; 101:7; Dan 1:21; 2:49; Hag 2:5; Luke 15:31; 22:28; Phil 4:1; 1 Jn 2:19, 27-28; 3:24; 2 Jn 1:9; Rev 2:10; 13:10

One of Jesus' favorite words was *menō,* often translated "remain," "stay," or "abide." It describes a profound, intimate, and enduring relationship. For example, Jesus said, "You are truly my disciples if you remain faithful to [*menō en,* 'stay in'] my teachings" (8:31). The idea is that a disciple's life is fully formed by Jesus' word. Jesus described how the Son is in the Father and the Father is in the Son (14:10-11). Likewise, when we remain in Christ, the Son is in us and we are in the Father and the Son (17:21). Both the Father and the Son come and make their home within his disciples. This mutual indwelling is precisely what it means that the disciple remains in Christ. We cannot gain the permanence of our relationship by our own effort; this relationship is only made permanent by the gracious initiative of God indwelling our lives through his Spirit. This means commitment on the part of both God and the disciple. The mutual indwelling between God and the believer is not a fleeting or temporary commitment, but an enduring, permanent, and eternal relationship (see 1 Jn 2:14, 17).

14:26 Jesus promised to send *the Holy Spirit* (see also 14:16; 15:26; 16:7; 16:12-14). • The Spirit will *teach . . . everything,* recalling Jesus' words and clarifying their meaning. John experienced this power as he wrote his Gospel (2:22); Christians experience this work of the Spirit as they read the Scriptures.

14:27 The Jewish greeting *peace* (Hebrew *shalom*) captured the spirit of Jesus' work on earth to restore humanity's relationship with God (Isa 9:6-7; 52:7; 57:19; Rom 5:1). The resurrection (14:28) and the Spirit were instrumental in achieving this work.

14:28 ***the Father, who is greater than I am:*** Jesus is subordinate to the Father (see also 5:19-20), and yet is also one with the Father (10:30).

14:30 The events unfolding in Jerusalem that led to the cross were not controlled by ***the ruler of this world,*** meaning Satan. The cross was not an accident, and Jesus was not a helpless victim. Rather, Jesus was obedient to God's plan.

15:1-27 Jesus prepared his disciples for his departure, instructing them to remain in close fellowship with him. The image of a grapevine illustrates both intimacy and fruitfulness. To sustain genuine spiritual life in the world, believers must remain intimately connected to Christ.

15:1 ***I am:*** See note on 6:35. The ***grapevine*** and the vineyard traditionally represented God's people, planted and tended by him in Israel (Ps 80:8-18; Isa 5:1-7; Jer 2:21; 12:10-11; Ezek 15:1-5; Hos 10:1-2). When Jesus used this image, he made an important departure: He declared that he is ***the true grapevine,*** and that a relationship with God requires attachment to him.

15:2-3 Gardeners cut away dead ***branches*** and trim healthy branches so they will produce more ***fruit.*** Fruitfulness is the result of life-giving connection to the vine.

15:4 The term ***remain*** (Greek *menō*) is key to understanding 15:4-10. A growing disciple, in whom the Father and the Son live through the Spirit, must be continuously connected to Christ (see 14:16-25; 15:26).

15:6 ***Anyone who does not remain*** in Christ is separated from the vine and its life. A living branch produces clusters of grapes (15:5). Connection with the vine allows the life of Jesus to flow fruitfully through the disciple. Those who claim to be attached to Christ but yield no fruit are ***useless*** and will ***be burned.***

15:7 Those whose lives are in harmony with Jesus ***may ask for anything*** because their prayers are controlled by his word. Their prayers will be answered and bring glory to God (14:10-13).

much fruit, you are my true disciples. This
brings great glory to my Father.
9"I have loved you even as the Father
has loved me. Remain in my [a]love. 10When
you obey my commandments, you remain
in my love, just as I obey my Father's commandments and remain in his love. 11I
have told you these things so that you will
be filled with my joy. Yes, your joy will overflow! 12This is my commandment: Love
each other in the same way I have loved
you. 13There is no greater [b]love than to lay
down one's life for one's friends. 14You are
my friends if you do what I command. 15I
no longer call you [c]slaves, because a master
doesn't confide in his [c]slaves. Now you are
my friends, since I have told you everything
the Father told me. 16You didn't choose me.
I chose you. I appointed you to go and produce lasting fruit, so that the Father will give
you whatever you ask for, using my name.
17This is my command: Love each other.

Jesus' Disciples and the World

18"If the world hates you, remember that it
hated me first. 19The world would love you
as one of its own if you belonged to it, but
you are no longer part of the world. I chose
you to come out of the world, so it hates you.
20Do you remember what I told you? 'A
slave is not greater than the master.' Since
they persecuted me, naturally they will persecute you. And if they had listened to me,
they would listen to you. 21They will do all
this to you because of me, for they have rejected the one who sent me. 22They would
not be guilty if I had not come and spoken
to them. But now they have no excuse for
their sin. 23Anyone who hates me also hates
my Father. 24If I hadn't done such miraculous signs among them that no one else
could do, they would not be guilty. But as it
is, they have seen everything I did, yet they
still hate me and my Father. 25This fulfills
what is written in their Scriptures: 'They
hated me without cause.'
26"But I will send you the [d]Advocate—the
Spirit of truth. He will come to you from the
Father and will testify all about me. 27And
you must also testify about me because you
have been with me from the beginning of
my ministry.

16 "I have told you these things so that
you won't abandon your faith. 2For
you will be expelled from the synagogues,
and the time is coming when those who kill
you will think they are doing a holy service
for God. 3This is because they have never
known the Father or me. 4Yes, I'm telling
you these things now, so that when they
happen, you will remember my warning. I
didn't tell you earlier because I was going to
be with you for a while longer.

The Work of the Holy Spirit

5"But now I am going away to the one who
sent me, and not one of you is asking where
I am going. 6Instead, you grieve because
of what I've told you. 7But in fact, it is best
for you that I go away, because if I don't,
the [e]Advocate won't come. If I do go away,

15:9 John 3:35
[a]*agapē* (0026) ‣John 15:13
15:10 John 14:15
15:11 John 17:13; 1 Jn 1:4
15:12 John 13:34
15:13 John 10:11; Rom 5:6-8
[b]*agapē* (0026) ‣Rom 5:5
15:15 [c]*doulos* (1401) ‣Rom 1:1
15:16 Rom 1:13; 1 Cor 3:12-14; Phil 1:22
15:18 John 7:7; 1 Jn 3:13
15:19 John 17:14; 1 Jn 4:5
15:21 Matt 5:11; 1 Pet 4:14
15:22 John 9:41
15:24 John 5:36; 9:41
15:25 *Ps 35:19; 69:4
15:26 John 14:17; 1 Jn 5:6-7
[d]*paraklētos* (3875) ‣John 16:7
15:27 John 21:24; 1 Jn 1:2; 4:14
16:2 John 9:22; Acts 22:3-4
16:3 John 15:21

15:8 ***True disciples*** will experience a transformed, fruit-bearing life because they live in a relationship of love with both Jesus and the Father (15:9-10).

15:10 Just as Jesus demonstrated his love for the Father by obeying his will (14:31), Jesus' disciples exhibit their love through obedience to him (13:34-35; 14:15; 1 Jn 2:5; 5:2-3).

15:12-13 ***This is my commandment: Love each other:*** See 13:34. • Jesus demonstrated his *love* by sacrificing his *life* at the cross.

15:14-16 Both Abraham and Moses were called *friends* of God (Exod 33:11; 2 Chr 20:7; Isa 41:8; Jas 2:23). This is the highest relationship possible between God and a person. Jesus chooses his friends (15:16), who demonstrate their friendship by obeying him.

15:15 The disciples of a rabbi were considered his servants or *slaves.* Jesus elevated his followers to a higher relationship as his *friends.*

15:18-27 Disciples must be like their master in every respect, both in showing love and obedience and in experiencing the antagonism of those who oppose their message (15:20-21; see ch 9; 11:16). If the darkness is opposed to the light (1:5), and if Jesus' followers are bearers of that light in the world (1 Jn 1:7; 2:9), they should expect the world to hate them in the way it hated Jesus (see 17:14). Jesus' disciples share his separation from and conflict with the world.

15:20 ***A slave is not greater than the master:*** See note on 13:16. Jesus' disciples should mirror him in every way, even in his experience of persecution and martyrdom.

15:22-24 ***But now they have no excuse:*** Jesus' ministry provided both words (15:22) and works (15:24) as evidence that pointed to God. Once people have heard and seen him, they are accountable.

15:25 ***in their Scriptures:*** Literally *in their law.* Ps 35:19; 69:4. • ***They hated me without cause:*** This OT citation reveals the unwarranted anger of those who belong to the darkness.

15:26 ***But I will send you the Advocate*** (or *Comforter,* or *Encourager,* or *Counselor;* Greek reads *Paraclete*)—***the Spirit of truth:*** See notes on 14:16-17. Like a legal advocate, the Holy Spirit counsels and protects Jesus' followers.

15:27 Disciples are not alone when they ***testify about*** Christ (Matt 28:20). The Spirit accompanies them, providing the words to say (Matt 10:19-20).

16:1-2 Jesus had outlined the coming conflicts (15:18-25) so that the disciples would not *abandon* their *faith* (literally *be caused to stumble*). The greatest obstacle his disciples would face was to stumble and renounce their faith before their Jewish opponents (see Matt 23:34; Luke 6:22), especially during the dark days ahead (see 12:35; 1 Jn 2:9-11).

16:7 ***the Advocate*** (or *Comforter,* or *Encourager,* or *Counselor;* Greek reads *Paraclete*): The Spirit was a gift awaiting Jesus' departure and glorification (7:37-39; 14:16, 26; 15:26; 16:12-14).

16:4
John 13:19
16:5
John 7:33; 13:36
16:7
John 14:26; 15:26
ᵉparaklētos (3875)
‣1 Jn 2:1
16:9
John 15:22
16:10
Acts 3:14; 7:52
Rom 1:17
1 Pet 3:18
16:11
John 12:31
16:13
John 14:17, 26
16:15
John 17:10
16:16
John 14:18-24
16:20
Mark 16:10
Luke 23:27
John 20:20
16:21
Isa 13:8; 21:3; 26:17
Acts 13:33
Col 1:18
16:22
Isa 66:14
John 20:20
16:23
John 14:20; 16:26
16:24
John 15:11
16:25
Ps 78:2
John 10:6
16:27
John 8:42; 14:21; 17:8
16:28
John 13:3
16:32
Zech 13:7
Matt 26:31, 56
John 8:29
16:33
John 14:27
Rom 5:1; 8:37
1 Jn 5:4

then I will send him to you. 8And when he
comes, he will convict the world of its sin,
and of God's righteousness, and of the coming judgment. 9The world's sin is that it
refuses to believe in me. 10Righteousness is
available because I go to the Father, and you
will see me no more. 11Judgment will come
because the ruler of this world has already
been judged.

12"There is so much more I want to tell
you, but you can't bear it now. 13When the
Spirit of truth comes, he will guide you into
all truth. He will not speak on his own but
will tell you what he has heard. He will tell
you about the future. 14He will bring me
glory by telling you whatever he receives
from me. 15All that belongs to the Father is
mine; this is why I said, 'The Spirit will tell
you whatever he receives from me.'

Sadness Will Be Turned to Joy

16"In a little while you won't see me anymore. But a little while after that, you will
see me again."

17Some of the disciples asked each other,
"What does he mean when he says, 'In a
little while you won't see me, but then you
will see me,' and 'I am going to the Father'?
18And what does he mean by 'a little while'?
We don't understand."

19Jesus realized they wanted to ask him
about it, so he said, "Are you asking yourselves what I meant? I said in a little while
you won't see me, but a little while after that
you will see me again. 20I tell you the truth,
you will weep and mourn over what is going
to happen to me, but the world will rejoice.
You will grieve, but your grief will suddenly
turn to wonderful joy. 21It will be like a
woman suffering the pains of labor. When
her child is born, her anguish gives way to
joy because she has brought a new baby into
the world. 22So you have sorrow now, but I
will see you again; then you will rejoice,
and no one can rob you of that joy. 23At that
time you won't need to ask me for anything.
I tell you the truth, you will ask the Father
directly, and he will grant your request because you use my name. 24You haven't done
this before. Ask, using my name, and you
will receive, and you will have abundant joy.

25"I have spoken of these matters in figures of speech, but soon I will stop speaking
figuratively and will tell you plainly all about
the Father. 26Then you will ask in my name.
I'm not saying I will ask the Father on your
behalf, 27for the Father himself loves you
dearly because you love me and believe that
I came from God. 28Yes, I came from the Father into the world, and now I will leave the
world and return to the Father."

29Then his disciples said, "At last you
are speaking plainly and not figuratively.
30Now we understand that you know everything, and there's no need to question you.
From this we believe that you came from
God."

31Jesus asked, "Do you finally believe?
32But the time is coming—indeed it's here
now—when you will be scattered, each one
going his own way, leaving me alone. Yet I
am not alone because the Father is with
me. 33I have told you all this so that you
may have peace in me. Here on earth you

16:8-11 One of the Spirit's roles is to *convict the world.* Convict is a legal term: The world had conducted its trial of Jesus, examining the evidence for his case (his signs and claims). Now the world would stand trial before the Spirit, and its guilt would be proven.

16:8 The Spirit unveils to the world the real nature of *its sin,* the truth about *righteousness* found only in God, and *the coming judgment,* which has already dawned on the world as light penetrating the darkness.

16:11 *Judgment* of sinners had already begun, for the *ruler of this world,* Satan, had *already been judged* (see 12:31). The world thought it was judging Jesus, but the opposite occurred.

16:13 The *Spirit of truth* (see notes on 14:16-17), who conveys truth from God, guides the judgment of the world. • The Spirit says only *what he has heard* from the Father. The Father, Son, and Spirit work in perfect unity (16:15). The disciples could expect the Spirit to reveal things they had not heard before about the present and *the future* (see 14:26).

16:16-33 *a little while:* This refrain reassured the disciples that their separation from Jesus would be short lived.

16:16 Jesus reassured the disciples that his departure (on the cross) would be short and his return (in the resurrection) would be soon. When they saw him *again,* the disciples would experience overwhelming joy and intimacy with him in the Spirit.

16:20 At the crucifixion, *the world* thought it had won a victory over the light. The shock of the cross would cause the disciples to *weep and mourn,* but their sorrow would change to *joy* when Jesus defeated the grave (20:20).

16:21 *the pains of labor:* This metaphor symbolizes anguish that is followed by God's blessing and wonder (cp. Isa 21:2-3; 26:16-21; 66:7-10; Jer 13:21).

16:23-24 *Ask . . . and you will receive:* Two notable effects of the resurrection are the joy of understanding and the joy of successful prayer. The disciples would no longer experience the confusion described in 16:16-18.

16:25 Jesus spoke using *figures of speech,* which could only be interpreted with God's help (1 Cor 1:18-25). With the coming of the Spirit, the disciples would understand.

16:26-27 After Jesus' resurrection, the Spirit brought intimacy, allowing individual disciples to *ask the Father* to meet their needs. (14:23).

16:27 *from God:* Some manuscripts read *from the Father.*

16:33 *But take heart, because I have overcome the world:* "Such a saying as this is worthy to be carried from Rome to Jerusalem on one's knees" (Martin Luther). Jesus' final words did not chastise, but brought comfort. Jesus promised peace (14:27) and joy (16:20, 22).

will have many trials and sorrows. But take
heart, because I have overcome the world."

Jesus' Final Prayer

17 After saying all these things, Jesus
looked up to heaven and said, "Father, the hour has come. Glorify your Son so
he can give glory back to you. 2For you have
given him authority over everyone. He gives
eternal life to each one you have given him.
3And this is the way to have eternal life—to
know you, the only true God, and Jesus
Christ, the one you sent to earth. 4I brought
glory to you here on earth by completing
the work you gave me to do. 5Now, Father,
bring me into the glory we shared before
the world began.

6"I have revealed you to the ones you
gave me from this world. They were always
yours. You gave them to me, and they have
kept your word. 7Now they know that everything I have is a gift from you, 8for I have
passed on to them the message you gave me.
They accepted it and know that I came from
you, and they believe you sent me.

9"My prayer is not for the world, but for
those you have given me, because they belong to you. 10All who are mine belong to
you, and you have given them to me, so they
bring me glory. 11Now I am departing from
the world; they are staying in this world, but
I am coming to you. Holy Father, you have
given me your name; now protect them by
the power of your name so that they will
be united just as we are. 12During my time
here, I protected them by the power of the
name you gave me. I guarded them so that
not one was lost, except the one headed for
destruction, as the Scriptures foretold.

13"Now I am coming to you. I told them
many things while I was with them in this
world so they would be filled with my joy.
14I have given them your word. And the
world hates them because they do not belong to the world, just as I do not belong to
the world. 15I'm not asking you to take them
out of the world, but to keep them safe from
the evil one. 16They do not belong to this
world any more than I do. 17Make them holy
by your truth; teach them your word, which
is truth. 18Just as you sent me into the world,
I am sending them into the world. 19And I
give myself as a holy sacrifice for them so
they can be made holy by your truth.

17:1 John 13:31
17:2 Matt 28:18; John 6:37, 39
17:3 Phil 3:8; 1 Jn 5:20
17:5 John 1:1-2; 17:24; Phil 2:6
17:6 John 17:26
17:8 John 13:3; 16:30
17:9 1 Jn 5:19
17:10 John 16:15
17:11 John 10:30; 17:21; Gal 3:28
17:12 Ps 41:9; John 6:39
17:13 John 7:33; 15:11
17:14 John 15:18-19
17:15 1 Jn 5:18
17:17 John 15:3; Eph 5:25-26
17:18 John 20:21
17:19 Heb 2:11

Now he added that his disciples can discover peace even when surrounded by threats; they can be tranquil despite those who are hostile to their faith.

17:1-26 This chapter records Jesus' longest prayer, which is often called his "high priestly prayer." It provides an intimate glimpse into his heart. In this prayer, which closes the farewell that began at 13:31, Jesus expressed his own concerns to his Father (17:1-8) and then turned to concerns for the church and its future (17:9-26).

17:1 ***Jesus looked up to heaven,*** assuming the traditional Jewish posture for prayer (11:41; Ps 123:1). He probably also raised his hands (Exod 9:33; 17:11; Ps 28:2). Prayers like this were said aloud so that followers could hear (11:41-42; 12:27-30; also Matt 11:25-30; Luke 10:21-22). • ***Father*** was Jesus' usual way to address God, which he did six times in this prayer (see also 11:41; 12:27). This title—unusual in Judaism—reflected Jesus' intimacy with God. • This ***hour*** included Jesus' betrayal, arrest, torture, death, and resurrection (see note on 12:23). • ***Glorify your Son:*** In the Gospel of John, the cross is a place of honor. Jesus' oneness with the Father means that if the Son is glorified, the Father will also be glorified.

17:2 All ***authority*** has been placed in Jesus' hands (3:35); he can give ***eternal life*** as only God can (3:15; 5:21, 25-26).

17:3 ***to know you:*** The Hebrew idea of knowing encompassed experience and intimacy, which for Christians means love for God and obedience to him. • ***sent to earth:*** Jesus originated in heaven and was returning there (17:5), so he exercises divine authority as the agent of God.

17:4 Jesus' miracles displayed God's ***glory*** for the world to see (1:14). This task was finished; Jesus' life and obedience had glorified God.

17:5 Jesus prayed to return to the position he had with God ***before the world began*** (1:1).

17:6 This verse summarizes Christ's mission. He revealed the true person of God to the world, gathered up God's people into his flock, and instructed them in obedience. The result of this work is the church. • ***have revealed you:*** Literally *have revealed your name;* also in 17:26.

17:8 Jesus revealed himself widely to the world. Those who embraced his ***message*** became children of God (1:12; 11:52), and he revealed God's word to them.

17:9-19 Jesus prayed for his disciples, who must carry on after his departure.

17:10 Just as the Son brings glory to the Father (17:1, 4-5), the disciples ***bring*** the Son ***glory*** (17:22). The love and obedience that brought glory to God in Jesus' life become features of his disciples' lives.

17:11 ***you have given me your name:*** Some manuscripts read *you have given me these* [i.e., *these disciples*]. • Jesus' first concern for his disciples was that ***they . . . be united*** with an intimacy similar to the oneness shared by Jesus and the Father.

17:12-13 ***I protected them by the power of the name you gave me:*** Some manuscripts read *I protected those you gave me, by the power of your name.* • Until now, Jesus had ***guarded*** his followers. Now he was concerned for their strength and survival in his absence, because the world would be hostile toward them (15:18-27) and their mission of challenging the world by heralding the truth (16:8-11). After Jesus' departure, the Spirit would protect them (15:26) and bring them joy.

17:14 God's ***word,*** which Jesus had ***given*** his disciples, also provides a defense against the world. The Spirit would preserve and recall God's word in the church (14:26), equipping the church for its encounter with the world.

17:16-18 Being ***holy*** refers to purity gained by separation from the world, and living a life so aligned with God that it reflects his passions. Disciples are set apart by God, equipped by the Spirit, and readied by God's word to enter the world without being victimized by its darkness.

17:19 ***I give myself as a holy sacrifice*** (literally *I sanctify myself*): Priests and

17:20 John 17:9
17:21 John 10:38; Gal 3:28
17:22 John 17:11
17:23 John 16:27; 17:5
17:24 John 1:14; 12:26
17:25 Matt 11:27
17:26 John 15:9
18:1 2 Sam 15:23; Matt 26:36; Mark 14:32
18:3-11 //Matt 26:47-56; //Mark 14:43-50; //Luke 22:47-53

[20]"I am praying not only for these disciples but also for all who will ever believe in
me through their message. [21]I pray that they
will all be one, just as you and I are one—as
you are in me, Father, and I am in you. And
may they be in us so that the world will believe you sent me.
[22]"I have given them the glory you gave
me, so they may be one as we are one. [23]I
am in them and you are in me. May they experience such perfect unity that the world
will know that you sent me and that you
love them as much as you love me. [24]Father,
I want these whom you have given me to be
with me where I am. Then they can see all
the glory you gave me because you loved me
even before the world began!
[25]"O righteous Father, the world doesn't
know you, but I do; and these disciples
know you sent me. [26]I have revealed you
to them, and I will continue to do so. Then
your love for me will be in them, and I will
be in them."

Jesus' Suffering and Death (18:1–19:42)

Jesus Is Betrayed and Arrested

John 18:1-12 // Matt 26:47-56 // Mark 14:43-52 // Luke 22:47-53

18 After saying these things, Jesus
crossed the Kidron Valley with
his disciples and entered a grove of olive
trees. [2]Judas, the betrayer, knew this place,
because Jesus had often gone there with
his disciples. [3]The leading priests and

The World (17:5-26)

John 1:9-10; 3:16-19; 7:7; 8:12; 12:47; 14:17-19, 27; 15:18-19; 16:7-9, 20, 33; Gen 6:11-12; Ps 2:1-6; 9:8; Isa 61:11; 66:16; Matt 5:14; 13:38-40; Luke 16:8; Acts 17:31; 1 Cor 1:20-28; 3:3; 6:2; 2 Cor 5:19; Eph 2:2; Col 2:20; Jas 4:4; 2 Pet 1:4; 2:20; 1 Jn 2:15-16; 4:3-5; Rev 17:18; 19:19

One of the most frequently used words in John is "world" (Greek *kosmos*). In Greek-speaking Jewish thought, *kosmos* refers to the heavens and the earth as created by God (Gen 1; see also John 1:3, 10; 17:5, 24). John extends the concept to include the world of humanity (e.g., 1:10; 3:16).

Although it was created as good, the human world is hostile to God (1:10-11; 3:19-20; 12:37-41). It is controlled by a darkness that cannot comprehend the light and resists the light (3:19). The world is dead and needs life (6:33, 51), yet it hates the one who can save it (7:7). The world is under the dominion of Satan (12:31), who will one day be judged.

God loves the world of humanity, despite its hostility and rebellion against him. Jesus died to take away the sin of the world (1:29; 3:16-17). God's love for the world he created stands alongside his necessary judgment of the world (3:18-21, 36; 5:27-30; 12:47-48). Christ's followers experience this same tension in their mission. We are called into the world to bring the message of God's love, but we will experience conflict, because the world will be hostile to our message (see 14:27-31; 15:18-27; 17:13-26).

prophets were similarly set apart for service to God (Lev 8:30; Jer 1:5). Jesus recommitted himself to his mission, acknowledging that he was set apart for the purpose of the cross. The disciples would benefit because his death would enable them to experience new holiness in a deep attachment to God.

17:20 Jesus was ***praying*** for other sheep who were not yet in his flock (10:16). These are the believers through the centuries who have come to faith through the witness of Jesus' disciples.

17:21 For believers, becoming ***one*** with one another is an outgrowth of the union they enjoy with Jesus himself, a union modeled on the oneness of the Father and the Son. • ***may they be in us:*** Through the power of the Spirit, believers would experience a profound spiritual intimacy with the Father and the Son and be transformed (14:20, 23; 1 Jn 4:13). • Disciples of Jesus represent him, so their conduct and relationships with each other reflect the credibility of Christ in ***the world.*** When there is disunity, infighting, and intolerance, their testimony to the world is unconvincing. When people observe the community of believers, they know that it represents Jesus; a unified, loving community convinces ***the world*** to ***believe*** (13:35; 1 Jn 3:11).

17:22 The community of believers should display the same ***glory*** that Jesus displayed from the Father.

17:23 ***that the world will know:*** If the church lives in the Spirit, reflects God's glory and love, and shows unity sustained by a shared knowledge of God, then its testimony will astonish ***the world.***

17:24 ***I want these . . . to be with me:*** Some day, Jesus' followers will see Jesus' true glory, the true love that has existed in heaven since the beginning of time (17:5). Jesus was returning to heaven, and he yearned to see his disciples there so that they might glimpse what no words on earth can describe.

17:26 All who accept the Son and embrace the Father will experience the kind of ***love*** known only between the Father and the Son. • ***I will be in them:*** Jesus wants to love his followers and indwell them with glory and joy unmatched by anything in the world.

18:1-40 After completing his farewell in the upper room (13:31–17:26), Jesus left the city and entered a garden just east of Jerusalem to pray. Here he was arrested, taken under guard into the city, and interrogated by the Jewish leaders. The climactic "time" that Jesus referred to repeatedly throughout the Gospel (see 2:4; note on 12:23) was now at hand.

18:1-2 ***Jesus crossed the Kidron Valley,*** a dry river valley (a *wadi*) outside Jerusalem's walls on the city's east edge. • The Garden of Gethsemane (Mark 14:32) was ***a grove of olive trees*** that grew along the west shoulder of the Mount of Olives (*gath shemaney* means "olive press" in Aramaic). Jesus liked this place and frequently prayed there (see 8:1; Luke 21:37; 22:39).

18:3 John's full description of the arresting party expands the picture from the other Gospels. The Temple authorities sent ***Roman soldiers and Temple guards;*** while the Temple guards made

Pharisees had given Judas a contingent of Roman soldiers and Temple guards to accompany him. Now with blazing torches, lanterns, and weapons, they arrived at the olive grove.

[4]Jesus fully realized all that was going to happen to him, so he stepped forward to meet them. "Who are you looking for?" he asked.

[5]"Jesus the Nazarene," they replied.

"I AM he," Jesus said. (Judas, who betrayed him, was standing with them.) [6]As Jesus said "I AM he," they all drew back and fell to the ground! [7]Once more he asked them, "Who are you looking for?"

And again they replied, "Jesus the Nazarene."

[8]"I told you that I AM he," Jesus said. "And since I am the one you want, let these others go." [9]He did this to fulfill his own statement: "I did not lose a single one of those you have given me."

[10]Then Simon Peter drew a sword and slashed off the right ear of Malchus, the high priest's slave. [11]But Jesus said to Peter, "Put your sword back into its sheath. Shall I not drink from the cup of suffering the Father has given me?"

[12]So the soldiers, their commanding officer, and the Temple guards arrested Jesus and tied him up.

Peter's First Denial of Jesus

John 18:15-18 // Matt 26:69-70 // Mark 14:66-68 // Luke 22:54-57

[13]First they took him to Annas, the father-in-law of Caiaphas, the high priest at that time. [14]Caiaphas was the one who had told the

18:4 John 6:64
18:9 John 6:39; 17:12
18:10 Luke 22:36, 38
18:11 Matt 20:22; 26:39 Mark 10:38; 14:36 Luke 22:42
18:12-15 //Matt 26:57-58 //Mark 14:53-54 //Luke 22:54
18:13 Luke 3:2 John 18:24
18:14 John 11:49-51

ANNAS AND CAIAPHAS (18:13-14, 19-24, 28)

John 11:49-53
Matt 26:3, 57-67
Mark 14:53-65
Luke 3:2
Acts 4:5-7

Annas and Caiaphas were both spoken of as high priests during the time of Jesus; they were instrumental in getting Jesus condemned to death.

Annas was the Jewish high priest about AD 6–15. Even after he was officially deposed by the Roman procurator of Judea, he retained considerable power and influence in the Jewish high council and was still spoken of as "high priest" fifteen to twenty years later (Luke 3:2; Acts 4:6)—perhaps because of the Jewish view that high priests retain their position for life. Five of his sons and his son-in-law Caiaphas became high priests after him. According to the Gospel of John, when Jesus was arrested, he was brought to Annas for his initial interrogation before he was turned over to Caiaphas for the official trial (18:13-24).

Caiaphas was the official Jewish high priest about AD 18–36. He worked closely with his powerful father-in-law, Annas. Caiaphas was the one who argued in the high council that it would be better for Jesus to be sacrificed than for the entire nation to be destroyed (11:49-50; cp. Matt 26:3-4). These prophetic words were given him by God because of his role as high priest (11:51-52). It was Caiaphas who tore his robes at Jesus' claim to be the Son of God (Matt 26:57, 65) and urged the high council to condemn him for blasphemy.

Not long after the execution of Jesus, the Jewish authorities became increasingly disturbed over the rapidly growing numbers of believers in Christ. Annas and Caiaphas also actively involved themselves in the interrogation of Peter and John over their healing a crippled beggar and their preaching about the resurrection of the dead (Acts 4:5-7).

the arrest, the Roman detachment stood by to prevent a riot. The Roman detachment was large enough to warrant a commander (18:12) and came armed, anticipating a struggle (18:10). Numerous men had claimed to be the Messiah, and often they had made politically explosive attempts to expel the Romans.

18:5 ***Jesus the Nazarene:*** Or *Jesus of Nazareth;* also in 18:7. • ***I AM he*** (or *"The 'I AM' is here"*; or *"I am the LORD"*; literally *I am;* also in 18:6, 8): Jesus identified himself by the divine name God had revealed to Moses on Mount Sinai (Exod 3:14; see also 4:26; 8:24, 58).

18:6 The soldiers and guards ***all drew back*** before the Lord (cp. Isa 6:5; Ezek 1:28; Dan 10:9; Acts 9:4; Rev 1:17). Even Roman soldiers, who were trained not to fall, ***fell to the ground*** before Christ. Although they submitted to God, they didn't really understand what had occurred and proceeded with the arrest.

18:8 ***I AM:*** Jesus used God's divine name for the second time (see note on 18:5).

18:9 ***his own statement:*** See 6:39; 17:12. • ***I did not lose a single one:*** Jesus continued to be a good shepherd, offering his life for the sheep and protecting them from the wolves (10:11-15). From the beginning, however, Judas Iscariot had not been a true disciple of Jesus (17:12).

18:10-11 ***Simon Peter drew a*** short ***sword*** or a long knife that was generally worn with everyday garments. • The Hebrew name ***Malchus*** means "king," a detail that John might have included for its wordplay on Jesus' true identity (see 18:36-37; 19:19). • ***Put your sword back:*** Jesus' mission was not to fight for his life, but to die for ours.

18:12-14 Jesus was bound by the soldiers and returned to Jerusalem. • ***First they took him to Annas,*** who had been the high priest and remained highly influential (five of his sons also became high priests). ***Caiaphas,*** his son-in-law, was the official ***high priest at that time*** (literally *that year*; see 18:24).

18:14 ***one man should die for the people:*** Caiaphas had previously made this political analysis (11:49-50). John points out the irony of this statement. Jesus' death did not bring Israel political salvation—it brought spiritual salvation to all who believe.

18:16-18
//Matt 26:69-70
//Mark 14:66-68
//Luke 22:55-57

18:18
Mark 14:54, 67

18:19-24
//Matt 26:59-68
//Mark 14:55-65
//Luke 22:63-71

18:19
'*archiereus* (0749)
‣Acts 5:27

18:20
Matt 26:55
John 7:26

18:22
John 19:3

18:23
Matt 5:39
Acts 23:2-5

18:24
Matt 26:3

18:25-27
//Matt 26:71-75
//Mark 14:69-72
//Luke 22:58-62

18:27
John 13:38

18:28-38
//Matt 27:1-2, 11-14
//Mark 15:1-5
//Luke 23:1-5

other Jewish leaders, "It's better that one
man should die for the people."
15 Simon Peter followed Jesus, as did another of the disciples. That other disciple
was acquainted with the high priest, so he
was allowed to enter the high priest's courtyard with Jesus. 16 Peter had to stay outside
the gate. Then the disciple who knew the
high priest spoke to the woman watching at
the gate, and she let Peter in. 17 The woman
asked Peter, "You're not one of that man's
disciples, are you?"
"No," he said, "I am not."
18 Because it was cold, the household servants and the guards had made a charcoal
fire. They stood around it, warming themselves, and Peter stood with them, warming
himself.

The High Priest Questions Jesus
John 18:19-24; cp. Matt 26:57-68 // Mark 14:53-65 // Luke 22:63-71

19 Inside, the 'high priest began asking Jesus
about his followers and what he had been
teaching them. 20 Jesus replied, "Everyone
knows what I teach. I have preached regularly in the synagogues and the Temple,
where the people gather. I have not spoken
in secret. 21 Why are you asking me this
question? Ask those who heard me. They
know what I said."
22 Then one of the Temple guards standing nearby slapped Jesus across the face. "Is
that the way to answer the high priest?" he
demanded.
23 Jesus replied, "If I said anything wrong,
you must prove it. But if I'm speaking the
truth, why are you beating me?"
24 Then Annas bound Jesus and sent him
to Caiaphas, the high priest.

Peter's Second and Third Denials
John 18:25-27 // Matt 26:71-75 // Mark 14:69-72 // Luke 22:58-65

25 Meanwhile, as Simon Peter was standing
by the fire warming himself, they asked
him again, "You're not one of his disciples,
are you?"
He denied it, saying, "No, I am not."
26 But one of the household slaves of the
high priest, a relative of the man whose
ear Peter had cut off, asked, "Didn't I see
you out there in the olive grove with Jesus?"
27 Again Peter denied it. And immediately a
rooster crowed.

Jesus' Trial before Pilate
John 18:28-38a // Matt 27:1-2, 11-14 // Mark 15:1-5 // Luke 23:1-5

28 Jesus' trial before Caiaphas ended in the
early hours of the morning. Then he was
taken to the headquarters of the Roman

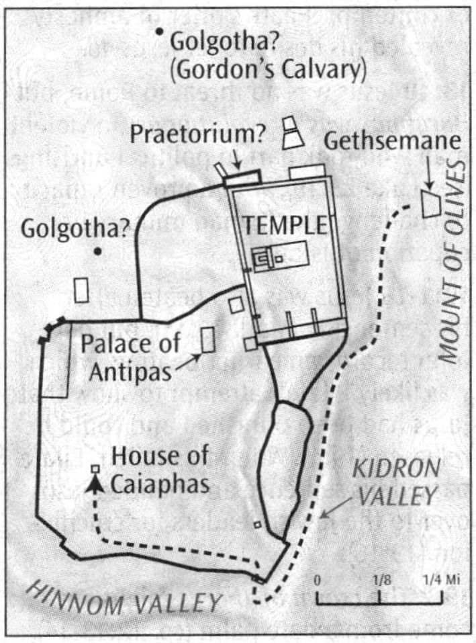

◀ **Jesus' Trial and Crucifixion (John 18:1–19:27; see also Matt 26:47–27:26; Mark 14:43–15:15; Luke 22:47–23:25).** After Jesus was arrested in GETHSEMANE, he was taken to the HOUSE OF CAIAPHAS the high priest. There the Jewish leaders decided to send him to Pilate (at the PRAETORIUM) to sentence him to death (18:28). Pilate sent Jesus to Herod (at the PALACE OF ANTIPAS?), who questioned Jesus and sent him back (Luke 23:6-12). Then Pilate sentenced Jesus to be crucified (19:16). • Regarding the location of GOLGOTHA, see note on 19:17; see also illustration of Jerusalem in Jesus' time, p. 1753.

18:15 ***That other disciple*** is unnamed, but was probably the "disciple Jesus loved" (13:23)—John, the author of this Gospel.

18:16-17 During Jesus' interrogation by Annas (18:12-14, 19-24), ***the woman watching at the gate*** asked ***Peter*** if he was ***one of that man's disciples.*** In contrast to Jesus, who stood up to his questioners and denied nothing, Peter quickly denied his link to Jesus three times (18:17, 25, 27).

18:19 The ***high priest began asking Jesus*** questions, but his inquiry was contrary to Jewish legal procedure. In Jewish court, the priest did not ask questions directly of the defendant, but accumulated evidence from witnesses to establish guilt (see Num 35:30; Deut 17:6; 19:15; cp. Matt 18:16). If Jesus said anything incriminating, Annas would later use it to testify against him at Jesus' trial. He was attempting to follow Roman practice by making Jesus incriminate himself, rather than gathering evidence through witnesses as Jewish law demanded.

18:20-21 Jesus' sharp answer, reminding Annas that everything was in the public record, unmasked the priest's attempt to follow Roman practice.

18:20 ***people:*** Literally *Jewish people;* also in 18:38.

18:22-23 When Jesus reminded Annas of correct judicial procedure, one of the ***Temple guards*** viewed it as insolence and ***slapped Jesus.*** However, Jesus knew the law and represented it truthfully. No witnesses were accusing him, and no evidence was being presented.

18:24 ***Annas*** was at an impasse—his probing had been unsuccessful. So he sent ***Jesus*** to ***Caiaphas*** to be prosecuted before the Sanhedrin, Jerusalem's judicial high council (see Mark 14:53–15:1).

18:25-27 ***He denied it:*** Peter's three denials were later echoed when Jesus invited him three times to reaffirm his love (21:15-17).

18:28 The trial before ***Caiaphas*** ended ***in the early hours of the morning.*** Since they did not have the power of capital punishment (18:31), the Sanhedrin needed to enlist Pilate, the Roman governor, to carry out an execution. • ***the headquarters of the Roman governor:*** Greek *the Praetorium;* also in 18:33. • ***it would defile them:*** They did not want to become ritually unclean by contact with Gentiles in Pilate's headquarters.

governor. His accusers didn't go inside because it would defile them, and they wouldn't be allowed to celebrate the Passover. 29So Pilate, the governor, went out to them and asked, "What is your charge against this man?"

30"We wouldn't have handed him over to you if he weren't a criminal!" they retorted.

31"Then take him away and judge him by your own law," Pilate told them.

"Only the Romans are permitted to execute someone," the Jewish leaders replied. 32(This fulfilled Jesus' prediction about the way he would die.)

33Then Pilate went back into his headquarters and called for Jesus to be brought to him. "Are you the king of the Jews?" he asked him.

34Jesus replied, "Is this your own question, or did others tell you about me?"

35"Am I a Jew?" Pilate retorted. "Your own people and their leading priests brought you to me for trial. Why? What have you done?"

36Jesus answered, "My Kingdom is not an earthly kingdom. If it were, my followers would fight to keep me from being handed over to the Jewish leaders. But my Kingdom is not of this world."

37Pilate said, "So you are a king?"

Jesus responded, "You say I am a king. Actually, I was born and came into the world to testify to the truth. All who love the truth recognize that what I say is true."

38"What is truth?" Pilate asked.

Jesus Is Sentenced to Death

John 18:38b–19:16 // Matt 27:15-31 // Mark 15:6-20 // Luke 23:13-25

Then he went out again to the people and told them, "He is not guilty of any crime. 39But you have a custom of asking me to release one prisoner each year at Passover. Would you like me to release this 'King of the Jews'?"

40But they shouted back, "No! Not this man. We want Barabbas!" (Barabbas was a revolutionary.)

19 Then Pilate had Jesus flogged with a lead-tipped whip. 2The soldiers wove a crown of thorns and put it on his head, and they put a purple robe on him. 3"Hail! King of the Jews!" they mocked, as they slapped him across the face.

4Pilate went outside again and said to the people, "I am going to bring him out to you now, but understand clearly that I find him not guilty." 5Then Jesus came out wearing the crown of thorns and the purple robe. And Pilate said, "Look, here is the man!"

18:32 Matt 20:19; John 12:32-33
18:33 Luke 23:3; John 19:9
18:36 Matt 26:53; Luke 17:21; John 6:15
18:37 John 8:47; 1 Jn 4:6
18:39–19:5 //Matt 27:15-31; //Mark 15:6-20; //Luke 23:13-25
19:1 Isa 50:6; 53:5
19:3 John 18:22
19:4 Luke 23:4; John 18:38

So Pilate, probably fearing a riot, went outside to meet them. • The ***Passover*** meal itself had occurred the night before (see 13:1; Mark 14:14-16). The following day, another meal began the weeklong Festival of Unleavened Bread (Lev 23:5-6).

18:29 ***Pilate***, the fifth Roman ***governor*** of Judea, ruled the country from AD 26 to 36. He usually lived on the coast in Caesarea, but kept troops stationed in a fortress in Jerusalem where he appeared personally for major festivals. He was a brutal ruler whose atrocities against the Jews were legendary (e.g., Luke 13:1; Josephus, *War* 2.9.2-4).

18:31-32 Pilate found the charges unsatisfying and told the Sanhedrin, ***judge him by your own law.*** Pilate saw this as a Jewish squabble, which he refused to investigate. The Jewish leaders, however, insisted that an execution was necessary. • ***fulfilled Jesus' prediction about the way he would die*** (see 12:32-33): The Jews would have employed stoning; the Romans used crucifixion. If Pilate delivered Jesus' sentence, he would be crucified.

18:33 ***Pilate*** was personally responsible for capital crimes in which the interests and security of the Roman empire were at stake, so he began his formal legal inquiry. • ***Are you the king of the Jews?*** To get the governor's attention, Caiaphas had charged that Jesus had urged people not to pay their taxes to the Roman government and had claimed to be a king (Luke 23:2). To Pilate, Jesus might have been just another Jewish terrorist–revolutionary (see Luke 23:18-19; Acts 5:36-37) with a head full of messianic notions and a band of well-armed followers.

18:34-35 Jesus' reply forced the governor to show the origin of his ***question.*** The Temple leadership was behind these charges. Pilate only wanted to know if Jesus was a rebel who might threaten Roman interests.

18:36-37 Jesus was willing to accept the title of ***king***, but he made it clear that he did not govern an ***earthly kingdom*** that might rival Rome. Jesus' kingship is ***not of this world.*** Rather than being a political ruler, he rules through the devotion and obedience of his followers.

18:38-39 ***What is truth?*** Truth was not a foreign idea to Pilate, but he did not wait for an answer to his question because he did not believe there was one. • Pilate returned to the council members waiting outside and delivered his verdict: ***not guilty.*** Although he referred to Jesus as ***"King of the Jews"*** (see also 19:19), the title meant nothing more to Pilate than a mocking expression of contempt. Pilate's offer of amnesty revealed his desire to let Jesus go.

18:40 Jesus was no threat to Rome, but ***Barabbas was a revolutionary***, a violent man who took part in political uprisings (see Luke 23:19), with a proven capacity to challenge the Roman military occupation of Israel.

19:1-16 Jesus was also beaten after his sentencing (Mark 15:15), but here John records an earlier beating, which was likely Pilate's attempt to show that Jesus had been punished and could be released (19:4). When this failed, Pilate passed his sentence and handed Jesus over to the Jewish leaders for crucifixion (19:16).

19:2 The ***crown of thorns*** might have come from a date palm (cp. 12:13-14), whose thorns can exceed twelve inches. There are Greek coin images showing such crowns, with the stems woven and the thorns radiating upward above the crown. • The ***purple robe*** was probably a soldier's robe—dark red to complete the picture of mock royalty.

19:4-6 Pilate's intention was ***to bring*** Jesus ***out*** to display the marks of his punishment to sway the crowd to let him go. After being flogged with a lead-tipped whip, Jesus was bleeding profusely. • Pilate announced his verdict

19:6 John 18:31
19:7 Lev 24:16; Matt 26:63-66
19:11 Rom 13:1
19:12 Luke 23:2; Acts 17:7
19:13 Matt 27:19
19:16-27 //Matt 27:32-44; //Mark 15:21-32; //Luke 23:26-43

[6]When they saw him, the leading priests and Temple guards began shouting, "Crucify him! Crucify him!"

"Take him yourselves and crucify him," Pilate said. "I find him not guilty."

[7]The Jewish leaders replied, "By our law he ought to die because he called himself the Son of God."

[8]When Pilate heard this, he was more frightened than ever. [9]He took Jesus back into the headquarters again and asked him, "Where are you from?" But Jesus gave no answer. [10]"Why don't you talk to me?" Pilate demanded. "Don't you realize that I have the power to release you or crucify you?"

[11]Then Jesus said, "You would have no power over me at all unless it were given to you from above. So the one who handed me over to you has the greater sin."

[12]Then Pilate tried to release him, but the Jewish leaders shouted, "If you release this man, you are no 'friend of Caesar.' Anyone who declares himself a king is a rebel against Caesar."

[13]When they said this, Pilate brought Jesus out to them again. Then Pilate sat down on the judgment seat on the platform that is called the Stone Pavement (in Hebrew, *Gabbatha*). [14]It was now about noon on the day of preparation for the Passover. And Pilate said to the people, "Look, here is your king!"

[15]"Away with him," they yelled. "Away with him! Crucify him!"

"What? Crucify your king?" Pilate asked.

"We have no king but Caesar," the leading priests shouted back.

[16]Then Pilate turned Jesus over to them to be crucified. So they took Jesus away.

The Crucifixion

John 19:17-24 // Matt 27:32-38 // Mark 15:21-27 // Luke 23:26-34

[17]Carrying the cross by himself, he went to the place called Place of the Skull (in

---

of *not guilty* a second time, but he was met with a strident call for Jesus' death (19:6).

19:6 Pilate knew that a riot could happen when a man popular with the masses was executed, so he shifted responsibility to *crucify* Jesus to the *Temple* leaders.

19:7 During the trial before Caiaphas, the charge of blasphemy—calling *himself the Son of God*—was determined to be Jesus' true crime (see Mark 14:61-65). • The leaders had already tried pitting Roman imperial interests against Jesus (18:33), and would do so again (19:12). Now they challenged the governor on another level: Pilate must keep the peace by upholding local *law,* even when it was irrelevant to Rome. Claiming to be God's son was not illegal, because Israel's kings did this (Ps 2:7; 89:22-27). However, Jesus claimed to have the divine authority of God himself (see 5:18), which they saw as blasphemy.

19:8-9 ***Pilate . . . was more frightened than ever:*** He was superstitious, and the idea of gods appearing in the world was not uncommon (Acts 14:11). He sensed that more than a political fight was going on, so he asked Jesus, ***Where are you from?*** He did not mean Jesus' birthplace, but whether Jesus was a divine man who had descended from heaven. • ***the headquarters:*** Greek *the Praetorium.* • Why ***Jesus gave no answer*** is unclear. Perhaps it was because Pilate would not have been able to understand the answer—that true power comes only from God, and God had empowered Jesus (cp. 19:11).

19:10-11 ***You would have no power over me:*** Although Pilate had ***the power to . . . crucify*** Jesus, it was only because God had given him this temporary power so Jesus could advance toward the cross (see 10:18).

19:12 Each time he had a conversation with Jesus, ***Pilate tried to release him:*** He kept trying, but his repeated efforts were fruitless. • ***"Friend of Caesar"*** is a technical term that refers to an ally of the emperor. It was an official title given to individuals such as senators who showed exceptional loyalty and service to the emperor. The Jewish leaders were implying that they would ruin Pilate's career by reporting that he was not working in Rome's interests. They probably knew that Pilate was also having a personal crisis. His patron in Rome, Sejanus (the chief administrator of the Empire under Tiberius Caesar), had fallen from favor and was executed in AD 31. Pilate had every reason to be afraid.

19:13 Pilate took the governor's ***judgment seat*** (Greek *bēma,* cp. Acts 25:6, "seat in court") to render his verdict. • The ***Stone Pavement*** was the platform holding the judgment seat; from there Pilate now spoke with the authority of his office.

19:14 ***the day of preparation for the Passover*** (or *the day of preparation during the Passover*): Here, Passover does not refer to the Jewish Passover meal, which had taken place the night before, but to the whole Festival of Unleavened Bread. It was now Friday, the day of preparation for the Passover Sabbath, which would begin at sundown (cp. Mark 15:42; Luke 23:54). • ***people:*** Literally *Jewish people;* also in 19:20.

19:15 The final words of the priests, ***"We have no king but Caesar,"*** stood in direct contradiction to the OT understanding that God was Israel's king (cp. Judg 8:23; 1 Sam 8:7; 10:19). Jerusalem and its leaders were in the process of killing their true king (18:37) while paying homage to Caesar, the pagan king of Rome.

19:16 ***Pilate turned Jesus over*** to the Roman garrison, who prepared Jesus for crucifixion by a second flogging (Mark 15:15), which brought him near death. Bleeding profusely, his clothes soaked in blood, his thorn-laced crown now digging deeply into his head, and nearly in shock, Jesus was marched to a site outside the city.

19:17 The vertical beam (Latin *staticulum*) of ***the cross*** was generally kept at the crucifixion site, and the victim was forced to carry only the heavy crossbeam (Latin *patibulum*). • Crucifixions were public executions that took place near major roadways. They were designed to shock and warn the people. • ***Place of the Skull*** (Hebrew and Aramaic *Golgotha;* Latin *calvariae,* "Calvary"): See map on p. 1809. Most archaeologists agree that Jesus' crucifixion was at the site of the present-day Church of the Holy Sepulchre, located in the Christian Quarter of the old walled city of Jerusalem (see "First-Century Jerusalem," p. 1753). An alternate site, Gordon's Calvary (north of the Damascus Gate), is a model of what the scene possibly looked like, but it holds only a tomb from the 500s BC and therefore cannot be the authentic site of Jesus' crucifixion and burial.

Hebrew, *Golgotha).* 18There they nailed
him to the cross. Two others were crucified
with him, one on either side, with Jesus between them. 19And Pilate posted a sign on
the cross that read, "Jesus of Nazareth, the
King of the Jews." 20The place where Jesus
was crucified was near the city, and the sign
was written in Hebrew, Latin, and Greek, so
that many people could read it.
21Then the leading priests objected and
said to Pilate, "Change it from 'The King
of the Jews' to 'He said, I am King of the
Jews.' "
22Pilate replied, "No, what I have written,
I have written."
23When the soldiers had crucified Jesus,
they divided his clothes among the four of
them. They also took his robe, but it was
seamless, woven in one piece from top to
bottom. 24So they said, "Rather than tearing it apart, let's throw dice for it." This
fulfilled the Scripture that says, "They divided my garments among themselves and
threw dice for my clothing." So that is what
they did.
25Standing near the cross were Jesus'
mother, and his mother's sister, Mary (the
wife of Clopas), and Mary Magdalene.
26When Jesus saw his mother standing
there beside the disciple he loved, he said to
her, "Dear woman, here is your son." 27And
he said to this disciple, "Here is your mother."
And from then on this disciple took her into
his home.

19:24 *Ps 22:18
19:25 Matt 27:55-56; Mark 15:40-41; Luke 8:2; 23:49
19:26 John 2:4; 13:23; 20:2; 21:7, 20

The Cross and Passover (19:17-36)

John 1:29, 36
Exod 12:1–13:16; 29:38-46
Num 9:1-14
Deut 16:1-8
2 Kgs 23:21-23
2 Chr 30:1-27
Ezra 6:19-21
Isa 53:7
Ezek 45:21-22
Matt 26:2, 17-19
Mark 14:17-31
Luke 22:14-30
Acts 8:32-35; 12:3-4
1 Cor 5:7-8
Heb 11:28
Rev 5:5-14

At the beginning of John's Gospel, John the Baptist introduced Jesus by calling him the "Lamb of God" (1:29, 36). This odd phrase might refer to the sacrificial lamb that was killed daily in the Temple (Exod 29:38-46) or to the sacrificial lamb of Isa 53:7 (cp. Acts 8:32-35; Rev 5:5-14). Both rituals of sacrifice spoke of rescue and forgiveness from sin.

However, this was not all that John had in mind. John presented Jesus as the Passover lamb whose death marks the central event of the Passover season (see Exod 12:46; Luke 22:7; 1 Cor 5:7). In the first century, Jews made a pilgrimage to Jerusalem each spring to celebrate the Passover and to reread the story of the Exodus (see Exod 12–15). When Israel was being rescued from Egypt, the blood of a lamb was sprinkled on the doorposts of each Jewish home in Egypt and saved those inside from death (Exod 12). Jews who came to Jerusalem to celebrate the Passover needed to supply a perfect young lamb for sacrifice. The animal could not be diseased or have broken bones.

Jesus used his final Passover meal to show that his sacrificial death would give new meaning to the festival (Mark 14:17-31). In John, the cross became an altar where Christ, the Passover lamb, was slain. Jesus' legs were not broken (19:33), fulfilling a Passover rule (19:36; Exod 12:46). Blood ran freely from his wound (19:34), showing that his life was being exchanged for others. Just as a lamb died to save the lives of Jewish families at the Passover in Egypt, so, too, this one death of the Son of God on the cross serves to bring salvation to the world.

19:18 None of the Gospel writers dwell on the details of being ***nailed . . . to the cross*** because they were well known and horrific. The soldiers used the cross as a means of torture; they wanted victims to survive for a while, in some cases for days. Because the Sabbath would begin at dusk (19:31), they expedited Jesus' crucifixion. Jesus had been thoroughly beaten with stone- or metal-tipped whips, so his back was thoroughly lacerated, and he was bleeding profusely.

19:19-22 *Pilate posted a sign on the cross:* It was customary for the Roman soldiers to provide a written public notice of the criminal's name and crimes. Perhaps as a final act of revenge against the Jewish high council, Pilate ordered that the sign should identify ***Jesus of Nazareth*** (or ***Jesus the Nazarene***) as ***the King of the Jews.*** Jesus' kingship was posted in three languages for the whole world to understand.

19:23-24 As was their common practice, the Roman soldiers ***divided his clothes.*** The soldiers gambled for his valuable ***robe,*** which was ***seamless,*** rather than dividing it up. • ***throw dice:*** Literally *cast lots.* • ***"They divided my garments among themselves and threw dice for my clothing":*** See Ps 22:18.

19:25-26 This is the only reference to Jesus' ***mother's sister*** in the NT. She might have been the wife of Zebedee and the mother of James and John (cp. Matt 27:56), which would make Jesus and John cousins. If so, it would help explain why Jesus assigned the ***disciple he loved*** (John) to care for Mary (John's aunt). • ***Mary (the wife of Clopas)*** is only mentioned here. She might be the same person as Mary the mother of James and Joseph (cp. Matt 27:56). • Jesus had healed ***Mary Magdalene,*** a woman from the village of Magdala (Mark 16:9; Luke 8:2). • ***Dear woman*** was a formal and polite form of address (see 2:4).

19:27 *Here is your mother:* Jesus employed a Jewish family law that assigned the care of one person to another. The scene had an additional significance: The people who were present represented the new community of the church that was born at the cross. Jesus wanted them to care for each other in obedience to his command to love one another (13:34; 15:12, 17).

19:28-29 *I am thirsty:* See Ps 22:15; 69:21. • The ***hyssop*** bush had been

19:28-37
//Matt 27:45-56
//Mark 15:33-41
//Luke 23:44-49

19:28
*Ps 22:15; 69:21

19:30
Job 19:26-27

19:31
Deut 21:22-23

19:35
John 20:30-31; 21:24
1 Jn 1:1

19:36
*Exod 12:46
Num 9:12
*Ps 34:20

19:37
*Zech 12:10
Rev 1:7

19:38-42
//Matt 27:57-61
//Mark 15:42-47
//Luke 23:50-56

19:39
John 3:1-2; 7:50

The Death of Jesus

John 19:28-30// Matt 27:45-56 // Mark 15:33-41 // Luke 23:44-49

28Jesus knew that his mission was now finished, and to fulfill Scripture he said, "I am
thirsty." 29A jar of sour wine was sitting
there, so they soaked a sponge in it, put it
on a hyssop branch, and held it up to his
lips. 30When Jesus had tasted it, he said, "It
is finished!" Then he bowed his head and released his spirit.
31It was the day of preparation, and
the Jewish leaders didn't want the bodies
hanging there the next day, which was the
Sabbath (and a very special Sabbath, because it was the Passover). So they asked
Pilate to hasten their deaths by ordering
that their legs be broken. Then their bodies could be taken down. 32So the soldiers
came and broke the legs of the two men crucified with Jesus. 33But when they came to
Jesus, they saw that he was already dead, so
they didn't break his legs. 34One of the soldiers, however, pierced his side with a spear,
and immediately blood and water flowed
out. 35(This report is from an eyewitness
giving an accurate account. He speaks the
truth so that you also can believe.) 36These
things happened in fulfillment of the Scriptures that say, "Not one of his bones will be
broken," 37and "They will look on the one
they pierced."

The Burial of Jesus

John 19:38-42 // Matt 27:57-61 // Mark 15:42-47 // Luke 23:50-56

38Afterward Joseph of Arimathea, who had
been a secret disciple of Jesus (because
he feared the Jewish leaders), asked Pilate
for permission to take down Jesus' body.
When Pilate gave permission, Joseph came
and took the body away. 39With him came

All dimensions are based on an average of actual rolling-stone tombs

Drawing based on "Reconstructing the Tomb of Christ from Archaeological and Literary Sources" by Eugenia L. Nitowski, Ph.D.

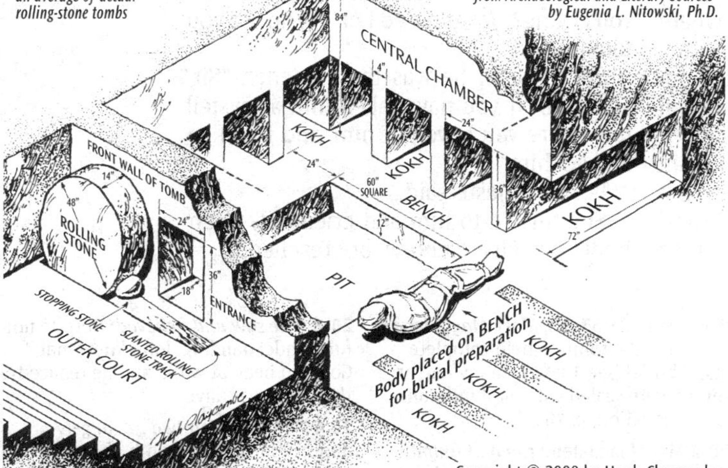

◀ **First-century Judean Tombs (John 19:41).** Joseph of Arimathea's tomb, where Jesus was buried (see Matt 27:57-60), was like other first-century Judean tombs. This drawing is based on sixty-one such "rolling-stone" tombs that have been discovered. These tombs, carved in limestone, were affordable only by wealthy families, and they were constructed according to the laws of Judaism (see *Mishnah Baba Batra* 6:8). After preparation for burial, bodies were placed in the KOKH (niche) which was then sealed with a rolling closure stone. Much later the dried bones were stored in ossuaries (stone boxes) within the tomb.

used in Egypt to brush lamb's blood on the doorposts and lintels during the first Passover (Exod 12:22). Jesus is God's Passover lamb (1:29, 36), and his blood likewise saves.

19:30 Jesus called out in triumph and exhaustion that he had ***finished*** the work he set out to do. On the cross he was not a victim, but a servant doing God's bidding.

19:31-33 The Jewish authorities, eager to complete the crucifixion before Sabbath began at dusk, asked Pilate to break ***the legs*** of the men. Breaking the legs with a mallet was common: It promoted asphyxiation and hemorrhaging, because the victim could no longer push himself up to breathe.

19:34 To confirm that Jesus was dead, a Roman soldier ***pierced his side with a spear.*** • ***blood and water flowed out:*** This has several levels of meaning: (1) The spear probably punctured Jesus' pericardium, the sac around the heart, releasing these fluids. (2) John might have been thinking of more Passover symbolism. The Passover lamb's blood had to flow as it died. (3) The living water, flowing from Jesus' side, reminds readers of earlier language that Jesus used to describe himself (see 7:37-39; "Living Water" at 4:10-14, p. 1777).

19:35 John was at the foot of the cross (19:26). He was not simply a collector of traditions about Jesus, but ***an eyewitness giving an accurate account*** of the events of Jesus' life (cp. 21:24). This same confidence can be seen in the opening of John's first letter (1 Jn 1:1-4) • ***can believe:*** Some manuscripts read *can continue to believe.*

19:36 ***"Not one of his bones will be broken":*** Exod 12:46; Num 9:12; Ps 34:20. The Passover lamb could have no broken bones; Jesus was the perfect Passover lamb (see also 1 Cor 5:7).

19:37 ***"They will look on the one they pierced":*** Zechariah 12:10 describes how Israel would look on a prophet or the Messiah and lament their own fatal lack of faith.

19:38 According to Luke, ***Joseph of Arimathea*** was a courageous man who was waiting for the Kingdom of God (Luke 23:50-51). He was a wealthy (Matt 27:57) and influential leader in Jerusalem and a member of the high council (Mark 15:43) who disagreed with the decision to kill Jesus. He asked Pilate for the favor of burying Jesus in his personal tomb. • Joseph was ***a secret disciple*** (cp. 12:42-43), but his bold deed brought him out in public support of Jesus.

Nicodemus, the man who had come to Jesus at night. He brought about seventy-five pounds of perfumed ointment made from myrrh and aloes. 40Following Jewish burial custom, they wrapped Jesus' body with the spices in long sheets of linen cloth. 41The place of crucifixion was near a garden, where there was a new tomb, never used before. 42And so, because it was the day of preparation for the Jewish Passover and since the tomb was close at hand, they laid Jesus there.

Jesus' Resurrection (20:1-31)

The Empty Tomb

John 20:1-10 // Matt 28:1-10 // Mark 16:1-8 // Luke 24:1-12

20 Early on Sunday morning, while it was still dark, Mary Magdalene came to the tomb and found that the stone had been rolled away from the entrance. 2She ran and found Simon Peter and the other disciple, the one whom Jesus loved. She said, "They have taken the Lord's body out of the tomb, and we don't know where they have put him!"

3Peter and the other disciple started out for the tomb. 4They were both running, but the other disciple outran Peter and reached the tomb first. 5He stooped and looked in and saw the linen wrappings lying there, but he didn't go in. 6Then Simon Peter arrived and went inside. He also noticed the linen wrappings lying there, 7while the cloth that had covered Jesus' head was folded up and lying apart from the other wrappings. 8Then the disciple who had reached the tomb first also went in, and he saw and believed—9for until then they still hadn't understood the Scriptures that said Jesus must rise from the dead. 10Then they went home.

Jesus Appears to Mary Magdalene

John 20:11-18; cp. Matt 28:8-10; Mark 16:9-11

11Mary was standing outside the tomb crying, and as she wept, she stooped and looked in. 12She saw two white-robed angels, one sitting at the head and the other at the foot of the place where the body of Jesus had been lying. 13"Dear woman, why are you crying?" the angels asked her.

"Because they have taken away my Lord," she replied, "and I don't know where they have put him."

14She turned to leave and saw someone standing there. It was Jesus, but she didn't recognize him. 15"Dear woman, why are you crying?" Jesus asked her. "Who are you looking for?"

She thought he was the gardener. "Sir," she said, "if you have taken him away, tell me where you have put him, and I will go and get him."

16"Mary!" Jesus said.

She turned to him and cried out, "[g]Rabboni!" (which is Hebrew for "Teacher").

19:40
Luke 24:12
John 20:5-7

20:1-8
//Matt 28:1-8
//Mark 16:1-8
//Luke 24:1-12

20:2
John 13:23

20:3
Luke 24:12

20:5
John 19:40

20:7
John 11:44

20:9
John 2:22

20:11-18
Mark 16:9-11

20:12
Mark 16:5
Luke 24:4

20:14
Mark 16:9
Luke 24:16
John 21:4

20:16
[g]*rhabbouni* (4462)
‣Matt 23:7

19:39 ***Nicodemus*** (see 3:1; 7:50), a member of the high council, understood that these bodies had to be buried before the upcoming Sabbath (19:31, 42). His public support, as with Joseph of Arimathea, might indicate that he, too, was becoming a disciple (see note on 7:49-51). • ***Myrrh*** was a commonly used aromatic powder. • The ***aloes*** were fragrant powdered sandalwood often used as perfume. • ***seventy-five pounds*** (Greek *100 litras* [32.7 kilograms]): This enormous amount of spices was appropriate for royalty; Jesus, the king, was given a royal burial.

19:41 ***a new tomb:*** More than 900 first-century burial tombs have been discovered in Judea, carved into the limestone hills (see illustration, p. 1813).

19:42 ***because it was the day of preparation for the Jewish Passover:*** Literally *because of the Jewish day of preparation;* see note on 19:14. The Sabbath was approaching, so Joseph and Nicodemus (19:38-39) would return to complete the burial process later.

20:1 ***Early on Sunday morning:*** Literally *On the first day of the week.* As a devoted follower of Jesus (see Luke 8:1-3; Matt 27:55-56), ***Mary Magdalene*** arrived at the tomb to help complete Jesus' burial (see 19:42). • Many Judean tombs were sealed with a rolling ***stone*** (see illustration, p. 1813).

20:2 Mary Magdalene ***ran and found Simon Peter.*** Her natural assumption was that someone had robbed the tomb and perhaps stolen the body—which was not an uncommon occurrence.

20:3-10 The ***other disciple*** was probably John, "the disciple Jesus loved," the author of this Gospel (see 13:23). He and ***Peter*** validated Mary's testimony by examining the tomb for themselves. John arrived first, but Peter entered first.

20:6-7 What Peter and John found in the tomb was remarkable. The ***linen wrappings*** (19:40) were on the burial bench (see note on 19:41). Jews also used a facial ***cloth*** for burials (cp. 11:44), which was rolled, wrapped under the chin, and tied on the top of the head. The apostles found this face cloth ***folded up*** on the bench. John's inclusion of these details counters any suggestion that grave robbers had taken Jesus' body; such costly garments would have been stolen in a robbery.

20:8-9 ***he saw and believed:*** Despite not fully understanding, John knew that God had been at work, and he realized that Jesus was alive.

20:11-13 Although ***two . . . angels*** appeared inside the tomb, the riddle of Jesus' disappearance remained unsolved (see Luke 24:4). • ***why are you crying?*** Sorrow was not the appropriate response in this moment.

20:14-15 Jesus, whom Mary mistook for ***the gardener,*** repeated the angel's question and added, ***Who are you looking for?*** Jesus' question was to provoke Mary's thinking: At this point Mary was looking for the body of Jesus, but she was about to meet the living Christ. Was she truly ready to meet her Lord?

20:16 When Jesus called ***Mary*** by name, she recognized him immediately (see 10:3-4).

20:17 Mary thought that with the resurrection, Jesus would resume normal relations with his disciples. She was trying to ***cling to*** the joy she discovered in her resurrected Lord. But his fellowship with her would come in a new form (20:22). Jesus had ***not yet ascended*** to complete his return to the Father, but the process

20:17 Matt 28:10; John 16:28; Rom 8:29; Col 1:18; Heb 2:11
20:19-23 //Matt 28:16-20 //Luke 24:36-49
20:20 John 16:20-22; 19:34
20:21 Matt 28:19; John 17:18
20:22 John 7:37-39; 14:16-18, 26
20:24 John 11:16

17"Don't cling to me," Jesus said, "for I haven't yet ascended to the Father. But go find my brothers and tell them, 'I am ascending to my Father and your Father, to my God and your God.' "
18Mary Magdalene found the disciples and told them, "I have seen the Lord!" Then she gave them his message.

Jesus Appears to His Disciples
John 20:19-23 // Luke 24:35-49

19That Sunday evening the disciples were meeting behind locked doors because they were afraid of the Jewish leaders. Suddenly, Jesus was standing there among them! "Peace be with you," he said. 20As he spoke, he showed them the wounds in his hands and his side. They were filled with joy when they saw the Lord! 21Again he said, "Peace be with you. As the Father has sent me, so I am sending you." 22Then he breathed on them and said, "Receive the Holy Spirit. 23If you forgive anyone's sins, they are forgiven. If you do not forgive them, they are not forgiven."

Jesus Appears to Thomas

24One of the twelve disciples, Thomas (nicknamed the Twin), was not with the others

THOMAS (20:24-28)

John 11:16; 14:5; 21:2; Matt 10:3; Mark 3:18; Luke 6:15; Acts 1:13

Thomas, also known as "the twin," was one of the twelve apostles (Matt 10:3; Mark 3:18; Luke 6:15; Acts 1:13). He is remembered for his unbelieving response to Jesus' resurrection.

Nothing is known of how Jesus first met and called Thomas to be his disciple. The only personal accounts of Thomas are found in the Gospel of John. Thomas voiced his willingness to follow Jesus, even if it meant death (11:16); he openly told Jesus that he didn't understand what he was saying (14:5); and he was one of the seven disciples who returned to fishing after the resurrection, when Jesus appeared to them (21:2).

When Jesus first appeared to his disciples after his death, Thomas was not present. When Thomas heard the report from the others, he did not believe it, insisting he would have to see the evidence of the crucifixion in Jesus' body with his own eyes and feel it with his own hands (20:19-23). A week later, when Jesus once again appeared to the disciples, he especially addressed Thomas, telling him to examine the marks of the nails and the spear in his body and challenging him to believe and not be skeptical. Thomas's response represents one of the strongest statements of Jesus' deity in the New Testament, and the culmination of the Gospel of John's portrayal of Jesus: "My Lord and my God!" (20:28).

Later tradition speaks of Thomas working as a missionary in the East: in Parthia (Eusebius), Persia (Jerome), and India (*Acts of Thomas*). The Mar Thoma church on the west coast of India traces its roots back to the early missionary work of Thomas. The historical reliability of these accounts is uncertain.

Thomas's name is unreliably linked to several later apocryphal writings: the *Acts of Thomas,* the *Infancy Gospel of Thomas,* the *Epistle to the Apostles,* the *Apocalypse of Thomas,* the *Book of Thomas the Athlete,* and especially the Coptic *Gospel of Thomas,* a Gnostic collection of Jesus' sayings.

was underway. Before his final departure, he would give the Holy Spirit (20:22; see 14:15-21, 26; 15:26-27; 16:5-15).

20:18 Mary was the first eyewitness to see *the Lord* following his resurrection. She not only saw him, she heard him and touched him (see 1 Jn 1:1-4). This great privilege was given to a woman whose broken life had experienced healing (Luke 8:2). In Jewish culture this was astounding; a woman could not even be a witness in court. No Jew in this period would make up such a story.

20:19 *That Sunday evening:* Literally *In the evening of that day, the first day of the week.* • *meeting behind locked doors:* The disciples feared prosecution for following Jesus. • *Peace be with you:* This was a standard Jewish greeting (see also 3 Jn 1:15), but Jesus was doing more than just greeting his disciples: he was offering the Messiah's peace (see Isa 9:6; 52:7) and delivering the gift of his Kingdom (see 14:27; 16:33).

20:20 The reality of Jesus' resurrection was quite clear. Jesus *showed them the wounds* from the nails and the spear. He did not feign death, but conquered it. He was no phantom, but a real man with a real body. He had been dead, but was now alive. Jesus was fully human both in life (1:14) and in his resurrection.

20:21 *I am sending you:* God had sent Jesus into the world to establish his Kingdom, and now Jesus was sending his disciples to carry on his mission. Christ's emissaries carry the truth of Jesus' words to the world (cp. 17:18).

20:22 Jesus commissioned the disciples and then empowered them with *the Holy Spirit.* The Spirit had not been given previously because Jesus had not yet been glorified (7:39). The glorified Jesus, resplendent in his resurrected body, poured the Spirit on his followers. This gift fulfilled many promises that the Spirit would be sent (14:16, 26; 15:26; 16:7, 13). It foreshadows the arrival of the Spirit's empowering presence at Pentecost (Acts 1:4-5; 2:1-47).

20:23 *If you forgive anyone's sins:* The ongoing work of Christ's followers parallels the work of Christ. Christ's followers do not distribute and withdraw God's forgiveness on a whim, but they follow Jesus' prompting through the Spirit (15:5), just as Jesus obeyed his Father (14:31).

20:24-25 *Thomas (nicknamed the Twin):* Literally *Thomas, who was called Didymus* (see also 11:16; 14:5). Thomas was absent when Jesus revealed himself. He remained skeptical despite the testimony of his friends, who had *seen the Lord.* Thomas demanded a concrete experience identical to theirs.

when Jesus came. 25They told him, "We have seen the Lord!"

But he replied, "I won't believe it unless I see the nail wounds in his hands, put my fingers into them, and place my hand into the wound in his side."

26Eight days later the disciples were together again, and this time Thomas was with them. The doors were locked; but suddenly, as before, Jesus was standing among them. "Peace be with you," he said. 27Then he said to Thomas, "Put your finger here, and look at my hands. Put your hand into the wound in my side. Don't be faithless any longer. Believe!"

28"My Lord and my God!" Thomas exclaimed.

29Then Jesus told him, "You believe because you have seen me. [h]Blessed are those who believe without seeing me."

Purpose of the Book

30The disciples saw Jesus do many other miraculous signs in addition to the ones recorded in this [i]book. 31But these are written so that you may continue to believe that Jesus is the Messiah, the Son of God, and that by believing in him you will have life by the power of his name.

4. EPILOGUE: THE WORD COMMISSIONS HIS FOLLOWERS (21:1-25)

The Miraculous Catch of Fish

21 Later, Jesus appeared again to the disciples beside the Sea of Galilee. This is how it happened. 2Several of the disciples were there—Simon Peter, Thomas (nicknamed the Twin), Nathanael from Cana in Galilee, the sons of Zebedee, and two other disciples.

3Simon Peter said, "I'm going fishing."

"We'll come, too," they all said. So they went out in the boat, but they caught nothing all night.

4At dawn Jesus was standing on the beach, but the disciples couldn't see who he was. 5He called out, "Fellows, have you caught any fish?"

"No," they replied.

6Then he said, "Throw out your net on the right-hand side of the boat, and you'll get some!" So they did, and they couldn't haul in the net because there were so many fish in it.

7Then the disciple Jesus loved said to Peter, "It's the Lord!" When Simon Peter heard that it was the Lord, he put on his tunic (for he had stripped for work), jumped into the water, and headed to shore. 8The others stayed with the boat and pulled the loaded net to the shore, for they were only about a hundred yards from shore. 9When they got there, they found breakfast waiting for them—fish cooking over a charcoal fire, and some bread.

10"Bring some of the fish you've just caught," Jesus said. 11So Simon Peter went aboard and dragged the net to the shore. There were 153 large fish, and yet the net hadn't torn.

20:28 John 1:1, 18; 10:30; 14:9; Phil 2:6; Col 2:9; Titus 2:13; 2 Pet 1:1; 1 Jn 5:20
20:29 1 Pet 1:8; [h]*makarios* (3107) ‣Acts 20:35
20:30 John 21:25; [i]*biblion* (0975) ‣John 21:25
20:31 John 3:15; 19:35; 1 Jn 5:13
21:2 John 1:45-51; 11:16; 20:24
21:3 Luke 5:5
21:4 Luke 24:16; John 20:14
21:6 Luke 5:4-7
21:7 Matt 14:29; John 13:23
21:9 John 18:18

20:26-27 ***Eight days later*** was Sunday, one week after Jesus' resurrection (it was customary to include the current day when counting forward). Jesus' appearance on the following Sunday helps explain the disciples' meeting on "the Lord's Day" (see Rev 1:10). • ***Peace be with you:*** This scene was exactly like Jesus' first appearance (20:19-20). Jesus had already heard Thomas's complaint and now answered directly. • ***Believe!*** Jesus challenged Thomas to believe in the resurrection like the others.

20:28 ***"My Lord and my God!"*** This was not an astonished exclamation but a proclamation of heartfelt belief. It concludes John's study of Jesus' deity that has framed the whole book (see 1:1-18).

20:29 Jesus points to the generations of Christians who, through the testimony of others, would ***believe without seeing.***

20:30-31 Many scholars view these words as the conclusion of John's Gospel, viewing ch 21 as an appendix. John's account is only a selection from Jesus' ***many . . . miraculous signs.***

20:31 ***that you may continue to believe:*** Some manuscripts use the present tense, indicating that John wrote to encourage believers. Other manuscripts read *that you may come to believe,* suggesting that John wrote to stimulate new faith (cp. 1:7).

21:1-25 This final chapter adds an account about the resurrected Jesus in Galilee (21:1-14) and records the exchange between Peter and Jesus concerning Peter's love (21:15-23). The chapter ends by summarizing the authority and importance of John's eyewitness report (21:24-25).

21:1 ***Sea of Galilee:*** Greek *Sea of Tiberias,* another name for the Sea of Galilee (see 6:1).

21:2 ***Several of the disciples*** returned to fishing in the Sea of Galilee. This was not a sign that their faith had weakened—even rabbis who regularly preached kept practicing their occupations (see Acts 18:3; 20:34; 1 Cor 4:12). • ***Thomas (nicknamed the Twin):*** Literally *Thomas, who was called Didymus.* • ***The sons of Zebedee*** were James and John (see Matt 4:21).

21:3 Fishing was usually successful in the early hours of the morning. However, this trip was useless and ***they caught nothing all night.***

21:4-5 ***Jesus was standing on the beach,*** but the men did not recognize him (cp. 20:11-16; Luke 24:13-53). • ***Fellows:*** Literally *Children.*

21:6 ***"Throw out your net on the right-hand side":*** Casting a net into the sea at random was futile. But when ***they did*** as the stranger said, the immense catch was immediate (21:11).

21:7 ***"It's the Lord!"*** John recognized Jesus, probably remembering that a miracle like this had happened before (Luke 5:1-11). • Peter, who ***had stripped*** off his clothes while working, ***put on his tunic*** in order to meet the Lord.

21:8 ***a hundred yards:*** Greek *200 cubits* [90 meters].

21:9 Cooked ***fish*** and ***bread*** were the mainstays of the Galilean diet; Jesus provided the men with breakfast. The ***charcoal fire*** is reminiscent of the scene of Peter's denials (18:18).

21:11 This miracle showed generous provision (as in 2:1-12; 6:1-15). No symbolism attaches to the number ***153.***

21:14
John 20:19, 26
21:15
Matt 26:33
21:16
Acts 20:28
Heb 13:20-21
1 Pet 5:2-3
[i]*poimainō* (4165)
‣Acts 20:28
21:17
John 13:37-38; 16:30
21:19
John 13:36
2 Pet 1:14
21:20
John 13:23, 25
21:22
Matt 16:27
21:24
John 15:27; 19:35
1 Jn 1:1-3
3 Jn 1:12
21:25
John 20:30
[k]*biblion* (0975)
‣2 Tim 4:13

12"Now come and have some breakfast!" Jesus said. None of the disciples dared to ask him, "Who are you?" They knew it was the Lord. 13Then Jesus served them the bread and the fish. 14This was the third time Jesus had appeared to his disciples since he had been raised from the dead.

Peter's Restoration

15After breakfast Jesus asked Simon Peter, "Simon son of John, do you love me more than these?"

"Yes, Lord," Peter replied, "you know I love you."

"Then feed my lambs," Jesus told him.

16Jesus repeated the question: "Simon son of John, do you love me?"

"Yes, Lord," Peter said, "you know I love you."

"Then [i]take care of my sheep," Jesus said.

17A third time he asked him, "Simon son of John, do you love me?"

Peter was hurt that Jesus asked the question a third time. He said, "Lord, you know everything. You know that I love you."

Jesus said, "Then feed my sheep.

18"I tell you the truth, when you were young, you were able to do as you liked; you dressed yourself and went wherever you wanted to go. But when you are old, you will stretch out your hands, and others will dress you and take you where you don't want to go." 19Jesus said this to let him know by what kind of death he would glorify God. Then Jesus told him, "Follow me."

20Peter turned around and saw behind them the disciple Jesus loved—the one who had leaned over to Jesus during supper and asked, "Lord, who will betray you?" 21Peter asked Jesus, "What about him, Lord?"

22Jesus replied, "If I want him to remain alive until I return, what is that to you? As for you, follow me." 23So the rumor spread among the community of believers that this disciple wouldn't die. But that isn't what Jesus said at all. He only said, "If I want him to remain alive until I return, what is that to you?"

Concluding Remarks

24This disciple is the one who testifies to these events and has recorded them here. And we know that his account of these things is accurate.

25Jesus also did many other things. If they were all written down, I suppose the whole world could not contain the [k]books that would be written.

21:12-13 ***None of the disciples dared to ask him, "Who are you?"*** Jesus' resurrected appearance was different. His offer of fish and bread removed all uncertainties (cp. 6:11; Luke 24:30).

21:14 This scene on the beach ***was the third time Jesus had appeared*** (see 20:11-23, 26-29).

21:15-17 ***do you love me?*** The three questions and affirmations mirror Peter's three denials (18:15-18, 25-27). Jesus invited Peter to reaffirm everything he had denied. • The Greek term translated *love* in Jesus' first two questions (*agapaō*) is different from the word in his third question (*phileō*). In each case, Peter answered with the second word (*phileō*). Most Greek scholars view the two words as synonyms in this situation. The focus of Jesus' exchange with Peter was not the quality of Peter's love, but Peter's commission to take care of Jesus' flock. Peter might be meditating on these events in 1 Pet 5:2-4.

21:15 ***more than these?*** Or *more than these others do?* Jesus was reminding Peter of his insistence that he would be more faithful and courageous than the others (13:37; Matt 26:33; Mark 14:29). He was urging Peter to examine himself.

21:17 ***feed my sheep:*** Jesus, who knows all things (1:42; 2:25; 16:30), understood that despite Peter's terrible failing, he still had faith and commitment to Jesus. These words called Peter to nurture and protect Christ's followers.

21:18 ***you will stretch out your hands:*** Jesus was probably predicting crucifixion, which according to tradition is how Peter died. • ***others*** (some manuscripts read *another one*) ***will dress you*** (literally *bind you*): Jesus alludes to captivity, bondage, and even crucifixion—victims were often tied to the cross.

21:19 Peter's life was a ministry tending the flock of God, and his martyrdom was a ***kind of death*** that glorifies God. • ***Follow me:*** This might require suffering and death (see 13:16; 15:18-21).

21:20-22 ***"What about him, Lord?"*** Peter asked Jesus about the fate of John, wondering if he, too, would experience martyrdom. Jesus' answer was abrupt: It was not Peter's business to know how or when John would die. Peter's only task was to follow Jesus, which John was already doing. This episode forms the core of John's concept of discipleship: What matters most for the disciple of Jesus is to follow him and do his will, come what may.

21:23 Jesus' words to Peter *spread*, causing some to conclude that John would not die until Jesus returned in his second coming. Jesus' rebuke to Peter (21:22) is repeated to answer that rumor. Those among ***the community of believers*** (literally *the brothers*) who believed this rumor were thus instructed to abandon any speculation about John. According to tradition, John died peacefully in Ephesus at an old age, surrounded by fellow believers.

21:24 ***This disciple is the one who testifies . . . and has recorded:*** John's Gospel is anchored in his personal experiences. It is not a story written from hearsay or speculation, but from the remembrance of a man who spent life-changing years with Jesus and recalled, with the help of the Holy Spirit (14:26), what Jesus said and did. • ***we know:*** This account of the life of Christ was not speculation or weak reminiscence. Rather, it was based on the confident knowledge of reliable eyewitness accounts.

21:25 ***the whole world could not contain the books:*** John ends his Gospel acknowledging that the story he has described is larger than anything he can imagine or fully communicate. Though it is glorious for us to read, John's account pales in comparison to the glory of the person it describes.

THE CHRONOLOGY OF THE Apostolic Age

Events in the apostolic age are difficult to date because few precise statements are made about time. Many events, however, can be correlated with known dates in the Roman world.

EVENTS IN THE APOSTOLIC CHURCH

Events from AD *30 to 50.* We know from Roman sources that Herod Agrippa I died in AD 44 (Acts 12:23), so his execution of the apostle James and imprisonment of Peter (Acts 12:2-17) must have happened before that date.

The famine prophesied by Agabus befell Palestine during the reign of Emperor Claudius (Acts 11:28-29). When the church in Antioch sent famine relief to the church in Jerusalem, Barnabas and Paul were appointed to carry the money (Acts 11:29-30). It was Paul's second trip to Jerusalem after his conversion. The Jewish historian Josephus dates the famine between AD 46 and 48.

While Paul was in Corinth on his second missionary journey, Gallio was governor of Achaia (Acts 18:12). An inscription discovered at nearby Delphi indicates that Gallio's term was AD 51–52. The incident in Acts 18:12-17 probably occurred at the beginning of Gallio's term. Paul then left Corinth not long afterward, probably in the summer or autumn of AD 52. Paul had spent eighteen months in Corinth (Acts 18:11), so he probably arrived in early AD 50. That arrival date is confirmed by Acts 18:2. When Paul came to Corinth, Aquila and Priscilla had recently been exiled from Rome. Claudius expelled Jews from Rome in AD 49.

Events from AD *50 to 70.* Festus replaced Felix as governor of Judea during Paul's imprisonment in Caesarea (Acts 24:27), probably in the summer of AD 59. This event helps us date events in the rest of the book of Acts. Paul's arrest (Acts 21:33) was about two years beforehand (AD 57). Earlier that spring, Paul had celebrated Passover in Philippi (Acts 20:6; April AD 57). Paul had just spent three months in Greece (Acts 20:3), probably the winter of AD 56–57 (see 1 Cor 16:6). Previously Paul had spent three years in Ephesus (Acts 20:31; AD 53~56).

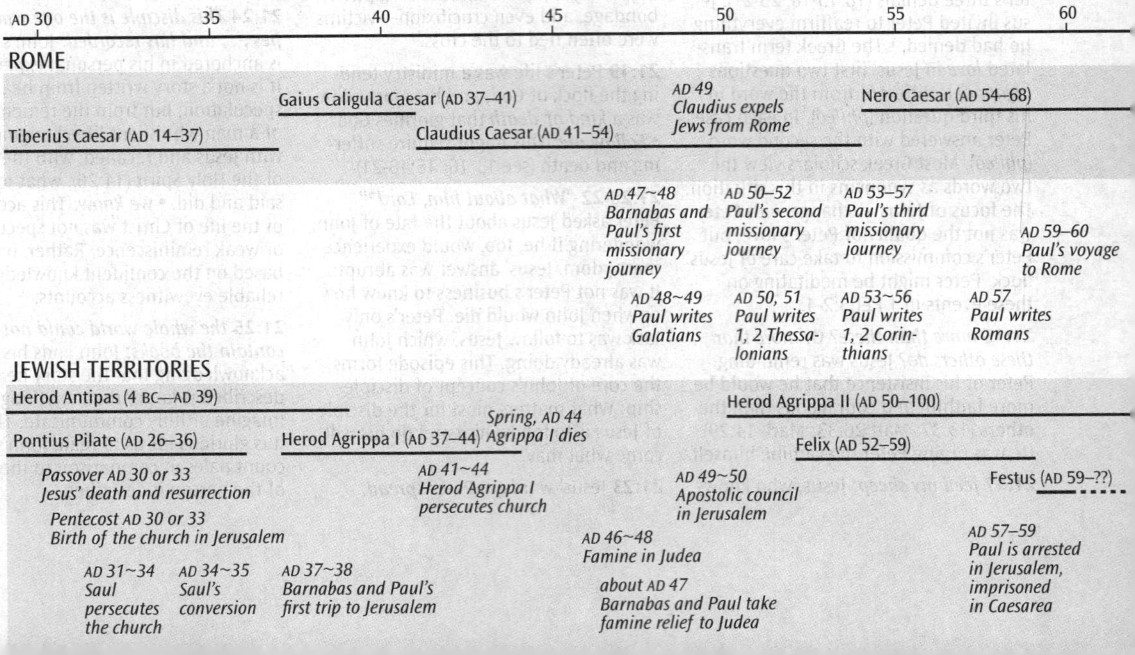

After Festus arrived in the summer of AD 59, Paul quickly stood trial and appealed to Caesar (Acts 25:1-12). The voyage to Rome most likely began in the fall of AD 59 (Acts 27:2) and ended early in AD 60 (Acts 28:11-16). Paul stayed in Rome "for the next two years" (Acts 28:30). The NT does not report the outcome of Paul's trial, but he was probably released and then recaptured and martyred in Rome along with Peter and many others during Nero's persecution (about AD 64~65; see "Introduction to Paul's Letters to Timothy and Titus," p. 2047).

In Jerusalem, James the brother of Jesus was stoned to death by the Jewish authorities in AD 62 (Josephus, *Antiquities* 20.9.1). Not long afterward, the church in Jerusalem left that doomed city and settled in Pella, one of the cities of the Decapolis east of the Jordan. Thus, when war broke out between the Jews and the Romans in AD 66, the Christians for the most part escaped its fury. That war ended in AD 70, when Jerusalem and the Temple were destroyed.

Events from AD 70 to 100. The NT and early Christians left few records of the period following the deaths of Peter and Paul and the destruction of Jerusalem. It is possible that both Matthew and Luke wrote after AD 70, but they did not write about the developments after AD 70. Similarly, the apostle John probably wrote his Gospel and three letters during the period before AD 90, but we learn few specifics about the late-first-century church from those writings. If Revelation was written in the early 90s AD, then it gives us a glimpse of what the churches in Asia Minor were facing during that time (see Revelation Introduction, "Date," p. 2164).

As the apostolic age came to a close, the church around the Mediterranean grew and developed, as it would continue to do after the last of the apostles had died and the leadership of the church passed on to the following generations (see "Introduction to the Time After the Apostles," pp. 2201–2205).

FURTHER READING

C. K. BARRETT, ED.
The New Testament Background (1995)

F. F. BRUCE
New Testament History (1983)

D. A. CARSON AND DOUGLAS J. MOO
An Introduction to the New Testament (2005)

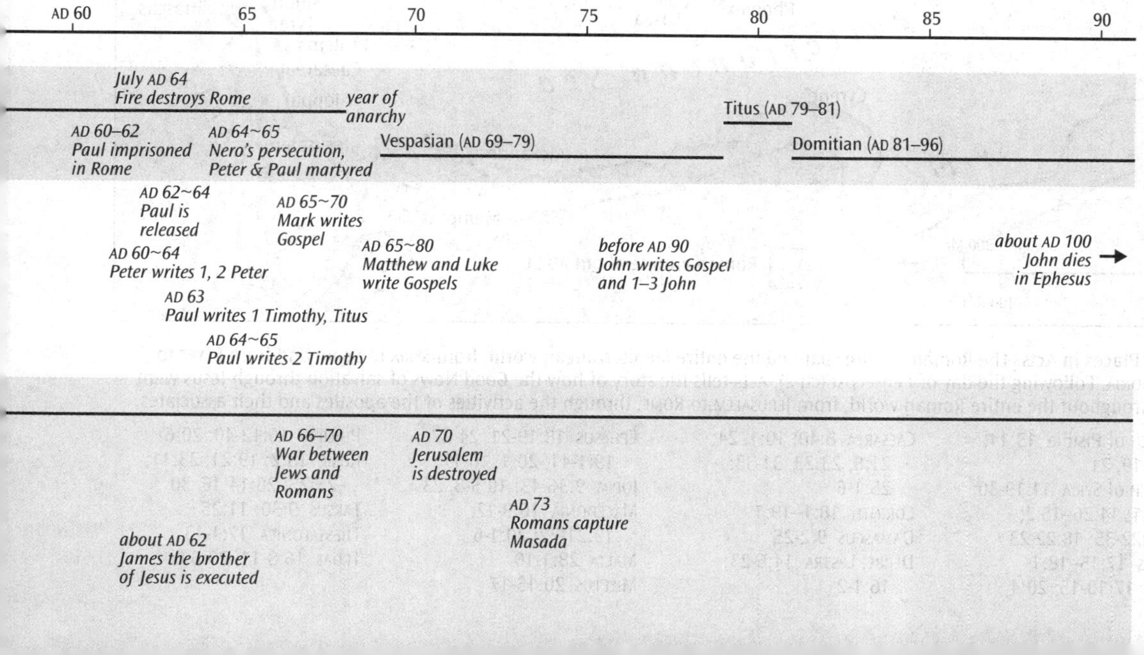

THE BOOK OF

ACTS

The book of Acts has a central role in the NT: It connects Jesus with the emerging Christian community, and the Gospels with the rest of the NT. It frames the proclamation of the Christian message in both Jewish and Gentile settings and underscores the key roles of Peter and Paul in the spread of the Good News throughout the Mediterranean. It is the story of a dynamic message with an outreach to all.

SETTING

Luke wrote at a time when the Good News about Jesus Christ was spreading from Jerusalem throughout the Mediterranean world. Luke was

▲ **Key Places in Acts.** The Roman empire spanned the entire Mediterranean world, from SYRIA to Spain and from EGYPT to MACEDONIA. Following the day of Pentecost (ch 2), Acts tells the story of how the Good News of salvation through Jesus went out throughout the entire Roman world, from JERUSALEM to ROME, through the activities of the apostles and their associates.

ANTIOCH of Pisidia 13:14; 14:19, 21
ANTIOCH of SYRIA 11:19-30; 13:1; 14:26–15:2; 15:22-35; 18:22-23
ATHENS 17:15–18:1
BEREA 17:10-15; 20:4
CAESAREA 8:40; 10:1, 24; 21:8; 23:23, 31-33; 25:1-6
CORINTH 18:1–19:1
DAMASCUS 9:2-25
DERBE, LYSTRA 14:6-23; 16:1-2
EPHESUS 18:19-21, 24-27; 19:1-41; 20:1, 16-17
JOPPA 9:36-43; 10:5-8, 23
MACEDONIA 16:9-12; 19:21-22; 20:1-6
MALTA 28:1-10
MILETUS 20:15-17
PHILIPPI 16:12-40; 20:6
ROME 18:2; 19:21; 23:11; 25:25; 28:14-16, 30
TARSUS 9:30; 11:25
THESSALONICA 17:1-13
TROAS 16:8-11; 20:5-6

probably a Gentile (non-Jew), and his material on Christian origins keeps the needs and outlook of the wider world in mind.

Luke began his presentation of the message of Christ with an account of Jesus' life (the Gospel of Luke). In the book of Acts, Luke describes how the Christian faith was carried across the Mediterranean world.

It was important for Luke to show that God's love and mercy reaches out to all people—"God shows no favoritism," as Peter told Cornelius (10:34). Christ is the only Savior (4:12), so all can believe in him for salvation and new life (16:31). Despite the tendency of Jewish Christians to keep God's grace to themselves, the church came to the united conclusion that Gentiles are fully included in God's promises (see 15:1-31). The message of the forgiveness of sins is for all nations.

OUTLINE

1:1-5
Prologue: The Promise of the Holy Spirit

1:6–5:42
The Church Begins in Jerusalem

6:1–12:25
The Church Grows From Jerusalem to Antioch

13:1–21:17
The Christian Message Goes to the Gentiles

21:18–26:32
Paul in Jerusalem and Caesarea

27:1–28:31
Paul Goes to Rome

SUMMARY

The apostles and other people of God were filled with the Spirit and empowered to carry out the Great Commission to all people. Acts highlights the ministries of Peter (chs 1–12) and Paul (chs 13–28).

Acts follows a geographical outline based on 1:8. The Christian message and community of believers spread in Jerusalem (1:1–8:3), in Palestine and Syria (8:4–12:25), and in the Gentile world throughout the Roman empire (13:1–28:31). The closing word in the Greek text of Acts (*akōlutōs,* "unhindered," 28:31) speaks of the unhindered spread of the gospel to Jews (3:1–5:42), Samaritans (6:1–8:40), "God-fearers" (8:26-40; 9:32–11:18), and Gentiles (11:19-30; 13:1–28:31).

PURPOSES OF ACTS

Biography. Peter, Stephen, James, and Paul were the principal figures leading the Christian movement.

History. The book describes the actual places where the Christian message was shared, and the reactions of local officials and citizens to it.

Geography. Acts shows how the message was taken from Jerusalem to Rome (1:8; 9:15).

Evangelism. Acts gives clear examples of how Christian leaders proclaimed the Good News to different audiences (note the speeches of chs 2–5, 7, 10, 13, 22, 26). Acts shows that the gospel is open to all—not only to Jews but also to Gentiles (including Samaritans, "God-fearers," and "converts to Judaism"; 2:8-11; 8:4-25; 10:1–11:18), and not only to men but also to women (5:14; 8:12; 16:13-15; 17:4, 12, 34; 18:26; 21:9).

TIMELINE

Passover, AD 30 or 33
Jesus' crucifixion and resurrection

Pentecost, AD 30 or 33
The birth of the church in Jerusalem

AD 31~34
Saul persecutes the church of Judea

AD 34~35
Saul's conversion near Damascus

AD 37~38
Barnabas and Paul's first trip to Jerusalem

AD 37–44
Herod Agrippa I rules Palestine

Spring AD 44
Death of Herod Agrippa I

AD 46~48
Famine in Judea

about AD 47
Barnabas and Paul travel to Jerusalem

AD 47~48
Barnabas and Paul's first missionary journey

AD 48~49
Paul writes Galatians

AD 49
Emperor Claudius expels Jews from Rome

AD 49~50
The council in Jerusalem

AD 50–100
Herod Agrippa II rules in Palestine

AD 50–52
Paul's second missionary journey

AD 50
Paul meets Priscilla and Aquila

about AD 50
Paul writes 1 Thessalonians from Corinth

AD 51–52
Gallio governs Achaia

about AD 51
Paul writes 2 Thessalonians

AD 52–59
Felix is governor of Judea

AD 53–57
Paul's third missionary journey

AD 53~56
Paul writes 1 Corinthians

AD 54–68
Nero as Emperor of Rome

about AD 56
Paul writes 2 Corinthians

about AD 57
Paul writes Romans

AD 57
Paul travels to Jerusalem

AD 57–59
Paul is imprisoned in Caesarea

about AD 59
Festus becomes governor of Judea

AD 59–60
Paul's journey to Rome

AD 60–62
Paul in prison in Rome
Peter writes 1 Peter

about 62 AD
James the brother of Jesus is stoned to death in Jerusalem

AD 62–64
Paul is released, travels freely

about AD 63
Paul writes 1 Timothy, Titus

before AD 64
Peter writes 2 Peter

July AD 64
Fire destroys Rome

AD 64~65
Peter is crucified in Rome

about AD 64~65?
Paul is imprisoned in Rome, writes 2 Timothy, is martyred

Politics. Acts presents a strong defense of the Christian faith to Jews (4:8-12; 7:2-53) and to Gentiles (e.g., Paul's defense before Felix, 24:10-21, and before Agrippa, 26:1-23). Luke argued that Christianity was entitled to the same protection Judaism enjoyed as a *religio licita* ("permitted religion") and that it represented no danger to the Roman state (18:15; 19:37; 23:29; 25:25; 26:32).

AUTHORSHIP

Luke was Paul's traveling companion (see 16:10 and note) and was with Paul during his later years (2 Tim 4:11). Several passages in Acts appear in the first person ("we"; 16:10-18; 20:5-15; 21:1-18; 27:1–28:16), which suggests that Luke was with Paul for parts of his journeys. In Col 4:14, Luke is referred to as the "beloved doctor" in connection with other non-Jews (cp. Col 4:11) who were working with Paul (see Phlm 1:24). Paul was grateful for Luke's love and support as a faithful co-worker and friend.

Luke was also apparently the author of the Gospel that bears his name. The theological viewpoint is consistent throughout both works. Each book highlights the historical character of God's action in redemption, the central role of the Holy Spirit, the central place of prayer, the importance of angels, and the fulfillment of OT promises in the life of Jesus and in the unfolding life of the Christian community. Luke was a theologian of holy history who saw God as governing the course of events for the outworking of the divine purpose.

As a responsible Hellenistic historian, Luke used good historical methods and described his procedures in detail, showing concern to write an accurate and orderly account of the truth of Christian origins (Luke 1:1-4). Where other sources can verify Luke's writings, he proves to have been careful and accurate in handling historical details. Luke was also a literary artist, a gifted storyteller who perceived and clearly portrayed the hand of God in the development of the Christian mission. He is one of the most important historical writers between Polybius, "the last of the great Greek historians" (100s BC), and Eusebius, the first major church historian (AD 275–339).

DATE AND PLACE OF WRITING

Acts was probably written in Rome, though Greece and Asia Minor are possible locations.

Acts is generally dated between the early 60s AD and the end of the expected life span of Paul's co-workers and traveling companions (mid-80s AD). Many scholars have opted for a date after AD 70, arguing that Luke used Mark as one of his sources and dating Mark in the late 60s. However, Acts makes no mention of the outcome of Paul's trial (about AD 62); the death of James, the Lord's brother (early 60s AD); the persecution of Christians carried out by Nero following the fire of Rome in AD 64; the deaths of Peter and Paul (about AD 64~65) and Nero (AD 68); the Jewish revolt (AD 66); or the destruction of Jerusalem (AD 70). Acts ends with Paul under house arrest (AD 60–62). Therefore, it seems more likely that Luke wrote Acts before AD 64. Those who date Acts after AD 70 would answer that Luke omits these events because they were not pertinent to his purpose (see 1:8; 9:15; 28:31).

RECIPIENTS AND DESTINATION

The book of Acts is the second volume of a two-part work (see 1:1-2; Luke 1:1-4). The prime recipient of Luke's Gospel and the book of Acts was Theophilus (1:1; Luke 1:3), whose name means "one who loves God." Theophilus is described by the title, "most honorable" (Luke 1:3), which is used elsewhere for Roman governors such as Felix and Festus (23:26; 24:2-3; 26:25). Theophilus may have been Luke's patron and benefactor. He was a Gentile who had received Christian instruction (Luke 1:4). Luke wanted him and others to have an accurate understanding of the Christian faith and of its spread into the Mediterranean world so they could be "certain of the truth" concerning Christianity (Luke 1:4).

LITERARY CHARACTERISTICS

The material of Acts is presented carefully and accurately (e.g., 11:28; 18:2), and this precision has often been affirmed by archaeology, geography, and related studies. Luke has combined historical accuracy and detail with a gift for vivid and dramatic descriptions (e.g., 5:17-32; 12:1-17; 14:8-20; 16:11-40; 27:1-44).

Acts is punctuated by powerful speeches of Peter, Stephen, James, and Paul (2:14-40; 7:2-53; 15:13-21; 22:3-21). The varied literary styles in Acts fit the cultural settings in a remarkable way. Peter's sermon on the day of Pentecost has a strongly Jewish character (2:14-40), while Paul's preaching before the cultured Greek philosophers in Athens uses the forms of Greek oratory (17:22-31). These characteristics all support the historical authenticity of the book.

The Book of Acts is more than first-century church history; it is a narrative about the Triune God on an unstoppable mission to the ends of the earth.

WILLIAM J. LARKIN
Acts in *Cornerstone Biblical Commentary,* vol. 12, p. 351

MEANING AND MESSAGE

Acts shows that the Christian faith truly fulfills God's promises in the Hebrew Scriptures (2:16-36; 4:11-12; 10:42-43; 13:16-41; 17:30-31; see Luke 24:25-27, 44-47). Christ brought salvation (8:35; 10:36; 16:17, 30-31). Prayer advances God's Kingdom (1:12-15; 2:1-4; 4:24-31; 12:5) while the Holy Spirit energizes and equips God's people to carry out their mission (1:8; 4:8, 31; 6:3, 5, 10; 7:55; 11:24; 13:9, 52).

Acts shows the importance of the individuals that God has chosen to carry his message and testify about Christ. At the beginning the apostles testified about the life and ministry of Jesus (1:22; 10:39-41; see Luke 1:2) and explained Jesus' significance in God's plan to redeem humanity (2:40; 3:15; 4:33; 10:42). Matthias was chosen to replace Judas in the company of the twelve apostles (1:12-26). Later, other Christian leaders shared in the task of testifying for their Lord; Stephen and Philip are two outstanding examples of bold witness to their faith (7:2-53; 8:4-40). Other Christians simply shared their faith as they had opportunity (e.g., 8:1-4; 11:19-21). Later, God called Paul to participate in this enterprise as his "chosen instrument to take my message to the Gentiles and to kings, as well as to the people of Israel" (9:15; 22:1-21; 26:2-23). Paul, like Peter, occupies a central role in Acts as a major witness for Christ.

The apostles proclaimed that the death and resurrection of Jesus was God's plan fulfilling Scripture (2:22-36; 3:15; 4:27-28, 33; 7:52; 8:32-35; 10:38-43; 13:26-39). Jesus was the one appointed to redeem humankind, so the apostles' message was, "Believe in the Lord Jesus and you will be saved" (16:31). God offers his grace and forgiveness to all. "There is peace with God through Jesus Christ, who is Lord of all" (10:36).

FURTHER READING

DARRELL BOCK
Acts (2007)

F. F. BRUCE
The Book of the Acts (1988)

WILLIAM J. LARKIN
Acts in *Cornerstone Biblical Commentary,* vol. 12 (2006)

I. HOWARD MARSHALL
Acts (1980)

I. H. MARSHALL AND D. PETERSON, EDS.
Witness to the Gospel: The Theology of Acts (1998)

J. STOTT
The Spirit, the Church, and the World (1990)

BEN WITHERINGTON III
The Acts of the Apostles (1998)

1. PROLOGUE (1:1-5)

The Promise of the Holy Spirit

1 In my first book I told you, Theophilus,
about everything Jesus began to do
and teach 2until the day he was taken up to
heaven after giving his chosen apostles further instructions through the Holy Spirit.
3During the forty days after his crucifixion,
he appeared to the apostles from time to
time, and he proved to them in many ways
that he was actually alive. And he talked to
them about the Kingdom of God.
4Once when he was eating with them, he
commanded them, "Do not leave Jerusalem
until the Father sends you the gift he promised, as I told you before. 5John baptized
with water, but in just a few days you will be
baptized with the Holy Spirit."

2. THE CHURCH BEGINS IN JERUSALEM (1:6–5:42)

The Coming of the Holy Spirit (1:6–2:47)

The Ascension of Jesus

Acts 1:6-11 // Mark 16:19-20 // Luke 24:50-53

6So when the apostles were with Jesus, they
kept asking him, "Lord, has the time come for
you to free Israel and restore our kingdom?"
7He replied, "The Father alone has the
authority to set those dates and times, and
they are not for you to know. 8But you will
receive power when the Holy Spirit comes
upon you. And you will be my witnesses,
telling people about me everywhere—in Jerusalem, throughout Judea, in Samaria, and
to the ends of the earth."
9After saying this, he was taken up into
a cloud while they were watching, and they
could no longer see him. 10As they strained
to see him rising into heaven, two white-
robed men suddenly stood among them.
11"Men of Galilee," they said, "why are you
standing here staring into heaven? Jesus
has been taken from you into heaven, but
someday he will return from heaven in the
same way you saw him go!"

Matthias Replaces Judas

Acts 1:18-19; cp. Matt 27:3-10

12Then the apostles returned to Jerusalem
from the Mount of Olives, a distance of half
a mile. 13When they arrived, they went to
the upstairs room of the house where they
were staying.
Here are the names of those who were
present: Peter, John, James, Andrew, Philip,
Thomas, Bartholomew, Matthew, James
(son of Alphaeus), Simon (the Zealot), and
Judas (son of James). 14They all met together
and were constantly united in prayer, along

1:1 Luke 1:3
1:2 Matt 28:19-20; Luke 24:49-51
1:3 Luke 24:33-36; John 20:19, 26; 21:1, 14
1:4 Luke 24:49; John 14:16-17, 26; Acts 2:33
1:5 Luke 3:16
1:7 Matt 24:36; 1 Thes 5:1-2
1:8 Luke 24:48; John 15:27; Acts 2:1-4
1:9 Mark 16:19
1:11 Rev 1:7
1:12 Luke 24:52
1:13 Matt 10:2-4; Mark 3:16-19; Luke 6:14-16
1:14 Acts 2:42

1:1-3 Here Luke summarizes his *first book*; the reference is to the Gospel of Luke, which Luke had previously written to *Theophilus* (Luke 1:3). Theophilus is elsewhere called "most honorable" (Luke 1:3)—the title indicates that he was a person of very high social standing (cp. Acts 23:26; 24:2; 26:25). He was probably a benefactor or patron who assisted Luke with the expenses of publication or distribution of his work (see note on Luke 1:3).

1:3 ***he proved to them in many ways that he was actually alive:*** The Gospels describe the evidence for Christ's resurrection: Jesus' tomb was empty (Luke 24:3-4), his grave clothes were undisturbed (John 20:3-9), and many people saw him (see Matt 28:1-20; Mark 16:1-8; Luke 24:1-53; John 20:11–21:23; 1 Cor 15:3-8). Jesus ***appeared to the apostles*** in part to overcome their doubt (Matt 28:17; Luke 24:17-24, 38, 41; John 20:27; see Mark 16:14) • The ***Kingdom of God*** was the central theme of Jesus' teaching (see 1:6-8; Matt 4:17; Mark 1:14-15; Luke 4:43).

1:4 ***until the Father sends you the gift he promised:*** See 2:1-13; cp. John 14:15-17.

1:5 ***baptized:*** See "Baptism" at 2:38, 41, p. 1828. • ***with water:*** Or *in water.* • ***with the Holy Spirit:*** Or *in the Holy Spirit.* Cp. 19:1-7.

1:6-11 Jesus' ascent into heaven (see also Luke 24:50-53) took place on the Mount of Olives (1:12; Luke 24:50). It was Jesus' last physical appearance—he was taken into heaven, where he will remain "until the time for the final restoration of all things" (3:21).

1:8 This key verse outlines the geographical extension of the Good News from its Jewish starting point in ***Jerusalem*** and ***Judea*** (1:6–8:1), out to ***Samaria*** (8:4-25), Antioch in Syria (11:19-30), and eventually throughout the Mediterranean world to Rome (13:1–28:31). Christ later gave a similar call to be his ***witnesses . . . to the ends of the earth*** to Saul of Tarsus (9:15), who had persecuted the Jewish Christians and then became the primary instrument for taking the Good News to the Gentiles. • The ***Holy Spirit*** was the source of ***power*** for all this evangelistic and missionary effort (see "The Holy Spirit's Presence" at 5:32, p. 1834).

1:10 Christ's *rising into heaven* indicates his elevation to a place of ultimate authority (see Eph 1:19-23; Phil 2:9-11).

1:11 Jesus promised to ***return from heaven in the same way*** (see Matt 24:30; Mark 13:26; John 14:3). Jesus has gone to heaven to prepare the place for his followers (John 12:26; 14:1-4; 2 Cor 5:4; Phil 3:21; Heb 6:20).

1:12 The witnesses of the ascension ***returned to Jerusalem*** with joy, worship, exhilaration, and praise to God (Luke 24:52), and with their doubts assuaged (see note on 1:3). • ***a distance of half a mile:*** Literally *a Sabbath day's journey.*

1:13-26 While the apostles waited for the promised gift of the Holy Spirit (1:4-5), the whole company of 120 disciples in Jerusalem engaged in earnest prayer (1:13-14), and then appointed an apostle to replace Judas Iscariot (1:15-26).

1:13 All eleven of the remaining apostles ***were present*** (cp. Matt 10:2-4; Mark 3:16-19; Luke 6:13-16). Judas Iscariot is omitted from this list on account of his betrayal and death (1:18-19).

1:14 The first disciples were ***united*** in worship, fellowship, and ***prayer*** (see also 2:42, 46-47; 4:24-31; 5:12; 12:5; 13:1-3). The faithful women who had been witnesses of Jesus' crucifixion and resurrection were present (Luke 23:49, 54-56; 24:1-10, 22). • ***The brothers of Jesus*** had not believed in him during his ministry (John 7:3-5; cp. Matt 12:46-49), but became his disciples after his resurrection (see "James, the Brother of Jesus" at 15:13-21, p. 1858).

1:16 Ps 41:9
1:17 John 6:70-71; Acts 1:24-25
1:18 Matt 27:3-8
1:20 *Ps 69:25; 109:8
1:21-22 Mark 1:9-11
1:22 [a]*anastasis* (0386) ‣Acts 2:31
1:24 Acts 6:6
1:25 [b]*apostolē* (0651) ‣Acts 2:42
1:26 Prov 16:33
2:1 Lev 23:15-21; Deut 16:9-11; Acts 1:14; 20:16
2:2 Acts 4:31
2:4 Mark 16:17; Acts 4:31; 10:44-46; 19:6; 1 Cor 12:10; 13:1

with Mary the mother of Jesus, several other
women, and the brothers of Jesus.
15During this time, when about 120 believers were together in one place, Peter
stood up and addressed them. 16"Brothers,"
he said, "the Scriptures had to be fulfilled
concerning Judas, who guided those who arrested Jesus. This was predicted long ago by
the Holy Spirit, speaking through King David. 17Judas was one of us and shared in the
ministry with us."
18(Judas had bought a field with the
money he received for his treachery. Falling
headfirst there, his body split open, spilling out all his intestines. 19The news of his
death spread to all the people of Jerusalem,
and they gave the place the Aramaic name
Akeldama, which means "Field of Blood.")
20Peter continued, "This was written in
the book of Psalms, where it says, 'Let his
home become desolate, with no one living
in it.' It also says, 'Let someone else take his
position.'
21"So now we must choose a replacement
for Judas from among the men who were
with us the entire time we were traveling
with the Lord Jesus—22from the time he
was baptized by John until the day he was
taken from us. Whoever is chosen will join
us as a witness of Jesus' [a]resurrection."
23So they nominated two men: Joseph
called Barsabbas (also known as Justus) and
Matthias. 24Then they all prayed, "O Lord,
you know every heart. Show us which of
these men you have chosen 25as an [b]apostle
to replace Judas in this ministry, for he has
deserted us and gone where he belongs."
26Then they cast lots, and Matthias was selected to become an apostle with the other
eleven.

The Holy Spirit Comes

2 On the day of Pentecost all the believers were meeting together in one place.
2Suddenly, there was a sound from heaven
like the roaring of a mighty windstorm, and
it filled the house where they were sitting.
3Then, what looked like flames or tongues
of fire appeared and settled on each of
them. 4And everyone present was filled

Jesus' Ascension (1:6-11)

Acts 3:20; 7:54-56
Matt 24:30
Mark 13:26
Luke 24:45-53
John 6:62; 13:1-3; 14:1-4, 27-28; 16:10, 16, 28; 20:17
2 Cor 5:4
Eph 1:19-23; 4:8-10
Phil 2:9-11
Heb 6:19-20

Jesus' ascension into heaven was a final commissioning service for the apostles (1:6-11; Luke 24:45-53). The ascension marks the beginning of the powerful ministry of the Holy Spirit through the church (Luke 24:49).

Christ's ascent to heaven indicates his elevation to ultimate power and authority (Eph 1:19-23; Phil 2:9-11). That Jesus was going to the Father is noted in other places (John 3:13; 6:62; 13:1-3; 14:3, 28; 16:10, 16, 28; 20:17; Eph 4:8-10). It occurred at the last of Jesus' physical appearances; after this he would remain in heaven until the "times of refreshment" (3:20).

The ascension reminds believers of Jesus' promised return (1:11; see Matt 24:30; Mark 13:26; John 13:3). The witnesses of the ascension went back to Jerusalem with joy and exhilaration, in praise and worship of Christ (Luke 24:52). They were convinced that their Lord would return again, physically and personally (1 Thes 4:16; 2 Thes 1:7-10; 2 Pet 3:10).

Jesus' ascension anticipates the believer's own glorious entrance into the presence of God, where Jesus has gone to prepare the way (John 12:26; 2 Cor 5:4; Phil 3:21; Heb 6:20).

1:15 ***believers:*** Literally *brothers.*

1:16-17 ***Scripture had to be fulfilled:*** See 1:20.

1:18-19 Matthew's account (Matt 27:3-10) is somewhat different; the two can be harmonized by considering the priests' purchase of the ***"Field of Blood"*** as acting in Judas's name. In addition, Judas may have committed suicide by hanging, but subsequently he fell ***headfirst*** and his ***body split open,*** perhaps when the rope broke.

1:20-21 ***'Let someone else take his position':*** Ps 69:25; 109:8. It was imperative that a ***replacement*** be found ***for Judas*** so that his position as the twelfth apostle would not remain empty. The new people of God, like Israel, were to have twelve designated and appointed leaders (see Matt 19:28; Luke 22:29-30).

1:21-22 To qualify for nomination as an apostle, a man had to have been ***with*** the other apostles ***the entire time*** of Jesus' public ministry, ***from the time he was baptized by John until*** his ascension.

1:23-26 With prayer (1:14, 24) and humble dependence on God to reveal his will, the apostles ***cast lots,*** using an established method of finding God's will (see Lev 16:8; Num 27:21; Deut 33:8; Josh 14:2; 18:3-10; Prov 16:33). ***Matthias was selected*** to replace Judas. After Pentecost, the Holy Spirit guided Jesus' followers through dreams, visions, and prophecies instead of through lots (cp. 2:17-18; 13:2; 16:7-10). • ***you know every heart:*** See also 1 Sam 16:6-7; 1 Kgs 8:39; 1 Chr 28:9; 2 Chr 6:30; Ps 7:9; 44:21; Jer 11:20; John 2:24-25; Rev 2:23.

2:1-4 Jews observed three great annual pilgrimage festivals, when many would go to the Temple in Jerusalem—Unleavened Bread (which includes Passover), ***Pentecost,*** and Shelters (see "Israel's Festivals," p. 235). The Festival of ***Pentecost*** came 50 days after Passover (when Jesus was crucified; see "The Cross and Passover" at John 19:17-36, p. 1812). On that decisive day, when the disciples were united and expectant as they gathered for prayer, the ***Holy Spirit*** came and ***filled*** the gathered believers.

with the Holy Spirit and began speaking
in other [c]languages, as the Holy Spirit gave
them this ability.
5At that time there were devout Jews
from every nation living in Jerusalem.
6When they heard the loud noise, everyone
came running, and they were bewildered to
hear their own languages being spoken by
the believers.
7They were completely amazed. "How
can this be?" they exclaimed. "These people are all from Galilee, 8and yet we hear
them speaking in our own native languages!
9Here we are—Parthians, Medes, Elamites,
people from Mesopotamia, Judea, Cappadocia, Pontus, the province of Asia, 10Phrygia,
Pamphylia, Egypt, and the areas of Libya
around Cyrene, visitors from Rome 11(both
Jews and converts to Judaism), Cretans,
and Arabs. And we all hear these people
speaking in our own [d]languages about the
wonderful things God has done!" 12They
stood there amazed and perplexed. "What
can this mean?" they asked each other.
13But others in the crowd ridiculed them,
saying, "They're just drunk, that's all!"

Peter Preaches to the Crowd

14Then Peter stepped forward with the
eleven other apostles and shouted to the
crowd, "Listen carefully, all of you, fellow
Jews and residents of Jerusalem! Make no
mistake about this. 15These people are not
drunk, as some of you are assuming. Nine
o'clock in the morning is much too early for
that. 16No, what you see was predicted long
ago by the prophet Joel:

17 'In the last days,' God says,
'I will pour out my Spirit upon all
people.
Your sons and daughters will prophesy.
Your young men will see visions,
and your old men will dream
dreams.
18 In those days I will pour out my Spirit
even on my servants—men and
women alike—
and they will prophesy.
19 And I will cause wonders in the heavens
above
and signs on the earth below—
blood and fire and clouds of smoke.
20 The sun will become dark,
and the moon will turn blood red
before that great and glorious day of
the LORD arrives.
21 But everyone who calls on the name of
the LORD
will be [e]saved.'

[c]*glōssa* (1100) ‣Acts 2:11

2:7 Acts 1:11

2:9 Acts 16:6; 19:10; 1 Pet 1:1

2:10 Matt 27:32; Acts 13:13; 16:6

2:11 [d]*glōssa* (1100) ‣Acts 10:46

2:13 1 Cor 14:23; Eph 5:18

2:17-21 *Joel 2:28-32

2:18 Num 11:29; 1 Cor 12:10

2:20 Matt 24:29

2:21 *Joel 2:32; Rom 10:13; [e]*sōzō* (4982) ‣Acts 2:47

2:22 John 3:2

2:4 ***everyone present was filled with the Holy Spirit:*** This event marks the coming of the Holy Spirit to fill Jesus' disciples, as he had promised, so that they could be powerful witnesses (1:4-5, 8). The Spirit's wisdom, energy, and power were the driving force behind the church's work and witness (e.g., 2:14-41, 43; 4:31; 9:17, 20; 13:9-12; see also Eph 5:18). • ***began speaking in other languages*** (or *in other tongues*): The Holy Spirit gave extraordinary communication that made it possible for people from other countries to hear in their own languages about what God had done (2:6-11). This passage is one of several references to speaking in "other languages" or "tongues" (see also 10:44-48; 19:6; 1 Cor 14:2-28; 14:39). Here, this supernatural gift reveals the energizing presence of God's Spirit and inaugurates the proclamation of the Good News to people of every nation.

2:5-11 Because Pentecost was a pilgrimage festival (see note on 2:1-4), Jews ***from every nation*** were present ***in Jerusalem*** at that time and were thus able to hear the Good News being proclaimed in ***their own languages.*** The Good News is for all people (2:38-39).

2:9-11 ***Parthians*** came from the region stretching from the Tigris River eastward to India. ***Medes*** (now called Kurds) were from Media, east of Mesopotamia and north of the Persian Gulf. ***Elamites*** were from Elam (now in Iran), north of the Persian Gulf and just east of the Tigris River. ***Mesopotamia*** lay between the Tigris and Euphrates rivers. ***Judea*** was well known as the Jewish homeland. ***Cappadocia, Pontus,*** and ***Asia*** were Roman provinces in Asia Minor (now in Turkey; see 1 Pet 1:1); Paul later taught and preached in some of these areas (see 16:6; 19:10, 26). ***Phrygia*** and ***Pamphylia*** were districts of Asia Minor later visited by Paul (13:13; 18:23). ***Egypt*** had a large Jewish population, particularly in the city of Alexandria (see 18:24). North Africa was also represented by ***Libya*** and ***Cyrene.*** ***Rome*** was the imperial capital and the home of thousands of Jews. The ***Cretans*** came from the island of Crete, located south-southeast of Greece, and the ***Arabs*** from the area south and east of Jerusalem. • The inclusion of all of these nations suggests how the Good News was going to go out to the ends of the earth (1:8).

2:11 ***converts to Judaism:*** See note on 13:43.

2:14-36 This is the first of about thirty speeches in Acts and one of the most important, standing as it does at the very inception of the church. It is a typical example of the preaching of the apostles, who proclaimed (1) that the OT promises had been fulfilled in the life, death, and resurrection of Jesus Christ, who is the promised Messiah; (2) that the apostles themselves were eyewitnesses of Jesus' entire public ministry and were his chosen representatives; (3) that people are called to repent of their sins and have faith in God through Christ; and (4) that salvation and the presence of the Holy Spirit are promised to those who respond affirmatively to this message of Good News. This basic message is echoed in the sermons of chs 3, 4, 5, 8, 10, and 13. The same themes characterized Paul's preaching (see 1 Cor 15:3-9). This message was repeatedly preached to both Jews and Gentiles throughout the Mediterranean world; all people are summoned to repent of their sins and turn to God through faith in Jesus Christ.

2:17-21 This passage quotes Joel 2:28-32. The prophet Joel predicted a wider exercise of the gifts of prophecy, including ***visions*** and ***dreams*** by both ***young*** and ***old***, both ***men and women*** in ***the last days*** (Joel 2:28-29). In Acts, on the day of Pentecost, Peter declared that Joel's prophecy was being fulfilled, signaling that "the last days" had arrived. See also "The Gift of Prophecy" at 21:9-11, p. 1873.

2:23
1 Pet 1:20
[f]prognōsis (4268)
‣Acts 2:25
2:24
Acts 3:15
2:25-28
*Ps 16:8-11
Acts 13:30-35
2:25
[g]prooraō (4308)
‣Acts 2:31
2:27
[h]hadēs (0086)
‣Acts 2:31
2:29
1 Kgs 2:10
Acts 13:36
2:30
2 Sam 7:12-14
*Ps 89:4; 132:11
2:31
*Ps 16:10
[i]prooraō (4308)
‣Rom 8:29
[j]christos (5547)
‣Acts 5:42
[k]anastasis (0386)
‣Acts 17:32
[a]hadēs (0086)
‣Jas 3:6
2:33
John 14:26
Acts 1:4, 8
Eph 4:8
Phil 2:9
Heb 1:3
2:34-35
*Ps 110:1
2:38
Mark 16:16
Acts 3:19; 8:12; 22:16
[b]baptizō (0907)
‣Acts 9:18
2:39
Isa 44:3; 57:19
Eph 2:13

22"People of Israel, listen! God publicly
endorsed Jesus the Nazarene by doing powerful miracles, wonders, and signs through
him, as you well know. 23But God knew what
would happen, and his [f]prearranged plan
was carried out when Jesus was betrayed.
With the help of lawless Gentiles, you nailed
him to a cross and killed him. 24But God released him from the horrors of death and
raised him back to life, for death could not
keep him in its grip. 25King David said this
about him:

'I [g]see that the LORD is always with me.
I will not be shaken, for he is right
beside me.
26 No wonder my heart is glad,
and my tongue shouts his praises!
My body rests in hope.
27 For you will not leave my soul among the
dead
or allow your Holy One to rot in the
[h]grave.
28 You have shown me the way of life,
and you will fill me with the joy of
your presence.'

29"Dear brothers, think about this! You
can be sure that the patriarch David wasn't
referring to himself, for he died and was
buried, and his tomb is still here among
us. 30But he was a prophet, and he knew
God had promised with an oath that one
of David's own descendants would sit on
his throne. 31David was [i]looking into the
future and speaking of the [j]Messiah's [k]resur-
rection. He was saying that God would not
leave him among the dead or allow his body
to rot in the [a]grave.

32"God raised Jesus from the dead, and we
are all witnesses of this. 33Now he is exalted
to the place of highest honor in heaven, at
God's right hand. And the Father, as he had
promised, gave him the Holy Spirit to pour
out upon us, just as you see and hear today.
34For David himself never ascended into
heaven, yet he said,

'The LORD said to my Lord,
"Sit in the place of honor at my right
hand
35 until I humble your enemies,
making them a footstool under your
feet." '

36"So let everyone in Israel know for certain that God has made this Jesus, whom you
crucified, to be both Lord and Messiah!"

37Peter's words pierced their hearts, and
they said to him and to the other apostles,
"Brothers, what should we do?"

38Peter replied, "Each of you must repent of your sins and turn to God, and be
[b]baptized in the name of Jesus Christ for
the forgiveness of your sins. Then you will
receive the gift of the Holy Spirit. 39This
promise is to you, and to your children,
and even to the Gentiles—all who have

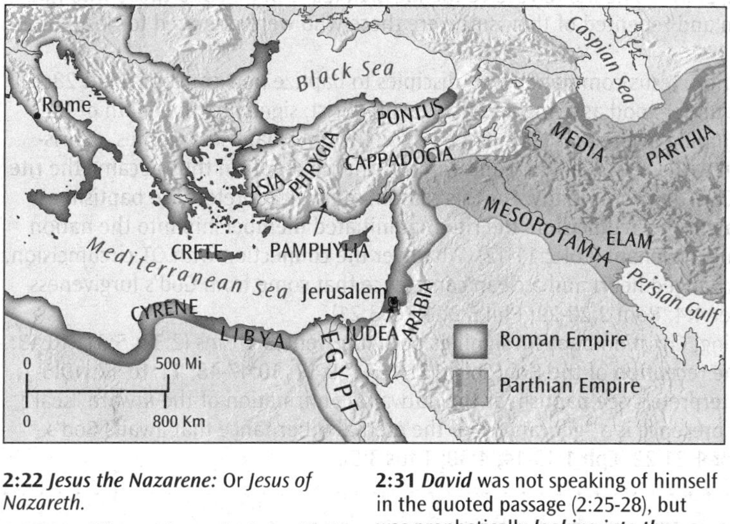

◂ **Nations at Pentecost (2:9-11).** When the Holy Spirit filled the believers, people from all over the ROMAN and PARTHIAN empires were in JERUSALEM for the celebration of Pentecost. Some of those who witnessed the believers "speaking in other languages" (2:3) were converted, and many of them eventually returned to their homelands, taking with them the message of Christ.

2:22 ***Jesus the Nazarene:*** Or *Jesus of Nazareth.*

2:23-28 While cruel men had crucified Jesus, this action had not defeated God's ***prearranged plan*** for salvation. In fact, God ***raised him back to life,*** which David had foretold (2:25-28, which quotes Ps 16:8-11, Greek version).

2:27 ***among the dead:*** Greek *in Hades;* also in 2:31. See note on Matt 11:23.

2:31 ***David*** was not speaking of himself in the quoted passage (2:25-28), but was prophetically ***looking into the future and speaking of the Messiah's resurrection.***

2:32-36 ***God raised Jesus from the dead, and we are all witnesses of this:*** The witness theme is often repeated in Acts (e.g., 3:15; 4:33; 5:32; 10:39-43). The capstone of this message is that God the Father, ***as he had promised,*** was now pouring out his ***Holy Spirit*** on the church through the risen Jesus. All Israel was called upon to recognize that God had acted decisively to make the crucified Jesus ***both Lord and Messiah!***

2:34-35 This passage quotes Ps 110:1, which Jesus fulfilled when he ***ascended into heaven*** (1:9).

2:37-38 ***Brothers, what should we do?*** Peter answered by strongly exhorting his listeners to ***repent of your sins and turn to God, and be baptized.*** See "Baptism" at 2:38, 41, p. 1828.

2:39 ***and even to the Gentiles:*** Or *and to people far in the future;* literally *and to those far away.*

been called by the Lord our God.” 40Then
Peter continued preaching for a long time,
strongly urging all his listeners, “Save yourselves from this crooked generation!”
41Those who believed what Peter said
were baptized and added to the church that
day—about 3,000 in all.

The Believers Form a Community

42All the believers devoted themselves to
the [c]apostles’ teaching, and to [d]fellowship,
and to sharing in meals (including the
Lord’s Supper), and to prayer.
43A deep sense of awe came over them
all, and the apostles performed many miraculous signs and wonders. 44And all the
believers met together in one place and
shared everything they had. 45They sold
their property and possessions and shared
the money with those in need. 46They
worshiped together at the Temple each day,
met in homes for the Lord’s Supper, and
shared their meals with great joy and generosity—47all the while praising God and
enjoying the goodwill of all the people. And
each day the Lord added to their fellowship
those who were being [e]saved.

The First Clash with Judaism (3:1–4:31)

Peter Heals a Crippled Beggar

3 Peter and John went to the Temple one
afternoon to take part in the three
o’clock prayer service. 2As they approached
the Temple, a man lame from birth was being carried in. Each day he was put beside
the Temple gate, the one called the Beautiful Gate, so he could beg from the people
going into the Temple. 3When he saw Peter
and John about to enter, he asked them for
some money.

2:40 Deut 32:5; Phil 2:15
2:42 Acts 20:7; [c]*apostolos* (0652) ‣ Acts 15:2; [d]*koinōnia* (2842) ‣ 1 Cor 1:9
2:44-45 Acts 4:32-37
2:47 Acts 4:4; 6:7; Rom 14:18; [e]*sōzō* (4982) ‣ Acts 4:12
3:1 Acts 10:3, 9, 30
3:2 Acts 14:8

Baptism (2:38, 41)

Acts 1:5, 22; 8:12-13, 16-17, 36-38; 9:18; 10:37, 47-48; 11:16; 13:24; 16:15, 33; 18:8, 25; 19:1-7; 22:16
Matt 3:6-16; 21:25; 28:19
Mark 1:4-9; 10:38-39; 11:30; 16:16
Luke 3:3-22; 7:29-30; 12:50; 20:4
John 1:25-36; 3:22-23, 26; 4:1-2; 10:40
Rom 6:3-4
1 Cor 1:13-17; 10:2; 12:13; 15:29
Gal 3:27
Eph 4:5
Col 2:12
Heb 6:2
1 Pet 3:21
1 Jn 5:6

Baptism was an important element of the Christian faith from the very beginning (2:38). Baptism is a ritual cleansing that signifies the removal of impurity and sin; it represents repentance from sin and turning to God for forgiveness and purification.

The words “baptism” and “baptize” were already used in Judaism to refer to a religious rite for cleansing. The law of Moses established the use of water to cleanse people from ceremonial defilement (Num 19:14-19). Later, Gentile converts to Judaism from pagan religions were admitted to Judaism only after fulfilling certain obligations, which included the study of the Torah, circumcision, and a ritual bath to wash away the impurities of the Gentile background.

John had thus preached “that people should be baptized to show that they had repented of their sins and turned to God to be forgiven” (Luke 3:3). John’s baptism was an aspect of his role in preparing people’s hearts to receive the Messiah (Luke 3:4-6), and those who had received his baptism and repented of their sins were those who were prepared for Jesus’ message (Luke 7:29-30).

After his resurrection, Jesus commanded his disciples to baptize new converts (Matt 28:19). Christian baptism is understood as dying and rising with Christ, signifying the death of the old life and the beginning of the new (Rom 6:1-4; Col 2:12). Thus baptism signifies a Christian’s spiritual union with Christ (Gal 3:27) and with his church. Baptism thus became the rite of initiation in the Christian community. For this reason, many interpreters see baptism as the Christian equivalent of circumcision, the rite that initiated membership into the nation of Israel under the old covenant (Col 2:11-12). Whatever the connection with OT circumcision, baptism signifies a changed heart and a clean conscience that come from God’s forgiveness (Deut 10:16; 30:6; Jer 4:4; Rom 2:28-29; Phil 3:3; 1 Pet 3:21).

As a ritual cleansing, Christian baptism signifies both forgiveness of sins (2:38; 5:31; 10:43; 13:38; 26:18) and the reception of the Holy Spirit (2:38, 41; 9:17; 10:47-48; 11:16-17; 19:5-7; Luke 3:16). Many interpreters see baptism as the outward confirmation of the inward “seal” of the Spirit, whose presence is a “guarantee” of the eternal inheritance that awaits God’s faithful people (2 Cor 1:21-22; Eph 1:13-14; 4:30; Titus 3:5).

2:42-47 Luke makes a clear connection between personal faith and membership in the Christian community. Life in this new community involved devotion to apostolic *teaching* of God’s Word, fellowship, *sharing*, joy, and praise, and it resulted in the Lord’s continuing to add to their number *those who were being saved.*

2:42 ***fellowship:*** Greek *koinōnia*, a close mutual relationship and participation in life together. • ***sharing in meals (including the Lord’s Supper):*** Literally *the breaking of bread;* also in 2:46. • At this stage, ***prayer*** probably included participation in the formal prayers of the Temple (see 3:1).

2:46 ***and generosity:*** Or *and sincere hearts.*

3:1-11 Jesus’ promise that his disciples would do even greater works than he had done (John 14:12; see Mark 16:20) was fulfilled in the signs, wonders, and mighty works of the apostles (2:43; 5:12; 8:4-8). Here, Peter clearly

3:4 Acts 13:9; 14:9
3:6 Acts 4:10
3:8 John 5:14
3:9 Acts 4:16, 21
3:10 John 9:8
3:11 John 10:23; Acts 5:12
3:13 *Exod 3:6, 15; Matt 22:32; Acts 5:30; 7:32
3:15 Acts 2:24; 5:30

4Peter and John looked at him intently, and Peter said, "Look at us!" 5The lame man looked at them eagerly, expecting some money. 6But Peter said, "I don't have any silver or gold for you. But I'll give you what I have. In the name of Jesus Christ the Nazarene, get up and walk!"

7Then Peter took the lame man by the right hand and helped him up. And as he did, the man's feet and ankles were instantly healed and strengthened. 8He jumped up, stood on his feet, and began to walk! Then, walking, leaping, and praising God, he went into the Temple with them.

9All the people saw him walking and heard him praising God. 10When they realized he was the lame beggar they had seen so often at the Beautiful Gate, they were absolutely astounded! 11They all rushed out in amazement to Solomon's Colonnade, where the man was holding tightly to Peter and John.

Peter Preaches in the Temple

12Peter saw his opportunity and addressed the crowd. "People of Israel," he said, "what is so surprising about this? And why stare at us as though we had made this man walk by our own power or godliness? 13For it is the God of Abraham, Isaac, and Jacob—the God of all our ancestors—who has brought glory to his servant Jesus by doing this. This is the same Jesus whom you handed over and rejected before Pilate, despite Pilate's decision to release him. 14You rejected this holy, righteous one and instead demanded the release of a murderer. 15You killed the author of life, but God raised him from the dead. And we are witnesses of this fact!

Church Growth (2:41-47)

Acts 1:8, 13-15; 2:41; 4:4, 23-37; 5:14, 27-33, 40-42; 6:1; 7:59; 8:4-40; 9:15, 31, 35, 42; 10:34, 36; 11:19-26; 14:22; 15:32, 41; 16:5, 19-25; 18:23; 21:20
1 Cor 4:16, 20
Phil 4:9
1 Thes 1:5-8
2 Thes 3:9
2 Tim 1:8; 2:1-9; 3:12

The book of Acts outlines the church's growth after Pentecost. In the early days there was *numerical* growth. Only 120 believers were present at the first prayer meeting seeking divine direction (1:13-15). After the mighty outpouring of the Holy Spirit on Pentecost, the number of Christians increased to about 3,000 (2:41). Many more believed the preaching of Peter and John, and the number grew to about 5,000 (4:4) and continued to rise (5:14; 6:1; 9:31; 21:20).

There is also ample evidence of *geographical* growth (1:8; 9:15). The church was not confined to Jerusalem, for the message spread to Lydda, Sharon, and Joppa on the Mediterranean coast (9:35, 42). The message of salvation in Christ also moved out from its Jewish base into Samaria (8:6, 12), then into Phoenicia, Cyprus, and Antioch (11:19-26). As Peter declared to Cornelius's household, "God shows no favoritism" (10:34). The message of Good News offers peace with God through Jesus Christ to all people (10:36).

With the increase in numbers and the geographical spread of the faith, the Christian communities also experienced growth in *spiritual* depth and vitality. Acts 2:42-47 vividly depicts this development in the inner life of the church, featuring earnest, united prayer in crises, generous sharing of possessions, courage during persecution, and boldness in witness (4:23-31, 32-37; 5:27-33, 40-42; 16:19-25). Philip's preaching and the manner of Stephen's death manifested a high standard of spiritual life and maturity (7:59; 8:4-40; 16:19-25). Church leaders encouraged and strengthened believers, made them more steadfast in their faith, enabled them to face persecution (14:22; 15:32, 41; 18:23; see 2 Tim 1:8; 2:1-9; 3:12), and lived by the standards they set for others (1 Cor 4:16, 20; Phil 4:9; 1 Thes 1:5-8; 2 Thes 3:9; 2 Tim 2:7). The church's sensitive handling of the Gentiles' inclusion also resulted in significant spiritual growth. "So the churches were strengthened in their faith and grew larger every day" (16:5).

exercised the power to heal ***in the name of Jesus Christ the Nazarene*** (3:6, 16). The cure was instant and undeniable (3:8), resulting in the man's ***praising God*** (3:8-9; cp. 2:47; 16:25; Luke 2:20; 17:15-18; 18:43; 19:37; 24:53). This is the first of many demonstrations of divine power given to disciples in Acts (4:24-31; 5:12; 6:8; 8:6; 9:33-42; 28:8).

3:6 ***The name of Jesus*** represents his identity and power to heal (see Mark 9:38-39). • ***Jesus Christ the Nazarene:*** Or *Jesus Christ of Nazareth.* • Some manuscripts do not include ***get up and.***

3:10-11 The ***Beautiful Gate*** was probably the Nicanor Gate, built of Corinthian bronze and located on the east side of the Temple (see Josephus, *War* 5.5.3). It was adorned in a costly manner, with richer and thicker plates of silver and gold upon its panels than other gates. • ***Solomon's Colonnade*** was a portico on the east side of the Temple (see Josephus, *War* 5.5.1-3; *Antiquities* 20.9.7).

3:12-26 The evangelistic speeches in the book of Acts focus on ***Jesus***, the crucified and risen Lord. They call people to repentance and faith in Jesus as the promised ***Messiah*** and the divinely appointed Judge (2:38; 3:19; 11:18; 17:30; 26:20). They also offer the same Good News for the people of Israel and the Gentile world—"there is peace with God through Jesus Christ, who is Lord of all" (10:36).

3:15 It was unfathomable to the Jewish mind that ***the author of life***, God himself, could be ***killed***. They didn't recognize Jesus as Messiah (cp. 13:27; Luke 23:34), and they did not realize that the Messiah would be divine (see John 1:1-18; cp. Dan 7:13-14).

16“Through faith in the name of Jesus,
this man was healed—and you know how
crippled he was before. Faith in Jesus’ name
has healed him before your very eyes.
17“Friends, I realize that what you and your
leaders did to Jesus was done in ignorance.
18But God was fulfilling what all the prophets had foretold about the Messiah—that he
must suffer these things. 19Now repent of
your sins and turn to God, so that your sins
may be wiped away. 20Then times of refreshment will come from the presence of the
Lord, and he will again send you Jesus, your
appointed Messiah. 21For he must remain
in heaven until the time for the final restoration of all things, as God promised long
ago through his holy prophets. 22Moses said,
‘The LORD your God will raise up for you a
Prophet like me from among your own people. Listen carefully to everything he tells
you.’ 23Then Moses said, ‘Anyone who will
not listen to that Prophet will be completely
cut off from God’s people.’
24“Starting with Samuel, every prophet
spoke about what is happening today. 25You
are the children of those prophets, and you
are included in the covenant God promised
to your ancestors. For God said to Abraham,
‘Through your descendants all the families on earth will be blessed.’ 26When God
raised up his servant, Jesus, he sent him
first to you people of Israel, to bless you by
turning each of you back from your sinful
ways.”

Peter and John before the Council

4 While Peter and John were speaking
to the people, they were confronted by
the priests, the captain of the Temple guard,
and some of the Sadducees. 2These leaders
were very disturbed that Peter and John
were teaching the people that through Jesus
there is a resurrection of the dead. 3They
arrested them and, since it was already evening, put them in jail until morning. 4But
many of the people who heard their message believed it, so the number of believers
now totaled about 5,000 men, not counting
women and children.
5The next day the council of all the rulers
and elders and teachers of religious law met
in Jerusalem. 6Annas the high priest was
there, along with Caiaphas, John, Alexander,
and other relatives of the high priest. 7They
brought in the two disciples and demanded,
“By what power, or in whose name, have you
done this?”
8Then Peter, filled with the Holy Spirit,
said to them, “Rulers and elders of our people, 9are we being questioned today because
we’ve done a good deed for a crippled man?
Do you want to know how he was healed?
10Let me clearly state to all of you and to all
the people of Israel that he was healed by
the powerful name of Jesus Christ the Nazarene, the man you crucified but whom God
raised from the dead. 11For Jesus is the one
referred to in the Scriptures, where it says,

‘The stone that you builders rejected
has now become the cornerstone.’

12There is salvation in no one else! God
has given no other name under heaven by
which we must be [f]saved.”
13The members of the council were
amazed when they saw the boldness of Peter and John, for they could see that they
were ordinary men with no special training

3:17 Luke 23:34; Acts 13:27; 1 Tim 1:13
3:18 Ps 22; 41:9; 69:4, 21; Isa 50:6; 53:4-11; Zech 12:10; 13:7; Luke 24:27, 44, 46
3:19 Acts 2:38; 26:20
3:21 Luke 1:70
3:22 *Deut 18:15, 18; John 1:20-21; 7:40-41, 52
3:23 Lev 23:29; Deut 18:19
3:25 *Gen 22:18; 26:4; Rom 9:4-8
3:26 Mark 7:27; Acts 13:46; Rom 1:16
4:1 Luke 22:4
4:3 Acts 5:18
4:4 Acts 4:21
4:6 Matt 26:3; Luke 3:2
4:7 Matt 21:23
4:10 Acts 2:24; 3:6
4:11 *Ps 118:22; Isa 28:16; Matt 21:42; 1 Pet 2:4, 7
4:12 Matt 1:21; Acts 10:43; 1 Tim 2:5; [f]*sōzō* (4982) ‣Rom 1:16
4:13 Matt 11:25

3:17 *Friends:* Literally *Brothers,* which was a common way to address one another (13:15, 26, 38; Gen 27:29; Lev 10:6; 25:46; Num 20:3; Deut 1:28; 24:7; Josh 22:3-4; 2 Sam 2:26; Ezek 11:15). • *in ignorance:* Cp. 17:30; 1 Tim 1:12-14. The Christian message challenges this ignorance and calls all people to respond in faith and repentance (2:38).

3:19 The Good News of forgiveness is more fully explained elsewhere (see 5:30-32; 10:36-43; 13:26-38; Luke 24:25-27, 45-47).

3:20-21 The message of Good News offers *refreshment* (see Matt 11:28-29). The second coming of Christ will be one of those *times of refreshment* from God, when he will *again send . . . Jesus* to his people.

3:22 Jesus fulfills the ancient promise of *a Prophet* like *Moses* (see Deut 18:15, 18; cp. John 6:14; 7:40).

3:23 Refusing to heed Jesus, God’s final *Prophet,* would have disastrous consequences (John 3:16, 17, 36). • This verse quotes Deut 18:19; Lev 23:29.

3:25 ***your descendants:*** Literally *your seed;* see Gen 12:3; 22:18. • ***all the families on earth will be blessed:*** God’s blessings on the covenant people were not intended to be selfishly hoarded, but were to be shared with the world.

4:1-22 Persecution was a common experience of God’s people throughout the Bible. God’s servants often faced hostility and opposition (Deut 30:7; 1 Kgs 18:13; Neh 4:1-3; Jer 37–38; Matt 23:34-37; Luke 11:49-51; 1 Thes 2:14-15). Jesus himself was persecuted (Luke 4:29; John 5:16), and he told his disciples to expect the same kind of treatment (Matt 10:23; 24:9; Mark 13:9; Luke 21:12; John 16:2), but he promised that the Holy Spirit would provide strength (1:8; Luke 12:11-12; 21:15). Acts records frequent times of persecution (4:3; 5:17-41; 7:54–8:3; 9:1-2; 11:19; 12:2; 13:50; 14:19; 16:19-24), but Acts also reiterates that the Holy Spirit empowers disciples to bear witness in such circumstances (2:44; 4:8-13; 6:10; 7:55). The boldness of Peter and John before the hostile high council exemplifies facing persecution with courage and power (4:20). See “Persecution,” facing page.

4:1 *Sadducees:* See “The Sadducees” at Matt 16:1-12, p. 1610.

4:4 ***5,000 men, not counting women and children:*** Literally *5,000 adult males;* see note on Matt 14:21.

4:10 ***Jesus Christ the Nazarene:*** Or *Jesus Christ of Nazareth.*

4:11 This verse quotes Ps 118:22.

4:13 ***ordinary men with no special training in the Scriptures:*** That is, they

4:15
Acts 5:34-35

4:16
John 11:47
Acts 3:6-10
[g]*sēmeion* (4592)
‣Acts 8:6

4:17-19
Acts 5:28-29

4:20
1 Jn 1:1, 3

4:24
*Exod 20:11
*Ps 146:6

4:25-26
*Ps 2:1-2

in the Scriptures. They also recognized them as men who had been with Jesus. 14But since they could see the man who had been healed standing right there among them, there was nothing the council could say. 15So they ordered Peter and John out of the council chamber and conferred among themselves.

16"What should we do with these men?" they asked each other. "We can't deny that they have performed a miraculous [g]sign, and everybody in Jerusalem knows about it. 17But to keep them from spreading their propaganda any further, we must warn them not to speak to anyone in Jesus' name again." 18So they called the apostles back in and commanded them never again to speak or teach in the name of Jesus.

19But Peter and John replied, "Do you think God wants us to obey you rather than him? 20We cannot stop telling about everything we have seen and heard."

21The council then threatened them further, but they finally let them go because they didn't know how to punish them without starting a riot. For everyone was praising God 22for this miraculous sign—the healing of a man who had been lame for more than forty years.

The Believers Pray for Courage

23As soon as they were freed, Peter and John returned to the other believers and told them what the leading priests and elders had said. 24When they heard the report, all the believers lifted their voices together in prayer to God: "O Sovereign Lord, Creator of heaven and earth, the sea, and everything in them—25you spoke long ago by the Holy Spirit through our ancestor David, your servant, saying,

'Why were the nations so angry?
Why did they waste their time with
futile plans?

Persecution (4:13-31)

Acts 5:17-42; 6:8–8:4; 9:1-31; 12:1-19; 14:1-7; 22:3-29; 23:12-31; 26:9-11
1 Kgs 18:2-15; 19:1-18
Neh 4:1-3
Jer 37–38
Matt 10:16-39; 13:20-21; 23:34-38; 24:9-14
Mark 10:29-31; 13:9-13
Luke 11:47-51; 12:11-12; 21:12-19
John 16:1-4
Gal 1:13
1 Thes 2:14-16
2 Tim 3:11-14
1 Pet 3:13-18

Persecution is a common experience of God's people. God's servants have often faced hostility and opposition (e.g., Deut 30:7; 1 Kgs 18:13; Neh 4:1-3; Jer 37–38; Matt 23:34-37; Luke 11:49-51; 1 Thes 2:14-15). Jesus also dealt with persecution (Luke 4:29; John 5:16). At the end of his earthly life, he endured mocking, beating, and a horrible death by crucifixion, and he told his disciples to expect the same kind of treatment (Matt 10:23; 24:9; Mark 13:9; Luke 21:12; John 16:2). He prepared his followers for such occasions, telling them that the Holy Spirit would give them the needed courage (1:8; Luke 12:11-12; 21:15).

The book of Acts documents the persecution of the earliest Christians, beginning with the hostility of the Jewish high council and the attacks of Saul of Tarsus on the early church prior to his encounter with Jesus near Damascus (8:3; 9:1-13, 21; 22:4; 26:9-11; see 1 Cor 15:9; Gal 1:13; Phil 3:6). Peter, John, Stephen, James, Paul, and Barnabas all suffered persecution (4:17-18; 5:17-18; 7:57-60; 12:1-4; 14:5-6). Jesus, in his parable of the farmer and the seed, noted the withering effects of persecution on those with shallow faith (Matt 13:21-22; Mark 4:5-7). Persecution purifies God's people and gives them the opportunity to conform more closely to the character of Jesus. The apostles' experiences in Acts bear out Paul's general statement: "Everyone who wants to live a godly life in Christ Jesus will suffer persecution" (2 Tim 3:12; see Mark 10:30).

Jesus told his disciples to expect to defend their faith in hostile settings (Matt 10:18-20; Luke 21:12-15), and the apostles and other leaders did so with courage and boldness (e.g., 4:8-12, 31; 5:29-32; 6:8-10; 8:4-40; 9:27). Christians are called to defend their faith courageously and graciously, explaining their convictions to those who ask questions (Col 4:6; 2 Tim 2:24, 25; 1 Pet 3:15).

were not scholars or ordained teachers—they were working men without higher education. The educated members of the Jewish high council were treated as authorities on the Scriptures and matters of religion, so it ***amazed*** them to see uneducated men speaking with such ***boldness*** about such matters.

4:15 ***the council chamber:*** Greek *the Sanhedrin.*

4:16-18 They recognize the miracle but still stubbornly tried to prevent the message. Jesus had encountered similar resistance (Matt 19:8; Mark 10:5; see also Deut 10:16; 30:6; Jer 4:4).

4:19-20 The apostles stated a principle that can guide God's people in dealing with hostile authorities (see also 5:40; cp. 1 Sam 15:22; Jer 7:23; Luke 20:20-26; Rom 13:1-7). Jesus had predicted that his disciples would encounter hostility and persecution (Luke 21:12-19).

4:23-31 The believers ***heard the report*** that their leaders had been threatened and commanded never again to speak about Jesus (4:18). The Christian movement was clearly under attack from the religious authorities, so they united in ***prayer.*** They turned to ***God,*** placing their troubles before him and asking him to make them bold in speaking the message and to divinely confirm its truth with ***signs and wonders.*** God dramatically answered their request.

26 The kings of the earth prepared for
battle;
the rulers gathered together
against the LORD
and against his Messiah.’
27“In fact, this has happened here in this
very city! For Herod Antipas, Pontius Pilate
the governor, the Gentiles, and the people
of Israel were all united against Jesus, your
holy servant, whom you anointed. 28But
everything they did was [h]determined beforehand according to your will. 29And now,
O Lord, hear their threats, and give us, your
servants, great boldness in preaching your
word. 30Stretch out your hand with healing
power; may miraculous signs and wonders
be done through the name of your holy servant Jesus.”
31After this prayer, the meeting place
shook, and they were all filled with the Holy
Spirit. Then they preached the word of God
with boldness.

The Fellowship of the Church (4:32–5:16)
The Believers Share Their Possessions

32All the believers were united in heart and
mind. And they felt that what they owned
was not their own, so they shared everything
they had. 33The apostles [i]testified powerfully to the resurrection of the Lord Jesus,
and God’s great blessing was upon them all.
34There were no needy people among them,
because those who owned land or houses
would sell them 35and bring the money to
the apostles to give to those in need.
36For instance, there was Joseph, the one
the apostles nicknamed Barnabas (which
means “Son of Encouragement”). He was
from the tribe of Levi and came from the
island of Cyprus. 37He sold a field he owned
and brought the money to the apostles.

Ananias and Sapphira Attempt to Deceive

5 But there was a certain man named
Ananias who, with his wife, Sapphira,
sold some property. 2He brought part of
the money to the apostles, claiming it was
the full amount. With his wife’s consent, he
kept the rest.
3Then Peter said, “Ananias, why have you
let [j]Satan fill your heart? You lied to the Holy
Spirit, and you kept some of the money for
yourself. 4The property was yours to sell or
not sell, as you wished. And after selling it,
the money was also yours to give away. How
could you do a thing like this? You weren’t
lying to us but to God!”
5As soon as Ananias heard these words,
he fell to the floor and died. Everyone who
heard about it was terrified. 6Then some
young men got up, wrapped him in a sheet,
and took him out and buried him.
7About three hours later his wife came
in, not knowing what had happened. 8Peter
asked her, “Was this the price you and your
husband received for your land?”
“Yes,” she replied, “that was the price.”
9And Peter said, “How could the two of
you even think of conspiring to test the
Spirit of the Lord like this? The young men
who buried your husband are just outside
the door, and they will carry you out, too.”
10Instantly, she fell to the floor and died.
When the young men came in and saw that
she was dead, they carried her out and buried her beside her husband. 11Great fear
gripped the entire church and everyone
else who heard what had happened.

4:27 Isa 61:1; Acts 3:13
4:28 Acts 2:23; [h]*proorizō* (4309) ‣Rom 8:29
4:29 Eph 6:19
4:30 Acts 5:12
4:31 Acts 2:4; 16:26
4:32 Acts 2:44
4:33-35 Acts 2:45-47
4:33 [i]*marturion* (3142) ‣1 Cor 1:6
4:36 Acts 9:27; 11:19-30; 12:25; 13:2
5:2 Acts 4:34-35, 37
5:3 Deut 23:21; John 13:2; [j]*satanas* (4567) ‣Rom 16:20
5:5 Acts 2:43
5:9 1 Cor 10:9

4:25-26 This passage quotes Ps 2:1-2, which describes the response of the Gentile nations to the Lord’s anointed king. In a similar manner, the Jews and Gentiles in Jerusalem had gathered together against Jesus and now against his followers.

4:26 ***his Messiah:*** Or *his anointed one;* or *his Christ.* The term “anointed one” originally referred to Israel’s anointed king; it came to refer to the Messiah, the coming King of Israel who would establish God’s Kingdom forever (2 Sam 7:14-16; Ps 89:36-37; Isa 9:6-7; 11:1-9; 61:1; Jer 23:5-6; 33:14-16; Luke 1:32-33).

4:28 God’s hand had been directing events all along in order to achieve his purpose. A similar awareness of God’s hand guiding the affairs of his people is found in the OT (cp. Ezra 7:6, 9, 28; 8:18, 31; Neh 2:8, 18; Eccl 9:1; Ezek 8:1; Rom 8:28; 1 Pet 5:6).

4:32-35 The sharing of early believers was remarkable (see also 2:44-45; cp. 6:1). Being ***united in heart and mind,*** they willingly offered anything they possessed to meet the needs of other believers. This sharing was voluntary and without coercion, and it related to pressing needs in the community and was prompted by Christian love and concern for one another.

4:36-37 ***Barnabas*** is held up as an example of generous, unselfish giving in response to the genuine needs in the Christian community (see “Barnabas,” facing page).

5:1-11 Luke is fond of balancing a positive example with a negative example. He has just recorded the remarkable story of Barnabas (4:36-37). Now Luke presents the opposite conduct of ***Ananias*** and ***Sapphira,*** who were tempted by the desire to be held in high regard. Ananias had not been forced to sell his property or to give the proceeds away. The couple’s sin was in their pretense and deception.

5:3-4 In ***lying*** about their ***property*** sale, Ananias was not just lying to others but ***to the Holy Spirit***—that is, ***to God.*** His actions compromised the transparent sincerity, unity, and integrity of the church at its very foundation, and thus he fell under the direct judgment of God (cp. Lev 10:1-5; Josh 7:16-26).

5:11 ***Great fear gripped the entire church and everyone else who heard what had happened:*** The sudden judgment on Ananias and then on Sapphira had a sobering effect on both the Christian community and those who heard about this incident (cp. Heb 10:31). Believers were forcefully reminded that they needed to be pure, and for non-Christians the believers’ integrity

5:12
Mark 16:15-20
John 10:23
Acts 3:10
Heb 2:4

5:13
Acts 2:47

5:14
[k]*pisteuō* (4100)
‣ Acts 18:8

5:17
Acts 4:1, 2

5:18
Acts 4:3

5:19
Acts 12:7-10
[a]*angelos* (0032)
‣ Acts 8:26

5:20
John 6:63, 68

The Apostles Heal Many

12 The apostles were performing many miraculous signs and wonders among the
people. And all the believers were meeting
regularly at the Temple in the area known
as Solomon's Colonnade. 13 But no one else
dared to join them, even though all the people had high regard for them. 14 Yet more and
more people [k]believed and were brought to
the Lord—crowds of both men and women.
15 As a result of the apostles' work, sick people were brought out into the streets on beds
and mats so that Peter's shadow might fall
across some of them as he went by. 16 Crowds
came from the villages around Jerusalem,
bringing their sick and those possessed by
evil spirits, and they were all healed.

The Second Clash with Judaism (5:17-42)

The Apostles Arrested and Rescued

17 The high priest and his officials, who
were Sadducees, were filled with jealousy.
18 They arrested the apostles and put them
in the public jail. 19 But an [a]angel of the Lord
came at night, opened the gates of the jail,
and brought them out. Then he told them,
20 "Go to the Temple and give the people this
message of life!"

BARNABAS (4:36-37)

Acts 9:26-28; 11:19-30; 13:1–15:40
Gal 2:1-14

Barnabas, like Stephen (see 6:5–8:2), is presented in Acts as a model Christian leader. A native of Cyprus, Barnabas was active in the Jerusalem church and demonstrated unselfish generosity in meeting the needs of the poorer members of that community (4:32-37). His given name was Joseph, but he was nicknamed Barnabas ("Son of Encouragement," 4:36), which indicates his character. He was a suitable person to give a fair and open-minded assessment of the new work in Antioch (11:19-22). Barnabas perceived God's blessing there and "encouraged the believers to stay true to the Lord" (11:23). His sterling character was clear in his transparent goodness, abundant faith, and Spirit-filled life and work (11:24). The leaders of the Antioch church chose him as their representative on the first missionary journey (13:1-3), confirming their recognition of his worth.

Barnabas's wisdom is clear in his trip to Tarsus to find Saul (11:25). Barnabas had been impressed by the boldness of Saul's preaching as a new Christian in Damascus and had taken him to the apostles, providing a vital introduction for a man who was under suspicion for his previous unrelenting attacks against believers. Through Barnabas's intervention, Saul obtained needed contact with the original apostles, received their acceptance, and preached fearlessly in Jerusalem until he was forced out of the city (9:26-30). Barnabas's trip was successful, and for a full year the two worked together in the Antioch church, drawing large crowds (11:26).

Barnabas was an impressive figure (note his reception in Lystra as Zeus, 14:8-18) and "a good man, full of the Holy Spirit and strong in faith" (11:24). He was John Mark's cousin and mentor and played a major role in giving John Mark a second chance to make good as a Christian leader (15:36-40).

Barnabas knew peer pressure, and he gave in to it on one occasion although he knew better (Gal 2:11-16). Paul's reminder to the Romans is helpful here: "Don't copy the behavior and customs of this world, but let God transform you into a new person by changing the way you think" (Rom 12:2). Barnabas wasn't perfect, but he was a Son of Encouragement to many and a generous, unselfish man who fostered growth in others and in the church.

was reestablished, so that once again "all the people had high regard for them" (5:13). Yet it also made outsiders wary of joining a movement with such high standards (5:13). This divine "pruning" (see John 15:1-11) helped new growth to follow (5:14; cp. 6:5-7; 11:24; 21:20).

5:12-16 As in Jesus' ministry, the apostles' preaching was accompanied by ***many miraculous signs and wonders,*** including convincing works of healing and exorcism (see also 6:8; cp. Matt 4:24; 9:35; Mark 1:32-34; Luke 4:40-41).

5:13 ***no one else dared to join them:*** Perhaps the high standards of belief or what had happened to Ananias and Sapphira (5:11) were daunting to the crowds. • ***though all the people had high regard for them:*** Christians were markedly different from the unbelievers around them.

5:16 *evil:* Literally *unclean.*

5:17-40 The success of the apostles' ministry again aroused strong opposition (cp. 4:1-3). The wealthy and powerful ***Sadducees*** controlled the Temple establishment and had a Temple police force at their disposal. They opposed belief in the resurrection (see "The Sadducees" at Matt 16:1-12, p. 1610) and were determined not to allow the apostles to proclaim their message about the resurrection of Jesus unchallenged. They also sensed that their hold on the Jewish people was loosening, so, ***filled with jealousy,*** they attacked the apostles.

5:19-20 The irony here is that the Sadducees denied the existence of angels (23:8). Angels frequently intervened in Acts (see also 10:3, 7, 22; 11:13; 12:6-11, 23; 27:23-24). Luke presents God as guiding his people in their ministry, using angels to accomplish his purpose.

21So at daybreak the apostles entered the
Temple, as they were told, and immediately
began teaching.
When the high priest and his officials arrived, they convened the high council—the
full assembly of the elders of Israel. Then
they sent for the apostles to be brought
from the jail for trial. 22But when the Temple guards went to the jail, the men were
gone. So they returned to the council and
reported, 23"The jail was securely locked,
with the guards standing outside, but when
we opened the gates, no one was there!"
24When the captain of the Temple guard
and the leading priests heard this, they were
perplexed, wondering where it would all
end. 25Then someone arrived with startling
news: "The men you put in jail are standing
in the Temple, teaching the people!"

The Apostles Arrested Again and Examined

26The captain went with his Temple guards
and arrested the apostles, but without violence, for they were afraid the people
would stone them. 27Then they brought the
apostles before the high council, where the
[b]high priest confronted them. 28"Didn't we
tell you never again to teach in this man's
name?" he demanded. "Instead, you have
filled all Jerusalem with your teaching
about him, and you want to make us responsible for his death!"
29But Peter and the apostles replied, "We
must obey God rather than any human authority. 30The God of our ancestors raised
Jesus from the dead after you killed him
by hanging him on a cross. 31Then God put
him in the place of honor at his right hand
as Prince and [c]Savior. He did this so the people of Israel would repent of their sins and
be forgiven. 32We are witnesses of these
things and so is the Holy Spirit, who is given
by God to those who obey him."
33When they heard this, the high council was furious and decided to kill them.
34But one member, a Pharisee named Gamaliel, who was an expert in religious law
and respected by all the people, stood up
and ordered that the men be sent outside

5:21 Acts 4:5-6
5:24 Acts 4:1
5:26 Matt 14:5; 21:26
5:27 [b]*archiereus* (0749) ‣Acts 23:2
5:28 Matt 23:35; 27:25 Acts 2:23; 4:18; 7:52
5:29 Acts 4:19
5:30 Acts 10:39
5:31 Acts 2:33, 38 Heb 2:10 [c]*sōtēr* (4990) ‣Acts 13:23
5:32 Luke 24:48 John 15:26-27
5:33 Acts 7:54
5:34 Acts 22:3

The Holy Spirit's Presence (5:32)

Acts 1:8, 16; 2:4, 41-47; 4:31; 6:1-7; 8:15, 17, 29; 9:15, 17, 31; 10:19-20; 11:12; 13:1-5; 14:3; 15:28; 16:6; 20:28
John 14:15-17, 26; 15:26; 16:7-15
1 Cor 2:13; 12:1-11
Eph 1:13-14
2 Tim 3:16-17
Heb 2:4; 3:7-11, 15; 9:8; 10:15-17
1 Pet 1:11-12
2 Pet 1:20-21

The book of Acts clearly highlights the presence and power of the Holy Spirit. Jesus spoke in advance of the Spirit's influence on the growth of the church (1:8; see John 14:15-17, 26; 15:26; 16:7-15). The Spirit's guidance was clear in the selection of Spirit-filled leaders to care for the needs of the Hellenistic widows (6:1-7) and in the appointing of Barnabas and Saul for missionary service (13:1-5). When the first church council met to consider the membership of Gentiles in the church, those present followed the Spirit's direction (15:28). Christian workers such as Stephen and Philip were filled with the Spirit and preached by his power (chs 6–8), and Paul's ministry was charged with the Spirit's energy from the beginning (9:17). In Acts, the growth, development, and expansion of the church took place entirely under the guidance and power of the Spirit (e.g., 2:4, 41-47; 4:31; 5:32; 8:15, 17, 29; 9:31). Because of the prominence of the Spirit's work in Acts, the book has often been called "the Acts of the Holy Spirit."

The Holy Spirit works in many ways. He gives and restores life (Gen 2:7; Ps 104:24-30; Ezek 37:1-14; Joel 2:28-32; Rom 8:9-11). He calls and commissions workers for the service of Christ (13:2; 20:28) and guides God's servants where and when he wants, to do as he desires (8:29; 9:15; 10:19-20; 11:12; 16:6; 1 Cor 2:13; 1 Pet 1:12). He inspired the writing of Scripture (2 Tim 3:16-17; 2 Pet 1:20-21), instructing the church in Christ's message (John 14:26; 1 Cor 12:3). He bears witness to the power of the Good News in signs and wonders (14:3; Heb 2:4), and teaches the truths of the Bible to God's people (1:16; Heb 9:8; 10:15-17; 1 Pet 1:11-12). He bears witness to Jesus and brings him glory (John 15:26; 16:14). He convicts people of their sinfulness and need for the Good News (John 16:8) and warns people against hardening their hearts (Heb 3:7-11, 15). He bestows gifts upon God's people (1 Cor 12:4-11), and he energizes and equips them to share the Good News, serve the Lord, and work for the Kingdom of God. (See also "The Holy Spirit's Work" at 1 Cor 12:1-11, p. 1945.)

5:21 ***high council:*** Greek *Sanhedrin;* also in 5:27, 41.

5:29 See note on 4:19-20.

5:30-32 ***We are witnesses of these things:*** The apostles, as witnesses, were required to testify to what they had seen and heard (see Lev 5:1; cp. Acts 1:8; Matt 28:18-20; Luke 24:44-49; John 20:21).

5:30 ***on a cross:*** Literally *on a tree.*

5:33-40 God once again thwarted the Jewish leaders' plans to stop the apostles—this time through the counsel of *Gamaliel.*

5:34 ***Gamaliel*** was an eminent *Pharisee,* a leader in the Jewish high council, and a famous teacher of the law. He was Paul's teacher during his rabbinical education (see 22:3).

5:36
Acts 21:38
5:37
Luke 2:1-2; 13:1-2
5:39
Prov 21:30
Isa 46:10
5:40
Matt 10:17
Mark 13:9
5:41
Matt 5:10-12
John 15:21
1 Pet 4:13
5:42
Acts 2:46
[d]*christos* (5547)
‣ Rom 8:35
6:1
Acts 2:45; 4:35
1 Tim 5:3
[e]*diakonia* (1248)
‣ Acts 6:4
6:2-4
Exod 18:13-26

the council chamber for a while. 35Then he said to his colleagues, "Men of Israel, take care what you are planning to do to these men! 36Some time ago there was that fellow Theudas, who pretended to be someone great. About 400 others joined him, but he was killed, and all his followers went their various ways. The whole movement came to nothing. 37After him, at the time of the census, there was Judas of Galilee. He got people to follow him, but he was killed, too, and all his followers were scattered.

38"So my advice is, leave these men alone. Let them go. If they are planning and doing these things merely on their own, it will soon be overthrown. 39But if it is from God, you will not be able to overthrow them. You may even find yourselves fighting against God!"

The Apostles Beaten, Threatened, and Released

40The others accepted his advice. They called in the apostles and had them flogged. Then they ordered them never again to speak in the name of Jesus, and they let them go.

41The apostles left the high council rejoicing that God had counted them worthy to suffer disgrace for the name of Jesus. 42And every day, in the Temple and from house to house, they continued to teach and preach this message: "Jesus is the [d]Messiah."

3. THE CHURCH GROWS FROM JERUSALEM TO ANTIOCH (6:1–12:25)

The Role of the Greek-Speaking Jews (6:1–8:40)

Seven Men Chosen to Serve

6 But as the believers rapidly multiplied, there were rumblings of discontent. The Greek-speaking believers complained about the Hebrew-speaking believers, saying that their widows were being discriminated against in the daily [e]distribution of food.

2So the Twelve called a meeting of all the

Leadership That Empowers (6:1-7)

Exod 19:6
Isa 61:6
Matt 20:25-28
1 Cor 12:4-11
Eph 4:11-12
1 Pet 2:5, 9; 4:10-11
Rev 1:6; 5:10; 20:6

In Acts 6 the new Christian community faced a crisis of leadership. The Hellenists, the Greek-speaking Jews in Jerusalem, were upset because the needs of their widows were being overlooked "in the daily distribution of food" (6:1). This disruption threatened the development of the church with "rumblings of discontent" (6:1) and had to be seriously addressed. Wisely, the apostles recognized the problem (6:2-3) and called for the selection of seven men to administer the food program (6:5-6). Many interpreters see the seven as the first deacons (see note on 6:2-6).

The apostles provided leadership that empowers by sensitively listening to genuine community needs. This wise handling of the issue, with the united, responsible action of both people and leaders, resulted in spiritual growth and increased the number of believers (6:7). Different gifts were recognized in the church and put to work for the common good (see 1 Cor 12:4-11; 1 Pet 4:10-11). A clear division of labor was agreed upon, with the apostles attending to preaching and teaching, and the material needs of the people being handled by other Spirit-filled leaders.

Every believer has the opportunity to exercise some kind of ministry. This usefulness of every Christian in the service of God is sometimes called the "priesthood of all believers" (1 Pet 2:5, 9; Rev 1:6; 5:10; see Exod 19:6; Isa 61:6; Rev 20:6). Not everyone has the same role, but all have the same calling to use their gifts in God's service.

God has given the church its leaders, not to "lord it over" other people, but to serve the community (Matt 20:25-28). The leaders of the church do well when they recognize both the needs of the community and those whom God has prepared to meet those needs. Good leaders recognize gifted people and help them develop, empowering the members of the body to use their God-given gifts (Eph 4:11-12).

5:36-37 This *Theudas* is otherwise unknown, although Josephus mentions a different man by that name who raised a revolt some years later (see Josephus, *Antiquities* 20.5.1). Theudas was a common Jewish name. • ***Judas of Galilee*** appears in Josephus as a rebel who opposed giving tribute to Caesar about AD 6 or 7, following the census of Quirinius (see Josephus, *Antiquities* 20.5.2; cp. Luke 2:2). His resistance, too, was crushed.

5:41 ***for the name of Jesus:*** Literally *for the name.*

6:1 ***The Greek-speaking believers*** were Jewish Christians who had lived elsewhere in the Greco-Roman world and probably observed some Greek customs. ***The Hebrew-speaking believers*** were more traditional Jews, native to Palestine, who spoke Hebrew or Aramaic and refrained from Greek customs. • ***believers:*** Literally *disciples;* also in 6:2, 7. • ***their widows were being discriminated against:*** This injustice threatened the growth and development of the church with ***rumblings of discontent,*** and had to be addressed.

6:2-6 Wisely, the apostles ***called a meeting of all the believers*** to address

believers. They said, "We apostles should spend our time teaching the [f]word of God, not running a food program. 3And so, brothers, select seven men who are well respected and are full of the Spirit and wisdom. We will give them this responsibility. 4Then we apostles can spend our time in prayer and [g]teaching the word."

5Everyone liked this idea, and they chose the following: Stephen (a man full of faith and the Holy Spirit), Philip, Procorus, Nicanor, Timon, Parmenas, and Nicolas of Antioch (an earlier convert to the Jewish faith). 6These seven were presented to the apostles, who prayed for them as they laid their hands on them.

7So God's message continued to spread. The number of believers greatly increased in Jerusalem, and many of the Jewish priests were converted, too.

Stephen Is Arrested

8Stephen, a man full of God's grace and power, performed amazing miracles and signs among the people. 9But one day some men from the Synagogue of Freed Slaves, as it was called, started to debate with him. They were Jews from Cyrene, Alexandria, Cilicia, and the province of Asia. 10None of them could stand against the wisdom and the Spirit with which Stephen spoke.

11So they persuaded some men to lie about Stephen, saying, "We heard him blaspheme Moses, and even God." 12This roused the people, the elders, and the teachers of religious law. So they arrested Stephen and brought him before the high council.

13The lying witnesses said, "This man is always speaking against the holy Temple and against the law of Moses. 14We have heard him say that this Jesus of Nazareth will destroy the Temple and change the customs Moses handed down to us."

15At this point everyone in the high council stared at Stephen, because his face became as bright as an angel's.

Stephen's Testimony before the Council

7 Then the high priest asked Stephen, "Are these accusations true?"

2This was Stephen's reply: "Brothers and fathers, listen to me. Our glorious God appeared to our ancestor Abraham in Mesopotamia before he settled in Haran. 3God told him, 'Leave your native land and your relatives, and come into the land that I will show you.' 4So Abraham left the land of the Chaldeans and lived in Haran until his father died. Then God brought him here to the land where you now live.

5"But God gave him no inheritance here, not even one square foot of land. God did promise, however, that eventually the whole land would belong to Abraham and his descendants—even though he had no children yet. 6God also told him that his descendants would live in a foreign land, where they would be oppressed as slaves for 400 years. 7'But I will punish the nation that enslaves them,' God said, 'and in the end they will come out and worship me here in this place.'

6:2 [f]*logos* (3056) ‣Acts 7:22
6:3 1 Tim 3:7-8
6:4 Acts 1:14 [g]*diakonia* (1248) ‣Rom 12:7
6:5 Acts 21:8
6:6 Num 8:10 Acts 1:24; 13:3 1 Tim 4:14
6:7 Acts 12:24; 19:20; 21:20
6:9 Matt 27:32
6:10 Luke 21:15
6:11 Matt 26:59-61
6:13 Acts 7:48; 21:28
6:14 John 2:19-21 Acts 21:21
7:2 Gen 11:31–12:1; 15:7 Acts 22:1
7:3 *Gen 12:1
7:4 Gen 12:5 Heb 11:8
7:5 Gen 12:7; 13:15; 15:2, 18; 17:8; 24:7
7:6 *Gen 15:13-14
7:7 Exod 3:12

---

the dispute. They recognized the seriousness of the problem, as well as their own priority of ***teaching the word of God***. The solution was to select wise and Spirit-filled men to oversee the food distribution. The community accepted the apostles' solution and chose good leaders from the ranks of the Greek-speaking believers (all of their names are Greek). These ***seven*** devoted themselves to this special ministry, allowing the ***apostles*** to ***spend*** their time ***in prayer and teaching the word***. • ***These seven*** men are sometimes called the first deacons because of the similarity of their role to the office of deacon (see 1 Tim 3:8-13). Although the Greek term translated "deacon" (Greek *diakonos*, "servant") is not used here, a related Greek word is translated ***running a food program*** (6:2; Greek *diakonein*, "to serve").

6:7 The result of the apostles' wise handling of the issue was growth and increase in ***the number of believers***, including ***many of the Jewish priests***. • This is the first of three places in Acts where Luke notes that ***God's message continued to spread*** (see also 12:24; 19:20). When real difficulties arose, God's message could overcome the challenges posed by internal strife, idolatry, and paganism, and the result was growth in the community. Acts is the story of the "unhindered" message of Good News (see 28:31).

6:8-15 The Jewish leaders did to ***Stephen*** as they had done to Jesus (cp. Matt 26:3-4, 59-66): They got someone ***to lie*** about him, accused him of blasphemy, incited a riot, arrested him, and posted false charges against him.

6:12 ***high council:*** Greek *Sanhedrin;* also in 6:15.

6:14 ***Jesus of Nazareth:*** Or *Jesus the Nazarene.*

6:15 ***His face became as bright as an angel's***, just as Moses' face had (6:14; see Exod 34:32-35). Stephen, like Moses, was bringing God's instruction to Israel (see also 2 Cor 3:7-18).

7:1-53 Stephen responded to the accusations by testifying about his Lord (cp. Luke 21:12-17). Instead of defending himself against their prosecution, he became a witness in God's prosecution of them, exposing their stubbornness and unfaithfulness to God. Stephen's recital of Israel's past reminded them of their repeated rejections of those whom God had sent. • Stephen's review of Israel's history has three principal parts, dealing with the work of the patriarchs (7:2-16), the ministry of Moses (7:17-43), and the role of the Tabernacle and the Temple (7:44-50). Stephen followed up his historical survey with a clear attack on the hardheartedness of his own people. With a prophetic challenge, he urged them to stop rebelling against the ***Holy Spirit*** and turn to God with repentance and faith.

7:2 ***Mesopotamia*** was the region now called Iraq. ***Haran*** was a city in what is now called Syria.

7:3 This verse quotes Gen 12:1.

7:5-7 This passage refers to Gen 12:7; 15:13-14; Exod 3:12.

7:8 Gen 17:10-14; 21:2-4; 25:26; 35:23-26
7:9 Gen 37:28; 39:2 Ps 105:17
7:10 Gen 41:37-43 Ps 105:21
7:11 Gen 41:54
7:12 Gen 42:1-2
7:13 Gen 45:1-4
7:14 Gen 45:9-10; 46:26-27 Deut 10:22
7:15 Gen 46:5-7; 49:33 Exod 1:6
7:16 Gen 23:16-20
7:17-18 *Exod 1:7-8 Ps 105:24
7:19 Exod 1:10-11, 22
7:20 Exod 2:2 Heb 11:23
7:21 Exod 2:3-10
7:22 1 Kgs 4:30 Isa 19:11 [h]*paideuō* (3811) ‣Acts 22:3 [i]*logos* (3056) ‣Acts 15:6
7:23-24 Exod 2:11-12
7:26-28 *Exod 2:13-14
7:29 Exod 2:15
7:30-31 Exod 3:1-4
7:32-34 *Exod 3:4-10
7:35 *Exod 2:14
7:36 Exod 7:3; 12:41
7:37 *Deut 18:15 Acts 3:22
7:38 Exod 19:1-6 Deut 32:45-47

8“God also gave Abraham the covenant of circumcision at that time. So when Abraham became the father of Isaac, he circumcised him on the eighth day. And the practice was continued when Isaac became the father of Jacob, and when Jacob became the father of the twelve patriarchs of the Israelite nation.

9“These patriarchs were jealous of their brother Joseph, and they sold him to be a slave in Egypt. But God was with him 10and rescued him from all his troubles. And God gave him favor before Pharaoh, king of Egypt. God also gave Joseph unusual wisdom, so that Pharaoh appointed him governor over all of Egypt and put him in charge of the palace.

11“But a famine came upon Egypt and Canaan. There was great misery, and our ancestors ran out of food. 12Jacob heard that there was still grain in Egypt, so he sent his sons—our ancestors—to buy some. 13The second time they went, Joseph revealed his identity to his brothers, and they were introduced to Pharaoh. 14Then Joseph sent for his father, Jacob, and all his relatives to come to Egypt, seventy-five persons in all. 15So Jacob went to Egypt. He died there, as did our ancestors. 16Their bodies were taken to Shechem and buried in the tomb Abraham had bought for a certain price from Hamor’s sons in Shechem.

17“As the time drew near when God would fulfill his promise to Abraham, the number of our people in Egypt greatly increased. 18But then a new king came to the throne of Egypt who knew nothing about Joseph. 19This king exploited our people and oppressed them, forcing parents to abandon their newborn babies so they would die.

20“At that time Moses was born—a beautiful child in God’s eyes. His parents cared for him at home for three months. 21When they had to abandon him, Pharaoh’s daughter adopted him and raised him as her own son. 22Moses was [h]taught all the wisdom of the Egyptians, and he was powerful in both [i]speech and action.

23“One day when Moses was forty years old, he decided to visit his relatives, the people of Israel. 24He saw an Egyptian mistreating an Israelite. So Moses came to the man’s defense and avenged him, killing the Egyptian. 25Moses assumed his fellow Israelites would realize that God had sent him to rescue them, but they didn’t.

26“The next day he visited them again and saw two men of Israel fighting. He tried to be a peacemaker. ‘Men,’ he said, ‘you are brothers. Why are you fighting each other?’

27“But the man in the wrong pushed Moses aside. ‘Who made you a ruler and judge over us?’ he asked. 28‘Are you going to kill me as you killed that Egyptian yesterday?’ 29When Moses heard that, he fled the country and lived as a foreigner in the land of Midian. There his two sons were born.

30“Forty years later, in the desert near Mount Sinai, an angel appeared to Moses in the flame of a burning bush. 31When Moses saw it, he was amazed at the sight. As he went to take a closer look, the voice of the LORD called out to him, 32‘I am the God of your ancestors—the God of Abraham, Isaac, and Jacob.’ Moses shook with terror and did not dare to look.

33“Then the LORD said to him, ‘Take off your sandals, for you are standing on holy ground. 34I have certainly seen the oppression of my people in Egypt. I have heard their groans and have come down to rescue them. Now go, for I am sending you back to Egypt.’

35“So God sent back the same man his people had previously rejected when they demanded, ‘Who made you a ruler and judge over us?’ Through the angel who appeared to him in the burning bush, God sent Moses to be their ruler and savior. 36And by means of many wonders and miraculous signs, he led them out of Egypt, through the Red Sea, and through the wilderness for forty years.

37“Moses himself told the people of Israel, ‘God will raise up for you a Prophet like me from among your own people.’ 38Moses was with our ancestors, the assembly of God’s people in the wilderness, when the angel spoke to him at Mount Sinai. And there

7:8 *the covenant of circumcision:* See Gen 17:9-14; see also “Circumcision” at 15:1-5, p. 1857.

7:13 ***Joseph revealed his identity to his brothers:*** Other manuscripts read *Joseph was recognized by his brothers.*

7:14 Compare this figure with the *seventy* mentioned in the Hebrew text of Gen 46:27. The number *seventy-five* is probably taken from the Septuagint (the Greek translation of the OT) for Gen 46:27. The Septuagint includes three descendants of Ephraim and two of Manasseh at Gen 46:20, making for a total of five more persons, whereas the Hebrew text does not include descendants for Joseph’s sons. The NT authors often quote from the Septuagint, which sometimes differs from the Hebrew Masoretic Text.

7:16 *a certain price:* Four hundred pieces of silver, according to Gen 23:16.

7:31-34 This passage refers to Exod 3:5-10.

7:37 This verse quotes Deut 18:15. *Moses* had prophesied that the Messiah would come, and it had happened as Moses said.

7:38 *to us:* Some manuscripts read *to you.*

Moses received life-giving words to pass on to us.

39"But our ancestors refused to listen to Moses. They rejected him and wanted to return to Egypt. 40They told Aaron, 'Make us some gods who can lead us, for we don't know what has become of this Moses, who brought us out of Egypt.' 41So they made an idol shaped like a calf, and they sacrificed to it and celebrated over this thing they had made. 42Then God turned away from them and abandoned them to serve the stars of heaven as their gods! In the book of the prophets it is written,

'Was it to me you were bringing
sacrifices and offerings
during those forty years in the
wilderness, Israel?
43 No, you carried your pagan gods—
the shrine of Molech,
the star of your god Rephan,
and the images you made to worship
them.
So I will send you into exile
as far away as Babylon.'

44"Our ancestors carried the Tabernacle with them through the wilderness. It was constructed according to the plan God had shown to Moses. 45Years later, when Joshua led our ancestors in battle against the nations that God drove out of this land, the Tabernacle was taken with them into their new territory. And it stayed there until the time of King David.

46"David found favor with God and asked for the privilege of building a permanent Temple for the God of Jacob. 47But it was Solomon who actually built it. 48However, the Most High doesn't live in temples made by human hands. As the prophet says,

7:39 Num 14:3
7:40 *Exod 32:1, 23
7:42-43 *Amos 5:25-27
7:44 Exod 25:9, 40; Heb 8:5; *tupos* (5179) ›Rom 5:14
7:45 Josh 3:14-17; 18:1; 23:9; 2 Sam 7:2, 6
7:46 2 Sam 7:2-16; 1 Kgs 8:17; Ps 132:1-5
7:47 1 Kgs 6:1-38; 8:17-21
7:48 2 Chr 2:6; Isa 57:15; Eph 2:22; 1 Pet 2:5

STEPHEN (6:5–8:2)

Acts 11:19; 22:20

Stephen, like Barnabas (see 4:36-37), was an exemplary early Christian who, as a result of the boldness of his witness, was arrested and killed by the Jewish authorities. He is known as the first Christian martyr.

A Hellenistic (Greek-speaking) Jewish Christian, Stephen was one of seven men chosen to help administer the distribution of food to needy Christians in Jerusalem (6:1-6). He was the most prominent of the seven and is singled out as a man "full of faith and the Holy Spirit" (6:5). Manifesting the grace and power of God in an unusual measure, he did miraculous things (6:8) and proved to be a bold and effective evangelist and defender of the faith (6:9-10). His witness was so powerful, he was soon arrested by the authorities and brought before the high council for interrogation (6:9-12).

When witnesses accused Stephen of speaking against the sacred Temple and the law of Moses (6:13-14; cp. Mark 13:2; John 2:19; 4:21), he defended himself before the Jewish high council (7:1-53). He spoke of Israel's long history of resisting God and his servants—first Moses and now the Prophet whom Moses had predicted (7:51-53). The Jewish authorities, infuriated by Stephen's bold accusations, dragged him outside the city and stoned him to death (7:54-60). As he died, Stephen prayed that they might be forgiven (7:60).

Stephen's bold witness gave rise to the first wave of persecution of the early Christians (8:1-3). But it resulted in the Good News spreading even wider as the believers fled Jerusalem and proclaimed the message of Jesus everywhere they went (8:4; 11:19-21). Stephen's death provides the first example of the maxim, "The blood of the martyrs is the seed of the church." His martyrdom marks the beginning of the spread of the Good News beyond the borders of Judaism, which ultimately made Christianity, more than any other faith, a worldwide religion. Stephen's strong expression of faith, even as he was dying, could have been a factor in the later conversion of Saul, who observed his stoning (7:58–8:1; see 22:19-20).

Stephen's life reminds us of the determined opposition that a faithful Christian witness can provoke. A bold testimony for Christ may be costly (see 22:20; Rev 2:10, 13), but there is no insuperable barrier to the growth of the church (see 8:1-3; Matt 16:18).

7:39-40 Just as the ancient Jews had *rejected* what *Moses* was saying, now Stephen was speaking to descendants who were still rejecting God's deliverers—in this case, Jesus, the ultimate deliverer.

7:42-43 This passage quotes Amos 5:25-27 (Greek version) to illustrate how the people of Israel rebelled against Moses (7:39-41). *Molech* was a Canaanite god to whom human sacrifices were offered (Lev 18:21; 20:2-5; 1 Kgs 11:7; 2 Kgs 23:10; Jer 32:35). *Rephan* was a star god identified with the planet Saturn, who was worshiped by the Israelites during their wilderness wanderings.

7:44 *the Tabernacle:* Literally *the tent of witness.*

7:46 *the God of Jacob:* Some manuscripts read *the house of Jacob.*

7:48-50 One of the charges was that Stephen was speaking against the Temple (cp. 6:14). The leading priests

7:49-50
*Isa 66:1-2
7:51
Exod 32:9; 33:3, 5
7:52
Matt 23:30-34
7:53
Gal 3:19
7:55
Heb 1:3, 13
7:56
Matt 3:16
7:58
Lev 24:14-16
Deut 17:7
7:59
Ps 31:5
Luke 23:46
7:60
Luke 23:34
8:1
Acts 7:58

49 'Heaven is my throne,
and the earth is my footstool.
Could you build me a temple as good as
that?'
asks the LORD.
'Could you build me such a resting place?
50 Didn't my hands make both heaven
and earth?'

51"You stubborn people! You are heathen
at heart and deaf to the truth. Must you forever resist the Holy Spirit? That's what your
ancestors did, and so do you! 52Name one
prophet your ancestors didn't persecute!
They even killed the ones who predicted the
coming of the Righteous One—the Messiah
whom you betrayed and murdered. 53You deliberately disobeyed God's law, even though
you received it from the hands of angels."
54The Jewish leaders were infuriated by
Stephen's accusation, and they shook their
fists at him in rage. 55But Stephen, full of the
Holy Spirit, gazed steadily into heaven and
saw the glory of God, and he saw Jesus standing in the place of honor at God's right hand.
56And he told them, "Look, I see the heavens
opened and the Son of Man standing in the
place of honor at God's right hand!"
57Then they put their hands over their
ears and began shouting. They rushed at
him 58and dragged him out of the city and
began to stone him. His accusers took off
their coats and laid them at the feet of a
young man named Saul.
59As they stoned him, Stephen prayed,
"Lord Jesus, receive my spirit." 60He fell to
his knees, shouting, "Lord, don't charge
them with this sin!" And with that, he died.

8 Saul was one of the witnesses, and he
agreed completely with the killing of
Stephen.

Persecution Scatters the Believers

A great wave of persecution began that day,
sweeping over the church in Jerusalem; and

Miracles (8:5-8)

Acts 4:29-31; 5:12-16; 6:8; 8:4-23; 9:32-42; 14:3-4; 26:8
Matt 19:23-26; 28:1-20
Mark 10:23-27
Luke 1:30-38; 18:24-27; 24:1-53
John 1:12-14; 3:2-8, 16; 20:1–21:25
Rom 5:1, 8; 8:32
Eph 2:4-5, 8-10
Heb 2:4
1 Pet 1:3-5
1 Jn 5:12-13

In the book of Acts, the activity of the living God is clearly seen in miraculous signs, wonders, and mighty works (4:29-31; 5:12-15; 6:8; 8:6-7; 9:34; 14:3). The Bible does not attempt to prove miracles, but simply reports them. Filled with the Holy Spirit, the apostles and other Christian leaders performed them. The miracles offer tangible evidence of the power and truth of the Christian message (14:3; see John 3:2; Heb 2:4).

The greatest miracles are (1) the coming of Jesus Christ as the Word of God in human flesh (John 1:14), (2) his glorious resurrection from the dead (Matt 28; Mark 16; Luke 24; John 20; see Acts 23:6; 26:8), and (3) the miracle of the new birth (John 3:3-8; Gal 2:20; Eph 2:8-10). The coming of Jesus into the world to be the Savior and to die for our sins shows us how much God loves us (John 3:16; Rom 5:8; 8:32; Eph 2:4-5; 1 Jn 3:1-2). The fact that God raised Jesus from the dead reveals God's power over death and gives us a living hope, the promise of eternal life (1 Pet 1:3-8). The person who puts faith in Jesus Christ as Savior and Lord receives eternal life (John 1:12; 3:36; Rom 5:1-2; 1 Jn 5:12-13). Miracles remind us of the truth that "nothing is impossible with God" (Luke 1:37; 18:27; cp. Matt 19:26; Mark 10:27).

and scribes controlled the Temple commerce and had a vital business interest in maintaining their enterprises unhindered (see Luke 19:45-48). That is why these leaders were so worried about the Temple despite the fact that God himself had said that ***the Most High doesn't live in temples made by human hands***.

7:49-50 This passage quotes Isa 66:1-2.

7:51 Stephen raised the same charge that God had raised against his people in the wilderness: that they were ***heathen*** (literally *uncircumcised*) ***at heart and deaf to truth***, because they were rejecting the gospel and obstinately resisting ***the Holy Spirit*** (see Exod 32:9; 33:3; 34:9; Deut 9:6, 13; 31:27; see also Ps 78:8; Zech 7:11-12).

7:54 ***they shook their fists at him in rage:*** Literally *they were grinding their teeth against him.*

7:55-56 ***Jesus standing . . . at God's right hand:*** Usually Jesus is described as seated in heaven at God's right hand (2:33-34; 5:31; Luke 20:42; 22:69; Rom 8:34; Eph 1:20; Col 3:1; Heb 1:3, 13; 10:12). One possible explanation is that Jesus was welcoming Stephen, the first martyr, to heaven with ***honor***. Stephen had confessed his Lord faithfully on earth, and now his Lord honored his promise to confess his faithful servant in heaven, standing as a witness to defend him (Matt 10:32; Luke 12:8). • ***the Son of Man standing:*** Cp. Dan 7:13-14. The Jewish leaders understood that Stephen was speaking of Jesus as the divine Son of Man (7:57), a title that speaks of Jesus' power and authority (cp. Rev 1:12-15).

7:57 ***they put their hands over their ears:*** They believed that the comparison of Jesus to the divine Son of Man (7:56) was horrible blasphemy.

7:58 ***Saul*** is later called Paul; see 13:9. Saul was the Hebrew form, Paul the Greek form of his name.

7:59-60 Stephen's prayer, ***Lord, don't charge them with this sin***, is strikingly similar to Jesus' prayer at his crucifixion (Luke 23:34). Jesus clearly taught his followers the importance of both forgiveness (Matt 6:14-15; Mark 11:25; see Luke 11:4; 17:3-4) and prayer (Luke 11:5-10; 18:1-8; see also Acts 1:12-15; 4:23-31; 12:5; Jas 5:16-18). The Lord answered Stephen's prayer affirmatively in the case of Saul (ch 9).

8:1-4 ***Saul:*** Cp. 9:1-2; 22:4; 26:9-11; Gal 1:13-14. The result of this ***great wave of persecution*** was that ***all the believers . . .***

all the believers except the apostles were
scattered through the regions of Judea and
Samaria. 2(Some devout men came and
buried Stephen with great mourning.) 3But
Saul was going everywhere to destroy the
church. He went from house to house, dragging out both men and women to throw
them into prison.

Philip Preaches in Samaria

4But the believers who were scattered
preached the Good News about Jesus wherever they went. 5Philip, for example, went
to the city of Samaria and told the people
there about the Messiah. 6Crowds listened
intently to Philip because they were eager
to hear his message and see the miraculous ksigns he did. 7Many evil spirits were
cast out, screaming as they left their victims. And many who had been paralyzed
or lame were healed. 8So there was great
joy in that city.

9A man named Simon had been a sorcerer there for many years, amazing the
people of Samaria and claiming to be someone great. 10Everyone, from the least to the
greatest, often spoke of him as "the Great
One—the Power of God." 11They listened
closely to him because for a long time he
had astounded them with his magic.

12But now the people believed Philip's
message of Good News concerning the Kingdom of God and the name of Jesus Christ.
As a result, many men and women were baptized. 13Then Simon himself believed and
was baptized. He began following Philip
wherever he went, and he was amazed by the
signs and great miracles Philip performed.

14When the apostles in Jerusalem heard
that the people of Samaria had accepted
God's message, they sent Peter and John
there. 15As soon as they arrived, they prayed
for these new believers to receive the Holy

8:3 Acts 9:1; 22:4; 26:9-11; 1 Cor 15:9; Gal 1:13
8:4 Acts 8:1; 11:19
8:5 Acts 6:5; 21:8
8:6 k*sēmeion* (4592) ‣Acts 15:12
8:7 Matt 10:1; Mark 6:7; 16:17
8:9 Acts 5:36; 13:6
8:12 Acts 2:38
8:13 Acts 19:11
8:14 Acts 8:1
8:15 Acts 2:38; 19:2

PHILIP THE EVANGELIST (8:4-13, 26-40)

Acts 6:5; 21:8-9

Philip, a prominent Hellenistic (Greek-speaking) Jewish Christian, was one of the first to take the Good News of Christ to those outside the borders of Judaism. Well respected among the early Christians, he was one of seven men chosen to administer the food-distribution program for needy believers in Jerusalem (6:1-6). Philip was a strong and effective evangelist in the power of the Spirit.

When Christians were forced to flee Jerusalem following the death of Stephen (8:4), Philip carried the Good News of Christ north to the ethnically-mixed city of Samaria. There he performed many miraculous healings and exorcisms, and people responded eagerly to his message (8:5-8). Many men and women were baptized, including a notorious sorcerer named Simon (8:9-13). Then, directed by an angel, Philip traveled southwest from Jerusalem toward Gaza (8:26). There, directed by the Spirit, he met the treasurer of Ethiopia, who was returning home after visiting Jerusalem (8:27). When the Ethiopian asked Philip to help him understand Isaiah 53, Philip told him the Good News about Jesus (8:28-35), then baptized the man by the roadside (8:36-38). Philip was then suddenly taken away by the Spirit of God to the town of Azotus (8:39-40), where he again preached the Good News. He traveled through all the coastal towns until he came to the large Roman city of Caesarea on the coast, where he settled down (8:40; 21:8-9).

Many years later, Paul spent a night in Philip's home in Caesarea (21:8). By this time Philip was known as Philip the Evangelist. He had raised four unmarried daughters, all of whom had the gift of prophecy (21:9).

Philip exemplifies early Christian evangelists, whom the Holy Spirit empowered and guided to authenticate their witness (see also 1:8; 3:4-8; 5:12-16; 6:8; 10:9-20; 13:2; 14:8; 16:6-10; 19:11-12; 20:9-12, 22-23). Philip submitted to the power and guidance of the Spirit, and God used him to take the Good News to those beyond the borders of Judaism.

were scattered. Rather than having their enthusiasm dampened, however, they simply spread the ***Good News about Jesus wherever they went.***

8:5-25 ***Philip:*** See "Philip the Evangelist," above.

8:7 ***evil:*** Literally *unclean.* • ***cast out . . . healed:*** Miracles often accompany evangelism in Acts (see note on 3:1-11).

8:9-24 ***Simon*** the ***sorcerer*** was a showman, dazzling the people of Samaria and making self-exalting claims. Simon's attempt to obtain spiritual power through payment gave the name *simony* to the later corrupt practice of buying and selling ordination to church leadership (cp. 1 Tim 6:9-10). Peter strongly rebuked Simon's ***wickedness.***

8:14-17 When ***the apostles*** sent two of their own to ***Samaria,*** it was an amazing step in overcoming prejudice (cp. Matt 10:5; Luke 9:52-54; John 4:9; 8:48). Then, it was even more amazing that ***Peter and John*** prayed that the new Samaritan believers would ***receive the Holy Spirit.*** This event parallels the day of Pentecost in Jerusalem (ch 2) and marks the spread of the Holy Spirit's power from Judea to Samaria (1:8).

8:16 Acts 10:44
8:17 Acts 6:6; 19:6
8:20 Matt 10:8; Acts 2:38
8:21 Ps 78:37
8:22 Acts 2:38
8:23 Deut 29:17-18; Isa 58:6
8:24 Exod 8:8; Num 21:7
8:26 Acts 5:19; 6:5; ᵃ*angelos* (0032) ‣Acts 10:3
8:27 1 Kgs 8:41-43; Ps 68:31; Isa 56:3-5; Zeph 3:10
8:32-33 *Isa 53:7-8
8:32 ᵇ*amnos* (0286) ‣1 Pet 1:19
8:35 Luke 24:27; Acts 18:28
8:36 Acts 10:47

Spirit. 16The Holy Spirit had not yet come
upon any of them, for they had only been
baptized in the name of the Lord Jesus.
17Then Peter and John laid their hands
upon these believers, and they received the
Holy Spirit.
18When Simon saw that the Spirit was
given when the apostles laid their hands on
people, he offered them money to buy this
power. 19"Let me have this power, too," he
exclaimed, "so that when I lay my hands on
people, they will receive the Holy Spirit!"
20But Peter replied, "May your money be
destroyed with you for thinking God's gift
can be bought! 21You can have no part in
this, for your heart is not right with God.
22Repent of your wickedness and pray to
the Lord. Perhaps he will forgive your evil
thoughts, 23for I can see that you are full of
bitter jealousy and are held captive by sin."
24"Pray to the Lord for me," Simon exclaimed, "that these terrible things you've
said won't happen to me!"
25After testifying and preaching the
word of the Lord in Samaria, Peter and John
returned to Jerusalem. And they stopped in
many Samaritan villages along the way to
preach the Good News.

Philip and the Ethiopian Eunuch

26As for Philip, an ᵃangel of the Lord said
to him, "Go south down the desert road
that runs from Jerusalem to Gaza." 27So
he started out, and he met the treasurer of
Ethiopia, a eunuch of great authority under
the Kandake, the queen of Ethiopia. The
eunuch had gone to Jerusalem to worship,
28and he was now returning. Seated in his
carriage, he was reading aloud from the
book of the prophet Isaiah.
29The Holy Spirit said to Philip, "Go over
and walk along beside the carriage."
30Philip ran over and heard the man reading from the prophet Isaiah. Philip asked,
"Do you understand what you are reading?"
31The man replied, "How can I, unless
someone instructs me?" And he urged Philip
to come up into the carriage and sit with
him.
32The passage of Scripture he had been
reading was this:

"He was led like a sheep to the slaughter.
And as a ᵇlamb is silent before the
shearers,
he did not open his mouth.
33 He was humiliated and received no justice.
Who can speak of his descendants?
For his life was taken from the earth."

34The eunuch asked Philip, "Tell me, was
the prophet talking about himself or someone else?" 35So beginning with this same
Scripture, Philip told him the Good News
about Jesus.
36As they rode along, they came to some
water, and the eunuch said, "Look! There's
some water! Why can't I be baptized?" 38He

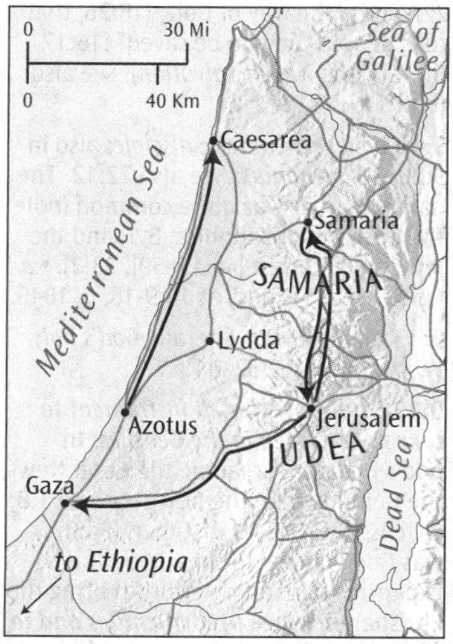

◀ **Philip's Ministry (8:4-40).** When persecution began sweeping over the church in JERUSALEM, Philip traveled north to SAMARIA, where he proclaimed the Good News and many people became believers. Later, God's Spirit directed Philip to go south toward GAZA. Along the way, he evangelized an Ethiopian eunuch. After the eunuch was baptized, the Spirit "snatched Philip away" to AZOTUS (8:39-40), where Philip continued preaching and traveling north to CAESAREA.

8:24 ***Simon*** recognized the need for Peter to intercede in prayer for him, but it is not clear that he repented and turned from his wickedness. His main concern was apparently to avoid the ***terrible*** consequences that Peter predicted when his wicked motives were exposed.

8:26-40 ***Philip*** obeyed the Holy Spirit's leading and then seized the opportunity to share the message of ***Good News*** with a ***eunuch*** on the ***desert road . . . from Jerusalem to Gaza***. This incident shows Philip's remarkable effectiveness as a Christian apologist and evangelist in his outreach for Christ and in his breaking down of barriers.

8:26 ***Go south:*** Or *Go at noon*. The Greek can be interpreted either way.

8:27 In the ancient world, ***a eunuch*** was an official, typically castrated, who served in a royal court (see 2 Kgs 9:30-32; Esth 1:10; 2:3, 14-15, 21; 4:4-5). Eunuchs were often scorned by Jews because they could not perpetuate the covenant family, and the law of Moses excluded men who had damaged genitals from the assembly of Israel (Deut 23:1; cp. Lev 21:17-23), but Isaiah spoke of God's acceptance of Gentiles and eunuchs (Isa 56:3-8; see also Matt 19:12). In the new covenant, all who have genuine faith have a place among the people of God. • The eunuch had traveled from Africa ***to Jerusalem to worship*** in the Temple, probably for one of the great Jewish festivals.

8:29 ***The Holy Spirit*** guides the servants of God in where, when, and what to preach, teach, or do (9:15; 10:19-20; 11:12; 16:6; 1 Cor 2:13; 1 Pet 1:12). See "The Holy Spirit's Presence" at 5:32, p. 1834.

8:32-33 ***The passage of Scripture*** was Isa 53:7-8 (Greek version), one of the Servant Songs of Isaiah, a passage that speaks of the suffering servant of the Lord.

8:36 Some manuscripts add verse 37, *"You can," Philip answered, "if you believe with all your heart." And the eunuch replied, "I believe that Jesus Christ is the Son of God."*

ordered the carriage to stop, and they went
down into the water, and Philip baptized
him.
39When they came up out of the water,
the Spirit of the Lord snatched Philip away.
The eunuch never saw him again but went
on his way rejoicing. 40Meanwhile, Philip
found himself farther north at the town of
Azotus. He preached the Good News there
and in every town along the way until he
came to Caesarea.

Saul's Conversion (9:1-31)

The Experience of Saul near Damascus

9 Meanwhile, Saul was uttering threats
with every breath and was eager to kill
the Lord's followers. So he went to the high
priest. 2He requested letters addressed to
the synagogues in Damascus, asking for
their cooperation in the arrest of any followers of the Way he found there. He wanted to
bring them—both men and women—back
to Jerusalem in chains.
3As he was approaching Damascus on
this mission, a light from heaven suddenly
shone down around him. 4He fell to the
ground and heard a voice saying to him,
"Saul! Saul! Why are you persecuting me?"
5"Who are you, lord?" Saul asked.
And the voice replied, "I am Jesus, the one
you are persecuting! 6Now get up and go
into the city, and you will be told what you
must do."
7The men with Saul stood speechless, for
they heard the sound of someone's voice
but saw no one! 8Saul picked himself up off
the ground, but when he opened his eyes
he was blind. So his companions led him
by the hand to Damascus. 9He remained
there blind for three days and did not eat
or drink.

The Role of Ananias

10Now there was a believer in Damascus
named Ananias. The Lord spoke to him in
a vision, calling, "Ananias!"
"Yes, Lord!" he replied.
11The Lord said, "Go over to Straight
Street, to the house of Judas. When you get
there, ask for a man from Tarsus named
Saul. He is praying to me right now. 12I have
shown him a vision of a man named Ananias coming in and laying hands on him so
he can see again."
13"But Lord," exclaimed Ananias, "I've
heard many people talk about the terrible
things this man has done to the believers
in Jerusalem! 14And he is authorized by the
leading priests to arrest everyone who calls
upon your name."
15But the Lord said, "Go, for Saul is my
chosen instrument to take my message
to the Gentiles and to kings, as well as to
the people of Israel. 16And I will show him
how much he must suffer for my name's
sake."

8:39 1 Kgs 18:12 2 Kgs 2:16 Ezek 3:12
9:1-29 //Acts 22:3-21; 26:9-18
9:1 Acts 8:3
9:2 Acts 9:14; 22:4
9:3 Acts 22:6-7; 26:12-13 1 Cor 15:8
9:5 Acts 5:39
9:7 Dan 10:7 Acts 22:9; 26:14
9:10 Acts 10:3; 11:5; 12:9; 22:12
9:11 Acts 21:39
9:13 Acts 26:10
9:15 Acts 13:2 Rom 1:1 Gal 1:15-16 1 Tim 1:12
9:16 Acts 20:23; 21:11 2 Cor 11:23-27

8:39-40 After ***the Spirit of the Lord snatched Philip away,*** Philip continued northward from ***Azotus*** (=Ashdod, 1 Sam 5:1-7; Neh 13:23-24; Isa 20:1) up the coast, preaching ***in every town along the way until he came to Caesarea***, where he settled (21:8). • ***Caesarea*** Maritima, a major seaport on the Mediterranean, was the seat of Roman government in Judea. It was built by Herod the Great about 22–9 BC and was named to honor Emperor Caesar Augustus.

9:1-19a The conversion of ***Saul*** of Tarsus on the ***Damascus*** road is of central importance to the narrative of Acts—Luke recounts the story three times (also 22:1-21; 26:1-29). Paul alludes to this experience several times in his letters (1 Cor 15:8-10; Gal 1:11-17; Phil 3:4-11; see 1 Tim 1:12-17). Saul's conversion was his prophetic call and commission as an apostle (9:15; 22:15, 21; 26:15-18). No one is beyond the power of God to reach, redeem, and use them for holy purposes—nothing is impossible with God (Luke 1:37). Paul was prepared through his training, upbringing, and experience to play a unique role in taking the gospel into the broader world as the "apostle to the Gentiles" (Rom 11:13; see 1 Cor 15:9; 2 Cor 12:11-12; Gal 1:1; Eph 3:8).

9:1 ***followers:*** Literally *disciples.*

9:2 The ***synagogues*** (Greek *sunagōgē,* "gathering place") were local Jewish meeting places. After the Exile, Jews began to meet in local synagogues as places of instruction and centers of worship. Synagogue services consisted of the reading of the Law and the Prophets, exposition of the Scriptures, prayer, praise, and thanksgiving (see 13:15; 15:21; Neh 9:5; Matt 6:5; Luke 4:16-21). Jesus attended, taught, preached, and performed miracles in synagogues (Matt 12:9-10; Mark 1:21, 39; Luke 4:16; 13:10-13; John 6:59; 18:20), as did the apostles (see 9:20; 13:5, 14; 14:1; 17:1, 10, 17; 18:4, 19, 26). • ***Damascus,*** the capital of Syria, was an important center with a long and distinguished past and the nearest major city outside of Palestine. It took from four to six days to reach Damascus from Jerusalem, a fact that highlights Saul's earnestness (9:1-5; see 22:4-8; 26:9-15). • The term ***the Way*** is used in Acts for Christianity (see 19:9, 23; 24:14, 22)—it is "the way of God" (18:26) that tells people "how to be saved" (16:17, literally *the way of salvation*). See also John 14:6; 2 Pet 2:2.

9:10 ***believer:*** Literally *disciple;* also in 9:26, 36. • ***Ananias:*** See also 22:12. The name Ananias was quite common (note the husband of Sapphira, 5:1, and the Jewish high priest [AD 47–59], 23:2). • ***a vision:*** See "Visions" at 10:9-16, p. 1846.

9:13 ***the believers:*** Literally *God's holy people;* also in 9:32, 41.

9:15 ***Saul is my chosen instrument to take my message to the Gentiles:*** In God's plan for spreading the Good News, the Gentiles were the next step (see 1:8; cp. chs 10–11). Saul of Tarsus (Paul) was God's choice to spearhead this expansive missionary effort to bring the Christian ***message to the Gentiles and to kings, as well as to the people of Israel.*** The rest of Acts illustrates Saul's (Paul's) faithfulness in carrying out this divine commission (e.g., 26:19-23).

9:16 As Jesus predicted, Paul suffered greatly for his faith (see 2 Cor 11:23-27; see Acts 13:45; 14:19; 16:22-27; 21:30-31; 26:21; 2 Tim 1:11-12).

9:17
Acts 13:52; 22:12-13
1 Cor 9:1; 15:8

9:18
ᶜ*baptizō* (0907)
‣ Acts 11:16

9:19
Acts 26:20

9:21
Acts 8:3

9:22
Acts 18:28

9:23
Acts 23:12

9:24
Acts 20:3; 23:16, 20
2 Cor 11:32

9:25
Josh 2:15
1 Sam 19:12
2 Cor 11:33

9:26
Acts 22:17-18
Gal 1:17-18

9:27
Acts 4:36

9:31
Acts 8:1

17So Ananias went and found Saul. He laid his hands on him and said, "Brother Saul, the Lord Jesus, who appeared to you on the road, has sent me so that you might regain your sight and be filled with the Holy Spirit." 18Instantly something like scales fell from Saul's eyes, and he regained his sight. Then he got up and was ᶜbaptized. 19Afterward he ate some food and regained his strength.

Saul in Damascus and Jerusalem

Saul stayed with the believers in Damascus for a few days. 20And immediately he began preaching about Jesus in the synagogues, saying, "He is indeed the Son of God!"

21All who heard him were amazed. "Isn't this the same man who caused such devastation among Jesus' followers in Jerusalem?" they asked. "And didn't he come here to arrest them and take them in chains to the leading priests?"

22Saul's preaching became more and more powerful, and the Jews in Damascus couldn't refute his proofs that Jesus was indeed the Messiah. 23After a while some of the Jews plotted together to kill him. 24They were watching for him day and night at the city gate so they could murder him, but Saul was told about their plot. 25So during the night, some of the other believers lowered him in a large basket through an opening in the city wall.

26When Saul arrived in Jerusalem, he tried to meet with the believers, but they were all afraid of him. They did not believe he had truly become a believer! 27Then Barnabas brought him to the apostles and told them how Saul had seen the Lord on the way to Damascus and how the Lord had spoken to Saul. He also told them that Saul had preached boldly in the name of Jesus in Damascus.

28So Saul stayed with the apostles and went all around Jerusalem with them, preaching boldly in the name of the Lord. 29He debated with some Greek-speaking Jews, but they tried to murder him. 30When the believers heard about this, they took him down to Caesarea and sent him away to Tarsus, his hometown.

Summary of the Church

31The church then had peace throughout Judea, Galilee, and Samaria, and it became stronger as the believers lived in the fear of

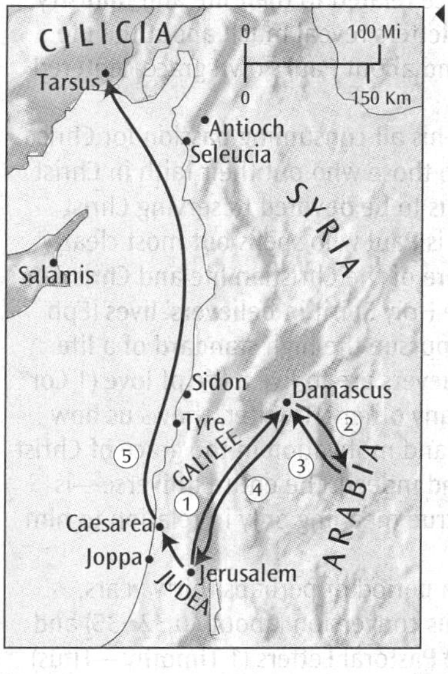

◀ **Saul's Conversion and Early Travels, AD 34~37 (9:1-31).** In his zeal to stamp out Christianity, Saul (1) traveled north toward DAMASCUS, where he intended to arrest believers, but along the way Christ appeared to him. In Damascus, Saul was baptized and began preaching about Jesus (9:20-23). During this time, Saul evidently (2) traveled to ARABIA and (3) back (see Gal 1:17). After three years in Damascus, he escaped a plot against his life and (4) went to JERUSALEM, where he finally met with the apostles (9:26-28; see Gal 1:18). There, too, he faced death threats, so after a visit of about two weeks he was taken to CAESAREA and (5) sailed to TARSUS, his hometown (9:29-30; see Gal 1:21), where he stayed for approximately ten years (AD 37~47; see 11:25-26).

9:17 Ananias's God-given role was to welcome Saul into the Christian family, beginning with laying hands on Saul to heal him and fill him ***with the Holy Spirit***.

9:19b ***believers:*** Literally *disciples;* also in 9:26, 38.

9:20-21 ***immediately he began preaching about Jesus***: The genuineness of Saul's encounter with the risen Christ is attested by the enthusiasm and boldness of his preaching. Saul's outspoken declaration provoked astonishment, for he was the very man who had created ***such devastation among Jesus' followers in Jerusalem***.

9:22-25 Despite the bewilderment of his hearers, Saul so compellingly presented the evidence for the claims of ***Jesus*** as ***Messiah*** that the non-believing ***Jews in Damascus*** found themselves unable to ***refute*** it. Apparently this went on for some time (see Gal 1:18), so some of the non-believing Jews launched a plot on his life, but he was spared when some believers let him down out of the city in ***a large basket***. Paul recounts this incident in 2 Cor 11:32-33.

9:25 ***some of the other believers:*** Literally *his disciples.*

9:26-28 ***When Saul arrived in Jerusalem***, the Christian community understandably did not immediately trust him, given his recent history of violently persecuting Christians (8:3; 9:1, 13; 22:3, 4; 26:9-11). Fortunately, ***Barnabas***, the "Son of Encouragement" (4:36), introduced the changed man to ***the apostles*** and explained his encounter with the Lord at ***Damascus***, his sense of call, and his subsequent boldness in preaching ***in the name of Jesus in Damascus***. Barnabas was able to convince the apostles that Saul's conversion was genuine, so Saul remained with the apostles in Jerusalem, where he ***preached boldly*** for his Lord. Paul recalls this visit in Gal 1:18-19.

9:29 Again Saul ***debated with some Greek-speaking Jews***, and again an assassination was planned (cp. 9:22-24).

9:30 After the ***believers*** (literally *brothers*) ***heard about*** the plot, Saul was once again sent away (cp. 9:25), this time ***to Tarsus, his hometown***, the capital of Cilicia (see map, left; see 21:39; 22:3; 23:34; cp. Gal 1:21).

9:31 This verse is one of several in Acts that detail the numerical and spiritual growth of the church (see also 2:41; 4:4; 5:14; 6:1, 7; 12:24; 21:20). • The first Christians were discovering the truth of the principle, "***the fear of the Lord***

THE APOSTLE PAUL (9:1-31)

Acts 7:58–8:3; 11:25-30; 12:25–28:31
Rom—Phlm
2 Pet 3:15-16

Paul was a leading persecutor of the early Christians who later became an apostle of Jesus Christ, the most illustrious of the early Christian missionaries, and the great apostle to the Gentiles. He has done more to shape Christianity than any other individual except Christ himself. We know about him from Luke's account of his conversion and ministry in Acts and from the thirteen letters bearing his name in the New Testament.

Paul was born in Tarsus to Jewish parents who were Roman citizens (through which he himself acquired Roman citizenship) and grew up in a traditional Jewish home. A tentmaker (or leatherworker) by trade, he was educated as a Pharisee by the well-known rabbi Gamaliel in Jerusalem. He became active in the violent persecution of Christians as a young man (22:3-5). But through a life-changing, personal revelation of the resurrected Jesus (9:3-6; 22:6-10), he was radically converted. He then dedicated the rest of his life to proclaiming Jesus as Savior and Lord throughout the Mediterranean world (see Gal 1:11-16). His dedication and hard work, especially among Gentiles (to whom he was specifically called), resulted in the founding of scores of churches during the first century. Most of his letters were written to these churches.

Paul's belief in Jesus as the Jewish Messiah set him apart from his Jewish contemporaries. His vision of Jesus (ch 9) brought him to the realization that Jesus' death and resurrection brings righteousness and life-transforming power to those who believe in him. Paul no longer understood righteousness in terms of the careful observance of the law of Moses, but as a gift from God to those who put their trust in Christ, the Savior who died for their sins (Rom 4:1-8). And he was convinced that this gift is for Gentiles as well as Jews (Rom 3:21-26).

Paul's thirteen letters deal with a wide range of issues, such as salvation and what Christians believe about Christ (Romans, Galatians, Ephesians, Colossians), specific problems in the church (1 Corinthians), the nature of Christian life and community (Ephesians, Colossians), and questions about Paul's own authority as an apostle (Galatians, 2 Corinthians). Some of his letters are intended to encourage young believers who are suffering for their faith (Philippians, 1 Thessalonians) or to correct false teachings (Galatians, Colossians, 2 Thessalonians). Still others are written to individuals, giving specific advice related to their life and ministry (1–2 Timothy, Titus, Philemon). Together, these thirteen letters reveal much about the life of the earliest Christians and the problems they faced, and about Paul's own grace-centered understanding of the Christian faith and life.

Paul's letters, with their strong focus on Christ, reflect his all-consuming passion for Christ and his twin convictions that (1) salvation is given only to those who put their faith in Christ as Savior (Gal 2:16), and (2) every part of a believer's life is to be devoted to serving Christ as Lord (Rom 14:7-9; 2 Cor 5:15). Of all the NT writers, it is Paul who spells out most clearly what salvation is (Rom 1–8) and gives us the fullest picture of the Christian life and Christian community. Paul's letters also highlight the power of the Holy Spirit in believers' lives (Eph 5:18; cp. Gal 2:20; Col 1:27). He encourages believers to pursue the high standard of a life that is truly like Christ (Rom 8:30; Eph 4:13, 15; 5:1). Believers are to live a life of love (1 Cor 13; Eph 5:2) and fully submit to Christ. Paul, more than any other NT writer, shows us how and why Christians must always find their deepest roots and motivation in the grace of Christ (Rom 12:1-2). For Paul, the whole of a believer's life—and indeed, the entire universe—is centered in Christ and Christ alone; everything finds its true meaning only in relation to him (Col 1:15-20; 2:6–3:4).

Luke's account of Paul's missionary life, which spans a period of perhaps thirty years, begins with Paul's preaching in Damascus shortly after his conversion (about AD 32~35) and ends with his imprisonment in Rome (AD 60–62). But the Pastoral Letters (1 Timothy—Titus) appear to be dated to a later time, and reliable later traditions affirm that Paul was released from prison (around AD 62) and continued his missionary activity. He was later rearrested and—after a lifetime of suffering as an evangelist for Christ—finally killed in Nero's persecution of Christians around AD 64~67. Paul's desire, not only to suffer as Christ suffered but also to die as Christ died, was thus fulfilled—with the sure hope of one day being resurrected, just as Christ was resurrected (Phil 3:10-11).

9:32 Acts 8:14
9:34 Acts 3:6; 4:10
9:35 Acts 2:41
9:36 1 Tim 2:10; Titus 3:8
9:40 1 Kgs 17:19-23; 2 Kgs 4:32-36; Matt 9:25; John 11:43
9:42 Acts 2:41
9:43 Acts 10:6
10:1-2 Acts 8:40; 27:1, 3

the Lord. And with the encouragement of
the Holy Spirit, it also grew in numbers.

The Mission of Peter to the Gentiles (9:32–11:18)

Peter Heals Aeneas and Raises Dorcas

32Meanwhile, Peter traveled from place to
place, and he came down to visit the believers in the town of Lydda. 33There he met a
man named Aeneas, who had been paralyzed and bedridden for eight years. 34Peter
said to him, "Aeneas, Jesus Christ heals you!
Get up, and roll up your sleeping mat!" And
he was healed instantly. 35Then the whole
population of Lydda and Sharon saw Aeneas
walking around, and they turned to the Lord.

36There was a believer in Joppa named
Tabitha (which in Greek is Dorcas). She was
always doing kind things for others and helping the poor. 37About this time she became
ill and died. Her body was washed for burial
and laid in an upstairs room. 38But the believers had heard that Peter was nearby at
Lydda, so they sent two men to beg him,
"Please come as soon as possible!"

39So Peter returned with them; and as
soon as he arrived, they took him to the
upstairs room. The room was filled with
widows who were weeping and showing
him the coats and other clothes Dorcas had
made for them. 40But Peter asked them all
to leave the room; then he knelt and prayed.
Turning to the body he said, "Get up, Tabitha." And she opened her eyes! When she
saw Peter, she sat up! 41He gave her his hand
and helped her up. Then he called in the widows and all the believers, and he presented
her to them alive.

42The news spread through the whole
town, and many believed in the Lord. 43And
Peter stayed a long time in Joppa, living with
Simon, a tanner of hides.

Cornelius Calls for Peter

10 In Caesarea there lived a Roman
army officer named Cornelius, who

Paul's Ministry (9:1-31).

Date	Event	References
AD 31~34	Saul persecutes the church of Judea	Acts 8:1-3; 9:1-2
AD 34~35	Saul's conversion near Damascus	Acts 9:3-19
AD 37~38	Barnabas and Saul's first trip to Jerusalem	Acts 9:26-30
about AD 47	Barnabas and Saul travel to Jerusalem with famine relief	Acts 11:29-30; 12:25
AD 47~48	Barnabas and Saul's first missionary journey	Acts 13:4–14:26
AD 48~49	Paul writes Galatians from Antioch	Galatians
AD 49~50	The council in Jerusalem	Acts 15:1-29
AD 50–52	Paul's second missionary journey	Acts 15:36–18:22
AD 53–57	Paul's third missionary journey	Acts 18:23–21:17
AD 57	Paul travels to Jerusalem and is arrested	Acts 21:1–23:11
AD 57–59	Paul is imprisoned in Caesarea	Acts 23:12–26:32
AD 59–60	Paul's voyage to Rome	Acts 27:1–28:16
AD 60–62	Paul is imprisoned in Rome	Acts 28:17-31
AD 62~64	Paul is released and travels freely	see Introduction to Paul's Letters to Timothy and Titus, "Date of Writing," p. 2047
about AD 64~65?	Paul is imprisoned and martyred in Rome	

is the foundation of true knowledge" (Prov 1:7; 9:10; cp. Job 28:28; Ps 111:10; Eccl 12:13; see Luke 7:16), and they were growing in their faith (cp. 2:43; 19:17).

9:32-43 These verses describe Peter's itinerant ministry in Judea, particularly along the seacoast. Exercising spiritual powers given to him by God, Peter performed wonderful works, including the healing of ***Aeneas*** and the raising of ***Dorcas***. Jesus had promised such signs and wonders to the disciples (John 14:12). • Typical of Luke's writing, the healing of a man is matched by the healing of a woman (see Luke 13:10-17; 14:1-6). The people in the area were deeply moved by these miracles, and many were drawn into the faith (9:35, 42).

9:36 The names ***Tabitha*** in Aramaic and ***Dorcas*** in Greek both mean "gazelle."

9:43 ***living with Simon, a tanner of hides:*** Tanning was an unclean business in Jewish eyes, which might suggest that Peter was not scrupulous in observing Jewish traditions (cp. Gal 2:11-14).

10:1-8 ***a Roman army officer:*** Literally *a centurion;* similarly in 10:22. A centurion was the highest-ranking non-commissioned officer in the Roman army; he was in charge of a *century,* a subdivision of roughly 100 men. Luke often describes centurions in favorable terms (10:22; 21:32; 22:25-26; 23:17, 23; 27:6, 11, 43; 28:16; Luke 7:1-10; 23:47). It was important for Luke to show that Christianity was not hostile to Roman officials or institutions and could, like Judaism, be permitted in the Roman empire (see Acts Introduction, "Purposes of Acts: Politics," p. 1822). • ***a captain of the Italian Regiment:*** A regiment included six centuries; a Roman legion was usually divided into ten regiments. The NT mentions the Italian Regiment and the Imperial Regiment (27:1).

was a captain of the Italian Regiment. 2He was a devout, God-fearing man, as was everyone in his household. He gave generously to the poor and prayed regularly to God. 3One afternoon about three o'clock, he had a vision in which he saw an [d]angel of God coming toward him. "Cornelius!" the angel said.

4Cornelius stared at him in terror. "What is it, sir?" he asked the angel.

And the angel replied, "Your prayers and gifts to the poor have been received by God as an offering! 5Now send some men to Joppa, and summon a man named Simon Peter. 6He is staying with Simon, a tanner who lives near the seashore."

7As soon as the angel was gone, Cornelius called two of his household servants and a devout soldier, one of his personal attendants. 8He told them what had happened and sent them off to Joppa.

Peter Visits Cornelius

9The next day as Cornelius's messengers were nearing the town, Peter went up on the flat roof to pray. It was about noon, 10and he was hungry. But while a meal was being prepared, he fell into a trance. 11He saw the sky open, and something like a large sheet was let down by its four corners. 12In the sheet were all sorts of animals, reptiles, and birds. 13Then a voice said to him, "Get up, Peter; kill and eat them."

14"No, Lord," Peter declared. "I have never eaten anything that our Jewish laws have declared impure and unclean."

15But the voice spoke again: "Do not call something unclean if God has made it clean." 16The same vision was repeated three times. Then the sheet was suddenly pulled up to heaven.

17Peter was very perplexed. What could the vision mean? Just then the men sent by Cornelius found Simon's house. Standing outside the gate, 18they asked if a man named Simon Peter was staying there.

19Meanwhile, as Peter was puzzling over the vision, the Holy Spirit said to him, "Three men have come looking for you. 20Get up, go downstairs, and go with them without hesitation. Don't worry, for I have sent them."

10:3
Acts 3:1
[d]*angelos* (0032)
‣Acts 12:7

10:4
2 Chr 7:15
Matt 25:40
Rev 8:4

10:6
Acts 9:43

10:9-32
//Acts 11:5-14

10:11
Ezek 1:1-3
Matt 3:16
Acts 7:56

10:14
Lev 11:1-47
Ezek 4:14

10:15
Matt 15:11
Rom 14:14, 17, 20
1 Cor 10:25
1 Tim 4:3-4
Titus 1:15

10:19
Acts 11:12; 13:2

10:20
Acts 15:7-9

Visions (10:9-16)

Acts 9:3-6, 10-16; 10:3-6, 30-32; 11:5-9; 16:9-10; 18:9-11; 22:6-10, 17-21; 23:11; 26:14-19
Gen 37:5-10; 40:1–41:36
Isa 6:1-13
Jer 14:14
Ezek 37:1-14
Dan 8:1-27; 9:21
Hos 12:10
Obad 1:1
Hab 2:3
Luke 1:8-20
2 Cor 12:1-10
Rev 1:9–22:7

Visions are important in the Bible (Jer 14:14; Dan 8:1-27; 9:21; Hos 12:10; Obad 1:1; Hab 2:3), and are closely related to other revelatory experiences such as dreams (Gen 37:5-10; 40:9-13). Classic examples include Ezekiel's vision of the valley of the dry bones (Ezek 37:1-14) and Isaiah's vision of God's throne (Isa 6).

Visions are prominent in Acts, and they are usually connected with prayer (9:11-12; 16:9, 10; 22:17-21; 23:11; see Luke 1:8-20). Cornelius was praying when an angel visited him (10:4, 30-32). The following day, Peter received a vision as he prayed (10:9-12; see 11:5-9). In the previous chapter of Acts, the visions of Paul and Ananias are connected with prayer and highlight God's involvement in their lives (9:3-6, 10-16). These visions are not chance coincidences but the providential outworking of God's saving purpose in the world.

Visions give divine direction and show Christian workers the way in which they should carry out the Great Commission (see 1:8; Matt 28:16-20; Luke 24:47; see also Mark 16:15; John 20:21-23). Paul had visions on the Damascus road at his conversion (9:5; 22:7-10; 26:14-19), on the threshold of his missionary advance into Europe (16:9), at Corinth (18:9, 10), in the Temple (22:17-18), and again in Jerusalem before he set out on his trip to Rome (23:11). Through visions God is active in guiding the affairs of the church and in extending its mission (see the notes on 10:3, 9-16; 22:17-22; 23:11; see also Gal 1:8-9 and note).

10:2 ***a devout, God-fearing man:*** Gentiles who are described as *God-fearing* were attracted to the high ethical standards of Judaism but were not prepared to accept the rite of circumcision or the full implications of the Jewish law by becoming full converts to Judaism (cp. 13:43). Christianity was an attractive option to Gentiles who worshiped God (18:7; see 13:48; 16:30; 17:4, 12, 17). These people would be wide open to the message of the gospel that announced that "there is peace with God through Jesus Christ" (10:36).

10:3 In Acts, visions are usually related to prayer (9:3-6, 10-16; 10:2-6, 9-12; 11:5-9; 12:9-17; 18:9-10; 22:17-21; 23:11). These visions are not chance coincidences, but expressions of God's saving work, providing divine direction and encouragement.

10:9-16 ***Peter*** received the same vision ***three times*** to confirm its truthfulness (see Gen 41:32; 2 Cor 13:1).

10:14 ***anything that our Jewish laws have declared impure and unclean*** (literally *anything common and unclean*): See Lev 11 for a description of animals that were clean and unclean for food.

10:17 ***Peter was very perplexed:*** The meaning of the vision would become clear through the events that followed (10:17-48; see 11:1-18): Peter should not hesitate to enter or even eat in the home of a Gentile because God has accepted Gentiles and cleansed them.

10:22
Acts 10:2

10:23
Acts 10:45; 11:12

10:24
Acts 8:40

10:25-26
Acts 14:13-15
Rev 19:10; 22:9

10:28
John 4:9
Acts 11:3; 15:9

10:30-33
Acts 10:1-8

10:34
Deut 10:17
Rom 2:11
Col 3:25

10:35
Acts 15:9

10:36
Rom 5:1
Eph 2:17
[e]*eirēnē* (1515)
› Rom 5:1

10:38
Luke 4:18-19

21 So Peter went down and said, "I'm the man you are looking for. Why have you come?"

22 They said, "We were sent by Cornelius, a Roman officer. He is a devout and God-fearing man, well respected by all the Jews. A holy angel instructed him to summon you to his house so that he can hear your message." 23 So Peter invited the men to stay for the night. The next day he went with them, accompanied by some of the brothers from Joppa.

24 They arrived in Caesarea the following day. Cornelius was waiting for them and had called together his relatives and close friends. 25 As Peter entered his home, Cornelius fell at his feet and worshiped him. 26 But Peter pulled him up and said, "Stand up! I'm a human being just like you!" 27 So they talked together and went inside, where many others were assembled.

28 Peter told them, "You know it is against our laws for a Jewish man to enter a Gentile home like this or to associate with you. But God has shown me that I should no longer think of anyone as impure or unclean. 29 So I came without objection as soon as I was sent for. Now tell me why you sent for me."

30 Cornelius replied, "Four days ago I was praying in my house about this same time, three o'clock in the afternoon. Suddenly, a man in dazzling clothes was standing in front of me. 31 He told me, 'Cornelius, your prayer has been heard, and your gifts to the poor have been noticed by God! 32 Now send messengers to Joppa, and summon a man named Simon Peter. He is staying in the home of Simon, a tanner who lives near the seashore.' 33 So I sent for you at once, and it was good of you to come. Now we are all here, waiting before God to hear the message the Lord has given you."

The Gentiles Hear the Good News

34 Then Peter replied, "I see very clearly that God shows no favoritism. 35 In every nation he accepts those who fear him and do what is right. 36 This is the message of Good News for the people of Israel—that there is [e]peace with God through Jesus Christ, who is Lord of all. 37 You know what happened throughout Judea, beginning in Galilee, after John began preaching his message of baptism. 38 And you know that God anointed Jesus of Nazareth with the Holy Spirit and with power. Then Jesus went around doing good and healing all who were oppressed by the devil, for God was with him.

The Good News (10:34-43)

Acts 2:14-40; 3:12-26; 8:4-8, 25-40; 13:16-41; 14:15; 15:7-9; 16:31; 17:16-31; 20:21; 26:22-23
Matt 4:23-24; 24:14
Mark 1:1, 14-15
Luke 3:15-18; 4:18-21; 7:21-23
Rom 1:1-5, 15-17; 10:15-17; 16:25-27
1 Cor 1:18; 15:3-8
2 Cor 4:3-7
Eph 1:13; 2:4-18
2 Thes 2:13-14
2 Tim 1:9-10; 2:8-13
Heb 4:1-16
1 Pet 1:3-12
Rev 14:6-7

The apostles proclaimed the Good News in a definite sequence. In summary, (1) the OT promises have been fulfilled in the life, death, and resurrection of Jesus Christ. (2) God has exalted Jesus by resurrecting him to be the head of the new Israel as the divinely appointed Messiah. (3) The apostles were witnesses of God's work in Jesus Christ, both as eyewitnesses of his public ministry and resurrection (13:31) and as his chosen advocates (1:22; 2:32; 3:15; 4:33; 5:32; 10:39-43). (4) The proper response to this Good News is repentance and faith (2:38; 3:19; 13:39, 48; 17:30, 34; 20:21; 26:20). (5) The Holy Spirit is promised to those who accept this offer of God's forgiveness and salvation from sin through Jesus Christ.

This basic message was repeatedly preached to many people, both Jews and Gentiles, throughout the Mediterranean world (note 1:8; 9:15; 28:31). It is echoed in the sermons of chs 2, 3, 4, 5, 8, 10, and 13. The same themes characterize Paul's preaching (e.g., 1 Cor 15:3-9).

All people are summoned to repentance from sin and faith in the saving power of Jesus (4:12; 13:38; 16:31)—through his death we can be "declared right with God" (13:39). Because the message is crucial to people's destiny, those who proclaim it are warned not to change it (13:40-42; see Heb 2:3).

10:25-26 ***Cornelius . . . worshiped him:*** This act must have been more than traditional obeisance to a high-ranking person. The Bible restricts worship to God alone (see 14:11-17; Exod 20:3; Deut 5:7; Matt 22:37-38; Mark 12:29-30; Luke 10:27; 1 Cor 10:14; Col 3:5; 1 Pet 4:3; 1 Jn 5:21; Rev 4:10; 9:20; 22:8-9). Peter was just a fellow ***human being*** whom Cornelius should not worship.

10:34-35 ***God shows no favoritism:*** See Deut 10:17; 2 Chr 19:7; Job 34:19; Luke 20:21; Rom 2:11; Gal 2:6; Col 3:25; 1 Pet 1:17. The application of this principle is the meaning of Peter's vision (10:9-16). • ***In every nation he accepts those who fear him and do what is right:*** See Rom 10:11-13.

10:36-43 Peter repeatedly underscores the importance of the apostolic ***witnesses*** to ***the message of Good News.*** The apostles ***ate and drank with*** Jesus (see Luke 24:41-43) and were eyewitnesses of his resurrection, so they could attest that he had conquered death (see 3:15; 4:33; 13:30-31). The original apostles were ***chosen in advance to be his witnesses*** (see 1:12-26); gradually, others such as Paul and Barnabas carried on this powerful preaching and teaching in the name of Jesus Christ (9:15; 14:1-3; 26:16).

39"And we apostles are witnesses of all
he did throughout Judea and in Jerusalem.
They put him to death by hanging him on
a cross, 40but God raised him to life on the
third day. Then God allowed him to appear,
41not to the general public, but to us whom
God had chosen in advance to be his witnesses. We were those who ate and drank
with him after he rose from the dead. 42And
he ordered us to preach everywhere and to
testify that Jesus is the one appointed by
God to be the judge of all—the living and
the dead. 43He is the one all the prophets
testified about, saying that everyone who
believes in him will have their sins forgiven
through his name."

The Gentiles Receive the Holy Spirit

44Even as Peter was saying these things, the
Holy Spirit fell upon all who were listening
to the message. 45The Jewish believers who
came with Peter were amazed that the gift
of the Holy Spirit had been poured out on
the Gentiles, too. 46For they heard them
speaking in other [f]tongues and praising
God.

Then Peter asked, 47"Can anyone object to
their being baptized, now that they have received the Holy Spirit just as we did?" 48So
he gave orders for them to be baptized in
the name of Jesus Christ. Afterward Cornelius asked him to stay with them for several
days.

Peter Explains His Actions

11 Soon the news reached the apostles
and other believers in Judea that
the Gentiles had received the word of God.
2But when Peter arrived back in Jerusalem,
the Jewish believers criticized him. 3"You
entered the home of Gentiles and even ate
with them!" they said.

4Then Peter told them exactly what had
happened. 5"I was in the town of Joppa," he
said, "and while I was praying, I went into
a trance and saw a vision. Something like a
large sheet was let down by its four corners
from the sky. And it came right down to
me. 6When I looked inside the sheet, I saw
all sorts of tame and wild animals, reptiles,
and birds. 7And I heard a voice say, 'Get up,
Peter; kill and eat them.'

8" 'No, Lord,' I replied. 'I have never eaten
anything that our Jewish laws have declared
impure or unclean.'

9"But the voice from heaven spoke again:
'Do not call something unclean if God has
made it clean.' 10This happened three times
before the sheet and all it contained was
pulled back up to heaven.

11"Just then three men who had been sent
from Caesarea arrived at the house where
we were staying. 12The Holy Spirit told me
to go with them and not to worry that they
were Gentiles. These six brothers here accompanied me, and we soon entered the
home of the man who had sent for us. 13He
told us how an angel had appeared to him
in his home and had told him, 'Send messengers to Joppa, and summon a man named
Simon Peter. 14He will tell you how you and
everyone in your household can be saved!'

15"As I began to speak," Peter continued,
"the Holy Spirit fell on them, just as he fell
on us at the beginning. 16Then I thought of

10:39 Luke 24:48
10:40-41 John 21:12-13
10:42 Matt 28:19; 2 Cor 5:10
10:43 Isa 53:11; Jer 31:34
10:44 Acts 11:15; 15:8
10:46 Mark 16:17; Acts 2:4; 19:6; [f]*glōssa* (1100) ➤Acts 19:6
10:47 Acts 8:36; 11:17
10:48 Acts 2:38; 19:5
11:3 Acts 10:28; Gal 2:12
11:5-14 //Acts 10:9-32
11:12 Acts 10:23, 45
11:13 Acts 10:30-32
11:14 Acts 10:22, 44; 16:31
11:15 Acts 2:4

10:39 ***on a cross:*** Literally *on a tree.*

10:41 ***the general public:*** Literally *the people.*

10:43 Based on what they had seen and heard (10:39-42), the apostles could proclaim that Jesus of Nazareth was indeed ***the one all the prophets testified about***. The whole plan of the Scriptures is profoundly centered in Christ (see Luke 24:25-27, 44-47; John 5:39). • The major point of their message was that ***everyone who believes in him will have their sins forgiven through his name*** (see Luke 24:47).

10:44-48 On the day of Pentecost, Peter told the assembly that if they would repent, turn to God, and be baptized in the name of Jesus for the forgiveness of sins, they would receive "the gift of the Holy Spirit" (2:38; cp. 19:1-7). As Cornelius and his household listened to Peter's message, ***the Holy Spirit fell upon*** them, too, and they were ***baptized*** (see "Baptism" at 2:38, 41, p. 1828). They received the Holy Spirit ***just as*** the Jews did, so clearly God had shown no partiality (10:34-35). This event parallels the day of Pentecost in Jerusalem (ch 2) and marks the spread of the Holy Spirit's power to Gentiles (1:8; 2:39).

10:45 ***The Jewish believers:*** Literally *The faithful ones of the circumcision.*

10:46 ***in other tongues:*** Or *in other languages.*

10:48 ***Cornelius asked*** Peter ***to stay with them for several days,*** perhaps because of his need for instruction in the Christian way.

11:1-18 Jews traditionally kept themselves separate and did not eat or associate socially with Gentiles (10:28; 22:21-22; see John 4:9, 27; 18:28; Gal 2:12-14). Therefore, when the Jewish believers in Jerusalem learned that ***Gentiles had received the word of God,*** they ***criticized*** Peter's unconventional actions and wanted an explanation, which Peter provided.

11:1 ***other believers:*** Literally *brothers.*

11:2 ***the Jewish believers:*** Literally *those of the circumcision.*

11:3 ***of Gentiles:*** Literally *of uncircumcised men.*

11:4-17 Peter reviewed the sequence of events, explaining that the whole development was the result of God's initiative (11:12). Peter had eaten with Gentiles because God had made it clear that he should (11:4-12). Peter had then observed the Holy Spirit's definite action of coming upon Gentiles, and he realized that they were being accepted and blessed by God just as Jewish believers had been (11:15-17; see 1:5). Peter was submitting to God's will in admitting Gentiles to the church.

11:8 ***anything that our Jewish laws have declared impure or unclean:*** Literally *anything common or unclean.*

11:16
Acts 1:5
[g]*baptizō* (0907)
‣Acts 16:15
11:17
Acts 10:47
11:18
Acts 13:48
[h]*metanoia* (3341)
‣Acts 20:21
11:19
Acts 8:1-4; 13:1; 14:25-27; 15:3
11:21
Luke 1:66
Acts 2:41
11:22
Acts 4:36
11:23
Acts 13:43; 14:26; 15:40; 20:24
11:24
Acts 2:41
11:25
*Acts 9:30
11:27
Acts 13:1; 15:32
11:28
Acts 21:10
11:29
Rom 15:26

the Lord's words when he said, 'John [g]bap-
tized with water, but you will be [g]baptized
with the Holy Spirit.' 17And since God gave
these Gentiles the same gift he gave us
when we believed in the Lord Jesus Christ,
who was I to stand in God's way?"
18When the others heard this, they
stopped objecting and began praising
God. They said, "We can see that God has
also given the Gentiles the privilege of [h]re-
penting of their sins and receiving eternal
life."

The Church in Antioch of Syria (11:19-30)

The Ministry of the Greek-Speaking Believers

19Meanwhile, the believers who had been
scattered during the persecution after
Stephen's death traveled as far as Phoenicia, Cyprus, and Antioch of Syria. They
preached the word of God, but only to Jews.
20However, some of the believers who went
to Antioch from Cyprus and Cyrene began
preaching to the Gentiles about the Lord
Jesus. 21The power of the Lord was with
them, and a large number of these Gentiles
believed and turned to the Lord.

The Ministry of Barnabas

22When the church at Jerusalem heard
what had happened, they sent Barnabas to
Antioch. 23When he arrived and saw this evidence of God's blessing, he was filled with
joy, and he encouraged the believers to stay
true to the Lord. 24Barnabas was a good man,
full of the Holy Spirit and strong in faith.
And many people were brought to the Lord.
25Then Barnabas went on to Tarsus to
look for Saul. 26When he found him, he
brought him back to Antioch. Both of them
stayed there with the church for a full year,
teaching large crowds of people. (It was at
Antioch that the believers were first called
Christians.)

The Ministry of the Church in Antioch

27During this time some prophets traveled
from Jerusalem to Antioch. 28One of them
named Agabus stood up in one of the meetings and predicted by the Spirit that a great
famine was coming upon the entire Roman
world. (This was fulfilled during the reign
of Claudius.) 29So the believers in Antioch
decided to send relief to the brothers and

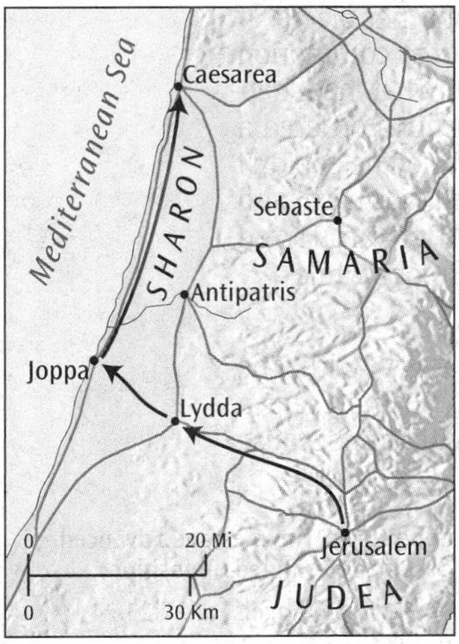

◂ **Peter's Early Ministry, AD 37~40 (9:32–11:18).** Sometime after meeting Saul in JERUSALEM (9:26-28; see Gal 1:18; about AD 37), Peter left Jerusalem and began traveling "from place to place." He first went to LYDDA (9:32-38) and then JOPPA, where he stayed "a long time" (9:39-43). He was there when the Lord sent messengers from Cornelius and prompted Peter to go to CAESAREA, where Cornelius and his household heard the Good News and believed (10:1-48). After staying a few days, Peter returned to Jerusalem and gave the church a report of what had happened (11:1-18).

11:16 *with water:* Or *in water.* • *with the Holy Spirit:* Or *in the Holy Spirit.*

11:18 Peter's logical, straightforward explanation convinced those who had objected—they recognized God's hand at work in the conversion of the Gentiles and their ***receiving eternal life.*** However, issues relating to the inclusion of Gentiles would soon provoke a major crisis (15:1-35; Paul's letter to the Galatians).

11:19-26 ***The persecution*** that followed ***Stephen's death*** forced believers into other areas (8:1-3), and they ***traveled as far as Phoenicia, Cyprus, and Antioch.*** • ***Antioch of Syria*** was a thriving cosmopolitan city, the third-largest in the Roman empire after Rome and Alexandria. Antioch was of central importance in the spread of the Christian message to the Gentile world.

11:20 This outreach effort on the part of Jewish ***believers . . . from Cyprus and Cyrene*** was the first systematic attempt to preach to Gentiles ***about the Lord Jesus.*** • ***the Gentiles:*** Greek *the Hellenists* (i.e., those who speak Greek); other manuscripts read *the Greeks.*

11:21-24 Once again, as had happened in the household of Cornelius, Gentiles ***turned to the Lord*** in considerable numbers. The explosion of Christian faith into the Gentile world had to remain in harmony with the church at Jerusalem, so the Jerusalem church ***sent Barnabas to Antioch*** to oversee developments there. He could see that ***God's blessing*** was on what was happening, so he endorsed it ***with joy.***

11:25-26 ***Barnabas*** recognized the special gifts that ***Saul*** possessed for preaching and ***teaching.*** His assessment of Saul's gifts was wise, and it resulted in a fruitful team ministry in Antioch.

11:26 ***Believers*** (literally *disciples;* also in 11:29) ***were first called Christians*** in Antioch. It was possibly a term of derision. The Greek text uses this term in only two other NT passages (26:28; 1 Pet 4:16). The NLT occasionally uses the term to clarify the meaning of the text (e.g., 1 Cor 7:12-15).

11:27-28 ***some prophets:*** See "The Gift of Prophecy" at 21:9-11, p. 1873. • ***Agabus:*** See also 21:10-12.

11:28 ***Claudius,*** nephew of Tiberius Caesar (Luke 3:1), was the Roman emperor in AD 41–54. His last wife was his niece Agrippina, whose son Nero he adopted.

11:29-30 The upshot of Agabus's prophecy was that the believers in Antioch decided to make a contribution to the Jewish believers—***the brothers and sisters*** (literally *the brothers*)—in Judea. The believers in Antioch gave as generously ***as they could*** and committed the responsibility for this financial aid to leaders they trusted, namely, to ***Barnabas*** and his fellow worker ***Saul.*** This unified love and support of Christians for one another was a tangible demonstration of the difference Christ had made in their lives. Paul describes this visit in his letter to the Galatians (Gal 2:1-10).

sisters in Judea, everyone giving as much as they could. 30This they did, entrusting their gifts to Barnabas and Saul to take to the elders of the church in Jerusalem.

Persecution in the Jerusalem Church (12:1-25)

The Martyrdom of James

12 About that time King Herod Agrippa began to persecute some believers in the church. 2He had the apostle James (John's brother) killed with a sword.

The Imprisonment and Escape of Peter

3When Herod saw how much this pleased the Jewish people, he also arrested Peter. (This took place during the Passover celebration.) 4Then he imprisoned him, placing him under the guard of four squads of four soldiers each. Herod intended to bring Peter out for public trial after the Passover. 5But while Peter was in prison, the church prayed very earnestly for him.

6The night before Peter was to be placed on trial, he was asleep, fastened with two chains between two soldiers. Others stood guard at the prison gate. 7Suddenly, there was a bright light in the cell, and an [i]angel of the Lord stood before Peter. The angel struck him on the side to awaken him and said, "Quick! Get up!" And the chains fell off his wrists. 8Then the angel told him, "Get dressed and put on your sandals." And he did. "Now put on your coat and follow me," the angel ordered.

9So Peter left the cell, following the angel. But all the time he thought it was a vision. He didn't realize it was actually happening. 10They passed the first and second guard posts and came to the iron gate leading to the city, and this opened for them all by itself. So they passed through and started walking down the street, and then the angel suddenly left him.

11Peter finally came to his senses. "It's really true!" he said. "The Lord has sent his angel and saved me from Herod and from what the Jewish leaders had planned to do to me!"

12When he realized this, he went to the home of Mary, the mother of John Mark, where many were gathered for prayer. 13He knocked at the door in the gate, and a servant girl named Rhoda came to open it. 14When she recognized Peter's voice, she was so overjoyed that, instead of opening the door, she ran back inside and told everyone, "Peter is standing at the door!"

15"You're out of your mind!" they said. When she insisted, they decided, "It must be his angel."

16Meanwhile, Peter continued knocking. When they finally opened the door and saw him, they were amazed. 17He motioned for them to quiet down and told them how the Lord had led him out of prison. "Tell James and the other brothers what happened," he said. And then he went to another place.

18At dawn there was a great commotion among the soldiers about what had happened to Peter. 19Herod Agrippa ordered a thorough search for him. When he couldn't be found, Herod interrogated the guards and sentenced them to death. Afterward Herod left Judea to stay in Caesarea for a while.

The Death of Herod Agrippa I

20Now Herod was very angry with the people of Tyre and Sidon. So they sent a delegation to make peace with him because

11:30 Acts 12:25; 1 Pet 5:1
12:2 Matt 4:21; 20:23; Mark 10:39
12:3 Exod 12:15; 23:15
12:4-10 Acts 5:18-25
12:5 Acts 1:14; Eph 6:18
12:7 Acts 5:19; [i]*angelos* (0032) ‣Acts 27:23
12:9 Acts 9:10
12:10 Acts 5:19; 16:26
12:11 Ps 34:7; Dan 3:28; 6:22; 2 Pet 2:9
12:12 Acts 12:25; 15:37; Col 4:10; 1 Pet 5:13
12:15 Matt 18:10
12:17 Acts 15:13; 21:18
12:19 Acts 8:40; 16:27

11:30 This is the first reference in Acts to *elders* as officers of the Christian church (see also 14:23; 15:2-23; 16:4; 20:17-35; 21:18; cp. 1 Tim 3:1-7; Titus 1:5-9).

12:1-5 Jesus had clearly predicted persecution and hardship for his followers (Luke 11:49-51). For the first time since Jesus' death, Roman authorities took direct violent action against the church. ***James,*** the brother of John, was one of the first called to be a disciple (Mark 1:16-20; Luke 5:1-11), and he was one of the first Christians to be martyred for his faith. • ***King Herod Agrippa:*** Literally *Herod the king.* He was the nephew of Herod Antipas and a grandson of Herod the Great. He attacked ***the church*** (cp. 12:20-23), a move that he found to be politically helpful with ***the Jewish people.*** The letter of James, the brother of Jesus, was probably written after this persecution to the scattered Christians (see 8:1-4; James Introduction, "Date of Writing," p. 2111).

12:3 ***the Passover celebration:*** Literally *the days of unleavened bread.*

12:4 Herod had Peter guarded by ***four squads*** of soldiers, making it humanly impossible for the apostle to escape (cp. 12:6). However, God was in charge, and nothing is too hard for him (cp. 4:27-31; Gen 18:14; Jer 32:17, 27; Matt 19:26; Mark 10:27; Luke 1:37; 18:27).

12:5 ***the church prayed very earnestly:*** God answers the earnest prayers of his people (12:6-17; see Luke 11:1-13; 18:1-8; cp. Matt 7:7-11; John 15:7; Phil 4:6-7; Jas 5:16; 1 Jn 3:22).

12:6-19 God, through ***an angel,*** led Peter out, reunited him with his praying friends, and sent him out to Caesarea to carry on the work of spreading the Good News. The message advanced despite determined opposition.

12:7-11 See "Angels" at 27:23-24, p. 1883.

12:11 ***the Jewish leaders:*** Or *the Jewish people.*

12:12 ***The home of Mary, the mother of John Mark,*** was evidently a gathering place for believers. John Mark later became a missionary colleague of Barnabas and Saul (12:25; see "John Mark" at 13:4-5, 13, p. 1852).

12:13-17 ***Rhoda*** was so surprised when Peter appeared that she left him standing at the closed ***door.*** Both she and the other believers were ***amazed*** by God's answer to their prayers (12:5).

12:18-23 When Peter couldn't be found after a careful ***search,*** Herod ***interrogated the guards*** and put them

12:22
Ezek 28:2
12:23
1 Sam 25:38
2 Sam 24:16-17
2 Kgs 19:35
Dan 5:20
12:24
Acts 6:7; 19:20
12:25
Acts 11:29-30
13:1
Acts 11:27
Rom 16:21
13:2
Acts 9:15
Gal 1:15-16

their cities were dependent upon Herod's country for food. The delegates won the support of Blastus, Herod's personal assistant,
21and an appointment with Herod was granted. When the day arrived, Herod put on his royal robes, sat on his throne, and made a speech to them.
22The people gave him a great ovation, shouting, "It's the voice of a god, not of a man!"
23Instantly, an angel of the Lord struck Herod with a sickness, because he accepted the people's worship instead of giving the glory to God. So he was consumed with worms and died.

The Success of the Mission
24Meanwhile, the word of God continued to spread, and there were many new believers.
25When Barnabas and Saul had finished their mission to Jerusalem, they returned, taking John Mark with them.

4. THE CHRISTIAN MESSAGE GOES TO THE GENTILES (13:1–21:17)
Paul and Barnabas's First Missionary Journey from Antioch (13:1–14:28)
Barnabas and Saul Are Commissioned

13 Among the prophets and teachers of the church at Antioch of Syria were Barnabas, Simeon (called "the black man"), Lucius (from Cyrene), Manaen (the childhood companion of King Herod Antipas), and Saul.
2One day as these men were worshiping the Lord and fasting, the Holy Spirit said, "Dedicate Barnabas and Saul for the special work to which I have called them."

HEROD AGRIPPA I (12:1-4, 18-23)

Herod Agrippa I was Herod the Great's grandson, Herod Antipas's nephew, and Herodias's brother (see genealogy, p. 1579). Agrippa I ruled the whole of Palestine for a short time following the death of Jesus, during the very early days of the Christian movement (AD 41–44).

While at school in Rome, Agrippa lived a wanton life, incurring many debts. At one point he stated that he wished his friend Gaius Caligula were emperor rather than Tiberius. This was reported to Tiberius, who imprisoned him. He remained in prison until Tiberius's death six months later.

Upon Caligula's accession to the throne, he rewarded Agrippa by releasing him and giving him Philip the Tetrarch's territories and the northern part of Lysanias's territory as well as the title of king. The title of king aroused the jealousy of Herodias, and Herod Antipas (her husband) was both critical and jealous of Agrippa. Agrippa responded by accusing Antipas of conspiracy and orchestrating Antipas's banishment. Agrippa then acquired all of Antipas's territories and property (AD 39).

When his friend Caligula died in AD 41, Agrippa curried the favor of the new emperor, Claudius, whereupon Claudius added Judea and Samaria to Agrippa's domain—territory once ruled by his grandfather, Herod the Great.

Agrippa was an active persecutor of the early Christians. He is remembered for killing the apostle James and having Peter arrested—acts which gained him the favor of the Jews (12:1-4). The Jews, for their part, liked him more than any of the other Herods. Agrippa died suddenly in AD 44 shortly after his subjects hailed him as a god (12:18-23; see Josephus, *Antiquities* 19.8.2; 19.9.1; *War* 2.11.5).

to ***death*** (cp. 16:27). However, Herod met his own painful end as a divine judgment on his conceit when he ***accepted the people's worship***. Josephus records the death of Herod Agrippa I in greater detail (Josephus, *Antiquities* 19.8.1-2).

12:24-25 Herod's demise from a terrible illness (12:23) contrasts with the growth of the Christian church and the unhindered message of Good News (28:31).

12:25 *mission to Jerusalem, they returned:* Or *mission, they returned to Jerusalem.* Other manuscripts read *mission, they returned from Jerusalem;* still others read *mission, they returned from Jerusalem to Antioch.*

13:1-3 The ***prophets and teachers of the church at Antioch*** spent significant time in worship and prayer, earnestly seeking the Lord's will as they fasted and opened themselves to divine direction. As they prayed, ***the Holy Spirit*** spoke to them, and they set apart ***Barnabas and Saul*** in clear recognition of God's call for them to carry out a ***special work*** in his name. The believers' inward journey in prayer and listening to God is matched by their outward journey in service, evangelism, and mighty works of healing and salvation.

13:1 *prophets and teachers:* See "The Gift of Prophecy" at 21:9-11, p. 1873; see also 1 Cor 12:28-29; Eph 4:11.

• The name ***Simeon*** suggests a Jewish background (see Gen 29:33; Luke 2:25; 3:30); he is also ***called "the black man"*** (literally *who was called Niger*), so he was probably of African descent. • ***Lucius*** is a Latin name; he came ***from Cyrene,*** the capital of Libya in North Africa. He was probably one of the preachers from Cyrene who had brought the Christian message to Antioch (11:20). • ***Manaen*** had been brought up with ***King Herod Antipas*** (literally *Herod the tetrarch*); he was probably Luke's source for insight into Antipas's thoughts and actions (see Luke 9:7-9). • ***Barnabas*** and ***Saul*** are prominently featured in the subsequent narrative.

3So after more fasting and prayer, the men
laid their hands on them and sent them on
their way.

Barnabas and Saul in Cyprus

4So Barnabas and Saul were sent out by the
Holy Spirit. They went down to the seaport
of Seleucia and then sailed for the island
of Cyprus. 5There, in the town of Salamis,
they went to the Jewish synagogues and
preached the word of God. John Mark went
with them as their assistant.
6Afterward they traveled from town to
town across the entire island until finally
they reached Paphos, where they met a
Jewish sorcerer, a false prophet named
Bar-Jesus. 7He had attached himself to the
governor, Sergius Paulus, who was an intelligent man. The governor invited Barnabas
and Saul to visit him, for he wanted to hear
the word of God. 8But Elymas, the sorcerer
(as his name means in Greek), interfered
and urged the governor to pay no attention
to what Barnabas and Saul said. He was trying to keep the governor from believing.
9Saul, also known as Paul, was filled with
the Holy Spirit, and he looked the sorcerer

13:3 Acts 6:6
13:5 Acts 9:20; 12:12
13:6 Matt 7:15; Acts 8:9
13:8 2 Tim 3:8
13:9 Acts 2:4

JOHN MARK (13:4-5, 13)

Acts 12:12, 25; 15:36-39
Col 4:10
2 Tim 4:11
Phlm 1:23-24
1 Pet 5:13

John Mark, writer of the earliest Gospel (the Gospel of Mark), was an assistant of three early missionaries—Barnabas, Paul, and Peter.

Mark was taken along as an assistant by Barnabas and Paul on their first missionary journey. However, for unknown reasons, he left them to return to Jerusalem before the trip was completed (12:25; 13:4-5, 13). Because of this, when Barnabas wanted to take him along on the second trip, Paul flatly refused. The sharp disagreement that resulted broke the team apart: Barnabas took Mark (his cousin) with him, and Paul chose Silas, and the two pairs went their separate ways (15:36-41).

Later, it appears that Paul and Mark were reconciled and that Mark once again served as his assistant. In Colossians, Paul refers to him as a co-worker and suggests that he may soon be sending him to visit the church in Colosse (Col 4:10; Phlm 1:24). Still later, when Paul was awaiting execution in prison in Rome, he asked Timothy to bring Mark with him, for he thought Mark would be helpful to him in his ministry (2 Tim 4:11).

Mark also appears to have assisted Peter when Peter was engaged in missionary work in Italy near the end of his life; early Christian tradition speaks of him as Peter's "interpreter." In one of Peter's letters, he speaks endearingly of Mark as his "son" who is with him (1 Pet 5:13). Early tradition says it was from Peter himself that Mark got the information for his account of the life and words of Jesus. Generally considered to be the earliest of all the Gospels, Mark's Gospel was almost certainly one of the key sources used by Matthew and Luke when they later wrote their own Gospels. For this reason, Mark's Gospel is one of the most influential of all the early Christian writings.

Mark's story reminds us that God can overcome human failings and restore rocky relationships for the sake of Christ and the Good News. Early failures do not disqualify a person from a life of effective service and even lasting significance.

13:3 ***the men laid their hands on them:*** This solemn act was only done *after more fasting and prayer;* the Pastoral Epistles warn against laying hands on a person to appoint that person as a Christian leader without due care and diligence (1 Tim 5:22). At this point, Barnabas and Saul were *sent . . . on their way* as missionaries of the church at Antioch.

13:4 Barnabas and Saul's first missionary journey was undertaken with a strong consciousness of *the Holy Spirit* as their guide. • *Seleucia* was Antioch's ancient *seaport,* located about twelve miles (20 km) west of the city at the mouth of the Orontes River. • Their journey took them westward by sea to *the island of Cyprus,* which was Barnabas's homeland (4:36).

13:5 Landing in *the town of Salamis* on the eastern end of Cyprus, they *went to the Jewish synagogues* (see note on 9:2), where the Jews could hear and respond to the Christian message. They would also meet converts to Judaism (see note on 13:43) and spiritually hungry Gentiles who are sometimes described as "God-fearers" (see note on 10:2).

13:6-12 At *Paphos* there was a power struggle with a *false prophet,* with the result that the power of God was manifested and the Roman governor *became a believer.*

13:6 *Paphos* was located on the southwest coast of Cyprus. As the leading city of Cyprus, it was of strategic importance. • ***a Jewish sorcerer . . . named Bar-Jesus:*** Such eastern magicians often exercised a tremendous influence in the Greco-Roman world.

13:7-8 ***The governor, Sergius Paulus, who was an intelligent man,*** was attracted to the teaching of Barnabas and Saul. But *Elymas* (the sorcerer's Greco-Roman name) recognized a challenge to his power and strongly opposed the message of Barnabas and Saul.

13:9 Luke makes the significant transition from the name *Saul* (a Hebrew name) to *Paul* (a Greco-Roman name), perhaps indicating that Paul was now on a predominantly Gentile mission. For the rest of the book of Acts, he is called Paul except when he recounts his conversion (as in 22:7, 13; 26:14).

13:10
Hos 14:9
Matt 13:38
John 8:44
13:11
2 Kgs 6:18
Acts 9:8
13:13
Acts 12:12; 15:38
13:14
Acts 14:19, 21
13:15
Acts 15:21
13:16
Acts 12:17; 13:26
13:17
Exod 6:6-7
Deut 7:6-8
13:18
Exod 16:35
Num 14:34
13:19
Deut 7:1
13:20
Judg 2:16
1 Sam 3:20
13:21
1 Sam 8:5; 9:1-2;
10:21-24
13:22
1 Sam 13:14
1 Sam 16:1, 13
13:23
2 Sam 7:12
Isa 11:1
Luke 2:11
sōtēr (4990)
‣ Eph 5:23
13:24
Mark 1:4-5

in the eye. 10Then he said, "You son of the devil, full of every sort of deceit and fraud, and enemy of all that is good! Will you never stop perverting the true ways of the Lord? 11Watch now, for the Lord has laid his hand of punishment upon you, and you will be struck blind. You will not see the sunlight for some time." Instantly mist and darkness came over the man's eyes, and he began groping around begging for someone to take his hand and lead him.

12When the governor saw what had happened, he became a believer, for he was astonished at the teaching about the Lord.

Paul and Barnabas in Antioch of Pisidia

13Paul and his companions then left Paphos by ship for Pamphylia, landing at the port town of Perga. There John Mark left them and returned to Jerusalem. 14But Paul and Barnabas traveled inland to Antioch of Pisidia.

On the Sabbath they went to the synagogue for the services. 15After the usual readings from the books of Moses and the prophets, those in charge of the service sent them this message: "Brothers, if you have any word of encouragement for the people, come and give it."

16So Paul stood, lifted his hand to quiet them, and started speaking. "Men of Israel," he said, "and you God-fearing Gentiles, listen to me.

17"The God of this nation of Israel chose our ancestors and made them multiply and grow strong during their stay in Egypt. Then with a powerful arm he led them out of their slavery. 18He put up with them through forty years of wandering in the wilderness. 19Then he destroyed seven nations in Canaan and gave their land to Israel as an inheritance. 20All this took about 450 years.

"After that, God gave them judges to rule until the time of Samuel the prophet. 21Then the people begged for a king, and God gave them Saul son of Kish, a man of the tribe of Benjamin, who reigned for forty years. 22But God removed Saul and replaced him with David, a man about whom God said, 'I have found David son of Jesse, a man after my own heart. He will do everything I want him to do.'

23"And it is one of King David's descendants, Jesus, who is God's promised ʲSavior of Israel! 24Before he came, John the Baptist preached that all the people of Israel

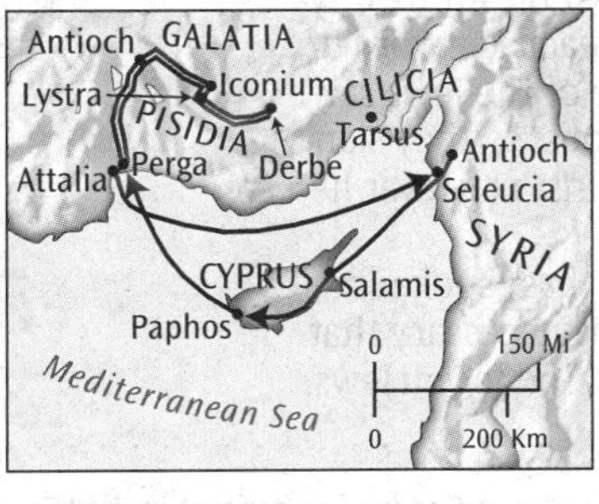

◂ **Barnabas and Paul's First Missionary Journey,** AD **47~48 (13:4–14:28).** Barnabas and Paul (Saul) founded new churches throughout the region of PISIDIA. It is likely that Paul's letter to the Galatians was addressed to these churches a short time after this first journey (see Galatians Introduction, p. 1976). Paul later returned to strengthen these churches during his second and third journeys (see maps, pp. 1859, 1869).

13:10-11 Paul, who became the chief spokesman, rebuked the sorcerer's fraudulent claims, exposed his deceit, and pronounced divine judgment (cp. 8:20-24). The sorcerer was ***instantly*** struck ***blind,*** a condition that lasted ***for some time,*** giving a strong demonstration of the truthfulness and superiority of the apostolic message over the bogus claims of the sorcerer.

13:12 The ***teaching about the Lord*** included a miraculous demonstration of divine power (cp. Mark 1:21-27), for it was a teaching about the living God (see 14:15).

13:13-14 ***Pamphylia*** and ***Pisidia*** were districts of the Roman province of Galatia, in what is now Turkey. They landed at the port of ***Perga.*** From here, major roads opened into the interior beyond the Taurus Mountains. • At this point, ***John Mark left*** the team for reasons that are not stated (see note on 15:36-41). Possibly he was unhappy that the Good News was moving out into Gentile lands; possibly he was homesick or otherwise unable to continue a difficult journey. Whatever the reason, he ***returned to*** the more familiar and comfortable Jewish surroundings of ***Jerusalem.***

13:14 ***Paul and Barnabas traveled inland*** into the high country, and came to ***Antioch of Pisidia*** (in the Roman province of Galatia in Asia Minor, not to be confused with Antioch in Syria). As was their custom, the apostles began at ***the synagogue*** (see note on 9:2; cp. 13:5; 14:1; 17:1, 2, 10, 17; 18:4, 19; 19:8).

13:15 After the ***usual*** Scriptures for the day had been read, one ***from the books of Moses*** (literally ***from the law***) and the other from ***the prophets*** (see Luke 4:16-28), the officials of the synagogue invited the visitors to speak ***any word of encouragement for the people.***

13:16-41 ***Paul*** accepted the invitation, motioned ***to quiet*** his audience (cp. 19:33; 21:40), and launched into a straightforward proclamation of ***the Good News.*** This is Paul's first great speech in Acts, and it provides a model of his preaching to a Jewish audience (see 22:1-21).

13:17-22 To establish common ground, Paul traced Jewish history from the Exodus onward, stressing the Jews' powerful deliverance from Egyptian bondage, the providential occupation of their inheritance in ***Canaan,*** the establishment of the monarchy, the removal of ***Saul,*** and the special place of ***David.***

13:18 ***He put up with them:*** Some manuscripts read ***He cared for them;*** cp. Deut 1:31.

13:22 David was ***a man after*** God's ***own heart*** despite his sins (e.g., 2 Sam 11–12). This verse quotes 1 Sam 13:14.

13:23-25 Paul here moved to the theme of his message: ***Jesus,*** one of ***David's descendants,*** was ***God's promised Savior of Israel.*** The Messiah's way had been prepared by ***John the Baptist,*** who insisted that ***Israel needed to repent . . . and turn to God and be baptized.*** John was a humble servant who simply cleared the ground for the one whose ***coming*** he announced.

needed to repent of their sins and turn to God and be baptized. 25As John was finishing his ministry he asked, 'Do you think I am the Messiah? No, I am not! But he is coming soon—and I'm not even worthy to be his slave and untie the sandals on his feet.'

26"Brothers—you sons of Abraham, and also you God-fearing Gentiles—this message of salvation has been sent to us! 27The people in Jerusalem and their leaders did not recognize Jesus as the one the prophets had spoken about. Instead, they condemned him, and in doing this they fulfilled the prophets' words that are read every Sabbath. 28They found no legal reason to execute him, but they asked Pilate to have him killed anyway.

29"When they had done all that the prophecies said about him, they took him down from the cross and placed him in a tomb. 30But God raised him from the dead! 31And over a period of many days he appeared to those who had gone with him from Galilee to Jerusalem. They are now his witnesses to the people of Israel.

32"And now we are here to bring you this Good News. The promise was made to our ancestors, 33and God has now fulfilled it for us, their descendants, by raising Jesus. This is what the second psalm says about Jesus:

'You are my Son.
Today I have become your Father.'

34For God had promised to raise him from the dead, not leaving him to rot in the grave. He said, 'I will give you the sacred blessings I promised to David.' 35Another psalm explains it more fully: 'You will not allow your Holy One to rot in the grave.' 36This is not a reference to David, for after David had done the will of God in his own generation, he died and was buried with his ancestors, and his body decayed. 37No, it was a reference to someone else—someone whom God raised and whose body did not decay.

38"Brothers, listen! We are here to proclaim that through this man Jesus there is forgiveness for your sins. 39Everyone who believes in him is declared right with God—something the law of Moses could never do. 40Be careful! Don't let the prophets' words apply to you. For they said,

41 'Look, you mockers,
be amazed and die!
For I am doing something in your own day,
something you wouldn't believe
even if someone told you about it.'"

42As Paul and Barnabas left the synagogue that day, the people begged them to speak about these things again the next week. 43Many Jews and devout converts to Judaism followed Paul and Barnabas, and the two men urged them to continue to rely on the grace of God.

Paul and Barnabas Turn to the Gentiles

44The following week almost the entire city turned out to hear them preach the word of the Lord. 45But when some of the Jews saw the crowds, they were jealous; so they slandered Paul and argued against whatever he said.

46Then Paul and Barnabas spoke out boldly and declared, "It was necessary that we first preach the word of God to you Jews.

13:25 Mark 1:7; John 1:20
13:27 Acts 3:17
13:28 Matt 27:22-23; Acts 3:14
13:29 Matt 27:59-60; Luke 23:52-53
13:30 Matt 28:6; Acts 2:24
13:31 Luke 24:48; Acts 1:11; 1 Cor 15:5
13:32 Rom 1:2-4
13:33 *Ps 2:7; Heb 1:5; 5:5
13:34 *Isa 55:3
13:35 *Ps 16:10
13:36 1 Kgs 2:10
13:37 Acts 2:24
13:39 Rom 3:28; 10:4
13:41 *Hab 1:5
13:45 Acts 8:6; 1 Pet 4:4; Jude 1:10
13:46 Acts 18:6

13:26-37 Paul reviewed the shameful treatment Jesus had received, involving unjust condemnation and death. *But God raised* Jesus *from the dead*, as attested by *witnesses.* This message provides good news, for through Jesus sinners can experience the forgiveness of sins. But this message must be met with faith, or dire consequences will follow.

13:29 *from the cross:* Literally *from the tree.*

13:31 The fact that Jesus was raised from the dead was well documented by *witnesses.*

13:33 *'You are my Son. Today I have become your Father':* Or *'Today I reveal you as my Son.'* Ps 2:7.

13:34 This verse quotes Isa 55:3.

13:35 This verse quotes Ps 16:10.

13:38-41 Paul appealed for them to believe the message about Jesus, through whom *there is forgiveness for your sins.*

13:38-39 English translations divide verses 38 and 39 in various ways.

13:39 Faith is prerequisite to being *declared right with God;* this was not provided for in *the law of Moses* (Ps 14:1-3; see Rom 3:9-20).

13:40-41 Paul closed his message with a strong warning (cp. Heb 2:3). The Good News must not be ignored, neglected, or rejected, or frightening consequences will follow.

13:41 This verse quotes Hab 1:5 (Greek version).

13:42-43 The message stirred up interest among the people, and *many* of them were converted.

13:43 Full *converts to Judaism* (also called *proselytes*) were Gentiles who had gone through the rite of circumcision to become full members of the Jewish community, observing the Jewish law (see also 2:11; 6:5; Matt 23:15). • *The grace of God* is a key concept in the NT to describe God's unmerited favor shown preeminently through Jesus Christ (see "The Grace of God" at 20:24, p. 1871).

13:44-49 The excitement caused by the apostles' preaching led to a mass turnout on the following week. This response provoked the jealousy of *some of the Jews* (cp. 5:17; 4:1-2), whose ability to win converts to Judaism (13:43) was being dwarfed by Paul's ministry. They verbally attacked Paul and his ministry (cp. 6:8-12; 18:6; 19:9; Matt 23:13). Paul met this hostility with a bold declaration that these Jews had had their opportunity to hear *the word of God*, and that since they had rejected it, the offer of salvation would now be given *to the Gentiles* (cp. 10:34-35), in accord with the Lord's *command* in Scripture. The local Gentiles welcomed the Good News and many responded to it, so the Lord's message was carried *throughout that region.*

But since you have rejected it and judged
yourselves unworthy of eternal life, we will
offer it to the Gentiles. 47For the Lord gave
us this command when he said,

'I have made you a light to the Gentiles,
to bring salvation to the farthest
corners of the earth.'"

48When the Gentiles heard this, they
were very glad and thanked the Lord for his
message; and all who were chosen for eternal life became believers. 49So the Lord's
message spread throughout that region.
50Then the Jews stirred up the influential
religious women and the leaders of the city,
and they incited a mob against Paul and Barnabas and ran them out of town. 51So they
shook the dust from their feet as a sign of
rejection and went to the town of Iconium.
52And the believers were filled with joy and
with the Holy Spirit.

Paul and Barnabas in Iconium

14 The same thing happened in Iconium. Paul and Barnabas went to the
Jewish synagogue and preached with such
power that a great number of both Jews
and Greeks became believers. 2Some of the
Jews, however, spurned God's message and
poisoned the minds of the Gentiles against
Paul and Barnabas. 3But the apostles stayed
there a long time, preaching boldly about
the grace of the Lord. And the Lord proved
their message was true by giving them
power to do miraculous signs and wonders.
4But the people of the town were divided in
their opinion about them. Some sided with
the Jews, and some with the apostles.
5Then a mob of Gentiles and Jews, along
with their leaders, decided to attack and
stone them. 6When the apostles learned
of it, they fled to the region of Lycaonia—to
the towns of Lystra and Derbe and the surrounding area. 7And there they preached
the Good News.

Paul and Barnabas in Lystra and Derbe

8While they were at Lystra, Paul and Barnabas came upon a man with crippled feet.
He had been that way from birth, so he had
never walked. He was sitting 9and listening
as Paul preached. Looking straight at him,
Paul realized he had faith to be healed. 10So
Paul called to him in a loud voice, "Stand up!"
And the man jumped to his feet and started
walking.
11When the crowd saw what Paul had
done, they shouted in their local dialect,
"These men are gods in human form!"
12They decided that Barnabas was the Greek
god Zeus and that Paul was Hermes, since
he was the chief speaker. 13Now the temple
of Zeus was located just outside the town.

13:47 *Isa 49:6; Luke 2:32
13:48 Rom 8:29-30; Eph 1:4-5, 11; 1 Pet 1:2
13:51 Matt 10:14; Mark 6:11; Luke 9:5; 10:11; Acts 18:6
13:52 1 Pet 1:8
14:1 Acts 13:45
14:2 2 Tim 3:11
14:3 Heb 2:4
14:4 Acts 28:24
14:5 Acts 14:19; 20:3; 2 Tim 3:11
14:6 Matt 10:23
14:8 Acts 3:2
14:10 Acts 3:8
14:11 Acts 28:6

13:47 This verse quotes Isa 49:6.

13:50-51 Jewish opposition once again forced ***Paul and Barnabas . . . out of town.*** They ***shook the dust from their feet as a sign of rejection,*** as Jesus had taught his disciples (see Matt 10:14-15; Mark 6:11-12; Luke 9:5-6; 10:10-11). That place was then treated as pagan territory, and other people were given access to the message of new life in Christ.

13:52 Despite probable harassment and persecution, ***the believers*** (literally *the disciples*) ***were filled with joy and with the Holy Spirit*** (cp. 5:41; 16:23-25; Matt 5:10-12; 2 Cor 8:2; 1 Thes 1:6).

14:1 The missionaries moved on to the next town, ***Iconium*** (now called Konya), located east of Pisidian Antioch on a high plateau in south central Asia Minor (*Iconium,* as well as *Lystra* and *Derbe* [14:6], were towns in what is now Turkey). Iconium enjoyed a favorable location on several key trade routes. • In their usual fashion, ***Paul and Barnabas*** began their ministry in the area by speaking powerfully in ***the Jewish synagogue,*** which led to a great response from ***both Jews and Greeks.***

14:2 Once again ***Paul and Barnabas*** faced hostile ***Jews*** who rejected the Christian ***message*** and also ***poisoned the minds of the Gentiles.***

14:3 The Spirit-inspired ***apostles*** were resilient to withstand the verbal attack against them, and they persisted in ***preaching*** the Good News that God's ***grace*** was available to Gentiles as well as to Jews. • ***boldly:*** Spirit-inspired boldness is evident throughout Acts (see 2:14; 4:9-10, 13; 7:2-53; 8:30-35; 9:27-28; 18:26; 19:8; 22:3-21; 23:1-6; 28:16-20, 23-31). • In addition, the Holy Spirit confirmed the Christian message with ***miraculous signs and wonders*** (cp. 5:12-16; 15:12; 16:18; 19:11).

14:4 The apostolic message required a decision about belief in Jesus, and ***opinion*** was clearly split. • Paul and Barnabas are called ***apostles*** for the first time (also in 14:14), extending the idea of apostleship beyond the Twelve. Their message was in continuity with that of the original apostles, and they were prepared to suffer hardship and persecution for it as the earlier apostles had done (5:41; 14:19; 20:24; 21:13-14; see also Rom 8:35-38; 2 Cor 4:8-17).

14:6 ***Lycaonia*** was a southern region of the Roman province of Galatia. Its major cities were Lystra, Derbe, Laranda, and Iconium. Acts reports two more visits by Paul to Lycaonia (16:1-5; 18:23). Paul's letter to the Galatians was probably addressed to scattered believers in the churches of Lycaonia (see Galatians Introduction, "Recipients," p. 1978). • ***Lystra*** was located roughly twenty-five miles (40 km) south-southwest of Iconium. • ***Derbe,*** situated about thirty miles (50 km) southeast of Lystra, was on the busy major road that stretched from Iconium and Lystra eastward to Tarsus, the capital of Cilicia.

14:8-20 Paul's healing of ***a man with crippled feet*** recalls a similar incident in 3:1-12. In Acts, the work of Paul parallels the work of Peter, and the many miraculous signs and wonders performed among the Jews were also performed among the Gentiles.

14:9 ***Paul realized he had faith to be healed:*** Paul, full of the Holy Spirit (9:17), sensed the man's spiritual openness and expectancy for divine help and intervention.

14:11-13 ***Zeus*** was the patron god of Lystra, and the city had a ***temple*** in his honor. They associated Barnabas with Zeus, perhaps because he was the more impressive figure, and ***Hermes*** was identified with ***Paul . . . since he was the chief speaker.*** The native people

So the priest of the temple and the crowd
brought bulls and wreaths of flowers to the
town gates, and they prepared to offer sacrifices to the apostles.
[14]But when the apostles Barnabas and
Paul heard what was happening, they tore
their clothing in dismay and ran out among
the people, shouting, [15]"Friends, why are
you doing this? We are merely human beings—just like you! We have come to bring
you the Good News that you should turn
from these [k]worthless things and turn to
the living God, who made heaven and earth,
the sea, and everything in them. [16]In the
past he permitted all the nations to go their
own ways, [17]but he never left them without
evidence of himself and his goodness. For
instance, he sends you rain and good crops
and gives you food and joyful hearts." [18]But
even with these words, Paul and Barnabas
could scarcely restrain the people from sacrificing to them.
[19]Then some Jews arrived from Antioch
and Iconium and won the crowds to their
side. They stoned Paul and dragged him out
of town, thinking he was dead. [20]But as the
believers gathered around him, he got up
and went back into the town. The next day
he left with Barnabas for Derbe.

Paul and Barnabas Return through Pisidia and Pamphylia

[21]After preaching the Good News in Derbe
and making many disciples, Paul and Barnabas returned to Lystra, Iconium, and
Antioch of Pisidia, [22]where they strengthened the believers. They encouraged them
to continue in the faith, reminding them
that we must suffer many hardships to enter
the Kingdom of God. [23]Paul and Barnabas
also appointed elders in every church. With
prayer and fasting, they turned the elders
over to the care of the Lord, in whom they
had put their trust. [24]Then they traveled
back through Pisidia to Pamphylia. [25]They
preached the word in Perga, then went
down to Attalia.

The Successful Return to the Antioch Church

[26]Finally, they returned by ship to Antioch
of Syria, where their journey had begun.
The believers there had entrusted them to
the grace of God to do the work they had
now completed. [27]Upon arriving in Antioch, they called the church together and
reported everything God had done through
them and how he had opened the door of
faith to the Gentiles, too. [28]And they stayed
there with the believers for a long time.

The Council at Jerusalem: Conflict over Gentiles (15:1-35)

The Challenge of the Judaizers

15 While Paul and Barnabas were at Antioch of Syria, some men from Judea
arrived and began to teach the believers:
"Unless you are circumcised as required by
the law of Moses, you cannot be saved."

The Debate in the Jerusalem Church

[2]Paul and Barnabas disagreed with them,
arguing vehemently. Finally, the church
decided to send Paul and Barnabas to Jerusalem, accompanied by some local believers,
to talk to the [a]apostles and elders about this
question. [3]The church sent the delegates to

14:15 Exod 20:11; Ps 146:6; Matt 16:16; Acts 10:26; 1 Thes 1:9; Rev 14:7
[k]*mataios* (3152) ‣1 Cor 3:20
14:16 Ps 81:12
14:17 Ps 147:8; Rom 1:20
14:19 Acts 13:45; 2 Cor 11:25; 2 Tim 3:11
14:22 2 Tim 3:12
14:26 Acts 13:1-3
14:27 1 Cor 16:9; Col 4:3; Rev 3:8
15:1 Lev 12:3; Gal 5:2
15:2 Acts 11:30; Gal 2:1-10
[a]*apostolos* (0652) ‣1 Cor 9:1
15:3 Acts 11:19; 14:27

of Lystra thought that they were being treated to a divine visitation similar to a past mythological appearance cited by the poet Ovid (in which the gods Zeus and Hermes came to visit the area but were unrecognized except by an old couple; see Ovid, *Metamorphoses* 8.616–724). So the people set out to honor these supposed gods.

14:13-18 *The apostles* opposed the people's idolatry and their attempt to ***offer sacrifices*** to them. They directed the people's worship ***to the living God;*** the apostles were his representatives as they brought ***the Good News*** of the Christian message.

14:15 *Friends:* Literally *Men.*

14:19-20 The crowd became fickle when ***some Jews arrived from Antioch and Iconium*** and easily turned the people against the apostles. • ***They stoned Paul and dragged him out of town:*** Paul later referred to this time of persecution as a lesson (2 Tim 3:11-12). • ***thinking he was dead:*** That Paul ***got up and went back into the town*** suggests that God miraculously healed him of his wounds.

14:20 *believers:* Literally *disciples;* also in 14:22, 28. • ***The next day he left:*** Paul later returned to Lystra on his second missionary journey (16:1).

14:22-23 The apostles were diligent in following up with those who had made a Christian profession of faith. These new disciples needed to be nurtured, supported, and encouraged (15:32, 41; 16:40; 18:23; see 1 Thes 3:2; 4:18; 5:14). • ***Paul and Barnabas . . . appointed elders:*** See "Church Leaders" at Titus 1:5-9, p. 2071.

14:26-28 As soon as Paul and Barnabas returned home to ***Antioch*** from their first missionary journey, they ***called the church together*** and gave a full report of their evangelism and discipleship. They humbly acknowledged divine guidance in opening ***the door of faith to the Gentiles*** (see 11:18; 1 Cor 16:9; 2 Cor 2:12). Similar reports (15:4, 12; 21:19) always stressed the activity of God as working through the ministries of his servants (see Rom 15:17-18; 1 Cor 3:5-9; 15:10-11).

15:1 These ***men from Judea*** were Jewish Christians who taught the necessity of circumcision (and with it, conversion to Judaism) in order to be saved. The central issue was how Gentiles were to be received into Christian fellowship. Paul wrote his letter to the Galatians about this time to counter the same teaching in Galatia (see Galatians Introduction, "Date," p. 1979). • ***believers:*** Literally *brothers;* also in 15:3, 23, 32, 33, 36, 40.

15:2-3 The Antioch church decided ***to send . . . delegates to Jerusalem*** to resolve this matter in discussion with ***the apostles and elders*** there. En route, the entourage visited believers ***in Phoenicia and Samaria,*** where the Christian faith had made substantial inroads (ch 8).

15:4-21 The first council of the church

15:5
Acts 15:11
[b]*nomos* (3551)
‣ Rom 2:12
15:6
[c]*logos* (3056)
‣ Rom 14:12
15:7-8
Acts 2:4; 10:44; 11:15
15:9
Acts 10:43
Rom 10:12
[d]*kardia* (2588)
‣ Acts 21:13
15:10
Matt 23:4
Gal 5:1
15:11
Rom 3:24
Eph 2:5-8
15:12
Acts 14:27; 15:4
[e]*sēmeion* (4592)
‣ Rom 15:19
15:13
Acts 12:17
15:14
Acts 15:7-9
15:16-17
*Amos 9:11-12
15:18
Isa 45:21

Jerusalem, and they stopped along the way in
Phoenicia and Samaria to visit the believers.
They told them—much to everyone's joy—
that the Gentiles, too, were being converted.
4 When they arrived in Jerusalem, Barnabas and Paul were welcomed by the
whole church, including the apostles and
elders. They reported everything God had
done through them. 5 But then some of
the believers who belonged to the sect of
the Pharisees stood up and insisted, "The
Gentile converts must be circumcised and
required to follow the [b]law of Moses."
6 So the apostles and elders met together
to resolve this [c]issue. 7 At the meeting, after a
long discussion, Peter stood and addressed
them as follows: "Brothers, you all know
that God chose me from among you some
time ago to preach to the Gentiles so that
they could hear the Good News and believe.
8 God knows people's hearts, and he confirmed that he accepts Gentiles by giving
them the Holy Spirit, just as he did to us. 9 He
made no distinction between us and them,
for he cleansed their [d]hearts through faith.
10 So why are you now challenging God by
burdening the Gentile believers with a yoke
that neither we nor our ancestors were able
to bear? 11 We believe that we are all saved
the same way, by the undeserved grace of
the Lord Jesus."
12 Everyone listened quietly as Barnabas
and Paul told about the miraculous [e]signs
and wonders God had done through them
among the Gentiles.
13 When they had finished, James stood
and said, "Brothers, listen to me. 14 Peter has
told you about the time God first visited
the Gentiles to take from them a people for
himself. 15 And this conversion of Gentiles
is exactly what the prophets predicted. As
it is written:

16 'Afterward I will return
and restore the fallen house of David.
I will rebuild its ruins
and restore it,
17 so that the rest of humanity might seek
the LORD,
including the Gentiles—
all those I have called to be mine.
The LORD has spoken—
18 he who made these things known so
long ago.'

Circumcision (15:1-5)

Acts 7:8; 15:19-21, 28-31; 16:2-3; 21:18-24
Gen 17:9-14
Lev 12:3
Josh 5:2-9
Jer 9:25-26
Luke 1:59; 2:21
John 7:22-24
Rom 2:25-29
1 Cor 7:17-19
Gal 2:3-5, 11-21; 5:6; 6:15
Phil 3:5-9
Col 2:11-23

Circumcision (cutting off the male foreskin) was widely practiced in the ancient Near East (Jer 9:25-26). For Jews, it had religious significance as the sign of the covenant that God had established with the people of Israel (7:8; Gen 17:9-14; Josh 5:2; John 7:22; *Sirach* 44:20). It was normally performed on the eighth day of a male infant's life (7:8; Gen 17:12; Lev 12:3; Luke 1:59). The NT notes the circumcision of John the Baptist, Jesus, Paul, and Timothy (16:3; Luke 1:59; 2:21; Phil 3:5). Circumcision became a metaphor for the renewal of a person's relationship with God (Deut 10:16; 30:6; Jer 4:4; Rom 2:28-29). In the late 40s AD, some Jewish Christians tried to require Gentile Christians to undergo circumcision (15:1, 5; see 21:20-21; Gal 2:4, 11-13), to which Paul and Barnabas objected (15:2). The ensuing church council at Jerusalem settled the matter in favor of not requiring Gentiles to be circumcised (15:19-21, 28-29).

Paul insisted that "it makes no difference whether or not a man has been circumcised" (1 Cor 7:19). "What is important is faith expressing itself in love" (Gal 5:6). In Galatians, Paul argued against vigorous Jewish opponents to insist that everyone enters God's family simply through faith in Jesus Christ (Gal 2:14-21). Circumcision is not required for acceptance by God (Gal 5:6). The cross of Christ is the way that sinners enter into covenant with God (Gal 2:14-21; Col 2:11-15).

met to resolve the dispute concerning Gentiles and circumcision (15:1-2).

15:5 These ***Pharisees*** were ***believers***, yet they retained their strong adherence to ***the law of Moses*** (see "The Pharisees" at Matt 3:7, p. 1581). Paul argued against their message most strenuously (see Gal 1:6-9; 2:14–3:14).

15:7-11 ***Peter***, no doubt remembering his own experience in the household of Cornelius (ch 10), argued that God had already ***confirmed*** his acceptance of the Gentiles without circumcision by ***giving them the Holy Spirit***. The ***undeserved grace of the Lord Jesus*** had been made available to all.

15:10 ***Gentile believers:*** Literally *disciples*.

15:13-19 ***James***, the brother of Jesus, declared that the conversion of the Gentiles was clearly in accord with Scripture. He argued forcefully that it was contrary to the divine will to put unnecessary requirements on the admission of the Gentiles.

15:14 ***Peter:*** Greek *Simeon*. Peter's given name was Simon (see Matt 16:17-19).

15:15-19 Because God's ***prophets*** had ***predicted*** the conversion and inclusion of ***the Gentiles***, James argued that the Gentiles should be accepted as Gentiles, without requiring them to practice Judaism (15:1).

15:16-18 This passage quotes Amos 9:11-12 (Greek version); Isa 45:21.
• ***house:*** Or *kingdom;* literally *tent*.

19"And so my judgment is that we should not make it difficult for the Gentiles who are turning to God. 20Instead, we should write and tell them to abstain from eating food offered to idols, from sexual immorality, from eating the meat of strangled animals, and from consuming blood. 21For these laws of Moses have been preached in Jewish synagogues in every city on every Sabbath for many generations."

The Decision of the Council

22Then the apostles and elders together with the whole church in Jerusalem chose delegates, and they sent them to Antioch of Syria with Paul and Barnabas to report on this decision. The men chosen were two of the church leaders—Judas (also called Barsabbas) and Silas. 23This is the letter they took with them:

"This letter is from the apostles and elders, your brothers in Jerusalem. It is written to the Gentile believers in Antioch, Syria, and Cilicia. Greetings!

24"We understand that some men from here have troubled you and upset you with their teaching, but we did not send them! 25So we decided, having come to complete agreement, to send you official representatives, along with our beloved Barnabas and Paul, 26who have risked their lives for the name of our Lord Jesus Christ. 27We are sending Judas and Silas to confirm what we have decided concerning your question.

28"For it seemed good to the Holy Spirit and to us to lay no greater burden on you than these few requirements: 29You must abstain from eating food offered to idols, from consuming blood or the meat of strangled animals, and from sexual immorality. If you do this, you will do well. Farewell."

15:20 Gen 9:4; Exod 20:3-4; Lev 3:17; Deut 12:16; 1 Cor 8:7; 10:7
15:21 Acts 13:15
15:22 Acts 15:27; 16:19; 1 Pet 5:12
15:24 Gal 1:7; 5:10
15:26 Acts 14:19; 1 Cor 15:30
15:29 Gen 9:4; Lev 17:10-14

JAMES, THE BROTHER OF JESUS (15:13-21)

Acts 12:17; 21:18-25; Matt 13:55; Mark 6:3; 1 Cor 15:7; Gal 2:9, 12; James; Jude 1:1

James, one of Jesus' brothers (Matt 13:55; Mark 6:3; Gal 1:19; cp. Jude 1:1), became the recognized leader of the church in Jerusalem shortly after Jesus' resurrection. He is traditionally recognized as the author of the book of James.

Though Jesus' brothers were initially skeptical of his claims (John 7:3-5), they later became believers (1:14). James's personal encounter with the resurrected Jesus (1 Cor 15:7) might have helped convince him. Two of Jesus' brothers (James and Jude) are known to have played significant roles in the early Christian community. James quickly rose to the position of leader of the church in Jerusalem. At the council in Jerusalem, James was instrumental in getting the Jewish church leaders to accept Gentile believers without requiring that they be circumcised—a decision of major importance for Paul and the early mission to Gentiles (15:13-21). Paul visited James in Jerusalem after his third missionary trip (21:18), just as he had done earlier, following his conversion (Gal 1:19).

Like most Jewish Christians, James continued to observe the law of Moses. He emphasized the need for believers to observe certain key laws when among Jews (15:20-21; 21:18-25). James acknowledged the validity of Paul's missionary calling and emphasis on salvation by faith alone (Gal 2:6-9), but many Jewish Christians did not. These Jewish believers demanded that Gentile converts be circumcised and observe the law of Moses in order to be saved.

James's Jewish background is reflected in his letter, which is full of practical advice for wise living, much of it in line with the traditional wisdom teaching of Jewish Scripture. One paragraph of his letter (Jas 5:1-6) reads very much like the work of the OT prophets (e.g., cp. Amos 5:21-24; 6:1-7).

James, titled "the Just" by his contemporaries, was apparently put to death for his faith by Jewish priests in Jerusalem (Josephus, *Antiquities* 20.9; Eusebius, *Church History* 2.23.4–18).

15:20 *Eating food offered to idols* is sinful if it involves knowingly partaking of an idolatrous sacrifice (see Exod 20:4; Deut 5:8; 1 Cor 8:4-13; 10:14-30; Rev 2:14, 20). • ***Sexual immorality*** was common in the Greek world but is always sinful (Exod 20:14; Deut 5:18; Gal 5:19). • ***eating the meat of strangled animals:*** God's law prohibits eating meat that has blood in it (Lev 17:13-14) or ***consuming blood*** (Lev 17:10-12), "for the life of every creature is in its blood" (Lev 17:14). Also, "It is the blood, given in exchange for a life, that makes purification possible" (see Lev 17:11 and note). This command was first given to Noah, the ancestor of Gentiles as well as Jews (Gen 9:4).

15:22-29 The Jerusalem church chose ***two of the church leaders*** (literally *leaders among the brothers*) ***to report*** its ***decision***. They took with them a letter ***from the apostles and elders . . . in Jerusalem*** explaining the terms of the agreement.

15:29 ***Farewell***: The letter to the churches includes this familiar Hellenistic greeting at the end of a letter, found only here in the NT. Paul often ended his letters on a more theological note (e.g., 1 Cor 16:23-24; 2 Cor 13:13; see Eph 6:23-24; Phil 4:23; Col 4:18; 1 Thes 5:23-28; 1 Tim 6:21).

15:32
Acts 11:27; 13:1
15:36
Acts 13:4, 13-14, 51; 14:1, 6, 24-25
15:37
Acts 12:12, 25
15:38
Acts 13:13
16:1
Acts 14:6
Phil 2:19-22
2 Tim 1:2, 5-6; 3:15
16:3
Gal 2:3-5

Joyful Return to the Antioch Church

30The messengers went at once to Antioch,
where they called a general meeting of the
believers and delivered the letter. 31And
there was great joy throughout the church
that day as they read this encouraging
message.
32Then Judas and Silas, both being prophets, spoke at length to the believers, encouraging and strengthening their faith.
33They stayed for a while, and then the believers sent them back to the church in
Jerusalem with a blessing of peace. 35Paul
and Barnabas stayed in Antioch. They and
many others taught and preached the word
of the Lord there.

Paul's Second Missionary Journey from Antioch (15:36–18:22)

Paul and Barnabas Separate

36After some time Paul said to Barnabas,
"Let's go back and visit each city where we
previously preached the word of the Lord,
to see how the new believers are doing."
37Barnabas agreed and wanted to take along
John Mark. 38But Paul disagreed strongly,
since John Mark had deserted them in Pamphylia and had not continued with them in
their work. 39Their disagreement was so
sharp that they separated. Barnabas took
John Mark with him and sailed for Cyprus.
40Paul chose Silas, and as he left, the believers entrusted him to the Lord's gracious care.
41Then he traveled throughout Syria and Cilicia, strengthening the churches there.

Paul Returns to Derbe and Lystra

16 Paul went first to Derbe and then
to Lystra, where there was a young
disciple named Timothy. His mother was
a Jewish believer, but his father was a
Greek. 2Timothy was well thought of by the
believers in Lystra and Iconium, 3so Paul
wanted him to join them on their journey.
In deference to the Jews of the area, he
arranged for Timothy to be circumcised
before they left, for everyone knew that his

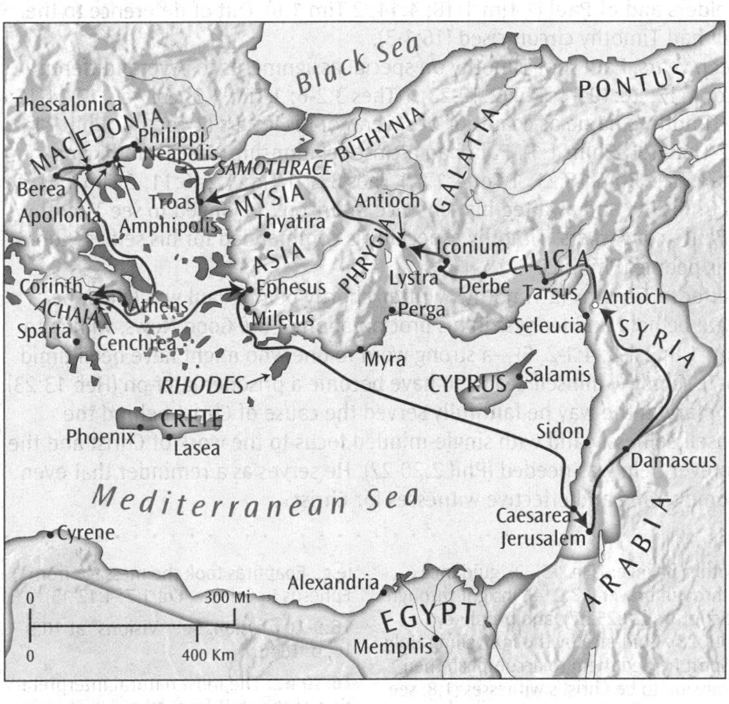

◀ **Paul's Second Missionary Journey, AD 50–52 (15:36–18:22).** After Paul and Barnabas returned to ANTIOCH to report the decision of the council in JERUSALEM (15:1-35; AD 49~50), Paul set off with Silas to visit the churches that had been established during his first journey (see 13:4–14:28; see map, p. 1853). But the journey turned out to be much vaster in reach: They traveled across PHRYGIA and MYSIA, over to MACEDONIA, and down to ACHAIA. Along the way, Paul and Silas established churches in PHILIPPI (16:11-40), THESSALONICA (17:1-9), BEREA (17:10-15), and finally CORINTH (18:1-11), where Paul stayed for over 1½ years (18:11) before returning to ANTIOCH by way of EPHESUS, CAESAREA, and JERUSALEM (18:18-22).

15:30-31 ***The believers*** **at** ***Antioch*** received the decision with ***great joy*** that conversion to Judaism and keeping all the requirements of the law of Moses was not required of them. The dispute had been resolved, so the work of teaching and preaching in Antioch could continue unimpeded.

15:33 Some manuscripts add verse 34, *But Silas decided to stay there.*

15:36-41 The discordant separation of Paul and Barnabas is indicated by a very strong word in Greek (***their disagreement was so sharp***). It was an honest disagreement between two godly men about whether John Mark (Barnabas's cousin, Col 4:10) should be given a second chance to accompany them on a mission journey after he ***had deserted them in Pamphylia*** (see 13:13). The rift between Paul and John Mark was eventually healed (2 Tim 4:11).

15:40-41 Following his disagreement with Barnabas over John Mark, ***Paul chose Silas*** as his partner for a second missionary journey through ***Syria and Cilicia***. The two men traveled overland to visit Derbe and Lystra, explaining the decision of the Jerusalem council and ***strengthening*** believers in their faith.

16:1-3 Paul returned to churches that he and Barnabas had established on their previous journey.

16:2 ***believers:*** Literally *brothers;* also in 16:40.

16:3 Paul had Timothy ***circumcised*** to enhance Timothy's acceptance and effectiveness as a Jew in Jewish circles (contrast Titus, who was a full Gentile, Gal 2:3). Elsewhere Paul clarified that it makes no difference to God whether we are circumcised or not circumcised (Rom 2:25-29; Gal 5:6; 6:15). Paul was prepared to use any legitimate means to communicate the Good News (1 Cor 9:20-21) to various audiences.

father was a Greek. 4Then they went from
town to town, instructing the believers to
follow the decisions made by the apostles
and elders in Jerusalem. 5So the churches
were strengthened in their faith and grew
larger every day.

A Call from Macedonia

6Next Paul and Silas traveled through the
area of Phrygia and Galatia, because the Holy
Spirit had prevented them from preaching
the word in the province of Asia at that time.
7Then coming to the borders of Mysia, they
headed north for the province of Bithynia,
but again the Spirit of Jesus did not allow
them to go there. 8So instead, they went on
through Mysia to the seaport of Troas.
9That night Paul had a vision: A man
from Macedonia in northern Greece was
standing there, pleading with him, "Come
over to Macedonia and help us!" 10So we
decided to leave for Macedonia at once, having concluded that God was calling us to
preach the Good News there.

Journey to Philippi

11We boarded a boat at Troas and sailed
straight across to the island of Samothrace,

16:5 Acts 9:31
16:7 Rom 8:9; Phil 1:19
16:8 2 Cor 2:12; 2 Tim 4:13
16:9 Rom 15:26
16:11 2 Cor 2:12

TIMOTHY (16:1-3)

Acts 17:14-15; 18:5; 19:22; 20:4
Rom 16:21
1 Cor 4:17; 16:10-11
2 Cor 1:1, 19
Phil 1:1; 2:19-23
Col 1:1
1 Thes 1:1; 3:2-6
2 Thes 1:1
1–2 Tim
Phm 1:1
Heb 13:23

Timothy traveled with Paul for much of his missionary career and was one of Paul's best-loved and most trusted assistants. Two of Paul's last letters were written to Timothy at a time when Timothy was providing leadership for the church in Ephesus, near the end of Paul's life.

Timothy had a devout mother and grandmother (2 Tim 1:5), and he was highly respected by the Christians in his hometown, Lystra, and in nearby Iconium. He joined Paul's missionary team on Paul's second missionary journey. Paul speaks of prophetic words that confirmed Timothy's selection. Timothy also received a special gifting for service through the laying on of the hands of the elders and of Paul (1 Tim 1:18; 4:14; 2 Tim 1:6). Out of deference to the Jews in the area, Paul had Timothy circumcised (16:1-3).

Over the next fifteen years, Paul sent Timothy on special assignments to several different churches (19:22; 1 Cor 4:17; 16:10-11; Phil 2:19-23; 1 Thes 3:2-6; 1 Tim 1:3; cp. Acts 17:14-15; 18:5). Paul included Timothy's name as coauthor of several of his letters (2 Cor 1:1; Phil 1:1; Col 1:1; 1 Thes 1:1; 2 Thes 1:1; Phlm 1:1). Paul had a close relationship with Timothy and held him in high regard (see Rom 16:21; 1 Cor 4:17; 1 Thes 3:2; 1 Tim 1:2; 6:11; 2 Tim 1:2). As Paul neared the end of his life and awaited his sentence in prison, he longed to see Timothy (2 Tim 1:3-4). Of all Paul's co-workers, Timothy especially is commended for his selfless concern for Christ and his people (Phil 2:20-22).

In Paul's second letter to Timothy (2 Timothy), written shortly before Paul was killed, he encouraged Timothy to be bold and fearless in his proclamation of the Good News, willing to suffer for Christ (2 Tim 1:8; 2:1-3; 4:1-2, 5)—a strong word to one who might have been timid by nature (2 Tim 1:6-7). Timothy himself seems to have become a prisoner later on (Heb 13:23).

Timothy was exemplary in the way he faithfully served the cause of Christ behind the scenes, devoting himself selflessly and with single-minded focus to the work of Christ and the people of Christ wherever help was needed (Phil 2:20-22). He serves as a reminder that even shy people may become strong and effective witnesses for Christ.

16:4-5 Paul and Silas faithfully communicated the ***decisions*** of the Jerusalem council. The wisdom of the decision was indicated as ***the churches were strengthened in their faith and grew larger every day*** (cp. 2:41; 4:4; 5:14; 6:1; 9:31; 21:20).

16:6-10 God directed the missionaries' travels: ***The Holy Spirit had prevented them*** from proceeding westward into the province of Asia, ***the Spirit of Jesus did not allow them to go*** north to ***Bithynia,*** and then ***Paul had a vision*** calling them to go northwest ***over*** the Aegean Sea ***to Macedonia***. God's Spirit guided his servants in Acts in a variety of ways, including divine visions (see also 9:10; 10:9-16; 22:18), direct intuition (cp. 8:29, 39; 10:19; 20:22), counsel with other believers (cp. 15:29), guidance through prayer (13:2, 4), insight through Scripture (28:25-27), and prophecy (11:28). Guidance by the indwelling Holy Spirit helped them to accomplish their mission to be Christ's witnesses (1:8; see also 4:8, 31; 11:24; 13:9).

16:6-7 ***Phrygia, Galatia, Asia, Mysia,*** and ***Bithynia*** were all districts in what is now Turkey.

16:8 ***Troas,*** a major port on the Aegean Sea, was one of the more significant cities in the Roman empire. Paul's strategy was often to visit principal places such as Troas, Athens, Corinth, and Ephesus. When the Christian faith had been planted in major centers, local Christian workers could carry it into outlying areas (e.g., Epaphras took the message from Ephesus to Colosse, Col 1:7; 4:12-13).

16:9-10 ***a vision:*** See "Visions" at 10:9-16, p. 1846.

16:10 ***we:*** The most natural interpretation of the shift from "they" to "we" is that Luke, the writer of this book, here joined Paul and accompanied him on his journey. From the "we" passages in Acts, we can infer Luke's itinerary with Paul: Luke apparently accompanied Paul from Troas to Philippi (16:10-17). Later Luke joined Paul again at Philippi and sailed with him to Troas, then to Miletus (20:5-15), then from Miletus to Jerusalem (21:1-18). After Paul's two-year imprisonment in Caesarea, Luke traveled with him to Rome (27:1–28:16).

16:12
Phil 1:1
1 Thes 2:2

16:14
Rev 1:11; 2:18, 24

16:15
[f]*baptizō* (0907)
‣Acts 19:3

16:16
Deut 18:10-11
1 Sam 28:3, 7

and the next day we landed at Neapolis.
12From there we reached Philippi, a major
city of that district of Macedonia and a Roman colony. And we stayed there several
days.

Lydia of Philippi Believes in Jesus

13On the Sabbath we went a little way
outside the city to a riverbank, where we
thought people would be meeting for prayer,
and we sat down to speak with some women
who had gathered there. 14One of them
was Lydia from Thyatira, a merchant of expensive purple cloth, who worshiped God.
As she listened to us, the Lord opened her
heart, and she accepted what Paul was saying. 15She was [f]baptized along with other
members of her household, and she asked
us to be her guests. "If you agree that I am
a true believer in the Lord," she said, "come
and stay at my home." And she urged us until we agreed.

Paul and Silas Imprisoned and Released

16One day as we were going down to the
place of prayer, we met a demon-possessed
slave girl. She was a fortune-teller who
earned a lot of money for her masters. 17She

LUKE (16:10)

Acts 1:1
Luke 1:3
Col 4:14
2 Tim 4:11
Phlm 1:24

Luke, a Gentile medical doctor who became a convert and trusted assistant of Paul in his missionary work, wrote both the Gospel of Luke and the Acts of the Apostles—one-quarter of the NT.

Though we know very little about Luke's background, he seems to have first encountered Paul and his preaching in western Asia Minor, where he became a convert. Leaving his home, he devoted his life to the service of Christ and the Good News as a dedicated assistant of Paul. Paul speaks of him warmly as "the beloved doctor" and one of his faithful "co-workers" (Col 4:14; Phlm 1:24). Luke is the only Christian who faithfully remained with Paul when Paul was awaiting execution in Rome (2 Tim 4:11). He is the only Gentile to have his writings included in the NT.

Accompanying Paul on his last trip to Jerusalem, Luke probably acquired the information for his Gospel and the early part of the book of Acts from people he interviewed in Judea when Paul was imprisoned there for two years. Having talked extensively with people who heard and saw Jesus, and having carefully studied what others had written about him, Luke then wrote his own careful account of Jesus' life and teachings (see Luke 1:1-4).

When Paul was sent by ship to Rome to have his case tried there, Luke accompanied him. While Paul was under house arrest, awaiting his trial, Luke might have used the time to write the book of Acts. The first fifteen chapters provide a chronological account of the earliest missionary work as told to him by the early followers of Christ and by Paul himself. But beginning in Acts 16:10—the point at which Luke joined Paul's team—he provides a direct eyewitness account. Acts emphasizes the way the Holy Spirit empowered and guided the early missionaries in their witness (1:4-5, 8) and ends with Paul still under house arrest in Rome (28:30-31).

We are indebted to Luke for many unique passages: his full account of Jesus' birth, descriptions of Jesus' ministry to women, many words about Jesus caring for the poor, and the only comprehensive account of the first thirty years of missionary activity—all carefully documented. Through Luke's writings we gain a much deeper appreciation of the crucial work of the Holy Spirit in the ministry of Jesus and the early missionaries.

16:11 *Samothrace* is a small mountainous *island* lying west-northwest of the Hellespont about twenty miles (32 km) from the coast of Thrace. • *Neapolis* (modern Kavala) was the seaport for Philippi and the eastern terminus of the famous *Via Egnatia* (the Egnatian Way), which ran from Rome to Asia.

16:12 At *Philippi,* about ten miles (17 km) inland from Neapolis, Paul began his missionary labors in Europe.

16:13-36 Luke gives his readers cameos of three lives touched by the Good News in Philippi: a wealthy woman (16:14-15), an exploited slave girl (16:16-21), and a middle-class officer (16:23-36).

16:13 The Jewish community at Philippi was too small to have a synagogue, which required ten adult males. Instead, Jews met *for prayer* in an open space by the Gangites (now called Angista) River that afforded privacy, quiet, and water for Jewish purification rites.

16:14-15 The first person changed by Christ in Philippi was *Lydia,* a successful businesswoman *from Thyatira* (modern Akhisar), a city of western Asia Minor famous for its woolen fabrics, weavers, and linens. Lydia responded to the message and *was baptized along with other members of her household* (cp. 16:32-33). • One of Lydia's first acts as a *true believer in the Lord* was to extend hospitality to the visiting missionaries. Hospitality is an important Christian virtue (Matt 25:31-46; Rom 12:13; 16:23; 1 Tim 3:2; Titus 1:8; Heb 13:2; 1 Pet 4:9; 3 Jn 1:5-8; cp. Gen 18:1-8; 19:1-3; 24:23-33).

16:16-18 The second portrait of a changed life in Philippi is of a *demon-possessed slave girl . . . a fortune-teller.*

followed Paul and the rest of us, shouting,
"These men are servants of the Most High
God, and they have come to tell you how to
be saved."
18 This went on day after day until Paul got
so exasperated that he turned and said to
the demon within her, "I command you in
the name of Jesus Christ to come out of her."
And instantly it left her.
19 Her masters' hopes of wealth were now
shattered, so they grabbed Paul and Silas
and dragged them before the authorities
at the marketplace. 20 "The whole city is
in an uproar because of these Jews!" they
shouted to the city officials. 21 "They are
teaching customs that are illegal for us Romans to practice."
22 A mob quickly formed against Paul and
Silas, and the city officials ordered them
stripped and beaten with wooden rods.
23 They were severely beaten, and then they
were thrown into prison. The jailer was ordered to make sure they didn't escape. 24 So
the jailer put them into the inner dungeon
and clamped their feet in the stocks.
25 Around midnight Paul and Silas were
praying and singing hymns to God, and the
other prisoners were listening. 26 Suddenly,
there was a massive earthquake, and the
prison was shaken to its foundations. All
the doors immediately flew open, and the
chains of every prisoner fell off! 27 The jailer
woke up to see the prison doors wide open.
He assumed the prisoners had escaped, so
he drew his sword to kill himself. 28 But Paul
shouted to him, "Stop! Don't kill yourself!
We are all here!"
29 The jailer called for lights and ran to
the dungeon and fell down trembling before Paul and Silas. 30 Then he brought them
out and asked, "Sirs, what must I do to be
saved?"
31 They replied, "Believe in the [g]Lord Jesus
and you will be saved, along with everyone
in your household." 32 And they shared the
word of the Lord with him and with all who
lived in his household. 33 Even at that hour
of the night, the jailer cared for them and
washed their wounds. Then he and everyone in his household were immediately
baptized. 34 He brought them into his house
and set a meal before them, and he and his
entire household rejoiced because they all
believed in God.
35 The next morning the city officials
sent the police to tell the jailer, "Let those
men go!" 36 So the jailer told Paul, "The city
officials have said you and Silas are free to
leave. Go in peace."
37 But Paul replied, "They have publicly
beaten us without a trial and put us in
prison—and we are Roman citizens. So now
they want us to leave secretly? Certainly not!
Let them come themselves to release us!"
38 When the police reported this, the city
officials were alarmed to learn that Paul

16:18 Mark 16:17; Acts 19:13
16:20 Acts 17:6
16:21 Esth 3:8
16:22 2 Cor 11:25; 1 Thes 2:2
16:25 Eph 5:19
16:26 Acts 5:19; 12:10
16:27 Acts 12:18-19
16:30 Acts 2:37
16:31 John 3:15; Acts 11:14; [g]*kurios* (2962) ‣ Eph 6:5
16:37 Acts 22:25
16:38 Acts 22:29

• Even though the ***demon within her*** was stating the truth, Paul, like Jesus, did not permit it to proclaim the Christian message (cp. Mark 1:25, 34; 3:11-12; Luke 4:35, 41). The Lord had commanded that the gospel be proclaimed by his disciples, not by opponents (Matt 28:18-20; Luke 24:46-49; John 20:21; Acts 1:8; 9:15; 26:15-18; see 22:15).

16:19-21 As in the ministry of Jesus, sometimes the Good News threatened established commercial interests (see also 19:25-27; Mark 5:1-20). The slave girl's exploiters viciously attacked the missionaries and ***dragged them before the authorities*** as criminals, blamed them for fomenting a disturbance, resorted to racial bias (***these Jews***), and appealed to the Philippians' pride (***us Romans;*** the Philippians prided themselves on being Roman citizens of a Roman colony). • ***customs that are illegal:*** By law, Jews were not permitted to make converts of Romans.

16:22-24 All reasonable security measures were taken to ensure that Paul and Silas ***didn't escape*** after they had been ***stripped and beaten with wooden rods*** (see 22:24-26; 2 Cor 6:5; 11:23-25). As at Christ's tomb (Matt 27:65), however, human effort did not prevent divine intervention.

16:25 ***Paul and Silas,*** like the persecuted apostles in Jerusalem, were joyful, "rejoicing that God had counted them worthy to suffer disgrace for the name of Jesus" (5:41).

16:26 The ***massive earthquake*** is reminiscent of the great earthquake at Jesus' resurrection (Matt 28:2-3).

16:27-36 Luke's third portrait in Philippi is of the Philippian ***jailer*** who, shaken by what had happened, responded in faith when challenged to accept ***the Lord Jesus*** and ***be saved.*** He was ***baptized*** with ***his household*** and rejoiced in his newfound faith as he reached out with hospitality to the preachers.

16:27 The Roman jailer clearly knew that his life could be forfeited if the prisoners for whom he was responsible escaped. This was standard practice (12:19; 27:42; cp. *Code of Justinian* 9.4.4).

16:29-30 ***Paul and Silas*** had impressed ***the jailer*** with their cheerful faith (16:25), their composure in crisis, and their concern for his well-being (16:28). Whatever the jailer's previous understanding of Paul's message, God touched his heart, and he cried out for divine help.

16:31-34 Paul and Silas directed the jailer to a faith in Christ that brings blessing both to him and his family. The whole household received Christian instruction, and their response was expressed in baptism (see "Baptism" at 2:38, 41, p. 1828) and the offering of hospitality to Paul and Silas.

16:37-39 Paul and Silas were both ***Roman citizens,*** so the beating and imprisonment (16:22-24) had been illegal. After the city officials learned of this, they were justifiably alarmed because they had committed a crime against Rome. • ***Let them come themselves to release us:*** Paul made use of his rights as a Roman citizen in order to clear his name and ensure that no disrepute would attach to the Christian message or those who accepted it. Luke intended to show that Christianity should enjoy the same status as Judaism in the Roman empire as a permitted religion—

16:39 Matt 8:34
16:40 Acts 16:14
17:1-9 1 Thes 1:1; 2:1-2; 2 Thes 1:1
17:2 Acts 9:20; 13:14; 17:10, 17
17:3 Luke 24:26; Acts 3:18; 9:22; 18:5
17:5 Rom 16:21; 1 Thes 2:14
17:6 Acts 16:20, 21
17:7 Luke 23:2; John 19:12
17:11 John 5:39
17:13 Acts 14:19
17:14 Matt 10:23
17:15 Acts 18:5; 1 Thes 3:1

and Silas were Roman citizens. 39So they came to the jail and apologized to them. Then they brought them out and begged them to leave the city. 40When Paul and Silas left the prison, they returned to the home of Lydia. There they met with the believers and encouraged them once more. Then they left town.

Paul Preaches in Thessalonica

17 Paul and Silas then traveled through the towns of Amphipolis and Apollonia and came to Thessalonica, where there was a Jewish synagogue. 2As was Paul's custom, he went to the synagogue service, and for three Sabbaths in a row he used the Scriptures to reason with the people. 3He explained the prophecies and proved that the Messiah must suffer and rise from the dead. He said, "This Jesus I'm telling you about is the Messiah." 4Some of the Jews who listened were persuaded and joined Paul and Silas, along with many God-fearing Greek men and quite a few prominent women.

5But some of the Jews were jealous, so they gathered some troublemakers from the marketplace to form a mob and start a riot. They attacked the home of Jason, searching for Paul and Silas so they could drag them out to the crowd. 6Not finding them there, they dragged out Jason and some of the other believers instead and took them before the city council. "Paul and Silas have caused trouble all over the world," they shouted, "and now they are here disturbing our city, too. 7And Jason has welcomed them into his home. They are all guilty of treason against Caesar, for they profess allegiance to another king, named Jesus."

8The people of the city, as well as the city council, were thrown into turmoil by these reports. 9So the officials forced Jason and the other believers to post bond, and then they released them.

Paul and Silas in Berea

10That very night the believers sent Paul and Silas to Berea. When they arrived there, they went to the Jewish synagogue. 11And the people of Berea were more open-minded than those in Thessalonica, and they listened eagerly to Paul's message. They searched the Scriptures day after day to see if Paul and Silas were teaching the truth. 12As a result, many Jews believed, as did many of the prominent Greek women and men.

13But when some Jews in Thessalonica learned that Paul was preaching the word of God in Berea, they went there and stirred up trouble. 14The believers acted at once, sending Paul on to the coast, while Silas and Timothy remained behind. 15Those escorting Paul went with him all the way to Athens; then they returned to Berea with instructions for Silas and Timothy to hurry and join him.

Paul Preaches in Athens

16While Paul was waiting for them in Athens, he was deeply troubled by all the idols

---

the Christian faith was compatible with the life of a Roman citizen. Accordingly, it was important to note that Paul made use of his rights as a Roman citizen (cp. 22:25-27) and was ready to use the privileges of citizenship to advance the cause of Christ in a hostile world.

16:40 This meeting in ***the home of Lydia*** bolstered the spirits of the Philippian Christians who had to deal with the fallout from the missionaries' work there.

17:1-9 After traveling through Macedonia to ***Thessalonica,*** Paul preached to the Jews first (Rom 1:16) in the synagogue. Here, as elsewhere, there was a mixed response.

17:1-3 ***Amphipolis*** was a Roman military post located on the Egnatian Way in the northeastern part of Macedonia. • ***Apollonia,*** named after the Greek god Apollo, was also situated on the Egnatian Way. • ***Thessalonica*** offered a starting point for ministry because it had ***a Jewish synagogue*** (see note on 9:2). Paul was able to preach for ***three*** consecutive ***Sabbaths,*** explaining ***the Scriptures*** and showing their fulfillment in Jesus.

17:4 ***God-fearing Greek men:*** See note on 10:2. • ***quite a few prominent women*** (some manuscripts read *quite a few of the wives of the leading men*): Luke regularly draws attention to women who joined the Christian movement (17:4, 12, 34; see also 5:14; 8:12; 16:13-15, 31-34; 18:26; 21:9).

17:5-7 Once again, the enemies of the Christian faith saw it as a disruptive threat (cp. 16:19-21). Ironically, ***they gathered some troublemakers*** and then accused Paul and Silas of causing ***trouble*** by disturbing the peace and committing ***treason against Caesar***—serious charges of threatening the stability of the empire (cp. Luke 23:2).

17:5 ***the crowd:*** Or *the city council.*

17:6 ***other believers:*** Literally *brothers;* also in 17:10, 14.

17:8-9 The charges did not hold up under scrutiny, so the officials ***released*** Paul and Silas after ***Jason and the other believers*** posted ***bond.*** Christianity, Luke contended, was politically harmless to the Roman empire and should therefore be recognized as a permitted religion and not subjected to political attack.

17:10-12 In light of the strong opposition in Thessalonica, ***the believers sent Paul and Silas to Berea,*** located about nineteen miles (30 km) west of Thessalonica. There the missionaries had a better reception than in Thessalonica. Many Jews came to faith, as well as ***many of the prominent Greek women and men.*** The Bereans were exemplary in their attitude, for they were ***open-minded*** and eager to learn, good listeners, diligent Bible students, and thoughtful people. Their resulting faith had a strong foundation.

17:13-15 Paul acknowledged the determination and persistence of this persecution when he wrote to the Thessalonians (1 Thes 2:14-16).

17:16-34 In this chapter, we see Paul presented as a model witness for Christ, engaging the thinkers of his day and challenging them with the Christian message. Paul quoted writers his

he saw everywhere in the city. 17He went to the synagogue to reason with the Jews and the God-fearing Gentiles, and he spoke daily in the public square to all who happened to be there.

18He also had a debate with some of the Epicurean and Stoic philosophers. When he told them about Jesus and his resurrection, they said, "What's this babbler trying to say with these strange ideas he's picked up?" Others said, "He seems to be preaching about some foreign gods."

19Then they took him to the high council of the city. "Come and tell us about this new teaching," they said. 20"You are saying some rather strange things, and we want to know what it's all about." 21(It should be explained that all the Athenians as well as the foreigners in Athens seemed to spend all their time discussing the latest ideas.)

22So Paul, standing before the council, addressed them as follows: "Men of Athens, I notice that you are very religious in every way, 23for as I was walking along I saw your many shrines. And one of your altars had this inscription on it: 'To an Unknown God.' This God, whom you worship without knowing, is the one I'm telling you about.

24"He is the God who made the world and everything in it. Since he is Lord of heaven and earth, he doesn't live in man-made temples, 25and human hands can't serve his needs—for he has no needs. He himself gives life and breath to everything, and he satisfies every need. 26From one man he created all the nations throughout the whole earth. He decided beforehand when they should rise and fall, and he determined their boundaries.

27"His purpose was for the nations to seek after God and perhaps feel their way toward him and find him—though he is not far from any one of us. 28For in him we live and move and exist. As some of your own poets have said, 'We are his offspring.' 29And since this is true, we shouldn't think of God as an idol designed by craftsmen from gold or silver or stone.

30"God overlooked people's ignorance about these things in earlier times, but now

17:17 Acts 18:19
17:18 1 Cor 1:22
17:23 John 4:22
17:24 1 Kgs 8:27; Isa 42:5; Acts 7:48
17:25 Ps 50:12; Isa 42:5
17:26 Deut 32:8
17:27 Isa 55:6; Jer 23:23-24
17:29 Isa 40:18-25; Rom 1:23
17:30 Acts 14:16

audience would be familiar with and showed the relevance of the gospel by dialoguing with them, critiquing their assumptions, and offering Jesus as a constructive alternative (see Col 1:28). Paul reminded these proud intellectuals that there is a living God to whom all human beings are answerable; that they will be judged by him through Jesus, whom God raised from the dead; and that they should therefore repent and put their faith in Jesus.

17:16-17 ***Athens,*** like Alexandria and Tarsus, prided itself on its intellectual sophistication in examining ideas and considering the different philosophies that were current at the time.

17:18 ***Epicurean . . . philosophers:*** Epicureanism was a popular school of Greek philosophy, founded by Epicurus (341–270 BC). Epicureans believed that the principal aim of life was to secure happiness. They thought of pleasure not in terms of sensual indulgence, as their critics charged, but in terms of tranquility. Their contemporaries often called them atheists; in their view, there were no gods to fear, and death simply marked the end of human existence. They sought their security in organized communities where they could live in contentment apart from society. • ***Stoic philosophers:*** Stoicism was founded by Zeno of Citium (335–263 BC) and became the most influential philosophy in the Greco-Roman world. It viewed the universe as permeated by Reason (sometimes referred to as God or Providence). Stoicism saw divine Reason as expressed in human reason and held that as humans made progress, they could advance from ignorance (the source of vice) to true knowledge (the source of virtue). They developed extensive lists of virtues and vices and produced detailed household codes to guide family behavior. Paul's teaching resembles that of the Stoics in his use of household codes and lists of virtues and vices (Gal 5:19-23; Eph 5:22-33; Col 3:18–4:1; 1 Tim 3:1-13; 5:1–6:1). However, Paul's message of Good News—focusing on the life, death, and ***resurrection*** of Jesus Christ—was ***strange*** and ***foreign*** to these Greek philosophers. • The air of superiority with which they addressed Paul as ***this babbler*** indicates their arrogance.

17:19 ***the high council of the city:*** Or *the most learned society of philosophers in the city.* Greek reads *the Areopagus.*

17:22-31 Paul's remarkable sermon in Athens reveals his versatility in preaching the Good News (Rom 11:14; 1 Cor 9:19-23; 10:33; cp. Acts 16:3; 17:2-3; 21:20-26). While Paul's Greek audience did not know the Scriptures or have a tradition of monotheism as the Jews did, they did have a rich intellectual heritage. So Paul established a point of contact on the basis of an Athenian inscription to an ***Unknown God.*** He then explained God's nature as the Creator (17:22-29), followed by God's purpose as the Redeemer (17:30-31). • As he did elsewhere in his own writings (see 1 Cor 15:33; Titus 1:12), Paul made use of the Greek poets. There are several points of connection in this sermon with the *Hymn to Zeus* by Cleanthes (about 315–240 BC). Paul was probably quoting Epimenides, who had declared about God, ***"In him we live and move and exist"*** (Epimenides, *Cretica,* about 600 BC). Paul also cited Aratus, a Stoic poet from Cilicia (about 315–240 BC), who had commented, ***"We are his offspring"*** (Aratus, *Phaenomena* 5). These allusions to their ***own poets*** established connections with his audience. Paul was then able to present the singular nature of God (17:29), and he stressed the coming judgment through Jesus Christ, whom God had raised from the dead. This message, while touching on Greek culture and philosophy, had a clear focus on Christ that presented the challenge of Christ to a cultured and intellectual but idolatrous people.

17:22 ***standing before the council:*** Traditionally rendered *standing in the middle of Mars Hill;* Greek reads *standing in the middle of the Areopagus.*

17:26 ***From one man:*** Literally *From one;* other manuscripts read *From one blood.*

17:28 ***some of your:*** Some manuscripts read *some of our.*

17:30 The idea of ***people's ignorance*** is carefully discussed both in the OT law (Lev 4:2, 22, 27; 5:15, 17; Num 15:25, 27) and in the NT (Eph 4:18; 1 Pet 1:14; 2:15; 2 Pet 3:5, 8). Paul was particularly fervent to overcome ignorance (see Rom 10:13-15; 11:25; 1 Cor 10:1; 12:1; 2 Cor 1:8; 1 Thes 4:13). The message of Good News overcomes ignorance and summons all who hear it to ***repent of their sins and turn to*** God (see 2:38).

17:31
Ps 96:13
Acts 10:42

17:32
[h]*anastasis* (0386)
‣1 Cor 15:12

18:2
Rom 16:3
1 Cor 16:19

18:3
Acts 20:34
1 Cor 4:12; 9:15
1 Thes 2:9

he commands everyone everywhere to
repent of their sins and turn to him. 31For
he has set a day for judging the world with
justice by the man he has appointed, and he
proved to everyone who this is by raising
him from the dead."
32When they heard Paul speak about the
[h]resurrection of the dead, some laughed in
contempt, but others said, "We want to hear
more about this later." 33That ended Paul's
discussion with them, 34but some joined him
and became believers. Among them were
Dionysius, a member of the council, a woman
named Damaris, and others with them.

Paul in Corinth

18 Then Paul left Athens and went to Corinth. 2There he became acquainted
with a Jew named Aquila, born in Pontus,
who had recently arrived from Italy with his
wife, Priscilla. They had left Italy when Claudius Caesar deported all Jews from Rome.
3Paul lived and worked with them, for they
were tentmakers just as he was.

PRISCILLA AND AQUILA (18:1-3)

Acts 18:18-19, 24-28
Rom 16:3-5
1 Cor 16:19
2 Tim 4:19

Priscilla and Aquila were a Christian couple with whom Paul lived and worked during his early days in Corinth. They were later active in Christian ministry and instrumental in bringing Apollos to a true understanding of Christ. They made a habit of opening their home in hospitality to other Christians.

Paul first met Priscilla and Aquila in Corinth, where they had newly arrived as a result of Claudius Caesar's deportation of all Jews from Rome (AD 49). Paul became acquainted with them and, because they were tentmakers (or possibly leatherworkers) like he was, Paul lived and worked with them during his first year and a half in Corinth (AD 50–52; Acts 18:1-3).

When Paul left Corinth, he took Priscilla and Aquila with him and left them in Ephesus (18:18-19) while he returned to Jerusalem and Antioch. When Apollos came through Ephesus later, enthusiastically preaching about Jesus in the synagogues, Priscilla and Aquila took him aside and explained to him more fully the truth of Christ. As a result of their training, Apollos went on to become a powerful evangelist and Christian apologist (18:24-28).

Later, Paul speaks of their home as a meeting place for Christians in Ephesus, and he sends their greeting with his own to the church in Corinth (1 Cor 16:19; cp. 2 Tim 4:19). Still later, it seems they returned to Rome (presumably after the relaxation of Claudius's edict), for they are the first of many to whom Paul sends his greetings when he writes to the church in Rome (Rom 16:3-5). Here, too, their home became a meeting place. It is clear that Paul felt a close bond of friendship with them and that he regarded their work for Christ highly—he speaks of them as "my co-workers in the ministry of Christ," and he refers to a time when they even risked their lives for him.

Priscilla and Aquila are examples of early Christians who, in the course of their daily work, were bold in bearing witness to Christ and active in ministering to his people—in this case, as a married couple dedicated to the service of Christ. The fact that Priscilla's name often occurs first (unusual for the time) might say something about the strong role she played in the couple's witness and ministry.

17:32 The Athenians listened carefully until ***Paul*** spoke of ***the resurrection of the dead*** (17:31); at that point some ***laughed*** or mocked, for the notion of resurrection was foolish to Greek ears (see 1 Cor 15:12-19). Similarly, the Jews in Jerusalem later listened carefully to Paul until he mentioned God's acceptance of the Gentiles (22:22). These are examples of how the message of Good News can offend people because of their prejudices (see 1 Cor 1:20-25).

17:34 ***some joined him and became believers:*** Paul's sermon was not without positive response. Two prominent converts are mentioned: ***Dionysius*** and ***Damaris.*** Luke often placed a man and a woman in juxtaposition (e.g., 5:1-11; 17:4, 12; Luke 14:1-6; 15:3-10). • Dionysius was ***a member of the council*** (Greek *an Areopagite*), the highest governing body of Athens.

18:1-17 Paul spent eighteen fruitful months preaching and teaching in ***Corinth,*** first in the synagogue and then ***next door*** in the house of ***Titius Justus*** (18:1-11). Then, in court, Paul won a significant victory over his enemies (18:12-17).

18:1 ***Athens*** and ***Corinth*** were major cities in Achaia, the region in the southern portion of the Greek peninsula. In Roman times, Greek political power in Achaia resided in ***Corinth,*** a prominent city-state and major commercial city. Corinth was notorious for its prostitution, immorality, and drunkenness (see 1 Corinthians Introduction, "Setting," p. 1924). Paul invested much time and effort establishing a Christian community in Corinth (see note on 16:8).

18:2-3 ***Aquila*** and ***Priscilla*** became an outstanding husband-and-wife team in the early church (see "Priscilla and Aquila," above). • The edict of ***Claudius Caesar*** that had ***deported all Jews from Rome*** around AD 49 is mentioned by the Roman historian Suetonius (*Life of Claudius* 25). • They earned their living as ***tentmakers*** (or ***leatherworkers***), as did Paul, who probably ***lived and worked with them*** during his year and a half in Corinth (18:11; see Rom 16:3-4; 1 Cor 16:19). • ***just as he was:*** Paul would have been trained as a tentmaker as a young man. It was Jewish custom to provide sons with a manual trade, including young men who intended to become rabbis or other professionals.

[4]Each Sabbath found Paul at the synagogue, trying to convince the Jews and
Greeks alike. [5]And after Silas and Timothy
came down from Macedonia, Paul spent all
his time preaching the word. He testified
to the Jews that Jesus was the Messiah. [6]But
when they opposed and insulted him, Paul
shook the dust from his clothes and said,
"Your blood is upon your own heads—I am
innocent. From now on I will go preach to
the Gentiles."
[7]Then he left and went to the home
of Titius Justus, a Gentile who worshiped
God and lived next door to the synagogue.
[8]Crispus, the leader of the synagogue, and
everyone in his household [i]believed in the
Lord. Many others in Corinth also heard
Paul, became [i]believers, and were baptized.
[9]One night the Lord spoke to Paul in a vision and told him, "Don't be afraid! Speak
out! Don't be silent! [10]For I am with you, and
no one will attack and harm you, for many
people in this city belong to me." [11]So Paul
stayed there for the next year and a half,
teaching the word of God.
[12]But when Gallio became governor of
Achaia, some Jews rose up together against
Paul and brought him before the governor
for judgment. [13]They accused Paul of "persuading people to worship God in ways that
are contrary to our law."
[14]But just as Paul started to make his
defense, Gallio turned to Paul's accusers
and said, "Listen, you Jews, if this were a
case involving some wrongdoing or a serious crime, I would have a reason to accept
your case. [15]But since it is merely a question
of words and names and your Jewish law,
take care of it yourselves. I refuse to judge
such matters." [16]And he threw them out of
the courtroom.
[17]The crowd then grabbed Sosthenes, the
leader of the synagogue, and beat him right
there in the courtroom. But Gallio paid no
attention.

Paul Visits Ephesus and Returns to Antioch

[18]Paul stayed in Corinth for some time after
that, then said good-bye to the brothers and
sisters and went to nearby Cenchrea. There
he shaved his head according to Jewish custom, marking the end of a vow. Then he set
sail for Syria, taking Priscilla and Aquila
with him.
[19]They stopped first at the port of Ephesus, where Paul left the others behind.
While he was there, he went to the synagogue to reason with the Jews. [20]They asked
him to stay longer, but he declined. [21]As
he left, however, he said, "I will come back
later, God willing." Then he set sail from
Ephesus. [22]The next stop was at the port of
Caesarea. From there he went up and visited

18:5 Acts 17:3; 18:28
18:6 Ezek 33:3-9; Matt 10:14; Acts 13:45-46; 20:26
18:8 1 Cor 1:14; [i]*pisteuō* (4100) ›Rom 1:17
18:9-10 Isa 41:10; Jer 1:18
18:15 John 18:31
18:17 Acts 18:8; 1 Cor 1:1
18:18 Num 6:18; Acts 21:24; Rom 16:1
18:19 Eph 1:1; Rev 1:11; 2:1
18:21 Jas 4:15
18:22 Acts 8:40; 11:19

18:4-6 Once again Paul followed his custom of ***preaching*** to ***the Jews*** first, and then reaching out to ***Gentiles*** after he met with rejection and opposition (13:42-49; see 3:25-26; 26:20; Rom 1:16; 2:10; 3:29, 30; 4:9-12). • Paul probably wrote his letters to the Thessalonian Christians ***after Silas and Timothy came down from Macedonia*** with a report of how things were going there (see 1 Thes 3:6; 2 Thessalonians Introduction, "Setting," p. 2040).

18:7 ***Titius Justus*** ("Titus the Just") was a ***Gentile who worshiped God*** (a "God-fearer"; see note on 10:2). Because Titus was a common Roman name, ***Justus*** differentiates him from the better-known Titus, Paul's co-worker (2 Cor 2:13; 7:6, 13; 8:6, 16, 23; Titus).

18:9-10 Paul had experienced real opposition in Corinth (18:6) and apparently was afraid of being attacked again, so the divine message was a comfort to him (cp. 23:11; Ps 34:4, 7, 19; Matt 28:20), encouraging him to persist in his public ministry and promising God's protection (cp. Ps 91:11; 2 Tim 4:17).

18:12-13 The ***governor of Achaia,*** Junio ***Gallio,*** was the older brother of the Roman philosopher Seneca (Seneca was a tutor to Emperor Nero). An inscription indicating that he was governor around AD 51–52 helps to date Paul's visit in Corinth to about that time.

18:14-17 Gallio's ruling indicated that the charges against Paul were unjustified. The Roman government had nothing to fear from acknowledging Christianity as a legal religion.

18:17 ***The crowd:*** Literally *Everyone;* other manuscripts read *All the Greeks.* • It is most likely that the Greeks beat ***Sosthenes*** to express their hostility to the Jews; it is possible that the Jews attacked their own synagogue leader because he was unsuccessful in pleading their case. Sosthenes may be the same man Paul later mentions as "our brother" (1 Cor 1:1), but it is uncertain, as the name was fairly common.

18:18 ***brothers and sisters:*** Literally *brothers;* also in 18:27. • ***Cenchrea*** was a seaport located on the Aegean Sea, roughly five miles (8 km) east of ***Corinth.*** It was here that Paul ***shaved his head according to Jewish custom*** to mark the completion of a temporary Nazirite *vow* (cp. 21:23-24; see Num 6:1-21; Judg 13:4-7; 16:1; Amos 2:11-12; Luke 1:15).

18:19-23 Paul made a quick stop at ***Ephesus,*** the most important city in the Roman province of Asia. There he ***left the others behind,*** including Priscilla and Aquila (18:26). He sailed to Judea, landing at ***Caesarea,*** the headquarters of the Roman forces of occupation. After a visit to ***the church at Jerusalem,*** Paul returned to ***Antioch,*** the church that had originally commissioned him. This marked the end of his second missionary journey. In Antioch, he spent a rewarding time of reporting what God had done through him and his colleagues, sharing the excitement and challenges of their work with the home church. Then ***after . . . some time,*** Paul began his third missionary journey. He went by land rather than by sea, traveling ***through Galatia and Phrygia*** and revisiting ***believers*** whom he had led to faith in Christ on his previous trips. It was important to him that these young converts not be left to founder and shipwreck their faith (see Eph 6:10-20; 1 Tim 1:18-20; 2 Tim 1:15; 4:10).

18:21 ***"I will come back later"*** (Some manuscripts read *"I must by all means be at Jerusalem for the upcoming festival, but I will come back later"*): Paul later spent significant time in Ephesus during his third missionary journey (19:1–20:1; see 19:8, 10).

18:23 Acts 16:6
18:24 Acts 19:1; 1 Cor 1:12; 4:6; 16:12; Titus 3:13
18:25 Acts 19:3
18:27 2 Cor 3:1
18:28 Acts 9:22

the church at Jerusalem and then went back to Antioch.

Paul's Third Missionary Journey from Antioch (18:23–21:17)

Paul Visits the Churches in Galatia and Phrygia

23After spending some time in Antioch,
Paul went back through Galatia and Phrygia, visiting and strengthening all the believers.

Apollos in Ephesus and Corinth

24Meanwhile, a Jew named Apollos, an eloquent speaker who knew the Scriptures well, had arrived in Ephesus from Alexandria in Egypt.
25He had been taught the way of the Lord, and he taught others about Jesus with an enthusiastic spirit and with accuracy. However, he knew only about John's baptism.
26When Priscilla and Aquila heard him preaching boldly in the synagogue, they took him aside and explained the way of God even more accurately.

27Apollos had been thinking about going to Achaia, and the brothers and sisters in Ephesus encouraged him to go. They wrote to the believers in Achaia, asking them to welcome him. When he arrived there, he proved to be of great benefit to those who, by God's grace, had believed.
28He refuted the Jews with powerful arguments in public debate. Using the Scriptures, he explained to them that Jesus was the Messiah.

APOLLOS (18:24–19:1)

1 Cor 1:10-12; 3:3-9; 4:1, 6-7; 16:12; 2 Cor 10:10; Titus 3:13

Apollos was a Hellenistic (Greek-speaking) Jew, well versed in Scripture, who became a strong evangelist and Christian apologist. A native of Alexandria in Egypt, where there was a large Jewish community, Apollos apparently came under the influence of John the Baptist's followers. He then became a bold and enthusiastic preacher of Jesus in Hellenistic synagogues, though he knew nothing of Christian baptism.

When Priscilla and Aquila heard Apollos preach in Ephesus, they invited him to their home and explained the way of Christ to him more fully. With the encouragement of the believers in Ephesus, who recognized his God-given gifts and ministry, Apollos then traveled on to Achaia (i.e., Corinth). There he greatly helped the believers as an effective defender of the Good News in public debate with the Jews, boldly demonstrating that Jesus is the Messiah predicted in Scripture (18:24-28).

A dynamic communicator, Apollos was popular with some of the Christians in Corinth because of his intellectual style and his powerful speaking abilities. As a result of his powerful ministry, some in Corinth were more drawn to Apollos than to Paul (1 Cor 1:11-12). When they began to criticize Paul for not matching up to Apollos (cp. 2 Cor 10:10), Paul was forced to defend himself and his simpler, unimpressive way of preaching the Good News. Significantly, Paul nowhere criticized Apollos himself. He called Apollos a fellow servant and was grateful for the follow-up work he had done—Apollos watered the seed that Paul had planted, and God blessed the work of both (1 Cor 3:5-9; 4:1). Paul only criticized the shallow perspectives and divisiveness of those drawn to Apollos for superficial reasons (1 Cor 1:10-12; 3:3-4; 4:6-7).

Perhaps Apollos's reluctance to return to Corinth from Ephesus (1 Cor 16:12) was due to concern over the divisions that resulted from his ministry. Yet Paul encouraged him. Several years later, when Apollos was ministering on the island of Crete, Paul encouraged Titus to make sure Apollos's needs were met as he set off to an unknown destination for further missionary service (Titus 3:13). Apollos, with his strong intellectual gifts and powerful speaking abilities, had a significantly different approach and style from that of Paul—yet both men proved effective and useful in the service of Christ.

18:22 ***the church at Jerusalem:*** Literally *the church.*

18:23–19:41 This section describes Paul's third missionary journey (about AD 53–57). Paul revisited Galatia and Phrygia, strengthening the disciples (18:23). He then traveled to Ephesus (19:1), where he remained for two years (19:10).

18:23 Paul wanted to keep in touch with earlier converts and strengthen their faith. • ***believers:*** Literally *disciples;* also in 18:27.

18:24-26 ***Apollos:*** See "Apollos," above. • ***Alexandria,*** the second-largest city in the Roman empire, was famous for its rhetorical tradition and the philosophical work of Philo. Apollos was ***an eloquent speaker*** with an excellent knowledge of ***the Scriptures*** (the OT). His knowledge about Jesus and the Holy Spirit was inadequate, though. He did not understand that believers could experience and enjoy the power of the Holy Spirit as a present energizing reality. Fortunately, ***Priscilla and Aquila*** took him aside and corrected his spiritual understanding.

18:25 ***with an enthusiastic spirit:*** Or *with enthusiasm in the Spirit.*

Paul's Ministry in Ephesus

19 While Apollos was in Corinth, Paul
traveled through the interior regions
until he reached Ephesus, on the coast,
where he found several believers. 2“Did you
receive the Holy Spirit when you believed?”
he asked them.

“No,” they replied, “we haven't even heard
that there is a Holy Spirit.”

3“Then what [j]baptism did you experience?” he asked.

And they replied, “The baptism of John.”

4Paul said, “John's baptism called for repentance from sin. But John himself told
the people to believe in the one who would
come later, meaning Jesus.”

5As soon as they heard this, they were baptized in the name of the Lord Jesus. 6Then
when Paul laid his hands on them, the
Holy Spirit came on them, and they spoke
in other [k]tongues and prophesied. 7There
were about twelve men in all.

8Then Paul went to the synagogue and
preached boldly for the next three months,
arguing persuasively about the Kingdom of
God. 9But some became stubborn, rejecting
his message and publicly speaking against
the Way. So Paul left the synagogue and
took the believers with him. Then he held
daily discussions at the lecture hall of Ty-
rannus. 10This went on for the next two
years, so that people throughout the province of Asia—both Jews and Greeks—heard
the word of the Lord.

11God gave Paul the power to perform
unusual miracles. 12When handkerchiefs
or aprons that had merely touched his
skin were placed on sick people, they were
healed of their diseases, and evil spirits
were expelled.

13A group of Jews was traveling from
town to town casting out evil spirits. They
tried to use the name of the Lord Jesus in
their incantation, saying, “I command you
in the name of Jesus, whom Paul preaches,
to come out!” 14Seven sons of Sceva, a leading priest, were doing this. 15But one time
when they tried it, the evil spirit replied, “I
know Jesus, and I know Paul, but who are
you?” 16Then the man with the evil spirit
leaped on them, overpowered them, and
attacked them with such violence that they
fled from the house, naked and battered.

17The story of what happened spread
quickly all through Ephesus, to Jews and
Greeks alike. A solemn fear descended on
the city, and the name of the Lord Jesus
was greatly honored. 18Many who became
believers confessed their sinful practices.
19A number of them who had been practicing sorcery brought their incantation
books and burned them at a public bonfire.
The value of the books was several million
dollars. 20So the message about the Lord
spread widely and had a powerful effect.

21Afterward Paul felt compelled by the
Spirit to go over to Macedonia and Achaia
before going to Jerusalem. “And after that,”
he said, “I must go on to Rome!” 22He sent
his two assistants, Timothy and Erastus,
ahead to Macedonia while he stayed awhile
longer in the province of Asia.

19:1 Acts 18:24
19:2 John 7:39; 20:22 Acts 8:16
19:3 Acts 18:25 [j]*baptizō* (0907) ‣Acts 22:16
19:4 Mark 1:4
19:5 Acts 8:12, 16; 10:48 Gal 3:27
19:6 Acts 2:4; 10:44, 46 [k]*glōssa* (1100) ‣Rom 14:11
19:8 Acts 28:23
19:10 Acts 20:31
19:11 Mark 16:20
19:12 Acts 5:15-16
19:13 Matt 12:27 Mark 9:38 Luke 9:49
19:15 Mark 1:24, 34 Luke 4:34, 41
19:17 Acts 5:5, 11
19:19 Deut 18:10-14
19:20 Acts 6:7; 12:24
19:21 Acts 23:11 Rom 15:25 1 Cor 16:5
19:22 Rom 16:23 2 Tim 4:20

19:1-7 ***Paul traveled*** to ***Ephesus*** after ***Apollos*** had left. Subsequently, Apollos returned to Ephesus while Paul was still working there (1 Cor 16:12). The two men had different personalities, gifts, and roles, but God worked through both of them. • Some ***believers*** (literally *disciples;* also in 19:9, 30) in Ephesus still had an inadequate understanding of the Christian faith (cp. 18:26) and did not ***receive the Holy Spirit when*** they ***believed.*** They had accepted ***John's baptism,*** which ***called for repentance from sin,*** but had not received Christian baptism, which included the gift of the Holy Spirit. When Paul had instructed them further, they were able to receive Christian baptism (19:5) and the Holy Spirit (19:6).

19:6 When Paul ***laid his hands on them*** they received the ***Holy Spirit, spoke in other tongues*** (or *in other languages*), and ***prophesied,*** thereby experiencing the same filling with God's power and presence that the disciples had received on the day of Pentecost (2:4, 11).

19:10 Paul probably wrote 1 Corinthians during this time (see 1 Corinthians Introduction, “Date and Occasion of Writing,” p. 1926).

19:11-12 Paul, like other Christian evangelists (3:1-11; 4:22; 5:12-16; 6:8; 8:6-7, 13; 9:33-42), performed ***unusual miracles.*** • ***evil spirits were expelled:*** As Jesus and Peter had done (cp. 5:16; Mark 1:21-34; Luke 4:31-37).

19:13-16 Paul's effectiveness is contrasted with the impotence of the traveling Jewish exorcists, who used ***the name of Jesus*** as though it were magical but did not have a relationship with him or the indwelling power of the Holy Spirit (cp. Matt 12:27; Mark 9:38-39; Luke 9:49-50; 11:19).

19:17-19 The contrast between Paul and the Jewish exorcists was not lost on the people of Ephesus, ***Jews and Greeks alike.*** The resulting ***fear*** caused the inhabitants to ***honor*** and respect ***the name of the Lord Jesus.*** It led many to confess and forsake ***their sinful practices,*** including ***sorcery.***

19:19 ***several million dollars:*** Literally *50,000 pieces of silver,* each of which was the equivalent of a day's wage.

19:20 Luke's summary of the success of the Good News in Ephesus is short but pungent (cp. 2:43-47; 5:14; 6:7; 9:31; 12:24; 16:5; see Rom 1:16). When the Christian faith overcame problems of internal dissension, idolatry, and pagan practices, it ***spread widely*** and grew rapidly.

19:21-22 ***felt compelled by the Spirit:*** Or *decided in his spirit.* No doubt Paul was troubled by what he had heard about the situation in Corinth (see 1 Corinthians Introduction, p. 1926). Instead of going immediately himself, ***he sent . . . Timothy,*** who was carrying a letter, 1 Corinthians, from Paul to the Corinthians (1 Cor 4:17; 16:10-11). Paul himself did ***go over to Macedonia and Achaia*** not long afterward (20:1-3). • ***“I must go on to Rome!”:*** Perhaps compelled by his proven strategy (see note on 16:8), Paul wanted to proclaim the Good News in the most significant city in the world.

19:23
2 Cor 1:8
19:24
Acts 16:16
19:26
Ps 115:4
Isa 44:10-20
Jer 10:3-5
Acts 17:29
1 Cor 8:4
19:28
Acts 18:19
19:29
Acts 20:4
Rom 16:23
1 Cor 1:14
Col 4:10
Phlm 1:24
19:32
Acts 21:34
19:33
1 Tim 1:20
[a]*apologeomai* (0626)
‣ Acts 22:1

The Riot in Ephesus

23About that time, serious trouble developed in Ephesus concerning the Way. 24It
began with Demetrius, a silversmith who
had a large business manufacturing silver
shrines of the Greek goddess Artemis. He
kept many craftsmen busy. 25He called them
together, along with others employed in similar trades, and addressed them as follows:

"Gentlemen, you know that our wealth
comes from this business. 26But as you have
seen and heard, this man Paul has persuaded
many people that handmade gods aren't
really gods at all. And he's done this not only
here in Ephesus but throughout the entire
province! 27Of course, I'm not just talking
about the loss of public respect for our business. I'm also concerned that the temple of
the great goddess Artemis will lose its influence and that Artemis—this magnificent
goddess worshiped throughout the province of Asia and all around the world—will
be robbed of her great prestige!"

28At this their anger boiled, and they
began shouting, "Great is Artemis of the
Ephesians!" 29Soon the whole city was
filled with confusion. Everyone rushed to
the amphitheater, dragging along Gaius and
Aristarchus, who were Paul's traveling companions from Macedonia. 30Paul wanted
to go in, too, but the believers wouldn't let
him. 31Some of the officials of the province,
friends of Paul, also sent a message to him,
begging him not to risk his life by entering
the amphitheater.

32Inside, the people were all shouting,
some one thing and some another. Everything was in confusion. In fact, most of them
didn't even know why they were there. 33The
Jews in the crowd pushed Alexander forward
and told him to explain the situation. He motioned for silence and tried to [a]speak. 34But
when the crowd realized he was a Jew, they
started shouting again and kept it up for
about two hours: "Great is Artemis of the Ephesians! Great is Artemis of the Ephesians!"

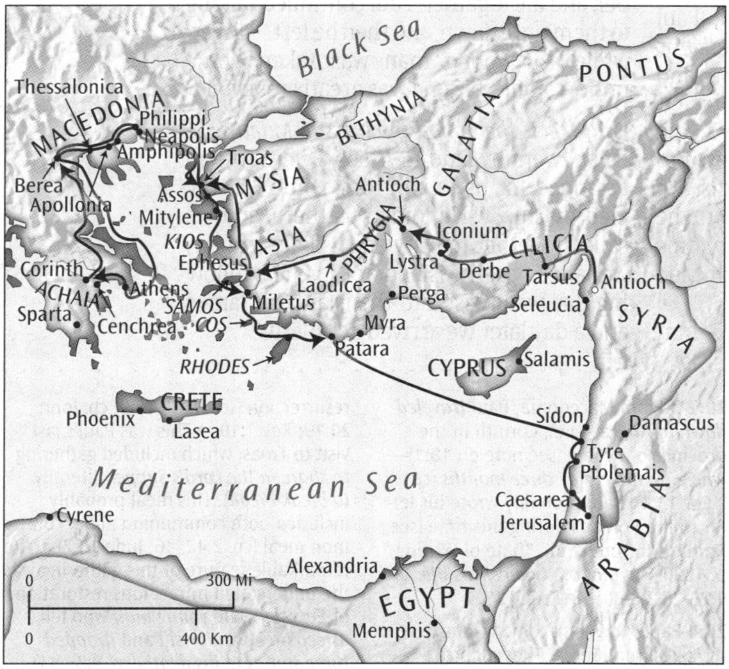

◂ **Paul's Third Missionary Journey, AD 53–57 (18:23–21:17).** Not long after finishing his second journey (18:22), Paul set out once again from ANTIOCH and traveled through GALATIA and PHRYGIA, "strengthening all the believers" (18:23). This time, however, he was able to go to EPHESUS, where he established the church and stayed for approximately three years (19:1–20:1). After traveling through MACEDONIA (20:1-2), Paul visited CORINTH for three months (20:2-3), then traveled back through Macedonia and TROAS (20:3-12). He visited the elders of Ephesus at MILETUS (20:16-38), and then sailed to TYRE (21:1-3) on his way to JERUSALEM, where he expected to be arrested (20:4-17).

19:23-41 The patron deity of *Ephesus* was ***the Greek goddess Artemis*** (otherwise known as Diana). Her birthplace was believed to be Ephesus, so Ephesus was the ***official guardian of the temple***. Twice annually, elaborate festivals were held in her honor with athletic, musical, and theatrical celebrations that included singing ***Great is Artemis of the Ephesians!*** The temple of Artemis at Ephesus was one of the seven wonders of the ancient world. Conversions to Christianity clearly damaged the worship of Artemis and the associated economic activity, but it became clear that Paul and his associates had committed no crime.

19:23 ***the Way:*** See note on 9:2.

19:24-34 ***Demetrius, a silversmith*** whose ***business*** was threatened by Paul's proclaiming faith in one God, whipped up a major riot against him.

19:24 ***Silver*** coins and ***shrines*** carrying the image of ***Artemis*** were minted in Ephesus; statuettes of the goddess were used in civic processions and are still sold there today.

19:27 ***all around the world:*** The ancient geographer Strabo reports that temples dedicated to Artemis existed in cities from Asia Minor (now Turkey) to what is now France and Spain (Strabo, *Geography* 3.4.8; 4.1.4).

19:29 Archaeologists have excavated the ***amphitheater*** where ***the whole city*** assembled; it held 24,000 people.

19:31 ***Some of the officials of the province*** (Greek *Asiarchai*, "rulers of Asia"): The "Asiarchs" were the appointed leaders in the Roman province of Asia. They served as civic benefactors and usually championed the emperor cult. Some of these officials in high places were ***friends of Paul***—Luke highlights that Christianity was attractive to people of high standing in society.

35At last the mayor was able to quiet
them down enough to speak. "Citizens of
Ephesus," he said. "Everyone knows that
Ephesus is the official guardian of the temple of the great Artemis, whose image fell
down to us from heaven. 36Since this is an
undeniable fact, you should stay calm and
not do anything rash. 37You have brought
these men here, but they have stolen nothing from the temple and have not spoken
against our goddess.
38"If Demetrius and the craftsmen have
a case against them, the courts are in session and the officials can hear the case at
once. Let them make formal charges. 39And
if there are complaints about other matters,
they can be settled in a legal assembly. 40I
am afraid we are in danger of being charged
with rioting by the Roman government,
since there is no cause for all this commotion. And if Rome demands an explanation,
we won't know what to say." 41Then he dismissed them, and they dispersed.

Paul Goes to Macedonia and Greece

20 When the uproar was over, Paul
sent for the believers and encouraged them. Then he said good-bye and
left for Macedonia. 2While there, he encouraged the believers in all the towns he
passed through. Then he traveled down to
Greece, 3where he stayed for months. He
was preparing to sail back to Syria when he
discovered a plot by some Jews against his
life, so he decided to return through Macedonia.
4Several men were traveling with him.
They were Sopater son of Pyrrhus from
Berea; Aristarchus and Secundus from Thessalonica; Gaius from Derbe; Timothy; and
Tychicus and Trophimus from the province
of Asia. 5They went on ahead and waited for
us at Troas. 6After the Passover ended, we
boarded a ship at Philippi in Macedonia and
five days later joined them in Troas, where
we stayed a week.

Paul's Final Visit to Troas

7On the first day of the week, we gathered
with the local believers to share in the
Lord's Supper. Paul was preaching to them,
and since he was leaving the next day, he
kept talking until midnight. 8The upstairs
room where we met was lighted with many
flickering lamps. 9As Paul spoke on and on,
a young man named Eutychus, sitting on the
windowsill, became very drowsy. Finally, he
fell sound asleep and dropped three stories
to his death below. 10Paul went down, bent
over him, and took him into his arms. "Don't
worry," he said, "he's alive!" 11Then they all
went back upstairs, shared in the Lord's Supper, and ate together. Paul continued talking
to them until dawn, and then he left. 12Mean-
while, the young man was taken home
unhurt, and everyone was greatly relieved.

Paul Meets the Ephesian Elders in Miletus

13Paul went by land to Assos, where he had
arranged for us to join him, while we traveled by ship. 14He joined us there, and we
sailed together to Mitylene. 15The next day
we sailed past the island of Kios. The following day we crossed to the island of Samos,
and a day later we arrived at Miletus.

19:37 Rom 2:22
20:1 Acts 16:9-10
20:3 Acts 9:23-24; 23:12; 2 Cor 11:26
20:4 Acts 16:1; 19:29; 21:29; Eph 6:21; 2 Tim 4:20; Titus 3:12
20:6 Acts 16:8, 10
20:7 Acts 2:42, 46; 1 Cor 16:2; Rev 1:10
20:10 1 Kgs 17:21; 2 Kgs 4:34; Matt 9:23-24
20:15 2 Tim 4:20

19:35-41 The demonstration was finally quelled only when the ***mayor*** intervened and ***dismissed*** the assembly to prevent the city from being charged by ***the Roman government*** with ***rioting***. This story demonstrates that Christians in the Roman world were entitled to legal due process.

19:35 The tradition that the ***image*** (statue) of ***Artemis*** had fallen ***from heaven*** might point to its having been carved from a meteor.

19:41 Some translations include v 41 as part of v 40.

20:1-2 ***believers:*** Literally *disciples.* • Paul traveled to ***Macedonia***, where he ***encouraged the believers in all the towns***, including Thessalonica, Philippi, and Berea. He also continued to gather the offering for the needy in Jerusalem (see Rom 15:25-28; 2 Cor 8:1–9:15). Titus met Paul in Macedonia with a report from Corinth, which prompted Paul to write 2 Corinthians and send Titus back carrying it (2 Cor 7:5-7; 8:6).

20:2-3 From Macedonia, Paul ***traveled down to Greece***—i.e., Corinth in the province of Achaia (see note on 18:1)—***where he stayed for three months*** (cp. 2 Cor 13:1). Paul probably wrote his letter to the Romans during this time (see Romans Introduction, "Date of Writing," p. 1890). • ***a plot . . . against his life:*** Cp. 9:23-25, 28-30; 23:12-35; 25:3.

20:4 Paul's traveling companions were disciples from Berea, Thessalonica, Derbe, and Asia, whom he was mentoring and equipping to lead (cp. 2 Tim 2:2).

20:5-15 This is another of the "we" passages in Acts (see note on 16:10). Luke apparently rejoined Paul at Philippi, where Luke had remained several years earlier, and journeyed with Paul to Jerusalem (21:1-18).

20:6 ***the Passover:*** Literally *the days of unleavened bread.*

20:7-12 ***On the first day of the week*** the early church commemorated Jesus' resurrection (see Mark 16:9; cp. John 20:19; Rev 1:10). • This was Paul's last visit to Troas, which included gathering ***to share in the Lord's Supper*** (literally *to break bread*). This meal probably included both communion and a common meal (cp. 2:42, 46; Jude 1:12). • The remarkable feature of this gathering was the understated miraculous restoration of ***Eutychus***, the ***young man*** who fell ***asleep*** on a ***windowsill*** and ***dropped three stories to his death*** (cp. 9:36-41).

20:11 ***shared in the Lord's Supper:*** Literally *broke the bread.*

20:13-15 ***Assos*** was a key city in Mysia on the east coast of the Aegean Sea. • ***Mitylene*** was the most strategic city on the island of Lesbos. • The island of ***Samos*** was of major importance on the trade routes from Asia Minor to the west and from the Aegean Sea to Egypt.

20:15 ***Samos, and:*** Some manuscripts read *Samos, and having stayed at Trogyllium.*

20:18
Acts 18:19-21; 19:1-41
20:21
Acts 2:38; 26:18
[b]*metanoia* (3341)
‣ Rom 2:4
20:22
Acts 19:21
20:23
Acts 9:16; 21:4, 11
20:24
Acts 21:13
2 Tim 4:7
20:26
Acts 18:6
20:28
Ps 74:2
John 21:15-17
1 Pet 5:2
[c]*poimainō* (4165)
‣ Eph 4:11
[d]*episkopos* (1985)
‣ Phil 1:1
20:29
Matt 7:15
John 10:12
20:30
1 Jn 2:19
20:31
Acts 19:10
20:32
Deut 33:3-4
Acts 26:18
Eph 1:18
Col 1:12; 3:24
1 Pet 1:4

16 Paul had decided to sail on past Ephesus, for he didn't want to spend any more
time in the province of Asia. He was hurrying to get to Jerusalem, if possible, in time
for the Festival of Pentecost. 17 But when
we landed at Miletus, he sent a message to
the elders of the church at Ephesus, asking
them to come and meet him.
18 When they arrived he declared, "You
know that from the day I set foot in the
province of Asia until now 19 I have done the
Lord's work humbly and with many tears.
I have endured the trials that came to me
from the plots of the Jews. 20 I never shrank
back from telling you what you needed to
hear, either publicly or in your homes. 21 I
have had one message for Jews and Greeks
alike—the necessity of [b]repenting from sin
and turning to God, and of having faith in
our Lord Jesus.
22 "And now I am bound by the Spirit to go
to Jerusalem. I don't know what awaits me,
23 except that the Holy Spirit tells me in city
after city that jail and suffering lie ahead.
24 But my life is worth nothing to me unless I
use it for finishing the work assigned me by
the Lord Jesus—the work of telling others
the Good News about the wonderful grace
of God.
25 "And now I know that none of you to
whom I have preached the Kingdom will
ever see me again. 26 I declare today that I
have been faithful. If anyone suffers eternal death, it's not my fault, 27 for I didn't
shrink from declaring all that God wants
you to know.
28 "So guard yourselves and God's people.
Feed and [c]shepherd God's flock—his church,
purchased with his own blood—over which
the Holy Spirit has appointed you as [d]elders.
29 I know that false teachers, like vicious
wolves, will come in among you after I leave,
not sparing the flock. 30 Even some men from
your own group will rise up and distort the
truth in order to draw a following. 31 Watch
out! Remember the three years I was with
you—my constant watch and care over you
night and day, and my many tears for you.
32 "And now I entrust you to God and the
message of his grace that is able to build
you up and give you an inheritance with all
those he has set apart for himself.

The Grace of God (20:24)

Acts 15:11; 20:32
Exod 33:17-19
Lev 26:9-13
Num 6:22-27
Ezra 9:8
Ps 30:5; 31:16
Isa 60:10; 61:1-3
Luke 4:18-19
Rom 5:15-17, 20-21; 6:1-2, 14; 12:6
1 Cor 1:3-9
2 Cor 6:1; 8:9; 12:9
Gal 2:21; 4:10; 5:3-6
Eph 1:3-8; 2:4-10
2 Tim 1:9; 2:1
Heb 2:9; 4:16; 13:9
1 Pet 5:5-6, 12
2 Pet 3:17-18

"Grace" is a key word in the Bible. It is used to indicate God's kindness and favor (e.g., 13:43; 14:26). The NT stresses that grace came through Jesus Christ (John 1:14, 16, 17). In Acts, God's great favor was initially experienced in the Jewish community (4:33); later, it became clear that God's grace in Jesus Christ extends to Gentiles as well (11:23; 15:8-9; 2 Cor 6:1; Gal 2:21; Eph 2:4-10; Titus 2:11). Signs and wonders attested the reality of God's grace at work among the Gentiles (14:3).

Paul's ministry proclaimed the Good News "about the wonderful grace of God" (20:24), and he encouraged Christians to continue in "the grace of God" as they remained faithful to their Lord (13:43). Second Peter similarly closes with a command for Christians to "grow in the grace" of Jesus Christ (2 Pet 3:18). When Paul left the Ephesian elders, he commended them "to God and the message of his grace," the divine message that was able to build them up and sustain them (20:32; see 15:40). God's grace is at the core of the Christian message and the Christian experience, from beginning to end.

20:16 *The Festival of Pentecost* was one of the three Jewish pilgrimage festivals (see note on 2:1-4).

20:17 *Miletus* was a major port on the western coast of Asia Minor at the mouth of the Meander River. It provided a place for Paul to meet briefly with the *elders* of Ephesus on his way to Jerusalem.

20:18-38 Paul's address to the elders of the church of Ephesus is a testimony regarding his life and ministry in Ephesus, calling for similar dedication from the leaders who would carry on the ministry. The sermon highlights Paul's integrity and pastoral *care* (20:18-21, 26, 31), speaks about the future (20:22-23, 25, 29-30), warns against *false teachers* (20:29-30), and exhorts the elders to be watchful and faithful (20:28, 31). Paul modeled sacrificial, conscientious, servant leadership.

20:22 *by the Spirit:* Or *by my spirit,* or *by an inner compulsion;* literally *by the spirit.*

20:23 *the Holy Spirit tells me:* See, e.g., 21:10-12.

20:26 *I have been faithful. If anyone suffers eternal death, it's not my fault:* Literally *I am innocent of the blood of all;* cp. Ezek 3:16-21.

20:28 Paul refers to the church as *God's people* and *God's flock* (cp. 1 Pet 2:25; 5:2, 4). Elsewhere the church is called *the body of Christ* (1 Cor 12:27; Eph 1:23; 4:12; Col 1:24); the *bride* of Christ (2 Cor 11:2; Rev 19:7; see Eph 5:25-32), *the temple of the living God,* (1 Cor 3:16; 2 Cor 6:16), *a chosen people, royal priests, a holy nation, God's very own possession* (1 Pet 2:9), and *God's field, God's building* (1 Cor 3:9). • *with his own blood:* Or *with the blood of his own [Son].* • Paul expected the *elders* (literally *overseers*) to feed and shepherd the church *over which the Holy Spirit* had appointed them as leaders (see 1 Tim 3:1-7; Titus 1:5-7; 1 Pet 5:1-4; cp. Acts 6:2-4).

20:29-30 *vicious wolves:* Paul's prophecy did in fact happen, prompting him to write to Timothy in Ephesus some five years later (see 1 Tim 1:3-7, 19-20; 4:1-5; see also Matt 7:15; 10:16; Mark 13:22; Luke 10:3; 2 Pet 2:1-22; 3:3).

33"I have never coveted anyone's silver or
gold or fine clothes. 34You know that these
hands of mine have worked to supply my
own needs and even the needs of those who
were with me. 35And I have been a constant
example of how you can help those in need
by working hard. You should remember the
words of the Lord Jesus: 'It is more [e]blessed
to give than to receive.'"

36When he had finished speaking, he
knelt and prayed with them. 37They all cried
as they embraced and kissed him good-bye.
38They were sad most of all because he had
said that they would never see him again.
Then they escorted him down to the ship.

Paul Travels from Miletus to Jerusalem

21 After saying farewell to the Ephesian elders, we sailed straight to
the island of Cos. The next day we reached
Rhodes and then went to Patara. 2There we
boarded a ship sailing for Phoenicia. 3We
sighted the island of Cyprus, passed it on
our left, and landed at the harbor of Tyre,
in Syria, where the ship was to unload its
cargo.

4We went ashore, found the local believers,
and stayed with them a week. These believers prophesied through the Holy Spirit that
Paul should not go on to Jerusalem. 5When
we returned to the ship at the end of the
week, the entire congregation, including
women and children, left the city and came
down to the shore with us. There we knelt,
prayed, 6and said our farewells. Then we
went aboard, and they returned home.

7The next stop after leaving Tyre was
Ptolemais, where we greeted the brothers
and sisters and stayed for one day. 8The
next day we went on to Caesarea and stayed
at the home of Philip the Evangelist, one
of the seven men who had been chosen to
distribute food. 9He had four unmarried
daughters who had the gift of prophecy.

10Several days later a man named Agabus,
who also had the gift of prophecy, arrived
from Judea. 11He came over, took Paul's belt,
and bound his own feet and hands with it.
Then he said, "The Holy Spirit declares, 'So
shall the owner of this belt be bound by the
Jewish leaders in Jerusalem and turned over
to the Gentiles.'" 12When we heard this, we
and the local believers all begged Paul not
to go on to Jerusalem.

13But he said, "Why all this weeping? You
are breaking my [f]heart! I am ready not only
to be jailed at Jerusalem but even to die for
the sake of the Lord Jesus." 14When it was
clear that we couldn't persuade him, we
gave up and said, "The Lord's will be done."

15After this we packed our things and left
for Jerusalem. 16Some believers from Caesarea accompanied us, and they took us to the
home of Mnason, a man originally from Cyprus and one of the early believers. 17When
we arrived, the brothers and sisters in Jerusalem welcomed us warmly.

5. PAUL IN JERUSALEM AND CAESAREA (21:18–26:32)

Paul in Jerusalem (21:18–23:35)

Paul's Meeting with the Jerusalem Church Leaders

18The next day Paul went with us to meet
with James, and all the elders of the Jerusalem church were present. 19After greeting
them, Paul gave a detailed account of the

20:33 1 Sam 12:3; 1 Cor 9:11; 2 Cor 7:2; 11:9; 12:14-17
20:34 Acts 18:3; 1 Cor 4:12; 1 Thes 2:9
20:35 1 Thes 4:11; [e]*makarios* (3107) ‣ Rom 4:7
20:36 Acts 21:5
20:37 Rom 16:16
21:1 Acts 16:10
21:4 Acts 20:23; 21:11
21:5 Acts 20:36
21:8 Acts 6:5; 8:26, 40; Eph 4:11; 2 Tim 4:5
21:9 Joel 2:28; Acts 2:17
21:10 Acts 11:28
21:11 Acts 20:23; 21:33
21:13 Acts 20:24; [f]*kardia* (2588) ‣ Rom 10:9
21:14 Matt 26:39
21:19 Acts 15:12

20:35 ***'It is more blessed to give than to receive':*** This saying of Jesus is not recorded in the Gospels.

20:38 The poignancy of the occasion was heightened by awareness that ***they would never see him again*** (20:25).

21:1-18 This "we" passage (see notes on 16:10; 20:5-15) covers Paul's journey from Miletus to Jerusalem at the close of the third missionary journey.

21:1 ***Cos*** was an island in the Aegean Sea with a major trade port. • ***Rhodes*** is a large Aegean island that featured the Colossus, a huge statue 100 feet (30 meters) tall that once stood at the entrance to the city. In Paul's time, the statue lay where it had fallen during an earthquake over 200 years earlier; it would not be removed for another 600 years. • ***Patara*** was the major port of Lycia, located on the coast opposite Rhodes.

21:2-3 ***Tyre*** was an important port in ***Phoenicia*** with a maritime empire of far-flung commercial interests (see Isa 23; Jer 25:15-38; 47; Zech 9; Matt 15:21-28; Mark 7:24-31).

21:4-6 The ***local believers*** (literally *disciples;* also in 21:16) at Tyre gave Paul a touching farewell that reveals deep Christian fellowship. • ***prophesied through the Holy Spirit that Paul should not go on to Jerusalem:*** The believers at Tyre clearly foresaw the danger in Paul's visiting Jerusalem and out of brotherly concern tried to dissuade him. Paul willingly accepted the risks in order to fulfill his apostolic mandate (cp. Phil 3:7-10). See also note on 21:11-14.

21:5 ***women:*** Or *wives.*

21:7 Paul visited ***Ptolemais,*** an important city on the coast of the Mediterranean, as he made his way from ***Tyre*** to Caesarea. • ***brothers and sisters:*** Literally *brothers;* also in 21:17.

21:8 ***Philip*** had the title of ***Evangelist*** due to his evangelistic activity (8:4-40; cp. Eph 4:11; 2 Tim 4:5).

21:9 Philip's daughters' ***gift of prophecy*** demonstrated the fulfillment of Joel's prophecy, as Peter had preached at Pentecost (2:17-21; Joel 2:28-32).

21:10 Luke juxtaposes female prophets (21:9) with a male prophet (see note on 17:34). ***Agabus,*** like the OT prophets, used symbolic actions to proclaim his message (see "Prophetic Sign Acts" at Ezek 4:1-17, p. 1319).

21:11-14 Despite Agabus's prediction of suffering and the believers' begging Paul not to go to Jerusalem, Paul was resolutely ready ***even to die for the sake of the Lord Jesus.*** Luke stresses Paul's courage, determination, and heroism as a Christian missionary who would let nothing interfere with his mission. See note on 21:4-6.

21:18-19 It was important for ***James*** and ***all the elders of the Jerusalem***

21:20 Acts 15:1, 5; Gal 3:10-11
21:21 Acts 16:3; Gal 2:3
21:23 Acts 18:18
21:24 Num 6:5, 13-20
21:25 Acts 15:19-29
21:26 Num 6:1-21; 1 Cor 9:20
21:27 Acts 24:18; 26:21
21:28 Matt 24:15; Acts 6:13; 24:5-6

things God had accomplished among the Gentiles through his ministry.

20 After hearing this, they praised God. And then they said, "You know, dear brother, how many thousands of Jews have also believed, and they all follow the law of Moses very seriously. 21 But the Jewish believers here in Jerusalem have been told that you are teaching all the Jews who live among the Gentiles to turn their backs on the laws of Moses. They've heard that you teach them not to circumcise their children or follow other Jewish customs. 22 What should we do? They will certainly hear that you have come.

23 "Here's what we want you to do. We have four men here who have completed their vow. 24 Go with them to the Temple and join them in the purification ceremony, paying for them to have their heads ritually shaved. Then everyone will know that the rumors are all false and that you yourself observe the Jewish laws.

25 "As for the Gentile believers, they should do what we already told them in a letter: They should abstain from eating food offered to idols, from consuming blood or the meat of strangled animals, and from sexual immorality."

Paul Is Arrested

26 So Paul went to the Temple the next day with the other men. They had already started the purification ritual, so he publicly announced the date when their vows would end and sacrifices would be offered for each of them.

27 The seven days were almost ended when some Jews from the province of Asia saw Paul in the Temple and roused a mob against him. They grabbed him, 28 yelling, "Men of Israel, help us! This is the man who preaches against our people everywhere and tells everybody to disobey the Jewish laws. He speaks against the Temple—and even defiles this holy place by bringing in

The Gift of Prophecy (21:9-11)

Acts 2:17-21; 11:27-28; 13:1; 15:32; 19:6; 20:23
Exod 15:20
Deut 13:1-5
Judg 4:4
1 Kgs 11:29-32
2 Kgs 22:14-20
Isa 20:2-6; 44:25
Jer 13:1-11; 23:25-32
Ezek 4:1-17; 13:2-9
Joel 2:28-32
Matt 7:15; 24:24
Rom 12:6
1 Cor 11:5; 12:4-11; 14:1-40
Eph 4:11-13
1 Thes 5:19-21
2 Pet 2:1
1 Jn 4:1-3
Rev 2:20-23; 19:10

In the early church, the gift of prophecy was not uncommon. As Peter had declared at Pentecost, the gift of prophecy was one of the results of the outpouring of God's Holy Spirit (2:17-21; see Joel 2:28-32). The book of Acts names a few Christian prophets (11:27-28; 13:1; 15:32; 21:9-11; see also *Martyrdom of Polycarp* 12:3; 16:2). One of the prophets was Agabus, whose function was similar to that of an OT prophet, performing symbolic acts (21:10-11; see 1 Kgs 11:29-32; Isa 20:2-6; Jer 13:1-11; "Prophetic Sign Acts" at Ezek 4:1-17, p. 1319) and predicting events to come (11:28; 21:10-11).

Philip the Evangelist was the father of four young women who "had the gift of prophecy" (21:9). The apostle Paul also acknowledged the prophetic gift of some Christian women (1 Cor 11:5). In the OT, most prophets were men, but several women are described as prophets: Miriam (Exod 15:20), Deborah (Judg 4:4), and Huldah (2 Kgs 22:14-20; 2 Chr 34:22-28). In the NT, the gift of prophecy is given to both men and women, and both young and old, as Peter signaled in his sermon at Pentecost (2:17-18).

Although prophecy sometimes involves foretelling the future (20:23; 21:10-11; see Rom 9:23-26; 1 Thes 4:13-17; 2 Thes 2:3-4), at its core prophecy is proclaiming God's word by preaching, exhorting, and explaining the will of God (15:32; 19:6; Rom 12:6; 1 Cor 14:3-4; 14:29-33; Rev 19:10). The gift of prophecy is clearly mentioned in 1 Corinthians and Ephesians as one of the gifts of the Holy Spirit and of Christ to the church (1 Cor 12:4-11; Eph 4:11). It is to be used for the benefit of believers (1 Cor 14:22).

Prophecy is always in need of testing (1 Thes 5:19-21), and the church is strongly warned against false prophets (1 Jn 4:1; Rev 2:20-23). When used faithfully and in submission to God's word and his Spirit, courageous proclamation of God's truth helps the church to determine what God's will is and inspires God's people to do it.

church to hear of Paul's successful mission ***among the Gentiles*** and for the mother church to continue to endorse this effort (21:20; see 15:7-21). Paul's report communicated that ***God had accomplished*** his purposes ***among the Gentiles through*** Paul's ***ministry***.

21:20-25 The Jerusalem church leaders urged Paul to strengthen his credibility by demonstrating that he was not teaching Jews ***to turn their backs on the laws of Moses***. At the same time, no attempt was made to force Jewish rules on Gentile converts—those terms had been set previously (15:22-29) and were simply to be honored.

21:26-36 The concerns of the Christian leaders (21:20-25) were evidently well based, for ***when their vows*** were almost completed, ***some Jews from the province of Asia*** raised a mob against Paul with false charges. They were intent on killing Paul, but the Roman ***commander*** rescued him.

21:28-29 ***Gentiles:*** Literally *Greeks*. It was a crime punishable by death to bring any non-Jew into the Temple

Gentiles." 29(For earlier that day they had seen him in the city with Trophimus, a Gentile from Ephesus, and they assumed Paul had taken him into the Temple.)

30The whole city was rocked by these accusations, and a great riot followed. Paul was grabbed and dragged out of the Temple, and immediately the gates were closed behind him. 31As they were trying to kill him, word reached the commander of the Roman regiment that all Jerusalem was in an uproar. 32He immediately called out his soldiers and officers and ran down among the crowd. When the mob saw the commander and the troops coming, they stopped beating Paul.

33Then the commander arrested him and ordered him bound with two chains. He asked the crowd who he was and what he had done. 34Some shouted one thing and some another. Since he couldn't find out the truth in all the uproar and confusion, he ordered that Paul be taken to the fortress. 35As Paul reached the stairs, the mob grew so violent the soldiers had to lift him to their shoulders to protect him. 36And the crowd followed behind, shouting, "Kill him, kill him!"

Paul Speaks to the Crowd

37As Paul was about to be taken inside, he said to the commander, "May I have a word with you?"

"Do you know Greek?" the commander asked, surprised. 38"Aren't you the Egyptian who led a rebellion some time ago and took 4,000 members of the Assassins out into the desert?"

39"No," Paul replied, "I am a Jew and a citizen of Tarsus in Cilicia, which is an important city. Please, let me talk to these people." 40The commander agreed, so Paul stood on the stairs and motioned to the people to be quiet. Soon a deep silence enveloped the crowd, and he addressed them in their own language, Aramaic.

22 "Brothers and esteemed fathers," Paul said, "listen to me as I offer my [g]defense." 2When they heard him speaking in their own language, the silence was even greater.

3Then Paul said, "I am a Jew, born in Tarsus, a city in Cilicia, and I was brought up and educated here in Jerusalem under Gamaliel. As his student, I was carefully [h]trained in our Jewish laws and customs. I became very zealous to honor God in everything I did, just like all of you today. 4And I persecuted the followers of the Way, hounding some to death, arresting both men and women and throwing them in prison. 5The high priest and the whole council of elders can testify that this is so. For I received letters from them to our Jewish brothers in Damascus, authorizing me to bring the Christians from there to Jerusalem, in chains, to be punished.

6"As I was on the road, approaching Damascus about noon, a very bright light from heaven suddenly shone down around me. 7I fell to the ground and heard a voice saying to me, 'Saul, Saul, why are you persecuting me?'

8" 'Who are you, lord?' I asked.

"And the voice replied, 'I am Jesus the Nazarene, the one you are persecuting.' 9The people with me saw the light but didn't understand the voice speaking to me.

10"I asked, 'What should I do, Lord?'

"And the Lord told me, 'Get up and go into

21:29 Acts 20:4; 2 Tim 4:20
21:32 Acts 23:27
21:33 Acts 20:23; Eph 6:20
21:36 Luke 23:18; John 19:15; Acts 22:22
21:39 Acts 9:11; 22:3
21:40 Acts 26:14
22:1 Acts 7:2; [g]*apologia* (0627) ‣Acts 24:10
22:3-21 //Acts 9:1-29; 26:9-18
22:3 Acts 5:34-40; Rom 10:2; [h]*paideuō* (3811) ‣1 Cor 11:32
22:4 Acts 8:3; 9:2
22:6 Acts 9:2-8; 26:12-13
22:9 Acts 9:7; 26:13

precincts beyond the Court of the Gentiles (see illustration, p. 1787; see also Josephus, *War* 5.5.2; 6.2.4). The Jews ***assumed*** that Paul had violated this sacred law by bringing ***Trophimus, a Gentile from Ephesus*** (literally *Trophimus, the Ephesian*; see also 20:4; 2 Tim 4:20), into the forbidden area.

21:30 This supposed desecration of the Temple aroused the fury of the Jewish populace. The ***Temple . . . gates were closed*** because they thought the Temple had been defiled by a Gentile.

21:31 ***commander:*** Or *tribune*, a Roman officer who commanded 1,000 men.

21:32 ***officers:*** Literally *centurions.*

21:34 The ***fortress*** of Antonia, a large military garrison built by Herod the Great on the northwest corner of the Temple Mount, accommodated the Roman cohort that was stationed there to keep the peace.

21:37-40 ***The commander*** had mistaken Paul for an ***Egyptian*** false messiah who had planned to seize power from the Romans around AD 54 (roughly three years earlier; see Josephus, *War* 2.13.5). Paul corrected the mistake, gained permission to speak to the people, and addressed the crowd in ***Aramaic*** (Or *Hebrew*), the common language of Judea. He gave a strong statement of his faith in Jesus as the Messiah (22:1-21).

22:1-21 Paul's premier defense of his life and faith before his own people in Jerusalem illustrates his flexibility as a missionary, just as his speech to the Greek philosophers in Athens had done (17:22-31; see 1 Cor 9:20-23). Paul begins by recognizing his kinship with his people, explaining his Jewish background and training under the noted rabbi ***Gamaliel*** the Elder and describing his zealous desire ***to honor God in everything***, which they shared (22:1-3). Paul then describes his persecution of Christians (22:4-5), the revelation of Jesus to him on the way to ***Damascus*** (22:6-10), and his conversion (22:11-16). Paul ends his speech by describing his conversation with the Lord in the Temple. The Lord had predicted the Jews' rejection of the message and had sent Paul to the ***Gentiles*** (22:17-21).

22:2 ***in their own language:*** Literally *in Aramaic*, or *in Hebrew.*

22:3 ***under Gamaliel:*** See note on 5:34.

22:8 ***Jesus the Nazarene:*** Or *Jesus of Nazareth.*

22:11 Acts 9:8
22:12 Acts 9:17
22:14 Acts 3:13; 1 Cor 15:8
22:15 Acts 26:16
22:16 Acts 2:38; Rom 10:13; 1 Cor 6:11; Heb 10:22; [i]*baptizō* (0907) ‣Rom 6:3
22:19 Acts 8:3; 22:4-5; 26:9-11
22:20 Acts 7:57–8:1
22:21 Acts 9:15; 13:2; Rom 15:15-16
22:22 Acts 21:36; 25:24
22:25 Acts 16:37
22:29 Acts 16:38
23:1 Acts 24:16; 1 Cor 4:4; 2 Cor 1:12; 1 Tim 3:9; Heb 13:18; 1 Pet 3:16, 21
23:2 John 18:22; Acts 24:1; [j]*archiereus* (0749) ‣Heb 4:14
23:3 Lev 19:15; Ezek 13:10-15; John 7:51
23:5 *Exod 22:28

Damascus, and there you will be told everything you are to do.’
11“I was blinded by the intense light and
had to be led by the hand to Damascus by my
companions. 12A man named Ananias lived
there. He was a godly man, deeply devoted
to the law, and well regarded by all the Jews
of Damascus. 13He came and stood beside
me and said, ‘Brother Saul, regain your sight.’
And that very moment I could see him!
14“Then he told me, ‘The God of our ancestors has chosen you to know his will and to
see the Righteous One and hear him speak.
15For you are to be his witness, telling everyone what you have seen and heard. 16What
are you waiting for? Get up and be [i]baptized.
Have your sins washed away by calling on
the name of the Lord.’
17“After I returned to Jerusalem, I was
praying in the Temple and fell into a trance.
18I saw a vision of Jesus saying to me, ‘Hurry!
Leave Jerusalem, for the people here won’t
accept your testimony about me.’
19“ ‘But Lord,’ I argued, ‘they certainly
know that in every synagogue I imprisoned
and beat those who believed in you. 20And I
was in complete agreement when your witness Stephen was killed. I stood by and kept
the coats they took off when they stoned
him.’
21“But the Lord said to me, ‘Go, for I will
send you far away to the Gentiles!’ ”
22The crowd listened until Paul said that
word. Then they all began to shout, “Away
with such a fellow! He isn’t fit to live!”
23They yelled, threw off their coats, and
tossed handfuls of dust into the air.

Paul Claims His Rights as a Roman Citizen

24The commander brought Paul inside and
ordered him lashed with whips to make
him confess his crime. He wanted to find
out why the crowd had become so furious.
25When they tied Paul down to lash him,
Paul said to the officer standing there, “Is
it legal for you to whip a Roman citizen who
hasn’t even been tried?”
26When the officer heard this, he went to
the commander and asked, “What are you
doing? This man is a Roman citizen!”
27So the commander went over and asked
Paul, “Tell me, are you a Roman citizen?”
“Yes, I certainly am,” Paul replied.
28“I am, too,” the commander muttered,
“and it cost me plenty!”
Paul answered, “But I am a citizen by
birth!”
29The soldiers who were about to interrogate Paul quickly withdrew when they
heard he was a Roman citizen, and the commander was frightened because he had
ordered him bound and whipped.

Paul before the High Council

30The next day the commander ordered the
leading priests into session with the Jewish
high council. He wanted to find out what
the trouble was all about, so he released
Paul to have him stand before them.

23 Gazing intently at the high council,
Paul began: “Brothers, I have always
lived before God with a clear conscience!”
2Instantly Ananias the [j]high priest commanded those close to Paul to slap him on
the mouth. 3But Paul said to him, “God will
slap you, you corrupt hypocrite! What kind
of judge are you to break the law yourself by
ordering me struck like that?”
4Those standing near Paul said to him,
“Do you dare to insult God’s high priest?”
5“I’m sorry, brothers. I didn’t realize he
was the high priest,” Paul replied, “for the

22:12-16 *Ananias:* See note on 9:17.

22:14 ***the Righteous One:*** See also 3:14; 7:52; 1 Jn 2:1. Righteousness was one of the Messiah’s characteristics (see Isa 32:1; 53:11).

22:16 ***be baptized. Have your sins washed away:*** See “Baptism” at 2:38, 41, p. 1828.

22:17-22 While Paul was praying ***in the Temple,*** he ***saw a vision of Jesus*** (literally *saw him*) telling him that the ***people*** of ***Jerusalem*** would not ***accept*** his ***testimony.*** The Lord then sent him ***to the Gentiles.*** The crowd’s response to this report (22:22-23) proved the point.

22:23 The crowd’s yelling, throwing off ***their coats,*** and tossing ***handfuls of dust into the air*** were probably ritual responses to perceived blasphemy. They opposed and tried to thwart Paul’s words that suggested the inclusion of Gentiles (22:21). Cp. Luke 4:16-30.

22:25-29 ***the officer:*** Literally *the centurion;* also in 22:26. • Paul claimed his status as a ***Roman citizen*** at this critical time when he was about to be tortured to make him confess his supposed crime. Roman citizenship was a valuable asset, and claiming it falsely was a capital offense. Its principal benefits were the prohibition of scourging and the right to appeal to the emperor (25:11). ***The commander was frightened*** at having nearly violated Roman law (cp. 16:35-39).

22:28 ***it cost me plenty!*** During the early part of the reign of Emperor Claudius (AD 41–54), Roman citizenship could be purchased, but it was expensive.

22:30 ***the Jewish high council:*** Greek *the Sanhedrin.*

23:1 In addressing ***the high council*** (Greek *the Sanhedrin;* also in 23:6, 15, 20, 28), Paul insisted on his personal integrity ***before God***—he had not violated God’s law or done the things they accused him of doing.

23:2 ***Ananias*** was the Jewish ***high priest*** from AD 47 to 58. • ***slap him:*** He apparently assumed that Paul was lying and tried to intimidate him.

23:3 ***you corrupt hypocrite*** (literally *you whitewashed wall*): Cp. Ezek 13:10-17; Matt 23:27.

23:5 Why Paul did not recognize the ***high priest*** is not known. • ***Paul replied*** by quoting Exod 22:28, acknowledging the respect to which the high priest was entitled by virtue of his office.

Scriptures say, 'You must not speak evil of
any of your rulers.'"
6Paul realized that some members of the
high council were Sadducees and some
were Pharisees, so he shouted, "Brothers, I
am a Pharisee, as were my ancestors! And I
am on trial because my [k]hope is in the resurrection of the dead!"
7This divided the council—the Pharisees
against the Sadducees—8for the Sadducees
say there is no resurrection or angels or
spirits, but the Pharisees believe in all of
these. 9So there was a great uproar. Some
of the teachers of religious law who were
Pharisees jumped up and began to argue
forcefully. "We see nothing wrong with
him," they shouted. "Perhaps a spirit or an
angel spoke to him." 10As the conflict grew
more violent, the commander was afraid
they would tear Paul apart. So he ordered
his soldiers to go and rescue him by force
and take him back to the fortress.
11That night the Lord appeared to Paul
and said, "Be encouraged, Paul. Just as you
have been a witness to me here in Jerusalem, you must preach the Good News in
Rome as well."

The Plan to Kill Paul

12The next morning a group of Jews got together and bound themselves with an oath
not to eat or drink until they had killed Paul.
13There were more than forty of them in
the conspiracy. 14They went to the leading
priests and elders and told them, "We have
bound ourselves with an oath to eat nothing until we have killed Paul. 15So you and
the high council should ask the commander
to bring Paul back to the council again. Pretend you want to examine his case more
fully. We will kill him on the way."
16But Paul's nephew—his sister's son—
heard of their plan and went to the fortress
and told Paul. 17Paul called for one of the
Roman officers and said, "Take this young
man to the commander. He has something
important to tell him."
18So the officer did, explaining, "Paul, the
prisoner, called me over and asked me to
bring this young man to you because he has
something to tell you."
19The commander took his hand, led him
aside, and asked, "What is it you want to tell
me?"
20Paul's nephew told him, "Some Jews are
going to ask you to bring Paul before the
high council tomorrow, pretending they
want to get some more information. 21But
don't do it! There are more than forty men
hiding along the way ready to ambush him.
They have vowed not to eat or drink anything until they have killed him. They are
ready now, just waiting for your consent."
22"Don't let anyone know you told me
this," the commander warned the young
man.

Paul Is Sent to Caesarea

23Then the commander called two of his officers and ordered, "Get 200 soldiers ready
to leave for Caesarea at nine o'clock tonight.
Also take 200 spearmen and 70 mounted
troops. 24Provide horses for Paul to ride, and
get him safely to Governor Felix." 25Then he
wrote this letter to the governor:

> 26"From Claudius Lysias, to his
> Excellency, Governor Felix: Greetings!
> 27"This man was seized by some Jews,
> and they were about to kill him when I
> arrived with the troops. When I learned
> that he was a Roman citizen, I removed
> him to safety. 28Then I took him to their
> high council to try to learn the basis of

23:6 Acts 26:5; Phil 3:5
[k]*elpis* (1680) ‣Rom 5:2
23:8 Matt 22:23; Mark 12:18; Luke 20:27
23:9 Acts 22:7; 25:25
23:11 Acts 18:9; 27:24; 28:23
23:12 1 Sam 14:24; Acts 9:23
23:14-15 Acts 25:3
23:16 Acts 21:34
23:23 Acts 8:40
23:27 Acts 21:30-33; 22:25-29
23:28 Acts 22:30

23:6 Paul focused on the key issue in his trial, the ***hope*** of ***resurrection*** from ***the dead.*** His preaching was simply the outworking of that hope and the fact of Jesus' resurrection, but the message was unacceptable to both groups of Jews because of its implications. ***Pharisees*** could not abide the inclusion of the Gentiles apart from circumcision and keeping the law of Moses (cp. 15:5; see "The Pharisees" at Matt 3:7, p. 1581), but that was what the resurrection of Jesus and the outpouring of the Spirit had provided (2:39; 10:34-48). ***Sadducees*** could not stand the proclamation of the resurrection at all (cp. 4:1-2; see "The Sadducees" at Matt 16:1-12, p. 1610).

23:7-10 Paul's statement (23:6) ***divided the council,*** with the ***Pharisees*** taking Paul's side against the ***Sadducees.*** The resulting ***uproar*** was so great that the commander rescued Paul and took him back into the ***fortress*** of Antonia.

23:11 At this critical juncture, Jesus encouraged Paul to continue as his faithful ***witness*** by assuring him that he would go to ***Rome*** (see 19:21).

23:12-15 The plan to kill Paul was desperate, as ***a group of Jews*** (literally *the Jews*), ***more than forty of them,*** took ***an oath to eat nothing until*** they had ***killed Paul*** (cp. 1 Sam 14:24-46; Matt 14:6-11; see also Deut 23:21-23; Matt 5:33-37; Jas 5:12).

23:16-22 ***Paul's nephew*** thwarted the murderous plot by reporting it to one of the ***Roman officers*** (literally *centurions;* also in 23:23).

23:23-35 A mounted escort took Paul safely to the Roman ***Governor Felix*** in ***Caesarea,*** the Roman headquarters for Judea. There Paul would have greater protection than in Jerusalem. The military operation was executed ***that night*** with secret efficiency and maximum security (23:31).

23:24 Antonius ***Felix*** was procurator (***Governor***) of Judea about AD 52–59, with responsibility for both military and civil affairs. Felix had a bad reputation (see 24:24-27) and was eventually recalled to Rome by Nero.

23:26-30 The letter of ***Claudius Lysias*** to ***Governor Felix*** is a typical Hellenistic letter, naming the writer and the person addressed, offering a greeting, and stating the business at hand (though there is no parting word of farewell;

23:29 Acts 18:14-15; 25:18-19; 26:31; 28:18
23:30 Acts 24:19; 25:16
23:33 Acts 8:40
23:34 Acts 6:9; 21:39; 22:3
23:35 Acts 25:16
24:1 Acts 23:2, 24-30, 35
24:3 Acts 23:26; 26:25
24:5 Mark 1:24; Acts 16:20; 17:6; 24:14
24:6 Acts 21:28, 30
24:9 1 Thes 2:16
24:10 [a]*apologeomai* (0626) ‣Acts 25:8
24:11 Acts 21:27
24:13 Acts 25:7
24:14 Acts 9:2; 26:22
24:15 Dan 12:2; Matt 22:31-32; John 5:28-29; Acts 23:6; 28:20
24:16 Acts 23:1

the accusations against him. 29I soon
discovered the charge was something
regarding their religious law—certainly
nothing worthy of imprisonment or
death. 30But when I was informed of a
plot to kill him, I immediately sent him
on to you. I have told his accusers to
bring their charges before you."

31So that night, as ordered, the soldiers
took Paul as far as Antipatris. 32They returned to the fortress the next morning,
while the mounted troops took him on to
Caesarea. 33When they arrived in Caesarea,
they presented Paul and the letter to Governor Felix. 34He read it and then asked Paul
what province he was from. "Cilicia," Paul
answered.

35"I will hear your case myself when your
accusers arrive," the governor told him.
Then the governor ordered him kept in the
prison at Herod's headquarters.

Paul in Caesarea (24:1–26:32)

Paul Appears before Felix

24 Five days later Ananias, the high
priest, arrived with some of the
Jewish elders and the lawyer Tertullus, to
present their case against Paul to the governor. 2When Paul was called in, Tertullus
presented the charges against Paul in the
following address to the governor:

"You have provided a long period of
peace for us Jews and with foresight have
enacted reforms for us. 3For all of this, Your
Excellency, we are very grateful to you. 4But
I don't want to bore you, so please give me
your attention for only a moment. 5We have
found this man to be a troublemaker who
is constantly stirring up riots among the
Jews all over the world. He is a ringleader of
the cult known as the Nazarenes. 6Further-
more, he was trying to desecrate the Temple
when we arrested him. 8You can find out
the truth of our accusations by examining
him yourself." 9Then the other Jews chimed
in, declaring that everything Tertullus said
was true.

10The governor then motioned for Paul to
speak. Paul said, "I know, sir, that you have
been a judge of Jewish affairs for many
years, so I gladly present my [a]defense before you. 11You can quickly discover that I
arrived in Jerusalem no more than twelve
days ago to worship at the Temple. 12My
accusers never found me arguing with anyone in the Temple, nor stirring up a riot in
any synagogue or on the streets of the city.
13These men cannot prove the things they
accuse me of doing.

14"But I admit that I follow the Way, which
they call a cult. I worship the God of our ancestors, and I firmly believe the Jewish law
and everything written in the prophets. 15I
have the same hope in God that these men
have, that he will raise both the righteous
and the unrighteous. 16Because of this, I
always try to maintain a clear conscience
before God and all people.

---

see note on 15:29). It summarizes the events that preceded it and explains the action taken; it also suggests that the commander has followed proper Roman judicial procedure. • The title ***his Excellency*** was often applied to persons of high social, political, or economic status (Luke 1:3).

23:31 ***Antipatris,*** a city rebuilt by Herod the Great in 9 BC on the Plain of Sharon, was a convenient military control point between Jerusalem and Caesarea.

23:35 ***The governor*** followed the proper protocol and waited for Paul's ***accusers*** to arrive before granting an official hearing. • ***Herod's headquarters*** (Greek *Herod's Praetorium*) was Herod the Great's palace at Caesarea; it subsequently became the residence of the Roman governors of Judea.

24:1-27 ***Tertullus*** presented a legal case against Paul in a Roman court on behalf of ***the high priest*** (24:1-9). Then Paul cheerfully made his ***defense*** and defended his faith (24:10-21), and the governor adjourned the hearing without a decision and ***left Paul in prison*** for two years (24:22-27).

24:1-4 ***some of the Jewish elders and the lawyer:*** Literally *some elders and an orator.* • ***Tertullus*** presented the case for the prosecution, beginning with the customary speech of praise intended to attract the attention and sympathy of the ***governor***, followed by the statement of charges (24:5-8).

24:5 ***Troublemaker*** (or *agitator*) was a charge of political sedition. A Roman court would have taken this charge very seriously (see 16:21; 17:7; 18:13). Similar accusations were made against Jesus before Pilate (Luke 23:2, 5, 14). • The term ***cult*** (or *party*, or *sect*) is used here in a negative sense to put Paul's religion under a pallor of suspicion if not illegality (see also 24:14).

24:6 ***trying to desecrate the Temple:*** See note on 21:28-29. • ***arrested him:*** Some manuscripts add an expanded conclusion to v 6, all of v 7, and an additional phrase in v 8: *We would have judged him by our law, 7but Lysias, the commander of the garrison, came and violently took him away from us, 8commanding his accusers to come before you.*

24:10-21 Paul's defense was that (1) he wasn't in Jerusalem long enough to incite a riot; (2) none of his accusers had ever seen him stirring up a riot; and (3) he worshiped in accord with ***Jewish law and everything written in the prophets.***

24:14 ***the Way:*** See note on 9:2. • Paul emphasized his common ground with his Jewish audience, including his ***worship,*** belief in ***the Jewish law,*** acceptance of ***the prophets,*** and hope in the resurrection (24:14, 15; see 24:21).

24:15 At the last judgment God ***will raise both the righteous and the unrighteous.*** Paul kept this final appointment with God constantly in mind (24:16). The fear of the "coming day of judgment" unnerved Felix in a subsequent conversation with Paul (24:25).

24:16 Paul stressed that he had acted with ***a clear conscience*** (see 20:27, 33; 23:1; 1 Cor 4:4; 2 Cor 1:12; 4:2; see 2 Tim 1:3). He had not departed from his Jewish heritage (24:14), and he had no fear of God's judgment (24:15).

17“After several years away, I returned to
Jerusalem with money to aid my people and
to offer sacrifices to God. 18My accusers
saw me in the Temple as I was completing a
purification ceremony. There was no crowd
around me and no rioting. 19But some Jews
from the province of Asia were there—and
they ought to be here to bring charges if
they have anything against me! 20Ask these
men here what crime the Jewish high council found me guilty of, 21except for the one
time I shouted out, ‘I am on trial before you
today because I believe in the resurrection
of the dead!’ ”

22At that point Felix, who was quite familiar with the Way, adjourned the hearing
and said, “Wait until Lysias, the garrison
commander, arrives. Then I will decide the
case.” 23He ordered an officer to keep Paul
in custody but to give him some freedom
and allow his friends to visit him and take
care of his needs.

24A few days later Felix came back with
his wife, Drusilla, who was Jewish. Sending
for Paul, they listened as he told them about
faith in Christ Jesus. 25As he reasoned with
them about righteousness and self-control
and the coming day of judgment, Felix became frightened. “Go away for now,” he
replied. “When it is more convenient, I’ll
call for you again.” 26He also hoped that
Paul would bribe him, so he sent for him
quite often and talked with him.

27After two years went by in this way, Felix was succeeded by Porcius Festus. And
because Felix wanted to gain favor with the
Jewish people, he left Paul in prison.

Paul Appears before Festus

25 Three days after Festus arrived in
Caesarea to take over his new responsibilities, he left for Jerusalem, 2where
the leading priests and other Jewish leaders
met with him and made their accusations
against Paul. 3They asked Festus as a favor
to transfer Paul to Jerusalem (planning to
ambush and kill him on the way). 4But Festus replied that Paul was at Caesarea and
he himself would be returning there soon.
5So he said, “Those of you in authority can
return with me. If Paul has done anything
wrong, you can make your accusations.”

6About eight or ten days later Festus returned to Caesarea, and on the following
day he took his seat in court and ordered
that Paul be brought in. 7When Paul arrived,
the Jewish leaders from Jerusalem gathered
around and made many serious accusations
they couldn’t prove.

8Paul [b]denied the charges. “I am not guilty
of any crime against the Jewish laws or the
Temple or the Roman government,” he said.

9Then Festus, wanting to please the Jews,
asked him, “Are you willing to go to Jerusalem and stand trial before me there?”

10But Paul replied, “No! This is the official
Roman court, so I ought to be tried right
here. You know very well I am not guilty
of harming the Jews. 11If I have done something worthy of death, I don’t refuse to die.
But if I am innocent, no one has a right to
turn me over to these men to kill me. I appeal to Caesar!”

12Festus conferred with his advisers and
then replied, “Very well! You have appealed
to Caesar, and to Caesar you will go!”

24:17 Acts 11:29-30; Rom 15:25-28; 1 Cor 16:1-4; 2 Cor 8:1-4; Gal 2:10
24:18 Acts 21:26-27
24:21 Acts 23:6
24:23 Acts 27:3; 28:16, 30
24:25 Acts 10:42; Gal 5:23; 2 Pet 1:6
24:27 Acts 25:9, 14
25:1 Acts 24:27
25:2 Acts 24:1; 25:15
25:3 Acts 23:15
25:5 Acts 23:30
25:6 Acts 25:17
25:7 Acts 24:5-6, 13
25:8 Acts 6:13; 24:12; 28:17
[b]*apologeomai* (0626) ‣Acts 25:16
25:9 Acts 24:27
25:10 Acts 25:21
25:11 Acts 26:32; 28:19

24:17 ***money to aid my people:*** See note on 20:1-2; see also Rom 15:25-29; 1 Cor 16:1-2; 2 Cor 9:1-7. • ***and to offer sacrifices to God:*** See 21:23-26.

24:20 ***the Jewish high council:*** Greek *the Sanhedrin.*

24:22 Perhaps *Felix* delayed his decision hoping that Paul would bribe him (24:26).

24:23 ***an officer:*** Literally *a centurion.* • It was in keeping with the proper treatment of a Roman citizen ***to give him some freedom and allow his friends to visit him and take care of his needs.***

24:24 ***Drusilla*** was the sister of Herod Agrippa II and Bernice (25:13; see genealogy, p. 1579); Drusilla had abandoned her former husband, Azizus the King of Emessa, and married *Felix.* Drusilla *was Jewish,* so in forsaking her original husband and marrying Felix she had disregarded God’s commands (Exod 20:14; Deut 5:18; cp. Mal 2:16; Mark 10:12). Josephus criticized her for this (*Antiquities* 20.7.1-2). Drusilla and her husband were confronted in their conversation with Paul by the prospect of judgment.

24:25 Paul’s words about ***righteousness, self-control,*** and coming divine ***judgment*** frightened *Felix,* who was notably corrupt (24:26-27; see notes on 23:24; 24:24).

24:26-27 Felix kept Paul in custody hoping for a ***bribe.*** When this failed and his own term ended, he left Paul in prison ***to gain favor with the Jewish people.***

24:27–25:5 Felix’s successor was ***Porcius Festus,*** appointed by Nero to be governor of Judea, about AD 59~62. Josephus describes Festus as a conscientious, honest administrator who was not able to stem the rising tide of Jewish unrest despite his strong action against the party of the Assassins (Josephus, *Antiquities* 20.8.10; cp. Acts 21:38). He resisted the Jewish leaders’ attempt to have Paul’s trial moved to Jerusalem, but he was not immune to their pressure (25:9).

25:7 The *serious accusations* were probably those raised previously (21:27-28; 24:5-9), but the accusations were unsupported by the evidence (24:10-13).

25:9 ***Festus, wanting to please the Jews:*** The governor would later state his official reason for delaying Paul’s trial and asking to move it to Jerusalem (25:17-20). His request was driven by politics, however, not justice.

25:10-11 Festus’s suggestion that Paul be tried in Jerusalem motivated the apostle’s ***appeal to Caesar.*** Paul was not afraid of death, but he objected to being turned over to a biased court intent on murder, not justice (25:7).

25:12 ***Festus*** granted Paul’s appeal. This fulfilled Paul’s conviction that he must see Rome (19:21; see also 23:11; 27:24; Rom 1:13-15; 15:22-29).

25:14 Acts 24:27
25:15 Acts 25:1-2
25:16 Acts 23:30
ᶜ*apologia* (0627)
‣Acts 26:1
25:18-19 Acts 18:14-15; 23:29
25:21 Acts 25:11-12
25:22 Acts 9:15
25:24 Acts 22:22
25:25 Luke 23:4
Acts 23:9

13A few days later King Agrippa arrived
with his sister, Bernice, to pay their respects
to Festus. 14During their stay of several
days, Festus discussed Paul's case with the
king. "There is a prisoner here," he told him,
"whose case was left for me by Felix. 15When
I was in Jerusalem, the leading priests and
Jewish elders pressed charges against him
and asked me to condemn him. 16I pointed
out to them that Roman law does not convict people without a trial. They must be
given an opportunity to confront their accusers and ᶜdefend themselves.
17"When his accusers came here for the
trial, I didn't delay. I called the case the very
next day and ordered Paul brought in. 18But
the accusations made against him weren't
any of the crimes I expected. 19Instead, it
was something about their religion and a
dead man named Jesus, who Paul insists is
alive. 20I was at a loss to know how to investigate these things, so I asked him whether
he would be willing to stand trial on these
charges in Jerusalem. 21But Paul appealed
to have his case decided by the emperor. So
I ordered that he be held in custody until I
could arrange to send him to Caesar."
22"I'd like to hear the man myself,"
Agrippa said.
And Festus replied, "You will—tomorrow!"

Paul Speaks to Agrippa

23So the next day Agrippa and Bernice arrived
at the auditorium with great pomp, accompanied by military officers and prominent
men of the city. Festus ordered that Paul be
brought in. 24Then Festus said, "King Agrippa
and all who are here, this is the man whose
death is demanded by all the Jews, both here
and in Jerusalem. 25But in my opinion he
has done nothing deserving death. However,
since he appealed his case to the emperor, I
have decided to send him to Rome.
26"But what shall I write the emperor?
For there is no clear charge against him. So
I have brought him before all of you, and especially you, King Agrippa, so that after we
examine him, I might have something to
write. 27For it makes no sense to send a prisoner to the emperor without specifying the
charges against him!"

HEROD AGRIPPA II (25:13–26:32)

Herod Agrippa II, son of Herod Agrippa I, succeeded his father as king and ruled in Palestine AD 50–100, eventually controlling approximately the same area as his great-grandfather, Herod the Great. Agrippa II was in control of the Temple treasury and could appoint the high priest. He was not popular among Jews on account of his incestuous relationship with his sister Bernice. The Romans consulted him on religious matters, which is probably why Festus invited him to hear the apostle Paul's defense at Caesarea (AD 59, Acts 25:13–26:32).

In May AD 66, the Jewish war against the Romans began (Josephus, *War* 2.14.4). When Agrippa's attempt to quell the revolt failed, he became a staunch ally of the Romans throughout the entire war (AD 66–70). During this time Nero committed suicide, the new emperor Galba was murdered, and Vespasian became the emperor. After pledging his allegiance to the new emperor, Agrippa remained with Titus, Vespasian's son, who was the general in charge of the war (Tacitus, *History* 5.81). After the fall of Jerusalem (Aug 6, AD 70), Agrippa was probably present to celebrate the destruction of his own people.

In AD 79 Vespasian died and Titus became emperor. Little is known of Agrippa's rule after this, except that he wrote to the historian Josephus, praising him for *The Jewish War,* and he purchased a copy of it (Josephus, *Life* 65; *Against Apion* 1.9.47–52).

Although the Talmud implies that Agrippa II had two wives (Babylonian Talmud, *Sukkah* 27a), Josephus gives no indication that he had any wives or children. He died around AD 100, and his death marks the end of the dynasty of the Herods.

25:13-22 ***King Agrippa arrived with his sister, Bernice:*** Literally *Agrippa the king and Bernice arrived.* Festus ***discussed Paul's case*** with Herod Agrippa II (ruled AD 50–100), who had come to Caesarea to make a courtesy call on the new governor.

25:16 It was a fundamental principle: ***Roman law*** did ***not convict people without a trial. They must be given an opportunity to confront their accusers and defend themselves*** (cp. 19:38-39). This put Roman judicial procedure in a favorable light for readers of Acts.

25:17 ***I didn't delay:*** In contrast with Felix, his predecessor (24:22-27).

25:18-20 These verses give Festus's official reasons for his actions; see also 25:9. There were no criminal accusations against Paul; the objections were ***about their religion*** and centered on Paul's claim that ***Jesus . . . is alive.***

25:23-27 Paul's hearing before ***King Agrippa*** was accompanied by all the pomp and circumstance appropriate for an official royal visit. The main purpose of the hearing was for Agrippa to advise Festus on what he should ***write*** in the appeal to Caesar, for there was ***no clear charge against*** Paul, and Festus himself believed Paul had ***done nothing deserving death.***

26

Then Agrippa said to Paul, "You may speak in your defense."

So Paul, gesturing with his hand, started his [d]defense: 2"I am fortunate, King Agrippa, that you are the one hearing my defense today against all these accusations made by the Jewish leaders, 3for I know you are an expert on all Jewish customs and controversies. Now please listen to me patiently!

4"As the Jewish leaders are well aware, I was given a thorough Jewish training from my earliest childhood among my own people and in Jerusalem. 5If they would admit it, they know that I have been a member of the Pharisees, the strictest sect of our religion. 6Now I am on trial because of my hope in the fulfillment of God's promise made to our ancestors. 7In fact, that is why the twelve tribes of Israel zealously worship God night and day, and they share the same hope I have. Yet, Your Majesty, they accuse me for having this hope! 8Why does it seem incredible to any of you that God can raise the dead?

9"I used to believe that I ought to do everything I could to oppose the very name of Jesus the Nazarene. 10Indeed, I did just that in Jerusalem. Authorized by the leading priests, I caused many believers there to be sent to prison. And I cast my vote against them when they were condemned to death. 11Many times I had them punished in the synagogues to get them to curse Jesus. I was so violently opposed to them that I even chased them down in foreign cities.

12"One day I was on such a mission to Damascus, armed with the authority and commission of the leading priests. 13About noon, Your Majesty, as I was on the road, a light from heaven brighter than the sun shone down on me and my companions. 14We all fell down, and I heard a voice saying to me in Aramaic, 'Saul, Saul, why are you persecuting me? It is useless for you to fight against my will.'

15" 'Who are you, lord?' I asked.

"And the Lord replied, 'I am Jesus, the one you are persecuting. 16Now get to your feet! For I have appeared to you to appoint you as my servant and witness. You are to tell the world what you have seen and what I will show you in the future. 17And I will rescue you from both your own people and the Gentiles. Yes, I am sending you to the Gentiles 18to open their eyes, so they may turn from darkness to light and from the power of Satan to God. Then they will receive forgiveness for their sins and be given a place among God's people, who are set apart by faith in me.'

19"And so, King Agrippa, I obeyed that vision from heaven. 20I preached first to those in Damascus, then in Jerusalem and throughout all Judea, and also to the Gentiles, that all must repent of their sins and turn to God—and prove they have changed by the good things they do. 21Some Jews arrested me in the Temple for preaching this, and they tried to kill me. 22But God has protected me right up to this present time so I can testify to everyone, from the least to the greatest. I teach nothing except what the prophets and Moses said would happen—23that the Messiah would suffer and be the first to rise from the dead, and in this way announce God's light to Jews and Gentiles alike."

24Suddenly, Festus shouted, "Paul, you are insane. Too much study has made you crazy!"

25But Paul replied, "I am not insane, Most Excellent Festus. What I am saying is the sober truth. 26And King Agrippa knows about these things. I speak boldly, for I am sure

26:1
[d]*apologeomai* (0626)
‣ Phil 1:7

26:4
Acts 22:3
Gal 1:13
Phil 3:5-6

26:6
Gen 3:15; 22:18; 26:4
Deut 18:15
Isa 7:14; 9:6-7
Jer 23:5-6; 33:14
Ezek 34:23; 37:24
Dan 9:24
Mal 3:1; 4:2
Acts 13:32; 23:6

26:7
Phil 3:11
1 Thes 3:10

26:8
Dan 12:2
Acts 23:6

26:9
John 15:21; 16:2
1 Tim 1:13

26:10
Acts 8:3; 22:4-5

26:12-18
//Acts 9:1-19; 22:6-16

26:14
Acts 9:7

26:16
Acts 22:14-15
Gal 1:12
Col 1:25
1 Tim 1:12

26:17
Acts 13:46-48; 22:21
Rom 11:13; 15:16
Gal 1:15-16; 2:7-9
1 Tim 2:7
2 Tim 1:11

26:18
Isa 35:5; 42:7, 16; 61:1
Luke 1:77, 79
Eph 1:11; 5:8
Col 1:13
1 Pet 2:9

26:20
Matt 3:8
Acts 9:19-29

26:21
Acts 21:30-31

26:22
Luke 24:27, 44

26:23
Isa 42:6; 49:6
Luke 24:46-47
Rom 1:3-4
1 Cor 15:20
Col 1:18
Rev 1:5

26:1-23 In his eloquent *defense* before King *Agrippa*, Paul argued that his preaching was completely consistent with the *Jewish* faith. The defense begins with a courteous acknowledgement of Agrippa's competence to hear the evidence (26:2-3), outlines the nature of Paul's background, Jewish training, and membership in the *Pharisees* (26:4-5), and explains that the charges against him are merely for believing the fulfillment of Jewish hopes for the resurrection (26:6-8). Paul then tells the story of his conversion from strong opponent of Christianity (26:9-11) through a vision on the way to *Damascus* (26:12-18; see 9:1-18). His preaching was nothing more than obeying this divine *vision* (26:19-20). Even though he encountered violent opposition from his fellow Jews (26:21), God *protected* him as he taught a message that the Jews should have embraced (26:22-23). This defense is a model for Christians put on trial for their faith (see 9:15; Luke 21:12-15).

26:9 *Jesus the Nazarene:* Or *Jesus of Nazareth.*

26:10 *many believers:* Literally *many of God's holy people.*

26:11 *to curse Jesus:* Literally *to blaspheme.*

26:12-18 See 9:1-18.

26:14 *Aramaic:* Or *Hebrew.* • *It is useless for you to fight against my will:* Literally *It is hard for you to kick against the oxgoads.*

26:17-18 Throughout his defense in this trial for his life, Paul also clearly set out the conditions for receiving new life in Christ (also in 26:20, 23; see Matt 10:19-20).

26:22-23 Paul stressed God's protection as he carried out his witness (cp. 3:18; 10:43; Luke 24:25-27, 44-47). Paul then called on his hearers to believe his message, that Jesus is the *Messiah* who fulfills the promises of the OT (see Luke 24:27, 44).

26:24 *Paul, you are insane:* Festus, a Roman, thought all this talk about the prophets and resurrection was *crazy* (cp. 17:18, 32), and he concluded that Paul must have driven himself mad with *too much study.*

26:24
1 Cor 4:10
26:26
John 18:20
Acts 26:3
26:31
Acts 23:9, 29
26:32
Acts 25:11
27:1
Acts 25:12
27:2
Acts 19:29; 20:4
27:3
Matt 11:21
Acts 24:23; 27:43; 28:2, 16

these events are all familiar to him, for they
were not done in a corner! 27King Agrippa,
do you believe the prophets? I know you
do—"
28Agrippa interrupted him. "Do you think
you can persuade me to become a Christian
so quickly?"
29Paul replied, "Whether quickly or not,
I pray to God that both you and everyone
here in this audience might become the
same as I am, except for these chains."
30Then the king, the governor, Bernice,
and all the others stood and left. 31As they
went out, they talked it over and agreed,
"This man hasn't done anything to deserve
death or imprisonment."
32And Agrippa said to Festus, "He could
have been set free if he hadn't appealed to
Caesar."

6. PAUL GOES TO ROME (27:1–28:31)

Paul's Journey to Rome (27:1–28:16)

The Journey to Cyprus and Crete

27 When the time came, we set sail for Italy. Paul and several other prisoners
were placed in the custody of a Roman officer named Julius, a captain of the Imperial
Regiment. 2Aristarchus, a Macedonian from
Thessalonica, was also with us. We left on a
ship whose home port was Adramyttium on
the northwest coast of the province of Asia;
it was scheduled to make several stops at
ports along the coast of the province.
3The next day when we docked at Sidon,

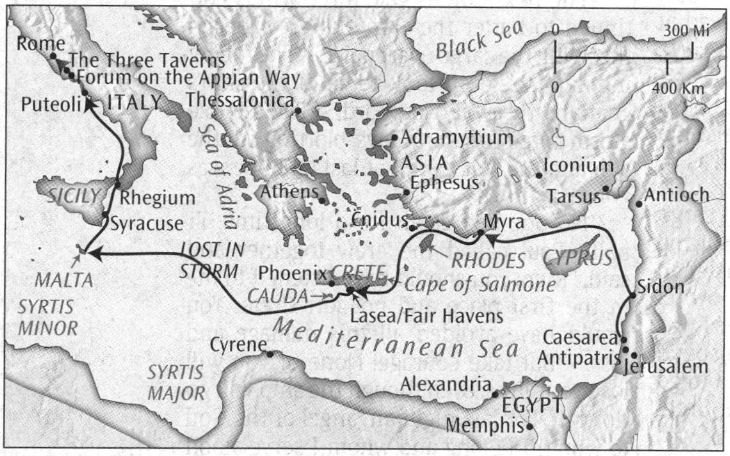

◀ **Paul's Journey to Rome, AD 59–60 (27:1–28:16).** Paul was arrested in Jerusalem and then imprisoned in Caesarea for over two years (AD 57–59). As a Roman citizen, he used the right of appeal to Caesar (25:10-11), so Festus sent him to Rome in late fall, AD 59. The sea and wind were dangerous at that time of year (27:1-12), and the voyage ended in shipwreck on Malta (27:13–28:1), where Paul and the rest of the company spent the winter (28:2-11). When the worst of winter was over in the spring, they traveled up to Rome (28:11-16; AD 60).

26:26 ***they were not done in a corner:*** The major events of the Christian faith were historical matters of public record that witnesses could attest as factually true. Agrippa could not invalidate Paul's statements of fact.

26:27-28 Paul's question put ***Agrippa*** in a bind: If he said he believed ***the prophets***, he knew Paul would press home the Christian message; if not, he would offend the devout Jews in his audience. Agrippa knew that Paul wasn't crazy and that Paul's testimony about Jesus was historically sound (26:26). So Agrippa evaded Paul's question and refused to face the claims of Christ, alleging that the statement given by Paul was too brief for him to arrive at a responsible decision.

26:28 ***"Do you think you can persuade me to become a Christian so quickly?"*** (or *"A little more, and your arguments would make me a Christian"*): This enigmatic remark might have been ironic, incredulous, scoffing, or brushing off Paul's challenge. It also might have been a direct statement of Paul's persuasiveness, or a direct statement about or genuine question of Paul's intention. It seems best to take Agrippa's reply as deliberately evasive: He didn't want to admit that he believed the prophets (26:27), for Paul had just made a strong case, and the next step would be to believe in Jesus as the promised Messiah to whom the prophets pointed. Agrippa didn't want to take that step. On the other hand, he didn't want to say that he didn't believe the prophets, for that would alienate the Jewish subjects to whose loyalties he wanted to appeal. His non-committal response underlines his discomfort with Paul's testimony.

26:29 Paul's bold answer shows his quickness in repartee. He challenges Agrippa and his whole audience about the value of knowing Christ and making a personal commitment to him.

26:31 The consensus of these rulers was that Paul had not ***done anything to deserve death or imprisonment;*** this verdict was given repeatedly by the Roman authorities that considered Paul's case (25:25; see Luke 23:4, 15, 22).

26:32 ***He could have been set free:*** The legal verdict was clear (26:31). But as a practical matter, ***if he hadn't appealed to Caesar,*** Paul might not have been alive (25:1-11). As it was, he was fulfilling God's purposes for him (23:11).

27:1–28:16 The vivid nautical language used throughout the account of Paul's journey to Rome yields one of the best available accounts of an ancient sea voyage. See map above. • This is the last "we" section in Acts (see also 16:10-17; 20:5-15; 21:1-18). During the two years of Paul's imprisonment, Luke had probably done much of the research for his Gospel throughout Judea and Galilee. Here, as a member of Paul's sailing party, he was an eyewitness participant in the danger at sea.

27:1 ***Roman officer:*** Literally ***centurion;*** similarly in 27:6, 11, 31, 43. ***Julius*** is otherwise unknown. • The ***Imperial Regiment*** (see note on 10:1) served in Syria during this time.

27:2 ***Aristarchus*** was a native of ***Thessalonica*** and a co-worker with Paul in Asia (see 19:29; 20:4, 6; Phlm 1:24). • ***Adramyttium*** was a port on the west coast of Asia Minor southeast of Troas. • ***Asia*** was a Roman ***province*** in what is now western Turkey.

27:3 ***Sidon,*** on the coast about 70 miles (110 km) north of Caesarea, was the first

Julius was very kind to Paul and let him go
ashore to visit with friends so they could
provide for his needs. 4Putting out to sea
from there, we encountered strong head-
winds that made it difficult to keep the
ship on course, so we sailed north of Cyprus between the island and the mainland.
5Keeping to the open sea, we passed along
the coast of Cilicia and Pamphylia, landing
at Myra, in the province of Lycia. 6There
the commanding officer found an Egyptian
ship from Alexandria that was bound for Italy, and he put us on board.

7We had several days of slow sailing,
and after great difficulty we finally neared
Cnidus. But the wind was against us, so we
sailed across to Crete and along the sheltered coast of the island, past the cape of
Salmone. 8We struggled along the coast
with great difficulty and finally arrived at
Fair Havens, near the town of Lasea. 9We
had lost a lot of time. The weather was becoming dangerous for sea travel because it
was so late in the fall, and Paul spoke to the
ship's officers about it.

10"Men," he said, "I believe there is trouble
ahead if we go on—shipwreck, loss of cargo,
and danger to our lives as well." 11But the
officer in charge of the prisoners listened
more to the ship's captain and the owner
than to Paul. 12And since Fair Havens was
an exposed harbor—a poor place to spend
the winter—most of the crew wanted to go
on to Phoenix, farther up the coast of Crete,
and spend the winter there. Phoenix was
a good harbor with only a southwest and
northwest exposure.

The Storm at Sea

13When a light wind began blowing from
the south, the sailors thought they could
make it. So they pulled up anchor and
sailed close to the shore of Crete. 14But the
weather changed abruptly, and a wind of
typhoon strength (called a "northeaster")
burst across the island and blew us out to
sea. 15The sailors couldn't turn the ship into
the wind, so they gave up and let it run before the gale.

16We sailed along the sheltered side of
a small island named Cauda, where with
great difficulty we hoisted aboard the lifeboat being towed behind us. 17Then the
sailors bound ropes around the hull of the
ship to strengthen it. They were afraid of being driven across to the sandbars of Syrtis
off the African coast, so they lowered the
sea anchor to slow the ship and were driven
before the wind.

18The next day, as gale-force winds continued to batter the ship, the crew began
throwing the cargo overboard. 19The following day they even took some of the ship's
gear and threw it overboard. 20The terrible
storm raged for many days, blotting out the
sun and the stars, until at last all hope was
gone.

21No one had eaten for a long time. Finally, Paul called the crew together and
said, "Men, you should have listened to me
in the first place and not left Crete. You
would have avoided all this damage and
loss. 22But take courage! None of you will
lose your lives, even though the ship will go
down. 23For last night an [e]angel of the God
to whom I belong and whom I serve stood
beside me, 24and he said, 'Don't be afraid,
Paul, for you will surely stand trial before
Caesar! What's more, God in his goodness
has granted safety to everyone sailing with
you.' 25So take courage! For I believe God. It

27:6 Acts 28:11
27:9 Lev 16:29-31
27:14 Mark 4:37
27:18 Jon 1:5
27:21 Acts 27:10
27:23 Acts 18:9; 23:11; 2 Tim 4:17; [e]*angelos* (0032) ‣ 1 Cor 4:9
27:24 Acts 23:11
27:25 Rom 4:20-21

port of call. ***Julius*** treated Paul kindly and allowed his local Christian ***friends*** to care for him.

27:4-6 Luke describes in detail the sea voyage north and then west along the southern coast of Asia Minor. • ***Myra*** was a regular stop for ***Egyptian*** grain ships ***bound for Italy***.

27:7 The ***great difficulty*** was due in part to the lateness of the season (27:9). • ***Cnidus*** was a seaport on the southwestern coast of Asia Minor near the island of Cos. • ***The cape of Salmone*** was located at the northeastern tip of ***Crete***, the largest of the Greek islands.

27:8 ***Fair Havens*** was a small bay on the southern side of the island of Crete.

27:9 ***because it was so late in the fall:*** Literally *because the fast was now already gone by.* This fast was associated with the Day of Atonement (*Yom Kippur*), which occurred in late September or early October. This was a ***dangerous*** time for a voyage on the Mediterranean.

27:10-11 Paul realized what would happen if they went on. He warned the ship's officers, but they and the Roman ***officer*** were unlikely to listen to an imprisoned Jewish rabbi with no experience as a seaman. Later, however, they would respect him more (27:30-36, 42-43).

27:12 The prevailing southeasterly winds made Fair Havens an unsafe place for ships to harbor in the winter, but ***Phoenix***, a town ***farther up the coast of Crete***, offered a better ***harbor***.

27:14-16 The storm, ***called a "northeaster,"*** was ***of typhoon strength***, very threatening to both the cargo and the crew. Forced to let the ship ***run before the gale***, they sailed past a small island called ***Cauda*** (some manuscripts read *Clauda*; it is known today as *Gaudos*), south of Crete.

27:17 Binding ropes around the ship's hull (called *frapping* in nautical terms) was intended ***to strengthen it*** against the tremendous pressure of the storm. • ***Syrtis*** refers to the shallow bays filled with ***sandbars*** off the coast of North Africa west of Cyrene (see map, p. 1881).

27:18-20 The violence and persistence of the storm led to ***throwing the cargo overboard*** (cp. Jon 1:5) and the crew's abandoning ***hope***.

27:21-26 Paul addressed the crew, first scolding them for not listening to him (27:10-12) and then encouraging them with the angel's assurance of survival for all of them.

27:26 Acts 28:1
27:34 Matt 10:30; Luke 12:7
27:35 Matt 14:19
27:38 Jon 1:5; Acts 27:18

will be just as he said. [26]But we will be shipwrecked on an island."

The Shipwreck at Malta

[27]About midnight on the fourteenth night
of the storm, as we were being driven
across the Sea of Adria, the sailors sensed
land was near. [28]They dropped a weighted
line and found that the water was 120 feet
deep. But a little later they measured again
and found it was only 90 feet deep. [29]At
this rate they were afraid we would soon be
driven against the rocks along the shore, so
they threw out four anchors from the back
of the ship and prayed for daylight.
[30]Then the sailors tried to abandon the
ship; they lowered the lifeboat as though
they were going to put out anchors from the
front of the ship. [31]But Paul said to the commanding officer and the soldiers, "You will
all die unless the sailors stay aboard." [32]So
the soldiers cut the ropes to the lifeboat and
let it drift away.
[33]Just as day was dawning, Paul urged
everyone to eat. "You have been so worried
that you haven't touched food for two weeks,"
he said. [34]"Please eat something now for your
own good. For not a hair of your heads will
perish." [35]Then he took some bread, gave
thanks to God before them all, and broke off
a piece and ate it. [36]Then everyone was encouraged and began to eat—[37]all 276 of us
who were on board. [38]After eating, the crew
lightened the ship further by throwing the
cargo of wheat overboard.
[39]When morning dawned, they didn't
recognize the coastline, but they saw a bay
with a beach and wondered if they could get

Angels (27:23-24)

Acts 5:19-20; 7:30-35, 53; 10:3-8; 12:6-11, 23
Ps 91:11
Dan 8:15-18; 9:21-23; 10:4–11:1; 12:1-2
Zech 1:8-13, 18-19; 2:3-5
Matt 1:20-24; 4:5-7, 11; 13:39-42, 49-50; 18:10; 24:31; 28:2-7
Mark 16:5-7
Luke 1:11-22, 26-38; 2:8-15; 9:26; 12:8
John 20:12-13
1 Cor 11:10
Gal 1:8; 3:19
Col 2:18
1 Thes 4:16
1 Tim 3:16; 5:21
Heb 1:5-14; 12:22; 13:2
2 Pet 2:4, 11
Jude 1:6, 9
Rev 1:1-2; 5:2, 11-12; 7:1-2; 8:3-8; 9:15; 10:7-9; 14:6-10; 16:1-12; 19:10, 17; 20:1; 22:6-9

In the book of Acts we frequently encounter the ministry of angels. On several occasions, an angel of the Lord made possible miraculous escapes from prison (5:19; 12:6-11). An angel offered a message of encouragement to Paul in the midst of a violent storm (27:23-24). An angel also directed Cornelius to seek the Good News from Peter (10:3, 7, 22; 11:13). On the other hand, we are told that an angel struck down Herod Agrippa "because he accepted the people's worship instead of giving the glory to God" (12:23). Throughout Acts, God was guiding his people in their ministry and using angels to accomplish his purpose.

The ministry of angels is also prominent in the Gospels. Angels announced the births of John the Baptist and Jesus (Luke 1–2) and ministered to Jesus after his temptation (Matt 4:5-7). Angels appeared at the empty tomb after the resurrection of Jesus (Matt 28:2, 5; Mark 16:5-7; Luke 24:23; John 20:12).

Throughout the Bible, angels are God's heavenly agents who carry out his purpose and communicate God's will to humanity (Gen 16:7; Num 22:22-34; Judg 13:13-21; 2 Kgs 1:3, 15; Zech 1:4-12; 12:8). Angels had a role in putting God's law into effect through Moses (7:30, 35, 38, 53; Gal 3:19). They are "spirits sent to care for people who will inherit salvation" (Heb 1:14). Angels dispense God's grace and sometimes administer his judgment (12:23; 2 Kgs 19:35; Rev 9:15; 16:1-12). Angels were witnesses of Christ's life (1 Tim 3:16), and they are now witnesses of the lives of God's people (1 Cor 11:10; 1 Tim 5:21). There are guardian angels who protect God's people (Matt 18:10; see also Ps 34:7; 91:11; Acts 12:11). Angels will accompany Christ when he returns (Matt 25:31; 2 Thes 1:7-8) and will participate in the final judgment (Matt 13:39, 41, 49-50; 16:27; 24:31; Mark 13:27; Luke 9:26; 12:8; 2 Thes 1:7).

Some angels have fallen into sin and are destined for eternal judgment (Matt 25:41; 2 Pet 2:4, 11; Jude 1:6). The only angels named in the Bible are Michael and Gabriel, who carry out special assignments (Dan 8:16, 18; 9:21; 10:12, 21; 12:1-2; Luke 1:19-20; 1 Thes 4:16; Jude 1:9).

Although angels are spiritual and heavenly beings, angels are not to be worshiped (Gal 1:8; Col 2:18; Rev 19:10; 22:8-9), because they are inferior to Christ (Heb 1:5-14). Their role is to be servants of God (Heb 1:14).

27:27 The *Sea of Adria* includes the central portion of the Mediterranean, south of Italy and Greece and between Malta and Crete. It is now known as the Ionian Sea.

27:28 *120 feet deep . . . 90 feet deep:* Greek *20 fathoms . . . 15 fathoms* [37 meters . . . 27 meters]; a fathom equaled six feet [1.85 meters].

27:30-32 This time the soldiers listened to Paul (cp. 27:10-11).

27:33-35 Paul's words and actions are those of a true leader who personally assesses a perilous situation, decides on action, and leads others in solving the problem (cp. Neh 1:1–3:32; contrast Jon 1). Paul's positive example and strong faith in God (27:22-25) encouraged the others to eat and take heart.

27:36-37 The food brought renewed strength and encouragement to the frightened and exhausted crew and prisoners. • ***all 276 of us:*** The exact number of persons onboard fits well with what is known of grain ships of the period.

27:39-41 They ***ran the ship aground*** on ***a shoal*** or reef.

to shore by running the ship aground. 40So they cut off the anchors and left them in the sea. Then they lowered the rudders, raised the foresail, and headed toward shore. 41But they hit a shoal and ran the ship aground too soon. The bow of the ship stuck fast, while the stern was repeatedly smashed by the force of the waves and began to break apart.

42The soldiers wanted to kill the prisoners to make sure they didn't swim ashore and escape. 43But the commanding officer wanted to spare Paul, so he didn't let them carry out their plan. Then he ordered all who could swim to jump overboard first and make for land. 44The others held on to planks or debris from the broken ship. So everyone escaped safely to shore.

Paul on the Island of Malta

28 Once we were safe on shore, we learned that we were on the island of Malta. 2The people of the island were very kind to us. It was cold and rainy, so they built a fire on the shore to welcome us.

3As Paul gathered an armful of sticks and was laying them on the fire, a poisonous snake, driven out by the heat, bit him on the hand. 4The people of the island saw it hanging from his hand and said to each other, "A murderer, no doubt! Though he escaped the sea, justice will not permit him to live." 5But Paul shook off the snake into the fire and was unharmed. 6The people waited for him to swell up or suddenly drop dead. But when they had waited a long time and saw that he wasn't harmed, they changed their minds and decided he was a god.

7Near the shore where we landed was an estate belonging to Publius, the chief official of the island. He welcomed us and treated us kindly for three days. 8As it happened, Publius's father was ill with fever and dysentery. Paul went in and prayed for him, and laying his hands on him, he healed him. 9Then all the other sick people on the island came and were healed. 10As a result we were showered with honors, and when the time came to sail, people supplied us with everything we would need for the trip.

The Trip from Malta to Rome

11It was three months after the shipwreck that we set sail on another ship that had wintered at the island—an Alexandrian ship with the twin gods as its figurehead. 12Our first stop was Syracuse, where we stayed three days. 13From there we sailed across to Rhegium. A day later a south wind began blowing, so the following day we sailed up the coast to Puteoli. 14There we found some believers, who invited us to spend a week with them. And so we came to Rome.

15The brothers and sisters in Rome had heard we were coming, and they came to meet us at the Forum on the Appian Way. Others joined us at The Three Taverns. When Paul saw them, he was encouraged and thanked God.

16When we arrived in Rome, Paul was permitted to have his own private lodging, though he was guarded by a soldier.

Paul's Ministry in Rome (28:17-31)

Paul's Meeting with the Jewish Community

17Three days after Paul's arrival, he called together the local Jewish leaders. He said to

27:41 2 Cor 11:25
27:43-44 Acts 27:22, 24
28:1 Acts 27:26, 39
28:4 Luke 13:2, 4
28:5 Mark 16:18; Luke 10:19
28:6 Acts 14:11
28:8 Jas 5:14-15
28:11 Acts 27:6
28:16 Acts 24:23; 27:3
28:17 Acts 24:12-13; 25:8

27:42-44 Even in a crisis, ***the prisoners*** remained the responsibility of ***the soldiers*** (see 12:19; 16:27; 27:32; see note on 16:27). Fortunately, ***the commanding officer*** intervened on their behalf. It was a clear indication of God's protection and favor that all 276 people made it ***safely to shore***, precisely fulfilling the angel's promise (see 27:24).

27:44 *or debris from the broken ship:* Or ***or were helped by members of the ship's crew.*** The Greek can be interpreted either way.

28:1 *Malta* was a major island under Roman control, about sixty miles (100 km) south of Sicily.

28:3-6 The locals of Malta understood ***justice*** as a personified power or deity carrying out judgment on a criminal. When nothing bad happened to Paul, the natives understood him as having power over snakes and concluded that he himself was a god (cp. 14:11-12). In fact, Paul's survival demonstrated God's protection (cp. Mark 16:17-18).

28:8-9 Cp. Luke 4:38-40.

28:10 Showing their gratefulness, the ***people supplied*** the ship's company with what they needed.

28:11-16 Luke, himself present on this journey (see note on 27:1–28:16), recorded Paul's itinerary from Malta to ***Rome*** with great geographical detail.

28:11 Another Egyptian ***ship*** from Alexandria took Paul and his companions on board after an interval of ***three months*** and the worst of the winter had passed. The ***twin gods*** were the Roman gods Castor and Pollux.

28:12 *Syracuse*, on the island of Sicily, was the capital of the eastern half of the island.

28:13-14 They sailed across the Straits of Messina to ***Rhegium*** on the southern tip of Italy. This port was a stopping place for ships traveling from the west coast of Italy to the eastern Mediterranean. • ***Puteoli*** (modern Pozzuoli) was a major port of entry for large grain ships bringing supplies from the east to Rome. Paul spent ***a week*** here with some local ***believers*** (literally ***brothers***) before moving on ***to Rome***.

28:15 Paul was greeted by ***brothers and sisters*** (literally ***brothers***) who met his party on the way up to Rome. • ***The Forum*** was about forty-three miles (70 km) from Rome. • ***The Three Taverns*** was about thirty-five miles (57 km) from Rome.

28:16 Paul was allowed ***to have his own . . . lodging***, apparently in ***private*** facilities, ***though he was guarded by a soldier***. Though Paul was traveling in chains, "the word of God cannot be chained" (2 Tim 2:9). Paul was possibly treated so well because of his social status or Roman citizenship (cp. 16:37-38; 22:25-28).

28:18 Acts 23:29
28:19 Acts 25:11
28:20 Acts 26:6
28:22 Acts 24:14
28:24 Acts 14:4
28:26-27 *Isa 6:9-10; John 12:39-40
28:28 Ps 67:2; 98:3; Luke 3:6; Acts 13:46
28:30 Acts 28:16

them, "Brothers, I was arrested in Jerusalem
and handed over to the Roman government,
even though I had done nothing against
our people or the customs of our ancestors.
18The Romans tried me and wanted to release me, because they found no cause for
the death sentence. 19But when the Jewish
leaders protested the decision, I felt it necessary to appeal to Caesar, even though I had
no desire to press charges against my own
people. 20I asked you to come here today
so we could get acquainted and so I could
explain to you that I am bound with this
chain because I believe that the hope of Israel—the Messiah—has already come."

21They replied, "We have had no letters
from Judea or reports against you from anyone who has come here. 22But we want to
hear what you believe, for the only thing we
know about this movement is that it is denounced everywhere."

23So a time was set, and on that day a
large number of people came to Paul's
lodging. He explained and testified about
the Kingdom of God and tried to persuade
them about Jesus from the Scriptures. Using the law of Moses and the books of the
prophets, he spoke to them from morning
until evening. 24Some were persuaded by
the things he said, but others did not believe.
25And after they had argued back and forth
among themselves, they left with this final
word from Paul: "The Holy Spirit was right
when he said to your ancestors through Isaiah the prophet,

26 'Go and say to this people:
When you hear what I say,
you will not understand.
When you see what I do,
you will not comprehend.
27 For the hearts of these people are
hardened,
and their ears cannot hear,
and they have closed their eyes—
so their eyes cannot see,
and their ears cannot hear,
and their hearts cannot understand,
and they cannot turn to me
and let me heal them.'

28So I want you to know that this salvation
from God has also been offered to the Gentiles, and they will accept it."

Paul's Unrestricted Preaching and Teaching
30For the next two years, Paul lived in Rome
at his own expense. He welcomed all who
visited him, 31boldly proclaiming the Kingdom of God and teaching about the Lord
Jesus Christ. And no one tried to stop him.

28:17-20 Conscious that the Good News was to be presented to the Jews first (13:46; Rom 1:16) and concerned that the false charges against him might already have reached Rome, Paul summoned ***the local Jewish leaders*** and gave an account of his life and work. He insisted that he was guilty of no criminal offense, but strong ***Jewish*** opposition had made it necessary for him ***to appeal*** to the emperor. Paul had nothing against his ***own people;*** rather, he wanted to explain his great conviction that ***the Messiah*** they had been expecting had ***already come*** in the person of Jesus of Nazareth.

28:21-22 The Jewish leaders assured Paul that they had received no ***reports against*** him, and they wanted ***to hear*** his explanation of ***this movement***.

28:23 Paul ***explained*** how ***Jesus*** fulfilled the OT hopes for ***the Kingdom of God,*** the master theme of Jesus' own preaching (Mark 1:14-15; see Matt 4:12-17; Luke 4:14-21, 43). Referring to ***the Scriptures,*** Paul presented the case for Jesus as the promised Messiah.

28:24 Paul's all-day message met a mixed response, as it had in other quarters (e.g., 13:40-51; 17:11-14).

28:25-28 Paul parted with scriptural words of warning that are often used in the NT to explain the Jewish rejection of the gospel (cp. Matt 13:14-15; Mark 4:12; Luke 8:10; John 12:38-40; see Rom 11:1-12, 25-32).

28:26-27 This passage quotes Isa 6:9-10 (Greek version).

28:28 Since Jews everywhere had been given an opportunity to accept the faith (13:46; see Rom 1:16), it was now time for ***the Gentiles*** to be offered ***this salvation.*** • Some manuscripts add v 29, *And when he had said these words, the Jews departed, greatly disagreeing with each other.*

28:30 ***at his own expense:*** Or *in his own rented quarters.*

28:31 Despite being under house arrest (28:16), Paul ***boldly*** proclaimed the Kingdom message. • ***And no one tried to stop him*** (Greek *akōloutōs,* "without hindrance"): This single word in Greek is the last word of the book of Acts and one of the keys to its meaning: God's word cannot be chained, even when its messengers are (2 Tim 2:9; see Phil 1:12-14). Acts is the story of an unhindered message of Good News, available to all people throughout the world, whether Jew, Gentile, proselyte, rich, or poor. The mission of proclaiming this message is accomplished in the power of the Spirit (1:8); it embraces Jews (3:1–5:42), Samaritans (8:1-25), converts to Judaism (2:11; 13:43), "God-fearers" (8:26-40; 9:32–11:18), and Gentiles (13:1–28:28). • Luke ends his account with Paul still under house arrest in Rome (about AD 60–62). Paul was later freed and traveled freely (see chart, p. 1845). According to tradition, Paul was imprisoned again in Rome in about AD 64 and was martyred there during Nero's persecution of believers.

INTRODUCTION TO THE
LETTERS OF PAUL

Paul wrote almost one-quarter of the New Testament. His thirteen letters to churches and individuals have been deeply influential in Christian belief and practice.

SETTING

Paul's early training and education (Acts 22:3; 26:4) instilled in him a zeal for his ancestral faith that led him to persecute the fledgling Christian movement (Acts 8:1-3). But Christ revealed himself to Paul on the road to Damascus, and his world was overturned (Acts 9).

After his conversion, Paul became one of the most passionate followers of Christ. He immediately began to proclaim Christ in Damascus (Acts 9:20) and then for a decade in his hometown (Acts 9:30). At the invitation of Barnabas, Paul moved to Antioch, where Jews and Gentiles were worshiping together (Acts 11:25-26). From there Paul was sent on three missionary journeys (Acts 13:1–14:28; 15:36–18:22; 18:23–21:17), during which vibrant churches were planted in Asia Minor, Macedonia, and Achaia.

Controversy, however, dogged Paul's steps. His insistence that Gentiles have full rights in the church without obligation to follow the law of Moses made him a target of Jewish opposition. Eventually, he was arrested in Jerusalem, imprisoned in Caesarea, and sent to Rome (Acts 21:27–28:16) to be tried before Caesar. After two years (Acts 28:30-31), Paul was released, only to be rearrested afterward and then executed during Nero's persecution (about AD 64~65).

LITERARY GENRE

Paul wrote letters, a well-known genre in his day. Greco-Roman letters ranged from short notes ("Dear Dad, please send money!") to longer public treatises. Paul's letters range along this spectrum. Even those letters written to individuals deal with issues that were significant for the churches (1 Timothy, 2 Timothy, Titus, Philemon). Toward the other end of the spectrum are Romans and Ephesians, each of which is more of a theological and pastoral treatise than a letter in any modern sense. The public nature of Paul's letters is also revealed in that his associates are sometimes mentioned as secondary authors.

Ancient letters usually followed a set form: address, greeting, body, conclusion. Paul follows this format, though he often expands it.

Ancient writers often employed a scribe, or *amanuensis,* to write down a letter, and Paul did, too (see, e.g., Rom 16:22). A trusted amanuensis would often have considerable freedom to choose the actual wording of a letter. The variation in Greek style that is found in the letters of Paul may owe something to the influence of an amanuensis.

AUTHORSHIP

Variations in style and theological emphasis have led some scholars to think that not all the NT letters attributed to Paul were actually written by him, but that some were written pseudonymously in his name. Many scholars believe that there are only seven authentic letters of Paul: Romans, 1 and 2 Corinthians, Galatians, Philippians, 1 Thessalonians, and Philemon.

This theory is improbable. There is no evidence from the ancient world that letters were ever written in another person's name—unless they were forgeries with the intent to deceive. The theory is also unnecessary, because the differences among the letters of Paul can be more naturally explained with the possible influence of an amanuensis as well as the natural adaptation of style and emphasis to audience and situation. Each of Paul's letters was written to deal with specific problems in a specific situation.

MEANING AND MESSAGE

Four themes occur repeatedly in Paul's letters. First, God (through Jesus Christ) has intervened in his fallen world to make things right again. Jesus' death and resurrection usher in "the last days" that the OT prophets anticipated. This time period will be brought to its climax when he returns.

Second, God offers sinful human beings the opportunity to be reconciled with him through Christ. People whose sin and rebellion have estranged them from God can be reconciled to him and declared righteous by believing in Jesus Christ.

Third, the Good News is for all kinds of people. Even though God's plan of salvation is unified from Adam to Christ, the coming of Christ broke down ethnic barriers. Jews and Gentiles alike need salvation, and they alike find salvation only through faith in Christ.

Fourth, Paul's letters were written to help believers understand and live out the meaning of their new life in Christ. Paul responded to false teachers who were leading people astray and dealt with misunderstandings that had arisen in the young churches. Paul therefore dealt with a wide spectrum of issues, some of which are quite similar to issues we still face.

Paul reminds us that Christ is Lord and wants to reign over every facet of our lives. The Holy Spirit empowers and guides us to live this new, Christ-centered life.

FURTHER READING

F. F. BRUCE
Paul, Apostle of the Heart Set Free (2000)

GERALD F. HAWTHORNE AND RALPH P. MARTIN, EDS.
Dictionary of Paul and his Letters (1993)

RICHARD N. LONGENECKER
The Ministry and Message of Paul (1971)

THOMAS R. SCHREINER
Paul: Apostle of God's Glory in Christ (2001)

PAUL'S LETTER TO THE

ROMANS

Romans has been called the greatest theological document ever written. In this letter, the apostle Paul explains the Good News—the climactic revelation of God to the world through his Son, the Lord Jesus Christ. Paul reflects on the human condition, on the meaning of our lives on earth, and on our hope for the world to come. He constantly moves us back to the fundamentals of God's truth revealed in Christ, and he teaches us to deal with the problems, failures, and disputes that characterize life in this world.

SETTING

We do not know who first brought the Good News to Rome. Perhaps Jews from Rome who were converted when God first poured out his Spirit on the day of Pentecost (see Acts 2:10) took the message back to their home city. Several "house churches" quickly grew up, made up primarily of converts from Judaism.

In AD 49, the Emperor Claudius expelled all Jews from Rome—including Jewish Christians (see Acts 18:2). Although Paul had never visited Rome (1:13), in his travels he met some of these Roman Christians, such as Priscilla and Aquila (16:3-4; cp. Acts 18:2).

Claudius's decree eventually lapsed, so by the time Paul wrote his letter to the Romans, many Jewish Christians had returned to Rome. However, in their absence the Gentile Christians had taken the lead in the Christian community in Rome. Therefore, when Paul wrote to the Roman Christians (probably about AD 57), the Roman Christian community was divided into two major factions. The Gentile Christians now comprised the majority group, and they were naturally less concerned about continuity with the OT or with the demands of the law of Moses than their Jewish brothers and sisters. They even looked down on the Jewish Christians (see 11:25). The minority Jewish Christians, for their part, reacted to the Gentile-Christian majority by insisting on adherence to certain aspects of the law of Moses. Paul wrote this letter to the Roman Christians to address this theological and social division, a schism that had at its heart the question of continuity and discontinuity between Jewish and Christian faith.

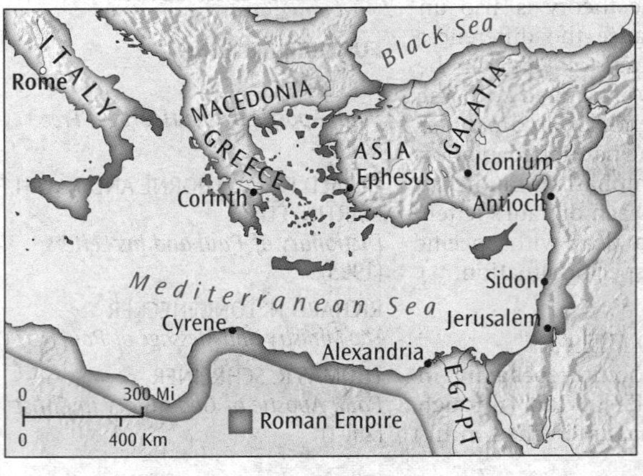

The Setting of Romans, about AD 57. Paul probably wrote Romans toward the end of his third missionary journey (Acts 18:23–19:41), perhaps from CORINTH. Paul had the opportunity to visit the Romans, as he hoped (1:10-15)—his third missionary journey ended in JERUSALEM, where he was imprisoned and eventually sent to ROME, where he arrived in AD 60 (Acts 28:11-15).

SUMMARY

In the introduction of the letter (1:1-17), Paul identifies himself and his readers (1:1-7), expresses thanks for the Roman Christians (1:8-15), and introduces the theme of the letter: the "Good News about Christ" (1:16-17).

Before elaborating on this Good News, Paul sets out the dark backdrop of universal human sinfulness that makes the Good News necessary. Both Gentiles (1:18-32) and Jews (2:1–3:8) have turned away from God's revelation of himself. All are "under the power of sin" and cannot be made right with God by anything they do (3:9-20).

Into this hopeless situation comes the Good News, which reveals a new "way to be made right" with God. God provided this new way by sending Jesus as a sacrifice for sin, and all human beings can gain the benefits of that sacrifice by faith (3:21-26). Paul highlights the centrality of faith and its nature in 3:27–4:25. He shows that faith excludes boasting and that it enables both Jews and Gentiles to have equal access to God's grace in Christ (3:27-31). He develops these same points through reference to Abraham (4:1-25).

In chs 5–8, Paul discusses the assurance or security of salvation. The assurance that believers will share God's glory (5:1-11) is based on the way in which Jesus Christ more than reversed the terrible effects of Adam's sin (5:12-21). Neither sin (6:1-23) nor the law (7:1-25) can prevent God from accomplishing his purposes for the believer. The Holy Spirit liberates believers from death (8:1-17) and assures them that the sufferings of this life will not keep them from the glory to which God has destined them (8:18-39).

OUTLINE

1:1-17
The Letter Opening

1:18–4:25
The Heart of the Gospel: Justification by Faith

5:1–8:39
The Assurance Provided by the Gospel: The Hope of Salvation

9:1–11:36
The Defense of the Gospel: The Problem of Israel

12:1–15:13
The Transforming Power of the Gospel: Christian Conduct

15:14–16:27
The Letter Closing

The Good News can only truly be "good news" if the message of Christ stands in continuity with God's promises in the OT. But the unbelief of so many Jews might show that God's promises to Israel are not being fulfilled (9:1-5). So, in chs 9–11, Paul demonstrates that God is being faithful to his promises. God had never promised salvation to all Jews, but only to a remnant (9:6-29). The Jews themselves are responsible for their predicament because they refuse to recognize the fulfillment of God's promises in Christ (9:30–10:21). Furthermore, God is faithfully preserving a remnant of Jewish believers (11:1-10), and God has still more to accomplish for his people Israel (11:11-36).

The Good News rescues people from the penalty of sin, and it also transforms a person's life. In 12:1–15:13, Paul turns his attention to the transforming power of the Good News. In keeping with God's mercies, this transformation demands a whole new way of thinking and living (12:1-2).

TIMELINE

Pentecost, AD 30 or 33
The birth of the church in Jerusalem

about AD 31 or 34
Probable founding of the church in Rome

AD 49
Emperor Claudius expels Jews from Rome

AD 53–57
Paul's third missionary journey

about AD 57
Paul writes Romans from Corinth

AD 57
Paul travels to Jerusalem and is arrested

AD 57–59
Paul is imprisoned in Caesarea

AD 59–60
Paul's voyage to Rome

AD 60–62
Paul is imprisoned in Rome

AD 62~64
Paul is released, travels freely

July AD 64
Fire destroys Rome

AD 64~65
Persecution of Christians under Nero
Peter is crucified in Rome

about AD 64~65?
Paul is imprisoned and martyred in Rome

The transformed life will be fleshed out in community harmony (12:3-8), manifestations of love (12:9-21; cp. 13:8-10), and submission to the government (13:1-7). The transformed life derives its power from the work God has already done, as well as from the work he has yet to do (13:11-14).

In 14:1–15:13, Paul tackles a specific issue that was a problem in the church at Rome. Christians were criticizing each other over various practices related to the OT law. Paul exhorts them to accept each other and to look to Christ's example of self-giving love as the model to emulate.

The letter format of Romans emerges again at the end, where Paul touches on his ministry and travel plans (15:14-33), greets and commends fellow workers and other Christians (16:1-16), and concludes with further references to fellow workers, a final warning, and a doxology (16:17-27).

DATE, PLACE, AND OCCASION OF WRITING

Paul probably wrote Romans during a three-month stay in Corinth near the end of his third missionary journey (Acts 20:2-3), around AD 57. The reference to Cenchrea in 16:1—a port city next to Corinth—identifies the geography more precisely. By this time, Paul had completed his missionary work in the eastern Mediterranean, and his visit to Jerusalem was imminent.

We can determine the general situation in which Romans was written by reviewing Paul's references to his prior ministry and his future travel plans (15:14-33). Four geographical references provide the framework: (1) Looking back, Paul declared that he had "fully presented the Good News of Christ from Jerusalem all the way to Illyricum" (15:19). Illyricum was a Roman province that occupied the same general area as modern-day Serbia and Croatia. Paul noted that he had planted churches in major cities from Jerusalem, through Asia Minor, and into Macedonia and Greece. This was the territory Paul and his companions covered on the three great missionary journeys recorded in Acts. (2) Paul's intermediate destination was Jerusalem, where he planned to deliver a "gift to the believers" (15:25). This gift was money that Paul had been collecting from the Gentile churches he had founded to assist the church in Jerusalem (15:26; see also 1 Cor 16:1-4; 2 Cor 8–9). (3) After visiting Jerusalem to deliver the collection, Paul planned to go to Rome (15:24). (4) A long stay with the Roman Christians was not Paul's final goal, as the language of 15:24 ("stop off") makes clear. His ultimate goal was Spain, where he could pursue his calling to plant churches in places "where the name of Christ has never been heard" (15:20, 24). This information points to a date near the end of the third missionary journey.

[Romans] is worthy not only that every Christian should know it word for word, by heart, but occupy himself with it every day, as the daily bread of the soul. It can never be read or pondered too much, and the more it is dealt with the more precious it becomes, and the better it tastes.

MARTIN LUTHER
"Preface to the Epistle to the Romans"

PAUL'S PURPOSE IN WRITING

Romans combines three specific purposes: to summarize Paul's theology, to solicit support for a future mission to Spain, and to bring unity to the church in Rome.

Paul saw himself standing at a critical juncture in his ministry (15:20). He had "fully presented" or fulfilled the Good News by taking it to a broad area of the eastern Mediterranean basin (15:19). He now stood ready to move to the far end of the Mediterranean to preach the

Good News in new territory. It is quite natural, then, that Paul took the occasion of his letter to the Romans to summarize his theology as he had hammered it out in the midst of controversy and trial for the previous twenty-five years.

In other words, Romans might be a summary of Paul's theology. Even so, this is not the whole of Paul's purpose in writing—it does not explain why Paul says so little in Romans about key theological ideas (e.g., the person of Christ, the church, the last days). Nor does it explain why Paul would have sent this summary of his theology to the church in Rome.

Another purpose emerges when we turn our attention to Paul's ultimate destination, Spain: Paul wanted to gather support from the Roman Christians for his new mission in a distant land. Paul's "sending church," Antioch, was thousands of miles from Spain. As the apostle sought a new church to partner with him, his attention naturally turned to the church in Rome (15:24). Therefore, it is likely that Paul sent this dense theological treatise to Rome because he wanted to explain who he was and what he believed. Because Paul's message had frequently been misunderstood, he became a controversial figure in the early church. He was undoubtedly aware that some Christians in Rome were suspicious of him and that he therefore must provide a careful and reasoned defense of his position on some of the most debated issues of the faith.

Finally, Paul wrote to a Christian community in Rome that was divided over the degree to which the OT law should continue to guide believers. Paul's long and explicit treatment of this problem (14:1–15:13) reveals that one of his purposes in writing was to heal this rift in the community in Rome.

In Romans, Paul presented the Good News as he had come to understand it. The heart of that Good News is the offer of salvation in Christ for all who believe. Paul explores the problem of human sin, the solution provided in the cross of Christ, and the assurance of glory that a living relationship with Christ provides. The message of the cross of Christ stands both in continuity with the OT (because its promises are truly fulfilled in Christ) and in discontinuity with it (as God in Christ inaugurates a new covenant that transcends the OT law).

The reasons why Romans is such a powerful piece of writing, and why it has been so influential in Christian history, are one and the same. . . . We see Paul the Jew wrestling with the implications of his own and his converts' experience of grace and Paul the Christian wrestling with the implications of his Jewish heritage. We see in Romans Paul operating at the interface between Pharisaic Judaism and Christianity, and the transition from the one to the other in process of being worked out.

JAMES D. G. DUNN
Romans, p. xvi

INTERPRETATION

Since the time of the Reformation, Romans has been read as a letter about the salvation of the individual. Following the lead of Martin Luther, whose own spiritual pilgrimage was closely tied to the theology of Romans, the Reformers (such as John Calvin and Ulrich Zwingli) saw in this letter the classic biblical expression of the truth that human beings are put right with God by their faith in Christ and not by their own effort. The Reformers viewed Paul as fighting against a legalistic Judaism that insisted that people had to obey the law to be saved. Jewish preoccupation with the law had led many Jews to presume that faithfulness to the law was sufficient for salvation (e.g., 10:1-4).

Many contemporary interpreters insist that this Reformation view of Romans left out important elements in understanding both the letter itself and first-century Judaism. Jews in Paul's day, it is argued, did not believe that they had to obey the law to be saved. They were already saved, through God's choosing them to be his people. Obeying the

law was the way they maintained their status as God's people. These interpreters say that Paul was not fighting against legalism but against exclusivism—against the Jewish claim that salvation was confined to Israel and was not to be shared with Gentiles. Accordingly, Paul shows how the Good News relates salvation through faith to the continuity of God's people from the OT to the NT and to the relationship of Jews and Gentiles in his own day.

This new approach to understanding Romans has much to commend it. Christian interpreters have sometimes missed the notes of grace and faith that are part of Jewish teaching. And Romans does have a lot to say about including Gentiles in God's people and the relationship between Jews and Gentiles in the church.

Ultimately, however, neither the Reformation view alone nor the contemporary view alone explains everything in Romans. They need to be combined if we are to appreciate the letter as a whole. At its most foundational level, Romans is about the Good News—and the Good News, first and foremost, is a message about how everyone can have a right relationship with God.

FURTHER READING

ROGER MOHRLANG
Romans in *Cornerstone Biblical Commentary,* vol. 14 (2007)

DOUGLAS J. MOO
The Epistle to the Romans (1996)

JOHN MURRAY
The Epistle to the Romans (1959, 1965)

THOMAS SCHREINER
Romans (1998)

JOHN R. W. STOTT
Romans: God's Good News for the World (1994)

1. THE LETTER OPENING (1:1-17)

Greetings from Paul

1 This letter is from Paul, a [a]slave of Christ
Jesus, chosen by God to be an apostle
and sent out to preach his [b]Good News.
2 God promised this Good News long ago
through his prophets in the holy Scriptures.
3 The Good News is about his Son. In his
earthly life he was born into King David's
family line, 4 and he was shown to be the Son
of God when he was raised from the dead
by the power of the Holy Spirit. He is Jesus
Christ our Lord. 5 Through Christ, God has
given us the privilege and authority as apostles
to tell Gentiles everywhere what God
has done for them, so that they will believe
and obey him, bringing glory to his name.
6 And you are included among those Gentiles
who have been [c]called to belong to
Jesus Christ. 7 I am writing to all of you in
Rome who are loved by God and are called
to be his own holy people.

May God our Father and the Lord Jesus
Christ give you grace and peace.

1:1 [a]*doulos* (1401) ‣Rom 6:20 [b]*euangelion* (2098) ‣Rom 1:16
1:2 Titus 1:2
1:3 Matt 1:1; 22:42
1:4 1 Cor 15:1-4, 12-23
1:5 Acts 9:15; 26:15-18
1:6 [c]*klētos* (2822) ‣Rom 8:28

1:1-17 These verses contain the normal features of NT letter introductions: an identification of the writer (1:1-6) and readers (1:7); a thanksgiving (1:8-15); and the theme of the letter (1:16-17).

1:1 ***slave of Christ Jesus:*** The word *slave* is used of important OT leaders of God's people, such as Moses (2 Kgs 18:12), Joshua (Josh 24:29), Elijah (2 Kgs 10:10), and David (2 Sam 7:8). The title underscores Paul's complete subservience to Christ as Lord. • ***sent out*** (literally *set apart*): Paul may be alluding to being "set apart" by God for his mission before he was born, as the prophet Jeremiah was (Jer 1:5). He may also be referring to God's call at the time of his Damascus Road conversion (Acts 9:15-16; cp. Acts 13:2), to preach the Good News to Jews and especially to Gentiles. • The ***Good News,*** or "gospel," is a recurrent topic in the opening of the letter (1:1, 9, 15, 16). Paul takes the word from the OT, where the Hebrew equivalent refers to the victory that God wins for his people (Isa 40:9; 41:27; 60:6; 61:1; Nah 1:15; see Joel 2:32).

1:3-4 In the Greek, these verses are in carefully structured parallel form; Paul might be quoting an early Christian creed or hymn about Jesus Christ as God's ***Son*** in order to establish common ground with the Roman Christians, whom he had never visited.

1:3 ***In his earthly life*** (literally *As regards the flesh*): Paul often uses "flesh" (Greek *sarx*) to refer to bodily existence in this world (e.g., 4:1; 8:3). • Paul refers to ***King David's family line*** because God promised that a descendant of David would be the Messiah and would be given an eternal kingdom (2 Sam 7:13-16; see Isa 9:7; Jer 33:15). Jesus was born into David's line (Matt 1:6; Luke 1:27, 32), so he was qualified to fulfill God's promise.

1:4 ***and he was shown to be*** (or *and was designated*): Although he eternally existed as the Son of God (1:3), Jesus' resurrection demonstrated him to be God's Son, revealing him in all his power and glory. • ***by the power of the Holy Spirit:*** Or *by the Spirit of holiness;* or *in the new realm of the Spirit.*

1:5 ***given us . . . apostles:*** Here Paul might have been thinking both of himself and of the other apostles, or he might be using an editorial plural to refer only to himself. • ***the privilege*** (or *the grace*): Privilege and ***authority*** could specify two separate things, but one might explain the other, as in the privilege of having apostolic authority. Paul always makes it clear that his distinctive authority is a gift from God (see also 15:15-16). • ***so that they will believe and obey him:*** This summary of Paul's purpose in preaching to Gentiles brackets the book of Romans, as he repeats the same idea in slightly different language at the end of the letter (16:26). Paul wanted Gentiles to believe in Jesus Christ; he underscored that believing in Jesus Christ as the Lord entails a commitment to obey him. Faith and obedience are not identical, but one does not occur without the other.

1:7 To be ***holy*** means to be set apart for God. This expression is used throughout the OT to describe Israel, God's chosen ***people*** (cp. Exod 19:6), whom God called from among all other nations to be his own. By calling the Gentile Christians ***his own holy people,*** Paul makes it clear that Gentiles are now fully included among God's people.

1:8
1 Thes 1:8
1:9
Phil 1:8-9
1:11
[d]*charisma* (5486)
‣Rom 12:6
1:14
1 Cor 9:16
1:15
Rom 15:20
1:16
Acts 3:26
1 Cor 1:18, 24
[e]*euangelion* (2098)
‣Rom 2:16
[f]*sōtēria* (4991)
‣Rom 8:24
1:17
*Hab 2:4
Rom 3:21-22
Gal 3:11
Heb 10:38
[g]*dikaiosunē* (1343)
‣Rom 3:21
[h]*pistis* (4102)
‣Rom 3:22
1:18
Eph 5:6
Col 3:6
[i]*orgē* (3709)
‣Rom 2:5
1:19
Acts 14:15-17;
17:24-28
1:20
Job 12:7-9
Ps 19:1

Thanksgiving and Occasion: Paul and the Romans

8 Let me say first that I thank my God
through Jesus Christ for all of you, because
your faith in him is being talked about all
over the world. 9 God knows how often I pray
for you. Day and night I bring you and your
needs in prayer to God, whom I serve with
all my heart by spreading the Good News
about his Son.

10 One of the things I always pray for is
the opportunity, God willing, to come at
last to see you. 11 For I long to visit you so I
can bring you some spiritual [d]gift that will
help you grow strong in the Lord. 12 When
we get together, I want to encourage you in
your faith, but I also want to be encouraged
by yours.

13 I want you to know, dear brothers and
sisters, that I planned many times to visit
you, but I was prevented until now. I want to
work among you and see spiritual fruit, just
as I have seen among other Gentiles. 14 For
I have a great sense of obligation to people
in both the civilized world and the rest of
the world, to the educated and uneducated
alike. 15 So I am eager to come to you in
Rome, too, to preach the Good News.

The Theme of the Letter: God's Good News

16 For I am not ashamed of this [e]Good News
about Christ. It is the power of God at work,
[f]saving everyone who believes—the Jew
first and also the Gentile. 17 This Good News
tells us how God makes us [g]right in his sight.
This is accomplished from start to finish by
[h]faith. As the Scriptures say, "It is through
[h]faith that a righteous person has life."

2. THE HEART OF THE GOSPEL: JUSTIFICATION BY FAITH (1:18–4:25)

All Persons are Accountable to God for Sin (1:18-32)

18 But God shows his [i]anger from heaven
against all sinful, wicked people who suppress the truth by their wickedness. 19 They
know the truth about God because he has
made it obvious to them. 20 For ever since
the world was created, people have seen
the earth and sky. Through everything God
made, they can clearly see his invisible qualities—his eternal power and divine nature. So
they have no excuse for not knowing God.

1:9 When Paul uses the phrase ***with all my heart*** (or *in my spirit*), he might be describing the influence of God's Holy Spirit on his own inner person. The word *spirit* also refers to the deepest part of a person, which the phrase *all my heart* expresses well.

1:11 ***some spiritual gift:*** Paul is probably referring to the spiritual benefit that he hopes his ministry will *bring* to the Roman Christians.

1:13 ***brothers and sisters*** (literally *brothers*): This Greek word (*adelphoi*) describes people who are in a familial relationship. Paul and other NT writers use this word to indicate that Christians are so intimately tied to one another in Christ that they are family. The word refers to both male and female Christians. • ***I was prevented until now:*** Paul wrote this letter when he was in Corinth toward the end of his third missionary journey (see Acts 20:2-4; cp. Rom 16:21-23). The need to plant and nourish churches in the eastern Mediterranean had occupied Paul up to this point. Before he could visit the Roman Christians, he first needed to return to Jerusalem to deliver a gift of money collected from the Gentile churches for the impoverished Jewish Christians (15:23-29).

1:14 ***to people in both the civilized world and the rest of the world*** (literally *to Greeks and barbarians*): The Greeks prided themselves on being sophisticated and cultured, while regarding people from other cultures as inferior. They mocked other peoples' poorly spoken Greek, claiming that they could only say "bar bar," a nonsense phrase from which our word *barbarian* comes. Paul uses this cultural divide to emphasize his intention to preach the Good News to all kinds of people.

1:16 Paul consistently emphasizes that the Good News is for ***everyone***. He also insists that God ***first*** chose the Jews to be his people, made promises to them, and gave them a unique place in the continuing plan of God (3:1-8; 9:1-5). They have a special responsibility to respond to the Good News and will be judged first if they turn away (2:9-10). • ***also the Gentile:*** Literally *also the Greek.*

1:17 ***how God makes us right in his sight*** (literally *the righteousness of God*): This key phrase appears eight times in Romans (see also 3:5, 21, 22, 25, 26; 10:3; the only other occurrence in Paul's writings is 2 Cor 5:21). The expression has OT roots, where God's righteousness refers to his character (as holy or faithful) or to an act of declaring his people sinless and perfect in his eyes (see especially Isa 46:13; 51:5-8). Paul uses the second meaning in this verse. The Good News has the power to save because it is the fulfillment of God's promise to vindicate his people. • The phrase ***makes us right*** comes from the law court. It does not mean "makes us good people"; it means "puts us in right standing before God." • ***"It is through faith that a righteous person has life"*** (or *"The righteous will live by faith"* Hab 2:4): The prophet Habakkuk had struggled to understand how God could use pagan nations to judge his own people Israel. God reminded Habakkuk that his true people—the *righteous*—need to live by faith. In chs 1–4, Paul repeatedly insists that only through faith can human beings be made right in God's sight.

1:18–3:20 Paul delays exploring the theme of righteousness through faith (see 3:21) until he first teaches about universal sinfulness. Gentiles (1:18-32) and Jews (2:1–3:8) are equally under sin's power and cannot find favor with God by any action of their own (3:9-20).

1:18 God's ***anger*** is not a spontaneous emotional outburst, but the holy God's necessary response to sin. The OT often depicts God's anger (Exod 32:10-12; Num 11:1; Jer 21:3-7) and predicts a decisive outpouring of God's wrath on human sin at the end of history. While Paul usually depicts God's anger as occurring in the end times (2:5, 8; 5:9; Col 3:6; 1 Thes 1:10), the present tense of ***shows*** refers to God's expressions of anger throughout human history. • ***who suppress the truth by their wickedness:*** Or *who, by their wickedness, prevent the truth from being known.*

21Yes, they knew God, but they wouldn't worship him as God or even give him thanks. And they began to think up foolish ideas of what God was like. As a result, their minds became dark and confused. 22Claiming to be wise, they instead became utter fools. 23And instead of worshiping the glorious, ever-living God, they worshiped idols made to look like mere people and birds and animals and reptiles.

24So God abandoned them to do whatever shameful things their hearts desired. As a result, they did vile and degrading things with each other's bodies. 25They traded the truth about God for a lie. So they worshiped and served the things God created instead of the Creator himself, who is worthy of eternal praise! Amen. 26That is why God abandoned them to their shameful desires. Even the women turned against the natural way to have sex and instead indulged in sex with each other. 27And the men, instead of having normal sexual relations with women, burned with lust for each other. Men did shameful things with other men, and as a result of this sin, they suffered within themselves the penalty they deserved.

28Since they thought it foolish to acknowledge God, he abandoned them to their foolish thinking and let them do things that should never be done. 29Their lives became full of every kind of wickedness, sin, greed, hate, envy, murder, quarreling, deception, malicious behavior, and gossip. 30They are backstabbers, haters of God, insolent, proud, and boastful. They invent new ways of sinning, and they disobey their parents. 31They refuse to understand, break their promises, are heartless, and have no mercy. 32They know God's justice requires that those who do these things deserve to die, yet they do them anyway. Worse yet, they encourage others to do them, too.

Jews are Accountable to God for Sin (2:1–3:8)

The Jews and the Judgment of God

2 You may think you can condemn such people, but you are just as bad, and you have no excuse! When you say they are wicked and should be punished, you are condemning yourself, for you who judge others do these very same things. 2And we know that God, in his justice, will punish anyone who does such things. 3Since you judge others for doing these things, why do you think you can avoid God's judgment when you do the same things? 4Don't you see how wonderfully kind, tolerant, and patient God is with you? Does this mean nothing to you? Can't you see that his kindness is intended to [j]turn you from your sin?

5But because you are stubborn and refuse to turn from your sin, you are storing up [k]terrible punishment for yourself. For a day of [k]anger is coming, when God's righteous judgment will be revealed. 6He will judge everyone according to what they have

1:21 2 Kgs 17:15; Eph 4:17-18
1:22 Jer 10:14; 1 Cor 1:20
1:23 Deut 4:15-19; Ps 106:20
1:24 Acts 14:16
1:26 1 Thes 4:5
1:27 Lev 18:22; 20:13; 1 Cor 6:9
1:30 2 Tim 3:2
1:31 2 Tim 3:3
1:32 Rom 6:23
2:1 Matt 7:1
2:4 Rom 9:22; 2 Pet 3:9, 15; [j]*metanoia* (3341) ‣2 Tim 2:25
2:5 Ps 110:5; [k]*orgē* (3709) ‣Rom 2:8
2:6 *Ps 62:12; Matt 16:27
2:7 Matt 25:46; 2 Tim 4:14

1:21 To *know God* in Scripture usually means to have an intimate, saving relationship with him (see 2 Cor 5:16; Gal 4:9; Phil 3:8, 10). Here, however, ***they knew God*** means that people knew about God. All people have some understanding of God through creation, yet they do not do what is right based on that knowledge. Rather than learn more about God, they worship gods of their own making.

1:24 When human beings exchanged the living God for idols, God ***abandoned them***, a point Paul makes twice more in this paragraph (1:26, 28). The word *abandon* includes a sense of "handing over," suggesting that God actively consigns people to the consequences of their sin.

1:26 ***women turned against the natural way:*** In this context, *natural way* refers to the nature of the world as God made it. As in the OT, Paul singles out homosexuality as a key illustration of how people have fallen away from worship of the true God (see Gen 19:1-28; Lev 18:22; 20:13; Deut 23:17-18). God created human beings as male and female, and engaging in homosexual activity is a violation of God's creative intention.

1:27 ***suffered within themselves the penalty they deserved:*** When people abandon the Creator's intentions, they are judged for their actions. This judgment can take many different forms, but the ultimate consequence is spiritual death (see 1:32).

1:28 ***thought it foolish:*** Sin affects our actions and even our thoughts. One of the serious consequences of turning away from God is an unsound mind; people can no longer use their minds as God intended.

1:29-31 This list of sins follows a popular Hellenistic literary form called a *vice list.* While not exhaustive, it reminds readers of various forms that evil might take.

1:32 To ***encourage others*** to sin is ***worse*** than sinning oneself (Jas 3:1; cp. *Testament of Asher* 6:2: "The two-faced are doubly punished because they both practice evil and approve of others who practice it; they imitate the spirits of error and join in the struggle against mankind").

2:1-5 ***You*** is singular in the Greek. Here, the *you* is a hypothetical complacent Jew, who feels superior to Gentiles and in no danger of judgment. Paul adopts a popular Hellenistic style called a *diatribe,* in which a writer tries to win over an audience to his views by portraying a debate between himself and a hypothetical opponent. • ***these very same things:*** Paul's point is that Jews, like Gentiles, turn from God's revelation to go their own way.

2:4 ***Can't you see that his kindness is intended to turn you from your sin?*** Behind Paul's question are Jewish passages (e.g., *Wisdom of Solomon* 12–15; cp. Jer 7:1-5; Amos 5:18-27) that portray a prevalent Jewish complacency toward judgment. Many Jews thought that because they were God's people, they did not need to worry about judgment, for their sins would not be punished as the sins of Gentiles would be. Paul emphasizes that God's grace was intended to turn the Jews from their sin, not to condone a sinful lifestyle.

2:6-11 Paul uses a *chiasm* ("X" arrangement) to make his point:

2:8
2 Thes 2:12
[a]*orgē* (3709)
‣ Eph 2:3

2:11
Gal 2:6
Eph 6:9
Col 3:25

2:12
[b]*nomos* (3551)
‣ Rom 7:7

2:13
Matt 7:21
John 13:17
Jas 1:22-25

2:14
Acts 10:35

2:16
Acts 10:42
Rom 16:25
2 Tim 2:8
[c]*euangelion* (2098)
‣ Rom 15:19

2:17
Mic 3:11

done. 7He will give eternal life to those who
keep on doing good, seeking after the glory
and honor and immortality that God offers.
8But he will pour out his [a]anger and wrath
on those who live for themselves, who refuse to obey the truth and instead live lives
of wickedness. 9There will be trouble and
calamity for everyone who keeps on doing
what is evil—for the Jew first and also for
the Gentile. 10But there will be glory and
honor and peace from God for all who do
good—for the Jew first and also for the Gentile. 11For God does not show favoritism.
12When the Gentiles sin, they will be
destroyed, even though they never had
God's written law. And the Jews, who do
have God's [b]law, will be judged by that [b]law
when they fail to obey it. 13For merely listening to the law doesn't make us right with
God. It is obeying the law that makes us
right in his sight. 14Even Gentiles, who do
not have God's written law, show that they
know his law when they instinctively obey
it, even without having heard it. 15They
demonstrate that God's law is written in
their hearts, for their own conscience and
thoughts either accuse them or tell them
they are doing right. 16And this is the [c]mes-
sage I proclaim—that the day is coming
when God, through Christ Jesus, will judge
everyone's secret life.

The Limitations of the Covenant

17You who call yourselves Jews are relying
on God's law, and you boast about your special relationship with him. 18You know what

Natural Revelation (1:19-21)

Ps 19:1-4
Acts 14:15-17;
17:24-29

When God speaks to people directly through his word, we call it *special revelation.* God also speaks to all people indirectly in *natural revelation,* through the world of nature he has created. Psalm 19, for example, proclaims that knowledge of God in creation is universal (see Ps 19:1-4).

Sadly, however, a saving response to God is anything but universal. Paul teaches in Romans 1–3 that as a result of Adam's sin, all people turn away from the knowledge of God that they find in the created world. Apart from God's grace, natural revelation only condemns people; as Paul states in 1:20, "They have no excuse for not knowing God."

God can still use natural revelation to awaken people to the reality of the one true God. When accompanied and empowered by the grace of God, the beauty and intricacy of the world can stimulate a search for the Creator. Paul appealed to natural revelation in Athens (Acts 17:16-31) as a bridge to preaching the Good News. God's revelation in the natural world and in human nature can stimulate people to search for the true God. And then, through the special revelation he has given in Scripture and in his Son, Jesus Christ, people can come to know him and experience his salvation.

A God judges everyone the same (2:6)
  B Life is the reward for doing good (2:7)
    C Wrath is the penalty for evil (2:8)
    C' Wrath for doing evil (2:9)
  B' Life for doing good (2:10)
A' God shows no favoritism (2:11)

2:7 ***He will give eternal life to those who keep on doing good:*** Paul makes it clear elsewhere that no one can receive eternal life except as God's gift through faith (3:20, 28; 4:1-8). Here, Paul is either referring to Christians whose good deeds (that result from faith) will be taken into account in God's judgment, or he is reminding readers of the absolute standard that God's own holiness establishes, since only by perfection can sinners hope to find acceptance before God. As the argument of the letter unfolds, Paul will show that no one is capable of meeting that standard.

2:8 ***Live for themselves*** translates a rare Greek word (*eritheia*) that seems to convey the idea of selfish ambition or strife. Using this word, Aristotle scolded the politicians of his day for seeking public office for selfish gain rather than from a desire to serve the people (Aristotle, *Politics* 5.3; see also 2 Cor 12:20; Gal 5:20; Phil 1:17; 2:3; Jas 3:14, 16).

2:9 ***also for the Gentile:*** Literally *also for the Greek;* also in 2:10.

2:12 ***destroyed:*** This common NT word describes the fate of the wicked after death (see also 9:22; 14:15; 1 Cor 1:18; 15:18; 2 Cor 2:15; 4:3; Phil 1:28; 3:19; 2 Thes 2:10; 1 Tim 6:9). Condemned sinners do not cease to exist, but they suffer eternal punishment, which includes the everlasting destruction of all good in their identity and experience. • ***the Jews, who do have God's law:*** The Jews were given the law of Moses, while the Gentiles ***never had God's written law.*** In the NT period, Jews emphasized their possession of the law as a mark of God's favor and even as a guarantee of salvation.

2:13 ***obeying the law . . . makes us right in his sight:*** Regarding the promise of righteousness through obedience, see 2:7; see also Jas 1:22.

2:14-15 The ***Gentiles*** who ***know his law when they instinctively obey it*** may be Gentile Christians, especially since ***written in their hearts*** (2:15) alludes to the prophecy of the new covenant (Jer 31:31-34). Or they could be non-Christian Gentiles who know God's general moral law through their consciences. In this case, Paul would be using the notion of *natural law* to show how all people could be held accountable for certain basic moral requirements.

2:16 ***secret life*** (literally *the hidden things*): Scripture frequently stresses that God will judge people according to their thoughts and intentions (see 1 Sam 16:7; Ps 139:1-2; Jer 17:10).

2:17-20 The boasting of the ***Jews*** reflects OT and Jewish teaching about the privileges and responsibilities God gave to Israel. God gave ***his law*** to Israel, entered into a ***special relationship*** with them, and commissioned them to be ***a light*** to the Gentiles (see Isa 42:6-7).

he wants; you know what is right because you have been taught his law. 19You are convinced that you are a guide for the blind and a light for people who are lost in darkness. 20You think you can instruct the ignorant and teach children the ways of God. For you are certain that God's law gives you complete knowledge and truth.

21Well then, if you teach others, why don't you teach yourself? You tell others not to steal, but do you steal? 22You say it is wrong to commit adultery, but do you commit adultery? You condemn idolatry, but do you use items stolen from pagan temples? 23You are so proud of knowing the law, but you dishonor God by breaking it. 24No wonder the Scriptures say, "The Gentiles blaspheme the name of God because of you."

25The Jewish ceremony of circumcision has value only if you obey God's law. But if you don't obey God's law, you are no better off than an uncircumcised Gentile. 26And if the Gentiles obey God's law, won't God declare them to be his own people? 27In fact, uncircumcised Gentiles who keep God's law will condemn you Jews who are circumcised and possess God's law but don't obey it.

28For you are not a true Jew just because you were born of Jewish parents or because you have gone through the ceremony of circumcision. 29No, a true Jew is one whose heart is right with God. And true circumcision is not merely obeying the letter of the law; rather, it is a change of heart produced by God's Spirit. And a person with a changed heart seeks praise from God, not from people.

God's Faithfulness and the Judgment of Jews

3 Then what's the advantage of being a Jew? Is there any value in the ceremony of circumcision? 2Yes, there are great benefits! First of all, the Jews were entrusted with the whole revelation of God.

3True, some of them were unfaithful; but just because they were unfaithful, does that mean God will be unfaithful? 4Of course not! Even if everyone else is a liar, God is true. As the Scriptures say about him,

> "You will be proved right in what you say,
> and you will win your case in court."

5"But," some might say, "our sinfulness serves a good purpose, for it helps people see how righteous God is. Isn't it unfair,

2:20 2 Tim 3:5
2:21 Matt 23:3-4
2:24 *Isa 52:5; Ezek 36:20
2:25 Gal 5:3
2:28 Matt 3:9; John 8:39; Gal 6:15
2:29 Deut 30:6; John 5:44; Rom 7:6; 2 Cor 3:6; 10:18; Phil 3:3; Col 2:11; 1 Pet 3:4
3:2 Deut 4:7-8; Ps 147:19-20; Acts 7:38
3:4 *Ps 51:4
3:5 Rom 5:8

Jews were not wrong to enjoy these blessings; their error was in failing to live up to their privileged position.

2:21-22 Paul again uses the diatribe style to expose the inconsistency of Jewish claims (see note on 2:1-5).

2:22 ***do you use items stolen from pagan temples?*** (literally *do you steal from temples?*): OT law prohibited Jews from having anything to do with pagan idols (see Deut 7:26), but first-century Jews did not strictly follow this law. Sometimes they stole idols and used or sold the precious metals.

2:24 Paul quotes Isa 52:5 (Greek version), where God's ***name*** is blasphemed because Israel is oppressed by pagan nations. Here, Paul uses that passage to demonstrate the failure of the Jews to live up to their responsibilities.

2:25 God instituted ***the Jewish ceremony of circumcision*** as a sign of his covenant with Abraham; it was to be performed on every male Israelite child (Gen 17:9-13; see Rom 4:11). Circumcision therefore represents God's covenant with his people Israel. The rite took on greater significance during the intertestamental period when the pagan king Antiochus IV Epiphanes tried to stamp out the Jewish faith by forbidding circumcision. The Jews resisted in the famous Maccabean Revolt (166–160 BC). After they restored the worship of the Lord in Israel, the Jews regarded circumcision as a highly prized mark of Jewish loyalty in the midst of a pagan culture.

2:26 ***won't God declare them to be his own people?*** Paul might be speaking of Gentile Christians who are God's people because they obey God's law, or he could be speaking hypothetically about what would happen if a Gentile perfectly obeyed God's law.

2:29 ***The letter of the law*** refers to the law of God written on tablets of stone (see 2 Cor 3:3), while ***God's Spirit*** now writes his law on people's hearts (Jer 31:33-34). Outward conformity is thus contrasted with obedience motivated by ***a change of heart.*** • ***seeks praise:*** Or *receives praise.*

3:1 ***what's the advantage of being a Jew?*** Paul moves his argument along by raising questions. After preaching the Good News for over twenty years, he knew what questions people would ask when they heard a particular teaching. His emphasis on the equality of Jews and Gentiles before God (ch 2) inevitably led people to ask whether he was eliminating all Jewish privileges. The question-and-answer style follows the pattern of the diatribe (see note on 2:1-5).

3:2 The advantage that Jews possessed was in having received God's word. • ***First of all:*** Paul never adds a second or a third point to the list he begins here. He might have forgotten to continue the list, or ***first of all*** might mean "most importantly." However, 9:4-5 provides a good indication of what a list of Jewish privileges would have included. • ***the whole revelation of God*** (literally *the oracles of God*): By using the word *oracles* (Greek *logia*), Paul highlights God's personal communication with his people (see Deut 33:9; Ps 105:19) through which he gives them special privileges and responsibilities.

3:4 ***Of course not!*** The Greek *mē genoito* is an emphatic negation, popular in the diatribe style that Paul uses here and in several other passages in Romans (see 3:6, 31; 6:2, 15; 7:7, 13; 9:14; 11:1, 11). • ***As the Scriptures say:*** Paul quotes Ps 51:4 (Greek version), where David confessed his sin in having an adulterous relationship with Bathsheba (see 2 Sam 11). God punished David, and David admitted that God was ***proved right*** and would ***win*** his ***case in court***—his punishment was entirely just. God is faithful to what he has said in the past—his entire revelation—and his words warn of punishment for sin even as they promise reward for obedience.

3:5-7 ***how would he be qualified to judge the world?*** Abraham asked a similar question: "Should not the Judge of all the earth do what is right?" (Gen 18:25). God punishes all sin, and he retains absolute righteousness as he does so. Even when God makes use of human sin for his own ends, that sin still deserves to be, and will be, punished (see 9:10-24).

3:7
Rom 9:19
3:8
Rom 6:1
3:9
Rom 1:18–2:24
[d]*hamartia* (0266)
‣ Rom 4:7
3:10-12
*Ps 14:1-3; 53:1-3
3:13
*Ps 5:9; 140:3
3:14
*Ps 10:7
3:15-17
*Isa 59:7-8
3:18
*Ps 36:1
3:19
Rom 2:12
3:20
Ps 143:2
Rom 4:15; 7:7
Gal 2:16; 3:11
3:21
Gen 15:6
Rom 1:2, 17; 9:30
[e]*dikaiosunē* (1343)
‣ Rom 4:3
3:22
Rom 4:11; 10:4, 12
Gal 2:16
Col 3:11
[f]*pisteuō* (4100)
‣ Rom 3:25

then, for him to punish us?" (This is merely
a human point of view.) 6Of course not!
If God were not entirely fair, how would
he be qualified to judge the world? 7"But,"
someone might still argue, "how can God
condemn me as a sinner if my dishonesty
highlights his truthfulness and brings him
more glory?" 8And some people even slander us by claiming that we say, "The more
we sin, the better it is!" Those who say such
things deserve to be condemned.

The Guilt of All Humanity (3:9-20)

9Well then, should we conclude that we
Jews are better than others? No, not at all,
for we have already shown that all people,
whether Jews or Gentiles, are under the
power of [d]sin. 10As the Scriptures say,

"No one is righteous—
not even one.
11 No one is truly wise;
no one is seeking God.
12 All have turned away;
all have become useless.
No one does good,
not a single one."
13 "Their talk is foul, like the stench from
an open grave.
Their tongues are filled with lies."
"Snake venom drips from their lips."
14 "Their mouths are full of cursing and
bitterness."
15 "They rush to commit murder.
16 Destruction and misery always follow
them.
17 They don't know where to find
peace."
18 "They have no fear of God at all."

19Obviously, the law applies to those to
whom it was given, for its purpose is to keep
people from having excuses, and to show
that the entire world is guilty before God.
20For no one can ever be made right with
God by doing what the law commands. The
law simply shows us how sinful we are.

Justification and the Righteousness of God (3:21-26)

21But now God has shown us a way to be
made [e]right with him without keeping the
requirements of the law, as was promised in
the writings of Moses and the prophets long
ago. 22We are made right with God by placing our faith in Jesus Christ. And this is true
for everyone who [f]believes, no matter who
we are.

3:8 *some people even slander us:* Paul is referring to misrepresentations about his teaching on justification by faith. If a person is made right with God by faith alone, through God's grace and apart from works, it could seem as if the Good News allows believers to sin because their sin is forgiven when confessed (see 6:1). One of Paul's purposes is to help the Roman Christians understand that such misunderstandings are without basis.

3:9 *No, not at all:* Paul's emphatic answer does not contradict his claim in 3:1-2 that Jews have an advantage. But that advantage has not done them any good because they have disobeyed God's word and incurred God's punishment. Jews, like Gentiles, have sinned against the revelation of God and stand condemned. • ***or Gentiles:*** Literally *or Greeks.* • ***under the power of sin*** (literally *under sin*): Being "under" something carries the sense of being under its power. The ultimate problem of human beings is not the fact of sin, but the more basic situation of being slaves to sin. The solution to this problem requires the liberation provided in Christ Jesus, who frees us from both the penalty and the power of sin.

3:10-18 The six quotations in these verses, drawn from various parts of the OT, all address human sinfulness. Paul follows the practice of rabbis who gathered together OT texts on similar themes in a practice called *pearl-stringing.*

3:10-12 This quotation from Ps 14:1-3; 53:1-3 (Greek version) directly supports the argument that all people are under the power of sin.

3:13-14 Paul here refers to sins of speech, mentioning a different organ of speech in each of the four lines (*talk* in 3:13 is literally *throat*).

3:13 These quotations are from Ps 5:9 (Greek version); 140:3.

3:14 This quotation is from Ps 10:7 (Greek version).

3:15-17 In this quotation from Isa 59:7-8, Paul addresses sins against others.

3:18 This concluding quotation from Ps 36:1 neatly ties up the whole series (3:10-18) by referring to the same Greek words that introduced the first quotation (*ouk estin,* "they have no" and "no one is").

3:19 Paul speaks of the entire OT as *the law* (see also 1 Cor 9:8, 9; 14:21, 34; Gal 4:21). • ***Those to whom it was given*** (literally *those in the law*) were the Jews, who were given the Scriptures. • How can Paul conclude that ***the entire world is guilty before God*** on the basis of evidence from the OT that Jews are sinful? He argues "from the greater to the lesser": If the law shows that the Jews, God's own people, are guilty, then how much more are the Gentiles, who have not had the benefit of God's instruction, also guilty.

3:20 ***By doing what the law commands*** refers to obeying the requirements of the law of Moses. While this phrase refers to Jews, the principle extends to all people. If Jews cannot be put in right relationship with God by obeying the law God gave them, certainly other people cannot establish such a relationship through good deeds.

3:21–4:25 Paul returns to the central theme of the ***righteousness*** of God that is revealed in Christ and is available to anyone who believes. The fundamental statement of this theology is in 3:21-26; Paul elaborates on it in 3:27-31, and illustrates it with the experience of Abraham in ch 4.

3:21-22 After a lengthy reminder of the power of sin (1:18–3:20), Paul returns to the theme presented in 1:17, the ***way to be made right with*** God (literally *the righteousness of God*). As in that verse, "the righteousness of God" is the way that God puts people in right relationship with himself. • ***without keeping the requirements of the law*** (literally *apart from the law*): The old covenant looked forward to the climactic revelation of God's righteousness in his Son. What God now accomplishes for us in Christ, he does apart from the covenant structure set up by the law of Moses (Heb 8:13). • ***the writings of Moses:*** Literally *the law.*

23For everyone has sinned; we all fall short
of God's [g]glorious standard. 24Yet God, with
undeserved [h]kindness, declares that we are
righteous. He did this through Christ Jesus
when he [i]freed us from the penalty for our
sins. 25For God presented Jesus as the [j]sacri-
fice for sin. People are made right with God
when they [k]believe that Jesus sacrificed
his life, shedding his blood. This sacrifice
shows that God was being fair when he held
back and did not punish those who sinned
in times past, 26for he was looking ahead
and including them in what he would do
in this present time. God did this to demonstrate his righteousness, for he himself is
fair and just, and he declares sinners to be
right in his sight when they believe in Jesus.

Justification "By Faith Alone" (3:27–4:25)

"By Faith Alone": Initial Statement

27Can we boast, then, that we have done anything to be accepted by God? No, because
our acquittal is not based on obeying the
law. It is based on faith. 28So we are made
right with God through faith and not by
obeying the law.

29After all, is God the God of the Jews
only? Isn't he also the God of the Gentiles?
Of course he is. 30There is only one God, and
he makes people right with himself only by
faith, whether they are Jews or Gentiles.
31Well then, if we emphasize faith, does
this mean that we can forget about the law?
Of course not! In fact, only when we have
faith do we truly fulfill the law.

"By Faith Alone": Abraham

4 Abraham was, humanly speaking, the
founder of our Jewish nation. What
did he discover about being made right
with God? 2If his good deeds had made him
acceptable to God, he would have had something to boast about. But that was not God's
way. 3For the Scriptures tell us, "Abraham
believed God, and God counted him as [a]righ-
teous because of his faith."

4When people work, their wages are not
a gift, but something they have earned.
5But people are counted as righteous, not
because of their work, but because of their
faith in God who forgives sinners. 6David
also spoke of this when he described the
happiness of those who are declared righteous without working for it:

7 "Oh, what [b]joy for those
whose disobedience is forgiven,
whose [c]sins are put out of sight.

3:23
[g]*doxa* (1391)
‣ 1 Cor 11:7

3:24
Eph 2:8
Heb 9:12
[h]*charis* (5485)
‣ Rom 5:2
[i]*apolutrōsis* (0629)
‣ Rom 8:23

3:25
Lev 16:10
Heb 9:12-14
1 Pet 1:19
1 Jn 4:10
[j]*hilastērion* (2435)
‣ Heb 2:17
[k]*pistis* (4102)
‣ Rom 5:1

3:27
Rom 2:17; 4:2
1 Cor 1:29-31

3:28
Acts 13:39

3:29
Rom 10:12
Gal 3:28

3:31
Matt 5:17

4:2
1 Cor 1:31

4:3
*Gen 15:6
Gal 3:6
Jas 2:23
[a]*dikaiosunē* (1343)
‣ Rom 4:9

4:4
Rom 11:6
Gal 2:16

3:24 ***undeserved kindness:*** God ***declares that we are righteous,*** not because he has to, but because he has freely chosen to give us his favor ***through Christ Jesus.*** Because we are helpless slaves of sin (3:9), our righteous status before God can never be earned (see 4:4-5). • ***through Christ Jesus when he freed us from the penalty for our sins*** (literally *through the redemption that is in Christ Jesus*): In Paul's day, *redemption* referred to the price paid to free a slave. God paid our redemption price with the blood of his own Son to rescue us from our slavery to sin (see 3:9). This language was used in the OT to refer to the Exodus, the first redemption of God's people from bondage (see 2 Sam 7:23). God promised that he would again redeem his people (Hos 13:14; Mic 4:10).

3:25 ***the sacrifice for sin*** (Greek *hilastērion*): This Greek word is used in the Greek OT to refer to the "atonement cover," the cover that rested on the Ark of the Covenant in the inner sanctuary of the Tabernacle. The atonement cover was prominent in the Day of Atonement ritual (Lev 16) and came to stand for the atonement ceremony itself. Paul characterizes Jesus Christ as God's provision of final atonement for his people. Jesus himself satisfies, or absorbs in himself, the anger of God against all sinful people (see 1:18). • ***those who sinned in times past:*** Paul refers to righteous OT people who were not punished for their sins as strict justice would require. Hebrews reminds us, "it is not possible for the blood of bulls and goats to take away sins" (Heb 10:4). How, then, could God forgive people in the OT? Paul answers that Jesus' sacrifice works backward in history as well as forward—through Christ, God provided for the full satisfaction of his righteous anger against human sin.

3:29-30 Paul uses the foundational Jewish commitment to monotheism to argue for universal access to God's forgiveness. If ***there is only one God,*** then he is equally the God of both Jews and Gentiles. All people must be able to come to God on the same terms, through ***faith.*** • ***whether they are Jews or Gentiles:*** Literally *whether they are circumcised or uncircumcised.*

3:31 ***we truly fulfill the law:*** Paul knows that some people will object to his insistence on faith apart from the law because it seems to dismiss the demands of the law. However, ***faith*** actually enables people to ***fulfill the law.*** The Holy Spirit is given to those who have faith, and he makes it possible for people to do as they should.

4:1 Jews in Paul's day revered ***Abraham*** as Israel's ***founder.*** Some Jewish texts claim that Abraham never sinned (*Prayer of Manasseh* 8; *Jubilees* 23:10). Others emphasize his obedience to the law of Moses as the basis for his relationship with God (*1 Maccabees* 2:52; *Sirach* 44:19-20). However, Paul demonstrates that Abraham's faith, not his obedience, established his status with God. Abraham's position as the founder of God's people demonstrates that justification by faith is central in God's plan.

4:3 Paul quotes Gen 15:6. In response to God's promise that he would have descendants as numerous as the stars in the sky, ***Abraham believed God.*** It was faith that established Abraham's relationship with God—not works (4:3-8), circumcision (4:9-12), the law (4:13-17), or the number of his descendants (4:18-21).

4:4-5 The logic of these verses is as follows: (1) The stated premise is that ***when people work,*** their pay is what ***they have earned,*** not a gift. (2) The unstated premise is that God is never indebted to his creatures (because they owe him everything), so anything he gives them is ***a gift*** (see also 9:14-16). (3) The conclusion is that therefore, people cannot be declared ***righteous*** before God because of their works.

4:7-8 This quotation from Ps 32:1-2 (Greek version) follows the Jewish custom of supporting a reference to the

4:7-8
*Ps 32:1-2
2 Cor 5:19
[b]makarios (3107)
‣Titus 2:13
[c]hamartia (0266)
‣Rom 5:12

4:9
Gen 15:6
Rom 3:30
[d]dikaiosunē (1343)
‣Rom 5:17

4:11
Gen 17:10-11
[e]patēr (3962)
‣1 Cor 1:3

4:13
Gen 18:18; 22:17-18
Gal 3:29

4:14
Gal 3:18

4:15
Rom 3:20; 7:12
1 Cor 15:55-56
Gal 3:10

4:16
Gal 3:7

[8] Yes, what [b]joy for those
whose record the LORD has cleared
of [c]sin."

[9]Now, is this blessing only for the Jews, or is it also for uncircumcised Gentiles? Well, we have been saying that Abraham was counted as [d]righteous by God because of his faith. [10]But how did this happen? Was he counted as righteous only after he was circumcised, or was it before he was circumcised? Clearly, God accepted Abraham before he was circumcised!

[11]Circumcision was a sign that Abraham already had faith and that God had already accepted him and declared him to be righteous—even before he was circumcised. So Abraham is the spiritual [e]father of those who have faith but have not been circumcised. They are counted as righteous because of their faith. [12]And Abraham is also the spiritual father of those who have been circumcised, but only if they have the same kind of faith Abraham had before he was circumcised.

[13]Clearly, God's promise to give the whole earth to Abraham and his descendants was based not on his obedience to God's law, but on a right relationship with God that comes by faith. [14]If God's promise is only for those who obey the law, then faith is not necessary and the promise is pointless. [15]For the law always brings punishment on those who try to obey it. (The only way to avoid breaking the law is to have no law to break!)

[16]So the promise is received by faith. It is given as a free gift. And we are all certain

God's Unified Plan of Salvation (3:21-26)

Rom 1:3-5, 16-17; 5:6-11; 8:1-4; 10:5-13; 11:26-27
Matt 1:21-23
Luke 1:46-55, 67-79
Acts 4:10-12; 10:34-43; 13:23-41
1 Cor 15:1-4
Gal 2:14-21; 3:5-14
Eph 1:3-14
Col 1:15-22
1 Tim 2:3-6
2 Tim 1:9-10
Heb 9:27-28

The continuity of God's unfolding plan of salvation is a central theme in Romans. In 3:21, Paul makes two important points about the new way of being "made right" with God that has been inaugurated in Jesus Christ. First, it does not depend on obeying the laws and regulations of the OT. Second, it was "promised in the writings of Moses and the prophets" (3:21). God has always planned to save the world through Jesus, and the entire OT was a preparation for that climactic moment in salvation history. In 1:2, Paul claims that "God promised this Good News long ago through his prophets in the holy Scriptures." Paul keeps returning to this theme of continuity, especially in chs 9–11, where he shows how God's dealings with Israel fit into that single, unfolding plan.

At the same time, Paul is also concerned to help us understand the discontinuity in God's single plan of salvation. That plan unfolds in stages. Now that the final stage in Christ has arrived, the prior stage—during which the law of Moses ruled over God's people—has been left behind. Paul repeatedly emphasizes that our new relationship with God stands separate from the law of Moses (see 6:14, 15; 7:4-6; 10:4). A similar point is made in John 1:17 and Heb 10:1. Paul's recurring focus in Romans on the nature of God's plan helps us to put the whole story of the Bible together in a way that honors both of its parts.

Law with a reference in the Prophets or the Writings. Paul also uses a Jewish exegetical technique of linking unrelated quotations with a key word. Here, ***record . . . has cleared*** translates the same Greek word as "counted" in 4:3.

4:9 ***is this blessing only for the Jews, or is it also for uncircumcised Gentiles?*** Literally *is this blessing only for the circumcised, or is it also for the uncircumcised?*

4:10 ***God accepted Abraham before he was circumcised!*** Paul's point is simple: God's declaration of Abraham's righteousness in Gen 15:6 could not have been based on his circumcision, which happened later (Gen 17). This point further demonstrates that God's acceptance and blessing is a free gift and not earned by works.

4:11-12 When God instituted circumcision, he called it "*a sign* of the covenant" between himself and Abraham (Gen 17:11). The covenant was *already* in place (Gen 12:1-3; 15:1-21; 17:1-8) *even before* Abraham *was circumcised* (Gen 17:9-14). This shows that the covenant was based on faith, not circumcision. ***So Abraham is the spiritual father*** of all people, whether *circumcised* (Jews) or uncircumcised (Gentiles), who *have the same kind of faith Abraham had*—that is, faith in God's promises (4:13-25).

4:13 ***the whole earth:*** God told Abraham that he would be the father of many nations (4:17; Gen 12:2; 13:16; 15:5; 17:4-6, 16-20; 22:17) and that he would be the means of blessing to all people (Gen 12:3; 18:18; 22:18; cp. Isa 55:3-5).

4:14 ***then faith is not necessary*** (literally *faith is emptied*): If works of obedience can be substituted for faith, then "faith is emptied" of its importance. Believing in God means acknowledging our unworthiness and depending entirely on God's mercy.

4:15 ***The only way to avoid breaking the law is to have no law to break!*** (literally *where there is no law, neither is there transgression*): Paul always uses the word "transgression" to denote disobedience of a clear commandment of God (see also 2:23; 5:14; Gal 3:19; 1 Tim 2:14). Transgression only exists where the law exists, which is why ***the law always brings punishment.*** The law that God gave to the Israelites specified requirements in great detail, which made the people more accountable for sin than before. So when they inevitably disobeyed the law, God brought more severe punishment upon them.

4:16 ***whether or not we live according to the law of Moses*** (literally *not only those who are of the law*): The Jews were *of the law* in that their covenant with God included the law of Moses and they were to live according to it.

to receive it, whether or not we live according to the law of Moses, if we have faith like Abraham's. For Abraham is the father of all who believe. 17 That is what the Scriptures mean when God told him, "I have made you the father of many nations." This happened because Abraham believed in the God who [f]brings the dead back to life and who creates new things out of nothing.

18 Even when there was no reason for hope, Abraham kept hoping—believing that he would become the father of many nations. For God had said to him, "That's how many descendants you will have!" 19 And Abraham's faith did not weaken, even though, at about 100 years of age, he figured his body was as good as dead—and so was Sarah's womb.

20 Abraham never wavered in believing God's promise. In fact, his faith grew stronger, and in this he brought glory to God. 21 He was fully convinced that God is able to do whatever he promises. 22 And because of Abraham's faith, God counted him as righteous. 23 And when God counted him as righteous, it wasn't just for Abraham's benefit. It was recorded 24 for our benefit, too, assuring us that God will also count us as righteous if we believe in him, the one who raised Jesus our Lord from the dead. 25 He was handed over to die because of our sins, and he was raised to life to make us [g]right with God.

3. THE ASSURANCE PROVIDED BY THE GOSPEL: THE HOPE OF SALVATION (5:1–8:39)

The Hope of Glory (5:1-21)

From Justification to Salvation

5 Therefore, since we have been made right in God's sight by [h]faith, we have [i]peace with God because of what Jesus Christ our Lord has done for us. 2 Because of our faith, Christ has brought us into this place of undeserved [j]privilege where we now stand, and we confidently and joyfully [k]look forward to sharing God's glory.

3 We can rejoice, too, when we run into problems and trials, for we know that they help us develop endurance. 4 And endurance develops strength of character, and character strengthens our confident hope of salvation. 5 And this hope will not lead to disappointment. For we know how dearly God loves us, because he has given us the Holy Spirit to fill our hearts with his [a]love.

6 When we were utterly helpless, Christ came at just the right time and died for us sinners. 7 Now, most people would not be willing to die for an upright person, though someone might perhaps be willing to die for a person who is especially good. 8 But God showed his great love for us by sending Christ to die for us while we were still sinners. 9 And since we have been made right in God's sight by the blood of Christ, he will certainly save us from God's condemnation.

4:17
*Gen 17:5
Isa 48:13
John 5:21
1 Cor 1:28
[f]*zōopoieō* (2227)
‣Rom 8:11

4:18
*Gen 15:5

4:19
Gen 17:17; 18:11
Heb 11:11

4:22
*Gen 15:6
Rom 4:3

4:24
1 Pet 1:21

4:25
Isa 53:4-5
Rom 8:32
1 Cor 15:17
2 Cor 5:15
1 Pet 1:21
[g]*dikaiōsis* (1347)
‣Rom 5:18

5:1
Acts 10:36
Rom 3:28
[h]*pistis* (4102)
‣Rom 10:17
[i]*eirēnē* (1515)
‣Rom 8:6

5:2
Eph 2:18; 3:12
[j]*charis* (5485)
‣Rom 5:21
[k]*elpis* (1680)
‣Rom 8:24

5:3
Matt 5:12
Jas 1:2-3

5:5
2 Cor 1:22
Gal 4:6
Eph 1:13
Phil 1:20
[a]*agapē* (0026)
‣Rom 8:39

5:6
Gal 4:4
Eph 5:2

4:17 This quotation is from Gen 17:5.

4:18 This quotation is from Gen 15:5.

4:24 ***raised . . . from the dead:*** Abraham experienced the life-giving power of God in the birth of his son, Isaac. Christians witness it in the resurrection of Jesus. Throughout history, salvation has been available only through faith in God, who makes and keeps his promises.

5:1–8:39 Paul now turns from the Good News about how people enter a relationship with God to the security of that relationship. Christians have a strong and unassailable promise because of God's work in Christ, God's love for them, and the power of the Holy Spirit. This theme frames the teaching of these chapters (5:1-11; 8:18-39) as Paul grounds that promise in the transfer of believers from the realm of Adam to the realm of Christ (5:12-21). No power—whether sin (ch 6), the law (ch 7), or death (8:1-13)—"will ever be able to separate us from the love of God" (8:39).

5:1 ***we have peace:*** In many manuscripts, the underlying Greek verb is indicative, as translated here. A number of other manuscripts use the subjunctive instead (*let us have peace*). • ***Peace with God*** does not refer to a mere feeling of peacefulness but to a real situation of peace. It is the end of hostilities between God and sinful human beings when they believe in Jesus Christ and the state of blessing and salvation that God promised his people in the end (see Isa 9:6-7; 52:7; Ezek 34:25; Nah 1:15).

5:2 ***undeserved privilege*** (or *grace*): So basic is God's grace (Greek *charis*) that Paul can use the word to sum up our present situation as believers. • ***Where we now stand*** indicates that God's grace is needed throughout the Christian life, not just at the beginning. • ***Sharing God's glory*** describes the content of Christian hope, which Paul introduces here and expounds more fully in 8:18-30. Behind Paul's use of the word *glory* (Greek *doxa*) is the Hebrew word *kabod,* which depicts God's majesty and overwhelming presence (see "The Glory of God" at Exod 24:15-17, p. 167). The prophets predict a day when God's glory will return to dwell in the midst of his people (see, e.g., Isa 60:1-2).

5:3-4 See also Jas 1:2-4; 1 Pet 1:6-7. The similarities in these passages indicate early Christian teaching common to all three of these writers.

5:5 ***this hope will not lead to disappointment*** (literally *will not put to shame*): In the OT, shame sometimes refers to a negative verdict from God's judgment (e.g., Isa 28:16, quoted in Rom 9:33). • ***he has given us the Holy Spirit to fill our hearts with his love:*** See Jer 31:33-34; Acts 2:17-21.

5:6 ***At just the right time*** might mean that God sent Christ at the time appointed in history, or that our condition as ***utterly helpless*** was the right time for God to demonstrate his love by sending his Son on our behalf.

5:9 ***The blood of Christ*** refers to Jesus' sacrificial death (3:25). In the Scriptures, *blood* is shorthand for a violent death (Lev 17:11), especially when that death atones for sins. • ***he will certainly save us from God's condemnation:*** Paul frequently speaks of salvation as the final deliverance of believers from God's wrath and the tribulations of this life (see 13:11).

5:8
John 3:16
1 Jn 4:10
5:9
Rom 1:18; 2:5, 8
5:10
Rom 8:34
2 Cor 5:18-19
Eph 2:3
[b]*katallassō* (2644)
‣Rom 5:11
5:11
[c]*katallagē* (2643)
‣Rom 11:15
5:12
Gen 3:1-19
1 Cor 15:21-22
[d]*hamartia* (0266)
‣Rom 6:1
5:14
[e]*tupos* (5179)
‣1 Cor 10:6
5:17
1 Cor 15:21
[f]*dikaiosunē* (1343)
‣Rom 5:21
5:18
1 Cor 15:22
[g]*dikaiōsis* (1347)
‣1 Cor 15:34

10For since our friendship with God was
[b]restored by the death of his Son while we
were still his enemies, we will certainly be
saved through the life of his Son. 11So now
we can rejoice in our wonderful new relationship with God because our Lord Jesus
Christ has [c]made us friends of God.

The Reign of Grace and Life

12When Adam sinned, [d]sin entered the
world. Adam's [d]sin brought death, so death
spread to everyone, for everyone sinned.
13Yes, people sinned even before the law was
given. But it was not counted as sin because
there was not yet any law to break. 14Still,
everyone died—from the time of Adam to
the time of Moses—even those who did not
disobey an explicit commandment of God,
as Adam did. Now Adam is a [e]symbol, a representation of Christ, who was yet to come.
15But there is a great difference between
Adam's sin and God's gracious gift. For the
sin of this one man, Adam, brought death
to many. But even greater is God's wonderful grace and his gift of forgiveness to many
through this other man, Jesus Christ. 16And
the result of God's gracious gift is very different from the result of that one man's sin. For
Adam's sin led to condemnation, but God's
free gift leads to our being made right with
God, even though we are guilty of many sins.
17For the sin of this one man, Adam, caused
death to rule over many. But even greater is
God's wonderful grace and his gift of [f]righ-
teousness, for all who receive it will live in
triumph over sin and death through this
one man, Jesus Christ.

18Yes, Adam's one sin brings condemnation for everyone, but Christ's one act of
righteousness brings a [g]right relationship

God's Grace (5:15-17, 20-21)

Rom 12:6
Exod 34:5-7
Ezra 9:8
Ps 84:11
Isa 60:10
Hos 14:1-9
Acts 15:11; 20:24
2 Cor 8:9; 12:9
Eph 1:6-7; 2:5-9
2 Tim 1:9
Titus 2:11; 3:7
Heb 4:16; 13:9
Jas 4:6
1 Pet 5:12

The grace of God is theological bedrock for Paul. He never tries to prove that God is gracious, but he assumes it as a fact when presenting the Good News to the Romans (see 3:24; 4:4-5, 16; 5:2, 15-21; 6:14-15; 11:5-6). Paul rules out any idea that we merit our salvation, because God acts by his grace (4:4-5). Our good works do not give us right standing with God—if they did, God would be obliged to reward us for our efforts, just as a worker earns a wage. Instead, he gives salvation as a gift to those he has chosen (11:5-6). Grace is so important to the Christian experience that Paul can refer simply to our "standing in" grace (cp. 5:2) and to our living under the power of grace (6:14-15). Grace now rules over us in the new age of redemption (5:20-21).

The apostle John makes the same point: "The law was given through Moses, but God's unfailing love [grace] and faithfulness came through Jesus Christ" (John 1:17). Neither John nor Paul meant that God's grace was not active in the OT, because God has always dealt graciously with his people. But the overwhelming power of God's grace is displayed for us in and through Jesus Christ.

5:10 ***saved through the life of his Son:*** Believers already share in the new life that Christ provided through his resurrection (6:11). Through this vital connection with Christ, believers will also be spared from God's wrath in the last day (see also Col 3:4).

5:12 ***Adam*** is both the name of the original man, Adam, and a Hebrew word that means "human." Paul emphasizes the solidarity of ***Adam*** with the human race. • ***sin entered the world:*** The significance that Paul ascribes to this act, and the parallel that he draws between Adam's sin and Christ's act of obedience on the cross, makes clear that Paul views Adam and his sin in the Garden of Eden as historical fact. • ***everyone sinned:*** Death is universal because sin is universal. It is not clear when or how everyone sinned, but Paul later attributes the condemnation of all people to the sin of Adam, their representative (5:18). • Jewish tradition is divided on the relationship between ***Adam's sin*** and the sin and death of human beings generally. Some texts emphasize a solidarity between Adam and all other people, as in "when Adam sinned a death was decreed against those who were to be born" (*2 Baruch* 23:4). Other texts insist that people die because of their own sin: "Adam is, therefore, not the cause, except only for himself, but each of us had become our own Adam" (*2 Baruch* 54:19).

5:13-14 Paul continues his explanation of "everyone sinned" (5:12) by stating that people who died between the times of Adam and Moses were not subject to specific commandments from God. Therefore, their condemnation was not only because of their own sin. It was because of their union with Adam, who sinned by violating ***an explicit commandment of God.***

5:15 Paul uses the word ***many*** in contrast with ***one.*** *Many* does not always mean *all,* but it can include all people if the context suggests it. Clearly, the many who suffer death because of ***Adam*** includes everyone (see 5:12), but Paul makes it clear elsewhere that the ***many*** who receive the ***gift of forgiveness*** through ***Jesus Christ,*** sadly, does not include everyone (see 11:1-5).

5:17 Both ***Adam*** and ***Jesus Christ*** committed a single act whose influence extends to all the people that they represent. Adam represents all people. People must ***receive*** the ***gift of righteousness*** to be represented by Christ.

5:18 ***Christ's one act of righteousness*** refers to his death on the cross, a righteous act because Christ chose to die in obedience to the Father's will (see John 10:18). • ***new life for everyone:*** Paul is not teaching that all people will experience the new life that Christ won through his death on the cross. New life is available to everyone through Christ, but not everyone receives it.

with God and new life for everyone. [19]Be-
cause one person disobeyed God, many
became sinners. But because one other
person obeyed God, many will be made righteous.
[20]God's law was given so that all people
could see how sinful they were. But as people sinned more and more, God's wonderful
grace became more abundant. [21]So just as
sin ruled over all people and brought them
to death, now God's wonderful [h]grace rules
instead, giving us [i]right standing with God
and resulting in eternal life through Jesus
Christ our Lord.

Freedom from Bondage to Sin (6:1-23)
"Dead to Sin" through Union with Christ

6 Well then, should we keep on [j]sinning
so that God can show us more and
more of his wonderful [k]grace? [2]Of course
not! Since we have died to sin, how can we
continue to live in it? [3]Or have you forgotten
that when we were [a]joined with Christ Jesus
in baptism, we [a]joined him in his death?
[4]For we died and were buried with Christ
by baptism. And just as Christ was raised
from the dead by the glorious power of the
Father, now we also may live new lives.
[5]Since we have been united with him in
his death, we will also be raised to life as he
was. [6]We know that our old sinful selves
were crucified with Christ so that sin might
lose its power in our lives. We are no longer
slaves to sin. [7]For when we died with Christ
we were set free from the power of sin.
[8]And since we died with Christ, we know
we will also live with him. [9]We are sure of
this because Christ was raised from the
dead, and he will never die again. Death no
longer has any power over him. [10]When he
died, he died once to break the power of sin.
But now that he lives, he lives for the glory
of God. [11]So you also should consider yourselves to be dead to the power of sin and
alive to God through Christ Jesus.
[12]Do not let sin control the way you live;
do not give in to sinful desires. [13]Do not
let any part of your body become an instrument of evil to serve sin. Instead, give
yourselves completely to God, for you were
dead, but now you have new life. So use your
whole body as an instrument to do what is
right for the glory of God. [14]Sin is no longer
your master, for you no longer live under the
requirements of the law. Instead, you live
under the freedom of God's grace.

Freed from Sin's Power to Serve Righteousness

[15]Well then, since God's grace has set us
free from the law, does that mean we can
go on sinning? Of course not! [16]Don't you realize that you become the slave of whatever

5:19 Phil 2:8
5:20 Rom 4:15; 7:8; Gal 3:19
5:21 Rom 6:23; [h]*charis* (5485) ‣Rom 6:1; [i]*dikaiosunē* (1343) ‣Rom 8:10
6:1 Rom 3:5-8; [j]*hamartia* (0266) ‣Rom 7:8; [k]*charis* (5485) ‣Gal 1:15
6:2 Rom 8:13; Col 2:20; 3:3
6:3 Gal 3:27; [a]*baptizō* (0907) ‣1 Cor 12:13
6:4 Eph 4:22-24; Col 2:12; 3:10
6:5 Phil 3:10-11; Col 2:12; 3:1
6:6 Gal 2:20; 5:24; Col 2:12
6:7 1 Pet 4:1
6:9 Acts 2:24
6:10 Heb 7:27
6:11 Rom 7:4; Col 2:20; 3:3
6:13 Rom 12:1; 2 Cor 5:14

5:20 Many Jews believed that the giving of the law to Israel reversed or mitigated the negative effects of Adam's sin, but Paul says that God's law magnified and illuminated their sins.

6:1 *Well then:* Because Paul has just proclaimed that God multiplies grace where sin increases (5:20), he knows that people will wonder whether this means that sin does not matter in the Christian life.

6:2 *we have died to sin:* As Paul makes clear in 6:3-10, our new relationship to sin is possible because of our vital connection with the death of Jesus. Just as dying means entrance into an entirely new state of being, our relationship with sin is now different because of Christ's death. To be "dead to sin" does not mean to be entirely insensitive to sin and temptation—believers are still involved in a battle with sin (6:12-14). However, Christians no longer have to live as helpless slaves to sin; they can choose not to sin (6:6, 14, 16-22).

6:3 *Baptism* is the rite of initiation into the Christian faith (see "Baptism" at Acts 2:38, 41, p. 1828). It sometimes symbolizes the entire conversion experience, so Paul refers to baptism as the means through which believers are joined to Christ in his death and resurrection (see also 6:4). However, baptism has no value apart from faith.

6:4 *we died and were buried with Christ:* The believer's power over sin and the ability to lead a new life stem from identification with Christ's death, burial, and resurrection (see 6:5, 8). From God's perspective, Jesus' death to sin (see 6:10) is ours as well. His rising to new life means that we also begin to lead a new life, and in the future our bodies will also be raised.

6:6 *our old sinful selves:* Our "old selves" are not a nature that we possess or just one part of who we are; it reflects who we were in Adam. All human beings were born "in Adam." As heirs of the sin and death that he introduced into the world (5:12), we were slaves to the power of sin. But as people who are now in Christ, we have gone through crucifixion with him (see also Gal 2:20). When he died on the cross, we also died to the dominating power of sin that ruled in our former selves.

6:8 *We will also live with him* refers to bodily resurrection with Christ (see 6:5). While believers are already raised with Christ spiritually (Eph 2:5-6; Col 2:13), we will also be raised bodily with him at the time of his coming in glory (2 Cor 4:14; Phil 3:21; 1 Thes 4:17; 2 Tim 2:11).

6:10 *he died once to break the power of sin:* Because we died with Jesus (6:4-5), we have also died to sin (6:2). Jesus was never under sin's power in the way that we are, because he had no sin nature from Adam and he never succumbed to temptation (2 Cor 5:21; Heb 4:15). However, when he became human, he entered the arena where sin holds sway, and he was truly vulnerable to sin.

6:12 *Do not let sin control the way you live:* Or *Do not let sin reign in your body, which is subject to death.*

6:14 *you no longer live under the requirements of the law:* With the Messiah's coming, the era governed by the law of Moses came to an end (see Gal 3:19-25). • *you live under the freedom of God's grace:* God's dealings with his people have always been characterized by grace, but grace dominates the new era in which Christians live in Christ. Cp. John 1:17.

6:15 *set us free from the law:* The law of Moses was the governing power of the old covenant era. Believers now live under the governing power of Christ himself.

6:14
Gal 5:18
6:16
John 8:34
2 Pet 2:19
6:17
2 Tim 1:13
6:18
John 8:32
6:19
[b]*hagiasmos* (0038)
‣Rom 6:22
6:20
[c]*doulos* (1401)
‣1 Cor 7:22
6:22
John 8:32
1 Cor 7:22
1 Pet 1:9; 2:16
[d]*hagiasmos* (0038)
‣1 Cor 1:30
6:23
John 3:16-21
Gal 6:8
7:2
1 Cor 7:39
7:3
Luke 16:18

you choose to obey? You can be a slave to
sin, which leads to death, or you can choose
to obey God, which leads to righteous living. 17Thank God! Once you were slaves of
sin, but now you wholeheartedly obey this
teaching we have given you. 18Now you are
free from your slavery to sin, and you have
become slaves to righteous living.
19Because of the weakness of your human
nature, I am using the illustration of slavery
to help you understand all this. Previously,
you let yourselves be slaves to impurity and
lawlessness, which led ever deeper into sin.
Now you must give yourselves to be slaves
to righteous living so that you will become
[b]holy.
20When you were [c]slaves to sin, you were
free from the obligation to do right. 21And
what was the result? You are now ashamed
of the things you used to do, things that end
in eternal doom. 22But now you are free
from the power of sin and have become
slaves of God. Now you do those things that
lead to [d]holiness and result in eternal life.
23For the wages of sin is death, but the free
gift of God is eternal life through Christ
Jesus our Lord.

Freedom from Bondage to the Law (7:1-25)
Released from the Law, Joined to Christ

7 Now, dear brothers and sisters—you
who are familiar with the law—don't you
know that the law applies only while a person is living? 2For example, when a woman
marries, the law binds her to her husband as
long as he is alive. But if he dies, the laws of
marriage no longer apply to her. 3So while
her husband is alive, she would be committing adultery if she married another man.
But if her husband dies, she is free from that

The Old Realm and the New (5:12–8:39)

Rom 14:17
Ps 2:1-10; 110:2; 145:13
Dan 2:31-45; 7:1-28
Matt 3:2; 6:10; 7:13; 8:11-12; 12:25-28; 13:44-52; 20:25-28
John 18:36
1 Cor 6:9-11; 15:20-28
Gal 5:16-26
Eph 1:3, 20; 2:6; 5:1-20
Col 1:13-14
Heb 6:4-5; 12:18-29
Rev 11:15; 12:10

Jews in Paul's day perceived a contrast between the "present evil age" and a "glorious age to come." Throughout Rom 5–8, Paul uses these contrasting realms to conceptualize our experience of salvation. The old realm is ruled by death (5:12-21), sin (ch 6), the law (ch 7), and sinful nature (8:1-11). The new realm is characterized by life (ch 5), righteous living (ch 6), grace (ch 6), and the Holy Spirit (ch 8). People's destinies are controlled by the realm to which they belong.

Each realm is headed by a man who represents its constituents. The old realm of sin and death is headed by Adam, the first man, while the new realm of forgiveness and life is headed by Christ. By nature, all human beings are in the old realm of sin and death and are represented by Adam, the first man—whose sin and death control the destiny of all people (5:12, 18-19). Those who put their faith in God through Christ are transferred by faith into the new realm of life. God appointed Jesus Christ as a "second Adam" (see 5:14). By obeying God and fulfilling God's will, Jesus won a decisive victory over the realm of sin that Adam had inaugurated (5:18-19). By receiving God's gift of grace (5:17), people accept Jesus as their head and look forward to eternal life.

Those who are in the new realm are identified with Christ and enjoy the benefits of union with him. They have "died with Christ," they have been "buried with Christ," and their present new life with Christ is an anticipation of the day when they will "live with him" forever (6:3-10).

6:16 ***righteous living*** (Greek *dikaiosunē*, "righteousness"): In the first part of Romans, Paul uses this Greek word in a judicial sense, referring (1) to the activity of God to set people in a right relationship with himself or (2) to the righteous standing that believers enjoy as a result of Christ's work (see, e.g., 1:17; 3:21-22; 4:3, 5). Here, Paul uses the same word as it is often used in the OT, meaning the right behavior that God demands from his people.

6:19 Paul uses the Greek word *sarx* (***human nature***, or *flesh*) to refer to the frailty and proneness to sin that characterizes humans. Paul uses the ***illustration of slavery*** to show the relationship of the human nature to sin.

6:20 ***free from the obligation to do right*** (literally *free from righteousness*): Paul means either that unbelievers feel no obligation to obey God or that they are unable to do so. But the freedom that they boast of actually makes them slaves to sin.

6:21 ***eternal doom*** (literally *death*): Throughout chs 5–8, Paul uses *death* to describe the eternal consequences of sin (5:12, 14, 15, 17, 21; 6:16, 23; 7:5, 9-10, 13, 24; 8:2, 6, 13). The language goes back to God's warning to Adam and Eve (Gen 2:17). This death is not primarily physical death; it denotes separation from the fellowship of God that, if not reversed through faith in Christ, will last forever.

7:1 ***brothers and sisters:*** Literally *brothers;* also in 7:4. See note on 1:13. • Both Jewish Christians and many of the Gentile Christians were ***familiar with the law.*** Jews were taught the law of Moses from birth. Many of the Gentiles in the church at Rome had been God-fearers, Gentiles who were interested in Judaism and attended the synagogue regularly. • ***the law applies only while a person is living:*** Paul may be paraphrasing a rabbinic saying: "If a person is dead, he is free from the Torah and the fulfilling of the commandments" (*Babylonian Shabbat* 30a; *baraita Shabbat* 151).

7:2-3 These verses are not an allegory, in which every element of the story has a theological counterpart. Paul simply cites an illustration to make two basic points: Death can release a person from obligation to the law, and freedom from one relationship can allow a person to establish a new one. Paul applies the illustration in 7:4.

law and does not commit adultery when she
remarries.
[4]So, my dear brothers and sisters, this is
the point: You died to the power of the law
when you died with Christ. And now you are
united with the one who was raised from
the dead. As a result, we can produce a harvest of good deeds for God. [5]When we were
controlled by our old nature, sinful desires
were at work within us, and the law aroused
these evil desires that produced a harvest of
sinful deeds, resulting in death. [6]But now
we have been released from the law, for we
died to it and are no longer captive to its
power. Now we can serve God, not in the
old way of obeying the letter of the law, but
in the new way of living in the Spirit.

The History and Experience of Jews under the Law

[7]Well then, am I suggesting that the [e]law of
God is sinful? Of course not! In fact, it was
the [e]law that showed me my sin. I would
never have known that coveting is wrong if
the [e]law had not said, "You must not covet."
[8]But [f]sin used this command to arouse
all kinds of covetous desires within me! If
there were no law, [f]sin would not have that
power. [9]At one time I lived without understanding the law. But when I learned the
command not to covet, for instance, the
power of sin came to life, [10]and I died. So I
discovered that the law's commands, which
were supposed to bring life, brought spiritual death instead. [11]Sin took advantage of
those commands and deceived me; it used
the commands to kill me. [12]But still, the [g]law
itself is holy, and its commands are holy and
right and good.
[13]But how can that be? Did the law, which
is good, cause my death? Of course not!
Sin used what was good to bring about my
condemnation to death. So we can see how
terrible sin really is. It uses God's good commands for its own evil purposes.
[14]So the trouble is not with the law, for
it is spiritual and good. The trouble is with
me, for I am all too human, a slave to sin. [15]I
don't really understand myself, for I want to
do what is right, but I don't do it. Instead, I
do what I hate. [16]But if I know that what I
am doing is wrong, this shows that I agree
that the law is good. [17]So I am not the one doing wrong; it is sin living in me that does it.
[18]And I know that nothing good lives in
me, that is, in my sinful nature. I want to
do what is right, but I can't. [19]I want to do
what is good, but I don't. I don't want to do
what is wrong, but I do it anyway. [20]But if I

7:4 Rom 6:6; 8:2; Gal 5:18; Col 2:14; 1 Pet 2:24
7:5 Rom 6:21; 8:8; Gal 5:19-21
7:6 2 Cor 3:6; Gal 5:22; Phil 3:3
7:7 *Exod 20:17; *Deut 5:21; Rom 4:15; [e]*nomos* (3551) ‣Rom 7:12
7:8 Rom 4:15; [f]*hamartia* (0266) ‣Rom 8:2
7:10 Lev 18:5; Rom 10:5; 2 Cor 3:7; Gal 3:12
7:11 Gen 3:13; Heb 3:13
7:12 1 Tim 1:8; [g]*nomos* (3551) ‣Rom 8:2
7:14 1 Kgs 21:20-25; Rom 3:9; 6:6
7:15 Gal 5:17
7:18 Gen 6:5; 8:21; John 3:6; Rom 8:3

7:4 Christians have ***died to the power of the law*** (literally *died to the law*) and so are no longer bound to it. Paul often refers to the law of Moses as representing the old regime of sin and death, but through union with Christ in his death, believers are set free.

7:5 ***When we were controlled by our old nature*** (literally *When we were in the flesh*): Although "flesh" can refer to the human body in a neutral sense (see 8:3, which speaks of Christ coming "in the flesh"), Paul more often uses the word negatively, to denote human existence apart from God. To be "in the flesh" is to be dominated by sin and its hostility to God. • ***the law aroused these evil desires:*** The law of God is a good thing in itself (see 7:12), but it arouses sinful tendencies by provoking the rebellion that is in people's hearts. When we are in rebellion against God, his commands spark in us a desire to do the exact opposite of what he commands.

7:6 ***the letter of the law*** (literally *the letter*): Paul uses the word *letter* to refer to the law, which was engraved on tablets of stone and consisted of individual *letters* (see 2:29; 2 Cor 3:5-7).

7:7-25 ***Well then*** (see note on 6:1): Paul has just said some rather negative things about the law, and he now explains how God's law is good in order to guard against any notion that it is evil in itself.

7:7 ***"You must not covet":*** See Exod 20:17; Deut 5:21.

7:8 ***sin used this command*** (literally *sin took an opportunity through this command*): The word *opportunity* is a military term for a position seized in enemy territory that becomes a base of operations (see 7:11). By expressing God's demands, the commandments stimulate rebellion in sinful human beings. The commandments of God become an occasion for sin to accomplish its deadly purposes. • ***sin would not have that power:*** The law, by clearly expressing God's will, makes people more accountable than they would be without it. The law of Moses did not solve Israel's sin problem but exposed and exacerbated it. This is always the effect that God's law, by itself, has on sinful human beings.

7:9 ***At one time I lived without understanding the law:*** Paul might be referring to his early childhood, before he came to understand the full demands of the law. • ***But when I learned the command:*** Paul's experience with the law as he grew to maturity exemplifies every person's experience with it. With the law, we have greater accountability to God, which brings the ***power of sin*** to life, and the result is greater judgment (7:10; see 4:15; 5:14, 20).

7:10 ***which were supposed to bring life:*** The OT promised a blessed and secure life to those who obeyed the law (e.g., Lev 18:5, quoted in Rom 10:5). However, human beings inherit from Adam a strong tendency to sin. Therefore, when God's commands come to us, we do not naturally obey them, but resist and disobey them. Instead of bringing life, the law only confirms and exposes our lost and helpless condition. We need a change of heart that the law cannot provide.

7:11 ***Sin . . . deceived me:*** The language is reminiscent of Gen 3:13—Paul might be thinking of the Fall.

7:17 ***I am not the one doing wrong:*** Paul is not evading responsibility for his sin (see also 7:20). Rather, he is saying that because he genuinely wants to do what the law commands, some other factor must be causing him to do just the opposite. That factor is ***sin living in me.*** Paul experiences a divide between his will and his actions.

7:18 ***my sinful nature*** (literally *my flesh;* also in 7:25): This phrase could refer to Paul's former state as an unredeemed person or to a part of Paul that remains tied to the world and resists the will of God. See note on 6:19.

7:21
Rom 8:2
7:22
Ps 1:2; 40:8
7:23
Gal 5:17
Jas 4:1
1 Pet 2:11
7:25
1 Cor 15:57
8:2
Gal 2:19; 5:1
[h]*nomos* (3551)
‣ Rom 10:4
[i]*hamartia* (0266)
‣ Rom 14:23
8:3
2 Cor 5:21
Heb 2:14; 4:15

do what I don't want to do, I am not really the one doing wrong; it is sin living in me that does it.

21I have discovered this principle of life—that when I want to do what is right, I inevitably do what is wrong. 22I love God's law with all my heart. 23But there is another power within me that is at war with my mind. This power makes me a slave to the sin that is still within me. 24Oh, what a miserable person I am! Who will free me from this life that is dominated by sin and death? 25Thank God! The answer is in Jesus Christ our Lord. So you see how it is: In my mind I really want to obey God's law, but because of my sinful nature I am a slave to sin.

Assurance of Eternal Life in the Spirit (8:1-30)

The Spirit of Life

8 So now there is no condemnation for those who belong to Christ Jesus. 2And because you belong to him, the [h]power of the life-giving Spirit has freed you from the [h]power of [i]sin that leads to death. 3The law of Moses was unable to save us because of the weakness of our sinful nature. So God did what the law could not do. He sent his

The Limitations of Law (7:1-25)

Rom 2:13-29; 3:19-21, 27-28; 4:13-16; 8:3-4, 7; 9:4, 31-32; 10:3-5
Deut 4:44-45; 5:1-33; 6:17-25
Josh 24:19-27
1 Kgs 2:3
Ezra 7:25-26
Ps 1:1-3; 19:7-14; 78:56-59; 119:36, 79, 88, 144
Isa 24:5; 26:4-8
Jer 31:33-34
Hos 4:6; 8:12
Hab 1:4
Matt 5:17-20; 7:12; 22:36-40
Mark 7:8-9; 12:28-34
Luke 16:16-17
John 1:16-17; 7:19
Acts 13:38-39
Gal 2:16-21; 3:2, 10-13, 17-25; 5:1-4
1 Tim 1:5-11
Heb 7:18-19; 8:7-13; 10:1-18
1 Jn 3:4-6

The law was central to God's old covenant with the people of Israel, and many Jews in Paul's day still saw it as critical to how God's people lived. Therefore, in Romans, Paul frequently deals with questions about the law. The pinnacle of his treatment comes in Rom 7, where Paul powerfully argues that the law of Moses, rather than having a positive effect on people's lives, stimulated sin and brought death (7:5).

Paul wants us to realize that the law is not at fault. God's law is good and holy (7:12), but it is powerless to change the human heart. Whether we conclude that Paul (in 7:14-25) is describing the experience of an unbeliever, a mature believer, or an immature believer, the point remains that human sin cannot be overcome by the law. God's law is given to people who, because of their connection with Adam, are already locked under sin's power. They may want to do what God tells them, but they find that they cannot (7:15-20). Deliverance can come only through a new and radical experience of God's power and grace in Jesus Christ (7:25). Through God's Spirit, Jesus rescues us "from the power of sin that leads to death" (8:2).

If God's good and holy law cannot rescue us from our predicament and save us, how much less helpful are all human laws that people rely on for religious or spiritual well-being. Whether those laws come from a religious figure, a tradition we have inherited, or a church we attend, none of them can change the human soul. They can tell us what to do, but they cannot empower us to do it. God's law can provide guidelines in the new life God has given us by grace, but it can never substitute for the power of God's grace, made available through the work of Christ.

7:21 ***principle of life*** (literally *law*): Paul is referring to a regular occurrence, such as when we speak of the "law of gravity." The struggle between wanting to ***do what is right*** and instead doing ***what is wrong*** reveals a regular pattern operating in the human sphere.

7:22 ***with all my heart*** (literally *in my inner person*): The Greeks used this phrase to denote the spiritual or immortal side of human beings (cp. 2 Cor 4:16; Eph 3:16).

7:23 ***another power. . . . This power*** (literally *another law. . . . This law*): Paul plays on the word *law* in these verses. Opposed to God's law (7:22) is another law, a ruling *power* that prevents Paul from submitting to God's law even though he fully agrees with it.

7:24 ***this life that is dominated by sin and death*** (literally *this body of death*): Sin is so invasive that it affects the whole person, particularly our interactions in the physical world.

8:1 ***So now there is no condemnation:*** Paul concludes from the argument of chs 5–7 that neither sin (ch 6) nor the law (ch 7) can keep believers from having eternal life (ch 5). Paul can triumphantly proclaim that ***those who belong to Christ Jesus*** need not fear that they will be condemned for their sins.

8:2 ***you belong . . . freed you:*** Some manuscripts read *I belong . . . freed me.* A scribe might have changed an original *you* into *I/me* at some point. • ***the power*** (literally *the law*) ***of the life-giving Spirit:*** This reference to *power* or *law* could refer to the law of Moses, which the Spirit can use to produce life. But because Paul does not portray the law as a life-giving entity, "law" here, as in 7:23, probably means *principle* or *power.* The Holy Spirit is a power that frees the believer from ***the power*** (literally *the law*) ***of sin that leads to death.***

8:3 ***our sinful nature:*** Literally *our flesh;* similarly in 8:4-9, 12. See note on 6:19. • ***in a body like the bodies we sinners have:*** Jesus identified with sinful people so that he could be their representative and redeem them. Paul also implies that Jesus' incarnate nature was not exactly like ours; born of a virgin through the power of the Holy Spirit, Jesus did not inherit a sinful nature from Adam. • ***a sacrifice for our sins:*** In the Greek OT, this phrase frequently describes a sin offering, and three of the eight NT occurrences also have this meaning (Heb 10:6, 8; 13:11). Christ was the sin offering that brought forgiveness and turned away God's wrath. God condemned sin in Christ, our substitute, so that we could escape condemnation.

own Son in a body like the bodies we sinners
have. And in that body God declared an end
to sin's control over us by giving his Son as a
sacrifice for our sins. 4He did this so that the
just requirement of the law would be fully
satisfied for us, who no longer follow our
[j]sinful nature but instead follow the Spirit.
5Those who are dominated by the sinful
nature think about sinful things, but those
who are controlled by the Holy Spirit think
about things that please the Spirit. 6So letting your sinful nature control your mind
leads to death. But letting the Spirit control your mind leads to life and [k]peace. 7For
the sinful nature is always hostile to God.
It never did obey God's laws, and it never
will. 8That's why those who are still under
the control of their sinful nature can never
please God.
9But you are not controlled by your sinful nature. You are controlled by the Spirit
if you have the Spirit of God living in you.
(And remember that those who do not have
the Spirit of Christ living in them do not belong to him at all.) 10And Christ lives within
you, so even though your body will die
because of sin, the [a]Spirit gives you life because you have been made [b]right with God.
11The Spirit of God, who raised Jesus from
the dead, lives in you. And just as God raised
Christ Jesus from the dead, he will [c]give life
to your mortal bodies by this same Spirit living within you.
12Therefore, dear brothers and sisters,
you have no obligation to do what your sinful nature urges you to do. 13For if you live
by its dictates, you will die. But if through
the power of the [d]Spirit you put to death the
deeds of your sinful nature, you will live.

The Spirit of Adoption

14For all who are led by the Spirit of God are
children of God.
15So you have not received a spirit that
makes you fearful slaves. Instead, you received God's Spirit when he [e]adopted you as
his own children. Now we call him, [f]"Abba,
Father." 16For his Spirit joins with our spirit
to affirm that we are God's children. 17And
since we are his children, we are his heirs.
In fact, together with Christ we are [g]heirs of
God's glory. But if we are to share his glory,
we must also share his suffering.

The Spirit of Glory

18Yet what we suffer now is nothing compared to the glory he will reveal to us later.

8:4 Gal 5:16, 25
[j]*sarx* (4561) ‣ 1 Cor 5:5
8:5 Gal 5:19-23
8:6 Gal 6:8
[k]*eirēnē* (1515) ‣ Rom 14:19
8:9 Gal 4:6
8:10 [a]*pneuma* (4151) ‣ Rom 8:13
[b]*dikaiosunē* (1343) ‣ Rom 10:10
8:11 [c]*zōopoieō* (2227) ‣ 1 Cor 15:22
8:13 Gal 6:8
Col 3:5
[d]*pneuma* (4151) ‣ 1 Cor 5:3
8:14 Gal 3:26
8:15 Gal 4:5-6
[e]*huiothesia* (5206) ‣ Rom 8:23
[f]*abba patēr* (0005, 3962) ‣ Gal 4:6
8:16 2 Cor 1:22
8:17 Gal 3:29; 4:7
[g]*sunklēronomos* (4789) ‣ Eph 3:6

8:4 ***just requirement of the law . . . fully satisfied for*** (Greek *en,* "in") ***us:*** The Greek preposition *en* might indicate that the law is fulfilled *in* us because of our connection with Jesus Christ, who perfectly fulfilled the law for us. It could also mean that by setting us free from sin's power, Jesus Christ enables us to please God and fulfill the true intention of the law. • As in the OT (see Gen 6:3, 12; Ps 78:39; Isa 40:6), ***sinful nature*** refers to human weakness and bondage to sin (also in 8:5-9, 12-13). Paul uses the phrase to describe the conflict between the ingrained human tendency to sin and the Holy Spirit.

8:5 ***think about sinful things:*** This phrase describes the general nature of a person's will, not just the mental process of thought (see also 12:3; 15:5; Phil 2:2, 5).

8:6 ***Peace*** here does not refer merely to peace of mind; instead, as opposed to ***death,*** it implies an objective state of peace with God (see note on 5:1).

8:9 ***You are controlled by the Spirit:*** In contrast to unbelievers, who continue to live under the domination of Adam's ***sinful nature,*** the Holy Spirit directs the lives of believers. The Spirit does not take away human initiative or make it impossible for believers to sin. However, as the most powerful force in believers' lives, the Spirit makes it possible for them to resist the continuing power of sin.

8:10 ***the Spirit gives you life*** (or *your spirit is alive*): The Spirit opposes sin (which leads to physical death) and brings resurrection from the dead.

8:11 ***by this same Spirit:*** The Holy Spirit is the agent of the resurrection of our ***bodies.*** Some manuscripts read "*because of* the same Spirit," which would mean that the Spirit is the guarantee that our bodies will be raised (cp. Eph 1:14).

8:12 ***brothers and sisters:*** Literally *brothers;* also in 8:29. See note on 1:13.

8:13 ***deeds of your sinful nature:*** Literally *deeds of the body.* • ***you will die:*** Death is the consequence of sin. Those who consistently yield to sin will suffer spiritual death (eternal condemnation). The presence of the Holy Spirit in the lives of believers makes it possible for them to turn away from sin. The result is eternal life (***you will live***).

8:14 ***children*** (literally *sons*) ***of God:*** In the OT, this phrase referred to Israel, the people God called to be his own (see especially Exod 4:22; Jer 3:19; 31:9; Hos 11:1). Paul uses it to remind believers that they enjoy an intimate relationship with God and that they will inherit many of the promises and blessings given to Israel. Christians are no longer minors or slaves, but mature children with full rights (see Gal 4:1-7).

8:15 ***you received God's Spirit when he adopted you as his own children*** (literally *you received a spirit of sonship*): According to Greco-Roman customs of adoption, a man had the right to adopt a son and to confer on that child all the legal rights and privileges that would be given to a natural child. This practice extended even to the imperial family. The Roman emperor Julius Caesar adopted Octavian as his heir; Octavian, using the name Augustus, later ruled the Roman empire. Paul's concept of adoption is also rooted in the OT and Judaism (Exod 4:22; Deut 1:31; Hos 11:1; see also Rom 9:4; Gal 4:5; Eph 1:5). • ***Abba*** is an Aramaic term for "father." This word was used in an intimate family context ("Daddy"). Jesus used this word to address God (Mark 14:36); all those who become children of God through Jesus have the privilege of addressing God in the same way.

8:17 Jesus is heir to all of God's promises (Mark 12:1-12; Gal 3:18-19; Heb 1:2), and as those who belong to Jesus, we ***share*** with him in that glorious inheritance. However, just as it was for Jesus, our path to ***glory*** is also marked by ***suffering.*** We experience the difficulties that come from striving to live righteously in a world dominated by sin (2 Cor 1:5; Phil 1:29; 3:10).

19For all creation is waiting eagerly for that future day when God will reveal who his children really are. 20Against its will, all creation was subjected to God's curse. But with eager hope, 21the creation looks forward to the day when it will join God's children in glorious [h]freedom from death and decay. 22For we know that all creation has been groaning as in the pains of childbirth right up to the present time. 23And we believers also groan, even though we have the Holy Spirit within us as a foretaste of future glory, for we long for our bodies to be released from sin and suffering. We, too, wait with eager hope for the day when God will give us our full rights as his [i]adopted children, including the [j]new bodies he has promised us. 24We were given this [k]hope when we were [a]saved. (If we already have something, we don't need to [k]hope for it. 25But if we look forward to something we don't yet have, we must wait patiently and confidently.)

26And the Holy Spirit helps us in our weakness. For example, we don't know what God wants us to pray for. But the Holy Spirit prays for us with groanings that cannot be expressed in words. 27And the Father who knows all hearts knows what the Spirit is saying, for the Spirit pleads for us believers in harmony with God's own will. 28And we know that God causes everything to work together for the good of those who love God and are [b]called according to his purpose for them. 29For God [c]knew his people in advance, and he [d]chose them to become like his Son, so that his Son would be the [e]firstborn among many brothers and sisters. 30And having [f]chosen them, he called them to come to him. And having called them, he gave them right standing with himself. And having given them right standing, he gave them his glory.

Nothing Can Separate Us from God's Love (8:31-39)

31What shall we say about such wonderful things as these? If God is for us, who can ever be against us? 32Since he did not spare even his own Son but gave him up for us all, won't he also give us everything else? 33Who dares accuse us whom God has chosen for his own? No one—for God himself has given us right standing with himself. 34Who then will condemn us? No one—for Christ Jesus died for us and was raised to life for us, and he is sitting in the place of honor at God's right hand, pleading for us.

35Can anything ever separate us from [g]Christ's love? Does it mean he no longer loves us if we have trouble or calamity, or are persecuted, or hungry, or destitute, or in danger, or threatened with death? 36(As the Scriptures say, "For your sake we are killed every day; we are being slaughtered like sheep.") 37No, despite all these things, overwhelming victory is ours through Christ, who loved us.

8:18
2 Cor 4:17
1 Pet 1:6-7

8:20
Gen 3:17-19

8:21
Acts 3:21
[h]*eleutheria* (1657)
‣1 Cor 10:29

8:23
[i]*huiothesia* (5206)
‣Rom 9:4
[j]*apolutrōsis* (0629)
‣1 Cor 1:30

8:24
Heb 11:1
[k]*elpis* (1680)
‣1 Cor 13:13
[a]*sōzō* (4982)
‣Rom 10:9

8:26
John 14:16

8:28
[b]*klētos* (2822)
‣Rom 11:29

8:29
1 Pet 1:2
[c]*proginōskō* (4267)
‣Rom 11:2
[d]*proorizō* (4309)
‣Rom 8:30
[e]*prōtotokos* (4416)
‣Col 1:15

8:30
[f]*proorizō* (4309)
‣1 Cor 2:7

8:31
Ps 118:6

8:34
1 Jn 2:1

8:35
[g]*christos* (5547)
‣2 Cor 5:10

8:36
*Ps 44:22

8:37
John 16:33
1 Jn 5:4

8:19-21 ***All creation*** includes animals, plants, and the earth itself. Paul follows OT precedent (see especially Ps 65:12-13; Isa 24:4; Jer 4:28; 12:4) by personifying the created world. • ***waiting eagerly . . . looks forward:*** Just as the entire world was harmed by Adam's fall into sin, it will share in the blessings that God has promised his people.

8:19 ***his children:*** Literally *his sons.*

8:22 The ***pains of childbirth*** is a metaphor for the longing of creation (see also Matt 24:8; Mark 13:8; John 16:20-22).

8:23 ***we believers also groan:*** "Groaning" expresses a frustrated longing for God's deliverance from the difficulties and oppression of this life (see Exod 3:7; Lam 1:22; Ezek 24:17; 2 Cor 5:2). • ***we have the Holy Spirit within us as a foretaste of future glory*** (literally *we have the first harvest of the Spirit*): In the OT, the phrase *first harvest* or *firstfruits* often describes the offering of the first and best part of a harvest to God (see Exod 23:19; Lev 2:12; 23:10; cp. 1 Cor 15:20, 23). The Holy Spirit is God's pledge that he will see his work in us through to its conclusion (see Eph 1:14). • ***wait with eager hope for the day when God will give us our full rights as his adopted children:*** Literally *wait anxiously for sonship.* Although we have already been *adopted* by God as his *children,* the *full rights* of that adoption—our inheritance (see 8:17)—are not yet ours. In this life, Christians live in tension between the "already" of redemption and the "not yet" of the glory to be revealed.

8:24 ***we don't need to hope for it:*** Some manuscripts read *we don't need to wait for it.*

8:26 ***groanings that cannot be expressed in words:*** This might refer to speech that does not take the form of human language, such as when believers, uncertain of what to pray, utter meaningless sounds in prayer. The groanings in question are the Spirit's, not ours. When we do not know how to pray, the Spirit is interceding for us before God.

8:27 ***for us believers:*** Literally *for God's holy people.*

8:28 ***And we know that God causes everything to work together:*** Some manuscripts read *And we know that everything works together.*

8:29 ***would be the firstborn:*** Or *would be supreme.*

8:30 ***gave them his glory:*** Elsewhere in this passage, the *glory* Christians will experience is consistently in the future (8:18, 21, 23). The past tense here refers to God's past decision to glorify us in the future. We have not yet entered into our inheritance, but the Father has irrevocably determined to give us his glory.

8:31 ***such wonderful things:*** Paul is referring to everything he has taught in chs 5–8 about the blessings and sense of assurance that believers receive from their relationship with God.

8:32 ***did not spare even his own Son:*** Behind this language is the story about Abraham's willingness to offer his only son, Isaac (Gen 22:12, 16). Isaac, however, was not actually sacrificed. God's not sparing his only Son went the full course: He handed him over to the shameful and painful death of crucifixion.

8:36 This quotation is from Ps 44:22.

38And I am convinced that nothing can
ever separate us from God's love. Neither
death nor life, neither angels nor demons,
neither our fears for today nor our worries
about tomorrow—not even the powers of
hell can separate us from God's love. 39No
power in the sky above or in the earth below—indeed, nothing in all creation will
ever be able to separate us from the [h]love
of God that is revealed in Christ Jesus our
Lord.

4. THE DEFENSE OF THE GOSPEL: THE PROBLEM OF ISRAEL (9:1–11:36)

Introduction: The Tension between God's Promises and Israel's Plight (9:1-5)

9 With Christ as my witness, I speak with
utter truthfulness. My conscience and
the Holy Spirit confirm it. 2My heart is filled
with bitter sorrow and unending grief 3for
my people, my Jewish brothers and sisters.
I would be willing to be forever cursed—cut
off from Christ!—if that would save them.
4They are the people of Israel, chosen to
be God's [i]adopted children. God revealed
his glory to them. He made covenants with
them and gave them his law. He gave them
the privilege of worshiping him and receiving his wonderful promises. 5Abraham,
Isaac, and Jacob are their ancestors, and
Christ himself was an Israelite as far as his
human nature is concerned. And he is God,
the one who rules over everything and is
worthy of eternal praise! Amen.

Defining the Promise (Part 1): God's Sovereign Election (9:6-29)

The Israel within Israel

6Well then, has God failed to fulfill his
promise to Israel? No, for not all who are
born into the nation of Israel are truly
members of God's people! 7Being descendants of Abraham doesn't make them truly
Abraham's children. For the Scriptures
say, "Isaac is the son through whom your
descendants will be counted," though Abraham had other children, too. 8This means
that Abraham's physical descendants are
not necessarily children of God. Only the
children of the promise are considered to
be Abraham's children. 9For God had promised, "I will return about this time next year,
and Sarah will have a son."

10This son was our ancestor Isaac. When
he married Rebekah, she gave birth to
twins. 11But before they were born, before
they had done anything good or bad, she received a message from God. (This message
shows that God chooses people according

8:38 John 10:28; Col 3:3
8:39 Rom 5:3-8; [h]*agapē* (0026) ‣Rom 13:10
9:1 1 Tim 2:7
9:2-3 Exod 32:32; Rom 10:1
9:4 Exod 4:22; Deut 4:13; 7:6; Eph 2:12; [i]*huiothesia* (5206) ‣Gal 4:5
9:5 John 1:1, 18; Rom 1:3; Titus 2:13; 2 Pet 1:1; 1 Jn 5:20
9:6 Num 23:19; Rom 2:28; Gal 6:16
9:7 *Gen 21:12; Heb 11:18
9:8 Rom 8:14; Gal 3:16; 4:23
9:9 *Gen 18:10, 14
9:10 Gen 25:21

8:38 *nor demons:* Literally *nor rulers.*

9:1–11:36 In this section, Paul takes up the problem raised by the unbelief of so many Jews. If God had promised salvation to Israel yet so few Jews were being saved, how could Jesus truly be the fulfillment of God's plan (9:1-5)? In his response to this objection, Paul cites the OT as evidence that God had always intended to save only a remnant of Israel (9:6-29), and he faults the Jews for refusing to embrace Christ (9:30–10:21). Paul then shows that God has not discarded Israel from his plan of salvation. Many Jews have already believed in Christ (11:1-10), and many more will believe in the future (11:12-26).

9:2-3 Paul does not explicitly say why he has such *bitter sorrow* for his *Jewish brothers and sisters.* Yet his willingness to become *cursed* on their behalf *if that would save them* makes clear that the failure of most Jews to respond to Jesus and be saved stimulated his agony (see also 10:1).

9:3 *my Jewish brothers and sisters:* Literally *my brothers.* Cp. note on 1:13. • *I would be willing to be forever cursed* (Greek *anathema*): *Anathema* is used in the Greek OT to translate a Hebrew expression that means "set apart for God," which usually has the negative sense of something destined to be destroyed as an offering to God (see Lev 27:28-29; Josh 6:17-18; 7:1, 11-13; 22:20; 1 Sam 15:3; 1 Chr 2:7). Paul knows that he cannot, in fact, be *cut off from Christ.* Paul is echoing the offer of Moses, who pled with God to kill him but to spare the people (Exod 32:30-32).

9:4 Up to this point in Romans, Paul has called the Jewish people *Jews.* His shift to *people of Israel,* here and throughout most of chs 9–11, is significant. *Jew* connotes national identity, but *Israel* emphasizes the covenant relationship of the people with God. • *chosen to be God's adopted children* (literally *chosen for sonship*): The OT called Israel God's *son* or *child* to emphasize that God had selected Israel to be his own people (e.g., Exod 4:22; Jer 3:19; 31:9; Hos 11:1). Israel's adopted status meant that they received God's blessing and promises, not that they were necessarily saved. • *covenants:* The OT includes several covenants between God and the people of Israel: one with Abraham (Gen 17), one with the nation through Moses at Mount Sinai (Exod 19–24), and one with David (2 Sam 7:8-16; 23:5). See also "God's Covenant Relationships" at Gen 12:1-9, p. 44.

9:5 *Christ* came from the people of Israel, and God first made his promises of salvation to them. • *And he is God, the one who rules over everything and is worthy of eternal praise! Amen.* Or *May God, the one who rules over everything, be praised forever. Amen.*

9:6 *are truly members of God's people* (literally *are Israel*): "Israel" can refer to the people of Israel in a biological sense, i.e., everyone descended from Jacob. But in the latter part of the OT and in Judaism, the idea of a "righteous remnant" within Israel developed (see "The Remnant" at Isa 11:10-16, p. 1126). On at least one occasion in the NT, Israel refers to everyone, Jew and Gentile, who belongs to God in a spiritual sense (Gal 6:16). Paul is stating that there is now an "Israel within Israel," a community consisting of both Jews and Gentiles who truly believe (cp. 11:16-17; Gal 6:16).

9:7 This quotation is from Gen 21:12, which God spoke to Abraham when he was reluctant to follow Sarah's advice to banish his son Ishmael, who was born to the slave woman Hagar. God assured Abraham that Sarah's child, Isaac, was the son through whom God's promises would be fulfilled.

9:9 This quotation is from Gen 18:10, 14.

9:10-11 *she gave birth to twins:* Literally *she conceived children through this one man.* No human circumstances differentiated Isaac's sons, Jacob and Esau. Not only were they born to the same mother, but they were also con-

9:12
*Gen 25:23
9:13
*Mal 1:2-3
9:14
Deut 32:4
9:15
*Exod 33:19
9:16
Eph 2:8
9:17
*Exod 9:16
9:18
Exod 4:21; 14:4
Josh 11:20
Rom 11:25
9:20
Isa 29:16; 45:9
9:21
Jer 18:6
2 Tim 2:20
9:22
Jer 50:25
9:23
Rom 8:30
9:24
Rom 3:29
9:25
*Hos 2:23
1 Pet 2:10

to his own purposes; 12he calls people, but
not according to their good or bad works.)
She was told, "Your older son will serve your
younger son." 13In the words of the Scriptures, "I loved Jacob, but I rejected Esau."

Objections Answered: The Freedom and Purpose of God

14Are we saying, then, that God was unfair?
Of course not! 15For God said to Moses,

"I will show mercy to anyone I choose,
and I will show compassion to anyone
I choose."

16So it is God who decides to show mercy.
We can neither choose it nor work for it.
17For the Scriptures say that God told
Pharaoh, "I have appointed you for the very
purpose of displaying my power in you and
to spread my fame throughout the earth."
18So you see, God chooses to show mercy to
some, and he chooses to harden the hearts
of others so they refuse to listen.
19Well then, you might say, "Why does God
blame people for not responding? Haven't
they simply done what he makes them do?"
20No, don't say that. Who are you, a mere
human being, to argue with God? Should
the thing that was created say to the one
who created it, "Why have you made me
like this?" 21When a potter makes jars out
of clay, doesn't he have a right to use the
same lump of clay to make one jar for deco-
ration and another to throw garbage into?
22In the same way, even though God has the
right to show his anger and his power, he
is very patient with those on whom his anger falls, who are destined for destruction.
23He does this to make the riches of his
glory shine even brighter on those to whom
he shows mercy, who were prepared in advance for glory.

God's Calling of a New People: Israel and the Gentiles

24And we are among those whom he selected, both from the Jews and from the
Gentiles.
25Concerning the Gentiles, God says in
the prophecy of Hosea,

God Is in Charge (9:5-24)

Rom 8:28
Deut 4:39; 7:7-8; 32:8, 39
Josh 2:11
1 Sam 2:6-8
2 Kgs 13:4-5; 17:18-20; 20:4-6
Ps 24:1-2; 84:11; 135:5-12
Isa 40:15-17; 42:8; 46:10
Jer 27:5-7
Dan 7:27-28
Hab 2:14
John 19:11
Acts 17:24-26
1 Cor 1:8-9
Col 1:15-20
2 Thes 1:11-12
Jude 1:24-25
Rev 1:7-8

We human beings always want to think that we are in charge. We think that we are the "captains of our souls"[1] and that by our decisions and actions we can determine what will happen. However, Scripture confronts us with quite a different scenario. Although human decisions and actions are significant, the will of God is vastly more important.

In Rom 9, Paul shows that God determines the course of salvation. Paul constantly explains the unexpected development of salvation history by appealing to what God has said and done. Human decisions alone cannot explain the situation, and God has said that he will show mercy to anyone he chooses (9:15). While theologians will continue to debate the role of God's action and the role of human decision in salvation, God's sovereignty stands out clearly.

The contemporary world has set God to the side and ignores the divine influence on the course of human affairs. But God's decisions really do direct the world as well as the personal histories of those who trust him. We can confidently affirm that "God causes everything to work together for the good of those who love God and are called according to his purpose for them" (8:28).

[1] "Invictus" by W. E. Henley (1849–1903).

ceived at the same time. Instead, Paul argues, the difference between them was of God's choosing.

9:12 ***"Your older son will serve your younger son":*** God spoke these words (Gen 25:23) to Rebekah before the twins were born. As the older of the twins, Esau was Isaac's natural heir. But Esau sold his birthright to Jacob and ceded his position to his brother in fulfillment of God's promise.

9:13 ***"I loved Jacob, but I rejected*** (literally *hated*) ***Esau":*** Paul quotes Mal 1:2-3, where ***Jacob,*** whose other name is Israel (Gen 32:28), stands for the nation of Israel, and ***Esau*** stands for Edom. Here, Paul is referring to them as individuals. Just as love can sometimes express a choice, so hate can express rejection. The story of Jacob and Esau illustrates how the sovereign God chooses his own people.

9:14-16 God's choice is not unfair because he owes nothing to his sinful creatures (see note on 4:4-5).

9:15 This quotation from Exod 33:19 focuses on God's nature: God is free from obligation or constraint in bestowing mercy on people.

9:17 ***God told Pharaoh:*** Paul quotes Exod 9:16 (Greek version). At God's direction, Moses had asked Pharaoh to let the people of Israel leave Egypt for their own land. When Pharaoh stubbornly refused, God displayed miracle after miracle to convince Israel, Pharaoh, and the Egyptians of God's power and authority (see Exod 6:7; 7:5; 9:14-16; 14:31).

9:18 ***he chooses to harden the hearts of others so they refuse to listen:*** Pharaoh refused to let Israel go because his heart was hardened. God hardened Pharaoh's heart (Exod 9:12), and Pharaoh hardened his own heart (Exod 8:15).

9:20-21 See Isa 29:16; 45:9-10.

9:24-26 God was free to select people ***from the Jews*** who would have a true spiritual relationship with him; similarly, he was also free to choose some ***from the Gentiles*** to be saved as well. Paul uses ***the prophecy of Hosea*** to

"Those who were not my people,
I will now call my people.
And I will love those
whom I did not love before."

26 And,

"Then, at the place where they were told,
'You are not my people,'
there they will be called
'children of the living God.'"

27 And concerning Israel, Isaiah the prophet
cried out,

"Though the people of Israel are as
numerous as the sand of the
seashore,
only a remnant will be saved.
28 For the LORD will carry out his sentence
upon the earth
quickly and with finality."

29 And Isaiah said the same thing in another
place:

"If the LORD of Heaven's Armies
had not spared a few of our children,
we would have been wiped out like Sodom,
destroyed like Gomorrah."

Understanding Israel's Plight: Christ as the Climax of Salvation History (9:30–10:21)

Israel, the Gentiles, and the Righteousness of God

30 What does all this mean? Even though
the Gentiles were not trying to follow God's
standards, they were made right with God.
And it was by faith that this took place.
31 But the people of Israel, who tried so hard
to get right with God by keeping the law,
never succeeded. 32 Why not? Because they
were trying to get right with God by keeping
the law instead of by trusting in him. They
[j]stumbled over the great rock in their path.
33 God warned them of this in the Scriptures
when he said,

"I am placing a stone in Jerusalem that
makes people [k]stumble,
a rock that makes them fall.
But anyone who trusts in him
will never be disgraced."

10 Dear brothers and sisters, the longing of my heart and my prayer to
God is for the people of Israel to be saved.
2 I know what enthusiasm they have for God,
but it is misdirected zeal. 3 For they don't
understand God's way of making people
right with himself. Refusing to accept God's
way, they cling to their own way of getting
right with God by trying to keep the law.
4 For Christ has already accomplished the
purpose for which the [a]law was given. As a
result, all who believe in him are made right
with God.
5 For Moses writes that the law's way of
making a person right with God requires
obedience to all of its commands. 6 But faith's

9:26 *Hos 1:10
9:27-28 *Isa 10:22-23; 28:22 *Hos 1:10
9:29 *Isa 1:9
9:30 Gal 2:16 Heb 11:7
9:31 Isa 51:1 Rom 10:2-3 Gal 5:4
9:32 Isa 8:14 [j]*proskomma* (4348) ›Rom 9:33
9:33 *Isa 28:16 Rom 10:11 1 Pet 2:6, 8 [k]*proskomma* (4348) ›Rom 14:13
10:2 Acts 22:3 Gal 1:14
10:3 Rom 9:31-32
10:4 Gal 3:24 [a]*nomos* (3551) ›1 Cor 14:21
10:5 Lev 18:5 Ezek 20:11, 13, 21 Rom 7:10

reinforce his point. Hosea predicted that God would renew his mercy to the ten northern tribes that had rebelled against God and were under his judgment. Paul saw a principle that applies to Gentiles as well. • ***Those who were not my people:*** see note on 10:19.

9:25 This quotation is from Hos 2:23.

9:26 ***children of the living God:*** Literally *sons of the living God.* Hos 1:10.

9:27-28 This quotation is from Isa 10:22-23 (Greek version). • ***only a remnant will be saved:*** So many Israelites had turned from God that the OT prophets spoke of a true spiritual Israel within the larger nation of Israel (see "The Remnant" at Isa 11:10-16, p. 1126). The remnant would receive salvation, while the rest of the Israelites would suffer condemnation.

9:29 This quotation is from Isa 1:9 (Greek version). • The destruction of the cities of *Sodom* and *Gomorrah* (Gen 19) is a poignant illustration of the reality and severity of God's judgment.

9:31 ***who tried so hard to get right with God by keeping the law*** (literally *who pursued the law of righteousness*): *Law of righteousness* is an idiom that means "righteousness through the law."

9:32-33 ***by keeping the law:*** Literally *by works.* • ***The great rock in their path*** is Christ. People either build on him by putting their faith in him, or they ***stumble*** over his message that faith, and not human works, is the key to getting ***right with God.***

9:33 This quotation is from Isa 8:14; 28:16 (Greek version). These two texts, along with Ps 118:22, are also quoted together in 1 Pet 2:6-8. The early church likely had a collection of messianic "stone" quotations from the OT that they used to illuminate the significance of Christ (see also Matt 21:42). • ***Jerusalem:*** Greek *Zion.*

10:1 ***Dear brothers and sisters:*** Literally *Brothers.* See note on 1:13.

10:2 ***Zeal*** denotes a passionate and commendable commitment to God and his purposes (see Num 25:6-13). But in Paul's day Jewish zeal was ***misdirected*** because it failed to understand that Jesus Christ is the pinnacle of God's plan. (For Paul's own misdirected zeal before his conversion to Christ, see Acts 9:1-2; Gal 1:13-14.)

10:3 ***God's way of making people right with himself:*** See 1:17; 3:21-26. Paul uses this phrase to explain Israel's failure in terms basic to the gospel. God manifested his righteousness through the ministry of Christ, but most Jews did not ***understand*** it, partly because they were so focused on the law as a way of securing their own righteousness.

10:4 ***For Christ has already accomplished the purpose for which the law was given*** (or *For Christ is the end of the law,* or *For Christ is the culmination of the law*): The function of the law was to point forward and prepare the way for the Messiah; Jesus' coming does not destroy the law but fulfills all of its requirements, so that the primary requirement for God's people is to ***believe in him*** (see 3:31; Matt 5:17-18).

10:5 ***requires obedience to all of its commands:*** See Lev 18:5, where these words encouraged the Israelites to obey the law in order to enjoy long life and prosperity in the land that God was giving them (see also Lev 26:3-13; Deut 28:1-14). Paul sees the implication that if people want to be right with God through the law, they can only do so by obeying all of it.

10:6-8
*Deut 30:12-14
10:9
Matt 10:32
[b]*kardia* (2588)
‣2 Cor 5:12
[c]*sōzō* (4982)
‣1 Cor 15:2
10:10
[d]*dikaiosunē* (1343)
‣Eph 5:9
10:11
*Isa 28:16
Rom 9:33
10:12
Acts 15:9
Eph 2:4-7
10:13
*Joel 2:32
Acts 2:21
10:15
*Isa 52:7
*Nah 1:15
10:16
*Isa 53:1
John 12:38
Heb 4:2
10:17
Gal 3:2, 5
Col 3:16
[e]*pistis* (4102)
‣Rom 14:1
10:18
*Ps 19:4
10:19
*Deut 32:21
10:20
*Isa 65:1
Rom 9:30
10:21
*Isa 65:2
Matt 23:37
11:1
Phil 3:5
11:2
1 Sam 12:22
[f]*proginōskō* (4267)
‣Gal 3:8

way of getting right with God says, "Don't say in your heart, 'Who will go up to heaven?' (to bring Christ down to earth). 7And don't say, 'Who will go down to the place of the dead?' (to bring Christ back to life again)." 8In fact, it says,

"The message is very close at hand;
it is on your lips and in your heart."

And that message is the very message about faith that we preach: 9If you confess with your mouth that Jesus is Lord and believe in your [b]heart that God raised him from the dead, you will be [c]saved. 10For it is by believing in your heart that you are made [d]right with God, and it is by confessing with your mouth that you are saved. 11As the Scriptures tell us, "Anyone who trusts in him will never be disgraced." 12Jew and Gentile are the same in this respect. They have the same Lord, who gives generously to all who call on him. 13For "Everyone who calls on the name of the LORD will be saved."

Israel's Accountability

14But how can they call on him to save them unless they believe in him? And how can they believe in him if they have never heard about him? And how can they hear about him unless someone tells them? 15And how will anyone go and tell them without being sent? That is why the Scriptures say, "How beautiful are the feet of messengers who bring good news!"

16But not everyone welcomes the Good News, for Isaiah the prophet said, "LORD, who has believed our message?" 17So [e]faith comes from hearing, that is, hearing the Good News about Christ. 18But I ask, have the people of Israel actually heard the message? Yes, they have:

"The message has gone throughout the earth,
and the words to all the world."

19But I ask, did the people of Israel really understand? Yes, they did, for even in the time of Moses, God said,

"I will rouse your jealousy through
people who are not even a nation.
I will provoke your anger through the
foolish Gentiles."

20And later Isaiah spoke boldly for God, saying,

"I was found by people who were not
looking for me.
I showed myself to those who were
not asking for me."

21But regarding Israel, God said,

"All day long I opened my arms to them,
but they were disobedient and
rebellious."

Summary: Israel, the "Elect," and the "Hardened" (11:1-10)

11 I ask, then, has God rejected his own people, the nation of Israel? Of course not! I myself am an Israelite, a descendant of Abraham and a member of the tribe of Benjamin.

2No, God has not rejected his own people, whom he [f]chose from the very beginning.

10:6-8 Here Paul quotes three phrases from Deut 30:12-14 dealing with the law, and he applies them to the Good News about Christ. We do not need to ***go up to heaven*** to find Christ (and thus to be made right with God), because God has already brought him ***down to earth*** as a man. Nor do we need to ***go down to the place of the dead*** to find Christ, because God has already raised him from the dead. To find Christ, we must simply believe in ***the message*** that is ***close at hand***.

10:11 See Isa 28:16 (Greek version).

10:12 ***and Gentile:*** Literally ***and Greek.***

10:13 Paul quotes Joel 2:32, where ***the LORD*** in Hebrew is ***Yahweh,*** the personal ***name*** of God (see Exod 3:15). However, as 10:12 makes clear, ***the Lord*** in Romans is Jesus Christ. This verse shows that Christians from the time of the apostles have associated Jesus with God.

10:14 It is natural to presume that the pronoun ***they*** refers to "all who call on him" from 10:12 or "everyone" from 10:13. While this verse probably does refer to all people, it also continues the accusation against Israel from 10:2-3 (see 10:18). Paul argues that Israel was in a position to know what God was doing through Jesus Christ, so they were culpable for their failure to understand or accept it. Israel was guilty both of failing to understand God's plan in light of Christ (10:3-4) and of focusing so much attention on the law that they missed Christ when he arrived (9:30-32).

10:15 This quotation is from Isa 52:7.

10:16 This quotation is from Isa 53:1.

10:18 ***Yes, they have:*** Paul quotes Ps 19:4 to show that the ***message*** of Good News was universally available through creation. And by the time Paul wrote Romans, early Christian missionaries had spread the Good News through most of the Roman empire. Most Jews would have had ample opportunity to hear the message.

10:19 ***rouse your jealousy . . . provoke your anger:*** This quotation from Deut 32:21 concerns God's punishment of Israel for their idolatry. In Paul's day, Israel remained guilty of idolatry because it put the law in place of God himself. God's punishment involved using the Gentiles, ***people who are not even a nation,*** to make Israel jealous and angry (11:12-32 elaborates on this theme).

10:20 This quotation is from Isa 65:1 (Greek version). In Isaiah, the words ***people who were not looking for me*** refer to the people of Israel. As in 9:25-26, Paul applies them to the Gentiles to show that God has opened the way for them to be a part of the people of God.

10:21 This quotation is from Isa 65:2 (Greek version).

11:2 ***chose from the very beginning:*** Before the people of Israel could do anything to earn their status, God selected them to be his people based

Do you realize what the Scriptures say
about this? Elijah the prophet complained
to God about the people of Israel and said,
3"LORD, they have killed your prophets and
torn down your altars. I am the only one left,
and now they are trying to kill me, too."
4And do you remember God's reply? He
said, "No, I have 7,000 others who have
never bowed down to Baal!"
5It is the same today, for a few of the
people of Israel have remained faithful
because of God's grace—his undeserved
kindness in choosing them. 6And since
it is through God's kindness, then it is not
by their good works. For in that case, God's
grace would not be what it really is—free
and undeserved.
7So this is the situation: Most of the people of Israel have not found the favor of
God they are looking for so earnestly. A few
have—the ones God has chosen—but the
hearts of the rest were hardened. 8As the
Scriptures say,

"God has put them into a deep sleep.
To this day he has shut their eyes so they
do not see,
and closed their ears so they do not
hear."

9Likewise, David said,

"Let their bountiful table become a
snare,
a trap that makes them think all is
well.
Let their blessings cause them to
stumble,
and let them get what they deserve.
10Let their eyes go blind so they cannot
see,
and let their backs be bent forever."

Defining the Promise (Part 2): The Future of Israel (11:11-32)

God's Purpose in Israel's Rejection

11Did God's people stumble and fall beyond
recovery? Of course not! They were disobedient, so God made salvation available to
the Gentiles. But he wanted his own people
to become jealous and claim it for themselves. 12Now if the Gentiles were enriched
because the people of Israel turned down
God's offer of salvation, think how much
greater a blessing the world will share when
they finally accept it.
13I am saying all this especially for you
Gentiles. God has appointed me as the apostle to the Gentiles. I stress this, 14for I want
somehow to make the people of Israel jealous of what you Gentiles have, so I might
save some of them. 15For since their rejection meant that God [g]offered salvation to
the rest of the world, their acceptance will
be even more wonderful. It will be life for
those who were dead!

The Interrelationship of Jews and Gentiles: Warning to Gentiles

16And since Abraham and the other patriarchs were holy, their descendants will also

11:3 *1 Kgs 19:10, 14
11:4 *1 Kgs 19:18
11:5 Rom 9:27
11:6 Rom 4:4
11:7 Rom 9:31
11:8 *Deut 29:4 *Isa 29:10 Matt 13:14 John 12:40 Acts 28:26-27
11:9-10 *Ps 69:22-23
11:11 Acts 13:46; 18:6
11:14 1 Cor 9:20 2 Tim 1:9
11:15 Luke 15:24, 32 Rom 5:10 [g]*katallagē* (2643) ‣1 Cor 7:11

on his grace alone. • ***Elijah the prophet:*** In 1 Kgs 19:1-18, the apostate King Ahab had slaughtered many of the Lord's prophets, and Ahab's wife Jezebel threatened Elijah with the same fate. Elijah fled to the wilderness, where he bemoaned his fate. God responded with the assurance that many faithful people remained. Paul found the present situation to be somewhat parallel. While many Jews did not believe, and some were even hostile, God was (and is) still working to preserve a believing remnant.

11:3 This quotation is from 1 Kgs 19:10, 14.

11:4 This quotation is from 1 Kgs 19:18.

11:5 ***for a few of the people of Israel*** (literally *for a remnant*): Paul returns to the OT concept of the remnant that he used in 9:27-29. This solid core of godly Israelites represents God's pledge of his continuing faithfulness to his promises and to his people.

11:7-8 ***the hearts of the rest were hardened:*** This is God's own work; God has ***put them into a deep sleep*** and ***shut their eyes.*** See Acts 13:46-48; 18:6.

11:8 This quotation is from Isa 29:10; Deut 29:4.

11:9-10 This quotation is from Ps 69:22-23 (Greek version).

11:11 ***so God made salvation available to the Gentiles:*** The offer of salvation to the Gentiles is the purpose, not just the result, of Israel's disobedience. Paul emphasizes that God had the salvation of Gentiles in view all along, and, ultimately, the salvation of many Jews as well. • ***he wanted his own people to become jealous:*** The theme of jealousy comes from Deut 32:21, which Paul quoted in 10:19. The sight of Gentiles enjoying the blessings of salvation that God had promised to Israel would spur Jews to desire salvation so they could participate in those blessings as well.

11:13-14 ***you Gentiles:*** Paul addresses the Gentile Christians in Rome with the practical goal of rebuking them for thinking too highly of themselves (11:20), especially in relation to their Jewish brothers and sisters. He shows that their enjoyment of salvation depends entirely on God's kindness (11:22), and that God's final goal is to stimulate repentance among the Jews (11:23). • ***I stress this:*** Paul devoted himself to the conversion of Gentiles because he knew that their salvation would ultimately lead to salvation for Jews as well.

11:15 The context emphasizes God's role in hardening many Jews (11:7-10), so the phrase ***their rejection*** likely means God's rejection of the unbelieving Jews. • ***their acceptance*** then refers to God's acceptance of Jews into his Kingdom (see also 14:3 and 15:7). • While the phrase ***life for those who were dead*** could refer to the new spiritual life that comes to the Jews as a result of their conversion to Christ (see 6:13), the language more naturally suggests the physical resurrection from the dead that occurs when Christ returns in glory (see, e.g., 1 Thes 4:13-18).

11:16 ***the entire batch of dough is holy because the portion given as an offering is holy:*** This imagery comes from Num 15:17-21, where God commanded the Israelites to take part of their first batch of dough and set it aside as a gift. God's

11:17
Jer 11:16
Eph 2:11-16
11:18
John 4:22
11:20
Rom 12:16
11:22
John 15:2, 14
Heb 3:14
11:23
2 Cor 3:14-16

be holy—just as the entire batch of dough is
holy because the portion given as an offering is holy. For if the roots of the tree are
holy, the branches will be, too.
17But some of these branches from
Abraham's tree—some of the people of
Israel—have been broken off. And you Gentiles, who were branches from a wild olive
tree, have been grafted in. So now you also
receive the blessing God has promised Abraham and his children, sharing in the rich
nourishment from the root of God's special
olive tree. 18But you must not brag about being grafted in to replace the branches that
were broken off. You are just a branch, not
the root.
19"Well," you may say, "those branches
were broken off to make room for me."
20Yes, but remember—those branches were
broken off because they didn't believe in
Christ, and you are there because you do believe. So don't think highly of yourself, but
fear what could happen. 21For if God did
not spare the original branches, he won't
spare you either.
22Notice how God is both kind and severe.
He is severe toward those who disobeyed,
but kind to you if you continue to trust in
his kindness. But if you stop trusting, you
also will be cut off. 23And if the people of
Israel turn from their unbelief, they will
be grafted in again, for God has the power
to graft them back into the tree. 24You, by
nature, were a branch cut from a wild olive

Jews and Gentiles (11:11-36)

Rom 1:5-6, 16-17; 2:9-10, 24-27; 3:9, 29-30; 9:25-33; 10:11-13; 15:7-13, 27
Deut 7:7-8; 32:19-21
Isa 9:1-3; 49:6
Matt 4:15-16; 8:10-12; 15:21-28
Luke 21:20-24
Acts 2:38-39; 10:45-46; 11:12-18; 13:42-49; 18:4-6; 26:15-18; 28:23-28
1 Cor 12:13
Gal 2:8-21; 3:8-9, 26-29
Eph 2:11-22; 3:6
Col 3:11

One of the key themes of Romans is that God has incorporated Gentiles into the people of God while remaining faithful to his promises to Israel. In 11:11-32, Paul describes God's plan to save all nations in four distinct stages:

1. *The Good News is proclaimed to the Jews, who respond (mostly) with unbelief.* In the central metaphor of the olive tree, "some of these branches from Abraham's tree . . . have been broken off" (11:17). This stage was already a matter of history and personal experience for Paul—although he shared the Good News with Jews in synagogues all over the eastern Mediterranean basin, many Jews rejected the message (see Acts 13:42-49; 18:4-6; 28:23-28).

2. *Many Gentiles respond to the message with faith.* As the natural branches were broken off, "branches from a wild olive tree have been grafted in" (11:17). After being resisted in the synagogue, Paul and the other apostles offered salvation to the Gentiles, and many responded affirmatively (see Acts 13:48-49; 26:15-18). By the time Paul wrote Romans, the church in Rome was largely a Gentile community.

3. *Many Jews respond to the Good News with faith.* In the future, the natural branches will be "grafted in again" (11:23). As Gentiles enjoy the blessings of salvation, Jews become jealous and respond to the Good News.

4. *God pours out great blessing on the world, including the resurrection from the dead.* When Jews finally turn to the Lord in greater numbers, there will be a "much greater blessing" (11:12), and the dead will be resurrected (11:15). The end of history will see a great community of both Jews and Gentiles praising God for his mercy. Then all people will see and understand the great wisdom and love of God (11:33-36).

promises to and blessings on Abraham, Isaac, and Jacob were like a down payment, guaranteeing the completion of God's work among his people.

11:17-24 In Paul's extended metaphor, ***God's special olive tree*** refers to the people of God. The image is a natural one, because the olive tree is the most widely cultivated fruit tree in the Mediterranean basin, and it was already used as a symbol of Israel in the OT (Jer 11:16; Hos 14:5-6). Paul refers to the Gentile Christians as ***branches from a wild olive tree*** because they were not originally included among the people of God.

11:18 ***You are just a branch, not the root:*** By the time Paul wrote to the church in Rome, it was composed mainly of Gentiles, a common situation in the early Christian communities. This dominant role led many Gentile Christians to brag about their status, while treating Jews and their religious heritage with disdain. Paul reminds the Gentile believers that they enjoy God's blessings only because they have been included in the one people of God, who are rooted in God's promises to Israel.

11:20 ***fear what could happen:*** In Scripture, fear often means a reverential awe of God that includes the recognition that we must one day stand before him in judgment (see 2 Cor 5:11; 7:1, 11, 15; Phil 2:12; Col 3:22).

11:21 ***he won't:*** Some manuscripts read *perhaps he won't.*

11:22 ***if you stop trusting, you also will be cut off:*** Scripture consistently emphasizes that only believers who persevere to the end will be saved. However, Paul's warning leads to debate over the theological implications of his statement. Some think that it implies that genuine believers can stop believing and therefore not be saved in the end. Others argue that we should not press the metaphor so far and that Paul is referring to people who appear to be believers but whose lack of real faith ultimately reveals itself.

11:24 ***by nature . . . contrary to nature:*** The usual method of enhancing the yield of olive trees involved grafting a shoot from a *cultivated tree* onto a wild olive tree to benefit from the wild tree's

tree. So if God was willing to do something contrary to nature by grafting you into his cultivated tree, he will be far more eager to graft the original branches back into the tree where they belong.

The Salvation of "All Israel"

25 I want you to understand this mystery, dear brothers and sisters, so that you will not feel proud about yourselves. Some of the people of Israel have hard hearts, but this will last only until the full number of Gentiles comes to Christ. 26 And so all Israel will be saved. As the Scriptures say,

"The one who rescues will come from
Jerusalem,
and he will turn Israel away from
ungodliness.
27 And this is my covenant with them,
that I will take away their sins."

28 Many of the people of Israel are now enemies of the Good News, and this benefits you Gentiles. Yet they are still the people he loves because he chose their ancestors Abraham, Isaac, and Jacob. 29 For God's gifts and his [h]call can never be withdrawn. 30 Once, you Gentiles were rebels against God, but when the people of Israel rebelled against him, God was merciful to you instead. 31 Now they are the rebels, and God's mercy has come to you so that they, too, will share in God's mercy. 32 For God has imprisoned everyone in disobedience so he could have mercy on everyone.

Conclusion: Praise to God in Light of His Awesome Plan (11:33-36)

33 Oh, how great are God's [i]riches and wisdom and knowledge! How impossible it is for us to understand his decisions and his ways!

34 For who can know the LORD's thoughts?
Who knows enough to give him
advice?
35 And who has given him so much
that he needs to pay it back?

36 For everything comes from him and exists by his power and is intended for his glory. All glory to him forever! Amen.

5. THE TRANSFORMING POWER OF THE GOSPEL: CHRISTIAN CONDUCT (12:1–15:13)

The Heart of the Matter: Total Transformation (12:1-2)

12 And so, dear brothers and sisters, I plead with you to give your bodies to God because of all he has done for you. Let them be a living and holy sacrifice—the kind he will find acceptable. This is truly

11:25 Luke 21:24
11:26-27 Ps 14:7; *Isa 59:20-21; Jer 31:31-34; Heb 8:8; 10:16
11:29 Heb 7:21; [h]*klēsis* (2821) ▸1 Cor 1:2
11:32 Gal 3:22; 1 Tim 2:4
11:33 Isa 45:15; 55:8; [i]*ploutos* (4149) ▸Eph 1:7
11:34 Job 15:8; 36:22; *Isa 40:13; Jer 23:18; 1 Cor 2:16
11:35 Job 41:11
11:36 1 Cor 8:6
12:1 1 Pet 2:5
12:2 Gal 1:4; Eph 4:23; Col 3:10; [j]*metamorphoō* (3339) ▸2 Cor 3:18; [k]*thelēma* (2307) ▸Rom 15:32
12:3 Prov 3:7; 1 Cor 12:11; Eph 4:7
12:4 1 Cor 12:12

vigor. By grafting wild olive branches (Gentiles) into the cultivated olive tree (the people of God), God has done what is contrary to nature.

11:25 ***dear brothers and sisters:*** Literally *brothers.* See note on 1:13. • Paul usually uses the word *mystery* to refer to an event of the last days that has already been determined by God. Such a *mystery* already exists in heaven, and is revealed to God's people in the Christian era (see 16:25; 1 Cor 2:1, 7; 4:1; 15:51; Eph 1:9; 3:3, 4, 9; 6:19; Col 1:26, 27; 2:2; 4:3; 1 Tim 3:9, 16). Here, the mystery is the relationship of Jews and *Gentiles* in the plan of salvation, which is at the heart of this entire passage (11:11-32).

11:26-27 The phrase *all Israel* could refer to the total of all believers, both Jewish and Gentile; with this meaning, *and so* would describe the way that God works to bring salvation to all his people. Alternatively, *all Israel* could refer to the total of all Jews destined to believe throughout the Christian era, or to a significant number of Jews who turn to Christ in the last days. With the last meaning, *and so* would have a sequential meaning—after the full number of Gentiles comes to Christ, *then* the full number of Jews will be saved. It does not mean all Jewish people (see 2:17-29) • ***As the Scriptures say:*** This quotation is from Isa 59:20-21; 27:9 (Greek version). • In the OT, ***The one who rescues*** is the Lord. Paul almost surely is referring to Jesus Christ (see 1 Thes 1:10). • ***from Jerusalem:*** Greek *from Zion.* The Hebrew text of Isa 59:20 says that the redeemer will come *to* Jerusalem. Paul might have changed the wording to represent Jesus' first coming from among the people of Israel or to speak of the second coming when Jesus will return from the heavenly Jerusalem (see Heb 12:22). • ***Israel:*** Literally *Jacob.*

11:31 ***will share:*** Other manuscripts read *will now share;* still others read *will someday share.*

11:32 ***have mercy on everyone:*** *Everyone* has the sense of "all kinds of people." In the context of Romans, and especially this chapter, it refers to the inclusion of Gentiles alongside Jews.

11:34 This quotation is from Isa 40:13 (Greek version).

11:35 See Job 41:11.

11:36 ***everything comes from him and exists by his power:*** This statement is similar to statements found among Greek Stoic philosophers in their descriptions of God. Paul regularly draws on literature from the Greco-Roman world to present and clarify the truth about God and his purposes (cp. Acts 17:24-29).

12:1–15:13 This section of Romans sets out the moral and ethical demands of the Good News. God's gift of salvation in Christ requires a response. God is not satisfied simply with forgiving our sin; he wants to transform our lives. Most of what Paul teaches concerning the moral duties of believers is paralleled in other letters. However, it also seems clear that he has chosen issues pertinent to the situation in Rome—most notably, the dispute between people who are weak in faith and people who are strong in faith (14:1–15:13).

12:1 ***dear brothers and sisters:*** Literally *brothers.* See note on 1:13. • ***Your bodies*** refers to the whole person in contact with the world, not just the physical body. • ***because of all he has done for you:*** As described in chs 1–11. • ***This is truly the way to worship him*** (or *This is your spiritual worship;* or *This is your reasonable service*): This phrase has at least three possible meanings: (1) Our sacrifice is *reasonable* in light of all God's mercies; (2) our sacrifice is *spiritual,* not the offering of an animal but of ourselves in spiritual service; or (3) our sacrifice is *intelligent,* offered with complete awareness of God's goodness to us.

12:5 1 Cor 12:27 Eph 4:25
12:6-8 1 Cor 12:4-11 1 Pet 4:10-11
12:6 [a]*charisma* (5486) ‣1 Cor 1:7
12:7 [b]*diakonia* (1248) ‣1 Cor 16:15
12:8 [c]*haplotēs* (0572) ‣2 Cor 8:2
12:9 Amos 5:15 1 Tim 1:5
12:10 John 13:34 Phil 2:3 1 Thes 4:9 2 Pet 1:7
12:12 Heb 10:32, 36
12:13 Heb 13:2
12:14 Matt 5:44
12:16 Prov 3:7 Isa 5:21

the way to worship him. 2 Don't copy the
behavior and customs of this world, but let
God [j]transform you into a new person by
changing the way you think. Then you will
learn to know God's [k]will for you, which is
good and pleasing and perfect.

Humility and Mutual Service (12:3-8)

3 Because of the privilege and authority
God has given me, I give each of you this
warning: Don't think you are better than
you really are. Be honest in your evaluation
of yourselves, measuring yourselves by the
faith God has given us. 4 Just as our bodies
have many parts and each part has a special
function, 5 so it is with Christ's body. We are
many parts of one body, and we all belong
to each other.

6 In his grace, God has given us different
[a]gifts for doing certain things well. So if God
has given you the ability to prophesy, speak
out with as much faith as God has given you.
7 If your gift is [b]serving others, [b]serve them
well. If you are a teacher, teach well. 8 If your
gift is to encourage others, be encouraging.
If it is giving, give [c]generously. If God has
given you leadership ability, take the responsibility seriously. And if you have a gift for
showing kindness to others, do it gladly.

Love and Its Manifestations (12:9-21)

9 Don't just pretend to love others. Really
love them. Hate what is wrong. Hold tightly
to what is good. 10 Love each other with genuine affection, and take delight in honoring
each other. 11 Never be lazy, but work hard
and serve the Lord enthusiastically. 12 Rejoice in our confident hope. Be patient in
trouble, and keep on praying. 13 When God's
people are in need, be ready to help them.
Always be eager to practice hospitality.

14 Bless those who persecute you. Don't
curse them; pray that God will bless them.
15 Be happy with those who are happy, and
weep with those who weep. 16 Live in harmony with each other. Don't be too proud to
enjoy the company of ordinary people. And
don't think you know it all!

12:2 *this world* (literally *this age*): The division of history into two ages was typical of the Jewish worldview. Early Christians adapted this point of view, identifying the coming of Christ as the time when the new age of salvation began. Unexpectedly, however, the new age did not bring an end to the old age. The old way of thinking and living continues, and it is a source of temptation even to Christians who seek to conform their lives to the values of the new age.

12:3 ***Because of the privilege and authority:*** Or *Because of the grace;* cp. 1:5. • ***by the faith God has given us:*** Or *by the faith God has given you;* or *by the standard of our God-given faith.* Whether Paul is referring to the amount of faith each of us has been given or to the Christian faith that we all hold in common, we need to assess ourselves accurately by this measure and not be vain about the abilities God has given us.

12:4-5 ***so it is with Christ's body:*** The parallel between the human body and the church—the body of Christ—is also found in 1 Cor 12. This metaphor provides an effective picture of unity and diversity in the church (cp. Livy, *History* 2.32; Epictetus, *Discourses* 2.10.4–5).

12:6 ***The ability to prophesy*** was one of the most important of the NT gifts (see also 1 Cor 12:28; Eph 4:11). Although prophets are mentioned in several passages in Acts as predicting the future (see Acts 11:28; 21:10-12), the prophet's most fundamental responsibility is to communicate God's message to the community of believers (1 Cor 12:3, 24-25, 29-30; see also 1 Cor 14). • ***as much faith as God has given you*** (literally *in proportion to the faith*): *Proportion* (Greek *analogia*) is a word drawn from mathematics and logic, where it refers to the correct proportions in a relationship among things, quantities, or ideas. Paul uses the phrase to remind prophets to make sure that their utterances are in right proportion to faith, whether the amount of individual faith the prophet has been given, or the Christian faith in general (see note on 12:3). This passage has given theology the phrase *the analogy of faith,* which refers to the importance of bringing the interpretation of any particular passage into line with the teaching of all of Scripture.

12:7 ***teacher:*** The gift of teaching comes third in the list of gifts in 1 Cor 12:28 and fifth in Eph 4:11. While prophets communicate to the community a message received directly from God, teachers address the church on the basis of studying the word of God.

12:8 ***give generously:*** See also 2 Cor 8:2; 9:11, 13.

12:9-21 The many injunctions in these verses do not follow a neat logical arrangement. The overall topic, stated at the beginning, is sincere *love.* Paul shows how we are to love both those inside the church (12:10, 13, 15-16) and those outside the church (12:14, 17-21).

12:10 ***with genuine affection:*** Literally *with brotherly love.* The key Greek word in this phrase connotes love of family. Christians are to *love each other* with the mutual love and commitment that are found within a healthy family.

12:11 ***but work hard and serve the Lord enthusiastically*** (or *but serve the Lord with a zealous spirit;* or *but let the Spirit excite you as you serve the Lord*): As Christians, we are to be passionate about our faith and eager to fulfill our ministry to others within the church.

12:12 The three commands in this verse are related. By rejoicing in ***confident hope,*** we can ***be patient in trouble.*** Continually ***praying*** is essential if we desire to have this attitude toward the difficulties of life (see also 8:24-27).

12:13 ***be ready to help them:*** The verb Paul uses is related to the familiar Greek word *koinōnia* ("fellowship"). When needs arise among our Christian brothers and sisters, we are not just to meet their needs; we should also enter into fellowship with these fellow Christians in ways that extend beyond material gifts.

12:14 The exhortations in this verse closely resemble two sayings of Jesus (Matt 5:44; Luke 6:27-28). Although Paul does not introduce the commands as a quotation, he is almost certainly alluding to these sayings of Christ. Perhaps the words were so well-known that he did not need to specify the source. The teaching of Rom 12–13 has many parallels with the teaching of Jesus.

12:16 All three exhortations in this verse use the Greek word *phroneō* (***think***). Paul addresses the need for right Christian thinking when it comes to our relationships with other Christians. • ***Live in harmony:*** Literally *Think the same things.* • ***Don't be too proud:*** Literally *Don't think arrogant things.*

17 Never pay back evil with more evil. Do
things in such a way that everyone can see
you are honorable. 18 Do all that you can to
live in peace with everyone.
19 Dear friends, never take revenge. Leave
that to the righteous anger of God. For the
Scriptures say,

"I will take revenge;
I will pay them back,"
says the LORD.

20 Instead,

"If your enemies are hungry, feed them.
If they are thirsty, give them
something to drink.
In doing this, you will heap
burning coals of shame on their heads."

21 Don't let evil conquer you, but conquer
evil by doing good.

The Christian and Secular Rulers (13:1-7)

13 Everyone must submit to governing
authorities. For all authority comes
from God, and those in positions of authority
have been placed there by God. 2 So anyone
who rebels against authority is rebelling
against what God has instituted, and they
will be punished. 3 For the authorities do not
strike fear in people who are doing right, but
in those who are doing wrong. Would you
like to live without fear of the authorities? Do
what is right, and they will honor you. 4 The
authorities are God's servants, sent for your
good. But if you are doing wrong, of course
you should be afraid, for they have the power
to punish you. They are God's servants, sent
for the very purpose of punishing those who
do what is wrong. 5 So you must submit to
them, not only to avoid punishment, but also
to keep a clear conscience.
6 Pay your taxes, too, for these same reasons. For government workers need to be
paid. They are [d]serving God in what they do.
7 Give to everyone what you owe them: Pay
your taxes and government fees to those
who collect them, and give respect and
honor to those who are in authority.

Love and the Law (13:8-10)

8 Owe nothing to anyone—except for your
obligation to love one another. If you
love your neighbor, you will fulfill the

12:17 Prov 3:4; 20:22; 1 Thes 5:15
12:19 *Deut 32:35
12:20 *Prov 25:21-22; Matt 5:44
13:1 Dan 2:21; John 19:11; Titus 3:1
13:3 1 Pet 2:13-14
13:5 1 Pet 2:13
13:6 [d]*leitourgos* (3011) ‣Rom 15:16
13:7 Matt 22:21; Mark 12:17; Luke 20:25
13:8 Matt 5:43; John 13:34
13:9 Exod 20:13-15, 17; *Lev 19:18; Deut 5:17-19, 21

12:18 *Do all that you can:* Paul recognizes that our efforts to live at peace with others will sometimes be frustrated by our own moral constraints or by other peoples' unwillingness to be reconciled to us.

12:19 This quotation is from Deut 32:35.

12:20-21 A simple act of Christian kindness can often bring a hostile person to repentance before God and restore fellowship between people.

12:20 This quotation is from Prov 25:21-22.

13:1-2 The basic command of 13:1-7 is to ***submit to governing authorities.*** In God's ordering of the world, we answer to ***those in positions of authority.*** Our submission to them will usually take the form of obedience. However, because God stands over all governments, our submission to governing authorities must always be in terms of our ultimate submission to God (see Acts 4:19-20). The Roman Christians might have been resisting government (see note on 13:6) based on a false understanding of the Good News, as if no longer copying "the behavior and customs of this world" (12:2) meant that they could ignore earthly institutions. • ***placed there by God:*** Scripture consistently teaches that God is actively involved in raising up and casting down human governments and leaders (1 Sam 2:6-10; 12:8; Prov 8:15-16; Isa 41:2-4; 45:1-7; Jer 21:7, 10; 27:5-6; Dan 2:21, 37-38; 4:17). God instituted governing authorities, so rebelling against them is rebelling against God, who will respond with judgment (13:2).

13:3 ***the authorities do not strike fear in people who are doing right:*** Paul presents a positive picture of the governing authorities, describing them in terms of what God has appointed them to do. He does not touch on situations where leaders punish those who do good and reward those who do evil, although he was certainly aware of such situations from OT and Jewish history, from the experience of Jesus and the other apostles, and from Greco-Roman affairs. Here, Paul confines himself to discussing the appropriate response to governing authorities who live according to their calling.

13:4 ***servants*** (Greek *diakonos*): The NT usually reserves this word to describe Christians who serve God in various capacities. However, it was also used in secular Greek to refer to a civic official. Whether they know it or not, governing authorities are serving God when they administer justice. • ***they have the power to punish you*** (literally *they do not bear the sword in vain*): The *sword* might simply be a metaphor for punishment of any kind, but some interpreters believe it suggests that human governments, under God's authority, have the right to carry out capital punishment.

13:5 The two reasons for submission sum up the argument of 13:1-4 in reverse order: ***to avoid punishment*** relates to 13:3-4, while ***to keep a clear conscience*** refers to 13:1-2. • The word *conscience* (Greek *suneidēsis*) refers to the painful knowledge of wrongdoing. Christians know about their duty to submit to governing authorities, and their failure to do so would bring the pain of a guilty conscience.

13:6 ***Pay your taxes:*** Jesus referred to paying taxes in his famous pronouncement about the disciples' relationship to government (Matt 22:21). A tax revolt occurred in Rome at about the time that Paul was writing, so Paul's whole discussion of the Christian's responsibility to government might have been sparked by his knowledge that Roman Christians were participating in this tax revolt (see Tacitus, *Annals* 13).

13:8-10 These verses discuss how believers relate to other people. If we truly love others, our actions will reflect all the commandments in the law that concern our relationships with other people.

13:8 The idea of ***obligation*** is the hinge that connects 13:1-7 and 13:8-10. Christians are to "give to everyone what [they] owe them" (13:7); and Christians always owe love to their neighbors. • ***Owe nothing to anyone:*** Debts are not sinful but should be avoided and, if incurred, should be promptly repaid so that the believer is free to serve in love (see Prov 22:7). • ***love one another:*** Believers are called to love all those they encounter (12:14-21; Luke 10:25-37), but the phrase especially emphasizes the love that each believer owes to other believers. • ***you will fulfill the requirements of God's law:*** This teaching closely follows Jesus' teaching in Matt 22:34-40.

13:10 Matt 22:39; John 13:34-35; Gal 5:13-14; [e]*agapē* (0026) ‣Rom 14:15
13:11 1 Cor 7:29-31; 1 Thes 5:5-6; Jas 5:8; 1 Pet 4:7
13:12 Eph 5:11; 6:13; 1 Thes 5:8
13:13 Luke 21:34; Eph 5:18
14:1 1 Cor 9:22; [f]*pistis* (4102) ‣Gal 2:20
14:2 1 Cor 10:25-27
14:3 Col 2:16
14:4 Matt 7:1
14:5 Gal 4:10
14:6 1 Cor 10:30
14:7 2 Cor 5:15; Gal 2:20
14:8 Phil 1:20; 1 Thes 5:10
14:9 Rev 1:18

requirements of God's law. 9For the commandments say, "You must not commit adultery. You must not murder. You must not steal. You must not covet." These—and other such commandments—are summed up in this one commandment: "Love your neighbor as yourself." 10[e]Love does no wrong to others, so [e]love fulfills the requirements of God's law.

Living in Light of the Day (13:11-14)

11This is all the more urgent, for you know how late it is; time is running out. Wake up, for our salvation is nearer now than when we first believed. 12The night is almost gone; the day of salvation will soon be here. So remove your dark deeds like dirty clothes, and put on the shining armor of right living. 13Because we belong to the day, we must live decent lives for all to see. Don't participate in the darkness of wild parties and drunkenness, or in sexual promiscuity and immoral living, or in quarreling and jealousy. 14Instead, clothe yourself with the presence of the Lord Jesus Christ. And don't let yourself think about ways to indulge your evil desires.

A Plea for Unity (14:1–15:13)

Do Not Condemn One Another!

14 Accept other believers who are weak in [f]faith, and don't argue with them about what they think is right or wrong. 2For instance, one person believes it's all right to eat anything. But another believer with a sensitive conscience will eat only vegetables. 3Those who feel free to eat anything must not look down on those who don't. And those who don't eat certain foods must not condemn those who do, for God has accepted them. 4Who are you to condemn someone else's servants? Their own master will judge whether they stand or fall. And with the Lord's help, they will stand and receive his approval.

5In the same way, some think one day is more holy than another day, while others think every day is alike. You should each be fully convinced that whichever day you choose is acceptable. 6Those who worship the Lord on a special day do it to honor him. Those who eat any kind of food do so to honor the Lord, since they give thanks to God before eating. And those who refuse to eat certain foods also want to please the Lord and give thanks to God. 7For we don't live for ourselves or die for ourselves. 8If we live, it's to honor the Lord. And if we die, it's to honor the Lord. So whether we live or die, we belong to the Lord. 9Christ died and rose again for this very purpose—to be Lord both of the living and of the dead.

13:9 ***"You must not commit adultery. . . . You must not covet":*** This quotation is from Exod 20:13-15, 17. • ***"Love your neighbor as yourself":*** This quotation is from Lev 19:18.

13:11 The NT often speaks of ***salvation*** as the final victory over sin and death that believers will experience when Jesus returns in glory (see 5:9-10).

13:12-13 ***the day of salvation:*** The word *day* reflects two sources. First, the OT repeatedly predicts the *day of the Lord* when God's plan culminates (see Isa 13:4-13; Jer 30:8-9; Joel 2:32; 3:18; Obad 1:15-18). Second, the tradition of moral instruction in the ancient world associated light/daytime with good and darkness/nighttime with evil. The Greeks, Romans, and ancient Jews all used this contrast. Because believers ***belong to the day*** they should be living out its values, avoiding the ***dark deeds*** that are typical of nighttime.

14:1–15:7 Paul moves to a specific issue that was causing conflict in the church at Rome. The church in Rome was embroiled in a dispute between people who were ***weak in faith*** and people who were strong (see 15:1) regarding certain practices. Throughout this section, Paul instructs believers to be tolerant toward others and their practices; he is convinced that people on both sides of the issue are genuine believers, and he does not think the issues they are fighting over are essential to the faith.

14:1 Being ***weak in faith*** means having scruples against doing certain things that Christian liberty would allow. In Rome, most of the weak in faith were Jewish Christians whose consciences did not give them liberty from certain requirements of Jewish law.

14:2 The weak in faith apparently believed that they should ***eat only vegetables.*** Their conviction probably stemmed from a concern to maintain Jewish ritual purity in the midst of a pagan culture. These Jewish Christians were following the lead of Daniel and his friends, who refused to eat the rich food and wine that the king of Babylon offered them (Dan 1:3-16). Other Jewish sources reveal that pious Jews often restricted their diets in pagan cultures because they could never be sure that meat had been slaughtered according to Jewish requirements.

14:3-4 ***look down on . . . condemn:*** The "strong," those who prided themselves on their enlightened freedom in Christ, looked with disdain on those they considered to be "weak." The weak, in turn—certain that they were following the true route to piety—condemned the strong for their laxness. These attitudes, over different issues, are mirrored throughout the history of the Christian church. • ***God has accepted them:*** Both the weak and the strong are genuine believers, welcomed by God into his family. Therefore, they have no right to treat each other as if they do not belong (14:4; see also 15:7).

14:5 ***some think one day is more holy than another day, while others think every day is alike:*** The reference is probably to Jewish festival days and to the Sabbath; cp. Col 2:16. With Christ's provision of salvation, observance of the Sabbath in its original form is not required of Christians.

14:7 As the Lord's servants (14:4), Christians are to look to God for guidance and seek to honor him in all things (14:8). Because we are ultimately accountable to him, our desire should always be to please him, not to ***live for ourselves.***

14:9 Paul refers to standard early Christian teaching on the significance of Jesus' death and resurrection (e.g., 2 Cor 5:15). • ***of the living and of the dead*** (literally *of the dead and of the living*): The original word order matches the sequence of Jesus' death and resurrection, the redemptive events that make Jesus our Lord.

10So why do you condemn another believer? Why do you look down on another
believer? Remember, we will all stand before the judgment seat of God. 11For the
Scriptures say,

"'As surely as I live,' says the LORD,
'every knee will bend to me,
and every [g]tongue will confess and
give praise to God.'"

12Yes, each of us will give a personal [h]ac-
count to God.

Do Not Cause Your Brother or Sister to Stumble!

13So let's stop condemning each other. Decide instead to live in such a way that you
will not cause another believer to [i]stumble
and fall.

14I know and am convinced on the authority of the Lord Jesus that no food, in and of
itself, is wrong to eat. But if someone believes
it is wrong, then for that person it is wrong.
15And if another believer is distressed by
what you eat, you are not acting in [j]love if
you eat it. Don't let your eating ruin someone for whom Christ died. 16Then you will
not be criticized for doing something you
believe is good. 17For the Kingdom of God
is not a matter of what we eat or drink, but
of living a life of goodness and peace and
joy in the Holy Spirit. 18If you serve Christ
with this attitude, you will please God, and
others will approve of you, too. 19So then,
let us aim for [k]harmony in the church and
try to build each other up.

20Don't tear apart the work of God over
what you eat. Remember, all foods are acceptable, but it is wrong to eat something
if it makes another person [a]stumble. 21It is
better not to eat meat or drink wine or do
anything else if it might cause another believer to stumble. 22You may believe there's
nothing wrong with what you are doing, but
keep it between yourself and God. Blessed
are those who don't feel guilty for doing
something they have decided is right. 23But
if you have doubts about whether or not
you should eat something, you are sinning
if you go ahead and do it. For you are not following your convictions. If you do anything
you believe is not right, you are [b]sinning.

Put Other People First!

15 We who are strong must be considerate of those who are sensitive about

14:10 2 Cor 5:10
14:11 [*]Isa 45:23; 49:18 [g]*glōssa* (1100) ‣1 Cor 12:10
14:12 Gal 6:5 [h]*logos* (3056) ‣Rom 15:18
14:13 Matt 7:1 [i]*proskomma* (4348) ‣Rom 14:20
14:14 Acts 10:15 1 Cor 8:7
14:15 1 Cor 8:11-13 [j]*agapē* (0026) ‣1 Cor 8:1
14:16 1 Cor 10:30
14:17 Gal 5:22
14:19 [k]*eirēnē* (1515) ‣1 Cor 14:33
14:20 Acts 10:15 1 Cor 8:9-12 [a]*proskomma* (4348) ‣1 Cor 1:23
14:21 1 Cor 8:13
14:22 1 Jn 3:21
14:23 [b]*hamartia* (0266) ‣1 Cor 15:56

14:10 ***another believer:*** Literally *your brother;* also in 14:10b, 13, 15, 21. See note on 1:13. • ***we will all stand before the judgment seat of God:*** Paul reminds the Roman Christians that it is God, not other Christians, who will ultimately judge all of us (cp. 2 Cor 5:10).

14:11 This quotation is from Isa 49:18; 45:23 (Greek version). In its original context, Isa 45:23 is surrounded by assertions of God's sovereignty (Isa 45:22, 24). Only the sovereign God has the right to stand in judgment (14:10, 12). • ***confess and give praise to God:*** Or *confess allegiance to God.*

14:13 This verse acts as a bridge. ***Let's stop condemning each other*** summarizes 14:1-12, while the concern about causing ***another believer to stumble and fall*** becomes the major emphasis of 14:14-23. • ***stumble and fall:*** This phrase originally applied to obstacles that could trip people as they walked, or to traps into which a person might fall. It is used metaphorically throughout the NT for behavior that might bring spiritual harm to another person (see 1 Cor 8:9, 13; 1 Jn 2:10; cp. Matt 21:42-44; Luke 20:17-18; Rom 9:32-33; 1 Pet 2:8).

14:14 ***no food, in and of itself, is wrong to eat*** (literally *nothing is common in itself*): The word *common* signals that the root concern that Paul was addressing was Jewish purity regulations. Jews described food as *common* if it was not clean (i.e., not kosher), thereby causing a Jew to become ritually impure (see Lev 11; cp. Mark 7:2, 5; Acts 10:14). Paul again follows the teaching of Jesus that "every kind of food is acceptable in God's eyes" (Mark 7:19). • ***for that person it is wrong:*** The truth that no food is wrong to eat was not easy for pious Jews to accept because they had been raised to honor God by avoiding certain foods. Paul urges those who are strong in faith not to force others to violate their consciences (cp. 1 Cor 8:1-13).

14:15 The word translated *ruin* (Greek *apollumi,* "destroy") is often applied to eternal damnation (see 2:12; Matt 10:28; 18:14; Luke 9:24; 13:2-5; John 3:16; 10:10, 28; 1 Cor 1:18-19; Jas 4:12; 2 Pet 3:9). By insisting on their freedom to eat whatever they want, the strong might cause sensitive Jewish Christians ***for whom Christ died*** to turn away from the faith.

14:20 ***The work of God*** refers both to the spiritual life of other Christians (14:15) and to the Christian community itself (14:19). The strong, with their dogged insistence on doing whatever they want, create division and disrupt God's intention to build a healthy and united community of believers.

14:21 ***or drink wine:*** Jews sometimes abstained from wine to avoid the appearance of ritual contamination, since wine was used in pagan religious celebrations (see Dan 1:3-16).

14:22 ***keep it between yourself and God:*** Paul did not contest the freedom of the strong believers, but he instructed them to limit the expression of their freedom out of love for fellow believers so that the whole Christian community could be built up. • ***Blessed are those who don't feel guilty:*** Guilt could come from harming the faith of the weak believers. Christian freedom is only worthwhile when it can be lived out without bringing such guilt.

14:23 ***If you do anything you believe is not right, you are sinning:*** God's word defines sin for us, yet sin also involves violating our conscience. The weak Christians in Rome did not yet believe in their own hearts that they could eat meat, drink wine, or ignore Jewish holy days; their consciences were still weak. They should not violate their consciences on these matters. Nor should the strong, by the power of their example or by their scorn, force weak Christians to do so.

15:1-4 ***We who are strong:*** Paul aligns himself with those he identifies as strong in faith, and he reveals that the division in the Roman church was not simply between Jews and Gentiles. Like Paul, some Jews had enlightened consciences and so were counted

15:2
1 Cor 9:19; 10:24
Gal 6:2
15:3
*Ps 69:9
15:4
2 Tim 3:16
[c]*paraklēsis* (3874)
‣ 1 Cor 14:31
15:5
1 Cor 1:10
2 Cor 1:3
15:6
Rev 1:6
15:8
Matt 15:24
Acts 3:25-26
2 Cor 1:20
15:9
*2 Sam 22:50
*Ps 18:49

things like this. We must not just please
ourselves. 2We should help others do what
is right and build them up in the Lord. 3For
even Christ didn't live to please himself. As
the Scriptures say, "The insults of those who
insult you, O God, have fallen on me." 4Such
things were written in the Scriptures long
ago to teach us. And the Scriptures give us
hope and [c]encouragement as we wait patiently for God's promises to be fulfilled.
5May God, who gives this patience and
encouragement, help you live in complete
harmony with each other, as is fitting for followers of Christ Jesus. 6Then all of you can
join together with one voice, giving praise
and glory to God, the Father of our Lord
Jesus Christ.

Receive One Another!

7Therefore, accept each other just as Christ
has accepted you so that God will be given
glory. 8Remember that Christ came as a
servant to the Jews to show that God is true
to the promises he made to their ancestors.
9He also came so that the Gentiles might give
glory to God for his mercies to them. That is
what the psalmist meant when he wrote:

"For this, I will praise you among the
Gentiles;
I will sing praises to your name."

Tolerance and Its Limits (14:1–15:13)

Rom 12:9-21
Ps 133:1-3
1 Cor 1:10; 6:1-20;
8:1-13; 10:1–11:1;
12:12-27; 13:1-8
2 Cor 6:14–7:1
Col 3:12-15
2 Tim 2:23-26

Paul pleads for tolerance between those who are weak in faith and those who are strong in faith, and he teaches that believers need to accept each other (14:1; 15:7). They should stop condemning and belittling each other. Rather, they should learn to worship God with a united voice and spirit (15:6).

Paul is addressing the specific issue of whether believers need to practice certain requirements of the OT law and of Jewish worship. Theologians have used the word *adiaphora* ("non-essentials") to describe beliefs or practices that are neither required nor prohibited by Scripture. On such issues, Christians must accommodate a variety of opinions.

Paul takes a very different approach when the Good News itself is at stake. In Galatians, for example, Paul confronts false teaching about the Good News by severely castigating the false teachers (Gal 1:6-9) and by warning readers that adopting false teaching will alienate them from Christ (Gal 5:4).

In our day, we need to be careful about what we tolerate and accommodate, and we need to be equally careful about what we decide is worthy of confrontation. Believers need to consider carefully the different issues they confront in their associations with other believers. If the basic truth of the Good News is not violated, we should not quarrel or be divided over such issues. Other issues, however, strike at the heart of the message of Good News. In these cases, Christians need to take a stand and be faithful to the Good News and to Christ. The way Paul himself dealt with a variety of issues in his own time can serve as a guide for dealing with conflicts and controversies in our time.

among the strong. Similarly, some Gentiles were so strongly influenced by Jewish teaching and tradition that they were among the weak in faith. • ***must be considerate of those who are sensitive about things like this:*** This phrase is reminiscent of Gal 6:2. Paul did not want the strong to simply put up with those who were weak in faith; rather the strong were to actively and sympathetically assist the weak in living out their Christian faith with integrity (see also Gal 5:13-15).

15:2 ***others*** (literally *the neighbor*): See Lev 19:18, quoted in 13:9. Love for others should govern the conduct of people who are strong in faith.

15:3 This quotation is from Ps 69:9. • A number of passages in the NT use Psalm 69 to describe Jesus' suffering (Matt 27:34; Mark 15:35-36; Luke 23:36; John 15:25; 19:28-29). Paul's quotation of just a small portion of that psalm evokes the whole experience of Jesus' suffering. • ***who insult you, O God, have fallen on me:*** Literally *who insult you have fallen on me.*

15:4 ***Such things were written in the Scriptures long ago to teach us:*** All that God caused to be recorded in the OT has supreme relevance to believers, who experience the fulfillment of God's plan.

15:5-6 ***live in complete harmony:*** This phrase (see note on 12:16) refers to the whole orientation of how someone thinks. A mindset of harmony is important for Christian unity (see 12:3-5, 16; Phil 2:2-5).

15:7 To ***accept each other*** means more than grudgingly putting up with each other. We are to welcome other believers, with all their flaws and sins, into our fellowship and treat them as family (see note on 12:10), ***just as Christ has accepted*** us, with all our flaws and sins, into his fellowship and family (5:8-11).

15:8-9 Through ***Christ***, God made it possible for ***Jews*** and ***Gentiles*** to join together to give glory to God in the new covenant people of God (see chs 9–11). The issue of Jewish–Gentile relationships was fundamental to the dispute in the Roman church (14:1–15:7).

15:8 ***servant to the Jews:*** Literally *servant of circumcision.*

15:9-12 These quotations from the OT all emphasize God's promise that ***Gentiles*** would join with Jews in praising God. Gentiles are now full members of God's people.

15:9 This quotation is from Ps 18:49.

10 And in another place it is written,

"Rejoice with his people,
you Gentiles."

11 And yet again,

"Praise the LORD, all you Gentiles.
Praise him, all you people of the
earth."

12 And in another place Isaiah said,

"The heir to David's throne will come,
and he will rule over the Gentiles.
They will place their hope on him."

13 I pray that God, the source of hope,
will fill you completely with joy and peace
because you trust in him. Then you will
overflow with confident hope through the
power of the Holy Spirit.

6. THE LETTER CLOSING (15:14–16:27)

Paul's Ministry and Travel Plans

14 I am fully convinced, my dear brothers
and sisters, that you are full of [d]goodness.
You know these things so well you can teach
each other all about them. 15 Even so, I have
been bold enough to write about some of
these points, knowing that all you need is
this reminder. For by God's grace, 16 I am
a [e]special messenger from Christ Jesus to
you Gentiles. I bring you the Good News so
that I might present you as an acceptable offering to God, made holy by the Holy Spirit.
17 So I have reason to be enthusiastic about
all Christ Jesus has done through me in my
service to God. 18 Yet I dare not boast about
anything except what Christ has done
through me, bringing the Gentiles to God
by my [f]message and by the way I worked
among them. 19 They were convinced by the
power of miraculous [g]signs and wonders
and by the power of God's Spirit. In this
way, I have fully presented the [h]Good News
of Christ from Jerusalem all the way to Illyricum.

20 My ambition has always been to preach
the Good News where the name of Christ
has never been heard, rather than where a
church has already been started by someone else. 21 I have been following the plan
spoken of in the Scriptures, where it says,

"Those who have never been told about
him will see,
and those who have never heard of
him will understand."

22 In fact, my visit to you has been delayed
so long because I have been preaching in
these places.

23 But now I have finished my work in
these regions, and after all these long years
of waiting, I am eager to visit you. 24 I am
planning to go to Spain, and when I do, I will
stop off in Rome. And after I have enjoyed
your fellowship for a little while, you can
provide for my journey.

15:10 *Deut 32:43
15:11 *Ps 117:1
15:12 *Isa 11:10; Rev 5:5; 22:16
15:14 2 Pet 1:12; [d]*agathōsunē* (0019) ‣Gal 5:22
15:15 Rom 1:5; 12:3
15:16 Phil 2:17; [e]*leitourgos* (3011) ‣2 Cor 9:12
15:17 Phil 3:3
15:18 Rom 1:5; [f]*logos* (3056) ‣Gal 5:14
15:19 Acts 19:11; 1 Cor 2:4; 1 Thes 1:5; [g]*sēmeion* (4592) ‣1 Cor 1:22; [h]*euangelion* (2098) ‣1 Cor 15:1
15:20 Rom 1:15; 1 Cor 3:10; 2 Cor 10:13, 15
15:21 *Isa 52:15
15:22 Rom 1:10-13; 1 Thes 2:18
15:23 Acts 19:21; Rom 1:10-11
15:24 1 Cor 16:6

15:10 This quotation is from Deut 32:43.

15:11 This quotation is from Ps 117:1.

15:12 This quotation is from Isa 11:10 (Greek version). • ***The heir to David's throne:*** Literally *The root of Jesse.* David was the son of Jesse.

15:14–16:27 This final section contains elements common at the end of NT letters: a discussion of travel plans (15:14-29), requests for prayer (15:30-33), references to ministry associates (16:1-2, 21-23), greetings (16:3-16), and a doxology (16:25-27). Only the warning about false teachers (16:17-19) is a non-standard feature in this conclusion.

15:14 ***dear brothers and sisters:*** Literally *brothers;* also in 15:30. See note on 1:13. • ***You know these things so well:*** Paul praises the Roman Christians, as he had in the opening of the letter (see 1:8-12), demonstrating a gracious manner toward a church he had neither founded nor visited.

15:15-16 ***by God's grace:*** Paul emphasized that his role as apostle and teacher was because God had chosen him to lead in the formation of the Christian church (see also 1:5; 12:3; 1 Cor 3:10; Gal 2:9; Eph 3:2, 7, 8).

15:16 ***special messenger:*** The Greek word (*leitourgos,* "servant" or "minister") could refer to almost any kind of servant, but Jews often applied the word to priests. Paul probably chose this word to emphasize the priestly nature of his ministry. • ***to you Gentiles:*** Paul stresses the Gentile flavor of the church in Rome (see also 1:6-7). This does not mean that there were no Jews in the church (see 16:3-16), but Gentiles had become the majority. • ***present you as an acceptable offering to God:*** Paul was fulfilling Isa 66:19-20.

15:19 ***God's Spirit:*** Other manuscripts read *the Spirit;* still others read *the Holy Spirit.* • ***I have fully presented the Good News of Christ:*** Paul was not claiming that the work of evangelism had been completed in these regions. His point was that churches had been planted in enough major population centers so that those churches could carry on the work of evangelism themselves. Paul's own distinctive ministry of planting foundational and strategic churches had been fulfilled. • ***from Jerusalem all the way to Illyricum:*** Illyricum was a region northeast of Italy, a Roman province that occupied most of the coastlands along the Adriatic Sea, from modern-day Albania to Croatia. An arc drawn from Jerusalem to Illyricum would include the areas where Paul had planted churches (southern Galatia, Asia Minor, Macedonia, and Greece).

15:21 This quotation is from Isa 52:15 (Greek version).

15:24 ***I am planning to go to Spain:*** In Paul's day, "Spain" included the entire Iberian Peninsula (modern Spain and Portugal). Parts of the peninsula had been occupied by the Romans since 200 BC, but only within Paul's lifetime had the area been organized into a Roman province. Paul saw Spain, at the far end of the Mediterranean, as his final target in fulfilling the promise of Isa 66:19-20. • ***you can provide for my journey:*** Spain was so far from Paul's previous sending church, Antioch in Syria, that he hoped the Roman church could serve as the logistical base for this future evangelistic effort.

15:25
Acts 19:21; 20:22
15:26
1 Cor 16:1
2 Cor 8:1; 9:2
15:27
1 Cor 9:11
15:29
Rom 1:10-11
15:30
2 Cor 1:11
Col 1:8; 4:12
15:31
2 Thes 3:2
15:32
Phlm 1:7
[i]*thelēma* (2307)
‣Eph 6:6
15:33
Rom 16:20
Heb 13:20
16:1
Acts 18:18
[j]*diakonos* (1249)
‣2 Cor 11:23
16:2
Phil 2:29
16:5
1 Cor 16:15, 19
Col 4:15
Phlm 1:2
[k]*ekklēsia* (1577)
‣1 Cor 1:2
16:7
Rom 16:11, 21
Col 4:10
Phlm 1:23

25But before I come, I must go to Jerusalem to take a gift to the believers there.
26For you see, the believers in Macedonia
and Achaia have eagerly taken up an offering for the poor among the believers in
Jerusalem. 27They were glad to do this because they feel they owe a real debt to them.
Since the Gentiles received the spiritual
blessings of the Good News from the believers in Jerusalem, they feel the least they can
do in return is to help them financially. 28As
soon as I have delivered this money and
completed this good deed of theirs, I will
come to see you on my way to Spain. 29And I
am sure that when I come, Christ will richly
bless our time together.

30Dear brothers and sisters, I urge you in
the name of our Lord Jesus Christ to join in
my struggle by praying to God for me. Do
this because of your love for me, given to
you by the Holy Spirit. 31Pray that I will be
rescued from those in Judea who refuse to
obey God. Pray also that the believers there
will be willing to accept the donation I am
taking to Jerusalem. 32Then, by the [i]will of
God, I will be able to come to you with a joyful heart, and we will be an encouragement
to each other.
33And now may God, who gives us his
peace, be with you all. Amen.

Paul Greets His Friends

16 I commend to you our sister Phoebe,
who is a [j]deacon in the church in
Cenchrea. 2Welcome her in the Lord as one
who is worthy of honor among God's people. Help her in whatever she needs, for she
has been helpful to many, and especially
to me.

3Give my greetings to Priscilla and Aquila,
my co-workers in the ministry of Christ
Jesus. 4In fact, they once risked their lives for
me. I am thankful to them, and so are all the
Gentile churches. 5Also give my greetings
to the [k]church that meets in their home.

Greet my dear friend Epenetus. He
was the first person from the province of
Asia to become a follower of Christ. 6Give
my greetings to Mary, who has worked so
hard for your benefit. 7Greet Andronicus

15:25-28 ***I must go to Jerusalem to take a gift to the believers there:*** During his third missionary journey, Paul collected donations from the Gentile churches to help the believers in Jerusalem and to draw the two wings of the first-century church closer together (see also 1 Cor 16:1-2; 2 Cor 8–9).

15:25 ***the believers:*** Literally *God's holy people;* also in 15:26, 31.

15:26 ***Macedonia*** and ***Achaia*** were the northern and southern regions of Greece. Paul founded churches in several prominent cities in Macedonia, including Philippi, Thessalonica, and Berea. In Achaia, Paul had preached in Athens and founded the church in Corinth (see Acts 16–18). • ***the poor among the believers in Jerusalem:*** Jewish Christians in Jerusalem were suffering from famines that had hit the area (see Acts 11:27-30), and also because their faith in Christ caused them to be ostracized from Jewish society.

15:27 ***they owe a real debt:*** Gentile Christians owe their spiritual existence to God's work among the Israelites (see 11:17-24).

15:31 ***Pray that I will be rescued from those in Judea who refuse to obey God:*** See Acts 21–22. God preserved Paul's life and used the circumstances of his arrest in Jerusalem to take him precisely where he planned to go—Rome. • ***the donation:*** Literally *the ministry;* other manuscripts read *the gift.*

15:33 Some manuscripts do not include *Amen.* One very early manuscript places the doxology (16:25-27) here. This has led some scholars to conclude that the original letter to the Romans consisted of only 1:1–15:33, but few now follow this theory. The best early manuscripts place the doxology at the end of ch 16, and the whole of ch 16 was most likely part of Paul's original letter to the Romans. See also note on 16:1-16.

16:1-16 Paul here commended and greeted twenty-seven Roman Christians, ten of whom were women. Women played important roles in the early church. • Paul had never been to Rome, which has led to some speculation as to how he knew so many people there. One theory is that ch 16 was actually part of another letter that Paul sent to Ephesus. However, we have no good manuscript evidence for a separate letter (cp. note on 15:33). Perhaps the answer is that Paul was able to greet so many people in Rome because he had encountered them during their travels away from Rome (see Romans Introduction, "Setting," p. 1888).

16:1 ***A deacon*** (Greek *diakonos,* "servant") refers both to a Christian who is recognized as a servant of Christ and specifically to someone who holds the office of deacon in a particular church (see Phil 1:1; 1 Tim 3:8-12; cp. Acts 6:1-6). • ***Cenchrea*** was located eight miles from Corinth and functioned as its port. Paul might have been writing this letter to the Romans from Corinth on a winter-long stop there near the end of his third missionary journey (see Acts 20:2-3).

16:2 ***she has been helpful to many:*** This phrase indicates the ancient role of the patron, a wealthy person who used influence and money to help people and causes (see "Work and Patronage" at 2 Thes 3:6-10, p. 2045). Phoebe was apparently a woman of wealth and influence who used her resources to help missionaries such as Paul.

16:3-16 Although Paul had never visited the Christian community in Rome, he established rapport with these believers by personally greeting many of the church's members. The names reveal that the Roman Christian community was very diverse—Jews and Gentiles, slaves and free, men and women all formed a new society in the church (see Gal 3:26-29).

16:3 ***Priscilla and Aquila*** were Paul's good friends (see "Priscilla and Aquila" at Acts 18:1-3, p. 1865). After leaving Rome around AD 49, they became his ***co-workers*** for an extended time in Corinth and Ephesus (see Acts 18–19). They had apparently returned to Rome by the time Paul wrote Romans (about AD 57).

16:5 ***the church that meets in their home:*** Early Christians did not have large buildings for their meetings—they met in private homes. The church in Rome was composed of a number of house churches where small groups of believers gathered for worship and instruction.

and Junia, my fellow Jews, who were in
prison with me. They are highly respected
among the apostles and became followers
of Christ before I did. 8Greet Ampliatus,
my dear friend in the Lord. 9Greet Urba-
nus, our co-worker in Christ, and my dear
friend Stachys.
10Greet Apelles, a good man whom Christ
approves. And give my greetings to the believers from the household of Aristobulus.
11Greet Herodion, my fellow Jew. Greet the
Lord's people from the household of Narcis-
sus. 12Give my greetings to Tryphena and
Tryphosa, the Lord's workers, and to dear
Persis, who has worked so hard for the Lord.
13Greet Rufus, whom the Lord picked out to
be his very own; and also his dear mother,
who has been a mother to me.
14Give my greetings to Asyncritus, Phle-
gon, Hermes, Patrobas, Hermas, and the
brothers and sisters who meet with them.
15Give my greetings to Philologus, Julia,
Nereus and his sister, and to Olympas
and all the believers who meet with them.
16Greet each other in Christian love. All
the churches of Christ send you their greetings.

Closing Remarks and Doxology

17And now I make one more appeal, my
dear brothers and sisters. Watch out for
people who cause divisions and upset people's faith by teaching things contrary to
what you have been taught. Stay away from
them. 18Such people are not serving Christ
our Lord; they are serving their own personal interests. By smooth talk and glowing
words they deceive innocent people. 19But
everyone knows that you are obedient to
the Lord. This makes me very happy. I want
you to be wise in doing right and to stay innocent of any wrong. 20The God of peace
will soon crush [a]Satan under your feet. May
the grace of our Lord Jesus be with you.
21Timothy, my fellow worker, sends you
his greetings, as do Lucius, Jason, and Sosip-
ater, my fellow Jews.
22I, Tertius, the one writing this letter for
Paul, send my greetings, too, as one of the
Lord's followers.
23Gaius says hello to you. He is my host
and also serves as host to the whole church.
Erastus, the city treasurer, sends you his
greetings, and so does our brother Quartus.
25Now all glory to God, who is able to make

16:10 Acts 11:14
16:11 Rom 16:7, 21
16:13 Mark 15:21; 2 Jn 1:1
16:16 1 Cor 16:20; 1 Thes 5:26; 1 Pet 5:14
16:17 1 Cor 5:9, 11; 2 Thes 3:6; 2 Tim 3:5; Titus 3:10; 2 Jn 1:10
16:18 Phil 3:19; Col 2:4; 2 Pet 2:3
16:19 Matt 10:16
16:20 Gen 3:15; [a]*satanas* (4567) ‣2 Cor 11:14
16:21 Acts 13:1; 16:1; 17:5
16:25 1 Cor 2:1; Eph 1:9; 3:3-5; Col 1:26-27; 2:2; 2 Tim 1:9-10; 1 Pet 1:20

16:7 In Greek, the name *Junia* could refer to a man named *Junias* or to a woman named *Junia.* Most interpreters understand *Junia* as a feminine name. Some late manuscripts accent the word so it reads *Junias,* a masculine name; still others read *Julia* (feminine). This section pairs masculine and feminine names to refer to husband-and-wife teams, so Junia was probably a woman. • *fellow Jews:* Or *compatriots;* also in 16:21. • ***who were in prison with me:*** When this occurred is uncertain. According to Acts, Paul had been imprisoned overnight in Philippi (Acts 16:19-28); after Romans was written, he would later be imprisoned for two years in Caesarea (Acts 24:27) and for two years in Rome (Acts 28:30-31). Paul was undoubtedly imprisoned on occasions not mentioned in Acts (see 2 Cor 11:23). • ***highly respected among the apostles:*** This phrase probably indicates that Andronicus and Junia were apostles—i.e., accredited missionaries of the church (see Acts 14:4, 14; 1 Cor 9:5-6; Gal 2:9).

16:10 This ***Aristobulus*** was probably the same man as the brother of Herod Agrippa I; Aristobulus was a member of the Roman aristocracy who lived in Rome many years prior to his death in AD 48 or 49 (see Josephus, *Antiquities* 18.8.4; *War* 2.11.6). His ***household*** probably refers to his family and their servants in Rome.

16:11 ***fellow Jew:*** Or *compatriot.*

16:13 This ***Rufus*** might be the individual mentioned as the son of Simon of Cyrene, who carried Christ's cross (see Mark 15:21).

16:14 ***brothers and sisters:*** Literally *brothers;* also in 16:17. See note on 1:13.

16:15 ***all the believers:*** Literally *all of God's holy people.*

16:16 ***in Christian love*** (literally *with a sacred kiss*): The kiss was a common way to ***greet*** another person in the ancient world and particularly among the Jews. It is mentioned frequently in the NT as a greeting (1 Cor 16:20; 2 Cor 13:12; 1 Thes 5:26; see 1 Pet 5:14); the kiss of peace became a standard feature of the Christian liturgy by the second century.

16:17 ***people who cause divisions:*** Paul had trouble with divisive false teachers elsewhere (see Galatians, Colossians, 1 Timothy), so he warned the Roman church about this danger.

16:20 ***The God of peace will soon crush Satan under your feet:*** Paul alludes to the curse that God pronounced upon the serpent after he had deceived Adam and Eve in the Garden of Eden (Gen 3:15). Christ, the offspring of Eve, will soon crush Satan under the feet of the church (cp. Matt 16:18-19). • ***Lord Jesus:*** Some manuscripts read *Lord Jesus Christ.*

16:21 ***Timothy*** was one of Paul's closest ministry associates (see "Timothy" at Acts 16:1-3, p. 1860). Timothy accompanied Paul on his second missionary journey (Acts 16:2-3) and was with Paul in Corinth while Paul wrote this letter to the Roman church (see Acts 20:2-4).

16:22 ***Tertius*** was the scribe (or *amanuensis*) who wrote the letter as Paul dictated. Most ancient letter writers employed such a scribe.

16:23 Some manuscripts add v 24, *May the grace of our Lord Jesus Christ be with you all. Amen.* Still others add this sentence after v 27.• This ***Erastus*** was probably the individual Paul sent from Ephesus to Macedonia during his third missionary journey (Acts 19:21-22; see 2 Tim 4:20). An inscription in Corinth mentions an Erastus who was a city magistrate, possibly the same Erastus mentioned here.

16:25-27 This doxology makes a very appropriate conclusion to Paul's letter and its argument, reprising many of the themes found at the very beginning (1:1-15). • The doxology is missing in two late manuscripts and is in different places in other manuscripts (after 14:23 and after 15:33). Therefore, these verses might have been added to Paul's letter at a later time. However, the majority of manuscripts do include the doxology at the end of the letter, and it uses vocabulary and themes common in the rest of the letter. Paul most likely wrote it himself as a conclusion to the letter.

[b]*apokalupsis* (0602)
‣ 1 Cor 1:7

16:26
Rom 1:2, 5

16:27
Rom 11:36

you strong, just as my Good News says. This
message about Jesus Christ has [b]revealed
his plan for you Gentiles, a plan kept secret
from the beginning of time. 26But now as
the prophets foretold and as the eternal
God has commanded, this message is made
known to all Gentiles everywhere, so that
they too might believe and obey him. 27All
glory to the only wise God, through Jesus
Christ, forever. Amen.

16:25 ***plan*** (literally *mystery*): For Paul, the *mystery* is the truth about God and his plan that was not clearly known in the OT era but which has been revealed in the NT era. While the OT predicted the conversion of Gentiles, it did not make clear that Gentiles would become equal members of the people of God without becoming proselytes of Judaism.

16:26 ***the prophets:*** Literally *the prophetic writings.* • ***so that they too might believe and obey him:*** Paul uses the same language about the mission to the Gentiles that he used in 1:5, creating a beautiful frame around the letter as a whole.

PAUL'S FIRST LETTER TO THE

CORINTHIANS

In this fascinating letter to a multiethnic church, we see some of the everyday problems the early Christians were dealing with. In Paul's advice on how to handle these problems, we find the deepest principles that shape his thinking about practical Christian living. These enduring principles—so different from the popular trends of Paul's time or ours—provide rich guidance for us as we deal with similar problems today.

SETTING

Corinth's widespread reputation as an important city full of vice was linked to its geography. The city was strategically located on the narrow four- to five-mile-wide isthmus separating mainland Greece from the Peloponnesus (the large southern peninsula). It profited from travelers passing north and south along the main overland route and from those sailing east and west between the Gulf of Corinth and the Saronic Gulf. To avoid the stormy hazards of the Mediterranean Sea, especially in wintertime, the owners of small commercial boats sailing between Italy and the eastern Mediterranean often had them dragged over the isthmus from one gulf to the other and spent a night or two in Corinth on the way. As a result, Corinth gained the notoriety of a port city and was widely known for prostitution and other vices. There was even a verb in Greek (*korinthiazomai*, "to act like a Corinthian") that referred to sexual immorality. It's not surprising that some of these problems made their way into the young church (see Paul's strong words about sexual immorality in 5:1-13; 6:12-20).

Old Corinth was conquered and destroyed by the Romans in 146 BC. It was rebuilt a century later as a Roman colony and populated

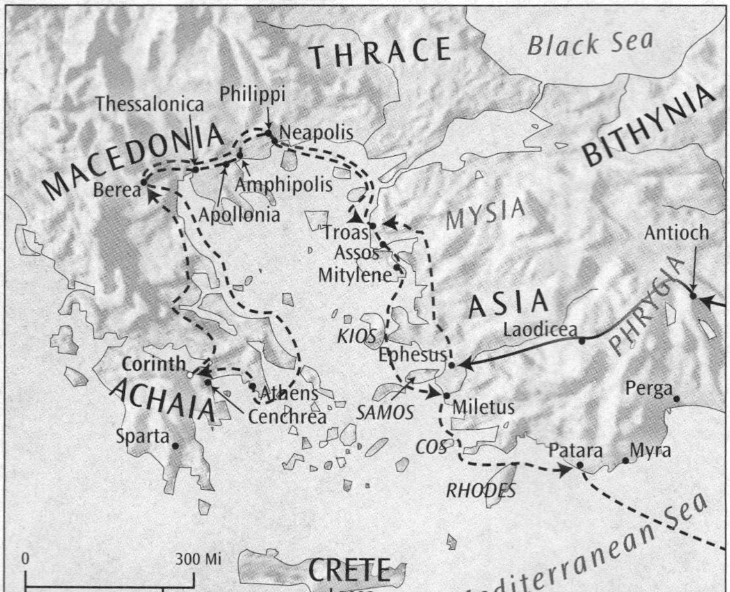

The Setting of 1 Corinthians, about AD 55. Paul wrote 1 Corinthians from EPHESUS during his third missionary journey (AD 53~57; see Acts 18:23–19:41). The church in CORINTH, which had been established during Paul's second missionary journey (AD 50–52; see Acts 15:36–18:22), was experiencing many difficulties during this time. The map shows Paul's third missionary journey as a solid line up to the writing of 1 Corinthians in Ephesus, and as a dashed line thereafter.

in large part by former Roman slaves. By the time of Paul's visit, it was a cosmopolitan city, with Romans, Greeks, Jews, and other ethnic groups from all over the Mediterranean, as well as international visitors passing through the city. As a result, the members of the young church were multi-ethnic. This surely contributed to the tensions and problems it experienced (see Paul's rebuke of their cliquishness in 1:10-12; 3:1-4).

Paul first arrived in the city during his second missionary trip (around AD 50), after his work in the northern province of Macedonia and Athens. Realizing that the city was strategic to his evangelistic efforts, he stayed in Corinth for eighteen months (AD 50–52; see Acts 18:1-17). When the Jews took him to court for breaking the law, the governor Gallio threw the case out because it was a religious dispute. Given the freedom to evangelize, Paul made a number of converts and began a church there before he left.

Over the next five years, Paul corresponded with the Corinthians several times on difficult issues and even visited them personally to sort out some of their problems. The present letter, written during the period AD 53–56, was sent from Ephesus, in the province of Asia (western Turkey), where Paul spent two to three years on his third missionary journey.

OUTLINE

1:1-9
Introduction

1:10–6:20
Paul Confronts Sin in the Church

7:1–16:4
Paul Answers the Corinthians' Questions

16:5-24
Conclusion

TIMELINE

AD 50–52
Paul's second missionary journey

AD 50
Paul meets Priscilla and Aquila in Corinth

about AD 50
Paul writes 1 Thessalonians from Corinth

AD 51–52
Gallio governs Achaia

about AD 51
Paul writes 2 Thessalonians from Corinth

AD 53–57
Paul's third missionary journey

AD 53~56
Paul writes 1 Corinthians from Ephesus

about AD 56
Paul writes 2 Corinthians from Macedonia

about AD 57
Paul writes Romans from Corinth

SUMMARY

Paul deals with a wide range of problems and questions facing the young church—some of which reflect the problems of the city itself—and he gives specific advice on dealing with them. Paul's advice reflects the fundamental principles underlying his view of the Christian life, principles rooted in the Good News itself. Paul addressed the following issues:

- Criticism of Paul's non-intellectual approach to evangelism (chs 1–4)
- A flagrant case of sexual immorality in the church (ch 5)
- The practice of taking fellow believers to court before pagan judges (ch 6)
- Problems of sexual immorality (ch 6)
- Questions about marriage, divorce, and staying single (ch 7)
- The question of whether believers are allowed to eat meat sacrificed to pagan idols (chs 8–10)
- The question of appropriate dress for women who minister publicly (ch 11)
- Irreverent and disrespectful behavior in receiving the Lord's Supper (ch 11)
- Distorted perspectives on spiritual gifts and their practice (chs 12–14)
- Skepticism about a future resurrection of the dead (ch 15)

AUTHORSHIP

Paul is widely accepted as the writer of 1 Corinthians. Though the authorship of a number of Paul's letters is disputed by some historical-critical

Paul's Corinth was at once the New York, Los Angeles, and Las Vegas of the ancient world . . . [and] the church was in many ways a mirror of the city.

GORDON FEE
The First Epistle to the Corinthians, p. 3

scholars, no one questions the authorship of 1 Corinthians. Some, however, question the authenticity of 14:34-35 (see note). In line with common practice of the ancient world, Paul used an amanuensis (secretary) to do the actual writing of this letter (see 16:21; see also Timothy and Titus Introduction, "Authorship," p. 2047).

DATE AND OCCASION OF WRITING

This letter to the Corinthian church was written on Paul's third missionary journey, during his two- to three-year stay in Ephesus (about AD 53–56; see Acts 19). Paul had written a previous letter to the church (see 5:9), and the Corinthians had replied, asking his advice on a number of points (see 7:1). He had also received reports and visitors from Corinth (see 1:11; 16:15-17), making him aware of a number of problems facing the young church. This letter, full of advice on specific issues, is his response. It may have been delivered by Stephanas, Fortunatus, and Achaicus (see 16:15-17) when they returned to Corinth.

Some problems apparently remained unresolved, resulting in a later personal visit to Corinth and a strongly worded letter that we do not have. Paul refers to these in the emotionally laden letter we know as 2 Corinthians, written from Macedonia shortly after he left Ephesus, in anticipation of yet another visit to the church (see 2 Cor 2:1-11; 7:8-10; 2 Corinthians Introduction, "Date and Occasion of Writing," p. 1956).

MEANING AND MESSAGE

In 1 Corinthians, we catch a fascinating glimpse of what life was like in the early church. We see some of the practical problems the early Christians faced as they lived in a pagan environment and how they dealt with them. Among the more theologically significant points are the following.

[First Corinthians is] an inexhaustible mine of Christian thought and life. Nowhere else in the NT is there a more many-sided embodiment of the imperishable principles and instincts which should inspire each member of the body of Christ for all time.

A. ROBERTSON
A Dictionary of the Bible, vol. 1, pp. 489-490

Motivation for Christian Behavior. Paul deals with problems in the churches from a thoroughly Christian point of view, rooted in the Good News of God's grace. In his thinking, Christian behavior is firmly grounded in Christian theology, in the message of Christ and the cross. The advice he gives on Christian living is not simply pragmatic, but solidly based on the relationship of believers to Christ. His own practical life has been revolutionized by his experience of God's grace in Christ.

So, for example, when Paul addresses issues of sexual immorality (chs 5, 6), he reminds the church that believers have been made new by the sacrifice of Christ and that they should live accordingly. His appeal for faithfulness is not that they should keep the law of Moses, but that they should understand what it means to be married to Christ and to be the sanctuary of the Holy Spirit (6:15-20).

When Paul discourages believers from taking one another to pagan law courts (6:1-8), he is in part concerned for the effect on their witness as Christians. He urges them to give up their rights out of love for others, as Christ did. The death of Christ has taught him that Christian love is sacrificial.

When Paul gives advice on marriage (ch 7), he encourages those who are unmarried to remain single so they can give themselves more fully to Christ's service. Christians are claimed by Christ and can no longer live only for themselves.

When he addresses the freedom of believers to eat meat sacrificed to pagan idols (chs 8, 10), he avoids formulating rules, asserting their liberty in Christ to eat anything. He emphasizes, however, that the

effect of one's actions on others is always more important than one's own rights, so believers should readily abstain from actions that would be detrimental to others. Like Christ, they are to be governed by sacrificial love in all their relationships.

Paul's practical advice is rooted in the Good News and in the relationship of believers to Christ. In his thinking, Christian behavior is a response of gratitude to the mercy and grace of God, shown in Christ and expressed in the Good News.

The whole of the believer's life is to express devotion to God and love for others (see 10:31-33). This is Paul's equivalent to Jesus' two great love commands (Matt 22:36-40; Luke 10:25-37). In this letter, we see more clearly than elsewhere how Paul applies these enduring principles to a wide range of practical problems.

Paul's Understanding of Evangelism. When Paul is criticized for his rather unpolished, non-intellectual approach to evangelism (chs 1–4), he emphasizes that only God can change a person's heart. The real power does not lie in the persuasive powers of human intellect and rhetoric, but in the message of God's grace and in the power of God's Spirit to renew and transform. Conversion is not a matter of one person changing another person's mind, but of God changing a person's heart.

Unity and Love in the Church. Unity among believers is important throughout this letter, as a number of the issues Paul deals with have apparently divided the church (see 1:10–4:21, cliques in the church; 6:1-12, lawsuits against fellow Christians; 8:1–11:1, different opinions on food sacrificed to idols; 11:2-16, different opinions on appropriate dress for women ministering publicly; 11:17-34, problems in taking the Lord's Supper). Bound together as fellow members of Christ's body by a common commitment to Christ as Lord and by the shared experience of God's Spirit, believers are to live together in unity. This letter, which includes Paul's classic chapter on Christian love (ch 13), highlights the importance of relating to other believers in sacrificial love, the kind of love shown by Christ himself.

Marriage, Divorce, and the Single Life. Paul has a high view of marriage and an even higher view of the single life (ch 7). The two ways of living are not ends in themselves, but alternate ways of serving Christ, which is the important thing.

The Lord's Supper. Along with the accounts in the synoptic Gospels, this letter sheds significant light on early Christian understanding and practice of the Lord's Supper, offering the only extended treatment in the NT (chs 10–11).

The Church As a Body. Paul understands the church as a dynamic, Spirit-led body made up of different parts, each with its own unique work to do (chs 12, 14). In these early days of the Christian movement, there is no distinction between clergy and laity, but different roles creating a complementary ministry of the Spirit's gifts when Christians gather. Each has a part to play in building up the body, and individuals are dependent on the Spirit to empower and guide them all in their ministries.

The Resurrection. Among the NT writings, this letter gives us the most complete discussion of resurrection (ch 15), including the fullest account of those who saw the resurrected Jesus, the rationale for a future resurrection, and the nature of resurrection bodies.

The most intensely practical of all St. Paul's letters. It was written to meet immediate needs of his converts.

A. H. MCNEILE
An Introduction to the Study of the New Testament, p. 136

FURTHER READING

WILLIAM BAKER
1 Corinthians in *Cornerstone Biblical Commentary*, vol. 15 (2009)

CRAIG L. BLOMBERG
1 Corinthians (1995)

GORDON D. FEE
The First Epistle to the Corinthians (1987)

ALAN F. JOHNSON
1 Corinthians (2004)

ANTHONY C. THISTLETON
The First Epistle to the Corinthians (2000)

1. INTRODUCTION (1:1-9)

Greetings from Paul

1 This letter is from Paul, chosen by the
will of God to be an apostle of Christ
Jesus, and from our brother Sosthenes.
2 I am writing to God's [a]church in Corinth,
to you who have been [b]called by God to be
his own holy people. He made you holy by
means of Christ Jesus, just as he did for all
people everywhere who call on the name of
our Lord Jesus Christ, their Lord and ours.
3 May God our [c]Father and the Lord Jesus
Christ give you grace and peace.

Paul Gives Thanks to God

4 I always thank my God for you and for the
gracious gifts he has given you, now that you
belong to Christ Jesus. 5 Through him, God
has enriched your church in every way—
with all of your eloquent words and all of
your knowledge. 6 This confirms that what I
[d]told you about Christ is true. 7 Now you have
every spiritual [e]gift you need as you eagerly
wait for the [f]return of our Lord Jesus Christ.
8 He will keep you strong to the end so that
you will be free from all blame on the day
when our Lord Jesus Christ returns. 9 God
will do this, for he is faithful to do what he
says, and he has invited you into [g]partner-
ship with his Son, Jesus Christ our Lord.

2. PAUL CONFRONTS SIN IN THE CHURCH (1:10–6:20)

Divisions in the Church (1:10–4:21)

The Problem of Competing Factions

10 I appeal to you, dear brothers and sisters,
by the authority of our Lord Jesus Christ, to
live in harmony with each other. Let there
be no divisions in the church. Rather, be of
one mind, united in thought and purpose.
11 For some members of Chloe's household
have told me about your quarrels, my dear
brothers and sisters. 12 Some of you are saying, "I am a follower of Paul." Others are
saying, "I follow Apollos," or "I follow Peter,"
or "I follow only Christ."

1:2 [a]*ekklēsia* (1577) ›1 Cor 10:32 [b]*klētos* (2822) ›1 Cor 1:26
1:3 [c]*patēr* (3962) ›2 Cor 1:3
1:5 2 Cor 8:7; 9:11
1:6 [d]*marturion* (3142) ›2 Thes 1:10
1:7 Phil 3:20 [e]*charisma* (5486) ›1 Cor 7:7 [f]*apokalupsis* (0602) ›1 Cor 14:6
1:8 Phil 1:6 1 Thes 3:13; 5:23 2 Thes 3:3
1:9 1 Jn 1:3 [g]*koinōnia* (2842) ›1 Cor 10:16
1:10 Rom 15:5
1:12 John 1:42 Acts 18:24

1:1-3 Paul commonly begins his letters with a few words about himself, followed by greetings and an invocation of grace and peace. In this, he follows the normal pattern of ancient Greek letters but expands it with Christian meaning.

1:1 ***An apostle of Christ Jesus*** was a missionary evangelist commissioned by Christ himself. • ***Sosthenes,*** Paul's co-worker, might be the same person as in Acts 18:17.

1:2 The ***church*** is comprised of those who are ***called by God to be his own holy people,*** those who belong to him and are dedicated to him. • ***Corinth*** was the capital city of Achaia, the southern region of the Greek peninsula. • They have been made holy ***by means of Christ Jesus*** (or *because you belong to Christ Jesus*; literally *in Christ Jesus*). God has set them apart for himself through the saving work of his Son and their faith relationship to him.

1:3 ***Grace and peace*** represent traditional Greek and Hebrew greetings. ***Grace*** is undeserved blessing that comes from the kindness of God. ***Peace*** is a sense of well-being and contentedness, rooted in the Good News and brought about by the Holy Spirit (see Gal 5:22). Together, the phrase conveys things understood as gifts from God (see Rom 5:1-2).

1:4-9 Paul thanks God for the spiritual gifts he sees in the lives of the Corinthian Christians and expresses his confidence that God will keep them safe to the end.

1:4 ***now that you belong to Christ Jesus*** (literally *in Christ Jesus*): Paul frequently uses the phrase *in Christ Jesus* to refer to the saving relationship believers have with Christ (e.g., Rom 3:24; Gal 2:4; Eph 3:6).

1:5 ***God*** had ***enriched*** the Corinthian ***church*** spiritually, specifically in ***eloquent words*** and ***knowledge.*** This probably refers to the spiritual messages and understanding (see 1:7) on which the church prided itself. *Word* and *knowledge* occur frequently in this letter: Paul acknowledges the abundant spiritual gifts that God has given the church in Corinth. Later, he corrects their distorted perspectives on these gifts (see 1:18–2:5; 3:18-20; chs 12–14).

1:7 ***every spiritual gift:*** See 12:8-10, 28.

1:8 Even though believers are saved from eternal condemnation (see Rom 8:1), they remain accountable to God for the way they live (see 3:12-15; 4:4-5; 2 Cor 5:10). Paul encourages his readers to live a holy life so that they will be found faultless when Christ returns (see Phil 1:6, 10; 1 Thes 3:13; 5:23-24).

1:9 ***God . . . is faithful:*** See 10:13; Deut 7:9; 1 Thes 5:24. • ***he has invited you:*** God has chosen them and brought them ***into partnership with his Son*** (cp. Rom 8:28-39).

1:10–15:58 The body of the letter is devoted to Paul's advice on specific problems and questions that had arisen in the Corinthian church.

1:10-17 The Corinthian believers were arguing over which of the leading evangelists (Paul, Apollos, Peter) was best. Paul rebukes them for their quarreling and worldly comparisons. As a minister of Christ and the Good News, he and the others are all channels through whom God works (see 3:1–4:7).

1:10 ***dear brothers and sisters*** (literally *brothers;* also in 1:11, 26): Paul uses this generic, traditional term of affection to address all the believers, not just the men. • ***I appeal to you:*** Paul motivates them ***by the authority of our Lord Jesus Christ,*** not by his own authority. • ***authority*** (literally *name*): In Jewish thought, a person's name carried the weight of the person's authority and reputation. • ***Let there be no divisions:*** His desire was not simply that they avoid divisiveness, but that they be so filled with the Spirit of Christ that they would ***be of one mind, united in thought and purpose*** (cp. Phil 2:2).

1:11 ***Chloe*** was a Corinthian woman, not mentioned elsewhere in Scripture.

1:12 The Christians in Corinth had formed factions loyal to different Christian leaders, but the leaders themselves do not seem to have been in conflict. ***Paul,*** as the one who had first brought the Good News to Corinth, would receive the loyalty of some. • ***Apollos,*** now with Paul (see 16:12), was an eloquent Alexandrian Jew who had become a powerful Christian evangelist and had ministered in Corinth (see Acts 18:24–19:1). He attracted followers because of his skillful oratory (perhaps in contrast to Paul) and his ability to interpret Scripture. See "Apollos" at Acts 18:24–19:1, p. 1867. • ***Peter:*** Greek *Cephas*; see also Matt 16:18; John 1:42. Peter was the primary early evangelist to the Jews. He represented a more traditional Jewish perspective and had a gift for speaking in front of crowds (see Acts 1:15-22; 2:14-40; 3:12-26; 4:8-12; 10:34-43). • ***I follow only Christ:*** This might refer to a group who disavowed allegiance to any human authority and viewed themselves as more holy than others.

1:13
Eph 4:5
1:18
Rom 1:16
2 Cor 2:15; 4:3
1:19
*Isa 29:14
1:20
Job 12:17
Isa 19:11-12; 44:25
1:21
Matt 11:25
1:22
Matt 12:38
[h]*sēmeion* (4592)
‣2 Cor 12:12
1:23
[i]*skandalon* (4625)
‣1 Cor 8:9
1:24
Col 2:3
1:25
2 Cor 13:4
1:26
Matt 11:25
John 7:48
Jas 2:1-5
[j]*klēsis* (2821)
‣Eph 1:18
1:28
Rom 4:17

13Has Christ been divided into factions?
Was I, Paul, crucified for you? Were any of
you baptized in the name of Paul? Of course
not! 14I thank God that I did not baptize any
of you except Crispus and Gaius, 15for now
no one can say they were baptized in my
name. 16(Oh yes, I also baptized the household of Stephanas, but I don't remember
baptizing anyone else.) 17For Christ didn't
send me to baptize, but to preach the Good
News—and not with clever speech, for fear
that the cross of Christ would lose its power.

The World's Wisdom and God's Wisdom

18The message of the cross is foolish to
those who are headed for destruction! But
we who are being saved know it is the very
power of God. 19As the Scriptures say,

> "I will destroy the wisdom of the wise
> and discard the intelligence of the
> intelligent."

20So where does this leave the philosophers, the scholars, and the world's brilliant
debaters? God has made the wisdom of this
world look foolish. 21Since God in his wisdom saw to it that the world would never
know him through human wisdom, he has
used our foolish preaching to save those
who believe. 22It is foolish to the Jews, who
ask for [h]signs from heaven. And it is foolish
to the Greeks, who seek human wisdom.
23So when we preach that Christ was crucified, the Jews are [i]offended and the Gentiles
say it's all nonsense.

24But to those called by God to salvation,
both Jews and Gentiles, Christ is the power
of God and the wisdom of God. 25This foolish plan of God is wiser than the wisest of
human plans, and God's weakness is stronger than the greatest of human strength.

26Remember, dear brothers and sisters,
that few of you were wise in the world's eyes
or powerful or wealthy when God [j]called you.
27Instead, God chose things the world considers foolish in order to shame those who
think they are wise. And he chose things
that are powerless to shame those who are
powerful. 28God chose things despised by

1:13 Paul asks three rhetorical questions, all expecting the obvious answer, "no." Christian devotion is to be given to Christ, not to his messengers.

1:14 ***Crispus and Gaius*** were two of Paul's earliest converts in Corinth. ***Crispus*** was a former leader of the synagogue in Corinth (see Acts 18:8), and ***Gaius*** later offered Paul the use of his home (see Rom 16:23). This might identify him with Titius Justus, an earlier convert to Judaism who lived next door to the synagogue (see Acts 18:7). His full Roman name would then be Gaius Titius Justus.

1:16 ***The household of Stephanas*** were the first converts in the province of Achaia (southern Greece; see 16:15). *Household* refers to all who lived in the house, which might include more than Stephanas's immediate family.

1:17 The important thing is not baptism, but the preaching of ***the Good News;*** baptism signifies people's response to the message (see "Baptism" at Acts 2:38, 41, p. 1828). • ***clever speech:*** Eloquence, or an appeal to human wisdom. • ***for fear that the cross of Christ would lose its power:*** Too much emphasis on eloquence and the persuasiveness of human reason can distract from the simple message that Christ died for people's sins so that they could be forgiven (2:1-5; 15:1-3).

1:18-31 Paul contrasts eloquence and human wisdom, which were highly valued by some of the Corinthians, and the foolish message of the cross—the expression of God's wisdom. The followers of Apollos, in particular (see 1:12), were probably attracted by his rhetorical abilities and intellectual approach to ministry (see Acts 18:24-28). In contrast, Paul emphasizes that the real power lies in the simple message of the cross of Christ.

1:18 The message that God is saving the world through a condemned criminal ***is foolish*** to unbelievers, for their eyes are blinded to the truth (2 Cor 4:4). For believers, whose eyes have been opened by God, ***the message of the cross*** has the ring of truth to it, and they know its ***power*** to convict the human heart (see 1:23-24; Rom 1:16). Unbelievers, still in their sin, are ***headed for destruction,*** for ultimate condemnation. Believers, whose sins have been forgiven, ***are being saved:*** They are on their way to eternal life and glory.

1:19 This quotation from Isa 29:14 shows God's estimation of mere human ***wisdom.***

1:20 In God's eyes, the human ***wisdom of this world*** is ***foolish.*** Divine wisdom lies in the message of the cross and in Jesus Christ (see 1:24, 30).

1:21 ***Human wisdom*** alone does not bring people to the true knowledge of God; that comes only through the message of the cross, which the world considers ***foolish,*** but which saves ***those who believe*** (cp. Matt 11:25).

1:22-24 Paul uses the words ***Greeks*** and ***Gentiles*** interchangeably to refer to non-Jews.

1:22 Unbelieving ***Jews*** wanted to see miraculous ***signs*** to validate the message (cp. Matt 12:38-39; 16:1-4; John 2:18, 23; 4:48). ***Greeks,*** renowned for their schools of philosophy, were only interested in ***human wisdom***—i.e., philosophical reasoning.

1:23 Regardless of what unbelieving ***Jews*** and ***Gentiles*** desired, Paul refused to give them anything but the simple message of the cross. To many Jews, the idea of a crucified Messiah was a contradiction in terms because crucifixion expressed not the power and blessing of God but his curse (see Gal 3:13; cp. Deut 21:23).

1:24 ***and Gentiles:*** Literally *and Greeks.* See note on 1:22-24.

1:25 What the unbelieving world considers ***foolish*** and weak—Christ and the message of the cross—is in reality ***wiser*** and ***stronger*** than anything the world has to offer. It solves the world's greatest problem, the problem of sin, and overcomes all the powers of evil that oppose human beings.

1:26 Socially and culturally, most Corinthian Christians were ordinary people; ***few*** were among the elite (cp. Matt 11:25). Only a few Christians, such as Erastus, the city treasurer in Corinth (see Rom 16:23), were ***wealthy*** (or ***high born***; cp. Jas 2:5).

1:27-29 God chose ***despised*** and humble people in order to demonstrate his judgment on human pride (cp. Rom 3:27; 4:2; 2 Cor 4:7-11; 12:8-10; Eph 2:9).

1:28 ***God chose things despised by the world:*** Or *God chose those who are low born.*

the world, things counted as nothing at all, and used them to bring to nothing what the world considers important. 29As a result, no one can ever boast in the presence of God.

30God has united you with Christ Jesus. For our benefit God made him to be wisdom itself. Christ made us right with God; he made us pure and [k]holy, and he [a]freed us from sin. 31Therefore, as the Scriptures say, "If you want to boast, boast only about the LORD."

The Power of the Message of the Cross

2 When I first came to you, dear brothers and sisters, I didn't use lofty words and impressive wisdom to tell you God's [b]secret plan. 2For I decided that while I was with you I would forget everything except Jesus Christ, the one who was crucified. 3I came to you in weakness—timid and trembling. 4And my message and my preaching were very plain. Rather than using clever and persuasive speeches, I relied only on the power of the Holy Spirit. 5I did this so you would trust not in human wisdom but in the power of God.

Paul's Message of Real Wisdom from the Spirit

6Yet when I am among mature believers, I do speak with words of wisdom, but not the kind of wisdom that belongs to this world or to the rulers of this world, who are soon forgotten. 7No, the wisdom we speak of is the mystery of God—his plan that was previously hidden, even though he [c]made it for our ultimate glory before the world began. 8But the rulers of this world have not understood it; if they had, they would not have crucified our glorious Lord. 9That is what the Scriptures mean when they say,

> "No eye has seen, no ear has heard,
> and no mind has imagined
> what God has prepared
> for those who love him."

10But it was to us that God revealed these things by his Spirit. For his Spirit searches out everything and shows us God's deep secrets. 11No one can know a person's thoughts except that person's own spirit, and no one can know God's thoughts except God's own Spirit. 12And we have received God's Spirit (not the world's spirit), so we can know the wonderful things God has freely given us.

13When we tell you these things, we do not use words that come from human wisdom. Instead, we speak words given to us by the Spirit, using the Spirit's words to explain spiritual truths. 14But people who aren't

1:29 Eph 2:9
1:30 Jer 23:5-6; Rom 3:24; 2 Cor 5:21; [k]*hagiasmos* (0038) ‣1 Thes 4:3; [a]*apolutrōsis* (0629) ‣Eph 1:7
1:31 *Jer 9:24; 2 Cor 10:17
2:1 [b]*mustērion* (3466) ‣1 Cor 15:51
2:3 2 Cor 10:1; Gal 4:13
2:6 Eph 4:13; Phil 3:15; Heb 5:14
2:7 Rom 16:25; [c]*proorizō* (4309) ‣Eph 1:5
2:8 Jas 2:1
2:9 *Isa 64:4; 65:17
2:10 Matt 11:25; 13:11; John 14:26; 15:26; 16:13-15; 1 Jn 2:27
2:11 Prov 20:27; Jer 17:9; Rom 11:33
2:12 John 16:13-15; Rom 8:15

1:30 When people are *united . . . with Christ Jesus,* God makes them righteous, *holy,* and free (see 6:11; Rom 3:21-26; 5:17-21). This work of Christ is an expression of God's *wisdom.*

1:31 This quotation is a paraphrase of Jer 9:24 (cp. 2 Cor 10:17). Because salvation is a result of God's sovereign power (2:5) and his decision to save his people, there is absolutely no room for human pride (see 1:29).

2:1-5 God's sovereign work made Paul's preaching effective. In his evangelism, Paul did not rely on the persuasive power of his intellect or his dynamic personality, but on the power of the Holy Spirit (see also note at 1:18-31).

2:1 ***When I first came to you:*** See Acts 18:1-17. • ***dear brothers and sisters:*** Literally *brothers.* See note on 1:10. • ***lofty words and impressive wisdom:*** Human wisdom and philosophy don't bring people to Christ (see 1:17, 21; 2:2). The message of the cross has its own power to convert the human heart (see 1:17; Rom 1:16; Gal 6:14). • ***God's secret plan:*** Literally *God's mystery;* other manuscripts read *God's testimony.* See note on 2:7.

2:3-4 Human *weakness* is no barrier to God's work (2 Cor 12:7-10). The real power is not in charismatic preaching, finesse of presentation, or logical persuasiveness (cp. 2 Cor 10:10), but in the *message* itself, centered on Christ and his death for our sins, and in the power of ***the Holy Spirit,*** who convicts the human heart.

2:6-16 Paul emphasizes God's ***wisdom*** in contrast to the world's wisdom. Real ***wisdom*** is not mere human wisdom but the wisdom of the Spirit, expressed in the so-called "foolishness" of the Good News (see 1:20-25).

2:6 Only the spiritually ***mature*** will recognize God's ***wisdom;*** many of the Corinthians would have been unable to recognize it (see 3:1-3). • ***The rulers of this world*** (see also 2:8) ***are soon forgotten*** because Christ now rules—his enemies have been defeated by his death on the cross (see 15:24-25; Col 2:15).

2:7 ***No, the wisdom we speak of is the mystery of God:*** Literally *But we speak God's wisdom in a mystery.* In Paul's writings, *mystery* often refers to a truth ***previously hidden*** but now revealed in the Good News of Christ and his saving work (see Rom 11:25-27; 1 Tim 3:9, 16). • ***before the world began:*** From the very beginning, it has been God's desire to save his chosen people through Christ (see Rom 16:25-26; Eph 1:9-12; 3:3-12; Col 1:25-27) and to bring them to ***ultimate glory*** in the coming age (see Rom 5:2; 8:18-21, 29-30; 1 Thes 2:12).

2:8 ***The rulers of this world*** are probably political rulers rather than spiritual authorities (see also 15:24; cp. Acts 3:14-15; 4:10; 5:29-32).

2:9 This quotation (cp. Isa 64:4) supports Paul's point (2:8): Those with no spiritual sensitivity do not understand God's work of redemption.

2:10-12 ***But:*** Some manuscripts read *For.* • ***it was to us:*** Those who believe in Christ and have thus received his Spirit (see 6:19; 12:13; Gal 3:2; Eph 1:13; Titus 3:5) are contrasted with the rulers of this world (2:8). ***God's deep secrets*** are not understood through secular wisdom or philosophy, but through ***God's own Spirit,*** who alone can reveal ***God's thoughts*** to his people (see 1 Jn 2:20, 27; cp. Matt 11:25-27). God has graciously given his Spirit to his people so they ***can know the wonderful things God has freely given*** them (cp. John 16:13-14).

2:13 ***using the Spirit's words to explain spiritual truths*** (or *explaining spiritual truths in spiritual language,* or *explaining spiritual truths to spiritual people*): Just as spiritual wisdom is different from ***human wisdom,*** so the way spiritual wisdom is taught must be different from the way human wisdom is taught. The communicating and learning of spiritual truth must be done in the dimension and power of the Spirit; it is not simply a rational, human exercise.

spiritual can't receive these truths from God's Spirit. It all sounds foolish to them and they can't understand it, for only those who are spiritual can understand what the Spirit means. [15]Those who are spiritual can evaluate all things, but they themselves cannot be evaluated by others. [16]For,

"Who can know the LORD's thoughts?
Who knows enough to teach him?"

But we understand these things, for we have the mind of Christ.

Paul and Apollos, Servants of Christ

3 Dear brothers and sisters, when I was with you I couldn't talk to you as I would to spiritual people. I had to talk as though you belonged to this world or as though you were infants in the Christian life. [2]I had to feed you with milk, not with solid food, because you weren't ready for anything stronger. And you still aren't ready, [3]for you are still controlled by your sinful nature. You are jealous of one another and quarrel with each other. Doesn't that prove you are controlled by your sinful nature? Aren't you living like people of the world? [4]When one of you says, "I am a follower of Paul," and another says, "I follow Apollos," aren't you acting just like people of the world?

[5]After all, who is Apollos? Who is Paul? We are only God's servants through whom you believed the Good News. Each of us did the work the Lord gave us. [6]I planted the seed in your hearts, and Apollos watered it, but it was God who made it grow. [7]It's not important who does the planting, or who does the watering. What's important is that God makes the seed grow. [8]The one who plants and the one who waters work together with the same purpose. And both will be rewarded for their own hard work. [9]For we are both God's workers. And you are God's field. You are God's building.

[10]Because of God's grace to me, I have laid the foundation like an expert builder. Now others are building on it. But whoever is building on this foundation must be very careful. [11]For no one can lay any foundation other than the one we already have—Jesus Christ.

[12]Anyone who builds on that foundation may use a variety of materials—gold, silver, jewels, wood, hay, or straw. [13]But on the judgment day, fire will reveal what kind of work each builder has done. The fire will show if a person's work has any value. [14]If the work survives, that builder will receive a reward. [15]But if the work is burned up, the builder will suffer great loss. The builder will be saved, but like someone barely escaping through a wall of flames.

2:13 2 Pet 1:20-21
2:14 John 8:47; 14:17; Jude 1:19
2:15 1 Jn 2:20
2:16 *Isa 40:13; Rom 11:34
3:1 Gal 6:1; Eph 4:14
3:2 Heb 5:12-13; 1 Pet 2:2
3:3 Rom 13:13
3:4 Gal 5:20
3:5 Acts 18:24; Rom 12:3, 6; 2 Cor 6:4
3:6 Acts 18:4-11
3:8 Ps 18:20; 62:12
3:9 Isa 61:3; Eph 2:20-22; 1 Pet 2:5
3:10 Rom 15:20
3:11 Isa 28:16; Eph 2:20; 1 Pet 2:4-6
3:13 2 Tim 1:12, 18; 4:8
3:15 Jude 1:23

2:14 ***people who aren't spiritual*** (or ***people who don't have the Spirit;*** or ***people who have only physical life***): Unbelievers, whose minds are blinded, function in the natural world and see life only through physical eyes (see 2 Cor 4:4). They cannot appreciate the significance of the Good News, for it is essentially a ***spiritual*** message.

2:15 ***Those who are spiritual:*** People who have the Spirit have a true understanding of divine revelation.

2:16 This quotation from Isa 40:13 (Greek version) shows how divine wisdom transcends the limitations of human reasoning (cp. Rom 11:34). • ***we have the mind of Christ:*** Linked to Christ, believers have the Spirit of Christ to reveal Christ's thinking to them.

3:1–4:7 Having contrasted human and spiritual wisdom, Paul now returns to the divisiveness in the Corinthian church (see 1:10-12), particularly their misplaced devotion to himself and Apollos.

3:1-4 Paul rebukes the Christians in Corinth for their spiritual immaturity.

3:1 ***Dear brothers and sisters:*** Literally *Brothers.* See note on 1:10. • The Corinthians' behavior was not that of the ***spiritual people*** (or ***people who have the Spirit***) whom Paul described in 2:15, but like that of unbelievers who are attracted to the wisdom and values of ***this world.*** • ***infants in the Christian life*** (literally ***infants in Christ***): Though they were converted, their lives and thinking did not reflect maturity in Christ and the transforming perspective of his spirit.

3:2 Because of the Corinthian Christians' lack of spiritual maturity, Paul was unable to speak about the deeper truths of life in Christ, the ***solid food*** (see 2:6-7) that is reserved for mature Christians. Instead, he had to restrict himself to ***milk,*** the basic teachings of the Good News (cp. Heb 5:12-14; 6:1-3; 1 Pet 2:2).

3:3 Their jealousy and quarreling (see 1:10-12) showed that they were ***still*** just like unbelievers, ***controlled by*** their ***sinful nature*** rather than by the Spirit of God (cp. 2 Cor 12:20; Gal 5:19-21).

3:4 Proudly identifying oneself with a preferred teacher (see 1:12) was common in Greek culture, but it is not in keeping with the mind of Christ (3:5-9; cp. Matt 23:8-10).

3:5-9 To identify oneself proudly as a follower of a human teacher is wrong because God does the real work of redemption, so he deserves the honor. • ***We are only God's servants:*** Cp. 2 Cor 4:5.

3:6 ***I planted:*** See Acts 18:1-11. • ***Apollos watered:*** See Acts 18:27–19:1.

3:10-17 All people are accountable to God for the way they serve Christ.

3:10 Paul ***laid the foundation*** when he first began the church in Corinth. ***Now others*** were ***building on it*** by what they were teaching the young Christians.

3:11 There can never be ***any*** other ***foundation*** for the church than ***Jesus Christ*** himself (see Isa 28:16; 1 Pet 2:4-8; cp. Rom 9:33), but the Corinthians were in danger of treating a human teacher as their foundation.

3:12-15 Some of the things that people build on the ***foundation*** of Christ will endure; other things will burn up in the fire of judgment (cp. Mal 4:1). On ***judgment day,*** the work of ***each builder*** who instructs the church will be assessed (cp. Jas 3:1; see also Rom 14:10-12; 2 Cor 5:10). Those whose teachings are faithful and true ***will receive a reward;*** the others ***will suffer great loss,*** not of their salvation but of their reward. They themselves ***will be saved,*** but just barely, like someone pulled to safety ***through a wall of flames*** (cp. Amos 4:11; Zech 3:2; Jude 1:23).

16 Don't you realize that all of you together
are the temple of God and that the Spirit of
God lives in you? 17 God will destroy anyone
who destroys this temple. For God's temple
is holy, and you are that temple.
18 Stop deceiving yourselves. If you think
you are wise by this world's standards, you
need to become a fool to be truly wise. 19 For
the wisdom of this world is foolishness to
God. As the Scriptures say,

"He traps the wise
in the snare of their own cleverness."

20 And again,

"The LORD knows the thoughts of the wise;
he knows they are [d]worthless."

21 So don't boast about following a particular human leader. For everything belongs
to you—22 whether Paul or Apollos or Peter,
or the world, or life and death, or the present and the future. Everything belongs to
you, 23 and you belong to Christ, and Christ
belongs to God.

Paul's Relationship with the Corinthians

4 So look at Apollos and me as mere servants of Christ who have been put [e]in
charge of explaining God's mysteries. 2 Now,
a person who is put in charge as a manager
must be faithful. 3 As for me, it matters very
little how I might be evaluated by you or
by any human authority. I don't even trust
my own judgment on this point. 4 My conscience is clear, but that doesn't prove I'm
right. It is the Lord himself who will examine me and decide.
5 So don't make judgments about anyone
ahead of time—before the Lord returns. For
he will bring our darkest secrets to light and
will reveal our private motives. Then God
will give to each one whatever praise is due.
6 Dear brothers and sisters, I have used
Apollos and myself to illustrate what I've
been saying. If you pay attention to what I
have quoted from the Scriptures, you won't
be proud of one of your leaders at the expense of another. 7 For what gives you the
right to make such a judgment? What do
you have that God hasn't given you? And if
everything you have is from God, why boast
as though it were not a gift?
8 You think you already have everything
you need. You think you are already rich.
You have begun to reign in God's kingdom
without us! I wish you really were reigning
already, for then we would be reigning with
you. 9 Instead, I sometimes think God has put
us apostles on display, like prisoners of war
at the end of a victor's parade, condemned
to die. We have become a spectacle to the
entire world—to people and [f]angels alike.

3:16 2 Cor 6:16
3:17 Eph 2:21-22
3:18 Isa 5:21; Gal 6:3
3:19 *Job 5:13
3:20 *Ps 94:11; [d]*mataios* (3152) ›1 Cor 15:17
3:21 Rom 8:32
3:22 Rom 8:38
4:1 Rom 16:25; [e]*oikonomos* (3623) ›1 Cor 9:17
4:2 Luke 12:42
4:4 Ps 143:2
4:5 Matt 7:1; 2 Cor 5:10; Rev 20:12
4:7 John 3:27; Rom 12:3, 6
4:8 Rev 3:17, 21
4:9 Rom 8:36; Heb 10:33; [f]*angelos* (0032) ›1 Cor 6:3
4:10 2 Cor 11:19

3:16-17 Christians must be very careful, both in what they teach and in how they relate to one another, because the body of believers is ***the temple of God***, the home of ***the Spirit of God*** who ***lives in*** (or ***among***) them (cp. Eph 2:21-22), and ***God's temple is holy*** (see 1:2). There are terrible consequences for ***anyone who destroys*** God's temple by such things as jealousy, argumentativeness, and divisiveness (see 3:3-4).

3:18-20 Here Paul returns to the contrast between human wisdom and divine wisdom (see 1:18-25). Using OT quotations, Paul encourages the Corinthians to be willing to appear foolish in the eyes of the world so that they may be ***truly wise*** in God's eyes.

3:19 This quotation is from Job 5:13.

3:20 This quotation is from Ps 94:11.

3:21-23 As the privileged children of God, they may now lay claim to ***everything—the world,*** and ***life and death***, and ***the present and the future*** (see Rom 8:38-39). So there is no point in claiming ***a particular human leader*** as their own.

3:22 ***Peter:*** Greek *Cephas.*

3:23 Just as they may now claim everything as their own, so ***Christ*** has claimed them for himself (see Rom 14:7-9), and in Christ they are ultimately claimed by ***God*** (see 6:19-20; 7:23).

4:1-5 Paul emphasizes his faithfulness and the genuineness of his motives as an apostle of Christ. But only God can judge the heart.

4:1 Paul and Apollos should not be viewed as leaders competing for a following, but as ***mere servants of Christ who have been put in charge of explaining God's mysteries.*** They were stewards entrusted with administration of the master's business (as in Luke 12:42); their whole life was devoted to their master's concerns, not to their own. • ***God's mysteries:*** See note on 2:7.

4:3-4 Paul's deepest desire was that he be found faithful before God. Human assessments of him—by himself or others—didn't matter.

4:5 ***don't make judgments about anyone:*** Only the Lord can fully know a person's heart, and when he returns, he will judge. Paul took God's judgment of his ministry very seriously (see 2 Cor 5:9-10; Phil 2:16; 1 Thes 2:19-20; cp. 2 Cor 1:14).

4:6-21 Paul again rebukes the Corinthian Christians for their arrogance (4:6-13) and then admonishes them as a father (4:14-21).

4:6 ***Dear brothers and sisters:*** Literally *Brothers.* See note on 1:10. • ***If you pay attention to what I have quoted from the Scriptures:*** Or *If you learn not to go beyond "what is written."* • ***you won't be proud:*** See also 1:29-31; 3:21; 4:18-19; 5:2, 6; 8:1; 13:4.

4:7 Pride in a particular leader results from failure to realize that ***everything*** is ***a gift*** from God. There is no room for pride; humble gratitude is the only appropriate attitude.

4:8-13 Paul ironically highlights the difference between himself and them. Their attitudes reflect the wisdom of the world; his, the wisdom of God. In their pride, the Corinthians thought they had arrived, but they actually had a long way to go (cp. Rev 3:17-18; contrast Phil 3:12-14). If they had truly arrived, they would be sharing more of the suffering that Paul experienced (4:11-13). In contrast to the Corinthians, who were so proud of their attainments and the respect they had from others, the apostles suffered scorn and contempt.

4:9 Like ***prisoners . . . condemned to die*** by facing wild animals in the amphitheater, the apostles were ***a spectacle.*** Paul gladly accepted suffering because God was using it to bring blessing to others (see 2 Cor 1:4-7; 4:7-12; Phil 2:17; Col 1:24).

4:11 Acts 23:2; Rom 8:35; 2 Cor 11:23-27
4:12 Matt 5:44; Acts 18:3; 1 Pet 3:9
4:13 Lam 3:45
4:14 2 Cor 6:13
4:15 Gal 4:19; [g]*paidagōgos* (3807) ‣Gal 3:24
4:16 Phil 3:17; 1 Thes 1:6
4:17 Acts 16:1; 19:22; 1 Tim 1:2
4:19 Acts 18:21; 2 Cor 1:15-16
4:21 2 Cor 1:23; 2:1
5:1 Lev 18:7-8; Deut 22:30; 27:20; Eph 5:3
5:3 Col 2:5; [h]*pneuma* (4151) ‣1 Cor 7:34
5:5 1 Tim 1:20; [i]*sarx* (4561) ‣Gal 3:3
5:6 Matt 16:6, 12; Gal 5:9; [j]*zumē* (2219) ‣1 Cor 5:7

10 Our dedication to Christ makes us look
like fools, but you claim to be so wise in
Christ! We are weak, but you are so powerful! You are honored, but we are ridiculed.
11 Even now we go hungry and thirsty, and
we don't have enough clothes to keep warm.
We are often beaten and have no home.
12 We work wearily with our own hands to
earn our living. We bless those who curse
us. We are patient with those who abuse us.
13 We appeal gently when evil things are said
about us. Yet we are treated like the world's
garbage, like everybody's trash—right up to
the present moment.

14 I am not writing these things to shame
you, but to warn you as my beloved children.
15 For even if you had ten thousand others to
[g]teach you about Christ, you have only one
spiritual father. For I became your father
in Christ Jesus when I preached the Good
News to you. 16 So I urge you to imitate me.

17 That's why I have sent Timothy, my beloved and faithful child in the Lord. He will
remind you of how I follow Christ Jesus, just
as I teach in all the churches wherever I go.

18 Some of you have become arrogant,
thinking I will not visit you again. 19 But I
will come—and soon—if the Lord lets me,
and then I'll find out whether these arrogant people just give pretentious speeches
or whether they really have God's power.
20 For the Kingdom of God is not just a lot
of talk; it is living by God's power. 21 Which
do you choose? Should I come with a rod to
punish you, or should I come with love and
a gentle spirit?

Sin in Relationships (5:1–6:20)

Paul Confronts Sexual Immorality and Spiritual Pride

5 I can hardly believe the report about
the sexual immorality going on among
you—something that even pagans don't do. I
am told that a man in your church is living in
sin with his stepmother. 2 You are so proud
of yourselves, but you should be mourning
in sorrow and shame. And you should remove this man from your fellowship.

3 Even though I am not with you in person,
I am with you in the [h]Spirit. And as though I
were there, I have already passed judgment
on this man 4 in the name of the Lord Jesus.
You must call a meeting of the church. I will
be present with you in spirit, and so will the
power of our Lord Jesus. 5 Then you must
throw this man out and hand him over to
Satan so that his [i]sinful nature will be destroyed and he himself will be saved on the
day the Lord returns.

6 Your boasting about this is terrible.
Don't you realize that this sin is like a little
[j]yeast that spreads through the whole batch

4:11-13 Paul reminds the Corinthians how much he had endured for Christ's sake (cp. 2 Cor 6:4-5; 11:23-28).

4:12 ***We work:*** To avoid being blamed by others for taking money, Paul preferred to support himself (9:3-18; Acts 18:3; 20:33-35). • ***We bless those who curse us:*** Paul's response was in line with Jesus' teaching (Matt 5:44-45; cp. Rom 12:14, 17-21).

4:14-21 Paul concludes this section on divisions in the church (1:10–4:21) with gentle words of fatherly admonition and warning.

4:14-16 As their ***spiritual father*** who first brought them the Good News, Paul affirms his genuine concern for their well-being (cp. 1 Thes 2:11-12). As his ***beloved children***, they should listen to their father and ***imitate*** his example and teachings (see 11:1; Gal 4:12; Phil 3:17; 4:9; 1 Thes 1:6; 2 Thes 3:7-9).

4:17 ***Timothy,*** Paul's ***child*** in the faith and one of his closest associates, was with Paul when he first preached the Good News in Corinth (see 2 Cor 1:19). Paul sent him to faithfully communicate what it means to ***follow Christ Jesus.*** See "Timothy" at Acts 16:1-3, p. 1860.

4:18-20 Because of his sending Timothy, some may have concluded that Paul lacked the courage to ***visit*** them himself, but in fact Paul was deeply engrossed in his work in Ephesus at this time (Acts 19:8-20; see note on Acts 19:10). He would indeed visit them soon (see 16:5-9; Acts 19:21-22; 20:1-3; cp. 2 Cor 1:15–2:4) and would confront those who publicly opposed him and show that they were nothing more than big talkers. His life and words would demonstrate the reality of ***God's power*** (see also 2:4).

5:1-8 Paul confronts ***sexual immorality*** in the church and instructs the Christians to expel a shameless offender from their fellowship.

5:1 ***sexual immorality:*** A man was having sex with ***his stepmother*** (literally *his father's wife*). Such behavior ***even pagans*** didn't do: It violated both the law of Moses (see Lev 18:7-8) and Roman law (Gaius, *Institutes* 1.63).

5:2 The Corinthian Christians were ***proud*** (see 4:8, 10, 18; 5:6), when they should have been ***mourning in sorrow and shame*** over such sin among them. • ***remove this man from your fellowship:*** This instruction might presuppose that the man had refused their appeals, or that such blatant sin required immediate discipline (cp. Matt 18:15-18).

5:3 ***in the Spirit*** (or *in spirit*): Paul's spiritual unity with them and the authority he had received from God through the Spirit were effective among them.

5:4 ***in the name of the Lord Jesus. You must call a meeting of the church:*** Or *In the name of the Lord Jesus, you must call a meeting of the church.* The punctuation of this verse is uncertain.

5:5 The instruction to ***throw this man out*** is not in the Greek text, but is implied from 5:2, 13. • ***and hand him over to Satan:*** Cp. 1 Tim 1:20. Those who are outside of God's church are under the power and control of Satan (see Eph 2:2; 1 Jn 5:19). • ***so that his sinful nature will be destroyed:*** (or *so that his body will be destroyed;* literally *for the destruction of the flesh*): *The flesh* may be interpreted figuratively as a reference to his evil desires or literally as his physical life (i.e., *so that he will die*). • ***and he himself*** (literally *and the spirit*) ***will be saved:*** Perhaps he would repent and not be condemned (cp. 2 Cor 2:5-8). • ***on the day the Lord returns:*** Literally *in the day of the Lord*, which includes the final judgment. • ***the Lord:*** Other manuscripts read *the Lord Jesus;* still others read *our Lord Jesus Christ.*

5:6-7 ***Yeast*** was often a symbol of ***sin*** (cp. Matt 16:6, 12; Mark 8:15; Luke 12:1; Gal 5:9). Jews ceremonially

of dough? 7Get rid of the old [k]"yeast" by removing this wicked person from among
you. Then you will be like a fresh batch of
dough made without yeast, which is what
you really are. Christ, our Passover Lamb,
has been sacrificed for us. 8So let us celebrate the festival, not with the old [a]bread of
wickedness and evil, but with the new bread
of sincerity and truth.

Disciplining Christians Who Sin

9When I wrote to you before, I told you not
to associate with people who indulge in
sexual sin. 10But I wasn't talking about unbelievers who indulge in sexual sin, or are
greedy, or cheat people, or [b]worship idols.
You would have to leave this world to avoid
people like that. 11I meant that you are not
to associate with anyone who claims to be
a believer yet indulges in sexual sin, or is
greedy, or worships idols, or is abusive, or is
a drunkard, or cheats people. Don't even eat
with such people.

12It isn't my responsibility to judge outsiders, but it certainly is your responsibility to
judge those inside the church who are sinning. 13God will judge those on the outside;
but as the Scriptures say, "You must remove
the evil person from among you."

Avoiding Lawsuits against Fellow Christians

6 When one of you has a dispute with
another believer, how dare you file a
lawsuit and ask a secular court to decide
the matter instead of taking it to other believers! 2Don't you realize that someday we
believers will judge the world? And since
you are going to judge the world, can't you
decide even these little things among yourselves? 3Don't you realize that we will judge
[c]angels? So you should surely be able to resolve ordinary disputes in this life. 4If you
have legal disputes about such matters, why
go to outside judges who are not respected
by the church? 5I am saying this to shame
you. Isn't there anyone in all the church who
is wise enough to decide these issues? 6But
instead, one believer sues another—right in
front of unbelievers!

7Even to have such lawsuits with one
another is a defeat for you. Why not just accept the injustice and leave it at that? Why
not let yourselves be cheated? 8Instead, you
yourselves are the ones who do wrong and
cheat even your fellow believers.

9Don't you realize that those who do
wrong will not inherit the Kingdom of God?
Don't fool yourselves. Those who indulge in
sexual sin, or who [d]worship idols, or commit
adultery, or are male prostitutes, or practice
homosexuality, 10or are thieves, or greedy
people, or drunkards, or are abusive, or
cheat people—none of these will inherit the
Kingdom of God. 11Some of you were once
like that. But you were cleansed; you were

5:7
Isa 53:7
1 Pet 1:19
[k]*zumē* (2219)
‣1 Cor 5:8

5:8
[a]*zumē* (2219)
‣Gal 5:9

5:10
John 17:15
[b]*eidōlolatrēs* (1496)
‣1 Cor 6:9

5:11
Rom 16:17
2 Thes 3:6
2 Jn 1:10

5:13
*Deut 17:7; 19:19; 21:21; 24:7

6:1
Matt 18:17

6:2
Dan 7:22
Luke 22:30
Rev 3:21

6:3
2 Pet 2:4
Jude 1:6
[c]*angelos* (0032)
‣1 Cor 11:10

6:7
Matt 5:39
1 Thes 5:15
1 Pet 3:9

6:8
1 Thes 4:6

6:9-10
Gal 5:19-21
Eph 5:5
Rev 22:15

6:9
[d]*eidōlolatrēs* (1496)
‣1 Cor 10:7

6:11
Acts 22:16
Rom 8:30

cleansed their homes of yeast before the annual Passover meal (Exod 12:19; 13:7). • ***Get rid of . . . this wicked person:*** Sin, if unaddressed, could spread throughout the church, just as ***yeast*** spreads throughout a ***batch of dough.***

5:7-8 Paul draws an analogy between the traditional Jewish ***Passover*** celebration and the sacrifice of ***Christ.*** In the Passover celebration, a ***lamb*** was sacrificed and unleavened bread was eaten (see Exod 12:1-27; 13:3-7). The sacrifice of Christ, which occurred at Passover (Matt 26:2; cp. John 1:29; 1 Pet 1:19), results in the removal of sin for believers. • ***has been sacrificed for us:*** Literally *has been sacrificed.* • ***not with the old bread:*** Literally *not with old leaven.* • ***but with the new bread:*** Literally *but with unleavened [bread].*

5:9-13 The church is to discipline anyone in the church who is known to be living in sin.

5:9 ***When I wrote to you before*** refers to an unknown earlier letter. • ***Sexual sin*** is any form of illicit sexual activity (see 6:9).

5:10 Paul generally encouraged believers not to separate themselves from the company of sinful unbelievers (e.g., 10:27).

5:11 Separation from a professing ***believer*** (literally *brother*) who was living in sin was intended to reinforce and maintain the high moral standards of the Christian community. The social pressure it exerted might also encourage repentance in an erring brother or sister (cp. 2 Thes 3:6, 14).

5:12-13 Christians are not called to ***judge*** (i.e., discipline) sin in unbelievers, but in believers. • ***as the Scriptures say:*** This quotation is from Deut 17:7.

6:1-11 When serious differences arise between two Christians, they are not to be settled by ***a secular court,*** but by ***other believers.***

6:1 ***other believers:*** Literally *God's holy people;* also in 6:2.

6:2-3 ***Someday we believers will judge the world***—and even ***angels***—as associates of the Son of Man, who is the ultimate Judge of all people (cp. Dan 7:13, 22, 27; Matt 19:28; John 5:27; Acts 17:31; Rev 3:21; 20:4). In light of this responsibility, Christians should be able to settle their disagreements over comparatively ***little things.***

6:4-6 ***I am saying this to shame you:*** It is a scandal for Christians to have to resolve their conflicts in secular courts, as if there were no one in the church sufficiently capable of resolving them.

6:6 ***one believer:*** Literally *one brother.* See note on 1:10.

6:7 ***Even to have such lawsuits with one another is a defeat for you:*** To sue a fellow believer reflects self-interest rather than concern for the welfare of others or the glory of God. • ***Why not just accept the injustice?*** Christians are called to follow the example of Christ's self-sacrifice (see Matt 5:38-42).

6:8 Far from following Christ's example or his teachings about sacrificial love, some of the Corinthian believers were cheating ***even*** their ***fellow believers*** (literally *even the brothers*). Both their actions and their attitudes were wrong.

6:9-11 Those who willingly sin have no share in the Kingdom of God. The lives of Christians must reflect the faith they confess.

6:9 ***Don't fool yourselves:*** Sin is deceptive; believers should not take it lightly, as if it were somehow acceptable (Jer 17:9). • Continuing to ***indulge*** unrepentantly ***in sexual sin*** indicates a heart that has not been renewed by the Holy

6:13
Col 2:22
1 Thes 4:3-5

6:14
Acts 2:24
Rom 6:5
Eph 1:19-20
1 Thes 4:16

6:16
*Gen 2:24
Matt 19:5

6:17
John 17:21-23
Rom 8:9-11, 16
2 Cor 3:17
Gal 2:20

made holy; you were made right with God
by calling on the name of the Lord Jesus
Christ and by the Spirit of our God.

Avoiding Sexual Sin

12You say, "I am allowed to do anything"—
but not everything is good for you. And
even though "I am allowed to do anything,"
I must not become a slave to anything. 13You
say, "Food was made for the stomach, and
the stomach for food." (This is true, though
someday God will do away with both of
them.) But you can't say that our bodies
were made for sexual immorality. They
were made for the Lord, and the Lord cares
about our bodies. 14And God will raise us
from the dead by his power, just as he raised
our Lord from the dead.
15Don't you realize that your bodies are
actually parts of Christ? Should a man take
his body, which is part of Christ, and join
it to a prostitute? Never! 16And don't you
realize that if a man joins himself to a prostitute, he becomes one body with her? For
the Scriptures say, "The two are united into
one." 17But the person who is joined to the
Lord is one spirit with him.

Holiness and Sexual Purity (6:9-20)

1 Cor 1:2; 7:1-9, 14
Gen 2:18-25
Lev 18:1-30; 20:10-24
Rom 12:1-2
Gal 5:16-24
Col 3:1-6
1 Thes 4:3-8
1 Pet 1:13-16
2 Pet 1:3-4

The NT writers emphasize the importance of holy living in the area of sexual relations. In contrast to the so-called sexual freedom of the Greco-Roman world, the sexual life of God's people is to be characterized by faithfulness and purity (1 Thes 4:3-8). Sexual relationships are to be restricted to marriage alone (1 Cor 7:1-9, 36-37; see also "Human Sexuality" at Gen 1:27-28, p. 23).

God has made Christians holy by the work of his Holy Spirit (1 Cor 6:11; 2 Thes 2:13), and they are therefore called to live as his own holy people (1 Cor 1:2). God has given them everything they need to live a holy life in this world (2 Pet 1:3-4). As a result, their way of life is to be distinctly different from that of the unholy world around them. Every part of their life is to reflect the transforming work of the Holy Spirit (Rom 12:2). It is therefore inappropriate for anyone who is united to Christ to have sexual relations with anyone outside of marriage. Such relations violate the Christian's body, which has become a sanctuary of the living God and is therefore claimed by God for himself (1 Cor 6:12-20).

Though homosexual activity was accepted in Greco-Roman culture, it is condemned throughout the Bible. In both the OT and the NT, homosexual activity is viewed as a perversion of God's intentions for men and women (Lev 18:22; 20:13; Rom 1:26-27; 1 Cor 6:9-11; 1 Tim 1:10).

Those who freely give themselves to illicit sexual relations, whether homosexual or heterosexual, will not inherit the Kingdom of God (1 Cor 6:9-10; Gal 5:19-21; Col 3:5-6), but will suffer God's judgment (see 2 Pet 2:1–3:13). As with all sin, though, forgiveness and cleansing are available for those who turn to Christ with faith and repentance (Acts 2:38; Rom 3:21-26). In every way, God's people are to live in holiness and godliness (2 Pet 3:11), in accord with the desires of their Creator and Judge.

Spirit. Sexual sins include *adultery* (see Exod 20:14; Matt 5:27-28) and practicing ***homosexuality*** (cp. Lev 18:22; 20:13; Rom 1:26-27; 1 Tim 1:10).

6:10 ***none of these will inherit the Kingdom of God:*** The repetition of this point (also 6:9) emphasizes the severe consequences of living in sin (for similar warnings, see Gal 5:19-21; Eph 5:5; cp. Col 3:5-6).

6:11 Following the strong warning of 6:9-10, Paul reaffirms his confidence in the genuineness of his readers' conversion. • ***you were cleansed*** (cp. Acts 22:16): Cleanliness is a metaphor for the righteousness that comes from forgiveness (see Titus 3:5). They ***were made holy*** by God himself (see 1:2). • They ***were made right with God*** by their identification with ***the Lord Jesus Christ*** and by the transforming work of ***the Spirit of our God***. God has forgiven them and views them as righteous (see Rom 1:17; 3:21-26), and their lives have really been changed for the good (see Titus 3:5-7).

6:12-20 Paul gives several reasons why Christians must not engage in sexual immorality.

6:12 ***"I am allowed to do anything"*** seems to have been a popular attitude among some Christians who were sexually immoral. Paul counters this attitude by emphasizing that not all things are helpful; true Christians must lead disciplined lives (cp. 10:23; Gal 5:13).

6:13-14 ***"Food was made for the stomach, and the stomach for food":*** This statement was apparently used by some Corinthian Christians to rationalize their sexual immorality on the analogy that "the body was made for sex, and sex for the body." It is a false analogy, because ***our bodies . . . were made for the Lord,*** and ***sexual immorality*** does not glorify him. In light of his concern for our bodies and the coming resurrection ***from the dead***, our bodies must be used for holy purposes in God's service.

6:15-17 To be a Christian is to be spiritually joined to Christ in both life and death (cp. Rom 6:3-11). As a result, believers' ***bodies*** have become ***parts of Christ*** (cp. 12:12-28; Rom 12:4-5). This spiritual union (cp. John 14:20; 17:21-23) means that they are not free to violate their bodies by physical union with a ***prostitute***.

6:16 This quotation is from Gen 2:24.

[18]Run from sexual sin! No other sin so clearly affects the body as this one does. For sexual immorality is a sin against your own body. [19]Don't you realize that your body is the temple of the Holy Spirit, who lives in you and was given to you by God? You do not belong to yourself, [20]for God bought you with a high price. So you must honor God with your body.

3. PAUL ANSWERS THE CORINTHIANS' QUESTIONS (7:1–16:4)

Marriage, Divorce, and Singleness (7:1-40)

7 Now regarding the questions you asked in your letter. Yes, it is good to abstain from sexual relations. [2]But because there is so much sexual immorality, each man should have his own wife, and each woman should have her own husband.

[3]The husband should fulfill his wife's sexual needs, and the wife should fulfill her husband's needs. [4]The wife gives authority over her body to her husband, and the husband gives authority over his body to his wife.

[5]Do not deprive each other of sexual relations, unless you both agree to refrain from sexual intimacy for a limited time so you can give yourselves more completely to prayer. Afterward, you should come together again so that Satan won't be able to [e]tempt you because of your lack of self-control. [6]I say this as a concession, not as a command. [7]But I wish everyone were single, just as I am. Yet each person has a special [f]gift from God, of one kind or another.

[8]So I say to those who aren't married and to widows—it's better to stay unmarried, just as I am. [9]But if they can't control themselves, they should go ahead and marry. It's better to marry than to burn with lust.

[10]But for those who are married, I have a command that comes not from me, but from the Lord. A wife must not leave her husband. [11]But if she does leave him, let her remain single or else be [g]reconciled to him. And the husband must not leave his wife.

[12]Now, I will speak to the rest of you, though I do not have a direct command from the Lord. If a Christian man has a wife who is not a believer and she is willing to continue living with him, he must not leave her. [13]And if a Christian woman has a husband who is not a believer and he is willing to continue living with her, she must not leave him. [14]For the Christian wife brings holiness to her marriage, and the Christian husband brings holiness to his marriage. Otherwise, your children would not be holy, but now they are holy. [15](But if the husband or wife who isn't a believer insists on leaving, let them go. In such cases the Christian

6:18 1 Thes 4:3-4
6:19 Rom 14:7-8; 1 Cor 3:16; 2 Cor 6:16
6:20 Phil 1:20; 1 Pet 1:18-19
7:1 1 Cor 7:8, 26
7:3 Exod 21:10; 1 Pet 3:7
7:5 1 Thes 3:5; [e]*peirazō* (3985) ›1 Cor 10:13
7:6 2 Cor 8:8
7:7 Matt 19:11-12; 1 Cor 9:5; 12:11; [f]*charisma* (5486) ›1 Cor 12:4
7:9 1 Tim 5:14
7:10 Mal 2:14-16; Matt 5:32; 19:9; Mark 10:10-12; Luke 16:18
7:11 [g]*katallassō* (2644) ›2 Cor 5:18
7:14 Mal 2:15
7:15 Rom 14:19

6:18-20 For Christians, the body is ***the temple of the Holy Spirit*** (see note on 3:16-17; cp. 2 Cor 6:16). Sexual sin violates this sacred sanctuary and the divine presence. • ***You do not belong to yourself:*** Christians can no longer claim their bodies as their own, as they have been ***bought . . . with a high price,*** the blood of Christ (cp. 7:23; Rev 5:9), and every part of their lives has been claimed by Christ for God's glory (see Rom 14:7-9; 2 Cor 5:14-15).

7:1–16:4 Paul now addresses ***the questions*** the Corinthians had ***asked*** him by ***letter,*** beginning with the question of marriage (cp. 7:25; 8:1; 12:1; 16:1).

7:1-40 Paul consistently states his strong conviction that true Christians, as slaves of Christ, are wholly claimed by Christ the Lord for his own service. Because of this, he recommends that Christians remain single, but concedes that getting married is no sin.

7:1 ***it is good to abstain from sexual relations*** (or *it is good to live a celibate life;* literally *It is good for a man not to touch a woman*): Both Paul and Jesus encouraged the ideal of a celibate life for God's sake (cp. Matt 19:10-12). Paul's emphasis on celibacy is shaped by his expectation that the end of the age is near (see 7:29-31).

7:2 Because of widespread ***sexual immorality,*** Paul encourages most Christians to get married (7:9). He tempers the ideal of the celibate life with awareness of physical realities.

7:3-4 Because of the temptation to sexual immorality, married Christians must always be considerate of the ***sexual needs*** of their spouses. Sexual intimacy is a mutual right for both spouses in a marriage and must not be withheld. Marriage means yielding the ***authority*** over one's body to one's spouse, though such authority is clearly not to be abused.

7:6-7 Paul's preference is singleness, but he recognizes that both marriage and the single life are among the gifts that God gives to various people.

7:8-9 Paul's general advice is that ***it's better to stay unmarried*** because of the opportunities it provides to serve Christ without distraction (7:32-35). But even with its distractions, an honorable marriage is much better than living a life dominated by unsatisfied sexual desire.

7:10-11 Paul advises Christian couples contemplating divorce. • ***a command that comes . . . from the Lord:*** This doesn't mean that Paul's other instructions (see 7:12, 25, 40) have less authority. It is an indication that this particular counsel is grounded in known sayings of Jesus (see Matt 5:32; 19:9; Mark 10:11-12; Luke 16:18). • ***But if she does leave him:*** Paul acknowledges that some couples have great difficulty in living together, but even in that case they must honor their marriage vows to be faithful to their spouse alone (see 7:27; Rom 7:2).

7:12-13 Paul now turns to the case of a Christian married to an unbeliever. • ***I do not have a direct command from the Lord:*** Paul knew of no saying of Jesus that was directly applicable, but his counsel is consistent: Believers must be faithful and honor their marriage commitment. • ***a Christian man:*** Literally *a brother.*

7:14 By remaining committed to the marriage, the Christian ***brings holiness*** to the unbelieving spouse. Such holiness extends to the ***children,*** who also benefit from the holiness of a Christian parent (cp. Mal 2:15). • ***the Christian husband:*** Literally *the brother.*

7:15 If the unbeliever breaks up the marriage, ***the Christian husband or wife*** (literally *the brother or sister*) is free to ***let them go.*** • ***has called you:*** Some manuscripts read *has called us.* • God's desire is that his people ***live in peace,***

7:16 Rom 11:14; 1 Pet 3:1
7:17 1 Cor 4:17; 14:33
7:18 Acts 15:1-19; Gal 5:2
7:19 Rom 2:25-27; Gal 5:6; 6:15; Col 3:11
7:22 John 8:36; Eph 6:6; 1 Pet 2:16; [h]*doulos* (1401) ‣Gal 1:10
7:23 1 Cor 6:20; 1 Pet 1:18
7:25 2 Cor 4:1; 1 Tim 1:12-13

husband or wife is no longer bound to
the other, for God has called you to live in
peace.) 16 Don't you wives realize that your
husbands might be saved because of you?
And don't you husbands realize that your
wives might be saved because of you?

17 Each of you should continue to live
in whatever situation the Lord has placed
you, and remain as you were when God
first called you. This is my rule for all the
churches. 18 For instance, a man who was
circumcised before he became a believer
should not try to reverse it. And the man
who was uncircumcised when he became
a believer should not be circumcised now.
19 For it makes no difference whether or not
a man has been circumcised. The important thing is to keep God's commandments.

20 Yes, each of you should remain as you
were when God called you. 21 Are you a slave?
Don't let that worry you—but if you get a
chance to be free, take it. 22 And remember,
if you were a [h]slave when the Lord called
you, you are now free in the Lord. And if
you were free when the Lord called you, you
are now a [h]slave of Christ. 23 God paid a high
price for you, so don't be enslaved by the
world. 24 Each of you, dear brothers and sisters, should remain as you were when God
first called you.

25 Now regarding your question about the
young women who are not yet married. I
do not have a command from the Lord for
them. But the Lord in his mercy has given
me wisdom that can be trusted, and I will
share it with you. 26 Because of the present crisis, I think it is best to remain as you
are. 27 If you have a wife, do not seek to end
the marriage. If you do not have a wife, do
not seek to get married. 28 But if you do

Belonging to Christ (7:20-24, 32-35)

1 Cor 6:19-20; Deut 9:26, 29; 32:9; 1 Kgs 8:53; Ps 2:8; 28:9; Ezek 18:4; Mark 8:34-36; 12:30; Rom 14:7-9; 2 Cor 5:14-15; Gal 2:19-20; 1 Pet 2:9-10

To many modern readers, the NT seems to portray an extreme view of the Christian life. Believers are called to forfeit their rights, suffer, and even die for the sake of Christ (Mark 8:34-36). They are to turn away from the things of the world that everybody else lives for (1 Jn 2:15-17) and even to despise their life in this world (John 12:24-25). So also Paul encourages them to give up the normal desires for marriage and family and remain single for Christ, if they have that spiritual gift (7:7).

What lies behind such an apparently extreme view of life? For Paul, it is the awareness that believers are claimed by Christ and so belong to him, body and soul. When Christ died, he bought them for himself (6:20). They must no longer live simply for themselves and their own desires (2 Cor 5:14-15). Having died to their own personal interests, they are called to live entirely for their Lord (Rom 14:7-9).

For true Christians, obedience to Christ is not an onerous burden, but a way to express their love and loyalty to the one who died for them (Mark 12:30). For the people of Christ, the whole of life is to be a joyful expression of thanks for the grace God has shown them in Jesus Christ. They gladly yield their lives to serve the one who gave up everything for them. By dying to themselves, they make it possible for him to live in and through them (Gal 2:19-20).

rather than in the intolerable conflict of a mixed marriage no longer desired by the non-Christian spouse.

7:16 There is always the hope that the believing mate will win the unbelieving mate to faith in Christ. However, the Greek text is ambiguous, and could also be interpreted as saying that there is no guarantee that the believing mate will ever win over the unbelieving spouse.

7:17-24 Paul states as a general principle that Christians should accept their God-given lot in life.

7:17 As a general rule, Christians should continue in the social ***situation*** in which they first became believers (see 7:20, 24).

7:18-19 Circumcision illustrates the general principle just stated (7:17). All Jewish males were circumcised. Some, seeking acceptance in Gentile society, attempted to reverse the procedure surgically (see *1 Maccabees* 1:14-15; Josephus, *Antiquities* 12.5.1), a practice Paul discourages. Circumcision has little importance (see also Rom 2:28-29; 4:9-12; Gal 5:2-6; 6:12-15; Phil 3:2-3), compared with keeping ***God's commandments,*** such as the commands to love God and others.

7:21-23 Slavery illustrates the general principle stated in 7:17, 20, 24. Slavery was widespread in the Greco-Roman world, and many Christian converts were slaves serving rich families. Like circumcision, one's own slavery is a relatively unimportant issue for the Christian. Even as a slave, the Christian is spiritually ***free*** from the power of sin, death, and the law (see Rom 6:14; 7:4-6; 8:2). And as a freeman, the believer is still ***a slave of Christ*** (see Eph 6:5-6; 1 Pet 2:16). • As one who has been purchased ***at a high price*** (see 6:20), the free Christian ought not to ***be enslaved by the world*** (literally *don't become slaves of people*).

7:24 ***dear brothers and sisters:*** Literally *brothers;* also in 7:29. See note on 1:10.

7:25-35 Paul gives three reasons why it is generally preferable for single people to remain ***unmarried.***

7:25-28 First, single people have fewer everyday ***problems*** than married people.

7:26 ***the present crisis:*** Or *the pressures of life.*

get married, it is not a sin. And if a young woman gets married, it is not a sin. However, those who get married at this time will have troubles, and I am trying to spare you those problems.

29But let me say this, dear brothers and sisters: The time that remains is very short. So from now on, those with wives should not focus only on their marriage. 30Those who weep or who rejoice or who buy things should not be absorbed by their weeping or their joy or their possessions. 31Those who use the things of the world should not become attached to them. For this world as we know it will soon pass away.

32I want you to be free from the concerns of this life. An unmarried man can spend his time doing the Lord's work and thinking how to please him. 33But a married man has to think about his earthly responsibilities and how to please his wife. 34His interests are divided. In the same way, a woman who is no longer married or has never been married can be devoted to the Lord and holy in body and in [i]spirit. But a married woman has to think about her earthly responsibilities and how to please her husband. 35I am saying this for your benefit, not to place restrictions on you. I want you to do whatever will help you serve the Lord best, with as few distractions as possible.

36But if a man thinks that he's treating his fiancée improperly and will inevitably give in to his passion, let him marry her as he wishes. It is not a sin. 37But if he has decided firmly not to marry and there is no urgency and he can control his passion, he does well not to marry. 38So the person who marries his fiancée does well, and the person who doesn't marry does even better.

39A wife is bound to her husband as long as he lives. If her husband dies, she is free to marry anyone she wishes, but only if he loves the Lord. 40But in my opinion it would be better for her to stay single, and I think I am giving you counsel from God's Spirit when I say this.

Rights and Self-Limitation (8:1–11:1)

Food Sacrificed to Idols

8 Now regarding your question about food that has been offered to idols. Yes, we know that "we all have knowledge" about this issue. But while knowledge makes us feel important, it is [j]love that strengthens the church. 2Anyone who claims to know all the answers doesn't really know very much. 3But the person who loves God is the one whom God recognizes.

4So, what about eating meat that has been offered to idols? Well, we all know that an idol is not really a god and that there is only one God. 5There may be so-called gods both in heaven and on earth, and some people actually worship many gods and many lords. 6But we know that there is only one God, the Father, who created everything, and we live for him. And there is only one Lord, Jesus Christ, through whom God made everything and through whom we have been given life.

7However, not all believers know this. Some are accustomed to thinking of idols

7:29 Rom 13:11
7:31 1 Jn 2:17
7:34 Luke 2:36-37; 1 Tim 5:5; [i]*pneuma* (4151) ‣ Eph 4:4
7:38 Heb 13:4
7:39 Rom 7:2; 2 Cor 6:14
7:40 1 Cor 7:6, 25
8:1 Acts 15:20, 29; [j]*agapē* (0026) ‣ 1 Cor 13:1
8:2 1 Cor 3:18; 13:8-9; Gal 6:3
8:3 Gal 4:9
8:4 Deut 4:35, 39; 6:4; 1 Cor 10:19
8:6 John 1:3; Acts 17:28; 1 Cor 12:5; Eph 4:5-6; Col 1:16
8:7 Rom 14:14; 1 Cor 10:28
8:8 Rom 14:17
8:9 Rom 14:1, 13, 21; 2 Cor 6:3; Gal 5:13; [k]*proskomma* (4348) ‣ 1 Cor 8:13

7:29-31 Second (see note on 7:25-35), because the end is near, Christians ought not let marriage and the things of the world be their dominant concerns. Their primary concern should be Christ and eternity.

7:32-35 Third (see note on 7:25-35), because marriage brings ***earthly responsibilities*** and ***divided*** interests, those who choose to remain single can devote their lives more fully to serving Christ.

7:36-38 Paul recommends celibate life in preference to marriage, but he allows for marriage if a person's sexual desires prove too much of a temptation. Those in firm ***control*** of their sexual desires are encouraged to choose the celibate life.

7:39 A widow may marry another man, but ***only if he loves the Lord*** (literally *only in the Lord*). Paul strongly discouraged the marriage of Christians to unbelievers (cp. 2 Cor 6:14-16).

8:1–11:1 Paul now addresses the Corinthians' ***question about food that has been offered to idols:*** Throughout the Greco-Roman world, there were temples and shrines dedicated to pagan gods. It was common for worshipers of those gods to offer animal sacrifices, and the excess meat was then sold in the market by pagan priests. The question inevitably arose as to whether Christians were free to eat such meat. Is meat taken from an animal that has been sacrificed to a pagan god inherently defiled? Paul makes no mention here of the prohibition made by the Jewish Christian leaders in Acts 15:20, 29, but emphasizes that one's actions must be governed, above all, by loving consideration of others. After introducing the topic (ch 8), he provides several illustrations of the principle of giving up one's rights for the sake of others (ch 9), and then gives his advice on three specific situations in which believers faced this issue.

8:1 ***"We all have knowledge"*** was apparently a common saying of the Corinthian Christians. The *knowledge* in question is religious knowledge, paraded by certain Christians who might have felt their superior understanding made them unaccountable to the opinions of others.

8:2-3 It is those who truly love God—not just those who ***know all the answers***—who are acknowledged by God as his own (see 13:12; Gal 4:9).
• ***the person who loves God is the one whom God recognizes:*** Some manuscripts read *the person who loves has full knowledge.*

8:4-6 In reality, the ***idols*** to which such meat is sacrificed are not gods, for ***there is only one God*** (Deut 6:4; cp. Deut 4:35, 39; 10:19-20). He is the Creator of everything, including the meat in question. The only ultimate reality is ***God, the Father,*** and the ***one Lord, Jesus Christ, through whom God made everything*** (cp. John 1:3; Col 1:16; Heb 1:2).

8:11 Rom 14:15, 20
8:12 Matt 18:6
8:13 Rom 14:21
[a]*skandalizō* (4624) ‣Gal 5:11
9:1 Acts 9:3; 18:9
1 Cor 15:8
1 Tim 2:7
2 Tim 1:11
[b]*apostolos* (0652) ‣1 Cor 12:28
9:2 2 Cor 3:2-3
[c]*sphragis* (4973) ‣Eph 1:13
9:4 Luke 10:8
1 Cor 9:13-14
9:5 Matt 8:14; 12:46
Mark 6:2-3
Luke 6:14
9:6 2 Thes 3:8-9
9:7 Deut 20:6
Prov 27:18
1 Cor 3:6, 8
2 Tim 2:4
9:9 *Deut 25:4
1 Tim 5:18
9:10 2 Tim 2:6
9:11 Rom 15:27
9:12 2 Cor 6:3; 11:7-12

as being real, so when they eat food that has been offered to idols, they think of it as the worship of real gods, and their weak consciences are violated. 8It's true that we can't win God's approval by what we eat. We don't lose anything if we don't eat it, and we don't gain anything if we do.

9But you must be careful so that your freedom does not cause others with a weaker conscience to [k]stumble. 10For if others see you—with your "superior knowledge"—eating in the temple of an idol, won't they be encouraged to violate their conscience by eating food that has been offered to an idol? 11So because of your superior knowledge, a weak believer for whom Christ died will be destroyed. 12And when you sin against other believers by encouraging them to do something they believe is wrong, you are sinning against Christ. 13So if what I eat [a]causes another believer to sin, I will never eat meat again as long as I live—for I don't want to cause another believer to [a]stumble.

Paul Gives Up His Rights

9 Am I not as free as anyone else? Am I not an [b]apostle? Haven't I seen Jesus our Lord with my own eyes? Isn't it because of my work that you belong to the Lord? 2Even if others think I am not an apostle, I certainly am to you. You yourselves are [c]proof that I am the Lord's apostle.

3This is my answer to those who question my authority. 4Don't we have the right to live in your homes and share your meals? 5Don't we have the right to bring a Christian wife with us as the other apostles and the Lord's brothers do, and as Peter does? 6Or is it only Barnabas and I who have to work to support ourselves?

7What soldier has to pay his own expenses? What farmer plants a vineyard and doesn't have the right to eat some of its fruit? What shepherd cares for a flock of sheep and isn't allowed to drink some of the milk? 8Am I expressing merely a human opinion, or does the law say the same thing? 9For the law of Moses says, "You must not muzzle an ox to keep it from eating as it treads out the grain." Was God thinking only about oxen when he said this? 10Wasn't he actually speaking to us? Yes, it was written for us, so that the one who plows and the one who threshes the grain might both expect a share of the harvest.

11Since we have planted spiritual seed among you, aren't we entitled to a harvest of physical food and drink? 12If you support others who preach to you, shouldn't we have an even greater right to be supported?

8:7 Many of the Corinthian believers, having grown up in the pagan world, viewed eating such meat as an expression of devotion to the god to whom the meat had been sacrificed. For such Christians, to eat meat presented to an idol would violate their ***weak consciences*** (see 8:10-12; 10:28-29; Rom 14:13-23).

8:8 The Corinthians' relationship with the living God was not affected by eating or not eating, whatever the source of the food (cp. Rom 14:17).

8:9-10 Believers must ***be careful*** that what they do (such as eating sacrificial meat) ***does not cause others . . . to stumble*** (cp. Rom 14:13, 20-21; Gal 5:13).

8:11 For believers to insist on eating food offered to idols because their ***superior knowledge*** assured them that they are free to eat such food could destroy less mature Christians (who understood eating this meat as an expression of worship of pagan gods). • ***believer:*** Literally *brother;* also in 8:13. See note on 1:10. • ***for whom Christ died:*** Cp. Rom 14:15.

8:12 To make immature ***believers*** (literally *brothers;* see note on 1:10) sin by violating their conscience is the same as ***sinning against Christ,*** who has claimed them for himself (cp. Matt 25:40, 45).

8:13 Personal rights must be subordinated to the larger commitment not ***to cause another believer to stumble.***

9:1-27 Continuing the argument begun in 8:1 (see note on 8:1–11:1), Paul cites personal examples of his giving up his own rights for the sake of other people.

9:1-2 These four rhetorical questions each expect a positive answer. The first, following his discussion in ch 8, is an assertion of Paul's freedom from Jewish ritual obligations—though, as he later emphasizes (see 9:19-23), he freely accommodates himself to the practices of Jews in his desire to win them to Christ. The other three rhetorical questions are assertions of Paul's apostolic authority, which was apparently being questioned by some in Corinth. • For those who might be skeptical, the reality of Paul's apostolic calling was verified by his firsthand encounter with ***Jesus our Lord*** on the road to Damascus (see 15:8; Acts 9:3-6, 17). Also, the Corinthians themselves, who came to faith through Paul's evangelism (see Acts 18:1-11), were ***proof*** (literally *the seal*) of his status as an ***apostle.***

9:3 ***my answer*** (literally *my defense*): This is a legal term for the argument made in response to accusations. • ***those who question my authority:*** Literally *those who examine me.* See 2 Cor 11–12 for another response to their challenge.

9:4 As an apostle, Paul had ***the right*** to expect food and housing from those to whom he ministered (cp. 9:14; Luke 10:7-8). Nevertheless, to avoid any possible criticism, he did not take advantage of this privilege (see 9:6, 12, 14-15, 18; 2 Cor 11:7-9; 12:13-14).

9:5 For the sake of Christ and the Good News, Paul had given up the right to have ***a Christian wife.*** • ***the Lord's brothers:*** See Mark 6:3 for their names. • ***Peter*** (Greek *Cephas*): Mark 1:30 also speaks of Peter as married.

9:7-10 These examples support Paul's point that he and other Christian workers had a right to be supported by those they served.

9:9 This quotation is from Deut 25:4.

9:12 Compared with other Christian workers supported by the Corinthians, Paul claimed ***an even greater right to be supported*** by them, because he was the one who first brought the Good News to them. But to avoid criticism, he had ***never used this right*** (see 9:6, 14-15, 18; cp. Acts 18:3; 2 Cor 11:7-9; 12:13-14).

But we have never used this right. We would
rather put up with anything than be an obstacle to the Good News about Christ.
13Don't you realize that those who work
in the temple get their meals from the offerings brought to the temple? And those who
serve at the altar get a share of the sacrificial offerings. 14In the same way, the Lord
ordered that those who preach the Good
News should be supported by those who
benefit from it. 15Yet I have never used any
of these rights. And I am not writing this to
suggest that I want to start now. In fact, I
would rather die than lose my right to boast
about preaching without charge. 16Yet
preaching the Good News is not something
I can boast about. I am compelled by God to
do it. How terrible for me if I didn't preach
the Good News!
17If I were doing this on my own initiative, I would deserve payment. But I have
no choice, for God has given me this sacred
[d]trust. 18What then is my pay? It is the opportunity to preach the Good News without
charging anyone. That's why I never demand
my rights when I preach the Good News.
19Even though I am a free man with no
master, I have become a slave to all people
to bring many to Christ. 20When I was with
the Jews, I lived like a Jew to bring the Jews
to Christ. When I was with those who follow the Jewish law, I too lived under that law.
Even though I am not subject to the law, I
did this so I could bring to Christ those who
are under the law. 21When I am with the
Gentiles who do not follow the Jewish law,
I too live apart from that law so I can bring
them to Christ. But I do not ignore the law of
God; I obey the law of Christ.
22When I am with those who are weak, I
share their weakness, for I want to bring the
weak to Christ. Yes, I try to find common
ground with everyone, doing everything I
can to save some. 23I do everything to spread
the Good News and share in its blessings.
24Don't you realize that in a race everyone
runs, but only one person gets the prize? So
run to win! 25All athletes are disciplined in
their training. They do it to win a prize that
will fade away, but we do it for an eternal
prize. 26So I run with purpose in every step.
I am not just shadowboxing. 27I discipline
my body like an athlete, training it to do
what it should. Otherwise, I fear that after
preaching to others I myself might be disqualified.

Lessons from Israel's Idolatry

10 I don't want you to forget, dear brothers and sisters, about our ancestors
in the wilderness long ago. All of them
were guided by a cloud that moved ahead
of them, and all of them walked through
the sea on dry ground. 2In the cloud and
in the sea, all of them were baptized as followers of Moses. 3All of them ate the same
spiritual food, 4and all of them drank the
same spiritual water. For they drank from

9:13 Num 18:8, 31
9:14 Matt 10:10; Gal 6:6; 1 Tim 5:17-18
9:15 Acts 18:3; 2 Cor 11:9-10
9:16 Acts 9:15; Rom 1:14
9:17 [d]*oikonomia* (3622) ‣Gal 4:2
9:19 Gal 5:13
9:20 Acts 16:3; 21:20-26
9:24 Heb 12:1
9:25 Jas 1:12; Rev 2:10; 3:11
9:27 2 Cor 13:5
10:1 Exod 13:21-22
10:2 Rom 6:3
10:3 Exod 16:4, 35; Deut 8:3; Ps 78:24-29; John 6:31-58
10:4 Exod 17:6; Num 20:11; Ps 78:15; John 6:53-58; 7:37; Rev 22:17; [e]*petra* (4073) ‣Rev 6:15
10:5 Num 14:23, 29-30; Ps 78:31; Heb 3:17; Jude 1:5

9:13 Paul might be referring to Levites and priests at God's ***temple*** in Jerusalem (see Deut 18:1-4; cp. Lev 6:16-17, 26; Num 18:8-32), but the pagan priests in temples around Corinth would have done similarly.

9:14 ***the Lord ordered:*** See Matt 10:10; Luke 10:7; see also Gal 6:6; 1 Tim 5:17-18.

9:15 Paul had never pressed his ***rights***, nor was he now seeking to do so. Rather, he was illustrating the importance of giving up one's rights for the sake of others (cp. 8:13).

9:16 ***compelled by God to do it:*** Acts 22:14-15; 26:16-18.

9:18 Paul's satisfaction came from preaching the Good News ***without charging anyone***. This is another example of the way Christians must be willing to give up their rights out of consideration for others (cp. 8:13).

9:19-23 Paul places himself in the position of a ***slave*** in the household. He shows how far he was willing to go in adjusting his lifestyle and behavior to that of the people to whom he was preaching in order to win them ***to Christ***.

9:21 ***the Gentiles who do not follow the Jewish law:*** Literally *those without the law*.

9:24-27 To illustrate how seriously the Corinthians must take the discipline of their salvation, Paul alludes to the familiar Isthmian games, an athletic competition held every two years in Corinth. • ***All athletes are disciplined:*** Strict self-discipline is required for athletes competing for a prize. In Paul's day, athletes endured months of rigorous training before competing. In the same way, strict self-discipline (cp. Gal 5:22-23) is required if a person is to gain the ***eternal prize*** of salvation. Christians must submit to the daily discipline of obeying Christ. • ***a prize that will fade away:*** Athletic prizes were often wreaths made out of laurel leaves (cp. 2 Tim 4:8; Jas 1:12; 1 Pet 5:4; Rev 2:10).

9:26 ***I am not just shadowboxing:*** Christians must engage in the real contest of obedience to Christ rather than merely going through the motions.

9:27 ***I fear that . . . I myself might be disqualified:*** Those who are disqualified from a sporting event have no hope of winning the prize. To avoid losing the eternal prize, Paul disciplined himself severely, like an athlete, so that he would not be led away from Christ into a life of sin (see 9:25; Heb 12:1).

10:1-22 After illustrating from his own life the key principle of giving up one's rights for the sake of others (ch 9), Paul turns back to the specific question of eating meat sacrificed to idols (8:1-13). He warns believers of God's wrath on those who sin, especially on those who engage in idolatry.

10:1-11 Even though the Israelites were God's people and experienced his salvation and provision (see Exod 13:21-22; 14:21-29), they still came under his judgment because of their disobedience.

10:1 ***dear brothers and sisters:*** Literally *brothers*. See note on 1:10.

10:2 ***all of them were baptized:*** Paul draws a parallel with the baptized Corinthians.

10:3-4 ***Spiritual food . . . spiritual water:*** God graciously and supernaturally provided food and water in the wilderness, especially for the people

10:6
Num 11:4, 34
[f]*tupos* (5179)
‣Phil 3:17

10:7
*Exod 32:6
[g]*eidōlolatrēs* (1496)
‣1 Cor 10:14

10:8
Num 25:1-9

10:9
Num 21:5-6

10:12
Matt 26:33-35, 69-75
Rom 11:20

10:13
2 Pet 2:9
[h]*peirasmos* (3986)
‣Gal 6:1

10:14
Mark 6:24
1 Jn 5:21
[i]*eidōlolatria* (1495)
‣Gal 5:20

10:16
Matt 26:26-28
[j]*koinōnia* (2842)
‣2 Cor 6:14

10:20
Deut 32:17
[k]*daimonion* (1140)
‣1 Tim 4:1

the spiritual [e]rock that traveled with them,
and that [e]rock was Christ. 5Yet God was not
pleased with most of them, and their bodies
were scattered in the wilderness.
6These things happened as a [f]warning to
us, so that we would not crave evil things as
they did, 7or [g]worship idols as some of them
did. As the Scriptures say, "The people celebrated with feasting and drinking, and they
indulged in pagan revelry." 8And we must
not engage in sexual immorality as some of
them did, causing 23,000 of them to die in
one day.
9Nor should we put Christ to the test, as
some of them did and then died from snake-
bites. 10And don't grumble as some of them
did, and then were destroyed by the angel of
death. 11These things happened to them as
examples for us. They were written down to
warn us who live at the end of the age.
12If you think you are standing strong,
be careful not to fall. 13The [h]temptations in
your life are no different from what others
experience. And God is faithful. He will not
allow the temptation to be more than you
can stand. When you are [h]tempted, he will
show you a way out so that you can endure.
14So, my dear friends, flee from the [i]wor-
ship of idols. 15You are reasonable people.
Decide for yourselves if what I am saying is
true. 16When we bless the cup at the Lord's Table, aren't we [j]sharing in the blood of Christ?
And when we break the bread, aren't we [j]shar-
ing in the body of Christ? 17And though we
are many, we all eat from one loaf of bread,
showing that we are one body. 18Think about
the people of Israel. Weren't they united by
eating the sacrifices at the altar?
19What am I trying to say? Am I saying
that food offered to idols has some significance, or that idols are real gods? 20No, not
at all. I am saying that these sacrifices are
offered to [k]demons, not to God. And I don't
want you to participate with [k]demons. 21You
cannot drink from the cup of the Lord and
from the cup of demons, too. You cannot

Giving Up Rights (9:1-23)

1 Cor 8:1-13; 10:23-24, 31-33; 13:4-7
Matt 5:38-48; 16:24-27; 19:16-22; 22:37-39
Rom 5:6-8; 13:8-10; 14:15-22; 15:1-5
Gal 5:6
Phil 2:3-4
2 Tim 2:9-13
Heb 11:24-26
1 Jn 4:9-12

Paul nowhere tells believers that they should defend their rights. On the contrary, he emphasizes that believers must always be willing to give up their rights for the sake of others. Believers are free from many of the rules that others feel bound by, but they must always be ready to give up their freedoms if their actions would cause someone else to sin (8:1-13; 10:23-33; Rom 14:15-22). Defending one's own personal rights is of little value to Paul.

Paul, like Jesus, sees loving others as one of the most important principles in life (13:1-13; Matt 5:43-44; 22:37-39; Rom 13:8-10; Gal 5:6). Real Christian love is always sacrificial (13:4-7), like Christ's own love. Believers ought never to focus on what is best for themselves, but on what is best for others (10:32-33). The sacrificial death of Christ for sinners (Rom 5:6-8) is the model that reveals the nature of true love (Rom 15:1-5; 1 Jn 4:9-12). The whole of a believer's life is to be an expression of Christ's sacrificial love. This will never be easy, for it means people must consider themselves dead to their own desires.

of Israel (see Exod 16:4-35; 17:1-7; Num 20:2-17). The Corinthians' situation was analogous. • ***The spiritual rock that traveled with them*** alludes to the rock that Moses struck to get water (Exod 17:1-7; Num 20:2-17). Early Jewish tradition understood both occurrences to involve the same rock that was traveling with them. • ***that rock was Christ:*** Paul's interpretation of Israel's experience provides a parallel between God's provision in the wilderness and the Lord's Supper (10:14-18; cp. John 4:14; 7:37-39; Rev 22:17). Both the Israelites and Christians share in the spiritual provisions of Christ; and just as the Israelites were therefore judged for their sins, so Christians will be judged if they sin (10:5-22).

10:6 ***evil things:*** see Num 11:4-6, 34.

10:7 ***worship idols:*** See Exod 32:6. • ***Feasting and drinking*** refers to celebrations in honor of pagan gods; ***pagan revelry*** suggests wild partying with drinking and sex.

10:8 See Num 25:1-9.

10:9 ***Nor . . . put Christ to the test:*** See Deut 6:16; Ps 78:18-20; Matt 4:7. • ***Christ:*** Some manuscripts read *the Lord,* which probably represents a scribe's attempt to harmonize with the OT context.

10:10 See Num 16:13-14, 41-49.

10:12-13 Paul gives the Corinthians a final warning against falling into sin (cp. Rom 11:20-22) and reminds them that ***God is faithful*** (see 1:9; cp. Deut 7:9; 1 Pet 4:19). God will not allow them to be ***tempted*** (or *tested;* cp. Jas 1:2-4) beyond their ability to endure, but will always provide ***a way out.***

10:14-22 Paul warns his readers against anything that might be interpreted as idolatry (cp. 1 Jn 5:21), which includes eating ***food*** in honor of a pagan god.

10:16-18 Paul affirms the spiritual meaning of sacred meals. In the Lord's Supper, believers share in ***the blood*** and ***body of Christ*** (see also 11:17-34; Matt 26:26-28; Mark 14:22-24; Luke 22:19-20). Sharing ***one loaf*** unites believers as ***one body*** in Christ, just as the pagans' religious meals unite them with the gods they worship (see 10:19-21).

10:19-20 ***Idols*** have no reality or life (see 8:4-6), and ***sacrifices*** made to them accomplish nothing. The sacrifices pagans make to idols are actually unknowingly made to ***demons*** (see Deut 32:16-17; Ps 106:37; Rev 9:20). Those who share in their religious meals are thereby uniting themselves with ***demons.***

10:21 Believers should avoid participating in religious meals eaten in a pagan temple (see 8:10), because those united to ***the Lord*** (Christ) cannot simultaneously be united to ***demons*** (see 2 Cor 6:14-16).

eat at the Lord's Table and at the table of demons, too. 22What? Do we dare to rouse the
Lord's jealousy? Do you think we are stronger than he is?

Specific Advice on Eating Sacrificial Food

23You say, "I am allowed to do anything"—
but not everything is good for you. You say,
"I am allowed to do anything"—but not everything is beneficial. 24Don't be concerned for
your own good but for the good of others.
25So you may eat any meat that is sold in
the marketplace without raising questions
of conscience. 26For "the earth is the LORD's,
and everything in it."
27If someone who isn't a believer asks
you home for dinner, accept the invitation if
you want to. Eat whatever is offered to you
without raising questions of conscience.
28(But suppose someone tells you, "This
meat was offered to an idol." Don't eat it, out
of consideration for the conscience of the
one who told you. 29It might not be a matter
of conscience for you, but it is for the other
person.) For why should my [a]freedom be
limited by what someone else thinks? 30If
I can thank God for the food and enjoy it,
why should I be condemned for eating it?
31So whether you eat or drink, or whatever you do, do it all for the glory of God.
32Don't give offense to Jews or Gentiles or
the [b]church of God. 33I, too, try to please
everyone in everything I do. I don't just do
what is best for me; I do what is best for others so that many may be saved. 11:1And you
should imitate me, just as I imitate Christ.

Instructions for Public Worship (11:2-34)

Appropriate Dress for Public Worship

11 2I am so glad that you always keep
me in your thoughts, and that you are
following the teachings I passed on to you.
3But there is one thing I want you to know:
The head of every man is Christ, the head
of woman is man, and the head of Christ is
God. 4A man dishonors his head if he covers his head while praying or prophesying.
5But a woman dishonors her head if she
prays or prophesies without a covering on
her head, for this is the same as shaving
her head. 6Yes, if she refuses to wear a head
covering, she should cut off all her hair! But

10:21 2 Cor 6:15-16
10:22 Deut 32:16, 21
10:24 Rom 15:1-2
10:25 Acts 10:15
10:26 *Ps 24:1
10:27 Luke 10:8
10:28 Rom 14:16
10:29 [a]*eleutheria* (1657) ‣2 Cor 3:17
10:30 1 Tim 4:4
10:31 Col 3:17
10:32 Matt 5:29; Acts 24:16; Rom 14:13; [b]*ekklēsia* (1577) ‣1 Cor 12:28
11:2 2 Thes 2:15; 3:6
11:3 Gen 3:16; Eph 5:23
11:5 Acts 21:9

10:22 To ignore Paul's advice on this matter is to rouse ***the Lord's jealousy*** and judgment, just as Israel did (see 10:6-11; Exod 20:5; Deut 32:21).

10:23–11:1 Paul closes the discussion begun in 8:1 with advice about when Christians may eat meat sacrificed to an idol, and when they should not (see note on 8:1–11:1). His advice reflects the principle of giving up one's rights out of love (see also 8:13–9:23).

10:23-24 ***You say:*** The NLT supplies these words—Paul is probably quoting a popular saying among the Corinthians and clarifying it. • ***"I am allowed to do anything"*** (literally *All things are lawful*): Paul qualifies the assertion of a Christian's freedom by emphasizing the importance of doing what is most beneficial for ***others*** (see 6:12; 10:32-33; Rom 14:13-15, 19-21; 15:1-2; cp. Phil 2:3-4).

10:26 This quotation is from Ps 24:1.

10:27-29a When Christians are invited for a meal with an unbeliever, the Christians are free to eat what is set before them unless warned that the meat has been ***offered to an idol.*** In that case, the Christian should refrain from eating it ***out of consideration for the conscience*** of the other person, who might misinterpret it or be hurt by believing that such eating honors the god to whom the meat has been sacrificed (see 8:7, 9-10; cp. Rom 14:13-15, 20-23).

10:29b-30 These two questions are difficult to understand in light of 10:28-29a. By placing 10:28-29a in parentheses, the NLT has interpreted these questions as expressing Paul's own convictions, following on from 10:27.

10:31-33 Paul concludes his discussion by summarizing the two principles that are to guide Christian behavior in issues like this: (1) Believers are to do everything ***for the glory of God*** (see Col 3:17; 1 Pet 4:11); (2) believers are not to ***give offense*** and should avoid doing anything that would harm another person's Christian faith (cp. 8:9, 13; 1 Jn 2:10). Christians' behavior is to be guided by what is best for others rather than by personal privilege (cp. Rom 14:13-15, 19-21; 15:1-2). These two basic principles lie at the heart of Paul's advice on practical Christian living in this letter.

10:32 ***Gentiles:*** Literally *Greeks.*

11:1 ***imitate me:*** Cp. 4:16; Phil 3:17.

11:2 ***the teachings I passed on to you:*** This language generally refers to an authoritative tradition of Christian teaching being passed down orally (see also 11:23; 15:1-3; 2 Thes 2:15).

11:3-16 Paul now addresses a woman's use of a head covering. Paul argues that women publicly praying or prophesying should wear a veil as an element of dressing modestly and appropriately in public worship (cp. 1 Tim 2:9; 1 Pet 3:3). Apparently some in Corinth were rejecting head coverings based on freedom in Christ. Paul's argument in favor of the custom is based on traditional social conventions, the Genesis account of Creation, and the watchful eye of ***angels.***

11:3 ***The head of every man is Christ, the head of woman is man, and the head of Christ is God:*** Or *The source of every man is Christ, the source of woman is man, and the source of Christ is God.* Or *Every man is responsible to Christ, a woman is responsible to her husband, and Christ is responsible to God.* The NLT gives the literal reading *head of,* which is a metaphor for either *source* or *authority.* The immediate context and Paul's overall teaching both favor understanding *head* in this context as meaning *authority* (see Gen 3:16; Eph 5:21-23; Col 3:18; 1 Pet 3:1).

11:4-6 In this passage, *head* is used in both a literal and a figurative sense. ***A man*** who ***covers his*** (physical) ***head*** when he prays ***dishonors his*** (spiritual) ***head,*** Christ. ***A woman*** who ***prays or prophesies without a covering on her*** (physical) ***head*** thereby ***dishonors her*** (spiritual) ***head,*** her husband. • The spiritual gift of ***prophesying*** is the God-given ability to speak a specific word from God, not merely to predict the future (cp. 12:10; 14:1-5; 1 Thes 5:20). • ***if she prays or prophesies:*** Women were allowed to engage in public praying and prophesying in the church (cp. Acts 21:9).

11:4 ***dishonors his head:*** Or *dishonors Christ.*

11:5 ***dishonors her head:*** Or *dishonors her husband.*

11:6 ***should wear a covering:*** Or *should have long hair,* a less likely interpretation.

11:7
Gen 1:26; 5:1; 9:6
Jas 3:9
[c]*doxa* (1391)
‣2 Cor 3:7

11:8
Gen 2:21-23
1 Tim 2:13

11:9
Gen 2:18

11:10
[d]*angelos* (0032)
‣Col 2:18

11:12
Rom 11:36

11:16
1 Cor 7:17; 10:32

11:18
1 Cor 1:10-12; 3:3

11:19
1 Jn 2:19

11:21
2 Pet 2:13
Jude 1:12

11:22
1 Cor 10:32
Jas 2:6

11:23-25
*Matt 26:26-28
*Mark 14:22-24
*Luke 22:17-20

11:25
1 Cor 10:16
2 Cor 3:6
[e]*diathēkē* (1242)
‣2 Cor 3:6

since it is shameful for a woman to have her hair cut or her head shaved, she should wear a covering.

7 A man should not wear anything on his head when worshiping, for man is made in God's image and reflects God's [c]glory. And woman reflects man's [c]glory. 8 For the first man didn't come from woman, but the first woman came from man. 9 And man was not made for woman, but woman was made for man. 10 For this reason, and because the [d]angels are watching, a woman should wear a covering on her head to show she is under authority.

11 But among the Lord's people, women are not independent of men, and men are not independent of women. 12 For although the first woman came from man, every other man was born from a woman, and everything comes from God.

13 Judge for yourselves. Is it right for a woman to pray to God in public without covering her head? 14 Isn't it obvious that it's disgraceful for a man to have long hair? 15 And isn't long hair a woman's pride and joy? For it has been given to her as a covering. 16 But if anyone wants to argue about this, I simply say that we have no other custom than this, and neither do God's other churches.

Order at the Lord's Supper

17 But in the following instructions, I cannot praise you. For it sounds as if more harm than good is done when you meet together. 18 First, I hear that there are divisions among you when you meet as a church, and to some extent I believe it. 19 But, of course, there must be divisions among you so that you who have God's approval will be recognized!

20 When you meet together, you are not really interested in the Lord's Supper. 21 For some of you hurry to eat your own meal without sharing with others. As a result, some go hungry while others get drunk. 22 What? Don't you have your own homes for eating and drinking? Or do you really want to disgrace God's church and shame the poor? What am I supposed to say? Do you want me to praise you? Well, I certainly will not praise you for this!

23 For I pass on to you what I received from the Lord himself. On the night when he was betrayed, the Lord Jesus took some bread 24 and gave thanks to God for it. Then he broke it in pieces and said, "This is my body, which is given for you. Do this to remember me." 25 In the same way, he took the cup of wine after supper, saying, "This cup is the new covenant between God and his people—an [e]agreement confirmed with my

11:7 ***man is made in God's image:*** See Gen 1:26-27.

11:10 ***because the angels are watching:*** Angels are guardians of the created order, appointed to ensure that everything is done according to God's plan (see Gen 19:1-21; 22:11-12; Exod 23:20; Num 22:22-23; Ps 34:7; 91:11; 103:20-21; Heb 1:7, 14). Believers are to do what is appropriate in the sight of fellow humans and God's observing angels (cp. 1 Tim 5:21). • ***should wear a covering on her head to show she is under authority:*** Or *should have authority over her own head;* literally *should have authority on* [or *over*] *her head.*

11:11-12 These verses qualify the preceding verses. Believers recognize that God has made men and women mutually dependent on one another. • ***Everything comes from God*** (cp. 8:6): Both men and women must ultimately submit to God, the head of all.

11:13 ***Is it right?*** This rhetorical question expects the answer "no."

11:14 ***Isn't it obvious?*** (literally *Doesn't nature itself teach you?*): In Paul's culture, men would never wear long hair.

11:15 Paul argues that social conventions regarding hair length express fundamental differences between men and women. • ***it has been given to her as a covering:*** Paul suggests that women's long hair, covering their head, shows that God intends women to have some type of "covering."

11:16 ***if anyone wants to argue about this:*** Some in the cosmopolitan Corinthian church did not agree with Paul. • Paul's final argument is that the use of a head covering was an established custom of the church. Most contemporary interpreters take this verse to mean that the custom was culturally based.

11:17-34 Paul addresses problems in the way the Corinthians were relating to each other and to the Lord while taking the Lord's Supper.

11:17 ***when you meet together:*** Early Christians met together in someone's home at least once a week, usually on the Lord's Day (see 16:2).

11:18 The ***divisions*** may be those spoken of in 1:10-12 (cp. Titus 3:10), or (more likely) the result of social discrimination when they shared meals (see 11:21-22, 33; Acts 6:1).

11:19 As translated, this ironic expression rebukes the Corinthian Christians' claims to superiority based on distinctions among them. Alternatively, Paul might be saying that though their divisiveness is clearly wrong, it will have the positive result of making clear who among them is truly faithful.

11:20-22 Some people were more concerned about eating their own supper than with ***the Lord's Supper.***

11:23 ***I pass on to you what I received from the Lord himself:*** This is one of the few explicit references in Paul's letters to traditions handed down from Christ (see also 7:10; 9:14; cp. 1 Thes 4:15-17). • ***On the night when he was betrayed:*** See Mark 14:43-46.

11:24 Jews and early Christians traditionally ***gave thanks*** to God for their food before eating (see note on Mark 14:22-25). • ***This is my body:*** Cp. John 6:32-35, 48-58. • ***which is given for you:*** Literally *which is for you;* other manuscripts read *which is broken for you.*

11:25 ***After supper*** might suggest that the main meal separated the breaking of the bread from the drinking of the cup (see Luke 22:20). • ***The new covenant*** is God's promise to forgive sins because of the sacrificial death of Jesus (cp. Jer 31:31-34; 32:40; Luke 22:20; Heb 7:22; 8:8-10; 9:15; 10:12-18; 12:24; 13:20). The blood of a sacrifice ***confirmed*** an ***agreement*** or covenant (see Exod 24:8; Zech 9:11; Heb 9:12; 13:20; cp. Rom 3:25; 5:9).

blood. Do this to remember me as often as
you drink it." 26For every time you eat this
bread and drink this cup, you are announcing the Lord's death until he comes again.
27So anyone who eats this bread or drinks
this cup of the Lord unworthily is guilty of
sinning against the body and blood of the
Lord. 28That is why you should examine
yourself before eating the bread and drinking the cup. 29For if you eat the bread or
drink the cup without honoring the body
of Christ, you are eating and drinking God's
judgment upon yourself. 30That is why
many of you are weak and sick and some
have even died.
31But if we would examine ourselves, we
would not be judged by God in this way.
32Yet when we are judged by the Lord, we
are being [f]disciplined so that we will not be
condemned along with the world.
33So, my dear brothers and sisters, when
you gather for the Lord's Supper, wait for
each other. 34If you are really hungry, eat
at home so you won't bring judgment upon
yourselves when you meet together. I'll give
you instructions about the other matters after I arrive.

Spiritual Gifts (12:1–14:40)

Different Spiritual Gifts

12 Now, dear brothers and sisters, regarding your question about the
special abilities the Spirit gives us. I don't
want you to misunderstand this. 2You know
that when you were still pagans, you were
led astray and swept along in worshiping
speechless idols. 3So I want you to know
that no one speaking by the Spirit of God
will curse Jesus, and no one can say Jesus is
Lord, except by the Holy Spirit.
4There are different kinds of spiritual
[g]gifts, but the same Spirit is the source
of them all. 5There are different kinds of
service, but we serve the same Lord. 6God
works in different ways, but it is the same
God who does the work in all of us.
7A spiritual gift is given to each of us so
we can help each other. 8To one person the
Spirit gives the ability to give wise advice; to
another the same Spirit gives a message of
special knowledge. 9The same Spirit gives
great faith to another, and to someone else
the one Spirit gives the gift of healing. 10He
gives one person the power to perform miracles, and another the ability to prophesy.

11:26 Luke 22:19
11:27 Heb 10:29
11:28 2 Cor 13:5
11:31 1 Jn 1:9
11:32 Ps 94:12; Heb 12:5-6
[f]*paideuō* (3811) ›Eph 6:4
11:34 1 Cor 4:19
12:1 1 Cor 14:1
12:2 Hab 2:18-19; 1 Thes 1:9
12:3 John 13:13; 1 Jn 4:2-3
12:4 Rom 12:6; Eph 4:4; Heb 2:4
[g]*charisma* (5486) ›1 Cor 12:28
12:6 Eph 4:6
12:7 1 Cor 14:26; Eph 4:12
12:8 1 Cor 2:6
12:9 Matt 17:19-20

11:26 In taking the Lord's Supper, Christians proclaim the saving significance of ***the Lord's death*** to those around them ***until he comes again*** (see 1:7-8; cp. 1 Thes 1:9-10; 3:12; 4:13-18; 5:23).

11:27 To take the Lord's Supper without recognizing its significance or with unconfessed sin in one's life is to take it ***unworthily*** (see 11:28-31). It is equivalent to ***sinning against the body and blood*** of the Lord himself; it treats his sacrificial death as trivial (cp. Heb 10:29). • ***is guilty of sinning against:*** Or *is responsible for.*

11:28 Before taking the Lord's Supper, Christians should confess their sins and consider what ***the bread*** and ***the cup*** signify (11:26).

11:29-30 In light of 11:27, ***the body of Christ*** (literally *the body;* other manuscripts read *the Lord's body*) is probably to be understood here as a reference to the death of Christ, not to the church, though some interpret it that way. • Those who ***eat the bread or drink the cup*** unworthily thereby invoke ***God's judgment*** upon themselves. Such judgment may be expressed in infirmities, sickness, and even death (cp. Acts 5:5, 10).

11:31 Self-judgment (which implies confession of sin and repentance) averts God's judgment.

11:32 When God's people are ***judged by the Lord*** and ***disciplined*** (cp. Deut 8:5; Heb 12:5-11), it is for their ultimate good, so that they ***will not be condemned with the world*** (see Eph 2:1-3).

11:33 ***dear brothers and sisters:*** Literally *brothers.* See note on 1:10.

11:34 ***after I arrive:*** Paul was planning to visit soon (4:19; 16:5-7).

12:1–14:40 The church at Corinth had placed too much emphasis on the gift of tongues (see 14:1-25, 27; cp. the lists in 12:8-10, 28, where Paul places tongues last), so Paul gives corrective advice regarding the value and use of spiritual gifts.

12:1-3 Paul introduces the topic, emphasizing the active presence of the ***Holy Spirit*** in believers.

12:1 ***dear brothers and sisters:*** Literally *brothers.* See note on 1:10.

12:2 ***pagans:*** Gentile unbelievers.

12:3 Paul gives two criteria for discerning the presence of the Spirit in worship. (1) Those who ***curse Jesus*** thereby express their rejection of Jesus and his message and thus cannot be ***speaking by the Spirit of God.*** (2) The presence of ***the Holy Spirit*** in believers' lives is shown by their sincere confession that ***Jesus is Lord.*** This is perhaps the earliest Christian creed (cp. Rom 10:9, 13; 2 Cor 4:5; Phil 2:11; 1 Jn 4:2-3).

12:4-11 Though believers are united in the Lord and his Spirit, God gives ***different kinds of spiritual gifts*** to different people so that they can fulfill ***different kinds of service*** to ***the same Lord*** (see also 7:7; 12:7-11, 28-31; Rom 12:6-8; Eph 4:11).

12:6 All the ***work*** believers do for God is in fact God working through them (see 15:10; 2 Cor 4:7; Gal 2:8; Phil 2:13; cp. Gal 2:20).

12:7 Spiritual gifts are not given for the individual recipients' benefit but to ***help each other*** (cp. 1 Pet 4:10-11).

12:8-10 This list of nine spiritual gifts is a representative rather than complete list (cp. 12:28-30; Rom 12:6-8; Eph 4:11).

12:8 God's ***Spirit*** gives supernatural wisdom or knowledge to some believers. • ***gives the ability to give wise advice:*** Or *gives a word of wisdom;* see 2:6-16. • ***gives a message of special knowledge:*** Or *gives a word of knowledge*; cp. 1:5; 8:1; 13:2, 8.

12:9 The spiritual gift of ***great faith*** is not the faith required for salvation but an unusual ability to trust God for special needs (see 13:2; Matt 17:19-20; cp. Acts 6:5; 11:24).

12:10 ***The ability to prophesy*** does not refer primarily to predicting the future, but to speaking a special message directly from God (see 11:4-5; 13:2, 8; 14:1-25, 29-33; 1 Thes 5:20; cp. Acts 13:1-2; 21:4, 10-11). • ***The ability to discern whether a message is from the Spirit of God or from another spirit*** is a necessary gift for any Christian community that is open to hearing a word directly from God (see 14:29; 1 Thes

12:10
Acts 2:4
Rom 12:6
1 Cor 14:26-32
Gal 3:5
1 Jn 4:1
[h]*glōssa* (1100)
‣1 Cor 12:30

12:11
Rom 12:6-8
Eph 4:5-7

12:12
Rom 12:4-5
1 Cor 10:17; 12:27

12:13
John 7:37-39
Gal 3:28
Eph 2:18
Col 3:11
[i]*baptizō* (0907)
‣1 Cor 15:29

12:18
1 Cor 12:28

He gives someone else the ability to discern
whether a message is from the Spirit of God
or from another spirit. Still another person
is given the ability to speak in unknown [h]lan-
guages, while another is given the ability to
interpret what is being [h]said. 11 It is the one
and only Spirit who distributes all these
gifts. He alone decides which gift each person should have.

The Church as One Body with Many Parts

12 The human body has many parts, but the
many parts make up one whole body. So
it is with the body of Christ. 13 Some of us
are Jews, some are Gentiles, some are slaves,
and some are free. But we have all been [i]bap-
tized into one body by one Spirit, and we all
share the same Spirit.
14 Yes, the body has many different parts,
not just one part. 15 If the foot says, "I am not
a part of the body because I am not a hand,"
that does not make it any less a part of the
body. 16 And if the ear says, "I am not part
of the body because I am not an eye," would
that make it any less a part of the body?
17 If the whole body were an eye, how would
you hear? Or if your whole body were an ear,
how would you smell anything?
18 But our bodies have many parts, and
God has put each part just where he wants
it. 19 How strange a body would be if it had
only one part! 20 Yes, there are many parts,
but only one body. 21 The eye can never say
to the hand, "I don't need you." The head
can't say to the feet, "I don't need you."
22 In fact, some parts of the body that
seem weakest and least important are actually the most necessary. 23 And the parts we
regard as less honorable are those we clothe

The Holy Spirit's Work (12:1-11)

1 Cor 2:9-16; 6:11, 19; 12:12-31; 14:1-33, 39-40
John 14:15-17, 26; 15:26; 16:7-15
Acts 1:8, 16; 2:4; 4:8, 31; 5:32; 6:1-7; 7:55; 8:15-17, 29, 39; 9:31; 13:1-5, 9; 14:3; 15:28; 16:6; 20:28
Rom 8:1-4, 9, 14-17, 26-29
2 Cor 1:22; 5:5
Gal 3:5; 5:16-18, 22-23
Eph 1:13-14; 5:18
2 Thes 2:13
2 Tim 3:16-17
Heb 2:4; 3:7-11, 15; 9:8; 10:15-17
1 Pet 1:11-12
2 Pet 1:20-21
1 Jn 2:20, 27

Different NT writers emphasized different aspects of the Holy Spirit's work. John, for example, highlighted the Spirit's role as teacher and revealer of God's thoughts and ways (John 14:17, 26; 15:26; 16:13-15; 1 Jn 2:20, 27). Luke focused on the Spirit's guidance and power for evangelism (Acts 1:8; 4:31; 8:29, 39) and the importance of being filled with the Holy Spirit (Acts 2:4; 4:8, 31; 7:55; 13:9). Paul, however, provides a comprehensive view of the Spirit's work.

According to Paul, God gives his Holy Spirit to all who come into a saving relationship with Jesus Christ (6:19; Eph 1:13-14; Gal 3:2-5). The Spirit brings new life in Christ. He affirms believers' salvation (6:11; 2 Thes 2:13) and their identity as children of God (Rom 8:9, 14-17).

The Holy Spirit gives Christians power over sin (Rom 8:1-4), power to live a fruitful life (Gal 5:22-23), and power for ministry (12:1-31). Believers are to be continuously "filled with the Spirit" (Eph 5:18), and though they experience the conflict between the flesh and the Spirit, they can please God by yielding to the Spirit's guidance and power (Gal 5:16-18).

The Holy Spirit enables Christians to understand God's thoughts and ways (2:9-16). He gives spiritual gifts to believers to help the church grow (ch 12). The Spirit leads and empowers their worship as they use the gifts that the Spirit has given them (14:26-33, 39-40).

The Spirit guarantees that believers will receive all the blessings that God has promised (2 Cor 1:22; 5:5; Eph 1:13-14). The Spirit helps believers and prays for them in their human weakness (Rom 8:26). The goal of the Spirit's work is to make them like Christ (Rom 8:28-29).

5:19-21; cp. Acts 16:16-18; 1 Jn 4:1-3). • For Paul, the ability to speak ***in unknown languages*** (or *in various tongues;* also in 12:28, 30) here refers to spiritual language that requires the spiritual gift of interpretation in order to be understood. By placing this gift near the bottom of the list (both here and in 12:28), Paul shows the lesser priority to be attached to the gift of tongues, with which the Corinthian church had become over-enamored (cp. 13:1, 8; 14:1-25, 27). • ***The ability to interpret*** does not refer to natural intellectual ability to translate, but to a spiritual ability to understand the meaning of the Spirit's message communicated through the gift of tongues (see 14:5, 13, 26-28).

12:11 The ***Spirit . . . decides which gift each person should have:*** See 12:4, 6, 18, 28. Paul paradoxically affirms both the sovereign choice of God in giving spiritual gifts, and the human responsibility to "earnestly desire the most helpful gifts" (12:31).

12:12-31 The church is like a ***body*** (see 12:27) composed of many different ***parts,*** each with its own function as determined by God (see 12:11, 18, 28; Rom 12:4-5).

12:13 Ethnic and social distinctions have no significance in the church (see Gal 3:28; Col 3:11). • ***Gentiles:*** Literally *Greeks.* • ***baptized into one body by one Spirit:*** Water baptism symbolizes a spiritual baptism in which the believer is united with Christ and the church by the work of the Holy Spirit (see "Baptism" at Acts 2:38, 41, p. 1828). • ***we all share the same Spirit:*** Literally *we were all given one Spirit to drink.*

12:14-21 These verses move from the image of a physical body to the image of the church as a spiritual body. Every part of the body is important and essential to its proper functioning. Believers should neither boast of their spiritual ministry nor belittle it in comparison to the ministries of other believers. God, who made the body, ***has put each part just where he wants it*** (12:18).

12:22-26 The seemingly weaker and less significant parts of the body are ***the most necessary*** and should be given special attention and respect so that the whole body will function well.

with the greatest care. So we carefully protect those parts that should not be seen,
24while the more honorable parts do not require this special care. So God has put the
body together such that extra honor and
care are given to those parts that have less
dignity. 25This makes for harmony among
the members, so that all the members care
for each other. 26If one part suffers, all the
parts suffer with it, and if one part is honored, all the parts are glad.
27All of you together are Christ's body,
and each of you is a part of it. 28Here are
some of the parts God has appointed for
the [j]church:

first are [k]apostles,
second are prophets,
third are teachers,
then those who do miracles,
those who have the [a]gift of healing,
those who can help others,
those who have the gift of leadership,
those who speak in unknown
languages.

29Are we all apostles? Are we all prophets? Are we all teachers? Do we all have the
power to do miracles? 30Do we all have the
gift of healing? Do we all have the ability
to speak in unknown [b]languages? Do we
all have the ability to interpret unknown
languages? Of course not! 31So you should
earnestly desire the most helpful gifts.

But now let me show you a way of life that
is best of all.

Love Is the Most Important Thing

13 If I could speak all the languages of
earth and of angels, but didn't [c]love
others, I would only be a noisy gong or a
clanging cymbal. 2If I had the gift of prophecy, and if I understood all of God's secret
plans and possessed all knowledge, and if I
had such faith that I could move mountains,
but didn't love others, I would be nothing.

12:27
Rom 12:5
Eph 1:23; 4:12
Col 1:18, 24

12:28
Rom 12:6-8
Eph 4:11-12
[j]*ekklēsia* (1577)
‣Eph 5:25
[k]*apostolos* (0652)
‣1 Cor 15:7
[a]*charisma* (5486)
‣1 Tim 4:14

12:30
[b]*glōssa* (1100)
‣1 Cor 13:8

13:1
1 Tim 1:5
[c]*agapē* (0026)
‣Gal 5:22

13:2
Matt 17:20; 21:21
Mark 11:23

13:3
Matt 6:2

13:4
1 Pet 4:8

13:5
Phil 2:4

13:6
2 Thes 2:12
2 Jn 1:4
3 Jn 1:3-4

The Church as a Dynamic Body (12:7-31)

1 Cor 14:26-33
Rom 12:4-8
Eph 1:23; 4:11-13
Col 1:24; 2:18-19
1 Tim 3:1-16

Paul viewed the church as the living body of Christ comprised of believers. Paul made no formal distinction between professional clergy and laity, with the ministry being done by the clergy. The community had leaders (see, e.g., 1 Tim 3:1-13), but every believer had a ministry in building up the body (12:12-31). When the early believers gathered together, usually in someone's home, everyone brought something from God to share with the others (14:26-33).

Paul understood God's Spirit as gifting people for their specific ministries (12:8-11, 28; Rom 12:6-8; Eph 4:11) and leading them when they came together for worship. Guided by the Spirit, every believer was to use their spiritual gifts for the benefit of the church. Paul wanted believers to be sensitive to the empowering of the Spirit in all that they did (14:26-33).

When believers meet together, every individual is important and each one has an active role to play. Believers must listen for God speaking his word—and be prepared to speak it—in all their relationships. Paul also calls for the others to "evaluate" what is said (14:26, 29). Every believer is a crucial part of the body, called to be actively involved in its growth.

12:25-26 The church is a unified body, so *harmony* and *care for each other* in the church is essential.

12:28-31 Paul lists some of the different individual roles given to people in the church (see also the list in 12:8-10; cp. Rom 12:6-8; Eph 4:11).

12:28 *Apostles* are specially commissioned emissaries of Christ in the world (see also Eph 4:11). • *Prophets* speak a word from God (see 12:10 and note; Eph 4:11; cp. Acts 13:1-2). • *Teachers* instruct others in the faith (Rom 12:7; Eph 4:11; cp. Acts 13:1). • *those who speak in unknown languages:* See note on 12:10.

12:29-30 These rhetorical questions all expect the answer, *Of course not!* Paul gently rebukes those who are jealous of others. Believers are to gratefully accept the gifts God has given them, and not to envy other gifts or elevate any gifts as more important than others (but see 12:31).

12:31 Believers are to *earnestly desire the most helpful gifts,* those that have the greatest potential to build up the church (see 14:12), while realizing that God is the one who distributes gifts as he chooses (12:11, 18, 28). Paul encourages the Corinthians to move beyond their desire for the gift of tongues (cp. 14:1-25, 27; see 12:10) because it has the least potential, of all the gifts, to build up the church. • *But now let me show you:* This statement transitions to Paul's description of love in ch 13. Love is *a way of life that is best of all.*

13:1-13 Paul interrupts his discussion of spiritual gifts (resumed in ch 14) to emphasize that *love* is more important than any spiritual gift (cp. 8:1-3). The most important thing for Christians is to become deeply and consistently loving people.

13:1-3 Spiritual gifts in themselves do not define our worth to God or to the church. In fact, apart from the expression of *love,* spiritual gifts are of no value.

13:1 *all the languages of earth* (literally *the tongues of men*) *and of angels:* Tongues was the spiritual gift most highly prized by the Corinthians (see also 12:10; 12:28; 14:1-25, 27). Some may have thought tongues to be the language of *angels;* in Acts, Luke uses the same term to refer to natural human languages (see Acts 2:4-13).

13:2 *If I . . . possessed all knowledge* possibly refers to the gift of "special knowledge" (12:8).

3 If I gave everything I have to the poor and even sacrificed my body, I could boast about it; but if I didn't love others, I would have gained nothing.

4 Love is patient and kind. Love is not jealous or boastful or proud 5 or rude. It does not demand its own way. It is not irritable, and it keeps no record of being wronged. 6 It does not rejoice about injustice but rejoices whenever the truth wins out. 7 Love never gives up, never loses faith, is always hopeful, and endures through every circumstance.

8 Prophecy and speaking in unknown [d]languages and special knowledge will become useless. But love will last forever! 9 Now our knowledge is partial and incomplete, and even the gift of prophecy reveals only part of the whole picture! 10 But when the time of [e]perfection comes, these partial things will become useless.

11 When I was a child, I spoke and thought and reasoned as a child. But when I grew up, I put away childish things. 12 Now we see things imperfectly, like puzzling reflections in a mirror, but then we will see everything with perfect clarity. All that I know now is partial and incomplete, but then I will know everything completely, just as God now knows me completely.

13 Three things will last forever—faith, [f]hope, and love—and the greatest of these is love.

The Gifts of Tongues and Prophecy

14 Let love be your highest goal! But you should also desire the special abilities the Spirit gives—especially the ability to prophesy. 2 For if you have the ability to speak in [g]tongues, you will be talking only to God, since people won't be able to

13:7 Prov 10:12; 1 Pet 4:8
13:8 [d]*glōssa* (1100) ‣1 Cor 14:2
13:10 Phil 3:12; [e]*teleios* (5046) ‣Eph 4:13
13:11 Ps 131:2
13:12 2 Cor 5:7; 1 Jn 3:2
13:13 Matt 22:37-40; Gal 5:5-6; 1 Thes 1:3; 1 Jn 4:16; [f]*elpis* (1680) ‣Eph 1:18
14:1 Rom 12:6; Eph 5:2
14:2 Acts 19:6; [g]*glōssa* (1100) ‣1 Cor 14:39

Loving Others (13:1-13)

Jesus speaks of loving one's neighbor as the second most important of the OT commandments (Mark 12:31). Love summarizes the entire OT law (Matt 7:12; 22:40; cp. Matt 9:9-13; 12:1-13; see Rom 13:8-10). Jesus criticized the Pharisees for their failure to show love (Matt 9:13; 12:7; 23:4, 13-14, 23). Love is the mark of a true follower of Jesus (John 13:34-35) and of an authentic experience of God (1 Jn 2:9-11; 3:11-18; 4:7-21).

For Paul, love is more important than any of the spiritual gifts and the most important virtue. Love "binds us all together in perfect harmony" (Col 3:14). Without love, ministry has limited value (13:1-3). Paul summed up the whole of the Christian ethics as "faith expressing itself in love" (Gal 5:6). Love is the central ethical expression of Christian faith, the primary fruit of the Spirit (Gal 5:22), and one of the most important motivations for ministry. The most important thing for believers to value and seek is to become a faithfully loving person.

Lev 19:18; Hos 6:6; Matt 7:12; 9:9-13; 12:1-13; 22:37-40; 23:2-4, 13, 23; John 13:34-35; Rom 13:8-10; Gal 5:6, 22-23; Col 3:12-14; 1 Jn 2:7-11; 3:11-18; 4:7-21

13:3 ***sacrificed my body, I could boast about it:*** Some manuscripts read *sacrificed my body to be burned;* it would have been easy for a copyist to change the text accidentally, because in Greek the two readings differ only by one letter. It is unclear which reading is to be preferred; however, the manuscripts supporting the reading *I could boast* are generally better. • ***I would have gained nothing:*** Even the most impressive sacrificial acts mean nothing if not motivated by love.

13:4-7 This description of Christian love emphasizes the willingness to give up one's own desires for the good of others (see also chs 8–10; Rom 5:6-8; 15:3; 2 Cor 8:9; Phil 2:4-8).

13:5 ***It does not demand its own way:*** Love is not self-centered, not concerned simply with its own interests (see Phil 2:4-8).

13:8-13 ***Love,*** in contrast to spiritual gifts, ***will last forever.***

13:8 ***in unknown languages*** (or *in tongues*): see note on 12:10. • ***Love will last forever,*** because God is love (cp. 1 Jn 4:7-12, 16).

13:9 None of the spiritual gifts gives us full understanding; unlike love, they are all limited in their benefits.

13:12 The contrast between *now* and ***then*** is between this age and the coming age. • ***Now we see things imperfectly, like puzzling reflections in a mirror:*** In Paul's day, mirrors were usually made of polished bronze, so the view was imperfect. Our perception in this life is limited and our understanding is ***partial and incomplete.*** • ***then:*** When the end comes and Christ establishes his eternal kingdom, ***we will see everything with perfect clarity*** (literally *[we will see] face to face*). Then the spiritual gifts that give knowledge will be unnecessary.

13:13 ***Faith, hope, and love*** are more important than spiritual gifts because they ***last forever*** (see also Rom 5:1-5; Gal 5:5-6; Col 1:4-5; 1 Thes 1:3; 5:8). Of the three, ***the greatest . . . is love,*** because love is the quintessential nature of God himself (see 1 Jn 4:7-12, 16-21). So love should epitomize our relationship with him and others.

14:1-25 Having emphasized the supreme importance of *love* (ch 13), Paul returns to the subject of spiritual gifts. Their relative value is defined by the benefit they give to others, which is characteristic of love (ch 13). In that light, Paul contrasts the over-valued gift of tongues with the more beneficial gift of prophecy.

14:1 Of all ***the special abilities the Spirit gives*** (see note on 12:1–14:40), Paul encourages the Corinthians to seek ***the ability to prophesy*** (see 12:10) because of its greater benefit to the church.

14:2-4 The problem with the gift of speaking ***in tongues*** (or ***in unknown languages;*** also in 14:4-5, 13-14, 18, 22, 26-28, 39; see 12:1, 10) is that hearers cannot readily ***understand*** the message; the gift of ***prophecy,*** however, is immediately intelligible and beneficial as a word from God that ***strengthens . . . encourages . . . and comforts*** those who hear.

understand you. You will be speaking by the power of the Spirit, but it will all be mysterious. 3But one who prophesies strengthens others, encourages them, and comforts them. 4A person who speaks in tongues is strengthened personally, but one who speaks a word of prophecy strengthens the entire church.

5I wish you could all speak in tongues, but even more I wish you could all prophesy. For prophecy is greater than speaking in tongues, unless someone interprets what you are saying so that the whole church will be strengthened.

6Dear brothers and sisters, if I should come to you speaking in an unknown language, how would that help you? But if I bring you a [h]revelation or some special knowledge or prophecy or teaching, that will be helpful. 7Even lifeless instruments like the flute or the harp must play the notes clearly, or no one will recognize the melody. 8And if the bugler doesn't sound a clear call, how will the soldiers know they are being called to battle?

9It's the same for you. If you speak to people in words they don't understand, how will they know what you are saying? You might as well be talking into empty space.

10There are many different languages in the world, and every language has meaning. 11But if I don't understand a language, I will be a foreigner to someone who speaks it, and the one who speaks it will be a foreigner to me. 12And the same is true for you. Since you are so eager to have the special abilities the Spirit gives, seek those that will strengthen the whole church.

13So anyone who speaks in tongues should pray also for the ability to interpret what has been said. 14For if I pray in tongues, my spirit is praying, but I don't understand what I am saying.

15Well then, what shall I do? I will pray in the spirit, and I will also pray in words I understand. I will sing in the spirit, and I will also sing in words I understand. 16For if you praise God only in the spirit, how can those who don't understand you praise God along with you? How can they join you in giving thanks when they don't understand what you are saying? 17You will be giving thanks very well, but it won't strengthen the people who hear you.

18I thank God that I speak in tongues more than any of you. 19But in a church meeting I would rather speak five understandable words to help others than ten thousand words in an unknown language.

20Dear brothers and sisters, don't be childish in your understanding of these things. Be innocent as babies when it comes to evil, but be mature in understanding matters of this kind. 21It is written in the [i]Scriptures:

"I will speak to my own people
  through strange languages
  and through the lips of foreigners.
But even then, they will not listen to me,"
  says the LORD.

22So you see that speaking in tongues is a sign, not for believers, but for unbelievers. Prophecy, however, is for the benefit of believers, not unbelievers. 23Even so, if unbelievers or people who don't understand these things come into your church meeting and hear everyone speaking in an unknown language, they will think you are crazy. 24But if all of you are prophesying, and unbelievers or people who don't understand these

14:3 Rom 14:19
14:4 1 Cor 14:18-19, 26-28
14:5 Num 11:29
14:6 Rom 6:17; Eph 1:17; [h]*apokalupsis* (0602) ‣1 Cor 14:26
14:8 Num 10:9; Jer 4:19; Ezek 33:1-6
14:12 Rom 14:19; 1 Cor 12:1
14:13 1 Cor 12:10
14:15 Eph 5:19; Col 3:16
14:16 1 Chr 16:36; Neh 8:6; Ps 106:48; Rev 5:14; 7:12
14:17 Rom 14:19
14:20 Eph 4:14; Heb 5:12
14:21 Deut 28:49; *Isa 28:11-12; [i]*nomos* (3551) ‣Gal 2:16
14:22 1 Cor 14:1
14:23 Acts 2:13
14:24 John 16:8
14:25 Isa 45:14; Zech 8:23
14:26 Rom 14:19; 1 Cor 12:7-10; Eph 4:12; 5:19; [j]*apokalupsis* (0602) ‣2 Cor 12:1

14:2 *speaking by the power of the Spirit:* Or *speaking in your spirit;* literally *speaking in spirit.*

14:4 The primary purpose of spiritual gifts is not self-edification, but the strengthening of ***the entire church*** (see 12:7; cp. 8:1; 14:12).

14:6 *Dear brothers and sisters:* Literally *Brothers;* also in 14:20, 26, 39. See note on 1:10. • ***in an unknown language:*** Or *in tongues;* also in 14:19, 23; see note on 12:10.

14:7-12 A message needs to be clearly intelligible if it is to communicate.

14:12 ***Special abilities*** from ***the Spirit*** are given to ***strengthen the whole church*** (see 12:7; 14:4; cp. Eph 4:15-16).

14:13 Paul does not forbid speaking in ***tongues*** (see 14:39), but ***the ability to interpret*** is crucial, especially in public worship (see 14:27-28).

14:14 Speaking in tongues engages the ***spirit*** of the speaker (because the Holy Spirit is speaking through the person) but not his mind (because the message is not rationally intelligible).

14:15-17 It is preferable both to worship ***in the spirit*** (or *in the Spirit*) and to use ***words I understand*** in worship and ministry because public worship should always bless both God and others. Speaking in tongues without interpretation, though it gives glory to God and edification to the speaker (14:4), fails to benefit others who are present. • ***praise God along with you*** (literally *say "amen" to your thanksgiving*): *Amen* was the traditional congregational response to a prayer.

14:18-19 Paul affirmed the personal value of speaking ***in tongues***, but speaking ***in a church meeting*** should ***help others***, not only the speaker.

14:20 To ***be mature in understanding*** such ***matters***, one must consider the purpose of spiritual gifts and not treat them as ends in themselves for one's own enjoyment.

14:21-25 *The Scriptures* (literally *the law*) refers here to the OT generally. Paul used this quotation from Isa 28:11-12 to show that ***speaking in tongues is a sign, not for believers, but for unbelievers.*** However, in 14:23-25, Paul argues that even unbelievers are more likely to be convicted by a word of prophecy than by speaking in tongues. His point is that, in public worship, the gift of prophecy is of greater usefulness than the gift of tongues.

14:27
1 Cor 14:2, 5, 13
14:29
1 Cor 12:10
1 Thes 5:19-21
14:31
[k]*parakaleō* (3870)
‣ Phil 2:1
14:32
1 Jn 4:1
14:33
[a]*eirēnē* (1515)
‣ Gal 5:22
14:34
Gen 3:16
1 Cor 11:3
Eph 5:22
Col 3:18
1 Tim 2:11-12
Titus 2:5
14:37
2 Cor 10:7
1 Jn 4:6
14:39
1 Cor 12:31
1 Thes 5:20
[b]*glōssa* (1100)
‣ Jas 3:8
14:40
1 Cor 14:33
Col 2:5
15:1
[c]*euangelion* (2098)
‣ 2 Cor 11:4
15:2
[d]*sōzō* (4982)
‣ 2 Cor 2:15
15:3
Isa 53:5-9
Luke 24:25-27
1 Pet 2:24

things come into your meeting, they will be
convicted of sin and judged by what you say.
25As they listen, their secret thoughts will
be exposed, and they will fall to their knees
and worship God, declaring, "God is truly
here among you."

Using Spiritual Gifts in Public Worship

26Well, my brothers and sisters, let's summarize.
When you meet together, one will
sing, another will teach, another will tell
some special [j]revelation God has given, one
will speak in tongues, and another will interpret
what is said. But everything that is
done must strengthen all of you.
27No more than two or three should speak
in tongues. They must speak one at a time,
and someone must interpret what they say.
28But if no one is present who can interpret,
they must be silent in your church meeting
and speak in tongues to God privately.
29Let two or three people prophesy, and
let the others evaluate what is said. 30But if
someone is prophesying and another person
receives a revelation from the Lord, the
one who is speaking must stop. 31In this
way, all who prophesy will have a turn to
speak, one after the other, so that everyone
will learn and be [k]encouraged. 32Remember
that people who prophesy are in control of
their spirit and can take turns. 33For God is
not a God of disorder but of [a]peace, as in all
the meetings of God's holy people.
34Women should be silent during the
church meetings. It is not proper for them
to speak. They should be submissive, just as
the law says. 35If they have any questions,
they should ask their husbands at home, for
it is improper for women to speak in church
meetings.
36Or do you think God's word originated
with you Corinthians? Are you the only
ones to whom it was given? 37If you claim to
be a prophet or think you are spiritual, you
should recognize that what I am saying is
a command from the Lord himself. 38But if
you do not recognize this, you yourself will
not be recognized.
39So, my dear brothers and sisters, be eager
to prophesy, and don't forbid speaking
in [b]tongues. 40But be sure that everything is
done properly and in order.

The Resurrection of the Dead (15:1-58)

The Resurrection of Christ

15 Let me now remind you, dear brothers
and sisters, of the [c]Good News I
preached to you before. You welcomed it
then, and you still stand firm in it. 2It is this
Good News that [d]saves you if you continue
to believe the message I told you—unless, of
course, you believed something that was
never true in the first place.
3I passed on to you what was most important
and what had also been passed on

14:25 *"God is truly here among you."* Paul is alluding to Isa 45:14.

14:26-40 Paul gives specific procedures for the use of spiritual gifts in the church and emphasizes that they are to be expressed in an orderly way. Among the early Christians, ***church meetings*** were not led by professional pastors or priests. Instead, everyone shared with the others what God had given them for strengthening the church.

14:26 ***will sing:*** Literally *has a psalm*, either to be sung alone or for the fellowship to sing together (cp. Eph 5:19; Col 3:16). • ***Everything that is done*** in public worship is to be for the purpose of strengthening the church (see 12:7; 14:4, 6, 12, 26; cp. 8:1).

14:27-28 For a church overly eager for the gift of ***tongues*** (see 12:10), Paul places limits on its public expression so it would be most helpful to the church: ***no more than two or three, . . . one at a time,*** and only if there is someone present ***who can interpret*** the message.

14:29-32 Public ***prophesying*** is to be expressed in an orderly way, sensitive to the guidance of the Spirit, so that everyone may benefit from it. ***The others*** are then to ***evaluate what is said*** to assess whether it is indeed a word from God (1 Thes 5:19-21). Those with a word of prophecy are to ***take turns***—prophecy is a divinely given word, but it is still subject to the ***control*** of the speaker.

14:33 The phrase ***as in all the meetings of God's holy people*** could instead be joined to the beginning of 14:34.

14:34-35 This aside in the discussion on using spiritual gifts reflects a perspective on women's roles similar to that of the Pastoral Letters (see "Women's Roles in the NT Church" at 1 Tim 2:11-15, p. 2053). Some manuscripts place 14:34-35 after 14:40. • Paul advises women to ***be silent*** and ***submissive*** in church meetings. This instruction is to be understood in light of 11:5, which clearly implies that women are permitted to pray and prophesy publicly. • ***just as the law says:*** Possibly referring to Gen 3:16.

14:36-37 Paul expected the Corinthians to take his apostolic word seriously, as ***a command from the Lord himself.*** • ***What I am saying*** probably refers to all of his teaching, especially as it relates to spiritual gifts.

14:38 Some manuscripts read *If you are ignorant of this, stay in your ignorance.*

14:39-40 Paul summarizes his discussion of spiritual gifts (chs 12–14).

15:1-58 Some people in the church had doubts about a future ***resurrection of the dead.*** Paul reassures them and, perhaps in response to their skeptical questions, discusses the nature of a resurrection body.

15:1-11 Paul summarizes the Good News that he preached.

15:1 ***dear brothers and sisters:*** Literally *brothers;* also in 15:31, 50, 58. See note on 1:10. • At the heart of ***the Good News*** stands the message of the atoning death and resurrection of Christ (see 15:3-4; Rom 5:8-10; 6:5-11).

15:2 ***if you continue to believe:*** Those who continue firm in their faith will be saved (cp. Matt 10:22; 24:13; John 15:6; Gal 5:4; Col 1:23; Heb 6:4-6; contrast 1 Cor 1:8; Rom 8:38-39; Phil 1:6; Heb 6:9). • ***unless, of course, you believed something that was never true in the first place:*** Or *unless you never believed it in the first place.*

15:3 The heart of the Good News is that ***Christ died for our sins*** (see Rom 3:24-25; 5:8-10; Gal 1:4; 1 Thes 5:9-10).

to me. Christ died for our sins, just as the Scriptures said. 4He was buried, and he was raised from the dead on the third day, just as the Scriptures said. 5He was seen by Peter and then by the Twelve. 6After that, he was seen by more than 500 of his followers at one time, most of whom are still alive, though some have died. 7Then he was seen by James and later by all the [e]apostles. 8Last of all, as though I had been born at the wrong time, I also saw him. 9For I am the least of all the apostles. In fact, I'm not even worthy to be called an apostle after the way I persecuted God's church.

10But whatever I am now, it is all because God poured out his special favor on me—and not without results. For I have worked harder than any of the other apostles; yet it was not I but God who was working through me by his grace. 11So it makes no difference whether I preach or they preach, for we all preach the same message you have already believed.

The Future Resurrection of the Dead

12But tell me this—since we preach that Christ rose from the dead, why are some of you saying there will be no [f]resurrection of the dead? 13For if there is no resurrection of the dead, then Christ has not been raised either. 14And if Christ has not been raised, then all our preaching is useless, and your faith is useless. 15And we apostles would all be lying about God—for we have said that God raised Christ from the grave. But that can't be true if there is no resurrection of the dead. 16And if there is no resurrection of the dead, then Christ has not been raised. 17And if Christ has not been raised, then your faith is [g]useless and you are still guilty of your sins. 18In that case, all who have died believing in Christ are lost! 19And if our hope in Christ is only for this life, we are more to be pitied than anyone in the world.

20But in fact, Christ has been raised from the dead. He is the first of a great harvest of all who have died.

21So you see, just as death came into the world through a man, now the resurrection from the dead has begun through another man. 22Just as everyone dies because we all belong to Adam, everyone who belongs to Christ will be [h]given new life. 23But there is an order to this resurrection: Christ was raised as the first of the harvest; then all who belong to Christ will be raised when he [i]comes back.

24After that the end will come, when he will turn the Kingdom over to God the Father, having destroyed every ruler and authority and power. 25For Christ must reign until he humbles all his enemies beneath his

15:4 Ps 16:10; Luke 24:25-27
15:5 Matt 28:16-17
15:7 Luke 24:33-37; [e]*apostolos* (0652) ‣2 Cor 12:11
15:8 Acts 9:3-6
15:9 Acts 8:3
15:12 Acts 17:32; 23:8; 2 Tim 2:18; [f]*anastasis* (0386) ‣Phil 3:10
15:15 Acts 2:24
15:17 Rom 4:25; [g]*mataios* (3152) ‣Titus 3:9
15:20 Col 1:18; 1 Pet 1:3; Rev 1:5
15:21 Rom 5:12, 18
15:22 Rom 5:14-18; [h]*zōopoieō* (2227) ‣1 Cor 15:36
15:23 1 Thes 4:16; [i]*parousia* (3952) ‣1 Thes 3:13
15:24 Dan 2:44; 7:14
15:25 Ps 110:1; Isa 9:7; Matt 22:44

15:4 ***just as the Scriptures said:*** See Ps 16:10; Hos 6:2; Jon 1:17; Matt 12:40; Acts 2:24-32.

15:5 ***He was seen by Peter*** (Greek *Cephas*): See Luke 24:34. • ***then by the Twelve:*** See Matt 28:16-17; Mark 16:14; Luke 24:36; John 20:19.

15:6 ***he was seen by more than 500:*** We have no other account of this event. • ***his followers:*** Literally *the brothers.* See note on 1:10. • ***most of whom are still alive:*** When this letter was written (around AD 53–56), the factuality of Christ's resurrection could be verified by consulting living eyewitnesses.

15:7 This ***James*** was almost certainly Jesus' brother, who became a leader of the Jerusalem church after Jesus' death (see Mark 6:3; John 7:1-5; Gal 1:19; cp. Acts 12:17; 15:13; 21:18).

15:8-9 ***as though I had been born at the wrong time*** (or *As though I were stillborn*): This phrase can refer to a miscarriage or stillbirth. Here it might express the unusual manner of Paul's conversion, or the derogatory view some opponents held of his apostleship, or his own sense of unworthiness to be an apostle. The overall emphasis is on the extraordinary grace of God to Paul as a former persecutor of Christ's people (see Gal 1:13; Phil 3:6; cp. Acts 8:3; 9:1-2). • ***I also saw him:*** Paul came face to face with the risen Christ at his conversion (see 9:1; Acts 9:3-6; Gal 1:15-16).

15:10 Paul's awareness of God's extraordinary ***special favor*** (literally *grace*) to him resulted in an extraordinary response on his part. But even that must be understood as an expression of ***God . . . working through me by his grace*** (see 2 Cor 4:7; Gal 2:20; Col 1:27).

15:11 The important thing is the ***message,*** not the messengers (cp. 1:10-12).

15:12-34 Paul now makes the case for a future ***resurrection.***

15:12-20 Christ's resurrection confirms the reality of the future resurrection.

15:12 Some believers in Corinth apparently had a difficult time accepting the Jewish notion of a bodily ***resurrection of the dead,*** preferring instead the Greek notion of the immortality of the soul (cp. Acts 17:18, 32).

15:14-18 If Christ has not risen from the dead, then Christian ***faith is useless.*** But in reality, Jesus' resurrection is proof that the sacrifice of Christ fully atoned for human sins (see 15:3). ***If Christ has not been raised,*** then human beings remain unforgiven, under the judgment of God—***still guilty of*** their ***sins*** (see Rom 3:19; Eph 2:1-3).

15:19 Without eternal life, faithful believers ***are more to be pitied than anyone in the world*** because they suffer persecution and deprivation. But they find their joy in anticipating what lies beyond this life, as did both Jesus (see Heb 12:2) and Paul (see 2 Cor 4:16-18; Phil 1:21-23; 3:7-11).

15:20 In the OT, the first crop was dedicated to God (see Exod 23:19). Christ's resurrection is ***the first of a great harvest*** of God's people who will be resurrected (see Col 1:18).

15:21-23 Adam's sin contrasts with Christ's resurrection (cp. 15:45-49).

15:24-28 Christ is the Lord of all things, even ***death*** itself. Nevertheless, he remains subordinate to ***God*** his ***Father.***

15:24 The phrase ***every ruler and authority and power*** refers to spiritual powers who oppose Christ (cp. Rom 8:38; Eph 1:21; Col 2:10, 15; 1 Pet 3:22).

15:25 This paraphrase of Ps 110:1 is applied to Jesus (cp. Heb 1:13). • ***beneath his feet:*** In the ancient Near East, victorious kings were depicted with their feet on the necks of their defeated enemies.

15:26
2 Tim 1:10
Rev 20:14; 21:4

15:27
*Ps 8:6
Matt 28:18
Eph 1:22

15:29
[j]*baptizō* (0907)
‣Gal 3:27

15:30-31
Rom 8:36
2 Cor 4:10-11; 11:26

15:32
*Isa 22:13
Luke 12:19-21
2 Cor 1:8

15:34
Eph 5:14
[k]*dikaiōs* (1346)
‣1 Thes 2:10

15:35
Ezek 37:3

15:36
John 12:24
[a]*zōopoieō* (2227)
‣1 Cor 15:45

feet. 26And the last enemy to be destroyed is
death. 27For the Scriptures say, "God has put
all things under his authority." (Of course,
when it says "all things are under his authority," that does not include God himself, who
gave Christ his authority.) 28Then, when all
things are under his authority, the Son will
put himself under God's authority, so that
God, who gave his Son authority over all
things, will be utterly supreme over everything everywhere.
29If the dead will not be raised, what
point is there in people being [j]baptized for
those who are dead? Why do it unless the
dead will someday rise again?
30And why should we ourselves risk our
lives hour by hour? 31For I swear, dear brothers and sisters, that I face death daily. This
is as certain as my pride in what Christ Jesus
our Lord has done in you. 32And what value
was there in fighting wild beasts—those
people of Ephesus—if there will be no resurrection from the dead? And if there is no
resurrection, "Let's feast and drink, for tomorrow we die!" 33Don't be fooled by those
who say such things, for "bad company corrupts good character." 34Think carefully
about what is [k]right, and stop sinning. For
to your shame I say that some of you don't
know God at all.

The Resurrection Body

35But someone may ask, "How will the dead
be raised? What kind of bodies will they
have?" 36What a foolish question! When
you put a seed into the ground, it doesn't
[a]grow into a plant unless it dies first. 37And
what you put in the ground is not the plant
that will grow, but only a bare seed of wheat

The Resurrection of the Dead (15:12-58)

Job 19:25-27
Ps 16:10; 49:15
Dan 12:2-3
Matt 16:21; 20:19; 28:1-10
Mark 12:18-27
John 3:13-16; 5:25-30; 6:39-40; 11:21-27
Acts 2:23-24; 3:14-15; 4:33; 10:39-41; 17:2-3; 24:15; 26:22-23
Rom 1:4; 4:25; 6:4-11; 8:10-11
2 Cor 1:8-9; 4:13-18; 5:1-10
Eph 1:19-20
Col 2:12; 3:1-4
1 Thes 4:13-18
1 Pet 1:3-6, 23
Rev 20:11-15; 21:1-7; 22:1-6

Jesus spoke of a future resurrection of all people—either to eternal life or to judgment (Mark 12:25-26; John 5:28-29; cp. Luke 20:34-36). He also promised that he would give new life to all who have believed in him (John 6:39-40, 44, 54; 11:25-26). When Christ returns, all his people will be resurrected to be with him forever (1 Thes 4:13-18; cp. 2 Cor 5:1-10).

This strong hope characterized the outlook of the early Christians. They were able to endure their suffering because their eyes were fixed on what lay beyond this life (2 Cor 4:16-18; Heb 12:2). They expected Jesus to return and resurrect their bodies. They looked forward to living with him forever (1 Pet 1:3-6, 23). Jesus' own bodily resurrection was the foundation of their Christian faith (15:12-20; Acts 4:33; see also 2 Cor 4:14).

The resurrection body will be fundamentally different from the body we experience in this life, with all its limitations and failings. Our resurrected bodies will be glorious, strong, immortal, and spiritual, like Christ's own resurrection body (15:35-58).

Because they are already joined to Christ, believers actually begin to experience resurrection existence here and now. They have already been "raised" with Christ; they have already been given "resurrection life" (Rom 6:4-11; 8:10-11; Col 2:12). As a result, their life is now centered in the spiritual realities of heaven, not the things of earth (Col 3:1-4). Believers can experience the transforming power of that new life here and now, the new life of the Spirit that frees them from the power of sin and death (Rom 8:1-4). In all the difficulties they face, their trust is not in themselves but in the resurrection power of God (2 Cor 1:9).

15:27 ***"God has put all things under his authority":*** See Ps 8:6; cp. Matt 22:44.

15:29 Some first-century Christians apparently practiced baptism-by-proxy for dead unbelievers whom they wished to be saved. Paul neither endorses nor condemns the practice; he simply uses it as evidence for belief in resurrection. There is no other reference to such a practice in early Christian literature.

15:30-32 The apostles' willingness to *risk* their *lives* was based on their conviction that there is life beyond death. If there is no resurrection, such suffering is pointless.

15:32 ***fighting wild beasts—those people of Ephesus*** (literally *fighting wild beasts in Ephesus*): Paul refers figuratively to his struggles with opponents in Ephesus (see 16:8; Acts 19:23-41; 2 Cor 1:8; 4:8-12; 11:23-28). Watching condemned prisoners *fighting wild beasts* and getting mauled to death was a common form of entertainment in the Roman world. • ***"Let's feast and drink, for tomorrow we die!"*** This quotation is from Isa 22:13.

15:33 ***"bad company corrupts good character":*** This quotation from the Greek poet Menander (300s BC) is a warning not to listen to those who are teaching wrong things.

15:34 ***some of you don't know God at all:*** Paul sharply rebukes those who prided themselves on their knowledge but remained skeptical of resurrection.

15:35-58 Paul discusses the nature of resurrection *bodies*, perhaps responding to skeptical questions. In the Greco-Roman world, belief in the immortality of the soul was common, but not belief in the resurrection of the body.

15:36 ***What a foolish question!*** Paul's strong response suggests that the question is skeptical. It might also imply that the answer is unknowable.

15:37-39 Just as the kind of seed determines the shape of the *plant* that grows, yet the plant does not resemble the seed, so the resurrection body will be unlike the present body, yet identifiable as belonging to the same person.

or whatever you are planting. 38 Then God
gives it the new body he wants it to have. A
different plant grows from each kind of
seed. 39 Similarly there are different kinds of
flesh—one kind for humans, another for animals, another for birds, and another for fish.
40 There are also bodies in the heavens
and bodies on the earth. The glory of the
heavenly bodies is different from the glory
of the earthly bodies. 41 The sun has one
kind of glory, while the moon and stars
each have another kind. And even the stars
differ from each other in their glory.
42 It is the same way with the resurrection
of the dead. Our earthly bodies are planted
in the ground when we die, but they will be
raised to live forever. 43 Our bodies are buried in brokenness, but they will be raised
in glory. They are buried in weakness, but
they will be raised in strength. 44 They are
buried as natural human bodies, but they
will be raised as spiritual bodies. For just as
there are natural bodies, there are also spiritual bodies.
45 The Scriptures tell us, "The first man,
Adam, became a living person." But the
last Adam—that is, Christ—is a [b]life-giving
Spirit. 46 What comes first is the natural
body, then the spiritual body comes later.
47 Adam, the first man, was made from the
dust of the earth, while Christ, the second
man, came from [c]heaven. 48 Earthly people
are like the earthly man, and heavenly people are like the heavenly man. 49 Just as we
are now like the earthly man, we will someday be like the heavenly man.
50 What I am saying, dear brothers and
sisters, is that our physical bodies cannot
inherit the Kingdom of God. These dying
bodies cannot inherit what will last forever.
51 But let me reveal to you a wonderful [d]se-
cret. We will not all die, but we will all be
transformed! 52 It will happen in a moment,
in the blink of an eye, when the last trumpet is blown. For when the trumpet sounds,
those who have died will be raised to live
forever. And we who are living will also be
transformed. 53 For our dying bodies must
be transformed into bodies that will never
die; our mortal bodies must be transformed
into immortal bodies.
54 Then, when our dying bodies have been
transformed into bodies that will never die,
this Scripture will be fulfilled:

"Death is swallowed up in victory.
55 O death, where is your victory?
O death, where is your sting?"

56 For [e]sin is the sting that results in death,
and the law gives [e]sin its power. 57 But thank
God! He gives us victory over sin and death
through our Lord Jesus Christ.
58 So, my dear brothers and sisters, be
strong and immovable. Always work enthusiastically for the Lord, for you know that
nothing you do for the Lord is ever useless.

The Collection for Jerusalem (16:1-4)

16 Now regarding your question about
the money being collected for God's
people in Jerusalem. You should follow the
same procedure I gave to the churches in

15:38 Gen 1:11
15:42 Dan 12:2-3
15:43 Phil 3:20-21; Col 3:4
15:45 *Gen 2:7; [b]*zōopoieō* (2227) ‣2 Cor 3:6
15:47 Gen 2:7; 3:19; John 3:13, 31; [c]*ouranos* (3772) ‣2 Cor 12:2
15:48 Phil 3:20-21
15:49 Gen 5:3; Rom 8:29
15:50 John 3:3, 5
15:51 2 Cor 5:2-4; Phil 3:21; 1 Thes 4:15-17; [d]*mustērion* (3466) ‣Eph 3:3
15:52 Matt 24:31
15:53 2 Cor 5:4
15:54 *Isa 25:8
15:55 *Hos 13:14
15:56 Rom 4:15; 5:12; [e]*hamartia* (0266) ‣Eph 2:1
15:57 Rom 8:37; 1 Jn 5:4
15:58 Rev 14:13
16:1 Acts 11:29; 24:17; Rom 15:25-26; 2 Cor 8:9; Gal 2:10

15:40-41 Everything that God has made has its own *glory*—its own unique beauty and magnificence. The resurrection body will be unlike anything else.

15:42-44 Just as growing plants differ from the seeds out of which they sprout, so resurrection bodies will be vastly unlike our mortal bodies.

15:45-49 *Adam* and *Christ* founded two distinct humanities: One is natural and earthly, enslaved to sin and death; the other is spiritual and heavenly, purified and destined for life. Adam represents *the natural* (physical) *body* and Christ *the spiritual* (resurrection) *body.* See also 15:21-22; Rom 5:12-21.

15:45-46 Just as Christ's *life-giving Spirit* supersedes the natural life, the spiritual body will supersede the physical body.

15:45 This quotation is from Gen 2:7.

15:47 ***made from the dust of the earth:*** Adam's earthly origin (Gen 2:7) is here contrasted with Christ's heavenly origin.

15:48 ***Earthly people*** (literally *those of the dust*): Like Adam, natural human beings are under the curse of sin and death. All return to dust (see Gen 3:19)—they all die. • ***heavenly people are like the heavenly man:*** Those who belong to Christ are like him in having an unending spiritual life.

15:49 Like ***the earthly man,*** Adam, we have physical bodies in this life. But ***we will someday be like*** (some manuscripts read *let us be like*) Christ, ***the heavenly man,*** experiencing the Kingdom of God in resurrection bodies (cp. Rom 6:4-14).

15:50 ***Physical bodies cannot inherit*** God's Kingdom. Only a spiritual, resurrected body can experience the Kingdom in all its fullness (cp. John 4:24).

15:51 The Good News reveals the previously unknown *secret* of resurrection. • ***We will not all die:*** Paul might have expected the future resurrection in his own lifetime (cp. 15:52; 1 Thes 4:15, 17).

15:52 Cp. 1 Thes 4:13-17.

15:54 ***bodies that will never die:*** Some manuscripts add *and our mortal bodies have been transformed into immortal bodies.* • ***"Death is swallowed up in victory":*** This quotation is from Isa 25:8. Resurrection defeats the ultimate enemy, ***death,*** just as the power of the Spirit enables believers to transcend sin here and now (see Rom 8:2, 11).

15:55 This quotation (Hos 13:14, Greek version) assures believers that they have nothing to fear from *death.* • Death is like the *sting* of a scorpion.

15:57 The death and resurrection of Christ end the dominating power of *sin* and *death* (see Rom 6:14; 8:2; 10:4).

15:58 ***Nothing you do for the Lord is ever useless:*** There will be eternal rewards for those who serve him faithfully (see 3:12-15).

16:1-4 Paul answers the Corinthians' ***question*** about the offering for poor Christians ***in Jerusalem*** (Acts 24:17; Rom 15:25-27; 2 Cor 8–9; Gal 2:10).

16:1 ***Galatia*** was a Roman province in Asia Minor (see Acts 16:6; 18:23).

Galatia. [2]On the first day of each week,
you should each put aside a portion of the
money you have earned. Don't wait until I
get there and then try to collect it all at once.
[3]When I come, I will write letters of recommendation for the messengers you choose
to deliver your gift to Jerusalem. [4]And if it
seems appropriate for me to go along, they
can travel with me.

4. CONCLUSION (16:5-24)

Paul's Final Instructions

[5]I am coming to visit you after I have been
to Macedonia, for I am planning to travel
through Macedonia. [6]Perhaps I will stay
awhile with you, possibly all winter, and
then you can send me on my way to my next
destination. [7]This time I don't want to make
just a short visit and then go right on. I want
to come and stay awhile, if the Lord will let
me. [8]In the meantime, I will be staying here
at Ephesus until the Festival of Pentecost.
[9]There is a wide-open door for a great work
here, although many oppose me.
[10]When Timothy comes, don't intimidate him. He is doing the Lord's work, just
as I am. [11]Don't let anyone treat him with
contempt. Send him on his way with your
blessing when he returns to me. I expect
him to come with the other believers.
[12]Now about our brother Apollos—I urged
him to visit you with the other believers, but
he was not willing to go right now. He will
see you later when he has the opportunity.
[13]Be on guard. Stand firm in the faith. Be
courageous. Be strong. [14]And do everything
with love.
[15]You know that Stephanas and his
household were the first of the harvest of
believers in Greece, and they are spending
their lives in [f]service to God's people. I urge
you, dear brothers and sisters, [16]to submit to
them and others like them who serve with
such devotion. [17]I am very glad that Stephanas, Fortunatus, and Achaicus have come
here. They have been providing the help
you weren't here to give me. [18]They have
been a wonderful encouragement to me, as
they have been to you. You must show your
appreciation to all who serve so well.

Paul's Final Greetings and Benediction

[19]The churches here in the province of Asia
send greetings in the Lord, as do Aquila and
Priscilla and all the others who gather in
their home for church meetings. [20]All the
brothers and sisters here send greetings to
you. Greet each other with Christian love.
[21]HERE IS MY GREETING IN MY OWN HAND-
WRITING—PAUL.
[22]If anyone does not love the Lord, that
person is cursed. Our Lord, come!
[23]May the grace of the Lord Jesus be with
you.
[24]My love to all of you in Christ Jesus.

16:2 Acts 20:7
16:5 Acts 19:21
16:6 Rom 15:24; Titus 3:13
16:7 Acts 18:21
16:8 Acts 2:1; 18:19
16:9 Acts 14:27; 19:8-10; 2 Cor 2:12
16:10 Acts 16:1
16:11 1 Tim 4:12
16:12 Acts 18:24
16:13 Eph 6:10; Phil 1:27; 4:1; 1 Thes 3:8
16:15 [f]*diakonia* (1248) ‣2 Cor 8:4
16:16 1 Thes 5:12
16:18 Phlm 1:7
16:19 Rom 16:5
16:20 Rom 16:16
16:21 Gal 6:11; Col 4:18; 2 Thes 3:17; Phlm 1:19
16:22 Gal 1:8-9
16:23 Rom 16:20

16:2 Christians met ***on the first day of each week*** (see Acts 20:7) rather than the last day of the week, as in the OT (Exod 20:8; 34:21; Isa 58:13-14). The first day was the "Lord's Day," the day of the Lord's resurrection (Mark 16:9; Luke 24:13-15; John 20:19; Rev 1:10). • The ***portion of the money you have earned*** is not specified; Paul later encouraged them to give as generously as they could (2 Cor 8:1-4; 9:6-13; cp. Luke 12:33-34; 21:1-4; 1 Tim 6:18-19).

16:4 Paul did in fact deliver the gift to Jerusalem (Rom 15:25-26).

16:5 Paul had traveled through ***Macedonia,*** a Roman province in the northern region of Greece, on his second missionary journey (Acts 15:36–18:22). • ***planning to travel through Macedonia:*** See Acts 19:21; 20:1-3; see also map, p. 1869.

16:6-7 ***possibly all winter:*** Paul evidently made this visit (cp. Acts 20:2-3).

16:8 Paul wrote this letter while in ***Ephesus*** (about AD 53–56; Acts 19:1–20:1). • ***Pentecost*** was in May or June.

16:10 ***When Timothy comes:*** See 4:17. Timothy was Paul's child in the faith and co-worker (see "Timothy" at Acts 16:1-3, p. 1860). • ***don't intimidate him:*** Timothy may have been shy (2 Tim 1:6-8).

16:11-12 ***with the other believers:*** Literally *with the brothers;* also in 16:12; see note on 1:10. It is not clear whom Paul meant. • ***Apollos:*** See note on 1:12.

16:13 ***Be courageous:*** Literally *Be men.*

16:15 ***in Greece:*** Literally *in Achaia,* the southern region of the Greek peninsula, which included Corinth. • ***dear brothers and sisters:*** Literally *brothers;* also in 16:20. See note on 1:10.

16:17 Together with ***Stephanas*** (see also 1:16; 16:15), ***Fortunatus*** and ***Achaicus*** had apparently traveled from Corinth to visit Paul in Ephesus.

16:19-24 As in other letters, Paul greets his friends and gives a benediction.

16:19 ***Asia*** was a Roman ***province*** in what is now western Turkey. • ***Aquila*** and ***Priscilla*** (Greek *Prisca*) had previously moved from Corinth to Ephesus, where Paul was writing this letter (see "Priscilla and Aquila" at Acts 18:1-3, p. 1865). • ***gather in their home:*** Aquila and Priscilla later continued this practice in Rome (see Rom 16:3-5).

16:20 ***with Christian love*** (literally *with a sacred kiss;* also in Rom 16:16; 2 Cor 13:12; 1 Thes 5:26; 1 Pet 5:14): A kiss on the cheek was a common greeting.

16:21 Paul takes up the pen and signs the letter in his ***own handwriting.*** As was common, Paul used a secretary to write this letter and others (see Rom 16:22; Gal 6:11; Col 4:18; 2 Thes 3:17).

16:22 To be ***cursed*** is to be condemned by God (see also Rom 9:3; Gal 1:8-9). • ***Our Lord, come!*** (from Aramaic, *Marana tha.* Some manuscripts read *Maran atha,* "Our Lord has come"): This phrase was sometimes used in early Christian prayers (see also Rev 22:20).

16:23-24 All of Paul's letters close with a benediction similar to this one. • Paul invokes ***grace*** at both the beginning and the end of this letter (see 1:3).

16:24 Some manuscripts add *Amen.*

PAUL'S SECOND LETTER TO THE CORINTHIANS

Second Corinthians reveals, more than any other letter, Paul's concern as a pastor. He passionately desires to win the Christians in Corinth back to himself, convinced that the Good News is above all a message of reconciliation. Paul faced criticism and accusations from fellow Christians who doubted him as a leader. Forced to defend himself, he opens his heart to this congregation to a degree not found in his other letters. Paul faced many dangers, including threats to his life, but being falsely accused by Christians he had won for Christ was one of his worst trials. This letter is a great source of encouragement and hope—both to Christian leaders when they are at an impasse over difficult congregations and when their role as leaders is challenged, and to the congregations themselves, who have Paul's example of how Christ loves his church.

SETTING

The apostle Paul first came to Corinth in the course of his second missionary journey (see Acts 18:1-20). The city was ancient even in Paul's day. It had developed into a strong, well-populated economic and urban center from the 500s BC. Under Roman occupation and influence since Julius Caesar reestablished it in 44 BC, it became a city of fine buildings, shops, theaters, and houses. Its trade, according to the geographer Strabo, brought much wealth, and Plutarch says that the city banks flourished. Artisans crafted bronze artifacts,

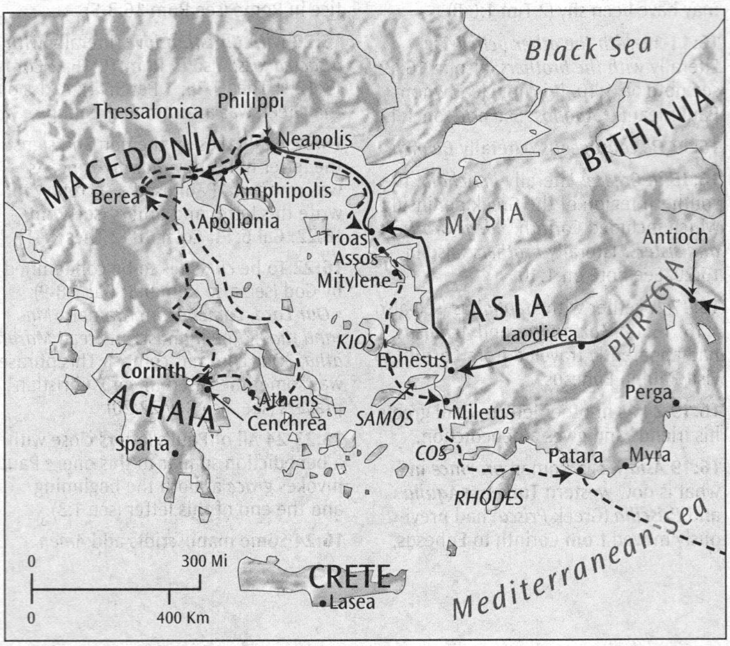

◀ **The Setting of 2 Corinthians, about AD 56.** After writing 1 Corinthians (see 1 Corinthians Introduction, p. 1924), Paul left Ephesus in AD 56 and traveled up to Macedonia; while there, he wrote 2 Corinthians to continue to address the serious difficulties the church in Corinth was facing. Shortly after writing 2 Corinthians, Paul traveled down to Corinth and spent three months there before finishing his journey. The map shows Paul's third missionary journey as a solid line up to the writing of 2 Corinthians in Macedonia, and as a dashed line thereafter.

pottery, and especially the terra cotta lamps that were well-known throughout the ancient world (see 4:7). Agriculture was also key to Corinth's prosperity, so Paul can use the imagery of field and farm to make a point in his teaching even though his readers were city dwellers (9:6-10; 1 Cor 3:6-9; 9:7, 10). Beginning in 27 BC, Achaia (southern Greece) had been controlled by the Roman senate because of Corinth's economic importance and geographical advantage.

The religious life of Corinth is well attested in contemporary writings. The Greek goddess Aphrodite (whom the Romans called Venus), the goddess of life, beauty, and passion, was a popular deity. Strabo speaks of her vast temple on a hill above the city as a center of prostitution, and the moral climate of Corinth was infamously degraded. Scholars are now cautious about this opinion, since the political rivalry between Corinth and nearby Athens might have motivated Strabo's denigrating remarks about Corinth. However, we know that Paul wrote Rom 1:18-32 while he was at Corinth (see Romans Introduction, "Date, Place, and Occasion of Writing," p. 1890; cp. Acts 20:2-3), and 2 Corinthians undeniably reflects his awareness of serious moral problems there (see 6:14-17; 12:19-21).

Into this city Paul brought the message of Christ. By God's grace and the ministry of his servant, a company of believers was established, and the nascent church grew. Paul's converts, whom he regarded as his children (6:13; 12:14; 1 Cor 4:15), were a mixed lot, a cross-section of cosmopolitan society in this city that was famous for its pretensions to wisdom and rhetoric, its popular culture, its trade, its two harbors, and its love of life. At the climax of his list of trials in 11:23-28, Paul writes: "Then, besides all this, I have the daily burden of my concern for all the churches." No congregation brought Paul more concern than the church at Corinth.

OUTLINE

1:1-11
Introduction

1:12–2:13
Paul's Travel Plans and Letter

2:14–7:16
Paul's Apostolic Ministry

8:1–9:15
The Relief Fund for Jerusalem

10:1–12:21
Paul Defends His Apostleship

13:1-14
Conclusion

SUMMARY

Arising out of challenges to Paul's apostolic authority and the infiltration of false teachers, 2 Corinthians handles a number of issues not raised in 1 Corinthians.

In the first half of 2 Corinthians (chs 1–6), Paul outlines his understanding of Christian service. Suffering for Christ's sake is a necessary part of service (ch 1), though it is hard to endure when we are offended by fellow Christians (ch 2). The message of Good News gives life in the Spirit and God's salvation, replacing the religion of the old covenant, though it has continuity with it (ch 3). The power of the message shows through the weakness of God's servants (ch 4) and centers in the death of God's Son, by

TIMELINE

AD 50–52
Paul's second missionary journey

AD 50
Paul meets Priscilla and Aquila in Corinth

about AD 50
Paul writes 1 Thessalonians from Corinth

about AD 51
Paul writes 2 Thessalonians from Corinth

AD 53–57
Paul's third missionary journey

AD 53~56
Paul writes 1 Corinthians from Ephesus

about AD 56
▸ **Paul writes 2 Corinthians from Macedonia**

about AD 57
Paul visits Corinth, where he writes Romans

AD 57
Paul travels to Jerusalem and is arrested

which we are restored to God's favor (ch 5). Christian living is marked by devotion and dedication that distinguish believers from the evils of the world (ch 6).

In chs 7–13 we see Paul as a caring pastor addressing a variety of themes. Paul explains how he came to write his letters to Corinth (ch 7). He reveals principles of giving and stewardship in discussing the collection for the Jerusalem church (chs 8–9), and he makes a spirited defense of his apostolic work against those who denigrated his status because of his weaknesses (chs 10–13).

AUTHOR

No one has seriously challenged Paul's authorship of 2 Corinthians. The sole exception is that 6:14–7:1 is sometimes regarded as a non-Pauline insertion, perhaps from a sect, since it is similar in terminology to the Dead Sea Scrolls. More likely it is simply a digression, or perhaps it has been taken from another of Paul's letters to Corinth and inserted here (see below under "Date and Occasion of Writing"). Either way, the material in it was most likely written by Paul himself to deal with the moral and spiritual situation in the church in Corinth.

DATE AND OCCASION OF WRITING

During his two- to three-year stay in Ephesus (AD 53~56), Paul wrote 1 Corinthians and sent it to the church in Corinth by the hand of Timothy (see 1 Cor 16:10-11; 1 Corinthians Introduction, "Date and Occasion of Writing," p. 1926). Apparently 1 Corinthians was not well-received, and some of the Corinthians were now questioning Paul's apostolic authority. This crisis was anticipated in 1 Cor 4:18-21, but the challenge became more vocal and aggressive. So Paul made a personal visit from Ephesus (2:1). This visit apparently failed to achieve its purpose, as Paul's opponents apparently withstood him. Humiliated before the church and insulted by a prominent member, Paul returned to Ephesus in great distress. He then wrote a "severe letter" and sent it with Titus to Corinth (2:3-13). This severe letter, which has been lost, was finally successful in bringing the Corinthians to repentance (7:8-10).

Paul's second letter to Corinth is very different from the first one. Something terrible had happened, and we feel his pain from the opening lines. . . . The letter itself comes through the tragedy and out into the sunlight, and has a lot to teach us as we make that journey from time to time ourselves.

N. T. WRIGHT
Paul for Everyone—2 Corinthians, p. x

Meanwhile, Paul left Ephesus after severe trials (Acts 19:23-41; cp. 2 Cor 1:8-11; 4:8-15; 6:4-10) and traveled to Macedonia (Acts 20:1). In Macedonia Paul found Titus, who had arrived from Corinth, and Titus gave Paul a very encouraging report about the situation there (7:5-7). In response to that report, Paul wrote 2 Corinthians (about AD 56) and sent it back to Corinth with Titus (8:6, 16-19). Paul then traveled on to Corinth himself, where he spent three months (see Acts 20:1-3).

THE UNITY OF 2 CORINTHIANS AS A LETTER

Although there is no question that Paul himself wrote 2 Corinthians, there are questions about whether it was all written and sent as one letter.

6:14–7:1. In 1 Cor 5:9, Paul mentions a letter that he had previously sent to Corinth dealing with the issue of associating with immoral people. Although this letter has been lost, some scholars believe that at least part of it is preserved as 2 Cor 6:14–7:1, which addresses the same subject. If 6:14–7:1 is a fragment of that previous letter, it might explain why this section seems to be inserted in the discussion, which

would otherwise flow naturally from 6:13 directly to 7:2. On the other hand, Paul often digressed while writing his letters, so it is also possible that 6:14–7:1 is simply a digression.

10:1–13:14. The last four chapters of 2 Corinthians are a puzzle. Some see them as part of Paul's "severe letter" (see 7:8); but that is not likely, since the Corinthians responded to his severe letter with repentance (7:9). The tone of chs 10–13 is more indignant and ironic. It is better to regard chs 10–13 as being written later than chs 1–9 in response to a new situation that arose following the coming of false teachers to Corinth (cp. 11:4, 12-15). The Corinthians had warmly received these teachers, who quickly reopened old wounds and insinuated that Paul was not a true apostle nor even a Christian at all (see 10:7, 10; 11:5; 12:11). When Paul sensed the danger, he wrote a blistering note full of irony, invective, ridicule, and self-defense. At the heart of chs 10–13 is Paul's "Fool's Speech" (11:16–12:10), in which he resorts to boasting because the need compels him (11:1, 16-17).

We cannot tell whether the letter preserved in chs 10–13 succeeded in warding off these threats and defending once more Paul's apostolic standing in Corinth. Paul followed up this letter with a visit (Acts 20:2) as he came to Greece, presumably Corinth. From there he sailed to Jerusalem with the money donated by the other churches, including Corinth. So it is possible that Paul's last letter was the most effective of all, and the Corinthians were finally won over. Forty years after the Corinthian correspondence, a letter known as *1 Clement,* written by a leader at Rome to the Corinthians, speaks warmly of Paul's ministry.

MEANING AND MESSAGE

The Minister's Job Description. The first half of the letter (chs 1-7) explains and describes the responsibilities and privileges of a leader. The message of Good News is new (ch 3) and must be validated by the lifestyle of those who proclaim it. The gospel brings reconciliation (ch 5).

The Heart of the Good News. Chapter 5 contains one of the fullest accounts of Paul's central message (5:18-21). Paul had already told the Corinthians that he came preaching Christ crucified (1 Cor 1:18–2:2). Now, in light of the situation that had developed at Corinth after Paul left for Ephesus, he explains how this message is to be applied. People are out of harmony with God because of sin, so God has acted in response to human need. God in Christ has dealt with the problem of sin and alienation by becoming human and taking our sin upon himself at the cross. Through Christ, we are restored to a relationship of peace and acceptance with God. We are urged to be reconciled to God (5:20) and to maintain our reconciliation with God. This relationship needs to be maintained throughout our lives, which implies loyalty to the Good News as Paul proclaimed it and separation from moral evils such as plagued the city of Corinth.

The Call to Holy Living. Running through this letter is a summons to holy life. The two governing images are of the church as a temple (6:14–7:1) and as a bride (11:2). Both images speak of purity and dedication. The Temple is the holy place where God is worshiped, so his people should be consecrated to this task. The bride of Christ should live in faithful relationship to her spouse.

We learn much more about Paul himself [in 2 Corinthians] than from any other of his letters.

ERNEST BEST
Second Corinthians, p. 3

FURTHER READING

PAUL BARNETT
2 Corinthians (1997)

C. K. BARRETT
A Commentary on the Second Epistle to the Corinthians (1974)

SCOTT J. HAFEMANN
2 Corinthians (2000)

C. G. KRUSE
The Second Epistle of Paul to the Corinthians (1987)

RALPH P. MARTIN WITH CARL N. TONEY
2 Corinthians in *Cornerstone Biblical Commentary,* vol. 15 (2009)

The Need for Generous Giving. Two lengthy chapters (chs 8–9) are devoted to a single theme. Those who are at strife among themselves at Corinth need to consider the needs of others, especially the poverty-stricken Jewish believers in Jerusalem. The incarnate Lord Jesus Christ is our supreme model for sacrificial giving (8:9).

Second Corinthians is a very human document that opens a window onto the inner life of the apostle Paul. For that reason, it has been called Paul's most personal letter. The apostle and the Good News are closely united throughout the epistle. What was at stake at Corinth was the essence of the Good News as expressed in the way of the cross. Paul's experience of suffering and weakness as an apostle was, to the believers in Corinth, a seeming contradiction to his authority. In fact, however, the essence of the Good News is for people to accept another person's suffering (Christ's, first and foremost) for their own good. This is still relevant to leadership and daily living among Christians today.

1. INTRODUCTION (1:1-11)

Greetings from Paul (1:1-2)

1 This letter is from Paul, chosen by the will of God to be an apostle of Christ Jesus, and from our brother Timothy.

I am writing to God's church in Corinth and to all of his holy people throughout Greece.

2May God our Father and the Lord Jesus Christ give you grace and peace.

Thanksgiving (1:3-11)

God Offers Comfort to All

3All praise to God, the [a]Father of our Lord Jesus Christ. God is our merciful [a]Father and the source of all comfort. 4He comforts us in all our troubles so that we can comfort others. When they are troubled, we will be able to give them the same comfort God has given us. 5For the more we suffer for Christ, the more God will shower us with his comfort through Christ. 6Even when we are weighed down with troubles, it is for your comfort and salvation! For when we ourselves are comforted, we will certainly comfort you. Then you can patiently endure the same things we suffer. 7We are confident that as you share in our sufferings, you will also share in the comfort God gives us.

God's Rescue of Paul

8We think you ought to know, dear brothers and sisters, about the trouble we went through in the province of Asia. We were crushed and overwhelmed beyond our ability to endure, and we thought we would never live through it. 9In fact, we expected to die. But as a result, we stopped relying on ourselves and learned to rely only on God, who raises the dead. 10And he did rescue us from mortal danger, and he will rescue us again. We have placed our confidence in him, and he will continue to rescue us. 11And you are helping us by praying for us. Then many people will give thanks because God has graciously answered so many prayers for our safety.

1:1 1 Cor 1:1; 2 Cor 1:19; Eph 1:1
1:2 Rom 1:7
1:3 Eph 1:3; 1 Pet 1:3; [a]*pater* (3962) ›Eph 1:3
1:4 Isa 51:12; 66:13; 2 Cor 7:6
1:5 2 Cor 4:10; Phil 3:10; Col 1:24
1:6 2 Cor 4:15
1:9 Jer 17:5, 7
1:10 2 Tim 4:18; 2 Pet 2:9
1:11 Rom 15:30; 2 Cor 4:15; Phil 1:19

1:1-2 Letters in the first century usually began by mentioning the writer's name and that of the person(s) addressed, followed by a greeting (see Acts 15:23; 23:25-26). Paul follows this pattern.

1:1 *Greece:* Greek *Achaia,* the southern region of the Greek peninsula. • Paul turns the usual, colorless "greetings" (Greek *chairein*) into a rich salutation by praying for God's ***grace*** (Greek *charis*) ***and peace*** on his readers. • Paul highlights his calling as an ***apostle;*** his status as God's appointed agent for establishing the church had been challenged at Corinth.

1:3-11 Paul now breaks into a jubilant thanksgiving. He is glad that, in spite of many troubles that have weighed upon him, he has had special ***comfort*** from God (1:4-7) and has been rescued from death in the province of Asia (1:8-11).

1:3 ***our merciful Father:*** God delights in showing favor to his people and in hearing his children's cry (Ps 145:18-19).

1:4-6 One purpose of suffering is to qualify Christ's servants to enter sympathetically into the experience of others. Paul is not an aloof pastor, remote from the people to whom he ministers.

1:6 ***it is for your comfort and salvation!*** Paul's sharing in their troubles and offering of encouragement promotes their spiritual well-being.

1:8-11 ***dear brothers and sisters:*** Literally ***brothers.*** Paul uses this traditional term of affection to address all the believers, not just the men. • ***The trouble we went through in the province of Asia*** is not easy to identify. One suggestion is the riot in Ephesus (Acts 19:23-41). Another is that Paul was tried in a civil court and faced the prospect of execution in Ephesus (1:9; see 1 Cor 15:32). Less likely is that he suffered an acute life-threatening illness. Paul was no stranger to ***mortal danger*** (1:10; see also 4:10-12; 6:9; 11:23), but he was marvelously rescued by divine assistance (1:11).

1:12
Acts 23:1
1 Cor 1:17
2 Cor 2:17; 4:15

1:14
2 Cor 5:12
Phil 2:16

1:15
Rom 1:11-13

1:16
Acts 19:21
1 Cor 16:5-6

1:17
2 Cor 5:16

1:19
Acts 18:5
Heb 13:8

1:20
Rom 15:8-9
Rev 3:14

1:21
1 Jn 2:20, 27

1:22
2 Cor 5:5
Eph 1:13-14; 4:30
[b]*arrabōn* (0728)
‣2 Cor 5:5

1:23
1 Cor 4:21

1:24
1 Cor 15:1

2:1
1 Cor 4:21
2 Cor 12:21

2:2
2 Cor 7:8

2:4
2 Cor 2:9; 7:8, 12

2. PAUL'S TRAVEL PLANS AND LETTER (1:12–2:13)

Paul's Change of Plans

12We can say with confidence and a clear conscience that we have lived with a God-given holiness and sincerity in all our dealings. We have depended on God's grace, not on our own human wisdom. That is how we have conducted ourselves before the world, and especially toward you. 13Our letters have been straightforward, and there is nothing written between the lines and nothing you can't understand. I hope someday you will fully understand us, 14even if you don't understand us now. Then on the day when the Lord Jesus returns, you will be proud of us in the same way we are proud of you.

15Since I was so sure of your understanding and trust, I wanted to give you a double blessing by visiting you twice—16first on my way to Macedonia and again when I returned from Macedonia. Then you could send me on my way to Judea.

17You may be asking why I changed my plan. Do you think I make my plans carelessly? Do you think I am like people of the world who say "Yes" when they really mean "No"? 18As surely as God is faithful, our word to you does not waver between "Yes" and "No." 19For Jesus Christ, the Son of God, does not waver between "Yes" and "No." He is the one whom Silas, Timothy, and I preached to you, and as God's ultimate "Yes," he always does what he says. 20For all of God's promises have been fulfilled in Christ with a resounding "Yes!" And through Christ, our "Amen" (which means "Yes") ascends to God for his glory.

21It is God who enables us, along with you, to stand firm for Christ. He has commissioned us, 22and he has identified us as his own by placing the Holy Spirit in our hearts as the [b]first installment that guarantees everything he has promised us.

23Now I call upon God as my witness that I am telling the truth. The reason I didn't return to Corinth was to spare you from a severe rebuke. 24But that does not mean we want to dominate you by telling you how to put your faith into practice. We want to work together with you so you will be full of joy, for it is by your own faith that you stand firm.

2 So I decided that I would not bring you grief with another painful visit. 2For if I cause you grief, who will make me glad? Certainly not someone I have grieved.

Paul's Tearful Letter

3That is why I wrote to you as I did, so that when I do come, I won't be grieved by the very ones who ought to give me the greatest joy. Surely you all know that my joy comes from your being joyful. 4I wrote that letter in great anguish, with a troubled heart and many tears. I didn't want to grieve you, but I wanted to let you know how much love I have for you.

1:12-14 Paul's travel plans and his unfulfilled promise of a visit to Corinth were criticized; he was charged with being fickle like persons of the world "who say 'Yes' when they really mean 'No'" (1:17). Before responding to that charge, he clarifies his motives in his ministry and in his letters.

1:12 ***holiness:*** Some manuscripts read *honesty.* The difference is only two letters in Greek (*hagiotēti*, "holiness"; *haplotēti*, "honesty").

1:14 ***the Lord Jesus:*** Some manuscripts read *our Lord Jesus.*

1:15–2:2 Paul had ***changed*** his travel ***plan.*** In 1 Cor 16:5, he expressed the hope of visiting Corinth after passing through ***Macedonia,*** which was in the northern region of Greece. Then he evidently promised to visit Corinth earlier (perhaps in his "severe letter," 7:8)—on his way north. Now he would have to go back to the original plan, and that earlier visit, bringing ***a double blessing,*** would not be happening after all.

1:17 Paul's apparent indecisiveness and failure to keep his promise were being criticized. Paul's protest is indignant.

1:18-22 It was bad enough that Paul's enemies at Corinth had attacked his character as unreliable and shifty (1:17). It was worse when they charged that his entire message was just as uncertain. In these verses Paul answers that allegation.

1:18-20 ***As surely as God is faithful:*** God can be trusted, as can his promises in Christ and his ministry through the apostles.

1:19 ***Silas*** (Greek *Silvanus*) was a well-known Christian leader from the church in Antioch (see Acts 15:22, 27, 32; 1 Thes 1:1; 2 Thes 1:1; 1 Pet 5:12).

1:20 God has put a seal of approval, ***with a resounding "Yes!"*** on the OT prophecies as they are fulfilled in Christ. Believers respond with ***"Amen,"*** meaning "confirmed and agreed."

1:21-22 Paul's ministry was enabled, ***commissioned*** (literally *anointed*), and endorsed by God, who equipped him for his work. • ***along with you:*** All believers are ***identified . . . as his own*** (literally *sealed*) by the Holy Spirit, who is God's gift to his people (see Rom 8:1-27; Gal 3:2-7; 5:5-6, 16-26; Eph 1:13-14). • ***First installment*** is a commercial term for a deposit or down payment, guaranteeing full possession (see 5:5; Eph 1:14).

1:23–2:2 ***God as my witness:*** This mild oath indicates that he is telling the truth (see 1 Sam 12:5; 20:12; Job 16:19; cp. Ruth 1:17; 1 Sam 14:44; 2 Sam 3:35; 1 Kgs 2:23; Jer 42:5). The real reason for Paul's change of travel plans was ***to spare*** them ***from a severe rebuke*** (1:23) and not inflict ***another painful visit*** on them (2:1).

2:1 Paul's previous ***visit*** had been very ***painful*** and had caused him great distress. This visit is not recorded in Acts; it apparently took place during Paul's three-year ministry in Ephesus (see Acts 19:8-22). During that visit, Paul severely rebuked the church (1:23) but was insulted by an unnamed man (2:5-11).

2:3-4 After his painful visit (2:1), Paul then wrote a letter with ***great anguish . . . and many tears*** that was intended for the Corinthians' good. That letter (see also 7:8-10) has evidently been lost. But it was effective in bringing about the needed repentance and change.

Forgiveness for the Sinner
5I am not overstating it when I say that the
man who caused all the trouble hurt all of
you more than he hurt me. 6Most of you
opposed him, and that was punishment
enough. 7Now, however, it is time to forgive
and comfort him. Otherwise he may be
overcome by discouragement. 8So I urge
you now to reaffirm your love for him.
9I wrote to you as I did to test you and
see if you would fully comply with my instructions. 10When you forgive this man, I
forgive him, too. And when I forgive whatever needs to be forgiven, I do so with
Christ's authority for your benefit, 11so that
Satan will not outsmart us. For we are familiar with his evil schemes.

Paul's Recent Travels
12When I came to the city of Troas to preach
the Good News of Christ, the Lord opened a
door of opportunity for me. 13But I had no
peace of mind because my dear brother Titus hadn't yet arrived with a report from
you. So I said good-bye and went on to Macedonia to find him.

3. PAUL'S APOSTOLIC MINISTRY (2:14–7:16)

Ministers of the New Covenant
14But thank God! He has made us his captives and continues to lead us along in
Christ's triumphal procession. Now he uses
us to spread the knowledge of Christ everywhere, like a sweet perfume. 15Our lives are
a Christ-like fragrance rising up to God. But
this fragrance is perceived differently by
those who are being [c]saved and by those
who are perishing. 16To those who are perishing, we are a dreadful smell of death and
doom. But to those who are being saved, we
are a life-giving perfume. And who is adequate for such a task as this?
17You see, we are not like the many hucksters who preach for personal profit. We
preach the word of God with sincerity and
with Christ's authority, knowing that God is
watching us.

3 Are we beginning to praise ourselves
again? Are we like others, who need
to bring you letters of recommendation, or
who ask you to write such letters on their
behalf? Surely not! 2The only letter of recommendation we need is you yourselves.
Your lives are a letter written in our hearts;
everyone can read it and recognize our
good work among you. 3Clearly, you are a
letter from Christ showing the result of our
ministry among you. This "letter" is written
not with pen and ink, but with the Spirit of
the living God. It is carved not on tablets of
stone, but on human hearts.
4We are confident of all this because of
our great trust in God through Christ. 5It is
not that we think we are qualified to do anything on our own. Our qualification comes
from God. 6He has enabled us to be ministers of his new [d]covenant. This is a covenant

2:5 1 Cor 5:1-2; 2 Cor 7:11
2:7 Gal 6:1; Eph 4:32
2:11 2 Cor 4:4; 1 Pet 5:8
2:12 Acts 14:27; 2 Cor 4:3
2:13 2 Cor 7:5-6
2:15 Num 15:3; 1 Cor 1:18; [c]*sōzō* (4982) ‣Eph 1:13
2:16 Luke 2:34; 2 Cor 3:5-6
2:17 2 Cor 1:12; 12:19
3:1 Acts 18:27; 2 Cor 5:12; 10:12
3:2 1 Cor 9:2
3:3 Exod 24:12; 31:18; 32:15-16; Prov 3:3; Jer 31:33; Ezek 36:26
3:5 1 Cor 15:10; 2 Cor 2:16
3:6 Jer 31:31; Luke 22:20; John 6:63; Rom 2:27; 7:6; 8:2; Gal 3:10; Heb 8:8-13; [d]*diathēkē* (1242) ‣2 Cor 3:14; [e]*zōopoieō* (2227) ‣Gal 3:21

2:5-11 These verses are the outcome of Paul's earlier visit and the insult he received. Following Paul's severe but tearful letter, the church condemned the behavior of ***the man who caused all the trouble*** and disciplined him (2:6). He repented, so now it was ***time to forgive and comfort him,*** as Paul had already done.

2:11 If we exercise forgiveness, as Paul did, ***Satan will not outsmart us*** by making us either too lax over sin or too rigorous in punishing offenders. • ***familiar with his evil schemes:*** Cp. 11:3, 14; Eph 6:11.

2:12-13 After the riot at Ephesus (Acts 19:1–20:1), Paul went to the seaport of ***Troas*** (Acts 20:5). He was impatient to get news from ***Titus*** about the result of the severe but tearful letter (2:4), and he crossed over to Macedonia in northern Greece ***to find him.***

2:14–7:4 At this point, the story about finding Titus breaks off, and will not be resumed until 7:5. Paul digresses to discuss his ministry as an apostle proclaiming the Good News.

2:14 Like ***captives*** in a Roman general's celebration march, Paul was ***in Christ's triumphal procession*** (cp. 1 Cor 4:9; Eph 4:7-11), carrying the marks of willing servitude (see Rom 1:1; Gal 6:17).

2:15-16 Incense was scattered along the parade route of a victorious Roman general, and it was received in one of two ways. For the captives, who were on their way to the arena and death, it was ***a dreadful smell of death and doom.*** For the victors, it was ***a life-giving perfume.*** So it is with the lives of those who proclaim the Good News, which either leads to eternal life or seals the fate of the person who rejects it (cp. 1 Cor 1:18).

2:17 Paul contrasts his service with that of his opponents. • ***the many hucksters:*** Some manuscripts read ***the rest of the hucksters.*** They ***preach for personal profit*** and adulterate the truth, like merchants in Paul's day who offered shoddy goods, or innkeepers who watered down the wine. By contrast, Paul preached ***with sincerity and with Christ's authority*** (cp. 1:12; 4:2). Paul's denial of mercenary motives reemerges in chs 11–12.

3:1-3 Paul's ministry was validated by the lives of those who were changed by the Good News rather than by a ***letter of recommendation*** (cp. Acts 18:27). Christ, the author of this transformation, used Paul to lead believers to him. The marks of genuineness are not in letters ***written . . . with pen and ink*** on parchment, but the fruit of ***the Spirit*** (Gal 5:22-23) in human lives and ***carved . . . on human hearts.***

3:2 ***our hearts:*** Some manuscripts read ***your hearts.***

3:4-18 The contrast between Paul's ministry and the others' ministries leads Paul to contrast the ***old covenant*** of written laws (Exod 31:18) with the ***new covenant*** written on human hearts (Jer 31:33).

3:4-6 ***The old written covenant*** is the religion of Moses as interpreted by the Jewish rabbis. It ***ends in death*** for adherents who see it as a way of salvation. The law is good (Rom 7:12-14), but those who use it to gain merit fail. It leads either to transgression or to pride;

3:7
Exod 34:29-35
[f]*doxa* (1391)
‣2 Cor 4:17
3:9
Deut 27:26
Rom 1:17; 3:21
3:10-11
Exod 34:29-30
John 17:10, 22
3:13
Exod 34:33-35
3:14
Acts 13:15
Rom 11:7-8
2 Cor 4:4
[g]*diathēkē* (1242)
‣Eph 2:12
3:16
Isa 25:7
Rom 11:23
3:17
John 8:36
Gal 4:6-7
[h]*eleutheria* (1657)
‣Gal 2:4
3:18
Rom 8:29
2 Cor 4:4, 6
[i]*metamorphoō* (3339)
‣Phil 3:21
4:2
2 Cor 2:17
1 Thes 2:5
4:3
1 Cor 1:18
2 Cor 3:14
4:4
Isa 6:10
John 12:39-41
Col 1:15
Heb 1:3
4:5
1 Cor 9:19
4:6
Gen 1:3
Ps 36:9
John 8:12; 12:46
Eph 5:8, 14
1 Pet 2:9
2 Pet 1:19
4:7
2 Tim 2:20
4:9
Rom 8:35
4:10
Rom 8:17
1 Cor 15:31
Gal 6:17
Phil 3:10
Col 1:24
2 Tim 2:11
1 Pet 4:13

not of written laws, but of the Spirit. The
old written covenant ends in death; but under the new covenant, the Spirit [e]gives life.

The Glory of the New Covenant

7 The old way, with laws etched in stone, led
to death, though it began with such [f]glory
that the people of Israel could not bear to
look at Moses' face. For his face shone with
the [f]glory of God, even though the brightness was already fading away. 8 Shouldn't
we expect far greater glory under the new
way, now that the Holy Spirit is giving life?
9 If the old way, which brings condemnation, was glorious, how much more glorious
is the new way, which makes us right with
God! 10 In fact, that first glory was not glorious at all compared with the overwhelming
glory of the new way. 11 So if the old way,
which has been replaced, was glorious, how
much more glorious is the new, which remains forever!
12 Since this new way gives us such confidence, we can be very bold. 13 We are not
like Moses, who put a veil over his face so
the people of Israel would not see the glory,
even though it was destined to fade away.
14 But the people's minds were hardened,
and to this day whenever the old [g]covenant
is being read, the same veil covers their
minds so they cannot understand the truth.
And this veil can be removed only by believing in Christ. 15 Yes, even today when
they read Moses' writings, their hearts
are covered with that veil, and they do not
understand.
16 But whenever someone turns to the
Lord, the veil is taken away. 17 For the Lord
is the Spirit, and wherever the Spirit of the
Lord is, there is [h]freedom. 18 So all of us
who have had that veil removed can see
and reflect the glory of the Lord. And the
Lord—who is the Spirit—makes us more
and more like him as we are [i]changed into
his glorious image.

Paul's Preaching Ministry

4 Therefore, since God in his mercy has
given us this new way, we never give up.
2 We reject all shameful deeds and under-
handed methods. We don't try to trick
anyone or distort the word of God. We tell
the truth before God, and all who are honest
know this.
3 If the Good News we preach is hidden
behind a veil, it is hidden only from people
who are perishing. 4 Satan, who is the god of
this world, has blinded the minds of those
who don't believe. They are unable to see
the glorious light of the Good News. They
don't understand this message about the
glory of Christ, who is the exact likeness of
God.
5 You see, we don't go around preaching
about ourselves. We preach that Jesus
Christ is Lord, and we ourselves are your
servants for Jesus' sake. 6 For God, who said,
"Let there be light in the darkness," has
made this light shine in our hearts so we
could know the glory of God that is seen in
the face of Jesus Christ.
7 We now have this light shining in our
hearts, but we ourselves are like fragile clay
jars containing this great treasure. This
makes it clear that our great power is from
God, not from ourselves.
8 We are pressed on every side by troubles,
but we are not crushed. We are perplexed,
but not driven to despair. 9 We are hunted
down, but never abandoned by God. We get
knocked down, but we are not destroyed.
10 Through suffering, our bodies continue
to share in the death of Jesus so that the life
of Jesus may also be seen in our bodies.
11 Yes, we live under constant danger of
death because we serve Jesus, so that the

either way, the law brings condemnation (3:9).

3:7-11 ***The old way:*** (Or *the old ministry;* also in 3:8-12): The old covenant had its moments of ***glory***, such as when ***Moses' face . . . shone*** from his communion with the Lord (Exod 34:29-35). • The ***old way*** has been ***replaced*** by ***the new way***, which is eternal (Heb 8:8-13).

3:12-15 The old covenant, represented by Moses' ***veil***, led to fear and did not remove spiritual blindness.

3:16-18 The believer who ***turns to the Lord*** has freedom in the ***Spirit***. We receive something Moses never knew as we become ***more and more like*** Christ (4:4; John 1:1-14; Col 1:15; Heb 1:1-4) ***and reflect the glory of the Lord.*** Divine glory in this present life leads to our being like Christ in the next life (Rom 8:29; Gal 4:19; Phil 3:21; 1 Jn 3:2).

4:1 ***This new way*** (or *This new ministry*) shows us God's ***mercy***. Paul felt privileged to have the ministry of sharing the message of Good News (1 Cor 15:9-11; 1 Tim 1:12-17).

4:2 Paul's ministry was marked by honesty, unlike some other preachers (2:17).

4:3-4 The ***Good News*** divides people into two categories: those who remain in darkness, and those who are enlightened by God (see Acts 26:18). God's action in bringing people to himself is a movement from a realm governed by darkness to the light of God's presence (Col 1:12-14; 1 Pet 2:9). ***The god of this world*** fights against the change that the Good News brings to people's hearts and ***minds***.

4:5 ***We preach that Jesus Christ is Lord:*** See also Rom 10:9-10; 1 Cor 12:3; Col 2:6.

4:7 ***We now have . . . this great treasure:*** Literally *We now have this treasure in clay jars*. The message of Good News is like ***great treasure***, but it is housed in ***fragile clay jars***—our weak bodies. This insight gives purpose to suffering (4:8–5:10).

4:11 Believers often share the humiliation of the Lord with confidence that they will also share in his triumphant risen life (4:14).

life of Jesus will be evident in our dying
bodies. 12So we live in the face of death, but
this has resulted in eternal life for you.
13But we continue to preach because we
have the same kind of faith the psalmist
had when he said, "I believed in God, so I
spoke." 14We know that God, who raised
the Lord Jesus, will also raise us with Jesus
and present us to himself together with you.
15All of this is for your benefit. And as God's
grace reaches more and more people, there
will be great thanksgiving, and God will receive more and more glory.
16That is why we never give up. Though
our bodies are dying, our spirits are being
renewed every day. 17For our present troubles are small and won't last very long. Yet
they produce for us a [i]glory that vastly outweighs them and will last forever! 18So we
don't look at the troubles we can see now;
rather, we fix our gaze on things that cannot be seen. For the things we see now will
soon be gone, but the things we cannot see
will last forever.

New Bodies

5 For we know that when this earthly tent
we live in is taken down (that is, when
we die and leave this earthly body), we will
have a house in heaven, an eternal body
made for us by God himself and not by human hands. 2We grow weary in our present
bodies, and we long to put on our heavenly
bodies like new clothing. 3For we will put on
heavenly bodies; we will not be spirits without bodies. 4While we live in these earthly
bodies, we groan and sigh, but it's not that
we want to die and get rid of these bodies

4:13 Ps 116:10
4:14 John 11:21-25; Acts 2:24; 1 Thes 2:19
4:15 2 Cor 1:3-6
4:16 Eph 3:16; Col 3:10
4:17 Rom 8:17-18; 1 Pet 1:6-7; [i]*doxa* (1391) ‣Phil 2:11
4:18 Rom 8:24; 2 Cor 5:7
5:1 1 Cor 15:47; 2 Cor 4:7; 2 Pet 1:13-14
5:2 Rom 8:23; 1 Cor 15:53-54
5:4 1 Cor 15:53-54

God's New Covenant (3:4-18)

2 Cor 4:4-6; Gen 9:1-17; 12:1-9; 15:1-21; Exod 19:3-6; 2 Sam 7:5-16; 1 Chr 10:13-14; Isa 59:20-21; 65:17-25; Jer 2:1–3:10; 31:31-34; Matt 26:27-29; Luke 22:20; 1 Cor 11:23-32; Heb 8:6-13; 9:11-28; 10:1-25; 12:18-24

Paul interprets the old covenant in light of his experience with Jesus Christ and the new covenant that Christ initiated (3:7-18), as prophesied in Jer 31:31-34. Using the creation story of Gen 1–2, Paul explains how the God of creation is also the God of the new creation in Jesus Christ, who shows his glory to those who believe (4:4-6; 5:17). God is now revealed in Christ, who brings God close to us. What that means is spelled out in various ways in this letter.

In the new covenant, God is our Father because he is the Father of our Lord Jesus Christ (1:3). He is the faithful God whose OT promises are fulfilled in the Messiah (1:18-22). He calls men and women into his family (6:18) and sustains them in times of trial because he is the merciful father and the God who gives encouragement (1:3).

God is the author of reconciliation (5:18-21), and the Father and the Son are bound together in this common purpose. Christ became the means by which God won the sinful world back to himself. Jesus Christ became one with sinful humankind (8:9), and released God's saving power and righteousness to restore the broken relationship between God and the world.

God works in human lives through his Holy Spirit. God's plan includes the promise of resurrection, when believers' mortal bodies will be transformed into glorified bodies (1 Cor 15:42-57). Paul gives a full account of this hope in 5:1-10.

Paul had a rich understanding of one God in three persons (see 13:14). The salvation brought by Christ the Son reveals the Father's love, and believers come to share in this by the Holy Spirit. The Spirit is life-giving (3:6, 17-18); he is the one who unites us to Christ and guarantees complete salvation in the resurrection (1:22; 5:5).

4:12 Through his life of danger and exposure to mortal peril (see 1 Cor 15:30), Paul was reinforcing the faith of the Christians in the churches that he founded (cp. Col 1:24; 2 Tim 2:10).

4:13-14 The secret of Paul's resilience was in ***the same kind of faith the psalmist had,*** which is centered in the living Lord. • ***"I believed in God, so I spoke":*** This quotation is from Ps 116:10.

4:14 ***who raised the Lord Jesus:*** Some manuscripts read *who raised Jesus.*

4:16-17 ***we never give up:*** This call to endurance is given with a reminder of what is in store in the future (5:1-10). The human body is in the process of ***dying*** in the normal course of growing old, and Paul was particularly worn away physically and emotionally (4:8-12). Yet he was ***being renewed every day***—his spirit's life was being rejuvenated and revitalized by the power of God. • ***our spirits are:*** Literally *our inner being is.*

4:18 If we ***look at the troubles we can see now,*** we grow faint; but when we see our lives in the light of eternal reality, we know that our troubles ***will soon be gone.***

5:1-10 The prospect of eternal hope is bright, with ***heavenly bodies*** replacing the ***dying bodies*** of this present life. The God of resurrection will also raise us and present us to himself with all believers (4:14). The immediate stimulus for this statement of resurrection hope was what Paul had to face in Ephesus (1:8-11). The frailty of his body reminded him of what lies beyond death, when ***this earthly tent we live in***—that is, our body—will be taken down in death and dissolution (see 1 Cor 15:42-57; Phil 3:20-21).

5:2 ***we long to put on our heavenly bodies:*** This is no death wish; Paul was yearning for the Lord's return when he would give new bodies to his people (1 Cor 15:51-58; Phil 3:20-21; 1 Thes 4:16-17).

5:3 ***we will not be spirits without bodies:*** Literally *we will not be naked.*

5:7 Our hope for future resurrection can only be known by faith (see Heb

5:5
Rom 8:23
2 Cor 1:22
Eph 1:13-14
[k]*arrabōn* (0728)
‣Eph 1:14
5:7
1 Cor 13:12
5:8
Phil 1:23
5:10
Matt 16:27
Acts 10:42
[a]*christos* (5547)
‣Gal 6:2
5:12
2 Cor 1:14; 3:1
[b]*kardia* (2588)
‣Gal 4:6
5:14
Rom 6:6-7
Gal 2:20
Col 3:3
5:15
Rom 14:7-9

that clothe us. Rather, we want to put on our
new bodies so that these dying bodies will
be swallowed up by life. 5God himself has
prepared us for this, and as a [k]guarantee he
has given us his Holy Spirit.
6So we are always confident, even though
we know that as long as we live in these bodies we are not at home with the Lord. 7For we
live by believing and not by seeing. 8Yes, we
are fully confident, and we would rather be
away from these earthly bodies, for then we
will be at home with the Lord. 9So whether
we are here in this body or away from this
body, our goal is to please him. 10For we
must all stand before [a]Christ to be judged.
We will each receive whatever we deserve
for the good or evil we have done in this
earthly body.

God's Ambassadors
11Because we understand our fearful responsibility to the Lord, we work hard to persuade
others. God knows we are sincere, and I hope
you know this, too. 12Are we commending
ourselves to you again? No, we are giving you
a reason to be proud of us, so you can answer
those who brag about having a spectacular
ministry rather than having a sincere [b]heart.
13If it seems we are crazy, it is to bring glory
to God. And if we are in our right minds, it
is for your benefit. 14Either way, Christ's love
controls us. Since we believe that Christ died
for all, we also believe that we have all died
to our old life. 15He died for everyone so that
those who receive his new life will no longer
live for themselves. Instead, they will live for
Christ, who died and was raised for them.

The Message of Reconciliation (5:18-21)

2 Cor 13:11
Ezek 45:15
Dan 9:24
Matt 5:24; 18:15
Acts 10:36
Rom 5:1-2; 8:6-9, 15-16; 12:18; 15:13
Eph 2:11-18
Col 1:19-22
Heb 2:17

Reconciliation is a term found throughout the Pauline letters with a wide range of meanings. In Rom 5:1-11, Paul concentrates on the cost of God's reconciling work in the death of his son. Colossians 1:15-20 is a hymn in praise of the cosmic scope of reconciliation, with the exalted Lord now ruler of all. In Eph 2:11-22, the emphasis is on the scope of reconciliation that embraces both Jews and Gentiles to form a united church with all hostility broken down like demolishing a wall of separation.

Paul's fullest exposition of the meaning of Jesus' death is in 2 Cor 5:18-21. Earlier, Paul had reminded the Corinthians of the centrality of the cross (1 Cor 15:3-5) but had not elaborated on the deepest meaning of that saving event. Now he explains what Christ's death on the cross means: Christ identified himself with human sin so that sinners might be restored to their family relationship with God. This reconciliation turns enemies into friends. The cost of this exchange is that "God made Christ, who never sinned, to be the offering for our sin, so that we could be made right with God through Christ" (5:21).

The event of Jesus' resurrection is also invested with tremendous significance. With the resurrection of Jesus and his triumph over death, a new world is born—a new era in which God's people have the promise of eternal fellowship with him (see 4:14–5:10). Those who have trusted in Christ for salvation have received the gift of the Holy Spirit, the guarantee of future salvation (5:5). They know that God has accepted them and will welcome them forever.

11:1, 3, 27), yet we do have Jesus' own resurrection and the presence of the Holy Spirit as evidence of what is to come (1 Cor 15:1-9; Eph 1:14).

5:9-10 The ***goal*** of the present life is ***to please him*** (see also Rom 12:1-2; 14:18; Col 1:10; 1 Thes 4:1). This ambition will be tested when we ***stand before Christ to be judged.*** The judge is also our advocate, so we are confident of acquittal (Rom 8:1, 33-34). Yet actions ***done in this earthly body*** will be assessed and called to account (Acts 17:31).

5:11–7:4 Paul now explains the main theme of his message, which is reconciliation—the turning of enemies into friends and the restoration of relationships. Paul's thinking is rooted in what God has done through Christ to reconcile sinners to himself (5:18-21). This exposition is framed by a defense of his own ministry (5:11-17) and an application of his message to the situation in Corinth (6:1–7:4).

5:11 One motive for Paul's ministry is ***fearful responsibility to the Lord***—not a cringing dread, but a healthy reverence (see "Fear of the LORD" at Prov 1:7, p. 1030).

5:12 ***proud of us:*** Some manuscripts read *proud of yourselves.* • Paul's opponents bragged ***about having a spectacular ministry*** outwardly, but they did not have ***a sincere heart*** (cp. 1 Sam 16:7; Rom 2:28-29).

5:13 ***if . . . we are crazy:*** This statement might imply a charge on Paul's previous visit to Corinth (2:1-2) that he was out of his mind when he proclaimed the simple Good News at Corinth (1 Cor 2:2).

5:14-17 Paul's doctrine of reconciliation arises from his conviction that (1) Christ ***died for*** all believers; (2) in Christ, believers also die to sin and self; and (3) now all believers should ***live for Christ.*** The new life in Christ thus leads to a fresh evaluation of other people and of Christ.

5:14 ***Christ's love controls us*** (or *urges us on*): This could refer either to believers' love for Christ or (more likely) to Christ's love for us, which urges believers on in making Christ known through their service (see 1 Cor 9:16). • ***Since we believe that Christ died for all, we also believe that we have all died to our old life:*** Literally *Since one died for all, then all died.*

16 So we have stopped evaluating others
from a human point of view. At one time
we thought of Christ merely from a human
point of view. How differently we know him
now! 17 This means that anyone who belongs
to Christ has become a new person. The old
life is gone; a new life has begun!
18 And all of this is a gift from God, who
brought us back to himself through Christ.
And God has given us this task of [c]reconcil-
ing people to him. 19 For God was in Christ,
reconciling the world to himself, no longer
counting people's sins against them. And he
gave us this wonderful message of [d]reconcil-
iation. 20 So we are Christ's ambassadors;
God is making his appeal through us. We
speak for Christ when we plead, [e]"Come
back to God!" 21 For God made Christ, who
never sinned, to be the offering for our sin,
so that we could be made right with God
through Christ.

6 As God's partners, we beg you not to
accept this marvelous gift of God's
kindness and then ignore it. 2 For God says,

"At just the right time, I heard you.
On the day of salvation, I helped you."

Indeed, the "right time" is now. Today is the
day of salvation.

Paul's Faithful Ministry

3 We live in such a way that no one will stumble because of us, and no one will find fault
with our ministry. 4 In everything we do, we
show that we are true ministers of God. We
patiently endure troubles and hardships and
calamities of every kind. 5 We have been
beaten, been put in prison, faced angry mobs,
worked to exhaustion, endured sleepless
nights, and gone without food. 6 We prove
ourselves by our purity, our understanding,
our patience, our kindness, by the Holy Spirit
within us, and by our sincere love. 7 We faithfully preach the truth. God's power is working
in us. We use the weapons of righteousness
in the right hand for attack and the left hand
for defense. 8 We serve God whether people
honor us or despise us, whether they slander
us or praise us. We are honest, but they call us
impostors. 9 We are ignored, even though we
are well known. We live close to death, but
we are still alive. We have been beaten, but
we have not been killed. 10 Our hearts ache,
but we always have joy. We are poor, but we
give spiritual riches to others. We own nothing, and yet we have everything.
11 Oh, dear Corinthian friends! We have
spoken honestly with you, and our hearts
are open to you. 12 There is no lack of love
on our part, but you have withheld your
love from us. 13 I am asking you to respond

5:16 2 Cor 10:4
5:17 Isa 65:17; Gal 6:15; Rev 21:5
5:18 Rom 5:10; [c]*katallagē* (2643) ‣2 Cor 5:19
5:19 Rom 3:24; 4:8; [d]*katallagē* (2643) ‣2 Cor 5:20
5:20 Eph 6:20; [e]*katallassō* (2644) ‣Rom 5:10
5:21 Isa 53:6, 9; Jer 23:6; Gal 3:13; Heb 4:15; 7:26; 1 Pet 2:22
6:1 1 Cor 3:9; 2 Cor 5:20
6:2 *Isa 49:8
6:3 1 Cor 8:9; 9:12
6:4 2 Cor 4:2
6:5 2 Cor 11:23-27
6:6 1 Tim 4:12
6:7 1 Cor 2:4; 2 Cor 10:4
6:8 Matt 27:63; 1 Cor 4:10, 13
6:9 Ps 118:18; 2 Cor 1:8-10; 4:10-11

5:16-17 ***merely from a human point of view:*** Paul might be reflecting on his belief ***at one time*** as a Pharisee that the Messiah would come to set the Jews free from political oppression. • ***How differently we know him now!*** Christ rose from the dead, ushered in the ***new*** creation (5:17), and was established as the redeemer from sin and Lord of the universe (Rom 1:3-4; Phil 2:6-11; Col 1:15-20).

5:18-21 God entrusts to his servants the ***message*** and ministry of reconciliation ***through Christ.*** • ***God has given us the task of reconciling people:*** Paul is speaking of his own ministry, but sharing ***this wonderful message*** is the responsibility of all believers. ***Christ's ambassadors*** call people to accept what God has done so they can be ***made right with God through Christ.*** • Christ paid the penalty for ***people's sins***—to take away all that stood between God and humans and to make us right with God.

5:20 The great privilege of believers is to be ***Christ's ambassadors*** (cp. Eph 6:20). • ***God is making his appeal through us:*** Paul doesn't say that he speaks for God; rather, God speaks his word through us. • Christ's redeeming work for sinners opens the way for them to ***"Come back to God!"*** and be reconciled with him (see Rom 5:1-11; Eph 2:11-22; Col 1:15-23). Christian witness has this appeal at its heart. Paul was also appealing to the rebellious Corinthians to come over to his side (see 6:1).

5:21 ***Christ*** became ***the offering for our sin*** (or ***sin itself;*** see Isa 53:10) on the cross when he took sin's penalty on himself and died a criminal's death. He did this, though he himself ***never sinned*** (John 8:46; 1 Pet 2:22; 1 Jn 3:5), so that we might be ***made right with God***—i.e., set in right relationship with God and accepted by him (see Gal 3:13).

6:1-2 To win over the disaffected believers at Corinth, Paul appeals to them to listen to him and Timothy as God's servants and messengers. • ***As God's partners:*** Literally *As we work together,* which leaves open the question whether Paul meant that they were working together in a team effort, or that they were working together with God.

6:2 This quotation from Isa 49:8 (Greek version) clinches the point that God's offer of ***salvation*** could secure reconciliation between Paul and the Corinthians; their reconciliation with Paul would follow naturally from their true acceptance of the Good News.

6:3-10 Paul gives a revealing picture of the hardships of his ministry (cp. 4:7-18). Nine trials are listed; many of these experiences from Paul's life are recorded in Acts (e.g., Acts 14:5-6, 19-20; 16:19-24; 21:30-36). Through their steadfast suffering for the Good News, Paul and Timothy (1:1) showed that they were ***true ministers of God.***

6:6-7 Paul describes the spirit with which he faced suffering, attributing his strength to the presence of ***the Holy Spirit within us*** (or ***our holiness of spirit***).

6:8-10 Paul's character as an apostle was often attacked; he and his colleagues were even called ***imposters.*** Yet he was ***honest*** in spite of people's attitudes. They must have thought that Paul was a nobody who could be safely ***ignored,*** a foolhardy person who ran unnecessary risks that made him as good as dead already. Paul rebuts each of their allegations with insight into spiritual reality.

6:11-13 Paul's impassioned plea reveals his inner feelings. • ***our hearts are open to you . . . Open your hearts to us!*** These sentiments are continued in 7:2 (see notes on 6:14–7:1; 7:2-4).

6:10 Acts 3:6; Rom 8:32; 1 Cor 3:21; 2 Cor 8:9
6:11 2 Cor 7:3
6:14 Eph 5:7, 11; 1 Jn 1:6; [f]*koinōnia* (2842) ‣2 Cor 8:4
6:16 *Lev 26:12; *Jer 32:38; *Ezek 37:27
6:17 *Isa 52:11; Ezek 20:34
6:18 *2 Sam 7:8, 14; Isa 43:6; Jer 31:9; [g]*pantokratōr* (3841) ‣Rev 1:8
7:1 1 Pet 1:15-16
7:3 Phil 1:7

as if you were my own children. Open your
hearts to us!

The Temple of the Living God

14 Don't team up with those who are unbelievers. How can righteousness be a partner
with wickedness? How can light [f]live with
darkness? 15 What harmony can there be
between Christ and the devil? How can a
believer be a partner with an unbeliever?
16 And what union can there be between
God's temple and idols? For we are the temple of the living God. As God said:

"I will live in them
and walk among them.
I will be their God,
and they will be my people.
17 Therefore, come out from among
unbelievers,
and separate yourselves from them,
says the LORD.
Don't touch their filthy things,
and I will welcome you.
18 And I will be your Father,
and you will be my sons and
daughters,
says the LORD [g]Almighty."

7 Because we have these promises, dear
friends, let us cleanse ourselves from
everything that can defile our body or spirit.
And let us work toward complete holiness
because we fear God.

Paul's Relationship with the Corinthians

2 Please open your hearts to us. We have
not done wrong to anyone, nor led anyone
astray, nor taken advantage of anyone. 3 I'm
not saying this to condemn you. I said before

The Church as God's Temple (6:14–7:1)

Exod 25:1-9; 2 Sam 7:12-16; 1 Kgs 8:12-53; 1 Chr 22:1-19; 2 Chr 6:20; Ezra 6:16-18; Ps 11:4; 27:4-6; Ezek 40:1–46:18; Zech 6:12-15; Matt 18:20; John 2:18-22; 14:20; 17:23; Rom 8:10; 1 Cor 3:10-17; 6:18-20; 9:11-14; Gal 2:20; Eph 2:20-22; 3:17-19; Col 1:27; Heb 3:6; 12:18-24; 1 Pet 2:4-9; Rev 1:12-16; 3:12, 20; 21:22

There are several pictures of the church as God's people. In 6:14–7:1, Paul portrays the church as the temple of God—a worshiping people whose dedication to God separates them from all that is not like him.

The imagery of the church as the temple of God has its roots in the OT. The promise to David and Solomon was that the Temple in Jerusalem would be a foretaste of God's abiding presence with his people (see 2 Sam 7:12-16; 1 Kgs 9:1-9). That Temple was completed in 960 BC, then destroyed in 586 BC. But the prophets of Israel looked forward to a new temple; they announced a message of hope that God would once again live among his people (see, e.g., Isa 56:7; Ezek 40:1–43:27). All these hopes were made good in the coming of Jesus (see John 1:14; 2:19-22; 4:21-24). He himself is God's temple, the place where God's holiness resides, and he calls his people to join him. Thus, God's people are to be a holy temple of God (see 6:16; 1 Cor 3:16-17; 6:19; Eph 2:21; 1 Pet 2:5; Rev 3:12).

Paul called on the Corinthians to realize their identity as God's "holy people" (1:1) in two ways: They were to separate themselves from moral evil, and they were to be dedicated to God in holy living and service. Christians are therefore urged, "Let us cleanse ourselves from everything that can defile our body or spirit. And let us work toward complete holiness because we fear God" (7:1).

6:14–7:1 The connection between 6:13 and 7:2 has led many scholars to conclude that 6:14–7:1 is an inserted fragment from another letter (perhaps the one mentioned in 1 Cor 5:9). However, this section might just as well be a digression in Paul's writing, a suitable challenge to the Corinthians to forsake their opposition to Paul and his message. Paul was anxious to see relationships restored; here, Paul draws a picture of believers in Christ forming a holy temple. Believers' identity as the temple of God motivates the need for harmony among them as well as separation from the impurity of unbelieving attitudes and behaviors. Paul therefore draws the contrast between Christian and pagan morality with quotations from the OT.

6:14 ***Don't team up with those who are unbelievers:*** This instruction alludes to the Jewish prohibition of certain mixtures (Lev 19:19; Deut 22:10). Paul was probably referring to how the Corinthians had been involving themselves in idolatrous practices (see 1 Cor 8–10; cp. 1 Cor 10:14-22).

6:15 ***the devil:*** Greek *Beliar;* various other manuscripts render this proper name of the devil as *Belian, Beliab,* or *Belial.* This Hebrew word means "worthless, good-for-nothing"; it came to be used in the intertestamental period as a name for Satan.

6:16 Believers together ***are the temple of the living God,*** indwelt by the Holy Spirit and thus holy (1 Cor 3:16; 1 Pet 2:1-10). • ***"I will live in them . . . and they will be my people":*** This quotation is from Lev 26:12; Ezek 37:27.

6:17 This quotation is from Isa 52:11; Ezek 20:34 (Greek version).

6:18 This quotation is from 2 Sam 7:14, though Paul adds ***and daughters*** (cp. Isa 43:6).

7:1 Paul wanted the church to be a holy people, filled with God's presence. • ***because we fear God:*** We should be reverent in the presence of a holy God (see note on 5:11).

7:2-4 ***Please open your hearts to us:*** Paul picks up his plea from 6:11-13 (see note on 6:14–7:1). Paul had a deep concern for the churches (11:28), expressed by seeking a close bond of fellowship. When he was misunderstood, he explained his actions, as he does here. • ***We have not . . . taken advantage of anyone:*** That is, by taking their money.

that you are in our hearts, and we live or die
together with you. 4 I have the highest confidence in you, and I take great pride in you.
You have greatly encouraged me and made
me happy despite all our troubles.

Paul's Joy at the Church's Repentance

5 When we arrived in Macedonia, there
was no rest for us. We faced conflict from
every direction, with battles on the outside and fear on the inside. 6 But God, who
encourages those who are discouraged,
encouraged us by the arrival of Titus. 7 His
presence was a joy, but so was the news he
brought of the encouragement he received
from you. When he told us how much you
long to see me, and how sorry you are for
what happened, and how loyal you are to
me, I was filled with joy!

8 I am not sorry that I sent that severe letter to you, though I was sorry at first, for I
know it was painful to you for a little while.
9 Now I am glad I sent it, not because it hurt
you, but because the pain caused you to repent and change your ways. It was the kind
of sorrow God wants his people to have, so
you were not harmed by us in any way. 10 For
the kind of sorrow God wants us to experience leads us away from sin and results in
salvation. There's no regret for that kind of
sorrow. But worldly sorrow, which lacks repentance, results in spiritual death.

11 Just see what this godly sorrow produced in you! Such earnestness, such
concern to clear yourselves, such indignation, such alarm, such longing to see me,
such zeal, and such a readiness to punish
wrong. You showed that you have done
everything necessary to make things right.
12 My purpose, then, was not to write about
who did the wrong or who was wronged. I
wrote to you so that in the sight of God you
could see for yourselves how loyal you are
to us. 13 We have been greatly encouraged
by this.

In addition to our own encouragement,
we were especially delighted to see how
happy Titus was about the way all of you
welcomed him and set his mind at ease. 14 I
had told him how proud I was of you—and
you didn't disappoint me. I have always told
you the truth, and now my boasting to Titus
has also proved true! 15 Now he cares for you
more than ever when he remembers the
way all of you obeyed him and welcomed
him with such fear and deep respect. 16 I am
very happy now because I have complete
confidence in you.

4. THE RELIEF FUND FOR JERUSALEM (8:1–9:15)

A Call to Generous Giving

8 Now I want you to know, dear brothers
and sisters, what God in his kindness
has done through the churches in Macedonia. 2 They are being tested by many
troubles, and they are very poor. But they
are also filled with abundant joy, which has
overflowed in rich [h]generosity.

3 For I can testify that they gave not only
what they could afford, but far more. And
they did it of their own free will. 4 They
begged us again and again for the privilege
of [i]sharing in the [j]gift for the believers in
Jerusalem. 5 They even did more than we
had hoped, for their first action was to give

7:4 2 Cor 8:24
7:5 2 Cor 2:13; 4:8
7:6 Isa 49:13; 2 Cor 1:3-4; 2:13
7:8 2 Cor 2:2-4
7:10 Matt 27:3-5
7:12 1 Cor 5:1-2; 2 Cor 2:3, 9
7:13 2 Cor 2:13
7:15 Phil 2:12
7:16 2 Cor 2:3; 2 Thes 3:4; Phlm 1:21
8:1 Acts 16:9
8:2 2 Cor 9:11; [h]*haplotēs* (0572) ‣2 Cor 9:11
8:4 Acts 24:17; Rom 15:26; 1 Cor 16:1, 3; [i]*koinōnia* (2842) ‣2 Cor 13:14; [j]*diakonia* (1248) ‣2 Cor 9:13

7:4 ***All our troubles*** might refer to Paul's many hardships (6:5) or his problems with the Corinthians themselves. Either way, he was filled with joy because the church's response had ***greatly encouraged*** him (as he explains in 7:5-16).

7:5-7 Paul's joy leads him to tell about his recent meeting with ***Titus***, whose ***presence was a joy*** when he joined Paul in Macedonia (see note on 2:14–7:4; Acts 20:1-2). • Initially, Paul had no ***rest*** (this Greek word is used in 2:13, where it is rendered "peace of mind") but only ***conflict, battles,*** and ***fear.*** Paul was deeply discouraged, but he received encouragement from ***God, who encourages those who are discouraged*** (cp. Ps 42:5-6). Titus arrived from Corinth with the news that Paul's letter (see 2:3-4) had done its work (7:8-16). This was the chief cause of Paul's ***joy.***

7:8-13a Paul ***was sorry at first*** that he had sent his previous letter (see 2:3-4). Now he was ***not sorry,*** realizing that the ***pain*** had been worthwhile, for the severe letter had brought the church in Corinth to ***repentance.*** They had rebuked the offending person—perhaps too strongly (see 2:6-11).

7:9-10 Two kinds of sorrow are mentioned: (1) ***Worldly sorrow*** that ***lacks repentance*** leads to ***spiritual death*** (e.g., see Matt 27:3-6; Heb 12:16-17). (2) Sorrow that ***leads us away from sin*** leads to ***salvation,*** as it did when the church in Corinth responded positively to Paul's rebuke.

7:13b-16 The way the Corinthians had welcomed and obeyed ***Titus*** as Paul's agent endeared the Corinthians to Titus and ***delighted*** Paul. The crisis at Corinth was over, and Paul had ***complete confidence*** that all was well.

7:13 ***his mind:*** Literally *his spirit.*

7:14 All along Paul had been optimistic, despite his fears, about the outcome of Titus's trip to Corinth.

8:1–9:15 Paul now turns his attention to the collection for the Jerusalem church (8:4; 9:1). This relief fund was intended to aid the poverty-stricken saints in the holy city (Acts 11:27-30; Rom 15:25-27, 31; Gal 2:10). Paul had earlier given instructions about this matter (1 Cor 16:1-2); now it was time to collect the funds (8:6). Paul hoped this gift from Gentile congregations to the Jewish church would cement relations between the two groups in the early Christian community.

8:1-2 ***dear brothers and sisters:*** Literally *brothers.* See note on 1:8-11. • ***The churches in Macedonia*** included the church in Philippi, which we know from Acts and Philippians was ***being tested by many troubles*** and was ***very poor.*** Yet they were generous in sending gifts to Paul and in supporting the collection (8:4-5; Phil 1:5; 2:25-30; 4:15-20).

8:4 ***for the believers:*** Literally *for God's holy people.*

8:6
2 Cor 12:13, 18

8:7
1 Cor 1:5; 16:1-2
2 Cor 9:8

8:9
Matt 8:20
Phil 2:6-7

8:10
2 Cor 9:2

8:12
Prov 3:27-28
Mark 12:43-44
2 Cor 9:7

8:14
Acts 4:34
2 Cor 9:12

8:15
*Exod 16:18

themselves to the Lord and to us, just as God
wanted them to do.
6 So we have urged Titus, who encouraged
your giving in the first place, to return to
you and encourage you to finish this ministry of giving. 7 Since you excel in so many
ways—in your faith, your gifted speakers,
your knowledge, your enthusiasm, and your
love from us—I want you to excel also in
this gracious act of giving.
8 I am not commanding you to do this.
But I am testing how genuine your love is
by comparing it with the eagerness of the
other churches.
9 You know the generous grace of our
Lord Jesus Christ. Though he was rich, yet
for your sakes he became poor, so that by
his poverty he could make you rich.
10 Here is my advice: It would be good for
you to finish what you started a year ago. Last
year you were the first who wanted to give,
and you were the first to begin doing it.
11 Now you should finish what you started. Let
the eagerness you showed in the beginning
be matched now by your giving. Give in proportion to what you have. 12 Whatever you
give is acceptable if you give it eagerly. And
give according to what you have, not what
you don't have. 13 Of course, I don't mean your
giving should make life easy for others and
hard for yourselves. I only mean that there
should be some equality. 14 Right now you
have plenty and can help those who are in
need. Later, they will have plenty and can
share with you when you need it. In this way,
things will be equal. 15 As the Scriptures say,

Christian Giving (8:1–9:15)

2 Cor 5:17-18
Exod 25:2; 35:5
Lev 25:35
Deut 15:7-11; 16:17
1 Chr 29:9
Prov 3:9-10; 11:24-26; 21:13; 28:27
Mal 3:8
Matt 5:42; 6:3-4; 10:8; 19:21
Luke 6:38; 11:41; 12:33-34; 18:22
Acts 11:29
1 Cor 13:3; 16:2-3
Phil 2:3-11

Second Corinthians speaks of men and women who had turned away from the evils of the world (1 Cor 12:2) but were in danger of relapsing into those immoral ways (12:20-21). Paul calls these believers to continually answer the summons of *dying to live* (5:14-15). Their desire should always be to please God, not themselves (5:15). This means that believers are called to live under Christ's lordship (4:5) and be motivated by his love (5:14).

Christian living therefore is marked by a forgiving spirit (2:10) and a generous concern for those in need (chs 8–9). The church at Corinth, already endowed with many spiritual gifts (1 Cor 1:7), is therefore encouraged "to excel also in this gracious act of giving" (8:7). They are asked to be responsive to human need as represented by the poor Jewish Christians in Jerusalem. It would be a sign that the Gentiles were one with the mother church in Jerusalem.

Such bountiful giving is a mark of true grace. We see its sublime expression in the Lord of glory, who by his poverty made us rich and became one with us (8:9; Phil 2:3-11). We have received his unmerited favor in salvation (9:8-11). Now we give sacrificially in response to "this gift too wonderful for words!" (9:15).

We may summarize Paul's teaching on Christian giving as follows:

(1) Our giving should spring from a willing mind and heart (8:12). Paul begins with motives (9:7), since all giving should hinge on why we give.

(2) True giving is a joy, in contrast with grudging gifts (9:5). There is joy in sowing seed, like a farmer who anticipates a crop (9:6-10); and there is joy in sharing with others in need (8:11-15).

(3) Christian giving is marked by generosity and may entail sacrifice, as it did for the Macedonians (8:1-7).

(4) The handling of financial gifts calls for honesty, integrity, and care. Paul was careful to deflect any suspicion of his colleagues who were sent to collect gifts from the churches (8:20-21). Those who handle monetary gifts in the church should, like those in 8:16-24, be persons of proven reputation and responsibility.

8:6 *Titus* would start taking up the collection when he returned to Corinth carrying this letter from Paul in Macedonia.

8:7 This is the key verse in Paul's exposition on Christian giving (8:1–9:15). The Corinthians had a reputation for spiritual gifts (1 Cor 1:5-7; 14:12). Now, they must be leaders ***in this gracious act of giving,*** which is a hallmark of true spirituality (cp. 1 Cor 13). God had been lavish in his goodness to the Corinthians, so they should be generous to the Jewish believers in their need (9:13). This would be recognized as a sign of unity in Christ. • ***your love from us:*** Some manuscripts read *your love for us.*

8:9 The model for generous giving is the ***Lord*** himself, who ***was rich*** in the Father's presence (John 17:5, 24) yet ***became poor*** by accepting a human existence and death on the cross (see Phil 2:6-11). By that self-giving sacrifice, ***he could make*** people ***rich*** with the blessings of salvation.

8:10 ***What you started a year ago*** was the collection of an offering for Jerusalem, prompted by 1 Cor 16:1-2. So this letter is to be dated at least one year after 1 Corinthians.

8:15 Paul quotes from Exod 16:18 to say that there is a mutual responsibility among Christians: Affluent believers (the Corinthians) should help poor believers (in Jerusalem) so that all may have enough.

"Those who gathered a lot had nothing
left over,
and those who gathered only a little
had enough."

Titus and His Companions

16But thank God! He has given Titus the
same enthusiasm for you that I have. 17Ti-
tus welcomed our request that he visit you
again. In fact, he himself was very eager to
go and see you. 18We are also sending another brother with Titus. All the churches
praise him as a preacher of the Good News.
19He was appointed by the churches to
accompany us as we take the offering to Jerusalem—a service that glorifies the Lord
and shows our eagerness to help.
20We are traveling together to guard
against any criticism for the way we are handling this generous gift. 21We are careful to
be honorable before the Lord, but we also
want everyone else to see that we are honorable.
22We are also sending with them another
of our brothers who has proven himself
many times and has shown on many occasions how eager he is. He is now even more
enthusiastic because of his great confidence in you. 23If anyone asks about Titus,
say that he is my partner who works with
me to help you. And the brothers with him
have been sent by the churches, and they
bring honor to Christ. 24So show them your
love, and prove to all the churches that our
boasting about you is justified.

The Collection for Christians in Jerusalem

9 I really don't need to write to you about
this ministry of giving for the believers
in Jerusalem. 2For I know how eager you
are to help, and I have been boasting to the
churches in Macedonia that you in Greece
were ready to send an offering a year ago. In
fact, it was your enthusiasm that stirred up
many of the Macedonian believers to begin
giving.
3But I am sending these brothers to be
sure you really are ready, as I have been
telling them, and that your money is all
collected. I don't want to be wrong in
my boasting about you. 4We would be
embarrassed—not to mention your own
embarrassment—if some Macedonian believers came with me and found that you
weren't ready after all I had told them! 5So I
thought I should send these brothers ahead
of me to make sure the [k]gift you promised
is ready. But I want it to be a willing [k]gift, not
one given grudgingly.
6Remember this—a farmer who plants
only a few seeds will get a small crop. But
the one who plants generously will get a
generous crop. 7You must each decide in
your heart how much to give. And don't give
reluctantly or in response to pressure. "For
God loves a person who gives cheerfully."
8And God will generously provide all you
need. Then you will always have everything
you need and plenty left over to share with
others. 9As the Scriptures say,

"They share freely and give generously to
the poor.
Their good deeds will be remembered
forever."

10For God is the one who provides seed for
the farmer and then bread to eat. In the
same way, he will provide and increase your
resources and then produce a great harvest
of generosity in you.
11Yes, you will be enriched in every way
so that you can always be [a]generous. And

8:16 2 Cor 2:14
8:18 2 Cor 12:18
8:19 Acts 14:23; 1 Cor 16:3-4
8:21 Prov 3:4; Rom 12:17
8:23 Phil 2:25
8:24 2 Cor 7:4
9:1 Acts 24:17; 2 Cor 8:4, 20
9:2 2 Cor 8:11-12, 19
9:3 1 Cor 16:2; 2 Cor 8:23
9:5 Phil 4:17; [k]*eulogia* (2129) ‣ Gal 3:14
9:6 Prov 11:24-25; 22:9; Gal 6:7, 9
9:7 Exod 25:2; Deut 15:7-10; 2 Cor 8:12
9:8 Phil 4:19
9:9 *Ps 112:9
9:10 Isa 55:10; Hos 10:12
9:11 2 Cor 1:11; 4:15; [a]*haplotēs* (0572) ‣ 2 Cor 9:13

8:18-24 Two other Christian men would travel with *Titus* to Corinth in order ***to guard against any criticism*** over the handling of the relief funds that they collected (8:20-21). Titus himself was a man of sterling character, whom ***all the churches*** praised. He and his companions would ensure that the money was properly handled. The identity of his two companions is unknown.

8:19 ***as we take the offering to Jerusalem:*** See 1 Cor 16:3-4.

8:23 ***have been sent by the churches:*** Literally *are apostles of the churches.*
• ***they bring honor to Christ:*** Paul's last phrase is even more expressive in Greek (literally *they are the glory of Christ*)—they are examples of Christians who reflect the Lord's splendor (3:1-18).

9:1-5 Two motives reinforce the spirit of love in giving: (1) to emulate the Macedonians, who in their poverty had been forthcoming in their generosity (9:2); and (2) not to shame Paul or themselves, since he had boasted about the Corinthians' generosity to the Macedonians (9:3-5). To ensure the timely gathering of the collection at Corinth, Paul would send the delegates (8:16-24) in advance to ***make sure the gift you promised is ready.***

9:1 ***about this ministry of giving for the believers in Jerusalem:*** Literally *about the offering for God's holy people.*

9:2 ***in Greece:*** Greek *in Achaia,* the southern region of the Greek peninsula. ***Macedonia*** was in the northern region of Greece.

9:6 Paul turns to agriculture for an illustration of the benefits of generosity. ***A farmer*** who expects a rich harvest must sow many seeds.

9:7 It is the spirit of giving that counts. ***"For God loves a person who gives cheerfully"*** (see note on Prov 22:8). Cheerfulness in giving is contrasted with giving ***reluctantly*** (literally *out of sorrow*) or ***in response to pressure.***

9:8-9 ***As the Scriptures say:*** The quotation from Ps 112:9 supports the assurance that God, who provides for all human needs, will reward generosity.

9:10-14 The Corinthians' ***generosity*** (literally *righteousness*) would be matched by God's generosity (9:10-11). It would also meet ***the needs*** of Jewish Christians (9:12), honor God (9:13), show believers in Jerusalem that their Gentile brothers and sisters were genuine believers (9:13), and result in the Jewish

9:12
2 Cor 8:14
[b]*leitourgia* (3009)
‣Phil 2:17

9:13
[c]*diakonia* (1248)
‣Eph 4:12
[d]*haplotēs* (0572)
‣2 Cor 11:3

10:1
1 Cor 2:3
2 Cor 10:10

10:2
1 Cor 4:21

10:4
Jer 1:10
Eph 6:13-17

10:5
Isa 2:11-12
1 Cor 1:19

10:6
2 Cor 2:9; 7:15

10:7
John 7:24
2 Cor 11:23

10:8
2 Cor 12:6; 13:10

10:10
1 Cor 1:17; 2:3
2 Cor 11:6
Gal 4:13-14

10:11
2 Cor 13:2, 10

10:12
2 Cor 3:1; 5:12

when we take your gifts to those who need
them, they will thank God. 12So two good
things will result from this ministry of [b]giv-
ing—the needs of the believers in Jerusalem
will be met, and they will joyfully express
their thanks to God.
13As a result of your [c]ministry, they will
give glory to God. For your [d]generosity to
them and to all believers will prove that you
are obedient to the Good News of Christ.
14And they will pray for you with deep affection because of the overflowing grace God
has given to you. 15Thank God for this gift
too wonderful for words!

5. PAUL DEFENDS HIS APOSTLESHIP (10:1–12:21)

Paul Defends His Authority

10 Now I, Paul, appeal to you with the
gentleness and kindness of Christ—
though I realize you think I am timid in
person and bold only when I write from far
away. 2Well, I am begging you now so that
when I come I won't have to be bold with
those who think we act from human motives.
3We are human, but we don't wage war
as humans do. 4We use God's mighty weapons, not worldly weapons, to knock down
the strongholds of human reasoning and to
destroy false arguments. 5We destroy every
proud obstacle that keeps people from
knowing God. We capture their rebellious
thoughts and teach them to obey Christ.
6And after you have become fully obedient,
we will punish everyone who remains disobedient.
7Look at the obvious facts. Those who
say they belong to Christ must recognize
that we belong to Christ as much as they do.
8I may seem to be boasting too much about
the authority given to us by the Lord. But
our authority builds you up; it doesn't tear
you down. So I will not be ashamed of using
my authority.
9I'm not trying to frighten you by my
letters. 10For some say, "Paul's letters are
demanding and forceful, but in person he
is weak, and his speeches are worthless!"
11Those people should realize that our actions when we arrive in person will be as
forceful as what we say in our letters from
far away.
12Oh, don't worry; we wouldn't dare say
that we are as wonderful as these other men

believers' intercessory prayer and *affection* for the Gentile believers (9:14). Paul envisioned a united, worldwide Christian church, composed of believing Jews and Gentiles who are all one in Christ Jesus (Gal 3:28; Eph 2:11-22), which would become a powerful witness to the Lord's work of reconciliation.

9:12 ***the believers in Jerusalem:*** Literally *God's holy people.*

9:15 ***this gift:*** Literally *his gift.*

10:1–13:13 In this section, Paul defends his ministry as an apostle. • These chapters pose several problems arising from a distinct change of tone and style. Chapters 1–9 are full of joy stemming from the reconciliation of sinners with God and of the Corinthians with Paul. Yet from this point on, Paul is on the defensive. These chapters are full of harsh words, bitter recriminations, passionate irony, and rebuke. The remarkable break at 10:1 has inspired a number of explanations: (1) These chapters might be a separate letter, perhaps the "severe letter" sent earlier to Corinth (2:3-4; 7:8-9). (2) It might be that, while the majority of the church members were obedient to the appeal for reconciliation, there was still a rebellious minority to whom Paul addressed these four chapters. (3) More likely, a new situation had arisen since Titus first brought back his glowing report of restored harmony (7:5-16). In this scenario, some anti-Paul missionaries had arrived in Corinth and launched a virulent campaign against the apostolic message of Good News (see 11:4, 13-15). They claimed that Paul was no real apostle or even a true Christian (10:7) and that he had no right to come to Corinth with the gospel message since it was territory that belonged to them (10:15-16). They brought an alien message (11:4) and exercised a domineering spirit. In short, they were doing Satan's work (11:13-15). Paul, summoned by hearing of this new situation, reasserts his apostolic authority and engages in a form of writing that is distasteful to him (11:1, 16-17; 12:1) by boasting of his weaknesses and trials. Paul's apostolic authority is real and powerful, yet it is conditioned and controlled by the love exhibited by the crucified Jesus (10:1; 13:4-10).

10:1-6 Paul states his own clear intentions and sincerity by defending himself against the suspicion that he is acting ***from human motives.***

10:1 ***you think I am timid in person:*** See 10:10. Paul could write ***bold*** letters at a distance, but they mistook his personal ***gentleness and kindness*** as weakness. However, they forgot that he had the authority of Christ (12:19; 13:3-5, 7, 10; 1 Cor 4:21).

10:3-5 A military metaphor enforces Paul's rebuttal: Paul's weapons have divine power over spiritual ***strongholds*** (see 4:3-4).

10:4-5 English translations divide verses 4 and 5 in various ways.

10:7-11 ***Look at the obvious facts:*** Or *You look at things only on the basis of appearance.* The rival teachers were evidently claiming to be Christ's representatives in some superior way that excluded Paul because of his weakness. Here he defines having true ***authority*** as distinct from being a domineering authoritarian. His authority was to build up God's people, not to demolish them (see 13:10), yet he intended to deal firmly with these rivals when he came to Corinth (see 13:1).

10:10 ***Paul's letters*** are sometimes difficult and ***demanding,*** as other Christians also found (cp. 2 Pet 3:16). • ***in person he is weak:*** Paul had no domineering presence, bulldozing people into submission (cp. 1:24; 1 Cor 2:1-5). The earliest descriptions of Paul's personal appearance (*Acts of Paul and Thecla,* around AD 200) depict him as "a man of small height, almost bald, with crooked legs, but with a good body and eyebrows meeting. His nose was hooked, full of grace, for sometimes he appeared like a man and sometimes had the face of an angel." • ***his speeches are worthless:*** Unlike Apollos (Acts 18:24), Paul was not an eloquent preacher or captivating orator when he came to Corinth (11:6; 1 Cor 2:3-4). His message, however, was charged with a power no human rhetoric could command, as it was given in the Holy Spirit.

10:12 Paul now charges his enemies with a set of false values, since they attached great importance to themselves.

who tell you how important they are! But
they are only comparing themselves with
each other, using themselves as the standard of measurement. How ignorant!
13We will not boast about things done
outside our area of authority. We will boast
only about what has happened within the
boundaries of the work God has given us,
which includes our working with you. 14We
are not reaching beyond these boundaries
when we claim authority over you, as if we
had never visited you. For we were the first
to travel all the way to Corinth with the
Good News of Christ.
15Nor do we boast and claim credit for
the work someone else has done. Instead,
we hope that your faith will grow so that
the boundaries of our work among you
will be extended. 16Then we will be able
to go and preach the Good News in other
places far beyond you, where no one else
is working. Then there will be no question
of our boasting about work done in someone else's territory. 17As the Scriptures say,
"If you want to boast, boast only about the
LORD."
18When people commend themselves,
it doesn't count for much. The important
thing is for the Lord to commend them.

Paul and the False Apostles

11 I hope you will put up with a little
more of my foolishness. Please bear
with me. 2For I am jealous for you with the
jealousy of God himself. I promised you as
a pure bride to one husband—Christ. 3But
I fear that somehow your [e]pure and undivided devotion to Christ will be corrupted,
just as Eve was deceived by the cunning
ways of the serpent. 4You happily put up
with whatever anyone tells you, even if they
preach a different Jesus than the one we
preach, or a different kind of Spirit than
the one you received, or a different kind of
[f]gospel than the one you believed.
5But I don't consider myself inferior
in any way to these "super apostles" who
teach such things. 6I may be unskilled as a
speaker, but I'm not lacking in knowledge.
We have made this clear to you in every possible way.
7Was I wrong when I humbled myself
and honored you by preaching God's Good
News to you without expecting anything in
return? 8I "robbed" other churches by accepting their contributions so I could serve
you at no cost. 9And when I was with you
and didn't have enough to live on, I did not
become a financial burden to anyone. For
the brothers who came from Macedonia
brought me all that I needed. I have never
been a burden to you, and I never will be.
10As surely as the truth of Christ is in me, no
one in all of Greece will ever stop me from
boasting about this. 11Why? Because I don't
love you? God knows that I do.

10:13 Rom 12:3
10:14 1 Cor 9:1
10:15 Rom 15:20; 2 Thes 1:3
10:16 Acts 19:21
10:17 *Jer 9:24; 1 Cor 1:31
10:18 Prov 27:2
11:1 2 Cor 5:13
11:2 Hos 2:19; Eph 5:26-27
11:3 Gen 3:1-6, 13; John 8:44; 1 Tim 2:14; Rev 12:9
[e]*haplotēs* (0572) ‣ Eph 6:5
11:4 Rom 8:15; Gal 1:6-8
[f]*euangelion* (2098) ‣ Gal 1:6
11:5 2 Cor 12:11; Gal 2:6
11:6 1 Cor 1:17; Eph 3:4
11:7 1 Cor 9:12, 18; 2 Cor 12:13
11:9 2 Cor 12:13
11:11 2 Cor 7:3; 12:15

10:13-16 Paul had not trespassed on the limits God set for his missionary service, ***which includes our working with you.*** So he justifies his integrity and authority, insisting that when he first came to Corinth (Acts 18:1-17) he did so in response to God's call. He was determined not to enter ***someone else's territory*** (see Rom 15:20), but Paul was ***the first to travel all the way to Corinth with the Good News of Christ.*** His more recent opponents visited the church much later (11:4), so their claim to Corinth as their territory was empty.

10:17-18 Paul quotes Jer 9:24 to the effect that all missionaries are directed by the Lord. So boasting ***doesn't count for much.*** Only as the Lord praises us for our service can success have any significance.

11:1-6 Paul finds it necessary, if distasteful, to justify his actions because of the close link he claims with the church (11:2) and because his enemies were enticing the Corinthian believers away from Christ.

11:1 Paul takes on an ironic tone in saying, ***I hope you will put up with a little more of my foolishness.*** He again asks with irony, ***Please bear with me*** (or ***But indeed you are putting up with me,*** a translation that makes the irony even more pointed).

11:2 The church is called to be ***a pure bride*** (literally ***a virgin***) ***to one husband—Christ.*** This metaphor goes back to the OT, where Israel is the bride of the Lord (Isa 54:5; 62:5). Paul saw himself as the best man who acted for the bridegroom (cp. John 3:29).

11:3 The false teachers were pulling the Corinthian believers away from ***pure and undivided devotion to Christ.*** In this they are doing the work of Satan, just as ***the serpent*** did in Eden (11:14; see Gen 3:4, 13).

11:4 The false missionaries in Corinth evidently preached a ***different Jesus, a different kind of Spirit,*** and ***a different kind of gospel than the one*** the Corinthians had ***believed.*** It is difficult to know exactly what these false teachers preached; most likely, they promoted a powerful, dominant Christ and sidelined the suffering of the cross. They probably saw themselves as equally powerful preachers, exempt from hardship and trial. Paul's message, by contrast, centered on Christ crucified (13:4), and Paul's own sufferings were a mark of true apostleship (12:1-12). The nature of this difference is the heart of Paul's defense of his apostleship in chs 10–13.

11:5-6 These false teachers claimed authority as ***"super apostles,"*** and they despised Paul's lack of sophisticated eloquence (10:10).

11:7 Paul was ***preaching God's Good News . . . without expecting anything in return.*** Paul's policy as a church planter (1 Cor 9:3-14) was to earn his living by his trade of tentmaking (Acts 18:3; 20:34) rather than being supported by the new churches (1 Thes 2:9; 2 Thes 3:8-9). His enemies in Corinth criticized him for this. In Greek thought, religious teachers could rightfully claim financial support; Paul's refusal provided his enemies with an argument that his apostleship was counterfeit.

11:8-9 Paul had ***accepted . . . contributions . . . from Macedonia***—i.e., Philippi (Phil 4:15-19). Paul's apparent inconsistency made the Corinthians suspicious of his motives or doubtful of his love toward them (11:11).

11:10 ***Greece:*** Greek *Achaia,* the southern region of the Greek peninsula.

11:12 1 Cor 9:12
11:13 Rev 2:2
11:14 [g]*satanas* (4567) ‣2 Cor 12:7
11:15 Phil 3:19
11:16 2 Cor 12:6
11:18 Phil 3:3-4
11:20 Gal 2:4; 4:9
11:21 2 Cor 10:10

12But I will continue doing what I have
always done. This will undercut those who
are looking for an opportunity to boast that
their work is just like ours. 13These people
are false apostles. They are deceitful workers who disguise themselves as apostles of
Christ. 14But I am not surprised! Even [g]Satan
disguises himself as an angel of light. 15So it
is no wonder that his servants also disguise
themselves as servants of righteousness. In
the end they will get the punishment their
wicked deeds deserve.

Paul's Many Trials

16Again I say, don't think that I am a fool to
talk like this. But even if you do, listen to me,
as you would to a foolish person, while I also
boast a little. 17Such boasting is not from the
Lord, but I am acting like a fool. 18And since
others boast about their human achievements, I will, too. 19After all, you think you are
so wise, but you enjoy putting up with fools!
20You put up with it when someone enslaves
you, takes everything you have, takes advantage of you, takes control of everything, and
slaps you in the face. 21I'm ashamed to say
that we've been too "weak" to do that!

But whatever they dare to boast about—
I'm talking like a fool again—I dare to boast

Apostolic Service (10:12-18)

2 Cor 2:17; 4:2; 6:3-12
Matt 10:5-42; 28:18-20
Mark 1:17; 2:14; 3:14-15
John 21:15-17
Acts 1:2-8, 20-26; 2:42-43; 4:33; 5:12; 6:2-4; 10:39-43; 14:3
Rom 1:5; 15:17-21
1 Cor 4:8-13; 12:28-29
Eph 2:20; 3:4-5; 4:11-13
1 Thes 2:7-12

In this letter, Paul reveals the heart of his ministry as an apostle. Paul was God's special messenger for the establishment and nurture of churches. His service was marked by seriousness and sincerity, and his message raises life and death issues (2:15-17). As a pioneer missionary, he took the Good News to places where Christ's name was not yet known (Rom 15:17-21).

Paul's message of Good News is clear and incisive (ch 5), and it was backed up and illustrated by his own life. All preachers are called to be persons of integrity (2:17; 4:2). As Paul carried the precious message (4:7), the cross of Jesus was both the foundation of his faith (5:18-21) and the pattern for his ministry to others (chs 11–12).

Paul's authority was apparently disputed, so he needed to offer a personal account of how God had called him as an apostle and established his ministry at Corinth (10:12-18). For those who demanded proof of Paul's credentials (13:3) and who criticized his weaknesses, he simply pointed to the cross of Jesus (13:4) and to the lessons he had learned from it (4:10). Paul needed divine grace to accomplish his work, being only too conscious of his own limitations and hardships. True apostolic authority expresses itself in human weakness reinforced by divine strength (12:1-10).

Paul also had the miraculous works to verify his claim to apostleship (12:12). These works impressed the Corinthians, but they were apparently not enough for the young church. Paul exercised his ministry "with all patience," not giving up when the Corinthians were difficult to deal with. This trait comes from Jesus, whose entire earthly ministry was marked by endurance (Heb 12:2-3). Paul's persistence with awkward people like the Corinthians is a sure sign of his calling from God.

Paul's example is a lesson for all those who are involved in Christian service: (1) Christian leaders should take criticism as a summons to self-examination, to see if any accusation is well-founded. (2) Christian leaders should be patient, as Paul was in his concern for the churches (11:28-29). (3) There is a place for reasoned defense and explanation of one's motives, such as Paul adopted (13:5-10); at the same time, Paul knew that the Lord was his ultimate and only true Judge (1 Cor 4:1-5).

11:12 Paul's motive in refusing to accept support from the Corinthians (11:7-11) was to show them what true Christian service is like in contrast to the ministry of ***those who*** were ***looking for an opportunity to boast***.

11:13-15 Paul fiercely condemns the false teachers in Corinth (cp. Gal 1:6-9). Although the false teachers wanted to claim that their work was just like Paul's (11:12), they were in fact ***false apostles*** and ***deceitful workers*** (cp. Phil 3:2). Just as Satan changed himself into ***an angel of light*** to deceive Eve (as described in the Jewish apocryphal book *The Life of Adam and Eve*), so ***his servants also disguise themselves as servants of righteousness***. Satan's servants claim to be God's servants, but their ***deeds*** are ***wicked***, and their ***punishment*** is sure (cp. 5:10).

11:16-29 Paul plays the part of a boastful ***fool*** (see also 12:11-13) so that he may present his true credentials as a suffering apostle. The intruders' arrogant spirit impels Paul to adopt a style of writing that matches their behavior, all in irony.

11:19 The Corinthians were proud of their capacity to understand deep religious issues, and they valued teachers who made a pretense of learning. Paul came with a different agenda (1 Cor 2:1-16).

11:20-21a The Corinthian church had welcomed the intruders even when they exploited and insulted them. They even saw Paul's refusal to exploit them as ***too "weak."***

11:21b-29 Rather than boasting about his strengths and successes like the false teachers did, Paul boasts in

about it, too. 22Are they Hebrews? So am I. Are they Israelites? So am I. Are they descendants of Abraham? So am I. 23Are they [h]servants of Christ? I know I sound like a madman, but I have served him far more! I have worked harder, been put in prison more often, been whipped times without number, and faced death again and again. 24Five different times the Jewish leaders gave me thirty-nine lashes. 25Three times I was beaten with rods. Once I was stoned. Three times I was shipwrecked. Once I spent a whole night and a day adrift at sea. 26I have traveled on many long journeys. I have faced danger from rivers and from robbers. I have faced danger from my own people, the Jews, as well as from the Gentiles. I have faced danger in the cities, in the deserts, and on the seas. And I have faced danger from men who claim to be believers but are not. 27I have worked hard and long, enduring many sleepless nights. I have been hungry and thirsty and have often gone without food. I have shivered in the cold, without enough clothing to keep me warm.

28Then, besides all this, I have the daily burden of my concern for all the churches. 29Who is weak without my feeling that weakness? Who is led astray, and I do not burn with anger?

30If I must boast, I would rather boast about the things that show how weak I am. 31God, the Father of our Lord Jesus, who is worthy of eternal praise, knows I am not lying. 32When I was in Damascus, the governor under King Aretas kept guards at the city gates to catch me. 33I had to be lowered in a basket through a window in the city wall to escape from him.

Paul's Vision and His Thorn in the Flesh

12 This boasting will do no good, but I must go on. I will reluctantly tell about visions and [i]revelations from the Lord. 2I was caught up to the third [j]heaven fourteen years ago. Whether I was in my body or out of my body, I don't know—only God knows. 3Yes, only God knows whether I was in my body or outside my body. But I do know 4that I was caught up to [k]paradise and heard things so astounding that they cannot be expressed in words, things no human is allowed to tell.

5That experience is worth boasting about, but I'm not going to do it. I will boast only about my weaknesses. 6If I wanted to boast, I would be no fool in doing so, because I

11:22 Rom 11:1; Phil 3:5
11:23 Rom 8:36; 1 Cor 15:10; 2 Cor 6:4-5; [h]*diakonos* (1249) ‣Phil 1:1
11:24 Deut 25:3
11:25 Acts 14:19; 16:22; 27:41
11:26 Acts 9:23; 14:5; 20:3; 21:31; Gal 2:4
11:27 1 Cor 4:11; 2 Cor 6:5
11:29 1 Cor 9:22
11:30 2 Cor 12:5
11:31 2 Cor 1:23
11:32-33 Acts 9:24-25
12:1 Gal 1:12; [i]*apokalupsis* (0602) ‣2 Cor 12:7
12:2 [j]*ouranos* (3772) ‣2 Cor 12:4
12:4 Luke 23:43; Rev 2:7; [k]*paradeisos* (3857) ‣Gal 1:8

weakness and defeat, pointing away from himself and toward God.

11:22 ***Are they Hebrews? So am I:*** A Jewish heritage was seen by Paul's opponents as a qualification for ministry (see Phil 3:5). • ***Are they Israelites? So am I:*** An Israelite was a member of the covenant community by circumcision (cp. John 1:47; Rom 9:4). Paul had this badge also and was in fact a Pharisee, a most devoted follower of Torah (Acts 26:4-5; Rom 11:1; Phil 3:5-6). • ***Are they descendants of Abraham?*** This is yet another of Paul's opponents' claims to God's favor based on ethnic identity. Elsewhere, Paul clarifies who can truly be called *Israelites* and *descendants of Abraham* (see Rom 2:28-29; Gal 3:16, 26-29). Here, he ironically adopts the erroneous perspective of his opponents to beat them at their own game.

11:23-27 ***I have served him far more!*** Paul's service to Christ had entailed Christlike sufferings and toils. Some of the difficulties in this litany are recorded in Acts.

11:23-24 ***in prison more often:*** E.g., see Acts 16:22-23. Clement of Rome says that Paul was imprisoned a total of seven times. • ***thirty-nine lashes:*** This punishment was prescribed in Deut 25:1-3. ***The Jewish leaders*** punished Paul as a renegade Jew, and he ***faced death again and again.***

11:25 ***Three times I was beaten with rods:*** Paul suffered this Roman punishment at Philippi, though as a Roman citizen he should have been exempted (Acts 16:22-24, 37). • ***Once I was stoned:*** At Lystra (Acts 14:19). • ***Three times I was shipwrecked:*** These events are otherwise unknown; Paul's shipwreck on the voyage to Rome would come later (Acts 27).

11:26-27 Paul's ***many long journeys*** are recorded in Acts 13–28. These trips involved facing ***danger*** and ***enduring*** hardship. • ***from men who claim to be believers but are not:*** literally *from false brothers.*

11:28 In addition to physical difficulties, Paul felt the ***burden*** of ***concern*** (or *anxiety*) ***for all the churches.*** No church gave Paul more cause for concern than Corinth.

11:30 ***the things that show how weak I am:*** Paul develops this theme in 12:1-10.

11:32-33 As a final "boast" of his weakness, Paul tells the story of his escape from ***Damascus*** a few years after his conversion (see Acts 9:23-25; Gal 1:15-18). • ***King Aretas*** IV of Nabataea controlled Damascus only after AD 37, following the death of the Emperor Tiberius (see Josephus, *Antiquities* 18.5.1-3); the mention of Aretas dates Paul's escape from Damascus between AD 37 and the end of Aretas's reign in AD 39 or 40.

12:1-7 Paul's accusers at Corinth leveled the charge that Paul did not have ecstatic spiritual experiences. He was no mystic, they said, but a plain person with no impressive gift (see 10:10). So even though Paul's authority did not come from ***visions and revelations from the Lord,*** he reveals his secret that he did, in fact, have such experiences.

12:1 ***This boasting will do no good:*** See note on 11:21b-29.

12:2 ***I was caught up*** (literally *I know a man in Christ who was caught up*): In Greek, Paul demurely uses third person to speak of himself. • ***The third heaven*** is a Jewish expression for the immediate presence of God. • ***fourteen years ago:*** That is, about AD 43.

12:3-4 Paul wasn't sure whether he was in a trance or actually taken to heaven. • ***But I do know that I was caught up:*** Literally *But I know such a man, that he was caught up;* see note on 12:2.

12:5-7a Paul could ***boast*** about his ***experience*** (12:2-4), but it was no source of confidence in his ministry. He never makes mystical experience a proof of

12:5 2 Cor 11:30
12:6 2 Cor 10:8
12:7 Job 2:6
[a]*apokalupsis* (0602) ‣Gal 1:12
[b]*satanas* (4567) ‣1 Thes 2:18
12:8 Matt 26:39, 44
12:9 Phil 4:13
12:10 2 Cor 6:4; 13:4
12:11 2 Cor 11:1, 5
[c]*apostolos* (0652) ‣Eph 4:11
12:12 Rom 15:19
[d]*sēmeion* (4592) ‣2 Thes 2:9
12:13 1 Cor 9:12, 18
2 Cor 11:7
12:14 1 Cor 4:14-15
2 Cor 13:1
12:15 2 Cor 11:11
Phil 2:17
1 Thes 2:8
12:16 2 Cor 11:9
12:18 2 Cor 8:6, 16-18
12:19 Rom 9:1
12:20 1 Cor 4:21
2 Cor 2:1-4
12:21 2 Cor 13:2

would be telling the truth. But I won't do
it, because I don't want anyone to give me
credit beyond what they can see in my life
or hear in my message, 7even though I have
received such wonderful [a]revelations from
God. So to keep me from becoming proud, I
was given a thorn in my flesh, a messenger
from [b]Satan to torment me and keep me
from becoming proud.

8Three different times I begged the Lord
to take it away. 9Each time he said, "My
grace is all you need. My power works best
in weakness." So now I am glad to boast
about my weaknesses, so that the power of
Christ can work through me. 10That's why I
take pleasure in my weaknesses, and in the
insults, hardships, persecutions, and troubles that I suffer for Christ. For when I am
weak, then I am strong.

Paul's Concern for the Corinthians

11You have made me act like a fool—boasting like this. You ought to be writing
commendations for me, for I am not at all
inferior to these "super [c]apostles," even
though I am nothing at all. 12When I was
with you, I certainly gave you [d]proof that
I am an apostle. For I patiently did many
[d]signs and wonders and miracles among
you. 13The only thing I failed to do, which
I do in the other churches, was to become a
financial burden to you. Please forgive me
for this wrong!

14Now I am coming to you for the third
time, and I will not be a burden to you. I
don't want what you have—I want you. After
all, children don't provide for their parents.
Rather, parents provide for their children.
15I will gladly spend myself and all I have
for you, even though it seems that the more
I love you, the less you love me.

16Some of you admit I was not a burden
to you. But others still think I was sneaky
and took advantage of you by trickery.
17But how? Did any of the men I sent to you
take advantage of you? 18When I urged Titus to visit you and sent our other brother
with him, did Titus take advantage of you?
No! For we have the same spirit and walk
in each other's steps, doing things the same
way.

19Perhaps you think we're saying these
things just to defend ourselves. No, we
tell you this as Christ's servants, and with
God as our witness. Everything we do, dear
friends, is to strengthen you. 20For I am
afraid that when I come I won't like what
I find, and you won't like my response. I
am afraid that I will find quarreling, jealousy, anger, selfishness, slander, gossip,
arrogance, and disorderly behavior. 21Yes, I
am afraid that when I come again, God will
humble me in your presence. And I will be
grieved because many of you have not given
up your old sins. You have not repented of

---

his apostolic authority—his *life* and his *message* must be the proof. He instead boasts about his *weaknesses* (11:23-33).

12:7b-10 We do not know what the ***thorn in*** Paul's ***flesh*** was (cp. Num 33:55; Ezek 28:24; Hos 2:6); we only know that its purpose was to ***keep*** him ***from becoming proud,*** to prick the bubble of pride. • It was ***a messenger from Satan***—that is, something or someone evil—so Paul prayed to the Lord ***to take it away.*** The Lord answered each petition the same way: ***"My grace is all you need. My power works best in weakness."*** Paul's human weakness was an opportunity for ***the power of Christ*** to ***work through*** him by God's grace. Paul accepted his suffering because Christ's strength showed itself through his weakness.

12:11-13 Paul reviews his apostolic credentials; he continues to play the role of ***a fool,*** making proud boasts because his detractors have forced him to do so (see note on 11:16-29). Paul, too, has a commission as ***an apostle,*** one sent by God himself, with all the ***signs*** to validate it.

12:11 Some manuscripts do not include ***boasting like this.*** • ***"super apostles":*** See 11:5.

12:12 Included in Paul's credentials was his ability to deal ***patiently*** with difficult people such as the Corinthians.

12:13 ***The only thing I failed to do*** refers to his not taking payment for his services (see 11:7-11). • ***Please forgive me this wrong!*** This request is ironic and tongue-in-cheek.

12:14-15 ***the third time:*** Paul's first visit was his initial evangelism at Corinth (Acts 18:1-18); the second was the unscheduled "painful visit" (2:1). Paul contemplates what he hopes will be a happier visit, but there is still some suspicion and a need to clear the air. • ***I will not be a burden:*** Paul did not want their money but rather that they would fully accept his authority. That is why he would ***gladly spend himself*** for them rather than accept payment from them.

12:16-18 Some of the Corinthians ***still*** believed that Paul had deceived them ***by trickery.*** They might have insinuated that Paul was helping himself to the proceeds of the collection for the Jerusalem church (chs 8–9). The answer to this charge is a reminder of the integrity of ***Titus*** and the ***other brother*** (see 8:18-24). The integrity of Paul and his associates should debunk such false charges.

12:19 Paul is not simply offering a defense of his conduct and motives; he wants to assure his ***dear friends*** of his genuine love and Christian service for the well-being of the church.

12:20-21 Paul feared encountering renewed rebellion and resistance during his upcoming visit, with the Corinthians relapsed into their old ways. • ***and you won't like my response:*** If Paul had to, he would deal sternly with flagrant sinners (cp. 1:23–2:24; 1 Cor 4:21).

12:21 Paul fears that ***God will humble me in your presence***—a reprise of the previous visit (2:1), when the Corinthians had rebuffed and humiliated Paul. • The vices listed were among the Corinthians' ***old sins*** (see 6:14–7:1; 1 Corinthians Introduction, "Setting," p. 1924).

your impurity, sexual immorality, and eagerness for lustful pleasure.

6. CONCLUSION (13:1-14)

Paul's Final Advice

13 This is the third time I am coming to
visit you (and as the Scriptures say,
"The facts of every case must be established
by the testimony of two or three witnesses").
2I have already warned those who had been
sinning when I was there on my second
visit. Now I again warn them and all others,
just as I did before, that next time I will not
spare them.
3I will give you all the proof you want
that Christ speaks through me. Christ is not
weak when he deals with you; he is powerful among you. 4Although he was crucified
in weakness, he now lives by the power of
God. We, too, are weak, just as Christ was,
but when we deal with you we will be alive
with him and will have God's power.
5Examine yourselves to see if your faith
is genuine. Test yourselves. Surely you know
that Jesus Christ is among you; if not, you
have failed the test of genuine faith. 6As you
test yourselves, I hope you will recognize
that we have not failed the test of apostolic
authority.
7We pray to God that you will not do what
is wrong by refusing our correction. I hope
we won't need to demonstrate our authority
when we arrive. Do the right thing before
we come—even if that makes it look like we
have failed to demonstrate our authority.
8For we cannot oppose the truth, but must
always stand for the truth. 9We are glad to
seem weak if it helps show that you are actually strong. We pray that you will become
mature.
10I am writing this to you before I come,
hoping that I won't need to deal severely
with you when I do come. For I want to
use the authority the Lord has given me to
strengthen you, not to tear you down.

Paul's Final Greetings

11Dear brothers and sisters, I close my let-

13:1 *Deut 19:15; Matt 18:16; 2 Cor 12:14; 1 Tim 5:19
13:2 2 Cor 1:23; 12:21
13:3 Matt 10:20; 1 Cor 5:4
13:4 Rom 1:4; 6:4; Phil 2:7-8; 1 Pet 3:18
13:5 John 14:20; 17:23, 26; Rom 8:10; 1 Cor 11:28; Gal 4:19; Col 1:27
13:8 1 Cor 13:6
13:9 1 Cor 2:3; 4:10
13:10 2 Cor 10:8, 11
13:11 Rom 15:33; Phil 4:4
13:12 Rom 16:16; 1 Cor 16:20; 1 Pet 5:14

13:1-2 Announcing his intention to return to Corinth *the third time* (see note on 12:14-15), Paul found confirmation of his plan in *the Scriptures.* The reason for this quotation from Deut 19:15 is not clear, but perhaps, given the context of Deut 19:15, Paul wanted to *warn them* that every transgression (listed in 12:20-21) would be judged on his arrival. The *two or three witnesses* against the Corinthian offenders were Paul's letters or visits and the promise of his coming *the third time.*

13:3-4 *Christ speaks through me:* Paul represented Christ to the Corinthian congregation, and he would exercise *God's power* in dealing with them. • Paul's weakness was patterned on the humiliation of Christ, who *was crucified in weakness* (see 8:9). Paul's judgment on the sinners would be tempered by the constraint of Christ's love (5:14-21). • *We, too, are weak:* Paul's humanity was frail, yet he could draw on Christ's strength (12:10).

13:5-6 The issue is clear cut: If they cannot recognize that *Jesus Christ* is living *among* (or *in*) them, they are the ones who *have failed the test of genuine faith* (literally *are disproved*). There is a play on words here: They were looking for "proof" of Paul's apostolic authority, but Paul urges them, *Test yourselves* (or *Prove yourselves*). The lack of Christ's presence would disprove their authenticity as Christians. But Paul himself has demonstrated that he has *not failed the test of apostolic authority* (literally *not been disproved*).

13:7-10 Whatever the problems Paul faced at Corinth, there is no doubt about his chief desire. He cherished the highest good for these people, that they would *become mature* and *strong.* Paul was always concerned to promote the welfare of his people, even when rebuking them.

13:7 *that you will not do what is wrong:* They would do this by embracing the false teachers who had appeared on the scene (11:5, 13-15; see note on 10:1–13:13). • *even if that makes it look like we have failed:* Paul's motivation in ministry is to be faithful, not to appear successful (1 Cor 4:2). He patterned his service on Jesus Christ himself (13:4), who was outwardly weak and an apparent failure in dying on the cross, but who is now victorious as he lives by the mighty power of God.

13:9 *become mature:* This Greek word sometimes carries the idea of *repair* or *completion,* of restoring something to its proper condition, as in a return to good health (a related word is used in 13:11, "grow to maturity"; Mark 1:19, "repair"; 1 Thes 3:10, "fill"; Heb 13:21, "equip"; 1 Pet 5:10, "restore").

13:10 Paul did not want *to deal severely* with the Corinthians by punishing the offenders (12:21). He wanted to exercise his apostolic *authority* in a positive way, but his ministry required him both to *strengthen* and to *tear . . . down* (cp. Jer 1:10). • *to strengthen you* (or *to build you up*): This is Paul's favorite expression for a stable Christian community (see Eph 4:12), in which the Lord lives both in and among the believers (13:5).

13:11-14 The letter's conclusion includes Paul's final appeal (13:11), greetings (13:12-13), and a blessing (13:14).

13:11 *Dear brothers and sisters:* Literally *Brothers.* See note on 1:8-11 • *These last words* are Paul's final instructions. • *Be joyful:* See also Phil 3:1; 4:4. • *Grow to maturity:* See note on 13:9—Paul's encouragement might be that they aim for restoration. • *Encourage each other:* The need for encouragement has been very prominent in 2 Corinthians, beginning with 1:3-7. • *Live in harmony:* Literally *Be of the same mind* (as in Phil 2:1-4).

13:12-13 *with Christian love* (literally *with a sacred kiss*): The kiss was a common Jewish form of salutation, not only a sign of personal affection. Common in the NT church (Rom 16:16; 1 Cor 16:20; 1 Thes 5:26; 1 Pet 5:14), it may have a significance in worship services in uniting fellow believers (the "kiss of peace"). The word for *sacred* (Greek *hagiō*) is the same word that is translated *God's people* (literally *the saints*; Greek *hagioi*) in the next sentence. • *God's people here* were the believers in the place from which Paul was writing in Macedonia.

13:13-14 Some English translations include v 13 as part of v 12, and then v 14 becomes v 13.

13:14 Paul closes his letter with a prayer and blessing. He invokes the three persons of the Trinity, with *the grace of the Lord Jesus Christ* (see 8:9) coming first. This is because we are

13:14
Rom 16:20
Phil 2:1
[e]*koinōnia* (2842)
‣Gal 2:9

ter with these last words: Be joyful. Grow to
maturity. Encourage each other. Live in harmony and peace. Then the God of love and
peace will be with you.
12 Greet each other with Christian love.
13 All of God's people here send you their
greetings.
14 May the grace of the Lord Jesus Christ,
the love of God, and the [e]fellowship of the
Holy Spirit be with you all.

always relying on Christ's sacrificial love, which reconciles us to *God* the Father (5:18-21) and unites us through the *fellowship of the Holy Spirit* with all our fellow believers. • ***The love of God*** provides for our needs and graciously restores us to his family. • ***The fellowship of the Holy Spirit*** means our fellowship with the Spirit, who joins Christians together into a unity (Eph 4:3; Phil 2:1).

PAUL'S LETTER TO THE GALATIANS

Is a person saved by faith alone, or by a combination of faith plus works? Paul's letter to the Galatians proclaims that salvation is through faith alone. It also emphasizes freedom in Christ to live by the power of the Spirit, knowing that our relationship with God is not based on our performance but on the finished work of Jesus Christ. So we are truly free, not to serve our sinful nature, but to love and serve our Lord and others.

SETTING

When Paul and Barnabas set out from Antioch of Syria on their first missionary journey, they headed across the northeast corner of the Mediterranean Sea through Cyprus, across the Taurus Mountains of Pamphylia, and into the south of the Roman province of Galatia. There Paul and Barnabas established churches in Antioch of Pisidia, Iconium, Lystra, and Derbe (Acts 13:13–14:28). Many believed the Good News, but the message also aroused opposition and persecution. Paul and Barnabas then returned to Antioch of Syria, reporting on what God had accomplished "and how he had opened the door of faith to the Gentiles, too" (Acts 14:27).

From the results of Paul's ministry in Galatia and from Peter's experience with Cornelius and his household in Caesarea (see Acts 10:1-48), it became clear that salvation was available to Gentiles as well as Jews on the basis of faith in Jesus Christ. Gentiles did not have to become Jews in order to become full members of God's family. They had only to put their faith in Jesus Christ for salvation.

Even so, in the period before the council in Jerusalem (AD 49 or 50; Acts 15), controversy over the relationship of Jews and Gentiles in the church became more heated. When Peter returned to Jerusalem from his groundbreaking work among Gentiles in Caesarea Philippi, he faced immediate criticism and pressure from Jewish compatriots who opposed his eating with uncircumcised Gentiles. He answered with an account of the Spirit's work, which temporarily stilled the criticism (Acts 11:1-18).

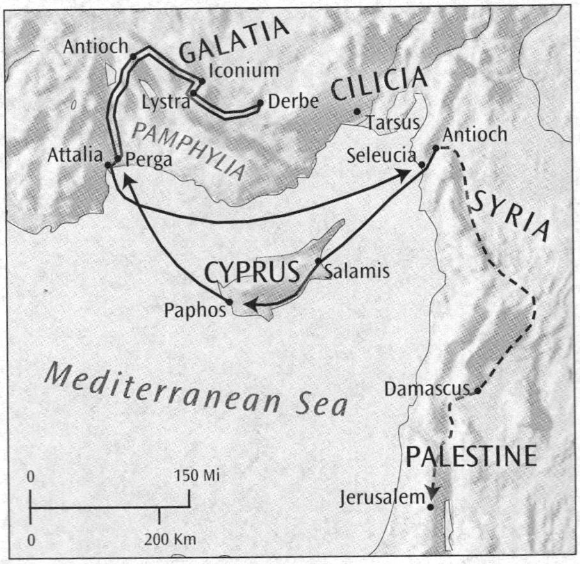

◂ **The Setting of Galatians, about AD 48.** Galatians was probably written from ANTIOCH, a short time after Barnabas and Paul's first missionary journey, to the churches that had recently been founded in the Roman province of GALATIA. At that time, the controversy over whether to circumcise Gentile believers was heating up and had not yet been resolved by the council in JERUSALEM (AD 49~50; Acts 15). The map shows the route of the first missionary journey (solid arrow) and the probable route Barnabas and Paul would take to Jerusalem (dashed arrow).

Some Jewish Christians continued to believe that Gentiles should practice Judaism in order to be Christians. Those who believed this are often referred to as "Judaizers." Some of the Judaizers went to Galatia and began claiming that Paul's teaching about the Good News was inadequate. They denigrated Paul's status as an apostle, declaring that he had learned the Good News from the "real" apostles in Jerusalem. They asserted that Paul had changed the message, and that his version of the gospel had never received the apostles' sanction. The Judaizers argued that Paul's law-free gospel was incomplete, and they claimed that the real gospel required Gentiles to be circumcised and to keep other aspects of the law.

Largely in response to the Judaizers' challenge, Paul wrote his letter to the Galatians.

OUTLINE

1:1-10
Introduction

1:11–2:21
Paul's Apostleship and Message

3:1–5:12
Justification by Faith

5:13–6:10
Life by the Spirit

6:11-18
Postscript

TIMELINE

Passover, AD 30 or 33
Jesus' crucifixion and resurrection

AD 31~34
Saul persecutes the church of Judea

AD 34~35
Saul's conversion near Damascus

AD 37~38
Barnabas and Paul's first trip to Jerusalem

about AD 47
Barnabas and Paul travel to Jerusalem with famine relief

AD 47~48
Barnabas and Paul's first missionary journey

AD 48~49
Paul writes Galatians from Antioch

AD 49~50
The council in Jerusalem

AD 50–52
Paul's second missionary journey

AD 53–57
Paul's third missionary journey

SUMMARY

After briefly identifying himself and greeting his recipients (1:1-5), Paul launches directly into his thesis: The Good News that he preaches is the only true Good News (1:6-7), he is a genuine apostle of Christ (1:1, 10), and his opponents will suffer God's judgment for their false message (1:8-9). The rest of the letter centers around these assertions.

Paul first demonstrates that he is a genuine apostle of Christ, preaching the true Good News (1:11–2:21). To this end, Paul reminds the Galatians of the kind of person he used to be (1:13-14) and recounts his conversion experience and his calling by God (1:15-16a). Paul received the Good News as a direct revelation from Christ (1:11-12) rather than from the other apostles in Jerusalem (1:16b-24). Still, the other apostles recognized Paul's apostleship and message (2:1-10), and they had nothing to add or change. Further, Paul was proven right in an instance when Peter and some others compromised the Good News contrary to their own principles (2:11-21).

Paul then makes an argument that his presentation of the Good News is scriptural and true (3:1–5:12). The Galatians had experienced the Spirit by faith (3:1-5), so they—like all who have faith in Christ—would experience the same blessing that Abraham received (3:6-9). By contrast, trying to be righteous by keeping the law only brings a curse (3:10-12). Christ rescued us from that curse and made God's blessing available to all who have faith in him (3:13-14). God's promise to Abraham shows that the promise is given on the basis of faith, not law (3:15-18). God's demand for righteousness was fulfilled by Christ, not by keeping the law, and those who have faith in Christ become recipients of God's promise to Abraham.

The law's purpose is not to make people righteous or to make them recipients of God's promises. Instead, it brings awareness of sin and points

to Christ and faith in him (3:19-22). Now that Christ has come, those who have faith in him are God's children and heirs of his promises (3:23–4:7). In light of this, the Galatians' return to trusting in the law was a dreadful return to slavery (4:8-11), so Paul personally appeals to them to reconsider (4:12-20). He draws an analogy between Hagar and Sarah and the old and new covenants, showing that Christ brings freedom, not slavery (4:21-31). God's people must live in freedom (5:1), reject reliance on obedience to the law for salvation (5:2-4), and live by faith (5:5-6), because a message of salvation through the law is not from God (5:7-12).

Finally, Paul shows the Galatians that Christian freedom is not a license to sin, as some might claim. Instead, it is the only way to overcome sin, to live in Christ's love, and to experience the Spirit's power (5:13–6:10). Freedom provides an opportunity to love rather than to sin (5:13-15), and the only way to overcome sin is to live by the power of the Holy Spirit (5:16-18). Living by human effort cannot overcome sin, because the sinful nature can produce only sinful actions (5:19-21). By contrast, living in the power of the Holy Spirit produces good fruit (5:22-23). Paul gives several examples of the Spirit's leading in the lives of God's children (5:24–6:10).

Paul ends his letter with a postscript in his own hand (6:11-18). He appeals again to the cross of Christ, bestows God's mercy and peace on those who follow his teaching, reasserts his apostolic authority, and closes with a benediction that extends "the grace of our Lord Jesus Christ" to the recipients of his letter.

> *Paul's Galatians is . . . like a lion turned loose in the arena of Christians. It challenges, intimidates, encourages, and focuses our attention on what is really essential. . . . How we deal with the issues it raises and the teachings it presents will in large measure determine how we think as Christians and how we live as Christ's own.*
>
> RICHARD LONGENECKER
> *Galatians*, p. lvii

AUTHOR

Galatians—with Romans and 1 and 2 Corinthians—has always been recognized as a genuine letter of Paul. It harmonizes well with the account of Paul's mission in Acts and the other letters, and it authentically reflects Paul's conflict with Jewish Christians who sought to make keeping the Jewish law a necessary element of Christian faith for Gentiles. Galatians has a message similar to that of Romans; but where Romans is grand and exalted, Galatians is intense and personal. Here we feel the heartbeat of Paul's care for the church.

RECIPIENTS

Some biblical scholars believe that Paul wrote to an ethnic group called "Galatians," who lived in north central Asia Minor and were related to Gauls and Celts. Others believe that the recipients of Paul's letter were groups of churches within the Roman province of Galatia, a much larger area than ethnic Galatia. The Roman province included in its southern districts all of the cities that Paul visited on his first missionary journey (Antioch of Pisidia, Iconium, Lystra, and Derbe).

Paul does not seem to have spent extended time in ethnic Galatia to the north (cp. Acts 16:6; 18:23), whereas we do have record of extensive and repeated missionary activity by Paul in the southern part of the Roman province of Galatia (Acts 13:13–14:25; 16:1-5). The available evidence suggests that the Galatians to whom Paul wrote this letter were most likely those whom Paul evangelized on his first missionary journey.

DATE

Paul wrote Galatians either shortly before the council at Jerusalem (Acts 15:1-29) in AD 49 or 50, or sometime after the council, perhaps during his third missionary journey (AD 53–57).

Traditionally, scholars saw Gal 2:1-10 as Paul's description of the council at Jerusalem. However, close examination reveals serious differences between Gal 2 and Acts 15. It is hard to reconcile Paul's account of two visits to Jerusalem (2:1) with the fact that the council in Acts 15 was really his third visit; neglecting to mention his second visit (Acts 11:30; 12:25) would seriously weaken Paul's argument that he had minimal contact with the apostles in Jerusalem. If this letter were written after the council, it would also be hard to imagine why Paul doesn't mention the council's decision, which directly addresses the issue in Galatians. After the council, in fact, Paul gladly carried news of its decision to the churches he visited (Acts 16:4). It is difficult to believe that 2:1-10 describes Acts 15 and that Galatians was written after the council at Jerusalem.

By contrast, there are relatively few difficulties in identifying the occasion described in Gal 2:1-10 with Acts 11:30 and 12:25. This would suggest that Paul wrote Galatians shortly before the council, perhaps in AD 48 or 49, just at the time when the controversy over circumcision was escalating in the church (see Acts 15:1-2).

MEANING AND MESSAGE

And now that the way of faith has come, we no longer need the law as our guardian. For you are all children of God through faith in Christ Jesus.

Galatians 3:25-26

The problem that arose in Galatia was a familiar one in the first-century church, and it remains a problem in the church today. Are we truly saved by the work of Jesus Christ on the cross, or is something more necessary on our part?

Paul's letter to the Galatians establishes the purity of the Good News—that salvation is available to all purely by faith in our Lord Jesus Christ and not by observing the law. It also establishes the unity of God's people: No division exists between Jews and Gentiles or between other classes of people. We all come to God and gain new life by the same means, through faith in Christ. Galatians establishes our liberty in Christ: We fulfill Christ's law not by human effort but by living in faith and love by the Holy Spirit. Finally, the letter establishes our need for the grace of God, which rescues us from the curse of sin, gives us new life and the promised Holy Spirit, and makes us God's children, empowered to fulfill Christ's law of love.

FURTHER READING

GERALD BORCHERT
Galatians in *Cornerstone Biblical Commentary*, vol. 14 (2007)

RONALD Y. K. FUNG
The Epistle to the Galatians (1988)

RICHARD N. LONGENECKER
Galatians (1990)

J. LOUIS MARTYN
Galatians (1997)

SCOT MCKNIGHT
Galatians (1995)

RICHARD B. HAYS
Galatians in *New Interpreter's Bible*, vol. 11 (2000)

1. INTRODUCTION (1:1-10)

Greetings from Paul

1 This letter is from Paul, an apostle. I was
not appointed by any group of people
or any human authority, but by Jesus Christ
himself and by God the Father, who raised
Jesus from the dead.
2All the brothers and sisters here join me
in sending this letter to the churches of Galatia.
3May God our Father and the Lord Jesus
Christ give you grace and peace. 4Jesus gave
his life for our sins, just as God our Father
planned, in order to rescue us from this evil
world in which we live. 5All glory to God forever and ever! Amen.

There Is Only One Good News

6I am shocked that you are turning away so
soon from God, who called you to himself
through the loving mercy of Christ. You
are following a different way that pretends
to be the [a]Good News 7but is not the Good
News at all. You are being fooled by those
who deliberately twist the truth concerning
Christ.
8Let God's curse fall on anyone, including us or even an angel from [b]heaven, who
preaches a different kind of Good News than
the one we preached to you. 9I say again
what we have said before: If anyone preaches
any other Good News than the one you welcomed, let that person be cursed.
10Obviously, I'm not trying to win the
approval of people, but of God. If pleasing
people were my goal, I would not be Christ's
[c]servant.

2. PAUL'S APOSTLESHIP AND MESSAGE (1:11–2:21)

Paul's Message Comes from Christ

11Dear brothers and sisters, I want you to understand that the gospel message I preach

1:1 Acts 20:24
1:3 Rom 1:7; Phil 1:2; Phlm 1:3
1:4 Rom 4:25; 1 Tim 2:6; Titus 2:14
1:5 Rom 11:36
1:6 2 Cor 11:4; [a]*euangelion* (2098) ‣Eph 1:13
1:7 Acts 15:1, 24
1:8 2 Cor 11:14; [b]*ouranos* (3772) ‣Eph 4:10
1:9 Deut 4:2; 12:32; 1 Cor 16:22; Rev 22:18
1:10 1 Thes 2:4; [c]*doulos* (1401) ‣Eph 6:5

1:1–2:21 Paul's opponents had questioned his integrity and authority as an apostle, so he opens his letter by defending his apostleship.

1:1-5 As in all his letters, Paul identifies himself and greets the recipients. This greeting is notable for (1) Paul's strong assertion of his apostolic authority (1:1); and (2) the lack of thanks, prayer, or praise, which are replaced by rebuke (1:6-10).

1:1 ***Paul, an apostle:*** Apostles were commissioned representatives having authority delegated by a sending agent, often a church body or council (e.g., 2 Cor 8:23; Phil 2:25). But Paul was not made an apostle by the Jerusalem church. Rather, he was directly commissioned ***by Jesus Christ himself*** and had Christ's authority (Acts 9:1-15; 26:12-20; see also Rom 1:5), which gave him equal authority with the other apostles. • Paul traced his commission to ***God the Father, who raised Jesus from the dead.*** The resurrection made Paul's commission possible.

1:2 ***the brothers and sisters*** (literally *brothers;* also in 1:11) ***here join me:*** Paul probably wrote from Antioch of Syria. Antioch was the hub of Paul's ministry and the earliest center of Gentile Christianity (see Acts 11:20-26). Paul did not stand alone (as his opponents in Galatia might have suggested), but in fellowship with a significant NT church. • ***The churches of Galatia*** were probably founded by Paul during his first missionary journey (Acts 13:4–14:26; see Galatians Introduction, "Recipients," p. 1978).

1:3-5 Paul followed the usual practice for first-century letters, including this greeting and wish of well-being as well as introducing the main topic, the Good News.

1:3 ***May God . . . give you grace and peace:*** This typical greeting by Paul (see also note on 1 Cor 1:3) uses elements of Greek and Hebrew greetings: "grace" (Greek *charis*), is similar to "greetings" (Greek *chairein*); "peace" mirrors Hebrew *shalom*. Thus Paul included both Jewish and Gentile Christians (cp. 3:28). The Galatians were at risk of losing God's grace and peace (3:1-4; 5:1-4). • ***God our Father and the Lord Jesus Christ:*** Some manuscripts read *God the Father and our Lord Jesus Christ.*

1:4-5 This summary of the Good News is the basis for the rebuke that follows (1:6-10). This might be a creed or confession of faith that Paul used to remind the Galatians of the message they had earlier embraced.

1:4 Because Jesus completely rescued us from ***our sins,*** there is no place for efforts to save ourselves. • Christian faith rescues us from ***this evil world in which we live*** (see 4:8-12; 5:13-26).

1:5 ***All glory*** must go ***to God*** for salvation, because it is his work alone.

1:6-10 ***I am shocked:*** In most of his letters, Paul followed his greeting with gratitude for his readers and a prayer for them (e.g., Rom 1:8-10; 1 Cor 1:4-5; Phil 1:3-6; Col 1:3-5; 2 Thes 1:3-12), but he found nothing to praise in the Galatian church.

1:6 The Galatians were ***turning away . . . from God*** by rejecting the Good News Paul proclaimed and looking instead to the law. God ***called*** them to himself ***through the loving mercy of Christ*** (some manuscripts read *through loving mercy*), not through the law (2:16). • ***God, who called you:*** Cp. 1:15; Rom 8:30; 9:24; 11:29. • ***a different way that pretends to be the Good News:*** Some were teaching that Gentile Christians had to be circumcised to be considered members of God's family. Paul rejected any requirement besides faith in Jesus (cp. 5:2-4).

1:7 The "different way" (1:6) was a distortion, ***not the Good News*** of salvation ***at all.*** The only way to be saved is by faith in Christ. Adding any requirements makes the message no longer the Good News. • ***those who deliberately twist the truth concerning Christ:*** The Judaizers knew they were changing the Good News to fit their views.

1:8-9 ***Let God's curse fall on anyone*** (literally *Let that person be anathema*): The Greek word *anathema* was often used to translate the Hebrew *kherem,* which in the OT means something dedicated to God for total destruction (see "Complete Dedication" at Lev 27:28-29, p. 244; cp. Rom 9:3; 1 Cor 12:3; 16:22). Paul was invoking God's strongest wrath on those who distort the Good News (1:7). • ***including us or even an angel from heaven:*** No one is authorized to change the Good News (cp. 2:6-10, 11-14).

1:9 The ***Good News . . . you welcomed*** was precisely the message Paul had preached to them (1:8; cp. 2 Thes 2:15).

1:10 The tone and content of this letter make it clear that ***trying to win the approval of people*** was not Paul's goal. Paul was probably criticized by the Judaizers for trying to please people by presenting only the part of the Good News pertaining to faith and grace, and not what they perceived to be the whole message including the law. • Being ***Christ's servant*** requires fidelity to Christ, regardless of how people respond (cp. Acts 5:29; Eph 6:5-6; 1 Thes 2:3-6).

1:11–2:21 The Judaizers who had come to Galatia preaching faith plus circumci-

1:11
1 Cor 15:1-3
1:12
1 Cor 2:10
Gal 1:1, 15-16
Eph 3:3
[d]*apokalupsis* (0602)
‣Eph 1:17
1:13
Acts 8:3; 9:21; 22:4-5; 26:4-11
1:14
Acts 22:3
1:15
Acts 9:15
[e]*charis* (5485)
‣Eph 1:6
1:16
Rom 1:17; 8:3, 10
Gal 2:9, 20
Col 1:27
1:18
Acts 9:22-23, 26-27
1:19
Matt 13:55
Acts 15:13
Gal 2:9, 12
1:23
Acts 9:20
2:1
Acts 15:2

is not based on mere human reasoning. 12I
received my message from no human source,
and no one taught me. Instead, I received it
by direct [d]revelation from Jesus Christ.
13You know what I was like when I followed the Jewish religion—how I violently
persecuted God's church. I did my best to destroy it. 14I was far ahead of my fellow Jews
in my zeal for the traditions of my ancestors.
15But even before I was born, God chose
me and called me by his marvelous [e]grace.
Then it pleased him 16to reveal his Son to
me so that I would proclaim the Good News
about Jesus to the Gentiles.
When this happened, I did not rush out
to consult with any human being. 17Nor did
I go up to Jerusalem to consult with those
who were apostles before I was. Instead, I
went away into Arabia, and later I returned
to the city of Damascus.
18Then three years later I went to Jerusalem to get to know Peter, and I stayed with
him for fifteen days. 19The only other apostle I met at that time was James, the Lord's
brother. 20I declare before God that what I
am writing to you is not a lie.
21After that visit I went north into the
provinces of Syria and Cilicia. 22And still
the Christians in the churches in Judea
didn't know me personally. 23All they knew
was that people were saying, "The one who
used to persecute us is now preaching the
very faith he tried to destroy!" 24And they
praised God because of me.

The Other Apostles Recognize Paul

2 Then fourteen years later I went back to
Jerusalem again, this time with Barnabas; and Titus came along, too. 2I went there
because God revealed to me that I should go.
While I was there I met privately with those
considered to be leaders of the church and
shared with them the message I had been
preaching to the Gentiles. I wanted to make

sion questioned Paul's apostleship and attempted to discredit his message. Paul defended his apostolic authority, demonstrating from past events that his message was the true Good News.

1:11 ***the gospel message I preach:*** Paul's message was that people are made right with God by grace through faith, not by obeying the law (see 2:16-17; Rom 10:9-13; Eph 2:8-9).

1:12 ***no human source . . . no one taught me:*** Jewish scholars primarily depended on teachers. The Judaizers argued that Paul had received his commission and message from the other apostles, but then had unfaithfully changed the message. • ***I received it by direct revelation from Jesus Christ*** (or *by the revelation of Jesus Christ*): See 1:17; Acts 9:3-15; 26:12-18. Paul's unique experience gave him distinctive authority and insight. But he learned other matters, such as the life of Christ, from others (e.g., 1:18; 1 Cor 11:23-26; 15:3-11).

1:13-14 To prove that his message did not come from human reason (1:11), Paul describes what he was like before he encountered Christ: He was a highly successful Jew (see Acts 8:1-3; 22:1-5; 26:4-5; Phil 3:4-7). His antagonism to ***God's church*** and strict adherence to Judaism demonstrated his faith in the law before Christ confronted him (1:15-16).

1:14 ***zeal for the traditions of my ancestors:*** Cp. Mark 7:6-13.

1:15-16a ***even before I was born:*** Cp. Jer 1:5; see also Ps 139:13-16; Isa 49:1-6; Rom 9:10-13. • ***God chose me and called me:*** For the account of Paul's conversion, see Acts 9:1-19; 22:1-21; 26:9-23. • Paul's calling was specifically to ***proclaim the Good News about Jesus to the Gentiles*** (2:7), and he even educated other apostles in what that means (e.g., 2:11-21). • ***to reveal his Son to me*** (or *to reveal his Son in me*): This might refer to Paul's encounter with Christ (Acts 9:1-19; cp. 1 Cor 9:1; 15:8); *in me* might also suggest an internal revelation (cp. 2:20; 4:6-7) and implies that Paul's changed heart revealed Christ to others.

1:16b-20 Paul was taught by the Lord directly and ***did not . . . consult with any human being*** (literally *with flesh and blood*), even the other ***apostles***. Paul was independent from the other apostles yet in harmony with them (2:1-10).

1:17 ***those who were apostles before I was:*** Paul put his own apostleship in the same category as the original disciples (see 1 Cor 9:1; 15:5-9; cp. Acts 1:22; 10:41). • Paul's trip to ***Arabia*** is not mentioned elsewhere; his understanding of the Good News was apparently formed during that time. Paul knew the OT Scriptures (see Acts 22:3), the claims of the first Christians (see Acts 8:1), and what others had told him since his conversion.

1:18-20 ***Peter*** and ***James*** had ***fifteen days*** to talk with Paul about his message, which was clearly in harmony with theirs. Paul did not receive a commission from the Jerusalem church—his apostleship did not derive from Jerusalem.

1:18 ***three years later*** (or *in the third year*): Either three years after Paul's conversion or after his return from Arabia. This event is probably the visit recorded in Acts 9:26-30. • ***to get to know Peter*** (Greek *Cephas*): Peter had something Paul did not: deep personal acquaintance with Jesus during Jesus' earthly ministry. • ***Fifteen days*** was much too short a time for Paul to become dependent on Peter as his mentor, but plenty of time for the content of each man's preaching to be thoroughly discussed.

1:20 ***I declare before God:*** Paul here takes an oath to emphasize the truthfulness of his account of his trip to Jerusalem.

1:21-22 Paul was not working under the supervision of the apostles in Jerusalem nor of the ***Christians . . . in Judea***.

1:23-24 Paul's conversion was a source of rejoicing in the Jerusalem church. This change (cp. 1:13-14) and his message were both the work of God (cp. Acts 9:31). Paul was not out of sync with the church in Jerusalem.

2:1-10 During Paul's second visit to Jerusalem, the other apostles affirmed his message. Traditionally, this passage has been seen as a description of the church council (Acts 15), but it is much more likely that Paul was talking about his previous visit to Jerusalem (Acts 11:30; 12:25; see Galatians Introduction, "Date," p. 1979).

2:1 Counting ***fourteen years*** from Paul's conversion (1:15-17), instead of from his previous visit (1:18), fits well with Acts. • That ***Barnabas*** was familiar to the Galatians suggests that the Galatians were evangelized during the first missionary journey (Acts 13:4–14:26; see Galatians Introduction, "Recipients," p. 1978). • ***Titus:*** See "Titus" at Titus 1:4; 2:1, p. 2073.

2:2 If 2:1-10 correlates with the visit of Acts 11:30, ***God*** might have ***revealed*** his will through Agabus's prophecy and

sure that we were in agreement, for fear
that all my efforts had been wasted and I
was running the race for nothing. 3And they
supported me and did not even demand
that my companion Titus be circumcised,
though he was a Gentile.
4Even that question came up only because
of some so-called Christians there—false
ones, really—who were secretly brought in.
They sneaked in to spy on us and take away
the [f]freedom we have in Christ Jesus. They
wanted to enslave us and force us to follow
their Jewish regulations. 5But we refused
to give in to them for a single moment. We
wanted to preserve the truth of the gospel
message for you.
6And the leaders of the church had nothing to add to what I was preaching. (By the
way, their reputation as great leaders made
no difference to me, for God has no favorites.) 7Instead, they saw that God had given
me the responsibility of preaching the gospel to the Gentiles, just as he had given Peter
the responsibility of preaching to the Jews.
8For the same God who worked through Peter as the apostle to the Jews also worked
through me as the apostle to the Gentiles.
9In fact, James, Peter, and John, who were
known as pillars of the church, recognized
the gift God had given me, and they accepted
Barnabas and me as their [g]co-workers. They
encouraged us to keep preaching to the Gentiles, while they continued their work with
the Jews. 10Their only suggestion was that
we keep on helping the poor, which I have
always been eager to do.

Paul's Dispute with Peter

11But when Peter came to Antioch, I had to
oppose him to his face, for what he did was
very wrong. 12When he first arrived, he ate
with the Gentile Christians, who were not

2:3
Acts 16:3

2:4
Gal 1:7; 5:1, 13
[f]*eleutheria* (1657)
‣Gal 5:1

2:5
Gal 1:6; 2:14

2:6
Deut 10:17
Acts 10:34
Rom 2:11
2 Cor 12:11

2:7
Acts 9:15; 22:21
1 Thes 2:4

2:9
Rom 1:5
[g]*koinōnia* (2842)
‣Phil 2:1

2:10
Acts 11:29-30; 24:17

2:12
Acts 11:2-3

---

the church's decision to send aid (Acts 11:27-29). • If Paul needed the endorsement of the leaders in Jerusalem, he would have met with them publicly; that they ***met privately*** indicates that no one thought he needed public endorsement. • ***those considered to be leaders of the church:*** Paul's tone downplays their importance, perhaps to counteract the false teachers' undue regard for them. • Paul ***shared*** his ***message*** with the apostles in Jerusalem, not for endorsement, but to ensure ***agreement,*** so that the church would not split into Jewish and Gentile factions. • ***for fear that all my efforts had been wasted:*** A split between Jewish and Gentile Christians would undermine the fundamental unity that Christ had secured (3:28).

2:3 The Jerusalem apostles affirmed Paul's message without qualification. They stood together on the same Good News—that God's grace comes through faith in Christ, not through keeping the law. Clearly the Jerusalem apostles did not think that circumcision was necessary for ***a Gentile*** (literally *a Greek*) like ***Titus.***

2:4-5 The false Christians entered the church ***there*** (either Jerusalem or Antioch) to subvert Paul's message that Gentiles are free from Jewish requirements such as circumcision.

2:4 By labeling ***some so-called Christians*** as ***false*** (literally *some false brothers*), Paul denied that they were Christians at all. They did not understand or truly receive the Good News, in contrast with the apostles in Jerusalem (2:3). • ***were secretly brought in:*** Paul implies that a larger group of Jewish "Christians" opposed his preaching (cp. Acts 15:5) and stood behind the false teachers who entered the Galatian church. • Requiring Gentile Christians to observe Jewish law would ***enslave*** them to regulations (see 3:23–4:11) and deny the Good News of Christ.

2:5 ***we refused to give in to them for a single moment:*** Titus was not circumcised (2:3) and Paul did not require circumcision of Gentile Christians. • ***to preserve the truth:*** The false teaching would destroy ***the gospel message*** by adding other requirements and impeaching the effectiveness of Christ's death and God's grace (cp. 2:11-21).

2:6-10 Paul's message was in harmony with the Jerusalem apostles, but their affirmation was not the source of Paul's authority (1:12, 16-20).

2:6 The Jerusalem apostles' ***reputation as great leaders*** was probably derived from their personal acquaintance with Jesus' earthly ministry, which did not give them greater apostolic authority than Paul had. What mattered most was Christ's personal commission (see 1 Cor 9:1; cp. 2 Cor 12:11-12). • ***God has no favorites:*** The Judaizers probably regarded the Jerusalem apostles' earthly relationship with Jesus as an advantage. Paul argues that such favoritism is inconsistent with God's character (cp. Lev 19:15-16; Deut 1:17; 2 Chr 19:7; Job 13:10; Ps 82:1-2; Prov 18:5; Mal 2:8-9).

2:7-8 The apostles in Jerusalem ***saw that*** Paul and Peter had different scopes of ministry (for Peter's, see Acts 1–5; 9–10; for Paul's, see Acts 13–28), but they both preached the same ***gospel.***

2:9 ***James:*** See "James, the Brother of Jesus" at Acts 15:13-21, p. 1858. • ***Peter:*** Greek *Cephas;* also in 2:11, 14. • ***they accepted Barnabas and me as their co-workers*** (literally *they gave me and Barnabas a right hand of fellowship*): This symbolic handshake showed full acceptance for Paul and Barnabas, their ministry, and their message.

2:10 The mention of ***helping the poor*** connects this narrative with Acts 11:30; 12:25. The Christians in Judea suffered years of deep poverty, and Paul was ***eager*** to have the Gentile churches alleviate some of that difficulty and build unity with the Jewish church (see Rom 15:25-27; 1 Cor 16:1-4; 2 Cor 8–9).

2:11-21 In Antioch, Peter and others compromised the Good News in contradiction of their own principles (this incident is not recorded in Acts). Paul's rebuke of Peter showed that Paul's apostleship was independent of Jerusalem and faithful to the Good News of Christ.

2:11 ***when Peter came to Antioch:*** This occasion, not recorded in Acts, probably occurred following the return of Paul and Barnabas from their first missionary journey (Acts 14:26-28). Paul probably wrote this letter soon afterward. • ***what he did was very wrong*** (or *he stood condemned*): Peter's actions were inconsistent with what he knew to be true—that God accepts Gentiles by faith, not by keeping the law (see Acts 10–11). • Paul ***had to oppose*** Peter ***to his face.*** Paul wanted to keep the Good News from being corrupted (2:21), which required showing publicly that Peter's own public action was wrong (cp. 1 Tim 5:20).

2:12 That Peter ***ate with the Gentile Christians*** was consistent with what God had shown him (Acts 10:9-16, 34-35). • The ***friends of James*** wanted to reassert Jewish scruples and prevent the free communion between

2:14 Acts 10:28
2:15 Phil 3:4-5
2:16 Acts 15:10-11; Rom 1:17; 3:20, 28; 8:3; Gal 3:11; Eph 2:8

circumcised. But afterward, when some friends of James came, Peter wouldn't eat with the Gentiles anymore. He was afraid of criticism from these people who insisted on the necessity of circumcision.
13As a result, other Jewish Christians followed Peter's hypocrisy, and even Barnabas was led astray by their hypocrisy.
14When I saw that they were not following the truth of the gospel message, I said to Peter in front of all the others, "Since you, a Jew by birth, have discarded the Jewish laws and are living like a Gentile, why are you now trying to make these Gentiles follow the Jewish traditions?
15"You and I are Jews by birth, not 'sinners' like the Gentiles.
16Yet we know that a person is made right with God by faith in

Righteousness by Faith (Gal 2:14-21)

Gal 3:11; Gen 15:6; Hab 2:4; Acts 10:1–11:18; Rom 1:17; Heb 10:38

The key issues for the church in Galatia were: How do people become acceptable to God? What do people need to do to earn God's favor? How do people become members of God's family?

For Paul, the answer was simple: There is nothing people can or need to do. Only Christ could do—and has done—what must be done to make people acceptable to God. So we should simply receive his gift, gratefully thank him for what he has done for us, and trust in him.

For Jewish Christians in the first century, it was hard to accept this answer. From the time of Abraham, their relationship with God had been defined by circumcision, the rite of cutting off the male foreskin (Gen 17:9-14). Every male who was part of God's family had to be circumcised, and those who neglected it were cut off from God's people. Those who had received circumcision were also expected to keep the laws regarding the Sabbath and what foods could be eaten, along with the rest of the law.

When the Christian faith moved from the Jewish to the Gentile world, it was natural for questions to arise. Do Christians need to be circumcised—and keep God's law in general—to be accepted as part of God's family? Or does God accept people purely on the basis of their faith in Christ's work on the cross? As Paul's mission to Gentiles advanced, these questions became pressing.

The apostle Peter understood from his vision in Joppa and his experience in Caesarea that God has accepted Gentiles *as Gentiles,* on the basis of their faith in Christ's finished work (Acts 10:9–11:18). They did not have to become Jewish by observing circumcision, for Christ provided them open access to God by faith. Peter and the Jerusalem church therefore welcomed Gentile believers into fellowship. But later, Peter temporarily withdrew from fellowship with Gentiles when some Jewish Christians criticized him (2:11-13). In response, Paul rebuked Peter for communicating that Gentiles must become Jews in order to be accepted by God (2:14-21).

No one is accepted by God and made righteous before him on the basis of keeping the law (2:16). Even Abraham was accounted as righteous and accepted by God because of his faith (3:6; Gen 15:6)—not because he was circumcised, which came later (Gen 17:9-14). Both Jews and Gentiles are accepted by God and made righteous before him on the basis of faith alone.

Gentiles and Jews from continuing. • ***Peter wouldn't eat with the Gentiles anymore:*** When Peter refused to share regular meals and the Lord's Supper (cp. 1 Cor 11:20-22, 33-34) with fellow Christians, he divided the Jewish and Gentile Christians and implied that the Jews' observances made them more acceptable to God. Peter's example, if uncorrected, would have undermined the Good News of salvation by grace through faith. • ***He was afraid:*** The friends of James intimidated Peter, who had previously withstood the same sort of ***criticism*** with power and eloquence (Acts 11:2-18). Peter might have been trying to avoid creating a barrier for the evangelism of Jews, or he might have been concerned for the safety and well-being of the Jewish Christians in Judea, who experienced persecution from non-Christian Jews (cp. 5:11; 6:12). In any case, his actions were inexcusable.

2:13 Peter's ***hypocrisy*** drew ***other Jewish Christians*** into error regarding the Good News.

2:14-21 The actions of Peter and the others implied that faith in Christ was not enough. Paul eloquently argues against such a compromise of the ***truth of the gospel message,*** showing that the law plays no role in defining a Christian's position before God, which is by grace through faith (Eph 2:8-9). • It is not clear where Paul's public rebuke of Peter ends and his message to the Galatians resumes (see note on 2:16). While Paul was recounting his address to Peter, he was also speaking to the Galatians. His rebuke of Peter was also a rebuke of them (see 3:1).

2:14 By ***living like a Gentile***—eating with Gentiles and not observing ***Jewish*** food ***laws***—Peter communicated God's acceptance of Gentiles on equal terms with Jews, on the basis of faith in Christ (see Acts 10:34-43; 11:17-18). • ***why are you now trying to make these Gentiles follow the Jewish traditions?*** Both Jews and Gentiles would draw this conclusion from Peter's actions.

2:15 Gentiles were ***'sinners'*** in that they did not have the law and could not obey God's commands. Paul was using the categories of Jewish thinking (cp. Matt 15:21-28; 26:45; Luke 6:32-34; 18:9-14) with strong irony in light of the sinful condition of all people (2:16; Rom 3:23).

2:16 Jews and Gentiles alike are sinners; the Good News requires both Jews and Gentiles to acknowledge that they

Jesus Christ, not by obeying the [h]law. And
we have believed in Christ Jesus, so that
we might be made right with God because
of our faith in Christ, not because we have
obeyed the [h]law. For no one will ever be
made right with God by obeying the [h]law."
17 But suppose we seek to be made right
with God through faith in Christ and then
we are found guilty because we have abandoned the law. Would that mean Christ has
led us into sin? Absolutely not! 18 Rather, I
am a sinner if I rebuild the old system of
law I already tore down. 19 For when I tried
to keep the [i]law, it condemned me. So I died
to the [i]law—I stopped trying to meet all its
requirements—so that I might live for God.
20 My old self has been crucified with Christ.
It is no longer I who live, but Christ lives in
me. So I live in this earthly body by [j]trusting
in the Son of God, who loved me and gave
himself for me. 21 I do not treat the grace of
God as meaningless. For if keeping the [k]law
could make us right with God, then there
was no need for Christ to die.

3. JUSTIFICATION BY FAITH (3:1–5:12)

The Law and Faith in Christ (3:1-14)

Personal Experience of the Spirit

3 Oh, foolish Galatians! Who has cast
an evil spell on you? For the meaning
of Jesus Christ's death was made as clear
to you as if you had seen a picture of his
death on the cross. 2 Let me ask you this one
question: Did you receive the Holy Spirit
by obeying the law of Moses? Of course
not! You received the Spirit because you believed the message you heard about Christ.
3 How foolish can you be? After starting your
Christian lives in the Spirit, why are you
now trying to become perfect by your own
[a]human effort? 4 Have you experienced so
much for nothing? Surely it was not in vain,
was it?

[h]*nomos* (3551) ‣Gal 2:19
2:19 Rom 6:10-14; 7:4; 2 Cor 5:15
[i]*nomos* (3551) ‣Gal 2:21
2:20 Rom 6:6; 8:37; Gal 1:4; 1 Tim 2:6; Titus 2:14
[j]*pistis* (4102) ‣Eph 2:8
2:21 [k]*nomos* (3551) ‣Gal 5:14
3:1 1 Cor 1:23; Gal 5:7
3:2 Rom 10:17
3:3 Gal 4:9
[a]*sarx* (4561) ‣Gal 5:19
3:4 2 Jn 1:8

are sinful (see Rom 2:1-5; 3:1-20) and in need of God's grace (Rom 3:21-26). Peter later demonstrated his agreement with this message (Acts 15:7-11). • Some translators hold that the quotation extends through v 14; others through v 16; and still others through v 21.

2:17-21 The false teachers probably claimed that Paul's law-free Good News would lead to lawlessness, that people would flaunt their sinfulness, and that ***Christ*** would thus be seen as leading people into sin (2:17). Paul shows that this is false, because those who place their faith in Christ are empowered by the Holy Spirit to live holy, God-honoring lives (see 5:13-26).

2:18 ***I am a sinner*** (or ***lawbreaker***): Turning away from faith and back to the law brings a person under the jurisdiction of the law, where all stand under God's judgment (Rom 3:10-12, 23-24; see Heb 6:1-8), and is itself a serious sin against Christ (5:2-4; cp. Heb 6:4-6). See also note on 2:19. • ***if I rebuild:*** By insisting on keeping Jewish laws concerning food and circumcision (2:11-13). • Christ ***tore down*** the ***system of law*** through his death (Eph 2:14-16).

2:19 ***when I tried to keep the law, it condemned me:*** Attempting to gain acceptance with God through keeping the law inevitably leads to sin (5:2-4; see Rom 7:5, 8-11), whereas living by the Spirit leads away from sin (5:16, 22-24; see "The Law and the Spirit" at 5:16-26, p. 1993). • ***I died to the law:*** The NLT adds an explanation that this means ***I stopped trying to meet all its requirements.*** Those who trust in Christ participate in his death (2:20); they are no longer under the law's judgment (see Rom 6:2, 10-11; 7:2-6), and they stop seeing the law as a means of their salvation. Instead, Christians ***live for God*** in a new relationship with God through Christ (3:23–4:11; see Rom 6:10-11; 14:7-8; 2 Cor 5:15).

2:20 A law-free Good News does not lead to lawlessness, as Paul's opponents argued (2:17), because lawlessness is a response of the unredeemed. The redeemed Christian ***has been crucified with Christ.*** (Some English translations put this sentence in v 19.) See also Col 2:11-14, 20-23. A Christian has laid aside the ***old self,*** which strove to achieve merit by keeping the law (cp. Rom 7:4-6). • ***It is no longer I who live, but Christ lives in me:*** Christians, having experienced Christ's death and resurrection (Rom 6:1-14), have new hearts (see Jer 31:31-34; 32:38-41; Ezek 11:19-20; 36:24-31) by the indwelling power of the Spirit (see Rom 8:9-11; Eph 3:16-19; Col 1:27; 3:1-17). • ***I live in this earthly body:*** Christianity does not teach that the body is evil or that we have to escape from this world to have fellowship with God. Instead, ***by trusting in the Son of God,*** we fulfill God's purposes for our lives. • ***who loved me and gave himself for me:*** Christ's self-giving love makes new life possible (1:4; Rom 8:32-39; 2 Thes 2:16-17).

2:21 Perhaps Paul's opponents in Galatia suggested that his message would make God's grace to Israel ***meaningless,*** since it was connected with the law (cp. Rom 3:1-2, 31). Instead, it was Paul's opponents who treated ***the grace of God as meaningless*** by voiding the ***need for Christ to die.***

3:1–5:12 Paul now defends the truth of his message—that right relationship with God comes by faith in Christ alone—and proves the fallacy of the message that Gentiles must keep the law in order to be acceptable to God.

3:1-9 Paul compares the Galatians' spiritual experience (3:1-5) with Abraham's (3:6-9), showing that they were made right with God in the same way, through faith and not through the law (Eph 2:8-9).

3:1 ***Oh, foolish Galatians!*** Their foolishness was both intellectual and spiritual (cp. Luke 24:25; see 1 Sam 25:1-38) as they turned away from Christ (1:6) and put faith in the law. • The Galatians were deceived by the teachers' ***evil spell*** (cp. Gen 3:1-7)—not literal witchcraft, but enticing arguments. • ***For the meaning of Jesus Christ's death was made as clear to you as if you had seen a picture of his death on the cross*** (literally *Before your eyes Jesus Christ was publicly portrayed as crucified*): Paul's proclamation of the Good News clearly portrayed Christ's death and explained its significance (see Rom 10:14-17).

3:2 The Galatians, like all Christians, ***received the Holy Spirit*** by faith in Christ, not ***by obeying the law of Moses*** (see Acts 2:38-39; Rom 8:9-11; 2 Cor 1:22; Eph 1:11-14; cp. Acts 10:44-48; 11:15-18). God accepted the Galatians because of their faith in ***the message . . . about Christ*** (cp. Rom 10:14-17), which made their turning to the law absurd (3:3-4).

3:3 ***by . . . human effort*** (literally ***by flesh***): Paul makes a pun: The Galatians were trying to ***become perfect*** by ***human effort*** through keeping the law about circumcising the ***flesh*** of the male foreskin.

3:4 ***Have you experienced*** (or ***suffered***) ***so much for nothing?*** This could refer to suffering, but what is known about the Galatian church does not suggest

3:5
1 Cor 12:10
3:6
*Gen 15:6
Rom 4:3
3:8
*Gen 12:3
Acts 3:25
[b]*proorao͂* (4308)
‣1 Pet 1:2
3:10
*Deut 27:26
Jer 11:3
3:11
*Hab 2:4
Rom 1:17
Heb 10:38
3:12
*Lev 18:5
Rom 10:5
3:13
*Deut 21:23
Gal 4:5
3:14
Joel 2:28
Acts 2:33
[c]*eulogia* (2129)
‣Eph 1:3
3:15
Heb 9:17
3:16
*Gen 12:7; 13:15;
17:7; 24:7

5 I ask you again, does God give you the
Holy Spirit and work miracles among you
because you obey the law? Of course not!
It is because you believe the message you
heard about Christ.

Faith the Same as Abraham's

6 In the same way, "Abraham believed God,
and God counted him as righteous because
of his faith." 7 The real children of Abraham,
then, are those who put their faith in God.
8 What's more, the Scriptures [b]looked forward to this time when God would declare
the Gentiles to be righteous because of
their faith. God proclaimed this good news
to Abraham long ago when he said, "All nations will be blessed through you." 9 So all
who put their faith in Christ share the same
blessing Abraham received because of his
faith.

Curse through Law, Blessing through Faith

10 But those who depend on the law to make
them right with God are under his curse,
for the Scriptures say, "Cursed is everyone
who does not observe and obey all the commands that are written in God's Book of the
Law." 11 So it is clear that no one can be made
right with God by trying to keep the law. For
the Scriptures say, "It is through faith that
a righteous person has life." 12 This way of
faith is very different from the way of law,
which says, "It is through obeying the law
that a person has life."
13 But Christ has rescued us from the
curse pronounced by the law. When he was
hung on the cross, he took upon himself the
curse for our wrongdoing. For it is written
in the Scriptures, "Cursed is everyone who
is hung on a tree." 14 Through Christ Jesus,
God has blessed the Gentiles with the same
[c]blessing he promised to Abraham, so that
we who are believers might receive the
promised Holy Spirit through faith.

The Law and God's Promise (3:15-29)

God's Promise to Abraham

15 Dear brothers and sisters, here's an example from everyday life. Just as no one can set
aside or amend an irrevocable agreement,
so it is in this case. 16 God gave the promises
to Abraham and his child. And notice that

this. Paul was probably referring to the spiritual experiences the Galatians had through the Holy Spirit (3:3, 5). Turning to the law for right standing with God would mean regarding the work of the Spirit as meaningless.

3:5 *work miracles:* See 1 Cor 12:4-11. The Holy Spirit is present with believers and in the church because of faith in ***the message . . . about Christ.***

3:6-9 Abraham's experience shows that faith has always been the basis for relationship with God and for receiving what God has promised.

3:6 This quote is from Gen 15:6, where God established his covenant with Abraham (see Gen 15:1-21; 17:1-27). This statement is foundational in defining God's relationship with humanity (see Hab 2:4; Rom 4:1-8, 17-22).

3:7 Gentile Christians—including the Galatians—are among ***the real children of Abraham,*** not by keeping the law of Moses, but by ***faith in God*** (see Rom 4:9-17, 23-25; cp. Matt 12:48-50).

3:8 ***the Scriptures looked forward:*** By faith, Abraham foresaw the coming Messiah (cp. John 8:56) and received the message that ***"All nations will be blessed through you"*** (Gen 12:3; 18:18; 22:18). Through Abraham's offspring, the Messiah, God would accept all nations on the same basis as Abraham himself—by faith.

3:10-12 By relying on circumcision, the Galatians depended ***on the law.*** Those who look to the law for right standing with God are under a ***curse.*** They cannot keep the whole law, so they cannot receive blessing under its terms.

3:10 Paul here quotes Deut 27:26, which summarized the curse that Israel would experience if they failed to keep all the stipulations of God's covenant (see Deut 27:9-26; cp. Deut 28:15-68; 31:26; Josh 1:8; Mal 2:2; see also Gen 3:14-19; 4:10-12). It is impossible for sinful human beings to obey God's will completely (see Rom 3:9-20).

3:11 *So it is clear* from Scripture, even if it was not clear to the Galatians or the false teachers who were insisting on circumcision for Gentile believers. • ***"It is through faith that a righteous person has life":*** Paul quotes Hab 2:4, in which the prophet was waiting in faith for God's promise to be fulfilled.

3:12 The ***law*** itself is not opposed to ***faith*** (see 3:19-25; Rom 7:7-13), but trying to be righteous by keeping the law opposes righteousness by faith in Christ. Paul quotes Lev 18:5 to show that ***life*** under the law comes by ***obeying*** rather than ***believing.*** Right standing with God is impossible on that basis (3:10-11).

3:13-14 In contrast with those who depend on the law (3:10-12), those who look to God through faith in Christ freely receive God's life and blessings.

3:13 *rescued us* (or *ransomed us*): Christ paid a ransom to buy back his people (see 4:4-5; 1 Pet 1:18-20). • ***"Cursed is everyone who is hung on a tree":*** Paul quotes Deut 21:23 (Greek version), in which executed criminals exposed for public shame were under God's curse (see note on Deut 21:22). Jesus, when he was crucified, ***took upon himself*** God's ***curse*** that should have fallen upon all sinners (cp. 2 Cor 5:21).

3:14 ***Christ Jesus*** has ***blessed the Gentiles with the same blessing . . . promised to Abraham,*** as described in 3:6-13. Paul equates this blessing with receiving ***the promised Holy Spirit*** (3:2-6; see also Rom 8:1-17, 23; Eph 1:13-14). • ***the promised Holy Spirit:*** Some manuscripts read *the blessing of the Holy Spirit.*

3:15-18 Christ, not the law, has fulfilled the promise and covenant given to Abraham.

3:15 ***Dear brothers and sisters:*** Literally *Brothers.* • An ***irrevocable agreement,*** such as a person's last will and testament, is unalterable after the person has died, and it must be executed exactly as written.

3:16 The ***promises to Abraham*** were primarily inherited by ***Abraham*** and ***his child*** (literally *his seed*)—the promised Messiah, the ultimate descendant of Abraham. "Seed" can refer to a single descendant or to many descendants (see notes on Gen 12:7; 13:15). Although the promise has a plural sense (see 3:29; Gen 13:15-16; 15:5-6; 17:7-8), this singular noun points to the one descendant, Christ, who completely fulfilled the promise. The heirs of the promise are not Jacob's physical children, but the spiritual children of Christ by the Spirit through faith. • ***children:*** Literally *seeds.*

the Scripture doesn't say "to his children,"
as if it meant many descendants. Rather,
it says "to his child"—and that, of course,
means Christ. 17This is what I am trying to
say: The agreement God made with Abraham could not be canceled 430 years later
when God gave the law to Moses. God would
be breaking his promise. 18For if the inheritance could be received by keeping the law,
then it would not be the result of accepting
God's promise. But God graciously gave it to
Abraham as a promise.

The Purpose of the Law

19Why, then, was the law given? It was given
alongside the promise to show people their
sins. But the law was designed to last only until the coming of the child who was promised.
God gave his law through angels to Moses,
who was the mediator between God and the
people. 20Now a mediator is helpful if more
than one party must reach an agreement.
But God, who is one, did not use a mediator
when he gave his promise to Abraham.

21Is there a conflict, then, between God's
law and God's promises? Absolutely not! If
the law could [d]give us new life, we could be
made right with God by obeying it. 22But
the Scriptures declare that we are all prisoners of sin, so we receive God's promise of
freedom only by believing in Jesus Christ.

God's Children through Faith

23Before the way of faith in Christ was available to us, we were placed under guard by
the law. We were kept in protective custody,
so to speak, until the way of faith was revealed.

24Let me put it another way. The law
was our [e]guardian until Christ came; it protected us until we could be made right with
God through faith. 25And now that the way
of faith has come, we no longer need the
law as our [f]guardian.

26For you are all children of God through
faith in Christ Jesus. 27And all who have
been united with Christ in [g]baptism have
put on Christ, like putting on new clothes.

3:17 Exod 12:40
3:18 Rom 4:14; 11:6
3:19 Exod 20:19; Deut 5:5; Acts 7:53; Heb 2:2
3:20 1 Tim 2:5
3:21 Rom 8:2-4; [d]*zōopoieō* (2227) ‣1 Pet 3:18
3:22 Rom 3:11-19; 11:32
3:24 Rom 10:4; [e]*paidagōgos* (3807) ‣Gal 3:25
3:25 [f]*paidagōgos* (3807) ‣1 Cor 4:15
3:27 Rom 6:3; 13:14; [g]*baptizō* (0907) ‣Eph 4:5
3:28 John 10:16; 17:21; 1 Cor 12:13; Eph 2:14-15; Col 3:11

3:17 Just as irrevocable agreements cannot be canceled (3:15), the terms of God's covenant with Abraham were not changed by the giving of ***the law***. • ***430 years:*** See note on Exod 12:40.

3:18 The ***inheritance*** (see 4:1-7) cannot come through ***keeping the law,*** because that would nullify ***God's promise*** to Abraham, which was by faith before the law.

3:19-22 Paul's argument so far might lead his readers to believe that the law had no purpose. Here, however, Paul emphasizes the law's proper role in order to correct false teaching about the law.

3:19 If people do not receive God's inheritance through the law, ***why, then, was the law given?*** It was ***to show people their sins*** and make it clear that sinful actions are offenses against God. People cannot rely on their own goodness to save them, but must turn to God in faith (see Rom 3:19-20; 4:15; 5:20; 7:7-13). • ***until the coming of the child who was promised:*** See 3:16. While the promise is permanent, the law was temporary. With Christ's coming, the law was fulfilled (see Matt 5:17-20; cp. Matt 3:13-15; John 19:30) and God's acceptance is based entirely on faith in Christ. • ***through angels:*** Deuteronomy 33:2 in the Greek version describes the Lord's coming from Sinai "with myriads of holy ones, angels with him at his right hand." See also Ps 68:17; Acts 7:38, 53; Heb 2:2. • ***Moses, who was the mediator:*** See Exod 20:19; Deut 5:24-27.

3:20 The law, given through angels and ***a mediator,*** required ***agreement*** between God and the people. The law was conditional, with blessings and curses attached to keeping or not keeping its statutes. In contrast, God ***gave his promise to Abraham*** directly; he ***did not use a mediator.*** It was God's unilateral and unconditional commitment. • ***God, who is one:*** Paul used the basic Jewish creed (Deut 6:4) to convince Gentile Christians not to become Jewish converts.

3:21-25 See Rom 7:7-13.

3:21 No ***conflict*** of purpose exists between law and promise, or between law and faith. Law partners with the promise in bringing people to faith in Christ. Law has its proper roles of declaring people prisoners of sin (3:19, 22) and of restraining sin (3:23-25). In Galatia, the Judaizers tried to convince Gentile Christians that the law could do something it was never intended to do—***give . . . new life*** and make people ***right with God***. God does these things on the basis of faith in his promise, which was fulfilled in Jesus Christ (see 3:22). • ***God's promises?*** Some manuscripts read *the promises?*

3:22 ***we are all prisoners of sin:*** See Rom 3:9; 7:1-13; 11:32. Keeping the law is of no use in bringing salvation; only ***believing in Jesus Christ*** can bring ***freedom***.

3:23-29 Paul contrasts the condition of God's people under the law before Christ with their condition now under Christ.

3:23 Because sin had imprisoned us (3:22), ***the law*** was a ***guard,*** keeping God's people in ***protective custody . . . until the way of faith*** in Christ ***was revealed.*** It made God's requirements explicit, and thus highlights the need for a Savior. The law also restrains sin by making the consequences of sin explicit.

3:24 The law is like a child's ***guardian*** (Greek *paidagōgos,* "tutor"). In Greco-Roman culture, a ***guardian*** was a faithful slave responsible for training and protecting the heir until he came of age.

3:25 ***the way of faith has come:*** The principle of righteousness by faith was always operative (cp. 3:6-9), but the object of that faith and the means of appropriating it are now clear to everyone through Jesus Christ. • ***we no longer need the law as our guardian:*** In Greco-Roman culture, a freeborn child who came of age was no longer under the discipline of a guardian, but was free to rule himself. So, too, those who are "of age" through faith in Christ are free from the guardianship of the law. They serve Christ directly as he leads by his word and Spirit.

3:26-29 Because of Christ, our condition under faith contrasts with our condition under the law (3:23-24).

3:26 Those who are ***children*** (literally *sons*) ***of God through faith in Christ Jesus*** (see also 4:4-7; John 1:12; Rom 9:8) have come of age as heirs of his promises (see 3:24-25, 29) and have received the down payment of that inheritance (3:14; Eph 1:14). The Galatians were foolish (3:1) in trying to gain access to God through circumcision. As God's children by faith, they already had the best possible access to God.

3:27 ***united with Christ in baptism:*** See Rom 6:3-4. Baptism represents death of an old life and birth into a new one. In the new life, the law's curse no longer has any force (cp. Rom 7:1-6). • ***have put***

3:29
Rom 8:17
4:2
[h]*oikonomos* (3623)
› Eph 1:10
4:3
Col 2:8, 20
4:4
Mark 1:15
John 1:14
Eph 1:10
Heb 2:14
4:5
Rom 8:15
Eph 1:5
[i]*huiothesia* (5206)
› Eph 1:5
4:6
Rom 8:15-16
[j]*kardia* (2588)
› Eph 4:18
[k]*abba patēr* (0005, 3962)
› Mark 14:36
4:7
Rom 8:17
4:8
1 Thes 1:9
4:9
Col 2:20
4:10
Rom 14:5
Col 2:16

28 There is no longer Jew or Gentile, slave or free, male and female. For you are all one in Christ Jesus. 29 And now that you belong to Christ, you are the true children of Abraham. You are his heirs, and God's promise to Abraham belongs to you.

Slavery and Freedom (4:1–5:1)

God's Heirs through Christ

4 Think of it this way. If a father dies and leaves an inheritance for his young children, those children are not much better off than slaves until they grow up, even though they actually own everything their father had. 2 They have to obey their [h]guardians until they reach whatever age their father set. 3 And that's the way it was with us before Christ came. We were like children; we were slaves to the basic spiritual principles of this world.

4 But when the right time came, God sent his Son, born of a woman, subject to the law. 5 God sent him to buy freedom for us who were slaves to the law, so that he could [i]adopt us as his very own children. 6 And because we are his children, God has sent the Spirit of his Son into our [j]hearts, prompting us to call out, [k]"Abba, Father." 7 Now you are no longer a slave but God's own child. And since you are his child, God has made you his heir.

Serving the Law: A Return To Slavery

8 Before you Gentiles knew God, you were slaves to so-called gods that do not even exist. 9 So now that you know God (or should I say, now that God knows you), why do you want to go back again and become slaves once more to the weak and useless spiritual principles of this world? 10 You are trying to earn favor with God by observing certain days or months or seasons or years. 11 I fear for you. Perhaps all my hard work with you was for nothing.

A Personal Appeal

12 Dear brothers and sisters, I plead with you to live as I do in freedom from these things,

on Christ, like putting on new clothes: Literally *have put on Christ.* Christ covers us and gives us a new identity. Cp. Col 3:12; 1 Thes 5:8.

3:28 ***There is no longer:*** Everyone comes to Christ and receives God's promises in exactly the same way (cp. 1 Cor 12:12-13; Eph 2:14; Col 3:11). • ***Jew or Gentile:*** Literally *Jew or Greek.* • ***male and female:*** Cp. Gen 1:27. • ***you are all one:*** The community of believers is one body, the body of Christ (see Rom 12:4-5; 1 Cor 12:27; Eph 2:15-16, 19-22). • ***in Christ Jesus:*** See Col 2:6–3:11.

3:29 Because Christ is the ideal descendant of Abraham (3:16), it follows that those who are one with Christ (3:27-28) are ***children*** (literally *seed*) ***of Abraham,*** and ***heirs*** of all that was promised to him.

4:1-7 Paul supports his argument that the law's purpose for God's children was fulfilled when Christ came, so that we are no longer bound by it.

4:1-3 A child inheriting an estate might receive a large fortune, but before coming of age, the child must obey ***guardians*** and trustees until the time set by the father. Similarly, before Christ came, God's people were under the guardianship of the law (see 3:23-24).

4:3 ***Before Christ came,*** God's people were like underage heirs to a large estate (4:1-2). They would inherit a great fortune (4:5), but they were still subject to their guardian (3:23-25). • ***the basic spiritual principles*** (or *powers;* also in 4:9) ***of this world:*** This probably refers to the principles of law that govern the world apart from Christ; these principles were fully expressed in the law of Moses (3:23-24; cp. 4:5).

4:4-5 God set ***the right time*** in the course of history for Christ to come (cp. Luke 4:18-19; Eph 4:8-10). • Christ was fully human (***born of a woman***) and ***subject to the law.*** Christ fulfilled the law (see Matt 3:13-15; 5:17) so that now God's ***children*** (literally *sons;* also in 4:6) have ***freedom*** and are no longer bound as ***slaves*** to it. • ***to buy freedom:*** By fulfilling the law and bearing its curse, Christ ransomed us from its claims (3:13; see also Rom 3:24; Col 1:13-14). • ***so that he could adopt us:*** See also Rom 8:15-17.

4:6 The Holy ***Spirit*** provides an inner testimony to assure us that ***we*** (literally *you*) are God's ***children*** (see Rom 8:16; Eph 1:13-14). • ***Abba, Father:*** *Abba* is an Aramaic term for "father." Those who have the ***Spirit of his Son*** are able to address God as Father, just as Christ did (Mark 14:36; cp. Matt 6:9).

4:7 ***child:*** Literally *son;* also in 4:7b.

4:8-11 Paul reminds the Galatians of their former paganism; he argues that practicing circumcision (and the law in general) would be a return to the same kind of slavery that they experienced ***before*** they ***knew God.***

4:8 The Gentile Galatians had previously practiced pagan idolatry; they worshiped the elements and the seasons (cp. Rom 1:25) and were ***slaves*** to the fear of offending these ***so-called gods*** (1 Cor 8:5-6).

4:9 ***now that you know God:*** Christians have a relationship with God that is like a child to a parent rather than a slave to a master (4:5-7). • ***why do you want to go back?*** Paul was perplexed (cp. 4:19-20) that Christians who had this standing would want to return to their old life of slavery. • ***now that God knows you:*** God is the agent of salvation and had taken the initiative in laying their souls bare (cp. Ps 139:1-6, 23-24; Luke 2:34-35; Heb 4:12) and forgiving them freely.• By turning to circumcision, the Galatians would be returning to the same ***useless spiritual principles of this world*** that they had known under paganism. In both cases, one must work to satisfy an unyielding master.

4:10-11 Circumcision was not the Galatians' only attempt to follow the law; it was one example of a whole way of thinking. They had also begun celebrating the Jewish festivals, thinking that it would make them more acceptable to God. To Paul, it was another indication that they did not understand, or had turned their backs on, the Good News of God's grace through Christ.

4:11 ***I fear for you:*** The Galatians were in danger of turning away from Christ by relying upon the law. If they did, Paul's ***hard work*** would have been ***for nothing.*** The Good News would have done them no good (cp. Heb 6:4-6; 2 Pet 2:20-22). See Acts 13:44–14:24 for a description of Paul's work for the sake of the Christians in that region.

4:12-20 Turning aside from scriptural arguments, Paul appeals personally to the Galatians by reminding them of their close relationship with him.

4:12 ***brothers and sisters:*** Literally *brothers;* also in 4:28, 31. • ***live as I do:***

for I have become like you Gentiles—free
from those laws.
You did not mistreat me when I first
preached to you. [13]Surely you remember
that I was sick when I first brought you the
Good News. [14]But even though my condition tempted you to reject me, you did not
despise me or turn me away. No, you took
me in and cared for me as though I were an
angel from God or even Christ Jesus himself. [15]Where is that joyful and grateful
spirit you felt then? I am sure you would
have taken out your own eyes and given
them to me if it had been possible. [16]Have
I now become your enemy because I am telling you the truth?
[17]Those false teachers are so eager to win
your favor, but their intentions are not good.
They are trying to shut you off from me so
that you will pay attention only to them. [18]If
someone is eager to do good things for you,
that's all right; but let them do it all the time,
not just when I'm with you.
[19]Oh, my dear children! I feel as if I'm going through labor pains for you again, and
they will continue until Christ is fully developed in your lives. [20]I wish I were with you
right now so I could change my tone. But at
this distance I don't know how else to help
you.

Hagar and Sarah, Slaves and Free

[21]Tell me, you who want to live under the
law, do you know what the law actually says?
[22]The Scriptures say that Abraham had two
sons, one from his slave wife and one from
his freeborn wife. [23]The son of the slave
wife was born in a human attempt to bring
about the fulfillment of God's promise. But
the son of the freeborn wife was born as
God's own fulfillment of his promise.
[24]These two women serve as an illus-

4:13 1 Cor 2:3
4:14 Matt 10:40
4:16 Amos 5:10
4:17 Gal 2:4, 12
4:19 Eph 4:13
4:22 Gen 16:15; 21:2-3
4:23 Rom 9:7-9

Paul, the scrupulous Jew, abandoned his own efforts at righteousness and received the free grace of God in Christ. Now he calls these Gentiles to adopt his position rather than take on the practices he had abandoned. Paul's exhortations throughout the rest of the letter (4:12–6:10) grow out of this single command. • ***You did not mistreat me:*** Likewise, the Galatians should not mistreat Paul now, but should continue in their warm acceptance of his ministry and message.

4:13-14 ***I was sick:*** Paul might have had a chronic physical ailment, but it is not certain what it was (cp. 2 Cor 12:7). Paul's ***condition*** was serious and apparently caused difficulty or even offense to the new church in Galatia. Physical trouble was often regarded by both Jews and Gentiles as a sign of God's judgment (cp. John 9:1-2; Acts 28:4). The Galatians saw past Paul's outward condition and received him as God's messenger (literally *angel;* Greek *angelos,* "angel, messenger"). • ***or even Christ Jesus himself:*** Cp. Luke 10:16.

4:15 The Galatians had been ***joyful and grateful*** in response to Paul's preaching of the Good News. • ***your own eyes:*** Some conclude from this phrase that Paul's eyes were diseased, but Paul might have been using ***eyes*** as a word-picture of a precious asset (cp. Deut 32:10; Ps 17:8; Matt 18:9). In their gratitude to Paul for the message of Good News, the Galatians ***would have . . . given*** him their most valuable possession.

4:16 The contrast couldn't be greater between the Galatians' acceptance of Paul and his message at the beginning of their Christian life, and their current suspicion or even rejection of him.

4:17 ***are so eager:*** The Greek word can have the positive meaning of zeal and eagerness or the negative meaning of jealousy and envy. The same word is also translated ***will pay attention*** and "is eager" (4:18). • ***They are trying to shut you off from me:*** Perhaps the Judaizers were so eager because they envied the Galatians' devotion to Paul and wanted it for themselves (cp. 2 Corinthians; see also Luke 11:46-52). Another possibility is that the Judaizers wanted the Galatians to become dependent on them as interpreters of the law.

4:18 Paul's statement might mean that it was fine for people to seek the Galatians' loyalty, but those other teachers were not in fact eager to do good things for them. Alternatively, this verse could be translated *It is good to be always sought eagerly for good things, and not just when I'm with you.* In this case it would mean that it was good for the Galatians to continue eagerly embracing Paul and his message and not change their attitude toward him in his absence.

4:19 The Galatians were Paul's spiritual ***children*** (cp. 1 Cor 4:14-15; Phlm 1:10). The process of bringing them to Christ had been like ***going through labor pains,*** a hard labor with a definite and joyful conclusion. Now Paul felt that it wasn't finished after all. • ***until Christ is fully developed in your lives:*** Paul uses wordplay, switching the metaphor so that the Galatians would give birth to Christ's image if they continued in the faith that Paul delivered to them. However, if they took up the law, they would produce a stillbirth. Paul must continue his hard work as a midwife in order to prevent this from happening.

4:20 Had Paul been personally present, he would have been able to "read" his hearers and thus shape his appeal to their exact spiritual and emotional condition. From afar, he wasn't sure if the ***tone*** he was using would be effective.

4:21-31 Paul now returns to arguing from Scripture, using the contrast between Hagar and Sarah and between their children. Paul argues for a similar contrast between those who are slaves under the law and those who are free in Christ. • Paul's argument uses the allegorical techniques of rabbinic Judaism (see note on 4:24). Having been trained as a rabbi (Acts 22:3), Paul could out-argue the Judaizers using their own methods.

4:21 ***do you know what the law actually says?*** They were trying to achieve righteousness by the law, but they did not truly understand its meaning (cp. Luke 24:25-27; 1 Tim 1:7).

4:22-23 ***The son of the slave-wife*** was Ishmael, born to Sarah's servant Hagar (see Gen 16:15). Sarah gave Hagar to Abraham ***in a human attempt*** to obtain the heir (see Gen 16:1-4) that God had promised (see Gen 15:1-6). Sarah's son, Isaac, was ***the son of the freeborn wife*** (see Gen 21:2-3); he was miraculously conceived as ***God's own fulfillment of his promise*** (see Gen 17:15-21).

4:24-25 Paul connects Abraham's human attempt to fulfill God's promises (4:23) with the human attempt in Galatia and elsewhere to attain salvation by keeping the law. Hagar's status as a slave-wife corresponds with Israel's ***enslaved*** status under the law. This status contrasts with the status of those who have faith in Christ (4:26-27).

4:24 ***serve as an illustration*** (literally *are being allegorized*): In allegorical

4:26 Heb 12:22 Rev 3:12; 21:2, 10
4:27 *Isa 54:1
4:28 Gal 3:29
4:29 Gen 21:9
4:30 Gen 21:10 John 8:35
4:31 Gal 3:29
5:1 John 8:32, 36 Acts 15:10 Gal 2:4 [a]*eleutheroō* (1659) ‣Gal 5:13
5:2 Acts 15:1

tration of God's two covenants. The first woman, Hagar, represents Mount Sinai where people received the law that enslaved them. [25]And now Jerusalem is just like Mount Sinai in Arabia, because she and her children live in slavery to the law. [26]But the other woman, Sarah, represents the heavenly Jerusalem. She is the free woman, and she is our mother. [27]As Isaiah said,

"Rejoice, O childless woman,
you who have never given birth!
Break into a joyful shout,
you who have never been in labor!
For the desolate woman now has more children
than the woman who lives with her husband!"

[28]And you, dear brothers and sisters, are children of the promise, just like Isaac. [29]But you are now being persecuted by those who want you to keep the law, just as Ishmael, the child born by human effort, persecuted Isaac, the child born by the power of the Spirit.

[30]But what do the Scriptures say about that? "Get rid of the slave and her son, for the son of the slave woman will not share the inheritance with the free woman's son." [31]So, dear brothers and sisters, we are not children of the slave woman; we are children of the free woman.

Freedom in Christ

5 So Christ has truly set us [a]free. Now make sure that you stay free, and don't get tied up again in slavery to the law.

Implications of Justification by Faith (5:2-12)

Gaining God's Favor

[2]Listen! I, Paul, tell you this: If you are counting on circumcision to make you right with God, then Christ will be of no benefit to you.

writing, every character and event is symbolic of a deeper meaning. Allegorical interpretations often ignore the historical meaning of the text and invent fanciful meanings. Here, by contrast, Paul understood the story correctly in its historical context and recognized the story as history. But he interpreted the characters of the historical story as symbolizing the current situation. Paul's opponents were apparently also using allegorical methods of interpretation, so Paul refuted faulty allegory with true allegory (cp. 1 Cor 9:22). • ***God's two covenants:*** The old covenant was formed through Moses; the new covenant came through Jesus Christ. • ***Hagar represents Mount Sinai:*** Just as Hagar was a slave-wife who represents human effort, ***Mount Sinai*** brought slavery to following the law.

4:25 ***And now Jerusalem is just like Mount Sinai in Arabia:*** Literally *And Hagar, which is Mount Sinai in Arabia, is now like Jerusalem;* other manuscripts read *And Mount Sinai in Arabia is now like Jerusalem.* • Both Hagar and Mount Sinai were symbols of ***Jerusalem,*** which stood for Judaism in Paul's day. Judaism continued to trust in the law and in physical descent from Abraham for their status before God (cp. John 8:31-59); they rejected Christ and continued to live ***in slavery to the law*** (3:23-24; 4:1-3). • ***Mount Sinai in Arabia:*** The traditional location for Mount Sinai is in the Sinai Peninsula in Egypt. However, some have suggested that ***in Arabia*** means that Mount Sinai was in Midian, where Moses once lived (see Exod 3:1; map, p. 122).

4:26 Just as Hagar represents slavery to human effort based on Mount Sinai (4:24-25), ***Sarah represents*** freedom in ***the heavenly Jerusalem,*** the ideal city of God. Abraham's true children by faith (3:29) now live in the reality of God's reign in Christ. • ***she is our mother:*** Sarah's child, Isaac, was the freeborn recipient of all of God's promises apart from the law. Similarly, Jews and Gentiles who live by faith in Christ are Sarah's true children—they receive God's promises to Abraham freely apart from the law (3:26-29; 4:4-7).

4:27 The quoted passage, Isa 54:1, promised Israel that they would be fruitful after the Exile. Because those who have faith in Christ are Sarah's children (4:26), they fulfill the promise that Sarah (the ***childless woman***) would be more abundantly fruitful than the slave-wife Hagar. To the Judaizers, those who don't follow the law may have been considered "barren," but through faith they are abundantly fruitful as the bride of Christ (2 Cor 11:2; Eph 5:31-33).

4:28-31 Paul applies the allegory of Hagar and Sarah (4:21-27) to the situation in Galatia. ***Isaac*** represents those who are born through God's ***promise*** (3:8) ***by the power of the Spirit*** (3:2-5; cp. Eph 1:13-14) and who trust in God for salvation through Christ by faith alone. ***Ishmael*** represents those who believe that ***human effort*** by keeping the law will make them acceptable to God (3:10-11). This identification would have been shocking to the Judaizers, who thought of themselves as the legitimate children of Abraham because of their insistence on law-keeping.

4:29 Ishmael ***persecuted*** Isaac, the child of the promise, at Isaac's weaning ceremony (see Gen 21:9). Similarly, in Galatia, ***those who want you to keep the law*** were persecuting those who trusted in God's promise, the message of God's grace through faith in Christ alone (cp. Acts 13:50-51; 14:1-7).

4:30-31 Sarah's demand regarding Ishmael, quoted from Gen 21:10, becomes a principle (see Gen 21:12) for dealing with the current ***son of the slave woman***—anyone who refuses to abandon slavery to the law. God does not allow those who seek righteousness through human effort to share in his inheritance (see Rom 9:30-33). Those who come to God through Christ alone, by faith and not by keeping the law, are ***children of the free woman*** who inherit God's blessings.

5:1 Paul succinctly summarizes his message to the Galatians, decrying their foolish behavior and offering a positive alternative—freedom. • ***So Christ has truly set us free:*** Christians are free to walk by faith in Christ alone (cp. Rom 8). • ***don't get tied up*** (literally *don't take on a yoke*): In Judaism, it was a duty and an honor to "take the yoke of the law." God's children in Christ are not called to bear this heavy burden (see Luke 11:46; Acts 15:10); instead, they enjoy Christ's yoke of freedom (Matt 11:28-30).

5:2-6 The Judaizers taught that keeping the law would earn God's favor (cp. Acts 15:1), but that path actually leads to alienation from God. Real righteousness comes to those who live in Christ by the power of the Spirit.

5:2 ***Paul*** reminded the Galatians of who was talking to them: the apostle of Christ who represented the Lord to the Gentiles and who had first proclaimed the Good News to them.

3I'll say it again. If you are trying to find
favor with God by being circumcised, you
must obey every regulation in the whole
law of Moses. 4For if you are trying to make
yourselves right with God by keeping the
law, you have been cut off from Christ! You
have fallen away from God's grace.
5But we who live by the Spirit eagerly wait
to receive by faith the righteousness God
has promised to us. 6For when we place our
faith in Christ Jesus, there is no benefit in
being circumcised or being uncircumcised.
What is important is faith expressing itself
in love.

A Law-Oriented Gospel Is False

7You were running the race so well. Who
has held you back from following the
truth? 8It certainly isn't God, for he is the
one who called you to freedom. 9This false
teaching is like a little [b]yeast that spreads
through the whole batch of dough! 10I am
trusting the Lord to keep you from believing false teachings. God will judge that
person, whoever he is, who has been confusing you.
11Dear brothers and sisters, if I were still
preaching that you must be circumcised—
as some say I do—why am I still being
persecuted? If I were no longer preaching
salvation through the cross of Christ, no one
would be [c]offended. 12I just wish that those
troublemakers who want to mutilate you by
circumcision would mutilate themselves.

4. LIFE BY THE SPIRIT (5:13–6:10)

Life in the Spirit (5:13-26)

Freedom and Love

13For you have been called to live in [d]free-
dom, my brothers and sisters. But don't
use your [d]freedom to satisfy your sinful
nature. Instead, use your freedom to serve
one another in love. 14For the whole [e]law
can be summed up in this one [f]command:
"Love your neighbor as yourself." 15But if
you are always biting and devouring one another, watch out! Beware of destroying one
another.

5:5 Rom 8:23-24
5:6 1 Cor 7:19; 1 Thes 1:3
5:7 1 Cor 9:24; Heb 12:1
5:8 Rom 8:28
5:9 1 Cor 5:6; [b]*zumē* (2219) ‣Matt 13:33
5:11 1 Cor 1:23; [c]*skandalon* (4625) ‣1 Pet 2:8
5:13 1 Pet 2:16; [d]*eleutheria* (1657) ‣Jas 1:25
5:14 *Lev 19:18; Rom 13:9; [e]*nomos* (3551) ‣Gal 5:18; [f]*logos* (3056) ‣Col 4:6
5:16 Rom 8:4-6
5:17 Rom 7:15-23

5:3 Those who seek righteousness through the law *must obey every regulation* of it (see 2:15-16; cp. Jas 2:10).

5:4 People who think circumcision is necessary for salvation are putting faith in the law and in themselves, not in Christ. Such people are ***cut off from Christ,*** outside of his grace (cp. Rom 5:2); they are under the judgment of the law. They have ***fallen away from*** the benefits of ***God's grace*** (cp. 1:6; 1 Pet 5:12).

5:5 The alternative to living by faith in the law is to ***live by*** complete reliance on ***the Spirit*** to make us pleasing to God. • ***eagerly wait to receive by faith the righteousness God has promised to us*** (or ***eagerly await by faith the hope that righteousness gives us***): We receive God's righteousness at our salvation (Rom 5:9-11; 10:10), in an ongoing way through the Spirit's sanctification (Rom 8:1-14), and fully at the resurrection when Christ returns (Rom 8:18-30). God's sole power provides righteousness and fulfills his promise (3:14, 22).

5:6 ***Faith in Christ Jesus*** provides access to all of God's favor and grace, so ***no*** further ***benefit*** is available through human effort. ***Faith*** is expressed by exercising ***love*** toward others (cp. Rom 13:10; 14:17-19; 2 Cor 8:8-13).

5:7 The life of faith is like ***running*** a ***race*** (cp. 1 Cor 9:24-27; Phil 3:13-14; 2 Tim 4:7-8). The law became a hindrance to the Galatians in this race rather than a help (cp. Luke 11:52).

5:8 The Galatians thought that their commitment to the law would please God, but ***God*** wasn't calling them to this slavery. God ***called*** them to ***freedom.***

5:9 This verse was apparently a well-known adage (literally *A little yeast makes the whole loaf rise;* cp. Matt 13:33; 16:6, 11-12; 1 Cor 5:6-7). A little reliance on the law for acceptance by God soon results in forgetting that Christ saves by *his* work alone.

5:10 ***that person, whoever he is:*** Perhaps Paul did not know who the false teachers were, or perhaps he meant that their credentials were unimportant (cp. 2:6). • ***confusing you:*** The false teaching distorted the Good News, so Paul wrote to clear up their thinking.

5:11 ***Dear brothers and sisters:*** Literally *Brothers;* similarly in 5:13. • ***if I were still preaching:*** This statement probably refers to Paul's preaching as an ardent zealot of Judaism before his conversion to Christ (1:13-14; Acts 7:58–8:3). As a Christian, Paul had never preached that Gentiles ***must be circumcised.*** • ***why am I still being persecuted?*** If Paul had been preaching a law-based religion, the Jewish zealots who persecuted him wherever he went would not have done so. The zealots found scandalous the complete rejection of the necessity of their laws (cp. Rom 9:33; 1 Cor 1:23).

5:12 ***mutilate themselves*** (or ***castrate themselves,*** or ***cut themselves off from you;*** literally *cut themselves off;* cp. Phil 3:2): Paul uses biting sarcasm and wordplay with multiple levels of meaning: (1) Paul might be alluding to pagan priests in the province of Galatia who castrated themselves in devotion to pagan gods. An insistence on circumcision for Christians is essentially no different. It involved cutting the flesh to become acceptable to God by physical deeds rather than by faith in Christ. (2) Depending on circumcision mutilated the false teachers' standing before God, so they might as well mutilate themselves physically. (3) In the old covenant, emasculated men were not allowed to enter the congregation (Deut 23:1); similarly, those who rely on circumcision have no place in the new covenant community. Paul probably wished that the Judaizers would *cut themselves off* by removing themselves from the community.

5:13–6:10 Having shown that justification comes by faith alone, Paul now addresses the question, "If we don't keep the law, then what will guide our conduct?" His answer is that righteousness comes from the Spirit. The Judaizers probably warned that Paul's message of ***freedom*** (5:1) would put believers on a slippery slope to moral ruin. Paul argues that freedom is not a license to sin, because ***love*** guides Christians. Liberty should be used ***to serve one another in love*** (cp. 2:20; 2 Cor 5:14-15).

5:14 ***the whole law can be summed up*** (or ***the whole law is fulfilled***): Christ's followers fulfill the law by exercising ***love*** toward every ***neighbor*** (Lev 19:18; see Matt 7:12; Luke 6:27-36; 10:25-37; John 13:34-35; 15:9-17; Rom 13:8-10).

5:15 The opposite of love is ***biting and devouring one another*** (cp. Ps 35:25; Prov 30:14; Jer 8:17). People who do not love are characterized by strife and bitterness. They will end up ***destroying one another,*** but love gives life to others (John 3:16; 15:12-13).

5:18
Rom 6:14; 8:14
[g]*nomos* (3551)
‣Gal 5:23

5:19
[h]*sarx* (4561)
‣Gal 5:24

5:20
[i]*eidōlolatria* (1495)
‣Eph 5:5

5:22
[j]*agapē* (0026)
‣Eph 4:2
[k]*eirēnē* (1515)
‣Eph 2:14
[a]*agathōsunē* (0019)
‣Eph 5:9

5:23
[b]*nomos* (3551)
‣Gal 6:2

The Spirit's Power

16 So I say, let the Holy Spirit guide your lives.
Then you won't be doing what your sinful
nature craves. 17 The sinful nature wants to
do evil, which is just the opposite of what
the Spirit wants. And the Spirit gives us desires that are the opposite of what the sinful
nature desires. These two forces are constantly fighting each other, so you are not
free to carry out your good intentions. 18 But
when you are directed by the Spirit, you are
not under obligation to the [g]law of Moses.

Results of the Sinful Nature

19 When you follow the desires of your [h]sin-
ful nature, the results are very clear: sexual
immorality, impurity, lustful pleasures,
20 [i]idolatry, sorcery, hostility, quarreling, jealousy, outbursts of anger, selfish ambition,
dissension, division, 21 envy, drunkenness,
wild parties, and other sins like these. Let
me tell you again, as I have before, that anyone living that sort of life will not inherit
the Kingdom of God.

Fruit of the Spirit

22 But the Holy Spirit produces this kind of
fruit in our lives: [j]love, joy, [k]peace, patience,
kindness, [a]goodness, faithfulness, 23 gentleness, and self-control. There is no [b]law
against these things!

Follow the Spirit's Leading

24 Those who belong to Christ Jesus have
nailed the passions and desires of their

5:16-26 A law-free faith will not lead to moral ruin because having the ***Holy Spirit*** to ***guide*** people's ***lives*** changes their hearts to follow the will of God and not sin (cp. Jer 31:33; Heb 8:10).

5:17 We cannot simply decide to keep the law and not sin: A war rages between God's Spirit and our ***sinful nature*** (see Rom 7:14-25; 1 Pet 2:11; cp. Gen 4:7). The answer is not human effort at law-keeping, but living by God's Spirit. When we are resurrected, we will finally be freed from sin (see Rom 8:18-25).

5:18 Those who are ***directed by the Spirit*** are under the Spirit's authority and not ***under obligation to the law***. They do not answer to the law but to the Spirit of God. It was not Paul's intent to justify civil disobedience (see Rom 13:1-7; Titus 3:1; cp. 1 Pet 2:13-17). He was addressing the means of obtaining spiritual righteousness before God.

5:19-26 These two lists contrast life dominated by the sinful nature (5:19-21) with life led by the Spirit (5:22-26). Living by the Spirit means observing a higher ethical standard than can be achieved under the law.

5:19 ***When you follow . . . the results are*** (literally *The works of the flesh are*): An emphasis on law-keeping and sinful actions both flow from trying to live apart from the power of God's Spirit. • ***very clear:*** Basic understanding of right and wrong is universal (cp. Rom 1:32; 2:14-15; 1 Cor 5:1), though some people suppress this awareness (Rom 1:18-21). • The list begins with ***sexual immorality;*** in contrast, the list of Christian virtues begins with love (5:22). All kinds of sexual misconduct was common (cp. Rom 1:24-27; 1 Cor 5:1; 6:15-18; 2 Cor 12:21; 2 Pet 3:10, 18). It was connected in paganism with fertility worship (cp. Rev 2:14, 20). • Moral ***impurity*** removes holiness and makes fellowship with a holy God impossible (see Matt 23:27; Rom 6:19; 2 Cor 12:21; Eph 5:3; Col 3:5; 1 Thes 4:7).

5:20 ***Idolatry,*** the worship of false gods, was common in Galatia and was often accompanied by ***sorcery*** (see Acts 19:19; cp. 1 Sam 15:23; Rev 9:21; 18:23; 21:8; 22:15) and sexual immorality (cp. 1 Cor 6:9, 15-20). • ***Hostility*** arises from angry pride rather than the Spirit's humility and love (5:22-23). • ***Quarreling*** refers not to standing up for what is right, but to stirring up discord and looking for a fight (1 Cor 3:3; 2 Cor 12:20; 1 Tim 6:4; Titus 3:9). Those who are guided by the Holy Spirit seek to speak the truth in love with a peacemaking attitude (5:22; Eph 4:15; 2 Tim 2:23-26). • ***Jealousy*** (Greek *zēlos,* "zeal") has both a positive sense ("passionate commitment") and, as here, a negative one ("intense desire for another's things"); cp. Jas 3:14-16. • ***Outbursts of anger*** (or *fits of rage*) contrast with self-control (5:23; see, e.g., Acts 19:28; 2 Cor 12:20; 1 Tim 3:3; Titus 1:7). • ***Selfish ambition*** (or *Selfishness*) is the antithesis of Christian love (cp. Rom 2:8; Phil 2:3; Jas 3:14, 16). • ***Division*** (Greek *haireseis,* "heresies, factions, sects") refers to people using differing beliefs or practices to divide the community (cp. 1 Cor 11:17-19; 2 Pet 2:1-3).

5:21 ***Drunkenness*** has no place in the Christian life (see Luke 21:34; 1 Cor 11:20-22; Eph 5:18). • ***wild parties:*** Festivals in honor of pagan gods were often accompanied by drunken orgies (cp. 1 Pet 4:3). • ***other sins like these:*** This list is only representative of the vices of the sinful nature (cp. Mark 7:20-23; Rom 1:29-31; 1 Cor 6:9-10; Eph 5:3-5; Col 3:5-8; 1 Tim 1:9-10; 2 Tim 3:2-5; Jas 3:13-18; Rev 21:8). People ***living that sort of life*** are not living by the Spirit, and thereby demonstrate no relationship with God by faith. Such people ***will not inherit the Kingdom of God:*** They are still slaves of their sinful nature (4:8-9, 22-25; cp. Rom 6:16-22; 1 Cor 6:9-10) and are not under God's rule.

5:22 Unlike following the sinful nature (5:19-21), letting the ***Holy Spirit*** guide (5:16) ***produces*** a life pleasing to God, which human effort and the law cannot do (cp. John 15:1-8). • These virtues directly address the factions in the church of Galatia. • ***love:*** The greatest Christian virtue encompasses all the others (1 Cor 13:4-7). Only the Spirit of God can produce in us love for those who hate us (Matt 5:43-48; Luke 6:35-36). • ***Joy*** produced by the Spirit does not depend on circumstances (Rom 15:13; 2 Cor 6:10; 8:2; 1 Thes 1:6). • ***Peace*** with God creates internal well-being (Rom 5:1; Eph 2:15; Phil 4:6-7; Col 1:20) that spills into our relationships with others so that we become peacemakers (Matt 5:9; Rom 8:6; 12:18; 14:17-19; 2 Cor 13:11; Eph 4:3; 6:15). • ***Patience*** (or *tolerance,* or *long-suffering*) gives us forbearance toward other people and endurance under unfavorable circumstances (Eph 4:2; 2 Tim 4:2; Jas 5:10-11). God is patient with us (Exod 34:6; Ps 103:8; Rom 2:4; 9:22; 1 Tim 1:16; 2 Pet 3:15) and promises his presence with those who are patient with others (Isa 57:15). • ***Kindness*** connotes generosity, a giving spirit that reflects how God treats us (Rom 2:4; 11:22; Titus 3:4-6). • ***goodness:*** Cp. Rom 15:14; Eph 5:9; 2 Thes 1:11. • ***Faithfulness*** (or *faith*) means exercising good faith and fidelity in our relationships, just as God does with us (1 Cor 1:9; 10:13; 2 Thes 3:3).

5:23 ***Gentleness*** is antithetical to the vices of 5:20 and requires strength (see Prov 15:1, 4; Matt 11:28-29; Eph 4:2). • ***self-control:*** The Holy Spirit does not give moral license but empowers people to avoid sin (cp. 5:13; Rom 6:14-18; 1 Thes 4:3-7; 1 Pet 2:16; see also Acts 24:25; Titus 1:8). • ***There is no law against these things!*** Paul is stating the obvious, but also making the point that those who are virtuous by the Spirit do not need law to govern them.

5:24 Those who have faith in Christ are ***crucified*** with him (cp. 2:19-20; Rom 6) and become new people (Rom 6:1-2;

[c]sinful nature to his cross and crucified them there. 25Since we are living by the Spirit, let us follow the Spirit's leading in every part of our lives. 26Let us not become conceited, or provoke one another, or be jealous of one another.

Practical Exhortations (6:1-10)

Dealing with Offenders

6 Dear brothers and sisters, if another believer is overcome by some sin, you who are godly should gently and humbly help that person back onto the right path. And be careful not to fall into the same [d]temptation yourself. 2Share each other's burdens, and in this way obey the [e]law of [f]Christ. 3If you think you are too important to help someone, you are only fooling yourself. You are not that important.

Work, Responsibility, and Rewards

4Pay careful attention to your own work, for then you will get the satisfaction of a job well done, and you won't need to compare yourself to anyone else. 5For we are each responsible for our own conduct.

6Those who are taught the word of God should provide for their teachers, sharing all good things with them.

Doing Good: Planting and Harvesting

7Don't be misled—you cannot mock the justice of God. You will always harvest what you plant. 8Those who live only to satisfy their own sinful nature will harvest decay and death from that sinful nature. But those who live to please the Spirit will harvest everlasting life from the Spirit. 9So let's not get tired of doing what is good. At just the right time we will reap a harvest of blessing if we don't give up. 10Therefore, whenever we have the opportunity, we should do good to everyone—especially to those in the family of faith.

5. POSTSCRIPT (6:11-18)

Final Appeal to the Cross of Christ

11NOTICE WHAT LARGE LETTERS I USE AS I WRITE THESE CLOSING WORDS IN MY OWN HANDWRITING.

12Those who are trying to force you to be circumcised want to look good to others. They don't want to be persecuted for teaching that the cross of [g]Christ alone can save. 13And even those who advocate circumcision don't keep the whole law themselves. They only want you to be circumcised so they can boast about it and claim you as their disciples.

14As for me, may I never boast about anything except the cross of our Lord Jesus

5:24 [c]*sarx* (4561) ‣ Eph 5:29
5:25 Rom 8:4
5:26 Phil 2:3
6:1 1 Cor 2:15; Jas 5:19-20; 1 Jn 5:16; [d]*peirazō* (3985) ‣ 1 Thes 3:5
6:2 Rom 15:1; [e]*nomos* (3551) ‣ Jas 1:25; [f]*christos* (5547) ‣ Gal 6:12
6:3 Rom 12:3; 1 Cor 3:18
6:4 2 Cor 13:5
6:5 Rom 14:12
6:6 1 Cor 9:11, 14
6:7 1 Cor 6:9; 2 Cor 9:6
6:8 Job 4:8; Rom 8:13
6:9 2 Thes 3:13
6:10 Eph 2:19
6:12 [g]*christos* (5547) ‣ Eph 3:4
6:13 Rom 2:25

2 Cor 5:17; Col 3:5-15): They have died to their ***sinful nature*** and to the law (2:19; Rom 7:4-6; 2 Cor 5:14; Col 3:1-4). • ***passions and desires:*** As in 5:19-21.

5:25 Christians do not live by the law but follow ***the Spirit's leading.***

5:26 The Galatian church was apparently having trouble with factions (see also note on 5:20; cp. 1 Cor 3) instead of following the Spirit's leading.

6:1-10 Living by the Spirit (5:13–6:10) results in doing good (6:1-5) and reaping rewards from one's work (6:6-10).

6:1-5 Paul outlines how to treat other Christians with love when they sin.

6:1 ***Dear brothers and sisters, if another believer:*** Literally *Brothers, if a man.* • Perhaps some of the Galatians were proud of their obedience to the law or their spiritual freedom and willpower. But those who are truly ***godly*** (literally *spiritual*) are not proud of their accomplishments but ***humbly help*** others. • ***be careful:*** We are all susceptible to ***the same temptation*** to sin (Rom 3:9-20).

6:2 Carrying ***each other's burdens*** (6:1) fulfills ***the law of Christ*** to love one another (5:13-14; see also Lev 19:18; Matt 22:36-40; John 13:34; 15:12; 1 Jn 3:23).

6:3 Those with a proud attitude wrongly assume they are ***too important*** to help the weak (see note on 6:1).

6:4 Instead of regarding ourselves as better than others, we should examine our ***own work*** and ensure that we obey Christ in everything (cp. 1 Cor 3:12-15).

6:5 If believers carry their own load (6:4), they will have no occasion to treat a brother or sister with contempt (6:3).

6:6-10 In financially supporting those who teach them God's message (6:6), believers harvest a spiritual crop.

6:6 Supporting Christian teachers applies 5:13 and 6:2 (cp. 1 Tim 5:17-18).

6:7 ***you cannot mock the justice of God:*** God cannot be fooled by spiritual pretenses. All people will ***harvest*** the consequences of their actions (***what you plant;*** see also Job 4:8; Ps 126:5; Prov 22:8; Hos 8:7; 10:12-15; Luke 19:21-23; 1 Cor 3:12-15; 9:11; 2 Cor 9:6).

6:8 Living ***to please the Spirit*** is only possible in the Spirit's power (3:3; 5:16). Those who trust in human effort and those who think they can do as they wish are in the same position: They live ***to satisfy their own sinful nature.*** Such people ***harvest decay and death.*** Those who live by the Spirit's power and trust in God ***will harvest everlasting life.***

6:9 ***Let's not get tired:*** Either by letting sinful behavior creep in or by grasping for a legal code of conduct rather than being in step with the Spirit (5:25). • ***At just the right time we will reap:*** This assurance is a source of strength for Christians to continue doing good work (cp. Rom 8:28). • ***if we don't give up:*** God's promises to believers require their steadfast perseverance in faith (see also Luke 18:1; 2 Cor 4:1).

6:10 ***Therefore:*** This statement forms an *inclusio* (bookends) for the section (5:13–6:10) by stating the same theme as 5:13: Freedom in the Spirit compels us to ***do good*** to others in love. • Doing good ***to those in the family of faith*** demonstrates God's faithfulness to his children: He provides for all their needs.

6:11-18 Paul took up the pen from his *amanuensis* (secretary) and added a postscript in his ***OWN HANDWRITING*** to show that the letter was authentically his and to make a final appeal.

6:12-13 For all of their theological reasoning, the false teachers' motivation was self-serving: They felt pressure from non-Christian Jews and were more concerned with their own reputation than with honoring God.

6:14 In contrast with the false teachers (6:12-13), Paul's motivation was to increase, not his own reputation, but God's glory. Boasting about law-keeping

6:14 Rom 6:2, 6; 1 Cor 2:2; Gal 2:20
6:15 1 Cor 7:19; 2 Cor 5:17; Gal 5:6
6:17 2 Cor 1:5; 4:10
6:18 Rom 16:20; 2 Tim 4:22

Christ. Because of that cross, my interest
in this world has been crucified, and the
world's interest in me has also died. 15It
doesn't matter whether we have been circumcised or not. What counts is whether
we have been transformed into a new creation. 16May God's peace and mercy be upon
all who live by this principle; they are the
new people of God.

Paul's Apostolic Authority

17From now on, don't let anyone trouble me
with these things. For I bear on my body the
scars that show I belong to Jesus.

Benediction

18Dear brothers and sisters, may the grace
of our Lord Jesus Christ be with your spirit.
Amen.

The Law and the Spirit (Gal 5:16-26)

Gal 3:2-5; 5:5; Num 11:16-17; 11:24-30; Jer 31:33-34; Luke 24:49; Acts 5:32; Rom 7:1–8:17; 2 Cor 3:7-18; Heb 12:14-29

An enduring question of the Christian faith is, Do Christians need to keep the OT law in order to become mature followers of Christ? Does following God's law provide sanctification?

When the Christians in Galatia had received the Good News of salvation through faith in Christ, they had also received the Holy Spirit as the guarantee of their status as believers. Not only had God given his Spirit to them, but he had also worked miracles among them (3:5). They knew from experience that the Holy Spirit has the power to make them new people, and Paul had taught them to rely on the Spirit to guide them.

Shortly after Paul left Galatia, Jewish-Christian teachers arrived who taught the need to observe God's law, both to be accepted by God and to be sanctified and become mature. They argued that Paul's approach to sanctification by the Spirit would lead to lawlessness and sin.

Paul responded (5:5, 16-26) that, just as God *accounts* us as righteous by faith, so also he *makes* us righteous by faith, through the working of the Spirit. Those who rely on the Spirit and follow his leading will not sin—God's Spirit will never lead people to sin.

The real problem is not a lack of understanding regarding right and wrong. Our God-given conscience tells us when we're doing wrong, and God's law makes the requirements of his righteousness even clearer (Rom 7:7-12). The real problem is that, by nature, our hearts are hard and sinful, and we lack the wisdom to know the right thing to do in a given situation. By nature, we are unable to apply God's word in a way that is consistent with faith in his love.

The law cannot ameliorate our condition (see "The Limitations of Law" at Rom 7:1-25, p. 1905). But when the Holy Spirit guides and controls us, he changes our hearts and guides us to do the things that please God (5:22-23; Rom 8:5-14). God's Spirit guides his people to fulfill his law in its true sense and intent. But fulfillment of the law is not the goal or focus—the law is just our guardian (3:24-25). The focus is on trusting God, relying on the Spirit, and loving others. God's Spirit gives us the will and the power to do these things and please God (see also "The Holy Spirit's Work" at 1 Cor 12:1-11, p. 1945).

would detract from recognition of *the cross of our Lord Jesus Christ.* • In the Greco-Roman world, *the cross* was a senseless scandal to those who did not believe (5:11; 1 Cor 1:23; cp. John 6:53-61), but it is the basis for a Christian's faith and hope (1 Cor 1:17-18; 15:3; Phil 2:8-11; Col 1:20-22; 2:14-15). • *Because of that cross:* Or *Because of him.*

6:15 The Galatians had missed the point of the Good News, that ***a new creation*** has come in Christ by the Spirit, not by human effort (cp. 2 Cor 5:16-17).

6:16 ***This principle*** is putting trust in Christ for salvation (6:14-15) • ***they are the new people of God*** (literally *and* [or *even*] *upon the Israel of God*): The Greek conjunction *kai* is most often translated "and," but it often means "even." If it means *and,* then the *Israel of God* is a separate group from *all who live by this principle;* if it means *even,* then they are the same group. The Jewish people still have an identity before God (Rom 9:1-5; 10:1-4; 11:1-32). Gentiles who believe have been grafted in, and Jews who disbelieve have been pruned out of the spiritual Israel (Rom 11:17-24; cp. Phil 3:2-3; Col 2:11-12). Paul thus considers all Christians to be the true Israel (see Rom 2:28-29; 9:6-8; cp. Gal 4:21-31). The phrase *the Israel of God* does not appear elsewhere in the NT or in other literature; perhaps the false teachers promised this identification to Gentiles who would accept circumcision. If so, then Paul turned their argument on its head: The Gentiles in Galatia didn't need circumcision, for they were already God's *Israel*—his true people—through faith in Christ.

6:17 ***don't let anyone trouble me with these things:*** No one has a right to criticize Paul or his message because of his proven status as Christ's servant. • Paul's ***scars*** (Greek *stigmata*) probably resulted from the severe persecution he had endured as a servant of Christ (see Acts 14:19; 2 Cor 6:4-10; 11:21-33). In contrast with the physical mark of circumcision that the false teachers in Galatia wanted to impose on Gentile Christians, Paul's scars of suffering were proof that he was Christ's servant (cp. Exod 21:6).

6:18 ***Dear brothers and sisters:*** Literally *Brothers.* • Paul prayed at the end as at the beginning (1:3-4). More than law, the Galatians needed ***the grace of our Lord Jesus Christ*** to be with their ***spirit.***

PAUL'S LETTER TO THE EPHESIANS

This beautiful letter, the favorite of many, is one of the gems of the NT. Paul is taken up with the overwhelming goodness that God in Christ has showered on believers, and with his amazing plan to unite Gentiles with Jews in a new community—the church, the body of Christ. Here we have one of the finest descriptions of the Christian life in the entire NT. Though written from prison, this letter is full of joy, praise, and thanksgiving. It is a fitting reply to the wonder of God's amazing grace in Christ, poured out in abundance on those chosen to know his love—Gentiles as well as Jews.

SETTING

Paul's third missionary journey (AD 53–57) centered on Ephesus, capital and port city of the Roman province of Asia on the western coast of what we now call Turkey. In Paul's time, Ephesus was the fourth-largest city in the Roman empire, with a population of perhaps 500,000. Many people visited the city to see the famous temple of Artemis.

After an initial brief visit (see Acts 18:19-21), Paul returned to spend between two and three years in this large and flourishing city (see Acts 19:1–20:1). It was a difficult time for him: He encountered much opposition and suffered much abuse (see Acts 19:21-41; 1 Cor 15:32; 2 Cor 1:8-9; 11:23-27). But during this time, people all over the province heard the Good News of Christ for the first time, and many small groups of believers sprang up, meeting together in homes, in villages and towns across the province (the seven churches addressed by Revelation probably originated during this time). Some of these churches (at Colosse, for example) were begun by Paul's converts, and had no firsthand acquaintance with Paul.

It is not clear how accurate their understanding of the gospel was, but we know from Paul's letter to the Colossians that some of them had encountered wrong teaching and distorted perceptions. In Ephesians, Paul is concerned with a perception that Gentile

The Setting of Ephesians. Paul was in prison when he wrote his letter to the Ephesians. It is unclear where he was—either in ROME, as traditionally thought, or perhaps in EPHESUS. It is also unclear exactly who were the recipients of the letter. It might have been intended for the Christians in Ephesus, or as an encyclical for all the churches in the province of Asia, including Ephesus.

Christians were inferior to or distinct from Jewish Christians, and not fully part of God's "new Israel." What gave rise to this misunderstanding is not clear—discrimination by Jewish Christians? Gentile aversion to Jewish Christians?—but it reflects traditional ethnic tensions between Jews and Gentiles throughout the Roman world. Paul was also concerned with a lack of awareness that God's people are to live in a distinctly different way from that of the surrounding world.

As spiritual father of these early converts, and as one commissioned by God to carry the Good News to the Gentiles, Paul was deeply concerned that the Ephesians have a correct understanding of all that God had given them in Christ and of the kind of life God wanted them to live in response. He writes a letter from prison that seems to be intended for several of these churches full of new converts.

With a heart full of praise for all that God has done, Paul beautifully summarizes the Good News of God's saving grace in Jesus Christ—emphasizing that it is for Gentiles as well as for Jews. He also gives practical instructions on how believers are to live in response, turning away from their former lives to become truly good and like Christ. There are no major, urgent problems addressed in this letter; it is a general summary of Paul's theological and moral teachings.

OUTLINE

1:1-2
Greetings from Paul

1:3–3:21
God's Amazing Grace

4:1–6:20
Living Like Christ

6:21-24
Final Greetings

TIMELINE

AD 53–57
Paul's third missionary journey

AD 53~56
Paul's ministry in Ephesus

AD 57
Paul travels to Jerusalem and is arrested

AD 57–59
Paul is imprisoned in Caesarea

AD 59
Festus becomes governor of Judea

AD 59–60
Paul's voyage to Rome

AD 60–62
Paul is imprisoned in Rome

SUMMARY

This letter summarizes the Good News of God's grace in Jesus Christ, emphasizing that it is for Gentiles as well as Jews (chs 1–3). It then gives specific instructions on how believers should live in response (chs 4–6).

Following a brief introduction (1:1-2), Paul praises God for the amazing grace that believers have received in Christ (1:3-14). In his sovereign love, God has chosen them, forgiven them, brought them into his family, made them his children, and promised them eternal blessings. In giving them his Spirit, he has marked them as his own so that they might praise his grace forever. Paul then prays that God will give them spiritual understanding to grasp the full depth of all that he has done for them (1:15-23). Though fully deserving of God's wrath, they have been saved by God's grace, not by anything they have done, but simply by being joined to Christ (2:1-10). As Gentiles, they were utterly alienated from God and his blessings, but in God's mercy, through the reconciling work of Christ, they have now been made members of God's family, fully equal to Jewish Christians. They are no longer outsiders (2:11-22).

Paul is the one commissioned by God to bring this wonderful Good News to them (3:1-13). His second prayer for them (3:14-21) is that God will give them spiritual power, strengthen them in their faith and love, enable them to understand Christ's saving love fully, and fill them with the life and power of God himself.

In response, they are to live a life of humility, grace, and love—a life worthy of their calling, as they use their God-given gifts to build up the body of Christ (4:1-16). They are to turn from the darkness of their former sinful ways and live an absolutely good life as children of light. Filled with kindness and love in the Holy Spirit, and following the example of Christ, their lives are to please God in all things (4:17–5:20).

All their relationships at home—between husbands and wives, parents and children, masters and slaves—are to be characterized by respect and love, as they live for Christ (5:21–6:9). Finally, they are warned to take on God's armor to protect themselves from the devil (6:10-20). Paul closes with some personal words and a benediction (6:21-24).

AUTHOR

Ephesians is traditionally ascribed to Paul, as are the other prison letters (Philippians, Colossians, and Philemon). However, on the basis of vocabulary, style, form, setting, purpose, and theological emphases, some have thought that Ephesians was written instead by a later disciple of Paul. Others see it as an original letter from Paul that has been reworked by a later editor. However, the letter is not at all incompatible with Paul's thought and style (note the similarities between Ephesians and Colossians), and there is no compelling reason to deny that Paul authored it.

The supposed differences with the undisputed letters of Paul can be explained by taking account of (1) variations in Paul's own vocabulary and style; (2) the different content of this letter (for example, chs 1–3 include extensive sections of blessing, praise, and prayer); (3) developments in Paul's own thinking; (4) Paul's use of secretaries (see Rom 16:22), who may have exercised some degree of freedom in putting his thoughts into their own words; and (5) the nature of Ephesians as a general letter sent to several churches, not just one.

Ephesians is breathtaking in its theological grasp of the scope of God's purposes in Christ for the church. It is a pastorally warm letter and spiritually sensitive in its advice, peaceable in tone and readily overflowing into joyful worship.

MAX TURNER
"Ephesians," *New Bible Commentary*, p. 1222

RECIPIENTS

Though traditionally understood to have been written to the church at Ephesus, this letter may have been written as a general letter to be circulated to a number of different churches in the Roman province of Asia. This opinion is based on (1) the omission of the introductory words *in Ephesus* (1:1) in many of the earliest manuscripts, and (2) the lack of personal greetings or references in Ephesians—a surprising omission if the letter was intended for the church in Ephesus, given Paul's extended stay in the city and personal acquaintance with the church there (see Acts 19:10; 20:31).

DATE AND PLACE OF WRITING

Ephesians is one of the prison letters (along with Philippians, Colossians, and Philemon), traditionally understood to have been written from Rome in AD 60–62 or shortly before Paul was executed around AD 64~65. This would place them among the last of Paul's writings. However, they might better be understood as having been written from prison in Ephesus. (In 2 Corinthians, written shortly after Paul left Ephesus, he refers to the strong opposition he encountered in the area, and mentions having been in prison many times; see 2 Cor 11:23-27.) If the prison letters were written from Ephesus, it would place them earlier in Paul's life, around AD 53~56.

MEANING AND MESSAGE

Praise for God's Grace. Perhaps more than any other book in the NT, Ephesians is filled with gratitude for the saving grace God has shown to those who believe in Jesus Christ. Solely by God's grace, believers have been chosen, forgiven, called into his family, made his children, promised his eternal blessings, and given the gift of his Holy Spirit to mark them as belonging to him forever (1:3-14). Salvation can never be viewed as something that is earned; it is a sheer gift (2:8-9). As a result, believers know they are called to praise God forever for his amazing grace (1:6, 12, 14). They can do nothing less, for they owe him everything.

The Condemned Nature of Human Beings. The awareness of grace that pervades the first three chapters of Ephesians is heightened by Paul's contrasting emphasis on sin and God's judgment upon it. What is true of his readers is true of everyone, since by nature all stand under God's judgment (see 2:1-3, 12, one of the strongest passages in the NT on how lost human beings are apart from Christ). Every human being stands guilty and condemned before the eternal judgment of God, who cannot tolerate sin. This concept seems troublingly harsh to modern ways of thinking; behind it stands a much stronger view of human sin and of the utter holiness of God than most Westerners today are used to. Since, apart from Christ, human beings are by nature driven by sin and subject to the devil, evangelism is an urgent issue in the NT (see Mark 16:15-16; cp. Rom 9:1-3; 10:1).

The Unity of the Church. With its emphasis on God's amazing plan to include Gentiles in his family (see 2:11–3:6), Ephesians reminds us that ethnic distinctions mean nothing to God and they should mean nothing to God's people (cp. Gal 3:28). Because God has joined people from all ethnic backgrounds together in his church (see 2:14-17; 3:6), believers should respond by warmly welcoming one another in humility, grace, and love, without consideration of ethnic differences (see 4:1-6; Rom 15:5-7). In the church, one's identity is defined only by one's faith in Christ.

Living Like Christ. In chs 4–6 (and Col 3–4), Paul gives us a beautiful picture of the Christian life as it ought to be lived. Believers are to turn away from the darkness of their former lives and, filled with the Holy Spirit, to live as new people of light, seeking only what is "good and right and true." They are to express gentleness, integrity, respect, kindness, and love to others. In relation to God, their lives are to be filled with purity, praise, and thanksgiving (see 4:17–5:20). Believers are to become like Christ and to reflect him in all they do and say (see 4:13, 15; Rom 8:29). In Christ, they have been created to be like God (see 4:24; 5:1-2).

Respect and Love at Home. In 5:21–6:9 (and Col 3:18–4:1), Paul emphasizes the importance of showing respect and love to those with whom one lives. On one hand, wives are to respect their husbands, children are to honor their parents, and slaves are to obey their masters. On the other hand, husbands are to love their wives, parents are to discipline their children gently, and masters are to be gracious to their slaves. The traditional cultural relationships are maintained and honored, while believers' attitudes are to be those of Christ.

Ephesians is, within the New Testament, the magna carta of the one, holy, apostolic, and catholic church.

MARKUS BARTH
"Ephesians," *Oxford Companion to the Bible*, p. 188

FURTHER READING

F. F. BRUCE
The Epistles to the Colossians, to Philemon, and to the Ephesians (1984)

HAROLD HOEHNER
Ephesians in Cornerstone Biblical Commentary, vol. 16 (2008)

ANDREW T. LINCOLN
Ephesians (1990)

PETER T. O'BRIEN
The Letter to the Ephesians (1999)

KLYNE SNODGRASS
Ephesians (1996)

Spiritual War. Eph 6:10-20 gives the fullest NT account of how believers are to protect themselves in their war against the devil. In this spiritual battle, believers cannot rely on their own resources, but must use the weapons the Lord supplies. Significantly, all of the weapons described—except the short-bladed sword—are defensive weapons. There is no picture here of Christians attacking the devil. Though the devil's opposition is to be taken seriously, Paul's view of the Christian life does not center on spiritual warfare in an aggressive or offensive sense.

1. GREETINGS FROM PAUL (1:1-2)

1 This letter is from Paul, chosen by the will of God to be an apostle of Christ Jesus.

I am writing to God's holy people in Ephesus, who are faithful followers of Christ Jesus.

2May God our Father and the Lord Jesus Christ give you grace and peace.

2. GOD'S AMAZING GRACE (1:3–3:21)

Spiritual Blessings in Christ

3All praise to God, the [a]Father of our Lord Jesus Christ, who has blessed us with every spiritual [b]blessing in the heavenly realms because we are united with Christ. 4Even before he made the world, God loved us and chose us in Christ to be holy and without fault in his eyes. 5God [c]decided in advance to [d]adopt us into his own family by bringing us to himself through Jesus Christ. This is what he wanted to do, and it gave him great pleasure. 6So we praise God for the glorious [e]grace he has poured out on us who belong to his dear Son. 7He is so [f]rich in kindness and grace that he [g]purchased our freedom with the blood of his Son and forgave our sins. 8He has showered his kindness on us, along with all wisdom and understanding.

9God has now revealed to us his mysterious plan regarding Christ, a plan to fulfill his own good pleasure. 10And this is the [h]plan: At the right time he will bring everything together under the authority of Christ—everything in heaven and on earth. 11Furthermore, because we are united with Christ, we have received an inheritance from God, for he [i]chose us in advance, and

1:3
[a]*patēr* (3962) ▸1 Thes 2:11
[b]*eulogia* (2129) ▸Heb 6:7

1:4
1 Pet 1:2, 20

1:5
[c]*proorizō* (4309) ▸Eph 1:11
[d]*huiothesia* (5206) ▸Rom 8:15

1:6
[e]*charis* (5485) ▸Eph 2:5

1:7
[f]*ploutos* (4149) ▸Eph 3:8
[g]*apolutrōsis* (0629) ▸Eph 1:14

1:10
[h]*oikonomia* (3622) ▸Eph 3:2

1:11
[i]*proorizō* (4309) ▸Acts 4:28

1:1-2 Paul follows the normal pattern of ancient Greek letters: He begins with a few words about himself followed by greetings. He expands this pattern in a Christian way by referring to his divine calling as an ***apostle***, by describing his recipients as ***God's holy people*** and as ***faithful followers*** of Christ, and by his invocation of ***grace and peace***.

1:1 The frequent emphasis on ***the will of God*** (see 1:5, 9, 11; 5:17; 6:6) underscores God's sovereignty in fulfilling his plan. • ***God's holy people:*** Literally *the holy ones*, who are dedicated to God (see also 1:15, 18; 2:19; 3:8, 18; 4:12; 5:3; 6:18). • The most ancient manuscripts do not include ***in Ephesus***, and there are no personal greetings in this letter. Many scholars believe that the letter was originally sent to be circulated to a number of churches in the area rather than to the church in Ephesus alone.

1:2 Paul usually invokes God's ***grace and peace*** on those to whom he is writing. ***Grace*** is undeserved blessing that comes from God's kindness; ***peace*** is a sense of well-being and contentedness rooted in the Good News and brought about by the Holy Spirit (see Gal 5:22). Both are gifts from ***God our Father and the Lord Jesus Christ*** (see Rom 5:1-2).

1:3–3:21 Ephesians is divided into two sections: Chapters 1–3 praise God for his amazing grace, and chs 4–6 instruct believers on how to live in grateful response.

1:3-14 Paul praises God for all the spiritual blessings he has graciously provided through Jesus Christ, for Gentiles as well as for Jews. • This section is a single, complex sentence in Greek—one of the longest in Paul's letters, with long sentences being typical of Paul's writing (also in 1:15-23; 2:1-7, 14-16; 3:1-7, 8-12, 14-19; Col 1:3-8, 9-20, 21-23, 24-29; 2:1-3, 8-15). The interwoven nature of these sentences reflects the interconnectedness of their ideas.

1:3 Paul describes ***every spiritual blessing in the heavenly realms*** in 1:4-8, 13-14. Paul's focus is not on physical blessings, but on what God has done through ***Christ*** to bring people into a saving relationship with himself.

1:4 God's people are ***holy and without fault in his eyes*** because they trust in Christ's atoning sacrifice for their sins (see 1:7; 5:25-27; Col 1:22; Titus 3:5-7; Jude 1:24).

1:5 ***God decided in advance to adopt us into his own family:*** By his sovereign initiative, God embraces and blesses as his children those who trust in Christ. They become heirs to all the promises God has made to his people (see 1:11, 14; 2:19; Rom 8:15-17, 29-30; Gal 4:5).

1:6 Believers ***praise God***, who has richly blessed them with his forgiving ***grace.*** • ***on us who belong to his dear Son:*** Literally *on us in the beloved. The beloved* is a Messianic title for Jesus; see Matt 3:17; 17:5; Col 1:13.

1:7 ***he purchased our freedom with the blood of his Son:*** Believers, who were once prisoners of sin, are free from God's judgment and from bondage to sin because of Christ's sacrificial death (see 1:14; 4:30; Rom 3:24; 1 Cor 6:20; Col 1:14; cp. Matt 26:28; Mark 10:45; Heb 9:11-12, 26; 1 Pet 1:18-19).

1:8-10 ***Wisdom and understanding*** come from the revelation of God's ***mysterious plan regarding Christ.*** In Paul's writings, *mysterious plan* (traditionally *mystery*) often refers to a divine truth formerly hidden but now revealed in the Good News (see 3:9). Here it refers to how God ***will bring everything together under the authority of Christ***, so that he may be universally recognized and respected as Lord (see Phil 2:9-11; Col 1:16-20, 26-27; 2:2, 19; 4:3). Ephesians focuses specifically on the inclusion of Gentiles as well as Jews in God's redeemed people (see 3:3-6; 6:19; cp. Rom 16:25-26).

1:11 ***we have received an inheritance from God*** (or *we have become God's inheritance*): Paul often talks about salvation as an *inheritance*, something

he makes everything work out according to
his plan.
12 God's purpose was that we Jews who
were the first to trust in Christ would
bring praise and glory to God. 13 And now
you Gentiles have also heard the truth, the
[j]Good News that God [k]saves you. And when
you believed in Christ, he [a]identified you
as his own by giving you the Holy Spirit,
whom he promised long ago. 14 The Spirit
is God's [b]guarantee that he will give us the
inheritance he promised and that he has
[c]purchased us to be his own people. He did
this so we would praise and glorify him.

Paul's Prayer for Spiritual Wisdom

15 Ever since I first heard of your strong faith
in the Lord Jesus and your love for God's
people everywhere, 16 I have not stopped
thanking God for you. I pray for you constantly, 17 asking God, the glorious Father of
our Lord Jesus Christ, to give you spiritual
wisdom and [d]insight so that you might grow
in your knowledge of God. 18 I pray that your
hearts will be flooded with light so that you
can understand the confident [e]hope he has
given to those he [f]called—his holy people
who are his rich and glorious inheritance.
19 I also pray that you will understand the
incredible greatness of God's power for us
who believe him. This is the same mighty
power 20 that raised Christ from the dead
and seated him in the place of honor at
God's right hand in the heavenly realms.
21 Now he is far above any ruler or authority
or power or leader or anything else—not
only in this world but also in the world to
come. 22 God has put all things under the
authority of Christ and has made him head
over all things for the benefit of the church.
23 And the church is his body; it is made full
and complete by Christ, who fills all things
everywhere with himself.

Made Alive with Christ

2 Once you were dead because of your disobedience and your many [g]sins. 2 You
used to live in sin, just like the rest of the
world, obeying the devil—the commander
of the powers in the unseen world. He is
the spirit at work in the hearts of those who
refuse to obey God. 3 All of us used to live

1:13
[j]*euangelion* (2098)
‣ Mark 1:1
[k]*sōtēria* (4991)
‣ Eph 2:8
[a]*sphragizō* (4972)
‣ Eph 4:30

1:14
[b]*arrabōn* (0728)
‣ 2 Cor 1:22
[c]*apolutrōsis* (0629)
‣ Eph 4:30

1:17
[d]*apokalupsis* (0602)
‣ Eph 3:3

1:18
[e]*elpis* (1680)
‣ Eph 2:12
[f]*klēsis* (2821)
‣ Eph 4:1

1:20
Acts 2:24

1:21
Phil 2:9
Col 1:16; 2:10

1:22
Col 1:18; 2:19

1:23
Col 1:19; 3:11

2:1
[g]*hamartia* (0266)
‣ 1 Tim 5:22

2:2
Col 3:7

promised to our spiritual ancestors and received by us (see Rom 8:17; Gal 3:29; 4:7; Col 1:12; 3:24). • Because God is sovereign, ***he makes everything work out according to his plan*** (cp. Rom 8:28-30).

1:12-13 ***we Jews . . . you Gentiles:*** Literally *we . . . you;* the reference to *Jews* and *Gentiles* is implied.

1:13 ***he identified you as his own*** (or *he put his seal on you*): Just as a *seal* signifies authentic ownership, the ***Holy Spirit*** in a believer's life signifies God's ownership (4:30; 2 Cor 1:22).

1:14 ***The Spirit is*** both ***God's guarantee*** of future blessings and a foretaste of eternal life and power. The believer's eternal ***inheritance*** includes everything ***he promised*** (see also 1:18; Rom 8:17; 2 Cor 1:22; 5:5; Gal 3:29; 4:7; Col 1:12; 3:24; Titus 3:7).

1:15-23 Paul prays that his readers may have the spiritual understanding to grasp the full significance of God's gifts (1:3-14).

1:15 ***your strong faith in the Lord Jesus and your love for God's people everywhere*** (some manuscripts read *your faithfulness to the Lord Jesus and to God's people everywhere*): Paul links faith in Christ with love for God's people. Personal faith in Christ brings salvation, and salvation is expressed, above all, by a life of love (see Gal 5:6; Col 1:4; 1 Thes 1:3; 3:6; 5:8; 2 Thes 1:3; 1 Tim 1:14; 2:15; Titus 2:2).

1:17 ***to give you spiritual wisdom*** (or *to give you the Spirit of wisdom*): The word *spirit* can refer either to the Holy Spirit or to the human spirit. • ***Knowledge of God*** is to know God personally and experientially, not just to know about him intellectually (see John 17:3).

1:18 ***Confident hope*** for believers is the anticipation of Christ's return and his future blessings that they will share. • ***called—his holy people who are his rich and glorious inheritance*** (or *called, and the rich and glorious inheritance he has given to his holy people*): Joined with Christ, believers become joint heirs with him of all God's promised blessings.

1:19-20 ***God's power for us who believe him*** is the power of his Spirit at work in and through his people, because they are joined to the resurrected Christ (see Rom 6:4-14; Col 2:12). Paul longed to experience the power of Christ's resurrection in his own life (Phil 3:10). • In biblical times, ***the place of honor*** was always at a person's ***right hand*** (Ps 110:1; Acts 7:56).

1:21 ***he is far above:*** Jesus' power and authority transcend all rival powers, whether human or spiritual, in this age and the coming age (see 3:10; 6:12; John 12:31; Rom 8:38-39; 1 Cor 15:24; Col 1:13; 2:10, 15; 1 Pet 3:22; Rev 12:7-9).

1:22 ***under the authority of Christ*** (literally *under his feet*): In pictures from the ancient Middle East, victorious kings have their feet on the necks of their defeated enemies. Paul is graphically picturing the way Christ has defeated all his enemies and reigns as king of all things (see Ps 110:1; 1 Cor 15:25-28).

1:23 ***it is made full and complete by Christ, who fills all things everywhere with himself*** (or *it is the full expression of the one who fills everything everywhere*): This difficult phrase probably means that the church, as ***his body,*** is the full expression of Christ in this world. His presence, which fills the entire universe (4:10), is reflected in and works through his body.

2:1-10 Paul reflects on the terrible situation of the believers before they believed in Christ and the grace of God that has spared them.

2:1-3 Paul's readers were once like ***dead*** people before God (see 2:5; Col 2:13). Because of their ***disobedience*** and ***sins,*** driven by the power of the ***devil,*** they were condemned along with ***the rest of the world*** to suffer God's judgment.

2:2 ***obeying the devil—the commander of the powers in the unseen world*** (literally *obeying the commander of the power of the air*): Human ***sin*** results from our being governed by ***the devil,*** the ***spirit*** who rules both the ***powers*** of evil in the spiritual realm (see 1:21; 6:11-12; cp. Col 1:13) and human beings ***who refuse to obey God*** (2 Cor 4:4; contrast Rom 8:2-14; Gal 5:22-23).

that way, following the passionate desires and inclinations of our sinful nature. By our very nature we were subject to God's [h]anger, just like everyone else.

4But God is so rich in [i]mercy, and he loved us so much, 5that even though we were dead because of our sins, he gave us life when he raised Christ from the dead. (It is only by God's [j]grace that you have been saved!) 6For he raised us from the dead along with Christ and seated us with him in the heavenly realms because we are united with Christ Jesus. 7So God can point to us in all future ages as examples of the incredible wealth of his grace and kindness toward us, as shown in all he has done for us who are united with Christ Jesus.

8God [k]saved you by his [a]grace when you [b]believed. And you can't take credit for this; it is a gift from God. 9Salvation is not a reward for the good things we have done, so none of us can boast about it. 10For we are God's masterpiece. He has created us anew in Christ Jesus, so we can do the good things he planned for us long ago.

Oneness and Peace in Christ

11Don't forget that you Gentiles used to be outsiders. You were called "uncircumcised heathens" by the Jews, who were proud of their circumcision, even though it affected only their bodies and not their hearts. 12In those days you were living apart from Christ. You were excluded from citizenship among the people of Israel, and you did not know the [c]covenant promises God had made to them. You lived in this world

2:3
[h]*orgē* (3709)
‣ Eph 4:31

2:4
John 3:16
[i]*eleos* (1656)
‣ Titus 3:5

2:5
Col 2:13
[j]*charis* (5485)
‣ Eph 2:8

2:6
Col 2:12

2:8
John 4:10
[k]*sōzō* (4982)
‣ 1 Thes 5:9
[a]*charis* (5485)
‣ 2 Thes 1:12
[b]*pistis* (4102)
‣ Phil 1:27

2:9
Rom 3:28
Titus 3:5

2:11
Col 2:11

God's Grace (2:8-9)

Eph 1:2-14; 2:12; 6:22-23
Rom 9:16; 11:6; 14:7-9
1 Cor 10:31
2 Cor 5:14-15

Christians live and die dependent on God's grace. Salvation is God's gift and can never be earned (2:8-9; Rom 9:16; 11:6). The most important things in life—forgiveness, a right relationship with God, acceptance into God's family as his child, eternal life, spiritual understanding, the transforming power of his Holy Spirit, the promise of God's blessing now and forever—are all gifts of God for those he has chosen and made his own by his grace (1:3-14). There is nothing we can do to get these things for ourselves.

In return, believers should live in recognition that they belong to God (Rom 14:7-9; 2 Cor 5:14-15). They joyfully praise God for his glorious grace (1:6, 12, 14; 1 Cor 10:31) because they know they owe God and his Son everything. Their entire lives reflect their gratitude for his grace.

Joy and thanksgiving are the appropriate response to God's grace (*joy, thanksgiving,* and *grace* are all related words in Greek). Everything in this life and the next hangs on grace. Without God's grace, we would be "without God and without hope" (2:12). That is why Paul begins and ends his letters with a prayer that God's people would have his grace and peace (e.g., 1:2; 6:22-24).

2:3 Unconverted people are naturally under the control of ***the passionate desires and inclinations of our sinful nature*** (see Rom 3:9-20, 23). Because of their sin, they are ***subject to God's anger,*** because God hates sin (see 5:6; Rom 1:18; 2:5, 8; 3:5, 19; 4:15; 5:9; 9:22; 12:19; 13:4-5; Col 3:6; 1 Thes 1:10; 2:16; 5:9).

2:4-10 By God's *mercy,* kindness, and love, those who are joined to Jesus Christ are saved from the terrible consequences of their sin and enjoy the benefits of Christ's resurrection.

2:5 ***gave us life when he raised Christ from the dead*** (literally *made us alive together with Christ*): Joined with Christ, believers share in his resurrection, now and in the future (see 2:6; Rom 6:4-14; Col 3:1-4). • ***It is only by God's grace that you have been saved:*** See 1:2; 2:8-9.

2:6 ***united with Christ Jesus:*** Because of this union, believers share God's glory and blessings, and experience resurrection both now and in the future (see Rom 6:4-14; Col 2:12-13; 3:1-4).

2:7 ***grace:*** See note on 1:2.

2:8-9 This is a concise summary of how a person is *saved.* It is a cardinal tenet of the Good News that people are made righteous through trust in Christ rather than through their own merit (see Rom 1:16-17; 3:24-25; Gal 2:16; cp. John 3:16, 36). ***Salvation is not a reward for the good things we have done*** (see Rom 3:21–4:8; 9:16; Gal 3:2-10; 5:1-6; cp. 2 Tim 1:9; Titus 3:5). Salvation is for those who trust Christ alone to save them. As a result, ***none of us can boast about it*** (cp. Rom 3:27; 4:2; 1 Cor 1:30-31; Gal 6:14).

2:10 ***He has created us anew in Christ Jesus, so we can do the good things he planned for us:*** Good works are the result, not the cause, of salvation. God's Spirit, working through a transformed heart, produces a good life (Gal 5:22-23).

2:11-22 Paul now focuses on the grace that God has given particularly to ***Gentiles*** (non-Jews), bringing them into his family and uniting them with Jews in a new, unified, multiethnic community—the body of Christ, the church. Paul's emphasis on the inclusion of Gentiles might suggest they were experiencing discrimination from Jewish Christians.

2:11 Traditionally, Jews disdained ***Gentiles,*** considering them ***"uncircumcised heathens"*** who were excluded from God's people (see Gen 17:9-14). Paul argues that judging people by ***their bodies and not their hearts*** is superficial—in Christ, physical ***circumcision*** means nothing (see Rom 2:28-29).

2:12 Before their conversion, Gentiles had no part in God's people or the ***covenant promises God had made to them;*** they were ***without God and without hope*** (see 4:18; Col 1:21).

2:12
[c]*diathēkē* (1242)
‣Heb 7:22
[d]*elpis* (1680)
‣Col 1:5

2:13
Col 1:20

2:14
[e]*eirēnē* (1515)
‣Phil 4:7

2:15
2 Cor 5:17
Gal 3:28
Col 1:21-22; 2:14

2:16
Col 1:20

2:17
Isa 57:19
Zech 9:10

without God and without [d]hope. 13 But now
you have been united with Christ Jesus.
Once you were far away from God, but now
you have been brought near to him through
the blood of Christ.
14 For Christ himself has brought [e]peace
to us. He united Jews and Gentiles into one
people when, in his own body on the cross,
he broke down the wall of hostility that separated us. 15 He did this by ending the system
of law with its commandments and regulations. He made peace between Jews and
Gentiles by creating in himself one new people from the two groups. 16 Together as one
body, Christ reconciled both groups to God
by means of his death on the cross, and our
hostility toward each other was put to death.
17 He brought this Good News of peace to
you Gentiles who were far away from him,
and peace to the Jews who were near. 18 Now
all of us can come to the Father through the
same Holy Spirit because of what Christ has
done for us.

A Temple for the Lord

19 So now you Gentiles are no longer strangers and foreigners. You are citizens along

The One Body of Christ (2:14–3:13)

Eph 1:9-10, 23; 2:7; 4:2-6, 11-16; 5:18-20, 23-29
Rom 8:29; 12:6-8
1 Cor 3:16-17; 6:16; 12:7-28
Gal 6:16
Col 1:18, 24, 27
1 Tim 3:15
1 Pet 2:5, 9-10

More than any other NT writing, Ephesians highlights the role of the church in God's amazing eternal plan. In Jesus Christ, God has revealed his desire to unite Gentiles with Jews in a new group of people, the church (1:9; 2:14-22; 3:6). The church is the community of those who recognize the lordship of Christ and submit to him (5:21-24). The church is part of God's plan to bring everything in heaven and on earth under the authority of Christ (1:9-10). Believers do not relate to God in isolation but as part of this new family.

The NT uses a number of images to describe the church:

- The church is *the Israel of God*—the "new people of God" (Gal 6:16) who belong to him (1 Pet 2:9-10) and who as his "holy priests" do his work in the world (1 Pet 2:5, 9).
- The church is *God's family* (2:19)—the "household of God" (1 Tim 3:15), made up of those who have been adopted as God's children and designated as his heirs.
- The church is *a holy temple for the Lord* (2:21-22)—the place where God lives by his Spirit (2:22; 4:6; 1 Cor 3:16-17; 2 Cor 6:16; Col 1:27).
- The church is the *body of Christ*—the full expression of Christ in the world, and Christ is its head (1:23; 4:15; 5:23-24; 1 Cor 12:12-27; Col 1:18, 24).
- The church is *Christ's pure bride*—the one he died for, cares for, and cherishes, who will live in union with him forever (5:25-29).

Because the church comprises people of different ethnic groups, it is to be a community of harmony and peace as believers live together in love, bound together by the shared experience of the Spirit (4:2-6). God's goal for the church is that it will achieve the fullest possible experience of unity, faith, spiritual understanding, and Christian maturity—to the full perfection of Christ (4:13, 15; cp. Rom 8:29), the likeness of God himself (4:24, 32; 5:1). To this end God has provided people in the church with many diverse gifts to build up the body and bring it to perfection (4:11-16; Rom 12:6-8; 1 Cor 12:7-11, 28). God's intention is that the church should be a showcase of his forgiving grace (2:7; 3:10), a community in which God's glory can be seen, and one devoted to the praise of that glory (3:21; 5:18-20).

2:13 Only by being ***united with Christ Jesus*** through trust in him can a person be reconciled to God (see Rom 5:10-12; 2 Cor 5:18-21). ***The blood of Christ***—his sacrificial death—makes this possible (see 1:7; Rom 3:24-25; 5:9; Col 1:20; cp. Heb 9:12-15; 1 Pet 1:19; 1 Jn 1:7; Rev 1:5; 5:9).

2:14 ***Christ himself has brought peace to us:*** Peace with God (2:16-17; Rom 5:1, 10-11, 18-21; Col 1:20-22) and between ***Jews and Gentiles*** (see 2:15-16; 4:3). • ***the wall of hostility that separated us:*** Social and religious practices traditionally divided Jews from Gentiles. A low wall around the Temple in Jerusalem marked the boundary beyond which Gentiles were not allowed to step (see illustration, p. 1787). It symbolized the distinction Jews drew between themselves and Gentiles.

2:15 ***ending the system of law:*** See Rom 10:4; Col 2:14; cp. Rom 6:14; 7:4-6. • The church is ***one new people,*** a community where love and acceptance are prized and ethnic distinctions are no longer a source of division (see Rom 15:7-12; Gal 3:28; cp. John 10:16).

2:16 Christ's ***death on the cross*** reconciles humans to God, and also Jews and Gentiles to each other.

2:17 ***far away . . . near:*** This verse possibly alludes to Isa 57:19. • The Greek text lacks the words ***Gentiles*** and ***Jews,*** but they are implied (see 2:13; see also note on 1:12-13).

2:18 Because of Christ's sacrifice for sins, both Jewish and Gentile believers receive the ***Holy Spirit,*** which makes it possible for them to approach God openly (see 3:12; cp. Acts 10:34-37, 44-48; 1 Pet 3:18).

2:19 ***Gentiles*** who believe ***are no longer strangers and foreigners*** (2:11-12, 17). Through Christ, they are fully accepted into ***God's family.*** They become children of God, just like believing Jews (see Rom 8:14-17).

with all of God's holy people. You are members of God's family. 20Together, we are his
house, built on the foundation of the apostles and the prophets. And the cornerstone
is Christ Jesus himself. 21We are carefully
joined together in him, becoming a holy
temple for the Lord. 22Through him you
Gentiles are also being made part of this
dwelling where God lives by his Spirit.

God's Mysterious Plan Revealed

3 When I think of all this, I, Paul, a prisoner of Christ Jesus for the benefit
of you Gentiles . . . 2assuming, by the way,
that you know God gave me the special [f]re-
sponsibility of extending his grace to you
Gentiles. 3As I briefly wrote earlier, God
himself [g]revealed his [h]mysterious plan to
me. 4As you read what I have written, you
will understand my insight into this plan
regarding [i]Christ. 5God did not reveal it to
previous generations, but now by his Spirit
he has revealed it to his holy apostles and
prophets.
6And this is God's plan: Both Gentiles
and Jews who believe the Good News [j]share
equally in the riches inherited by God's
children. Both are part of the same body,
and both enjoy the promise of blessings because they belong to Christ Jesus. 7By God's
grace and mighty power, I have been given
the privilege of serving him by spreading
this Good News.
8Though I am the least deserving of all
God's people, he graciously gave me the
privilege of telling the Gentiles about the
endless [k]treasures available to them in
Christ. 9I was chosen to explain to everyone
this mysterious [a]plan that God, the Creator
of all things, had kept secret from the beginning.
10God's purpose in all this was to use the
church to display his wisdom in its rich
variety to all the unseen rulers and authorities in the heavenly places. 11This was his
eternal plan, which he carried out through
Christ Jesus our Lord.
12Because of Christ and our faith in him,
we can now come boldly and confidently
into God's presence. 13So please don't lose
heart because of my trials here. I am suffering for you, so you should feel honored.

2:20 Ps 118:22; Isa 28:16; 1 Pet 2:4-8
2:21 1 Cor 3:16
3:2 Acts 9:15; [f]*oikonomia* (3622) ‣ Eph 3:9
3:3 [g]*apokalupsis* (0602) ‣ 1 Pet 1:13; [h]*mustērion* (3466) ‣ Eph 5:32
3:4 [i]*christos* (5547) ‣ Col 3:16
3:6 [j]*sunklēronomos* (4789) ‣ Heb 11:9
3:7 Col 1:25
3:8 [k]*ploutos* (4149) ‣ Eph 3:16
3:9 [a]*oikonomia* (3622) ‣ Col 1:25
3:10 Rom 11:33; 1 Cor 2:7; 1 Pet 1:12
3:12 Heb 4:16
3:14 Phil 2:10

2:20 *Apostles* are missionary evangelists commissioned by God. • Here, ***prophets*** appear to be NT prophets, not OT ones (see 3:5; 4:11; see also 1 Cor 12:10, 28-29; 14:1-5, 22-24, 29-32, 39; cp. Acts 13:1; 19:6; 21:9, 10). In both the OT and NT, prophets are not primarily predictors of the future but are empowered to speak a message from God (see 1 Cor 12:10). • The church is built on the ***foundation of the apostles and the prophets*** (or *on the foundation laid by the apostles and prophets*)—that is, on their faithful witness to the saving message of Christ (see Rev 21:14; cp. Matt 16:18). However, ***the cornerstone is Christ Jesus himself,*** the Messiah, Savior, and Lord (cp. 1 Cor 3:11). The cornerstone is the most important stone in a building's foundation (see Isa 28:16; Mark 12:10; Acts 4:11; 1 Pet 2:6-7).

2:21 ***Joined together*** in Christ, Gentile and Jewish Christians become ***a holy temple for the Lord,*** because the Lord himself is among his people (see Matt 18:20; 28:20; 1 Cor 3:16; 1 Pet 2:4-5).

3:1-13 Paul now describes his own role in God's eternal plan: to proclaim God's grace to the Gentiles.

3:1 ***When I think of all this:*** Paul has written about the amazing salvation that God's grace has brought to undeserving sinners who are under his judgment, and about the incredible revelation that Gentiles can also be included in God's new family, the people of God (chs 1–2). • ***a prisoner of Christ Jesus:*** Paul wrote this letter while imprisoned for his witness to Christ among the Gentiles. • ***for the benefit of you Gentiles . . . :*** Paul resumes this thought in v 14: "When I think of all this, I fall to my knees and pray to the Father."

3:2-13 Paul interrupts his thought in 3:1 to discuss his own role in God's plan. When Paul was first converted, he was given ***the special responsibility of extending*** God's ***grace to*** the ***Gentiles*** (see Acts 9:15-16; 22:14-15, 21; 26:17-18; Rom 1:5; 11:13-14; 15:15-18; Gal 1:15-16; 2:7-9; Col 1:25-27; 1 Tim 2:7; 2 Tim 4:17).

3:3 What Paul ***briefly wrote earlier*** is a reference either to 1:9-10 (cp. 2:11-22) or to an unknown letter. • Paul's understanding of God's ***mysterious plan*** (see note on 1:8-10) came as ***God himself revealed*** it to him (see 1:9-10; Gal 1:11-12, 15-17; cp. Acts 9:3-6; 1 Cor 12:1, 7; Gal 2:2).

3:5 ***his holy apostles:*** See 1:1. • The order of the terms ***apostles and prophets*** (see 2:20) suggests that Paul is speaking of NT, not OT, ***prophets.*** In both the OT and the NT, the gift of prophecy is less concerned with predicting the future than with speaking a special word from God (see 1 Cor 12:10).

3:6 ***God's plan*** that has now been revealed to Paul is that the ***Gentiles*** are now included in God's family, the ***body*** of Christ, just as ***Jews*** are. They ***share equally*** in God's eternal blessings. • ***because they belong to Christ Jesus:*** Or *because they are united with Christ Jesus.*

3:7 ***grace:*** See note on 1:2. • ***serving him:*** Paul speaks of himself as a servant of the ***Good News*** (see also Col 1:23), of God (1 Cor 3:5; 2 Cor 6:4), of Christ (2 Cor 11:23), of the church (Col 1:25), and of the new covenant (2 Cor 3:6).

3:8 Paul considered himself ***the least deserving of all God's people*** (literally *the least of God's people*) because he was once an ardent persecutor of believers (see 1 Cor 15:9; 1 Tim 1:12-16). • ***the endless treasures available to them in Christ:*** See 1:3-14.

3:9 Some manuscripts do not include *to everyone.*

3:10 ***The church*** is meant to showcase to the entire universe God's ***wisdom in its rich variety,*** as expressed in his plan of redemption (see Rom 11:33-36). • ***the unseen rulers and authorities in the heavenly places:*** See 1:21 and note.

3:12 ***Because of Christ and our faith in him:*** Or *Because of Christ's faithfulness.* • ***We can come boldly and confidently into God's presence,*** not because of good deeds that we have done, but because of Christ's all-sufficient sacrifice for our sins (see 2:18; Heb 4:14-16; 10:19-23; 1 Pet 3:18; 1 Jn 4:14).

3:13 ***my trials here:*** Paul is writing from jail, as a prisoner (see 3:1). He knows that ***suffering*** is to be expected and that it works for good in a believer's life (see Rom 5:3-5; Col 1:24; 1 Thes 3:3; 2 Tim 3:12; Jas 1:2-4).

3:16
[b]*ploutos* (4149)
‣Phil 4:19
3:17
John 14:23
Col 2:7
3:18
John 1:16
Rom 8:39
3:19
Col 2:9-10
4:1
[c]*klēsis* (2821)
‣2 Thes 1:11
4:2
[d]*agapē* (0026)
‣Eph 4:15
4:3
Col 3:14-15
4:4
[e]*pneuma* (4151)
‣Phil 1:27
4:5
[f]*baptisma* (0908)
‣Col 2:12
4:6
Rom 11:36
4:7
Rom 12:3
1 Cor 12:7
4:8
*Ps 68:18
Col 2:15

Paul's Prayer for Spiritual Growth

14When I think of all this, I fall to my knees
and pray to the Father, 15the Creator of
everything in heaven and on earth. 16I pray
that from his glorious, unlimited [b]resources
he will empower you with inner strength
through his Spirit. 17Then Christ will make
his home in your hearts as you trust in him.
Your roots will grow down into God's love
and keep you strong. 18And may you have
the power to understand, as all God's people
should, how wide, how long, how high, and
how deep his love is. 19May you experience
the love of Christ, though it is too great to
understand fully. Then you will be made
complete with all the fullness of life and
power that comes from God.

20Now all glory to God, who is able,
through his mighty power at work within
us, to accomplish infinitely more than we
might ask or think. 21Glory to him in the
church and in Christ Jesus through all generations forever and ever! Amen.

3. LIVING LIKE CHRIST (4:1–6:20)

The Body of Christ (4:1-16)

Unity in the Body

4 Therefore I, a prisoner for serving the
Lord, beg you to lead a life worthy of
your [c]calling, for you have been called by
God. 2Always be humble and gentle. Be patient with each other, making allowance
for each other's faults because of your
[d]love. 3Make every effort to keep yourselves
united in the Spirit, binding yourselves together with peace. 4For there is one body
and one [e]Spirit, just as you have been called
to one glorious hope for the future. 5There
is one Lord, one faith, one [f]baptism, 6and
one God and Father, who is over all and in
all and living through all.

Gifts for Building Up the Church

7However, he has given each one of us a special gift through the generosity of Christ.
8That is why the Scriptures say,

"When he ascended to the heights,

3:14-21 Paul closes this section (1:3–3:21) with a second prayer for his readers. The first (1:15-23) was for their spiritual understanding, the second (3:14-21) is for their spiritual growth and empowerment.

3:14 ***When I think of all this, I fall to my knees and pray:*** Paul resumes what he started to say at the beginning of the chapter (see 3:1). • ***the Father:*** Some manuscripts read *the Father of our Lord Jesus Christ.*

3:15-16 ***the Creator of everything in heaven and on earth*** (or ***from whom every family in heaven and on earth takes its name***): There is a play on words between *Father* (Greek *patēr,* 3:14) and *family* (Greek *patria*). God is the Creator of everything, including every family—angelic or human, Gentile or Jew (see 2:14-22; 3:6). So he is the source of ***glorious, unlimited resources*** that he gladly gives his children.

3:17 Having ***Christ . . . make his home in your hearts*** is the source of spiritual power for life and ministry (see John 14:16-17, 23; 15:4-5; Gal 2:20).

3:18 ***how wide, how long, how high, and how deep his love is:*** Christ's love is great in every dimension (cp. Rom 8:38-39).

3:19 ***May you experience*** (literally *know*) ***the love of Christ:*** The whole Christian life is based on the experience and personal knowledge of God's grace and love in Jesus Christ (see Rom 12:1). • ***it is too great to understand fully:*** Christ's love is much greater than ordinary human love (see Rom 5:6-8). • The believer's life is ***made complete*** when it is filled ***with all the fullness of life and power*** by the presence of Christ within (see 1:23; Gal 2:20; Col 1:27). The believer then is conformed to his image and reflects God (see 4:14, 24; 5:1-2; Rom 8:29; 2 Cor 3:16-18).

3:20-21 This doxology concludes the first section of the letter (see also Rom 16:25-27; Gal 1:5; 1 Tim 1:17; 2 Tim 4:18; Jude 1:24-25).

3:20 ***all glory to God:*** Because of the grace God has shown in Jesus Christ, he deserves nothing less. • The ***mighty power at work within us*** is the power of the living God that raised Christ from the dead (see 1:19-20). By that power, he is able ***to accomplish infinitely more than we might ask or think,*** because God is at work in the lives of his children (see Rom 8:31-39; Phil 4:13; Col 1:29).

3:21 ***The church***—the community of believers, both Jews and Gentiles—is to be the reflection and full expression of the ***glory*** of God.

4:1–6:20 ***Therefore:*** Ephesians divides into two sections, the first devoted to explaining the Good News, the second to drawing out the implications for Christian living. This arrangement reflects Paul's belief that believers' lives should be a response of gratitude for God's grace.

4:1-6 God's saving grace for both Jews and Gentiles should be reflected in how the two groups relate to each other in the church: They are to accept each other warmly, just as God has accepted them.

4:1 ***I, a prisoner for serving the Lord:*** See note on 3:1. • Though salvation can never be earned, believers are to live in a manner ***worthy*** of their ***calling*** to salvation (see Phil 1:27; Col 1:10; 1 Thes 2:12). • ***called by God:*** See 1:4-5, 11.

4:2 ***humble . . . gentle . . . patient:*** Believers are to be like Christ in how they treat others (see Col 3:12-14; cp. Gal 6:2).

4:3 ***binding yourselves together with peace:*** Paul's emphasis on God's acceptance of Gentiles as well as Jews (2:11–3:6) is now applied ethically: Jews and Gentiles are to accept one another in the church (see Col 3:14-15).

4:4-6 These three verses might have been taken from a creedal statement. • Whatever their ethnic differences, Jewish and Gentile Christians share ***one Lord*** and ***one faith,*** so they should live together in unity. • Christ's ***one body*** is the church (see 1:23; 2:16). • ***One God and Father, who is over all:*** See 1 Cor 8:6; 15:28. • ***in all and living through all:*** God is especially present in believers' lives (see 1 Cor 6:19; 2 Cor 13:5; Gal 2:20; Col 1:27; cp. John 14:16-17, 23; 15:4-5).

4:7-16 Though believers share a common faith, God has given different special abilities to ***each*** individual believer for building up the church.

4:7 ***a special gift:*** Literally *a grace.* ***He has given each one of us*** a gift of his grace for building up the community of believers (see 1 Cor 12:7; cp. Rom 12:6; 1 Cor 12:11).

4:8 This verse quotes Ps 68:18. • ***He led a crowd of captives*** may refer to Christ's victory over spiritual powers (see 1:21-22; Col 2:15), or to his capture of disobedient sinners and making them believers through the power of the Good News message. • Christ ***gave gifts to his people*** (see 4:11-12).

he led a crowd of captives
and gave gifts to his people.”
9 Notice that it says “he ascended.” This
clearly means that Christ also descended to
our lowly world. 10 And the same one who
descended is the one who ascended higher
than all the [g]heavens, so that he might fill
the entire universe with himself.
11 Now these are the gifts Christ gave to
the church: the [h]apostles, the prophets, the
evangelists, and the [i]pastors and teachers.
12 Their responsibility is to equip God’s people to do his [j]work and build up the church,
the body of Christ. 13 This will continue until we all come to such unity in our faith and
knowledge of God’s Son that we will be [k]ma-
ture in the Lord, measuring up to the full
and complete standard of Christ.
14 Then we will no longer be immature
like children. We won’t be tossed and
blown about by every wind of new teaching.
We will not be influenced when people try
to trick us with lies so clever they sound like
the truth. 15 Instead, we will speak the truth
in [a]love, growing in every way more and
more like Christ, who is the head of his body,
the church. 16 He makes the whole body fit
together perfectly. As each part does its
own special work, it helps the other parts
grow, so that the whole body is healthy and
growing and full of love.

The Light of Christ (4:17–5:14)
Living as Children of Light

17 With the Lord’s authority I say this: Live
no longer as the Gentiles do, for they are
hopelessly confused. 18 Their minds are full
of darkness; they wander far from the life
God gives because they have closed their
minds and hardened their [b]hearts against
him. 19 They have no sense of shame. They
live for lustful pleasure and eagerly practice
every kind of impurity.
20 But that isn’t what you learned about
Christ. 21 Since you have heard about Jesus
and have learned the truth that comes from
him, 22 throw off your old sinful nature and
your former way of life, which is corrupted
by lust and deception. 23 Instead, let the
Spirit renew your thoughts and attitudes.
24 Put on your new nature, created to be like
God—truly righteous and holy.
25 So stop telling lies. Let us tell our neighbors the truth, for we are all parts of the
same body. 26 And “don’t sin by letting anger control you.” Don’t let the sun go down
while you are still angry, 27 for anger gives a
foothold to the [c]devil.

4:9 John 3:13
4:10 [g]*ouranos* (3772) ▸2 Pet 3:13
4:11 [h]*apostolos* (0652) ▸1 Tim 2:7; [i]*poimēn* (4166) ▸Heb 13:20
4:12 [j]*diakonia* (1248) ▸Col 4:17
4:13 [k]*teleios* (5046) ▸Col 3:14
4:15 [a]*agapē* (0026) ▸Phil 1:9
4:17 Rom 1:21
4:18 [b]*kardia* (2588) ▸1 Tim 1:5
4:22 Jas 1:21
4:23 Rom 12:2
4:25 Zech 8:16
4:26 *Ps 4:4
4:27 [c]*diabolos* (1228) ▸Eph 6:11
4:28 1 Thes 4:11
4:29 Matt 12:36

4:9-10 *to our lowly world* (or *to the lowest parts of the earth*): Some understand this phrase as referring to the tomb, to the world of the dead (cp. Matt 12:40; 1 Pet 3:18-20), or to the coming of the Spirit at Pentecost. Instead, it probably refers to the incarnation, when ***Christ** . . . **descended*** from heaven and became a man (see John 1:14; 3:13; Phil 2:7-8).

4:11 In his letters, Paul has four different lists of God’s gifts (see also Rom 12:4-8; 1 Cor 12:8-10, 28), none of which is comprehensive. Here the focus is on the gifts of leadership most needed for the growth of the church. • ***Apostles*** are divinely commissioned missionary evangelists. • ***Prophets*** speak messages from God for his people (see “The Gift of Prophecy” at Acts 21:9-11, p. 1873). • ***Evangelists*** proclaim the Good News. • ***Pastors*** (literally *shepherds*) care for God’s people (see 1 Tim 3:1-7). • ***Teachers*** expound Scripture and God’s truths to the church. • ***Pastors and teachers*** might refer to separate ministries or to two aspects of the same ministry.

4:12 God’s gifts are given so that believers will ***build up the church*** (see 1 Cor 12:7; cp. 1 Pet 2:5). • ***to equip God’s people to do his work:*** All believers are called to active Christian service.

4:13 The goal of ministry is for the whole Christian community to understand and experience the Christian ***faith*** more deeply and gain a deeper ***knowledge of God’s Son.*** In this way, believers will be ***mature in the Lord*** (see 1 Cor 2:6; 14:20; Phil 3:15; Col 1:28; 4:12; cp. Heb 5:14; Jas 1:4; 3:2). The ***standard*** of maturity is ***Christ*** himself; the Spirit’s transforming work is to make people fully like Christ (Rom 8:29).

4:14 ***We won’t be tossed and blown about:*** Mature Christians, with a well-grounded knowledge of the Good News and of Christ himself, will be able to discern and resist false ***teaching*** (see Gal 1:6-7; 3:1; Col 2:8-23; 1 Tim 1:3-7; 4:1-3; 6:3-5, 20; 2 Tim 4:3-4; Titus 1:11).

4:16 ***Each part*** of the ***body*** plays an important role and ***helps the other parts grow.*** Christ, the head of the body, works through the individual parts, ***makes*** them ***fit together,*** and is the ultimate source of growth (see Col 2:19). • When all believers are ministering effectively, ***the whole body*** will be ***healthy and growing and full of love*** (cp. 1 Cor 8:1). Love is the most important factor in Christian growth (1 Cor 13:1-13).

4:17–5:20 Paul gives believers specific guidelines for living a new life in Christ.

4:17 God’s people are called to a way of life that is different from that of ***the Gentiles*** (pagans, unbelievers) of the world.

4:18 ***Their minds are full of darkness*** because their ***minds*** are ***closed*** and ***hearts*** are hard (see 2 Cor 4:4).

4:19 ***no sense of shame:*** The hardness of unbelievers’ hearts is reflected in their moral insensitivity and sexual immorality (see Rom 1:21-31).

4:20-24 ***What you learned about Christ*** is ***the truth that comes from him.*** He gives true understanding (cp. John 14:6) and calls his people to an entirely new way of life (cp. Rom 6:3-14; 13:12-14; Col 3:8-10).

4:24 A believer has a ***new nature:*** God’s Spirit expresses his life within the believer (see Col 3:10; cp. Gen 1:26; Rom 12:1-2; Gal 5:22-23). The transforming work of God’s Spirit is part of the gift of salvation (2:8-10).

4:25 ***Let us tell our neighbors the truth:*** Cp. Zech 8:16. • ***for we are all parts of the same body:*** See Rom 12:5; 1 Cor 12:12-13, 27.

4:26-27 ***“don’t sin by letting anger control you”*** (literally *“be angry and do not sin”*): This verse quotes Ps 4:4 (Greek version). The literal form of the quotation cannot be used to justify anger, ***for anger gives a foothold to the devil*** (cp. Jas 1:20). God’s people are to be gentle and gracious, not harsh or angry (see 4:31-32). • ***Don’t let the sun go down while you are still angry:*** Anger must quickly be resolved, not allowed to stew.

4:30
[d]*sphragizō* (4972)
‣2 Tim 2:19
[e]*apolutrōsis* (0629)
‣Col 1:14

4:31
[f]*orgē* (3709)
‣Eph 5:6
[g]*blasphēmia* (0988)
‣Col 3:8

4:32
Matt 6:12; 18:23-33
Col 3:12-13

5:2
John 13:34
Gal 1:4; 2:20

5:3-4
Col 3:5, 8

5:5
[h]*eidōlolatrēs* (1496)
‣Col 3:5

5:6
[i]*orgē* (3709)
‣Col 3:8

5:8
John 8:12

5:9
[j]*agathōsunē* (0019)
‣2 Thes 1:11
[k]*dikaiosunē* (1343)
‣Eph 6:14

28 If you are a thief, quit stealing. Instead, use your hands for good hard work, and then give generously to others in need. 29 Don't use foul or abusive language. Let everything you say be good and helpful, so that your words will be an encouragement to those who hear them.

30 And do not bring sorrow to God's Holy Spirit by the way you live. Remember, he has [d]identified you as his own, guaranteeing that you will be saved on the day of [e]redemption.

31 Get rid of all bitterness, rage, [f]anger, harsh words, and [g]slander, as well as all types of evil behavior. 32 Instead, be kind to each other, tenderhearted, forgiving one another, just as God through Christ has forgiven you.

Living in the Light

5 Imitate God, therefore, in everything you do, because you are his dear children. 2 Live a life filled with love, following the example of Christ. He loved us and offered himself as a sacrifice for us, a pleasing aroma to God.

3 Let there be no sexual immorality, impurity, or greed among you. Such sins have no place among God's people. 4 Obscene stories, foolish talk, and coarse jokes—these are not for you. Instead, let there be thankfulness to God. 5 You can be sure that no immoral, impure, or greedy person will inherit the Kingdom of Christ and of God. For a greedy person is an [h]idolater, worshiping the things of this world.

6 Don't be fooled by those who try to excuse these sins, for the [i]anger of God will fall on all who disobey him. 7 Don't participate in the things these people do. 8 For once you were full of darkness, but now you have light from the Lord. So live as people of light! 9 For this light within you produces only what is [j]good and [k]right and true.

The Old Life and the New Life (4:17–5:20)

Rom 6:3-14; 12:1-2
Gal 5:19-23
Phil 3:12-13

When people become believers in Christ, they are joined to Jesus Christ and begin to share in his experience and benefits, including his death and resurrection. Their old life dies with Christ, and they rise to new life by his power within them (see Rom 6:3-14).

This is all the work of God, who transforms them by his Spirit. Their minds are renewed (see Rom 12:2), their desires and actions change, and their lives begin to reflect the fruit of his Spirit (Gal 5:22-23). They become different people, gradually growing into the likeness of Christ.

Believers are also responsible for living out Christ's death and resurrection (see Phil 3:10-13). They are to turn away from their old life that was full of darkness and embrace a new life full of light (4:17–5:20). Using the imagery of clothing, Paul calls believers to *put off* the old, sinful life driven by the devil and to *put on* a new, pure life directed by the Holy Spirit. As they do so, they recognize their reliance on God's grace and power.

Believers must actively turn from their old lives to live in a new way that pleases God; it is God's gracious working in their hearts that gives them the desire and power to do so.

4:28 Christians are to be hard-working people who have integrity and care for others (cp. 1 Thes 4:11; 2 Thes 3:6-12).

4:29 Believers are to learn new patterns of speech to ***be an encouragement*** to others (see also 5:3-4, 12).

4:30 Believers must not alienate ***God's Holy Spirit,*** who identifies them as belonging to God (cp. Mark 3:29; Acts 5:3-5, 9; 1 Thes 4:8; Heb 6:4-8). • ***has identified you as his own*** (or *has put his seal on you*): The presence of the Spirit both confirms and guarantees the future redemption of believers (see 1:13-14; Rom 8:16-17; 2 Cor 1:22; 1 Jn 4:13).

4:32 ***Forgiving*** fellow believers is a natural and good response to experiencing God's forgiving grace in Christ (cp. Col 3:12-13; 1 Jn 4:19).

5:1 ***Imitate God . . . in everything you do:*** Primarily by expressing love (5:2; cp. Matt 5:44-45, 48). • ***because you are his dear children:*** Just as children follow their parents' example, believers should follow God's example (1 Cor 4:14-17).

5:2 Christ's ***love*** is shown especially in his offering himself ***as a sacrifice for us*** (cp. 5:25; John 15:13; Rom 5:8). Christian love is motivated by and modeled after Christ's sacrificial love (see Phil 2:5-8). • ***He loved us:*** Some manuscripts read *He loved you.* • Paul draws on OT imagery, where the smell of a burning *sacrifice* was ***a pleasing aroma to God*** (see Lev 1:9; 2:2; cp. Rom 12:1).

5:3-5 ***God's people*** (literally *holy ones*) must have a holy lifestyle, avoiding the immorality common among unbelievers (cp. 4:19; Col 3:5).

5:4 The speech of God's people is to be characterized by ***thankfulness to God*** (see 4:29; 5:3, 12).

5:5 Many similar statements describe the kind of ***person*** who will not ***inherit the Kingdom of . . . God:*** See 1 Cor 6:9-10; Gal 5:19-21; Rev 22:15; cp. Col 3:5-6. • ***For a greedy person is an idolater:*** The things greedy people desire become their gods (see Matt 6:24).

5:6 ***The anger of God will fall*** at his final judgment (see Rom 1:18; Col 3:5-6; cp. John 3:36).

5:7 ***Don't participate:*** Cp. 2 Cor 6:14–7:1.

5:8 ***Darkness*** is ignorance of God and his ways and being dominated by sin (see 4:18). • ***Light from the Lord*** is Christ's Good News (see John 8:12). ***As people of light,*** believers live in fellowship with God, in whom there is no darkness (see 1 Jn 1:5-7; 5:9; cp. Matt 5:14-16; John 8:12; 12:35-36, 46; Rom 13:12; 2 Cor 6:14; 1 Thes 5:4-8; 1 Pet 2:9).

5:9 God's people are to do ***what is good and right and true,*** in harmony with God's ***light*** (cp. Rom 12:2; some early manuscripts read *Spirit* instead of *light;* cp. 4:22-24; Matt 7:16-20; Gal 5:22-23).

[10]Carefully determine what pleases
the Lord. [11]Take no part in the worthless
deeds of evil and darkness; instead, expose
them. [12]It is shameful even to talk about
the things that ungodly people do in secret.
[13]But their evil intentions will be exposed
when the light shines on them, [14]for the
light makes everything visible. This is why
it is said,

"Awake, O sleeper,
rise up from the dead,
and Christ will give you light."

Living by the Spirit's Power (5:15-20)

[15]So be careful how you live. Don't live like
fools, but like those who are wise. [16]Make
the most of every opportunity in these
evil days. [17]Don't act thoughtlessly, but
understand what the Lord wants you to
do. [18]Don't be drunk with wine, because
that will ruin your life. Instead, be filled
with the Holy Spirit, [19]singing psalms and
hymns and spiritual songs among yourselves, and making music to the Lord in
your hearts. [20]And give thanks for everything to God the Father in the name of our
Lord Jesus Christ.

Relationships in Christ (5:21–6:9)

Wives and Husbands

[21]And further, submit to one another out of
reverence for Christ.
[22]For wives, this means submit to your
husbands as to the Lord. [23]For a husband is
the head of his wife as Christ is the head of
the church. He is the [a]Savior of his body, the
church. [24]As the church submits to Christ,
so you wives should submit to your husbands in everything.
[25]For husbands, this means love your
wives, just as Christ loved the [b]church. He
gave up his life for her [26]to make her holy
and clean, washed by the cleansing of God's
word. [27]He did this to present her to himself as a glorious church without a spot or
wrinkle or any other blemish. Instead, she
will be holy and without fault. [28]In the same
way, husbands ought to love their wives as
they love their own bodies. For a man who
loves his wife actually shows love for himself. [29]No one hates his own [c]body but feeds
and cares for it, just as Christ cares for the
church. [30]And we are members of his body.
[31]As the Scriptures say, "A man leaves his
father and mother and is joined to his wife,

5:11 Rom 13:12
5:13 John 3:20-21
5:14 Isa 52:1; 60:1; John 5:25; Rom 13:11
5:16 Col 4:5
5:18 Prov 20:1; 23:31
5:19 Col 3:16
5:21 1 Pet 5:5
5:22 Gen 3:16
5:23 [a]*sōtēr* (4990) ‣Phil 3:20
5:25 [b]*ekklēsia* (1577) ‣Col 1:18
5:26 John 15:3; 17:17; Titus 3:5; Heb 10:22
5:27 Col 1:22
5:29 [c]*sarx* (4561) ‣Heb 5:7
5:30 1 Cor 6:15; 12:27
5:31 *Gen 2:24; Matt 19:5

5:10 ***Carefully determine what pleases the Lord:*** The point is to obey God's will, not simply to understand it (cp. Rom 12:2; Phil 1:10).

5:11 ***expose them:*** By the light shining from their lives (cp. John 3:20-21; Rom 13:12; 1 Pet 2:9), not by verbally accusing or condemning people (see 1 Cor 5:9-13).

5:13-14 ***"Awake, O sleeper":*** This might be a fragment from an unknown Christian song, perhaps based on texts in Isaiah (cp. Isa 26:19; 52:1; 60:1). It calls on God's people to turn from their sinful darkness and live in the full ***light*** of ***Christ.***

5:15 ***Fools*** have no understanding of God and his ways, but ***those who are wise*** do know God and understand his ways (see Job 28:28; Prov 1:7; 2:1-22).

5:16 ***Make the most of every opportunity:*** See also Col 4:5. • ***in these evil days:*** See Matt 24:6-12, 15-22; 2 Thes 2:3-10.

5:18 ***The Holy Spirit,*** not ***wine,*** should dominate believers' lives (see Prov 23:29-35; cp. Acts 2:15-18). • ***be filled:*** The grammar here suggests that believers' lives are to be continuously filled with and governed by the Holy Spirit.

5:19-20 Lives filled with the Holy Spirit will be expressed in ***singing . . . and making music*** (Col 3:16-17). Joyful praise, worship, and giving ***thanks*** are fitting responses to God's saving grace. • ***among yourselves:*** Singing together builds up the body of Christ. • The ***Lord*** hears the ***music*** in our ***hearts.*** • ***in the name of our Lord Jesus Christ:*** Jesus Christ is our mediator and representative as we approach God (cp. John 14:13-14; 16:23-27; Rev 22:4).

5:21–6:9 Paul gives specific instructions on how believers are to relate to one another in a Christian home (see also Col 3:18–4:1; 1 Pet 2:18–3:7). Love and respect are to characterize all relationships in the body of Christ as an expression of believers' commitment to the Lord himself. • ***And further, submit:*** The verb form links it with the command to ***be filled*** (5:18).

5:21 ***submit to one another:*** This general instruction (cp. Phil 2:3) applies to all three relationships that Paul discusses: wives and husbands (5:22-33), children and their parents (6:1-4), and slaves and their masters (6:5-9). For believers, submission is not expressed out of fear or desire for personal gain, but ***out of reverence for Christ.***

5:22-33 Christian ***wives*** are to ***submit*** to their ***husbands,*** showing them respect. At least as important, Christian ***husbands*** are to ***love*** their ***wives*** (see Col 3:18-19). Christian marriages become a reflection of the union and relationship between the Lord and the church.

5:22 Submission is part of the life to which the wives' Christian commitment calls them (see 1 Cor 11:3-10; 14:34-35; Col 3:18; 1 Tim 2:11-12; Titus 2:5; 1 Pet 3:1-6).

5:23-24 ***a husband is the head of his wife:*** To be the head is to have authority (see 1 Cor 11:3). • ***Christ is the head of the church:*** See 1:22; 4:15; Col 1:18; 2:10, 19.

5:25-33 Christian husbands are to love their wives ***just as Christ loved the church***—that is, sacrificially, for Christ ***gave up his life for her*** (5:2; cp. Col 3:19; 1 Pet 3:7).

5:26 ***washed by the cleansing of God's word*** (literally ***washed by water with the word***): The church has been cleansed by the message of Good News. God has forgiven the sins of his people through Christ's sacrificial death (John 15:3; cp. Titus 3:5; 1 Pet 3:21).

5:27 ***a glorious church without a . . . blemish:*** The church's sins have been forgiven through Christ's sacrifice, and her life is purified by the Holy Spirit. As a result, the church stands ***holy and without fault*** before God. Cp. 1:4; 2 Cor 11:2; Col 1:22; Rev 19:7-8; 21:2.

5:28-29 Husbands should prize and cherish their wives, for in marriage the two have become one (see 5:31).

5:31 This verse quotes Gen 2:24. The unity of husband and wife should motivate the husband to care for his wife.

5:32
[d]*mustērion* (3466)
‣ Eph 6:19

5:33
1 Pet 3:1-2, 5

6:1
Col 3:20

6:2-3
*Exod 20:12
*Deut 5:16
Matt 15:4

6:4
[e]*paideia* (3809)
‣ 2 Tim 2:25

6:5-7
//Col 3:22-23
Titus 2:9-10

6:5
[f]*doulos* (1401)
‣ Phil 1:1
[g]*kurios* (2962)
‣ Phil 2:11
[h]*haplotēs* (0572)
‣ Col 3:22

6:6
[i]*thelēma* (2307)
‣ Col 4:12

6:8
Col 3:24-25

6:9
Job 31:13-14
Col 4:1

6:11
[j]*diabolos* (1228)
‣ 1 Tim 3:7

and the two are united into one." 32 This is
a great [d]mystery, but it is an illustration of
the way Christ and the church are one. 33 So
again I say, each man must love his wife as
he loves himself, and the wife must respect
her husband.

Children and Parents

6 Children, obey your parents because
you belong to the Lord, for this is the
right thing to do. 2 "Honor your father and
mother." This is the first commandment
with a promise: 3 If you honor your father
and mother, "things will go well for you, and
you will have a long life on the earth."
4 Fathers, do not provoke your children
to anger by the way you treat them. Rather,
bring them up with the [e]discipline and instruction that comes from the Lord.

Slaves and Masters

5 [f]Slaves, obey your earthly [g]masters with
deep respect and fear. Serve them [h]sin-
cerely as you would serve Christ. 6 Try to
please them all the time, not just when they
are watching you. As slaves of Christ, do the
[i]will of God with all your heart. 7 Work with
enthusiasm, as though you were working
for the Lord rather than for people. 8 Remember that the Lord will reward each one
of us for the good we do, whether we are
slaves or free.

9 Masters, treat your slaves in the same
way. Don't threaten them; remember, you
both have the same Master in heaven, and
he has no favorites.

The Whole Armor of God (6:10-20)

10 A final word: Be strong in the Lord and in
his mighty power. 11 Put on all of God's armor so that you will be able to stand firm
against all strategies of the [j]devil. 12 For we
are not fighting against flesh-and-blood
enemies, but against evil rulers and authorities of the unseen world, against mighty
powers in this dark world, and against evil
spirits in the heavenly places.

13 Therefore, put on every piece of God's
armor so you will be able to resist the enemy in the time of evil. Then after the battle
you will still be standing firm. 14 Stand your
ground, putting on the belt of truth and the

5:32 ***it is an illustration:*** Both the unity of husband and wife and the unity of ***Christ and the church*** are ***a great mystery*** (see note on 1:8-10).

5:33 Paul summarizes his teaching on the relationship between husbands and wives (5:22-33). Christian marriages should be marked by ***love*** and ***respect.***

6:1-4 The relationship between parents and children is to be a reflection of their devotion to the Lord. Christian children are to obey their parents, and Christian parents are to discipline their children gently (see Col 3:20-21).

6:1 ***Children, obey your parents because you belong to the Lord:*** Or *Children, obey your parents who belong to the Lord;* some manuscripts read simply *Children, obey your parents.*

6:2-3 These verses quote Exod 20:12; Deut 5:16. Children who honor and respect their parents also honor and respect God himself, and blessings follow.

6:4 ***Fathers*** often ***provoke*** their ***children to anger*** by being harsh or unjust (see Col 3:21). Parents should give their children ***the discipline and instruction that comes from the Lord*** (or ***the discipline and instruction about the Lord***) so that they will learn a way of living that is good and pleases God. Such discipline is not to be excessive, but loving and gentle so that children are not turned from the Lord but are drawn to him (cp. Heb 12:5-11).

6:5-9 The relationship between slaves and masters (and, by analogy, between employees and employers) is to be shaped by their commitment to the Lord and their desire to build one another up in Christ. Christian slaves are to obey their masters, and Christian masters are to treat their slaves kindly (see Col 3:22–4:1). • Paul was not promoting slavery but teaching Christians to live with it as a fact of life in that culture (for Paul's treatment of slavery, see Philemon Introduction, "Meaning and Message," p. 2078).

6:5 Obedient service to ***earthly masters*** expresses a Christian slave's service to ***Christ*** (see Col 3:22-23; 1 Tim 6:1-2; Titus 2:9-10; 1 Pet 2:18-23).

6:6-7 ***As slaves of Christ:*** As those who have been bought by the blood of Christ, believers no longer belong to themselves (see 1 Cor 6:19-20; 7:22; cp. Rom 1:1; Gal 1:10; Phil 1:1). For Christian slaves, ***the will of God*** is that they honor him by serving their human masters faithfully and ***with enthusiasm.***

6:8 The master of all believers is ***the Lord,*** and he ***will reward*** those who are faithful (see 1 Cor 3:12-15).

6:9 ***in the same way:*** That is, with integrity and concern for their welfare (see Col 4:1). • ***Don't threaten them:*** Christian masters, too, will be held accountable by ***the same Master in heaven*** for their lives on earth. Pleasing him requires treating their slaves humanely and kindly. • ***he has no favorites:*** God judges all people by the same standard (see Deut 10:17; Acts 10:34; Rom 2:11; Col 3:25).

6:10-20 Paul's ***final word*** is to remind the believers of the devil's opposition and urge them to protect themselves with ***all of God's armor.***

6:11 ***Put on all of God's armor:*** See Rom 13:12; 2 Cor 10:4-5. It is only by the Lord's protection that a believer can ***stand firm against all strategies of the devil*** (cp. 1 Pet 5:8-9).

6:12 ***For we:*** Some manuscripts read *For you.* • Believers should not consider human beings to be their ***enemies.*** Instead, the opposition they face comes from the ***unseen world*** of spiritual evil, and Christ has authority over that realm (see 1:21-22).

6:13 ***God's armor*** gives believers the ability to ***resist*** the attacks of the devil ***in the time of evil***—when evil seems to prevail—and to keep ***standing firm.***

6:14-17 Paul uses the physical armor worn by Roman soldiers as imagery for spiritual armor used by believers. Most of this equipment is to defend, not to attack. Paul's focus is not on the precise functions of each piece but on God's gifts. Grounding in Christ and Scripture provides protection and ability to ***stand your ground*** (cp. Jas 4:7; 1 Pet 5:8-9).

6:14 ***God's righteousness:*** Either the righteousness God credits to those who believe in Christ, or the righteous

body armor of God's [k]righteousness. 15For shoes, put on the peace that comes from the Good News so that you will be fully prepared. 16In addition to all of these, hold up the shield of faith to stop the fiery arrows of the devil. 17Put on salvation as your helmet, and take the sword of the Spirit, which is the word of God.

18Pray in the Spirit at all times and on every occasion. Stay alert and be persistent in your prayers for all believers everywhere.

19And pray for me, too. Ask God to give me the right words so I can boldly explain God's [a]mysterious plan that the Good News is for Jews and Gentiles alike. 20I am in chains now, still preaching this message as God's ambassador. So pray that I will keep on speaking boldly for him, as I should.

4. FINAL GREETINGS (6:21-24)

21To bring you up to date, Tychicus will give you a full report about what I am doing and

6:14
[k]*dikaiosunē* (1343)
›Phil 3:9

6:15
Isa 52:7

6:16
1 Jn 5:4

6:17
Isa 59:17
1 Thes 5:8

6:18
Rom 8:26-27
Phil 4:6
1 Thes 5:17

6:19
[a]*mustērion* (3466)
›Col 1:26

Overcoming the Devil (6:10-20)

Eph 2:2; 4:27
Matt 6:13; 13:19
Acts 5:3-5
Rom 8:38-39
1 Cor 5:5; 15:24
2 Cor 4:4
Col 1:13; 2:10, 15
1 Thes 2:18
Jas 4:7
1 Pet 3:22; 5:8
1 Jn 2:14; 3:8; 4:4; 5:18-19
Rev 2:10; 12:7-9, 11-12, 17

The NT writers were convinced of the reality of evil and the dangers of the spiritual world. So they took Satan (the evil one, the devil) seriously as a real threat. The devil not only inhibits the work of God's people (see 1 Thes 2:18; Rev 2:10), but he "prowls around like a roaring lion, looking for someone to devour" (see 1 Pet 5:8).

The entire unbelieving world is subject to the power of sin and the devil (see 2:2; 1 Jn 5:19). As the "god of this world," the devil can blind the minds of unbelievers (see 2 Cor 4:4; cp. Matt 13:19). Although Satan opposes God and seeks to destroy his people (Rev 12:12, 17), Jesus came to destroy Satan's work (1 Jn 3:8). God turns what the devil intends for evil into good; for example, when believers are expelled from the Christian fellowship, they are exposed to the devil's destructive power so that they might repent and be saved (see 1 Cor 5:5).

Christians are to stand firm and resist the devil (4:27; Jas 4:7), praying for God's deliverance (Matt 6:13) and availing themselves of the armor that God provides for their defense (6:10-20). Those who yield to Satan's influence suffer the consequences (see Acts 5:3-5). But believers who walk with Christ are secure because they know that the cross has broken the devil's power (see Rom 8:38-39; 1 Cor 15:24; Col 1:13; 2:10, 15; 1 Pet 3:22; Rev 12:7-9) and that the Lord protects them (see 1 Jn 5:18). They also know that the Holy Spirit within them is greater than the devil (see 1 Jn 4:4). By the word of God, they can overcome the evil one (see 1 Jn 2:14; cp. Rev 12:11).

Although believers need to be wary of the devil and protect themselves from his power, they need not live in fear. The power of the devil is no match for the power of God. In the NT, the Christian life is not centered on spiritual warfare, but on a joyful life of obedience in the Spirit.

way of life brought about by the transforming work of the Spirit of God in believers' lives. The one implies the other.

6:15 *For shoes, put on the peace that comes from the Good News* (or *For shoes, put on the readiness to preach the Good News of peace with God;* see Isa 52:7): In this context, the focus is on letting one's life be governed by the peace that the Good News gives (see Rom 5:1).

6:16 *Faith* is trust in Christ as Savior or trust in God to meet one's needs in evil times. • ***fiery arrows:*** Paul graphically pictures the nature of temptation to sin (cp. Matt 6:13; 26:41; 1 Cor 10:13; Jas 1:12-15). Arrows were sometimes dipped in pitch and ignited before being shot. • ***the devil:*** Literally *the evil one.*

6:17 *Put on salvation as your helmet:* Protect the mind with the assurance that God has indeed saved and given eternal life to those who believe in Christ. • ***The sword of the Spirit*** pictures using ***the word of God*** to respond to an attack, either with the Good News or with the spoken or written word of God more generally (cp. Jer 23:29; Heb 4:12).

6:18 Paul contrasts purely mental prayer with prayer ***in the Spirit,*** prayer that arises from the Spirit of God within (see 1 Cor 14:15; Jude 1:20; cp. Rom 8:26-27). • ***at all times and on every occasion:*** Believers are to make prayer a way of life and turn the whole of life into prayer (see Phil 4:6-7; 1 Thes 5:17)—not simply for themselves, but ***for all believers everywhere*** (literally *for all of God's holy people*). • ***Stay alert and be persistent:*** Because the danger of the devil is constant.

6:19-20 *explain God's mysterious plan that the Good News is for Jews and Gentiles alike* (literally *explain the mystery of the Good News;* some manuscripts read simply *explain the mystery*): Paul's missionary calling was primarily to the Gentiles, to help them realize that they are now accepted by God and welcomed into his church. • ***mysterious plan:*** See notes on 1:8-10; 3:3. • ***I am in chains now:*** Though writing as a prisoner (see 3:1; 4:1), Paul knew that his calling as ***God's ambassador*** (cp. 2 Cor 5:20) was to ***keep on speaking boldly for him.***

6:21-24 Paul closes with some personal words and a benediction that repeats the desires expressed at the beginning of the letter.

6:22
Col 4:7-9
6:23
Gal 6:16
2 Thes 3:16

how I am getting along. He is a beloved
brother and faithful helper in the Lord's
work. 22I have sent him to you for this very
purpose—to let you know how we are doing
and to encourage you.

23Peace be with you, dear brothers and sisters, and may God the Father and the Lord
Jesus Christ give you love with faithfulness.
24May God's grace be eternally upon all who
love our Lord Jesus Christ.

6:23-24 *Peace . . . love . . . faithfulness . . . grace:* These qualities, highlighted at the beginning of the letter (1:2, 15), are what Paul most desired for believers. • *dear brothers and sisters:* Literally *brothers.* Paul uses this generic term to refer to both male and female believers. • *be eternally upon all who love our Lord Jesus Christ:* Or *be upon all who love our Lord Jesus Christ eternally.*

PAUL'S LETTER TO THE

PHILIPPIANS

How do you live as a Christian in a non-Christian world? How do you respond when those around you are hostile to your faith? Paul wrote this poignant letter to encourage the persecuted Christians of the church in Philippi and to strengthen them in the difficulties they faced. Paul wrote while in prison—he, too, was suffering for his faith—but he wrote with joy, demonstrating that a Christian can be passionate for Christ regardless of the circumstances.

SETTING

Philippi was a small Roman colony in the province of Macedonia in northeastern Greece. Located about ten miles inland from the Aegean Sea, Philippi was important because of its strategic position on the Via Egnatia, the major east–west Roman route through Macedonia.

Philippi was the first town of Greece to hear the Good News of Christ from Paul on his second missionary journey (about AD 50; see Acts 16:11-40). From the beginning, there was opposition to Paul's preaching. During his brief stay there, he was thrown into prison and then asked to leave town, but not before a group of new believers had been established (Acts 16:35-40).

Perhaps six years later (AD 56~57) on his third missionary trip, Paul visited Philippi again (see Acts 20:1-6). After that, it is possible that he never saw the Philippian Christians again (but see 1 Tim 1:3, about AD 63).

Paul later wrote Philippians while in prison. Epaphroditus had brought a monetary gift to Paul from the Philippians and was returning to Philippi, so Paul sent this warm letter of encouragement along for the church. Aware that the Philippians were being persecuted, he wanted to support and strengthen them, in part by sharing with them his experience as a prisoner for Christ's sake.

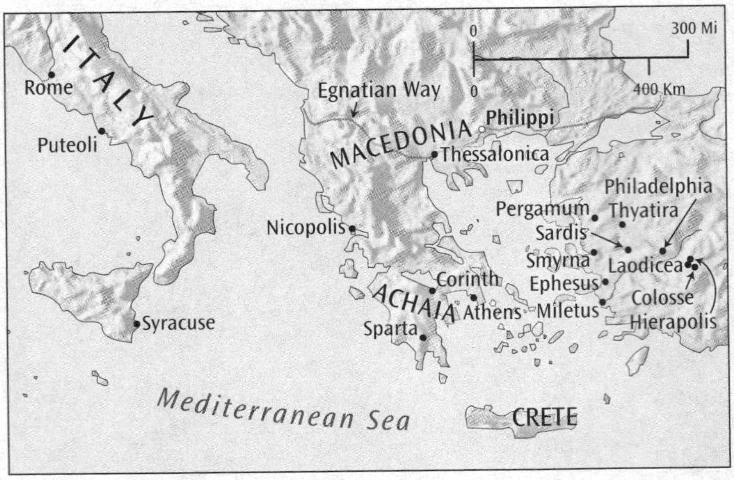

The Setting of Philippians. PHILIPPI was located on the EGNATIAN WAY, a major Roman trade road through MACEDONIA. Paul founded the church there on his second missionary journey (AD 50–52; Acts 15:36–18:22) and visited again during his third missionary journey (about AD 56; see Acts 20:1-2). When Paul wrote to the Philippians, he was in prison, but it is uncertain when or where.

SUMMARY

This letter addresses no major theological or moral problems. It is a warm letter of encouragement sent to a church suffering for its faith.

After a brief introduction (1:1-2), Paul affirms his gratitude to God for the Philippians and prays for their spiritual growth (1:3-11). He then talks about his own experience of imprisonment and the way it has resulted in the spread of the Good News (1:12-19). Paul's greatest desire is to live and die for Christ, whatever his situation (1:20-26). The Philippians, too, must be strong in their faith as they suffer for Christ (1:27-30). They should warmly support one another, remembering the example of Christ, who gave up everything in sacrificing his life for theirs (2:1-18). Paul, too, is willing to do this.

Eager to know how the Philippians are doing and to tell them how he is, Paul will soon be sending Epaphroditus and Timothy to them, both of whom have proven their willingness to suffer for Christ (2:19-30).

Paul next warns the Philippians about Jewish-Christian propaganda requiring adherence to the law of Moses (3:1-3). He recounts his own conversion from Judaism and the Mosaic law. The only important thing now is Christ—knowing Christ and his righteousness, sharing in his suffering and death, and experiencing his resurrection power both now and in the future (3:4-11). All believers are to be single-minded in pursuing full life in Christ (3:12–4:1).

In closing, Paul encourages the Philippians to fill their lives with joy, prayer, and thanksgiving, and to focus their minds on God's good gifts, even in their persecution (4:2-9). He thanks them for the gift they have sent. He tells them that he has learned to be content regardless of his circumstances, and implies that they, too, should learn to live this way (4:1-20). As usual, Paul ends his letter with praise to God, greetings to the believers, and an invocation of the Lord's grace (4:21-23).

OUTLINE

1:1-11
Opening Greetings

1:12-26
Paul's Personal Circumstances

1:27–2:18
The Life in Christ

2:19-30
Plans for Timothy and Epaphroditus

3:1–4:9
Warning against Enemies and Dangers

4:10-20
Thanks for Their Gifts

4:21-23
Final Greetings

DATE AND PLACE OF WRITING

There is no consensus on where or when the Prison Letters (Ephesians, Philippians, Colossians, and Philemon) were written, though all of them speak of having been written from prison. They have traditionally been linked to Rome, where Paul was imprisoned twice (AD 60–62 and around AD 64~65). More recently, scholars have made a case for Ephesus (AD 53~56). During Paul's two- to three-year stay in that city, he experienced much opposition and suffering (see Acts 19:23-41; 2 Cor 11:23-28).

LITERARY UNITY

In order to account for sudden changes of content and tone in the writing (see especially 3:2–4:3 and 4:10-20), some have suggested that Philippians

TIMELINE

AD 50–52
Paul's second missionary journey

AD 53–57
Paul's third missionary journey

AD 59–60
Paul's voyage to Rome

AD 60–62
Paul is imprisoned in Rome, then released

about AD 64~65?
Paul is imprisoned and martyred in Rome

Joy is how believers who know Christ and whose futures are guaranteed by Christ respond in the context of present difficulties. . . . Christ is the gospel; Christ is Savior and Lord; thus Christ is our life; Christ is our way of life; Christ is our future; Christ is our joy.

GORDON FEE
Paul's Letter to the Philippians, p. 53

One of the most positive and delightful of Paul's letters, setting out the sheer joy of the gospel.

ALISTER E. MCGRATH
The NIV Bible Companion, p. 402

is actually a combination of several different letters or fragments joined by an anonymous editor. An early Christian writer, Polycarp, also spoke of "letters" of Paul to the Philippians. Many others, however, judge this to be a single coherent letter, written by Paul, who in his letters often changes the subject unexpectedly to address new issues.

MEANING AND MESSAGE

Paul writes from prison to Christians who are experiencing opposition, encouraging them to imitate his life and attitudes. By speaking of his own courage, commitment, confidence, and contentment even in prison, Paul encourages the Philippians to respond similarly as they face opposition. In doing so, he shows us that a Christian life of joy, peace, contentment, prayer, thanksgiving, and devotion to Christ can transcend all circumstances.

Though Paul is in prison, he is not ashamed but rejoices that it has resulted in a greater spread of the Good News. He desires to be bold for Christ, whatever the consequences, for he knows he is called to live for Christ and he feels privileged to suffer for Christ (see 1:12-26).

Even in prison, Paul can say that his deepest desire is to be completely filled with Christ's life. Paul is ready to share in Christ's suffering and death, and eager to experience the full power of his resurrection. Then, whatever happens, he will one day be raised from the dead like Christ (3:7-14). Meanwhile, Paul has learned to be content whatever his lot in life. He relies on Christ and has found Christ's strength sufficient in even the most trying situations (4:11-13).

Paul urges the Philippians to be full of joy in the Lord as they experience opposition. They are not to worry about anything, but to pray for all their needs with a heart full of gratitude to God. In this way, they will experience the deep peace of God (see 4:4-9).

FURTHER READING

MARKUS BOCKMUEHL
Epistle to the Philippians (2006)

PHILIP W. COMFORT
Philippians in *Cornerstone Biblical Commentary*, vol. 16 (2008)

GORDON FEE
Paul's Letter to the Philippians (1995)

GERALD F. HAWTHORNE AND RALPH MARTIN
Philippians (2004)

PETER T. O'BRIEN
Epistle to the Philippians (1991)

MOISÉS SILVA
Philippians (2005)

1. OPENING GREETINGS (1:1-11)

Greetings from Paul

1 This letter is from Paul and Timothy, [a]slaves of Christ Jesus.
I am writing to all of God's holy people in Philippi who belong to Christ Jesus, including the [b]elders and [c]deacons.
2May God our Father and the Lord Jesus Christ give you grace and peace.

Paul's Thanksgiving and Prayer

3Every time I think of you, I give thanks to
my God. 4Whenever I pray, I make my requests for all of you with joy, 5for you have
been my partners in spreading the Good
News about Christ from the time you first
heard it until now. 6And I am certain that
God, who began the good work within you,
will continue his work until it is finally

1:1 Acts 16:1; 2 Cor 1:1; Col 1:1; Phlm 1:1
[a]*doulos* (1401) ‣Col 3:11
[b]*episkopos* (1985) ‣1 Tim 3:1
[c]*diakonos* (1249) ‣Col 1:7

1:2-3 Rom 1:7-8

1:1-2 Paul introduces his letter by listing the names of the senders and recipients of his letter, then giving an invocation of grace and peace.

1:1 *Timothy* was one of Paul's most trusted co-workers and messengers (see "Timothy" at Acts 16:1-3, p. 1860). He is listed as co-sender, as he is for five other letters (2 Cor, Col, 1 Thes, 2 Thes, Phlm). • ***slaves of Christ Jesus:*** As those who belong entirely to Christ, they were completely devoted to his service (see 2:20-21). • ***God's holy people*** have been made holy in God's sight by Christ's redeeming work (see Eph 1:4, 7; 5:25-27; Col 1:22), and they are being sanctified by the transforming work of the Holy Spirit in their lives (cp. 4:21). • ***Philippi*** was a Roman colony in the province of Macedonia. The church in Philippi was the first Christian community in Greece (see Acts 16:11-40). • In the early church, ***elders*** (or *overseers;* or *bishops*) usually provided spiritual leadership, while ***deacons*** attended to practical matters (see 1 Tim 3:1-13). There were no professional pastors or priests as there are today (cp. 1 Cor 14:26-31).

1:2 ***Grace*** is undeserved blessing that comes from God; ***peace*** is well-being and contentedness rooted in the Good News and brought about by the Holy Spirit (see Gal 5:22). These qualities are gifts from ***God our Father and the Lord Jesus Christ*** (see Rom 5:1-2).

1:3-11 Following his usual practice, Paul thanks God for the recipients and prays for them.

1:4-6 Paul's ***joy*** derived from how the Philippians had joined him as ***partners in spreading the Good News*** and from his confidence that God would ***continue*** his ***good work*** in them.

1:5 Their partnership included financial support (see 4:10-20).

1:6 ***God, who began the good work within you:*** God takes the initiative

1:6 1 Cor 1:8
1:7 2 Cor 7:3; [d]*apologia* (0627) ‣ Phil 1:16
1:8 Rom 1:9
1:9 1 Thes 3:12; [e]*agapē* (0026) ‣ Col 3:14
1:10 Rom 12:2; 1 Cor 1:8
1:11 John 15:4
1:12 2 Tim 2:9
1:13 Acts 28:30-31; Eph 3:1; 4:1
1:14 Phil 1:20
1:15 Phil 2:3
1:16 [f]*apologia* (0627) ‣ 1 Pet 3:15
1:17 Acts 21:33
1:19 2 Cor 1:11
1:20 Rom 5:5; 14:8; 1 Cor 6:20; Eph 6:19
1:21 Gal 2:20; Col 1:27
1:22 Rom 1:13
1:23 2 Cor 5:8; 2 Tim 4:6
1:26 Phil 2:24

finished on the day when Christ Jesus returns.
7So it is right that I should feel as I do
about all of you, for you have a special place
in my heart. You share with me the special
favor of God, both in my imprisonment and
in [d]defending and confirming the truth of
the Good News. 8God knows how much I
love you and long for you with the tender
compassion of Christ Jesus.
9I pray that your [e]love will overflow more
and more, and that you will keep on growing in knowledge and understanding. 10For
I want you to understand what really matters, so that you may live pure and blameless
lives until the day of Christ's return. 11May
you always be filled with the fruit of your
salvation—the righteous character produced in your life by Jesus Christ—for this
will bring much glory and praise to God.

2. PAUL'S PERSONAL CIRCUMSTANCES (1:12-26)

Paul's Joy That Christ Is Preached

12And I want you to know, my dear brothers
and sisters, that everything that has happened to me here has helped to spread the
Good News. 13For everyone here, including
the whole palace guard, knows that I am in
chains because of Christ. 14And because
of my imprisonment, most of the believers
here have gained confidence and boldly
speak God's message without fear.
15It's true that some are preaching out
of jealousy and rivalry. But others preach
about Christ with pure motives. 16They
preach because they love me, for they know
I have been appointed to [f]defend the Good
News. 17Those others do not have pure
motives as they preach about Christ. They
preach with selfish ambition, not sincerely,
intending to make my chains more painful
to me. 18But that doesn't matter. Whether
their motives are false or genuine, the message about Christ is being preached either
way, so I rejoice. And I will continue to rejoice. 19For I know that as you pray for me
and the Spirit of Jesus Christ helps me, this
will lead to my deliverance.

Paul's Life for Christ

20For I fully expect and hope that I will
never be ashamed, but that I will continue to
be bold for Christ, as I have been in the past.
And I trust that my life will bring honor to
Christ, whether I live or die. 21For to me,
living means living for Christ, and dying is
even better. 22But if I live, I can do more fruitful work for Christ. So I really don't know
which is better. 23I'm torn between two desires: I long to go and be with Christ, which
would be far better for me. 24But for your
sakes, it is better that I continue to live.
25Knowing this, I am convinced that I will
remain alive so I can continue to help all of
you grow and experience the joy of your
faith. 26And when I come to you again, you
will have even more reason to take pride
in Christ Jesus because of what he is doing
through me.

to work his salvation in people (see Rom 9:16; Eph 1:3-8, 11; 2:4-10), so he can be trusted to *continue his work* of changing people into the likeness of his Son (see Rom 8:29; Eph 4:13, 15).

1:7 ***You share with me the special favor of God:*** Perhaps their lives were blessed because of Paul's suffering and witness; perhaps they had suffered together with him (see 1:29).

1:9-10 ***Love*** is a fruit of Christ's Spirit within them (Rom 5:5; Gal 5:22). • ***growing in knowledge and understanding:*** In this way, believers can understand ***what really matters*** (see Rom 12:2) and ***live pure and blameless lives until the day of Christ's return*** (cp. 1 Thes 3:12-13; 5:23).

1:11 ***with the fruit of your salvation . . . by Jesus Christ:*** Literally *with the fruit of righteousness through Jesus Christ.* • ***Righteous character*** cannot be produced by human effort; it comes only through the Spirit of Christ working in people's hearts. • ***Glory and praise to God*** is the ultimate purpose for which God's people live (see Eph 1:6, 12, 14).

1:12-19 Paul rejoiced that his imprisonment had resulted in the spread of the Good News.

1:12 ***my dear brothers and sisters:*** Literally *brothers*, a generic term commonly used to address both men and women. • ***Everything that has happened to me here*** refers to Paul's imprisonment. • ***has helped to spread the Good News:*** See Acts 28:17-31 for an example of this.

1:13 ***The whole palace guard*** (literally *including all the Praetorium*) were workers in the emperor's or provincial governor's official residence (see 4:22). • Paul was in prison ***because of Christ***—that is, because of preaching the Good News of Christ (cp. Acts 21:26–28:31).

1:14 As a result of Paul's courage and boldness, ***the believers*** (literally *the brothers in the Lord;* see note on 1:12) had become more daring and less fearful in proclaiming ***God's message*** (some manuscripts read *the message*). Paul's boldness was contagious.

1:15-18 ***some are preaching out of jealousy and rivalry:*** They evidently were believers who were critical of Paul (cp. 2 Cor 10–13; Gal 4:12-20; 5:7-12). Even so, the message about Christ was being preached, so Paul rejoiced.

1:19 ***this will lead to my deliverance:*** Paul expected to be released from prison soon (see 1:25-26; 2:24; contrast 2 Tim 4:6, written from prison at a later time when Paul expected death).

1:21 ***dying is even better:*** For believers, death holds no fear, for death leads directly into the presence of Christ (see 1:23; cp. John 5:24; 11:25-26; Rom 8:38-39).

1:23 ***I long to go and be with Christ:*** Death leads believers immediately into the Lord's presence (cp. 3:20-21; 1 Cor 15:20-23, 51-52; 2 Cor 5:1-8; 1 Thes 4:13-17).

1:25 The well-being of the church is more important to Paul than his own desire to be with Christ. • ***experience the joy of your faith:*** Believers are encouraged to find joy even in the midst of suffering (see 4:4; John 15:11, 20; 16:20-24; 1 Thes 5:16).

3. THE LIFE IN CHRIST (1:27–2:18)

Live as Citizens of Heaven

27 Above all, you must live as citizens of
heaven, conducting yourselves in a manner worthy of the Good News about Christ.
Then, whether I come and see you again or
only hear about you, I will know that you are
standing together with one [g]spirit and one
purpose, fighting together for the [h]faith,
which is the Good News. 28 Don't be intimidated in any way by your enemies. This
will be a sign to them that they are going to
be destroyed, but that you are going to be
saved, even by God himself. 29 For you have
been given not only the privilege of trusting
in Christ but also the privilege of suffering
for him. 30 We are in this struggle together.
You have seen my struggle in the past, and
you know that I am still in the midst of it.

Have the Attitude of Christ

2 Is there any [i]encouragement from belonging to Christ? Any comfort from
his love? Any [j]fellowship together in the
Spirit? Are your hearts tender and compassionate? 2 Then make me truly happy by
agreeing wholeheartedly with each other,
loving one another, and working together
with one mind and purpose.

3 Don't be selfish; don't try to impress others. Be humble, thinking of others as better
than yourselves. 4 Don't look out only for
your own interests, but take an interest in
others, too.

5 You must have the same attitude that
Christ Jesus had.

6 Though he was God,
 he did not think of equality with God
 as something to cling to.
7 Instead, he gave up his divine privileges;
 he took the humble position of a slave
 and was born as a human being.
When he appeared in human form,
8 he humbled himself in obedience to
 God

1:27
Eph 4:1
[g]*pneuma* (4151)
‣1 Thes 5:23
[h]*pistis* (4102)
‣1 Thes 1:3

1:28
2 Tim 2:11
Heb 13:6

1:29
Matt 5:11-12
Acts 5:41

1:30
Acts 16:16-40
1 Thes 2:2

2:1
[i]*paraklēsis* (3874)
‣Col 2:2
[j]*koinōnia* (2842)
‣Phil 3:10

2:2
1 Pet 3:8

2:3
Gal 5:26
1 Pet 5:5

2:4
1 Cor 10:24

2:6
John 1:1-2; 5:18

2:7
John 1:14
Rom 8:3
2 Cor 8:9

Living for Christ (1:21)

Phil 3:7-11, 20
Rom 6:3-14; 8:14-17; 12:1; 14:7-9
1 Cor 6:19
2 Cor 5:14-15
Gal 2:19-20
Eph 1:11, 14

From prison Paul writes, "To me, living means living for Christ" (1:21). Why are believers called to devote their lives to Christ?

1. *Believers acknowledge that they owe everything to Christ,* especially their salvation. Devoting their life to his service expresses their eternal indebtedness and gratitude (see Rom 12:1).

2. *Believers acknowledge Christ as their master and Lord* and submit to Christ's rule in their lives. They recognize that they belong to the Lord and no longer live simply for themselves (see Rom 14:7-9; 2 Cor 5:14-15).

3. *Believers now share in Christ's death and resurrection*—they have died to themselves and have risen with him (see Rom 6:3-14; cp. Gal 2:19-20). They have a new identity in Christ (3:20; Rom 8:14-17; Eph 1:11, 14).

4. *Believers recognize that everything of value is found in Christ.* Things of the world that once seemed important have lost their attraction; nothing compares to the infinite value of knowing Christ (3:7-11; Eph 1:3–3:21; Col 1:15–3:4).

1:27-30 Paul encourages the Philippian Christians to live in a way that is *worthy of the Good News* (cp. Eph 4:1; Col 1:10; 1 Thes 2:12), particularly by standing strong despite persecution.

1:27 As foreigners in this world, the Philippian believers are to *live as citizens of heaven* (cp. 3:20; 1 Pet 2:9-11).

1:28 ***a sign to them that they are going to be destroyed, but that you are going to be saved:*** As translated, the persecutors would be convicted by the Philippians' example. The same Greek phrase could also be translated *a sign to them that you are going to be destroyed, but a sign to you that you are going to be saved.* By that interpretation, the persecutors would remain blind to the truth (cp. 2 Cor 2:15-16).

1:29 ***the privilege of suffering:*** What the world considers dishonorable, Christians consider an honor because it is *for him*—it honors Christ.

1:30 ***We are in this struggle together:*** Both Paul and the Philippians faced strong opposition—Paul was in prison, and the Philippians were being persecuted. • ***You have seen my struggle in the past:*** See Acts 16:11-40; cp. 1 Thes 2:2.

2:1-11 In the midst of their persecution, Paul encourages the Philippians to be united and to live a humble life like Christ.

2:1-2 ***Is there . . . ?*** These rhetorical questions expect positive answers. Those who have a real experience of Christ should live together in harmony and *love.*

2:3-4 ***Don't be selfish:*** Self-centeredness is antithetical to genuine care for others (cp. 2:20-21; 1 Cor 10:24; Gal 5:26).

2:6-11 This early Christian hymn is about Christ's preexistence and divine nature, incarnation and death, exaltation and lordship.

2:6 ***Though he was God:*** Or *Being in the form of God;* see John 1:1-3; 17:5; Col 1:15.

2:7 ***he gave up his divine privileges*** (literally *he emptied himself*): The rest of 2:7-8 explains this ultimate expression of divine self-denial (cp. 2 Cor 8:9). • ***the humble position of a slave*** (or *the form of a slave*): Paul might have been thinking of Isa 52:13–53:12. • ***and was born as a human:*** See John 1:14; 1 Tim 3:16. • ***When he appeared in human form:*** Some English translations put this phrase in v 8.

2:8 ***in obedience to God:*** It was God's will that Jesus die for the sins of humanity (see Isa 53:7; Matt 26:39; John 3:16; 10:17-18; Rom 5:8, 19; 8:3;

2:8
John 10:17-18
2:9
Eph 1:20-21
2:10
Isa 45:23
2:11
John 13:13
[k]*kurios* (2962)
‣ Phil 3:20
[a]*doxa* (1391)
‣ Phil 3:21
2:13
Heb 13:21
2:14
1 Cor 10:10
2:15
John 12:36
Eph 5:1
2:16
1 Thes 2:19
2:17
Rom 15:16
2 Tim 4:6
[b]*leitourgia* (3009)
‣ Heb 1:7

and died a criminal's death on a
cross.
9 Therefore, God elevated him to the place
of highest honor
and gave him the name above all other
names,
10 that at the name of Jesus every knee
should bow,
in heaven and on earth and under the
earth,
11 and every tongue confess that Jesus
Christ is [k]Lord,
to the [a]glory of God the Father.

Shine Brightly for Christ
12Dear friends, you always followed my instructions when I was with you. And now
that I am away, it is even more important.
Work hard to show the results of your
salvation, obeying God with deep reverence and fear.
13For God is working in you,
giving you the desire and the power to do
what pleases him.
14Do everything without complaining
and arguing,
15so that no one can criticize
you. Live clean, innocent lives as children
of God, shining like bright lights in a world
full of crooked and perverse people.
16Hold
firmly to the word of life; then, on the day
of Christ's return, I will be proud that I did
not run the race in vain and that my work
was not useless.
17But I will rejoice even if I
lose my life, pouring it out like a liquid offering to God, just like your faithful [b]service is
an offering to God. And I want all of you to
share that joy.
18Yes, you should rejoice, and
I will share your joy.

The Divine Nature of Christ (2:6-11)

Isa 53:3-12
John 1:1-2, 10-14; 3:14-17
Rom 5:9-10
Col 1:15-22; 2:9, 13-14
Heb 1:1-3; 2:14, 17; 10:9-14
Rev 5:8-14

Philippians 2:6-11, often called the Christ Hymn, reveals early Christian beliefs about the nature of Jesus Christ. This hymn affirms that the early Christians believed in the preexistence and divine nature of Christ (see also Col 1:15-20; 2:9; cp. John 1:1-2; Heb 1:1-3). Christ is not simply another human prophet. He was present with God the Father from the very beginning, and he is the one through whom the universe was created. As the Son of God, he shares the nature of God himself.

The hymn also affirms that Jesus Christ came to earth in an act of immense humility—the infinite God became human (2:7; see Col 1:15; John 1:10-14; Heb 2:14, 17). Jesus Christ, the glorious Creator of the universe, died as a sacrificial offering for the sins of human beings so that we might be forgiven and be reconciled to God (2:8; see John 3:14-17; Rom 5:9-10; Col 1:20, 22; 2:13-14; Heb 1:3; 10:9-14), as the Scriptures had foretold (see Isa 53:3-12).

This hymn also affirms that God raised Jesus from the dead, has given him "the place of highest honor" in heaven (2:9), and conferred on him the title "Lord" (2:11; cp. Col 1:18). One day, all created beings will bow before him and acknowledge that he is Lord of the entire universe (2:9-11), deserving of the worship that God alone is worthy to receive (see Rev 5:8-14).

Heb 5:8; 1 Jn 4:9-10, 14). • ***a criminal's death on a cross:*** In the Roman empire, crucifixion was a cruel and humiliating punishment for criminals.

2:9 As a result of Christ's humble obedience, ***God elevated him to the place of highest honor;*** see Acts 1:9-10; cp. Acts 2:32-33; 7:55-56. • ***the name above all other names:*** Jesus has supreme authority and power (2:10-11; cp. Matt 28:18; John 17:5; Acts 2:33-36; Heb 2:9; 12:2).

2:10-11 The entire creation, including spiritual powers and angels, humans on ***earth,*** and those who have died, will one day acknowledge the authority of ***Jesus Christ*** as ***Lord*** (see Eph 1:9-10, 21; Col 1:20-25; 1 Pet 3:22). • ***every tongue confess*** (cp. Isa 45:23; Rom 14:11): This does not imply universal salvation, because not all will confess him as Lord freely out of love and devotion. • ***Lord,*** a divine title representing the OT name Yahweh, is frequently applied to Jesus in the NT.

2:12-18 Paul encourages believers to remain firm in their faith and to live faithful, obedient, and pure lives modeled after Christ.

2:12 ***obeying God*** (see John 3:36; Rom 1:5): Believers must reckon with God's judgment like everyone else (cp. 1 Cor 3:10-13), so they must live before him obediently, ***with deep reverence and fear.***

2:13 ***For God is working in you:*** God empowers and energizes believers' lives (see John 15:5; 1 Cor 12:6; 15:10; 2 Cor 3:5; 1 Thes 2:13). Both ***the desire and the power to do what pleases him*** come from God.

2:14 ***Complaining and arguing*** arise from self-centeredness (see 1 Cor 10:10; 1 Pet 4:9; Jude 1:16), whereas believers are called to sacrificial love (2:4).

2:15 ***shining like bright lights:*** Believers are to draw people to God by their lives (see Matt 5:13-16). • ***in a world full of crooked and perverse people:*** See Deut 32:5; Rom 1:18-32; 3:10-23.

2:16 ***Hold firmly to the word of life:*** Believers must maintain their faith in Christ's life-giving Good News. God is faithful, but they, too, must remain faithful (1:6; 2:12-13). • ***run the race:*** Paul frequently uses athletic language as a metaphor for the Christian life (see 3:12-14; 1 Cor 9:24, 26; Gal 2:2; 5:7; 2 Tim 4:7).

2:17-18 ***I will rejoice even if I lose my life, pouring it out like a liquid offering to God*** (literally *I will rejoice even if I am to be poured out as a liquid offering*): Both Jews and pagans often poured out a libation of wine either on a sacrifice or at the base of the altar in honor of the deity. Paul's entire life was an offering to God (cp. Rom 12:1; 15:16). • ***Faithful service*** is a cause for rejoicing, because nothing done for God is in vain (see 1 Cor 15:58).

4. PLANS FOR TIMOTHY AND EPAPHRODITUS (2:19-30)

Paul Commends Timothy

19If the Lord Jesus is willing, I hope to send
Timothy to you soon for a visit. Then he can
cheer me up by telling me how you are getting along. 20I have no one else like Timothy,
who genuinely cares about your welfare.
21All the others care only for themselves
and not for what matters to Jesus Christ.
22But you know how Timothy has proved
himself. Like a son with his father, he has
served with me in preaching the Good
News. 23I hope to send him to you just as
soon as I find out what is going to happen
to me here. 24And I have confidence from
the Lord that I myself will come to see you
soon.

Paul Commends Epaphroditus

25Meanwhile, I thought I should send Epaphroditus back to you. He is a true brother,
co-worker, and fellow soldier. And he was
your messenger to help me in my need. 26I
am sending him because he has been longing to see you, and he was very distressed
that you heard he was ill. 27And he certainly
was ill; in fact, he almost died. But God had
mercy on him—and also on me, so that I
would not have one sorrow after another.
28So I am all the more anxious to send
him back to you, for I know you will be glad
to see him, and then I will not be so worried
about you. 29Welcome him with Christian
love and with great joy, and give him the
honor that people like him deserve. 30For
he risked his life for the work of Christ, and
he was at the point of death while doing for
me what you couldn't do from far away.

5. WARNING AGAINST ENEMIES AND DANGERS (3:1–4:9)

The Priceless Value of Knowing Christ

3 Whatever happens, my dear brothers
and sisters, rejoice in the Lord. I never
get tired of telling you these things, and I do
it to safeguard your faith.
2Watch out for those dogs, those people
who do evil, those mutilators who say you
must be circumcised to be saved. 3For we
who worship by the Spirit of God are the
ones who are truly circumcised. We rely on
what Christ Jesus has done for us. We put
no confidence in human effort, 4though I
could have confidence in my own effort if
anyone could. Indeed, if others have reason
for confidence in their own efforts, I have
even more!
5I was circumcised when I was eight days
old. I am a pure-blooded citizen of Israel
and a member of the tribe of Benjamin—a
real Hebrew if there ever was one! I was a
member of the Pharisees, who demand the
strictest obedience to the Jewish law. 6I was
so zealous that I harshly persecuted the

2:20 1 Cor 16:10
2:21 1 Cor 10:24
2:22 1 Cor 4:17; 1 Tim 1:2
2:24 Phil 1:25-26
2:25 Phil 4:18
2:26 Phil 1:8
2:29 1 Cor 16:16, 18; 1 Tim 5:17
2:30 1 Cor 16:17
3:1 Phil 2:18; 4:4
3:2 Ps 22:16, 20; Rev 22:15
3:3 John 4:21-24; Rom 2:29; Gal 6:15; Col 2:11
3:5 Luke 1:59; 2:21; Acts 23:6; Rom 11:1; 2 Cor 11:22
3:6 Acts 8:3; 22:4; 26:9-11; Rom 10:5; Gal 1:13
3:7 Matt 13:44; Luke 14:33
3:8 John 17:3; Eph 4:13; 2 Pet 3:18

2:19-24 Paul commends ***Timothy,*** whom he hopes to send to the Philippians in the near future. Timothy had accompanied Paul on his first trip to Philippi (see Acts 16:1-3, 12; 17:15; 18:5; cp. Acts 19:22). Timothy stood out as a person whose whole life was sacrificially devoted to ***what matters to Jesus Christ*** and to the ***welfare*** of his people.

2:23 *What is going to happen to me here* possibly refers to the outcome of Paul's trial.

2:24 Paul had ***confidence*** that he would soon be freed from prison and be able to visit the Philippians (see 1:19, 25-26).

2:25-30 Paul commends ***Epaphroditus*** (see also 4:18), a messenger from the church at Philippi whom he was now sending back to them, perhaps carrying this letter. • The description ***fellow soldier*** suggests the difficulties, opposition, and dangers encountered in Christ's work.

2:27 Epaphroditus's recovery from a nearly fatal illness is attributed to God's ***mercy,*** both on Epaphroditus and on Paul, who was already suffering in prison.

2:29-30 *Welcome him with Christian love:* Literally *Welcome him in the Lord.* • Epaphroditus deserved their ***honor,*** for ***he risked his life*** for Christ on their behalf (for the importance of showing honor, cp. Rom 10:12; 13:7; Eph 5:33; 6:2; 1 Tim 5:17; 6:1; 1 Pet 2:17; 3:7).

3:1 *my dear brothers and sisters:* Literally *brothers;* also in 3:13, 17. See note on 1:12. • ***rejoice in the Lord:*** This theme is resumed in 4:4 (see also 1:18; 2:17-18, 28; 4:10). • The phrase ***these things*** (literally *the same things*) is ambiguous: it may refer to (1) the immediately preceding encouragement to ***rejoice in the Lord***; (2) the earlier encouragement to follow Christ's example (2:1-18); (3) Paul's exhortation in general; or (4) the following warning about threats to their faith.

3:2-11 Paul warns the believers against being influenced by Jewish Christians who argued that circumcision is necessary for salvation. He then talks about his own conversion from Judaism to Christ.

3:2 *those dogs, . . . those mutilators:* Here Paul reverses the traditional Jewish practice of referring to Gentiles as *dogs* (cp. Mark 7:27-28). Paul's strongest insults are directed against Jews who preached that Gentiles must be circumcised in order to be saved (cp. 2 Cor 11:13-15; Gal 1:6-9; 5:1-6, 12).

3:3 *worship by the Spirit of God:* some manuscripts read *worship God in spirit;* one early manuscript reads *worship in spirit* (cp. John 4:24). • Circumcision was understood as identifying a true man of God (see Gen 17:10-14), but those who put their trust in Christ are ***the ones who are truly circumcised*** in heart (see Rom 2:28-29; cp. Jer 4:4; Eph 2:11; Col 2:11-13).

3:4 *in my own effort* (literally *in the flesh*): Paul uses *flesh* for self-reliance and human effort in contrast to reliance on Christ and empowerment by the Spirit.

3:5-6 If anyone could rely on Jewish credentials, Paul could: He practiced ***the strictest obedience to the Jewish law*** and was extremely ***zealous*** for the Jewish religion.

3:5 *circumcised when I was eight days old:* See Gen 17:12; Lev 12:3; Luke 1:59; 2:21. • Paul was ***a member of the Pharisees,*** the Jewish sect known for its strict observance of the law (see Acts 23:6; 26:5; see also "The Pharisees" at Matt 3:7, p. 1581).

3:6 *I harshly persecuted the church* (see Acts 8:1-3; 9:1-2, 21; Gal 1:13):

3:9
Rom 1:17; 3:21-22; 9:30; 10:3
Gal 2:16
2 Pet 1:1
[c]*dikaiosunē* (1343)
‣1 Tim 6:11

3:10
Rom 6:3-5; 8:17, 29
Gal 6:17
[d]*anastasis* (0386)
‣Heb 11:35
[e]*koinōnia* (2842)
‣Phlm 1:6

3:11
1 Cor 15:23

3:13
Luke 9:62

3:14
1 Cor 9:24
2 Tim 4:7-8
Heb 12:1

3:15
1 Cor 2:6
Phil 1:9-10

3:17
1 Cor 4:16
1 Pet 5:3
[f]*tupos* (5179)
‣1 Thes 1:7

church. And as for righteousness, I obeyed the law without fault.

[7]I once thought these things were valuable, but now I consider them worthless because of what Christ has done. [8]Yes, everything else is worthless when compared with the infinite value of knowing Christ Jesus my Lord. For his sake I have discarded everything else, counting it all as garbage, so that I could gain Christ [9]and become one with him. I no longer count on my own [c]righteousness through obeying the law; rather, I become righteous through faith in Christ. For God's way of making us [c]right with himself depends on faith. [10]I want to know Christ and experience the mighty power that [d]raised him from the dead. I want to suffer [e]with him, sharing in his death, [11]so that one way or another I will experience the resurrection from the dead!

Pressing toward the Goal

[12]I don't mean to say that I have already achieved these things or that I have already reached perfection. But I press on to possess that perfection for which Christ Jesus first possessed me. [13]No, dear brothers and sisters, I have not achieved it, but I focus on this one thing: Forgetting the past and looking forward to what lies ahead, [14]I press on to reach the end of the race and receive the heavenly prize for which God, through Christ Jesus, is calling us.

[15]Let all who are spiritually mature agree on these things. If you disagree on some point, I believe God will make it plain to you. [16]But we must hold on to the progress we have already made.

[17]Dear brothers and sisters, pattern your lives after mine, and learn from those who follow our [f]example. [18]For I have told you

Christian Joy (3:1; 4:4)

John 15:11; 16:24
Rom 5:3-4; 8:28
Gal 5:22
Eph 5:18
1 Thes 5:16

In this letter to a persecuted church, Paul urges Christians to be filled with joy (see 3:1; 4:4), just as he does the persecuted Thessalonian believers ("always be joyful," 1 Thes 5:16). In the last hours of his life, Jesus also desired that his disciples "be filled with [his] joy" (see John 15:11; 16:24).

Superficial happiness is dependent on circumstances. Christian joy is clearly different; it is rooted in a person's relationship with the Lord, and it is resilient even in the midst of suffering and death. Joy comes in knowing that whatever happens, God will use everything for our ultimate good (see Rom 5:3-4; 8:28). Believers also have joy from the dynamic presence of God's Spirit in their hearts (see Gal 5:22). The real secret to a joyful life is in being continuously "filled with the Holy Spirit" (Eph 5:18). The life and attitude of believers are not defined by outward circumstances, but by their relationship with the living God.

His actions demonstrated his zeal for Judaism, to which the Good News of Jesus was seen as a threat. • Paul's ***righteousness***, as judged by human standards, was another indication of his zeal for ***the law*** (see also Gal 1:14; for Paul's later Christian view, cp. Rom 3:23; 7:14-25).

3:7-8 As a Christian, Paul now regarded ***these things*** (3:5-6) as ***worthless because of what Christ has done:*** A believer's relationship with God is defined by ***knowing Christ*** (cp. 3:10; John 17:3) and nothing else. The only important thing is to ***gain Christ***, thus receiving the gift of eternal salvation (cp. John 3:16; 1 Jn 5:11-13). By comparison, all other things are meaningless ***garbage*** (or *excrement*).

3:9 Paul here summarizes the contrast between his understanding of salvation and that of his opponents (3:2). • Believers ***become one with*** Christ by trusting him for salvation and sharing his life (cp. John 15:1-5). • We ***become righteous***, not by observing the law of Moses, but ***through faith in Christ*** (or *through the faithfulness of Christ*). This is ***God's way of making us right with himself:*** Salvation cannot be earned, but only received as a free gift (see Rom 1:17; 3:21-26; 4:5-8; Gal 2:16; Eph 2:8-9).

3:10 ***to know Christ:*** In knowing him, a person knows and is accepted by God (cp. 3:7-8; John 1:12-13; 17:3). • Believers ***experience the mighty power that raised him from the dead***, both now and in eternity (see Rom 6:4-14; 8:10-11; Col 3:1-4). • ***to suffer with him, sharing in his death:*** Joined to Christ, a believer has the privilege of experiencing his life and death (see 1:29; 2 Cor 4:10-12; Col 1:24; 1 Pet 4:13-16).

3:11 To ***experience the resurrection from the dead*** is to be saved from judgment and receive eternal life (see Rev 20:4-6). Paul was aware of God's holiness and the severity of the final judgment (Rev 20:11-15); he knew he must persevere in his pursuit of Christ and salvation (cp. Gal 5:5).

3:12–4:1 Using himself as an example, Paul encourages the Philippians to pursue Christ and the hope of heaven with determination and strength.

3:13-14 ***not achieved it:*** Some manuscripts read *not yet achieved it.* • ***the race:*** See note on 2:16. • Paul was willing to give up everything else for the ultimate goal, ***the heavenly prize*** of eternal life.

3:15 Those who are ***spiritually mature*** (cp. 1 Cor 2:6; 3:1) will share Paul's perspective that eternal things are most important in life (3:12-14; cp. 2 Cor 4:16-18).

3:16 ***hold on to the progress we have already made:*** There must be no slipping or reversal; as believers, our conduct must be consistent with our spiritual understanding.

3:17 ***pattern your lives after mine:*** Paul's serious pursuit of Christ and the life to which God had called him (3:7-14; 4:9; 1 Cor 4:6, 16-17; 11:1; 2 Thes 3:7-9) contrasts markedly with that of the enemies of Christ who are described next (3:18-19).

3:18 The identity of the ***enemies*** is not known; they might have been (1) Jews or Jewish Christians proud of their

often before, and I say it again with tears in my eyes, that there are many whose conduct shows they are really enemies of the cross of Christ. 19They are headed for destruction. Their god is their appetite, they brag about shameful things, and they think only about this life here on earth. 20But we are citizens of heaven, where the [g]Lord Jesus Christ lives. And we are eagerly waiting for him to return as our [h]Savior. 21He will take our weak mortal bodies and [i]change them into [j]glorious bodies like his own, using the same power with which he will bring everything under his control.

4 Therefore, my dear brothers and sisters, stay true to the Lord. I love you and long to see you, dear friends, for you are my joy and the crown I receive for my work.

Words of Encouragement

2Now I appeal to Euodia and Syntyche. Please, because you belong to the Lord, settle your disagreement. 3And I ask you, my true partner, to help these two women, for they worked hard with me in telling others the Good News. They worked along with Clement and the rest of my co-workers, whose names are written in the Book of Life.

4Always be full of joy in the Lord. I say it again—rejoice! 5Let everyone see that you are considerate in all you do. Remember, the Lord is coming soon.

6Don't worry about anything; instead, pray about everything. Tell God what you need, and thank him for all he has done. 7Then you will experience God's [k]peace, which exceeds anything we can understand. His peace will guard your hearts and minds as you live in Christ Jesus.

8And now, dear brothers and sisters, one final thing. Fix your thoughts on what is true, and honorable, and right, and pure, and lovely, and admirable. Think about things that are [a]excellent and worthy of praise. 9Keep putting into practice all you learned and received from me—everything you heard from me and saw me doing. Then the God of [b]peace will be with you.

6. THANKS FOR THEIR GIFTS (4:10-20)

10How I praise the Lord that you are concerned about me again. I know you have always been concerned for me, but you

3:19
Rom 8:5-6; 16:18

3:20
Col 3:1-3
Heb 12:22-23
[g]*kurios* (2962)
›2 Thes 3:16
[h]*sōtēr* (4990)
›1 Tim 4:10

3:21
1 Cor 15:24-28, 43-53
[i]*metaschēmatizō* (3345)
›Matt 17:2
[j]*doxa* (1391)
›Luke 2:14

4:3
Rev 3:5; 20:12, 15

4:5
Heb 10:37
Jas 5:8-9

4:6
Matt 6:25
1 Pet 5:7

4:7
Isa 26:3
John 14:27
[k]*eirēnē* (1515)
›Phil 4:9

4:8
[a]*aretē* (0703)
›1 Pet 2:9

4:9
Rom 15:33; 16:20
1 Cor 14:33
1 Thes 5:23
[b]*eirēnē* (1515)
›Col 3:15

4:10
2 Cor 11:9

circumcision (as in 3:2), whose emphasis on observant Judaism contradicted *the cross of Christ*; (2) pseudo-believers living a worldly, immoral life (cp. 3:19); or (3) professing believers who had rejected Paul's cross-centered view of the Good News. Christ's crucifixion as a criminal was scandalous and offensive to many (see 1 Cor 1:23; cp. Rom 9:33; 1 Pet 2:8).

3:19 ***Their god is their appetite*** may refer to their greed, their sensuality, or their self-interest (cp. Rom 16:18). • ***they brag about shameful things:*** This is best understood as a reference to immorality rather than to pride in being circumcised. • Eternal ***destruction*** is the ultimate judgment of God for those who reject Christ and live self-centered, sinful lives (see 2 Thes 1:8-9; cp. Phil 1:28; Matt 7:13; Rom 9:22; 1 Cor 1:18; 2 Thes 2:10; 1 Tim 6:9; 2 Pet 2:3, 13; Jude 1:10; Rev 11:18). • They are unable to see beyond ***this life*** (cp. John 12:25; 1 Jn 2:15-17).

3:20 By contrast, believers who know their home is in ***heaven*** (see Eph 2:19) with ***the Lord Jesus Christ*** fill their minds with thoughts of heaven (see Col 3:1-2; cp. 1 Cor 15:19; 1 Pet 2:11) and Christ's ***return*** (see 1 Cor 1:7; Titus 2:13).

3:21 ***change them into glorious bodies:*** See 1 Cor 15:42-54; cp. Rom 8:23. • ***he will bring everything under his control:*** See 1 Cor 15:24-27.

4:1 ***my dear brothers and sisters:*** Literally *brothers;* also in 4:8. See note on 1:12. • ***stay true to the Lord*** (literally *stand in the Lord*): Cp. 1:27. • Their continuing faithfulness to Christ was a deep source of *joy* to Paul and the *crown* for his hard work (see 1 Thes 2:19-20).

4:2-9 Before closing, Paul addresses a small conflict in the church and writes a few words of encouragement.

4:2 ***because you belong to the Lord, settle your disagreement:*** The Lord's people are to live together in harmony (see 2:2; 1 Cor 1:10; Eph 4:1-3, 31-32; Col 3:12-15). The nature of the dispute between ***Euodia and Syntyche*** is unknown.

4:3 ***my true partner*** or ***loyal Syzygus***: The Greek word *suzuge* is either a proper name or a description; this person is unknown. • Nothing more is known of ***Clement.*** • Those ***whose names are written in the Book of Life*** are true believers, destined to receive eternal life (see Luke 10:20; Rev 3:5; 13:8; 17:8; 20:12, 15; 21:27; cp. Exod 32:32; Ps 69:28; Dan 12:1).

4:4-6 ***rejoice! . . . pray . . . thank him:*** Cp. 1 Thes 5:16-18; both passages are addressed to persecuted churches; see also Rom 12:12.

4:4 In Paul's letters, *joy* and rejoicing are a response to the Good News (see Eph 5:19-20). Joy is not dependent on circumstances; believers find joy ***in the Lord*** even in the midst of suffering. • ***rejoice!*** See 2:18; 3:1; Rom 12:12, 15; 1 Thes 5:16.

4:5 Believers are to be ***considerate*** in their responses to others, even in persecution. They can afford to leave justice in God's hands because they know ***the Lord is coming soon*** (cp. Jas 5:8-9).

4:6 Believers need not ***worry about anything*** because the heavenly Father loves his children and cares about their needs, and he has invited his children to ***pray about everything*** (see Matt 6:25-34; 7:9-11; Rom 12:12; Eph 6:18; 1 Thes 5:17; 1 Pet 5:7).

4:7 The life of trusting God (4:6) brings ***God's peace*** (see also Isa 26:3; John 14:27; Col 3:15).

4:8 Paul urges the Philippians to focus on God's good gifts so that, even during suffering and persecution, their lives will be exemplary and their minds and hearts will be filled with peace (4:7, 9).

4:9 ***all you learned and received from me:*** Everything Paul had taught them by word or example about the kind of life God desires (see 3:17; 1 Cor 4:6, 16-17; 2 Thes 3:7-9).

4:10-20 In closing, Paul thanks the Philippians for the gift they had sent him by the hand of Epaphroditus.

4:10 Why they ***didn't have the chance to help*** him earlier is not clear.

4:11 1 Tim 6:6
4:12 1 Cor 4:11; 2 Cor 11:9
4:13 2 Cor 12:9-10
4:14 Heb 10:33-34
4:15 2 Cor 11:8-9
4:16 Acts 17:1; 1 Thes 2:9
4:17 1 Cor 9:11
4:18 2 Cor 9:12
4:19 2 Cor 9:8; ^c*ploutos* (4149) ‣1 Tim 6:17
4:20 Rom 11:36
4:23 Gal 6:18; 2 Tim 4:22

didn't have the chance to help me. [11]Not
that I was ever in need, for I have learned
how to be content with whatever I have. [12]I
know how to live on almost nothing or with
everything. I have learned the secret of living in every situation, whether it is with a
full stomach or empty, with plenty or little.
[13]For I can do everything through Christ,
who gives me strength. [14]Even so, you have
done well to share with me in my present
difficulty.

[15]As you know, you Philippians were
the only ones who gave me financial help
when I first brought you the Good News
and then traveled on from Macedonia. No
other church did this. [16]Even when I was in
Thessalonica you sent help more than once.
[17]I don't say this because I want a gift from
you. Rather, I want you to receive a reward
for your kindness.

[18]At the moment I have all I need—and
more! I am generously supplied with the
gifts you sent me with Epaphroditus. They
are a sweet-smelling sacrifice that is acceptable and pleasing to God. [19]And this same
God who takes care of me will supply all
your needs from his glorious ^c riches, which
have been given to us in Christ Jesus.

[20]Now all glory to God our Father forever
and ever! Amen.

7. FINAL GREETINGS (4:21-23)

[21]Give my greetings to each of God's holy
people—all who belong to Christ Jesus. The
brothers who are with me send you their
greetings. [22]And all the rest of God's people
send you greetings, too, especially those in
Caesar's household.

[23]May the grace of the Lord Jesus Christ
be with your spirit.

4:11-12 As a slave of Christ, Paul has learned to ***be content*** with ***every situation,*** whether he had ***plenty or little.*** His life was filled with the joy that comes from doing the will of God whatever the cost.

4:13 ***through Christ*** (literally *through the one*): With Christ's help, Paul had the strength to *do everything*. In everything, especially while enduring suffering, Paul relied on the strength of Christ, who lived in him and worked through him (see 2 Cor 1:8-10; 4:7-12; 12:8-10; Gal 2:20; Col 1:27).

4:14 The Philippians' generosity and care were commendable, especially given Paul's *present difficulty* in prison.

4:15 ***the only ones who gave me financial help:*** By contrast, Paul determined not to accept financial help from the Corinthians because it would have damaged the reputation of the Good News in their eyes (1 Cor 9:11-18; 2 Cor 11:7-12). He did not face such a problem with the Philippians. • ***when I first brought you the Good News:*** See Acts 16:11-40.

4:16 After leaving Philippi (4:15) Paul had gone to *Thessalonica* (see Acts 17:1-8; cp. 1 Thes 2:1-14).

4:17 ***I don't say this because I want a gift from you:*** Paul preferred to support himself (see Acts 18:3; 1 Cor 4:12; 9:3-18; 2 Cor 11:7-11; 12:14-15). • The ***reward*** would be a blessing from God.

4:18 ***Epaphroditus*** (see also 2:25-30) had carried ***the gifts*** from Philippi. • Their gifts were ***a sweet-smelling sacrifice:*** In the OT, acceptable offerings were a pleasant fragrance to God (see Lev 1:9, 13, 17; 2:2, 9; 3:5, 16; cp. Rom 12:1; Eph 5:2).

4:20 Having reflected on God's glorious blessings, Paul concludes appropriately with an expression of praise to God.

4:22 ***Those in Caesar's household*** were believers employed in the service of the Roman government—perhaps those whom Paul had evangelized while in prison. They might have been ***especially*** close to Paul and concerned for him in prison (see 1:13).

4:23 In closing, Paul usually invokes ***the grace of the Lord Jesus Christ*** on those to whom he writes (see also 1:2). Believers depend on Christ's grace to save and sustain them. • The ***spirit*** is the part of the person that relates directly to God.

PAUL'S LETTER TO THE COLOSSIANS

The letter to the Colossians is a beautiful blend of theology and practice. It combines some of the deepest and most sublime teaching about Christ with very basic instruction. As strongly as any other book in the NT, Colossians reminds us that Christ must always be preeminent in a Christian's affections and worship.

SETTING

The city of Colosse was located about 120 miles (193 kilometers) east of Ephesus, in Asia Minor (modern-day Turkey).

Paul mentions Epaphras as the one who first brought the Good News to the Colossians (1:7). Epaphras was probably converted during Paul's three-year ministry in Ephesus. Ephesus was the commercial and governmental center for the whole province, which included Colosse. Luke tells us that during Paul's time in Ephesus, "people throughout the province of Asia . . . heard the word of the Lord" (Acts 19:10). While Paul had not visited Colosse (2:1), he was the spiritual "father" of Epaphras and thus the spiritual "grandfather" of their church. So he wrote with both apostolic authority and personal concern.

When Colossians was written, Epaphras was visiting Paul in prison (4:12). He had told Paul about some of the difficulties the young church was going through. He was especially concerned about some false teachers in Colosse who were emphasizing the importance of "spiritual rulers and authorities" and "spiritual powers of this world," and thus were detracting from Christ's preeminence. Paul wrote to address these issues.

SUMMARY

Colossians divides into two parts, with chs 1–2 focused on theology and chs 3–4 on practical matters.

Paul's greetings (1:1-2) are followed by a thanksgiving section (1:3-14), a typical way of opening a NT letter. Then, to make his key theological point, Paul quotes and adapts a hymn about the supremacy of Christ (1:15-20), then makes a practical

The Setting of Colossians. The church in COLOSSE was founded by a believer named Epaphras (see 1:7), who had probably heard the Good News in EPHESUS, either during or after Paul's ministry there (see Acts 19:1–20:1). Paul sent this letter by the hand of Epaphras, who was visiting Paul in prison.

application (1:21-23) before discussing his own ministry as apostle to the Gentiles (1:24–2:5). He then returns to his main point, urging the Colossians to maintain their allegiance to Christ Jesus, the one who provides for their spiritual life (2:6-15). The theological part of the letter concludes with a warning not to become preoccupied with rules as a means to spiritual fulfillment (2:16-23).

The more practical part of the letter (chs 3–4) opens with a general call to turn from sin and embrace the new life in Christ (3:1-11). Paul follows this with instructions for the Christian community (3:12-17) and family life (3:18–4:1). The letter concludes with an exhortation to prayer (4:2-6) and remarks about co-workers and other Christians (4:7-18).

DATE AND OCCASION OF WRITING

Remember my chains. *Colossians 4:18*

Colossians, along with Ephesians, Philemon, and Philippians, are called "prison letters." All four were written while Paul was in jail for preaching about Jesus Christ (see 4:18). Ephesians, Colossians, and Philemon are closely related, having probably been written from the same place at about the same time (either Rome or Ephesus—see Ephesians Introduction, "Date and Place of Writing," p. 1996). These three letters share common themes and vocabulary and were written to people in the same part of the world: Colosse was only about 120 miles east of Ephesus in the Roman province of Asia Minor, and Philemon was a resident of Colosse.

Paul mentioned some of the same co-workers in each of the prison letters. In his letter to Philemon, he explained why he was sending Onesimus, Philemon's runaway slave, back to him. Onesimus also traveled with the letter to the Colossians (4:9). In both Colossians (4:7) and Ephesians (Eph 6:21), Paul said that Tychicus would give the churches more detailed information about Paul's situation. So Tychicus was probably the messenger who carried these three letters to their destinations in Asia Minor.

OUTLINE

1:1-2
Introduction: Greetings from Paul

1:3–2:23
The Good News about Christ

3:1–4:6
Living the New Life in Christ

4:7-18
Conclusion: Paul's Final Instructions and Greetings

THE FALSE TEACHING

Paul wrote to the Colossians because false teachers were disturbing the church. Colosse was an important commercial center on one of the main Roman roads in its region, so the city would have been exposed to ideas from many religions and philosophies. Like many false teachings, the "Colossian heresy" was probably a mixture of various attitudes and ideas that were in the air at the time. We cannot identify these false teachers or the details of their particular teaching, but we can see some characteristics: (1) The false teachers were apparently insisting on the observance of

TIMELINE

Passover, AD 30 or 33
Jesus' crucifixion and resurrection

AD 50–52
Paul's second missionary journey

AD 53–57
Paul's third missionary journey

AD 53~56
Paul's ministry in Ephesus, founding of the church in Colosse

AD 59–60
Paul's voyage to Rome

AD 60–62
Paul is imprisoned in Rome, then released

about AD 64~65?
Paul is imprisoned and martyred in Rome

Those who are incorporated into [Christ] have come to fullness of life in him who is master over every principality and power.

PETER T. O'BRIEN
Colossians, Philemon, p. xxxix

Sabbath and new moon festivals (2:16), which suggests some Jewish input in their viewpoint; (2) they were preoccupied with following various rules, particularly pertaining to the body (asceticism); and (3) their emphasis on spiritual beings was typical of many religious movements of the period. The basic problem is clear: The teaching did not regard Christ as the center and origin of all religious experience. Any teaching or philosophy that fails to do so is not the Good News.

MEANING AND MESSAGE

In his letter to the Colossians, Paul steers a young Christian church back to the apostles' message of the Good News about Christ. To counter the influence of false teaching, Paul insisted that Christ is supreme (literally *firstborn*; see note on 1:15) over all beings in creation, both spiritual and physical. Jesus is the one in whom the very fullness of God resides. Jesus is also the only ultimate source of spiritual growth, the center from which all true spiritual experience must radiate (2:19). The false teachers were deriving their emphasis on rules from something other than Christ, and this meant that the rules could not produce spiritual benefit (2:23). In this case, Paul argues, addition means subtraction: Trying to add anything to Christ leads to subtracting the power that he alone gives to lead the Christian life.

Christ has reconciled us to the God in whom we now live, so all of our spiritual needs are fulfilled by Christ. We need no one and nothing else for true spiritual fulfillment.

Paul urged the Colossians to avoid putting too much stock in ritual practices (2:16-23). Instead, all Christians should identify with Christ in his death and resurrection (2:11, 19-20; 3:1-4) and let the Good News, as preached by the apostles, mold their thinking and behavior. Colossians reminds us that we must keep Christ at the center of all that we do, in our own spiritual journey and in the life of the church. Adding to Christ is inevitably a distortion of true Christian faith.

FURTHER READING

PETER DAVIDS
Colossians in *Cornerstone Biblical Commentary*, vol. 16 (2008)

DAVID E. GARLAND
Colossians/Philemon (1998)

PETER T. O'BRIEN
Colossians, Philemon (1982)

MARIANNE MEYE THOMPSON
Colossians & Philemon (2005)

N. T. WRIGHT
The Epistles of Paul to the Colossians and to Philemon (1987)

1. INTRODUCTION: GREETINGS FROM PAUL (1:1-2)

1 This letter is from Paul, chosen by the will of God to be an apostle of Christ Jesus, and from our brother Timothy.

2 We are writing to God's holy people in the city of Colosse, who are faithful brothers and sisters in Christ.

May God our Father give you grace and peace.

2. THE GOOD NEWS ABOUT CHRIST (1:3–2:23)

Paul's Thanksgiving and Prayer

3 We always pray for you, and we give thanks
to God, the Father of our Lord Jesus Christ.
4 For we have heard of your faith in Christ
Jesus and your love for all of God's people,
5 which come from your confident [a]hope of
what God has reserved for you in heaven.
You have had this expectation ever since

1:1 1 Cor 1:1; Eph 1:1
1:2 Rom 1:7
1:4 Eph 1:15
1:5 Eph 1:13; 1 Pet 1:4; [a]*elpis* (1680) 1 Thes 5:8
1:6 Rom 1:13

1:1 *Timothy* was one of Paul's closest co-workers (see "Timothy" at Acts 16:1-3, p. 1860). So close was their relationship and so significant Timothy's ministry that Paul included him as one of the senders of this letter as well as of 2 Corinthians, Philippians, 1 and 2 Thessalonians, and Philemon.

1:2 *Colosse* was situated in the Lycus River valley in western Asia Minor, about 120 miles (193 kilometers) east of Ephesus and 10 miles (16 kilometers) east of Laodicea. Its location on an important Roman road meant that it was influenced by the social and religious currents of the time. • ***brothers and sisters:*** Literally *brothers,* a generic term commonly used to refer to both men and women.

1:3-14 This opening section begins with a thanksgiving, typical of NT letters. Paul thanks God for the Colossians' progress in the faith and prays that they might understand it even better. With this prayer, Paul hints at his concern about the influence of false teachers.

1:4 ***God's people*** (literally *holy ones,* or *saints*): In the NT, all Christians are *saints,* people who have been specially set apart by God as his own holy people (3:12).

1:5 The Colossian Christians' ***confident hope*** gives them a secure foundation for their faith and love (1:4). • ***What God has reserved*** for believers has not yet been fully revealed, but it already exists ***in heaven***.

1:7
Col 4:12
Phlm 1:23
[b]*diakonos* (1249)
‣Col 1:23
1:9
Eph 1:15-17
1:10
Eph 4:1
Phil 1:27
1 Thes 2:12
1:11
Eph 3:16
1:12
Acts 26:18
Eph 5:20
1:13
Matt 3:17
Acts 26:18
Eph 1:6; 2:2; 6:12
1:14
Eph 1:7
[c]*apolutrōsis* (0629)
‣Heb 9:15
1:15
John 1:1, 18; 14:9
2 Cor 4:4
Heb 1:3
Rev 3:14
[d]*prōtotokos* (4416)
‣Col 1:18
1:16
John 1:3
Heb 1:2
1:17
John 1:1; 8:58
1:18
Acts 4:2; 26:23
Eph 1:22-23
Rev. 1:5
[e]*ekklēsia* (1577)
‣Col 4:15
[f]*prōtotokos* (4416)
‣Heb 1:6

you first heard the truth of the Good News.
6 This same Good News that came to you
is going out all over the world. It is bearing
fruit everywhere by changing lives, just as
it changed your lives from the day you first
heard and understood the truth about God's
wonderful grace.
7 You learned about the Good News from
Epaphras, our beloved co-worker. He is
Christ's faithful [b]servant, and he is helping
us on your behalf. 8 He has told us about the
love for others that the Holy Spirit has given
you.
9 So we have not stopped praying for you
since we first heard about you. We ask God
to give you complete knowledge of his will
and to give you spiritual wisdom and understanding. 10 Then the way you live will
always honor and please the Lord, and your
lives will produce every kind of good fruit.
All the while, you will grow as you learn to
know God better and better.
11 We also pray that you will be strengthened with all his glorious power so you will
have all the endurance and patience you
need. May you be filled with joy, 12 always
thanking the Father. He has enabled you to
share in the inheritance that belongs to his
people, who live in the light. 13 For he has rescued us from the kingdom of darkness and
transferred us into the Kingdom of his dear
Son, 14 who [c]purchased our freedom and forgave our sins.

Christ Is Supreme

15 Christ is the visible image of the
invisible God.
He existed before anything was
created and is [d]supreme over all
creation,
16 for through him God created
everything
in the heavenly realms and on earth.
He made the things we can see
and the things we can't see—
such as thrones, kingdoms, rulers, and
authorities in the unseen world.
Everything was created through him
and for him.
17 He existed before anything else,
and he holds all creation together.
18 Christ is also the head of the [e]church,
which is his body.
He is the beginning,
[f]supreme over all who rise from the
dead.
So he is first in everything.
19 For God in all his fullness
was pleased to live in Christ,

1:6 ***bearing fruit everywhere by changing lives:*** The ***Good News*** is effective to change lives and bring about spiritual growth (cp. 1:10).

1:7 ***Epaphras*** (see also 4:12-13; Phlm 1:23) was probably converted when Paul ministered in Ephesus (see Acts 19:10) and then returned to Colosse to bring the ***Good News*** to his own town. • ***he is helping us on your behalf:*** Or *he is ministering on your behalf;* some manuscripts read *he is ministering on our behalf.*

1:9-10 Paul prays that God would grant his readers deeper understanding of the Good News and its full expression in their lives. Spiritual growth yields a clearer and deeper comprehension of Christian truth and conduct that pleases the Lord, through which a believer will have the endurance and patience to stand firm against evil (1:11).

1:11 ***all the endurance and patience you need. May you be filled with joy:*** Or *all the patience and endurance you need with joy.* The Greek can be interpreted either way.

1:12-13 ***always thanking the Father:*** Humble gratitude to God for salvation is a powerful antidote to the lure of false teaching (see also 2:7; 3:17; 4:2). • The ***inheritance*** is what God has promised his people (e.g., see Deut 3:28; Ps 33:12; Ezek 44:28). In the NT, *the inheritance* consists of salvation and final deliverance (see also Eph 1:11; Titus 3:7; Heb 9:15).

1:14 ***who purchased our freedom:*** Some manuscripts add *with his blood.*

1:15-20 Paul presents Jesus as the supreme creator (1:15-17) and redeemer (1:18-20). The series of short statements, the exalted conceptions of Christ, and the parallelism in language and thought strongly suggest that these verses quote an early Christian hymn about Jesus that Paul applied to the situation of the Colossian Christians.

1:15 ***visible image:*** In the Greek translation of the OT, *eikōn* ("image, representation") is used to refer to human beings having been made in the image of God (Gen 1:26-27) and also to the wisdom figure in Jewish writings (see *Wisdom* 7:25-26). The NT writers speak about ***Christ*** as God's wisdom to help explain his significance (cp. 1 Cor 1:24, 30). • ***He existed before anything was created and is supreme over all creation*** (or *He is the firstborn of all creation*): This phrase figured prominently in early Christian debates about the nature of Christ. *Firstborn* does not mean he was created; it is a title, drawn from the OT, indicating supremacy of rank and priority in time (see, e.g., Ps 89:27).

1:16 ***Thrones, kingdoms, rulers, and authorities in the unseen world*** refer to various spiritual powers. This line emphasizes Christ's supremacy over these beings who were getting so much attention from the false teachers (see 2:18). • ***Everything was created through him and for him:*** Christ is both the one through whom all things were created and the goal of all creation.

1:18 ***head of the church***: The Greek word *kephalē* (head) usually has the sense of *authority over* or *chief* when Paul uses it as a metaphor (see also 2:10, 19; 1 Cor 11:3-10; Eph 4:15; 5:23). • ***which is his body:*** The metaphor of the church as Christ's body expresses the essential unity of Christ and the church (see also 1:24; 2:19; 3:15; Eph 1:23; 2:16; 4:4, 12; 5:23, 30). • ***supreme over all who rise from the dead*** (or *the firstborn from the dead*): See note on 1:15.

1:19 ***God in all his fullness*** emphasizes that God has chosen to reveal himself fully in Jesus Christ. Seeing Jesus and understanding him therefore means seeing and understanding God (see John 14:6-11). The false teachers seemed to be saying that Christians needed to look to other spiritual beings to find out more about God (see 1:16, 20). But Christ is sufficient for all our knowledge of God (cp. 2:8-9).

20 and through him God reconciled
everything to himself.
He made peace with everything in
heaven and on earth
by means of Christ's blood on the
cross.

Reconciliation in Christ

21 This includes you who were once far away
from God. You were his enemies, separated
from him by your evil thoughts and actions.
22 Yet now he has reconciled you to himself
through the death of Christ in his physical
body. As a result, he has brought you into
his own presence, and you are holy and
blameless as you stand before him without
a single fault.
23 But you must continue to believe this
truth and stand firmly in it. Don't drift away
from the assurance you received when you
heard the Good News. The Good News has
been preached all over the world, and I, Paul,
have been appointed as God's [g]servant to
proclaim it.

Paul's Work for the Church

24 I am glad when I suffer for you in my body,
for I am participating in the sufferings of
Christ that continue for his body, the church.
25 God has given me the [h]responsibility of
serving his church by proclaiming his entire
message to you. 26 This message was kept [i]se-
cret for centuries and generations past, but
now it has been revealed to God's people.
27 For God wanted them to know that the
riches and glory of Christ are for you Gentiles, too. And this is the secret: Christ lives
in you. This gives you assurance of sharing
his glory.
28 So we tell others about Christ, warning
everyone and teaching everyone with all
the wisdom God has given us. We want to
present them to God, perfect in their relationship to Christ. 29 That's why I work and
struggle so hard, depending on Christ's
mighty power that works within me.

2 I want you to know how much I have
agonized for you and for the church
at Laodicea, and for many other believers
who have never met me personally. 2 I want
them to be [j]encouraged and knit together
by strong ties of love. I want them to have
complete confidence that they understand
God's mysterious plan, which is Christ himself. 3 In him lie hidden all the treasures of
wisdom and knowledge.
4 I am telling you this so no one will deceive you with well-crafted arguments. 5 For
though I am far away from you, my heart is
with you. And I rejoice that you are living as
you should and that your faith in Christ is
strong.

Freedom from Rules and New Life in Christ

6 And now, just as you accepted Christ Jesus
as your Lord, you must continue to follow
him. 7 Let your roots grow down into him,
and let your lives be built on him. Then your
faith will grow strong in the truth you were
taught, and you will overflow with thankfulness.
8 Don't let anyone capture you with empty
philosophies and high-sounding nonsense

1:21 Rom 5:10; Eph 2:3, 12
1:22 Rom 7:4; Eph 1:4; 5:27
1:23 Eph 3:17; Col 1:5-6; [g]*diakonos* (1249) ‣Col 4:7
1:24 Phil 2:17; 3:10; 2 Tim 1:8
1:25 Eph 3:2; [h]*oikonomia* (3622) ‣1 Tim 1:4
1:26 Rom 16:25-26; Eph 3:3, 5, 9-10; [i]*mustērion* (3466) ‣Col 4:3
1:27 Rom 8:10; Eph 3:9-11
1:28 Eph 4:13
1:29 Eph 1:19; 3:7; Phil 4:13
2:1 Col 4:12-13
2:2 Matt 11:25-27; Eph 1:18-19; Col 2:19; [j]*parakaleō* (3870) ‣1 Thes 5:11
2:3 Isa 11:2; Rom 11:33; Eph 3:8, 19
2:5 1 Cor 5:3-4
2:6 Col 1:10
2:7 Eph 3:17
2:8 Col 2:4; 1 Tim 6:20

1:20 Through Christ, God has ***reconciled everything to himself,*** reestablishing his rule over all creation, including both the spiritual and the earthly realms.

1:21-23 Paul applies the truth of 1:15-20 to the Colossian Christians. As people who have been reconciled to God, they enjoy a new spiritual status and need to stand firm in the truth they have been taught.

1:21 The phrase ***once far away from God*** probably refers to their condition as Gentiles (see Eph 2:12).

1:22 The Colossians, like all believers, were ***holy and blameless*** in God's sight not because of their own perfection but because they had been ***reconciled*** with God through Christ's ***death.***

1:23 ***preached all over the world*** (literally ***preached to every creature under heaven***): The point of Paul's hyperbole (exaggeration for emphasis) is that centers for preaching the Good News had been established in key cities throughout the Roman world (see also 1:6).

1:24–2:5 Paul considers his own role in the widespread preaching of the Good News (1:23).

1:24 ***I am participating in the sufferings of Christ*** (literally ***I am filling up what is lacking in the sufferings of Christ***): While the redemptive suffering of Christ is unique and completely finished, Christ still suffers through his people in a world hostile to the message of redemption. Christ and his church will continue to suffer until God's purposes in this world are complete (see also Mark 13:19-23; Rom 8:17-18; 1 Thes 3:3).

1:26 The concept of a ***secret,*** hidden at one time and then revealed, is based upon Jewish apocalyptic ideas. Jewish thinkers conceived of God's entire plan as already existing in heaven, hidden until God should draw back the curtain and reveal it. The Good News, especially for the Gentiles, had been kept secret until it was revealed in Christ. See "The Secret of the Good News," facing page.

1:28 ***perfect:*** Or ***mature.***

2:1-5 Paul introduces his concern to strengthen his relationship with the Colossians, whom he had not met, and to counter the heretical ideas which threatened their Christian community. • Laodicea was located twenty miles northwest of Colosse.

2:2 ***God's mysterious plan:*** See 1:26; ***Christ himself*** personifies this plan.

2:3 Paul builds on 1:15-20: Christ alone is sufficient for our spiritual understanding.

2:6-15 In the face of the false teachers' enticing arguments, Paul exhorts the Colossians to stand firm in their faith in Christ, for ***in Christ lives all the fullness of God*** and their spiritual experience is complete in him.

2:8 The Greek word *philosophia* referred to everything from the metaphysics of Plato to the religious teaching of cults. Paul does not condemn philosophy per se, but only ***empty*** philosophical speculation that stands opposed to the Good News. • ***the spiritual powers of this***

2:9
John 1:14
Col 1:19
2:10
Eph 1:21-22; 3:19
2:12
Rom 6:5
Eph 1:19-20; 2:6
[k]*baptismos* (0909)
‣Heb 6:2
2:13
Eph 2:1, 5
2:14
Eph 2:15
1 Pet 2:24
2:15
John 12:31
2:16
Rom 14:3, 5

that come from human thinking and from
the spiritual powers of this world, rather
than from Christ.
9 For in Christ lives all the
fullness of God in a human body.
10 So you
also are complete through your union with
Christ, who is the head over every ruler and
authority.
11 When you came to Christ, you were "circumcised," but not by a physical procedure.
Christ performed a spiritual circumcision—
the cutting away of your sinful nature.
12 For you were buried with Christ when
you were [k]baptized. And with him you were
raised to new life because you trusted the
mighty power of God, who raised Christ
from the dead.
13 You were dead because of your sins and
because your sinful nature was not yet cut
away. Then God made you alive with Christ,
for he forgave all our sins.
14 He canceled
the record of the charges against us and
took it away by nailing it to the cross.
15 In
this way, he disarmed the spiritual rulers
and authorities. He shamed them publicly
by his victory over them on the cross.
16 So don't let anyone condemn you for
what you eat or drink, or for not celebrating
certain holy days or new moon ceremonies

The Secret of the Good News (1:26-27)

Col 2:2; 4:3
Rom 11:25; 16:25
1 Cor 2:1, 7; 15:51
Eph 1:9; 3:1-9; 5:32; 6:19

In Paul's letters, the word *secret* (sometimes translated *mystery*) is applied to the Good News. Sometimes *secret* is used as an abbreviation for the Good News itself (2:2; 4:3; 1 Cor 2:1; Eph 1:9; 6:19). Frequently, as in 1:26, Paul claims that the secret had been hidden in the past but has now been revealed (see also Rom 16:25; 1 Cor 2:7; Eph 3:9). Paul does not mean by this that the Good News is a secret that has to be probed. He adapts the term from Jewish apocalyptic teaching (the term *apocalyptic* is from a Greek word that means "uncovering" or "revelation"; the same word is used as the name for the book of Revelation). In the apocalyptic perspective, the plan God has mapped out for all of history already exists in his mind but is hidden from human eyes until God chooses to disclose it. For Paul, the secret plan has now been disclosed in Christ, and it is broadcast through the world by his apostles.

Through the OT prophets, God foretold many elements of the Good News, but he kept some aspects of it hidden until he revealed them in the NT era. These include the full participation of Gentiles as fellow-heirs with Jews (1:27; Eph 3:1-9); the indwelling of Christ in believers (1:27; 2:2); and the union of Christ and the church, as illustrated by the union of husband and wife (Eph 5:32). But some elements of God's plan are still hidden and await further revelation, such as the salvation of all Israel (Rom 11:25) and the transfiguration of Christians at the time of Christ's return (1 Cor 15:51).

world: or *the spiritual principles of the world;* also in 2:20): This phrase may refer to elementary teaching that is characteristic of this world (see Heb 5:12), or to spiritual beings who were thought to have a decisive influence on the course of events (see also 2:15, 20; Gal 4:3).

2:9 ***in Christ lives all the fullness of God in a human body:*** Or *in him dwells all the completeness of the Godhead bodily.* The Greek can be interpreted either way.

2:11 ***Christ performed a spiritual circumcision:*** Spiritual conversion to Christ is the Christian counterpart to physical circumcision. • ***the cutting away of your sinful nature*** (literally *the cutting away of the body of the flesh*): Just as Jewish boys have the flesh of their foreskin cut off to mark their initiation into the people of God, so believers have metaphorical *flesh* (translated *sinful nature*) cut off when they come to Christ.

2:12 ***you were buried with Christ when you were baptized:*** As in a roughly parallel passage (Rom 6:3-6), Paul assumes a strong identity between believers and Christ. In God's sight, we really were *with Christ* when he was buried and ***raised***, so we experience the benefits of what Christ did for us. Paul can link that identification with Christ to baptism because water baptism was so closely related to conversion in the early church.

2:14 ***the record of charges against us:*** The Greek phrase suggests an IOU that we have all signed. Since we are unable to pay what we owe, it stands *against us.* The law of God required obedience that people are unable to give, but God has forgiven our debt through the work of Christ (2:13).

2:15 ***he disarmed:*** Or *he stripped off.* • ***He shamed them publicly*** (literally *he led [them] in triumphal procession*): The Roman army would celebrate a great victory with a triumphal procession. The victorious Roman general would lead the humiliated captives from his campaign into the conquered city. The image vividly captures the glorious victory that God, through the cross of Christ, has won over all hostile spiritual powers (see also Eph 4:7-11).

2:16-23 Paul repudiates the false teachers and their demands, explaining why their appeal comes from ***human teachings*** (see 2:8). They advocated various rules of conduct that had no basis in Christ.

2:16 ***what you eat or drink:*** Religious teachings that prohibited certain kinds of food and drink were widespread in the ancient world. The OT does not prohibit drinking alcohol, but many pious Jews who lived in pagan cultures did abstain (cp. Dan 1:8-16). • Many ancient religious groups, including the Jews, celebrated the ***new moon*** with various ***ceremonies*** (see Num 10:10; Ps 81:3; Isa 1:13). • Jewish ***Sabbaths*** were set forth in the law of Moses and celebrated by Jews as an essential part of their religion (see chart, p. 235). Christians could continue to observe the Sabbath if they wanted to, but Paul insists that Christians have liberty on this matter (see Rom 14:5) and that it is wrong for anyone to insist on Sabbath observance as a necessary expression of Christian piety.

or Sabbaths. [17]For these rules are only shadows of the reality yet to come. And Christ
himself is that reality. [18]Don't let anyone condemn you by insisting on pious self-denial
or the worship of [a]angels, saying they have
had visions about these things. Their sinful
minds have made them proud, [19]and they
are not connected to Christ, the head of the
body. For he holds the whole body together
with its joints and ligaments, and it grows as
God nourishes it.
[20]You have died with Christ, and he has
set you free from the spiritual powers of
this world. So why do you keep on following
the rules of the world, such as, [21]"Don't handle! Don't taste! Don't touch!"? [22]Such rules
are mere human teachings about things
that deteriorate as we use them. [23]These
rules may seem wise because they require
strong devotion, pious self-denial, and severe bodily discipline. But they provide no
help in conquering a person's evil desires.

3. LIVING THE NEW LIFE IN CHRIST (3:1–4:6)

Living the New Life

3 Since you have been raised to new life
with Christ, set your sights on the realities of heaven, where Christ sits in the place
of honor at God's right hand. [2]Think about
the things of heaven, not the things of earth.
[3]For you died to this life, and your real life
is hidden with Christ in God. [4]And when
Christ, who is your life, is revealed to the
whole world, you will share in all his glory.
[5]So put to death the sinful, earthly things
lurking within you. Have nothing to do with
sexual immorality, impurity, lust, and evil
desires. Don't be greedy, for a greedy person is an [b]idolater, worshiping the things
of this world. [6]Because of these sins, the
anger of God is coming. [7]You used to do
these things when your life was still part of
this world. [8]But now is the time to get rid
of [c]anger, rage, malicious behavior, [d]slander,
and dirty language. [9]Don't lie to each other,
for you have stripped off your old sinful nature and all its wicked deeds. [10]Put on your
new nature, and be renewed as you learn to
know your Creator and become like him.
[11]In this new life, it doesn't matter if you
are a Jew or a Gentile, circumcised or uncircumcised, barbaric, uncivilized, [e]slave, or
free. Christ is all that matters, and he lives
in all of us.

New Relationships

[12]Since God chose you to be the holy people
he loves, you must clothe yourselves with
tenderhearted mercy, kindness, humility,
gentleness, and patience. [13]Make allowance
for each other's faults, and forgive anyone

2:17 Heb 8:5; 10:1
2:18 [a]*angelos* (0032) ‣Heb 1:4
2:19 Eph 1:22; 4:15-16
2:20 Gal 4:3, 9
2:22 Matt 15:9
3:1 Matt 6:33
3:4 1 Cor 15:43; 1 Jn 3:2
3:5 Gal 5:19-21; [b]*eidōlolatria* (1495) ‣1 Pet 4:3
3:7 Eph 2:2
3:8 Eph 4:25-31; 5:4; [c]*orgē* (3709) ‣Rev 6:17; [d]*blasphēmia* (0988) ‣1 Tim 1:20
3:9 Eph 4:25
3:10 Rom 12:2; Eph 2:10; 4:24
3:11 1 Cor 12:13; [e]*doulos* (1401) ‣Phlm 1:16
3:12 Eph 4:2, 32
3:13 Eph 4:32; 5:2

2:17 The *reality* of Christ was anticipated by the OT rituals, which Paul calls *shadows* (see also Heb 10:1).

2:18 ***the worship of angels*** (or ***worshiping with angels***): People in the first century were fascinated with spiritual beings. Some Jews believed that angels were present during their times of worship, and some might even have worshiped them. • The false teachers were evidently *saying* they had *had visions* that established certain rituals as requirements for the community.

2:20 ***You have died with Christ:*** Christ's death on the cross marked his victory over the spiritual powers (2:15), so we who participate in his death have likewise been set ***free from the*** evil ***spiritual powers of this world*** (see 2:8).

2:23 ***they provide no help:*** Not only are such rules rooted in the world rather than in Christ (2:19), they are also ineffective ***in conquering a person's evil desires.***

3:1-11 Paul summons the Colossians to a new way of thinking that results in a new lifestyle.

3:1 ***set your sights on the realities of heaven:*** Christians live on earth, but because they have been raised with Christ, their true being is oriented to the spiritual realm over which Christ rules. In contrast, the rules and regulations of the false teachers focused on the earthly realm (2:22).

3:3-4 ***you died to this life:*** See 2:20. • What is now ***hidden*** will one day be ***revealed*** (cp. 1:26). We cannot now see that Christ is enthroned at the right hand of God and that we have been raised to new life with Christ. But by faith in the Good News, we know that these things are true. When Christ returns in glory, his supremacy will be evident to all and our relationship to him will be a direct experience.

3:4 ***your life:*** Some manuscripts read *our life.*

3:5 ***So put to death:*** Our death to this life (3:3) must be made real in the way that we live day by day. • ***a greedy person is an idolater:*** Greedy people pursue the objects of their greed—money, sex, power, possessions—in the place of God, with the hope of finding satisfaction in those things.

3:6 ***coming:*** Some manuscripts read *coming on all who disobey him.* In the Greek text, these words occur verbatim in Eph 5:6, so it is possible that an early scribe added them here, either intentionally or accidentally.

3:8 ***get rid of*** (literally ***take off***): Taking off clothes is a metaphor for ridding our lives of practices that interfere with our walk with the Lord (see Rom 13:12; Eph 4:22, 25; Heb 12:1; Jas 1:21; 1 Pet 2:1).

3:9-10 ***your old sinful nature . . . your new nature:*** Paul contrasts old and new identities (see also Rom 5:12-21; 6:6; Eph 4:22-24). Believers strip off their old life and put on Christ's new life, allowing him to be Lord and to guide the way they live.

3:11 ***a Gentile:*** Literally *a Greek.* • ***barbaric, uncivilized:*** Literally *Barbarian, Scythian.* The Greeks mocked people from other cultures for their inability to speak Greek well, claiming they could only say "bar bar" (hence the word *barbarian*). The Scythians were tribes that had settled on the north coast of the Black Sea and were widely viewed as fierce and crude (see Josephus, *Against Apion* 2.38). All such distinctions do not ***matter*** in our relationship with God through ***Christ.***

3:12-17 Paul describes the nature of the new life of people who have been raised with Christ (3:1). Their virtues and activities contribute to the peace and strength of the Christian community.

3:14
[f]*agapē* (0026)
‣1 Thes 3:12
[g]*teleiotēs* (5047)
‣Heb 6:1

3:15
John 14:27
Eph 2:14-16
[h]*eirēnē* (1515)
‣Heb 12:14

3:16
[i]*christos* (5547)
‣Matt 2:4

3:17
1 Cor 10:31

3:18-20
Eph 5:22–6:4
1 Pet 3:7

3:21-25
//Eph 6:4-8

3:22
[j]*haplotēs* (0572)
‣Rom 12:8

3:25
Acts 10:34

4:1
Lev 25:43
Eph 6:9

who offends you. Remember, the Lord
forgave you, so you must forgive others.
14Above all, clothe yourselves with [f]love,
which binds us all together in [g]perfect harmony. 15And let the [h]peace that comes from
Christ rule in your hearts. For as members
of one body you are called to live in peace.
And always be thankful.
16Let the message about [i]Christ, in all its
richness, fill your lives. Teach and counsel
each other with all the wisdom he gives.
Sing psalms and hymns and spiritual songs
to God with thankful hearts. 17And whatever you do or say, do it as a representative
of the Lord Jesus, giving thanks through
him to God the Father.

Instructions for Christian Households

18Wives, submit to your husbands, as is fitting for those who belong to the Lord.
19Husbands, love your wives and never
treat them harshly.
20Children, always obey your parents, for
this pleases the Lord. 21Fathers, do not aggravate your children, or they will become
discouraged.
22Slaves, obey your earthly masters in
everything you do. Try to please them all
the time, not just when they are watching
you. Serve them [j]sincerely because of your
reverent fear of the Lord. 23Work willingly
at whatever you do, as though you were
working for the Lord rather than for people. 24Remember that the Lord will give you
an inheritance as your reward, and that the
Master you are serving is Christ. 25But if
you do what is wrong, you will be paid back
for the wrong you have done. For God has
no favorites.

4 Masters, be just and fair to your slaves.
Remember that you also have a Master—in heaven.

Legalism (2:16-23)

Matt 23:13-33
Mark 7:1-15
Gal 2:14-21

At the time of Christ and the early church, Jews made much of rules and laws in their understanding of religion. This was natural to them because God had given his law to the Jewish people as a mark of his favor upon them and as a way for them to ratify the covenant agreement he had made with them. However, many Jews added to the laws that God had given his people, trying to develop rules for virtually every situation in which they might find themselves. Their motivation was often a positive desire not to transgress any of God's laws. As Jesus often pointed out, however, the rules developed by rabbis sometimes became obstacles to obeying God's rules (Mark 7:1-15). Furthermore, many Jews thought that following the law would automatically endear them to God.

Paul apparently confronted a situation of this kind in 2:16-23. False teachers, influenced by Jewish beliefs, were insisting that Christians follow certain rules as a way of expressing their faith. Paul criticized this in light of faith in Christ. As the culmination of all God's plans and purposes, Christ is the center of all true piety. This does not mean that rules for conduct are inherently bad. Some rules, such as the prohibition on lying (3:9), clearly manifest an aspect of Christ's character. Paul also had no problem with individual Christians imposing rules on themselves that they think are conducive to their own growth in Christ (cp. Rom 14:5; 1 Cor 8). But they must not require others to obey these self-imposed rules.

3:15 Just as Christ is one, so there can be only *one body* of Christ (see 1:18; Eph 4:4-6). Allegiance to Jesus as Lord must transcend differences and will result in *peace* (harmonious relationships).

3:16 ***Psalms and hymns and spiritual songs*** are songs of praise and worship (see 1 Cor 14:26; Eph 5:19). The prototype is the book of Psalms.

3:17 ***as a representative of the Lord Jesus*** (literally *in the name of the Lord Jesus*): In the Bible, a person's name represents that person. To do something *in the name of the Lord Jesus* is therefore to act in a way that is in harmony with his identity and under his authority.

3:18–4:1 This series of exhortations is called a *household code.* Paul gives instructions to wives (3:18), husbands (3:19), children (3:20), fathers (3:21), slaves (3:22-25), and masters (4:1). Such codes appear in Greco-Roman writers and elsewhere in the NT (see Eph 5:22–6:9; 1 Pet 2:18–3:7).

3:18 To ***submit*** is to recognize one's place under someone else in a social order. Such submission always implies that God is at the top and that his will is paramount (cp. Acts 4:19-20; 5:29).

3:19 The exhortation to wives to submit to their ***husbands*** is immediately followed by a command to the husbands to *love* their ***wives*** (see also Eph 5:25-30; 1 Pet 3:7).

3:22-24 ***Slaves*** have ***earthly masters*** whom they must obey. Slavery was central to the life and economy of the ancient world, and the NT never attacks the practice as such. However, Christian faith establishes relationships that change the nature of the social structure (see Phlm 1:15-16).
• ***and that the Master you are serving is Christ:*** Or *and serve Christ as your Master.* All Christians, both slave and free, serve a higher Master, whose will is paramount.

4:1 ***Masters:*** Christian slave owners had to recognize that they, too, were slaves bound to obey Jesus Christ, their Master ***in heaven*** who treats all people with dignity and grace.

An Encouragement for Prayer
[2]Devote yourselves to prayer with an alert
mind and a thankful heart. [3]Pray for us, too,
that God will give us many opportunities to
speak about his [k]mysterious plan concerning Christ. That is why I am here in chains.
[4]Pray that I will proclaim this message as
clearly as I should.

[5]Live wisely among those who are not
believers, and make the most of every opportunity. [6]Let your [a]conversation be gracious
and attractive so that you will have the right
response for everyone.

4. CONCLUSION: PAUL'S FINAL INSTRUCTIONS AND GREETINGS (4:7-18)

[7]Tychicus will give you a full report about
how I am getting along. He is a beloved
brother and faithful [b]helper who serves
with me in the Lord's work. [8]I have sent
him to you for this very purpose—to let you
know how we are doing and to encourage
you. [9]I am also sending Onesimus, a faithful
and beloved brother, one of your own people. He and Tychicus will tell you everything
that's happening here.

[10]Aristarchus, who is in prison with me,
sends you his greetings, and so does Mark,
Barnabas's cousin. As you were instructed
before, make Mark welcome if he comes
your way. [11]Jesus (the one we call Justus)
also sends his greetings. These are the only
Jewish believers among my co-workers;
they are working with me here for the Kingdom of God. And what a comfort they have
been!

[12]Epaphras, a member of your own
fellowship and a servant of Christ Jesus,
sends you his greetings. He always prays
earnestly for you, asking God to make you
strong and perfect, fully confident that you
are following the whole [c]will of God. [13]I
can assure you that he prays hard for you
and also for the believers in Laodicea and
Hierapolis.

[14]Luke, the beloved doctor, sends his
greetings, and so does Demas. [15]Please give
my greetings to our brothers and sisters at
Laodicea, and to Nympha and the [d]church
that meets in her house.

[16]After you have read this letter, pass it on
to the church at Laodicea so they can read it,

4:2 Eph 6:18; 1 Thes 5:17
4:3 [k]*mustērion* (3466) ‣1 Tim 3:9
4:4 Eph 6:20
4:5 Eph 5:15-16
4:6 Eph 4:29; 1 Pet 3:15; [a]*logos* (3056) ‣Heb 4:12
4:7 [b]*diakonos* (1249) ‣1 Tim 3:8
4:9 Phlm 1:10
4:10 Acts 12:12; 15:37; 19:29; 20:4; 27:2
4:12 Phlm 1:23; [c]*thelēma* (2307) ‣1 Thes 4:3
4:14 2 Tim 4:10-11; Phlm 1:24
4:15 Rom 16:5; [d]*ekklēsia* (1577) ‣Jas 2:2
4:16 1 Thes 5:27; 2 Thes 3:14

4:2-6 NT letters often end with an exhortation to pray, along with requests for prayer.

4:2 *with an alert mind*: The Greek verb behind this phrase is used in the NT of the need for Christians to be watchful in light of Christ's return (Matt 24:42; 25:13; Mark 13:35, 37; 1 Thes 5:6; Rev 3:3; 16:15).

4:3 ***that God will give us many opportunities*** (literally *that God might open for us a door*): An open door is a metaphor for an opportunity to proclaim the Good News (see also Acts 14:27; 1 Cor 16:9; 2 Cor 2:12). • ***his mysterious plan concerning Christ:*** See 1:26-27; 2:2. • ***That is why I am here in chains:*** Paul's dedication to preaching the Good News had led to his imprisonment (see Colossians Introduction, "Date and Occasion of Writing," p. 2021).

4:5 ***make the most of every opportunity*** (literally *buy up the time*): Like people who are buying up a product offered at a good price, Christians are to "buy up" every opportunity God gives them to share the Good News and to serve others.

4:6 ***attractive*** (literally *seasoned with salt*): Salt is both a seasoning and a preservative (see Matt 5:13). Paul might be encouraging Christians to speak to unbelievers in words that are well chosen and winsome. The rabbis occasionally referred to wisdom as *salt,* so Paul might also be exhorting Christians to speak wisely.

4:7-18 Most NT letters end with a series of greetings and references to co-workers and travel plans, but this part of Colossians is longer than normal. Paul, being unable to travel, might have been seeking to ensure that the Colossians maintain connections with his co-workers. This would help them not to fall for the enticements of the false teachers.

4:7 ***Tychicus*** was from the province of Asia, where Colosse was located (Acts 20:4). He worked with Paul especially in that province (Eph 6:21; 2 Tim 4:12). He was later sent to work with Titus in Crete (Titus 3:12). Tychicus probably carried this letter along with the letters known as Ephesians and Philemon.

4:9 ***Onesimus*** was the runaway slave whom Paul was sending back to his master Philemon (see Philemon).

4:10-14 Of the six people named, five are also mentioned in Phlm 1:23-24.

4:10 ***Aristarchus*** was a common name, but he was probably the same man from Thessalonica (Acts 19:29; 20:4) who accompanied Paul on his voyage to Rome (Acts 27:2). Acts does not suggest that *Aristarchus* was also under arrest, so perhaps he was ***in prison with*** Paul voluntarily, sharing his confinement in order to encourage him and assist him in ministry. • ***Mark, Barnabas's cousin,*** had gone with Barnabas and Paul on their first missionary journey, but had left them before the journey was finished (Acts 13:13). That desertion led to a split between Paul and Barnabas as the second journey was about to begin (Acts 15:37-40). Paul and Mark were apparently now reconciled (see also 2 Tim 4:11; Phlm 1:24). • ***As you were instructed before:*** There is no other record of this communication.

4:11 ***Jesus (the one we call Justus)*** is mentioned only here in the NT. The surname *Justus* is included because *Jesus* (which means *the Lord saves*) was a common name among Jews in the first century.

4:13 ***Laodicea and Hierapolis*** were the two most important cities in the Lycus River valley. The fact that Epaphras prayed for the believers in Colosse and in these nearby cities suggests that he was the pioneering evangelist in all three cities.

4:14 ***Luke, the beloved doctor,*** is well known as the author of Acts and the gospel bearing his name (see "Luke" at Acts 16:10, p. 1861). This verse is the sole evidence for two facts about Luke: He was a doctor, and he was not a Jewish believer (see 4:10-11). • In contrast to the other people mentioned in this passage, no details are given about ***Demas.*** Perhaps Paul did not know him well. Demas later deserted Paul (2 Tim 4:10).

4:15 ***brothers and sisters:*** Literally *brothers.* • ***Nympha and the church that meets in her house:*** In the first two centuries of the Christian church,

4:17
[e]*diakonia* (1248)
‣2 Tim 4:5

4:18
2 Thes 3:17

too. And you should read the letter I wrote to them.

17And say to Archippus, "Be sure to carry out the [e]ministry the Lord gave you."

18HERE IS MY GREETING IN MY OWN HANDWRITING—PAUL.

Remember my chains.

May God's grace be with you.

almost all believers met for worship in private homes. Nothing else is known of Nympha.

4:16 ***you should read the letter I wrote to them***: Various attempts have been made over the years to identify the letter to the Laodiceans with a NT letter or fragment, but it is most likely that Paul's letter to the Laodicean church has been lost.

4:17 ***Archippus:*** See also Phlm 1:2. We have no way of knowing more about ***the ministry the Lord gave*** him.

4:18 ***HERE IS MY GREETING IN MY OWN HANDWRITING—PAUL:*** Like most ancient letters, Colossians was probably dictated by Paul to a scribe, or *amanuensis,* who would have been trained to write neatly and compactly. As a way of authenticating the letter, Paul added his own handwritten greeting at the end (cp. Paul's comment in 2 Thes 2:2).

PAUL'S FIRST LETTER TO THE THESSALONIANS

What chance did the Thessalonian church have? As recent converts to Christianity, they lacked a full understanding of the faith and suffered severe persecution. Could the fledgling believers withstand the antagonistic social climate? First Thessalonians tells of new believers who remained firm in their faith despite tremendous opposition and great disadvantages. The letter reminds us that faithful leaders, good teaching, and obedience are important, and it presents a clear vision of God as powerfully active in the lives of those he has called through the Good News of Jesus Christ.

SETTING

Thessalonica, the major city of Macedonia, enjoyed the good will of Rome and the Roman citizens who settled there. The city was not subject to Roman taxation, could mint its own coins, and was not obliged to garrison Roman troops within the city walls. It prospered as a political and commercial center whose influence extended throughout the province of Macedonia and beyond.

The mixed population of Thessalonica included Macedonians, Romans, Jews, and other peoples who traveled through the city. Many of the Romans who settled there became wealthy benefactors in the town. The Jewish population was large enough to have a synagogue (Acts 17:1).

Luke reported the evangelization of Thessalonica in Acts 17:1-9. When Paul preached in the synagogue, some Jews converted to Christ. Most of the converts in Thessalonica, however, were Roman or Macedonian Gentiles who abandoned idolatry to follow Christ (1:9).

The Jews who did not accept the Good News started a riot against the apostles

The Setting of 1–2 Thessalonians, about AD 50. During his second missionary journey (shown), Paul established the church in THESSALONICA as he made his way through MACEDONIA, but he was forced to leave the city very quickly (see Acts 17:1-9). He probably wrote 1 Thessalonians from CORINTH after being encouraged by Timothy's report (3:1-8). Not long after, Paul wrote 2 Thessalonians to address further issues that had arisen.

and accused Paul and Silas of causing civil disturbance (Acts 17:4-7). The accusation was calculated to generate maximum opposition by taking advantage of the Romans' intolerance of social unrest. As a consequence, Paul and his companions were forced to leave the city after a short time.

Paul left a church that was at most a few months old in the faith. It was already experiencing persecution (1:6; 2:14; 3:3-4). The Christians in Thessalonica had not received all the teaching they needed, nor did they have mature leadership to oversee the church. As Paul traveled on to Berea, Athens, and finally Corinth (Acts 17:10–18:1), he was deeply concerned about the welfare of the Thessalonian church. His repeated attempts to return to the city were blocked by severe circumstances that he attributed to Satan (2:17-18).

While in Athens, Paul could no longer bear his anxiety over the church. He sent Timothy back to Thessalonica to strengthen the believers and to be sure that they had not abandoned their faith (3:1-2, 5). While Paul was in Corinth, Timothy returned from Thessalonica with the good news that the Thessalonian believers continued in faith and love and were standing firm despite the opposition they faced (3:6-8; Acts 18:5). First Thessalonians explodes with the joy Paul experienced upon hearing this report. It expresses his thankfulness to God for their faithfulness and his prayer that he might return to see them again and establish them more fully in the faith (3:9-11).

OUTLINE

1:1
Greetings

1:2-10
Opening Thanksgiving

2:1–3:13
The Reception of the Good News in Thessalonica

4:1–5:22
Exhortations and Teachings

5:23-28
Final Prayers and Greetings

SUMMARY

First Thessalonians is a letter of thanksgiving to God for the faith, love, and hope of the young Thessalonian church (1:2-3; 2:13; 3:9). Paul, however, also presents some of his concerns. Paul and his companions had preached the Good News in the city, then left abruptly and failed to return. In the ancient world there were many traveling orators who only sought money and fame. In 2:1–3:13, Paul defends his motives and ministry—he had not come looking for fame or fortune. He sincerely cared for the Thessalonian believers. He longed to see the church and had tried unsuccessfully to "come back" (2:17-20). Paul also affirms his care by reminding them that he had sent Timothy back to strengthen them and to find out about their welfare (3:1-5). Paul recounts how greatly comforted he was by the news Timothy brought (3:6-8), and he tells the church about his thanksgiving to God for them and his prayer that he might see them again (3:9-13).

Timothy's report also informed Paul that some in the congregation had ignored Paul's teaching about sexual morality. In response, Paul emphasizes God's will for them to be holy (4:1-8). In addition, certain individuals within the church were refusing to work, ignoring the teaching

TIMELINE

AD 47~48
Barnabas and Paul's first missionary journey

AD 48~49
Paul writes Galatians from Antioch

AD 49~50
The council in Jerusalem

AD 50–52
Paul's second missionary journey

about AD 50
Paul and Silas establish the Thessalonian church

about AD 50–52
Paul in Corinth

about AD 50
▸ Paul writes 1 Thessalonians from Corinth

July 1, AD 51
Gallio named proconsul of Achaia

about AD 51
Paul writes 2 Thessalonians from Corinth

Spring AD 52
Paul leaves Corinth for Syria

AD 53–57
Paul's third missionary journey

and example of the apostles in this regard (4:11-12; 5:14; see 2 Thes 3:6-15).

Timothy's report also included some questions from the Thessalonians. First, what would happen to believers who died before Christ's return? Paul answers that such people will be the first to be raised from the dead and will be caught up with the living to meet the Lord at the time of his royal appearing (4:13-18). Second, the Thessalonians wanted to know when Christ would return and bring about the final consummation. Paul replies that the day will come at an unexpected moment, like a thief in the night (5:1-11). They should be prepared by living in faith, love, and hope.

The letter closes with several exhortations on living a life that pleases God. Paul reminds the church to honor its emerging leaders (5:12-13). In addition, Paul instructs the Thessalonians that they should not reject prophecies but evaluate them (5:19-22). The letter concludes with a blessing that expresses Paul's absolute confidence in God's faithfulness and work in their lives (5:23-24).

Perhaps the most important issue that makes this letter timely is its disarming awareness of God. First Thessalonians is about faith, love, and hope, not as human attributes but as gifts that spring from God alone. It is God who calls into faith, God who enables human love, and God toward whom hope is directed.

BEVERLY ROBERTS GAVENTA
First and Second Thessalonians, p. 9

AUTHOR

First Thessalonians opens (1:1) with the names of Silas and Timothy, cofounders of the church in Thessalonica, alongside the name of Paul, the apostle to the Gentiles (Rom 11:13; Gal 1:16). The letter is mostly written in the first person plural ("we"), indicating that Silas and Timothy might have had a real part in the letter's composition. Paul only occasionally steps out individually to express his particular concerns (2:18; 3:5; 5:27). Joint composition of letters was known in the ancient world. For example, in his letter *Ad Atticum,* Cicero refers to "letters—both that which you wrote in conjunction with others and the one you wrote in your own name." However, the final command in 5:27 suggests that Paul had the major hand in writing, whatever the role of his companions may have been.

DATE AND OCCASION OF WRITING

Paul wrote this epistle from Corinth during his second missionary journey (Acts 16–18) after Timothy returned from visiting the Thessalonian church (3:6; Acts 18:5). Gallio was named as proconsul of the Roman province of Achaia in AD 51, during Paul's stay in Corinth (Acts 18:11-12). Therefore, Paul probably wrote this letter during the latter part of AD 50. First Thessalonians is one of Paul's earliest epistles, second only to Galatians.

MEANING AND MESSAGE

First Thessalonians provides a look into the life and struggles of a new congregation of believers. These new converts were greatly disadvantaged because the founders of their church were absent. The new believers were experiencing great hostility from their own countrymen because of their faith (1:6; 2:14; 3:3-4). Paul believed they were under attack by Satan, the tempter (3:5), who had also hindered him from visiting them again (2:18). When Timothy returned from visiting them, Paul was overjoyed to discover that the Thessalonians were exhibiting the character of people truly converted to Christ. Their lives were marked by faith, love, and hope (1:3; 3:6; 5:8). They helped to spread the Good News throughout the surrounding regions (1:8)

and became examples for other believers of true faith in the midst of suffering (1:6-7).

What enabled the Thessalonians to stand firm in faith in the face of great adversity? Some might attribute such perseverance to simple resolve, good upbringing, or just "blind faith." Paul emphasizes that believers are chosen by God (1:4). The Good News is the divine message and witness of God's power (1:5). When people receive this message, it continues to work powerfully in them (2:13). Genuine conversion means turning to the true God in repentance and serving him while awaiting the return of his Son from heaven (1:9-10). Although the Christians in Thessalonica were young in the faith, separated from their church founders, and suffering for their conversion to Christ, God was at work in them. Such strength of faith is the work of Christ (3:8, 13).

Still, these new Christians needed to grow in moral character and theological understanding. Paul had warned the Thessalonians about sexual immorality, but some dismissed his teaching (4:3-8). They did not understand that their belief in Christ's resurrection was their source of hope in the face of the bitter reality of death (4:13-18). They were confused about when Christ would return (5:1-11). Some in the church did not heed Paul's teaching about work (4:11; 5:14), and others were not properly respecting the emerging leaders in the church (5:12-13). Some Thessalonians were repressing prophecy in the church (5:19-22).

Although correction may seem distasteful, we need it for proper moral and theological growth. Paul, as a wise pastor, writes this letter to help the Thessalonian believers with these issues. His hope is that the letter will address these problems until he is able to return (3:10). In the end, every leader should entrust believers to God's work in their lives (5:23) since he is faithful (5:24).

FURTHER READING

GREGORY BEALE
1–2 Thessalonians (2003)

PHILIP W. COMFORT
1 Thessalonians in *Cornerstone Biblical Commentary,* vol. 16 (2008)

GENE L. GREEN
The Letters to the Thessalonians (2002)

ABRAHAM J. MALHERBE
Letters to the Thessalonians (2000)

I. HOWARD MARSHALL
The First and Second Epistles to the Thessalonians (1991)

CHARLES WANAMAKER
The Epistles to the Thessalonians (1990)

1:1 Acts 17:1
1:2 Rom 1:8-10; 2 Thes 1:11
1:3 Col 1:4-5; [a]*pistis* (4102) ‣1 Tim 4:6
1:4 Col 3:12
1:5 1 Cor 2:4-5; 4:20
1:6 Acts 17:1-9; 1 Cor 4:16

1. GREETINGS (1:1)
Greetings from Paul

1 This letter is from Paul, Silas, and Timothy.
We are writing to the church in Thessalonica, to you who belong to God the Father and the Lord Jesus Christ.
May God give you grace and peace.

2. OPENING THANKSGIVING (1:2-10)

2 We always thank God for all of you and
pray for you constantly. 3 As we pray to our
God and Father about you, we think of your
[a]faithful work, your loving deeds, and the enduring hope you have because of our Lord Jesus Christ.
4 We know, dear brothers and sisters, that
God loves you and has chosen you to be his
own people. 5 For when we brought you the
Good News, it was not only with words but also with power, for the Holy Spirit gave you full assurance that what we said was true. And you know of our concern for you from the way we lived when we were with
you. 6 So you received the message with joy
from the Holy Spirit in spite of the severe

1:1 Ancient letters began with the name of the author, the name of the recipients, and a salutation. • ***Paul, Silas, and Timothy*** were the founders of this church (Acts 17:1-9). • ***Silas:*** Greek *Silvanus,* the Greek form of the name. • The greeting ***grace and peace*** summarizes the believer's experience of the Good News.

1:2-10 After thanking God for the faith, love, and hope of the Thessalonian believers (1:2-3), Paul recalls how the Good News was proclaimed to them (1:4-5) and how they accepted its message (1:6-10). Paul returns to these themes in 2:1-12 and 2:13-16.

1:2 ***We always thank God for all of you*** is the first of three thanksgivings for the church (see 2:13; 3:9).

1:3 The reason for Paul's gratitude was the Thessalonians' ***faithful work, loving deeds,*** and ***enduring hope*** (or *confidence;* see 3:6; 5:8; 2 Thes 1:3-4).

1:4 ***dear brothers and sisters:*** Literally *brothers,* a generic term that refers to both male and female believers.

1:5 God called the Thessalonians through hearing the ***Good News*** (2 Thes 2:13-14). The ***Holy Spirit*** convinced the hearers that the message was true (1 Cor 2:4-5; 1 Pet 1:12). • ***with power, for the Holy Spirit gave you full assurance:*** Or *with the power of the Holy Spirit, so you can have full assurance.*

1:6 Because they accepted the Good News, the Thessalonians experienced ***severe suffering*** from their contemporaries (2:14; 3:3-4). Yet as they followed the model of the apostles and of the

suffering it brought you. In this way, you imitated both us and the Lord. 7 As a result, you
have become an [b]example to all the believers in Greece—throughout both Macedonia
and Achaia.
8 And now the word of the Lord is ringing
out from you to people everywhere, even beyond Macedonia and Achaia, for wherever
we go we find people telling us about your
faith in God. We don't need to tell them
about it, 9 for they keep talking about the
wonderful welcome you gave us and how
you turned away from idols to serve the living and true God. 10 And they speak of how
you are looking forward to the coming of
God's Son from heaven—Jesus, whom God
raised from the dead. He is the one who has
rescued us from the terrors of the coming
judgment.

3. THE RECEPTION OF THE GOOD NEWS IN THESSALONICA (2:1–3:13)

Paul Defends the Character of His Visit

2 You yourselves know, dear brothers and
sisters, that our visit to you was not a
failure. 2 You know how badly we had been
treated at Philippi just before we came to you
and how much we suffered there. Yet our
God gave us the courage to declare his Good
News to you boldly, in spite of great opposition. 3 So you can see we were not preaching
with any deceit or impure motives or trickery.
4 For we speak as messengers approved
by God to be entrusted with the Good
News. Our purpose is to please God, not people. He alone examines the motives of our
hearts. 5 Never once did we try to win you
with flattery, as you well know. And God is
our witness that we were not pretending to
be your friends just to get your money! 6 As
for human praise, we have never sought it
from you or anyone else.
7 As apostles of Christ we certainly had
a right to make some demands of you, but
instead we were like children among you.
Or we were like a mother feeding and caring for her own children. 8 We loved you
so much that we shared with you not only
God's Good News but our own lives, too.
9 Don't you remember, dear brothers and
sisters, how hard we worked among you?
Night and day we toiled to earn a living so
that we would not be a burden to any of you
as we preached God's Good News to you.
10 You yourselves are our witnesses—and
so is God—that we were devout and [c]honest
and faultless toward all of you believers.
11 And you know that we treated each of you
as a [d]father treats his own children. 12 We
pleaded with you, encouraged you, and
urged you to live your lives in a way that God

1:7
[b]*tupos* (5179)
›2 Thes 3:9
1:8
Rom 1:8
2 Thes 3:1
1:9
Acts 14:15
1 Cor 12:2
1:10
Phil 3:20
1 Thes 5:9
Titus 2:13
Heb 9:28
Rev 1:7
2:1
1 Thes 1:5, 9
2:2
Acts 16:22; 17:2
Phil 1:30
2:3
2 Cor 4:2
2 Pet 1:16
2:4
Gal 1:10
1 Tim 1:11
2:5
Acts 20:33
2:7
2 Tim 2:24
2:8
2 Cor 12:15
2:9
Acts 18:3
2 Cor 11:9
2 Thes 3:8
2:10
1 Thes 1:5
[c]*dikaiōs* (1346)
›Titus 2:12
2:11
1 Cor 4:14
[d]*patēr* (3962)
›1 Tim 5:1

Lord himself (Matt 5:11-12; Rom 8:17; 12:12; Phil 2:17), they received ***joy from the Holy Spirit*** (1 Pet 4:13-14).

1:7-8 ***ringing out:*** The example of the Thessalonians' faith and their proclamation of the Good News was heard throughout the provinces of ***Macedonia*** and ***Achaia*** (the northern and southern regions of Greece).

1:9 Among the Gentiles, the message of the apostles was an exhortation to turn from false idols ***to serve the living and true God,*** who created all things (Acts 14:11-18; 17:22-31; 19:23-41). In a pluralistic religious environment, the call to forsake ancestral gods was unusual (cp. Jer 10:8-10; 1 Cor 8:4-6).

1:10 The resurrection of Jesus ***from the dead*** was the core of the apostles' preaching (4:14; Acts 2:32; 3:15; 10:40; 13:29-30; 1 Cor 15:3-8) and the foundation for confidence in Jesus' return (see 5:9; 2 Thes 1:6-10).

2:1–3:13 The body of this letter begins by discussing Paul's and his associates' character (2:1-12) and the way the Thessalonians received the Good News (2:13-16). It then emphasizes Paul's sincere care for the church, telling of his attempts to return to visit them (2:17-20) and his decision to send Timothy to them when he himself could not come (3:1-5). Finally, it tells of Paul's joy over Timothy's good report (3:6-9) and his prayers to get back to the church himself (3:10-13). This lengthy defense is Paul's response to criticisms of his abrupt departure and prolonged absence.

2:1 ***dear brothers and sisters:*** Literally ***brothers;*** also in 2:9, 14, 17. See note on 1:4. • The Greek word translated ***visit*** often refers to entry into a city. Ancient orators were known for their grand entrances into a town. Paul's entrance to Thessalonica should be judged by its credible results rather than its lack of pomp or ceremony.

2:2 Despite the dishonor and pain Paul and Silas had suffered in Philippi (Acts 16:19-40), they showed ***courage*** by preaching confidently in Thessalonica.

2:4 In the ancient world, those ***entrusted*** with a public office had to be tested and ***approved.*** The Thessalonians (2:3) and ***God*** served as two witnesses to the purity of Paul's ***motives.***

2:5 ***Flattery*** was a common means of getting financial gain from others. Paul denies that he flattered the Thessalonians in order to be given ***money.*** He again calls both the Thessalonians and ***God*** as witnesses (cp. 2:10; Deut 19:15; 2 Cor 13:1; 1 Tim 5:19).

2:7 ***we were like children:*** Some manuscripts read ***we were gentle.*** Paul and his associates did not wield their apostolic authority to make ***demands*** (cp. Matt 20:25-28).

2:9 Paul and his associates engaged in manual labor to support themselves while in the city (cp. Acts 18:1-4; 1 Cor 9:12-18) as an example to the Thessalonians (2 Thes 3:8-9) and to avoid becoming an economic ***burden*** to them.

2:10 Both God and the Thessalonians were ***witnesses*** (see 2:5) that Paul's conduct was ***devout and honest,*** terms used in ancient literature to describe obedience to both divine and human laws.

2:11 In the ancient world, the moral instruction of children was a fundamental obligation of fathers. Roman fathers could be harsh, but Plutarch advised Greek fathers to use praise, reason, exhortations, and good counsel when teaching children to avoid vice and embrace virtue. Paul describes himself as this kind of ***father*** to the Thessalonians.

2:12 What ***God would consider worthy*** is a life lived in harmony with the high standards he expects of those called

2:12 Eph 4:1; Col 1:10; 1 Pet 1:15
2:13 1 Thes 1:2; 2 Thes 2:13
2:14 Acts 17:5; 1 Thes 1:6
2:15 Luke 24:20; Acts 2:23; 7:52
2:16 Matt 23:32-33; Acts 13:45, 50; 17:5; 20:3; 21:27; 24:9
2:17 1 Cor 5:3; 1 Thes 3:10
2:18 Rom 1:13; 15:22; [e]*satanas* (4567) ‣ Rev 2:24
2:19 Phil 2:16; 1 Thes 3:13; 2 Thes 1:4; Rev 1:7; 22:12
2:20 2 Cor 1:14
3:1 Acts 17:15
3:2 Acts 16:1-3
3:3 2 Tim 3:12
3:4 1 Thes 2:14
3:5 Matt 4:3; Phil 2:16; [f]*peirazō* (3985) ‣ 1 Tim 6:9
3:6 Acts 18:5
3:7 2 Thes 1:4

would consider worthy. For he called you to
share in his Kingdom and glory.

The Thessalonians Receive the Good News

13Therefore, we never stop thanking God
that when you received his message from
us, you didn't think of our words as mere
human ideas. You accepted what we said as
the very word of God—which, of course, it
is. And this word continues to work in you
who believe.
14And then, dear brothers and sisters,
you suffered persecution from your own
countrymen. In this way, you imitated the
believers in God's churches in Judea who,
because of their belief in Christ Jesus, suffered from their own people, the Jews.
15For some of the Jews killed the prophets,
and some even killed the Lord Jesus. Now
they have persecuted us, too. They fail to
please God and work against all humanity
16as they try to keep us from preaching the
Good News of salvation to the Gentiles. By
doing this, they continue to pile up their
sins. But the anger of God has caught up
with them at last.

Paul's Desire to Return to Thessalonica

17Dear brothers and sisters, after we were
separated from you for a little while (though
our hearts never left you), we tried very
hard to come back because of our intense
longing to see you again. 18We wanted very
much to come to you, and I, Paul, tried again
and again, but [e]Satan prevented us. 19After
all, what gives us hope and joy, and what will
be our proud reward and crown as we stand
before our Lord Jesus when he returns? It is
you! 20Yes, you are our pride and joy.

Paul Sends Timothy to Thessalonica

3 Finally, when we could stand it no longer, we decided to stay alone in Athens,
2and we sent Timothy to visit you. He is our
brother and God's co-worker in proclaiming the Good News of Christ. We sent him
to strengthen you, to encourage you in your
faith, 3and to keep you from being shaken
by the troubles you were going through.
But you know that we are destined for such
troubles. 4Even while we were with you,
we warned you that troubles would soon
come—and they did, as you well know.
5That is why, when I could bear it no longer, I sent Timothy to find out whether your
faith was still strong. I was afraid that the
[f]tempter had gotten the best of you and that
our work had been useless.

Timothy Returns and Reports to Paul

6But now Timothy has just returned, bringing us good news about your faith and love.
He reports that you always remember our
visit with joy and that you want to see us as
much as we want to see you. 7So we have
been greatly encouraged in the midst of our
troubles and suffering, dear brothers and
sisters, because you have remained strong

(4:7) to share ***his Kingdom and glory*** (Rom 8:17-18; Col 1:27; 2 Thes 2:14).

2:13 Paul gives thanks a second time (see 1:2; 3:9) because the Thessalonians accepted the message of the apostles—not just as a human philosophy, but as ***the very word of God*** (1:5; 2 Thes 2:14; 2 Cor 5:20).

2:14 The evidence that the Thessalonian believers accepted the word of God was that they ***suffered persecution*** (1:6). This followed the pattern of the apostles, the ***churches in Judea*** (Acts 8:1), and Christ himself.

2:15 Paul was not anti-Jewish; out of love for his own people, he prayed for their salvation (Rom 9:1-5; 10:1). But he was aware of the role ***some of the Jews*** had in the deaths of God's messengers, including Jesus (1 Kgs 19:10; Acts 7:52). Now they had ***persecuted*** the apostolic messengers in Thessalonica (Acts 17:10; 2 Cor 11:26).

2:16 The mission to the ***Gentiles*** was one of the most important issues in the early church (Acts 11:18; 13:46-49; 28:28; Rom 1:16). • Judgment comes when sins ***pile up*** to their complete measure (Gen 15:16; Dan 8:23; cp. Matt 23:31-36).

2:17 ***separated:*** Paul describes his unplanned departure from Thessalonica (see Acts 17:10) as depriving these new believers of their spiritual parents. However, this absence was not neglect. As evidenced by Paul's attempts to return to the church, the separation was unintentional (cp. Phil 1:7; Col 2:5).

2:18 ***again and again:*** Paul made repeated attempts to return to the Thessalonian church. Despite the opposition of ***Satan*** (see Rom 16:20; 2 Cor 2:11; Eph 6:10-12), both Timothy (3:1, 5) and Paul (Acts 20:1-3) were eventually able to visit the church again.

2:19 In the Greek and Roman world, a ***crown*** was given to those who received great civic honor or who were victorious in athletic games.

2:20 Paul views the Thessalonian believers—not his own accomplishments—as the source of his ***pride***, or renown, and his ***joy*** (3:9).

3:1-5 After preaching in Berea, Paul had departed from Macedonia and sailed to Athens, instructing Silas and Timothy to join him soon (Acts 17:13-15). Timothy returned to Thessalonica (3:2), as Paul's anxiety for the Thessalonian church had intensified (3:1, 5).

3:2 ***and God's co-worker:*** Other manuscripts read *and God's servant;* still others read *and a co-worker,* or *and a servant and co-worker for God,* or *and God's servant and our co-worker.*

3:3 ***we are destined for such troubles:*** Suffering for the faith is often part of a Christian's life (1:6; 2:14; Phil 1:29; 1 Pet 1:6; 2:21; 3:17; 4:19).

3:5 Paul was concerned that Satan, ***the tempter*** (Mark 1:13; 1 Cor 7:5), had undermined the Thessalonians' ***faith*** (3:2, 6, 8) and rendered his ***work*** among them futile (Gal 2:2; Phil 2:16).

3:6 Paul wrote 1 Thessalonians from Corinth just after Timothy ***returned*** from Thessalonica (3:1, 5; Acts 18:5). Timothy's report provided ***good news*** about the Thessalonians' ***faith and love,*** steadfastness (3:8), and hope (1:3; see also 5:8; 2 Thes 1:3-4).

3:7 ***dear brothers and sisters:*** Literally *brothers.* See note on 1:4.

in your faith. 8It gives us new life to know
that you are standing firm in the Lord.
9How we thank God for you! Because of
you we have great joy as we enter God's presence. 10Night and day we pray earnestly for
you, asking God to let us see you again to fill
the gaps in your faith.

Paul Prays to Return to Thessalonica

11May God our Father and our Lord Jesus
bring us to you very soon. 12And may the
Lord make your [g]love for one another and
for all people grow and overflow, just as
our love for you overflows. 13May he, as a
result, make your hearts strong, blameless,
and holy as you stand before God our Father
when our Lord Jesus [h]comes again with all
his holy people. Amen.

4. EXHORTATIONS AND TEACHINGS (4:1–5:22)

Living to Please God (4:1-2)

4 Finally, dear brothers and sisters, we
urge you in the name of the Lord Jesus
to live in a way that pleases God, as we have
taught you. You live this way already, and
we encourage you to do so even more. 2For
you remember what we taught you by the
authority of the Lord Jesus.

Avoiding Sexual Sin (4:3-8)

3God's [i]will is for you to be [j]holy, so stay
away from all sexual sin. 4Then each of you
will control his own body and live in [k]holi-
ness and honor—5not in lustful passion
like the pagans who do not know God and
his ways. 6Never harm or cheat a Christian
brother in this matter by violating his wife,
for the Lord avenges all such sins, as we
have solemnly warned you before. 7God has
called us to live [a]holy lives, not impure lives.
8Therefore, anyone who refuses to live by
these rules is not disobeying human teaching but is rejecting God, who gives his Holy
Spirit to you.

Paul Responds to the Thessalonians' Questions (4:9–5:11)

Love in God's Family

9But we don't need to write to you about the
importance of loving each other, for God
himself has taught you to love one another.
10Indeed, you already show your love for all

3:8 1 Cor 16:13
3:12 Phil 1:9; [g]*agapē* (0026) ‣Phlm 1:5
3:13 Zech 14:5; 1 Cor 1:8; 2 Thes 1:7; [h]*parousia* (3952) ‣1 Thes 4:15
4:1 Eph 4:1
4:3 Heb 10:10; 1 Pet 1:16; [i]*thelēma* (2307) ‣1 Thes 5:18; [j]*hagiasmos* (0038) ‣1 Thes 4:4
4:4 1 Cor 7:2; [k]*hagiasmos* (0038) ‣1 Thes 4:7
4:6 1 Cor 6:8
4:7 Lev 11:44; 2 Thes 2:13-14; 1 Pet 1:15; [a]*hagiasmos* (0038) ‣2 Thes 2:13
4:8 Rom 5:5; 1 Jn 3:24
4:9 Jer 31:33-34; John 6:45; 13:34; 1 Jn 2:20, 27

3:8 Paul was distressed by his present circumstances (3:7) and deeply concerned for the church (3:1, 5). He was relieved to learn that the Thessalonians remained strong and were ***standing firm in the Lord*** even though they were also suffering (2:14; 3:3-4).

3:11 Paul's prayer to return to Thessalonica ***very soon*** (3:10) is directed both to the ***Father*** and the ***Lord Jesus***, implying Jesus' divinity.

3:12 A characteristic of this church was their ***love for one another*** as members of God's family (4:9; 2 Thes 1:3-4). Paul prays that their love will ***grow and overflow*** toward those outside the Christian community (cp. 5:15; Gal 6:10; 2 Tim 2:24; Titus 3:2) even in the face of persecution.

3:13 In the final part of this prayer (3:11-13), Paul prays that their ***hearts***—their conduct and moral resolve (Matt 5:8; Acts 15:9; Heb 10:22)—might be ***strong, blameless, and holy.*** • When Jesus ***comes,*** he will be accompanied by ***all his holy people,*** possibly a reference to angels (Deut 33:2; Ps 89:5, 7; Dan 4:13; 8:13; Matt 13:41; Mark 8:38; 13:26-27; 2 Thes 1:7).

4:1–5:22 The second part of the body of the letter concerns Timothy's news about the church and the questions the believers had for Paul. Paul addresses the problem of sexual immorality (4:3-8) before responding to the Thessalonians' questions about love for other Christians (4:9-12), the destiny of believers who have died (4:13-18), and the timing of the day of the Lord (5:1-11). Paul takes up a variety of exhortations on topics such as leadership and community relations (5:12-15), relationship with the Lord (5:16-18), and prophecy (5:19-22).

4:1-2 ***dear brothers and sisters:*** Literally *brothers;* also in 4:10, 13. See note on 1:4. • ***we urge you:*** Paul's exhortation ***in the name of the Lord Jesus*** emphasizes the authority of his teaching. • ***you remember what we taught:*** Ancient letters frequently included reminders of what the recipients already knew. Paul reminds the Thessalonians of matters that required their obedience (4:11; 2 Thes 3:4, 6, 10, 12).

4:3 ***God's will is for you to be holy:*** The foundation of Christian ethics is not philosophical speculation about virtue but doing God's will (Rom 12:1-2; Eph 6:6; Heb 10:36; 13:20-21). Holiness (4:4, 7) embraces all of a person's life (5:23); here it involves staying away from ***sexual sin*** (Greek *porneia,* any sexual union outside marriage).

4:4 ***will control his own body:*** Or *will know how to take a wife for himself;* or *will learn to live with his own wife;* literally *will know how to possess his own vessel.* • Self-control brings ***honor*** from others (Rom 12:10) and from God (Rom 2:7; 1 Pet 5:4, 6).

4:5 Willful ignorance of ***God and his ways*** is the root of moral corruption (Rom 1:18-32; Eph 4:17-18). • ***lustful passion:*** Sexual immorality was tolerated in the Mediterranean world. Prostitution was allowed, but sexual relations with another man's wife were prohibited. Roman marriage customs barred women, but not men, from extramarital affairs. By contrast, Jewish and Christian authors alike prohibited all sexual involvement outside of marriage (Acts 15:20; 1 Cor 6:12-20; Col 3:5-6).

4:6 ***Never harm or cheat a Christian brother in this matter by violating his wife:*** Literally *Never harm or cheat a brother in this matter.*

4:7 ***holy . . . not impure:*** Cp. 1:4; 2:12; 5:23-24; 2 Thes 2:13-14; 1 Pet 1:15-16.

4:8 Rejecting Paul's teaching on these matters was the same as ***rejecting God.*** • The ***Holy Spirit*** empowers Christians to live in accord with God's will (Ezek 36:27; Rom 8:1-4; Gal 5:16; 1 Jn 3:24).

4:9–5:11 Paul responds to a series of questions from the Thessalonians (cp. 1 Cor 7:1) concerning love for one another (4:9-12), the destiny of deceased believers (4:13-18), and when the day of the Lord would come (5:1-11).

4:9 ***about the importance of loving each other:*** Literally *about brotherly love.* • ***God himself has taught you to love one another*** (cp. Isa 54:13) through the teaching of Jesus (John 13:34-35), the cross (Rom 5:8; Eph 5:1-2), and the Holy Spirit (Rom 5:5; Gal 5:22).

4:10 The Thessalonian believers demonstrated ***love*** toward ***all the believers*** (literally *all the brothers*; see note on 1:4) in the province of ***Macedonia*** (Philippi and Berea; see also 1:7-8) through economic aid (cp. 2 Cor 8:1-5).

4:10 2 Thes 3:4
4:11 Eph 4:28; 2 Thes 3:10-12
4:12 Mark 4:11
4:13 Eph 2:12
4:14 Rom 14:9; 1 Cor 15:3-4, 12
4:15 1 Cor 7:10, 25; 15:52; [b]*parousia* (3952) ‣1 Thes 5:23
4:16 Matt 24:30; 1 Cor 15:52; 2 Thes 1:7
4:17 Acts 1:9; Rev 11:12

the believers throughout Macedonia. Even
so, dear brothers and sisters, we urge you to
love them even more.
11 Make it your goal to live a quiet life,
minding your own business and working
with your hands, just as we instructed you
before. 12 Then people who are not Christians will respect the way you live, and you
will not need to depend on others.

Believers Who Have Died

13 And now, dear brothers and sisters, we
want you to know what will happen to the
believers who have died so you will not
grieve like people who have no hope. 14 For
since we believe that Jesus died and was
raised to life again, we also believe that
when Jesus returns, God will bring back
with him the believers who have died.
15 We tell you this directly from the Lord:
We who are still living when the Lord [b]re-
turns will not meet him ahead of those
who have died. 16 For the Lord himself will
come down from heaven with a commanding shout, with the voice of the archangel,
and with the trumpet call of God. First, the
Christians who have died will rise from their
graves. 17 Then, together with them, we who
are still alive and remain on the earth will
be caught up in the clouds to meet the Lord
in the air. Then we will be with the Lord forever. 18 So encourage each other with these
words.

The Last Things (4:13–5:11)

Mark 13:1-37; 2 Thes 2:1-12

The Thessalonian believers heartily embraced Paul's teaching about the day of the Lord and Christ's second coming, but this instruction generated questions and speculations about the end times. What would happen to believers who died before Jesus' return (4:13-18)? When would the day of the Lord come (5:1-11)? Would believers suffer the wrath of God (1:10; 5:9)? Paul calms the congregation by clarifying the points in question (4:13–5:11) and reminding them of the teaching they had already received.

Although Paul expected Jesus' return to happen during his lifetime (4:15), he also recognized that the final event would come at an unpredictable moment, "like a thief in the night" (5:2). The way to be ready for the end is not by knowing the date but by living with Christian alertness. The Thessalonians also needed to understand the deaths of fellow believers. Paul says nothing about the condition of believers between their death and the return of Christ. Instead, he emphasizes the resurrection of believers. Just as Christ was raised, those who died as believers will be raised when he returns. In fact, they will rise from the dead first and then be caught up together with the living believers to meet Christ in his royal coming.

Despite Paul's efforts to clarify the Christian hope, the Thessalonian believers became confused by false teaching that the day of the Lord had already begun (2 Thes 2:2). As a counterpoint to this false teaching, Paul addressed the issue further in his second letter to the young church (see 2 Thes 2:1-12).

4:11 To *live a quiet life* is to be respectable and not cause problems in the community. • ***working with your hands:*** Paul had previously *instructed* through his teaching (see 2 Thes 3:10) and personal example (2 Thes 3:7-9) that they should earn their own living.

4:12 Self-sufficiency and decorum would win the recognition and *respect* of ***people who are not Christians*** (see Rom 13:13; 1 Cor 5:12-13; Col 4:5).

4:13 ***the believers who have died*** (literally *those who have fallen asleep;* also in 4:14): Sleep was a common euphemism for death in Greek, Jewish, and Christian literature (Dan 12:2; Matt 27:52). Personal existence continues after death (Luke 23:40-43; Acts 7:55-60; 2 Cor 5:6-10; Phil 1:20-24; Rev 6:9-11); those who have died await the resurrection (1 Cor 15:23). • ***grieve like people who have no hope:*** Ancient letters of comfort exhorted mourners not to be overcome with grief because they could do nothing to avert death. Paul does not prohibit grief (cp. John 16:6, 20; Phil 2:27) but calls Christian mourners to abandon the kind of grief typical of those who have no hope in God.

4:14 The central Christian creed, ***that Jesus died and was raised to life again,*** is the foundation for hope in the face of death, guaranteed by the resurrection of Christ (1 Cor 15). • ***God will bring back*** refers to the resurrection of believers (4:16).

4:15 ***directly from the Lord:*** Jesus' own teaching provided the source of Paul's assurance for the Thessalonians (see Matt 24:29-31, 40-41) • ***not . . . ahead:*** Paul wants the Thessalonians to know that, ***when the Lord returns,*** the dead will not be at a disadvantage but will participate equally in the resurrection. • In referring to Jesus' coming, Paul uses a Greek term (*parousia*) commonly used to describe the coming of the emperor to a city with great pomp and celebration (see 4:17). • ***those who have died:*** Literally *those who have fallen asleep.* See note on 4:13.

4:16 ***with the trumpet call of God:*** God's trumpet will herald the resurrection, just as it previously announced the rescue of Israel (Zeph 1:16; Zech 9:14). In the future it will announce the gathering of God's chosen people from the "farthest ends of the earth and heaven" (Matt 24:31; cp. 1 Cor 15:52). • ***the Christians who have died:*** Literally *the dead in Christ.*

4:17 ***to meet:*** This alludes to the custom of sending an official delegation to greet a visiting dignitary and accompany him as he enters the city (Matt 25:6, 10; Acts 28:15-16).

4:18 The purpose of Paul's teaching about the end is so believers will ***encourage each other*** in the face of death. He is not promoting speculation about the end times.

The Day of the Lord

5 Now concerning how and when all this
will happen, dear brothers and sisters,
we don't really need to write you. 2For you
know quite well that the day of the Lord's return will come unexpectedly, like a thief in
the night. 3When people are saying, "Everything is peaceful and secure," then disaster
will fall on them as suddenly as a pregnant
woman's labor pains begin. And there will
be no escape.
4But you aren't in the dark about these
things, dear brothers and sisters, and you
won't be surprised when the day of the Lord
comes like a thief. 5For you are all children
of the light and of the day; we don't belong
to darkness and night. 6So be on your guard,
not asleep like the others. Stay alert and be
clearheaded. 7Night is the time when people sleep and drinkers get drunk. 8But let
us who live in the light be clearheaded, protected by the armor of faith and love, and
wearing as our helmet the [c]confidence of
our salvation.
9For God chose to [d]save us through our
Lord Jesus Christ, not to pour out his anger
on us. 10Christ died for us so that, whether
we are dead or alive when he returns, we
can live with him forever. 11So [e]encourage
each other and build each other up, just as
you are already doing.

Final Exhortations (5:12-22)

12Dear brothers and sisters, honor those
who are your leaders in the Lord's work.
They work hard among you and give you
spiritual guidance. 13Show them great respect and wholehearted love because of
their work. And live peacefully with each
other.
14Brothers and sisters, we [f]urge you to
warn those who are lazy. Encourage those
who are timid. Take tender care of those
who are weak. Be patient with everyone.
15See that no one pays back evil for evil,
but always try to do good to each other and
to all people.
16Always be joyful. 17Never stop praying.

5:1 Matt 24:36
5:2 Matt 24:42-44; 2 Pet 3:10
5:3 Jer 6:13-14; Matt 24:37-39
5:5 John 12:36; Eph 5:9
5:8 Eph 6:14, 17; [c]*elpis* (1680) ‣Titus 2:13
5:9 [d]*sōtēria* (4991) ‣2 Thes 2:13
5:10 Rom 14:8-9
5:11 [e]*parakaleō* (3870) ‣1 Thes 5:14
5:12 1 Tim 5:17
5:14 2 Thes 3:6-7, 11; [f]*parakaleō* (3870) ‣2 Thes 3:12
5:15 Prov 20:22; Rom 12:17; 1 Pet 3:9

5:1 Questions such as ***how and when all this will happen*** occupied the thoughts of both Jewish and Christian people (Dan 12:6; Matt 24:3; Luke 17:20; Acts 1:6; 1 Pet 1:10-11). • ***dear brothers and sisters:*** Literally *brothers;* also in 5:4, 12, 14, 25, 26, 27.

5:2 ***For you know quite well:*** Paul reminds them of the teaching they had already received (3:3-4). • The ***day of the Lord's return*** is the time when God will come to judge humanity (Isa 13:6, 9; Ezek 30:3) and save his people (Joel 2:21-32; 3:18; Zech 14:1-21). • ***like a thief in the night:*** Cp. Matt 24:43-44; Luke 12:39-40; 2 Pet 3:10; Rev 3:3; 16:15.

5:3 ***"Everything is peaceful and secure":*** The expression "peace and safety" was common during the era of the *pax Romana* (Roman peace). One ancient author spoke of "comfort in the time of peace and security in the time of war." God's ultimate judgment, however, comes without warning and is inescapable.

5:4 The ***day of the Lord*** will not surprise believers—not because they know the date of his coming, but because they are spiritually prepared. • ***comes like a thief:*** Some manuscripts read *comes upon you as if you were thieves.*

5:5 As ***children of the light,*** the Thessalonian believers were saved from darkness (John 12:36; Acts 26:18; Eph 5:8; 1 Pet 2:9). • ***of the day:*** They belong to God's new order (Rom 13:12). • ***darkness and night:*** These refer to an immoral life (see 5:6-8).

5:6 ***Stay alert and be clearheaded*** echoes Jesus' call to be morally prepared because the disciples will not know the day of his return (Matt 24:42, 44; 25:13; cp. 1 Pet 1:13).

5:7 ***Sleep*** refers to moral indifference (5:6) and ***drunk*** is a metaphor for those who do not exercise self-control; they will be surprised by the day of the Lord (5:4; Matt 24:48-51).

5:8 ***Armor . . . helmet*** (Isa 59:17; Eph 6:11-17): The armament is the moral life (Rom 13:12; 2 Cor 6:7; 10:3-5; 2 Tim 2:3-4). The Christian soldier is equipped with the virtues of ***faith, love,*** and ***confidence*** (see 1:3; 3:6; 1 Cor 13:13; 2 Thes 1:3-4).

5:9 God's ***anger*** (1:10; 2:16; Rom 5:9; cp. 2 Thes 1:6-10; 2:8) represents the carrying out of his judgment against evil. However, God destined believers for salvation, not wrath (2 Thes 2:13-14), and they will escape the terrors of the day of the Lord (5:1-3).

5:10 The promise that believers will ***live with him forever*** is based on Christ's resurrection (4:14). • ***dead or alive:*** A reference to living and deceased believers (4:13-15) rather than people's moral condition (as in 5:6-7).

5:11 Paul wants the Thessalonians to use the instruction about the end to ***encourage*** and ***build each other up*** (see 4:18), not to fuel speculation about the timing of the Lord's return.

5:12 ***honor*** (or *know*): This may be a call either to honor church leaders or to recognize the emerging leaders in the church (1 Cor 16:15-16). True ***leaders . . . work hard*** (1 Tim 4:10; 5:17) and govern to serve (Matt 20:25-28). They preside over, as well as help and protect, the church (Rom 16:1-2; 1 Tim 3:4-5, 12). • ***give you spiritual guidance:*** Leaders correct both moral and doctrinal errors (Acts 20:31; 1 Cor 4:14; Col 1:28).

5:13 Leaders were to receive honor and ***love*** not because of their high position but ***because of their work.*** • ***live peacefully:*** Teaching about community peace and harmony was a standard topic in ancient moral instruction. Harmony between believers and leaders was especially important because of the persecution the church suffered (2:14).

5:14 The responsibility for the moral progress of the congregation does not rest solely with the leaders (4:18; 5:11). Paul urged the church to ***warn those who are lazy,*** that is, those who were "disorderly," and who did not live by the apostles' instructions (see 2 Thes 3:6-15). • ***Take tender care of those who are weak,*** or those who have no economic or social power. Greek society denigrated the weak. • Instead of being irritable, believers should ***be patient*** in their relationships (Gal 5:23; Eph 4:2).

5:15 Jesus and the apostles warned against retaliation (Matt 5:38-48; Luke 6:27-36; Rom 12:17-21; 1 Pet 3:9). The Roman author Seneca, by contrast, considered revenge legitimate and necessary as a way of restoring social honor lost because of ill treatment from others. Paul calls Christians ***to do good***—both to members of the church (***each other***) and to those outside the Christian community (***to all people***), including their persecutors (2:14; see 3:12; Gal 6:10).

5:17 ***Never stop praying*** means not giving up (1:2; Luke 18:1; Rom 12:12; Eph 6:18); it does not mean praying at every moment.

5:18
Eph 5:20
[g]*thelēma* (2307)
‣Heb 10:36
5:20
1 Cor 14:1, 39
5:21
1 Jn 4:1
5:23
[h]*pneuma* (4151)
‣Heb 4:12
[i]*parousia* (3952)
‣Jas 5:7
5:24
1 Cor 1:9

18 Be thankful in all circumstances, for this
is God's [g]will for you who belong to Christ
Jesus.
19 Do not stifle the Holy Spirit. 20 Do not
scoff at prophecies, 21 but test everything
that is said. Hold on to what is good. 22 Stay
away from every kind of evil.

5. FINAL PRAYERS AND GREETINGS (5:23-28)

23 Now may the God of peace make you holy
in every way, and may your whole [h]spirit and
soul and body be kept blameless until our
Lord Jesus Christ [i]comes again. 24 God will
make this happen, for he who calls you is
faithful.
25 Dear brothers and sisters, pray for us.
26 Greet all the brothers and sisters with
Christian love.
27 I command you in the name of the Lord
to read this letter to all the brothers and
sisters.
28 May the grace of our Lord Jesus Christ
be with you.

5:18 ***Be thankful:*** God is sovereign and can redeem any situation (Rom 8:28).

5:19 ***Do not stifle the Holy Spirit:*** Paul exhorts the Thessalonian believers not to put out the Spirit's fire (Matt 3:11; Acts 2:3; 2 Tim 1:6) by prohibiting prophecy in the church (Jer 20:9; 1 Jn 4:1-2).

5:20-21 Prophecy, meant to build up the church (1 Cor 14:1-4), should not be rejected. Instead, the Thessalonians should ***test*** the ***prophecies*** (1 Cor 12:10; 14:29) to discern their origin, to check their agreement with the teaching of the apostles (2 Thes 2:2; 1 Jn 4:1-3), and to gauge the character of those who utter the prophecies (Matt 7:15-20). Early Christian teaching said, "Not everyone who speaks about spiritual things is a prophet, but only if the person's conduct is like the Lord" (*Didache* 11:8). They should ***hold on to what is good***—namely, prophecies that have been tested and found to be genuine.

5:22 They should reject ***every kind of evil,*** especially false prophecies (5:19-21).

5:23-28 Greek and Roman letters ended with a wish for the good health of the recipient. Jewish letters concluded with a peace blessing. Paul closes with a Christian variation on these practices.

5:23 God enables Christians to live a ***holy*** life (3:11-13). His sanctifying work extends to the ***spirit and soul and body,*** the totality of human life (cp. Matt 10:28; Mark 12:30; 1 Cor 7:34).

5:24 ***God will make this happen:*** Paul bases his confidence on the ***faithful*** character of God (1 Cor 1:9; 2 Thes 3:3; 2 Tim 2:13; 1 Jn 1:9).

5:26 ***with Christian love*** (literally *with a holy kiss;* see also Rom 16:16; 1 Cor 16:20; 2 Cor 13:12; 1 Pet 5:14): Kissing on the cheek or forehead was a common form of greeting that reflected such sentiments as honor, friendship, and love among family members (Mark 14:44-45; Luke 7:36-47; 15:20; Acts 20:37).

5:27 ***read this letter:*** Public reading of Scripture was practiced both in the synagogue (Luke 4:16; Acts 13:15) and the church (1 Tim 4:13). Similarly, Paul's letters were to be read aloud to the whole congregation (Col 4:16).

5:28 Paul improves the customary greeting by adding a blessing of ***grace*** at the end of his correspondence (Rom 16:20; 1 Cor 16:23; Gal 6:18; Eph 6:24; 2 Thes 3:18).

PAUL'S SECOND LETTER TO THE THESSALONIANS

The believers in Thessalonica had faced persecution since their conversion, but now it was more severe. A false teaching declared that the day of the Lord had already come, and some believers even quit working. What do you say to people whose lives move from bad to worse? Paul's second letter to this new church addresses their troubling problems.

The Christian view of history . . . is linear, and neither circular nor cyclical. We believe that it will come to a planned end, a grand finale, consisting of the Parousia, the Resurrection, the Judgment, and the Kingdom. That these events are history's goal is plain in both Paul's letters to the Thessalonians.

JOHN R. W. STOTT
The Message of 1 & 2 Thessalonians

SETTING

From the time of their conversion, the Thessalonian Christians had experienced hostility (1 Thes 1:6; 2:14), and Paul had worried whether they would retain their faith (1 Thes 3:5). When Paul wrote 1 Thessalonians, they had stood firm in faith, love, and hope (1 Thes 1:3; 3:6-8).

After Paul sent his first letter, the situation in the Thessalonian church deteriorated and the persecution intensified. What Paul had previously written was being countered by a false teaching that said that the day of the Lord had already come (2:2). Paul wrote 2 Thessalonians after receiving this news (2:2; 3:11) in order to give this church a divine perspective.

SUMMARY

Second Thessalonians opens with the customary greeting (1:1-2), then quickly moves to thanksgiving for their faith, love, and persevering hope, which had become a model for other congregations (1:3-4). Noting their suffering, Paul says that God will judge their persecutors and bring reward to the Thessalonians (1:5-10). Paul gives thanks for this church and prays that God will continue to make them worthy of his calling (1:11-12). In spite of their troubles, Paul is confident in God's work among them.

Paul counters the false teaching that "the day of the Lord has already begun" (2:1-2) and urges the church not to be deceived by this doctrine (2:3). He outlines events that will precede Christ's coming, when the church will be gathered to meet him (2:1-12). First, there will be rebellion against God (2:3). Then will come "the man of lawlessness," who will claim to be divine and demand worship (2:3-4). Although he will be empowered by Satan and will deceive many, Jesus will destroy him (2:8-12).

Although many will be deceived by the man of lawlessness, Paul is confident that God chose and called the Thessalonian Christians, and he urges them to stand firm (2:13-15). Paul concludes his discussion on final events with a prayer for the church (2:16-17) and a request that they pray for him as he preaches the Good News (3:1-2). His confidence in the church is based on God's handiwork in them (3:3-5).

In the closing section (3:6-18), Paul returns to an issue that he had addressed in the first letter. Some believers were refusing to work, despite Paul's instruction and example, so Paul calls on the church to discipline them (3:6-10). He also addresses these idle members directly, telling them to get to work (3:11-12). He commands the church to treat these slackers as errant Christians rather than hostile enemies (3:14-15) and he encour-

ages the church to continue its generosity toward those in genuine need (3:13). He closes the letter with prayers and a final greeting (3:16-18).

AUTHORSHIP

Paul's name is in the letter opening (1:1), and at the conclusion, Paul adds a note in his own hand to guarantee the letter's authenticity (3:17). As in 1 Thessalonians, the names of Silas and Timothy, the cofounders of this church, are included alongside Paul's, indicating that they stood behind the contents of the letter and probably shared in its writing. Most of the first person pronouns in the letter are plural ("we"), suggesting that Silas and Timothy had real input into the letter and that their names were not included simply as a courtesy. However, the final greeting in Paul's own writing emphasizes that he is the primary author, personally responsible for the contents of the letter.

The early church unanimously affirmed that 2 Thessalonians was a genuine letter of the apostle Paul. The book is in harmony with Paul's other writings. Nearly all scholars today recognize Paul as the author of this letter.

OUTLINE

1:1-2
Greetings

1:3-12
Opening Thanksgiving

2:1-17
The Time of the Day of the Lord

3:1-5
Request for Prayer

3:6-15
Disorderly Christians

3:16-18
Final Blessing and Greetings

RECIPIENTS

The recipients of the letter were the same as those who received 1 Thessalonians: "the church in Thessalonica, . . . you who belong to God our Father and the Lord Jesus Christ" (1:1). Many were artisans who earned their living by manual labor (3:6-12) or were clients of rich patrons (see "Work and Patronage" at 3:6-10, p. 2045). They were not people who had great wealth.

MEANING AND MESSAGE

Wars are often fought on multiple fronts. This was certainly the case with the conflict in the church at Thessalonica. With persecutors assailing the church, false doctrine circulating, and unruly members refusing to work, the battle lines were numerous. In his response, however, Paul never embraces despair or exasperation. He is very clear in his teaching and correction. He intends for his words to strengthen the troubled church, stop the false teaching, and correct the errant members.

The value of Paul's second letter to the Thessalonians is not merely in figuring out how events will occur at the end of human history. Such has often been the approach to the second chapter of this letter. Second Thessalonians is primarily a pastoral letter from Paul that provides hope and confidence in God when the world has gone mad. Christ reigns now, and Christ will be triumphant in the end.

TIMELINE

AD 47~48
Barnabas and Paul's first missionary journey

AD 48~49
Paul writes Galatians from Antioch

AD 49~50
The council in Jerusalem

AD 50–52
Paul's second missionary journey

about AD 50
Paul and Silas establish the Thessalonian church

about AD 50–52
Paul in Corinth

about AD 50
Paul writes 1 Thessalonians from Corinth

July 1, AD 51
Gallio named proconsul of Achaia

about AD 51
▸ **Paul writes 2 Thessalonians from Corinth**

AD 53–57
Paul's third missionary journey

FURTHER READING

GREGORY BEALE
1–2 Thessalonians (2003)

PHILIP W. COMFORT
2 Thessalonians in *Cornerstone Biblical Commentary*, vol. 16 (2008)

GENE L. GREEN
The Letters to the Thessalonians (2002)

ABRAHAM J. MALHERBE
Letters to the Thessalonians (2000)

I. HOWARD MARSHALL
The First and Second Epistles to the Thessalonians (1991)

CHARLES WANAMAKER
The Epistles to the Thessalonians (1990)

1. GREETINGS (1:1-2)

1 This letter is from Paul, Silas, and Timothy.
We are writing to the church in Thessalonica, to you who belong to God our Father
and the Lord Jesus Christ.
2May God our Father and the Lord Jesus
Christ give you grace and peace.

2. OPENING THANKSGIVING (1:3-12)

Encouragement during Persecution

3Dear brothers and sisters, we can't help
but thank God for you, because your faith
is flourishing and your love for one another
is growing. 4We proudly tell God's other
churches about your endurance and faithfulness in all the persecutions and hardships
you are suffering. 5And God will use this
persecution to show his justice and to make
you worthy of his Kingdom, for which you
are suffering. 6In his justice he will pay back
those who persecute you.
7And God will provide rest for you who
are being persecuted and also for us when
the Lord Jesus appears from heaven. He will
come with his mighty angels, 8in flaming
fire, bringing judgment on those who don't
know God and on those who refuse to obey
the Good News of our Lord Jesus. 9They will
be punished with eternal destruction, forever separated from the Lord and from his
glorious power. 10When he comes on that
day, he will receive glory from his holy people—praise from all who believe. And this
includes you, for you believed [a]what we told
you about him.

Prayer for the Thessalonians

11So we keep on praying for you, asking
our God to enable you to live a life worthy
of his [b]call. May he give you the power to
accomplish all the [c]good things your faith
prompts you to do. 12Then the name of our
Lord Jesus will be honored because of the
way you live, and you will be honored along
with him. This is all made possible because
of the [d]grace of our God and Lord, Jesus
Christ.

3. THE TIME OF THE DAY OF THE LORD (2:1-17)

Response to False Teaching

2 Now, dear brothers and sisters, let us
clarify some things about the coming
of our Lord Jesus Christ and how we will
be gathered to meet him. 2Don't be so easily shaken or alarmed by those who say that

1:1 1 Thes 1:1
1:2 Rom 1:7
1:3 1 Thes 1:2; 2 Thes 2:13
1:5 Phil 1:28; 1 Thes 2:12
1:6 Rev 6:10
1:7 Matt 25:31; 1 Thes 4:16
1:8 Ps 79:6; Isa 66:15; Jer 10:25
1:9 Isa 2:10, 19, 21; 1 Thes 5:3; 2 Thes 2:8
1:10 John 17:10; 1 Thes 3:13; [a]*marturion* (3142) ‣1 Tim 2:6
1:11 1 Thes 1:3; [b]*klēsis* (2821) ‣2 Tim 1:9; [c]*agathōsunē* (0019) ‣Rom 15:14
1:12 Isa 66:5; Mal 1:11; [d]*charis* (5485) ‣2 Tim 2:1
2:1 1 Thes 4:13-17

1:1-2 Paul follows ancient letter writing customs, but instead of the normal greeting (Greek *chairein*) he blesses them with ***grace*** (Greek *charis*) and ***peace***.

1:1 *Silas:* Greek *Silvanus,* the Greek form of the name.

1:2 ***God our Father*** (some manuscripts read *God the Father*) ***and the Lord Jesus Christ*** are coequal as the source of ***grace and peace***. The Thessalonians' hope was bound to God's grace (2:16), and even in persecution they could experience God-given peace (3:16).

1:3-10 After thanking God for the Thessalonian church (1:3-4), Paul writes about persecution (1:4), which had intensified since his first letter (1 Thes 1:6; 2:14; 3:3-4). God will relieve their suffering (1:5-10) and judge their persecutors.

1:3 ***Dear brothers and sisters:*** Literally *Brothers,* a generic term that refers to both male and female believers. • ***thank God:*** Paul begins with thanksgiving for the Thessalonians' ***faith, love,*** and "endurance" (1:4). These fundamental Christian virtues (see 1 Cor 13:13; Col 1:4-5; Heb 10:21-24; 1 Pet 2:1-22) were maturing in the church despite the persecution they endured (1:5).

1:4 Paul's boasting to ***other churches*** about the Thessalonians' ***endurance and faithfulness*** would stimulate the church's resolve to endure and remain faithful in the face of great hostility (1 Thes 2:14; 3:3-4).

1:5 Those called by God to enter his ***Kingdom*** will suffer for it (Acts 14:22; 1 Thes 2:12).

1:7 *rest:* Relief from suffering. • Elsewhere, Paul speaks of Christ's "coming" (2:1; 1 Thes 2:19; 3:13; 4:15; 5:23); here, he speaks of the event as the "appearing" or "unveiling" of ***the Lord Jesus,*** who cannot currently be seen physically (cp. 1 Pet 1:7-8; 4:13).

1:9 ***They will be punished*** for rejecting the message about Christ (1:8). • ***Eternal destruction*** (see 1 Thes 5:3; 1 Tim 6:9) is irrevocable. • ***Separated from the Lord*** refers to the source of the judgment to come (Isa 2:10, 19, 21).

1:10 *that day:* The day of the Lord (2:2; 1 Thes 5:2-4).

1:11-12 Paul assures the Thessalonian believers of God's promised justice, both for them and their persecutors (1:5-10). Because future deliverance means carrying out present responsibilities, Paul prays that they will be found worthy at Christ's return.

1:11 ***enable you to live a life worthy of his call:*** Paul had previously reminded the Thessalonians that God called them to conduct themselves "in a way that God would consider worthy" (1 Thes 2:12; see also Eph 4:1; Phil 1:27; Col 1:10). • Paul prayed that God would ***give*** the Thessalonian Christians ***power*** to live and work in a manner that would please God.

1:12 Though the ***name of our Lord Jesus*** was rejected by the Thessalonians' persecutors (1:8), Jesus will ultimately be glorified because of the lives of the believers. Further, they will be ***honored along with him*** (2:14; 1 Thes 2:12; cp. Rom 8:17-18; Col 3:4). Cp. Isa 66:5. • ***of our God and Lord, Jesus Christ:*** Or *of our God and our Lord Jesus Christ.*

2:1-12 False teaching about the day of the Lord had disturbed the Thessalonian church (2:1-2). Paul reminds them (2:5) that two events will precede that day: a great apostasy and the unveiling of the man of lawlessness (2:3-12). Christ will destroy this man when he returns (2:3, 8), and those who have been deceived will also be judged (2:9-12).

2:1 ***dear brothers and sisters:*** Literally *brothers;* also in 2:13, 15. See note on 1:3. • At ***the coming of our Lord Jesus Christ*** (1:7-10; 1 Thes 2:19; 3:13; 4:15–5:2, 23), all of his people will be ***gathered to meet him***. This will occur at the resurrection and rapture of the church (1 Thes 4:13-18).

2:2 The Thessalonian Christians previously asked Paul when the ***day of the***

2:2
2 Thes 2:15; 3:17
2:3
1 Tim 4:1
2:4
Isa 14:13-14
1 Cor 8:5
2:7
1 Jn 4:3
2:8
Job 4:9
Isa 11:4
Rev 19:15
[e]*epiphaneia* (2015)
‣1 Tim 6:14
2:9
Matt 24:24
Rev 13:13

the day of the Lord has already begun. Don't
believe them, even if they claim to have had
a spiritual vision, a revelation, or a letter supposedly from us. [3]Don't be fooled by what
they say. For that day will not come until
there is a great rebellion against God and
the man of lawlessness is revealed—the one
who brings destruction. [4]He will exalt himself and defy everything that people call
god and every object of worship. He will
even sit in the temple of God, claiming that
he himself is God.
[5]Don't you remember that I told you about
all this when I was with you? [6]And you know
what is holding him back, for he can be revealed only when his time comes. [7]For this
lawlessness is already at work secretly, and
it will remain secret until the one who is
holding it back steps out of the way. [8]Then
the man of lawlessness will be revealed, but
the Lord Jesus will kill him with the breath
of his mouth and destroy him by the [e]splen-
dor of his coming.
[9]This man will come to do the work of

"He Will Come" (1:7-10)

2 Thes 2:1-12
Matt 25:1-46
Acts 1:6-7
1 Thes 4:13–5:11

When Christ comes, he will destroy the enemies of the Good News and rescue persecuted believers (1:7-10). This future event calls for a present response. Those who obey the Good News can have confidence of rescue. Those who disobey will experience everlasting destruction.

Although Paul carefully lays out the events that will precede the day of the Lord, such as apostasy and the appearing of the man of lawlessness (2:1-12; 1 Thes 4:13-18), he does not fix the Thessalonians' attention here. Rather, he reminds them of these events (2:5) in order to refute the false teaching circulating among them. Paul assures the Thessalonian Christians that the Lord will judge evil (2:8) and that those who have believed the lie will perish (2:9-12).

God's choosing and calling of believers is their hope and comfort (2:13-14). They can stand firm in the present as they face the future (2:14-15). The final consummation of all things—the "day of the Lord" (2:2)—will come when least expected, like "a thief in the night" (1 Thes 5:2). Only the Father knows when that day will be (Acts 1:6-7). The present is not a time for speculation but for hope and solid confidence. Setting dates and times is not the way Christians should approach questions about the end. Scripture teaches about final things (*eschatology*) to give hope in the midst of trouble and perspective on present life and conduct.

Lord would come (1 Thes 5:1-11). Now a false teaching that this day had ***already begun*** (cp. 2 Tim 2:18) was causing them to waver in faith and become frightened. • ***a spiritual vision, a revelation, or a letter:*** The source of the teaching might have been a false prophecy (cp. 1 Jn 4:1-2), an erroneous sermon, or a letter falsely attributed to Paul.

2:3 Two events will precede ***that day*** of the Lord (2:2). • Both Jewish and Christian theology predicted ***a great rebellion against God*** before the end (Matt 24:11-14; 1 Tim 4:1). • The ***man of lawlessness*** (some manuscripts read *the man of sin*) is without or against law; his character is defined by sin. • ***the one who brings destruction*** (or *the one destined for destruction;* literally *the son of destruction*): The emphasis is on the lawless man's own destruction (2:8) rather than on the destruction he brings.

2:4 ***exalt himself:*** Like other Roman cities, Thessalonica constructed temples for the worship of the emperor. This cult was the prototype of the worship described here. • ***He will even sit in the temple of God:*** The profaning of the Temple in Jerusalem by Antiochus Epiphanes in 167 BC (see Dan 9:27; 11:31; 12:11) may have prefigured the event predicted here (Matt 24:15; Mark 13:14). Or it may refer to the attempt of the emperor Caligula, called "the new god manifest," to erect his own image in the Temple in AD 40. Alternatively, the *temple* may be an imperial temple (*of God* could be *of the god*) erected in honor of the lawless man and not necessarily a rebuilt temple in Jerusalem. • ***claiming that he himself is God*** (Ezek 28:2-10): The ascription of divine titles to the emperor was common in the first century.

2:6 ***what is holding him back:*** This has been variously identified as God, the Holy Spirit, the church, the gospel, Paul, the emperor, the Roman empire, or the government. Alternatively, the term may refer to something or someone who comes before the man of lawlessness, an agent of the lawlessness active at that time (2:7-8); in Greek literature, this term could describe demonic possession. This figure would prepare the way for the man of lawlessness ***when his time comes*** (2:3, 8).

2:7 The power of the coming man of lawlessness (2:3-6) ***is already at work secretly,*** like the antichrists of 1 Jn 2:18. • ***secretly*** (Greek *mustērion*): A descriptor commonly used of rituals in the mystery religions (see 2:6). • ***at work:*** This connotes supernatural intervention, whether divine (1 Thes 2:13) or, as here, evil (2:9; Eph 2:2). • ***The one who is holding it back*** could refer to one who is in opposition to the man of lawlessness; to one who is possessed; or to Satan, the one who possesses (2:9; see note on 2:6).

2:8 Paul announces the doom of ***the man of lawlessness*** (cp. 2:3). Although this figure claims to be divine, places his cult above all other worship (2:4), and receives power from Satan (2:9), ***the Lord Jesus will*** violently and utterly ***destroy him*** (Isa 11:4). • ***splendor:*** A reference to Christ's epiphany (1 Tim 6:14; 2 Tim 1:10; 4:1, 8; Titus 2:13), an alternative description of Christ's coming (2:1; 1 Thes 2:19; 3:13; 4:15; 5:23) or unveiling (1:7). In ancient literature, an *epiphany* was the appearance of a deity or a demonstration of divine power that evoked worship.

2:9 As Christ will appear in royal and divine power (his *parousia;* 2:1, 8; 1 Thes 2:19; 3:13; 4:15; 5:23), this figure similarly ***will come*** (*parousia*) with a royal entrance. • To ***do the work*** implies supernatural, Satanic action (see note on 2:7; 1 Thes 2:13, 18; 3:5).

Satan with counterfeit power and [f]signs and miracles. 10He will use every kind of evil deception to fool those on their way to destruction, because they refuse to love and accept the truth that would save them. 11So God will cause them to be greatly deceived, and they will believe these lies. 12Then they will be condemned for enjoying evil rather than believing the truth.

Thanks for God's Calling

13As for us, we can't help but thank God for you, dear brothers and sisters loved by the Lord. We are always thankful that God chose you to be among the first to experience [g]salvation—a salvation that came through the Spirit who makes you [h]holy and through your belief in the truth. 14He called you to salvation when we told you the Good News; now you can share in the glory of our Lord Jesus Christ.

Call to Stand Firm

15With all these things in mind, dear brothers and sisters, stand firm and keep a strong grip on the teaching we passed on to you both in person and by letter.

A Blessing

16Now may our Lord Jesus Christ himself and God our Father, who loved us and by his grace gave us eternal comfort and a wonderful hope, 17comfort you and strengthen you in every good thing you do and say.

4. REQUEST FOR PRAYER (3:1-5)

3 Finally, dear brothers and sisters, we ask you to pray for us. Pray that the Lord's message will spread rapidly and be honored wherever it goes, just as when it came to you. 2Pray, too, that we will be rescued from wicked and evil people, for not everyone is a believer. 3But the Lord is faithful; he will strengthen you and guard you from the evil one. 4And we are confident in the Lord that you are doing and will continue to do the things we commanded you. 5May the Lord lead your hearts into a full understanding and expression of the love of God and the patient endurance that comes from Christ.

5. DISORDERLY CHRISTIANS (3:6-15)

Paul's Exhortation and Example

6And now, dear brothers and sisters, we give you this command in the name of our Lord Jesus Christ: Stay away from all believers who live idle lives and don't follow the tradition they received from us. 7For you know that you ought to imitate us. We were not idle when we were with you. 8We never accepted food from anyone without paying

[f]*sēmeion* (4592) ‣Heb 2:4
2:10 1 Cor 1:18
2:11 Rom 1:24, 28; 2 Tim 4:4
2:12 Rom 1:18, 32; 2:8
2:13 Deut 33:12; Eph 1:4
[g]*sōtēria* (4991) ‣2 Tim 1:9
[h]*hagiasmos* (0038) ‣1 Tim 2:15
2:14 1 Thes 4:7; 5:9
2:15 1 Cor 11:2; 16:13
2:16 John 3:16
2:17 1 Thes 3:2; 5:11
3:1 1 Thes 1:8; 5:25
3:2 Rom 15:31
3:3 1 Cor 1:9
3:4 1 Thes 4:10
3:5 1 Chr 29:18
3:6 Rom 16:17; 1 Cor 11:2
3:8 Acts 18:3; 1 Thes 2:9
3:9 Matt 10:10; 1 Cor 9:4, 6

2:11 As seen elsewhere in Scripture (Exod 9:12; 2 Chr 18:22), God sometimes hands people over to the power of the sin or deception they have desired in place of the truth (Rom 1:24, 26, 28; 11:8).

2:12 ***They will be condemned*** (see 1:6-9) by God's judicial verdict for not ***believing the truth*** (2:10), instead believing the lie of the man of lawlessness (2:9-10).

2:13 ***chose you to be among the first:*** Some manuscripts read *chose you from the very beginning.*

2:14 ***He called you to salvation:*** God calls his chosen ones to himself (1:11; 1 Thes 2:12; 4:7; 5:24) through the preaching of ***the Good News.*** • Those who suffer because of their faith will ultimately ***share in the glory of our Lord Jesus Christ*** (Rom 5:2; 8:17-18; Col 1:27; 1 Thes 2:12).

2:15 Ever since the founding of the Thessalonian church, Paul had been concerned for the stability of their faith (1 Thes 3:2, 5, 8; 4:1-2) and their adherence to his ***teaching*** (3:6; 1 Cor 11:2; 15:3; see Jude 1:3).

2:16 ***Eternal comfort and . . . hope*** transcend both death and uncertainty about the immediate future.

2:17 Paul's prayer echoes the purpose of Timothy's visit to the church—to ***strengthen*** and encourage the Thessalonian believers in their faith (1 Thes 3:2). • To ***comfort you*** does not merely mean to *console,* but to *exhort* or *encourage* them because of their fears and doubts (2:1-12; 1 Thes 4:18; 5:11).

3:1-5 Before taking up the final topic of the letter (3:6-15), Paul requests prayer (3:1-2) and assures the Thessalonians of God's providence in troubles (3:3-5).

3:1 ***dear brothers and sisters:*** Literally *brothers;* also in 3:6, 13. See note on 1:3. • ***pray:*** The prayer that the gospel would ***spread rapidly*** recalls Ps 147:15. Paul merges the image with reference to the games (see 1 Cor 9:24-26; Gal 2:2) in which a victor was ***honored.***

3:2 Paul, too, suffered for the Good News (2 Cor 6:5; 11:23-26; 1 Thes 2:2). His prayer to ***be rescued*** echoes Isa 25:4.

3:3 The sufferings the Thessalonians faced were caused by ***the evil one*** (or by *evil;* see 2:9; cp. 1:4-6; 1 Thes 1:6; 2:14).

3:5 The prayer that God would ***lead*** (literally *make straight*) their ***hearts*** reflects an OT expression (1 Chr 29:18; Prov 23:19). Christians are expected to ***love*** as God loves and practice ***patient endurance*** as Christ endured.

3:6-15 In his previous letter, Paul had addressed the problem of lazy members of the church who refused to work (1 Thes 4:11-12; 5:14). Some had ignored his message and example, so he gives additional instruction for dealing with these members.

3:6 Paul's ***command*** is given by the authority of the ***Lord Jesus Christ*** (1 Thes 4:2). • Church members should shun Christians who ***live idle lives*** (see 3:7, 11-13; 1 Thes 5:14). To ***stay away from*** the lazy would make a strong impression on them (Matt 18:17; Rom 16:17; 1 Cor 5:9-13), promoting shame (3:14) and repentance, but stopping short of excommunication (3:15). • ***from all believers:*** Literally *from every brother.* See note on 1:3. • ***they received:*** Some manuscripts read *you received.*

3:7 Teaching by example was highly regarded in the ancient world. Paul himself provided an example by working for his own food (3:8; 1 Thes 2:9).

3:8 ***without paying for it:*** Although Paul taught that workers in the Christian church could receive pay for their labor (3:9; see Matt 10:10; 1 Cor 9:7-14; 1 Tim 5:17-18), he did not take advantage of that privilege (1 Thes 2:9). See "Work and Patronage," facing page.

[i]*tupos* (5179)
‣1 Tim 4:12
3:10
1 Thes 4:11
3:11
1 Tim 5:13
3:12
1 Thes 4:11
[j]*parakaleō* (3870)
‣2 Tim 4:2
3:15
Gal 6:1
1 Thes 5:14
3:16
Rom 15:33
[k]*kurios* (2962)
‣1 Pet 3:6
3:17
1 Cor 16:21
Gal 6:11
Col 4:18
Phlm 1:19

for it. We worked hard day and night so we
would not be a burden to any of you. 9We
certainly had the right to ask you to feed us,
but we wanted to give you an [i]example to
follow. 10Even while we were with you, we
gave you this command: "Those unwilling
to work will not get to eat."

Paul's Commands

11Yet we hear that some of you are living
idle lives, refusing to work and meddling
in other people's business. 12We command
such people and [j]urge them in the name of
the Lord Jesus Christ to settle down and
work to earn their own living. 13As for the
rest of you, dear brothers and sisters, never
get tired of doing good.

14Take note of those who refuse to obey
what we say in this letter. Stay away from
them so they will be ashamed. 15Don't think
of them as enemies, but warn them as you
would a brother or sister.

6. FINAL BLESSING AND GREETINGS (3:16-18)

16Now may the [k]Lord of peace himself give
you his peace at all times and in every situation. The [k]Lord be with you all.

17HERE IS MY GREETING IN MY OWN HAND-
WRITING—PAUL. I DO THIS IN ALL MY LETTERS
TO PROVE THEY ARE FROM ME.

18May the grace of our Lord Jesus Christ
be with you all.

Work and Patronage (3:6-10)

Matt 10:10
1 Cor 9:13-16
Phil 4:15-16
1 Thes 2:5, 9; 4:11-12; 5:14

When Paul first visited Thessalonica, he taught the believers to work for a living rather than being dependent by demanding support or becoming clients of non-Christian patrons.

Yet some of the Thessalonians refused to work. Paul dealt with these idle Christians in his first letter (1 Thes 4:11-12; 5:14) but they remained entrenched and had not changed their ways. Why did they refuse to work? Possibly, these believers so vividly expected a quick return of the Lord that they gave up all work. Paul's teaching about the coming of the Lord, however, never contradicted his basic instruction about the necessity of work (3:6, 10).

These idle Christians may have been clients of prominent patrons. Patronage was a fundamental feature of the Roman economic world. Rich patrons often supported numerous clients in various ways, such as by giving them food or money and by representing them in public assembly. Having numerous clients increased the honor of a patron. However, being a client brought social obligations that Paul would have wanted the Thessalonian believers to avoid, especially because their patrons were most likely not Christians.

Paul set for the Thessalonians an example of self-reliance. While he was among them, he supported himself (3:7-8; 1 Thes 2:9). Although Paul believed that "those who work deserve to be fed" (Matt 10:10; 1 Cor 9:13-16), he did not receive support from the Thessalonians (he did accept offerings from the Philippians, Phil 4:15-16). Paul wanted the Thessalonians to know that he did not come to them as a smooth talker hoping for monetary gain (1 Thes 2:5, 9). He wanted them to understand from his example how they themselves should live.

3:9 Paul had distanced himself from others in the culture who were motivated by fame and money (1 Thes 2:5).

3:10 Work is the appropriate way to gain a living (see Gen 3:17-19; Ps 128:2; Prov 10:4). Paul absolves the church of the responsibility of feeding other believers who refuse to work.

3:12 Paul underscores the strength of the command by appealing to the authority of the ***Lord Jesus*** (as in 3:6; 1 Thes 4:1-2). • ***settle down:*** I.e., lead a quiet life instead of being involved in meddlesome activities (see 1 Thes 4:11).

3:13 ***doing good:*** The Thessalonians were exhorted to reach out and help those in genuine need (see Gal 6:9-10), in contrast with those who are lazy and dependent (3:7-8, 10).

3:14 Paul hoped that the disobedient Christians would be ***ashamed*** and repent (see note on 3:6) in response to being shunned by the community.

3:15 ***Don't think of them as enemies:*** In the ancient world, social relations with enemies were broken off and punitive action was initiated against them. Paul warns the Thessalonians that discipline against disobedient Christians (3:14) should not result in this kind of attack. Rather, the church should treat them as members of the family, with the hope that they would correct their conduct (1 Thes 5:12, 14). • ***a brother or sister:*** Literally *as a brother.* See note on 1:3.

3:16 The final prayer echoes Jesus' blessing in John 14:27 (cp. Num 6:26) and contrasts with the situation these believers faced in Thessalonica (1:4-10; 1 Thes 2:14). Paul was always conscious of the ***Lord*** Jesus' presence ***with*** his people (Rom 15:33; Phil 4:9).

3:17 A secretary had written this letter for Paul (Rom 16:22; 1 Pet 5:12). Now Paul takes the pen to add a final greeting in his own hand (cp. 1 Cor 16:21; Gal 6:11; Col 4:18; Phlm 1:19). Because he suspected that a letter he had not written was circulating under his name (2:2), he emphasizes this authenticating procedure ***to prove*** this letter is from him.

3:18 Ancient letters frequently ended with a wish for health or prosperity, but Paul's blessing is much grander: He calls on the ***Lord Jesus Christ*** to grant ***grace*** to the recipients (see 1 Thes 5:28).

INTRODUCTION TO PAUL'S LETTERS TO
TIMOTHY AND TITUS

The "Pastoral Epistles" (1–2 Timothy and Titus) were written following Paul's release from the imprisonment described in Acts 28. They are the only letters from Paul that survive from this last period of his life. In 1 Timothy and Titus, Paul works through two of his associates to stabilize churches in Ephesus and Crete. In 2 Timothy, Paul is again in a Roman prison. Aware that his life is nearing its end, he is concerned that the mission he began should continue after he is gone.

SETTING

Having been released from prison in Rome (Acts 28, AD 60–62), Paul resumed his apostolic mission, continuing his earlier activities in Dalmatia, Greece, and east to Asia and Galatia. Paul was conscious that his apostolic career was closing, and he sought to set the churches in order before his departure (1 Tim 3:15).

AUTHORSHIP

A widespread view is that these letters were not written by Paul. There are several good reasons, however, to believe that Paul is the author.

(1) Until the 1800s, there was no hesitation in ascribing these letters to Paul. This includes early church fathers whose native language was Greek and who were very familiar with Paul's other letters.

(2) The early church would never have accepted these letters had they suspected the letters of being falsely signed in Paul's name.

(3) Paul's style in these letters is different from elsewhere, but it might be a result of the distinctive situations Paul was addressing. It also might result from the use of a different *amanuensis* (scribe) for these letters.

These letters, from a distinctive period of Paul's life and career, are still true to Paul and complement his other writings. It is reasonable to affirm Paul's authorship and overreaching to exclude it.

DATE OF WRITING

In 2 Timothy, Paul is jailed in Rome at the end of his life. This would seem to place the letters of 1 Timothy and Titus—written while Paul was still moving freely—in the time leading up to his arrest. How do these details fit with Acts?

One possibility is that 2 Timothy was written during the Roman imprisonment of Acts 28. In this case, all three letters would fit into Luke's historical account in the book of Acts, and Paul would have been executed at the end of that imprisonment (Acts 28:30; AD 62).

There are early reports, however, that Paul was released from the Roman imprisonment (e.g., *1 Clement* 5:6-7, AD 95~97; see also Eusebius, *Church History* 2.22, AD 325). He engaged in further work, possibly went to Spain, and was then rearrested and executed in Rome during Nero's persecution of Christians (about AD 64~65). The letters to Timothy and Titus were then written during this later period.

In support of this approach, there is no reason that these letters must be fitted into the history recorded in Acts. Also, the activities of Paul and his delegates in 1 Timothy and Titus do not correspond to the details in Acts, nor does the imprisonment of 2 Timothy sound like the imprisonment of Acts 28. Finally, the distinctive style and content of these letters is less puzzling if they were written at a different time from Paul's other letters.

THE FALSE TEACHERS

It is very difficult to draw a clear picture of the false teachers, but there are clues. Their teaching had ascetic elements (see 1 Tim 4:3; Titus 1:15) and a Jewish focus (see 1 Tim 1:7; Titus 1:10, 14; 3:9). It claimed special knowledge (1 Tim 6:20; Titus 1:16), asserted that the resurrection of the believers had already taken place (2 Tim 2:18), disrupted relationships (2 Tim 3:6-7; Titus 1:11), and might have emphasized salvation by works (2 Tim 1:9; Titus 3:5). Paul's strong response suggests a need to make corrections regarding the doctrine of Christ (see 1 Tim 2:5-6; 3:16; 2 Tim 2:8) and the last days (see 1 Tim 4:1-5; 2 Tim 2:18; 3:1-9; Titus 2:11-14). The false teachers opposed Paul's message, promoted immorality, and undercut the church's mission. Thus, good leaders were needed (see Titus 1:10-13; 2:6-8, 15).

MEANING & MESSAGE

The letters to Timothy and Titus are not handbooks of church government, but they do provide insight into the organization of the earliest churches. They are rare snapshots of church leadership making adaptations in response to needs.

These letters incorporate summaries of essential apostolic doctrines (e.g., 1 Tim 3:16; Titus 3:4-7), which Paul wanted his readers to preserve faithfully and make central to their lives.

In these letters, Paul makes a strong appeal to live the new life in Christ. He challenges the whole church to carry the Good News forward faithfully, proclaiming the message and living out God's presence in the world.

FURTHER READING

LINDA BELLEVILLE
1 Timothy in *Cornerstone Biblical Commentary*, vol. 17 (2008)

GORDON FEE
1 and 2 Timothy, Titus (1984, 1988)

LUKE TIMOTHY JOHNSON
Letters to Paul's Delegates (1996)

JON LAANSMA
2 Timothy, Titus in *Cornerstone Biblical Commentary*, vol. 17 (2008)

WILLIAM MOUNCE
The Pastoral Epistles (2000)

PAUL'S FIRST LETTER TO

TIMOTHY

During the final phase of Paul's apostolic career, a serious disruption was troubling a long-established Christian church: Some church leaders had become false teachers. Paul had warned that this would happen (Acts 20:29-31), and now their impact was threatening the life and well-being of the community. A skillful person was needed to restore order to God's household. Paul gave this task to Timothy, his trusted delegate.

SETTING

Paul's first contact with Ephesus, during his second missionary journey (Acts 18:19-21), gave no opportunity for significant work. During his third journey, he returned to the city and served a couple of years (Acts 19, around AD 53~56). Later, when Paul was on his way to Jerusalem, he had opportunity to stop at Miletus and speak to the elders from Ephesus, who met him there (Acts 20:17-38). Paul traveled to Jerusalem, was arrested, was later transferred to Caesarea, and was then sent to Rome, where he stayed under house arrest for approximately two years (Acts 21–28; AD 60–62). When he was released from prison, he reembarked on his missionary journeys, possibly directed toward Spain (see Rom 15:24, 28), although it is just as possible that the imprisonment changed Paul's orientation back eastward.

Paul was still involved with the Ephesian church during this period. Timothy had accompanied Paul for much of his original ministry there (Acts 19:22) and had now been delegated the task of dealing with new and troubling developments in Ephesus (1:3). False teachers were upsetting households (cp. 2:15; 3:4-5; 5:11-15; Titus 1:11). Repercussions in the surrounding society (see 2:2) were bringing the church and the gospel into disrepute. Paul wrote Timothy to guide him in correcting errant behavior and in preventing false teachers from gaining another foothold.

◀ **The Setting of 1 Timothy, about AD 63.** Timothy had accompanied Paul on his second missionary journey (Acts 16:1-3; 17:14-15; 18:5) and was with Paul in EPHESUS during his third journey (Acts 19:22). After Paul's imprisonment in Rome (AD 60–62), he evidently sent Timothy back to EPHESUS while Paul himself went to visit the churches in MACEDONIA (see 1:3). Paul then wrote to Timothy to help him make corrections in the Ephesian church (3:14-15).

SUMMARY

After directing Timothy to deal with the would-be teachers of the law (1:3-20), Paul gives guidance on conduct in God's household with respect to prayer, women's teaching, and leadership (2:1–3:13). These three areas had been harmed by the false teachers. Paul makes clear what he is trying to accomplish and explains why and how it must be done (3:14–4:16). Then he resumes his instructions on godly conduct concerning old and young people, widows, elders, and masters (5:1–6:2). These areas, too, had been distorted by false teaching. Finally, Paul returns to the need to deal with the false teachers themselves, this time centering on issues of wealth and profit (6:2-21).

OUTLINE

1:1-2
Salutation from Paul

1:3-17
Dealing with False Teaching

1:18-20
The Responsibility to Act

2:1–3:13
Right Conduct in God's Household

3:14–4:16
Right Teaching and Timothy's Task

5:1–6:2a
Right Conduct in God's Household

6:2b-21a
Dealing with False Teaching

6:21b
Closing Blessing

DATE OF WRITING

Most likely, 1 Timothy was written after Paul's first imprisonment in Rome (Acts 28). If, however, 1 Timothy is dated within the time frame of Acts, then Acts 20:1-3 provides a possible window. Another option is during a possible time gap between Acts 19:20, 21. On balance, however, these earlier periods are less plausible for 1 Timothy than a time period after Acts 28 (see Introduction to Paul's Letters to Timothy and Titus, "Date of Writing," p. 2047).

LITERARY GENRE

This letter has characteristics similar to a Greco-Roman *mandatum principis* ("commandment of a ruler"), in which "a superior writes to a representative or delegate with instructions concerning the delegate's mission."[1] Though addressed to the delegate, such mandates were intended to be public rather than private. This literary form was commonly used in situations such as Timothy's. It authorized the delegate and established a public norm of conduct to which he could be held accountable by those in his charge. Though Paul and Timothy had a close personal relationship, the content and formal tone of 1 Timothy are in keeping with its literary genre.

MEANING AND MESSAGE

First Timothy is not primarily an essay on church government and gender policies. It is a passionate and masterful advocacy for the Good News of Jesus Christ, its ongoing progress in the world, and the new life which it creates and promotes (see 3:14-16).

[1] Luke Timothy Johnson, *The First and Second Letters to Timothy* (New York: Doubleday, 2001), 139.

TIMELINE

AD 34~35
Saul's conversion near Damascus

AD 53~56
Paul's ministry in Ephesus

AD 60–62
Paul is imprisoned in Rome

AD 62~64
Paul's further ministry, including Crete and Ephesus

about AD 63
Paul writes 1 Timothy and Titus from Macedonia

about AD 64~65?
Paul is imprisoned, writes 2 Timothy, and is martyred in Rome

The need for wise dealing with questions of church arrangements and Christian discipline is ever present, and [the Pastoral] Epistles have constantly supplied Christian leaders with sober practical advice in these matters.

DONALD GUTHRIE
The Pastoral Epistles,
p. 62

God's household was Paul's immediate concern. Just as the surrounding society expected orderly conduct in the family household—with roles and decorum and notions of honor and shame—so it was with the household of God. God's household adapts to the social and economic structures of society, reflecting widely accepted standards of honor and propriety as well as the social structures themselves. At the same time, where proper and necessary, God's household runs counter to society, reflecting very different and even countercultural values and practices. The formation of God's household is dynamic, not mathematical. Salvation is begun but is not complete. God's household is in the world, but not of it. That world remains God's good creation (4:3-4; 6:17), but the world is transient and is in its last, difficult, evil-ridden days (4:1; 2 Tim 3:1). God's household exists in the world and reflects the new creation.

Paul's primary concern was with the mission of the church to advance the Good News in the world and promote the will of God (see 2:4-7). God's people should do what supports that mission (2:1–3:13; 5:1–6:2; see 1 Cor 9:19-23). The false teachers were, by contrast, talking foolishness and damaging the integrity of the church, so Paul directed most of his words toward right conduct. The condensed summaries of the Good News (1:15; 2:5-6; 3:16; 6:13-16) indicate what was actually under assault—the right understanding of salvation in the present age. This "deposit" (see note on 6:20) is what must be preserved, skillfully taught, and passed along with godly life as its outcome.

FURTHER READING

LINDA BELLEVILLE
1 Timothy in *Cornerstone Biblical Commentary*, vol. 17 (2009)

GORDON FEE
1 and 2 Timothy, Titus (1988)

LUKE TIMOTHY JOHNSON
Letters to Paul's Delegates (1996)

I. HOWARD MARSHALL
The Pastoral Epistles (1999)

WILLIAM MOUNCE
The Pastoral Epistles (2000)

1. SALUTATION FROM PAUL (1:1-2)

1 This letter is from Paul, an apostle of
Christ Jesus, appointed by the command of God our Savior and Christ Jesus,
who gives us hope.
2 I am writing to Timothy, my true son in
the faith.
May God the Father and Christ Jesus our
Lord give you grace, mercy, and peace.

2. DEALING WITH FALSE TEACHING (1:3-17)

Silencing False Teachers

3 When I left for Macedonia, I urged you to
stay there in Ephesus and stop those whose
teaching is contrary to the truth. 4 Don't
let them waste their time in endless discussion of myths and spiritual pedigrees.
These things only lead to meaningless

1:1 Col 1:27; Titus 1:3; 3:4
1:2 Acts 16:1; 1 Cor 4:17; 2 Tim 1:2; Titus 1:4
1:3 Acts 20:1; Gal 1:6-7
1:4 Titus 3:9

1:1-2 This opening has the standard components of a letter: sender, recipient, and greeting. Additions to the basic pattern underscore Paul's authoritative message (see also Rom 1:1-7; 1 Cor 1:1-3; Gal 1:1-5; Titus 1:1-4).

1:1 ***Our Savior***, here used of God, applies equally to ***Christ Jesus*** (1:15; 2:3-4; see 2 Tim 1:9-10; Titus 1:3-4; 2:10, 13). • ***Hope*** is based on God in contrast to other objects such as wealth (4:10; 5:5; 6:17).

1:2 ***Timothy*** was currently in Ephesus as Paul's delegate (see 1 Timothy Introduction, "Setting," p. 2048). See also "Timothy" at Acts 16:1-3, p. 1860. • Timothy was Paul's ***true son in the faith*** (see Phil 2:20; cp. Titus 1:4), but probably not Paul's direct convert (see Acts 16:1).

1:3-11 Paul's greetings are usually followed by thanksgiving or blessing to God; Greco-Roman letters often did the same. First Timothy and Titus probably do not include this because of their character as official letters authorizing a delegate (see 1 Timothy Introduction, "Literary Genre," p. 2049). Instead, Paul first addresses his concern to silence the false teachers.

1:3 ***stop those . . . contrary to the truth:*** Just as Paul had previously warned (Acts 20:29-31), false teachers came into the church ***in Ephesus;*** this letter was written to help Timothy to deal with them.

1:4 ***in endless discussion . . . meaningless speculations*** (literally *in myths and endless genealogies, which cause speculation*): Paul might be dismissing their teaching as trivial, or he might be rejecting the fanciful nature of their interpretations (1:7; see also 2 Tim 4:3-4; Titus 1:14; 3:9; 2 Pet 1:16) and their justification of immoral behavior (1:8-11; 4:1-2, 7; see also Titus 1:15-16). • ***spiritual pedigrees*** (literally *endless genealogies*): In Judaism, one's genealogy established one's spiritual pedigree; the false teachers might have been preoccupied with this. They were probably also exploiting OT genealogies (Gen 2–4, 5) in fanciful interpretations of the law. • ***which don't help people live a life of faith in God*** (literally *rather than a stewardship of God in faith*): The Greek uses an important word ("stewardship," "household management") that has to do with the household (see 3:15); this phrase can be translated in a number of ways, such as faithfulness to God's household management or faithfulness in managing God's household.

[a]*oikonomia* (3622)
‣ Titus 1:7

1:5
Rom 13:10
Gal 5:14
2 Tim 1:5
[b]*kardia* (2588)
‣ 1 Pet 1:22

1:6
2 Tim 2:23
Titus 1:10

1:8
Rom 7:12, 16

1:9
Gal 3:19; 5:23

1:10
2 Tim 4:3
Titus 1:9; 2:1

1:11
Gal 2:7

1:12
Acts 9:15
Gal 1:15-16
Phil 4:13

1:13
Luke 23:34
Acts 8:3; 26:9
1 Cor 15:9

1:14
Rom 5:20
2 Tim 1:13

1:15
Luke 15:2; 19:10
Rom 5:8

1:17
Rom 16:27

1:19
2 Tim 4:7

speculations, which don't help people live a
[a]life of faith in God.
[5]The purpose of my instruction is that
all believers would be filled with love that
comes from a pure [b]heart, a clear conscience,
and genuine faith. [6]But some people have
missed this whole point. They have turned
away from these things and spend their
time in meaningless discussions. [7]They
want to be known as teachers of the law of
Moses, but they don't know what they are
talking about, even though they speak so
confidently.
[8]We know that the law is good when used
correctly. [9]For the law was not intended for
people who do what is right. It is for people
who are lawless and rebellious, who are
ungodly and sinful, who consider nothing
sacred and defile what is holy, who kill their
father or mother or commit other murders.
[10]The law is for people who are sexually immoral, or who practice homosexuality, or
are slave traders, liars, promise breakers, or
who do anything else that contradicts the
wholesome teaching [11]that comes from the
glorious Good News entrusted to me by our
blessed God.

Parenthesis: Gratitude for God's Mercy

[12]I thank Christ Jesus our Lord, who has
given me strength to do his work. He considered me trustworthy and appointed me
to serve him, [13]even though I used to blaspheme the name of Christ. In my insolence,
I persecuted his people. But God had mercy
on me because I did it in ignorance and unbelief. [14]Oh, how generous and gracious our
Lord was! He filled me with the faith and
love that come from Christ Jesus.
[15]This is a trustworthy saying, and everyone should accept it: "Christ Jesus came
into the world to save sinners"—and I am
the worst of them all. [16]But God had mercy
on me so that Christ Jesus could use me as
a prime example of his great patience with
even the worst sinners. Then others will realize that they, too, can believe in him and
receive eternal life. [17]All honor and glory to
God forever and ever! He is the eternal King,
the unseen one who never dies; he alone is
God. Amen.

3. THE RESPONSIBILITY TO ACT (1:18-20)

[18]Timothy, my son, here are my instructions
for you, based on the prophetic words spoken about you earlier. May they help you
fight well in the Lord's battles. [19]Cling to your
faith in Christ, and keep your conscience
clear. For some people have deliberately

1:5 ***The purpose of my instruction:*** Paul seeks godliness that flows out of sound faith and renewal (see Titus 3:5; see also 1 Cor 13; Col 3:14). • In 1 Timothy and Titus, all allusions to a ***clear conscience*** are in contrast to the false teachers' dead consciences (e.g., 1:19; 4:2; Titus 1:15).

1:6-11 Paul now elaborates on the false teachers and turns their subject matter against them.

1:6 ***Some people*** is probably a put-down, demoting the false teachers to a general class of opponents of the Good News (cp. Rom 3:8; 1 Cor 4:18; 2 Cor 3:1; Gal 1:7). • They were professing believers who had ***missed*** the ***whole point*** of the Good News and had ***turned away.***

1:7 Their aspirations to be ***teachers of the law of Moses*** were ironic; their handling of the law was deficient in the light of the Good News, and they neither understood nor fulfilled the law (see 1:8-11).

1:8 See Rom 7:11-16; Gal 3:19–4:7; 2 Tim 3:15-17.

1:9 ***the law was not intended for people who do what is right:*** As a general principle, the virtuous person needs no law. For Christians, a righteous life results from faith apart from the law (see Gal 5:16-26; Eph 2:11-14; Titus 2:11-14; cp. Rom 8:1-17; Jas 2:14-16).

1:10 This list portrays the ultimate tendencies of the false teachers' teachings, their underlying spiritual state, and the superior righteousness of the Good News (see Matt 5:20; Gal 5:22-23). • ***slave traders:*** Or *kidnappers.* • ***that contradicts the wholesome*** (or *sound, healthy*) ***teaching:*** See also 6:3-4; 2 Tim 1:13; 4:3; Titus 1:9, 13; 2:1, 8. This addition to the list is both a closing generalization and a powerful assertion. Righteousness is now defined more perfectly by the Good News than by the law, but law still speaks to all that is opposed to the Good News. The false teachers' reliance on the law, therefore, underscores their departure from Paul's teaching.

1:11 Titus 2:11-14 gives a fuller version of Paul's idea here.

1:12-17 This expression of gratitude is a parenthesis from Paul's charge to Timothy (1:3-11, 18-20). Triggered by the mention of Paul's role (1:11), it gives perspective on the source of Paul's thankfulness and provides a model for its readers. When talking about his own work, Paul directs glory to God and makes it plain that he is doing God's work (see also 2 Cor 1:21-22; 2:14-17; 3:4-6; 4:7; 12:9-10).

1:15 ***This is a trustworthy saying:*** This expression recurs only in the letters to Timothy and Titus (3:1; 4:8-9; 2 Tim 2:11-13; Titus 3:4-8). These sayings are probably quotations from tradition that Paul has adapted to the current situation; here, in addition to the way the saying underscores the mercy shown to Paul, it probably corrects the false teachers. The emphasis of this saying falls on Christ's entrance into history for the salvation of sinners, which was probably being marginalized by the false teachers, who emphasized law (1:7), special knowledge (6:20; cp. Titus 1:16), and stipulations such as those in 4:3 (cp. Col 2:16-23).

1:18-20 Paul continues his charge to Timothy (1:3-11), who is to draw upon available resources, remain faithful, and consider two bad examples. The church (also part of the audience; see 1 Timothy Introduction, "Literary Genre," p. 2049) should expect Paul's delegate to do these things.

1:18 ***the prophetic words spoken about you earlier:*** This was probably at Timothy's commissioning (see 4:14; 2 Tim 1:6; cp. Acts 13:2-3).

1:19 See also 1:5-6; 6:20-21; 2 Tim 2:15-18. ***Conscience*** is viewed as a kind of gyroscope; keeping it ***clear*** (or *good*) means ensuring that it is not destroyed (see note on 4:2).

violated their consciences; as a result, their faith has been shipwrecked. 20Hymenaeus and Alexander are two examples. I threw them out and handed them over to Satan so they might learn not to [c]blaspheme God.

4. RIGHT CONDUCT IN GOD'S HOUSEHOLD (2:1–3:13)

Holy Prayer and Right Teaching

2 I urge you, first of all, to pray for all people. Ask God to help them; intercede on their behalf, and give thanks for them. 2Pray this way for kings and all who are in authority so that we can live peaceful and quiet lives marked by godliness and dignity. 3This is good and pleases God our Savior, 4who wants everyone to be saved and to understand the truth. 5For there is only one God and one Mediator who can reconcile God and humanity—the man Christ Jesus. 6He gave his life to [d]purchase freedom for everyone. This is the [e]message God gave to the world at just the right time. 7And I have been chosen as a preacher and [f]apostle to teach the Gentiles this message about faith and truth. I'm not exaggerating—just telling the truth.

8In every place of worship, I want men to pray with holy hands lifted up to God, free from anger and controversy.

9And I want women to be modest in their appearance. They should wear decent and appropriate clothing and not draw attention to themselves by the way they fix their hair or by wearing gold or pearls or expensive clothes. 10For women who claim to be devoted to God should make themselves attractive by the good things they do.

11Women should learn quietly and submissively. 12I do not let women teach men or have authority over them. Let them listen quietly. 13For God made Adam first,

1:20 1 Cor 5:5; 2 Tim 2:17; 4:14
[c]*blasphēmeō* (0987) ›2 Tim 3:2
2:1 Eph 6:18; Phil 4:6
2:6 Gal 1:4; 2:20
[d]*antilutron* (0487) ›Titus 2:14
[e]*marturion* (3142) ›2 Tim 1:8
2:7 Acts 9:15
[f]*apostolos* (0652) ›2 Pet 3:2
2:8 Ps 24:3-6; 63:4
2:9 1 Pet 3:3-5
2:11 1 Cor 14:34
2:12 Eph 5:22
2:13 Gen 1:27; 2:7, 22
2:14 Gen 3:1-6, 13

1:20 ***Hymenaeus and Alexander*** might have been elders in Ephesus (see also 2 Tim 2:17; 4:14; cp. Acts 19:33; 20:29-31). • Paul ***handed them over to Satan*** by removing them from the church, the realm of the Spirit's oversight (see also 2 Tim 2:25-26; Job 2:6; Matt 18:17-20; 1 Cor 5:2-5; 2 Cor 2:5-11). • ***blaspheme God:*** They attacked and defamed the true Good News, and thus God himself (see 1:13; cp. 6:1; Titus 2:5; 2 Pet 2:2).

2:1–3:13 Paul moves to the areas of conduct in God's household that were affected by the false teachers (3:15). Community life had been corrupted in worship and gender roles (2:1-15) and leadership (3:1-13).

2:1-15 This unit deals first with prayer (2:1-7) and with the deportment of men and women (2:8-10). It closes with the question of women and teaching (2:11-15).

2:1-7 Here, prayer focuses on the church's mission, which suggests that the false teachers had brought the church into disrepute in the wider society (cp. 3:6-7; 6:1; Titus 2:5) and hampered its mission to the *Gentiles.*

2:1 ***all people:*** The prayers of the false teachers and their disciples were evidently not consonant with God's will to save all kinds of people (2:3-4).

2:2 ***all who are in authority:*** Those who had the power to persecute or to protect the church (see also Rom 13:1-7; 1 Pet 2:13-17). • ***live peaceful and quiet lives:*** The point was not for Christians to blend in and be unnoticed, but to display the beauty of the Good News and allow the church's mission to proceed without unnecessary complications (cp. 2 Tim 3:12; 1 Pet 3:13-17). • The word ***godliness*** and its cognates (also at 3:16; 4:7-8; 5:4; 6:3, 5-6, 11) sum up the beliefs, attitudes, and lifestyles that accord with right and reverential knowledge of God, obedience, and authentic worship.

2:5-6 Compact teachings, as in this passage, occur throughout the letters to Timothy and Titus (see also 3:16; 2 Tim 1:9-10; 2:8, 11-13; Titus 3:4-7). They might be adapted bits of creeds, hymns, or prayers that were known to the churches. The doctrines referenced probably relate to Paul's trouble with the false teachers; it appears that their teaching undercut the universal appeal of the Good News and the effectiveness of the Gentile mission. The false teachers also had a deficient understanding of Jesus and his salvation.

2:5 There is ***one God*** and therefore one mission encompassing all people (Rom 3:29-30; Gal 3:26-29). Using the phrase *one God* suggests a fundamental declaration of Christian faith, analogous to the basics of Jewish faith (Deut 6:4). • There is ***one Mediator*** of God's covenant, ***the man Christ Jesus.*** He is fully human and fully God, and thus able to reconcile ***God and humanity*** (see 1 Cor 8:6; Eph 4:5-6).

2:6 See Mark 10:45; Gal 4:4-5; Titus 1:3; 2:14.

2:8 Genuine prayer had evidently deteriorated among the Ephesians due to the false teachers' influence (see 6:4-5; 1:4; cp. 2 Tim 3:1-5; Titus 3:9-11). • ***holy hands lifted up:*** Cp. Isa 1:15-17. An ancient posture of praise and supplication (see Exod 9:29; 1 Kgs 8:22, 54; Neh 8:6; Ps 28:2; Luke 24:50). • ***free from anger and controversy:*** Cp. Jas 3:8-12.

2:9-10 The subject is still community prayer. • ***to be modest in their appearance*** (or *to pray in modest apparel*): Christian women must praise God rather than seek to be praised by people (cp. 1 Pet 3:3-5). They are to do good deeds for others, not focus on enhancing their appearance or being sexually seductive. Jewelry and ***expensive clothes*** imply wealth (see 6:5-10, 17-19), which might have played into the power struggles Timothy had to combat (2:11-15).

2:11-15 Paul is still talking about women in the assembly—here, in their relationship to public teaching (cp. 1 Cor 11:2-16; 14:33-36; 2 Cor 11:3).

2:12 ***teach men or have authority over them:*** The relationship between teaching and authority depends on how both are understood. Women did teach (Titus 2:3-5), but there are no clear NT examples or endorsements of women teaching men in church meetings (cp. Acts 18:26; 1 Cor 14:34-35; Phil 4:3). We know it was happening in some of the churches only by way of Paul's opposing responses. Women did prophesy (Acts 2:17-18; 21:9; 1 Cor 11:5), but some types of prophecy might not have been seen as authoritative teaching (Acts 11:28; 21:10-11; 1 Cor 14:29). • ***have authority over them*** (or *usurp their authority*): This verb can denote either a domineering attitude or simply the exercise of authority.

2:13 The most common understanding of this verse is that Paul believes social roles are attached to the man being created ***first*** (Gen 2:7, 22; 1 Cor 11:8-12). Paul's logic has usually been tied to the leading role of the firstborn son in the OT. However, there are exceptions to the rule of firstborn even in Scripture (see Gen 27–28). And while gender retains its distinctions in the NT, there is also an element of equality in Christ (Gal 3:28; see also 1 Cor 11:11-12; 12:13; Eph 5:21; Col 3:11). • It is also possible that the heretics asserted a reversal of gender

2:15 [g]*hagiasmos* (0038) ‣Heb 12:14
3:1 [h]*episkopē* (1984) ‣1 Tim 3:2

and afterward he made Eve. [14]And it was
not Adam who was deceived by Satan. The
woman was deceived, and sin was the result. [15]But women will be saved through
childbearing, assuming they continue to
live in faith, love, [g]holiness, and modesty.

Faithful Leadership

3 This is a trustworthy saying: "If someone aspires to be an [h]elder, he desires

Women's Roles in the NT Church (2:11-15)

Gen 2:23-24; Acts 18:26; Rom 16:1-7; 1 Cor 11:2-16; 14:34-35; Gal 3:28

Paul's words regarding women's roles in the church were intended to correct what was happening in Ephesus, but the extent to which this passage applies to other situations is a subject of discussion. The possible understandings include the following three.

Universal Interpretation. Galatians 3:28 ("There is no longer . . . male and female") does not negate creational gender distinctions and roles. Even if Gal 3:28 represents the ideal of equality in God's eternal Kingdom, gender roles should still be ordered as outlined in 1 Tim 2:11-15 for as long as this creation continues. By way of comparison, Matt 22:30 discusses the status of marriage in the new creation—it differs from the structure of this creation outlined in Gen 2:23-24, and it applies to the present life only in a special and limited sense (see 4:3-5; Matt 19:11-12; 1 Cor 7:29-35). The structure of the new creation will be fully realized in the coming age, and it is not the ideal for the present time. Therefore, Christian women in all times and places must recognize their role in the created order of God. They must not teach men or exercise authority over men in the church (see also 1 Cor 11:2-16; 14:34-35).

Polemical Interpretation. Paul was addressing a particular situation created by the false teaching within the Ephesian church (see 1:18-20; 4:1-5; cp. 2 Tim 3:6). Evidence suggests that this teaching was disturbing family relationships (see 2:15; 4:3; Titus 1:11). It is possible that Ephesian women, caught up in the local heresy, were abusing Gen 1–3 in their teaching. They might have been asserting female domination in the final resurrection (which, according to some of the Ephesians, had already occurred; 2 Tim 2:18) and accentuated Adam's blame for the Fall. Paul corrects their misreadings by alluding to the biblical text, but his point is not to make a universal statement about the status of women in the church. His concern is merely to silence the false teachers in Ephesus, including the women among them. First Timothy 2:11-15 entails a rebuke with loss of privilege specifically for those false teachers.

Cultural Interpretation. Paul's argument was not necessarily directed to a local problem in Ephesus, but it presupposes a strongly patriarchal society, both in concern for public decorum (women in their place, showing proper honor to men) and in handling Gen 2:7, 22. This shows that Christians must respect cultural norms insofar as possible in their evangelistic mission (1 Cor 9:19-23). In addition, most women in that society had limited training as teachers. Their society, in contrast to many 21st century societies, usually educated women poorly. Because of that culture's patriarchal structure, women would not normally have qualified as teachers and leaders. First Timothy 2:11-15, therefore, shows that properly qualified people should lead and teach. At the same time, there is a tendency in Paul (e.g., Gal 3:28; 1 Cor 11:5) and in the early church (e.g., Acts 18:26; Rom 16:1-7) toward the full engagement of women in ministry, which makes it unlikely that Paul was issuing a universal limitation here. Cultures that do not operate according to patriarchal norms would apply Paul's principle in very different ways. An egalitarian culture, as in contemporary western society, would see men and women as sharing equal roles in the church.

status in Christ relative to the surrounding culture, giving an objectionable dominance to women. Paul's allusion would then function to discredit this assertion and reestablish balance.

2:14 See Gen 3:6, 13; cp. 2 Cor 11:3.

2:15 ***will be saved through childbearing*** (or *will be saved by accepting their role as mothers,* or *will be saved by the birth of the Child*): The most likely explanation for this statement is that the false teachers had stirred up trouble in households (see 1 Timothy Introduction, "Setting," p. 2048), and Paul was calling these women back to proper relations within their homes, in keeping with the truth of the Good News (see 1:4-5; 4:1-5). In so doing they would *be saved* in the ultimate sense (see 4:16; cp. 3:13). This verse might allude to Gen 3:15-16, suggesting a reversal of the curse, either through normal childbirth or the birth of the Messiah.

3:1-13 The topic shifts to church leadership by elders (3:1-7) and deacons (3:8-13). Timothy's role in the appointments is less clear than that of Titus (see 5:17-22; Titus 1:5), possibly because the church in Ephesus was more mature and thus better able to manage the process (cp. Acts 6:2-6). The criteria listed here pertain to character rather than function and are partly a response to the local heretics. Reading this letter in the churches would make the criteria public and demonstrate the unfitness of the heretics for leadership.

3:1 ***trustworthy saying:*** See note on 1:15. • ***an elder*** (or *an overseer,* or *a bishop;* also in 3:2, 6): The translation assumes that "overseer" and "elder"

an honorable position.” 2So an [i]elder must
be a man whose life is above reproach. He
must be faithful to his wife. He must exercise self-control, live wisely, and have a good
reputation. He must enjoy having guests in
his home, and he must be able to teach. 3He
must not be a heavy drinker or be violent.
He must be gentle, not quarrelsome, and
not love money. 4He must manage his own
family well, having children who respect
and obey him. 5For if a man cannot manage
his own household, how can he take care of
God’s church?
6An elder must not be a new believer,
because he might become proud, and the
devil would cause him to fall. 7Also, people
outside the church must speak well of him
so that he will not be disgraced and fall into
the [j]devil’s trap.
8In the same way, [k]deacons must be well
respected and have integrity. They must not
be heavy drinkers or dishonest with money.
9They must be committed to the [a]mystery
of the faith now revealed and must live
with a clear conscience. 10Before they are
appointed as deacons, let them be closely examined. If they pass the test, then let them
serve as deacons.
11In the same way, their wives must be respected and must not [b]slander others. They
must exercise self-control and be faithful
in everything they do.
12A [c]deacon must be faithful to his wife,
and he must manage his children and household well. 13Those who do well as deacons
will be rewarded with respect from others
and will have increased confidence in their
faith in Christ Jesus.

5. RIGHT TEACHING AND TIMOTHY’S TASK (3:14–4:16)

The Truths of Our Faith

14I am writing these things to you now, even
though I hope to be with you soon, 15so that
if I am delayed, you will know how people
must conduct themselves in the household
of God. This is the church of the living God,
which is the pillar and foundation of the
truth.
16Without question, this is the great [d]mys-
tery of our faith:

Christ was revealed in a human body
and vindicated by the Spirit.
He was seen by angels
and announced to the nations.

3:2-7 Titus 1:6-9

3:2 [i]*episkopos* (1985) ‣Titus 1:7

3:7 2 Cor 8:21; 2 Tim 2:26; [j]*diabolos* (1228) ‣1 Tim 3:11

3:8 [k]*diakonos* (1249) ‣1 Tim 3:12

3:9 1 Tim 1:19; [a]*mustērion* (3466) ‣1 Tim 3:16

3:11 [b]*diabolos* (1228) ‣2 Tim 3:3

3:12 [c]*diakonos* (1249) ‣1 Tim 4:6

3:15 Matt 16:16-18; Eph 2:19-21

3:16 Isa 7:14; Matt 4:11; John 1:14; Acts 1:9; Rom 1:3-4; 1 Jn 4:2-3; 5:6; [d]*mustērion* (3466) ‣Mark 4:11

4:1 John 16:13; 2 Tim 3:1; 2 Pet 3:3

(see note on 5:17) are the same office (see Titus 1:5-7). In the Greco-Roman world, an overseer was a religious, civic, or military supervisor.

3:2 ***whose life is above reproach:*** This is the most general prerequisite for a community leader and public representative (see 3:7, 10; 5:7; 6:14; Titus 1:6-7; 2:8). • ***must be faithful to his wife*** (or *must have only one wife,* or *must be married only once;* literally *must be the husband of one wife;* also in 3:12): This assumes but does not require a married male. It mainly addresses purity and faithfulness in the marriage relationship, something that could not be taken for granted in the surrounding culture; it probably does not prohibit remarriage after the death of a spouse (see 5:9), nor does it address the issue of polygamy. See also 3:12; Titus 1:6; cp. 1 Tim 5:9. • ***enjoy having guests in his home*** (literally *be hospitable*): Hospitality was an important duty and a respected virtue in the ancient world. Any traveling Christian would seek out and probably stay with fellow believers (see 2 Jn 1:10-11; 3 John). In addition, first-century churches often met in private homes (see Col 4:15; Phlm 1:2).

3:3 ***must not be a heavy drinker:*** Literally *must not drink too much wine;* similarly in 3:8.

3:4-5 The church as a household (3:15) overlapped with the family ***household.*** An overseer’s capacity to ***manage*** in one sphere reflected his capability in the other (see also 3:12; 5:17; Rom 12:8; 1 Thes 5:12). • The Greco-Roman household was united by familial bonds characterized by mutual responsibilities, roles, and stewardship. The household included the blood relatives living together along with other dependents, such as household servants.

3:6 ***he might become proud, and the devil would cause him to fall:*** Or *he might fall into the same judgment as the devil.*

3:7 Paul expected Christians to live in a way that could be respected by ***people outside the church*** (see also 1 Tim 6:1; Titus 2:5-10). • The ***trap*** might pertain to the false teachers (see 1:20; 5:14-15; 6:9; 2 Tim 2:26).

3:8-13 The Greek word translated *deacon* (“servant, assistant, courier, agent”) and its cognates (“service, to serve”) are commonly used for service of any kind (e.g., 4:6; Matt 22:13; John 2:5; 12:26; Rom 13:4; 1 Cor 3:5). As designating an office in the church, it occurs only in 3:8-13; Phil 1:1; and (maybe) Rom 16:1. This passage concentrates on character rather than activities. See also note on Acts 6:1-6.

3:8 ***must not be . . . dishonest with money*** (3:3): Greed is disreputable and improper (6:6-10, 17-19; Eph 5:3; Col 3:5), especially for those who lead in the church (3:9; see Titus 1:7).

3:11 ***their wives*** (or *the women deacons;* the Greek word can be translated *women* or *wives*): In favor of *their wives,* 3:8-13 is a discussion of male deacons; switching to “women deacons” would disrupt the flow of thought. However, there might have been women deacons in the early church (see Rom 16:1). In that case, this verse might parallel 3:8.

3:14–4:16 This section addresses how Timothy should occupy himself until Paul arrives (3:14-15; 4:13).

3:15 ***household of God:*** The earliest churches were house churches (Rom 16:5; 1 Cor 16:19; Col 4:15; Phlm 1:2) that reflected the codes of conduct of Greco-Roman households (see note on 3:4-5). Violating these norms brought disrepute, disgrace, and shame on the entire household and its head. The same is true for the church (cp. Eph 2:19-22; Heb 3:6; 10:21; 1 Pet 4:17). • ***the church . . . is the pillar and foundation of the truth:*** This idea may anticipate the transition from the time of the apostles to the period after their deaths (cp. Gal 2:9; Rev 3:12). The church must be active rather than defensive in upholding ***the truth*** in the world (cp. 2 Cor 10:3-6).

3:16 The short hymn or creed in this verse shows the theological richness

[e]*daimonion* (1140)
‣Jas 2:19

4:2
Eph 4:19

4:3
Gen 9:3
Rom 14:6
1 Cor 10:30-31

4:4
Gen 1:31
Acts 10:15

4:6
2 Tim 3:15
[f]*diakonos* (1249)
‣Matt 20:26
[g]*pistis* (4102)
‣Heb 6:1

4:7
2 Tim 2:16
Titus 1:14

4:9
1 Tim 1:15

4:10
1 Tim 2:3-4
[h]*sōtēr* (4990)
‣2 Tim 1:10

He was believed in throughout the world
and taken to heaven in glory.

The Holy Spirit's Warning about False Teachers

4 Now the Holy Spirit tells us clearly that in the last times some will turn away from the true faith; they will follow deceptive spirits and teachings that come from [e]demons. 2These people are hypocrites and liars, and their consciences are dead.

3They will say it is wrong to be married and wrong to eat certain foods. But God created those foods to be eaten with thanks by faithful people who know the truth. 4Since everything God created is good, we should not reject any of it but receive it with thanks. 5For we know it is made acceptable by the word of God and prayer.

The Heart and Life of the Servant of Christ Jesus

6If you explain these things to the brothers and sisters, Timothy, you will be a worthy [f]servant of Christ Jesus, one who is nourished by the message of [g]faith and the good teaching you have followed. 7Do not waste time arguing over godless ideas and old wives' tales. Instead, train yourself to be godly. 8"Physical training is good, but training for godliness is much better, promising benefits in this life and in the life to come." 9This is a trustworthy saying, and everyone should accept it. 10This is why we work hard and continue to struggle, for our hope is in the living God, who is the [h]Savior of all people and particularly of all believers.

The NT Household (3:5)

1 Tim 2:8-15; 3:12, 15; 5:1-2, 8; 6:1-2
Eph 5:21–6:9
Col 3:18–4:1
Titus 2:1–3:8
1 Pet 2:13–3:7; 4:17; 5:1-5

The household was the basic unit of Greco-Roman society; it was believed that the stability of the state rested upon the stability of the household. Roles and responsibilities were well defined and deeply ingrained. The central concern was to maintain the "natural" ordering of authority and subordination, the violation of which would lead to degradation and corruption. In this framework, the husband-father-master was over all. The public space of society and government belonged to men, the private space of the home belonged to women. It was not uncommon for Greco-Roman orators to accuse new foreign cults (as Christianity was perceived) of corrupting and destabilizing society, precisely by threatening the structure of the household.

The NT household codes (see 2:8-15; 5:1-2; 6:1-2; Titus 2:1–3:8; cp. Eph 5:22–6:9; Col 3:18–4:1; 1 Pet 2:13–3:7; 5:1-5) were therefore not innovations, even if these catalogs were adapted by the apostles to fit the Christian faith and to address particular needs. In practice, the Christian faith would result in the significant modification of cultural norms. Yet wisdom and loving restraint were needed, because heedlessly violating cultural norms created destructive upheaval and threatened to bring disrepute, disgrace, and shame on the entire household—including Christ, its head. This was precisely the effect of the false teachers in Ephesus. In this context, the NT household codes guided Christian communities toward a life that (1) silenced the accusations of unbelievers that Christianity was a threat to the state; and (2) served as a compelling, winsome witness to the truth.

of early Christian worship. • ***mystery of our faith*** (or *mystery of godliness*): See note on 2:2. • ***Christ*** (literally *He who;* other manuscripts read *God*): Jesus Christ is the only source of godliness. • ***vindicated by the Spirit*** (or *vindicated in his spirit*): Christ's resurrection (Rom 1:4) answers the apparent weakness of his life and death as a human, and affirms his teaching. • ***seen by angels:*** This emphasizes Jesus' sovereign rule in the heavenly realm (see also Eph 1:21; Phil 2:9-11; Heb 1:3-4; 1 Pet 3:22; Rev 5:8-14). • ***announced to the nations:*** Christ's provision of salvation and sovereign rule must be proclaimed and accepted in the earthly realm as well (cp. 2:1-7). • ***believed in throughout the world:*** The mission to the nations is successful, but it does not guarantee universal acceptance. • Christ was ***taken to heaven*** (Luke 24:51; Acts 1:2, 11, 22) and was exalted ***in glory*** (cp. Acts 7:55-56). Christ's saving work is crowned with success in the world and with glory in heaven.

4:1-5 Paul's sound teaching (3:16) contrasts with the false teachings that he denounces.

4:1 The early church regarded itself as already in ***the last times*** (see Acts 2:16-17; Heb 1:2; cp. 2 Thes 2:7; 1 Jn 2:18-23).

4:2 ***are dead*** (literally *are seared*): Dead ***consciences*** either don't function or function wickedly, rendering judgments that oppose the truth of the gospel (see also Titus 1:15; Rom 1:28-32).

4:5 ***made acceptable:*** Or *made holy.*

4:6-16 Timothy must respond to the false teachers (cp. 2 Tim 3:1–4:5).

4:6 ***brothers and sisters:*** Literally *brothers,* a generic term that refers to both male and female believers. • The training of the ***worthy servant*** involves a whole pattern of conduct, modeled by Paul and based on sound doctrine. ***Good teaching*** unifies word and deed, belief and behavior (cp. 3:10, 14-15; Phil 4:9).

4:8-9 ***physical training . . . godliness:*** Cp. 1 Cor 9:24-27; Col 2:23. • ***benefits in this life . . . the life to come:*** Cp. 4:16; 6:6-8; Mark 10:29-30; Eph 6:2-3. • ***trustworthy saying:*** See note on 1:15.

4:10 ***continue to struggle:*** Some manuscripts read *continue to suffer.* • ***God . . . the Savior:*** See note on 1:1.

11 Teach these things and insist that
everyone learn them. 12 Don't let anyone
think less of you because you are young. Be
an [i]example to all believers in what you say,
in the way you live, in your love, your faith,
and your purity. 13 Until I get there, focus
on reading the Scriptures to the church, encouraging the believers, and teaching them.
14 Do not neglect the spiritual [j]gift you received through the prophecy spoken over
you when the elders of the church laid their
hands on you. 15 Give your complete attention to these matters. Throw yourself into
your tasks so that everyone will see your
progress. 16 Keep a close watch on how you
live and on your teaching. Stay true to what
is right for the sake of your own salvation
and the salvation of those who hear you.

6. RIGHT CONDUCT IN GOD'S HOUSEHOLD (5:1–6:2a)

Honoring Older People and Spiritual Siblings

5 Never speak harshly to an older man,
but appeal to him respectfully as you
would to your own [k]father. Talk to younger
men as you would to your own brothers.
2 Treat older women as you would your
mother, and treat younger women with all
purity as you would your own sisters.

Honoring Widows

3 Take care of any widow who has no one
else to care for her. 4 But if she has children
or grandchildren, their first responsibility
is to show godliness at home and repay their
parents by taking care of them. This is something that pleases God.
5 Now a true widow, a woman who is truly
alone in this world, has placed her hope in
God. She prays night and day, asking God for
his help. 6 But the widow who lives only for
pleasure is spiritually dead even while she
lives. 7 Give these instructions to the church
so that no one will be open to criticism.
8 But those who won't care for their
relatives, especially those in their own
household, have denied the true faith. Such
people are worse than unbelievers.
9 A widow who is put on the list for support must be a woman who is at least sixty
years old and was faithful to her husband.
10 She must be well respected by everyone
because of the good she has done. Has she
brought up her children well? Has she been
kind to strangers and served other believers humbly? Has she helped those who are
in trouble? Has she always been ready to do
good?
11 The younger widows should not be on
the list, because their physical desires will
overpower their devotion to Christ and they
will want to remarry. 12 Then they would be
guilty of breaking their previous pledge.
13 And if they are on the list, they will learn
to be lazy and will spend their time gossiping from house to house, meddling in other
people's business and talking about things
they shouldn't. 14 So I advise these younger widows to marry again, have children,
and take care of their own homes. Then

4:11 1 Tim 5:7
4:12 Titus 2:15; [i]*tupos* (5179) ›Titus 2:7
4:13 1 Tim 3:14
4:14 Acts 6:6; 8:17; 2 Tim 1:6; [j]*charisma* (5486) ›2 Tim 1:6
5:1 Lev 19:32; Titus 2:2, 6; [k]*patēr* (3962) ›Heb 12:9
5:4 Eph 6:2; 1 Tim 2:3
5:5 Luke 2:36-37; 1 Pet 3:5
5:6 Luke 15:24; Jas 5:5
5:10 Gen 18:3-5; Acts 9:36
5:13 2 Thes 3:11
5:14 1 Cor 7:9

4:12 ***Be an example:*** Only those whose lives are shaped by the Good News are worthy teachers of it (cp. 2 Tim 3:10-11; Titus 2:7; Heb 13:7). The false teachers were not.

4:14 ***laid their hands on you:*** The gesture signified recognition, authorization, and blessing (see Acts 13:1-3; 6:6). This was probably the same event as in 2 Tim 1:6-7 (see 1:18; cp. Rom 12:6-8; 1 Cor 12:7-11; Eph 4:7-13). Paul's ministry and that of his delegates was under the authority of the church.

5:1–6:2a Conduct in God's household (see 3:15) relates to old and young (5:1-2), widows (5:3-16), elders (5:17-25), and slaves (6:1-2a). Proper honor within the household cuts across social boundaries.

5:1 ***an older man:*** Or *an elder.*

5:3-16 A ***widow*** without wealth or family was alone in a world that did not provide for her. The Christian community was expected to care for such widows among its members (see Deut 10:17-19; Isa 1:17; cp. Acts 6:1-6; Jas 1:27). There is no certain evidence of a religious order of widows in the first-century church, only of a ministry of care for community members without means.

5:3 ***Take care of:*** Or *Honor.*

5:5 The only recourse for a ***widow*** who was ***truly alone*** was ***hope in God*** (Ps 68:5; 146:9).

5:6 Some widows in Ephesus were living ***only for pleasure,*** more interested in receiving than in giving (see also 6:17-19; Jas 5:5). They did not need support.

5:8 ***Faith*** is not mere belief but a whole way of life (see Jas 2:14-26).

5:9 ***at least sixty:*** Young widows required a different approach (5:11-15). Young and old were customarily divided at around forty; elders would probably have been over fifty (see Titus 2:2). • ***was faithful to her husband*** (literally *was the wife of one husband*): The grammar is identical in 3:2, 12; Titus 1:6.

5:10 ***and served other believers humbly*** (literally *and washed the feet of God's holy people*): See Gen 18:4; Luke 7:44; John 13:1-17.

5:11-15 Young widows still in their childbearing years required a different approach. Paul was concerned that the false teachers were leading them *astray.*

5:11-12 If Paul was concerned about remarriage to unbelievers (cp. 5:14), ***their previous pledge*** would refer to their Christian faith, which they would surrender upon entering a pagan marriage; such a marriage would probably have alienated them from Christ. It is also possible that Paul and the church recognized a special category of "sacred widowhood" (see 5:5; cp. Acts 9:36-37), entered by a vow that Paul refers to as the *previous pledge.*

5:13 Too seldom do those who are fully supported by the church invest their lives in remarkable piety (cp. 2:9-10; 5:10). Abusing the church's support does not help them or the Good News (cp. 5:14). • ***talking about things they shouldn't:*** The wording suggests involvement in the false teaching (5:15; cp. 2 Thes 3:11-13; Titus 1:11).

5:14 Paul is advising younger widows to remarry—and to marry believers (5:11-

5:15
1 Tim 1:19-20
5:17
Phil 2:29
1 Thes 5:12
5:18
*Deut 25:4
Matt 10:10
*Luke 10:7
1 Cor 9:9
5:19
Matt 18:16
5:20
Deut 13:11
Eph 5:11
5:21
1 Tim 6:13
5:22
1 Tim 4:14
[a]*hamartia* (0266)
‣ Heb 9:26
5:23
1 Tim 3:8
5:24-25
Rev 14:13
6:1
Eph 6:5
Titus 2:9-10
6:2
Phlm 1:16
6:3
1 Tim 1:3, 10
6:4
2 Tim 2:14

the enemy will not be able to say anything
against them. 15For I am afraid that some
of them have already gone astray and now
follow Satan.
16If a woman who is a believer has relatives who are widows, she must take care of
them and not put the responsibility on the
church. Then the church can care for the
widows who are truly alone.

Rewarding and Disciplining Church Elders

17Elders who do their work well should be respected and paid well, especially those who
work hard at both preaching and teaching.
18For the Scripture says, "You must not muzzle an ox to keep it from eating as it treads
out the grain." And in another place, "Those
who work deserve their pay!"
19Do not listen to an accusation against an
elder unless it is confirmed by two or three
witnesses. 20Those who sin should be reprimanded in front of the whole church; this
will serve as a strong warning to others.
21I solemnly command you in the presence of God and Christ Jesus and the
highest angels to obey these instructions
without taking sides or showing favoritism
to anyone.
22Never be in a hurry about appointing a
church leader. Do not share in the [a]sins of
others. Keep yourself pure.
23Don't drink only water. You ought to
drink a little wine for the sake of your stomach because you are sick so often.
24Remember, the sins of some people are
obvious, leading them to certain judgment.
But there are others whose sins will not be
revealed until later. 25In the same way, the
good deeds of some people are obvious.
And the good deeds done in secret will
someday come to light.

Honoring Masters

6 All slaves should show full respect for
their masters so they will not bring
shame on the name of God and his teaching.
2If the masters are believers, that is no excuse for being disrespectful. Those slaves
should work all the harder because their
efforts are helping other believers who are
well loved.

7. DEALING WITH FALSE TEACHING (6:2b-21a)

Godliness and Contentment

Teach these things, Timothy, and encourage everyone to obey them. 3Some people
may contradict our teaching, but these are
the wholesome teachings of the Lord Jesus
Christ. These teachings promote a godly life.
4Anyone who teaches something different
is arrogant and lacks understanding. Such
a person has an unhealthy desire to quib-
ble over the meaning of words. This stirs
up arguments ending in jealousy, division,

12; cp. 2:15). • ***not . . . say anything against them:*** Their actions were hurting their testimony for the Good News (see 1 Thes 4:11-12; Titus 2:8).

5:15 ***now follow Satan:*** They had committed apostasy, renouncing Christ, probably in connection with the false teachers (1:6-7; cp. 3:6-7; Heb 2:1) and their self-indulgence (5:6, 13).

5:16 Individual Christian households maintained their function and identity within the church (cp. 2:15; 3:15). They were not eclipsed by the church, although the household of God is primary to the identity of the believing community (see Mark 3:31-35).

5:17-25 As in Judaism, ***elders*** (see 3:1-7; Titus 1:5-9) were usually older men who were leaders in the community. The letters to Timothy and Titus recognize an office of elders, as here (see also 4:14; Titus 1:5), but the word is also used generally for older men in the community (as in 5:1). See "Church Leaders" at Titus 1:5-9, p. 2071.

5:17-18 ***should be respected and paid well*** (literally *should be worthy of double honor*): Cp. Gal 6:6. There is no evidence of a paid clergy at this time; the word used here is never used for a continuous salary, though it does imply something beyond a show of respect. The quotations from ***Scripture*** (Deut 25:4; Luke 10:7) suggest gifts of money.

5:19-21 The climate created by the false teachers may have led to spurious charges against the leaders of the community. This passage follows the outline of Deut 19:15-21. • ***two or three witnesses:*** See Deut 17:6; 19:15; Matt 18:16; 2 Cor 13:1; Heb 10:28.

5:20 ***Those who sin:*** This term refers either to one who is (rightly) accused or to one making a (false) accusation (Deut 19:16-19). • The ***others*** are either the other elders or the rest of the church (cp. Deut 19:20; Acts 5:1-11).

5:21 ***God and Christ Jesus and the highest angels*** constitute three witnesses (5:19). Angels are associated with God's judgment (Dan 7:9-10; Matt 13:49; 25:31, 41; Luke 9:26; 2 Thes 1:7).

5:22 ***about appointing a church leader:*** Literally *about the laying on of hands;* see 4:14. • ***Do not share in the sins of others:*** Those who commission an elder are responsible for his conduct.

5:23 Possibly the concern with purity (5:22) was being taken too far with respect to ***wine*** (see 3:3; Num 6:1-21) or food (1 Cor 10:21). Wine may have been considered medicinal.

5:24-25 These two proverbial statements summarize 5:17-23 and point to God's ***judgment***.

6:1 Both unbelieving and believing masters should be treated with ***respect,*** which will bring honor rather than ***shame*** to God's ***name*** (see note on 5:1–6:2).

6:2a ***other believers:*** Literally *brothers;* see note on 4:6.

6:2b-21 The last major section of the letter returns to the need for Timothy to confront the false teachers. The whole section has a similar structure to 1:3-20.

6:2b-10 This paragraph exposes the false teachers' desire ***to become wealthy***.

6:4 ***This stirs up arguments:*** This is the same problem as in 1:4 (see also 2 Tim 2:23-24; Titus 3:9).

slander, and evil suspicions. 5These people
always cause trouble. Their minds are corrupt, and they have turned their backs on
the truth. To them, a show of godliness is
just a way to become wealthy.
6Yet true godliness with contentment is
itself great wealth. 7After all, we brought
nothing with us when we came into the
world, and we can't take anything with us
when we leave it. 8So if we have enough
food and clothing, let us be content.
9But people who long to be rich fall into
[b]temptation and are trapped by many foolish and harmful desires that plunge them
into ruin and destruction. 10For the love
of money is the root of all kinds of evil.
And some people, craving money, have
wandered from the true faith and pierced
themselves with many sorrows.

Parenthesis: The Charge to Timothy

11But you, Timothy, are a man of God; so run
from all these evil things. Pursue [c]righteous-
ness and a godly life, along with faith, love,
perseverance, and gentleness. 12Fight the
good fight for the true faith. Hold tightly
to the eternal life to which God has called
you, which you have confessed so well before many witnesses. 13And I charge you
before God, who gives life to all, and before
Christ Jesus, who gave a good testimony
before Pontius Pilate, 14that you obey this
command without wavering. Then no one
can find fault with you from now until our
Lord Jesus Christ [d]comes again. 15For at just
the right time Christ will be revealed from
heaven by the blessed and only almighty
God, the King of all kings and Lord of all
lords. 16He alone can never die, and he lives
in light so brilliant that no human can approach him. No human eye has ever seen
him, nor ever will. All honor and power to
him forever! Amen.

Managing for Life

17Teach those who are rich in this world not
to be proud and not to trust in their [e]money,
which is so unreliable. Their trust should
be in God, who richly gives us all we need
for our enjoyment. 18Tell them to use their
money to do good. They should be rich in
good works and generous to those in need,
always being ready to share with others.
19By doing this they will be storing up their
treasure as a good foundation for the future
so that they may experience true life.

6:5 2 Tim 3:8; 4:4; Titus 1:14
6:6 Phil 4:11-12; Heb 13:5
6:7 Job 1:21; Eccl 5:15
6:8 Prov 30:8; Heb 13:5
6:9 Prov 23:4; 28:22
[b]*peirasmos* (3986) ‣Heb 4:15
6:11 2 Tim 2:22
[c]*dikaiosunē* (1343) ‣2 Tim 3:16
6:12 1 Cor 9:25-26; 2 Tim 4:7
6:13 John 18:33-37
6:14 1 Thes 3:13
[d]*epiphaneia* (2015) ‣2 Tim 1:10
6:15 Deut 10:17; Rev 17:14
6:16 Exod 33:20; Ps 104:2; John 1:18; 5:26
6:17
[e]*ploutos* (4149) ‣Jas 5:2

6:5 ***have turned their backs on the truth:*** Literally *having been robbed of the truth;* see 2 Tim 2:18; 3:7, 8; 4:4; Titus 1:14. • ***a show of godliness is just a way to become wealthy*** (see 2:2; 3:8; 4:8; 6:3; see also 2 Tim 3:2; Acts 8:9-25): Just how these false teachers thought they would profit is not clear. In the wider culture there were many itinerant teachers who taught for pay. Abuse was common and often deserved the accusation that someone's teaching was for "gain and glory." Perhaps the false teachers of 1 Timothy were bringing this practice into the church or espousing some version of a prosperity gospel. They appear to have had an influence on wealthy believers (6:17-19), and possibly on women in particular (2:9; 5:6).

6:6 ***with contentment:*** This is not just a philosophical outlook but real dependence on the sufficiency of Christ. See 4:8; 2 Cor 9:8; 12:7-10; Phil 4:10-13; Heb 13:5.

6:11-16 Before ending the discussion of wealth, Paul exhorts Timothy to live beyond reproach, commanding him to flee from desire for wealth.

6:12 The promise of ***eternal life*** moderates the appeal of wealth (cp. 6:19). • Paul is probably referring to the time when Timothy ***confessed*** his faith at baptism.

6:13 Paul emphasizes the historical nature of Christ's mediating work (see 2:5-6). The ***testimony*** of ***Christ Jesus*** at his trial ***before Pontius Pilate*** (Matt 27:11-14; Luke 23:1-4; John 18:33-38; 19:9-11) holds up his example as an incentive for Timothy to remain steadfast under pressure.

6:14 ***until our Lord Jesus Christ comes again*** (literally *until the appearance of our Lord Jesus Christ*): Christ's comings, both past (2 Tim 1:10; Titus 2:11) and future (2 Tim 4:1, 8; Titus 2:13), are described in the letters to Timothy and Titus as "epiphanies" or "appearances." An ***epiphany*** is a divine intervention in a particular historical moment. The church is positioned between these past and future appearances of Christ. Christ's first, saving epiphany made possible a new life; his future epiphany will achieve final salvation. Though the present is evil (the "last days," 4:1-3; 2 Tim 3:1-9), our anticipation of Christ's appearance creates accountability for living a godly life in the present. By contrast, the false teachers advocated sinful behaviors because they assumed the resurrection had already occurred (2 Tim 2:18). In response, Paul makes clear that salvation has begun but is not yet complete. The conduct of God's household requires responsible living in the light of Christ's past, present, and future saving work (3:15-16; Titus 2:11-14).

6:15-16 ***At just the right time*** (cp. 2:6), God will complete the salvation promised to us before the world began (2 Tim 1:9; Titus 1:2), which Christ enacted in his first appearance (2:6; Titus 1:3). The saving work of Christ is positioned within God's sovereign and eternal purposes. This thought expands into worship of God our Savior (cp. 1:17). • This material might be quoted from a baptismal confession (see note on 6:12).

6:17-19 In light of 6:11-16, it is folly to treasure the transient wealth of this age (Jas 5:3). It is better to store up ***treasure*** for the coming age through ***trust*** in God and by being ***rich in good works and generous*** in love for others (see 1:5).

6:17-18 ***for our enjoyment:*** Christian hope does not lead to asceticism or communism but to the management of resources (Gen 1:28-30; 2:15), which we are to use for enjoyment (see 4:3-5; Ps 145:16; Acts 14:17) and for sharing Christ's love with others (see Luke 12:16-34; 2 Cor 8–9).

6:20-21 This brief but pointed exhortation summarizes and shows the importance of Timothy's task in Ephesus (cp. 1:18-20; 2 Tim 1:13-14).

6:20 ***what God has entrusted to you*** (literally *the deposit*): The Good News is a deposit entrusted to the church and its leaders for safekeeping (1:15; 2:5-6; 3:16). It encompasses the whole pattern of conduct that follows from it (2 Tim 1:13-14; 3:10-11). It stabilizes and puri-

6:19
Matt 6:20
6:20
2 Tim 1:14; 2:16
6:21
2 Tim 2:18

Guarding the Deposit

[20]Timothy, guard what God has entrusted to you. Avoid godless, foolish discussions with those who oppose you with their so-called knowledge. [21]Some people have wandered from the faith by following such foolishness.

8. CLOSING BLESSING (6:21b)

May God's grace be with you all.

fies the church when it is buffeted by counterfeits in the polluted environment of difficult times (2 Tim 3:1). The deposit belongs to the "tradition" of the church (see 2 Tim 2:2; 1 Cor 11:23-25; 15:1-8; 2 Thes 2:15; 3:6). It requires creative and faithful interpretation to meet changing circumstances and problems (see 2 Tim 1:12-14).

6:21 The letter closes abruptly. Evidently there was no need of directions for the mission (cp. Titus 3:12-14) and greetings were unnecessary or unsuitable (cp. Titus 3:15; Rom 16:3-16). • ***you all:*** The letter was sent to Timothy but was intended to be read to the whole church (see 1 Timothy Introduction, "Literary Genre," p. 2049).

PAUL'S SECOND LETTER TO TIMOTHY

Back in a Roman prison, Paul realized that he had reached the end of his race. His life, modeled on the death and resurrection of Jesus Christ, was nearing its conclusion, so Paul commissioned his delegate Timothy to carry on his work. When Paul died at the hands of the Romans, he had composed this letter as his own epitaph (see 4:7-8) and empowered the church to carry on in his absence. The mission of the Good News would continue.

SETTING

Following Paul's conversion (Acts 9:1-19), his work as an apostle to the world extended from Jerusalem in the east to as far west as Italy (Acts 28:30-31; Rom 15:19), including considerable time in Asia Minor, and especially Ephesus (Acts 19:1–20:1, 31). This period ended when Paul was arrested in Jerusalem (Acts 21:27-36), detained in Caesarea (Acts 23:23–26:32), and imprisoned in Rome (Acts 28:16-31). Paul was eventually released and engaged in further ministry; he wrote 1 Timothy and Titus during this time. He was then arrested and imprisoned in Rome a second time (2 Tim 1:8, 16-17; 2:9).

This letter, written from prison in Rome, came during the concluding episode of Paul's life (see 4:6-18). It was written to Timothy, Paul's faithful co-worker and delegate. Timothy was in the province of Asia at that time, probably in Ephesus (4:13, 19). Paul was asking him to come to Rome as soon as possible. If Timothy proved faithful, he would experience suffering and persecution also.

SUMMARY

After the traditional salutation (1:1-2), thanksgiving, and prayer (1:3-4), Paul charges Timothy to suffer with him for the Good News (1:5-18). The resources for doing so include Timothy's spiritual heritage and the Good News itself, as illustrated by Paul's life and by both good and bad examples.

Paul then charges Timothy again (2:1-13) to be strong and to endure suffering along with Paul. Again, Timothy's

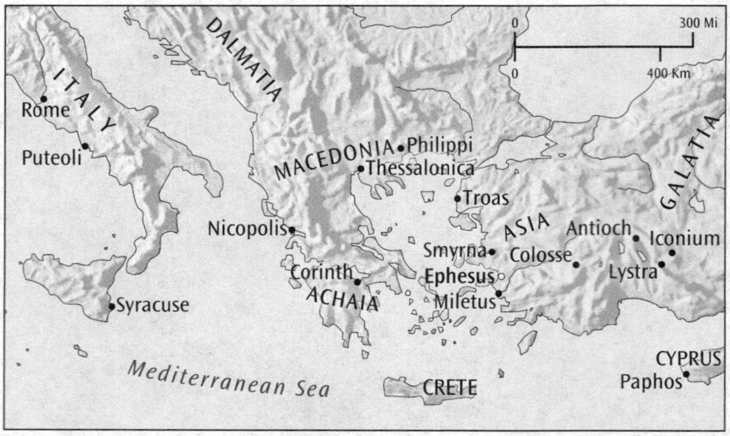

The Setting of 2 Timothy, AD 64~65. When Paul wrote his second letter to Timothy, he had been imprisoned in ROME for the second time and was facing execution. He wrote to Timothy, who was probably still in EPHESUS (see 1 Timothy Introduction, p. 2048), to summon Timothy to Rome.

obedience is to be motivated by reflection on the Good News and on Paul's example. Paul instructs Timothy on conducting his ministry among the false teachers (2:14-26).

The perspective then broadens to set Timothy's task in the context of the last days (3:1–4:8). These days will be difficult, but God will deal with troublemakers just as he has in the past. Timothy is to stay on track with the faith he has inherited and remain rooted in the Scriptures. He is to carry out his ministry with a sense of urgency in light of his hope and the increasing resistance of his listeners. He is not to be afraid of suffering for the Lord, and he is to consider Paul's work as completed. Timothy must step into the gap and regard Paul as an example to follow.

The letter closes with an appeal for Timothy to come to Rome as soon as possible (4:9-18). Paul gives greetings, news, and a final urging for Timothy to make his journey to Rome before winter (4:19-21). Then Paul closes with a blessing (4:22).

OUTLINE

1:1-2
Salutation from Paul

1:3-4
Thanksgiving and Prayer

1:5-18
Charge to Be Faithful

2:1-13
Charge to Be Strong and Endure Suffering

2:14-26
Dealing with Opposition

3:1–4:8
Charge in Light of the Last Days

4:9-22
Paul's Final Words

DATE OF WRITING

It is possible that 2 Timothy was written during Paul's first imprisonment in Rome (Acts 28). The evidence, however, gives stronger support to a later date, during a second imprisonment in Rome that resulted in Paul's death (see Introduction to Paul's Letters to Timothy and Titus, "Date of Writing," p. 2047).

OCCASION

We do not know the details of Paul's second arrest. Possibly Alexander (4:14-15), a heretic that Paul had disciplined earlier (1 Tim 1:20), had a hand in the arrest (see 4:16-18). It might have occurred in Asia Minor (1:15); if so, Paul's heretical opponents—the false teachers discussed in 1 Timothy and Titus—were not just making idle threats. The struggle in which Paul and Timothy were engaged (2:3; 4:7; 1 Tim 1:18; 6:12) was not simply metaphorical or spiritual. The directions on prayer for civil authorities (1 Tim 2:1-7; cp. Titus 3:1) may be understood as relating to wider problems created for the churches by false teachers, problems that resulted in Paul's final arrest and execution for the Good News. The false teachers were still on the prowl (2:14–3:9; 4:14-15). Paul viewed his ministry as being completed and knew that his death was imminent (4:6-8), so he was summoning Timothy to Rome to receive his mantle of leadership.[1]

[1] See Philip H. Towner, "The Portrait of Paul and the Theology of 2 Timothy: The Closing Chapter of the Pauline Story," *Horizons in Biblical Theology* 21 (1999): 150-170.

TIMELINE

AD 34~35
Saul's conversion near Damascus

AD 47~48
Barnabas and Paul's first missionary journey
Timothy's conversion

AD 53~56
Paul's ministry in Ephesus

AD 60–62
Paul is imprisoned in Rome

AD 62~64
Paul is released, travels freely

about AD 63
Paul writes 1 Timothy and Titus from Macedonia

about AD 64~65?
Paul is imprisoned, writes 2 Timothy, and is martyred in Rome

FURTHER READING

GORDON FEE
1 and 2 Timothy, Titus (1988)

LUKE TIMOTHY JOHNSON
Letters to Paul's Delegates (1996)

JON LAANSMA
2 Timothy in *Cornerstone Biblical Commentary,* vol. 17 (2009)

I. HOWARD MARSHALL
The Pastoral Epistles (1999)

WILLIAM MOUNCE
The Pastoral Epistles (2000)

MEANING AND MESSAGE

The apostle Paul had not only proclaimed the Good News of the death and resurrection of Jesus Christ; he had personally enacted it. The Good News gives rise to a way of life that takes up the cross and follows Jesus in the life-giving power of his resurrection. Paul had modeled his life after Christ's, and now his death was at hand. God's work will be completed right up to the day of Christ's return (1:12), yet the continuing responsibility of God's servants is great. Paul passed the torch to Timothy and challenged him to carry Paul's work forward.

In this letter, all who take up the cross and follow Jesus are charged to complete the ministry that God has given them, through the life-giving power of Christ's resurrection.

1. SALUTATION FROM PAUL (1:1-2)

1 This letter is from Paul, chosen by the
will of God to be an apostle of Christ
Jesus. I have been sent out to tell others
about the life he has promised through
faith in Christ Jesus.
2 I am writing to Timothy, my dear son.
May God the Father and Christ Jesus our
Lord give you grace, mercy, and peace.

2. THANKSGIVING AND PRAYER (1:3-4)

3 Timothy, I thank God for you—the God
I serve with a clear conscience, just as my
ancestors did. Night and day I constantly
remember you in my prayers. 4 I long to see
you again, for I remember your tears as we
parted. And I will be filled with joy when we
are together again.

3. CHARGE TO BE FAITHFUL (1:5-18)

Timothy's Spiritual Heritage

5 I remember your genuine faith, for you
share the faith that first filled your grandmother Lois and your mother, Eunice. And
I know that same faith continues strong in
you. 6 This is why I remind you to fan into
flames the spiritual [a]gift God gave you
when I laid my hands on you. 7 For God has
not given us a spirit of fear and timidity, but
of power, love, and self-discipline.

The Commission of the Good News

8 So never be ashamed to [b]tell others about
our Lord. And don't be ashamed of me, either, even though I'm in prison for him.
With the strength God gives you, be ready
to suffer with me for the sake of the Good
News. 9 For God [c]saved us and called us to
live a holy [d]life. He did this, not because we
deserved it, but because that was his plan
from before the beginning of time—to show
us his grace through Christ Jesus. 10 And
now he has made all of this plain to us by the
[e]appearing of Christ Jesus, our [f]Savior. He

1:1 John 5:24; Titus 1:1; 1 Jn 5:10-11, 20
1:2 1 Tim 1:2
1:3 Acts 23:1; 24:16; Rom 1:8-10
1:4 Acts 20:37; 2 Tim 4:9
1:5 Acts 16:1
1:6 1 Tim 4:14; [a]*charisma* (5486) ‣1 Pet 4:10
1:7 Rom 8:15
1:8 Rom 1:16; Eph 3:1; 2 Tim 2:3; [b]*marturion* (3142) ‣Matt 8:4
1:9 Rom 8:28; 11:14; Eph 2:8-9; Titus 3:5; [c]*sōzō* (4982) ‣2 Tim 2:10; [d]*klēsis* (2821) ‣2 Pet 1:10

1:1-2 See note on 1 Tim 1:1-2.

1:1 ***the life he has promised:*** See Rom 4:13-17. This letter to Timothy celebrates Christ's resurrection (2:8) and the life which results from it (1:10) as the answer to the suffering and death of the godly (3:12). Paul's own life demonstrates this hope (4:17-18).

1:3-4 Thanksgiving and prayer are standard sections of Paul's letters (e.g., Rom 1:8-12; Col 1:3-14; contrast Gal 1:6-10).

1:3 ***just as my ancestors did:*** See Phil 3:5; cp. Deut 6:4-9. • ***with a clear conscience:*** This might be in relation to heresy (see 2:17-18; see also 1 Tim 1:5) or to Paul's previous legal self-defense (see Acts 23:1; 24:14-16).

1:4 Paul begins urging Timothy to come to him (see note on 1:5-14). • ***your tears:*** The two may have last ***parted*** when Paul was transferred to Rome under arrest (cp. Acts 20:37-38; 21:12-14).

1:5-14 Paul gently but firmly summons Timothy to Rome (see also 4:9, 21; cp. 1 Tim 1:3-11, 12-17). Suffering seemed certain if Timothy remained faithful, and Paul wanted to strengthen Timothy's resolve. • The allusions to the Spirit in 1:6-7 and 1:14 form an *inclusio* (literary bookends) around this section.

1:5 On Timothy's parentage, see Acts 16:1-3; 1 Tim 1:2. • ***Faith*** means Christian faith, but Timothy's Jewish heritage through his ***grandmother*** and ***mother*** explains how he was rooted in OT instruction (3:14-15). Their Christian faith was an example for him to follow.

1:6 ***fan into flames:*** The Spirit's work is not automatic—it must be cultivated (see Eph 5:18-21; 1 Thes 5:19-20; cp. Acts 4:31; 7:55; 13:9). • The ***spiritual gift*** is the Holy Spirit's enablement for ministry (see 1 Cor 12–14; cp. Acts 6:3, 5; 11:24). • ***when I laid my hands on you:*** Paul and the elders (1 Tim 4:14) had ordained Timothy for ministry with the ceremonial laying on of hands.

1:8 This verse summarizes the letter. Timothy would probably experience suffering (2:3; 3:12; 4:5; see Heb 13:23) both in coming to Rome and in his subsequent ministry as Paul's successor.

1:9-10 This passage underscores the importance of obedience (1:8) and strengthens Timothy for it (cp. 1 Tim 1:15; 2:5-6). • ***God saved us . . . Christ Jesus, our Savior:*** God and Christ are described interchangeably in the role of Savior (see 1 Tim 1:1; 2:3-4). • ***called us to live a holy life:*** Salvation and godliness are linked (see 1 Tim 3:14-16; 5:8; Titus 2:11-14; 3:4-7; Eph 2:10). • ***not because we deserved it:*** We deserve condemnation (see Rom 3:23-24; 5:6-11; Eph 2:8-9; Titus 3:5). • ***that was his plan from before the beginning of time:*** See Titus 1:2; John 17:24; Eph 1:4, 11; 1 Pet 1:20; Rev 13:8. Salvation is completely removed from human merit and located exclusively in the gracious working of God.

1:10
1 Cor 15:54
[e]*epiphaneia* (2015)
‣2 Tim 4:1
[f]*sōtēr* (4990)
‣Titus 1:3

1:11
1 Tim 2:7

1:12
1 Tim 6:20

1:13
Rom 6:17
1 Tim 1:14

1:14
Rom 8:9, 11, 16
Gal 4:6

1:15
2 Tim 4:10, 16

1:16
2 Tim 4:19

1:18
Heb 6:10

2:1
Eph 6:10
[g]*charis* (5485)
‣Titus 2:11

2:2
2 Tim 1:13

2:3
2 Tim 1:8; 4:5

2:5
1 Cor 9:25

2:6
1 Cor 9:7, 10

2:8
Acts 2:24
Rom 1:3

2:9
Eph 3:1
Phil 1:12-14

2:10
Col 1:24
[h]*sōtēria* (4991)
‣2 Tim 3:15

broke the power of death and illuminated
the way to life and immortality through the
Good News. [11]And God chose me to be a
preacher, an apostle, and a teacher of this
Good News.

Paul's Pattern

[12]That is why I am suffering here in prison.
But I am not ashamed of it, for I know the
one in whom I trust, and I am sure that he is
able to guard what I have entrusted to him
until the day of his return.

[13]Hold on to the pattern of wholesome
teaching you learned from me—a pattern
shaped by the faith and love that you have
in Christ Jesus. [14]Through the power of the
Holy Spirit who lives within us, carefully
guard the precious truth that has been entrusted to you.

Examples, Bad and Good

[15]As you know, everyone from the province
of Asia has deserted me—even Phygelus
and Hermogenes.

[16]May the Lord show special kindness
to Onesiphorus and all his family because
he often visited and encouraged me. He
was never ashamed of me because I was
in chains. [17]When he came to Rome, he
searched everywhere until he found me.
[18]May the Lord show him special kindness
on the day of Christ's return. And you know
very well how helpful he was in Ephesus.

4. CHARGE TO BE STRONG AND ENDURE SUFFERING (2:1-13)

Be Strong in Grace and Faithfulness

2 Timothy, my dear son, be strong
through the [g]grace that God gives you
in Christ Jesus. [2]You have heard me teach
things that have been confirmed by many
reliable witnesses. Now teach these truths
to other trustworthy people who will be
able to pass them on to others.

Endure Suffering

[3]Endure suffering along with me, as a good
soldier of Christ Jesus. [4]Soldiers don't get
tied up in the affairs of civilian life, for then
they cannot please the officer who enlisted
them. [5]And athletes cannot win the prize
unless they follow the rules. [6]And hardwork-
ing farmers should be the first to enjoy the
fruit of their labor. [7]Think about what I am
saying. The Lord will help you understand
all these things.

Suffer with Christ, As Paul Has Done

[8]Always remember that Jesus Christ, a descendant of King David, was raised from the
dead. This is the Good News I preach. [9]And
because I preach this Good News, I am suffering and have been chained like a criminal. But the word of God cannot be chained.
[10]So I am willing to endure anything if it
will bring [h]salvation and eternal glory in
Christ Jesus to those God has chosen.

1:10 God's gift of grace has been *made . . . plain* in history by ***Christ Jesus*** (see Rom 16:26; 1 Pet 1:20). • ***by the appearing:*** See note on 1 Tim 6:14. • ***broke the power of death:*** See 1 Cor 15:26; 2 Thes 2:8; Heb 2:14. • ***the way to life:*** See 1:1; 1 Cor 15:53-54; Titus 1:2. • ***through the Good News:*** Salvation is provided by Christ, but its effects are mediated through proclamation of the Good News (see Titus 1:2-3; Rom 1:16-17; 10:14-15).

1:12 Paul had complete confidence as he faced his own death (see 4:17-18; Rom 1:16; 2 Cor 4:8-9; Phil 1:20); it was an example for Timothy to follow (see 1:8). • ***what I have entrusted to him*** (or *what has been entrusted to me;* literally *my deposit*): *My deposit* might be either the Good News that had been entrusted to Paul (see 1 Tim 6:20) or Paul's life and ministry that he had committed to God.

1:14 Timothy must ***guard the precious truth*** (literally *guard the good deposit;* see notes on 1:12; 3:10-11) by faithfully proclaiming it and preventing false teachers from distorting it (see note on 2:2; see also 1 Tim 6:20).

1:15-18 Using the examples of others, both negative and positive, Paul continues urging Timothy to be faithful and to come to Rome without fear.

1:15 ***everyone . . . has deserted me:*** The desertion took place either in Rome or in ***the province of Asia*** when Paul was arrested. Paul might have seen this as another way his life followed the pattern of Christ's (see Matt 26:31, 56). • ***Phygelus and Hermogenes*** are otherwise unknown. The context (1:11-14) might imply that they were church leaders who sided with Paul's opponents.

2:1-13 Timothy is again told to ***be strong*** and to endure suffering along with Paul (2:1-7; see 1:8). Timothy's obedience should be motivated by reflecting on the Good News and on Paul's example (2:8-13).

2:1 ***Timothy, my dear son*** (literally *Therefore you, my child*): In the Greek, *therefore* links this phrase back to 1:15-18 and the emphatic *you* is in contrast to those examples.

2:2 The ***many reliable witnesses*** would confirm the validity and veracity of Paul's teaching (see also 3:10-11). • ***teach these truths*** (literally *entrust these things*): This verb is a cognate of *deposit* (1:12, 14). Timothy's own guarding of the deposit includes entrusting it to faithful people.

2:4-7 In rapid-fire sequence, Paul quotes maxims about single-minded struggling and laboring.

2:8-13 Paul's suffering (1:12) reflects the suffering of Jesus Christ and points to the cross and resurrection as the inner meaning of that Good News (see 1:8). Paul's suffering, like Christ's, was instrumental in bringing salvation to others. Christ gives his approval to those who suffer and endure with him.

2:8 ***Jesus Christ, a descendant of King David, was raised from the dead:*** Cp. Rom 1:3-4. Suffering with Christ should be viewed from the perspective of the resurrection to come.

2:9 ***like a criminal:*** Paul was identifying with Jesus' death (2:11; Phil 3:10-11). • ***the word of God cannot be chained:*** Both Paul and the Good News would be victorious through the power of Christ's resurrection (see 4:17-18; see also 2 Cor 12:8-10; Phil 1:12-14).

11 This is a trustworthy saying:

If we die with him,
we will also live with him.
12 If we endure hardship,
we will reign with him.
If we deny him,
he will deny us.
13 If we are unfaithful,
he remains faithful,
for he cannot deny who he is.

5. DEALING WITH OPPOSITION (2:14-26)

Avoid Useless Words

14 Remind everyone about these things, and
command them in God's presence to stop
fighting over words. Such arguments are useless, and they can ruin those who hear them.
15 Work hard so you can present yourself to God and receive his approval. Be a
good worker, one who does not need to be
ashamed and who correctly explains the
word of truth.
16 Avoid worthless, foolish
talk that only leads to more godless behavior.
17 This kind of talk spreads like cancer,
as in the case of Hymenaeus and Philetus.
18 They have left the path of truth, claiming
that the resurrection of the dead has already
occurred; in this way, they have turned some
people away from the faith.

God's Truth

19 But God's truth stands firm like a foundation stone with this [i]inscription: "The LORD
knows those who are his," and "All who belong to the LORD must turn away from evil."

Stay Pure

20 In a wealthy home some utensils are made
of gold and silver, and some are made of
wood and clay. The expensive utensils are
used for special occasions, and the cheap
ones are for everyday use.
21 If you keep
yourself pure, you will be a special utensil
for honorable use. Your life will be clean,
and you will be ready for the Master to use
you for every good work.
22 Run from anything that stimulates
youthful lusts. Instead, pursue righteous
living, faithfulness, love, and peace. Enjoy
the companionship of those who call on the
Lord with pure hearts.

Patiently Teach

23 Again I say, don't get involved in foolish,
ignorant arguments that only start fights.
24 A servant of the Lord must not quarrel
but must be kind to everyone, be able to
teach, and be patient with difficult people.
25 Gently [j]instruct those who oppose the
truth. Perhaps God will [k]change those people's hearts, and they will learn the truth.

2:11 Rom 6:2-11; 1 Thes 5:10
2:12 Matt 10:33; Rom 8:17; 1 Pet 4:13
2:13 Num 23:19; Rom 3:3; 1 Cor 1:9
2:14 1 Tim 1:4; 6:4; Titus 3:9
2:17 1 Tim 1:20
2:18 1 Tim 1:19; 6:21
2:19 *Num 16:5; Isa 52:11; John 10:14; [i]*sphragis* (4973) ‣Rev 5:1
2:20 Rom 9:21
2:21 2 Tim 3:17
2:22 1 Tim 6:11
2:23 1 Tim 4:7
2:24 1 Tim 3:2-3; Titus 1:7
2:25 [j]*paideuō* (3811) ‣2 Tim 3:16; [k]*metanoia* (3341) ‣Heb 6:1

2:11 ***a trustworthy saying:*** See notes on 1 Tim 1:15; 2:5-6.

2:13 ***he remains faithful:*** This could mean that (1) he allows those who have stumbled an opportunity for repentance; (2) he faithfully judges unbelievers in accord with his unchanging will; (3) he himself is an example of faithfulness for his people to follow; and/or (4) he will faithfully accomplish his purposes in history, to save those who trust in him through the Good News (1:12; 2:19). See also Rom 3:3-4; 1 Cor 10:13; 1 Jn 1:9.

2:14-26 Timothy must insist on the teaching of 2:8-13 and steer clear of the teaching and conduct of the false teachers. The heresy was probably the same as in 1 Tim 6:20-21.

2:15 ***who correctly explains*** (literally *who guides along a straight path*): The NLT relates this verse to right interpretation of ***the word of truth.*** Another possibility is that Timothy should keep to his purpose in teaching the word (see 1 Tim 1:4) and not turn aside by engaging in the false teachers' controversies (2:16).

2:17 ***cancer:*** Literally *gangrene.* • ***Hymenaeus*** was earlier teamed with Alexander (1 Tim 1:20); both of them were still wreaking havoc (4:14-15). • ***Philetus*** was Hymenaeus's new accomplice.

2:18 ***claiming that the resurrection of the dead has already occurred:*** Cp. 2 Thes 2:2. These false teachers might have twisted Paul's own teaching on the resurrection of the dead (Rom 6:5; Gal 2:20; Eph 1:3; 2:6; 5:14; Col 2:12; 3:1-4) by teaching that they already fully participated in the heavenly life, and perhaps that physical resurrection would not occur. They could have concluded from this that one's conduct in the body (i.e., morality) was irrelevant, since their mortal bodies could have no impact on their eternal spirits. Or, they could have gone the other way, toward world-denying asceticism (1 Tim 4:3; see Col 2:8, 16-23), with the idea that enjoyment of material things is inappropriate for resurrected, spiritual persons. These teachers might have understood from Jesus' teachings (see Matt 19:10-12; 22:30) that marriage should be prohibited (1 Tim 4:3). Their teachings on the OT law (1 Tim 1:7-11) might have led to the promotion of certain taboos. Their teachings might have involved an overly aggressive promotion of equality (see 3:6; cp. Gal 3:28; 1 Tim 2:11-15) in the belief that the age to come was already here. Their teaching might have focused exclusively on resurrection power, which would contradict Paul's message of suffering and the cross (see 1:8, 12; 2:8-13; cp. 1 Cor 4:8-13; 2 Cor 12:8-10). Whatever its exact form, Paul describes their teaching as "worthless, foolish talk" (2:16).

2:19 Paul assures Timothy that the false teaching will not win (see 3:9), and he reinforces the call to purity. • ***foundation stone:*** This metaphor emphasizes immunity to destruction (Isa 28:16) and might reflect a temple (see also 1 Tim 3:15; 1 Cor 3:11; Eph 2:20; 1 Pet 2:4-7; Rev 21:14). • ***The LORD knows:*** This quotation alludes to Num 16:5 (Greek version). • ***All who belong to the LORD must turn away from evil:*** See Isa 52:11; cp. Num 16:26-27; Lev 24:16; Ps 6:8.

2:20-21 Building on 2:19, Paul uses imagery about the ***utensils*** in a ***wealthy home*** (see Rom 9:21). Within God's household one should endeavor to be like a utensil that is cherished rather than one that is treated with contempt.

2:22 ***those who call on the Lord:*** Cp. Ps 99:6; Joel 2:32; Acts 2:21; 9:14, 21; 22:16; Rom 10:12-13; 1 Cor 1:2. • ***with pure hearts:*** Cp. 1 Tim 1:5.

2:24 ***A servant of the Lord:*** See Titus 1:1; cp. Isa 42:1-2; 50:6; 53:7; Matt 12:14-21. • ***be able to teach, and be patient:*** See 1 Tim 3:2-3; Titus 3:2.

2:25 ***Gently instruct:*** Cp. 1 Cor 4:21; 2 Cor 10:1; 1 Thes 5:14; 2 Thes 3:14-15; Titus 3:10-11; Jude 1:22-23.

2:26
1 Tim 3:7
3:1
1 Tim 4:1
Jude 1:18
3:2-3
Rom 1:29-31
3:2
[a]*blasphēmos* (0989)
‣Jude 1:8
3:3
[b]*diabolos* (1228)
‣Titus 2:3
3:6
Jude 1:4
3:8
1 Tim 6:5
3:10
1 Tim 4:6
3:11
Ps 34:19
Acts 13:14, 50-51;
14:5, 19
3:12
John 15:20
Acts 14:22
3:14
2 Tim 1:13; 2:2
3:15
John 5:39
[c]*sōtēria* (4991)
‣Titus 3:5
3:16
Rom 15:4
2 Pet 1:20-21
[d]*paideia* (3809)
‣Titus 2:12
[e]*dikaiosunē* (1343)
‣2 Pet 2:21
3:17
1 Tim 6:11
2 Tim 2:21
4:1
Acts 10:42

26Then they will come to their senses and
escape from the devil's trap. For they have
been held captive by him to do whatever he
wants.

6. CHARGE IN LIGHT OF THE LAST DAYS (3:1–4:8)

Understand the Dangers of the Last Days

3 You should know this, Timothy, that in
the last days there will be very difficult
times. 2For people will love only themselves
and their money. They will be boastful and
proud, [a]scoffing at God, disobedient to their
parents, and ungrateful. They will consider
nothing sacred. 3They will be unloving and
unforgiving; they will [b]slander others and
have no self-control. They will be cruel
and hate what is good. 4They will betray
their friends, be reckless, be puffed up with
pride, and love pleasure rather than God.
5They will act religious, but they will reject
the power that could make them godly. Stay
away from people like that!

6They are the kind who work their way into
people's homes and win the confidence of
vulnerable women who are burdened with
the guilt of sin and controlled by various
desires. 7(Such women are forever following new teachings, but they are never able
to understand the truth.) 8These teachers
oppose the truth just as Jannes and Jambres
opposed Moses. They have depraved minds
and a counterfeit faith. 9But they won't get
away with this for long. Someday everyone
will recognize what fools they are, just as
with Jannes and Jambres.

Remain Faithful to What You Know

10But you, Timothy, certainly know what I
teach, and how I live, and what my purpose
in life is. You know my faith, my patience,
my love, and my endurance. 11You know
how much persecution and suffering I
have endured. You know all about how I
was persecuted in Antioch, Iconium, and
Lystra—but the Lord rescued me from all
of it. 12Yes, and everyone who wants to live
a godly life in Christ Jesus will suffer persecution. 13But evil people and impostors will
flourish. They will deceive others and will
themselves be deceived.

14But you must remain faithful to the
things you have been taught. You know they
are true, for you know you can trust those
who taught you. 15You have been taught the
holy Scriptures from childhood, and they
have given you the wisdom to receive the
[c]salvation that comes by trusting in Christ
Jesus. 16All Scripture is inspired by God and
is useful to teach us what is true and to make
us realize what is wrong in our lives. It corrects us when we are wrong and [d]teaches us
to do what is [e]right. 17God uses it to prepare
and equip his people to do every good work.

Charge to Carry Out the Ministry

4 I solemnly urge you in the presence of
God and Christ Jesus, who will someday judge the living and the dead when he

3:1–4:8 Timothy must stay on course through ***difficult times*** ahead.

3:1-5 Paul describes what people will be like in ***the last days*** (see also 1 Tim 4:1-5; 2 Pet 2:1-22; 3:3; Jude 1:18), which had already begun (3:5, 6-9).

3:5 ***People like that*** (3:2-4) had rejected sound teaching and cut themselves off from ***the power that could make them godly*** (see 1 Tim 1:5-11; Col 2:16-23).

3:6-7 ***and win the confidence of*** (literally *and take captive*): The effect of the false teachers on households and ***women*** is a consistent concern of the letters to Timothy and Titus (Titus 1:11; see 1 Tim 2:11-15; 3:4-5; 5:14-15). Whether or not the false teachers targeted women, they apparently were successful with some of them.

3:8 ***Jannes and Jambres*** are, according to tradition, the names of the Egyptian sorcerers who ***opposed Moses*** (see Exod 7:8-13; 8:18; 9:11).

3:11 Timothy was from ***Lystra***, near ***Antioch*** and ***Iconium***, so he knew ***all about*** what Paul had suffered (see Acts 13:14, 45-51; 14:1-8, 19-22), though he was recruited after these events (Acts 16:1-3). • ***the Lord rescued me:*** Paul could attest from his own life that the Lord would accomplish his purposes through his faithful servant (see 4:6-8, 17-18; Ps 22:19-22; 34:19; Dan 3:17-18; 2 Cor 1:8-10; 2 Pet 2:7-9).

3:14-15 ***from childhood:*** Timothy's Jewish grandmother and mother, Lois and Eunice (see Acts 16:1-3), provided his education in the OT ***Scriptures*** (see 1:5), and their lives reinforced their teaching. • The OT Scriptures give ***the wisdom to receive . . . Christ Jesus.*** In turn, Jesus Christ is needed to understand the OT Scriptures fully.

3:16-17 These verses elaborate on 3:15 by explaining Scripture's effectiveness, its source, and the ways that it gives wisdom to live out our salvation. Paul was speaking of the OT, but his statement applies to ***all Scripture***, including the NT (see, e.g., 2 Pet 3:15-16).

3:16 The fact that ***Scripture is inspired by God*** (literally *God-breathed*, breathed out by God's own speech; see also Heb 4:12-13; 2 Pet 1:20-21) does not negate the active involvement of the human authors. But it does affirm that God is fully responsible for his word. Scripture is true, reliable, authoritative, permanent, and powerful because it comes from God himself. Its message is coherent, and it is consistent in its testimony about Jesus Christ (see Luke 24:25-27, 44; John 5:39-40; Acts 3:24; 1 Cor 15:3-4). Thus it has the power to bring salvation and elicit faith. It must not be abused, as the false teachers had been doing (4:2-4; 1 Tim 1:4-7; cp. 2 Pet 3:16), but must be taught properly (2:2, 15). • As a consequence of inspiration, all Scripture is ***useful.*** Both the OT and the NT are together our guide and teacher in life.

3:17 Paul makes it clear that salvation (3:15) results in godliness (see Gal 1:4; 5:16-26; Eph 2:8-10).

4:1-8 Timothy stood in the ***presence of God*** and was to work in view of Jesus' coming to ***judge*** and ***set up his Kingdom*** (see 1 Tim 5:21; 6:13-14). Christ's appearing will bring cleansing (2:19), accountability (3:8-9), salvation, vindication, and reward (4:8, 18). See also 1 Cor 3:10-15; 4:4-5; 2 Cor 5:10.

4:1 ***judge the living and the dead:*** See Matt 25:31-46; Acts 10:42; Rom 14:7-12;

[f]appears to set up his Kingdom: [2]Preach
the word of God. Be prepared, whether the
time is favorable or not. Patiently correct,
rebuke, and [g]encourage your people with
good teaching.
[3]For a time is coming when people will
no longer listen to sound and wholesome
teaching. They will follow their own desires
and will look for teachers who will tell them
whatever their itching ears want to hear.
[4]They will reject the truth and chase after
myths.
[5]But you should keep a clear mind in
every situation. Don't be afraid of suffering for the Lord. Work at telling others the
Good News, and fully carry out the [h]minis-
try God has given you.
[6]As for me, my life has already been
poured out as an offering to God. The time
of my death is near. [7]I have fought the good
fight, I have finished the race, and I have remained faithful. [8]And now the prize awaits
me—the crown of righteousness, which the
Lord, the righteous Judge, will give me on
the day of his return. And the prize is not
just for me but for all who eagerly look forward to his [i]appearing.

7. PAUL'S FINAL WORDS (4:9-22)

Appeal for Timothy to Come

[9]Timothy, please come as soon as you can.
[10]Demas has deserted me because he loves
the things of this life and has gone to Thessalonica. Crescens has gone to Galatia, and
Titus has gone to Dalmatia. [11]Only Luke is
with me. Bring Mark with you when you
come, for he will be helpful to me in my [j]min-
istry. [12]I sent Tychicus to Ephesus. [13]When
you come, be sure to bring the coat I left
with Carpus at Troas. Also bring my [k]books,
and especially my papers.

Warning about Alexander

[14]Alexander the coppersmith did me much
harm, but the Lord will judge him for what
he has done. [15]Be careful of him, for he
fought against everything we said.

Account of Paul's First Trial

[16]The first time I was brought before the
judge, no one came with me. Everyone abandoned me. May it not be counted against
them. [17]But the Lord stood with me and
gave me strength so that I might preach the
Good News in its entirety for all the Gentiles
to hear. And he rescued me from certain

[f]*epiphaneia* (2015)
‣2 Tim 4:8

4:2
1 Tim 5:20
[g]*parakaleō* (3870)
‣Titus 2:15

4:4
1 Tim 1:4

4:5
[h]*diakonia* (1248)
‣2 Tim 4:11

4:6
Phil 2:17

4:7
1 Cor 9:24-27
1 Tim 6:12

4:8
Phil 3:14
Rev 2:10
[i]*epiphaneia* (2015)
‣Titus 2:13

4:11
Col 4:10, 14
[j]*diakonia* (1248)
‣Acts 6:1

4:13
[k]*biblion* (0975)
‣Rev 1:11

4:14
1 Tim 1:20

4:16
Acts 7:60

4:17
Ps 22:21
Dan 6:22
Acts 9:15

Rev 20:11-15. • ***when he appears*** (literally *his epiphany*): See note on 1 Tim 6:14; see also 2 Tim 1:10; 4:8; Titus 2:11-13; 3:4.

4:5-8 Paul effectively hands the mantle of leadership to Timothy (cp. Deut 31:7-8; 34:9; 2 Kgs 2:1-18).

4:5 This final charge summarizes what has been said before (1:6-14; 2:1-15, 24-26; 3:12).

4:6-8 Paul's faithfulness, vindication, and reward are a model and a challenge to others—particularly Timothy—to follow Paul's example after he is gone.

4:6 Paul pictures his death as a drink ***offering*** that is ***poured out . . . to God*** (see Exod 29:40-41; Lev 23:13; Num 28:7; Phil 2:17); this offering participates in Christ's own sacrifice (see Col 1:24; see also Rom 12:1).

4:7 Paul had ***remained faithful*** to the trust that was committed to him (see notes on 1:12; 1 Tim 6:20; cp. Acts 20:24). He had preserved the integrity of the Christian faith and wanted Timothy to follow his example (see 2:3-7; 1 Tim 1:18; 6:12; cp. Rom 15:30-31; 1 Cor 9:25-27; Heb 12:1; Jude 1:3).

4:8 Only one thing remained for Paul: the victor's ***crown*** (see also Jas 1:12; 1 Pet 5:4; Rev 2:10; 3:11). • If we live expecting that Christ is indeed coming again, we can ***eagerly look forward to his appearing*** (see 1 Tim 6:14) to set up his kingdom (4:1). If we don't follow Christ's commands, we cannot look forward to his coming as Judge and King.

4:9 Paul makes explicit his summons for ***Timothy*** to come to Rome (see 1:4).

4:10 ***Demas:*** See Col 4:14; Phlm 1:24. • ***deserted:*** See also 4:16-17; cp. Ps 22:1; Mark 15:34. • Loving ***the things of this life*** contrasts with the anticipation of Christ's glorious return (4:8). • ***Crescens*** is otherwise unknown; his and Titus's absence seems to have heightened Paul's isolation. • ***Titus*** was Paul's effective and reliable co-worker (see "Titus" at Titus 1:4; 2:1, p. 2073). Perhaps he had ***gone to Dalmatia*** (northwest of modern-day Greece) on a mission for Paul.

4:11 ***Luke,*** the author of Luke and Acts (see Luke and Acts Introductions, "Authorship," pp. 1696, 1822), accompanied Paul in his journeys at various times (see "Luke" at Acts 16:10, p. 1861). It is often supposed that Luke was with Paul as his physician (Col 4:14). Luke was the ***only*** one of Paul's co-workers who was continuously present with him. Thus Paul wished for Timothy to come quickly. • ***Mark:*** See "John Mark" at Acts 13:4-5, 13, p. 1852. • Paul's assessment that ***he will be helpful to me*** tells a story of forgiveness and redemption (see Acts 13:13; 15:36-40; see also Col 4:10; Phlm 1:24).

4:12 ***Tychicus*** was apparently a Greek (implied in Col 4:7-8, 10-11) from Asia Minor (see also Acts 20:4; Eph 6:21-22; Col 4:7-8; Titus 3:12). He was possibly going ***to Ephesus*** to deliver the present letter and take over for Timothy (assuming that Timothy was in Ephesus; see notes on 4:13, 19).

4:13 Paul's arrest and transfer to Rome apparently did not allow him to gather his things. • ***the coat:*** Winter was coming (4:21). • ***Carpus*** might have been Paul's host in Troas. The reference to ***Troas*** implies that Timothy was still in Ephesus and would travel through Troas, a port town. • ***my books . . . my papers:*** These writings may have included Scriptures, personal notes, letters addressed to Paul, copies of Paul's own letters, and other Christian and Jewish materials. • ***my papers:*** Literally *the parchments.*

4:14 Alexander was a common name (cp. Mark 15:21; Acts 4:6; 19:33). ***Alexander the coppersmith*** was probably the same person as in 1 Tim 1:20. • ***did me much harm:*** Apparently he did more than merely oppose Paul's teaching. Perhaps he had a hand in Paul's arrest.

4:16 ***The first time I was brought before the judge:*** A Roman trial was divided between an initial, preliminary investigation and the trial proper. Paul was probably referring to the first of these. It could also refer to his first imprisonment in Rome (Acts 28; see 2 Timothy Introduction, "Date of Writing," p. 2061). • ***Everyone abandoned me:*** See note on 4:10.

4:17 ***so that I might preach the Good***

4:18 Ps 121:7; Rom 11:36
4:19 Acts 18:2
4:20 Acts 19:22; 20:4; Rom 16:23
4:22 Rom 16:20; Gal 6:18

death. 18Yes, and the Lord will deliver me
from every evil attack and will bring me
safely into his heavenly Kingdom. All glory
to God forever and ever! Amen.

Final Greetings and Blessing

19Give my greetings to Priscilla and Aquila
and those living in the household of Onesiphorus.
20Erastus stayed at Corinth, and
I left Trophimus sick at Miletus.
21Do your best to get here before winter.
Eubulus sends you greetings, and so do Pudens, Linus, Claudia, and all the brothers
and sisters.
22May the Lord be with your spirit. And
may his grace be with all of you.

The Mantle of Leadership (4:1-5)

Pattern your lives after mine, and learn from those who follow our example. Philippians 3:17

2 Tim 1:8, 12; 2:3, 10-12; Mark 10:35-45; John 8:39; 13:15; Acts 20:35; 2 Cor 4:8-12; Eph 5:2; Phil 3:10, 17; Col 1:24; 1 Thes 1:6-7; 2 Thes 3:9; 1 Tim 1:16; 4:12; Titus 2:7; Heb 6:12; 13:7; 1 Pet 2:21; 5:1-4

For Paul, the essence of good leadership was to provide an example that mirrored Christ's own example. The cross of Christ was central for Paul, and it had a total claim on his life. When he said, "I want to suffer with him, sharing in his death" (Phil 3:10; see Col 1:24), he was speaking of more than emotional turmoil or even of dealing with sin. He meant suffering violently and bodily. Paul endured suffering for the sake of those to whom he proclaimed the Good News, always putting their salvation before his own physical well-being (2:10; 2 Cor 4:8-12). Paul's life was a proclamation of Christ crucified, of God's power through Paul's weakness (2 Cor 12:8-10), and of God's wisdom despite human foolishness (1 Cor 1:18-31). As Paul summoned Timothy to take up the mantle of leadership (4:1-5), he was also summoning Timothy to suffer with him (1:8; 2:3; 4:5), scorning the shame of the cross (1:8, 12, 16).

The mantle of Christian leadership is the garb of a servant who suffers for those he leads (Mark 10:35-45). If leadership does not orbit faithfully around Christ as its self-giving center, it ceases to be leadership in Christ and fails to understand the Good News. But leadership that is modeled after Christ gains a reward at Christ's future coming, when those who have died with him will live with him and those who endure hardship will reign with him (2:11-12).

News: Paul had turned his defense in court into proclamation of the Good News—just as in his earlier experiences (Acts 22–24; 26:1-29; see also 2 Tim 2:9-10; Phil 1:12-14). • ***for all the Gentiles to hear:*** Paul sensed that he had completed his task (4:7-8). The OT specifically anticipates the conversion of the nations (e.g., Ps 22:27-29). • ***from certain death*** (literally *from the mouth of a lion*): The lion is often a metaphor for enemies (see Ps 7:2; 35:17; cp. Dan 6; Heb 11:33). Here, it might refer to literal lions in the amphitheater, to the emperor, to the false teachers, or to Satan (1 Pet 5:8; cp. Ps 22:21).

4:18 God would continue to strengthen Paul and keep him strong in the faith (4:7) to the end of his life (see 1:12). • The Lord's ***heavenly Kingdom*** contrasts with the earthly kingdom that was about to pass judgment on Paul (see also 4:1; 1 Cor 15:48-49; Heb 12:18-29). • ***All glory . . . Amen:*** Paul's doxology in the face of execution expresses confidence that God's glory will be upheld (cp. 1 Tim 1:17; 6:15-16). • ***to God*** (literally *to him*): The Greek suggests that this praise is ascribed to "the Lord" of the preceding sentence—namely, to Jesus (cp. Titus 2:13).

4:19-21 As in several of Paul's epistles, the letter closes with greetings and final instructions (e.g., Rom 16:1-23; 1 Cor 16:19-21; 2 Cor 13:12).

4:19 ***Priscilla and Aquila*** had been in Ephesus (Acts 18:26; 1 Cor 16:19) and were probably there at this time (see "Priscilla and Aquila" at Acts 18:1-3, p. 1865). They had also lived in Rome (Acts 18:2; Rom 16:3), where Paul currently was. This might imply that Timothy was still in Ephesus (see 1 Tim 1:3). • Paul appreciatively mentions ***Onesiphorus*** in 1:16 as having ministered to him in prison.

4:20 ***Erastus*** was a resident of Corinth (Acts 19:22; Rom 16:23). Modern excavations have found an inscription at Corinth mentioning an Erastus who was the city treasurer; he was probably the same man. • ***Trophimus*** (Acts 20:4; 21:29) was an Ephesian associated with Tychicus (4:12).

4:21 ***before winter:*** Paul was probably concerned there would be an extended delay if Timothy missed this chance to travel in the fall (see 1:4; 4:9). Winter closed travel across the Adriatic Sea from November to March (see Acts 27:12). Paul might also have been concerned to receive his coat (4:13) for the unheated prison. ***Eubulus*** is not mentioned elsewhere in the NT, but he was obviously well known to Timothy. • ***Pudens*** was a name used in upper class families. • Eusebius and Irenaeus later identified ***Linus*** as the first bishop of Rome. • ***Claudia*** is not mentioned elsewhere in the NT. • ***brothers and sisters:*** Literally *brothers*, a generic term that refers to both male and female believers.

4:22 The precise phrasing here is unique, perhaps to emphasize what had already been said in 1:6-8; 2:1 (cp. Gal 6:18; Phil 4:23; Phlm 1:25). • ***with all of you:*** This letter would be read publicly.

PAUL'S LETTER TO

TITUS

The letter to Titus gives us a powerful understanding of the church in Crete as it was beginning to grow and also an insightful glimpse into Paul's work there. These people were new converts in a culture where conduct was very crude. Paul, the aged missionary, demonstrates a mature finesse in adapting the Good News to the spiritual condition and circumstances of these believers in Crete.

SETTING

A group from Crete had been in Jerusalem during Pentecost at the birth of the Christian church (Acts 2:11). Some of these might have carried the Christian faith back to the island at that time, but this letter to Titus suggests that the church on Crete had been recently founded as a result of Paul's mission (see 1:5; 3:15). The only other mention of Crete in the NT comes during Paul's transfer to Rome as a prisoner (Acts 27:7-21), but he did not have an opportunity to become active in Crete at that time. Most likely, Paul's work in Crete began after the events of Acts 28 (AD 60–62) and before his final Roman imprisonment (about AD 64~65?).

As during his first missionary journey out of Antioch, Paul had begun the church in Crete without appointing leaders. As with those earliest churches, he now wanted leaders to be established (cp. Acts 14:23), although in this case he delegated the responsibility to Titus, a longtime co-worker. Paul was headed for Nicopolis on the west coast of modern Greece, and he wanted Titus to join him there when Artemas or Tychicus had arrived on the island of Crete (3:12). Paul's plan to winter at Nicopolis suggests that he planned to sail westward from there when spring arrived (see 2 Tim 4:21), probably heading for Italy and possibly Spain (Rom 15:24, 28).

The Setting of Titus, about AD 63. Paul wrote to Titus, who was stationed in CRETE, around the same time as he wrote his first letter to Timothy in EPHESUS (see 1 Timothy Introduction, p. 2048). Paul's instructions to Titus reflect the rough cultural environment in which he was working.

On Crete, the degenerate culture was negatively influencing the believers in the young church. False teachers were also troubling the community, seemingly like those mentioned in 1 and 2 Timothy. As Paul's delegate to Crete, Titus had to set this church in order before the arrival of Artemas or Tychicus. Above all, he needed to assign elders in each city. When this was completed, he would depart and join Paul.

SUMMARY

The letter to Titus is all business, setting the tone for Titus himself to follow. Each section of the body (1:5–3:11) is composed in a pattern of command, rationale, and charge. Paul consistently repeats this pattern—whether addressing the appointment of elders (1:5-16), right conduct among members of the household of faith (2:1-15), or right conduct in society at large (3:1-11). The rationale for Paul's commands in the first section, on leadership, is that the community is threatened by false teachers and needs decisive leadership. In the next two sections, on right conduct, the commands are based on the rationale of God's grace and mercy and its provisions.

OUTLINE

1:1-4
Salutation from Paul

1:5-16
Leadership in Crete

2:1-15
Relationships in the Church

3:1-11
Relationship with Society

3:12-15
Paul's Closing

DATE OF WRITING

All three of the letters to Timothy and Titus were written at about the same time, addressing three distinct situations and yet sharing significant historical and theological elements. It is possible that Paul wrote these letters, including the one to Titus, during the period prior to his arrest in Acts 21, but a date sometime after the imprisonment of Acts 28 is more likely (see Introduction to Paul's Letters to Timothy and Titus, "Date of Writing," p. 2047).

SITUATION AT CRETE

The study of Greek mythology at Crete has given us insight into the situation Paul faced there.[1] According to Cretan mythology, the god Zeus was once a mere human who lived and died on Crete but who had achieved godhood through the benefits he gave to humans (see note on 1:12). The idea of a great human benefactor being exalted to the status of god by virtue of good deeds contradicts the Good News. God graciously lowered himself to humanity in Jesus Christ—"our great God and Savior" (2:13)—and offers salvation through pure mercy (3:5).

LITERARY GENRE

Like 1 Timothy, this letter has characteristics similar to a Greco-Roman *mandatum principis* ("commandment of a ruler")—see 1 Timothy Introduction, "Literary Genre," p. 2049.

[1] See Reggie M. Kidd, "Titus as *Apologia*: Grace for Liars, Beasts, and Bellies," *Horizons in Biblical Theology* 21 (1999), 185-209.

TIMELINE

AD 34~35
Saul's conversion near Damascus

AD 53~56
Paul's ministry in Ephesus

AD 60–62
Paul is imprisoned in Rome

AD 62~64
Paul is released, travels freely, including Crete and Ephesus

about AD 63
Paul writes 1 Timothy and Titus from Macedonia

about AD 64~65?
Paul is imprisoned, writes 2 Timothy, and is martyred in Rome

The writer is . . . dealing with communities in a fairly early stage of Christian life. . . . To secure [a civilized] character the foundation is laid in sound, wholesome teaching.

WALTER LOCK
The Pastoral Epistles, p. 123

This is a proof of the virtue of Titus, that [Paul] did not require many words, but a short remembrance.

JOHN CHRYSOSTOM
The Homilies of St. John Chrysostom

COMPARISON WITH 1 & 2 TIMOTHY

Although Crete is some distance from the church in Ephesus (the recipients of 1 & 2 Timothy), there are some intriguing parallels between the two situations. The characterization of the false teachers and their teaching (1:10-16) suggests that quite similar teachings were being confronted in both places (see 1 Tim 1:4-7; 4:1-4; 2 Tim 3:1-7; 4:3-4).

That said, the situation on Crete as addressed in Titus is not identical to that of Ephesus in 1 & 2 Timothy. The church in Crete was new, whereas the church in Ephesus was long established. Crete was socially less civilized than Ephesus. The newness of the church in Crete might explain the absence of a widows list (1 Tim 5:3-16) and deacons (1 Tim 3:8-13). The differences in the troublemakers might account for silence on the subject of women teachers (see 1 Tim 2:11-15). The criteria for leaders (1:6-9), as well as the standards of conduct for members of the community (see 2:3-4), might represent a lowering of the bar to accommodate new converts from an uncouth background. Finally, the stress on guarding the "deposit," so important in Timothy (1 Tim 1:18; 6:20; 2 Tim 1:12-14; 2:2), is absent in Titus.

MEANING AND MESSAGE

Central to this letter is the realization that the Christian community should enact God's saving grace, which has been shown to the world in the person and work of Jesus Christ. The community's behavior among its members, and in relation to those outside, should be consistent with the way that God had dealt with it. Christians must embody God's grace in the world and toward the world. In so doing, they will advance the Good News within their territory and culture (2:10-11; 3:2-3, 8; see Matt 5:14-16).

The drama of the divine salvation of humanity invites participation. As Christ's followers, we must become players in this performance of grace. Our communities should promote godly lives because the appearance of grace, in the person of Christ, has taught us how to live and has made such living possible (2:1-15). As believers, we must also conduct ourselves properly in a fallen world, with hearts bent on the salvation of others. We must bear in mind our former lives—remembering how God has dealt with us, has given us salvation, and has provided for our godliness (3:1-11).

FURTHER READING

GORDON FEE
1 and 2 Timothy, Titus (1988)

LUKE TIMOTHY JOHNSON
Letters to Paul's Delegates (1996)

JON LAANSMA
Titus in *Cornerstone Biblical Commentary*, vol. 17 (2009)

I. HOWARD MARSHALL
The Pastoral Epistles (1999)

WILLIAM MOUNCE
The Pastoral Epistles (2000)

1. SALUTATION FROM PAUL (1:1-4)

1 This letter is from Paul, a slave of God
and an apostle of Jesus Christ. I have
been sent to proclaim faith to those God has
chosen and to teach them to know the truth
that shows them how to live godly lives.
2This truth gives them confidence that they
have eternal life, which God—who does not
lie—promised them before the world began. 3And now at just the right time he has
revealed this message, which we announce
to everyone. It is by the command of God
our [a]Savior that I have been entrusted with
this work for him.

1:1 1 Tim 2:4
1:2 2 Tim 1:1, 9; Titus 3:7
1:3 1 Tim 1:1, 11; Titus 2:10
[a]*sōtēr* (4990) ‣ Titus 1:4

1:1-4 The opening of Titus, like that of 1 Timothy (1 Tim 1:1-2), establishes Paul's authority for his delegate.

1:1 *to proclaim faith to:* Or *to strengthen the faith of.* • *and to teach . . . godly lives:* See 2:11-14; 1 Tim 6:3.

1:2 The *confidence that they have eternal life* enables God's people to live in the present in light of the future (see 2:11-14; 3:7-8). • *God—who does not lie:* The true God contrasts with popular Cretan conceptions (see note on 1:12). This statement also underlines God's plan of salvation as unchanging (1:1): God can be trusted to fulfill his promises (see Num 23:19; 1 Sam 15:29; Rom 3:3-4).

1:3 *at just the right time:* The initiative is entirely with God, who carries out his plan on his own timetable by his own will (see 3:5; 1 Tim 2:6; 2 Tim 1:10). • *God our Savior:* In 1:4, Jesus is also called "our Savior," identifying Jesus with God (see 2:10, 13; 3:4, 6).

1:4
2 Cor 2:13
2 Tim 4:10
[b]*sōtēr* (4990)
‣Titus 3:6

1:5
Acts 14:23

1:6-9
//1 Tim 3:2-7
2 Tim 2:24-26

1:7
1 Cor 4:1
[c]*episkopos* (1985)
‣1 Pet 2:25
[d]*oikonomos* (3623)
‣Luke 16:1

1:9
1 Tim 1:10
2 Tim 4:3
Titus 2:1

4I am writing to Titus, my true son in the
faith that we share.
May God the Father and Christ Jesus our
[b]Savior give you grace and peace.

2. LEADERSHIP IN CRETE (1:5-16)

Command: Appoint Leaders

5I left you on the island of Crete so you
could complete our work there and appoint
elders in each town as I instructed you. 6An
elder must live a blameless life. He must be
faithful to his wife, and his children must
be believers who don't have a reputation
for being wild or rebellious. 7An [c]elder is a
[d]manager of God's household, so he must
live a blameless life. He must not be arrogant or quick-tempered; he must not be a
heavy drinker, violent, or dishonest with
money.
8Rather, he must enjoy having guests in
his home, and he must love what is good. He
must live wisely and be just. He must live a
devout and disciplined life. 9He must have
a strong belief in the trustworthy message
he was taught; then he will be able to encourage others with wholesome teaching

Church Leaders (1:5-9)

Titus 2:15
Acts 6:1-6; 13:1-3; 14:23; 15:4-35
1 Cor 12:28-30; 14:26-33
Eph 4:11-13
1 Tim 3:1-13; 4:11-16; 5:17-22
2 Tim 2:2, 25-26

Spontaneity and spiritual giftedness characterized the first church gatherings (see 1 Cor 11:4-5; 14:26-33). The apostles exercised general oversight of the Christian communities (Acts 6:2; 8:14; 14:23) together with the elders in Jerusalem (Acts 15:4, 6, 22-23), whose function was drawn from the Jewish synagogue and Greco-Roman models. The titles and functions of Christian leaders in communities outside of Jerusalem appear to have been fluid (e.g. Acts 6:1-6; 13:1-3), but local leaders were dependent on the apostles when possible. Teachers and prophets also had important roles in guiding the church (see Acts 2:17-18; 11:27-30; 1 Cor 14:26-40). Churches were often founded before their leaders were appointed (1:5; Acts 14:23). Such appointments were almost certainly related to spiritual gifting (e.g. 1 Cor 12:28-30; Eph 4:11) and (in some situations) to age.

There were always community leaders, whether or not they occupied a formal office. In the letters to Timothy and Titus, however, there is a strong emphasis on elders (see note on 1 Tim 5:17), overseers (see note on 1:7), and deacons (see note on 1 Tim 3:8-13). How these offices developed over the years is unclear, and even the practices described in 1 Timothy and Titus might not have been universal. Elders in Ephesus and on Crete may have carried more of the teaching role because the false teachers had to be decisively counteracted. Otherwise, the norms of 1 Cor 14:26-40 might have prevailed. These letters are more concerned with ensuring that the Good News be faithfully transmitted than with perpetuating a form of government (see note on 1 Tim 6:20).

The apostle Paul exercised influence and control over his entire mission field, but there is no evidence that he intended to build or leave a regional or mission-wide infrastructure of governance. Apparently the overseers were to carry on the teaching and disciplinary role of Paul and his delegates without the wider responsibilities and authority of the apostles. As leaders of the local church, they wielded real and distinctive authority (see 1 Tim 4:11-16; 5:19-22; 2 Tim 2:14-19, 25-26; Titus 2:15; 3:10-11; 1 Cor 5:3-5).

1:4 *Titus* was Paul's delegate in dealing with the church in Crete. • ***my true son:*** The wording authorizes the delegate (as in 1 Tim 1:2).

1:5-16 Strong, faithful leadership was needed in the churches of Crete to address the danger of false teachers (1:10-16). This part of Titus's task dovetails with the larger concern of the letter: to shape a community that bears witness to Christ by embodying God's grace in its conduct. Cp. 1 Tim 3:1-7.

1:5-9 Titus was directed to appoint leaders in order to ***complete our work there***—i.e., to establish the church (cp. 1 Tim 3:1-13). Deacons are not mentioned, possibly because these were new, small churches. • These leadership qualities might be an accommodation to the newness of these converts and the roughness of their culture. It is assumed that the elders will be male (see 1 Tim 3:4-5).

1:5 *Crete* was located in the Mediterranean, south of the Aegean Sea. It was an important location for travel and trade by sea, so it had a mix of influences, including a Jewish population. Some from Crete had been at Pentecost (Acts 2:11), but this letter seems to deal with an infant church. • ***elders in each town:*** There may have been more than one house church in a given town and possibly more than one elder in a given house church. Clearly, there were churches in at least two towns and the leadership was specific to each town.

1:6 ***must live a blameless life:*** See 1 Tim 3:2, 10. • ***must be faithful to his wife:*** Or *must have only one wife,* or *must be married only once;* literally *must be the husband of one wife.* See note on 1 Tim 3:2. • ***children:*** See 1 Tim 3:4-5, 12. • ***wild or rebellious:*** This probably reflects Cretan culture with its low moral standards (1:12).

1:7 ***An elder*** (or *An overseer,* or *A bishop*) ***is a manager of God's household:*** See 1:11; 2:2-10; 1 Tim 1:4; 3:4-5, 12, 15; 2 Tim 2:20-21. • These qualities indicate that an elder should not be running with the Cretan masses (see 1:12). • ***must not be a heavy drinker:*** Literally *must not drink too much wine.*

1:9 The elders had a leading role in teaching the community. This may have been necessary in dealing with the

and show those who oppose it where they
are wrong.

Rationale: The Rebellion of False Teachers

10For there are many rebellious people who
engage in useless talk and deceive others.
This is especially true of those who insist
on circumcision for salvation. 11They must
be silenced, because they are turning whole
families away from the truth by their false
teaching. And they do it only for money.
12Even one of their own men, a prophet
from Crete, has said about them, "The people of Crete are all liars, cruel animals, and
lazy gluttons."

Charge: Reprove Them! (1:13-16)

13This is true. So reprimand them sternly to
make them strong in the faith. 14They must
stop listening to Jewish myths and the commands of people who have turned away
from the truth.
15Everything is pure to those whose
hearts are pure. But nothing is pure to those
who are corrupt and unbelieving, because
their minds and consciences are corrupted.
16Such people claim they know God, but
they deny him by the way they live. They are
detestable and disobedient, worthless for
doing anything good.

3. RELATIONSHIPS IN THE CHURCH (2:1-15)

Command: Promote Right Conduct in God's Household

2 As for you, Titus, promote the kind of
living that reflects wholesome teaching.
2Teach the older men to exercise self-control, to be worthy of respect, and to live
wisely. They must have sound faith and be
filled with love and patience.
3Similarly, teach the older women to
live in a way that honors God. They must
not [e]slander others or be heavy drinkers.
Instead, they should teach others what is
good. 4These older women must train the
younger women to love their husbands and
their children, 5to live wisely and be pure,
to work in their homes, to do good, and to
be submissive to their husbands. Then they
will not bring shame on the word of God.

1:10 1 Tim 1:6
1:13 1 Tim 5:20
1:14 Col 2:22; 1 Tim 1:4; 4:7
1:15 Matt 15:10-11; Rom 14:14-20
1:16 1 Jn 1:6; 2:4
2:1 1 Tim 1:10; Titus 1:9
2:3 1 Tim 3:8, 11; [e]*diabolos* (1228) ‣Jas 4:7
2:5 Eph 5:22; 1 Tim 5:14
2:7 1 Tim 4:12; [t]*tupos* (5179) ‣Heb 8:5
2:8 1 Pet 2:12
2:9 Eph 6:5

immediate threat to these particular communities (as also in Ephesus; see 1 Tim 3:1). • Only with ***a strong belief*** in the Good News would an elder ***be able to*** provide ***wholesome teaching.*** Paul's specific concerns are addressed in 2:1–3:11, in light of the problems mentioned in 1:10-16 and 3:9-11 (see also 1 Tim 1:10). • Titus had a similar role (cp. 1:13; 2:15; 3:10-11). The local leadership would carry on where Paul and his delegates left off. • ***Those who oppose it*** are described in 1:10-16.

1:10-16 In a native population of troublemakers, Titus would need to exercise a firm hand to rid these Christian communities of corruption and make them healthy in the faith (1:13-16).

1:10 ***rebellious people:*** The same Greek word is used of children in 1:6. • ***those who insist on circumcision for salvation*** (literally *those of the circumcision*): This probably refers to Jewish Christians; the Greek phrase leaves open whether or not they required circumcision of Gentiles. The Jewish flavor of this false teaching is suggested in 1:14-15 and 3:9.

1:11 ***turning whole families away:*** This also happened in Ephesus (cp. 1 Tim 4:3; 2 Tim 2:18; 3:6). • ***only for money:*** Elders must not have this characteristic (1:7; see also 1 Tim 6:5-10; 2 Cor 2:17; 1 Pet 5:2).

1:12 ***one of their own men, a prophet from Crete has said:*** This quotation is from Epimenides of Knossos, a philosopher who lived on Crete around the 500s BC. • ***all liars:*** This charge was directed specifically at the Cretan claim to have Zeus's tomb on the island. According to Cretan mythology, the god Zeus was once a mere human who lived and died on Crete (his tomb was said to be there) but who had achieved godhood through his patronage (i.e., gifts and benefits) to humans. Some Greek moralists opposed this legend and characterized it as a lie. A quote from Alexandria in the 200s BC reads: "Cretans are always liars. For a tomb, O Lord, Cretans build for you; but you do not die, for you are forever." One of Crete's own prophets (Epimenides) had the same assessment, and Paul cites his voice of conscience approvingly (1:13; see Acts 17:28), for the God who does not lie (1:2) stands in opposition to the lies of such myths. • ***liars . . . animals . . . gluttons:*** It was believed that Cretan immorality resulted from their belief about Zeus; religious lies had given rise to moral corruption. Paul later counters these vices by presenting the contrasting virtues (2:12). He calls the Cretans to reach ethical ideals that are extolled in human society generally but were absent on Crete, as bemoaned by their own prophet. They would reach these ideals only through the gospel of Jesus Christ (2:11-14). • ***lazy gluttons:*** Cretans were known to do anything for a little cash. They were famous as mercenaries and as insatiate consumers. They reputedly saw no shame in greed (see Phil 3:19). • Paul applies the quotation more directly to the current false teachers than to Cretan culture generally; the false teachers carried on this Cretan tradition of immorality built on falsehood.

1:13 ***This is true:*** See note on 1:12. • Being ***strong in the faith*** is here defined as rejecting false teachings (cp. 1:9).

1:14 ***Jewish myths:*** See 3:9; 1 Tim 1:4; 4:7; 2 Tim 4:4. • ***have turned away from the truth:*** This was apostasy, not mere unbelief. See 1 Tim 1:6-7.

1:15-16 These two verses comment on the people of 1:14 and their commands, while transitioning to a discussion of wholesome teaching (2:1–3:11).

1:15 Cp. 1 Tim 4:3-5.

1:16 Sound teaching and godliness are always linked together in the letters to Timothy and Titus (see 1 Tim 1:7-11; 3:15-16; 5:24-25; 2 Tim 3:5, 9). Similarly, the ungodly *way they live* is connected with false teaching. • ***anything good:*** This contrasts with 3:1.

2:1-15 ***Wholesome teaching*** was especially urgent on account of the false teachers, who had wreaked havoc on "whole families" (1:11). In 2:1-10, Paul addresses different groups within the household of faith, showing his concern for the public testimony of the church (2:5, 8, 10; see also 1 Tim 5:1–6:2). Paul then elaborates on the coming of Christ (2:11-14) before giving a direct charge to Titus (2:15).

2:3 ***be heavy drinkers:*** Literally *be enslaved to much wine.*

2:4-5 Cp. 1 Tim 5:9-10.

2:5 ***to work in their homes:*** Some manuscripts read *to care for their homes.*

2:11
2 Tim 1:9-10
[g]*charis* (5485)
‣1 Pet 3:7

2:12
[h]*paideuō* (3811)
‣Heb 12:6
[i]*dikaiōs* (1346)
‣1 Pet 2:23

2:13
Phil 3:20
[j]*elpis* (1680)
‣Heb 7:19
[k]*makarios* (3107)
‣Jas 1:12

6 In the same way, encourage the young
men to live wisely. 7 And you yourself must
be an [f]example to them by doing good works
of every kind. Let everything you do reflect
the integrity and seriousness of your teaching.
8 Teach the truth so that your teaching
can't be criticized. Then those who oppose
us will be ashamed and have nothing bad to
say about us.

9 Slaves must always obey their masters
and do their best to please them. They must
not talk back 10 or steal, but must show themselves to be entirely trustworthy and good.
Then they will make the teaching about
God our Savior attractive in every way.

Rationale: The Instruction of God's Grace

11 For the [g]grace of God has been revealed,
bringing salvation to all people. 12 And we
are [h]instructed to turn from godless living
and sinful pleasures. We should live in this
evil world with wisdom, [i]righteousness, and
devotion to God, 13 while we look forward
with [j]hope to that [k]wonderful day when
the glory of our great God and Savior, Jesus

TITUS (1:4; 2:1)

2 Cor 2:13; 7:6, 13-14; 8:6, 16-17, 23; 12:18
Gal 2:1, 3
2 Tim 4:10

Titus was a Gentile convert who served as one of Paul's trusted assistants. One of Paul's last letters was addressed to him, when Titus was helping to consolidate the church in Crete. Titus is an example of the Gentile converts who were so deeply touched by the Good News of Christ that they left their homes and devoted their lives to assisting Paul in the proclamation of the Good News.

We know nothing about Titus's background or conversion; his name is not mentioned in Acts. We first hear of him as a Gentile believer who accompanied Paul and Barnabas to Jerusalem (Gal 2:1). Significantly, Paul emphasized that Titus was not compelled to be circumcised (Gal 2:3).

Later, as a trusted member of Paul's team, Titus was sent on special assignments. He was the one sent by Paul to Corinth to deal with a difficult situation there (apparently carrying the demanding letter mentioned in 2 Cor 2:4, 9; 7:8-9). This task required both tact and strong leadership (Titus's personality seems to have been stronger than Timothy's; see 1 Cor 16:10-11; 2 Cor 7:15). When Titus returned to Paul with good news (2 Cor 7:6-7, 13-15), Paul sent him back to Corinth carrying the letter we call 2 Corinthians to encourage the believers to complete their money-raising project for the poor believers in Jerusalem. It was an assignment he eagerly accepted because of his love for the Christians in Corinth (2 Cor 7:15; 8:6, 16-17). Paul speaks of him as a person of integrity, like Paul himself (2 Cor 8:23; 12:18).

A few years later, following Paul's first trial in Rome and subsequent release, Paul left Titus on the island of Crete to help consolidate the church. While Titus was there, Paul wrote his letter to Titus, giving him advice on choosing church leaders and encouraging him to teach and model godly behavior. Paul then asked Titus to meet him at Nicopolis (in Achaia), where Paul hoped to spend the winter (3:12). Later, shortly before he was killed in Rome, Paul wrote that Titus had gone to Dalmatia (along the Adriatic coast, northwest of modern-day Greece), probably for ministry there (2 Tim 4:10).

The church historian Eusebius refers to the early tradition that Titus eventually settled in Crete, serving as the bishop there until he was quite old (Eusebius, *Church History* 3.4.6).

2:9-10 The purpose of these commands is to ***make the teaching about God . . . attractive*** (see 1 Tim 6:1-2).

2:11-15 ***For:*** The commands of 2:1-10 are here grounded in the past and future coming of Christ. God's grace is a model for the church's own conduct, even as salvation by grace makes a good life possible and creates people devoted to good works (see also 3:3-7).

2:11 ***has been revealed*** (literally *has appeared*): See note on 1 Tim 6:14. • ***salvation to all people:*** Paul intends that God's grace will fully accomplish its ends among the Cretans and that, in doing so, it will enlist them into God's saving work of evangelism (2:12; see 1 Tim 2:1-7; 4:10).

2:12 ***we are instructed:*** The emphasis of this instruction falls on the positive virtues: ***wisdom, righteousness, and devotion to God.*** In Greco-Roman writings, these three virtues represent virtuous conduct in general. These virtues counter the Cretan vices listed in 1:12 and are transformed into thoroughly Christian qualities (see 2:13). • Paul exhorts the Cretans to bring these virtues to life, in order to make plain to their compatriots that a virtuous life derives only from the appearance of God's grace in Jesus Christ.

2:13 ***we look forward:*** This implies ***hope*** as well as future accountability, both of which stimulate godly conduct in the present. • ***will be revealed:*** This phrase translates a prominent Greek word in the letters to Timothy and Titus ("epiphany" or "appearing"; also 2:11; see note on 1 Tim 6:14). • ***great God and Savior:*** This is one of the few places in the NT where Jesus Christ is called "God" outright (see also John 1:1; 20:28; Rom 9:5; Heb 1:8; 2 Pet 1:1; possibly John 1:18). Yet this claim is entirely consistent with the roles and attributes of Christ and the worship that he receives. Possibly this designation is used here to insist that Christ is not a mere human promoted to membership in the pantheon of gods (see note on 1:12). At the time of this

Christ, will be [a]revealed. 14He gave his life to [b]free us from every kind of sin, to cleanse us, and to make us his very own people, totally committed to doing good deeds.

Charge: Teach and Encourage

15You must teach these things and [c]encourage the believers to do them. You have the authority to correct them when necessary, so don't let anyone disregard what you say.

4. RELATIONSHIP WITH SOCIETY (3:1-11)

Command: Promote Right Conduct in Society

3 Remind the believers to submit to the government and its officers. They should be obedient, always ready to do what is good. 2They must not slander anyone and must avoid quarreling. Instead, they should be gentle and show true humility to everyone.

Rationale: The Example of God's Mercy

3Once we, too, were foolish and disobedient. We were misled and became slaves to many lusts and pleasures. Our lives were full of evil and envy, and we hated each other.

4But—"When God our Savior revealed his kindness and love, 5he [d]saved us, not because of the righteous things we had done, but because of his [e]mercy. He washed away our sins, giving us a new birth and new life through the Holy Spirit. 6He generously poured out the Spirit upon us through Jesus Christ our [f]Savior. 7Because of his grace he declared us righteous and gave us confidence that we will inherit eternal life."

Charge: Insist on Wholesome Teaching, Reject Quarrels

8This is a trustworthy saying, and I want you to insist on these teachings so that all who trust in God will devote themselves to doing good. These teachings are good and beneficial for everyone.

9Do not get involved in foolish discussions about spiritual pedigrees or in quarrels and fights about obedience to Jewish laws. These things are [g]useless and a waste of time. 10If people are causing divisions among you, give a first and second warning. After that, have nothing more to do with them. 11For people like that have turned away from the truth, and their own sins condemn them.

5. PAUL'S CLOSING (3:12-15)

Final Instructions

12I am planning to send either Artemas or

[a]*epiphaneia* (2015) ▸2 Thes 2:8

2:14 Exod 19:5; Deut 7:6; Eph 2:10; 1 Pet 2:9; [b]*lutroō* (3084) ▸1 Pet 1:18

2:15 1 Tim 4:12; [c]*parakaleō* (3870) ▸Heb 3:13

3:1 Rom 13:1; 1 Pet 2:13-14

3:3 1 Cor 6:11; Eph 5:8

3:5 John 3:5; Eph 2:4, 8; 1 Pet 1:3; [d]*sōzō* (4982) ▸1 Pet 2:2; [e]*eleos* (1656) ▸Jas 2:13

3:6 Joel 2:28; Rom 5:5; [f]*sōtēr* (4990) ▸2 Pet 1:1

3:7 Rom 3:24

3:9 2 Tim 2:14, 16, 23; [g]*mataios* (3152) ▸Jas 1:26

3:10 Matt 18:15-17; Rom 16:17

---

letter, Christians were insisting more and more that Christ alone, rather than rulers and emperors, should be called divine.

2:14 Salvation produces a people who have the desire and capacity for the good deeds outlined in 2:2-10. • ***He gave his life:*** See also 1 Tim 2:6. • ***to free us:*** See Gal 3:22; 4:4-5; cp. Exod 6:6-8. • The phrase ***his very own people*** recalls the formation of Israel as a nation (see Exod 19:5; Deut 7:6; 14:2). Those who follow Christ are now God's people—his nation—and the Spirit leads them to keep God's covenant. • ***totally committed to doing good deeds:*** See 1:16; Eph 2:10.

3:1-11 The emphasis on wholesome teaching (1:9; 2:1) continues; Paul turns now to the relationship of the Christian community with society at large (cp. 1 Tim 2:2-4). As in 2:1-15, God's instructions for his people (3:1-2) are based on his dealings with them (3:3-7; cp. note on 2:11-15). Paul then instructs Titus to avoid fruitless disputes and to insist on beneficial teaching (3:8-11).

3:1 Paul might be telling ***the believers*** to make a clear distinction between themselves and the unruly common masses. Alternatively, the troublemakers (1:10-15; 3:10) might have adopted unruly behaviors that stemmed from their erroneous teachings (as is likely the case in 1 Tim 2:1-7). • On relations to ***government . . . officers,*** see 1 Tim 2:2; Rom 13:1-7.

3:3 Humility (3:2) is fitting, considering our state when God's kindness and love came to us (3:4; see Eph 2:1-4; 5:8; Col 3:7; 1 Pet 4:3).

3:4-7 This passage might be a summary or quote from traditional teaching (see 1 Tim 1:15; 2:5-6).

3:4 We should behave toward our compatriots as God acted toward us—in ***kindness and love.*** God's salvation makes this possible. • ***revealed*** (literally *appeared*): The Greek word relates to the coming of Christ (also in 2:11, 13; see note on 1 Tim 6:14).

3:5 ***not because . . . but because:*** The contrast is between human actions that might be thought to merit salvation and God's grace (see Gal 2:16). Salvation is through faith in God's ***mercy*** alone (Eph 2:8). • ***He washed away our sins, giving us a new birth*** (literally *He saved us through the washing of regeneration*): See Ezek 16:9; John 3:1-15; Eph 5:26; Heb 10:22; 2 Pet 1:9. • ***and new life through the Holy Spirit*** (literally *and renewing of the Holy Spirit*): This signifies a complete departure from the life of sin and death and a transfer into the realm of life and purity (see also Rom 12:2; 2 Cor 5:17; Col 3:10).

3:6 ***Christ our Savior:*** Cp. 3:4; see note on 1:3.

3:7 The first half of this verse sums up 3:4-6. The second half supplies the purpose for what God did. • ***declared us righteous:*** See Rom 3:20-28; Gal 2:16-17. • ***inherit eternal life:*** The Spirit (3:5) is often linked with our status as heirs (see Rom 8:15-17; 1 Cor 6:9-11; Gal 4:6-7; Eph 1:13-14).

3:8 The ***trustworthy saying*** is 3:4-7 (cp. 1 Tim 1:15).

3:9-11 See 1:10-16; cp. 1 Tim 1:4, 7.

3:9 ***spiritual pedigrees:*** Or *spiritual genealogies.*

3:10-11 ***have nothing more to do with . . . people like that:*** This refers to incorrigibly quarrelsome and divisive people (see 1:11, 13).

3:12-15 The letter closes with news (3:12), a final exhortation (3:13-14), greetings, and a blessing (3:15).

3:12 Evidently ***Artemas or Tychicus*** would be Titus's replacement on Crete. Since Tychicus was in fact sent to Ephesus (see 2 Tim 4:12), Artemas might have been the one who went to Crete. • ***Nicopolis:*** Several cities had this name; this was most likely a major city on the western coast of the Greek peninsula. Paul had possibly worked here before (see Rom 15:19, which mentions Paul's activity even further west).

3:12
Acts 20:4
2 Tim 4:9, 21
3:13
Acts 18:24
3:14
Eph 4:28
Titus 2:14; 3:8
3:15
Col 4:18

Tychicus to you. As soon as one of them arrives, do your best to meet me at Nicopolis,
for I have decided to stay there for the winter. 13Do everything you can to help Zenas
the lawyer and Apollos with their trip. See
that they are given everything they need.
14Our people must learn to do good by meeting the urgent needs of others; then they
will not be unproductive.

Greetings and Blessing

15Everybody here sends greetings. Please
give my greetings to the believers—all who
love us.

May God's grace be with you all.

3:13 ***Zenas*** and ***Apollos*** were involved in spreading the Good News, and they might have been the couriers of this letter to Titus. • ***Zenas*** was probably an expert in Roman law or a Roman jurist (the same word for ***lawyer*** is in Luke 7:30; 10:25); his pagan name ("gift of Zeus") makes it unlikely that he was an expert in Jewish law. • ***Apollos*** is presumably the same man as in Acts 18:24; 19:1; 1 Cor 1:12; 3:4-6, 22; 4:6; 16:12 (see "Apollos" at Acts 18:24–19:1, p. 1867). • ***everything they need:*** See 1 Tim 3:2; 3 Jn 1:5-8; cp. Rom 15:24; 1 Cor 16:6, 11; 2 Cor 1:16.

3:14 This final exhortation is connected to the responsibility to take care of Zenas and Apollos (see Rom 12:13; Eph 4:28; 1 Thes 4:11; 1 Tim 5:8, 16; 6:18). • ***Our people must*** involve themselves in the life-giving ministry of the Good News rather than in the ***unproductive*** speculations of the false teachers.

3:15 ***you all:*** The letter was addressed to Titus (1:4), but the whole church was the audience for the letter (see Titus Introduction, "Literary Genre," p. 2069).

PAUL'S LETTER TO PHILEMON

This little letter, the shortest and most personal of Paul's letters, shows how attitudes and relationships are transformed by Christ. It was written on behalf of Onesimus, a runaway slave, as he returned to Philemon, his master. Paul encouraged Philemon to go beyond the traditional master–slave relationship by welcoming Onesimus back as a beloved brother in Christ. With these reconciling words, Paul reminds us that all relationships among Christians, regardless of a person's social standing, are transformed by the love of Christ.

SETTING

A slave named Onesimus seems to have run away from his Christian master, Philemon. His master resided in Colosse, a small town in the Roman province of Asia (now western Turkey) about 100 miles (160 kilometers) east of Ephesus. When Onesimus ran away, he might have stolen some of his master's things. Somehow Onesimus came into contact with Paul, who was in prison, and became a believer through Paul's ministry. When Paul became aware that Onesimus was a runaway slave, he encouraged him to return to his master.

Slavery was widespread in the Roman world and, by law, captured runaways had to be returned to their owners. They often faced severe punishment, such as whipping, branding, or execution, as an example to other slaves. However, Philemon was a well-respected Christian leader and a gracious, loving person. Paul wrote this letter to Philemon from prison and sent it with Onesimus to ensure a warm Christian welcome for the runaway on what might have been a rather fearful return to his master. The letter resembles a letter of recommendation and carries the full weight of Paul's apostolic authority.

We do not know what happened when Onesimus returned. Some fifty or sixty years later, however, in a letter written to the Christians at Ephesus by the Christian martyr Ignatius, the name

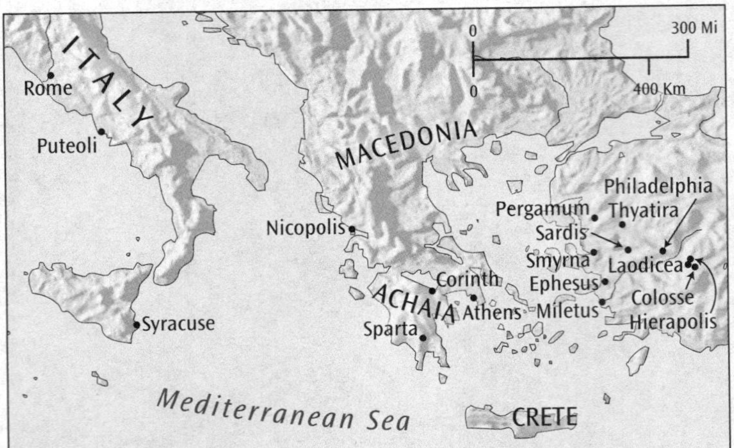

The Setting of Philemon. Onesimus, a slave, had run away from his master, Philemon, a believer in COLOSSE. Paul, who was in prison, was now sending Onesimus back to Philemon with this personal note. Onesimus traveled with Tychicus, who carried Paul's letter to the Colossians (see Col 4:7-9).

Onesimus appears again, this time as the name of the highly-regarded bishop of the province of Asia. We cannot be sure it was the same person, but it is quite possible that, because of his close association with Paul, the young slave rose to prominence in the church and eventually became bishop of the entire province. It is a reminder that traditional class distinctions are of no significance in the church of Jesus Christ.

TIMELINE

AD 53~56
Paul's ministry in Ephesus

AD 57–59
Paul is imprisoned in Caesarea

AD 59–60
Paul's voyage to Rome

AD 60–62
Paul is imprisoned in Rome

about AD 64~65?
Paul is imprisoned and martyred in Rome

SUMMARY

Paul encourages Philemon to treat Onesimus no longer simply as a slave but as a genuine brother in Christ. Using his traditional opening (vv 1-3), Paul introduces himself, greets Philemon, his family, and the church that meets in their home, and invokes grace and peace upon them. Paul then thanks God for the good things he has heard about Philemon, especially his trust in the Lord Jesus and the love he has shown to so many of God's people (vv 4-7).

Paul then makes his appeal for Onesimus (vv 8-22). Though formerly a runaway, Onesimus has now become a believer in Christ and has proven himself to be a changed person. Paul asks Philemon to be gracious and forgiving in welcoming his slave back. Paul's real desire is for Onesimus to stay with him, to assist him in his ministry from prison. Although he has the apostolic authority to demand that Philemon release him for that purpose, he refuses to use that authority, desiring that such an expression of mercy come from Philemon himself and not be forced. But Paul clearly hints that Philemon should consider freeing his slave for the work of the Good News.

The letter ends in a customary way (vv 23-25). Paul sends greetings to Philemon from various Christians, then invokes the grace of Christ upon him and all those in his home.

OUTLINE

vv 1-3
Introduction and Greetings from Paul

vv 4-7
Paul's Thanksgiving and Prayer

vv 8-22
Paul's Appeal for Onesimus

vv 23-25
Paul's Final Greetings

The Christian liberty of which Paul was the outspoken champion certainly had its social consequences, but it existed only "in Christ." Such liberty was not to be attained by any superficial changes in the structure of Graeco-Roman social and economic life.

G. B. CAIRD
Paul's Letters from Prison, p. 216

OCCASION OF WRITING

Though the traditional interpretation is that Onesimus was a runaway slave, other possibilities have been posed. For example, Onesimus might have been sent as a messenger to Paul or he might have turned to Paul to mediate a problem that had arisen between him and his master. In reality, we do not know why he left his master's home, but the traditional interpretation fits the letter well.

DATE AND PLACE OF WRITING

It is traditionally believed that Paul wrote the prison letters (Ephesians, Philippians, Colossians, and Philemon) when he was in prison in Rome (AD 60–62 or about AD 64~65). It is also quite possible that these letters were written from Ephesus during an earlier imprisonment. See Ephesians Introduction, "Date and Place of Writing," p. 1996.

This epistle gives us a masterful and tender illustration of Christian love.

MARTIN LUTHER
Preface to the Epistle of Saint Paul to Philemon

MEANING AND MESSAGE

This letter is a vivid illustration of the way that attitudes and relationships are transformed in Christ. Those who know Christ are to see people through the eyes of love and to express that love in their relationships with others.

Paul's appeal to Philemon reminds us that, as Christians, we must always be willing to forgive one another. No matter how much we have been wronged by others, we must be quick to give them a warm-hearted welcome and show them our acceptance and love.

In the church of Christ, traditional social distinctions, such as the relationship between slave and master, must be transcended. We must show genuine love to all Christians, regardless of their economic or cultural status, education, ethnicity, or gender (cp. Gal 3:28; Col 3:11). Paul's desire to reconcile Philemon and Onesimus is an example of such love.

Many people have wondered why Paul did not explicitly call for Onesimus's freedom or for the abolition of slavery as an institution. In the Roman world, slavery was widespread; it was an integral part of society, and the whole of society was built on it. Paul, like most early Christians, seems to have accepted the traditional structures of society, including slavery. The mission of the early Christians was not to overthrow the structures of society but to see people converted and built up in Christ. Proclaiming the Good News of salvation would result in lives and relationships being transformed by Christ within the fellowship of the church.

Though Paul did not call explicitly for Onesimus's release, he clearly hinted that he would like to see him freed for the work of the Good News. In his consistent emphasis on the importance of Christians living together in forgiveness and mutual love, he was planting the seeds that would one day result in the overthrow of slavery as an institution.

FURTHER READING

PETER DAVIDS
Philemon in *Cornerstone Biblical Commentary*, vol. 16 (2008)

DAVID E. GARLAND
Colossians/Philemon (1998)

PETER T. O'BRIEN
Colossians, Philemon (1982)

MARIANNE MEYE THOMPSON
Colossians and Philemon (2005)

N. T. WRIGHT
Colossians & Philemon (2007)

Introduction and Greetings from Paul (vv 1-3)

This letter is from Paul, a prisoner for preaching the Good News about Christ Jesus, and
from our brother Timothy.
I am writing to Philemon, our beloved co-
worker, [2]and to our sister Apphia, and to our
fellow soldier Archippus, and to the church
that meets in your house.
[3]May God our Father and the Lord Jesus
Christ give you grace and peace.

Paul's Thanksgiving and Prayer (vv 4-7)

[4]I always thank my God when I pray for
you, Philemon, [5]because I keep hearing
about your faith in the Lord Jesus and your
[a]love for all of God's people. [6]And I am
praying that you will put into action the

1:1
Eph 4:1
Phil 1:7
Phlm 1:9, 23

1:2
Rom 16:5
Phil 2:25
Col 4:17

1:4
Rom 1:8-9

1:5
[a]*agapē* (0026)
› 1 Pet 4:8

vv 1-3 ***Paul*** usually begins with a short introduction followed by greetings and the invocation of ***grace and peace.***

v 1 ***Paul, a prisoner:*** It is traditionally thought that Paul was writing from prison in Rome, but it is also possible that he was writing earlier from Ephesus, much closer to Philemon's home in Colosse (see Philemon Introduction, "Date and Place of Writing," p. 2077). • ***Timothy*** was one of Paul's closest co-workers (see "Timothy" at Acts 16:1-3, p. 1860). • ***co-worker:*** Philemon was active in ministry for Christ.

v 2 This is not a private letter to Philemon alone but is addressed also to his family and church. • ***Apphia*** was probably Philemon's wife. • ***soldier:*** The servant of Christ is involved in a war and must be prepared to stand firm in the face of opposition (Eph 6:10-17). • ***Archippus*** was probably Philemon's son (also mentioned in Col 4:17). • ***the church that meets in your house:*** The early Christians met together in private homes (see also Rom 16:5; 1 Cor 16:19; Col 4:15). • Throughout this letter, *you* and *your* are singular except in vv 3, 22, 25.

v 3 ***You*** is plural, referring to all those mentioned in v 2. • ***Grace and peace*** represent traditional Greek and Hebrew greetings, respectively; they are now understood as gifts from God (cp. Rom 5:1-2).

vv 4-7 In his letters, Paul usually thanks God for the faith and love of his readers and mentions his prayers for them (Rom 1:8-12; 1 Cor 1:4-9; 2 Cor 1:3-11; contrast Gal 1:6-10). Ancient Greek letters occasionally included a section of thanksgiving following the greeting.

v 5 It is by ***faith*** in Christ that we are saved, and it is by ***love*** for fellow Christians that we live out our salvation.

v 6 This verse can be translated in different ways. Paul is hinting that Philemon should be gracious toward Onesimus in light of God's goodness to Philemon (cp. vv 10, 17-19).

1:6
Phil 1:9
[b]koinōnia (2842)
›Heb 13:16
1:7
2 Cor 7:4, 13
1:9
Eph 3:1; 4:1
Phil 1:7
1:10
1 Cor 4
Col 4
1:
..or 16:21
1:22
Phil 1:25-26; 2:24
1:23
Col 1:7; 4:10
1:24
Acts 12:12; 19:29; 27:2
Col 4:10, 14
2 Tim 4:10
1:25
Gal 6:18
2 Tim 4:22

...rosity that comes from your faith as
[b]...nderstand and experience all the good
...gs we have in Christ. 7Your love has
...en me much joy and comfort, my brother,
...r your kindness has often refreshed the
...earts of God's people.

Paul's Appeal for Onesimus (vv 8-22)

8That is why I am boldly asking a favor of
you. I could demand it in the name of Christ
because it is the right thing for you to do.
9But because of our love, I prefer simply
to ask you. Consider this as a request from
me—Paul, an old man and now also a prisoner for the sake of Christ Jesus.
10I appeal to you to show kindness to my
child, Onesimus. I became his father in
the faith while here in prison. 11Onesimus
hasn't been of much use to you in the past,
but now he is very useful to both of us. 12I
am sending him back to you, and with him
comes my own heart.
13I wanted to keep him here with me
while I am in these chains for preaching
the Good News, and he would have helped
me on your behalf. 14But I didn't want to do
anything without your consent. I wanted
you to help because you were willing, not because you were forced. 15It seems you lost
Onesimus for a little while so that you could
have him back forever. 16He is no longer
like a [c]slave to you. He is more than a [c]slave,
for he is a beloved brother, especially to me.
Now he will mean much more to you, both
as a man and as a brother in the Lord.
17So if you consider me your partner, welcome him as you would welcome me. 18If
he has wronged you in any way or owes you
anything, charge it to me. 19I, PAUL, WRITE
THIS WITH MY OWN HAND: I WILL REPAY IT.
AND I WON'T MENTION THAT YOU OWE ME
YOUR VERY SOUL!
20Yes, my brother, please do me this favor
for the Lord's sake. Give me this encouragement in Christ.
21I am confident as I write this letter that
you will do what I ask and even more! 22One
more thing—please prepare a guest room
for me, for I am hoping that God will answer
your prayers and let me return to you soon.

Paul's Final Greetings (vv 23-25)

23Epaphras, my fellow prisoner in Christ
Jesus, sends you his greetings. 24So do
Mark, Aristarchus, Demas, and Luke, my co-
workers.
25May the grace of the Lord Jesus Christ
be with your spirit.

---

vv 8-9 The reason ***why*** Paul was ***asking a favor*** was Philemon's reputation as a gracious, loving person (vv 5-7). Paul ***could demand it*** by his authority as Christ's apostle, but ***love*** leads Paul to request rather than demand. • ***Paul, an old man:*** Paul appeals to the respect due to older people as well as to his status as ***a prisoner for the sake of Christ Jesus*** (or *a prisoner of Christ Jesus*), which would only increase a fellow Christian's respect.

v 10 ***show kindness:*** In the Roman world, runaway slaves could be treated harshly with whipping, branding, or even execution, at the owner's discretion. • ***Onesimus*** was Paul's spiritual ***child*** because he became a believer through Paul's ministry.

v 11 ***Onesimus*** means "useful." • ***hasn't been of much use*** (literally *useless*) . . . ***very useful:*** This might be a play on words (cp. v 20). Onesimus was ***now*** serving others and proclaiming the Good News. At last he had become what his name means.

vv 13-14 Paul hints at his desire that Philemon choose to free Onesimus to serve as Paul's helper (also v 21). The Christian life is a free response to God's grace (Rom 12:1; Eph 4:1; Col 3:12-13).

v 15 ***you lost Onesimus*** (literally *he went away*): This might be a euphemism for running away, in order not to mention Onesimus's offense directly. • ***so that you could have him back forever:*** It is implied that God providentially arranged events to lead to Onesimus's salvation.

v 16 Though Onesimus was still legally Philemon's ***slave,*** Philemon must think of him as ***a beloved brother*** and be committed to his well-being. • ***both as a man and as a brother in the Lord:*** Brotherhood in Christ must now transform their whole relationship in both the natural and spiritual realms.

v 18 Onesimus might have stolen some things from Philemon's home or had a debt to pay off when he ran away.

v 19 Paul guarantees his promise with his signature. He typically dictated his letters to a secretary; on occasion, as here, he wrote something in his OWN HAND. • ***YOUR VERY SOUL:*** That is, his salvation. Philemon owed Paul much more than anything Onesimus might have owed him. Whether this means Philemon was converted directly or indirectly through Paul's preaching is not clear (cp. Col 1:7).

v 20 ***do me this favor:*** Or *let me have this benefit;* Greek *onaimēn* ("favor, benefit") might be a play on the name Onesimus, which can mean "beneficial" (cp. v 11).

v 21 ***and even more:*** Paul might be hinting that he would like to see Onesimus released (cp. vv 13-14), or he might simply be expressing confidence in Philemon's kindness.

v 22 Paul's request for ***a guest room*** in anticipation of his visit reinforces his request that Philemon treat Onesimus kindly. At his coming, he would see how Onesimus had been treated.

vv 23-25 Paul usually closes his letters with greetings from others and a benediction. Cp. Col 4:7-18; Paul's letters to the Colossians and to Philemon were probably carried to Colosse at the same time by Tychicus and Onesimus.

v 23 ***Epaphras*** was a native of Colosse who first brought the Good News to Philemon and his family (Col 1:7; 4:12).

v 24 These men are also mentioned at the end of Colossians (Col 4:10, 14). • ***co-workers:*** They helped Paul spread the Good News. • ***Mark:*** See "John Mark" at Acts 13:4-5, 13, p. 1852. • ***Aristarchus*** was a faithful associate of Paul for many years (Acts 19:29; 20:4; 27:2). • ***Demas*** was a co-worker who later abandoned Paul (2 Tim 4:10). • ***Luke:*** See "Luke" at Acts 16:10, p. 1861.

v 25 ***grace:*** See note on v 3.

THE LETTER TO THE HEBREWS

Have you ever known a person who turned his or hei back on Christ and the church and simply walked away Perhaps you have struggled to maintain your own Christ commitment in the face of disillusionment, spiritual confusion, or loss of perspective. The book of Hebrews renews our perspective by pointing us to Christ. It provides light to help struggling Christians see Jesus clearly.

SETTING

As Christianity spread throughout the Mediterranean world, the first followers of Jesus Christ faced grave challenges. The pagan society misunderstood and mistrusted both Christians and Jews and considered them "atheists" because they did not believe in the Greek or Roman gods. Opposition to Christianity also arose from within traditional Judaism. Many Jews rejected Jesus as the Messiah and held interpretations of the OT Scriptures that conflicted with those embraced by the Christian movement. Those who converted to faith in Christ from various backgrounds often paid a high price in their jobs, family connections, friendships, and other social associations. Persecution of Christians was common.

The believers to whom Hebrews was addressed probably belonged to a group of house churches in Rome in the early 60s AD. The Christian community in Rome was founded in the AD 30s when those present at Pentecost (Acts 2:10) made their way home. Rome had over a million people, including a large population of Jews (40,000–60,000). Roman believers had demonstrated courage and endurance (10:32-34), but by the time Hebrews was written, the spiritual fervor of some had grown cold (5:11-14), and their theological perspective was skewed (2:1). Some had even abandoned Christ and the church (6:4-8).

SUMMARY

Hebrews was written as an energetic and highly crafted pastoral response to the needs of struggling people. In the style of a first-century sermon, the author alternates between *exposition* on the person and work of Christ and *exhortation* of the hearers to respond with obedience and endurance. By a detailed exposition on God's Son, and with warnings, challenges, examples, and reminders of God's faithfulness, the author calls his readers to endure in following Christ.

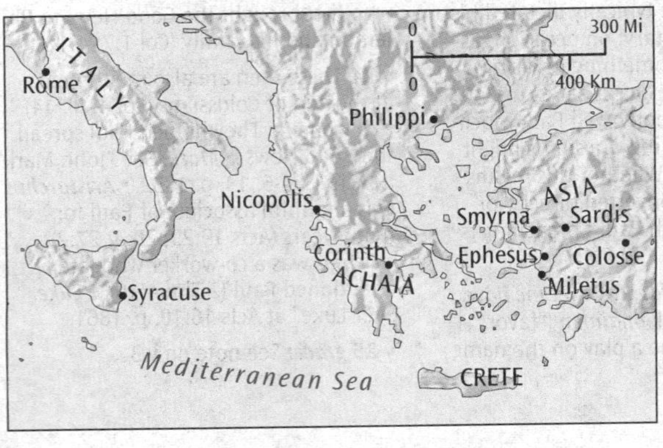

The Setting of Hebrews. The letter to the Hebrews was probably written to Christians in Rome (see "Recipients," p. 2082). Many of the recipients were Jewish Christians who were being tempted to return to Judaism. It is uncertain who wrote the letter or where its author was located at the time.

Following an introduction to the whole sermon (1:1-4), the author's exposition of Christ's superiority develops in two great movements. The first movement (1:5–2:18) explains the Son's relationship to the angels. The angels are servants (1:6-7, 14), but the exalted Son (1:13), with his unique relationship with the Father (1:5), is the Lord, creator, and sustainer of the universe—indeed, he is God (1:8-12). The author exhorts the hearers to pay careful attention to the message of salvation they have been taught (2:1-4), then resumes his exposition. The exalted Christ's position was temporarily lower than the angels when he became human (2:5-9); Jesus took on flesh and blood in order to die to set us free (2:10-18).

The first movement is followed by an exhortation (3:1–4:13) focusing primarily on the need for faithful obedience and a continued promise of rest for God's people.

The second movement of the exposition (4:14–10:18) addresses the position of the Son, our High Priest, in relation to the OT sacrificial system, with 4:14-16 as the introduction. The author addresses the Son's appointment as the superior High Priest (5:1-10) and confronts the community with their spiritual immaturity (5:11–6:20). A discussion of Melchizedek's superiority to the Levitical priests (7:1-10) lays the groundwork for presenting Jesus as the superior High Priest according to the order of Melchizedek (7:11-28). In short, Jesus was not appointed according to the conventions of the OT law, which said that priests should come from the tribe of Levi. Rather, he was appointed by God, with an oath, on the basis of his indestructible life. The book then considers the superior offering of this appointed High Priest (8:3–10:18). Like the earthly priests, this superior priest had to make an offering for sins, but his offering was a new covenant offering (8:7-13) that was superior to the old (9:1–10:18).

The final main section (10:19–13:25) is an exhortation challenging the hearers to respond in faithfulness to the message about Christ. The book ends with a benediction and a formal conclusion (13:20-25).

OUTLINE

1:1-4
Introduction: The Son Is God's Final Word

1:5–2:18
The Son and the Angels

3:1–4:13
Exhortations to Faithfulness

4:14–10:18
The Son and the Sacrificial System

10:19–13:19
Exhortations to Faithfulness

13:20-25
Benediction and Conclusion

AUTHORSHIP

Unlike many other letters of the NT, Hebrews does not begin by identifying its author and recipients; many scholars today believe that this is because the book was originally written as a sermon. Since the earliest centuries of the church, the question of Hebrews' authorship has been much discussed. The book circulated with Paul's letters, and some church fathers in the eastern half of the Mediterranean world (such as Origen and Clement of Alexandria) argued that Paul was the author. Others, especially around Rome, did not think Paul had written the book.

TIMELINE

early 60s AD
James, the brother of Jesus, is stoned to death in Jerusalem

AD 60–62
Paul is imprisoned in Rome

AD 62~64
Paul is released, travels freely

July AD 64
Fire destroys Rome

AD 64~65
Persecution of Christians under Nero
Peter is crucified in Rome

about AD 64~65?
Paul is imprisoned and martyred in Rome

AD 66–70
War between Romans and Jews at Jerusalem

AD 70
Jerusalem and the Temple are destroyed

Hebrews is a delight for the person who enjoys puzzles.
WILLIAM L. LANE
Hebrews 1–8, p. xlvii

Almost all scholars today agree that Paul was not the author of Hebrews. First, In 2:3, the author depicts himself as having received the Good News from the original witnesses who followed Christ, and this does not sound at all like Paul (see Rom 1:1; 1 Cor 15:8; Gal 1:11-16). Second, the style, theological images, and vocabulary are quite different from Paul's; for example, Hebrews uses 169 words not found elsewhere in the NT.

Through the centuries, many other possible authors for the book have been suggested, such as Philip, Priscilla, Luke, Barnabas, Jude, and Clement of Rome. One of the most popular ideas, since Martin Luther first made the suggestion, is that Apollos wrote it. Luke describes Apollos in Acts 18:24-26 as an eloquent man from Alexandria who was a powerful orator and preacher of the OT.

Although we cannot identify the author of Hebrews with certainty, a careful study of the book reveals much about him. First, the excellent Greek in which the book is written and its expertly crafted forms of expression point to a highly educated person. Second, the author of Hebrews must have been a dynamic preacher, one trained in interpretation and exposition, who had memorized large portions of the OT. Third, and most importantly, this author was a deeply concerned Christian leader who addressed his readers urgently and with passion. Hebrews is not simply a theological treatise, but a pastoral appeal that vies for the hearts and minds of those who are challenged in their Christian commitment.

RECIPIENTS

In 13:24, the author writes, "Greet all your leaders and all the believers there. The believers from Italy send you their greetings." The author seems to have been writing back to Italy, and probably to Rome, sending greetings from Italian Christians who had traveled abroad.

Those addressed in this letter seem to have had some background in Jewish worship. The author's use of the OT and his theological concepts would have been familiar to those of the synagogue in the Mediterranean world. This does not necessarily mean that all of the recipients were Jews, since many Gentiles were in the synagogue as "God-fearers" who worshiped the God of Israel.

*Hebrews remains something of a sleeping giant, a neglected **tour de force** within the New Testament canon. It is undeniably one of the most difficult New Testament books, and whether in spite of that or because of it, one of the most rewarding.*

J. RAMSEY MICHAELS
Hebrews in Cornerstone Biblical Commentary, vol. 16

OCCASION OF WRITING

Some in the Christian community were evidently struggling to maintain their commitment as they were being persecuted. Passages such as 10:32-39 suggest that this group of believers, which had faced persecution in the past, was facing it again. In the crucible of having to stand for Christ and the church in the face of public opposition, some were faltering spiritually and others had apparently turned their backs on the faith altogether. The author thus challenges this group of professed Christ-followers to endure in their public profession of Christ.

If we are correct that Rome is the destination for this book, this word of exhortation might have been precipitated by the persecution that occurred under the emperor Nero, whose intense persecution and martyrdom of Christians in the mid-60s AD is well-known. It is also possible that Hebrews was written after AD 70. At the time Hebrews was written, none in the community had faced martyrdom (12:4), but the pressure of persecution was on the rise.

MEANING AND MESSAGE

God has spoken about his Son and through his Son (1:1-3), and there are dire consequences for those who do not listen and respond with obedience to that word (2:1-3). In the end, Jesus, the creator and sustainer of the universe (1:2-3), will put away the created order like a person rolls up an article of old clothing (1:10-12).

Jesus is supremely worthy of our commitment, worship, and endurance in the faith, superior to the angels (1:5-14), to Moses (3:1-6), and to the Levitical priesthood of the old covenant (5:1-10; 7:1-28).

Jesus has made a new, heavenly covenant, offering himself once for all through his own death (8:3–10:18). Therefore, Jesus provides us with a superior basis for persevering in the Christian life. In his incarnation he endured as a faithful Son (3:1-6; 5:7-8; 12:1-2), and in his exaltation he reigns as the supreme Lord of the universe (1:2-4, 8-13); both give us hope for our future.

We can look to positive examples of others who have been faithful in their journey to God's eternal city (see 6:13-15; 10:32-39; 11:1-40), and to negative examples of those who fell through disobedience (see 3:7-19; 6:4-8). And we can embrace God's promises to us concerning our inheritance as his children (4:3-11; 6:13-20; 12:22-24).

Because of Jesus, we can live as faithful members of the Christian community in our relationships and in our worship (13:1-17). Our perseverance in the Christian faith will be directly proportional to the clarity with which we understand who Jesus is and what he has accomplished on our behalf.

FURTHER READING

F. F. BRUCE
The Epistle to the Hebrews (1990)

DAVID DESILVA
Perseverance in Gratitude (2000)

GEORGE H. GUTHRIE
Hebrews (1998)

WILLIAM L. LANE
Hebrews, 2 vols. (1991)

J. RAMSEY MICHAELS
Hebrews in *Cornerstone Biblical Commentary,* vol. 17 (2009)

1:2
Ps 2:8
Matt 21:33-38
John 1:3
1 Pet 1:20
1:3
Ps 110:1
John 14:9
Col 1:15
1:4
Eph 1:21
Phil 2:9-10
[a]*angelos* (0032)
› 1 Pet 3:22

1. INTRODUCTION: THE SON IS GOD'S FINAL WORD (1:1-4)

1 Long ago God spoke many times and
in many ways to our ancestors through
the prophets. 2 And now in these final days,
he has spoken to us through his Son. God
promised everything to the Son as an inheritance, and through the Son he created
the universe. 3 The Son radiates God's own
glory and expresses the very character
of God, and he sustains everything by the
mighty power of his command. When he
had cleansed us from our sins, he sat down
in the place of honor at the right hand of the
majestic God in heaven. 4 This shows that
the Son is far greater than the [a]angels, just
as the name God gave him is greater than
their names.

1:1-4 Ancient sermons often began with an introduction meant to grab the hearer's attention and introduce the sermon's main topics. In Hebrews, the first four verses form a single, eloquent Greek sentence built around the main clause, ***God . . . has spoken.*** Most English translations present these verses as several sentences for ease of reading.

1:1-2 ***Long ago. . . . And now:*** These verses deal with two time periods in which God has spoken, addressing the differences between the two eras in parallel fashion.

1:1 ***Long ago,*** in Jewish theology, referred to the time before the Messiah's coming. For the author of Hebrews, this primarily meant the OT era. Throughout that past era, ***God spoke many times and in many ways***—through dreams, visions, mighty acts, stories, commands, exhortations, angelic appearances, and appearances of God himself. • ***The prophets*** were all those through whom God gave his revelation (see 2 Pet 1:19-21).

1:2 ***These final days*** refers to the historical era inaugurated at Christ's coming (see Isa 2:2; Acts 2:17). Whereas the revelation of the OT era came in a wide variety of forms over time, God's ultimate revelation was given ***through his Son,*** Jesus (see 2:3-4). • ***as an inheritance:*** Christ is God's royal heir; the author probably had Ps 2:8 in mind.

1:3 The word translated ***radiates,*** found only here in the NT, includes an idea of intense brightness. ***God's own glory*** is the glorious manifestation of his presence (Exod 16:7; 33:18; Isa 40:5). The Son's glory is an expression of God's glory—the Son of God manifests the person and presence of God (Luke 9:32; John 1:14; 2:11; 17:5; Rom 8:17). • The term translated ***expresses,*** used only here in the NT, was used of a distinguishing mark imprinted on an object such as a coin. The Son gives a clear picture of ***the very character of God*** (John 1:18; Phil 2:6; Col 1:15). • ***the mighty power of his command*** (literally *his powerful word*): God's word is the powerful, dynamic force that created and governs the world (11:3; Ps 33:6-11). Elsewhere the Son is called "the Word of God" (Rev 19:13; see also John 1:1-18). • ***cleansed us from our sins:*** See 9:11–10:18. • ***he sat down:*** This clause is an allusion to Ps 110:1 (see also 1:13; 8:1; 10:12; 12:2), which foretold the exaltation of Christ after his suffering (see Matt 22:44; Acts 2:33; 1 Cor 15:25). ***The right hand*** of God indicates high honor, rank, and position (see 1 Kgs 2:19; Ps 16:11; 45:4, 9; 80:17).

1:4 The Son's exalted position ***shows that the Son is far greater than the angels*** in status or rank. First-century Jews were fascinated with angels and held them in high esteem, so the

2. THE SON AND THE ANGELS (1:5–2:18)

Jesus, the Divine Son (1:5–2:4)

The Son Is Greater Than the Angels

5For God never said to any angel what he
said to Jesus:

"You are my Son.
Today I have become your Father."

God also said,

"I will be his Father,
and he will be my Son."

6And when he brought his [b]supreme Son
into the world, God said,

"Let all of God's angels worship him."

7Regarding the angels, he says,

"He sends his angels like the winds,
his [c]servants like flames of fire."

8But to the Son he says,

"Your throne, O God, endures forever and
ever.

1:5 *Ps 2:7 *2 Sam 7:14
1:6 *Deut 32:43 *Ps 8:4 [b]*prōtotokos* (4416) ‣Heb 11:28
1:7 *Ps 104:4 [c]*leitourgos* (3011) ‣Heb 1:14
1:8-9 *Ps 45:6-7

The Superiority of the Son (1:1-14)

Heb 3:1-6; 7:1–10:18, 34; 11:16, 35, 40 Ps 110:1

The author of Hebrews argues for the superiority of the Son as to his *person* and his *ministry*. The superiority of the Son's *person* is presented primarily in 1:1–3:6. In the book's introduction (1:1-4), the Son is presented as the creator, sustainer, and heir of the universe (1:2-3), one who "radiates God's own glory and expresses the very character of God" (1:3), and the exalted one, who has achieved the cleansing of sins and now has a status "far greater than the angels" (1:3-4).

In 1:5-14 and 2:5-18, the Son is shown to be superior to the angels. He has a unique relationship with the Father (1:5) and is the ruler, creator, and terminator of the created order (1:8-12). The angels have a status that is inferior to him, and they worship him (1:6-7). Scripture exalts him to the highest possible position of honor at the Father's right hand (1:13; Ps 110:1), so now he has authority over all things (2:5-8).

In 3:1-6, the author builds on the hearers' great respect for Moses to make the case for the even greater respect due the Son. Like Moses, the Son was faithful in his ministry to the people of God. Yet the Son deserves more glory and praise than Moses, for he is identified with God the Father and is the ultimate builder of God's house (3:3-4). The Son is ultimately in charge of God's people (3:5-6).

The passages that focus on the superiority of the Son's *ministry* are found primarily in 7:1–10:18. Through his superior high priesthood, Jesus has brought in a "better hope" (7:19), grounded in a "better covenant" (7:22), based on "better promises" (8:6), through which he performs a ministry "superior" to that of the priests of the old covenant (8:6). His ministry under the new covenant is a "better system" because of the superiority of Christ's sacrifice (9:10, 23; see also 12:24). His ministry causes new covenant believers to anticipate "better things" in terms of their inheritance (10:34), a "better . . . heavenly homeland" (11:16), and a "better life after the resurrection" (11:35). For new covenant believers in Christ, God has something "better" that could only be anticipated by their old covenant counterparts (11:40).

author of Hebrews establishes the Son's superiority to them. • ***just as the name . . . is greater:*** Cp. 2 Sam 7:8-14. Some commentators believe that the title "Son" is the *name* implied here. Others think the name is *Yahweh*, the covenant name of God in the OT (Exod 3:14-15; cp. Phil 2:9-11).

1:5-14 In these ten verses, the author uses a variety of OT texts to show that Jesus is superior to the angels. Among ancient Jewish and Christian interpreters, OT passages were strung together one after the other in "chain quotations" (called "pearl stringing") to convince the hearers or readers of a certain theological point by presenting a lot of scriptural evidence together.

1:5 ***God . . . said:*** This verse quotes Ps 2:7 and 2 Sam 7:14. By exalting Jesus to his right hand (see Acts 1:9-11; 2:32-36; 7:55-56), the Father proclaimed his unique relationship with the Son. • ***Today I have become your Father*** (or *Today I reveal you as my Son*): Jesus did not *become* the Son at the exaltation—he had been involved in creation (1:2)—but the exaltation verified his identity to all.

1:6 ***when he brought his supreme Son into the world, God said*** (or *when he again brings his supreme Son* [or *firstborn Son*] *into the world, God will say*): The *supreme* (or *firstborn*) *Son* shared the authority of the father, inherited most of his property, and was especially favored. In the NT, "firstborn" most frequently refers to Christ's supremacy both in the church and in the created order; his resurrection is often given as the evidence for this status (Acts 13:33; Rom 1:4; 8:29; Col 1:15, 18; Rev 1:5; cp. Heb 12:23, where believers are called firstborn children). • ***"Let all of God's angels worship him":*** This quotation from Deut 32:43 demonstrates the lower status of the angels in that they worship the Son (see also Ps 97:7).

1:7 This verse quotes Ps 104:4 (Greek version) to show that the angels are messengers or *servants* and, therefore, of a lesser rank than the Son, whom they serve. • In the OT, *angels* are sometimes associated with *winds* and *fire* (see Exod 3:2; Judg 6:21; 13:16, 20; 2 Sam 22:11; Ps 18:10; 35:5), which is why angels are mentioned in connection with God's lordship over nature.

1:8-9 These verses, quoting Ps 45:6-7, proclaim ***the Son*** as the divine, just, eternal, anointed King of the universe. • ***to the Son he says:*** Jesus is addressed

1:10-12
*Ps 102:25-27
Rev 6:14; 11:15

1:13
Ps 110:1
Matt 22:44

1:14
Ps 34:7; 91:11
[d]*leitourgikos* (3010)
‣Heb 8:2

2:2
Deut 33:2
Acts 7:38, 53
Gal 3:19

You rule with a scepter of justice.
9 You love justice and hate evil.
Therefore, O God, your God has
anointed you,
pouring out the oil of joy on you more
than on anyone else."

10 He also says to the Son,

"In the beginning, Lord, you laid the
foundation of the earth
and made the heavens with your
hands.
11 They will perish, but you remain forever.
They will wear out like old clothing.
12 You will fold them up like a cloak
and discard them like old clothing.
But you are always the same;
you will live forever."

13 And God never said to any of the angels,

"Sit in the place of honor at my right hand
until I humble your enemies,
making them a footstool under your
feet."

14 Therefore, angels are only [d]servants—spirits sent to care for people who will inherit salvation.

A Warning against Drifting Away

2 So we must listen very carefully to
the truth we have heard, or we may
drift away from it. 2 For the message God

Consequences of Apostasy (2:1-4)

Heb 6:4-8; 10:26-31
Num 16
Deut 13
2 Kgs 17:5-23
Ezek 8
Matt 24:10-13
Gal 1:6-9
2 Tim 3:1-9
2 Pet 2
1 Jn 2:18-19

Although it is not a popular theme, the Bible is clear that disobeying God has severe consequences (see, e.g., Gen 9:5-6; Num 35:16-21; Lev 20:10; Zech 5:4). Those who oppose God's will and rule will ultimately be excluded from his life-giving presence (Isa 66:14-24). Sadly, opposition to God is not limited to those outside the community of faith; the Bible tells of many people who seemed to know God but turned away (Num 16; Deut 13; 2 Kgs 17:5-23; Ezek 8). God brings just consequences to those who turn away from him (Job 11:20; Prov 1:24-31; Jer 11:11). Jesus also spoke of those who fall away and their judgment (Matt 5:22; 16:27; 23:13; 24:10-13; 25:41-46), and the writers of the NT follow his lead (Gal 1:6-9; 2 Tim 3:1-9; 2 Pet 2; 1 Jn 2:18-19).

Several passages in Hebrews warn that those who fail to take God's word seriously are in deep spiritual trouble and will face the judgment of God (see 2:1-4; 4:12-13; 6:4-8; 10:26-31; 12:25-29). Scholars have understood the nature of the *apostasy* (falling away) and judgment described in the "warning passages" of Hebrews in various ways, including: (1) Some have understood the warnings to be hypothetical, suggesting that the harshness serves simply to shock the hearers out of spiritual lethargy, with no impending judgment in view. (2) A second position holds that those with whom the author was concerned were Jewish and had not yet converted to Christianity. Thus they were under God's judgment because they were not yet a part of the new covenant. (3) A third view proclaims that the "apostates" in view were Christians who, because of their spiritual condition, faced God's judgment as believers, but were in no danger of actually losing their salvation. (4) A fourth view suggests that the apostates had been full members of the Christian community and had experienced the full reality of the Christian faith but had now turned their backs on Christ and the Church. (5) A fifth view is that, rather than having been true believers, the apostates showed that they never really knew Christ in the first place.

Ultimately, warnings of judgment are an expression of God's grace, seeking to turn the rebellious person to the ways of God. Taking the consequences of rebellion seriously can help us build resolve in faithfully following Jesus.

as **God**; in 1:9, ***your God*** is a reference to God the Father. • ***pouring out the oil of joy:*** Olive oil was used to anoint kings of Israel at the inauguration of their rule (1 Sam 10:1; 1 Kgs 19:15-16). God ***has anointed*** his Son, Jesus Christ, as King.

1:10-12 These verses, quoting Ps 102:25-27, celebrate the Son as both the creator and the one who brings the created order to an end. All created things ***will wear out like old clothing***, and the Son will ***discard them*** (cp. 2:5; 2 Pet 3:13; Rev 21:1). By contrast, the Son of God ***will live forever***.

1:13 In climactic fashion, the author ends his string of OT quotations (see note on 1:5-14) by quoting from Ps 110:1 in celebration of Christ's exaltation (see also notes on Luke 20:42-43; 22:69; 1 Cor 15:25; Eph 1:19-22).
• The image of the Son's ***enemies*** as ***a footstool under*** his ***feet*** represents their absolute subjugation (see 2:8). In the ancient world, a victorious king would place his foot on the neck or back of an enemy as a symbolic act of domination.

1:14 ***Therefore, angels are only servants:*** The author restates his conclusion. God sends out the angels ***to care for*** his people, ***who will inherit salvation*** at the end of the age (see 9:28).

2:1-4 The author makes an argument from lesser to greater: If, in the lesser situation of the OT era, people who rejected God's word as delivered by angels were severely punished, how

delivered through angels has always stood
firm, and every violation of the law and
every act of disobedience was punished.
3 So what makes us think we can escape
if we ignore this great salvation that was
first announced by the Lord Jesus himself
and then delivered to us by those who
heard him speak? 4 And God confirmed
the message by giving [e]signs and wonders
and various miracles and gifts of the Holy
Spirit whenever he chose.

Jesus, the Man (2:5-18)

The Son Temporarily Lower Than Angels

5 And furthermore, it is not angels who will
control the future world we are talking
about. 6 For in one place the Scriptures say,

"What are mere mortals that you should
think about them,
or a son of man that you should care
for him?
7 Yet you made them only a little lower
than the angels
and crowned them with glory and
honor.
8 You gave them authority over all things."

Now when it says "all things," it means nothing is left out. But we have not yet seen all
things put under their authority. 9 What we
do see is Jesus, who was given a position "a
little lower than the angels"; and because he
suffered death for us, he is now "crowned
with glory and honor." Yes, by God's grace,
Jesus tasted death for everyone.

The Son of God Became Human

10 God, for whom and through whom everything was made, chose to bring many
children into glory. And it was only right
that he should make Jesus, through his suffering, a perfect leader, fit to bring them
into their salvation.

2:3 Heb 1:2; 10:29
2:4 Mark 16:20
[e]*sēmeion* (4592)
‣ Rev 13:13
2:6-8 Ps 8:4-6
2:8 1 Cor 15:27
2:9 Phil 2:6-9
2:10 Luke 24:26, 46
Rom 11:36
Heb 5:9

much greater the punishment will be for those who now reject the word of salvation that has been delivered by the Son himself and confirmed by the Holy Spirit.

2:1 ***The truth we have heard*** is the message of salvation delivered through Christ (2:3). • ***Drift away*** pictures a ship getting off course. Here it speaks of getting off track spiritually due to not listening ***very carefully*** to the Good News.

2:2 According to Jewish tradition, ***the message God delivered,*** the law given on Mount Sinai (see Acts 7:38; Gal 3:19), was delivered ***through angels.*** • ***Violation of the law*** was punished (see Exod 22:19; Lev 20:10; Num 35:16-21), and punishment was inescapable (Prov 1:24-31; Jer 11:11).

2:3 ***So what makes us think we can escape?*** Here the author presses the full force of the danger of turning away from Christ and his salvation. There is no escape from punishment for those who walk away, and the punishment will be of the greatest severity (cp. 6:4-12; 10:26-31; 12:29; Rom 2:5; 1 Thes 2:16). • ***Salvation*** refers to God's acts on behalf of his people. For example, God saved his people through the exodus from Egypt (Deut 26:5-9). In the NT, salvation primarily refers to Christ's work of rescuing people from the penalty of sin and giving them new life by his sacrificial death on the cross (5:9-10). This salvation was ***first announced by the Lord Jesus himself*** (e.g., Matt 4:17; 9:35; Mark 1:15; Luke 13:1-5). He ***then delivered*** (or *validated*) the message through ***those who heard him speak*** (e.g., Mark 6:12; Acts 2:38; 3:19-20).

2:4 ***God confirmed the message*** (literally *God bore witness*): God himself confirmed the validity of the message of Christ and his followers ***by giving signs and wonders and various miracles and gifts of the Holy Spirit*** (see Acts 2:22; Rom 15:19; 2 Cor 12:12).

2:5-9 The author of Hebrews uses Ps 8:4-6 to transition from the discussion of Christ's exalted divinity (1:5-14) to the discussion of his humanity (2:10-18). Ps 8 is often presented with Ps 110:1 (see 1:13) to speak of the submission of created things to Christ (see 1 Cor 15:25-27; Eph 1:20-23). Christ is the consummate human being. In his exaltation, he fulfills what fallen humanity could not: true dominion over the created order.

2:5 ***it is not angels:*** Cp. 1:13.

2:6-8 These verses quote Ps 8:4-6 (Greek version). Ps 8 speaks of the position God has given humanity, but the author of Hebrews applies it as a prediction about Christ, who is the fulfillment and representative head of humanity.

2:6 ***What are mere mortals:*** These two lines of the psalm proclaim God's special attention to human beings. • ***a son of man*** (or *the Son of Man*): The phrase *son of man* speaks of human existence; it parallels *mere mortals* in the previous line. In the Gospels Jesus referred to himself with this phrase (see "The Son of Man" at Matt 8:18-22, p. 1593).

2:7 ***them:*** Literally *him.* This refers to humanity in general and is applied specifically to Christ (see note on 2:6-8). • Christ became ***only a little lower than the angels*** (or *lower than the angels for only a little while*), like other human beings (see also Phil 2:5-8). As a result of his suffering, he was ***crowned . . . with glory and honor*** (see 2:9; Phil 2:9-11). • At the end of this verse some manuscripts add *You gave them charge of everything you made.*

2:8 ***You gave them authority over all things*** (literally *You have put all things under his feet*): See note on 2:6-8. • ***nothing is left out:*** All things are ultimately subject to Christ and the church, but ***we have not yet seen*** the complete expression of this reality—it will be consummated at the end of the age.

2:9 ***What we do see is Jesus:*** How can the church persevere when evil and death are still in the world? We look to Jesus both in his human life in ***a position "a little lower than the angels"*** and in his exaltation, ***now "crowned with glory and honor."*** His suffering as a human being led to his exaltation (see Phil 2:5-11; cp. Isa 52:13–53:12). See also 12:1-13.

2:10-18 At least four reasons why the Son of God became human are implied in this passage. First, ***it was only right:*** It is consistent with what we know of God's character that he would accomplish salvation in this way (2:10). Second, Jesus had to become ***human*** to die (2:14). Third, high priests, as detailed in the OT law, had to come from among God's ***people*** (2:17). Fourth, Jesus became a sympathetic priest, experiencing the ***suffering and testing*** we know as humans (2:18).

2:10 ***children*** (literally *sons*): The author plays off his use of the title *Son* for Jesus throughout the section, here referring to the people of God as *sons.* The translation *children* makes it clear that this term refers to all God's people, male and female. • The term translated ***leader*** had a wide range of meanings in the ancient world, including *founder, hero, champion, prince, captain, leader,* or *scout.* Jesus is a leader in that he blazed a trail for those who are saved, leading them to glory.

[11]So now Jesus and the ones he makes
holy have the same Father. That is why Jesus
is not ashamed to call them his brothers and
sisters. [12]For he said to God,

"I will proclaim your name to my
brothers and sisters.
I will praise you among your
assembled people."

[13]He also said,

"I will put my trust in him,"
that is, "I and the children God has
given me."

[14]Because God's children are human beings—made of flesh and blood—the Son
also became flesh and blood. For only as a
human being could he die, and only by dying could he break the power of the devil,
who had the power of death. [15]Only in this
way could he set free all who have lived their
lives as slaves to the fear of dying.
[16]We also know that the Son did not
come to help angels; he came to help the
descendants of Abraham. [17]Therefore, it
was necessary for him to be made in every
respect like us, his brothers and sisters, so
that he could be our merciful and faithful
High Priest before God. Then he could
[f]offer a sacrifice that would take away the
sins of the people. [18]Since he himself has
gone through suffering and testing, he is
able to help us when we are being tested.

3. EXHORTATIONS TO FAITHFULNESS (3:1–4:13)

Jesus Is Greater Than Moses

3 And so, dear brothers and sisters who
belong to God and are partners with
those called to heaven, think carefully about
this Jesus whom we declare to be God's messenger and High Priest. [2]For he was faithful
to God, who appointed him, just as Moses
served faithfully when he was entrusted
with God's entire house.
[3]But Jesus deserves far more glory than
Moses, just as a person who builds a house
deserves more praise than the house itself.
[4]For every house has a builder, but the one
who built everything is God.
[5]Moses was certainly faithful in God's
house as a servant. His work was an illustration of the truths God would reveal later.
[6]But Christ, as the Son, is in charge of God's
entire house. And we are God's house, if we
keep our courage and remain confident in
our hope in Christ.

2:11 Matt 12:50; 28:10; John 20:17; Rom 8:29; Heb 10:10; 13:12
2:12 *Ps 22:22
2:13 *Isa 8:17-18; John 17:11-12
2:14 John 1:14; Rom 8:3; 1 Cor 15:54-57; 2 Tim 1:10; 1 Jn 3:8
2:17 Phil 2:7; Heb 3:1; 4:15; 5:1; 1 Jn 2:2; 4:10; [f]*hilaskomai* (2433) ‣Heb 9:5
2:18 Heb 4:15; 5:2
3:1 Heb 2:17; 4:14
3:2 Num 12:7-8
3:3 2 Cor 3:7-11
3:5 Exod 14:31; Num 12:7
3:6 Eph 2:19-22; 1 Tim 3:15; 1 Pet 2:5

2:11 ***have the same Father*** (literally *are all out of one*): Based on the family terminology in the context, the phrase can be understood as referring to God. However, the author might have been thinking of Abraham as a common ancestor (see 2:16) or of human nature as a common experience (*out of one nature*). • ***brothers and sisters*** Literally *brothers;* also in 2:12; see note on 3:1.

2:12 This verse quotes Ps 22:22, commenting on the phrase ***brothers and sisters*** in 2:11. Psalm 22 contains profound messianic prophecies concerning the sufferings of Christ (Ps 22:1, 7-8, 16-18; see Matt 27:35, 43; John 19:23-24, 31-36). Psalm 22:22 shows the solidarity of the righteous sufferer (Jesus) with the people of God in praising God for his help.

2:13 This verse quotes Isa 8:17-18, which comes from a broader messianic context (cp. Isa 8:14 with Rom 9:33; 1 Pet 2:8). • ***I will put my trust in him*** here declares Jesus' trust in the Father. • ***I and the children God has given me*** indicates a close relationship between Jesus and the children of God.

2:14-15 The death of ***the Son*** of God as a sacrifice for sin served to ***break the power of the devil:*** It made the devil's ***power of death*** ineffective (1 Cor 15:56). • ***who had:*** Or *who has.* • Philo, a first-century Jewish philosopher, wrote that "nothing is so calculated to enslave the mind as fearing death" (Philo, *That Every Good Person Is Free* 3.22). Through his sacrificial death, Christ set free those who were ***slaves to the fear of dying.***

2:16 ***descendants of Abraham:*** Jesus' sacrifice on the cross was for the heirs of God's promises to Abraham, rather than for the ***angels.***

2:17-18 These verses introduce Jesus' role as ***our merciful and faithful High Priest,*** which is fully discussed in the central section of Hebrews (4:14–10:25). • ***It was necessary for him*** to share our humanity (see 5:1). • ***like us, his brothers and sisters:*** Literally *like the brothers;* see note on 3:1.

3:1-6 The author compares Jesus to Moses, setting Jesus forward as the supreme example of faithfulness. The great status of Moses, a revered figure in Judaism, is used to show the incomparable greatness of Jesus.

3:1 ***And so, dear brothers and sisters who belong to God:*** Literally *And so, holy brothers.* Speakers and writers of the ancient world often addressed religious gatherings as "brothers," referring to both men and women. • ***think carefully about this Jesus:*** Focusing on Jesus is a primary means of persevering in the faith (2:9; 12:1-2). • ***God's messenger*** (literally *God's apostle*): This description might be highlighting the Son's role in bearing a proclamation of God's name and message (2:12; Matt 10:40; Mark 9:37; Luke 10:16).

3:2 Jesus ***was faithful to God*** and to the task to which the Father had appointed him (5:7-10; 12:1-3; Phil 2:5-11), ***just as Moses*** had been (Num 12:7). Many Jews of the first century regarded Moses as the greatest person in history, of even higher status than the angels. • ***entire house:*** Some manuscripts do not include *entire.*

3:3-6 ***Jesus deserves far more glory*** for two reasons. First, ***a person who builds a house deserves more praise than the house itself.*** The Messiah is the one who builds God's house (see 2 Sam 7:13). The implication is that Moses is part of the house (i.e., God's people) that God has built. Second, whereas Moses was ***a servant*** in God's house, ***Christ, as the Son,*** is the heir ***in charge of God's entire house.*** Sons have greater status than household servants.

3:6 We are part of Christ's house ***if we keep our courage.*** The author could not give unqualified assurance to those who were drifting away from Christ and the church. Those who persevere in the faith have assurance that they are part of God's house (see 3:14; Rom 8:9, 17; 11:22; 2 Cor 13:5; Col 1:22-23). • Some manuscripts add *faithful to the end* at the end of this verse.

Do Not Be Like the Rebels in the Wilderness
7 That is why the Holy Spirit says,

"Today when you hear his voice,
8 don't harden your hearts
as Israel did when they rebelled,
when they tested me in the
wilderness.
9 There your ancestors tested and tried my
patience,
even though they saw my miracles for
forty years.
10 So I was angry with them, and I said,
'Their hearts always turn away from me.
They refuse to do what I tell them.'
11 So in my anger I took an oath:
'They will never enter my place of rest.' "

12 Be careful then, dear brothers and sisters.
Make sure that your own hearts are not evil
and unbelieving, turning you away from
the living God. 13 You must [g]warn each other
every day, while it is still "today," so that
none of you will be deceived by sin and hardened against God. 14 For if we are faithful to
the end, trusting God just as firmly as when
we first believed, we will share in all that belongs to Christ. 15 Remember what it says:

"Today when you hear his voice,
don't harden your hearts
as Israel did when they rebelled."

16 And who was it who rebelled against
God, even though they heard his voice?
Wasn't it the people Moses led out of Egypt?
17 And who made God angry for forty years?
Wasn't it the people who sinned, whose
corpses lay in the wilderness? 18 And to
whom was God speaking when he took an
oath that they would never enter his rest?
Wasn't it the people who disobeyed him?
19 So we see that because of their unbelief
they were not able to enter his rest.

Promised Rest for God's People

4 God's promise of entering his rest still
stands, so we ought to tremble with
fear that some of you might fail to experience it. 2 For this good news—that God has
prepared this rest—has been announced
to us just as it was to them. But it did them
no good because they didn't share the faith
of those who listened to God. 3 For only we
who believe can enter his rest. As for the others, God said,

3:7-11 *Ps 95:7-11
3:8 Exod 17:7
3:11 Num 14:21-23
3:13 Eph 4:22; [g]*parakaleō* (3870) ›Rom 15:4
3:14 Heb 3:6
3:15 *Ps 95:7-8
3:16-18 Num 14:1-35
3:17 Num 14:29; 1 Cor 10:5
3:18 Num 14:22-23
4:2 1 Thes 2:13
4:3 *Ps 95:11

3:7-19 This passage presents, "as a warning to us" (1 Cor 10:6), the negative example of those who wandered in the wilderness for forty years and died there. The wilderness wanderings represent disobedience to God and its consequences (see Num 32:7-11; Deut 1:19-35; Ps 106:24-26).

3:7-11 These verses quote Ps 95:7-11.

3:8 ***Israel . . . rebelled*** and ***tested*** God in places such as Massah and Meribah, where there was a shortage of water (Exod 17:1-7; Num 20:2-13), and especially at Kadesh, where the disobedient Israelites refused to enter the Promised Land (3:10; see Num 14:1-25; Deut 1:19-46; Ps 106).

3:9-10 Despite seeing the ***miracles*** God had performed on their behalf, the people of Israel ***tested*** God's ***patience*** by refusing to trust him in the wilderness (Num 14:11, 22). The essence of their rebellion was that ***their hearts always*** turned ***away*** from God—they did not desire to obey him. The result was that God ***was angry with them.***

3:11 Rebellion has consequences. • God's ***anger*** is not merely an emotional reaction; it is his just displeasure toward sin (John 3:36; Rom 1:18; 1 Thes 2:16). • God's ***oath*** (see 6:13-20; 7:20-22, 28) was that they would ***never enter*** Canaan, the ***place of rest*** from their wanderings (Deut 1:19-46; 3:20; 12:10; Josh 1:13).

3:12-19 The author of Hebrews discusses the terms *heart, day, today, hear, enter, rest, unbelief,* and *oath,* all drawn from Ps 95. Bible teachers of the ancient world would cite and then explain an OT text, often highlighting significant words from the text, just as preachers do today. This form of exposition was called *midrash.*

3:12 ***dear brothers and sisters:*** Literally *brothers;* see note on 3:1. • ***hearts . . . not evil and unbelieving:*** An evil heart stubbornly sets its will against the Lord due to unbelief, causing a person to turn ***away from the living God.***

3:13 Using the word ***"today"*** from Ps 95:7, the author challenges his hearers to ***warn each other every day*** against the deceptive and hardening power of ***sin.***

3:14 ***For if we are faithful:*** Those who persevere in the faith have assurance that they are indeed part of God's family (see 3:6; Rom 8:9, 17; 11:22; 2 Cor 13:5; Col 1:22-23).

3:15 This verse again quotes Ps 95:7-8, the exhortation from that portion of the psalm. It sums up the author's own exhortation in 3:12-14, focusing on the importance of listening and responding favorably to God's ***voice.***

3:16-19 These verses contain a rapid-fire series of questions and answers, a common rhetorical technique. The three questions follow the progression of ideas found in Ps 95:8-11: The people of Israel rebelled against God, God was angry, and God took an oath that they would never enter his rest. The answers are taken from other OT passages that focus on the Israelites' rebellion in the wilderness (Num 14; Deut 9; Ps 106). The author drives home the terrible cost of disobedience to God.

3:19 ***Unbelief*** and disobedience are closely associated in Hebrews and in the OT passages being discussed (Num 14:11; Deut 9:23; Ps 78:22, 32). As a consequence of disobedience, ***they were not able to enter his rest*** by entering the land of Canaan (Deut 3:20; 12:10; Josh 1:13).

4:1-2 The author transitions to the ***promise*** that the faithful will enter God's ***rest*** and exhorts his listeners to take this promise seriously. Hearing is not enough: It must be combined with ***faith.***

4:1 To ***fear*** God means to experience an appropriate reverence, even awe, for God and his will. It would be the worst of tragedies to ***fail to experience*** what God has promised.

4:2 ***This good news*** is the message of salvation (2:3-4). • ***they didn't share the faith of those who listened to God:*** Some manuscripts read *they didn't combine what they heard with faith.* In either case, the hearers were deficient in faith, distrusting God's word of promise.

4:3 People ***who believe*** the Good News are the true heirs of God's ***rest,*** the salvation that God offers through Christ's sacrifice. • ***God said:*** The quotation of

4:4 *Gen 2:2
4:5 *Ps 95:11
4:6 Heb 3:18
4:7 *Ps 95:7-8
4:8 Josh 22:4
4:10 Gen 2:2; Rev 14:13

"In my anger I took an oath:
'They will never enter my place of
rest.'"
even though this rest has been ready since
he made the world. 4We know it is ready because of the place in the Scriptures where it
mentions the seventh day: "On the seventh
day God rested from all his work." 5But in
the other passage God said, "They will never
enter my place of rest."
6So God's rest is there for people to enter,
but those who first heard this good news
failed to enter because they disobeyed God.
7So God set another time for entering his
rest, and that time is today. God announced
this through David much later in the words
already quoted:

"Today when you hear his voice,
don't harden your hearts."

8Now if Joshua had succeeded in giving
them this rest, God would not have spoken
about another day of rest still to come. 9So
there is a special rest still waiting for the
people of God. 10For all who have entered
into God's rest have rested from their labors, just as God did after creating the
world. 11So let us do our best to enter that

God's Sabbath Rest (4:1-11)

Gen 2:1-3; Exod 16:21-29; 20:8-11; 31:13-16; Lev 16:29-31; Isa 52:7; 54:13-14; 56:2, 4; 57:2, 21; 58:13; Ezek 20:20; Matt 11:28-30; Mark 2:23-28; Luke 8:48; John 14:27; Acts 10:36; Rom 5:1; 15:13; 2 Cor 5:19-21; Eph 2:17; Col 1:20; 2:16; 3:15; 2 Pet 1:2

The concept of God's Sabbath rest, found in 4:1-11, has been a theological puzzle for commentators. The concept has various connotations from the OT, including the Promised Land as a place to rest from slavery and wandering and the Sabbath day as a weekly day of rest. In 3:7-19, the author of Hebrews expounds on Ps 95:7-11, offering the wilderness wanderers as an example of those who failed to enter God's rest because of their disobedience. Yet, what is this "rest" they failed to enter, which still remains for the people of God (4:1-3)? The author of Hebrews clearly had more in mind than the physical land as the place of "special rest" (4:8-9).

The author adds Gen 2:2, another passage that speaks of "God's rest," to the discussion (4:4). God's "special rest" is something that he prepared since the foundation of the world (4:3) and it relates to ceasing from one's own work as God did from his (4:10). Further, the rest can be entered by those who "hear his voice," don't harden their hearts, and believe the Good News (4:1-3, 7). What is this rest that the author has in mind?

In the OT, the Day of Atonement is called a "Sabbath day of complete rest" (Lev 16:29-31). On that day, people ceased completely from their own work. In the new covenant, Jesus as our Great High Priest has offered a once-for-all sacrifice that decisively dealt with sin (5:1-4; 9:7, 11-28). He has provided the final Day of Atonement sacrifice, and he thus offers people a spiritual rest, which they enter by believing this Good News.

God's rest that is available through Jesus has two aspects. First, those who believe in him have ceased from their own works—they no longer work for God's acceptance, but they trust in Christ's finished work (Eph 2:8-9) and enjoy the blessings of peace with God (John 14:27; Acts 10:36; Rom 5:1; 2 Cor 5:19-21). Second, they look forward to an eternal life of rest and enjoyment in God's presence (Isa 26:19; Rev 14:13). Jesus Christ gives complete and perfect rest (Matt 11:28-30).

Ps 95:11 reminds the reader that the unbelieving rebels in the wilderness would ***never enter*** God's ***place of rest*** (cp. 11:8, 10, 14-16; 12:22-24). • ***since he made the world:*** God's rest means much more than physical entry into Canaan (see note on 4:4).

4:4 This verse quotes Gen 2:2 to demonstrate that the promised rest was established when ***God rested*** at creation.

4:5 This quotation of Ps 95:11 reiterates the point made in 4:3.

4:6 ***So God's rest is there:*** Building on the discussion in 4:3-5, the author is about to argue that the promised *rest* is still available (4:7-10). But those who wandered in the wilderness, even though they ***heard*** the ***good news*** that the Promised Land was open to them, ***failed to enter because they disobeyed God*** (see Num 14:1-25; Deut 1:19-46; Ps 106).

4:7 ***So God set another time . . . and that time is today:*** The logic here is that ***David*** wrote Ps 95 ***much later*** than the wilderness debacle, so God's ***rest*** cannot be limited to that earlier generation. The ***words already quoted*** are from Ps 95:7-8; these words encourage us not to ***harden*** our ***hearts*** when hearing God's ***voice*** so that we might enter the rest that the people in the wilderness were denied. This opportunity is available ***today*** (see 3:13).

4:8 ***Joshua*** is the same name as *Jesus* (Greek *Iēsous*, Hebrew *Yehoshua'*). It is normally translated *Joshua* in the OT and *Jesus* in the NT (see also note on Exod 17:9). The author is making a wordplay on Jesus' and Joshua's shared name. Joshua did lead God's people into the Promised Land (Josh 3–4), but God had more in mind when he promised his people ***rest***. God's ultimate rest is provided by Jesus (3:13-14; 4:3, 9-11, 14-16).

4:9 ***a special rest*** (or ***a Sabbath rest***): Jesus' sacrifice functioned as a Day of Atonement sacrifice (5:1-3; 9:13-22; see Lev 23:26-28, 32). Through Christ's sacrifice, God's promised rest for his people is available.

4:10 ***have rested from their labors:*** See Exod 20:8-11. • ***just as God did:*** Gen 2:2.

4:11 ***let us do our best to enter:*** Failure to respond to the Good News with active obedience to God's voice (4:1-2)

rest. But if we disobey God, as the people of
Israel did, we will fall.
12For the [h]word of God is alive and
powerful. It is sharper than the sharpest
two-edged sword, cutting between soul
and [i]spirit, between joint and marrow. It exposes our innermost thoughts and desires.
13Nothing in all creation is hidden from
God. Everything is naked and exposed before his eyes, and he is the one to whom we
are accountable.

4. THE SON AND THE SACRIFICIAL SYSTEM (4:14–10:18)

Christ Is Our High Priest (4:14-16)

14So then, since we have a great [j]High Priest
who has entered heaven, Jesus the Son of
God, let us hold firmly to what we believe.
15This High Priest of ours understands our
weaknesses, for he faced all of the same
[k]testings we do, yet he did not sin. 16So let
us come boldly to the throne of our gracious God. There we will receive his mercy,
and we will find grace to help us when we
need it most.

Christ Is a Priest in the Line of Melchizedek (5:1–7:28)

The Son Appointed as High Priest

5 Every [a]high priest is a man chosen to
represent other people in their dealings
with God. He presents their gifts to God
and offers sacrifices for their sins. 2And
he is able to deal gently with ignorant and
wayward people because he himself is subject to the same weaknesses. 3That is why
he must offer sacrifices for his own sins as
well as theirs.
4And no one can become a high priest
simply because he wants such an honor.
He must be called by God for this work,
just as Aaron was. 5That is why Christ did
not honor himself by assuming he could
become [b]High Priest. No, he was chosen by
God, who said to him,

> "You are my Son.
> Today I have become your Father."

6And in another passage God said to him,

> "You are a priest forever in the order of
> Melchizedek."

4:12 Jer 23:29; 1 Cor 14:24-25; [h]*logos* (3056) ‣Heb 13:7; [i]*pneuma* (4151) ‣Matt 12:18
4:13 Ps 33:13-15
4:14 [j]*archiereus* (0749) ‣Heb 5:1
4:15 2 Cor 5:21; [k]*peirazō* (3985) ‣Jas 1:12
5:1 Heb 2:17; 7:27; 8:3; [a]*archiereus* (0749) ‣Heb 5:5
5:2 Heb 2:17; 4:15
5:3 Lev 9:7; 16:6; Heb 7:27; 9:7
5:4 Exod 28:1
5:5 *Ps 2:7; Acts 13:33; Heb 1:5; [b]*archiereus* (0749) ‣Heb 5:10
5:6 *Ps 110:4

---

will have an outcome analogous to the outcome for the wilderness wanderers: ***we will fall.*** • ***us . . . we . . . we:*** Obedience is not simply a personal matter; God's people have a communal responsibility for obedience and should support each other in that endeavor (cp. 3:13; 10:25; 12:15).

4:12-13 Echoing the call to hear God's voice (3:7, 15; 4:7; quoted from Ps 95:7), the author gives a beautiful epigram on the power and penetration of God's ***word.*** • ***alive and powerful:*** God's word is an active, effective force. The word that created and governs the cosmos (1:2-3) can deal powerfully with people. • ***the sharpest two-edged sword:*** God's word is able to penetrate the darkest recesses of people's lives, exposing their ***innermost thoughts and desires*** (cp. Eph 6:17; Rev 1:16; 2:12, 16; 19:15).

4:13 To be ***naked and exposed*** speaks figuratively of being vulnerable, helpless, or unprotected. The guilty are not able to hide from God's penetrating word of judgment (cp. Rev 3:17).

4:14-16 These key verses conclude the exhortation begun at 3:1 and introduce the lengthy treatment of Jesus' role as High Priest (4:14–10:25).

4:14 This verse effectively summarizes the whole message and challenge of Hebrews; the high priesthood of ***Jesus the Son of God*** is the basis for endurance in the Christian faith. • ***a great High Priest:*** Israel's high priest was the main leader in the worship of God and the primary mediator between God and the people (see Exod 31:10; Lev 4:3; 2 Kgs 12:10; 2 Chr 26:20). • ***who has entered heaven:*** The earthly high priests entered God's presence in the Most Holy Place once a year on the Day of Atonement (Lev 16:1-25). By contrast, Jesus, our High Priest, has entered God's presence in heaven, and there he remains (7:26; 9:11-12, 23-26). • ***let us hold firmly:*** An enduring commitment to active belief in and allegiance to Jesus (see also Col 2:19; 2 Thes 2:15; Rev 2:13, 25; 3:11).

4:15 Our High Priest ***understands our weaknesses,*** our human pull toward sin, because ***he faced all of the same testings we do.*** He was tempted with all the essential aspects of sin, such as lust, greed, unforgiveness, and dishonesty. This makes him compassionate as our High Priest (5:2). • ***yet he did not sin:*** Jesus is unlike the earthly high priests, who had to make offerings for their own sins before they could make offerings for the people (5:3; 7:26-28; see also 1 Pet 2:22-23).

4:16 The verb translated ***let us come*** could be translated to indicate ongoing action: *let us continually come.* • As our compassionate High Priest, Jesus has opened the way for people to enter God's presence ***boldly*** (see 6:19-20; 10:19-23), where we can obtain his ***mercy*** and ***grace to help us when we need it most.***

5:1-10 This section addresses the appointment of the Son of God as a superior High Priest. The focal text is Ps 110:4, which reveals God's oath that the Son would be a priest forever in the order of Melchizedek.

5:1 ***Every high priest:*** This phrase introduces requirements for high priests in general. • ***a man:*** The high priest was one of the people, so Jesus had to become human (see 2:17-18). • A second requirement for high priests was that they would ***represent other people*** by offering ***sacrifices*** on their behalf (7:25-28). Only the high priest could offer the sacrifice on the Day of Atonement (Exod 29:1-46; Lev 16:1-25).

5:2 A high priest was ***able to deal gently*** with those who sin because ***he himself*** was ***subject to the same weaknesses,*** i.e., he was sinful (5:3; cp. 4:15).

5:3 On the Day of Atonement the high priest was required to ***offer sacrifices*** for himself and his household prior to offering sacrifices for the people (Lev 16:11).

5:4 The role of ***high priest*** is by God's appointment rather than human enlistment (see Exod 28:1; Lev 8:1-12; Num 16:1-26).

5:5-6 The author brings Ps 2:7 and Ps 110:4 together based on shared language—both passages have ***God*** speaking to his ***Son.*** The exalted Son, who came to earth as a human (chs 1–2), is the one God has appointed to a unique high priesthood.

5:5 This verse quotes Ps 2:7. • ***Today I have become your Father:*** Or *Today I reveal you as my Son.*

5:6 This verse quotes Ps 110:4.

5:7
Mark 14:32-42
[c]*sarx* (4561)
‣Matt 16:17
5:8
Phil 2:8
5:9
Isa 45:17
5:10
Ps 110:4
[d]*archiereus* (0749)
‣Heb 7:26
5:12
1 Cor 3:2
5:13
Eph 4:14
5:14
1 Cor 2:6
6:1
[e]*teleiotēs* (5047)
‣Jas 1:4
[f]*metanoia* (3341)
‣2 Pet 3:9
[g]*pistis* (4102)
‣Heb 11:1

7While Jesus was here on [c]earth, he offered prayers and pleadings, with a loud cry
and tears, to the one who could rescue him
from death. And God heard his prayers because of his deep reverence for God. 8Even
though Jesus was God's Son, he learned obedience from the things he suffered. 9In this
way, God qualified him as a perfect High
Priest, and he became the source of eternal
salvation for all those who obey him. 10And
God designated him to be a [d]High Priest in
the order of Melchizedek.

A Call to Spiritual Growth

11There is much more we would like to say
about this, but it is difficult to explain, especially since you are spiritually dull and don't
seem to listen. 12You have been believers
so long now that you ought to be teaching
others. Instead, you need someone to teach
you again the basic things about God's word.
You are like babies who need milk and cannot eat solid food. 13For someone who lives
on milk is still an infant and doesn't know
how to do what is right. 14Solid food is for
those who are mature, who through training
have the skill to recognize the difference between right and wrong.

6 So let us stop going over the basic teachings about Christ again and again. Let
us go on instead and become [e]mature in
our understanding. Surely we don't need
to start again with the fundamental importance of [f]repenting from evil deeds and
placing our [g]faith in God. 2You don't need

God's Word (4:12)

Heb 1:1-4; 6:13-20; 11:3
Gen 1:3-28
Deut 8:3
Ps 12:6; 19:8; 119:11, 89, 105
Isa 40:8
Jer 15:16; 23:29; 36:2
Matt 5:18; 7:24
John 1:1-14; 5:24
2 Tim 3:16
1 Pet 1:25
2 Pet 1:19-21

A foundational truth in Hebrews is that God has spoken. In fact, the author of Hebrews, in line with other Jewish preachers of the era, presents the OT as coming from the lips of God, introducing those texts with "God says . . ." or something similar. God may speak a word of promise (6:14) or a word of punishment (3:11; 4:11-12); he may tell us something about himself or his Son (see 1:5-12) or reveal some aspect of his will (see 8:7-13; 10:5-7). God's word created the universe and still governs it (1:3; 11:3; Gen 1:3-28).

In the past, God's word came through angels or prophets, but now it has come preeminently in the person of Jesus, God's Son (1:1-4; 2:3-4; cp. John 1:1-14). The word is to be heard, heeded, obeyed, and believed as a source of hope.

Through his word, God initiates relationship with us and wants us to listen to him and respond in faith (Gen 15:6; John 1:12). His word is authoritative and intentional, and it gives profound hope because God can be trusted to keep his promises (6:13-20).

5:7-10 Jesus' suffering was a foundation for his superior priesthood. The Son's humiliation and suffering preceded his exaltation (2:9; Phil 2:5-11).

5:7 The phrase ***with a loud cry and tears*** is probably an allusion to Christ's suffering in the Garden (see Matt 26:36-46; Mark 14:32-42; Luke 22:40-46). ***God heard his prayers*** in the sense of affirming his righteousness and suitability for his role as high priest. Jesus' faithful devotion is being presented as an example for the readers (cp. 12:2-3).

5:8 *he learned obedience from the things he suffered:* Jesus was not disobedient before his suffering, but he walked his path of human experience—all the way to his death on the cross—in complete submission to the Father's will. We are expected to travel the same path (12:1-11).

5:9 *God qualified him as a perfect High Priest:* As used in Hebrews, *perfect* means "complete" or "mature" (see 2:10; 5:14; 7:11; 9:9-11). Jesus, through his sufferings, was qualified to be ***the source of eternal salvation for all those who obey him.*** • ***High Priest*** is not in the Greek text, but it is implied. • As the Son obeyed the Father (5:8), submitting completely to the Father's will, so those who come to him for *salvation* must *obey him.*

5:10 *a High Priest in the order of Melchizedek:* See 7:1-28.

5:11–6:20 After beginning to discuss Jesus' appointment as High Priest (5:1-10), the author confronts his audience with a series of exhortations (5:11–6:20). Such a shift in a sermon or discourse was meant to focus the hearers' attention.

5:11–6:3 This exhortation deals with the recipients' spiritual lethargy.

5:11 *spiritually dull:* The Greek term means "sluggish, dimwitted, negligent, lazy."

5:12 Their lack of spiritual vitality was especially shocking since they had been ***believers so long:*** they ought to have been spiritual leaders who were ***teaching others*** from their wealth of knowledge and Christian experience. • ***the basic things:*** The most rudimentary aspects of the Christian faith (see 6:1-3). • ***about God's word:*** Or *about the oracles of God.* • The imagery of ***milk*** and ***solid food*** (or *meat*) was used to distinguish basic from advanced education, and immature from mature students.

5:14 Being able ***to recognize the difference between right and wrong*** is a defining characteristic of spiritual maturity.

6:1-3 In light of the hearers' immaturity (5:11-14), the author urges them to move beyond ***basic teachings.*** The six basic teachings here were all foundational elements of Jewish instruction. The author might be challenging them to move beyond these basic teachings to ***further understanding*** about the person of Christ, which he elaborates in 7:1–10:25.

6:1 *Let us go on:* Or *Let us be carried on,* suggesting that God initiates growth to maturity (Phil 2:12-13) and that it is an ongoing process. • ***Repenting*** and ***faith*** are the basic commitments that initiate a person to the new covenant and constitute the basic posture of a Christian's life (see Acts 20:21). • ***evil deeds:*** Literally *dead works.*

further instruction about [h]baptisms, the
laying on of hands, the resurrection of the
dead, and eternal judgment. 3And so, God
willing, we will move forward to further understanding.
4For it is impossible to bring back to repentance those who were once enlightened—
those who have experienced the good things
of heaven and shared in the Holy Spirit, 5who
have tasted the goodness of the word of God
and the power of the age to come—6and who
then turn away from God. It is impossible to
bring such people back to repentance; by
rejecting the Son of God, they themselves
are nailing him to the cross once again and
holding him up to public shame.
7When the ground soaks up the falling
rain and bears a good crop for the farmer,
it has God's [i]blessing. 8But if a field bears
thorns and thistles, it is useless. The farmer
will soon condemn that field and burn it.
9Dear friends, even though we are talking
this way, we really don't believe it applies to
you. We are confident that you are meant
for better things, things that come with salvation. 10For God is not unjust. He will not
forget how hard you have worked for him
and how you have shown your love to him

6:2
Acts 4:2; 6:6; 17:18, 32
[h]*baptismos* (0909)
› 1 Pet 3:21

6:3
Acts 18:21

6:4
John 4:10
Eph 2:8
Heb 10:32

6:5
Ps 34:8
1 Pet 2:3

6:6
Heb 10:26, 29
2 Pet 2:21
1 Jn 5:16

6:7
[i]*eulogia* (2129)
› Jas 3:10

Maturity (5:11-14)

Heb 6:1-3; 10:14; 12:1-2
1 Cor 2:6; 3:1-3; 14:20
2 Cor 13:9-11
Eph 4:11-16
Col 4:12
1 Pet 2:1-3

The author of Hebrews was concerned with the spiritual immaturity of his audience. He wanted to give them real spiritual meat, but they were acting like spiritual babies who needed basic nourishment rather than deeper teaching (5:13). They had not been listening to the word of God. They had been believers long enough to be teaching others (5:12), but a growing insensitivity had rendered them spiritually dull (5:11; cp. 1 Cor 3:1-3). They lacked maturity to discern the basic difference between right and wrong (5:14).

The author challenged them to move on to maturity so he could present them with deeper truths of the faith (6:1-3). As elsewhere in the NT, maturity in Hebrews has to do with one's ability to discern spiritual truth (1 Cor 2:6). Christians are exhorted to be mature in their thinking (1 Cor 14:20). The body of Christ is growing to maturity through the equipping of believers and by growing in knowledge of the Son of God (Eph 4:11-16). The result is a united community of faith in which love and truth further build up the body of Christ.

Spiritual maturity is not an automatic result of time. It results from focused listening to the word of God and living out that word in fellowship with the community.

6:2 The term ***baptisms*** (or ***washings***) is plural, so it must mean more than just Christian baptism. Instruction about various washings was prevalent in first-century Judaism (see Matt 15:2; Mark 7:3). The author might also have in mind the cleansing rituals of the OT (cp. 9:13; 10:22). • The ***laying on of hands*** was associated with healing (Mark 5:22-23; Luke 13:13), ritual blessing (Matt 19:13, 15), reception of the Holy Spirit (Acts 8:17; 9:17; 19:6), and acknowledgement of a person's ministry (Acts 6:6; 13:3). • ***resurrection of the dead:*** See "The Resurrection of the Dead" at 1 Cor 15:12-58, p. 1951. • ***eternal judgment:*** See Rev 20:11-15.

6:3 The author is implicitly exhorting his readers to maturity, not only in their ***understanding*** but in everything (cp. 4:11; 5:14; 10:23-39; 12:1-13).

6:4-8 This passage, one of the most difficult in the NT, gives a harsh warning about those who have left the Christian faith. Those who have fallen away from Christ and the church are like those who fell in the wilderness (3:15-19): The lack of faith shown in such apostasy results in devastating judgment (cp. 10:26-31).

6:4 In Greek, the word ***impossible*** begins the sentence for emphasis—it absolutely cannot happen (see also 6:18; 10:4; 11:6). • They were ***once enlightened*** when they "first learned about Christ" (see 10:32 and note). • The ***good things of heaven*** might allude to the manna given from heaven (Exod 16:4, 15; Ps 78:24) as an image of spiritual blessings.

6:5 *tasted the goodness of the word of God:* These people had heard the word of God preached (2:3-4; 4:1-2) and had seen its effects. • ***the power of the age to come:*** They had witnessed signs and wonders when they heard the Good News (2:4; cp. Exod 7:3-4; Deut 7:19; Ps 66:3; 77:15-20; 78:9-16; 1 Cor 10:1-13).

6:6 *then turn* (or ***fall***) ***away:*** The image is reminiscent of the wilderness wanderers who turned away from obeying God and fell in the desert (3:17; 4:11; Num 14:1-4, 29-30). • ***to bring such people back to repentance:*** They had repented before, but had no fruit from their repentance (6:7-8). When people turn their back on Christ and his superior sacrifice, ***it is impossible*** for them to find any other means of repentance. • ***Rejecting the Son of God*** constitutes ***nailing him to the cross once again.*** Crucifixion was the ultimate instrument of rejection and humiliation in the Greco-Roman world and brought ***public shame.*** Those who turned away from Christ had in effect joined those who stood before the cross shouting insults, insisting that Jesus was not really the Messiah and Son of God but was instead worthy of shame (see Matt 27:39-44).

6:7-8 *ground:* Good, productive land is an image of blessing, contrasted with the curse of unproductive land that ***bears thorns and thistles.*** To ***burn*** such a field is an image of judgment (2 Sam 23:4-7; Isa 10:17; 33:12; Ezek 19:12-13; Matt 3:10).

6:9-12 Having confronted his readers with a stern warning (6:4-8), the author now softens that warning by greeting them as ***dear friends,*** expressing confidence in them, and giving them further encouragement.

6:9 *We are confident:* Skilled speakers and writers express confidence in those they address to motivate them (cp. Rom 15:14). • The author is confident that his hearers' lives give evidence of a true relationship with God, including ***salvation.*** In the NT, salvation primarily refers to Christ's work on the cross (5:9-10; see also note on 2:3); Hebrews places emphasis on the consummation of salvation at the end of the age (9:28).

6:10 *He will not forget how hard you*

6:8
Gen 3:17-18
6:10
Matt 10:40, 42
1 Thes 1:3
6:11
Heb 3:6; 10:22
6:12
Heb 10:36; 13:7
6:13
Gen 22:16
6:14
*Gen 22:17
6:15
Gen 21:1-5
6:16
Exod 22:11
6:18
Num 23:19
Titus 1:2
6:19
Heb 9:2-12
6:20
Ps 110:4

by caring for other believers, as you still
do. 11 Our great desire is that you will keep
on loving others as long as life lasts, in order to make certain that what you hope for
will come true. 12 Then you will not become
spiritually dull and indifferent. Instead, you
will follow the example of those who are
going to inherit God's promises because of
their faith and endurance.

God's Promises Bring Hope

13 For example, there was God's promise to
Abraham. Since there was no one greater to
swear by, God took an oath in his own name,
saying:

14 "I will certainly bless you,
and I will multiply your descendants
beyond number."

15 Then Abraham waited patiently, and he
received what God had promised.

16 Now when people take an oath, they
call on someone greater than themselves to
hold them to it. And without any question
that oath is binding. 17 God also bound himself with an oath, so that those who received
the promise could be perfectly sure that he
would never change his mind. 18 So God has
given both his promise and his oath. These
two things are unchangeable because it is
impossible for God to lie. Therefore, we
who have fled to him for refuge can have
great confidence as we hold to the hope that
lies before us. 19 This hope is a strong and
trustworthy anchor for our souls. It leads us
through the curtain into God's inner sanctuary. 20 Jesus has already gone in there for us.

Endurance (6:12)

Heb 12:1-10
Rom 5:3-4
1 Cor 4:12
2 Thes 1:4
Jas 1:2-4; 5:11
1 Pet 2:20

Hebrews was written for people who were experiencing great difficulties because of their Christian commitment, and they needed endurance—the ability to bear up patiently under difficult circumstances. Life is not easy under the best of circumstances, and commitment to Christ in a hostile world brings its own share of suffering.

The recipients of Hebrews were experiencing harassment, loss of property, and imprisonment, all of which they had suffered at some point in the past (10:32-34). Thus they needed to "hold firmly" to what they believed "without wavering" (4:14; 10:23) and to endure while anticipating the fulfillment of God's promises (6:12; 10:36). Like runners in a race, they needed to stay on the path of obedience. Like true children of a loving father, they were to receive the Lord's discipline in order to grow in holiness (12:1-10).

Hebrews joins a chorus of NT voices affirming that endurance in following Jesus is needed for effective ministry (1 Cor 4:12), to face hardship (2 Thes 1:4; 2 Tim 4:5; 1 Pet 2:20), and for growth toward maturity (Rom 5:3-4; Jas 1:2-4). God shows his compassion to those who endure (Jas 5:11).

have worked: In showing that they love God and his people, their works bear witness to their true relationship with God (Rom 2:6-7; 1 Cor 3:13-15; Jas 2:14-20). God remembers (Exod 2:24; 1 Chr 16:15; Ps 106:45) and acknowledges those who are truly his. • ***for other believers:*** Literally *for God's holy people.*

6:11 ***keep on loving others*** (literally *show the same eager commitment*): Love of other believers is a hallmark of genuine Christian faith (Jas 2:15-16; 1 Jn 3:16-20). Through diligence and focused commitment, they can ***make*** their ***hope*** in Christ absolutely ***certain.*** Assurance of salvation comes through perseverance.

6:12 A focused commitment (6:10-11) is the antidote to being ***spiritually dull*** (5:11-12). By loving God and others, we ***follow the example*** of great people of the faith. The author puts a great deal of emphasis on both ***faith and endurance*** as normal requirements for God's people (see 11:4-38).

6:13-20 This passage focuses on the reliability of God's faithfulness to his promises. The theme of God's oath is developed with an illustration (6:13-15), followed by a general principle (6:16), followed by the main point: God has sworn a significant oath (6:17-18), which gives us hope because it shows that Jesus is our permanent High Priest (6:19-20).

6:13-14 ***Abraham*** was the premier exemplar of faith: He continued to believe that God would give him a son, then was willing to sacrifice that son in obedience to God (11:17-19; Gen 15:1-5; 22:1-14). In response to Abraham's faith, ***God took an oath,*** assuring Abraham that he would ***bless*** him and ***multiply*** his ***descendants.***

6:14 This verse quotes Gen 22:17.

6:15 ***what God had promised:*** Through Isaac, God made Abraham into a great nation (Exod 1:7).

6:16 It is a general principle in human relationships that when ***people take an oath,*** the ***oath is binding.*** If in human contexts oaths give assurance that something is true, an oath from God ought to inspire much greater confidence (6:17-19). • ***someone greater than themselves:*** Cp. 6:13.

6:17-18 ***God also bound himself with an oath:*** See 7:20-22. God's oath makes it clear that ***he would never change his mind . . . because it is impossible for God to lie*** (see Ps 110:4). • We have ***fled to him for refuge,*** like those in the OT era who killed someone accidentally (Num 35:9-34; Deut 4:41-43); Christ is like a city of refuge, where believers escape God's wrath. Christ's followers, therefore, have ***great confidence.***

6:19-20 Christian ***hope is a strong and trustworthy anchor for our souls.*** In the first century, an anchor was an image of stability and safety. • ***through the curtain:*** A curtain separated the outer room of the sanctuary, into which only priests could go, from the inner room, the Most Holy Place (Exod 25:10-40). Only the high priest could go into the Most Holy Place,

He has become our eternal High Priest in
the order of Melchizedek.

Melchizedek Is Greater Than Abraham and the Levites

7 This Melchizedek was king of the city
of Salem and also a priest of God Most
High. When Abraham was returning home
after winning a great battle against the
kings, Melchizedek met him and blessed
him. 2Then Abraham took a tenth of all he
had captured in battle and gave it to Melchizedek. The name Melchizedek means
"king of justice," and king of Salem means
"king of peace." 3There is no record of his father or mother or any of his ancestors—no
beginning or end to his life. He remains a
priest forever, resembling the Son of God.
4Consider then how great this Melchizedek was. Even Abraham, the great patriarch
of Israel, recognized this by giving him a
tenth of what he had taken in battle. 5Now
the law of Moses required that the priests,
who are descendants of Levi, must collect
a tithe from the rest of the people of Israel,
who are also descendants of Abraham. 6But
Melchizedek, who was not a descendant of
Levi, collected a tenth from Abraham. And
Melchizedek placed a blessing upon Abraham, the one who had already received the
promises of God. 7And without question,
the person who has the power to give a blessing is greater than the one who is blessed.
8The priests who collect tithes are men
who die, so Melchizedek is greater than they
are, because we are told that he lives on. 9In
addition, we might even say that these Levites—the ones who collect the tithe—paid
a tithe to Melchizedek when their ancestor
Abraham paid a tithe to him. 10For although
Levi wasn't born yet, the seed from which
he came was in Abraham's body when Melchizedek collected the tithe from him.

Jesus, a Priest in the Line of Melchizedek

11So if the priesthood of Levi, on which the
law was based, could have achieved the perfection God intended, why did God need

7:1-2 Gen 14:17-20
7:3 Ps 110:4
7:4 Gen 14:20
7:5 Num 18:21, 26
7:6 Rom 4:13
7:7 Gen 14:19
7:8 Heb 5:6; 6:20
7:11 Ps 110:4; Heb 5:6; 7:17

and only once per year on the Day of Atonement (Exod 29:1-46; Lev 16:1-25). Because of Jesus' extraordinary high priesthood, he ***has already gone in there for us*** into the presence of God as ***our eternal High Priest,*** and he leads us in with him (10:19-23). • ***the order of Melchizedek:*** This phrase introduces the discussion in 7:1-28.

7:1-28 Chapter 7 develops the main topic introduced in 5:1-10: Jesus' appointment as a high priest in the order of Melchizedek.

7:1-10 This section proclaims the superiority of Melchizedek's priesthood over that of the Levites, based primarily on Gen 14:17-20.

7:1 ***king of . . . Salem:*** See Gen 14:18 and note. • ***also a priest of God Most High:*** Unlike the Hebrew kings, Melchizedek combined the offices of king and priest, thus foreshadowing the Messiah. • ***winning a great battle against the kings:*** See Gen 14:1-17.

7:2 Abraham was giving ***a tenth*** to the Lord by giving it to ***Melchizedek,*** his priest. This act anticipates the giving of tithes under the law (Lev 27:30, 32) and becomes a key point in the author's argument (7:4). • ***Melchi-*** (Hebrew *melek*) means ***king.*** • ***-zedek*** (Hebrew *tsedeq*) means ***justice*** or ***righteousness.*** • ***Salem*** (Hebrew *shalom*) means ***peace.*** It was common for rabbis to bring out the theological significance of a biblical figure's name by making associations between the name and other Hebrew terms.

7:3 That we have ***no record*** of Melchizedek's ***father or mother or any of his ancestors*** is significant in light of the ancestral requirement upon which the Levite priesthood was based. He appears from nowhere—it is as though there is ***no beginning or end to his life.*** The author is interpreting Gen 14:17-20 in light of Ps 110:4, which also understands Melchizedek as representing an eternal priesthood. • ***He remains a priest forever:*** This contrasts with a Levite, whose priesthood ended when he died (7:8, 23). • ***resembling the Son of God:*** Melchizedek was not an OT appearance of Jesus. Rather, his priesthood and that of Jesus had characteristics in common, in light of Ps 110:4.

7:4 The point of this section (7:1-10) is to have the readers ***consider . . . how great this Melchizedek was*** by comparing him to the descendants of Levi. Melchizedek was so great that ***Abraham*** gave him ***a tenth*** of the spoils of ***battle*** (Gen 14:20).

7:5-6a Collecting the ***tithe*** was a requirement and an honor for the ***priests*** under ***the law of Moses*** (Num 18:21-32). • ***from the rest of the people of Israel*** (literally *from their brothers*): The reference is to the people of Israel as a whole. • Although ***Melchizedek*** was ***not a descendant of Levi,*** he ***collected a tenth from Abraham,*** the ancestor of the Levites. This demonstrates Melchizedek's eminence over both Abraham and his descendants, including the priests (7:8-10).

7:6b-7 ***Melchizedek placed a blessing upon Abraham:*** Gen 14:19-20; this is an example of the kind of blessing that a superior would give a subordinate—e.g., a father would bless his son, and a priest would bless his people (Num 6:22-27; see "Blessing" at Gen 48:8-20, p. 113). The power to give a blessing demonstrates that Melchizedek ***is greater than*** Abraham.

7:8 Melchizedek's "immortality" (7:3) is one aspect of his superiority to the Levites: The Levites ***are men who die,*** but Melchizedek ***lives on.***

7:9-10 ***we might even say:*** The author recognizes that what he is about to say, that the ***Levites . . . paid a tithe to Melchizedek,*** is not literally true, since ***Levi wasn't born yet.*** Rather, Abraham represented all his descendants in paying his tithe to Melchizedek. Levi was united with Abraham because ***the seed from which he came was in Abraham's body.*** All the people issuing from Abraham were one with him. Thus, his act could be considered their act.

7:11-28 Having argued for Melchizedek's superiority to the Levites (7:1-10), the author now argues that Jesus, our high priest like Melchizedek, is also superior to the Levitical priests of the old covenant.

7:11 ***Perfection*** in Hebrews does not mean ***flawless,*** but ***reaching a desired goal*** (see note on 5:9). The priesthood under the old covenant could not achieve all that ***God intended*** for a covenant relationship with his people. That is why God needed ***to establish a different priesthood.*** • ***the order of Levi and Aaron:*** Literally *the order of Aaron.*

7:14
Gen 49:10
Isa 11:1
Matt 1:3; 2:6
Luke 3:33
Rom 1:3
Rev 5:5

7:17
*Ps 110:4
Heb 5:6; 6:20

7:18
Rom 8:3

7:19
Rom 3:20
Heb 9:9; 10:19-22
[j]*elpis* (1680)
‣1 Pet 1:3

7:21
*Ps 110:4
Heb 5:6; 6:20; 7:17

7:22
Heb 8:6; 12:24
[k]*diathēkē* (1242)
‣Heb 8:6

7:24
Isa 9:6-7
Rev 1:18

7:25
Rom 8:34
1 Jn 2:1

7:26
2 Cor 5:21
Heb 4:14
[a]*archiereus* (0749)
‣Heb 8:1

7:27
Lev 9:7; 16:6, 11, 15
Eph 5:2
Heb 9:12

7:28
Heb 2:10; 5:1-2

to establish a different priesthood, with a
priest in the order of Melchizedek instead
of the order of Levi and Aaron?
[12]And if the priesthood is changed, the
law must also be changed to permit it. [13]For
the priest we are talking about belongs to a
different tribe, whose members have never
served at the altar as priests. [14]What I mean
is, our Lord came from the tribe of Judah,
and Moses never mentioned priests coming
from that tribe.
[15]This change has been made very clear
since a different priest, who is like Melchizedek, has appeared. [16]Jesus became a priest,
not by meeting the physical requirement
of belonging to the tribe of Levi, but by the
power of a life that cannot be destroyed.
[17]And the psalmist pointed this out when
he prophesied,

"You are a priest forever in the order of
Melchizedek."

[18]Yes, the old requirement about the priesthood was set aside because it was weak and
useless. [19]For the law never made anything
perfect. But now we have confidence in a
better [j]hope, through which we draw near
to God.
[20]This new system was established with a
solemn oath. Aaron's descendants became
priests without such an oath, [21]but there
was an oath regarding Jesus. For God said
to him,

"The LORD has taken an oath and will not
break his vow:
'You are a priest forever.' "

[22]Because of this oath, Jesus is the one who
guarantees this better [k]covenant with God.
[23]There were many priests under the
old system, for death prevented them from
remaining in office. [24]But because Jesus
lives forever, his priesthood lasts forever.
[25]Therefore he is able, once and forever, to
save those who come to God through him.
He lives forever to intercede with God on
their behalf.
[26]He is the kind of [a]high priest we need
because he is holy and blameless, unstained
by sin. He has been set apart from sinners
and has been given the highest place of
honor in heaven. [27]Unlike those other high
priests, he does not need to offer sacrifices
every day. They did this for their own sins
first and then for the sins of the people. But
Jesus did this once for all when he offered
himself as the sacrifice for the people's sins.
[28]The law appointed high priests who were
limited by human weakness. But after the
law was given, God appointed his Son with

7:12 According to the law given to Moses, the appointed priests were descendants of Aaron (Exod 28:41-43; 29:9). The ***priesthood is changed*** because Jesus is now the High Priest. Thus, God himself had *changed* the *law* concerning priests.

7:13-14 Jesus ***belongs to a different tribe:*** Under the old covenant, priests came from the tribe of Levi, whereas Jesus was from ***the tribe of Judah.***

7:15-17 ***This change*** of how God appoints priests (7:11-14) has been made ***very clear*** by the appointment of Jesus as a ***different priest.*** He, ***like Melchizedek,*** is ***a priest forever:*** Jesus' resurrection from the dead shows that he has ***the power of a life that cannot be destroyed.*** Because his priesthood ***in the order of Melchizedek*** is superior to that of the Levites (7:1-10), he supersedes them as priest.

7:17 This verse quotes Ps 110:4.

7:18 ***The old requirement about the priesthood*** was membership in the family of Aaron (see Exod 28:41-43). • ***set aside:*** See 7:15-17. • ***because it was weak and useless:*** As explained in the verses that follow (7:19-28).

7:19-28 The weakness of the priesthood under the old covenant is highlighted in that those priests died (thus discontinuing their office) and were themselves sinful. In contrast, Jesus, the new High Priest, never sinned and will never die, making him a more effective and permanent High Priest.

7:19 ***the law never made anything perfect:*** The law never accomplished what God planned to accomplish through the superior high priesthood of Jesus—namely, completely removing sin and guaranteeing eternal salvation. This gives believers ***confidence in a better hope*** in relationship with God. We can ***draw near to God*** without fearing condemnation.

7:20-21 ***This new system*** refers to God's way of appointing a priest. • God's ***solemn oath*** is expressed in the quote from Ps 110:4.

7:22 Legally, ***the one who guarantees*** (literally *the guarantee* or *the guarantor*) refers to the person who bears the risk of another person's investment or debt. Because of God's ***oath,*** Jesus' priesthood is unassailable, so our ***covenant*** relationship ***with God*** is secure. Having Jesus as the guarantor makes the new covenant ***better.***

7:23-24 Of necessity, the old covenant had a succession of ***many priests*** because each of them died. In contrast, Jesus' ***priesthood lasts forever*** (literally *is permanent*): This term refers to something that cannot be changed, such as the sun's daily trek through the sky or the constant turning of the seasons.

7:25 ***able, once and forever, to save*** (or *able to save completely*): Since Jesus ***lives forever,*** the salvation he brings also lasts forever. To draw near to an eternal God, we need an eternal priest. • Jesus will ***intercede*** or ***appeal*** to God for us as our High Priest of the new covenant, and his intercession is never-ending (see 9:11-28; 10:21-22; Rom 8:31-34).

7:26-27 Jesus is ***unstained by sin*** and ***set apart from sinners*** (cp. 4:15), which makes him superior to the priests of the old covenant, who had to deal with ***their own sins*** as well as those ***of the people*** (see also 5:1-3). • ***has been given the highest place of honor in heaven*** (or *has been exalted higher than the heavens*): This is an affirmation of his uniqueness as High Priest (cp. 2:9; 5:9; Phil 2:5-11). • ***once for all:*** This does not mean *once for all people* but rather *once, never to be repeated.*

7:28 This verse echoes 5:1-3 and sums up the entire discussion of Christ's appointment as High Priest (5:1-10; 7:1-28). • ***Limited by human weakness*** refers primarily to human sinfulness and mortality (5:2-3; 7:18, 23-27). • ***God appointed his Son with an oath:*** See

an oath, and his Son has been made the perfect High Priest forever.

Christ's New Covenant Offering (8:1–10:18)
The Superior Ministry of Our High Priest

8 Here is the main point: We have a
[b]High Priest who sat down in the place
of honor beside the throne of the majestic
God in heaven. 2 There he [c]ministers in the
heavenly Tabernacle, the true place of worship that was built by the Lord and not by
human hands.
3 And since every high priest is required
to offer gifts and sacrifices, our High Priest
must make an offering, too. 4 If he were here
on earth, he would not even be a priest, since
there already are priests who offer the gifts
required by the law. 5 They serve in a system
of worship that is only a copy, a shadow of
the real one in heaven. For when Moses was
getting ready to build the Tabernacle, God
gave him this warning: "Be sure that you
make everything according to the [d]pattern I
have shown you here on the mountain."
6 But now Jesus, our High Priest, has been
given a [e]ministry that is far superior to the
old priesthood, for he is the one who mediates for us a far better [f]covenant with God,
based on better promises.
7 If the first covenant had been faultless,
there would have been no need for a second
covenant to replace it. 8 But when God found
fault with the people, he said:

"The day is coming, says the LORD,
when I will make a new covenant
with the people of Israel and Judah.
9 This covenant will not be like the one
I made with their ancestors
when I took them by the hand
and led them out of the land of Egypt.
They did not remain faithful to my
covenant,
so I turned my back on them, says the
LORD.
10 But this is the new covenant I will make
with the people of Israel on that day,
says the LORD:
I will put my laws in their minds,
and I will write them on their hearts.
I will be their God,
and they will be my people.

8:1
Heb 1:3; 2:17; 4:14; 6:20; 7:26; 9:11
[b]*archiereus* (0749)
‣Heb 9:11

8:2
Heb 9:11
[c]*leitourgos* (3011)
‣Heb 8:6

8:3
Heb 5:1

8:5
*Exod 25:40; 26:30
Col 2:17
Heb 9:23
[d]*tupos* (5179)
‣1 Pet 5:3

8:6
Heb 7:22; 9:15; 12:24
[e]*leitourgia* (3009)
‣Heb 9:21
[f]*diathēkē* (1242)
‣Heb 9:15

8:7
Heb 7:11

8:8-12
*Jer 31:31-34

8:10
Heb 10:16

Ps 110:4, the key OT passage behind 7:11-28. • *perfect . . . forever:* The words ***High Priest*** are not in the Greek text but are implied in the context. • In Hebrews, the term *perfect* means *complete* or *mature* (see 2:10; 5:9; 7:11; 9:9-11); the Son, through his sacrificial death and resurrection, has become completely qualified to serve as our eternal High Priest, and his priesthood lasts *forever.*

8:1–10:18 This passage on Jesus' superior offering argues that his ministry as the heavenly High Priest is superior to that of earthly priests.

8:1-2 The first two verses of ch 8 transition from the discussion just completed and anticipate the discussion to come. • ***Here is the main point:*** The author is referring back to the appointment of Jesus as a superior High Priest (5:1-10; 7:1-28). • ***he ministers in the heavenly Tabernacle*** (or *tent;* also in 8:5): This anticipates the theme of Jesus' superior offering that is covered in the rest of this section (8:3–10:18). Unlike the Levitical priests who served in an earthly tent or building, Jesus' sacrifice is superior because he serves in ***the true place of worship,*** the very presence of God in heaven (8:5; 9:11, 24; 10:12).

8:3 ***every high priest is required to offer gifts and sacrifices:*** Making offerings is a general requirement of priests, so Jesus also had to offer a sacrifice. • This verse reiterates what is stated in the first verse of the previous discussion (5:1), indicating another major movement in the book.

8:4 ***If he were here on earth:*** Under the old order Jesus ***would not even be a priest,*** as previously discussed (see 7:13-14). But Jesus is in heaven, which makes his priestly service distinct from and superior to that of the priests of the old covenant (8:5; 9:11, 24; 10:12).

8:5 ***a copy, a shadow:*** The earthly place of worship was an imitation that pointed to ***the real one in heaven.*** That is why ***God*** warned ***Moses*** to make it ***according to the pattern*** (see Exod 25:40; 26:30; cp. Acts 7:44). Judaism and early Christianity both spoke of a heavenly Temple within a heavenly Jerusalem, which would come down to earth at the end of the age (see Rev 21:2). Hebrews suggests that this heavenly place of worship was shown to Moses so he would know how to build the earthly Tabernacle. It is the heavenly Temple, however, in which Jesus ministers as High Priest.

8:6 ***the one who mediates:*** A mediator works with two parties to bring them to agreement. Christ's work of sacrifice established the ***covenant*** relationship between people and God. • ***a far better covenant with God:*** See "The New Covenant," facing page. This covenant is better because it is ***based on better promises*** (see 8:7-13).

8:7-13 The author quotes Jer 31:31-34, an OT prophecy concerning the new covenant that includes a number of striking promises. Establishing the superiority of the new covenant lays a foundation for the argument in 9:1–10:18 that the Son's offering under the new covenant was superior to the offerings of the old covenant.

8:7 The ***first covenant,*** made at Sinai, was not ***faultless.*** It was not the end of God's plan, because it didn't solve human weaknesses (see 7:11-28; 8:9).

8:8 ***found fault with the people:*** Because the people were unable to keep the terms of the old covenant (see note on 8:7), God made a ***new covenant.***

8:9 God ***made*** a covenant ***with their ancestors*** at Sinai (Exod 19:1-8; 24:7-8; 34:27-28; Deut 4:13). • ***I took them by the hand:*** In rescuing his people from ***the land of Egypt,*** God ***led them*** as a parent might lead a child that could not fend for itself (see Exod 12–14). • ***They did not remain faithful:*** See 3:7-19; Num 14:1-38; Deut 9; Ps 106. • ***so I turned my back on them:*** The covenant warned that if the people turned away, God would turn away from them (see Deut 28:15-68; 30:11-20; 1 Kgs 8:22-53; 2 Chr 6:12-42).

8:10 Under the old covenant, the people were commanded to take the words of the law to heart (Deut 32:46), and the kings of Israel and Judah were judged on whether or not they followed the law of God wholeheartedly (2 Kgs 10:31; 2 Chr 31:21). A difference in the ***new covenant*** is that God's ***laws*** would be in people's ***minds*** and ***on their hearts.*** People would have renewed hearts and minds, with God's law as an intrinsic, internal motivation. • ***on that day:*** Literally *after those days.*

8:11 John 6:45
8:12 Heb 10:17
8:13 Heb 12:24
9:1 Exod 25:8
9:2 Exod 25:23-40; 26:1-30 Lev 24:5
9:3 Exod 26:31-33
9:4 Exod 16:33; 25:10-16; 30:1-6 Num 17:8-10 Deut 10:3-5

11 And they will not need to teach their
neighbors,
nor will they need to teach their
relatives,
saying, 'You should know the LORD.'
For everyone, from the least to the
greatest,
will know me already.
12 And I will forgive their wickedness,
and I will never again remember their
sins."

13When God speaks of a "new" covenant, it means he has made the first one obsolete. It is now out of date and will soon disappear.

Old Covenant Worship

9 That first covenant between God and Israel had regulations for worship and a place of worship here on earth.
2There were two rooms in that Tabernacle. In the first room were a lampstand, a table, and sacred loaves of bread on the table. This room was called the Holy Place.
3Then there was a curtain, and behind the curtain was the second room called the Most Holy Place.
4In that room were a gold incense altar and a wooden chest called the Ark of the Covenant, which was covered with gold on all sides. Inside the Ark were a gold jar containing manna, Aaron's staff that sprouted leaves, and the

The New Covenant (8:7-13)

Heb 7:22; 8:6; 12:24 Jer 31:31-34 Ezek 37:1-14 Matt 5:17-20; 26:27-28 2 Cor 3:1-18

A covenant is a binding agreement and relationship between two parties. God is a covenant-making God; he forms agreements and relationships with people. God made a covenant with Noah and his family (Gen 6:18; 9:9), and later with all the creatures of the earth (Gen 9:11-17). God covenanted with Abraham to give him and his descendants the land of Canaan and to multiply those descendants greatly (Gen 15:18; 17:2-21). God reiterated and expanded this covenant at Mount Sinai with the whole nation of Israel (Exod 19–20), promising to be their God and challenging them to be obedient to him. This covenant was often broken, with the people failing to live up to their obligations (see Exod 32; Jer 11:10; 34:18; Mal 2:8). God also made a covenant with David that his descendants would be established forever as kings (2 Sam 7:9-16).

The OT also speaks of a new covenant to be established with God's people (Jer 31:31-34), a covenant in which the people would all know God, would have the law of God internalized by receiving God's Spirit (Ezek 37:1-14; 2 Cor 3:1-18), and would be decisively forgiven for their sins (8:7-12). With his sacrificial death, Jesus established this new covenant between God and those who respond in faith. He is the guarantor and mediator of this covenant, established by indisputable promises of God (7:22; 8:6; 12:24). God has called us to a covenant relationship with himself, a meaningful agreement in which we know God, have his laws written on our hearts, and have our sins decisively forgiven by the sacrifice of Christ.

8:11 ***their relatives:*** Literally *their brother.* • All those in the new covenant ***know the LORD;*** intimate personal relationship with the Lord is in the very nature of the new covenant.

8:12 A final characteristic of the new covenant is that God would ***forgive their wickedness*** and ***never again remember their sins.*** The blood of Jesus cleanses his people completely from sin (9:13-15; 10:14-18, 22; 1 Jn 1:7).

8:13 The word *new* in ***"new" covenant*** emphasizes that, once God had enacted this covenant, the Sinai covenant was considered *old* or ***obsolete,*** and was thus *out of date.* Its time of usefulness was over and its termination was imminent.

9:1–10:18 This section argues that Christ's death, the sacrifice in the new covenant, is superior to the sacrifices in the old covenant. In 9:1-10, the author describes aspects of worship under the ***regulations*** of the old covenant (see Exod 28–29; Lev 1–10; 16–17). In 9:11–10:18, these regulations are contrasted with Christ's superior offering.

9:1-5 These verses describe the ***Tabernacle***, Israel's ***place of worship*** before the Temple was constructed.

9:2 Israel's ***Tabernacle*** (or *tent;* also in 9:11, 21) was a tent with ***two rooms*** (see Exod 25–31, 35–40). • ***a lampstand:*** Exod 25:31-40; 26:35. • ***a table:*** Exod 25:23-30. • The priests went into the ***Holy Place*** daily in their ritual duties (9:6; see Exod 28:43; Num 28:3-8).

9:3 At the back of the first room of the Tabernacle was a ***curtain*** that separated the first room from the ***second room*** (literally *second tent*) ***called the Most Holy Place*** (Exod 26:31-33). This curtain was a sacred barrier: Only the high priest could go behind it into the Most Holy Place, and only once a year on the Day of Atonement (9:7; see Exod 30:6, 10; Lev 16:2-34; 23:27-32).

9:4 The ***gold incense altar*** probably stood just outside the inner curtain (Exod 30:1-10); its location is ambiguous at points in the OT, but it was closely associated with the Most Holy Place (Exod 30:6; Lev 16:13; 1 Kgs 6:22). • Since it represented the presence of God, the ***Ark of the Covenant*** was the most important item in the Tabernacle (see Exod 25:10-22). • The ***gold jar containing manna*** was a reminder of God's provision in the wilderness (Exod 16:32-34). • ***Aaron's staff that sprouted leaves*** (see Num 17:1-11) was a reminder not to rebel against God's chosen leaders (Num 17:10; cp. Heb 13:17). • The ***stone tablets of the covenant*** held the Ten Commandments and were to remind the people of the terms by which they were to live out the covenant (Exod 25:16; 31:18; Deut 9:9–10:5).

stone tablets of the covenant. [5]Above the Ark were the cherubim of divine glory, whose wings stretched out over the Ark's [g]cover, the place of atonement. But we cannot explain these things in detail now.

[6]When these things were all in place, the priests regularly entered the first room as they performed their religious duties. [7]But only the high priest ever entered the Most Holy Place, and only once a year. And he always offered blood for his own sins and for the sins the people had committed in ignorance. [8]By these regulations the Holy Spirit revealed that the entrance to the Most Holy Place was not freely open as long as the Tabernacle and the system it represented were still in use.

[9]This is an [h]illustration pointing to the present time. For the gifts and sacrifices that the priests offer are not able to cleanse the consciences of the people who bring them. [10]For that old system deals only with food and drink and various cleansing ceremonies—physical regulations that were in effect only until a better system could be established.

Christ Is the Perfect Sacrifice

[11]So Christ has now become the [i]High Priest over all the good things that have come. He has entered that greater, more perfect Tabernacle in heaven, which was not made by human hands and is not part of this created world. [12]With his own blood—not the blood of goats and calves—he entered the Most Holy Place once for all time and secured our redemption forever.

[13]Under the old system, the blood of goats and bulls and the ashes of a young cow could cleanse people's bodies from ceremonial impurity. [14]Just think how much more the blood of Christ will purify our consciences from sinful deeds so that we can worship the living God. For by the power of the eternal Spirit, Christ offered himself to God as a perfect sacrifice for our sins. [15]That is why he is the one who mediates a new [j]covenant between God and people, so that all who are called can receive the eternal inheritance God has promised them. For Christ died to [k]set them free from the penalty of the sins they had committed under that first [j]covenant.

9:5 Exod 25:17-22
[g]*hilastērion* (2435) ▸1 Jn 2:2

9:6 Num 18:2-6

9:7 Exod 30:10
Lev 16:2, 14-15
Heb 5:2-3

9:8 John 14:6
Heb 10:19-20

9:9 Heb 5:1; 10:1-2
[h]*parabolē* (3850) ▸Matt 13:3

9:10 Lev 11:2, 25; 15:8
Num 6:3; 19:13

9:11 Heb 8:2; 10:1
[i]*archiereus* (0749) ▸Heb 13:11

9:12 Heb 7:27

9:13 Lev 16:3, 14-15
Num 19:9, 17

9:14 Heb 6:1
1 Pet 3:18
1 Jn 1:7

9:15 1 Tim 2:5
Heb 7:22
[j]*diathēkē* (1242) ▸Heb 12:24
[k]*apolutrōsis* (0629) ▸Heb 11:35

9:5 ***The cherubim of divine glory*** were statues of angels formed into the Ark's cover. This category of angels is especially associated with God's glorious presence (Gen 3:24; Ps 80:1; 99:1; Isa 37:16). The ***Ark's cover*** itself was ***the place of atonement,*** on which the blood from the Day of Atonement sacrifice was to be sprinkled (Lev 16:14-16). • ***But we cannot explain these things in detail now:*** The main focus of the discussion is the offering of sacrifices under the old covenant (9:6-10).

9:6-8 The worship practices in the Holy Place, the ***first room*** (literally *first tent*) of the Tabernacle (9:2), were the duty of the priests, who kept the lamps lit and the sacred loaves of bread replenished (Exod 27:20-21; Lev 24:8).

9:7 The yearly duty was carried out on the Day of Atonement, when ***the high priest*** offered sacrifices for ***the sins*** not covered by other sacrifices during the previous year (Lev 16:1-25).

9:8 ***was not freely open:*** Free entrance into the presence of God was not available to all of the people under the old covenant system. • The outer room of ***the Tabernacle*** (or *the first room;* literally *the first tent;* see 9:2), which served as a sacred barrier keeping the people from the presence of God in ***the Most Holy Place,*** was symbolic of the whole system. Under that system, people were kept out of God's presence rather than led into it.

9:9 ***This is an illustration:*** The problem with ***the gifts and sacrifices*** of the old covenant is that they were ***not able to cleanse the consciences of the people***—they could not remove people's guilt before a holy God (cp. 9:14; 10:2, 22; 13:18).

9:10 The ***old system*** dealt only with ***physical regulations,*** but it could not deal with the condition of the heart (8:10; 10:21-24). Consequently, it was provisional, only intended to last until Christ could come and establish a ***better system*** (9:11–10:18).

9:11–10:18 The author now contrasts the old system (9:1-10) with the superior sacrifice made by Christ as High Priest: The blood of Christ's offering was his own blood, not the blood of animals (9:13-22; cp. 9:7); Christ's offering was made in the heavenly Tabernacle, not the earthly one (9:23-24; cp. 9:1-5); and Christ's offering, rather than being made continually, was made just one time (9:25–10:18; cp. 7:27; 9:6-7).

9:11 ***Christ has now become the High Priest over all the good things*** of the new covenant. He was appointed by God in accord with Ps 110:4 (5:1-10; 7:1-28) and offered a superior offering. • ***that have come:*** Some manuscripts read *that are about to come,* either from the perspective of the old covenant era or looking forward to the culmination of God's plan in the future. • Christ's sacrifice is superior because of where it was made: in ***that greater, more perfect Tabernacle in heaven*** rather than the earthly Tabernacle (see 8:5 and note).

9:12 Christ's offering is superior because it was made ***with his own blood*** rather than ***the blood of goats and calves*** (e.g., cp. Lev 16:3-5). • Christ's offering is superior because ***he entered the Most Holy Place once for all time.*** Unlike the sacrifices in the old covenant, which had to be made year after year (10:1), Jesus' sacrificial death only had to be made once and was decisive in securing ***our redemption forever.***

9:13 The ***ashes of a young cow*** were used with water to ***cleanse people's bodies from ceremonial impurity*** (see Num 19:1-22).

9:14 ***how much more:*** This is an argument from lesser to greater; the logic is that if something is true in a lesser situation, it will be even more true in a greater situation (see also 2:1-4; 12:25-29). If the blood of animals had some effect in cleansing, the blood of Christ will be much more effective. • ***will purify our consciences:*** Christ's sacrifice, unlike the sacrifices of the old covenant, removes the paralyzing guilt that keeps us from God by decisively cleansing us ***from sinful deeds*** (literally *from dead works*).

9:15 ***the one who mediates:*** This term refers to an arbiter in a difficult legal dispute or political disagreement. In the old covenant, Moses and the angels were understood as mediators between God and the people (Gal 3:19-20). In the ***new covenant,*** Christ ***mediates*** the relationship between ***God and people*** by his sacrificial death (8:6; 12:24; Rom 6:23; 1 Tim 2:5; 1 Pet 3:18) and ongoing intercession (7:25).

9:18-19 Exod 24:6-8 Lev 14:4 Num 19:6
9:20 *Exod 24:8 Matt 26:28
9:21 Lev 8:15, 19 [a]*leitourgia* (3009) ‣ Luke 1:23
9:22 Lev 17:11
9:23 Heb 8:5
9:24 Rom 8:34 Heb 8:2; 9:12 1 Jn 2:1
9:25 Heb 9:7; 10:19
9:26 1 Cor 10:11 Heb 7:27 1 Pet 3:18 [b]*hamartia* (0266) ‣ Heb 12:1
9:27 Gen 3:19
9:28 Isa 53:12 Phil 3:20 Heb 7:27 1 Pet 2:24
10:1 Col 2:17 Heb 7:19; 8:5; 9:11

16 Now when someone leaves a will, it is
necessary to prove that the person who
made it is dead. 17 The will goes into effect
only after the person's death. While the person who made it is still alive, the will cannot
be put into effect.

18 That is why even the first covenant
was put into effect with the blood of an
animal. 19 For after Moses had read each
of God's commandments to all the people,
he took the blood of calves and goats, along
with water, and sprinkled both the book of
God's law and all the people, using hyssop
branches and scarlet wool. 20 Then he said,
"This blood confirms the covenant God has
made with you." 21 And in the same way,
he sprinkled blood on the Tabernacle and
on everything used for [a]worship. 22 In fact,
according to the law of Moses, nearly everything was purified with blood. For without
the shedding of blood, there is no forgiveness.

23 That is why the Tabernacle and everything in it, which were copies of things in
heaven, had to be purified by the blood of
animals. But the real things in heaven had
to be purified with far better sacrifices
than the blood of animals.

24 For Christ did not enter into a holy
place made with human hands, which was
only a copy of the true one in heaven. He
entered into heaven itself to appear now
before God on our behalf. 25 And he did
not enter heaven to offer himself again and
again, like the high priest here on earth
who enters the Most Holy Place year after
year with the blood of an animal. 26 If that
had been necessary, Christ would have had
to die again and again, ever since the world
began. But now, once for all time, he has appeared at the end of the age to remove [b]sin
by his own death as a sacrifice.

27 And just as each person is destined to
die once and after that comes judgment,
28 so also Christ died once for all time as a
sacrifice to take away the sins of many people. He will come again, not to deal with our
sins, but to bring salvation to all who are eagerly waiting for him.

Christ's Sacrifice Once for All

10 The old system under the law of
Moses was only a shadow, a dim preview of the good things to come, not the
good things themselves. The sacrifices under that system were repeated again and

9:16-22 The author gives a general principle about the nature of wills or covenants (9:16-17), which he then expounds in light of the inauguration of the first covenant (9:18-22).

9:16 ***a will:*** Or *a covenant;* also in 9:17; see also 8:6, 8, 9, 10; 9:4, 15, 20; 10:16. • This verse could also be translated *Now when someone makes a covenant, it is necessary to ratify it with the death of a sacrifice.*

9:18-19 ***was put into effect:*** Exodus 24:3-8 records Moses' inauguration of the old covenant with the blood of the sacrifice. • Some manuscripts do not include ***and goats.*** • Hebrews alone among ancient sources states that Moses sprinkled ***the book of God's law*** (cp. Exod 24:6-8). • ***Hyssop branches*** have blue flowers and strongly aromatic leaves; they were used with sacrifices for cleansing (Exod 12:22; Lev 14:4; Num 19:6, 18).

9:20 ***"This blood confirms the covenant God has made with you"*** (Exod 24:8): Jesus used similar language at the Lord's Supper, referring to his own death (Matt 26:28; Mark 14:24; 1 Cor 11:25).

9:21 ***he sprinkled blood:*** See Exod 24:3-8; Lev 16:14-19.

9:22 Many of the rituals of cleansing in ***the law of Moses*** involved the death of a sacrificial animal; ***blood*** was involved both in the rites of cleansing (see Exod 29:12; 30:10; Lev 4:6, 17; 16:14-19; Num 19:4) and in making atonement (see "Atonement" at Lev 16:1-34, p. 223). The ***shedding*** of Christ's blood established the new covenant, providing permanent purification and complete ***forgiveness*** of sins (8:12; 10:15-18; Matt 26:28; Eph 1:7).

9:23 This verse argues from lesser to greater (see note on 9:14). Just as ***heaven*** is greater than the earthly ***Tabernacle***, so Christ's sacrifice ***had to be . . . far better*** than the earthly sacrifices. • ***That is why:*** See 9:16-22; Lev 16:14-19. • ***copies of things in heaven:*** See note on 8:5. • ***in heaven, had to be purified:*** Just as the Tabernacle had to be cleansed because of the sin of the Israelites (Lev 16:16-19), the heavenly Tabernacle required that the uncleanness be removed from those who would enter heaven under the new covenant.

9:24 Under the new covenant, ***Christ*** did not offer his sacrifice in the earthly Tabernacle. Rather, he ***entered into*** the very presence of God in ***heaven*** to act ***on our behalf.*** His sacrifice makes him a much better mediator to bring us into a right relationship with God (2 Cor 5:19-21).

9:25-26 Under the old covenant, the sacrifice on the Day of Atonement had to be made ***again and again*** (Lev 16:29-34). Christ's superior sacrifice was made ***once for all time.***

9:26 ***If that had been necessary:*** The author makes an argument using *reductio ad absurdum* (reduction to absurdity), logically showing that Christ's one-time sacrifice must be permanently effective. Since Christ himself is the ***sacrifice*** as well as the high priest, if his offering were made every year as with the earthly high priests, he would have to ***die again and again.*** But of course this is absurd; so, clearly, Christ died ***once for all time . . . to remove sin.*** • ***the age:*** Literally *the ages.*

9:27-28 ***each person is destined to die once:*** It is a necessary consequence of Christ's humanity that he ***died once.*** • Christ's first coming was to ***take away the sins of many people.*** When ***he will come again,*** it will not be to deal with sins, since that has already been accomplished. Instead, he will ***bring salvation to all who are eagerly waiting for him*** (see note on Gal 5:5).

10:1 ***The old system under the law of Moses*** (literally *The law*), like the Tabernacle itself (8:5), ***was only a shadow, a dim preview*** of a greater reality—namely, ***the good things*** that Christ inaugurated in the new covenant. Under the old covenant, ***sacrifices*** had to be ***repeated again and again*** because they were not able to cleanse worshipers permanently or in such a way that they could come into the presence of God perpetually.

again, year after year, but they were never
able to provide perfect cleansing for those
who came to worship. 2If they could have
provided perfect cleansing, the sacrifices
would have stopped, for the worshipers
would have been purified once for all time,
and their feelings of guilt would have disappeared.
3But instead, those sacrifices actually reminded them of their sins year after year.
4For it is not possible for the blood of bulls
and goats to take away sins. 5That is why,
when Christ came into the world, he said to
God,

"You did not want animal sacrifices or
sin offerings.
But you have given me a body to offer.
6 You were not pleased with burnt
offerings
or other offerings for sin.
7 Then I said, 'Look, I have come to do your
will, O God—
as is written about me in the
Scriptures.' "

8First, Christ said, "You did not want animal
sacrifices or sin offerings or burnt offerings or other offerings for sin, nor were
you pleased with them" (though they are required by the law of Moses). 9Then he said,
"Look, I have come to do your will." He cancels the first covenant in order to put the
second into effect. 10For God's will was for
us to be made holy by the sacrifice of the
body of Jesus Christ, once for all time.
11Under the old covenant, the priest
stands and ministers before the altar day
after day, offering the same sacrifices again
and again, which can never take away sins.
12But our High Priest offered himself to
God as a single sacrifice for sins, good for
all time. Then he sat down in the place of
honor at God's right hand. 13There he waits
until his enemies are humbled and made a
footstool under his feet. 14For by that one
offering he forever made perfect those who
are being made holy.
15And the Holy Spirit also testifies that
this is so. For he says,

16 "This is the new covenant I will make
with my people on that day, says the
LORD:
I will put my laws in their hearts,
and I will write them on their
minds."

17Then he says,

"I will never again remember
their sins and lawless deeds."

18And when sins have been forgiven, there
is no need to offer any more sacrifices.

10:3 Lev 16:34; Heb 9:7
10:4 Lev 16:15, 21; Heb 9:13
10:5-7 *Ps 40:6-8
10:8 *Ps 40:6
10:10 Eph 5:2; Heb 7:27; 9:12, 28; 1 Pet 2:24
10:11 Heb 5:1
10:12 Ps 110:1; Matt 22:44; Col 3:1; Heb 1:3
10:13 Ps 110:1
10:15 Heb 3:7
10:16-17 *Jer 31:33-34

10:2 The perpetual nature of the sacrifices demonstrates their inadequacy. ***If*** the sacrifices of the old covenant had offered true, lasting purity, they ***would have stopped.*** • ***their feelings of guilt would have disappeared:*** Cp. 9:9, 14; 10:22; 13:18.

10:3 ***Instead*** of removing guilt, the ongoing sacrifices ***actually reminded*** those who wished to come near to God, ***year after year,*** that they were guilty before God.

10:4 The ***blood of bulls and goats*** in the sacrifices of the old covenant offered a degree of cleansing (9:13, 23), but that cleansing was limited in that it could not ***take away sins.*** It could not eradicate sin in a way that would offer permanent cleansing and peace with God (see Acts 10:36; Rom 5:1; 11:26-27).

10:5-7 These verses quote Ps 40:6-8 (Greek version). Psalm 40:1-11 is a hymn of praise to God in which the psalmist confesses his desire to do God's will. The author of Hebrews understands ***Christ*** (literally *he;* also in 10:8) to be the speaker.

10:5 ***But you have given me a body to offer:*** God had prepared the psalmist to be obedient, ready to do God's will; Hebrews now applies this idea to Christ. For Hebrews, the preparation of a human *body*, specifically Christ's body, shows that God would use it as a superior sacrifice.

10:8-10 The author follows the flow of thought in the psalm with great precision. • ***First, Christ said, "You did not want animal sacrifices . . .":*** The author of Hebrews understands this as God's rejection of the old system of sacrifices. • ***Then he said, "Look, I have come to do your will":*** The author of Hebrews takes this to be Christ's willingness to be the supreme sacrifice for sins. • The author of Hebrews concludes that because of Christ's sacrifice, God has canceled the first covenant—***God's will,*** as shown by Ps 40:6-8, was that Christ would die for sins as a ***sacrifice,*** and this only had to be done ***once for all time.***

10:11-14 Christ's superior offering was decisive, in contrast with the sacrifices made by the priests of the old covenant.

10:11 ***the priest stands:*** See Deut 18:5. • ***day after day:*** E.g., 2 Chr 13:11.

10:12-13 Christ's sacrifice contrasts with that of the earthly high priests in that he ***offered himself to God as a . . . sacrifice,*** rather than offering animal sacrifices. • After the sacrifice was accomplished, ***he sat down in the place of honor*** (see Ps 110:1). Instead of standing daily like the priests of the old covenant (10:11), ***he waits until his enemies are humbled and made a footstool under his feet*** (Ps 110:1).

10:14 ***made perfect:*** See notes on 7:11, 28. • ***those who are being made holy:*** What the author has in mind is complete purification from sins.

10:15-17 The author again quotes from Jer 31:33-34 (see 8:7-12) to support the statement in 10:14, that Christ's one offering under the new covenant has made worshipers perfect forever. • ***on that day:*** Literally *after those days.* • God's ***laws*** have now been placed ***in their hearts*** and ***on their minds.*** This has internalized believers' relationship with God. • ***I will never again remember their sins and lawless deeds:*** As the author has shown (9:11–10:14), the superior sacrifice of Christ has made this new covenant reality possible.

10:18 The logical conclusion ***when sins have been forgiven***—that is, when sins have been taken away completely and permanently (10:1-4, 11)—is that ***there is no need to offer any more sacrifices.*** Thus, the superior sacrifice of Christ has made the entire sacrificial system of the old covenant obsolete.

10:19 Eph 3:12; Heb 4:16; 9:25
10:20 John 4:10, 14; Heb 6:19; 9:8
10:21 Heb 2:17; 3:6
10:22 Ezek 36:25; Eph 5:26
10:23 1 Cor 1:9; 10:13; Heb 3:6
10:25 Acts 2:42; Heb 3:13
10:26 Heb 6:4-8; 2 Pet 2:20
10:27 Isa 26:11
10:28 Deut 17:6
10:30 *Deut 32:35-36; Ps 135:14
10:31 2 Cor 5:11

5. EXHORTATIONS TO FAITHFULNESS (10:19–13:19)

A Call to Persevere

19And so, dear brothers and sisters, we can boldly enter heaven's Most Holy Place because of the blood of Jesus. 20By his death, Jesus opened a new and life-giving way through the curtain into the Most Holy Place. 21And since we have a great High Priest who rules over God's house, 22let us go right into the presence of God with sincere hearts fully trusting him. For our guilty consciences have been sprinkled with Christ's blood to make us clean, and our bodies have been washed with pure water.

23Let us hold tightly without wavering to the hope we affirm, for God can be trusted to keep his promise. 24Let us think of ways to motivate one another to acts of love and good works. 25And let us not neglect our meeting together, as some people do, but encourage one another, especially now that the day of his return is drawing near.

Faithfulness and Judgment

26Dear friends, if we deliberately continue sinning after we have received knowledge of the truth, there is no longer any sacrifice that will cover these sins. 27There is only the terrible expectation of God's judgment and the raging fire that will consume his enemies. 28For anyone who refused to obey the law of Moses was put to death without mercy on the testimony of two or three witnesses. 29Just think how much worse the punishment will be for those who have trampled on the Son of God, and have treated the blood of the covenant, which made us holy, as if it were common and unholy, and have insulted and disdained the Holy Spirit who brings God's mercy to us. 30For we know the one who said,

"I will take revenge.
I will pay them back."

He also said,

"The LORD will judge his own people."

31It is a terrible thing to fall into the hands of the living God.

32Think back on those early days when you first learned about Christ. Remember how you remained faithful even though it

10:19-25 The author of Hebrews repeats words and concepts from 4:14-16 to mark off and summarize the central section (4:14–10:18) and to introduce the exhortations that follow, offering a concise statement of the message of Hebrews: The new covenant, established by Jesus' superior ministry, gives us a superior basis for drawing near to God and for persevering in the Christian life.

10:19 ***dear brothers and sisters:*** Literally *brothers;* see note on 3:1. • The earthly ***Most Holy Place*** was not freely accessible (see note on 9:3). Now, however, the very presence of God in heaven (9:11, 24) is open ***because of the blood of Jesus*** in his sacrificial death (9:11–10:18).

10:20 ***By his death*** (literally *Through his flesh*): Jesus' death has ***opened a new and life-giving way*** for us ***through the curtain,*** an allusion to the curtain separating the first and second rooms of the Tabernacle (see 9:1-5). Believers now enter the ***Most Holy Place*** of God's presence through Jesus' sacrificial death.

10:21 Jesus, as Messiah, is the ***High Priest*** and king ***who rules over God's house,*** the people of God (see 3:1-6; 2 Sam 7:13).

10:22 ***sincere hearts:*** Under the new covenant, believers have transformed hearts (8:10; 10:16; Jer 31:31-34). • ***fully trusting him:*** Christ's work on our behalf gives us confidence that God will welcome us into his ***presence.*** • ***our guilty consciences have been sprinkled . . . our bodies have been washed:*** Christ's sacrificial death has provided complete cleansing from sin (see 9:13-14, 19-23).

10:23 We are to ***hold tightly to the hope we affirm,*** that Christ's death is effective in winning us right relationship with God.

10:24 ***Acts of love and good works*** characterize true Christian commitment (6:10; 10:32-34; Gal 5:13; 1 Thes 1:3; Rev 2:19).

10:25 Some in this Christian community had evidently begun to ***neglect*** their ***meeting together*** in regular worship, perhaps to avoid persecution (10:32-39). • Our motivating one another to love and good works should be done in light of ***the day of his return,*** Christ's second coming (9:28; Luke 12:42-46; 1 Cor 5:5; 1 Thes 5:2; 2 Pet 3:10; 1 Jn 2:28).

10:26-31 The author interjects a strong warning concerning the danger of rejecting God's Son and his authoritative word. The warning challenges hearers to respond with a commitment to follow Christ.

10:26-27 ***deliberately:*** Open rebellion against God's laws was described as "sinning with a high hand" (see note on Num 15:30-31). Here the author has in mind specifically a rejection of Christ and his work. Christ's sacrifice for sins has done away with the sacrificial system of the old covenant (9:11–10:18). If a person rejects the Son's sacrifice, ***there is no*** other ***sacrifice***—nowhere else to go—for forgiveness. A person who rejects Christ can only expect ***judgment*** as one of God's ***enemies*** (cp. Isa 26:10-11).

10:28-29 The author argues from lesser to greater (see note on 9:14). The lesser situation is the old punishment of ***death*** for a person ***who refused to obey the law of Moses*** (see Deut 13:6-11). The greater situation concerns those who reject Christ and treat him with contempt. • ***how much worse the punishment:*** Eternal damnation is the fate awaiting those who have rejected Christ (see "Consequences of Apostasy" at 2:1-4, p. 2085). • ***The blood of the covenant, which made us holy,*** is Christ's perfect sacrifice (9:11–10:18). • ***insulted and disdained the Holy Spirit:*** Those who reject the Spirit's prompting and mercy deny the validity of the Good News and the superiority of Christ and his saving work (cp. Mark 3:22-30).

10:30-31 ***"I will take revenge. I will pay them back":*** Deut 32:35. • ***"The LORD will judge his own people":*** Deut 32:36; cp. 1 Pet 4:17-18. • That God ***will pay them back*** and ***will judge his own people*** shows the dreadful circumstances of those who have rejected Christ. Once God moves to judge a person, no one can rescue that person out of God's hand (Deut 32:39).

10:32-39 The harsh warning (10:26-31) is followed by a word of encouragement. The hearers' own faithfulness in the past is used as a positive example for them to follow now.

10:32 ***when you first learned about Christ*** (literally *when you were first enlightened*): The author reminds his

meant terrible suffering. 33Sometimes you were exposed to public ridicule and were beaten, and sometimes you helped others who were suffering the same things. 34You suffered along with those who were thrown into jail, and when all you owned was taken from you, you accepted it with joy. You knew there were better things waiting for you that will last forever.

35So do not throw away this confident trust in the Lord. Remember the great reward it brings you! 36Patient endurance is what you need now, so that you will continue to do God's [c]will. Then you will receive all that he has promised.

37 "For in just a little while,
the Coming One will come and not delay.
38 And my righteous ones will live by faith.
But I will take no pleasure in anyone who turns away."

39But we are not like those who turn away from God to their own destruction. We are the faithful ones, whose souls will be saved.

Great Examples of Faith and Endurance

11 [d]Faith is the confidence that what we hope for will actually happen; it gives us assurance about things we cannot see. 2Through their faith, the people in days of old earned a good reputation.

3By faith we understand that the entire universe was formed at God's command, that what we now see did not come from anything that can be seen.

4It was by faith that Abel brought a more acceptable offering to God than Cain did. Abel's offering gave evidence that he was a righteous man, and God showed his approval of his gifts. Although Abel is long dead, he still speaks to us by his example of faith.

5It was by faith that Enoch was taken up to heaven without dying—"he disappeared, because God took him." For before he was taken up, he was known as a person who pleased God. 6And it is impossible to please God without faith. Anyone who wants to come to him must believe that God exists and that he rewards those who sincerely seek him.

10:33
1 Cor 4:9
1 Thes 2:14

10:34
Heb 13:3

10:36
Heb 9:15
[c]*thelēma* (2307)
›1 Pet 2:15

10:37-38
*Hab 2:3-4
Rom 1:17
Gal 3:11

11:1
Rom 8:24
Heb 3:6, 14
[d]*pistis* (4102)
›Jas 2:14

11:3
Gen 1:1-31
Ps 33:6, 9
John 1:3
Rom 1:19-20
Heb 1:2

11:4
Gen 4:3-10

11:5
Gen 5:22-24

11:6
Heb 7:19

readers of ***those early days,*** shortly after the community embraced Christianity, when their faith was tested. At that time, they ***remained faithful*** in the face of ***terrible suffering.*** Suffering is normal for a person who identifies with Christ and his community (13:12-13; Acts 9:16; Rom 8:17; 1 Cor 4:12-13; Phil 1:29; Jas 1:2-4).

10:33 ***public ridicule:*** They were insulted and disgraced. • ***beaten:*** They were abused physically. • At times they were direct recipients of abuse, and at times they stood with ***others who were suffering.***

10:34 ***those who were thrown into jail:*** Prisoners were dependent on friends and family for the most basic daily needs (cp. 13:3). • ***when all you owned was taken from you:*** At times, the Roman government evicted groups of people from their homes and forced them to leave a city (see Acts 18:2-3). These Christians had faced this kind of persecution in the past and ***accepted it with joy*** (cp. Rom 5:3; Jas 1:2-4; 1 Pet 1:6). They anticipated ***better things . . . that will last forever*** (see 11:35). God promises rewards to those who persevere faithfully.

10:35-36 Based on their exemplary faithfulness in the past (10:32-34), the author urges them not to ***throw away this confident trust in the Lord.*** The word translated *confident trust* is also used in Hebrews to speak of *boldness* in entering the presence of God (4:16; 10:19; cp. 3:6). Those who remain faithful receive a ***great reward*** (see 1:14; 6:12; 9:15; Jas 1:12). ***Patient endurance*** is the key response needed in the face of persecution, as the author argues in 10:32–12:17.

10:37-38 These verses quote Hab 2:3-4 to contrast the righteous and the wicked as they face God's judgment (cp. Rom 1:17; Gal 3:11). • ***my righteous ones will live by faith:*** Or *my righteous ones will live by their faithfulness;* literally *my righteous one will live by faith.*

10:39 The author ends this section with a statement of confidence in his hearers (see note on 6:9).

11:1-40 In presenting readers with a long catalog of faith-filled heroes, ch 11 builds up overwhelming evidence that the life of faith is the only real way to live for God. The writer repeats the phrase ***by faith*** to drive this main message into the minds and hearts of his hearers. The examples follow a pattern: (a) the phrase *by faith,* (b) the name of the person, (c) the event or action which demonstrated faith, and (d) the outcome.

11:1 Before presenting the list of examples, the author defines what *faith is:* It is acting on what God has revealed about his will and character. • The ***confidence*** of faith is based on the God who fulfills his promises. • The word translated ***assurance*** means an active certainty that what God has promised will come to pass despite our not yet seeing it.

11:2 ***earned a good reputation:*** Scripture speaks favorably about their lives of faith (see also 11:39).

11:3 ***That the entire universe was formed at God's command*** is a basic belief of Jewish and Christian theology (see Gen 1:1-3). God created everything that ***we now see.*** A life of faith understands that, by analogy, God's promises are real and will be called into reality by God himself, even if they are unseen at present.

11:4 ***Abel:*** See Gen 4:3-5. • ***evidence that he was a righteous man:*** Cp. 10:38. • ***he still speaks to us:*** The story of his faith challenges us, and his blood bears witness to his righteousness and to the injustice of his murder (see 12:24).

11:5 ***Enoch was taken up to heaven*** and thus did not face a normal death (see Gen 5:21-24). • ***"he disappeared, because God took him":*** Gen 5:24.

11:6 ***it is impossible to please God without faith:*** The author alludes to 10:38, which quotes Hab 2:4. • Faith must include believing ***that God exists and that he rewards those who sincerely seek him.*** In life's difficulties, readers are challenged to trust in God and to anticipate the fulfillment of his promises.

11:7 Gen 6:13-22; Rom 3:22; 1 Pet 3:20
11:8 Gen 12:1-5; Acts 7:2-4
11:9 Gen 12:8; [e]*sunklēronomos* (4789) ▸1 Pet 3:7
11:10 Heb 12:22; Rev 21:2
11:11 Gen 17:19; 21:1-3
11:12 Gen 15:5-6; 22:17; Rom 4:19
11:13 Gen 23:4; Matt 13:17; Heb 11:39
11:14 Heb 13:14
11:15 Gen 24:6-8
11:16 Gen 26:24; Exod 3:6, 15

7 It was by faith that Noah built a large
boat to save his family from the flood. He
obeyed God, who warned him about things
that had never happened before. By his faith
Noah condemned the rest of the world, and
he received the righteousness that comes
by faith.
8 It was by faith that Abraham obeyed
when God called him to leave home and go
to another land that God would give him
as his inheritance. He went without knowing where he was going. 9 And even when
he reached the land God promised him,
he lived there by faith—for he was like a
foreigner, living in tents. And so did Isaac
and Jacob, who [e]inherited the same promise. 10 Abraham was confidently looking
forward to a city with eternal foundations,
a city designed and built by God.
11 It was by faith that even Sarah was able
to have a child, though she was barren and
was too old. She believed that God would
keep his promise. 12 And so a whole nation
came from this one man who was as good
as dead—a nation with so many people
that, like the stars in the sky and the sand
on the seashore, there is no way to count
them.
13 All these people died still believing
what God had promised them. They did
not receive what was promised, but they
saw it all from a distance and welcomed it.
They agreed that they were foreigners and
nomads here on earth. 14 Obviously people
who say such things are looking forward to
a country they can call their own. 15 If they
had longed for the country they came from,
they could have gone back. 16 But they were
looking for a better place, a heavenly homeland. That is why God is not ashamed to be
called their God, for he has prepared a city
for them.

Faith (11:1-40)

Heb 10:22, 38; Gen 15:6; 2 Chr 20:20; Hab 2:4; Matt 9:29; 21:21; Luke 8:50; John 3:16, 36; 5:24; 11:25; 12:46; 20:30-31; Rom 5:1; 10:9, 17; Gal 3:6; 5:6; 1 Tim 1:19; 6:12; Jas 1:5-6; 2:14-26; 1 Jn 3:23; 5:4

Hebrews 11 is one of the most extensive essays on faith in the NT and one of the most loved sections of Scripture, yet misconceptions about faith abound. Some see faith as meaning any form of spirituality ("he is a person of faith"). Others understand it as a resolute belief that something good is going to happen to them, a ticket to health and wealth. Still others think that faith is a blind leap against known facts. None of these constitutes biblical faith.

Instead, faith involves confident action in response to what God has made known (11:1-3). As seen in the examples listed in ch 11, faith comes into play in a variety of life's circumstances. The results of faith also are various. Some people get rescued, achieve success in life, and get some of what God has promised in their lifetimes. Others get mocked, beaten, tortured, put in prison, and killed. Faith is sometimes rewarded sooner and sometimes later, but people of faith anticipate the rewards because of their confidence in God's character.

What does it mean to live by faith? It means that, in our various circumstances, we live out our belief "that God exists and that he rewards those who sincerely seek him" (11:6). Those who live by faith take confident action based on what God has revealed about his character, seeking to do his will in all things.

11:7 The story of ***Noah*** (see Gen 6:1–9:17) further demonstrates that faith involves obedience in the face of the unseen. • ***things that had never happened before:*** Namely, ***the flood.*** Noah's faith ***condemned the rest of the world*** by bearing witness to God's reality and his desire for holiness.

11:8 ***Abraham obeyed:*** See Gen 12:1-2. He, too, acted in the face of what he could not yet see, since ***he went without knowing where he was going.***

11:9-10 ***he lived there by faith:*** Abraham himself did not experience the inheritance of the land of promise. Rather, he ***was like a foreigner, living in tents*** (see Gen 12:10–13:18). • ***so did Isaac and Jacob:*** This life of faith was continued in the next two generations: They received the ***same promise*** and hoped in God, but did not experience what God had promised. • ***city with eternal foundations:*** Abraham did not settle in the Canaanite cities but followed the will of God in faithful obedience, anticipating a heavenly city.

11:11 ***It was by faith that even Sarah was able to have a child, though she was barren and was too old. She believed:*** Or *It was by faith that he [Abraham] was able to have a child, even though Sarah was barren and he was too old. He believed.* Textual variants make it difficult to determine whether Sarah or Abraham is the subject of this verse. Either way, Sarah's ability to have a child far past the normal age of childbearing is in view (see Gen 15:6; 18:10-15; 21:1-7).

11:12 ***this one man who was as good as dead:*** Abraham was very old, yet he became the source for ***a whole nation.*** Faith involves believing that God is able to answer his promises seemingly out of nothing. • ***like the stars . . . and the sand:*** See Gen 22:17. God fulfilled the promise (Exod 1:7).

11:13-16 The author pauses to point out general principles evident in the lives he has highlighted thus far.

11:13 Abraham's family lived in the land of promise as ***foreigners and nomads*** (see Gen 23:4; cp. 1 Chr 29:15; Ps 39:12; 1 Pet 2:11).

11:14-16 Abraham's family was obviously not longing for the ***country they came from,*** since if that had been the case, ***they could have gone back.*** Their posture of faith demonstrates a longing for ***a better place.*** Their hope was ultimately in God, who rewarded their faith by preparing ***a heavenly . . . city for them.***

17 It was by faith that Abraham offered
Isaac as a sacrifice when God was testing
him. Abraham, who had received God's
promises, was ready to sacrifice his [f]only
son, Isaac, 18 even though God had told
him, "Isaac is the son through whom your
descendants will be counted." 19 Abraham
reasoned that if Isaac died, God was able to
bring him back to life again. And in a sense,
Abraham did receive his son back from the
dead.

20 It was by faith that Isaac promised
blessings for the future to his sons, Jacob
and Esau.

21 It was by faith that Jacob, when he was
old and dying, blessed each of Joseph's sons
and bowed in worship as he leaned on his
staff.

22 It was by faith that Joseph, when he
was about to die, said confidently that the
people of Israel would leave Egypt. He even
commanded them to take his bones with
them when they left.

23 It was by faith that Moses' parents hid
him for three months when he was born.
They saw that God had given them an unusual child, and they were not afraid to
disobey the king's command.

24 It was by faith that Moses, when he
grew up, refused to be called the son of
Pharaoh's daughter. 25 He chose to share
the oppression of God's people instead
of enjoying the fleeting pleasures of sin.
26 He thought it was better to suffer for the
sake of Christ than to own the treasures of
Egypt, for he was looking ahead to his great
reward. 27 It was by faith that Moses left the
land of Egypt, not fearing the king's anger.
He kept right on going because he kept his
eyes on the one who is invisible. 28 It was by
faith that Moses commanded the people of
Israel to keep the Passover and to sprinkle
blood on the doorposts so that the angel of
death would not kill their [g]firstborn sons.

29 It was by faith that the people of Israel
went right through the Red Sea as though
they were on dry ground. But when the Egyptians tried to follow, they were all drowned.

30 It was by faith that the people of Israel
marched around Jericho for seven days, and
the walls came crashing down.

31 It was by faith that Rahab the prostitute
was not destroyed with the people in her
city who refused to obey God. For she had
given a friendly welcome to the spies.

32 How much more do I need to say? It

11:17 Gen 22:1-10; Jas 2:21; [f]*monogenēs* (3439) ▸1 Jn 4:9
11:18 *Gen 21:12
11:19 Rom 4:21
11:20 Gen 27:27-29
11:21 Gen 47:31; 48:8-20
11:22 Gen 50:24-25; Exod 13:19
11:23 Exod 1:16, 22; 2:2
11:24 Exod 2:10-12
11:26 Heb 13:13
11:27 Exod 12:50-51
11:28 Exod 12:21-30; [g]*prōtotokos* (4416) ▸Heb 12:23
11:29 Exod 14:21-31
11:30 Josh 6:12-21
11:31 Josh 2:8-13; 6:20-25; Jas 2:25
11:32 Judg 4–13; 1 Sam 1:20; 16:1, 13

11:17-31 Great examples of faith take the reader from Abraham's family to Rahab. These examples build up evidence that faith is the only appropriate response to God.

11:17-19 ***Abraham offered Isaac:*** See Gen 22:1-18. God never intended for Abraham to offer his son but ***was testing*** Abraham's faith, which he expressed through his obedience.

11:18 This verse quotes Gen 21:12.

11:19 ***Abraham reasoned:*** The resurrection of Isaac was the only answer to Abraham's dilemma. In Gen 22:5, Abraham expressed confidence that Isaac would return with him.

11:20 ***Isaac promised blessings:*** See Gen 27:27-40; the only part of the story that can be considered a blessing for Esau is that he would eventually shake off his subservience to his brother. Esau was later blessed by Jacob's riches (Gen 33:8-11).

11:21 ***Jacob*** passed the ritual blessing on to ***Joseph's sons,*** Ephraim and Manasseh (Gen 48:8-22). • ***bowed in worship:*** Gen 47:31. The phrase ***as he leaned on his staff*** comes from the Greek translation of the OT.

11:22 Joseph's prophecy and command (see Gen 50:24-25) showed faith that God would keep his promises.

11:23 ***Moses' parents:*** See Exod 2:1-2. • ***unusual*** (or ***attractive,*** or ***beautiful***): This word refers to something of superior quality. Their insight that Moses was extraordinary led them to act by faith in God. • ***the king's command:*** Exod 1:22.

11:24-25 ***Moses, when he grew up:*** See Exod 2:11-15. Moses took a public stand with the people of Israel rather than continuing ***to be called the son of Pharaoh's daughter,*** who had adopted him (Exod 2:3-10). Therefore, ***he chose to share the oppression of God's people,*** as the readers of this letter were being called to do (see 10:32-34).

11:26 ***the treasures of Egypt:*** The New Kingdom of Egypt (about 1550–1069 BC) was an era of phenomenal wealth and political power. Moses evidently had a greater ***reward*** in mind.

11:27 Like his forefather Abraham, ***Moses*** acted in ***faith*** by leaving ***the land of Egypt,*** with which he was familiar, and walked into an unknown future (Exod 2:15). • ***not fearing the king's anger:*** Rather than watching the king, he ***kept his eyes on the one who is invisible***—God.

11:28 ***Moses commanded . . . the Passover:*** See Exod 12:1-27. The first Passover (Exod 12:28-30) initiated the Exodus (Exod 12:31-42, 50-51) and instituted the annual Passover observance as a memorial (Exod 12:43-49; 13:1-16). • ***to sprinkle blood:*** The sprinkling of the blood of sacrifices under the old covenant was parallel to the sprinkling of Christ's blood (see 9:12-14, 18-22).

11:29 The rescue ***through the Red Sea*** (see Exod 13:17–14:21) constitutes the greatest moment of deliverance in Israel's history. The people's fear and accusation at the time (Exod 14:10-12) do not obviously exemplify ***faith,*** but the people went forward when told to do so despite their fear. The episode demonstrates that obedience is central to faith.

11:30 The conquest of ***Jericho*** (Josh 5:13–6:27) offers another example of great faith, as the people acted in obedience to God's unusual instructions.

11:31 ***Rahab the prostitute*** (Josh 2:1-24; 6:25) showed faith in the power of the God of Israel by protecting the spies who came to her home (cp. Jas 2:25). As a result, she and her family were ***not destroyed*** but joined the community of Israel. In fact, Rahab was an ancestor of Jesus (Matt 1:5).

11:32-40 In a rapid series of examples, the author gives an overview of other faithful people through the rest of the old covenant era. In 11:32-35a, the outcome of faith is deliverance and victory. In 11:35b-38, however, faith brought severe persecution and even martyrdom. The result for both groups was that God honored them with a good reputation because of their faith (11:39).

11:33
1 Sam 17:34-36
Dan 6:1-27

11:34
Judg 7:1-22
Dan 3:19-27

11:35
1 Kgs 17:17-24
2 Kgs 4:25-37
[h]*anastasis* (0386)
‣1 Pet 1:3
[i]*apolutrōsis* (0629)
‣Luke 21:28

11:36
Gen 39:20
Jer 20:2; 37:15

11:37
1 Kgs 19:10
2 Chr 24:20-22

11:38
1 Kgs 18:4; 19:9

11:40
Rom 11:26
Rev 6:11

12:1
1 Cor 9:24
Phil 3:12-14
[j]*hamartia* (0266)
‣Jas 1:15

12:2
Ps 110:1
Phil 2:8-9
Heb 2:9-10
1 Pet 1:11

would take too long to recount the stories
of the faith of Gideon, Barak, Samson, Jephthah, David, Samuel, and all the prophets.
[33]By faith these people overthrew kingdoms,
ruled with justice, and received what God
had promised them. They shut the mouths
of lions, [34]quenched the flames of fire, and
escaped death by the edge of the sword.
Their weakness was turned to strength.
They became strong in battle and put whole
armies to flight. [35]Women received their
loved ones [h]back again from death.

But others were tortured, refusing to
turn from God in order to be [i]set free. They
placed their hope in a better life after the
[h]resurrection. [36]Some were jeered at, and
their backs were cut open with whips. Others were chained in prisons. [37]Some died by
stoning, some were sawed in half, and others were killed with the sword. Some went
about wearing skins of sheep and goats,
destitute and oppressed and mistreated.
[38]They were too good for this world, wandering over deserts and mountains, hiding
in caves and holes in the ground.

[39]All these people earned a good reputation because of their faith, yet none of them
received all that God had promised. [40]For
God had something better in mind for us,
so that they would not reach perfection
without us.

Endure by Keeping Your Eyes on Jesus

12 Therefore, since we are surrounded
by such a huge crowd of witnesses to
the life of faith, let us strip off every weight
that slows us down, especially the [j]sin that
so easily trips us up. And let us run with endurance the race God has set before us. [2]We
do this by keeping our eyes on Jesus, the
champion who initiates and perfects our
faith. Because of the joy awaiting him, he
endured the cross, disregarding its shame.
Now he is seated in the place of honor beside God's throne. [3]Think of all the hostility
he endured from sinful people; then you

11:32 ***How much more do I need to say?*** The author makes a transition to his concluding summary, which begins with six heroes of faith from the time of the judges and the united monarchy. ***Gideon*** defeated the Midianites with torches and jars (Judg 7:7-25). ***Barak*** routed Sisera and the Canaanites (Judg 4:8-16). ***Samson,*** though weak in moral fiber, was used by God to fight the Philistines on behalf of Israel (Judg 13:1–16:31). ***Jephthah*** won victory over the Amorites and Ammonites (Judg 10:6–12:7). ***David,*** the only king in the group, loved God and, for the most part, led an exemplary life of faith (1 Sam 16—1 Kgs 1). ***Samuel*** was an important transitional leader between the judges and the monarchy; he heard God's voice and obeyed his will (1 Sam 1–15). • The statement ***all the prophets*** includes Elijah, Elisha, and the "writing prophets" from Isaiah to Malachi. The prophets often exhibited great faith in the face of hostility.

11:33 ***overthrew kingdoms:*** During the time of the judges and the reign of David, Israel defeated many of their enemies. David and Solomon and a few others ***ruled with justice*** (see 2 Sam 8:15; 1 Kgs 10:9). • ***shut the mouths of lions:*** See Dan 6:1-23.

11:34 ***quenched the flames of fire:*** See Dan 3:16-30. • ***escaped death by the edge of the sword:*** E.g., Elijah and Jeremiah (see 1 Kgs 19:2; 2 Kgs 1; Jer 26:10-16; 38:1-13).

11:35 Elijah and Elisha both brought women's ***loved ones back again from death*** (see 1 Kgs 17:17-24; 2 Kgs 4:17-37). • ***But others were tortured:*** Faith does not always have a positive outcome in this life. The author might be alluding to the 170s and 160s BC, when many Jews suffered and died rather than forsake their faith (see, e.g., *1 Maccabees* 1:20-64).

11:37 According to tradition, the prophet Jeremiah ***died by stoning*** and the prophet Isaiah was ***sawed in half.*** (At this point, some manuscripts add *some were tested.*)

11:38 ***too good for this world:*** Their hope was in God more than in the pleasures and comforts of this world.

11:39-40 The way to live as God's people under the new covenant is to live as ***all these people*** did under the old covenant: by ***faith*** in God's promises, enduring any difficulties faced in this world. • ***earned a good reputation:*** God has borne witness to their faithfulness (see also 11:2). • ***yet none of them received all that God had promised:*** They all died prior to Christ's promised coming; the ***something better*** began with Christ's sacrificial work (8:3–10:18) and anticipates the future culmination of God's plan for his people. • ***would not reach perfection:*** See notes on 5:9; 7:11. Jesus has fulfilled God's goal of bringing his people into relationship with him.

12:1-17 The author challenges his hearers to endure in following Jesus, the supreme example of faithfulness, by imitating him in his suffering (12:1-4), by enduring under God's discipline (12:5-13), and by living in peace with others (12:14-17).

12:1 ***huge crowd of witnesses:*** The host of faithful followers of God (ch 11) bear witness to the truth that God blesses ***the life of faith.*** • ***let us strip off every weight:*** In Greco-Roman literature, a race is a metaphor for the need for endurance in life. Just as extra weight hinders a runner, ***sin . . . trips us up.*** It entangles us and restricts us from moving by faith.

12:2 Jesus is the supreme example of faithful endurance (3:1). Our endurance in the Christian life will depend on our ***keeping our eyes on Jesus***—staying focused on him and his work on our behalf. • ***Jesus, the champion who initiates and perfects our faith*** (or *Jesus, the originator and perfecter of our faith*): Jesus has accomplished everything necessary for faith under the new covenant to be a reality. • ***Because of the joy:*** Or *Instead of the joy.* • ***disregarding its shame:*** Crucifixion was the most shameful form of execution, meant to humiliate and torture the person crucified. It was used only for slaves and criminals who were not Roman citizens. Christ treated that shame as if it were nothing. • ***seated in the place of honor:*** The author again alludes to Ps 110:1 (see also 1:3, 13; 8:1; 10:12); through endurance, Jesus reached the place of ultimate honor at the right hand of God.

12:3 ***Think of all the hostility he endured from sinful people*** (some manuscripts read *Think of how people hurt themselves by opposing him*): The recipients of Hebrews had ***become weary*** and were about to ***give up***—they were emotionally fatigued because of the persecution they were facing. The key to their endurance was to focus on Jesus, who had been through even worse hostility.

won't become weary and give up. 4 After
all, you have not yet given your lives in your
struggle against sin.

Endure God's Loving Discipline

5 And have you forgotten the encouraging
words God spoke to you as his children? He
said,

"My child, don't make light of the LORD's
discipline,
and don't give up when he corrects you.
6 For the LORD [k]disciplines those he loves,
and he punishes each one he accepts
as his child."

7 As you endure this divine discipline, remember that God is treating you as his own
children. Who ever heard of a child who
is never disciplined by its father? 8 If God
doesn't discipline you as he does all of his
children, it means that you are illegitimate
and are not really his children at all. 9 Since
we respected our earthly [a]fathers who [b]dis-
ciplined us, shouldn't we submit even more
to the discipline of the [a]Father of our spirits,
and live forever?

10 For our earthly fathers disciplined us
for a few years, doing the best they knew
how. But God's discipline is always good for
us, so that we might share in his holiness.
11 No discipline is enjoyable while it is happening—it's painful! But afterward there
will be a peaceful harvest of right living for
those who are trained in this way.

12 So take a new grip with your tired
hands and strengthen your weak knees.
13 Mark out a straight path for your feet so
that those who are weak and lame will not
fall but become strong.

Endure by Rejecting a Corrupt Life

14 Work at living in [c]peace with everyone, and
work at living a [d]holy life, for those who are
not holy will not see the Lord. 15 Look after
each other so that none of you fails to receive
the grace of God. Watch out that no poisonous root of bitterness grows up to trouble
you, corrupting many. 16 Make sure that no
one is immoral or godless like Esau, who
traded his birthright as the firstborn son for
a single meal. 17 You know that afterward,
when he wanted his father's blessing, he was
rejected. It was too late for repentance, even
though he begged with bitter tears.

Contrast Between Two Covenants

18 You have not come to a physical mountain,
to a place of flaming fire, darkness, gloom,
and whirlwind, as the Israelites did at

12:4 Heb 10:32-34
12:5-6 *Prov 3:11-12
12:6 Rev 3:19; [k]*paideuō* (3811) ‣Heb 12:9
12:7 Deut 8:5; 2 Sam 7:14
12:8 1 Pet 5:9
12:9 Isa 38:16; [a]*patēr* (3962) ‣Jas 1:17; [b]*paideutēs* (3810) ‣Rev 3:19
12:10 2 Pet 1:4
12:11 Jas 3:17-18
12:12 Isa 35:3
12:13 Prov 4:26
12:14 Rom 14:19; [c]*eirēnē* (1515) ‣1 Pet 3:11; [d]*hagiasmos* (0038) ‣1 Pet 1:2
12:15 Deut 29:17-18; Heb 4:1
12:16 Gen 25:29-34
12:17 Gen 27:30-40

12:4 ***not yet given your lives:*** This community had not yet faced martyrdom for the faith. (This is one reason to date Hebrews prior to Nero's persecution in the mid-60s AD.) If Jesus could endure a shameful death, the hearers should be able to endure lesser persecution.

12:5-6 In these verses, ***the encouraging words*** are quoted from Prov 3:11-12 (Greek version), a passage that regards hardship as ***the LORD's*** loving ***discipline*** for his ***children*** (literally *sons;* also in 12:7, 8; see note on 2:10). God can turn a wide variety of trials and difficulties to our good, training us in righteousness and holy character. • ***child:*** Literally *son;* also in 12:7.

12:7-8 ***disciplined by its father:*** Fathers from Greco-Roman as well as Jewish families were involved in day-to-day aspects of raising their children. Discipline was seen as a necessary, healthy, and important component of preparing the child for adulthood. A lack of fatherly discipline—in this case, a lack of hardships in life—is a mark of illegitimacy, not a blessing.

12:9 The author argues from lesser to greater (see note on 9:14). Here, the lesser situation is the respect shown to an earthly father when he is giving discipline. We should ***submit even more to the discipline of the Father of our spirits*** in the more important context of our relationship with God. We should adopt a posture of yielding to God as to a good Father, trusting that he is helping us grow even through painful circumstances. • ***and live forever?*** Or *and really live?*

12:10-11 There are at least two limitations on an earthly father's discipline. First, his discipline, or education, is only ***for a few years*** (literally *for a few days*)—children eventually leave home. Second, earthly fathers were ***doing the best they knew how*** from their limited perspectives. By contrast, God's discipline lasts throughout life and ***is always good for us,*** based on his limitless knowledge and love. His goal is ***that we might share in his holiness.*** Although it is ***painful,*** discipline brings about ***a peaceful harvest of right living.*** It brings God's children into a state conducive to harmonious relationships and doing what is right (see also Rom 5:3-4; 8:17, 28; 2 Cor 4:17; Phil 1:12-14; Jas 1:2-4; 1 Pet 1:7; 4:14).

12:12-13 The author, alluding to Isa 35:3-8 and Prov 4:26, encourages those who are emotionally and spiritually exhausted. According to Isa 35, God is in the process of defeating his enemies and is making a ***straight path*** for the righteous so that they ***will not fall.***

12:14 Those who are ***living a holy life*** have confident hope of seeing ***the Lord*** (see 1 Jn 2:28; 3:21; 4:17).

12:15 The ***poisonous root of bitterness*** alludes to people turning their backs on God's covenant to serve other gods (Deut 29:18). Bitterness can corrupt the church.

12:16 Ancient Jewish literature describes Esau as sexually ***immoral*** because he was married to the Hittite women Judith and Basemath (Gen 26:34; see *Jubilees* 25:1; Philo, *On the Virtues* 208). • Esau's lack of regard for his birthright (Gen 25:29-34) was ***godless.*** His willingness to give up God's blessings for immediate satisfaction illustrates the opposite of faith.

12:17 Hebrews sees Esau's disregard for his inheritance (12:16) and his loss of the ***blessing*** (Gen 27:30-40) as intrinsically related. The result was ***bitter tears.*** By analogy, those who reject an inheritance through Christ's new covenant have only bitterness in their future.

12:18-24 This passage contrasts the old covenant with the new. The old covenant, represented by Mount Sinai (12:18-21), is depicted as impersonal, intimidating, and unapproachable; it booms, flashes, and terrifies. The new covenant, represented by Mount Zion (12:22-24), is depicted as relational, welcoming, and celebratory.

12:18 ***to a physical mountain:*** Literally *to something that can be touched.* The descriptions of ***Mount Sinai*** come

12:18-19
Exod 19:16–20:21
12:20
*Exod 19:12-13
12:21
Deut 9:19
12:22
Gal 4:26-28
Rev 5:11; 21:2
12:23
[e]*prōtotokos* (4416)
› Rev 1:5
12:24
Gen 4:10
Heb 10:22
[f]*diathēkē* (1242)
› Heb 13:20
12:26
Exod 19:18
*Hag 2:6
12:27
2 Pet 3:10
12:28
Dan 2:44
12:29
Deut 4:24; 9:3
13:1
Rom 12:10
13:2
Gen 18:1-8; 19:1-3
13:3
Matt 25:36
Col 4:18
Heb 10:34
13:4
1 Cor 7:38

Mount Sinai. 19For they heard an awesome
trumpet blast and a voice so terrible that
they begged God to stop speaking. 20They
staggered back under God's command: "If
even an animal touches the mountain, it
must be stoned to death." 21Moses himself
was so frightened at the sight that he said, "I
am terrified and trembling."
22No, you have come to Mount Zion, to
the city of the living God, the heavenly Jerusalem, and to countless thousands of angels
in a joyful gathering. 23You have come to
the assembly of God's [e]firstborn children,
whose names are written in heaven. You
have come to God himself, who is the judge
over all things. You have come to the spirits
of the righteous ones in heaven who have
now been made perfect. 24You have come
to Jesus, the one who mediates the new [f]cov-
enant between God and people, and to the
sprinkled blood, which speaks of forgiveness instead of crying out for vengeance
like the blood of Abel.

A Final Warning

25Be careful that you do not refuse to listen
to the One who is speaking. For if the people
of Israel did not escape when they refused
to listen to Moses, the earthly messenger, we
will certainly not escape if we reject the One
who speaks to us from heaven! 26When God
spoke from Mount Sinai his voice shook the
earth, but now he makes another promise:
"Once again I will shake not only the earth
but the heavens also." 27This means that all
of creation will be shaken and removed, so
that only unshakable things will remain.
28Since we are receiving a Kingdom that
is unshakable, let us be thankful and please
God by worshiping him with holy fear and
awe. 29For our God is a devouring fire.

Practical Instructions

13 Keep on loving each other as brothers and sisters. 2Don't forget to show
hospitality to strangers, for some who have
done this have entertained angels without
realizing it! 3Remember those in prison, as
if you were there yourself. Remember also
those being mistreated, as if you felt their
pain in your own bodies.
4Give honor to marriage, and remain
faithful to one another in marriage. God

directly from God's encounter with Israel at that mountain (see Exod 19:16-22; 20:18-21; Deut 4:11-12; 5:23-27). The images communicate separation from a holy God.

12:19 The ***awesome trumpet blast and a voice*** terrified the people (see Exod 19:16, 19; 20:18; Deut 4:12) so that ***they begged God to stop speaking*** (Exod 20:19).

12:20 ***God's command*** is quoted from Exod 19:13.

12:21 ***"I am terrified and trembling":*** Deut 9:19.

12:22 ***No:*** There is a strong contrast between the old and the new covenant. Believers have now come to wonderful ***Mount Zion***, which is closely associated with Jerusalem and represents God's dwelling place. • ***heavenly Jerusalem:*** See note on 8:5. • The new covenant constitutes a relationship with God by which we experience his presence with joy, peace, and fellowship.

12:23 The word translated ***assembly*** is usually translated "church"; it speaks of God's assembled people. • ***God's firstborn children*** refers to people who are members of the new covenant (cp. 1:6; 2:10-13). • The concept that God's people have their ***names . . . written in heaven*** speaks of God's special attention to his people (see also Exod 32:32; Ps 69:28; Isa 4:3; Dan 12:1; Luke 10:20; Phil 4:3; Rev 3:5). • For God's children, ***God*** as ***judge*** is the vindicator of his people (cp. Ps 9:8; 58:11; 82:11; 94:2; Isa 11:4; Jer 22:16). • Those who have already died ***have now been made perfect*** by the sacrifice of Christ (10:14).

12:24 ***Jesus*** is the mediator of ***the new covenant*** (8:7-13; 9:11-14; 10:15-18). His ***sprinkled blood***, used as the sacrifice for sins, ***speaks of forgiveness.*** • ***The blood of Abel*** cried out to God from the ground, demanding ***vengeance*** for his murder by Cain (Gen 4:10). By contrast, Jesus' blood cries out that the price for sins has been paid for those in the new covenant (10:16-18).

12:25-29 As the final warning in the book (see 2:1-4; 4:12-13; 6:4-8; 10:26-31), this passage plays off the image of God speaking in 12:18-24.

12:25 God is ***the One who is speaking*** his revealed word in his Son, Jesus (1:1-3). The author argues from lesser to greater (see note on 9:14): Moses' warning the people under the old covenant is the lesser situation, and God's warning us from heaven is the greater situation. If people did not escape judgment when they were warned by Moses, those who reject the message of the Son of God will certainly not escape punishment.

12:26-27 ***shook the earth:*** Exod 19:18; Judg 5:5; Ps 68:8; 77:18. • ***"Once again I will shake not only the earth but the heavens also":*** Quoting Hag 2:6, the author emphasizes that ***all of creation will be shaken and removed*** at the judgment at the end of the age (1 Cor 7:31; 2 Pet 3:10, 12; Rev 21:1).

12:28-29 God deserves ***holy fear and awe.*** • ***our God is a devouring fire:*** This quotation from Deut 4:24 speaks at once of God's awesome power and of his right to judge.

13:1-6 This series of practical guidelines is similar to other ethics lists in the NT. It describes how to love others in the community of faith, a strong ethical foundation for all of life.

13:1 ***Keep on loving each other as brothers and sisters:*** Literally *Continue in brotherly love* (see Rom 12:10; 1 Thes 4:9; 1 Pet 1:22; 2 Pet 1:7). This instruction applies to everyone in the Christian community (see note on 3:1).

13:2 ***Hospitality*** is another foundational principle in Jewish and Christian ethics (1 Pet 4:9; see also Matt 10:11; Acts 16:15; Titus 3:13; Phlm 1:22; 3 Jn 1:5-8). In the first century, most people did not stay at inns when traveling. • ***Some . . . have entertained angels:*** See Gen 18:2-15; Judg 13:2-23.

13:3 ***Remember those in prison:*** Prisoners often depended on family members and friends for their most basic needs. Christians were challenged to provide comfort, food, prayer, and other necessities for those imprisoned because of their faith (13:18-19; Matt 25:36; Col 4:18; 2 Tim 1:16).

13:4 ***Give honor to marriage*** means to protect it and hold it as highly valuable. • ***Immoral*** refers to all sexually illicit

will surely judge people who are immoral
and those who commit adultery.
5Don't love money; be satisfied with what
you have. For God has said,

"I will never fail you.
I will never abandon you."

6So we can say with confidence,

"The LORD is my helper,
so I will have no fear.
What can mere people do to me?"

7Remember your leaders who taught you
the [g]word of God. Think of all the good that
has come from their lives, and follow the example of their faith.
8Jesus Christ is the same yesterday, today, and forever.
9So do not be attracted by
strange, new ideas. Your strength comes
from God's grace, not from rules about food,
which don't help those who follow them.
10We have an altar from which the priests
in the Tabernacle have no right to eat.
11Under the old system, the [h]high priest brought
the blood of animals into the Holy Place as
a sacrifice for sin, and the bodies of the animals were burned outside the camp.
12So
also Jesus suffered and died outside the
city gates to make his people holy by means
of his own blood.
13So let us go out to him,
outside the camp, and bear the disgrace he
bore.
14For this world is not our permanent
home; we are looking forward to a home yet
to come.
15Therefore, let us offer through Jesus
a continual sacrifice of praise to God, proclaiming our allegiance to his name.
16And
don't forget to do good and to [i]share with
those in need. These are the sacrifices that
please God.
17Obey your spiritual leaders, and do
what they say. Their work is to watch over
your souls, and they are accountable to God.
Give them reason to do this with joy and not
with sorrow. That would certainly not be for
your benefit.

13:5
Gen 28:15
*Deut 31:5
Josh 1:5

13:6
*Ps 118:6

13:7
Heb 6:12
[g]*logos* (3056)
‣1 Jn 1:1

13:8
Heb 1:12

13:9
Eph 4:14
Col 2:7, 16

13:11
Lev 4:12, 21; 16:27
[h]*archiereus* (0749)
‣Luke 3:2

13:12
John 19:17
Heb 9:12

13:13
Heb 11:26

13:14
Heb 11:10; 12:22

13:15
Ps 50:14
Hos 14:2
1 Pet 2:5

13:16
Phil 4:18
[i]*koinōnia* (2842)
‣1 Jn 1:6

behavior. • *Adultery* breaks the marriage vow by engaging in sexual activity outside the marriage relationship.

13:5 ***Don't love money:*** See 1 Tim 6:6-10. Instead, the believer is to ***be satisfied*** with what God has provided. Perhaps some in the community were under financial strain (see 10:32-34). The promises of God still stand: ***"I will never fail you. I will never abandon you"*** (see Deut 31:6, 8).

13:6 This quotation from Ps 118:6 offers the response of faith: ***The LORD is my helper,*** so we can ***have no fear*** of what ***people*** might do.

13:7-19 This middle section of ch 13 is bracketed by references to the community's leaders (13:7, 17-19). Rabbis often used this technique, called *inclusio,* in which similar words or phrases were used to mark the beginning and ending of a unit, much as we would use a subheading in a book today. This section hints at several difficulties in the church to which Hebrews was originally addressed.

13:7 ***Remember your leaders:*** The word *leaders* was used for military, political, and religious leaders. These leaders, evidently founders of this community, ***taught . . . the word of God*** to them—a basic responsibility of those who lead (see 1 Tim 3:2; 2 Tim 2:15; Titus 1:9). Their ***lives*** and ***faith*** were an ***example*** to ***follow.***

13:8 Though the community was facing new challenges, ***Jesus Christ is the same,*** and his Good News does not change. • ***yesterday:*** Jesus was the Father's agent in creation (1:2, 10). • ***today:*** Jesus currently sits at the Father's right hand (1:13; 7:26-28; 10:12). He will rule the universe ***forever*** (1:8, 10-12).

13:9-10 Since Jesus does not change (13:8), it is unwise for a believer to be ***attracted by strange, new ideas.*** The false teachings in view seemed to involve ***rules about food.*** In some branches of Judaism, certain ritual meals were understood as providing God's grace to those participating. Some in the community might have been tempted to abandon the Christian community by participating in Jewish fellowship meals. These Jewish meals at times encouraged participants to focus on the Jerusalem altar. The author reminds his hearers that ***we have an altar*** of which those under the old covenant have no part—Christ's sacrifice (7:27-28; 8:13; 9:11-14; 10:11-14). • ***Tabernacle:*** Or *tent.*

13:11-12 The author describes the sacrifice on the Day of Atonement (Lev 16:1-28), in which ***animals were burned outside the camp*** (Lev 16:27). By analogy, ***Jesus suffered and died outside the city gates*** of Jerusalem. He was the supreme Day of Atonement sacrifice (9:11-14, 24-28; 10:1-4).

13:13 ***let us go out to him, outside the camp:*** We should stand with Jesus, identifying with him and rejecting the apparent safety and comfort of standing with the world against him. In standing with Christ, we ***bear the disgrace he bore*** (6:5-6; 12:1-3).

13:14 Like Abraham's family (11:9-16), we are not ultimately invested in the ***world,*** for it ***is not our permanent home.*** We are looking for ***a home yet to come,*** the heavenly city of Jerusalem (12:22).

13:15-16 In light of Jesus' decisive, sacrificial work on our behalf, we still have ***sacrifices*** to offer: ***praise*** and obedience. Because Christ has eradicated the sacrificial system of the old covenant through the sacrifice of himself (7:27-28; 8:13; 9:11-14; 10:11-14), ***these are the sacrifices that please God.***

13:15 ***sacrifice of praise:*** This probably refers to a peace offering (Lev 7:11-14). The person bringing the offering had to be made ritually clean before the offering could be made. Our thank offering to God can be ***continual*** because Jesus has made us clean for all time. When we give thanks to Jesus continually, we are ***proclaiming our allegiance to his name.***

13:16 ***to do good and to share with those in need:*** These are basic Christian ***sacrifices*** (6:10; 10:24, 34; 13:1-3); they characterize life in the Christian community.

13:17 The relationship between the ***spiritual leaders*** and the members of the church may have been strained, so the author exhorts the members to ***obey*** them ***and do what they say.*** • The Greek word translated *obey* can also mean *follow, place confidence in,* or *be persuaded by.* • Christian leaders ***watch over*** people's ***souls*** (Acts 20:28-31; 1 Pet 5:1-4), a role that carries grave responsibility, making them ***accountable to God*** (Jas 3:1). • The word ***sorrow*** could be translated *groaning;* it speaks of emotional burden and stress. Having leaders who are stressed and burdened because of an unruly church does not ***benefit*** the church.

13:17
Acts 20:28
13:18
Acts 24:16
13:20
Jer 32:40
Ezek 37:26
John 10:11
[j]*poimēn* (4166)
‣1 Pet 2:25
[k]*diathēkē* (1242)
‣Matt 26:28
13:21
Rom 11:36
Phil 2:13
13:22
1 Pet 5:12
13:23
Acts 16:1
13:25
Col 4:18
Titus 3:15

18Pray for us, for our conscience is clear
and we want to live honorably in everything
we do. 19And especially pray that I will be
able to come back to you soon.

6. BENEDICTION AND CONCLUSION (13:20-25)

20 Now may the God of peace—
who brought up from the dead our
Lord Jesus,
the great [j]Shepherd of the sheep,
and ratified an eternal [k]covenant with
his blood—
21 may he equip you with all you need
for doing his will.
May he produce in you,
through the power of Jesus Christ,
every good thing that is pleasing to him.
All glory to him forever and ever!
Amen.

22I urge you, dear brothers and sisters, to
pay attention to what I have written in this
brief exhortation.
23I want you to know that our brother
Timothy has been released from jail. If he
comes here soon, I will bring him with me
to see you.
24Greet all your leaders and all the believers there. The believers from Italy send you
their greetings.
25May God's grace be with you all.

Love in the Christian Community (13:1-6)

Heb 6:10; 10:24
Lev 19:18
Matt 22:39
John 13:34
Rom 12:10; 13:8
1 Cor 13
1 Thes 4:9
1 Pet 1:22
2 Pet 1:7
1 Jn 2:10; 3:10; 4:7

The relational aspects of life in community are not always easy, and the group to whom Hebrews was written seems to have been struggling with unity (see 13:7-17). The answer to relational discord in the Christian community is to exercise love toward our brothers and sisters in Christ. This command is grounded in the teaching of Jesus (Matt 22:39; John 13:34; see Lev 19:18), is expressed by Paul (Rom 13:8; 1 Cor 13), and is found elsewhere in the NT (1 Pet 1:22; 1 Jn 2:10; 3:10; 4:7). Loving others in the body of Christ is central to a Christian ethic (Rom 12:10; 1 Thes 4:9; 2 Pet 1:7).

The author of Hebrews reminds his readers to love one another (6:10; 10:24). Christians are to relate to one another in such a way that our communities of faith are characterized by acts of love. In 13:1-6, the command to love comes to concrete expression. Here, as elsewhere in the NT, love refers not to an emotion but to a commitment to meet others' needs. Love means showing hospitality, caring for the needs of those who are persecuted and in prison, being faithful in one's marriage, and rejecting a life motivated by money.

Great confusion exists in the world about the nature of love and the character of the Christian church. Therefore, there is a great need for the church to live out the Lord's command to "Keep on loving each other as brothers and sisters" (13:1).

13:18-19 ***Pray for us:*** The author asks for prayer for himself using the "authorial plural" (see also 5:11; 6:9). • ***our conscience is clear:*** Cp. 2 Cor 1:11-12; 4:2.

13:20-21 Benedictions were an important element of letters, speeches, and sermons. The author of Hebrews weaves a number of important themes from the book into his benediction. • The image of ***our Lord Jesus*** as ***the great Shepherd of the sheep*** (cp. Ps 23) communicates God's provision for and protection of his people (see also John 10:11-18; 1 Pet 2:25) and is specifically tied here to ***an eternal covenant.***

13:21 ***in you:*** Some manuscripts read *in us.*

13:22 ***dear brothers and sisters*** (literally *brothers*): See note on 3:1. • ***this brief exhortation:*** This probably indicates that Hebrews was a sermon (cp. the same term in Acts 13:14-15, translated "encouragement").

13:23 This ***Timothy*** may have been Paul's traveling companion (see "Timothy" at Acts 16:1-3, p. 1860); if so, his imprisonment is not mentioned elsewhere in the NT. He clearly knows the author and the recipients of this letter.

13:24-25 The book closes with a formal greeting and a blessing. • ***all the believers there:*** Literally *all of God's holy people.* ***The believers from Italy*** probably suggests that the author is writing back to Rome from elsewhere in the Mediterranean world; some scholars, however, have thought that the author was writing from Rome.

THE LETTER OF JAMES

How can we be faithful friends of God like Abraham? Can we resist the pressures of the world, our rebellious human impulses, and the influence of the devil? Can Christians live together in peace as we seek solutions to life's problems? James addresses these issues in his letter as he seeks to motivate Christians to develop a mature and consistent faith and to show how Christians can have loyal friendship with God and with one another.

SETTING

James, Jesus' brother, writes as the leader of the Jerusalem church to Jewish Christians who have been scattered by persecution. He encourages them to endure their trials with Christian fortitude and to exhibit consistent Christian character.

The recipients of this letter were Jewish Christians (1:1; 2:1) who had been scattered by the persecutions which began with the stoning of Stephen (Acts 8:1; 11:19). They lived among the Jews who had been "scattered abroad" in the Diaspora (1:1; John 7:35), which had its origins in the Assyrian dispersion of Israel (the northern kingdom) in 722–721 BC and in the Babylonian exile of Judah (the southern kingdom) in 586 BC. This dispersion later included many Jews who traveled extensively during the Greek and Roman empires (4:13; Acts 13:14; 17:1). By the middle of the first century, there were Jewish communities all over the Greco-Roman world.

SUMMARY

The letter of James is written with a pastor's perspective, and it focuses more on ethics than any other book of the NT. The letter contains teachings based on the law as understood through the life and teaching of Jesus (1:25; 2:8). James also reflects Jesus' own teachings, especially as later recorded in Matthew's "Sermon on the Mount" (Matt 5–7) and Luke's "Sermon on the Plain" (Luke 6:20-49).

AUTHORSHIP

The letter of James was written by one of Jesus' brothers (see further "James, the Brother of Jesus" at Acts 15:13-21, p. 1858). Like the other sons of Joseph and Mary (Matt 13:55), James (Greek *Iakōbos*) bore the name of an Israelite hero: Jacob (Hebrew *Ya'aqob*; Greek *Iakōb*). After Jesus' resur-

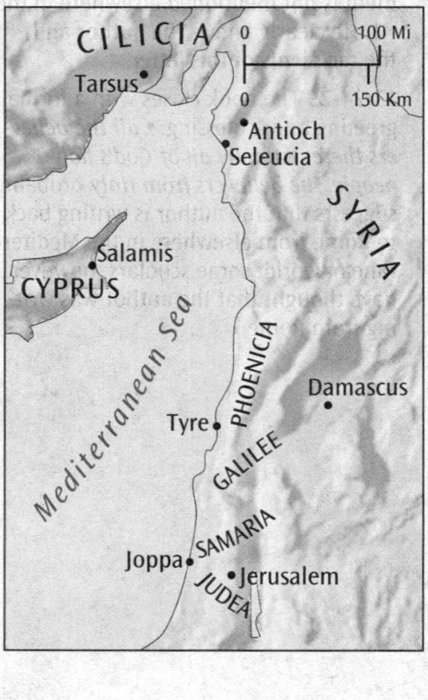

◀ **The Setting of James, about AD 46.** James, one of Jesus' brothers, was a leader of the church in JERUSALEM. The believers from Jerusalem had been scattered in the early 40s AD as a result of persecution (see Acts 8:1-3; 12:1-4). The scattered believers traveled throughout JUDEA, SAMARIA, and PHOENICIA, and to ANTIOCH in SYRIA and CYPRUS (see Acts 11:19).

rection, James became a believer (cp. 1 Cor 15:7) and rose to a position of leadership in the Jerusalem church (see Acts 15:13-22).

During Jesus' public ministry, neither James nor the other siblings were followers of Jesus. They had even tried to end his ministry and bring him home to his responsibilities as eldest son (Mark 3:31-35; cp. John 7:3-5). A personal resurrection appearance convinced James that Jesus was the Christ (1 Cor 15:7), and he was with the others in the upper room when the Spirit was given on Pentecost (Acts 1:14; 2:1-3). James became the leader of the Jerusalem church after Peter's arrest and departure from Jerusalem (Acts 12:1-3; 15:13-21; 21:18; Gal 1:19; 2:9).

OUTLINE

1:1
Greetings from James

1:2-18
Faith and Endurance

1:19-27
Listening and Doing

2:1-26
Poverty and Generosity

3:1–4:3
Speech and Conflict

4:4-10
Drawing Close to God

4:11–5:6
Warnings

5:7-20
Final Exhortations

DATE AND LOCATION OF WRITING

The letter of James is one of the earliest books in the NT, written after the persecution under Herod Agrippa (AD 44, Acts 12:1-5), yet prior to Galatians (AD 48~49) and the council in Jerusalem (AD 49~50). It reflects an early period prior to the conflict over circumcising Gentile converts and before the development of false teachings in other Christian communities. It was a time when *synagogue* ("meeting," 2:2) and *church* (5:14) were interchangeable terms, as were *law* and *word* (1:23, 25).

That this letter was written from Jerusalem is deduced from information in Acts and Galatians about James's location (Acts 15:13-22; 21:18; Gal 1:18-19; 2:9, 12). The book contains allusions appropriate to Palestine, including references to the scorching heat (1:11); salty water springs (3:11); the cultivation of figs, olives, and grapevines (3:12); the imagery of the sea (1:6; 3:4); and the early and later rains (5:7).

LITERARY CHARACTER

The letter of James is written in good Koiné Greek, the common Greek of the Greco-Roman world. It reflects the Hellenistic influences on Galilee and Palestine, as well as the enculturation of Jewish readers in the Diaspora. James writes with grammatical accuracy, has a wide vocabulary, and has an elegant feel for the rhythms and sounds of words. There are clear allusions to the Greek translation of the OT (e.g., 4:6), with some imagery from the Hellenistic world.

James uses many oratorical devices, such as fraternal appeals (1:2; 2:1; 3:1; 4:11), rhetorical questions (2:5; 3:11-12; 4:1), imperative exhortations (1:16; 3:1; 5:16), metaphors and illustrations (2:26; 3:3-5; 4:14), and aphorisms that summarize a paragraph (2:13, 17; 3:18; 4:17).

TIMELINE

Passover, AD 30 or 33
Jesus' crucifixion and resurrection

Pentecost, AD 30 or 33
The birth of the church in Jerusalem

AD 34~35
Saul's conversion near Damascus

AD 41~44
Persecution of Christians by Herod Agrippa I

AD 44~49
James writes to the "twelve tribes"

AD 47~48
Barnabas and Paul's first missionary journey

AD 49~50
The council in Jerusalem

early 60s AD
James, the brother of Jesus, is stoned to death in Jerusalem

about AD 64~65?
Paul is martyred in Rome

AD 70
Jerusalem and the Temple are destroyed

James distinctively emphasizes friendship as the ideal relationship with God.

WILLIAM R. BAKER
Personal Speech-Ethics in the Epistle of James, p. 288

[James] takes us . . . back to the infancy of the Christian Church, to the purple dawn of Christian enthusiasm and the first glow of Christian love.

J. B. ADAMSON
The Epistle of James, p. 21

MEANING AND MESSAGE

James's primary concern is for his readers to maintain undivided faith and loyalty toward God (1:6). They were under pressure from a society that oppressed them economically (2:6) and abused them for their faith in Jesus Christ (2:7). James recommends patient endurance (1:3), submission to God (4:7), and sharing in the ministries of the church (5:13-20). These will result in perfection (1:4), honor (4:10), and a glorious life (1:12) at the coming of Jesus Christ (5:8).

The Law. As leader of the Jerusalem church, James maintained proper respect for the law of Moses and for Jewish traditions, such as the purification ceremonies after a vow (Acts 21:18-25). James also expressed a sympathetic understanding of the Gentile mission when he concluded that Gentiles could be recognized as Christians without first becoming proselytes to Judaism. He based this on God's covenant with Noah (Acts 15:19-22; see Gen 9:1-17). In his letter, we find James both upholding the law (1:25) and at the same time hinting at its reinterpretation through Jesus the Messiah (2:8-11).

Jewishness. This is one of the most Jewish letters in the NT. James uses the symbols of Judaism with little criticism (contrast Matt 5:21-22) and uses the primary identity markers of Judaism without redefinition (contrast Rom 2:29). James addresses the readers as the "twelve tribes" (1:1) and identifies their church gathering as a synagogue (2:2) with its elders (5:14) and teachers (3:1). He refers to the law of Moses repeatedly (1:25; 2:8-12; 4:11), cites the foundational creed of Israel (the *Shema*, 2:19), and names God as "the Lord of Heaven's Armies" (5:4), a common OT title for God. James also uses the literary elements of OT wisdom literature (1:5; 3:13, 17) and prophetic exhortations (4:13; 5:1). He appeals to Israel's heroes (Abraham, 2:21, 23; Rahab, 2:25; Job, 5:11; Elijah, 5:17). He does not, however, explicitly mention the ceremonial elements of Judaism, such as the Sabbath, circumcision, or food laws.

Works. The apparent differences between James and Paul regarding "good works" must be understood in their differing historical and theological contexts. Paul emphasized that people could not get right with God by "obeying the law" (Rom 3:20, 28; Gal 2:16) or, indeed by anything that they might do (Rom 4:3-5). Only God, through his initiative of grace, could overcome the problem of human sin; a person must respond to him by faith. Both Paul and James believed this, but they differed in their emphasis. Paul emphasized that works of the law do not produce salvation (Eph 2:8-9), and so he opposed circumcision of Gentiles (Rom 4:5; Gal 2:11-12; 5:2-6).

James, however, was addressing Jewish Christian communities. He speaks of "good works" as charitable deeds (2:14-18, 21-24). Good deeds are faithful obedience; they are the evidence of a genuine relationship with God based on faith. True biblical faith will always produce good deeds pleasing to God. James emphasizes that faith cannot be reduced to a mere affirmation of truth (2:19), and faithfulness does not allow for divided allegiance between God and the world (1:8; 4:4, 7).

The letter of James gives us insight into very early communities of Christian Jews. It also helps us understand how Christians should live when they are a minority group in the midst of an oppressive, non-Christian society. It is alive with godly counsel for us today.

FURTHER READING

LUKE TIMOTHY JOHNSON
James (1995)

RALPH MARTIN
James (1989)

DOUGLAS J. MOO
James (2000)

1:2-3 1 Pet 1:6-7
1:4 [a]*teleios* (5046) ›Jas 3:2
1:5 Prov 2:3-6; Matt 7:7
1:6 Matt 21:22
1:10-11 Isa 40:6-7; 1 Pet 1:24
1:12 Rev 2:10; 3:11; [b]*makarios* (3107) ›1 Pet 3:14; [c]*peirasmos* (3986) ›Jas 1:13
1:13 [d]*peirazō* (3985) ›1 Pet 4:12
1:14 Prov 19:3
1:15 [e]*hamartia* (0266) ›Jas 5:15
1:16 1 Cor 6:9
1:17 Gen 1:16; Ps 136:7; Matt 7:11; [f]*patēr* (3962) ›1 Jn 2:13
1:18 John 1:13; 1 Pet 1:23

1. GREETINGS FROM JAMES (1:1)

1 This letter is from James, a slave of God
and of the Lord Jesus Christ.
I am writing to the "twelve tribes"—Jewish believers scattered abroad.
Greetings!

2. FAITH AND ENDURANCE (1:2-18)

2 Dear brothers and sisters, when troubles
come your way, consider it an opportunity
for great joy. 3 For you know that when your
faith is tested, your endurance has a chance
to grow. 4 So let it grow, for when your endurance is [a]fully developed, you will be [a]perfect
and complete, needing nothing.
5 If you need wisdom, ask our generous
God, and he will give it to you. He will not rebuke you for asking. 6 But when you ask him,
be sure that your faith is in God alone. Do
not waver, for a person with divided loyalty
is as unsettled as a wave of the sea that is
blown and tossed by the wind. 7 Such people
should not expect to receive anything from
the Lord. 8 Their loyalty is divided between
God and the world, and they are unstable in
everything they do.
9 Believers who are poor have something
to boast about, for God has honored them.
10 And those who are rich should boast that
God has humbled them. They will fade away
like a little flower in the field. 11 The hot sun
rises and the grass withers; the little flower
droops and falls, and its beauty fades away.
In the same way, the rich will fade away
with all of their achievements.
12 God [b]blesses those who patiently endure [c]testing and temptation. Afterward
they will receive the crown of life that God
has promised to those who love him. 13 And
remember, when you are being [d]tempted,
do not say, "God is [d]tempting me." God is
never tempted to do wrong, and he never
[d]tempts anyone else. 14 Temptation comes
from our own desires, which entice us and
drag us away. 15 These desires give birth to
[e]sinful actions. And when [e]sin is allowed to
grow, it gives birth to death.
16 So don't be misled, my dear brothers
and sisters. 17 Whatever is good and perfect
comes down to us from God our [f]Father,
who created all the lights in the heavens. He
never changes or casts a shifting shadow.
18 He chose to give birth to us by giving us
his true word. And we, out of all creation, became his prized possession.

1:1 ***James:*** See "James, the Brother of Jesus" at Acts 15:13-21, p. 1858. • By identifying his readers as ***the "twelve tribes,"*** James affirms Christianity's continuity with Israel's heritage. The Exile had dispersed the twelve tribes, but Jewish interpreters looked forward to God reuniting them (see *Psalms of Solomon* 17:26-28; *Testament of Benjamin* 9:2; cp. Ezek 37:15-28; Matt 19:28). Christ has spiritually brought an end to Israel's exile and reunited the tribes. • Jews ***scattered abroad*** (Greek *diaspora*) were living outside Palestine (John 7:35; Acts 2:5; 8:1; 11:19). • ***Greetings!*** (Greek *chairein*): This greeting is typical in first-century Greek letters (Acts 15:23; 23:26) and interpersonally (Matt 26:49; Luke 1:28).

1:2-4 Enduring troubles and temptations is a recurring theme (1:12-15; 5:7-12). Failure to endure is "wandering from the truth" that requires being "saved from death" (5:19-20).

1:2 ***Dear brothers and sisters:*** Literally *My brothers;* also in 1:16, 19. See note on 2:1. • James uses a wordplay: ***joy*** (Greek *chara*) in 1:2 is related to *greetings* in 1:1.

1:5-8 James introduces ***wisdom*** as a recurring theme (cp. 3:13-18).

1:6 ***Do not waver, for a person with divided loyalty:*** The Greek is often translated *Do not doubt, for a person who doubts,* but the sense here is of a person whose loyalty is divided between God and the world (see 1:8).

1:8 ***Their loyalty is divided between God and the world*** (literally *They are double-minded*): James might have created the Greek word used here. He emphasizes the need for confidence in God alone.

1:9-11 Poverty and wealth are a recurring theme (cp. 2:1-26; 4:13–5:11). James does not promise material wealth to the righteous poor but announces a future reversal in heaven.

1:9 ***Believers who are:*** Literally *The brother who is;* see note on 2:1. • ***something to boast about:*** In the NT, boasting is usually viewed negatively (3:14; 4:16; Eph 2:9), but here it means boasting about what God has done (2:5; Rom 15:18; 1 Cor 1:31; Gal 6:14).

1:10 ***those who are rich should boast:*** With irony, James is describing the dreadful fate of the ungodly rich who elevate themselves by oppressing poor and vulnerable people (see 2:6-8; 5:1-6).

1:12-27 James addresses the same three topics as in 1:2-11, adding a new dimension to each topic. External testing (1:2-4) becomes internal temptation (1:11-18); the need for wisdom (1:5-8) is related to controlling angry speech (1:19-21); and poverty/wealth relate to the need to act upon God's word (1:22-25). The section then summarizes these themes (1:26-27).

1:12 ***Those who love him*** are faithful and obedient (cp. 1:22-25; 2:5; Deut 7:9; 1 Jn 5:2).

1:13 ***do not say:*** James is using *diatribe,* in which an imaginary opponent presents a contrary opinion. In this way he is able to voice the readers' possible objection and immediately refute it (also in 2:3, 16, 18; 4:13). • ***God is never tempted to do wrong:*** Or *God should not be put to a test by evil people;* the alternate translation dulls the parallelism with ***he never tempts.***

1:14 Like hooks for fishing or traps for hunting, ***desires . . . entice us*** into sin and ***drag us away*** from faithfulness to God.

1:15 When evil desires conceive, they give birth to ***sinful actions*** (literally *sin,* personified as an infant). When the infant sin is ***allowed to grow*** to full maturity, it ***gives birth to death,*** in opposition to "the crown of [eternal] life" (1:12).

1:17 ***from God our Father, who created all the lights in the heavens*** (literally *from above, from the Father of lights*): God is *the Father of lights* since he created everything in the heavens (Gen 1:3, 14-17). In contrast to the moving lights in the heavens, God ***never changes or casts a shifting shadow*** (some manuscripts read *He never changes, as a shifting shadow does*).

1:18 God's ***true word*** is the Good News (1:21-23; 1 Pet 1:23-25). • ***give birth:*** The imagery of a mother giving birth shows the full scope of God's parental love for his children (cp. Luke 13:34; John 1:13; 3:3-8; 1 Pet 1:23). • ***we, out of all creation, became his prized possession:*** Literally *we became a kind of firstfruit of his creatures* (cp. Exod 23:16; Lev 23:9-14; 1 Cor 15:20; Col 1:18). Christians are examples of the ultimate restoration of all creation (Rom 8:20-22).

3. LISTENING AND DOING (1:19-27)

19 Understand this, my dear brothers and
sisters: You must all be quick to listen, slow
to speak, and slow to get angry. 20 Human
anger does not produce the righteousness
God desires. 21 So get rid of all the filth and
evil in your lives, and humbly accept the
word God has planted in your hearts, for it
has the power to save your souls.

22 But don't just listen to God's word. You
must do what it says. Otherwise, you are
only fooling yourselves. 23 For if you listen
to the word and don't obey, it is like glancing
at your face in a mirror. 24 You see yourself,
walk away, and forget what you look like.
25 But if you look carefully into the perfect
[g]law that sets you [h]free, and if you do what it
says and don't forget what you heard, then
God will bless you for doing it.

26 If you claim to be religious but don't
control your tongue, you are fooling yourself, and your religion is [i]worthless. 27 Pure
and genuine religion in the sight of God the
Father means caring for orphans and widows in their distress and refusing to let the
world corrupt you.

4. POVERTY AND GENEROSITY (2:1-26)

A Warning against Prejudice

2 My dear brothers and sisters, how can
you claim to have faith in our glorious
Lord Jesus Christ if you favor some people
over others?

2 For example, suppose someone comes
into your [j]meeting dressed in fancy clothes
and expensive jewelry, and another comes
in who is poor and dressed in dirty clothes.
3 If you give special attention and a good
seat to the rich person, but you say to the
poor one, "You can stand over there, or else
sit on the floor"—well, 4 doesn't this discrimination show that your judgments are
guided by evil motives?

5 Listen to me, dear brothers and sisters.
Hasn't God chosen the poor in this world to
be rich in faith? Aren't they the ones who
will inherit the Kingdom he promised to
those who love him? 6 But you dishonor
the poor! Isn't it the rich who oppress you
and drag you into court? 7 Aren't they the
ones who slander Jesus Christ, whose noble
name you bear?

8 Yes indeed, it is good when you obey the
royal law as found in the Scriptures: "Love

1:19 Prov 10:19; 15:1
1:21 Eph 1:13; 4:22; Col 1:28; 1 Pet 2:1
1:22 Matt 7:21, 26; Rom 2:13
1:25 John 13:17; 1 Pet 2:16; [g]*nomos* (3551) ‣Jas 2:10; [h]*eleutheria* (1657) ‣Jas 2:12
1:26 Ps 34:13; [i]*mataios* (3152) ‣1 Pet 1:18
2:1 Prov 24:23; Acts 10:34; 1 Cor 2:8
2:2 [j]*sunagōgē* (4864) ‣Rev 1:20
2:4 John 7:23-24
2:5 Luke 6:20; 21:1-4; 1 Cor 1:26-28
2:7 Acts 11:26; 1 Pet 4:16
2:8 *Lev 19:18; Matt 7:12; Rom 13:8

1:20 *Human anger:* Literally *A man's anger.* • *the righteousness:* Or *the justice.*

1:21 *get rid of:* Literally *put off,* like filthy clothing; cp. Eph 4:22; 1 Pet 2:1. • ***the word God has planted . . . has the power to save your souls:*** James emphasizes that Christians are called to respond to a word that God himself has put within our very beings (in fulfillment of Jer 31:31-34). • The soul refers to the whole person (so also in 5:20; see Gen 2:7; 1 Pet 3:20).

1:22-23 In several places, James appears to be reflecting on Jesus' teachings. These verses reflect the teaching of Jesus (Matt 7:24, 26; Luke 6:46, 49).

1:22 *don't just listen to God's word:* Reading the scriptures was an important part of worship (Luke 4:16-17; Acts 13:13-16; Col 4:16; 1 Tim 4:13). Since most people could not read and copies were not readily available, they listened to the readings in public worship.

1:24 *forget what you look like:* The problem is not the poor quality of an ancient mirror but the inattention of the viewer (cp. Matt 7:24-27).

1:25 *law that sets you free:* God's word gives us new birth and salvation (1:18, 21) but demands that we ***do what it says*** (1:22-25).

1:26-27 ***control*** (literally *bridle*) ***your tongue:*** James uses the graphic image of the bridle in a horse's mouth to imply the relationship between speech and a whole body of behaviors (cp. 3:1-13).

• ***Orphans and widows*** were the most helpless members of ancient society. They were dependent upon the care of others, since the husband and father was the means of economic support and social contact (Exod 22:22-24; Deut 10:18). Christians are called to take care of the helpless (cp. 1 Tim 5:3-16). • In James, ***the world*** stands in opposition to God (cp. 3:15; 4:4; Rom 12:2; 1 Jn 2:15-17).

2:1-4 James gives a realistic illustration to enforce his prohibition against favoring the wealthy.

2:1 *dear brothers and sisters* (literally *brothers;* also in 2:5, 14): The Greek word used here means *fellow Christians* of either sex. James frequently begins a new section with this affectionate greeting (1:2, 16; 2:14; 3:1; 5:7, 19), soliciting their loyal response. • James contrasts ***our glorious Lord Jesus Christ*** with the glory of a well-dressed man (2:2). Christ's glory includes his resurrection, exaltation, and second coming.

2:2 *your meeting* (literally *your synagogue*): This word refers to the gathering of people rather than the building in which they met. • The ***fancy clothes and expensive jewelry*** of the rich, in contrast to the ***dirty clothes*** of the poor, symbolize the contrast in socioeconomic status.

2:3-4 It is natural to ***give special attention*** to wealthy people because of their social status, political power, and potential generosity as patrons. By serving and publicly honoring the wealthy, the church could gain whatever economic benefits they wished to give. James warns that ***this discrimination*** reflects ***evil motives,*** a division between loyalty to God (1:6) and a desire for the benefits of worldly wealth (4:4).

2:5 *Listen to me:* Employing this rhetorical device for emphasis (see Deut 6:3; Amos 3:1; Matt 13:18; Acts 15:13), James presents his argument against favoring the rich. • ***Hasn't God chosen the poor?*** God's special concern for the poor is reflected in the OT (Exod 23:11; 1 Sam 2:8; Ps 12:5) and in the ministries of Jesus and Paul (Luke 4:18; 6:20; 1 Cor 1:26-28). This concern was emphasized by the Jerusalem church (Gal 2:9-10), of which James was the leader. • ***inherit the Kingdom:*** The Kingdom of God was central to the teaching of Jesus (Matt 12:8; Mark 1:15; Luke 17:21). Christ already rules from his place at the right hand of the Father, yet his Kingdom will be fully realized only when the Son of Man comes (Matt 25:31, 34; 1 Cor 15:24-28).

2:7 ***slander Jesus Christ, whose noble name you bear*** (literally *slander the noble name spoken over you*): The name *spoken over you* is Jesus Christ (2:1). It is a sign of ownership, pronounced at the time of conversion and baptism.

2:8-13 James applies biblical evidence to counter the common practice of favoring rich and powerful people.

2:8 Christians are to *obey* (literally *fulfill*) ***the royal law,*** just as Jesus fulfilled the law by his coming (Matt 5:17) and his teaching (Matt 22:34-40). • The law is

2:10
Matt 5:19
[k]*nomos* (3551)
‣Jas 4:11

2:11
*Exod 20:13-14
*Deut 5:17-18

2:12
[a]*eleutheria* (1657)
‣1 Pet 2:16

2:13
Matt 18:32-35
Luke 6:38
[b]*eleos* (1656)
‣Jas 3:17

2:14
[c]*pistis* (4102)
‣Jas 2:20

2:16
1 Jn 3:17-18

2:18
Matt 7:16-17

2:19
[d]*daimonion* (1140)
‣Rev 16:14

2:20
[e]*pistis* (4102)
‣1 Jn 3:23

2:21
Gen 22:9, 12

2:22
Heb 11:17

your neighbor as yourself." 9But if you favor some people over others, you are committing a sin. You are guilty of breaking the law. 10For the person who keeps all of the [k]laws except one is as guilty as a person who has broken all of God's laws. 11For the same God who said, "You must not commit adultery," also said, "You must not murder." So if you murder someone but do not commit adultery, you have still broken the law.

12So whatever you say or whatever you do, remember that you will be judged by the law that sets you [a]free. 13There will be no mercy for those who have not shown [b]mercy to others. But if you have been merciful, God will be [b]merciful when he judges you.

Faith without Good Deeds Is Dead

14What good is it, dear brothers and sisters, if you say you have [c]faith but don't show it by your actions? Can that kind of [c]faith save anyone? 15Suppose you see a brother or sister who has no food or clothing, 16and you say, "Good-bye and have a good day; stay warm and eat well"—but then you don't give that person any food or clothing. What good does that do?

17So you see, faith by itself isn't enough. Unless it produces good deeds, it is dead and useless.

18Now someone may argue, "Some people have faith; others have good deeds." But I say, "How can you show me your faith if you don't have good deeds? I will show you my faith by my good deeds."

19You say you have faith, for you believe that there is one God. Good for you! Even the [d]demons believe this, and they tremble in terror. 20How foolish! Can't you see that [e]faith without good deeds is useless?

21Don't you remember that our ancestor Abraham was shown to be right with God by his actions when he offered his son Isaac on the altar? 22You see, his faith and his actions worked together. His actions

Faith and Faithfulness (2:14-26)

Gen 17:1; 22:1-19
Lev 22:31
1 Sam 2:9
Hab 2:4
John 15:2
Rom 2:6
Gal 5:6; 6:5-10
Eph 2:8-10
Phil 2:12-13
Heb 11:1-40

James's conspicuous emphasis on faithfulness to God argues for charitable deeds as an expression of faith (2:14-26). A faith relationship with God cannot be based merely on believing a true statement (2:19). Saving faith (2:14) results in actions (1:22-25) which emulate God, who generously gives good gifts (1:5, 17; 4:6). Faith and good deeds are inseparable. As with Abraham, good deeds show that a person has complete faith (1:4) and is righteous before God (2:23; Gen 15:6).

Our Lord taught (Matt 5:16) and modeled faith that does good deeds, and Paul also affirmed the need for good deeds (Rom 2:6; Gal 6:5-10; Eph 2:10; Phil 2:12-13; 1 Thes 1:3). Christians are to endure testings (1:3) and temptations (1:13-14), receive wisdom (1:5-6), inherit the Kingdom (2:5), pray for the sick, receive forgiveness (5:15), and rescue the wanderer (5:20). All of these things can be understood as "faith expressing itself in love" (Gal 5:6).

called *royal* because it belongs to the Kingdom (2:5) and was articulated by our glorious Lord (King). • ***as found in the Scriptures:*** James changes from a general reference to the law to a specific written commandment from the holiness code (Lev 19:1-37). It specifies how our love for God is to be expressed in relationships with other people (see Lev 19:18; Deut 6:5). • ***"Love your neighbor as yourself":*** This quotation from Lev 19:18 requires identifying with the neighbor as though the neighbor were yourself.

2:9 Favoritism violates the command to love one's neighbor (2:8).

2:11 This verse quotes Exod 20:13-14; Deut 5:17-18.

2:12 ***The law . . . sets you free*** from the controlling power of sin (see 1:25 and note) and thereby promotes endurance and growth toward perfection (1:3-4).

2:13 James concludes this section (2:1-13) by correlating divine mercy with human mercy (see also Matt 6:14-15; Eph 4:32).

2:14-26 James explains why Christians need to be concerned about the judgment of their actions (2:12-13): Real faith must be accompanied by good deeds (see 1:22-25).

2:14 ***if you say you have faith:*** James writes to Christians who need to be stimulated to produce *actions* that should arise from genuine faith. Paul makes the same point (see, e.g., Gal 5:6) but often criticizes people for trying to base their relationship with God on what they do (Rom 3:20, 28; 4:3-5; Gal 2:16; 3:1-14).

2:15-16 ***Suppose you see:*** As in 2:2-4, James gives an illustration of "faith" that is useless. • ***no food or clothing:*** In first-century Palestine and the Roman world in general, many poverty-stricken persons lacked the bare necessities of life. • ***stay warm and eat well:*** This sentence probably expresses a presumption that God would provide the needs of the poor person. The speaker might suppose that he needs only to express his faith to make it happen. But without his participation (action), it is an empty wish.

2:18-19 James demonstrates the futility of believing that something is true without acting upon it. • ***Now someone may argue:*** James presents another diatribe (see note on 1:13), in which he presents a hypothetical counterargument that one person may have the gift of faith while another person has the gift of works (see 1 Cor 12:7-9).

2:19 ***that there is one God:*** Some manuscripts read *that God is one;* see Deut 6:4, which is the basic confession of Israel's faith. • ***the demons believe:*** They know that there is one God, and he is their enemy (Mark 1:24).

2:20-26 James demonstrates from Scripture that genuine faith finds expression in action.

2:22 This verse explains 2:21 so it won't be misunderstood: Abraham was not justified by ***his actions*** alone; instead, ***his faith and his actions worked together.*** This describes the full scope of Abraham's faithful response to God throughout his life (see Gen 12:1-4; 18:1-27).

made his faith complete. 23And so it happened just as the Scriptures say: "Abraham
believed God, and God counted him as righteous because of his faith." He was even
called the friend of God. 24So you see, we
are shown to be right with God by what we
do, not by faith alone.
25Rahab the prostitute is another example. She was shown to be right with God by
her actions when she hid those messengers
and sent them safely away by a different road.
26Just as the body is dead without breath,
so also faith is dead without good works.

5. SPEECH AND CONFLICT (3:1–4:3)

Controlling the Tongue

3 Dear brothers and sisters, not many
of you should become teachers in the
church, for we who teach will be judged
more strictly. 2Indeed, we all make many
mistakes. For if we could control our tongues,
we would be [f]perfect and could also control
ourselves in every other way.
3We can make a large horse go wherever
we want by means of a small bit in its mouth.
4And a small rudder makes a huge ship
turn wherever the pilot chooses to go, even
though the winds are strong. 5In the same
way, the tongue is a small thing that makes
grand speeches.
But a tiny spark can set a great forest on
fire. 6And the tongue is a flame of fire. It is a
whole world of wickedness, corrupting your
entire body. It can set your whole life on fire,
for it is set on fire by [g]hell itself.
7People can tame all kinds of animals, birds,
reptiles, and fish, 8but no one can tame the
[h]tongue. It is restless and evil, full of deadly
poison. 9Sometimes it praises our Lord and
Father, and sometimes it curses those who
have been made in the image of God. 10And
so [i]blessing and cursing come pouring out of
the same mouth. Surely, my brothers and sisters, this is not right! 11Does a spring of water
bubble out with both fresh water and bitter
water? 12Does a fig tree produce olives, or a
[j]grapevine produce figs? No, and you can't
draw fresh water from a salty spring.

True Wisdom Comes from God

13If you are wise and understand God's ways,
prove it by living an honorable life, doing
good works with the humility that comes
from wisdom. 14But if you are bitterly jealous and there is selfish ambition in your
heart, don't cover up the truth with boasting

2:23
*Gen 15:6
Isa 41:8
Rom 4:3-5

2:25
Josh 2:4, 6, 15
Heb 11:31

3:1
Luke 12:48
Rom 2:21

3:2
[f]*teleios* (5046)
‣Matt 5:48

3:3
Ps 32:9

3:5
Prov 26:20

3:6
Prov 16:27
Matt 12:36-37; 15:11, 18-19
[g]*geenna* (1067)
‣Rev 1:18

3:8
Ps 140:3
Rom 3:13
[h]*glōssa* (1100)
‣Mark 16:17

3:9
Gen 1:26-27; 5:1
1 Cor 11:7

3:10
[i]*eulogia* (2129)
‣1 Pet 3:9

3:12
Matt 7:16
[j]*ampelos* (0288)
‣Matt 26:29

3:14
2 Cor 12:20

2:23 *it happened just as the Scriptures say* (literally *the Scripture was fulfilled*): James saw the offering of Isaac (Gen 22) as the fulfillment of Abraham's pledge of faith and God's declaration of Abraham's righteousness (quoted from Gen 15:6). • ***He was even called the friend of God:*** See Isa 41:8. James emphasizes the nature of faith as a relationship of undivided loyalty (1:5-8; 4:4; John 15:15).

2:24 ***not by faith alone:*** That is, not like the demons who merely believe something is true (2:19), but by a belief that results in generous deeds like those of God himself (1:17). Though some have thought that this teaching contradicts what Paul taught, it does not. Paul does not speak against good deeds themselves, but about trying to receive forgiveness of sins because of good deeds (Rom 3:28; Gal 2:16). Just as Paul understands that love and generosity necessarily issue from a true faith (Gal 5:6), so also James knows that good deeds can result only from authentic faith that results in a commitment to God (2:18, 26).

2:25 James presents ***Rahab the prostitute*** (see Josh 2:1) as his second example of good works that must accompany genuine faith. She declared her belief that the Lord God of Israel was the only God (Josh 2:9-11), and her faith was made perfect ***by her actions*** when she provided hospitality and a means of escape to the Israelite spies (Josh 2:1-6; 6:25; Heb 11:31).

2:26 ***Good works*** are as necessary to ***faith*** as ***breath*** is to a physical ***body*** (Gen 2:7). We cannot have one without the other. • ***without breath:*** Or *without spirit.*

3:1 ***Dear brothers and sisters:*** Literally *My brothers;* also in 3:10. See note on 2:1. • Becoming ***teachers*** was one way to improve social status in the early church (1 Cor 12:28; Eph 4:11; 1 Tim 5:17; cp. Acts 5:34). Such honor would compensate for the shame imposed upon Christians as social outsiders (2:6-7). But the conspicuous role of teachers symbolizes the power of human speech to benefit or harm the church.

3:2 ***we all:*** James's primary concern is with the speech of church members as they influence interpersonal relationships (3:9-10, 14; 4:1-3).

3:6 ***It is a whole world of wickedness:*** The tongue acts as an agent of the whole unrighteous world which is opposed to God (1:27; 4:4). • ***for it is set on fire by hell itself:*** Or *for it will burn in hell* (Greek *Gehenna*). *Gehenna* is the place of eternal punishment (Matt 5:22, 30; 23:15), in contrast to *Hades,* the abode of the dead (Luke 16:23; Acts 2:31). The reference to ***hell*** is an allusion to the devil (4:7; Matt 5:22; John 8:44) as the ultimate source of evil speech.

3:8 ***no one can tame the tongue:*** The tongue has an astonishing capacity for committing evil. If its evil is motivated by hell (3:6), it certainly cannot be tamed by mere human effort. • ***full of deadly poison:*** This might allude to the serpent in the Garden of Eden (Gen 3:1), who is identified with the devil (Rev 20:2).

3:9 ***praises . . . curses:*** Praising ***our Lord and Father*** is the best activity of the tongue, whereas cursing ***those*** made in his ***image*** is one of the worst, because it is an implicit curse on God himself (Gen 1:26-27; 9:6).

3:11 Some springs, especially in the upper sources of the Jordan River, did produce ***fresh water and bitter water;*** such brackish springs could not support a town. Similarly, if a person's speech mixes foul with sweet, it will not build up the community.

3:12 ***from a salty spring:*** Literally *from salt.*

3:13 ***If you are wise and understand:*** The wisdom that comes from God (1:5) is not mere intellectual skill nor the collection of information, it is practical insight and spiritual understanding which expresses itself in moral uprightness, as described in 3:17-18 (see also Job 28:28; Prov 1:2-4; 2:10-15).

3:14 The ***truth*** is that wisdom cannot be associated with jealousy and ***selfish ambition.*** Only in humility can we receive God's true word (1:18, 21).

3:16
1 Cor 3:3
Gal 5:20-21
3:17
Luke 6:36
Rom 12:9
[k]*eleos* (1656)
‣ Matt 9:13
3:18
Prov 11:18
Isa 32:17
Matt 5:9
Phil 1:11
4:2
1 Jn 3:15
4:3
1 Jn 3:22; 5:14
4:4
John 15:19
1 Jn 2:15
4:5
1 Cor 6:19
2 Cor 6:16
4:6
*Prov 3:34
Matt 23:12
1 Pet 5:5
4:7
Eph 6:12
1 Pet 5:6-9
[a]*diabolos* (1228)
‣ 1 Pet 5:8
4:8
Isa 1:16
Zech 1:3
Mal 3:7
4:9
Luke 6:25
4:10
1 Pet 5:6
4:11
Matt 7:1-5
[b]*nomos* (3551)
‣ Matt 7:12

and lying. 15 For jealousy and selfishness are not God's kind of wisdom. Such things are earthly, unspiritual, and demonic. 16 For wherever there is jealousy and selfish ambition, there you will find disorder and evil of every kind.

17 But the wisdom from above is first of all pure. It is also peace loving, gentle at all times, and willing to yield to others. It is full of [k]mercy and good deeds. It shows no favoritism and is always sincere. 18 And those who are peacemakers will plant seeds of peace and reap a harvest of righteousness.

Conflict from Selfish Prayer

4 What is causing the quarrels and fights among you? Don't they come from the evil desires at war within you? 2 You want what you don't have, so you scheme and kill to get it. You are jealous of what others have, but you can't get it, so you fight and wage war to take it away from them. Yet you don't have what you want because you don't ask God for it. 3 And even when you ask, you don't get it because your motives are all wrong—you want only what will give you pleasure.

6. DRAWING CLOSE TO GOD (4:4-10)

Seek God's Favor

4 You adulterers! Don't you realize that friendship with the world makes you an enemy of God? I say it again: If you want to be a friend of the world, you make yourself an enemy of God. 5 What do you think the Scriptures mean when they say that the spirit God has placed within us is filled with envy? 6 But he gives us even more grace to stand against such evil desires. As the Scriptures say,

"God opposes the proud
but favors the humble."

Resist the Devil

7 So humble yourselves before God. Resist the [a]devil, and he will flee from you. 8 Come close to God, and God will come close to you. Wash your hands, you sinners; purify your hearts, for your loyalty is divided between God and the world. 9 Let there be tears for what you have done. Let there be sorrow and deep grief. Let there be sadness instead of laughter, and gloom instead of joy. 10 Humble yourselves before the Lord, and he will lift you up in honor.

7. WARNINGS (4:11–5:6)

Warning against Judging Others

11 Don't speak evil against each other, dear brothers and sisters. If you criticize and judge each other, then you are criticizing and judging God's [b]law. But your job is to obey the [b]law, not to judge whether [b]it

---

3:15 The wisdom that is *earthly* is not part of the good creation; it is the opposite of heavenly wisdom because it excludes God. It is *unspiritual* because it does not acknowledge or respond to God's Spirit (1 Cor 2:14; Jude 1:19). It is *demonic* since it comes from the devil, the ultimate source of this destructive wisdom (3:6; 4:6; 1 Tim 4:1).

3:18 James uses an agricultural image to emphasize the benefits of living by the wisdom from above: Those who plant ***seeds of peace*** in relationships will enjoy a luxuriant ***harvest of righteousness*** (or *of good things*, or *of justice*) in those relationships (cp. Matt 5:9).

4:1 ***quarrels and fights*** (literally *wars and battles*): James uses military imagery to declare that their own ***evil desires at war within*** them were the immediate cause of the battles among church members. James uses the Greek word translated *evil desires* again in 4:3 (translated "pleasure") to enclose the entire paragraph and indicate the source of conflict and unanswered prayer (Luke 8:14; Titus 3:3).

4:2 ***you scheme and kill:*** Killing was the extreme, but logical, outcome of their rapacious attitude. Some of James's readers might have followed the Jewish Zealot movement and engaged in murder to benefit their cause. Hostile attitudes and violent methods do not provide satisfaction—***you can't get*** what you want by them.

4:4-10 James explains the causes of conflict: love for the world, divided loyalty, and arrogant criticism (4:11-12). He gives exhortations which will rectify these causes and lead to peace.

4:4 ***You adulterers*** (literally *You adulteresses*): James uses this prophetic imagery (see, e.g., Jer 3:6; Hos 3:1) because his readers were seeking what ***friendship with the world*** could give them—social acceptance (2:1-4), prestige (3:1), or wealth (4:13). Divided loyalty toward God (4:8) is like adultery against one's spouse. • In the ancient world, ***friend*** was used as a title for special and exclusive relationships (Luke 23:12, Herod and Pilate; John 19:12, Pilate as "friend of Caesar"; see also *1 Maccabees* 2:18; 6:28). Both Moses (Exod 33:11) and Abraham were called friends of God (2:23; 2 Chr 20:7; Isa 41:8; cp. John 15:15). • The ***world*** consists of society that is opposed to ***God*** and his kingdom. The world is guided by earthly wisdom, not heavenly (3:15-17), and is characterized by evil desires, fighting, and killing (4:2-3).

4:5 ***Scriptures . . . say:*** James summarizes one of the messages of Scripture, ***that the spirit God has placed within us is filled with envy*** (or *that God longs jealously for the human spirit he has placed within us*, or *that the Holy Spirit, whom God has placed within us, opposes our envy*).

4:6 ***"God opposes the proud but favors the humble":*** Prov 3:34 (Greek version).

4:7 ***Resist the devil:*** See also Eph 6:11; 1 Pet 5:8.

4:8 ***Come close to God:*** This is the language of friendship (2:23) and loyalty (1:6-8). • ***Wash your hands . . . purify your hearts:*** The language of ceremonial cleansing is applied to the inner purity of one's actions and intentions (cp. Mark 7:1-23).

4:10 To those who ***humble*** themselves before him, God gives ***honor*** in place of the shame of their persecution and oppression (2:6-7).

4:11-12 These verses reflect on Matt 7:1 and Luke 6:37 (see note on 1:22-23).

4:11 ***Don't speak evil against each other:*** This exhortation for peace in the Christian community requires that Christians not slander each other. Slandering one's neighbor is the same as slandering ***God's law,*** because the law prohibits slander and demands love

applies to you. 12 God alone, who gave the
law, is the Judge. He alone has the power to
save or to destroy. So what right do you have
to judge your neighbor?

Warning about Self-Confidence

13 Look here, you who say, "Today or tomorrow we are going to a certain town and will
stay there a year. We will do business there
and make a profit." 14 How do you know
what your life will be like tomorrow? Your
life is like the morning fog—it's here a little
while, then it's gone. 15 What you ought to
say is, "If the Lord wants us to, we will live
and do this or that." 16 Otherwise you are
boasting about your own plans, and all such
boasting is evil.
17 Remember, it is sin to know what you
ought to do and then not do it.

Warning to the Rich

5 Look here, you rich people: Weep and
groan with anguish because of all the
terrible troubles ahead of you. 2 Your [c]wealth
is rotting away, and your fine clothes are
moth-eaten rags. 3 Your gold and silver have
become worthless. The very wealth you
were counting on will eat away your flesh
like fire. This treasure you have accumulated will stand as evidence against you on
the day of judgment. 4 For listen! Hear the
cries of the field workers whom you have
cheated of their pay. The wages you held
back cry out against you. The cries of those
who harvest your fields have reached the
ears of the LORD of Heaven's Armies.
5 You have spent your years on earth in luxury, satisfying your every desire. You have
fattened yourselves for the day of slaughter.
6 You have condemned and killed innocent
people, who do not resist you.

8. FINAL EXHORTATIONS (5:7-20)

Patience and Endurance

7 Dear brothers and sisters, be patient as you
wait for the Lord's [d]return. Consider the
farmers who patiently wait for the rains in
the fall and in the spring. They eagerly look
for the valuable harvest to ripen. 8 You, too,
must be patient. Take courage, for the coming of the Lord is near.
9 Don't grumble about each other, brothers and sisters, or you will be judged. For
look—the Judge is standing at the door!
10 For examples of patience in suffering,
dear brothers and sisters, look at the prophets who spoke in the name of the Lord. 11 We
give great honor to those who endure under
suffering. For instance, you know about Job,
a man of great endurance. You can see how
the Lord was kind to him at the end, for the
Lord is full of tenderness and mercy.
12 But most of all, my brothers and sisters,
never take an oath, by heaven or earth or

4:12 Rom 2:1; 14:4
4:13-14 Prov 27:1; Luke 12:18-20
4:15 Acts 18:21
4:17 Luke 12:47
5:1 Prov 11:4, 28
5:2 Matt 6:19; [c]*ploutos* (4149) ‣ Mark 4:19
5:3 Matt 27:3-5; Luke 12:15-21
5:4 Lev 19:13; Deut 24:14-15; Ps 18:6
5:5 Jer 12:3; 25:34; Luke 16:19-23
5:7 Deut 11:14; Jer 5:24; Joel 2:23; [d]*parousia* (3952) ‣ 2 Pet 3:4
5:8 Rom 13:11-12; Heb 10:37
5:9 Matt 24:33; 1 Cor 4:5
5:10 Matt 5:12
5:11 Job 1:20-22; 2:7-10; 42:10-17; Ps 103:8
5:12 Matt 5:34-37

---

for one's neighbor (2:8; Lev 19:16-18; Matt 7:1-5). • ***dear brothers and sisters:*** Literally *brothers;* see note on 2:1.

4:13-16 Itinerant merchants depended on personal assertiveness as a solution to their poverty and low social status. James urges greater recognition of God's providence and warns against arrogantly planning events which one cannot really control.

4:15 The ***Lord*** has authority over life and death (Deut 32:39; 1 Sam 2:6; Matt 10:28).

4:16 Christians may boast about what God has done (1:9-10), but not about their own arrogant ***plans,*** which assume that God has no claim or authority over their lives.

4:17 ***Remember:*** This verse is probably a maxim that James expected his readers to recognize. Its source is unknown, but it is consistent with the teaching of Scripture (cp. Deut 24:15; Prov 3:27-28; Matt 25:41-46; Luke 12:47).

5:1-6 This section denounces the ***rich people*** for their greed and arrogant oppression of the poor (Lev 19:13). James warns them to repent while they can; if they do not, they will face ***terrible troubles . . . on the day of judgment.***

5:2 The ***wealth*** and ***fine clothes*** are so excessive that they deteriorate from lack of use; their destruction is a sign of the anticipated judgment.

5:3 Material wealth, represented by ***gold*** and ***silver,*** is ***worthless*** in the face of God's ***judgment.*** In fact, it ***will stand as evidence against*** them because it was unjustly gotten (5:4) and wickedly used (5:5-6).

5:4 These rich people (5:1) were exploitive landowners. Like those in 2:6 who oppressed and dragged Christians into court, they were exploiting the day laborers whose work was to ***harvest*** their ***fields.*** • ***cries . . . have reached the ears of the LORD:*** God hears the prayers of the oppressed (see Deut 24:14-15). Even while the laborers are still suffering, the Lord has heard (see Exod 3:7). • ***the LORD of Heaven's Armies*** (1 Sam 17:45; Ps 103:20-21; Rom 9:29): This title emphasizes God's power to act when the oppressed cannot.

5:6 ***killed innocent people*** (or ***killed the Righteous One***): In this context, the phrase most likely refers to innocent people such as the oppressed laborers in this paragraph rather than to Jesus (cp. Acts 3:14; 7:52). • ***who do not resist you:*** Or *Don't they resist you?* or *Doesn't God oppose you?* or *Aren't they now accusing you before God?*

5:7-8 ***Dear brothers and sisters:*** Literally *Brothers;* also in 5:9, 10, 12, 19. See note on 2:1. • ***be patient:*** This is the ultimate resolution for the poor in their economic pressures and for the unjust treatment by the wicked rich (5:1-6; see 2:6-7). Even though the poor have been marginalized and oppressed, they must not give up nor strike out at their oppressors. At ***the Lord's return,*** the faithful will receive their final reward (Isa 40:10; Luke 6:20-35; 1 Cor 15:23; 1 Pet 1:17; 5:4; Rev 22:12).

5:9 ***the Judge is standing at the door!*** The coming of Christ is imminent.

5:10 This verse reflects on Matt 5:11 and Luke 6:23 (see note on 1:22-23).

5:11 ***Job*** was ***a man of great endurance*** because he remained faithful to God throughout his hardships (Job 1:20-21; 2:9-10) despite his complaints (Job 3:1-26; 12:1-3; 16:1-3).

5:12 ***never take an oath:*** Because the churches were having such severe verbal conflicts (4:1-3, 11-12), James calls upon them to avoid the pitfalls of

5:13
Col 3:16
5:14
[e]*aleiphō* (0218)
▸Matt 6:17
5:15
[f]*hamartia* (0266)
▸1 Jn 1:9
5:16
Matt 18:15-18
1 Jn 1:9
5:17
1 Kgs 17:1-7
Luke 4:25
5:18
1 Kgs 18:42-45
5:19
Matt 18:15
5:20
Prov 10:12
1 Pet 4:8

anything else. Just say a simple yes or no, so that you will not sin and be condemned.

The Power of Prayer

[13]Are any of you suffering hardships? You
should pray. Are any of you happy? You
should sing praises. [14]Are any of you sick?
You should call for the elders of the church to come and pray over you, [e]anointing you
with oil in the name of the Lord. [15]Such a
prayer offered in faith will heal the sick, and the Lord will make you well. And if you have committed any [f]sins, you will be forgiven.

[16]Confess your sins to each other and pray for each other so that you may be healed. The earnest prayer of a righteous person has great power and produces wonderful
results. [17]Elijah was as human as we are, and yet when he prayed earnestly that no rain would fall, none fell for three and a half
years! [18]Then, when he prayed again, the sky sent down rain and the earth began to yield its crops.

Restore Wandering Believers

[19]My dear brothers and sisters, if someone among you wanders away from the truth
and is brought back, [20]you can be sure that whoever brings the sinner back will save that person from death and bring about the forgiveness of many sins.

The Future Coming of the Lord (5:7-9)

1 Sam 2:10
Ps 2:7-12; 96:11-13
Isa 26:21
Mic 1:3
Matt 16:27
Luke 12:35-48; 18:8
John 5:22-30
Acts 10:42
1 Cor 4:5
1 Jn 2:28

James announces the future coming of the Lord as Judge (5:7-9; cp. Isa 26:21; Mic 1:3). There will be a day of judgment (5:3). God, who gave the law, is the Judge who has the power to save and destroy (4:12). Those who oppress Christians and slander Jesus Christ (2:6-7) will be slaughtered (5:5-6). Those who follow Christ will be judged by the law that was intended to set them free (2:12) if they neglect to show mercy (2:13), befriend the world (4:4), sin through speech and strife (4:11; 5:9), or live to satisfy evil desires (4:1, 16).

The Lord's coming influences present realities. God already honors the faithful poor and humiliates the exploitative rich (1:9-10; 5:2-3). Christians have already become God's prized possession as God is restoring all things (1:18). James declares that we should obey the royal law of the messianic kingdom (2:8), to which Christians have become heirs (2:5).

The coming of the Lord may not be immediate, so James exhorts Christians to endure (1:4) and wait patiently for Christ's return (5:7-8). Christians will receive the crown of eternal life (1:12) and reap the harvest of righteousness sown by a life of faithfulness to God (3:18).

In view of impending judgment, James exhorts Christians to resist the devil and to humble themselves before God (4:7). We must grieve over sin, live with pure intentions and behavior (4:8-9), and rescue any Christian brother or sister who is headed toward death (5:19-20). Like Elijah, we must practice faith, prayer, and confession (5:13-17). Like Job, we must endure suffering to learn how kind the Lord is at the end (4:10; 5:11).

deceitful oaths by not using any oaths at all (Matt 5:33-37). To swear an oath in the name of the Lord was to call upon him to enforce the oath (Gen 31:53; 1 Kgs 8:31-32). When people swore ***by heaven or earth*** they were either feigning reverence while avoiding the use of the divine name, or they were being deceitful with clever verbiage (see Matt 23:16-22). Peter used an oath deceitfully (Matt 26:71-73), but Paul used an oath to confirm his assertions (Rom 1:9; 2 Cor 1:23), which suggests that the prohibition of oaths is not absolute.

5:14 ***The elders of the church*** were responsible for the well-being of a local assembly of Christians. Elders were selected because of their relative age and their qualifications as Christian leaders (Acts 14:23; 20:17, 28; 1 Pet 5:1-4; cp. 1 Tim 3:1-7; Titus 1:5-9). • At this early stage in the development of the church (AD 40s; see James Introduction, "Date and Location of Writing," p. 2111), the word ***church*** is apparently a nontechnical term meaning "congregation, assembly" (cp. Matt 18:17). • The act of ***anointing . . . with oil*** symbolizes divine blessing and healing (Isa 1:6; Matt 6:17; Mark 6:13; Luke 10:34).

5:15 ***a prayer offered in faith will heal the sick:*** This proverb is a generally true statement, subject to the will of God. Only prayers that embody true ***faith*** will be answered affirmatively by the Lord, and faith for a particular healing is a gift that comes from God. See also Mark 9:23; John 14:13-14; 15:7, 16; 16:23-27; 1 Jn 3:22; 5:14-15. • ***if you have committed any sins:*** James suggests that some illnesses might be caused by sin, and it is important that the sin also be confessed and ***forgiven*** (5:16; see Mark 2:3-12; John 5:14).

5:17 ***Elijah . . . prayed:*** See 1 Kgs 17:1; 18:41-46. • ***three and a half years*** (see 1 Kgs 18:1; Luke 4:25) is a round figure, half of seven, which symbolizes a period of judgment (cp. Dan 12:7; Rev 11:2).

5:19-20 These verses end the letter as a bookend (*inclusio*) counterbalancing the exhortation to endurance in 1:2-4.

5:20 To ***save*** a sinner ***from death*** refers not merely to physical death but to eternal death, the punishment of departing from the truth of the Good News of Jesus Christ (see 1:12, 15; cp. Heb 6:4-8). If the sinful person listens and repents, eternal punishment will be averted (see also Gal 6:1; Jude 1:22-24).

THE FIRST LETTER OF PETER

First Peter has the single focus of encouraging Christians to exhibit faithfulness under the pressure arising from persecution. The believers to whom Peter wrote were in the midst of such "fiery trials." The culture in which they lived scorned their faith, criticized their morality, and mocked their hope. Peter calls on readers to respond to this pressure with a renewed commitment to live out the grace of God, both to please God and to bear witness to his grace.

SETTING

Many people in the ancient world regarded Christians as strange, superstitious, and disloyal to Roman society. They gathered in secret, practiced strange rituals (such as the Lord's Supper, widely misunderstood as involving bloody sacrifice), and practiced a countercultural lifestyle. They often refused to serve in the Roman army because they would not take an oath to the emperor. This refusal to go along with the prevailing culture created tensions even more than it does in the modern world. Christians were often discriminated against and accused of misbehavior and were even brought into court on trumped-up charges.

This is the situation that 1 Peter addresses. Believers were undergoing very difficult trials (1:6; 4:12), and non-Christians were saying evil things about them (4:4; see 3:16). The Christians were tempted to retaliate in kind and repay harsh words with harsh words. They were also tempted to compromise their godly lifestyle because of the grief it caused them.

Peter was well aware of these temptations, so his letter encourages Christians to view the accusations and unfair treatment as an opportunity to bear witness to Jesus Christ. By following the example of their own Lord, who lived an exemplary life before all and refused to revile those who reviled him, Christians can practice a lifestyle of true evangelism.

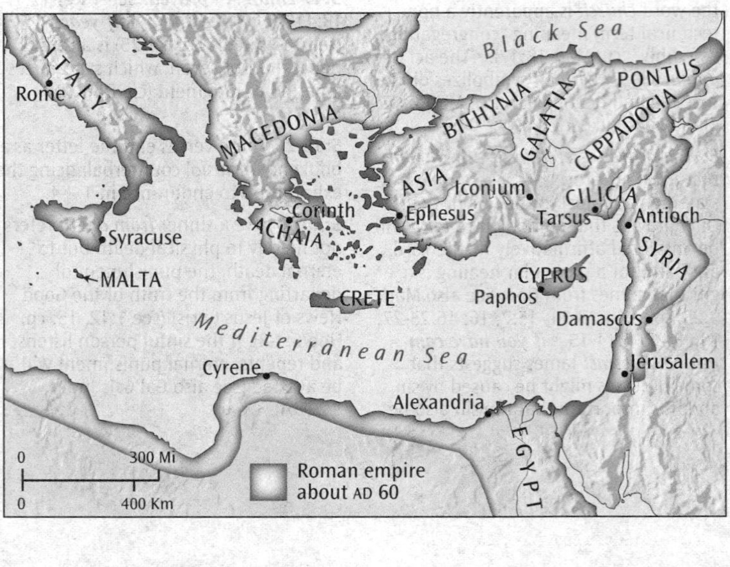

◀ **The Setting of 1 Peter, early 60s AD.** Peter was apparently in ROME toward the end of his life when he wrote this letter to encourage persecuted Christians in the provinces of PONTUS, GALATIA, CAPPADOCIA, ASIA, and BITHYNIA.

SUMMARY

After a typical opening for a letter (1:1-2), Peter exhorts his readers in the first section (1:3–2:12) to regard their present temporary suffering

as strengthening their faith and preparing them to receive salvation (1:3-9). This salvation is so great that prophets predicted it and angels investigate it (1:10-12). This gift of salvation should result in a life of holiness that recognizes the cost at which God purchased our salvation (1:13-21). The first section concludes with a call for love and patience toward fellow Christians (1:22–2:3) and a reminder of our status as the new covenant people of God (2:4-12).

The second part of the letter (2:13–3:12) exhorts Christians to live within recognized authority structures as a witness to a hostile world. Christians are to accept the authority of government (2:13-17), Christian slaves are to accept the authority of their masters (2:18-25), and Christian wives are to accept the authority of their husbands (3:1-6). Husbands are to respond by honoring their wives (3:7). This section ends with general exhortations to behave in a way that God rewards (3:8-12).

The third section (3:13–4:11) begins with a challenge to respond to social pressures with honorable and respectful behavior, even when it results in abuse (3:13-17). Peter reminds us that our hope of redemption is secure because of Christ's life, death, resurrection, and ascension (3:18-22). Peter renews his call to abandon the ways and values of the world around us (4:1-6), and concludes with various exhortations (4:7-11).

The fourth section of the letter (4:12–5:11) opens with a final call to stand firm in the midst of suffering (4:12-19). Peter then concludes with a charge to elders (5:1-4), younger men (5:5), and the church at large (5:5-11). The letter ends with customary greetings (5:12-14).

OUTLINE

1:1-2
Greetings

1:3–2:12
Salvation and the Call to Holiness

2:13–3:12
Living under Authority

3:13–4:11
Doing Good in the Face of Suffering

4:12–5:11
Concluding Exhortations

5:12-14
Final Greetings

AUTHOR AND RECIPIENTS

The opening verse of the letter identifies the apostle Peter as the author and the recipients as Christians living in "the provinces of Pontus, Galatia, Cappadocia, Asia, and Bithynia." These Roman provinces occupied the northern portion of Asia Minor, the peninsula that today forms most of Turkey. We have no record of Peter's visiting this area, nor does the letter indicate such a visit. We have little information about Peter's movements and activities after his initial days of ministry in Jerusalem and Judea (Acts 1–12). Luke tells us that after being miraculously rescued from prison, Peter "went to another place" (Acts 12:17). Speculations abound, but we simply don't know where that place was. Peter was back for the council in Jerusalem (Acts 15; AD 49~50) and apparently spent some time ministering in Corinth (see 1 Cor 1:12; 9:5). He was also in Antioch at some point (Gal 2:11-16). Christian tradition places Peter in Rome at the end of his life, where he suffered a martyr's death at the hands of the emperor Nero (probably AD 64 or 65).

TIMELINE

Passover, AD 30 or 33
Jesus' crucifixion and resurrection

Pentecost, AD 30 or 33
The birth of the church in Jerusalem

AD 41~44
Persecution of Christians by Herod Agrippa I, Peter is imprisoned

AD 49~50
The council in Jerusalem

AD 60–62
▸ Peter writes 1 Peter from Rome

before AD 64
Peter writes 2 Peter from Rome

AD 64~65
Persecution of Christians under Nero,
Peter is crucified in Rome
Paul is martyred in Rome

[First Peter is among] the true and noblest books of the New Testament [and contains] the true kernel and marrow of all the books.

MARTIN LUTHER
Preface to the New Testament

[First Peter is] a microcosm of Christian faith and duty, the model of a pastoral charge.

E. G. SELWYN
The First Epistle of Peter, p. 1

PLACE OF WRITING

The apostle was evidently in Rome when he wrote this letter. "Your sister church here in Babylon" (5:13) is almost certainly a reference to the church in Rome. The ancient city of Babylon, well-known from later OT books, was small and insignificant in Peter's day (the first century AD), and it would be surprising if Peter had ever traveled so far east. But because the ancient city of Babylon had been so dominant in the 600s–500s BC, the name came to symbolize the center of world power and cultural influence. The book of Revelation thus uses Babylon as a code word for Rome (see Rev 17:5 and note), and Peter was probably doing the same. If Peter wrote this letter from Rome, then it was probably written toward the end of his life. This supposition is confirmed by the presence of Mark with Peter (see 5:13), whom Christian tradition places in Rome with Peter in the late 50s and early 60s AD. We can surmise, then, that Peter wrote this letter from Rome in the early 60s AD.

OCCASION OF WRITING

Peter's letter was motivated by the severe trials that the Christians in northern Asia Minor were suffering. Attempts have sometimes been made to identify the situation and date of 1 Peter by connecting the letter to a known official persecution. The letter, however, does not suggest that the Christians were being subjected to an official, state-sponsored program of persecution. Most often, pressures came from the general populace, sometimes aided and abetted by local officials.

MEANING AND MESSAGE

First Peter encourages Christians to maintain a life of holiness in the midst of the pressures created by the non-Christian, and often anti-Christian, atmosphere in which they live. Peter pursues three key ideas. First, believers must understand that we have experienced the salvation that God promised through his prophets and which the angels are "eagerly watching" (1:12; see 1:5, 10). We are God's own children (1:14), born again through God's powerful word (1:23). We are the stones that God is using to construct a new, spiritual temple (2:5) and a chosen people called out of darkness into light (2:9-10). Because we enjoy all these privileges, we have become foreigners and aliens in this world (1:1, 17; 2:12). Christians live in the world but do not belong to the world.

The second key idea is that Christians, who are God's people, need to pursue a lifestyle that embodies the values of heaven, not the values of this world. As God's children, Christians need to imitate their Father and become holy, as he is holy (1:15-16). We need to love each other (1:22) and have respect for authorities. Peter sums all this up in his call to "do good," even and especially to those who abuse and cause difficulty (3:16-17; 4:19).

The third key idea is that believers have become a holy people because of Christ. His death and resurrection provide the foundation for our new identity (1:18-19; 3:18), and his victory over evil powers gives us hope and confidence (1:3-9; 3:19-22). Christ provided for our salvation and our holiness and has also given us an example to imitate. Christ did not retaliate when he was criticized, persecuted, and even executed (2:21-25). We are to follow in his footsteps, refuse to retaliate, and use our trials as an occasion to testify about the grace and power of God.

FURTHER READING

KAREN JOBES
1 Peter (2005)

SCOT MCKNIGHT
1 Peter (1996)

THOMAS SCHREINER
1–2 Peter, Jude (2003)

1:1
Jas 1:1
2 Pet 1:1
1:2
Rom 8:29
Heb 12:24
[a]*prognōsis* (4268)
‣ 1 Pet 1:20
[b]*hagiasmos* (0038)
‣ Rom 6:19
1:3
Titus 3:5
[c]*anagennaō* (0313)
‣ 1 Pet 1:23
[d]*anastasis* (0386)
‣ Rev 20:5
[e]*elpis* (1680)
‣ 1 Pet 3:15
1:4
Acts 20:32
Col 1:5, 12
1:5
Phil 4:7
1:6
Rom 5:2
Jas 1:2
1:7
Job 23:10
Prov 17:3
Isa 48:10
Jas 1:3
1:8
John 20:29
2 Cor 5:7
1:9
Rom 6:22
1:10
Matt 13:17; 26:24
1:11
Ps 22
Isa 53
Luke 24:26
Acts 16:7
2 Pet 1:21
1:12
Acts 2:2-4
Eph 3:10

1. GREETINGS (1:1-2)

1 This letter is from Peter, an apostle of
Jesus Christ.
I am writing to God's chosen people who
are living as foreigners in the provinces
of Pontus, Galatia, Cappadocia, Asia, and
Bithynia. [2]God the Father [a]knew you and
chose you long ago, and his Spirit has made
you [b]holy. As a result, you have obeyed him
and have been cleansed by the blood of
Jesus Christ.
May God give you more and more grace
and peace.

2. SALVATION AND THE CALL TO HOLINESS (1:3–2:12)

The Hope of Eternal Life (1:3-12)

Salvation, Trials, and Hope

[3]All praise to God, the Father of our Lord
Jesus Christ. It is by his great mercy that
we have been [c]born again, because God
[d]raised Jesus Christ from the dead. Now we
live with great [e]expectation, [4]and we have
a priceless inheritance—an inheritance that
is kept in heaven for you, pure and undefiled, beyond the reach of change and decay.
[5]And through your faith, God is protecting
you by his power until you receive this salvation, which is ready to be revealed on the
last day for all to see.
[6]So be truly glad. There is wonderful
joy ahead, even though you have to endure
many trials for a little while. [7]These trials
will show that your faith is genuine. It is
being tested as fire tests and purifies gold—
though your faith is far more precious than
mere gold. So when your faith remains
strong through many trials, it will bring you
much praise and glory and honor on the day
when Jesus Christ is revealed to the whole
world.
[8]You love him even though you have
never seen him. Though you do not see him
now, you trust him; and you rejoice with a
glorious, inexpressible joy. [9]The reward for
trusting him will be the salvation of your
souls.

The Greatness of Salvation

[10]This salvation was something even the
prophets wanted to know more about when
they prophesied about this gracious salvation prepared for you. [11]They wondered
what time or situation the Spirit of Christ
within them was talking about when he told
them in advance about Christ's suffering
and his great glory afterward.
[12]They were told that their messages
were not for themselves, but for you. And
now this Good News has been announced
to you by those who preached in the power
of the Holy Spirit sent from heaven. It is all
so wonderful that even the angels are eagerly watching these things happen.

1:1 ***to God's chosen people:*** Peter opens his letter to suffering Christians by reminding them of the status they enjoy because of God's act on their behalf (1:2). • ***living as foreigners*** (literally *exiles of the dispersion*): An exile had been uprooted from his or her homeland and taken to live in a foreign country. Peter uses the concept metaphorically to remind Christians that they are living in a world dominated by anti-Christian values and ways of life. • ***Pontus, Galatia, Cappadocia, Asia, and Bithynia*** were Roman provinces in what is now Turkey (see map, p. 2120). They might be listed in the order of the route that a messenger would have followed while carrying the letter to the various churches.

1:2 ***knew you and chose you:*** When God knows a person, it means that he chooses that person. He chose to enter into relationship with his people before they knew him (cp. Rom 8:29; 11:2).

1:3-9 In most NT letters, the greeting is followed by a section of thanksgiving or praise. Peter praises God that his mercy brings new spiritual life, which produces confident expectation about the future despite sufferings in the meantime.

1:3 ***born again:*** New birth is a way of describing Christian conversion (cp. John 3:1-13; Jas 1:18; 1 John 2:29; 3:9; 4:7; 5:1, 4, 18). This Greek word, which occurs again in 1:23, brackets the message of ch 1.

1:4 The language of *inheritance* frequently refers to what God has promised his people. Originally applied to the land of Israel (see Deut 3:28), the *inheritance* came to mean the people of God and God's presence with them (see Ps 33:12; Ezek 44:28). In the NT, the inheritance is the spiritual benefit and eternal salvation that God promises to his people (see Eph 1:11; Heb 9:15).

1:5 ***until you receive this salvation:*** In the NT, *salvation* often refers to final rescue from sin and death at the time of Christ's return. This hope encourages believers to persevere to the end (see also 1:9, 10; 2:2; 4:18). • ***ready to be revealed:*** The future revealing of God's salvation contrasts with the present hiddenness of God and his purposes (see also 1:7, 13).

1:6 ***So be truly glad:*** Or *So you are truly glad.*

1:7 ***will show that your faith is genuine:*** Faith, like ***gold***, is purified as it is tested. • The NLT understands ***praise and glory and honor*** as being given by God to the faithful Christian. The phrase could also mean that a faithful Christian life brings *praise and glory and honor* to God.

1:9 ***salvation of your souls:*** The Greek word translated *souls* often refers to the whole person and not just to some part or aspect of the person (Matt 20:28; Mark 8:35). Salvation affects our whole person, not the inner person only.

1:10-12 Our salvation is very great: The OT ***prophets*** predicted it, and ***angels*** long to investigate it.

1:11 ***They wondered:*** Much was revealed about the future to the OT prophets, but they did not know precisely when or how the salvation they predicted would come about. • The Greek translated ***what time*** could also mean *what person.* The prophets knew that a Messiah would come and that he would suffer before he was glorified, but they did not know who that Messiah would be.

1:12 ***eagerly watching:*** The same Greek word is used of the disciples when they peered into Jesus' empty tomb (Luke 24:12; John 20:5, 11).

A Call to Holy Living (1:13–2:3)

A Call to Holiness

13So think clearly and exercise self-control. Look forward to the gracious salvation
that will come to you when Jesus Christ is
[f]revealed to the world. 14So you must live
as God's obedient children. Don't slip back
into your old ways of living to satisfy your
own desires. You didn't know any better
then. 15But now you must be holy in everything you do, just as God who chose you is
holy. 16For the Scriptures say, "You must be
holy because I am holy."
17And remember that the heavenly Father to whom you pray has no favorites. He
will judge or reward you according to what
you do. So you must live in reverent fear of
him during your time as "foreigners in the
land." 18For you know that God [g]paid a ransom to save you from the [h]empty life you
inherited from your ancestors. And the ransom he paid was not mere gold or silver. 19It
was the precious blood of Christ, the sinless,
spotless [i]Lamb of God. 20God [j]chose him as
your ransom long before the world began,
but he has now revealed him to you in these
last days.
21Through Christ you have come to trust
in God. And you have placed your faith and
hope in God because he raised Christ from
the dead and gave him great glory.

Living in Love with Fellow Believers

22You were cleansed from your sins when
you obeyed the truth, so now you must show
sincere love to each other as brothers and
sisters. Love each other deeply with all your
[k]heart.
23For you have been [a]born again, but not
to a life that will quickly end. Your new life
will last forever because it comes from the
eternal, living word of God. 24As the Scriptures say,

"People are like grass;
their beauty is like a flower in the
field.
The grass withers and the flower fades.
25 But the word of the Lord remains
forever."

And that word is the Good News that was
preached to you.

2 So get rid of all evil behavior. Be done
with all deceit, hypocrisy, jealousy, and
all unkind speech. 2Like newborn babies,
you must crave pure spiritual milk so that
you will grow into a full experience of [b]sal-
vation. Cry out for this nourishment, 3now
that you have had a taste of the Lord's kindness.

God's New People (2:4-12)

4You are coming to Christ, who is the living
cornerstone of God's temple. He was rejected by people, but he was chosen by God
for great honor.
5And you are living stones that God is
building into his spiritual temple. What's
more, you are his holy priests. Through the

1:13 1 Thes 5:6
[f]*apokalupsis* (0602) ‣1 Pet 4:13

1:14 Rom 12:2

1:15 2 Cor 7:1

1:16 *Lev 11:44-45; 19:2

1:18 [g]*lutroō* (3084) ‣Matt 20:28
[h]*mataios* (3152) ‣Acts 14:15

1:19 John 1:29
Heb 9:14
[i]*amnos* (0286) ‣John 1:29

1:20 Eph 1:4
[j]*proginōskō* (4267) ‣Acts 2:23

1:21 John 14:6

1:22 John 13:34
[k]*kardia* (2588) ‣Matt 5:8

1:23 John 1:13; 3:3
Heb 4:12
[a]*anagennaō* (0313) ‣John 3:3

1:24-25 *Isa 40:6-8

2:1 Eph 4:22, 31

2:2 1 Cor 3:2
Heb 5:12-13
[b]*sōtēria* (4991) ‣1 Pet 3:21

2:3 *Ps 34:8

2:4 Ps 118:22
Isa 28:16

1:13-21 New birth and the hope of salvation require that Christians live as God's people, separating themselves from the values of the world and emulating the holiness of God, who redeemed them.

1:13 *think clearly* (literally *gird the loins of your mind*): In Peter's day, a man had to tuck the hem of his long robe into his belt before he could work or run.

1:15-16 ***"You must be holy because I am holy":*** See Lev 11:44-45; 19:2; 20:7. That God's people must be holy as God is holy is a common refrain in Scripture (see also Ezek 20:12; Eph 1:4; 1 Thes 4:3; Rev 22:11).

1:17 Christians' citizenship is in heaven (1:1; see Phil 3:20); they live in this world as ***"foreigners in the land"*** who are uncomfortable with its values and who long for their true home.

1:18 A ***ransom*** is ***paid*** for the release of a captive. Slaves could sometimes pay a ransom and be released from their master. Christ's death is the price God paid to release people from captivity to sin (1:19).

1:19 ***the sinless, spotless Lamb of God:*** The Passover *Lamb* had to be without defect (Exod 12:5); Christ, who fulfills the meaning of the Passover, was without defect or sin (cp. Heb 4:14-16; 7:26-28).

1:20 With Christ's coming, OT promises of redemption are being fulfilled and the *last days* have begun.

1:22–2:3 Following his call for holiness (1:13-21), Peter specifies how believers must live in a loving way with fellow Christians.

1:22 ***must show sincere love to each other as brothers and sisters:*** Literally *must have brotherly love.* See note on 5:9. • ***with all your heart:*** Some manuscripts read *with a pure heart.*

1:24-25 These verses quote Isa 40:6-8.

2:2 Believers, who have been "born again" (1:23), are to be ***like newborn babies*** in naturally and regularly craving ***pure spiritual milk.*** Elsewhere in the NT, *milk* (in contrast to solid food) stands for elementary Christian teaching (1 Cor 3:2; Heb 5:12-13). This does not imply that Peter's readers are new believers, however; here, it probably refers to God's word in general.

2:3 ***now that you have had a taste of the Lord's kindness:*** The words are taken from Ps 34:8. Peter quotes this psalm again in 3:10-12.

2:4-10 Throughout the letter, Peter encourages the suffering believers by reminding them of their exalted spiritual status. In this paragraph, he presents the Christian community as the new temple built on the foundation of Christ, and as heirs of the blessings granted to God's covenant people.

2:4 ***rejected by people, but he was chosen by God for great honor:*** This is an allusion to Ps 118:22, which is quoted in 2:7.

2:5 God's people themselves constitute the ***spiritual temple*** where God dwells (1 Cor 3:16). Jesus compared his body to a "temple" (John 2:19-22), and the church is called the "body of Christ" (Eph 4:12). God no longer manifests himself in a particular place but in the people who belong to him and praise his good-

2:5
Exod 19:6
Isa 61:6
Eph 2:21-22
1 Tim 3:15
Heb 13:15
Rev 1:6
2:6
*Isa 28:16
2:7
*Ps 118:22
2:8
*Isa 8:14
c*proskomma* (4348)
‣Matt 5:29
2:9
*Exod 19:5-6
Isa 43:20-21
d*aretē* (0703)
‣2 Pet 1:3

mediation of Jesus Christ, you offer spiritual sacrifices that please God.
6As the Scriptures say,

"I am placing a cornerstone in
Jerusalem,
chosen for great honor,
and anyone who trusts in him
will never be disgraced."

7Yes, you who trust him recognize the honor God has given him. But for those who reject him,

"The stone that the builders rejected
has now become the cornerstone."

8And,

"He is the stone that makes people
[c]stumble,
the rock that makes them fall."

They stumble because they do not obey God's word, and so they meet the fate that was planned for them.

9But you are not like that, for you are a chosen people. You are royal priests, a holy nation, God's very own possession. As a result, you can show others the [d]goodness of God, for he called you out of the darkness into his wonderful light.

The Holiness of God's Redeemed People (1 Pet 1:15-18)

Lev 10:3; 11:44-45; 19:2
Isa 29:17-24
1 Cor 6:9-20
Heb 12:1-13
Rev 21:5-8; 22:14-15

God called on the people of Israel to be holy because he had ransomed them from their slavery in Egypt. He has also ransomed us (1:18) through Jesus Christ, who paid the price to release us from slavery to sin and death. God has paid the ultimate price to set us free: He has given "the precious blood of Christ, the sinless, spotless Lamb of God" (1:19). He has purchased our freedom from our "empty way of life" that has no meaning. That is the kind of life we experience before coming to Christ.

At the heart of the lifestyle that God demanded of his people under the old covenant was the requirement that they be "holy" as God is holy (see Lev 19:2). God had rescued them from the domination of a cruel, foreign nation who served other gods; now they were to live as God's people in the new land to which he was bringing them.

Peter applies the same requirement to God's people of the new covenant, those who have come to him through faith in Jesus Christ: "You must be holy in everything you do, just as God who chose you is holy" (1:15). This holiness has both a negative and a positive side. Negatively, to be holy is to *separate from* this world, to avoid the ways of thinking and acting that characterize people who do not know God. We turn away from our old sinful, pre-Christian lifestyle. As a result, God's people truly are "foreigners in the land" (1:17)—they are different from those who have not experienced God's redemption. Positively, to be holy is also to *be separate for* God; it means that we imitate our Father and live out the values of our new homeland, the Kingdom of God.

Christians have been set free from the old, meaningless life and its values. We have to stop following the way of life that we inherited from our "ancestors" (1:18) and live as obedient children of our heavenly Father (1:14). Our Father has not only redeemed us in his love; he also, like a human father, disciplines his children. He will judge us "according to what we do" (1:17). For this reason, we must live before God in "reverent fear," recognizing his holiness and majesty, and seeking by faith to express his holy character in our lives. The life of holiness is not merely an option for believers: While we are justified by our faith, this faith is never a faith that is "alone." Authentic faith must always reveal itself in works of holiness that please our Father.

ness (see 2:10). • As God's ***holy priests*** (literally *holy priesthood*) in the new covenant, Christians offer not animal sacrifices but ***spiritual sacrifices*** such as praising God, praying, and doing good (see Rom 12:1; Heb 13:15-16).

2:6-8 The three OT quotations in these verses each identify Christ as some kind of stone: the ***cornerstone*** on which the new temple is built (2:6); the ***cornerstone*** that God, despite peoples' rejection, has elevated to be the keystone of his redemptive plan (2:7); and the ***stone that makes people stumble*** (2:8). Jesus quotes Ps 118:22 (Matt 21:42), and Paul quotes both Isa 8:14 and 28:16 (Rom 9:33). Likely these three quotations were brought together very early as a combined OT testimony to the nature and significance of Jesus the Messiah.

2:6 This verse quotes Isa 28:16 (Greek version). • ***in Jerusalem:*** Greek *in Zion.*

2:7 This verse quotes Ps 118:22.

2:8 This verse quotes Isa 8:14. • ***they meet the fate that was planned for them*** (literally *for which they were appointed*): It is not clear whether these people were appointed by God to unbelief or whether they were, because of their unbelief, appointed by God to suffer condemnation.

2:9 Peter applies descriptions of the Israelites in the OT (see, e.g., Exod 19:5-6) to his primarily Gentile audience, indicating that they—like all Christians—are truly God's people in the new covenant era. • ***royal priests:*** Literally *a royal priesthood.*

10 "Once you had no identity as a people;
now you are God's people.
Once you received no mercy;
now you have received God's mercy."

11 Dear friends, I warn you as "temporary
residents and foreigners" to keep away from
worldly desires that wage war against your
very souls. 12 Be careful to live properly among
your unbelieving neighbors. Then even if
they accuse you of doing wrong, they will see
your honorable behavior, and they will give
honor to God when he judges the world.

3. LIVING UNDER AUTHORITY (2:13–3:12)

Respecting People in Authority

13 For the Lord's sake, respect all human authority—whether the king as head of state,
14 or the officials he has appointed. For the
king has sent them to punish those who do
wrong and to honor those who do right.
15 It is God's [e]will that your honorable
lives should silence those ignorant people
who make foolish accusations against you.
16 For you are [f]free, yet you are God's slaves,
so don't use your freedom as an excuse to
do evil. 17 Respect everyone, and love your
Christian brothers and sisters. Fear God,
and respect the king.

Instructions for Slaves

18 You who are slaves must accept the
authority of your masters with all respect.
Do what they tell you—not only if they are
kind and reasonable, but even if they are
cruel. 19 For God is pleased with you when
you do what you know is right and patiently
endure unfair treatment. 20 Of course, you
get no credit for being patient if you are
beaten for doing wrong. But if you suffer
for doing good and endure it patiently, God
is pleased with you.
21 For God called you to do good, even if it
means suffering, just as Christ suffered for
you. He is your example, and you must follow in his steps.

22 He never sinned,
nor ever deceived anyone.
23 He did not retaliate when he was
insulted,
nor threaten revenge when he
suffered.
He left his case in the hands of God,
who always judges [g]fairly.
24 He personally carried our sins
in his body on the cross
so that we can be dead to sin
and live for what is right.
By his wounds
you are healed.
25 Once you were like sheep
who wandered away.
But now you have turned to your
[h]Shepherd,
the [i]Guardian of your souls.

2:10
*Hos 1:6, 9; 2:23
Rom 9:25; 10:19

2:11
Rom 13:14
Gal 5:16
Jas 4:1

2:12
Phil 2:15
Titus 2:14

2:13-14
Rom 13:1-7
Titus 3:1

2:15
[e]*thelēma* (2307)
›1 Pet 3:17

2:16
Gal 5:13
[f]*eleutheria* (1657)
›2 Pet 2:19

2:17
Prov 24:21
Rom 12:10; 13:7

2:18
Eph 6:5
Jas 3:17

2:21
Matt 16:24
Acts 14:22
1 Pet 3:9, 18

2:22
*Isa 53:9
2 Cor 5:21

2:23
Isa 53:7
1 Pet 3:9
[g]*dikaiōs* (1346)
›Rom 4:25

2:24
*Isa 53:4-5, 12

2:25
*Isa 53:6
Heb 13:20
1 Pet 5:4
[h]*poimēn* (4166)
›1 Pet 5:2
[i]*episkopos* (1985)
›1 Pet 5:2

2:10 This verse quotes Hos 1:6, 9; 2:23.

2:11-12 These verses are transitional. They can be viewed as the finale to the first section of the letter or as the opening statement of the second part of the letter. They enunciate the letter's central theme: Christians living in hostile territory need to live out the principles of the Good News so that they can win other people to the Lord.

2:11 ***"temporary residents and foreigners":*** Believers belong not to this world but to the Kingdom of Heaven (see 1:1, 17).

2:12 ***when he judges the world*** (or *on the day of visitation*): This phrase is used in the Greek OT to describe the time when God will visit his enemies to judge them (Isa 10:3; Jer 6:15).

2:13–3:7 This section revolves around the key phrase *respect* (or *submit to*) ***all human authority***, which Peter applies to several relationships: Christians should accept the authority of those in government (2:13-17), Christian slaves should accept the authority of their masters (2:18-25), and Christian wives should accept the authority of their husbands (3:1-6). Peter seems to be following an early Christian usage of the traditional household code, in which a series of instructions was given for different members of the household (cp. Eph 5:21–6:9; Col 3:18–4:1; 1 Tim 5:1–6:2; Titus 2:1-10).

2:13 In Peter's day, ***the king*** was the Roman emperor. Christians were suffering in the hands of the state and would soon suffer more intensely under Nero.

2:14 ***to punish those who do wrong and honor those who do right:*** Cp. Rom 13:3-4.

2:17 ***love your Christian brothers and sisters:*** Literally *love the brotherhood;* see note on 5:9. • ***Fear God, and respect the king:*** Peter might be reflecting on Jesus' balanced statement about the Christian's duty to both God and the government (see Matt 22:21).

2:18-20 The slave was legally bound and could not change his or her master, whereas the modern employee has the right to stop working for a cruel employer. Of course, some employees may not be able to change their situation, in which case Peter's advice to slaves is very applicable to employees today.

2:18 Many ***slaves*** in the Roman empire held responsible positions and had a decent income, but most were harshly treated and all were deprived of legal status and rights. • ***with all respect*** (or *because you fear God;* literally *with all fear*): Peter might be calling on slaves to fear God (see 2:17; cp. 1:17) or the master's punishment, but he often speaks this way about the respectful attitude Christians must have toward others (3:16).

2:21-25 While there is no explicit change of address here, the general character of these verses makes them applicable to all believers. • These verses might incorporate an early Christian hymn or confession about Christ (2:22-25). Its focus is on the redemptive sufferings of Christ in language drawn largely from Isaiah 52:13–53:12.

2:21 ***suffered:*** Some manuscripts read *died.*

2:22 This verse quotes Isa 53:9.

2:24 ***he personally carried our sins:*** This phrase alludes to Isa 53:4, 11-12. • ***By his wounds you are healed:*** The physical suffering of Christ has freed us from slavery to sin (cp. Isa 53:5). Matthew applies similar language from Isa 53:4 to the physical healings performed by Jesus (Matt 8:17).

3:1 Eph 5:22
3:3 Isa 3:18-23; 1 Tim 2:9
3:4 Rom 2:29
3:5 1 Tim 5:5
3:6 Gen 18:12; [j]*kurios* (2962) ‣2 Pet 2:20
3:7 Eph 5:25; Col 3:19; [k]*sunklēronomos* (4789) ‣Rom 8:17; [a]*charis* (5485) ‣Rev 22:21
3:8 Rom 15:5; Eph 4:2, 32
3:9 Matt 5:44; Rom 12:17

Instructions for Wives

3 In the same way, you wives must accept the authority of your husbands. Then, even if some refuse to obey the Good News, your godly lives will speak to them without any words. They will be won over [2]by observing your pure and reverent lives.

[3]Don't be concerned about the outward beauty of fancy hairstyles, expensive jewelry, or beautiful clothes. [4]You should clothe yourselves instead with the beauty that comes from within, the unfading beauty of a gentle and quiet spirit, which is so precious to God. [5]This is how the holy women of old made themselves beautiful. They trusted God and accepted the authority of their husbands. [6]For instance, Sarah obeyed her husband, Abraham, and called him her [j]master. You are her daughters when you do what is right without fear of what your husbands might do.

Instructions for Husbands

[7]In the same way, you husbands must give honor to your wives. Treat your wife with understanding as you live together. She may be weaker than you are, but she is your [k]equal partner in God's [a]gift of new life. Treat her as you should so your prayers will not be hindered.

Instructions for All Christians

[8]Finally, all of you should be of one mind. Sympathize with each other. Love each other as brothers and sisters. Be tenderhearted, and keep a humble attitude. [9]Don't repay evil for evil. Don't retaliate with insults when people insult you. Instead, pay them back with a blessing. That is what God

The New Community (2:4-10)

Gen 12:3; Exod 19:4-6; Deut 7:6; 2 Chr 5:13-14; Isa 11:1-16; John 1:14; 1 Cor 3:9-17; 6:19; 2 Cor 6:16-18; Eph 2:19-22; Rev 3:12; 21:1-3, 22

In this passage, Peter draws our attention to the importance of the Christian community, an emphasis that sometimes gets lost in individualistic cultures. Though Christians are individually converted and born again to a new life (1:23; see 2:2), we are not intended to remain in isolation. God's purpose is to build us together as "living stones" in his "spiritual temple" (2:5). God no longer inhabits a building on Mount Zion in Jerusalem; he now lives in and among his people by the Holy Spirit.

The promise that God would rebuild his temple (see Ezek 40–48) has been fulfilled as God dwells among his people (see John 1:14), who themselves constitute the "temple" under the new covenant. Only as we join together in worship, praise, and service will we function in the way God intended. Christians enjoy together the wonderful blessing of being the people God has chosen to carry out his mission to the world.

The church is now (2:9) what Israel was originally, a "chosen people" (see Deut 7:6), "royal priests," "a holy nation" (see Exod 19:6), and "God's very own possession" (see Exod 19:5). With that privileged status comes responsibility: to proclaim God to the nations. As we join in harmonious worship and together serve in various ministries, we "show others the goodness of God" (2:9).

3:1-7 The last of Peter's three exhortations about accepting authority (2:13–3:7) concerns wives and husbands (cp. Eph 5:21-33; Col 3:18-19).

3:1 ***accept the authority of*** (literally *submit to;* also in 2:13, 18): Wives are instructed to acknowledge that God has appointed the husband as head of the relationship (see Eph 5:22-25). Submission in the ancient world took the form of obedience (see 3:6). God also intends the husband to be a loving and respectful head (3:7; see Eph 5:25-30). However, Peter focuses especially on wives with pagan husbands who would potentially be hostile toward their wives' faith. • ***without any words:*** Peter urges Christian wives to evangelize their husbands through their submissive and appropriate behavior.

3:3-4 ***fancy hairstyles, expensive jewelry, or beautiful clothes:*** Peter has sometimes been interpreted as if he condemns any form of female ornamentation, but this is not his purpose. Instead, he insists that Christian women should not be noticed for the beauty of clothing and jewels but for the interior ***beauty*** of ***a gentle and quiet spirit.*** See also 1 Tim 2:9-10.

3:6 ***and called him her master:*** See Gen 18:12. Peter views this address as indicative of Sarah's overall attitude toward Abraham. • ***without fear of what your husbands might do:*** Christian wives married to unbelievers frequently found themselves pressured, both subtly and overtly, to abandon Christian principles and values. Peter urges them to continue to ***do what is right.***

3:7 ***In the same way:*** Like slaves and wives (2:18–3:6), husbands also have a particular responsibility within the household. • ***She may be weaker than you are:*** Peter was probably thinking of the woman's physical strength and perhaps her social status. Since women are typically physically weaker than men and were often less able to assert themselves in that society, the husband had the duty of protecting and caring for his wife. • ***your equal partner in God's gift of new life:*** The husband's headship is balanced and informed by the equal status that men and women have before God (see also Gal 3:26-29). • The ***prayers*** of a husband are ***hindered*** if he does not give exceptional honor to his wife (cp. Jas 4:3).

3:8-12 ***Finally:*** This is the last in a series of exhortations to different groups (2:13–3:12). Here, ***all*** believers must respond to others—believers (3:8) and unbelievers (3:9-12)—with love.

3:8 ***Love each other as brothers and sisters:*** Literally *Show brotherly love;* see note on 5:9.

has called you to do, and he will [b]bless you
for it. 10 For the Scriptures say,

"If you want to enjoy life
and see many happy days,
keep your tongue from speaking evil
and your lips from telling lies.
11 Turn away from evil and do good.
Search for [c]peace, and work to
maintain it.
12 The eyes of the Lord watch over those
who do right,
and his ears are open to their prayers.
But the Lord turns his face
against those who do evil."

4. DOING GOOD IN THE FACE OF SUFFERING (3:13–4:11)

Suffering for Doing Good (3:13-22)

Keeping a Clear Conscience

13 Now, who will want to harm you if you are
eager to do good? 14 But even if you suffer
for doing what is right, God will [d]reward you
for it. So don't worry or be afraid of their
threats. 15 Instead, you must worship Christ
as Lord of your life. And if someone asks
about your Christian [e]hope, always be ready
to [f]explain it. 16 But do this in a gentle and
respectful way. Keep your conscience clear.
Then if people speak against you, they will
be ashamed when they see what a good life
you live because you belong to Christ. 17 Remember, it is better to suffer for doing good,
if that is what God [g]wants, than to suffer for
doing wrong!

Christ's Death and Victory

18 Christ suffered for our sins once for all
time. He never sinned, but he died for
sinners to bring you safely home to God. He
suffered physical death, but he was [h]raised
to life in the Spirit.
19 So he went and preached to the spirits
in prison— 20 those who disobeyed God long
ago when God waited patiently while Noah
was building his boat. Only eight people
were saved from drowning in that terrible
flood. 21 And that water is a picture of [i]bap-
tism, which now [j]saves you, not by removing
dirt from your body, but as a response to
God from a clean conscience. It is effective
because of the resurrection of Jesus Christ.
22 Now Christ has gone to heaven. He is
seated in the place of honor next to God,
and all the [k]angels and authorities and powers accept his authority.

[b]*eulogia* (2129) ‣Rev 5:12

3:10-12 *Ps 34:12-16

3:11 [c]*eirēnē* (1515) ‣Matt 10:34

3:14-15 Isa 8:12-13

3:14 [d]*makarios* (3107) ‣Rev 1:3

3:15 Col 4:6
[e]*elpis* (1680) ‣Acts 23:6
[f]*apologia* (0627) ‣Acts 19:33

3:17 [g]*thelēma* (2307) ‣1 Jn 2:17

3:18 Eph 2:18
Heb 9:26, 28
[h]*zōopoieō* (2227) ‣John 5:21

3:20 Gen 6:1–7:24

3:21 Heb 9:13; 10:22
[i]*baptisma* (0908) ‣Matt 3:11
[j]*sōzō* (4982) ‣Acts 2:21

3:22 Matt 28:18
Mark 16:19
Heb 1:4, 6; 4:14
[k]*angelos* (0032) ‣Rev 1:20

3:9 ***and he will bless you for it:*** By blessing others, we receive a blessing from God.

3:10-12 Peter underscores the relationship between conduct and blessing by quoting Ps 34:12-16. This psalm is prominent in early Christian teaching (see also 2:3; Heb 12:14). The text focuses on curbing sins of speech, resisting evil, and doing good. It also highlights the promise of blessing for obedience.

3:13-17 This short paragraph emphasizes the Christian response to suffering—following Christ's example (3:18).

3:13 Generally speaking, no one ***will want to harm*** someone who is doing good, but sometimes Christians do suffer even when they do good (3:14; see 1:6; 4:12-19).

3:14-15 ***or be afraid of their threats:*** See Isa 8:13, where God exhorts the prophet to fear nothing except the Lord. • ***worship Christ as Lord:*** By fearing Christ, they will be free from fear of their human persecutors.

3:16 ***But do this in a gentle and respectful way:*** Some English translations put this sentence in v 15.

3:18-22 As in 2:21-25, Peter again appeals to Christ, who was righteous and yet suffered, as an example for believers facing persecution (3:13-17). The unique work of Christ on our behalf reminds suffering Christians that they have a secure foundation for hope and confidence.

3:18 ***Christ suffered:*** Some manuscripts read *Christ died.* • ***He suffered physical death*** (literally *death in the flesh*), ***but he was raised to life in the Spirit*** (or *in spirit*): *Flesh* and *spirit* are often contrasted (e.g., Rom 7:5-6; 8:2-11). Here, *flesh* stands for ordinary human life; ***the Spirit*** stands for the new realm inaugurated through Christ's death and resurrection. Christ died in the old realm, and came to life in the new realm.

3:19-20 This difficult passage has been widely interpreted in three ways: (1) One interpretation holds that it refers to the *spirits* of people who have died and that Christ, after his resurrection, preached the Good News to these *spirits.* However, the idea that people might hear the Good News and respond after their deaths is not found elsewhere in the NT, and this meaning of *spirits* is not the most likely. (2) A second interpretation sees 3:19-20 as describing Christ's preaching through *Noah* to people who are now spirits *in prison.* This interpretation does justice to 3:20, but does not fit well in the discussion of Christ's death and resurrection (3:18). (3) In the third interpretation, *the spirits in prison* are evil spiritual beings. Jewish tradition, based on Gen 6:1-3, held that many angels fell in the time of Noah (see also Jude 1:6; *1 Enoch* 6–10). Peter's point would then be that Christ proclaimed his victory over the evil spiritual powers after his resurrection (cp. 3:22).

3:20 ***Only eight people:*** That is, Noah, his wife, their three sons, and their wives (Gen 6:18; 8:18). • ***saved from drowning in that terrible flood:*** Literally *saved through water.*

3:21 ***a picture of baptism:*** Peter might mean that, as the *water* floated the boat in which Noah and his family were saved, so *baptism* saves believers. Or he might mean that, as Noah and his family passed through *water* to safety, so Christians pass through the waters of *baptism* to salvation. Finally, he might mean that, as the *water* judged sin in Noah's day, so the water of *baptism* washes away the sins of Christians. • Peter does not mean that water baptism *saves* a person regardless of that person's heart. He adds that baptism *saves* only ***as a response to God from*** (or *as an appeal to God for*) ***a clean conscience,*** thus making clear that only people exercising faith toward God will benefit from baptism.

3:22 ***all the angels and authorities and powers accept his authority:*** In the ancient world, spiritual beings were widely believed to directly affect the course of affairs on earth. Christians needed to be reminded that Christ has already won his victory over these spiritual powers. It means that we don't need to fear even the spiritual realm (cp. 3:14).

4:1
Rom 6:7
Gal 2:20
4:2
Rom 6:2
4:3
Rom 13:13
Eph 2:2
[a]*eidōlolatria* (1495)
‣Rev 21:8
4:5
Acts 10:42
4:7
Rom 13:11-12
4:8
Prov 10:12
Jas 5:20
[b]*agapē* (0026)
‣1 Jn 4:7
4:10
Rom 12:6-8
Eph 4:11-12
[c]*charisma* (5486)
‣Rom 1:11

Living for God (4:1-11)

4 So then, since Christ suffered physical
pain, you must arm yourselves with the
same attitude he had, and be ready to suffer, too. For if you have suffered physically
for Christ, you have finished with sin. 2You
won't spend the rest of your lives chasing
your own desires, but you will be anxious to
do the will of God. 3You have had enough in
the past of the evil things that godless people enjoy—their immorality and lust, their
feasting and drunkenness and wild parties,
and their terrible [a]worship of idols.
4Of course, your former friends are surprised when you no longer plunge into the
flood of wild and destructive things they
do. So they slander you. 5But remember that
they will have to face God, who will judge
everyone, both the living and the dead.
6That is why the Good News was preached
to those who are now dead—so although
they were destined to die like all people,
they now live forever with God in the Spirit.
7The end of the world is coming soon.
Therefore, be earnest and disciplined in
your prayers. 8Most important of all, continue to show deep [b]love for each other, for
[b]love covers a multitude of sins. 9Cheerfully
share your home with those who need a
meal or a place to stay.
10God has given each of you a [c]gift from
his great variety of spiritual gifts. Use them

Suffering in Christian Perspective (4:12-19)

Isa 48:10; 52:13–53:12; 63:7-9
Mark 10:35-40
Acts 5:41; 9:16; 14:22
Rom 8:17-23
2 Cor 1:5-7; 4:10; 12:10
Phil 1:29
Col 1:24
1 Thes 2:14
2 Thes 1:5
2 Tim 3:12
Heb 2:9-10; 5:8; 13:12
Jas 5:11-13

First Peter is focused almost exclusively on Christian suffering, especially unjust persecution at the hands of people hostile to the faith. The several themes about suffering that are woven throughout the letter find their climactic expression in 4:12-19. Peter makes the following points about suffering:

1. We should not be surprised when suffering comes (4:12). Christians who live a countercultural lifestyle in obedience to God should expect the culture to respond with hostility. We should expect mockery, discrimination, trumped-up charges, and even violence.
2. God has a purpose for us in suffering: It brings us into fellowship with Christ, who suffered before he was glorified (4:13; see also Rom 8:17).
3. By suffering in fellowship with Christ, we can be confident of enjoying the glory that he has already won (4:13; see Rom 8:17).
4. We need to commit ourselves to doing what is right when we face suffering (4:19). Our difficulties can always provide an excuse for sinning, but when difficulties come our way, we must live exemplary Christian lives, characterized by love for others.
5. Our loving response to enemies in the midst of trials can be a powerful opportunity to share our faith. By treating our persecutors with love and kindness, we can make our faith respectable and even attractive to them.
6. We need to remember in our trials that God is both sovereign and faithful (4:19). He controls all the circumstances of life, and we don't need to fear that a trial will come our way apart from God's oversight or will.

4:1-6 Peter urges Christians to decisively turn their backs on the former sinful way of life from which Christ in his suffering delivered us.

4:1 ***since Christ suffered physical pain:*** Peter introduced this idea in 3:18; he now indicates its significance in Christian experience. In our own physical sufferings, we are to imitate Christ's ***attitude*** (see 2:21-24). • ***For if you have suffered physically for Christ, you have finished with sin*** (or *For the one* [or *One*] *who has suffered physically has finished with sin*): Our suffering with Christ shows that we have identified with him (see Rom 8:17). Those who identify with Christ experience the victory over the power of sin that he won on the cross (Rom 6:1-10).

4:3 ***godless people*** (literally *the Gentiles*): Peter takes this term from his Jewish heritage to describe those who do not know God.

4:6 ***preached to those who are now dead*** (literally *preached even to the dead*): Peter refers to people now dead who were exposed to the Good News while alive; he does not envision a chance to repent after death. If they responded in faith to the message in life, they can be confident that, ***although they were destined to die like all people*** (or *although people had judged them worthy of death*), they will ***live forever with God in the Spirit*** (or *in spirit*).

4:7-11 With this paragraph of miscellaneous exhortations, Peter concludes the third major section of the letter (3:13–4:11).

4:7 ***The end of the world is coming soon***: At Christ's coming, the "last days" predicted by the OT prophets had begun (see 1:10-12). The next event in salvation history is the second coming of Christ, which will bring the *end* of the world as we know it. The *end* could come at any time; therefore, Christians must always be ready for it (see also Phil 4:5; Jas 5:8; Rev 1:3; 22:10).

4:8 By its nature, ***love*** overlooks ***sins*** committed against us by others (see Prov 10:12; Matt 18:21-22; 1 Cor 13:4-7). Peter might also mean that our attitude of love, because it displays our relationship with Christ, ***covers*** our own sins and causes them to be forgiven (see Luke 7:47).

4:10 ***his great variety of spiritual gifts:*** See Rom 12:6-8; 1 Cor 12:1-31; Eph 4:7-16. • ***Use*** (literally *manage*) ***them well:*** Believers are like managers: They have been entrusted by God, their Master, with gifts to be used to glorify him.

well to serve one another. 11 Do you have the
gift of speaking? Then speak as though God
himself were speaking through you. Do you
have the gift of helping others? Do it with
all the strength and energy that God supplies. Then everything you do will bring
glory to God through Jesus Christ. All glory
and power to him forever and ever! Amen.

5. CONCLUDING EXHORTATIONS (4:12–5:11)

Suffering for Being a Christian

12 Dear friends, don't be surprised at the
fiery [d]trials you are going through, as if
something strange were happening to you.
13 Instead, be very glad—for these trials
make you partners with Christ in his suffering, so that you will have the wonderful
joy of seeing his glory when it is [e]revealed
to all the world.

14 So be happy when you are insulted for
being a Christian, for then the glorious
Spirit of God rests upon you. 15 If you suffer,
however, it must not be for murder, stealing, making trouble, or prying into other
people's affairs. 16 But it is no shame to
suffer for being a Christian. Praise God for
the privilege of being called by his name!
17 For the time has come for judgment, and
it must begin with God's household. And if
judgment begins with us, what terrible fate
awaits those who have never obeyed God's
Good News? 18 And also,

> "If the righteous are barely saved,
> what will happen to godless sinners?"

19 So if you are suffering in a manner that
pleases God, keep on doing what is right,
and trust your lives to the God who created
you, for he will never fail you.

Advice for Elders and Young Men

5 And now, a word to you who are elders
in the churches. I, too, am an elder and
a witness to the sufferings of Christ. And
I, too, will share in his glory when he is revealed to the whole world. As a fellow elder,
I appeal to you: 2 [f]Care for the flock that God
has entrusted to you. [g]Watch over it willingly, not grudgingly—not for what you will
get out of it, but because you are eager to
serve God. 3 Don't lord it over the people assigned to your care, but lead them by your
own good [h]example. 4 And when the [i]Great
Shepherd appears, you will receive a crown
of never-ending glory and honor.

5 In the same way, you younger men must
accept the authority of the elders. And all of
you, serve each other in humility, for

> "God opposes the proud
> but favors the humble."

6 So humble yourselves under the mighty
power of God, and at the right time he will
lift you up in honor. 7 Give all your worries
and cares to God, for he cares about you.

8 Stay alert! Watch out for your great enemy, the [j]devil. He prowls around like a
roaring lion, looking for someone to devour.
9 Stand firm against him, and be strong in
your faith. Remember that your Christian
brothers and sisters all over the world are

4:11
1 Cor 10:31

4:12
[d]*peirasmos* (3986)
‣ Matt 6:13

4:13
2 Cor 1:5
[e]*apokalupsis* (0602)
‣ Rev 1:1

4:14
Matt 5:11
John 15:20-21

4:15
1 Thes 4:11

4:16
Acts 5:41

4:17
2 Thes 1:8

4:18
*Prov 11:31

4:19
Ps 31:5

5:2
John 21:16
Acts 20:28
[f]*poimainō* (4165)
‣ 1 Pet 5:4
[g]*episkopeō* (1983)
‣ Acts 20:28

5:3
Matt 20:25-28
2 Cor 1:24
[h]*tupos* (5179)
‣ Acts 7:44

5:4
Heb 13:20-21
[i]*archipoimēn* (0750)
‣ Rev 19:15

5:5
*Prov 3:34
Jas 4:6

5:6
Jas 4:10

5:7
Ps 55:22
Matt 6:25

5:8
Job 1:7
[j]*diabolos* (1228)
‣ Rev 12:9

4:11 ***All glory and power to him forever and ever! Amen:*** This doxology has led some to suggest that one original letter of Peter ended here and that another one was added to it. Doxologies in the NT do appear at the end of letters (Rom 16:25-27; Phil 4:20; Heb 13:21; 2 Pet 3:18; Jude 1:24-25), but also at the end of sections within letters (Rom 11:36; Gal 1:5; Eph 3:21; 1 Tim 1:17). Since there is no textual evidence for the existence of two separate letters, it is better to assume that this doxology marks the end of a major section of the letter.

4:12-19 Peter instructs Christians one last time about the way to face the trials that will inevitably come.

4:12 ***don't be surprised:*** Christians, especially those seeking to lead godly lives, can expect to face the hostility of a sinful world (see John 16:33; Acts 14:22; Rom 8:17; Phil 1:29).

4:13 Christians are called to suffer with Christ in order to be glorified with him (see also Rom 8:17).

4:14 ***be happy when you are insulted*** (literally *you are blessed when you are reproached*): This verse reflects Jesus' teaching in Matt 5:11-12. • ***for being a Christian:*** Literally *for the name of Christ.* • ***for then the glorious Spirit of God:*** Or *for the glory of God, which is his Spirit.* • At the end of 4:14, some manuscripts add *On their part he is blasphemed, but on your part he is glorified.*

4:16 Although evidence is very fragmentary, it is likely that the label ***Christian*** (cp. Acts 11:26) was originally a convenient way of summarizing the alleged superstitious practices and immoral character attributed to Jesus' followers.

4:17 God's ***judgment*** is often pictured as beginning ***with God's household***—i.e., with his own people—as a means of purifying them (Jer 25:29; Ezek 9:5-6; Mal 3:1-6).

4:18 This verse quotes Prov 11:31 (Greek version).

5:1-14 Peter ends the letter with final exhortations to *elders* (5:1-4), to *younger men* (5:5), and to the church as a whole (5:5-11). These exhortations are followed by final greetings and a closing (5:12-14).

5:1-4 ***Elders*** were the spiritual leaders of the early churches (see also Acts 14:23; 20:17; 1 Tim 5:17-19; Titus 1:5; Jas 5:14). By calling himself a ***fellow elder,*** Peter identifies with them in their responsibilities and with the charge that he gives them.

5:2 ***Care for the flock*** (literally *Shepherd the flock*): Our word *pastor* comes from NT imagery of a shepherd pasturing his flock.

5:5 ***You younger men:*** This phrase, in contrast to the elders, might refer to a particular class of ministers, perhaps elders in training or those who assisted the elders in various ways. But probably it simply denotes the younger men in the church (see, for example, 1 Jn 2:12-14). • ***"God opposes the proud but favors the humble":*** Prov 3:34 (Greek version).

5:9 ***your Christian brothers and sisters:***

5:9
Eph 6:11-13
Jas 4:7

5:10
1 Thes 2:12
2 Tim 2:10

5:12
Acts 15:22
Heb 13:22

5:13
Acts 12:12

5:14
Rom 16:16
Eph 6:23

going through the same kind of suffering
you are.
10 In his kindness God called you to share
in his eternal glory by means of Christ Jesus.
So after you have suffered a little while, he
will restore, support, and strengthen you,
and he will place you on a firm foundation.
11 All power to him forever! Amen.

6. FINAL GREETINGS (5:12-14)

12 I have written and sent this short letter to
you with the help of Silas, whom I commend
to you as a faithful brother. My purpose in
writing is to encourage you and assure you
that what you are experiencing is truly part
of God's grace for you. Stand firm in this
grace.
13 Your sister church here in Babylon
sends you greetings, and so does my son
Mark. 14 Greet each other with Christian
love.

Peace be with all of you who are in Christ.

Literally *your brothers,* a generic term often used to refer to both male and female believers. • ***all over the world:*** Persecution was not confined to the churches of Asia Minor. In various forms and with varying intensity, Christians were persecuted almost everywhere the Good News about Jesus Christ was preached. Peter reminds his readers of this to console them and encourage them to emulate those who had successfully endured the test of suffering.

5:10 ***a little while:*** Sufferings on this earth—while sometimes appearing to be endless—are in fact only momentary compared with the glorious eternity that believers will spend with God (cp. 1:6; Rom 8:18; 2 Cor 4:16-18).

5:12 ***with the help of:*** This phrase identifies Silas as the *amanuensis,* the person who wrote the words as Peter directed. • ***Silas*** (Greek *Silvanus*): Silas is the shortened form of Silvanus; both names refer to the same individual. Silas was Paul's constant colleague after the time of the council in Jerusalem (Acts 15:40; 16:19; 17:10, 14-15; 18:5; 2 Cor 1:19; 1 Thes 1:1; 2 Thes 1:1). We are not sure how Silas ended up with Peter in Rome, but he may have traveled with or followed Paul (Acts 27–28).

5:13 ***Your sister church here in Babylon:*** Literally *The elect one in Babylon.* Babylon was probably symbolic for Rome. Like Rome, Babylon was a great city, the capital of an empire. Babylon held sway over much of the ancient Near East in the 500s BC. As a great city and the capital of the empire that burned Jerusalem and took many captive Israelites back to the city, Babylon was regarded as the power center of a world hostile to God's people. For this reason, the book of Revelation uses "Babylon" as a metaphor or code word for Rome. Peter probably also used the title in the same way. • ***Mark,*** also called John Mark, was another co-worker of the apostle Paul (see "John Mark" at Acts 13:4-5, 13, p. 1852). Mark wrote the Gospel of Mark, which is generally thought to be based on Peter's teachings.

5:14 ***with Christian love:*** Literally *with a kiss of love.* See note on Rom 16:16.

THE SECOND LETTER OF

PETER

Second Peter discusses the need to grow in Christ's grace and warns against false teaching that threatens that growth. Many world views, religious perspectives, and cultural values clamor for attention. This letter warns against compromising the Christian faith by mixing it with ideas that are foreign to Christianity. We need to take this warning seriously.

2 Peter and Jude, written as they were to meet problems very like our own, have [much] to teach us. So long as sin needs to be exposed, so long as man needs to be reminded that persistent wrongdoing ends in ruin, that lust is self-defeating, that intellectualism devoid of love is a barren thing, and that Christian theology has no right to outrun the "faith once delivered to the saints," these Epistles will remain uncomfortably, burningly relevant.

E. M. B. GREEN
The Second Epistle General of Peter and the General Epistle of Jude, p. 11

SETTING

As its name suggests, 2 Peter was almost certainly the second NT letter written by the apostle Peter (see "Authorship," below), probably written to the same group of Christians as 1 Peter (see 3:1; map, p. 2120). We do not know if Peter ever visited Asia Minor—the NT tells us little about his movements after he departed from Jerusalem around AD 44 (Acts 12:17). We know that Peter was in Rome in the early 60s AD (see note on 1 Pet 5:13). Presumably, he wrote 2 Peter from Rome shortly after 1 Peter. Early Christian tradition indicates that Peter died under the emperor Nero in AD 64 or 65.

SUMMARY

In the letter opening (1:1-15), Peter identifies himself and his readers (1:1-2) and introduces his main concern, that his readers will grow in their knowledge of God and of Christ (1:3-11). He urgently tells them he does not have long to live (1:12-15).

Chapter 2 is the central focus of this letter, where Peter profiles and condemns false teachers. Peter prepares for this denunciation by emphasizing the certainty of Christ's return in glory (1:16-21). The false teachers were evidently skeptical about Christ's return and final judgment.

Peter denounces the false teachers (2:1-22) in four stages: He predicts the coming of false teachers (2:1-3), he insists that God will judge them while rescuing the righteous (2:4-10a), he declares the false teachers' sins (2:10b-16), and he pronounces their doom (2:17-22).

After further insisting that Christ will, indeed, return in glory to transform the world (3:1-13), Peter concludes the letter as he began, by praying that his readers will "grow in the grace and knowledge of our Lord and Savior Jesus Christ" (3:18; see 1:3-11).

AUTHORSHIP

The author identifies himself as Simon Peter (1:1), one of Jesus' apostles (see "Simon Peter" at Matt 14:28-31, p. 1609). Peter claims that "this is my second letter to you" (3:1). The first letter was probably 1 Peter.

In many ways, however, 2 Peter is dissimilar from 1 Peter while containing striking similarities to the letter of Jude (see below). Because of this, some interpreters think that someone else wrote 2 Peter in his name. This conclusion is unnecessary, because 2 Peter is dealing with a very different situation than is 1 Peter, so naturally the language and concepts differ. Moreover, it is possible that Silas (Peter's scribe mentioned in 1 Pet 5:12)

was responsible for some of the wording of 1 Peter and that Peter used a different scribe in 2 Peter.

RELATIONSHIP TO JUDE

It is undeniable that 2 Peter and Jude have some kind of literary relationship. The two letters use too many of the same unusual expressions for the similarities to be coincidental or a matter of a shared oral tradition (cp. 2 Pet 2:3 // Jude 1:4; 2 Pet 2:4 // Jude 1:6; 2 Pet 2:6 // Jude 1:7; 2 Pet 2:10 // Jude 1:8; 2 Pet 2:11 // Jude 1:9; 2 Pet 2:13, 17 // Jude 1:12; 2 Pet 3:3 // Jude 1:8). This relationship can be explained in one of three ways: (1) Jude borrowed from 2 Peter; (2) 2 Peter borrowed from Jude; or (3) both 2 Peter and Jude borrowed from a common literary source, now lost. Option 2 is the most popular, although option 1 is equally possible. Option 3 is least likely, simply because it is more complicated and unnecessary. Whichever author did the borrowing was apparently faced with a very similar situation and found what the other had written to be appropriate to his own purposes. Such borrowing was not uncommon in the ancient world; rather than being considered plagiarism, it was considered a compliment.

OUTLINE

1:1-15
The Letter Opening

1:16-21
The Certainty of Christ's Return

2:1-22
The Danger of False Teachers

3:1-13
The Day of the Lord Is Coming

3:14-16
A Final Call to Godliness

3:17-18
The Letter Closing: Peter's Final Words

FALSE TEACHERS

The false teachers that Peter denounces cannot be identified with any known heresy in the ancient church. With their immorality and skepticism, these false teachers were libertines: They assumed that God's grace gave them the liberty to do anything they wanted to do (2:19-20). They had no use for authority (see 2:10-11). They engaged in "sins of the flesh" such as illicit sex, excess drinking and eating, and greed (2:13-20). They might have been precursors to the later, second-century Gnostic heresy.

MEANING AND MESSAGE

Second Peter is a vital reminder of how dangerous it is to deviate from the truth. The church must always be on guard against those who twist the truth of the Good News and whose lives so sadly misrepresent it.

This letter is dominated by concern over the presence of false teachers in the church. Although these profligates were claiming to be Christians (2:1, 21-22), Peter leaves no doubt that in reality they were destined for condemnation as rebels against the Lord (2:3, 10). Peter writes this letter to warn his readers to reject these false teachers and their teaching, and to remain faithful to the Good News.

TIMELINE

Passover, AD 30 or 33
Jesus' crucifixion and resurrection

AD 49~50
The council in Jerusalem

AD 60–62
Paul is imprisoned in Rome
Peter writes 1 Peter from Rome

before AD 64
▸ Peter writes 2 Peter from Rome

AD 64~65
Persecution of Christians under Nero
Peter is crucified in Rome

FURTHER READING

PETER DAVIDS
The Letters of 2 Peter & Jude (2006)

GENE L. GREEN
2 Peter & Jude (2008)

DOUGLAS MOO
2 Peter & Jude (1996)

THOMAS SCHREINER
1–2 Peter, Jude (2003)

1. THE LETTER OPENING (1:1-15)

Greetings from Peter

1 This letter is from Simon Peter, a slave
and apostle of Jesus Christ.
I am writing to you who share the same
precious faith we have. This faith was given
to you because of the justice and fairness of
Jesus Christ, our God and [a]Savior.
[2]May God give you more and more grace
and peace as you grow in your knowledge of
God and Jesus our Lord.

Growing in Faith

[3]By his divine power, God has given us
everything we need for living a godly life.
We have received all of this by coming to
know him, the one who called us to himself by means of his marvelous glory and
[b]excellence. [4]And because of his glory and
excellence, he has given us great and precious promises. These are the promises
that enable you to share his divine nature
and escape the world's corruption caused
by human desires.
[5]In view of all this, make every effort to
respond to God's promises. Supplement your
faith with a generous provision of [c]moral
excellence, and [c]moral excellence with knowledge, [6]and knowledge with self-control, and
self-control with patient endurance, and
patient endurance with godliness, [7]and godliness with brotherly affection, and brotherly
affection with love for everyone.
[8]The more you grow like this, the more
productive and useful you will be in your
knowledge of our Lord Jesus Christ. [9]But
those who fail to develop in this way are
shortsighted or blind, forgetting that they
have been cleansed from their old sins.
[10]So, dear brothers and sisters, work
hard to prove that you really are among
those God has [d]called and chosen. Do these
things, and you will never fall away. [11]Then
God will give you a grand entrance into the
eternal Kingdom of our Lord and Savior
Jesus Christ.

Peter's Situation

[12]Therefore, I will always remind you about
these things—even though you already
know them and are standing firm in the
truth you have been taught. [13]And it is only
right that I should keep on reminding you
as long as I live. [14]For our Lord Jesus Christ
has shown me that I must soon leave this
earthly life, [15]so I will work hard to make
sure you always remember these things after I am gone.

2. THE CERTAINTY OF CHRIST'S RETURN (1:16-21)

Peter's Own Eyewitness Testimony

[16]For we were not making up clever stories when we told you about the powerful
coming of our Lord Jesus Christ. We saw
his majestic splendor with our own eyes

1:1 Rom 1:1, 12; Titus 2:13; 1 Pet 1:1; [a]*sōtēr* (4990) ‣2 Pet 2:20
1:2 2 Pet 3:18; Jude 1:2
1:3 1 Pet 2:9; [b]*aretē* (0703) ‣2 Pet 1:5
1:4 2 Cor 7:1; Jas 1:27
1:5 Col 2:3; [c]*aretē* (0703) ‣Phil 4:8
1:6 Acts 24:25; 1 Cor 9:25; Gal 5:22
1:7 John 13:34-35; Rom 12:10; 1 Pet 1:22
1:8 John 15:2; Col 1:10; 2 Pet 1:2-3
1:9 Eph 5:26; 1 Jn 2:11
1:10 Rom 8:28; Jude 1:24; [d]*klēsis* (2821) ‣Jude 1:1
1:11 2 Tim 4:18; 2 Pet 3:18
1:12 1 Jn 2:21; Jude 1:5

1:1 ***Simon*** (Greek *Symeon*) was one of the most common Jewish names in the first century. Jesus gave him the name ***Peter*** (Matt 16:17-18). Many people in the Greco-Roman world would use both their given name in their native language and also a Greek name, since Greek was the *lingua franca* (see note on Acts 7:58). • ***a slave . . . of Jesus Christ:*** In the OT, important leaders of God's people are called servants of the Lord (Josh 14:7; 24:29; 2 Kgs 10:10). The title underscores Peter's submission to Christ and suggests that he had an important role in God's plan. • ***We*** probably refers to Jewish Christians; the recipients were mostly Gentile Christians. In the new covenant, Gentile and Jewish Christians ***share the same precious faith*** and are on an equal footing as God's people (see Gal 3:26-29). • ***because of the justice and fairness:*** Or *in the righteousness.* • This is one of the few places in the NT where ***Jesus Christ*** is called ***God*** (see also John 1:1; 20:28; Rom 9:5; Titus 2:13; Heb 1:8; 1 Jn 5:20).

1:3-11 An explanation of all that ***God has given us*** in Christ (1:3-4) forms the basis for an urgent exhortation to grow in the knowledge of Christ (1:5-11).

1:3 ***By his divine power, God has*** (literally *His divine power has*): The name of ***God*** does not occur in the Greek text; Peter could be referring to the *divine power* of "Jesus our Lord" (1:2).

1:4 ***enable you to share his divine nature:*** Peter probably did not mean that our souls are merged with God but that believers share God's qualities (cp. Lev 11:44; Matt 5:43-48; Eph 4:24; 5:1).

1:5-7 The stair-step structure of these verses, with each virtue leading to another, is a common literary device called a *sorites.* The sequence in such passages is not stressed—e.g., Peter does not imply that ***moral excellence*** must come before ***knowledge.*** Yet ***love*** is the pinnacle of the virtues (1:7).

1:10 ***dear brothers and sisters:*** Literally *brothers,* a term that refers to both male and female believers. • ***Work hard to prove*** (literally *Be zealous to make certain*): Peter did not mean that our being ***chosen*** by God for salvation depends on what we do, but that our zeal to grow in Christian virtue confirms that we have, indeed, been chosen by God.

1:12-15 Peter was writing at the end of his life, so 2 Peter is similar to a popular Jewish genre called the *testament,* in which an old and respected leader gives final instructions to his children or others on his deathbed (cp. Deut 31–33; Josh 24). This genre is especially well-known from a Jewish book called *The Testaments of the Twelve Patriarchs.*

1:13 ***as long as I live:*** Literally *as long as I am in this tent* [or *tabernacle*].

1:14 This prophecy might have come in a vision, but it is more likely that Peter was recalling Jesus' prophecy about his death (John 21:18-19). • ***I must soon leave this earthly life*** (literally *I must soon put off my tent* [or *tabernacle*]).

1:16-21 Peter's denunciation of the false teachers (ch 2) is framed by this teaching about the certainty of Jesus' return (see also 3:1-13). The false teachers were probably denying the reality of Christ's return and judgment. Peter's eyewitness experience (1:16-18) and the intrinsic reliability of scriptural prophecy (1:19-21) make Christ's return a certainty.

1:16-18 ***clever stories*** (literally *cleverly invented myths*): The false teachers were probably charging that the message of Christ's return was just an edifying fable with no factual truth. • ***We saw his majestic splendor with our own eyes:*** At Jesus' transfiguration (Matt 17:1-9; Mark 9:2-8; Luke 9:28-36), which prefigured

1:13-14 John 13:36; 21:18-19; 2 Cor 5:1, 4
1:16-18 Matt 17:1-6; Mark 13:26; Luke 9:28-32
1:19 Ps 119:105; Luke 1:78; 2 Cor 4:6; 1 Pet 1:10-12; Rev 22:16
1:21 John 14:26; 1 Cor 2:13; 2 Tim 3:16
2:1 Deut 13:1-3; Matt 7:15; 1 Tim 4:1; Jude 1:4
2:2 Jude 1:4
2:3 Rom 16:18; 1 Thes 2:5
2:4 Gen 6:1-4; //Jude 1:6; Rev 20:1-2
2:5 Gen 6:5–8:18; 1 Pet 3:20
2:6 Gen 19:24; Matt 10:15; Rom 9:29; //Jude 1:7
2:7 Gen 19:1-16
2:9 //Jude 1:6

17 when he received honor and glory from God the Father. The voice from the majestic glory of God said to him, "This is my dearly loved Son, who brings me great joy." 18 We ourselves heard that voice from heaven when we were with him on the holy mountain.

The Reliability of Scriptural Prophecy

19 Because of that experience, we have even greater confidence in the message proclaimed by the prophets. You must pay close attention to what they wrote, for their words are like a lamp shining in a dark place—until the Day dawns, and Christ the Morning Star shines in your hearts. 20 Above all, you must realize that no prophecy in Scripture ever came from the prophet's own understanding, 21 or from human initiative. No, those prophets were moved by the Holy Spirit, and they spoke from God.

3. THE DANGER OF FALSE TEACHERS (2:1-22)

2 But there were also false prophets in Israel, just as there will be false teachers among you. They will cleverly teach destructive heresies and even deny the Master who bought them. In this way, they will bring sudden destruction on themselves. 2 Many will follow their evil teaching and shameful immorality. And because of these teachers, the way of truth will be slandered. 3 In their greed they will make up clever lies to get hold of your money. But God condemned them long ago, and their destruction will not be delayed.

4 For God did not spare even the angels who sinned. He threw them into hell, in gloomy pits of darkness, where they are being held until the day of judgment. 5 And God did not spare the ancient world—except for Noah and the seven others in his family. Noah warned the world of God's righteous judgment. So God protected Noah when he destroyed the world of ungodly people with a vast flood. 6 Later, God condemned the cities of Sodom and Gomorrah and turned them into heaps of ashes. He made them an example of what will happen to ungodly people. 7 But God also rescued Lot out of Sodom because he was a righteous man who was sick of the shameful immorality of the wicked people around him. 8 Yes, Lot was a righteous man who was tormented in his soul by the wickedness he saw and heard day after day. 9 So you see, the Lord knows how to rescue godly people from their trials, even while keeping the wicked under punishment until the day of

Christ's return by revealing Jesus as the glorious King. Peter's confidence was not based on human speculation but on eyewitness experience.

1:17 ***"This is my dearly loved Son, who brings me great joy":*** See Matt 17:5; Mark 9:7; Luke 9:35.

1:19 The word *Day* is capitalized because it is shorthand for *the day of the Lord,* the time when God intervenes in history to save his people and judge his enemies (see Isa 13:4-12; Joel 2:1-32; Zeph 2:1-3). The first coming of Christ inaugurated the day of the Lord's salvation for his people. A future day of the Lord's judgment on his enemies is yet to come. • ***Christ the Morning Star:*** The planet Venus, known as the "morning star," often appears above the eastern horizon just before dawn. Peter reverses the order of natural events: The dawning of the day of the Lord leads to the Morning Star's shining in the hearts of believers. • ***shines:*** Or *rises.*

1:20-21 ***came from the prophet's own understanding*** (or *is a matter of one's own interpretation*): The point is probably that the prophets were not left on their own to interpret the visions that God gave them. God made the meaning clear to the prophets, so that they could prophesy clearly and reliably.

2:1-3 Alongside authentic prophets (1:20-21), there have always been ***false*** prophets who receive God's judgment.

2:1 ***They will:*** Peter's use of the future tense in 2:1-3 does not imply that false prophets had not yet come, but it alludes to Jesus' prediction that false teachers would arise (Matt 24:11, 24; Mark 13:22; cp. Acts 20:29-31; 2 Tim 3:1-6). The false teachers who had arisen fulfilled that prediction. • ***deny the Master who bought them:*** The false teachers might have been overtly renouncing Christ, but it is more likely that their immoral conduct constituted a denial of Christ (cp. Titus 1:16).

2:2 One of the saddest effects of false teaching is that ***the way of truth will be slandered*** by a watching world. By their immoral and greedy conduct, false teachers bring shame on Christ.

2:4-10a Three OT examples of judgment show that God will vindicate those who remain faithful to him and will condemn those who deny him, including the false teachers (see 2:3).

2:4 The first example of judgment is ***the angels who sinned:*** The widespread Jewish tradition was that "the sons of God" in Gen 6:1-5 (understood as angels) had intercourse with women and were therefore judged by God at that time (see *1 Enoch* 6–10; cp. 1 Pet 3:19-20; Jude 1:6). • ***hell:*** Greek *Tartarus.* • ***in gloomy pits of darkness*** (some manuscripts read *in chains of gloom*): This description of the underworld was popular in the ancient world and is probably metaphorical.

2:5 The second example of judgment is that ***God did not spare the ancient world*** at the time of ***Noah.*** In the flood, God destroyed all human life apart from Noah and ***his family*** (see Gen 6–8).

2:6 The third example of judgment is that ***God condemned the cities of Sodom and Gomorrah.*** The people of these cities were so immoral that God rained down sulfur from heaven to destroy them (Gen 19:24). Peter focuses on the result of this action: The cities were turned into ***heaps of ashes.***

2:7-8 Even though the OT does not portray ***Lot*** as a very ***righteous man*** (see "Lot" at Gen 19:1-38, p. 58), he remained basically faithful to the Lord; Jewish tradition also portrays him as righteous (see *Wisdom of Solomon* 10:6; 19:17).

2:9 ***the Lord knows how to rescue godly people from their trials:*** As illustrated by Noah's family (2:5) and Lot (2:7), the Lord is faithful to his own people. Peter's readers needed assurance that their struggles to live godly lives in the face of false teaching and the world's scorn would be rewarded.

final judgment. 10He is especially hard on
those who follow their own twisted sexual
desire, and who despise authority.
These people are proud and arrogant,
daring even to scoff at supernatural beings
without so much as trembling. 11But the
angels, who are far greater in power and
strength, do not dare to bring from the
Lord a charge of blasphemy against those
supernatural beings.
12These false teachers are like unthinking
animals, creatures of instinct, born to be
caught and destroyed. They scoff at things
they do not understand, and like animals,
they will be destroyed. 13Their destruction is their reward for the harm they have
done. They love to indulge in evil pleasures
in broad daylight. They are a disgrace and a
stain among you. They delight in deception
even as they eat with you in your fellowship
meals. 14They commit adultery with their
eyes, and their desire for sin is never satisfied. They lure unstable people into sin, and
they are well trained in greed. They live under God's curse. 15They have wandered off
the right road and followed the footsteps
of Balaam son of Beor, who loved to earn
money by doing wrong. 16But Balaam was
stopped from his mad course when his donkey rebuked him with a human voice.
17These people are as useless as dried-
up springs or as mist blown away by the
wind. They are doomed to blackest darkness. 18They brag about themselves with
empty, foolish boasting. With an appeal to
twisted sexual desires, they lure back into
sin those who have barely escaped from
a lifestyle of deception. 19They promise
[e]freedom, but they themselves are slaves
of sin and corruption. For you are a slave to
whatever controls you. 20And when people
escape from the wickedness of the world by
knowing our [f]Lord and [g]Savior Jesus Christ
and then get tangled up and enslaved by sin
again, they are worse off than before. 21It
would be better if they had never known
the way to [h]righteousness than to know it
and then reject the command they were
given to live a holy life. 22They prove the
truth of this proverb: "A dog returns to its
vomit." And another says, "A washed pig returns to the mud."

4. THE DAY OF THE LORD IS COMING (3:1-13)

3This is my second letter to you, dear
friends, and in both of them I have tried
to stimulate your wholesome thinking and
refresh your memory. 2I want you to remember what the holy prophets said long ago
and what our Lord and Savior commanded
through your [i]apostles.

2:10 //Jude 1:7-8, 16, 18
2:11 //Jude 1:9
2:12 //Jude 1:10
2:13 1 Cor 11:20-21; //Jude 1:12
2:14 Eph 2:3
2:15 Num 22:5-7, 17; Deut 23:5; //Jude 1:11; Rev 2:14
2:16 Num 22:21-28
2:17 //Jude 1:12-13
2:18 //Jude 1:16
2:19 John 8:34; Rom 6:16; [e]*eleutheria* (1657) ‣Rom 8:21
2:20 Matt 12:45; [f]*kurios* (2962) ‣Rev 22:21; [g]*sōtēr* (4990) ‣2 Pet 3:18
2:21 Ezek 18:24; Heb 6:4-6; 10:26; [h]*dikaiosunē* (1343) ‣1 Jn 2:29
2:22 *Prov 26:11
3:2 //Jude 1:17; [i]*apostolos* (0652) ‣Rev 2:2

2:10a ***twisted sexual desire:*** The reference is to illicit sexual desire generally and probably to homosexuality in particular (cp. reference to Sodom and Gomorrah, 2:6). • The false teachers were so arrogant that they refused to listen to any ***authority*** but their own.

2:10b-16 This profile of the false teachers focuses more on how they were living than on what they were teaching.

2:10b ***supernatural beings:*** Literally *glorious ones,* which are probably evil angels, in contrast to the angels of 2:11. It is wrong to ***scoff*** even at evil angels, because they bear the mark of their glorious origin—they have real power and pose a real threat to humans.

2:11 Even ***angels . . . do not dare*** to charge evil ***supernatural beings*** with blasphemy, but the false teachers were so arrogant that they did not hesitate to do so. • ***from the Lord:*** Other manuscripts read *to the Lord;* still others do not include this phrase at all.

2:13 ***They delight in deception even as they eat with you in your fellowship meals:*** Cp. Jude 1:12. Christians often ate fellowship meals together in celebration of the Lord (see Acts 2:46; 6:1). The false teachers were using these mealtimes as opportunities to deceive true believers. Some manuscripts read *They delight* (or *revel,* or *carouse*) *in their fellowship meals as they eat with you.* If this reading is correct, they were using the fellowship meals for self-indulgence (cp. 1 Cor 11:20-22).

2:15 ***Balaam son of Beor*** (some manuscripts read *Balaam son of Bosor*): See Num 22–24. • ***who loved to earn money by doing wrong:*** Despite consulting with God about what he should do, Balaam was determined to go his own way in hopes of receiving Balak's money. The OT account hints at Balaam's greed, and Jewish tradition developed this theme (see *Numbers Rabbah* 20:10; *Mishnah Avot* 5:22; Philo, *Moses* 1:266-268).

2:17-22 Peter continues his description of the false teachers by explaining their effect on other people.

2:18 ***those who have barely escaped:*** The false teachers cleverly targeted new converts, people who had only recently committed themselves to Christ.

2:19 One of the great lures of false teaching through the centuries has been the ***promise*** of ***freedom*** from authority, but such freedom is illusory (Rom 6:16). The false teachers, while reveling in their freedom from authority (see 2:10), were in fact ***slaves*** to ***sin and corruption.***

2:20 ***they are worse off than before:*** The false teachers or their followers had known the truth, but their deliberate rejection of that truth put them in a far worse situation than when they ignorantly lived in sin (see "Consequences of Apostasy" at Heb 2:1-4, p. 2085).

2:22 ***"A dog returns to its vomit":*** Prov 26:11. Dogs were not seen as friendly family pets but as wild and filthy beasts. • ***"A washed pig returns to the mud":*** This proverb might go back to a popular book of sayings called *Ahiqar* from around 500 BC, which reads, "My son, you have been to me like the pig who went into the hot bath with people of quality, and when it came out of the hot bath, it saw a filthy hole and went down and wallowed in it" (*Ahiqar* 8:18).

3:1-13 Peter shifts from denunciation of false teachers to exhortation of believers. The false teachers' skepticism about Christ's return required clear teaching. Christians need to hold onto the apostolic message about the day of judgment and live godly lives in anticipation of that day.

3:1 ***This is my second letter to you:*** The previous letter was probably 1 Peter.

3:2 ***The holy prophets*** of the OT predicted the day of the Lord, when God would judge his enemies (see note on 1:19). • ***what our Lord and Savior commanded:*** Jesus had taught the church ***through*** the ***apostles.***

3:3 1 Tim 4:1; //Jude 1:18
3:4 Isa 5:19; Jer 17:15; [j]*parousia* (3952) ‣ 1 Jn 2:28
3:5 Gen 1:6-9; Rom 1:19-21; Heb 11:3
3:6 Gen 7:11-21
3:7 Matt 10:15; 2 Thes 1:7-8
3:8 Ps 90:4
3:9 Hab 2:3; Rom 2:4; 1 Tim 2:4; [k]*metanoia* (3341) ‣ Mark 1:4
3:10 Matt 24:43-44; 1 Thes 5:2; Rev 3:3; 16:5
3:12 Ps 50:3; 1 Cor 1:7
3:13 Isa 60:21; 65:17; Rev 21:1, 27; [a]*ouranos* (3772) ‣ Rev 2:7
3:14 1 Thes 3:13; 1 Pet 1:7
3:15 Rom 2:4
3:17 1 Cor 10:12; Rev 2:5
3:18 Rom 11:36; 2 Tim 4:18; [b]*sōtēr* (4990) ‣ 1 Jn 4:14

[3]Most importantly, I want to remind you that in the last days scoffers will come, mocking the truth and following their own desires. [4]They will say, "What happened to the promise that Jesus is [j]coming again? From before the times of our ancestors, everything has remained the same since the world was first created."

[5]They deliberately forget that God made the heavens by the word of his command, and he brought the earth out from the water and surrounded it with water. [6]Then he used the water to destroy the ancient world with a mighty flood. [7]And by the same word, the present heavens and earth have been stored up for fire. They are being kept for the day of judgment, when ungodly people will be destroyed.

[8]But you must not forget this one thing, dear friends: A day is like a thousand years to the Lord, and a thousand years is like a day. [9]The Lord isn't really being slow about his promise, as some people think. No, he is being patient for your sake. He does not want anyone to be destroyed, but wants everyone to [k]repent. [10]But the day of the Lord will come as unexpectedly as a thief. Then the heavens will pass away with a terrible noise, and the very elements themselves will disappear in fire, and the earth and everything on it will be found to deserve judgment.

[11]Since everything around us is going to be destroyed like this, what holy and godly lives you should live, [12]looking forward to the day of God and hurrying it along. On that day, he will set the heavens on fire, and the elements will melt away in the flames. [13]But we are looking forward to the new [a]heavens and new earth he has promised, a world filled with God's righteousness.

5. A FINAL CALL TO GODLINESS (3:14-16)

[14]And so, dear friends, while you are waiting for these things to happen, make every effort to be found living peaceful lives that are pure and blameless in his sight.

[15]And remember, our Lord's patience gives people time to be saved. This is what our beloved brother Paul also wrote to you with the wisdom God gave him—[16]speaking of these things in all of his letters. Some of his comments are hard to understand, and those who are ignorant and unstable have twisted his letters to mean something quite different, just as they do with other parts of Scripture. And this will result in their destruction.

6. THE LETTER CLOSING: PETER'S FINAL WORDS (3:17-18)

[17]I am warning you ahead of time, dear friends. Be on guard so that you will not be carried away by the errors of these wicked people and lose your own secure footing. [18]Rather, you must grow in the grace and knowledge of our Lord and [b]Savior Jesus Christ.

All glory to him, both now and forever! Amen.

3:3 ***in the last days:*** Peter was not merely predicting an event in the future; he was speaking about his readers' situation. In the NT, *the last days* refers to the period from Jesus' first coming to his second coming (see Acts 2:17; Heb 1:2). It is the time when God's promises are fulfilled. • ***scoffers will come:*** See Prov 1:22; 9:7-8; 13:1. Rather than using evidence and logic to argue, scoffers belittle and make fun of the truth.

3:4 ***From before the times of our ancestors:*** The false teachers were probably claiming that, for all of God's promises to intervene in history, things had not really changed and never would.

3:5 Creation is the first evidence that the false teachers were wrong: Change does happen. If God made the world, he certainly can destroy it. • ***brought the earth out from the water:*** See Gen 1:2, 6-10.

3:7 The OT associates ***fire*** with the day of the Lord (see Isa 30:30; 66:15-16).

3:8 Peter alludes to Ps 90:4. God operates according to his time scale. He will send his Son in his own good time.

3:10 The ***very elements themselves*** might refer to the basic components of the physical universe or to the sun, moon, and stars. • ***will be found to deserve judgment:*** Literally *will be found;* other manuscripts read *will be burned up;* one early manuscript reads *will be found destroyed.* The Greek text is difficult; the reading followed by the NLT probably means that creation *will appear before* God at the time of judgment, and he will find it to deserve his judgment.

3:12 ***looking forward to the day of God and hurrying it along:*** God's people can hasten the end by their repentance and godly living (cp. Acts 3:19-20). • ***the elements will melt away:*** Cp. Mic 1:3-4; see also Isa 63:19–64:1.

3:13 ***the new heavens and new earth:*** See Isa 65:17; 66:22; Rev 21.

3:15 ***our beloved brother Paul:*** The NT tells us little about the relationship between Peter and Paul. Because of the dispute in Antioch (Gal 2:11-14), it is sometimes thought that the two were hostile to one another, but the NT paints a different picture. Peter and Paul essentially agreed about the Good News for the Gentiles (Acts 11:2-18; 15:7-11). Silas and Mark were associates of both Paul and Peter (see 1 Pet 5:12-13). According to tradition, both apostles were martyred in Rome during the same persecution by Nero in the mid-60s AD.

3:16 Peter probably knew of ***all*** but one or two of Paul's ***letters*** by this time. Peter's language implies that he considered the letters of Paul to belong in the category of ***Scripture.***

3:17-18 Peter restates his purpose: to protect his readers from false teachers so that they can ***grow*** in ***grace.*** He ends with a doxology to ***our Lord and Savior Jesus Christ.***

THE FIRST LETTER OF JOHN

John's Gospel explains how Jesus Christ came to offer eternal life; his first letter tells how to know, by our experience and behavior, that we have eternal life. John's Gospel tells us how Jesus came to reveal the Father; his letter shows how we can be confident in our relationship with him. John's Gospel relates how Jesus gives the Spirit to each one who is born again; his letter explains daily life in the Spirit. John's Gospel encourages Jesus' disciples to practice spiritual unity by loving one another; his letter clarifies how to put that love into action.

SETTING

John and the other apostles were probably forced to leave Jerusalem by AD 68, if not earlier, due to the mounting persecution against the church and the siege of Jerusalem by Roman armies. Sometime later (probably after AD 70), John migrated to the Roman province of Asia (the western region of modern Turkey) and began a successful ministry, primarily among the Gentiles. By AD 90, John had written his Gospel for these believers to whom he had been ministering.

Soon after this, some members of the Christian community left to form a rival group. These rivals were a heretical faction that promoted teachings about Jesus Christ that later characterized Gnosticism, such as denying that Jesus was God in the flesh (see 4:1-3). By leaving the fellowship of the apostles, they demonstrated that they did not genuinely belong to God's family (2:18-19). However, the effects of their false teachings still lingered in the minds of the faithful, so John wrote this letter to clear the air of these falsehoods, to bring the believers back to the basics of the Christian life, and to reinforce their faith.

The Setting of 1 John, late 80s AD. When the apostle John left Jerusalem (probably in the late 60s AD), he seems to have settled in EPHESUS in the province of ASIA. He wrote his three letters (1–3 John) to the churches in Asia.

Another heresy that John confronted was promoted by Cerinthus, who taught that Jesus was not born to a virgin but was a normal human being born to Joseph and Mary and was more righteous, prudent, and wise than other men. Cerinthus taught that at Jesus' baptism, "the Christ" descended upon him in the form of a dove from the supreme Ruler; he then proclaimed the unknown Father and performed miracles. At last "the Christ" departed from the man "Jesus," and then Jesus (but not "the Christ") suffered and rose again, while "the Christ" remained untouched, inasmuch as he was a spiritual being. John specifically refutes the heresy of Cerinthus in 5:5-8.

John wrote this epistle to encourage believers in the Roman province of Asia to remain steadfast in Christ, and he denounced those who had not remained in the apostolic fellowship. This first letter went out to the churches under John's care around AD 85–90 (including the churches that are mentioned in Rev 1:11).

OUTLINE

1:1–2:11
Experiencing Christian Fellowship

2:12–3:10
Maintaining True Fellowship

3:11–4:21
Loving One Another

5:1-21
Living in Fellowship

SUMMARY

John stressed that Christians must maintain loyalty to Jesus' apostles—those who had followed Jesus during his life and had known him personally—in order to safeguard against pseudo-spirituality and heresy. John urged his Christian readers to:

1. maintain loyalty in fellowship toward the apostles and thus to have fellowship with God, who is light, by living in the light he gives us;
2. confess their sins to God and thus know the advocacy of Jesus Christ, the righteous one;
3. esteem Jesus Christ as the Word of life, the Son of God;
4. love God, who is love, and love other Christians;
5. remain in Christ, become like Christ, and purify themselves of worldly lusts;
6. know and experience God personally and understand the truth through the Spirit;
7. discern false teaching by the aid of the Spirit and recognize the spirit of false prophets and of the antichrist; and
8. enjoy eternal life.

AUTHOR

Some scholars have suggested that a Christian elder named John, but not the apostle, was the author of these letters. They make this judgment on the basis of a quotation from Papias (bishop of Hierapolis in the province of Asia, AD 100–130), who mentioned John the apostle and then later mentioned John the elder (see Eusebius, *Church History* 3.39.4). But most evangelical scholars think that John the apostle and John the elder are the

TIMELINE

Passover, AD 30 or 33
Jesus' crucifixion and resurrection

by AD 68
The apostles leave Jerusalem

about AD 70?
John settles in Asia Minor

before AD 90
John writes the Gospel of John

John writes 1–3 John

AD 60s or 90s
John writes Revelation

about AD 100
John dies peacefully in Ephesus

AD 100~130
Papias is bishop of Hierapolis

same person (cp. 2 Jn 1:1; 3 Jn 1:1). The writing style of John's Gospel is undeniably similar to that of these three letters. The apostle John was an eyewitness of Jesus and one of the very first to follow him. In John's Gospel, John is called "the one whom Jesus loved" (John 13:23; 19:26; 20:2; 21:7, 20). He was one of the twelve disciples and a very close friend to Jesus. The author's claim to be an eyewitness is as strong in the letters (see 1:1-4) as it is in the Gospel (John 1:14; 19:35). The author of 1 John claims to have personally heard, seen, and touched the eternal Word made flesh (1:1-4).

MEANING AND MESSAGE

First John is a natural extension of John's Gospel. John's Gospel shows that it was Jesus' mission to reveal God the Father and to bring believers into union with the Father and the Son through the Spirit. John's first letter emphasizes how Christians experience God in daily life, as demonstrated by their relationships with the other members of the church community. We must exhibit our love for God by loving one another. This command came straight from Jesus (John 14:24; 15:17), and John repeated it often (2:7; 3:11, 23; 2 Jn 1:5-6). Since God is love, all who claim to know God must love other Christians.

To love other Christians, however, does not mean accepting everything they say or all that independent teachers teach. There were people in the breakaway churches denying that Jesus is the Christ, the unique Son of God, or that he had come as a human being. All such people are antichrists when they deny the true humanity and the full deity of Jesus Christ. This letter warns strongly against those who teach such heresy and lead Christians away from fellowship with the true apostles of Christ.

History shows that many heretical movements have infiltrated the church, but the truth has withstood these assaults. We need to be wary of teachings that are contrary to the teaching of the apostles; the word of God and the Holy Spirit are our guides.

FURTHER READING

DANIEL AKIN
1–3 John (2001)

PHILIP W. COMFORT AND WENDELL C. HAWLEY
1 John in *Cornerstone Biblical Commentary*, vol. 13 (2007)

I. HOWARD MARSHALL
The Epistles of John (1978)

STEPHEN SMALLEY
1–3 John (1984)

JOHN R. W. STOTT
The Letters of John (1988)

1:1
John 1:1, 4, 14
1 Jn 4:14
[a]*logos* (3056)
‣Rev 1:2

1:2
John 1:1-4; 19:35; 20:30-31

1:4
John 15:11; 16:24

1:5
John 1:9; 8:12
1 Tim 6:16

1:6
John 3:19-21
2 Cor 6:14
[b]*koinōnia* (2842)
‣Acts 2:42

1:7
Ephesians 5:8-9

1:9
Ps 32:5
Prov 28:13
[c]*hamartia* (0266)
‣Matt 26:28

2:1
Rom 8:34
1 Tim 2:5
Heb 7:25; 9:24
[d]*paraklētos* (3875)
‣John 14:16

1. EXPERIENCING CHRISTIAN FELLOWSHIP (1:1–2:11)

Prologue: Fellowship with Jesus Christ

1 We proclaim to you the one who existed
from the beginning, whom we have
heard and seen. We saw him with our own
eyes and touched him with our own hands.
He is the [a]Word of life. 2This one who is life
itself was revealed to us, and we have seen
him. And now we testify and proclaim to
you that he is the one who is eternal life.
He was with the Father, and then he was revealed to us. 3We proclaim to you what we
ourselves have actually seen and heard so
that you may have fellowship with us. And
our fellowship is with the Father and with
his Son, Jesus Christ. 4We are writing these
things so that you may fully share our joy.

Living in the Light

5This is the message we heard from Jesus and
now declare to you: God is light, and there is
no darkness in him at all. 6So we are lying
if we say we have [b]fellowship with God but
go on living in spiritual darkness; we are not
practicing the truth. 7But if we are living in
the light, as God is in the light, then we have
fellowship with each other, and the blood of
Jesus, his Son, cleanses us from all sin.
8If we claim we have no sin, we are only
fooling ourselves and not living in the truth.
9But if we confess our [c]sins to him, he is
faithful and just to forgive us our [c]sins and
to cleanse us from all wickedness. 10If we
claim we have not sinned, we are calling
God a liar and showing that his word has no
place in our hearts.

2 My dear children, I am writing this to
you so that you will not sin. But if anyone does sin, we have an [d]advocate who
pleads our case before the Father. He is

1:1-4 This poetic prologue reflects the message of the prologue to John's Gospel (John 1:1-18). • The *we* that occurs throughout the prologue refers to John and the other apostles, and perhaps to other Christians who had *seen* and *touched* Jesus Christ. The apostles were the first eyewitnesses of Jesus and had personal fellowship with God through him. John, representing the apostles, now invites readers to join in that fellowship.

1:1 *We proclaim to you the one who existed from the beginning:* Literally *What was from the beginning.* That is, from before time began, eternally (John 8:58). When Jesus came in the flesh (John 1:14), the apostles *saw him . . .* ***and touched him.*** This affirmation that they actually touched ***the Word of life*** is important because Gnosticism and Docetism (early Christian heresies) denied that Christ was truly a human being (see 4:2-3). Jesus, the Son of God, is the personal expression of the invisible God, and the giver of eternal life (John 1:1-4).

1:2 *life itself* (Greek *zōē*): Throughout the NT, this word is used to designate the eternal life of God (Eph 4:18). This life resides in Christ, and he makes it available to all who believe in him. • ***This one . . . was revealed to us:*** Jesus, the Christ, was known to his apostles as a human being during his earthly ministry.

1:3 *what we . . . have actually seen:* The Word of life had, as a man, revealed God to the apostles. • ***our fellowship is with the Father and with his Son:*** Once the Spirit regenerated the apostles, they entered into spiritual fellowship with the Father and the Son. • ***you may have fellowship with us:*** Whoever entered into fellowship with the apostles by associating with them while they were alive, or enters now by remaining in their teaching, has fellowship with the Father and the Son through them.

1:4 *so that you may fully share our joy* (or *so that our joy may be complete;* some manuscripts read *your joy*): The *joy* that the apostles have comes from their fellowship with God the Father and the Son (1:3). Readers will *share* this joy when they enter into the same fellowship.

1:5–2:6 Here John focuses on the first aspect of living in fellowship with God. ***Living in the light*** means that the believers will see that they are sinners, but they will also realize that Jesus is their Advocate to make them right with God (see Eph 5:6-13).

1:5 *from Jesus:* Literally *from him.* • ***God is light:*** This *light* shone through Jesus Christ to all he came in contact with, to expose their sin and to illumine the moral nature and character of God (see John 1:4-5, 9; 3:19-21; 8:12; 9:5; 12:35-36, 46). In John, "light" represents God's holiness and revelation. It is the opposite of false teaching and undisciplined living, which is "darkness" (1:6).

1:6 This is the first of several instances in which John challenges the claims of the Gnostics, who had broken away from the apostolic fellowship and were thus ***living in spiritual darkness.*** They claimed to have ***fellowship with God*** but did not express his character, which is light. Jesus had warned the Jewish leaders of his day not to let the light they thought they had be darkness (Matt 6:23)—their religious beliefs had blinded them to the spiritual illumination they could have received from Christ. In like manner, these Gnostic teachers thought they were enlightened but were actually darkened by their so-called illuminations. They claimed to have spiritual experiences from God, yet they rejected fellowship with the ones who had actually seen God in the flesh, namely, John and the other apostles.

1:7 Believers have ***fellowship*** with each other and with God as they live ***in the light.*** People cannot say they commune with God and then refuse to have fellowship with God's people. This was the case with the Gnostics. The apostles of Christ had known Jesus Christ as God-in-the-flesh and were continuing to have spiritual fellowship with him (1:3).

1:8 *If we claim we have no sin:* This is the second false claim of the Gnostics (see 1:6). They claimed that they were or could be sinless since Christ had abolished their sins once and for all—their higher knowledge would lift them above the realm of sin. But Christians do still sin when they live in their old nature (see Rom 7:14-25). The true Christian both acknowledges this sin (1:9) and trusts in Christ to take it away.

1:9 To maintain continual fellowship with God, we need to ***confess our sins to him.*** Forgiveness and cleansing are guaranteed because God is ***faithful*** to his promises and because he acts on the basis of his justice. Christ's death for our sins fulfills God's justice and acquits us of our guilt.

1:10 *If we claim we have not sinned, we are calling God a liar:* God's word emphasizes the permeating and penetrating nature of sin (see note on 1:8).

2:1 In order to live "in the light" (1:5-7), one must confess sin (1:9) and stop

Jesus Christ, the one who is truly righteous. 2 He himself is the [e]sacrifice that atones for our sins—and not only our sins but the sins of all the world.

3 And we can be sure that we know him if we obey his commandments. 4 If someone claims, "I know God," but doesn't obey God's commandments, that person is a liar and is not living in the truth. 5 But those who obey God's word truly show how completely they love him. That is how we know we are living in him. 6 Those who say they live in God should live their lives as Jesus did.

A New Commandment

7 Dear friends, I am not writing a new commandment for you; rather it is an old one you have had from the very beginning. This old commandment—to love one another—is the same message you heard before. 8 Yet it is also new. Jesus lived the truth of this commandment, and you also are living it. For the darkness is disappearing, and the true light is already shining.

9 If anyone claims, "I am living in the light," but hates a Christian brother or sister, that person is still living in darkness. 10 Anyone who loves another brother or sister is living in the light and does not cause others to stumble. 11 But anyone who hates another brother or sister is still living and walking in darkness. Such a person does not know the way to go, having been blinded by the darkness.

2. MAINTAINING TRUE FELLOWSHIP (2:12–3:10)

John's Purpose in Writing

12 I am writing to you who are God's
children
because your sins have been forgiven
through Jesus.
13 I am writing to you who are [f]mature in
the faith
because you know Christ, who existed
from the beginning.
I am writing to you who are young in the
faith
because you have won your battle
with the evil one.
14 I have written to you who are God's
children
because you know the Father.
I have written to you who are mature in
the faith
because you know Christ, who existed
from the beginning.
I have written to you who are young in
the faith
because you are strong.
God's word lives in your hearts,
and you have won your battle with the
evil one.

Do Not Love This World

15 Do not love this world nor the things it offers you, for when you love the world, you do not have the love of the Father in you. 16 For the world offers only a craving for

2:2 John 1:29; Rom 3:25; Heb 2:17; 1 Jn 4:10
[e]*hilasmos* (2434) ‣1 Jn 4:10
2:3 1 Jn 3:22, 24
2:5 John 14:21, 23; 1 Jn 3:24; 4:13; 5:2
2:6 Matt 11:29; John 13:15; 1 Pet 2:21
2:7 John 13:34; 1 Jn 2:24; 3:11; 2 Jn 1:5-6
2:8 John 1:9; 13:34; Rom 13:12; Eph 5:8; 1 Thes 5:5
2:9 1 Jn 3:10, 15-16
2:10 Ps 119:165; Rom 14:13
2:11 John 12:35; 2 Cor 4:4; 2 Pet 1:9; 1 Jn 2:9; 3:15
2:12 1 Cor 6:11
2:13 John 1:1; 16:33; 1 Jn 1:1; 4:4; 5:18
[f]*patēr* (3962) ‣1 Jn 2:23
2:14 John 1:1-2; Eph 6:10; 1 Jn 1:1; 1:10
2:15 Rom 12:2; Jas 4:4

---

sinning. John emphasized sin in ch 1 in order to make believers despise their sin and avoid it. • ***if anyone does sin:*** Believers should repudiate sin, but they should not fear confessing sins to God. • ***advocate*** (Greek *paraklētos,* "one who is called to our side" as comforter or advocate): Christ is our defense attorney, representing us before the Father in heaven (see Rom 8:26-34; cp. John 14:16). • ***Jesus Christ, the . . . righteous:*** We, in contrast, are sinful. Because Christ fulfilled the law and paid sin's penalty for us, he can plead for us on the basis of justice as well as mercy. When God raised Christ from the dead, he accepted once for all Christ's plea for our acquittal (see Rom 4:23-25). "The righteousness of Christ stands on our side; for God's righteousness is, in Jesus Christ, ours" (Martin Luther).

2:2 ***sacrifice that atones:*** The Greek *hilasmos* means "appeasement by means of sacrifice" (cp. 4:10). Christ satisfied God's justice by dying in our place (Rom 3:25).

2:3-6 Obedience is one clear indication that we know Christ and belong to him. If we do not obey Christ, it is obvious that we do not belong to him or love him. • As we obey Christ and his ***commandments,*** our love for God and our knowledge of him will grow toward completeness and maturity. We will ***live . . . as Jesus did,*** in union with God and showing love for others.

2:7-11 The disciples had the ***old*** commandment (to love one another) ***from the very beginning,*** from Jesus himself (John 13:34-35) and from the OT (Lev 19:18, 33-34).

2:8 ***Yet it is also new:*** Jesus' command provided the new basis for their love in his own demonstration of love to the disciples (John 13:1-17). • ***the darkness is disappearing and the true light is already shining:*** The light of the Good News expels darkness. Darkness cannot overcome it, especially where believers are ***living out*** the love that is in Christ.

2:9-11 Another indication of truly knowing Christ is one's treatment of other Christians. John is again pointing to those who claim to be spiritually enlightened but separate themselves from other Christians with an attitude of superiority. John defines such an attitude as hatred.

2:9 ***hates a Christian brother or sister:*** Literally *hates his brother;* similarly in 2:11. *Brother* is a generic term often used to refer to both male and female believers.

2:10 ***loves another brother or sister:*** Literally *loves his brother.* • ***To cause others to stumble*** can also mean to ensnare or entrap them. The Greek word *skandalon* means a trap or a block in someone's path. The Gnostics, who taught falsehood about Christ, were hindering people by ensnaring them in error and darkness. • ***living in the light:*** A godly life will help, not hinder, the faith of other Christians.

2:12-14 John gives three classes of believers at various stages of spiritual maturity: ***God's children,*** the ***young in the faith*** (literally *young people*), and the ***mature in the faith*** (literally *fathers*).

2:12 ***through Jesus:*** Literally *through his name.*

2:13 ***to you who are mature in the faith:*** Or *to you fathers;* also in 2:14.

2:15-17 The ***world*** is a morally evil system that is under the influence of Satan and is opposed to God and to

2:16
Rom 13:14
Eph 2:3
2:17
Matt 7:21
1 Cor 7:31
[g]*thelēma* (2307)
‣ Mark 3:35
2:18
Matt 24:24
[h]*antichristos* (0500)
‣ 1 Jn 2:22
2:19
Acts 20:30
1 Cor 11:19
2:22
[i]*antichristos* (0500)
‣ 1 Jn 4:3
2:23
John 8:19; 17:3
[j]*patēr* (3962)
‣ Matt 5:16
2:24
2 Jn 1:9
2:25
John 3:15; 6:40; 17:3
2:27
John 14:16, 26; 16:13
1 Cor 2:10-12
2:28
Col 3:4
1 Thes 2:19
[k]*parousia* (3952)
‣ Matt 24:3
2:29
[a]*dikaiosunē* (1343)
‣ Rom 1:17
3:1
John 1:12-13
Eph 1:4-5
3:2
Rom 8:19, 29
2 Cor 3:18
Phil 3:21
3:3
2 Cor 7:1
3:4
Matt 7:23

physical pleasure, a craving for everything
we see, and pride in our achievements and
possessions. These are not from the Father,
but are from this world. 17And this world
is fading away, along with everything that
people crave. But anyone who does what
[g]pleases God will live forever.

Warning about Antichrists

18Dear children, the last hour is here. You
have heard that the [h]Antichrist is coming,
and already many such [h]antichrists have
appeared. From this we know that the last
hour has come. 19These people left our
churches, but they never really belonged
with us; otherwise they would have stayed
with us. When they left, it proved that they
did not belong with us.
20But you are not like that, for the Holy
One has given you his Spirit, and all of you
know the truth. 21So I am writing to you
not because you don't know the truth but
because you know the difference between
truth and lies. 22And who is a liar? Anyone
who says that Jesus is not the Christ. Anyone who denies the Father and the Son is
an [i]antichrist. 23Anyone who denies the Son
doesn't have the [j]Father, either. But anyone
who acknowledges the Son has the [j]Father
also.

Remaining Faithful in Fellowship

24So you must remain faithful to what you
have been taught from the beginning. If
you do, you will remain in fellowship with
the Son and with the Father. 25And in this
fellowship we enjoy the eternal life he promised us.
26I am writing these things to warn you
about those who want to lead you astray.
27But you have received the Holy Spirit,
and he lives within you, so you don't need
anyone to teach you what is true. For the
Spirit teaches you everything you need to
know, and what he teaches is true—it is not
a lie. So just as he has taught you, remain in
fellowship with Christ.
28And now, dear children, remain in
fellowship with Christ so that when he [k]re-
turns, you will be full of courage and not
shrink back from him in shame.
29Since we know that Christ is righteous,
we also know that all who do what is [a]right
are God's children.

Living as Children of God

3 See how very much our Father loves us,
for he calls us his children, and that is
what we are! But the people who belong to
this world don't recognize that we are God's
children because they don't know him.
2Dear friends, we are already God's children,
but he has not yet shown us what we will be
like when Christ appears. But we do know
that we will be like him, for we will see him
as he really is. 3And all who have this eager
expectation will keep themselves pure, just
as he is pure.
4Everyone who sins is breaking God's law,

Christ's Kingdom on this earth (2:16; 3:1; 4:4; 5:19; John 12:31; 15:18; Eph 6:11-12; Jas 4:4). The world appeals to people's fleshly desires and thereby diverts them from God. Those who are ***from this world*** need God to redeem them from it.

2:18 ***Antichrist*** literally means "instead of Christ"; he claims for himself what belongs to Christ and poses as a substitute for Christ (cp. 2 Thes 2:3 and Rev 13:1-10). • ***many such antichrists have appeared:*** They are the false teachers who deny that Jesus is the Christ, God's Son (2:22-23), God in the flesh (4:2; 2 Jn 1:7).

2:19 ***These people left our churches:*** This is John's first direct statement about the false teachers. At one point, they had been part of the church community, in fellowship with John and the other apostles. Then they left that fellowship and evidently formed a separate, exclusive community based on their false teachings about Jesus (see 4:1; 2 Jn 1:7; 3 Jn 1:9-10). • ***they never really belonged with us:*** True believers would have stayed in fellowship with the apostles and remained faithful to their teachings.

2:20-23 ***for the Holy One has given you his Spirit:*** The Holy Spirit gives believers the ability to understand and recognize spiritual truth (see Isa 61:1; Acts 10:38; 2 Cor 1:21-22). Those who have the Spirit ***know the truth*** about the Father and the Son and can detect what does not accord with the truth of the apostles' teaching.

2:20 ***But you are not like that, for the Holy One has given you his Spirit:*** Literally *But you have an anointing from the Holy One.*

2:22 John marks out as ***a liar*** any false teacher who denies that Jesus is the Christ, the Son of God, the unique revealer of the Father (4:2). • ***not the Christ:*** Or *not the Messiah.* • ***an antichrist:*** Or *the antichrist.*

2:24-25 John instructs his readers to resist the lies of such antichrists and to ***remain faithful*** to the truth that he and the other apostles have proclaimed to them. If they would do this, then they would ***remain in fellowship with the Son and with the Father*** and have assurance of ***eternal life*** (John 3:15, 36; 6:40, 47, 57; 17:2-3).

2:27 ***received the Holy Spirit:*** Literally *received the anointing from him.* • ***For the Spirit:*** Literally *For the anointing.*

2:28-29 To ***remain in fellowship with Christ*** means, in part, not being misled by any kind of false teaching. If John's readers listen to the false teachers, they will not be in fellowship with Christ and will have reason to ***shrink back from him in shame*** when he returns, because of the judgment coming upon them.

3:1-3 When Christ returns, ***we will be like him, for we will see him as he really is.*** God's children bear the image of Christ and will share in his glory (see Rom 8:18-30). • Those who have this hope ***keep themselves pure,*** seeking to become more like Christ in anticipation of his glorious appearing. It is partly for this reason that God's children will not be ashamed when Christ comes (2:29).

3:4-10 This section discusses what it means to live a pure life (3:3). Being ***born into God's family*** demands

for all sin is contrary to the law of God. 5And you know that Jesus came to take away our sins, and there is no sin in him. 6Anyone who continues to live in him will not sin. But anyone who keeps on sinning does not know him or understand who he is.

7Dear children, don't let anyone deceive you about this: When people do what is right, it shows that they are righteous, even as Christ is righteous. 8But when people keep on sinning, it shows that they belong to the devil, who has been sinning since the beginning. But the Son of God came to destroy the works of the devil. 9Those who have been born into God's family do not make a practice of sinning, because God's life is in them. So they can't keep on sinning, because they are children of God. 10So now we can tell who are children of God and who are children of the devil. Anyone who does not live righteously and does not love other believers does not belong to God.

3. LOVING ONE ANOTHER (3:11–4:21)

Showing We Love One Another

11This is the message you have heard from the beginning: We should love one another. 12We must not be like Cain, who belonged to the evil one and killed his brother. And why did he kill him? Because Cain had been doing what was evil, and his brother had been doing what was righteous. 13So don't be surprised, dear brothers and sisters, if the world hates you.

14If we love our Christian brothers and sisters, it proves that we have passed from death to life. But a person who has no love is still dead. 15Anyone who hates another brother or sister is really a murderer at heart. And you know that murderers don't have eternal life within them.

16We know what real love is because Jesus gave up his life for us. So we also ought to give up our lives for our brothers and sisters. 17If someone has enough money to live well and sees a brother or sister in need but shows no compassion—how can God's love be in that person?

18Dear children, let's not merely say that we love each other; let us show the truth by our actions. 19Our actions will show that we belong to the truth, so we will be confident when we stand before God. 20Even if we feel guilty, God is greater than our feelings, and he knows everything.

21Dear friends, if we don't feel guilty, we can come to God with bold confidence. 22And we will receive from him whatever we ask because we obey him and do the things that please him.

23And this is his commandment: We must [b]believe in the name of his Son, Jesus Christ, and love one another, just as he commanded us. 24Those who obey God's

3:5 John 1:29; 2 Cor 5:21
3:6 Rom 6:14
3:8 John 8:44
3:10 John 1:12-13
3:11 John 13:34; 15:12, 17; 2 Jn 1:5
3:12 Gen 4:3-8
3:13 John 15:18; 17:14
3:14 John 5:24
3:15 Matt 5:21-22; John 8:44; Gal 5:20-21
3:16 John 13:1; 15:13; Phil 2:17; 1 Thes 2:8
3:17 Deut 15:7-8; Jas 2:15-16
3:18 Rom 12:9; Jas 1:22
3:19 John 18:37
3:20 John 21:17
3:21 Rom 5:1
3:22 Matt 7:7; John 8:29; 14:13
3:23 John 6:29; 13:34
[b]*pisteuō* (4100) ▸John 8:30

purification; a life of sin—a continual lack of purity—is evidence that someone is not really God's child. Sin is incompatible with the new nature derived from the new birth. John wants believers to *do what is right,* and thus demonstrate that they are joined to Christ and his righteousness. Those who are children of God *do not make a practice of sinning,* but this differs from the sort of "sinlessness" that the false teachers claimed (see 1:5-10 and notes).

3:6 *continues to live in him* (Greek *menō*): This indicates "abiding" and "remaining" (John 15:1-8) in contrast to departing into falsehood. To the extent that we live in continual, dependent fellowship with Christ and in faithfulness to the apostles' teachings, we *will not sin.* • *keeps on sinning:* This verb denotes sin as an ongoing, repeated action. John was not saying that anyone who sins once *does not know* God (i.e., has no relationship with God). But if we persist in sin, we demonstrate a lack of relationship with God.

3:8 *destroy:* This does not mean "to annihilate" but "to break down" (see Eph 2:14), "to undo," or "to render ineffective." Christ did not obliterate Satan; he came to undo *the works of the devil* by freeing people from sin and its awful consequences.

3:9-10 *because God's life:* Literally *because his seed.* • To *live righteously* means to live in a right relationship with God. (This is in contrast to the false teachers, who held that life in the spirit could not be contaminated by any behavior in a physical body.) This does not mean that we live perfect lives (1:8), but that we keep ourselves in a good relationship with God (1:9).

3:10 *does not love other believers:* Literally *does not love his brother;* see note on 2:9.

3:11-22 John now focuses on the believers' need to love one another (see John 13:34).

3:12-13 *Cain had been doing what was evil:* Cain was jealous that Abel received approval from God; this jealousy led to murder (Gen 4:8). Hatred is judged, just as the outward act that results from it (see Matt 5:21-22).

3:13 *dear brothers and sisters:* Literally *brothers;* see note on 2:9.

3:14 Having *love* for *our Christian brothers and sisters* (literally *the brothers;* similarly in 3:16) is tangible evidence that we have experienced rebirth in Christ and will have eternal *life* rather than *death* (i.e., condemnation; see Rom 6:23; Jas 5:20; Rev 21:8).

3:15 *hates another brother or sister:* Literally *hates his brother;* see note on 2:9.

3:16-18 Christ's example shows that *real love* involves self-sacrifice. We do this by becoming truly concerned about the needs of other Christians and by unselfishly giving time, effort, prayer, possessions, and even our lives to supply those needs.

3:17 *sees a brother or sister:* Literally *sees his brother;* see note on 2:9.

3:19-22 Those who truly love (3:16-18) have confidence that God accepts them because real love is primary evidence of real faith and of new life in Christ (see 4:7-8).

3:23-24 John here gives a new criterion for discerning who has the Spirit. The Spirit is not the possession of an elite who are enlightened without their lives being changed. Instead, the Spirit

3:24 Rom 8:9
4:1 Acts 17:11; 1 Thes 5:21; 1 Jn 2:18
4:2 John 1:14; 1 Cor 12:3
4:3 2 Jn 1:7; [c]*antichristos* (0500) ‣2 Jn 1:7
4:4 John 12:31; Rom 8:31
4:5 John 15:19; 17:14, 16
4:6 John 8:47; 14:17; 1 Cor 14:37; 1 Tim 4:1
4:7 [d]*agapē* (0026) ‣Jude 1:12
4:9 John 3:16; [e]*monogenēs* (3439) ‣Luke 7:12
4:10 Rom 5:8, 10; [f]*hilasmos* (2434) ‣Luke 18:13
4:11 Matt 18:33
4:12 John 1:18; 14:23; 1 Tim 6:16
4:13 Rom 8:9
4:14 John 1:14; 3:17; 4:42; [g]*sōtēr* (4990) ‣Jude 1:25
4:15 John 6:69

commandments remain in fellowship with
him, and he with them. And we know he
lives in us because the Spirit he gave us lives
in us.

Discerning False Prophets

4 Dear friends, do not believe everyone
who claims to speak by the Spirit. You
must test them to see if the spirit they have
comes from God. For there are many false
prophets in the world. 2This is how we know
if they have the Spirit of God: If a person
claiming to be a prophet acknowledges that
Jesus Christ came in a real body, that person has the Spirit of God. 3But if someone
claims to be a prophet and does not acknowledge the truth about Jesus, that person is not
from God. Such a person has the spirit of
the [c]Antichrist, which you heard is coming
into the world and indeed is already here.
4But you belong to God, my dear children.
You have already won a victory over those
people, because the Spirit who lives in you
is greater than the spirit who lives in the
world. 5Those people belong to this world,
so they speak from the world's viewpoint,
and the world listens to them. 6But we belong to God, and those who know God listen
to us. If they do not belong to God, they
do not listen to us. That is how we know if
someone has the Spirit of truth or the spirit
of deception.

God Is Love

7Dear friends, let us continue to love one
another, for [d]love comes from God. Anyone
who loves is a child of God and knows God.
8But anyone who does not love does not
know God, for God is love.
9God showed how much he loved us by
sending his [e]one and only Son into the world
so that we might have eternal life through
him. 10This is real love—not that we loved
God, but that he loved us and sent his Son as
a [f]sacrifice to take away our sins.
11Dear friends, since God loved us that
much, we surely ought to love each other.
12No one has ever seen God. But if we love
each other, God lives in us, and his love is
brought to full expression in us.
13And God has given us his Spirit as proof
that we live in him and he in us. 14Further-
more, we have seen with our own eyes and
now testify that the Father sent his Son to
be the [g]Savior of the world. 15All who confess that Jesus is the Son of God have God
living in them, and they live in God. 16We
know how much God loves us, and we have
put our trust in his love.
God is love, and all who live in love live
in God, and God lives in them. 17And as we
live in God, our love grows more perfect. So
we will not be afraid on the day of judgment,
but we can face him with confidence because we live like Jesus here in this world.

---

comes to all believers and stimulates obedient discipleship (Gal 5:22-23).

4:1-6 Those who *belong to God* (4:4) can distinguish spiritual truth from error, because the Spirit's presence (3:23-24) teaches them (see 2:20, 27; John 14:15-26; 16:5-15). Yet John provides concrete tests for the believers to apply so that there will be no confusion. These tests are a starting point for true teachers, not an exhaustive set; they were designed to address the false teachings that were being promoted in the churches of John's readers.

4:1 ***everyone who claims to speak by the Spirit*** (literally *every spirit*): The teachers who left John's churches claimed to be ***prophets***, but the true prophet is an instrument for the Holy Spirit's messages (Acts 4:25; 1 Tim 4:1; Rev 19:10). Every speaker should be tested against what the Holy Spirit has said through the apostles (4:2-3, 6).

4:2 ***If a person claiming to be a prophet*** (literally *If a spirit;* similarly in 4:3): John outlines a doctrinal test for prophets and teachers. Those who have the Spirit of God confess ***that Jesus Christ came in a real body.*** In other words, they must affirm the full reality that Jesus is both fully man and fully God. Prophets and teachers who deny these basic teachings are antichrists (2:18). Certain false teachers in John's day (the Docetists) taught that Jesus Christ only seemed to have a human body but did not really have one. They thereby denied that God became flesh; see 1:1-3; John 1:14).

4:5 The ***world's viewpoint*** is one of systematic evil, opposed to God (2:15-17).

4:6 John tests the reality of a person's Christianity by whether they listen to and agree with the teachings of the apostles. • The ***Spirit of truth*** is the Holy Spirit (John 14:17, 26; 15:26; 16:13-15), who teaches the truth about Christ (2:20, 27). • False prophets have ***the spirit of deception,*** the spirit of antichrist, which leads people away from Christ (see note on 2:22). Therefore, union with the historic body of Christ and the consensus of teaching that began with the apostles is a sign of fidelity to Christ's work in the world.

4:7-21 John explains the source of a Christian's love and its outworking.

4:8 ***God is love,*** the source and embodiment of all love. This concept and the concept that "God is light" (1:5) form the foundation on which John writes this letter.

4:9-10 Jesus Christ, sent from God the Father, embodied and demonstrated God's love in his life on earth and in his sacrificial death on the cross as an atoning ***sacrifice.***

4:11-12 Those who have received God's love cannot help but spontaneously ***love*** those who have done the same. As this love flows through us to ***each other,*** it becomes evident that we love God.

4:15 Those who believe in Christ ***have God living in them, and they live in God.*** The Father and the Son experience this fellowship (John 10:38; 14:10; 17:21). Experiencing God in this way is a special privilege for believers (see John 14:20; 15:5; 17:21-24).

4:17 ***our love grows more perfect:*** The Greek word translated *grows more perfect* does not mean flawless, but mature and complete. We mature as our relationship with God grows, and God's love makes our love complete. • Experiencing and expressing God's love and doing what it requires does not *make* us acceptable to God, but it does give us the assurance that we *have been* accepted, and our fears of the final ***judgment*** melt away.

18 Such love has no fear, because perfect
love expels all fear. If we are afraid, it is for
fear of punishment, and this shows that we
have not fully experienced his perfect love.
19 We love each other because he loved us
first.

20 If someone says, "I love God," but hates
a Christian brother or sister, that person is
a liar; for if we don't love people we can see,
how can we love God, whom we cannot see?
21 And he has given us this command: Those
who love God must also love their Christian
brothers and sisters.

4. LIVING IN FELLOWSHIP (5:1-21)

Faith in the Son of God

5 Everyone who believes that Jesus is
the Christ has become a child of God.
And everyone who loves the Father loves
his children, too. 2 We know we love God's
children if we love God and obey his commandments. 3 Loving God means keeping
his commandments, and his commandments are not burdensome. 4 For every
child of God defeats this evil world, and we
achieve this victory through our faith. 5 And
who can win this battle against the world?
Only those who believe that Jesus is the Son
of God.

6 And Jesus Christ was revealed as God's
Son by his baptism in water and by shedding his blood on the cross—not by water
only, but by water and blood. And the Spirit,
who is truth, confirms it with his testimony.
7 So we have these three witnesses—8 the
Spirit, the water, and the blood—and all
three agree. 9 Since we believe human testimony, surely we can believe the greater
testimony that comes from God. And God
has testified about his Son. 10 All who believe in the Son of God know in their hearts
that this testimony is true. Those who don't
believe this are actually calling God a liar
because they don't believe what God has testified about his Son.

Knowing We Have Life

11 And this is what God has testified: He has
given us eternal life, and this life is in his Son.
12 Whoever has the Son has life; whoever
does not have God's Son does not have life.

13 I have written this to you who believe
in the name of the Son of God, so that you
may know you have eternal life. 14 And we
are confident that he hears us whenever we
ask for anything that pleases him. 15 And
since we know he hears us when we make
our requests, we also know that he will give
us what we ask for.

Keeping from Sin

16 If you see a Christian brother or sister sinning in a way that does not lead to death, you
should pray, and God will give that person

4:18 Rom 8:15
4:20 1 Jn 2:4; 3:17
4:21 Matt 5:43; 22:37-39
5:1 John 1:13; 3:3; 8:42
5:2 1 Jn 2:3
5:3 Deut 30:11; Matt 11:30; John 14:15
5:5 Rom 8:37
5:6 John 1:31-34; 14:7; 19:34-35
5:9 Matt 3:16-17; John 5:32-37; 8:17-18
5:10 John 3:33; Rom 8:16; Gal 4:6; 1 Jn 1:10
5:11 John 1:4; 1 Jn 2:25; 4:9; 5:13, 20
5:12 John 3:15-16, 36; 5:24; 14:6; 17:2-3; 2 Jn 1:9
5:13 John 20:31
5:14 Matt 7:7; John 14:13; 15:7
5:16 Jer 7:16; 14:11-12; Matt 12:31; Heb 6:4-6; 10:26

4:18 ***perfect love expels all fear:*** As we live with Christ and grow more mature and complete in God's love, we have confidence in facing the day of judgment, which will be terrifying for those who don't know God (Acts 24:25; Rom 2:16). • Based on consciousness of guilt, ***fear*** anticipates a deserved ***punishment,*** producing dread that is itself a foretaste of that punishment. Christ died to set us free from this dread (Heb 2:14-15).

4:19 ***We love each other:*** Literally *We love.* Other manuscripts read *We love God;* still others read *We love him.* • God ***loved us first,*** while we were sinners, not only after we gave sin up (Rom 8:5-11). God started the process; when he loved us he enabled us to respond to him in love and to extend that love to other Christians.

4:20 ***hates a Christian brother or sister:*** Literally *hates his brother;* see note on 2:9.

4:21 ***Those who love God must also love their Christian brothers and sisters:*** Literally *The one who loves God must also love his brother.*

5:1-5 Those who believe that ***Jesus is the Christ*** (or *the Messiah*) and ***the Son of God*** have been born spiritually as ***children*** of God (see John 20:31). Such people are empowered by the Spirit of God to love him and other Christians, and by their faith to obey God and overcome the evil temptations of ***the world.*** Through ***faith,*** they can love God and live in obedience to him.

5:6 ***And Jesus Christ was revealed as God's Son by his baptism in water and by shedding his blood on the cross*** (literally *This is he who came by water and blood*): John's contemporary, the heretic Cerinthus, taught that "the Christ" descended as a spirit on the man Jesus when he was baptized but left him before he died. The truth is that Jesus' baptism and death confirmed his identity as the Christ, the Son of God. Jesus of Nazareth was and is truly the Christ, the Son of God, from the beginning and forever.

5:7-8 ***three witnesses:*** The ***Spirit*** descended on Christ at his baptism (see John 1:32-34). The ***water*** is the water in which Christ was baptized (see Matt 3:13-15; Mark 1:9-11). The ***blood*** is the blood that Christ shed at his crucifixion (see Mark 15:37-39). ***All three*** proclaim Jesus as God's Son (5:6). • After the phrase *three witnesses,* a few very late manuscripts add *in heaven—the Father, the Word, and the Holy Spirit, and these three are one. And we have three witnesses on earth.* The longer version was written in Latin several centuries after John to explain the three elements (water, blood, and Spirit) as symbols of the Trinity. This explanation found its way into some Latin editions of 1 John, including later copies of the Latin Vulgate. Eventually, Erasmus translated it into Greek and included it in what became the *Textus Receptus,* the "received text," which is why it was included in the King James Version. The longer version cannot be found in any Greek manuscript prior to the 1700s and was never cited by any of the early fathers of the church. For these reasons, few modern English translations recognize the longer version as part of the authentic text.

5:11-12 ***Whoever has the Son has life:*** Those who have the Son of God living in them have God's ***eternal life*** now—they enjoy the presence of God's Spirit (2:20, 25, 27) and they have the guarantee of eternity with God (see Eph 1:13-14).

5:16 ***a Christian brother or sister:*** Literally *a brother;* see note on 2:9. • Sins that ***lead to death*** are those involving apostasy (see Matt 12:31-32; Heb 6:4-6). In the context of this letter, apos-

5:18
John 10:28-29
5:19
John 17:15
5:20
Luke 24:45
John 1:1, 4; 17:3
Rom 9:5
Rev 3:7
5:21
1 Cor 10:14
1 Thes 1:9

life. But there is a sin that leads to death,
and I am not saying you should pray for
those who commit it. 17All wicked actions
are sin, but not every sin leads to death.
18We know that God's children do not
make a practice of sinning, for God's Son
holds them securely, and the evil one cannot touch them. 19We know that we are
children of God and that the world around
us is under the control of the evil one.
20And we know that the Son of God has
come, and he has given us understanding
so that we can know the true God. And now
we live in fellowship with the true God because we live in fellowship with his Son,
Jesus Christ. He is the only true God, and he
is eternal life.
21Dear children, keep away from anything that might take God's place in your
hearts.

tasy involves leaving the apostolic faith and joining a heretical, anti-Christian movement such as those denounced in John's letters (see also "Consequences of Apostasy" at Heb 2:1-4, p. 2085).

5:17 ***not every sin leads to death:*** Those that do not involve ultimate apostasy can end in repentance and restoration (see Jas 5:20).

5:20 The NLT interprets the phrase ***the true God*** (literally *the one who is true*) as referring to God, since the next phrase refers to ***his Son, Jesus Christ***. John is also saying that Jesus Christ ***is the only true God*** (see John 1:1, 18; 20:28; Rom 9:5; Titus 2:13; 2 Pet 1:1). • To have ***fellowship with*** Jesus Christ is to have eternal life, because ***he is eternal life*** (5:12; see John 1:4; 3:16; 14:6; 20:31).

5:21 In closing, John exhorts his flock to ***keep away from anything that might take God's place in your hearts*** (literally *keep yourselves from idols*). In the context of 1 John, the primary idol would be any false teaching that takes people away from Jesus Christ, who is at once fully man and fully God.

THE SECOND LETTER OF JOHN

Second John is the shortest book in the NT, only thirteen verses. In antiquity, the entire letter would have fit on one sheet of papyrus. The first letter of John elaborated the principles of continuing in the truth, loving fellow believers, and watching out for false teachers. This letter gives us an example of applying these principles to a concrete situation.

SETTING

The setting of 2 John is similar to that of 1 John (see 1 John Introduction, "Setting," p. 2138). False teachers had been traveling in Asia Minor, teaching a heresy about Jesus known as Docetism. These deceivers refused to acknowledge that Jesus, the divine Christ, had a physical, human body, and they were persuading others to think the same way. These deceivers were probably the same heretics John alludes to in his first letter. Some of the members of the church, influenced by this teaching, had broken away to form a new sect. The apostle John was exhorting the believers in Asia Minor to be strong in their faith in the apostolic message of Jesus Christ, in their grasp of the truth, and in their love for one another.

SUMMARY

This personal letter begins with a greeting (vv 1-3) and then states John's wishes (vv 4-11). Above all, John wanted his readers to continue to love other Christians and to live in the eternal truth. John warns the Christians about false teachers who might come among them, and he encourages them to hold on to the apostles' teachings concerning Jesus Christ so that they will receive their full reward. At the same time, he commands them not to welcome false teachers into their meetings or their homes or to help them in any way. They should not even wish them well; to do so would be to participate in their heresy.

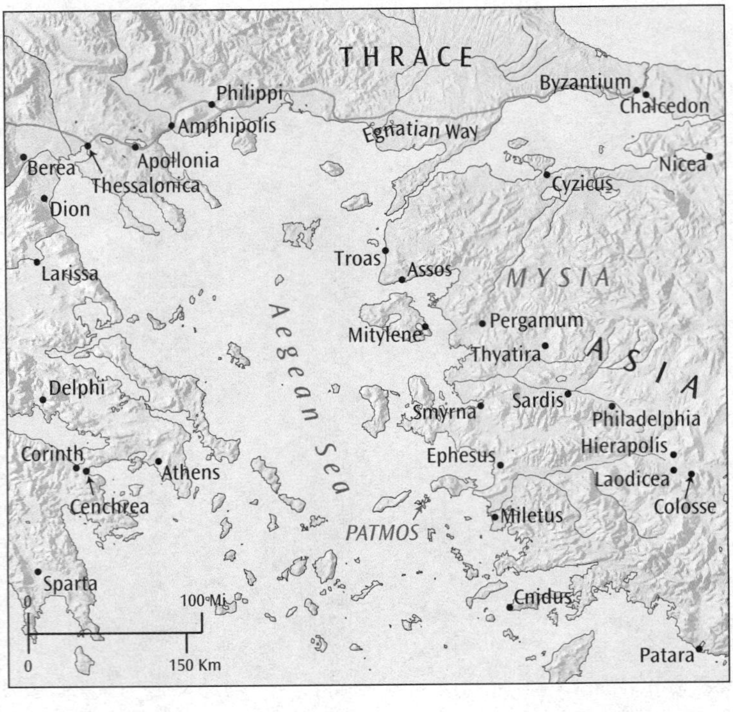

The Setting of 2 John, late 80s AD. When the apostle John left Jerusalem (probably in the late 60s AD), he seems to have settled in EPHESUS in the province of ASIA. He wrote his three letters (1–3 John) to the churches in Asia.

John closes his letter with a promise to visit soon and with greetings to the whole church.

AUTHOR

Some scholars have thought that the John who penned this letter (v 1) was a different John from the apostle. They think this because of a quotation from Papias, who was bishop of Hierapolis in Asia Minor (AD 100~130):

> If anywhere one came my way who had been a follower of the elders, I would inquire about the words of the elders—what Andrew and Peter had said, or what Thomas or James or John or Matthew or any other of the Lord's disciples; and I would inquire about the things which Aristion and the elder John, the Lord's disciples, are saying.

This quote has led some to think that Papias was speaking of two different people named John, but that is not necessarily the case. Papias noted what the "elders" (including the apostles, such as John) *had said* about Jesus and what two of the Lord's disciples (Aristion and John) were still *saying* (present tense). The apostle John lived to be a very old man, so old that even Papias had heard him speak in person. It is reasonable to conclude that the "elder" of 1–3 John is the same as the apostle John.

OUTLINE

vv 1-3
Greetings

vv 4-11
Encouragement to Live in the Truth

vv 12-13
Concluding Words

RECIPIENTS

The recipients of 2 John were a "chosen lady and . . . her children" (v 1). This might refer to a specific woman named Kyria and her biological children (the Greek word *kuria*, "lady," can be a proper name). However, it is likely that John was speaking about a particular local church ("the chosen lady") and its individual members ("her children"; cp. 1 Pet 5:13). If so, 2 John was sent to one of the churches in Asia Minor, for these were the churches under his authority. Since the author identifies himself at the beginning of this epistle as "the elder," the recipients were likely a fellowship of Christians under his care.

MEANING AND MESSAGE

> *Genuine Christian missionaries . . . may be recognized both by the message they bring and by the motive which inspires them. If they faithfully proclaim the doctrine of Christ, and if they have set out not for gain but for the sake of the name, then they should be both received and helped forward on their journey.*
>
> JOHN R. W. STOTT, *The Letters of John*, p. 202

The message of 2 John is twofold. First, the members of the Christian community must love one another (v 5). The outworking of this love follows Jesus' commands (v 6). Second, John warns the church about false teachers who needed to be exposed, avoided, and shunned.

TIMELINE

Passover, AD 30 or 33
Jesus' crucifixion and resurrection

by AD 68
The apostles leave Jerusalem

about AD 70?
John settles in Asia Minor

before AD 90
John writes the Gospel of John

▸ **John writes 1–3 John**

AD 60s or 90s
John writes Revelation

about AD 100
John dies peacefully in Ephesus

AD 100~130
Papias is bishop of Hierapolis

FURTHER READING

DANIEL AKIN
1–3 John (2001)

PHILIP W. COMFORT AND WENDELL C. HAWLEY
2 John in *Cornerstone Biblical Commentary*, vol. 13 (2007)

I. HOWARD MARSHALL
The Epistles of John (1978)

STEPHEN SMALLEY
1–3 John (1984)

JOHN R. W. STOTT
The Letters of John (1988)

Many of the NT Epistles were written to deal with heresy. This is true of several of Paul's letters: Galatians (Gal 1:6), Colossians (Col 2:16-23), 2 Thessalonians (2 Thes 2:1-3), and 1 Timothy (1 Tim 4:1; 6:20-21). Peter wrote his second letter to counter false teachers (2 Pet 2:1-22), and Jude wrote his letter (Jude 1:3-4) for the same reason. John's letters, likewise, were written as antidotes to the poisonous effects of false teachings, such as Gnosticism and Docetism, that were infecting many of the early churches.

Greetings (vv 1-3)

1 This letter is from John, the elder.
I am writing to the chosen lady and to her
children, whom I love in the truth—as does
everyone else who knows the truth—2 because the truth lives in us and will be with
us forever.
3 Grace, mercy, and peace, which come
from God the Father and from Jesus Christ—
the Son of the Father—will continue to be
with us who live in truth and love.

Encouragement to Live in the Truth (vv 4-11)

Live in the Truth

4 How happy I was to meet some of your children and find them living according to the
truth, just as the Father commanded.
5 I am writing to remind you, dear friends,
that we should love one another. This is not
a new commandment, but one we have had
from the beginning. 6 Love means doing
what God has commanded us, and he has
commanded us to love one another, just as
you heard from the beginning.

The Nature of Christ

7 I say this because many deceivers have
gone out into the world. They deny that
Jesus Christ came in a real body. Such a person is a deceiver and an [a]antichrist. 8 Watch
out that you do not lose what we have
worked so hard to achieve. Be diligent so
that you receive your full reward. 9 Anyone
who wanders away from this teaching has
no relationship with God. But anyone who
remains in the teaching of Christ has a relationship with both the Father and the Son.
10 If anyone comes to your meeting and
does not teach the truth about Christ, don't
invite that person into your home or give
any kind of encouragement. 11 Anyone who

1:1 1 Jn 3:18-19; 3 Jn 1:1
1:2 John 8:32; 14:17; 1 Jn 1:8; 3:18-19
1:3 1 Tim 1:2
1:4 3 Jn 1:3-4
1:5 John 13:34; 15:12; 1 Jn 2:7
1:6 John 14:15, 23-24; 1 Jn 2:5, 7; 4:7-12; 5:3
1:7 1 Tim 4:1-5; 2 Pet 2:1-3; 1 Jn 2:18, 26; 4:1-3; [a]*antichristos* (0500) ‣Matt 24:24
1:8 Matt 10:41-42; 1 Cor 3:8-9
1:9 John 8:31; 1 Jn 2:23
1:10 Rom 16:17; Eph 5:11

---

vv 1-3 John begins with a standard introduction for a personal letter. • John mentions *truth* four times in this brief introduction and once in v 4. John wanted his readers to know and live out the truths about *Jesus Christ* and their relationship with him and not to be led astray by false teachers.

v 1 ***This letter is from John, the elder*** (literally *From the elder*): The translators have added *John* for clarification; John refers to himself as *the elder* to affirm his authority in the church. • ***to the chosen lady*** (Greek *kuria*) ***and to her children:*** Or *to the church God has chosen and its members.* The Greek word *kuria* could be the name of a specific individual; more likely, it refers to a particular local church and its believers (cp. v 13). • ***whom I love in the truth:*** This either means "truly love" (see vv 5-6) or, more likely, it refers to love between those who profess the same truth about Christ in contrast to the lies of the false teachers (v 7; see 1 Jn 2:21-23). John emphasizes the pronoun *I* to contrast sharply with the lovelessness of the false teachers, who rejected the true church.

v 2 Christian love is rooted in knowing ***the truth.*** The truth that ***lives in us*** is more than just facts or doctrine; it is the presence of God (see John 14:15-17), who ***will be with us forever.***

v 3 ***Grace, mercy, and peace*** are blessings of which John is confident for those ***who live in truth and love,*** and who demonstrate by their actions that they are God's children.

vv 4-11 John now applies the truth and love that he mentioned in the introduction (vv 1-3) to the readers' situation. Living in truth and love means maintaining fellowship with true Christians (vv 4-6), but also discerning false teachers and refusing to listen to them or help them (vv 7-11; see 1 John Introduction, "Setting," p. 2138).

v 5 ***I am writing to remind you, dear friends:*** Literally *I urge you, lady.* See note on v 1.

v 7 ***many deceivers have gone out into the world:*** Docetists were denying that Jesus Christ came in a real body. John refuted this heresy in his first letter (see 1 Jn 4:2-3). • ***Jesus Christ came:*** Or *Jesus Christ will come.* • A false teacher is ***a deceiver,*** because he misleads unwary believers, ***and an antichrist,*** because he distracts and leads people away from the true Christ. By using the apocalyptic symbol of the antichrist, John signals the severity of the heresy and the ultimate judgment upon false teachers.

v 8 ***we*** (some manuscripts read *you*): This word refers to the apostles and their co-workers. The apostles taught the truth and defended it against heresies, and believers (referred to as *you*) are admonished to protect their faith from teaching that could destroy them (v 9).

v 9 ***Anyone who wanders away from this teaching*** (literally *everyone going beyond and not remaining in the teaching*): To *go beyond* is to contradict the apostolic teachings about Jesus Christ and believe things about Jesus that were not taught by the apostles. This is a warning to the church not to listen to the false teachers.

vv 10-11 Believers should not *invite that person,* who does not teach the truth about Christ, into their homes. The early churches met in homes (see Acts 2:46; 5:42; 8:3; 12:5, 12; Col 4:15; Phlm 1:2), so this could refer to inviting false teachers to a meeting of the church. It could also refer to giving any form of hospitality to false teachers, which would help their mission. The only way to deal with them was to not accept them into the fellowship.

1:11
1 Tim 5:22
1:12
Num 12:8
1 Jn 1:4
3 Jn 1:13-14

encourages such people becomes a partner in their evil work.

Concluding Words (vv 12-13)

12I have much more to say to you, but I don't want to do it with paper and ink. For I hope to visit you soon and talk with you face to face. Then our joy will be complete.

13Greetings from the children of your sister, chosen by God.

v 12 Our English idiom *face to face* has the same meaning as the Greek idiom used here (literally *mouth to mouth;* see also 3 Jn 1:14). • ***Then our joy will be complete:*** Our relationship with Christ is not merely a private experience; we experience the fullest joy in harmonious fellowship with other believers.

v 13 ***from the children of your sister*** (or *from the members of your sister church*): This probably refers to the sister church in Ephesus and its members, with whom John was staying (see v 1). John lived in that region and served as elder for several churches.

THE THIRD LETTER OF JOHN

Gaius and Demetrius were two men who remained faithful to the church and to the apostle John. Another man, Diotrephes, was improperly controlling the church and rejecting the apostle and his emissaries. This small personal letter provides a window into some issues of leadership and conflict in the early churches.

SETTING

The apostle John wrote this letter in the same time period as 1 John and 2 John. Some teachers and leaders, claiming to be spiritual, taught a different doctrine about Christ and did not make the same disciplinary demands upon the members of their churches (see 1 John Introduction, p. 2138). They assumed their own authority and refused the authority of John. They also perverted the teaching of the apostles. Diotrephes was one of those who had broken away from the apostolic fellowship (cp. 1 Jn 2:18-19). As a leader in one of the local churches, he rejected John's authority and refused to accept the teachers John sent to the church. He even excommunicated those in the church who did receive them and provide them with hospitality.

Knowing this situation, John wrote this letter to Gaius, a faithful member of that church, encouraging him to continue welcoming and hosting John's emissaries and to remain faithful to John's teaching and fellowship.

SUMMARY

Of all the NT letters, 3 John is most typical of personal letters in first-century Greece and Rome. As with all the letters of this era, 3 John begins (vv 1-4) with an identification of the writer ("the elder") and the recipient ("Gaius"), followed by a wish for his welfare.

In the body of this letter (vv 5-12), John commends Gaius and reproves Diot-

◀ **The Setting of 3 John, late 80s AD.** When the apostle John left Jerusalem (probably in the late 60s AD), he seems to have settled in EPHESUS in the province of ASIA. He wrote his three letters (1–3 John) to the churches in Asia.

rephes. Gaius acted commendably in welcoming the traveling teachers, and these had in turn reported to John that Gaius was living according to the truth. This gave John great joy. John commends Gaius for giving hospitality to the traveling teachers who worked "on behalf of the Name" of the Lord Jesus Christ (see note on v 7) and encourages him to continue giving them this hospitality.

OUTLINE

vv 1-4
Greetings

vv 5-12
Caring for the Lord's Workers

vv 13-15
Final Words

In contrast to Gaius, a church leader named Diotrephes earned the apostle's censure (vv 9-10). Diotrephes' love for prestigious leadership caused him to rebuff John's authority and to persuade others to do the same. Diotrephes even excommunicated those who didn't follow his own leadership. Gaius is warned not to submit to the aggressive leadership of Diotrephes or be influenced by his bad example.

AUTHOR AND DATE

There is no doubt that 3 John is a real letter from the elder to his friend Gaius, fitting in with the pattern of ancient letter-writing, but transformed by Christian usage.

I. HOWARD MARSHALL *The Epistles of John*, p. 9

The author of this epistle calls himself "the elder" (see v 1), a position of authority because of his age and especially because he was a disciple of Christ. Most think that this is John the apostle, an elderly man and an elder of the churches in Asia Minor during the last decades of the first century (see 1 John and 2 John Introductions, pp. 2138, 2148). Third John was probably written during the same period as 1 John and 2 John, before AD 90.

MEANING AND MESSAGE

It is clear from the less polemical tone of 3 John that truth and love were two of the fundamental terms in [John's] theology, and it would not be difficult to write a summary of his thought centered on these two terms.

I. HOWARD MARSHALL, *The Epistles of John*, p. 52

John's third letter is concerned with a problem introduced in 1 John: Some church leaders followed false teaching and ignored the authority of the apostles. Diotrephes is a clear example of one who falsely claimed to know the truth. By rejecting those sent by John, Diotrephes was destroying the unity of the church. He did not love other Christians and he rejected those who truly knew Jesus Christ. We cannot claim to love God and the truth if we don't love apostolic teaching and if we don't join in fellowship with God's church, the members of the Father's family.

TIMELINE

Passover, AD 30 or 33
Jesus' crucifixion and resurrection

by AD 68
The apostles leave Jerusalem

about AD 70?
John settles in Asia Minor

before AD 90
John writes the Gospel of John
▸ **John writes 1–3 John**

AD 60s or 90s
John writes Revelation

about AD 100
John dies peacefully in Ephesus

AD 100~130
Papias is bishop of Hierapolis

FURTHER READING

DANIEL AKIN
1–3 John (2001)

PHILIP W. COMFORT AND WENDELL C. HAWLEY
3 John in *Cornerstone Biblical Commentary*, vol. 13 (2007)

I. HOWARD MARSHALL
The Epistles of John (1978)

STEPHEN SMALLEY
1–3 John (1984)

JOHN R. W. STOTT
The Letters of John (1988)

Greetings (vv 1-4)

1 This letter is from John, the elder.
I am writing to Gaius, my dear friend,
whom I love in the truth.
2 Dear friend, I hope all is well with you
and that you are as healthy in body as you
are strong in spirit. 3 Some of the traveling
teachers recently returned and made me
very happy by telling me about your faithfulness and that you are living according to
the truth. 4 I could have no greater joy than
to hear that my children are following the
truth.

Caring for the Lord's Workers (vv 5-12)

Encouragement for Gaius

5 Dear friend, you are being faithful to God
when you care for the traveling teachers who
pass through, even though they are strangers to you. 6 They have told the church here
of your loving friendship. Please continue
providing for such teachers in a manner
that pleases God. 7 For they are traveling for
the Lord, and they accept nothing from people who are not believers. 8 So we ourselves
should support them so that we can be their
partners as they teach the truth.

Reproof for Diotrephes

9 I wrote to the church about this, but Diotrephes, who loves to be the leader, refuses
to have anything to do with us. 10 When I
come, I will report some of the things he is
doing and the evil accusations he is making
against us. Not only does he refuse to welcome the traveling teachers, he also tells
others not to help them. And when they do
help, he puts them out of the church.

Approval of Demetrius

11 Dear friend, don't let this bad example
influence you. Follow only what is good. Remember that those who do good prove that
they are God's children, and those who do
evil prove that they do not know God.
12 Everyone speaks highly of Demetrius,
as does the truth itself. We ourselves can
say the same for him, and you know we
speak the truth.

1:1 2 Jn 1:1
1:3 2 Jn 1:4
1:4 1 Cor 4:15; Gal 4:19; 1 Jn 2:1
1:5 Rom 12:13; Heb 13:2; 1 Pet 4:10
1:6 Col 1:10; Titus 3:13
1:7 Matt 10:9-14; Mark 6:8-13; Luke 9:3-5; 10:4-11; Acts 20:33, 35
1:9 Matt 20:27
1:10 John 9:22, 34; 2 Jn 1:12; 3 Jn 1:5
1:11 Ps 34:14; 1 Jn 2:29; 3:6, 9-10
1:12 John 19:35; 21:24

vv 1-4 John begins his *letter* with a conventional greeting, which includes the identification of the author and addressee, a salutation (*dear friend*), a wish for the recipient's welfare, and gratitude for some aspect of the friendship.

v 1 ***This letter is from John, the elder*** (literally *From the elder*): The translators have added *John* (see note on 2 Jn 1:1). • There are several people named ***Gaius*** in the NT (see Acts 19:29; 20:4; Rom 16:23; 1 Cor 1:14); it was a popular name in the Greco-Roman world.

v 3 The *traveling teachers* (literally *brothers;* also in vv 5, 10) were probably John's emissaries who traveled from church to church, teaching the Good News and encouraging Christians (see vv 5, 10). • ***you are living according to the truth:*** Gaius was faithful to the apostolic gospel of Jesus Christ. The false teachers denied the reality of the incarnation or the sacrificial death of Jesus Christ (cp. 1 Jn 4:1-3).

v 4 As in 2 John (see 2 Jn 1:1-4), John's emphasis is on knowing and ***following the truth*** in contrast to Diotrephes and his followers (v 9).

vv 5-8 John now encourages Gaius to continue supporting the traveling teachers whom John had sent out (v 3).

v 5 Gaius provided hospitality for ***the traveling teachers*** (literally *the brothers*) sent by John from church to church to affirm the apostles' teaching about Christ (vv 7-8). By doing this, Gaius showed that he had received the truth from the apostles and that he was thus *faithful to God*.

v 6 ***The church here*** was most likely in Ephesus, where John was probably staying. Ephesus was an important port city in the province of Asia, and the fourth-largest city in the Roman empire. It became an important city for the Christian community (Acts 18:19–19:41; 1 Tim 1:3; 1 Pet 1:1; Rev 2:1-7).

vv 7-8 ***For they are traveling for the Lord*** (literally *They went out on behalf of the Name*): The writer did not need to identify whose name this was because all the early Christians knew that *the Name* represented Jesus Christ (see Acts 5:41). • The traveling teachers had chosen to ***accept nothing*** offered to them ***from people who are not believers*** (literally *from Gentiles*), but to rely fully on the churches for their support. Christians who support legitimate traveling teachers become ***their partners as they teach the truth*** (see Matt 10:41-42; Phil 4:15-19).

vv 9-12 In these verses, John condemns Diotrephes and presents Demetrius as the model of a faithful Christian who lives according to the truth. Gaius is urged to emulate Demetrius.

v 9 ***I wrote to the church about this:*** This could refer to 1 John or to a letter that is now lost. • ***Diotrephes*** was full of pride and self-importance (cp. 1 Tim 3:6), motivated by selfish ambition. • ***refuses to have anything to do with us:*** This dissidence was one of the key issues John dealt with in 1 John (see, e.g., 1 Jn 2:19; 4:5-6). Diotrephes rejected the teachers sent by John and excommunicated any members of the church who did accept them. He wanted to rule the local church without answering to any outside authority.

v 11 ***those who do evil:*** Diotrephes was condemned for his failure to live by the Christian rule of love (1 Jn 3:10-14). This was how Gaius could be sure that Diotrephes was not living according to the truth. This applies to all who refuse to accept the apostolic teaching about Jesus Christ and refuse to live in fellowship with others who do. • ***they do not know God:*** Literally *they have not seen God.*

v 12 ***Demetrius*** was the very opposite of Diotrephes, a prime example of one who knows the truth and practices it (v 3). The placement of Demetrius's name at the end of the letter suggests that he was the one who carried John's letter to Gaius (cp. Col 4:7-9; 1 Pet 5:12). • ***you know we speak the truth:*** John wished to protect his honor as a reliable elder over these churches rather than being shamed by any possible usurpation by Diotrephes and other false teachers.

vv 13-15 As in 2 John, the conclusion of 3 John shows John's desire to make a personal visit and see to the instructions of this letter.

v 13 ***pen and ink*** (literally *ink and reed*): In antiquity, writing was typically done with a stylus shaped from a reed and black carbon ink (see also 2 Jn 1:12).

v 14 Our English idiom ***face to face***

1:13 Num 12:8; 2 Jn 1:12
1:14 2 Jn 1:12

Final Words (vv 13-15)

13 I have much more to say to you, but I don't want to write it with pen and ink. 14 For I hope to see you soon, and then we will talk face to face.

15 Peace be with you.

Your friends here send you their greetings. Please give my personal greetings to each of our friends there.

parallels the Greek idiom used here (literally *mouth to mouth;* see also 2 Jn 1:12).

v 15 John closes his letter with his farewell and with greetings to others.

• Some English translations combine vv 14 and 15 into v 14. • ***Peace be with you:*** This was a traditional greeting among the Jews (Matt 10:12; Luke 10:5-6), which had taken on heightened significance for Christians because Jesus used it after his resurrection (John 20:19-21, 26). • ***give my personal greetings*** (literally *greet by name*): Gaius was to greet the ***friends***—that is, those who accept the apostolic gospel and live according to the truth (cp. vv 3-4).

THE LETTER OF

JUDE

The very brief letter of Jude has a single focus: to warn believers against succumbing to false teaching. Jude helps Christians stay true to the faith by painting a grim and gloomy picture of deviant teachers. Arrogant, immoral, and greedy, these teachers are destined for the terrible judgment God has in store for all who deny and defy him. Who would want to follow such people to their condemnation? This is the question that Jude puts before us in this letter. In a world with so many distorted ideas about Christianity, we need to be reminded of the dangers of false teaching.

SETTING

Jude wrote this letter to combat false teachers in the early church. Jude focuses less on what these people were teaching than on the way they were living; at the heart of Jude's critique is the charge that they were libertines—they assumed that God's grace revealed in Christ gave them the freedom to do whatever they pleased (v 4). They had no respect for authority (see vv 8-9). They engaged in many sinful behaviors (vv 16, 19). These profligates, who claimed to be Christians (v 4), were effectively denying the Lord and were therefore destined for the condemnation of all who rebel against the Lord.

SUMMARY

This brief letter is oriented entirely around an outbreak of false teaching. After the letter opening (vv 1-2), Jude explains the situation prompting his letter (vv 3-4): The imminent danger posed by the false teachers required that he write a very different kind of letter from the one he had planned to write.

In vv 5-16, Jude elaborates on the character of these false teachers. This section unfolds in an *A-B-A'* sequence. Jude first uses three scriptural examples to illustrate the condemnation that the false teachers face (*A*, vv 5-10). He then cites three more scriptural examples to castigate them for their ungodly attitudes and behavior (*B*, vv 11-13). At the end of this section, he returns to their condemnation, citing Jewish tradition to hammer home his indictment (*A'*, vv 14-16).

Jude then appeals directly to his readers (vv 17-23), urging them to hold fast to God's truth and to reach out to believers who might be tempted to follow the false teachers. The letter ends with a notable doxology (vv 24-25).

[The Letter of Jude] is packed with sound words of heavenly grace.

ORIGEN
Introduction to Matthew 17

AUTHOR

Jude identifies himself as "a brother of James" (v 1). This James is almost certainly the "Lord's brother" (Gal 1:19; see Mark 6:3 // Matt 13:55)

who became a leader of the Jerusalem church (Acts 15:13-21; 21:18) and wrote the letter of James. Jude was therefore also a brother of Jesus (Jude is spelled "Judas" in Mark 6:3 // Matt 13:55). Jude and the other brothers of Jesus did not follow Jesus during his earthly ministry (John 7:5), but evidently became believers after the resurrection (see 1 Cor 15:7) and traveled to spread the message about the resurrected Lord (1 Cor 9:5).

OUTLINE

vv 1-2
Greetings from Jude

vv 3-4
Jude's Purpose in Writing

vv 5-16
The Danger of False Teachers

vv 17-23
A Call to Remain Faithful

vv 24-25
A Prayer of Praise

DATE AND DESTINATION

We know so little about Jude that we cannot pin down a date or destination of the letter. It was probably written after AD 45, to allow time for the kind of false teaching described here to develop. It was probably written before AD 90, when even a young brother of Jesus would have been old. The close relationship between 2 Peter and Jude suggests that the two might have been written at about the same time (see 2 Peter Introduction, "Relationship to Jude," p. 2133).

MEANING AND MESSAGE

False Teachers. False teachers of many varieties have disturbed God's people over the years. Jude's letter is a powerful reminder of their potential to harm the community and a stark depiction of their terrible fate. Jude's description of the false teachers makes dynamic use of OT and Jewish traditions. Jude compares the false teachers to the rebellious Israelites in the wilderness (v 5), to the angels who rebelled against God (v 6), and to the sinners of Sodom and Gomorrah (v 7). The false teachers are like Cain (see Gen 4), Balaam (see Num 22–24), and Korah (see Num 16). Like all of them, false teachers are rebels against the Lord and will experience his judgment.

Defending the Faith. In v 3, Jude implies that there is a defined body of doctrine in the early church to which all Christians need to adhere. Paul assumes the same thing when he urges Timothy to "guard what God has entrusted to you" (1 Tim 6:20; see 2 Tim 1:14).

To be a Christian means to have faith in God and love for others; it also means to confess gladly the truth that God has revealed in Jesus Christ. We cannot truly express faith in God unless we acknowledge the truth that he has revealed. For this reason, early Christians, even in the NT period, formulated creeds to summarize the essentials of Christian truth (e.g., 1 Tim 3:16). These creeds were often crafted to counteract a false teaching. If we are to heed Jude's call to "defend the faith," we need to know just what that faith is. Too many Christians spend too much energy in debating nonessential details and too little in learning the essentials well. Only by learning the essentials will the faithful be able to explain their faith to others and to guard Christian truth from false teaching.

TIMELINE

Passover, AD 30 or 33
Jesus' crucifixion and resurrection

Pentecost, AD 30 or 33
The birth of the church in Jerusalem

AD 49~50
The council in Jerusalem

early 60s AD
James the brother of Jesus is stoned to death in Jerusalem

before AD 64
Peter writes 2 Peter from Rome

AD 64~65
Persecution of Christians under Nero, Peter is crucified in Rome

AD 70
Jerusalem and the Temple are destroyed

FURTHER READING

PETER DAVIDS
The Letters of 2 Peter & Jude (2006)

GENE L. GREEN
2 Peter & Jude (2008)

DOUGLAS MOO
2 Peter & Jude (1996)

THOMAS SCHREINER
1–2 Peter, Jude (2003)

Greetings from Jude (vv 1-2)

1This letter is from Jude, a slave of Jesus
Christ and a brother of James.
I am writing to all who have been [a]called
by God the Father, who loves you and keeps
you safe in the care of Jesus Christ.
2May God give you more and more mercy,
peace, and love.

Jude's Purpose in Writing (vv 3-4)

3Dear friends, I had been eagerly planning
to write to you about the salvation we all
share. But now I find that I must write
about something else, urging you to defend
the faith that God has entrusted once for all
time to his holy people. 4I say this because
some ungodly people have wormed their
way into your churches, saying that God's
marvelous grace allows us to live immoral
lives. The condemnation of such people
was recorded long ago, for they have denied
our only Master and Lord, Jesus Christ.

The Danger of False Teachers (vv 5-16)

5So I want to remind you, though you already know these things, that Jesus first
rescued the nation of Israel from Egypt,
but later he destroyed those who did not
remain faithful. 6And I remind you of the
angels who did not stay within the limits of
authority God gave them but left the place
where they belonged. God has kept them
securely chained in prisons of darkness,
waiting for the great day of judgment. 7And
don't forget Sodom and Gomorrah and
their neighboring towns, which were filled
with immorality and every kind of sexual
perversion. Those cities were destroyed by
fire and serve as a warning of the eternal
fire of God's judgment.
8In the same way, these people—who
claim authority from their dreams—live
immoral lives, defy authority, and [b]scoff at
supernatural beings. 9But even Michael,
one of the mightiest of the angels, did not
dare accuse the devil of blasphemy, but simply said, "The Lord rebuke you!" (This took
place when Michael was arguing with the
devil about Moses' body.) 10But these people
scoff at things they do not understand. Like
unthinking animals, they do whatever their
instincts tell them, and so they bring about
their own destruction. 11What sorrow
awaits them! For they follow in the footsteps
of Cain, who killed his brother. Like Balaam,
they deceive people for money. And like Korah, they perish in their rebellion.
12When these people eat with you in
your fellowship meals commemorating

1:1 Matt 13:55
[a]*klētos* (2822) ‣Matt 22:14
1:2 2 Pet 1:2
1:3 1 Tim 6:12
1:4 Gal 2:4; 2 Pet 2:1-2
1:5 Exod 14:21-31; Num 14:29-37; 1 Cor 10:5-10
1:6 //2 Pet 2:4, 9
1:7 Gen 19:4-25; Matt 10:15; //2 Pet 2:6, 10
1:8 //2 Pet 2:10
[b]*blasphēmeō* (0987) ‣Rev 13:1
1:9 Dan 10:13, 21; 12:1; Zech 3:2; //2 Pet 2:11; Rev 12:7
1:10 //2 Pet 2:12
1:11 Gen 4:3-8; Num 16:1-35; 31:16; //2 Pet 2:15-16; 1 Jn 3:12; Rev 2:14
1:12 Ezek 34:8; 1 Cor 11:20-22; //2 Pet 2:13

---

vv 1-2 In a typical letter opening, Jude identifies himself and his audience and prays for them. • ***keeps you safe in the care of Jesus Christ*** (or *keeps you for Jesus Christ*): This description introduces an important emphasis (see also vv 21, 24) and gives assurance in the context of false teaching.

v 1 ***Jude*** (or *Judas*) is the Greek equivalent of the Hebrew name "Judah." It was a common name; this Jude was ***a brother of James***, who was a brother of Jesus (see Jude Introduction, "Author," p. 2156). • ***a slave of Jesus Christ:*** Jude acknowledges that he is under Jesus' lordship in every area of life. The title also carries honor: The great OT leaders of God's people were also called *slaves* or *servants* of God (see Josh 14:7; 2 Kgs 18:12; Ezek 34:23). • ***to all who have been called:*** It is unclear who the specific recipients of Jude's letter were.

vv 3-4 In place of the thanksgiving that usually comes at this point in a NT letter (see Rom 1:8-14; 1 Cor 1:4-9), Jude explains his central purpose. False teaching was a potent danger to the faith of his readers (see vv 22-23).

v 3 In the NT, "faith" usually refers to the act of believing, while ***the faith*** refers to the content of Christian belief.

v 4 Abusing ***God's marvelous grace*** by saying that it ***allows us to live immoral lives*** is a constant temptation (cp. Rom 6).

vv 5-16 This section elaborates on the "condemnation recorded long ago" (1:4) by applying to the false teachers OT examples of God's judgment.

v 5 ***Jesus:*** As in the best manuscripts; various other manuscripts read *[the] Lord*, or *God*, or *Christ;* one reads *God Christ.* The preexistent *Jesus* rescued the people of Israel from Egypt and later destroyed the unfaithful (cp. 1 Cor 10:4). • After rescuing ***the nation of Israel from Egypt***, God led them toward the Promised Land. Most of the people did not trust the Lord to protect them. Because of their unbelief, God sentenced that generation (except Joshua and Caleb) to wander in the wilderness until they died (see Num 14).

v 6 ***The angels*** might refer to the fall of Satan and his angelic followers, but no OT passage clearly describes this event (see notes on Isa 14:12-17; Ezek 28:11-19). Jude was probably referring to Gen 6:1-4; Jewish tradition understood the "sons of God" in Gen 6 to be wicked angels and viewed their intercourse with women as the cause of their ***judgment*** (see *1 Enoch* 6–10; see also notes on 1 Pet 3:19-20; 2 Pet 2:4). Jude later (vv 14-15) quotes directly from *1 Enoch.*

v 7 God's judgment on ***Sodom and Gomorrah*** had become proverbial (see Gen 18:17–19:26; Luke 17:26-29). • ***neighboring towns:*** Deuteronomy 29:23 mentions Admah and Zeboiim. • ***Every kind of sexual perversion*** probably refers to homosexuality (Gen 19:5-10).

v 8 ***supernatural beings:*** Literally *glorious ones*, which are probably evil angels. In the OT and in Judaism, angels were given a prominent role in the judgment. The false teachers might have been downplaying the reality of a judgment to come (see v 18; 2 Pet 3:3-4) or denying the glorious origin of these fallen angels (cp. 2 Pet 2:10).

v 9 ***Michael, one of the mightiest of the angels*** (literally *Michael, the archangel*): In Jewish tradition, "archangel" was the highest rank of angel (see also 1 Thes 4:16). Michael is mentioned several other times in Scripture (Dan 10:13, 21; 12:1; Rev 12:7); the story about him fighting with ***the devil about Moses' body*** is not in the OT but is preserved in Jewish tradition (see *Assumption of Moses*).

v 11 ***Cain:*** See Gen 4:1-16. • ***Balaam:*** See note on 2 Pet 2:15. • ***Korah:*** See Num 16:1-35.

v 12 The early Christians celebrated the Lord's Supper as part of shared ***fellowship meals*** with one another. • ***they are like dangerous reefs that can shipwreck you:*** Or *they are contaminants among you;* or *they are stains.*

v 13 The planets were considered to be ***wandering stars*** because they moved

[c]*agapē* (0026)
‣Rev 2:4
1:13
Isa 57:20
Phil 3:19
//2 Pet 2:17
1:15
2 Pet 2:6-9
1:16
//2 Pet 2:10, 18
1:17
Heb 2:3
2 Pet 3:2
1:18
//2 Pet 3:3
1:19
1 Cor 2:14-15
1:20
Eph 6:18
Col 2:7
1 Thes 5:11
1:21
2 Tim 1:18
Titus 2:13
Heb 9:28
1:23
Amos 4:11
Zech 3:2-5
Rev 3:4
1:24
Rom 16:25
2 Cor 4:14
Phil 1:10
1 Thes 5:23
1:25
Rom 16:27
2 Pet 3:18
[d]*sōtēr* (4990)
‣Luke 1:47

the Lord's [c]love, they are like dangerous
reefs that can shipwreck you. They are like
shameless shepherds who care only for
themselves. They are like clouds blowing
over the land without giving any rain. They
are like trees in autumn that are doubly
dead, for they bear no fruit and have been
pulled up by the roots. [13]They are like wild
waves of the sea, churning up the foam of
their shameful deeds. They are like wandering stars, doomed forever to blackest
darkness.

[14]Enoch, who lived in the seventh generation after Adam, prophesied about these
people. He said, "Listen! The Lord is coming
with countless thousands of his holy ones
[15]to execute judgment on the people of the
world. He will convict every person of all
the ungodly things they have done and for
all the insults that ungodly sinners have spoken against him."

[16]These people are grumblers and complainers, living only to satisfy their desires.
They brag loudly about themselves, and
they flatter others to get what they want.

A Call to Remain Faithful (vv 17-23)

[17]But you, my dear friends, must remember
what the apostles of our Lord Jesus Christ
said. [18]They told you that in the last times
there would be scoffers whose purpose
in life is to satisfy their ungodly desires.
[19]These people are the ones who are creating divisions among you. They follow their
natural instincts because they do not have
God's Spirit in them.

[20]But you, dear friends, must build each
other up in your most holy faith, pray in the
power of the Holy Spirit, [21]and await the
mercy of our Lord Jesus Christ, who will
bring you eternal life. In this way, you will
keep yourselves safe in God's love.

[22]And you must show mercy to those
whose faith is wavering. [23]Rescue others
by snatching them from the flames of judgment. Show mercy to still others, but do so
with great caution, hating the sins that contaminate their lives.

A Prayer of Praise (vv 24-25)

[24]Now all glory to God, who is able to keep
you from falling away and will bring you
with great joy into his glorious presence
without a single fault. [25]All glory to him
who alone is God, our [d]Savior through Jesus
Christ our Lord. All glory, majesty, power,
and authority are his before all time, and in
the present, and beyond all time! Amen.

across the sky in seemingly irregular patterns. The false teachers wandered, and God condemned their sin.

vv 14-15 ***Enoch*** was an early descendant of Adam (see Gen 5:18-24; 1 Chr 1:3); the comment in Gen 5:24 apparently means that Enoch did not die but was taken directly to heaven (cp. 2 Kgs 2:1-13; see Heb 11:5). This extraordinary commendation from God and the almost complete silence of Scripture about him make Enoch a fascinating character. There are a number of legends about him in Jewish literature, and at least two books of apocalyptic visions written between the OT and the NT are attributed to him (*1–2 Enoch*). • ***"Listen! . . .":*** The quotation comes from Jewish literature (*1 Enoch* 1:9).

vv 17-23 After condemning the false teachers, Jude again encourages his readers directly (see vv 3-4). They had been warned by the apostles about false teaching (vv 17-19). They should encourage each other in the faith (vv 20-21) and reach out to those who might be going astray through the false teachers' influence (vv 22-23).

v 17 ***what the apostles of our Lord Jesus Christ said:*** Such predictions are in Acts 20:29-30; 1 Tim 4:1-3; 2 Tim 3:1-5.

v 18 ***in the last times:*** The coming of Jesus as Messiah inaugurated the last stage of God's plan, when the fulfillment of OT prophecies about the last days began to take place. For this reason, Jude applies the apostles' prophecy about the last times to the immediate crisis created by the false teachers (v 19).

v 20 ***your most holy faith:*** As in v 3, *faith* refers to what Christians believe, the doctrinal and ethical core of Christian identity, which false teachers threaten. Believers must therefore devote themselves to it. • ***pray in the power of the Holy Spirit:*** Literally *pray in the Holy Spirit.*

vv 22-23 The NLT accepts the manuscript tradition that includes three commands in these verses, corresponding to three categories of people: (1) those whose faith is wavering, (2) those who need to be snatched from the flames of judgment, and (3) others who need to be shown mercy. Some manuscripts have only two categories of people: (1) those whose faith is wavering and thus need to be snatched from judgment, and (2) those who need to be shown mercy. The text adopted in the NLT follows the pattern of threes that Jude uses elsewhere (vv 5-7, 11).

v 22 ***must show mercy to:*** Some manuscripts read *must reprove.* • ***those whose faith is wavering:*** Some believers were in the early stages of doubt because of what the false teachers were saying.

v 23 ***Rescue others:*** Some believers were so open to the false teachers that they were in imminent danger of condemnation. • ***Show mercy to still others:*** The third group probably consists of the false teachers themselves or those who had subscribed to the false teachers' program. Showing mercy might have meant praying for them (cp. Matt 5:44). • ***with great caution, hating the sins that contaminate their lives*** (literally *with fear, hating even the clothing stained by the flesh*): Believers need to exercise *great caution* when showing mercy to false teachers and those who have fallen into their sinful ways, because their sins can be enticing. Cp. Zech 3:1-4; Rev 3:4.

vv 24-25 Jude concludes his letter with one of the most stirring doxologies in Scripture, and one quoted very often in liturgical settings. Jude's wording makes it especially appropriate for his readers: They needed a renewed vision of God who could *keep* them *from falling away*, from succumbing to the enticing doctrine of false teachers. He has the ***glory, majesty, power, and authority*** to bring them safely into his glorious presence forever.

THE BOOK OF REVELATION

John's Apocalypse is a magnificent and wonderfully designed message of the salvation that is available in Jesus Christ. The book blesses all who ponder it and sternly warns those who oppose Christ and the Good News and those who are shallow in their Christian walk. The unfolding drama of the book stretches the imagination while bearing witness to God's supreme power. Its visions describe the plight of Christians, God's judgments on their persecutors, and eternal hope and promise for God's faithful people.

SETTING

Revelation was probably written in the AD 90s, or it could have been written in the AD 60s. During these periods, Christians experienced increasing pressure and persecution. By the 90s, the Jews had condemned Christianity in their councils at Jamnia (AD 70–85). They then reported Christians to Roman authorities as religious deviants who did not deserve protection under the religious licensing laws that allowed Jews to practice their faith. At the same time, Rome demanded absolute loyalty to the emperor. At that point, there may have been no official persecution in the empire as a whole, but in the pro-Roman province of Asia (modern-day Turkey), those who refused to worship the emperor were persecuted harshly.

In the face of such persecution, Revelation dramatically reminded Christians of the source of their hope and vindication and firmly challenged them to remain faithful. The Christians in the province of Asia may have appeared weak and powerless to the world, but Revelation repeatedly reminded them, as it still reminds us, that the God they served is Almighty. God controls history; he has accomplished our salvation and continues to work out his purposes.

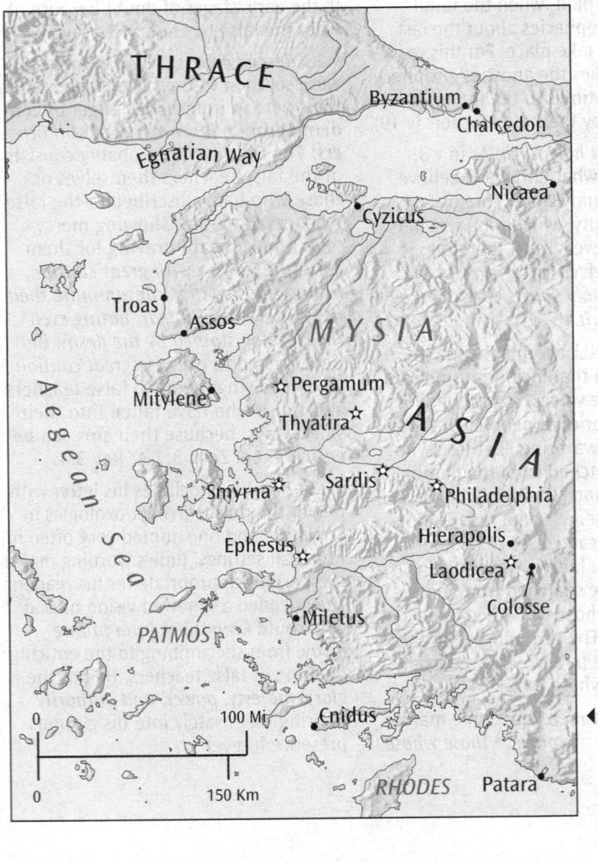

The Setting of Revelation. The apostle John wrote Revelation during a period of intense persecution against the churches in ASIA, while he himself had been exiled to the island of PATMOS. He sent Revelation to seven churches in Asia (marked on the map with stars).

SUMMARY

Revelation begins in an unusual way, with three separate introductions. John first

spells out the visionary nature of the book (1:1-3); there is then a letter salutation (1:4-8) followed by a historical introduction (1:9-11). The book then describes a vision of Jesus (1:12-20). In letters to seven churches in the province of Asia, Christ personally addresses the believers and the life of the churches (2:1–3:22). Following these letters, chs 4–5 set the stage for the drama that follows by displaying God's sovereign majesty and picturing Jesus as both a lion and a lamb.

The heart of the book (chs 6–16) describes the drama in three acts of judgment. In the first act (6:1–8:1), Christ opens seven seals that result in seven judgments. This act also contains the first interlude (7:1-17), which shows God's people being protected from harm.

The second act portrays seven angels blowing seven trumpets (8:2–11:19) in a second view of judgment on the world. The sixth trumpet is followed by a mysterious second interlude (10:1-10) in which an angel, a little scroll, and seven secretive thunders provide an opening for a bittersweet picture of two witnesses who proclaim God's message (11:1-14). The final trumpet presents heaven, the coming kingdom of Christ the Lord (11:15-19).

Following the second act, Revelation shifts to a series of three great signs and symbolic portraits. Revelation 12 depicts the cosmic battle between good and evil and the birth of the promised deliverer, Christ, whom God rescues from Satan's destructive intentions (12:1-10). Although defeated, Satan—portrayed as a dragon—continues to create havoc among God's people (12:11-17). The book next introduces two other beasts, who with the dragon form a false "evil trinity" in the world (13:1-18). These evil forces contrast starkly with the Lamb of God and his faithful servants standing on Mount Zion, the place of God's redemption and rule (14:1-5). Three angels deliver God's message of coming judgment and the destruction of the evil forces (14:6-20).

The third and final act of judgment involves seven plagues (16:1-21). John introduces it with a joint song by Moses and the Lamb (15:1-8). After the plagues, John narrates the end of the great prostitute, Babylon (or Rome, 17:1-18). While the world mourns the passing of this supposed source of security (18:1-19), heaven, the apostles, and the prophets rejoice at its destruction (18:20-24) with songs of God's

OUTLINE

1:1-11
Introduction in Three Parts

1:12-20
Vision of the Son of Man

2:1–3:22
Messages to the Seven Churches

4:1–5:14
Introduction to the Drama

6:1–8:1
Act I: Seven Seals of Judgment

8:2–11:19
Act II: Seven Trumpets of Judgment

12:1–14:20
The Two Sides of the Great Conflict

15:1–16:21
Act III: Seven Bowls of Judgment

17:1–19:10
Babylon the Great

19:11–20:15
Triumph and Judgment

21:1–22:5
The New Jerusalem

22:6-21
Epilogue: Jesus Is Coming

TIMELINE

586 BC
Babylon destroys Jerusalem

536 BC
Temple rebuilding begins and is halted

520–515 BC
Temple rebuilding resumes and is completed

167 BC
Antiochus defiles the Temple, Mattathias revolts at Modin

63 BC
Roman general Pompey violates the Temple

27 BC—AD 14
Augustus as emperor of Rome

about 6~4 BC
Birth of Jesus

AD 11–12
Tiberius reigns in the provinces

AD 14–37
Tiberius as emperor of Rome

Passover, AD 30 or 33
Jesus' crucifixion and resurrection

AD 37–41
Gaius Caligula as emperor of Rome

AD 41–54
Claudius as emperor of Rome

AD 54–68
Nero as emperor of Rome

July AD 64
Fire destroys Rome

AD 64~65
Persecution of Christians under Nero

AD 69–79
Vespasian as emperor of Rome

AD 70
Jerusalem and the Temple are destroyed

AD 79–81
Titus as emperor of Rome

AD 81–96
Domitian as emperor of Rome

AD 135
End of Bar Kokhba revolt, complete destruction of Jerusalem

victory (19:1-10). God's enemies have no chance of success against the Lord of lords. The beasts (the power structures of the world) and all who follow them meet their just end in the lake of fire when Jesus destroys his enemies in the battle of Armageddon (19:11-21). While the devil is imprisoned (20:1-3), the saints of God enjoy a respite as they reign with Christ on earth (20:4-6). Despite Satan's all-out attempt to defeat God in battle, he too is thrown into the lake of fire (20:7-10). All who follow the dragon are judged before the throne of God, and death—humanity's greatest nemesis—is terminated (20:11-15).

Finally, John paints a marvelous picture of heaven, stretching the human imagination with design, size, and symbolic images (chs 21–22). With their vision of hope, these scenes make a fitting conclusion to Revelation and to the entire Bible. The Spirit and the church invite all readers to come and receive God's eternal promise (22:17). The book closes with the ongoing prayer of Christians: "Come, Lord Jesus!" (22:20).

INTERPRETING REVELATION

The book of Revelation is an exciting work that has bewildered many readers, perhaps because of its nature as both a prophecy and an apocalypse (see "Apocalyptic Writing," facing page). John Calvin, the Swiss reformer, wrote commentaries on every book in the Bible except Revelation, which indicates that he wasn't confident that he fully understood the book. Similarly, Martin Luther did not think that Revelation taught enough about justification by faith; therefore, he assigned Revelation a sub-canonical status, not viewing it as authoritative for doctrine but only for Christian life. In light of the interpretive difficulties, many Christian teachers follow suit by avoiding the book of Revelation entirely, or only speak about the letters to the churches.

Through the centuries, interpreters have argued over the meaning of Revelation. Some have used their interpretations of the book to categorize as apostate or heretical other Christians who don't share their views. Others spend months and years searching the book for information about recent and upcoming events. The notes in this study Bible tend to interpret the visions as reflecting the Roman empire and the world and experience of the original churches to whom it was first written. The entire drama and message of the book, however, reveals great treasures to encourage believers of all eras in their faith.

> *The fundamental perspective of the book is the exhortation to endure persecution on the basis of the transcendent reality of God's kingdom in the present as grounded in God's control of the future.*
>
> GRANT R. OSBORNE
> *Revelation*, p. 14-15

THE NATURE OF REVELATION

The entire Bible is inspired by God (see 2 Tim 3:15-17; 2 Pet 1:20-21). Some books, such as Romans, the historical books, and some of the prophets, primarily address the *intellect*. Other books, such as the Psalms and other poetical writings, engage the *emotions*. The book of Revelation, however, appeals to the *imagination* (as do some OT works, such as Ezekiel and parts of Daniel and Zechariah). Revelation speaks through visions, images, and figurative language rather than logical reasoning. The book sometimes presents the literal and the symbolic in intriguing combinations. It resists being treated as a system of end-times doctrines, as those who have tried to systematize it have often discovered.

Because of its nature, reading Revelation requires imagination. It is like entering the realm of dreams with God and discovering that they contain a marvelous message from him. Instead of trying to fit all of

Revelation's scenes into a logical system, readers will benefit from picture-thinking. For example, when John says that "all the green grass was burned" (8:7) and then later says that the locusts are instructed not to "harm the grass" (9:4), such statements seem contradictory. The incongruity, however, is resolved when we realize that John is describing what he saw in two different visions and that the two visions are not meant to narrate a sequence of events—they are meant to portray God's message in pictures. Similarly, we read in the vision of heaven that "the Temple of God was opened" (11:19), but later we find "no temple" there (21:22). Again, the focus of each vision is different; readers must not try to read one vision into another but instead concentrate on the main point of each vision in its own terms. Early readers, familiar with the logic of metaphors, understood the nature of picture-thinking. Just as they knew not to read one of Jesus' parables into another, they avoided trying to systematize or conflate John's visions.

APOCALYPTIC WRITING

Through word pictures and visions, John magnificently transports our minds to the realm of imagination. John was not alone in writing this way—he used a familiar kind of literature to convey his message. These imaginative works are called "apocalyptic" (Greek "uncover") because they claim to reveal a new vision of reality. Such works were often written during times of great stress and persecution as tracts for bad times. Apocalyptic writings often used symbolic names, numbers, and descriptions as a "code" so that outside readers (particularly enemies) who did not possess the key to the code would not understand the implications of the message. The work would seem to them like double talk or nonsense. In Revelation, for instance, Babylon is used as a code for Rome (17:5-9).

The OT contains examples of apocalyptic literature in Daniel and Zechariah (see Daniel Introduction, "Daniel as Literature: Daniel as Apocalyptic Literature," p. 1391; Zechariah Introduction, "Literary Genre," p. 1526). In Jewish apocalyptic literature, God is usually pictured as transcendent and fully in control of history, even when the situation might seem bleak to readers. God's message is usually presented through visions, dreams, or journeys to cosmic or spiritual realms. These revelations gave seers, dreamers, interpreters, and prophets messages of hope and salvation for God's people and messages of judgment on God's enemies. The prophets were obliged to share their messages with others—particularly with God's people, who were under persecution and in distress. Readers understood that the promises of hope would not be fulfilled immediately; these promises were generally expressed as part of a coming cataclysmic judgment in which God would destroy his enemies and bring final bliss to his people. Meanwhile, God's people were to remain faithful and persevere in the face of suffering, understanding that God would soon deliver them. All of these features find expression in Revelation.

As a seer or a visionary, John also refers to his work as a "prophecy" (1:3; 22:7); he does not mean that it is prophecy simply in a predictive sense, but in the OT sense of proclaiming a word from God that is addressed to his people. John's prophetic visions emphasize that God's answer to distressing times will not be entirely realized until the end of history and in the coming eternity.

The Revelation is by common consent one of the most difficult of all the books of the Bible. . . . Modern readers find it strange. They are moreover not usually attracted by the fantastic schemes of prophecy which some exegetes find in it, and whose ingenuity is matched only by their improbability.

LEON MORRIS
Revelation, p. 17

AUTHOR

Many Jewish apocalypses were written after the close of the OT canon, at a time when Jews believed that prophecy had ceased and that the word of the Lord for them was primarily to be found in the Law and the Prophets. These Jewish writers therefore wrote under the names of earlier godly persons such as Ezra, Baruch, Enoch, Isaiah, and even Adam so that their writings would gain credibility and acceptance. These works are called *pseudepigrapha* (literally "false writings") because they were written under pseudonyms. Similarly, in the post-apostolic era, fanciful writers and false teachers returned to this practice by using the names of earlier followers of Jesus (such as Peter, James, John, and even Mary) to gain a hearing from Christians.

By contrast, the books collected in the NT were written under their authors' own names (see Rom 1:1; 2 Thes 3:17) or were legitimately apostolic even though they do not claim an author by name (e.g., Matthew, Hebrews). The author of Revelation identifies himself simply as John (1:1, 4, 9). In the early church, this John was generally identified as the apostle John, who refers to himself in the Gospel bearing his name as "the disciple Jesus loved" (John 13:23; 19:26; 20:2; 21:7); in his epistles, he calls himself "the elder" (3 Jn 1:1). John received the visions presented in Revelation while he was a political and religious prisoner on Patmos, a rocky island used as a Roman prison off the western coast of Asia Minor near Ephesus (1:9).

It is important to realize that we know no more about the second coming than Jesus' Jewish disciples did about the first. They too thought they were reading the Scriptures rightly. . . . In interpreting the symbols of the book, we first need the "hermeneutics of humility" to realize we "see things imperfectly as in a poor mirror" (1 Cor 13:12).

GRANT R. OSBORNE
Revelation, p. 16

DATE

Revelation was probably written during the concluding years of Domitian's reign (AD 94–96) or immediately following (AD 96–99). The eight kings (17:7-11) may refer to the eight Roman emperors from Augustus to Domitian (see chart, p. 2191). It is also possible that Revelation was written during the AD 60s, when Nero was persecuting the church and killing Christians. During these times, Christians were experiencing significant anguish and persecution (13:7). John called his readers to endurance and faithfulness (13:10). While some have argued that the persecution was more perceived than actual, Revelation seems to suggest real, physical persecution (2:9, 13; 3:9).

RECIPIENTS

The recipients of Revelation were the churches in the Roman province of Asia (the western part of modern Turkey). The seven cities mentioned in chs 1–3 were joined by a triangular road system forming something like a mail route. These cities all lie in ruins today except for Smyrna, which is now the bustling modern seaport of Izmir, Turkey. The order of the cities in the seven letters is geographical and follows the route a courier probably took as he carried the book to each church to be read.

MEANING AND MESSAGE

Revelation portrays the stark nature of evil while emphasizing how God's sovereign hand is always present and at work to accomplish his purposes on behalf of his people. Even evil can only do what God allows (e.g., 6:3-4, 7-8; 13:5-7). Jesus is "the Alpha and the Omega" (1:8), the Lord over all history from beginning to end. Ultimately the powers of evil are futile. Satan has already lost the war (12:12); he can merely imitate and pervert what God does.

Revelation clarifies that what is done on earth has eternal consequences. God's suffering servants may sometimes wonder whether Jesus is powerful enough to accomplish God's purpose of salvation (6:9-10). Despite all the evil in the world, however, Revelation assures readers that the crucified and resurrected Lamb of God is truly the powerful Lion of the tribe of Judah (5:5-6). He is fully worthy to receive our praise (5:12), as he is united with the eternal God (5:13-14). Although the ways of the world result in war, violence, economic imbalance, and death (6:1-8), and although some people seem to profit from alignments with evil (13:15-17), they will ultimately reap distress and doom (18:9-24). God's people may be persecuted and die for their faith (13:7), but they will ultimately triumph with Christ (14:1-3) because they have been marked by the seal of God (7:4) and have been granted the white robe of victory (6:11; 7:9). They will have access to their heavenly dwelling (21:7), will continually praise God and the Lamb (7:10), and will live forever (22:5). Revelation reminds readers that the great victory over the powers of evil has already been won at the cross (5:5-6). Armageddon is not the final defeat of Satan but a desperate act of defiance by a foe who is already defeated. While Satan is allowed to kill the saints (13:7), they have already conquered him through Christ and their own witness (12:11).

The message for Christians who suffer at the hands of Satan's servants is not to weep or be afraid (1:17-18; 5:5) but to endure their suffering faithfully (13:10). With God they will prevail (1:6-7; 11:17-18). People will ultimately be judged by what they do and how they act (20:12), and God will bless those who pay attention to the words of this book (1:3; 22:7). The saints are therefore called to persevere faithfully in order to be victorious (2:7, 11, 17, 26; 3:5, 12, 21). Revelation calls them to obey God, maintain their witness (12:17; 22:7), endure patiently (13:10; 14:12), and remain vigilant (16:15; 17:14) in the face of persecution, knowing that cowards will face eternal punishment along with evildoers (21:8).

FURTHER READING

DENNIS JOHNSON
Triumph of the Lamb (2001)

LEON MORRIS
Revelation (1987)

ROBERT H. MOUNCE
The Book of Revelation (1998)

GRANT R. OSBORNE
Revelation (2002)

1:1
Dan 2:28-29, 45
John 12:49; 17:8
[a]*apokalupsis* (0602)
‣ Luke 2:32
[b]*doulos* (1401)
‣ Matt 20:27

1:2
[c]*logos* (3056)
‣ Rev 19:13

1:3
[d]*makarios* (3107)
‣ Rev 22:7

1:4
Exod 3:14

1. INTRODUCTION IN THREE PARTS (1:1-11)

Prologue

1 This is a [a]revelation from Jesus Christ,
which God gave him to show his [b]ser-
vants the events that must soon take place.
He sent an angel to present this revelation
to his [b]servant John, 2who faithfully reported everything he saw. This is his report
of the [c]word of God and the testimony of
Jesus Christ.
3God [d]blesses the one who reads the
words of this prophecy to the church, and
he blesses all who listen to its message and
obey what it says, for the time is near.

Letter Introduction: John's Greeting to the Seven Churches

4This letter is from John to the seven
churches in the province of Asia.
Grace and peace to you from the one who
is, who always was, and who is still to come;

1:1-11 Revelation opens with a three-part introduction, including a prologue (1:1-3), a letter introduction (1:4-8), and a historical introduction (1:9-11).

1:1 The word *revelation* (Greek *apokalupsis*) introduces the book's visionary nature as apocalyptic writing (see Revelation Introduction, "Apocalyptic Writing," p. 2163). God communicates his inspired message through mysterious symbols, numbers, and word pictures. • ***from*** (or *of*) ***Jesus Christ:*** He is both the source and the main subject of the book. • ***the events that must soon*** (or *suddenly*, or *quickly*) ***take place:*** Cp. 3:11; 22:6-7; Luke 18:8; Rom 16:20.

1:2 ***reported*** (Greek *martureō*) . . . ***testimony*** (Greek *marturia*): These closely related Greek words indicate an authentic witness and emphasize that the sacrificial witness of Jesus and the authentic testimony of John are the basis for the revelation.

1:3 ***God blesses:*** Revelation contains seven promises of blessing (1:3; 14:13; 16:15; 19:9; 20:6; 22:7, 14). • ***listen . . . and obey:*** Authentic hearing entails obedience.

1:4-8 The second introduction (see note on 1:1-11) is in the style of a Greek letter.

1:4 ***To the seven churches*** does not mean that there were only seven churches in the Roman ***province of Asia*** but that these seven churches represent the entire group. • ***Asia*** was a

from the sevenfold Spirit before his throne;
5and from Jesus Christ. He is the faithful
witness to these things, the [e]first to rise
from the dead, and the ruler of all the kings
of the world.

All glory to him who loves us and has
freed us from our sins by shedding his
blood for us. 6He has made us a Kingdom
of priests for God his Father. All glory and
power to him forever and ever! Amen.

7 Look! He comes with the clouds of heaven.
And everyone will see him—
even those who pierced him.
And all the nations of the world
will mourn for him.
Yes! Amen!

8"I am the Alpha and the Omega—the
beginning and the end," says the Lord God.
"I am the one who is, who always was, and
who is still to come—the [f]Almighty One."

Historical Introduction

9I, John, am your brother and your partner
in suffering and in God's Kingdom and in
the patient endurance to which Jesus calls
us. I was exiled to the island of Patmos for
preaching the word of God and for my testimony about Jesus. 10It was the Lord's Day,
and I was worshiping in the Spirit. Suddenly, I heard behind me a loud voice like
a trumpet blast. 11It said, "Write in a [g]book
everything you see, and send it to the seven
churches in the cities of Ephesus, Smyrna,
Pergamum, Thyatira, Sardis, Philadelphia,
and Laodicea."

2. VISION OF THE SON OF MAN (1:12-20)

12When I turned to see who was speaking
to me, I saw seven gold lampstands. 13And
standing in the middle of the lampstands
was someone like the Son of Man. He was
wearing a long robe with a gold sash across
his chest. 14His head and his hair were
white like wool, as white as snow. And his
eyes were like flames of fire. 15His feet were
like polished bronze refined in a furnace,

1:5 Ps 89:27; Isa 40:2; Col 1:18
[e]*prōtotokos* (4416) ‣Luke 2:7
1:6 Exod 19:6; Isa 61:6; 1 Pet 2:5, 9
1:7 Dan 7:13; Zech 12:10; Matt 24:30; John 19:34, 37
1:8 Amos 3:13; 4:13
[f]*pantokratōr* (3841) ‣Rev 4:8
1:9 Phil 4:14; 2 Tim 2:12
1:11 Rev 1:2, 19; 2:1, 8, 12, 18; 3:1, 7, 14
[g]*biblion* (0975) ‣Rev 5:1
1:12 Zech 4:2
1:13 Dan 7:13; 10:5
1:14 Dan 7:9; 10:6
1:15 Ezek 1:24; 43:2

Roman province in what is now western Turkey. • ***Grace and peace*** is a typical Christian greeting (see notes on 2 Cor 1:1-2; 2 Thes 1:1-2). The order of the two words is consistent in the NT, suggesting that peace follows from God's grace. • ***who is, who always was, and who is still to come:*** God controlled the past, will surely control the future, and is sovereign over every present crisis (see also 1:8; 4:8; 11:17; 16:5). • ***the sevenfold Spirit*** (literally *the seven spirits*): Some argue that the "seven spirits" are seven angels, but the phrase fits between references to God the Father (1:4) and to God the Son (1:5), making this passage a description of the Trinity (see Matt 28:19; John 14:26; 15:26; 2 Cor 13:14; 1 Pet 1:2). The number seven acknowledges the Holy Spirit's perfection (cp. Zech 4:2, 6, 10).

1:5a John gives three descriptions of ***Jesus Christ.*** (1) As ***the faithful witness,*** Jesus is our model for proclaiming the Good News of salvation (1:2). (2) The truth that Jesus was ***the first to rise from the dead*** is foundational to Christian faith (1 Cor 15:14, 17). (3) As ***ruler of all the kings of the world*** (see also 17:14; 19:16), he is the absolute Lord of everything. Inhabitants of the Roman world were expected to declare Caesar as absolute lord; many early Christians died for their conviction that Jesus alone holds that position.

1:5b-6 In this doxology, John gives reasons for praising Jesus. • Doxologies often conclude with the confessional ***Amen*** (see Rom 11:36; Phil 4:20), which expresses affirmation.

1:8 ***"I am the Alpha and the Omega—the beginning and the end"*** (literally *I am the Alpha and the Omega*): *I am* is the name of God in the OT (Exod 3:13-14; 6:2; Deut 6:4). Jesus applied this name to himself (cp. John 4:26). *Alpha* and *Omega* are the first and last letters of the Greek alphabet; they signify that God's actions are all-encompassing. God is fully in control.

1:9-11 This third introduction (see note on 1:1-11) is historical; it shows God communicating with humanity in historical events. God gave John a significant mission while in exile.

1:9 ***your brother and your partner:*** Though separated from other Christians by his imprisonment, John shared a sense of community with them ***in suffering,*** based on hope in ***God's Kingdom*** and a willingness to endure. • The Roman fortress on ***the island of Patmos*** housed prisoners and exiles. Patmos was in a group of islands that protected the thriving seaport of Miletus. • ***for preaching . . . and for my testimony:*** In typical Semitic parallelism, the second statement means essentially the same as the first. By John's time, Jews were persuading Roman authorities that Christianity was different from Judaism and therefore not an authorized religion.

1:10 ***the Lord's Day:*** This designation was used in the Roman world to refer to celebrations in honor of Caesar, but Christians used it to refer to their weekly worship, celebrating Jesus' resurrection. The earliest Christians worshiped in Jewish synagogues on the Sabbath, the last day of the week (Acts 18:4), but by the time of Revelation, they were excluded from synagogues and gathered on the day that commemorated the resurrection, the first day of the week (see note on Luke 24:1; see also Acts 20:7). • ***in the Spirit:*** Or *in spirit.* • The ***loud voice like a trumpet blast*** was an announcement of the Lord's coming.

1:11 ***Write . . . and send:*** God authorized John as a prophet and herald of his revelation (see 22:8, 10; cp. Isa 6:8-9; Jer 2:1-2; Ezek 2:1-3; 34:1-2). • ***in a book:*** Or *on a scroll.*

1:12-20 John's first vision is a symbolic picture of Christ as the wise, secure, and powerful agent of God who always cares for his people.

1:12 ***I turned to see who was speaking:*** This statement refers to the loud voice of 1:10. • ***seven gold lampstands:*** The lighted menorah was a symbol of God's presence among his people (Exod 27:21; Lev 24:1-4) and of his all-seeing eyes in the world (Zech 4:10).

1:13 ***like the Son of Man*** (or *like a son of man.* See Dan 7:13): *Son of Man* is a title Jesus used for himself (see Matt 8:20; 9:6; 16:13; Mark 2:28; 9:9; 14:41; John 1:51; 3:13; 5:27). • The ***long robe*** and ***gold sash*** give Christ an authoritative appearance (see 19:13-16; Dan 10:5). The robe was a priestly garment symbolizing purity and holiness.

1:14 ***White*** hair represents wisdom and maturity; this vision reflects Daniel's vision of the Ancient One (Dan 7:9). • His ***eyes . . . like flames of fire*** pierce through pretense; the One who knows everything will judge everyone (see Dan 10:6; Heb 4:13).

1:15 ***Refined*** or hardened ***bronze*** in the ***feet*** implies stability, firmness, and

1:16
Isa 49:2
1:17
Isa 44:6; 48:12
Dan 8:18
1:18
[h]*hadēs* (0086)
‣Rev 20:13
1:19
Isa 48:6
1:20
[i]*angelos* (0032)
‣Matt 4:11
[j]*ekklēsia* (1577)
‣Matt 16:18
2:2
2 Cor 11:13
1 Jn 4:1

and his voice thundered like mighty ocean
waves. [16]He held seven stars in his right
hand, and a sharp two-edged sword came
from his mouth. And his face was like the
sun in all its brilliance.
[17]When I saw him, I fell at his feet as if
I were dead. But he laid his right hand on
me and said, "Don't be afraid! I am the First
and the Last. [18]I am the living one. I died,
but look—I am alive forever and ever! And I
hold the keys of death and the [h]grave.
[19]"Write down what you have seen—both
the things that are now happening and the
things that will happen. [20]This is the meaning of the mystery of the seven stars you
saw in my right hand and the seven gold
lampstands: The seven stars are the [i]angels
of the seven [j]churches, and the seven lampstands are the seven [j]churches.

3. MESSAGES TO THE SEVEN CHURCHES (2:1–3:22)

The Message to Ephesus, a Loyal Church

2 "Write this letter to the angel of the
church in Ephesus. This is the message
from the one who holds the seven stars in
his right hand, the one who walks among
the seven gold lampstands:
[2]"I know all the things you do. I have
seen your hard work and your patient

Letters to the Seven Churches (2:1–3:22)

In the letters to the seven churches of Asia (chs 2–3), John uses a single literary pattern. Each letter begins with an address to the "angel of the church" in a particular city, followed by an aspect of Christ's appearance taken from the vision of the Son of Man (1:12-16). Christ states that he knows each church and describes the state of the church in that city. He then gives advice or judgment for the church along with a promised reward for obedience. Each time, Christ emphasizes the need for full attention to the Spirit's message to the churches.

It is common for interpreters to separate the seven letters into seven distinct messages and to make them symbolic of seven types of people or seven distinct periods of time. The seven letters, however, actually form a single unified message for the church in all times and places, taking into account all its spots and wrinkles. In other words, any single body of Christians might be similar to one of these churches, and each community contains people who are like the Christians from these churches. Christ invites every community of believers to examine itself in the light of these messages.

security (cp. Dan 10:6). • The thundering *voice* suggests God's power—when he speaks, he will be heard (cp. Ezek 43:2).

1:16 The *seven stars* represent the complete church. The church is secure in the *right hand* (i.e., in the acceptance and blessing) of the Son of Man. • The *sharp . . . sword* coming *from his mouth* is his effective message and his judgment (see 19:15; Gen 3:24; Eph 6:17; Heb 4:12). Jesus proclaims both grace and judgment, but here the emphasis is that he carries out judgment (see 2:12, 16; 19:15, 21; cp. Isa 11:4).

1:17 ***When I saw him, I fell . . . dead:*** Terror and a dead faint, if not death itself (see Exod 33:20), frequently result when someone sees God (see Isa 6:1-5; Matt 28:4). The Lord graciously responds by the touch of his *right hand* (cp. Matt 25:34) and the words *"Don't be afraid!"* (cp. Luke 1:13), indicating both grace and acceptance. • ***I am:*** The phrase identifies Jesus as God (see note on 1:8).

1:18 ***the living one:*** Because the Son of Man (1:13) has conquered death, he holds *the keys of death* and controls the outcome of our greatest fear (see 20:14; Heb 2:14-15). Jesus has complete authority to provide hope in a hostile world. • ***and the grave:*** Greek *and Hades.* See note on 6:7-8.

1:19 ***Write:*** In the vision, God gives instructions for what John is to do on his behalf (see Isa 6:9-10). • ***what you have seen—both the things that are now happening and the things that will happen*** (or *what you have seen and what they mean—the things that have already begun to happen*): This vision's purpose is to help the church (1:20) to understand the present and the future from God's perspective.

1:20 John is to record what he sees because Revelation is an instructive word for the *churches.* • The *angels* (or *messengers;* Greek *angelos*) ***of the seven churches*** could be (1) the guardian angels of these churches (cp. Matt 18:10; Acts 12:15); (2) the leading officials of the churches (cp. Matt 11:10, where "messenger" is *angelos*); or (3) a personification of the *ethos* of the church. The best understanding is probably a combination of 1 and 3.

2:1–3:22 The seven messages to the seven churches reflect the state of Christ's church when Revelation was written, and it is similar today. God still calls Christians to faithfulness and integrity. Those who heed Christ's message will reap God's promised rewards; those who fail to do so will be judged.

2:1-7 The letter to ***the church in Ephesus*** addresses tradition-bound Christians who are faithful but have lost their early, zealous love for Christ and for each other (see 2:5).

2:1 ***Write . . . to the angel:*** This repeated command that introduces each of the seven letters suggests the importance of the message. • ***the angel:*** Or *the messenger;* also in 2:8, 12, 18. See note on 1:20. • ***Ephesus*** had become the main city of the Roman province of Asia. It contained the temple of Artemis (see Acts 19:23-35) and became the richest banking center in that part of the world. The people of Ephesus were very independent; they declined help from Alexander in rebuilding their temple after it was destroyed (300s BC), arguing adroitly that one god should not stoop to build a temple to another god (see Strabo, *Geography* 14.1.22). The Ephesians' protective pride also led to the uproar against Paul (Acts 19:23-41).

2:2-3 ***I know:*** This repeated refrain (2:9, 13, 19; 3:1, 8, 15) shows Christ's

endurance. I know you don't tolerate evil
people. You have examined the claims
of those who say they are [k]apostles but
are not. You have discovered they are
liars. 3 You have patiently suffered for me
without quitting.
4 "But I have this complaint against
you. You don't [a]love me or each other as
you did at first! 5 Look how far you have
fallen! Turn back to me and do the works
you did at first. If you don't repent, I will
come and remove your lampstand from
its place among the churches. 6 But this
is in your favor: You hate the evil deeds
of the Nicolaitans, just as I do.
7 "Anyone with ears to hear must listen
to the Spirit and understand what he is
saying to the churches. To everyone who
is victorious I will give fruit from the
tree of life in the [b]paradise of God.

The Message to Smyrna, a Suffering Church

8 "Write this letter to the angel of the church
in Smyrna. This is the message from the
one who is the First and the Last, who was
dead but is now alive:
9 "I know about your suffering and
your poverty—but you are rich! I know
the blasphemy of those opposing you.
They say they are Jews, but they are
not, because their synagogue belongs
to Satan. 10 Don't be afraid of what you
are about to suffer. The devil will throw
some of you into prison to test you. You
will suffer for ten days. But if you remain
faithful even when facing death, I will
give you the crown of life.
11 "Anyone with ears to hear must
listen to the Spirit and understand what
he is saying to the churches. Whoever
is victorious will not be harmed by the
second death.

The Message to Pergamum, a Compromising Church

12 "Write this letter to the angel of the church
in Pergamum. This is the message from the
one with the sharp two-edged sword:
13 "I know that you live in the city where
Satan has his throne, yet you have
remained loyal to me. You refused to

[k]*apostolos* (0652) ‣Matt 10:2

2:3
John 15:21

2:4
Jer 2:2
Matt 24:12
[a]*agapē* (0026) ‣John 5:42

2:5
Rev 2:16, 22; 3:3, 19

2:6
Ps 139:21
Rev 2:15

2:7
Gen 2:8-9; 3:22-24
Ezek 31:8-9
Rev 22:2, 14
[b]*paradeisos* (3857) ‣Rev 3:12

2:8
Rev 1:11, 17-18

2:9
2 Cor 6:10; 11:14-15
Rev 3:9

2:10
Dan 1:12-14
Jas 1:12
Rev 3:9; 17:14

2:11
Rev 2:7; 20:6, 14

2:12
Rev 1:16; 2:16

2:13
Rev 14:12

total knowledge of his people, their activities, and their circumstances.
• The Ephesian Christians had a correct theology marked by perseverance and faithfulness. They had ***examined*** various ***claims***, exercised discipline on ***evil people***, could tell what is true and what is false, and had ***patiently suffered*** for their faith in Christ.

2:4 ***You don't love me or each other as you did at first*** (literally *You have lost your first love*): When the church was first established, their love for Christ and for each other had been strong. Struggles with false teachers and persecution had caused that original love to grow cold. Correct theology, action, and even suffering (2:2-3) are just an empty shell of Christian life if dynamic love is absent (1 Cor 13).

2:5 Christ calls even those who keep the faith to ***turn back*** to him and ***repent*** of cold-heartedness. The warning, ***I will come and remove your lampstand***, means that they would lose their status as a church; God would treat them as he did the apostates within Israel (see Rom 11).

2:6 Not much is known of ***the Nicolaitans***, but their teaching (2:15) seems to link them with those who ate food sacrificed to idols and who were involved in sexual immorality, behavior prohibited by the council in Jerusalem (see Acts 15:20, 29). Irenaeus argued (about AD 180) that the Nicolaitans were dependent on Nicolas (Acts 6:3-5) and that John's writings were directed against the heresies of the Nicolaitans who followed Cerinthus (see 1 John Introduction, "Setting," p. 2138).

2:7 The reward for obedience is ***fruit from the tree of life***—that is, eternal life (22:2; Gen 3:22).

2:8-11 The letter to ***the church in Smyrna*** pictures suffering Christians under intense pressures who need a message of assurance. Smyrna typifies a small church that remains faithful to God despite difficult circumstances.

2:8 The seaport village of ***Smyrna*** had been destroyed and rebuilt several times. Like Christ, the city had been ***dead*** but was ***now alive.*** It is the only city of the seven that has survived to this day (Izmir, Turkey).

2:9 Jesus connected material ***poverty*** with the blessing of being ***rich*** in God's Kingdom (Matt 5:3, 10-12; Luke 6:20).
• ***Jews*** who had no faith are condemned for aligning themselves with ***Satan*** in hostile opposition to the Christian faith (3:9; see John 8:44; Acts 14:2-5; 17:13; 18:6; 20:3; Gal 5:11; 1 Thes 2:14-16). At the Jewish council of Jamnia, the Jews excluded Christians as unholy heretics. John was not anti-Semitic; he was a Jew describing the actions of fellow Jews against Jewish and Gentile Christians.

2:10 John saw ***the devil*** as the source of human hostility against Christians.
• The period of their suffering would be ***ten days***, symbolizing a limited time of persecution (see 1 Pet 1:6). If they would ***remain faithful***, their reward would be the ***crown*** of eternal ***life.*** • ***when facing death:*** John's pupil, Polycarp, was a martyr in Smyrna in the mid-100s AD.

2:11 Faithfulness until death is described as being ***victorious;*** overcoming ***the second death*** means receiving eternal life (see 20:5-6, 14; 21:8).

2:12-17 The letter to ***the church in Pergamum*** portrays Christians who are tempted to compromise their morality and their loyalty to God. The city of Pergamum was the earliest capital of the Roman province of Asia. It contained a famous library, and its citizens developed the use of animal skins as writing materials.

2:12 Christ's ***sharp two-edged sword*** indicates that these Christians would receive the Lord's most severe judgment (see 2:16; see note on 1:16). The ***two-edged sword*** was the Roman symbol of authority, which typified Pergamum as capital of the province. If the church failed, the true governor of the city (Christ) would turn his authority against them.

2:13 The ***throne*** of ***Satan*** might refer to the altar of Zeus on the mountain above the city or to emperor worship at the temple of Augustus. For many years, the Roman proconsul had his throne there, and the great temple of Athena and other shrines were also located in Pergamum. Its description as ***Satan's city*** might also refer to the temple of Asclepius, whose symbol was coiled snakes. The city was dedicated to the

2:14
Num 31:16
1 Cor 6:13
2 Pet 2:15
Jude 1:11
2:15
Rev 2:6
2:16
2 Thes 2:8
Rev 1:16; 2:5; 22:7, 12, 20
2:17
Ps 78:24
Isa 62:2; 65:15
John 6:49-58
Rev 3:12; 19:12
2:18
Dan 10:6
Rev 1:14-15
2:19
Rev 2:2
2:20
1 Kgs 16:31
2 Kgs 9:7, 22
2:21
Rev 9:20
2:22
Rev 17:2
2:23
Prov 24:12
Jer 17:10
Matt 16:27
Luke 16:15
Rom 8:27
2:24
ᶜ*satanas* (4567)
‣ Rev 20:2
2:25
Rev 3:11
2:26-27
Ps 2:8-9
Matt 10:22
Rev 12:5

[redacted] Antipas, my faithful
[redacted]artyred among you there
in Sa[redacted]'s city.

14 “But I have a few complaints against you. You tolerate some among you whose teaching is like that of Balaam, who showed Balak how to trip up the people of Israel. He taught them to sin by eating food offered to idols and by committing sexual sin. 15 In a similar way, you have some Nicolaitans among you who follow the same teaching. 16 Repent of your sin, or I will come to you suddenly and fight against them with the sword of my mouth.

17 “Anyone with ears to hear must listen to the Spirit and understand what he is saying to the churches. To everyone who is victorious I will give some of the manna that has been hidden away in heaven. And I will give to each one a white stone, and on the stone will be engraved a new name that no one understands except the one who receives it.

The Message to Thyatira, an Overly Tolerant Church

18 “Write this letter to the angel of the church in Thyatira. This is the message from the Son of God, whose eyes are like flames of fire, whose feet are like polished bronze:

19 “I know all the things you do. I have seen your love, your faith, your service, and your patient endurance. And I can see your constant improvement in all these things.

20 “But I have this complaint against you. You are permitting that woman—that Jezebel who calls herself a prophet—to lead my servants astray. She teaches them to commit sexual sin and to eat food offered to idols. 21 I gave her time to repent, but she does not want to turn away from her immorality.

22 “Therefore, I will throw her on a bed of suffering, and those who commit adultery with her will suffer greatly unless they repent and turn away from her evil deeds. 23 I will strike her children dead. Then all the churches will know that I am the one who searches out the thoughts and intentions of every person. And I will give to each of you whatever you deserve.

24 “But I also have a message for the rest of you in Thyatira who have not followed this false teaching (‘deeper truths,’ as they call them—depths of ᶜSatan, actually). I will ask nothing more of you 25 except that you hold tightly to what you have until I come. 26 To all who are victorious, who obey me to the very end,

Roman pantheon and emperor worship. • *Antipas* is otherwise unknown.

2:14-15 *Some* in Pergamum were syncretists, combining Christianity with paganism and engaging in immoral activities. John compares them to *Balaam*, who lured *Israel* into *sin* (see Num 25:1-3; 2 Pet 2:15; Jude 1:11).

2:17 Those who remain faithful to Christ will receive *manna*, nourishment from heaven (see Exod 16:11-36). • *hidden away in heaven:* During the Exodus, a jar of manna was placed in the Ark of the Covenant (Exod 16:33-36). Jewish tradition said that at the coming of the Messiah, the Ark would reappear and manna would be eaten at the messianic banquet. Jesus is the bread from heaven and the bread of life (John 6:32-35; cp. Exod 16:4-21). • A *white stone* was often given to victors at the games, and it was common for special banquets or festivities to use a white stone for admission. It therefore suggests acceptance and victory. • The *new name* probably refers to the recipient's transformed nature in Christ (see Gen 17:5; 32:28; John 1:42).

2:18-29 The letter to *the church in Thyatira* confronts Christians who mix Christianity with pagan practices and a worldly lifestyle.

2:18 *Thyatira* was an outpost city known for its many trade guilds, including weavers and dyers (Acts 16:14). • The flaming *eyes* of the *Son of God* indicate penetrating perception; the solid *feet* portray Christ's stability, in vivid contrast to the nearby Colossus of Rhodes, which had once been thought to be firmly planted until an earthquake destroyed it.

2:19 Christ emphasizes knowing and seeing all things as he praises the Thyatirans.

2:20-21 The mention of *Jezebel,* who led Israel into pagan idolatry and immorality (1 Kgs 16:31-33; 21:5-26), indicates a serious problem. Like the OT queen who led the pagan cult of Baal (see 1 Kgs 16:31; 18:4; 19:1-3), this unknown Jezebel called *herself a prophet* but was leading God's people into various forms of *immorality*, including sexual misconduct and straying from God into idolatrous alliances and actions (Exod 34:15-16; Ps 106:39; Isa 57:7-8).

2:21 Through messengers such as John, Christ had given this false prophet opportunity to *repent* of her sinful teachings and actions, but like many, she had refused (cp. 9:20-21).

2:22-23 Christ's judgment on this "Jezebel" and her followers comes in three stages: (1) Jezebel is *on a bed of suffering* (literally *a bed*); (2) her followers *will suffer greatly*; and (3) *her children* will die (cp. Acts 5:5, 10; 1 Cor 11:30). This judgment echoes the plagues on Egypt that ended with the deaths of Egypt's firstborn sons (see Exod 12:29-30). • God sees *thoughts and intentions* (see Jer 17:10; Acts 1:24; Heb 4:12-13), and he gives whatever sentence people *deserve* (see 22:12; Jer 17:10; Matt 16:27).

2:24 The *depths of Satan* might be a striking reference to the Gnostic god named "Depth" (*Bythos*), who with his partner "Silence" (*Sigē*) formed a philosophic godhead. Gnosticism placed great emphasis on secret knowledge.

2:26-28 Christ promises that those who are obedient will share *authority* with him, as symbolized by the *iron rod* that will *smash* the opposition *like clay pots* (quoting Ps 2:8-9, Greek version; cp. Rev 12:5; 19:15). • The *morning star*

To them I will give authority over all
the nations.
27 They will rule the nations with an iron
rod
and smash them like clay pots.

28They will have the same authority I
received from my Father, and I will also
give them the morning star!
29"Anyone with ears to hear must
listen to the Spirit and understand what
he is saying to the churches.

The Message to Sardis, a Dead Church

3 "Write this letter to the angel of the
church in Sardis. This is the message
from the one who has the sevenfold Spirit
of God and the seven stars:

"I know all the things you do, and that
you have a reputation for being alive—
but you are dead. 2Wake up! Strengthen
what little remains, for even what is left
is almost dead. I find that your actions
do not meet the requirements of my God.
3Go back to what you heard and believed
at first; hold to it firmly. Repent and turn
to me again. If you don't wake up, I will
come to you suddenly, as unexpected as
a thief.
4"Yet there are some in the church in
Sardis who have not soiled their clothes
with evil. They will [illegible]
white, for they are wort[illegible]re
victorious will be clothed in white. I will
never erase their names from the Book
of Life, but I will announce before my
Father and his angels that they are mine.
6"Anyone with ears to hear must listen
to the Spirit and understand what he is
saying to the churches.

The Message to Philadelphia, a Weak but Obedient Church

7"Write this letter to the angel of the church
in Philadelphia.

This is the message from the one who is
holy and true,
the one who has the key of David.
What he opens, no one can close;
and what he closes, no one can open:
8"I know all the things you do, and I have
opened a door for you that no one can
close. You have little strength, yet you
obeyed my word and did not deny me.
9Look, I will force those who belong
to Satan's synagogue—those liars who
say they are Jews but are not—to come
and bow down at your feet. They will
acknowledge that you are the ones I love.
10"Because you have obeyed my
command to persevere, I will protect you

2:28 Rev 22:16
2:29 Rev 2:7
3:1 Rev 1:4, 11, 16; 3:8, 15
3:3 Matt 24:42-44; Luke 22:32; 1 Thes 5:2-6; 2 Pet 3:10; Rev 2:5; 16:15
3:4 Jude 1:23; Rev 3:5; 4:4; 6:11; 19:14
3:5 Exod 32:32-33; Ps 69:28; Matt 10:32; Luke 12:8; Rev 13:8; 17:8; 20:12
3:6 Rev 2:7
3:7 Job 12:14; Isa 22:22; Matt 16:19
3:8 Acts 14:27; Rev 2:13
3:9 Isa 43:4; 49:23; 2 Cor 11:14-15; Rev 2:9
3:10 2 Pet 2:9; Rev 2:10

is the planet Venus, which signals the coming of a new day. Here it refers to the promise of resurrection at Christ's return (22:16; 2 Pet 1:19).

3:1-6 The letter to ***the church in Sardis*** warns Christians who are reputed to be spiritually alive (when actually dead) that without genuine transformation they face God's judgment.

3:1 ***the angel*** (or ***the messenger;*** also in 3:7, 14): See note on 1:20. • ***Sardis,*** nearly 50 miles (80 kilometers) east of Smyrna on the southeast highway from Pergamum and Thyatira, was home to a large colony of prosperous Jews, called "Sephardic" after the city's ancient name. Its fortified acropolis gave its inhabitants an overconfident sense of security. • ***the sevenfold Spirit*** (literally *the seven spirits*): See note on 1:4. • ***a reputation for being alive—but you are dead:*** Other churches may have believed that the Sardian Christians comprised a dynamic church, but their secularism revealed their lack of spiritual life.

3:2-3 The church of Sardis needed to ***wake up*** or it would ***suddenly*** fall. The city of Sardis had fallen when the forces of Cyrus (549/546 BC) and of Antiochus III (189 BC) made ***unexpected*** attacks through a secret tunnel and caught the watchmen off guard. The same would be true of the Christians there if they did not ***meet the requirements of . . . God*** (see 20:12; Eph 2:10; Jas 2:20). • ***as a thief:*** Like the invaders in the city's history, this phrase pictures the sudden return of Christ (see 16:15; Matt 24:43; 1 Thes 5:2; 2 Pet 3:10).

3:4 ***Soiled . . . clothes*** represent an impure life (Zech 3:4), while ***white*** clothes depict purity (see 6:11; 7:13-14; 22:14). • ***Walk*** expresses how a person lives (see Gen 17:1; Ps 81:13; 82:5; Rom 8:4; Gal 5:16).

3:5 Having one's name recorded in ***the Book of Life*** (see 20:12-15; Dan 7:10) symbolizes having assurance of God's acceptance and eternal life (see 17:8; 20:12; Phil 4:3; see also Luke 10:20). For God to ***erase*** a name implies condemnation and eternal death (see Exod 32:32-33; Ps 69:28).

3:7-13 The letter to ***the church in Philadelphia*** encourages Christians who seem to be weak and powerless to realize that their true strength is in Christ. This comforting message includes no words of disapproval. The Kingdom of God does not depend on human strength or wisdom but on God's power and authority.

3:7 ***Philadelphia*** was situated in the foothills of the Timolus Mountains, open to fertile plains in the east. The city repeatedly experienced severe earthquakes that left it weak and impoverished. • This verse quotes phrases from Isa 22:22. • ***key of David:*** Jesus the Messiah is successor to David's royal line. As the gatekeeper of heaven, Jesus has authority to ***open*** and ***close*** the way to heaven (cp. Matt 16:19).

3:8 ***I know:*** See note on 2:2-3. • ***little strength:*** Like the city of Philadelphia itself (see note on 3:7), the Christians there were not prosperous, and they lacked status and power. But Christ had ***opened a door*** for them (see 3:7) to claim his status and authority. In spite of their weakness, the Philadelphia church ***obeyed*** Christ's ***word*** and ***did not deny*** him under pressure.

3:9 ***those who belong to Satan's synagogue:*** The Christians in Philadelphia had suffered maltreatment by anti-Christian Jews (see note on 2:9). • ***bow down at your feet:*** In the ancient world, captives were often forced to prostrate themselves before their conquerors (see Isa 49:23; 60:14). The church's human enemies will ultimately ***acknowledge that*** Christians ***are the ones*** God loves.

3:10 Jesus will ***protect*** Christians who ***persevere*** through trials (cp. Isa 43:2-4; John 10:27-28; 1 Cor 10:13; Heb 6:18-19).

3:11
Rev 2:25; 22:7, 12, 20

3:12
Ezek 48:35
Gal 4:26
Rev 21:2, 10
[d]*ouranos* (3772)
‣Rev 16:11

3:13
Rev 2:7

3:14
John 1:3
2 Cor 1:20
Col 1:15-18
Rev 1:5

3:15
Rom 12:11

from the great time of testing that will
come upon the whole world to test those
who belong to this world. 11 I am coming
soon. Hold on to what you have, so that
no one will take away your crown. 12 All
who are victorious will become pillars
in the Temple of my God, and they will
never have to leave it. And I will write on
them the name of my God, and they will
be citizens in the city of my God—the
new Jerusalem that comes down from
[d]heaven from my God. And I will also
write on them my new name.
13 "Anyone with ears to hear must
listen to the Spirit and understand what
he is saying to the churches.

The Message to Laodicea, a Lukewarm and Uncommitted Church

14 "Write this letter to the angel of the
church in Laodicea. This is the message
from the one who is the Amen—the faithful
and true witness, the beginning of God's
new creation:
15 "I know all the things you do, that you
are neither hot nor cold. I wish that you
were one or the other! 16 But since you
are like lukewarm water, neither hot nor

Security, Warnings, and the Call to Obedience (3:5)

Rev 2:5, 10-11, 16-17; 3:5, 10-12; 18:4; 20:12; 21:7-8; 22:11-12
Gen 15:1, 13-16
1 Sam 12:22-25
1 Kgs 9:4-9
Jer 18:7-10
John 10:27-30; 15:6
Rom 11:13-32
1 Cor 10:6-12
Heb 6:4-8, 18-20; 13:6
Jas 1:25

The thought of one's name being erased from the Book of Life (3:5) may raise questions of security for some Christians. While the NT is filled with words of assurance (e.g., 1:5-6, 17-18; 3:10; 7:16-17; 22:14; John 10:27-30; 1 Cor 10:13; Heb 6:18-20), it also contains stern warnings. We often dislike and avoid the warnings because they threaten our sense of security. Yet this concern for security is the precise reason that the NT writers issued their warnings that stressed the importance of obedience, faithfulness, and endurance (e.g., 2:5; 3:11; 13:10; John 15:6; 1 Cor 10:6-12; Heb 6:4-8).

This call to obedience was nothing new. God repeatedly called the people of Israel to be faithful (e.g., Gen 12:1-2; 15:1-18; 22:17-18; 28:13-14; 1 Sam 12:19-25; 15:10-11; 28:16-19; 2 Sam 7:11-16; 1 Kgs 9:4-9). All the promises and predictions of God are conditioned upon faithfulness and obedience (see especially Jer 18:7-10). Paul realized that the disobedience of Israel had led to the Gentiles' inclusion among the people of God. He clearly warned Gentile Christians not to become overconfident (Rom 11:13-32); the promise of God is unchanged, but human disobedience brings judgment. Humble obedience and dependence on God are the basis for genuine security.

At the time when the NT was written, it was costly and threatening to be a Christian. The book of Revelation promises a secure hope for Christians despite the threat of death, but this hope is set clearly within the context of warnings about judgment (21:8, 27; 22:15). The call to faithfulness and obedience is a major theme in Revelation (see 2:5, 10-11,16-17, 26-29; 3:2, 12, 18, 21-22; 7:14; 13:9-10, 12; 16:15; 18:4; 20:12; 21:7; 22:3, 7, 11-12). The NT clearly affirms that with God's help, faithful Christians will persevere to the end (see 3:10; Heb 13:6; Jas 1:25).

• ***The great time of testing*** refers to the end times, when the world experiences tribulation.

3:11 *soon:* Or *suddenly*, or *quickly.* • Christians must ***hold on;*** they must persevere in difficulty so they will not lose their ***crown,*** their expected reward.

3:12 ***Victorious*** Christians are secure in God's household since, like ***pillars, . . . they will never have to leave it.*** • ***The name of . . . God*** that is inscribed ***on them*** portrays God's ownership and the security Christians thus enjoy (see 7:4; 14:1). • The ***new Jerusalem*** is not a realm constructed by humans, but God's gift ***from heaven*** (21:2-10). • A ***new name*** was a sign of God's blessing (see also 2:17); Abram, Jacob, Simon, and others were given new names (Gen 17:5; 32:28; John 1:42).

3:14-22 The letter to ***the church in Laodicea*** castigates lukewarm Christians whose inconsistent lives stand for nothing but themselves. They sicken Christ to the point of his spitting them from his mouth.

3:14 ***Laodicea,*** situated 40 miles (65 kilometers) southeast of Philadelphia, was the economic and judicial center of a metropolitan region that included Colosse and Hierapolis. The citizens of Laodicea were very proud of their self-sufficiency. After a severe earthquake (AD 60), Laodicea refused aid from Rome and rebuilt their city themselves (Tacitus, *Annals* 14.27), making it very beautiful. • ***the Amen:*** Used as an oath, "Amen" is a promise of truth (Isa 65:16). Jesus is the truth (John 8:32; 14:6), and his message is authenticated by the truthfulness and reliability of his word. • The description of Christ as ***the faithful and true witness*** declares that he knew them as they really were: Though wealthy and proud of their status and accomplishments, they were not measuring up to God's expectations. • ***the beginning:*** Or *the ruler,* or *the source.*

3:15-16 ***neither hot nor cold:*** The hot springs in Hierapolis were famous for their healing qualities. Colosse was equally famous for its cold, refreshing springs. In contrast, the water available in Laodicea was smelly and ***lukewarm.*** Such water is distasteful; Jesus was saying that the church's indecisive commitment to him was revolting.

cold, I will spit you out of my mouth!
17You say, 'I am rich. I have everything
I want. I don't need a thing!' And you
don't realize that you are wretched
and miserable and poor and blind and
naked. 18So I advise you to buy gold
from me—gold that has been purified
by fire. Then you will be rich. Also buy
white garments from me so you will
not be shamed by your nakedness, and
ointment for your eyes so you will be
able to see. 19I correct and [e]discipline
everyone I love. So be diligent and turn
from your indifference.
20"Look! I stand at the door and knock.
If you hear my voice and open the door,
I will come in, and we will share a meal
together as friends. 21Those who are
victorious will sit with me on my throne,
just as I was victorious and sat with my
Father on his throne.
22"Anyone with ears to hear must
listen to the Spirit and understand what
he is saying to the churches."

4. INTRODUCTION TO THE DRAMA (4:1–5:14)

The Stage: Worship in Heaven

4 Then as I looked, I saw a door standing
open in heaven, and the same voice I
had heard before spoke to me like a trumpet blast. The voice said, "Come up here,
and I will show you what must happen after
this." 2And instantly I was in the Spirit, and I
saw a throne in heaven and someone sitting
on it. 3The one sitting on the throne was
as brilliant as gemstones—like jasper and
carnelian. And the glow of an emerald circled his throne like a rainbow. 4Twenty-four
thrones surrounded him, and twenty-four
elders sat on them. They were all clothed in
white and had gold crowns on their heads.
5From the throne came flashes of lightning
and the rumble of thunder. And in front of
the throne were seven torches with burning
flames. This is the sevenfold Spirit of God.
6In front of the throne was a shiny sea of
glass, sparkling like crystal.
In the center and around the throne were

3:17 Hos 12:8; Zech 11:5; 1 Cor 4:8
3:18 1 Pet 1:7
3:19 Prov 3:12; 1 Cor 11:32; Heb 12:6; [e]*paideuō* (3811) ▸Acts 7:22
3:20 John 14:23
3:21 Matt 19:28
4:1 Exod 19:20, 24; Ezek 1:1; Dan 2:28-29, 45
4:2 1 Kgs 22:19; Isa 6:1; Ezek 1:26-27
4:3 Ezek 1:26-28
4:4 Isa 24:23; Rev 11:16; 19:4
4:5 Exod 19:16; Ezek 1:13; Zech 4:2; Rev 1:4; 5:6

3:17 Although Christians in Laodicea felt prosperous and self-sufficient (see note on 3:14), Jesus accurately saw their ***wretched and miserable and poor*** spiritual condition.

3:18 Jesus' prescription for Laodicea required a complete change of attitude from self-reliance to dependence on God. • ***buy gold from me:*** Materially, they could buy whatever they wanted, but they needed to acquire the treasures of heaven so they would have spiritual riches through faith in Christ. • ***purified by fire:*** While material wealth will not withstand God's purging ***by fire*** (cp. 1 Cor 3:12-15), spiritual wealth has eternal value. • ***White garments*** represent spiritual purity. Black wool cloth and garments were prized exports of the city of Laodicea. This famous black wool cloth was a source of Laodicea's material wealth; it probably represents the Laodiceans' proud and unredeemed spiritual condition. • Laodicea's material prosperity was also due to their well-known Phrygian eye ***ointment,*** which may have been used there in the eye clinic associated with the famed physician Demosthenes Philalethes. The Laodiceans needed to buy ***ointment*** from Christ through faith. Only his eye salve would enable them to ***see*** their sin and repent.

3:19 Christ will ***correct and discipline*** those whom he loves (Prov 3:11-12; Heb 12:5-6), rather than rejecting them. His faithfulness extends even to the unfaithful (2 Tim 2:13).

3:20 A person or a church must ***hear*** Jesus knocking and ***open the door*** to him. Christ provides a pattern of revival for a church that has grown spiritually weak and out of fellowship with him. Simply opening the door can renew their former bond. • ***We will share a meal:*** A shared meal symbolizes acceptance, deep friendship, and a covenant relationship (19:9; see Gen 18:1-5, 16-19; Exod 12:1-31; 18:12; Matt 26:26-30).

3:21 The reward for ***victorious*** and obedient faith is to ***sit with*** Christ on his ***throne.*** Christians do not become divine, but they share in Christ's victorious reign (20:4, 6; 22:5; Col 3:1-4; 2 Tim 2:12).

4:1–5:14 This section introduces the visions and judgments to come. John presents God in his heavenly court—the scene of the drama of Revelation (4:1-11)—and the Lamb, who has a central role (5:1-14). John contrasts the majesty of God with the so-called majesty of Caesar. God's power and splendor is unequaled by the ceremonial court of any earthly ruler.

4:1-11 The description of God's throne room stretches the imagination. It builds on the visions of Isa 6:1-4, Ezek 1:4-28, and Dan 7:9-10, where God is seen enthroned in power and majesty. God's throne dominates Revelation, and the worship in the rest of the book flows from this scene. God's magnificence, grace, and glory are fundamental to the church's worship.

4:1 ***Then . . . I saw:*** This introductory phrase (see also 7:9; 15:5; 18:1; cp. 19:1) does not signal chronological sequence but the beginning of a new visionary experience. • ***Come up here:*** The ***voice*** of the Lord invites John to look at things from God's perspective.

4:2 By being ***in the Spirit*** (or ***in spirit***), John could experience spiritual realities (see 1:10; 17:3; 21:10; Ezek 11:1) and grasp insights about God's presence, the heavenly realm, and God's intentions in history.

4:3 Rather than painting a visual picture of God (Exod 20:4; Deut 4:15-19), John uses ***gemstones*** and the ***rainbow*** (Gen 9:8-17; Ezek 1:28) to suggest God's qualities. The rainbow speaks of God's grace as it recalls God's covenant with Noah (Gen 9:13-17) that he would never again destroy the earth with water. In Revelation, however, we see the earth destroyed by fire (cp. Gen 19:24-29).

4:4 The ***twenty-four elders*** on their ***thrones*** probably represent all of God's people. They might correlate to the twelve tribes of the old covenant and the twelve apostles of the new (see 21:12-14), although some have identified them with the twenty-four divisions of the Israelite priesthood (1 Chr 24:1-19). In the drama, they act as an antiphonal chorus (alternating groups of speakers or singers).

4:5 The ***thunder*** that follows ***flashes of lightning*** is God's call to attention (see 8:5; 11:19; 16:18). • ***in front of the throne were seven torches:*** In ancient times, torches were set before rulers to show their authority. These torches ***with burning flames*** represent the perfect ***Spirit of God.*** • ***This is the sevenfold Spirit:*** Literally *They are the seven spirits;* see note on 1:4.

4:6 ***a shiny sea of glass, sparkling like crystal:*** The most eye-catching part

4:6-7 Ezek 1:5-22; 10:12, 14; Rev 15:7; 19:4
4:8 Isa 6:2; Ezek 1:18; 10:12; ^f pantokratōr (3841) ›Rev 11:17
4:9 Dan 4:34; Rev 4:2; 5:1
4:10 Rev 4:4; 5:8, 14
4:11 Rev 10:6

four living beings, each covered with eyes,
front and back. 7The first of these living
beings was like a lion; the second was like
an ox; the third had a human face; and the
fourth was like an eagle in flight. 8Each of
these living beings had six wings, and their
wings were covered all over with eyes, inside and out. Day after day and night after
night they keep on saying,

"Holy, holy, holy is the Lord God, the
[f]Almighty—
the one who always was, who is, and
who is still to come."

9Whenever the living beings give glory and
honor and thanks to the one sitting on the
throne (the one who lives forever and ever),
10the twenty-four elders fall down and worship the one sitting on the throne (the one
who lives forever and ever). And they lay
their crowns before the throne and say,

11"You are worthy, O Lord our God,
to receive glory and honor and power.

Symbolic Numbers (4:4)

Rev 1:16; 2:10; 6:1; 7:1, 4-8; 12:1, 3; 13:1; 17:3-14; 20:2-7; 21:12-21; Gen 2:2-3; 4:15; 15:13; 41:53-54; Exod 20:6; 25:31-37; 32:15; Lev 16:14; 23:16; 2 Sam 24:13; 1 Kgs 4:26; 17:21; 18:31, 43-44; Job 1:2; Ps 90:4; Jer 15:3; 49:36; Ezek 14:21; Dan 4:16, 23-25; 7:3, 17, 24; Zech 4:2; 6:1; Matt 10:1-5; 12:40; 18:21-22; Mark 6:7; Luke 15:8; Acts 6:3; 10:16; 1 Cor 8:6; Eph 4:4-6; 2 Pet 3:8

The numbers used in Revelation (and elsewhere in Scripture) have often inspired wild speculation. An understanding of the symbolism of numbers in the ancient world can help ground our interpretation. Such symbolism, however, is not rigid or exact, so great care must be exercised, when numbers are used in interpretation, not to push fanciful predictions about future events.

The number *one* can refer to God's oneness (Deut 6:4; Gal 3:20; Jas 2:19). *Two* is the minimum number required to give a legitimate witness (11:3; Deut 17:6), and *three* can imply divine representation (1:4-5; Gen 18:1-2; 2 Cor 13:14). *Four* can stand for the known world, represented in Revelation by living creatures, horsemen, winds, and angels (4:6-8; 6:1-8; 7:1) and in Genesis by *four* rivers (Gen 2:10-14). When *three* and *four* are added to make *seven,* they represent perfection or divine fulfillment, indicating that God and the world are in harmony. The multiplication of *three* by *four* yields *twelve,* the number used in Revelation to represent God's people. The number *five* and its multiples, such as *ten,* represent human completeness (e.g., *five* fingers per hand); and *six* carries a negative sense or implication of evil, being neither humanly complete (*five*) nor divinely complete (*seven*).

Multiples of *ten* (e.g., *forty*) are a symbolic way to indicate *many*, whereas *three sixes* (666) imply supreme evil. *One thousand* is regarded as the foundational large number; 12,000 is the foundational large religious number; and 144,000 is the supreme religious number that represents the complete people of God (7:4; 14:1). The number 10,000 and its multiples are probably best transliterated from Greek as *myriads*, since they really mean "a huge number" rather than a precise count. The numbers *eight, nine,* and *eleven* carry little symbolic significance.

While some of the numbers in the Bible have symbolic meanings, using numbers to speculate on the time of Christ's return or of the end of the world is highly dubious—only God possesses that knowledge (Mark 13:32). God did not intend for the symbolic numbers in Revelation to help us predict the future; rather, they help to explain the significance of the visions. Because the numbers are symbolic, sometimes translations into contemporary sizes, distances, and numbers for our ease of reading can result in the loss of theological significance. The use of these symbolic numbers can illuminate a vision's relationship to the world, the people of God, and either perfection or imperfection.

of ancient theaters was the glistening mosaic where the speaking orchestra was positioned to provide perspective (cp. 15:2-4). • The ***four living beings*** represent the whole created order. • ***covered with eyes:*** This phrase probably indicates that they had knowledge or understanding. In the ancient world, figures were covered with a particular feature to emphasize that quality (e.g., statues of Artemis were covered with breasts to emphasize fertility). Cp. Ezek 1:18.

4:7 These four creatures symbolize four types of beings: ***a lion*** represents wild animals, ***an ox*** represents domesticated animals, ***a human*** represents humanity, and ***an eagle*** represents the birds (cp. Ezek 1:10). These four figures are drawn from Ezek 1 (cherubim) and Isa 6 (seraphim). They probably represent the best of creation as worshiping God. Missing from this worldwide orchestra are fish, which ancient people associated with the evil sea (see 21:1), and insects, represented by locusts in the evil kingdom (see 9:1-11).

4:8 *day and night:* The four beings ceaselessly praised God's basic characteristics: his holiness, his power (***the Almighty***), and his eternity (see note on 1:4). • ***Holy, holy, holy*** comes from Isa 6:3 and is the highest worship affirmation in Scripture. To double something makes it emphatic; to triple it makes it ultimate.

4:9-11 The antiphonal chorus of twenty-four elders provides divine perspective on creation. • ***The one sitting on the throne*** is typical Jewish indirection to avoid speaking God's name.

4:11 *You are worthy:* This phrase is never used of God in the OT but was frequently used in Rome during emperor worship. As emphasized here, only

For you created all things,
and they exist because you created
what you pleased."

A Dramatic Introduction: The Lamb Opens the Scroll

5 Then I saw a [g]scroll in the right hand of
the one who was sitting on the throne.
There was writing on the inside and the
outside of the scroll, and it was sealed with
seven [h]seals. 2And I saw a strong angel, who
shouted with a loud voice: "Who is worthy
to break the seals on this scroll and open it?"
3But no one in heaven or on earth or under
the earth was able to open the scroll and
read it.
4Then I began to weep bitterly because
no one was found worthy to open the scroll
and read it. 5But one of the twenty-four elders said to me, "Stop weeping! Look, the
Lion of the tribe of Judah, the heir to David's
throne, has won the victory. He is worthy to
open the scroll and its seven seals."
6Then I saw a Lamb that looked as if it
had been slaughtered, but it was now standing between the throne and the four living
beings and among the twenty-four elders.
He had seven horns and seven eyes, which
represent the sevenfold Spirit of God that
is sent out into every part of the earth. 7He
stepped forward and took the scroll from
the right hand of the one sitting on the
throne. 8And when he took the scroll, the
four living beings and the twenty-four elders fell down before the Lamb. Each one
had a harp, and they held gold bowls filled
with incense, which are the prayers of God's
people. 9And they sang a new song with
these words:

"You are worthy to take the scroll
and break its seals and open it.
For you were slaughtered, and your
blood has ransomed people for
God
from every tribe and language and
people and nation.
10 And you have caused them to become
a Kingdom of priests for our God.
And they will reign on the earth."

11Then I looked again, and I heard the
voices of thousands and millions of angels
around the throne and of the living beings
and the elders. 12And they sang in a mighty
chorus:

"Worthy is the Lamb who was
slaughtered—
to receive power and riches
and wisdom and strength
and honor and glory and [i]blessing."

5:1 Isa 29:11; Ezek 2:9-10; Dan 12:4; Rev 5:7
[g]*biblion* (0975) ‣ Rev 17:8
[h]*sphragis* (4973) ‣ Rev 20:3
5:2 Rev 10:1; 18:21
5:3 Phil 2:10
5:5 Gen 49:9; Isa 11:1, 10; Heb 7:14; Rev 22:16
5:6 Isa 53:7; Zech 4:10; John 1:29, 36; Rev 1:4; 4:5
5:7 Rev 5:1
5:8 Rev 4:4, 6; 8:3-4; 14:2; 15:2
5:9 Ps 144:9; Rev 14:3
5:10 Exod 19:6; 1 Pet 2:5-9; Rev 1:6; 20:4
5:11 Dan 7:10; Heb 12:22; Rev 4:4, 6
5:12 1 Chr 29:11; Isa 53:7; John 1:29, 36; Rev 4:11
[i]*eulogia* (2129) ‣ Rev 7:12

God deserves worship. • ***you created all things:*** Many in the ancient world believed that the gods were too busy to be concerned with humans. But God is Almighty in more than a philosophical sense; he is involved as Creator and ***Lord***. In Revelation, creation affirms that God is in sovereign control of the world (see 3:14; 10:6; 14:7; 21:1). • ***they exist because you created what you pleased:*** God had a purpose for everything that he created.

5:1-14 John introduces the Lamb, Jesus Christ, the central figure of Revelation and God's chosen agent for accomplishing his purposes.

5:1 The ***scroll*** (or ***book;*** also in 5:2-5, 7-9), like a dramatic script, details God's plan for the world (Ps 139:16). • ***The right hand*** represents God's gracious authority and power (see 1:17, 20). • The ***writing on the inside and the outside*** means that God's plans for history are full and complete. • ***sealed with seven seals:*** God has put his purposes for history in an impermeable safe (Isa 29:11-12; Dan 8:26). His purposes will be completed only when the seals are broken (see 5:4).

5:2-3 At first, ***no one*** in the entire universe seemed to have the divine authority or power to answer the angel's call.

5:4 John wept because even though the revelation had been promised to him, he thought he would be denied knowledge of the divine script—God's plan for history (4:1; see 10:4). John's weeping highlights the significance of the anticipated revelation.

5:5 Designations for Jesus as ***the Lion of . . . Judah*** (see Gen 49:9-10) and ***the heir to David's throne*** (literally ***the root of David;*** see Isa 11:10) are OT metaphors for the Messiah (see Jer 23:5; 30:9; John 7:42). • Because Jesus ***won the victory*** at the cross (John 16:33), he is the only one ***worthy to open the scroll*** and reveal God's purposes (4:11; 5:2, 12). God's plan for history centers around Jesus and what he has done. His relationship to the scroll indicates his control of history.

5:6 The Jews expected the Messiah to appear as a conquering lion. Instead, Jesus came as ***a Lamb*** (John 1:29, 36; Acts 8:32-35; 1 Cor 5:7; 1 Pet 1:19). The Lamb that ***had been slaughtered*** but ***was now standing*** refers to Jesus' death and resurrection. • The Lamb's ***seven horns*** represent his complete power, and the ***seven eyes*** represent his complete knowledge (see Zech 4:10). He is also fully related to the perfect ***Spirit of God*** (1:4). • ***which represent the sevenfold Spirit:*** Literally ***which are the seven spirits;*** see note on 1:4.

5:8 ***fell down before the Lamb:*** The crucified and risen Christ has divine authority to initiate the events of this age; he is fully worthy of worship. • The ***prayers of God's people*** become a significant basis for the judgments and plagues (6:9-11; 8:2-5).

5:9-10 The whole created order joins in ***a new song*** of praise to the Lamb (cp. 14:1-5; Ps 149:1; Isa 42:10). • The Lamb is ***worthy*** because, through his sacrifice, he won the right to ***break*** the ***seals*** of the ***scroll*** and enact God's purposes in history. • The song summarizes the implications of the Good News about Jesus (1 Pet 1:18-25).

5:10 The description of God's people as ***a Kingdom of priests*** who will enjoy ultimate victory and will ***reign*** with Christ reflects the images of Jesus as both King (Rom 1:3) and High Priest (Heb 6:20). • ***they will reign:*** Some manuscripts read ***they are reigning.***

5:11-12 A huge angelic ***chorus*** numbering ***thousands and millions*** provides an antiphonal response; all heaven responds to creation's confession of Christ's sacrifice.

5:12 This doxology ascribes to Jesus divine honors that are reserved for God alone (see 4:11; 5:13; 7:12).

5:13 Phil 2:10 Rev 4:11; 5:7
5:14 Rev 4:6, 9-10
6:1 Rev 5:1, 6
6:2 Zech 1:8; 6:1-3 Rev 14:14; 19:11-12
6:3 Rev 4:7
6:4 Zech 1:8; 6:2 Matt 10:34
6:5 Dan 5:27 Zech 6:2, 6-8 Rev 4:7
6:6-7 Rev 4:6-7

13 And then I heard every creature in
heaven and on earth and under the earth
and in the sea. They sang:

"Blessing and honor and glory and power
belong to the one sitting on the
throne
and to the Lamb forever and ever."

14 And the four living beings said, "Amen!"
And the twenty-four elders fell down and
worshiped the Lamb.

5. ACT I: SEVEN SEALS OF JUDGMENT (6:1–8:1)

The Lamb Breaks the First Six Seals (6:1-17)

Seals 1–4: The Riders of War, Violence, Economic Imbalance, and Death

6 As I watched, the Lamb broke the first
of the seven seals on the scroll. Then I
heard one of the four living beings say with
a voice like thunder, "Come!" 2 I looked up
and saw a white horse standing there. Its
rider carried a bow, and a crown was placed
on his head. He rode out to win many battles and gain the victory.
3 When the Lamb broke the second
seal, I heard the second living being say,
"Come!" 4 Then another horse appeared, a
red one. Its rider was given a mighty sword
and the authority to take peace from the
earth. And there was war and slaughter
everywhere.
5 When the Lamb broke the third seal, I
heard the third living being say, "Come!" I
looked up and saw a black horse, and its
rider was holding a pair of scales in his
hand. 6 And I heard a voice from among the
four living beings say, "A loaf of wheat bread

The Theater and Revelation (4:1–5:14)

This passage plays a distinctive role in Revelation. It introduces a divine drama and highlights the significance of God's agent (the Messiah) in world history. These two chapters also set the stage for the great drama about the world, the reality of judgment, and the victory that comes through the Lamb. Understanding the ancient theater can help us to understand these chapters that communicate their message dramatically in a series of tableaus (scenes).

These chapters open by describing God on his heavenly throne (4:1-3). In the ancient theater, a divine persona was placed in a central box or throne high above the stage. This actor clarified the significance of each scene for the audience through positive and negative comments or solved dilemmas in the script when they became too complex for the characters on stage to handle. In Revelation, readers should similarly watch for scenes where God or his messengers interpret or intervene to advance the message.

The ancient drama took place on the stage below the divine figure. Between the stage and the audience, an orchestra of speakers voiced the emotional climate of the play. In Revelation, the four living creatures have a similar role (4:6-8). The twenty-four elders (representatives of the old and new covenants; 4:4) provide an antiphonal chorus (alternating groups of speakers or singers) and the historical setting for this great drama. God supplies the script, and only his special agent, the Lamb, can open it (5:1-5; 6:1).

5:13 The second antiphonal response resounds from *every creature,* even those *under the earth* (the place of the dead) and *in the sea* (usually associated with evil), possibly implying a mandatory response even by those in rebellion against God (Isa 45:23-25; Rom 14:11; Phil 2:10-11).

5:14 The dramatic introduction of *the Lamb* (5:1-14) closes with the *living beings* (4:6-9). Their *Amen* affirms the truth of what John had seen, as *the twenty-four elders* prostrate themselves in worship.

6:1–16:21 Three sets of seven judgments—the seals, trumpets, and bowls—form the core of Revelation. Some suggest that the judgments form a chronological sequence from beginning to end, with each set of judgments flowing from the seventh judgment of the previous set for a total of twenty-one successive judgments. More likely, the relationship is cyclical (as in other Jewish apocalyptic works; cp. Dan 2, 7, 8, 11), with each set conveying increasing intensity and adding new details of God's judgment on those who rebel against him. In this perspective, all three cycles end at the same chronological point, with the return of Christ.

6:1–8:1 The Lamb breaks the seven seals to reveal the significance of history from God's perspective.

6:1-8 The four horses and their riders (see Zech 1:8-11; 6:1-8) sum up the power structures of the world; their activities primarily lead to war, violence, economic imbalance, and death. It is pointless to put our hope in these power structures.

6:1 *scroll:* Or *book.*

6:2 While some have understood the *rider* on *a white horse* to be Christ, as in 19:11, the only similarity between these two images is the horse. The four riders represent the destructive, senseless world and show no redeeming qualities. • The *bow* was typical Greco-Roman military hardware; here it is a symbol of war. • *win many battles . . . gain the victory:* The double use of the Greek word *nikaō* (conquer) confirms that this rider is powerful. The focus on war and conquest illustrates human depravity.

6:3-4 The *red* horse represents bloody violence on the earth. Although peace was what the Roman empire promised (the *pax Romana*), widespread violence was the horrible reality. This rider represents *slaughter,* including civil upheavals and ethnic cleansing.

6:5-6 The *black horse* represents economic and social dysfunction, indicated by *scales* used in commerce. Rampant

or three loaves of barley will cost a day's pay.
And don't waste the olive oil and wine."
7When the Lamb broke the fourth seal, I
heard the fourth living being say, "Come!" 8I
looked up and saw a horse whose color was
pale green. Its rider was named Death, and
his companion was the Grave. These two
were given authority over one-fourth of the
earth, to kill with the sword and famine and
disease and wild animals.

Seal 5: The Martyrs and Their Haunting Question

9When the Lamb broke the fifth seal, I saw
under the altar the souls of all who had
been martyred for the word of God and for
being faithful in their testimony. 10They
shouted to the Lord and said, "O Sovereign
Lord, holy and true, how long before you
judge the people who belong to this world
and avenge our blood for what they have
done to us?" 11Then a white robe was given
to each of them. And they were told to rest
a little longer until the full number of their
brothers and sisters—their fellow servants
of Jesus who were to be martyred—had
joined them.

Seal 6: The Cosmic End

12I watched as the Lamb broke the sixth seal,
and there was a great earthquake. The sun
became as dark as black cloth, and the moon
became as red as blood. 13Then the stars
of the sky fell to the earth like green figs
falling from a tree shaken by a strong wind.
14The sky was rolled up like a scroll, and all
of the mountains and islands were moved
from their places.
15Then everyone—the kings of the earth,
the rulers, the generals, the wealthy, the powerful, and every slave and free person—all
hid themselves in the caves and among the
[j]rocks of the mountains. 16And they cried
to the mountains and the rocks, "Fall on us
and hide us from the face of the one who
sits on the throne and from the wrath of the
Lamb. 17For the great day of their [k]wrath
has come, and who is able to survive?"

First Interlude (7:1-17)

God's People Will Be Preserved

7 Then I saw four angels standing at the
four corners of the earth, holding back
the four winds so they did not blow on the

6:8 Jer 14:12; 15:2-3; Hos 13:14
6:9 Exod 29:12; Lev 4:7
6:10 Ps 79:10; Zech 1:12; Luke 18:7
6:11 Heb 11:40
6:12 Joel 2:10; Matt 24:29
6:13 Isa 34:4
6:14 Ps 46:2; 2 Pet 3:10
6:15 Isa 2:10, 19, 21; Jer 4:29; [j]*petra* (4073) ›Matt 7:24
6:16 Hos 10:8; Luke 23:30
6:17 Joel 2:11; Zeph 1:14-15; Mal 3:2; [k]*orgē* (3709) ›Rev 16:19

inflation is shown by the cost of the staples of life: ***A loaf of wheat bread or three loaves of barley will cost a day's pay*** (Greek *A choinix* [1 quart or 1 liter] *of wheat for a denarius, and 3 choinix of barley for a denarius.* A denarius was equivalent to a laborer's full day's wage). Yet the prices of luxuries such as ***oil and wine*** would remain unchanged. It is an image of social and economic imbalance. • ***don't waste:*** Or *don't harm.*

6:7-8 With ***the fourth seal*** comes a ghastly looking horse. In the ancient world, ***pale green*** was the color for depicting a corpse. • ***the Grave:*** Greek *Hades.* In Greek thought, Hades was the underworld abode of bodiless beings. The Hebrew idea of *Sheol,* the place of the dead (1 Sam 28:15), was similar. • The killing of ***one-fourth*** of those on earth indicates that the final judgment has not yet arrived (contrast 6:16-17). • This fourfold set of woes (***sword and famine and disease and wild animals;*** cp. Ezek 14:21) summarizes the tragedies of earthly existence. The world cannot offer hope to humanity. • ***disease:*** Literally *death.*

6:9-11 In counterpoint to the world's destructive ways (6:1-8), ***the fifth seal*** introduces Christian martyrs who ask how God intends to deal with evil.

6:9 Rather than follow the world's destructive ways, the martyrs gave their lives ***for the word of God.***

6:10 The martyrs ***shouted*** to the ***Sovereign Lord*** because they trusted in his power to redress their grievances. • ***how long:*** Is God slow to act? Will justice be done? God does act decisively (see 6:12-14); his wrath (6:16-17) must be understood in terms of justice, fairness, and righteousness (see Exod 34:5-7; Neh 9:17; Ps 103:8; 145:8; Joel 2:13; Jon 4:2; Rom 2:6-11). • ***avenge our blood:*** This cry for God's justice follows the pattern of OT imprecatory (vengeance) psalms (see "Prayers for Vengeance" at Ps 137, p. 1017; cp. Ps 6:3; 74:10; 79:5; 80:4). It also reflects the covenant curses of Deut 28:53-57; 32:35 (quoted in Rom 12:19).

6:11 ***A white robe*** is symbolic of the martyrs' victory and of God's full acceptance. • ***they were told to rest:*** Death is a state of rest (cp. John 11:11-12) in which martyrs await God's justice. • ***the full number:*** Only God knows how many Christians will be martyred before the end. In his sovereignty, God will fulfill his purposes through his children who are ***martyred*** and will vindicate them at the appropriate time. • ***their brothers and sisters:*** Literally *their brothers,* a generic term that refers to both male and female believers.

6:12-17 The opening of ***the sixth seal*** offers a glimpse into the end of the created order.

6:12-14 These cataclysmic signs are associated in Scripture with the day of the Lord, when God's judgment will overturn the whole created order (see Isa 13:4-12; 34:1-4; Joel 2:1-32; Zeph 2:1-3; Mark 13:1-37).

6:15-17 ***hid themselves:*** In the face of God's judgment, unredeemed people will be terrified and seek a safe hiding place, but in vain (Isa 2:19-21; Ezek 38:20; Hos 10:8; Luke 23:30). The prophets repeatedly warned that ***the great day*** would be a day of ***wrath*** and judgment (Isa 13:6-11; Joel 1:15; Amos 5:18; Zeph 1:14-15). • The ultimate question concerning God's judgment is, ***Who is able to survive?*** (Mal 3:2). God's children will rejoice to see him (5:13-14; 14:3-5) because they understand God's response to the martyrs' cry for vengeance (6:9-11), and they themselves have nothing to fear from God's judgment (Acts 10:34-36; Rom 5:1-2). Those who have persecuted God's people, however, will quake in fear as they face ***the wrath of the Lamb.***

7:1-17 Three interludes occur in chs 6–16 (7:1-17; 10:1–11:14; 12:1–14:20) to define the place of God's holy people and to provide perspective on the previous scenes. In this first interlude before the seventh seal is broken, two visions communicate how God protects his people and assures them of his calling.

7:1-8 The interlude's first vision shows how God protects his faithful followers from ultimate ***harm.***

7:1-3 ***Wait!*** God calls for a temporary halt by the ***four angels*** of destruction. • ***The seal of the living God*** implies membership in God's household; God owns and protects his people (2 Cor 1:22; Eph 1:13-14). In the ancient

7:1 Jer 49:36; Ezek 37:9; Dan 7:2; Zech 6:5; Matt 24:31
7:2 Rev 9:4
7:3 Ezek 9:4, 6; Rev 9:4; 14:1; 22:4
7:4 Rev 14:1, 3
7:9 Rev 3:5; 5:9
7:10 Rev 5:13; 12:10; 19:1; 22:3
7:11 Rev 4:4, 6, 10
7:12 Rev 5:12-14; [a]*eulogia* (2129) ‣2 Cor 9:5
7:13 Rev 6:11; 7:9
7:14 Dan 12:1; Rev 6:11; 22:14
7:15 Rev 4:9; 11:19; 22:3
7:16 Isa 49:10

earth or the sea, or even on any tree. 2And I
saw another angel coming up from the east,
carrying the seal of the living God. And he
shouted to those four angels, who had been
given power to harm land and sea, 3"Wait!
Don't harm the land or the sea or the trees
until we have placed the seal of God on the
foreheads of his servants."

4And I heard how many were marked
with the seal of God—144,000 were sealed
from all the tribes of Israel:

5 from Judah 12,000
from Reuben 12,000
from Gad 12,000
6 from Asher 12,000
from Naphtali 12,000
from Manasseh 12,000
7 from Simeon 12,000
from Levi 12,000
from Issachar 12,000
8 from Zebulun 12,000
from Joseph 12,000
from Benjamin 12,000

Praise from the Great Crowd

9After this I saw a vast crowd, too great to
count, from every nation and tribe and people
and language, standing in front of the throne
and before the Lamb. They were clothed in
white robes and held palm branches in their
hands. 10And they were shouting with a great
roar,

"Salvation comes from our God who sits
on the throne
and from the Lamb!"

11And all the angels were standing around
the throne and around the elders and the
four living beings. And they fell before the
throne with their faces to the ground and
worshiped God. 12They sang,

"Amen! [a]Blessing and glory and wisdom
and thanksgiving and honor
and power and strength belong to our
God
forever and ever! Amen."

13Then one of the twenty-four elders
asked me, "Who are these who are clothed
in white? Where did they come from?"

14And I said to him, "Sir, you are the one
who knows."

Then he said to me, "These are the ones
who died in the great tribulation. They have
washed their robes in the blood of the Lamb
and made them white.

15 "That is why they stand in front of God's
throne
and serve him day and night in his
Temple.
And he who sits on the throne
will give them shelter.
16 They will never again be hungry or thirsty;
they will never be scorched by the
heat of the sun.

world, sealing or tattooing was a sign of ownership. • The ***angel . . . carrying the seal*** identified God's people, answering the question of who would survive God's wrath (6:17; see Ezek 9:3-8; John 17:14-15) and furthering the promise of protection (3:10; see also 11:1-2).

7:4-8 Who are the *144,000*? This listing of the ***tribes of Israel*** does not exactly correlate with the twelve physical tribes. Instead, it communicates that God knows precisely which people on earth belong to him. By the AD 90s, Israel's twelve tribes no longer existed; ten tribes were dispersed when Assyria conquered the northern kingdom of Israel (2 Kgs 17). The early Christian church regarded itself symbolically as the Israel of God (Matt 19:28; Rom 2:28-29; 9:6-8; Gal 3:29; 6:16; Phil 3:3). The *144,000* probably represent all faithful Christians (cp. 14:1-5; 21:12-17). The list begins appropriately with Judah (the royal tribe of Jesus) but substitutes Manasseh (one of the two tribes of Joseph) for Dan. The tribe of Dan fell into idolatry (Judg 18:14-31; 1 Kgs 12:25-30), and early Christians regarded it as the epitome of evil.

7:9-17 The interlude's second vision shows heaven with an innumerable crowd rejoicing because they are secure in Christ and all tears and sorrows have ended.

7:9 This *vast crowd* of believers (7:14) is *too great to count,* fulfilling God's promises to Abraham (Gen 15:5; 17:4-5; Rom 4:16-24; Gal 3:29). • ***White robes*** (6:11) and ***palm branches*** (John 12:13) are ancient symbols of victory and success, adding to the celebration that occurs after God ends the hostile world.

7:10 Ancient victory parades, heralding the accomplishments of conquerors, included loud chants. The shout of ***Salvation*** ("victory," "deliverance") honors God's triumph and prepares readers for his reign.

7:11-12 The ***angels, elders,*** and ***four living beings*** all prostrated themselves before God and responded together in a sevenfold (i.e., comprehensive) doxology to recognize God's eternal nature. The doxology is preceded and followed by ***Amen***—a powerful affirmation of God's victory.

7:14 ***who died in*** (literally *who came out of*): See 6:9; 20:4. • ***the great tribulation*** (or *the great suffering*): A time of horrible and distressing events (see 1:9; 2:9-10; Deut 4:30-31; Matt 24:21-22; Acts 14:22). • ***They have washed their robes in the blood of the Lamb:*** This description symbolizes Christ's redeeming death for them. • ***made them white:*** This description expresses their victory over sin and death and their acceptance by God into eternal life.

7:15 ***serve him day and night:*** Service to God is the continual duty of Christians. • God's ***Temple*** symbolizes his presence (also 11:19; cp. 21:22).

7:16-17 For desert-dwellers, ***life-giving water*** and relief from the scorching ***sun*** represent paradise (see also 21:6; 22:1, 17; Ps 23:1-2; Ezek 47:1-12; John 7:37-38). • ***on the throne*** (literally *on the center of the throne*): The ***Lamb*** is closely identified with God. • Christ's designation as the ***Shepherd*** of God's people (cp. Ps 23; Matt 15:24; John 10:3, 11, 14; Heb 13:20; 1 Pet 2:25) means that he protects and provides for the sheep, bringing hope and salvation to his people (see Ezek 34:11-16, 23-24).

17 For the Lamb on the throne
will be their Shepherd.
He will lead them to springs of
life-giving water.
And God will wipe every tear from
their eyes."

The Lamb Breaks Seal 7: Silence (8:1)

8 When the Lamb broke the seventh seal
on the scroll, there was silence throughout heaven for about half an hour.

6. ACT II: SEVEN TRUMPETS OF JUDGMENT (8:2–11:19)

Introduction to the Trumpets (8:2-5)

2 I saw the seven angels who stand before
God, and they were given seven trumpets.
3 Then another angel with a gold incense
burner came and stood at the altar. And a
great amount of incense was given to him to
mix with the prayers of God's people as an
offering on the gold altar before the throne.
4 The smoke of the incense, mixed with the
prayers of God's holy people, ascended up
to God from the altar where the angel had
poured them out. 5 Then the angel filled the
incense burner with fire from the altar and
threw it down upon the earth; and thunder
crashed, lightning flashed, and there was a
terrible earthquake.

The First Four Trumpets (8:6-13)

6 Then the seven angels with the seven trumpets prepared to blow their mighty blasts.
7 The first angel blew his trumpet, and
hail and fire mixed with blood were thrown
down on the earth. One-third of the earth
was set on fire, one-third of the trees were
burned, and all the green grass was burned.
8 Then the second angel blew his trumpet,
and a great mountain of fire was thrown
into the sea. One-third of the water in the
sea became blood, 9 one-third of all things
living in the sea died, and one-third of all
the ships on the sea were destroyed.
10 Then the third angel blew his trumpet,
and a great star fell from the sky, burning
like a torch. It fell on one-third of the rivers
and on the springs of water. 11 The name of
the star was Bitterness. It made one-third of
the water bitter, and many people died from
drinking the bitter water.
12 Then the fourth angel blew his trumpet,
and one-third of the sun was struck, and
one-third of the moon, and one-third of the
stars, and they became dark. And one-third
of the day was dark, and also one-third of
the night.
13 Then I looked, and I heard a single eagle crying loudly as it flew through the air,

7:17
Ps 23:1-5
Isa 25:8; 49:10
John 10:11, 14
Rev 21:4, 6; 22:1

8:1
Rev 6:1-17

8:2
Rev 9:1, 13; 11:15

8:3
Exod 30:1-3
Rev 9:13

8:4
Ps 141:2
Rev 5:8; 8:3

8:5
Exod 19:16-19
Lev 16:12
Rev 4:5; 11:19; 16:18

8:7
Exod 9:23-25
Ezek 38:22

8:8
Jer 51:25
Rev 16:3

8:9
Exod 7:20-21

8:10
Isa 14:12
Rev 6:13; 9:1; 16:4

8:11
Jer 9:15

8:12
Exod 10:21
Ezek 32:7-8
Rev 6:12-13

8:13
Rev 3:10; 9:12

9:1
Isa 14:12
Luke 8:31; 10:18
Rev 17:8; 20:1

8:1 The opening of ***the seventh seal*** concludes the first act and dramatically initiates ***silence,*** which suggests the mystery of God in his dealings with the world (10:4; 1 Kgs 19:11-12). Perhaps the mysterious silence here is analogous to God's rest on the seventh day of creation (Gen 2:1-3; see also "God's Sabbath Rest" at Heb 4:1-11, p. 2089). • ***scroll:*** Or *book.* • ***half an hour:*** This brief hush precedes the unfolding of the second act of divine judgment when God will answer the prayers of his people.

8:2–11:19 The second cycle of judgments is structured around ***seven trumpets.*** Like the first cycle (6:1–8:1), this one contains an interlude (10:1–11:14; cp. 7:1-17) and ends with a glimpse of God's eternal Kingdom (11:15-19; see 7:9–8:1). • The trumpet judgments are reminiscent of the ten plagues of Egypt (Exod 7:14–11:10) and have the same purpose—to show the powerlessness of earthly gods (or satanic powers) and to demonstrate beyond doubt the power and sovereignty of God.

8:2-6 This scene of preparation in heaven introduces the seven trumpets of judgment and continues the theme of God's receiving and answering prayer (5:8; 6:9-11).

8:2 The dramatic sounding of ***trumpets*** by ***angels*** heralds an approaching end (see Isa 27:13; Zech 9:14; Matt 24:31; 1 Cor 15:52; 1 Thes 4:16).

8:3-4 ***The prayers of God's people*** ask for God's ultimate justice and judgment (6:10-11; see also 5:8; Ezra 9:5-6; Ps 141:2; Dan 9:21). The mixture of ***incense*** and ***prayers*** that reaches God's presence shows that God hears their prayers (see 6:9-11) and is prepared to act.

8:5 The action of ***the angel,*** as he throws ***fire . . . down upon the earth,*** signals the dramatic beginning of God's judgment (see Gen 19:24; Exod 9:23; Lev 10:2; Deut 9:3; 2 Kgs 1:10). • ***thunder . . . lightning . . . earthquake:*** These earthly portents remind us of God's power, presence, and judgment (also 11:19; 16:18; see Exod 19:18-19; 1 Kgs 19:11-12; Isa 29:6).

8:7-12 Each of the first four trumpets affects ***one-third*** of its target (see Ezek 5:1-4, 12; Zech 13:8). The point is not to convey an exact measurement; instead, it indicates that God's judgment on the earth is beginning but has not reached its zenith. Together, the first four trumpets form a unified message of judgment on the whole physical world (as with 6:1-8).

8:7 ***Hail and fire mixed with blood*** signal the destruction of plant life, as did the seventh plague on Egypt (see Exod 9:13-35; Joel 2:31; Acts 2:19). • ***all the green grass was burned:*** Nothing escapes God's judgment. • This vision need not be harmonized with 9:4 because each scene is self-contained and communicates its own message.

8:8-9 ***water . . . became blood:*** This judgment is similar to the first plague on Egypt (see Exod 7:14-25; Ps 78:44). • The ***mountain of fire*** suggests something similar to the eruption of Mount Vesuvius in AD 79 that brought bloody destruction to ships and sea life (see Pliny the Younger, *Letters* 6.16.1-22).

8:10-11 The ***star*** named ***Bitterness*** (literally *wormwood,* a shrubby plant yielding a bitter extract) is symbolic rather than physical. Bitter water is connected with judgment from early in Israel's national experience (Exod 15:22-26; Num 5:18; Jer 9:13-16; 23:15). The message is that wide-scale judgment has begun.

8:12 ***the fourth angel:*** On the fourth day of creation, God made ***the sun . . . the moon, and . . . the stars*** (Gen 1:14-19). • ***the day was dark:*** This judgment replicates the ninth plague in Egypt (Exod 10:21-23).

8:13 The ancients regarded the ***eagle*** as a symbolic messenger of God (see *4 Ezra* 11:7-8; *2 Baruch* 77:19-26). • ***Terror, terror, terror:*** A threefold announcement

"Terror, terror, terror to all who belong to this world because of what will happen when the last three angels blow their trumpets."

Trumpets 5–6: The First Two Terrors (9:1-21)

The Fifth Trumpet Brings the First Terror

9 Then the fifth angel blew his trumpet, and I saw a star that had fallen to earth from the sky, and he was given the key to the shaft of the bottomless pit. 2When he opened it, smoke poured out as though from a huge furnace, and the sunlight and air turned dark from the smoke.

3Then locusts came from the smoke and descended on the earth, and they were given power to sting like scorpions. 4They were told not to harm the grass or plants or trees, but only the people who did not have the seal of God on their foreheads. 5They were told not to kill them but to torture them for five months with pain like the pain of a scorpion sting. 6In those days people will seek death but will not find it. They will long to die, but death will flee from them!

7The locusts looked like horses prepared for battle. They had what looked like gold crowns on their heads, and their faces looked like human faces. 8They had hair like women's hair and teeth like the teeth of a lion. 9They wore armor made of iron, and their wings roared like an army of chariots rushing into battle. 10They had tails that stung like scorpions, and for five months they had the power to torment people. 11Their king is the angel from the bottomless pit; his name in Hebrew is *Abaddon*, and in Greek, *Apollyon*—the Destroyer.

12The first terror is past, but look, two more terrors are coming!

The Sixth Trumpet Brings the Second Terror

13Then the sixth angel blew his trumpet, and I heard a voice speaking from the four horns of the gold altar that stands in the presence of God. 14And the voice said to the sixth angel who held the trumpet, "Release the four angels who are bound at the great Euphrates River." 15Then the four angels who had been prepared for this hour and day and month and year were turned loose to kill one-third of all the people on earth. 16I heard the size of their army, which was 200 million mounted troops.

17And in my vision, I saw the horses and

9:2 Gen 19:28; Exod 19:18; Joel 2:2, 10
9:3 Exod 10:12-15; Rev 9:5, 10
9:4 Ezek 9:4, 6; Rev 7:3
9:6 Job 3:21; Rev 6:16
9:7 Joel 2:4-5
9:8 Joel 1:6
9:9 Joel 2:5
9:11 Job 26:6; 28:22; Prov 15:11; Rev 9:1
9:12 Rev 8:13
9:13 Exod 30:1-3; Rev 8:3
9:14 Gen 15:18; Rev 7:1; 16:12
9:15 Rev 8:7-12; 9:18; 20:7
9:17 Job 41:10-12

would be recognized as a message from God (see Acts 10:16). • The *terror* (Greek *ouai*) that sounded like an eagle's screech was directed against humans of ***this world*** who were not among God's faithful people (6:10; 9:4, 20).

9:1-21 The fifth and sixth trumpets demonstrate how God's judgment impacts the people of the world and detail how futile it is to resist God. While these judgments should lead to repentance, they do not. Sin has such control over people that they choose to worship the evil forces that torture and murder them rather than repent and turn to God.

9:1-12 The ***fifth . . . trumpet***, the first of the three terrors (8:13), brings the judgment of locusts from ***the bottomless pit*** (or *the abyss*, or *the underworld;* also in 9:11), a place of horror. Ancient cultures viewed the oceanic depths, or the "abyss," as a dwelling place of demonic forces (see note on Gen 1:2).

9:2 ***The smoke*** from the pit turned the sky ***dark***, as in the plague on Egypt (Exod 10:21-29; see Matt 27:45).

9:3-4 The ***locusts . . . from the smoke*** with their ***power to sting like scorpions*** are fiercer than those of the Egyptian plague (see Exod 10:14-15). Rather than eating plants, these locusts are like stinging *scorpions* that viciously attack people. Only people without the ***seal of God*** (see 7:1-8) receive this painful judgment. While the stings cause painful torture, they are not life-threatening (9:5-6).

9:5 ***torture them for five months:*** This time period is a symbolically complete number based on the fingers on a hand. It is also the normal life span of locusts, suggesting that their entire purpose was to torture people.

9:7-10 While some see these ***locusts*** as symbolic of attack helicopters, missiles, or other modern armaments, they come from the "bottomless pit" rather than from human engineering. The description of these creatures, derived from the physical appearance of locusts, is intended to cause revulsion and terror. • Their ***gold crowns*** indicate that their torment dominates much of the earth.

9:11 The ***king*** of the locusts is identified in three ways: (1) as ***the angel from the bottomless pit*** (probably different from the fallen star, 9:1, who unlocked the abyss rather than coming from it); (2) as ***Abaddon*** ("destruction"), often paired with death (see Job 28:22; Ps 88:11); and (3) as ***Apollyon—the Destroyer*** (see 1 Cor 10:10). • Although John makes no direct connection between the devil and this king of the locusts, the prince of demons is linked with Satan in the Gospels (Mark 3:22-26; see Matt 12:24-27; Luke 11:15-18). The NT also identifies the devil as the prince of this world (John 12:31; 14:30; 16:11) and as the prince of the power of the air (Eph 2:2), so he probably represents Satan. There is also a connection with the Roman emperor Domitian, whose patron god Apollo was symbolized by the locust.

9:13-14 The ***four horns of the gold altar*** (see 8:3) are introduced with the sixth trumpet blast. Many excavations have uncovered altars with pointed horns at their four corners (see note on Exod 27:2; see illustrations, pp. 173, 176). • The ***voice*** carries the authority ***of God*** in the command to ***release the four angels***. • These angels have been ***bound***, suggesting their evil nature (cp. 20:2; *1 Enoch* 10; contrast 7:1). Their location ***at the great Euphrates River*** probably refers to Assyria and Babylon, empires that had devastated the kingdoms of Israel and Judah and thus were symbols of destruction (see 2 Kgs 17:22-24; 25:1-11).

9:15 ***hour and day and month and year:*** The fourfold time designation for releasing ***the four angels*** confirms that even evil forces must observe God's timing.

9:16 The relationship of the four angels to ***their army*** is not clear. • ***200 million:*** This figure represents an innumerable multitude. Even at its greatest strength, the ancient Roman army with twenty-one legions numbered only about 126,000 soldiers. It is unproductive to use this number in attempting to identify any specific country with such an overwhelming destructive force.

the riders sitting on them. The riders wore
armor that was fiery red and dark blue and
yellow. The horses had heads like lions,
and fire and smoke and burning sulfur billowed from their mouths. [18]One-third of
all the people on earth were killed by these
three plagues—by the fire and smoke and
burning sulfur that came from the mouths
of the horses. [19]Their power was in their
mouths and in their tails. For their tails had
heads like snakes, with the power to injure
people.
[20]But the people who did not die in these
plagues still refused to repent of their evil
deeds and turn to God. They continued to
worship demons and idols made of gold, silver, bronze, stone, and wood—idols that can
neither see nor hear nor walk! [21]And they
did not repent of their murders or their
witchcraft or their sexual immorality or
their thefts.

Second Interlude (10:1–11:14)
The Angel and the Small Scroll

10 Then I saw another mighty angel coming down from heaven, surrounded
by a cloud, with a rainbow over his head.
His face shone like the sun, and his feet
were like pillars of fire. [2]And in his hand
was a small scroll that had been opened. He
stood with his right foot on the sea and his
left foot on the land. [3]And he gave a great
shout like the roar of a lion. And when he
shouted, the seven thunders answered.
[4]When the seven thunders spoke, I was
about to write. But I heard a voice from
heaven saying, "Keep secret what the seven
thunders said, and do not write it down."
[5]Then the angel I saw standing on the
sea and on the land raised his right hand
toward heaven. [6]He swore an oath in the
name of the one who lives forever and ever,
who created the heavens and everything in
them, the earth and everything in it, and the
sea and everything in it. He said, "There will
be no more delay. [7]When the seventh angel
blows his trumpet, God's mysterious plan
will be fulfilled. It will happen just as he announced it to his servants the prophets."
[8]Then the voice from heaven spoke to me
again: "Go and take the open scroll from the
hand of the angel who is standing on the
sea and on the land."
[9]So I went to the angel and told him to
give me the small scroll. "Yes, take it and eat
it," he said. "It will be sweet as honey in your
mouth, but it will turn sour in your stomach!" [10]So I took the small scroll from the
hand of the angel, and I ate it! It was sweet
in my mouth, but when I swallowed it, it
turned sour in my stomach.

9:20 Deut 4:28; 32:17; Ps 115:4-7; Dan 5:23; Mic 5:13; Acts 7:41; 1 Cor 10:19-20; Rev 2:21
9:21 Rev 16:9, 11, 21
10:1 Matt 17:2; Rev 1:15-16; 4:3; 5:2; 18:1
10:2 Rev 10:8
10:3 Ps 29:3-9; Rev 4:5
10:4 Dan 8:26; 12:4, 9; Rev 22:10
10:5 Deut 32:40; Dan 12:7
10:6 Gen 14:19, 22; Exod 20:11; Neh 9:6; Ps 146:6; Rev 4:11; 14:7; 16:17
10:7 Dan 9:6, 10; Amos 3:7; Rev 11:15
10:8 Rev 10:2
10:9 Jer 15:16; Ezek 2:8–3:3
10:11 Jer 1:9-10; 25:30; Rev 5:9

9:17-19 The *riders* had *armor* in colors that matched the *plagues* of their horses, with *red* for *fire, blue* for *smoke*, and *yellow* for *sulfur*—all of which are signs of judgment in Scripture (see 14:10-11; 19:20; Gen 19:24-28; Ps 11:6; Ezek 38:22; Luke 17:29). • The *horses* are reminiscent of the terrifying monsters of Greek tales pictured on ancient buildings and celebrated in ancient dramas. • *One-third:* See note on 8:7-12.

9:20-21 Even when humans are faced with *plagues* and death, repentance is not automatic. People tend to continue in their *evil deeds* and to *worship demons and idols*—things that belong to the created order—rather than worshiping the Creator (see 13:4; 14:9-10; Rom 1:25; 1 Cor 8:4; 10:19-22). • *murders . . . witchcraft . . . immorality . . . thefts:* What people worship parallels the ways in which they live (see 21:8; 22:15; Rom 1:23, 29-32). • Revelation portrays the extent to which depravity controls unbelievers. It is not logical to worship powers and beings that torture and kill oneself and one's friends; the powers of sin and rebellion against God are deceptively captivating.

10:1–11:14 This interlude between the sixth and seventh trumpets is divided into two parts: (1) the seven thunders and the small scroll (10:1-11), and (2) the two witnesses (11:1-13). The interlude ends with the announcement that the second terror is finished (11:14).

10:1 *another mighty angel* (see 5:2; 7:2; cp. 1:12-16): This angel appears similar to the huge bronze Colossus that stood as a symbol of human power in the harbor of Rhodes for several decades before it was toppled by an earthquake in the late 200s BC. The statue still lay broken at the time that John wrote Revelation. It was about 100 feet tall and represented the sun god, Helios. The angel was *surrounded by a cloud*, suggesting that he dwarfed the Rhodes statue and, by implication, all idols. The *rainbow over his head* is a reminder that the enthroned God is encircled by a rainbow (4:3), a biblical symbol of God's covenant with humanity (Gen 9:8-17).

10:2-3 Although the *scroll* (or *book;* also in 10:8-10) is *small*, it is not unimportant. It reveals a small yet critical part of God's purposes in events still to come before eternity begins. • *he gave a great shout:* Cp. Job 37:2-5; Ps 18:13; 29:3-4.

10:4 Revelation reveals God's intentions in the world without eliminating the mystery of God's ways. The martyrs did not receive an immediate answer to their cries (6:10), the meaning of the seventh seal is cloaked in silence (8:1), and here *the seven thunders* are kept *secret* (cp. Dan 12:9). • *Keep secret:* Literally *Seal up.*

10:5-6 While raising one's *right hand* is common in taking *an oath* today, it is rare in biblical literature (cp. Gen 14:22; 24:9; Dan 12:7). • When making an oath, Jews were very careful not to swear lightly by God's *name* (see Exod 20:7). Jesus also rebuked insincere oath-taking (see Matt 5:33-37; 23:16-22). When God swore an oath, he did so in his own name as the highest possible point of reference (see Gen 22:16; Ps 89:35-36; Jer 22:5; Heb 6:13-18).

10:7 *angel blows his trumpet:* See 1 Cor 15:51-54; 1 Thes 4:16. • *God's mysterious plan* for the world is no surprise; *the prophets* who served God in the past warned that the day of the Lord would come (see Joel 2:1-3, 10-11; Amos 5:18-20; Zeph 1:14-18).

10:8-10 As in Ezekiel's experience, the *scroll* tasted *sweet* in the *mouth* (Ezek 3:1-3; see Jer 15:16; see also Ps 19:10; 119:103). The experiences yet to come for God's people would be sweet, including the victory of God's plan and the vindication of his people. John's *sour . . . stomach* resembles the effects of Ezekiel's hard message for Israel (Ezek 3:8-9). The process of bringing God's plan to fruition involves hardship.

11:1 Ezek 40:3; Rev 21:15
11:2 Ezek 40:17-19; Luke 21:24; Rev 12:6; 13:5
11:3 Rev 2:13
11:4 Zech 4:3, 11, 14

11 Then I was told, "You must prophesy
again about many peoples, nations, languages, and kings."

The Two Prophetic Witnesses

11 Then I was given a measuring stick, and I was told, "Go and measure the Temple of God and the altar, and count the number of worshipers.
2 But do not measure the outer courtyard, for it has been turned over to the nations. They will trample the holy city for 42 months.
3 And I will give power to my two witnesses, and they will be clothed in burlap and will prophesy during those 1,260 days."
4 These two prophets are the two olive

The Purpose of the Judgments (9:20-21)

Exod 6:6; 12:12; Lev 26:25; 2 Kgs 17:7-23; Ps 103:6; Prov 16:11; Isa 13:11; 26:21; 59:18; Jer 5:1-9; Ezek 11:21; 39:21-24; Zeph 1:12; Mal 3:5; Luke 12:47; John 5:30; Rom 2:2-11; Heb 2:1-4; 10:29

What is the purpose of the judgments in Revelation? Are they meant to bring about redemption or are they simply intended to destroy? Revelation gives us some clues:

- At the end of the sixth seal, in spite of all the plagues, people "still refused to repent of their evil deeds and turn to God" (9:20-21). For some people, it does not seem to matter what happens to them—they will not change even under pressure.
- The tormented sufferers of the fifth trumpet sought death rather than looking to God (9:6). Many prefer to die rather than to admit their sin.
- In the sixth seal (6:12-17), the people cried for the rocks to fall and hide them from "the wrath of the Lamb" (6:16). Their seeking escape from judgment shows their fear rather than trusting in God.
- Revelation emphasizes the ultimate justice of God (16:5-7) and the principle of retribution. Believers and unbelievers alike will receive exactly what they deserve (see 2:23; 11:18; 14:13; 18:6; 20:12-13; 22:12).
- The judgments are God's partial answer to the prayers of the saints for retribution. Judgment occurs in God's time, not ours (6:9-11; 8:2-5).
- The judgments, like the plagues on Egypt, disprove the power of the earthly gods and of God's enemies (Exod 7:8-12; 12:12; cp. Rev 13:4-17; 19:20-21; 20:9-10).
- The judgments are a part of God's mission and offer a last chance to repent (14:6-7; see 9:20-21; 16:9, 11, 21).

Even though God has made it clear that sin is wrong and judgment is coming (Rom 1:24, 26, 28 and 3:9-18), many people still refuse to repent and accept God's grace (Rom 1:32; 3:24-26). Even in the final days, when God sends his witnesses to prophesy concerning the coming destruction (11:4-6), many people will prefer to align themselves with evil forces and will gloat over the demise of God's prophets (11:10). Those who thus oppose God and flee from him will eventually be excluded from his presence.

Judgment against disobedience and evil ways (see Rom 1:18-28) is inevitable, even in the church (2:5, 16; 3:3, 16). God, however, patiently waits for repentance and offers his grace (2:7, 16-17, 22; 3:3, 20).

10:11 Unlike Ezekiel, who prophesied for Israel alone, John *must prophesy . . . about* (or *against*) all the people of the world. There is debate whether "about" or "against" is the best translation; "about" allows for both promise and judgment (see both at 21:24-27).

11:1-13 This section pictures the willful rejection of God's continuing call for repentance. The many attempts to silence his witnesses ultimately fail, and God triumphs. • Many attempts have been made to identify the *two witnesses* of this chapter. Moses and Elijah, who appeared with Jesus at the transfiguration (Matt 17:3; Mark 9:4; Luke 9:30), are likely candidates (see 11:6); they represent the law and the prophets. Others have suggested Enoch and Elijah because they did not die (see Gen 5:21-24; 2 Kgs 2:11-12). Other possibilities include Peter and Paul, or James and John. More important than their identities is their role of confirming God's message by the testimony of "two or three witnesses" (see Deut 17:6). God provides a twofold witness to the world about the impending judgment, making it clear that his word is certain to be fulfilled (Deut 19:15; Matt 18:15-16).

11:1 The instructions to ***measure the Temple*** are reminiscent of Ezekiel's visions (see Ezek 40:1–42:20; 43:13-17). The Jerusalem Temple was destroyed by the Romans in AD 70; these details symbolize God's precise knowledge of and care for his people who belong to him (cp. 7:2-4; Zech 2:1-5).

11:2-3 ***The outer courtyard*** in the Jerusalem Temple, outside the stone warning fence, was regarded as the place for the Gentile ***nations***. John makes a clear distinction between the people God recognizes and those he does not. • The ***42 months*** and ***1,260 days*** refer to a period of three and a half years, or a broken seven (see notes on Dan 7:24-25; 8:26; 9:24-27). John repeatedly uses these time designations in Revelation when persecution is evident and evil appears to dominate the world. God's people will be secure in him (see note on 11:1) even though God allows evil forces to persecute them (see 13:7; Mark 10:30).

11:3 During the period of persecution, God will not abandon the world but will send his ***two witnesses*** to proclaim the coming judgment, just as God sent Jonah to Nineveh (Jon 1:2; 4:11). • Clothing made of ***burlap*** was symbolic of mourning or repentance (see Gen 37:34; 2 Sam 3:31; Neh 9:1; Esth 4:1; Jon 3:6).

trees and the two lampstands that stand before the Lord of all the earth. 5If anyone tries to harm them, fire flashes from their mouths and consumes their enemies. This is how anyone who tries to harm them must die. 6They have power to shut the sky so that no rain will fall for as long as they prophesy. And they have the power to turn the rivers and oceans into blood, and to strike the earth with every kind of plague as often as they wish.

7When they complete their testimony, the beast that comes up out of the bottomless pit will declare war against them, and he will conquer them and kill them. 8And their bodies will lie in the main street of Jerusalem, the city that is figuratively called "Sodom" and "Egypt," the city where their Lord was crucified. 9And for three and a half days, all peoples, tribes, languages, and nations will stare at their bodies. No one will be allowed to bury them. 10All the people who belong to this world will gloat over them and give presents to each other to celebrate the death of the two prophets who had tormented them.

11But after three and a half days, God breathed life into them, and they stood up! Terror struck all who were staring at them. 12Then a loud voice from heaven called to the two prophets, "Come up here!" And they rose to heaven in a cloud as their enemies watched.

13At the same time there was a terrible earthquake that destroyed a tenth of the city. Seven thousand people died in that earthquake, and everyone else was terrified and gave glory to the God of heaven.

14The second terror is past, but look, the third terror is coming quickly.

Trumpet 7: The Third Terror (11:15-19)

15Then the seventh angel blew his trumpet, and there were loud voices shouting in heaven:

"The world has now become the
Kingdom of our Lord and of his
Christ,
and he will reign forever and ever."

16The twenty-four elders sitting on their thrones before God fell with their faces to the ground and worshiped him. 17And they said,

"We give thanks to you, Lord God, the
[b]Almighty,
the one who is and who always was,
for now you have assumed your great
power
and have begun to reign.

11:5 2 Sam 22:9; 2 Kgs 1:10; Jer 5:14
11:6 Exod 7:17-20; 1 Kgs 17:1
11:7 Dan 7:21; Rev 13:1, 7
11:8 Isa 1:9-10
11:9 Ps 79:2-3
11:11 Ezek 37:5, 10
11:12 2 Kgs 2:11; Acts 1:9; Rev 4:1
11:13 Ezek 38:19-20; Rev 16:9, 11
11:14 Rev 8:13; 9:12
11:15 Ps 10:16; Dan 2:44; 7:14, 27; Rev 10:7; 12:10; 16:17
11:16 Rev 4:4, 10
11:17 Amos 3:13; 4:13; Rev 1:8; 19:6
[b]*pantokratōr* (3841) ›Rev 15:3

11:4 *two olive trees and . . . two lampstands:* See note on 1:12; see also Exod 25:31-40; Zech 4:2-6.

11:5 In one of the psalms, God is portrayed with *fire* coming from his mouth, a picture of judgment on his enemies (Ps 18:8; see also 2 Sam 22:9). Cp. Elijah, 2 Kgs 1:1-15.

11:6 These two witnesses were given *power* to stop the *rain* and bring down plagues, as were Elijah (see 1 Kgs 17:1; 18:41-46) and Moses (see Exod 7:14-24; 8:1–11:10).

11:7-8 When the witnesses finish *their testimony,* the scene changes dramatically. *The beast* (cp. 13:1) is introduced for the first time; it is associated with *the bottomless pit* (or *the abyss,* or *the underworld*; see 9:1, 11; 17:8). Like all enemies of God, the beast engages in *war* against God's witnesses, and he kills them.

11:8 *their bodies will lie in the main street:* Evil is so vindictive that it even desecrates the dead. • *Jerusalem* (literally *the great city*): The designation "the great city" would have immediately suggested Rome to early readers (16:19; 17:18; 18:10, 16, 18-19, 21). But John also describes it as the city *where their Lord was crucified* as well as *Sodom* and *Egypt*—all places that were hostile to God and his people (see also 17:5, 9). • *where their Lord was crucified:* There is a direct connection between how the Lord was treated by evil forces and the experience of persecuted Christians (see Acts 9:5).

11:9 Leaving people's *bodies* out for public display was a way to dishonor them after their death (see 1 Sam 31:10; the usual Roman custom was to leave bodies hanging after crucifixion). • *peoples, tribes, languages, and nations:* All the peoples of the world are represented in this exhibition.

11:10 *All the people . . . will gloat* and *celebrate:* God's enemies despise and reject his messengers.

11:11 The death of the two witnesses is not the end of their ministry. God was not defeated in the death of Jesus and he will not be defeated in the slaughter of his witnesses. The God of the resurrection *breathed life* into the dead so that they *stood up* (see Ezek 37:3-5, 10), leaving no doubt about God's power. • *Terror struck:* It is a fearful experience for sinful humans to face the power of the living God (see Heb 10:31).

11:12 *they rose to heaven in a cloud:* The event is reminiscent of the ascent of Jesus (see Acts 1:9) and others (see 2 Kgs 2:11-12; 1 Thes 4:17).

11:13 An *earthquake* often accompanies key moments in biblical history (see Exod 19:18; 1 Kgs 19:11-12; Matt 27:51). • *Seven thousand:* The number who *died* shows God's involvement in judgment (contrast 1 Kgs 19:18). • *everyone else . . . gave glory to the God of heaven:* Those who survived the earthquake were forced to acknowledge God's power and sovereignty over the world (see Phil 2:9-11).

11:15-19 The *seventh* trumpet ("the third terror," 11:14; see also 9:12) presents a scene of final judgment and the eternal Kingdom. As in 7:9-17, this scene provides a dramatic window into the ultimate Christian hope with God. In the midst of judgment, the reader is reminded of eternity with God.

11:15 *Loud voices* in the court of *heaven* sing a victory hymn; the earth has been transformed into the realm of *our Lord* and *his Christ* (or *his Messiah*), who is enthroned as king *forever.*

11:16-18 *The twenty-four elders,* representing the people of God, confirm God's victorious enthronement (see note on 4:4). Their worship acknowledges God's sovereign rule as *the Almighty* (see 4:10-11; 5:8-10).

11:17 The thanksgiving prayer describes God as *the one who is and who always was;* the description "is still to come" (see 1:4, 8) no longer applies, because in this scene eternity has come and God has *begun to reign.*

11:18
Ps 2:1
Rev 10:7; 19:5; 20:12
11:19
2 Chr 5:7
Rev 4:5; 15:5
12:2
Isa 26:17; 66:6-9
Mic 4:10
12:3
Dan 7:7, 24
Rev 13:1; 17:3, 7, 12, 16
12:4
Dan 8:10
12:5
Ps 2:9
Rev 2:27; 19:15
12:6
Rev 11:2; 13:5
12:7
Dan 10:13; 12:1
Jude 1:9
Rev 12:3
12:9
Gen 3:1
Zech 3:1-2
Matt 4:10
Luke 10:18
Rev 12:3; 20:2-10
[c]*diabolos* (1228)
‣ Rev 20:2
12:10
Job 1:9-11
Zech 3:1
Rev 7:10; 11:15

18 The nations were filled with wrath,
but now the time of your wrath has come.
It is time to judge the dead
and reward your servants the prophets,
as well as your holy people,
and all who fear your name,
from the least to the greatest.
It is time to destroy
all who have caused destruction on the earth."

19 Then, in heaven, the Temple of God was
opened and the Ark of his covenant could be
seen inside the Temple. Lightning flashed,
thunder crashed and roared, and there was
an earthquake and a terrible hailstorm.

7. THE TWO SIDES OF THE GREAT CONFLICT (12:1–14:20)

The Woman and the Dragon

12 Then I witnessed in heaven an event
of great significance. I saw a woman
clothed with the sun, with the moon beneath her feet, and a crown of twelve stars
on her head. 2 She was pregnant, and she
cried out because of her labor pains and the
agony of giving birth.
3 Then I witnessed in heaven another
significant event. I saw a large red dragon
with seven heads and ten horns, with seven
crowns on his heads. 4 His tail swept away
one-third of the stars in the sky, and he threw
them to the earth. He stood in front of the
woman as she was about to give birth, ready
to devour her baby as soon as it was born.
5 She gave birth to a son who was to rule
all nations with an iron rod. And her child
was snatched away from the dragon and
was caught up to God and to his throne.
6 And the woman fled into the wilderness,
where God had prepared a place to care for
her for 1,260 days.
7 Then there was war in heaven. Michael
and his angels fought against the dragon
and his angels. 8 And the dragon lost the battle, and he and his angels were forced out
of heaven. 9 This great dragon—the ancient
serpent called the [c]devil, or Satan, the one
deceiving the whole world—was thrown
down to the earth with all his angels.
10 Then I heard a loud voice shouting
across the heavens,

"It has come at last—
salvation and power
and the Kingdom of our God,
and the authority of his Christ.
For the accuser of our brothers and sisters
has been thrown down to earth—

11:18 ***The nations were filled with wrath*** when they refused to do as God commanded (see Ps 2). But things will *now* be different because God's ***wrath has come.*** God will ***reward*** his ***holy people*** (see 22:12) with new life as his children (see John 1:12; 20:31). • ***fear your name:*** God's name implies his nature; fearing God's name means accepting who he is (see "Fear of the LORD" at Prov 1:7, p. 1030). • The end of the age will be the ***time to destroy*** those who have not accepted God's love (see John 3:16-20). They will go into the lake of fire (20:15). This doom of God's enemies is the third and final terror (11:14).

11:19 This verse provides a dramatic conclusion to the first half of Revelation and a link to the second half. • In this scene, the ***Temple*** and the ***Ark*** are symbols of God's presence; the earthly Ark was the copy of the design of the Ark in heaven (see Exod 25:40; Heb 8:5).

12:1–14:20 The people of God, portrayed as a woman who brings forth the Messiah, are under attack by the devil even though he has already been defeated (12:1-17). With his two minions, the beast and the false prophet, Satan attempts to continue controlling the world (13:1-18) before the final confrontation with the Lord (14:1-20).

12:1-17 Satan (pictured as a dragon) plots to challenge God's purposes but is thwarted. Having failed in direct confrontation with God and Christ, he attempts to attack God's people. Three brief scenes present an overview of the story (12:1-6), followed by elaborations of the war in heaven (12:7-9) and the war on earth (12:13-17).

12:1 The number ***twelve*** suggests that the ***woman*** represents God's people (cp. 12:15-17; see Jer 2:32; 2 Cor 11:2; Eph 5:32), from whom came the Messiah. This woman is marked by God's glory in contrast with the prostitute (see 17:1-6), who is destined for destruction.

12:2 The symbolic woman going through the ***agony*** of ***labor*** portrays Christ's birth, reflecting the biblical theme of Israel's trauma while waiting to be delivered (see Isa 26:16-18; Jer 4:31; Mic 4:9-10; John 16:21).

12:3-4 The ***large red dragon*** represents Satan (see 12:9). • ***seven heads and ten horns:*** The numbers represent a mixture of divine and created powers (see 17:7-14). • The historic battle between evil and the people of God is staged in cosmic dimensions (see Gen 3:1-7, 14-15; Job 1:9-12). • Herod's desire to kill Jesus embodied Satan's attempt ***to devour her baby*** after ***it was born*** (see Matt 2:7-8, 16).

12:5 Jesus was the ***son who was to rule all nations*** (see Luke 1:31-33; 2:30-32; cp. Ps 2:6-12). • Although Jesus was killed by agents of the devil, he was ***snatched away from the dragon*** and raised from the dead (Matt 28:6; Mark 10:33-34; 16:6; 1 Cor 15:3-4). Jesus' entire life on earth, from his birth to his death and resurrection, is compressed into this scene. • ***caught up to God and to his throne:*** See Acts 1:9-11.

12:6 Like the people of Israel who were spiritually refined in ***the wilderness*** (see Hos 2:14-15; Acts 7:38-45) and in exile (see Isa 5:13; Ezek 12:1-3), the Christian church must face its own wilderness. Revelation presents messages of endurance and perseverance in the face of trouble and shows that God provides places of refuge and avenues of escape for his people (cp. 1 Cor 10:13).

12:7-9 This scene clarifies the dragon's identity and power. • God dispatches ***Michael,*** the warrior archangel (see Dan 12:1; Jude 1:9), to confront ***the dragon and his angels.*** God does not have to engage in the battle himself (see Matt 26:53), and Satan is defeated.

12:10-11 ***his Christ:*** Or *his Messiah.* • ***brothers and sisters*** (literally *brothers*; see note on 6:11): Satan's defeat is encouraging for Christians who, like the recipients of Revelation, are not ***afraid to die*** (see John 12:24-26).

the one who accuses them
before our God day and night.
11 And they have defeated him by the
blood of the Lamb
and by their testimony.
And they did not love their lives so much
that they were afraid to die.
12 Therefore, rejoice, O heavens!
And you who live in the heavens,
rejoice!
But terror will come on the earth and
the sea,
for the devil has come down to you in
great anger,
knowing that he has little time."

13 When the dragon realized that he had
been thrown down to the earth, he pursued
the woman who had given birth to the male
child. 14 But she was given two wings like
those of a great eagle so she could fly to the
place prepared for her in the wilderness.
There she would be cared for and protected
from the dragon for a time, times, and half
a time.

15 Then the dragon tried to drown the
woman with a flood of water that flowed
from his mouth. 16 But the earth helped
her by opening its mouth and swallowing
the river that gushed out from the mouth
of the dragon. 17 And the dragon was angry
at the woman and declared war against the
rest of her children—all who keep God's
commandments and maintain their testimony for Jesus.

18 Then the dragon took his stand on the
shore beside the sea.

The Beast out of the Sea

13 Then I saw a beast rising up out of the
sea. It had seven heads and ten horns,
with ten crowns on its horns. And written
on each head were names that [d]blasphemed
God. 2 This beast looked like a leopard, but
it had the feet of a bear and the mouth of a
lion! And the dragon gave the beast his own
power and throne and great authority.

3 I saw that one of the heads of the beast
seemed wounded beyond recovery—but
the fatal wound was healed! The whole
world marveled at this miracle and gave allegiance to the beast. 4 They worshiped the
dragon for giving the beast such power, and
they also worshiped the beast. "Who is as
great as the beast?" they exclaimed. "Who
is able to fight against him?"

5 Then the beast was allowed to speak
great blasphemies against God. And he was
given authority to do whatever he wanted
for forty-two months. 6 And he spoke terrible words of blasphemy against God,
slandering his name and his dwelling—that
is, those who dwell in heaven. 7 And the
beast was allowed to wage war against God's
holy people and to conquer them. And he
was given authority to rule over every tribe

12:11 Rev 2:10; 6:9; 7:14; 15:2
12:12 Rev 8:13; 18:20
12:14 Exod 19:4; Dan 7:25; 12:7; Rev 17:3, 18
12:17 Rev 1:2; 11:7; 13:7
13:1 Dan 7:2-8; Rev 17:12
[d]*blasphēmia* (0988) ‣Matt 15:19
13:2 Dan 7:4-6; Rev 2:13; 12:3
13:3 2 Thes 2:9-12; Rev 17:8
13:4 Exod 15:11
13:5 Dan 7:8, 11, 20, 25; 11:36; 2 Thes 2:4; Rev 11:2
13:6 Rev 12:12
13:7 Rev 5:9; 11:7

12:13 ***When the dragon realized:*** The scene picks up from 12:9.

12:14 ***two wings . . . of a great eagle*** (see Exod 19:4-6; Deut 32:10-11; Isa 40:29-31): God strengthens his people; he does not promise that they will escape persecution or death. • ***from the dragon:*** Literally *from the serpent;* also in 12:15. See 12:9. • ***a time, times, and half a time:*** Usually understood as three and a half years (see 11:2-3).

12:15-16 John pictures Satan as Leviathan (cp. Job 41:1) trying to destroy God's people (the woman; see note on 12:1). The protective ***earth*** responds and the waters of chaos are contained, as at creation (cp. Gen 1:2, 6-7, 9-10).

12:17 The ***dragon*** turns his hostility against the woman's ***children*** (believers) who ***keep God's commandments*** and continue in ***their testimony for Jesus.***

12:18–13:18 John portrays the dragon's conduct of his war (12:17) through two beasts who with Satan form an evil trinity.

12:18 ***Then the dragon took his stand:*** Literally *Then he took his stand;* some manuscripts read *Then I took my stand.* Some translations put this entire sentence into 13:1. • ***on the shore beside the sea:*** By contrast, the Lamb stands on the rock of Zion (14:1).

13:1-10 The first beast is the second member of the evil trinity (see note on 12:18–13:18) and should probably be identified with Roman power (see "Four World Empires" at Dan 2:1-45; 7:1-28, p. 1395).

13:1 The ***beast*** emerges from ***the sea*** (symbolizing evil). Like the dragon, it has ***seven heads and ten horns*** (see 12:3). The ***crowns*** represent its political and military power (cp. 17:3, 7-11; Dan 7:7, 19-20) and indicate that Satan is the head of this beast's empire.

13:2 Satan makes the beast a pseudo-deity by giving it his ***power, throne,*** and ***authority.*** In the first century, Roman emperors increasingly claimed divinity.

13:3 Satan often imitates God. Here ***the beast*** mimics the death and resurrection of Jesus. • That ***one of the heads*** had been fatally ***wounded*** but ***was healed*** has led to its identification with Nero. A tradition emerged that the emperor Nero (AD 54–68) was so evil that he either did not really die or would be reincarnated as another tyrant like Domitian (AD 81–96). In 17:9-10, the beast's seven heads are linked both to *seven hills* (Rome) and to *seven kings.*

13:5-8 The four characteristics of ***the beast*** are that he (1) blasphemes God, (2) has ***authority*** for a limited time, (3) makes ***war*** against God's people, and (4) rules the world. But God is in control.

13:5 The ***forty-two months*** are the three and a half years of persecution and evil domination (see note on 11:2-3).

13:6 ***and his dwelling—that is, those who dwell in heaven:*** Some manuscripts read *and his dwelling and all who dwell in heaven.*

13:7 The beast's ***authority*** extends over all the ***people*** of the world.

13:8 Those who ***worshiped the beast*** receive its mark (13:15-17) and are not listed in the ***Book of Life*** (see 20:12). • ***not written in the Book of Life before the world was made—the Book that belongs to the Lamb who was slaughtered:*** Or *not written in the Book of Life that belongs to the Lamb who was slaughtered before the world was made.*

13:9-10 The scene (13:1-10) ends with a dramatic conclusion patterned on

13:8
Dan 12:1
13:9
Rev 2:7
13:10
Jer 15:2; 43:11
Matt 26:52
Heb 6:12
13:11
Rev 13:1, 4
13:12
Rev 14:9-10; 19:20
13:13
1 Kgs 18:24-39
Matt 24:24
2 Thes 2:9
Rev 19:20
ᵉsēmeion (4592)
‣ Matt 12:38
13:14
2 Thes 2:9
Rev 12:9; 13:3, 12
13:15
Dan 3:3-6
Rev 20:4
13:16
Rev 14:9; 19:18
13:17
Rev 14:9, 11; 16:2; 19:20; 20:4
13:18
Rev 17:9

and people and language and nation. [8]And
all the people who belong to this world worshiped the beast. They are the ones whose
names were not written in the Book of Life
before the world was made—the Book that
belongs to the Lamb who was slaughtered.

[9] Anyone with ears to hear
should listen and understand.
[10] Anyone who is destined for prison
will be taken to prison.
Anyone destined to die by the sword
will die by the sword.

This means that God's holy people must endure persecution patiently and remain faithful.

Another Beast out of the Earth

[11]Then I saw another beast come up out
of the earth. He had two horns like those
of a lamb, but he spoke with the voice of a
dragon. [12]He exercised all the authority
of the first beast. And he required all the
earth and its people to worship the first
beast, whose fatal wound had been healed.
[13]He did astounding ᵉmiracles, even making fire flash down to earth from the sky
while everyone was watching. [14]And with
all the miracles he was allowed to perform
on behalf of the first beast, he deceived all
the people who belong to this world. He
ordered the people to make a great statue
of the first beast, who was fatally wounded
and then came back to life. [15]He was then
permitted to give life to this statue so that
it could speak. Then the statue of the beast
commanded that anyone refusing to worship it must die.

[16]He required everyone—small and great,
rich and poor, free and slave—to be given a
mark on the right hand or on the forehead.
[17]And no one could buy or sell anything
without that mark, which was either the
name of the beast or the number representing his name. [18]Wisdom is needed here.
Let the one with understanding solve the

The Antichrist (13:11)

2 Thes 2:3-10
1 Jn 2:18, 22; 4:2-3
2 Jn 1:7

The term "antichrist" appears only in John's letters (1 Jn 2:18, 22; 4:3; 2 Jn 1:7). John expected many antichrists to appear in history (1 Jn 2:18), all of whom would deny that Jesus was both divine and human (1 Jn 2:22; 4:2-3; 2 Jn 1:7).

In Revelation 13, the hostile spirit opposed to Christ is personified by "another beast" who serves the dragon (Satan) and the first beast. The number of this antichrist, 666, probably stood for Nero and perhaps for the emperor Domitian (see note on 17:8). Emperor worship was a pseudo-religion that stood in opposition to proclaiming Christ as Lord.

Whether John expected a final antichrist even greater than a political figure like Nero or Domitian is uncertain. Either way, Christians must take seriously the presence of evil and its opposition to Christ in the people and power structures of the world. Resisting these enemies may lead to persecution and even death. Our hope rests in victory through Christ.

Jer 15:2; 43:11. ***Anyone with ears to hear*** must pay attention, because judgment is coming (cp. 2:7, 11, 17).

13:10 ***God's holy people*** are summoned to ***endure*** and ***remain faithful*** while experiencing temporary ***persecution***.

13:11-18 ***another beast:*** This second beast, the third member of the evil trinity (see note on 12:18–13:18), is later called the "false prophet" (16:13). As a high priest of false religion, he leads the world into worshiping the first beast and the dragon (see also 16:13-14).

13:11 The ***beast*** is portrayed as ***a lamb***, the same symbol used to represent Christ (see 5:6-13; 7:9-17; 14:1-4), but this lamb ***spoke*** like ***a dragon***. The image is of a fraudulent messiah. • The ***two horns*** might stand for two emperors, perhaps Nero and Domitian.

13:12-15 The second beast derives its power from ***the first beast***, which in turn answers to the dragon (13:4).

13:12 ***he required . . . people to worship the first beast:*** Imperial Rome demanded worship of the emperor Domitian. • ***whose fatal wound had been healed:*** This description might refer to Domitian, who was viewed as the reincarnation of Nero (see note on 13:3). The image is a picture of the constant reemergence of evil, particularly in the latter days (see note on 17:8).

13:13-15 In NT times, false prophets astounded people with reports of divine visitations and of idols speaking for the gods they represented (see Acts 16:16-18; 1 Cor 12:2-3). Such practices involved worship of demons (see 1 Cor 10:20-21) and were epitomized in the Roman emperor cult. Those who refused to conform were put to death.

13:14-15 ***he was allowed. . . . He was then permitted:*** God never relinquishes ultimate authority. These creatures of evil have been allowed to rebel against God, but they are not in control.

13:16-17 ***small and great, rich and poor, free and slave:*** All humanity is required to accept the beast's evil ***mark*** of ownership (see 14:9, 11; 19:20; 20:4), a precondition for all commerce (the right to ***buy or sell***). The text does not explicitly tell us what the mark is or looks like. • ***On the right hand or on the forehead*** suggests the branding of slaves—the beast owns them. • ***the number representing his name:*** In both Hebrew and Greek, letters of the alphabet represent numbers, which gave names a numerical value (13:18).

13:18 ***Wisdom is needed:*** John is giving a clue to help his readers ***solve the meaning*** of the beast's ***number***. • ***of a man*** (or ***of humanity***): John hides the man's identity, perhaps because revealing the name would place him and his readers in danger (cp. use of Babylon as a symbol for Rome, 17:9). • The number ***666*** (some manuscripts read *616*) represents supernatural evil (see

meaning of the number of the beast, for it
is the number of a man. His number is 666.

The Lamb and the 144,000

14 Then I saw the Lamb standing on
Mount Zion, and with him were
144,000 who had his name and his Father's
name written on their foreheads. 2And I
heard a sound from heaven like the roar of
mighty ocean waves or the rolling of loud
thunder. It was like the sound of many harp-
ists playing together.
3This great choir sang a wonderful
new song in front of the throne of God
and before the four living beings and the
twenty-four elders. No one could learn this
song except the 144,000 who had been redeemed from the earth. 4They have kept
themselves as pure as virgins, following the
Lamb wherever he goes. They have been
purchased from among the people on the
earth as a special offering to God and to the
Lamb. 5They have told no lies; they are without blame.

The Three Angels Proclaim Judgment and Blessing

6And I saw another angel flying through
the sky, carrying the eternal Good News
to proclaim to the people who belong to
this world—to every nation, tribe, language,
and people. 7"Fear God," he shouted. "Give
glory to him. For the time has come when
he will sit as judge. Worship him who made
the heavens, the earth, the sea, and all the
springs of water."
8Then another angel followed him
through the sky, shouting, "Babylon is fallen—
that great city is fallen—because she made
all the nations of the world drink the wine of
her passionate immorality."
9Then a third angel followed them, shouting, "Anyone who worships the beast and
his statue or who accepts his mark on the
forehead or on the hand 10must drink the
wine of God's anger. It has been poured full
strength into God's cup of wrath. And they
will be tormented with fire and burning sulfur in the presence of the holy angels and
the Lamb. 11The smoke of their torment will
rise forever and ever, and they will have no
relief day or night, for they have worshiped
the beast and his statue and have accepted
the mark of his name."
12This means that God's holy people must
endure persecution patiently, obeying his
commands and maintaining their faith in
Jesus.
13And I heard a voice from heaven saying,
"Write this down: Blessed are those who die

14:1 Rev 3:12; 7:4
14:2 Rev 1:15; 19:6
14:3 Rev 4:4, 6
14:4 2 Cor 11:2; Rev 5:9; 7:17
14:5 Ps 32:2; Isa 53:9; Zeph 3:13; 1 Pet 2:22
14:6 Rev 5:9
14:7 Acts 4:24; Rev 15:4
14:8 Isa 21:9; Jer 51:8; Rev 16:19; 17:5; 18:2, 10
14:9 Rev 13:12-17
14:10 Ps 75:8; Isa 51:17, 22-23; Jer 25:15; Rev 16:19; 19:20; 20:10; 21:8
14:11 Isa 34:10; Rev 13:12-17
14:12 Rev 2:13; 12:17; 13:10
14:13 Heb 4:10

"Symbolic Numbers" at 4:4, p. 2173). John might have used the transliteration *Caesar Neron* (a Hebrew spelling of the name) to arrive at the number 666. Later scribes, who spoke Greek but not Hebrew, corrected the number to 616 in some manuscripts, probably to match the name's numerical value in Greek.

14:1-5 The true *Lamb* and his followers starkly contrast with the evil trinity.

14:1 *standing* (see 5:6; note on 12:18). • *144,000:* God's righteous remnant (see note on 7:4-8). • The brand on *their foreheads* (contrast 13:16-17) is the *name* of both *the Lamb* and *his Father,* reflecting the union of Jesus and the Father (see John 5:20-23; 14:5-10; 17:22).

14:2-3 *This great choir sang a . . . new song* that only those *who had been redeemed from the earth* could *learn.* These people had died and were already with the Lord, which might explain why John did not include the content of their refrain for readers still in the battle of life (cp. 2 Cor 12:4).

14:4-5 These warriors were ritually *pure* (unpolluted) and morally *without blame.* • *They have kept themselves as pure as virgins* (literally *They are virgins who have not defiled themselves with women*): Referring to men as *virgins* is a metaphor for the faithfulness of God's people. The image might refer to the church as the virgin bride of Christ (see 2 Cor 11:2; Eph 5:25-27); it also suggests that the church constitutes soldiers in a holy war that are required to keep themselves chaste (see Deut 23:9-10; 1 Sam 21:5). • These faithful people are *a special offering* (literally *firstfruits;* see Exod 13:14-16; 23:19; Lev 23:9-14; Num 3:40-51; 18:15-20; Luke 2:22-24) who *have been purchased* for God. • *They have told no lies:* John teaches that liars will never enter heaven (21:8, 27; 22:15; see also John 8:44). The followers of Jesus speak and live the truth (see also John 8:32; 14:6).

14:6-13 Three angels are *flying through the sky* with messages from God.

14:6-7 The first *angel* proclaims *the eternal Good News,* which includes the message that God *will sit as judge*—the end is near, so this message provides a last-chance summons to repentance.

14:8 *Babylon* is probably a cryptic designation for Rome (see 16:19; 17:5-9); it represents earthly power and corruption. The coming of God as judge (14:7) includes the end of earthly powers.

14:9-11 The *third angel* announces God's judgment (14:7) on the counterfeit worship of the *beast and his statue* (see 13:12-18; 19:20; 20:4). God's response to the rebellion against his reign is *anger* or *wrath,* pictured as a *cup* of bitter *wine* (see 16:1-21; 19:15). • *fire and burning sulfur . . . smoke:* This description of judgment (see also 19:20; 20:10, 14-15) echoes God's judgment of Sodom and Gomorrah (Gen 18:16–19:28). • Those condemned to a fiery end will suffer *in the presence of the holy angels and the Lamb* (cp. Luke 16:22-24).

14:12 The threat of *persecution* and death was very real to the Christians first reading this letter, so John calls God's people to obedience and faithfulness (see 2:10; 3:10; 12:17; 13:10).

14:13 A dramatic *voice from heaven* once again instructs John to *write* (see 1:11, 19; 21:5; cp. 10:4). • *Blessed are those who die in the Lord:* God desires that those who endure persecution be with him and enjoy his blessings and *rest.* • The mention of *hard work* and *good deeds* in connection with eternal reward foreshadows the assigning of rewards based on works (20:12).

14:14
Dan 7:13
Rev 1:13

14:15
Joel 3:13
Matt 13:39-40
Mark 4:29

14:18
Joel 3:13
Rev 6:9; 14:15

14:19
Isa 63:2-6
Rev 19:15

14:20
Gen 49:11
Isa 63:3
Lam 1:15
Rev 19:15

15:1
Lev 26:21
Rev 15:6; 16:1; 21:9

15:2
Rev 4:6

15:3
Exod 15:1
Deut 32:1-4
Ps 145:17
Jer 10:7
Amos 3:13; 4:13
Rev 1:8; 4:8
[f]*pantokratōr* (3841)
‣ Rev 16:7

15:4
Ps 86:9
Jer 10:6-7
Mal 1:11

15:5
Rev 11:19

in the Lord from now on. Yes, says the Spirit,
they are blessed indeed, for they will rest
from their hard work; for their good deeds
follow them!"

The Harvest of the Earth

[14]Then I saw a white cloud, and seated on
the cloud was someone like the Son of Man.
He had a gold crown on his head and a
sharp sickle in his hand.
[15]Then another angel came from the
Temple and shouted to the one sitting on
the cloud, "Swing the sickle, for the time of
harvest has come; the crop on earth is ripe."
[16]So the one sitting on the cloud swung his
sickle over the earth, and the whole earth
was harvested.
[17]After that, another angel came from
the Temple in heaven, and he also had a
sharp sickle. [18]Then another angel, who had
power to destroy with fire, came from the altar. He shouted to the angel with the sharp
sickle, "Swing your sickle now to gather the
clusters of grapes from the vines of the
earth, for they are ripe for judgment." [19]So
the angel swung his sickle over the earth and
loaded the grapes into the great winepress
of God's wrath. [20]The grapes were trampled
in the winepress outside the city, and blood
flowed from the winepress in a stream about
180 miles long and as high as a horse's bridle.

8. ACT III: SEVEN BOWLS OF JUDGMENT (15:1–16:21)

The Song of Moses and of the Lamb (15:1-4)

15 Then I saw in heaven another marvelous event of great significance. Seven
angels were holding the seven last plagues,
which would bring God's wrath to completion. [2]I saw before me what seemed to be
a glass sea mixed with fire. And on it stood
all the people who had been victorious over
the beast and his statue and the number representing his name. They were all holding
harps that God had given them. [3]And they
were singing the song of Moses, the servant
of God, and the song of the Lamb:

"Great and marvelous are your works,
O Lord God, the [f]Almighty.
Just and true are your ways,
O King of the nations.
[4] Who will not fear you, Lord,
and glorify your name?
For you alone are holy.
All nations will come and worship before
you,
for your righteous deeds have been
revealed."

The Open Temple and the Seven Angels (15:5-8)

[5]Then I looked and saw that the Temple in
heaven, God's Tabernacle, was thrown wide

14:14-20 Two brief scenes portray God's judgment.

14:14 ***like the Son of Man*** (or *like a son of man;* see Dan 7:13): "Son of Man" is a title Jesus used for himself (see Matt 8:20; 9:6; 12:8; Mark 2:10; 9:31; Luke 9:22; 22:69; John 3:13-14). • A ***gold crown*** is a symbol of status or power, clearly distinguishing Jesus from the angels (see 4:4; 6:2; 9:7; 12:3; 13:1). • The ***sharp sickle*** is symbolic of God's harvest of judgment (see 14:17-18; see also Jer 51:33; Hos 6:11; Mic 4:12-13).

14:15-18 The ***Temple*** and the ***altar*** represent God's presence (see 9:13; 11:19; 16:7).

14:18-20 The ***ripe . . . grapes*** (see Amos 8:2) that are ***trampled in the winepress*** emphasize God's power to judge (see 19:15; Joel 3:13). • Winepresses were built outside cities and towns; here, ***the city*** is Jerusalem. The bloody river of death stretched about ***180 miles*** (Greek *1,600 stadia* [300 kilometers]): God's enemies stand no chance when the Son of Man comes in judgment. The carnage here is closely linked with the final battle in 19:17-21; God is just and fair in giving people exactly what they deserve (see 16:5-7).

15:1–16:21 The third and final cycle of seven judgments (see note on 6:1–16:21) is introduced with a vision of God's victorious people singing a hymn of praise (15:2-4). Then a scene of the Temple is presented (15:5-8), from which angels emerge bearing the bowls of God's judgment upon the earth (16:1-21).

15:1 This cycle of ***seven last plagues*** (15:1–16:21) brings ***God's wrath*** against his enemies ***to completion*** (see 16:17; Amos 1–2; Rom 1:18–2:16). Revelation returns later to the subjects of God's wrath (19:15-21).

15:2 The ***glass sea mixed with fire*** symbolizes victory through testing. Those ***who had been victorious over the beast*** (see 13:1-8, 15-18) hold ***harps*** that represent ultimate peace. Their place ***on*** the ***glass sea*** (cp. 4:6) symbolizes their endurance in the ***fire*** of persecution (cp. Ps 66:12; Isa 43:2; Dan 3:8-30).

15:3-4 The ***song of Moses*** and ***the Lamb*** signifies that God's will is united in the old and new covenants.

15:3 The ***Lord God, the Almighty*** (see also 1:8; 4:8; 11:17; 16:7; 19:6; 21:22): For persecuted Christians, the message that God is all-powerful provides great comfort and security. • The truth that God is also ***just and true*** is the foundation of human integrity in the midst of a confused, unjust, and dishonest world. • God is the supreme, universal ***King of the nations*** (some manuscripts read *King of the ages*), not a localized deity attached to one nation or to a human monarch with limited authority.

15:4 ***Who will not fear . . . and glorify your name?*** This rhetorical question (cp. Jer 10:7) assumes that only a fool would fail to do so (cp. 14:7; 16:9; see Ps 14:1; 53:1). • God ***alone*** is ***holy:*** See 16:5; Lev 11:44; 1 Pet 1:16. God's holiness is the basis for our worship and salvation. • ***All nations will . . . worship:*** Some will be forced to acknowledge God (cp. Phil 2:10-11), but all will recognize that God's ***deeds*** and judgments ***have been revealed*** and are ***righteous*** and just.

15:5-6 ***God's Tabernacle*** implies God's presence (see John 1:14); even the plagues have their source in God's presence. Christ's sacrifice (Matt 27:51; Mark 15:38; Heb 6:19-20; 10:19-20) removed the veil between God and humanity (see Exod 26:31-35; Lev 16:1-34). Now those who do not belong to Christ experience the full force of God's presence (see 20:11-15; Isa 13:4-12; Zeph 2:1-3; Mal 3:2-3). • ***white linen*** (other manuscripts read *white stone;* still others read *white [garments] made of linen*): Linen, a symbol of purity, was also worn by the priests when performing their

open. 6The seven angels who were holding
the seven plagues came out of the Temple.
They were clothed in spotless white linen
with gold sashes across their chests. 7Then
one of the four living beings handed each
of the seven angels a gold bowl filled with
the wrath of God, who lives forever and ever.
8The Temple was filled with smoke from
God's glory and power. No one could enter
the Temple until the seven angels had completed pouring out the seven plagues.

The Seven Bowls of the Seven Plagues (16:1-21)

The First Bowl: Malignant Sores

16 Then I heard a mighty voice from the
Temple say to the seven angels, "Go
your ways and pour out on the earth the
seven bowls containing God's wrath."
2So the first angel left the Temple and
poured out his bowl on the earth, and horrible, malignant sores broke out on everyone
who had the mark of the beast and who worshiped his statue.

The Second and Third Bowls: Waters Turned to Blood

3Then the second angel poured out his bowl
on the sea, and it became like the blood of a
corpse. And everything in the sea died.
4Then the third angel poured out his bowl
on the rivers and springs, and they became
blood. 5And I heard the angel who had authority over all water saying,

"You are just, O Holy One, who is and
who always was,
because you have sent these
judgments.
6 Since they shed the blood
of your holy people and your prophets,
you have given them blood to drink.
It is their just reward."

7And I heard a voice from the altar, saying,

"Yes, O Lord God, the [g]Almighty,
your judgments are true and just."

The Fourth and Fifth Bowls: Scorching Sun and Smothering Darkness

8Then the fourth angel poured out his bowl
on the sun, causing it to scorch everyone
with its fire. 9Everyone was burned by this
blast of heat, and they cursed the name of
God, who had control over all these plagues.
They did not repent of their sins and turn to
God and give him glory.
10Then the fifth angel poured out his bowl
on the throne of the beast, and his kingdom
was plunged into darkness. His subjects
ground their teeth in anguish, 11and they
cursed the God of [h]heaven for their pains
and sores. But they did not repent of their
evil deeds and turn to God.

15:6 Lev 26:21; Rev 1:13
15:7 Rev 4:6, 9
15:8 Exod 40:34; 1 Kgs 8:10-11; 2 Chr 5:13-14; Isa 6:4
16:1 Isa 66:6; Zeph 3:8; Rev 11:19; 15:1
16:2 Exod 9:9-11; Rev 8:7; 13:15-17
16:3 Exod 7:17-21; Rev 8:8-9
16:4 Exod 7:17-21; Ps 78:44; Rev 8:10
16:5 Rev 1:4, 8; 4:8; 11:17
16:6 Ps 79:3; Isa 49:26; Matt 23:35
16:7 Rev 1:8; 6:9; 14:18; 15:3; 19:2
[g]*pantokratōr* (3841) ‣Rev 16:14
16:8 Rev 6:12; 8:12
16:9 Rev 11:13
16:10 Exod 10:21; Isa 8:22; Rev 8:12; 9:2; 13:2
16:11 Rev 9:20-21
[h]*ouranos* (3772) ‣Rev 21:1

duties (see Exod 28:39-43; Lev 16:4, 23; see also Ezek 9:2-3; Dan 12:6-7). The function of these angels is not intercession; they are agents of judgment. The linen therefore represents the purity and justice of God's judgment. • The ***gold sashes across their chests*** probably symbolize their divine mission as ministers of justice on God's behalf (cp. 1:13).

15:7 ***the four living beings:*** See 4:6-8. • ***a gold bowl:*** These bowls are probably like the offering pans that were used in ancient worship (see Exod 37:16).

15:8 ***The Temple was filled with smoke*** as a symbol of ***God's glory and power*** (Isa 6:4; see Exod 19:16-18; 40:34-35; 1 Kgs 8:10-13).

16:1-21 These ***seven bowls*** filled with God's wrath represent the final judgments on the world; with the seventh bowl, ***"It is finished!"*** is shouted from God's throne (16:17; cp. John 19:30).

16:1 The ***mighty voice*** probably belongs to God (also in 6:6; 9:13; 16:17; 18:4; 19:5; see Isa 66:6).

16:2 The ***malignant sores*** are reminiscent of the sixth plague of Egypt (Exod 9:9-11). • ***mark of the beast:*** See 13:13-17; 14:9-10.

16:3-4 The plagues of the ***second*** and ***third*** bowls are similar to the first plague of Egypt (Exod 7:17-21). Perhaps John had in mind that much of Rome's food and wealth came by sea. After Julius Caesar rid the sea of pirates, shipping became Rome's lifeblood. Its end would mean economic death for the empire (see 18:17-19).

16:5-6 ***the angel who had authority over all water:*** Angels and archangels are portrayed as having special roles in the hierarchy of heaven (see Dan 8:16; 9:21; 10:13, 21; 12:1; Luke 1:19, 26; see also *1 Enoch* 66:1-2). This angel confirms ***these judgments*** as coming from God, who is both ***just*** and ***holy.***

16:6 Punishment of God's enemies is a ***just reward*** because they killed God's ***holy people*** and ***prophets.*** Because they have ***shed . . . blood,*** they must ***drink . . . blood.*** The principle of *lex talionis* (the law of retribution), the basis of Roman and Jewish jurisprudence, means that God is completely just in judging and rewarding people on the basis of what they have done (see 2:23; 11:18; 14:13; 18:6; 20:12, 13; 22:12).

16:7 ***I heard a voice from the altar*** (literally *I heard the altar*): The antiphonal response to the angel's proclamation (16:5-6) affirms God's authority and justice. This doxology in the midst of judgment reminds persecuted Christians that God truly cares about his suffering servants and fulfills his own purpose in everything.

16:8-9 The ***fourth . . . bowl*** is unlike any of the plagues of Egypt or the earlier seals or trumpets. • ***Everyone was burned:*** Contrast 7:16. Yet the recipients of this judgment refused to ***repent*** or ***give*** God ***glory*** (see 9:20-21; 16:11; cp. 14:6-7); they even ***cursed the name of God.***

16:10-11 ***the throne of the beast:*** John might be alluding to Rome, the political power of his time. Built on seven hills (17:9), Rome's empire spanned the sea (13:1) and ruled the world (13:7). • ***plunged into darkness:*** Similar to the ninth plague of Egypt (Exod 10:22) and to the fourth trumpet (8:12). • ***ground their teeth*** [literally *gnawed their tongues*] . . . ***cursed the God of heaven:*** Both pain and hostility motivated these responses to punishment (cp. Matt 8:12; 13:42, 50; 22:13; 24:51; 25:30; Luke 13:28).

16:12 Isa 11:15-16; 44:27 Jer 50:38; 51:36 Rev 9:14
16:13 Rev 12:3; 13:1, 11-17
16:14 Rev 6:17; 17:14; 19:19 [i]*daimonion* (1140) ‣Matt 10:8 [j]*pantokratōr* (3841) ‣Rev 19:6
16:15 1 Thes 5:2 Rev 3:3, 18
16:16 Judg 5:19 2 Kgs 9:27; 23:29 Zech 12:11
16:17 Isa 66:6 Rev 11:15; 21:6
16:18 Dan 12:1 Matt 24:21 Rev 4:5; 6:12
16:19 Rev 14:8, 10 [k]*orgē* (3709) ‣Rev 19:15
16:20 Rev 6:14; 20:11
16:21 Exod 9:23-25 Rev 11:19; 16:9, 11
17:1 Jer 51:13 Rev 17:15; 19:2
17:2 Jer 51:7 Rev 14:8; 18:3

The Sixth Bowl: Deceitful Spirits and Armageddon

12 Then the sixth angel poured out his
bowl on the great Euphrates River, and it
dried up so that the kings from the east
could march their armies toward the west
without hindrance. 13 And I saw three evil
spirits that looked like frogs leap from the
mouths of the dragon, the beast, and the
false prophet. 14 They are [i]demonic spirits
who work miracles and go out to all the rulers of the world to gather them for battle against the Lord on that great judgment day of God the [j]Almighty.

> 15 "Look, I will come as unexpectedly as
> a thief! Blessed are all who are watching
> for me, who keep their clothing ready so
> they will not have to walk around naked
> and ashamed."

16 And the demonic spirits gathered all the rulers and their armies to a place with the Hebrew name *Armageddon.*

The Seventh Bowl: God's Judgment

17 Then the seventh angel poured out his
bowl into the air. And a mighty shout came
from the throne in the Temple, saying, "It is
finished!" 18 Then the thunder crashed and
rolled, and lightning flashed. And a great
earthquake struck—the worst since people
were placed on the earth. 19 The great city
of Babylon split into three sections, and the cities of many nations fell into heaps of rubble. So God remembered all of Babylon's sins, and he made her drink the cup that was filled with the wine of his fierce [k]wrath.
20 And every island disappeared, and all the
mountains were leveled. 21 There was a terrible hailstorm, and hailstones weighing as much as seventy-five pounds fell from the sky onto the people below. They cursed God because of the terrible plague of the hailstorm.

9. BABYLON THE GREAT (17:1–19:10)

The Great Prostitute (17:1-18)

17 One of the seven angels who had poured out the seven bowls came over and spoke to me. "Come with me," he said, "and I will show you the judgment that is going to come on the great prostitute, who rules over many waters. 2 The kings of the world
have committed adultery with her, and the people who belong to this world have been made drunk by the wine of her immorality."

16:12 The *Euphrates,* the largest *river* in Mesopotamia, stood between Babylon and Israel and formed the eastern boundary of the Roman empire. If it *dried up,* it would allow *kings from the east* to move their armies westward (cp. 9:13-16). From John's perspective as an ancient Jewish writer, these armies would always be identified with Mesopotamia rather than with countries farther east such as China or India.

16:13-14 Three agents of deceit, *evil* (literally *unclean*) *spirits* in the form of *frogs,* represent the *demonic* role of the evil trinity. Although the powers of evil *battle against the Lord,* it is *God the Almighty,* not any evil power, who is in control.

16:15 Readers are warned to *look* because the Lord will *come as unexpectedly as a thief* (see also 3:3; Matt 24:43; 25:13; 1 Thes 5:2; 2 Pet 3:10). Being ready for his coming requires preparation; those who are not prepared will not have the proper *clothing* and will find themselves *naked* (see Matt 22:11-13). This imagery recalls the two failing churches: lifeless Sardis, which is told to "wake up" (3:2), and lukewarm Laodicea, which is advised to obtain proper clothing (3:18).

16:16 The name *Armageddon* (or *Harmagedon*) is probably derived from *har* ("mountain," "hill") plus *Megiddo,* which was one of the three cities fortified by Solomon along with Gezer in the south and Hazor in the north (1 Kgs 9:15). The fortress of Megiddo stood on a hill in the largest pass through the Carmel range, strategically guarding the Jezreel Valley. The city was situated on the Via Maris, the main highway between Egypt and Mesopotamia. Many armies used this route, and the site became known as a bloody battlefield. It was here, for instance, that Pharaoh Neco, on his way to fight the Assyrians, killed Josiah (2 Kgs 23:29). Armageddon thus became a symbolic term epitomizing the final conflict between God and the forces of evil.

16:17 When *the seventh . . . bowl* is poured out, an unexpected event occurs. The enemies of God had assembled themselves for battle, but when the decisive moment arrives, instead of the battle comes the shout, *"It is finished!"* Jesus uttered these same words from the cross when he had finished his work (John 19:30). No one can ultimately fight God. Therefore, this scene pictures an end to rebellion against God. What remains are various descriptions of the end.

16:18-20 The catastrophic events of this judgment scene recapitulate the scenes portraying the destruction of the world (6:12-14; 11:13). They also foreshadow the final judgment (20:11-15) when the earth will be dismantled to make way for the new creation (21:1; cp. Isa 45:2; Rom 8:19-22).

16:21 Despite the severity of these plagues, the people of the world again *cursed God* rather than recognizing his reason for the judgments (see 9:20; 16:9, 11). • The *terrible hailstorm* is a reminder of the seventh plague on Egypt (Exod 9:23-24). • *seventy-five pounds:* Greek *1 talent* [34 kilograms].

17:1–19:10 The great drama in this section focuses on the powers that are hostile to God and responsible for the persecution and suffering of God's people. Rome's power was captivating to many (17:6); John purposely defines Rome's sins and provides God's assessment (17:3-18) before outlining its fall (18:1-24) and heaven's response (19:1-10).

17:1 *One of the . . . angels* of judgment addresses John and summons him to a new scene in which he sees the coming *judgment* of *the great prostitute, who rules over many waters.* Rome, located on the Tiber River, controlled the seats of power and water trade routes throughout the Mediterranean, from the British Isles to the Euphrates River.

17:2 *Adultery with her* is a biblical image for serving other gods (see, e.g., Exod 34:12-16; Judg 2:17; Hos 2). • *drunk by . . . her immorality:* Drunkenness in Scripture often depicts nations that indulge in wanton and immoral behavior (see 18:3, 9; Jer 25:27; 51:7; Lam 4:21; Ezek 23:33).

3So the angel took me in the Spirit into
the wilderness. There I saw a woman sitting
on a scarlet beast that had seven heads and
ten horns, and blasphemies against God
were written all over it. 4The woman wore
purple and scarlet clothing and beautiful
jewelry made of gold and precious gems
and pearls. In her hand she held a gold goblet full of obscenities and the impurities
of her immorality. 5A mysterious name
was written on her forehead: "Babylon the
Great, Mother of All Prostitutes and Obscenities in the World." 6I could see that she
was drunk—drunk with the blood of God's
holy people who were witnesses for Jesus. I
stared at her in complete amazement.

7"Why are you so amazed?" the angel
asked. "I will tell you the mystery of this
woman and of the beast with seven heads
and ten horns on which she sits. 8The beast
you saw was once alive but isn't now. And
yet he will soon come up out of the bottomless pit and go to eternal destruction. And
the people who belong to this world, whose
names were not written in the [a]Book of Life
before the world was made, will be amazed
at the reappearance of this beast who had
died.

9"This calls for a mind with understanding: The seven heads of the beast represent
the seven hills where the woman rules. They
also represent seven kings. 10Five kings
have already fallen, the sixth now reigns,
and the seventh is yet to come, but his reign
will be brief.

11"The scarlet beast that was, but is no
longer, is the eighth king. He is like the other
seven, and he, too, is headed for destruction.
12The ten horns of the beast are ten kings
who have not yet risen to power. They will
be appointed to their kingdoms for one
brief moment to reign with the beast.
13They will all agree to give him their power
and authority. 14Together they will go to war
against the Lamb, but the Lamb will defeat
them because he is Lord of all lords and
King of all kings. And his called and chosen
and faithful ones will be with him."

15Then the angel said to me, "The waters
where the prostitute is ruling represent
masses of people of every nation and language. 16The scarlet beast and his ten horns
all hate the prostitute. They will strip her
naked, eat her flesh, and burn her remains
with fire. 17For God has put a plan into
their minds, a plan that will carry out his

17:3 Rev 1:10; 12:6; 13:1
17:4 Jer 51:7; Ezek 28:13
17:5 Rev 17:2, 7
17:6 Rev 16:6; 18:24
17:8 Dan 12:1; Rev 11:7; 13:1, 3; [a]*biblion* (0975) ‣Rev 20:12
17:9 Rev 13:18
17:12 Dan 7:20, 24; Rev 18:10, 17, 19
17:14 Matt 22:14; 1 Tim 6:15; Rev 16:14; 19:16
17:15 Rev 13:7; 17:1
17:16 Lev 21:9; Ezek 16:37, 39; Rev 18:8, 19
17:17 Rev 10:7; 17:13

17:3-4 John is carried *in the Spirit* (or *in spirit*) *into the wilderness,* his way of describing a visionary experience (see 1:10; 4:2). He sees a depiction of Rome's moral corruption and excessive luxury (see 18:12-13, 16) that illustrates how such wealth can become an abomination to God. • The *beast* here is like the second figure in the evil trinity (see 13:1-4). • ***blasphemies against God:*** See 13:5-6. • ***purple and scarlet:*** Clothing in these two colors indicated royalty and carnality, respectively. • ***a gold goblet:*** See Jer 51:7.

17:5 Using code language, John was probably referring to Rome (see 17:9) as ***Babylon the Great, Mother of All Prostitutes.*** Babylon was a symbol of the idolatries and demonic *obscenities* of the world. As *Mother,* she had produced offspring who copied her character. Rome, like Babylon, prostituted herself to false gods and led other nations into adultery and idolatry.

17:6 ***God's holy people . . . were witnesses for Jesus*** to the point of shedding their *blood* (see 16:6; Heb 12:4). In John's time, Rome was responsible for this persecution.

17:7 In response to John's amazement, *the angel* prepares him to understand the *mystery* (17:8-14).

17:8-11 The destruction within this vision contrasts with the destiny of the people of God in the new heaven and earth (see 21:1-4).

17:8 ***The beast . . . was once alive but isn't now . . . will soon come up:*** When Domitian became emperor (AD 81–96), he was as evil as Nero (both were fierce persecutors of the church), and many thought he was the embodiment of Nero's spirit, if not Nero himself (perhaps similar to the way that John the Baptist was considered to embody Elijah's spirit; see Mal 4:5; Matt 11:14; Luke 1:17; John 1:21). • ***you saw:*** The past tense indicates that the angel's interpretation took place after John's vision. • ***was once alive but isn't now:*** This contrasts with God, "who is, who always was, and who is still to come" (1:4, 8). • ***the bottomless pit*** (or *the abyss,* or *the underworld*): See note on 9:1-12. • In contrast to God's people, the ***people*** of ***this world*** are ***not written in the Book of Life*** (see 20:11-15). They ***will be amazed*** by the apparent resurrection of the beast (see note on 17:10-11; see also 13:13-17).

17:9 ***The seven heads of the beast represent the seven hills*** on which Rome was built (see note on 16:10-11). • ***the woman:*** see 17:3-6.

17:10-11 ***five kings have already fallen:*** If these kings represent Roman emperors, and the starting point for numbering them is the switch from a republic to an empire with Augustus (29 BC—AD 14), then the fifth in line would be Nero (AD 54–68), ***the sixth*** would be Vespasian, and ***the seventh*** would be Titus. ***The eighth king*** would then be Domitian. • ***that was, but is no longer:*** Early commentators argued that Domitian was an embodiment of Nero's spirit (see note on 17:8). • ***like the other seven:*** This apparently invincible ruler was also ***headed for destruction.***

17:12-13 The ***ten horns,*** symbolic of the world kingdoms that follow ***the beast,*** rule simultaneously under his direction. While these verses have caused speculation concerning a ten-nation confederacy (from the client kingdoms of Rome, to the states opposed to the Holy Roman empire, to the European Union), these conjectures are beside the point, which is that all nations opposed to God will be defeated (17:14).

17:14 Whatever power they amass, the beast and ten kings (17:11-12) have no hope of winning because Jesus is ***Lord of all lords*** (see 19:11-16). Those God has ***called and chosen*** and who remain ***faithful*** to him will stand ***with him*** as victors.

17:15-16 While ***the prostitute*** rules over the ***masses,*** it does not bring her victory. Instead, the ***beast*** hates and kills the great prostitute. Satan strikes even those he uses for his evil purposes.

17:17 John provides another reminder that God is in control; God puts ***a plan*** into the ***minds*** of the enemy that will fulfill the Lord's divine ***purposes*** (e.g., Exod 7:3; 35:31-35; Ezra 7:27; Rom 9:18, 21).

17:18 Rev 16:19
18:1 Ezek 43:2; Rev 10:1
18:2 Isa 13:19-22; 21:9; 34:10-11; Jer 50:39; Rev 14:8
18:3 Rev 17:2
18:4 Gen 19:15; Isa 48:20; 52:11; Jer 51:6, 9, 45; 2 Cor 6:17
18:5 Gen 18:20; Jer 51:9; Rev 16:19
18:6 Ps 137:8; Jer 50:15, 29; Rev 17:4
18:7 Isa 47:8
18:8 Isa 47:9; Jer 50:31-34; Rev 17:16
18:9 Ezek 26:16; Rev 17:2
18:10 Ezek 26:17; Rev 14:8

purposes. They will agree to give their authority to the scarlet beast, and so the words of God will be fulfilled.
18And this woman you saw in your vision represents the great city that rules over the kings of the world."

Seven Songs: The Fall of Babylon (18:1-24)

Song 1: A Taunt Song

18 After all this I saw another angel come down from heaven with great authority, and the earth grew bright with his splendor.
2He gave a mighty shout:

"Babylon is fallen—that great city is fallen!
  She has become a home for demons.
She is a hideout for every foul spirit,
  a hideout for every foul vulture
  and every foul and dreadful animal.
3 For all the nations have fallen
  because of the wine of her passionate immorality.
The kings of the world
  have committed adultery with her.
Because of her desires for extravagant luxury,
  the merchants of the world have grown rich."

Song 2: A Call to Flee

4Then I heard another voice calling from heaven,

"Come away from her, my people.
  Do not take part in her sins,
  or you will be punished with her.
5 For her sins are piled as high as heaven,
  and God remembers her evil deeds.
6 Do to her as she has done to others.
  Double her penalty for all her evil deeds.
She brewed a cup of terror for others,
  so brew twice as much for her.
7 She glorified herself and lived in luxury,
  so match it now with torment and sorrow.
She boasted in her heart,
  'I am queen on my throne.
I am no helpless widow,
  and I have no reason to mourn.'
8 Therefore, these plagues will overtake her in a single day—
  death and mourning and famine.
She will be completely consumed by fire,
  for the Lord God who judges her is mighty."

Songs 3–5: Three Laments

9And the kings of the world who committed adultery with her and enjoyed her great luxury will mourn for her as they see the smoke rising from her charred remains.
10They will stand at a distance, terrified by her great torment. They will cry out,

"How terrible, how terrible for you,
  O Babylon, you great city!
In a single moment
  God's judgment came on you."

Emperor	Reign
1. Augustus	27 BC—AD 14
2. Tiberius	AD 14–37
3. Gaius Caligula	AD 37–41
4. Claudius	AD 41–54
5. Nero	AD 54–68
year of anarchy	*AD 68–69*
6. Vespasian	AD 69–79
7. Titus	AD 79–81
8. Domitian	AD 81–96

▲ **Roman Emperors, 27 BC—AD 96 (17:10-11).**

18:1-24 This chapter contains seven poetic responses to the fall of Babylon (or Rome; see note on 17:5).

18:1-3 The angel's powerful taunt song is the first poetic response. Ancient taunt songs derided a defeated enemy (see Isa 13:19-22; 34:10-17). In these taunts, the fall of Babylon (or Rome; see note on 14:8) is portrayed as a traumatic event for subservient kingdoms and especially for those who had profited from her luxury. The sacking of Rome by the Goths and Visigoths (AD 400s) brought the prosperous empire to an end.

18:1 This *angel* derived his splendor *from heaven.* The word *splendor* is normally used for the divine presence.

18:2 ***Babylon is fallen:*** See Isa 21:9. Once a beautifully dressed woman (see 17:4), Babylon (Rome) became a desolate den for ***demons*** and unclean birds such as ***vultures*** (cp. Isa 13:20-22; Jer 4:23-31; 50:39). • ***foul:*** Literally *unclean.* • Some manuscripts condense the last two lines to read *a hideout for every foul [unclean] and dreadful vulture.*

18:3 ***have fallen:*** Some manuscripts read *have drunk.* • ***committed adultery with her:*** See note on 17:2. • ***extravagant luxury:*** Rome plundered conquered nations of their wealth before God's justice fell on her.

18:4-8 This second poetic response (see note on 18:1-24) is a warning ***from heaven*** to flee the doomed city.

18:4 ***Do not take part in her sins:*** Association with the evil city could lead to being identified with it in punishment and even involved with it in its sins (see Gen 13:8-13; 19:1-29; cp. Jer 51:6, 45).

18:5 ***God remembers:*** His response may seem slow (Ps 103:8; 145:8; Joel 2:13; Jon 4:2), but God is not weak, and he does not forget either good or evil (16:19; Gen 19:29; 1 Sam 1:19).

18:6 ***Double her penalty*** (or *Give her an equal penalty*): The severity of some sins required a double recompense (see Exod 22:4, 7, 9; cp. Isa 40:2; Jer 16:18; 17:18). • ***brew twice as much:*** Or *brew just as much.*

18:7 ***I am queen:*** Cp. Ezek 28:1-2.

18:8 The ***plagues*** (18:2-3) are a reminder that destruction was not merely a human action; it is the ***Lord God who judges her.*** He ***is mighty,*** able to accomplish what he promises.

18:9-19 These three laments highlight the grief of those who profited most from the wicked city's rich lifestyle (cp. Ezek 27).

18:9-10 The ***kings of the world*** lament as they ***mourn*** the loss of the ***luxury*** they had obtained from alliance with the wicked city.

18:10 With a ***terrified*** sense of separation and abandonment (see 18:15, 17), the kings ***stand at a distance*** in a futile attempt to avoid punishment.

11The merchants of the world will weep
and mourn for her, for there is no one left
to buy their goods. 12She bought great quantities of gold, silver, jewels, and pearls; fine
linen, purple, silk, and scarlet cloth; things
made of fragrant thyine wood, ivory goods,
and objects made of expensive wood; and
bronze, iron, and marble. 13She also bought
cinnamon, spice, incense, myrrh, frankincense, wine, olive oil, fine flour, wheat, cattle,
sheep, horses, chariots, and bodies—that is,
human slaves.

14 "The fancy things you loved so much
are gone," they cry.
"All your luxuries and splendor
are gone forever,
never to be yours again."

15The merchants who became wealthy by
selling her these things will stand at a distance, terrified by her great torment. They
will weep and cry out,

16 "How terrible, how terrible for that great
city!
She was clothed in finest purple and
scarlet linens,
decked out with gold and precious
stones and pearls!
17 In a single moment
all the wealth of the city is gone!"

And all the captains of the merchant
ships and their passengers and sailors and
crews will stand at a distance. 18They will
cry out as they watch the smoke ascend,
and they will say, "Where is there another
city as great as this?" 19And they will weep
and throw dust on their heads to show their
grief. And they will cry out,

"How terrible, how terrible for that great
city!
The shipowners became wealthy
by transporting her great wealth on
the seas.
In a single moment it is all gone."

Song 6: A Summons to Rejoice

20 Rejoice over her fate, O heaven
and people of God and apostles and
prophets!
For at last God has judged her
for your sakes.

Song 7: Babylon's Destruction

21Then a mighty angel picked up a boulder
the size of a huge millstone. He threw it into
the ocean and shouted,

"Just like this, the great city Babylon
will be thrown down with violence
and will never be found again.
22 The sound of harps, singers, flutes, and
trumpets
will never be heard in you again.
No craftsmen and no trades
will ever be found in you again.
The sound of the mill
will never be heard in you again.
23 The light of a lamp
will never shine in you again.
The happy voices of brides and grooms
will never be heard in you again.
For your merchants were the greatest in
the world,
and you deceived the nations with
your sorceries.
24 In your streets flowed the blood of the
prophets and of God's holy people
and the blood of people slaughtered
all over the world."

Songs of Victory in Heaven (19:1-10)

Four Hallelujahs

19 After this, I heard what sounded like
a vast crowd in heaven shouting,

18:11 Ezek 27:27, 36; Rev 18:3
18:12-13 Ezek 27:12-22
18:15 Ezek 27:36
18:16 Rev 17:4
18:17 Ezek 27:27-29; Rev 17:16
18:18 Ezek 27:32; Rev 13:4
18:19 Ezek 27:30-34
18:20 Jer 51:48; Rev 12:12; 19:2
18:21 Jer 51:63-64
18:22 Ezek 26:13
18:23 Jer 7:34; 16:9; 25:10; Nah 3:4
18:24 Jer 51:49; Matt 23:35-37; Rev 16:6; 17:6
19:1 Rev 4:11; 7:10; 12:10

18:11-17a ***The merchants of the world*** sing the second lament (18:14; see note on 18:9-19). They profited from the Roman economy (18:12-13), but their trade ceased as the great city was swiftly destroyed.

18:12-13 This cargo list suggests the extent of the wealth Rome pillaged from the rest of its empire (cp. Ezek 27:12-24). Some of the most expensive products in the ancient world are mentioned in this indictment of ostentatious materialism and pride.

18:13 ***bodies:*** Rome developed a huge slave market, which some historians have estimated at nearly 20% of the population.

18:14-17a The merchants would lament the fall of Rome (see note on 18:1-3) because it would *forever* end their accustomed *luxuries.* Material goods can be swept aside *in a single moment.*

18:17b-19 ***all the captains:*** Seafarers sing the third lament (see note on 18:9-19). Their mourning focuses on the breakdown of communication and transportation. During the reign of Julius Caesar, the Mediterranean was cleared of pirates and trade blossomed under the region's Roman law enforcement. The swift loss of Roman authority would upset the system of trade.

18:20 The laments (18:9-19) stimulate a call for *heaven* to *rejoice.* The *people of God* are not to grieve, because the judgment was for their *sakes;* they had suffered persecution from the evil forces represented by the great city.

18:21-24 The songs responding to Babylon's fall (18:1-24) conclude with a portrayal of the city's doom.

18:21 ***a boulder the size of a huge millstone:*** Heavy millstones, shaped for grinding olives or grain, were used throughout the ancient world. Jesus also spoke of using such stones in judgment (see Matt 18:6). The dramatically thrown boulder signified that the power of Rome was forever *thrown down.*

18:23 Cp. Jer 25:10-11.

18:24 ***your streets:*** Literally *her streets.*

19:1-10 This section expands the message of the sixth song of response

19:2
Rev 6:10; 16:7; 17:1
19:3
Isa 34:10
Rev 14:11
19:4
Rev 4:4, 6, 10
19:5
Ps 115:13; 134:1; 135:1
Rev 11:18
19:6
Rev 11:15
[b]*pantokratōr* (3841)
‣Rev 19:15
19:7
Matt 22:2; 25:10
Eph 5:32
Rev 21:2, 9
19:8
Isa 61:10
Rev 15:4, 6
19:9
Luke 14:15
Rev 21:5; 22:6
19:10
Acts 10:25-26
Rev 22:8-9
19:11
Isa 11:4
Rev 3:14
19:12
Rev 1:14; 2:17

"Praise the LORD!
Salvation and glory and power belong to our God.
2 His judgments are true and just.
He has punished the great prostitute who corrupted the earth with her immorality.
He has avenged the murder of his servants."

3And again their voices rang out:

"Praise the LORD!
The smoke from that city ascends forever and ever!"

4Then the twenty-four elders and the four living beings fell down and worshiped God, who was sitting on the throne. They cried out, "Amen! Praise the LORD!"
5And from the throne came a voice that said,

"Praise our God,
all his servants,
all who fear him,
from the least to the greatest."

6Then I heard again what sounded like the shout of a vast crowd or the roar of mighty ocean waves or the crash of loud thunder:

"Praise the LORD!
For the Lord our God, the [b]Almighty, reigns.
7 Let us be glad and rejoice,
and let us give honor to him.
For the time has come for the wedding feast of the Lamb,
and his bride has prepared herself.
8 She has been given the finest of pure white linen to wear."
For the fine linen represents the good deeds of God's holy people.

John and the Angel, Servants of God

9And the angel said to me, "Write this: Blessed are those who are invited to the wedding feast of the Lamb." And he added, "These are true words that come from God."
10Then I fell down at his feet to worship him, but he said, "No, don't worship me. I am a servant of God, just like you and your brothers and sisters who testify about their faith in Jesus. Worship only God. For the essence of prophecy is to give a clear witness for Jesus."

10. TRIUMPH AND JUDGMENT (19:11–20:15)

The Rider on the White Horse

11Then I saw heaven opened, and a white horse was standing there. Its rider was named Faithful and True, for he judges fairly and wages a righteous war.
12His eyes were like flames of fire, and on his head were many crowns. A name was written on him that no one understood except himself.

(18:20; see note on 18:1-24), which called for rejoicing. Various groups direct praises to the Lord. The praises can be divided into two sections: thankfulness for the destruction of the evildoers (19:1-4) and thankfulness for the reward of God's people (19:5-8).

19:1-2 This scene focuses on what John *heard* rather than on what he saw. The first three-part praise comes from ***a vast crowd*** (cp. 7:9-10).

19:1 ***Praise the LORD:*** Literally *Hallelujah;* also in 19:3, 4, 6. *Hallelujah* is the transliteration of a Hebrew term that means "Praise the LORD."

19:2 ***true and just*** (see 15:3; 16:7): In his righteous justice, God kept his promise of judging ***the great prostitute,*** who represents moral and spiritual corruption and persecution of God's people.

19:3 ***The smoke from that city:*** God's people praise him once again as they see the evil city's demise (cp. 14:11).

19:4 In response to the first two praises (19:1-3), the ***elders*** and the ***living beings*** (see ch 4) again prostrate themselves before the enthroned ***God*** (see 4:10; 5:8, 14; 7:11). • ***Amen!*** See note on 5:14.

19:6-8 The focus of the final thunderous ***Praise the LORD!*** is that God ***reigns*** as ***the Almighty*** in complete supremacy (see 1:8; 4:8; 11:17; 15:3; 16:7, 14; 19:15; 21:22).

19:6 ***the Lord our God:*** Some manuscripts read *the Lord God.*

19:7 ***the wedding feast of the Lamb:*** This event—the wedding of the Messiah with his bride, the church (see Isa 54:5; 61:10; Jer 31:32; Ezek 16:7-14; Hos 2:16-20; Mark 2:19-20; 2 Cor 11:2)—symbolizes complete victory and eternal fellowship.

19:8 ***finest . . . linen:*** See note on 15:5-6. • ***the good deeds of God's holy people:*** See Eph 2:8-10; 2 Tim 3:16-17; Jas 2:18-22.

19:9 ***Blessed are those:*** This fourth blessing in Revelation (see 1:3; 14:13; 16:15) affirms the hope of the faithful. • ***who are invited:*** God is in control and determines who will participate. • ***wedding feast*** (cp. 19:17): Jesus often used meals to explain the Kingdom (Matt 22:1-13; Luke 14:7-24) and he ordained a meal for the church (Mark 14:22-25; 1 Cor 11:23-26). • ***These are true words:*** This oath asserts the reliability of the message.

19:10 The angel issues a stern warning against misdirected worship (cp. 22:8-9). • ***brothers and sisters:*** Literally *brothers;* see note on 6:11. • ***is to give a clear witness for Jesus:*** Or *is the message confirmed by Jesus.*

19:11–20:15 The drama moves into its climactic scenes: God's enemies are defeated and punished in two episodes (19:11-21; 20:7-10). Meanwhile, the faithful experience a 1,000-year resurrection (20:1-6) followed by the final judgment (20:11-15).

19:11-16 ***Then I saw:*** John describes a new vision of Jesus Christ as the holy warrior and conquering King (see 14:1; see also Exod 15:1-7; Ps 24:8; 78:49-50; Isa 59:16-17).

19:11 The ***rider*** is both a judge and a ***righteous*** warrior (see Isa 11:1-5). He is ***named Faithful and True:*** He embodies God's authenticity and reliability (see 19:2; 21:5-6).

19:12 ***His eyes were like flames of fire:*** See 1:14-16; Dan 10:6. • Christ, wearing ***many crowns,*** is contrasted with the dragon, whose seven heads were each crowned (see 12:3).

13He wore a robe dipped in blood, and his
title was the [c]Word of God. 14The armies
of heaven, dressed in the finest of pure
white linen, followed him on white horses.
15From his mouth came a sharp sword to
strike down the nations. He will [d]rule them
with an iron rod. He will release the fierce
[e]wrath of God, the [f]Almighty, like juice flowing from a winepress. 16On his robe at his
thigh was written this title: King of all kings
and Lord of all lords.
17Then I saw an angel standing in the sun,
shouting to the vultures flying high in the
sky: "Come! Gather together for the great
banquet God has prepared. 18Come and
eat the flesh of kings, generals, and strong
warriors; of horses and their riders; and of
all humanity, both free and slave, small and
great."
19Then I saw the beast and the kings of the
world and their armies gathered together to
fight against the one sitting on the horse and
his army. 20And the beast was captured, and
with him the false prophet who did mighty
miracles on behalf of the beast—miracles
that deceived all who had accepted the mark
of the beast and who worshiped his statue.
Both the beast and his false prophet were
thrown alive into the fiery lake of burning
sulfur. 21Their entire army was killed by the
sharp sword that came from the mouth of the
one riding the white horse. And the vultures
all gorged themselves on the dead bodies.

The Thousand Years

20 Then I saw an angel coming down
from heaven with the key to the
bottomless pit and a heavy chain in his
hand. 2He seized the dragon—that old serpent, who is the [g]devil, [h]Satan—and bound

19:13
Isa 63:1-3
John 1:1, 14
1 Jn 1:1-2
[c]*logos* (3056)
‣Luke 16:2

19:14
Rev 3:4

19:15
Isa 11:4; 63:3
2 Thes 2:8
[d]*poimainō* (4165)
‣Matt 2:6
[e]*orgē* (3709)
‣Mark 3:5
[f]*pantokratōr* (3841)
‣Rev 21:22

19:17-18
Ezek 39:17-20

19:20
Isa 30:33
Dan 7:11
Rev 13:12-16; 20:10, 14-15; 21:8

20:1
Rev 1:18; 10:1

20:2
[g]*diabolos* (1228)
‣Rev 20:10
[h]*satanas* (4567)
‣Rev 20:7

The Worship of Angels (19:10)

Acts 27:23-24
2 Cor 5:19-21
1 Tim 2:5-6
Heb 1:5-14; 7:24-25

Angels have a servant role and are not to be worshiped (19:10; see also Heb 1:5-14). But Jewish tradition had developed the concept of angels as mediators with God. In pre-Christian Judaism, God's *transcendence* or "otherness" was emphasized to such an extent that people felt the need for mediators to communicate with him. In this context, angels grew in importance.

For Christians, Christ has a unique role as mediator between God and humans. Interest in angels or deceased saints to communicate with God get in the way of honoring Christ alone as the mediator between God and human beings (1 Tim 2:5-6; see also 2 Cor 5:19-21; Heb 7:24-25). God still has angelic messengers, but they are creatures who serve him, not divine beings to be worshiped. Faithful saints of the past, including Mary, are human beings. They may be honored in our Christian memories but they have no claim to divinity, and they should never be worshiped. God alone is worthy of our prayers and our worship.

19:13 ***He wore a robe dipped in blood:*** This description may refer to (1) the blood of Christ's enemies, signifying his total victory (Isa 63:2-4); or (2) Christ's sacrificial death for humanity (1:7). • The ***Word of God*** is John's distinctive designation for Jesus (see John 1:1, 14).

19:14 Christ's ***armies of heaven,*** dressed in victorious ***white*** and riding ***on white horses,*** contrast with the locust forces of the abyss (9:3-11), the three frog-like evil spirits (16:13), and the defeated armies at Armageddon (16:16; see also 19:19).

19:15 ***From his mouth . . . a sharp sword:*** See 1:16; Heb 4:12; see also Isa 49:2; 2 Thes 2:8. • The ***iron rod*** represents Christ's power as ruler and as supreme shepherd (see Ps 2:9; 23:4). • ***God, the Almighty:*** See 1:8; 4:8; 11:17; 16:7, 14; 21:22. • His ***fierce wrath*** will crush his enemies like grapes in ***a winepress*** (Isa 63:2-4).

19:16 ***On his robe at his thigh:*** Or *On his robe and thigh.* • ***King . . . and Lord:*** See 1:5; 15:3; 17:14.

19:17-19 ***Gather together for the great banquet:*** This feast upon ***the flesh*** of the ***armies gathered together to fight against*** Christ is contrasted with "the wedding feast of the Lamb" (19:7). The enemies that form for battle are quickly destroyed (19:20-21; see also 14:17-20; 16:16-21). Two feasts—the marriage supper of the Lamb (19:7-8) and the "great supper" of God's judgment (19:17-18, 21)—provide two perspectives on the end of time. They illustrate the two sides of the Good News: grace and judgment, reward and punishment (cp. John 3:16-18).

19:20 ***beast . . . false prophet:*** See 13:1-10. • The ***fiery lake of burning sulfur*** provides a picture of eternal punishment (see 20:10, 14-15; 21:8; see also Isa 66:24; Matt 13:41, 49-50; Mark 9:43, 48). • God's enemies are ***thrown*** into the ***fiery lake.*** The two beasts (19:20) are followed by the dragon (20:10) and then by death (20:14) and unsaved humans (20:15).

19:21 The ***entire army*** of enemies is dispatched by the ***sword*** from Christ's ***mouth*** (see 1:16; 2:12, 16; see also Isa 11:4; 49:2; 2 Thes 2:8). While one side of God's word (grace) leads to repentance, the other side (judgment) carries out the death sentence.

20:1-10 There are three parts to this passage: the binding of Satan (20:1-3), the reign of God's holy people (20:4-6), and the release of Satan for his final attempt at a battle (20:7-10). Four themes emerge: (1) Satan's war is futile—he cannot withstand even an angel; (2) God's holy people will be vindicated and glorified; (3) God will have the final victory; and (4) even when sinful and depraved human beings experience Christ's good purposes in the world, they still flock after Satan when he gains even a small amount of freedom to act.

20:1-2 Like the OT "angel of the LORD" (see Gen 16:7-11; 22:15; Exod 3:2; Num 22:22-34; Judg 2:1-4; 6:11-22), the ***angel coming down from heaven*** has God's authority, symbolized by the ***key*** that controls ***the bottomless pit*** (or *the abyss,* or *the underworld;* also in 20:3) and the power to put ***chains*** on God's great enemy (cp. 12:7-9) for ***a thousand years.*** See "The Thousand Years (The Millennium)," facing page.

20:3
2 Pet 2:4
Jude 1:6
[l]*sphragizō* (4972)
‣Rev 22:10

20:4
Dan 7:9, 22, 27
Matt 19:28

20:5
Ezek 37:10
Luke 14:14
[j]*anastasis* (0386)
‣Matt 22:28

20:6
1 Pet 2:5, 9

20:7
[k]*satanas* (4567)
‣Matt 4:10

20:8
Ezek 38:2

him in chains for a thousand years. 3The angel threw him into the bottomless pit, which
he then shut and [l]locked so Satan could not
deceive the nations anymore until the thousand years were finished. Afterward he
must be released for a little while.
4Then I saw thrones, and the people sitting on them had been given the authority
to judge. And I saw the souls of those who
had been beheaded for their testimony
about Jesus and for proclaiming the word
of God. They had not worshiped the beast
or his statue, nor accepted his mark on their
foreheads or their hands. They all came to
life again, and they reigned with Christ for
a thousand years.
5This is the first [j]resurrection. (The rest of
the dead did not come back to life until the
thousand years had ended.) 6Blessed and
holy are those who share in the first resurrection. For them the second death holds no
power, but they will be priests of God and
of Christ and will reign with him a thousand
years.

The Final Defeat of Satan

7When the thousand years come to an end,
[k]Satan will be let out of his prison. 8He will
go out to deceive the nations—called Gog
and Magog—in every corner of the earth.
He will gather them together for battle—a
mighty army, as numberless as sand along

The Thousand Years (The Millennium) (20:1-10)

Revelation 20 describes the 1,000-year reign of Christ on earth. Three perspectives regarding how the millennium relates to the coming of Christ have been held by Christian groups with an equally high regard for Scripture as God's inspired, authoritative word:

1. *Premillennialism:* Christ will return before the millennium to inaugurate a literal 1,000-year rule on earth with his holy people before the final judgment.

2. *Amillennialism:* 1,000 years is a metaphor representing the current age between Christ's first and second comings. Christ reigns spiritually with his people. At the end of this age, Christ will return, execute the final judgment, and inaugurate his eternal Kingdom.

3. *Postmillennialism:* The Good News will triumph on earth, and Christ will establish through the church an age of peace on earth. Then Christ will return and inaugurate his eternal Kingdom.

Differences over these perspectives have caused conflict among Christians. Many have forsaken Christian fellowship with those who hold a different opinion. True Christian humility and love (1 Pet 3:8), however, would never let such differences disrupt Christian fellowship.

All believers can agree with the overall message of Revelation: Christ will visibly return and rule in an actual new heaven and earth. A real spiritual warfare is taking place. Hell, like heaven, is real, and all people will be judged by God's standards. The prophecies of Revelation offer hope to God's people in the midst of pain, suffering, and confusion in the world.

20:3 This incarceration, portrayed as ***the bottomless pit,*** is a preliminary defeat for Satan and the powers of evil. Various NT passages describe the impact of Christ's work on Satan (Luke 10:17-20; Acts 10:38; 26:18; Rom 16:20; Eph 6:11; Jas 4:7; see Matt 12:24; 16:19; 18:18; John 12:31; 1 Jn 3:8). Christ's presence with his people binds evil powers (see 2 Thes 2:7), reminding persecuted Christians that there is a future with God. • ***so Satan could not deceive:*** Deception is the trademark of the devil, who is a liar (see John 8:44; 1 Jn 3:8); no liar will enter heaven (21:8, 27; 22:15). The faithful believers who experience Christ's reign will not be deceived. • The ***little while*** might be the equivalent of the symbolic three and a half years (see 11:2-3, 9-11; 12:14; 13:5)—it is a limited time.

20:4 ***thrones . . . people sitting on them:*** This portrayal of a heavenly tribunal includes the elders (4:4) on thrones (see Dan 7:9-10), the victorious martyrs (see Dan 7:22), and all God's people. • ***beheaded for . . . Jesus:*** Beheading was a common form of execution for Roman citizens. • The faithful who resisted receiving the ***mark*** of ***the beast*** (13:16-17) will judge the condemned (see 1 Cor 6:2-3) on thrones similar to those of the worshiping elders (see 4:10-11; 5:8-10; 11:16).

20:5-6 John contrasts ***the first resurrection*** with ***the second death*** (see 20:12-15; cp. John 5:29).

20:6 ***Blessed:*** This fifth blessing of Revelation (see also 1:3; 14:13; 16:15; 19:9; 22:7, 14) focuses on the promised reward of life. God's faithful people (20:4) will ***reign with*** Christ as ***priests of God*** (see also 1:6; 5:10).

20:7-10 Satan's all-out attempt to conquer God's people is followed by his fiery demise. This passage has two major purposes: (1) to show God's absolute justice, because Satan and his followers are worthy of punishment and will never change; and (2) to show the depravity of people who follow Satan. In spite of viewing the nature of Christ's reign in the world for many years, they still flock to Satan's standard when he is freed. These factors are the basis for the judgment at the great white throne (20:11-15).

20:7-8 When free to act (20:7), ***Satan*** still seeks ***to deceive.*** He will ***gather*** a ***mighty army*** (cp. Ezek 38–39) in a final attempt to overwhelm God's people (20:9).

20:8 Jewish traditions vary regarding the locations of ***Gog and Magog.*** They are symbolically to the north (see Jer 1:14-15), the direction from which the enemies traditionally approached Megiddo and Jerusalem. The names represent nations and rulers from ***every corner of the earth*** that oppose God's people (see Ezek 38–39). • ***He will gather them together for battle:*** Repeating the earlier scenes in which God's enemies assemble for battle (16:16; 19:19), Satan here makes a last-ditch attempt to confront God and his forces.

the seashore. 9And I saw them as they went
up on the broad plain of the earth and surrounded God's people and the beloved city.
But fire from heaven came down on the attacking armies and consumed them.
10Then the [a]devil, who had deceived them,
was thrown into the fiery lake of burning sulfur, joining the beast and the false prophet.
There they will be tormented day and night
forever and ever.

The Final Judgment

11And I saw a great white throne and the
one sitting on it. The earth and sky fled
from his presence, but they found no place
to hide. 12I saw the dead, both great and
small, standing before God's throne. And
the [b]books were opened, including the
[b]Book of Life. And the dead were judged according to what they had done, as recorded
in the [b]books. 13The sea gave up its dead,
and death and the [c]grave gave up their dead.
And all were judged according to their
deeds. 14Then death and the [d]grave were
thrown into the lake of fire. This lake of fire
is the second death. 15And anyone whose
name was not found recorded in the Book
of Life was thrown into the lake of fire.

11. THE NEW JERUSALEM (21:1–22:5)

Introduction to the New Jerusalem

21 Then I saw a new [e]heaven and a new
earth, for the old [e]heaven and the
old earth had disappeared. And the sea was
also gone. 2And I saw the holy city, the new
Jerusalem, coming down from God out of
heaven like a bride beautifully dressed for
her husband.
3I heard a loud shout from the throne,
saying, "Look, God's home is now among
his people! He will live with them, and they
will be his people. God himself will be with
them. 4He will wipe every tear from their
eyes, and there will be no more death or sorrow or crying or pain. All these things are
gone forever."
5And the one sitting on the throne said,
"Look, I am making everything new!" And
then he said to me, "Write this down, for
what I tell you is trustworthy and true."
6And he also said, "It is finished! I am the
Alpha and the Omega—the Beginning and

20:10
[a]*diabolos* (1228)
‣ Matt 4:1

20:11-12
Dan 7:9-10
Matt 25:31-46

20:12
Exod 32:32
Dan 12:1
[b]*biblion* (0975)
‣ Rev 21:27

20:13
Isa 26:19
Matt 16:27
John 5:28-29
[c]*hadēs* (0086)
‣ Rev 20:14

20:14
1 Cor 15:26, 55
[d]*hadēs* (0086)
‣ Matt 5:22

21:1
Isa 65:17; 66:22
2 Pet 3:13
[e]*ouranos* (3772)
‣ Matt 3:2

21:2
Isa 52:1; 61:10
Heb 11:10; 12:22

21:3
2 Chr 6:18
Ezek 37:27
Zech 2:10
2 Cor 6:16

21:4
Isa 25:8; 35:10; 65:19

20:9 Again, no battle occurs (see 16:16-21; 19:19-21), because ***fire from heaven came down . . . and consumed them*** as it did Sodom (Gen 19:24; see also 2 Kgs 1:10-12; Ezek 38:22-23; 39:6). The enemies of God cannot stand against him.

20:10 ***they will be tormented . . . forever:*** Rebellion against God has eternal consequences. While the concept of unending punishment repulses some, it is the message of Revelation and of Scripture generally that God will deal sternly with sin and rebellion by those who reject Christ's saving work (see Matt 13:42; 25:41-46; John 3:18, 36; Rom 2:7). Perhaps more than any book in Scripture, Revelation illustrates that the unrepentant persist in their rebellion despite the consequences (9:20-21; 16:9-11; cp. Luke 16:31). Revelation also emphasizes that God is just and deals with sin as it deserves.

20:11-15 This segment portrays a court hearing at which the dead are judged on the basis of their works. God's response to eternal rebellion is eternal punishment.

20:12 ***books were opened:*** See Ps 56:8; Dan 7:10. • ***The Book of Life*** holds the names of faithful people who have experienced God's saving power (Mal 3:16; see Rev 3:5; 13:8; 17:8; 20:15); they are probably the same ones as those who experience the "first resurrection" (20:5-6). • ***And the dead were judged:*** The works of both the redeemed and the unredeemed will be judged (see 22:12; Matt 16:27; 25:31-46).

20:13 ***the grave:*** Greek *Hades;* also in 20:14. See note on 6:7-8.

20:14 The expression ***death and the grave*** refers to the reality of death; it is the last enemy that God will destroy (see 21:4; 1 Cor 15:26). • The ***lake of fire*** portrays the horrible end of God's enemies who will not experience the "first resurrection" (see 20:5-6; cp. Matt 25:41; Luke 16:24; Jude 1:7).

21:1–22:9 The final scenes of the new heaven and earth are striking pictures of a new community and home for God's people that is fashioned and given by God. These scenes help to lift the spirits of persecuted Christians. John lays out his basic vision (21:1-6) and follows it with two expansions: (1) In 21:9-27, he presents the new Jerusalem as the site of holy perfection; (2) in 22:1-5, he describes the new Jerusalem as the ultimate Garden of Eden that Adam and Eve could have experienced had they not sinned.

21:1 The vision involves God's creation of the new ***heaven*** and ***earth*** (contrast Gen 1:1 with Isa 65:17; 66:22). The ***old*** creation has ***disappeared***—it was subject to decay (see Rom 8:20-21; 2 Pet 3:7, 10). • ***the sea was also gone:*** The sea was associated with chaos or the abyss (see note on 9:1-12) and was sometimes portrayed as a roaring monster (see Ps 46:3; 74:14; see also Job 3:8; 41:1-34; Luke 21:25). The new creation will be free from all such evil.

21:2 ***coming down from God:*** The new creation is a gift from God. In the beginning, God created everything good, and in the end, God will create a new, unbroken world. • This picture of ***Jerusalem*** as a beautiful ***bride*** (see Isa 61:10) contrasts starkly with the vision of Babylon (or Rome) as the prostitute (17:4-5; 18:2-3; see note on 21:9–22:9).

21:3 ***God's home is now among his people!*** OT and NT expectations are fully and finally realized. Ever since humanity sinned (Gen 3), separation from God has been humanity's greatest problem (Gen 3:23). God has repeatedly called his people to himself through the prophets, through Jesus his Son, and through the presence of the Spirit (see Gen 17:8; Exod 29:45-46; Ps 46:4-5; 95:7; Jer 7:23; 31:33; Ezek 34:14; 37:27; Zech 8:8; John 14:2-3; 17:24). In the new heaven and new earth, God's people will finally experience ultimate and everlasting fellowship with God. • ***God himself will be with them:*** Some manuscripts read *God himself will be with them, their God.*

21:4 ***no more death or sorrow or crying or pain:*** See Isa 25:8; 1 Cor 15:54. God's people will know the creative wholeness and salvation that Christ brings (see 2 Cor 5:17; Gal 6:15).

21:6 God restates Jesus' final words from the cross, ***It is finished!*** (John 19:30; cp. 16:17), connecting Christ's death with the assurance of eternal life. • ***I am the Alpha and the Omega:*** With the first and last letters of the Greek alphabet, John portrays God as encompassing total reality and total truth. God was from the ***Beginning*** (see Gen 1:1; cp. John 1:1-2) and is also the

21:5 Isa 43:19; 2 Cor 5:17
21:7 2 Sam 7:14; Rom 8:14; 2 Cor 6:16
21:8 Ps 5:6; 1 Cor 6:9; Eph 5:5; [f]*eidōlolatrēs* (1496) ‣Rev 22:15
21:10 Ezek 40:1-2
21:11 Isa 60:1-2, 19; Ezek 43:2
21:12 Exod 28:21; Ezek 48:30-34
21:14 Eph 2:20; Heb 11:10
21:15 Ezek 40:3, 5
21:16-17 Ezek 48:16-17
21:19 Exod 28:17-20; Isa 54:11-12; Ezek 28:13
21:21 Isa 54:12
21:22 John 4:21-24; 17:21-24; [g]*pantokratōr* (3841) ‣2 Cor 6:18

the End. To all who are thirsty I will give
freely from the springs of the water of life.
7All who are victorious will inherit all these
blessings, and I will be their God, and they
will be my children.
8"But cowards, unbelievers, the corrupt,
murderers, the immoral, those who practice witchcraft, [f]idol worshipers, and all
liars—their fate is in the fiery lake of burning sulfur. This is the second death."

Vision of the New Jerusalem

9Then one of the seven angels who held
the seven bowls containing the seven last
plagues came and said to me, "Come with
me! I will show you the bride, the wife of
the Lamb."
10So he took me in the Spirit to a great,
high mountain, and he showed me the holy
city, Jerusalem, descending out of heaven
from God. 11It shone with the glory of God
and sparkled like a precious stone—like jasper as clear as crystal. 12The city wall was
broad and high, with twelve gates guarded
by twelve angels. And the names of the
twelve tribes of Israel were written on the
gates. 13There were three gates on each
side—east, north, south, and west. 14The
wall of the city had twelve foundation stones,
and on them were written the names of the
twelve apostles of the Lamb.
15The angel who talked to me held in his
hand a gold measuring stick to measure the
city, its gates, and its wall. 16When he measured it, he found it was a square, as wide
as it was long. In fact, its length and width
and height were each 1,400 miles. 17Then
he measured the walls and found them to
be 216 feet thick (according to the human
standard used by the angel).
18The wall was made of jasper, and the
city was pure gold, as clear as glass. 19The
wall of the city was built on foundation
stones inlaid with twelve precious stones:
the first was jasper, the second sapphire,
the third agate, the fourth emerald, 20the
fifth onyx, the sixth carnelian, the seventh
chrysolite, the eighth beryl, the ninth topaz,
the tenth chrysoprase, the eleventh jacinth,
the twelfth amethyst.
21The twelve gates were made of pearls—
each gate from a single pearl! And the main
street was pure gold, as clear as glass.
22I saw no temple in the city, for the Lord
God [g]Almighty and the Lamb are its temple.

End (see 1:8; 22:13). • Because Christ is supreme and in charge of all things (see Rom 9:5; 1 Cor 15:28; Eph 1:22-23; 4:5-6), he dispenses *the water of life* to all who are *thirsty* for it (see note on 7:16-17; see also Isa 55:1; John 4:10; 7:37-38).

21:7 ***All who are victorious:*** God's ***children*** who persevere in life ***will inherit*** his ***blessings***. Adoption is a covenant relationship; the language of adoption certifies their privileges and responsibilities (cp. Gen 17:8; 2 Sam 7:14-16; Jer 31:33; Ezek 34:24).

21:8 This vice list summarizes sins described throughout Revelation. These sins characterize people who have not experienced adoption by God; their fate is the ***fiery lake*** (see Rom 1:29-32; Gal 5:19-21; 2 Tim 3:2-5; cp. Exod 20:13-17; see also note on Rev 20:10). • ***all liars:*** John apparently viewed deception as the root of sin; elsewhere he describes Satan as the "father of lies" (John 8:44; 1 Jn 2:4; see Rev 14:5; 21:27; 22:15; cp. Matt 12:34).

21:9–22:9 This symbolic vision of the new Jerusalem uses vivid word pictures to describe ***the bride, the wife of the Lamb***—all those who respond to Christ's message of salvation (see 21:2; 22:17; Eph 5:22-32).

21:10 ***in the Spirit:*** Or *in spirit.* • ***a great, high mountain:*** In Scripture, experiences with God frequently take place on the mountains (cp. Ezek 40:2; see also Exod 3:1; 19:10-25; Deut 34:1-4; 1 Kgs 18:20-40; 19:8-18; Matt 5:1; 15:29; 17:1; 24:3; 28:16). • ***the holy city . . . descending out of heaven from God:*** God's presence and eternal life cannot be reached by human effort but are received as a gift (Eph 2:8-9; cp. 2 Cor 5:1).

21:11 Like the true people of God, the ***glory*** of the city reflects God's glory (cp. Exod 34:29-35; 2 Cor 3:7-11). • ***Jasper*** (see also 4:3; 21:11, 18) is opaque on earth; the heavenly jasper is ***clear as crystal,*** having a transparency that mirrors God's purity and integrity.

21:12-14 In this vision, ***the twelve tribes of Israel*** represent the redeemed people of God (see 7:4-8; see also Rom 9:6-7). The foundation for this community of God's redeemed is ***the twelve apostles of the Lamb.*** In Jesus, God's promise to bless all of the families of the earth through Abraham has been fully realized (Gen 12:3).

21:15-17 ***measure the city:*** Measuring defines accepted boundaries (contrast the unmeasured section of the Temple, 11:2; see also Ezek 40:3–42:20).

21:16 The city is described as a perfect cube. Each dimension is ***1,400 miles*** (Greek *12,000 stadia* [2,220 kilometers]); the number *12,000* symbolically represents the people of God (see "Symbolic Numbers" at 4:4, p. 2173).

21:17 In the ancient world, ***walls*** were important not only to the defense and boundary of a city, but also to its status. That these walls are ***216 feet thick*** (Greek *144 cubits* [65 meters]) indicates the strength of God's redeemed people. The measurement of *144 cubits* again uses a multiple of 12 to represent God's people. A cubit was the length of a man's forearm, with a standard length of about 18 inches.

21:18 The ***wall*** is built of ***jasper*** (see note on 21:11; cp. 4:3). The city is fashioned in ***gold,*** which is not opaque like earthly gold; rather, like God's transformed people, the heavenly gold is ***clear*** and ***pure***.

21:19 The ***twelve precious stones*** adorning the ***foundation stones*** of the city's ***wall*** are a reminder of the twelve stones on the high priests' breastplate that represented the people of God (see Exod 28:17-20). • The identification of some of these gemstones is uncertain.

21:21 Things that are precious and luxurious on earth are common building materials in heaven.

21:22 ***I saw no temple:*** This apparent conflict with earlier visions (11:19; 14:15-17) is resolved by understanding each visionary picture in Revelation as a separate symbolic representation of God's presence. There is no longer any need for a temple in heaven because God is present with his people.

23 And the city has no need of sun or moon,
for the glory of God illuminates the city, and
the Lamb is its light. 24 The nations will walk
in its light, and the kings of the world will enter the city in all their glory. 25 Its gates will
never be closed at the end of day because
there is no night there. 26 And all the nations
will bring their glory and honor into the city.
27 Nothing evil will be allowed to enter, nor
anyone who practices shameful idolatry and
dishonesty—but only those whose names
are written in the Lamb's [h]Book of Life.

22 Then the angel showed me a river
with the water of life, clear as crystal, flowing from the throne of God and of
the Lamb. 2 It flowed down the center of the
main street. On each side of the river grew
a tree of life, bearing twelve crops of fruit,
with a fresh crop each month. The leaves
were used for medicine to heal the nations.
3 No longer will there be a curse upon
anything. For the throne of God and of the
Lamb will be there, and his servants will worship him. 4 And they will see his face, and
his name will be written on their foreheads.
5 And there will be no night there—no need
for lamps or sun—for the Lord God will
shine on them. And they will reign forever
and ever.

12. EPILOGUE: JESUS IS COMING (22:6-21)

6 Then the angel said to me, "Everything
you have heard and seen is trustworthy and
true. The Lord God, who inspires his prophets, has sent his angel to tell his servants
what will happen soon."

7 "Look, I am coming soon! [i]Blessed are
those who obey the words of prophecy
written in this book."

8 I, John, am the one who heard and saw
all these things. And when I heard and saw
them, I fell down to worship at the feet of
the angel who showed them to me. 9 But he
said, "No, don't worship me. I am a servant
of God, just like you and your brothers the
prophets, as well as all who obey what is
written in this book. Worship only God!"
10 Then he instructed me, "Do not [j]seal

21:23-24 Isa 60:3, 5, 19-20
21:25 Isa 60:11
21:26 Ps 72:10-11
21:27 Isa 52:1
[h]*biblion* (0975) ‣ Matt 19:7
22:1 Ezek 47:1; Joel 3:18; Zech 14:8; John 7:37-39
22:2 Gen 2:9; Ezek 47:12
22:3 Zech 14:11
22:4 Ps 17:15; 42:2; Matt 5:8
22:5 Isa 60:19-20; Dan 7:18, 27; Zech 14:7
22:7 [i]*makarios* (3107) ‣ Matt 5:3
22:10 [j]*sphragizō* (4972) ‣ Matt 27:66

21:23 The vitality, energy, and life of the city are not in institutions or physical sources of power and light, but in ***the glory of God*** and the Lamb. The ***sun*** and ***moon*** were features of the first creation (Gen 1:14-19; see Isa 60:19-20). • ***the Lamb is its light:*** Jesus is the light of the world (see John 8:12; 9:5; 12:35-36).

21:24-25 ***The nations:*** God's promise to Abraham is fulfilled (Gen 12:3; see Isa 2:3). • In Revelation, ***the kings of the world*** usually refer to God's enemies (6:15; 17:18; 18:3, 9). Now that the enemies have been destroyed (16:9, 11; 19:1-2, 19-21), the picture is of God's ***glory*** as reflected in those people who have repented (14:6-7; cp. 11:13) and walk with God (5:9; 15:4). • The ***gates*** that are ***never . . . closed*** contrast with the ancient scene in which closed gates protected cities from enemies, particularly at night. The people enjoy peace and security in God's supremacy (see Isa 60:11). God's enemies have been destroyed, and fear and failure have ended (see Zech 14:7; John 11:8-10; 12:35-36).

21:27 ***Nothing evil*** (or ***ceremonially unclean***): Spiritual impurity is a basic concern in Revelation (see 21:8). Evil is generalized as ***idolatry and dishonesty*** (see 14:5; 21:8; 22:15). Those who fail to appear in the ***Book of Life*** are excluded from the city of God. Only those ***whose names are written*** in the Book of Life, the pure of heart (Matt 5:8), will see God.

22:1-2 This part of John's vision of the city deals with God's provision of water and food for his people (cp. Exod 16:4, 22-24; Ezek 47:1-12; John 4:10; 6:32-35). Although God originally made a "garden of delight" (Eden) for Adam and Eve, they disobeyed him and lost it (Gen 2–3). Now Eden is refashioned and united to the celestial city as God's marvelous gift for his faithful people.

22:1 ***the water of life:*** See 7:17; John 4:10-15; cp. Exod 17:1-7; Isa 55:1; Ezek 47:1-10; Zech 14:8.

22:2 Although humans were denied access to the ***tree of life*** after they sinned (see Gen 3:22-24), it is now freely available. The tree ***on each side of the river*** (cp. Ezek 47:12) shows that there is no wrong side of the river in heaven. The tree produces ***twelve crops of fruit*** (or ***twelve kinds of fruit***) ***each month,*** demonstrating God's constant provision.

22:3 ***No longer . . . a curse:*** Ever since the first sin (Gen 3:14-19), humanity has been cursed because of their rebellion against God (see 1 Cor 16:22). Now rebellion, sin, and the curse are gone forever. • ***his servants will worship him:*** Revelation gives glimpses of authentic worship (see 4:1–5:14; 7:9-17).

22:4 The human fears of death and of seeing God (see Gen 16:13; 32:30; Judg 6:22; Isa 6:5) will be removed. God's people will bear his name and ***will see his face*** with joy (see Matt 5:8; 2 Cor 3:18; 1 Jn 3:2-3).

22:5 ***They will reign*** with God ***forever*** (see 20:4; see also 5:10) in his radiant light that banishes ***night*** and the ***need for lamps*** (see Isa 60:19-20).

22:6-21 This epilogue to Revelation contains utterances by an angel (22:6, 8-11) and Christ (22:7, 12-19) followed by a concluding plea for Christ's return (22:20) and a closing benediction (22:21). The epilogue has a number of direct verbal connections with the introduction to the book (1:1-11), and it sums up important themes such as encouraging faithful perseverance, warning evildoers, affirming the authenticity of the prophetic message, and restating the nearness of Christ's return.

22:6 ***Everything*** that John records in Revelation is ***trustworthy and true*** because ***God,*** who has all authority (cp. Matt 28:18), ***has sent*** the messenger. But it does not mean these visions are easy to understand. • ***The Lord God, who inspires his prophets:*** Or ***The Lord, the God of the spirits of the prophets.*** • ***soon:*** Or *suddenly,* or *quickly;* also in 22:7, 12, 20.

22:7 ***Blessed:*** The sixth blessing of Revelation (see 1:3; 14:13; 16:15; 19:9; 20:6; 22:14) is for ***those who obey.*** Obedience is key to God's blessing. • ***book:*** Or *scroll;* also in 22:9-10, 18-19.

22:8-9 The earlier warning against false worship (see 19:10) is reiterated when John again falls ***at the feet of the angel. Only God*** deserves our ***worship*** (cp. John the Baptist in relation to Jesus; John 1:6-8, 26-27; 3:27-35).

22:10 ***Do not seal up:*** The angel expands John's initial instruction to "write in a book" (1:11) and warns against curtailing its communication. Although

22:11 Dan 12:10
22:12 Matt 16:27
22:14 Gen 2:9; 3:22 Ezek 47:12
22:15 1 Cor 6:9-10 Gal 5:19-21 [k]*eidōlolatrēs* (1496) ‣1 Cor 5:10
22:16 Num 24:17 Isa 11:1, 10
22:17 Isa 55:1 John 7:37-39
22:18 Deut 4:2; 12:32 Prov 30:6
22:20 1 Cor 16:22
22:21 Rom 16:20 2 Thes 3:18 [a]*charis* (5485) ‣Luke 2:40 [b]*kurios* (2962) ‣Matt 3:3

up the prophetic words in this book, for
the time is near. [11]Let the one who is doing
harm continue to do harm; let the one who
is vile continue to be vile; let the one who
is righteous continue to live righteously; let
the one who is holy continue to be holy."

[12]"Look, I am coming soon, bringing
my reward with me to repay all people
according to their deeds. [13]I am the
Alpha and the Omega, the First and the
Last, the Beginning and the End."

[14]Blessed are those who wash their robes.
They will be permitted to enter through
the gates of the city and eat the fruit from
the tree of life. [15]Outside the city are the
dogs—the sorcerers, the sexually immoral,
the murderers, the [k]idol worshipers, and all
who love to live a lie.

[16]"I, Jesus, have sent my angel to give you
this message for the churches. I am both
the source of David and the heir to his
throne. I am the bright morning star."

[17]The Spirit and the bride say, "Come."
Let anyone who hears this say, "Come." Let
anyone who is thirsty come. Let anyone
who desires drink freely from the water of
life. [18]And I solemnly declare to everyone
who hears the words of prophecy written in
this book: If anyone adds anything to what
is written here, God will add to that person
the plagues described in this book. [19]And if
anyone removes any of the words from this
book of prophecy, God will remove that person's share in the tree of life and in the holy
city that are described in this book.

[20]He who is the faithful witness to all
these things says, "Yes, I am coming soon!"

Amen! Come, Lord Jesus!

[21]May the [a]grace of the [b]Lord Jesus be
with God's holy people.

some things are sealed—God does not reveal everything (cp. 10:4)—what has been written must be communicated so that people will understand the seriousness of the message and that ***the time is near*** (see 1:1, 3; 22:6-7; cp. Dan 12:4).

22:11 ***Vile*** people who refuse to accept God's forgiveness will ***continue to be vile*** (see 16:9), yet John reminds the ***righteous*** to maintain their integrity. This verse is a warning to evildoers, and it calls the righteous to recognize the crucial significance of Christ's return relative to their commitments and their actions.

22:12 Christ is ***coming soon . . . to repay all people,*** not just on the basis of their profession of faith, but ***according to their deeds*** (see 2:23; 11:18; 14:13; 20:12-13; see also Prov 24:12; Matt 16:27; 2 Cor 5:10). Not every statement of belief is genuine (John 2:23-25); faith will show itself in actions (Jas 2:14-26). We are indeed saved by the grace and power of God in Christ. Our works do not save us, but they do indicate the seriousness of our confession and provide a just basis for our ultimate reward or punishment.

22:14 ***Blessed are those:*** In response to the connection between actions and ultimate results (22:12), the seventh blessing of Revelation (see also 1:3; 14:13; 16:15; 19:9; 20:6; 22:7) promises acceptance for ***those who wash their robes***—those who have been purified by trusting in Christ and following him faithfully (3:5; 6:11; 7:9-10, 14; 19:13; Eph 5:26; Heb 10:22). • ***enter through the gates of the city:*** See note on 21:24-25.

22:15 This verse again lists those who are not admitted to contrast with those admitted in 22:14 (see 21:8, 27; 22:11). These unrepentant sinners remain ***outside the city;*** it is another warning to those who do not repent that they will not be allowed to enter the city of God (22:14). • The reference to sinners as ***dogs*** was a familiar Jewish designation for rejected outsiders (see Matt 7:6; Phil 3:2; also 2 Sam 3:8; 2 Kgs 8:13); Jews used this term to refer to Gentiles (see Mark 7:26-28).

22:16 ***I am both the source of David and the heir to his throne*** (literally *I am the root and offspring of David*): ***Jesus*** validates the ***message*** of Revelation (cp. John 21:24) by swearing that he is simultaneously *the source of David* (see 5:5; Isa 11:10) and David's *heir* (see Ezek 37:23-24; Rom 1:3). • The ***morning star*** was a name for the Messiah (see Num 24:17; 2 Pet 1:19; cp. Luke 1:78-79).

22:17 ***Come*** is a repeated invitation and a confession (see 22:20). • ***the bride:*** The Lamb's wife (see 21:9) is the church, the people of God. • The ***thirsty*** can ***drink freely*** from God's provision (see 21:6; 22:1; Ps 42:1; Isa 55:1; John 4:10-14).

22:18-19 ***I solemnly declare:*** John issues an oath to protect the integrity of the book of Revelation. He declares a curse upon anyone who alters the contents of the book or its message (cp. Deut 4:2; 12:32). The curse contrasts with the statement of blessing on all who read aloud, listen to, and obey the prophecy (1:3). At the time Revelation was written, scribes would sometimes alter books to suit their own views. Early Christians quickly developed means of authenticating both messages and messengers (see John 21:24; 1 Cor 16:21; Gal 6:11; Col 4:18; 2 Thes 3:17; 1 Jn 4:1-3). • Since the time of the early church, the scope and content of the NT has been established as the measure of the Christian proclamation (see "After the Apostles," p. 2201). Yet the church continues to be plagued by those who would attempt to reconstruct the borders of Scripture by adding other works that they believe are of equal status with the Bible or by arguing that certain segments of the Bible are unreliable creations of human effort and perception. The genuine church has rejected and will continue to reject efforts to redefine the boundaries of the canon as human and even demonic attempts to alter the basis of the Christian faith.

22:20 ***I am coming soon!*** See 3:11. • ***Come, Lord Jesus!*** Paul uttered the same response (1 Cor 16:22; see also Phil 4:5).

22:21 Revelation closes with a benediction similar to those in Paul's letters (e.g., Rom 15:33; 1 Cor 16:23-24). • The fitting final sentence invokes ***the grace of the Lord Jesus,*** the foundation of our forgiveness and the basis of our eternal hope. • ***be with God's holy people:*** Other manuscripts read *be with all;* still others read *be with all of God's holy people.* Some manuscripts add *Amen.*

INTRODUCTION TO THE TIME
AFTER THE APOSTLES

The most pertinent issue that Christians faced at the end of the first century and into the second was that of self-identity. Ever since the council of apostles met in Jerusalem (Acts 15), Christians had wrestled with distinguishing their faith from contemporary Judaism and Greco-Roman religious culture. With the death of the apostles and their disciples, the eyewitnesses of Jesus were gone. With greater urgency many believers asked, "Who are we?" The process of answering this question pushed believers for the following centuries to clarify and define their own unique identity.

By the end of the first century AD, scores of documents were circulating that claimed to be written by one or more of the original disciples.[1] All Christian groups drew on the Hebrew Scriptures, but the writings of the apostles were still in process of being compiled into a collection that most churches would accept as equal in authority to the OT. Every Christian group appealed to apostolic authority: Jewish Christians honored the Gospel of Matthew and *The Gospel of the Nazarenes* (now lost); Gnostics heralded the Gospel of John and a variety of esoteric documents; followers of Marcion promoted the apostle Paul as the preferred interpreter of Jesus; and so on. How could believers recognize which documents were to be considered Scripture? What parts of Christian doctrine and practice should function as authoritative standards for Christians? What documents should be considered "canonical"—that is, which documents authoritatively reflected the church's faith and canon of belief? These were the questions at stake for determining genuine apostolic teaching.

THE FIRST "CANON"

The language and concept of *canon* preceded Christianity's use of it. The word meant a plumb line or a stick for making measurements. It came to be used figuratively in the Greco-Roman world to mean a standard or norm by which other things are judged, whether it be artwork, an idea, or a moral principle.

It is with this usage in mind that the first appearance of a "canon" in a Christian context occurs. In Gal 6:15-16, Paul reminds the Galatians that in relationship to Christ, it doesn't matter whether or not a man has been circumcised. Rather than measuring oneself by the law of circumcision, "what counts is whether we have been transformed into a new creation" through faith in Christ's redemption. Paul then says, "May God's peace and mercy be upon all who live by this principle" (Greek *kanōn*). The mention of canon here has nothing to do with a list of authoritative texts; instead, it refers to a standard of belief and behavior based on Christ. Earlier, Paul probably referred to this same canon when he complained about those Jewish Christians at Antioch who separated themselves from the Gentiles and thus "were not following the truth of the gospel message" (Gal 2:14). Elsewhere Paul similarly speaks of an existing standard of faith that correlates with his message of Good News (see 1 Cor 15:1-8; 2 Tim 1:13-14; 2:2). This "pattern of wholesome teaching" was by no means something Paul dreamed up—he had received it from the Lord (1 Cor 11:23; 15:3; Gal 1:15-17), and he passed it on with the intent that Christians would follow that pattern and pass it on to others (1 Thes 4:1-2; 1 Tim 6:20; 2 Tim 1:13-14; 2:2).

Paul was describing the process by which the faith was being transmitted well before the NT canon was codified. There was indeed a canon of teaching, as the above passages show. The first canon was a standard body of teaching handed down through the apostles' preaching. This teaching described the revelation of God in Christ, as seen through his incarnate life, crucifixion, death, burial, resurrection, and ascension to heaven. There was also some initial arrangement for devotion and worship in the life of the church (see, e.g., Acts 2:42) and for the appointing of leaders in the church (see, e.g., 1 Tim 3:1-13).

THE POSTAPOSTOLIC CHURCH

After the death of the apostles, the concern to preserve apostolic truth was no less active than it had been earlier. Every postapostolic Christian writer acknowledged the supreme and unique authority of the Scriptures, and postapostolic writers submitted themselves to the authority of the apostolic documents. For them, the apostles were the teachers *par excellence,* having unique authority.

The early postapostolic (i.e., the patristic) church, however, was not a different entity from the apostolic church, as if somehow detached from the Christian community of the first century. For the Christians who lived the apostolic faith in the years after the death of the apostles, there was not a radical break in how the churches were preaching, teaching, and defending the Christian faith. The points of continuity from one century into the next were far greater than the differences. The ancient church had an integrity and coherence that ran from the earliest days after Pentecost, through the NT, and into the postapostolic period.

The leaders of the patristic church

[1] Such as the *Gospel of James* and the *Apocalypse of Peter,* accepted as Scripture by some churches but eventually rejected for their questionable teaching.

were aware of the need for clarifying the connection of the present churches with the apostolic legacy. *Apostolicity*, or that which is apostolic, pertained to the continuation of what the apostles taught and to the ability to trace a historical lineage back to those churches actually founded by the apostles. It was therefore important that Polycarp, the bishop of Smyrna, was called "an apostolic and prophetic teacher" (*Martyrdom of Polycarp* 16.2; about AD 156). He had been a disciple of the apostle John and was said to have faithfully preserved and transmitted the teaching given to him by the apostles. Twenty years later, Irenaeus of Lyons argued against Gnostic groups that the true churches are only those churches that stand in the succession of the "tradition which originates from the apostles, and which is preserved by means of the succession of elders" (Irenaeus, *Against Heresies* 3.2-4). The reality of the church's faith required an identifiable connection with the apostles.

THE CANON OF APOSTOLIC DOCTRINE

The way of faithfulness to the gospel was further defined and lived out by those we call the "fathers" of the church. The church fathers of the earliest centuries can be considered authors and exponents of a founding tradition. Protestants might insist that tradition is not revelation, yet they will agree that the early tradition was an element of the Holy Spirit's providential working to define and preserve the Christian faith and the church in its integrity. Even as the Spirit continues to incorporate new expressions of the church's faith, hope, and love into the body of Christ, it does so always under the guidance of Scripture and in "conversation" with the patristic tradition. We may not be familiar with the terminology used by the postapostolic fathers of the church, or we might object to their use of Platonic or Stoic categories. Nevertheless, the patristic tradition became an indelible part of the Christian faith upon which all theology, spirituality, and exegesis has been built. Practically speaking, this tradition has functioned as a canon of Christian belief, especially through the doctrinal and confessional achievements of the church during the fourth and fifth centuries. This "canon of belief" has operated ever since as the historical and theological precedent for all subsequent Christian doctrinal formulations.

This description of the patristic tradition as "canon" is not meant to equate the authority of the church fathers with that of the Bible. Any of the ancient church fathers would have been horrified to find their written legacy being placed on par with Holy Scripture. The patristic tradition is not revelatory in the way that Scripture is revelatory. Still, the Christian tradition that was birthed in the apostolic era and formulated throughout the following 400 years has been regarded as the foundation upon which the church's history has been built. Each period of church history has made its unique contributions and will continue to do so, but the early church was unique for giving Christianity the tradition, the canons of Scripture and doctrine.

Historically, it is through the ancient church fathers that the NT canon was set, the basic professions of faith were composed, and Christian doctrine and theology were defined in response to contemporary culture and heresy. It was also they who formulated the first reflective responses to Scripture within daily pastoral experience and teaching.

SCRIPTURE AND TRADITION

For most of church history, Scripture and tradition were perceived as compatible. Tradition was the distillation of biblical truth and always existed alongside Scripture. For example, in response to a religious leader whose group vaunted themselves as true Christians but rejected the truly human birth of Christ, Augustine replied, "The catholic [i.e., universally held] doctrine, which is also the apostolic doctrine, is that our Lord and Savior Jesus Christ is both the Son of God in his divine nature and the Son of David after the flesh. . . . This teaching represents the 'plainest statement in

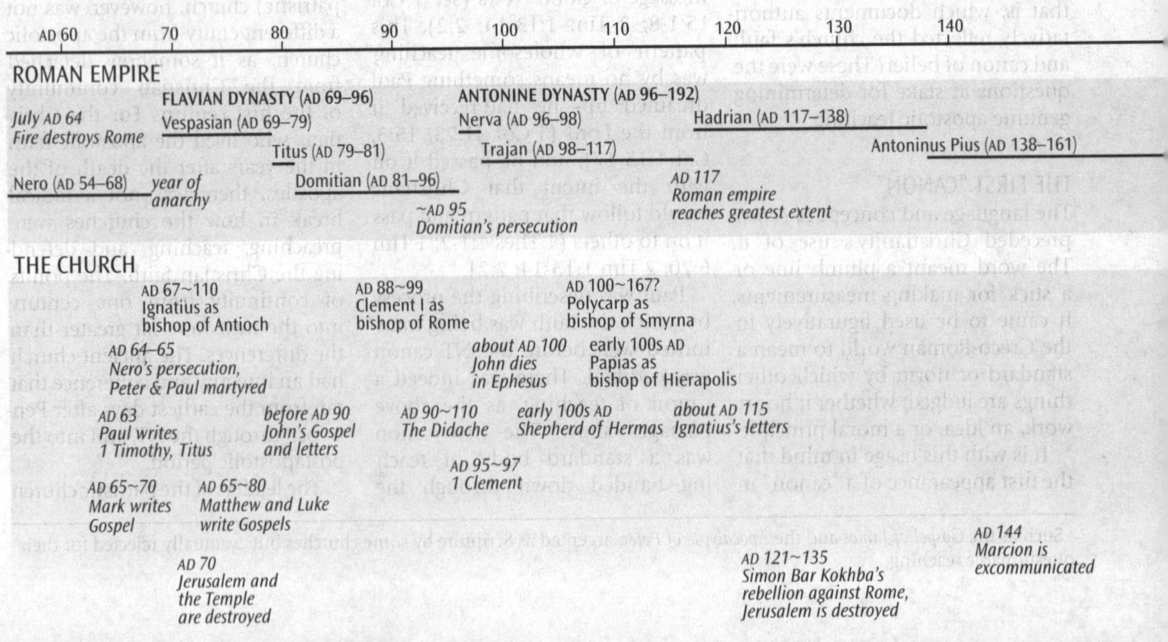

Holy Scripture'" (Augustine, *Reply to Faustus the Manichaean* 23.5). Tradition and the Bible are like streams coming out of the same spring. Like the work of the Holy Spirit in the church, both tradition and Scripture are necessary elements of the Christian faith.

In the ancient church, the practice of reading and hearing Scripture did not occur without the tradition. A Christian writer at the end of the first century addressed a letter to the church at Corinth in order to encourage believers there to avoid worldly practices and to seek heartfelt repentance. In this exhortation, the writer told the church leaders to embrace "the glorious and holy canon of our tradition" (*1 Clement* 7:2-4). This writer frequently cites the OT as declaring the Good News of Jesus Christ, but he displays no knowledge of an operational NT canon. Implicit to the writer's argument is that the apostolic understanding is achieved only when Scripture is read through the lenses of the "canon of our tradition." Only then does accurate theological and spiritual interpretation become possible. Tradition was not from outside the faith but was regarded as the essential teaching of the Bible.

Scripture was the authoritative anchor of the tradition's content, and the tradition stood as the primary interpreter of Scripture. In other words, the tradition was not a novel set of beliefs and practices added to Scripture, as if it were a separate source of divine revelation. It instead expressed the ancient consensus of the church fathers regarding the meaning of Scripture.

It was in fact the tradition, provided through the apostles' preaching, that formed the basis of the NT and served as the guide for interpreting the OT. As the body of this tradition developed over the next 400 years, it was understood as bearing witness to and interpreting Scripture. The baptismal formulas, catechisms, doctrinal summaries, and later creeds were valued as accurately representing the intent of Scripture. Augustine said, when he was instructing new converts, "Whatever you hear in the Creed is contained in the inspired books of Holy Scripture" (Augustine, *Sermon* 212.2). To describe the tradition was inevitably to speak about the message of Scripture.

THE CANONIZATION OF NT TEXTS

The concept of possessing an authoritative canon emerged gradually out of the worship and life of the early churches. With regard to Christian texts, the primary issue on the minds of early believers was inspiration, not canonization. Christian interests followed the Jewish attitude toward the Hebrew Bible. Creating an exclusive list of authoritative books wasn't as important as determining which texts were and were not "inspired by God" (2 Tim 3:16). As a result, writers from the first to early second century would refer to a particular writing as "Scripture" without wondering whether it was "canonical."

There was not very much doubt about the divine inspiration of the words and deeds of Jesus as accounted in the four Gospels, nor of many of the apostolic letters. But by the middle of the second century there were a growing number of other texts that were regarded by many churches as inspired, such as *The Epistle of Barnabas, 1 Clement,* and a puzzling apocalyptic work known as *The Shepherd of Hermas* that enjoyed widespread acceptance. These and other writings appear in some collections of biblical books by the fourth century, but none were read as Scripture in every church.

There was no single principle at work in the canonization process. There was no council of Christian leaders that met and decided which books should be in the Bible. Multiple issues were involved. Certainly, apostolic authorship and the antiquity of a text were important. Authors who were closer to the life of Jesus were believed to have a more reliable account than later writers. But the resemblance of a book's theological content to the church's canon of faith was undoubtedly more important than any other factor.

A good example is the case of Serapion, bishop of the church in

AD 150 — 160 — 170 — 180 — 190 — 200 — 210 — 220 — 230 — 240 — 250

SEVERAN DYNASTY (AD 193–235)

Marcus Aurelius (AD 161–180)

Septimius Severus (AD 193–211)

Alexander Severus (AD 222–235)

Commodus (AD 180–192)

Caracalla (AD 211–217)

MILITARY ANARCHY (AD 235–284)

AD 165
Justin is martyred

Macrinus (AD 217–218)

AD 235
Hippolytus is martyred

Elagabalus (AD 218–222)

AD 150~200
Irenaeus as bishop of Lyons

AD 169~183
Theophilus as bishop of Antioch

AD 190~211
Serapion as bishop of Antioch

AD ??–235
Hippolytus as bishop of Rome

about AD 156
Polycarp is martyred

AD 190~203
Serapion rejects The Gospel of Peter

AD 203~231
Origen teaches at Alexandria

AD 158
Justin Martyr's Apology

about AD 170
Tatian's Diatessaron

AD 178
Irenaeus's Against Heresies

about AD 190
Melito of Sardis lists OT books

about AD 215
Hippolytus's Apostolic Tradition

AD 250
Origen's First Principles

AD 231~254
Origen in exile

about AD 200
Tertullian's Apologeticum

AD 207~208
Tertullian's Against Marcion

AD 207~225
Tertullian of Carthage adopts Montanism

AD 200s~300s
Desert Fathers in Egypt

Antioch (around AD 190~203). He complained that *The Gospel of Peter* was being read as Scripture in the worship services of some other churches.[2] This document carried docetic ideas about Christ, which means that Christ's physical reality was downplayed or denied. Such a view was largely associated with the Gnostic systems and unacceptable for most churches. Serapion argued against attributing scriptural status to *The Gospel of Peter* because it was heretical, denying the humanity of Christ and thus "the true faith." He called for the ultimate rejection of this gospel, not because it was absent in a list of scriptural books, but because it violated the traditional faith of the church.

The terminology of "canon" or "rule" is virtually never used for sacred books until later in the fourth century, and even then, there is only sparse mention. The earliest Christians did not trouble themselves about the canonical status of texts.[3] Marcion's insistence (about AD 120) that only the Pauline epistles and an edited version of Luke's Gospel presented true Christianity is usually overinterpreted to mean that Marcion was propounding a scriptural canon and thereby instigated the early church to do likewise. However, we know of no writer during the second or third centuries who responded to Marcion's considerable theological challenge with a fixed canon of books. Justin, Irenaeus, Tertullian, and the many others who responded to Marcion attacked his position by highlighting the canon of truth, the rule of faith. It is true that the majority of churches were using the four Gospels, Acts, the letters of Paul, and some other letters as Scripture by the early second century AD, and they found Marcion's edited "Bible" unacceptable. Still, there was no consensus about the extent or parameters of the biblical books. Opposition to Marcion, therefore, was not and could not have been in the form of an "orthodox" canon of texts.

The Gnostics, similarly, were faulted with an inability to understand the Bible, not because they were using the wrong texts, but because they failed to understand the right tradition and thereby misinterpreted the texts. In the words of Clement of Alexandria, the Gnostics were guilty of not explaining Scripture according to the "canon of truth."

The process of NT canonization occurred primarily in the context of the believing community. Canonical "testing" took place within the give-and-take of church life. Determination of the shape and content of the NT canon, just like the theological canon, occurred as the NT text was received and consistently affirmed by the churches. We cannot simply point to a church council that decided the issue of the biblical books once and for all. None of the major church councils, east or west, addressed the matter of biblical canonization.[4] Instead, the church's understanding of "Scripture" and "canon" slowly melded into a single entity: an exclusive, closed collection of inspired books.

The infrequent references to a normative list of texts suggest that Christian churches were not anxiously looking to create a canon; they were seeking to hear God's word in the Scripture readings during worship and to ascertain which readings conveyed this word. Public reading of Scripture is mentioned explicitly by Paul in 1 Timothy 4:13 as an activity intended for the whole church. In the process of liturgically reading in assembly, authoritative weight was accrued by certain texts that lent to their canonization. It was in this manner that the church ultimately came to reject, for example, *The Gospel of Peter* and *The Gospel*

[2] The fragment is preserved in Eusebius, *Church History* 6.12. [3] F. F. Bruce, *The Canon of Scripture*, 255. [4] A small council that met at Rome in AD 382 is thought to have first enumerated the canonical books of both Testaments in a document known as the Tome of Damasus. Damasus was bishop of Rome (AD 366–384), and he convened councils of bishops in order to set church policy throughout Italy. But it is doubtful that the list of biblical books, which one manuscript also calls the "Decree of Gelasius on Which Books Should and Should Not Be Received," is actually from the proceedings of the council.

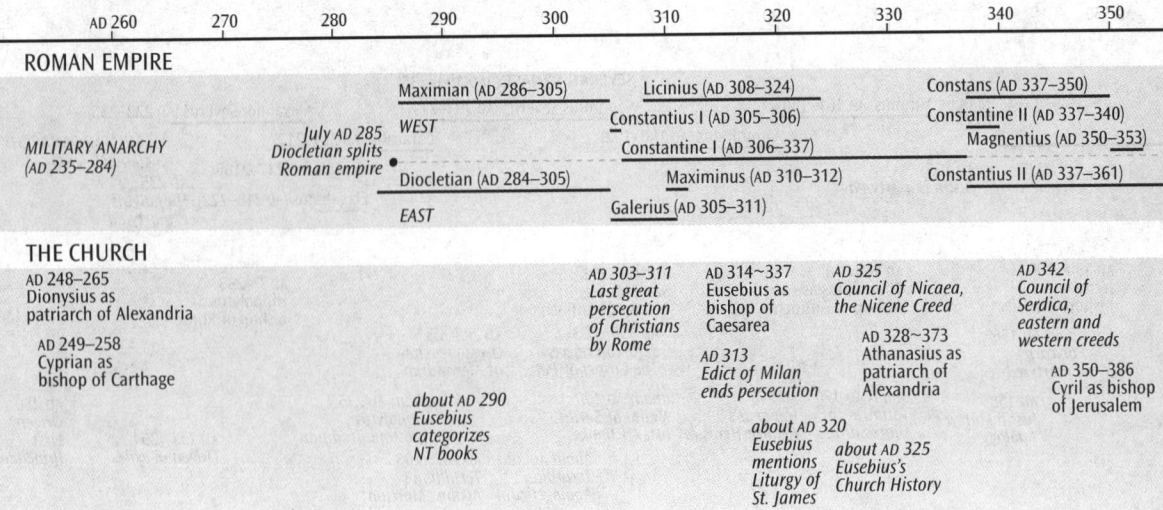

AD 260 — 270 — 280 — 290 — 300 — 310 — 320 — 330 — 340 — 350

ROMAN EMPIRE

MILITARY ANARCHY (AD 235–284)

July AD 285 Diocletian splits Roman empire

WEST

Maximian (AD 286–305)

Constantius I (AD 305–306)

Licinius (AD 308–324)

Constantine I (AD 306–337)

Constans (AD 337–350)

Constantine II (AD 337–340)

Magnentius (AD 350–353)

EAST

Diocletian (AD 284–305)

Galerius (AD 305–311)

Maximinus (AD 310–312)

Constantius II (AD 337–361)

THE CHURCH

AD 248–265 Dionysius as patriarch of Alexandria

AD 249–258 Cyprian as bishop of Carthage

about AD 290 Eusebius categorizes NT books

AD 303–311 Last great persecution of Christians by Rome

AD 314~337 Eusebius as bishop of Caesarea

AD 313 Edict of Milan ends persecution

about AD 320 Eusebius mentions Liturgy of St. James

AD 325 Council of Nicaea, the Nicene Creed

about AD 325 Eusebius's Church History

AD 328~373 Athanasius as patriarch of Alexandria

AD 342 Council of Serdica, eastern and western creeds

AD 350–386 Cyril as bishop of Jerusalem

of Thomas whereas it continued to embrace Matthew, Mark, Luke, and John.

The churches eventually came to a consensus, and the NT canon was formalized: In AD 367, Athanasius of Alexandria gave the first official list of the twenty-seven books that are accepted today, and regional councils in Hippo (AD 393) and Carthage (AD 397) affirmed this list.

THE PILLARS OF THE CHRISTIAN FAITH

The faith articulated during the first 500 years set into place the pillars of authority on which Christians have relied: the theological canon of apostolicity (the tradition, the cardinal doctrines and confessions), the apostolic canon of Scripture (the Bible), and the community of faith itself (the church). Like a three-legged stool, these elements served as the foundation for determining true doctrine. Such an arrangement acted like spiritual checks and balances that guided the early church in its decision-making and served to protect the church from those seductive voices who offered new or special revelation or an alien interpretation of Scripture. Whatever authority a Christian leader claimed, it had to be based on this apostolic faith.

IT HAS BEEN RIGHTLY SAID that the "Book of the People" came to us from the "People of the Book." In other words, the church's faith, and the acknowledgment of specific books as canonical, occurred through their use and acknowledgment within living and believing communities. Whether in written or oral forms, the determination for declaring something canonical did not simply drop out of heaven, nor was it set in place by the decrees of church councils. The Christian Bible is intimately related to communities who first received and used its texts. Any historical consideration we may give to the authority and canonization of the biblical texts must take into account the believing community that recognized it as such. The Christian Bible first arose within the Christian church, it was first interpreted in the church, and it is acknowledged by the church. We cannot, therefore, divorce the development of the biblical canon from the role that the earliest Christian assemblies and meetings played in the canonization process. Just as God was revealed in Jesus Christ, in the process of canonizing the tradition and the NT the divine was revealed through the human.

FURTHER READING

CRAIG D. ALLERT
A High View of Scripture? (2007)

MARK HUSBANDS AND JEFFREY P. GREENMAN, EDS.
Ancient Faith for the Church's Future (2008)

JOHN J. O'KEEFE AND R. R. RENO
Sanctified Vision: An Introduction to Early Christian Interpretation of the Bible (2005)

ROBERT E. WEBBER
Ancient-Future Faith: Rethinking Evangelicalism for a Postmodern World (1999)

D. H. WILLIAMS
Retrieving the Tradition and Renewing Evangelicalism: A Primer for Suspicious Protestants (1999)
Tradition, Scripture and Interpretation: A Sourcebook of the Ancient Church (2006)

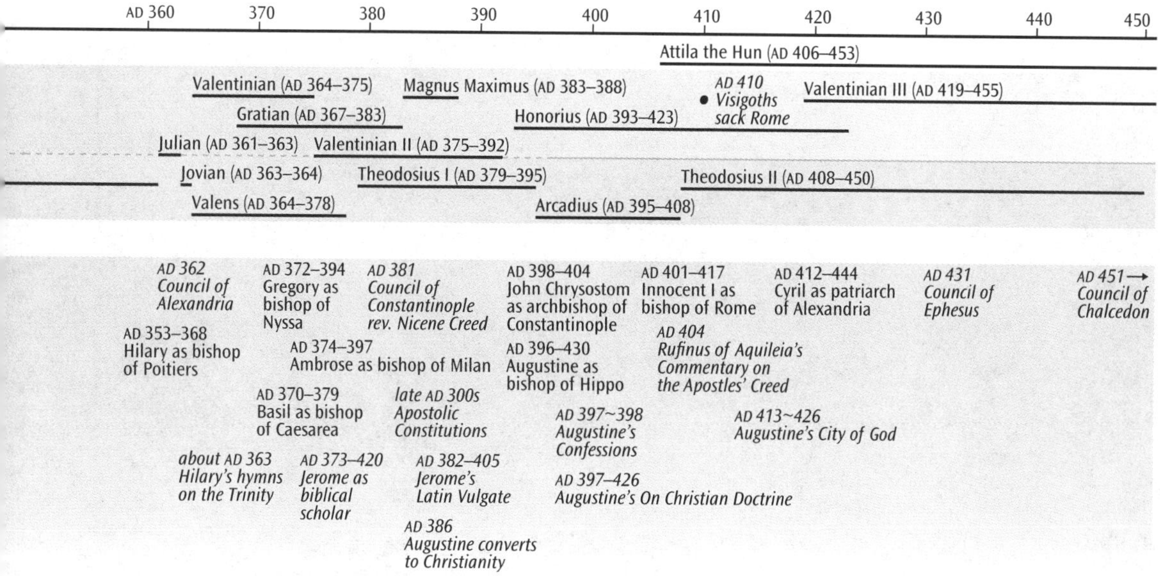

REFERENCE HELPS

NLT STUDY BIBLE
READING PLAN

It is possible to study the *NLT Study Bible* without a reading plan—simply start reading! Having a reading plan, though, can help you measure your progress—just as it is useful to have a road map while taking a long journey.

The following reading plan divides the *NLT Study Bible* into daily readings. Each book of the Bible has an introduction reading, which is followed (except in the shortest books) by one to four reading segments of just the Bible text (listed like this: **Gen 1–11**). Reading through the book introduction and Bible text first will give you the "big picture" for that book of the Bible. Then there are short readings for the Bible text with the accompanying features. There are also readings for the section introductions and for the chronology and background articles.

If you follow this reading plan and study one section each day, five days per week, you will read through the *NLT Study Bible* in five years. That sounds like a long time, but it turns out to be a realistic pace. Studying the Bible is not a sprint but a life journey with a daily rhythm of Bible reading, study, meditation, and prayer.

It is possible to work through the *NLT Study Bible* more quickly or more slowly than this. If you read six days per week rather than five, you will finish in four years, two months. You can finish twice as quickly by reading and studying two sections per day. Whatever pace you choose, we encourage you not just to read but also to question, reflect, meditate, and pray about what you have read. Use a Bible journal to record your discoveries, thoughts, questions, and prayers (see "Keep a Journal," p. A18). Follow some of the cross-references to other passages. You might even choose to go twice as slowly to spend more time on each passage.

There are a variety of ways to work through the *NLT Study Bible.* You could simply read through it from beginning to end, pp. 1– 2205. You could also move around, reading a book at a time from various places. Another possibility is to read a section of the Bible at a time, beginning with the section introduction and then moving through each book in that section. You could also read the Bible chronologically; the "Master Timeline" on pp. A20 – 25 shows how the different books of the Bible are related in history, and the chronology articles give an overview of each era in biblical history. We encourage you to follow whatever sequence makes the most sense to you.

We wish you well on your journey through the *NLT Study Bible* and pray for God's blessings along the way. Please tell us about your experiences at www.NLTStudyBible.com, or feel free to send us an e-mail at NLTStudyBible@tyndale.com.

☐ *Introduction to the Old Testament*
☐ *Old Testament Background*
☐ *Introduction to the Pentateuch*

GENESIS
☐ *Gen Introduction*
☐ **Gen 1–11**
☐ **Gen 12–34**
☐ **Gen 35–50**
☐ Gen 1:1-13
☐ Gen 1:14–2:3
☐ Gen 2:4-25
☐ Gen 3:1-24
☐ Gen 4:1-24
☐ Gen 4:25–5:32
☐ Gen 6:1-22
☐ Gen 7:1-24
☐ Gen 8:1-22
☐ Gen 9:1-29
☐ Gen 10:1-32
☐ Gen 11:1-32
☐ Gen 12:1-20
☐ Gen 13:1-18
☐ Gen 14:1-24
☐ Gen 15:1-21
☐ Gen 16:1-16
☐ Gen 17:1-27
☐ Gen 18:1-33
☐ Gen 19:1-38
☐ Gen 20:1-18
☐ Gen 21:1-34
☐ Gen 22:1-19
☐ Gen 22:20–23:20
☐ Gen 24:1-67
☐ Gen 25:1-34
☐ Gen 26:1-35
☐ Gen 27:1-40
☐ Gen 27:41–28:22
☐ Gen 29:1-30
☐ Gen 29:31–30:24
☐ Gen 30:25–31:21
☐ Gen 31:22-55
☐ Gen 32:1-32
☐ Gen 33:1-20
☐ Gen 34:1-31
☐ Gen 35:1-29
☐ Gen 36:1–37:1
☐ Gen 37:2-36
☐ Gen 38:1-30
☐ Gen 39:1–40:23
☐ Gen 41:1-57
☐ Gen 42:1-38
☐ Gen 43:1-34
☐ Gen 44:1-34
☐ Gen 45:1-28
☐ Gen 46:1-34
☐ Gen 47:1-31
☐ Gen 48:1-22
☐ Gen 49:1-33
☐ Gen 50:1-26

☐ *Chronology of Abraham to Joshua*

EXODUS
☐ *Exod Introduction*
☐ **Exod 1–12**
☐ **Exod 13–24**
☐ **Exod 25–40**
☐ Exod 1:1-22
☐ Exod 2:1-25
☐ Exod 3:1-22
☐ Exod 4:1-28
☐ Exod 4:29–5:23
☐ Exod 6:1–7:7
☐ Exod 7:8–8:19
☐ Exod 8:20–9:35
☐ Exod 10:1–11:10
☐ Exod 12:1-30
☐ Exod 12:31–13:16
☐ Exod 13:17–14:31
☐ Exod 15:1-21
☐ Exod 15:22–16:36
☐ Exod 17:1–18:27
☐ Exod 19:1-25
☐ Exod 20:1-21
☐ Exod 20:22–21:36
☐ Exod 22:1-31
☐ Exod 23:1-33
☐ Exod 24:1-18
☐ Exod 25:1-30
☐ Exod 25:31–27:19
☐ Exod 27:20–28:43
☐ Exod 29:1-46
☐ Exod 30:1-38
☐ Exod 31:1-18
☐ Exod 32:1-35
☐ Exod 33:1-23
☐ Exod 34:1-35
☐ Exod 35:1–36:38
☐ Exod 37:1–38:31
☐ Exod 39:1-43
☐ Exod 40:1-38

LEVITICUS
☐ *Lev Introduction*
☐ **Lev 1–15**
☐ **Lev 16–27**
☐ Lev 1:1-17
☐ Lev 2:1-16
☐ Lev 3:1-17
☐ Lev 4:1-35
☐ Lev 5:1-13
☐ Lev 5:14–6:7
☐ Lev 6:8-30
☐ Lev 7:1-38
☐ Lev 8:1-36
☐ Lev 9:1-24
☐ Lev 10:1-20
☐ Lev 11:1-47
☐ Lev 12:1–13:46
☐ Lev 13:47–14:32
☐ Lev 14:33–15:33
☐ Lev 16:1-34
☐ Lev 17:1-16
☐ Lev 18:1-30
☐ Lev 19:1-37
☐ Lev 20:1-27
☐ Lev 21:1–22:33
☐ Lev 23:1-22
☐ Lev 23:23-44
☐ Lev 24:1-23
☐ Lev 25:1-22
☐ Lev 25:23-55
☐ Lev 26:1-46
☐ Lev 27:1-34

NUMBERS
☐ *Num Introduction*
☐ **Num 1–12**
☐ **Num 13–24**
☐ **Num 25–36**
☐ Num 1:1–2:34
☐ Num 3:1-51
☐ Num 4:1-49
☐ Num 5:1-31
☐ Num 6:1-27

☐ Num 7:1-89
☐ Num 8:1-26
☐ Num 9:1-23
☐ Num 10:1-32
☐ Num 10:33–11:30
☐ Num 11:31–12:16
☐ Num 13:1-33
☐ Num 14:1-25
☐ Num 14:26-45
☐ Num 15:1-41
☐ Num 16:1-35
☐ Num 16:36–17:13
☐ Num 18:1-32
☐ Num 19:1-22
☐ Num 20:1-29
☐ Num 21:1-35
☐ Num 22:1-20
☐ Num 22:21-41
☐ Num 23:1-30
☐ Num 24:1-25
☐ Num 25:1-18
☐ Num 26:1-65
☐ Num 27:1-23
☐ Num 28:1-31
☐ Num 29:1-40
☐ Num 30:1-16
☐ Num 31:1-54
☐ Num 32:1-42
☐ Num 33:1-49
☐ Num 33:50–34:29
☐ Num 35:1-34
☐ Num 36:1-13

DEUTERONOMY

☐ *Deut Introduction*
☐ **Deut 1–11**
☐ **Deut 12–22**
☐ **Deut 23–34**
☐ Deut 1:1-18
☐ Deut 1:19-46
☐ Deut 2:1-37
☐ Deut 3:1-29
☐ Deut 4:1-31
☐ Deut 4:32-49
☐ Deut 5:1-33
☐ Deut 6:1-25
☐ Deut 7:1-26
☐ Deut 8:1-20
☐ Deut 9:1-29
☐ Deut 10:1-22
☐ Deut 11:1-32
☐ Deut 12:1-32
☐ Deut 13:1-18
☐ Deut 14:1-29
☐ Deut 15:1-23
☐ Deut 16:1-17
☐ Deut 16:18–17:20
☐ Deut 18:1-22
☐ Deut 19:1-21
☐ Deut 20:1-20
☐ Deut 21:1-23
☐ Deut 22:1-30
☐ Deut 23:1-25
☐ Deut 24:1-22
☐ Deut 25:1-19
☐ Deut 26:1-19
☐ Deut 27:1-26
☐ Deut 28:1-68
☐ Deut 29:1-29
☐ Deut 30:1-20
☐ Deut 31:1-29
☐ Deut 31:30–32:47
☐ Deut 32:48–33:29
☐ Deut 34:1-12

☐ *Introduction to the OT Historical Books*

JOSHUA

☐ *Josh Introduction*
☐ **Josh 1–12**
☐ **Josh 13–24**
☐ Josh 1:1-18
☐ Josh 2:1-24
☐ Josh 3:1–4:24
☐ Josh 5:1-15
☐ Josh 6:1-27
☐ Josh 7:1-26
☐ Josh 8:1-35
☐ Josh 9:1-27
☐ Josh 10:1-43
☐ Josh 11:1–12:24
☐ Josh 13:1-33
☐ Josh 14:1-15
☐ Josh 15:1-63
☐ Josh 16:1–17:18
☐ Josh 18:1–19:51
☐ Josh 20:1-9
☐ Josh 21:1-45
☐ Josh 22:1-34
☐ Josh 23:1-16
☐ Josh 24:1-33

☐ *Chronology of the Time of the Judges*

JUDGES

☐ *Judg Introduction*
☐ **Judg 1–10**
☐ **Judg 11–21**
☐ Judg 1:1-36
☐ Judg 2:1-23
☐ Judg 3:1-31
☐ Judg 4:1-24
☐ Judg 5:1-31
☐ Judg 6:1-40
☐ Judg 7:1-25
☐ Judg 8:1-35
☐ Judg 9:1-57
☐ Judg 10:1-18
☐ Judg 11:1-40
☐ Judg 12:1-15
☐ Judg 13:1-25
☐ Judg 14:1-20
☐ Judg 15:1-20
☐ Judg 16:1-31
☐ Judg 17:1-13
☐ Judg 18:1-31
☐ Judg 19:1-30
☐ Judg 20:1-48
☐ Judg 21:1-25

RUTH

☐ *Ruth Introduction* **& Ruth 1–4**
☐ Ruth 1:1-22
☐ Ruth 2:1-23
☐ Ruth 3:1-18
☐ Ruth 4:1-22

1 SAMUEL

☐ *1 Sam Introduction*
☐ **1 Sam 1–15**
☐ **1 Sam 16–31**
☐ 1 Sam 1:1–2:11
☐ 1 Sam 2:12-36
☐ 1 Sam 3:1–4:1a
☐ 1 Sam 4:1b-22
☐ 1 Sam 5:1–7:2
☐ 1 Sam 7:3–8:22
☐ 1 Sam 9:1–10:16
☐ 1 Sam 10:17–11:15
☐ 1 Sam 12:1-25
☐ 1 Sam 13:1-23
☐ 1 Sam 14:1-52
☐ 1 Sam 15:1-35
☐ 1 Sam 16:1-23
☐ 1 Sam 17:1-58
☐ 1 Sam 18:1-30
☐ 1 Sam 19:1-24
☐ 1 Sam 20:1-42
☐ 1 Sam 21:1–22:2
☐ 1 Sam 22:3-23
☐ 1 Sam 23:1-29
☐ 1 Sam 24:1-22
☐ 1 Sam 25:1-44
☐ 1 Sam 26:1-25
☐ 1 Sam 27:1–28:2
☐ 1 Sam 28:3-25
☐ 1 Sam 29:1-11
☐ 1 Sam 30:1-31
☐ 1 Sam 31:1-13

2 SAMUEL

☐ *2 Sam Introduction*
☐ **2 Sam 1–12**
☐ **2 Sam 13–24**
☐ 2 Sam 1:1-27
☐ 2 Sam 2:1–3:5
☐ 2 Sam 3:6-39
☐ 2 Sam 4:1–5:10
☐ 2 Sam 5:11–6:23
☐ 2 Sam 7:1-29
☐ 2 Sam 8:1-18
☐ 2 Sam 9:1-13
☐ 2 Sam 10:1-19
☐ 2 Sam 11:1-27
☐ 2 Sam 12:1-31
☐ 2 Sam 13:1-39
☐ 2 Sam 14:1-33
☐ 2 Sam 15:1-37
☐ 2 Sam 16:1-23
☐ 2 Sam 17:1-29
☐ 2 Sam 18:1-33
☐ 2 Sam 19:1-43
☐ 2 Sam 20:1-26
☐ 2 Sam 21:1-22
☐ 2 Sam 22:1-51
☐ 2 Sam 23:1-39
☐ 2 Sam 24:1-25

☐ *Chronology of Israel's Monarchy*

1 KINGS

☐ *1 Kgs Introduction*
☐ **1 Kgs 1–11**
☐ **1 Kgs 12–22**
☐ 1 Kgs 1:1-53
☐ 1 Kgs 2:1-46
☐ 1 Kgs 3:1-28
☐ 1 Kgs 4:1-34
☐ 1 Kgs 5:1-18
☐ 1 Kgs 6:1-38
☐ 1 Kgs 7:1-40
☐ 1 Kgs 7:41–8:21
☐ 1 Kgs 8:22-53
☐ 1 Kgs 8:54–9:9
☐ 1 Kgs 9:10-28
☐ 1 Kgs 10:1-29
☐ 1 Kgs 11:1-43
☐ 1 Kgs 12:1-33
☐ 1 Kgs 13:1-34
☐ 1 Kgs 14:1-31
☐ 1 Kgs 15:1-31
☐ 1 Kgs 15:32–16:28
☐ 1 Kgs 16:29–17:24
☐ 1 Kgs 18:1-46
☐ 1 Kgs 19:1-21
☐ 1 Kgs 20:1-43
☐ 1 Kgs 21:1-29
☐ 1 Kgs 22:1-53

2 KINGS

☐ *2 Kgs Introduction*
☐ **2 Kgs 1–12**
☐ **2 Kgs 13–25**
☐ 2 Kgs 1:1-18
☐ 2 Kgs 2:1-25
☐ 2 Kgs 3:1-27
☐ 2 Kgs 4:1-37
☐ 2 Kgs 4:38–5:27
☐ 2 Kgs 6:1-33
☐ 2 Kgs 7:1-20
☐ 2 Kgs 8:1-29
☐ 2 Kgs 9:1-37
☐ 2 Kgs 10:1-36
☐ 2 Kgs 11:1-20
☐ 2 Kgs 11:21–12:21
☐ 2 Kgs 13:1-25
☐ 2 Kgs 14:1-29
☐ 2 Kgs 15:1-31
☐ 2 Kgs 15:32–16:20
☐ 2 Kgs 17:1-41
☐ 2 Kgs 18:1-16
☐ 2 Kgs 18:17–19:37
☐ 2 Kgs 20:1-21
☐ 2 Kgs 21:1-26
☐ 2 Kgs 22:1-20
☐ 2 Kgs 23:1-20
☐ 2 Kgs 23:21-34
☐ 2 Kgs 23:35–24:20a
☐ 2 Kgs 24:20b–25:30

1 CHRONICLES

☐ *1 Chr Introduction*
☐ **1 Chr 1–16**
☐ **1 Chr 17–29**
☐ 1 Chr 1:1–2:55
☐ 1 Chr 3:1–5:26
☐ 1 Chr 6:1–7:40
☐ 1 Chr 8:1–9:44
☐ 1 Chr 10:1–11:47
☐ 1 Chr 12:1–13:14
☐ 1 Chr 14:1–15:29
☐ 1 Chr 16:1-43
☐ 1 Chr 17:1-27
☐ 1 Chr 18:1-17
☐ 1 Chr 19:1-19
☐ 1 Chr 20:1-8
☐ 1 Chr 21:1-30
☐ 1 Chr 22:1-19
☐ 1 Chr 23:1–24:31
☐ 1 Chr 25:1–26:32
☐ 1 Chr 27:1-34
☐ 1 Chr 28:1-21
☐ 1 Chr 29:1-30

2 CHRONICLES

☐ *2 Chr Introduction* **& 2 Chr 1–12**
☐ **2 Chr 13–24**
☐ **2 Chr 25–36**
☐ 2 Chr 1:1-17
☐ 2 Chr 2:1–3:14
☐ 2 Chr 3:15–5:1
☐ 2 Chr 5:2-14
☐ 2 Chr 6:1-42
☐ 2 Chr 7:1-22
☐ 2 Chr 8:1-18
☐ 2 Chr 9:1-31
☐ 2 Chr 10:1-19
☐ 2 Chr 11:1-23
☐ 2 Chr 12:1-16
☐ 2 Chr 13:1-22
☐ 2 Chr 14:1-15
☐ 2 Chr 15:1-19
☐ 2 Chr 16:1-14
☐ 2 Chr 17:1-19
☐ 2 Chr 18:1-34
☐ 2 Chr 19:1–21:1
☐ 2 Chr 21:2-20
☐ 2 Chr 22:1–23:21
☐ 2 Chr 24:1-27
☐ 2 Chr 25:1-28
☐ 2 Chr 26:1-23
☐ 2 Chr 27:1–28:27
☐ 2 Chr 29:1-36
☐ 2 Chr 30:1–31:21
☐ 2 Chr 32:1-33
☐ 2 Chr 33:1-25
☐ 2 Chr 34:1-33
☐ 2 Chr 35:1-27
☐ 2 Chr 36:1-23

☐ *Chronology of Israel's Exile and Return*

EZRA

☐ *Ezra Introduction* **& Ezra 1–10**
☐ Ezra 1:1–2:70
☐ Ezra 3:1-13
☐ Ezra 4:1-24
☐ Ezra 5:1–6:22
☐ Ezra 7:1-28
☐ Ezra 8:1-36
☐ Ezra 9:1-15
☐ Ezra 10:1-44

NEHEMIAH

☐ *Neh Introduction*
☐ **Neh 1–13**
☐ Neh 1:1–2:20
☐ Neh 3:1-32
☐ Neh 4:1-23
☐ Neh 5:1-19
☐ Neh 6:1-19
☐ Neh 7:1-73
☐ Neh 8:1-18
☐ Neh 9:1-38
☐ Neh 10:1-39
☐ Neh 11:1-36
☐ Neh 12:1-47
☐ Neh 13:1-31

ESTHER

☐ *Esth Introduction* **& Esth 1–10**
☐ Esth 1:1–2:23

☐ Esth 3:1–4:17
☐ Esth 5:1–6:14
☐ Esth 7:1–8:17
☐ Esth 9:1–10:3

☐ *Introduction to the Books of Poetry and Wisdom*

JOB
☐ *Job Introduction & Job 1–14*
☐ **Job 15–28**
☐ **Job 29–42**
☐ Job 1:1-22
☐ Job 2:1–3:26
☐ Job 4:1–5:27
☐ Job 6:1–7:21
☐ Job 8:1-22
☐ Job 9:1-35
☐ Job 10:1-22
☐ Job 11:1-20
☐ Job 12:1-25
☐ Job 13:1–14:22
☐ Job 15:1-35
☐ Job 16:1-22
☐ Job 17:1-16
☐ Job 18:1-21
☐ Job 19:1-29
☐ Job 20:1-29
☐ Job 21:1-34
☐ Job 22:1-30
☐ Job 23:1-17
☐ Job 24:1-25
☐ Job 25:1–26:14
☐ Job 27:1-23
☐ Job 28:1-28
☐ Job 29:1-25
☐ Job 30:1-31
☐ Job 31:1-40
☐ Job 32:1-22
☐ Job 33:1-33
☐ Job 34:1-37
☐ Job 35:1–36:21
☐ Job 36:22–37:24
☐ Job 38:1-41
☐ Job 39:1–40:2
☐ Job 40:3–41:34
☐ Job 42:1-17

PSALMS
☐ *Ps Introduction*
☐ Ps 1
☐ Ps 2
☐ Pss 3–4
☐ Pss 5–6
☐ Ps 7
☐ Ps 8
☐ Pss 9–10
☐ Pss 11–12
☐ Pss 13–15
☐ Pss 16–17
☐ Ps 18
☐ Ps 19
☐ Pss 20–21
☐ Ps 22
☐ Ps 23
☐ Ps 24
☐ Ps 25
☐ Pss 26–27
☐ Pss 28–29
☐ Pss 30–31
☐ Pss 32–33
☐ Ps 34
☐ Ps 35
☐ Ps 36
☐ Ps 37
☐ Pss 38–39
☐ Ps 40
☐ Ps 41
☐ Pss 42–43
☐ Ps 44
☐ Pss 45–46
☐ Pss 47–48
☐ Ps 49
☐ Ps 50
☐ Ps 51
☐ Pss 52–53
☐ Pss 54–55
☐ Pss 56–57
☐ Pss 58–59
☐ Pss 60–61
☐ Pss 62–63
☐ Pss 64–65
☐ Pss 66–67
☐ Ps 68
☐ Ps 69
☐ Pss 70–71
☐ Ps 72
☐ Ps 73
☐ Ps 74
☐ Pss 75–76
☐ Ps 77
☐ Ps 78
☐ Pss 79–80
☐ Pss 81–83
☐ Pss 84–85
☐ Ps 86
☐ Pss 87–88
☐ Ps 89
☐ Ps 90
☐ Ps 91
☐ Pss 92–93
☐ Pss 94–95
☐ Pss 96–97
☐ Pss 98–100
☐ Pss 101–102
☐ Ps 103
☐ Ps 104
☐ Ps 105
☐ Ps 106
☐ Ps 107
☐ Pss 108–109
☐ Ps 110
☐ Pss 111–112
☐ Pss 113–115
☐ Pss 116–118
☐ Ps 119:1-56
☐ Ps 119:57-112
☐ Ps 119:113-176
☐ Pss 120–123
☐ Pss 124–127
☐ Pss 128–130
☐ Pss 131–132
☐ Pss 133–135
☐ Pss 136–137
☐ Pss 138–139
☐ Pss 140–142
☐ Pss 143–144
☐ Pss 145–147
☐ Pss 148–150

PROVERBS
☐ *Prov Introduction*
☐ **Prov 1–9**
☐ Prov 1:1-33
☐ Prov 2:1-22
☐ Prov 3:1-35
☐ Prov 4:1-27
☐ Prov 5:1-23
☐ Prov 6:1-35
☐ Prov 7:1-27
☐ Prov 8:1-36
☐ Prov 9:1-18
☐ Prov 10:1-32
☐ Prov 11:1-31
☐ Prov 12:1-28
☐ Prov 13:1-25
☐ Prov 14:1-35
☐ Prov 15:1-33
☐ Prov 16:1-33
☐ Prov 17:1-28
☐ Prov 18:1-24
☐ Prov 19:1-29
☐ Prov 20:1-30
☐ Prov 21:1-31
☐ Prov 22:1-29
☐ Prov 23:1-35
☐ Prov 24:1-34
☐ Prov 25:1-28
☐ Prov 26:1-28
☐ Prov 27:1-27
☐ Prov 28:1-28
☐ Prov 29:1-27
☐ Prov 30:1-33
☐ Prov 31:1-31

ECCLESIASTES
☐ *Eccl Introduction*
☐ **Eccl 1–12**
☐ Eccl 1:1–2:11
☐ Eccl 2:12–3:15
☐ Eccl 3:16–4:16
☐ Eccl 5:1-20
☐ Eccl 6:1–7:14
☐ Eccl 7:15–8:17
☐ Eccl 9:1–10:4
☐ Eccl 10:5–11:6
☐ Eccl 11:7–12:14

SONG OF SONGS
☐ *Song Introduction*
☐ **Song 1–8**
☐ Song 1:1–2:17
☐ Song 3:1–5:1
☐ Song 5:2–6:10
☐ Song 6:11–8:14

☐ *Introduction to the Books of the Prophets*

ISAIAH
☐ *Isa Introduction*
☐ **Isa 1–19**
☐ **Isa 20–39**
☐ **Isa 40–53**
☐ **Isa 54–66**
☐ Isa 1:1-20
☐ Isa 1:21-31
☐ Isa 2:1-22
☐ Isa 3:1-15
☐ Isa 3:16–5:7
☐ Isa 5:8-30
☐ Isa 6:1-13
☐ Isa 7:1-25
☐ Isa 8:1-22
☐ Isa 9:1-21
☐ Isa 10:1-19
☐ Isa 10:20-34
☐ Isa 11:1-16
☐ Isa 12:1–13:22
☐ Isa 14:1-27
☐ Isa 14:28–15:9
☐ Isa 16:1-14
☐ Isa 17:1–18:7
☐ Isa 19:1–20:6
☐ Isa 21:1-17
☐ Isa 22:1-25
☐ Isa 23:1-18
☐ Isa 24:1-23
☐ Isa 25:1-12
☐ Isa 26:1-21
☐ Isa 27:1-13
☐ Isa 28:1-29
☐ Isa 29:1-24
☐ Isa 30:1-17
☐ Isa 30:18-33
☐ Isa 31:1-9
☐ Isa 32:1-20
☐ Isa 33:1-24
☐ Isa 34:1-17
☐ Isa 35:1-10
☐ Isa 36:1-22
☐ Isa 37:1-20
☐ Isa 37:21-38
☐ Isa 38:1-22
☐ Isa 39:1-8
☐ Isa 40:1-11
☐ Isa 40:12-31
☐ Isa 41:1-29
☐ Isa 42:1-25
☐ Isa 43:1-28
☐ Isa 44:1-28
☐ Isa 45:1-25
☐ Isa 46:1–47:15
☐ Isa 48:1-22
☐ Isa 49:1-26
☐ Isa 50:1-11
☐ Isa 51:1-23
☐ Isa 52:1-12
☐ Isa 52:13–53:12
☐ Isa 54:1-17
☐ Isa 55:1-13
☐ Isa 56:1–57:2
☐ Isa 57:3-21
☐ Isa 58:1-14
☐ Isa 59:1-21
☐ Isa 60:1-22
☐ Isa 61:1–62:12
☐ Isa 63:1-19
☐ Isa 64:1-12
☐ Isa 65:1-25
☐ Isa 66:1-24

JEREMIAH
☐ *Jer Introduction*
☐ **Jer 1–20**
☐ **Jer 21–33**
☐ **Jer 34–52**
☐ Jer 1:1-19
☐ Jer 2:1-37
☐ Jer 3:1–4:2
☐ Jer 4:3-31
☐ Jer 5:1-31
☐ Jer 6:1-30
☐ Jer 7:1-34
☐ Jer 8:1–9:2
☐ Jer 9:3-26
☐ Jer 10:1-25
☐ Jer 11:1-23
☐ Jer 12:1-17
☐ Jer 13:1-27
☐ Jer 14:1-22
☐ Jer 15:1-21
☐ Jer 16:1-21
☐ Jer 17:1-27
☐ Jer 18:1–19:15
☐ Jer 20:1–21:10
☐ Jer 21:11–22:23
☐ Jer 22:24–23:8
☐ Jer 23:9-40
☐ Jer 24:1–25:14
☐ Jer 25:15-38
☐ Jer 26:1-24
☐ Jer 27:1-22
☐ Jer 28:1-17
☐ Jer 29:1-32
☐ Jer 30:1-24
☐ Jer 31:1-40
☐ Jer 32:1-44
☐ Jer 33:1-26
☐ Jer 34:1-22
☐ Jer 35:1-19
☐ Jer 36:1-32
☐ Jer 37:1-21
☐ Jer 38:1-28
☐ Jer 39:1-18
☐ Jer 40:1–41:18
☐ Jer 42:1–43:13
☐ Jer 44:1-30
☐ Jer 45:1–46:12
☐ Jer 46:13-28
☐ Jer 47:1–48:10
☐ Jer 48:11-47
☐ Jer 49:1-39
☐ Jer 50:1-20
☐ Jer 50:21-46
☐ Jer 51:1-35
☐ Jer 51:36-64
☐ Jer 52:1-34

LAMENTATIONS
☐ *Lam Introduction & Lam 1–5*
☐ Lam 1:1-22
☐ Lam 2:1-22
☐ Lam 3:1-66
☐ Lam 4:1–5:22

EZEKIEL
☐ *Ezek Introduction*
☐ **Ezek 1–16**
☐ **Ezek 17–32**
☐ **Ezek 33–48**
☐ Ezek 1:1-28
☐ Ezek 2:1–3:15
☐ Ezek 3:16–4:8
☐ Ezek 4:9–5:17
☐ Ezek 6:1–7:27
☐ Ezek 8:1-18
☐ Ezek 9:1-11
☐ Ezek 10:1–11:13
☐ Ezek 11:14–12:20
☐ Ezek 12:21–13:23
☐ Ezek 14:1-23
☐ Ezek 15:1–16:34
☐ Ezek 16:35-63
☐ Ezek 17:1-24
☐ Ezek 18:1-32
☐ Ezek 19:1-14
☐ Ezek 20:1-44

- ☐ Ezek 20:45–21:17
- ☐ Ezek 21:18-32
- ☐ Ezek 22:1-31
- ☐ Ezek 23:1-21
- ☐ Ezek 23:22-49
- ☐ Ezek 24:1-27
- ☐ Ezek 25:1-17
- ☐ Ezek 26:1-21
- ☐ Ezek 27:1-36
- ☐ Ezek 28:1-26
- ☐ Ezek 29:1-21
- ☐ Ezek 30:1-26
- ☐ Ezek 31:1-18
- ☐ Ezek 32:1-32
- ☐ Ezek 33:1-33
- ☐ Ezek 34:1-31
- ☐ Ezek 35:1-15
- ☐ Ezek 36:1-38
- ☐ Ezek 37:1-28
- ☐ Ezek 38:1-23
- ☐ Ezek 39:1-29
- ☐ Ezek 40:1-43
- ☐ Ezek 40:44–41:26
- ☐ Ezek 42:1-20
- ☐ Ezek 43:1-27
- ☐ Ezek 44:1-31
- ☐ Ezek 45:1-25
- ☐ Ezek 46:1-24
- ☐ Ezek 47:1-23
- ☐ Ezek 48:1-35

DANIEL

- ☐ *Dan Introduction*
- ☐ **Dan 1–12**
- ☐ Dan 1:1-21
- ☐ Dan 2:1-49
- ☐ Dan 3:1-30
- ☐ Dan 4:1-37
- ☐ Dan 5:1-31
- ☐ Dan 6:1-28
- ☐ Dan 7:1-28
- ☐ Dan 8:1-27
- ☐ Dan 9:1-27
- ☐ Dan 10:1–11:1
- ☐ Dan 11:2-45
- ☐ Dan 12:1-13

HOSEA

- ☐ *Hos Introduction*
- ☐ **Hos 1–14**
- ☐ Hos 1:1–2:23
- ☐ Hos 3:1–4:19
- ☐ Hos 5:1–6:11
- ☐ Hos 7:1–8:14
- ☐ Hos 9:1–10:15
- ☐ Hos 11:1–12:14
- ☐ Hos 13:1–14:9

JOEL

- ☐ *Joel Introduction* **& Joel 1–3**
- ☐ Joel 1:1–2:17
- ☐ Joel 2:18–3:21

AMOS

- ☐ *Amos Introduction* **& Amos 1–9**
- ☐ Amos 1:1–2:16
- ☐ Amos 3:1–4:13
- ☐ Amos 5:1–6:14
- ☐ Amos 7:1–8:14
- ☐ Amos 9:1-15

OBADIAH

- ☐ *Obad Introduction*
- ☐ Obad 1:1-21

JONAH

- ☐ *Jon Introduction* **& Jon 1–4**
- ☐ Jon 1:1–2:10
- ☐ Jon 3:1–4:11

MICAH

- ☐ *Mic Introduction* **& Mic 1–7**
- ☐ Mic 1:1–2:13
- ☐ Mic 3:1–5:15
- ☐ Mic 6:1–7:20

NAHUM

- ☐ *Nah Introduction* **& Nah 1–3**
- ☐ Nah 1:1–2:10
- ☐ Nah 2:11–3:19

HABAKKUK

- ☐ *Hab Introduction* **& Hab 1–3**
- ☐ Hab 1:1–2:20
- ☐ Hab 3:1-19

ZEPHANIAH

- ☐ *Zeph Introduction* **& Zeph 1–3**
- ☐ Zeph 1:1–2:3
- ☐ Zeph 2:4–3:20

HAGGAI

- ☐ *Hag Introduction*
- ☐ Hag 1:1–2:23

ZECHARIAH

- ☐ *Zech Introduction*
- ☐ **Zech 1–14**
- ☐ Zech 1:1–2:13
- ☐ Zech 3:1–6:15
- ☐ Zech 7:1–8:23
- ☐ Zech 9:1-17
- ☐ Zech 10:1–11:17
- ☐ Zech 12:1–13:9
- ☐ Zech 14:1-21

MALACHI

- ☐ *Mal Introduction* **& Mal 1–4**
- ☐ Mal 1:1–2:16
- ☐ Mal 2:17–4:6

- ☐ *Historical Background of the Intertestamental Period*
- ☐ *Introduction to the New Testament*
- ☐ *Introduction to the Four Gospels*
- ☐ *Chronology of the Life of Jesus*

MATTHEW

- ☐ *Matt Introduction*
- ☐ **Matt 1–7**
- ☐ **Matt 8–18**
- ☐ **Matt 19–28**
- ☐ Matt 1:1-25
- ☐ Matt 2:1-23
- ☐ Matt 3:1-17
- ☐ Matt 4:1-25
- ☐ Matt 5:1-20
- ☐ Matt 5:21-48
- ☐ Matt 6:1-34
- ☐ Matt 7:1-29
- ☐ Matt 8:1-27
- ☐ Matt 8:28–9:13
- ☐ Matt 9:14-38
- ☐ Matt 10:1-25
- ☐ Matt 10:26–11:1
- ☐ Matt 11:2-24
- ☐ Matt 11:25–12:21
- ☐ Matt 12:22-50
- ☐ Matt 13:1-33
- ☐ Matt 13:34-58
- ☐ Matt 14:1-36
- ☐ Matt 15:1-28
- ☐ Matt 15:29–16:12
- ☐ Matt 16:13-28
- ☐ Matt 17:1-27
- ☐ Matt 18:1-20
- ☐ Matt 18:21-35
- ☐ Matt 19:1-30
- ☐ Matt 20:1-17
- ☐ Matt 20:18-34
- ☐ Matt 21:1-22
- ☐ Matt 21:23-46
- ☐ Matt 22:1-22
- ☐ Matt 22:23–23:12
- ☐ Matt 23:13-39
- ☐ Matt 24:1-28
- ☐ Matt 24:29-51
- ☐ Matt 25:1-30
- ☐ Matt 25:31-46
- ☐ Matt 26:1-30
- ☐ Matt 26:31-56
- ☐ Matt 26:57–27:2
- ☐ Matt 27:3-31
- ☐ Matt 27:32-66
- ☐ Matt 28:1-20

MARK

- ☐ *Mark Introduction*
- ☐ **Mark 1–8**
- ☐ **Mark 9–16**
- ☐ Mark 1:1-13
- ☐ Mark 1:14-45
- ☐ Mark 2:1-28
- ☐ Mark 3:1-30
- ☐ Mark 3:31–4:9
- ☐ Mark 4:10-34
- ☐ Mark 4:35–5:20
- ☐ Mark 5:21–6:6a
- ☐ Mark 6:6b-29
- ☐ Mark 6:30-56
- ☐ Mark 7:1-30
- ☐ Mark 7:31–8:21
- ☐ Mark 8:22–9:1
- ☐ Mark 9:2-13
- ☐ Mark 9:14-37
- ☐ Mark 9:38–10:16
- ☐ Mark 10:17-45
- ☐ Mark 10:46–11:14
- ☐ Mark 11:15-33
- ☐ Mark 12:1-27
- ☐ Mark 12:28-44
- ☐ Mark 13:1-20
- ☐ Mark 13:21-37
- ☐ Mark 14:1-26
- ☐ Mark 14:27-52
- ☐ Mark 14:53-72
- ☐ Mark 15:1-32
- ☐ Mark 15:33-47
- ☐ Mark 16:1-20

LUKE

- ☐ *Luke Introduction*
- ☐ **Luke 1–7**
- ☐ **Luke 8–16**
- ☐ **Luke 17–24**
- ☐ Luke 1:1-38
- ☐ Luke 1:39-80
- ☐ Luke 2:1-24
- ☐ Luke 2:25-52
- ☐ Luke 3:1-14
- ☐ Luke 3:15-38
- ☐ Luke 4:1-30
- ☐ Luke 4:31–5:11
- ☐ Luke 5:12-39
- ☐ Luke 6:1-26
- ☐ Luke 6:27-49
- ☐ Luke 7:1-35
- ☐ Luke 7:36– 8:15
- ☐ Luke 8:16-39
- ☐ Luke 8:40–9:9
- ☐ Luke 9:10-36
- ☐ Luke 9:37-50
- ☐ Luke 9:51–10:20
- ☐ Luke 10:21-42
- ☐ Luke 11:1-28
- ☐ Luke 11:29-54
- ☐ Luke 12:1-34
- ☐ Luke 12:35-59
- ☐ Luke 13:1-35
- ☐ Luke 14:1-35
- ☐ Luke 15:1-32
- ☐ Luke 16:1-31
- ☐ Luke 17:1-37
- ☐ Luke 18:1-34
- ☐ Luke 18:35–19:27
- ☐ Luke 19:28-48
- ☐ Luke 20:1-26
- ☐ Luke 20:27–21:4
- ☐ Luke 21:5-24
- ☐ Luke 21:25-38
- ☐ Luke 22:1-38
- ☐ Luke 22:39-71
- ☐ Luke 23:1-25
- ☐ Luke 23:26-56
- ☐ Luke 24:1-34
- ☐ Luke 24:35-53

JOHN

- ☐ *John Introduction*
- ☐ **John 1–7**
- ☐ **John 8–14**
- ☐ **John 15–21**
- ☐ John 1:1-18
- ☐ John 1:19-51
- ☐ John 2:1-25
- ☐ John 3:1-36
- ☐ John 4:1-38
- ☐ John 4:39–5:15
- ☐ John 5:16-47
- ☐ John 6:1-21
- ☐ John 6:22-71
- ☐ John 7:1-36
- ☐ John 7:37–8:11
- ☐ John 8:12-30
- ☐ John 8:31-59
- ☐ John 9:1-34
- ☐ John 9:35–10:21
- ☐ John 10:22-42
- ☐ John 11:1-44
- ☐ John 11:45–12:19
- ☐ John 12:20-50
- ☐ John 13:1-38
- ☐ John 14:1-31
- ☐ John 15:1-27
- ☐ John 16:1-33
- ☐ John 17:1-26
- ☐ John 18:1-27
- ☐ John 18:28–19:16
- ☐ John 19:17-42
- ☐ John 20:1-23
- ☐ John 20:24-31
- ☐ John 21:1-25

- ☐ *Chronology of the Apostolic Age*

ACTS

- ☐ *Acts Introduction* **& Acts 1–9**
- ☐ **Acts 10–18**
- ☐ **Acts 19–28**
- ☐ Acts 1:1-26
- ☐ Acts 2:1-21
- ☐ Acts 2:22-47
- ☐ Acts 3:1-26
- ☐ Acts 4:1-31
- ☐ Acts 4:32–5:16
- ☐ Acts 5:17-42
- ☐ Acts 6:1–7:29
- ☐ Acts 7:30-60
- ☐ Acts 8:1-25
- ☐ Acts 8:26-40
- ☐ Acts 9:1-30
- ☐ Acts 9:31-43
- ☐ Acts 10:1-33
- ☐ Acts 10:34–11:18
- ☐ Acts 11:19–12:2
- ☐ Acts 12:3-25
- ☐ Acts 13:1-12
- ☐ Acts 13:13-43
- ☐ Acts 13:44–14:20
- ☐ Acts 14:21–15:21
- ☐ Acts 15:22-41
- ☐ Acts 16:1-15
- ☐ Acts 16:16-40
- ☐ Acts 17:1-15
- ☐ Acts 17:16-34
- ☐ Acts 18:1-23
- ☐ Acts 18:24–19:22
- ☐ Acts 19:23–20:6
- ☐ Acts 20:7-38
- ☐ Acts 21:1-25
- ☐ Acts 21:26–22:23
- ☐ Acts 22:24–23:22
- ☐ Acts 23:23–24:27
- ☐ Acts 25:1-27
- ☐ Acts 26:1-32
- ☐ Acts 27:1-26
- ☐ Acts 27:27–28:10
- ☐ Acts 28:11-31

- ☐ *Introduction to the Letters of Paul*

ROMANS

- ☐ *Rom Introduction*
- ☐ **Rom 1–8**

- ☐ **Rom 9–16**
- ☐ Rom 1:1-17
- ☐ Rom 1:18-32
- ☐ Rom 2:1-16
- ☐ Rom 2:17–3:8
- ☐ Rom 3:9-31
- ☐ Rom 4:1-25
- ☐ Rom 5:1-21
- ☐ Rom 6:1-23
- ☐ Rom 7:1-25
- ☐ Rom 8:1-17
- ☐ Rom 8:18-39
- ☐ Rom 9:1-23
- ☐ Rom 9:24-33
- ☐ Rom 10:1-21
- ☐ Rom 11:1-18
- ☐ Rom 11:19-36
- ☐ Rom 12:1-8
- ☐ Rom 12:9-21
- ☐ Rom 13:1-14
- ☐ Rom 14:1-23
- ☐ Rom 15:1-13
- ☐ Rom 15:14-33
- ☐ Rom 16:1-27

1 CORINTHIANS
- ☐ *1 Cor Introduction*
- ☐ **1 Cor 1–8**
- ☐ **1 Cor 9–16**
- ☐ 1 Cor 1:1-17
- ☐ 1 Cor 1:18-31
- ☐ 1 Cor 2:1-16
- ☐ 1 Cor 3:1-23
- ☐ 1 Cor 4:1-21
- ☐ 1 Cor 5:1-13
- ☐ 1 Cor 6:1-20
- ☐ 1 Cor 7:1-25
- ☐ 1 Cor 7:26-40
- ☐ 1 Cor 8:1-13
- ☐ 1 Cor 9:1-27
- ☐ 1 Cor 10:1-30
- ☐ 1 Cor 10:31–11:16
- ☐ 1 Cor 11:17-34
- ☐ 1 Cor 12:1-11
- ☐ 1 Cor 12:12-31
- ☐ 1 Cor 13:1-13
- ☐ 1 Cor 14:1-25
- ☐ 1 Cor 14:26-40
- ☐ 1 Cor 15:1-34
- ☐ 1 Cor 15:35-58
- ☐ 1 Cor 16:1-24

2 CORINTHIANS
- ☐ *2 Cor Introduction*
- ☐ **2 Cor 1–13**
- ☐ 2 Cor 1:1-24
- ☐ 2 Cor 2:1-17
- ☐ 2 Cor 3:1-18
- ☐ 2 Cor 4:1-18
- ☐ 2 Cor 5:1-21
- ☐ 2 Cor 6:1–7:1
- ☐ 2 Cor 7:2-16
- ☐ 2 Cor 8:1-24
- ☐ 2 Cor 9:1-15
- ☐ 2 Cor 10:1-18
- ☐ 2 Cor 11:1-33
- ☐ 2 Cor 12:1-21
- ☐ 2 Cor 13:1-14

GALATIANS
- ☐ *Gal Introduction* & **Gal 1–6**
- ☐ Gal 1:1-10
- ☐ Gal 1:11–2:10
- ☐ Gal 2:11-21
- ☐ Gal 3:1-14
- ☐ Gal 3:15-29
- ☐ Gal 4:1-20
- ☐ Gal 4:21–5:1
- ☐ Gal 5:2-12
- ☐ Gal 5:13-26
- ☐ Gal 6:1-10
- ☐ Gal 6:11-18

EPHESIANS
- ☐ *Eph Introduction* & **Eph 1–6**
- ☐ Eph 1:1-23
- ☐ Eph 2:1-18
- ☐ Eph 2:19–3:13
- ☐ Eph 3:14–4:16
- ☐ Eph 4:17-32
- ☐ Eph 5:1-20
- ☐ Eph 5:21–6:9
- ☐ Eph 6:10-24

PHILIPPIANS
- ☐ *Phil Introduction* & **Phil 1–4**
- ☐ Phil 1:1-26
- ☐ Phil 1:27–2:11
- ☐ Phil 2:12–3:1
- ☐ Phil 3:2–4:1
- ☐ Phil 4:2-23

COLOSSIANS
- ☐ *Col Introduction* & **Col 1–4**
- ☐ Col 1:1-14
- ☐ Col 1:15–2:5
- ☐ Col 2:6-23
- ☐ Col 3:1–4:1
- ☐ Col 4:2-18

1 THESSALONIANS
- ☐ *1 Thes Introduction* & **1 Thes 1–5**
- ☐ 1 Thes 1:1-10
- ☐ 1 Thes 2:1-20
- ☐ 1 Thes 3:1–4:8
- ☐ 1 Thes 4:9-18
- ☐ 1 Thes 5:1-28

2 THESSALONIANS
- ☐ *2 Thes Introduction* & **2 Thes 1–3**
- ☐ 2 Thes 1:1-12
- ☐ 2 Thes 2:1-17
- ☐ 2 Thes 3:1-18

- ☐ *Introduction to Paul's Letters to Timothy and Titus*

1 TIMOTHY
- ☐ *1 Tim Introduction* & **1 Tim 1–6**
- ☐ 1 Tim 1:1-20
- ☐ 1 Tim 2:1-15
- ☐ 1 Tim 3:1-16
- ☐ 1 Tim 4:1-16
- ☐ 1 Tim 5:1–6:2a
- ☐ 1 Tim 6:2b-21

2 TIMOTHY
- ☐ *2 Tim Introduction* & **2 Tim 1–4**
- ☐ 2 Tim 1:1-18
- ☐ 2 Tim 2:1-26
- ☐ 2 Tim 3:1–4:8
- ☐ 2 Tim 4:9-22

TITUS
- ☐ *Titus Introduction* & **Titus 1–3**
- ☐ Titus 1:1-16
- ☐ Titus 2:1-15
- ☐ Titus 3:1-15

PHILEMON
- ☐ *Phlm Introduction*
- ☐ Phlm 1:1-25

HEBREWS
- ☐ *Heb Introduction*
- ☐ **Heb 1–13**
- ☐ Heb 1:1-14
- ☐ Heb 2:1-18
- ☐ Heb 3:1-19
- ☐ Heb 4:1-13
- ☐ Heb 4:14–5:14
- ☐ Heb 6:1-12
- ☐ Heb 6:13–7:10
- ☐ Heb 7:11-28
- ☐ Heb 8:1-13
- ☐ Heb 9:1-10
- ☐ Heb 9:11-28
- ☐ Heb 10:1-18
- ☐ Heb 10:19-39
- ☐ Heb 11:1-16
- ☐ Heb 11:17-40
- ☐ Heb 12:1-17
- ☐ Heb 12:18-29
- ☐ Heb 13:1-25

JAMES
- ☐ *Jas Introduction* & **Jas 1–5**
- ☐ Jas 1:1-27
- ☐ Jas 2:1-26
- ☐ Jas 3:1–4:3
- ☐ Jas 4:4–5:6
- ☐ Jas 5:7-20

1 PETER
- ☐ *1 Pet Introduction* & **1 Pet 1–5**
- ☐ 1 Pet 1:1-21
- ☐ 1 Pet 1:22–2:12
- ☐ 1 Pet 2:13–3:7
- ☐ 1 Pet 3:8-22
- ☐ 1 Pet 4:1-19
- ☐ 1 Pet 5:1-14

2 PETER
- ☐ *2 Pet Introduction* & **2 Pet 1–3**
- ☐ 2 Pet 1:1-21
- ☐ 2 Pet 2:1-22
- ☐ 2 Pet 3:1-18

1 JOHN
- ☐ *1 Jn Introduction* & **1 Jn 1–5**
- ☐ 1 Jn 1:1–2:11
- ☐ 1 Jn 2:12-29
- ☐ 1 Jn 3:1-24
- ☐ 1 Jn 4:1-21
- ☐ 1 Jn 5:1-21

2 JOHN
- ☐ *2 Jn Introduction*
- ☐ 2 Jn 1:1-13

3 JOHN
- ☐ *3 Jn Introduction*
- ☐ 3 Jn 1:1-15

JUDE
- ☐ *Jude Introduction*
- ☐ Jude 1:1-25

REVELATION
- ☐ *Rev Introduction*
- ☐ **Rev 1–11**
- ☐ **Rev 12–22**
- ☐ Rev 1:1-20
- ☐ Rev 2:1-17
- ☐ Rev 2:18–3:6
- ☐ Rev 3:7-22
- ☐ Rev 4:1-11
- ☐ Rev 5:1-14
- ☐ Rev 6:1-17
- ☐ Rev 7:1-17
- ☐ Rev 8:1-13
- ☐ Rev 9:1-21
- ☐ Rev 10:1-11
- ☐ Rev 11:1-19
- ☐ Rev 12:1-18
- ☐ Rev 13:1-18
- ☐ Rev 14:1-20
- ☐ Rev 15:1–16:11
- ☐ Rev 16:12–17:18
- ☐ Rev 18:1-24
- ☐ Rev 19:1-21
- ☐ Rev 20:1-15
- ☐ Rev 21:1-27
- ☐ Rev 22:1-21

- ☐ *Introduction to the Time after the Apostles*

DICTIONARY AND INDEX FOR HEBREW AND GREEK WORD STUDIES

The *NLT Study Bible* includes over 200 Hebrew and Greek word studies throughout the Bible text. These word studies give readers a glimpse into the inner workings of the New Living Translation and open a small window to the original languages of the Bible.

HOW TO DO WORD STUDIES WITH THE *NLT STUDY BIBLE*

While reading through the Bible text, you will find at various places a superscript letter attached to the front of an English word. In the cross-reference column, there is a transliteration of the Hebrew or Greek word or phrase that underlies the translation at that point, along with the *Strong's* number(s) in parentheses (see below) and the location of the next reference in that Hebrew or Greek word chain. If you follow the reference chain, eventually you will read through all of the marked instances of that word or group of words in the entire study Bible. Doing so is a good way to begin doing Hebrew and Greek word studies.

Another way to use the tool is to systematically study a particular word from those listed below. Here we have listed and defined all of the words that are included in the Hebrew and Greek word-study chains.

The references in the chains are selective and do not represent all of the places where a Hebrew or Greek word occurs in the Bible; we chose a limited number of instances in order to show the variety of usage for a given term or group of terms. If you want to do a complete study of a biblical word, it would be a good idea to read most or all instances, which you can find with *Strong's Concordance* (see below) or a similar tool.

You can take your study of Hebrew and Greek words further by obtaining a copy of *Strong's Exhaustive Concordance of the Bible.* Dr. James Strong first published his exhaustive concordance of the King James Version in 1890, and the system he created for referring to every individual word in Hebrew and Greek by a number has been tremendously helpful for English readers who want to do word studies in the original languages. The *Strong's* numbering system has become the de facto standard for English language word-study tools. There is a wide variety of other publications and software tools available with which you can take your study of any Hebrew or Greek term further.

This dictionary and index is organized using the *Strong's* numbering system, named for the system used in *Strong's Concordance.* For any word you find while reading the text, you will simply have to use the *Strong's* number to find the brief definition and full chain. Please note that there are separate numbers and lists for the Hebrew words in the OT and the Greek words in the NT.

If you follow the entire word chain, note each context in which the word occurs and how it has been translated. You will get a good feel for the range of uses that each word can have, and you will get a unique glimpse into the inner workings of the NLT.

HEBREW AND GREEK WORD STUDIES

Because the Bible was originally written in ancient languages that are quite different from our own, the Hebrew and Greek words of the original text are often seen as strange and wonderful. Sometimes, Greek and Hebrew words are portrayed as though they are somehow a special or "divine" language containing more significant meaning than normal languages like English. In truth, biblical Greek and Hebrew are normal human languages, with words that are similar to the words of any language.

Words are complex animals. Consider, for example, the word *animal* in the previous sentence. In most contexts, that word conjures up images of wildlife. In this particular instance, however, it means something quite different. Words have a dynamic relationship to meaning, neither confined to a dictionary entry nor free to mean anything at all. Few readers whose mother tongue is English would have misunderstood the meaning of the sentence, "Words are complex animals," but it could certainly cause confusion for a reader whose knowledge of English is minimal.

When confronted with a word from any foreign language, especially an ancient one like the Hebrew or Greek of the Bible, people can misunderstand if they aren't careful to study the word in a way that makes sense with how language is used. Some common mistakes that are made in studying words in the biblical languages include the following:

- *Assuming a word means more than it does.* When faced with the range of meanings a given word can have, sometimes interpreters are tempted to think that *every* instance of that word contains *all* of the possible

meanings. While it is true that sometimes a writer will purposefully use a word to mean more than one thing, it is not common. Normally, a word has *one* meaning in a given context. For instance, not every instance of the Greek ***sarx*** (4561) has to do with the sin nature. An important part of original-language Bible study is to discern which meaning a term probably has in a given context.

- *Understanding words by their roots.* Many words share common roots, but this does not necessarily mean their meanings are related. The meaning of a word is related to how it is used in the language, not where it came from. The Greek ***ekklēsia*** (1577) comes from two words that mean "to call" (*kaleō*) and "out of" (*ek*). This does not mean that *ekklēsia* means "called out of," any more than the English word *goodbye* means "it's good that you're leaving." It is important to understand the meaning of the word from its usage rather than its roots.
- *Confusing synonyms.* Many words share common meanings, or at least have very similar meanings in specific contexts. An example in English is "choose" and "select." In many cases, the difference is negligible, and a writer could choose between them without changing the meaning at all. But in some contexts the selection is meaningful. In this tool, we sometimes string synonyms together in a single chain, but that does not mean they are completely interchangeable. Each word must be considered on its own terms in each context.
- *Failing to appreciate the difference between words and concepts.* Words are only tools to communicate meaning, so any one word will never be sufficient to get a complete picture of an important concept. If you want to understand the concept of "truth" in the Bible, Hebrew ***'emeth*** (0571) is a good place to start, but to limit study to a word alone will miss important components of the biblical picture of truth. Each concept must be studied as whole, going beyond the study of words.

Please tell us about your experiences using this word study index at www.NLTStudyBible.com, or send us an e-mail at NLTStudyBible@tyndale.com.

HEBREW WORDS

'abal (0056): *mourn.* This verb expresses an attitude of deep sorrow. Often mourning is accompanied by weeping and other physical manifestations of grief or more formal mourning rites.
SEE Gen 37:34; Exod 33:4; 1 Sam 6:19; 2 Sam 13:37; 1 Chr 7:22; Ezra 10:6; Neh 1:4; Isa 3:26; 66:10; Dan 10:2; Amos 9:5

'adonay Yahweh (0136, 3068): *Sovereign* LORD. A compound name and title of God that combines his covenant name, *Yahweh,* with the title *'adonay* ("my lord, my master"). This title occurs over 280 times in the OT and emphasizes God's power and authority as well as his gracious relationship with his people.
SEE Gen 15:2; Deut 3:24; Josh 7:7; Judg 6:22; 2 Sam 7:18; Ps 73:28; Isa 61:1; Ezek 2:4; Amos 3:7; Hab 3:19; Zeph 1:7

'iwweleth (0200): *foolishness.* This noun is often presented as the opposite of wisdom. It indicates a lack of wisdom and understanding, with overtones of moral deficiency rather than simply intellectual failure.
SEE Ps 69:5; Prov 12:23; 14:17, 24; 15:14, 21; 17:12; 22:15; 26:4, 5

'el (0410), ***'elohim*** (0430): *God.* These two related words are both used to refer to God. Similar to the English word *god,* these words are also used to refer to deity generally (i.e., a god) or other supernatural beings. They can be used to address God directly ("O God, hear my prayer"), as part of a description of God ("the living God," "my God"), or in describing false gods ("the gods of the Egyptians").
SEE Exod 3:6; Num 23:21; Josh 24:2; Ps 16:1; 17:6; 36:7; 40:17; 85:4, 8; Isa 42:5

'aman (0539): *believe.* This verb denotes trust. It often involves the active decision to believe in the veracity or trustworthiness of an idea or person but can also signify an ongoing state of belief and the action associated with that faith. The word is often used to refer to faith in God and his promises, though not exclusively.
SEE Gen 15:6; 45:26; Exod 14:31; Num 14:11; Ps 106:12; 119:66; Prov 14:15; Isa 28:16; 53:1; Jon 3:5

'amen (0543): *amen, let it be so.* This word is an affirmation of the truth of what has been said. It can express either the firm belief that something is true ("Yes!") or the desire that something will happen ("let it be so"). It is also used as a formulaic response in praising God, sometimes doubled for emphasis.
SEE Num 5:22; Deut 27:15; 1 Kgs 1:36; 1 Chr 16:36; Neh 5:13; 8:6; Ps 41:13; Isa 65:16; Jer 11:5

'emeth (0571): *truth, faithfulness.* This word has many nuances around the central idea of truth. It can represent the concept of truth as opposed to falsehood; it can refer to the faithfulness or reliability of a person or standard. It is also used in phrases such as "the true God."
SEE Exod 34:6; Ps 25:5; 26:3; 86:11; 119:142, 151, 160; Prov 16:6; Isa 38:3; Dan 10:21

'ap (0639): *anger.* This word denotes anger or extreme displeasure toward a person, group, or state of affairs. It is morally neutral, as it is used both for foolish, selfish anger and for righteous anger at injustice. It also means "nose, nostrils"; the flaring of nostrils and reddening of the nose when a person is angry led to the usage of this word to denote anger.
SEE Num 32:13; Deut 7:4; Judg 6:39; 2 Sam 12:5; 2 Kgs 23:26; Ps 6:1; Prov 27:4; 29:8, 22; Isa 12:1; Hab 3:8

'arbeh (0697): *locust.* This word refers to a desert migratory locust in the mature wing stage. These insects can swarm in vast, inordinate numbers, covering scores of square miles and even blotting out broad daylight.
SEE Exod 10:4, 12; Lev 11:22; Deut 28:38; Judg 6:5; 1 Kgs 8:37; Ps 78:46; Prov 30:27; Joel 1:4; 2:25; Nah 3:15

'aron (0727): *ark, chest.* This noun refers to a container for objects. It is generally a rectangular box. Its most common usage is for the Ark of the Covenant, but it can also refer to a coffin or a contribution chest. It is not the same word used for Noah's large boat, even though it is traditionally called an "ark" in English.
SEE Gen 50:26; Exod 25:22; 40:20; Num 10:33; 1 Sam 3:3; 2 Sam 6:6; 1 Kgs 8:1; 2 Kgs 12:9; 1 Chr 28:2; Ps 132:8; Jer 3:16

'arek 'appayim (0750, 0639): *slow to anger.* Rendered literally, this idiom would be "long of nose," but it means the attitude or emotion of patience. It pertains to not being easily or quickly angered in a potentially hostile situation. It is often used to describe a person of high moral quality and is a repeated component of God's character. Cp. ***'ap*** (0639).
SEE Exod 34:6; Num 14:18; Neh 9:17; Ps 86:15; 103:8; 145:8; Prov 14:29; 15:18; 16:32; Joel 2:13; Jon 4:2; Nah 1:3

'erets (0776): *earth, land.* This noun refers to any solid geographic area as contrasted

to the sky or bodies of water. It is used in several idiomatic ways as well, such as in the phrase "the heavens and earth," meaning "the entire created order." Sometimes the word can refer specifically to a region or territory of the world, as in "the land" promised to Abraham and his descendants.
SEE *Gen 1:1; 9:11; 12:1; 13:17; 15:18; 28:13; Num 13:27; Deut 4:39; Josh 1:15; 23:14, 16; Ps 24:1; 47:2; 97:5; Isa 65:17; 66:22*

'ashrey (0835): *happy, blessed.* This word points to a heightened state or condition of joy and rejoicing, implying very favorable circumstances and enjoyment. It may be implied that it is a state to be envied or highly desired. This "blessed" is somewhat different from divine favor (a blessing).
SEE *Job 5:17; Ps 1:1; 32:1; 34:8; 41:1; 84:5, 12; 94:12; 106:3; Prov 3:13; 14:21; 28:14; Isa 30:18*

bakhar (0977): *choose.* This verb denotes making a distinguishing selection, often between items of similar features or qualities. It can refer to human or divine choices. Some contexts have the same general meaning but a different focus; such "choice" is based on a relationship or special loving concern.
SEE *Exod 18:25; Deut 7:6; 14:2; 21:5; 1 Sam 2:28; 10:24; 17:40; 1 Chr 28:5; Ps 78:68; 135:4; Isa 40:20; 43:10*

beliya'al (1100): *worthlessness, wickedness.* This noun can mean "worthless," referring to an object that is ruined or devastated. Another meaning is a person who is actively evil, "worthless" in relation to the standard of right living. It is often used in phrases such as "children of wickedness," meaning troublesome people.
SEE *Deut 13:13; Judg 19:22; 1 Sam 1:16; 2:12; 25:17, 25; 2 Sam 22:5; Ps 18:4; 101:3; Prov 6:12; 19:28*

ben 'adam (1121, 0120), ***bar 'anash*** (1247, 0606): *son of man.* This phrase simply means "human being." There is no specific gender in view; it is a way of pointing to the essential human quality of a person. Occasionally there is a diminutive sense (e.g., God is not a mere *ben 'adam*). It is also a messianic term in some contexts. In Dan 7:13, the Aramaic *bar 'anash* is equivalent to the Hebrew *ben 'adam*.
SEE *Num 23:19; Job 25:6; 35:8; Ps 8:4; 80:17; 90:3; Isa 56:2; Jer 49:18; Ezek 2:1; Dan 7:13; 8:17*

ben 'el (1121, 0410), ***ben 'elohim*** (1121, 0430): *sons of God.* This phrase means a being or entity that has its origin in God's creative power. It can refer to humans in relationship with God or to supernatural beings that are in the presence of God, including angels. In some contexts, it refers to a "heavenly court" (e.g., Job 1:6).
SEE *Gen 6:2; Job 1:6; 2:1; 38:7; Ps 29:1; 89:6; Hos 1:10*

ba'al (1168): *lord, Baal.* This noun means one who is a ruler, owner, or master of another person or people. It can refer to humans in various controlling social and political relationships. It also came to be a title for pagan deities in and around Canaan.
SEE *1 Kgs 16:31; 18:19, 40; 2 Kgs 10:18; 11:18; Hos 2:8, 13, 16*

bar 'anash (1247, 0606): See ***ben 'adam*** (1121, 0120)

bara' (1254): *create.* This verb means to generate something into existence. It implies craftsmanship, yet the focus is often on bringing objects into existence. This same word can also describe making something out of existing materials or re-creating something into something new.
SEE *Gen 1:1, 27; 2:3; 6:7; Ps 51:10; 148:5; Eccl 12:1; Isa 40:28; 43:15; 65:17; Mal 2:10*

berith (1285): *covenant.* This noun refers to a binding agreement, a contract between at least two parties. A covenant can be between human parties (such as nations, friends, rulers and subjects, etc.) or between God and a human person or group. *Covenant* is an important defining concept in the relationship between God and his people.
SEE *Gen 9:9; 15:18; 17:2; Exod 19:5; Num 25:12; Deut 29:1; 33:9; Josh 24:25; 2 Kgs 11:17; 23:3; 2 Chr 29:10; Ezra 10:3; Isa 42:6; 55:3; Jer 31:31; 33:21; Ezek 37:26; Hos 2:18; Mal 2:4*

barak (1288), ***berakah*** (1293): *bless, blessing.* The verb (*barak*) means either divine speech that bestows success or prosperity, or human vocalization of a desire that God would bless a person. In some contexts, it is virtually a synonym for praise (e.g., "bless God"). The related noun (*berakah*) means an oath that results in prosperity, peace, freedom, safety, etc.
SEE *Gen 2:3; 12:2; 49:28; Num 6:23; 22:6; Deut 30:19; 33:1; 1 Kgs 8:14; 2 Chr 6:3; Ezek 34:26; Mal 3:10*

ga'al (1350): *redeem.* This verb means to reclaim a person or thing. Often it is an economic transaction, such as buying property back from a creditor or purchasing freedom for an enslaved family member. Another meaning is a relative attempting to right a wrong against a family member. See ***go'el*** (1350).
SEE *Lev 25:25; 27:13; Num 35:12; Ps 77:15; 103:4; 107:2; Isa 43:1; 63:9; Jer 31:11; Lam 3:58; Hos 13:14; Mic 4:10*

go'el (1350): *family redeemer.* The family redeemer is a close family member who is obligated to buy an object or person from indenture, slavery, or otherwise harsh circumstances. It is also a title for God, who removes his people from a dangerous bondage and reclaims them as his own. This word is a noun form of the verb ***ga'al*** (1350), but it is used as a distinct word with its own meaning.
SEE *Ruth 2:20; 3:9; 4:6; Job 19:25; Ps 19:14; Isa 41:14; 44:6, 24; 54:5; 60:16; 63:16; Jer 50:34*

garash (1644): See ***kerituth*** (3748)

dod (1730): *beloved.* This describes a person in a romantic, sensual relationship. It can also mean the act of physical lovemaking itself or a figurative description referring to Jerusalem and God as lovers.
SEE *Prov 7:18; Song 1:2, 4; 4:10, 16; 7:12; Ezek 16:8; 23:17*

dam (1818): *blood.* This noun refers to lifeblood. Its meaning is often equivalent to life, so "to pour out blood" means "to kill."
SEE *Gen 9:4; 49:11; Lev 3:17; 17:11; Deut 12:23; 2 Kgs 21:16; Ps 94:21; Ezek 33:4*

hebel (1892): *vapor, meaningless.* This noun meaning "mist, vapor, breath" is often used figuratively to signify something as transitory, worthless, or meaningless.
SEE *Ps 39:5, 6; Eccl 1:2, 14; 2:1; 3:19; 4:4; 5:7; 6:2; 7:6; 8:10; 9:9; 11:8; 12:8; Isa 49:4; Jon 2:8*

hagah (1897): *ponder.* This verb means to cogitate on something by talking to oneself either internally or audibly. It is also used to describe the cooing of a dove and the growling of a lion, and can refer to discussing a plan with other people or occasionally simply speaking about something.
SEE *Josh 1:8; Ps 1:2; 35:28; 37:30; 38:12; 63:6; 77:12; 143:5*

halal (1984): *praise.* This verb refers to speaking of the excellence or greatness of something or someone. When referring to a deity, it is an aspect of worship, whether to a false god or to the true God.
SEE *Judg 16:24; 2 Chr 5:13; 20:19; 29:30; Ps 22:22; 109:30; 113:1; 119:164; 135:3; 147:12; 150:1; Prov 27:2; 28:4; 31:30; Jer 20:13*

zabakh (2076), ***zebakh*** (2077): *sacrifice.* This verb (*zabakh*) refers to killing a living thing for the purpose of worship or relationship to a deity. The cognate noun (*zebakh*) means the thing itself that is killed and presented to the deity, often a small domestic mammal such as a sheep or goat.
SEE *Gen 46:1; Exod 22:20; 23:18; Num 15:8; Deut 15:21; Josh 22:27; 1 Kgs 8:5; Ps 4:5; 51:17; Prov 21:27; Isa 1:11; Hos 6:6; 13:2; Mal 1:8, 14*

zadon (2087): *pride.* This noun means the state or condition of having an inflated attitude of oneself. It is overconfidence to the point of moral failure.
SEE *Deut 17:12; 1 Sam 17:28; Prov 11:2; 13:10; 21:24; Jer 49:16; 50:31, 32; Ezek 7:10; Obad 1:3*

zakar (2142): *remember.* This verb means a recollection of some information or memory, often with an associated meaning of relationship to the object remembered. Often this remembrance is intended to trigger action as much as thought.
SEE *Gen 8:1; Exod 2:24; Lev 26:45; Num 10:9; 15:39; Deut 5:15; Judg 16:28; 1 Sam 1:19; 2 Kgs 20:3; Ps 22:27; 115:12; 119:55; 137:1; Isa 64:9; Jer 15:15*

zamar (2167): *sing, praise.* This verb means the act of using the voice and/or instruments to make music and so "sing and play music." In the book of Psalms this action refers to the joyful singing of glory, praise, and thanksgiving to God.
SEE *1 Chr 16:9; Ps 21:13; 27:6; 30:12; 33:2;*

47:7; 66:2; 71:22; 92:1; 138:1; 146:2; 147:1; 149:3

zaqen (2205): *elder.* This noun means "old person," but it is usually used to mean a civic or religious leader. Another meaning is a dignitary of a king's court.
SEE *Exod 12:21; Lev 4:15; Num 11:25; Deut 19:12; 21:3, 20; 22:15; 25:8; 32:7; Josh 20:4; Ruth 4:11; Ps 105:22; 107:32; 119:100; Prov 31:23*

zera' (2233): *seed, offspring.* This noun refers to plant seed and human or animal sperm. It is commonly used figuratively to refer to a child or a descendant.
SEE *Gen 3:15; 12:7; 26:3; 35:12; 48:4; Exod 32:13; Deut 34:4; Josh 24:3; 2 Sam 7:12; Ps 89:4; Isa 53:10; Jer 33:26*

khag (2282): *feast, festival.* This noun refers to a regular celebration by a religious group. The celebration often has common rites, themes, and ceremonies associated with it; a pilgrimage is often part of the festival.
SEE *Exod 23:15, 16; Deut 16:10, 14, 16; 2 Chr 30:21; Ezra 6:22; Ps 81:3; Isa 30:29; Amos 8:10*

khadash (2318): *renew.* This verb means to return an object to a condition or state that is the same as a prior condition. It can refer to the restoration or reaffirmation of relationship between people or groups.
SEE *1 Sam 11:14; 2 Chr 24:4; Ps 51:10; 103:5; 104:30; Isa 61:4; Lam 5:21*

khazon (2377): *vision.* This noun refers to a prophetic communication from God, i.e., a revelation or vision. There is usually a focus on the visual (nonverbal) aspects of the communication, and it is not entirely unlike a dream, though they are distinguished.
SEE *1 Sam 3:1; 2 Chr 32:32; Prov 29:18; Isa 29:7; Jer 14:14; Dan 1:17; 8:1; 9:24; Hos 12:10; Hab 2:2*

khata' (2398), ***khet'*** (2399): *sin.* The verb (*khata'*) means violating a standard, law, or agreement, usually implying guilt and penalty for that violation. The noun (*khet'*) refers to the offense itself.
SEE *Gen 39:9; Exod 10:16; Deut 20:18; 1 Sam 12:23; 14:33; Neh 9:29; Ps 41:4; 119:11; Isa 1:4; Lam 3:39; Dan 9:5; Hos 4:7*

khokmah (2451): *wisdom.* This noun means the capacity to understand information and situations, and thus have skill in applied living. It is similar to discernment and perception. Another meaning is the ability to construct and craft items, a kind of skillful understanding.
SEE *Exod 36:1; 1 Kgs 4:29; Ps 111:10; Prov 13:10; 14:6; 16:16; 17:24; 29:3, 15; Eccl 1:16; Isa 11:2; Jer 9:23*

khesed (2617): *faithful love, unfailing kindness.* This noun refers to an unconditional, highly favorable disposition toward an object. Different contexts highlight different elements: love, mercy, kindness, loyalty, faithfulness, etc. The word is often used in a covenantal or relational context to mean love with freely chosen obligations.
SEE *Exod 20:6; Josh 2:12; Ruth 1:8; 2 Sam 9:1; 1 Kgs 3:6; Ps 25:6; 51:1; 57:10; 103:4; Prov 3:3; Lam 3:22; Zech 7:9*

kharam (2763), ***kherem*** (2764): *set apart, devoted [to destruction].* The verb (*kharam*) means excluding an object from use and devoting it to God. Sometimes it entails setting the object aside, but other times it entails complete destruction. The cognate noun (*kherem*) means the thing itself that is devoted.
SEE *Exod 22:20; Lev 27:28; Num 21:2; Deut 7:2, 26; Josh 6:21; 7:12; 1 Sam 15:3; Isa 43:28; Mal 4:6*

yadah (3034): *praise, confess.* This verb signifies speaking out loud concerning the praiseworthiness of God or a person. It can also refer to the verbal confession of sins and wrongs. In some contexts, the elements of praise and confession are combined.
SEE *Lev 16:21; 2 Chr 5:13; Ezra 10:1; Neh 1:6; Ps 7:17; 30:12; 32:5; 49:18; 86:12; 100:4; 109:30; 136:1; Dan 9:4*

yidde'oni (3049): *soothsayer, spirit of the dead.* This noun means one who contacts the underworld through a spirit. It can also refer directly to the spirit of the dead as the object of a soothsayer's craft.
SEE *Lev 19:31; 20:6, 27; Deut 18:11; 1 Sam 28:3, 9; 2 Kgs 21:6; 23:24; 2 Chr 33:6; Isa 8:19; 19:3*

Yahweh 'adonay (3068, 0136): See ***'adonay Yahweh*** (0136, 3068)

yakhal (3176): *hope.* This verb indicates a confident expectation for the future with a sense of anticipation and certainty while waiting for the outcome.
SEE *Job 13:15; Ps 33:18; 42:11; 119:43, 114; 130:7; 131:3; Isa 51:5; Lam 3:21; Mic 7:7*

yare' (3372), ***yir'ah*** (3374): *fear, respect.* The verb (*yare'*) and the cognate noun (*yir'ah*) both refer to being afraid. Sometimes it refers to feeling fear about an existing situation, and in other contexts it is more an anticipation than an emotion. It can also signify respect and high honor toward a person.
SEE *Exod 1:17; Lev 19:14; 25:17; Deut 5:5; 10:20; 17:19; 1 Sam 7:7; 21:12; 2 Kgs 17:35; Ps 86:11; 112:1; Jon 1:9*

yeshu'ah (3444), ***yasha'*** (3467): *salvation, save.* The verb (*yasha'*) means removing an object from a dangerous situation or the state of being delivered from distress. In some contexts, it has added associations to a loving relationship with God. The related noun (*yeshu'ah*) refers to the salvation that the verb enacts.
SEE *Exod 14:13; 15:2; Ps 6:4; 34:18; 67:2; 74:12; Isa 30:15; 33:22; 43:12; 45:20, 22; 51:8; 59:1; Jer 17:14; Ezek 37:23; Zech 8:7*

kabod (3519): *impressiveness, glory.* This noun has a literal meaning, "a heavy item," which is not often used. The figurative meaning of something that is highly valued is more common. In theological contexts, this word often describes God and his attributes.
SEE *Gen 31:1; Exod 16:10; Num 14:10; 1 Sam 4:21; 2 Chr 32:27; Ps 4:2; 24:7; 145:5; Prov 11:16; 25:2; Isa 4:2; 6:3; 40:5; Ezek 10:18; Mal 2:2*

kohen (3548): *priest.* This noun refers to a person who performs religious rites and rituals. In ancient Israel, all priests were descended from Aaron (the brother of Moses) of the tribe of Levi. The priests' relatives, the Levites, helped them lead Israel's worship.
SEE *Gen 14:18; Exod 18:1; 19:6; Lev 1:5; Num 3:6; 5:16; Deut 17:9; 18:3; 1 Sam 2:35; Jer 33:18; Joel 2:17; Mic 3:11; Zech 6:13; Mal 2:7*

kisse' (3678): *chair, throne.* This noun refers to a piece of furniture that can be sat upon. It can refer to a common chair or to the special chair of a ruler. By extension, it sometimes refers to the sovereign authority of a ruler.
SEE *2 Sam 7:13; 1 Kgs 10:18; Ps 93:2; 103:19; Prov 16:12; 20:28; 29:14; Isa 6:1; 9:7; 66:1; Ezek 1:26; Zech 6:13*

kapar (3722): *atone.* This verb means the removal of guilt incurred by wrongdoing. In some contexts the focus seems to be on the means of forgiveness. Making atonement averts punishment and makes further relationship with the offended person possible.
SEE *Exod 32:30; Lev 4:26; 9:7; Num 15:25, 28; 35:33; 1 Sam 3:14; Ps 65:3; 78:38; 79:9; Prov 16:6; Dan 9:24*

kerub (3742), ***sarap*** (8314): *cherub, seraph.* These nouns both refer to a winged class of supernatural beings. They are often in groups, and so the plural forms are familiar (cherubim/seraphim). They both function as attendants to God, either in close proximity or as his representative.
SEE *Gen 3:24; Exod 25:18, 20; Num 7:89; 1 Sam 4:4; 2 Sam 22:11; 1 Kgs 6:23; Isa 6:2, 6; 14:29; Ezek 10:5, 15; 28:14*

kerituth (3748), ***garash*** (1644), ***shalakh*** (7971): *divorce.* These three related words all refer to the ending of a marriage, usually pictured as a man dismissing his wife. The noun *kerituth* focuses on the written notice from a husband to a wife of impending divorce. The verb *garash* refers to the dissolution ("banishment") of the marriage bond. The verb *shalakh* is the divorce ("dismissing") of the former spouse.
SEE *Lev 21:7, 14; 22:13; Deut 22:19, 29; 24:1, 3; 2 Sam 13:16; Isa 50:1; Jer 3:1, 8; Ezek 44:22*

leb (3820), ***lebab*** (3824): *heart.* These synonyms refer to the heart, literally and figuratively. Figuratively, the heart is the seat of a person's inner feelings, thoughts, inclinations, and choices. The word is also used to refer to the middle of a space, e.g., the heart of the sea.
SEE *Gen 42:28; Exod 15:8; Deut 6:5; 8:2; 29:19; 2 Sam 17:10; 1 Kgs 3:12; 1 Chr 29:17; 2 Chr 12:14; Ps 7:9; 28:7; 86:12; 141:4; Prov 21:4; Jer 17:9; Dan 11:28*

magen (4043): *shield.* This noun refers to a warrior's relatively small defensive weapon that protects from attack of physical blows from an enemy. It can also refer to an ornamental piece in a shield-like shape. Figuratively, it means protection or defense.
SEE *Gen 15:1; Deut 33:29; 2 Sam 1:21;*

22:31; 1 Kgs 10:17; 14:27; 2 Chr 14:8; 26:14; Ps 3:3; 7:10; 28:7; 84:9, 11; 89:18; Prov 2:7; 30:5; Isa 21:5; Ezek 23:24

mal'ak (4397): *messenger, angel.* This noun refers to a messenger who is acting as an agent of the sender. Often it means a supernatural being who serves God in many ways, including giving messages. The "angel of the LORD" refers to a unique messenger of God who is closely identified with God.
SEE Gen 16:7; 19:1; 28:12; 48:16; Exod 3:2; Num 22:22; Josh 6:17; Judg 13:3; 2 Sam 14:17; 2 Kgs 19:35; 2 Chr 32:21; Job 33:23; Ps 34:7; 78:49; 91:11; 103:20; 148:2; Zech 3:1; 12:8

melek (4428): *king.* This noun means a male royal ruler, a king. In ancient society, the king often embodied political, social, religious, and military authority. The word is also used as a title for God, the King over all.
SEE Exod 1:8; 1 Sam 18:6; 2 Sam 5:3; 1 Kgs 1:34; 4:1; Ps 2:2; 5:2; 24:9; 33:16; 47:2; Prov 16:12; 19:12; Eccl 8:2; Isa 33:22; 43:15; Ezek 37:22

man (4478): *manna.* This noun refers to a food given by God to provide for his people. The word also means "What is it?" The food received its name because the people didn't know what it was when they first saw it.
SEE Exod 16:15, 31, 33, 35; Num 11:6, 7, 9; Deut 8:3, 16; Josh 5:12; Neh 9:20; Ps 78:24

ma'aser (4643): *tithe.* This word meaning "one-tenth" is almost always used in connection with an offering of some kind. The word often refers directly to the offering itself, whether cattle, produce, or money.
SEE Gen 14:20; Lev 27:30, 31; Num 18:21; Deut 12:6, 17; 14:23; 2 Chr 31:5, 12; Mal 3:8, 10

mashakh (4886): *anoint.* This verb means rubbing oil onto a thing or person as part of a ceremony of dedication for service. The focus is often on the ceremony of dedication or consecration itself, not the materials used in the ceremony.
SEE Exod 40:9; Lev 8:11, 12; 1 Sam 10:1; 15:1, 17; 16:13; 1 Kgs 1:34; 19:16; 1 Chr 29:22; Ps 45:7; 89:20; Isa 61:1

mishkan (4908): *dwelling, tent, tabernacle.* This noun means a portable building. It can refer to a nomad's tent home. It often refers to the beautiful, large worship tent as the dwelling place of God's glory, the Tabernacle. The word can also be used to stand for the concept of God's presence rather than the Tabernacle itself.
SEE Exod 25:9; 35:11; Lev 8:10; 17:4; 2 Sam 7:6; 1 Chr 21:29; 23:26; Ps 26:8; 43:3; 46:4; 74:7; 78:60

mashal (4912): *saying, proverb, aphorism.* This noun refers to many forms of pithy communication that function as a unit, such as a slogan, maxim, parable, allegory, song, or riddle. They usually express wisdom in a compact form, but the length varies.
SEE 1 Sam 10:12; 24:13; 1 Kgs 4:32; Job 13:12; Ps 78:2; Prov 1:1, 6; 10:1; 25:1; 26:7; Eccl 12:9; Ezek 24:3

mishpat (4941): *justice.* This noun means fairness in disputes, based on an authoritative common law or principle. Other meanings include court, law, judgment, or prescription, all associated with justice in legal and social matters. It often refers to God and his character.
SEE Gen 18:25; Ps 9:16; 33:5; 37:30; 48:11; 103:6; 106:3; Prov 12:5; 21:15; Isa 30:18; 51:4; 56:1; Mic 3:1; 6:8; Hab 1:4

nabi' (5030), ***nebi'ah*** (5031): *prophet.* These nouns refer to a person (male, *nabi'*; female, *nebi'ah*) who proclaims an authorized message for God or a false god. It is usually an office of leadership, similar to priests and judges.
SEE Gen 20:7; Exod 7:1; 15:20; Deut 13:1; 18:15, 18, 20, 22; Judg 4:4; 1 Sam 10:10; 1 Kgs 18:19; 2 Chr 34:22; Neh 6:14; Ps 51:TITLE; 74:9; Isa 8:3; Jer 6:13; 7:25; Hos 9:7; Amos 7:14; Mal 4:5

nepesh (5315): *soul, life, self.* This noun has a wide range of meaning, encompassing much of the immaterial part of a being. It is similar to "spirit," which is also related to the inner person, but *nepesh* often has more connection to the physical, animate life, including the seat of cravings and desires. Often this word is simply an equivalent for the personal pronoun (i.e., "my soul" = "me").
SEE Gen 1:20; 2:7; Deut 12:23; Job 7:11; Ps 6:3; 19:7; 23:3; 25:1; 34:2; 35:9; 42:1; 57:1; 62:1; 63:5; 86:4; 103:1; 119:20; Prov 13:4; Isa 26:8

netser (5342): See ***tsemakh*** (6780)

nasa' (5375): *lift, forgive.* This verb can mean physically lifting or picking up an object and moving it away. It can also mean to remove guilt and the penalty that goes with wrongdoing.
SEE Gen 50:17; Exod 10:17; 32:32; 34:7; Josh 24:19; 1 Sam 15:25; Ps 32:1, 5; 85:2; 99:8; Hos 14:2; Mic 7:18

'ebed (5650): *slave, servant.* This noun refers to a person of lower social status who is subject to another person for service or labor. The *'ebed* could be an owned slave, an indentured servant, a military subordinate, or a political subject. Sometimes a worshiper is referred to as the *'ebed* of God.
SEE Exod 20:10; 21:2, 5, 20, 26, 32; Lev 25:6, 39, 44; Deut 23:15; 2 Kgs 10:23; Ps 116:16; 119:65, 124; Prov 11:29; 12:9; 17:2; 30:10; Isa 42:1; 53:11

'olam (5769): *forever.* This word can mean a continuous, unlimited amount of time, often with a focus on the future. Another meaning is more limited: "the rest of a lifetime." Yet another meaning is a long time in the past.
SEE Gen 3:22; 9:16; 21:33; Deut 33:15; 2 Sam 7:13; Ps 10:16; 30:12; 44:8; 90:2; 92:8; 100:5; 110:4; 119:44, 89, 142; Eccl 3:11; 12:5; Isa 45:17; 51:11; Dan 12:2

'azab (5800): *abandon.* This verb means to leave something or someone behind. One can abandon an object, a person, a principle, or a commitment. Sometimes *'azab* has the connotation of leaving behind something or someone originally held dear.
SEE Josh 1:5; 24:16; Judg 2:12; 1 Sam 12:10; 1 Kgs 11:33; 2 Kgs 17:16; 22:17; 2 Chr 15:2; Ps 9:10; 22:1; 27:10; Prov 4:6; Jer 2:13; Ezek 9:9; Dan 11:30

'elyon (5945): *most high.* This word describes something having supremely high elevation or status. It is used as a descriptive title for God, with a focus on his very high status as supreme over all.
SEE Gen 14:20; Num 24:16; Deut 32:8; Ps 7:17; 46:4; 47:2; 50:14; 78:35; 82:6; 91:1; 97:9; Isa 14:14; Lam 3:38

'anaw (6035): *humble.* This word means a condition of sincere and straightforward behavior with a lack of arrogance and pride.
SEE Num 12:3; Ps 25:9; 37:11; 147:6; 149:4; Prov 3:34; Isa 29:19; Zeph 2:3

palal (6419): *intercede, pray.* This verb means to make a spoken request on behalf of oneself or others, often by asking God for something in prayer. Such prayer can be vocal or internal, personal or public.
SEE Gen 20:17; Deut 9:26; 1 Sam 1:10; 1 Kgs 8:35; 2 Kgs 6:18; 20:2; 2 Chr 7:14; Neh 2:4; 4:9; Ps 32:6; 72:15; Isa 45:20; Jer 32:16; Jon 2:1

pesakh (6453): *Passover.* This noun refers to the Passover sacrifice, meal, and festival. Passover is a memorial to God's rescue of his people from the plague of the firstborn and to their rescue from Egypt in general.
SEE Exod 12:11, 21, 27, 43, 48; Deut 16:1; Josh 5:10; 2 Kgs 23:21; 2 Chr 30:18; 35:18; Ezra 6:19; Ezek 45:21

pesha' (6588): *transgression.* This noun means a moral failure, with a focus on the rebellious nature of the offense. This word assumes that a standard or law is in place; a person guilty of *pesha'* is a lawbreaker.
SEE Gen 50:17; Exod 34:7; Ps 32:1, 5; 51:3; 103:12; Prov 10:12, 19; 17:19; 28:13; Isa 53:5; Amos 5:12

tsaba' (6635): *army.* This noun usually means a military group as a large fighting unit. While it can refer to human armies, in the OT it often refers to the angel armies of heaven. It is part of an expressive title for God, the LORD of Heaven's Armies.
SEE Deut 4:19; 17:3; Josh 5:14; 1 Sam 17:45; 1 Kgs 22:19; Ps 24:10; 80:19; 103:21; Isa 6:5; 13:4; Amos 4:13; 9:5

tsedeq (6664): *justice, righteousness.* This noun means doing what is just and right, either as a moral attribute or in accord with a legal or moral standard. It can refer to people's treatment of one another, but it is also a character quality of the LORD, flowing from his moral purity. God has lovingly revealed his standard in his word, and he desires it be kept as a matter of *tsedeq*.
SEE Lev 19:15, 36; Deut 16:20; Ps 9:8; 23:3; 35:28; 45:7; 97:2; 119:75, 123; Isa 11:4; 45:8; 62:2; Zeph 2:3

tsur (6697): *rock.* This noun refers to a large mass of rock, from boulders to mountains. The word has numerous connotative meanings as well, such as strength, hiding,

protective refuge, and stability. It also occurs as a title or description of God.
SEE *Exod 33:22; Deut 32:4, 13, 18, 31; 1 Sam 2:2; 2 Sam 23:3; Job 14:18; Ps 18:46; 27:5; 31:2; 61:2; 62:7; 73:26; 78:35; 89:26; 92:15; 144:1; Isa 26:4; 51:1*

tsemakh (6780), **netser** (5342): *branch, bud.* These nouns refer to the sprout, bud, or new growth of a living plant. They are also titles for the Messiah, the king from the lineage of David.
SEE *Isa 4:2; 11:1; Jer 23:5; 33:15; Zech 3:8; 6:12*

qahal (6951): *assembly.* This noun refers to a public gathering of people. It can refer to a socioreligious community with common customs, rituals, and leadership structures, such as the congregation of Israel, but it can also refer to a crowd gathered for any purpose.
SEE *Gen 28:3; 35:11; Deut 23:2; 1 Kgs 8:55; 2 Chr 29:28; 30:25; Ps 22:22, 25; 26:5; 89:5; 149:1; Joel 2:16*

qana' (7065), **qanna'** (7067), **qin'ah** (7068): *jealous, jealousy.* These words indicate a strong desire and deep devotion to an object or person with the expectation that the relationship will be exclusive and faithful. Sometimes this commitment entails a response of anger based on a real or perceived breach of exclusivity in the relationship. God is often described as jealous, passionately desiring the faithfulness of his people.
SEE *Gen 37:11; Exod 20:5; 34:14; Deut 4:24; Job 5:2; Prov 3:31; 14:30; 24:19; Joel 2:18; Zeph 1:18; 3:8; Zech 1:14*

rahab (7293): *sea monster, Rahab.* This noun refers to a legendary sea monster or dragon defeated by God in combat long ago. Mythically, God forcefully controlled chaos by smiting Rahab at creation. In another related image, God shows mastery over the sea in the Exodus. The word became a poetic symbol for Egypt and other oppressive human powers.
SEE *Job 9:13; 26:12; Ps 87:4; 89:10; Isa 30:7; 51:9*

ruakh (7307): *breath, wind, spirit.* This noun refers physically to wind and breath. It is figuratively used to refer to immaterial things. It can mean spirit, either as the immaterial part of a person or as the spirit of God. It can also mean a pervading sense or condition (e.g., a spirit of wisdom).
SEE *Gen 1:2; 45:27; Exod 31:3; Num 11:25; Deut 34:9; 1 Sam 16:15; 2 Sam 23:2; 2 Kgs 2:15, 16; Ps 32:2; 51:11; 104:30; Eccl 12:7; Isa 4:4; 11:2; 26:9; 28:6; 32:15; 61:1; 63:10; Mic 2:7; Zech 4:6*

rum (7311): *exalted.* Physically, this word refers to an object being raised to higher elevation. It often means that a person or object has an elevated status for admirers or worshipers. Often the greatness of the honored object is extolled. It can also refer to God exalting the needy by improving their social or economic status.
SEE *Exod 15:2; 1 Sam 2:7; 2 Sam 22:47; Neh 9:5; Ps 30:1; 34:3; 57:5; 89:16; 99:2, 5; 118:28; Prov 14:34; Isa 6:1*

rakham (7355): *have compassion.* This verb means to have a feeling of strong affection for someone, usually based on a prior relationship. The word has a special focus on mercy or pity toward a person in difficult circumstances. It is often characterized as unconditional love.
SEE *Exod 33:19; 2 Kgs 13:23; Ps 103:13; 116:5; Isa 30:18; 49:10, 13; 54:8; Lam 3:32; Hos 2:23; Zech 10:6*

ra'ah, ro'eh, ro'ah (7462): *shepherd.* This verb means caring for a flock of sheep or similar animals—leading the flock to pasture, giving personal care to individual sheep, and defending them from predators. The participle forms of the verb (male, *ro'eh*; female, *ro'ah*) function as nouns, meaning "shepherd." Figuratively, a ruler or God can be called a shepherd as an image of caring leadership.
SEE *Gen 29:9; 48:15; 49:24; Exod 3:1; 1 Sam 16:11; 1 Chr 11:2; Ps 23:1; 78:72; Isa 40:11; Jer 3:15; Ezek 34:2; Amos 3:12; Zech 13:7*

she'ol (7585): *grave, underworld.* This noun names the realm of death, perceived as a place under the earth. It is seen as a joyless place of darkness, silence, inactivity, and physical decay or decomposition. All dead, righteous and wicked, are seen as abiding in *she'ol.*
SEE *Gen 37:35; Num 16:30; 1 Sam 2:6; Job 7:9; 17:16; 26:6; Ps 16:10; 49:14; 89:48; 116:3; 139:8; Prov 5:5; 23:14; Isa 38:18; Hos 3:14; Jon 2:2*

shabbath (7676): *Sabbath.* This noun refers to a periodic time of complete rest and cessation from work. The seventh day of the week is called the Sabbath day. The seventh year is called the Sabbath year, a time for the land to rest from planting and harvesting. Other periodic times of rest are similarly called Sabbaths.
SEE *Exod 16:23; 20:11; 31:15, 16; Lev 23:32; 25:2; Num 15:32; Deut 5:12; 2 Chr 36:21; Neh 13:15; Isa 56:2; Jer 17:21; Ezek 20:20*

shadday (7706): *Almighty.* This word is a title for God with a focus on his absolute power. It is traditionally transliterated *Shaddai.* Sometimes the word **'el** (0410) is added to create the title *El Shaddai,* translated as "God Almighty."
SEE *Gen 17:1; 28:3; 35:11; 48:3; 49:25; Exod 6:3; Job 22:25; 37:23; 40:2; Ps 68:14; 91:1; Joel 1:15*

shub (7725): *return, repent.* This verb means to return to an earlier state. It can refer to physical movement or a change in condition, behavior, or belief. The focus is sometimes on turning away from a negative thing, sometimes on returning to what is good. It often begins a renewal of relationship, especially with God.
SEE *Deut 30:10; 2 Kgs 23:35; 2 Chr 15:4; 19:4; 36:13; Job 36:10; Ps 22:27; Isa 55:7; Jer 5:3; 15:19; Ezek 14:6; 18:30, 32; Zech 1:6*

khawah (7812): *bow down, worship.* This verb means bowing down in obeisance to another's superior status. Sometimes it refers to the simple showing of respect to another human being of perceived superior position. It can also refer to worship of God.
SEE *Gen 22:5; 42:6; Exod 4:31; Num 25:2; Deut 5:9; 29:26; Neh 8:6; Ps 29:2; Isa 46:6; 66:23; Zech 14:16*

satan (7854): *adversary, Satan.* This noun means a person who opposes someone in an adversarial manner, either verbally or physically. It is also used as a name for the devil, a supernatural creature who is an enemy of God and humanity.
SEE *1 Kgs 11:14; 1 Chr 21:1; Job 1:6, 9, 12; 2:2, 4; Ps 109:6; Zech 3:1, 2*

shalom (7965): *peace.* This noun means holistic peace and well-being. There can be associations of satisfaction, contentment, and feelings of wholeness. It can apply to individuals as well as groups.
SEE *Josh 9:15; Judg 6:24; 1 Chr 22:9; Ps 4:8; 29:11; 34:14; 119:165; 122:6; Prov 3:17; 12:20; Eccl 3:8; Isa 9:6; 59:8; Zech 8:19*

shalakh (7971): See **kerituth** (3748)

simkhah (8057): *joy.* This noun means an attitude of happiness and cheerfulness, usually referring to the transcendent joy and jubilance of a relationship with God.
SEE *1 Kgs 1:40; 1 Chr 29:22; Job 20:5; Ps 16:11; 30:11; 51:8; 97:11; Prov 10:28; 15:23; 21:15; Isa 29:19; 55:12; 61:7*

shamayim (8064): *heavens.* This noun means the area above the earth. It can refer to the sky, sometimes conceived of as a place where rain and clouds are stored. It can refer to the area of the celestial bodies, what we call *space.* It can also refer to the abode or dwelling place of God, sometimes perceived as regions above the skies.
SEE *Gen 1:1; Exod 16:4; 2 Kgs 1:10; 2 Chr 30:27; Job 11:8; 26:11; Ps 11:4; 19:1; 50:6; 108:4; Isa 14:12; 34:4; 51:6; 55:9; 65:17; Jer 23:24; Mal 3:10*

shama' (8085): *listen, obey.* This verb means to listen to someone and, as an extension of listening, to submit to doing what is asked or required. It often refers to the action of obeying the commands and instructions of God.
SEE *Deut 4:30; 11:27; 13:4; 28:1; 30:10; Josh 1:18; 1 Sam 15:22; 1 Kgs 12:24; 2 Kgs 22:13; Neh 9:16; Eccl 7:21; Isa 42:24; Dan 9:10; Zech 6:15*

shapat (8199): *decide, judge.* This verb means making a decision, often in a legal context, with the implication that the one judging has the authority and power to enforce the decisions. The participle form (*shopet*) refers to a judge who is in the position to make such judgments.
SEE *Gen 18:25; Exod 2:14; 18:26; Lev 19:15; Deut 25:1; Judg 2:16; Ruth 1:1; 1 Sam 8:1; Ps 7:11; 9:4; 75:7; 82:1; Prov 31:9; Eccl 3:17; Isa 1:26; 33:22; Jer 11:20; Mic 7:3*

sarap (8314): See **kerub** (3742)

sharath (8334): *serve, minister.* This verb means to serve another. It can refer to servants serving the rich and powerful, to attendants or protégés serving important

religious figures, or to the attendants of God serving with religious practices, rites, and ceremonies.
SEE *Exod 24:13; Num 1:50; Deut 10:8; 1 Sam 2:11, 18; 1 Kgs 19:21; Ps 103:21; Isa 61:6; Jer 33:22*

todah (8426): *thanksgiving.* This noun refers to concrete declarations of thanksgiving in the context of worship, often by way of song or sacrifice. When giving thanks to God, statements of his greatness and exaltation accompany the thanks.
SEE *Lev 7:15; 22:29; Josh 7:19; Neh 12:27, 31; Ps 26:7; 42:4; 50:23; 100:4; 107:22; Jer 30:19; 33:11; Jon 2:9*

torah (8451): *instruction, law.* This noun means an instruction which is imparted to a student, child, or covenant partner, with a focus on directing the thinking and behavior of the recipient. It usually refers to God's instructions to his people in general. It can also refer to Genesis through Deuteronomy as a unit, the written code given through Moses, or one law in particular.
SEE *Exod 13:9; 18:20; Deut 30:10; 31:9; 32:46; Josh 1:8; Neh 9:13; Job 22:22; Ps 1:2; 19:7; 40:8; 119:1, 18, 34, 97, 113, 174; Isa 5:24; Hab 1:4*

tekhinnah (8467): *plea for mercy.* This noun means a verbal request or plea for mercy or favor for self or others, as a kind of imploring prayer. It is a humble request, often of a servant to a master, with no particular claim that the request must be fulfilled.
SEE *1 Kgs 8:28, 38, 45, 54; 9:3; Ps 6:9; 55:1; 119:170; Jer 36:7; Dan 9:20*

tamim (8549): *complete, blameless.* This word pertains to something that is completely intact, free from blemishes or defects. Often the focus is on moral goodness, being guiltless and thus not liable for sin. It also often describes an animal that is suitable for sacrifice.
SEE *Gen 6:9; 17:1; Exod 12:5; Deut 32:4; 2 Sam 22:24; Job 12:4; Ps 15:2; 18:25; 19:7; 119:1, 80; Prov 11:20; 28:10*

GREEK WORDS

abba patēr (0005, 3962): *Abba, father.* This phrase combines two words that both mean "father." *Abba* is a transliteration of an Aramaic term of endearment used by children to address their father ("Daddy"). *Patēr* is the standard Greek word to refer to a father. This phrase is used in the NT only as a title for God, with a focus on God's role as our caregiver and authority.
SEE *Mark 14:36; Rom 8:15; Gal 4:6*

agathōsunē (0019): *goodness, generosity.* This noun refers to a general positive moral quality. There is an implication of good actions, such as generosity, springing from this moral quality. See also ***aretē*** (0703).
SEE *Rom 15:14; Gal 5:22; Eph 5:9; 2 Thes 1:11*

agapē (0026): *love.* This noun means the attitude or emotion of deep affection for another person, with a focus on loving action and not feelings alone. This love is extolled as a cardinal virtue. The word *agapē* can also refer to a common meal connected to worship for early Christians.
SEE *John 5:42; 15:9, 13; Rom 5:5; 8:39; 13:10; 14:15; 1 Cor 8:1; 13:1; Gal 5:22; Eph 4:2, 15; Phil 1:9; Col 3:14; 1 Thes 3:12; Phlm 1:5; 1 Pet 4:8; 1 Jn 4:7; Jude 1:12; Rev 2:4*

angelos (0032): *messenger, angel.* This noun refers to someone who serves as an envoy, often with a message to deliver. While it can refer to a human messenger, in the NT it usually refers to angels, heavenly beings created by God to serve him and his creation. Some angels are fallen and are also known as "demons."
SEE *Matt 4:11; 22:30; 25:41; 26:53; 28:2; Mark 8:38; Luke 16:22; 24:23; Acts 5:19; 8:26; 10:3; 12:7; 27:23; 1 Cor 4:9; 6:3; 11:10; Col 2:18; Heb 1:4; 1 Pet 3:22; Rev 1:20*

hagiasmos (0038): *sanctification.* This noun means dedication to God, both in faithfulness to him and in active service. There is a sense of process toward godliness, with *hagiasmos* being the goal and the result, which is possible through the work of Jesus and his Spirit.
SEE *Rom 6:19, 22; 1 Cor 1:30; 1 Thes 4:3, 4, 7; 2 Thes 2:13; 1 Tim 2:15; Heb 12:14; 1 Pet 1:2*

hadēs (0086), ***geenna*** (1067): *grave, place of the dead, hell.* Similar to the Hebrew ***she'ol*** (7585), *hadēs* is a place below the surface of the earth, the habitation of the dead for both the righteous and unrighteous. *Geenna* is a more specific Aramaic term that pictures this place as one of judgment and punishment, i.e., hell.
SEE *Matt 5:22, 29; 11:23; 16:18; 18:9; 23:33; Mark 9:43; Luke 12:5; 16:23; Acts 2:27, 31; Jas 3:6; Rev 1:18; 20:13, 14*

aleiphō (0218): *anoint.* This verb means applying oil or something similar onto someone, usually to mark dedication of the person to a purpose or as an act of devotion. Additionally, it is a welcoming act of hospitality for a guest and a folk remedy for illness.
SEE *Matt 6:17; Mark 6:13; Luke 7:38, 46; John 12:3; Jas 5:14*

hamartia (0266): *sin.* This noun is a general term for sin, any action or attitude that is contrary to the will of God and the revealed standards of God.
SEE *Matt 26:28; Luke 1:77; 3:3; Rom 3:9; 4:7; 5:12; 6:1; 7:8; 8:2; 14:23; 1 Cor 15:56; Eph 2:1; 1 Tim 5:22; Heb 9:26; 12:1; Jas 1:15; 5:15; 1 Jn 1:9*

amnos (0286): *lamb.* This noun refers to a lamb, a small sheep. In the NT this word figuratively refers to Jesus as the Lamb of God, an acceptable sacrifice without blemish or defect.
SEE *John 1:29, 36; Acts 8:32; 1 Pet 1:19*

ampelos (0288): *vine.* This noun refers to a fruit-bearing vine, particularly a grapevine, with the associated meanings of life and new growth. Jesus refers to himself as the true vine.
SEE *Matt 26:29; Mark 14:25; Luke 22:18; John 15:1, 5; Jas 3:12*

anagennaō (0313), ***anōthen gennaō*** (0509, 1080): *born again, born from above.* These two related concepts mean to be "born again," signifying a change from one state of being into another. Rather than a physical change, a person's spirit is renewed or comes alive by the work of the Holy Spirit. The phrase *anōthen gennaō* is ambiguous and could mean either "born again" or "born from above."
SEE *John 3:3, 7, 31; 1 Pet 1:3, 23*

anastasis (0386): *resurrection.* This noun means bodily resurrection to life after having been dead. It usually refers to the resurrection of Jesus Christ and the future resurrection of which Jesus is the firstfruits.
SEE *Matt 22:28; Mark 12:18; John 5:29; 11:24; Acts 1:22; 2:31; 17:32; 1 Cor 15:12; Phil 3:10; Heb 11:35; 1 Pet 1:3; Rev 20:5*

antilutron (0487): See ***lutron*** (3083)

antichristos (0500): See ***pseudochristos*** (5580)

anōthen gennaō (0509, 1080): See ***anagennaō*** (0313)

haplotēs (0572): *generosity, sincerity.* This noun means the positive moral quality of being genuine and authentic as an expression of singularity in purpose and motivation. It can also mean giving to another in a free-handed manner, with the implication that the giving is sincere and not with duplicitous purposes.
SEE *Rom 12:8; 2 Cor 8:2; 9:11, 13; 11:3; Eph 6:5; Col 3:22*

apokalupsis (0602): *revelation.* This noun means a state or action of making something known, usually with the implication that it had been hidden or unknown. It is also the Greek title of the book of Revelation.
SEE *Luke 2:32; Rom 16:25; 1 Cor 1:7; 14:6, 26; 2 Cor 12:1, 7; Gal 1:12; Eph 1:17; 3:3; 1 Pet 1:13; 4:13; Rev 1:1*

apologeomai (0626), ***apologia*** (0627): *defense.* This verb (*apologeomai*) and its cognate noun (*apologia*) mean to respond to accusation or blame by giving a rational, logical defense. To defend with an *apologia* is not to give excuses; it is to give reasons.
SEE *Acts 19:33; 22:1; 24:10; 25:8, 16; 26:1; Phil 1:7, 16; 1 Pet 3:15*

apolutrosis (0629): *redemption.* This noun refers to buying the freedom of a slave or captive by paying a ransom. In the NT, it is used figuratively of the results of Christ's work, releasing people from the power of sin and death.
SEE *Luke 21:28; Rom 3:24; 8:23; 1 Cor 1:30; Eph 1:7, 14; 4:30; Col 1:14; Heb 9:15; 11:35*

apostolos (0652), ***apostolē*** (0651): *apostle.* This noun means a person who functions as a special messenger. In the NT it usually refers to those personally commissioned by Jesus, sent out for disciple-making in all nations. It is also used of those who are commissioned by the church as its messengers or representatives. The office of being an apostle is called "an apostleship" (*apostolē*).
SEE *Matt 10:2; Acts 1:25; 2:42; 15:2; 1 Cor 9:1; 12:28; 15:7; 2 Cor 12:11; Eph 4:11; 1 Tim 2:7; 2 Pet 3:2; Rev 2:2*

aretē (0703): *exceptional virtue, miracle.* This noun means the moral and ethical quality of goodness, with an emphasis on moral excellence. It is conceptually related to ***agathōsunē*** (0019), only more specific. This word can also mean a manifestation of the power of God.
SEE *Phil 4:8; 1 Pet 2:9; 2 Pet 1:3, 5*

arrabōn (0728): *deposit, pledge.* This noun means the deposit or pledge that guarantees the completion of a transaction between two parties. It is used figuratively of the Holy Spirit, whose presence guarantees the promise of eternal life to those who believe the Good News.
SEE *2 Cor 1:22; 5:5; Eph 1:14*

archiereus (0749): *high priest.* This noun refers to a leading priest among other priests. When plural, it refers to a class of religious leaders in association with other kinds of religious leaders. In first-century Judaism, there was one particular *archiereus* with the highest status, *the* high priest.
SEE *Luke 3:2; John 18:19; Acts 5:27; 23:2; Heb 4:14; 5:1, 5, 10; 7:26; 8:1; 9:11; 13:11*

archipoimēn (0750): See ***poimēn*** (4166)

baptizō (0907), ***baptisma*** (0908), ***baptismos*** (0909): *baptize, baptism.* These words refer to a water-washing ceremony. This practice of baptism is not uniquely Christian, but it is an integral part of initiation into the Christian faith. It can also refer to initiatory experiences not related to water at all, such as baptism in the Holy Spirit.
SEE *Matt 3:11; 28:19; Mark 16:16; Acts 2:38; 9:18; 11:16; 16:15; 19:3; 22:16; Rom 6:3; 1 Cor 12:13; 15:29; Gal 3:27; Eph 4:5; Col 2:12; Heb 6:2; 1 Pet 3:21*

beelzeboul (0954): *Beelzebub.* This word most likely refers to a name or title of Satan as lord over the kingdom of demons, as applied by both Jesus and his opposition. The Greek is *beelzeboul* ("lord of filth"), but it is traditionally rendered in English as Beelzebub ("lord of flies").
SEE *Matt 10:25; 12:24, 27; Mark 3:22; Luke 11:15, 18, 19*

biblion (0975): *book, scroll.* This noun means a common sheet of "paper" consisting of the inner bark from the papyrus plant, dried, flattened, crisscrossed, and gummed together. It can refer to a document on a single sheet, but usually it refers to sheets formed into a long scroll. In most cases the focus is on the contents written on the paper.
SEE *Matt 19:7; Luke 4:17; John 20:30; 21:25; 2 Tim 4:13; Rev 1:11; 5:1; 17:8; 20:12; 21:27*

blasphēmia (0988), ***blasphēmeō*** (0987), ***blasphēmos*** (0989): *blaspheme, blasphemy.* These words refer to abusive, slanderous, insulting, or otherwise untrue speech about someone so as to harm their reputation. In many NT contexts, the focus is on such talk about God and its disastrous consequences.
SEE *Matt 15:19; Mark 2:7; 3:28; 7:22; Luke 12:10; John 10:33; Eph 4:31; Col 3:8; 1 Tim 1:20; 2 Tim 3:2; Jude 1:8; Rev 13:1*

geenna (1067): See ***hadēs*** (0086)

glōssa (1100): *tongue.* This noun refers to the physical tongue. By extension, it also refers to a language, the common speech of a community. Sometimes *glōssa* is used to refer to groups of people defined by their language, or it can figuratively mean the effect speech can have.
SEE *Mark 16:17; Acts 2:4, 11; 10:46; 19:6; Rom 14:11; 1 Cor 12:10, 30; 13:8; 14:2, 39; Jas 3:8*

daimonion (1140): *demon.* This noun refers to a fallen angel, a limited, created being. Demons are evil beings, perverse to all that is good and just. Though subservient to God, they have the power to harass and inhabit other creatures.
SEE *Matt 10:8; 12:24; Mark 7:26; 16:17; Luke 4:33; 8:2, 30; 9:1; 1 Cor 10:20; 1 Tim 4:1; Jas 2:19; Rev 16:14*

diabolos (1228): *slanderous, devil.* This noun means one who slanders or accuses. While it can refer to a wicked human, it usually refers to the supernatural being the devil, who was the tempter in the Garden of Eden and in the desert with Jesus.
SEE *Matt 4:1; 25:41; John 8:44; Eph 4:27; 6:11; 1 Tim 3:7, 11; 2 Tim 3:3; Titus 2:3; Jas 4:7; 1 Pet 5:8; Rev 12:9; 20:2, 10*

diathēkē (1242): *covenant.* This noun refers to a person's last will and testament or to other solemn agreements involving benefits and responsibilities to all involved parties. In the NT, the word is often used as an equivalent to Hebrew ***berith*** (1285), especially in theological contexts.
SEE *Matt 26:28; Mark 14:24; Luke 22:20; 1 Cor 11:25; 2 Cor 3:6, 14; Eph 2:12; Heb 7:22; 8:6; 9:15; 12:24; 13:20*

diakonia (1248): *ministry, service.* This noun means the act of giving help and assistance to others. This service can often involve ignoble or lowly tasks. While it can refer to common household tasks, it often refers to service to others or to God.
SEE *Acts 6:1, 4; Rom 12:7; 1 Cor 16:15; 2 Cor 8:4; 9:13; Eph 4:12; Col 4:17; 2 Tim 4:5, 11*

diakonos (1249): *assistant, deacon.* This noun refers to a person who performs ***diakonia*** (1248). In addition to referring to a servant in general, in the NT it often refers to a servant of God and his people. It can also refer to an office in the Christian community. While this office has some status as a church leader, the focus is on humble service to God and meeting others' needs.
SEE *Matt 20:26; Rom 16:1; 2 Cor 11:23; Phil 1:1; Col 1:7, 23; 4:7; 1 Tim 3:8, 12; 4:6*

dikaiosunē (1343): *righteousness.* This noun means being in accord with a standard of justice; in the NT that standard is defined by God's own character. In individual contexts, the focus of the word can be on standing before God, practical living, internal motivations, etc.
SEE *Rom 1:17; 3:21; 4:3, 9; 5:17, 21; 8:10; 10:10; Eph 5:9; 6:14; Phil 3:9; 1 Tim 6:11; 2 Tim 3:16; 2 Pet 2:21; 1 Jn 2:29*

dikaiōs (1346), ***dikaiōsis*** (1347): *justly, justification.* These words are related to the concept of being in right relationship with God; see also ***dikaiosunē*** (1343). The noun *dikaiōsis* refers to a state of being, the result of an accomplished act. The adverb *dikaiōs* is a way of describing a person or action as being characterized by righteousness.
SEE *Rom 4:25; 5:18; 1 Cor 15:34; 1 Thes 2:10; Titus 2:12; 1 Pet 2:23*

doxa (1391): *glory.* This noun means radiance or splendor, with a strong association of importance and display of power. It refers to eye-catching, wondrous beauty, perhaps with a focus on the object shining or reflecting light. Glory means ascribing honor or giving praise, emphasizing that the person being honored is powerful, beautiful, and important.
SEE *Luke 2:14; 4:6; 9:32; 12:27; John 1:14; Rom 3:23; 1 Cor 11:7; 2 Cor 3:7; 4:17; Phil 2:11; 3:21*

doulos (1401): *slave.* This noun refers to a person who is the property of another person. A slave can be bought, sold, inherited, leased, or jointly owned. This language is also used figuratively to identify something that exercises power over a person, e.g., "slave to sin." In the NT, believers are often identified as slaves of Christ Jesus, with an emphasis on their identity with, obedience to, and humble service for their master.
SEE *Matt 20:27; John 13:16; 15:15; Rom 1:1; 6:20; 1 Cor 7:22; Gal 1:10; Eph 6:5; Phil 1:1; Col 3:11; Phlm 1:16; Rev 1:1*

eidōlolatria (1495), ***eidōlolatrēs*** (1496): *idolatry, idolater.* These words describe the worship of idols, often with an association to other immoral behaviors. Idolatry may involve items other than hand-fashioned idols; for example, a lust for wealth to replace God amounts to idolatry. An idolater (*eidōlolatrēs*) is a person who practices idolatry.
SEE *1 Cor 5:10; 6:9; 10:7, 14; Gal 5:20; Eph 5:5; Col 3:5; 1 Pet 4:3; Rev 21:8; 22:15*

eirēnē (1515): *peace.* This noun means a state of concord, peace, and harmony among parties. There is no necessary implication of a previous state of discord. The word can also signify an internal sense of well-being. It often refers to the peace between God and human beings made possible through Christ.
SEE *Matt 10:34; Luke 2:14; John 14:27; Acts 10:36; Rom 5:1; 8:6; 14:19; 1 Cor 14:33; Gal 5:22; Eph 2:14; Phil 4:7, 9; Col 3:15; Heb 12:14; 1 Pet 3:11*

ekklēsia (1577), ***sunagōgē*** (4864): *assembly, congregation, church.* This noun means a gathered group, usually for the purpose of

a political or religious meeting. In the NT, it usually refers to a local community gathered around faith in Jesus: the church. It does not refer to a building but rather the people who make up the community.
SEE *Matt 16:18; 18:17; Rom 16:5; 1 Cor 1:2; 10:32; 12:28; Eph 5:25; Col 1:18; 4:15; Jas 2:2; Rev 1:20*

eleos (1656): *mercy.* This noun means gracious compassion or kindness for someone in need. Mercy is differentiated from kindness; while kindness can be to anyone, mercy is for those in need. It can also mean legal clemency. It can refer to God's mercy to human beings.
SEE *Matt 9:13; 23:23; Luke 1:50; 10:37; Eph 2:4; Titus 3:5; Jas 2:13; 3:17*

eleutheria (1657), ***eleutheroō*** (1659): *freedom, set free.* This noun means to be in a state of liberty, free from outside control, often with an implication of prior confinement, oppression, slavery, or constraints. The verb *eleutheroō* describes the act of liberation.
SEE *Rom 8:21; 1 Cor 10:29; 2 Cor 3:17; Gal 2:4; 5:1, 13; Jas 1:25; 2:12; 1 Pet 2:16; 2 Pet 2:19*

elpis (1680): *hope.* This noun means looking forward to something with confident expectation. It can refer to common expectations, such as a farmer expecting a share of a harvest. In the NT it often refers to ultimate, eternal hope grounded in God and his saving activity.
SEE *Acts 23:6; Rom 5:2; 8:24; 1 Cor 13:13; Eph 1:18; 2:12; Col 1:5; 1 Thes 5:8; Titus 2:13; Heb 7:19; 1 Pet 1:3; 3:15*

episkopos (1985), ***episkopeō*** (1983), ***episkopē*** (1984): *overseer, oversee.* These words refer to a person who is a guardian, supervisor, or overseer for a group. In the NT, it indicates a role or office in a local church. The nouns *episkopos* and *episkopē* refer to the person and the office respectively. The verb *episkopeō* describes the work of serving as an overseer.
SEE *Acts 20:28; Phil 1:1; 1 Tim 3:1, 2; Titus 1:7; 1 Pet 2:25; 5:2*

epiphaneia (2015): *appearing.* This noun refers to the appearance of something previously hidden, unknown, or unrecognized. In the NT it refers to the appearance of Jesus and his Kingdom.
SEE *2 Thes 2:8; 1 Tim 6:14; 2 Tim 1:10; 4:1, 8; Titus 2:13*

euangelion (2098): *gospel, Good News.* This noun means a message with a positive, public focus. In most NT contexts *euangelion* refers to the specific message about what God has done in and through Jesus, the Good News. It can also refer to one of the first four books of the NT, the four Gospels.
SEE *Mark 1:1, 14, 15; Rom 1:1, 16; 2:16; 15:19; 1 Cor 15:1; 2 Cor 11:4; Gal 1:6; Eph 1:13*

eulogia (2129): *praise, blessing.* This noun can mean to speak of something in favorable terms. It can also mean to speak to God and ask him to impart his favor on an object or person. Such a blessing can also refer to some tangible gift rather than simply speech.
SEE *2 Cor 9:5; Gal 3:14; Eph 1:3; Heb 6:7; Jas 3:10; 1 Pet 3:9; Rev 5:12; 7:12*

zumē (2219): *leaven.* This noun refers to a substance used as an agent for fermenting dough, with the associated meaning of a change agent that is subtle and gradual, yet thorough.
SEE *Matt 13:33; 16:6, 11; Mark 8:15; Luke 12:1; 13:21; 1 Cor 5:6, 7, 8; Gal 5:9*

zōopoieō (2227): *make alive.* This verb means to give life to something. In the NT it refers to the new, supernatural life that God gives to his people, both in the present and at the future resurrection of the dead.
SEE *John 5:21; 6:63; Rom 4:17; 8:11; 1 Cor 15:22, 36, 45; 2 Cor 3:6; Gal 3:21; 1 Pet 3:18*

thelēma (2307): *will, desire.* This noun means the purpose or intention in someone's mind or emotions (a desire), or a part of the inner person (the will). Often it refers to the will of God.
SEE *Mark 3:35; Rom 12:2; 15:32; Eph 6:6; Col 4:12; 1 Thes 4:3; 5:18; Heb 10:36; 1 Pet 2:15; 3:17; 1 Jn 2:17*

hilaskomai (2433), ***hilasmos*** (2434), ***hilastērion*** (2435): *atonement, propitiation, expiation.* These words refer to the means by which sins and offenses are forgiven. The result of atonement is mercy and reconciliation between the sinner and the one wronged. In the NT, these words refer to Jesus' atoning sacrifice. *Hilastērion* can also mean the "place of atonement," referring to the cover of the Ark.
SEE *Luke 18:13; Rom 3:25; Heb 2:17; 9:5; 1 Jn 2:2; 4:10*

kardia (2588): *heart.* This noun means the inner person. It is closely related to soul, mind, and spirit. In some contexts there is an emphasis on thinking and understanding; in others the emphasis is on feeling and desiring; in still others the focus is on making choices. The word can also denote the central area of something or the physical organ, but these meanings are less common in the NT.
SEE *Matt 5:8; 15:18; Mark 12:30; John 14:1; Acts 15:9; 21:13; Rom 10:9; 2 Cor 5:12; Gal 4:6; Eph 4:18; 1 Tim 1:5; 1 Pet 1:22*

katallagē (2643), ***katallassō*** (2644): *reconciliation.* These words mean the reestablishment of a friendly relationship after it had been seriously disrupted or broken. There is a focus on the change in the relationship from a negative to a positive condition.
SEE *Rom 5:10, 11; 11:15; 1 Cor 7:11; 2 Cor 5:18, 19, 20*

klēsis (2821), ***klētos*** (2822): *calling.* These words mean an invitation to someone to accept responsibilities for a particular task or a new relationship. God calls/invites the believer to relationship with him or to a particular role in his Kingdom. While *klēsis* refers to the invitation itself, *klētos* is used to describe a person who has already been called.
SEE *Matt 22:14; Rom 1:6; 8:28; 11:29; 1 Cor 1:2, 26; Eph 1:18; 4:1; 2 Thes 1:11; 2 Tim 1:9; 2 Pet 1:10; Jude 1:1*

koinōnia (2842): *fellowship.* This noun means an association of close mutual relationship and involvement with another; it is an alliance with another person or group, formal or informal. There is an implication of intimacy, singleness of purpose, trust of one another, sharing of material goods, and harmony rather than hostility.
SEE *Acts 2:42; 1 Cor 1:9; 10:16; 2 Cor 6:14; 8:4; 13:14; Gal 2:9; Phil 2:1; 3:10; Phlm 1:6; Heb 13:16; 1 Jn 1:6*

kurios (2962): *lord.* This noun means master, lord, or owner in social and economic contexts; generally, it refers to a social superior. When addressing such a superior, "sir" is an appropriate rendering. When Jesus is the referent, the title has more significant implications and is appropriately rendered "Lord." Sometimes, this word functions as the Greek equivalent to the Hebrew divine name Yahweh (which Jewish people pronounced using the Hebrew word meaning "lord").
SEE *Matt 3:3; 12:8; 27:63; Mark 12:9; Acts 16:31; Eph 6:5; Phil 2:11; 3:20; 2 Thes 3:16; 1 Pet 3:6; 2 Pet 2:20; Rev 22:21*

leitourgia (3009), ***leitourgikos*** (3010), ***leitourgos*** (3011): *service, ministry.* The general noun (*leitourgia*) usually refers to religious ceremonial service to God. It can also refer to specialized practical and material service to others. A *leitourgos* is one who does such service, and *leitourgikos* indicates ongoing engagement in service.
SEE *Luke 1:23; Rom 13:6; 15:16; 2 Cor 9:12; Phil 2:17; Heb 1:7, 14; 8:2, 6; 9:21*

logos (3056): *word.* This noun refers to an idea that finds concrete expression. The primary focus is on the content of the communication, though the action of speaking can also be in view. It can refer to a single word, a command, a literary work, a financial statement, a line of reasoning, a summary of a person's thought, and many more things. It is also a title of Jesus Christ, the *logos*, as the culmination of God's revelation to humanity.
SEE *Luke 16:2; 21:33; John 1:1, 14; Acts 6:2; 7:22; 15:6; Rom 14:12; 15:18; Gal 5:14; Col 4:6; Heb 4:12; 13:7; 1 Jn 1:1; Rev 1:2; 19:13*

lutron (3083), ***lutroō*** (3084), ***antilutron*** (0487): *ransom.* The verb (*lutroō*) means to liberate something or someone, often through payment. The nouns (*lutron* and *antilutron*) refer to the ransom or payment itself. In the NT these words refer to the substitutionary work of Jesus by which his people find relationship to him as God and Savior.
SEE *Matt 20:28; Mark 10:45; Luke 24:21; 1 Tim 2:6; Titus 2:14; 1 Pet 1:18*

makarios (3107): *blessed.* This adjective pertains to a state or condition of joy and happiness. It implies that the blessed person is in favorable, pleasant, and fulfilling circumstances. It can range from emotional joy to a more sedate, virtuous attitude. There is also often an implication that the person is in a right covenant relationship with God. See also Hebrew ***'ashrey*** (0835).
SEE *Matt 5:3; Luke 6:20; 11:28; John 20:29;*

Acts 20:35; Rom 4:7; Titus 2:13; Jas 1:12; 1 Pet 3:14; Rev 1:3; 22:7

marturion (3142): *witness.* This noun refers to something that serves as testimony or proof of an idea. It can refer to speech, actions, or even objects that confirm something.
SEE *Matt 8:4; Luke 9:5; Acts 4:33; 1 Cor 1:6; 2 Thes 1:10; 1 Tim 2:6; 2 Tim 1:8*

mataios (3152): *futile, worthless.* This adjective relates to being useless on the basis of being empty or hollow. Things that are *mataios* have no value at all.
SEE *Acts 14:15; 1 Cor 3:20; 15:17; Titus 3:9; Jas 1:26; 1 Pet 1:18*

messias (3323): See ***christos*** (5547)

metamorphoō (3339), ***metaschēmatizō*** (3345): *transform.* These verbs mean to change fundamentally and completely from one state to another. It can refer to a physical transformation or to an inward change of character or mind-set. With *metaschēmatizō*, there can be an implication that the change is deceptive and false, but not in every instance.
SEE *Matt 17:2; Mark 9:2; Rom 12:2; 2 Cor 3:18; Phil 3:21*

metanoia (3341): *repentance.* This noun means the action or condition of change, especially of behavior and opinions. In the NT it usually refers to changing from a sinful state to a righteous standard. Repentance is not merely regret about something, it is a change of perspective that results in changed actions.
SEE *Mark 1:4; Luke 3:8; 5:32; 24:47; Acts 11:18; 20:21; Rom 2:4; 2 Tim 2:25; Heb 6:1; 2 Pet 3:9*

metaschēmatizō (3345): See ***metamorphoō*** (3339)

monogenēs (3439): *unique, one and only.* This word indicates something that is the only representative of its kind, with the implication that it is special or extraordinary in some way. It can refer to a unique child, special to the parents, whether or not the child is an only child.
SEE *Luke 7:12; 8:42; 9:38; John 1:14, 18; 3:16, 18; Heb 11:17; 1 Jn 4:9*

mustērion (3466): *secret.* This noun means a secret that has been kept from general knowledge. Such secrets are often known only by a small, privileged group. In the NT, God's secret was known only to God and revealed through Jesus Christ. It is often translated "mystery," but the Greek word has no implication of inscrutability, only of what is not yet known or revealed.
SEE *Mark 4:11; 1 Cor 2:1; 15:51; Eph 3:3; 5:32; 6:19; Col 1:26; 4:3; 1 Tim 3:9, 16*

nomos (3551): *law.* This noun means a governing principle or set of rules, whether legal, moral, social, logical, or practical. It can refer to established statutory law, such as the Roman law. In the NT it often refers to written Scripture—an individual law from the Pentateuch, the Mosaic law system as a whole, the Pentateuch as a whole, or even the entire OT.
SEE *Matt 7:12; 23:23; Luke 16:17; 24:44; Acts 15:5; Rom 2:12; 7:7, 12; 8:2; 10:4; 1 Cor 14:21; Gal 2:16, 19, 21; 5:14, 18, 23; 6:2; Jas 1:25; 2:10; 4:11*

oikonomia (3622), ***oikonomos*** (3623): *stewardship, manager.* These nouns refer, respectively, to a person (*oikonomos*) who manages a household, business, or other significant responsibility and to that person's responsibilities or stewardship (*oikonomia*). Sometimes *oikonomia* refers to a grand plan. The *oikonomos* is generally a person of authority who is accountable to a superior.
SEE *Luke 16:1; 1 Cor 4:1; 9:17; Gal 4:2; Eph 1:10; 3:2, 9; Col 1:25; 1 Tim 1:4; Titus 1:7*

orgē (3709): *anger.* This noun means a strong feeling of displeasure and antagonism, often the response to a standard being violated. This anger can range from an appropriate response of anger against injustice to sinful, selfish anger.
SEE *Mark 3:5; John 3:36; Rom 1:18; 2:5, 8; Eph 2:3; 4:31; 5:6; Col 3:8; Rev 6:17; 16:19; 19:15*

ouranos (3772), ***paradeisos*** (3857): *heaven, paradise.* The noun *ouranos* means a region above the earth in contrast to regions on the earth and below it. It can refer to at least three spaces: the sky, space, and heaven. The noun *paradeisos* is more specific in referring to the future abode of God's people in the afterlife, translated "paradise."
SEE *Matt 3:2; 16:3; Luke 23:43; 1 Cor 15:47; 2 Cor 12:2, 4; Gal 1:8; Eph 4:10; 2 Pet 3:13; Rev 2:7; 3:12; 16:11; 21:1*

paidagōgos (3807): *tutor, guardian.* This noun means a person who has responsibility for a minor. The guardian was to be respected by the child and could impose discipline as necessary. This person was often a slave and was not usually a teacher formally, although instruction was usually involved.
SEE *1 Cor 4:15; Gal 3:24, 25*

paideuō (3811), ***paideia*** (3809), ***paideutēs*** (3810): *instruct, discipline.* These related words mean the teaching and molding of a student according to a behavioral standard. The verb (*paideuō*) describes the action, and *paideutēs* is one who trains and guides. It can refer to formal training, but often it refers to a parent's disciplining, training, and correcting his child. Such training at times should be gentle, yet it also includes discipline.
SEE *Acts 7:22; 22:3; 1 Cor 11:32; Eph 6:4; 2 Tim 2:25; 3:16; Titus 2:12; Heb 12:6, 9; Rev 3:19*

pantokratōr (3841): *almighty.* This is a title for God with a focus on his unlimited power over all things. This title is likely related to a similar OT title for God; see Hebrew ***tsaba'*** (6635).
SEE *2 Cor 6:18; Rev 1:8; 4:8; 11:17; 15:3; 16:7, 14; 19:6, 15; 21:22*

parabolē (3850): *parable, proverb.* This noun refers to a maxim or a story with a symbolic meaning. It is usually relatively short. Jesus' parables are often true to life, but they do not represent actual historical events. Another use of *parabolē* is of a past event that serves as an archetype or symbolic foreshadowing of a later realization (Heb 9:9).
SEE *Matt 13:3, 10; Mark 4:2, 33; Luke 5:36; 12:41; 15:3; 18:1; 21:29; Heb 9:9*

paradeisos (3857): See ***ouranos*** (3772)

parakaleō (3870), ***paraklēsis*** (3874): *encourage, request.* The verb (*parakaleō*) can mean to give comfort to another person, to urge a person toward action or a new thought pattern, to urgently request something, to cheer someone up, and so on. Generally, a positive attitude and desire to help is implied. The noun (*paraklēsis*) refers to the act itself of encouraging, requesting, etc.
SEE *Rom 15:4; 1 Cor 14:31; Phil 2:1; Col 2:2; 1 Thes 5:11, 14; 2 Thes 3:12; 2 Tim 4:2; Titus 2:15; Heb 3:13*

paraklētos (3875): *comforter, helper, advocate.* This noun is a person who helps or enables another person; see ***parakaleō*** (3870). Sometimes *paraklētos* has a legal meaning, referring to an advocate in a courtroom setting. It became a title for the Holy Spirit, whose role includes encouraging, strengthening, and supporting God's people.
SEE *John 14:16, 26; 15:26; 16:7; 1 Jn 2:1*

parousia (3952): *presence, coming.* This noun refers to the presence of a person in a particular place with a focus on the event of the person's arrival. In the NT the word often refers to the future coming of Jesus Christ in glory.
SEE *Matt 24:3, 37; 1 Cor 15:23; 1 Thes 3:13; 4:15; 5:23; Jas 5:7; 2 Pet 3:4; 1 Jn 2:28*

patēr (3962): *father.* This noun refers to a male parent, a father. As an extension of this meaning, it can refer to an ancestor, a spiritual leader in a community, a great religious leader from the past (e.g., Abraham), etc. God has revealed himself as the Father of his people.
SEE *Matt 5:16; 6:9; 7:11; Rom 4:11; 1 Cor 1:3; 2 Cor 1:3; Eph 1:3; 1 Thes 2:11; 1 Tim 5:1; Heb 12:9; Jas 1:17; 1 Jn 2:13, 23*

peirazō (3985), ***peirasmos*** (3986): *tempt, try.* This verb (*peirazō*) and its cognate noun (*peirasmos*) can mean trying to learn more about the character, nature, or viability of someone or something. A person who is tested often becomes a better, more mature person because of the test. These words can also mean temptation, attempting to cause someone to fail and sin.
SEE *Matt 6:13; Mark 1:13; 14:38; Luke 4:2; 1 Cor 7:5; 10:13; Gal 6:1; 1 Thes 3:5; 1 Tim 6:9; Heb 4:15; Jas 1:12, 13; 1 Pet 4:12*

petra (4073), ***petros*** (4074): *rock.* The noun *petra* means "rock." It can be any kind of natural stone, ranging from a boulder to a large rock formation or even bedrock suitable to be the foundation for a large building. In the NT, *petros* is Jesus' nickname for Simon, one of the twelve disciples.
SEE *Matt 7:24; 16:18; Mark 15:46; Luke 6:48; John 1:42; 1 Cor 10:4; Rev 6:15*

pisteuō (4100), ***pistis*** (4102): *believe, faith.* This verb (*pisteuō*) and the related noun

(*pistis*) refer to confidence that something is real, with a strong implication that action will ensue from this belief. While faith can be rather mundane (e.g., believing a report, 1 Cor 11:18), in the NT it almost always refers to faith in God or Christ. Such faith entails active belief, entrusting oneself completely to God.
SEE *John 8:30; 12:11; Acts 5:14; 18:8; Rom 1:17; 3:22, 25; 5:1; 10:17; 14:1; Gal 2:20; Eph 2:8; Phil 1:27; 1 Thes 1:3; 1 Tim 4:6; Heb 6:1; 11:1; Jas 2:14, 20; 1 Jn 3:23*

ploutos (4149): *wealth.* This noun means an abundance of possessions and economic prosperity. It can refer to an abundance of anything. In the NT it often refers to the heavenly riches of relationship with God.
SEE *Mark 4:19; Rom 11:33; Eph 1:7; 3:8, 16; Phil 4:19; 1 Tim 6:17; Jas 5:2*

pneuma (4151): *spirit.* This noun can refer to air in motion, either as wind or as breath. It can refer to an incorporeal part of a person, an essential part of life and a central component of the mind and personality. It can also refer to a noncorporeal being, either good or evil. It often refers to the Spirit of God.
SEE *Matt 12:18; Rom 8:10, 13; 1 Cor 5:3; 7:34; Eph 4:4; Phil 1:27; 1 Thes 5:23; Heb 4:12*

poimēn (4166), ***archipoimēn*** (0750), ***poimainō*** (4165): *shepherd.* These words relate to taking care of sheep. They figuratively refer to someone who is in a leadership position, such as over a community or nation; a shepherd has authority, provides protection, and cares for the flock. The action of shepherding is *poimainō,* while *poimēn* refers to the shepherd. The related word *archipoimēn* means a shepherd of high status among other shepherds, a chief shepherd.
SEE *Matt 2:6; 9:36; 26:31; Mark 6:34; Luke 2:8; John 10:11, 12; 21:16; Acts 20:28; Eph 4:11; Heb 13:20; 1 Pet 2:25; 5:2, 4; Rev 19:15*

proginōskō (4267), ***prognōsis*** (4268), ***prooraō*** (4308): *foreknow, foresee.* The verb *proginōskō* means to know or choose something in advance. The noun *prognōsis* refers to the advanced knowledge itself. The verb *prooraō* has a similar meaning, referring to seeing something in advance without the implication of choice.
SEE *Acts 2:23, 25, 31; Rom 8:29; 11:2; Gal 3:8; 1 Pet 1:2, 20*

proorizō (4309): *predestine.* This verb means deciding on something beforehand. In the NT, it refers to God's making plans, decisions, and choices in a prior time.
SEE *Acts 4:28; Rom 8:29, 30; 1 Cor 2:7; Eph 1:5, 11*

proskomma (4348): See ***skandalizō*** (4624)

prōtotokos (4416): *firstborn.* This noun refers to a parent's firstborn child. As an extension of this literal meaning, it can refer to a person who holds a special status as preeminent.
SEE *Luke 2:7; Rom 8:29; Col 1:15, 18; Heb 1:6; 11:28; 12:23; Rev 1:5*

rhabbi (4461), ***rhabbouni*** (4462): *teacher, rabbi.* This noun refers to a Jewish instructor and academic expert in interpreting the Jewish Scriptures. It was a position of honor and respect, though not necessarily a formal office.
SEE *Matt 23:7; 26:49; Mark 9:5; 10:51; John 1:38, 49; 3:2; 11:8; 20:16*

sarx (4561): *flesh.* This noun refers to the soft tissue of a human or animal. By extension, it can mean the entire physical body or simply human existence in general. It sometimes means the external parts of human life, only those that can be observed directly without reference to internal or spiritual realities. Still another meaning is the reasoning, appetites, and desires that relate to the sinful nature, at odds with our redeemed life in God.
SEE *Matt 16:17; 26:41; John 1:14; 3:6; Rom 8:4; 1 Cor 5:5; Gal 3:3; 5:19, 24; Eph 5:29; Heb 5:7*

satanas (4567): *Satan.* This noun can refer to an adversary in general, but in the NT it functions as a title for the devil, the great adversary of God and his people.
SEE *Matt 4:10; 16:23; Luke 10:18; John 13:27; Acts 5:3; Rom 16:20; 2 Cor 11:14; 12:7; 1 Thes 2:18; Rev 2:24; 20:2, 7*

sēmeion (4592): *sign.* This noun means a distinguishing mark or indication that authenticates something as real or genuine. It can be as mundane as a signature or a prearranged signal. This word can also refer to a supernatural miracle or act of power that causes wonder and amazement and stamps the event as God's work.
SEE *Matt 12:38; 24:30; Mark 16:17; Acts 4:16; 8:6; 15:12; Rom 15:19; 1 Cor 1:22; 2 Cor 12:12; 2 Thes 2:9; Heb 2:4; Rev 13:13*

skandalizō (4624), ***skandalon*** (4625), ***proskomma*** (4348): *offend, stumbling block.* These words refer to an object that trips a person (*proskomma*) or a trap (*skandalon*). The verb *skandalizō* means to cause someone to trip or stumble. Figuratively, these words refer to causing offense or sin.
SEE *Matt 5:29; 16:23; 18:6; Rom 9:32, 33; 14:13, 20; 1 Cor 1:23; 8:9, 13; Gal 5:11; 1 Pet 2:8*

sunklēronomos (4789): *coheirs.* This noun means a person inherits something along with someone else, often with the sense that the coheir is included as a gracious gift. The second party is a full participant in the inheritance, receiving the same benefit as the original heir.
SEE *Rom 8:17; Eph 3:6; Heb 11:9; 1 Pet 3:7*

sunagōgē (4864): See ***ekklēsia*** (1577)

sphragizō (4972), ***sphragis*** (4973): *seal.* The noun (*sphragis*) refers to an engraved object used as a mark to show possession, acceptance, or closing off an object. The verb (*sphragizō*) is the action of setting such a seal. These words can have a figurative sense, indicating approval or guarantee that one person represents another.
SEE *Matt 27:66; 1 Cor 9:2; Eph 1:13; 4:30; 2 Tim 2:19; Rev 5:1; 20:3; 22:10*

sōzō (4982), ***sōtēria*** (4991): *save, salvation.* This verb (*sōzō*) and noun (*sōtēria*) mean the state or action of delivering or rescuing another from a dangerous situation. The danger can be physical or figurative. In the NT, it usually refers to divine salvation for a fallen creation and humanity.
SEE *Acts 2:21, 47; 4:12; Rom 1:16; 8:24; 10:9; 1 Cor 15:2; 2 Cor 2:15; Eph 1:13; 2:8; 1 Thes 5:9; 2 Thes 2:13; 2 Tim 1:9; 2:10; 3:15; Titus 3:5; 1 Pet 2:2; 3:21*

sōtēr (4990): *savior.* This noun refers to a person who delivers or rescues another from a dangerous circumstance. In the NT it refers to God saving his people from the results of sin, God's wrath, death, and hell.
SEE *Luke 1:47; 2:11; John 4:42; Acts 5:31; 13:23; Eph 5:23; Phil 3:20; 1 Tim 4:10; 2 Tim 1:10; Titus 1:3, 4; 3:6; 2 Pet 1:1; 2:20; 3:18; 1 Jn 4:14; Jude 1:25*

sōtēria (4991): See ***sōzō*** (4982)

teleios (5046), ***teleiotēs*** (5047): *perfect, complete, mature.* This word describes something that lacks nothing and has come to complete maturity in a particular area. When applied to morality, it means not lacking any moral quality and that each moral quality is fully developed. The noun *teleiotēs* is the state of such completion, perfection, and maturity.
SEE *Matt 5:48; 1 Cor 13:10; Eph 4:13; Col 3:14; Heb 6:1; Jas 1:4; 3:2*

tupos (5179): *example, type.* This noun means a pattern or model which is to be replicated or reproduced. It can refer to a statue, the image from a signet ring, building plans, etc. Figuratively, it can refer to a model or pattern of some kind of behavior. It can also refer to a model or prototype, prefiguring a person to come.
SEE *Acts 7:44; Rom 5:14; 1 Cor 10:6; Phil 3:17; 1 Thes 1:7; 2 Thes 3:9; 1 Tim 4:12; Titus 2:7; Heb 8:5; 1 Pet 5:3*

huiothesia (5206): *adoption.* This noun refers to adoption, with an emphasis that the child has full inheritance rights and the same status as a natural child.
SEE *Rom 8:15, 23; 9:4; Gal 4:5; Eph 1:5*

hupokritēs (5273): *pretender, hypocrite.* This noun refers to a person who pretends to be something that he or she is not. Its original meaning was a stage actor, but this meaning is not found in the NT. In the NT, the focus is on the sin of simulation and pretext, especially referring to those who presume they are righteous and condemn others.
SEE *Matt 6:2, 5; 15:7; 22:18; 23:13; 24:51; Mark 7:6; Luke 6:42; 13:15*

charis (5485): *grace.* This noun means showing kindness toward someone, often with gifts and benefits as part of the beneficent relationship. The word can be used as a greeting or a simple thank you. It often refers to God's basic relationship of favor and kindness to human beings, especially his children.
SEE *Luke 2:40; Rom 3:24; 5:2, 21; 6:1; Gal 1:15; Eph 1:6; 2:5, 8; 2 Thes 1:12; 2 Tim 2:1; Titus 2:11; 1 Pet 3:7; Rev 22:21*

charisma (5486): *gift.* This noun refers to a gift generously and freely given as an

expression of the giver's favor. In the NT, it often refers to spiritual gifts given by God to believers for various purposes within the body of Christ.
SEE Rom 1:11; 12:6; 1 Cor 1:7; 7:7; 12:4, 28; 1 Tim 4:14; 2 Tim 1:6; 1 Pet 4:10

christos (5547), ***messias*** (3323): *Christ, Messiah.* These related words mean a person who has been anointed. The Greek word is *christos;* the word *messias* is a Greek transliteration from Hebrew ***mashakh*** (4886), and it has the same meaning. The word is used as a title for the king who has God's authority and approval. The NT identifies Jesus as this king, so in some contexts, Christ can function as a proper name for Jesus.
SEE Matt 2:4; Luke 2:11; John 1:17, 41; 4:25; Acts 2:31; 5:42; Rom 8:35; 2 Cor 5:10; Gal 6:2, 12; Eph 3:4; Col 3:16

pseudochristos (5580), ***antichristos*** (0500): *false christ, antichrist.* These nouns refer to people opposed to God, either by falsely posing as divine agents or by actively disparaging God or Christ. An *antichristos* is likely a religious leader who is clearly in opposition to Christ. A *pseudochristos* falsely claims to be anointed by God. The concept of antichrist is commonly connected to the "man of lawlessness" (*anomos*, 2 Thes 2:8).
SEE Matt 24:24; Mark 13:22; 1 Jn 2:18, 22; 4:3; 2 Jn 1:7

SUBJECT INDEX
FOR THE STUDY MATERIALS

The *NLT Study Bible* contains over one million words of study materials alongside the Bible text. To help you find what you are looking for, we have designed this index to be as comprehensive and easy-to-use as possible.

Each entry and subentry is followed by a list of references to the *NLT Study Bible* notes and features. Under each topic heading, we have placed the main features having to do with that topic first—for instance, Abraham's PROFILE is listed immediately following his name. All other features are listed in order of page number. References to study notes are indicated by passage references. The page number for a given feature follows the feature name or reference.

Please note that this index does not list every topic that occurs in the Bible text but only those that appear in the notes and features. Although the *NLT Study Bible* materials do not cover every topic in Scripture, they do cover many of the important ones for the student of the Bible. If you would like to find a word or phrase in the Bible text itself, we encourage you to use the Dictionary/Concordance that begins on p. 2369.

The Subject Index can be used in conjunction with your Bible reading and study. If you see a word or concept during your reading that you would like to study further, you might find more information about it here. In this manner, the index can be used to do topical studies. Also, if you wish to read all of the special features, such as the PROFILES, you can look under the topic heading for that type of feature (*See* CHARTS; DIAGRAMS; ILLUSTRATIONS; MAPS; PROFILES; THEMES; TIMELINES). For these listings, we break the usual page-order rule and list the features alphabetically.

Please tell us about your experiences using this Subject Index by visiting us at www.NLTStudyBible.com, or send us an email at NLTStudyBible@tyndale.com. We look forward to hearing from you.

A

B

H

I

K

M

Q

R

S

T

W

NLT DICTIONARY / CONCORDANCE

A

AARON First high priest of Israel; elder brother and spokesman of Moses (Exod 4:14-31; 7:1-2); confronted Pharaoh with Moses (Exod 5–12); held up Moses' hands during battle (Exod 17:8-15); led Israel while Moses was absent (Exod 24:14); priestly clothing and accessories (Exod 28); his ordination (Exod 29; Lev 8); his failure with the gold calf (Exod 32; Acts 7:40); spoke against Moses, then interceded on behalf of sister, Miriam (Num 12:1-16); helped stop the plague (Num 16:45-48); priesthood confirmed (Num 17; Heb 5:1-4); failed at Meribah and was denied entry to Promised Land (Num 20:1-13); died (Num 20:22-29; 33:38-39).

ABANDON, ABANDONED, ABANDONS (v) to desert or forsake
Josh 1:5 . . . will not fail you or **a** you.
Josh 24:16 . . . We would never **a** the LORD
Ezra 9:9 . . . God did not **a** us in our slavery.
Neh 9:31 . . . completely or **a** them forever.
Ps 22:1 . . . why have you **a-ed** me?
Ps 37:25 . . . never seen the godly **a-ed**
Ps 37:28 . . . he will never **a** the godly.
Prov 15:10 . . . Whoever **a-s** the right path
Matt 27:46 . . . why have you **a-ed** me?
John 16:1 . . . you won't **a** your faith.
Rom 1:24 . . . So God **a-ed** them to do
Rom 1:28 . . . **a-ed** them to their foolish
2 Cor 4:9 . . . down, but never **a-ed** by God.
Heb 13:5 . . . I will never **a** you.

ABASED (KJV)
Ezek 21:26 . . . mighty will be *brought down.*
Matt 23:12 . . . themselves will be *humbled*
Phil 4:12 . . . how to *live on almost nothing*

ABEL Son of Adam and Eve, brother of Cain (Gen 4:1-2); his offering accepted (Gen 4:4; Heb 11:4); murdered by Cain (Gen 4:8; Matt 23:35; Luke 11:51; Heb 12:24; 1 Jn 3:11-12; Jude 1:11); replaced by Seth (Gen 4:25).

ABHOR (v) to hate or loathe
Ps 119:163 . . . I hate and **a** all falsehood,

ABIDE(TH), ABIDING (KJV)
Luke 2:8 . . . shepherds *staying* in the fields
John 12:46 . . . no longer *remain* in the dark
John 15:4 . . . be fruitful unless you *remain*

ABILITY, ABILITIES (n) talent, aptitude, or skill
Exod 35:34 . . . the **a** to teach their skills
Dan 6:3 . . . because of Daniel's great **a,**
Acts 2:4 . . . Spirit gave them this **a.**
1 Cor 12:1 . . . special **a-ies** the Spirit gives
1 Cor 14:1 . . . special **a-ies** the Spirit gives—
1 Cor 14:12 . . . special **a-ies** the Spirit gives,
2 Cor 1:8 . . . beyond our **a** to endure,

ABLE (adj) marked by power, intelligence, competence, skill, giftedness
Deut 16:17 . . . must give as they are **a,**
Dan 3:17 . . . whom we serve is **a** to save
Rom 8:39 . . . ever be **a** to separate us from
Rom 16:25 . . . to God, who is **a** to
Eph 3:20 . . . all glory to God, who is **a,**
Eph 6:13 . . . you will be **a** to resist
2 Tim 1:12 . . . that he is **a** to guard
2 Tim 2:24 . . . be **a** to teach, and
Jude 1:24 . . . to God, who is **a** to keep

ABOLISH (v) to destroy; to annul
Matt 5:17 . . . did not come to **a** the law

ABOUND(ED) (KJV)
Prov 28:20 . . . person will *get a rich reward*
Matt 24:12 . . . Sin will *be rampant everywhere*
Rom 5:15 . . . *even greater* is God's wonderful grace
Rom 5:20 . . . grace *became more abundant*
2 Cor 8:7 . . . *excel* also in this gracious act

ABOVE (adv or prep) in a higher position, superior
Ps 95:3 . . . a great King **a** all gods.
Ps 99:2 . . . exalted **a** all the nations.
Luke 12:31 . . . Seek the Kingdom of God **a** all
Eph 1:21 . . . he is far **a** any ruler or authority
Phil 2:9 . . . the name **a** all other names,
1 Tim 3:2 . . . a man whose life is **a** reproach.
Jas 3:17 . . . wisdom from **a** is first of all pure.

ABRAHAM (ABRAM) Father of the nation of Israel (Isa 51:2; John 8:37-59); friend of God (Isa 41:8); father of all people of faith (Gen 12–25; Rom 4; Heb 11); made covenant with the LORD (Gen 12:1-3; 13:14-17; 15:12-21; 22:15-18; 50:24; Exod 2:24; 32:13; Lev 26:42; 2 Kgs 13:23; 1 Chr 16:16; Neh 9:8; Ps 105:9; Luke 1:73; Acts 3:25; Gal 3:17-20; Heb 6:13); descendant of Terah from Ur (Gen 11:27-31); husband of Sarah (Sarai) (Gen 11:29); called to leave home (Gen 12:1-9; Acts 7:2-4; Heb 11:8-10); went to Egypt and deceived the Pharaoh (Gen 12:10-20); chose Canaan over the Jordan Plain (Gen 13); rescued Lot from enemies (Gen 14:11-16); blessed by Melchizedek (Gen 14:18-24; Heb 7:1); covenant restated by God (Gen 15); faith counted as righteousness (Gen 15:6; Rom 4:3; Gal 3:6-9; Jas 2:21-23); given son (Ishmael) by Hagar (Gen 16); circumcision commanded (Gen 17; Rom 4:9-12); name changed to "Abraham" (Gen 17:5; Neh 9:7); son promised to Sarah (Gen 17:16; 18:10); welcomed heavenly visitors (Gen 18:1-15); bargained to save Sodom and Gomorrah (Gen 18:16-33); deceived Abimelech (Gen 20); named as a prophet (Gen 20:7); given son (Isaac) by Sarah (Gen 21:1-7; Heb 11:11-12); sent Hagar and Ishmael away (Gen 21:9-14; Gal 4:21-31); offered Isaac as test (Gen 22:1-19; Heb 11:17-19; Jas 2:21); secured burial ground for Sarah (Gen 23); found a wife for Isaac (Gen 24); descendants through wife Keturah (Gen 25:1-6); died (Gen 25:7-11).

ABSTAIN (v) to refrain from, forgo
Exod 19:15 . . . then **a** from having sexual intercourse.
Acts 15:20 . . . **a** from eating food offered to idols,

ABUNDANCE (n) great quantity, affluence; more than ample
Job 36:31 . . . giving them food in **a.**
Ps 66:12 . . . a place of great **a.**
Jer 31:14 . . . The priests will enjoy **a,**
Matt 13:12 . . . have an **a** of knowledge.
Matt 25:29 . . . they will have an **a.**
John 1:16 . . . From his **a** we have all

ABUNDANT (adj) marked by great plenty, abounding
Deut 28:11 . . . livestock, and **a** crops.
Ps 68:9 . . . You sent **a** rain, O God
Jer 31:12 . . . good gifts—the **a** crops
John 16:24 . . . you will have **a** joy.
2 Cor 8:2 . . . are also filled with **a** joy,

ABUSE (n) strong condemnation or disapproval
Mark 15:29 . . . shouted **a,** shaking their heads

ABUSE (v) to injure or damage physically or verbally
1 Cor 4:12 . . . patient with those who **a** us.

ABUSIVE (adj) using harsh, insulting language; characterized by wrong or improper use or action
1 Cor 5:11 . . . worships idols, or is **a,**
1 Cor 6:10 . . . drunkards, or are **a,** or
Eph 4:29 . . . use foul or **a** language.

ABYSS (KJV)
Luke 8:31 . . . send them into the *bottomless pit*
Rev 9:1 . . . the shaft of the *bottomless pit*
Rev 9:11 . . . the angel from the *bottomless pit*

ACACIA (n) several species of shrubs and trees, some of which are found in the Holy Land, yielding highly durable wood
Exod 25:10 . . . make an Ark of **a** wood
Exod 27:1 . . . Using **a** wood, construct a square altar
Josh 2:1 . . . the Israelite camp at **A** Grove.

ACCEPT, ACCEPTED, ACCEPTS (v) to receive willingly
Gen 4:4 . . . The LORD **a-ed** Abel
Gen 4:7 . . . be **a-ed** if you do what is right.
Deut 16:19 . . . Never **a** a bribe, for bribes
Job 42:8 . . . I will **a** his prayer
Job 42:9 . . . the LORD **a-ed** Job's prayer.
Eccl 5:18 . . . to **a** their lot in life.

Luke 4:24 . . . no prophet is **a-ed** in his
Luke 10:16 . . . who **a-s** your message
John 1:12 . . . believed him and **a-ed** him,
John 17:8 . . . They **a-ed** it and know that
Rom 11:12 . . . when they finally **a** it.
Gal 2:9 . . . they **a-ed** Barnabas and me
Col 2:6 . . . just as you **a-ed** Christ Jesus
1 Tim 1:15 . . . everyone should **a** it:
1 Tim 4:9 . . . everyone should **a** it.
Jas 1:21 . . . **a** the word God has planted

ACCEPTABLE (adj) capable or worthy of being accepted; welcome, pleasing, favorable
Mark 7:19 . . . every kind of food is **a**
Rom 4:2 . . . had made him **a** to God,
Rom 12:1 . . . the kind he will find **a.**
Rom 14:20 . . . all foods are **a,** but it is
2 Cor 8:12 . . . is **a** if you give it eagerly.
1 Tim 4:5 . . . made **a** by the word of God

ACCIDENTALLY (adv) unintentionally, by mistake
Josh 20:9 . . . who **a** killed another person
Matt 23:24 . . . so you won't **a** swallow a gnat,

ACCOMPLISH, ACCOMPLISHES (v) to perform, do to completion
Eccl 2:11 . . . hard to **a,** it was all so meaningless
Isa 55:11 . . . fruit. It will **a** all I want it to,
Matt 5:17 . . . No, I came to **a** their purpose.
John 6:63 . . . Human effort **a-es** nothing.
Eph 3:20 . . . within us, to **a** infinitely more
2 Thes 1:11 . . . power to **a** all the good things

ACCOUNT (n) description of facts, conditions, or events; a report
Gen 2:4 . . . This is the **a** of the creation
Gen 5:1 . . . the written **a** of the descendants
Gen 6:9 . . . the **a** of Noah and his family.
Gen 10:1 . . . This is the **a** of the families
Gen 37:2 . . . This is the **a** of Jacob and
Rom 14:12 . . . give a personal **a** to God.

ACCOUNTABLE (adj) subject to giving an account; answerable
Heb 4:13 . . . the one to whom we are **a.**
Heb 13:17 . . . and they are **a** to God.

ACCURATE (adj) conforming exactly to truth or to a standard; free from error, correct
Lev 19:36 . . . and weights must be **a.**
Deut 25:13 . . . You must use **a** scales
Prov 11:1 . . . delights in **a** weights.
Prov 22:21 . . . take an **a** report to those
John 21:24 . . . account of these things is **a.**

ACCURSED (KJV)
Deut 21:23 . . . anyone who is hung is *cursed*
Josh 6:18 . . . things *set apart for destruction*
1 Cor 12:3 . . . will *curse* Jesus, and no one
Gal 1:9 . . . let that person be *cursed*

ACCUSATION, ACCUSATIONS (n) a charge of wrongdoing, often false
Ps 4:2 . . . will you make groundless **a-s?**
Luke 3:14 . . . extort money or make false **a-s.**
1 Tim 5:19 . . . Do not listen to an **a**

ACCUSE, ACCUSED, ACCUSES, ACCUSING (v) to charge with fault or offense; to blame
Job 22:4 . . . he **a-s** you and brings judgment
Ps 27:12 . . . For they **a** me of things
Dan 6:5 . . . grounds for **a-ing** Daniel
Luke 23:14 . . . **a-ing** him of leading a revolt.
John 5:45 . . . it isn't I who will **a**
John 7:7 . . . because I **a** it of doing evil.
John 8:46 . . . can truthfully **a** me of sin?
Acts 18:13 . . . **a-d** Paul of "persuading
Rom 2:15 . . . and thoughts either **a** them
Rom 8:33 . . . Who dares **a** us whom God
Rev 12:10 . . . who **a-s** them before our God

ACCUSER, ACCUSERS (n) one who charges another of wrongdoing
Deut 19:18 . . . If the **a** has brought false
Isa 50:8 . . . Where are my **a-s?**
Luke 12:58 . . . the way to court with your **a,**
Rev 12:10 . . . the **a** of our brothers

ACKNOWLEDGE, ACKNOWLEDGES (v) to express a gratitude of debt; to recognize as valid; to confess (wrongdoing)
Jer 3:13 . . . Only **a** your guilt. Admit
Matt 10:32 . . . Everyone who **a-s** me
Luke 12:8 . . . Son of Man will also **a**
Rom 1:28 . . . thought it foolish to **a** God,
1 Jn 2:23 . . . anyone who **a-s** the Son
1 Jn 4:3 . . . and does not **a** the truth

ACQUAINTED (v) to make familiar; to know firsthand
Isa 53:3 . . . sorrows, **a** with deepest grief.
Acts 18:2 . . . **a** with a Jew named Aquila,

ACQUIT, ACQUITTING (v) to free from the penalty of a guilty action; (used theologically) to justify or make right with God
2 Chr 6:23 . . . **A** the innocent because of
Prov 17:15 . . . **A-ting** the guilty and

ACT (v) to behave; to take action or do something
Ps 119:126 . . . it is time for you to **a,**
Eccl 6:8 . . . how to **a** in front of others?

ACTION, ACTIONS (n) a thing done, deed; an exercise of will
Jer 4:18 . . . Your own **a-s** have brought this
Phlm 1:6 . . . put into **a** the generosity
Rev 3:2 . . . **a-s** do not meet the requirements

ACTIVITY (n) a pursuit in which a person is active; quality or state of being active
Eccl 3:1 . . . for every **a** under heaven.

ADAM First man (Gen 1:26–2:25; Rom 5:14; 1 Tim 2:13-14); son of God (Luke 3:38); sinned (Gen 3:1-19; Hos 6:7; Rom 5:12-21); descendants of (Gen 5); died (Gen 5:5; 1 Cor 15:22-49).

ADD, ADDED (v) to make or serve as an addition
Deut 4:2 . . . Do not **a** to or subtract from
Deut 12:32 . . . You must not **a** anything to
Prov 30:6 . . . Do not **a** to his words,
Eccl 3:14 . . . Nothing can be **a-ed** to it
Matt 6:27 . . . worries **a** a single moment
Luke 12:25 . . . worries **a** a single moment
Acts 2:47 . . . each day the Lord **a-ed** to their
Rev 22:18 . . . God will **a** to that person

ADEQUATE (adj) suitable for a task; suitable
2 Cor 2:16 . . . who is **a** for such a task as this?

ADMIT (v) to acknowledge, confess
Hos 5:15 . . . until they **a** their guilt
John 12:42 . . . But they wouldn't **a** it

ADMINISTRATOR (n) one who administers, especially governmental affairs
Num 3:32 . . . chief **a** over all the Levites
Isa 37:2 . . . And he sent Eliakim the palace **a**

ADMONISH(ED) (KJV)
Eccl 12:12 . . . give you *some further advice*
Jer 42:19 . . . Don't forget this *warning* I
2 Thes 3:15 . . . *warn* them as you would
Heb 8:5 . . . God *gave* him this *warning*

ADMONITION (KJV)
1 Cor 10:11 . . . written down *to warn us*
Eph 6:4 . . . *instruction* that comes from the Lord
Titus 3:10 . . . a first and second *warning*

ADOPT, ADOPTED (v) to take another's child into one's own family
Rom 8:15 . . . when he **a-ed** you as his own
Rom 8:23 . . . rights as his **a-ed** children,
Rom 9:4 . . . to be God's **a-ed** children.
Gal 4:5 . . . so that he could **a** us as
Eph 1:5 . . . decided in advance to **a** us

ADULTERER, ADULTERERS (n) one who commits adultery
Job 24:15 . . . The **a** waits for the twilight,
Jas 4:4 . . . You **a-s!** Don't you realize

ADULTEROUS (adj) prone to adultery or idolatry
Mark 8:38 . . . in these **a** and sinful days,

ADULTERY (n) unlawful sexual relations between a married and an unmarried person; symbolic of idolatry
Exod 20:14 . . . You must not commit **a.**
Deut 5:18 . . . You must not commit **a.**
Prov 6:32 . . . who commits **a** is an utter fool,
Matt 5:27 . . . You must not commit **a.**
Matt 19:18 . . . You must not commit **a.**
Mark 10:11 . . . someone else commits **a**
Luke 18:20 . . . You must not commit **a.**
John 8:4 . . . caught in the act of **a.**
1 Cor 6:9 . . . **a,** or are male prostitutes,

ADVANTAGE (n) benefit; upper hand
Exod 17:11 . . . in his hand, the Israelites had the **a.**
Lev 25:17 . . . not taking **a** of each other.
Rom 3:1 . . . Then what's the **a** of being a Jew?
Rom 7:11 . . . Sin took **a** of those commands
2 Cor 7:2 . . . astray, nor taken **a** of anyone.

ADVERSARY, ADVERSARIES (n) enemy, opponent
2 Sam 19:22 . . . Why have you become my **a**
Esth 7:6 . . . Haman is our **a** and our enemy.
Ps 89:23 . . . beat down his **a-ies** before him
Matt 5:25 . . . on the way to court with your **a,**

ADVERSITY (n) affliction, misfortune, woe
Job 36:15 . . . gets their attention through **a.**
Isa 30:20 . . . gave you **a** for food and suffering

ADVICE (n) recommendation regarding a decision or course of conduct; counsel
1 Kgs 12:8 . . . rejected the **a** of
2 Chr 10:8 . . . rejected the **a** of
Prov 12:5 . . . **a** of the wicked is
Prov 12:26 . . . godly give good **a** to their
Prov 15:22 . . . Plans go wrong for lack of **a;**
Isa 44:25 . . . I cause the wise to give bad **a,**
Rom 11:34 . . . enough to give him **a?**

ADVISE (v) to give advice; to counsel
Ps 32:8 . . . I will **a** you and watch over
1 Tim 5:14 . . . I **a** these younger widows
Rev 3:18 . . . I **a** you to buy gold from me—

ADVISERS (n) one who gives advice; counselor
1 Sam 28:23 . . . his **a** joined the woman in

1 Kgs 12:14 . . . counsel of his younger **a.**
Esth 1:13 . . . consulted with his wise **a**,
Prov 11:14 . . . safety in having many **a.**
Prov 29:12 . . . all his **a** will be wicked.

ADVOCATE (n) one who pleads the cause of another; defender
see also HOLY SPIRIT
Job 16:19 . . . My **a** is there on high.
John 14:16 . . . he will give you another **A**,
John 14:26 . . . the Father sends the **A**
John 15:26 . . . I will send you the **A**—
John 16:7 . . . if I don't, the **A** won't come.
1 Jn 2:1 . . . an **a** who pleads our case

AFFECTION (n) tender attachment; a positive feeling
Rom 12:10 . . . each other with genuine **a**,
2 Pet 1:7 . . . godliness with brotherly **a**,

AFFIRM (v) to validate; to confirm
John 3:33 . . . can **a** that God is true.
Rom 8:16 . . . **a** that we are God's children.
Heb 10:23 . . . hope we **a**, for God can

AFFLICT, AFFLICTED (v) relating to, characterized by, or given to persistent suffering or anguish
Deut 28:61 . . . LORD will **a** you
1 Sam 5:12 . . . were **a-ed** with tumors;

AFFORD (v) to have enough money or other assets
Lev 5:7 . . . if you cannot **a** to bring a sheep,
2 Cor 8:3 . . . what they could **a**, but far more.

AFRAID (adj) fearful or apprehensive about an unwanted or uncertain situation
Gen 3:10 . . . I was **a** because I was naked.
Gen 26:24 . . . Do not be **a**, for I am
Exod 3:6 . . . he was **a** to look at God.
Deut 1:21 . . . Don't be **a**!
Deut 20:1 . . . your own, do not be **a.**
Ps 23:4 . . . I will not be **a**, for you are
Isa 10:24 . . . do not be **a** of the Assyrians
Isa 41:10 . . . Don't be **a**, for I am
Isa 43:1 . . . Do not be **a**, for I have
Matt 8:26 . . . Why are you **a**?
Matt 10:31 . . . So don't be **a**;
Mark 5:36 . . . Don't be **a.**
John 14:27 . . . don't be troubled or **a.**
2 Tim 4:5 . . . Don't be **a** of suffering
1 Pet 3:14 . . . don't worry or be **a**

AFRESH (adv) from a fresh beginning; anew, again
Lam 3:23 . . . his mercies begin **a** each

AGAINST (prep) in opposition or hostility to; contrary to
Ps 41:9 . . . has turned **a** me.
Ps 78:19 . . . even spoke **a** God himself,
Matt 6:12 . . . those who sin **a** us.
Matt 10:35 . . . to set a man **a** his father,
Matt 12:30 . . . actually working **a** me.
Acts 26:14 . . . for you to fight **a** my will.
Rom 11:30 . . . you Gentiles were rebels **a** God,
1 Cor 8:12 . . . you are sinning **a** Christ.
1 Pet 5:9 . . . Stand firm **a** him,

AGED (adj) showing the effects or characteristics of increasing age
Job 12:12 . . . Wisdom belongs to the **a**,
Prov 17:6 . . . crowning glory of the **a**;

AGES (n) long period of time; a generation; a measure of history, geology, or culture
Prov 8:23 . . . I was appointed in **a** past,
Jer 23:40 . . . infamous throughout the **a.**
Eph 2:7 . . . in all future **a** as examples

AGGRAVATE (v) to cause anger by persistent goading; to produce inflammation in
Col 3:21 . . . do not **a** your children,

AGONY (n) extreme pain and suffering
Ps 6:2 . . . Lord, for my bones are in **a.**
Luke 22:44 . . . he was in such **a** of spirit that

AGREE, AGREED, AGREEING (v) to admit, concede
Matt 18:19 . . . If two of you **a** here on
Luke 7:29 . . . **a-d** that God's way was right,
Rom 7:16 . . . that I **a** that the law is good.
Phil 2:2 . . . make me truly happy by **a-ing**

AID (v) to give assistance
Acts 24:17 . . . with money to **a** my people

AIM (v) to direct to or toward a specified object or goal
Rom 14:19 . . . **a** for harmony in the church

AIR (n) empty space, nothingness; atmosphere
1 Thes 4:17 . . . meet the Lord in the **a.**

ALABASTER (adj) a compact, fine-textured, usually white and translucent plaster often carved into vases and ornaments
Matt 26:7 . . . with a beautiful **a** jar
Mark 14:3 . . . with a beautiful **a** jar
Luke 7:37 . . . she brought a beautiful **a** jar

ALARM (n) a signal that warns or alerts
Num 10:9 . . . sound the **a** with the trumpets.
2 Cor 7:11 . . . such indignation, such **a**,

ALCOHOL (n) drink (as wine or beer) containing ethanol
Prov 20:1 . . . **a** leads to brawls.
Isa 5:22 . . . boast about all the **a** they

ALCOHOLIC (adj) containing alcohol
Num 6:3 . . . give up wine and other **a**

ALERT (adj) quick to perceive and act
Isa 21:7 . . . the watchman be fully **a.**
Mark 13:33 . . . be on guard! Stay **a**!
1 Pet 5:8 . . . Stay **a**! Watch out for

ALIEN (KJV)
Exod 18:3 . . . a *foreigner* in a foreign
Job 19:15 . . . I am like a *foreigner* to them
Eph 2:12 . . . You were *excluded from citizenship*

ALIENATED (KJV)
Ezek 48:14 . . . traded or *used by others*
Eph 4:18 . . . *wander far from* the life God
Col 1:21 . . . were once *far away from God*

ALIVE (adj) animate, having life; active; aware
Gen 45:7 . . . keep you and your families **a**
Ps 41:2 . . . them and keeps them **a.**
Luke 24:23 . . . Jesus is **a**!
Acts 1:3 . . . ways that he was actually **a.**
Rom 6:11 . . . the power of sin and **a** to God
Rev 2:8 . . . who was dead but is now **a**:

ALLELUIA (KJV)
Rev 19:1 . . . shouting, *"Praise the Lord!*
Rev 19:3 . . . rang out: *"Praise the Lord!*
Rev 19:4 . . . "Amen! *Praise the Lord!"*
Rev 19:6 . . . *"Praise the Lord!* For the Lord

ALLOTMENT, ALLOTMENTS (n) share, portion, provision
Num 18:21 . . . Instead of an **a** of land, I will
Josh 13:32 . . . These are the **a-s** Moses had
Jer 13:25 . . . your **a**, the portion I have assigned

ALLOWANCE (n) the act of admitting or conceding; permission
Eph 4:2 . . . **a** for each other's faults

ALLOW, ALLOWED (v) to admit or concede; to permit
1 Cor 6:12 . . . though "I am **a-ed** to
1 Cor 10:23 . . . I am **a-ed** to do anything
2 Cor 12:4 . . . no human is **a-ed** to tell.

ALMIGHTY (n) having absolute power over all; God
see also (HEAVEN'S) ARMIES
Gen 17:1 . . . I am El-Shaddai—'God **A.**'
Exod 6:3 . . . as El-Shaddai—'God **A**'—
Ruth 1:20 . . . **A** has made life very bitter
Job 6:14 . . . without any fear of the **A.**
Job 33:4 . . . breath of the **A** gives me life.
Ps 91:1 . . . rest in the shadow of the **A.**
Rev 4:8 . . . the **A**—the one who always was,
Rev 15:3 . . . O Lord God, the **A.**
Rev 19:6 . . . our God, the **A**, reigns.

ALONE (adj) isolated or solitary; solely or exclusively; without aid or support
John 5:44 . . . the one who **a** is God.

ALONGSIDE (adv) at the side; in parallel position, close by
Gal 3:19 . . . It was given **a** the promise

ALPHA (n) first letter of Greek alphabet; figurative of beginning or first one
Rev 1:8 . . . I am the **A** and the Omega—
Rev 21:6 . . . I am the **A** and the Omega—
Rev 22:13 . . . I am the **A** and the Omega,

ALTAR, ALTARS (n) high places of worship on which sacrifices are offered or incense is burned
Gen 8:20 . . . Noah built an **a** to the LORD,
Gen 12:7 . . . Abram built an **a** there
Gen 22:9 . . . Abraham built an **a** and
Gen 26:25 . . . Isaac built an **a** there
Exod 27:1 . . . construct a square **a** 7½ feet
Exod 30:1 . . . make another **a** of acacia
Exod 37:25 . . . incense **a** of acacia wood.
Josh 8:30 . . . Joshua built an **a** to the LORD,
Josh 22:10 . . . a large and imposing **a.**
1 Sam 7:17 . . . Samuel built an **a** to the
2 Chr 4:1 . . . made a bronze **a** 30 feet long,
2 Chr 4:19 . . . Temple of God: the gold **a**;
2 Chr 32:12 . . . only at the **a** at the Temple
2 Chr 33:16 . . . restored the **a** of the LORD
Ezra 3:2 . . . rebuilding the **a** of the God
Isa 6:6 . . . coal he had taken from the **a**
Matt 5:23 . . . presenting a sacrifice at the **a**
Acts 17:23 . . . your **a-s** had this inscription
Heb 13:10 . . . an **a** from which the priests
Rev 6:9 . . . I saw under the **a** the souls

ALTERED (v) to make change or become different; to modify
John 10:35 . . . the Scriptures cannot be **a.**

ALWAYS (adv) at all times; forever, perpetually
1 Kgs 2:4 . . . will **a** sit on the throne
Ps 16:8 . . . the LORD is **a** with me.
Ps 52:8 . . . will **a** trust in God's unfailing
Ps 102:27 . . . But you are **a** the same;
Ps 106:3 . . . and **a** do what is right.
Prov 23:7 . . . They are **a** thinking about
Isa 16:5 . . . He will **a** do what is just
Matt 28:20 . . . I am with you **a**, even to
Mark 14:7 . . . You will **a** have the poor
John 12:8 . . . you will not **a** have me.
1 Pet 3:15 . . . **a** be ready to explain it.

AMAZED (v) to fill with wonder, astound
Matt 7:28 . . . were **a** at his teaching

Mark 7:37 . . . They were completely **a** and
Mark 10:24 . . . This **a** them. But Jesus
Luke 2:33 . . . Jesus' parents were **a** at
Acts 2:7 . . . They were completely **a.**

AMAZING (adj) causing amazement, great wonder, or surprise
1 Chr 16:24 . . . about the **a** things he does.
Ps 96:3 . . . about the **a** things he does.
Ps 126:2 . . . What **a** things the LORD has

AMBASSADOR, AMBASSADORS (n) an authorized representative or messenger
2 Cor 5:20 . . . So we are Christ's **a-s;**
Eph 6:20 . . . this message as God's **a.**

AMBITION (n) aspiration to achieve a particular goal, good or bad
Gal 5:20 . . . anger, selfish **a,** dissension,
Phil 1:17 . . . They preach with selfish **a,**
Jas 3:14 . . . there is selfish **a** in your heart,

ANCESTOR, ANCESTORS (n) one from whom a person is descended; forefather
Exod 3:15 . . . God of your **a-s**—the God of
Deut 19:14 . . . markers your **a-s** set up
Isa 9:7 . . . throne of his **a** David for all
Isa 43:27 . . . your first **a** sinned against me;
Mark 11:10 . . . Kingdom of our **a** David!
Luke 1:32 . . . the throne of his **a** David.
Rom 9:5 . . . Abraham, Isaac, and Jacob are their **a-s,**
Gal 1:14 . . . for the traditions of my **a-s.**
Heb 1:1 . . . to our **a-s** through the prophets.

ANCHOR (n) a reliable or principal support; mainstay
Heb 6:19 . . . trustworthy **a** for our souls.

ANCIENT (adj) having the qualities of age or long existence; old
Dan 7:22 . . . until the **A** One—the Most High—
Mark 7:3 . . . required by their **a** traditions.

ANDREW One of the 12 disciples; listed second (Matt 10:2; Luke 6:14) and fourth (Mark 3:18; 13:3; Acts 1:13); came from Bethsaida (John 1:44); brother of Simon Peter (Matt 4:18); former fisherman (Mark 1:16); follower of John the Baptist who introduced Peter to Jesus (John 1:40-44).

ANGEL, ANGELS (n) human or superhuman agent or messenger of God
Exod 23:20 . . . I am sending an **a**
2 Sam 24:16 . . . and said to the death **a,**
Ps 91:11 . . . will order his **a-s** to protect
Matt 4:6 . . . will order his **a-s** to protect
Matt 28:2 . . . an **a** of the Lord came down
Luke 1:26 . . . God sent the **a** Gabriel
Luke 2:9 . . . an **a** of the Lord appeared
Luke 20:36 . . . they will be like **a-s.**
Acts 12:7 . . . The **a** struck him on the side
1 Cor 6:3 . . . we will judge **a-s?**
2 Cor 11:14 . . . disguises himself as an **a**
Gal 1:8 . . . or even an **a** from heaven,
Heb 1:6 . . . all of God's **a-s** worship him.
Heb 2:7 . . . a little lower than the **a-s**
Heb 13:2 . . . entertained **a-s** without
1 Pet 1:12 . . . the **a-s** are eagerly watching
2 Pet 2:4 . . . even the **a-s** who sinned.
Jude 1:6 . . . *I remind you of the* **a-s**

ANGELIC (adj) having or displaying characteristics of an angel
2 Sam 22:11 . . . on a mighty **a** being, he flew,
Ps 18:10 . . . on a mighty **a** being, he flew,

ANGER (n) a strong feeling of displeasure
Exod 34:6 . . . slow to **a** and filled with
Num 14:18 . . . slow to **a** and filled with
Deut 9:19 . . . furious **a** of the LORD,
Deut 29:28 . . . In great **a** and fury
2 Kgs 22:13 . . . LORD's great **a** is burning
Ps 30:5 . . . his **a** lasts only a moment,
Ps 78:38 . . . Many times he held back his **a**
Rom 1:18 . . . God shows his **a** from heaven
Rom 2:5 . . . a day of **a** is coming,
Eph 4:26 . . . by letting **a** control you.
1 Thes 5:9 . . . pour out his **a** on us.
Jas 1:20 . . . Human **a** does not produce
Rev 14:10 . . . the wine of God's **a.**

ANGRY (adj) feeling or showing anger; wrathful
Exod 32:11 . . . so **a** with your own people
Neh 9:17 . . . merciful, slow to become **a,**
Ps 103:8 . . . merciful, slow to get **a**
Prov 22:24 . . . Don't befriend **a** people
Jon 4:2 . . . slow to get **a** and filled
Matt 5:22 . . . if you are even **a** with
Mark 10:14 . . . he was **a** with his disciples.
John 3:36 . . . under God's **a** judgment.
Acts 4:25 . . . Why were the nations so **a?**
Jas 1:19 . . . to speak, and slow to get **a.**

ANGUISH (n) extreme pain, distress, or anxiety
Isa 53:11 . . . by his **a,** he will be satisfied.
Zeph 1:15 . . . of terrible distress and **a,**
Matt 24:21 . . . greater **a** than at any time
Luke 16:24 . . . I am in **a** in these flames.
Rev 16:10 . . . ground their teeth in **a,**

ANIMAL, ANIMALS (n) any of a kingdom of living things that typically differ from plants
Gen 1:24 . . . livestock, small **a-s** that scurry
Gen 6:19 . . . a pair of every kind of **a**—
Gen 7:8 . . . all the various kinds of **a-s**—
Deut 14:4 . . . These are the **a-s** you may eat:
1 Kgs 4:33 . . . **a-s,** birds, small creatures,
Job 12:7 . . . ask the **a-s,** and they will teach
Ps 73:22 . . . like a senseless **a** to you.
Isa 43:20 . . . The wild **a-s** in the fields

ANNIHILATED (v) to cause to cease to exist; to kill
Esth 3:13 . . . and **a** on a single day.

ANNOUNCE, ANNOUNCED, ANNOUNCING (v) to proclaim; to tell news
Jer 51:10 . . . let us **a** in Jerusalem
Matt 9:35 . . . and **a-ing** the Good News
Mark 15:26 . . . **a-ed** the charge against him.
Acts 26:23 . . . **a** God's light to Jews and
Rev 10:7 . . . as he **a-d** it to his servants the prophets.

ANNUAL (adj) occurring or happening every year or once a year
Exod 30:10 . . . a regular, **a** event
Judg 21:19 . . . the **a** festival of the LORD
1 Sam 1:21 . . . their **a** trip to offer a sacrifice
1 Sam 20:6 . . . for an **a** family sacrifice.
2 Chr 8:13 . . . the three **a** festivals—

ANOINT, ANOINTED, ANOINTING (v) to smear or rub with oil; used for healing or consecration to sacred duty; used for grooming or burial; figurative for divine appointment
see also ANOINTED ONE
Exod 30:26 . . . oil to **a** the Tabernacle,
Exod 30:30 . . . **A** Aaron and his sons
Lev 8:12 . . . **a-ing** him and making him holy
1 Sam 15:1 . . . told me to **a** you as king
2 Sam 2:4 . . . David and **a-ed** him king over
2 Sam 23:1 . . . man **a-ed** by the God of Jacob,
Ps 23:5 . . . honor me by **a-ing** my head
Ps 92:10 . . . You have **a-ed** me with
Isa 61:1 . . . the LORD has **a-ed** me
Dan 9:24 . . . and to **a** the Most Holy Place.
Acts 10:38 . . . you know that God **a-ed** Jesus
Heb 1:9 . . . your God has **a-ed** you,
Jas 5:14 . . . pray over you, **a-ing** you with oil

ANOINTED ONE (n) one chosen by divine election
see also MESSIAH
1 Sam 2:10 . . . the strength of his **a.**"
1 Sam 26:9 . . . the LORD's **a?**
Ps 132:17 . . . my **a** will be a light for
Dan 9:25 . . . a ruler—the **A**—
Isa 45:1 . . . says to Cyrus, his **a,**

ANSWER, ANSWERED (v) something spoken or written in reply to a question; a solution of a problem
Ps 6:9 . . . the LORD will **a** my prayer.
Ps 34:4 . . . LORD, and he **a-ed** me.
Jon 2:2 . . . trouble, and he **a-ed** me.

ANTICHRIST, ANTICHRISTS (n) opponent of Christ; the personification of evil
1 Jn 2:18 . . . heard that the **A** is coming,
1 Jn 2:18 . . . many such **a-s** have appeared.
1 Jn 4:3 . . . has the spirit of the **A,**
2 Jn 1:7 . . . deceiver and an **a.**

ANTS (n) any of a family of colonial hymenopterous insects
Prov 6:6 . . . from the **a,** you lazybones.

ANXIETY, CARE(S) (KJV)
Ps 139:23 . . . know my *anxious thoughts*
Phil 4:6 . . . Don't *worry* about anything
1 Pet 5:7 . . . your *worries and cares* to God,

APOSTLE, APOSTLES (n) messengers or "sent ones"; generally but not exclusively applied to the original twelve followers of Christ and to Paul
Mark 3:14 . . . and called them his **a-s.**
Acts 1:26 . . . selected to become an **a**
Acts 5:2 . . . part of the money to the **a-s,**
Acts 8:18 . . . **a-s** laid their hands on
Rom 11:13 . . . the **a** to the Gentiles.
1 Cor 9:1 . . . Am I not an **a?**
1 Cor 9:2 . . . I am the Lord's **a.**
1 Cor 12:28 . . . first are **a-s,** second are,
2 Cor 12:12 . . . I am an **a.**
Eph 2:20 . . . on the foundation of the **a-s**
Eph 4:11 . . . the **a-s,** the prophets,
2 Tim 1:11 . . . to be a preacher, an **a,**
Rev 21:14 . . . of the twelve **a-s** of the Lamb.

APPEAR, APPEARED, APPEARING, APPEARS (v) to come out of hiding and show up in public view; to make one's presence known
Gen 1:9 . . . so dry ground may **a.**
Num 14:10 . . . presence of the LORD **a-ed**
Deut 33:16 . . . **a-ed** in the burning bush.
Mal 3:2 . . . and face him when he **a-s?**
Matt 1:20 . . . angel of the Lord **a-ed** to him
Matt 24:30 . . . will **a** in the heavens,
Luke 2:9 . . . angel of the Lord **a-ed** among
Luke 16:15 . . . You like to **a** righteous
Phil 2:7 . . . When he **a-ed** in human form,
2 Thes 1:7 . . . the Lord Jesus **a-s** from
2 Tim 1:10 . . . by the **a-ing** of Christ Jesus,
2 Tim 4:1 . . . **a-s** to set up his Kingdom:
Heb 9:24 . . . **a** now before God on our
Heb 9:26 . . . **a-ed** at the end of the age

1 Pet 5:4 . . . when the Great Shepherd **a-s,**
1 Jn 3:2 . . . will be like when Christ **a-s.**

APPEARANCE (n) external show; the outward or visible aspect
Isa 53:2 . . . or majestic about his **a,**

APPETITE (n) the desire to eat; an inherent craving
Prov 13:2 . . . have an **a** for violence.
Prov 16:26 . . . good for workers to have an **a;**
Phil 3:19 . . . Their god is their **a,**

APPLES (n) the fleshy, usually rounded, red, yellow, or green edible fruit of a tree
Prov 25:11 . . . golden **a** in a silver basket.

APPLY (v) to bring into action; to put to use especially for some practical purpose
Prov 22:17 . . . **a** your heart to my instruction.

APPOINT, APPOINTED, APPOINTING (v) to ordain or designate; to name officially
Deut 1:15 . . . **a-ed** them to serve as judges
2 Sam 7:11 . . . the time I **a-ed** judges to rule
Prov 8:23 . . . I was **a-ed** in ages past,
John 15:16 . . . I chose you. I **a-ed** you
Rom 11:13 . . . God has **a-ed** me as the
1 Tim 5:22 . . . about **a-ing** a church leader.
Titus 1:5 . . . work there and **a** elders

APPOINTED (adj) marked by being fixed or set officially
Exod 23:15 . . . annually at the **a** time
Lev 23:2 . . . the LORD's **a** festivals,
Dan 11:27 . . . come at the **a** time.
Matt 8:29 . . . before God's **a** time?"
Acts 3:20 . . . Jesus, your **a** Messiah.

APPRECIATE (v) to value or admire highly
Prov 28:23 . . . people **a** honest criticism

APPRECIATION (n) an expression of admiration, approval, or gratitude
1 Cor 16:18 . . . must show your **a** to all

APPROACH (v) to draw closer to; to come very near to
1 Tim 6:16 . . . no human can **a** him.

APPROPRIATE (adj) especially suitable or compatible; fitting
Deut 25:2 . . . lashes **a** to the crime.
1 Tim 2:9 . . . wear decent and **a** clothing

APPROVAL (n) an act or instance of approving
Ps 90:17 . . . LORD our God show us his **a**
John 6:27 . . . the seal of his **a.**
Rom 14:4 . . . stand and receive his **a.**
1 Cor 11:19 . . . you who have God's **a**
2 Tim 2:15 . . . and receive his **a.**
Heb 11:4 . . . God showed his **a** of his gifts.

APPROVE, APPROVED, APPROVES (v) to have or express a favorable opinion of; to attest
Gen 7:2 . . . animal I have **a-ed** for eating
Prov 12:2 . . . LORD **a-s** of those who
Rom 14:18 . . . and others will **a** of you,
Rom 16:10 . . . a good man whom Christ **a-s.**
1 Thes 2:4 . . . speak as messengers **a-ed**

ARARAT (n) a mountain on the far east border of modern Turkey; the mountain Noah's ark rested on after the Flood
Gen 8:4 . . . to rest on the mountains of **A.**

ARCHANGEL, ARCHANGELS (n) a leader and chief angel; biblically designated as Michael
Dan 10:13 . . . one of the **a-s,** came to help
Dan 12:1 . . . At that time Michael, the **a**
1 Thes 4:16 . . . with the voice of the **a,**

ARCHER (n) one who uses a bow and arrow
Prov 26:10 . . . like an **a** who shoots at random.

ARCHITECT (n) a person who designs buildings and advises in their construction; a person who designs and guides a plan or undertaking
Prov 8:30 . . . I was the **a** at his side.

ARGUE, ARGUING (v) to contend or disagree in words; to dispute
Job 13:8 . . . Will you **a** God's case
Job 40:2 . . . to **a** with the Almighty?
Prov 25:9 . . . When **a-ing** with your neighbor,
Isa 45:9 . . . those who **a** with their Creator.
Rom 14:1 . . . and don't **a** with them
1 Cor 11:16 . . . anyone wants to **a**

ARGUMENT, ARGUMENTS (n) the act or process of arguing; discourse intended to persuade
Job 32:3 . . . to answer Job's **a-s.**
Job 36:3 . . . I will present profound **a-s**
Prov 26:17 . . . in someone else's **a**
1 Tim 6:4 . . . This stirs up **a-s**
2 Tim 2:14 . . . Such **a-s** are useless,

ARK (n) commonly, a portable wooden chest, box, or coffer; specifically, of Noah, a ship the size of a light cruiser; of the Covenant, a sacred housing for the Law of Moses
Exod 25:21 . . . inside the **A** the stone
Deut 10:5 . . . tablets in the **A** of the
1 Kgs 8:9 . . . Nothing was in the **A** except
1 Chr 13:9 . . . his hand to steady the **A.**
Rev 11:19 . . . the **A** of his covenant

ARM, ARMS (n) upper limb of the body; extension or projection of; lineage; figurative of power or might
Num 11:23 . . . Has my **a** lost its power?
Deut 4:34 . . . a powerful **a,** and terrifying
Deut 7:19 . . . strong hand and powerful **a**
Deut 33:27 . . . everlasting **a-s** are under
Ps 44:3 . . . it was not their own strong **a**
Ps 98:1 . . . his holy **a** has shown
Isa 40:11 . . . carry the lambs in his **a-s,**
Isa 65:2 . . . opened my **a-s** to a rebellious
Jer 27:5 . . . powerful **a** I made the earth
Mark 10:16 . . . took the children in his **a-s**
1 Pet 4:1 . . . you must **a** yourselves with

ARMAGEDDON (n) the gathering place for the final battle between God's forces and Satan's forces associated with Christ's second coming
Rev 16:16 . . . with the Hebrew name **A.**

ARMOR (n) weapons of war or self-defense; figurative of spiritual resources
Ps 91:4 . . . are your **a** and protection.
Isa 59:17 . . . righteousness as his body **a**
Jer 46:4 . . . and prepare your **a.**
Rom 13:12 . . . put on the shining **a**
Eph 6:11 . . . Put on all of God's **a**
Eph 6:13 . . . put on every piece of God's **a**
1 Thes 5:8 . . . protected by the **a** of faith

ARMY, ARMIES (n) large band of men organized and armed for war; any large multitude devoted to a cause
Ps 33:16 . . . best-equipped **a** cannot save
Ps 84:12 . . . LORD of Heaven's **A-ies,**
Isa 6:3 . . . LORD of Heaven's **A-ies!**
Isa 45:13 . . . LORD of Heaven's **A-ies,**
Isa 51:15 . . . the LORD of Heaven's **A-ies.**
Joel 2:2 . . . great and mighty **a** appears.
Joel 2:5 . . . like a mighty **a** moving into
Joel 2:11 . . . This is his mighty **a,**
Hag 1:5 . . . LORD of Heaven's **A-ies** says:
Zech 8:6 . . . LORD of Heaven's **A-ies** says:
Rev 19:14 . . . The **a-ies** of heaven,
Rev 19:19 . . . the horse and his **a.**

AROMA (n) a distinctive, pervasive, and usually pleasant or savory smell; a distinctive quality or atmosphere
Gen 8:21 . . . LORD was pleased with the **a**
Exod 29:18 . . . it is a pleasing **a,**
Lev 3:16 . . . a special gift of food, a pleasing **a**
Eph 5:2 . . . a pleasing **a** to God.

ARREST, ARRESTED, ARRESTING (v) to take or keep in custody by authority of law
Dan 6:16 . . . gave orders for Daniel to be **a-ed**
Matt 10:19 . . . When you are **a-ed,** don't
Mark 14:44 . . . to **a** when I greet him with a kiss.
Mark 14:49 . . . Why didn't you **a** me in the Temple?
Luke 20:20 . . . so he would **a** Jesus.
Acts 22:4 . . . to death, **a-ing** both men

ARROGANCE (n) a feeling or an impression of superiority manifested in an overbearing manner or presumptuous claims
1 Sam 2:3 . . . Don't speak with such **a!**
Prov 8:13 . . . I hate pride and **a,**
Isa 16:6 . . . its pride and **a** and rage.
2 Cor 12:20 . . . slander, gossip, **a,**

ARROGANT (adj) exaggerating or disposed to exaggerate one's own worth or importance in an overbearing manner
Ps 31:23 . . . harshly punishes the **a.**
Ps 119:78 . . . upon the **a** people who lied
1 Tim 6:4 . . . is **a** and lacks understanding.
Titus 1:7 . . . not be **a** or quick-tempered;

ARROW, ARROWS (n) a missile weapon shot from a bow and usually having a slender shaft, a pointed head, and feathers at the butt
Ps 64:3 . . . their bitter words like **a-s.**
Ps 64:7 . . . with his **a-s,** suddenly striking
Ps 91:5 . . . the **a** that flies in the day.
Ps 127:4 . . . like **a-s** in a warrior's hands.
Eph 6:16 . . . the fiery **a-s** of the devil.

ASCEND, ASCENDED (v) to go or move up
Ps 68:18 . . . When you **a-ed** to the heights,
Isa 14:13 . . . I will **a** to heaven
John 6:62 . . . Son of Man **a** to heaven again?
John 20:17 . . . I haven't yet **a-ed** to the Father.
Acts 2:34 . . . never **a-ed** into heaven,
Eph 4:8 . . . When he **a-ed** to the heights,

ASHAMED (adj) feeling shame, guilt, or disgrace
Ps 69:6 . . . be **a** because of me,
Jer 31:19 . . . I was thoroughly **a** of all I did
Jer 48:13 . . . were **a** of their gold calf
Mark 8:38 . . . If anyone is **a** of me
Luke 9:26 . . . If anyone is **a** of me
Rom 1:16 . . . I am not **a** of this Good News
2 Tim 1:8 . . . So never be **a** to tell others
2 Tim 2:15 . . . who does not need to be **a**

ASHES (n) burnt residue or remains of the dead, or anything ruined; denotes grief, repentance, or humiliation
Job 42:6 . . . sit in dust and **a**
Matt 11:21 . . . throwing **a** on their heads

ASK, ASKED, ASKING, ASKS (v) to seek information; to call on for an answer; to make a request
1 Sam 10:22 . . . So they **a-ed** the LORD,

Prov 18:6 . . . they are **a-ing** for a beating.
Isa 8:19 . . . Let's **a** the mediums
Matt 7:7 . . . Keep on **a-ing,** and you will receive
Luke 6:30 . . . Give to anyone who **a-s;**
Luke 11:9 . . . will receive what you **a** for.
John 17:15 . . . I'm not **a-ing** you
Eph 3:20 . . . more than we might **a** or
Phlm 1:21 . . . do what I **a** and even more!
1 Jn 5:14 . . . whenever we **a** for anything

ASLEEP (adj) state of bodily rest; figurative for physical death or spiritual dullness
see also DIE, SLEEP
Judg 4:21 . . . Sisera fell **a** from exhaustion,
1 Kgs 18:27 . . . away on a trip, or is **a** and
Matt 9:24 . . . isn't dead; she's only **a.**"
Matt 26:40 . . . disciples and found them **a.**
John 11:11 . . . Lazarus has fallen **a,** but
1 Thes 5:6 . . . be on your guard, not **a** like

ASSEMBLY (n) a company of persons gathered for deliberation and legislation, worship, or entertainment
Ps 35:18 . . . in front of the great **a.**
Ps 149:1 . . . praises in the **a** of the faithful.

ASSIGN, ASSIGNED (v) to transfer (property) to another, especially in trust or for the benefit of creditors; to appoint as a duty or task
Gen 47:11 . . . So Joseph **a-ed** the best land
Deut 32:8 . . . When the Most High **a-ed** lands
Josh 13:14 . . . Moses did not **a** any allotment

ASSOCIATE (v) to join as a partner, friend, or companion; to keep company with
Prov 13:20 . . . **a** with fools and get in
Prov 22:24 . . . or **a** with hot-tempered
Prov 24:21 . . . Don't **a** with rebels,
Acts 10:28 . . . like this or to **a** with you.
1 Cor 5:9 . . . not to **a** with people who
1 Cor 5:11 . . . are not to **a** with anyone

ASSURANCE (n) the act or action of giving confidence to or making sure or certain
Col 1:27 . . . This gives you **a** of sharing
1 Thes 1:5 . . . full **a** that what we said

ASSURE (v) to make certain or reassure
Mark 10:29 . . . I **a** you that everyone who has
Luke 23:43 . . . I **a** you, today you will be with
John 3:5 . . . I **a** you, no one can enter
John 5:25 . . . I **a** you that the time is coming,

ASTRAY (adv) off the right path or route; in error, away from what is desirable or proper
Prov 20:1 . . . Those led **a** by drink
Isa 47:10 . . . 'knowledge' have led you **a,**
Jer 50:6 . . . shepherds have led them **a**
1 Jn 2:26 . . . who want to lead you **a.**

ASTROLOGERS (n) one who studies the stars and planets to foresee or foretell future events by their positions and aspects
Isa 47:13 . . . all your **a,** those stargazers
Dan 2:2 . . . enchanters, sorcerers, and **a,**

ATE (v) *see also* EAT
Gen 3:6 . . . some of the fruit and **a** it.
Ezek 3:3 . . . And when I **a** it, it tasted as
Matt 15:37 . . . **a** as much as they wanted.
Rev 10:10 . . . I **a** it! It was sweet

ATHLETE, ATHLETES (n) a person who is trained or skilled in exercises, sports, or games requiring physical strength, agility, or stamina
Ps 19:5 . . . like a great **a** eager to run
1 Cor 9:25 . . . All **a-s** are disciplined
1 Cor 9:27 . . . body like an **a,** training it
2 Tim 2:5 . . . **a-s** cannot win the prize unless

ATONE, ATONES (v) to supply satisfaction for; to make amends; to reconcile
see also FORGIVE
Dan 9:24 . . . their sin, to **a** for their guilt,
1 Jn 2:2 . . . sacrifice that **a-s** for our sins—

ATONEMENT (n) reconciliation; reparation for an offense or injury; cleansing
see also FORGIVENESS
Exod 25:17 . . . cover—the place of **a**—
Lev 23:27 . . . Day of **A** on the tenth day
2 Chr 29:24 . . . to make **a** for the sins
Prov 16:6 . . . faithfulness make **a** for sin.

ATTACK, ATTACKED (v) to set upon or work against forcefully; to assail with unfriendly or bitter words
1 Sam 17:48 . . . Goliath moved closer to **a,**
Joel 3:19 . . . they **a-ed** the people of Judah
Zech 10:2 . . . **a-ed** because they have no
2 Tim 4:18 . . . deliver me from every evil **a**

ATTENTION (n) the act or state of applying the mind to an object or thought
Exod 23:13 . . . Pay close **a** to all my
Prov 4:20 . . . pay **a** to what I say.
Prov 5:1 . . . My son, pay **a** to my wisdom;
Acts 18:17 . . . Gallio paid no **a.**
1 Tim 4:15 . . . Give your complete **a** to

ATTITUDE, ATTITUDES (n) a mental position with regard to a fact or state; a feeling or emotion toward a fact or state
Eph 4:23 . . . your thoughts and **a-s.**
Phil 2:5 . . . have the same **a** that Christ
1 Pet 3:8 . . . keep a humble **a.**
1 Pet 4:1 . . . with the same **a** he had,

ATTRACT, ATTRACTED (v) to pull to or draw toward oneself or itself; to draw by appeal to natural or excited interest, emotion, or aesthetic sense
Isa 53:2 . . . nothing to **a** us to him.
Heb 13:9 . . . **a-ed** by strange, new ideas.

ATTRACTIVE (adj) arousing interest or pleasure; having the power to attract
Prov 19:22 . . . Loyalty makes a person **a.**
Col 4:6 . . . conversation be gracious and **a**
1 Tim 2:10 . . . make themselves **a** by the
Titus 2:10 . . . God our Savior **a** in every

AUTHORITY, AUTHORITIES (n) the right to govern; the freedom or ability to act; one entrusted with the right to govern
Matt 28:18 . . . been given all **a** in heaven
Luke 10:19 . . . have given you **a** over
John 5:22 . . . absolute **a** to judge,
Acts 1:7 . . . **a** to set those dates and times,
Rom 13:1 . . . submit to governing **a-ies.**
Rom 13:1 . . . For all **a** comes from God,
Rom 13:2 . . . anyone who rebels against **a**
Rom 13:3 . . . without fear of the **a-ies?**
1 Cor 4:3 . . . by any human **a.**
1 Cor 15:24 . . . ruler and **a** and power.
Eph 1:22 . . . things under the **a** of Christ
Eph 3:10 . . . all the unseen rulers and **a-ies**
Eph 6:12 . . . against evil rulers and **a-ies**
Col 2:10 . . . every ruler and **a.**
Col 2:15 . . . the spiritual rulers and **a-ies.**
1 Tim 2:2 . . . all who are in **a** so that
Titus 2:15 . . . You have the **a** to correct
1 Pet 2:18 . . . accept the **a** of your masters
1 Pet 3:1 . . . accept the **a** of your husbands.
1 Pet 3:22 . . . the angels and **a-ies** and
1 Pet 5:5 . . . accept the **a** of the elders.
Jude 1:6 . . . the limits of **a** God gave them

AVENGE, AVENGES (v) to take revenge or punish an evildoer
Deut 32:43 . . . **a** the blood of his servants;
1 Thes 4:6 . . . the Lord **a-s** all such sins,
Rev 6:10 . . . **a** our blood for what they have

AVENGER (n) one who seeks revenge or to punish an evildoer
Num 35:27 . . . **a** finds him outside the city

AVOID, AVOIDING (v) to keep away from; to depart or withdraw from
Prov 4:24 . . . **A** all perverse talk;
Prov 14:16 . . . are cautious and **a** danger;
Prov 16:6 . . . By fearing the LORD, people **a**
Prov 20:3 . . . **A-ing** a fight is a mark
Eccl 7:18 . . . fears God will **a** both
Rom 2:3 . . . think you can **a** God's

AWAKE (v) to cease sleeping; to become aroused or active again
see also WAKE
Ps 17:15 . . . When I **a,** I will see
Eph 5:14 . . . "**A,** O sleeper, rise up

AWARE (adj) having or showing realization, perception, or knowledge
Exod 34:29 . . . he wasn't **a** that

AWARENESS (n) the state of realization or perception
Hab 2:14 . . . filled with an **a** of the glory

AWAY (adv) in another direction; by a long distance or interval
1 Thes 4:3 . . . stay **a** from all sexual sin.
2 Tim 3:5 . . . Stay **a** from people like that!
1 Pet 2:11 . . . keep **a** from worldly desires

AWE (n) an emotion variously combining dread, respect, and wonder that is inspired by authority or the sacred
see also FEAR, REVERENCE
1 Kgs 3:28 . . . people were in **a** of the king,
Ps 119:120 . . . I stand in **a** of your
Luke 5:26 . . . with great wonder and **a,**
Acts 2:43 . . . sense of **a** came over them
Heb 12:28 . . . holy fear and **a.**

AWESOME (adj) characterized by reverential fear; expressive of or inspiring awe
see also MARVELOUS, WONDERFUL
Exod 34:10 . . . the **a** power I will display
Deut 7:21 . . . a great and **a** God.
2 Sam 7:23 . . . You performed **a** miracles
Neh 1:5 . . . the great and **a** God
Job 10:16 . . . display your **a** power
Ps 47:2 . . . Most High is **a.**
Ps 65:5 . . . answer our prayers with **a**
Ps 99:3 . . . your great and **a** name.
Ps 106:22 . . . such **a** deeds at the Red Sea.
Ps 131:1 . . . too **a** for me to grasp.
Dan 9:4 . . . a great and **a** God!

AX (n) a cutting tool that is used especially for felling trees and chopping and splitting wood
2 Kgs 6:6 . . . Then the **a** head floated
Prov 25:18 . . . hitting them with an **a,**

B

BAAL (n) a fertility and nature god of the Canaanites and Phoenicians
1 Kgs 18:25 . . . said to the prophets of **B,**
1 Kgs 19:18 . . . bowed down to **B** or kissed
Rom 11:4 . . . have never bowed down to **B!**

BABY, BABIES (n) infant child; youngest of a group; figurative of new or immature Christians
Exod 2:7 . . . women to nurse the **b** for you?

Luke 1:44 . . . **b** in my womb jumped for
Luke 2:12 . . . find a **b** wrapped snugly
Luke 2:16 . . . the **b**, lying in the manger.
Acts 7:19 . . . abandon their newborn **b-ies**
1 Cor 14:20 . . . Be innocent as **b-ies** when
1 Pet 2:2 . . . Like newborn **b-ies**, you must

BABYLON (n) capital city of the Babylonian Empire; a city devoted to materialism and sensual pleasure; biblical writers used as model of paganism and idolatry
Ps 137:1 . . . Beside the rivers of **B**, we sat
Jer 29:10 . . . will be in **B** for seventy years.
Jer 51:37 . . . **B** will become a heap of ruins,
Rev 14:8 . . . shouting, "**B** is fallen—

BACKSLIDERS, BACKSLIDING (KJV)
Prov 14:14 . . . *Backsliders* get what they deserve
Jer 3:22 . . . I will heal your *wayward* hearts
Jer 31:22 . . . wander, my *wayward* daughter
Hos 14:4 . . . I will heal you of your *faithlessness*

BAD (adj) poor, inadequate; morally objectionable; disagreeable, unpleasant
Job 2:10 . . . of God and never anything **b**?
Eccl 12:14 . . . thing, whether good or **b**.
Isa 45:7 . . . good times and **b** times.

BALAAM Pagan prophet, summoned to curse the Israelites but instead blessed them (Num 22–24; also Deut 23:3-5; 2 Pet 2:15-16; Jude 1:11; Rev 2:14); died (Num 31:8; Josh 13:22).

BALANCES (n) an instrument for weighing; a means of judging or deciding
see also SCALES
Dan 5:27 . . . you have been weighed on the **b**

BALD (adj) lacking a natural or usual covering (as of hair or vegetation); bare, unadorned
Mic 1:16 . . . Make yourselves as **b** as a vulture,

BALDY (n) a derogatory nickname for someone who is bald
2 Kgs 2:23 . . . "Go away, **b**!" they chanted.

BANNER (n) a piece of cloth attached by one edge to a staff and used by a leader as his emblem
Exod 17:15 . . . "the LORD is my **b**").
Isa 11:10 . . . will be a **b** of salvation

BANQUET, BANQUETS (n) a sumptuous feast, especially a ceremonious meal in honor of a person, occasion, or achievement
Song 2:4 . . . He escorts me to the **b** hall;
Matt 24:38 . . . enjoying **b-s** and parties

BAPTISM, BAPTISMS (n) a Christian ordinance; a washing with water to demonstrate cleansing from sin, linked with repentance and admission into the community of faith; figurative of an ordeal or initiation
Matt 3:16 . . . After his **b**, as Jesus came up
Luke 3:7 . . . crowds came to John for **b**,
Acts 19:3 . . . what **b** did you experience?
Rom 6:3 . . . joined with Christ Jesus in **b**,
Gal 3:27 . . . united with Christ in **b**
Eph 4:5 . . . one Lord, one faith, one **b**,
Heb 6:2 . . . further instruction about **b-s**,
1 Pet 3:21 . . . that water is a picture of **b**,

BAPTIST (n) one who baptizes
Matt 11:11 . . . greater than John the **B**.
Mark 1:4 . . . messenger was John the **B**.

BAPTIZE, BAPTIZED, BAPTIZING (v) to engage in the ordinance of baptism (see above)
see also WASH
Matt 3:13 . . . River to be **b-d** by John.
Matt 28:19 . . . of all the nations, **b-ing**
Mark 1:4 . . . that people should be **b-d**
Mark 1:8 . . . will **b** you with the Holy Spirit!
Mark 10:38 . . . suffering I must be **b-d** with?
Luke 3:3 . . . that people should be **b-d**
Luke 3:16 . . . I **b** you with water;
Luke 3:21 . . . Jesus himself was **b-d**.
John 1:28 . . . where John was **b-ing**.
John 1:31 . . . I have been **b-ing** with water
John 1:33 . . . is the one who will **b** with
John 3:22 . . . with them there, **b-ing** people.
John 3:26 . . . is also **b-ing** people.
John 4:1 . . . was **b-ing** and making more
John 4:2 . . . Jesus himself didn't **b** them—
John 10:40 . . . where John was first **b-ing**
Acts 1:5 . . . will be **b-d** with the Holy Spirit.
Acts 1:22 . . . time he was **b-d** by John
Acts 2:41 . . . **b-d** and added to the church
Acts 8:12 . . . and women were **b-d**.
Acts 8:38 . . . water, and Philip **b-d** him.
Acts 11:16 . . . will be **b-d** with the Holy
Acts 16:15 . . . She was **b-d** along with
Acts 16:33 . . . were immediately **b-d**.
Acts 19:5 . . . **b-d** in the name of the Lord
1 Cor 1:13 . . . you **b-d** in the name of Paul?
1 Cor 1:14 . . . I did not **b** any of you
1 Cor 1:16 . . . **b-d** the household of
1 Cor 10:2 . . . were **b-d** as followers
1 Cor 15:29 . . . **b-d** for those who are dead?
Col 2:12 . . . when you were **b-d**.

BARN (n) a usually large building for the storage of farm products, feed, animals, and/or equipment
Matt 13:30 . . . the wheat in the **b**.

BARREN (adj) unproductive, unfruitful, especially in childbearing
Heb 11:11 . . . she was **b** and was too old.

BASKET (n) a receptacle made of interwoven material; any of various lightweight, usually wood, containers
Exod 2:3 . . . she got a **b** made of papyrus
Acts 9:25 . . . lowered him in a large **b**
2 Cor 11:33 . . . in a **b** through a window

BARNABAS Levite believer from Cyprus, generous giver of property (Acts 4:36-37); encourager of Paul (Acts 9:26-29); missionary with Paul (Acts 11:22-30; 12:25; 13:1-3); at Jerusalem council (Acts 15:1-2, 12); disagreed with Paul over John Mark (Acts 15:36-40; *see also* 1 Cor 9:6; Col 4:10).

BATCH (n) the quantity baked at one time
Rom 11:16 . . . the entire **b** of dough is holy
1 Cor 5:6 . . . through the whole **b** of dough?
1 Cor 5:7 . . . like a fresh **b** of dough
Gal 5:9 . . . through the whole **b** of dough!

BATH (n) a washing or soaking (as in water or steam) of all or part of the body
2 Sam 11:2 . . . unusual beauty taking a **b**.

BATHED (v) to take a bath; to give a bath to
John 13:10 . . . A person who has **b** all over

BATHSHEBA Committed adultery with King David, widow of Uriah the Hittite (2 Sam 11–12); mother of Solomon, her second son with David (1 Kgs 1–2; 1 Chr 3:5).

BATTLE, BATTLES (n) a combat between two persons; a general encounter between armies, ships of war, aircraft; an extended contest, struggle, or controversy
1 Sam 17:47 . . . This is the LORD's **b**,
1 Sam 18:17 . . . the LORD's **b-s**.
1 Sam 25:28 . . . the LORD's **b-s**.
2 Kgs 14:8 . . . Come and meet me in **b**!
2 Chr 32:8 . . . to fight our **b-s** for us!
Ps 24:8 . . . LORD, invincible in **b**.
Rev 16:14 . . . gather them for **b** against
Rev 20:8 . . . gather them together for **b**—

BEAR (v) to carry or support; to give as testimony; to give birth to or produce
see also BORN
Gen 4:13 . . . too great for me to **b**!
Ps 38:4 . . . too heavy to **b**.
John 15:2 . . . branches that do **b** fruit
Heb 13:13 . . . and **b** the disgrace he bore.

BEAR (n) a large, heavy mammal with shaggy hair, rudimentary tail, and plantigrade feet
Isa 11:7 . . . cow will graze near the **b**.
Dan 7:5 . . . it looked like a **b**.

BEARD, BEARDS (n) the hair that grows on a man's face often excluding the mustache
Lev 19:27 . . . or trim your **b-s**.
Isa 50:6 . . . who pulled out my **b**.

BEAST, BEASTS (n) devilish creature(s) ravishing the earth during the Tribulation; animals, as distinguished from plants or humans; a contemptible person
Dan 7:3 . . . Then four huge **b-s** came up
Dan 7:6 . . . authority was given to this **b**.
1 Cor 15:32 . . . fighting wild **b-s**—those
Rev 13:18 . . . number of the **b**, for it is
Rev 16:2 . . . had the mark of the **b**
Rev 19:20 . . . accepted the mark of the **b**

BEATEN (v) stricken repeatedly so as to inflict pain
see also FLOGGED, WHIPPED
Acts 16:23 . . . They were severely **b**,
2 Cor 11:25 . . . Three times I was **b**
1 Pet 2:20 . . . if you are **b** for doing wrong.

BEAUTIFUL (adj) lovely, handsome, or pleasing to the eye; excellent
Gen 2:9 . . . trees that were **b**
Gen 6:2 . . . sons of God saw the **b**
Prov 11:22 . . . A **b** woman who lacks
Eccl 3:11 . . . everything **b** for its own time.
Isa 53:2 . . . was nothing **b** or majestic
Lam 2:15 . . . the city called 'Most **B**
Acts 3:2 . . . the one called the **B** Gate,
Rom 10:15 . . . How **b** are the feet of

BEAUTY (n) a particularly graceful, ornamental, or excellent quality; the quality in a person or thing that gives pleasure to the senses
2 Sam 11:2 . . . a woman of unusual **b**
Ps 50:2 . . . the perfection of **b**, God shines
Prov 31:30 . . . and **b** does not last;
Isa 28:1 . . . but its glorious **b** will fade
Jas 1:11 . . . and its **b** fades away.
1 Pet 1:24 . . . their **b** is like a flower
1 Pet 3:4 . . . **b** of a gentle and quiet spirit,

BED (n) a piece of furniture on or in which to lie and sleep; a place for sleeping
Deut 6:7 . . . when you are going to **b**
Song 3:1 . . . as I lay in **b**, I yearned
Luke 17:34 . . . will be asleep in one **b**;

BEDROCK (n) the solid rock underlying loosely arranged surface materials (as soil)
Matt 7:25 . . . it is built on **b**.

BEG, BEGGED, BEGGING (v) to ask for charity or mercy; to ask earnestly for
Ps 37:25 . . . their children **b-ging** for bread.
Ps 80:14 . . . Come back, we **b** you,
Mal 1:9 . . . Go ahead, **b** God to
2 Cor 12:8 . . . different times I **b-ged** the Lord

BEGINNING (n) the point at which something starts; the first part; the origin, source
Gen 1:1 . . . In the **b** God created
John 1:1 . . . In the **b** the Word already
Rom 16:25 . . . secret from the **b** of time.
1 Jn 1:1 . . . one who existed from the **b,**
Rev 21:6 . . . the **B** and the End.
Rev 22:13 . . . the **B** and the End.

BEHEMOTH (n) Hebrew word that could mean elephant, crocodile, hippopotamus, water buffalo, or mythological monster; a mighty animal created as an example of the power of God
Job 40:15 . . . a look at **B,** which I made,

BELIEF (n) the content of one's conviction on a matter; confidence in or reliance upon the truth of a matter
1 Thes 2:14 . . . because of their **b** in Christ
2 Thes 2:13 . . . through your **b** in the truth.
Titus 1:9 . . . **b** in the trustworthy message

BELIEVE, BELIEVED, BELIEVES, BELIEVING (v) to trust in; to hold a firm conviction about; to accept as true, genuine, or real
see also FAITH, TRUST
Gen 15:6 . . . Abram **b-d** the LORD,
Prov 14:15 . . . simpletons **b** everything
Isa 53:1 . . . Who has **b-d** our message?
Matt 27:42 . . . we will **b** in him!
Mark 9:23 . . . is possible if a person **b-s.**
Mark 9:24 . . . I do **b,** but help me
Mark 15:32 . . . we can see it and **b** him!
Luke 8:12 . . . prevent them from **b-ing**
Luke 24:25 . . . You find it so hard to **b**
John 1:7 . . . so that everyone might **b**
John 1:12 . . . all who **b-d** him and accepted
John 3:16 . . . everyone who **b-s** in him
John 4:41 . . . hear his message and **b.**
John 5:38 . . . because you do not **b** me—
John 6:69 . . . We **b,** and we know you are
John 7:5 . . . his brothers didn't **b** in him.
John 7:39 . . . to everyone **b-ing** in him.
John 9:35 . . . asked, "Do you **b** in the Son
John 9:38 . . . Yes, Lord, I **b!**
John 10:37 . . . Don't **b** me unless
John 11:25 . . . Anyone who **b-s** in me
John 11:27 . . . **b-d** you are the Messiah,
John 11:40 . . . see God's glory if you **b?**
John 12:37 . . . did not **b** in him.
John 12:38 . . . who has **b-d** our message?
John 13:19 . . . you will **b** that I AM
John 14:11 . . . Or at least **b** because of the
John 14:12 . . . anyone who **b-s** in me
John 16:30 . . . **b** that you came from God.
John 17:21 . . . world will **b** you sent me.
John 19:35 . . . so that you also can **b.**
John 20:8 . . . and he saw and **b-d**—
John 20:29 . . . **b** because you have seen
John 20:31 . . . and that by **b-ing** in him
Acts 10:43 . . . that everyone who **b-s** in him
Acts 13:8 . . . keep the governor from **b-ing.**
Acts 16:31 . . . **B** in the Lord Jesus and
Acts 19:4 . . . **b** in the one who would come
Acts 26:27 . . . do you **b** the prophets?
Acts 27:25 . . . For I **b** God.
Rom 1:16 . . . saving everyone who **b-s**—
Rom 3:22 . . . for everyone who **b-s,** no
Rom 3:25 . . . **b** that Jesus sacrificed his life,
Rom 4:3 . . . tell us, "Abraham **b-d** God,
Rom 4:20 . . . never wavered in **b-ing** God's
Rom 10:9 . . . **b** in your heart that God
Rom 10:10 . . . For it is by **b-ing** in your heart
Rom 10:14 . . . unless they **b** in him?
Rom 14:23 . . . anything you **b** is not right,
Rom 16:26 . . . they too might **b** and obey
1 Cor 1:21 . . . to save those who **b.**
1 Cor 15:2 . . . **b-d** something that was never
2 Cor 5:7 . . . by **b-ing** and not by seeing.
2 Cor 5:14 . . . Since we **b** that Christ
Gal 3:2 . . . because you **b-d** the message
Gal 3:6 . . . same way, "Abraham **b-d** God,
Eph 2:8 . . . his grace when you **b-d.**
Col 1:23 . . . continue to **b** this truth
1 Thes 4:14 . . . For since we **b** that Jesus
2 Thes 2:11 . . . and they will **b** these lies.
2 Thes 2:12 . . . enjoying evil rather than **b-ing**
1 Tim 3:16 . . . He was **b-d** in throughout the
Heb 3:14 . . . firmly as when we first **b-d,**
Heb 11:6 . . . must **b** that God exists
Heb 11:13 . . . still **b-ing** what God had
Jas 2:19 . . . you **b** that there is one God.
1 Jn 3:23 . . . We must **b** in the name
1 Jn 4:1 . . . friends, do not **b** everyone
1 Jn 5:1 . . . Everyone who **b-s** that Jesus is
1 Jn 5:10 . . . All who **b** in the Son

BELIEVER, BELIEVERS (n) one who accepts something as true, genuine, or real; one who trusts in or has a firm conviction about
Matt 18:15 . . . If another **b** sins
Acts 2:44 . . . all the **b-s** met together
Acts 4:32 . . . All the **b-s** were united
Acts 6:1 . . . as the **b-s** rapidly multiplied,
Acts 6:7 . . . number of **b-s** greatly increased
Acts 13:48 . . . for eternal life became **b-s.**
Acts 14:22 . . . they strengthened the **b-s.**
Acts 15:2 . . . accompanied by some local **b-s,**
Acts 15:23 . . . to the Gentile **b-s** in Antioch,
Acts 15:32 . . . to the **b-s,** encouraging
Acts 16:15 . . . I am a true **b** in the Lord,
Acts 20:2 . . . there, he encouraged the **b-s**
Acts 21:25 . . . As for the Gentile **b-s,**
Rom 8:27 . . . the Spirit pleads for us **b-s**
Rom 14:13 . . . cause another **b** to stumble
Rom 14:15 . . . if another **b** is distressed
Rom 14:21 . . . cause another **b** to stumble.
Rom 15:27 . . . the **b-s** in Jerusalem,
1 Cor 6:2 . . . someday we **b-s** will judge
1 Cor 10:27 . . . who isn't a **b** asks you
1 Cor 14:22 . . . tongues is a sign, not for **b-s,**
2 Cor 6:15 . . . can a **b** be a partner with an
2 Cor 11:26 . . . claim to be **b-s** but are not.
Col 4:5 . . . among those who are not **b-s,**
2 Thes 3:6 . . . away from all **b-s** who live idle
1 Tim 3:6 . . . An elder must not be a new **b,**
1 Tim 4:12 . . . Be an example to all **b-s**
1 Tim 5:16 . . . a woman who is a **b**
1 Jn 3:10 . . . and does not love other **b-s**

BELITTLE (v) to cause (a person or thing) to seem little or less; to speak slightingly of
Prov 11:12 . . . foolish to **b** one's neighbor;
Prov 14:21 . . . a sin to **b** one's neighbor;

BELLY (n) abdomen; the stomach and its adjuncts
Gen 3:14 . . . crawl on your **b,** groveling
Dan 2:32 . . . its **b** and thighs were bronze,
Matt 12:40 . . . in the **b** of the great fish

BELONG, BELONGED, BELONGS (v) to be the property of a person or thing
Lev 25:55 . . . people of Israel **b** to me.
Lev 27:30 . . . **b-s** to the LORD and
Ps 22:28 . . . royal power **b-s** to the LORD.
John 8:47 . . . Anyone who **b-s** to God
John 15:19 . . . if you **b-ed** to it,
Rom 1:6 . . . called to **b** to Jesus
Rom 12:5 . . . we all **b** to each other.
2 Cor 10:7 . . . who say they **b** to Christ
Gal 5:24 . . . Those who **b** to Christ
1 Thes 5:5 . . . we don't **b** to darkness
2 Tim 2:19 . . . All who **b** to the LORD
1 Pet 3:16 . . . because you **b** to Christ.
1 Jn 4:6 . . . If they do not **b** to God,

BELOVED (adj) dearly loved; dear to the heart
Ps 60:5 . . . rescue your **b** people.
Matt 12:18 . . . He is my **B,** who pleases me.
1 Cor 4:14 . . . as my **b** children.
1 Cor 4:17 . . . Timothy, my **b** and faithful
Eph 6:21 . . . a **b** brother and faithful helper
Col 1:7 . . . Epaphras, our **b** co-worker.
Col 4:9 . . . a faithful and **b** brother,
Col 4:14 . . . Luke, the **b** doctor,
Phlm 1:1 . . . to Philemon, our **b** co-worker,
Phlm 1:16 . . . he is a **b** brother,
2 Pet 3:15 . . . our **b** brother Paul also wrote
Rev 20:9 . . . God's people and the **b** city.

BENEFICIAL (adj) conferring benefits; conducive to personal or social well-being
Titus 3:8 . . . good and **b** for everyone.

BENEFIT, BENEFITS (n) advantages or blessings; something that promotes well-being
Prov 12:14 . . . Wise words bring many **b-s,**
Acts 18:27 . . . he proved to be of great **b** to
2 Cor 4:15 . . . this is for your **b.**

BENEFIT, BENEFITS (v) to be useful or profitable to; to favor (another) or gain (for oneself)
Job 36:28 . . . and everyone **b-s.**
Prov 9:12 . . . you will be the one to **b.**
Luke 9:25 . . . what do you **b** if you gain
1 Cor 9:14 . . . by those who **b** from it.

BENJAMIN Second son of Jacob and Rachel, the youngest of Jacob's 12 sons; never knew his mother (Gen 35:16-20); taken to Egypt against Jacob's wishes (Gen 43:3-17); gave his name to a tribe of Israel; his tribe was blessed (Gen 49:27; Deut 33:12), numbered (Num 1:36-37), allotted land and cities (Josh 18:11-28); civil war nearly wiped them out (Judg 20–21); 12,000 will be marked by God (Rev 7:8).

BESEECH(ING), BESOUGHT (KJV)
Deut 3:23 . . . I *pleaded with* the LORD
Ps 118:25 . . . LORD, *please* give us success
Jon 1:14 . . . *pleaded,* "don't make us die
Matt 8:5 . . . officer came and *pleaded with* him
2 Cor 12:8 . . . I *begged* the Lord to take it away

BESIDE (prep) by the side of
Ps 16:8 . . . he is right **b** me.
Ps 109:31 . . . he stands **b** the needy,

BEST (adj) excelling all others
Ps 122:9 . . . seek what is **b** for you,
1 Cor 12:31 . . . life that is **b** of all.
Heb 4:11 . . . do our **b** to enter that rest.

BESTOWED (KJV)
Isa 63:7 . . . he has *granted* according

BETHLEHEM (n) a city about five miles south of Jerusalem in the hill country of Judah; the ancestral home of King David and the birthplace of Jesus Christ
Ruth 1:19 . . . When they came to **B,**

1 Sam 16:1 . . . go to **B.**
2 Sam 23:15 . . . the well by the gate in **B.**
Mic 5:2 . . . **B** Ephrathah, are only a small
Matt 2:1 . . . Jesus was born in **B** in Judea,
Matt 2:6 . . . you, O **B** in the land of Judah,

BETRAY, BETRAYED (v) to turn one's back on a friend; to deliver to an enemy by treachery; to lead astray, seduce
Num 5:6 . . . men or women—**b** the LORD
Deut 32:51 . . . both of you **b-ed** me
Jer 38:22 . . . They have **b-ed** and misled you.
Mal 2:10 . . . Then why do we **b** each other,
Matt 10:21 . . . A brother will **b** his brother
Matt 24:10 . . . and **b** and hate each other.
Matt 26:21 . . . one of you will **b** me.
Matt 27:4 . . . I have **b-ed** an innocent man.
Luke 6:16 . . . (who later **b-ed** him).
John 18:5 . . . Judas, who **b-ed** him,

BETRAYER (n) one who violates a trust or loyalty
Matt 26:46 . . . Look, my **b** is here!
John 18:2 . . . Judas, the **b,** knew this place,

BETTER (adj) more attractive, favorable, or commendable; more advantageous or effective
Ps 63:3 . . . unfailing love is **b** than life
Matt 5:20 . . . unless your righteousness is **b**
Phil 1:21 . . . and dying is even **b.**

BEWARE (v) to take heed or be careful
Mark 8:15 . . . **B** of the yeast of the Pharisees

BIRD, BIRDS (n) any of a class of warm-blooded vertebrates distinguished by having the body more or less covered with feathers and the forelimbs modified as wings
Prov 27:8 . . . **b** that strays from its nest.
Eccl 10:20 . . . **b** might deliver your
Matt 8:20 . . . and **b-s** have nests,
Luke 9:58 . . . and **b-s** have nests,

BIRTH (n) the emergence of a new individual from the body of its parent; beginning, start
Gen 25:24 . . . the time came to give **b,**
Ps 58:3 . . . even from **b** they have lied
Matt 24:8 . . . only the first of the **b** pains,
John 3:6 . . . Spirit gives **b** to spiritual life.
Titus 3:5 . . . giving us a new **b** and new life
Jas 1:15 . . . it gives **b** to death.

BIRTHRIGHT (KJV)
Gen 25:31 . . . me your *rights as the firstborn son*
1 Chr 5:1 . . . *birthright* was given to the
Heb 12:16 . . . his *birthright as the firstborn son*

BITTER (adj) expressive of severe pain, grief, or regret; distasteful
Exod 12:8 . . . eat it along with **b** salad greens
Prov 27:7 . . . **b** food tastes sweet to the
Prov 30:23 . . . a **b** woman who finally gets
Jas 3:11 . . . both fresh water and **b** water?

BITTERNESS (n) an intense or severe expression or feeling of pain, grief, or regret; exhibiting intense animosity
Prov 14:10 . . . Each heart knows its own **b,**
Prov 17:25 . . . **b** to the one who gave them
Rom 3:14 . . . full of cursing and **b.**
Eph 4:31 . . . Get rid of all **b,** rage,

BLACK (adj) of the color black; very dark in color
Zech 6:6 . . . The chariot with **b** horses
Rev 6:5 . . . I looked up and saw a **b** horse,

BLAME (n) an expression of disapproval or reproach; responsibility for something believed to deserve censure
1 Cor 1:8 . . . free from all **b** on the day
Rev 14:5 . . . they are without **b.**

BLAMELESS (adj) characterized by being free from sin and fault
see also INTEGRITY, RIGHTEOUS
Gen 6:9 . . . only **b** person living on earth
Job 1:8 . . . **b**—a man of complete integrity.
Ps 18:23 . . . I am **b** before God;
Prov 13:6 . . . guards the path of the **b,**
Prov 29:10 . . . The bloodthirsty hate **b**
Phil 1:10 . . . live pure and **b** lives
Col 1:22 . . . and you are holy and **b**
1 Thes 5:23 . . . kept **b** until our Lord
Titus 1:6 . . . must live a **b** life.
2 Pet 3:14 . . . pure and **b** in his sight.

BLASPHEME, BLASPHEMED, BLASPHEMES, BLASPHEMING (v) to dishonor or revile God; to speak of or address with irreverence
Lev 24:11 . . . son of an Israelite woman **b-ed**
Lev 24:16 . . . Anyone who **b-s** the Name
Num 15:30 . . . have **b-ed** the LORD,
Isa 52:5 . . . My name is **b-ed** all day long.
Dan 11:36 . . . even **b-ing** the God of gods.
Mark 3:29 . . . who **b-s** the Holy Spirit
Luke 12:10 . . . who **b-s** the Holy Spirit
Acts 6:11 . . . We heard him **b** Moses,
Rom 2:24 . . . Gentiles **b** the name of God
1 Tim 1:13 . . . to **b** the name of Christ.
1 Tim 1:20 . . . learn not to **b** God.
Rev 13:1 . . . were names that **b-ed** God.

BLASPHEMER (n) one who dishonors or reviles God; one who speaks or addresses with irreverence
Lev 24:14 . . . Take the **b** outside the camp,
Lev 24:23 . . . took the **b** outside the camp

BLASPHEMOUS (adj) impiously irreverent; profane
2 Kgs 19:6 . . . by this **b** speech against me
Isa 37:6 . . . by this **b** speech against me

BLASPHEMY, BLASPHEMIES (n) the words or actions that dishonor God; the act of insulting or showing contempt or lack of reverence for God
Neh 9:18 . . . They committed terrible **b-ies.**
Mark 3:28 . . . all sin and **b** can be forgiven,
Mark 14:64 . . . You have all heard his **b.**
John 10:33 . . . for any good work, but for **b!**
2 Pet 2:11 . . . a charge of **b** against those
Rev 13:5 . . . to speak great **b-ies** against God.
Rev 13:6 . . . words of **b** against God,
Rev 17:3 . . . and **b-ies** against God were

BLESS, BLESSED, BLESSES (v) to confer prosperity or happiness upon; to honor in worship; to offer approval or encouragement; to bring pleasure or divine favor
Gen 1:22 . . . Then God **b-ed** them,
Gen 12:3 . . . I will **b** those who **b** you
Gen 22:18 . . . of the earth will be **b-ed**—
Ps 16:7 . . . I will **b** the LORD who guides
Prov 31:28 . . . Her children stand and **b**
Matt 5:3 . . . God **b-es** those who are poor
Matt 5:7 . . . God **b-es** those who are merciful,
Matt 5:9 . . . God **b-es** those who work for
Matt 5:11 . . . God **b-es** you when people mock
Acts 20:35 . . . **b-ed** to give than to receive.
Jas 1:12 . . . God **b-es** those who patiently
Rev 22:7 . . . **B-ed** are those who obey

Rev 22:14 . . . **B-ed** are those who wash their robes.

BLESSING, BLESSINGS (n) happiness; praise; divine favor or heavenly reward; the antidote to cursings
Josh 8:34 . . . **b-s** and curses Moses
Prov 13:21 . . . **b-s** reward the righteous.
John 12:13 . . . **B-s** on the one who comes in
Acts 4:33 . . . God's great **b** was upon them
Acts 11:23 . . . evidence of God's **b,**
Rom 15:27 . . . spiritual **b-s** of the Good
Eph 3:6 . . . both enjoy the promise of **b-s**
Rev 7:12 . . . **B** and glory and wisdom

BLIND (adj) sightless; lacking spiritual discernment
Matt 11:5 . . . the **b** see, the lame walk,
Matt 15:14 . . . **b** guides leading the **b,**
Mark 10:46 . . . **b** beggar named
Luke 6:39 . . . Can one **b** person lead

BLINDED (v) to withhold light from or pull wool over; to be without sight
John 12:40 . . . The Lord has **b** their eyes
2 Cor 4:4 . . . god of this world, has **b** the

BLINK (n) glimpse, glance; a usually involuntary shutting and opening of the eye
1 Cor 15:52 . . . moment, in the **b** of an eye,

BLOOD (n) fluid in the circulatory system; signifies human life; kinfolk; of animals, used in priestly sacrifices; of Christ, effective for the forgiveness of sins; on hands or head, symbolic of guilt
Exod 12:13 . . . When I see the **b,** I will pass
Deut 12:23 . . . But never consume the **b,**
Isa 1:11 . . . no pleasure from the **b** of bulls
Mark 14:24 . . . my **b,** which confirms the
John 6:53 . . . and drink his **b,** you cannot
Acts 15:20 . . . and from consuming **b.**
1 Cor 11:25 . . . confirmed with my **b.**
Eph 1:7 . . . with the **b** of his Son
Eph 2:13 . . . through the **b** of Christ.
Heb 9:7 . . . offered **b** for his own sins
Heb 9:20 . . . This **b** confirms the covenant
1 Pet 1:2 . . . cleansed by the **b** of Jesus
1 Pet 1:19 . . . the precious **b** of Christ,
1 Jn 1:7 . . . the **b** of Jesus, his Son, cleanses
Rev 1:5 . . . by shedding his **b** for us.
Rev 5:9 . . . your **b** has ransomed people
Rev 7:14 . . . in the **b** of the Lamb
Rev 12:11 . . . by the **b** of the Lamb
Rev 19:13 . . . He wore a robe dipped in **b,**

BLOT (v) to wipe out, destroy; to erase or cover up
Ps 51:1 . . . **b** out the stain of my sins.
Isa 43:25 . . . I alone—will **b** out your sins

BOAST, BOASTED, BOASTING (v) to puff oneself up in speech, brag
Isa 20:5 . . . and **b-ed** of their allies in Egypt!
Jer 9:23 . . . the wise **b** in their wisdom,
Rom 2:17 . . . **b** about your special
1 Cor 1:31 . . . **b, b** only about the Lord.
2 Cor 8:24 . . . our **b-ing** about you is justified.
2 Cor 10:13 . . . We will **b** only about
Gal 6:14 . . . **b** about anything except
Eph 2:9 . . . none of us can **b** about it.
Jas 1:9 . . . poor have something to **b** about,
Jas 4:16 . . . **b-ing** about your own plans,

BOASTFUL (adj) bragging, overproud, vainglorious
Ps 12:3 . . . and silence their **b** tongues.
1 Cor 13:4 . . . Love is not jealous or **b** or proud

BOAT, BOATS (n) a small vessel for travel on water; ship
Gen 6:14 . . . Build a large **b** from cypress
Luke 5:3 . . . Stepping into one of the **b-s**,

BOAZ 1. Family redeemer and husband of the widow Ruth; ancestor of David in the family line of Jesus (Ruth 2–4; especially 4:1-10, 18-21; *see also* 1 Chr 2:12-15; Matt 1:5; Luke 3:23).
2. Pillar's name at front of the Jerusalem Temple (1 Kgs 7:15-22).

BODILY (adj) of or relating to the body
Col 2:23 . . . and severe **b** discipline.

BODY, BODIES (n) one's physical essence; a corpse; a group of people
see also FLESH
Job 19:26 . . . in my **b** I will see God!
Ps 49:14 . . . Their **b-ies** will rot in the grave,
Isa 26:19 . . . their **b-ies** will rise again!
Matt 26:41 . . . willing, but the **b** is weak!
Mark 14:22 . . . Take it, for this is my **b.**
Rom 12:4 . . . our **b-ies** have many parts
1 Cor 6:15 . . . that your **b-ies** are actually
1 Cor 6:19 . . . that your **b** is the temple
1 Cor 6:20 . . . honor God with your **b.**
1 Cor 11:24 . . . my **b,** which is given for
1 Cor 12:13 . . . into one **b** by one Spirit,
1 Cor 15:44 . . . as spiritual **b-ies.**
2 Cor 5:1 . . . eternal **b** made for us by God
2 Cor 5:2 . . . to put on our heavenly **b-ies**
2 Cor 5:4 . . . so that these dying **b-ies** will
Eph 1:23 . . . the church is his **b;**
Eph 3:6 . . . Both are part of the same **b,**
Eph 5:28 . . . love their own **b-ies.**
Eph 5:30 . . . are members of his **b.**
Col 1:24 . . . for his **b,** the church.

BOLD (adj) fearless before danger; self-assured, confident; prominent
2 Sam 7:27 . . . been **b** enough to pray
1 Chr 17:25 . . . been **b** enough to pray
Phil 1:20 . . . continue to be **b** for Christ,

BOLDLY (adv) showing or requiring a fearless daring spirit
Acts 26:26 . . . I speak **b,** for I am sure
Eph 3:12 . . . **b** and confidently into God's
Heb 4:16 . . . let us come **b** to the throne
Heb 10:19 . . . **b** enter heaven's Most Holy

BOLDNESS (n) fearlessness before danger; self-assurance; confidence; prominence
Acts 4:13 . . . they saw the **b** of Peter
Acts 4:29 . . . give us, your servants, great **b**

BONE, BONES (n) one of the hard parts of the skeleton
Gen 2:23 . . . This one is **b** from my **b,**
Ps 22:14 . . . all my **b-s** are out of joint.
Ps 22:17 . . . I can count all my **b-s.**
Ezek 37:1 . . . a valley filled with **b-s.**
John 19:36 . . . Not one of his **b-s** will be

BOOK, BOOKS (n) a long written or printed literary composition; written records, register, or accounting
Josh 1:8 . . . Study this **B** of Instruction
Ps 69:28 . . . names from the **B** of Life;
Ps 139:16 . . . recorded in your **b.**
Eccl 12:12 . . . for writing **b-s** is endless,
Dan 7:10 . . . and the **b-s** were opened.
Dan 12:1 . . . name is written in the **b**
John 21:25 . . . could not contain the **b-s**
Phil 4:3 . . . are written in the **B** of Life.
Rev 3:5 . . . names from the **B** of Life,
Rev 20:12 . . . including the **B** of Life.
Rev 20:12 . . . as recorded in the **b-s.**
Rev 21:27 . . . in the Lamb's **B** of Life.

BORN (v) to give birth to or produce; to be productive; spiritually, to renew or confirm a commitment of faith
see also BEAR
Ps 51:5 . . . For I was **b** a sinner—
Eccl 3:2 . . . A time to be **b** and a time to die.
Isa 9:6 . . . For a child is **b** to us,
Luke 2:11 . . . the Lord—has been **b** today
John 3:3 . . . unless you are **b** again,
John 3:7 . . . You must be **b** again.
1 Pet 1:3 . . . we have been **b** again,
1 Pet 1:23 . . . you have been **b** again,

BORROWER, BORROWERS (n) one who takes with the implied or expressed intention of returning the same; to borrow (money) with the intention of returning the same plus interest
Prov 22:7 . . . the **b** is servant to the lender.
Isa 24:2 . . . lenders and **b-s,** bankers and

BOSS (n) one who directs or supervises workers
Eccl 10:4 . . . If your **b** is angry at you,
Luke 16:3 . . . Now what? My **b** has fired me

BOTTOMLESS (adj) unfathomable; boundless, unlimited
Luke 8:31 . . . into the **b** pit.
Rev 9:1 . . . shaft of the **b** pit.
Rev 9:11 . . . the angel from the **b** pit;
Rev 11:7 . . . out of the **b** pit
Rev 17:8 . . . up out of the **b** pit
Rev 20:1 . . . the key to the **b** pit
Rev 20:3 . . . into the **b** pit,

BOUGHT (v) *see also* BUY
Job 28:15 . . . It cannot be **b** with gold.
1 Cor 6:20 . . . God **b** you with a high price.
2 Pet 2:1 . . . the Master who **b** them.

BOUND (v) to confine, restrain, or restrict as if with bonds; to put under an obligation
Acts 20:22 . . . now I am **b** by the Spirit
Rev 20:2 . . . and **b** him in chains

BOUNDARY (n) border, limit; dividing line
Num 34:3 . . . The southern **b** will begin
Prov 22:28 . . . moving the ancient **b** markers

BOUNTIFUL (adj) given or provided abundantly; generous
Ps 65:11 . . . year with a **b** harvest;
Ps 68:10 . . . with a **b** harvest, O God,

BOUNTY (n) crop yield; generosity
Deut 33:16 . . . gifts of the earth and its **b,**

BOW, BOWED, BOWS (v) to bend the head, body, or knee in reverence, submission, or shame
Gen 47:31 . . . Jacob **b-ed** humbly
Deut 5:9 . . . You must not **b** down to them
1 Kgs 1:16 . . . Bathsheba **b-ed** down before
1 Kgs 19:18 . . . never **b-ed** down to Baal
2 Chr 29:29 . . . everyone with him **b-ed** down
2 Chr 29:30 . . . and **b-ed** down in worship.
Esth 3:2 . . . would **b** down before Haman
Ps 72:9 . . . nomads will **b** before him;
Ps 95:6 . . . let us worship and **b** down.
Isa 44:15 . . . an idol and **b-s** down in front
Mic 6:6 . . . Should we **b** before God
Rom 11:4 . . . never **b-ed** down to Baal!
Phil 2:10 . . . every knee should **b,** in heaven

BOWL (n) a concave vessel often used for holding food or liquids
Prov 15:17 . . . A **b** of vegetables with
Luke 8:16 . . . covers it with a **b** or hides

BOY, BOYS (n) a male child from birth to puberty
Gen 21:17 . . . God has heard the **b** crying
Gen 22:12 . . . Don't lay a hand on the **b!**
Exod 1:18 . . . you allowed the **b-s** to live?
1 Sam 2:11 . . . the **b** served the LORD
1 Sam 3:8 . . . who was calling the **b.**
Matt 17:18 . . . rebuked the demon in the **b,**

BRAG (v) to talk boastfully
Prov 27:1 . . . Don't **b** about tomorrow,
Amos 4:5 . . . so you can **b** about it
2 Cor 5:12 . . . you can answer those who **b**

BRANCH, BRANCHES (n) limb of a (family) tree; part of a complex body (of knowledge); figurative of offspring and of disciples (of Christ and his disciples)
Isa 4:2 . . . the **b** of the LORD will be beautiful
Dan 4:21 . . . nested in its **b-es.**
Zech 3:8 . . . bring my servant, the **B.**
John 15:2 . . . **b** of mine that doesn't
John 15:4 . . . a **b** cannot produce fruit if
John 15:5 . . . you are the **b-es.**
Rom 11:20 . . . those **b-es** were broken off
Rom 11:21 . . . not spare the original **b-es,**

BREAD (n) basic staple in diet of ancient Israel; signifies livelihood
see also FOOD
Exod 23:15 . . . Festival of Unleavened **B.**
Prov 20:17 . . . Stolen **b** tastes sweet,
Mark 14:22 . . . Jesus took some **b** and
Luke 4:3 . . . stone to become a loaf of **b.**
Luke 9:13 . . . only five loaves of **b**
John 6:48 . . . Yes, I am the **b** of life!
John 6:51 . . . I am the living **b**
1 Cor 10:16 . . . when we break the **b,**
1 Cor 11:23 . . . the Lord Jesus took some **b**
1 Cor 11:26 . . . eat this **b** and drink

BREAK, BREAKING (v) to fracture; to shatter; to violate or transgress; to burst forth; to separate into parts; to force a way through; to disperse
see also BROKE
Lev 26:15 . . . and if you **b** my covenant
Prov 25:15 . . . soft speech can **b** bones.
Matt 5:33 . . . You must not **b** your vows;
1 Cor 10:16 . . . And when we **b** the bread,
1 Jn 3:4 . . . who sins is **b-ing** God's law,

BREAKFAST (n) first meal of the day, especially taken in the morning
Prov 31:15 . . . to prepare **b** for her

BREATH (n) air inhaled and exhaled in breathing; a spoken sound, utterance; a slight indication, suggestion
Gen 2:7 . . . He breathed the **b** of life
Exod 15:8 . . . At the blast of your **b,**
Ps 18:15 . . . at the blast of your **b,**
Ps 144:4 . . . we are like a **b** of air;

BREATHED (v) to inhale and exhale freely; to blow softly
Gen 2:7 . . . He **b** the breath of life
Mark 15:37 . . . and **b** his last.
John 20:22 . . . Then he **b** on them

BREVITY (n) shortness of duration
Ps 90:12 . . . to realize the **b** of life,

BRIBE (n) something that serves to induce or influence
Deut 16:19 . . . Never accept a **b,**

BRIBERY (n) the act or practice of giving or taking a bribe
Job 15:34 . . . homes, enriched through **b,**

BRICKS (n) units for building or paving, made of mud and often a binding agent such as straw; in the ancient world bricks

were baked or sun dried
Gen 11:3 . . . Let's make **b** and harden
Exod 5:7 . . . any more straw for making **b.**
Exod 5:13 . . . Meet your daily quota of **b,**
Isa 9:10 . . . replace the broken **b** of our ruins
Nah 3:14 . . . making **b** to repair the walls.

BRIDE (n) a woman just married or about to be married
2 Cor 11:2 . . . as a pure **b** to one husband—
Rev 19:7 . . . **b** has prepared herself.
Rev 21:2 . . . like a **b** beautifully dressed
Rev 21:9 . . . the **b,** the wife of the Lamb.
Rev 22:17 . . . Spirit and the **b** say, "Come."

BRIDEGROOM (n) a man just married or about to be married
Ps 19:5 . . . like a radiant **b** after
Matt 25:1 . . . and went to meet the **b.**
Matt 25:5 . . . When the **b** was delayed,

BRIDESMAIDS (n) women attendants of a bride
Matt 25:1 . . . will be like ten **b** who

BRIDLE (n) the headgear consisting of a bit and reigns with which a horse or other animal is governed
Prov 26:3 . . . a donkey with a **b,** and a fool

BRIGHTNESS (n) the quality or state of being bright; luminance; radiance
Ps 18:12 . . . shielded the **b** around him
Isa 24:23 . . . the **b** of the sun will fade,

BRILLIANT (adj) very bright, glittering; striking, distinctive
Hab 3:4 . . . His coming is as **b** as
1 Tim 6:16 . . . he lives in light so **b** that

BROAD (adj) extending far and wide; spacious
Matt 7:13 . . . highway to hell is **b,**

BROKE, BROKEN (v) *see also* BREAK
Josh 9:20 . . . if we **b** our oath.
1 Kgs 19:10 . . . have **b-n** their covenant
Ps 34:20 . . . not one of them is **b-n!**
Ps 51:17 . . . not reject a **b-n** and repentant
Eccl 4:12 . . . braided cord is not easily **b-n.**
Eccl 12:6 . . . the golden bowl is **b-n.**
Matt 26:26 . . . Then he **b** it in pieces
Mark 14:22 . . . Then he **b** it in pieces
Luke 20:18 . . . stone will be **b-n** to pieces,
John 19:36 . . . of his bones will be **b-n,**
Rom 11:20 . . . those branches were **b-n** off
1 Cor 11:24 . . . Then he **b** it in pieces
2 Tim 1:10 . . . He **b** the power of death
Jas 2:10 . . . who has **b-n** all of God's laws.

BROKENHEARTED (n) those overcome by grief or despair
Ps 34:18 . . . The LORD is close to the **b;**
Ps 109:16 . . . he hounded the **b** to death.
Ps 147:3 . . . He heals the **b** and

BROTHER, BROTHERS (n) male family members with the same parents; kinsmen in the extended family, church, or nation; co-workers in ministry; fellow believers, followers, or friends in Christ
Ps 133:1 . . . **b-s** live together in harmony!
Prov 18:24 . . . friend sticks closer than a **b.**
Prov 27:10 . . . to ask your **b** for assistance.
Mark 3:33 . . . Who are my **b-s?**
Mark 10:29 . . . given up house or **b-s** or
John 7:5 . . . even his **b-s** didn't believe
Heb 2:11 . . . ashamed to call them his **b-s**
Heb 13:1 . . . each other as **b-s** and sisters.
Jas 2:15 . . . you see a **b** or sister
Jas 4:11 . . . evil against each other, dear **b-s**
1 Pet 1:22 . . . each other as **b-s** and sisters.
1 Pet 3:8 . . . Love each other as **b-s** and
1 Jn 2:9 . . . a Christian **b** or sister,
1 Jn 3:16 . . . for our **b-s** and sisters.
1 Jn 3:17 . . . sees a **b** or sister in need
1 Jn 4:20 . . . hates a Christian **b** or sister,
1 Jn 4:21 . . . love their Christian **b-s** and
Rev 12:10 . . . the accuser of our **b-s** and

BROTHERLY (adj) natural or becoming to brothers; affectionate
2 Pet 1:7 . . . godliness with **b** affection,

BROUGHT (v) to carry, lead, or otherwise cause something to move toward an end
Jer 40:2 . . . has **b** this disaster on this land,
Eph 2:17 . . . He **b** this Good News

BUILD, BUILDING, BUILDS, BUILT (v) to erect or construct; to edify or encourage; to increase, enlarge
Gen 6:14 . . . **B** a large boat from cypress
1 Kgs 6:14 . . . Solomon finished **b-ing** the
Neh 4:17 . . . who were **b-ing** the wall.
Ps 127:1 . . . Unless the LORD **b-s** a house,
Prov 14:1 . . . A wise woman **b-s** her home,
Prov 16:12 . . . his rule is **b-t** on justice.
Hag 1:9 . . . busy **b-ing** your own fine houses.
Matt 7:24 . . . **b-s** a house on solid rock
Matt 16:18 . . . rock I will **b** my church,
Rom 14:19 . . . try to **b** each other up.
1 Cor 3:10 . . . Now others are **b-ing** on it.
1 Cor 3:12 . . . Anyone who **b-s** on that
2 Cor 10:8 . . . But our authority **b-s** you up;
Eph 2:20 . . . **b-t** on the foundation of the
Eph 4:12 . . . do his work and **b** up the church,
Col 2:7 . . . let your lives be **b-t** on him.
1 Thes 5:11 . . . and **b** each other up,
Heb 3:3 . . . as a person who **b-s** a house
1 Pet 2:5 . . . God is **b-ing** into his spiritual
Jude 1:20 . . . friends, must **b** each other up

BUILDER, BUILDERS (n) one who builds
Ps 118:22 . . . The stone that the **b-s** rejected
Mark 12:10 . . . stone that the **b-s** rejected
Acts 4:11 . . . The stone that you **b-s** rejected
1 Cor 3:10 . . . like an expert **b.**
1 Cor 3:14 . . . that **b** will receive a reward.
Heb 3:4 . . . For every house has a **b,**
1 Pet 2:7 . . . The stone that the **b-s** rejected

BUILDING (n) a walled structure built for permanent use; figurative of the Church
1 Cor 3:9 . . . You are God's **b.**

BULL, BULLS (n) a male, adult, uncastrated bovine
Lev 4:3 . . . a young **b** with no defects.
Heb 10:4 . . . the blood of **b-s** and goats

BURDEN, BURDENS (n) a (usually) heavy load to be borne—physically, emotionally, or spiritually
Ps 38:4 . . . a **b** too heavy to bear.
Matt 11:28 . . . weary and carry heavy **b-s,**
Matt 11:30 . . . the **b** I give you is light.
Acts 15:28 . . . to lay no greater **b** on you
2 Cor 11:9 . . . a financial **b** to anyone.
2 Cor 11:28 . . . the daily **b** of my concern
2 Cor 12:14 . . . I will not be a **b** to you.
Gal 6:2 . . . Share each other's **b-s,**
1 Thes 2:9 . . . so that we would not be a **b**
2 Thes 3:8 . . . so we would not be a **b**

BURDENED (v) to load; to oppress
Isa 43:23 . . . I have not **b** and wearied you
Isa 43:24 . . . Instead, you have **b** me
2 Tim 3:6 . . . are **b** with the guilt of sin

BURGLAR (n) one who enters a building with the intent to commit a crime
Luke 12:39 . . . when a **b** was coming,

BURLAP (n) a coarse, heavy, plain-woven fabric usually of jute or hemp used for bagging and wrapping
Dan 9:3 . . . I also wore rough **b**
Matt 11:21 . . . clothing themselves in **b**

BURN, BURNED, BURNING (v) to consume by fire; to be emotionally excited or agitated; to produce or undergo discomfort or pain
see also BURNING, BURNT
Exod 27:20 . . . keep the lamps **b-ing**
Lev 6:9 . . . must be kept **b-ing** all night.
Deut 7:5 . . . and **b** their idols.
Ps 79:5 . . . will your jealousy **b** like fire?
Isa 30:27 . . . far away, **b-ing** with anger,
Jer 23:29 . . . Does not my word **b** like fire?
Rom 1:27 . . . **b-ed** with lust for each other.
1 Cor 7:9 . . . to marry than to **b** with lust.

BURNER, BURNERS (n) the part of a fuel-burning device where the flame or heat is produced
Lev 16:12 . . . an incense **b** with burning coals
Num 16:6 . . . prepare your incense **b-s.**

BURNING (adj) being on fire
see also BURN, BURNT
Prov 25:22 . . . heap **b** coals of shame
Rom 12:20 . . . heap **b** coals of shame
Rev 19:20 . . . fiery lake of **b** sulfur.

BURNISHED (adj) shiny or lustrous from rubbing; polished
1 Kgs 7:45 . . . these things of **b** bronze
Ezek 1:7 . . . shone like **b** bronze.

BURNT (adj) marked by alteration or destruction by fire
see also BURN
Gen 22:2 . . . sacrifice him as a **b** offering
Exod 18:12 . . . brought a **b** offering
Lev 1:3 . . . present as a **b** offering
Josh 8:31 . . . they presented **b** offerings
Judg 6:26 . . . Sacrifice the bull as a **b**
Judg 13:16 . . . a **b** offering as a sacrifice
1 Kgs 3:4 . . . sacrificed 1,000 **b** offerings.
Ezra 3:2 . . . to sacrifice **b** offerings

BURY, BURIED (v) to deposit (a dead body) in the earth or in a tomb; figurative of denying oneself and submitting to Christ
Deut 34:6 . . . The LORD **b-ied** him
Ruth 1:17 . . . and there I will be **b-ied.**
Mark 6:29 . . . get his body and **b-ied** it in
Luke 9:60 . . . dead **b** their own dead!
Luke 23:30 . . . plead with the hills, '**B** us.'
Rom 6:4 . . . and were **b-ied** with Christ
1 Cor 15:4 . . . **b-ied,** and he was raised
Col 2:12 . . . For you were **b-ied** with Christ

BUSH (n) a low, densely branched shrub
Exod 3:2 . . . fire from the middle of a **b.**
Mark 12:26 . . . story of the burning **b?**
Luke 20:37 . . . wrote about the burning **b.**
Acts 7:35 . . . him in the burning **b,**

BUSINESS (n) role or function; economic dealings; affair or matter
Gen 40:8 . . . Interpreting dreams is God's **b,**
Ps 112:5 . . . conduct their **b** fairly.
1 Thes 4:11 . . . minding your own **b** and
2 Thes 3:11 . . . meddling in other people's **b.**
1 Tim 5:13 . . . meddling in other people's **b**

BUSY (adj) engaged in action; occupied
1 Kgs 20:40 . . . I was **b** doing something
Eccl 11:6 . . . keep **b** all afternoon,
Hag 1:9 . . . **b** building your own fine houses.

BUY, BUYS (v) to purchase; to redeem; to hire, bribe
see also BOUGHT
Prov 31:16 . . . to inspect a field and **b-s** it;
Rev 13:17 . . . no one could **b** or sell

C

CAESAR (n) a title applied to several emperors of the Roman Empire
Matt 22:21 . . . to **C** what belongs to **C**,

CALF (n) the young of a domestic cow
Exod 32:4 . . . it into the shape of a **c**.
Luke 15:23 . . . kill the **c** we have been
Acts 7:41 . . . made an idol shaped like a **c**,

CALL, CALLED, CALLING, CALLS (v) to make a request or demand; to designate or name
see also CHOSE, CHOSEN
Gen 2:23 . . . She will be **c-ed** 'woman,'
1 Kgs 18:24 . . . **c** on the name of your god,
2 Kgs 5:11 . . . leprosy and **c** on the name
2 Chr 7:14 . . . who are **c-ed** by my name
Ps 147:4 . . . stars and **c-s** them all by name.
Isa 40:26 . . . **c-ing** each by its name.
Isa 45:3 . . . the one who **c-s** you by name.
Isa 56:7 . . . Temple will be **c-ed** a house of
Hos 11:1 . . . I **c-ed** my son out of Egypt.
Joel 2:32 . . . everyone who **c-s** on the name
Matt 2:15 . . . I **c-ed** my Son out of Egypt.
Matt 9:13 . . . I have come to **c** not those
Matt 22:14 . . . many are **c-ed**, but few are
Matt 22:43 . . . **c** the Messiah 'my Lord'?
Mark 2:17 . . . I have come to **c** not those
Mark 10:49 . . . Come on, he's **c-ing** you!
Luke 1:32 . . . **c-ed** the Son of the Most High.
Luke 23:15 . . . this man has done **c-s**
Acts 2:21 . . . everyone who **c-s** on the name
Acts 2:39 . . . have been **c-ed** by the Lord
Acts 9:14 . . . arrest everyone who **c-s** upon
Acts 22:16 . . . sins washed away by **c-ing** on
Rom 1:6 . . . **c-ed** to belong to Jesus
Rom 8:28 . . . **c-ed** according to his purpose
Rom 10:12 . . . to all who **c** on him.
Rom 10:13 . . . Everyone who **c-s** on the
Rom 11:29 . . . **c** can never be withdrawn.
1 Cor 1:2 . . . who have been **c-ed** by God
1 Cor 1:2 . . . **c** on the name of our Lord
1 Cor 1:24 . . . **c-ed** by God to salvation,
1 Cor 7:17 . . . when God first **c-ed** you.
Gal 1:6 . . . so soon from God, who **c-ed** you
Gal 5:13 . . . been **c-ed** to live in freedom,
Eph 1:18 . . . to those he **c-ed**—his holy
Col 3:15 . . . you are **c-ed** to live in peace.
1 Thes 2:12 . . . **c-ed** you to share in his
1 Thes 4:7 . . . God has **c-ed** us to live holy
1 Thes 5:24 . . . he who **c-s** you is faithful.
2 Tim 2:22 . . . those who **c** on the Lord
Heb 9:15 . . . all who are **c-ed** can receive
1 Pet 2:9 . . . he **c-ed** you out of the darkness
1 Pet 3:9 . . . what God has **c-ed** you to do,
1 Pet 5:10 . . . God **c-ed** you to share in his
2 Pet 1:10 . . . are among those God has **c-ed**

CALLING (n) a strong inner impulse toward a particular course of action; an occupation or vocation
Eph 4:1 . . . to lead a life worthy of your **c**,

CALM (v) to make still; to free from agitation, excitement, or disturbance
Zeph 3:17 . . . he will **c** all your fears.

CALVARY (KJV)
Luke 23:33 . . . place called *The Skull*,

CAME (v) *see also* COME
John 1:17 . . . faithfulness **c** through Jesus
Heb 7:14 . . . our Lord **c** from the tribe of

CAMEL (n) either of two large ruminant mammals used as draft and saddle animals in desert regions especially of Africa and Asia
Matt 19:24 . . . easier for a **c** to go through
Matt 23:24 . . . but you swallow a **c**!

CANAAN (n) region along the Mediterranean Sea taken and settled by the Israelites
Num 33:51 . . . Jordan River into the land of **C**,
1 Chr 16:18 . . . **C** as your special possession.
Ps 105:11 . . . **C** as your special possession.
Acts 13:19 . . . he destroyed seven nations in **C**

CANCEL, CANCELED (v) to destroy the force, effectiveness, or validity of; to annul
Deut 15:1 . . . year you must **c** the debts
Matt 15:6 . . . so you **c** the word of God
Col 2:14 . . . He **c-ed** the record of the charges

CANDLE (n) a usually molded or dipped mass of wax or tallow containing a wick that may be burned
Isa 42:3 . . . or put out a flickering **c**.
Matt 12:20 . . . or put out a flickering **c**.

CANDLESTICK(S) (KJV)
Exod 25:31 . . . Make a *lampstand* of pure,
Dan 5:5 . . . palace, near the *lampstand*.
Matt 5:15 . . . a lamp is placed on a *stand*
Heb 9:2 . . . a *lampstand*, a table, and sacred
Rev 1:12 . . . I saw seven gold *lampstands*

CANOPY (n) a cover (as of cloth) fixed or carried above a person of high rank or a sacred object; a protective covering
2 Kgs 16:18 . . . he also removed the **c** that
Isa 4:5 . . . He will provide a **c** of cloud
Isa 51:16 . . . stretched out the sky like a **c**
Jer 43:10 . . . will spread his royal **c** over them.

CAPSTONE, HEADSTONE (KJV)
Ps 118:22 . . . become the *cornerstone*
Zech 4:7 . . . the *final stone* of the Temple
Matt 21:42 . . . now become the *cornerstone*.
Luke 20:17 . . . now become the *cornerstone*.

CAPTIVE (adj) (people) taken and held against their will
Prov 5:22 . . . is held **c** by his own sins;
Acts 8:23 . . . and are held **c** by sin.
2 Tim 2:26 . . . they have been held **c**

CAPTIVES (n) a prisoner
Ps 68:18 . . . you led a crowd of **c**.
Isa 60:11 . . . led as **c** in a victory
Isa 61:1 . . . that **c** will be released
Luke 4:18 . . . that **c** will be released,

CAPTIVITY (n) imprisonment, exile; subjection or subservience
Deut 28:41 . . . they will be led away into **c**.

CAPTURE, CAPTURED (v) an act of catching, winning, or gaining control by force, stratagem, or guile
1 Sam 4:11 . . . The Ark of God was **c-ed**,
2 Sam 5:7 . . . David **c-ed** the fortress of Zion,
Song 4:9 . . . You have **c-ed** my heart,
2 Cor 10:5 . . . We **c** their rebellious
Col 2:8 . . . **c** you with empty philosophies

CARCASS (n) a dead body; corpse
Judg 14:9 . . . honey from the **c** of the lion.
Matt 24:28 . . . vultures shows there is a **c**

CARE, CARED, CARES, CARING (v) to feel interest or concern; to attend to or provide for the needs, operation, or treatment of
Deut 1:31 . . . LORD your God **c-d** for you
Ps 8:4 . . . human beings that you should **c**
Ps 37:17 . . . LORD takes **c** of the godly.
Ps 65:9 . . . take **c** of the earth and
Ps 116:15 . . . **c-s** deeply when his loved ones
Ps 138:6 . . . is great, he **c-s** for the humble,
Prov 12:10 . . . godly **c** for their animals,
Prov 27:23 . . . into **c-ing** for your herds,
Isa 53:8 . . . No one **c-d** that he died without
Jer 23:2 . . . Instead of **c-ing** for my flock
Matt 6:30 . . . if God **c-s** so wonderfully for
Matt 25:36 . . . sick, and you **c-d** for me.
Luke 10:34 . . . an inn, where he took **c** of
John 10:13 . . . really **c** about the sheep.
John 12:25 . . . who **c** nothing for their life
John 21:16 . . . Then take **c** of my sheep,
Eph 5:29 . . . just as Christ **c-s** for the church.
Phil 2:21 . . . others **c** only for themselves
1 Thes 2:7 . . . **c-ing** for her own children.
1 Tim 5:14 . . . take **c** of their own homes.
1 Tim 5:16 . . . she must take **c** of them and
Heb 2:6 . . . that you should **c** for him?
1 Pet 5:2 . . . **C** for the flock that God
1 Pet 5:7 . . . and cares to God, for he **c-s**

CAREFUL (adj) marked by wary caution; meticulous
Exod 34:12 . . . **c** never to make a treaty
Lev 18:4 . . . and be **c** to obey my decrees,
Lev 22:2 . . . be very **c** with the sacred gifts
Lev 26:3 . . . are **c** to obey my commands,
Deut 4:9 . . . But watch out! Be **c** never to
Deut 6:3 . . . and be **c** to obey.
Deut 8:1 . . . Be **c** to obey all the commands
Deut 12:1 . . . **c** to obey when you live in
Deut 12:28 . . . Be **c** to obey all my
Josh 1:7 . . . and very courageous. Be **c**
Josh 23:11 . . . be very **c** to love the LORD
2 Kgs 21:8 . . . Israelites will be **c** to obey
1 Cor 8:9 . . . be **c** so that your freedom
1 Cor 10:12 . . . strong, be **c** not to fall.
Eph 5:15 . . . So be **c** how you live.

CAREFULLY (adv) scrupulously attentive
Deut 11:13 . . . **c** obey all the commands
2 Kgs 18:6 . . . he **c** obeyed all the commands
Prov 5:1 . . . attention to my wisdom; listen **c**
1 Cor 15:34 . . . **c** about what is right, and stop
Heb 2:1 . . . must listen very **c** to the truth
Heb 3:1 . . . think **c** about this Jesus

CARNAL(LY) (KJV)
Rom 7:14 . . . *all too human*, a slave to sin
Rom 8:6 . . . letting your *sinful nature* control
1 Cor 3:3 . . . still *controlled by your sinful nature*
2 Cor 10:4 . . . not *worldly* weapons

CAROUSE, CAROUSING (v) to drink liquor freely or excessively
Prov 23:20 . . . Do not **c** with drunkards
Luke 21:34 . . . your hearts be dulled by **c-ing**

CARPENTER (n) a worker who builds or repairs wooden structures or their structural parts
Matt 13:55 . . . He's just the **c**'s son,
Mark 6:3 . . . He's just a **c**, the son of Mary

CARRY, CARRIED, CARRIES (v) to transport or convey; to sustain the weight of; to bring to a successful end
Exod 19:4 . . . how I **c-ied** you on eagles'
Lev 16:22 . . . will **c** all the people's sins
Deut 32:11 . . . to take them up and **c-ied**
Ps 68:19 . . . For each day he **c-ies** us in his
Ps 103:20 . . . ones who **c** out his plans,
Isa 40:11 . . . **c** the lambs in his arms,
Isa 53:4 . . . it was our weaknesses he **c-ied;**
Isa 63:9 . . . He lifted them up and **c-ied** them
Luke 14:27 . . . do not **c** your own cross
Col 4:17 . . . Be sure to **c** out the ministry
1 Pet 2:24 . . . He personally **c-ied** our sins
2 Pet 3:17 . . . not be **c-ied** away by the errors

CAST, CASTING (v) to toss (dice); to drive out
Lev 16:8 . . . He is to **c** sacred lots to
Matt 10:1 . . . authority to **c** out evil spirits
Matt 12:26 . . . if Satan is **c-ing** out Satan,

CATCH (v) to get entangled; to seize and hold firmly
see also CAUGHT
Luke 5:4 . . . let down your nets to **c** some fish.

CATTLE (n) bovine animals on a farm or ranch
Ps 50:10 . . . I own the **c** on a thousand

CAUGHT (v) *see also* CATCH
Gen 22:13 . . . saw a ram **c** by its horns
Prov 6:2 . . . and are **c** by what you said—
2 Cor 12:2 . . . I was **c** up to the third heaven
1 Thes 4:17 . . . will be **c** up in the clouds

CAUTION (n) prudent forethought to minimize risk; precaution; warning
Jude 1:23 . . . do so with great **c**, hating the sins

CEASE (v) to come to an end; to discontinue
Lam 3:22 . . . His mercies never **c.**

CELEBRATE, CELEBRATED, CELEBRATING (v) to perform (a sacrament or ceremony) publicly and with appropriate rites; to observe a notable occasion with festivities
Exod 10:9 . . . together in **c-ing** a festival
Exod 12:47 . . . Israel must **c** this Passover
Exod 13:5 . . . You must **c** this event in this
Exod 23:14 . . . **c** three festivals in my
Exod 34:18 . . . **c** the Festival of
Exod 34:22 . . . **c** the Festival of the Final
Num 9:2 . . . **c** the Passover at the
Deut 16:1 . . . your God, **c** the Passover
2 Sam 6:21 . . . so I **c** before the LORD.
2 Kgs 23:21 . . . **c** the Passover to the LORD
2 Chr 30:1 . . . to **c** the Passover.
2 Chr 30:13 . . . **c** the Festival of
2 Chr 30:23 . . . **c-d** joyfully for another
Neh 8:12 . . . to **c** with great joy
Esth 8:15 . . . people of Susa **c-d** the new
Esth 9:19 . . . villages **c** an annual festival
Esth 9:21 . . . to **c** an annual festival
Matt 25:21 . . . Let's **c** together!
Luke 15:23 . . . We must **c** with a feast,
Luke 15:32 . . . We had to **c** this happy day.
John 18:28 . . . to **c** the Passover.
Col 2:16 . . . for not **c-ing** certain holy days
Rev 11:10 . . . to **c** the death of the two prophets

CELEBRATION, CELEBRATIONS (n) a party or festival in honor of a religious ceremony or holiday; the observation of a notable occasion with festivities
Num 9:3 . . . regulations concerning this **c.**
2 Sam 6:12 . . . City of David with a great **c.**
Esth 8:17 . . . had a great **c** and declared
Jer 31:13 . . . young—will join in the **c.**
Joel 1:16 . . . No joyful **c-s** are held in the
Zech 8:19 . . . **c** for the people of Judah.
John 11:55 . . . for the Jewish Passover **c,**

CENSUS (n) count of population, sometimes including assessment of property value
2 Sam 24:1 . . . to harm them by taking a **c.**
Luke 2:1 . . . decreed that a **c** should be taken

CENTURION (KJV)
Matt 8:5 . . . *Roman officer* came and pleaded
Luke 7:2 . . . slave of a *Roman officer* was sick
Acts 10:1 . . . *Roman army officer* named Cornelius

CEPHAS (n) rock; Aramaic name of Simon Peter, given to him by Christ
John 1:42 . . . called **C"** (which means

CEREMONIAL (adj) marked by, involved in, or belonging to ceremony; stressing careful attention to form and detail
Lev 14:2 . . . seeking **c** purification from a
John 2:6 . . . used for Jewish **c** washing.
John 3:25 . . . Jew over **c** cleansing.
Heb 9:13 . . . bodies from **c** impurity.

CEREMONIALLY (adv) in accordance with law and custom
Lev 4:12 . . . the camp that is **c** clean,
Lev 6:11 . . . to a place that is **c** clean.
Lev 10:14 . . . eaten in any place that is **c** clean.
Lev 12:2 . . . she will be **c** unclean for seven
Lev 13:3 . . . pronounce the person **c** unclean.
Lev 15:13 . . . he will be **c** clean.
Lev 15:33 . . . intercourse with a woman who is **c**
Lev 21:1 . . . **c** unclean by touching
Lev 22:3 . . . any of your descendants is **c**
Num 5:2 . . . who has become **c** unclean by
Num 9:6 . . . the men had been **c** defiled
Num 18:11 . . . your family who is **c** clean
Num 19:7 . . . **c** unclean until evening.
Num 19:18 . . . someone who is **c** clean must
Deut 12:22 . . . whether **c** clean or unclean,
Deut 14:7 . . . so they are **c** unclean for you.
1 Sam 20:26 . . . made David **c** unclean.

CEREMONY, CEREMONIES (n) a formal act or series of acts prescribed by ritual, protocol, or convention
Exod 12:25 . . . continue to observe this **c.**
Exod 12:26 . . . ask, 'What does this **c** mean?'
Neh 12:27 . . . to assist in the **c-ies.**
Acts 24:18 . . . completing a purification **c.**
Heb 9:10 . . . and various cleansing **c-ies**—

CERTAIN (adj) assured in mind or action; dependable, reliable; known or proved to be true, indisputable
Josh 23:13 . . . know for **c** that the LORD
Eccl 7:14 . . . nothing is **c** in this life.
Luke 1:4 . . . so you can be **c** of the truth
Phil 1:6 . . . **c** that God, who began the good
Heb 6:11 . . . to make **c** that what you hope

CHAFF (n) the seed coverings and other debris separated from the seed in threshing grain; something comparatively worthless
Ps 1:4 . . . worthless **c,** scattered by the wind.
Ps 35:5 . . . Blow them away like **c** in the
Dan 2:35 . . . like **c** on a threshing floor.
Matt 3:12 . . . separate the **c** from the

CHAIN, CHAINS (n) metal links or rings connected to one another and used for various purposes
Prov 1:9 . . . a **c** of honor around your neck.
Acts 26:29 . . . as I am, except for these **c-s"**
Eph 6:20 . . . I am in **c-s** now, still preaching
Col 4:18 . . . Remember my **c-s.**
2 Tim 1:16 . . . because I was in **c-s.**

CHAINED (v) to fasten, bind, or connect with or as with a chain; to obstruct
2 Tim 2:9 . . . the word of God cannot be **c.**
Jude 1:6 . . . securely **c** in prisons of darkness,

CHALLENGE (v) to put to a test or trial; to dispute with
Jer 49:19 . . . like me, and who can **c** me?

CHANCE (n) something that happens unpredictably without discernible human intention or observable cause, luck; a situation favoring some purpose, opportunity
1 Sam 18:21 . . . another **c** to see him killed
Eccl 9:11 . . . all decided by **c,** by being
Jer 15:6 . . . giving you another **c.**
Phil 4:10 . . . didn't have the **c** to help

CHANGE, CHANGED, CHANGES (v) to make different or transform; to shift, exchange, or transfer
Exod 32:14 . . . the LORD **c-d** his mind about
1 Sam 10:6 . . . be **c-d** into a different person.
1 Sam 15:29 . . . human that he should **c**
Ps 93:5 . . . Your royal laws cannot be **c-d.**
Isa 14:27 . . . who can **c** his plans?
Jer 33:25 . . . than I would **c** my laws
Jon 3:9 . . . Perhaps even yet God will **c** his mind
Mal 3:6 . . . I am the LORD, and I do not **c.**
2 Cor 3:18 . . . we are **c-d** into his glorious
Heb 6:17 . . . he would never **c** his mind.
Jas 1:17 . . . never **c-s** or casts a shifting

CHARACTER (n) moral excellence and firmness; main or essential nature
Rom 5:4 . . . develops strength of **c,**
1 Cor 15:33 . . . corrupts good **c.**
Heb 1:3 . . . expresses the very **c** of God,

CHARGE, CHARGES (n) management, supervision; obligation, requirement; a formal assertion of illegality or statement of complaint
Deut 19:18 . . . brought false **c-s** against
Ps 8:6 . . . gave them **c** of everything you
Prov 23:11 . . . bring their **c-s** against you.
Isa 50:8 . . . dare to bring **c-s** against me
Mic 6:2 . . . will bring **c-s** against Israel.
1 Cor 4:1 . . . in **c** of explaining God's
1 Cor 4:2 . . . in **c** as a manager must be

CHARGE, CHARGED, CHARGING (v) to impose a financial burden on; to command, instruct, or exhort with authority
Ps 119:4 . . . You have **c-d** us to keep your commandments
1 Cor 9:18 . . . the Good News without **c-ing**
Phlm 1:18 . . . owes you anything, **c** it to me.

CHARIOT, CHARIOTS (n) a two-wheeled horse-drawn battle car of ancient times used also in processions and races
2 Kgs 2:11 . . . suddenly a **c** of fire appeared,
2 Kgs 6:17 . . . with horses and **c-s** of fire.
Ps 20:7 . . . boast of their **c-s** and horses,
Ps 68:17 . . . thousands of **c-s,** the LORD came
Ps 104:3 . . . You make the clouds your **c;**

CHARITY (KJV)
1 Cor 8:1 . . . *love* that strengthens the church
1 Cor 13:1 . . . but didn't *love* others, I would
Col 3:14 . . . clothe yourselves with *love,*
1 Tim 4:12 . . . in your *love,* your faith, and
2 Pet 1:7 . . . affection with *love* for everyone

CHARM (n) something worn about the person to ward off evil or ensure good fortune; a trait that fascinates, allures, or delights
Prov 17:8 . . . A bribe is like a lucky **c;**
Prov 31:30 . . . **C** is deceptive, and beauty

CHASTE (KJV)
2 Cor 11:2 . . . as a *pure* bride to one husband—
Titus 2:5 . . . to live wisely and be *pure*
1 Pet 3:2 . . . *pure* and reverent lives

CHASTEN(ED) (KJV)
Ps 6:1 . . . or *discipline* me in your rage
Prov 19:18 . . . *Discipline* your children
1 Cor 11:32 . . . *being disciplined* so that we
Heb 12:11 . . . No *discipline* is enjoyable
Rev 3:19 . . . I correct and *discipline*

CHEAT, CHEATED, CHEATING, CHEATS (v) to deprive of something valuable by deceit or fraud; to practice fraud or trickery
Gen 31:7 . . . he has **c-ed** me, changing my
1 Sam 12:3 . . . Have I ever **c-ed** any of you?
1 Sam 12:4 . . . have never **c-ed** or oppressed
Amos 8:5 . . . get back to **c-ing** the helpless.
Mal 3:8 . . . You have **c-ed** me of the tithes
Mark 10:19 . . . You must not **c** anyone.
Mark 12:40 . . . they shamelessly **c** widows
1 Cor 5:10 . . . are greedy, or **c** people,
1 Cor 5:11 . . . is a drunkard, or **c-s** people.
1 Cor 6:7 . . . not let yourselves be **c-ed?**
1 Cor 6:8 . . . who do wrong and **c** even
1 Cor 6:10 . . . abusive, or **c** people—

CHEEK (n) the fleshy side of the face below the eye and above and to the side of the mouth
Matt 5:39 . . . slaps you on the right **c,**
Luke 6:29 . . . offer the other **c** also.

CHEERFUL (adj) full of good spirits; merry, ungrudging
Prov 15:30 . . . A **c** look brings joy
Prov 17:22 . . . A **c** heart is good medicine,

CHEERFULLY (adv) marked by or suggestive of lighthearted ease of mind and spirit; cheerily, gladly
2 Cor 9:7 . . . loves a person who gives **c.**
1 Pet 4:9 . . . **C** share your home with those

CHEERS (v) to instill with hope, joy, hilarity, or comfort
Prov 12:25 . . . encouraging word **c** a person

CHERISH (v) to hold dear; to feel or show affection for
Ps 102:14 . . . **c** even the dust in her streets.
Prov 19:8 . . . people who **c** understanding

CHERUBIM (n) winged angelic beings, often associated with worship and praise of God
Gen 3:24 . . . God stationed mighty **c** to the
Exod 25:19 . . . Mold the **c** on each end
1 Sam 4:4 . . . enthroned between the **c.**
1 Kgs 6:23 . . . He made two **c** of wild olive
Isa 37:16 . . . between the mighty **c!**
Ezek 10:1 . . . over the heads of the **c.**

CHEST (n) a wooden box or container; the trunk or rib cage of the human body
Exod 25:10 . . . a sacred **c** 45 inches long,
2 Kgs 12:9 . . . a hole in the lid of a large **c**
Zech 13:6 . . . those wounds on your **c?**
Rev 1:13 . . . with a gold sash across his **c.**

CHESTPIECE (n) a breastplate attached to the front of an ephod worn by the high priest
Exod 28:15 . . . make a **c** to be worn for

CHILD, CHILDREN (n) an unborn or recently born person; a young person between infancy and youth, not yet of age; offspring or descendants
see also SON(S)
Exod 20:5 . . . family is affected—even **c-ren**
Deut 24:16 . . . sins of their **c-ren,** nor **c-ren**
Deut 32:46 . . . as a command to your **c-ren**
1 Kgs 3:26 . . . Give her the **c**—please do
Job 1:5 . . . Perhaps my **c-ren** have sinned
Ps 8:2 . . . You have taught **c-ren** and infants
Prov 20:7 . . . blessed are their **c-ren** who
Prov 23:13 . . . discipline your **c-ren.**
Prov 29:15 . . . To discipline a **c** produces
Prov 31:28 . . . Her **c-ren** stand and bless
Isa 7:14 . . . The virgin will conceive a **c!**
Isa 9:6 . . . For a **c** is born to us,
Isa 54:13 . . . I will teach all your **c-ren,**
Mal 4:6 . . . hearts of **c-ren** to their fathers.
Matt 1:23 . . . The virgin will conceive a **c!**
Matt 5:9 . . . will be called the **c-ren** of God.
Matt 18:3 . . . and become like little **c-ren,**
Mark 9:37 . . . welcomes a little **c** like this
Mark 10:14 . . . Let the **c-ren** come to me.
Mark 10:16 . . . took the **c-ren** in his arms
Luke 1:42 . . . and your **c** is blessed.
Luke 6:35 . . . as **c-ren** of the Most High,
Luke 18:15 . . . their little **c-ren** to Jesus
John 1:12 . . . to become **c-ren** of God.
John 12:36 . . . become **c-ren** of the light.
Acts 2:39 . . . to your **c-ren,** and even to the
Rom 9:26 . . . called '**c-ren** of the living God.'
1 Cor 13:11 . . . and reasoned as a **c.**
Gal 3:26 . . . you are all **c-ren** of God
Eph 3:6 . . . riches inherited by God's **c-ren.**
Eph 6:1 . . . **C-ren,** obey your parents
Eph 6:4 . . . not provoke your **c-ren** to anger
Col 3:21 . . . do not aggravate your **c-ren,**
1 Tim 3:4 . . . having **c-ren** who respect and
1 Tim 3:12 . . . manage his **c-ren** and
1 Tim 5:10 . . . brought up her **c-ren** well?
Heb 12:7 . . . treating you as his own **c-ren.**
1 Jn 4:7 . . . Anyone who loves is a **c** of God
1 Jn 5:4 . . . every **c** of God defeats this evil
1 Jn 5:18 . . . God's **c-ren** do not make a

CHILDISH (adj) of, relating to, or befitting a child; marked by or suggestive of immaturity
1 Cor 13:11 . . . I put away **c** things.
1 Cor 14:20 . . . and sisters, don't be **c**

CHILDLESS (adj) a person characterized by lack of children; barren
Ps 113:9 . . . He gives the **c** woman a family,
Isa 54:1 . . . Sing, O **c** woman, you who
Gal 4:27 . . . Rejoice, O **c** woman, you who

CHILDLIKE (adj) resembling, suggesting, or appropriate to a child; marked by innocence, trust, and ingenuousness
Ps 116:6 . . . protects those of **c** faith;
Matt 11:25 . . . revealing them to the **c.**

CHOOSE, CHOOSES (v) to decide; to have a preference for; to select freely and after consideration
see also CALL, CHOSE
Deut 30:19 . . . Oh, that you would **c** life, so
Josh 24:15 . . . **c** today whom you will serve.
Eccl 10:2 . . . A wise person **c-s** the right road;
Jer 27:5 . . . things of mine to anyone I **c.**
Dan 4:25 . . . gives them to anyone he **c-s.**
John 15:16 . . . You didn't **c** me.
Rom 9:11 . . . God **c-s** people according to
Rom 9:18 . . . he **c-s** to harden the hearts of

CHOSE, CHOSEN (v) *see also* CALL, CHOOSE, CHOSEN
Matt 22:14 . . . called, but few are **c-n.**
John 15:16 . . . didn't choose me. I **c** you.
Rom 1:1 . . . **c-n** by God to be an apostle
Rom 8:29 . . . **c** them to become like his
1 Cor 1:1 . . . Paul, **c-n** by the will of God
1 Cor 1:27 . . . **c** things that are powerless
Eph 1:4 . . . loved us and **c** us in Christ
Eph 1:11 . . . God, for he **c** us in advance,
2 Thes 2:13 . . . thankful that God **c** you
1 Pet 1:15 . . . as God who **c** you is holy.
2 Pet 1:10 . . . God has called and **c-n.**

CHOSEN (adj) selected or marked for special favor or privilege; elect
see also CALLED
1 Chr 16:22 . . . Do not touch my **c** people,
Isa 41:8 . . . my **c** one, descended from Abraham
Mark 13:20 . . . for the sake of his **c** ones
Luke 23:35 . . . God's Messiah, the **C** One.
John 1:34 . . . that he is the **C** One of God.
1 Pet 1:1 . . . writing to God's **c** people
1 Pet 2:9 . . . for you are a **c** people.

CHRIST (n) Son of God, Messiah, Anointed One
see also JESUS, MESSIAH
John 1:17 . . . Faithfulness came through Jesus **C.**
Rom 1:4 . . . He is Jesus **C** our Lord.
Rom 3:22 . . . by placing our faith in Jesus **C.**
Rom 5:1 . . . what Jesus **C** our Lord has done
Rom 5:6 . . . **C** came at just the right time
Rom 5:11 . . . **C** has made us friends of God.
Rom 6:4 . . . as **C** was raised from the dead
Rom 6:23 . . . eternal life through **C** Jesus
Rom 7:4 . . . when you died with **C.**
Rom 8:1 . . . who belong to **C** Jesus.
Rom 8:34 . . . **C** Jesus died for us and
Rom 8:35 . . . separate us from **C**'s love?
Rom 14:9 . . . **C** died and rose again for this
Rom 15:5 . . . fitting for followers of **C** Jesus.
Rom 15:20 . . . where the name of **C** has never
1 Cor 1:2 . . . the name of our Lord Jesus **C,**
1 Cor 1:13 . . . Has **C** been divided into
1 Cor 1:17 . . . cross of **C** would lose its power.
1 Cor 1:23 . . . preach that **C** was crucified,
1 Cor 1:30 . . . God has united you with **C**
1 Cor 5:7 . . . **C,** our Passover Lamb,
1 Cor 6:15 . . . his body, which is part of **C,**
1 Cor 8:12 . . . you are sinning against **C.**
1 Cor 9:19 . . . to bring many to **C.**
1 Cor 10:4 . . . that rock was **C.**

1 Cor 10:9 . . . Nor should we put **C** to the test,
1 Cor 11:3 . . . and the head of **C** is God.
1 Cor 12:27 . . . you together are **C**'s body,
1 Cor 15:3 . . . **C** died for our sins,
2 Cor 1:5 . . . the more we suffer for **C**, the
2 Cor 3:3 . . . you are a letter from **C**
2 Cor 3:14 . . . removed only by believing in **C**.
2 Cor 5:10 . . . stand before **C** to be judged.
2 Cor 5:14 . . . **C**'s love controls us.
2 Cor 5:20 . . . we are **C**'s ambassadors;
Gal 1:7 . . . twist the truth concerning **C**.
Gal 2:4 . . . the freedom we have in **C** Jesus.
Gal 2:21 . . . need for **C** to die.
Gal 3:13 . . . But **C** has rescued us
Gal 4:19 . . . continue until **C** is fully developed
Gal 5:4 . . . you have been cut off from **C**!
Gal 5:24 . . . Those who belong to **C** Jesus have
Eph 1:3 . . . because we are united with **C**.
Eph 1:10 . . . under the authority of **C**—
Eph 1:20 . . . that raised **C** from the dead
Eph 2:10 . . . created us anew in **C** Jesus,
Eph 2:20 . . . the cornerstone is **C** Jesus
Eph 4:7 . . . through the generosity of **C**.
Eph 4:32 . . . God through **C** has forgiven you.
Eph 5:21 . . . out of reverence for **C**.
Eph 5:23 . . . head of his wife as **C** is the head
Eph 5:25 . . . wives, just as **C** loved the
Phil 1:21 . . . living means living for **C**,
Phil 1:23 . . . with **C**, which would be far better
Phil 1:29 . . . the privilege of trusting in **C**
Phil 2:5 . . . the same attitude that **C** Jesus had.
Phil 3:18 . . . enemies of the cross of **C**.
Col 1:22 . . . through the death of **C**
Col 2:2 . . . mysterious plan, which is **C**
Col 2:6 . . . accepted **C** Jesus as your Lord,
Col 2:13 . . . God made you alive with **C**,
Col 3:1 . . . raised to new life with **C**,
Col 3:3 . . . real life is hidden with **C** in God.
Col 3:15 . . . peace that comes from **C**
1 Thes 5:9 . . . through our Lord Jesus **C**,
1 Tim 1:15 . . . **C** Jesus came into the world
1 Tim 2:5 . . . humanity—the man **C** Jesus.
2 Tim 1:10 . . . by the appearing of **C** Jesus,
2 Tim 2:3 . . . as a good soldier of **C** Jesus.
2 Tim 2:10 . . . eternal glory in **C** Jesus
2 Tim 3:12 . . . a godly life in **C** Jesus will
2 Tim 3:15 . . . by trusting in **C** Jesus.
2 Tim 4:1 . . . of God and **C** Jesus, who will
Titus 2:13 . . . and Savior, Jesus **C**, will be
Heb 3:14 . . . share in all that belongs to **C**.
Heb 6:1 . . . teachings about **C** again and
Heb 9:14 . . . the blood of **C** will purify
Heb 9:28 . . . **C** died once for all time
Heb 10:10 . . . body of Jesus **C**, once for all
Heb 13:8 . . . Jesus **C** is the same yesterday,
1 Pet 1:11 . . . the Spirit of **C** within them
1 Pet 1:19 . . . blood of **C**, the sinless,
1 Pet 2:21 . . . just as **C** suffered for you.
1 Pet 3:15 . . . you must worship **C** as Lord
1 Pet 4:13 . . . partners with **C** in his suffering,
2 Pet 1:16 . . . coming of our Lord Jesus **C**.
1 Jn 2:1 . . . He is Jesus **C**, the one who is
1 Jn 2:22 . . . says that Jesus is not the **C**.
1 Jn 4:2 . . . that Jesus **C** came in a real
1 Jn 5:1 . . . Jesus is the **C** has become
1 Jn 5:20 . . . fellowship with his Son, Jesus **C**.
Rev 1:1 . . . from Jesus **C**, which God gave
Rev 1:5 . . . and from Jesus **C**.
Rev 20:4 . . . and they reigned with **C** for
Rev 20:6 . . . God and of **C** and will reign

CHRISTIAN, CHRISTIANS (n) one who professes belief in and follows the teachings of Jesus Christ; believer
Acts 11:26 . . . believers were first called **C-s**.
Acts 26:28 . . . persuade me to become a **C**
Gal 2:4 . . . some so-called **C-s**
1 Thes 4:12 . . . people who are not **C-s**
1 Pet 4:14 . . . insulted for being a **C**,
1 Pet 4:16 . . . to suffer for being a **C**.
1 Pet 5:9 . . . your **C** brothers and sisters

CHURCH, CHURCHES (n) "assembly" or "called ones"; the body of believers gathered to worship Jesus (not the building in which they meet)
Matt 16:18 . . . this rock I will build my **c**,
Matt 18:17 . . . take your case to the **c**.
Acts 16:5 . . . the **c-es** were strengthened
Acts 20:28 . . . shepherd God's flock—his **c**,
1 Cor 15:9 . . . way I persecuted God's **c**.
Gal 1:13 . . . I violently persecuted God's **c**.
Eph 5:23 . . . Christ is the head of the **c**.
Col 1:18 . . . head of the **c**, which is his
Col 1:24 . . . continue for his body, the **c**.
2 Thes 1:4 . . . tell God's other **c-es** about
Rev 1:20 . . . angels of the seven **c-es**,

CIRCUMCISE, CIRCUMCISED, CIRCUMCISING (v) to cut off the foreskin of a male child
Gen 17:10 . . . among you must be **c-d**.
Gen 17:12 . . . **c-d** on the eighth day after his
Josh 5:3 . . . Joshua made flint knives and **c-d**
John 7:23 . . . correct time for **c-ing** your son
Acts 21:21 . . . not to **c** their children
Rom 4:11 . . . even before he was **c-d**.
1 Cor 7:19 . . . or not a man has been **c-d**.

CIRCUMCISION (n) the condition of being circumcised; the ceremony signifying Israel's covenant with God; act symbolic of cleansing
Rom 2:25 . . . **c** has value only if you obey
Rom 2:29 . . . true **c** is not merely
Gal 5:2 . . . If you are counting on **c** to make

CIRCUMSTANCES (n) a condition, fact, or event accompanying, conditioning, or determining another
1 Thes 5:18 . . . Be thankful in all **c**, for this

CITIZEN, CITIZENS (n) a person owing allegiance to and deriving protection from a sovereign state
Acts 22:28 . . . But I am a **c** by birth!
Eph 2:19 . . . You are **c-s** along with
Phil 3:20 . . . But we are **c-s** of heaven,

CITIZENSHIP (n) the status of being a citizen; membership in a community
Eph 2:12 . . . excluded from **c** among

CLAIM, CLAIMS (v) to assert in the face of possible contradiction; to take as the rightful owner
Eccl 8:17 . . . no matter what they **c**.
Song 7:10 . . . and he **c-s** me as his own.
Isa 62:4 . . . LORD delights in you and will **c** you
Jas 1:26 . . . **c** to be religious but don't control
1 Jn 1:10 . . . If we **c** we have not sinned,
1 Jn 2:9 . . . If anyone **c-s**, "I am living in the

CLAP, CLAPPED (v) to strike (the hands) together repeatedly usually in applause
2 Kgs 11:12 . . . everyone **c-ped** their hands
Ps 47:1 . . . Come, everyone! **C** your hands!
Ps 98:8 . . . Let the rivers **c** their hands
Isa 55:12 . . . trees of the field will **c**
Nah 3:19 . . . hear of your destruction will **c**

CLAY (n) an earthy material that is pliable when moist but hard when fired and is used for brick, tile, and pottery
Isa 45:9 . . . Does the **c** dispute with the one
Isa 64:8 . . . **c**, and you are the potter.
Lam 4:2 . . . are now treated like pots of **c**
Dan 2:33 . . . of iron and baked **c**.
Rom 9:21 . . . to use the same lump of **c**
2 Cor 4:7 . . . **c** jars containing this great
2 Tim 2:20 . . . are made of wood and **c**.

CLEAN (adj) unadulterated, pure; without guilt or moral corruption; without ceremonial defilement; fit for use or human consumption
see also PURE
Lev 10:10 . . . unclean and what is **c**.
Ps 51:2 . . . Wash me **c** from my guilt.
Ps 51:7 . . . and I will be **c**; wash me,
Ps 51:10 . . . Create in me a **c** heart, O God.
John 13:10 . . . you disciples are **c**, but not all
Acts 10:15 . . . if God has made it **c**.
2 Tim 2:21 . . . Your life will be **c**,

CLEANSE, CLEANSED, CLEANSES (v) to make clean, pure, holy
see also PURIFY, WASH
Ps 19:12 . . . **C** me from these hidden
Prov 20:9 . . . Who can say, "I have **c-d** my
Jer 4:14 . . . O Jerusalem, **c** your heart
Acts 15:9 . . . he **c-d** their hearts through
1 Cor 6:11 . . . were **c-d**; you were made holy;
2 Cor 7:1 . . . let us **c** ourselves from
Titus 2:14 . . . **c** us, and to make us his
Heb 1:3 . . . he had **c-d** us from our sins,
Heb 9:13 . . . of a young cow could **c**
1 Pet 1:2 . . . and have been **c-d** by the blood
1 Pet 1:22 . . . You were **c-d** from your sins
2 Pet 1:9 . . . that they have been **c-d**
1 Jn 1:7 . . . blood of Jesus, his Son, **c-s** us
1 Jn 1:9 . . . and to **c** us from all wickedness.

CLEAR, CLEARED (v) to free from what obstructs or is unneeded
Ps 32:2 . . . whose record the LORD has **c-ed**
John 1:23 . . . **C** the way for the Lord's coming!
Rom 4:8 . . . whose record the LORD has **c-ed**

CLEARHEADED (adj) having or showing a clear understanding; able to think clearly
1 Thes 5:6 . . . Stay alert and be **c**.

CLEVER (adj) mentally quick and resourceful; marked by wit or ingenuity
Job 15:5 . . . are based on **c** deception.
Isa 5:21 . . . and think themselves so **c**.
Eph 4:14 . . . lies so **c** they sound like the truth.
2 Pet 1:16 . . . we were not making up **c** stories

CLEVERNESS (n) the state of being mentally quick and resourceful; showing wit or ingenuity
1 Cor 3:19 . . . in the snare of their own **c**.

CLING (v) to adhere as if glued firmly; to hold or hold on tightly or tenaciously
Deut 10:20 . . . worship him and **c** to him.
Deut 13:4 . . . listen to his voice, and **c** to
Matt 10:39 . . . If you **c** to your life,
Luke 8:15 . . . who hear God's word, **c** to it,
John 20:17 . . . "Don't **c** to me," Jesus
Phil 2:6 . . . as something to **c** to.

CLOSE, CLOSED, CLOSES (v) to draw near; to contract, fold, swing, or slide so as to leave no opening
Gen 7:16 . . . Then the LORD **c-d** the door
Prov 28:27 . . . who **c** their eyes to poverty
Isa 22:22 . . . no one will be able to **c** them;
Acts 28:27 . . . and they have **c-d** their eyes—
Rev 3:7 . . . what he **c-s,** no one can open:
Rev 21:25 . . . Its gates will never be **c-d**

CLOSE, CLOSER (adv) being near in time, space, effect, or degree
Exod 3:5 . . . Do not come any **c-r,**
Ps 34:18 . . . is **c** to the brokenhearted;
Ps 148:14 . . . of Israel who are **c** to him.
Prov 18:24 . . . sticks **c-r** than a brother.
Isa 40:11 . . . in his arms, holding them **c**

CLOTHED (v) to dress; to endow especially with power or a quality
Ps 30:11 . . . mourning and **c** me with joy,
Prov 31:25 . . . She is **c** with strength
Rev 7:9 . . . They were **c** in white robes
Rev 7:13 . . . these who are **c** in white?

CLOTHES (n) cloth articles of personal use that can be worn and washed
Deut 8:4 . . . forty years your **c** didn't wear out,
Isa 50:9 . . . old **c** that have been eaten by
Matt 6:25 . . . food and drink, or enough **c**
Matt 27:35 . . . soldiers gambled for his **c**
John 19:23 . . . they divided his **c**
Gal 3:27 . . . like putting on new **c.**

CLOTHING (n) garments in general; covering
Gen 3:21 . . . God made **c** from animal skins
Deut 22:5 . . . woman must not put on men's **c,**
Ps 22:18 . . . and throw dice for my **c.**
Matt 6:28 . . . And why worry about your **c?**
1 Tim 6:8 . . . food and **c,** let us be content.

CLOUD, CLOUDS (n) a visible mass of particles of condensed vapor suspended in the atmosphere
1 Kgs 18:44 . . . I saw a little **c** about the
Ps 68:4 . . . praises to him who rides the **c-s.**
Ps 108:4 . . . faithfulness reaches to the **c-s.**
Isa 19:1 . . . Egypt, riding on a swift **c.**
Dan 7:13 . . . coming with the **c-s** of heaven.
Mark 13:26 . . . coming on the **c-s** with great
Luke 21:27 . . . Son of Man coming on a **c**
1 Thes 4:17 . . . up in the **c-s** to meet the Lord
Rev 1:7 . . . He comes with the **c-s** of heaven.
Rev 14:14 . . . I saw a white **c,** and seated on

COALS (n) a piece of glowing carbon or charred wood; ember
Prov 25:22 . . . heap burning **c** of shame
Rom 12:20 . . . heap burning **c** of shame

COARSE (adj) crude or unrefined in taste, manners, or language; harsh, raucous, or rough in tone
Eph 5:4 . . . **c** jokes—these are not for you.

COAT (n) an outer garment worn on the upper body
Matt 5:40 . . . give your **c,** too.
Luke 6:29 . . . your **c,** offer your shirt

COIN, COINS (n) a usually flat piece of metal issued by governmental authority as money
Mark 12:15 . . . Show me a Roman **c,**
Mark 12:42 . . . dropped in two small **c-s.**
Luke 12:6 . . . sparrows—two copper **c-s?**
Luke 15:8 . . . woman has ten silver **c-s**

COLLAPSE (v) to cave or fall in or give way
Matt 7:25 . . . it won't **c** because it is built
Luke 6:49 . . . it will **c** into a heap of ruins.

COLLECTED (v) to bring together into one body or place
Hos 13:12 . . . Ephraim's guilt has been **c,**
1 Cor 16:1 . . . about the money being **c**

COLT (n) a young male animal of the horse family
Zech 9:9 . . . riding on a donkey's **c.**

COME, COMES, COMING (v) to originate, arise; to move or journey to a vicinity with a specified purpose; to happen, occur
see also CAME
Ps 121:1 . . . does my help **c** from there?
Prov 12:21 . . . No harm **c-s** to the godly,
1 Thes 3:13 . . . our Lord Jesus **c-s** again
Heb 9:28 . . . He will **c** again,
Heb 13:7 . . . good that has **c** from their
Jas 5:8 . . . for the **c-ing** of the Lord
Rev 7:10 . . . Salvation **c-s** from our God

COMFORT (n) consolation in time of trouble or worry; solace
Gen 24:67 . . . she was a special **c** to him
Job 10:20 . . . I may have a moment of **c**
Ps 94:19 . . . your **c** gave me renewed hope
Zech 10:2 . . . falsehoods that give no **c.**
2 Cor 1:5 . . . shower us with his **c**
2 Cor 1:7 . . . share in the **c** God gives us.
Col 4:11 . . . And what a **c** they have been!

COMFORT, COMFORTED, COMFORTS (v) to give strength and hope to; to console
Gen 37:35 . . . he refused to be **c-ed.**
Ruth 2:13 . . . You have **c-ed** me by speaking
Job 2:11 . . . traveled from their homes to **c**
Job 42:11 . . . consoled him and **c-ed** him
Ps 69:20 . . . one would turn and **c** me.
Ps 86:17 . . . O LORD, help and **c** me.
Ps 119:50 . . . it **c-s** me in all my troubles.
Ps 119:52 . . . O LORD, they **c** me.
Isa 40:1 . . . **C, c** my people,
Isa 49:13 . . . the LORD has **c-ed** his people
Isa 51:3 . . . The LORD will **c** Israel again
Isa 51:12 . . . I, am the one who **c-s** you.
Isa 51:19 . . . Who is left to **c** you?
Isa 52:9 . . . the LORD has **c-ed** his people.
Isa 61:1 . . . to **c** the brokenhearted
Isa 66:13 . . . as a mother **c-s** her child.
Lam 1:2 . . . there is no one left to **c** her.
Lam 1:17 . . . but no one **c-s** her.
Zech 1:17 . . . the LORD will again **c** Zion
Matt 5:4 . . . mourn, for they will be **c-ed.**
1 Cor 14:3 . . . encourages them, and **c-s**
2 Cor 1:4 . . . He **c-s** us in all our troubles
2 Cor 1:4 . . . so that we can **c** others.
2 Cor 1:6 . . . when we ourselves are **c-ed,**
2 Cor 1:6 . . . we will certainly **c** you.
2 Cor 2:7 . . . forgive and **c** him.

COMFORTER (KJV)
John 14:16 . . . another *Advocate,* who will
John 14:26 . . . sends the *Advocate* as my
John 15:26 . . . the *Advocate*—the Spirit of
John 16:7 . . . if I don't, the *Advocate* won't

COMMAND, COMMANDS (n) an order given; religious instruction
see also COMMANDMENT
Exod 20:6 . . . who love me and obey my **c-s.**
Exod 24:12 . . . the instructions and **c-s**
Lev 22:31 . . . keep all my **c-s**
Num 15:39 . . . and obey all the **c-s**
Deut 4:2 . . . or subtract from these **c-s**
Deut 6:6 . . . wholeheartedly to these **c-s**
Deut 7:9 . . . who love him and obey his **c-s.**
Deut 8:1 . . . Be careful to obey all the **c-s**
Deut 11:1 . . . decrees, regulations, and **c-s.**
Deut 11:27 . . . if you obey the **c-s** of the
Deut 28:1 . . . keep all his **c-s** that I am giving
Deut 32:46 . . . as a **c** to your children
Josh 1:9 . . . my **c**—be strong and
1 Kgs 8:58 . . . obey all the **c-s,** decrees,
1 Kgs 8:61 . . . obey his decrees and **c-s,**
1 Chr 28:7 . . . if he continues to obey my **c-s**
Neh 1:5 . . . who love him and obey his **c-s,**
Job 36:10 . . . **c-s** that they turn from evil.
Ps 33:9 . . . It appeared at his **c.**
Ps 78:7 . . . and obeying his **c-s.**
Ps 103:20 . . . listening for each of his **c-s.**
Ps 112:1 . . . and delight in obeying his **c-s.**
Ps 119:32 . . . I will pursue your **c-s,**
Ps 119:47 . . . How I delight in your **c-s!**
Ps 119:73 . . . the sense to follow your **c-s.**
Ps 119:96 . . . your **c-s** have no limit.
Ps 119:127 . . . I love your **c-s** more than
Ps 119:143 . . . I find joy in your **c-s.**
Ps 119:172 . . . all your **c-s** are right.
Ps 119:176 . . . I have not forgotten your **c-s.**
Prov 3:1 . . . Store my **c-s** in your heart.
Prov 6:23 . . . For their **c** is a lamp
Eccl 12:13 . . . Fear God and obey his **c-s,**
Isa 48:18 . . . you had listened to my **c-s!**
Dan 9:4 . . . who love you and obey your **c-s.**
Matt 28:20 . . . disciples to obey all the **c-s**
John 15:17 . . . my **c:** Love each other.
Acts 17:30 . . . he **c-s** everyone everywhere to
Rom 7:8 . . . sin used this **c** to arouse
Rom 7:9 . . . I learned the **c** not to covet,
Rom 7:12 . . . law itself is holy, and its **c-s** are
1 Cor 14:37 . . . saying is a **c** from the Lord
Gal 5:14 . . . summed up in this one **c:**
2 Thes 3:6 . . . we give you this **c**
2 Pet 2:21 . . . reject the **c** they were given

COMMAND, COMMANDED, COMMANDING (v) to issue a charge or directive
Gen 7:5 . . . everything as the LORD **c-ed**
Exod 7:6 . . . did just as the LORD had **c-ed**
Exod 19:7 . . . everything the LORD had **c-ed**
Deut 6:1 . . . LORD your God **c-ed** me to teach
Deut 6:24 . . . our God **c-ed** us to obey
Deut 15:11 . . . why I am **c-ing** you to share
John 15:14 . . . my friends if you do what I **c.**
2 Tim 2:14 . . . **c** them in God's presence
2 Pet 3:2 . . . Savior **c-ed** through your
1 Jn 3:23 . . . just as he **c-ed** us.
2 Jn 1:4 . . . just as the Father **c-ed.**

COMMANDER (n) one in an official position of command or control
Eph 2:2 . . . the **c** of the powers in the unseen

COMMANDMENT, COMMANDMENTS (n) a gracious provision of God's law or covenant, obeyed as an act of love and devotion
see also COMMAND
Exod 34:28 . . . Ten **C-s**—on the stone
Deut 4:13 . . . his covenant—the Ten **C-s**
Deut 10:4 . . . LORD wrote the Ten **C-s** on
Ps 103:18 . . . of those who obey his **c-s!**
Ps 111:7 . . . all his **c-s** are trustworthy.
Ps 111:10 . . . who obey his **c-s** will grow

Ps 119:93 . . . I will never forget your **c-s,**
Prov 19:16 . . . the **c-s** and keep your life;
Matt 5:19 . . . if you ignore the least **c**
Matt 19:17 . . . eternal life, keep the **c-s.**
Matt 22:36 . . . the most important **c**
Matt 22:38 . . . the first and greatest **c.**
Mark 10:19 . . . you know the **c-s:**
Mark 12:28 . . . **c-s,** which is the most
Luke 18:20 . . . you know the **c-s:**
John 13:34 . . . a new **c:** Love each other.
John 14:15 . . . If you love me, obey my **c-s.**
Rom 13:9 . . . in this one **c:** "Love your
1 Cor 7:19 . . . is to keep God's **c-s.**
Eph 2:15 . . . law with its **c-s** and regulations.
Eph 6:2 . . . the first **c** with a promise:
Heb 9:19 . . . had read each of God's **c-s**
1 Jn 2:3 . . . we know him if we obey his **c-s.**
1 Jn 3:24 . . . Those who obey God's **c-s**
1 Jn 5:3 . . . God means keeping his **c-s,**
Rev 12:17 . . . who keep God's **c-s** and

COMMEND, COMMENDING (v) to entrust for care or preservation; to praise
Rom 16:1 . . . I **c** to you our sister Phoebe,
2 Cor 5:12 . . . Are we **c-ing** ourselves to you
2 Cor 10:18 . . . When people **c** themselves,

COMMENDATIONS (n) a praiseworthy citation
2 Cor 12:11 . . . ought to be writing **c** for me,

COMMIT, COMMITS, COMMITTED, COMMITTING (v) to carry into action deliberately, perpetrate; to obligate or pledge oneself
Deut 30:20 . . . **c-ting** yourself firmly to him.
2 Chr 16:9 . . . hearts are fully **c-ted** to him.
2 Chr 17:6 . . . deeply **c-ted** to the ways
Prov 6:32 . . . the man who **c-s** adultery
Prov 29:22 . . . a hot-tempered person **c-s**
Matt 5:28 . . . has already **c-ted** adultery
Matt 5:32 . . . causes her to **c** adultery.
Matt 19:9 . . . someone else **c-s** adultery—
Mark 10:11 . . . someone else **c-s** adultery
Mark 10:19 . . . You must not **c** adultery.
Luke 16:18 . . . her husband **c-s** adultery.
Rom 13:9 . . . You must not **c** adultery.
Titus 2:14 . . . totally **c-ted** to doing good
Jas 2:11 . . . You must not **c** adultery,
Rev 18:3 . . . world have **c-ted** adultery with
Rev 18:9 . . . the world who **c-ted** adultery

COMMON (adj) characterized by a lack of privilege or special status; belonging to or shared by two or more individuals or things or all members of a group
Lev 10:10 . . . what is sacred and what is **c,**
1 Cor 9:22 . . . I try to find **c** ground with

COMMUNITY (n) a unified body of individuals
Num 20:1 . . . whole **c** of Israel arrived

COMPANION , COMPANIONS (n) a close friend or fellow participant
Ps 55:13 . . . my **c** and close friend.
Ps 55:20 . . . As for my **c,** he betrayed his
Prov 16:29 . . . mislead their **c-s,** leading

COMPANY (n) association with another, fellowship; companions, associates
Prov 21:16 . . . end up in the **c** of the dead.
Prov 24:1 . . . or desire their **c.**
Rom 12:16 . . . to enjoy the **c** of ordinary
1 Cor 15:33 . . . for "bad **c** corrupts good

COMPASSION (n) sympathy, usually granted because of unusual or distressing circumstances
Exod 34:6 . . . The God of **c** and mercy!
Ps 51:1 . . . Because of your great **c,**
Ps 86:15 . . . a God of **c** and mercy, slow to
Ps 145:9 . . . He showers **c** on all
Isa 49:13 . . . and will have **c** on them
Isa 63:15 . . . your mercy and **c** now?
Lam 3:32 . . . brings grief, he also shows **c**
Hos 2:19 . . . unfailing love and **c.**
Mic 7:19 . . . you will have **c** on us.
Zech 10:6 . . . because of my **c.**
Mark 1:41 . . . Moved with **c,** Jesus reached
Mark 6:34 . . . and he had **c** on them
Luke 15:20 . . . with love and **c,** he ran to
Rom 9:15 . . . show **c** to anyone I choose.

COMPASSIONATE (adj) having or showing compassion; sympathetic
Ps 103:13 . . . tender and **c** to those who
Ps 112:4 . . . They are generous, **c,**
Ps 145:8 . . . is merciful and **c,** slow to
Joel 2:13 . . . he is merciful and **c,** slow to
Luke 6:36 . . . You must be **c,** just as your
Phil 2:1 . . . Are your hearts tender and **c?**

COMPELLED (v) to drive or urge forcefully or irresistibly
1 Cor 9:16 . . . I am **c** by God to do it.

COMPENSATION (n) something that constitutes an equivalent or recompense
Prov 6:35 . . . He will accept no **c,**

COMPLACENCY (n) self-satisfaction especially when accompanied by unawareness of actual dangers or deficiencies
Prov 1:32 . . . destroyed by their own **c.**
Isa 32:11 . . . throw off your **c.**

COMPLACENT (adj) self-satisfied; unconcerned
Jer 49:31 . . . attack that **c** nation,
Zeph 1:12 . . . who sit **c** in their sins.

COMPLAINED, COMPLAINING (v) to express grief, pain, or discontent; to make a formal accusation or charge
Exod 15:24 . . . the people **c** and turned
Num 14:2 . . . in the wilderness!" they **c.**
Num 14:29 . . . Because you **c** against me,
John 6:43 . . . Jesus replied, "Stop **c-ing**
Phil 2:14 . . . Do everything without **c-ing**

COMPLAINERS (n) one who complains
Jude 1:16 . . . grumblers and **c,** living only

COMPLAINT (n) a formal allegation against a party
Mic 6:2 . . . listen to the LORD's **c!**

COMPLETE (adj) having all necessary parts, elements, or steps
Eph 4:13 . . . full and **c** standard of Christ.
Jas 2:22 . . . made his faith **c.**
2 Jn 1:12 . . . joy will be **c.**

COMPREHEND (v) to grasp the nature, significance, or meaning of
Matt 13:14 . . . I do, you will not **c.**

COMPREHENSION (n) the act or action of grasping with the intellect; understanding
Ps 147:5 . . . is beyond **c!**

CONCEAL, CONCEALED (v) to prevent disclosure or recognition of; to place out of sight
Prov 25:2 . . . God's privilege to **c**
Prov 28:13 . . . People who **c** their sins will
Luke 8:17 . . . everything that is **c-ed** will be

CONCEIT (n) excessive appreciation of one's own worth or virtue
Ps 36:2 . . . In their blind **c,** they cannot

CONCEITED (adj) having or showing an excessively high opinion of oneself
Gal 5:26 . . . us not become **c,** or provoke

CONCEIVE, CONCEIVED (v) to become pregnant; to devise or imagine
Gen 29:31 . . . Rachel could not **c.**
Ps 7:14 . . . The wicked **c** evil; they are
Matt 1:20 . . . was **c-d** by the Holy Spirit.
Luke 1:7 . . . Elizabeth was unable to **c,**
Luke 1:31 . . . You will **c** and give birth

CONCERN, CONCERNS (n) affair or business; an uneasy state of blended interest, uncertainty, and apprehension
Job 19:4 . . . that is my **c,** not yours.
1 Cor 7:32 . . . free from the **c-s** of this life.
2 Cor 7:11 . . . such **c** to clear yourselves,
2 Cor 11:28 . . . the daily burden of my **c**

CONCERN, CONCERNED (v) to involve; to be a care, trouble, or distress to
1 Sam 23:21 . . . someone is **c-ed** about me!
Ps 131:1 . . . I don't **c** myself with matters
1 Cor 10:24 . . . be **c-ed** for your own good
Phil 4:10 . . . have always been **c-ed** for me,

CONCUBINE, CONCUBINES (n) a woman living in a man's household, though not married; of lower family status than the wife
Judg 19:1 . . . from Bethlehem in Judah to be his **c.**
2 Sam 3:7 . . . one of his father's **c-s,**
2 Sam 5:13 . . . David married more **c-s** and
2 Sam 16:22 . . . sex with his father's **c-s.**
2 Sam 21:11 . . . what Rizpah, Saul's **c,** had
1 Chr 1:32 . . . Keturah, Abraham's **c,**
1 Chr 7:13 . . . of Jacob's **c** Bilhah.

CONDEMN, CONDEMNED, CONDEMNING, CONDEMNS (v) to declare guilty; to sentence or doom
Job 15:6 . . . Your own mouth **c-s** you, not I.
Job 40:8 . . . my justice and **c** me just to
Ps 37:33 . . . or let the godly be **c-ed**
Ps 102:20 . . . to release those **c-ed** to die.
Prov 12:2 . . . **c-s** those who plan wickedness.
Prov 17:15 . . . guilty and **c-ing** the innocent—
Isa 53:8 . . . Unjustly **c-ed,** he was led away.
Matt 12:7 . . . not have **c-ed** my innocent
Matt 12:37 . . . acquit you or **c** you.
Matt 12:41 . . . on judgment day and **c** it,
Matt 27:3 . . . Jesus had been **c-ed** to die,
Luke 11:31 . . . on judgment day and **c** it,
John 8:10 . . . even one of them **c** you?
Rom 2:1 . . . think you can **c** such people,
Rom 2:1 . . . you are **c-ing** yourself,
Rom 3:7 . . . how can God **c** me as a sinner
Rom 3:8 . . . deserve to be **c-ed.**
Rom 8:34 . . . Who then will **c** us? No one—
Rom 14:3 . . . foods must not **c** those who
Rom 14:13 . . . So let's stop **c-ing** each other.
1 Cor 4:9 . . . a victor's parade, **c-ed** to die.
2 Cor 7:3 . . . saying this to **c** you.
Col 2:16 . . . So don't let anyone **c** you
Jas 5:6 . . . You have **c-ed** and killed
Jas 5:12 . . . not sin and be **c-ed.**

CONDEMNATION (n) conviction of guilt; censure or blame
Rom 5:9 . . . save us from God's **c.**
Rom 5:18 . . . Adam's one sin brings **c**
Rom 7:13 . . . bring about my **c** to death.
Rom 8:1 . . . there is no **c** for those who
2 Cor 3:9 . . . which brings **c,** was glorious,

CONDUCT (n) a mode or standard of personal behavior especially as based on moral principles
Prov 20:11 . . . act, whether their **c** is pure,
Jer 32:19 . . . You see the **c** of all people,
Gal 6:5 . . . responsible for our own **c.**

CONDUCT, CONDUCTED, CONDUCTING (v) to cause (oneself) to act or behave in a particular and controlled manner; to direct or take part in the management or operation of
Exod 18:20 . . . them how to **c** their lives.
Ps 112:5 . . . lend money generously and **c**
2 Cor 1:12 . . . how we have **c-ed** ourselves
Phil 1:27 . . . of heaven, **c-ing** yourselves in a
1 Tim 3:15 . . . **c** themselves in the

CONFESS, CONFESSED, CONFESSES, CONFESSING (v) to admit or acknowledge (sin or faith)
1 Sam 7:6 . . . **c-ed** that they had sinned
Ezra 10:11 . . . So now **c** your sin to
Ps 32:3 . . . I refused to **c** my sin,
Ps 32:5 . . . Finally, I **c-ed** all my sins
Ps 38:18 . . . But I **c** my sins;
Ps 66:18 . . . If I had not **c-ed** the sin in my
Dan 9:4 . . . to the LORD my God and **c-ed:**
Dan 9:20 . . . praying and **c-ing** my sin
Matt 18:15 . . . **c-es** it, you have won
Mark 1:5 . . . And when they **c-ed** their sins,
Rom 10:10 . . . by **c-ing** with your mouth
Rom 14:11 . . . every tongue will **c** and give
Phil 2:11 . . . and every tongue **c** that Jesus
1 Tim 6:12 . . . which you have **c-ed** so well
Jas 5:16 . . . **C** your sins to each other
1 Jn 1:9 . . . But if we **c** our sins to him,

CONFESSION, CONFESSIONS (n) a disclosure of one's sins; a formal statement of religious beliefs
Ezra 10:1 . . . and made this **c,** weeping
Hos 14:2 . . . your **c-s,** and return

CONFIDENCE (n) faith or belief that one will act in a right, proper, or effective way; a feeling or consciousness of one's powers; a quality or state of being certain
Ps 146:3 . . . Don't put your **c** in powerful
Isa 30:15 . . . In quietness and **c** is your
2 Cor 8:22 . . . of his great **c** in you.
Phil 1:14 . . . believers here have gained **c**
Phil 2:24 . . . And I have **c** from the Lord
Phil 3:4 . . . I could have **c** in my own
Col 2:2 . . . want them to have complete **c**
1 Thes 5:8 . . . as our helmet the **c** of our
Titus 1:2 . . . This truth gives them **c**
Heb 11:1 . . . Faith is the **c** that what we
2 Pet 1:19 . . . we have even greater **c**
1 Jn 4:17 . . . but we can face him with **c**

CONFIDENT (adj) full of conviction, certain; trustful
Ps 27:13 . . . Yet I am **c** I will see the
Ps 57:7 . . . My heart is **c** in you, O God;
2 Cor 3:4 . . . We are **c** of all this
Eph 1:18 . . . can understand the **c** hope
Col 1:5 . . . **c** hope of what God has reserved
Col 4:12 . . . fully **c** that you are following
2 Thes 3:4 . . . And we are **c** in the Lord
Heb 3:6 . . . keep our courage and remain **c**

CONFIDENTLY (adv) acting with confidence
Ps 112:7 . . . they **c** trust the LORD
Rom 5:2 . . . we **c** and joyfully look forward
Eph 3:12 . . . boldly and **c** into God's

CONFIRM, CONFIRMED, CONFIRMING, CONFIRMS (v) to strengthen; to remove doubt by authoritative statement or action
Gen 6:18 . . . I will **c** my covenant with you.
Gen 9:17 . . . sign of the covenant I am **c-ing**
Gen 17:21 . . . will be **c-ed** with Isaac,
Heb 9:20 . . . This blood **c-s** the covenant

CONFLICT (n) fight, battle, war
Prov 13:10 . . . Pride leads to **c;**
Prov 17:1 . . . filled with feasting—and **c.**
Gal 3:21 . . . Is there a **c,** then, between

CONFUSED (v) to confound, stupify, perplex; the state of being confounded, stupified, perplexed
Gen 11:9 . . . where the Lord **c** the people
Matt 9:36 . . . they were **c** and helpless,
Rom 1:21 . . . their minds became dark and **c.**

CONGRATULATE (v) to express pleasure to (a person) on the occasion of success or good fortune
2 Sam 19:7 . . . go out there and **c** your troops,

CONGREGATION (n) an assembly or gathering (not church)
Ps 107:32 . . . exalt him publicly before the **c**

CONQUER, CONQUERED, CONQUERING (v) to gain or acquire by force of arms
see also OVERCOME
Gen 22:17 . . . descendants will **c** the cities
Num 13:30 . . . We can certainly **c** it!
Prov 16:32 . . . than to **c** a city.
Dan 2:44 . . . never be destroyed or **c-ed.**
Matt 16:18 . . . of hell will not **c** it.
Rom 12:21 . . . Don't let evil **c** you,
Col 2:23 . . . no help in **c-ing** a person's evil

CONQUEROR (n) one who subdues, defeats, or vanquishes
Mic 1:15 . . . I will bring a **c** to capture

CONSCIENCE, CONSCIENCES (n) one's moral sensitivity or scruples
2 Sam 24:10 . . . census, David's **c** began to
Acts 24:16 . . . maintain a clear **c** before God
Rom 14:2 . . . with a sensitive **c** will eat
1 Cor 8:7 . . . their weak **c-s** are violated.
1 Cor 8:10 . . . to violate their **c** by eating
1 Cor 10:25 . . . raising questions of **c.**
1 Tim 1:5 . . . a clear **c,** and genuine faith.
1 Tim 1:19 . . . and keep your **c** clear.
Titus 1:15 . . . minds and **c-s** are corrupted.
Heb 9:9 . . . are not able to cleanse the **c-s**
Heb 9:14 . . . will purify our **c-s** from sinful
Heb 10:22 . . . guilty **c-s** have been sprinkled
Heb 13:18 . . . for our **c** is clear
1 Pet 3:16 . . . Keep your **c** clear.
1 Pet 3:21 . . . to God from a clean **c.**

CONSCIENTIOUS (adj) scrupulous, meticulous, careful
2 Chr 29:34 . . . been more **c** about purifying

CONSECRATE, CONSECRATED (v) to devote irrevocably to God by a solemn ceremony; to make or declare sacred
see also DEDICATE, DEVOTE, ORDAINED
Exod 40:9 . . . all its furnishings to **c** them
Lev 19:24 . . . the entire crop must be **c-d**
2 Chr 29:31 . . . you have **c-d** yourselves

CONSIDER (v) to think about carefully; to come to judge or classify; to regard
Job 37:14 . . . Stop and **c** the wonderful
Rom 6:11 . . . **c** yourselves to be dead
Jas 1:2 . . . troubles come your way, **c** it

CONSIDERATE (adj) thoughtful of the rights and feelings of others
Phil 4:5 . . . see that you are **c** in all you

CONSOLE, CONSOLING (v) to alleviate the grief or sense of loss; to offer just reward
John 11:19 . . . had come to **c** Martha and Mary
John 11:31 . . . at the house **c-ing** Mary

CONSTANT (adj) marked by steadfast faithfulness; continually occurring or recurring
Ps 119:98 . . . they are my **c** guide.
Prov 27:15 . . . is as annoying as **c** dripping
Luke 18:5 . . . with her **c** requests!

CONSTRUCT (v) to build
1 Kgs 6:1 . . . he began to **c** the Temple

CONSULT (v) to ask the advice or opinion of; to confer
Gal 1:16 . . . rush out to **c** with any human

CONSUME, CONSUMED (v) to engage fully, engross
Ps 69:9 . . . Passion for your house has **c-d**
John 2:17 . . . Passion for God's house will **c**

CONTAIN (v) to keep within limits; to restrain or control
1 Kgs 8:27 . . . heavens cannot **c** you.
John 21:25 . . . world could not **c** the books

CONTAMINATE (v) to soil, corrupt, or infect
Jude 1:23 . . . the sins that **c** their lives.

CONTEMPT (n) the act of despising; arousing disgust, scorn, or disdain
Gen 25:34 . . . showed **c** for his rights
Ps 119:51 . . . The proud hold me in utter **c,**
Prov 18:3 . . . scandalous behavior brings **c.**
Mal 1:6 . . . ever shown **c** for your name?

CONTENT, CONTENTED (adj) feeling or showing satisfaction with one's possessions, status, or situation; pleased
Josh 7:7 . . . If only we had been **c**
1 Kgs 4:20 . . . They were very **c-ed,**
Prov 13:25 . . . godly eat to their hearts' **c,**
Luke 3:14 . . . And be **c** with your pay.
Phil 4:11 . . . I have learned how to be **c**
1 Tim 6:8 . . . food and clothing, let us be **c.**

CONTENTMENT (n) the quality or state of being contented
1 Tim 6:6 . . . godliness with **c** is

CONTINUAL (adj) continuing indefinitely in time
Prov 15:15 . . . life is a **c** feast.

CONTINUALLY (adv) in continual or steadily recurring manner
1 Chr 16:11 . . . **c** seek him.

CONTINUE, CONTINUED, CONTINUES (v) to maintain without interruption a condition, course, or action
Ps 100:5 . . . unfailing love **c-s** forever,
Jer 32:20 . . . have **c-d** to do
Acts 13:43 . . . **c** to rely on
Acts 14:22 . . . encouraged them to **c**
Rom 11:22 . . . if you **c** to trust in
Col 1:23 . . . But you must **c** to believe
Col 2:6 . . . you must **c** to follow
1 Tim 2:15 . . . assuming they **c** to live in
1 Jn 3:6 . . . who **c-s** to live in him
Rev 22:11 . . . **c** to be holy.

CONTRACT (n) a binding agreement between two or more persons or parties
Exod 21:8 . . . who broke the **c** with her.

CONTRIBUTIONS (n) a payment imposed by authorities for a special purpose; the act of giving to a common fund or store
Mark 12:43 . . . who are making **c.**

CONTRITE (adj) feeling or showing sorrow or remorse for a sin
see also HUMBLE, REPENTANT
Isa 66:2 . . . have humble and **c** hearts,

CONTROL, CONTROLS (v) to exercise restraining or directing influence over; to rule
Job 37:15 . . . know how God **c-s** the storm

Rom 6:12 . . . Do not let sin **c**
Rom 8:6 . . . letting the Spirit **c** your mind
Rom 8:8 . . . still under the **c** of
1 Cor 7:9 . . . they can't **c** themselves,
1 Cor 7:37 . . . and he can **c** his passion,
2 Cor 5:14 . . . Christ's love **c-s** us.
Jas 1:26 . . . but don't **c** your tongue,
Jas 3:2 . . . could also **c** ourselves
2 Pet 2:19 . . . a slave to whatever **c-s** you.

CONTROVERSY, CONTROVERSIES (n) a dispute or quarrel
Acts 26:3 . . . customs and **c-ies.**
1 Tim 2:8 . . . from anger and **c.**

CONVERTED (v) to bring over from one belief, view, or party to another
Acts 6:7 . . . priests were **c**, too.
Acts 15:3 . . . the Gentiles, too, were being **c.**

CONVICT, CONVICTED (v) to find or prove guilty of an offense
Prov 24:25 . . . for those who **c** the guilty;
John 7:51 . . . Is it legal to **c** a man
John 16:8 . . . he will **c** the world of
1 Cor 14:24 . . . they will be **c-ed** of sin
Jude 1:15 . . . He will **c** every person

CONVICTIONS (n) strongly held beliefs or principles
Rom 14:23 . . . you are not following your **c.**

CONVINCE, CONVINCED (v) to persuade to a belief, consent, or course of action
Exod 4:31 . . . people of Israel were **c-d**
Acts 18:4 . . . to **c** the Jews and Greeks
Rom 2:19 . . . are **c-d** that you are a guide
Rom 8:38 . . . I am **c-d** that nothing
Rom 14:14 . . . I know and am **c-d**
Rom 15:14 . . . I am fully **c-d,**
Phil 1:25 . . . I am **c-d** that I will

COPY (n) an imitation or reproduction of an original work; a duplicate
Heb 8:5 . . . that is only a **c,**
Heb 9:24 . . . was only a **c** of

COPY (v) to duplicate; to model oneself on
Deut 17:18 . . . he must **c** for himself
Rom 12:2 . . . Don't **c** the behavior and

CORD (n) a long, slender, flexible material usually consisting of several strands woven together
Eccl 4:12 . . . for a triple-braided **c**

CORNERSTONE (n) a stone forming a corner or angle in a wall; foundation
Ps 118:22 . . . now become the **c.**
Mark 12:10 . . . now become the **c.**
Acts 4:11 . . . now become the **c.**
Eph 2:20 . . . And the **c** is Christ
1 Pet 2:7 . . . now become the **c.**

CORRECT, CORRECTED, CORRECTING, CORRECTS (v) to set right with remedies, revisions, or reforms
Job 5:17 . . . joy of those **c-ed** by God!
Ps 141:5 . . . If they **c** me,
Prov 3:12 . . . For the LORD **c-s** those
Prov 9:8 . . . don't bother **c-ing** mockers;
Prov 19:25 . . . if you **c** the wise,
Jer 5:3 . . . refused to be **c-ed.**
Jer 10:24 . . . Do not **c** me in anger,
2 Tim 3:16 . . . It **c-s** us when we
2 Tim 4:2 . . . Patiently **c,** rebuke,
Titus 2:15 . . . the authority to **c** them
Heb 12:5 . . . give up when he **c-s** you.

CORRECTION (n) a rebuke or punishment; the action of making right
Prov 10:17 . . . those who ignore **c**
Prov 12:1 . . . it is stupid to hate **c.**
Prov 15:5 . . . learns from **c** is wise.
Prov 15:10 . . . whoever hates **c** will die.
Prov 15:32 . . . if you listen to **c,**
Zeph 3:2 . . . it refuses all **c.**

CORRUPT (adj) morally degenerate and perverted; depraved
Gen 6:11 . . . the earth had become **c**
Ps 14:1 . . . They are **c,**
Ps 14:3 . . . all have become **c.**
Prov 19:28 . . . A **c** witness
Luke 9:41 . . . faithless and **c** people!

CORRUPT, CORRUPTED, CORRUPTS (v) to change from good to bad, physically or morally
Eccl 7:7 . . . and bribes **c** the heart.
1 Cor 15:33 . . . bad company **c-s** good
Titus 1:15 . . . and consciences are **c-ed.**
Jas 1:27 . . . let the world **c** you.

CORRUPTION (n) impairment of integrity, virtue, or moral principle; depravity, decay
2 Pet 1:4 . . . the world's **c** caused
2 Pet 2:19 . . . slaves of sin and **c.**

CORRUPTLY (adv) marked by moral perversion and degeneracy
Deut 32:5 . . . they have acted **c**

COST (n) loss or penalty incurred especially in gaining something; price
Num 16:38 . . . sinned at the **c** of their lives,
Luke 14:28 . . . calculating the **c**

COST (v) to require effort, suffering, or loss
Prov 7:23 . . . it would **c** him his life.
Rev 6:6 . . . barley will **c** a day's pay.

COUNCIL (n) a group elected or appointed as an advisory or legislative body
Acts 17:19 . . . to the high **c** of the city.
Acts 17:22 . . . standing before the **c,**
Acts 17:34 . . . a member of the **c,**

COUNSEL (n) advice; policy, plan, or action
Ps 37:30 . . . godly offer good **c;**
Ps 73:24 . . . guide me with your **c,**
Ps 107:11 . . . scorning the **c** of the
Prov 27:9 . . . The heartfelt **c** of a friend
1 Cor 7:40 . . . I am giving you **c**

COUNSEL (v) to advise
Col 3:16 . . . Teach and **c** each other

COUNSELOR (n) one who gives advice or wisdom
see also ADVOCATE, HOLY SPIRIT
Isa 9:6 . . . Wonderful **C,** Mighty God,

COUNT, COUNTED, COUNTING, COUNTS (v) to number; to consider
Gen 15:6 . . . and the LORD **c-ed** him as
Ps 22:17 . . . I can **c** all my bones.
Ps 130:5 . . . yes, I am **c-ing** on him.
Ps 147:4 . . . He **c-s** the stars
Prov 20:25 . . . and only later **c-ing** the cost.
Acts 5:41 . . . **c-ed** them worthy to suffer
Rom 4:9 . . . Abraham was **c-ed** as righteous
Rom 4:24 . . . that God will also **c** us
Rom 5:13 . . . it was not **c-ed** as sin
2 Cor 5:19 . . . no longer **c-ing** people's sins
Gal 3:6 . . . and God **c-ed** him as righteous
Jas 2:23 . . . and God **c-ed** him as righteous

COUNTENANCE (KJV)
Gen 4:6 . . . Why do you *look* so dejected
Num 6:26 . . . LORD *show you his favor*
1 Sam 16:7 . . . Don't judge by his *appearance*
Prov 15:13 . . . glad heart makes a happy *face*
Luke 9:29 . . . *appearance of his face* was transformed

COURAGE (n) mental or moral strength
Judg 5:21 . . . March on with **c,** my soul!
2 Chr 15:8 . . . he took **c**
Dan 11:25 . . . stir up his **c** and raise a
Mark 6:50 . . . Take **c!** I am here!
Acts 27:22 . . . But take **c!**
Heb 3:6 . . . if we keep our **c**
Jas 5:8 . . . Take **c,** for the coming
1 Jn 2:28 . . . be full of **c** and not shrink

COURAGEOUS (adj) having or characterized by courage; brave
Deut 31:6 . . . So be strong and **c!**
Josh 1:6 . . . Be strong and **c,**
2 Sam 10:12 . . . Be **c!**
2 Chr 32:7 . . . Be strong and **c!**
Ps 31:24 . . . be strong and **c,**
1 Cor 16:13 . . . Be **c.**

COURT, COURTS (n) a place for the administration of justice; an open space enclosed by buildings
Ps 82:1 . . . presides over heaven's **c;**
Ps 84:10 . . . single day in your **c-s**
Ps 96:8 . . . come into his **c-s.**
Ps 100:4 . . . go into his **c-s**
Prov 22:22 . . . exploit the needy in **c.**
Prov 25:8 . . . to go to **c.**
Isa 3:13 . . . takes his place in **c**
Amos 5:15 . . . **c-s** into true halls of justice.
Zech 8:16 . . . verdicts in your **c-s**
Matt 5:25 . . . are on the way to **c**

COURTROOM (n) a room in which a court of law is held
Eccl 3:16 . . . evil in the **c.**

COURTYARD (n) enclosed area adjacent to a building
Exod 27:9 . . . make the **c** for the Tabernacle,
Exod 27:18 . . . the entire **c** will be 150 feet long
Matt 26:69 . . . sitting outside in the **c.**

COVENANT, COVENANTS (n) a mutual agreement or contract (between persons, between nations, or between God and humanity) with conditions and consequences spelled out
see also PROMISE, VOW
Gen 9:9 . . . hereby confirm my **c**
Gen 17:2 . . . I will make a **c** with you,
Exod 19:5 . . . and keep my **c,**
Deut 4:13 . . . He proclaimed his **c**—
Judg 2:1 . . . never break my **c**
1 Kgs 8:21 . . . which contains the **c**
2 Kgs 23:2 . . . Book of the **C**
2 Chr 6:14 . . . You keep your **c**
Neh 1:5 . . . keeps his **c** of unfailing love
Ps 105:8 . . . stands by his **c**—
Prov 2:17 . . . and ignores the **c**
Isa 61:8 . . . an everlasting **c** with them.
Jer 31:31 . . . make a new **c** with the people
Hos 10:4 . . . make **c-s** they don't intend
Mal 3:1 . . . messenger of the **c,**
Mark 14:24 . . . confirms the **c**
Luke 22:20 . . . new **c** between God and his
Rom 9:4 . . . He made **c-s** with them
1 Cor 11:25 . . . new **c** between God and his
2 Cor 3:6 . . . under the new **c,**
Heb 8:6 . . . a far better **c** with God,
Heb 9:15 . . . mediates a new **c** between
Heb 12:24 . . . the new **c** between God and

COVER (n) something that is placed over or about another thing; lid or top piece
Exod 25:17 . . . make the Ark's **c**—
Exod 25:21 . . . put the atonement **c**
Lev 16:2 . . . the atonement **c.**

COVER, COVERED, COVERING, COVERS (v) to hide from sight or knowledge; to lay or spread something over; to lie over
Gen 3:7 . . . to **c** themselves.
Exod 33:22 . . . and **c** you with my hand
Job 29:14 . . . Righteousness **c-ed** me
Ps 85:2 . . . you **c-ed** all their sins.
Ps 91:4 . . . He will **c** you with
Isa 6:2 . . . they **c-ed** their faces,
Matt 10:26 . . . everything that is **c-ed**
1 Cor 11:4 . . . if he **c-s** his head while
1 Cor 11:13 . . . without **c-ing** her head?
2 Cor 3:15 . . . their hearts are **c-ed**
Jas 3:14 . . . don't **c** up the truth
1 Pet 4:8 . . . love **c-s** a multitude of sins.

COVERING (n) something that covers or conceals
1 Cor 11:5 . . . without a **c** on her head,
1 Cor 11:15 . . . given to her as a **c.**

COVET, COVETED, COVETING (v) to inordinately desire unjust gain or another's property
see also DESIRE
Exod 20:17 . . . not **c** your neighbor's wife,
Exod 34:24 . . . so no one will **c**
Deut 7:25 . . . must not **c** the silver or gold
Acts 20:33 . . . **c-ed** anyone's silver or gold
Rom 7:7 . . . have known that **c-ing** is wrong
Rom 13:9 . . . You must not **c.**

COWARDS (n) one who shows disgraceful fear or timidity
Rev 21:8 . . . But **c**, unbelievers, the

COWS (n) the mature female of cattle
Gen 41:2 . . . he saw seven fat, healthy **c**

CRAFTSMAN, CRAFTSMEN (n) a worker who practices a trade or handicraft
Isa 45:16 . . . All **c-en** who make idols
Jer 10:3 . . . and a **c** carves an idol.

CRAFTSMANSHIP (n) the product of a craftsman that demonstrates his skill
Ps 19:1 . . . the skies display his **c.**

CRAVE, CRAVED, CRAVES (v) to want greatly; to yearn for
Num 11:4 . . . began to **c** the good things
Num 11:34 . . . people who had **c-d** meat
Ps 78:18 . . . the foods they **c-d.**
Ps 78:29 . . . gave them what they **c-d.**
Prov 31:4 . . . should not **c** alcohol.
Gal 5:16 . . . your sinful nature **c-s.**
1 Pet 2:2 . . . **c** pure spiritual milk
1 Jn 2:17 . . . everything that people **c.**

CRAVING (n) an intense, urgent, or abnormal desire or longing
Ps 78:30 . . . they satisfied their **c**,
Prov 10:3 . . . satisfy the **c** of the wicked.
1 Jn 2:16 . . . world offers only a **c**

CREATE, CREATED, CREATING (v) to bring into being; to form, make, or produce
see also FORMED, MADE, MAKE
Gen 1:1 . . . God **c-d** the heavens
Gen 1:27 . . . male and female he **c-d** them;
Gen 6:7 . . . human race I have **c-d** from
Ps 51:10 . . . **C** in me a clean heart
Ps 104:30 . . . life is **c-d**, and you renew
Prov 8:22 . . . before he **c-d** anything else.
Isa 43:1 . . . the LORD who **c-d** you.
Isa 43:7 . . . I who **c-d** them.
Isa 45:8 . . . I, the LORD, **c-d** them.
Isa 54:16 . . . I have **c-d** the blacksmith
Isa 65:17 . . . I am **c-ing** new heavens and
John 1:3 . . . **c-d** everything through him,
Rom 1:20 . . . since the world was **c-d,**
Rom 1:25 . . . served the things God **c-d**
Rom 9:20 . . . the thing that was **c-d** say
Eph 2:10 . . . He has **c-d** us anew
Eph 2:15 . . . by **c-ing** in himself
Eph 4:24 . . . **c-d** to be like God—
Col 1:16 . . . Everything was **c-d** through
1 Tim 4:3 . . . But God **c-d** those foods
Heb 1:2 . . . through the Son he **c-d**
1 Pet 4:19 . . . to the God who **c-d** you,
Rev 4:11 . . . For you **c-d** all things,
Rev 10:6 . . . who **c-d** the heavens

CREATION (n) something that is created; the world; the act of bringing the world into existence
Gen 2:3 . . . from all his work of **c.**
Mark 10:6 . . . from the beginning of **c.**
Rom 8:19 . . . For all **c** is waiting
Rom 8:39 . . . nothing in all **c** will ever
Gal 6:15 . . . into a new **c.**
Col 1:17 . . . holds all **c** together.
Heb 12:27 . . . all of **c** will be shaken
Jas 1:18 . . . we, out of all **c**,
Rev 3:14 . . . of God's new **c:**

CREATOR (n) maker; one who creates
see also MAKER
Gen 14:19 . . . God Most High, **C** of heaven
Job 40:19 . . . only its **C** can threaten
Eccl 12:1 . . . to forget your **C.**
Isa 40:28 . . . the **C** of all the earth.
Isa 45:9 . . . argue with their **C.**
Isa 51:13 . . . the LORD, your **C**,
Jer 51:19 . . . He is the **C** of everything
Rom 1:25 . . . instead of the **C** himself,
Eph 3:9 . . . the **C** of all things,
Eph 3:15 . . . the **C** of everything

CREATURE, CREATURES (n) something created either animate or inanimate
Lev 17:14 . . . the life of any **c** is in
Ps 104:24 . . . full of your **c-s.**

CREDIT (n) honor, recognition, or acknowledgment
Luke 6:33 . . . should you get **c?**
1 Pet 2:20 . . . no **c** for being patient

CRETE (n) an island in the Mediterranean Sea
Acts 27:12 . . . up the coast of **C**,
Titus 1:12 . . . "The people of **C** are all liars,

CRIME, CRIMES (n) a grave offense; criminal activity
Deut 22:26 . . . no **c** worthy of death
Judg 19:30 . . . Such a horrible **c** has
1 Sam 20:1 . . . What is my **c?** How have I
Job 31:11 . . . lust is a shameful sin, a **c**
Ps 52:1 . . . about your **c-s**, great warrior?
Luke 11:48 . . . join in their **c** by
Luke 23:41 . . . deserve to die for our **c-s,**

CRIMINAL, CRIMINALS (n) one who has broken the law
Ps 59:2 . . . Rescue me from these **c-s;**
Isa 53:9 . . . he was buried like a **c;**
Luke 23:32 . . . Two others, both **c-s,**

CRIMSON (n) any of several deep purplish reds
Isa 1:18 . . . Though they are red like **c**,

CRIPPLED (adj) lame, physically disabled
2 Sam 9:3 . . . He is **c** in both feet.
Luke 14:13 . . . invite the poor, the **c**, the lame,
Acts 14:8 . . . came upon a man with **c** feet.

CRITIC (n) one who expresses an opinion on a matter involving a judgment of its value, truth, righteousness, beauty, or technique
Job 40:2 . . . You are God's **c**, but do you

CRITICISM (n) a critical observation or remark; critique
Prov 15:31 . . . listen to constructive **c**,
Prov 25:12 . . . valid **c** is like a gold
Prov 28:23 . . . people appreciate honest **c**
Prov 29:1 . . . refuses to accept **c**
2 Cor 8:20 . . . guard against any **c**

CRITICIZE, CRITICIZED, CRITICIZING (v) to find fault with; to point out the faults of
Job 34:29 . . . who can **c** him?
Eccl 7:5 . . . be **c-d** by a wise person
Rom 14:16 . . . not be **c-d** for doing
Phil 2:15 . . . no one can **c** you.
Titus 2:8 . . . teaching can't be **c-d.**
Jas 4:11 . . . **c-ing** and judging God's law.

CROOKED (adj) not straight, twisted; dishonest, evil
Ps 125:5 . . . those who turn to **c** ways,
Prov 5:6 . . . staggers down a **c** trail
Prov 8:8 . . . nothing devious or **c** in it.
Prov 10:9 . . . those who follow **c** paths
Prov 21:8 . . . The guilty walk a **c** path;
Eccl 7:13 . . . what he has made **c?**
Isa 59:8 . . . have mapped out **c** roads,

CROP, CROPS (n) the product or yield after a harvest
Exod 23:16 . . . bring me the first **c-s**
Prov 28:3 . . . that destroys the **c-s.**
Hos 10:12 . . . harvest a **c** of love.
Matt 13:8 . . . they produced a **c** that was
Matt 21:41 . . . his share of the **c**

CROSS (n) an upright post used as an instrument of death in ancient times; the means by which atonement was made between God and humanity
Mark 8:34 . . . take up your **c**,
Luke 9:23 . . . take up your **c** daily,
Acts 2:23 . . . you nailed him to a **c**
Acts 5:30 . . . hanging him on a **c.**
1 Cor 1:18 . . . message of the **c** is
Gal 3:1 . . . death on the **c.**
Gal 6:12 . . . that the **c** of Christ alone
Phil 2:8 . . . criminal's death on a **c.**
Col 1:20 . . . Christ's blood on the **c.**
Heb 12:2 . . . he endured the **c**,
1 Pet 2:24 . . . his body on the **c**

CROSSED (v) to fold one (arm) over the other
Gen 48:14 . . . But Jacob **c** his arms

CROSSROADS (n) the place of intersection of two or more roads
Jer 6:16 . . . Stop at the **c** and look

CROUCHING (v) to lie close to the ground with the legs bent
Gen 4:7 . . . Sin is **c** at the door,

CROW, CROWED, CROWS (v) to make the loud shrill sound characteristic of a rooster
Matt 26:34 . . . before the rooster **c-s,**
Matt 26:74 . . . the rooster **c-ed.**

CROWD, CROWDS (n) a large number of persons especially when collected together
Exod 23:2 . . . by the **c** to twist justice.
Matt 9:36 . . . When he saw the **c-s,**
Heb 12:1 . . . such a huge **c** of witnesses
Rev 19:1 . . . like a vast **c** in heaven

CROWDED (v) to push or force
Mark 4:19 . . . the message is **c** out

CROWN, CROWNS (n) top of the head; a cap or headdress worn by victors, priests, or royalty
Prov 16:31 . . . Gray hair is a **c** of glory;
Song 3:11 . . . He wears the **c** his mother
Isa 61:3 . . . will give a **c** of beauty

Isa 62:3 . . . a splendid **c** in the hand
Zech 9:16 . . . like jewels in a **c.**
Matt 27:29 . . . thorn branches into a **c**
Mark 15:17 . . . thorn branches into a **c**
John 19:2 . . . wove a **c** of thorns
John 19:5 . . . wearing the **c** of thorns
Phil 4:1 . . . and the **c** I receive
1 Thes 2:19 . . . our proud reward and **c**
Jas 1:12 . . . will receive the **c** of life
Rev 2:10 . . . will give you the **c** of life.
Rev 3:11 . . . take away your **c.**
Rev 4:4 . . . had gold **c-s** on their heads.
Rev 4:10 . . . lay their **c-s** before the throne
Rev 12:3 . . . with seven **c-s** on his heads.
Rev 14:14 . . . He had a gold **c** on his head
Rev 19:12 . . . on his head were many **c-s.**

CROWNED, CROWNS (v) to place a crown on the head of; to bless or adorn
Ps 8:5 . . . and **c-ed** them with
Ps 149:4 . . . he **c-s** the humble
Prov 14:18 . . . are **c-ed** with knowledge.
Isa 51:11 . . . **c-ed** with everlasting joy.
Heb 2:7 . . . and **c-ed** them with
Heb 2:9 . . . **c-ed** with glory and honor.

CRUCIFIXION (n) the execution or death of a person on a cross
Matt 23:34 . . . you will kill some by **c,**
John 19:41 . . . The place of **c** was near

CRUCIFY, CRUCIFIED (v) to execute or nail to the cross; to put to death
Matt 26:2 . . . handed over to be **c-ied.**
Matt 27:22 . . . **C** him!
Matt 27:44 . . . who were **c-ied** with him
Mark 15:13 . . . **C** him!
Mark 15:27 . . . revolutionaries were **c-ied**
Mark 15:32 . . . who were **c-ied** with Jesus
Mark 16:6 . . . who was **c-ied.**
Luke 23:21 . . . **C** him! **C** him!
Luke 23:23 . . . that Jesus be **c-ied,**
Luke 23:33 . . . criminals were also **c-ied**—
Luke 24:20 . . . and they **c-ied** him.
John 19:6 . . . **C** him! **C** him!
John 19:10 . . . to release you or **c** you?
John 19:20 . . . where Jesus was **c-ied**
John 19:32 . . . the two men **c-ied** with Jesus.
Acts 4:10 . . . the man you **c-ied**
Rom 6:6 . . . were **c-ied** with Christ
1 Cor 1:13 . . . Was I, Paul, **c-ied** for you?
1 Cor 1:23 . . . preach that Christ was **c-ied,**
1 Cor 2:8 . . . would not have **c-ied**
2 Cor 13:4 . . . he was **c-ied** in weakness,
Gal 5:24 . . . and **c-ied** them there.
Rev 11:8 . . . where their Lord was **c-ied.**

CRUEL (adj) disposed to inflict pain or suffering; devoid of human feelings
2 Tim 3:3 . . . They will be **c** and hate
1 Pet 2:18 . . . even if they are **c.**

CRUELTY (n) the quality or state of being cruel; inhuman treatment
Prov 11:17 . . . your **c** will destroy you.

CRUSH, CRUSHED (v) to squeeze or force by pressure so as to alter or destroy; to oppress or burden grievously
Ps 34:18 . . . whose spirits are **c-ed.**
Prov 31:8 . . . justice for those being **c-ed.**
Isa 42:3 . . . will not **c** the weakest reed
Isa 42:13 . . . and **c** all his enemies.
Isa 53:5 . . . **c-ed** for our sins.
Matt 26:38 . . . My soul is **c-ed** with grief
Luke 10:19 . . . scorpions and **c** them.
Rom 16:20 . . . will soon **c** Satan
2 Cor 1:8 . . . We were **c-ed** and overwhelmed
2 Cor 4:8 . . . but we are not **c-ed.**

CRY, CRIES (n) entreaty, appeal; an inarticulate utterance of distress, rage, or pain
Exod 2:23 . . . their **c** rose up to God.
Ps 5:2 . . . Listen to my **c** for help,
Ps 34:15 . . . open to their **c-ies** for help.
Ps 40:1 . . . and heard my **c.**
Ps 142:6 . . . Hear my **c,** for I am
Prov 21:13 . . . to the **c-ies** of the poor

CRY, CRIED (v) to shout; to beg or beseech; to shed tears often noisily
Exod 14:10 . . . They **c-ied** out to the LORD,
Josh 24:7 . . . When your ancestors **c-ied** out
Judg 3:9 . . . people of Israel **c-ied** out
Judg 4:3 . . . people of Israel **c-ied** out
Judg 6:6 . . . Then the Israelites **c-ied** out
Judg 10:12 . . . you **c-ied** out to me
Ps 18:6 . . . in my distress I **c-ied** out
Eccl 3:4 . . . A time to **c** and a time
Lam 2:18 . . . **C** aloud before the LORD,
Hab 2:11 . . . walls **c** out against you,

CULTIVATE (v) to foster the growth of; to encourage
Job 4:8 . . . plant trouble and **c** evil

CUP (n) a drinking vessel; figurative of human vessel; token of tangible consolation, salvation of Christ, wrath of God, drunkenness, or fate
Ps 23:5 . . . My **c** overflows
Matt 26:39 . . . let this **c** of suffering
Matt 26:42 . . . If this **c** cannot be
Mark 10:39 . . . drink from my bitter **c**
Mark 14:23 . . . And he took a **c** of wine
Mark 14:36 . . . take this **c** of suffering
Luke 22:20 . . . This **c** is the new covenant
John 18:11 . . . from the **c** of suffering
1 Cor 10:16 . . . When we bless the **c**
1 Cor 10:21 . . . from the **c** of the Lord
1 Cor 11:25 . . . took the **c** of wine after
1 Cor 11:25 . . . This **c** is the new covenant

CUP-BEARER (n) one who tasted and served wine to a king
Gen 40:1 . . . Pharaoh's chief **c**
Neh 1:11 . . . I was the king's **c.**

CURE (n) recovery or relief from a disease; a complete or permanent solution
Jer 30:15 . . . wound that has no **c?**
Luke 8:43 . . . she could find no **c.**

CURE, CURED (v) to restore to health, soundness, or normality
Isa 30:26 . . . and **c** the wounds
Matt 11:5 . . . the lepers are **c-d,**
John 5:10 . . . said to the man who was **c-d,**

CURSE, CURSES, CURSING (n) a condemnation or judgment
Num 5:23 . . . priest will write these **c-s**
Josh 8:34 . . . blessings and **c-s** Moses had
Rom 8:20 . . . was subjected to God's **c.**
Gal 3:10 . . . right with God are under his **c,**
Gal 3:13 . . . the **c** for our wrongdoing.
Rom 3:14 . . . full of **c-ing** and bitterness.
Jas 3:10 . . . and **c-ing** come pouring out
Rev 22:3 . . . No longer will there be a **c**

CURSE, CURSES (v) to pronounce a sentence; to afflict; to call upon a supernatural power to bring injury upon; to utter profane language against
Gen 8:21 . . . will never again **c** the ground
Gen 12:3 . . . **c** those who treat you
Prov 3:33 . . . **c-s** the house of the wicked,
Matt 5:22 . . . And if you **c** someone,
Rom 12:14 . . . Don't **c** them;
1 Cor 12:3 . . . will **c** Jesus, and no one
Jas 3:9 . . . and sometimes it **c-s** those who

CURSED (adj) being under or deserving a curse
Gen 3:17 . . . the ground is **c** because
Deut 21:23 . . . anyone who is hung is **c**
Deut 27:16 . . . **C** is anyone who dishonors
Deut 27:18 . . . **C** is anyone who leads
Deut 27:20 . . . **C** is anyone who has sexual
Deut 27:24 . . . **C** is anyone who attacks a
Deut 27:26 . . . **C** is anyone who does not
Prov 28:27 . . . poverty will be **c.**
Gal 3:10 . . . **C** is everyone who does not
Gal 3:13 . . . **C** is everyone who is hung

CURTAIN (n) a hanging screen usually capable of being drawn back or up
Isa 40:22 . . . the heavens like a **c**
Mark 15:38 . . . And the **c** in the sanctuary

CUT OFF (v) separated; isolated
Gen 17:14 . . . fails to be circumcised will be **c**
Ps 31:22 . . . "I am **c** from the Lord!"
Prov 21:28 . . . false witness will be **c,** but a
Ezek 21:4 . . . will **c** both the righteous
Hos 10:7 . . . Samaria and its king will be **c**
Zech 13:8 . . . in the land will be **c** and die
Rom 9:3 . . . **c** from Christ!—if that
Gal 5:4 . . . keeping the law, you have been **c**

D

DAILY (adv) every day
Deut 17:19 . . . read it **d** as long as he
Acts 17:17 . . . spoke **d** in the public square

DAN 1. First son of Jacob and Bilhah (Gen 30:3-6), who gave his name to a tribe of Israel; his tribe was blessed (Gen 49:16-17; Deut 33:22), numbered (Num 1:39), allotted land and cities (Josh 19:40-47); took the town of Laish and renamed it Dan (Judg 18).
2. Town at the northern boundary of Israel (Judg 20:1), earlier known as Laish; captured and renamed by Danites (Josh 19:47); became a center for idolatry (1 Kgs 12:28-30); attacked by Ben-hadad (1 Kgs 15:20).

DANCE, DANCING (n) a series of rhythmic bodily movements usually performed to music
Ps 30:11 . . . into joyful **d-ing.**
Mark 6:22 . . . a **d** that greatly pleased

DANCE, DANCED (v) to move in a rhythmic manner, usually to music
2 Sam 6:14 . . . David **d-d** before the LORD
Eccl 3:4 . . . and a time to **d.**
Matt 11:17 . . . and you didn't **d,**

DANGER (n) harm or damage
Ps 57:1 . . . until the **d** passes by.
Prov 22:3 . . . prudent person foresees **d**
Matt 5:22 . . . in **d** of being brought
Rom 8:35 . . . or in **d,** or threatened
2 Cor 1:10 . . . did rescue us from mortal **d,**
2 Cor 11:26 . . . I have faced **d** from rivers

DANGEROUS (adj) able or likely to inflict injury or harm
Prov 29:25 . . . Fearing people is a **d** trap,

DANIEL 1. Prophet of Judah (southern kingdom), exiled to Babylon; also called "Belteshazzar" (Dan 1:6-7); refused food of the Babylonian court (Dan 1:8-17); interpreted dreams (Dan 2) and writing on a wall (Dan 5:12-29); survived in lion's den (Dan 6:1-23); recorded visions (Dan 7–12);

identified as a hero of renown (Ezek 14:14, 20; 28:3).
2. Son of David (1 Chr 3:1), also called "Kileab" (2 Sam 3:3).

DARK, DARKEST (adj) devoid or partially devoid of light; wholly or partially black
Exod 20:21 . . . approached the **d** cloud
Ps 23:4 . . . walk through the **d-est** valley,
Song 1:6 . . . because I am **d**—
Song 5:10 . . . My lover is **d** and dazzling,
Joel 2:31 . . . The sun will become **d,**
Acts 2:20 . . . The sun will become **d,**
2 Pet 1:19 . . . lamp shining in a **d** place—

DARKENED (v) to make dark
Matt 24:29 . . . the sun will be **d,**

DARKNESS (n) the state of being devoid of light; nightfall; in spiritual terms, secret, closed, blinded, or evil; place of punishment (hell)
Gen 1:2 . . . and **d** covered the deep waters.
Gen 1:4 . . . the light from the **d.**
Ps 18:28 . . . my God, lights up my **d.**
Matt 4:16 . . . people who sat in **d**
Luke 23:44 . . . it was about noon, and **d** fell
John 1:5 . . . light shines in the **d,**
John 3:19 . . . people loved the **d** more
John 12:35 . . . the **d** will not overtake
2 Cor 4:6 . . . Let there be light in the **d,**
2 Cor 6:14 . . . can light live with **d?**
Eph 5:8 . . . once you were full of **d,**
Eph 5:11 . . . deeds of evil and **d;**
1 Pet 2:9 . . . called you out of the **d**
1 Jn 1:5 . . . there is no **d** in him at all.
1 Jn 2:9 . . . is still living in **d.**
Jude 1:6 . . . chained in prisons of **d,**

DARLING (n) a dearly loved person
Song 2:10 . . . Rise up, my **d!**
Jer 31:20 . . . my son, my **d** child?" says

DAUGHTER, DAUGHTERS (n) the female offspring or adopted offspring of parents
Gen 19:36 . . . Lot's **d-s** became pregnant
Num 36:10 . . . The **d-s** of Zelophehad
Judg 11:40 . . . the fate of Jephthah's **d.**
Esth 2:7 . . . raised her as his own **d.**
Joel 2:28 . . . sons and **d-s** will prophesy.
Mark 5:34 . . . said to her, "**D,** your faith
Mark 7:29 . . . the demon has left your **d.**

DAVID King of Israel (united kingdom); son of Jesse, in the family line of Jesus (Ruth 4:17-22; Matt 1:1; Luke 3:31); anointed king (1 Sam 16:1-13); skillful musician to Saul (1 Sam 16:14-23; 18:10); David and Goliath (1 Sam 17); faithful friendship with Jonathan (1 Sam 18:1-4); envied by Saul; loved by the people (1 Sam 18:5-16); married Michal (1 Sam 18:17-30); wives and children (2 Sam 3:2-5; 5:13-16; 1 Chr 3:1-9); fled from Saul (1 Sam 19–23); ate used "Bread of the Presence" (1 Sam 21:1-6; Matt 12:3-4); dealings with the Philistines (1 Sam 21:10-14; 27–30); spared Saul twice (1 Sam 22–24; 26); married widow Abigail (1 Sam 25:2-42); lamented death of Saul and Jonathan (2 Sam 1); contended with Saul's dynasty (2 Sam 2–4); anointed king of Judah (2 Sam 2:1-7); lamented Abner's death (2 Sam 3:31-39); made king over all Israel (2 Sam 5:1-5); victories over the Philistines (2 Sam 5:17-25; 21:15-22; 1 Chr 14:8-17; 20:4-8); made Jerusalem the royal city (2 Sam 5:6-16); moved Ark to Jerusalem (2 Sam 6); eternal covenant with God (2 Sam 7; 1 Chr 17); showed loyal love to Mephibosheth (2 Sam 9); committed adultery with Bathsheba (2 Sam 11–12; Pss 32; 51); plotted Uriah's death (2 Sam 11:14-25); rebuked by Nathan (2 Sam 12:1-12); repented of affair and intrigue (2 Sam 12:13); rebellion and death of Absalom (2 Sam 14–18); lamented Absalom's death (2 Sam 18:33–19:8); rebellion and death of Sheba (2 Sam 20); judged for taking census (2 Sam 24:1-25); made Solomon next king (1 Kgs 1:28–2:9); final words to Solomon (1 Kgs 2:1-9); died (1 Kgs 2:10-12); preparations for the Temple (1 Chr 22–29).

DAWN (n) first appearance of light in the morning followed by sunrise
Exod 14:24 . . . But just before **d** the LORD
Ps 37:6 . . . radiate like the **d,** and the
Prov 4:18 . . . gleam of **d,** which shines ever
Prov 31:15 . . . gets up before **d** to prepare
Amos 4:13 . . . the light of **d** into darkness
Acts 20:11 . . . talking to them until **d,**

DAWNS (v) to begin to grow light as the sun rises
Hos 10:15 . . . day of judgment **d,** the king
2 Pet 1:19 . . . until the Day **d,** and Christ

DAY, DAYS (n) the time of light between one night and the next; a specified time or period; a 24-hour time period
Gen 1:5 . . . called the light "**d**" and the
Gen 2:2 . . . On the seventh **d** God had
Exod 16:30 . . . the seventh **d.**
Lev 23:28 . . . it is the **D** of Atonement,
Josh 1:8 . . . Meditate on it **d** and night so
2 Kgs 7:9 . . . This is a **d** of good news,
Ps 23:6 . . . pursue me all the **d-s** of my life,
Ps 84:10 . . . A single **d** in your
Ps 118:24 . . . This is the **d** the LORD has
Isa 13:9 . . . coming—the terrible **d** of his
Jer 46:10 . . . this is the **d** of the LORD,
Jer 50:31 . . . Your **d** of reckoning
Hos 3:5 . . . In the last **d-s,** they will
Joel 1:15 . . . How terrible that **d** will be!
Joel 2:31 . . . great and terrible **d** of the
Amos 5:20 . . . Yes, the **d** of the LORD
Zeph 1:14 . . . That terrible **d** of the
Zech 14:1 . . . Watch, for the **d** of the LORD
Zech 14:7 . . . be continuous **d!**
Mal 4:5 . . . great and dreadful **d** of the
Matt 24:38 . . . In those **d-s** before the
Luke 11:3 . . . Give us each **d** the food we
Acts 2:17 . . . 'In the last **d-s,**' God says,
Rom 14:5 . . . some think one **d** is more holy
1 Cor 5:5 . . . be saved on the **d** the Lord
2 Cor 4:16 . . . renewed every **d.**
1 Thes 5:2 . . . the **d** of the Lord's return
1 Thes 5:4 . . . surprised when the **d** of the
2 Thes 2:2 . . . say that the **d** of the Lord
2 Tim 3:1 . . . in the last **d-s** there will be
Heb 1:2 . . . now in these final **d-s,** he has
2 Pet 3:3 . . . in the last **d-s** scoffers will
2 Pet 3:10 . . . But the **d** of the Lord
Rev 16:14 . . . that great judgment **d** of God

DAZZLING (adj) characterized by shining brilliantly or arousing admiration
Job 37:22 . . . is clothed in **d** splendor.
Song 5:10 . . . My lover is dark and **d,**
Mark 9:3 . . . his clothes became **d** white,

DEACON, DEACONS (n) a servant; an officer of the church
see also ELDERS
Phil 1:1 . . . the elders and **d-s.**
1 Tim 3:8 . . . **d-s** must be well respected
1 Tim 3:10 . . . they are appointed as **d-s,**
1 Tim 3:12 . . . A **d** must be faithful
1 Tim 3:13 . . . Those who do well as **d-s**

DEAD (n) the state of being dead (physically or spiritually); (un)believers who have died
Matt 8:22 . . . the spiritually **d** bury their
Luke 24:46 . . . rise from the **d** on the third
1 Cor 15:29 . . . If the **d** will not
Rev 20:12 . . . I saw the **d,** both great and

DEAD (adj) without (physical or spiritual) life; fatal; useless; unresponsive
Rom 6:11 . . . be **d** to the power of sin
Eph 2:1 . . . Once you were **d** because of
Jas 2:17 . . . good deeds, it is **d** and useless.
1 Pet 2:24 . . . that we can be **d** to sin and
Rev 2:8 . . . Last, who was **d** but is now

DEAF (adj) lacking or deficient in the sense of hearing
Ps 94:9 . . . Is he **d**—the one who made

DEAR (adj) highly valued; precious
1 Cor 10:14 . . . my **d** friends, flee from
2 Cor 7:1 . . . these promises, **d** friends,
Eph 5:1 . . . you are his **d** children.
2 Tim 1:2 . . . to Timothy, my **d** son.
Jas 1:16 . . . don't be misled, my **d** brothers
1 Jn 4:4 . . . to God, my **d** children.
3 Jn 1:1 . . . to Gaius, my **d** friend, whom I
Jude 1:20 . . . But you, **d** friends, must

DEATH (n) the cessation of (physical or spiritual) life; personification and consequence of evil
Exod 21:12 . . . must be put to **d.**
Ruth 1:17 . . . anything but **d** to separate
Prov 11:19 . . . evil people find **d.**
Prov 14:12 . . . it ends in **d.**
Prov 23:14 . . . save them from **d.**
Isa 38:17 . . . have rescued me from **d**
Acts 2:24 . . . for **d** could not keep him
Rom 5:12 . . . brought **d,** so **d** spread to
Rom 6:23 . . . the wages of sin is **d,**
Rom 7:24 . . . dominated by sin and **d?**
1 Cor 15:21 . . . see, just as **d** came into the
1 Cor 15:26 . . . enemy to be destroyed is **d.**
2 Cor 3:6 . . . written covenant ends in **d;**
Gal 3:1 . . . the meaning of Jesus Christ's **d**
2 Tim 1:10 . . . power of **d** and illuminated
Heb 2:14 . . . the power of **d.**
Heb 9:17 . . . after the person's **d.**
1 Jn 5:16 . . . there is a sin that leads to **d,**
Rev 2:11 . . . by the second **d.**
Rev 20:6 . . . them the second **d** holds no
Rev 20:14 . . . is the second **d.**
Rev 21:4 . . . be no more **d** or sorrow or
Rev 21:8 . . . This is the second **d.**

DEBATERS (n) one who contends or argues
1 Cor 1:20 . . . world's brilliant **d?**

DEBAUCHERY (KJV)
Rom 13:13 . . . promiscuity and *immoral living*
2 Cor 12:21 . . . *eagerness for lustful pleasure*
Gal 5:19 . . . impurity, *lustful pleasures*
1 Pet 4:3 . . . their *immorality* and lust, their

DEBT, DEBTS (n) what is owing; sense of obligation
Deut 15:1 . . . cancel the **d-s** of everyone
Deut 15:3 . . . This release from **d,** however,
Deut 15:9 . . . year for canceling **d-s** is close
1 Sam 22:2 . . . trouble or in **d** or who were
2 Kgs 4:7 . . . pay your **d-s,** and
Prov 22:26 . . . another person's **d** or put up
Neh 10:31 . . . will cancel all **d-s** owed to us.
Matt 18:25 . . . to pay the **d.**
Matt 18:27 . . . and forgave his **d.**
Matt 18:30 . . . in prison until the **d** could
Matt 18:32 . . . you that tremendous **d**
Luke 7:42 . . . canceling their **d-s.**
Luke 7:43 . . . canceled the larger **d.**

DEBTORS (n) one who owes a debt
Hab 2:7 . . . Suddenly, your **d** will take

DECAY (n) a wasting or wearing away
Rom 8:21 . . . freedom from death and **d.**
1 Pet 1:4 . . . the reach of change and **d.**

DECAY, DECAYED (v) to undergo decomposition
Job 19:26 . . . my body has **d-ed,** yet in my
Acts 13:37 . . . whose body did not **d.**

DECEIT (n) fraud; trickery; lying
Mark 7:22 . . . greed, wickedness, **d,** lustful
Acts 13:10 . . . of every sort of **d** and fraud,
1 Pet 2:1 . . . done with all **d,** hypocrisy,

DECEITFUL (adj) not honest; misleading, deceptive
Isa 59:13 . . . planning our **d** lies.
2 Cor 11:13 . . . They are **d** workers who

DECEIVE, DECEIVED, DECEIVES, DECEIVING (v) to lead astray; to cause to accept as true what is false
Gen 3:13 . . . "The serpent **d-d** me," she
Prov 10:31 . . . the tongue that **d-s** will be
Prov 14:8 . . . but fools **d** themselves.
Prov 26:24 . . . but they're **d-ing** you.
Matt 24:24 . . . so as to **d,** if possible, even
Mark 13:6 . . . They will **d** many.
Rom 7:11 . . . those commands and **d-d** me;
Rom 16:18 . . . they **d** innocent people.
1 Cor 3:18 . . . Stop **d-ing** yourselves.
2 Cor 11:3 . . . as Eve was **d-d** by the cunning
Col 2:4 . . . so no one will **d** you with
1 Tim 2:14 . . . The woman was **d-d,** and sin
2 Tim 3:13 . . . They will **d** others and will
2 Tim 3:13 . . . will themselves be **d-d.**
Heb 3:13 . . . you will be **d-d** by sin
Rev 20:3 . . . Satan could not **d** the nations
Rev 20:10 . . . devil, who had **d-d** them, was

DECEIVER, DECEIVERS (n) one who leads astray; one who causes another to accept as true what is false
Ps 101:7 . . . will not allow **d-s** to serve in
Matt 27:63 . . . remember what that **d** once said
2 Jn 1:7 . . . because many **d-s** have gone
2 Jn 1:7 . . . Such a person is a **d** and an

DECENT (adj) conforming to the standards of propriety or morality; modest
1 Tim 2:9 . . . should wear **d** and appropriate

DECEPTION (n) something that deceives; trick; the act of deceiving
Isa 28:15 . . . refuge made of lies and **d.**
Dan 8:25 . . . He will be a master of **d**
Rom 1:29 . . . quarreling, **d,** malicious
Eph 4:22 . . . corrupted by lust and **d.**
2 Thes 2:10 . . . kind of evil **d** to fool those
1 Jn 4:6 . . . truth or spirit of **d.**

DECEPTIVE (adj) tending or having power to deceive; misleading
Prov 31:30 . . . Charm is **d,** and beauty
1 Tim 4:1 . . . will follow **d** spirits and

DECIDE, DECIDED, DECIDES (v) to make a final choice or judgment about; to select as a course of action
1 Sam 14:7 . . . whatever you **d.**
Job 14:5 . . . You have **d-d** the length of
Ps 75:7 . . . he **d-s** who will rise and
Rom 14:13 . . . **D** instead to live
Rom 14:22 . . . they have **d-d** is right.
1 Cor 2:2 . . . For I **d-d** that while I
1 Cor 6:2 . . . can't you **d** even these
1 Cor 12:11 . . . He alone **d-s** which gift
2 Cor 9:7 . . . You must each **d** in your heart

DECISION, DECISIONS (n) a determination arrived at after consideration; conclusion
Joel 3:14 . . . waiting in the valley of **d.**
Mic 3:11 . . . You rulers make **d-s** based on
Rom 11:33 . . . to understand his **d-s** and his

DECLARE, DECLARED, DECLARING (v) to make known formally, officially, or explicitly; to state emphatically, affirm; to make evident, show
Deut 25:1 . . . and the judges **d** that one is
Ps 71:8 . . . praising you; I **d** your glory
Ps 92:15 . . . They will **d,** "The LORD
Prov 31:31 . . . deeds publicly **d** her praise.
Dan 4:24 . . . what the Most High has **d-d**
Mark 7:19 . . . saying this, he **d-d** that every
Acts 20:27 . . . didn't shrink from **d-ing** all that
Rom 4:6 . . . who are **d-d** righteous without
Heb 3:1 . . . Jesus whom we **d** to be God's

DECREE, DECREES (n) an order usually having the force of law; a foreordaining will
Exod 15:25 . . . them the following **d**
Exod 15:26 . . . and keeping all his **d-s,** then I
Exod 18:20 . . . Teach them God's **d-s,**
Lev 18:4 . . . to obey my **d-s,** for I am the
Num 15:15 . . . to the same **d-s.**
Deut 4:1 . . . to these **d-s** and regulations
1 Kgs 3:3 . . . and followed all the **d-s** of his
1 Chr 16:17 . . . it to Jacob as a **d,**
Ps 2:7 . . . proclaims the LORD's **d:**
Ps 119:12 . . . LORD; teach me your **d-s.**
Ps 119:54 . . . Your **d-s** have
Ps 148:6 . . . His **d** will never be

DECREED (v) to determine or order judicially; to command by or as if by decree
Dan 9:24 . . . sets of seven has been **d**
Luke 2:1 . . . Augustus, **d** that a census

DEDICATE, DEDICATED (v) to devote to the worship of a divine being; to set apart to a definite use
see also CONSECRATE, DEVOTE, ORDAINED
Exod 13:2 . . . **D** to me every firstborn
Num 6:9 . . . the hair they have **d-d** will be
Num 6:18 . . . the hair that had been **d-d**
Num 18:6 . . . a gift to you, **d-d** to the LORD
1 Kgs 8:63 . . . Israel **d-d** the Temple
Neh 3:1 . . . which they **d-d,** and the Tower
Luke 2:23 . . . he must be **d-d** to the LORD.

DEDICATION (n) an act or rite of dedicating to a diving being or to sacred use
John 10:22 . . . the Festival of **D.**

DEED, DEEDS (n) a signed instrument containing some legal transfer, bargain, or contract; a usually illustrious act or action; feat, exploit
see also WORKS
Ps 45:4 . . . perform awe-inspiring **d-s!**
Ps 66:3 . . . awesome are your **d-s!**
Ps 71:24 . . . your righteous **d-s** all day
Ps 88:12 . . . your wonderful **d-s?**
Ps 96:3 . . . his glorious **d-s** among the
Ps 105:2 . . . his wonderful **d-s.**
Prov 31:31 . . . Let her **d-s** publicly declare
Isa 64:6 . . . our righteous **d-s,** they are
Jer 32:10 . . . and sealed the **d** of purchase
Matt 5:16 . . . let your good **d-s** shine out for
Rom 4:2 . . . If his good **d-s** had made him
2 Cor 9:9 . . . Their good **d-s** will be
Col 3:9 . . . all its wicked **d-s.**
Jas 2:18 . . . my faith by my good **d-s.**
Jas 2:20 . . . without good **d-s** is useless?

DEEP, DEEPER (adj) extending far downward from some surface or area; situated well within the boundaries; difficult to penetrate or comprehend
Gen 1:2 . . . covered the **d** waters.
Rom 6:19 . . . which led ever **d-er** into sin.
1 Cor 2:10 . . . shows us God's **d** secrets.

DEEPLY (adv) in an intense, profound manner
Ps 116:15 . . . The LORD cares **d**
Isa 66:11 . . . Drink **d** of her glory

DEER (n) a mammal with usually brownish fur and antlers borne by the males
Ps 42:1 . . . As the **d** longs for streams of

DEFEAT (n) an overthrow especially of an army in battle; loss, destruction
Ps 25:2 . . . enemies rejoice in my **d.**
1 Cor 6:7 . . . with one another is a **d**

DEFEAT, DEFEATED, DEFEATS (v) to destroy; to win victory over
Ps 129:2 . . . they have never **d-d** me.
1 Jn 5:4 . . . child of God **d-s** this evil
Rev 12:11 . . . And they have **d-d** him by the
Rev 17:14 . . . the Lamb will **d** them

DEFEND, DEFENDING, DEFENDS (v) to maintain or support in the face of argument or hostile criticism; to drive danger or attack away from
Deut 33:7 . . . strength to **d** their cause;
Ps 10:14 . . . You **d** the orphans.
Ps 34:7 . . . he surrounds and **d-s** all who
Ps 72:4 . . . Help him to **d** the poor,
Ps 106:8 . . . saved them—to **d** the honor of
Phil 1:7 . . . and in **d-ing** and confirming the
Phil 1:16 . . . been appointed to **d** the Good
Jude 1:3 . . . urging you to **d** the faith

DEFENDER (n) one who guards and protects
Ps 68:5 . . . the fatherless, **d** of widows—
Prov 22:23 . . . the LORD is their **d.**
Isa 51:22 . . . your God and **D,** says:

DEFENSE (n) the act of defending
Ps 35:23 . . . Rise to my **d!**

DEFIED, DEFYING (v) to challenge to combat, dare; to disregard
1 Sam 17:45 . . . whom you have **d-ied.**
Isa 37:23 . . . Whom have you been **d-ing**

DEFILE, DEFILED, DEFILES, DEFILING (v) to make unclean—either physically, sexually, ethically, or ceremonially
Num 6:7 . . . must not **d** themselves,
Num 15:39 . . . desires and **d-ing** yourselves,
Ezek 23:7 . . . idols and **d-ing** herself.
Ezek 44:7 . . . In this way, you **d-d** my Temple
Matt 15:11 . . . you are **d-d** by the words
Mark 7:23 . . . they are what **d** you.
Acts 21:28 . . . even **d-s** this holy place
2 Cor 7:1 . . . that can **d** our body or

DEFLECTS (v) to turn aside; deviate
Prov 15:1 . . . A gentle answer **d** anger,

DELAY (n) the state of being delayed; putting off; wait
Rev 10:6 . . . There will be no more **d.**

DELAY, DELAYED (v) to put off; to postpone
Eccl 5:4 . . . don't **d** in following through,
Matt 25:5 . . . When the bridegroom was **d-ed,**
Heb 10:37 . . . will come and not **d.**

DELIBERATE (adj) characterized by awareness of the consequences
Ps 19:13 . . . servant from **d** sins!

DELICACIES (n) indulgences; something pleasing to eat that is considered rare or luxurious
Ps 141:4 . . . share in the **d** of those who
Prov 23:6 . . . don't desire their **d.**

DELIGHT, DELIGHTS (n) source of great pleasure; joy
Ps 36:8 . . . your river of **d-s.**
Ps 40:6 . . . You take no **d** in sacrifices
Ps 119:111 . . . they are my heart's **d.**
Prov 8:30 . . . I was his constant **d,**
Isa 58:13 . . . and speak of it with **d**
Jer 15:16 . . . my joy and my heart's **d,**
Mal 3:12 . . . your land will be such a **d,**
Mark 12:37 . . . to him with great **d.**

DELIGHT, DELIGHTED, DELIGHTING, DELIGHTS (v) to enjoy
Exod 4:14 . . . He will be **d-ed** to see you.
2 Sam 22:20 . . . because he **d-s** in me.
Ps 1:2 . . . But they **d** in the law of
Ps 18:19 . . . he rescued me because he **d-s**
Ps 27:4 . . . **d-ing** in the LORD's
Ps 37:4 . . . Take **d** in the LORD,
Ps 119:70 . . . I **d** in your instructions.
Prov 3:12 . . . a child in whom he **d-s.**
Prov 11:1 . . . he **d-s** in accurate weights.
Prov 11:20 . . . he **d-s** in those with integrity.
Song 8:10 . . . he is **d-ed** with what he sees.
Isa 11:3 . . . He will **d** in obeying
Isa 65:19 . . . and **d** in my people.
Isa 66:3 . . . **d-ing** in their detestable sins—
Jer 9:24 . . . I **d** in these things.

DELIGHTFUL (adj) highly pleasing
Prov 3:17 . . . guide you down **d** paths;
Song 2:3 . . . sit in his **d** shade and taste

DELIVER (v) to save, liberate, set free from
Ps 82:4 . . . **d** them from the grasp of evil
2 Tim 4:18 . . . **d** me from every evil attack

DELIVERANCE (n) freedom from harm, salvation
Esth 4:14 . . . **d** and relief for the Jews will arise
Isa 51:1 . . . "Listen to me, all who hope for **d**
Phil 1:19 . . . this will lead to my **d.**

DEMON-POSSESSED (adj) characterized by the possession or control of demons
Matt 4:24 . . . if they were **d** or epileptic
Matt 8:16 . . . That evening many **d** people
Matt 8:33 . . . happened to the **d** men.
Matt 9:32 . . . When they left, a **d** man who
Matt 12:22 . . . Then a **d** man, who was
Mark 1:32 . . . many sick and **d** people were
Mark 5:16 . . . about the **d** man and
Luke 8:36 . . . others how the **d** man had

DEMON, DEMONS (n) an agent of the Devil; an evil spirit
Deut 32:17 . . . They offered sacrifices to **d-s,**
Matt 8:31 . . . So the **d-s** begged, "If you cast
Matt 9:34 . . . by the prince of **d-s.**
Matt 11:18 . . . He's possessed by a **d.**
Matt 12:24 . . . he can cast out **d-s.**
Matt 12:28 . . . if I am casting out **d-s** by the
Matt 17:18 . . . Jesus rebuked the **d**
Mark 1:34 . . . But because the **d-s** knew who
Mark 5:15 . . . by the legion of **d-s.**
Mark 5:18 . . . been **d** possessed begged
Mark 7:29 . . . the **d** has left your daughter.
Mark 9:38 . . . to cast out **d-s,** but we told
Mark 16:9 . . . cast out seven **d-s.**
Mark 16:17 . . . will cast out **d-s** in my name,
Luke 4:33 . . . possessed by a **d**—an evil
Luke 7:33 . . . He's possessed by a **d.**
Luke 8:2 . . . he had cast out seven **d-s;**
Luke 8:30 . . . with many **d-s.**
Luke 8:33 . . . Then the **d-s** came out of the
Luke 8:38 . . . freed from the **d-s** begged
Luke 9:49 . . . to cast out **d-s,** but we told
Luke 10:17 . . . Lord, even the **d-s** obey us
Luke 11:14 . . . Jesus cast out a **d** from
Luke 11:19 . . . They cast out **d-s,** too, so they
Luke 11:20 . . . casting out **d-s** by the power
John 8:49 . . . Jesus said, "I have no **d** in me.
John 10:21 . . . possessed by a **d!**
Rom 8:38 . . . neither angels nor **d-s,**
1 Cor 10:20 . . . to participate with **d-s.**
1 Cor 10:21 . . . the cup of **d-s,** too.
1 Cor 10:21 . . . the table of **d-s,** too.
1 Tim 4:1 . . . teachings that come from **d-s.**
Rev 9:20 . . . to worship **d-s** and idols made
Rev 18:2 . . . become a home for **d-s.**

DEMONIC (adj) of, relating to, or suggestive of a demon
Jas 3:15 . . . unspiritual, and **d.**
Rev 16:14 . . . They are **d** spirits who work

DEMONSTRATE (v) to show clearly
Ezek 39:21 . . . **d** my glory to the nations.
Rom 3:26 . . . to **d** his righteousness,

DEN (n) the lair of a wild, usually predatory, animal; a center of secret activity
Dan 6:16 . . . thrown into the **d** of lions.
Matt 21:13 . . . into a **d** of thieves!

DENY, DENIED, DENIES (v) to disavow or refuse to accept as true; to refuse to grant
Exod 23:6 . . . you must not **d** justice to the
Deut 27:19 . . . is anyone who **d-ies** justice
Prov 30:9 . . . I may **d** you and say,
Matt 10:33 . . . everyone who **d-ies** me
Matt 26:35 . . . I will never **d** you!
Matt 26:70 . . . But Peter **d-ied** it
Luke 12:9 . . . anyone who **d-ies** me
Luke 22:34 . . . you will **d** three times
John 18:25 . . . He **d-ied** it, saying,
Acts 4:16 . . . We can't **d** that they
1 Tim 5:8 . . . have **d-ied** the true faith.
2 Tim 2:12 . . . **d** him, he will **d** us.
Titus 1:16 . . . **d** him by the way they live.
2 Pet 2:1 . . . and even **d** the Master who
1 Jn 2:22 . . . Anyone who **d-ies** the Father
1 Jn 2:23 . . . Anyone who **d-ies** the Son
Jude 1:4 . . . they have **d-ied** our only Master
Rev 3:8 . . . and did not **d** me.

DEPEND (v) to place reliance or trust
Prov 3:5 . . . do not **d** on your own
Jer 49:11 . . . widows, too, can **d** on me
Gal 3:10 . . . But those who **d** on the law

DEPOSIT (v) to place especially for safekeeping
Matt 25:27 . . . why didn't you **d** my money in

DEPRAVED (adj) characterized by moral corruption or evil; perverted
2 Tim 3:8 . . . They have **d** minds and

DEPRESSION (n) a state of feeling sad; dejection
Ps 143:7 . . . answer me, for my **d** deepens.

DEPRIVE (v) to withhold something from; to remove
Isa 10:2 . . . They **d** the poor
1 Cor 7:5 . . . Do not **d** each other of

DEPTHS (n) a deep place in a body of water; the quality of being deep
Ps 130:1 . . . From the **d** of despair,
Mic 7:19 . . . them into the **d** of the ocean!

DESCENDANT, DESCENDANTS (n) those who came or originated from; offspring, children
see also OFFSPRING, SON(S)
Gen 12:7 . . . give this land to your **d-s.**
Gen 13:16 . . . will give you so many **d-s** that,
Gen 17:9 . . . You and all your **d-s** have this
Deut 30:19 . . . you and your **d-s** might live!
Isa 53:8 . . . he died without **d-s,** that his
Isa 53:10 . . . he will have many **d-s.**
Jer 23:5 . . . I will raise up a righteous **d**
Matt 1:1 . . . the Messiah, a **d** of David and
Acts 3:25 . . . Through your **d-s** all the
Rom 4:18 . . . That's how many **d-s** you will
Rom 9:8 . . . Abraham's physical **d-s** are not

DESCEND, DESCENDED, DESCENDING (v) to pass from a higher place or level to a lower one
Matt 3:16 . . . Spirit of God **d-ing** like a dove
Mark 1:10 . . . the Holy Spirit **d-ing** on him like
Eph 4:9 . . . that Christ also **d-ed** to our

DESECRATE, DESECRATED (v) to profane something holy or treat it with contempt
Neh 13:18 . . . Sabbath to be **d-d** in this way!
Isa 56:6 . . . and do not **d** the Sabbath day

DESECRATION (n) violation of something sacred; profanation; blasphemy
Dan 11:31 . . . object that causes **d.**
Dan 12:11 . . . object that causes **d** is set
Matt 24:15 . . . causes **d** standing in the

DESERT, DESERTS (n) arid land with usually sparse vegetation
see also WILDERNESS
Prov 21:19 . . . better to live alone in the **d**
Isa 32:2 . . . like streams of water in the **d**
Isa 43:20 . . . giving them water in the **d.**
2 Cor 11:26 . . . cities, in the **d-s,** and on the

DESERTED (v) to abandon
Matt 26:56 . . . all the disciples **d** him and
2 Tim 1:15 . . . of Asia has **d** me—even

DESERVE, DESERVED, DESERVES (v) to be worthy, fit, or suitable for some reward or requital; to merit
Judg 9:16 . . . the honor he **d-s** for all he
2 Sam 12:5 . . . do such a thing **d-s** to die!
Neh 9:33 . . . gave us only what we **d-d.**
Ps 103:10 . . . with us, as we **d.**
Prov 14:14 . . . Backsliders get what they **d;**
Dan 9:18 . . . not because we **d** help,
Zech 1:6 . . . received what we **d-d** from the
Luke 7:4 . . . If anyone **d-s** your help,
Acts 26:31 . . . done anything to **d** death or
Rom 3:8 . . . who say such things **d** to be
Rom 11:9 . . . get what they **d.**
2 Cor 11:15 . . . their wicked deeds **d.**
1 Tim 5:18 . . . Those who work **d** their pay!
Heb 3:3 . . . But Jesus **d-s** far more

DESIRABLE (adj) attractive; worth seeking or doing
Ps 19:10 . . . They are more **d** than gold,

DESIRE, DESIRES (n) conscious impulse toward something that promises enjoyment or satisfaction in its attainment; longing, craving
Job 17:11 . . . My heart's **d-s** are broken.
Ps 10:3 . . . brag about their evil **d-s;**
Ps 37:4 . . . give you your heart's **d-s.**

Ps 145:19 . . . He grants the **d-s** of those who
Song 6:12 . . . my strong **d-s** had taken me
Mark 4:19 . . . wealth, and the **d** for other
Rom 1:26 . . . to their shameful **d-s.**
Rom 6:12 . . . not give in to sinful **d-s.**
Rom 7:5 . . . sinful **d-s** were at work
Rom 13:14 . . . indulge your evil **d-s.**
Gal 5:24 . . . the passions and **d-s** of their
Phil 2:13 . . . you the **d** and the power
Col 2:23 . . . a person's evil **d-s.**
Col 3:5 . . . lust, and evil **d-s.**
1 Tim 6:9 . . . and harmful **d-s** that plunge
2 Tim 4:3 . . . follow their own **d-s** and will
Jas 1:14 . . . from our own **d-s,** which entice
Jas 4:1 . . . from the evil **d-s** at war within
1 Pet 2:11 . . . from worldly **d-s** that wage
1 Pet 4:2 . . . chasing your own **d-s,**
2 Pet 2:10 . . . their own twisted sexual **d,**
2 Pet 2:18 . . . twisted sexual **d-s,** they lure
2 Pet 3:3 . . . following their own **d-s.**
Jude 1:18 . . . their ungodly **d-s.**

DESIRE, DESIRED, DESIRES (v) to long or hope for; to wish or request
see also COVET
Gen 3:16 . . . And you will **d** to control
Ps 51:6 . . . But you **d** honesty from
Ps 51:16 . . . You do not **d** a sacrifice,
Prov 8:11 . . . Nothing you **d** can compare
Prov 21:10 . . . Evil people **d** evil;
Rom 1:24 . . . things their hearts **d-d.**
1 Cor 12:31 . . . earnestly **d** the most
1 Cor 14:1 . . . you should also **d** the special
1 Tim 3:1 . . . an elder, he **d-s** an honorable
Jas 1:20 . . . righteousness God **d-s.**
Rev 22:17 . . . Let anyone who **d-s** drink

DESOLATE (adj) deserted; joyless; alone; barren
Isa 54:1 . . . For the **d** woman now has
Gal 4:27 . . . For the **d** woman now has

DESPAIR (n) utter loss of hope
Ps 40:2 . . . out of the pit of **d,**
Ps 79:8 . . . on the brink of **d.**
Ps 130:1 . . . the depths of **d,** O LORD,
Isa 61:3 . . . praise instead of **d.**
2 Cor 4:8 . . . but not driven to **d.**

DESPISE, DESPISED, DESPISES (n) to scorn or regard as unworthy, sometimes with malice or outrage
2 Sam 12:9 . . . you **d-d** the word of the LORD
Job 5:17 . . . Do not **d** the discipline
Job 9:21 . . . to me—I **d** my life.
Ps 22:6 . . . I am scorned and **d-d** by all!
Prov 1:7 . . . but fools **d** wisdom and
Prov 12:8 . . . a warped mind is **d-d.**
Prov 15:5 . . . Only a fool **d-s** a parent's
Prov 15:20 . . . foolish children **d** their
Prov 29:27 . . . The righteous **d** the unjust;
Prov 30:17 . . . and **d-s** a mother's
Isa 53:3 . . . He was **d-d,** and we did not
Mic 7:6 . . . For the son **d-s** his father.
Luke 16:13 . . . to one and **d** the other.
Gal 4:14 . . . you did not **d** me or
2 Pet 2:10 . . . and who **d** authority.

DESTINED (v) to decree beforehand; to predetermine
Luke 2:34 . . . This child is **d** to cause
Heb 9:27 . . . each person is **d** to die once

DESTINY (n) a predetermined course of events; fate or fortune
Ps 73:17 . . . understood the **d** of the
Eccl 9:2 . . . The same **d** ultimately awaits

DESTITUTE (adj) lacking possessions and resources; suffering extreme poverty
Ps 82:3 . . . of the oppressed and the **d.**
Ps 102:17 . . . prayers of the **d.**
Rom 8:35 . . . or hungry, or **d,** or in
Heb 11:37 . . . **d** and oppressed

DESTROY, DESTROYED, DESTROYING, DESTROYS (v) to kill; to cause devastation or ruin
see also PERISH
Gen 6:17 . . . that will **d** every living
Gen 9:11 . . . will a flood **d** the earth.
Num 32:15 . . . responsible for **d-ing** this
Deut 28:63 . . . find pleasure in **d-ing** you.
Josh 10:40 . . . He completely **d-ed** everyone
Prov 6:32 . . . fool, for he **d-s** himself.
Prov 10:21 . . . fools are **d-ed** by their lack
Prov 10:29 . . . but it **d-s** the wicked.
Prov 11:3 . . . dishonesty **d-s** treacherous
Prov 11:9 . . . the godless **d** their friends,
Prov 18:9 . . . as someone who **d-s** things.
Prov 18:24 . . . "friends" who **d** each other,
Prov 29:1 . . . will suddenly be **d-ed** beyond
Isa 11:4 . . . his mouth will **d** the wicked.
Dan 2:44 . . . never be **d-ed** or conquered.
Jon 3:9 . . . fierce anger from **d-ing** us.
Jon 4:2 . . . turn back from **d-ing** people.
Matt 10:28 . . . God, who can **d** both soul
Luke 9:25 . . . but are yourself lost or **d-ed?**
John 10:10 . . . and kill and **d.**
Rom 2:12 . . . they will be **d-ed,** even though
1 Cor 3:17 . . . anyone who **d-s** this temple.
1 Cor 5:5 . . . nature will be **d-ed** and he
1 Cor 8:11 . . . died will be **d-ed.**
1 Cor 15:24 . . . **d-ed** every ruler and
1 Cor 15:26 . . . enemy to be **d-ed** is death.
2 Cor 4:9 . . . are not **d-ed.**
Gal 5:15 . . . Beware of **d-ing** one another.
Heb 7:16 . . . that cannot be **d-ed.**
2 Pet 2:12 . . . be caught and **d-ed.**
2 Pet 3:7 . . . people will be **d-ed.**
Jude 1:5 . . . but later he **d-ed** those who did
Rev 11:18 . . . It is time to **d** all who have

DESTRUCTION (n) the state or fact of being destroyed, ruin; place of punishment (hell)
Ps 1:6 . . . leads to **d.**
Prov 16:18 . . . Pride goes before **d,**
1 Cor 1:18 . . . are headed for **d!**
2 Thes 1:9 . . . punished with eternal **d,**
2 Thes 2:3 . . . the one who brings **d.**
1 Tim 6:9 . . . into ruin and **d.**
2 Pet 2:3 . . . their **d** will not be delayed.
Rev 17:8 . . . and go to eternal **d.**

DESTRUCTIVE (adj) designed or tending to hurt or destroy; ruinous
1 Pet 4:4 . . . and **d** things they do.
2 Pet 2:1 . . . cleverly teach **d** heresies and

DETERMINE, DETERMINED, DETERMINES (v) to decide; to resolve
Exod 28:30 . . . objects used to **d** the LORD's
Ezra 7:10 . . . because Ezra had **d-d** to study
Ps 17:3 . . . I am **d-d** not to sin in
Ps 119:30 . . . I have **d-d** to live by
Ps 119:112 . . . I am **d-d** to keep your
Prov 4:23 . . . it **d-s** the course of your life.
Prov 16:9 . . . but the LORD **d-s** our steps.
Dan 1:8 . . . But Daniel was **d-d** not to
Dan 11:36 . . . what has been **d-d** will surely
Matt 12:34 . . . heart **d-s** what you say.
Luke 22:22 . . . it has been **d-d** that the Son
Acts 4:28 . . . was **d-d** beforehand according

DETEST, DETESTS (v) to loathe; to denounce
Prov 8:7 . . . the truth and **d** every kind of
Prov 12:22 . . . The LORD **d-s** lying lips,
Prov 15:8 . . . The LORD **d-s** the sacrifice
Prov 15:26 . . . The LORD **d-s** evil plans,
Prov 16:5 . . . The LORD **d-s** the proud;
Prov 20:10 . . . the LORD **d-s** double
Prov 24:9 . . . everyone **d-s** a mocker.

DETESTABLE(adj) arousing or meriting intense dislike; abominable
Lev 11:10 . . . They are **d** to you.
Prov 3:32 . . . wicked people are **d** to the
Prov 17:15 . . . both are **d** to the LORD.
Prov 21:27 . . . an evil person is **d,**
Luke 16:15 . . . What this world honors is **d**

DEVIL (n) Satan; enemy of God and of everything good; destroyer, tempter, adversary
see also SATAN
Matt 4:1 . . . tempted there by the **d.**
Matt 4:11 . . . Then the **d** went away,
Matt 13:39 . . . among the wheat is the **d.**
Matt 25:41 . . . prepared for the **d** and his
Luke 4:2 . . . tempted by the **d** for forty
Luke 4:13 . . . When the **d** had finished
Luke 8:12 . . . to have the **d** come and take
John 6:70 . . . but one is a **d.**
John 13:2 . . . **d** had already prompted
Eph 4:27 . . . foothold to the **d.**
Eph 6:11 . . . strategies of the **d.**
Eph 6:16 . . . fiery arrows of the **d.**
2 Tim 2:26 . . . escape from the **d's** trap.
Jas 4:7 . . . Resist the **d,** and he
1 Jn 3:8 . . . the works of the **d.**
1 Jn 3:10 . . . children of the **d.**
Jude 1:9 . . . accuse the **d** of blasphemy,
Rev 12:9 . . . called the **d,** or Satan,

DEVOTE, DEVOTED (v) to commit by a solemn act
see also CONSECRATE, DEDICATE
2 Chr 31:4 . . . could **d** themselves fully
Acts 2:42 . . . the believers **d-d** themselves to
Col 4:2 . . . **D** yourselves to prayer

DEVOTED (adj) characterized by loyalty and devotion
1 Kgs 18:3 . . . (Obadiah was a **d** follower of
Ps 86:2 . . . for I am **d** to you.
Matt 6:24 . . . you will be **d** to one and
1 Tim 2:10 . . . claim to be **d** to God should

DEVOTION (n) religious fervor; being ardently dedicated and loyal
1 Chr 29:3 . . . of my **d** to the Temple
2 Chr 32:32 . . . his acts of **d** are recorded
2 Chr 35:26 . . . his acts of **d** (carried out
1 Cor 16:16 . . . serve with such **d.**
2 Cor 11:3 . . . and undivided **d** to Christ
Col 2:23 . . . they require strong **d,** pious
1 Tim 5:11 . . . overpower their **d** to Christ

DEVOUR, DEVOURED, DEVOURING, DEVOURS (v) to consume by eating; to destroy (as if by eating); to enjoy avidly
2 Sam 11:25 . . . The sword **d-s** this one
Isa 66:24 . . . the worms that **d** them will
Jer 15:16 . . . your words, I **d-ed** them.
Jer 30:16 . . . you will be **d-ed,** and all your
Gal 5:15 . . . biting and **d-ing** one another,
1 Pet 5:8 . . . for someone to **d.**

DEVOURING (adj) characterized by consuming or destroying ravenously
Deut 4:24 . . . your God is a **d** fire; he is a
Heb 12:29 . . . our God is a **d** fire.

DEVOUT (adj) very religious; devoted
Luke 2:25 . . . was righteous and **d** and was
Acts 2:5 . . . time there were **d** Jews from
Acts 10:2 . . . He was a **d,** God-fearing man,
Acts 10:7 . . . servants and a **d** soldier,
Acts 13:43 . . . Many Jews and **d** converts to
Titus 1:8 . . . must live a **d** and disciplined

DEW (n) moisture condensed upon cool surfaces especially at night
Judg 6:37 . . . is wet with **d** in the morning

DICE (n) a small cube marked on each face with numbers and used usually for games and gambling by being shaken and thrown
Ps 22:18 . . . throw **d** for my clothing
Matt 27:35 . . . his clothes by throwing **d.**

DIE, DIED, DIES (v) to pass from physical life; to cease from existence
see also DYING, PERISH
Gen 2:17 . . . you are sure to **d.**
Gen 3:3 . . . if you do, you will **d.**
Esth 4:16 . . . If I must **d**, I must **d.**
Job 2:9 . . . Curse God and **d.**
Prov 5:23 . . . He will **d** for lack of
Prov 11:7 . . . When the wicked **d**, their
Prov 11:10 . . . when the wicked **d.**
Prov 23:13 . . . They won't **d** if you
Eccl 7:2 . . . After all, everyone **d-s**—so the
Isa 22:13 . . . drink, for tomorrow we **d!**
Isa 66:24 . . . that devour them will never **d,**
Jer 31:30 . . . All people will **d** for their
Matt 26:52 . . . will **d** by the sword.
Mark 9:48 . . . the maggots never **d** and the
Luke 16:22 . . . The rich man also **d-d** and
John 13:37 . . . I'm ready to **d** for you.
Rom 4:25 . . . handed over to **d** because of
Rom 5:6 . . . the right time and **d-d** for us
Rom 5:7 . . . be willing to **d** for a person
Rom 5:8 . . . by sending Christ to **d** for us
Rom 5:14 . . . Still, everyone **d-d**—from the
Rom 6:7 . . . For when we **d-d** with Christ we
Rom 6:10 . . . When he **d-d**, he **d-d** once
Rom 7:2 . . . But if he **d-s**, the laws of
Rom 7:6 . . . the law, for we **d-d** to it and
Rom 14:8 . . . whether we live or **d**, we
1 Cor 7:39 . . . If her husband **d-s**, she is free
1 Cor 9:15 . . . I would rather **d** than lose
1 Cor 15:6 . . . though some have **d-d.**
1 Cor 15:18 . . . all who have **d-d** believing in
1 Cor 15:22 . . . Just as everyone **d-s** because
1 Cor 15:32 . . . for tomorrow we **d!**
1 Cor 15:36 . . . plant unless it **d-s** first.
1 Cor 15:42 . . . in the ground when we **d,**
1 Cor 15:51 . . . will not all **d**, but we will
2 Cor 5:15 . . . for Christ, who **d-d** and was
Col 2:20 . . . You have **d-d** with Christ,
1 Thes 4:16 . . . who have **d-d** will rise from
1 Thes 5:10 . . . Christ **d-d** for us so
1 Tim 6:16 . . . He alone can never **d,**
2 Tim 2:11 . . . saying: If we **d** with him,
Heb 9:27 . . . is destined to **d** once and
1 Pet 3:18 . . . sinned, but he **d-d** for sinners

DIFFERENCE (n) the quality or state of being different; a significant change in or affect on a situation
2 Chr 12:8 . . . know the **d** between serving
Ezek 22:26 . . . teach my people the **d**
Gal 2:6 . . . leaders made no **d** to me,

DIFFERENT (adj) not the same as; dissimilar; another
Lev 19:19 . . . woven from two **d** kinds of
1 Sam 10:6 . . . into a **d** person.
Dan 7:24 . . . king will arise, **d** from the
Rom 12:6 . . . God has given us **d** gifts for
1 Cor 12:4 . . . There are **d** kinds of
1 Cor 12:6 . . . God works in **d** ways, but it
2 Cor 11:4 . . . if they preach a **d** Jesus than
Gal 1:8 . . . who preaches a **d** kind of Good

DIFFICULT (adj) hard to understand; hard to do or carry out; hard to manage or overcome
Deut 30:11 . . . **d** for you to understand,
2 Kgs 2:10 . . . have asked a **d** thing," Elijah
Acts 15:19 . . . should not make it **d** for the
2 Tim 3:1 . . . will be very **d** times.

DIFFICULTY (n) the quality or state of being difficult; trouble
Phil 4:14 . . . in my present **d.**

DIGNITY (n) the quality or state of being worthy, honored, or esteemed
Prov 31:25 . . . with strength and **d**, and she

DILIGENT (adj) characterized by steady, earnest, and energetic effort; painstaking
Ezra 4:22 . . . Be **d**, and don't
Prov 12:27 . . . but the **d** make use of

DILIGENTLY (adv) in a diligent manner
Deut 6:17 . . . You must **d** obey the

DINING (v) to take or give a dinner
Prov 23:1 . . . While **d** with a ruler,

DINNER (n) the principal meal of the day
1 Cor 10:27 . . . believer asks you home for **d,**

DIRECT, DIRECTED, DIRECTS (v) to regulate the activities or course of
Gen 18:19 . . . that he will **d** his sons and
Gen 24:51 . . . as the LORD has **d-ed.**
Job 38:31 . . . Can you **d** the movement of
Prov 20:24 . . . The LORD **d-s** our steps,
Jer 13:2 . . . as the LORD **d-ed** me, and I put
Gal 5:18 . . . when you are **d-ed** by the Spirit,

DISAPPEAR, DISAPPEARED, DISAPPEARING (v) to pass from view; to cease to be
1 Kgs 20:40 . . . the prisoner **d-ed!**
Job 17:11 . . . My hopes have **d-ed.**
Ps 37:20 . . . they will **d** like smoke.
Prov 26:20 . . . and quarrels **d** when gossip
Isa 29:14 . . . of the intelligent will **d.**
Isa 51:6 . . . the skies will **d** like smoke,
Matt 5:18 . . . until heaven and earth **d,**
Matt 24:35 . . . Heaven and earth will **d,**
Mark 13:31 . . . Heaven and earth will **d,**
Luke 16:17 . . . and earth to **d** than for the
John 5:13 . . . for Jesus had **d-ed** into the
Heb 8:13 . . . and will soon **d.**
1 Jn 2:8 . . . the darkness is **d-ing**, and the

DISAPPOINTED (v) to fail to meet the expectation or hope of; to frustrate
Prov 23:18 . . . hope will not be **d.**

DISAPPOINTMENT (n) the state or emotion of being frustrated, failed, or let down
Rom 5:5 . . . not lead to **d.**

DISARMED (v) to make harmless
Col 2:15 . . . this way, he **d** the spiritual

DISASTER, DISASTERS (n) a sudden calamitous event bringing great damage, loss, or destruction; a sudden or great misfortune or failure
Exod 32:12 . . . this terrible **d** you have
Deut 31:17 . . . will say, 'These **d-s** have come
Deut 31:21 . . . when great **d-s** come down
Ps 91:6 . . . nor the **d** that strikes at
Prov 3:25 . . . not be afraid of sudden **d**
Prov 27:10 . . . When **d** strikes,
Jer 17:17 . . . the day of **d.**
Jer 29:11 . . . plans for good and not for **d,**
1 Thes 5:3 . . . then **d** will fall on them

DISCERNMENT (n) the quality of being able to grasp and comprehend what is obscure
Ps 119:125 . . . Give **d** to me,
Prov 1:4 . . . knowledge and **d** to the young.
Prov 5:2 . . . you will show **d**, and your
Prov 8:12 . . . knowledge and **d.**
Prov 28:11 . . . a poor person with **d** can see

DISCIPLE, DISCIPLES (n) student or follower of some doctrine or teacher
Matt 28:19 . . . go and make **d-s** of all the
Mark 16:20 . . . the **d-s** went everywhere and
Luke 6:13 . . . all of his **d-s** and chose twelve
Luke 14:26 . . . you cannot be my **d.**
Luke 14:33 . . . become my **d** without
John 6:66 . . . many of his **d-s** turned away
John 8:31 . . . are truly my **d-s** if you remain
John 13:5 . . . to wash the **d-s'** feet, drying
John 13:23 . . . The **d** Jesus loved
John 15:8 . . . fruit, you are my true **d-s.**
John 19:26 . . . there beside the **d** he loved,
John 21:7 . . . Then the **d** Jesus loved
John 21:20 . . . the **d** Jesus loved—

DISCIPLINE (n) punishment; instruction
Deut 11:2 . . . the **d** of the LORD
Prov 10:17 . . . People who accept **d** are on
Prov 13:1 . . . child accepts a parent's **d;**
Prov 13:24 . . . spare the rod of **d** hate their
Prov 15:32 . . . If you reject **d**, you only
Heb 12:5 . . . of the LORD's **d**, and don't
Heb 12:11 . . . No **d** is enjoyable

DISCIPLINE, DISCIPLINED, DISCIPLINES (v) to punish or correct with love; to exercise self-control
Deut 8:5 . . . as a parent **d-s** a child,
Deut 8:5 . . . LORD your God **d-s** you for your
Ps 38:1 . . . in your anger or **d** me in your
Ps 39:11 . . . When you **d** us for our
Ps 119:67 . . . wander off until you **d-d** me;
Ps 119:75 . . . you **d-d** me because I needed
Prov 15:10 . . . right path will be severely **d-d;**
Jer 30:11 . . . I will **d** you, but with
Jer 31:18 . . . saying, 'You **d-d** me severely,
1 Cor 9:25 . . . All athletes are **d-d** in their
1 Cor 9:27 . . . I **d** my body like
1 Cor 11:32 . . . we are being **d-d** so that we
Heb 12:6 . . . For the LORD **d-s** those he
Heb 12:7 . . . who is never **d-d** by its father?
Heb 12:9 . . . fathers who **d-d** us, shouldn't
1 Pet 4:7 . . . be earnest and **d-d** in your

DISCOURAGED (v) to dissuade or hinder; to deprive of courage or confidence
Deut 31:8 . . . be afraid or **d**, for the LORD
2 Sam 11:25 . . . not to be **d**," David said.
1 Chr 28:20 . . . afraid or **d**, for the LORD
Isa 41:10 . . . Don't be **d**, for I am
2 Cor 7:6 . . . who are **d**, encouraged us by
Col 3:21 . . . will become **d.**

DISCOURAGEMENT (n) the state of being discouraged
2 Cor 2:7 . . . may be overcome by **d.**

DISCRETION (n) cautious reserve in speech; prudent or modest in behavior and dress
Prov 11:22 . . . woman who lacks **d** is like a

DISCRIMINATION (n) prejudiced outlook, action, or treatment
see also FAVORITISM, PARTIALITY
Jas 2:4 . . . doesn't this **d** show that your

DISEASE, DISEASES (n) sickness, malady
Exod 4:6 . . . a severe skin **d.**
2 Chr 16:12 . . . a serious foot **d.**
Ps 91:6 . . . not dread the **d** that stalks
Ps 103:3 . . . heals all my **d-s.**
Matt 9:35 . . . every kind of **d** and illness.
Matt 10:1 . . . every kind of **d** and illness.
Luke 4:40 . . . matter what their **d-s** were,

DISGRACE (n) loss of grace, favor, or honor; source of shame
Prov 11:2 . . . Pride leads to **d**, but with
Prov 14:34 . . . but sin is a **d** to any people.

Acts 5:41 . . . worthy to suffer **d** for the
Heb 13:13 . . . and bear the **d** he bore.

DISGRACE, DISGRACED (v) to cause to lose favor or standing; to be a source of shame to
Ps 25:3 . . . trusts in you will ever be **d-d,**
Ps 37:19 . . . will not be **d-d** in hard times;
Prov 29:15 . . . but a mother is **d-d** by an
Matt 1:19 . . . did not want to **d** her
Rom 9:33 . . . in him will never be **d-d.**
Rom 10:11 . . . in him will never be **d-d.**
1 Tim 3:7 . . . will not be **d-d** and fall into

DISGRACEFUL (adj) bringing or involving disgrace
Prov 12:4 . . . a **d** woman is like cancer
Prov 17:2 . . . over the master's **d** son and
1 Cor 11:14 . . . it's **d** for a man to have

DISGUISES (v) to mask the identity of; to use pretense or deception
2 Cor 11:14 . . . Even Satan **d** himself as an

DISGUSTS (v) to provoke loathing, repugnance, or aversion
Isa 1:13 . . . of your offerings **d** me!

DISHONEST (adj) characterized by lack of truth, honesty, or trustworthiness
Lev 19:35 . . . Do not use **d** standards when
Prov 20:23 . . . not pleased by **d** scales.
Luke 16:8 . . . to admire the **d** rascal for
Luke 16:10 . . . But if you are **d** in little

DISHONESTLY (adv) in a shameful, unfair, or deceptive manner
Hab 2:9 . . . houses with money gained **d!**

DISHONESTY (n) lack of honesty or integrity
Jer 22:17 . . . eyes only for greed and **d!**
Jer 23:14 . . . commit adultery and love **d.**
Rom 3:7 . . . sinner if my **d** highlights his
Rev 21:27 . . . idolatry and **d**—but only

DISHONOR, DISHONORED, DISHONORING, DISHONORS (v) to degrade or bring shame upon
Exod 21:17 . . . Anyone who **d-s** father or
Exod 22:28 . . . You must not **d** God or
Lev 20:19 . . . This would **d** a close
Deut 27:16 . . . is anyone who **d-s** father or
Ezra 4:14 . . . see the king **d-ed** in this way,
Lam 2:2 . . . **d-ing** the kingdom and its
John 8:49 . . . my Father—and you **d** me.
Rom 2:23 . . . the law, but you **d** God by
1 Cor 11:4 . . . A man **d-s** his head if
1 Cor 11:5 . . . a woman **d-s** her head if
Jas 2:6 . . . But you **d** the poor!

DISMAYED (v) to cause to lose courage or resolution; to be upset or perturbed
Ps 49:16 . . . So don't be **d** when the wicked

DISOBEDIENCE (n) refusal or neglect to obey
Ps 32:1 . . . those whose **d** is forgiven,
Rom 11:32 . . . imprisoned everyone in **d**

DISOBEDIENT (adj) refusing or neglecting to obey
Neh 9:26 . . . they were **d** and rebelled
2 Cor 10:6 . . . everyone who remains **d.**
Titus 1:16 . . . detestable and **d,** worthless

DISOBEY, DISOBEYED, DISOBEYING (v) to fail to obey
Judg 2:2 . . . But you **d-ed** my command.
1 Kgs 13:26 . . . man of God who **d-ed** the
2 Chr 24:20 . . . says: Why do you **d** the
Neh 9:29 . . . and obstinate and **d-ed** your
Esth 3:3 . . . Why are you **d-ing** the king's
Dan 9:11 . . . Israel has **d-ed** your instruction
Acts 7:53 . . . You deliberately **d-ed** God's
Rom 1:30 . . . and they **d** their parents.
Rom 5:19 . . . Because one person **d-ed** God,
Eph 5:6 . . . fall on all who **d** him.
Heb 3:18 . . . the people who **d-ed** him?
Heb 4:6 . . . enter because they **d-ed** God.
Heb 4:11 . . . But if we **d** God, as the
1 Pet 3:20 . . . those who **d-ed** God long ago

DISORDER (n) lack of order; confusion
1 Cor 14:33 . . . not a God of **d** but of peace,
Jas 3:16 . . . you will find **d** and evil of

DISORDERLY (adj) in a manner that lacks order; turbulently
2 Cor 12:20 . . . arrogance, and **d** behavior.

DISPLAY (n) a presentation of something in open view; exhibition
1 Cor 4:9 . . . apostles on **d,** like prisoners

DISPLAYED, DISPLAYING (v) to put or spread before the view; to make evident
Neh 9:10 . . . You **d** miraculous signs
Isa 5:16 . . . The holiness of God will be **d**
Isa 63:12 . . . whose power was **d** when Moses
Rom 9:17 . . . very purpose of **d-ing** my power

DISPLEASED (v) to incur the disapproval or dislike of
2 Sam 11:27 . . . But the LORD was **d** with
Prov 24:18 . . . LORD will be **d** with you and

DISPUTE, DISPUTES (n) verbal controversy; quarrel or debate
Prov 18:18 . . . it settles **d-s** between
1 Cor 6:1 . . . you has a **d** with another

DISSENSION (n) disagreement; discord
Gal 5:20 . . . selfish ambition, **d,** division,

DISTINCTION (n) the distinguishing of a difference; division
Acts 15:9 . . . He made no **d** between us and

DISTORT (v) to twist out of the true meaning or proportion
Acts 20:30 . . . rise up and **d** the truth in

DISTRACTED (v) to divert one's attention
Luke 10:40 . . . But Martha was **d** by the big

DISTRACTIONS (n) something that distracts
1 Cor 7:35 . . . with as few **d** as possible.

DISTRESS (n) a troubling or painful situation; a state of danger or desperate need
Exod 3:7 . . . their cries of **d** because of
Job 36:16 . . . to a place free from **d.**
Ps 18:6 . . . But in my **d** I cried out
Ps 118:5 . . . In my **d** I prayed to
Ps 143:11 . . . bring me out of this **d.**
Jas 1:27 . . . and widows in their **d**

DISTRESSED (v) to subject one to grief or misery
Rom 14:15 . . . another believer is **d** by

DISTURB (v) to interfere with; to interrupt
Ezra 6:7 . . . Do not **d** the construction of

DIVIDE, DIVIDED (v) to separate into parts; to distribute; to make distinctions
Ps 22:18 . . . They **d** my garments
Luke 12:51 . . . have come to **d** people
1 Cor 1:13 . . . Has Christ been **d-d** into
Jas 4:8 . . . your loyalty is **d-d** between God

DIVINATION (n) the attempt through ritual means to know the future or other hidden knowledge
Num 24:1 . . . he did not resort to **d** as before.
2 Kgs 21:6 . . . He practiced sorcery and **d,**

DIVINE (adj) of, relating to, or preceding directly from God or a god
Prov 29:18 . . . not accept **d** guidance,
Rom 1:20 . . . power and **d** nature.
2 Pet 1:4 . . . to share his **d** nature

DIVISION, DIVISIONS (n) act or process of dividing, separating, distributing; a portion, part, grouping, or distinction
1 Cor 1:10 . . . there be no **d-s** in the church.
1 Cor 11:18 . . . that there are **d-s** among
Gal 5:20 . . . selfish ambition, dissension, **d,**
Titus 3:10 . . . are causing **d-s** among you,

DIVORCE (n) the action or an instance of legally dissolving a marriage
Deut 24:1 . . . a letter of **d,** hands it to
Mal 2:16 . . . "For I hate **d!**" says the
Matt 19:8 . . . Moses permitted **d** only as a

DIVORCE, DIVORCED, DIVORCES (v) to dissolve a marriage; to end a relationship
Lev 21:7 . . . a woman who is **d-d** from her
Lev 21:14 . . . who is **d-d,** or a woman
Lev 22:13 . . . a widow or is **d-d** and has no
Num 30:9 . . . is a widow or is **d-d,** she must
Deut 22:19 . . . and he may never **d** her.
1 Chr 8:8 . . . After Shaharaim **d-d** his wives
Jer 3:1 . . . If a man **d-s** a woman and
Jer 3:8 . . . saw that I **d-d** faithless Israel
Matt 5:31 . . . A man can **d** his wife by
Matt 5:32 . . . a man who **d-s** his wife, unless
Matt 5:32 . . . who marries a **d-d** woman also
Mark 10:2 . . . be allowed to **d** his wife?
Mark 10:11 . . . Whoever **d-s** his wife and
Mark 10:12 . . . if a woman **d-s** her husband
Luke 16:18 . . . a man who **d-s** his wife and
Luke 16:18 . . . marries a woman **d-d** from

DOCTOR, DOCTORS (n) a person skilled or specializing in healing arts
Matt 9:12 . . . don't need a **d**—sick people
Mark 5:26 . . . great deal from many **d-s,**

DOG, DOGS (n) a carnivorous (usually domestic) mammal similar to wolves and coyotes
Prov 26:11 . . . As a **d** returns to its
Eccl 9:4 . . . to be a live **d** than a dead
Matt 15:26 . . . throw it to the **d-s.**
Phil 3:2 . . . Watch out for those **d-s,**
2 Pet 2:22 . . . this proverb: "A **d** returns to

DONKEY (n) a domestic mammal smaller than the horse and having long ears
Num 22:30 . . . same **d** you have ridden
Matt 21:5 . . . riding on a **d**—riding on a
2 Pet 2:16 . . . when his **d** rebuked him

DOOMED (adj) condemned; certain failure or destruction of
Isa 6:5 . . . I am **d,** for I am

DOOR, DOORS (n) a barrier by which an entry is closed and opened; a means of access or participation
Ps 24:7 . . . Open up, ancient **d-s,** and let
Matt 7:7 . . . the **d** will be opened to you.
Luke 13:24 . . . enter the narrow **d** to God's
Acts 14:27 . . . had opened the **d** of faith to
1 Cor 16:9 . . . is a wide-open **d** for a great
2 Cor 2:12 . . . opened a **d** of opportunity
Rev 3:20 . . . stand at the **d** and knock.

DOORPOSTS (n) the two sides of a doorway, similar to a door frame
Deut 6:9 . . . Write them on the **d** of

DOUBLE-EDGED (adj) having two cutting edges
Prov 5:4 . . . dangerous as a **d** sword.

DOUBT, DOUBTS (n) uncertainty of belief or opinion; lack of confidence; distrust
Mark 11:23 . . . have no **d** in your heart.
Luke 24:38 . . . hearts filled with **d?**
Rom 14:23 . . . if you have **d-s** about whether

DOUBT (v) to distrust; to be uncertain
Matt 14:31 . . . Why did you **d** me?
Matt 21:21 . . . faith and don't **d,** you

DOVE, DOVES (n) a small wild pigeon, often symbolic of gentleness
Gen 8:8 . . . also released a **d** to see if
Matt 3:16 . . . like a **d** and settling on him.
Matt 10:16 . . . snakes and harmless as **d-s.**

DOWNTRODDEN (adj) suffering oppression
Ps 74:21 . . . Don't let the **d** be humiliated

DRAGON (n) a huge serpent
Rev 12:7 . . . fought against the **d** and his
Rev 20:2 . . . He seized the **d**—that old

DRAW, DRAWING, DRAWS (v) to pull; to bring in or gather; to come steadily or gradually
John 6:44 . . . who sent me **d-s** them to me,
John 12:32 . . . I will **d** everyone to myself.
Heb 10:25 . . . day of his return is **d-ing** near.

DREAD (n) great fear; extreme uneasiness in the face of a disagreeable prospect
Isa 51:13 . . . remain in constant **d** of human

DREADFUL (adj) causing great and oppressive fear; inspiring awe or reverence
Job 25:2 . . . powerful and **d.**

DREAM, DREAMS (n) a strongly desired goal or purpose; a series of thoughts, images, or emotions occurring during sleep
Prov 13:12 . . . sick, but a **d** fulfilled is a
Prov 13:19 . . . pleasant to see **d-s** come true,
Eccl 5:3 . . . gives you restless **d-s;**

DREAM (v) to have a dream
Joel 2:28 . . . old men will **d** dreams,
Acts 2:17 . . . old men will **d** dreams.

DRESSED (v) to put on clothing
Exod 12:11 . . . Be fully **d,** wear your
Ps 104:2 . . . You are **d** in a robe
Isa 61:10 . . . For he has **d** me with the

DRINK, DRINKING, DRINKS (v) to swallow; to partake of alcoholic beverages
1 Sam 1:13 . . . she had been **d-ing.**
Isa 5:22 . . . who are heroes at **d-ing** wine
Isa 12:3 . . . you will **d** deeply from
Matt 26:27 . . . Each of you **d** from it,
Mark 16:18 . . . **d** anything poisonous,
John 4:13 . . . Anyone who **d-s** this water will
John 6:54 . . . my flesh and **d-s** my blood has
Rom 14:17 . . . we eat or **d,** but of living a
1 Cor 11:27 . . . this bread or **d-s** this cup of
Rev 14:10 . . . **d** the wine of God's anger.
Rev 22:17 . . . who desires **d** freely from

DRINKER, DRINKERS (n) a person who drinks alcoholic beverages
1 Tim 3:3 . . . not be a heavy **d** or be violent.
1 Tim 3:8 . . . not be heavy **d-s** or dishonest
Titus 2:3 . . . or be heavy **d-s.**

DRIVE (v) to exert inescapable or coercive pressure on; to force
Exod 23:30 . . . I will **d** them out a little
Num 33:52 . . . you must **d** out all the people
Josh 13:13 . . . failed to **d** out the people of
Josh 23:13 . . . will no longer **d** them out of

DROUGHT (n) a period of prolonged dryness
1 Kgs 18:1 . . . in the third year of the **d,**
Jer 17:8 . . . by long months of **d.**

DROWNED (v) to suffocate by submersion especially in water
Exod 15:4 . . . officers are **d** in the Red
Matt 18:6 . . . neck and be **d** in the depths
Heb 11:29 . . . they were all **d.**

DRUNK (adj) having the faculties impaired by alcohol; intoxicated
Acts 2:15 . . . These people are not **d,** as

DRUNKARD, DRUNKARDS (n) one who is habitually drunk
Prov 23:20 . . . not carouse with **d-s** or feast
Matt 11:19 . . . glutton and a **d,** and a friend
1 Cor 5:11 . . . or is a **d,** or cheats people.
1 Cor 6:10 . . . greedy people, or **d-s,** or are

DRUNKENNESS
Ezek 23:33 . . . **D** and anguish will fill you,
Rom 13:13 . . . darkness of wild parties and **d**

DRY (adj) free or relatively free from a liquid, especially water
Gen 1:9 . . . so **d** ground may appear.
Exod 14:16 . . . of the sea on **d** ground.
Josh 3:17 . . . Covenant stood on **d** ground
Isa 53:2 . . . a root in **d** ground.

DULL (adj) slow in action, sluggish; slow in perception or sensibility
Heb 6:12 . . . not become spiritually **d** and

DUST (n) specks or clumps of earthy matter; ground or earth
Gen 2:7 . . . man from the **d** of the ground.
Gen 3:19 . . . were made from **d,** and to **d**
Ps 22:15 . . . laid me in the **d** and left me
Eccl 3:20 . . . they return to **d.**
Matt 10:14 . . . shake its **d** from your feet
1 Cor 15:47 . . . from the **d** of the earth,

DUTY, DUTIES (n) moral or legal obligation; assigned service or task
Eccl 8:3 . . . Don't try to avoid doing your **d,**
Eccl 12:13 . . . is everyone's **d.**
Dan 8:27 . . . performed my **d-ies** for the

DWELLING (n) a shelter (as a house) in which one lives; residence
see also HOME, HOUSE
Exod 15:17 . . . your own **d,** the sanctuary,
Eph 2:22 . . . made part of this **d** where God

DWELLS (v) to stay for a time; to live as a resident
see also LIVE(S)
Ps 26:8 . . . glorious presence **d.**

DYING (v) *see also* DIE
John 11:25 . . . even after **d.**
2 Cor 4:16 . . . our bodies are **d,** our spirits
Phil 1:21 . . . for Christ, and **d** is even

DYNASTY (n) a succession of rulers of the same line of descent
see also HOUSE
1 Chr 17:17 . . . a lasting **d!**

E

EAGER (adj) marked by enthusiastic or impatient desire or interest
Rom 15:23 . . . I am **e** to visit you.
1 Cor 14:39 . . . sisters, be **e** to prophesy,
1 Pet 5:2 . . . because you are **e** to serve

EAGERLY (adv) in an enthusiastic or impatient manner
Rom 8:19 . . . creation is waiting **e** for that

EAGERNESS (n) the state or quality of enthusiasm for a desire or interest
Ps 119:36 . . . Give me an **e** for your laws

EAGLE, EAGLES (n) any of various large diurnal birds of prey noted for their strength, size, keenness of vision, and powers of flight
Deut 32:11 . . . Like an **e** that rouses her chicks
Isa 40:31 . . . soar high on wings like **e-s.**
Rev 4:7 . . . was like an **e** in flight.
Rev 12:14 . . . wings like those of a great **e**

EARN, EARNED (v) to receive as return for effort or work done
2 Thes 3:12 . . . **e** their own living.
Heb 11:2 . . . **e-ed** a good reputation.

EARNEST (adj) characterized by or proceeding from an intense and serious state of mind; ardent or fervent
Jas 5:16 . . . The **e** prayer of a righteous
1 Pet 4:7 . . . be **e** and disciplined

EARNESTLY (adv) in a manner that is intense and serious; fervently
2 Chr 15:15 . . . they **e** sought after God,
Col 4:12 . . . He always prays **e** for you,

EARNINGS (n) pay; wages
Prov 31:16 . . . with her **e** she plants a vineyard.

EARRING, EARRINGS (n) an ornament for the ear and especially the earlobe
Exod 35:22 . . . gold—brooches, **e-s,** rings
Prov 25:12 . . . valid criticism is like a gold **e**

EARS (n) the external organ for hearing, expressing the entire faculty of understanding
Prov 2:2 . . . Tune your **e** to wisdom,
Eccl 5:1 . . . your **e** open and your mouth shut.
2 Tim 4:3 . . . whatever their itching **e** want

EARTH (n) the planet on which we live
Gen 1:1 . . . created the heavens and the **e.**
Gen 7:24 . . . floodwaters covered the **e**
Gen 14:19 . . . Creator of heaven and **e.**
Job 26:7 . . . and hangs the **e** on nothing.
Job 38:4 . . . I laid the foundations of the **e?**
Ps 108:5 . . . your glory shine over all the **e.**
Prov 8:23 . . . first, before the **e** began.
Prov 8:26 . . . had made the **e** and fields
Isa 6:3 . . . The whole **e** is filled with his glory!
Isa 40:22 . . . God sits above the circle of the **e.**
Isa 44:23 . . . O depths of the **e!**
Isa 55:9 . . . higher than the **e,** so my ways
Isa 65:17 . . . new heavens and a new **e,**
Isa 66:1 . . . and the **e** is my footstool.
Jer 23:24 . . . in all the heavens and **e?**
Hab 2:20 . . . Let all the **e** be silent
Matt 5:18 . . . until heaven and **e** disappear, not
Matt 5:35 . . . do not say, 'By the **e!'**
Matt 6:10 . . . your will be done on **e,**
Matt 16:19 . . . Whatever you forbid on **e**
Matt 28:18 . . . in heaven and on **e.**
Luke 2:14 . . . and peace on **e**
Acts 4:24 . . . Creator of heaven and **e,**
Acts 7:49 . . . the **e** is my footstool.
Rom 8:39 . . . or in the **e** below—

1 Cor 10:26 . . . the **e** is the Lord's,
Eph 3:15 . . . in heaven and on **e.**
Phil 2:10 . . . in heaven and on **e** and under
Col 3:2 . . . not the things of **e.**
Heb 1:10 . . . laid the foundation of the **e**
2 Pet 3:13 . . . and new **e** he has promised,
Rev 20:11 . . . The **e** and sky fled
Rev 21:1 . . . a new heaven and a new **e,**
Rev 21:1 . . . the old **e** had disappeared.

EARTHLY (adj) belonging to the earth; mundane or worldly; temporal or temporary; human
Rom 1:3 . . . In his **e** life he was born
Col 3:5 . . . put to death the sinful, **e** things

EARTHQUAKE, EARTHQUAKES (n) a shaking or trembling of the earth
Matt 24:7 . . . There will be famines and **e-s**
Matt 28:2 . . . there was a great **e!**
Rev 6:12 . . . there was a great **e.**

EAST (n) the general direction of the sunrise
Gen 2:8 . . . a garden in Eden in the **e,**
Ps 103:12 . . . far from us as the **e** is from

EASTERN (adj) coming from the east
Matt 2:1 . . . wise men from **e** lands arrived

EASY (adj) causing or involving little difficulty or discomfort
Matt 11:30 . . . For my yoke is **e** to bear,

EAT, EATEN, EATING, EATS (v) to ingest, chew, and swallow in turn
see also ATE
Gen 2:16 . . . You may freely **e** the fruit
Gen 3:11 . . . Have you **e-en** from the tree
Deut 14:4 . . . the animals you may **e:**
Isa 65:25 . . . The lion will **e** hay
Jer 31:29 . . . parents have **e-en** sour grapes,
Matt 26:26 . . . Take this and **e** it,
Luke 15:2 . . . sinful people—even **e-ing** with
John 6:52 . . . give us his flesh to **e?**
John 6:54 . . . anyone who **e-s** my flesh and
Acts 10:13 . . . kill and **e** them.
Acts 10:14 . . . I have never **e-en** anything
Rom 14:15 . . . Don't let your **e-ing** ruin
1 Cor 8:4 . . . So, what about **e-ing** meat that
1 Cor 8:10 . . . **e-ing** in the temple of an idol,
1 Cor 10:31 . . . So whether you **e** or drink,
1 Cor 11:26 . . . every time you **e** this bread
1 Cor 11:27 . . . anyone who **e-s** this bread or

EDEN (n) the garden where Adam and Eve first lived
Gen 2:8 . . . a garden in **E** in the east,
Ezek 28:13 . . . in **E,** the garden of God.

EDIFY, EDIFYING (KJV)
1 Cor 10:23 . . . but not everything is *beneficial*
1 Cor 14:5 . . . will be *strengthened*
1 Cor 14:17 . . . won't *strengthen* the people
Eph 4:12 . . . work and *build up* the church,

EFFORT, EFFORTS (n) conscious exertion of power; hard work; a serious attempt
2 Chr 31:21 . . . **e-s** to follow God's laws
Ps 90:17 . . . make our **e-s** successful.
Gal 3:3 . . . by your own human **e?**
Eph 4:3 . . . Make every **e** to keep
2 Pet 1:5 . . . make every **e** to respond
2 Pet 3:14 . . . make every **e** to be found

EGYPT (n) the country in the northeast corner of Africa that extended from the Mediterranean Sea on the north to the Nile River on the south
Gen 46:6 . . . his entire family went to **E—**
Exod 3:11 . . . people of Israel out of **E?**
Exod 12:40 . . . Israel had lived in **E**
Hos 11:1 . . . I called my son out of **E.**
Matt 2:15 . . . I called my Son out of **E.**
Heb 11:27 . . . Moses left the land of **E,**

ELDER, ELDERS (n) older, wise man; ruling body of decision makers invested with authority by virtue of their age, character, or experience
see also DEACONS
Acts 14:23 . . . appointed **e-s** in every church.
Acts 15:2 . . . talk to the apostles and **e-s**
Acts 20:17 . . . a message to the **e-s** of the
Acts 20:28 . . . appointed you as **e-s.**
Phil 1:1 . . . including the **e-s** and deacons.
1 Tim 3:1 . . . aspires to be an **e,** he desires
1 Tim 3:2 . . . an **e** must be a man whose life is
1 Tim 4:14 . . . **e-s** of the church laid their
1 Tim 5:19 . . . against an **e** unless it is
Titus 1:6 . . . An **e** must live a blameless life.
Titus 1:7 . . . An **e** is a manager of God's
Jas 5:14 . . . call for the **e-s** of the church
1 Pet 5:1 . . . a word to you who are **e-s**
1 Pet 5:1 . . . I, too, am an **e** and a witness
1 Pet 5:5 . . . the authority of the **e-s.**
2 Jn 1:1 . . . letter is from John, the **e.**
3 Jn 1:1 . . . letter is from John, the **e.**
Rev 4:10 . . . the twenty-four **e-s** fall down

ELDERLY (n) a rather old person
Lev 19:32 . . . the **e,** and show respect

ELECT (KJV)
Isa 42:1 . . . my *chosen one,* who pleases me
Matt 24:31 . . . gather his *chosen ones* from all
Rom 8:33 . . . *us whom God has chosen* for his
Col 3:12 . . . *chose* you to be the holy people
2 Tim 2:10 . . . Jesus to *those God has chosen*

ELEMENTS (n) any of four substances air, water, fire, and earth
2 Pet 3:10 . . . the very **e** themselves
2 Pet 3:12 . . . the **e** will melt away

ELIJAH Powerful prophet in Israel (northern kingdom); proclaimed drought (1 Kgs 17:1; Jas 5:17); hid and was fed by ravens (1 Kgs 17:2-6); performed miracles for widow (1 Kgs 17:8-24; Luke 4:25); proclaimed truth to King Ahab (1 Kgs 18:1-15); defeated Baal and his prophets on Mount Carmel (1 Kgs 18:16-40); brought rain (1 Kgs 18:41-46; Jas 5:17); ran for his life (1 Kgs 19:3); served by angels (1 Kgs 19:1-9); given assurance by God (1 Kgs 19:9-18); put mantle on Elisha (1 Kgs 19:19-21); condemned by Ahab (1 Kgs 21:17-29); whirlwind and fire took him into heaven (2 Kgs 2:11); return prophesied and expected (Mal 4:5-6; Matt 11:14; Luke 1:17; John 1:25); compared to John the Baptist (Matt 17:9-13; Mark 9:9-13; Luke 1:17); appeared at Jesus' Transfiguration (Matt 17:1-8; Mark 9:1-8).

ELISHA Powerful prophet in Israel (northern kingdom) who replaced Elijah (1 Kgs 19:16-21); inherited Elijah's cloak (2 Kgs 2:1-18); asked for double measure of spirit (2 Kgs 2:9); witnessed Elijah's departure (2 Kgs 2:11-12); healed bad water (2 Kgs 2:19-22); cursed 42 mockers (2 Kgs 2:23-25); prophesied victory over Moab (2 Kgs 3:11-27); provided abundant oil for widow (2 Kgs 4:1-7); raised child to life (2 Kgs 4:32-37); made stew edible (2 Kgs 4:38-41); fed a multitude with few loaves (2 Kgs 4:42-44); healed Naaman's leprosy (2 Kgs 5:14-15); made an ax head float (2 Kgs 6:1-7); prophesied the availability of food (2 Kgs 7:1); prophesied death of Ben-hadad (2 Kgs 8:7-15); died (2 Kgs 13:20); bones produced miracle after death (2 Kgs 13:21).

ELIZABETH Mother of John the Baptist, cousin of Mary the mother of Jesus (Luke 1:5-66).

EMBARRASSED (v) to become anxiously self-conscious
Luke 14:9 . . . you will be **e,** and you will

EMBARRASSMENT (n) the state of being anxiously self-conscious
2 Cor 9:4 . . . not to mention your own **e—**

EMPLOYER (n) one who provides with a job that pays wages
Luke 16:5 . . . owed money to his **e** to come and

EMPOWER, EMPOWERED (v) to give official authority or legal power to; to enable
Luke 11:18 . . . You say I am **e-ed** by Satan.
Eph 3:16 . . . resources he will **e** you with

EMPTINESS (n) a void; containing nothing
Job 15:31 . . . for **e** will be their only
Isa 40:17 . . . nothing—mere **e** and froth

EMPTY (adj) containing nothing; having no purpose or result; destitute of effect or force
Gen 1:2 . . . formless and **e,** and darkness
Deut 32:47 . . . not **e** words—they are your life!
Job 26:7 . . . the northern sky over **e** space
Isa 45:18 . . . not to be a place of **e** chaos.
Jer 4:23 . . . and it was **e** and formless.
Luke 1:53 . . . the rich away with **e** hands.
1 Cor 14:9 . . . be talking into **e** space.
1 Pet 1:18 . . . to save you from the **e** life
2 Pet 2:18 . . . with **e,** foolish boasting.

EMPTY-HANDED (adj) having, bringing, or gaining nothing
Eccl 5:15 . . . as naked and **e** as on the day

ENABLE, ENABLED (v) to make possible, provide an opportunity for
2 Cor 3:6 . . . **e-ed** us to be ministers of his
2 Thes 1:11 . . . to **e** you to live a life worthy
2 Pet 1:4 . . . **e** you to share his divine

ENCOURAGE, ENCOURAGED, ENCOURAGES, ENCOURAGING (v) to inspire with courage, spirit, or hope; to spur on
Isa 41:7 . . . The carver **e-s** the goldsmith,
Acts 11:23 . . . and he **e-d** the believers
Acts 15:32 . . . length to the believers, **e-ing**
Acts 20:1 . . . sent for the believers and **e-d**
Acts 28:15 . . . he was **e-d** and thanked God.
Rom 1:12 . . . I also want to be **e-d** by yours.
Rom 12:8 . . . your gift is to **e** others,
1 Cor 8:12 . . . other believers by **e-ing**
1 Cor 14:3 . . . strengthens others, **e-s** them,
2 Cor 7:6 . . . who **e-s** those who are
2 Cor 7:6 . . . **e-d** us by the arrival of Titus.
2 Cor 7:13 . . . have been greatly **e-d** by this.
Eph 6:22 . . . how we are doing and to **e**
Col 4:8 . . . how we are doing and to **e** you.
1 Thes 2:12 . . . pleaded with you, **e-d** you,
1 Thes 3:2 . . . to strengthen you, to **e** you
1 Thes 3:7 . . . we have been greatly **e-d** in
1 Thes 5:11 . . . So **e** each other
1 Thes 5:14 . . . **E** those who are timid.
Titus 1:9 . . . he will be able to **e** others
Heb 12:5 . . . you forgotten the **e-ing** words
1 Pet 5:12 . . . purpose in writing is to **e** you
2 Jn 1:11 . . . Anyone who **e-s** such people

ENCOURAGEMENT (n) the act of encouraging; the state of being encouraged
Rom 15:5 . . . who gives this patience and **e,**
1 Cor 16:18 . . . a wonderful **e** to me,
2 Cor 7:13 . . . In addition to our own **e,**
Eph 4:29 . . . an **e** to those who hear them.
Phil 2:1 . . . any **e** from belonging to Christ?
Phlm 1:20 . . . Give me this **e** in Christ.

END, ENDS (n) the point where something ceases to exist; death and destruction; the goal or result toward which some action or agent is heading
Ps 65:8 . . . live at the **e-s** of the earth stand
Eccl 3:11 . . . work from beginning to **e.**
Isa 30:8 . . . stand until the **e** of time
Isa 49:6 . . . bring my salvation to the **e-s**
Matt 24:13 . . . the one who endures to the **e**
Matt 24:14 . . . and then the **e** will come.
Matt 24:31 . . . farthest **e-s** of the earth
1 Cor 15:24 . . . After that the **e** will come,
Phil 3:14 . . . press on to reach the **e** of
Rev 21:6 . . . the Beginning and the **E.**
Rev 22:13 . . . the Beginning and the **E.**

END, ENDING, ENDS (v) to come to an end; to die
1 Sam 12:23 . . . sin against the LORD by **e-ing**
Prov 14:12 . . . but it **e-s** in death.
Prov 14:13 . . . the laughter **e-s,** the grief
Prov 29:23 . . . Pride **e-s** in humiliation,
Isa 9:7 . . . its peace will never **e.**
Eph 2:15 . . . by **e-ing** the system of law

ENDANGER (v) to bring into danger or peril
Prov 22:25 . . . be like them and **e** your soul.

ENDLESS (adj) being or seeming to be without end
Eccl 12:12 . . . writing books is **e,**
Amos 5:24 . . . an **e** river of righteous
Eph 3:8 . . . the **e** treasures available

ENDURANCE (n) the ability to withstand hardship or adversity
see also PERSEVERANCE
Rom 5:3 . . . they help us develop **e.**
Col 1:11 . . . have all the **e** and patience
2 Thes 1:4 . . . your **e** and faithfulness
Heb 12:1 . . . let us run with **e** the race
Jas 1:3 . . . when your faith is tested, your **e**
2 Pet 1:6 . . . self-control with patient **e,**
Rev 1:9 . . . in the patient **e** to which Jesus

ENDURE, ENDURED, ENDURES, ENDURING (v) to withstand, suffer, or persevere
see also PERSEVERE
Ps 89:2 . . . Your faithfulness is as **e-ing** as
Ps 136:1 . . . faithful love **e-s** forever.
Matt 10:22 . . . everyone who **e-s** to the end
Mark 13:13 . . . one who **e-s** to the end
1 Cor 13:7 . . . **e-s** through every
2 Cor 1:6 . . . Then you can patiently **e**
2 Cor 6:4 . . . patiently **e** troubles and
2 Tim 2:3 . . . **E** suffering along with me,
2 Tim 2:12 . . . If we **e** hardship,
2 Tim 3:11 . . . suffering I have **e-d.**
Heb 12:2 . . . he **e-d** the cross,
Heb 12:3 . . . hostility he **e-d** from sinful
Heb 12:7 . . . As you **e** this divine discipline,
Jas 1:12 . . . who patiently **e** testing and
Jas 5:11 . . . those who **e** under suffering.
1 Pet 2:19 . . . patiently **e** unfair treatment.
Rev 13:10 . . . must **e** persecution patiently

ENEMY, ENEMIES (n) foe—personal, national, or spiritual
Ps 23:5 . . . the presence of my **e-ies.**
Ps 62:7 . . . a rock where no **e** can reach me.
Prov 16:7 . . . even their **e-ies** are at peace
Prov 24:17 . . . rejoice when your **e-ies** fall;
Prov 25:21 . . . If your **e-ies** are hungry,
Prov 27:6 . . . than many kisses from an **e.**
Isa 51:13 . . . fear the anger of your **e-ies?**
Isa 59:18 . . . repay his **e-ies** for their evil
Matt 5:44 . . . love your **e-ies!** Pray for those
Luke 6:35 . . . Love your **e-ies!** Do good to
Luke 10:19 . . . over all the power of the **e,**
Rom 5:10 . . . while we were still his **e-ies,**
Rom 12:20 . . . If your **e-ies** are hungry,
1 Cor 15:25 . . . until he humbles all his **e-ies**
1 Cor 15:26 . . . the last **e** to be destroyed
Phil 3:18 . . . they are really **e-ies** of the cross
Jas 4:4 . . . makes you an **e** of God?
1 Pet 5:8 . . . Watch out for your great **e,**

ENERGY (n) vigorous exertion of power; effort
Ezra 5:8 . . . with great **e** and success.
John 6:27 . . . Spend your **e** seeking the eternal

ENGAGED (adj) pledged to be married; betrothed
Matt 1:18 . . . His mother, Mary, was **e** to

ENGAGEMENT (n) a pledge to marry; betrothal
Matt 1:19 . . . to break the **e** quietly.

ENJOY, ENJOYED, ENJOYING (v) to have a good time; to experience; to take pleasure in
see also HAPPY, JOY
Deut 6:2 . . . you will **e** a long life.
Neh 9:25 . . . grew fat and **e-ed** themselves
Eccl 5:19 . . . good health to **e** it.
Eccl 5:20 . . . so busy **e-ing** life that
Eccl 8:15 . . . eat, drink, and **e** life.
2 Tim 2:6 . . . the first to **e** the fruit
Heb 11:25 . . . **e-ing** the fleeting pleasures
1 Pet 3:10 . . . If you want to **e** life

ENJOYABLE (adj) of or relating to having a good time; pleasurable
Heb 12:11 . . . No discipline is **e** while

ENJOYMENT (n) an attitude, circumstance, or favorable response to a stimulus that tends to make one gratified or happy; delight; joy
1 Tim 6:17 . . . all we need for our **e.**

ENQUIRE (KJV)
1 Sam 28:7 . . . a medium, so I can go and *ask*
2 Kgs 1:2 . . . the god of Ekron, to *ask*

ENRICH, ENRICHED (v) to make rich or richer; to enhance
Prov 31:11 . . . she will greatly **e** his life.
2 Cor 9:11 . . . you will be **e-ed** in every way

ENSLAVE, ENSLAVED (v) to reduce to slavery; to subjugate
Gal 2:4 . . . They wanted to **e** us and force us
2 Pet 2:20 . . . get tangled up and **e-d** by sin

ENSURE (v) to make sure, certain, or safe; to guarantee
Prov 31:8 . . . **e** justice for those being crushed.

ENTER, ENTERED, ENTERING, ENTERS (v) to go or come in
Ps 100:4 . . . **E** his gates
Matt 5:20 . . . you will never **e** the Kingdom
Matt 7:13 . . . **e** God's Kingdom only
Matt 19:23 . . . rich person to **e** the
Mark 9:43 . . . **e** eternal life with only
Mark 10:23 . . . for the rich to **e** the
Luke 11:52 . . . prevent others from **e-ing.**
Luke 13:24 . . . Work hard to **e** the narrow
Luke 18:17 . . . like a child will never **e** it.
John 3:5 . . . no one can **e** the Kingdom
John 10:2 . . . who **e-s** through the gate
Rom 5:12 . . . When Adam sinned, sin **e-ed**
Heb 3:11 . . . will never **e** my place of rest.
Heb 4:1 . . . God's promise of **e-ing** his rest
Heb 4:11 . . . do our best to **e** that rest.
Heb 9:12 . . . of goats and calves—he **e-ed**

ENTERTAIN, ENTERTAINS (v) to provide entertainment for; to amuse
Ps 45:8 . . . music of strings **e-s** you.
Hos 7:3 . . . The people **e** the king

ENTERTAINMENT (n) amusement or diversion provided especially by performers
Dan 6:18 . . . refused his usual **e**

ENTHRONED (v) to seat ceremonially on a throne or in a place associated with power and authority
1 Sam 4:4 . . . **e** between the cherubim.
2 Kgs 19:15 . . . **e** between the mighty
1 Chr 13:6 . . . **e** between the cherubim.
Ps 22:3 . . . you are holy, **e** on the praises
Ps 113:5 . . . God, who is **e** on high?
Isa 37:16 . . . God of Israel, you are **e**

ENTHUSIASM (n) strong excitement of feeling; zeal, fervor, passion
Neh 4:6 . . . the people had worked with **e.**
Prov 19:2 . . . **E** without knowledge
Rom 10:2 . . . I know what **e** they have
2 Cor 8:7 . . . your **e,** and your love
2 Cor 8:16 . . . Titus the same **e** for you
2 Cor 9:2 . . . your **e** that stirred up
Eph 6:7 . . . Work with **e,**

ENTHUSIASTIC (adj) filled with or marked by zeal, fervor, or passion
Ps 45:15 . . . a joyful and **e** procession
Acts 18:25 . . . about Jesus with an **e** spirit
Rom 15:17 . . . I have reason to be **e** about

ENTICE, ENTICED, ENTICES (v) to tempt; to lure
Deut 13:6 . . . someone secretly **e-s** you—
Job 31:27 . . . secretly **e-d** in my heart
Prov 1:10 . . . if sinners **e** you, turn your back
Prov 7:21 . . . and **e-d** him with her flattery.
Jas 1:14 . . . our own desires, which **e** us

ENTRUST, ENTRUSTED (v) to commit to another with confidence
Ps 31:5 . . . I **e** my spirit into your hand.
Luke 12:48 . . . has been **e-ed** with much,
Luke 23:46 . . . I **e** my spirit into your
Acts 15:40 . . . left, the believers **e-ed** him
Acts 20:32 . . . And now I **e** you to God
Rom 3:2 . . . Jews were **e-ed** with the whole
1 Thes 2:4 . . . to be **e-ed** with the Good News.
1 Tim 1:11 . . . Good News **e-ed** to me
2 Tim 1:14 . . . truth that has been **e-ed** to you.
1 Pet 5:2 . . . flock that God has **e-ed** to you.

ENVY (n) discontent or resentment because of another's success, advantages, or superiority
see also JEALOUSY
Mark 7:22 . . . lustful desires, **e,** slander,
Rom 1:29 . . . sin, greed, hate, **e,** murder,
Gal 5:21 . . . **e,** drunkenness, wild parties,
Titus 3:3 . . . full of evil and **e,** and we hated
Jas 4:5 . . . within us is filled with **e?**

ENVY (v) to feel or show envy; to begrudge
Prov 3:31 . . . Don't **e** violent people
Prov 24:1 . . . Don't **e** evil people

EPILEPTIC (adj) relating to, affected with, or having characteristics of epilepsy
Matt 4:24 . . . were demon-possessed or **e** or

EQUAL (adj) like in quantity, quality, nature, or status
John 5:18 . . . making himself **e** with God.
2 Cor 8:14 . . . In this way, things will be **e.**

EQUIP (v) to prepare; to furnish for service or action
Eph 4:12 . . . to **e** God's people to do
2 Tim 3:17 . . . to prepare and **e** his people
Heb 13:21 . . . **e** you with all you need

ERASE (v) to blot out, cause to disappear
Ps 34:16 . . . **e** their memory from the earth.
Rev 3:5 . . . never **e** their names from the Book

ESCAPE (n) evasion of something undesirable
1 Thes 5:3 . . . there will be no **e.**

ESCAPE, ESCAPED, ESCAPING (v) to avoid; to get free of or break away from
Ps 89:48 . . . can **e** the power of the grave.
Ps 139:7 . . . I can never **e** from your Spirit!
Matt 23:33 . . . will you **e** the judgment
1 Cor 3:15 . . . barely **e-ing** through a wall of
Heb 2:3 . . . think we can **e** if we ignore
Heb 12:25 . . . we will certainly not **e** if we
2 Pet 2:18 . . . those who have barely **e-d**
2 Pet 2:20 . . . **e** from the wickedness

ESTABLISH, ESTABLISHED (v) to institute permanently; to set up; to bring into existence
1 Kgs 9:5 . . . will **e** the throne of your dynasty
Ps 89:4 . . . I will **e** your descendants as kings
Prov 8:28 . . . when he **e-ed** springs
Isa 16:5 . . . God will **e** one of David's

ESTEEM (n) the regard in which one is held; worth; value
2 Chr 18:1 . . . enjoyed great riches and high **e,**
Prov 22:1 . . . being held in high **e** is better

ESTHER Jewish exile who became queen of Persia, also known as "Hadassah" (Esth 1:1); cousin of Mordecai (Esth 2:7); brought into king's harem (Esth 2:8-9); crowned queen (Esth 2:17); agreed to help Jews (Esth 4:14-17); invited king to a banquet (Esth 5:1-8); revealed Haman's plan (Esth 7:3-6); rescued the Jews (Esth 8:8); established Festival of Purim (Esth 9:18-32).

ETERNAL (adj) having infinite duration; valid or existing at all times
see also EVERLASTING, FOREVER
Gen 9:16 . . . will remember the **e** covenant
Exod 3:15 . . . my **e** name, my name to
Lev 24:8 . . . a requirement of the **e**
Num 18:19 . . . an **e** and unbreakable
Ps 119:142 . . . Your justice is **e,**
Jer 50:5 . . . with an **e** covenant
Dan 4:34 . . . and his kingdom is **e.**
Dan 7:14 . . . His rule is **e**—
Matt 18:8 . . . better to enter **e** life with
Matt 19:16 . . . must I do to have **e** life?
Matt 25:41 . . . into the **e** fire
Matt 25:46 . . . away into **e** punishment,
Mark 3:29 . . . a sin with **e** consequences.
Luke 10:25 . . . should I do to inherit **e** life?
Luke 18:18 . . . should I do to inherit **e** life?
John 3:15 . . . in him will have **e** life.
John 3:16 . . . not perish but have **e** life.
John 3:36 . . . believes in God's Son has **e**
John 5:29 . . . will rise to experience **e** life,
John 5:39 . . . you think they give you **e** life.
John 6:68 . . . the words that give **e** life.
John 12:50 . . . his commands lead to **e** life;
John 17:2 . . . He gives **e** life
Rom 1:20 . . . **e** power and divine nature
Rom 5:21 . . . resulting in **e** life through
Rom 6:23 . . . free gift of God is **e** life
Rom 9:5 . . . is worthy of **e** praise! Amen.
Rom 16:26 . . . the **e** God has commanded,
Eph 3:11 . . . This was his **e** plan,
2 Thes 1:9 . . . punished with **e** destruction,
1 Tim 6:12 . . . Hold tightly to the **e** life
Titus 3:7 . . . we will inherit **e** life.
Heb 5:9 . . . source of **e** salvation
Heb 9:15 . . . **e** inheritance God has
Heb 13:20 . . . an **e** covenant with his blood—
1 Pet 1:23 . . . from the **e,** living word
1 Pet 5:10 . . . to share in his **e** glory
1 Jn 1:2 . . . he is the one who is **e** life.
1 Jn 2:25 . . . we enjoy the **e** life he
1 Jn 5:20 . . . and he is **e** life.
Jude 1:7 . . . the **e** fire of God's judgment.
Jude 1:21 . . . who will bring you **e** life.

ETERNALLY (adv) in an endless, infinite manner
Eph 6:24 . . . May God's grace be **e** upon all

ETERNITY (n) immortality; infinite time
Eccl 3:11 . . . has planted **e** in the human
Isa 57:15 . . . who lives in **e,** the Holy One,
John 12:25 . . . will keep it for **e.**

EUNUCH, EUNUCHS (n) male attendant, often castrated, implying singular devotion to a master
Isa 56:4 . . . I will bless those **e-s** who keep
Matt 19:12 . . . some have been made **e-s** by
Acts 8:27 . . . The **e** had gone to Jerusalem

EVALUATE, EVALUATED (v) to determine the significance, worth, or value of
1 Cor 2:15 . . . Those who are spiritual can **e**
1 Cor 2:15 . . . cannot be **e-d** by others.
1 Cor 4:3 . . . **e-d** by you or by any human
1 Cor 14:29 . . . let the others **e** what is said.

EVALUATION (n) the determination of the significance, worth, or value of
Rom 12:3 . . . in your **e** of yourselves,

EVANGELIST, EVANGELISTS (n) preacher of the gospel
Acts 21:8 . . . Philip the **E,** one of the seven
Eph 4:11 . . . apostles, the prophets, the **e-s,**

EVE First woman and mother of all people; created from Adam's rib (Gen 2:21-23; 1 Tim 2:13); deceived by the serpent (Gen 3:1-13; 2 Cor 11:3); named "Eve" by Adam (Gen 3:20); cursed with painful childbirth (Gen 3:16; 4:1); descendants of (Gen 5).

EVENING (n) the latter part and close of the day
Gen 1:5 . . . And **e** passed and morning came,

EVER-LIVING (adj) eternal; immortal
Rom 1:23 . . . the glorious, **e** God,

EVER (adv) always; at any time
Exod 15:18 . . . will reign forever and **e!**
Ps 145:1 . . . praise your name forever and **e.**
Dan 7:18 . . . they will rule forever and **e.**
John 1:18 . . . No one has **e** seen God.
Phil 4:20 . . . forever and **e!** Amen.
2 Tim 4:18 . . . glory to God forever and **e!**
Heb 1:8 . . . endures forever and **e.**
1 Pet 4:11 . . . to him forever and **e!** Amen.
1 Jn 4:12 . . . No one has **e** seen God.
Rev 1:6 . . . to him forever and **e!** Amen.
Rev 1:18 . . . I am alive forever and **e!**
Rev 22:5 . . . they will reign forever and **e.**

EVERLASTING (adj) continuing indefinitely
see also ETERNAL, FOREVER
Gen 17:7 . . . This is the **e** covenant:
Gen 48:4 . . . as an **e** possession.
2 Sam 23:5 . . . made an **e** covenant with
Ps 139:24 . . . lead me along the path of **e** life.
Isa 9:6 . . . God, **E** Father, Prince of Peace.
Isa 35:10 . . . crowned with **e** joy.
Isa 40:28 . . . The LORD is the **e** God,
Isa 54:8 . . . But with **e** love
Isa 55:3 . . . an **e** covenant with you.
Isa 60:19 . . . God will be your **e** light,
Isa 60:20 . . . the LORD will be your **e** light.
Isa 61:7 . . . and **e** joy will be yours.
Isa 61:8 . . . an **e** covenant with them.
Jer 10:10 . . . the living God and the **e** King!
Jer 31:3 . . . with an **e** love.
Ezek 16:60 . . . establish an **e** covenant with
Dan 4:34 . . . His rule is **e,**
Dan 9:24 . . . to bring in **e** righteousness,
Dan 12:2 . . . to **e** life and some to shame
Gal 6:8 . . . will harvest **e** life from the

EVERYTHING (pron) all that exists; all that relates to the subject
Ps 145:17 . . . is righteous in **e** he does;
Matt 6:6 . . . your Father, who sees **e,**
Mark 12:44 . . . has given **e** she had to live on.
Acts 2:44 . . . and shared **e** they had.
2 Cor 1:22 . . . **e** he has promised
2 Cor 6:10 . . . and yet we have **e.**
Heb 13:18 . . . to live honorably in **e** we do.

EVIDENCE (n) an outward sign; proof
Acts 11:23 . . . **e** of God's blessing,
Heb 11:4 . . . **e** that he was a righteous man,

EVIL (adj) bad, sinful, or morally reprehensible; of the devil
Gen 6:5 . . . was consistently and totally **e.**
Exod 32:22 . . . know how **e** these people
Ps 51:4 . . . what is **e** in your sight.
Ps 140:8 . . . not let **e** people have their way.
Prov 15:26 . . . The LORD detests **e** plans,
Matt 6:13 . . . rescue us from the **e** one.
Matt 12:45 . . . spirits more **e** than itself,
Matt 15:19 . . . from the heart come **e**
Mark 7:21 . . . heart, come **e** thoughts,
Luke 11:24 . . . When an **e** spirit leaves
John 17:15 . . . them safe from the **e** one.
Acts 19:13 . . . casting out **e** spirits.
Rom 2:9 . . . keeps on doing what is **e**—
Rom 13:14 . . . to indulge your **e** desires.
1 Cor 5:13 . . . remove the **e** person from
Eph 5:16 . . . in these **e** days.
Col 3:5 . . . lust, and **e** desires.
2 Thes 3:3 . . . guard you from the **e** one.
1 Tim 6:4 . . . slander, and **e** suspicions.
2 Tim 3:13 . . . **e** people and impostors
1 Jn 2:13 . . . your battle with the **e** one.
1 Jn 3:12 . . . Cain, who belonged to the **e** one
1 Jn 5:18 . . . the **e** one cannot touch

EVIL (n) something that brings sorrow, distress, or misfortune
Gen 2:9 . . . of the knowledge of good and **e.**
Gen 3:5 . . . knowing both good and **e.**
Judg 6:1 . . . The Israelites did **e**
Ps 5:5 . . . for you hate all who do **e.**
Ps 14:4 . . . Will those who do **e** never learn?

Ps 34:13 . . . tongue from speaking **e**
Ps 37:27 . . . Turn from **e** and do good,
Ps 45:7 . . . You love justice and hate **e.**
Ps 53:4 . . . Will those who do **e** never learn?
Ps 92:15 . . . There is no **e** in him!
Ps 101:4 . . . and stay away from every **e.**
Ps 125:5 . . . with those who do **e.**
Prov 6:18 . . . a heart that plots **e,**
Prov 8:13 . . . fear the LORD will hate **e.**
Prov 11:27 . . . search for **e,** it will find you!
Prov 13:6 . . . but the **e** are misled by sin.
Prov 17:13 . . . repay good with **e, e** will
Prov 20:30 . . . cleanses away **e;** such
Isa 5:20 . . . those who say that **e** is good
Isa 13:11 . . . punish the world for its **e**
Jer 23:14 . . . who are doing **e** so that
Hab 1:13 . . . cannot stand the sight of **e.**
Mal 3:15 . . . those who do **e** get rich,
Matt 5:45 . . . to both the **e** and the good,
Luke 13:27 . . . all you who do **e.**
John 3:20 . . . All who do **e** hate the light
Rom 12:21 . . . Don't let **e** conquer you,
1 Cor 14:20 . . . babies when it comes to **e,**
1 Thes 5:15 . . . no one pays back **e** for **e,**
1 Thes 5:22 . . . away from every kind of **e.**
1 Tim 6:10 . . . the root of all kinds of **e.**
2 Tim 2:19 . . . must turn away from **e.**
Heb 1:9 . . . You love justice and hate **e.**
Jas 1:21 . . . get rid of all the filth and **e**
Jas 3:8 . . . It is restless and **e,**
1 Pet 2:16 . . . as an excuse to do **e.**
1 Pet 3:9 . . . Don't repay **e** for **e.**
1 Pet 3:11 . . . Turn away from **e** and do
3 Jn 1:11 . . . those who do **e** prove that they

EVIL-MINDED (adj) having an evil disposition or evil thoughts
Ps 119:115 . . . Get out of my life, you **e** people,

EVILDOERS (n) one who does evil
Ps 92:7 . . . like weeds and **e** flourish,
Ps 92:9 . . . perish; all **e** will be scattered.
Ps 94:16 . . . will stand up for me against **e?**
Prov 21:15 . . . it terrifies **e.**
Prov 24:19 . . . Don't fret because of **e;**

EXALT, EXALTED, EXALTING, EXALTS (v) to elevate; to glorify; to raise in rank or power
see also GLORIFY, HONOR
Exod 15:2 . . . and I will **e** him!
2 Sam 22:47 . . . of my salvation, be **e-ed!**
Neh 9:5 . . . May it be **e-ed** above all blessing
Job 36:7 . . . kings and **e-s** them forever.
Ps 18:46 . . . God of my salvation be **e-ed!**
Ps 30:1 . . . I will **e** you, LORD,
Ps 92:8 . . . O LORD, will be **e-ed** forever.
Ps 97:9 . . . you are **e-ed** far above all gods.
Ps 107:32 . . . Let them **e** him publicly
Ps 145:1 . . . I will **e** you, my God and King,
Dan 11:36 . . . as he pleases, **e-ing** himself
Luke 14:11 . . . those who **e** themselves will
Acts 2:33 . . . is **e-ed** to the place of highest
2 Thes 2:4 . . . He will **e** himself

EXAMINE, EXAMINED, EXAMINES, EXAMINING (v) to test the condition of; to inspect closely
1 Chr 29:17 . . . you **e** our hearts
Ps 11:4 . . . **e-ing** every person on earth.
Ps 11:5 . . . The LORD **e-s** both
Ps 17:3 . . . **e-d** my heart in the night.
Ps 139:1 . . . LORD, you have **e-d** my heart
Prov 5:21 . . . **e-ing** every path he takes.
Prov 21:2 . . . the LORD **e-s** their heart.
Jer 11:20 . . . you **e** the deepest thoughts
Jer 17:10 . . . and **e** secret motives.
Lam 3:40 . . . let us test and **e** our ways.
1 Cor 4:4 . . . Lord himself who will **e**
1 Cor 11:28 . . . you should **e** yourself
2 Cor 13:5 . . . **E** yourselves to see
1 Thes 2:4 . . . He alone **e-s** the motives

EXAMPLE, EXAMPLES (n) one that serves as a pattern to be or not to be imitated
John 13:15 . . . given you an **e** to
1 Cor 10:11 . . . happened to them as **e-s** for
2 Thes 3:9 . . . give you an **e** to follow.
Titus 2:7 . . . **e** to them by doing good
Heb 13:7 . . . and follow the **e** of their faith.
Jas 5:10 . . . For **e-s** of patience in suffering,
1 Pet 2:21 . . . He is your **e,** and you must

EXCEEDS (v) to be greater than or superior to
Phil 4:7 . . . **e** anything we can understand.

EXCEL (v) to surpass in accomplishment or achievement
2 Cor 8:7 . . . **e** also in this gracious act of

EXCELLENCE (n) something that gives especial worth or value
2 Pet 1:5 . . . a generous provision of moral **e,**

EXCELLENT (adj) very good of its kind; superior
Phil 4:8 . . . Think about things that are **e**

EXCHANGE (n) the act of giving or taking one thing for another
Lev 17:11 . . . blood, given in **e** for a life,

EXCHANGED (v) to part with for a substitute
Job 28:19 . . . cannot be **e** for it.
Jer 2:11 . . . my people have **e** their glorious God
Hos 4:7 . . . They have **e** the glory of God

EXCUSE (n) the apology or justification offered
John 15:22 . . . they have no **e** for their sin.
Rom 1:20 . . . no **e** for not knowing God.
Rom 2:1 . . . and you have no **e!**
1 Pet 2:16 . . . your freedom as an **e**

EXCUSE (v) to overlook, justify, or make an apology for
Exod 34:7 . . . But I do not **e** the guilty.
Eph 5:6 . . . those who try to **e** these sins,

EXECUTED (v) to put to death
Num 35:16 . . . the murderer must be **e.**
Deut 21:22 . . . and is **e** and hung on a tree,

EXECUTION (n) a putting to death especially as a legal penalty
Num 35:31 . . . murder and subject to **e;**

EXHAUST (v) to consume entirely
Isa 7:13 . . . Must you **e** the patience of my God

EXHAUSTION (n) fatigue, tiredness, collapse
2 Cor 6:5 . . . worked to **e,** endured

EXHORT(ATION) (KJV)
Rom 12:8 . . . If your gift is to *encourage*
1 Thes 2:3 . . . not *preaching* with any deceit
Heb 3:13 . . . You must *warn* each other

EXILE, EXILES (n) the state of forced absence from one's country or home; a person who is in exile
2 Kgs 25:11 . . . took as **e-s** the rest of
2 Kgs 25:21 . . . sent into **e** from their land.
Ezra 2:1 . . . the Jewish **e-s** of the provinces
Jer 52:27 . . . were sent into **e** from their land.

EXILED (v) to banish or expel
2 Kgs 17:6 . . . of Israel were **e** to Assyria.
2 Kgs 17:23 . . . So Israel was **e** from their land

EXISTS (v) to have real being whether material or spiritual
Heb 11:6 . . . must believe that God **e**

EXORCISTS (n) one who expels evil spirits
Luke 11:19 . . . what about your own **e?**

EXPELLED, EXPELS (v) to force to leave
Ezek 28:16 . . . I **e** you, O mighty guardian,
1 Jn 4:18 . . . perfect love **e-s** all fear.

EXPENSES (n) financial costs
1 Cor 9:7 . . . has to pay his own **e?**

EXPENSIVE (adj) involving high cost
Mark 14:3 . . . alabaster jar of **e** perfume
Luke 7:25 . . . a man dressed in **e** clothes?
John 12:3 . . . a twelve-ounce jar of **e** perfume
1 Tim 2:9 . . . gold or pearls or **e** clothes.

EXPERIENCE (v) to learn by or have direct observation or participation
Deut 28:2 . . . You will **e** all these blessings
Eph 3:19 . . . May you **e** the love of Christ,

EXPLAIN, EXPLAINED, EXPLAINS (v) to make plain or understandable; to give the reason or cause
Gen 2:24 . . . This **e-s** why a man leaves his
Neh 8:8 . . . and clearly **e-ed** the meaning
Matt 19:5 . . . This **e-s** why a man leaves his
Acts 17:3 . . . He **e-ed** the prophecies
Acts 18:28 . . . **e-ed** to them that Jesus was
Eph 6:19 . . . **e** God's mysterious plan
2 Tim 2:15 . . . correctly **e-s** the word of
1 Pet 3:15 . . . always be ready to **e** it.

EXPLOIT (v) to make use of meanly or unfairly for one's own advantage
Exod 22:22 . . . must not **e** a widow or an orphan.
Prov 22:22 . . . or **e** the needy in court.

EXPLOITED (n) one unfairly used for another's advantage
Isa 11:4 . . . fair decisions for the **e.**

EXPLORE (v) to investigate, study, or analyze
Num 13:2 . . . Send out men to **e** the land
Num 32:8 . . . to **e** the land.

EXPOSE, EXPOSED, EXPOSES, EXPOSING (v) to make known; to display
Prov 20:27 . . . **e-ing** every hidden motive.
Lam 4:22 . . . your many sins will be **e-d.**
John 3:20 . . . fear their sins will be **e-d.**
Eph 5:11 . . . instead, **e** them.
Heb 4:12 . . . It **e-s** our innermost thoughts
Heb 4:13 . . . is naked and **e-d** before his eyes,

EXTENDS (v) to stretch out to the fullest length; to proffer
Ps 119:90 . . . faithfulness **e** to every
Prov 31:20 . . . She **e** a helping hand

EXTINGUISH (v) to cause to cease burning
John 1:5 . . . the darkness can never **e** it.

EXTOL(LED) (KJV)
Ps 30:1 . . . will *exalt* you, LORD, for you
Ps 66:17 . . . to him for help, *praising* him
Ps 68:4 . . . *Sing loud praises* to him who
Isa 52:13 . . . he will be *highly exalted*

EXTORTION (n) the act or practice of obtaining money or property by illegal power
Lev 6:4 . . . or the money you took by **e,**

EXTREME (adj) situated at the farthest possible point from a center
Josh 15:21 . . . of Edom in the **e** south
Ezek 46:19 . . . a place at the **e** west end
Ezek 48:1 . . . Dan is in the **e** north

EXTREMES (n) something situated at or marking one end or the other of a range
Eccl 7:18 . . . will avoid both **e.**

EXULT (v) to be extremely joyful; to rejoice
Ps 89:16 . . . They **e** in your righteousness.

EYE, EYES (n) organ of (physical and spiritual) sight
Exod 21:24 . . . an **e** for an **e,**
Deut 16:19 . . . bribes blind the **e-s** of
Job 36:7 . . . never takes his **e-s** off the
Ps 119:18 . . . Open my **e-s** to see
Ps 119:37 . . . Turn my **e-s** from worthless
Ps 123:1 . . . I lift my **e-s** to you,
Prov 4:25 . . . and fix your **e-s** on what
Matt 5:29 . . . **e**—causes you to lust,
Matt 5:38 . . . An **e** for an **e,**
Matt 6:22 . . . When your **e** is good,
1 Cor 2:9 . . . when they say, "No **e** has seen,
Heb 12:2 . . . by keeping our **e-s** on Jesus,
2 Pet 1:16 . . . with our own **e-s**
Rev 21:4 . . . wipe every tear from their **e-s,**

EYELIDS (n) the movable fold of skin and muscle that closes over the eyeball
2 Kgs 9:30 . . . painted her **e** and fixed her hair

EYEWITNESS (n) one who sees an occurrence or object
Luke 1:2 . . . They used the **e** reports

EZEKIEL Prophet of Judah (southern kingdom) and priest (Ezek 1:3); exiled to Babylon near the Kebar River (Ezek 3:15).

EZRA Postexilic priestly reformer in time of Artaxerxes (Ezra 7; 10; Neh 8; 12); descendant of Seraiah (Ezra 7:1); skillful, learned teacher of the Law (Ezra 7:6); determined to study and obey the Law (Ezra 7:10); served as priest (Ezra 7:11); restored Temple and its worship (Ezra 7–8); corrected pagan intermarriage (Ezra 9–10); dedicated Jerusalem's repaired walls (Neh 12).

F

FACE (n) in or into direct contact or confrontation (as in "face to face"); countenance; presence; the front part of the head
Gen 32:30 . . . I have seen God **f** to **f,**
Exod 33:11 . . . speak to Moses **f** to **f,**
Exod 34:29 . . . his **f** had become radiant
Num 12:8 . . . I speak to him **f** to **f,**
Deut 31:17 . . . hiding my **f** from them,
Judg 6:22 . . . angel of the LORD **f** to **f!**
2 Chr 7:14 . . . and seek my **f** and turn from
Ps 4:6 . . . Let your **f** smile on us,
Ps 17:15 . . . I will see you **f** to **f**
Ps 67:1 . . . May his **f** smile with favor on us.
Luke 9:29 . . . appearance of his **f** was
2 Cor 3:7 . . . For his **f** shone with the glory
Rev 1:16 . . . And his **f** was like the sun
Rev 22:4 . . . they will see his **f,**

FACE, FACED, FACING (v) to confront; to be confronted by
Ps 112:8 . . . **f** their foes triumphantly.
Ps 116:6 . . . I was **f-ing** death, and he saved
2 Cor 6:5 . . . **f-d** angry mobs,

FADE, FADING (v) to lose freshness, strength, or vitality
Isa 40:7 . . . and the flowers **f**
1 Cor 9:25 . . . to win a prize that will **f**
2 Cor 3:7 . . . brightness was already **f-ing**
2 Cor 3:13 . . . it was destined to **f** away.
Jas 1:11 . . . the rich will **f** away
1 Jn 2:17 . . . this world is **f-ing** away,

FAIL, FAILED, FAILS (v) to disappoint; to fall short; to weaken; to miss performing an expected service; to be unsuccessful
Num 23:19 . . . spoken and **f-ed** to act?
Deut 31:6 . . . He will neither **f** you
Josh 23:14 . . . Not a single one has **f-ed!**
1 Kgs 8:56 . . . Not one word has **f-ed**
Ps 77:8 . . . his promises permanently **f-ed?**
Luke 13:24 . . . try to enter but will **f.**
Luke 22:32 . . . faith should not **f.**
Rom 9:6 . . . has God **f-ed** to fulfill his promise
2 Cor 13:5 . . . if not, you have **f-ed** the test
2 Cor 13:6 . . . we have not **f-ed** the test
Heb 12:15 . . . none of you **f-s** to receive
Heb 13:5 . . . I will never **f** you.
1 Pet 4:19 . . . he will never **f** you.

FAINT (adj) lacking strength or vigor
Jon 4:8 . . . grew **f** and wished to die.

FAINT (v) to become weak or lose courage in body or spirit
Isa 40:31 . . . will walk and not **f.**

FAIR (adj) free from self-interest, prejudice, or favoritism; beautiful
Prov 1:3 . . . do what is right, just, and **f.**
Song 2:13 . . . away with me, my **f** one!
Isa 11:4 . . . make **f** decisions for the
Rom 3:25 . . . God was being **f** when he
Rom 3:26 . . . he himself is **f** and just,
Col 4:1 . . . be just and **f** to your slaves.

FAIRNESS (n) the quality of being free from self-interest, prejudice, or favoritism
Ps 9:8 . . . rule the nations with **f.**
Ps 98:9 . . . and the nations with **f.**
Ps 99:4 . . . you have established **f.**
Isa 9:7 . . . will rule with **f** and justice

FAITH (n) reliance, loyalty, or complete trust in God; a system of religious beliefs
see also BELIEVE, TRUST
Exod 14:31 . . . They put their **f** in the LORD
Isa 7:9 . . . Unless your **f** is firm,
Matt 9:2 . . . Seeing their **f,** Jesus said
Matt 9:29 . . . Because of your **f,** it will
Matt 15:28 . . . your **f** is great.
Matt 17:20 . . . **f** even as small as a mustard
Matt 21:22 . . . if you have **f,** you will receive
Mark 10:52 . . . for your **f** has healed you.
Luke 5:20 . . . Seeing their **f,** Jesus said
Luke 7:50 . . . Your **f** has saved you;
Luke 8:48 . . . your **f** has made you well.
Luke 12:28 . . . Why do you have so little **f?**
Luke 17:6 . . . **f** even as small as a mustard
Luke 18:8 . . . find on the earth who have **f?**
John 16:1 . . . won't abandon your **f.**
Acts 6:5 . . . full of **f** and the Holy Spirit
Acts 14:9 . . . he had **f** to be healed.
Acts 14:27 . . . opened the door of **f** to the
Acts 16:5 . . . strengthened in their **f** and grew
Acts 24:24 . . . told them about **f** in Christ
Rom 1:8 . . . your **f** in him is being talked about
Rom 1:12 . . . to encourage you in your **f,**
Rom 1:17 . . . from start to finish by **f.**
Rom 1:17 . . . through **f** that a righteous
Rom 3:28 . . . right with God through **f**
Rom 3:30 . . . right with himself only by **f,**
Rom 3:31 . . . only when we have **f**
Rom 4:5 . . . because of their **f** in God
Rom 4:9 . . . because of his **f.**
Rom 4:12 . . . same kind of **f** Abraham had
Rom 4:13 . . . with God that comes by **f.**
Rom 4:14 . . . then **f** is not necessary
Rom 4:16 . . . the promise is received by **f.**
Rom 4:16 . . . if we have **f** like Abraham's.
Rom 4:19 . . . And Abraham's **f** did not weaken,
Rom 4:20 . . . In fact, his **f** grew stronger,
Rom 5:1 . . . made right in God's sight by **f,**
Rom 5:2 . . . Because of our **f,** Christ has
Rom 10:8 . . . message about **f** that we preach:
Rom 10:17 . . . So **f** comes from hearing,
Rom 12:6 . . . speak out with as much **f** as
Rom 14:1 . . . believers who are weak in **f,**
1 Cor 12:9 . . . gives great **f** to another,
1 Cor 13:13 . . . **f,** hope, and love—
1 Cor 15:14 . . . and your **f** is useless.
1 Cor 16:13 . . . Stand firm in the **f.**
2 Cor 1:24 . . . put your **f** into practice.
2 Cor 13:5 . . . failed the test of genuine **f.**
Gal 1:23 . . . the very **f** he tried to destroy!
Gal 3:9 . . . all who put their **f** in Christ
Gal 3:11 . . . **f** that a righteous person
Gal 3:12 . . . This way of **f** is very different
Gal 3:14 . . . Holy Spirit through **f.**
Gal 3:23 . . . the way of **f** in Christ was available
Gal 3:24 . . . made right with God through **f.**
Gal 3:25 . . . the way of **f** has come,
Gal 3:26 . . . children of God through **f** in Christ
Gal 5:5 . . . wait to receive by **f**
Eph 1:15 . . . heard of your strong **f** in the Lord
Eph 4:5 . . . one Lord, one **f,** one baptism,
Eph 6:16 . . . hold up the shield of **f**
Phil 1:25 . . . experience the joy of your **f.**
Phil 3:9 . . . righteous through **f** in Christ.
Col 1:4 . . . we have heard of your **f** in Christ
1 Thes 1:8 . . . telling us about your **f** in God.
1 Thes 3:5 . . . your **f** was still strong.
1 Thes 3:10 . . . fill the gaps in your **f.**
2 Thes 1:3 . . . because your **f** is flourishing
1 Tim 1:4 . . . live a life of **f** in God.
1 Tim 1:19 . . . Cling to your **f** in Christ,
1 Tim 3:9 . . . mystery of the **f** now
1 Tim 4:1 . . . will turn away from the true **f;**
1 Tim 6:10 . . . have wandered from the true **f**
1 Tim 6:12 . . . good fight for the true **f.**
2 Tim 1:5 . . . remember your genuine **f,**
2 Tim 2:18 . . . away from the **f.**
2 Tim 3:10 . . . You know my **f,** my patience,
Titus 1:1 . . . have been sent to proclaim **f**
Titus 1:13 . . . make them strong in the **f.**
Titus 2:2 . . . must have sound **f** and be filled
Phlm 1:5 . . . hearing about your **f** in the Lord
Phlm 1:6 . . . that comes from your **f**
Heb 4:2 . . . they didn't share the **f**
Heb 6:1 . . . and placing our **f** in God.
Heb 6:12 . . . because of their **f** and endurance.
Heb 10:38 . . . will live by **f.**
Heb 11:5 . . . It was by **f** that Enoch
Heb 11:7 . . . It was by **f** that Noah
Heb 11:8 . . . It was by **f** that Abraham
Heb 11:23 . . . It was by **f** that Moses' parents
Heb 11:29 . . . It was by **f** that the people
Heb 12:2 . . . perfects our **f.**
Jas 1:3 . . . when your **f** is tested,
Jas 2:5 . . . be rich in **f?**
Jas 2:14 . . . Can that kind of **f** save anyone?
Jas 2:17 . . . **f** by itself isn't enough.

Jas 2:18 . . . Some people have **f**;
Jas 2:20 . . . **f** without good deeds
Jas 2:22 . . . made his **f** complete.
Jas 2:24 . . . not by **f** alone.
Jas 2:26 . . . so also **f** is dead
Jas 5:15 . . . prayer offered in **f** will heal
1 Pet 1:21 . . . have placed your **f** and hope
2 Pet 1:1 . . . the same precious **f** we have.
Jude 1:3 . . . defend the **f** that God
Jude 1:20 . . . in your most holy **f**,

FAITHFUL (adj) firm in adherence, utterly loyal
see also LOYAL, TRUSTWORTHY, UNFAILING
Deut 7:9 . . . He is the **f** God who keeps his
1 Sam 2:9 . . . will protect his **f** ones,
1 Sam 20:14 . . . me with the **f** love of the
2 Sam 22:26 . . . you show yourself **f**; to those
1 Kgs 8:61 . . . you be completely **f** to the
1 Kgs 15:14 . . . remained completely **f** to
2 Kgs 20:3 . . . have always been **f** to you
Ps 18:25 . . . you show yourself **f**;
Ps 71:22 . . . because you are **f** to your
Ps 89:8 . . . You are entirely **f**.
Ps 89:49 . . . with a **f** pledge.
Ps 143:1 . . . you are **f** and righteous.
Isa 38:3 . . . have always been **f** to you and
Hos 11:12 . . . God and is **f** to the Holy One.
Zech 8:3 . . . be called the **F** City;
Zech 8:8 . . . I will be **f** and just toward
Matt 24:45 . . . A **f**, sensible
Matt 25:21 . . . You have been **f** in handling
Matt 25:23 . . . my good and **f** servant.
Luke 12:42 . . . Lord replied, "A **f**, sensible
Luke 16:10 . . . If you are **f** in little
1 Cor 4:17 . . . my beloved and **f** child in the
2 Cor 1:18 . . . as God is **f**, our word to you
Eph 1:1 . . . who are **f** followers of Christ
Phil 2:17 . . . just like your **f** service is
Col 4:7 . . . brother and **f** helper who
Col 4:9 . . . Onesimus, a **f** and beloved
1 Thes 1:3 . . . we think of your **f** work,
1 Thes 5:24 . . . calls you is **f**.
2 Thes 3:3 . . . But the Lord is **f**; he will
1 Tim 3:2 . . . He must be **f** to his wife.
1 Tim 3:11 . . . and be **f** in everything they
1 Tim 5:9 . . . old and was **f** to her husband.
2 Tim 4:7 . . . I have remained **f**.
Heb 2:17 . . . merciful and **f** High Priest
Heb 3:2 . . . For he was **f** to God, who
Heb 8:9 . . . They did not remain **f** to my
Heb 13:4 . . . marriage, and remain **f** to one
1 Jn 1:9 . . . to him, he is **f** and just to
Rev 1:5 . . . He is the **f** witness to these
Rev 2:10 . . . But if you remain **f** even when
Rev 3:14 . . . is the Amen—the **f** and true
Rev 17:14 . . . chosen and **f** ones will be

FAITHFUL (n) those who practice faith
Ps 149:1 . . . assembly of the **f**.
Ps 149:5 . . . Let the **f** rejoice that he

FAITHFULLY (adv) in a manner that is firm, regular, and steady
Deut 7:12 . . . regulations and **f** obey them,
1 Kgs 8:25 . . . and **f** follow me
2 Chr 32:1 . . . Hezekiah had **f** carried out
Neh 13:14 . . . all that I have **f** done for
Isa 61:8 . . . I will **f** reward my people for

FAITHFULNESS (n) the quality of steadfast loyalty or firm adherence to promises
Exod 34:6 . . . unfailing love and **f**.
Ps 25:10 . . . with unfailing love and **f**
Ps 36:5 . . . your **f** reaches beyond
Ps 57:10 . . . Your **f** reaches to the clouds.
Ps 92:2 . . . your **f** in the evening,
Ps 100:5 . . . **f** continues to each
Prov 14:22 . . . unfailing love and **f**.
Prov 16:6 . . . love and **f** make atonement
Prov 20:28 . . . love and **f** protect the king;
Isa 38:18 . . . no longer hope in your **f**.
Lam 3:23 . . . Great is his **f**;
Gal 5:22 . . . kindness, goodness, **f**,
Eph 6:23 . . . give you love with **f**.
2 Thes 1:4 . . . your endurance and **f**
2 Tim 2:22 . . . pursue righteous living, **f**,

FAITHLESS (adj) disloyal; lacking trust
Ps 78:57 . . . and were as **f** as their parents.
Jer 3:8 . . . I divorced **f** Israel because
Jer 3:11 . . . Even **f** Israel is less guilty than
Jer 3:12 . . . Israel, my **f** people, come home
Matt 17:17 . . . You **f** and corrupt people!
Mark 9:19 . . . You **f** people!
John 20:27 . . . Don't be **f** any longer.

FALL, FALLEN, FALLING (v) to collapse; to drop down (wounded or dead); to become lower in degree or level; to come by assignment or inheritance; to descend; to stumble or stray (morally)
2 Sam 1:19 . . . the mighty heroes have **f-en**!
Ps 37:24 . . . they will never **f**,
Ps 69:9 . . . those who insult you have **f-en** on
Prov 10:8 . . . babbling fools **f** flat on their
Prov 24:17 . . . when your enemies **f**;
Isa 14:12 . . . How you are **f-en** from heaven,
Matt 13:21 . . . They **f** away as soon as
Luke 10:18 . . . I saw Satan **f** from heaven
Rom 3:23 . . . we all **f** short of
Rom 14:13 . . . believer to stumble and **f**.
Gal 5:4 . . . have **f-en** away from God's grace.
2 Pet 1:10 . . . and you will never **f** away.
Jude 1:24 . . . able to keep you from **f-ing** away

FALSE (adj) intentionally untrue; dishonest; misleading; unwise; faithless
Prov 12:17 . . . a **f** witness tells lies.
Isa 44:25 . . . I expose the **f** prophets as
Matt 24:11 . . . And many **f** prophets will
Mark 13:22 . . . For **f** messiahs and **f**
2 Cor 11:13 . . . These people are **f** apostles.
Titus 1:11 . . . by their **f** teaching.
2 Pet 2:1 . . . were also **f** prophets in Israel,
1 Jn 4:1 . . . many **f** prophets in the world.
Rev 16:13 . . . and the **f** prophet.
Rev 19:20 . . . beast and his **f** prophet were
Rev 20:10 . . . the beast and the **f** prophet.

FALSEHOOD (n) a lie; the practice of lying
Ps 119:163 . . . hate and abhor all **f**,

FALSELY (adv) in an untrue, deceptive, or misleading manner
Exod 20:16 . . . must not testify **f** against
Mark 10:19 . . . not steal. You must not testify **f**.

FAME (n) popular acclaim
Exod 9:16 . . . spread my **f** throughout the earth.
Ps 49:12 . . . but their **f** will not last.
Ps 102:12 . . . Your **f** will endure
Isa 66:19 . . . heard of my **f** or seen my glory.

FAMILY, FAMILIES (n) a household unit of related people, as in a clan
see also HOUSEHOLD
Josh 24:15 . . . my **f**, we will serve the LORD.
Ps 68:6 . . . God places the lonely in **f-ies**;
Mark 3:25 . . . a **f** splintered by feuding
Luke 9:61 . . . let me say good-bye to my **f**.
Luke 12:52 . . . **f-ies** will be split apart,
Gal 6:10 . . . to those in the **f** of faith.
Eph 2:19 . . . members of God's **f**.
1 Tim 3:4 . . . manage his own **f** well,
Titus 1:11 . . . whole **f-ies** away from the truth
1 Jn 3:9 . . . who have been born into God's **f**

FAMINE (n) extreme scarcity of food
Gen 12:10 . . . a severe **f** struck the land
Gen 26:1 . . . A severe **f** now struck the
Gen 41:30 . . . seven years of **f** so great
Ruth 1:1 . . . a severe **f** came upon the land.
1 Kgs 18:2 . . . the **f** had become very
Amos 8:11 . . . I will send a **f** on the land—

FAMOUS (adj) widely known; honored for achievement
Gen 11:4 . . . This will make us **f**
Gen 12:2 . . . bless you and make you **f**,
Isa 63:12 . . . making himself **f** forever?

FANCY (adj) not plain; ornamental
1 Pet 3:3 . . . outward beauty of **f** hairstyles,

FANTASIES (n) created unrealistic or improbable mental images; daydream
Prov 12:11 . . . who chases **f** has no sense.

FAR (adv) at a considerable distance in space or degree
Ps 22:19 . . . Lord, do not stay **f** away!
Ezek 11:15 . . . are **f** away from the Lord
Eph 2:13 . . . you were **f** away from God,
Col 1:21 . . . were once **f** away from God

FARMER (n) one who cultivates crops or raises animals for food
Isa 28:24 . . . Does a **f** always plow and never
Isa 55:10 . . . producing seed for the **f**
Matt 13:18 . . . the parable about the **f** planting
2 Cor 9:6 . . . a **f** who plants only a few seeds
2 Cor 9:10 . . . seed for the **f** and then bread

FARTHEST (adj) most distant, especially in space or time
Acts 13:47 . . . bring salvation to the **f** corners

FAST, FASTING (v) to abstain from food
Ps 35:13 . . . denied myself by **f-ing** for
Matt 6:16 . . . when you **f**, don't make it
Acts 13:2 . . . worshiping the Lord and **f-ing**,

FATE (n) an inevitable and often adverse outcome or end
Prov 1:19 . . . the **f** of all who are greedy
Eccl 9:3 . . . suffers the same **f**.
1 Pet 2:8 . . . the **f** that was planned for them.

FATHER, FATHERS (n) male parent; ancestor(s); characteristic of a mentor or provider relationship; name and role for God in relation to the children he fosters/adopts; originator or creator
see also PARENT
Gen 2:24 . . . a man leaves his **f** and mother
Gen 17:4 . . . make you the **f** of a multitude
Exod 20:12 . . . Honor your **f** and mother.
Exod 21:15 . . . Anyone who strikes **f** or
Deut 32:6 . . . he your **F** who created you?
2 Sam 7:14 . . . I will be his **f**, and he
Ps 2:7 . . . Today I have become your **F**.
Ps 89:26 . . . You are my **F**, my God,
Prov 10:1 . . . wise child brings joy to a **f**;
Prov 23:22 . . . Listen to your **f**,
Isa 9:6 . . . Everlasting **F**, Prince of Peace.
Isa 63:16 . . . you would still be our **F**.
Jer 3:19 . . . forward to your calling me '**F**,'

Ezek 22:10 . . . sleep with their **f-s'** wives
Mal 2:10 . . . children of the same **F?**
Mal 4:6 . . . will turn the hearts of **f-s**
Matt 5:16 . . . will praise your heavenly **F.**
Matt 6:9 . . . Our **F** in heaven, may your
Matt 6:14 . . . heavenly **F** will forgive
Matt 10:37 . . . If you love your **f** or mother
Matt 11:27 . . . no one truly knows the **F**
Matt 15:4 . . . Honor your **f** and mother,
Matt 16:27 . . . in the glory of his **F**
Matt 19:5 . . . a man leaves his **f** and mother
Matt 19:29 . . . or **f** or mother or children
Matt 23:9 . . . is your spiritual **F.**
Luke 1:17 . . . hearts of the **f-s** to their
Luke 9:59 . . . and bury my **f.**
John 4:21 . . . you worship the **F** on this
John 5:17 . . . My **F** is always working,
John 5:20 . . . For the **F** loves the Son
John 6:44 . . . come to me unless the **F**
John 6:65 . . . unless the **F** gives them
John 8:19 . . . you don't know who my **F** is.
John 8:41 . . . God himself is our true **F.**
John 10:38 . . . understand that the **F** is in me,
John 14:6 . . . come to the **F** except through
John 14:21 . . . love me, my **F** will love
John 15:8 . . . brings great glory to my **F.**
John 15:23 . . . also hates my **F.**
John 20:17 . . . ascending to my **F** and
Acts 13:33 . . . Today I have become your **F.**
Rom 4:11 . . . Abraham is the spiritual **f**
Rom 4:16 . . . Abraham is the **f** of all who
Rom 8:15 . . . we call him, "Abba, **F.**"
2 Cor 6:18 . . . I will be your **F,** and you
Eph 5:31 . . . man leaves his **f** and mother
Eph 6:2 . . . Honor your **f** and mother.
Eph 6:4 . . . **F-s,** do not provoke
Phil 2:11 . . . to the glory of God the **F.**
Col 3:21 . . . **F-s,** do not aggravate
Heb 12:7 . . . is never disciplined by its **f?**
Heb 12:9 . . . earthly **f-s** who disciplined
1 Jn 1:3 . . . fellowship is with the **F** and
1 Jn 2:15 . . . the love of the **F** in you.
1 Jn 2:22 . . . who denies the **F** and the Son
1 Jn 3:1 . . . See how very much our **F** loves
Rev 3:21 . . . sat with my **F** on his throne.

FATHERLESS (adj) without a father; orphaned
see also ORPHAN
Ps 68:5 . . . Father to the **f,** defender of

FATTENING (v) to feed (as a stock animal) and make fat for slaughter
Luke 15:23 . . . calf we have been **f.**

FAULT (n) lack or error; moral weakness less serious than a vice
1 Sam 29:3 . . . never found a single **f** in
Prov 17:9 . . . when a **f** is forgiven,
Acts 20:26 . . . it's not my **f,**
2 Cor 6:3 . . . no one will find **f** with our
Eph 5:27 . . . she will be holy and without **f.**
Jude 1:24 . . . without a single **f.**

FAULTLESS (adj) having no fault; irreproachable
1 Thes 2:10 . . . honest and **f** toward all of you

FAVOR, FAVORS (n) gracious kindness; approval from a superior; a special privilege or right granted or conceded
see also GRACE
Gen 6:8 . . . Noah found **f** with the LORD.
Exod 34:9 . . . if it is true that I have found **f**
1 Sam 2:26 . . . and grew in **f** with the LORD
Prov 3:4 . . . you will find **f** with both God
Prov 18:22 . . . receives **f** from the LORD.
Prov 19:6 . . . Many seek **f-s** from a ruler;
Zech 11:7 . . . named one **F** and the other
Luke 1:30 . . . you have found **f** with God!
Luke 2:40 . . . and God's **f** was on him.
Luke 2:52 . . . and in **f** with God
Luke 4:19 . . . the time of the LORD's **f**
Rom 11:7 . . . have not found the **f** of God
Phil 1:7 . . . with me the special **f** of God,

FAVOR, FAVORING (v) to show partiality toward
Lev 19:15 . . . justice in legal matters by **f-ing**
Jas 2:9 . . . But if you **f** some people over

FAVORITE (adj) having special favor or liking
Gen 27:4 . . . Prepare my **f** dish,

FAVORITES (n) a person specially loved, trusted, or provided with favors
see also PARTIALITY
Job 32:21 . . . I won't play **f**
Matt 22:16 . . . and don't play **f.**
Gal 2:6 . . . for God has no **f.**
Eph 6:9 . . . he has no **f.**
Col 3:25 . . . For God has no **f.**

FAVORITISM (n) the showing of special favor; partiality
see also DISCRIMINATION, PARTIALITY
Prov 24:23 . . . **f** when passing judgment.
Mal 2:9 . . . **f** in the way you carry out
Acts 10:34 . . . that God shows no **f.**
Rom 2:11 . . . God does not show **f.**
Jas 3:17 . . . It shows no **f** and is always

FEAR, FEARS (n) dread or alarm in facing danger; profound reverence and awe
2 Sam 23:3 . . . who rules in the **f** of God,
Ps 2:11 . . . Serve the LORD with reverent **f,**
Ps 34:4 . . . freed me from all my **f-s.**
Prov 1:33 . . . untroubled by **f** of harm.
Heb 13:6 . . . will have no **f.**

FEAR, FEARED, FEARING, FEARS (v) to have reverential awe of God; to be afraid or apphrehensive
Deut 6:13 . . . You must **f** the LORD your
Deut 8:6 . . . walking in his ways and **f-ing**
Deut 13:4 . . . your God and **f** him alone.
Deut 31:12 . . . learn to **f** the LORD your God
Josh 4:24 . . . might **f** the LORD your God
1 Sam 12:14 . . . if you **f** and worship
2 Chr 26:5 . . . taught him to **f** God.
Neh 5:15 . . . But because I **f-ed** God,
Neh 7:2 . . . a faithful man who **f-ed** God
Job 1:1 . . . He **f-ed** God
Job 1:8 . . . He **f-s** God and stays away from
Ps 34:7 . . . and defends all who **f** him.
Ps 46:2 . . . not **f** when earthquakes come
Ps 61:5 . . . for those who **f** your name.
Ps 76:7 . . . you are greatly **f-ed!**
Ps 103:17 . . . with those who **f** him.
Ps 128:1 . . . joyful are those who **f** the
Prov 8:13 . . . All who **f** the LORD will
Prov 28:14 . . . those who **f** to do wrong,
Prov 31:30 . . . a woman who **f-s** the LORD
Isa 25:3 . . . nations will **f** you.
Jer 2:19 . . . your God and not to **f** him.
Mal 3:16 . . . those who **f-ed** the LORD spoke
Mal 4:2 . . . for you who **f** my name,
2 Cor 7:1 . . . because we **f** God.
Rev 11:18 . . . and all who **f** your name,

FEARFUL (adj) very great—used as an intensive
2 Cor 5:11 . . . our **f** responsibility to the Lord,

FEAST (n) an elaborate meal; banquet
Ps 23:5 . . . You prepare a **f** for me
Prov 15:15 . . . life is a continual **f.**
Luke 15:29 . . . goat for a **f** with my friends.

FEAST, FEASTING (v) to enjoy a good meal
Esth 9:17 . . . with a day of **f-ing** and gladness.
Prov 17:1 . . . a house filled with **f-ing**—and
Prov 23:20 . . . or **f** with gluttons,
Isa 22:13 . . . You **f** on meat and drink wine.

FED (v) *see also* FEED
Deut 8:16 . . . He **f** you with manna
Ezek 3:2 . . . my mouth, and he **f** me the scroll.
John 6:26 . . . want to be with me because I **f**

FEED, FEEDS (v) to give food to; to eat; to provide something essential to the development, sustenance, maintenance, or operation of
see also FED
Prov 15:14 . . . while the fool **f-s** on trash.
Prov 22:9 . . . because they **f** the poor.
Jer 50:19 . . . own land, to **f** in the fields
Matt 6:26 . . . your heavenly Father **f-s** them.
Matt 14:16 . . . you **f** them.
Matt 25:42 . . . and you didn't **f** me.
John 6:57 . . . anyone who **f-s** on me will live
John 21:15 . . . Then **f** my lambs,
John 21:17 . . . Then **f** my sheep.
Rom 12:20 . . . enemies are hungry, **f** them.

FEEL (v) to perceive by physical sensation
Ps 115:7 . . . have hands but cannot **f,**

FEET (n) *see also* FOOT
Ps 22:16 . . . pierced my hands and **f.**
Ps 40:2 . . . He set my **f** on solid ground
Ps 73:2 . . . My **f** were slipping,
Ps 119:105 . . . a lamp to guide my **f**
Isa 52:7 . . . are the **f** of the messenger
Matt 10:14 . . . shake its dust from your **f**
Luke 24:39 . . . Look at my **f.**
John 13:5 . . . began to wash the disciples' **f,**
John 13:14 . . . wash each other's **f.**
Rom 10:15 . . . beautiful are the **f** of
Rom 16:20 . . . crush Satan under your **f.**
1 Cor 15:25 . . . his enemies beneath his **f.**
Heb 1:13 . . . a footstool under your **f.**
Heb 12:13 . . . a straight path for your **f**

FELLOWSHIP (n) friendship; association; company; partnership
Gen 5:24 . . . walking in close **f** with God.
1 Cor 5:2 . . . remove this man from your **f.**
2 Cor 13:14 . . . and the **f** of the Holy Spirit
1 Jn 1:3 . . . you may have **f** with us.
1 Jn 1:3 . . . And our **f** is with the Father and
1 Jn 1:6 . . . we say we have **f** with God but
1 Jn 2:27 . . . remain in **f** with Christ.

FEMALE (adj) of, relating to, or being a woman
Gen 1:27 . . . male and **f** he created them.
Gen 5:2 . . . He created them male and **f,**
Mark 10:6 . . . God made them male and **f**
Gal 3:28 . . . slave or free, male and **f.**

FERTILE (adj) capable of sustaining abundant growth; productive
Mark 4:8 . . . other seeds fell on **f** soil,

FESTIVAL, FESTIVALS (n) a time of celebration marked by special observances
Lev 23:2 . . . the LORD's appointed **f-s,**
Isa 30:29 . . . at the holy **f-s.**
Amos 5:21 . . . religious **f-s** and solemn
Zech 14:18 . . . of Egypt refuse to attend the **f,**
1 Cor 5:8 . . . let us celebrate the **f,**

FESTIVE (adj) joyful, gay
Isa 61:3 . . . **f** praise instead of despair.

FEVER (n) a rise of body temperature above the normal
Job 30:30 . . . my bones burn with **f.**
Matt 8:14 . . . sick in bed with a high **f.**
Luke 4:38 . . . very sick with a high **f.**
John 4:52 . . . his **f** suddenly disappeared!
Acts 28:8 . . . was ill with **f** and dysentery.

FEW (adj) not many, a low number of
Prov 17:27 . . . wise person uses **f** words;
Matt 9:37 . . . is great, but the workers are **f.**
Matt 22:14 . . . many are called, but **f** are

FIANCÉE (n) a woman engaged to be married
1 Cor 7:36 . . . treating his **f** improperly

FIELD, FIELDS (n) an open land area free of woods and buildings; an area of cleared land used for cultivation
Lev 19:9 . . . along the edges of your **f-s,**
Ruth 2:2 . . . into the harvest **f-s** to pick
Isa 40:6 . . . the flowers in a **f.**
Matt 6:28 . . . Look at the lilies of the **f**
Matt 13:44 . . . hidden in a **f.**
Luke 2:8 . . . staying in the **f-s** nearby,
John 4:35 . . . The **f-s** are already ripe
1 Cor 3:9 . . . And you are God's **f.**
1 Pet 1:24 . . . like a flower in the **f.**

FIERY (adj) consisting of fire
Eph 6:16 . . . to stop the **f** arrows of the devil.

FIG, FIGS (n) an oblong or pear-shaped syconium fruit of a tree of the mulberry family; a fruit-producing plant which could be either a tall tree or a low-spreading shrub
Gen 3:7 . . . they sewed **f** leaves together
Judg 9:10 . . . they said to the **f** tree,
Prov 27:18 . . . workers who tend a **f** tree
Mic 4:4 . . . grapevines and **f** trees,
Zech 3:10 . . . grapevine and **f** tree.
Matt 21:19 . . . a **f** tree beside the road.
Luke 13:6 . . . man planted a **f** tree in his
Jas 3:12 . . . Does a **f** tree produce olives,
Jas 3:12 . . . or a grapevine produce **f-s?**

FIGHT, FIGHTS (n) a hostile encounter; a struggle for a goal or an objective
Prov 15:18 . . . person starts **f-s;** a cool
Prov 20:3 . . . Avoiding a **f** is a mark of
Prov 29:22 . . . An angry person starts **f-s;**
2 Tim 4:7 . . . fought the good **f,**
Jas 4:1 . . . causing the quarrels and **f-s**

FIGHT, FIGHTING, FIGHTS (v) to actively oppose or combat, as with weapons; to gain by struggle
see also FOUGHT
Exod 14:14 . . . LORD himself will **f** for you.
Josh 23:10 . . . LORD your God **f-s** for you,
1 Sam 17:32 . . . I'll go **f** him!
1 Sam 25:28 . . . are **f-ing** the LORD's battles.
Neh 4:20 . . . our God will **f** for us!
Prov 28:25 . . . Greed causes **f-ing;**
Ps 35:1 . . . **F** those who **f** against me.
Isa 49:25 . . . I will **f** those who **f** you,
1 Cor 15:32 . . . value was there in **f-ing** wild
Phil 1:27 . . . one purpose, **f-ing** together for
1 Tim 6:12 . . . **F** the good fight
Jas 4:2 . . . so you **f** and wage war

FILL, FILLED, FILLS (v) to occupy the whole of; to supply fully; to spread through
Gen 1:28 . . . **F** the earth and govern it.
Exod 34:6 . . . **f-ed** with unfailing love
1 Kgs 8:11 . . . presence of the LORD **f-ed**
Ps 81:10 . . . and I will **f** it with good things.
Ps 107:9 . . . the thirsty and **f-s** the hungry
Ps 119:64 . . . unfailing love **f-s** the earth;
Ps 123:3 . . . have had our **f** of contempt.
Isa 6:3 . . . whole earth is **f-ed** with his glory!
Joel 2:13 . . . and **f-ed** with unfailing love.
Jon 4:2 . . . and **f-ed** with unfailing love.
Hag 2:7 . . . I will **f** this place with glory,
Luke 1:15 . . . be **f-ed** with the Holy Spirit,
Luke 1:41 . . . was **f-ed** with the Holy Spirit.
Luke 1:67 . . . **f-ed** with the Holy Spirit
Luke 2:40 . . . He was **f-ed** with wisdom,
Luke 24:49 . . . Holy Spirit comes and **f-s**
Acts 2:4 . . . was **f-ed** with the Holy Spirit
Acts 2:28 . . . you will **f** me with the joy
Acts 4:8 . . . **f-ed** with the Holy Spirit,
Acts 4:31 . . . all **f-ed** with the Holy Spirit.
Acts 9:17 . . . be **f-ed** with the Holy Spirit.
Acts 13:9 . . . was **f-ed** with the Holy Spirit,
Rom 5:5 . . . Holy Spirit to **f** our hearts
Rom 15:13 . . . **f** you completely with joy
Eph 1:23 . . . by Christ, who **f-s** all things
Eph 5:18 . . . be **f-ed** with the Holy Spirit,
Col 3:16 . . . in all its richness, **f** your lives.

FILTH (n) moral corruption or defilement
Isa 4:4 . . . wash the **f** from beautiful Zion

FILTHY (adj) covered with, containing, or characterized by foul or putrid matter or moral corruption
Isa 6:5 . . . I have **f** lips, and I live
Isa 64:6 . . . they are nothing but **f** rags.
Zech 3:4 . . . Take off his **f** clothes.
2 Cor 6:17 . . . Don't touch their **f** things,

FINANCIAL (adj) relating to money
2 Cor 11:9 . . . did not become a **f** burden

FIND, FINDS (v) to attain or reach (a goal or conclusion); to discover by searching or effort; to experience
see also FOUND
1 Chr 28:9 . . . seek him, you will **f** him.
Job 23:3 . . . knew where to **f** God,
Prov 3:13 . . . the person who **f-s** wisdom,
Prov 8:17 . . . who search will surely **f** me.
Prov 8:35 . . . For whoever **f-s** me **f-s** life
Prov 11:27 . . . you will **f** favor;
Prov 31:10 . . . Who can **f** a virtuous and
Isa 55:6 . . . while you can **f** him.
Jer 6:16 . . . will **f** rest for your souls.
Matt 7:7 . . . seeking, and you will **f.**
Matt 7:8 . . . Everyone who seeks, **f-s.**
Matt 10:39 . . . your life for me, you will **f** it.
Luke 11:9 . . . and you will **f.**
Luke 11:10 . . . Everyone who seeks, **f-s.**
Luke 15:4 . . . that is lost until he **f-s** it?
Luke 15:8 . . . search carefully until she **f-s** it?

FINEST (adj) superior in kind, quality, or appearance
Isa 55:2 . . . will enjoy the **f** food.
Jer 3:19 . . . the **f** possession in the world.

FINGER, FINGERS (n) any of the five terminating members of the hand; figurative for the power of God
Exod 8:19 . . . This is the **f** of God!
Exod 31:18 . . . written by the **f** of God.
Deut 9:10 . . . had written with his own **f**
Luke 16:24 . . . dip the tip of his **f** in water
John 8:6 . . . wrote in the dust with his **f.**
John 20:25 . . . in his hands, put my **f-s** into

FINISH (n) the end
Rom 1:17 . . . from start to **f** by faith.

FINISH, FINISHED, FINISHING (v) to bring to completion; to bring to an end
Gen 2:2 . . . God had **f-ed** his work of creation,
John 4:34 . . . and from **f-ing** his work.
John 19:30 . . . he said, "It is **f-ed!"**
Acts 20:24 . . . I use it for **f-ing** the work
2 Cor 8:11 . . . Now you should **f** what you
2 Tim 4:7 . . . I have **f-ed** the race,
Rev 20:3 . . . the thousand years were **f-ed.**

FIRE, FIRES (n) hot flame and burning light; symbolic of hell; severe trial or ordeal
Exod 3:2 . . . **f** from the middle of a bush.
Exod 13:21 . . . a pillar of **f.**
Dan 3:25 . . . walking around in the **f**
Matt 3:11 . . . the Holy Spirit and with **f.**
Matt 5:22 . . . are in danger of the **f-s** of hell.
Matt 18:8 . . . be thrown into eternal **f**
Mark 9:43 . . . the unquenchable **f-s** of hell
Mark 9:49 . . . be tested with **f.**
Luke 3:16 . . . with the Holy Spirit and with **f.**
Acts 2:3 . . . tongues of **f** appeared and
1 Cor 3:13 . . . The **f** will show
Heb 12:29 . . . God is a devouring **f.**
Jas 3:6 . . . it is set on **f** by hell itself.

FIRM (adj) securely or solidly fixed in place; not weak or uncertain
Isa 7:9 . . . Unless your faith is **f,**
2 Cor 1:21 . . . to stand **f** for Christ.
2 Cor 1:24 . . . your own faith that you stand **f.**
Eph 6:13 . . . will still be standing **f.**
1 Thes 3:8 . . . you are standing **f** in the Lord.
2 Thes 2:15 . . . brothers and sisters, stand **f**
1 Pet 5:9 . . . Stand **f** against him,

FIRMAMENT (KJV)
Gen 1:7 . . . this *space* to separate the waters
Ps 19:1 . . . *skies* display his craftsmanship
Ezek 1:22 . . . surface like the *sky,* glittering
Dan 12:3 . . . will shine as bright as the *sky*

FIRST (adj) preceding all others in time, order, or importance
Gen 1:5 . . . morning came, marking the **f** day.
Isa 44:6 . . . I am the **F** and the Last;
Isa 48:12 . . . God, the **F** and the Last.
Matt 22:38 . . . the **f** and greatest
Mark 9:35 . . . wants to be **f** must take last
Mark 13:10 . . . Good News must **f** be
Rom 1:16 . . . Jew **f** and also the Gentile.
Rom 2:9 . . . Jew **f** and also for the Gentile.
1 Cor 15:45 . . . The **f** man, Adam,
Eph 6:2 . . . the **f** commandment with a
1 Tim 2:13 . . . God made Adam **f,**
Heb 10:9 . . . He cancels the **f** covenant
1 Jn 4:19 . . . because he loved us **f.**
Rev 1:17 . . . I am the **F** and the Last.
Rev 22:13 . . . and the Omega, the **F** and the

FIRSTBEGOTTEN (KJV)
Heb 1:6 . . . his *supreme* Son into the world

FIRSTBORN (n) eldest; the most prominent; the rightful heir
Gen 25:34 . . . for his rights as the **f.**
Exod 11:5 . . . All the **f** sons will die
Exod 13:2 . . . every **f** among the Israelites.
Exod 34:19 . . . The **f** of every animal
Exod 34:20 . . . buy back every **f** son.
Ps 89:27 . . . I will make him my **f** son,
Mic 6:7 . . . sacrifice our **f** children to pay
Heb 12:23 . . . the assembly of God's **f**

FIRSTFRUITS (KJV)
Exod 23:16 . . . the *first crops* of your harvest
Exod 23:19 . . . bring the *very best* of
Lev 2:14 . . . *first portion* of your harvest

Lev 23:10 . . . you harvest its *first crops,*
Num 28:26 . . . the *first* of your new grain
Rev 14:4 . . . as a *special offering* to God

FISH (n) any of numerous cold-blooded aquatic vertebrates
Jon 1:17 . . . had arranged for a great **f**
Matt 12:40 . . . in the belly of the great **f**
Luke 9:13 . . . loaves of bread and two **f,**
John 6:9 . . . five barley loaves and two **f.**

FISH, FISHED, FISHING (v) to attempt to catch fish
Mark 1:16 . . . for they **f-ed** for a living.
Mark 1:17 . . . how to **f** for people!
Luke 5:10 . . . you'll be **f-ing** for people!

FISHERMEN (n) those who engage in fishing as an occupation or for pleasure
Ezek 26:5 . . . a rock in the sea, a place for **f**

FISHERS (KJV)
Isa 19:8 . . . *fishermen* will lament for lack of work
Jer 16:16 . . . *fishermen* who will catch
Matt 4:19 . . . show you *how to fish* for people

FLAME, FLAMES (n) a state of blazing combustion; burning zeal or passion
Isa 5:24 . . . and dry grass shrivels in the **f,**
1 Cor 3:15 . . . escaping through a wall of **f-s.**
2 Tim 1:6 . . . fan into **f-s** the spiritual gift
Rev 1:14 . . . his eyes were like **f-s** of fire.

FLAMING (adj) blazing; intense
Isa 4:5 . . . and smoke and **f** fire at night,
2 Thes 1:8 . . . in **f** fire, bringing judgment on
Heb 12:18 . . . to a place of **f** fire, darkness,

FLASHED (v) to break forth in or like a sudden flame; to give off light suddenly
1 Kgs 18:38 . . . the fire of the LORD **f** down
Dan 10:6 . . . His face **f** like lightning,

FLATTER (v) to praise excessively out of self-interest
Job 32:21 . . . or try to **f** anyone.
Prov 29:5 . . . To **f** friends is
Dan 11:32 . . . He will **f** and win over those
Jude 1:16 . . . they **f** others to get what they want.

FLATTERING (adj) characterized by excessive praise out of self-interest
Ps 12:2 . . . speaking with **f** lips
Ps 12:3 . . . cut off their **f** lips
Prov 26:28 . . . and **f** words cause ruin.

FLATTERY (n) insincere or excessive praise
Job 32:22 . . . For if I tried **f,** my Creator
Ps 5:9 . . . tongues are filled with **f.**
Prov 28:23 . . . criticism far more than **f.**
1 Thes 2:5 . . . try to win you with **f,**

FLEE (v) to run away; to shun
1 Cor 10:14 . . . **f** from the worship of idols.
Jas 4:7 . . . and he will **f** from you.

FLEECE (n) the wool obtained from a sheep at one sheering
Judg 6:37 . . . If the **f** is wet with dew

FLEETING (adj) passing swiftly
Ps 39:4 . . . how **f** my life is.

FLESH (n) the meaty part of animal and human bodies
see also BODY, HUMAN
Gen 2:23 . . . and **f** from my **f!**
John 6:51 . . . so the world may live, is my **f.**
1 Cor 15:39 . . . different kinds of **f**—

FLIGHT (n) an act or instance of running away
Deut 32:30 . . . put ten thousand to **f,**

FLIRTING (v) to behave amorously without serious intent
Isa 3:16 . . . **f** with her eyes,

FLOCK, FLOCKS (n) a group of animals assembled or herded together; a group under the guidance of a leader
Isa 40:11 . . . feed his **f** like a shepherd.
Jer 10:21 . . . and their **f-s** are scattered.
Jer 31:10 . . . as a shepherd does his **f.**
Zech 11:17 . . . who abandons the **f!**
Matt 26:31 . . . the **f** will be scattered.
Luke 2:8 . . . guarding their **f-s** of sheep.
Luke 12:32 . . . don't be afraid, little **f.**
John 10:16 . . . one **f** with one shepherd.
Acts 20:28 . . . shepherd God's **f**—

FLOGGED (v) to beat with a rod or whip
Deut 25:2 . . . is sentenced to be **f,**
John 19:1 . . . Pilate had Jesus **f**
Acts 5:40 . . . and had them **f.**

FLOOD, FLOODS (n) a rising and over-flowing of a body of water; the destruction of the world by water during the time of Noah
Gen 7:7 . . . the boat to escape the **f**—
Prov 27:4 . . . cruel, and wrath is like a **f,**
Matt 24:38 . . . In those days before the **f,**
Luke 6:49 . . . the **f-s** sweep down against
2 Pet 2:5 . . . ungodly people with a vast **f.**

FLOUR (n) a product consisting of finely milled wheat
Lev 2:1 . . . must consist of choice **f.**
Num 7:13 . . . choice **f** moistened with olive oil.
Luke 17:35 . . . grinding **f** together at the mill;

FLOURISH, FLOURISHING (v) to grow luxuriantly; to prosper or thrive
Ps 72:7 . . . all the godly **f** during his reign.
Ps 92:7 . . . and evildoers **f,** the will be
Ps 92:12 . . . the godly will **f** like palm trees
Prov 14:11 . . . the tent of the godly will **f.**
Prov 28:28 . . . meet disaster, the godly **f.**
Isa 35:7 . . . reeds and rushes will **f**
2 Thes 1:3 . . . your faith is **f-ing**

FLOW, FLOWING, FLOWS (v) to proceed smoothly and readily; to abound
Exod 3:8 . . . land **f-ing** with milk and honey—
Exod 33:3 . . . land that **f-s** with milk and
Num 13:27 . . . land **f-ing** with milk and honey.
Josh 5:6 . . . a land **f-ing** with milk and honey.
Ps 119:171 . . . Let praise **f** from my lips,
Jer 32:22 . . . land **f-ing** with milk and honey.
Lam 1:16 . . . I weep; tears **f** down my cheeks.
John 7:38 . . . living water will **f** from his
Rev 22:1 . . . **f-ing** from the throne of God

FLOWER, FLOWERS (n) the blossom of a plant
Job 14:2 . . . We blossom like a **f** and then
Isa 40:6 . . . as quickly as the **f-s** in a field.
Isa 40:7 . . . **f-s** fade beneath the breath
Jas 1:10 . . . like a little **f** in the field.

FOCUS (v) to concentrate attention or effort
1 Tim 4:13 . . . **f** on reading the Scriptures

FOES (n) adversary, opponent, or enemy
Ps 112:8 . . . face their **f** triumphantly.

FOLLOW, FOLLOWED, FOLLOWING, FOLLOWS (v) to pursue or run after; to imitate; to obey
Deut 1:36 . . . because he has **f-ed** the LORD
Deut 5:32 . . . **f-ing** his instructions
Josh 14:14 . . . he wholeheartedly **f-ed** the
1 Kgs 3:3 . . . loved the LORD and **f-ed**
2 Chr 10:14 . . . and **f-ed** the counsel
Prov 4:27 . . . feet from **f-ing** evil.
Prov 10:9 . . . those who **f** crooked paths
Isa 57:2 . . . For those who **f** godly paths
Isa 65:2 . . . But they **f** their own evil paths
Matt 4:20 . . . at once and **f-ed** him.
Matt 7:24 . . . listens to my teaching and **f-s**
Matt 8:19 . . . I will **f** you wherever you go.
Matt 8:22 . . . **F** me now. Let the
Matt 9:9 . . . got up and **f-ed** him.
Matt 16:24 . . . take up your cross, and **f**
Matt 19:27 . . . given up everything to **f** you.
Matt 26:58 . . . Meanwhile, Peter **f-ed** him
Mark 1:17 . . . Come, **f** me, and I will show
Luke 9:23 . . . your cross daily, and **f** me.
Luke 17:23 . . . go out and **f** them.
Luke 18:43 . . . **f-ed** Jesus, praising God.
John 8:12 . . . If you **f** me, you won't have to
John 10:4 . . . they **f** him because they know
John 10:27 . . . know them, and they **f** me.
John 12:26 . . . to be my disciple must **f** me,
John 21:19 . . . Jesus told him, "**F** me."
1 Cor 1:12 . . . or "I **f** only Christ."
1 Cor 4:17 . . . of how I **f** Christ Jesus,
Gal 5:7 . . . you back from **f-ing** the truth?
Gal 5:25 . . . **f** the Spirit's leading
Phil 2:12 . . . you always **f-ed** my instructions
Phil 3:17 . . . those who **f** our example.
2 Thes 3:6 . . . and don't **f** the tradition
1 Pet 2:21 . . . must **f** in his steps.
Rev 14:4 . . . as virgins, **f-ing** the Lamb

FOLLOWER, FOLLOWERS (n) one who follows the teachings of another; a disciple
1 Kgs 18:3 . . . was a devoted **f** of the LORD.
Matt 10:42 . . . one of the least of my **f-s,**
Matt 18:20 . . . together as my **f-s,** I am there
Acts 9:21 . . . Jesus' **f-s** in Jerusalem?

FOLLY (KJV)
Prov 14:18 . . . clothed with *foolishness*
Prov 26:11 . . . a fool repeats his *foolishness*
Eccl 2:13 . . . Wisdom is better than *foolishness*
Isa 9:17 . . . they all speak *foolishness*
2 Tim 3:9 . . . recognize what *fools* they are

FOOD (n) something that nourishes, sustains, or supplies energy and vitality
see also BREAD
Lev 11:2 . . . the ones you may use for **f.**
Prov 25:21 . . . hungry, give them **f** to eat.
Isa 58:7 . . . Share your **f** with the hungry,
Dan 1:8 . . . defile himself by eating the **f**
Matt 6:11 . . . today the **f** we need,
Matt 6:25 . . . Isn't life more than **f,**
Mark 7:19 . . . every kind of **f** is acceptable
John 6:55 . . . my flesh is true **f,** and my
John 13:18 . . . eats my **f** has turned against
Acts 15:20 . . . abstain from eating **f**
Rom 14:6 . . . kind of **f** do so to honor
1 Tim 6:8 . . . have enough **f** and clothing,
Jas 2:15 . . . who has no **f** or clothing,

FOOL, FOOLS (n) one deficient in intellectual, practical, or moral sense
1 Sam 25:25 . . . He is a **f,** just as his name
Ps 14:1 . . . Only **f-s** say in their hearts,
Prov 6:32 . . . commits adultery is an utter **f,**
Prov 10:8 . . . babbling **f-s** fall flat on
Prov 10:23 . . . wrong is fun for a **f,**
Prov 17:7 . . . are not fitting for a **f;**
Prov 17:16 . . . to pay tuition to educate a **f,**
Prov 26:1 . . . associated with **f-s** than snow

Prov 26:7 . . . A proverb in the mouth of a **f**
Prov 29:11 . . . **F-s** vent their anger,
Prov 29:20 . . . more hope for a **f** than for
Rom 1:22 . . . became utter **f-s.**
1 Cor 3:18 . . . need to become a **f** to be
2 Cor 11:21 . . . I'm talking like a **f** again—
Eph 5:15 . . . Don't live like **f-s,**
2 Tim 3:9 . . . will recognize what **f-s** they are,

FOOL, FOOLED, FOOLING (v) to trick or deceive
Ps 119:118 . . . are only **f-ing** themselves.
Jer 7:4 . . . don't be **f-ed** by those who promise
1 Cor 15:33 . . . Don't be **f-ed** by those who
Gal 6:3 . . . you are only **f-ing** yourself.
Eph 5:6 . . . Don't be **f-ed** by those who try to
2 Thes 2:3 . . . Don't be **f-ed** by what they say.
Jas 1:22 . . . are only **f-ing** yourselves.
Jas 1:26 . . . you are **f-ing** yourself,
1 Jn 1:8 . . . we are only **f-ing** ourselves

FOOLISH (adj) lacking in sense, judgment, or discretion; irreverent
Prov 26:4 . . . the **f** arguments of fools,
Prov 26:17 . . . else's argument is as **f**
Rom 1:28 . . . abandoned them to their **f**
1 Cor 1:18 . . . the cross is **f** to those who
1 Cor 1:27 . . . world considers **f** in order to
1 Cor 2:14 . . . It all sounds **f** to them
Eph 5:4 . . . Obscene stories, **f** talk,
1 Tim 6:20 . . . Avoid godless, **f** discussions
Titus 3:9 . . . not get involved in **f** discussions

FOOLISHNESS (n) aimless behavior befitting a fool
Prov 19:3 . . . ruin their lives by their own **f**
Prov 22:15 . . . heart is filled with **f,**
Eccl 10:1 . . . so a little **f** spoils great
Mark 7:22 . . . pride, and **f.**

FOOT (n) the end of the leg upon which an individual stands
see also FEET
Josh 1:3 . . . Wherever you set **f,**
Matt 18:8 . . . with only one hand or one **f**
Luke 4:11 . . . won't even hurt your **f**
1 Cor 12:15 . . . If the **f** says,
Rev 10:2 . . . and his left **f** on the land.

FOOTHOLD (n) a strategic position enabling further advance or advantage
Eph 4:27 . . . anger gives a **f** to the devil.

FOOTSTOOL (n) a low stool used to support the feet
Ps 110:1 . . . making them a **f** under
Isa 66:1 . . . throne, and the earth is my **f.**
Matt 5:35 . . . the earth is his **f.**
Acts 7:49 . . . the earth is my **f.**
Heb 1:13 . . . making them a **f** under
Heb 10:13 . . . and made a **f** under

FORBID, FORBIDDEN (v) to command against
Matt 16:19 . . . Whatever you **f** on earth
Matt 16:19 . . . will be **f-den** in heaven,
Matt 18:18 . . . whatever you **f** on earth
1 Cor 14:39 . . . don't **f** speaking in

FORCE (n) violence, compulsion, or constraint exerted upon or against a person or thing
Zech 4:6 . . . is not by **f** nor by strength,

FORCE, FORCED (v) to compel by physical, moral, or intellectual means
Matt 27:32 . . . soldiers **f-d** him to carry
John 6:15 . . . were ready to **f** him to be

FORCEFUL (adj) possessing or filled with force; effective
2 Cor 10:10 . . . letters are demanding and **f,**

(FORE)FATHERS (KJV)
Exod 10:6 . . . *ancestors* seen a plague like
Num 11:12 . . . swore to give their *ancestors*
Jer 11:10 . . . the sins of their *forefathers*
Matt 23:32 . . . what your *ancestors* started

FOREHEAD, FOREHEADS (n) the part of the face above the eyes
Exod 13:9 . . . on your hand or your **f.**
Deut 6:8 . . . wear them on your **f**
1 Sam 17:49 . . . the Philistine in the **f.**
Rev 9:4 . . . seal of God on their **f-s.**
Rev 13:16 . . . right hand or on the **f.**
Rev 14:1 . . . written on their **f-s.**

FOREIGN (adj) related to or dealing with other nations; pagan
see also STRANGE
2 Chr 14:3 . . . He removed the **f** altars and
2 Chr 33:15 . . . also removed the **f** gods and
Isa 28:11 . . . through **f** oppressors

FOREIGNER, FOREIGNERS (n) nonresident, alien, or sojourner
see also STRANGER
Exod 22:21 . . . not mistreat or oppress **f-s**
Exod 23:9 . . . must not oppress **f-s.**
Lev 24:22 . . . to the **f-s** living among you.
Neh 9:2 . . . separated themselves from all **f-s**
Ps 119:19 . . . I am only a **f** in the land
Hos 7:8 . . . mingle with godless **f-s,**
Luke 17:18 . . . glory to God except this **f?**
1 Cor 14:11 . . . I will be a **f** to someone
Eph 2:19 . . . no longer strangers and **f-s.**
1 Pet 1:1 . . . living as **f-s** in the provinces
1 Pet 2:11 . . . temporary residents and **f-s**

FOREKNOW, FOREKNEW, FOREKNOWLEDGE (KJV)
Acts 2:23 . . . God *knew what would happen*
Rom 8:29 . . . God *knew* his people *in advance*
Rom 11:2 . . . whom he *chose from the very beginning*
1 Pet 1:2 . . . Father *knew you and chose you* long

FOREORDAINED (KJV)
1 Pet 1:20 . . . *chose* him *as* your ransom

FORESKIN (n) flap of skin covering the tip of the penis
Gen 17:11 . . . cut off the flesh of your **f** as
Exod 4:25 . . . touched his feet with the **f** and
Lev 12:3 . . . the boy's **f** must be circumcised.

FORETASTE (n) a small anticipatory sample
Rom 8:23 . . . as a **f** of future glory,

FORETOLD (v) to tell beforehand; to predict
Rom 16:26 . . . as the prophets **f**

FOREVER (adv) for a limitless time; continually
see also ETERNAL, EVERLASTING
Gen 3:22 . . . they will live **f!**
Gen 17:8 . . . be their possession **f,**
2 Sam 7:26 . . . name be honored **f**
1 Chr 17:24 . . . be established and honored **f**
1 Chr 29:10 . . . be praised **f** and ever!
Ezra 9:12 . . . prosperity to your children **f.**
Ps 9:7 . . . the LORD reigns **f,**
Ps 21:4 . . . of his life stretch on **f.**
Ps 28:9 . . . in your arms **f.**
Ps 37:28 . . . keep them safe **f,**
Ps 61:8 . . . sing praises to your name **f**
Ps 73:26 . . . he is mine **f.**
Ps 79:13 . . . will thank you **f** and ever,
Ps 86:12 . . . glory to your name **f,**
Ps 92:8 . . . will be exalted **f.**
Ps 100:5 . . . unfailing love continues **f,**
Ps 103:17 . . . the LORD remains **f** with
Ps 107:1 . . . faithful love endures **f.**
Ps 110:4 . . . are a priest **f**
Ps 111:8 . . . They are **f** true,
Ps 112:9 . . . be remembered **f.**
Ps 119:152 . . . laws will last **f.**
Ps 146:6 . . . every promise **f.**
Isa 32:17 . . . and confidence **f.**
Isa 51:6 . . . but my salvation lasts **f.**
Isa 60:15 . . . make you beautiful **f,**
Isa 63:12 . . . making himself famous **f?**
Jer 25:5 . . . you and your ancestors **f.**
Dan 2:44 . . . and it will stand **f.**
Dan 4:3 . . . kingdom will last **f,** his rule
Dan 7:27 . . . kingdom will last **f,**
John 6:51 . . . eats this bread will live **f;**
1 Cor 13:8 . . . But love will last **f!**
1 Cor 13:13 . . . Three things will last **f**—
1 Cor 15:42 . . . will be raised to live **f.**
1 Cor 15:50 . . . inherit what will last **f.**
2 Cor 4:17 . . . and will last **f!**
2 Cor 4:18 . . . cannot see will last **f.**
1 Thes 4:17 . . . will be with the Lord **f.**
2 Thes 1:9 . . . destruction, **f** separated
Heb 5:6 . . . a priest **f** in the order
Heb 7:17 . . . a priest **f** in the order
Heb 7:24 . . . Jesus lives **f,**
Heb 9:12 . . . secured our redemption **f.**
Heb 13:8 . . . yesterday, today, and **f.**
1 Pet 1:25 . . . word of the Lord remains **f.**
1 Jn 2:17 . . . will live **f.**
Rev 22:5 . . . they will reign **f** and ever.

FORGAVE (v) *see also* FORGIVE
Ps 78:38 . . . was merciful and **f** their sins
Luke 7:42 . . . so he kindly **f** them both,
Eph 1:7 . . . his Son and **f** our sins.
Col 1:14 . . . our freedom and **f** our sins.
Col 2:13 . . . with Christ, for he **f** all our

FORGET, FORGETTING (v) to slip from remembrance; to disregard intentionally; to cease from remembering
see also FORGOT
Deut 4:9 . . . careful never to **f**
Ps 78:7 . . . hope anew on God, not **f-ting**
Ps 119:16 . . . and not **f** your word.
Prov 3:1 . . . My child, never **f**
Eccl 12:1 . . . cause you to **f** your Creator.
Jer 2:32 . . . a young woman **f** her jewelry?
Luke 12:6 . . . God does not **f** a single one
Rom 3:31 . . . we can **f** about the law?
Phil 3:13 . . . **F-ting** the past and looking
Heb 13:16 . . . And don't **f** to do good
Jas 1:24 . . . walk away, and **f**
Jas 1:25 . . . and don't **f** what you heard,
2 Pet 1:9 . . . **f-ting** that they have been
2 Pet 3:8 . . . must not **f** this one thing,

FORGIVE, FORGIVEN, FORGIVES, FORGIVING (v) to pardon or acquit of sins
see also ATONE, FORGAVE
Gen 50:17 . . . Please **f** your brothers
Exod 23:21 . . . he will not **f** your rebellion.
Exod 34:7 . . . I **f** iniquity, rebellion,
Exod 34:9 . . . but please **f** our iniquity and
Num 14:18 . . . **f-ing** every kind of sin
Num 14:19 . . . just as you have **f-n** them
1 Sam 3:14 . . . never be **f-n** by sacrifices
1 Kgs 8:34 . . . hear from heaven and **f**
Ps 65:3 . . . by our sins, you **f** them all.

Ps 79:9 . . . Save us and **f** our sins
Ps 86:5 . . . so good, so ready to **f,**
Ps 103:3 . . . He **f-s** all my sins
Prov 17:9 . . . when a fault is **f-n,**
Isa 22:14 . . . you will never be **f-n** for this
Isa 38:17 . . . and **f-n** all my sins.
Isa 55:7 . . . for he will **f** generously.
Jer 31:34 . . . I will **f** their wickedness,
Dan 9:19 . . . O Lord, hear. O Lord, **f.**
Hos 14:2 . . . **F** all our sins and
Matt 6:12 . . . and **f** us our sins,
Matt 6:14 . . . If you **f** those who sin
Matt 6:15 . . . if you refuse to **f** others,
Matt 9:6 . . . authority on earth to **f** sins.
Matt 18:21 . . . how often should I **f**
Matt 26:28 . . . to **f** the sins of many.
Mark 2:7 . . . Only God can **f** sins!
Mark 2:10 . . . authority on earth to **f** sins.
Mark 3:29 . . . will never be **f-n.**
Mark 11:25 . . . first **f** anyone you are
Mark 11:25 . . . will **f** your sins,
Luke 5:21 . . . Only God can **f** sins!
Luke 5:24 . . . authority on earth to **f** sins.
Luke 6:37 . . . **F** others, and you will be
Luke 7:47 . . . a person who is **f-n** little
Luke 7:49 . . . he goes around **f-ing** sins?
Luke 11:4 . . . **f** us our sins, as we
Luke 17:3 . . . if there is repentance, **f.**
Luke 17:4 . . . asks forgiveness, you must **f.**
Luke 23:34 . . . Father, **f** them,
John 20:23 . . . If you **f** anyone's sins,
Acts 5:31 . . . repent of their sins and be **f-n.**
Acts 8:22 . . . Perhaps he will **f** your evil
Rom 4:5 . . . faith in God who **f-s** sinners.
Rom 4:7 . . . whose disobedience is **f-n,**
2 Cor 2:7 . . . time to **f** and comfort
2 Cor 2:10 . . . When you **f** this man,
Col 3:13 . . . so you must **f** others.
Heb 8:12 . . . I will **f** their wickedness,
1 Jn 1:9 . . . is faithful and just to **f** us

FORGIVENESS (n) aquittal or pardon of sins
see also ATONEMENT, MERCY
Neh 9:17 . . . you are a God of **f,**
Luke 24:47 . . . There is **f** of sins for all
Acts 13:38 . . . this man Jesus there is **f**
Rom 5:15 . . . his gift of **f** to many
Heb 9:22 . . . of blood, there is no **f.**
Jas 5:20 . . . bring about the **f** of many sins.

FORGOT, FORGOTTEN (v) *see also* FORGET
Deut 32:18 . . . **f** the God who had given
Ps 44:20 . . . If we had **f-ten** the name
Ps 78:11 . . . They **f** what he had done—
Ps 106:13 . . . how quickly they **f**
Ps 119:176 . . . not **f-ten** your commands.
Isa 17:10 . . . You have **f-ten** the Rock
Isa 51:13 . . . Yet you have **f-ten** the LORD,
Hos 8:14 . . . Israel has **f-ten** its Maker

FORMED (v) to create, fashion, or give shape to something
see also CREATE(D), MADE, MAKE
Gen 2:7 . . . the LORD God **f** the man
Gen 2:19 . . . LORD God **f** from the ground
Ps 94:9 . . . the one who **f** your eyes?
Isa 49:5 . . . the one who **f** me
Jer 1:5 . . . knew you before I **f** you
Heb 11:3 . . . universe was **f** at God's

FORMLESS (adj) lacking order or arrangement; having no physical existence
Gen 1:2 . . . The earth was **f** and empty,
Jer 4:23 . . . and it was empty and **f.**

FORNICATION (KJV)
Isa 23:17 . . . *be a prostitute* to all kingdoms
Matt 19:9 . . . wife has been *unfaithful*
1 Cor 5:1 . . . *sexual immorality* going on
1 Cor 6:18 . . . *sexual immorality* is a sin
Jude 1:7 . . . were filled with *immorality*

FORSAKE (v) to renounce or turn away from entirely
1 Chr 28:9 . . . But if you **f** him, he will
Job 28:28 . . . to **f** evil is real understanding.

FORTRESS (n) a fortified place; a place of security or survival
see also REFUGE
2 Sam 22:2 . . . my **f,** and my savior;
Ps 27:1 . . . The LORD is my **f,**
Ps 71:3 . . . my rock and my **f.**
Ps 144:2 . . . and my **f,** my tower of safety,
Prov 18:10 . . . LORD is a strong **f;**
Zeph 3:6 . . . devastating their **f** walls and

FORTUNE-TELLER, FORTUNE-TELLERS (n) one who professes to foretell future events
Jer 29:8 . . . your prophets and **f-s** who are
Acts 16:16 . . . She was a **f** who earned a lot

FORTUNE-TELLING (n) the act of one foretelling future events by occultic means
Lev 19:26 . . . not practice **f** or witchcraft.

FORTY (adj) the number 40
Gen 7:4 . . . for **f** days and **f** nights,
Exod 16:35 . . . Israel ate manna for **f** years
Exod 24:18 . . . **f** days and **f** nights.
Num 14:34 . . . wilderness for **f** years—
Matt 4:2 . . . For **f** days and **f** nights
Acts 1:3 . . . the **f** days after his crucifixion,
Acts 13:18 . . . **f** years of wandering

FOUGHT (v) *see also* FIGHT
Gen 32:28 . . . because you have **f** with God
Josh 10:14 . . . Surely the LORD **f** for Israel
2 Tim 4:7 . . . I have **f** the good fight,

FOUND (v) *see also* FIND
2 Kgs 22:8 . . . I have **f** the Book of the Law
2 Kgs 23:24 . . . Hilkiah the priest had **f**
2 Chr 15:15 . . . after God, and they **f**
Luke 15:6 . . . I have **f** my lost sheep.
Luke 15:9 . . . because I have **f** my lost coin.
Luke 15:24 . . . but now he is **f.**
Jas 2:8 . . . the royal law as **f** in the
Rev 5:4 . . . because no one was **f** worthy

FOUNDATION (n) basis upon which something is built, supported, or added to; substructure
Prov 1:7 . . . Fear of the LORD is the **f**
Prov 9:10 . . . the LORD is the **f** of wisdom.
Isa 28:16 . . . placing a **f** stone in Jerusalem,
Luke 6:49 . . . a house without a **f.**
Eph 2:20 . . . built on the **f** of the apostles
1 Tim 3:15 . . . pillar and **f** of the truth.
2 Tim 2:19 . . . stands firm like a **f** stone
Heb 1:10 . . . you laid the **f** of the earth

FOUNTAIN (n) source; spring of water
Isa 12:3 . . . from the **f** of salvation!
Zech 13:1 . . . a **f** to cleanse them

FOXES (n) any of various carnivorous mammals of the dog family with shorter legs, pointed muzzles, and long bushy tails
Song 2:15 . . . Catch all the **f,** those little **f,**
Luke 9:58 . . . **F** have dens to live in,

FRAGRANCE (n) a sweet or delicate odor
see also PERFUME
2 Cor 2:15 . . . are a Christ-like **f** rising up

FRANKINCENSE (n) an aromatic gum resin obtained from the Boswellia tree
Matt 2:11 . . . gifts of gold, **f,** and myrrh.

FRAUD (n) an act of deceiving or misrepresenting; trickery
Lev 6:2 . . . you steal or commit **f,**
Acts 13:10 . . . every sort of deceit and **f,**

FREE (adj) not bound, confined, or detained by force; without restraint, inhibition, or cost; possessing the rights of citizenship
John 8:32 . . . the truth will set you **f.**
John 8:36 . . . sets you **f,** you are truly **f.**
Rom 6:7 . . . we were set **f** from the power
Rom 6:18 . . . you are **f** from your slavery
Gal 3:28 . . . slave or **f,** male and female.
Jas 1:25 . . . the perfect law that sets you **f,**
1 Pet 2:16 . . . For you are **f,** yet

FREED, FREES (v) to relieve or rid of what restrains, confines, restricts, or embarrasses
Ps 116:16 . . . **f-d** me from my chains.
Ps 146:7 . . . The LORD **f-s** the prisoners.
Isa 61:1 . . . prisoners will be **f-d.**
Rom 3:24 . . . he **f-d** us from the penalty
1 Cor 1:30 . . . and he **f-d** us from sin.
Rev 1:5 . . . and has **f-d** us from our sins

FREEDOM (n) liberation from slavery, restraint, or the power of another
Ps 119:45 . . . I will walk in **f,** for I have
2 Cor 3:17 . . . the Lord is, there is **f.**
Gal 2:4 . . . take away the **f** we have in Christ
Gal 4:5 . . . sent him to buy **f** for us
Gal 5:13 . . . don't use your **f** to satisfy
Eph 1:7 . . . purchased our **f** with the blood
1 Pet 2:16 . . . don't use your **f** as an excuse

FRIEND, FRIENDS (n) intimate associate; a favored companion
Prov 16:28 . . . separates the best of **f-s.**
Prov 17:9 . . . on it separates close **f-s.**
Prov 20:6 . . . Many will say they are loyal **f-s,**
Prov 27:6 . . . Wounds from a sincere **f** are
Prov 28:7 . . . with wild **f-s** bring shame
Prov 29:5 . . . To flatter **f-s** is to lay a trap
Isa 41:8 . . . from Abraham my **f,**
Zech 13:6 . . . was wounded at my **f-s'** house!
John 11:3 . . . Lord, your dear **f** is very sick.
John 15:13 . . . one's life for one's **f-s.**
John 15:14 . . . You are my **f-s** if you do
John 15:15 . . . Now you are my **f-s,**
John 19:12 . . . you are no '**f** of Caesar.'
Jas 2:23 . . . even called the **f** of God.
Jas 4:4 . . . want to be a **f** of the world,

FRIENDSHIP (n) association of familiarity and companionship
Prov 3:32 . . . he offers his **f** to the godly.
Rom 5:10 . . . since our **f** with God was
Jas 4:4 . . . you realize that **f** with the world

FRIGHTENED (v) to terrify; to make afraid
Heb 12:21 . . . was so **f** at the sight

FRINGE (n) the edge; the threads hanging from cut or raveled edges
Matt 9:20 . . . touched the **f** of his robe,

FROGS (n) a leaping aquatic amphibian with smooth, moist skin; strong, long hind legs; and webbed feet
Exod 8:2 . . . I will send a plague of **f**
Rev 16:13 . . . spirits that looked like **f**

FRUIT (n) a product of plant growth; product or result
Ps 1:3 . . . bearing **f** each season.
Isa 11:1 . . . new Branch bearing **f** from
Dan 4:12 . . . loaded with **f** for all to eat.
Matt 3:10 . . . not produce good **f** will be
Matt 7:20 . . . can identify a tree by its **f,**
Matt 12:33 . . . is bad, its **f** will be bad.
John 15:2 . . . that doesn't produce **f,**
John 15:16 . . . go and produce lasting **f,**
Gal 5:22 . . . produces this kind of **f**

Phil 1:11 . . . the **f** of your salvation—
2 Tim 2:6 . . . first to enjoy the **f**
Rev 22:2 . . . bearing twelve crops of **f,**

FRUITFUL (adj) bearing fruit (product of a tree or plant); abundant (at producing work or in bearing children)
Gen 1:22 . . . Be **f** and multiply.
Gen 9:1 . . . Be **f** and multiply.
Gen 35:11 . . . Be **f** and multiply.
Ps 128:3 . . . will be like a **f** grapevine,
Jer 2:7 . . . brought you into a **f** land
Phil 1:22 . . . do more **f** work for Christ.

FRUSTRATES (v) to impede or obstruct; to make invalid or with no effect
Ps 33:10 . . . The LORD **f** the plans

FULFILL, FULFILLED, FULFILLS (v) to complete or perform as promised; to measure up or satisfy
Ps 57:2 . . . to God who will **f** his purpose
Dan 9:4 . . . You always **f** your covenant
Matt 2:15 . . . This **f-ed** what the Lord had
Matt 2:23 . . . This **f-ed** what the prophets
Matt 13:35 . . . **f-ed** what God had spoken
Matt 27:9 . . . This **f-ed** the prophecy of
Luke 4:21 . . . has been **f-ed** this very day!
Luke 24:44 . . . Psalms must be **f-ed.**
John 18:9 . . . this to **f** his own statement:
John 19:28 . . . and to **f** Scripture he said,
Acts 1:16 . . . Scriptures had to be **f-ed**
Rom 3:31 . . . do we truly **f** the law.
Rom 13:8 . . . you will **f** the requirements
Rom 13:10 . . . love **f-s** the requirements
Eph 1:9 . . . plan to **f** his own good pleasure.

FULFILLMENT (n) the act of bringing to completion as promised
John 19:36 . . . happened in **f** of the Scriptures

FULL (adj) possessing or containing a great amount
Deut 34:9 . . . was **f** of the spirit of wisdom,
Luke 4:1 . . . Then Jesus, **f** of the Holy Spirit,
Acts 6:3 . . . **f** of the Spirit and wisdom.
Acts 6:5 . . . Stephen (a man **f** of faith and
Acts 7:55 . . . Stephen, **f** of the Holy Spirit,
Acts 11:24 . . . man, **f** of the Holy Spirit

FULLNESS (n) the quality or state of containing all that is wanted, needed, or possible
Eph 3:19 . . . with all the **f** of life and
Col 1:19 . . . God in all his **f** was pleased
Col 2:9 . . . lives all the **f** of God

FUN (n) providing entertainment, amusement, or enjoyment
Prov 10:23 . . . Doing wrong is **f** for a fool,
Prov 14:9 . . . Fools make **f** of guilt,

FUNDAMENTAL (adj) primary; basic; central
Heb 6:1 . . . the **f** importance of repenting

FUNERAL (adj) of, relating to, or constituting the observances held for a dead person
2 Sam 1:17 . . . David composed a **f** song
Luke 7:32 . . . so we played **f** songs,

FUNERALS (n) the observances held for a dead person
Eccl 7:2 . . . Better to spend your time at **f**

FURIOUS (adj) exhibiting or goaded by anger
Judg 14:19 . . . But Samson was **f**
2 Sam 12:5 . . . David was **f.**
Jer 21:5 . . . You have made me **f!**

FURNACE (n) an enclosed structure in which heat is produced
Dan 3:6 . . . be thrown into a blazing **f.**
Matt 13:42 . . . throw them into the fiery **f,**

FURY (n) wrath; fierceness; rage
Exod 15:7 . . . You unleash your blazing **f;**
Deut 29:28 . . . In great anger and **f**
Jer 32:37 . . . will scatter them in my **f.**

FUTILITY (n) uselessness; a useless act or gesture
Job 7:3 . . . months of **f,** long and weary

FUTURE (adj) existing or occurring at a later time
Rom 8:19 . . . waiting eagerly for that **f** day

FUTURE (n) time that is to come; what is going to happen
Num 24:14 . . . do to your people in the **f.**
Ps 31:15 . . . My **f** is in your hands.
Ps 37:37 . . . a wonderful **f** awaits those
Isa 42:9 . . . tell you the **f** before it happens.
Isa 46:10 . . . can tell you the **f** before it
Jer 29:11 . . . to give you a **f** and a hope.
Jer 31:17 . . . There is hope for your **f,**

G

GABRIEL Angel who stands in God's presence; seen in Daniel's visions (Dan 8:16-18; 9:21); announced birth of John the Baptist (Luke 1:11-20); announced birth of Jesus (Luke 1:26-28).

GAIN (n) winnings or profits
Isa 56:11 . . . intent on personal **g.**

GAIN, GAINED, GAINS (v) to acquire or win; to profit or increase
Prov 3:13 . . . one who **g-s** understanding.
Prov 11:16 . . . gracious woman **g-s** respect,
Mark 8:36 . . . **g** the whole world but lose your
Luke 9:25 . . . **g** the whole world but are
1 Cor 13:3 . . . I would have **g-ed** nothing.

GALILEE (n) a Roman province of Palestine during the time of Jesus
Isa 9:1 . . . a time in the future when **G**
Matt 4:15 . . . beyond the Jordan River, in **G**
Matt 26:32 . . . I will go ahead of you to **G**
Matt 28:10 . . . my brothers to leave for **G,**

GARBAGE (n) food waste; discarded or useless material
1 Cor 4:13 . . . treated like the world's **g,**
Phil 3:8 . . . counting it all as **g,**

GARDEN (n) a planted area where fruits, vegetables, and flowers are cultivated
Gen 2:8 . . . God planted a **g** in Eden
Gen 2:15 . . . God placed the man in the **G**
1 Kgs 4:25 . . . had its own home and **g.**
Song 4:12 . . . my private **g,** my treasure,
Isa 58:11 . . . will be like a well-watered **g,**
Jer 31:12 . . . life will be like a watered **g,**
Ezek 28:13 . . . in Eden, the **g** of God.

GARDENER (n) one who takes care of a garden
John 15:1 . . . my Father is the **g.**

GARMENT, GARMENTS (n) an article of clothing
Exod 28:2 . . . Make sacred **g-s** for Aaron
Lev 16:23 . . . he must take off the linen **g-s**
Lev 16:24 . . . put on his regular **g-s,** and go
Ps 102:26 . . . You will change them like a **g**
John 19:24 . . . divided my **g-s** among

GATE, GATES (n) opening in a (city) wall or fence, consisting of a door and protected by defensive structures (as towers); the place of judicial decisions, town criers, and marketplace trade; entrance
Esth 6:10 . . . sits at the **g** of the palace.
Ps 24:7 . . . Open up, ancient **g-s!**
Ps 100:4 . . . Enter his **g-s** with thanksgiving;
Isa 62:10 . . . Go out through the **g-s!**
Matt 7:13 . . . only through the narrow **g.**
John 10:1 . . . going through the **g,**
John 10:2 . . . who enters through the **g**
John 10:7 . . . I am the **g** for the sheep.
Heb 13:12 . . . died outside the city **g-s**
Rev 21:21 . . . **g-s** were made of pearls—
Rev 21:21 . . . each **g** from a single pearl!

GATEKEEPER (n) one who guards or tends a gate
Ps 84:10 . . . a **g** in the house of my God

GATHER, GATHERED, GATHERING (v) to bring together; to reap or harvest; to assemble
Exod 16:18 . . . Those who **g-ed** a lot
Jer 23:3 . . . will **g** together the remnant
Zech 14:2 . . . I will **g** all the nations
Matt 24:31 . . . they will **g** his chosen ones
Matt 25:26 . . . **g-ed** crops I didn't cultivate,
Matt 25:32 . . . the nations will be **g-ed** in his
Mark 13:27 . . . to **g** his chosen ones
Luke 3:17 . . . **g-ing** the wheat into his barn
Luke 13:34 . . . wanted to **g** your children
2 Cor 8:15 . . . say, "Those who **g-ed** a lot
2 Thes 2:1 . . . we will be **g-ed** to meet him.
Rev 16:16 . . . demonic spirits **g-ed** all

GAVE (v) *see also* GIVE
John 3:16 . . . he **g** his one and only Son,
Rom 8:32 . . . **g** him up for us all,
Gal 2:20 . . . loved me and **g** himself for me.
1 Tim 2:6 . . . He **g** his life to purchase

GENERATION, GENERATIONS (n) the whole body of individuals born about the same time (nation or racial group); the period of time during which those individuals lived (also, age or era); offspring
Gen 17:7 . . . from **g** to **g.**
Exod 20:6 . . . love for a thousand **g-s**
Num 32:13 . . . the entire **g** that sinned
Judg 2:10 . . . After that **g** died,
1 Chr 16:15 . . . to a thousand **g-s.**
Ps 71:18 . . . your power to this new **g,**
Ps 100:5 . . . continues to each **g.**
Ps 102:12 . . . endure to every **g.**
Ps 102:18 . . . recorded for future **g-s,**
Ps 105:8 . . . to a thousand **g-s.**
Ps 119:90 . . . extends to every **g,**
Ps 145:4 . . . Let each **g** tell its children
Ps 146:10 . . . throughout the **g-s.**
Prov 27:24 . . . not be passed to the next **g.**
Isa 41:4 . . . summoning each new **g**
Lam 5:19 . . . from generation to **g.**
Joel 1:3 . . . down from **g** to generation.
Matt 12:39 . . . Only an evil, adulterous **g**
Mark 13:30 . . . this **g** will not pass
Luke 1:48 . . . all **g-s** will call me blessed.
Luke 11:29 . . . This evil **g** keeps asking me
Acts 2:40 . . . this crooked **g!**
Eph 3:5 . . . did not reveal it to previous **g-s,**
Eph 3:21 . . . through all **g-s** forever and ever!

GENEROSITY (n) the quality or fact of being magnanimous, kindly, or openhanded; abundance
Acts 2:46 . . . meals with great joy and **g**—
2 Cor 9:10 . . . a great harvest of **g** in you.

Eph 4:7 . . . through the **g** of Christ.
Phlm 1:6 . . . put into action the **g** that

GENEROUS (adj) magnanimous, kindly; liberal in giving; abundant
Deut 15:8 . . . Instead, be **g** and lend
Ps 37:26 . . . godly always give **g** loans to
2 Cor 9:6 . . . will get a **g** crop.
1 Tim 6:18 . . . **g** to those in need,

GENTILE, GENTILES (n) non-Jewish individuals or nations, often connoting heathens or pagans
see also NATION(S)
Isa 49:6 . . . I will make you a light to the **G-s,**
Luke 21:24 . . . period of the **G-s** comes
Acts 10:45 . . . out on the **G-s,** too.
Acts 14:27 . . . faith to the **G-s,** too.
Acts 15:14 . . . God first visited the **G-s**
Acts 21:25 . . . As for the **G** believers,
Acts 28:28 . . . also been offered to the **G-s,**
Rom 1:16 . . . and also the **G.**
Rom 2:9 . . . and also for the **G.**
Rom 3:9 . . . all people, whether Jews or **G-s,**
Rom 3:29 . . . God of the **G-s?**
Rom 10:12 . . . Jew and **G** are the same
Rom 11:11 . . . available to the **G-s.**
Rom 15:9 . . . so that the **G-s** might give glory
Rom 15:27 . . . **G-s** received the spiritual
Gal 2:2 . . . preaching to the **G-s.**
Gal 2:8 . . . apostle to the **G-s.**
Gal 2:9 . . . keep preaching to the **G-s,**
Gal 3:8 . . . God would declare the **G-s** to be
Gal 3:14 . . . blessed the **G-s** with the same
Gal 3:28 . . . no longer Jew or **G,** slave or
Eph 3:8 . . . the privilege of telling the **G-s**
Col 3:11 . . . a Jew or a **G,** circumcised or

GENTLE (adj) kind; mild-mannered; soft
1 Kgs 19:12 . . . sound of a **g** whisper.
Prov 15:1 . . . A **g** answer deflects anger,
Prov 15:4 . . . **G** words are a tree of life;
Matt 11:29 . . . am humble and **g** at heart,
1 Cor 4:21 . . . love and a **g** spirit?
Eph 4:2 . . . be humble and **g.** Be patient
1 Tim 3:3 . . . must be **g,** not quarrelsome,
Titus 3:2 . . . be **g** and show true humility
Jas 3:17 . . . **g** at all times,

GENTLENESS (n) mildness of manners or disposition
Gal 5:23 . . . **g,** and self-control.
Col 3:12 . . . kindness, humility, **g,** and
1 Tim 6:11 . . . perseverance, and **g.**

GENUINE (adj) actual, true, authentic, sincere
John 1:47 . . . here is a **g** son of Israel—
2 Cor 8:8 . . . I am testing how **g** your love
Phil 1:18 . . . motives are false or **g,**
2 Tim 1:5 . . . I remember your **g** faith,

GETHSEMANE (n) the garden where Jesus often went for prayer, rest, or fellowship; the site where Judas betrayed Jesus before the crucifixion
Matt 26:36 . . . to the olive grove called **G,**
Mark 14:32 . . . to the olive grove called **G,**

GHOST, GHOSTS (n) the soul of a dead person believed to appear to the living in bodily likeness
Luke 24:39 . . . I am not a **g,** because **g-s**

GIDEON Judge of Israel, also called "Jerubbaal" (Judg 6–8; 7:1; Heb 11:32); called by angel of the Lord (Judg 6:11-16); cut down Baal's altar (Judg 6:25-32); used fleece for guidance (Judg 6:36-40); led Israel against Midianite oppressors (Judg 7:1–8:21); refused kingship (Judg 8:22-23); made an "ephod" (Judg 8:24-28); died (Judg 8:29-35).

GIFT, GIFTS (n) a present from people to people (often a bribe); a sacrifice from people to God; anything given voluntarily or at no cost; that which is given from God, enabling or empowering his people
Prov 18:16 . . . Giving a **g** can open doors;
Matt 2:11 . . . and gave him **g-s** of gold,
Luke 11:13 . . . how to give good **g-s** to your
Rom 4:16 . . . given as a free **g.**
Rom 5:15 . . . and God's gracious **g.**
Rom 6:23 . . . free **g** of God is eternal
Rom 11:29 . . . For God's **g-s** and his call
1 Cor 12:4 . . . kinds of spiritual **g-s,**
1 Cor 12:7 . . . A spiritual **g** is given
1 Cor 12:31 . . . the most helpful **g-s.**
2 Cor 9:5 . . . I want it to be a willing **g,**
2 Cor 9:15 . . . Thank God for this **g**
Gal 2:9 . . . recognized the **g** God had
Eph 2:8 . . . it is a **g** from God.
Eph 4:8 . . . and gave **g-s** to his people.
2 Tim 1:6 . . . the spiritual **g** God gave you
Heb 2:4 . . . **g-s** of the Holy Spirit
1 Pet 3:7 . . . equal partner in God's **g**
1 Pet 4:10 . . . of spiritual **g-s.**

GIRL (n) a female child from birth to adulthood
2 Kgs 5:2 . . . was a young **g** who had been
Mark 5:41 . . . which means "Little **g,** get up!"

GIVE, GIVEN, GIVES, GIVING (v) to grant, bestow, convey, offer, provide, or designate; to yield or produce; to suffer the loss of (life)
Exod 30:15 . . . poor must not **g** less.
1 Sam 1:28 . . . **g-ing** him to the LORD,
Ps 112:9 . . . share freely and **g** generously
Ps 119:130 . . . your word **g-s** light,
Prov 21:26 . . . love to **g!**
Prov 23:26 . . . O my son, **g** me your heart.
Isa 9:6 . . . a son is **g-n** to us.
Matt 7:11 . . . heavenly Father **g** good gifts
Matt 16:19 . . . And I will **g** you the keys
Matt 22:30 . . . marry nor be **g-n** in marriage.
Mark 6:7 . . . by two, **g-ing** them authority
Luke 11:13 . . . know how to **g** good gifts to
Luke 14:33 . . . my disciple without **g-ing** up
Luke 22:19 . . . body, which is **g-n** for you.
John 1:17 . . . the law was **g-n** through Moses,
John 5:21 . . . so the Son **g-s** life to anyone
John 13:34 . . . So now I am **g-ing** you a new
John 14:27 . . . And the peace I **g** is a gift
Acts 5:32 . . . Spirit, who is **g-n** by God
Acts 14:3 . . . was true by **g-ing** them power
Acts 15:8 . . . Gentiles by **g-ing** them the Holy
Acts 20:35 . . . is more blessed to **g** than to
Rom 2:7 . . . He will **g** eternal life
Rom 5:5 . . . because he has **g-n** us the Holy
Rom 8:32 . . . won't he also **g** us everything
Rom 10:12 . . . Lord, who **g-s** generously
Rom 12:8 . . . is giving, **g** generously.
Rom 14:12 . . . each of us will **g** a personal
1 Cor 9:17 . . . God has **g-n** me this sacred
1 Cor 11:24 . . . body, which is **g-n** for you.
1 Cor 15:57 . . . thank God! He **g-s** us victory
2 Cor 3:6 . . . the Spirit **g-s** life.
2 Cor 8:6 . . . this ministry of **g-ing.**
2 Cor 9:7 . . . how much to **g.**
Eph 4:7 . . . However, he has **g-n** each one of
Eph 4:28 . . . and then **g** generously to
1 Thes 4:8 . . . rejecting God, who **g-s**
1 Tim 6:17 . . . God, who richly **g-s** us all we
1 Jn 4:13 . . . And God has **g-n** us his Spirit

GLAD (adj) joyful or happy, often with shouts
Ps 16:9 . . . my heart is **g,** and I rejoice.
Ps 32:11 . . . LORD and be **g,** all you who
Ps 69:32 . . . at work and be **g.**
Ps 97:1 . . . coastlands be **g.**
Ps 104:15 . . . wine to make them **g,**
Ps 118:24 . . . will rejoice and be **g** in it.
Prov 10:8 . . . The wise are **g** to be
Prov 27:11 . . . make my heart **g.**
Isa 35:1 . . . and desert will be **g**
Zeph 3:14 . . . O Israel! Be **g** and rejoice
Matt 5:12 . . . Be very **g!**
John 11:15 . . . for your sakes, I'm **g** I wasn't
Acts 13:48 . . . they were very **g**
1 Cor 12:26 . . . the parts are **g.**
2 Cor 2:2 . . . will make me **g?**
Rev 19:7 . . . Let us be **g** and rejoice,

GLADNESS (n) the quality or state of joy or delight; happiness
Ps 40:16 . . . with joy and **g** in you.
Ps 90:15 . . . Give us **g** in proportion to
Isa 35:10 . . . filled with joy and **g.**
Jer 48:33 . . . Joy and **g** are gone
Zeph 3:17 . . . in you with **g.**

GLEAMING (adj) shining with or as if with moderate brightness
Ezek 1:27 . . . he looked like **g** amber,
2 Sam 23:4 . . . clouds, like the **g** of the sun

GLORIFY, GLORIFIED, GLORIFIES, GLORIFYING (v) to bestow honor or praise (as in worship); to magnify
see also EXALT, HONOR
Ps 147:12 . . . **G** the LORD,
Isa 26:8 . . . desire is to **g** your name.
Isa 42:12 . . . the whole world **g** the LORD;
Dan 4:37 . . . praise and **g** and honor the
Luke 2:20 . . . flocks, **g-ing** and praising
John 8:50 . . . no wish to **g** myself, God is
John 13:31 . . . God will be **g-ied**
John 17:1 . . . **G** your Son so
John 21:19 . . . of death he would **g** God.
2 Cor 8:19 . . . a service that **g-ies** the Lord
Eph 1:14 . . . would praise and **g** him.
Rev 15:4 . . . you, Lord, and **g** your name?

GLORIOUS (adj) possessing or deserving special honor; splendid or magnificent
Exod 15:6 . . . O LORD, is **g** in power.
Exod 33:18 . . . show me your **g** presence.
Deut 32:3 . . . the LORD; how **g** is our God!
1 Chr 16:28 . . . the LORD is **g** and strong.
Neh 9:5 . . . prayed: "May your **g** name be
Job 37:5 . . . God's voice is **g** in the
Ps 45:3 . . . You are so **g,** so majestic!
Ps 76:4 . . . You are **g** and more majestic
Ps 96:3 . . . Publish his **g** deeds among the
Ps 149:9 . . . This is the **g** privilege of
Isa 55:5 . . . of Israel, have made you **g.**
Isa 63:15 . . . from your holy, **g** home,
Dan 8:9 . . . east and toward the **g** land of
Dan 11:45 . . . between the **g** holy mountain
Matt 19:28 . . . sits upon his **g** throne,
Acts 2:20 . . . that great and **g** day of the
Acts 7:2 . . . Our **g** God appeared to
Rom 1:23 . . . worshiping the **g,** ever-living
Rom 3:23 . . . of God's **g** standard.
Rom 8:21 . . . children in **g** freedom from
2 Cor 3:9 . . . how much more **g** is the new
2 Cor 3:10 . . . first glory was not **g** at all
2 Cor 3:18 . . . into his **g** image.

Eph 1:6 . . . God for the **g** grace he has
Eph 1:17 . . . asking God, the **g** Father of
Eph 3:16 . . . that from his **g**, unlimited
Eph 5:27 . . . himself as a **g** church without
Phil 3:21 . . . them into **g** bodies like his
Phil 4:19 . . . from his **g** riches, which have
Col 1:11 . . . with all his **g** power so you
Jas 2:1 . . . faith in our **g** Lord Jesus
1 Pet 1:8 . . . with a **g**, inexpressible joy.
1 Pet 4:14 . . . for then the **g** Spirit of God
Jude 1:24 . . . into his **g** presence without a

GLORY (n) honor bestowed; splendor or magnificence; a distinguishing quality, asset, or attribute
Exod 16:10 . . . awesome **g** of the LORD
Num 14:21 . . . filled with the LORD's **g**,
Josh 7:19 . . . My son, give **g** to the LORD,
1 Sam 4:21 . . . said, "Israel's **g** is gone."
Ps 8:5 . . . them with **g** and honor.
Ps 19:1 . . . proclaim the **g** of God.
Ps 29:1 . . . LORD for his **g** and strength.
Ps 44:8 . . . O God, we give **g** to you
Ps 57:11 . . . May your **g** shine over all the
Ps 71:8 . . . I declare your **g** all day
Ps 86:12 . . . I will give **g** to your name
Ps 108:5 . . . May your **g** shine over all the
Ps 145:12 . . . the majesty and **g** of your
Prov 16:31 . . . is a crown of **g**; it is gained
Isa 6:3 . . . earth is filled with his **g**!
Isa 24:16 . . . songs that give **g** to the
Isa 35:2 . . . display his **g**, the splendor
Isa 42:8 . . . not give my **g** to anyone else,
Isa 48:11 . . . not share my **g** with idols!
Isa 66:11 . . . Drink deeply of her **g** even
Isa 66:19 . . . they will declare my **g** to the
Ezek 44:4 . . . saw that the **g** of the LORD
Matt 16:27 . . . angels in the **g** of his Father
Matt 25:31 . . . comes in his **g**, and all the
Mark 13:26 . . . great power and **g**.
Luke 2:14 . . . **G** to God in highest heaven,
Luke 9:26 . . . and in the **g** of the Father
Luke 9:32 . . . they saw Jesus' **g** and the two
Luke 21:27 . . . power and great **g**.
John 1:14 . . . have seen his **g**, the glory of
John 7:39 . . . not yet entered into his **g**.
John 11:40 . . . you would see God's **g** if
John 12:23 . . . enter into his **g**.
John 12:41 . . . the Messiah's **g**.
John 14:13 . . . the Son can bring **g** to the
John 16:14 . . . will bring me **g** by telling
John 17:22 . . . given them the **g** you gave
Acts 3:13 . . . who has brought **g** to his
Rom 2:7 . . . seeking after the **g** and honor
Rom 2:10 . . . there will be **g** and honor and
Rom 3:7 . . . and brings him more **g**?
Rom 4:20 . . . in this he brought **g** to God.
Rom 8:17 . . . heirs of God's **g**.
Rom 8:18 . . . compared to the **g** he will
Rom 8:30 . . . gave them his **g**.
Rom 9:4 . . . God revealed his **g** to them.
Rom 9:23 . . . riches of his **g** shine even
Rom 9:23 . . . in advance for **g**.
Rom 15:6 . . . giving praise and **g** to God,
Rom 15:9 . . . Gentiles might give **g** to God
Rom 16:27 . . . All **g** to the only
1 Cor 2:7 . . . for our ultimate **g** before the
1 Cor 10:31 . . . all for the **g** of God.
1 Cor 15:43 . . . will be raised in **g**.
2 Cor 1:20 . . . to God for his **g**.
2 Cor 3:7 . . . shone with the **g** of God, even
2 Cor 3:10 . . . In fact, that first **g** was not
2 Cor 4:4 . . . about the **g** of Christ, who is
2 Cor 4:17 . . . for us a **g** that vastly
Eph 1:12 . . . bring praise and **g** to God.
Phil 1:11 . . . will bring much **g** and praise
Phil 2:11 . . . is Lord, to the **g** of God the
Phil 4:20 . . . Now all **g** to God our
1 Thes 2:12 . . . Kingdom and **g**.
2 Thes 2:14 . . . share in the **g** of our Lord
1 Tim 1:17 . . . All honor and **g** to God
1 Tim 3:16 . . . to heaven in **g**.
2 Tim 4:18 . . . All **g** to God forever
Titus 2:13 . . . when the **g** of our great God
Heb 1:3 . . . God's own **g** and expresses the
Heb 2:9 . . . crowned with **g** and honor.
Heb 3:3 . . . far more **g** than Moses, just
1 Pet 1:7 . . . much praise and **g** and honor
1 Pet 1:21 . . . gave him great **g**.
1 Pet 5:4 . . . of never-ending **g** and honor.
2 Pet 1:3 . . . means of his marvelous **g** and
2 Pet 1:17 . . . from the majestic **g** of God
Jude 1:25 . . . All **g**, majesty, power,
Rev 4:9 . . . beings give **g** and honor and
Rev 4:11 . . . God, to receive **g** and honor
Rev 5:12 . . . honor and **g** and blessing.
Rev 5:13 . . . and honor and **g** and power
Rev 11:13 . . . terrified and gave **g** to the
Rev 16:9 . . . God and give him **g**.
Rev 21:11 . . . shone with the **g** of God and
Rev 21:23 . . . for the **g** of God
Rev 21:26 . . . will bring their **g** and honor

GLUTTON, GLUTTONS (n) one given habitually to greedy and voracious eating and drinking
Prov 23:20 . . . or feast with **g-s**,
Matt 11:19 . . . He's a **g** and a drunkard,
Titus 1:12 . . . cruel animals, and lazy **g-s**.

GNASHING (v) to grate or grind one's teeth together as an expression of hatred, scorn, or utter despair
Matt 8:12 . . . be weeping and **g** of teeth.

GNAT, GNATS (n) any of various small usually biting dipteran flies
Exod 8:16 . . . swarms of **g-s** throughout the
Matt 23:24 . . . swallow a **g**, but you swallow

GOAL (n) the end toward which effort is directed; aim
1 Cor 14:1 . . . be your highest **g**!
2 Cor 5:9 . . . our **g** is to please him.
1 Thes 4:11 . . . Make it your **g** to live a

GOAT, GOATS (n) any of various hollow-horned ruminant mammals with backwardly arching horns, a short tail, and usually straight hair
Gen 15:9 . . . a three-year-old female **g**,
Gen 30:32 . . . all the sheep and **g-s** that are
Gen 37:31 . . . killed a young **g** and dipped
Lev 16:9 . . . sin offering the **g** chosen by
Num 7:16 . . . and a male **g** for a sin
Num 7:17 . . . rams, five male **g-s**, and five
Isa 11:6 . . . with the baby **g**.
Dan 8:5 . . . a male **g** appeared from the
Matt 25:32 . . . the sheep from the **g-s**.
Heb 10:4 . . . blood of bulls and **g-s**

GOD, GODS (n) eternal, infinite Spirit; Creator, Redeemer, sovereign Lord; impotent pagan diety; image of pagan diety (made of wood, metal, or stone)
see also IDOL(S)
Gen 1:1 . . . In the beginning **G** created
Gen 1:27 . . . In the image of **G** he created
Gen 3:1 . . . Did **G** really say you must not
Gen 6:2 . . . The sons of **G** saw the
Gen 14:18 . . . a priest of **G** Most High,
Gen 17:1 . . . El-Shaddai—'**G** Almighty.'
Gen 22:12 . . . I know that you truly fear **G**.
Gen 50:20 . . . **G** intended it all for good.
Exod 20:5 . . . am a jealous **G** who will not
Exod 22:28 . . . must not dishonor **G** or curse
Exod 32:4 . . . these are the **g-s** who brought
Exod 34:6 . . . The **G** of compassion
Deut 6:4 . . . LORD is our **G**, the LORD
Deut 23:5 . . . LORD your **G** loves you.
Deut 32:16 . . . by worshiping foreign **g-s**; they
Deut 32:39 . . . There is no other **g** but me!
Deut 33:27 . . . The eternal **G** is
Josh 24:19 . . . a holy and jealous **G**.
1 Kgs 8:23 . . . there is no **G** like you
1 Kgs 18:21 . . . if Baal is **G**, then follow
2 Kgs 19:15 . . . You alone are **G** of all
Ezra 9:9 . . . unfailing love our **G** did not
Neh 1:5 . . . awesome **G** who keeps
Ps 19:1 . . . proclaim the glory of **G**.
Ps 22:1 . . . My **G**, my **G**, why have
Ps 42:2 . . . I thirst for **G**, the living **G**.
Ps 42:8 . . . praying to **G** who gives
Ps 51:10 . . . a clean heart, O **G**.
Ps 82:6 . . . say, 'You are **g-s**; you are all
Ps 100:3 . . . the LORD is **G**!
Ps 139:23 . . . Search me, O **G**, and know
Prov 24:12 . . . For **G** understands all
Eccl 12:13 . . . conclusion: Fear **G** and obey
Isa 9:6 . . . Mighty **G**, Everlasting Father,
Isa 43:10 . . . I alone am **G**.
Dan 6:16 . . . May your **G**, whom you
Jon 4:2 . . . compassionate **G**, slow to
Mic 6:8 . . . walk humbly with your **G**.
Mic 7:18 . . . Where is another **G** like you,
Nah 1:2 . . . a jealous **G**, filled with
Mark 2:7 . . . Only **G** can forgive
Mark 3:35 . . . Anyone who does **G's** will is
Mark 15:34 . . . My **G**, my **G**, why
Luke 2:14 . . . Glory to **G** in highest
Luke 10:9 . . . The Kingdom of **G** is near
Luke 16:13 . . . cannot serve both **G** and
Luke 20:38 . . . So he is the **G** of the living,
John 1:1 . . . Word was with **G**
John 1:18 . . . One, who is himself **G**, is near
John 1:29 . . . The Lamb of **G** who
John 3:16 . . . For **G** loved the world so
John 10:34 . . . I say, you are **g-s**!
John 14:1 . . . Trust in **G**, and trust also
Acts 5:29 . . . We must obey **G** rather than
Acts 12:24 . . . word of **G** continued to
Acts 19:26 . . . aren't really **g-s** at all.
Rom 1:16 . . . the power of **G** at work,
Rom 3:23 . . . short of **G's** glorious
Rom 5:1 . . . have peace with **G** because
Rom 5:5 . . . know how dearly **G** loves us,
Rom 6:23 . . . free gift of **G** is eternal
Rom 8:17 . . . are heirs of **G's** glory.
Rom 12:2 . . . learn to know **G's** will for you,
1 Cor 1:18 . . . the very power of **G**.
1 Cor 1:25 . . . foolish plan of **G** is wiser
1 Cor 6:20 . . . you must honor **G** with your
1 Cor 14:33 . . . not a **G** of disorder but
2 Cor 10:4 . . . We use **G's** mighty weapons,
Gal 3:6 . . . believed **G**, and **G** counted him
Eph 2:10 . . . For we are **G's** masterpiece.
Eph 5:1 . . . Imitate **G**, therefore, in
Phil 2:6 . . . equality with **G** as something
Phil 4:7 . . . you will experience **G's** peace,
Col 2:9 . . . the fullness of **G** in a human
1 Thes 5:18 . . . for this is **G's** will
1 Tim 2:5 . . . is only one **G** and one
Titus 1:2 . . . **G**—who does not lie—
Heb 6:18 . . . is impossible for **G** to lie.
Heb 7:19 . . . we draw near to **G**.
Heb 11:6 . . . believe that **G** exists
Jas 2:19 . . . there is one **G**.
Jas 2:23 . . . Abraham believed **G**, and **G**
Jas 4:8 . . . Come close to **G**, and **G**
1 Pet 2:15 . . . It is **G's** will that your
1 Pet 5:5 . . . for "**G** opposes the proud
1 Jn 1:5 . . . declare to you: **G** is light,
1 Jn 4:21 . . . Those who love **G** must also

Rev 19:6 . . . the Lord our **G,** the Almighty,
Rev 21:23 . . . glory of **G** illuminates the

GOD-BREATHED (KJV)
2 Tim 3:16 . . . Scripture is *inspired by God*

GOD-FEARING (adj) having a reverent feeling toward God; devout
Acts 10:2 . . . was a devout, **G** man,
Acts 10:22 . . . is a devout and **G** man,
Acts 13:26 . . . and also you **G** Gentiles—this
Acts 17:4 . . . along with many **G** Greek men
Acts 17:17 . . . Jews and the **G** Gentiles,

GODDESS (n) a female god
Acts 19:27 . . . of the great **g** Artemis will

GODLESS (adj) not acknowledging a deity or divine law
see also UNGODLY
Job 20:5 . . . joy of the **g** has been only
Hos 7:8 . . . mingle with **g** foreigners,
1 Tim 6:20 . . . Avoid **g,** foolish
2 Tim 2:16 . . . to more **g** behavior.
Titus 2:12 . . . to turn from **g** living and
1 Pet 4:3 . . . things that **g** people enjoy—
1 Pet 4:18 . . . will happen to **g** sinners?

GODLINESS (n) devotion to God; piety
see also RIGHTEOUSNESS
Prov 16:8 . . . Better to have little, with **g,**
1 Tim 4:8 . . . but training for **g** is much
1 Tim 5:4 . . . to show **g** at home
1 Tim 6:6 . . . Yet true **g** with contentment

GODLY (adj) marked by or showing reverence for God and devotion to worship
see also RIGHTEOUS, UPRIGHT
Ps 31:23 . . . LORD, all you **g** ones!
Ps 34:9 . . . LORD, you his **g** people,
Prov 16:31 . . . by living a **g** life.
Prov 23:24 . . . The father of **g** children has
Acts 22:12 . . . He was a **g** man, deeply
Gal 6:1 . . . you who are **g** should gently
1 Tim 6:3 . . . promote a **g** life.
2 Tim 3:12 . . . to live a **g** life in Christ
Titus 1:1 . . . how to live **g** lives.
2 Pet 2:9 . . . how to rescue **g** people from
2 Pet 3:11 . . . what holy and **g** lives you

GODLY (n) people who are righteous or devout
Ps 1:5 . . . no place among the **g.**
Ps 37:21 . . . but the **g** are generous givers.
Ps 37:30 . . . The **g** offer good counsel;
Ps 68:3 . . . But let the **g** rejoice.
Ps 118:20 . . . LORD, and the **g** enter there.
Prov 3:32 . . . friendship to the **g.**
Prov 10:11 . . . The words of the **g** are a
Prov 10:20 . . . The words of the **g** are like
Prov 10:28 . . . The hopes of the **g** result in
Prov 11:5 . . . The **g** are directed by
Prov 11:28 . . . But the **g** flourish like
Prov 13:9 . . . The life of the **g** is full of
Prov 20:7 . . . The **g** walk with
Prov 21:15 . . . Justice is a joy to the **g,**
Prov 28:1 . . . the **g** are as bold as lions.

GOLD (n) a valuable yellow malleable metal especially used in coins and jewelry
1 Kgs 20:3 . . . Your silver and **g** are mine,
Ps 19:10 . . . more desirable than **g,**
Ps 119:127 . . . even the finest **g.**
Prov 3:14 . . . are better than **g.**
Matt 2:11 . . . gifts of **g,** frankincense,
Rev 3:18 . . . advise you to buy **g** from me—

GOLGOTHA (n) a hill just outside Jerusalem; the place where Jesus was crucified
Matt 27:33 . . . a place called **G**
Mark 15:22 . . . a place called **G**
John 19:17 . . . (in Hebrew, **G**).

GOLIATH Great Philistine warrior killed by David (1 Sam 17:4, 8, 23; 21:9; 22:10; 2 Sam 21:19; 1 Chr 20:5).

GOMORRAH (n) one of the five "cities of the plain" located in the Valley of Siddim; God destroyed this city by fire for its extreme wickedness
Gen 19:24 . . . on Sodom and **G.**
Matt 10:15 . . . and **G** will be better
2 Pet 2:6 . . . of Sodom and **G** and turned
Jude 1:7 . . . forget Sodom and **G** and their

GOOD (adj) kind; profitable; excellent; fitting or appropriate; morally right
Gen 1:4 . . . that the light was **g.**
Gen 1:31 . . . it was very **g!**
Gen 2:18 . . . It is not **g** for the man to
2 Chr 7:3 . . . He is **g!** His faithful
2 Chr 31:20 . . . was pleasing and **g** in the
Ps 34:8 . . . see that the LORD is **g.**
Ps 119:68 . . . You are **g** and do only
Eccl 7:20 . . . earth is always **g** and never
Isa 5:20 . . . that evil is **g** and **g** is
Isa 45:7 . . . I send **g** times and
Mic 6:8 . . . told you what is **g,** and this is
Matt 5:29 . . . eye—even your **g** eye—causes
Matt 19:17 . . . One who is **g.**
Matt 22:10 . . . they could find, **g** and bad
Matt 25:21 . . . Well done, my **g** and
Mark 3:4 . . . the law permit **g** deeds on the
Mark 10:18 . . . God is truly **g.**
Luke 6:45 . . . person produces **g** things from
Luke 6:45 . . . treasury of a **g** heart,
Luke 8:15 . . . seeds that fell on the **g** soil
Luke 14:34 . . . Salt is **g** for seasoning.
Luke 18:19 . . . God is truly **g.**
Luke 19:17 . . . You are a **g** servant.
John 10:11 . . . I am the **g** shepherd.
Rom 7:12 . . . and right and **g.**
Rom 7:16 . . . that the law is **g.**
Rom 7:18 . . . know that nothing **g** lives in
Rom 7:19 . . . do what is **g,** but I don't.
Rom 12:2 . . . you, which is **g** and pleasing
Rom 12:9 . . . Hold tightly to what is **g.**
1 Cor 6:12 . . . not everything is **g** for you.
1 Cor 7:1 . . . Yes, it is **g** to abstain
1 Cor 15:33 . . . corrupts **g** character.
Gal 6:9 . . . doing what is **g.**
Eph 2:10 . . . so we can do the **g** things he
Phil 1:6 . . . who began the **g** work within
1 Thes 5:21 . . . to what is **g.**
1 Tim 4:4 . . . everything God created is **g,**
1 Tim 6:12 . . . Fight the **g** fight
2 Tim 3:17 . . . people to do every **g** work.
2 Tim 4:7 . . . I have fought the **g** fight,
Titus 3:8 . . . These teachings are **g**
Heb 10:24 . . . of love and **g** works.
Heb 12:10 . . . is always **g** for us,
Jas 2:8 . . . indeed, it is **g** when you obey

GOOD (n) something that is excellent, profitable, or morally right; advancement of prosperity or well-being; something useful or beneficial
Gen 2:9 . . . the knowledge of **g** and evil.
Gen 3:22 . . . knowing both **g** and evil.
Gen 50:20 . . . God intended it all for **g.**
1 Sam 26:23 . . . reward for doing **g** and for
Ps 14:1 . . . not one of them does **g!**
Ps 53:3 . . . No one does **g,** not a single
Prov 3:27 . . . Do not withhold **g** from those
Prov 11:27 . . . If you search for **g,** you will
Prov 31:12 . . . She brings him **g,** not harm,
Isa 55:2 . . . does you no **g?**
Jer 13:23 . . . you start doing **g,** for you
Jer 32:39 . . . for their own **g** and for the
Matt 5:45 . . . evil and the **g,** and he sends
Rom 3:12 . . . No one does **g,** not a single
Rom 8:28 . . . together for the **g** of those
Rom 13:4 . . . sent for your **g.**
1 Cor 10:24 . . . but for the **g** of others.
Gal 6:10 . . . we should do **g** to everyone—
Eph 6:8 . . . each one of us for the **g** we do,
1 Tim 5:10 . . . because of the **g** she has
Heb 13:16 . . . forget to do **g** and to share
1 Pet 2:20 . . . suffer for doing **g** and endure
1 Pet 3:17 . . . suffer for doing **g,** if that

GOODNESS (n) the beneficial quality of something; kindness
Ps 145:7 . . . the story of your wonderful **g;**
Isa 63:7 . . . in his great **g** to Israel,
Rom 14:17 . . . a life of **g** and peace and joy
Rom 15:14 . . . that you are full of **g.**

GOSPEL (KJV)
Mark 1:1 . . . the *Good News* about Jesus
Luke 4:18 . . . anointed me to bring *Good News*
Rom 1:16 . . . not ashamed of this *Good News*
Rom 10:15 . . . feet of messengers who bring *good news*
Gal 3:8 . . . God proclaimed this *good news*

GOSSIP (n) rumor or report revealing personal or sensational facts about others
Prov 16:28 . . . of strife; **g** separates the
Prov 26:20 . . . disappear when **g** stops.
2 Cor 12:20 . . . slander, **g,** arrogance,

GOSSIP, GOSSIPING (v) to relate rumors or reports about others
Ps 15:3 . . . who refuse to **g** or harm their
1 Tim 5:13 . . . spend their time **g-ing**

GOVERN (v) to exercise continuous sovereign authority over; to control or rule
Gen 1:16 . . . larger one to **g** the day,
Gen 1:28 . . . the earth and **g** it.
Gen 49:16 . . . Dan will **g** his people, like
Job 34:17 . . . Could God **g** if he hated
Ps 67:4 . . . because you **g** the nations

GOVERNMENT (n) the organization or agency through which a political unit exercises authority
Isa 9:6 . . . The **g** will rest on his
Rom 13:6 . . . For **g** workers need
Titus 3:1 . . . to submit to the **g** and its

GRACE (n) God's free and unmerited favor toward sinful humanity
see also FAVOR
Acts 6:8 . . . full of God's **g** and power,
Acts 14:3 . . . about the **g** of the Lord.
Acts 15:11 . . . by the undeserved **g** of the
Acts 20:32 . . . message of his **g** that is able
Rom 5:15 . . . is God's wonderful **g** and his
Rom 5:21 . . . now God's wonderful **g** rules
Rom 6:1 . . . of his wonderful **g?**
Rom 11:5 . . . of God's **g**—his undeserved
Rom 12:6 . . . In his **g,** God has
1 Cor 3:10 . . . Because of God's **g** to me,
1 Cor 16:23 . . . May the **g** of the Lord
2 Cor 4:15 . . . And as God's **g** reaches more
2 Cor 9:14 . . . of the overflowing **g** God has
Gal 1:15 . . . by his marvelous **g.**
Gal 2:21 . . . do not treat the **g** of God as
Gal 5:4 . . . away from God's **g.**
Eph 1:7 . . . in kindness and **g** that he
Eph 2:5 . . . only by God's **g** that you have
Eph 2:7 . . . wealth of his **g** and kindness
Eph 2:8 . . . saved you by his **g** when you
Eph 3:2 . . . of extending his **g** to you
Eph 3:7 . . . By God's **g** and mighty
Phil 4:23 . . . May the **g** of the Lord
2 Thes 1:12 . . . because of the **g** of our God

2 Thes 2:16 . . . and by his **g** gave us eternal
1 Tim 1:2 . . . Lord give you **g**, mercy,
2 Tim 1:9 . . . show us his **g** through Christ
2 Tim 2:1 . . . strong through the **g** that God
2 Tim 4:22 . . . And may his **g** be with all of
Titus 2:11 . . . For the **g** of God has
Titus 3:7 . . . Because of his **g** he declared
Titus 3:15 . . . May God's **g** be with you
Heb 4:16 . . . and we will find **g** to help us
Heb 12:15 . . . to receive the **g** of God.
Heb 13:9 . . . comes from God's **g**, not from
Heb 13:25 . . . May God's **g** be with you all.
Jas 4:6 . . . gives us even more **g** to stand
1 Pet 5:12 . . . Stand firm in this **g**.
2 Pet 3:18 . . . grow in the **g** and knowledge
Rev 22:21 . . . May the **g** of the Lord

GRACIOUS (adj) abounding in grace and kindness; merciful, compassionate
2 Kgs 13:23 . . . the LORD was **g** and merciful
Ps 145:13 . . . he is **g** in all he
Prov 11:16 . . . A **g** woman gains
John 1:16 . . . received one **g** blessing after
2 Cor 8:7 . . . also in this **g** act of giving.
Col 4:6 . . . your conversation be **g** and
1 Tim 1:14 . . . and **g** our Lord
1 Pet 1:10 . . . about this **g** salvation
1 Pet 1:13 . . . to the **g** salvation that will

GRAFTED (v) to unite a shoot or bud with a growing plant so they grow as one
Rom 11:18 . . . not brag about being **g** in to

GRANDCHILDREN (n) the child of one's son or daughter
1 Tim 5:4 . . . children or **g**, their first

GRANDMOTHER (n) the mother of one's father or mother
2 Tim 1:5 . . . first filled your **g** Lois and

GRANT (n) property transferred by deed or writing
Josh 14:3 . . . already given a **g** of land to

GRANT, GRANTED (v) to permit as a right, privilege, or favor; to consent to carry out for a person
Prov 10:24 . . . of the godly will be **g-ed**.
Isa 26:12 . . . LORD, you will **g** us peace;
Matt 15:28 . . . Your request is **g-ed**." And her
John 15:7 . . . and it will be **g-ed!**

GRAPES (n) a smooth-skinned juicy greenish-white to deep red or purple berry
Gen 40:10 . . . it produced clusters of ripe **g**
Lev 19:10 . . . not pick up the **g** that fall
Num 6:3 . . . not eat **g** or raisins
Num 13:23 . . . single cluster of **g** so large
Deut 32:32 . . . Their **g** are poison
Job 15:33 . . . a vine whose **g** are harvested
Isa 5:4 . . . expected sweet **g**, why did
Isa 63:3 . . . my enemies as if they were **g**
Matt 7:16 . . . **g** from thornbushes, or figs
Rev 14:19 . . . **g** into the great winepress

GRAPEVINE (n) the vine on which grapes grow
Ps 128:3 . . . a fruitful **g**, flourishing
Isa 36:16 . . . from your own **g** and fig tree
John 15:1 . . . am the true **g**, and my Father

GRASS (n) green plants that grow from the ground and are suitable for grazing animals
Isa 40:6 . . . people are like the **g**.
1 Pet 1:24 . . . The **g** withers and

GRAVE, GRAVES (n) burial place; euphemism for Hades, hell, or Sheol
Ps 5:9 . . . from an open **g**.
Ps 49:15 . . . power of the **g**.
John 5:28 . . . dead in their **g-s** will hear the
Acts 2:27 . . . rot in the **g**.
Rom 3:13 . . . from an open **g**.
Rev 20:13 . . . death and the **g** gave up their

GRAVECLOTHES (n) strips of cloth wrapped around a corpse in preparation for burial
John 11:44 . . . and feet bound in **g**, his face

GREAT, GREATER, GREATEST (adj) huge; remarkable in magnitude, degree, or effectiveness
Deut 10:17 . . . He is the **g** God, the mighty
2 Sam 24:14 . . . his mercy is **g**.
Ps 107:8 . . . LORD for his **g** love and for
Ps 147:5 . . . How **g** is our LORD!
Dan 9:4 . . . you are a **g** and awesome God!
Matt 12:41 . . . someone **g-er** than Jonah is
Matt 12:42 . . . **g-er** than Solomon
Matt 19:30 . . . who are the **g-est** now will be
Matt 22:38 . . . first and **g-est** commandment.
John 3:30 . . . He must become **g-er**
John 15:13 . . . There is no **g-er** love than to
1 Cor 13:13 . . . and the **g-est** of these is love.
Rev 20:11 . . . I saw a **g** white throne and

GREED (n) a selfish and excessive desire for more of something (as money) than is needed
Prov 15:27 . . . **G** brings grief
Rom 1:29 . . . of wickedness, sin, **g**, hate,
2 Pet 2:3 . . . In their **g** they will make up
2 Pet 2:14 . . . well trained in **g**.

GREEDY (adj) having or showing a selfish desire for wealth and possessions
1 Sam 8:3 . . . for they were **g** for money.
Prov 1:19 . . . all who are **g** for money;
Prov 21:26 . . . people are always **g**
1 Cor 6:10 . . . are thieves, or **g** people,
Eph 5:5 . . . For a **g** person is an
Col 3:5 . . . Don't be **g**, for a **g**

GREEKS (n) a native or inhabitant of Greece
1 Cor 1:22 . . . And it is foolish to the **G**,

GREEN (adj) of the color green; pleasantly alluring
Ps 23:2 . . . lets me rest in **g** meadows;

GREET (v) to address with expressions of kind wishes upon meeting or arrival
Rom 16:16 . . . **G** each other in Christian
1 Cor 16:20 . . . **G** each other with
2 Cor 13:12 . . . **G** each other with
1 Thes 5:26 . . . **G** all the brothers
1 Pet 5:14 . . . **G** each other with

GREW (v) *see also* GROW
Luke 1:80 . . . John **g** up and became
Luke 2:52 . . . Jesus **g** in wisdom
Acts 9:31 . . . Spirit, it also **g** in numbers.
Acts 16:5 . . . faith and **g** larger every day.

GRIEF (n) deep and poignant distress due to bereavement; a cause of suffering
Job 16:5 . . . take away your **g**.
Ps 10:14 . . . the trouble and **g** they cause.
Prov 10:1 . . . a foolish child brings **g** to a
Prov 15:27 . . . Greed brings **g** to the
John 16:20 . . . your **g** will suddenly turn
Rom 9:2 . . . sorrow and unending **g**

GRIEVE, GRIEVED (v) to feel, show, or cause distress, vexation, sorrow, or regret
Eccl 3:4 . . . A time to **g** and a time
Isa 63:10 . . . rebelled against him and **g-d**
Lam 3:20 . . . time, as I **g** over my loss.
1 Thes 4:13 . . . so you will not **g** like people

GROAN, GROANING, GROANINGS (n) a deep moan indicative of pain, grief, or annoyance
Exod 2:24 . . . God heard their **g-ing**, and he
Ps 90:9 . . . years with a **g**.
Rom 8:26 . . . for us with **g-ings** that cannot be

GROAN, GROANING (v) to utter a deep moan indicative of pain, grief, or annoyance
Job 35:9 . . . They **g** beneath the power
Rom 8:22 . . . creation has been **g-ing** as
Rom 8:23 . . . believers also **g**, even though
2 Cor 5:4 . . . bodies, we **g** and sigh,

GROUND (n) soil, earth, or territory
Gen 1:10 . . . called the dry **g** "land" and
Gen 3:17 . . . the **g** is cursed because of you.
Gen 4:2 . . . Cain cultivated the **g**.
Gen 4:10 . . . cries out to me from the **g!**
Exod 3:5 . . . standing on holy **g**.
Exod 15:19 . . . sea on dry **g!**
Isa 53:2 . . . like a root in dry **g**.
Matt 10:29 . . . fall to the **g** without your

GROW, GROWING, GROWS (v) to become; to spring up and develop to maturity
see also GREW
Isa 40:31 . . . run and not **g** weary.
1 Cor 3:6 . . . God who made it **g**.
Eph 4:16 . . . is healthy and **g-ing** and full of
Phil 1:25 . . . all of you **g** and experience
Col 2:19 . . . it **g-s** as God nourishes it.
2 Thes 1:3 . . . one another is **g-ing**.
Jas 1:15 . . . when sin is allowed to **g**,
2 Pet 3:18 . . . Rather, you must **g** in the

GRUDGE (n) a feeling of deep-seated resentment or ill will
Mark 11:25 . . . you are holding a **g** against,

GRUMBLE (v) to mutter in discontent
1 Cor 10:10 . . . And don't **g** as some
Jas 5:9 . . . Don't **g** about each other

GRUMBLERS (n) one who mutters in discontent
Jude 1:16 . . . people are **g** and complainers,

GUARANTEE (n) an assurance for the fulfillment of a condition
2 Cor 5:5 . . . and as a **g** he has given us

GUARANTEED, GUARANTEEING, GUARANTEES (v) to assure that some agreement or condition will be fulfilled; to give security for
Ps 111:9 . . . He has **g** his covenant
2 Cor 1:22 . . . first installment that **g-s**
Eph 4:30 . . . **g-ing** that you will be saved
Heb 7:22 . . . is the one who **g-s** this better

GUARD (adj) defensively watchful; alert
2 Pet 3:17 . . . Be on **g** so that you

GUARD, GUARDING, GUARDS (v) to protect by watchful attention; to watch over
see also KEEP
Prov 4:23 . . . **G** your heart
Prov 7:2 . . . as you **g** your own eyes.
Prov 24:12 . . . He who **g-s** your soul knows
Luke 2:8 . . . fields nearby, **g-ing** their flocks
Phil 4:7 . . . His peace will **g** your hearts
2 Thes 3:3 . . . and **g** you from

GUARDIAN (n) one who has the care of the person or property of another
Gen 4:9 . . . Am I my brother's **g?**
Gal 3:25 . . . the law as our **g**.
1 Pet 2:25 . . . your Shepherd, the **G** of your

GUIDANCE (n) direction or counsel provided by another person
2 Chr 26:5 . . . as the king sought **g** from

Prov 24:6 . . . go to war without wise **g;**
Prov 29:18 . . . do not accept divine **g,**

GUIDE, GUIDED, GUIDES, GUIDING (v) to direct, supervise, or influence usually to a particular end
Exod 13:21 . . . He **g-d** them during the
Exod 15:13 . . . In your might, you **g** them
Deut 1:33 . . . **g-ing** you with a pillar of fire
Ps 16:7 . . . bless the LORD who **g-s** me;
Ps 23:3 . . . He **g-s** me along
Ps 32:8 . . . I will **g** you along
Ps 139:10 . . . your hand will **g** me,
John 16:13 . . . he will **g** you into all
Gal 5:16 . . . let the Holy Spirit **g** your lives.

GUIDES (n) one who leads or directs another's way
Matt 23:16 . . . Blind **g!** What sorrow
Matt 23:24 . . . Blind **g!** You strain

GUILT (n) the state or feeling of one who has committed an offense
Job 6:29 . . . Stop assuming my **g,** for I
Ps 32:2 . . . the LORD has cleared of **g,**
Ps 38:4 . . . My **g** overwhelms me—
Ps 51:2 . . . Wash me clean from my **g.**
Isa 6:7 . . . Now your **g** is removed,
Dan 9:24 . . . atone for their **g,** to bring

GUILTY (adj) justly chargeable with wrongdoing
Lev 19:17 . . . not be held **g** for their sin.
Rom 3:19 . . . entire world is **g** before God.
1 Cor 11:27 . . . **g** of sinning against
1 Jn 3:20 . . . if we feel **g,** God is greater
1 Jn 3:21 . . . we don't feel **g,** we can come

H

HAGAR Sarah's Egyptian servant and rival, mother of Ishmael (Gen 16); sent away by Abraham, son's cries heard by God (Gen 21:9-21); Paul's analogy using Hagar and Sarah (Gal 4:24-25).

HAIL (n) precipitation in the form of small balls of ice and snow
Exod 9:19 . . . die when the **h** falls.
Ps 18:12 . . . rained down **h** and
Rev 8:7 . . . his trumpet, and **h** and fire

HAIR, HAIRS (n) a slender threadlike outgrowth of the skin of an animal or human
Lev 19:27 . . . Do not trim off the **h** on your
2 Sam 18:9 . . . his **h** got caught in the tree.
Matt 10:30 . . . And the very **h-s** on your head
1 Cor 11:6 . . . to have her **h** cut or her head
1 Cor 11:14 . . . man to have long **h?**
1 Cor 11:15 . . . And isn't long **h** a woman's
Rev 1:14 . . . His head and his **h** were white

HAIRSTYLES (n) a way of wearing the hair
1 Pet 3:3 . . . outward beauty of fancy **h,**

HAIRY (adj) covered with hair
Gen 27:11 . . . Esau, is a **h** man, and my skin

HALF (n) either of two equal parts that compose something
see also HALVES
Exod 30:13 . . . (This payment is **h** a shekel,
1 Kgs 3:25 . . . to one woman and **h** to the
1 Kgs 10:7 . . . not heard the **h** of it!
Esth 5:3 . . . if it is **h** the kingdom!
Dan 7:25 . . . a time, times, and **h** a time.
Mark 6:23 . . . ask, up to **h** my kingdom!

HALLELUJAH (KJV)
Rev 19:1 . . . shouting, *"Praise the Lord!*
Rev 19:3 . . . voices rang out: *"Praise the Lord!*
Rev 19:4 . . . "Amen! *Praise the Lord!"*
Rev 19:6 . . . *"Praise the Lord!* For the Lord

HALLOW(ED) (KJV)
Exod 20:11 . . . Sabbath day and *set it apart as holy*
Lev 25:10 . . . *Set* this year *apart as holy*
1 Kgs 9:3 . . . *set* this Temple *apart to be holy*
Matt 6:9 . . . *may* your name *be kept holy*

HALVES (n) *see also* HALF
Gen 15:17 . . . between the **h** of the carcasses.
Jer 34:18 . . . between its **h** to solemnize

HAND, HANDS (n) the end of the arm that serves as a grasping and handling tool for humans; symbolic of power
Gen 47:29 . . . Put your **h** under my
Exod 15:6 . . . Your right **h,** O LORD,
Exod 29:10 . . . will lay their **h-s** on its head.
Exod 33:22 . . . cover you with my **h** until
1 Kgs 13:4 . . . king's **h** became paralyzed
Ps 22:16 . . . have pierced my **h-s** and feet.
Ps 24:4 . . . Only those whose **h-s** and hearts
Ps 32:4 . . . your **h** of discipline
Ps 44:3 . . . It was your right **h** and
Ps 63:4 . . . lifting up my **h-s** to you in prayer.
Ps 75:8 . . . a cup in his **h** that is full
Ps 110:1 . . . at my right **h** until I humble
Ps 137:5 . . . let my right **h** forget how to
Ps 145:16 . . . you open your **h,** you satisfy
Isa 40:12 . . . the oceans in his **h?**
Isa 41:13 . . . by your right **h**—I, the LORD
Isa 55:12 . . . will clap their **h-s!**
Isa 64:8 . . . formed by your **h.**
Dan 10:10 . . . Just then a **h** touched me
Matt 5:30 . . . And if your **h**—even your
Matt 6:3 . . . don't let your left **h** know what
Matt 18:8 . . . with only one **h** or one foot
Matt 26:64 . . . at God's right **h** and coming
Mark 12:36 . . . at my right **h** until I humble
Acts 6:6 . . . they laid their **h-s** on them.
Acts 7:55 . . . at God's right **h.**
Acts 8:18 . . . laid their **h-s** on people,
Acts 13:3 . . . men laid their **h-s** on them
Acts 19:6 . . . Paul laid his **h-s** on them,
Acts 28:8 . . . and laying his **h-s** on him,
1 Thes 4:11 . . . working with your **h-s,**
1 Tim 2:8 . . . pray with holy **h-s** lifted up
1 Tim 4:14 . . . church laid their **h-s** on you.
2 Tim 1:6 . . . when I laid my **h-s** on you.
Heb 1:13 . . . at my right **h** until I humble
Rev 13:16 . . . mark on the right **h** or on the

HANDED (v) to yield control of
Rom 4:25 . . . He was **h** over to die
1 Tim 1:20 . . . threw them out and **h** them over

HANDFUL (n) a small quantity or number
Eccl 4:6 . . . to have one **h** with quietness

HANDSOME (adj) having a pleasing and usually impressive appearance; beautiful
Gen 39:6 . . . Joseph was a very **h** and well-built
1 Sam 16:12 . . . dark and **h,** with beautiful
2 Sam 14:25 . . . as the most **h** man in all Israel.
1 Kgs 1:6 . . . he was very **h.**
Ezek 23:6 . . . commanders dressed in **h** blue,

HANGED, HANGING, HANGS (v) to suspend; to execute (on a tree or gallows)
see also HUNG
Job 26:7 . . . **h-s** the earth on nothing.
Matt 27:5 . . . went out and **h-ed** himself.
Acts 10:39 . . . death by **h-ing** him on a cross,

HAPPINESS (n) a state of well-being and contentment; joy
Deut 24:5 . . . **h** to the wife he has married.
Job 7:7 . . . never again feel **h.**
Job 9:25 . . . a glimpse of **h.**
Ps 86:4 . . . Give me **h,** O LORD,
Ps 119:35 . . . that is where my **h** is found.
Eccl 8:15 . . . **h** along with all the hard work
Isa 65:18 . . . Jerusalem as a place of **h.**
Luke 6:24 . . . you have your only **h** now.

HAPPY (adj) expressing, reflecting, or suggestive of happiness
see also BLESSED
Deut 16:14 . . . festival will be a **h** time
Ps 113:9 . . . making her a **h** mother.
Prov 15:13 . . . A glad heart makes a **h** face;
Prov 15:15 . . . for the **h** heart, life is
Prov 23:25 . . . she who gave you birth be **h.**
Eccl 9:7 . . . drink your wine with a **h** heart,
Zech 10:7 . . . will be made **h** as if by wine.
Rom 12:15 . . . Be **h** with those who are **h,**
Phil 2:2 . . . make me truly **h** by agreeing
Jas 5:13 . . . Are any of you **h?**

HARBOR (n) a part of a body of water where ships dock; a place of security and comfort
Ps 107:30 . . . brought them safely into **h!**

HARD (adj) lacking in responsiveness, unfeeling; demanding the exertion of energy
Rom 11:25 . . . of Israel have **h** hearts,
Rev 2:2 . . . I have seen your **h** work and

HARD, HARDER (adv) with great or utmost effort or energy
Prov 13:4 . . . those who work **h**
Acts 20:35 . . . in need by working **h.**
Rom 16:12 . . . has worked so **h**
1 Cor 15:10 . . . worked **h-er** than any of
2 Cor 11:23 . . . worked **h-er,** been put in
1 Thes 5:12 . . . They work **h** among you
2 Thes 3:8 . . . We worked **h** day and night

HARD-HEARTED (adj) lacking in sympathetic understanding; unfeeling
Deut 15:7 . . . do not be **h** or tightfisted

HARDEN, HARDENED (v) to make callous or unfeeling
Exod 4:21 . . . But I will **h** his heart
Exod 10:20 . . . LORD **h-ed** Pharaoh's heart
Ps 95:8 . . . Don't **h** your hearts as Israel did
Isa 6:10 . . . **H** the hearts of these people.
Matt 13:15 . . . hearts of these people are **h-ed,**
John 12:40 . . . and **h-ed** their hearts—
Eph 4:18 . . . minds and **h-ed** their hearts
Heb 3:8 . . . don't **h** your hearts as Israel did

HARDSHIPS (n) something that causes or entails suffering or privation
Acts 14:22 . . . must suffer many **h** to enter
2 Cor 6:4 . . . troubles and **h** and calamities
2 Thes 1:4 . . . and **h** you are suffering.
Jas 5:13 . . . Are any of you suffering **h?**

HARLOT (KJV)
Gen 38:15 . . . thought she was a *prostitute*
Josh 2:1 . . . a *prostitute* named Rahab
Hos 4:15 . . . you, Israel, are a *prostitute*
Matt 21:31 . . . *prostitutes* will get into the Kingdom
Rev 17:5 . . . Mother of All *Prostitutes* and

HARM (n) physical or mental damage; injury, hurt
Ps 37:8 . . . it only leads to **h.**
Prov 3:29 . . . Don't plot **h** against your
Prov 19:23 . . . and protection from **h.**
Prov 31:12 . . . brings him good, not **h,** all
1 Cor 11:17 . . . more **h** than good is done

HARM, HARMED, HARMS (v) to injure or hurt
Ps 121:6 . . . sun will not **h** you by day,
Jer 10:5 . . . they can neither **h** you nor do
Zech 2:8 . . . who **h-s** you **h-s** my most
Rev 2:11 . . . will not be **h-ed** by the second

HARMLESS (adj) lacking capacity or intent to injure
Matt 10:16 . . . shrewd as snakes and **h** as

HARMONY (n) tranquility; agreement; unity
Zech 6:13 . . . will be perfect **h** between his
Rom 12:16 . . . Live in **h** with each other.
Rom 14:19 . . . aim for **h** in the church
Rom 15:5 . . . live in complete **h** with each
1 Cor 12:25 . . . This makes for **h**
2 Cor 6:15 . . . What **h** can there be
2 Cor 13:11 . . . Live in **h** and peace.
Col 3:14 . . . together in perfect **h.**

HARP, HARPS (n) a plucked stringed instrument
Gen 4:21 . . . all who play the **h** and flute.
1 Sam 16:23 . . . would play the **h.**
Ps 33:2 . . . on the ten-stringed **h.**
Ps 98:5 . . . with the **h** and melodious song,
Ps 137:2 . . . our **h-s,** hanging them
Ps 144:9 . . . a ten-stringed **h.**
Ps 147:7 . . . sing praises to our God with a **h.**
Ps 150:3 . . . praise him with the lyre and **h!**
Rev 5:8 . . . Each one had a **h,** and they held

HARSH (adj) causing a disagreeable or painful sensory reaction; unduly exacting
Prov 15:1 . . . **h** words make tempers flare.
Eph 4:31 . . . rage, anger, **h** words,

HARVEST, HARVESTS (n) the time or fruit of reaping or gathering in a crop—physically or spiritually
Deut 16:15 . . . blesses you with bountiful **h-s**
Matt 9:37 . . . The **h** is great, but
John 4:35 . . . fields are already ripe for **h.**
1 Cor 15:23 . . . raised as the first of the **h;**
2 Cor 9:10 . . . great **h** of generosity
Gal 6:9 . . . we will reap a **h** of blessing
Heb 12:11 . . . peaceful **h** of right living
Jas 3:18 . . . reap a **h** of righteousness.
Rev 14:15 . . . the time of **h** has come;

HARVEST, HARVESTS (v) to gather in (a crop); to reap
Gen 8:22 . . . there will be planting and **h,**
Job 4:8 . . . and cultivate evil will **h**
Prov 10:5 . . . wise youth **h-s** in the summer,
Gal 6:8 . . . sinful nature will **h** decay and

HARVESTER, HARVESTERS (n) one who gathers in (a crop)
Ruth 2:3 . . . to gather grain behind the **h-s.**
John 4:36 . . . planter and the **h** alike!

HASTE (n) rash or headlong action; swiftness
Prov 19:2 . . . **h** makes mistakes.

HASTY (adj) done or made in a hurry; impatient; speedy
Prov 21:5 . . . **h** shortcuts lead to poverty.
Eccl 5:2 . . . don't be **h** in bringing matters

HATE, HATED, HATES, HATING (v) to feel extreme enmity toward; to have a strong aversion to
Ps 45:7 . . . love justice and **h** evil.
Prov 1:22 . . . you fools **h** knowledge?
Prov 6:16 . . . six things the LORD **h-s**—
Prov 13:5 . . . The godly **h** lies;
Prov 15:27 . . . those who **h** bribes will live.
Prov 26:28 . . . A lying tongue **h-s** its victims,
Prov 28:16 . . . but one who **h-s** corruption
Mal 2:16 . . . "For I **h** divorce!"
Matt 5:43 . . . and **h** your enemy.
Matt 24:9 . . . be **h-d** all over the world
Luke 6:22 . . . when people **h** you
John 3:20 . . . All who do evil **h** the light
John 15:18 . . . remember that it **h-d** me
2 Tim 3:3 . . . be cruel and **h** what is good.
Heb 1:9 . . . You love justice and **h** evil.
1 Jn 2:9 . . . **h-s** a Christian brother or sister,
1 Jn 4:20 . . . **h-s** a Christian brother or sister,
Jude 1:23 . . . **h-ing** the sins that contaminate

HATERS (n) one who feels or expresses enmity or aversion
Rom 1:30 . . . They are backstabbers, **h** of God,

HATRED (n) strong emotional aversion
Lev 19:17 . . . Do not nurse **h** in your heart
Prov 26:24 . . . People may cover their **h**

HAUGHTY (adj) blatantly and disdainfully proud
Prov 6:17 . . . **h** eyes, a lying tongue,
Prov 21:24 . . . are proud and **h;** they act

HAY (n) herbage and especially grass mowed and cured for fodder
1 Cor 3:12 . . . jewels, wood, **h,** or straw.

HEAD, HEADS (n) top part of the body that contains the brain; one in charge; person, individual
Gen 3:15 . . . He will strike your **h,** and
Lev 26:13 . . . walk with your **h-s** held high.
Ps 22:7 . . . shake their **h-s,** saying,
Ps 23:5 . . . by anointing my **h** with oil.
Ps 133:2 . . . over Aaron's **h,** that ran
Prov 25:22 . . . coals of shame on their **h-s,**
Matt 27:39 . . . shaking their **h-s** in mockery.
John 19:2 . . . thorns and put it on his **h,**
Acts 18:6 . . . your own **h-s**—I am innocent.
Rom 12:20 . . . coals of shame on their **h-s.**
Eph 1:22 . . . and has made him **h** over all
Eph 5:23 . . . as Christ is the **h** of the
Rev 4:4 . . . crowns on their **h-s.**
Rev 14:14 . . . He had a gold crown on his **h**
Rev 19:12 . . . on his **h** were many crowns.

HEADCLOTH (n) portion of burial garb covering the head and face
John 11:44 . . . wrapped in a **h.**

HEAL, HEALED, HEALING, HEALS (v) to mend, cure, make whole; to restore to health
Gen 20:17 . . . and God **h-ed** Abimelech,
Exod 15:26 . . . I am the LORD who **h-s** you.
Num 12:13 . . . I beg you, please **h** her!
Deut 32:39 . . . one who wounds and **h-s;**
2 Chr 30:20 . . . prayer and **h-ed** the people.
Job 5:18 . . . his hands also **h.**
Ps 6:2 . . . **H** me, LORD,
Ps 103:3 . . . and **h-s** all my diseases.
Ps 107:20 . . . his word and **h-ed** them,
Prov 3:8 . . . will have **h-ing** for your body
Prov 13:17 . . . messenger brings **h-ing.**
Isa 6:10 . . . and turn to me for **h-ing.**
Isa 30:26 . . . LORD begins to **h** his people
Isa 57:18 . . . but I will **h** them anyway!
Isa 57:19 . . . the LORD, who **h-s** them.
Jer 8:18 . . . My grief is beyond **h-ing;**
Jer 17:14 . . . O LORD, if you **h** me, I will
Jer 17:14 . . . I will be truly **h-ed;**
Jer 30:13 . . . No medicine can **h** you.
Hos 6:1 . . . now he will **h** us.
Hos 7:1 . . . I want to **h** Israel, but its
Hos 14:4 . . . Then I will **h** you of your
Zech 11:16 . . . nor **h** the injured,
Mal 4:2 . . . with **h-ing** in his wings.
Matt 4:23 . . . And he **h-ed** every kind
Matt 8:7 . . . will come and **h** him.
Matt 8:16 . . . and he **h-ed** all the sick.
Matt 9:35 . . . he **h-ed** every kind of disease
Matt 10:8 . . . **H** the sick, raise the
Matt 15:30 . . . Jesus, and he **h-ed** them all.
Matt 17:16 . . . they couldn't **h** him.
Mark 1:34 . . . So Jesus **h-ed** many people
Mark 3:2 . . . If he **h-ed** the man's
Mark 3:10 . . . He had **h-ed** many people
Mark 5:28 . . . touch his robe, I will be **h-ed.**
Mark 6:5 . . . sick people and **h** them.
Mark 6:13 . . . and **h-ed** many sick
Mark 6:56 . . . who touched him were **h-ed.**
Mark 10:52 . . . your faith has **h-ed** you.
Luke 4:23 . . . Physician, **h** yourself
Luke 4:40 . . . his hand **h-ed** every one.
Luke 6:7 . . . If he **h-ed** the man's
Luke 8:50 . . . faith, and she will be **h-ed.**
Luke 10:9 . . . **H** the sick, and tell them
Luke 13:14 . . . indignant that Jesus had **h-ed**
Luke 14:3 . . . **h** people on the Sabbath
Luke 14:4 . . . the sick man and **h-ed** him
Luke 17:19 . . . Your faith has **h-ed** you.
Luke 18:42 . . . Your faith has **h-ed** you.
Luke 22:51 . . . man's ear and **h-ed** him.
John 4:47 . . . to Capernaum to **h** his son,
John 7:23 . . . angry with me for **h-ing** a man
John 12:40 . . . and have me **h** them.
Acts 3:16 . . . this man was **h-ed**—
Acts 4:9 . . . want to know how he was **h-ed?**
Acts 4:14 . . . see the man who had been **h-ed**
Acts 4:22 . . . sign—the **h-ing** of a man
Acts 8:7 . . . or lame were **h-ed.**
Acts 9:34 . . . Jesus Christ **h-s** you! Get up,
Acts 10:38 . . . and **h-ing** all who were
Acts 28:8 . . . his hands on him, he **h-ed**
Acts 28:27 . . . turn to me and let me **h**
1 Cor 12:28 . . . the gift of **h-ing,**
1 Cor 12:30 . . . have the gift of **h-ing?**
Jas 5:16 . . . so that you may be **h-ed.**
1 Pet 2:24 . . . By his wounds you are **h-ed.**
Rev 13:3 . . . fatal wound was **h-ed!**
Rev 13:12 . . . wound had been **h-ed.**

HEALING (adj) marked by restoring to original purity or integrity
Luke 6:19 . . . **h** power went out from him,
Acts 4:30 . . . your hand with **h** power;

HEALTH (n) the general condition of the body
Ps 38:3 . . . my **h** is broken because of
Ps 38:7 . . . and my **h** is broken.
Prov 15:30 . . . makes for good **h.**
Isa 38:16 . . . You restore my **h**
Jer 30:17 . . . I will give you back your **h**

HEALTHY, HEALTHIER (adj) enjoying good health and vigor of body, mind, or spirit
Ps 73:4 . . . bodies are so **h** and strong.
Prov 16:24 . . . the soul and **h** for the body.
Dan 1:15 . . . friends looked **h-ier** and better
Zech 11:16 . . . nor feed the **h.** Instead,

Matt 9:12 . . . he said, "**H** people don't need
Mark 2:17 . . . **H** people don't need
Luke 5:31 . . . answered them, "**H** people
Eph 4:16 . . . whole body is **h** and growing
3 Jn 1:2 . . . that you are as **h** in body as

HEAP (v) to pile in great quantity; to load heavily
Prov 25:22 . . . You will **h** burning coals of
Rom 12:20 . . . you will **h** burning coals of

HEAR, HEARD, HEARING (v) to perceive sound; to listen with attention; to be informed of; to take testimony from and make a legal decision
see also LISTEN
Gen 3:8 . . . and his wife **h-d** the LORD God
Exod 2:24 . . . God **h-d** their groaning,
Deut 1:16 . . . judges, 'You must **h** the cases
Josh 7:9 . . . people living in the land **h**
1 Kgs 8:30 . . . May you **h** the humble
2 Chr 7:14 . . . I will **h** from heaven and will
Neh 1:11 . . . O LORD, please **h** my prayer!
Ps 5:1 . . . O LORD, **h** me as I pray;
Ps 89:1 . . . Young and old will **h** of your
Isa 29:18 . . . the deaf will **h** words read
Isa 30:21 . . . own ears will **h** him.
Isa 40:28 . . . Have you never **h-d?**
Isa 59:1 . . . too deaf to **h** you call.
Dan 10:12 . . . has been **h-d** in heaven.
Matt 5:21 . . . have **h-d** that our ancestors
Matt 5:43 . . . You have **h-d** the law
Matt 11:5 . . . cured, the deaf **h,** the dead
Matt 13:14 . . . When you **h** what I say,
Mark 4:12 . . . When they **h** what I say,
Luke 7:22 . . . cured, the deaf **h,** the dead
John 8:26 . . . what I have **h-d** from the one
Acts 2:6 . . . When they **h-d** the loud noise,
Acts 13:7 . . . he wanted to **h** the word of
Rom 10:14 . . . how can they **h** about him
Rom 10:17 . . . faith comes from **h-ing,**
1 Cor 2:9 . . . no ear has **h-d,** and no mind
1 Cor 12:17 . . . how would you **h?**
Heb 3:7 . . . Today when you **h** his voice,
2 Jn 1:6 . . . just as you **h-d** from the
Rev 3:20 . . . If you **h** my voice and
Rev 22:8 . . . I, John, am the one who **h-d**

HEART, HEARTS (n) figuratively, the seat of emotions, thoughts, and intentions; personality, disposition; courage; love, affection; central or most vital part of something
Gen 6:6 . . . It broke his **h.**
Exod 4:21 . . . will harden his **h** so he
Exod 35:21 . . . All whose **h-s** were stirred
Deut 6:5 . . . LORD your God with all your **h,**
Deut 9:10 . . . from the **h** of the fire
Deut 20:3 . . . Do not lose **h** or panic
Deut 28:65 . . . will cause your **h** to tremble,
Josh 22:5 . . . with all your **h** and all your
Josh 23:14 . . . Deep in your **h-s** you know
1 Sam 1:15 . . . pouring out my **h**
1 Sam 10:9 . . . God gave him a new **h,**
1 Sam 12:20 . . . the LORD with all your **h,**
1 Sam 13:14 . . . a man after his own **h.**
1 Sam 16:7 . . . but the LORD looks at the **h.**
1 Kgs 8:48 . . . with their whole **h** and soul
1 Kgs 11:2 . . . turn your **h-s** to their gods.
1 Kgs 11:3 . . . turn his **h** away from the LORD.
1 Kgs 14:8 . . . followed me with all his **h**
2 Kgs 23:3 . . . with all his **h** and soul.
1 Chr 22:19 . . . God with all your **h** and soul.
2 Chr 6:38 . . . with their whole **h** and soul
2 Chr 22:9 . . . sought the LORD with all his **h.**
2 Chr 34:31 . . . with all his **h** and soul.
Ezra 1:5 . . . God stirred the **h-s** of the priests
Job 4:5 . . . when trouble strikes, you lose **h.**
Ps 9:1 . . . praise you, LORD, with all my **h;**
Ps 14:1 . . . say in their **h-s,** "There is no
Ps 19:14 . . . meditation of my **h**
Ps 24:4 . . . whose hands and **h-s** are pure,
Ps 27:8 . . . my **h** responds, "LORD,
Ps 36:1 . . . within their **h-s.** They have no
Ps 42:11 . . . Why is my **h** so sad?
Ps 45:1 . . . Beautiful words stir my **h.**
Ps 51:10 . . . Create in me a clean **h,** O God.
Ps 57:7 . . . my **h** is confident.
Ps 73:7 . . . everything their **h-s** could ever
Ps 73:26 . . . the strength of my **h;**
Ps 108:1 . . . with all my **h!**
Ps 111:1 . . . thank the LORD with all my **h**
Ps 119:2 . . . with all their **h-s.**
Ps 119:11 . . . hidden your word in my **h,**
Ps 119:58 . . . With all my **h** I want your
Ps 119:145 . . . I pray with all my **h;**
Ps 139:23 . . . and know my **h;** test me and
Prov 3:3 . . . deep within your **h.**
Prov 4:23 . . . Guard your **h** above all else,
Prov 13:12 . . . deferred makes the **h** sick,
Prov 14:30 . . . A peaceful **h** leads to a
Prov 15:13 . . . a broken **h** crushes the
Prov 15:30 . . . look brings joy to the **h;**
Prov 17:22 . . . A cheerful **h** is good
Prov 20:9 . . . have cleansed my **h;** I am pure
Prov 23:15 . . . wise, my own **h** will rejoice!
Prov 27:23 . . . and put your **h** into caring
Song 4:9 . . . captured my **h,** my treasure,
Song 5:2 . . . I slept, but my **h** was awake,
Song 5:4 . . . and my **h** thrilled within me.
Song 8:6 . . . Place me like a seal over your **h,**
Isa 1:5 . . . and your **h** is sick.
Isa 6:10 . . . Harden the **h-s** of these people.
Isa 42:4 . . . or lose **h** until justice
Jer 3:15 . . . shepherds after my own **h,**
Jer 3:22 . . . your wayward **h-s.**
Jer 9:26 . . . have uncircumcised **h-s.**
Jer 20:9 . . . burns in my **h** like a fire.
Jer 32:39 . . . will give them one **h** and one
Ezek 44:7 . . . who have no **h** for God.
Joel 2:12 . . . Give me your **h-s.** Come with
Matt 5:8 . . . those whose **h-s** are pure,
Matt 5:28 . . . adultery with her in his **h.**
Matt 11:29 . . . I am humble and gentle at **h,**
Matt 12:34 . . . whatever is in your **h**
Matt 15:19 . . . For from the **h** come evil
Matt 18:35 . . . from your **h.**
Matt 22:37 . . . God with all your **h,** all your
Mark 11:23 . . . have no doubt in your **h.**
Mark 12:30 . . . God with all your **h,** all your
Mark 12:33 . . . love him with all my **h** and
Luke 6:45 . . . treasury of a good **h,**
Luke 10:27 . . . God with all your **h,** all your
Luke 12:34 . . . desires of your **h** will also
Luke 24:38 . . . Why are your **h-s** filled with
John 5:38 . . . your **h-s,** because you do not
Acts 1:24 . . . you know every **h.** Show us
Acts 4:32 . . . were united in **h** and mind.
Acts 8:21 . . . this, for your **h** is not right
Acts 15:8 . . . God knows people's **h-s,** and
Acts 16:14 . . . Lord opened her **h,** and she
Acts 28:27 . . . hear, and their **h-s** cannot
Rom 1:9 . . . with all my **h** by spreading
Rom 2:15 . . . written in their **h-s,** for their
Rom 2:29 . . . changed **h** seeks praise
Rom 10:9 . . . believe in your **h** that God
2 Cor 2:4 . . . with a troubled **h** and many
2 Cor 7:2 . . . Please open your **h-s** to us.
2 Cor 9:7 . . . decide in your **h** how much to
Eph 1:18 . . . I pray that your **h-s** will be
Eph 3:13 . . . don't lose **h** because of my
Eph 5:19 . . . music to the Lord in your **h-s.**
Eph 6:6 . . . of God with all your **h.**
Phil 1:7 . . . place in my **h.** You share with
1 Tim 1:5 . . . comes from a pure **h,** a clear

HEARTLESS (adj) lacking feeling; cruel
Rom 1:31 . . . promises, are **h,** and have no

HEATHEN, HEATHENS (n) one who does not worship the true God; uncivilized; without religion
Acts 7:51 . . . You are **h** at heart and deaf to the.
Eph 2:11 . . . called "uncircumcised **h-s**" by

HEAVEN, HEAVENS (n) sky and stars above; God's dwelling place; abode of eternal bliss
Deut 30:12 . . . is not kept in **h,** so distant
Job 41:11 . . . Everything under **h** is mine.
Ps 18:16 . . . down from **h** and rescued me;
Ps 71:19 . . . to the highest **h-s.** You have
Ps 108:4 . . . than the **h-s.** Your faithfulness
Matt 11:25 . . . Father, Lord of **h** and earth,
Matt 24:30 . . . appear in the **h-s,** and there
Rom 10:6 . . . go up to **h?**' (to bring Christ
2 Cor 12:2 . . . to the third **h** fourteen years
Heb 9:24 . . . He entered into **h** itself to

HEAVENLY (adj) celestial; of or pertaining to God in the highest
Ps 29:1 . . . the LORD, you **h** beings;

HEIR, HEIRS (n) one who succeeds to a hereditary title; one who inherits
see also INHERITANCE
Isa 11:10 . . . In that day the **h** to David's
Rom 8:17 . . . with Christ we are **h-s** of God's

HELL (n) abode of the dead; place of punishment; personification of evil; lowest place one can go
see also UNDERWORLD
Matt 5:22 . . . of the fires of **h.**
Matt 16:18 . . . all the powers of **h** will not
Matt 23:33 . . . judgment of **h?**
Mark 9:43 . . . fires of **h** with two hands.
Luke 12:5 . . . throw you into **h.**
Jas 3:6 . . . on fire by **h** itself.
2 Pet 2:4 . . . threw them into **h,** in gloomy

HELMET (n) any of various protective head coverings usually made of hard metal
Isa 59:17 . . . and placed the **h** of salvation
Eph 6:17 . . . salvation as your **h,** and take

HELP (n) aid, assistance
2 Sam 22:36 . . . your **h** has made me great.
Ps 30:2 . . . I cried to you for **h,** and you
Ps 33:20 . . . He is our **h** and our shield.
Ps 108:12 . . . for all human **h** is useless.
Isa 30:18 . . . wait for his **h.**
Isa 38:14 . . . looking to heaven for **h.** I am
Phil 4:16 . . . you sent **h** more than once.

HELP, HELPED, HELPING, HELPS (v) to give assistance or support; to rescue or save
Exod 23:5 . . . Instead, stop and **h.**
Deut 2:36 . . . our God also **h-ed** us conquer
1 Sam 7:12 . . . the LORD has **h-ed** us!
Ps 46:1 . . . always ready to **h** in times of
Ps 72:12 . . . he will **h** the oppressed,
Ps 145:14 . . . The LORD **h-s** the fallen
Prov 11:4 . . . Riches won't **h** on the
Prov 14:31 . . . their Maker, but **h-ing** the poor
Prov 19:17 . . . If you **h** the poor,
Isa 41:10 . . . strengthen you and **h** you.
Isa 44:10 . . . that cannot **h** him one bit?
Jer 51:9 . . . We would have **h-ed** her if we
Lam 4:16 . . . he no longer **h-s** them.
Mark 9:24 . . . but **h** me overcome

Acts 9:36 . . . for others and **h-ing** the poor.
Acts 16:9 . . . to Macedonia and **h** us!
Rom 12:13 . . . be ready to **h** them.
1 Cor 12:28 . . . those who can **h** others,
2 Cor 6:2 . . . salvation, I **h-ed** you.
Gal 6:1 . . . and humbly **h** that person back
1 Tim 5:10 . . . Has she **h-ed** those who
2 Tim 2:7 . . . Lord will **h** you understand
Heb 10:33 . . . you **h-ed** others who
1 Pet 4:11 . . . the gift of **h-ing** others?

HELPER (n) one who gives aid; co-worker
Gen 2:18 . . . I will make a **h** who is just
Ps 70:5 . . . You are my **h** and my savior;
Ps 115:9 . . . He is your **h** and your shield.
Heb 13:6 . . . The LORD is my **h,** so I will

HELPFUL (adj) of service or assistance; useful
Job 22:2 . . . Can even a wise person be **h**
Prov 10:32 . . . the godly speak **h** words,
1 Cor 12:31 . . . desire the most **h** gifts.
Eph 4:29 . . . be good and **h,** so that your

HELPLESS (adj) without any aid, comfort, protection, or chance of success
Ps 9:12 . . . cares for the **h.** He does not
Ps 10:12 . . . not ignore the **h!**
Ps 34:2 . . . let all who are **h** take heart.
Ps 35:10 . . . Who else protects the **h**
Amos 2:7 . . . They trample **h** people in the
Matt 9:36 . . . confused and **h,** like sheep
Rom 5:6 . . . were utterly **h,** Christ came

HEN (n) a female chicken especially over a year old
Matt 23:37 . . . together as a **h** protects her
Luke 13:34 . . . together as a **h** protects her

HEROD 1. Herod the Great, ruler of Palestine at birth of John the Baptist and Jesus (Luke 1:5); tried to kill baby Jesus (Matt 2:1-18); died (Matt 2:19).
2. Herod Antipas, tetrarch of Galilee (Luke 3:1), son of Herod the Great; arrested and beheaded John the Baptist (Matt 14:1-12; Mark 1:14; 6:14-29; Luke 3:19-20; 9:7-9); tried Jesus (Luke 23:7-15).
3. Herod Agrippa I, grandson of Herod the Great; killed the apostle James (Acts 12:1-2); arrested Peter (Acts 12:3-19); died (Acts 12:21-23).
4. Herod Agrippa II, great-grandson of Herod the Great; spoke at Paul's trial (Acts 25–26).

HEROES (n) an object of extreme admiration
Ps 16:3 . . . in the land are my true **h!**

HEZEKIAH King of Judah (southern kingdom) (2 Kgs 18–20; 2 Chr 29–32); reformed the Temple and its worship (2 Chr 29:20-36); offered effective prayer during war against Assyria (2 Kgs 19:14-19; 2 Chr 32:1-23; Isa 36:14-20); became sick but was healed (2 Kgs 20:1-11; 2 Chr 32:24-26; Isa 38:1-22); showed kingdom's treasures to Babylonians (2 Kgs 20:12-19; 2 Chr 32:31; Isa 39); died (2 Kgs 20:20-21; 2 Chr 32:32-33).

HID, HIDDEN (v) *see also* HIDE
Ps 119:11 . . . I have **h-den** your word
Matt 13:35 . . . explain things **h-den** since the
Matt 13:44 . . . discovered **h-den** in a field.
Matt 13:44 . . . he **h** it again and
Matt 25:25 . . . your money, so I **h** it in the
Mark 4:22 . . . that is **h-den** will eventually be
1 Cor 2:7 . . . was previously **h-den,** even
Col 3:3 . . . real life is **h-den** with Christ in
Heb 11:23 . . . that Moses' parents **h** him

HIDE, HIDING (v) to shield; to seek protection; to put or remain out of sight
see also HID
Deut 31:17 . . . abandon them, **h-ing** my face
1 Sam 10:22 . . . "He is **h-ing** among the
Ps 27:5 . . . he will **h** me in his
Ps 57:1 . . . I will **h** beneath the shadow
Ps 143:9 . . . run to you to **h** me.
Jer 16:17 . . . cannot hope to **h** from me.
Matt 11:25 . . . thank you for **h-ing** these

HIGH, HIGHER, HIGHEST (adj) foremost in rank, dignity, or standing; having large extension upward; of greater degree or value than average, usual, or expected
Gen 14:18 . . . of God Most **H,** brought Abram
Gen 14:22 . . . LORD, God Most **H,** Creator of
Ps 113:4 . . . his glory is **h-er** than the heavens.
Isa 14:14 . . . be like the Most **H.**
Dan 4:17 . . . that the Most **H** rules over
Mark 5:7 . . . Son of the Most **H** God?
Phil 2:9 . . . the place of **h-est** honor and gave
Heb 7:1 . . . of God Most **H.** When Abraham

HIGHLIGHTS (v) to throw a strong light on
Rom 3:7 . . . sinner if my dishonesty **h** his

HIGHWAY (n) a main direct road
Isa 40:3 . . . Make a straight **h** through the
Matt 7:13 . . . The **h** to hell is broad

HILLS (n) a usually rounded natural elevation of land lower than a mountain
1 Kgs 20:23 . . . are gods of the **h;**
Ps 50:10 . . . the cattle on a thousand **h.**
Isa 40:4 . . . mountains and **h.** Straighten
Hos 10:8 . . . plead with the **h,** "Fall on
Matt 24:16 . . . flee to the **h.**
Luke 3:5 . . . mountains and **h** made level.
Luke 23:30 . . . plead with the **h,** 'Bury us.'
Rev 17:9 . . . the seven **h** where the woman

HILLTOP (n) the highest part of a hill
Matt 5:14 . . . a city on a **h** that cannot be

HINDER, HINDERED (v) to delay, impede, or prevent action
1 Sam 14:6 . . . for nothing can **h** the LORD.
1 Pet 3:7 . . . will not be **h-ed.**

HIRE (v) to engage the personal services of for pay
Luke 15:15 . . . a local farmer to **h** him,

HOARD, HOARDING (v) to keep to oneself
Prov 11:26 . . . those who **h** their grain,
Eccl 5:13 . . . **H-ing** riches harms

HOLD, HOLDING, HOLDS (v) to keep under restraint; to have or maintain in the grasp; to keep from falling or moving; to have in the mind or express as a judgment, opinion, or belief; to maintain control of
2 Kgs 4:16 . . . you will be **h-ing** a son in
Ps 3:3 . . . the one who **h-s** my head high.
Ps 37:24 . . . for the LORD **h-s** them by the
Ps 39:1 . . . I will **h** my tongue when
Ps 63:8 . . . right hand **h-s** me securely.
Prov 27:16 . . . **h** something with greased
Isa 40:11 . . . **h-ing** them close to his heart.
Isa 48:9 . . . name, I will **h** back my anger
Matt 4:6 . . . And they will **h** you up with
Mark 11:25 . . . forgive anyone you are **h-ing**
Col 1:17 . . . and he **h-s** all creation
Col 2:19 . . . For he **h-s** the whole body
Heb 4:14 . . . God, let us **h** firmly to what
Heb 10:23 . . . Let us **h** tightly without

HOLINESS (n) sanctity or purity
Exod 15:11 . . . glorious in **h,** awesome in
Deut 32:51 . . . to demonstrate my **h** to the
Ps 29:2 . . . the splendor of his **h.**
Luke 1:75 . . . in **h** and righteousness for
1 Cor 7:14 . . . wife brings **h** to her
2 Cor 1:12 . . . a God-given **h** and sincerity
1 Thes 4:4 . . . and live in **h** and honor—
1 Tim 2:15 . . . faith, love, **h,** and modesty.
Heb 12:10 . . . share in his **h.**

HOLY (adj) consecrated or set aside for sacred use (as opposed to pagan or common use); standing apart from sin and evil; characteristic of God, especially the third person of the Trinity
see also PURE
Gen 2:3 . . . and declared it **h,** because it
Exod 3:5 . . . are standing on **h** ground.
Exod 19:6 . . . priests, my **h** nation.
Exod 26:33 . . . separate the **H** Place
Exod 29:37 . . . be absolutely **h,**
Exod 30:10 . . . LORD's most **h** altar.
Exod 31:13 . . . the LORD, who makes you **h.**
Lev 11:45 . . . you must be **h** because I am
Lev 19:8 . . . for defiling what is **h** to the
Lev 20:7 . . . set yourselves apart to be **h,**
Lev 20:26 . . . You must be **h** because I,
Lev 21:12 . . . for he has been made **h** by the
Lev 22:32 . . . the LORD who makes you **h.**
Lev 27:9 . . . LORD will be considered **h.**
Deut 5:12 . . . by keeping it **h,** as the LORD
Josh 5:15 . . . where you are standing is **h.**
Josh 24:19 . . . he is a **h** and jealous God.
1 Chr 16:35 . . . we can thank your **h** name
Neh 11:1 . . . in Jerusalem, the **h** city.
Ps 22:3 . . . Yet you are **h,** enthroned on
Ps 30:4 . . . Praise his **h** name.
Ps 99:3 . . . Your name is **h!**
Ps 105:3 . . . Exult in his **h** name; rejoice,
Ps 111:9 . . . What a **h,** awe-inspiring name
Prov 9:10 . . . of the **H** One results in good
Isa 6:3 . . . to each other, "**H, h, h**
Isa 40:25 . . . my equal?" asks the **H** One.
Isa 54:5 . . . your Redeemer, the **H** One of
Isa 66:20 . . . them to my **h** mountain in
Dan 7:18 . . . But in the end, the **h** people
Dan 9:24 . . . anoint the Most **H** Place.
Zech 14:5 . . . and all his **h** ones with him.
Matt 24:15 . . . in the **H** Place.
Mark 1:24 . . . —the **H** One of God
Luke 1:35 . . . baby to be born will be **h,**
Luke 1:49 . . . Mighty One is **h,** and he has
Luke 4:34 . . . you are—the **H** One of God
Luke 11:2 . . . may your name be kept **h.**
John 6:69 . . . you are the **H** One of God.
John 17:17 . . . Make them **h** by your
Acts 13:35 . . . not allow your **H** One to rot
Rom 7:12 . . . the law itself is **h,** and its
Rom 14:5 . . . day is more **h** than another
Rom 15:16 . . . made **h** by the **H** Spirit.
1 Cor 1:2 . . . be his own **h** people.
1 Cor 1:30 . . . made us pure and **h,**
1 Cor 3:17 . . . God's temple is **h,** and you
1 Cor 6:11 . . . you were made **h;** you were
1 Cor 7:14 . . . children would not be **h,** but
Eph 1:4 . . . in Christ to be **h** and without
Eph 2:21 . . . becoming a **h** temple for
Eph 4:24 . . . righteous and **h.**
Eph 5:26 . . . to make her **h** and clean,
Col 1:22 . . . and you are **h** and blameless
1 Thes 3:13 . . . blameless, and **h** as you
1 Thes 4:7 . . . called us to live **h** lives,
1 Thes 5:23 . . . make you **h** in every
2 Thes 1:10 . . . from his **h** people—praise

1 Tim 2:8 . . . to pray with **h** hands lifted
2 Tim 1:9 . . . called us to live a **h** life.
2 Tim 3:15 . . . taught the **h** Scriptures from
Heb 2:11 . . . ones he makes **h** have the same
Heb 10:14 . . . those who are being made **h.**
Heb 10:19 . . . heaven's Most **H** Place
Heb 10:29 . . . which made us **h,** as if it
Heb 13:12 . . . make his people **h** by means
1 Pet 1:16 . . . You must be **h** because I am
1 Pet 2:5 . . . you are his **h** priests.
1 Pet 2:9 . . . priests, a **h** nation, God's
1 Pet 3:5 . . . is how the **h** women of old
2 Pet 1:18 . . . on the **h** mountain.
2 Pet 2:21 . . . to live a **h** life.
2 Pet 3:11 . . . like this, what **h** and godly
Rev 3:7 . . . one who is **h** and true,
Rev 4:8 . . . on saying, "**H, h, h** is
Rev 15:4 . . . you alone are **h.** All nations
Rev 20:6 . . . Blessed and **h** are those who
Rev 22:11 . . . continue to be **h.**

HOLY GHOST (KJV)
Matt 1:18 . . . the power of the *Holy Spirit*
Matt 3:11 . . . baptize you with the *Holy Spirit*
Matt 28:19 . . . the Son and the *Holy Spirit*
Luke 3:22 . . . *Holy Spirit,* in bodily form,
1 Jn 5:7-8 . . . three witnesses—the *Spirit*

HOLY SPIRIT (n) the third person of the Holy Trinity
see also ADVOCATE, COUNSELOR
Luke 11:13 . . . give the **H** to those
2 Cor 5:5 . . . given us his **H.**
Eph 1:13 . . . **H,** whom he promised
Eph 4:30 . . . sorrow to God's **H**
1 Thes 4:8 . . . gives his **H** to you

HOME (n) one's place of residence; place of origin, destiny, or comfort; family-style social unit
see also DWELLING, HOUSE
Deut 11:19 . . . when you are at **h** and
1 Chr 16:43 . . . turned and went **h** to bless
Ps 46:4 . . . God, the sacred **h** of the Most
Prov 3:33 . . . but he blesses the **h** of the
Prov 27:8 . . . person who strays from **h**
Matt 10:11 . . . stay in his **h** until you
Luke 10:7 . . . move around from **h**
Luke 19:9 . . . has come to this **h** today,
John 14:2 . . . in my Father's **h.** If this
John 14:23 . . . make our **h** with each
Acts 16:15 . . . stay at my **h.**
Rom 16:5 . . . meets in their **h.** Greet my
Eph 3:17 . . . will make his **h** in your
1 Tim 5:4 . . . show godliness at **h**
Heb 13:14 . . . not our permanent **h;** we are
1 Pet 4:9 . . . share your **h** with those who

HOMELAND (n) area set aside to be a state for a people of a particular national, cultural, or racial origin
2 Sam 7:10 . . . And I will provide a **h** for my

HOMETOWN (n) the city or town where one was born or grew up
Matt 13:57 . . . in his own **h** and among his
Luke 4:24 . . . is accepted in his own **h.**
John 4:44 . . . is not honored in his own **h.**

HOMOSEXUALITY (n) erotic activity with another of the same sex
1 Cor 6:9 . . . prostitutes, or practice **h,**
1 Tim 1:10 . . . or who practice **h,** or are

HONEST (adj) truthful; genuine; reputable; marked by integrity
Exod 18:21 . . . some capable, **h** men
2 Kgs 12:15 . . . were **h** and trustworthy
Ps 37:37 . . . those who are **h** and good,
Prov 12:17 . . . An **h** witness tells
Prov 28:6 . . . Better to be poor and **h** than
Jer 5:1 . . . find even one just and **h** person,
Matt 22:16 . . . we know how **h** you are.
1 Thes 2:10 . . . devout and **h** and faultless

HONESTY (n) fairness and straightforwardness of conduct; sincerity
Ps 51:6 . . . But you desire **h** from the
Prov 11:5 . . . are directed by **h;** the wicked
Jer 5:3 . . . searching for **h.** You struck

HONEY (n) a sweet liquid substance produced by bees; symbolic of abundance or delight in God's word
Exod 3:8 . . . with milk and **h**—the land
1 Sam 14:26 . . . dare touch the **h**
Ps 19:10 . . . sweeter than **h,** even **h**
Ps 119:103 . . . they are sweeter than **h.**
Isa 7:15 . . . yogurt and **h.**
Rev 10:9 . . . be sweet as **h** in your mouth,

HONEYCOMB (n) a mass of hexagonal wax cells in a honeybee nest that stores honey
Song 5:1 . . . and eat **h** with my honey.

HONOR, HONORS (n) having a renowned reputation or social standing; physical or spiritual blessing (from God); a showing of merited respect
Ps 8:5 . . . crowned them with glory and **h.**
Ps 104:1 . . . are robed with **h** and majesty.
Prov 3:35 . . . The wise inherit **h,** but fools
Prov 15:33 . . . humility precedes **h.**
Prov 25:27 . . . not good to seek **h-s**
Isa 53:12 . . . I will give him the **h-s** of a
Isa 55:13 . . . will bring great **h** to the
Luke 14:8 . . . don't sit in the seat of **h.**
Eph 1:20 . . . the place of **h** at God's right
Heb 13:4 . . . Give **h** to marriage,
1 Pet 2:6 . . . chosen for great **h,** and
1 Pet 2:12 . . . they will give **h** to God when
1 Pet 3:7 . . . husbands must give **h** to
2 Pet 1:17 . . . when he received **h** and glory
Rev 4:9 . . . give glory and **h** and thanks
Rev 19:7 . . . and let us give **h** to him.

HONOR, HONORED, HONORING, HONORS (v) of God, to reverence his majesty; of man, to respect or esteem; to confer honor upon
Exod 20:12 . . . **H** your father and mother.
1 Kgs 8:43 . . . Temple I have built **h-s**
Neh 1:11 . . . who delight in **h-ing** you.
Ps 29:1 . . . **H** the LORD, you
Ps 45:11 . . . **h** him, for he is your LORD.
Ps 46:10 . . . I will be **h-ed** by every nation.
Ps 47:9 . . . He is highly **h-ed** everywhere.
Prov 14:31 . . . helping the poor **h-s** him.
Isa 66:5 . . . the LORD be **h-ed!**
Matt 15:4 . . . God says, '**H** your father and
Mark 6:4 . . . A prophet is **h-ed** everywhere
Luke 16:15 . . . What this world **h-s**
John 5:23 . . . that everyone will **h** the Son,
John 12:26 . . . the Father will **h** anyone who
Rom 12:10 . . . delight in **h-ing** each other.
Rom 13:3 . . . and they will **h** you.
1 Cor 6:20 . . . So you must **h** God with your
1 Cor 12:26 . . . if one part is **h-ed,** all the
Eph 6:2 . . . **H** your father and mother
Col 1:10 . . . the way you live will always **h**
1 Thes 5:12 . . . and sisters, **h** those who are
2 Thes 1:12 . . . be **h-ed** along with him.
Titus 2:3 . . . a way that **h-s** God.

HONORABLE (adj) characterized by integrity; upright
Rom 12:17 . . . everyone can see you are **h.**
2 Cor 8:21 . . . to see that we are **h.**
Phil 4:8 . . . is true, and **h,** and right,
1 Pet 2:12 . . . will see your **h** behavior,

HOOKS (n) a pole bearing a curved blade for pruning plants
Isa 2:4 . . . into pruning **h.** Nation will
Joel 3:10 . . . your pruning **h** into spears.
Mic 4:3 . . . into pruning **h.** Nation will

HOPE, HOPES (n) confident trust with the expectation of fulfillment
1 Sam 9:20 . . . focus of all Israel's **h-s.**
Job 31:16 . . . crushed the **h-s** of widows?
Ps 10:17 . . . LORD, you know the **h-s** of the
Ps 42:5 . . . I will put my **h** in God!
Ps 112:10 . . . slink away, their **h-s** thwarted.
Ps 119:49 . . . to me; it is my only **h.**
Ps 119:74 . . . I have put my **h** in your word.
Prov 10:24 . . . the **h-s** of the godly will be
Prov 13:12 . . . **H** deferred makes the heart
Zech 9:12 . . . prisoners who still have **h!**
Rom 5:4 . . . our confident **h** of salvation.
Rom 8:20 . . . curse. But with eager **h,**
Rom 12:12 . . . Rejoice in our confident **h.**
Rom 15:4 . . . give us **h** and encouragement
Rom 15:13 . . . God, the source of **h,** will
1 Cor 13:13 . . . faith, **h,** and love—
1 Cor 15:19 . . . And if our **h** in Christ is
Eph 2:12 . . . without God and without **h.**
1 Thes 1:3 . . . and the enduring **h** you have
1 Tim 4:10 . . . struggle, for our **h** is in the
Heb 10:23 . . . wavering to the **h** we affirm,
1 Pet 3:15 . . . about your Christian **h,**

HOPE (v) to desire with expectation of obtainment
Rom 8:24 . . . don't need to **h** for it.

HOPEFUL (adj) full of or inclined to hope
1 Cor 13:7 . . . is always **h,** and endures

HORN, HORNS (n) a bony material arising from the head of many animals; a projection on the four corners of the altar in the tabernacle and Temple; a symbol of power and might
Exod 19:13 . . . when the ram's **h** sounds a
Exod 27:2 . . . so that the **h-s** and altar are
Judg 7:19 . . . blew the rams' **h-s** and broke
Dan 7:8 . . . This little **h** had eyes
Dan 7:24 . . . Its ten **h-s** are ten kings
Amos 2:2 . . . and the ram's **h** sounds.
Zech 9:14 . . . sound the ram's **h** and attack
Rev 5:6 . . . He had seven **h-s** and seven
Rev 12:3 . . . heads and ten **h-s,** with seven
Rev 13:1 . . . heads and ten **h-s,** with ten
Rev 17:3 . . . and ten **h-s,** and blasphemies

HORROR (n) painful and intense fear, dread, or aversion
Jer 2:12 . . . shrink back in **h** and dismay,

HORSE (n) a large solid-hoofed herbivorous mammal often used for working or riding
Ps 147:10 . . . strength of a **h** or in human
Prov 26:3 . . . Guide a **h** with a
Zech 1:8 . . . on a red **h** that was standing
Rev 6:2 . . . saw a white **h** standing there.
Rev 6:4 . . . Then another **h** appeared,
Rev 6:5 . . . saw a black **h,** and its rider
Rev 6:8 . . . and saw a **h** whose color was
Rev 19:11 . . . and a white **h** was standing

HOSANNA (KJV)
Matt 21:9 . . . *Praise God* in highest heaven!
Matt 21:15 . . . *Praise God* for the Son of David
Mark 11:9 . . . *Praise God!* Blessings on the one
Mark 11:10 . . . *Praise God* in highest heaven
John 12:13 . . . *Praise God!* Blessings on the

HOSPITALITY (n) generous and cordial treatment, reception, or disposition
Matt 25:38 . . . and show you **h?**

Luke 10:7 . . . Don't hesitate to accept **h,**
Rom 12:13 . . . be eager to practice **h.**

HOSTILE (adj) openly opposed or resisting
Rom 8:7 . . . nature is always **h** to God.

HOSTILITY (n) deep-seated ill will; enmity
Gen 3:15 . . . I will cause **h** between you
Lev 26:28 . . . I will give full vent to my **h.**
Gal 5:20 . . . sorcery, **h,** quarreling,
Eph 2:14 . . . the wall of **h** that separated
Eph 2:16 . . . our **h** toward each other was
Heb 12:3 . . . of all the **h** he endured from

HOUR (n) a (short) unit or passage of time; moment
John 12:27 . . . save me from this **h'?**
John 13:1 . . . knew that his **h** had come
John 17:1 . . . Father, the **h** has come.

HOUSE, HOUSES (n) living quarters; a family including ancestors, descendants, and kindred extended family unit, including ancestors and descendants
see also DWELLING, DYNASTY, HOME, TEMPLE
Exod 12:22 . . . doorframes of your **h-s.**
Exod 12:27 . . . he passed over the **h-s** of the
Exod 20:17 . . . your neighbor's **h.**
2 Sam 7:11 . . . he will make a **h** for you—
Ps 23:6 . . . live in the **h** of the LORD
Ps 27:4 . . . to live in the **h** of the LORD
Ps 69:9 . . . for your **h** has consumed me,
Ps 127:1 . . . Unless the LORD builds a **h,**
Isa 54:2 . . . Enlarge your **h;**
Amos 5:11 . . . beautiful stone **h-s,** you will
Matt 7:24 . . . who builds a **h** on solid rock.
Matt 19:29 . . . given up **h-s** or brothers or
Mark 11:17 . . . be called a **h** of prayer for
John 2:17 . . . for God's **h** will consume me.

HOUSEHOLD (n) a social unit composed of those living together in the same dwelling; family
see also FAMILY
Exod 12:3 . . . one animal for each **h.**
Acts 16:31 . . . everyone in your **h.**
1 Tim 3:5 . . . manage his own **h,**
1 Tim 3:12 . . . children and **h** well.
1 Tim 3:15 . . . themselves in the **h** of God.
1 Pet 4:17 . . . begin with God's **h.**

HOUSETOPS (n) roof
Matt 10:27 . . . shout from the **h** for all to

HUMAN (adj) of, relating to, or characteristic of men and women collectively; mortal; finite
see also FLESH
Gen 1:26 . . . Let us make **h** beings in our
Gen 3:22 . . . Look, the **h** beings have
Gen 9:6 . . . If anyone takes a **h** life,
Ps 9:20 . . . they are merely **h.**
Ps 33:13 . . . sees the whole **h** race.
Ps 89:47 . . . futile this **h** existence!
John 1:14 . . . So the Word became **h**
John 2:24 . . . because he knew **h** nature.
John 8:15 . . . judge me by **h** standards,
Rom 6:19 . . . weakness of your **h** nature,
1 Cor 2:5 . . . trust not in **h** wisdom but in
1 Cor 2:13 . . . come from **h** wisdom.
2 Cor 3:3 . . . of stone, but on **h** hearts.
2 Cor 10:3 . . . We are **h,** but we
Gal 3:3 . . . by your own **h** effort?
Col 2:9 . . . of God in a **h** body.
1 Thes 2:13 . . . words as mere **h** ideas.
Heb 7:28 . . . limited by **h** weakness.
2 Pet 1:21 . . . or from **h** initiative.

HUMAN, HUMANS (n) a Homo sapiens; mankind
Gen 6:3 . . . Spirit will not put up with **h-s**
Isa 2:22 . . . trust in mere **h-s.** They are as
Jer 17:5 . . . trust in mere **h-s,** who rely on

HUMANITY (n) the quality or state of being human; the human race
Job 14:1 . . . How frail is **h!** How short
Zech 2:13 . . . Be silent before the LORD, all **h,**

HUMBLE (adj) not proud or haughty; can imply lower social or economic status; meek or gentle
Num 12:3 . . . Moses was very **h—**
Ps 138:6 . . . cares for the **h,** but he keeps
Ps 149:4 . . . he crowns the **h** with victory.
Zech 9:9 . . . yet he is **h,** riding on a
Matt 5:5 . . . those who are **h,**
Matt 11:29 . . . I am **h** and gentle at
Matt 21:5 . . . He is **h,** riding on a
Eph 4:2 . . . Always be **h** and gentle.
Phil 2:3 . . . Be **h,** thinking of
Jas 4:6 . . . but favors the **h.**
1 Pet 3:8 . . . and keep a **h** attitude.

HUMBLE, HUMBLED, HUMBLES (v) to not think too highly of oneself; to bring low or prostrate
Isa 26:5 . . . He **h-s** the proud and
Luke 14:11 . . . themselves will be **h-d,**
Luke 18:14 . . . will be **h-d,** and those who
2 Cor 11:7 . . . wrong when I **h-d** myself
Phil 2:8 . . . he **h-d** himself in obedience
Jas 1:10 . . . that God has **h-d** them.
Jas 4:10 . . . **H** yourselves before the Lord,
1 Pet 5:6 . . . So **h** yourselves under

HUMBLY (adv) in an unhaughty, unproud manner; in an insignificant or unpretentious manner
Zeph 2:3 . . . and to live **h.** Perhaps even
Acts 20:19 . . . I have done the Lord's work **h**
1 Tim 5:10 . . . served other believers **h?**

HUMILIATE, HUMILIATED (v) to shame or mortify
Deut 21:14 . . . for you have **h-ed** her.
2 Sam 22:28 . . . watch the proud and **h**
Ps 18:27 . . . but you **h** the proud

HUMILIATION (n) shame, mortification, disgrace, dishonor
Job 19:5 . . . using my **h** as evidence
Ps 44:15 . . . the constant **h;** shame is
Prov 29:23 . . . ends in **h,** while humility

HUMILITY (n) show of submission or meekness; quality or state of being humble
Prov 11:2 . . . but with **h** comes wisdom.
Prov 15:33 . . . **h** precedes honor.
Prov 22:4 . . . True **h** and fear
Col 3:12 . . . kindness, **h,** gentleness,
Jas 3:13 . . . works with the **h** that comes
1 Pet 5:5 . . . each other in **h,** for "God

HUNDRED (n) the number 100
Matt 13:8 . . . and even a **h** times as much as
Luke 8:8 . . . that was a **h** times as much as

HUNG (v) *see also* HANG
Deut 21:23 . . . anyone who is **h** is cursed
Luke 19:48 . . . all the people **h** on every word
Gal 3:13 . . . When he was **h** on the cross,

HUNGER (n) a craving or urgent need for food
Ps 145:16 . . . you satisfy the **h** and thirst

HUNGRY (adj) feeling a strong desire for food; a craving for anything
Prov 25:21 . . . If your enemies are **h,**
Matt 15:32 . . . to send them away **h,**
Matt 25:35 . . . For I was **h,** and you fed me.
Luke 1:53 . . . He has filled the **h** with good
Luke 6:21 . . . you who are **h** now, for you
John 6:35 . . . never be **h** again.
Rom 8:35 . . . or are persecuted, or **h,** or
Rom 12:20 . . . enemies are **h,** feed them.
Rev 7:16 . . . never again be **h** or thirsty;

HUNT, HUNTED (v) to pursue with intent to capture
Ps 119:86 . . . Protect me from those who **h** me
2 Cor 4:9 . . . We are **h-ed** down,

HURT, HURTING, HURTS (v) to wound, injure, or damage
1 Chr 16:22 . . . and do not **h** my prophets.
Ps 15:4 . . . promises even when it **h-s.**
Eccl 8:9 . . . the power to **h** each other.
Lam 3:33 . . . he does not enjoy **h-ing** people
Matt 4:6 . . . you won't even **h** your foot on
Mark 16:18 . . . it won't **h** them.

HUSBAND, HUSBANDS (n) male partner in a marriage; head of family; protector and provider; figurative of Christ
Ruth 1:11 . . . could grow up to be your **h-s?**
Prov 12:4 . . . is a crown for her **h,**
Prov 31:28 . . . Her **h** praises her:
Jer 3:20 . . . wife who leaves her **h.**
Rom 7:2 . . . binds her to her **h** as long as
1 Cor 7:3 . . . The **h** should fulfill
1 Cor 7:10 . . . not leave her **h.**
1 Cor 7:39 . . . is bound to her **h** as long as
2 Cor 11:2 . . . bride to one **h**—Christ.
Gal 4:27 . . . lives with her **h!**
Eph 5:22 . . . means submit to your **h-s** as to the
Eph 5:23 . . . For a **h** is the head
Eph 5:25 . . . For **h-s,** this means
Eph 5:28 . . . the same way, **h-s** ought to love
Col 3:18 . . . submit to your **h-s,** as is
Col 3:19 . . . **H-s,** love your
1 Tim 5:9 . . . faithful to her **h.**
Titus 2:4 . . . to love their **h-s** and their
1 Pet 3:1 . . . the authority of your **h-s.**
1 Pet 3:7 . . . same way, you **h-s** must give

HYMN, HYMNS (n) a song of praise to God
Ps 40:3 . . . to sing, a **h** of praise to our
Matt 26:30 . . . they sang a **h** and went out
Mark 14:26 . . . they sang a **h** and went out
Acts 16:25 . . . praying and singing **h-s**
Eph 5:19 . . . psalms and **h-s** and spiritual
Col 3:16 . . . psalms and **h-s** and spiritual

HYPOCRISY (n) feigning to be what one is not; pretense of piety
Matt 23:28 . . . your hearts are filled with **h**
Mark 12:15 . . . saw through their **h**
Gal 2:13 . . . followed Peter's **h,** and even
Gal 2:13 . . . led astray by their **h.**
1 Pet 2:1 . . . all deceit, **h,** jealousy,

HYPOCRITE, HYPOCRITES (n) a person who portrays a false appearance of religion; a person who acts in contradiction to his or her stated beliefs; pretender
Matt 6:16 . . . make it obvious, as the **h-s**
Matt 7:5 . . . **H!** First get rid of the log
Matt 23:13 . . . and you Pharisees. **H-s!**
Luke 6:42 . . . the log in your own eye? **H!**
Luke 13:15 . . . Lord replied, "You **h-s!**
1 Tim 4:2 . . . These people are **h-s** and liars,

HYSSOP (n) an aromatic shrub of the species of marjoram and a member of the mint family that has clusters of yellow flowers
Exod 12:22 . . . Brush the **h** across the
John 19:29 . . . put it on a **h** branch, and held it

I

IDEAS (n) a formulated thought or opinion; notion or concept
Ps 73:20 . . . you will laugh at their silly **i**
Ps 81:12 . . . living according to their own **i.**

IDENTIFY, IDENTIFIED (v) to establish the distinguishing character or personality of; to conceive as united (as in spirit, outlook, or principle)
Matt 7:16 . . . You can **i** them by their fruit,
Matt 12:33 . . . A tree is **i-ied** by its fruit.
Eph 1:13 . . . believed in Christ, he **i-ied** you

IDLE (adj) not employed or useful for work; inactive, lazy
2 Thes 3:6 . . . believers who live **i** lives
2 Thes 3:7 . . . not **i** when we were with you.
2 Thes 3:11 . . . you are living **i** lives,

IDLENESS (n) a state of unemployment, inactivity, or laziness
Prov 19:15 . . . but **i** leaves them hungry.
Eccl 10:18 . . . **i** leads to a leaky house.

IDOL, IDOLS (n) a representation or symbol of a false god
Exod 20:4 . . . make for yourself an **i**
Deut 27:15 . . . who carves or casts an **i**
1 Sam 15:23 . . . as bad as worshiping **i-s.**
Isa 40:19 . . . Can he be compared to an **i**
Isa 44:9 . . . who worship **i-s** don't know
Isa 44:15 . . . makes an **i** and bows down
Isa 44:17 . . . and makes his god: a carved **i!**
Isa 44:19 . . . who made the **i** never stops to
Hab 2:18 . . . What good is an **i** carved
Acts 15:20 . . . eating food offered to **i-s,**
Rom 1:23 . . . worshiped **i-s** made to look
1 Cor 6:9 . . . or who worship **i-s**, or commit
1 Cor 8:1 . . . has been offered to **i-s.**
1 Cor 8:4 . . . an **i** is not really a god
Rev 2:14 . . . sin by eating food offered to **i-s**

IDOLATER (n) worshiper of idols; one who worships an undeserving object blindly
Eph 5:5 . . . a greedy person is an **i,**
Col 3:5 . . . a greedy person is an **i,**

IDOLATRY (n) the worship of a physical object as a god; immoderate attachment or devotion to something
Gal 5:20 . . . pleasures, **i**, sorcery,

IGNORANT (adj) resulting from or showing lack of knowledge, comprehension, or intelligence; unaware, uninformed
Job 38:2 . . . questions my wisdom with such **i**
Heb 5:2 . . . with **i** and wayward people
1 Pet 2:15 . . . lives should silence those **i**
2 Pet 3:16 . . . are **i** and unstable have twisted

IGNORE (v) to refuse to take notice of
Ps 9:12 . . . He does not **i** the cries of
Ps 9:17 . . . all the nations who **i** God.
Ps 10:12 . . . Do not **i** the helpless!
Prov 13:18 . . . If you **i** criticism,
Heb 2:3 . . . if we **i** this great salvation

ILL-TEMPERED (adj) having a cross or surly disposition; quarrelsome
1 Sam 25:17 . . . He's so **i** that no

ILLEGITIMATE (adj) not recognized as lawful offspring
Heb 12:8 . . . means that you are **i** and are not

ILLUMINATES (v) to supply or brighten with light
Rev 21:23 . . . the glory of God **i** the city,

IMAGE (n) a God-given likeness or reflection; a tangible or visible representation
Gen 1:26 . . . make human beings in our **i,**
Gen 1:27 . . . human beings in his own **i.**
Gen 9:6 . . . made human beings in his own **i.**
Col 1:15 . . . Christ is the visible **i** of the
Jas 3:9 . . . have been made in the **i** of God.

IMAGINE, IMAGINED (v) to form a mental image of; to suppose or guess
Gen 6:5 . . . **i-d** was consistently and totally
Job 37:5 . . . can't even **i** the greatness
1 Cor 2:9 . . . no mind has **i-d** what God has

IMITATE, IMITATED (v) to follow as a pattern, model, or example; to resemble; to mimic
1 Cor 4:16 . . . I urge you to **i** me.
1 Cor 11:1 . . . should **i** me, just as I **i**
1 Thes 1:6 . . . In this way, you **i-d** both us and
1 Thes 2:14 . . . you **i-d** the believers
2 Thes 3:7 . . . that you ought to **i** us.

IMMANUEL (n) Hebrew name meaning "God is with us"
Isa 7:14 . . . to a son and will call him **I**
Isa 8:8 . . . one end to the other, O **I.**
Matt 1:23 . . . a son, and they will call him **I,**

IMMATURE (adj) lacking complete growth, development, or maturity
Eph 4:14 . . . no longer be **i** like children.

IMMORAL (adj) characterized by conflicting with traditionally (biblically) held moral principles; sinful or impure
Prov 2:16 . . . save you from the **i** woman,
Prov 6:24 . . . keep you from the **i** woman,
Prov 22:14 . . . an **i** woman is a dangerous
Luke 7:37 . . . a certain **i** woman from
Rom 13:13 . . . promiscuity and **i** living,
Eph 5:5 . . . be sure that no **i**, impure,
1 Tim 1:10 . . . people who are sexually **i,**
Jude 1:4 . . . grace allows us to live **i** lives.
Rev 22:15 . . . the sorcerers, the sexually **i,**

IMMORALITY (n) the quality or state of being immoral; an immoral act or practice
Matt 15:19 . . . all sexual **i**, theft, lying,
Acts 15:29 . . . animals, and from sexual **i.**
1 Cor 6:13 . . . made for sexual **i.**
1 Cor 6:18 . . . **i** is a sin against
1 Cor 7:2 . . . there is so much sexual **i,**
Gal 5:19 . . . very clear: sexual **i**, impurity,
2 Pet 2:7 . . . who was sick of the shameful **i**
Jude 1:7 . . . towns, which were filled with **i**

IMMORTAL (adj) exempt from death; imperishable
1 Cor 15:53 . . . transformed into **i** bodies.

IMMORTALITY (n) unending existence; lasting fame
Rom 2:7 . . . and honor and **i**
2 Tim 1:10 . . . the way to life and **i**

IMMOVABLE (adj) incapable of being moved; steadfast, unyielding
1 Cor 15:58 . . . be strong and **i.** Always work

IMPALED (v) to torture or kill by fixing on a sharp stake
Esth 7:10 . . . they **i** Haman on the pole

IMPARTIAL (adj) not partial or biased; treating all equally
Deut 1:17 . . . and **i** in your judgments.
Matt 22:16 . . . **i** and don't play favorites.

IMPATIENT (adj) restless or short of temper especially under irritation, delay, or opposition
Zech 11:8 . . . I became **i** with these sheep,

IMPORTANT (adj) marked by or indicative of significant worth or consequence
Matt 23:23 . . . ignore the more **i** aspects of
Matt 23:23 . . . do not neglect the more **i**
Mark 12:29 . . . The most **i** commandment
Mark 12:33 . . . I know it is **i** to love him
1 Cor 7:19 . . . The **i** thing is to keep God's
1 Cor 15:3 . . . what was most **i** and what
Gal 5:6 . . . What is **i** is faith expressing

IMPOSSIBLE (adj) incapable of being or occurring
Zech 8:6 . . . this may seem **i** to you now,
Luke 1:37 . . . For nothing is **i** with God.
Heb 6:4 . . . it is **i** to bring back
Heb 11:6 . . . it is **i** to please God

IMPOSTORS (n) one who assumes false identity or title for the purpose of deception
2 Cor 6:8 . . . are honest, but they call us **i.**
2 Tim 3:13 . . . evil people and **i** will flourish.

IMPRESS, IMPRESSED (v) to gain the admiration or interest of
Dan 1:19 . . . **i-ed** him as much as Daniel,
Phil 2:3 . . . don't try to **i** others. Be humble

IMPRESSION (n) an often indistinct or imprecise notion or remembrance
Luke 19:11 . . . to correct the **i** that the Kingdom

IMPRESSIVE (adj) having the power to excite attention, awe, or admiration
Ps 107:24 . . . his **i** works on the deepest seas.

IMPURE (adj) ritually unclean; lewd, unchaste
Acts 11:8 . . . have declared **i** or unclean.
Eph 5:5 . . . no immoral, **i**, or greedy person
1 Thes 2:3 . . . with any deceit or **i** motives
1 Thes 4:7 . . . live holy lives, not **i** lives.

IMPURITY, IMPURITIES (n) something that is impure or makes something else impure; the quality or state of being impure
Prov 25:4 . . . Remove the **i-ies** from silver,
Gal 5:19 . . . very clear: sexual immorality, **i,**
Col 3:5 . . . to do with sexual immorality, **i,**

INCENSE (n) material used to produce a fragrant odor when burned
Exod 30:1 . . . acacia wood for burning **i.**
Exod 30:38 . . . Anyone who makes **i**
Exod 40:5 . . . Place the gold **i** altar
Ps 141:2 . . . Accept my prayer as **i** offered
Heb 9:4 . . . In that room were a gold **i** altar
Rev 5:8 . . . held gold bowls filled with **i,**
Rev 8:3 . . . great amount of **i** was given
Rev 8:4 . . . smoke of the **i**, mixed with the

INCORRUPTIBLE (KJV)
1 Cor 15:52 . . . will be raised *to live forever.*
1 Pet 1:4 . . . *beyond the reach of* change and *decay.*

INCREASE, INCREASED, INCREASES (v) to become progressively greater (as in size, amount, number, or intensity)
1 Sam 2:10 . . . he **i-s** the strength of his anointed
Ps 62:10 . . . if your wealth **i-s**, don't make it
Luke 17:5 . . . Show us how to **i** our faith.
Acts 6:7 . . . number of believers greatly **i-d**

INCREDIBLE (adj) too extraordinary and improbable to be believed; amazing, extraordinary
Acts 26:8 . . . does it seem **i** to any of you
Eph 2:7 . . . examples of the **i** wealth of

INCURABLE (adj) unlikely to be changed or corrected
Jer 30:12 . . . Your injury is **i**—a terrible

INDEPENDENT (adj) not requiring or relying on others; not subject to control by others
1 Cor 11:11 . . . women are not **i** of men,
1 Cor 11:11 . . . men are not **i** of women.

INDULGE, INDULGED, INDULGES (v) to take unrestrained pleasure in
Rom 1:26 . . . **i-d** in sex with each other.
Rom 13:14 . . . ways to **i** your evil desires.
1 Cor 5:9 . . . people who **i** in sexual sin.
1 Cor 5:11 . . . claims to be a believer yet **i-s**

INEXPRESSIBLE (adj) not capable of being expressed; indescribable
1 Pet 1:8 . . . rejoice with a glorious, **i** joy.

INFANTS (n) a child in the first period of (physical or spiritual) life
Ps 8:2 . . . and **i** to tell of your strength,
Matt 21:16 . . . and **i** to give you praise.
1 Cor 3:1 . . . were **i** in the Christian life.

INFINITE (adj) subject to no limitation or external determination
Phil 3:8 . . . when compared with the **i** value

INFLUENCE, INFLUENCED (v) to sway; to affect or modify
Luke 20:21 . . . **i-d** by what others think.
3 Jn 1:11 . . . bad example **i** you.

INFLUENTIAL (adj) exerting or possessing the power or capacity of causing an effect in indirect ways
Ruth 2:1 . . . there was a wealthy and **i** man

INHERIT, INHERITED (v) to receive as a legacy or promise; to take possession as a rightful heir
Matt 5:5 . . . they will **i** the whole earth.
Matt 25:34 . . . **i** the Kingdom prepared
Mark 10:17 . . . I do to **i** eternal life?
1 Cor 6:9 . . . will not **i** the Kingdom
Eph 3:6 . . . share equally in the riches **i-ed**
Eph 5:5 . . . impure, or greedy person will **i**
Rev 21:7 . . . All who are victorious will **i**

INHERITANCE (n) the acquisition of a possession, condition, or trait from past generations; something that is or may be inherited
Ps 16:6 . . . What a wonderful **i!**
Ps 33:12 . . . people he has chosen as his **i.**
Ps 61:5 . . . an **i** reserved for those who fear
Gal 4:30 . . . will not share the **i**
Eph 1:14 . . . give us the **i** he promised
Col 3:24 . . . give you an **i** as your reward,
Heb 9:15 . . . receive the eternal **i** God has

INIQUITY, INIQUITIES (KJV)
Ps 51:9 . . . Remove the stain of my *guilt*
Isa 6:7 . . . your *guilt* is removed,
Isa 53:6 . . . laid on him the *sins* of us all.
1 Cor 13:6 . . . not rejoice about *injustice*
Rev 18:5 . . . God remembers her *evil deeds*

INJURE, INJURED (v) to do an injustice to; to harm or impair
Prov 8:36 . . . those who miss me **i** themselves.
Ezek 34:16 . . . I will bandage the **i-ed** and
Zech 11:16 . . . nor heal the **i-ed,** nor feed

INJUSTICE (n) unfairness; wrongs
1 Cor 6:7 . . . accept the **i** and leave it
1 Cor 13:6 . . . It does not rejoice about **i**

INK (n) a colored, usually liquid, material for writing and printing
2 Cor 3:3 . . . is written not with pen and **i,**

INNOCENCE (n) freedom from guilt or sin through being unacquainted with evil; blamelessness
Gen 20:5 . . . I acted in complete **i!**
2 Sam 22:25 . . . He has seen my **i.**
Hos 8:5 . . . will you be incapable of **i?**

INNOCENT (adj) regarded as righteous; free from guilt or sin; unaware or ignorant
Job 13:18 . . . I will be proved **i.**
Job 34:5 . . . Job also said, 'I am **i,**
Ps 7:8 . . . for I am **i,** O Most High!
Ps 26:1 . . . Declare me **i,** O LORD, for I
Ps 143:2 . . . no one is **i** before you.
Matt 27:4 . . . I have betrayed an **i** man.
Matt 27:24 . . . I am **i** of this man's blood.
Rom 16:18 . . . they deceive **i** people.

INQUIRE (v) to ask about or look into
Deut 12:30 . . . Do not **i** about their gods,
Deut 32:7 . . . **I** of your elders
1 Chr 21:30 . . . to go there to **i** of God

INSIGHT (n) the power or act of seeing into a situation; discernment
Ps 19:8 . . . are clear, giving **i** for living.
Prov 7:4 . . . make **i** a beloved member
Eph 1:17 . . . and **i** so that you might grow

INSOLENCE (n) the quality or state of being overbearing or impudent
1 Tim 1:13 . . . In my **i,** I persecuted his people.

INSPECT (v) to view closely in critical appraisal
Prov 31:16 . . . She goes to **i** a field

INSPIRATION (n) guidance by divine influence
Matt 22:43 . . . under the **i** of the Spirit

INSPIRED (adj) to influence, move, or guide by divine influence
2 Tim 3:16 . . . All Scripture is **i** by God

INSTINCT, INSTINCTS (n) a natural or inherent aptitude, impulse, or capacity
2 Pet 2:12 . . . creatures of **i,** born to be caught
Jude 1:10 . . . whatever their **i-s** tell them,
Jude 1:19 . . . They follow their natural **i-s**

INSTITUTED (v) to originate and get established; to set going
Rom 13:2 . . . rebelling against what God has **i,**

INSTRUCT, INSTRUCTED, INSTRUCTS (v) to provide with authoritative information or advice; to teach, train, or direct
Exod 4:12 . . . I will **i** you in what to say.
Deut 2:1 . . . just as the LORD had **i-ed** me,
Deut 4:36 . . . so he could **i** you.
Josh 11:9 . . . chariots, as the LORD had **i-ed.**
Josh 11:23 . . . as the LORD had **i-ed** Moses.
Ps 105:22 . . . He could **i** the king's aides
Prov 9:9 . . . **I** the wise, and they will be even
Prov 10:8 . . . The wise are glad to be **i-ed,**
Prov 21:11 . . . if you **i** the wise,
Acts 8:31 . . . unless someone **i-s** me?
2 Tim 2:25 . . . Gently **i** those who oppose
Titus 2:12 . . . **i-ed** to turn from godless living

INSTRUCTION, INSTRUCTIONS (n) a command or principle intended especially as a general rule of action; an order; directions; the action, practice, or profession of teaching
see also COMMANDMENT(S), LAW(S)
Exod 34:32 . . . Moses gave them all the **i-s**
Deut 31:11 . . . you must read this Book of **I**
Josh 1:7 . . . Be careful to obey all the **i-s**
Josh 1:8 . . . Study this Book of **I**
Ps 19:7 . . . The **i-s** of the LORD are perfect,
Ps 40:8 . . . your **i-s** are written on my heart.
Ps 119:97 . . . Oh, how I love your **i-s!**
Prov 4:13 . . . Take hold of my **i-s;**
Prov 7:2 . . . Guard my **i-s** as you guard
Prov 8:33 . . . Listen to my **i** and be wise.
Prov 23:12 . . . Commit yourself to **i;**
Isa 40:14 . . . need **i** about what is good?
Jer 31:33 . . . put my **i-s** deep within
Zech 7:12 . . . they could not hear the **i-s**
1 Tim 1:5 . . . purpose of my **i** is that all
1 Tim 1:18 . . . here are my **i-s** for you,

INSTRUMENT, INSTRUMENTS (n) a device used to produce music; one used by another as a means or aid; a means whereby something is achieved, performed, or furthered
Dan 3:7 . . . at the sound of the musical **i-s,**
Hab 3:19 . . . accompanied by stringed **i-s.)**
Acts 9:15 . . . Saul is my chosen **i**
Rom 6:13 . . . part of your body become an **i**

INSULT, INSULTS (n) a gross indignity
Job 20:3 . . . I've had to endure your **i-s,**
Ps 69:7 . . . For I endure **i-s** for your sake;
Ps 69:9 . . . the **i-s** of those who insult you
Ps 69:20 . . . Their **i-s** have broken my heart,
Prov 9:7 . . . will get an **i** in return.
Prov 22:10 . . . and **i-s** will disappear.
Rom 15:3 . . . The **i-s** of those who insult you,
2 Cor 12:10 . . . and in the **i-s,** hardships,
Jude 1:15 . . . all the **i-s** that ungodly sinners

INSULT, INSULTED (v) to treat with insolence, indignity, or contempt
Prov 12:16 . . . stays calm when **i-ed.**
Prov 20:20 . . . **i** your father or mother,
Prov 30:9 . . . and thus **i** God's holy name.
Heb 10:29 . . . have **i-ed** and disdained
1 Pet 2:23 . . . not retaliate when he was **i-ed,**
1 Pet 3:9 . . . insults when people **i** you.
1 Pet 4:14 . . . be happy when you are **i-ed**

INTEGRITY (n) honesty; without compromise or corruption
Job 2:3 . . . a man of complete **i.**
Job 2:9 . . . still trying to maintain your **i?**
Job 27:5 . . . I will defend my **i** until I die.
Ps 25:21 . . . May **i** and honesty protect me,
Ps 26:11 . . . I live with **i.** So redeem
Ps 111:8 . . . faithfully and with **i.**
Ps 119:1 . . . Joyful are people of **i,**
Prov 2:7 . . . shield to those who walk with **i.**
Prov 10:9 . . . People with **i** walk safely,
Titus 2:7 . . . you do reflect the **i**

INTELLIGENCE (n) the ability to learn or understand; mental acuteness
Isa 29:14 . . . the **i** of the intelligent will
1 Cor 1:19 . . . the **i** of the intelligent.

INTELLIGENT (adj) having or indicating a high or satisfactory degree of mental capacity
Job 32:8 . . . that makes them **i.**
Prov 17:28 . . . mouths shut, they seem **i.**

INTERCEDE, INTERCEDED (v) to mediate or plead another's case for justice or mercy
Isa 53:12 . . . of many and **i-d** for rebels.
1 Tim 2:1 . . . **i** on their behalf, and
Heb 7:25 . . . lives forever to **i** with God

INTEREST, INTERESTS (n) a charge for borrowed money; the profit in goods or money that is made on invested capital; a feeling that accompanies or causes special attention to an object
Lev 25:36 . . . Do not charge **i** or make a profit
Deut 23:20 . . . You may charge **i** to foreigners,
Deut 23:20 . . . not charge **i** to Israelites,
Neh 5:10 . . . stop this business of charging **i.**
Ps 15:5 . . . lend money without charging **i,**
Prov 28:8 . . . Income from charging high **i**
Matt 25:27 . . . I could have gotten some **i**
1 Cor 7:34 . . . His **i-s** are divided.
Phil 2:4 . . . look out only for your own **i-s,**

INTERMARRY, INTERMARRYING (v) to marry each other; to marry within a group
Deut 7:3 . . . You must not **i** with them.
Ezra 9:14 . . . **i-ing** with people who

INTERPRET, INTERPRETS (v) to explain; to translate
Gen 41:15 . . . a dream you can **i** it.
Matt 16:3 . . . how to **i** the weather
1 Cor 12:30 . . . to **i** unknown languages?
1 Cor 14:5 . . . unless someone **i-s** what you
1 Cor 14:13 . . . **i** what has been said.
1 Cor 14:26 . . . another will **i** what is said.
1 Cor 14:27 . . . must **i** what they say.
1 Cor 14:28 . . . is present who can **i,**

INTIMIDATED (v) to make timid or fearful
Phil 1:28 . . . Don't be **i** in any way

INVADED (v) to enter for conquest or plunder
2 Kgs 17:5 . . . king of Assyria **i** the entire
2 Kgs 24:1 . . . Nebuchadnezzar of Babylon **i**

INVENT (v) to devise by thinking; to find or discover . . .
Rom 1:30 . . . They **i** new ways of sinning,

INVISIBLE (adj) hidden; imperceptible
Rom 1:20 . . . see his **i** qualities—
Col 1:15 . . . visible image of the **i** God.
Heb 11:27 . . . his eyes on the one who is **i.**

INVITATION (n) an often formal request to be present or participate
1 Cor 10:27 . . . accept the **i** if you want to.

INVITE, INVITED (v) to request the presence or participation of; to welcome
Matt 25:35 . . . a stranger, and you **i-d** me
Luke 14:12 . . . For they will **i** you back,
Rev 19:9 . . . Blessed are those who are **i-d**

IRON (n) metal used in instruments of war, farming, and building; symbolic of strength for both security and destruction
Ps 2:9 . . . break them with an **i** rod
Prov 27:17 . . . As **i** sharpens **i,** so
Dan 2:33 . . . its legs were **i,** and its feet
Rev 2:27 . . . rule the nations with an **i** rod
Rev 12:5 . . . nations with an **i** rod.
Rev 19:15 . . . rule them with an **i** rod.

IRRITABLE (adj) easily exasperated or excited
1 Cor 13:5 . . . It is not **i,** and it keeps

ISAAC Patriarch, son of Abraham; promised by God (Gen 17:16-22; 18:14); born (Gen 21:1-7; 1 Chr 1:28; Acts 7:8); recipient of divine covenant (Gen 17:21; 26:2-5); offered to God by Abraham (Gen 22:1-19; Heb 11:17-19); took Rebekah as wife (Gen 24:67); inherited wealth (Gen 25:5); prayed for wife to have children (Gen 25:20-21); father of twins, Esau and Jacob (Gen 25:24; 1 Chr 1:34); preferred Esau (Gen 25:28); dealings with Abimelech (Gen 26:1-31); tricked into blessing Jacob (Gen 27:1-29); died (Gen 35:27-29); father of a nation (Deut 29:13; Rom 9:7, 10); often mentioned in NT (Luke 3:34; Gal 4:28; Heb 11:9, 17-20; Jas 2:21).

ISAIAH Prophet of Judah (southern kingdom) who prophesied during the reigns of four consecutive kings (Isa 1:1); called by God in a vision (Isa 6); prophesied Immanuel's coming (Isa 7–11); prophesied to Hezekiah (2 Kgs 19–20; Isa 36–38); recorded history of kings (2 Chr 26:22; 32:32); often quoted in NT (Matt 3:3; 4:14; 8:17; 12:17; 13:14; 15:7; Luke 4:17; John 12:38; Acts 8:28; 28:25; Rom 9:27; 10:16, 20).

ISLAND (n) a small tract of land surrounded on all sides by water
Rev 1:9 . . . I was exiled to the **i** of Patmos
Rev 16:20 . . . And every **i** disappeared,

ISRAEL (n) 1. Another name for Jacob (Gen 32:28); *see* JACOB.
2. The united kingdom of Israel, including all twelve tribes, as ruled by Saul, David, and Solomon.
3. The northern kingdom of Israel, including the ten northern tribes, in contrast to Judah (southern kingdom) (*see* 2 Sam 19:41-43).
Exod 3:9 . . . cry of the people of **I** has
Exod 12:37 . . . **I** left Rameses and started
Exod 16:1 . . . **I** set out from Elim
Exod 28:29 . . . **I** on the sacred chestpiece
Exod 31:16 . . . **I** must keep the Sabbath day
Exod 39:42 . . . **I** followed all of the LORD's
Lev 25:55 . . . the people of **I** belong to me.
Num 6:23 . . . **I** with this special blessing:
Num 9:17 . . . **I** would break camp and follow
Num 20:22 . . . community of **I** left Kadesh
Num 27:12 . . . I have given the people of **I.**
Num 35:10 . . . instructions to the people of **I.**
Deut 10:12 . . . **I,** what does the LORD your
Josh 21:3 . . . **I** gave the Levites the following
Judg 17:6 . . . In those days **I** had no king;
1 Sam 3:20 . . . And all **I,** from Dan
1 Sam 4:21 . . . said, "**I's** glory is gone."
1 Sam 15:26 . . . rejected you as king of **I.**
1 Sam 18:16 . . . all **I** and Judah loved David
2 Sam 14:25 . . . handsome man in all **I.**
1 Kgs 1:35 . . . him to be ruler over **I**
1 Kgs 12:1 . . . **I** had gathered to make him king.
1 Kgs 19:18 . . . preserve 7,000 others in **I**
2 Kgs 17:24 . . . replacing the people of **I.**
1 Chr 11:4 . . . and all **I** went to Jerusalem
1 Chr 21:1 . . . Satan rose up against **I**
2 Chr 9:8 . . . Because God loves **I**
Ps 73:1 . . . Truly God is good to **I,**
Ps 98:3 . . . to love and be faithful to **I.**
Isa 44:6 . . . says—**I's** King and Redeemer,
Isa 44:21 . . . you are my servant, O **I.**
Jer 2:3 . . . In those days **I** was holy
Jer 31:2 . . . I will give rest to the people of **I.**
Jer 31:9 . . . For I am **I's** father,
Jer 31:31 . . . covenant with the people of **I**
Ezek 3:17 . . . as a watchman for **I.**
Hos 1:10 . . . **I's** people will be like the sands
Hos 3:1 . . . LORD still loves **I,** even though
Amos 4:12 . . . in judgment, you people of **I!**
Amos 8:2 . . . Like this fruit, **I** is ripe
Mic 5:2 . . . a ruler of **I** will come from you,
Mal 1:5 . . . far beyond **I's** borders!
Matt 2:6 . . . the shepherd for my people **I.**
Matt 10:6 . . . people of **I**—God's lost sheep.
Matt 15:24 . . . lost sheep—the people of **I.**
Mark 12:29 . . . Listen, O **I!**
Acts 1:6 . . . time come for you to free **I**
Acts 9:15 . . . as well as to the people of **I.**
Rom 9:4 . . . **I,** chosen to be God's adopted
Rom 9:6 . . . **I** are truly members of God's
Rom 9:27 . . . **I** are as numerous as the sand
Rom 9:31 . . . **I,** who tried so hard to get
Rom 10:1 . . . the people of **I** to be saved.
Rom 11:7 . . . **I** have not found the favor of God
Rom 11:26 . . . And so all **I** will be saved.
Eph 2:12 . . . citizenship among the people of **I,**
Heb 8:8 . . . covenant with the people of **I**
Rev 7:4 . . . sealed from all the tribes of **I:**
Rev 21:12 . . . **I** were written on the gates.

ISRAELITE, ISRAELITES (n) *see also* JEW(S)
Exod 1:7 . . . the **I-s,** had many children
Exod 16:12 . . . heard the **I-s'** complaints.
Lev 25:46 . . . never treat your fellow **I-s** this
Num 10:12 . . . **I-s** set out from the wilderness
Josh 1:2 . . . lead these people, the **I-s,** across
Josh 7:1 . . . LORD was very angry with the **I-s.**
Judg 2:7 . . . **I-s** served the LORD throughout
Judg 3:12 . . . **I-s** did evil in the LORD's sight,
Judg 6:1 . . . **I-s** did evil in the LORD's sight.
Judg 10:16 . . . **I-s** put aside their foreign
Rom 11:1 . . . I myself am an **I,** a descendant
2 Cor 11:22 . . . Are they **I-s?** So am I.

ITALY (n) a long boot-shaped country that juts into the Mediterranean Sea
Acts 27:1 . . . we set sail for **I.**
Heb 13:24 . . . believers from **I** send

J

JACOB Patriarch, son of Isaac, grandson of Abraham; younger twin son of Issac and Rebekah (Gen 25:23–35:26; 48–49); also known as "Israel" (Gen 32:28); favored by Rebekah (Gen 25:28); bought Esau's birthright for a meal (Gen 25:29-34); deceived Isaac to receive his blessing (Gen 27:1-29); fled from Esau (Gen 27:41-45); married inside of clan (Gen 28:1-5); Jacob's ladder (Gen 28:12); covenant extended to Jacob in a dream (Gen 28:13-15); wives and concubines, Rachel favored (Gen 29:1-30); children (Gen 29:31–30:24; 35:16-26); prospered at his uncle Laban's expense (Gen 30:25-43); fled from Laban (Gen 31); name changed to "Israel" (Gen 32:22-32); reconciled with Esau (Gen 33); favored Rachel's oldest son Joseph (Gen 37:3); overwhelmed by loss of Joseph (Gen 37:33-35); migrated to Egypt (Gen 46:5-7); blessed Joseph's sons (Gen 48); blessed his own sons (Gen 49:1-28); died (Gen 49:33); buried (Gen 50:1-14); often mentioned in NT (John 4:5-6, 12; Acts 7:8-15; Rom 9:13; Heb 11:20-21).

JAMES 1. One of the 12 disciples, brother of John, son of Zebedee (Matt 10:2; Mark 3:17); called by Jesus (Matt 4:21; Luke 5:10); zealous for the Lord (Luke 9:54); wanted honor (Mark 10:35-45); witnessed the Transfiguration (Matt 17:1-9; Mark 9:2-8; Luke 9:28-36); killed by Herod Agrippa I (Acts 12:2).
2. One of the 12 disciples, son of Alphaeus (Matt 10:3; Mark 3:18; Luke 6:15); called "the younger" (Mark 15:40).
3. Half-brother of Jesus (Matt 13:55; Mark 6:3; Luke 24:10; 1 Cor 15:7; Gal 1:19; 2:9, 12), brother of Jude (Jude 1:1); leader of Jerusalem Council (Acts 15:13; 21:18); with select group before Pentecost (Acts 1:13); wrote letter (Jas 1:1).
4. Father of the apostle Judas, not Iscariot (Luke 6:16).
5. Son of a certain Mary, perhaps the same as the "son of Alphaeus" (Matt 27:56).

JAR, JARS (n) an open container, typically made of clay in the ancient world
John 12:3 . . . **j** of expensive perfume
John 19:29 . . . A **j** of sour wine was
2 Cor 4:7 . . . like fragile clay **j-s** containing

JAVELIN (n) a light spear thrown as a weapon of war or in hunting
1 Sam 17:45 . . . sword, spear, and **j**, but I

JAWBONE (n) either of two bony structures that border the mouth
Judg 15:15 . . . the **j** of a recently killed donkey.

JEALOUS (adj) intolerant of rivalry or unfaithfulness; hostile toward a rival
Exod 20:5 . . . am a **j** God who will not
Exod 34:14 . . . whose very name is **J**,
Prov 6:34 . . . **j** husband will be furious,
Nah 1:2 . . . a **j** God, filled with vengeance
Rom 11:14 . . . **j** of what you Gentiles have,
1 Cor 13:4 . . . Love is not **j** or boastful
Gal 5:26 . . . provoke one another, or be **j**
Jas 3:14 . . . if you are bitterly **j** and there is

JEALOUSY (n) a jealous feeling, disposition, or attitude
Prov 27:4 . . . but **j** is even more dangerous.
Rom 10:19 . . . I will rouse your **j**
Rom 13:13 . . . or in quarreling and **j**.
1 Cor 10:22 . . . dare to rouse the Lord's **j**?
2 Cor 11:2 . . . you with the **j** of God
Gal 5:20 . . . **j**, outbursts of anger,
1 Tim 6:4 . . . arguments ending in **j**,
1 Pet 2:1 . . . with all deceit, hypocrisy, **j**,

JEERED, JEERS (v) to scoff; to taunt
Job 27:23 . . . **j-s** at them and mocks them.
Heb 11:36 . . . Some were **j-ed** at,

JEHOVAH (KJV)
Exod 6:3 . . . did not reveal my name, *Yahweh*,
Ps 83:18 . . . you alone are called *the* LORD
Isa 12:2 . . . The LORD *GOD* is my strength
Isa 26:4 . . . the LORD *GOD* is the eternal

JEREMIAH Prophet of Judah (southern kingdom) from Anathoth (Jer 11:18-23); marital status single (Jer 16:2); put in stocks (Jer 20:1-6); threatened by priests and prophets (Jer 26:8); brought death to false prophet (Jer 28:16-17); writings burned (Jer 36); imprisoned in dungeon (Jer 37:15); removed from the dungeon by King Zedekiah (Jer 37:21); lowered into cistern (Jer 38:1-6); set free by invaders (Jer 39:11–40:6); taken to Egypt (Jer 43); mentioned in NT (Matt 2:17; 27:9).

JERICHO (n) a city in the plain of the Jordan Valley at the foot of the ascent to the Judean mountains
Num 22:1 . . . across from **J**.
Josh 3:16 . . . near the town of **J**.
Josh 5:10 . . . at Gilgal on the plains of **J**,
Luke 10:30 . . . from Jerusalem down to **J**,
Heb 11:30 . . . around **J** for seven days,

JERUSALEM (n) sacred city and well-known capital of Palestine during Bible times
Josh 10:1 . . . Adoni-zedek, king of **J**, heard that
Josh 15:8 . . . where the city of **J** is located.
Judg 1:8 . . . Judah attacked **J** and captured it,
2 Sam 5:5 . . . **J** he reigned over all Israel
2 Sam 11:1 . . . David stayed behind in **J**.
1 Kgs 9:15 . . . terraces, the wall of **J**,
1 Kgs 10:26 . . . and some near him in **J**.
1 Kgs 14:25 . . . came up and attacked **J**.
2 Kgs 8:17 . . . he reigned in **J** eight years.
2 Kgs 12:1 . . . He reigned in **J** forty years.
2 Kgs 14:2 . . . reigned in **J** twenty-nine years.
2 Kgs 15:2 . . . he reigned in **J** fifty-two years.
2 Kgs 16:2 . . . he reigned in **J** sixteen years.
2 Kgs 18:2 . . . reigned in **J** twenty-nine years.
2 Kgs 19:31 . . . will spread out from **J**,
2 Kgs 21:12 . . . I will bring such disaster on **J**
2 Kgs 22:1 . . . he reigned in **J** thirty-one years.
2 Kgs 23:31 . . . he reigned in **J** three months.
2 Kgs 24:8 . . . he reigned in **J** three months.
2 Kgs 24:14 . . . Nebuchadnezzar took all of **J**
2 Kgs 24:20 . . . anger against the people of **J**
2 Kgs 25:9 . . . and all the houses of **J**.
1 Chr 21:16 . . . reaching out over **J**.
2 Chr 3:1 . . . the Temple of the LORD in **J**
2 Chr 9:1 . . . she came to **J** to test him
2 Chr 20:15 . . . all you people of Judah and **J**!
2 Chr 29:8 . . . has fallen upon Judah and **J**.
2 Chr 36:19 . . . tore down the walls of **J**,
Ezra 2:1 . . . but now they returned to **J**
Ezra 4:12 . . . who came here to **J** from Babylon
Ezra 6:12 . . . who has chosen the city of **J**
Ezra 9:9 . . . a protective wall in Judah and **J**.
Neh 1:3 . . . The wall of **J** has been torn
Neh 3:8 . . . They left out a section of **J**
Neh 11:1 . . . of the people were living in **J**,
Neh 12:43 . . . joy of the people of **J** could be
Ps 9:11 . . . the LORD who reigns in **J**.
Ps 51:18 . . . rebuild the walls of **J**.
Ps 74:2 . . . remember **J**, your home here
Ps 79:1 . . . made **J** a heap of ruins.
Ps 87:2 . . . He loves the city of **J** more than
Ps 102:13 . . . arise and have mercy on **J**—
Ps 122:2 . . . standing inside your gates, O **J**.
Ps 122:6 . . . Pray for peace in **J**.
Ps 125:2 . . . **J**, so the LORD surrounds
Ps 128:5 . . . May you see **J** prosper
Ps 137:3 . . . Sing us one of those songs of **J**!
Ps 137:5 . . . If I forget you, O **J**,
Ps 147:2 . . . The LORD is rebuilding **J**
Ps 147:12 . . . Glorify the LORD, O **J**!
Isa 1:1 . . . saw concerning Judah and **J**.
Isa 3:1 . . . take away from **J** and Judah
Isa 4:3 . . . who survive the destruction of **J**
Isa 27:13 . . . return to **J** to worship the LORD
Isa 31:5 . . . will hover over **J** and protect it
Isa 40:2 . . . Speak tenderly to **J**.
Isa 51:11 . . . They will enter **J** singing,
Isa 52:1 . . . beautiful clothes, O holy city of **J**,
Isa 52:8 . . . they see the LORD returning to **J**.
Isa 62:7 . . . he makes **J** the pride of the earth.
Jer 2:2 . . . Go and shout this message to **J**.
Jer 4:5 . . . Shout to Judah, and broadcast to **J**!
Jer 6:6 . . . siege ramps against the walls of **J**.
Jer 9:11 . . . I will make **J** into a heap of ruins,
Jer 23:14 . . . the prophets of **J** are even worse!
Jer 26:18 . . . **J** will be reduced to ruins!
Jer 39:1 . . . came with his army to besiege **J**.
Jer 51:50 . . . think about your home in **J**.
Lam 1:7 . . . **J** remembers her ancient splendor.
Dan 6:10 . . . windows open toward **J**.
Dan 9:2 . . . **J** must lie desolate for seventy
Dan 9:12 . . . a disaster as happened in **J**.
Dan 9:25 . . . command is given to rebuild **J**
Joel 3:16 . . . from Zion and thunder from **J**,
Amos 2:5 . . . fortresses of **J** will be destroyed.
Obad 1:11 . . . and cast lots to divide up **J**,
Mic 4:2 . . . his word will go out from **J**.
Zeph 3:16 . . . the announcement to **J** will be,
Zech 1:17 . . . Zion and choose **J** as his own.
Zech 2:4 . . . **J** will someday be so full
Zech 8:8 . . . home again to live safely in **J**.
Zech 8:22 . . . nations will come to **J** to seek
Zech 9:10 . . . and the warhorses from **J**.
Zech 12:10 . . . and on the people of **J**.
Zech 14:8 . . . waters will flow out from **J**,
Matt 20:18 . . . going up to **J**, where the Son
Matt 21:10 . . . city of **J** was in an uproar
Matt 23:37 . . . **J**, the city that kills the
Mark 10:33 . . . going up to **J**, where the Son
Luke 2:22 . . . parents took him to **J**
Luke 2:41 . . . Jesus' parents went to **J**
Luke 4:9 . . . Then the devil took him to **J**,
Luke 9:31 . . . about to be fulfilled in **J**.
Luke 13:34 . . . O **J**, **J**, the city that kills
Luke 18:31 . . . to **J**, where all the predictions
Luke 21:20 . . . you see **J** surrounded
Luke 24:47 . . . nations, beginning in **J**:
Acts 1:8 . . . about me everywhere—in **J**,
Acts 6:7 . . . believers greatly increased in **J**,
Acts 20:22 . . . bound by the Spirit to go to **J**.
Acts 23:11 . . . a witness to me here in **J**,
Rom 9:33 . . . I am placing a stone in **J**
Rom 11:26 . . . rescues will come from **J**,
Rom 15:19 . . . from **J** all the way to Illyricum.
Gal 4:25 . . . **J** is just like Mount Sinai
Gal 4:26 . . . Sarah, represents the heavenly **J**.
Heb 12:22 . . . living God, the heavenly **J**,
Rev 21:10 . . . he showed me the holy city, **J**,

JESUS *see also* CHRIST, MESSIAH
Family line (Matt 1:1-17; Luke 3:23-38); birth announced (Matt 1:18-25; Luke 1:26-38); born in Bethlehem (Luke 2:1-20); circumcised, officially named, and presented at Temple (Luke 2:21-40); visited by Magi (Matt 2:1-12); escape to and return

from Egypt (Matt 2:13-23); amazed the Temple scholars (Luke 2:41-50); summary of youth (Luke 2:51-52); baptized by John (Matt 3:13-17; Mark 1:9-11; Luke 3:21-22; John 1:32-34); tempted by Satan (Matt 4:1-11; Mark 1:12-13; Luke 4:1-13); ministered in Galilee (Matt 4:12–18:35; Mark 1:14–9:50); transfigured on a mountain (Matt 17:1-13; Mark 9:2-13; Luke 9:28-36; 2 Pet 1:16-18); triumphal entry (Matt 21:1-11; Mark 11:1-11; Luke 19:28-44; John 12:12-19); the Last Supper (Matt 26:17-35; Mark 14:12-31; Luke 22:7-38; John 13–17); betrayed and tried (Matt 26:36–27:31; Mark 14:32–15:20; Luke 22:39–23:25; John 18:1–19:16); crucified, died, and was buried (Matt 27:32-66; Mark 15:21-47; Luke 23:26-56; John 19:17-42); rose again and appeared to followers (Matt 28; Mark 16; Luke 24; John 20–21; Acts 1:1-11; 7:55-56; 9:3-6; 1 Cor 15:1-8; Rev 1:1-20); ascended to heaven (Mark 16:19; Luke 24:50-53; John 1:51; Acts 1:9; Eph 4:8).

JEW, JEWS (n) a name applied first to the people living in the southern kingdom of Judah; broadly, a descendant of Abraham *see also* ISRAELITE(S)
Esth 3:13 . . . property of the **J-s** would be
Zech 8:23 . . . clutch at the sleeve of one **J**.
Matt 2:2 . . . the newborn king of the **J-s?**
John 19:3 . . . Hail! King of the **J-s!**
Acts 20:21 . . . message for **J-s** and Greeks
Acts 21:39 . . . I am a **J** and a citizen of
Rom 1:16 . . . everyone who believes—the **J**
Rom 2:28 . . . you are not a true **J**
Rom 9:24 . . . from the **J-s** and from
Rom 10:12 . . . **J** and Gentile are the same
1 Cor 9:20 . . . with the **J-s**, I lived like a **J**
1 Cor 12:13 . . . **J-s**, some are Gentiles,
Gal 2:8 . . . Peter as the apostle to the **J-s**
Gal 2:14 . . . **J** by birth, have discarded
Gal 3:28 . . . There is no longer **J** or Gentile,
Eph 3:6 . . . Gentiles and **J-s** who believe
Col 3:11 . . . **J** or a Gentile, circumcised or

JEWEL, JEWELS (n) a precious stone; gem
Prov 3:22 . . . They are like **j-s** on a necklace.
Song 4:9 . . . with a single **j** of your necklace.
Isa 61:10 . . . or a bride with her **j-s**.
Zech 9:16 . . . in his land like **j-s** in a crown.
1 Cor 3:12 . . . gold, silver, **j-s**, wood, hay,

JEWELRY (n) objects of precious metal worn for personal adornment
Prov 25:12 . . . earring or other gold **j**.
Jer 2:32 . . . a young woman forget her **j?**
Ezek 16:11 . . . I gave you lovely **j**, bracelets,

JEWISH (adj) of, relating to, or characteristic of the Jews
Esth 2:5 . . . a **J** man in the fortress of Susa
John 3:10 . . . You are a respected **J** teacher,

JEZEBEL Queen of Israel (northern kingdom), daughter of Ethbaal, king of Sidon; evil, influential wife of King Ahab (1 Kgs 21:25); Baal worshiper (1 Kgs 16:31-33); tried to kill all the Lord's prophets (1 Kgs 18:4, 13); vowed to kill Elijah (1 Kgs 19:1-2); arranged murder to get vineyard for Ahab (1 Kgs 21:1-16); death foretold and fulfilled (1 Kgs 1:23; 2 Kgs 9:10, 30-37).

JOB Man who feared God and had integrity (Job 1:1-5); slandered and attacked by Satan (Job 1:6–2:10); debated suffering with his "friends" (Job 3–37); enlightened by vision of the Lord (Job 38–41); restored to peace and prosperity (Job 42); example of righteousness (Ezek 14:14, 20); example of endurance in suffering (Jas 5:11).

JOHN 1. The Baptist, son of Zechariah and Elizabeth (Luke 1:5-25, 57-80); called to prepare the way for the Messiah (Isa 40:3-5; Luke 3:1-6; John 1:19-28); called to preach and baptize (Matt 3:1-12; Mark 1:1-8); preached repentance (Luke 3:7-20); baptized Jesus (Matt 3:13-17; Luke 3:21-22); confirmed Jesus' ministry (Matt 3:11-12; Mark 1:7-8; Luke 3:15-18; John 3:22-36; 5:33); ministry compared to Elijah (Mal 4:5; Matt 11:11-19; Mark 9:11-13; Luke 7:24-35); arrested and beheaded by Herod Antipas (Matt 14:1-12; Mark 6:14-29; Luke 9:7-9).
2. One of the 12 disciples, brother of James, son of Zebedee (Matt 10:2; Mark 3:17); witnessed the Transfiguration (Matt 17:1-9; Mark 9:2-8; Luke 9:28-36); inner circle of Jesus' followers (Matt 17:1; Mark 5:37; 9:2; 13:3; Luke 8:51; 9:28; Gal 2:9); with Peter, healed a man and was arrested (Acts 3–4); with Peter, rebuked sorcerer (Acts 8:14-25); wrote fourth Gospel (John 13:23-25; *see also* 20:2; 21:20-25), letters of John (the "elder," 2 Jn 1:1; 3 Jn 1:1), and Revelation (the "servant," Rev 1:1, 9; 22:8).
3. *See* MARK, also known as John Mark.

JOIN, JOINED, JOINS (v) to put or bring into close association or relationship; to take part in a collective activity
Ps 26:5 . . . I refuse to **j** in with the wicked.
Dan 11:34 . . . who **j** them will not be sincere.
Zech 2:11 . . . will **j** themselves to the LORD
Matt 19:6 . . . what God has **j-ed** together.
Mark 10:9 . . . what God has **j-ed** together.
Rom 6:3 . . . **j-ed** with Christ Jesus in baptism,
Rom 8:16 . . . his Spirit **j-s** with our spirit
Rom 15:30 . . . **j** in my struggle by praying
1 Cor 6:16 . . . if a man **j-s** himself to
Eph 2:21 . . . carefully **j-ed** together in him,

JOINT (n) the point of contact between bone and the parts surrounding and supporting it
Ps 22:14 . . . all my bones are out of **j**.
Heb 4:12 . . . between **j** and marrow.

JOKE, JOKES (n) something said or done to provoke laughter
Ps 44:14 . . . made us the butt of their **j-s**;
Ps 89:41 . . . he has become a **j** to his
Eph 5:4 . . . coarse **j-s**—these are not

JOKING (v) to jest; to kid
Gen 19:14 . . . men thought he was only **j**.
Prov 26:19 . . . and then says, "I was only **j**."

JONAH Prophet of Israel (northern kingdom), in the days of Jeroboam II (2 Kgs 14:25); swallowed by great fish (Jon 1:17); survived and then preached to Nineveh (Jon 3); mentioned by Jesus as a sign (Matt 12:39-41; 16:4; Luke 11:29-32).

JORDAN (n) the name of the longest and most important river in Palestine
Josh 4:22 . . . crossed the **J** on dry ground.
Matt 3:6 . . . them in the **J** River.
Matt 4:15 . . . sea, beyond the **J** River, in
Mark 1:9 . . . him in the **J** River.

JOSEPH 1. Oldest son of Jacob and Rachel (Gen 30:24); loved by Jacob—hated by brothers (Gen 37:3-4); dreamer of dreams (Gen 37:5-11); captured to be killed, but sold into slavery (Gen 37:20, 27-28); faithfully served Egyptian master (Gen 39:3); wrongfully accused and imprisoned (Gen 39); interpreted dreams of royal staff (Gen 40); interpreted dreams of Pharaoh, then ruled Egypt (Gen 41:4-44); prepared Egypt for famine (Gen 41:46-57); tested brothers, revealed identity, and reconciled with them (Gen 42–45); brought his father Jacob and family to Egypt (Gen 46–47); sons, Ephraim and Manasseh, blessed by Jacob (Gen 48); Joseph blessed by Jacob (Gen 49:22-26; Deut 33:13-17); reassured his brothers (Gen 50:15-21); died (Gen 50:22-26; Heb 11:22); remembered as one chosen and helped by God (Acts 7:9-18); 12,000 descendants will be marked by God (Rev 7:8).
2. Husband of Mary the mother of Jesus; accepted supernatural pregnancy of Mary (Matt 1:16-25); had no relations with Mary until birth of Jesus (Matt 1:25); was present at birth and dedication of Jesus (Luke 2:4-38); fled to Egypt, then Nazareth (Matt 2:13-22); descendant of David in the family line of Jesus (Luke 3:23); Jesus called his son (Luke 4:22; John 1:45; 6:42).

JOSHUA Son of Nun, who led Israel into Promised Land (Acts 7:45; Heb 4:8); commanded by Moses to fight Amalek (Exod 17:8-16); assistant to Moses (Exod 24:13); explored Canaan (Num 13:8); demonstrated faith in his report (Num 14:6-9); allowed to enter Promised Land (Num 14:30; Deut 1:38); became Israel's leader after Moses (Num 27:18-23; Deut 31:1-18); went with Moses up the mountain of God (Exod 24:13); assumed command (Josh 1); sent spies to Jericho (Josh 2); led Israel across the Jordan (Josh 3–4); established memorial stones (Josh 4); circumcised the people (Josh 5:2-9); conquered Jericho (Josh 6) and Ai (Josh 7–8); uncovered Achan's sin (Josh 7:10-26); made pact with the Gibeonites (Josh 9); sun stood still (Josh 10:1-15); conquered southern Canaan (Josh 10:28-43); conquered northern Canaan (Josh 11–12); divided the land (Josh 13–22); gave final words to Israel (Josh 23); made covenant at Shechem (Josh 8:30-35; 24:1-28); died (Josh 24:29-30).

JOURNEY (n) an act or instance of traveling from one place to another
Judg 18:6 . . . the LORD is watching over your **j**.
Ezra 8:21 . . . give us a safe **j**
Rom 15:24 . . . provide for my **j**.

JOY, JOYS (n) the emotion evoked by well-being, success, or good fortune
Deut 16:15 . . . be a time of great **j** for all.
1 Sam 18:6 . . . danced for **j** with tambourines
1 Chr 16:27 . . . and **j** fill his dwelling.
1 Chr 29:22 . . . with great **j** that day.
Ezra 3:12 . . . however, were shouting for **j**.
Neh 8:10 . . . **j** of the LORD is your strength!
Neh 8:17 . . . they were all filled with great **j!**
Esth 9:22 . . . and their mourning into **j**.
Job 3:22 . . . filled with **j** when they finally die,
Job 8:21 . . . your lips with shouts of **j**.
Ps 1:1 . . . **j-s** of those who do not follow the
Ps 2:12 . . . **j** for all who take refuge in him!
Ps 9:2 . . . filled with **j** because of you.
Ps 19:8 . . . are right, bringing **j** to the heart.

Ps 21:1 . . . He shouts with **j**
Ps 28:7 . . . my heart is filled with **j.**
Ps 30:11 . . . and clothed me with **j,**
Ps 32:2 . . . what **j** for those whose record
Ps 33:12 . . . **j** for the nation whose God
Ps 41:1 . . . **j-s** of those who are kind
Ps 42:4 . . . singing for **j** and giving thanks
Ps 45:7 . . . pouring out the oil of **j** on you
Ps 46:4 . . . A river brings **j** to the city
Ps 51:12 . . . to me the **j** of your salvation,
Ps 65:8 . . . you inspire shouts of **j.**
Ps 65:13 . . . They all shout and sing for **j!**
Ps 71:23 . . . I will shout for **j** and sing
Ps 92:4 . . . I sing for **j** because of what
Ps 98:4 . . . in praise and sing for **j!**
Ps 105:43 . . . his people out of Egypt with **j,**
Ps 106:5 . . . Let me rejoice in the **j**
Ps 119:92 . . . hadn't sustained me with **j,**
Ps 126:2 . . . with laughter, and we sang for **j.**
Ps 132:9 . . . loyal servants sing for **j.**
Ps 132:16 . . . servants will sing for **j.**
Ps 145:7 . . . with **j** about your righteousness.
Prov 10:1 . . . A wise child brings **j**
Prov 11:10 . . . shout for **j** when the wicked die.
Prov 14:10 . . . no one else can fully share its **j.**
Prov 15:20 . . . Sensible children bring **j** to
Prov 21:15 . . . Justice is a **j** to the godly,
Prov 23:25 . . . your father and mother **j!**
Prov 29:6 . . . righteous escape, shouting for **j.**
Isa 12:6 . . . shout his praise with **j!**
Isa 16:9 . . . no more shouts of **j** over your
Isa 16:10 . . . gone the **j** of harvest.
Isa 26:19 . . . will rise up and sing for **j!**
Isa 35:10 . . . crowned with everlasting **j.**
Isa 42:11 . . . Let the people of Sela sing for **j;**
Isa 49:13 . . . Sing for **j,** O heavens!
Isa 51:11 . . . filled with **j** and gladness.
Isa 52:8 . . . watchmen shout and sing with **j,**
Isa 56:7 . . . fill them with **j** in my house
Isa 60:15 . . . beautiful forever, a **j** to all
Isa 61:7 . . . everlasting **j** will be yours.
Isa 65:14 . . . My servants will sing for **j,** but
Jer 31:13 . . . young women will dance for **j,**
Jer 31:13 . . . turn their mourning into **j.**
Jer 33:11 . . . the sounds of **j** and laughter.
Jer 48:33 . . . treads the grapes with shouts of **j.**
Jer 49:25 . . . a city of **j,** will be forsaken!
Joel 1:12 . . . And the people's **j** has dried up
Matt 2:10 . . . they were filled with **j!**
Matt 28:8 . . . but also filled with great **j,**
Mark 1:11 . . . Son, and you bring me great **j.**
Mark 4:16 . . . and immediately receive it with **j.**
Luke 1:14 . . . have great **j** and gladness,
Luke 1:44 . . . in my womb jumped for **j.**
Luke 2:10 . . . bring great **j** to all people.
Luke 6:23 . . . be happy! Yes, leap for **j!**
Luke 10:21 . . . with the **j** of the Holy Spirit,
Luke 24:41 . . . filled with **j** and wonder.
John 15:11 . . . you will be filled with my **j.**
John 16:20 . . . turn to wonderful **j.**
John 16:24 . . . and you will have abundant **j.**
John 20:20 . . . **j** when they saw the Lord!
Acts 2:28 . . . you will fill me with the **j**
Acts 2:46 . . . their meals with great **j**
Acts 11:23 . . . he was filled with **j,**
Acts 13:52 . . . believers were filled with **j**
Acts 15:3 . . . to everyone's **j**—that the Gentiles,
Rom 14:17 . . . and **j** in the Holy Spirit.
Rom 15:13 . . . with **j** and peace because
2 Cor 1:24 . . . so you will be full of **j,**
2 Cor 2:3 . . . ought to give me the greatest **j.**
2 Cor 2:3 . . . **j** comes from your being joyful.
2 Cor 6:10 . . . but we always have **j.**
2 Cor 7:7 . . . I was filled with **j!**
Gal 5:22 . . . fruit in our lives: love, **j,** peace,
Phil 1:4 . . . requests for all of you with **j,**
Phil 1:25 . . . experience the **j** of your faith.
Phil 4:1 . . . you are my **j** and the crown I
1 Thes 1:6 . . . received the message with **j**
1 Thes 2:19 . . . what gives us hope and **j,**
1 Thes 2:20 . . . Yes, you are our pride and **j.**
1 Thes 3:9 . . . we have great **j**
2 Tim 1:4 . . . with **j** when we are together
Heb 10:34 . . . you accepted it with **j.**
Heb 12:2 . . . Because of the **j** awaiting him,
Heb 13:17 . . . reason to do this with **j**
Jas 1:2 . . . it an opportunity for great **j.**
1 Pet 1:8 . . . a glorious, inexpressible **j.**
1 Pet 4:13 . . . the wonderful **j** of seeing his
1 Jn 1:4 . . . you may fully share our **j.**

JOYFUL (adj) characterized by gladness or delight
Ps 30:11 . . . my mourning into **j** dancing.
Ps 66:1 . . . Shout **j** praises to God, all the
Ps 98:6 . . . a **j** symphony before the LORD,
Ps 137:3 . . . insisted on a **j** hymn:
Rom 15:32 . . . come to you with a **j** heart,
Gal 4:15 . . . Where is that **j** and grateful spirit
Gal 4:27 . . . Break into a **j** shout, you who have
1 Thes 5:16 . . . Always be **j.**
Heb 12:22 . . . angels in a **j** gathering.

JOYOUS (adj) characterized by gladness or delight
2 Chr 29:30 . . . offered **j** praise and bowed
Neh 12:43 . . . were offered on that **j** day,
Isa 61:3 . . . for ashes, a **j** blessing instead
Jer 33:11 . . . along with the **j** songs of people

JUBILEE (n) a year of celebration, emancipation, and restoration
Lev 25:11 . . . fiftieth year will be a **j**

JUDAH 1. Fourth son of Jacob and Leah (Gen 29:35), who gave his name to a tribe of Israel; interceded for Joseph (Gen 37:26-27); failed to uphold daughter-in-law Tamar's rights (Gen 38:1-30); offered himself as slave and ransom (Gen 44:18-34); given the family birthright by Jacob (Gen 49:3-10); his tribe was numbered (Num 1:26-27), allotted land and cities (Josh 15:1-63), led the conquest of Canaan (Judg 1:2); 12,000 will be marked by God (Rev 7:7).
2. The southern kingdom of Judah, including the tribes of Judah and Benjamin, in contrast to Israel (northern kingdom) (*see* 2 Sam 12:8).

JUDAISM (n) the cultural, social, and religious beliefs and practices of the Jews
Acts 13:43 . . . devout converts to **J** followed Paul

JUDAS 1. One of the 12 disciples, also known as "Iscariot" (Mark 3:19; Luke 6:16); criticized Mary (John 12:3-6); foretold as betrayer (John 6:70-71; 13:21-30); made deal for 30 pieces of silver (Matt 26:14-15; *see also* Mark 14:10); identified as a thief (John 12:6); entered by Satan (Luke 22:3; John 13:27); betrayed Jesus with kiss (Mark 14:43-45); had remorse and committed suicide (Matt 27:3-10; Acts 1:18); his position refilled (Acts 1:20-26).
2. Brother of James and half-brother of Jesus, also known as "Jude" (Matt 13:55; Mark 6:3; Jude 1:1).
3. One of the 12 disciples, son of James, likely also called Thaddaeus (Matt 10:3; Mark 3:18), not Iscariot (John 14:22); *see also* Luke 6:16; Acts 1:13.

JUDEA (n) the Greco-Roman name for the land of Judah
Matt 2:1 . . . was born in Bethlehem in **J,**
Matt 24:16 . . . in **J** must flee to the hills.
Luke 3:1 . . . Pilate was governor over **J;**
Acts 1:8 . . . throughout **J,** in Samaria,
Acts 9:31 . . . had peace throughout **J,**
1 Thes 2:14 . . . in God's churches in **J**

JUDGE, JUDGES (n) a public official authorized to decide issues brought before a court; one of a cycle of charismatic deliverers of ancient Israel
Deut 17:12 . . . to reject the verdict of the **j**
Judg 2:16 . . . LORD raised up **j-s** to rescue
Judg 2:18 . . . the LORD raised up a **j**
1 Sam 7:6 . . . Samuel became Israel's **j.**)
1 Sam 7:15 . . . continued as Israel's **j**
Ps 50:6 . . . God himself will be the **j.**
Isa 33:22 . . . the LORD is our **j,** our lawgiver,
Acts 7:35 . . . you a ruler and **j** over us?
Acts 10:42 . . . **j** of all—the living and
Rev 14:7 . . . he will sit as **j.**

JUDGE, JUDGED, JUDGES, JUDGING (v) to form an evaluation of; to decide as a judge; to govern or rule; to punish or condemn; to form a negative opinion about
1 Sam 16:7 . . . Don't **j** by his appearance or
1 Sam 24:12 . . . the LORD **j** between us.
2 Chr 19:7 . . . **j** with integrity, for the LORD
Ps 7:8 . . . The LORD **j-s** the nations.
Ps 9:4 . . . For you have **j-d** in my favor;
Ps 9:8 . . . He will **j** the world
Ps 82:8 . . . Rise up, O God, and **j** the earth,
Ps 96:10 . . . He will **j** all peoples fairly.
Ps 96:13 . . . He will **j** the world with justice,
Prov 16:10 . . . he must never **j** unfairly.
Prov 29:14 . . . If a king **j-s** the poor fairly,
Isa 11:3 . . . He will not **j** by appearance
Isa 66:16 . . . He will **j** the earth,
Matt 7:1 . . . Do not **j** others, and you
Matt 16:27 . . . will **j** all people according
Matt 19:28 . . . thrones, **j-ing** the twelve
John 3:18 . . . been **j-d** for not believing
John 5:22 . . . the Father **j-s** no one.
John 5:22 . . . absolute authority to **j,**
John 5:27 . . . authority to **j** everyone
John 5:30 . . . I **j** as God tells me.
John 12:31 . . . time for **j-ing** this world
John 12:47 . . . not **j** those who hear me
Acts 17:31 . . . he has set a day for **j-ing**
Rom 2:16 . . . Jesus, will **j** everyone's secret
Rom 3:6 . . . be qualified to **j** the world?
1 Cor 6:2 . . . we believers will **j** the world?
1 Cor 11:31 . . . we would not be **j-d**
2 Cor 5:10 . . . stand before Christ to be **j-d.**
2 Tim 4:1 . . . Jesus, who will someday **j**
Heb 10:30 . . . The LORD will **j** his own
Heb 13:4 . . . **j** people who are immoral
Jas 2:13 . . . God will be merciful when he **j-s**
Jas 3:1 . . . we who teach will be **j-d** more
Jas 4:11 . . . criticizing and **j-ing** God's law.
Jas 4:12 . . . So what right do you have to **j**
1 Pet 1:17 . . . He will **j** or reward you
1 Pet 2:23 . . . God, who always **j-s** fairly.
Rev 19:11 . . . **j-s** fairly and wages a righteous
Rev 20:4 . . . given the authority to **j.**
Rev 20:12 . . . the dead were **j-d** according to

JUDGMENT, JUDGMENTS (n) a ruling or moral decision by a ruler (often God), a judge, or an individual; the process of forming an opinion or evalution by discerning and comparing
see also JUSTICE
Deut 1:17 . . . impartial in your **j-s.**
1 Sam 3:13 . . . warned him that **j** is coming
Ps 1:5 . . . be condemned at the time of **j.**
Ps 37:13 . . . he sees their day of **j** coming.
Ps 51:4 . . . your **j** against me is just.
Prov 4:1 . . . Pay attention and learn good **j,**
Prov 4:7 . . . else you do, develop good **j.**
Prov 9:10 . . . results in good **j.**
Isa 3:14 . . . comes forward to pronounce **j**
Jer 11:20 . . . you make righteous **j-s,**
Jer 25:31 . . . His cry of **j** will reach
Dan 9:11 . . . curses and **j-s** written in
Hos 6:5 . . . with **j-s** as inescapable as light.
Joel 3:12 . . . LORD, will sit to pronounce **j**
Matt 5:21 . . . murder, you are subject to **j.**
Matt 11:24 . . . will be better off on **j** day
Matt 12:36 . . . on **j** day for every idle word
Matt 12:41 . . . this generation on **j** day
John 5:30 . . . **j** is just, because I carry out
John 8:16 . . . if I did, my **j** would be correct
John 16:8 . . . and of the coming **j.**
Acts 24:25 . . . coming day of **j,**
1 Cor 4:3 . . . I don't even trust my own **j**
1 Cor 4:5 . . . don't make **j-s** about anyone
1 Cor 11:29 . . . eating and drinking God's **j**
2 Thes 1:8 . . . **j** on those who don't know
Heb 9:27 . . . and after that comes **j,**
1 Pet 4:17 . . . And if **j** begins with us,
2 Pet 2:9 . . . until the day of final **j.**
2 Pet 3:7 . . . being kept for the day of **j,**
Jude 1:6 . . . waiting for the great day of **j.**
Rev 16:7 . . . your **j-s** are true and just.

JUST (adj) conforming to a standard of correctness; faithful to the original design; honest, fair, upright
see also RIGHT, RIGHTEOUS
Gen 18:19 . . . by doing what is right and **j.**
Deut 32:4 . . . Everything he does is **j**
2 Sam 8:15 . . . did what was **j** and right
Neh 9:13 . . . and instructions that were **j,**
Job 37:23 . . . he is **j** and righteous,
Ps 33:5 . . . He loves whatever is **j** and good;
Ps 92:15 . . . The LORD is **j!** He is
Ps 119:121 . . . I have done what is **j**
Prov 1:3 . . . do what is right, **j,** and fair.
Prov 2:9 . . . will understand what is right, **j,**
Prov 12:5 . . . The plans of the godly are **j;**
Isa 16:5 . . . He will always do what is **j**
Isa 59:8 . . . or what it means to be **j**
Jer 22:3 . . . Be fair-minded and **j.**
Ezek 18:5 . . . and does what is **j** and right.
Dan 4:37 . . . All his acts are **j** and true,
Matt 5:45 . . . rain on the **j** and the unjust
1 Jn 1:9 . . . he is faithful and **j** to forgive
Rev 15:3 . . . **J** and true are your ways,
Rev 16:5 . . . You are **j,** O Holy One,
Rev 16:7 . . . your judgments are true and **j.**
Rev 19:2 . . . His judgments are true and **j.**

JUSTICE (n) the administration of law that determines what is right, based on principles of equity and correctness, and rewards accordingly; the quality of being just, impartial, or fair
see also JUDGMENT, RIGHTEOUSNESS
Exod 23:2 . . . by the crowd to twist **j.**
Lev 19:15 . . . Do not twist **j** in legal matters
Deut 16:19 . . . never twist **j**
Deut 32:36 . . . LORD will give **j** to his
1 Sam 8:3 . . . bribes and perverted **j.**
1 Kgs 3:11 . . . governing my people with **j**
1 Kgs 7:7 . . . Hall of **J,** where he sat to hear
2 Chr 9:8 . . . so you can rule with **j**
Job 8:3 . . . Does God twist **j?**
Job 19:7 . . . I protest, but there is no **j.**
Job 31:6 . . . weigh me on the scales of **j,**
Job 34:17 . . . God govern if he hated **j?**
Ps 9:8 . . . He will judge the world with **j**
Ps 10:18 . . . You will bring **j** to the orphans
Ps 36:6 . . . your **j** like the ocean depths.
Ps 45:4 . . . defending truth, humility, and **j.**
Ps 45:7 . . . You love **j** and hate evil.
Ps 72:1 . . . Give your love of **j** to the king,
Ps 82:3 . . . Give **j** to the poor
Ps 96:13 . . . He will judge the world with **j,**
Ps 98:9 . . . **j,** and the nations with fairness.
Ps 99:4 . . . You have acted with **j**
Ps 103:6 . . . **j** to all who are treated
Ps 146:7 . . . He gives **j** to the oppressed
Prov 16:12 . . . his rule is built on **j.**
Prov 19:28 . . . makes a mockery of **j;**
Prov 29:26 . . . but **j** comes from the LORD.
Prov 31:9 . . . and see that they get **j.**
Isa 1:17 . . . Seek **j.** Help the oppressed.
Isa 1:27 . . . Zion will be restored by **j;**
Isa 5:16 . . . will be exalted by his **j.**
Isa 10:2 . . . They deprive the poor of **j**
Isa 28:17 . . . with the measuring line of **j**
Isa 33:5 . . . make Jerusalem his home of **j**
Isa 42:1 . . . He will bring **j** to the nations.
Isa 51:4 . . . my **j** will become a light
Isa 59:9 . . . there is no **j** among us,
Isa 59:14 . . . **j** is nowhere to be found.
Isa 61:8 . . . I, the LORD, love **j.**
Jer 4:2 . . . you could do so with truth, **j,**
Jer 9:24 . . . who brings **j** and righteousness
Jer 21:12 . . . Give **j** each morning
Jer 30:11 . . . discipline you, but with **j;**
Lam 3:36 . . . if they twist **j** in the courts—
Hos 2:19 . . . righteousness and **j,**
Amos 5:7 . . . You twist **j,** making it a bitter
Amos 5:15 . . . courts into true halls of **j.**
Amos 6:12 . . . when you turn **j** into poison
Mic 3:8 . . . I am filled with **j** and strength
Hab 1:4 . . . there is no **j** in the courts.
Zeph 3:5 . . . Day by day he hands down **j,**
Mal 2:17 . . . Where is the God of **j?**
Matt 5:6 . . . who hunger and thirst for **j,**
Matt 12:18 . . . proclaim **j** to the nations.
Matt 23:23 . . . aspects of the law—**j,**
Luke 11:42 . . . ignore **j** and the love of God.
Luke 18:3 . . . Give me **j** in this dispute
Acts 8:33 . . . humiliated and received no **j.**
Acts 17:31 . . . **j** by the man
Rom 2:2 . . . God, in his **j,** will punish
2 Thes 1:5 . . . persecution to show his **j**
2 Thes 1:6 . . . In his **j** he will pay back
Heb 1:8 . . . You rule with a scepter of **j.**
Heb 7:2 . . . Melchizedek means "king of **j,**"
Heb 11:33 . . . ruled with **j,**

JUSTIFY, JUSTIFIED (v) to prove to be just, right, or reasonable; to acquit or absolve
see also RIGHT, RIGHTEOUS
Luke 10:29 . . . wanted to **j** his actions,
Luke 18:14 . . . returned home **j-ied**
2 Cor 8:24 . . . boasting about you is **j-ied.**

K

KEEP, KEEPING, KEEPS, KEPT (v) to be faithful to; to have in control; to refrain from granting, giving, or allowing; to cause to remain in a given place, situation, or condition; to refrain from revealing; to maintain or preserve
see also GUARD, OBEY, PROTECT
Exod 12:42 . . . the LORD **k-pt** his promise
Exod 20:8 . . . Sabbath day by **k-ing** it holy.
Exod 31:13 . . . Be careful to **k** my Sabbath
Deut 5:12 . . . Sabbath day by **k-ing** it holy,
Deut 7:8 . . . **k-ing** the oath he had sworn
Deut 7:9 . . . God who **k-s** his covenant for a
Deut 7:12 . . . your God will **k** his covenant
2 Chr 6:14 . . . You **k** your covenant
2 Chr 34:31 . . . to obey the LORD by **k-ing**
Neh 1:5 . . . God who **k-s** his covenant of
Ps 15:4 . . . **k** their promises even when
Ps 116:14 . . . I will **k** my promises to
Ps 119:100 . . . **k-pt** your commandments.
Ps 121:7 . . . The LORD **k-s** you from
Ps 130:3 . . . LORD, if you **k-pt** a record of
Ps 146:6 . . . He **k-s** every promise
Prov 10:19 . . . and **k** your mouth
Prov 15:3 . . . **k-ing** his eye on
Prov 21:23 . . . your tongue and **k**
Eccl 3:6 . . . A time to **k** and a time to
John 17:6 . . . and they have **k-pt** your word.
Acts 2:24 . . . death could not **k** him in its
Rom 10:3 . . . by trying to **k** the law.
Rom 14:22 . . . **k** it between yourself
1 Cor 1:8 . . . He will **k** you strong
1 Cor 7:19 . . . **k** God's commandments.
1 Cor 13:5 . . . it **k-s** no record
Eph 4:3 . . . effort to **k** yourselves united
1 Tim 5:22 . . . **K** yourself pure.
2 Tim 4:5 . . . But you should **k** a clear mind
Heb 11:27 . . . going because he **k-pt** his eyes
Jas 2:10 . . . the person who **k-s** all of the
1 Pet 1:4 . . . **k-pt** in heaven for you, pure and
1 Jn 5:3 . . . means **k-ing** his commandments,
Jude 1:21 . . . **k** yourselves safe in God's love.
Rev 12:17 . . . **k** God's commandments

KEY, KEYS (n) instrument that opens (or locks) doors or gates; symbolic of authority, power, and control
Matt 16:19 . . . the **k-s** of the Kingdom
Rev 1:18 . . . And I hold the **k-s** of death and
Rev 20:1 . . . with the **k** to the bottomless

KILL, KILLED, KILLING, KILLS (v) to take or deprive of life
Gen 4:8 . . . Abel, and **k-ed** him.
Exod 2:12 . . . Moses **k-ed** the Egyptian
Exod 21:12 . . . assaults and **k-s** another
Lev 24:21 . . . whoever **k-s** another person
2 Sam 2:26 . . . always be **k-ing** each other?
Neh 9:26 . . . they **k-ed** your prophets
Job 13:15 . . . God might **k** me, but I
Ps 44:22 . . . for your sake we are **k-ed**
Prov 6:17 . . . hands that **k** the innocent,
Eccl 3:3 . . . A time to **k** and a time to
Matt 10:28 . . . who want to **k** your body;
Matt 16:21 . . . He would be **k-ed,**
Mark 10:34 . . . flog him with a whip, and **k**
Luke 11:48 . . . They **k-ed** the prophets,
Acts 3:15 . . . You **k-ed** the author
Rom 8:36 . . . For your sake we are **k-ed**
1 Tim 1:9 . . . who **k** their father or mother
1 Jn 3:12 . . . evil one and **k-ed** his brother.

KIND (adj) affectionate, loving; of a sympathetic or helping nature; gentle
Luke 6:35 . . . for he is **k** to those who are
1 Cor 13:4 . . . is patient and **k.** Love is not
Eph 4:32 . . . Instead, be **k** to each other,
2 Tim 2:24 . . . but must be **k** to everyone,

KIND, KINDS (n) nature, family, type, or category
Gen 1:12 . . . and trees of the same **k.**

1 Cor 12:4 . . . different **k-s** of spiritual gifts,
1 Tim 6:10 . . . root of all **k-s** of evil.

KINDNESS (n) a kind deed; affection; the quality or state of being kind
Ps 106:7 . . . his many acts of **k** to them.
Rom 2:4 . . . his **k** is intended to turn you
Rom 3:24 . . . with undeserved **k,** declares
Rom 12:8 . . . gift for showing **k** to others,
2 Cor 6:1 . . . marvelous gift of God's **k**
2 Cor 8:1 . . . God in his **k** has done through
2 Cor 10:1 . . . gentleness and **k** of Christ—
Gal 5:22 . . . peace, patience, **k,** goodness,
Eph 2:7 . . . his grace and **k** toward us,
Col 3:12 . . . mercy, **k,** humility,
Titus 3:4 . . . revealed his **k** and love,
1 Pet 2:3 . . . a taste of the Lord's **k.**

KING, KINGS (n) a sovereign ruler (often God); chief among competitors
Deut 17:14 . . . We should select a **k** to rule
Judg 17:6 . . . In those days Israel had no **k;**
1 Sam 8:5 . . . Give us a **k** to judge us
1 Sam 11:15 . . . they made Saul **k.**
2 Sam 2:4 . . . and anointed him **k** over the
2 Kgs 19:15 . . . of all the **k-s** of the earth.
Ps 44:4 . . . You are my **K** and my God.
Ps 68:32 . . . to God, you **k-s** of the earth.
Ps 72:11 . . . All **k-s** will bow
Ps 97:1 . . . The LORD is **k!**
Isa 32:1 . . . a righteous **k** is coming!
Isa 37:16 . . . of all the **k-s** of the earth.
Dan 2:21 . . . he removes **k-s** and sets
Dan 4:17 . . . the Most High rules over the **k-s**
Dan 4:37 . . . and honor the **K** of heaven.
Dan 7:24 . . . Its ten horns are ten **k-s**
Zeph 3:8 . . . to gather the **k-s** of the earth
Zech 9:9 . . . Look, your **k** is coming to you.
Matt 27:11 . . . Are you the **k** of the Jews?
John 1:49 . . . Son of God—the **K** of Israel!
John 12:13 . . . Hail to the **K** of Israel!
Acts 17:7 . . . to another **k,** named Jesus.
1 Tim 1:17 . . . is the eternal **K,** the unseen
1 Tim 6:15 . . . the **K** of all **k-s** and
1 Pet 2:13 . . . the **k** as head of state,
Rev 1:5 . . . of all the **k-s** of the world.
Rev 17:14 . . . all lords and **K** of all **k-s.**
Rev 19:16 . . . **K** of all **k-s** and Lord

KINGDOM (n) rule or realm; dominion of a king
Exod 19:6 . . . will be my **k** of priests,
1 Kgs 11:31 . . . to tear the **k** from the hand
1 Chr 28:7 . . . make his **k** last forever.
Ps 145:11 . . . glory of your **k;**
Matt 3:2 . . . for the **K** of Heaven is near.
Matt 4:23 . . . Good News about the **K.**
Matt 5:10 . . . right, for the **K** of Heaven is
Matt 5:19 . . . great in the **K** of Heaven.
Matt 6:10 . . . May your **K** come soon.
Matt 7:21 . . . will enter the **K** of Heaven.
Matt 8:12 . . . for whom the **K** was prepared—
Matt 10:7 . . . them that the **K** of Heaven is
Matt 11:12 . . . until now, the **K** of Heaven
Matt 12:26 . . . His own **k** will not
Matt 13:11 . . . secrets of the **K** of Heaven,
Matt 13:38 . . . represents the people of the **K.**
Matt 13:43 . . . their Father's **K.** Anyone with
Matt 13:45 . . . Again, the **K** of Heaven is
Matt 13:52 . . . a disciple in the **K** of Heaven
Matt 16:28 . . . Son of Man coming in his **K.**
Matt 18:4 . . . greatest in the **K** of Heaven.
Matt 19:12 . . . sake of the **K** of Heaven.
Matt 19:23 . . . to enter the **K** of Heaven.
Matt 20:1 . . . For the **K** of Heaven is
Matt 21:43 . . . I tell you, the **K** of God will
Matt 23:13 . . . shut the door of the **K** of Heaven
Matt 24:14 . . . Good News about the **K** will be
Matt 25:34 . . . inherit the **K** prepared for
Mark 3:24 . . . A **k** divided by
Mark 4:11 . . . secret of the **K** of God.
Mark 4:30 . . . I describe the **K** of God?
Mark 9:1 . . . they see the **K** of God arrive
Mark 10:15 . . . doesn't receive the **K** of God
Mark 10:24 . . . to enter the **K** of God.
Mark 11:10 . . . on the coming **K** of our
Mark 13:8 . . . and **k** against **k.**
Mark 15:43 . . . waiting for the **K** of God to
Luke 4:43 . . . Good News of the **K** of God in
Luke 7:28 . . . least person in the **K** of God
Luke 8:10 . . . secrets of the **K** of God.
Luke 9:11 . . . taught them about the **K** of God,
Luke 9:60 . . . preach about the **K** of God.
Luke 10:9 . . . tell them, 'The **K** of God is
Luke 10:11 . . . know this—the **K** of God is
Luke 11:17 . . . he said, "Any **k** divided
Luke 11:20 . . . the **K** of God has arrived
Luke 12:31 . . . Seek the **K** of God
Luke 13:18 . . . What is the **K** of God like?
Luke 14:15 . . . a banquet in the **K** of God!
Luke 17:20 . . . When will the **K** of God
Luke 17:21 . . . For the **K** of God is
Luke 18:24 . . . to enter the **K** of God!
Luke 18:29 . . . for the sake of the **K** of God,
Luke 21:10 . . . and **k** against **k.**
Luke 22:16 . . . fulfilled in the **K** of God.
Luke 22:29 . . . granted me a **K,** I now grant
Luke 23:42 . . . come into your **K.**
John 3:3 . . . you cannot see the **K** of God.
John 3:5 . . . no one can enter the **K** of God
John 18:36 . . . But my **K** is not of
Acts 1:3 . . . talked to them about the **K** of God.
Acts 1:6 . . . restore our **k?**
Acts 8:12 . . . News concerning the **K** of God
Acts 19:8 . . . about the **K** of God.
Acts 28:23 . . . testified about the **K** of God
Rom 14:17 . . . For the **K** of God is
1 Cor 4:20 . . . For the **K** of God is
1 Cor 6:10 . . . will inherit the **K** of God.
1 Cor 15:24 . . . will turn the **K** over to God
1 Cor 15:50 . . . cannot inherit the **K** of God.
Gal 5:21 . . . will not inherit the **K** of God.
Eph 5:5 . . . will inherit the **K** of Christ
Col 4:11 . . . with me here for the **K** of God.
1 Thes 2:12 . . . to share in his **K** and glory.
2 Thes 1:5 . . . worthy of his **K,** for which
2 Tim 4:18 . . . his heavenly **K.** All glory to
Heb 12:28 . . . we are receiving a **K** that is
Jas 2:5 . . . inherit the **K** he promised to
2 Pet 1:11 . . . into the eternal **K** of our
Rev 1:6 . . . made us a **K** of priests for
Rev 5:10 . . . to become a **K** of priests for
Rev 11:15 . . . now become the **K** of our Lord
Rev 12:10 . . . power and the **K** of our God,
Rev 16:10 . . . his **k** was plunged into darkness.

KINSMAN-REDEEMER (KJV)
Ruth 3:9 . . . my *family redeemer*
Ruth 3:12 . . . of your *family redeemers*
Ruth 4:1 . . . the *family redeemer* he had

KISS, KISSES (n) a greeting or caress with the lips; an expression of affection
Prov 27:6 . . . better than many **k-es** from an
Song 7:9 . . . May your **k-es** be as
Mark 14:45 . . . and gave him the **k.**
Luke 22:48 . . . the Son of Man with a **k?**

KISS, KISSING (v) to caress with the lips
Song 1:2 . . . **K** me and **k** me again,
Song 8:1 . . . Then I could **k** you no matter
Luke 7:38 . . . Then she kept **k-ing** his feet and

KNEE, KNEES (n) the joint in the middle part of the leg; when bent, symbolic of submission or defeat
Isa 35:3 . . . those who have weak **k-s.**
Isa 45:23 . . . Every **k** will bend to me,
Luke 5:8 . . . he fell to his **k-s** before Jesus
Rom 14:11 . . . every **k** will bend to me,
Eph 3:14 . . . I fall to my **k-s** and pray to
Phil 2:10 . . . at the name of Jesus every **k**
Heb 12:12 . . . strengthen your weak **k-s.**

KNEEL, KNELT (v) to bend the knee; to fall or rest on the knees; usually a gesture of submission, defeat, or reverence
2 Chr 6:13 . . . then he **k-lt** in front of
Ps 95:6 . . . Let us **k** before the LORD
Dan 6:10 . . . went home and **k-lt** down
Matt 8:2 . . . approached him and **k-lt**
Matt 9:18 . . . came and **k-lt** before him.
Matt 17:14 . . . came and **k-lt** before Jesus
Matt 27:29 . . . **k-lt** before him in mockery
Luke 22:41 . . . stone's throw, and **k-lt** down
Acts 20:36 . . . speaking, he **k-lt** and prayed
Acts 21:5 . . . There we **k-lt,** prayed,

KNEW (v) *see also* KNOW
Matt 7:23 . . . reply, 'I never **k** you.
John 2:24 . . . because he **k** human nature.
John 19:28 . . . Jesus **k** that his mission
Acts 2:23 . . . But God **k** what would
Rom 1:21 . . . Yes, they **k** God,
Rom 8:29 . . . God **k** his people in advance,
1 Pet 1:2 . . . God the Father **k** you and

KNIT (v) to link firmly or closely
Ps 139:13 . . . **k** me together in my mother's womb
Col 2:2 . . . encouraged and **k** together by

KNOCK, KNOCKING, KNOCKS (v) to strike sharply
Matt 7:7 . . . Keep on **k-ing,** and the door
Matt 7:8 . . . to everyone who **k-s,** the door
Luke 11:9 . . . Keep on **k-ing,** and the door
Rev 3:20 . . . I stand at the door and **k.**

KNOW, KNOWING, KNOWN, KNOWS (v) to be intimately familiar with; to discern, recognize, regard, acknowledge, pay heed to, approve, learn
see also KNEW
Gen 3:5 . . . be like God, **k-ing** both good
Gen 3:22 . . . become like us, **k-ing** both good
Gen 22:12 . . . for now I **k** that you truly
Exod 6:7 . . . Then you will **k** that I am the
Deut 18:21 . . . How will we **k** whether or not
Deut 29:29 . . . God has secrets **k-n** to no
Josh 23:14 . . . Deep in your hearts you **k**
Job 19:25 . . . for me, I **k** that my Redeemer
Ps 9:10 . . . Those who **k** your name trust
Ps 19:2 . . . after night they make him **k-n.**
Ps 44:21 . . . for he **k-s** the secrets of
Ps 46:10 . . . Be still, and **k** that I am
Ps 94:10 . . . doesn't he also **k** what you
Ps 94:11 . . . The LORD **k-s** people's thoughts;
Ps 103:14 . . . For he **k-s** how weak we are;
Ps 119:168 . . . you **k** everything I do.
Ps 139:2 . . . You **k** when I sit
Ps 139:23 . . . O God, and **k** my heart;
Isa 12:4 . . . Let them **k** how mighty
Jer 9:24 . . . that they truly **k** me and
Jer 31:34 . . . will **k** me already,

Dan 11:32 . . . the people who **k** their God
Matt 6:3 . . . don't let your left hand **k** what
Matt 10:29 . . . without your Father **k-ing** it.
Matt 11:27 . . . no one truly **k-s** the Father
Mark 12:24 . . . you don't **k** the Scriptures,
Luke 11:13 . . . if you sinful people **k** how to
Luke 13:25 . . . will reply, 'I don't **k** you
Luke 16:15 . . . but God **k-s** your hearts.
Luke 23:34 . . . they don't **k** what they are
John 3:11 . . . you what we **k** and have seen,
John 4:42 . . . Now we **k** that he
John 6:69 . . . we **k** you are the Holy One
John 7:28 . . . Yes, you **k** me, and you
John 8:14 . . . For I **k** where I came
John 8:32 . . . And you will **k** the truth,
John 10:4 . . . because they **k** his voice.
John 10:27 . . . I **k** them, and they follow
John 13:17 . . . Now that you **k** these things,
John 14:7 . . . If you had really **k-n** me,
John 16:30 . . . we understand that you **k**
John 17:23 . . . the world will **k** that you sent
John 21:15 . . . Peter replied, "you **k** I love
Acts 1:24 . . . O Lord, you **k** every heart.
Rom 1:19 . . . They **k** the truth
Rom 7:18 . . . And I **k** that nothing good
Rom 8:26 . . . we don't **k** what God wants us
Rom 8:27 . . . the Father who **k-s** all hearts
Rom 11:34 . . . For who can **k** the LORD's
Rom 12:16 . . . And don't think you **k** it all!
Rom 16:26 . . . message is made **k-n** to all
1 Cor 2:11 . . . no one can **k** God's thoughts
1 Cor 13:12 . . . All that I **k** now is partial
2 Cor 4:6 . . . so we could **k** the glory of
Gal 4:9 . . . now that you **k** God (or should
Phil 3:10 . . . I want to **k** Christ and
Col 1:10 . . . you learn to **k** God better and
1 Thes 3:3 . . . But you **k** that we
1 Thes 5:2 . . . For you **k** quite well
2 Thes 1:8 . . . on those who don't **k** God
1 Tim 1:7 . . . but they don't **k** what they
1 Tim 3:15 . . . you will **k** how people must
2 Tim 1:12 . . . I **k** the one in whom I trust,
2 Tim 2:19 . . . The LORD **k-s** those who are
Heb 8:11 . . . greatest, will **k** me already.
Heb 11:8 . . . He went without **k-ing** where he
Jas 1:3 . . . For you **k** that when your faith
Jas 4:14 . . . How do you **k** what your life
Jas 4:17 . . . it is sin to **k** what you ought
1 Pet 2:19 . . . do what you **k** is right and
2 Pet 2:21 . . . they had never **k-n** the way to
1 Jn 2:3 . . . we can be sure that we **k** him
1 Jn 2:4 . . . claims, "I **k** God," but
1 Jn 2:5 . . . is how we **k** we are living in
1 Jn 2:11 . . . person does not **k** the way to
1 Jn 2:29 . . . Since we **k** that Christ
1 Jn 3:1 . . . they don't **k** him.
1 Jn 3:2 . . . But we do **k** that we will be
1 Jn 3:24 . . . And we **k** he lives in us
1 Jn 4:6 . . . is how we **k** if someone has
1 Jn 4:7 . . . is a child of God and **k-s** God.
1 Jn 4:8 . . . does not **k** God, for God
1 Jn 5:13 . . . that you may **k** you have eternal
1 Jn 5:15 . . . And since we **k** he hears us
1 Jn 5:20 . . . And we **k** that the Son of
Rev 3:15 . . . I **k** all the things you do,

KNOWLEDGE (n) the fact or condition of being aware of something, of having information, or of being learned; information, wisdom
Gen 2:9 . . . the tree of the **k** of good and
Gen 2:17 . . . the tree of the **k** of good and
Prov 1:7 . . . foundation of true **k**, but fools
Prov 2:6 . . . From his mouth come **k** and
Prov 3:20 . . . By his **k** the deep
Prov 8:10 . . . **k** rather than pure gold.
Prov 14:6 . . . **k** comes easily to those with
Prov 18:15 . . . Their ears are open for **k**.
Isa 11:2 . . . the Spirit of **k** and the fear
Luke 11:52 . . . the key to **k**
Rom 2:20 . . . gives you complete **k**
1 Cor 12:8 . . . gives a message of special **k**.
1 Cor 13:2 . . . and possessed all **k**,
1 Cor 13:9 . . . Now our **k** is partial
2 Cor 2:14 . . . to spread the **k** of Christ
Eph 1:17 . . . grow in your **k** of God.
Eph 4:13 . . . our faith and **k** of God's Son
Phil 1:9 . . . will keep on growing in **k** and
Col 1:9 . . . to give you complete **k** of his
Col 2:3 . . . treasures of wisdom and **k**.
Heb 10:26 . . . we have received **k** of the
2 Pet 1:5 . . . and moral excellence with **k**,
2 Pet 1:8 . . . **k** of our Lord Jesus Christ.
2 Pet 3:18 . . . the grace and **k** of our Lord

L

LABOR (adj) of or relating to manual labor; of or relating to the physical activities of giving birth
1 Kgs 12:4 . . . Lighten the harsh **l** demands
Gal 4:19 . . . I'm going through **l** pains for

LABOR (n) work that produces goods and services; the physical activities of giving birth
Ps 128:2 . . . enjoy the fruit of your **l**.
Isa 54:1 . . . you who have never been in **l**.
Gal 4:27 . . . have never been in **l**!

LACK (n) the fact or state of being wanting or deficient; absence
Prov 5:23 . . . die for **l** of self-control;
Prov 15:22 . . . go wrong for **l** of advice;
1 Cor 7:5 . . . because of your **l** of self-control.

LACK, LACKED, LACKING (v) to be deficient, missing, or short; to have need of something
Deut 2:7 . . . and you have **l-ed** nothing.
Deut 28:48 . . . naked, and **l-ing** in everything.
Neh 9:21 . . . and they **l-ed** nothing.
Prov 28:27 . . . the poor will **l** nothing,

LAID (v) *see also* LAY
Isa 53:6 . . . Yet the LORD **l** on him the
Acts 6:6 . . . as they **l** their hands on them.
Acts 8:18 . . . the apostles **l** their hands on
1 Tim 4:14 . . . elders of the church **l** their
2 Tim 1:6 . . . when I **l** my hands on

LAKE (n) a considerable inland body of standing water
Matt 8:24 . . . a fierce storm struck the **l**,
Luke 8:33 . . . into the **l** and drowned.
John 6:25 . . . on the other side of the **l**
Rev 19:20 . . . into the fiery **l** of burning
Rev 20:14 . . . This **l** of fire is

LAKESHORE (n) the land bordering a lake
Mark 4:1 . . . Jesus began teaching by the **l**.

LAMB, LAMBS (n) a young sheep that is less than one year old
Exod 12:21 . . . pick out a **l** or young goat
Isa 53:7 . . . He was led like a **l** to the
Mark 14:12 . . . the Passover **l** is sacrificed,
Luke 10:3 . . . out as **l-s** among wolves.
John 1:29 . . . and said, "Look! The **L** of God
John 21:15 . . . "Then feed my **l-s**," Jesus
Acts 8:32 . . . And as a **l** is silent before
1 Pet 1:19 . . . sinless, spotless **L** of God.
Rev 5:6 . . . Then I saw a **L** that looked as
Rev 5:12 . . . Worthy is the **L** who was
Rev 7:14 . . . robes in the blood of the **L**
Rev 15:3 . . . the song of the **L**:
Rev 17:14 . . . to war against the **L**, but the
Rev 19:9 . . . to the wedding feast of the **L**.
Rev 21:23 . . . and the **L** is its light.

LAME (adj) having a disabled body part as to impair freedom of movement
Isa 33:23 . . . Even the **l** will take
Isa 35:6 . . . The **l** will leap like a
Matt 11:5 . . . blind see, the **l** walk,
Matt 15:31 . . . the **l** were walking,
Luke 14:21 . . . the blind, and the **l**.
Heb 12:13 . . . weak and **l** will not fall

LAMP, LAMPS (n) a source of intellectual or spiritual illumination; any of various devices for producing light
2 Sam 22:29 . . . O LORD, you are my **l**.
Ps 18:28 . . . You light a **l** for me.
Ps 119:105 . . . Your word is a **l** to guide my
Prov 6:23 . . . For their command is a **l**
Prov 31:18 . . . her **l** burns late
Matt 6:22 . . . Your eye is a **l** that
Matt 25:1 . . . who took their **l-s**
Matt 25:7 . . . got up and prepared their **l-s**.
Luke 8:16 . . . No one lights a **l** and then
Luke 12:35 . . . and keep your **l-s** burning,
Rev 22:5 . . . no need for **l-s** or sun—for the

LAMPSTAND, LAMPSTANDS (n) a support that holds a lamp
Exod 25:31 . . . Make the entire **l** and its
2 Chr 4:7 . . . cast ten gold **l-s** according to
Zech 4:2 . . . a solid gold **l** with a bowl of
Zech 4:11 . . . on each side of the **l**,
Heb 9:2 . . . In the first room were a **l**,
Rev 1:12 . . . I saw seven gold **l-s**.
Rev 1:20 . . . the seven gold **l-s**:
Rev 2:5 . . . and remove your **l** from its

LAND (n) the solid part of the surface of the earth; a portion of the earth's solid surface distinguishable by boundaries or ownership
Gen 1:10 . . . the dry ground "**l**" and the
Gen 15:18 . . . I have given this **l** to your
Exod 6:8 . . . you into the **l** I swore to
Deut 8:7 . . . you into a good **l** of flowing
Ps 37:11 . . . will possess the **l** and will

LANGUAGE, LANGUAGES (n) audible, meaningful sound; dialect or manner of speech peculiar to a certain people; a special language gift given by the Holy Spirit
see also TONGUE(S)
Gen 11:9 . . . the people with different **l-s**.
Isa 28:11 . . . speak a strange **l**!
Mark 16:17 . . . they will speak in new **l-s**.
Acts 2:4 . . . speaking in other **l-s**, as the
1 Cor 12:28 . . . speak in unknown **l-s**.
1 Cor 12:30 . . . to interpret unknown **l-s**?
1 Cor 13:8 . . . in unknown **l-s** and special
1 Cor 14:19 . . . in an unknown **l**.
Eph 4:29 . . . or abusive **l**. Let everything
Col 3:8 . . . slander, and dirty **l**.
Rev 5:9 . . . every tribe and **l** and people
Rev 7:9 . . . and tribe and people and **l**,
Rev 14:6 . . . nation, tribe, **l**, and people.

LAP (v) to take in food or drink with the tongue
Judg 7:5 . . . and **l** it up with their tongues

LASCIVIOUSNESS (KJV)
Mark 7:22 . . . deceit, *lustful desires*, envy,
2 Cor 12:21 . . . and *eagerness for lustful pleasure*

Gal 5:19 . . . impurity, *lustful pleasures*
Eph 4:19 . . . They live for *lustful pleasure*
1 Pet 4:3 . . . their *immorality* and lust,

LAST, LASTING (adj) following all the rest; being the only remaining; belonging to the final stage; of or relating to being continuous in time; existing or continuing a long while
Prov 10:25 . . . have a **l-ing** foundation.
Isa 41:4 . . . First and the **L.** I alone
Isa 44:6 . . . First and the **L;** there is no
Isa 48:12 . . . God, the First and the **L.**
John 15:16 . . . to go and produce **l-ing** fruit,
Acts 2:17 . . . 'In the **l** days,' God says,
1 Cor 15:26 . . . And the **l** enemy to be
1 Cor 15:52 . . . **l** trumpet is blown.
2 Tim 3:1 . . . that in the **l** days there will
2 Pet 3:3 . . . that in the **l** days scoffers
Jude 1:18 . . . you that in the **l** times there
Rev 1:17 . . . I am the First and the **L.**
Rev 22:13 . . . the Omega, the First and the **L,**

LASTS (v) to continue in time
Ps 30:5 . . . For his anger **l** only a moment,

LAUGH, LAUGHED, LAUGHS (v) to show mirth or joy or to despise or mock something with a chuckle or explosive vocal sound
Gen 17:17 . . . **l-ed** to himself in disbelief.
Gen 18:12 . . . So she **l-ed** silently to herself
Ps 2:4 . . . the one who rules in heaven **l-s.**
Ps 37:13 . . . the LORD just **l-s,** for he sees
Ps 59:8 . . . But LORD, you **l** at them.
Prov 31:25 . . . and she **l-s** without fear of
Eccl 3:4 . . . and a time to **l.** A time to
Luke 6:21 . . . for in due time you will **l.**
Luke 6:25 . . . awaits you who **l** now,

LAUGHTER (n) a chuckle or explosive vocal sound; cause for merriment
Gen 21:6 . . . God has brought me **l.**
Ps 126:2 . . . We were filled with **l,** and we
Eccl 2:2 . . . So I said, "**L** is silly.
Jer 7:34 . . . happy singing and **l** in the
Jas 4:9 . . . instead of **l,** and gloom

LAVER(S) (KJV)
Exod 30:18 . . . Make a bronze *washbasin*
Lev 8:11 . . . *washbasin* and its stand,
1 Kgs 7:38 . . . ten smaller bronze *basins*
2 Chr 4:14 . . . carts holding the *basins*

LAVISH (v) to expend or bestow with profusion
Exod 34:7 . . . I **l** unfailing love

LAW, LAWS (n) words of Moses; a binding decree; a universal principle; governing authority
see also COMMANDMENT(S), INSTRUCTION(S), REGULATIONS, TEACHING(S)
2 Chr 17:9 . . . the Book of the **L**
Ps 1:2 . . . delight in the **l** of the LORD,
Ps 93:5 . . . Your royal **l-s** cannot be
Ps 119:14 . . . rejoiced in your **l-s** as much as
Ps 119:36 . . . for your **l-s** rather than a love
Ps 119:125 . . . I will understand your **l-s.**
Ps 119:152 . . . days that your **l-s** will last
Matt 5:17 . . . to abolish the **l** of Moses or
Matt 5:19 . . . who obeys God's **l-s**
Matt 22:40 . . . The entire **l** and all the
Matt 23:23 . . . of the **l**—justice, mercy,
Mark 7:8 . . . ignore God's **l** and substitute
Luke 11:52 . . . experts in religious **l!**
Luke 23:56 . . . rested as required by the **l.**
Luke 24:44 . . . written about me in the **l**
John 1:17 . . . For the **l** was given
Rom 2:12 . . . be judged by that **l** when they
Rom 2:15 . . . that God's **l** is written in
Rom 2:20 . . . that God's **l** gives you
Rom 2:25 . . . if you don't obey God's **l,**
Rom 3:19 . . . Obviously, the **l** applies to
Rom 3:21 . . . requirements of the **l,** as was
Rom 3:28 . . . not by obeying the **l.**
Rom 4:13 . . . his obedience to God's **l,**
Rom 4:16 . . . according to the **l** of Moses,
Rom 5:13 . . . was not yet any **l** to break.
Rom 6:15 . . . has set us free from the **l,**
Rom 7:4 . . . power of the **l** when you died
Rom 7:5 . . . the **l** aroused these evil desires
Rom 7:8 . . . If there were no **l,** sin would
Rom 7:12 . . . But still, the **l** itself is
Rom 7:22 . . . I love God's **l** with all my
Rom 7:25 . . . I really want to obey God's **l,**
Rom 8:3 . . . did what the **l** could not do.
Rom 8:4 . . . requirement of the **l** would be
Rom 8:7 . . . did obey God's **l-s,** and it
Rom 9:4 . . . gave them his **l.** He gave them
Rom 9:31 . . . with God by keeping the **l,**
Rom 10:4 . . . for which the **l** was given.
Rom 13:10 . . . requirements of God's **l.**
1 Cor 9:9 . . . For the **l** of Moses
1 Cor 9:21 . . . I obey the **l** of Christ.
2 Cor 3:6 . . . not of written **l-s,** but of the
Gal 2:16 . . . by obeying the **l.** And we have
Gal 2:19 . . . So I died to the **l**—I stopped
Gal 3:2 . . . by obeying the **l** of Moses?
Gal 3:5 . . . because you obey the **l?**
Gal 3:11 . . . by trying to keep the **l.**
Gal 3:19 . . . But the **l** was designed
Gal 3:21 . . . If the **l** could give us
Gal 3:23 . . . placed under guard by the **l.**
Gal 4:21 . . . live under the **l,** do you know
Gal 5:3 . . . in the whole **l** of Moses.
Gal 5:14 . . . the whole **l** can be summed
Gal 6:2 . . . this way obey the **l** of Christ.
Eph 2:15 . . . the system of **l** with its
Phil 3:6 . . . I obeyed the **l** without fault.
1 Tim 1:8 . . . know that the **l** is good when
Heb 10:1 . . . under the **l** of Moses
Jas 1:25 . . . into the perfect **l** that sets
Jas 2:8 . . . obey the royal **l** as found in
Jas 2:10 . . . all of the **l-s** except one is as

LAWGIVER (n) one who gives a code of laws to a people
Isa 33:22 . . . is our judge, our **l,** and our

LAWLESS (adj) not regulated by law; not restrained or controlled by law; unruly
Acts 2:23 . . . the help of **l** Gentiles,
Heb 10:17 . . . their sins and **l** deeds.

LAWLESSNESS (n) the quality or state of not being restrained or controlled by law
2 Thes 2:3 . . . the man of **l** is revealed—
2 Thes 2:7 . . . For this **l** is already
2 Thes 2:8 . . . Then the man of **l** will be

LAWSUITS (n) an act or instance of suing
1 Cor 6:7 . . . Even to have such **l** with one

LAY, LAYING (v) to put or set down
see also LAID
Exod 29:10 . . . his sons will **l** their hands
Lev 1:4 . . . **L** your hand on
Lev 4:15 . . . must then **l** their hands on
Num 8:10 . . . of Israel must **l** their hands
Num 27:18 . . . in him, and **l** your hands on
Acts 8:19 . . . so that when I **l** my hands on
Heb 6:2 . . . the **l-ing** on of hands,
Rev 4:10 . . . And they **l** their crowns

LAZINESS (n) a disinclination to activity or exertion
Prov 31:27 . . . suffers nothing from **l.**
Ezek 16:49 . . . gluttony, and **l,** while the

LAZY (adj) disinclined to activity or exertion; not energetic or vigorous
Prov 12:27 . . . **L** people don't
Prov 20:4 . . . Those too **l** to plow in the
Rom 12:11 . . . Never be **l,** but work
1 Tim 5:13 . . . they will learn to be **l**
Titus 1:12 . . . animals, and **l** gluttons.

LAZYBONES (n) a lazy person
Prov 6:6 . . . from the ants, you **l.**

LEAD, LEADING, LEADS (v) to guide by direction or example; to go at the head of; to result in
see also LED
Deut 27:18 . . . anyone who **l-s** a blind
Deut 31:2 . . . no longer able to **l** you.
Josh 1:6 . . . one who will **l** these people
2 Chr 1:10 . . . knowledge to **l** them
Ps 25:9 . . . He **l-s** the humble in
Ps 73:24 . . . with your counsel, **l-ing** me to a
Prov 6:22 . . . counsel will **l** you.
Prov 14:30 . . . A peaceful heart **l-s** to a
Prov 19:23 . . . Fear of the LORD **l-s** to life,
Isa 11:6 . . . little child will **l** them all.
Matt 15:14 . . . blind guides **l-ing** the blind,
John 10:3 . . . by name and **l-s** them out.
Rom 6:16 . . . to sin, which **l-s** to death,
Rom 6:22 . . . things that **l** to holiness and
1 Tim 5:24 . . . **l-ing** them to certain judgment.
Rev 7:17 . . . He will **l** them to

LEADER, LEADERS (n) a person who has commanding authority or influence; chief among others
1 Sam 13:14 . . . to be the **l** of his people,
Prov 17:26 . . . to flog **l-s** for being honest.
Jer 51:46 . . . **l-s** fight against each other.
Matt 20:26 . . . a **l** among you must be
Mark 10:43 . . . a **l** among you must be
Luke 22:26 . . . **l** should be like a servant.
Acts 13:27 . . . Jerusalem and their **l-s** did not
1 Thes 5:12 . . . who are your **l-s** in the Lord's
Heb 13:7 . . . Remember your **l-s** who taught
Heb 13:17 . . . Obey your spiritual **l-s,** and do
3 Jn 1:9 . . . to be the **l,** refuses to have

LEADERSHIP (n) the office or position of a leader; capacity to lead
Num 33:1 . . . under the **l** of Moses
1 Cor 12:28 . . . those who have the gift of **l,**

LEAP, LEAPED (v) to spring from (or as if from) the ground
Isa 35:6 . . . The lame will **l** like a deer,
Luke 1:41 . . . Elizabeth's child **l-ed** within

LEARN, LEARNED, LEARNS (v) to come to know or realize; to acquire knowledge, skill, or behavioral tendency
Deut 4:10 . . . Then they will **l** to fear me
Deut 5:1 . . . so you may **l** them and obey
Prov 9:9 . . . and they will **l** even more.
Prov 18:15 . . . are always ready to **l.**
Isa 1:17 . . . **L** to do good.
Isa 26:9 . . . will people **l** what is right.
Isa 29:13 . . . man-made rules **l-ed** by rote.
Matt 2:7 . . . and he **l-ed** from them the time
John 6:45 . . . listens to the Father and **l-s**
Phil 4:9 . . . all you **l-ed** and received from
Phil 4:11 . . . have **l-ed** how to be content
Col 1:10 . . . grow as you **l** to know God
1 Tim 2:11 . . . Women should **l** quietly and
2 Tim 1:13 . . . teaching you **l-ed** from me—
Heb 5:8 . . . he **l-ed** obedience from the

LEAST (adj) lowest in importance or position
Matt 19:30 . . . will be **l** important then,
Mark 10:31 . . . will be **l** important then,

LEATHER (adj) of or relating to animal skin dressed for use
2 Kgs 1:8 . . . he wore a **l** belt around his
Matt 3:4 . . . he wore a **l** belt around his

LEAVEN (KJV)
Exod 12:20 . . . anything made with *yeast*
Exod 13:7 . . . any *yeast* at all found within
Matt 13:33 . . . of Heaven is like the *yeast*
Matt 16:6 . . . the *yeast* of the Pharisees
1 Cor 5:6 . . . this sin is like a little *yeast*

LED (v) *see also* LEAD
Ps 68:18 . . . the heights, you **l** a crowd of
Isa 53:7 . . . He was **l** like a lamb
Jer 11:19 . . . like a lamb being **l** to the
Luke 4:1 . . . He was **l** by the Spirit
Acts 8:32 . . . He was **l** like a sheep
Rom 8:14 . . . all who are **l** by the Spirit
Eph 4:8 . . . the heights, he **l** a crowd of

LEFT (adj) of, relating to, situated on, or being the side of the body in which the heart is mostly located
Matt 6:3 . . . don't let your **l** hand know

LEFT (n) the location or direction of the left side
Josh 1:7 . . . or to the **l.** Then you will be
Josh 23:6 . . . either to the right or to the **l.**
Isa 30:21 . . . to the right or to the **l.**
Matt 25:33 . . . and the goats at his **l.**
Matt 25:41 . . . those on the **l** and say, 'Away

LEFT (v) to depart from; to allow to remain
Isa 53:6 . . . We have **l** God's paths
Ezek 34:8 . . . and **l** the sheep to starve.

LEFTOVERS (n) something that remains unused or unconsumed
Matt 14:20 . . . picked up twelve baskets of **l.**

LEGION (n) a very large number; multitude
Mark 5:9 . . . My name is **L,** because there

LEND, LENDING (v) to give for temporary use on condition that the same or its equivalent be returned
Lev 25:37 . . . interest on money you **l**
Deut 15:8 . . . and **l** them whatever
Ps 15:5 . . . Those who **l** money without
Prov 19:17 . . . you are **l-ing** to the LORD—
Luke 6:34 . . . Even sinners will **l** to other

LENDER, LENDERS (n) one who loans to another
Exod 22:25 . . . as a money **l** would.
Prov 22:7 . . . borrower is servant to the **l.**
Isa 24:2 . . . and sellers, **l-s** and borrowers,

LENGTHENS (v) to make longer; to extend
Prov 10:27 . . . of the LORD **l** one's life,

LEPERS (n) one who suffers from a severe contagious skin and nerve disease
Matt 11:5 . . . lame walk, the **l** are cured,
Luke 17:12 . . . ten **l** stood at a distance,

LEPROSY (n) a chronic infectious disease affecting the skin and peripheral nerves which causes loss of sensation, paralysis, and deformities
Num 12:10 . . . as white as snow from **l.**
2 Kgs 5:1 . . . he suffered from **l.**
2 Kgs 7:3 . . . four men with **l** sitting at
2 Chr 26:21 . . . King Uzziah had **l** until the

LESSON (n) something learned by study or experience; an instructive example
Lev 26:23 . . . to learn the **l** and continue
Prov 6:6 . . . Take a **l** from the ants,

LETTER, LETTERS (n) a piece of written communication
Deut 24:1 . . . he writes her a **l** of divorce,
2 Cor 3:2 . . . Your lives are a **l** written in
2 Cor 10:10 . . . Paul's **l-s** are demanding
2 Thes 3:14 . . . obey what we say in this **l.**
2 Pet 3:16 . . . have twisted his **l-s** to mean

LEVEL (v) to make flat
Isa 40:4 . . . valleys, and **l** the mountains

LEVI 1. Third son of Jacob and Leah (Gen 29:34), who gave his name to a tribe of Israel; violently avenged his sister Dinah (Gen 34); cursed for his violent temper (Gen 49:5-7); his tribe was blessed (Deut 33:8-11), chosen for priestly service (Num 3–4), numbered (Num 3:39; 26:62), allotted cities, but not land (Josh 13:14; *see also* Num 18:21-32); 12,000 will be marked by God (Rev 7:7).
2. *See* MATTHEW, also known as Levi.

LEVIATHAN (n) a sea monster represented as a cruel enemy defeated by God
Job 41:1 . . . Can you catch **L** with a hook
Ps 74:14 . . . crushed the heads of **L** and
Isa 27:1 . . . and punish **L,** the swiftly

LEWDNESS (n) that which lacks legal or moral restraints; sexual obscenity or vulgarity
Ezek 23:27 . . . stop to the **l** and prostitution
Ezek 24:13 . . . impurity is your **l** and

LIAR, LIARS (n) a person who deceives by telling untruths or falsehoods
Ps 63:11 . . . while **l-s** will be silenced.
Ps 116:11 . . . These people are all **l-s!**
Prov 17:4 . . . **l-s** pay close attention to
Prov 29:12 . . . pays attention to **l-s,** all his
Prov 30:6 . . . expose you as a **l.**
Isa 57:4 . . . of sinners and **l-s!**
John 8:44 . . . **l** and the father of lies.
Rom 3:4 . . . everyone else is a **l,** God is true.
1 Tim 1:10 . . . are slave traders, **l-s,**
Titus 1:12 . . . are all **l-s,** cruel animals,
1 Jn 1:10 . . . calling God a **l** and showing
1 Jn 2:4 . . . that person is a **l** and is not
1 Jn 4:20 . . . that person is a **l;** for if we
1 Jn 5:10 . . . calling God a **l** because they
Rev 3:9 . . . synagogue—those **l-s** who say
Rev 21:8 . . . and all **l-s**—their fate is in

LIBERATORS (n) one who frees or sets at liberty
Neh 9:27 . . . you sent them **l** who rescued

LICK (v) to draw the tongue over
Isa 49:23 . . . before you and **l** the dust

LIE, LIES (n) an untrue or inaccurate statement; something that misleads or deceives
Ps 7:14 . . . give birth to **l-s.**
Ps 24:4 . . . and never tell **l-s.**
Ps 34:13 . . . lips from telling **l-s!**
Prov 12:17 . . . a false witness tells **l-s.**
Prov 30:8 . . . never to tell a **l.**
John 8:44 . . . the father of **l-s.**
Rom 1:25 . . . about God for a **l.**
Rom 3:13 . . . filled with **l-s.**
Eph 4:14 . . . to trick us with **l-s** so clever
Eph 4:25 . . . So stop telling **l-s.**
2 Thes 2:11 . . . they will believe these **l-s.**
1 Pet 3:10 . . . and your lips from telling **l-s.**
2 Pet 2:3 . . . make up clever **l-s** to get hold
1 Jn 2:21 . . . between truth and **l-s.**
Rev 14:5 . . . They have told no **l-s;**

LIE, LIED, LIES (v) to make an untrue statement with intent to deceive; to create a false or misleading impression
see also LYING
Lev 6:3 . . . lost property and **l** about it,
Job 31:5 . . . Have I **l-d** to anyone or
Ps 58:3 . . . even from birth they have **l-d**
Ps 89:35 . . . in my holiness I cannot **l:**
Prov 24:28 . . . don't **l** about them.
Prov 26:19 . . . who **l-s** to a friend
Jer 7:9 . . . commit adultery, **l,** and burn
Matt 5:11 . . . persecute you and **l**
Col 3:9 . . . Don't **l** to each other,
Titus 1:2 . . . God—who does not **l**

LIFE (n) the quality that distinguishes a vital and functional being from a dead body; period from birth to death; a way or manner of living; spiritual existence transcending death; salvation
see also LIVES
Gen 1:30 . . . everything that has **l.**
Gen 2:7 . . . He breathed the breath of **l**
Gen 2:9 . . . the tree of **l** and the tree of
Gen 9:5 . . . who takes another person's **l.**
Gen 9:6 . . . a human **l,** that person's **l**
Exod 21:23 . . . the injury: a **l** for a **l,**
Num 35:31 . . . payment for the **l** of someone
Deut 19:21 . . . be **l** for **l,** eye for eye,
Deut 30:19 . . . choice between **l** and death,
Deut 32:39 . . . kills and gives **l;** I am the
1 Sam 2:6 . . . both death and **l;** he brings
Ps 23:6 . . . the days of my **l,** and I will
Ps 69:28 . . . the Book of **L;** don't let them
Ps 91:16 . . . with a long **l** and give them
Ps 139:24 . . . the path of everlasting **l.**
Prov 3:2 . . . your **l** will be satisfying.
Prov 6:26 . . . will cost you your **l.**
Prov 13:3 . . . have a long **l;** opening your
Prov 15:4 . . . Gentle words are a tree of **l;**
Prov 21:21 . . . will find **l,** righteousness,
Prov 28:16 . . . will have a long **l.**
Isa 53:8 . . . that his **l** was cut short in
Isa 55:3 . . . you will find **l.** I will make
Lam 3:58 . . . you have redeemed my **l.**
Dan 12:2 . . . to everlasting **l** and some to
Matt 7:14 . . . But the gateway to **l** is very
Matt 18:8 . . . to enter eternal **l** with only
Matt 20:28 . . . and to give his **l** as a ransom
Mark 8:35 . . . to hang on to your **l,**
Mark 10:45 . . . and to give his **l** as a ransom
Luke 6:9 . . . a day to save **l** or to destroy
Luke 9:24 . . . give up your **l** for my sake,
Luke 12:25 . . . single moment to your **l?**
John 1:4 . . . The Word gave **l** to everything
John 3:15 . . . will have eternal **l.**
John 4:14 . . . giving them eternal **l.**
John 5:24 . . . passed from death into **l.**
John 5:39 . . . they give you eternal **l.**
John 6:27 . . . the eternal **l** that the Son of
John 6:35 . . . I am the bread of **l.**
John 6:47 . . . who believes has eternal **l.**
John 6:53 . . . have eternal **l** within you.
John 6:68 . . . the words that give eternal **l.**
John 10:10 . . . a rich and satisfying **l.**
John 10:15 . . . So I sacrifice my **l** for the
John 10:28 . . . give them eternal **l,** and they
John 12:25 . . . nothing for their **l** in this
John 14:6 . . . the truth, and the **l.**
John 17:2 . . . He gives eternal **l** to each
John 20:31 . . . you will have **l** by the power
Acts 3:15 . . . You killed the author of **l,**
Rom 1:17 . . . a righteous person has **l.**
Rom 2:7 . . . will give eternal **l** to those
Rom 4:25 . . . he was raised to **l** to make us
Rom 5:10 . . . be saved through the **l** of his
Rom 5:18 . . . God and new **l** for everyone.
Rom 5:21 . . . in eternal **l** through Jesus
Rom 6:13 . . . now you have new **l.**
Rom 6:22 . . . result in eternal **l.**
Rom 6:23 . . . is eternal **l** through Christ
Rom 8:6 . . . mind leads to **l** and peace.

Rom 8:11 . . . he will give **l** to your mortal
Rom 8:38 . . . death nor **l**, neither angels
2 Cor 3:6 . . . the Spirit gives **l**.
2 Cor 4:10 . . . so that the **l** of Jesus may
Gal 3:11 . . . a righteous person has **l**.
Gal 3:21 . . . give us new **l**, we could be
Gal 6:8 . . . harvest everlasting **l** from
Eph 2:5 . . . he gave us **l** when he raised
Eph 4:1 . . . to lead a **l** worthy of your
Phil 2:16 . . . Hold firmly to the word of **l**;
Phil 4:3 . . . written in the Book of **L**.
Col 3:3 . . . and your real **l** is hidden
1 Tim 1:16 . . . and receive eternal **l**.
1 Tim 4:8 . . . and in the **l** to come.
1 Tim 6:19 . . . may experience true **l**.
2 Tim 1:9 . . . called us to live a holy **l**.
2 Tim 3:12 . . . to live a godly **l** in Christ
Titus 3:5 . . . new **l** through the Holy Spirit.
Heb 7:16 . . . power of a **l** that cannot be
Jas 1:12 . . . the crown of **l** that God has
1 Pet 3:7 . . . God's gift of new **l**.
1 Pet 3:10 . . . want to enjoy **l** and see many
1 Pet 3:16 . . . see what a good **l** you live
2 Pet 1:3 . . . for living a godly **l**.
1 Jn 1:1 . . . He is the Word of **l**.
1 Jn 3:14 . . . have passed from death to **l**.
1 Jn 3:16 . . . gave up his **l** for us.
1 Jn 5:20 . . . is eternal **l**.
Jude 1:21 . . . bring you eternal **l**.
Rev 3:5 . . . their names from the Book of **L**,
Rev 13:8 . . . in the Book of **L** before the
Rev 17:8 . . . in the Book of **L** before the
Rev 20:12 . . . the Book of **L**. And the dead
Rev 21:27 . . . in the Lamb's Book of **L**.
Rev 22:1 . . . with the water of **l**, clear as
Rev 22:2 . . . a tree of **l**, bearing twelve
Rev 22:14 . . . eat the fruit from the tree of **l**.
Rev 22:17 . . . from the water of **l**.
Rev 22:19 . . . in the tree of **l** and in the

LIFE-GIVING (adj) giving or having power to give life and spirit; invigorating
Prov 10:11 . . . the godly are a **l** fountain;
Prov 16:22 . . . Discretion is a **l** fountain to
Rom 8:2 . . . the power of the **l** Spirit has
1 Cor 15:45 . . . Christ—is a **l** Spirit.
2 Cor 2:16 . . . we are a **l** perfume.
Rev 7:17 . . . to springs of **l** water.

LIFETIME (n) the duration of the existence of a living being or thing
Ps 30:5 . . . his favor lasts a **l**!
Ps 39:5 . . . My entire **l** is just a
Luke 16:25 . . . that during your **l** you had

LIFT, LIFTED, LIFTING, LIFTS (v) to raise from a lower to a higher position; to raise in rank or condition
Lev 23:11 . . . the priest will **l** it up
1 Sam 2:7 . . . some down and **l-s** others up.
Neh 8:6 . . . Amen!" as they **l-ed** their hands.
Ps 28:2 . . . I **l** my hands toward your holy
Ps 63:4 . . . **l-ing** up my hands to you in prayer.
Ps 89:13 . . . Your right hand is **l-ed** high in
Ps 113:7 . . . He **l-s** the poor from the dust
Ps 123:1 . . . I **l** my eyes to
Ps 134:2 . . . **L** up holy hands
Lam 1:9 . . . no one to **l** her out.
Lam 3:41 . . . Let us **l** our hearts and
John 3:14 . . . Son of Man must be **l-ed** up,
John 8:28 . . . When you have **l-ed** up the Son
John 12:32 . . . And when I am **l-ed** up
1 Tim 2:8 . . . with holy hands **l-ed** up to God,
Jas 4:10 . . . he will **l** you up in honor.
1 Pet 5:6 . . . he will **l** you up in honor.

LIGHT, LIGHTS (n) daylight; brightness; illumination; celestial body; spiritual enlightenment; exposure to the truth and justice
Gen 1:3 . . . "Let there be **l**," and there
Gen 1:14 . . . God said, "Let **l-s** appear in the sky
Exod 13:21 . . . and he provided **l** at night
Job 38:19 . . . Where does **l** come from,
Ps 27:1 . . . The LORD is my **l** and my
Ps 56:13 . . . in your life-giving **l**.
Ps 119:105 . . . my feet and a **l** for my path.
Ps 132:17 . . . will be a **l** for my people.
Ps 139:12 . . . Darkness and **l** are the
Isa 2:5 . . . us walk in the **l** of the LORD!
Isa 42:6 . . . you will be a **l** to guide the
Isa 45:7 . . . I create the **l** and make the
Isa 49:6 . . . make you a **l** to the Gentiles,
Matt 5:14 . . . You are the **l** of the world—
Luke 2:32 . . . He is a **l** to reveal God to
Luke 11:33 . . . its **l** can be seen by all
John 1:4 . . . life brought **l** to everyone.
John 1:9 . . . who is the true **l**, who gives
John 3:20 . . . All who do evil hate the **l**
John 3:21 . . . come to the **l** so others can
John 8:12 . . . I am the **l** of the world.
John 9:5 . . . I am the **l** of the world.
John 12:46 . . . I have come as a **l** to shine
Acts 13:47 . . . made you a **l** to the Gentiles,
2 Cor 4:6 . . . said, "Let there be **l** in the
2 Cor 6:14 . . . can **l** live with darkness?
2 Cor 11:14 . . . as an angel of **l**.
Eph 1:18 . . . be flooded with **l** so that you
Eph 5:8 . . . live as people of **l**!
Phil 2:15 . . . like bright **l-s** in a world
1 Thes 5:5 . . . children of the **l** and of the
1 Tim 6:16 . . . he lives in **l** so brilliant
1 Pet 2:9 . . . into his wonderful **l**.
1 Jn 1:5 . . . God is **l**, and there is
1 Jn 1:7 . . . living in the **l**, as God is in
1 Jn 2:9 . . . I am living in the **l**,
Rev 21:23 . . . city, and the Lamb is its **l**.

LIGHT, LIGHTS (v) to brighten; to ignite something
Ps 18:28 . . . The LORD, my God, **l-s** up my
Luke 8:16 . . . No one **l-s** a lamp and

LIGHTNING (n) the flashing of light produced by a discharge of atmospheric electricity
Exod 9:23 . . . **l** flashed toward the earth.
Exod 20:18 . . . saw the flashes of **l** and the
Dan 10:6 . . . face flashed like **l**, and his
Matt 24:27 . . . For as the **l** flashes in the
Matt 28:3 . . . face shone like **l**, and his
Luke 10:18 . . . from heaven like **l**!
Rev 4:5 . . . came flashes of **l** and the

LIKE (prep) similar in appearance, character, quality
Gen 1:26 . . . to be **l** us. They will
Ps 86:8 . . . No pagan god is **l** you, O LORD.
Isa 14:14 . . . and be **l** the Most High.
Luke 13:18 . . . Kingdom of God **l**?
Rom 8:3 . . . Son in a body **l** the bodies we
Rom 8:29 . . . chose them to become **l** his Son,

LIKENESS (n) copy; resemblance; appearance
2 Cor 4:4 . . . is the exact **l** of God.

LINEN (adj) made of flax
Lev 16:4 . . . **l** undergarments worn next to
Prov 31:24 . . . makes belted **l** garments
Mark 15:46 . . . a long sheet of **l** cloth.
John 20:6 . . . noticed the **l** wrappings lying

LINEN (n) cloth made of flax and noted for its strength, coolness, and luster
Prov 31:22 . . . dresses in fine **l** and purple
Rev 15:6 . . . in spotless white **l** with gold
Rev 19:8 . . . of pure white **l** to wear.

LION, LIONS (n) a wild beast with a threatening roar; symbolic of a strong and fierce enemy
Isa 11:7 . . . The **l** will eat hay like a cow.
Isa 65:25 . . . The **l** will eat hay like a cow.
Dan 6:7 . . . thrown into the den of **l-s**.
Dan 7:4 . . . was like a **l** with eagles'
1 Pet 5:8 . . . like a roaring **l**, looking for
Rev 5:5 . . . Look, the **L** of the tribe of

LIPS (n) the fleshy, muscular folds that surround the mouth; symbolic of speech
Ps 140:3 . . . drips from their **l**.
Prov 12:22 . . . The LORD detests lying **l**,
Isa 6:5 . . . I have filthy **l**, and I live
Matt 15:8 . . . honor me with their **l**,
Rom 3:13 . . . venom drips from their **l**.
1 Pet 3:10 . . . evil and your **l** from telling

LISTEN, LISTENED, LISTENING (v) to hear something with thoughtful attention
see also HEAR
Deut 6:4 . . . **L**, O Israel! The LORD
Deut 18:15 . . . You must **l** to him.
1 Sam 3:9 . . . LORD, your servant is **l-ing**.
Neh 8:3 . . . All the people **l-ed** closely to
Ps 95:7 . . . If only you would **l** to his voice
Prov 12:15 . . . but the wise **l** to others.
Prov 18:13 . . . Spouting off before **l-ing** to
Isa 6:9 . . . to this people, '**L** carefully,
Dan 9:6 . . . We have refused to **l** to your
Mark 9:7 . . . dearly loved Son. **L** to him.
Luke 10:39 . . . the Lord's feet, **l-ing** to
Luke 16:31 . . . If they won't **l** to Moses and
John 10:27 . . . My sheep **l** to my
John 15:20 . . . And if they had **l-ed** to me,
Rom 2:13 . . . For merely **l-ing** to the law
1 Tim 2:12 . . . Let them **l** quietly.
Jas 1:19 . . . be quick to **l**, slow to speak,
1 Jn 4:6 . . . they do not **l** to us.
Rev 1:3 . . . he blesses all who **l** to its
Rev 2:7 . . . to hear must **l** to the Spirit

LIVE, LIVED, LIVES, LIVING (v) to be alive or come to life; to endure a period of time (a life span); to attain eternal life; to dwell; to subsist; to continue alive; to conduct or pass one's life
see also DWELLS
Gen 3:22 . . . Then they will **l** forever!
Exod 20:12 . . . Then you will **l** a long, full
Lev 26:11 . . . I will **l** among you,
Deut 6:2 . . . as long as you **l**.
Deut 8:3 . . . that people do not **l** by bread
Job 14:14 . . . Can the dead **l** again?
Job 19:25 . . . that my Redeemer **l-s**, and he
Ps 23:6 . . . and I will **l** in the house of
Ps 37:3 . . . Then you will **l** safely in the
Ps 61:4 . . . Let me **l** forever in your
Ps 104:33 . . . as long as I **l**. I will praise
Prov 21:19 . . . It's better to **l** alone in the
Isa 33:14 . . . Who can **l** with this
Isa 45:18 . . . He made the world to be **l-d** in,
Amos 5:6 . . . to the LORD and **l**!
Hab 2:4 . . . the righteous will **l** by their
Zech 2:11 . . . I will **l** among you,
Matt 4:4 . . . People do not **l** by bread
John 14:19 . . . Since I **l**, you also will **l**.
Acts 17:28 . . . For in him we **l** and move
Rom 2:8 . . . on those who **l** for themselves,
Rom 6:10 . . . he **l-s**, he **l-s** for the glory
Rom 8:11 . . . same Spirit **l-ing** within you.
Rom 13:13 . . . we must **l** decent lives
Rom 14:7 . . . For we don't **l** for ourselves
1 Cor 3:16 . . . Spirit of God **l-s** in you?
2 Cor 5:7 . . . For we **l** by believing

2 Cor 6:16 . . . said: "I will **l** in them and
Gal 2:20 . . . no longer I who **l**, but Christ
Gal 5:25 . . . Since we are **l-ing** by the Spirit,
Col 1:19 . . . was pleased to **l** in Christ,
Col 2:5 . . . that you are **l-ing** as you should
1 Thes 4:11 . . . your goal to **l** a quiet life,
1 Thes 5:13 . . . And **l** peacefully with
1 Tim 2:2 . . . so that we can **l** peaceful and
1 Tim 4:16 . . . close watch on how you **l**
2 Tim 3:12 . . . who wants to **l** a godly life
Heb 10:38 . . . righteous ones will **l** by faith.
Heb 12:14 . . . and work at **l-ing** a holy life,
1 Pet 1:17 . . . So you must **l** in reverent
1 Jn 1:7 . . . But if we are **l-ing** in the light,
1 Jn 4:16 . . . God, and God **l-s** in them.

LIVES (n) *see also* LIFE
Exod 23:26 . . . I will give you long, full **l**.
1 Thes 2:8 . . . but our own **l**, too.
1 Tim 2:2 . . . and quiet **l** marked by
1 Pet 3:2 . . . pure and reverent **l**.
1 Pet 4:2 . . . rest of your **l** chasing your

LIVING (adj) having life; active, functioning
Gen 2:7 . . . man became a **l** person.
Gen 6:17 . . . destroy every **l** thing that
Jer 2:13 . . . the fountain of **l** water.
Matt 22:32 . . . God of the **l**, not the dead.
John 4:10 . . . would give you **l** water.
John 6:51 . . . I am the **l** bread that came
Rom 12:1 . . . Let them be a **l** and holy
Heb 10:31 . . . the hands of the **l** God.
Rev 1:18 . . . I am the **l** one.

LIVING (n) conduct or manner of life
Phil 1:21 . . . to me, **l** means living for
2 Tim 2:22 . . . righteous **l**, faithfulness,

LOAF (n) a shaped or molded mass of bread
see also LOAVES
1 Cor 10:17 . . . all eat from one **l** of bread,

LOAN, LOANS (n) money lent at interest
Deut 15:2 . . . must cancel the **l-s** they have
Deut 15:9 . . . refuse someone a **l**
Deut 24:6 . . . as security for a **l**, for the
Ps 37:26 . . . give generous **l-s** to others,

LOANED (v) to lend
Luke 7:41 . . . A man **l** money to two

LOAVES (n) *see also* LOAF
Mark 6:41 . . . took the five **l** and two fish,
Mark 8:6 . . . took the seven **l**, thanked God
Luke 11:5 . . . to borrow three **l** of bread.

LOCKED (v) to fasten in or out or to make secure or inaccessible by means of locks
Job 38:10 . . . For I **l** it behind barred
John 20:26 . . . doors were **l**; but suddenly,

LOCUSTS (n) a short-horned grasshopper
Exod 10:4 . . . a swarm of **l** on your country.
Joel 2:25 . . . and the cutting **l**. It was I
Matt 3:4 . . . he ate **l** and wild honey.
Rev 9:3 . . . Then **l** came from

LODGING (n) a temporary place to stay
Luke 2:7 . . . there was no **l** available for

LOFTY (adj) elevated in character, spirit, and status; rising to a great height
Isa 6:1 . . . sitting on a **l** throne,
Isa 57:15 . . . The high and **l** one who lives

LOG (n) a usually bulky piece or length of a tree
Matt 7:3 . . . you have a **l** in your own?
Luke 6:41 . . . you have a **l** in your own?

LONG (adj) extending over a considerable time or space
Deut 5:33 . . . will live **l** and prosperous
1 Cor 11:14 . . . man to have **l** hair?
Eph 3:18 . . . how wide, how **l**, how high,

LONG, LONGING, LONGS (v) to feel a strong desire or craving; to yearn
Job 7:2 . . . a worker who **l-s** for the shade,
Ps 42:1 . . . As the deer **l-s** for streams of
Ps 42:1 . . . of water, so I **l** for you,
Ps 63:1 . . . my whole body **l-s** for you in
Ps 119:131 . . . **l-ing** for your commands.
Luke 16:21 . . . lay there **l-ing** for scraps from
Phil 1:8 . . . I love you and **l** for you with
Phil 2:26 . . . he has been **l-ing** to see you,

LONGING (n) a strong desire, especially for something unattainable; craving
Rom 10:1 . . . the **l** of my heart and
2 Cor 7:11 . . . such alarm, such **l** to see me,
1 Thes 2:17 . . . of our intense **l** to see you

LONGSUFFERING (KJV)
Exod 34:6 . . . I am *slow to anger* and filled
Num 14:18 . . . LORD is *slow to anger*
Ps 86:15 . . . mercy, *slow to get angry*
Gal 5:22 . . . love, joy, peace, *patience*,
Eph 4:2 . . . Be *patient* with each other

LOOK (n) glance
Prov 15:30 . . . A cheerful **l** brings joy to

LOOK, LOOKED, LOOKING, LOOKS (v) to direct the eyes; to examine; to see; to make sure or take care (that something is done); to regard with contempt; to seem; to search
Gen 19:17 . . . And don't **l** back or
Gen 19:26 . . . But Lot's wife **l-ed** back as she
Exod 3:6 . . . was afraid to **l** at God.
1 Sam 6:19 . . . they **l-ed** into the Ark
1 Sam 16:7 . . . LORD **l-s** at the heart.
Ps 34:5 . . . Those who **l** to him for
Ps 113:6 . . . He stoops to **l** down on heaven
Ps 123:2 . . . We keep **l-ing** to the LORD
Isa 65:1 . . . but no one was **l-ing** for me.
Dan 10:5 . . . I **l-ed** up and saw a man
Hab 3:6 . . . When he **l-s**, the nations
Zech 12:10 . . . They will **l** on me
Matt 5:28 . . . who even **l-s** at a woman
Mark 16:6 . . . You are **l-ing** for Jesus
Luke 9:62 . . . plow and then **l-s** back is not
Luke 22:61 . . . turned and **l-ed** at Peter.
John 4:23 . . . The Father is **l-ing** for those
John 17:1 . . . Jesus **l-ed** up to heaven
Rom 14:10 . . . Why do you **l** down
Phil 2:4 . . . Don't **l** out only
Heb 11:16 . . . they were **l-ing** for a better
Jas 1:25 . . . But if you **l** carefully into
2 Pet 3:12 . . . **l-ing** forward to the day
Rev 5:6 . . . I saw a Lamb that **l-ed** as if it

LOOSE (adv) in an unrigidly fastened or unsecure manner
Isa 33:23 . . . sails hang **l** on broken masts

LORD (n) traditionally rendered Jehovah (Hebrew *Yahweh*); the sovereign God Almighty
see also YAHWEH
Gen 2:4 . . . When the **L** God made
Gen 4:4 . . . The **L** accepted Abel
Gen 15:6 . . . Abram believed the **L**, and
Gen 22:14 . . . the **L** will provide
Gen 31:49 . . . May the **L** keep watch
Exod 6:2 . . . I am Yahweh—'the **L**.'
Exod 15:26 . . . I am the **L** who heals you.
Exod 40:34 . . . the glory of the **L** filled
Lev 20:26 . . . because I, the **L**, am holy.
Lev 23:4 . . . these are the **L**'s appointed
Num 6:24 . . . May the **L** bless you and
Num 14:18 . . . The **L** is slow to anger
Num 14:21 . . . filled with the **L**'s glory,
Num 14:41 . . . disobeying the **L**'s orders
Deut 5:9 . . . I, the **L** your God, am a jealous
Deut 6:5 . . . love the **L** your God with all
Deut 6:18 . . . good in the **L**'s sight,
Deut 10:13 . . . obey the **L**'s commands
Deut 10:20 . . . must fear the **L** your God
Deut 11:1 . . . must love the **L** your God
Deut 29:29 . . . The **L** our God has secrets
Deut 30:20 . . . obey the **L**, you will live
Josh 23:11 . . . to love the **L** your God.
2 Sam 22:2 . . . sang: "The **L** is my rock,
2 Sam 22:31 . . . All the **L**'s promises prove
2 Kgs 22:2 . . . pleasing in the **L**'s sight
2 Kgs 22:8 . . . Law in the **L**'s Temple!
1 Chr 17:1 . . . Ark of the **L**'s Covenant is
2 Chr 16:9 . . . The eyes of the **L** search
Neh 9:6 . . . You alone are the **L**.
Job 38:1 . . . Then the **L** answered Job
Ps 1:6 . . . For the **L** watches over
Ps 12:6 . . . The **L**'s promises are pure,
Ps 18:30 . . . All the **L**'s promises prove
Ps 23:1 . . . The **L** is my shepherd;
Ps 24:1 . . . The earth is the **L**'s,
Ps 34:3 . . . tell of the **L**'s greatness;
Ps 34:8 . . . see that the **L** is good.
Ps 89:1 . . . sing of the **L**'s unfailing love
Ps 92:13 . . . to the **L**'s own house.
Ps 95:6 . . . kneel before the **L** our maker,
Ps 97:1 . . . The **L** is king!
Ps 99:5 . . . Exalt the **L** our God!
Ps 100:5 . . . For the **L** is good.
Ps 107:1 . . . thanks to the **L**, for he is
Ps 118:8 . . . better to take refuge in the **L**
Ps 118:23 . . . This is the **L**'s doing,
Ps 121:2 . . . help comes from the **L**, who
Ps 145:3 . . . Great is the **L**!
Ps 145:17 . . . The **L** is righteous
Ps 146:7 . . . The **L** frees the prisoners.
Ps 147:11 . . . No, the **L**'s delight is
Prov 3:5 . . . Trust in the **L** with all your
Prov 3:9 . . . Honor the **L** with your
Prov 3:11 . . . reject the **L**'s discipline,
Prov 12:22 . . . The **L** detests lying
Prov 15:33 . . . Fear of the **L**
Prov 19:21 . . . the **L**'s purpose will prevail.
Prov 21:2 . . . the **L** examines their heart.
Prov 31:30 . . . a woman who fears the **L** will
Isa 6:3 . . . holy is the **L** of Heaven's
Isa 24:14 . . . praise the **L**'s majesty.
Isa 30:9 . . . to the **L**'s instructions.
Isa 42:8 . . . I am the **L**; that is my name!
Isa 43:11 . . . I, am the **L**, and there is
Isa 49:4 . . . leave it all in the **L**'s hand;
Isa 53:6 . . . Yet the **L** laid on him
Isa 53:10 . . . was the **L**'s good plan
Isa 55:13 . . . honor to the **L**'s name;
Isa 61:2 . . . time of the **L**'s favor
Isa 66:15 . . . See, the **L** is coming
Jer 8:7 . . . do not know the **L**'s laws.
Jer 17:10 . . . But I, the **L**, search all
Jer 31:11 . . . For the **L** has redeemed
Jer 48:10 . . . to do the **L**'s work,
Jer 51:7 . . . cup in the **L**'s hands,
Ezek 7:19 . . . day of the **L**'s anger.
Ezek 44:4 . . . the glory of the **L** filled
Joel 1:15 . . . The day of the **L** is near,
Joel 3:18 . . . from the **L**'s Temple, watering
Jon 2:9 . . . salvation comes from the **L**
Mic 4:1 . . . mountain of the **L**'s house
Mic 6:2 . . . listen to the **L**'s complaint!
Nah 1:2 . . . The **L** is a jealous God,
Nah 1:7 . . . The **L** is good, a strong
Hab 2:16 . . . cup of the **L**'s judgment,
Zeph 2:3 . . . yet the **L** will protect
Matt 3:3 . . . way for the **L**'s coming!
Matt 4:7 . . . not test the **L** your God.
Matt 4:10 . . . must worship the **L** your God

Matt 22:37 . . . must love the **L** your God
Mark 1:3 . . . way for the **L**'s coming!
Mark 12:11 . . . This is the **L**'s doing,
John 1:23 . . . way for the **L**'s coming!
Acts 2:21 . . . name of the **L** will be saved.
Rom 10:13 . . . name of the **L** will be saved.
Rom 11:34 . . . can know the **L**'s thoughts?
1 Cor 10:26 . . . the earth is the **L**'s,
Heb 12:5 . . . of the **L**'s discipline,

LORD, LORDS (n) honored one or a superior; master (to a slave); king or ruler; God or Jesus
see also LORD
Deut 10:17 . . . of gods and **L** of **l-s**.
Neh 4:14 . . . Remember the **L**, who is
Isa 6:1 . . . I saw the **L**. He was sitting
Dan 9:19 . . . O **L**, listen and act!
Matt 12:8 . . . Son of Man is **L**, even
Luke 1:38 . . . I am the **L**'s servant.
Acts 10:36 . . . Christ, who is **L** of all.
Acts 16:31 . . . Believe in the **L** Jesus
Rom 10:9 . . . that Jesus is **L** and believe
1 Cor 8:6 . . . only one **L**, Jesus Christ,
1 Cor 11:26 . . . announcing the **L**'s death
1 Cor 12:3 . . . say Jesus is **L**, except
Eph 4:5 . . . There is one **L**, one faith,
Phil 2:11 . . . Jesus Christ is **L**,
Col 2:6 . . . Jesus as your **L**, you must
1 Thes 5:2 . . . day of the **L**'s return
1 Tim 6:15 . . . kings and **L** of all **l-s**.
Jas 5:8 . . . the coming of the **L** is near.
1 Pet 2:3 . . . taste of the **L**'s kindness.
1 Pet 3:15 . . . worship Christ as **L** of
Rev 4:8 . . . holy, holy is the **L** God,
Rev 4:11 . . . are worthy, O **L** our God,
Rev 19:16 . . . kings and **L** of all **l-s**.
Rev 22:20 . . . Amen! Come, **L** Jesus!

LOSE, LOSES (v) to fail to keep, sustain, or maintain; to damn
Matt 10:39 . . . cling to your life, you will **l**
Mark 8:36 . . . whole world but **l** your own
Luke 15:8 . . . silver coins and **l-s** one.
Luke 17:33 . . . cling to your life, you will **l**
John 6:39 . . . I should not **l** even one of
2 Jn 1:8 . . . you do not **l** what we have

LOSS (n) the act of losing possession; deprivation
1 Cor 3:15 . . . the builder will suffer great **l**.

LOST (adj) no longer possessed or known; lacking assurance of eternal salvation
Jer 50:6 . . . have been **l** sheep.
Ezek 34:16 . . . will search for my **l** ones
Luke 15:4 . . . and one of them gets **l**,
Luke 15:6 . . . I have found my **l** sheep.
Luke 15:9 . . . have found my **l** coin.
Luke 15:24 . . . He was **l**, but now he

LOTS (n) small stones or other devices used for making choices, much like throwing dice or drawing straws
Josh 18:10 . . . Joshua cast sacred **l** in the
Obad 1:11 . . . wealth and cast **l** to divide
Acts 1:26 . . . they cast **l**, and Matthias was

LOUD (adj) marked by intensity or volume of sound
Isa 54:1 . . . Break into **l** and joyful song,

LOVE (n) the ultimate expression of God's loyalty, purity, and mercy extended toward his people—to be reflected in human relationships of brotherly concern, marital fidelity, and adoration of God; a beloved person
Gen 24:12 . . . unfailing **l** to my master,
Gen 32:10 . . . unfailing **l** and faithfulness
Gen 34:3 . . . he fell in **l** with her, and he
Gen 39:21 . . . showed him his faithful **l**.
Exod 20:6 . . . unfailing **l** for a thousand
Exod 34:6 . . . filled with unfailing **l** and
Num 14:18 . . . with unfailing **l**, forgiving
Num 14:19 . . . unfailing **l**, please pardon
Deut 5:10 . . . unfailing **l** for a thousand
Deut 7:9 . . . his unfailing **l** on those who
Deut 10:15 . . . the objects of his **l**.
Deut 10:18 . . . He shows **l** to the
Deut 10:19 . . . must show **l** to foreigners,
Judg 16:4 . . . Samson fell in **l** with a woman
1 Sam 18:20 . . . had fallen in **l** with David,
1 Kgs 8:23 . . . and show unfailing **l** to all
1 Kgs 10:9 . . . LORD's eternal **l** for Israel,
1 Chr 16:41 . . . for "his faithful **l** endures
1 Chr 29:18 . . . See to it that their **l**
2 Chr 5:13 . . . His faithful **l** endures
2 Chr 20:21 . . . faithful **l** endures forever!
Ezra 3:11 . . . His faithful **l** for Israel
Job 37:13 . . . to show his unfailing **l**.
Ps 6:4 . . . because of your unfailing **l**.
Ps 13:5 . . . I trust in your unfailing **l**.
Ps 18:50 . . . you show unfailing **l** to your
Ps 21:7 . . . The unfailing **l** of the
Ps 23:6 . . . and unfailing **l** will pursue
Ps 25:6 . . . and unfailing **l**, which you
Ps 25:10 . . . leads with unfailing **l** and
Ps 26:3 . . . of your unfailing **l**, and I
Ps 31:7 . . . in your unfailing **l**, for you
Ps 31:16 . . . your unfailing **l**, rescue me.
Ps 32:10 . . . but unfailing **l** surrounds
Ps 33:5 . . . the unfailing **l** of the
Ps 33:18 . . . who rely on his unfailing **l**.
Ps 33:22 . . . your unfailing **l** surround us,
Ps 36:5 . . . Your unfailing **l**, O LORD, is
Ps 36:10 . . . Pour out your unfailing **l** on
Ps 40:10 . . . of your unfailing **l** and
Ps 40:11 . . . Let your unfailing **l** and
Ps 42:8 . . . his unfailing **l** upon me,
Ps 48:9 . . . on your unfailing **l** as we
Ps 51:1 . . . your unfailing **l**. Because of
Ps 57:3 . . . send forth his unfailing **l** and
Ps 57:10 . . . For your unfailing **l** is as
Ps 59:10 . . . In his unfailing **l**, my God
Ps 59:16 . . . your unfailing **l**. For you
Ps 59:17 . . . shows me unfailing **l**.
Ps 62:12 . . . unfailing **l**, O LORD, is yours.
Ps 66:20 . . . his unfailing **l** from me.
Ps 69:16 . . . LORD, for your unfailing **l** is
Ps 77:8 . . . his unfailing **l** gone forever?
Ps 85:7 . . . us your unfailing **l**, O LORD,
Ps 86:5 . . . full of unfailing **l** for all
Ps 86:15 . . . filled with unfailing **l** and
Ps 88:11 . . . your unfailing **l**?
Ps 89:1 . . . LORD's unfailing **l** forever!
Ps 89:14 . . . Unfailing **l** and truth
Ps 89:49 . . . is your unfailing **l**?
Ps 90:14 . . . with your unfailing **l**, so we
Ps 92:2 . . . your unfailing **l** in the
Ps 100:5 . . . His unfailing **l** continues
Ps 101:1 . . . sing of your **l** and justice,
Ps 103:4 . . . crowns me with **l** and tender
Ps 103:11 . . . his unfailing **l** toward those
Ps 103:17 . . . But the **l** of the LORD
Ps 106:1 . . . His faithful **l** endures
Ps 106:45 . . . because of his unfailing **l**.
Ps 107:31 . . . for his great **l** and for the
Ps 107:43 . . . the faithful **l** of the LORD.
Ps 108:4 . . . your unfailing **l** is higher
Ps 109:26 . . . because of your unfailing **l**.
Ps 115:1 . . . for your unfailing **l** and
Ps 118:1 . . . His faithful **l** endures
Ps 119:41 . . . give me your unfailing **l**,
Ps 119:76 . . . let your unfailing **l** comfort
Ps 119:124 . . . deal with me in unfailing **l**,
Ps 130:7 . . . LORD there is unfailing **l**.
Ps 138:2 . . . your unfailing **l** and faithfulness;
Ps 143:12 . . . your unfailing **l**, silence all
Ps 147:11 . . . put their hope in his unfailing **l**.
Prov 5:19 . . . be captivated by her **l**.
Prov 14:22 . . . will receive unfailing **l** and
Prov 16:6 . . . Unfailing **l** and
Prov 20:28 . . . is made secure through **l**.
Prov 21:21 . . . and unfailing **l** will find
Prov 27:5 . . . better than hidden **l**!
Song 1:4 . . . We praise your **l** even more
Song 1:7 . . . Tell me, my **l**, where are you
Song 1:16 . . . so handsome, my **l**, pleasing
Song 2:7 . . . not to awaken **l** until the
Song 2:17 . . . to me, my **l**, like a gazelle
Song 3:4 . . . I found my **l**!
Song 4:10 . . . Your **l** delights me,
Song 4:16 . . . your garden, my **l**; taste its
Song 5:5 . . . door for my **l**, and my hands
Song 5:8 . . . tell him I am weak with **l**.
Song 7:6 . . . How pleasing, my **l**, how full
Song 7:12 . . . will give you my **l**.
Song 8:4 . . . not to awaken **l** until the
Song 8:6 . . . For **l** is as strong as death,
Song 8:7 . . . cannot quench **l**, nor can
Song 8:14 . . . Come away, my **l**!
Isa 55:3 . . . the unfailing **l** I promised to
Isa 63:7 . . . LORD's unfailing **l**.
Isa 63:9 . . . In his **l** and mercy he
Jer 2:25 . . . I'm in **l** with these
Jer 9:24 . . . demonstrates unfailing **l** and
Jer 16:5 . . . taken away my unfailing **l**
Jer 31:3 . . . with an everlasting **l**.
Jer 33:11 . . . His faithful **l** endures
Lam 3:22 . . . The faithful **l** of the
Lam 3:32 . . . the greatness of his unfailing **l**.
Dan 9:4 . . . of unfailing **l** to those who
Hos 1:7 . . . I will show **l** to the people
Hos 2:19 . . . and justice, unfailing **l** and
Hos 2:23 . . . I will show **l** to those I
Hos 6:4 . . . For your **l** vanishes like the
Hos 6:6 . . . want you to show **l**, not offer
Hos 11:4 . . . my ropes of kindness and **l**.
Hos 12:6 . . . Act with **l** and justice,
Joel 2:13 . . . filled with unfailing **l**.
Jon 4:2 . . . filled with unfailing **l**.
Zeph 3:17 . . . With his **l**, he will
Zech 8:17 . . . Stop your **l** of telling
Mark 10:21 . . . Jesus felt genuine **l** for him.
John 5:42 . . . have God's **l** within you.
John 15:9 . . . Remain in my **l**.
John 15:10 . . . remain in his **l**.
John 15:13 . . . is no greater **l** than to lay
John 17:26 . . . Then your **l** for me will
Rom 5:5 . . . fill our hearts with his **l**.
Rom 5:8 . . . showed his great **l** for us by
Rom 8:35 . . . us from Christ's **l**?
Rom 8:39 . . . us from the **l** of God that is
Rom 13:10 . . . **L** does no wrong
Rom 13:10 . . . to others, so **l** fulfills the
Rom 14:15 . . . not acting in **l** if you eat
Rom 15:30 . . . because of your **l** for me,
1 Cor 4:21 . . . I come with **l** and a gentle
1 Cor 8:1 . . . it is **l** that strengthens the
1 Cor 13:13 . . . faith, hope, and **l**—and the
1 Cor 13:13 . . . greatest of these is **l**.
2 Cor 2:4 . . . know how much **l** I have for
2 Cor 2:8 . . . to reaffirm your **l** for him.
2 Cor 5:14 . . . Either way, Christ's **l** controls
2 Cor 8:7 . . . and your **l** from us—I want
2 Cor 8:24 . . . show them your **l**, and prove
Gal 5:22 . . . **l**, joy, peace, patience,
Eph 1:15 . . . Jesus and your **l** for God's
Eph 3:17 . . . down into God's **l** and keep
Eph 3:18 . . . how deep his **l** is.
Eph 4:15 . . . the truth in **l**, growing in
Eph 5:2 . . . filled with **l**, following the

Eph 6:23 . . . give you **l** with faithfulness.
Phil 1:9 . . . that your **l** will overflow
Col 1:4 . . . Jesus and your **l** for all of
Col 1:8 . . . told us about the **l** for others
Col 2:2 . . . strong ties of **l.**
1 Thes 3:6 . . . your faith and **l.**
1 Thes 3:12 . . . the Lord make your **l** for one
1 Thes 5:13 . . . and wholehearted **l** because of
2 Thes 3:5 . . . expression of the **l** of God
1 Tim 1:5 . . . be filled with **l** that comes
1 Tim 2:15 . . . in faith, **l,** holiness,
1 Tim 4:12 . . . live, in your **l,** your faith,
1 Tim 6:10 . . . For the **l** of money is the
1 Tim 6:11 . . . with faith, **l,** perseverance,
2 Tim 1:7 . . . but of power, **l,** and
2 Tim 1:13 . . . the faith and **l** that you have
2 Tim 2:22 . . . living, faithfulness, **l,** and
2 Tim 3:10 . . . my patience, my **l,** and my
Titus 2:2 . . . filled with **l** and patience.
Titus 3:4 . . . revealed his kindness and **l,**
Heb 10:24 . . . to acts of **l** and good works.
1 Pet 4:8 . . . for **l** covers a multitude
1 Pet 5:14 . . . with Christian **l.**
1 Jn 3:14 . . . who has no **l** is still dead.
1 Jn 3:16 . . . know what real **l** is because
1 Jn 4:7 . . . for **l** comes from God.
1 Jn 4:8 . . . for God is **l.**
1 Jn 4:10 . . . This is real **l**—not that we
1 Jn 4:16 . . . put our trust in his **l.**
1 Jn 4:16 . . . God is **l,** and all who
1 Jn 4:17 . . . live in God, our **l** grows more
1 Jn 4:18 . . . because perfect **l** expels all
Jude 1:12 . . . commemorating the Lord's **l,**
Jude 1:21 . . . safe in God's **l.**
Rev 2:19 . . . have seen your **l,** your faith,

LOVE, LOVED, LOVES, LOVING (v) to hold dear; to feel a lover's passion, devotion, or tenderness for; to feel affection or experience desire; to like or desire actively
Gen 22:2 . . . Isaac, whom you **l** so much—
Gen 29:32 . . . my husband will **l** me.
Exod 21:5 . . . may declare, 'I **l** my master,
Lev 19:34 . . . as you **l** yourself.
Deut 4:37 . . . Because he **l-d** your ancestors,
Deut 6:5 . . . And you must **l** the LORD your
Deut 7:8 . . . that the LORD **l-s** you, and he
Deut 7:13 . . . He will **l** you and
Deut 11:13 . . . and if you **l** the LORD your
Deut 13:3 . . . if you truly **l** him with all
Deut 15:16 . . . because he **l-s** you and
Deut 21:15 . . . son of the wife he does not **l.**
Deut 23:5 . . . LORD your God **l-s** you.
Deut 30:6 . . . that you will **l** him with all
Deut 30:16 . . . to **l** the LORD
Deut 30:20 . . . this choice by **l-ing** the LORD
Deut 30:20 . . . And if you **l** and obey the
Deut 33:3 . . . Indeed, he **l-s** his people;
Josh 23:11 . . . be very careful to **l** the LORD
Judg 14:16 . . . said, "You don't **l** me;
Judg 16:15 . . . tell me, 'I **l** you,' when you
1 Sam 18:1 . . . for Jonathan **l-d** David.
2 Sam 12:24 . . . The LORD **l-d** the child
2 Sam 19:6 . . . You seem to **l** those who hate
1 Kgs 3:3 . . . Solomon **l-d** the LORD and
1 Kgs 11:1 . . . King Solomon **l-d** many foreign
2 Chr 2:11 . . . the LORD **l-s** his people
2 Chr 19:2 . . . the wicked and **l** those who
Neh 1:5 . . . with those who **l** him and obey
Neh 13:26 . . . **l-d** him and made him king
Ps 11:5 . . . those who **l** violence.
Ps 11:7 . . . righteous LORD **l-s** justice.
Ps 18:1 . . . I **l** you, LORD;
Ps 26:8 . . . I **l** your sanctuary,
Ps 36:10 . . . on those who **l** you;
Ps 40:16 . . . those who **l** your salvation
Ps 44:3 . . . helped them, for you **l-d** them.
Ps 45:7 . . . You **l** justice and
Ps 52:3 . . . You **l** evil more
Ps 52:4 . . . You **l** to destroy
Ps 70:4 . . . those who **l** your salvation
Ps 78:68 . . . Mount Zion, which he **l-d.**
Ps 89:28 . . . I will **l** him and be
Ps 89:33 . . . I will never stop **l-ing** him nor
Ps 91:14 . . . rescue those who **l** me.
Ps 97:10 . . . You who **l** the LORD,
Ps 98:3 . . . his promise to **l** and be
Ps 119:48 . . . I honor and **l** your commands.
Ps 119:97 . . . how I **l** your instructions!
Ps 119:113 . . . but I **l** your instructions.
Ps 119:119 . . . no wonder I **l** to obey your
Ps 119:127 . . . I **l** your commands more
Ps 119:140 . . . that is why I **l** them so much.
Ps 122:6 . . . May all who **l** this city
Ps 145:20 . . . all those who **l** him, but he
Ps 146:8 . . . The LORD **l-s** the godly.
Prov 3:12 . . . corrects those he **l-s,** just as
Prov 8:17 . . . I **l** all who **l** me.
Prov 8:21 . . . Those who **l** me inherit
Prov 8:36 . . . All who hate me **l** death.
Prov 9:8 . . . and they will **l** you.
Prov 12:1 . . . you must **l** discipline; it is
Prov 15:17 . . . with someone you **l** is better
Prov 17:19 . . . Anyone who **l-s** to quarrel
Prov 18:21 . . . those who **l** to talk
Prov 19:8 . . . wisdom is to **l** oneself;
Prov 21:17 . . . Those who **l** pleasure
Prov 22:11 . . . Whoever **l-s** a pure
Prov 30:19 . . . how a man **l-s** a woman.
Eccl 3:8 . . . A time to **l** and a time
Eccl 9:9 . . . the woman you **l** through all
Song 1:3 . . . the young women **l** you!
Song 3:2 . . . search for the one I **l.**
Song 3:3 . . . Have you seen the one I **l?**
Isa 1:23 . . . All of them **l** bribes and
Isa 56:6 . . . serve him and **l** his name, who
Isa 61:8 . . . I, the LORD, **l** justice.
Jer 2:2 . . . long ago, how you **l-d** me and
Jer 8:2 . . . my people have **l-d,** served,
Jer 31:20 . . . but I still **l** him.
Hos 2:1 . . . The ones I **l.**
Hos 2:4 . . . I will not **l** her children,
Hos 2:23 . . . to those I called 'Not **l-d.**'
Hos 9:15 . . . I will **l** them no
Hos 11:1 . . . was a child, I **l-d** him, and I
Hos 12:7 . . . scales—they **l** to cheat.
Amos 4:5 . . . you Israelites **l** to do," says
Amos 5:15 . . . Hate evil and **l** what is good;
Mic 6:8 . . . is right, to **l** mercy, and to
Mal 1:2 . . . "I have always **l-d** you," says
Matt 5:43 . . . that says, '**L** your neighbor'
Matt 5:44 . . . But I say, **l** your enemies!
Matt 5:46 . . . If you **l** only those
Matt 6:24 . . . hate one and **l** the other;
Matt 10:37 . . . If you **l** your father or
Matt 19:19 . . . **L** your neighbor
Matt 22:37 . . . You must **l** the LORD your
Mark 12:6 . . . his son whom he **l-d** dearly.
Mark 12:30 . . . you must **l** the LORD your
Mark 12:33 . . . it is important to **l** him with
Mark 12:33 . . . and to **l** my neighbor as
Luke 6:27 . . . I say, **l** your enemies!
Luke 6:32 . . . If you **l** only those who
Luke 6:35 . . . **L** your enemies!
Luke 10:27 . . . You must **l** the LORD your
Luke 10:27 . . . And, '**L** your neighbor
Luke 16:13 . . . hate one and **l** the other;
John 3:16 . . . For God **l-d** the world so
John 3:35 . . . The Father **l-s** his Son
John 5:20 . . . For the Father **l-s** the Son and
John 8:42 . . . you would **l** me, because I
John 10:17 . . . The Father **l-s** me because I
John 11:36 . . . See how much he **l-d** him!
John 12:25 . . . Those who **l** their life
John 12:43 . . . For they **l-d** human praise more
John 13:1 . . . He had **l-d** his disciples during
John 13:34 . . . **L** each other.
John 13:34 . . . as I have **l-d** you, you should
John 14:21 . . . are the ones who **l** me.
John 14:28 . . . If you really **l-d** me, you
John 14:31 . . . know that I **l** the Father.
John 17:23 . . . and that you **l** them as much
John 17:24 . . . gave me because you **l-d** me
John 19:26 . . . beside the disciple he **l-d,**
John 20:2 . . . one whom Jesus **l-d.**
John 21:15 . . . do you **l** me more than
John 21:16 . . . son of John, do you **l** me?
John 21:20 . . . the disciple Jesus **l-d**—the one
Rom 8:28 . . . of those who **l** God and are
Rom 8:37 . . . through Christ, who **l-d** us.
Rom 9:13 . . . Scriptures, "I **l-d** Jacob, but I
Rom 9:25 . . . And I will **l** those whom I did
Rom 12:10 . . . **L** each other with genuine
1 Cor 2:9 . . . for those who **l** him.
1 Cor 13:2 . . . but didn't **l** others, I would
1 Cor 16:22 . . . anyone does not **l** the Lord,
2 Cor 9:7 . . . For God **l-s** a person
2 Cor 12:15 . . . the more I **l** you, the less
Gal 2:20 . . . of God, who **l-d** me and gave
Eph 1:4 . . . God **l-d** us and chose us
Eph 2:4 . . . mercy, and he **l-d** us so much,
Eph 5:25 . . . this means **l** your wives, just
Eph 5:25 . . . just as Christ **l-d** the church.
Eph 5:28 . . . a man who **l-s** his wife actually
Eph 5:33 . . . love his wife as he **l-s** himself,
Phil 1:16 . . . preach because they **l** me,
Phil 2:2 . . . each other, **l-ing** one another,
1 Thes 1:4 . . . God **l-s** you and has chosen
1 Thes 4:10 . . . urge you to **l** them even
2 Thes 2:10 . . . they refuse to **l** and accept
2 Thes 2:16 . . . our Father, who **l-d** us and
1 Tim 3:3 . . . and not **l** money.
1 Tim 6:2 . . . believers who are well **l-d.**
2 Tim 3:2 . . . people will **l** only themselves
Titus 1:8 . . . and he must **l** what is good.
Titus 2:4 . . . women to **l** their husbands
Titus 3:15 . . . believers—all who **l** us.
Heb 12:6 . . . disciplines those he **l-s,**
Heb 13:1 . . . Keep on **l-ing** each other as
Heb 13:5 . . . Don't **l** money;
Jas 2:5 . . . to those who **l** him?
1 Pet 1:8 . . . You **l** him even though
1 Pet 2:17 . . . Respect everyone, and **l** your
1 Pet 3:8 . . . **L** each other
2 Pet 2:15 . . . **l-d** to earn money by doing
1 Jn 2:5 . . . how completely they **l** him.
1 Jn 2:10 . . . Anyone who **l-s** another brother
1 Jn 3:1 . . . how very much our Father **l-s** us,
1 Jn 3:14 . . . If we **l** our Christian
1 Jn 4:9 . . . how much he **l-d** us by sending
1 Jn 4:10 . . . not that we **l-d** God, but that
1 Jn 4:11 . . . since God **l-d** us that much,
1 Jn 4:11 . . . surely ought to **l** each other.
1 Jn 4:19 . . . We **l** each other
1 Jn 4:19 . . . because he **l-d** us first.
1 Jn 4:20 . . . someone says, "I **l** God," but
1 Jn 4:20 . . . how can we **l** God, whom we
1 Jn 5:1 . . . And everyone who **l-s** the Father
Jude 1:1 . . . God the Father, who **l-s** you and
Rev 1:5 . . . glory to him who **l-s** us and has
Rev 2:4 . . . You don't **l** me or each other
Rev 3:9 . . . you are the ones I **l.**

Rev 3:19 . . . discipline everyone I **l.**
Rev 12:11 . . . they did not **l** their lives so
Rev 22:15 . . . and all who **l** to live a lie.

LOVE, LOVED, LOVING (adj) of or relating to a strong affection for another; affectionate, painstaking
Ps 88:18 . . . my companions and **l-d** ones.
Ps 127:2 . . . gives rest to his **l-d** ones.
Ezek 33:32 . . . who sings **l** songs with a
Mark 1:11 . . . are my dearly **l-d** Son, and you
Mark 9:7 . . . is my dearly **l-d** Son.
1 Thes 1:3 . . . work, your **l-ing** deeds, and the

LOVELY (adj) eliciting love by moral or ideal worth; beautiful
Phil 4:8 . . . pure, and **l,** and admirable.

LOVER, LOVERS (n) one who loves; two persons in love with each other; a person with whom one has sexual relations
Ps 99:4 . . . Mighty King, **l** of justice,
Song 2:9 . . . My **l** is like a
Song 5:2 . . . I heard my **l** knocking and
Ezek 16:33 . . . gifts to your **l-s,** bribing them
Ezek 16:39 . . . who are your **l-s,** and they will
Hos 2:5 . . . run after other **l-s** and sell

LOVINGKINDNESS (KJV)
Ps 25:6 . . . *unfailing love,* which you have
Ps 40:11 . . . Let your *unfailing love* and
Ps 63:3 . . . *unfailing love* is better than life
Ps 143:8 . . . your *unfailing love* each morning
Isa 63:7 . . . according to his *mercy and love*

LOWER, LOWEST (adj) of lesser position, rank, or order
Ps 8:5 . . . only a little **l-er** than God and
Luke 14:10 . . . Instead, take the **l-est** place at
Heb 2:7 . . . them only a little **l-er** than the

LOWLY (adj) humble in manner or spirit; of or relating to a low social or economic rank
Ps 37:11 . . . The **l** will possess
Ezek 21:26 . . . Now the **l** will be

LOYAL (adj) unswerving in allegiance; faithful
see also FAITHFUL, TRUSTWORTHY
1 Sam 26:23 . . . and for being **l,**
2 Sam 2:6 . . . May the LORD be **l** to you in
1 Chr 12:33 . . . and completely **l** to David.
Ps 31:23 . . . those who are **l** to him,
Ps 51:10 . . . Renew a **l** spirit within
Prov 17:17 . . . A friend is always **l,** and a
Prov 20:6 . . . say they are **l** friends,

LOYALTY, LOYALTIES (n) the quality or state or an instance of being loyal
Judg 8:35 . . . Nor did they show any **l** to
Ps 119:113 . . . I hate those with divided **l-ies,**
Prov 19:22 . . . **L** makes a person

LUKE The beloved doctor (Col 4:14); faithful co-worker of Paul (2 Tim 4:11; Phlm 1:23-24); noted fact-gatherer and writer of the third Gospel and the book of Acts.

LURE (n) enticement, appeal, attraction
Mark 4:19 . . . the **l** of wealth,

LURE (v) to draw with a hint of pleasure or gain
2 Pet 2:18 . . . they **l** back into sin those

LUST, LUSTS (n) usually intense or un-bridled sexual desire; an intense longing
1 Cor 7:9 . . . than to burn with **l.**
Eph 4:22 . . . corrupted by **l** and deception.
Col 3:5 . . . immorality, impurity, **l,** and
2 Tim 2:22 . . . stimulates youthful **l-s.**
Titus 3:3 . . . to many **l-s** and pleasures.

LUST, LUSTED (v) to have an intense (sexual) desire
Prov 6:25 . . . Don't **l** for her
Ezek 23:5 . . . Then Oholah **l-ed** after other

LUSTFUL (adj) excited by lust; lecherous
Mark 7:22 . . . deceit, **l** desires, envy,
Gal 5:19 . . . impurity, **l** pleasures,
Eph 4:19 . . . They live for **l** pleasure and

LUXURY (n) a condition of abundance or great ease and comfort
Prov 21:17 . . . those who love wine and **l**
Jas 5:5 . . . your years on earth in **l,**

LYING (adj) marked by or containing falsehoods; false
Prov 6:17 . . . haughty eyes, a **l** tongue,
Prov 12:22 . . . The LORD detests **l** lips,
Prov 21:6 . . . Wealth created by a **l** tongue
Prov 26:28 . . . A **l** tongue hates

LYING (v) *see also* LIE
Mic 6:12 . . . are so used to **l** that their
Matt 15:19 . . . immorality, theft, **l,** and
Acts 5:4 . . . You weren't **l** to us but
1 Cor 15:15 . . . would all be **l** about God—

M

MACEDONIA (n) a mountainous country north of Greece in the Balkan Peninsula
Acts 16:9 . . . A man from **M** in northern

MAD (adj) insane; carried away by intense anger
Deut 28:34 . . . You will go **m** because of

MADE (v) *see also* CREATE(D), FORMED, MAKE
Gen 1:7 . . . God **m** this space to separate
Gen 1:16 . . . He also **m** the stars.
Gen 1:25 . . . **m** all sorts of wild animals,
Gen 1:31 . . . God looked over all he had **m,**
Gen 2:4 . . . LORD God **m** the earth and
Gen 2:22 . . . LORD God **m** a woman
Gen 6:6 . . . LORD was sorry he had ever **m**
Gen 9:6 . . . God **m** human beings in his
Exod 20:11 . . . the LORD **m** the heavens,
Deut 32:6 . . . Has he not **m** you and
2 Chr 2:12 . . . **m** the heavens and
Job 10:9 . . . that you **m** me from dust—
Ps 95:5 . . . sea belongs to him, for he **m** it.
Ps 115:15 . . . who **m** heaven and earth.
Prov 22:2 . . . The LORD **m** them both.
Eccl 3:11 . . . God has **m** everything
Isa 27:11 . . . the one who **m** them will
Isa 43:7 . . . I have **m** them for my glory.
Isa 57:16 . . . all the souls I have **m.**
Jer 51:15 . . . The LORD **m** the earth
Jon 1:9 . . . God of heaven, who **m** the sea
Matt 19:4 . . . **m** them male and female.
Matt 19:28 . . . when the world is **m** new
1 Cor 11:9 . . . man was not **m** for woman,
2 Cor 5:1 . . . an eternal body **m** for us by
1 Tim 2:13 . . . For God **m** Adam first,
Heb 4:3 . . . since he **m** the world.
Rev 13:8 . . . before the world was **m**—
Rev 14:7 . . . him who **m** the heavens,

MAGIC (adj) having seemingly supernatural qualities or powers
Ezek 13:20 . . . all your **m** charms,

MAGICIANS (n) ones skilled in extraordinary power or influence seemingly from a supernatural source; sorcerers
Exod 7:11 . . . Egyptian **m** did the same
Dan 2:2 . . . called in his **m,** enchanters,

MAGNIFICENT (adj) grand or lavish; strikingly beautiful or impressive
Num 14:19 . . . In keeping with your **m,**
1 Chr 22:5 . . . must be a **m** structure,
Ps 48:2 . . . It is high and **m;**
Isa 63:14 . . . and gained a **m** reputation.

MAJESTIC (adj) having or exhibiting majesty; grand, stately
Ps 8:1 . . . your **m** name fills the earth!
Ps 29:4 . . . the voice of the LORD is **m.**
Ps 145:5 . . . I will meditate on your **m,**
Isa 53:2 . . . nothing beautiful or **m** about
Heb 1:3 . . . hand of the **m** God in heaven.
Heb 8:1 . . . the throne of the **m** God
2 Pet 1:16 . . . saw his **m** splendor with our
2 Pet 1:17 . . . from the **m** glory of God

MAJESTY (n) greatness or splendor of quality or character; sovereign power, authority, or dignity
Exod 15:7 . . . In the greatness of your **m,**
1 Chr 16:27 . . . and **m** surround him;
Job 40:10 . . . splendor, your honor and **m.**
Ps 21:5 . . . with splendor and **m.**
Ps 68:34 . . . His **m** shines down on Israel;
Ps 93:1 . . . is king! He is robed in **m.**
Ps 145:12 . . . about the **m** and glory of
Isa 2:10 . . . and the glory of his **m.**
Isa 26:10 . . . no notice of the LORD's **m.**
Jude 1:25 . . . All glory, **m,** power, and

MAKE, MAKES, MAKING (v) to create, prepare, or fashion; to force; to bring about; to render
see also CREATE(D), FORMED, MADE
Gen 1:26 . . . Let us **m** human beings in our
Gen 2:18 . . . will **m** a helper who is just
Exod 4:11 . . . Who **m-s** a person's mouth?
Exod 25:40 . . . you **m** everything
Lev 16:34 . . . **m-ing** them right with the
Ps 19:7 . . . **m-ing** wise the simple.
Ps 139:14 . . . **m-ing** me so wonderfully
Prov 13:12 . . . Hope deferred **m-s** the heart
Isa 8:14 . . . stone that **m-s** people stumble,
Isa 29:16 . . . "He didn't **m** me"?
Isa 44:10 . . . fool would **m** his own god—
Jer 18:4 . . . jar he was **m-ing** did not turn out
Jer 23:16 . . . **m-ing** up everything they say.
Jer 31:31 . . . when I will **m** a new covenant
Matt 28:19 . . . **m** disciples of all
John 5:18 . . . **m-ing** himself equal with God.
Rom 14:20 . . . it **m-s** another person stumble.
1 Cor 3:7 . . . that God **m-s** the seed grow.
Heb 8:5 . . . you **m** everything according to
1 Pet 2:8 . . . stone that **m-s** people stumble,

MAKER (n) one who makes; God
see also CREATOR
Ps 95:6 . . . before the LORD our **m,**
Ps 149:2 . . . Israel, rejoice in your **M.**
Prov 17:5 . . . mock the poor insult their **M;**
Isa 45:9 . . . clay pot argue with its **m?**
Hos 8:14 . . . Israel has forgotten its **M**

MALE (adj) of, relating to, or being of the male sex
Gen 1:27 . . . **m** and female he created them.
Matt 19:4 . . . God made them **m** and female.
Gal 3:28 . . . slave or free, **m** and female.

MALICIOUS (adj) given to, marked by, or arising from a desire to cause pain, injury, or distress to another

Rom 1:29 . . . deception, **m** behavior,
Col 3:8 . . . of anger, rage, **m** behavior,

MAMMON (KJV)
Matt 6:24 . . . serve both God and *money*
Luke 16:9 . . . your *worldly resources* to benefit
Luke 16:11 . . . untrustworthy about *worldly wealth,*

MAN (n) an adult male human; individual, person
Gen 2:7 . . . the **m** from the dust
Gen 2:15 . . . the **m** in the Garden
Gen 2:18 . . . for the **m** to be alone.
Gen 2:23 . . . she was taken from **'m.'**
Gen 2:25 . . . **m** and his wife were both
Gen 3:9 . . . God called to the **m,** "Where
Isa 53:3 . . . rejected—a **m** of sorrows,
1 Cor 11:3 . . . of every **m** is Christ,
1 Cor 11:3 . . . the head of woman is **m,**
1 Cor 15:45 . . . The first **m,** Adam,
Eph 5:31 . . . A **m** leaves his father and
1 Tim 2:5 . . . the **m** Christ Jesus.

MAN-MADE (adj) manufactured, created, or constructed by human beings
Matt 15:9 . . . teach **m** ideas as commands from

MANAGE, MANAGING (v) to handle or direct with a degree of skill
Luke 12:42 . . . of **m-ing** his other household
1 Tim 3:4 . . . **m** his own family well,
1 Tim 3:12 . . . he must **m** his children

MANAGER (n) a person who conducts business or household affairs
Luke 16:1 . . . a **m** handling his affairs.
1 Cor 4:2 . . . as a **m** must be faithful.
Titus 1:7 . . . a **m** of God's household,

MANGER (n) a trough or open box in a stable designed to hold feed for livestock
Luke 2:7 . . . cloth and laid him in a **m,**
Luke 2:12 . . . strips of cloth, lying in a **m.**

MANNA (n) in Hebrew, the word means "What is it?"; miraculous supply of food given to Israel in the wilderness; symbolic of spiritual nourishment
Exod 16:31 . . . Israelites called the food **m.**
Deut 8:16 . . . He fed you with **m** in the
John 6:49 . . . Your ancestors ate **m** in the
Rev 2:17 . . . some of the **m** that has been

MANNER (n) a mode of procedure or way of acting
Phil 1:27 . . . in a **m** worthy of the Good News

MANSIONS (n) a very large house
Isa 5:9 . . . even beautiful **m** will be empty.
Amos 3:15 . . . their winter **m** and their summer

MARANATHA (KJV)
1 Cor 16:22 . . . *Our Lord, come!*

MARCH (v) to move along steadily usually with a rhythmic stride and in step with others; to advance or proceed
Josh 6:4 . . . you are to **m** around the town
Isa 42:13 . . . The LORD will **m** forth

MARK Son of Mary of Jerusalem (Acts 12:12); traveled with Barnabas and Paul (Acts 12:25; 13:5); returned to Jerusalem (Acts 13:13); went to Cyprus with Barnabas (Acts 15:37-39); in Paul's greetings, called "helpful" (Col 4:10; 2 Tim 4:11; Phlm 1:24); Peter's "son" (1 Pet 5:13).

MARK (n) an impression (as a scratch, scar, or stain) made on something; a distinguishing trait or quality
Gen 4:15 . . . LORD put a **m** on Cain
Rev 13:16 . . . given a **m** on the right hand or

MARKETPLACE, MARKETPLACES (n) an open square or place in town where markets or public sales are held
Matt 23:7 . . . as they walk in the **m-s,**
John 2:16 . . . my Father's house into a **m!**

MARRIAGE (adj) of or relating to marriage
Gen 49:4 . . . you defiled my **m** couch.
Mal 2:14 . . . the wife of your **m** vows.

MARRIAGE (n) the state of being lawfully united to a person of the opposite sex as husband or wife; an act of marrying
Matt 22:30 . . . marry nor be given in **m.**
Rom 7:2 . . . laws of **m** no longer apply
1 Cor 7:14 . . . brings holiness to her **m,**
1 Cor 7:27 . . . do not seek to end the **m.**
Heb 13:4 . . . Give honor to **m,** and remain

MARRY, MARRIED, MARRIES, MARRYING (v) to take a spouse according to law or custom
Exod 21:10 . . . who has **m-ied** a slave wife
Deut 24:4 . . . first husband may not **m** her
Deut 24:5 . . . newly **m-ied** man must not be
Deut 25:5 . . . husband's brother should **m**
Ezra 10:10 . . . By **m-ing** pagan women,
Hos 1:2 . . . Go and **m** a prostitute, so that
Matt 1:18 . . . to be **m-ied** to Joseph.
Matt 19:9 . . . divorces his wife and **m-ies**
Matt 22:30 . . . will neither **m** nor be given
Mark 12:23 . . . all seven were **m-ied** to her.
Luke 16:18 . . . his wife and **m-ies** someone
Rom 7:2 . . . when a woman **m-ies,** the law
1 Cor 7:9 . . . better to **m** than to burn
1 Cor 7:28 . . . if you do get **m-ied,** it is not
1 Cor 7:33 . . . a **m-ied** man has to think
1 Tim 5:14 . . . these younger widows to **m**

MARTYRED (v) to put to death for adhering to a belief, faith, or profession
Rev 6:9 . . . who had been **m** for the word

MARVELING (v) to become filled with surprise, wonder, or amazed curiosity
Luke 9:43 . . . everyone was **m** at

MARVELOUS (adj) astonishing; miraculous, supernatural
Ps 9:1 . . . tell of all the **m** things
Rev 15:1 . . . heaven another **m** event
Rev 15:3 . . . Great and **m** are your works,

MARY 1. Mother of Jesus; the foretold virgin (Matt 1:16-25; Luke 1:26-38); psalmist of the Magnificat (Luke 1:46-56); gave birth in Bethlehem (Luke 2:5-20); at first sign (miracle) of Jesus (John 2:1-5); at the cross (John 19:25-27); in upper room after the ascension (Acts 1:14); Jesus assigned her care to John (John 19:25-27).
2. Mary Magdalene, former demoniac, supporter of Jesus (Luke 8:1-3); was at the cross and Jesus' burial (Matt 27:55-61; Mark 15:40-47; John 19:25); saw angel after resurrection (Matt 28:1-10; Mark 16:1-9; Luke 24:10); saw Jesus after resurrection (John 20:1-18).
3. Sister of Martha and Lazarus (Luke 10:38-42; John 11; 12:1-8).
4. Mother of James and Joseph (Matt 27:56; Mark 15:40, 47; 16:1).
5. Mother of John Mark (Acts 12:12).
6. A woman in Rome greeted by Paul (Rom 16:6).

MASTER, MASTERS (n) one in authority or leadership; employer; teacher; lord or Lord
Jer 3:14 . . . the LORD, "for I am your **m.**
Matt 10:24 . . . are not greater than their **m.**
Luke 16:13 . . . No one can serve two **m-s.**
Rom 6:14 . . . Sin is no longer your **m,**
Eph 6:5 . . . obey your earthly **m-s** with deep
Col 3:22 . . . Slaves, obey your earthly **m-s**
1 Tim 6:1 . . . full respect for their **m-s**
1 Tim 6:2 . . . If the **m-s** are believers,
2 Tim 2:21 . . . ready for the **M** to use you
Titus 2:9 . . . always obey their **m-s** and do
1 Pet 2:18 . . . the authority of your **m-s**
2 Pet 2:1 . . . deny the **M** who bought them.
Jude 1:4 . . . denied our only **M** and Lord,

MAT (n) a large thick pad or cushion
Mark 2:9 . . . pick up your **m,** and walk'?
Acts 9:34 . . . and roll up your sleeping **m!**

MATTHEW One of the 12 disciples (Matt 10:3; Mark 3:18; Luke 6:15; Acts 1:13); former tax collector who followed Jesus (Matt 9:9-10); also known as "Levi" (Mark 2:14).

MATURE (adj) of or relating to a condition of full development or to attaining a desired or final state
1 Cor 2:6 . . . I am among **m** believers,
1 Cor 14:20 . . . but be **m** in understanding
2 Cor 13:9 . . . that you will become **m.**
Eph 4:13 . . . we will be **m** in the Lord,
Phil 3:15 . . . all who are spiritually **m** agree
Heb 6:1 . . . **m** in our understanding.
1 Jn 2:13 . . . who are **m** in the faith

MATURITY (n) the quality or state of being fully developed
Luke 8:14 . . . And so they never grow into **m.**
2 Cor 13:11 . . . Grow to **m.** Encourage each

MEADOWS (n) a grassy land area
Ps 23:2 . . . He lets me rest in green **m;**

MEAL, MEALS (n) a portion of food eaten usually at designated times in the day to satisfy appetite; an act or time of eating
Heb 12:16 . . . firstborn son for a single **m.**
Jude 1:12 . . . with you in your fellowship **m-s**

MEAN-SPIRITED (adj) exhibiting or characterized by meanness of spirit
Deut 15:9 . . . Do not be **m** and refuse someone

MEAN, MEANS (v) to serve or intend to convey, show, or indicate
Gen 41:16 . . . But God can tell you what it **m-s**
Rom 3:3 . . . that **m** God will be unfaithful?

MEANING (n) the thing that is conveyed especially by language
Neh 8:8 . . . and clearly explained the **m**

MEANINGLESS (adj) having no meaning; lacking any significance
Eccl 1:2 . . . **m,"** says the Teacher,
Eccl 8:14 . . . not all that is **m** in our world.
1 Tim 1:6 . . . their time in **m** discussions.

MEASURE, MEASURED, MEASURING (v) to gauge or regulate the specific dimensions of; to have a specified measurement; to regulate by a standard
Ps 145:3 . . . No one can **m** his greatness.
Isa 40:28 . . . No one can **m** the depths
Jer 31:37 . . . heavens cannot be **m-d** and
Ezek 45:3 . . . area, **m** out a portion of land
Dan 5:27 . . . balances and have not **m-d** up.

Zech 2:2 . . . I am going to **m** Jerusalem,
Luke 12:15 . . . Life is not **m-d** by how much
Eph 4:13 . . . mature in the Lord, **m-ing** up
Rev 11:1 . . . Go and **m** the Temple

MEASURES (n) an instrument or utensil for measuring; a system of standard units of measure
Deut 25:14 . . . must use full and honest **m.**
Prov 20:10 . . . unequal **m**—the LORD detests

MEAT (n) animal tissue considered especially as food
Rom 14:21 . . . better not to eat **m** or drink
1 Cor 8:13 . . . sin, I will never eat **m** again
1 Cor 10:25 . . . may eat any **m** that is sold

MEDDLING (v) to interest oneself in what is not one's concern; to interfere without right or propriety
2 Thes 3:11 . . . refusing to work and **m** in
1 Tim 5:13 . . . **m** in other people's

MEDIATE, MEDIATES (v) to act as an intermediary agent in bringing, effecting, or communicating; to interpose
Job 16:21 . . . to **m** between God and me,
Isa 2:4 . . . LORD will **m** between nations
Heb 8:6 . . . the one who **m-s** for us a far
Heb 9:15 . . . who **m-s** a new covenant
Heb 12:24 . . . Jesus, the one who **m-s**

MEDIATOR (n) one who mediates
Job 9:33 . . . If only there were a **m** between
1 Tim 2:5 . . . one God and one **M** who can

MEDICINE (n) a substance or preparation used in treating disease; something that affects well-being
Prov 17:22 . . . A cheerful heart is good **m,**
Jer 8:22 . . . Is there no **m** in Gilead?
Rev 22:2 . . . The leaves were used for **m**

MEDITATE, MEDITATING (v) to contemplate, reflect, or ponder
see also PONDER, THINK
Gen 24:63 . . . walking and **m-ing** in the fields,
Ps 1:2 . . . LORD, **m-ing** on it day and night.
Ps 48:9 . . . O God, we **m** on your unfailing
Ps 63:6 . . . **m-ing** on you through the night.
Ps 119:23 . . . but I will **m** on your decrees.
Ps 119:27 . . . **m** on your wonderful deeds.
Ps 119:48 . . . I **m** on your decrees.
Ps 145:5 . . . I will **m** on your majestic,

MEDITATION (n) the act or process of meditating
Ps 19:14 . . . words of my mouth and the **m**

MEDIUMS (n) a psychic; one through whom it is thought the dead communicate with the living
Lev 20:27 . . . who act as **m** or who consult

MELCHIZEDEK King of Salem, priest of the God Most High (Gen 14:18); blessed Abram and accepted his tithe (Gen 14:19-20); associated with mysterious priesthood (Ps 110:4; Heb 7:11).

MELODIOUS (adj) having a pleasant melody
Ps 98:5 . . . the harp and **m** song,

MELODY (n) a sweet or agreeable succession or arrangement of sounds
Ps 92:3 . . . harp and the **m** of the lyre.

MELT, MELTS (v) to dissolve or disintegrate; to disappear as if by dissolving
Jer 9:7 . . . **m** them down in a crucible
Amos 9:5 . . . touches the land and it **m-s,**

MEMBERS (n) one of the individuals composing a group; a part of a whole
see also PARTS
Eph 5:30 . . . And we are **m** of his body.
Col 3:15 . . . For as **m** of one body

MERCIFUL (adj) compassionate; forgiving
Deut 4:31 . . . your God is a **m** God;
Ps 78:38 . . . Yet he was **m** and forgave
Dan 4:27 . . . and be **m** to the poor.
Dan 9:9 . . . our God is **m** and forgiving,
Matt 5:7 . . . God blesses those who are **m,**
Luke 1:54 . . . and remembered to be **m.**
Heb 2:17 . . . **m** and faithful High Priest
Jas 2:13 . . . God will be **m** when he judges

MERCY, MERCIES (n) a blessing that is an act of divine favor or compassion; withholding of the punishment or judgment our sins deserve
see also COMPASSION, FORGIVENESS
Exod 34:6 . . . God of compassion and **m!**
2 Sam 24:14 . . . for his **m** is great.
Neh 9:27 . . . In your great **m,** you sent
Job 41:3 . . . beg you for **m** or implore
Ps 28:6 . . . he has heard my cry for **m.**
Ps 103:4 . . . me with love and tender **m-ies.**
Ps 119:77 . . . with your tender **m-ies** so I
Ps 119:156 . . . how great is your **m;**
Isa 14:1 . . . LORD will have **m** on
Isa 49:10 . . . LORD in his **m** will lead
Isa 60:10 . . . I will now have **m** on you
Lam 3:22 . . . His **m-ies** never cease.
Dan 9:18 . . . because of your **m.**
Jon 2:8 . . . their backs on all God's **m-ies.**
Mic 6:8 . . . do what is right, to love **m,**
Matt 5:7 . . . for they will be shown **m.**
Matt 9:13 . . . I want you to show **m,**
Matt 18:33 . . . just as I had **m** on you?
Matt 23:23 . . . law—justice, **m,** and faith.
Rom 9:15 . . . I will show **m** to anyone
Rom 9:18 . . . God chooses to show **m**
Rom 11:32 . . . have **m** on everyone.
2 Cor 4:1 . . . God in his **m** has given us
Gal 1:6 . . . through the loving **m** of Christ.
Eph 2:4 . . . But God is so rich in **m,** and
1 Tim 1:13 . . . But God had **m** on me
Titus 3:5 . . . but because of his **m.**
Heb 4:16 . . . we will receive his **m,**
Heb 10:29 . . . who brings God's **m** to us.
Jas 2:13 . . . will be no **m** for those
Jas 3:17 . . . It is full of **m** and good
1 Pet 1:3 . . . by his great **m** that we
Jude 1:22 . . . show **m** to those whose faith

MERCYSEAT (KJV)
Heb 9:5 . . . the *Ark's cover, the place of atonement.*

MESSAGE (n) a communication in writing, in speech, or by signals; an underlying theme or idea
Isa 53:1 . . . Who has believed our **m?**
Isa 62:11 . . . LORD has sent this **m**
John 12:38 . . . who has believed our **m?**
Acts 5:20 . . . give the people this **m** of life!
Acts 10:36 . . . This is the **m** of Good News
Rom 10:16 . . . who has believed our **m?**
1 Cor 1:18 . . . The **m** of the cross
2 Cor 5:19 . . . wonderful **m** of reconciliation.
Titus 1:9 . . . belief in the trustworthy **m**
2 Pet 1:19 . . . confidence in the **m** proclaimed

MESSENGER, MESSENGERS (n) one who bears a message or does an errand
Prov 13:17 . . . a reliable **m** brings healing.
Prov 25:13 . . . Trustworthy **m-s** refresh like
Isa 52:7 . . . feet of the **m** who brings good
Isa 66:19 . . . who survive to be **m-s** to the
Mal 3:1 . . . my **m,** and he will prepare
Matt 11:10 . . . am sending my **m** ahead
Rom 10:15 . . . feet of **m-s** who bring good
Rom 15:16 . . . a special **m** from Christ
2 Cor 12:7 . . . **m** from Satan to torment
Phil 2:25 . . . he was your **m** to help me
1 Thes 2:4 . . . speak as **m-s** approved by God
Heb 3:1 . . . to be God's **m** and High Priest.

MESSIAH, MESSIAHS (n) the one anointed by God to deliver His people and establish His kingdom
see also CHRIST, JESUS
Matt 24:24 . . . false **m-s** and false
Mark 13:22 . . . false **m-s** and false
John 1:41 . . . him, "We have found the **M**"
John 4:25 . . . I know the **M** is coming—

METHUSELAH The oldest man, who lived 969 years; the son of Enoch, who never died (Gen 5:21-24); the father of Lamech (Gen 5:25-27).

MICHAEL Ruling angel (Jude 1:9; Rev 12:7); great defender-prince in the visions of Daniel (Dan 10:13, 21; 11:1; 12:1).

MIDNIGHT (n) the middle of the night
Exod 12:29 . . . at **m,** the Lord struck down
Acts 16:25 . . . Around **m** Paul and Silas were

MIDWIVES (n) a person who assists women in childbirth
Exod 1:17 . . . because the **m** feared God,

MIGHT (n) the power, energy, or intensity of which one is capable
Josh 9:9 . . . heard of the **m** of the LORD
2 Sam 6:14 . . . the LORD with all his **m,**
Ps 54:1 . . . Defend me with your **m.**
Isa 11:2 . . . the Spirit of counsel and **m,**
Isa 63:15 . . . and the **m** you used to show

MIGHTY, MIGHTIER, MIGHTIEST (adj) powerful; great or imposing in size or extent
Gen 49:24 . . . hands of the **M** One of Jacob,
Deut 10:17 . . . God, the **m** and awesome
Deut 34:12 . . . With **m** power, Moses
2 Sam 23:8 . . . David's **m-iest** warriors.
2 Chr 20:6 . . . You are powerful and **m;**
Neh 9:32 . . . and **m** and awesome God,
Job 9:4 . . . For God is so wise and so **m.**
Job 36:5 . . . He is **m** in both power and
Ps 24:8 . . . LORD, strong and **m;**
Ps 47:5 . . . ascended with a **m** shout.
Ps 50:1 . . . LORD, the **M** One, is God,
Ps 71:16 . . . I will praise your **m** deeds,
Ps 77:12 . . . thinking about your **m** works.
Ps 89:27 . . . son, the **m-iest** king on earth.
Ps 93:4 . . . But **m-ier** than the violent raging
Ps 93:4 . . . LORD above is **m-ier** than these!
Ps 95:4 . . . and the **m-iest** mountains.
Ps 145:4 . . . children of your **m** acts;
Ps 145:12 . . . will tell about your **m** deeds
Ps 150:2 . . . Praise him for his **m** works;
Prov 24:5 . . . wise are **m-ier** than the strong,
Isa 9:6 . . . Wonderful Counselor, **M** God,
Isa 60:16 . . . your Redeemer, the **M** One of
Zeph 3:17 . . . He is a **m** savior.
Eph 1:19 . . . This is the same **m** power
Eph 6:10 . . . in the Lord and in his **m**
Heb 1:3 . . . sustains everything by the **m**
1 Pet 5:6 . . . yourselves under the **m**
Jude 1:9 . . . Michael, one of the **m-iest** of the angels,

MILE (n) a unit of distance equal to 5,280 feet
Matt 5:41 . . . gear for a **m**, carry it two

MILK (n) from goats, used for food and drink; figurative of abundant produce, prosperity, spiritual food, or salvation
Exod 3:8 . . . flowing with **m** and honey—
1 Cor 3:2 . . . feed you with **m**, not with
1 Pet 2:2 . . . must crave pure spiritual **m**

MILLSTONE (n) either of two circular stones used for grinding (as grain)
Luke 17:2 . . . into the sea with a **m** hung

MIND, MINDS (n) the part of humans that engages in conscious thinking, feeling, and decision making; in the Bible, mind is akin to the heart, not the brain
Num 23:19 . . . he does not change his **m.**
1 Sam 15:29 . . . nor will he change his **m,**
Mark 12:30 . . . all your soul, all your **m,**
Luke 24:45 . . . opened their **m-s**
Acts 4:32 . . . were united in heart and **m.**
Rom 8:6 . . . Spirit control your **m**
1 Cor 1:10 . . . be of one **m**, united in
1 Cor 2:9 . . . heard, and no **m** has imagined
2 Cor 4:4 . . . has blinded the **m-s** of those
Col 2:18 . . . sinful **m-s** have made them
2 Tim 4:5 . . . clear **m** in every situation.
Heb 8:10 . . . I will put my laws in their **m-s,**
Heb 10:16 . . . I will write them on their **m-s.**

MINDING (v) to be concerned about
1 Thes 4:11 . . . live a quiet life, **m** your own

MINISTERS (n) agent; one who serves or assists another of higher rank
2 Cor 3:6 . . . to be **m** of his new covenant.

MINISTRY (n) exercise of one's gifts and resources
2 Cor 9:12 . . . from this **m** of giving—
2 Cor 9:13 . . . As a result of your **m**, they
Heb 8:6 . . . a **m** that is far superior to

MIRACLE, MIRACLES (n) an extraordinary event manifesting divine intervention in human affairs
Exod 3:20 . . . performing all kinds of **m-s**
Exod 7:9 . . . demand, 'Show me a **m.**'
Deut 13:1 . . . they promise you signs or **m-s,**
Job 9:10 . . . He performs countless **m-s.**
Ps 105:5 . . . he has performed, his **m-s,**
Ps 106:2 . . . the glorious **m-s** of the LORD?
Jer 32:19 . . . and do great and mighty **m-s.**
Matt 7:22 . . . and performed many **m-s**
Matt 13:54 . . . and the power to do **m-s?**
Mark 6:2 . . . power to perform such **m-s?**
Mark 9:39 . . . No one who performs a **m**
Luke 19:37 . . . wonderful **m-s** they had
Luke 23:8 . . . to see him perform a **m.**
John 7:21 . . . I did one **m** on the Sabbath,
Acts 2:22 . . . by doing powerful **m-s,**
Acts 8:13 . . . **m-s** Philip performed.
Acts 19:11 . . . to perform unusual **m-s.**
1 Cor 12:28 . . . those who do **m-s**, those
2 Cor 12:12 . . . and **m-s** among you.
Gal 3:5 . . . Spirit and work **m-s** among you
Heb 2:4 . . . and various **m-s** and gifts of

MIRACULOUS (adj) working or able to work miracles; supernatural
Ps 106:7 . . . the LORD's **m** deeds.
Matt 12:39 . . . would demand a **m**
John 9:16 . . . sinner do such **m** signs?
John 12:37 . . . despite all the **m** signs Jesus
John 20:30 . . . do many other **m** signs
Acts 2:43 . . . performed many **m** signs
Acts 4:16 . . . have performed a **m** sign,
Rom 15:19 . . . of **m** signs and wonders

MIRROR (n) a polished or smooth surface (as of glass) that forms images by reflection
1 Cor 13:12 . . . puzzling reflections in a **m,**
Jas 1:23 . . . glancing at your face in a **m.**

MISERABLE (adj) being in a pitiable state of distress or unhappiness
Rom 7:24 . . . Oh, what a **m** person I am!

MISERY (n) a state of suffering or discomfort; a state of great unhappiness and emotional distress
Judg 10:16 . . . And he was grieved by their **m.**
Rom 3:16 . . . Destruction and **m** always follow

MISFORTUNE (n) bad luck; a distressing or unfortunate incident or event
Prov 17:5 . . . who rejoice at the **m** of others
Obad 1:12 . . . people of Judah suffered such **m.**

MISLEAD, MISLED (v) to lead astray; to deceive
Prov 13:6 . . . the evil are **m-ed** by sin.
Prov 16:29 . . . **m** their companions,
Matt 24:4 . . . Don't let anyone **m** you,
Gal 6:7 . . . Don't be **m-ed**—you cannot
Jas 1:16 . . . So don't be **m-ed**, my dear

MISTREAT, MISTREATED (v) to treat badly; to abuse
Exod 22:21 . . . You must not **m** or oppress
Prov 19:26 . . . Children who **m** their father
Heb 13:3 . . . those being **m-ed**, as if you

MISUSE (v) to use incorrectly; to mistreat or abuse
Exod 20:7 . . . must not **m** the name of
Deut 5:11 . . . must not **m** the name of
Ps 139:20 . . . your enemies **m** your name.

MOCK, MOCKED, MOCKS (v) to treat with contempt or ridicule; to mimic in sport or derision
Job 11:3 . . . When you **m** God, shouldn't
Ps 22:7 . . . Everyone who sees me **m-s** me.
Ps 89:51 . . . Your enemies have **m-ed** me,
Prov 3:34 . . . The LORD **m-s** the mockers
Prov 30:17 . . . The eye that **m-s** a father and
Mic 6:16 . . . with contempt, **m-ed** by all
Matt 5:11 . . . blesses you when people **m**
Matt 27:41 . . . the elders also **m-ed** Jesus.
Mark 10:34 . . . They will **m** him, spit on
Luke 6:22 . . . and exclude you and **m** you
Gal 6:7 . . . cannot **m** the justice of God.

MOCKER, MOCKERS (n) one who mocks
Ps 1:1 . . . sinners, or join in with **m-s.**
Prov 3:34 . . . The LORD mocks the **m-s**
Prov 9:7 . . . Anyone who rebukes a **m** will
Prov 20:1 . . . Wine produces **m-s**; alcohol

MOCKERY (n) a subject of laughter, derision, or sport; insulting or contemptuous action or speech
1 Kgs 9:7 . . . object of **m** and ridicule
Isa 50:6 . . . not hide my face from **m** and
Joel 2:17 . . . become an object of **m.**
Matt 27:29 . . . in **m** and taunted,

MODEL (n) an example for imitation or emulation
Ezek 28:12 . . . were the **m** of perfection,

MODESTY (n) propriety in dress, speech, or conduct; freedom from conceit or vanity
1 Tim 2:15 . . . faith, love, holiness, and **m.**

MOLTEN (adj) made by melting and casting
Exod 34:17 . . . not make any gods of **m** metal

MOMENT (n) a comparatively brief period of time; instant
Ps 30:5 . . . lasts only a **m**, but his favor
Prov 11:18 . . . get rich for the **m,**
Isa 54:7 . . . For a brief **m** I abandoned you,
Isa 66:8 . . . come forth in a mere **m?**
Matt 6:27 . . . your worries add a single **m**
Gal 2:5 . . . give in to them for a single **m.**

MONEY (n) officially coined or stamped metal or paper currency
see also POSSESSION(S), RICHES, TREASURE(S), WEALTH
2 Chr 24:10 . . . gladly brought their **m** and
Eccl 5:10 . . . who love **m** will never have
Matt 6:24 . . . serve both God and **m.**
Luke 3:14 . . . Don't extort **m** or make false
1 Tim 3:3 . . . and not love **m.**
1 Tim 6:10 . . . love of **m** is the root of all
1 Tim 6:17 . . . and not to trust in their **m,**
1 Jn 3:17 . . . If someone has enough **m**

MONTH, MONTHS (n) a measure of time corresponding nearly to the period of the moon's revolution and amounting to approximately 4 weeks or 30 days
Ezek 47:12 . . . will be a new crop every **m,**
Gal 4:10 . . . certain days or **m-s** or seasons
Rev 11:2 . . . trample the holy city for 42 **m-s.**
Rev 13:5 . . . he wanted for forty-two **m-s.**
Rev 22:2 . . . fruit, with a fresh crop each **m.**

MOON (n) a celestial body that orbits the earth
Josh 10:13 . . . and the **m** stayed in place
Ps 121:6 . . . harm you by day, nor the **m** at
Ps 148:3 . . . Praise him, sun and **m!**
Joel 2:31 . . . the **m** will turn blood red
Hab 3:11 . . . The sun and **m** stood still
Matt 24:29 . . . the **m** will give no light,
Acts 2:20 . . . the **m** will turn blood red
Col 2:16 . . . or new **m** ceremonies
Rev 21:23 . . . city has no need of sun or **m,**

MORE (adv) to a greater or higher degree
Ps 73:25 . . . I desire you **m** than anything
1 Pet 1:2 . . . give you **m** and **m** grace

MORNING STAR (n) a bright planet (as Venus) seen in the eastern sky before or at sunrise
2 Pet 1:19 . . . and Christ the **M** shines
Rev 2:28 . . . give them the **m!**
Rev 22:16 . . . I am the bright **m.**

MORNING (n) the time from sunrise to noon
Gen 1:5 . . . evening passed and **m** came,
Ps 5:3 . . . Listen to my voice in the **m,**
Lam 3:23 . . . mercies begin afresh each **m.**

MORTAL (adj) subject to death
Gen 6:3 . . . for they are only **m** flesh.
Rom 8:11 . . . will give life to your **m** bodies
1 Cor 15:53 . . . our **m** bodies must be

MORTALS (n) a human being
Ps 8:4 . . . mere **m** that you should think
Ps 144:3 . . . mere **m** that you should think

MOSES Deliverer of Israel from Egypt, lawgiver, servant of God; "drawn out" of the Nile, raised in Pharaoh's house (Exod 2:1-10); killed an Egyptian and fled to Midian (Exod 2:11-15; Acts 7:24); married Zipporah and had a child (Exod 2:16-22); saw the LORD at the burning bush (Exod 3:1–4:17); returned to Egypt (Exod 4:18-31); conflict with Pharaoh and the 10 plagues (Exod 5–11); brother of Aaron and Miriam (1 Chr 6:3); Passover and the Exodus (Exod 12–14; 1 Cor 10:2); song of salvation and praise (Exod 15:1-21; Rev 15:3); heavenly provisions

(Exod 15:22–17:7); raised arms to defeat enemies (Exod 17:8-16); delegated judgeships (Exod 18); received the Law at Sinai (Exod 19–23; John 1:17; Heb 12:21); received Tabernacle plans (Exod 25–31); broke tablets at gold calf incident (Exod 32); received new tablets (Exod 33–34); face glowed with the LORD's glory (Exod 34:29-35; 2 Cor 3:13-15); directed the building of the Tabernacle (Exod 35–40); anointed Tabernacle and Aaronic priesthood (Lev 8–9); opposed by Aaron and Miriam, interceded for sister (Num 12); interceded for Israel when they refused to enter Canaan (Num 14:11-25); Korah's rebellion (Num 16); water at Meribah (Num 20:1-13); denied entrance to Promised Land (Num 20:12; Deut 1:37; 3:23-28); bronze snake healed (Num 21:4-9; John 3:14); succeeded by Joshua (Num 27:12-23; Deut 31:1-8); received additional laws (Num 28–30); gave concluding messages to Israel (Deut 1–33); gave final blessings to the tribes (Deut 33; *see also* Gen 49); died and was exalted (Deut 34; Heb 3:2); wrote a psalm (Ps 90); recorded book of the Law (Ezra 3:2; Neh 13:1; Luke 24:44).

MOTHER (n) a female parent; a woman in authority
see also PARENT
Gen 2:24 . . . a man leaves his father and **m**
Gen 3:20 . . . she would be the **m** of all who
Exod 20:12 . . . Honor your father and **m.**
Deut 21:18 . . . not obey his father or **m,**
Judg 5:7 . . . Deborah arose as a **m**
Prov 10:1 . . . brings grief to a **m.**
Prov 23:22 . . . don't despise your **m**
Isa 66:13 . . . as a **m** comforts her child.
Matt 10:35 . . . a daughter against her **m,**
Matt 10:37 . . . father or **m** more than you
Matt 12:48 . . . Who is my **m?**
Mark 10:19 . . . Honor your father and **m.**
John 19:27 . . . disciple, "Here is your **m."**
Eph 5:31 . . . A man leaves his father and **m**
Eph 6:2 . . . Honor your father and **m.**

MOTHER-IN-LAW (n) the mother of one's spouse
Ruth 2:19 . . . Ruth told her **m** about the man
Matt 10:35 . . . daughter-in-law against her **m.**

MOTHS (n) insects whose larvae eat wool, fur, or feathers
Matt 6:19 . . . on earth, where **m** eat them

MOTIVES (n) something (as a need or desire) that causes a person to act
1 Chr 29:17 . . . all this with good **m,**
Ps 26:2 . . . Test my **m** and my heart.
Prov 16:2 . . . LORD examines their **m.**
Jer 17:10 . . . hearts and examine secret **m.**
1 Cor 4:5 . . . will reveal our private **m.**
Phil 1:18 . . . Whether their **m** are false or
1 Thes 2:3 . . . with any deceit or impure **m**
1 Thes 2:4 . . . He alone examines the **m** of
Jas 4:3 . . . because your **m** are all wrong—

MOUNT (n) a high hill; mountain
Exod 17:6 . . . on the rock at **M** Sinai
Exod 19:18 . . . **M** Sinai was covered with smoke
Zech 14:4 . . . the **M** of Olives will split
Matt 24:3 . . . Jesus sat on the **M** of Olives
Luke 22:39 . . . as usual to the **M** of Olives

MOUNTAIN, MOUNTAINS (n) a landmass that projects conspicuously above its surroundings and is higher than a hill
Exod 24:18 . . . on the **m** forty days
Deut 5:4 . . . At the **m** the LORD
Ps 36:6 . . . is like the mighty **m-s,**
Ps 121:1 . . . I look up to the **m-s—**
Isa 14:13 . . . preside on the **m** of the gods
Matt 17:20 . . . say to this **m,** 'Move
Mark 9:2 . . . led them up a high **m**
Mark 9:9 . . . went back down the **m,**
Luke 23:30 . . . beg the **m-s,** 'Fall on us,'
1 Cor 13:2 . . . faith that I could move **m-s,**
2 Pet 1:18 . . . with him on the holy **m.**
Rev 6:16 . . . they cried to the **m-s** and

MOUNTAINTOPS (n) the summit of a mountain
Isa 42:11 . . . shout praises from the **m!**

MOURN (v) to feel or express grief or sorrow
Gen 50:11 . . . watched them **m**
Zech 12:10 . . . have pierced and **m**
Matt 5:4 . . . God blesses those who **m,**

MOURNING (n) the act of sorrowing; a period of time during which signs of grief are shown
Ps 30:11 . . . my clothes of **m** and clothed
Isa 60:20 . . . Your days of **m** will come to
Isa 61:3 . . . instead of **m,** festive praise
Jer 31:13 . . . I will turn their **m** into joy.
Zech 8:19 . . . times of **m** you have kept

MOUTH, MOUTHS (n) the natural opening through which food passes into the body of an animal; voice, speech
Ps 10:7 . . . Their **m-s** are full of cursing,
Ps 19:14 . . . words of my **m** and
Prov 13:3 . . . opening your **m** can ruin
Isa 51:16 . . . have put my words in your **m**
Isa 53:7 . . . he did not open his **m.**
Isa 59:3 . . . and your **m** spews corruption.
Jer 31:29 . . . their children's **m-s** pucker
Matt 4:4 . . . word that comes from the **m**
Rom 3:14 . . . Their **m-s** are full of cursing
Rom 10:9 . . . **m** that Jesus is Lord
Rev 2:16 . . . with the sword of my **m.**

MOVE, MOVED, MOVES, MOVING (v) to change the place or position of; to go from one place to another in continuous motion; to carry on one's life or activities in a specified environment; to stir the emotions or passions of; to prompt to the doing of something
Exod 35:21 . . . and whose spirits were **m-d**
Deut 19:14 . . . steal anyone's land by **m-ing**
Deut 23:14 . . . LORD your God **m-s** around
Prov 4:15 . . . Turn away and keep **m-ing.**
Prov 23:10 . . . cheat your neighbor by **m-ing**
Isa 54:10 . . . For the mountains may **m**
Acts 17:28 . . . For in him we live and **m**
1 Cor 13:2 . . . faith that I could **m**
2 Pet 1:21 . . . were **m-d** by the Holy Spirit,

MUD (n) soft, wet earth
Ps 40:2 . . . pit of despair, out of the **m**
John 9:6 . . . spread the **m** over the blind

MUDDYING (v) to soil or stain with or as if with mud
Prov 25:26 . . . a fountain or **m** a spring.

MULTIPLY, MULTIPLIED (v) to increase greatly in extent or number
Gen 1:22 . . . Be fruitful and **m.**
Acts 6:1 . . . the believers rapidly **m-ied,**

MULTITUDE (n) a great number
1 Pet 4:8 . . . love covers a **m** of sins.

MURDER (n) the personal, intentional killing of another person
Matt 5:21 . . . If you commit **m,**
Rom 1:29 . . . hate, envy, **m,** quarreling,

MURDER, MURDERED, MURDERS (v) to kill (a human being) unlawfully and with premeditated malice
Gen 9:5 . . . **m-s** a fellow human must die.
Exod 20:13 . . . You must not **m.**
Deut 5:17 . . . You must not **m.**
Matt 23:31 . . . who **m-ed** the prophets.
Acts 7:52 . . . whom you betrayed and **m-ed.**
Rom 13:9 . . . You must not **m.**
Jas 2:11 . . . You must not **m.**

MURDERER, MURDERERS (n) one who commits the crime of murder
Num 35:16 . . . **m** must be executed.
Ps 5:6 . . . LORD detests **m-s** and deceivers.
Ps 26:9 . . . condemn me along with **m-s.**
Ps 59:2 . . . save me from these **m-s.**
Ezek 18:10 . . . a robber or **m** and refuses
1 Jn 3:15 . . . brother or sister is really a **m**
Rev 21:8 . . . the corrupt, **m-s,** the immoral,
Rev 22:15 . . . the sexually immoral, the **m-s,**

MUSIC (n) vocal, instrumental, or mechanical sounds having rhythm, melody, or harmony
Judg 5:3 . . . I will make **m** to the LORD,
1 Chr 6:31 . . . lead the **m** at the house of
Neh 12:27 . . . and with the **m** of cymbals,
Ps 45:8 . . . the **m** of strings entertains
Amos 5:23 . . . to the **m** of your harps.
Eph 5:19 . . . and making **m** to the Lord

MUSICAL (adj) of or relating to music
1 Chr 23:5 . . . praise the LORD with the **m**
2 Chr 23:13 . . . with **m** instruments
Neh 12:36 . . . the **m** instruments
Dan 3:5 . . . and other **m** instruments,
Dan 3:15 . . . of the **m** instruments.

MUSICIAN, MUSICIANS (n) a composer, conductor, or performer of music; instrumentalist
1 Chr 6:33 . . . Heman the **m** was from
1 Chr 9:33 . . . **m-s,** all prominent Levites,
1 Chr 15:16 . . . were singers and **m-s** to sing
1 Chr 15:19 . . . The **m-s** Heman, Asaph,
2 Chr 9:11 . . . lyres and harps for the **m-s.**
2 Chr 34:12 . . . were skilled **m-s,**
2 Chr 35:15 . . . **m-s,** descendants of

MUSTARD (n) a plant whose seeds are used as a condiment and for oil; in Jesus' time, the smallest seed known
Matt 13:31 . . . is like a **m** seed planted
Matt 17:20 . . . as small as a **m** seed,
Mark 4:31 . . . is like a **m** seed planted

MUTILATORS (n) one who cripples or maims
Phil 3:2 . . . **m** who say you must be

MUZZLE (v) to fit with a fastening or covering for the mouth of an animal to prevent eating or biting
Deut 25:4 . . . You must not **m** an ox
1 Tim 5:18 . . . You must not **m** an ox

MYRRH (n) an aromatic extract from a stiff-branched tree with white flowers and plum-like fruit
Song 1:13 . . . My lover is like a sachet of **m**
Matt 2:11 . . . gold, frankincense, and **m.**
Mark 15:23 . . . wine drugged with **m,**
John 19:39 . . . ointment made from **m** and
Rev 18:13 . . . incense, **m,** frankincense,

MYSTERIOUS (adj) exciting wonder, curiosity, or surprise while baffling efforts to comprehend or identify; of, relating to, or constituting mystery
1 Cor 14:2 . . . Spirit, but it will all be **m.**

Eph 1:9 . . . now revealed to us his **m** plan
Eph 3:3 . . . revealed his **m** plan to me.
Eph 6:19 . . . explain God's **m** plan that the
Col 2:2 . . . they understand God's **m** plan,
Col 4:3 . . . about his **m** plan concerning
Rev 10:7 . . . God's **m** plan will be fulfilled.

MYSTERY, MYSTERIES (n) something not understood or beyond understanding; a religious truth that one can know only by revelation and cannot fully understand
see also SECRET(S)
Dan 4:9 . . . and that no **m** is too great
Rom 11:25 . . . to understand this **m**,
1 Cor 2:7 . . . speak of is the **m** of God—
1 Cor 4:1 . . . explaining God's **m-ies.**
1 Tim 3:9 . . . to the **m** of the faith
1 Tim 3:16 . . . the great **m** of our faith:
Rev 1:20 . . . the **m** of the seven stars
Rev 17:7 . . . tell you the **m** of this woman

MYTHS (n) a popular belief or tradition that has grown up around something or someone
1 Tim 1:4 . . . in endless discussion of **m**
2 Tim 4:4 . . . and chase after **m.**
Titus 1:14 . . . listening to Jewish **m**

N

NAILED, NAILING (v) to fasten with or as if with a nail
Matt 27:35 . . . had **n-ed** him to the cross,
Mark 15:24 . . . soldiers **n-ed** him to the
Acts 2:23 . . . you **n-ed** him to a cross
Col 2:14 . . . away by **n-ing** it to the cross.
Heb 6:6 . . . are **n-ing** him to the cross

NAKED (adj) not covered by clothing; nude
Gen 2:25 . . . man and his wife were both **n**,
Job 1:21 . . . and I will be **n** when I leave.
Eccl 5:15 . . . the end of our lives as **n**

NAME, NAMES (n) a word or phrase that constitutes the distinctive designation of a person or thing; reputation
see also REPUTATION
Gen 2:19 . . . the man chose a **n** for each
Exod 3:15 . . . my **n** to remember
Exod 28:9 . . . on them the **n-s** of the tribes
Exod 34:14 . . . whose very **n** is Jealous,
Lev 24:11 . . . blasphemed the **N**
Deut 18:5 . . . minister in the LORD's **n**
Deut 28:58 . . . awesome **n** of the LORD
1 Chr 17:8 . . . will make your **n** as famous
2 Chr 7:14 . . . called by my **n** will humble
Ps 8:1 . . . your majestic **n** fills the earth!
Ps 23:3 . . . paths, bringing honor to his **n.**
Ps 34:3 . . . let us exalt his **n** together.
Ps 66:2 . . . Sing about the glory of his **n!**
Ps 103:1 . . . I will praise his holy **n.**
Ps 138:2 . . . I praise your **n** for your
Ps 147:4 . . . stars and calls them all by **n.**
Isa 40:26 . . . calling each by its **n.**
Isa 42:8 . . . I am the LORD; that is my **n!**
Jer 15:16 . . . I bear your **n**, O LORD
Dan 12:1 . . . people whose **n** is written in
Joel 2:32 . . . calls on the **n** of the LORD
Mic 5:4 . . . majesty of the **n** of the LORD
Zech 14:9 . . . one LORD—his **n** alone
Mal 1:6 . . . have shown contempt for my **n!**
Matt 24:5 . . . come in my **n**, claiming, 'I am
Matt 28:19 . . . baptizing them in the **n** of
Luke 10:20 . . . your **n-s** are registered
Luke 11:2 . . . may your **n** be kept holy.
John 16:24 . . . Ask, using my **n**, and you
Acts 2:21 . . . calls on the **n** of the LORD
Acts 4:12 . . . no other **n** under heaven
Rom 10:13 . . . calls on the **n** of the LORD
Phil 2:9 . . . gave him the **n** above all
Phil 2:10 . . . that at the **n** of Jesus every
Phil 4:3 . . . whose **n-s** are written in the Book
Heb 12:23 . . . **n-s** are written in heaven.
Jas 5:14 . . . with oil in the **n** of the Lord.
Rev 2:17 . . . stone will be engraved a new **n**
Rev 3:5 . . . erase their **n-s** from the Book
Rev 3:12 . . . write on them the **n**
Rev 20:15 . . . whose **n** was not found
Rev 21:27 . . . **n-s** are written in the Lamb's

NAME (v) to give a name to; to call
Matt 1:21 . . . you are to **n** him Jesus,

NARROW (adj) of slender width
Matt 7:13 . . . only through the **n** gate.
Matt 7:14 . . . the gateway to life is very **n**

NATION, NATIONS (n) group of people defined by geography or ethnicity
see also GENTILE(S), PEOPLE(S)
Gen 12:2 . . . I will make you into a great **n.**
Gen 17:4 . . . father of a multitude of **n-s!**
Gen 17:16 . . . the mother of many **n-s.**
Gen 25:23 . . . will become two **n-s.**
Gen 28:3 . . . multiply and become many **n-s!**
Exod 19:6 . . . of priests, my holy **n.**
Deut 15:6 . . . You will rule many **n-s**, but
Deut 28:10 . . . the **n-s** of the world will see
Ps 2:8 . . . you the **n-s** as your inheritance,
Ps 22:28 . . . He rules all the **n-s.**
Ps 46:10 . . . I will be honored by every **n.**
Ps 66:7 . . . every movement of the **n-s;**
Ps 68:30 . . . Scatter the **n-s** that delight in
Ps 87:6 . . . the LORD registers the **n-s,**
Ps 99:2 . . . exalted above all the **n-s.**
Ps 113:4 . . . LORD is high above the **n-s;**
Prov 14:34 . . . Godliness makes a **n** great,
Isa 11:10 . . . The **n-s** will rally to him,
Isa 34:1 . . . listen, O **n-s** of the earth.
Isa 40:15 . . . for all the **n-s** of the world
Isa 42:1 . . . He will bring justice to the **n-s.**
Isa 52:15 . . . And he will startle many **n-s.**
Isa 56:7 . . . a house of prayer for all **n-s.**
Isa 60:12 . . . the **n-s** that refuse to serve
Isa 66:8 . . . Has a **n** ever been born in a
Ezek 37:22 . . . divided into two **n-s** or into
Joel 3:2 . . . my people among the **n-s,**
Amos 9:12 . . . **n-s** I have called to be mine.
Mic 4:3 . . . disputes between strong **n-s**
Mic 5:7 . . . take their place among the **n-s.**
Zeph 3:8 . . . stand and accuse these evil **n-s.**
Hag 2:7 . . . I will shake all the **n-s,**
Zech 8:13 . . . Among the other **n-s**, Judah
Zech 12:2 . . . makes the nearby **n-s** stagger
Matt 12:18 . . . proclaim justice to the **n-s.**
Matt 24:14 . . . so that all **n-s** will hear it;
Matt 28:19 . . . make disciples of all the **n-s,**
Mark 11:17 . . . house of prayer for all **n-s,**
Acts 4:25 . . . Why were the **n-s** so angry?
Gal 3:8 . . . All **n-s** will be blessed through
1 Pet 2:9 . . . royal priests, a holy **n,**
Rev 5:9 . . . and language and people and **n.**
Rev 14:6 . . . to every **n**, tribe, language,
Rev 21:24 . . . The **n-s** will walk in its light,
Rev 22:2 . . . for medicine to heal the **n-s.**

NATIVITY (KJV)
Gen 11:28 . . . the land of his *birth*
Jer 46:16 . . . to the land of our *birth.*

NATURAL (adj) having a physical or real existence as contrasted with one that is spiritual, intellectual, or fictitious
1 Cor 15:44 . . . as there are **n** bodies,

NATURE (n) inherent character or essence; given by God at birth
Rom 1:20 . . . eternal power and divine **n.**
Rom 8:4 . . . follow our sinful **n**
Rom 8:7 . . . For the sinful **n** is always
Gal 5:19 . . . the desires of your sinful **n,**
Gal 5:24 . . . desires of their sinful **n** to
2 Pet 1:4 . . . share his divine **n** and escape

NAZARENE, NAZARENES (n) a native or resident of Nazareth
Matt 2:23 . . . He will be called a **N.**
Acts 24:5 . . . of the cult known as the **N-s.**
Acts 26:9 . . . the very name of Jesus the **N.**

NAZARETH (n) a town of lower Galilee where Jesus spent his boyhood years
Matt 4:13 . . . He went first to **N,**
Mark 14:67 . . . those with Jesus of **N.**
Mark 16:6 . . . looking for Jesus of **N**, who
John 1:46 . . . anything good come from **N?**

NAZIRITE (n) a person consecrated to God by a vow to avoid drinking wine, cutting the hair, and being defiled by the presence of a corpse
Num 6:2 . . . take the special vow of a **N,**
Judg 13:7 . . . be dedicated to God as a **N**

NECK (n) the part of the body that connects the head and the torso
Prov 6:21 . . . Tie them around your **n.**
Matt 18:6 . . . millstone tied around your **n**

NECKLACE (n) an ornament worn around the neck
Prov 3:22 . . . They are like jewels on a **n.**

NEED, NEEDS (n) a condition requiring supply or relief; poverty; obligation; a lack of something requisite, desirable, or useful
1 Kgs 8:59 . . . according to each day's **n-s.**
Ps 79:8 . . . compassion quickly meet our **n-s,**
Ps 112:9 . . . give generously to those in **n.**
Prov 11:26 . . . who sells in time of **n.**
Prov 30:8 . . . just enough to satisfy my **n-s.**
Matt 6:2 . . . give to someone in **n,**
Acts 2:45 . . . the money with those in **n.**
Acts 20:35 . . . you can help those in **n** by
Rom 12:13 . . . God's people are in **n,**
1 Cor 7:3 . . . fulfill his wife's sexual **n-s,**
Eph 4:28 . . . give generously to others in **n.**
Phil 4:19 . . . will supply all your **n-s** from his
Titus 3:14 . . . by meeting the urgent **n-s**

NEED, NEEDED, NEEDING (v) to require; to be necessary; to be in want
Ps 34:9 . . . fear him will have all they **n.**
Ps 119:75 . . . disciplined me because I **n-ed**
Phil 4:6 . . . Tell God what you **n**, and
Heb 4:16 . . . grace to help us when we **n** it
Jas 1:4 . . . complete, **n-ing** nothing.
Jas 1:5 . . . If you **n** wisdom, ask our

NEEDLE (n) a small slender instrument that has an eye for thread at one end and is used for sewing
Matt 19:24 . . . go through the eye of a **n**

NEEDY (adj) poverty-stricken; marked by want of affection, attention, or emotional support
1 Sam 2:8 . . . **n** from the garbage dump.
Ps 9:18 . . . the **n** will not be ignored
Ps 68:10 . . . you provided for your **n**
Ps 69:33 . . . LORD hears the cries of the **n;**
Prov 22:22 . . . or exploit the **n** in court.
Prov 31:20 . . . opens her arms to the **n.**

NEGLECT (v) to disregard; to overlook; to ignore
Deut 12:19 . . . careful never to **n** the Levites

Deut 14:27 . . . And do not **n** the Levites
Ezra 4:22 . . . and don't **n** this matter,
Neh 10:39 . . . together not to **n** the Temple
Luke 11:42 . . . do not **n** the more important
1 Tim 4:14 . . . Do not **n** the spiritual

NEHEMIAH Cupbearer of the Persian king Artaxerxes (Neh 1:11); governor of Israel (Neh 5:14; 8:9); prayed for restoration (1:4); king commissioned him to rebuild Jerusalem's walls (Neh 2:8); rebuilt walls over opposition (Neh 2:9–6:19); reestablished worship (Neh 8:1-18); prayer of praise and confession (Neh 9); wall of Jerusalem dedicated (Neh 12:27-43).

NEIGHBOR, NEIGHBORS (n) one living or located near another; fellow man
Lev 19:18 . . . but love your **n** as yourself.
Ps 15:3 . . . to gossip or harm their **n-s**
Prov 24:28 . . . your **n-s** without cause;
Prov 27:10 . . . better to go to a **n** than
Jer 31:34 . . . not need to teach their **n-s,**
Mark 12:31 . . . Love your **n** as yourself.
Luke 10:29 . . . And who is my **n?**
Rom 13:8 . . . If you love your **n,** you will
Gal 5:14 . . . Love your **n** as yourself.
Eph 4:25 . . . Let us tell our **n-s** the truth,
Heb 8:11 . . . not need to teach their **n-s,**
Jas 2:8 . . . Love your **n** as yourself.

NET, NETS (n) a meshed fabric made of ropes used for catching fish, birds, insects, or other animals
Ps 66:11 . . . You captured us in your **n**
Ps 141:10 . . . wicked fall into their own **n-s,**
Hab 1:15 . . . caught in their **n-s** while they
Matt 4:20 . . . they left their **n-s** at once and
Matt 13:47 . . . is like a fishing **n** that was
John 21:6 . . . Throw out your **n** on the

NEVER (adv) at no time; not in any degree; not under any condition
1 Chr 29:18 . . . their love for you **n** changes.
Ps 89:33 . . . But I will **n** stop loving him
Ps 111:3 . . . His righteousness **n** fails.
John 14:16 . . . who will **n** leave you.
Rom 11:29 . . . his call can **n** be withdrawn.
Rom 12:11 . . . **N** be lazy, but work hard
1 Cor 15:2 . . . something that was **n** true

NEVER-ENDING (adj) unceasing
1 Chr 16:17 . . . of Israel as a **n** covenant:
Ps 105:10 . . . of Israel as a **n** covenant:
Luke 3:17 . . . burning the chaff with **n** fire.

NEW (adj) fresh; original; different than before; unfamiliar
Ps 98:1 . . . Sing a **n** song to the LORD,
Jer 31:31 . . . I will make a **n** covenant with
Ezek 36:26 . . . I will give you a **n** heart,
Mark 16:17 . . . will speak in **n** languages.
Luke 22:20 . . . cup is the **n** covenant
Rom 6:4 . . . we also may live **n** lives.
Rom 12:2 . . . you into a **n** person
1 Cor 11:25 . . . cup is the **n** covenant
2 Cor 3:6 . . . but under the **n** covenant,
2 Cor 5:17 . . . is gone; a **n** life has begun!
Gal 6:15 . . . into a **n** creation.
Eph 4:24 . . . Put on your **n** nature,
Col 3:10 . . . Put on your **n** nature,
Heb 8:8 . . . when I will make a **n** covenant
Heb 9:15 . . . mediates a **n** covenant
Heb 12:24 . . . the **n** covenant
2 Pet 3:13 . . . **n** heavens and **n** earth he
Rev 2:17 . . . a **n** name that no one
Rev 21:1 . . . **n** heaven and a **n** earth,

NEWBORN (adj) recently born
1 Pet 2:2 . . . Like **n** babies, you must crave

NEWS (n) a report of recent events; "Good News": the Gospel of Jesus Christ
Isa 40:9 . . . of good **n,** shout from the
Matt 4:23 . . . the Good **N** about
Mark 1:15 . . . sins and believe the Good **N!**
Luke 4:43 . . . I must preach the Good **N**
Acts 13:32 . . . to bring you this Good **N.**
Acts 14:21 . . . preaching the Good **N**
Rom 1:16 . . . not ashamed of this Good **N**
Rom 10:17 . . . the Good **N** about Christ.
Rom 15:16 . . . I bring you the Good **N**
Rom 16:25 . . . just as my Good **N** says.
1 Cor 1:17 . . . to preach the Good **N**—
1 Cor 9:12 . . . an obstacle to the Good **N**
1 Cor 9:16 . . . preach the Good **N!**
1 Cor 9:23 . . . to spread the Good **N**
1 Cor 15:1 . . . the Good **N** I preached
2 Cor 4:4 . . . glorious light of the Good **N.**
2 Cor 9:13 . . . obedient to the Good **N**
2 Cor 11:7 . . . preaching God's Good **N**
Gal 1:7 . . . is not the Good **N** at all.
Eph 6:15 . . . comes from the Good **N**
Phil 1:27 . . . worthy of the Good **N**
Col 1:5 . . . heard the truth of the Good **N.**
Col 1:23 . . . Good **N** has been preached
1 Thes 2:4 . . . entrusted with the Good **N.**
2 Thes 1:8 . . . obey the Good **N** of our Lord
2 Tim 1:10 . . . through the Good **N.**
2 Tim 4:5 . . . telling others the Good **N,**
Rev 14:6 . . . the eternal Good **N**

NIGHT, NIGHTS (n) period of darkness between sunset and sunrise; figurative of suffering and sorrow or the reign of sin and immorality
Gen 1:16 . . . smaller one to govern the **n.**
Exod 13:21 . . . provided light at **n**
Job 35:10 . . . who gives songs in the **n?**
Ps 1:2 . . . meditating on it day and **n.**
Ps 19:2 . . . **n** after **n** they make him
Ps 77:6 . . . my **n-s** were filled with joyful
Jon 1:17 . . . fish for three days and three **n-s.**
Matt 4:2 . . . days and forty **n-s** he fasted
Matt 12:40 . . . for three days and three **n-s.**
Luke 2:8 . . . That **n** there were shepherds
2 Cor 6:5 . . . endured sleepless **n-s,** and gone
1 Thes 5:2 . . . like a thief in the **n.**
1 Thes 5:5 . . . belong to darkness and **n.**
Rev 21:25 . . . there is no **n** there.

NINETY-NINE (n) the number 99
Matt 18:13 . . . than over the **n** that didn't
Luke 15:7 . . . to God than over **n** others

NOAH Builder of great boat, survivor of the Flood (Gen 6–9; Matt 24:37-38; Luke 17:26-27; Heb 11:7; 1 Pet 3:20; 2 Pet 2:5); family line (Gen 5:25-32); found favor with God (Gen 6:8); enacted covenant between God and all creatures (Gen 9:1-17); made wine and became drunk (Gen 9:18-23); gave blessings and curse to descendants (Gen 9:24-27); considered righteous (Ezek 14:14, 20).

NONSENSE (n) words or language having no meaning or intelligible ideas; things of no importance or value
Luke 24:11 . . . sounded like **n** to the men,
1 Cor 1:23 . . . the Gentiles say it's all **n.**
Col 2:8 . . . high-sounding **n** that come from

NOOSE (n) a loop with a slipknot that binds closer the more it is drawn
Job 41:1 . . . or put a **n** around its jaw?

NORMAL (adj) occurring naturally
Rom 1:27 . . . **n** sexual relations with women,

NOSTRILS (n) either of the external openings of the nose
Gen 2:7 . . . breath of life into the man's **n,**

NOTES (n) melody, song; tones
1 Cor 14:7 . . . harp must play the **n** clearly,

NOTHING (pron) not any thing
Neh 9:21 . . . wilderness, and they lacked **n.**
Eccl 5:5 . . . better to say **n** than to make
Jas 1:4 . . . perfect and complete, needing **n.**

NOTICE (n) a warning or intimation of something; announcement
Matt 5:31 . . . giving her a written **n** of divorce.

NOTICED (v) to treat with attention
Job 1:8 . . . Satan, "Have you **n** my servant
Job 2:3 . . . Satan, "Have you **n** my servant

NOTORIOUS (adj) generally known and talked of; famous
Hab 1:7 . . . They are **n** for their cruelty

NOURISHMENT (n) food, nutriment; sustenance
Rom 11:17 . . . in the rich **n** from the root

NUMBERED (v) to restrict to a definite number
Ps 39:4 . . . Remind me that my days are **n**—

NUMEROUS (adj) consisting of great numbers; many
Ps 40:5 . . . plans for us are too **n** to list.

O

OATH (n) an appeal to God to witness the truth of some statement
Ps 95:11 . . . in my anger I took an **o:**
Ps 110:4 . . . LORD has taken an **o**
Ezek 20:42 . . . I promised with a solemn **o**
Heb 6:16 . . . people take an **o,** they call
Heb 7:20 . . . established with a solemn **o.**
Heb 7:21 . . . was an **o** regarding Jesus.
Jas 5:12 . . . never take an **o,** by heaven

OBEDIENCE (n) an act or instance of obeying; the quality or state of being obedient
Judg 2:17 . . . who had walked in **o** to the
1 Sam 15:22 . . . **O** is better than sacrifice,
Phil 2:8 . . . he humbled himself in **o** to God
Heb 5:8 . . . learned **o** from the things he

OBEDIENT (adj) submissive to authority; willing to obey
Luke 2:51 . . . with them and was **o** to them.
Rom 16:19 . . . that you are **o** to the Lord.
2 Cor 9:13 . . . that you are **o** to the Good
2 Cor 10:6 . . . you have become fully **o,**
1 Pet 1:14 . . . as God's **o** children.

OBEY, OBEYED, OBEYING, OBEYS (v) to follow the commands or guidance of; to conform to or comply with
see also KEEP
Gen 22:18 . . . because you have **o-ed** me.
Exod 20:6 . . . love me and **o** my commands.
Lev 18:4 . . . be careful to **o** my decrees,
Lev 25:18 . . . decrees and **o** my regulations.
Deut 4:2 . . . Just **o** the commands of the
Deut 5:27 . . . we will listen and **o.**
Deut 6:17 . . . diligently **o** the commands of
Deut 6:25 . . . when we **o** all the commands
Deut 11:1 . . . and **o** all his requirements,
Deut 11:22 . . . Be careful to **o** all these
Deut 13:4 . . . **O** his commands, listen to his
Deut 26:16 . . . to **o** them wholeheartedly.
Deut 28:1 . . . If you fully **o** the LORD

Deut 30:2 . . . if you **o** with all your heart
Deut 30:12 . . . so we can hear it and **o?**
Deut 30:20 . . . love and **o** the LORD,
Josh 1:7 . . . to **o** all the instructions Moses
Josh 22:5 . . . all his ways, **o** his commands,
1 Sam 7:3 . . . to **o** only the LORD;
1 Kgs 8:61 . . . May you always **o** his decrees
2 Kgs 17:13 . . . **O** my commands and
2 Kgs 18:6 . . . **o-ed** all the commands
2 Kgs 23:3 . . . pledged to **o** the LORD
Neh 1:5 . . . love him and **o** his commands,
Job 36:11 . . . they listen and **o** God,
Ps 111:10 . . . All who **o** his commandments
Ps 119:17 . . . I may live and **o** your word.
Ps 119:129 . . . No wonder I **o** them!
Eccl 8:2 . . . **O** the king since you vowed
Eccl 12:13 . . . and **o** his commands,
Isa 11:3 . . . delight in **o-ing** the LORD.
Jer 32:33 . . . not receive instruction or **o.**
Jer 42:6 . . . For if we **o** him, everything
Jer 43:4 . . . refused to **o** the LORD's
Dan 9:4 . . . love you and **o** your commands.
Dan 9:10 . . . We have not **o-ed** the LORD
Jon 3:3 . . . This time Jonah **o-ed** the LORD's
Mic 5:15 . . . nations that refuse to **o** me.
Matt 5:19 . . . anyone who **o-s** God's laws
Matt 8:27 . . . the winds and waves **o** him!
Matt 19:20 . . . **o-ed** all these commandments,
Matt 28:20 . . . to **o** all the commands
Luke 8:21 . . . hear God's word and **o** it.
John 3:36 . . . who doesn't **o** the Son
John 8:51 . . . anyone who **o-s** my teaching
John 14:15 . . . **o** my commandments.
Acts 4:19 . . . to **o** you rather than him?
Acts 5:29 . . . We must **o** God rather than
Rom 1:5 . . . believe and **o** him,
Rom 2:27 . . . possess God's law but don't **o**
Rom 3:28 . . . and not by **o-ing** the law.
Rom 6:16 . . . of whatever you choose to **o?**
Rom 6:17 . . . wholeheartedly **o** this
Rom 15:31 . . . in Judea who refuse to **o** God.
2 Cor 10:5 . . . teach them to **o** Christ.
Gal 2:16 . . . Christ, not by **o-ing** the law.
Gal 3:2 . . . by **o-ing** the law of Moses?
Gal 3:10 . . . and **o** all the commands
Eph 2:2 . . . who refuse to **o** God.
Eph 6:1 . . . Children, **o** your parents
Eph 6:5 . . . Slaves, **o** your earthly masters
2 Thes 3:14 . . . who refuse to **o** what we
1 Tim 3:4 . . . who respect and **o** him.
Titus 2:9 . . . Slaves must always **o** their
Heb 11:8 . . . that Abraham **o-ed** when God
Heb 11:31 . . . who refused to **o** God.
Jas 2:8 . . . good when you **o** the royal law
1 Pet 1:2 . . . you have **o-ed** him and have
1 Pet 1:22 . . . when you **o-ed** the truth,
1 Pet 2:8 . . . they do not **o** God's word,
1 Jn 3:22 . . . because we **o** him and do
Rev 22:7 . . . Blessed are those who **o** the

OBLIGATION (n) something one is bound to do; duty, responsibility
Rom 1:14 . . . a great sense of **o** to people
Rom 8:12 . . . no **o** to do what your sinful
Rom 13:8 . . . except for your **o** to love one

OBSERVE, OBSERVES (v) to notice or consider; to keep or comply with; to watch carefully
Exod 12:24 . . . your descendants must **o** forever.
Lev 25:2 . . . the land itself must **o** a Sabbath
Deut 5:12 . . . **O** the Sabbath day by keeping
Deut 16:13 . . . **o** the Festival of Shelters
Ps 33:14 . . . From his throne he **o-s** all who
Acts 21:24 . . . **o** the Jewish laws.
Gal 3:10 . . . everyone who does not **o**

OBSOLETE (adj) no longer in use or no longer useful
Heb 8:13 . . . he has made the first one **o.**

OBSTINATE (adj) unreasonably persistent; stubborn
Isa 48:4 . . . how stubborn and **o** you are
Ezek 3:8 . . . as **o** and hard-hearted as

OCCUPY (v) to take or hold possession or control of; to reside in as an owner or tenant
Deut 1:8 . . . Go in and **o** it, for it is
Deut 4:14 . . . are about to enter and **o.**

OFFEND, OFFENDED, OFFENDS (v) to violate, wrong, insult, or hurt; to cause difficulty, discomfort, or injury
Ps 139:24 . . . anything in me that **o-s** you,
1 Cor 1:23 . . . the Jews are **o-ed** and the
Gal 5:11 . . . Christ, no one would be **o-ed.**
Col 3:13 . . . and forgive anyone who **o-s** you.

OFFENSE, OFFENSES (n) a cause or occasion of sin; the act of displeasing or affronting
Isa 44:22 . . . I have scattered your **o-s**
Matt 18:15 . . . and point out the **o.**
1 Cor 10:32 . . . Don't give **o** to Jews or

OFFER, OFFERED, OFFERING (v) to present for acceptance as an act of worship or devotion; to sacrifice
Ps 4:5 . . . **O** sacrifices in the right spirit,
Ps 116:12 . . . What can I **o** the LORD
Mic 6:7 . . . Should we **o** him thousands of
1 Cor 10:20 . . . sacrifices are **o-ed** to demons,
Eph 5:2 . . . He loved us and **o-ed** himself
Heb 7:27 . . . when he **o-ed** himself
Heb 9:14 . . . Christ **o-ed** himself to God
Heb 9:25 . . . to **o** himself again and again,
Heb 10:11 . . . **o-ing** the same sacrifices again
Heb 11:17 . . . that Abraham **o-ed** Isaac
Heb 13:15 . . . let us **o** through Jesus
Jas 5:15 . . . a prayer **o-ed** in faith will heal

OFFERING, OFFERINGS (n) a sacrifice ceremonially offered as a part of worship; a contribution to the support of a church
Gen 22:8 . . . a sheep for the burnt **o,**
1 Sam 13:9 . . . Bring me the burnt **o**
1 Sam 15:22 . . . burnt **o-s** and sacrifices
Ps 40:6 . . . no delight in sacrifices or **o-s.**
Ps 141:2 . . . hands as an evening **o.**
Isa 53:10 . . . his life is made an **o** for sin,
Hos 6:6 . . . more than I want burnt **o-s.**
Mal 3:8 . . . cheated me of the tithes and **o-s**
Mark 12:33 . . . all of the burnt **o-s**
Rom 15:26 . . . taken up an **o** for the poor
Phil 2:17 . . . faithful service is an **o**
Heb 10:5 . . . animal sacrifices or sin **o-s.**
Heb 10:14 . . . that one **o** he forever made
Heb 11:4 . . . Abel's **o** gave evidence that he

OFFICER (n) one who holds a position of authority or command in the armed forces
Matt 8:5 . . . a Roman **o** came and pleaded
Luke 7:2 . . . slave of a Roman **o** was sick
Acts 10:1 . . . army **o** named Cornelius,
Acts 27:1 . . . a Roman **o** named Julius,

OFFSPRING (n) children or descendants
see also DESCENDANT(S)
Gen 3:15 . . . between your **o** and her **o.**
Acts 17:28 . . . said, 'We are his **o.**'

OIL (n) liquid produced from olives used in biblical times for lamp fuel, anointing, trade, and dressing wounds; often symbolic of the Holy Spirit
Exod 29:7 . . . anointing **o** over his head.
Exod 30:25 . . . to make a holy anointing **o.**
1 Sam 10:1 . . . **o** and poured it over Saul's
1 Sam 16:13 . . . **o** he had brought and
Ps 23:5 . . . anointing my head with **o.**
Ps 133:2 . . . as precious as the anointing **o**
Heb 1:9 . . . pouring out the **o** of joy

OINTMENT, OINTMENTS (n) a salve for application to the skin
Isa 1:6 . . . any soothing **o-s** or bandages.
Rev 3:18 . . . and **o** for your eyes so you

OLD, OLDER (adj) dating from the remote past; advanced in years or age
1 Kgs 12:8 . . . rejected the advice of the **o-er**
2 Cor 3:11 . . . So if the **o** way, which
1 Tim 5:2 . . . Treat **o-er** women as you would
Titus 2:2 . . . Teach the **o-er** men to exercise

OLIVE, OLIVES (n) a Mediterranean evergreen tree with berries that ripen black; the berries of an olive tree
Gen 8:11 . . . evening with a fresh **o** leaf
Jer 11:16 . . . a thriving **o** tree, beautiful
Zech 4:3 . . . And I see two **o** trees,
Zech 14:4 . . . the Mount of **O-s** will split
Matt 24:3 . . . Jesus sat on the Mount of **O-s.**
Rom 11:17 . . . of God's special **o** tree.
Rom 11:24 . . . cut from a wild **o** tree.
Jas 3:12 . . . Does a fig tree produce **o-s,** or
Rev 11:4 . . . prophets are the two **o** trees

OMEGA (n) the last letter of the Greek alphabet
Rev 1:8 . . . I am the Alpha and the **O**—
Rev 21:6 . . . I am the Alpha and the **O**—
Rev 22:13 . . . I am the Alpha and the **O,**

ONE (adj) being a single unit or thing; being in agreement or union
2 Chr 30:12 . . . giving them all **o** heart
Phil 2:2 . . . working together with **o** mind

ONE (n) a single person or thing
Gen 2:24 . . . the two are united into **o.**
Jas 2:10 . . . all of the laws except **o**

ONIONS (n) a plant with a large pungent, edible bulb
Num 11:5 . . . melons, leeks, **o,** and garlic

OPEN-MINDED (adj) receptive to arguments or ideas
Acts 17:11 . . . people of Berea were more **o**

OPENED (v) to spread out; to unfold
Isa 65:2 . . . All day long I **o** my arms
Rom 10:21 . . . All day long I **o** my arms

OPINIONS (n) a view, judgment, or appraisal formed in the mind about a particular matter
1 Kgs 18:21 . . . hobbling between two **o?**

OPPONENTS (n) one who takes an opposite position; adversary, rival
Prov 18:18 . . . disputes between powerful **o.**

OPPORTUNITY (n) a favorable circumstance or advantage
2 Cor 11:12 . . . looking for an **o** to boast
Gal 6:10 . . . have the **o,** we should do good
Col 4:5 . . . make the most of every **o.**

OPPOSE, OPPOSED, OPPOSES (v) to set onself against or opposite someone or something; to resist
Exod 23:22 . . . **o** those who **o** you.

Ps 8:2 . . . enemies and all who **o** you.
Ps 35:1 . . . **o** those who **o** me.
Acts 26:11 . . . was so violently **o-d** to them
Gal 2:11 . . . I had to **o** him to his face,
1 Tim 6:20 . . . with those who **o**
2 Tim 2:25 . . . instruct those who **o**
Titus 1:9 . . . show those who **o** it
Titus 2:8 . . . who **o** us will be ashamed
Jas 4:6 . . . God **o-s** the proud but favors
1 Pet 5:5 . . . God **o-s** the proud but favors

OPPRESS, OPPRESSED, OPPRESSES, OPPRESSING (v) to crush or burden by abuse of power or authority
Exod 22:21 . . . not mistreat or **o** foreigners
Ps 9:9 . . . a shelter for the **o-ed,** a refuge
Ps 14:6 . . . frustrate the plans of the **o-ed,**
Ps 82:3 . . . uphold the rights of the **o-ed** and
Ps 146:7 . . . He gives justice to the **o-ed**
Prov 22:16 . . . gets ahead by **o-ing** the poor
Prov 28:16 . . . no understanding will **o**
Prov 31:5 . . . not give justice to the **o-ed.**
Isa 1:17 . . . Seek justice. Help the **o-ed.**
Isa 3:5 . . . People will **o** each other—
Isa 58:3 . . . you keep **o-ing** your workers.
Ezek 18:12 . . . **o-es** the poor and helpless,
Dan 7:25 . . . defy the Most High and **o** the
Amos 2:7 . . . shove the **o-ed** out of the way.
Amos 5:12 . . . **o** good people by taking
Zech 7:10 . . . Do not **o** widows, orphans,
Luke 4:18 . . . that the **o-ed** will be set free,
Jas 2:6 . . . the rich who **o** you and drag

OPPRESSION (n) unjust or cruel exercise of power or authority
Judg 2:18 . . . burdened by **o** and suffering.
Ps 72:14 . . . redeem them from **o** and
Ps 119:134 . . . Ransom me from the **o** of
Isa 58:9 . . . Remove the heavy yoke of **o.**
Heb 11:25 . . . chose to share the **o** of God's

OPPRESSORS (n) one who abuses power or authority to crush or burden others
Ps 72:4 . . . and to crush their **o.**
Eccl 4:1 . . . The **o** have great power,
Jer 22:3 . . . rescue them from their **o.**

ORDAINED (v) to appoint someone to a specific duty or office
see also CONSECRATE(D), DEDICATE(D)
Ezek 28:14 . . . I **o** and anointed you

ORDER, ORDERS (n) a rank, class, or special group in a community or society; a command
Ps 110:4 . . . in the **o** of Melchizedek.
Joel 2:11 . . . they follow his **o-s.**
Mark 1:27 . . . spirits obey his **o-s!**
Heb 5:10 . . . in the **o** of Melchizedek.

ORDER (v) to command
Ps 91:11 . . . For he will **o** his angels
Matt 4:6 . . . He will **o** his angels

ORPHAN, ORPHANS (n) a child deprived by death of one or usually both parents
see also FATHERLESS
Exod 22:22 . . . not exploit a widow or an **o.**
Deut 10:18 . . . **o-s** and widows receive
Deut 24:17 . . . among you and to **o-s,**
Deut 24:19 . . . **o-s,** and widows.
Ps 10:14 . . . in you. You defend the **o-s.**
Ps 82:3 . . . justice to the poor and the **o;**
Prov 23:10 . . . the land of defenseless **o-s.**
John 14:18 . . . will not abandon you as **o-s**—
Jas 1:27 . . . caring for **o-s** and widows in

OUTSIDE (prep) used as a function word to indicate position on the outer side of
1 Tim 3:7 . . . Also, people **o** the church

OUTSMART (v) to get the better of; to outwit
2 Cor 2:11 . . . Satan will not **o** us.

OUTWARD, OUTWARDLY (adj or adv) superficial, having to do with external appearance or circumstance only
1 Sam 16:7 . . . People judge by **o** appearance,
Matt 23:28 . . . **o-ly** you look like righteous
1 Pet 3:3 . . . concerned about the **o** beauty

OUTWEIGHS (v) to exceed in weight, value, or importance
2 Cor 4:17 . . . glory that vastly **o** them and

OVERCOME (v) to get the better of; to overwhelm
see also CONQUER, VICTORY
Ps 119:133 . . . will not be **o** by evil.
Mark 9:24 . . . but help me **o** my unbelief!
John 16:33 . . . because I have **o** the world.
2 Cor 2:7 . . . may be **o** by discouragement.

OVERFLOW, OVERFLOWED, OVERFLOWS (v) to fill a space to capacity and spread beyond its limits; to flow over bounds
Ps 23:5 . . . My cup **o-s** with blessings.
Ps 65:11 . . . even the hard pathways **o** with
Prov 3:10 . . . vats will **o** with good wine.
John 15:11 . . . Yes, your joy will **o!**
Rom 15:13 . . . you will **o** with confident
2 Cor 8:2 . . . joy, which has **o-ed** in rich
Phil 1:9 . . . I pray that your love will **o**
Col 2:7 . . . you will **o** with thankfulness.

OVERJOYED (adj) feeling great joy
Dan 6:23 . . . The king was **o** and ordered
Acts 12:14 . . . she was so **o** that,

OVERLOOKING (v) to look past; to ignore or excuse
Prov 19:11 . . . they earn respect by **o** wrongs.
Mic 7:18 . . . **o** the sins of his special people?

OVERSEER(S) (KJV)
2 Chr 2:18 . . . and 3,600 as *foremen*
Neh 11:22 . . . *chief officer* of the Levites
Prov 6:7 . . . or *governor* or ruler to make
Acts 20:28 . . . appointed you as *elders*
1 Tim 3:1 . . . an *elder* must be a man whose
1 Pet 2:25 . . . Shepherd, the *Guardian* of

OVERSHADOW (v) to cast a shadow over
Luke 1:35 . . . power of the Most High will **o**

OVERWHELMED, OVERWHELMING, OVERWHELMS (v) to overpower in thought or feeling; to submerge; to overthrow
2 Sam 22:5 . . . waves of death **o-ed** me;
Job 19:27 . . . I am **o-ed** at the thought!
Ps 38:4 . . . My guilt **o-s** me—it is
Ps 65:3 . . . we are **o-ed** by our sins,
Ps 90:7 . . . we are **o-ed** by your fury.
Isa 61:10 . . . I am **o-ed** with joy in
Mark 9:15 . . . they were **o-ed** with awe,
2 Cor 1:8 . . . We were crushed and **o-ed**
2 Cor 3:10 . . . with the **o-ing** glory

OWE (v) to be under obligation to pay or repay in return for something received
Rom 13:7 . . . Give to everyone what you **o**
Phlm 1:19 . . . that you **o** me your very soul!

OWN (adj) belonging to oneself or itself
Luke 18:9 . . . in their **o** righteousness
1 Cor 13:5 . . . does not demand its **o** way.
Titus 2:14 . . . to make us his very **o** people,

OWN (v) to have or hold as property
Gen 28:4 . . . May you **o** this land

OX, OXEN (n) a domestic bovine mammal
Deut 25:4 . . . not muzzle an **o** to keep it
1 Kgs 7:25 . . . base of twelve bronze **o-en,**
1 Kgs 19:20 . . . Elisha left the **o-en**
Isa 1:3 . . . **o** knows its owner, and a
Ezek 1:10 . . . the face of an **o** on the left
1 Cor 9:9 . . . not muzzle an **o** to keep it
1 Tim 5:18 . . . not muzzle an **o** to keep it
Rev 4:7 . . . the second was like an **o;**

P

PACT (n) an agreement or covenant between two or more parties
1 Sam 23:18 . . . renewed their solemn **p** before

PAGAN (adj) of or relating to a pagan
1 Sam 17:26 . . . Who is this **p** Philistine

PAGAN, PAGANS (n) a follower of a false god or religion; one who delights in sensual pleasures and material goods
Ps 106:35 . . . they mingled among the **p-s**
Isa 2:6 . . . have made alliances with **p-s.**
Matt 5:47 . . . Even **p-s** do that.
Matt 18:17 . . . treat that person as a **p**
1 Cor 5:1 . . . something that even **p-s** don't
1 Cor 12:2 . . . when you were still **p-s,** you

PAID (v) *see also* PAY
1 Cor 7:23 . . . God **p** a high price for you,
Col 3:25 . . . be **p** back for the wrong
1 Tim 5:17 . . . should be respected and **p**

PAIN, PAINS (n) physical, mental, or emotional suffering; the spasms of childbirth
Job 6:10 . . . Despite the **p,** I have not
Ps 73:14 . . . every morning brings me **p.**
Jer 4:19 . . . my heart—I writhe in **p!**
Matt 24:8 . . . only the first of the birth **p-s,**
John 16:21 . . . suffering the **p-s** of labor.
Rom 8:22 . . . in the **p-s** of childbirth
Gal 4:19 . . . going through labor **p-s** for you
1 Thes 5:3 . . . woman's labor **p-s** begin.
Heb 13:3 . . . as if you felt their **p** in your
Rev 21:4 . . . death or sorrow or crying or **p.**

PAINFUL (adj) feeling or giving pain
Gen 5:29 . . . the **p** labor of farming
Prov 17:21 . . . **p** to be the parent of a fool;
2 Cor 2:1 . . . grief with another **p** visit.
Heb 12:11 . . . while it is happening—it's **p!**

PALACE, PALACES (n) the official residence of a chief of state (as a monarch or president)
2 Sam 7:2 . . . living in a beautiful cedar **p,**
Jer 22:6 . . . concerning Judah's royal **p:**
Matt 11:8 . . . expensive clothes live in **p-s.**
Luke 7:25 . . . live in luxury are found in **p-s.**

PALM, PALMS (n) a long feathery leaf from any of various mostly tropical or subtropical trees; the part of the human hand between the base of the fingers and wrist
Isa 49:16 . . . on the **p-s** of my hands.
John 12:13 . . . took **p** branches and went
Rev 7:9 . . . and held **p** branches

PAMPERED (v) to treat with extreme or excessive care and attention
Prov 29:21 . . . A servant **p** from childhood

PANIC (n) a sudden unreasoning terror often accompanied by mass flight
1 Sam 14:15 . . . Suddenly, **p** broke out
Zech 14:13 . . . by the LORD with great **p.**

PANIC (v) to be affected with panic
Deut 20:3 . . . Do not lose heart or **p**
Mark 13:7 . . . threats of wars, but don't **p.**

PAPERS (n) a piece of paper containing writing or print; documents
Jer 32:16 . . . had given the **p** to Baruch,
2 Tim 4:13 . . . books, and especially my **p.**

PARABLE, PARABLES (n) a brief narrative story told with earthly analogies to illustrate a spiritual truth
Ps 78:2 . . . I will speak to you in a **p.**
Matt 13:35 . . . I will speak to you in **p-s.**
Luke 8:10 . . . I use **p-s** to teach the

PARADE (n) a public procession
1 Cor 4:9 . . . at the end of a victor's **p,**

PARADISE (n) an intermediate place where the souls of the righteous await resurrection and the final judgment
Luke 23:43 . . . you will be with me in **p.**
2 Cor 12:4 . . . that I was caught up to **p**

PARALYZED (adj) characterized by the inability to move
Matt 9:2 . . . Jesus said to the **p** man,
Mark 2:3 . . . men arrived carrying a **p** man
John 5:3 . . . blind, lame, or **p**—

PARDON, PARDONED (v) to allow (an offense) to pass without punishment; to forgive
Num 14:19 . . . **p** the sins of this people,
Deut 29:20 . . . LORD will never **p** such
2 Kgs 5:18 . . . may the LORD **p** me
2 Chr 30:18 . . . LORD, who is good, **p**
Isa 40:2 . . . gone and her sins are **p-ed.**
Jer 5:7 . . . How can I **p** you?
Joel 3:21 . . . I will **p** my people's crimes,
Joel 3:21 . . . which I have not yet **p-ed;**

PARENT, PARENTS (n) one who produces and cares for offspring
see also FATHER, MOTHER
Exod 20:5 . . . I lay the sins of the **p-s** upon
Prov 13:1 . . . child accepts a **p's** discipline;
Jer 31:29 . . . **p-s** have eaten sour grapes,
Ezek 18:19 . . . child pay for the **p's** sins?
Matt 10:21 . . . will rebel against their **p-s**
Rom 1:30 . . . and they disobey their **p-s.**
Eph 6:1 . . . Children, obey your **p-s**
Col 3:20 . . . always obey your **p-s,**

PART, PARTS (n) portion or segment; role
see also MEMBER(S)
Rom 12:5 . . . We are many **p-s** of one body,
1 Cor 6:15 . . . are actually **p-s** of Christ?
1 Cor 12:18 . . . each **p** just where he wants
1 Cor 12:28 . . . **p-s** God has appointed for
Gal 5:25 . . . Spirit's leading in every **p** of our
Eph 4:25 . . . we are all **p-s** of the same body.

PARTIAL (adj) inclined to favor one party more than the other; of or relating to a part rather than the whole
Lev 19:15 . . . or being **p** to the rich
1 Cor 13:10 . . . **p** things will become

PARTIALITY (n) the quality or state of being partial
see also FAVORITES, FAVORITISM
Deut 10:17 . . . God, who shows no **p** and
Deut 16:19 . . . twist justice or show **p.**
2 Chr 19:7 . . . perverted justice, **p,**

PARTICIPATE (v) to have a part or share in something; to take part
1 Cor 10:20 . . . to **p** with demons.
Eph 5:7 . . . **p** in the things these people

PARTNER, PARTNERS (n) a person with whom one shares an intimate relationship; one associated with another, especially in action
Mal 2:14 . . . she remained your faithful **p,**
2 Cor 6:14 . . . can righteousness be a **p**
Phil 1:5 . . . **p-s** in spreading the Good
1 Pet 3:7 . . . but she is your equal **p** in
1 Pet 4:13 . . . trials make you **p-s** with
3 Jn 1:8 . . . be their **p-s** as they teach
Rev 1:9 . . . your **p** in suffering and in God's

PARTNERSHIP (n) the state of being a partner
1 Cor 1:9 . . . into **p** with his Son,

PARTY, PARTIES (n) a social gathering
Luke 15:24 . . . So the **p** began.
Rom 13:13 . . . of wild **p-ies** and drunkenness,
1 Pet 4:3 . . . and drunkenness and wild **p-ies,**

PASS, PASSED (v) to move, proceed, go; to go away; to move past
Exod 12:13 . . . the blood, I will **p** over you.
Exod 33:22 . . . my hand until I have **p-ed**
1 Kgs 19:11 . . . there, the LORD **p-ed**
1 Cor 7:31 . . . it will soon **p** away.
2 Pet 3:10 . . . the heavens will **p** away

PASSION, PASSIONS (n) intense, driving, or overmastering feeling or conviction; ardent affection; sexual desire
Isa 59:17 . . . himself in a cloak of divine **p.**
Zech 8:2 . . . with **p** for Jerusalem!
1 Cor 7:37 . . . he can control his **p,** he does
Gal 5:24 . . . Jesus have nailed the **p-s**
1 Thes 4:5 . . . lustful **p** like the pagans

PASSIONATE (adj) capable of, affected by, or expressing intense feeling
2 Kgs 19:31 . . . **p** commitment of the LORD
Isa 9:7 . . . **p** commitment of the LORD
Isa 37:32 . . . **p** commitment of the LORD
Zech 1:14 . . . Mount Zion is **p** and strong.
Zech 8:2 . . . Mount Zion is **p** and strong;

PASSOVER (n) a festival that commemorated the Hebrew departure from Egypt in haste
Num 9:2 . . . celebrate the **P**
Deut 16:1 . . . celebrate the **P** each year
Ezra 6:19 . . . returned exiles celebrated **P.**
Mark 14:12 . . . **P** lamb is sacrificed,
Heb 11:28 . . . to keep the **P** and to sprinkle

PASTORS (n) a spiritual overseer
Eph 4:11 . . . and the **p** and teachers.

PASTURE, PASTURES (n) land or a plot of land used for grazing
Ps 100:3 . . . his people, the sheep of his **p.**
John 10:9 . . . freely and will find good **p-s.**

PATH, PATHS (n) course, route; a way of life, conduct, or thought
1 Kgs 8:36 . . . follow the right **p,**
Ps 23:3 . . . He guides me along right **p-s,**
Ps 27:11 . . . Lead me along the right **p,**
Prov 2:13 . . . to walk down dark **p-s.**
Prov 3:6 . . . show you which **p** to take.
Prov 5:21 . . . examining every **p** he takes.
Prov 8:20 . . . in **p-s** of justice.
Prov 14:12 . . . a **p** before each person that
Isa 48:17 . . . leads you along the **p-s**
Hos 14:9 . . . **p-s** of the LORD are true
2 Tim 2:18 . . . have left the **p** of truth,
Heb 12:13 . . . Mark out a straight **p**

PATHWAY (n) path, course
Ps 32:8 . . . along the best **p** for your life.

PATIENCE (n) the power or capacity to endure without complaint something difficult or disagreeable; forbearance, longsuffering
Rom 15:5 . . . May God, who gives this **p**
Gal 5:22 . . . joy, peace, **p,** kindness,
Col 1:11 . . . endurance and **p** you need.
Col 3:12 . . . humility, gentleness, and **p.**
2 Tim 3:10 . . . my faith, my **p,** my love,
Titus 2:2 . . . and be filled with love and **p.**
Jas 5:10 . . . examples of **p** in suffering,
2 Pet 3:15 . . . Lord's **p** gives people time

PATIENT (adj) bearing pains or trials calmly or without complaint; steadfast despite opposition, difficulty, or adversity; not hasty or impetuous
Rom 2:4 . . . and **p** God is with you?
Rom 12:12 . . . Be **p** in trouble,
1 Cor 4:12 . . . We are **p** with those who
1 Cor 13:4 . . . Love is **p** and kind.
1 Thes 5:14 . . . Be **p** with everyone.
Jas 5:8 . . . You, too, must be **p.**

PATIENTLY (adv) in a patient manner
Ps 40:1 . . . I waited **p** for the LORD
1 Pet 3:20 . . . God waited **p** while Noah
Rev 14:12 . . . endure persecution **p,**

PATTERN (n) a form or model proposed for imitation
Exod 25:40 . . . according to the **p**
Exod 26:30 . . . the **p** you were shown
2 Tim 1:13 . . . Hold on to the **p**
Heb 8:5 . . . according to the **p**

PAUL Pharisee and Roman citizen (Acts 22:3); from city of Tarsus (Acts 9:11; Phil 3:5); became apostle (Gal 1) to the Gentiles (Rom 11:13); also known as "Saul" (Acts 7:58; 13:9); supported stoning of Stephen (Acts 8:1); attacked early Christians (Acts 8:1-3; 9:1-2; Gal 1:13); converted on road to Damascus (Acts 9:1-9; 22:6-16; 26:12-18); preached in Damascus (Acts 9:20-22); escaped over the wall in basket (Acts 9:23-25); escaped to Jerusalem, then to Tarsus (Acts 9:26-30); saw visions in Arabia (Gal 1:17); with Barnabas in Antioch (Acts 11:22-26); sent to Jerusalem (Acts 11:27-30); first missionary journey: Cyprus and Galatia (Acts 13–14); advocate for Gentile believers (Acts 15:1-5); testified at Jerusalem Council (Acts 15:12); split with Barnabas over John Mark (Acts 15:36-41); second missionary journey with Silas: northern and southern Greece, western Asia (Acts 15:36–18:22); received call to Macedonia (Acts 16:6-10); Philippi, Thessalonica, Berea (Acts 16–17); Athens, Corinth (Acts 17–18); third missionary journey: returned to northern and southern Greece, western Asia (Acts 18:23–21:14); Corinth, Ephesus, Macedonia, Troas—to Jerusalem (Acts 18–21); farewell to Ephesian elders (Acts 20:13-38); journey to Rome (Acts 21–28); falsely arrested and in hands of mob (Acts 21:26–22:21); saved by Roman custody (Acts 22:22-29; 23:10); before the Jewish high council (Acts 23:1-11); relocated to Caesarea (Acts 23:12-35); trial before Felix (Acts 24); appealed to Caesar before Festus (Acts 25:1-12), before Herod Agrippa (Acts 25:13–26:32); sailed to Rome, was shipwrecked (Acts 27); arrived in Rome (Acts 28); pattern of self-denial (1 Cor 9); his gospel message (Rom 1–5; Gal 3–6); catalog of trials (2 Cor 11:22-33); his goal (Phil 3:7-15); last known written words (2 Tim 4); intervened for returning slave

(Phlm 1:8-22); wrote letters: Romans through Philemon (see verse 1 of each book).

PAVEMENT (n) a surface covered firmly and solidly with material (as asphalt or concrete)
John 19:13 . . . that is called the Stone **P**

PAY (n) something paid for a purpose and especially as a salary or wage
1 Tim 5:18 . . . who work deserve their **p**!

PAY, PAYS (v) to suffer the consequences of an act; to requite according to what is deserved; to make due return to for services or goods rendered
see also PAID
Exod 22:3 . . . A thief who is caught must **p**
Deut 32:35 . . . I will **p** them back.
Ps 137:8 . . . Happy is the one who **p-s** you
Matt 22:17 . . . to **p** taxes to Caesar or not?
Rom 12:19 . . . I will **p** them back,
1 Thes 5:15 . . . no one **p-s** back evil
2 Thes 1:6 . . . he will **p** back those who

PAYMENT (n) the act of paying; something that is paid
Deut 15:2 . . . must not demand **p**
Deut 27:25 . . . anyone who accepts **p**
Hos 9:7 . . . the day of **p** is here.

PEACE (n) a state of tranquility or quiet; a pact or agreement to end hostilities between those who have been at war or in a state of enmity; harmony in personal relations, especially with God; a state of security or order within a community; freedom from disquieting or oppressive thoughts or emotions
Exod 20:24 . . . and **p** offerings, your sheep
Lev 26:6 . . . I will give you **p** in the land,
Num 6:26 . . . his favor and give you his **p**.
Deut 20:10 . . . offer its people terms for **p**.
1 Sam 7:14 . . . there was **p** between Israel
1 Kgs 5:4 . . . God has given me **p** on every
1 Chr 22:9 . . . a son who will be a man of **p**.
2 Chr 14:7 . . . has given us **p** on every side.
Job 3:26 . . . I have no **p**, no quietness.
Job 25:2 . . . He enforces **p** in the heavens.
Ps 34:14 . . . Search for **p**, and work to
Ps 37:37 . . . awaits those who love **p**.
Ps 120:7 . . . I search for **p**;
Ps 147:14 . . . He sends **p** across your nation
Prov 12:20 . . . hearts that are planning **p**!
Eccl 3:8 . . . for war and a time for **p**.
Isa 9:6 . . . Everlasting Father, Prince of **P**.
Isa 32:17 . . . righteousness will bring **p**.
Isa 48:22 . . . there is no **p** for the wicked,
Isa 52:7 . . . good news of **p** and salvation,
Jer 6:14 . . . They give assurances of **p** when
Jer 46:27 . . . return to a life of **p** and quiet,
Ezek 34:25 . . . I will make a covenant of **p**
Zech 8:19 . . . So love truth and **p**.
Matt 5:9 . . . blesses those who work for **p**,
Mark 9:50 . . . live in **p** with each other.
Luke 1:79 . . . guide us to the path of **p**.
John 16:33 . . . you may have **p** in me.
Rom 5:1 . . . by faith, we have **p** with God
Rom 8:6 . . . your mind leads to life and **p**.
1 Cor 14:33 . . . God of disorder but of **p**,
Gal 5:22 . . . love, joy, **p**, patience,
Eph 2:14 . . . Christ himself has brought **p**
Eph 2:15 . . . made **p** between Jews and
Eph 2:17 . . . Good News of **p** to you Gentiles
Eph 6:15 . . . put on the **p** that comes from
Phil 4:7 . . . experience God's **p**,
1 Thes 5:23 . . . God of **p** make you holy
2 Thes 3:16 . . . Lord of **p** himself give you
2 Tim 2:22 . . . faithfulness, love, and **p**.
Heb 13:20 . . . the God of **p**—who brought
Jas 3:17 . . . It is also **p** loving, gentle
1 Pet 3:11 . . . Search for **p**, and work to

PEACEFUL (adj) quiet, tranquil; devoid of violence or force; of or relating to a state or time of peace
Ps 23:2 . . . leads me beside **p** streams.
Prov 14:30 . . . A **p** heart leads to a healthy
1 Thes 5:3 . . . Everything is **p** and secure,
1 Tim 2:2 . . . we can live **p** and quiet lives
Heb 12:11 . . . a **p** harvest of right living
2 Pet 3:14 . . . effort to be found living **p**

PEACEMAKER, PEACEMAKERS (n) one who makes peace especially by reconciling parties at variance
Acts 7:26 . . . He tried to be a **p**.
Jas 3:18 . . . **p-s** will plant seeds of peace

PEARL, PEARLS (n) a white translucent jewel created within certain species of mollusks
Matt 7:6 . . . throw your **p-s** to pigs!
Matt 13:45 . . . on the lookout for choice **p-s**.
1 Tim 2:9 . . . or by wearing gold or **p-s**
Rev 21:21 . . . were made of **p-s**—
Rev 21:21 . . . each gate from a single **p**!

PENALTY (n) disadvantage, loss, or hardship due to some action
Job 34:36 . . . you deserve the maximum **p**
Rom 3:24 . . . freed us from the **p**

PENNY (n) the smallest monetary unit
Matt 5:26 . . . you have paid the last **p**.
Luke 12:59 . . . paid the very last **p**.

PENTECOST (n) a Jewish feast celebrated on the 50th day after the Feast of Unleavened Bread; the day God sent the Holy Spirit after Christ's resurrection
Acts 2:1 . . . the day of **P** all the believers
Acts 20:16 . . . in time for the Festival of **P**.
1 Cor 16:8 . . . until the Festival of **P**.

PEOPLE, PEOPLES (n) human beings making up a group or assembly or linked by a common interest; clan or nation; humanity
see also NATION(S)
Exod 5:1 . . . says: Let my **p** go
Exod 8:23 . . . between my **p** and your **p**.
Exod 19:5 . . . among all the **p-s** on earth;
Exod 19:8 . . . all the **p** responded together,
Exod 33:13 . . . nation is your very own **p**.
Lev 26:12 . . . and you will be my **p**.
Num 14:11 . . . How long will these **p**
Deut 7:6 . . . you are a holy **p**, who belong
Deut 14:1 . . . are the **p** of the LORD
Deut 32:9 . . . For the **p** of Israel belong
Deut 33:29 . . . **p** saved by the LORD?
Ruth 1:16 . . . Your **p** will be my **p**,
2 Chr 7:20 . . . uproot the **p** from this land
Neh 1:10 . . . The **p** you rescued by your
Neh 8:1 . . . the **p** assembled with a unified
Ps 33:12 . . . whose **p** he has chosen
Ps 53:6 . . . When God restores his **p**,
Ps 94:14 . . . will not reject his **p**;
Ps 96:10 . . . He will judge all **p-s** fairly.
Ps 135:14 . . . will give justice to his **p**
Isa 2:2 . . . **p** from all over the world
Isa 6:10 . . . Harden the hearts of these **p**.
Isa 40:1 . . . Comfort, comfort my **p**,
Isa 49:13 . . . LORD has comforted his **p**
Isa 52:6 . . . I will reveal my name to my **p**,
Isa 53:8 . . . for the rebellion of my **p**.
Isa 55:4 . . . my power among the **p-s**.
Jer 2:11 . . . Yet my **p** have exchanged their
Jer 2:32 . . . my **p** have forgotten me.
Jer 7:16 . . . Pray no more for these **p**,
Jer 32:27 . . . of all the **p-s** of the world.
Dan 8:24 . . . and devastate the holy **p**.
Dan 9:24 . . . decreed for your **p**
Hos 1:10 . . . You are not my **p**,
Hos 2:23 . . . Now you are my **p**.
Mic 4:1 . . . **p** from all over the world
Mic 4:3 . . . LORD will mediate between **p-s**
Matt 4:19 . . . show you how to fish for **p**!
Mark 7:6 . . . **p** honor me with their lips,
Mark 8:27 . . . Who do **p** say I am?
Luke 1:68 . . . visited and redeemed his **p**.
John 11:50 . . . should die for the **p**
John 18:14 . . . should die for the **p**.
Rom 9:25 . . . Those who were not my **p**,
Rom 11:1 . . . **p**, the nation of Israel?
2 Cor 6:16 . . . and they will be my **p**.
Gal 6:16 . . . they are the new **p** of God.
Eph 1:14 . . . purchased us to be his own **p**.
Eph 1:18 . . . he called—his holy **p**
Eph 2:15 . . . creating in himself one new **p**
Eph 4:8 . . . and gave gifts to his **p**.
2 Tim 2:2 . . . trustworthy **p** who will
2 Tim 3:17 . . . and equip his **p** to do every
Titus 2:11 . . . bringing salvation to all **p**.
Titus 2:14 . . . make us his very own **p**,
Heb 4:9 . . . waiting for the **p** of God.
1 Pet 2:9 . . . for you are a chosen **p**.
1 Pet 2:10 . . . now you are God's **p**.
Rev 5:8 . . . prayers of God's **p**.
Rev 10:11 . . . again about many **p-s**,
Rev 18:4 . . . from her, my **p**.
Rev 19:8 . . . of God's holy **p**.
Rev 21:3 . . . home is now among his **p**!

PERFECT (adj) being entirely without fault or defect; corresponding to an ideal standard or abstract concept; mature, pure, complete
Deut 32:4 . . . the Rock; his deeds are **p**.
Ps 19:7 . . . instructions of the LORD are **p**,
Ps 119:138 . . . laws are **p** and completely
Matt 5:48 . . . you are to be **p**, even as
John 17:23 . . . experience such **p** unity
Gal 3:3 . . . become **p** by your
Col 4:12 . . . God to make you strong and **p**,
Heb 2:10 . . . suffering, a **p** leader,
Heb 5:9 . . . as a **p** High Priest,
Heb 7:19 . . . law never made anything **p**.
Heb 9:11 . . . greater, more **p** Tabernacle
Heb 9:14 . . . as a **p** sacrifice for our sins.
Heb 10:14 . . . he forever made **p** those
Heb 12:23 . . . who have now been made **p**.
Jas 1:25 . . . look carefully into the **p** law
1 Jn 4:18 . . . because **p** love expels all fear.

PERFECT, PERFECTED, PERFECTS (v) to bring to final form; to refine or improve
Ezek 16:14 . . . splendor and **p-ed** your beauty,
Heb 12:2 . . . champion who initiates and **p-s**

PERFECTION (n) flawlessness; maturity; an exemplification of supreme excellence
Job 37:16 . . . with wonderful **p** and skill?
Ps 50:2 . . . Mount Zion, the **p** of beauty,
1 Cor 13:10 . . . when the time of **p** comes,
Phil 3:12 . . . I have already reached **p**.
Heb 7:11 . . . achieved the **p** God intended,
Heb 11:40 . . . not reach **p** without us.

PERFORM, PERFORMED, PERFORMING (v) to carry out; to do
Exod 3:20 . . . **p-ing** all kinds of miracles
2 Sam 7:23 . . . You **p-ed** awesome miracles
John 10:41 . . . John didn't **p** miraculous

PERFUME (n) a substance that emits a pleasant odor
Eccl 7:1 . . . more valuable than costly **p**.

Mark 14:3 . . . and poured the **p** over his head.
2 Cor 2:14 . . . everywhere, like a sweet **p.**
2 Cor 2:16 . . . saved, we are a life-giving **p.**

PERISH, PERISHING (v) to become destroyed or ruined physically or spiritually; to die
see also DESTROY, DIE
Ps 102:26 . . . They will **p,** but you remain
John 3:16 . . . believes in him will not **p** but
John 10:28 . . . they will never **p.**
2 Cor 2:15 . . . by those who are **p-ing.**
2 Cor 4:3 . . . from people who are **p-ing.**
Jude 1:11 . . . they **p** in their rebellion.

PERMANENT (adj) continuing or enduring without fundamental or marked change; lasting
Num 25:13 . . . a **p** right to the priesthood,

PERMIT, PERMITTED (v) to consent to; to authorize; to make possible
Matt 16:19 . . . whatever you **p** on earth
Matt 18:18 . . . whatever you **p** on earth
Matt 19:8 . . . "Moses **p-ted** divorce

PERPLEXED (v) to make unable to grasp something clearly; to puzzle
Luke 21:25 . . . **p** by the roaring seas and

PERSECUTE, PERSECUTED, PERSECUTING (v) to harass or punish in a manner designed to injure, grieve, or afflict; to cause to suffer because of belief
Ps 140:12 . . . help those they **p;**
Matt 5:10 . . . blesses those who are **p-d**
Matt 5:11 . . . when people mock you and **p**
Matt 5:12 . . . prophets were **p-d**
Matt 5:44 . . . Pray for those who **p** you!
Matt 13:21 . . . **p-d** for believing God's
John 15:20 . . . they **p-d** me, naturally
John 15:20 . . . they will **p** you.
Acts 9:4 . . . Why are you **p-ing** me?
Rom 8:35 . . . or are **p-d,** or hungry,
Rom 12:14 . . . Bless those who **p** you.
1 Cor 15:9 . . . the way I **p-d** God's church.
2 Thes 1:7 . . . for you who are being **p-d**

PERSECUTION, PERSECUTIONS (n) the condition of being persecuted, harassed, or annoyed
Mark 10:30 . . . along with **p.**
2 Cor 12:10 . . . insults, hardships, **p-s,**
2 Thes 1:4 . . . all the **p-s** and hardships
2 Thes 1:5 . . . God will use this **p** to show
2 Tim 3:11 . . . You know how much **p** and
2 Tim 3:12 . . . in Christ Jesus will suffer **p.**
Rev 13:10 . . . must endure **p** patiently

PERSECUTORS (n) one who persecutes
Ps 142:6 . . . Rescue me from my **p,**

PERSEVERANCE (n) enduring hardships with patience; steadfastness
see also ENDURANCE
1 Tim 6:11 . . . along with faith, love, **p,** and

PERSEVERE (v) to persist in a state, enterprise, or undertaking in spite of counterinfluences, opposition, or discouragement
see also ENDURE
Rev 3:10 . . . obeyed my command to **p,**

PERSISTENCE (n) the action, quality, or state of continuing resolutely in the face of obstacles
Luke 11:8 . . . because of your shameless **p.**

PERSON (n) human, individual
Ps 119:9 . . . How can a young **p** stay pure?
2 Cor 5:17 . . . to Christ has become a new **p.**
Heb 9:27 . . . just as each **p** is destined to die

PERSUADE, PERSUADED (v) to move by argument or entreaty to a belief, position, or course of action
Prov 25:15 . . . Patience can **p** a prince,
Acts 19:26 . . . Paul has **p-d** many people
Acts 28:23 . . . tried to **p** them about Jesus
Acts 28:24 . . . were **p-d** by the things he

PERSUASIVE (adj) tending to persuade
Prov 16:21 . . . and pleasant words are **p.**
Prov 16:23 . . . the words of the wise are **p.**
1 Cor 2:4 . . . clever and **p** speeches,

PERVERSE (adj) corrupt; improper, incorrect; perverted
Lev 18:23 . . . This is a **p** act.
Lev 20:12 . . . They have committed a **p** act
Phil 2:15 . . . in a world full of crooked and **p**

PERVERT, PERVERTED (v) to cause to turn aside or away from what is good, true, or morally right; to corrupt
1 Sam 8:3 . . . bribes and **p-ed** justice.
Prov 17:23 . . . secret bribes to **p** the course

PETER Leader of the 12 disciples, also known as "Simon son of John" (John 21:17) and "Cephas" (John 1:42); called to "fish for people" (Matt 4:18-20; Mark 1:16-20; Luke 5:1-11; *see also* John 21:3); mother-in-law healed (Matt 8:14-15; Mark 1:29-31; Luke 4:38-39); called to preach (Mark 1:36-39); brother of Andrew (Matt 10:2; Mark 3:16; Luke 6:14; Acts 1:13); present at raising of the dead (Mark 5:37; Luke 8:51); walked on water (Matt 14:22-33; Mark 6:45-52; John 6:15-21); identified Jesus as the Christ (Matt 16:13-20; Mark 8:27-30; Luke 9:18-20; *see also* John 6:68-69); rebuked by Jesus for lack of heavenly perspective (Matt 16:21-23; Mark 8:32-33; *see also* John 13:6-11); witnessed the Transfiguration (Matt 16:28–17:8; Mark 9:1-13; Luke 9:28-36; 2 Pet 1:16-20); noticed the withered fig tree (Mark 11:21; *see also* Matt 21:20); his denial predicted by Jesus (Matt 26:31-35; Mark 14:27-31; Luke 22:31-34; John 13:36-38); in Gethsemane (Matt 26:36-46; Mark 14:32-42; Luke 22:39-46); cut off ear of Malchus (Matt 26:51; Mark 14:47; Luke 22:50); denied Jesus—then wept (Matt 26:69-75; Mark 14:66-72; Luke 22:54-62; John 18:15-27); visited empty tomb (Luke 24:12; John 20:1-10; *see also* Matt 28:1-8); saw Jesus (Luke 24:34; 1 Cor 15:5); told by Jesus to shepherd his flock (John 21:15-19); in upper room before Pentecost (Acts 1:13); preached at Pentecost (Acts 2); performed miracles (Acts 3:1-10; 5:14-16; 9:32-43); preached at Temple (Acts 3:11-26); preached before Jewish high council (Acts 4:1-22); prophesied death of Ananias and Sapphira (Acts 5:1-11); preached again before Jewish high council (Acts 5:29-32); rebuked power seeker (Acts 8:14-25); healed sick (Acts 9:32-34); raised dead (Acts 9:36-43); introduced Gentiles to gospel (Acts 10–11); rescued by angel from prison (Acts 12:3-19); preached grace at Jerusalem Council (Acts 15); became pillar of the church (Gal 2:9); was correctable (Gal 2:14); wrote letters (1 Pet 1:1; 2 Pet 1:1); had believing wife (1 Cor 9:5).

PHARAOH (n) a ruler of ancient Egypt
Gen 12:15 . . . praises to **P,** their king,
Gen 41:14 . . . went in and stood before **P.**
Exod 14:4 . . . to display my glory through **P**
Exod 14:17 . . . will be displayed through **P**

PHARISEE, PHARISEES (n) a religious and political party in Palestine in New Testament times known for strict observance of rites and ceremonies of the written law and for insistence on the validity of their own oral traditions concerning the law
Matt 5:20 . . . **P-s,** you will never enter
Matt 16:6 . . . of the yeast of the **P-s**
Matt 23:13 . . . and you **P-s.** Hypocrites!
John 3:1 . . . religious leader who was a **P.**
Acts 23:6 . . . **P,** as were my ancestors!

PHILIP 1. One of the 12 disciples (Matt 10:3; Mark 3:18; Luke 6:14; John 1:43-48; 12:21-22; 14:8; Acts 1:13).
2. Deacon and evangelist (Acts 6:5; Acts 8:5-25); with the Ethiopian eunuch (Acts 8:26-40); hosted Paul in Caesarea (Acts 21:8-9).
3. Son of Herod the Great and Cleopatra of Jerusalem, half-brother of Antipas and Archelaus; tetrarch of the regions north of Galilee (Luke 3:1).
4. Son of Herod the Great and Mariamne; first husband of Herodias, who left him for Herod Antipas (Matt 14:3; Mark 6:17). (He also was half-brother to Archelaus and Antipas.)

PHILISTINE, PHILISTINES (n) a native or inhabitant of ancient Philistia
1 Sam 4:1 . . . was at war with the **P-s.**
1 Sam 17:1 . . . **P-s** now mustered their
1 Sam 17:26 . . . get for killing this **P**
1 Sam 31:1 . . . the **P-s** attacked Israel,

PHILOSOPHERS (n) a person who seeks wisdom or enlightenment; scholar, thinker
1 Cor 1:20 . . . leave the **p,** the scholars,

PHILOSOPHIES (n) a theory underlying or regarding a sphere of activity or thought
Col 2:8 . . . capture you with empty **p**

PHYSICAL (adj) having material existence; of or relating to the body
John 1:13 . . . reborn—not with a **p** birth
Col 1:22 . . . of Christ in his **p** body.
1 Tim 4:8 . . . **P** training is good, but
1 Tim 5:11 . . . **p** desires will overpower
1 Jn 2:16 . . . a craving for **p** pleasure

PICTURE (n) a representation, image, or copy
1 Pet 3:21 . . . water is a **p** of baptism,

PIERCE, PIERCED (v) to make a hole through; to stab
Exod 21:6 . . . and publicly **p** his ear
Ps 22:16 . . . have **p-d** my hands and feet.
Zech 12:10 . . . me whom they have **p-d**
Luke 2:35 . . . sword will **p** your very soul.
John 19:37 . . . look on the one they **p-d.**
Rev 1:7 . . . even those who **p-d** him.

PIG, PIGS (n) a wild or domestic swine
Matt 7:6 . . . Don't throw your pearls to **p-s!**
Mark 5:11 . . . a large herd of **p-s** feeding
Luke 15:15 . . . his fields to feed the **p-s.**
2 Pet 2:22 . . . washed **p** returns to the mud.

PIGEONS (n) any of the family of birds with a stout body, rather short legs, and smooth and compact plumage
Lev 5:11 . . . turtledoves or two young **p,**
Luke 2:24 . . . turtledoves or two young **p.**

PILATE The procurator (Roman governor) in Palestine at the time of the crucifixion of Christ (Luke 3:1). "Pontius" was his family name; he questioned Jesus and found him

innocent; later, influenced by the Jewish leaders, he sentenced him to execution (Matt 27; Mark 15; Luke 23; John 18–19).

PILGRIM(S) (KJV)
Heb 11:13 . . . *nomads* here on earth
1 Pet 2:11 . . . as "temporary residents and *foreigners*"

PILLAR, PILLARS (n) a column or shaft standing alone as a monument or supporting a superstructure; miraculous cloud by day and fire by night; memorial pile of stones; a supporting, integral, or upstanding member of a group
Gen 19:26 . . . she turned into a **p** of salt.
Exod 13:21 . . . night with a **p** of fire.
Exod 24:4 . . . set up twelve **p-s,** one for
Deut 1:33 . . . by night and a **p** of cloud by
Judg 16:26 . . . my hands against the **p-s**
Gal 2:9 . . . known as **p-s** of the church,
1 Tim 3:15 . . . **p** and foundation of
Rev 3:12 . . . victorious will become **p-s**

PINIONS (n) a bird's wings
Deut 32:11 . . . carried them safely on his **p.**

PIOUS (adj) marked by or showing reverence for God and devotion to worship; religious
Isa 58:2 . . . Yet they act so **p!**
Col 2:18 . . . insisting on **p** self-denial
Col 2:23 . . . strong devotion, **p** self-denial,

PIT (n) a hole, shaft, or cavity in the ground; a place or situation of misery, futility, or degradation
Ps 40:2 . . . me out of the **p** of despair,
Luke 14:5 . . . or your cow falls into a **p,**

PITCH (n) a black or dark sticky substance
Exod 2:3 . . . waterproofed it with tar and **p.**

PITIED (v) to feel pity for
1 Cor 15:19 . . . we are more to be **p** than

PITY (n) sympathetic sorrow for one suffering, distressed, or unhappy
Judg 2:18 . . . For the LORD took **p** on
Ps 17:10 . . . They are without **p.**
Ps 69:20 . . . would show some **p;**
Ps 72:13 . . . He feels **p** for the weak
Isa 27:11 . . . show them no **p** or mercy.
Hos 13:14 . . . I will not take **p** on them.

PLAGUE, PLAGUES (n) a disastrous evil, affliction, or epidemic of infectious disease, issued by God in judgment
2 Chr 6:28 . . . or a **p** or crop disease
Luke 21:11 . . . will be famines and **p-s**
Rev 21:9 . . . the seven last **p-s** came
Rev 22:18 . . . add to that person the **p-s**

PLAGUED (v) to smite, infest, or afflict with disease, calamity, or natural evil
Ps 73:5 . . . they're not **p** with problems

PLAN, PLANS (n) a detailed formulation of a program of action; goal, aim
see also PURPOSE
Ps 2:1 . . . waste their time with futile **p-s?**
Ps 33:10 . . . frustrates the **p-s** of the
Ps 40:5 . . . **p-s** for us are too numerous
Isa 30:1 . . . You make **p-s** that are contrary
Isa 32:6 . . . and make evil **p-s.**
Jer 29:11 . . . I know the **p-s** I have for you
Acts 2:23 . . . his prearranged **p** was carried
Acts 4:25 . . . waste their time with futile **p-s?**
Acts 7:44 . . . according to the **p** God had
Rom 16:25 . . . **p** kept secret from
Eph 3:9 . . . this mysterious **p** that God,
Eph 3:11 . . . This was his eternal **p,**
2 Tim 1:9 . . . **p** from before the beginning

PLANNED, PLANNING (v) to devise or project the realization or achievement of
Prov 12:20 . . . hearts that are **p-ning** peace!
Isa 25:1 . . . You **p-ned** them long ago,
Jer 23:20 . . . has finished all he has **p-ned.**
Eph 2:10 . . . do the good things he **p-ned**

PLANT (n) a young tree, vine, shrub, or herb planted or suitable for planting
Matt 15:13 . . . **p** not planted by
1 Cor 15:36 . . . it doesn't grow into a **p**

PLANT, PLANTED, PLANTING, PLANTS (v) to put or set (seeds or plants) in the ground for growth; to establish or settle
Gen 2:8 . . . the LORD God **p-ed** a garden
Gen 8:22 . . . there will be **p-ing** and harvest,
Ps 1:3 . . . like trees **p-ed** along the riverbank,
Ps 126:5 . . . who **p** in tears will harvest
Prov 22:8 . . . who **p** injustice will harvest
Prov 31:16 . . . earnings she **p-s** a vineyard.
Hos 10:12 . . . **P** the good seeds
Amos 9:15 . . . I will firmly **p** them there
Matt 6:26 . . . They don't **p** or harvest or
Matt 13:3 . . . A farmer went out to **p** some
Matt 13:18 . . . about the farmer **p-ing**
1 Cor 3:6 . . . **p-ed** the seed in your hearts,
1 Cor 3:7 . . . who does the **p-ing,**
1 Cor 9:7 . . . What farmer **p-s** a vineyard
1 Cor 15:42 . . . earthly bodies are **p-ed**
2 Cor 9:6 . . . a farmer who **p-s** only a few
Jas 1:21 . . . accept the word God has **p-ed**
Jas 3:18 . . . will **p** seeds of peace

PLANTER (n) one who cultivates plants
John 4:36 . . . What joy awaits both the **p** and

PLAY, PLAYED (v) to perform music; to engage in sport or recreation
1 Sam 16:23 . . . David would **p** the harp.
Ps 87:7 . . . The people will **p** flutes
Ps 137:5 . . . forget how to **p** the harp.
Isa 11:8 . . . baby will **p** safely near the hole
Luke 7:32 . . . so we **p-ed** funeral songs,

PLEA, PLEAS (n) an earnest entreaty; appeal
1 Kgs 8:28 . . . prayer and my **p,** O LORD
Ps 102:17 . . . He will not reject their **p-s.**

PLEAD, PLEADING, PLEADS (v) to entreat or appeal earnestly; to argue a case or cause
Job 9:15 . . . I could only **p** for mercy.
Lam 3:56 . . . Listen to my **p-ing!**
Hos 10:8 . . . and **p** with the hills,
Acts 16:9 . . . **p-ing** with him, "Come over
Rom 8:27 . . . the Spirit **p-s** for us
Rom 8:34 . . . right hand, **p-ing** for us.
2 Cor 5:20 . . . speak for Christ when we **p,**

PLEASANT (adj) having qualities that tend to give pleasure; agreeable
Gen 49:15 . . . and how **p** the land,
Ps 16:6 . . . given me is a **p** land.
Prov 16:21 . . . and **p** words are persuasive.
Isa 5:7 . . . of Judah are his **p** garden.

PLEASE, PLEASED, PLEASES (v) to make glad; to satisfy; to like or wish; to be the will or pleasure of
Deut 12:25 . . . doing what **p-s** the LORD.
Ps 135:6 . . . The LORD does whatever **p-s**
Prov 16:7 . . . people's lives **p** the LORD,
Isa 42:1 . . . my chosen one, who **p-s** me.
Matt 12:18 . . . my Beloved, who **p-s** me.
Luke 2:14 . . . those with whom God is **p-d.**
Luke 10:21 . . . Yes, Father, it **p-d** you to do
John 8:29 . . . I always do what **p-s** him.
Rom 8:8 . . . sinful nature can never **p** God.
Rom 14:18 . . . this attitude, you will **p** God,
2 Cor 5:9 . . . our goal is to **p** him.
Gal 6:8 . . . live to **p** the Spirit will harvest
Eph 5:10 . . . determine what **p-s** the
Phil 2:13 . . . power to do what **p-s** him.
Col 1:10 . . . always honor and **p** the Lord,
Col 1:19 . . . God in all his fullness was **p-d**
1 Thes 2:4 . . . Our purpose is to **p** God,
1 Thes 2:15 . . . They fail to **p** God
1 Tim 2:3 . . . is good and **p-s** God our
1 Tim 5:4 . . . is something that **p-s** God.
Heb 10:6 . . . not **p-d** with burnt offerings
Heb 11:6 . . . to **p** God without faith.
Heb 13:16 . . . sacrifices that **p** God.
1 Pet 2:19 . . . God is **p-d** with you when
1 Jn 2:17 . . . does what **p-s** God will live
Rev 4:11 . . . you created what you **p-d.**

PLEASING (adj) giving pleasure; agreeable
Lev 1:9 . . . a special gift, a **p** aroma
Ps 19:14 . . . of my heart be **p** to you,
Ps 104:34 . . . my thoughts be **p** to him,
Eccl 7:26 . . . who are **p** to God will escape
Rom 12:2 . . . is good and **p** and perfect.
Phil 4:18 . . . is acceptable and **p** to God.

PLEASURE, PLEASURES (n) desire, inclination; a source of delight or joy; sensual gratification
Ps 5:4 . . . you take no **p** in wickedness;
Ps 16:3 . . . I take **p** in them!
Ps 16:11 . . . the **p-s** of living with you
Isa 1:11 . . . I get no **p** from the blood of
Luke 8:14 . . . cares and riches and **p-s**
Eph 1:9 . . . a plan to fulfill his own good **p.**
1 Tim 5:6 . . . widow who lives only for **p**
2 Tim 3:4 . . . and love **p** rather than God.
Titus 2:12 . . . living and sinful **p-s.**
Titus 3:3 . . . slaves to many lusts and **p-s.**
Heb 11:25 . . . the fleeting **p-s** of sin.
Jas 4:3 . . . want only what will give you **p.**

PLEDGE (n) a binding promise or agreement to do or forbear
1 Tim 5:12 . . . breaking their previous **p.**

PLENTY (n) the full or more-than-adequate amount or supply
Ps 17:14 . . . May their children have **p,**
Prov 12:11 . . . A hard worker has **p** of food,
2 Cor 8:14 . . . now you have **p** and can help
2 Cor 9:8 . . . **p** left over to share with others.

PLOT, PLOTS (v) to plan or contrive especially secretly; to scheme
Prov 3:29 . . . **p** harm against your neighbor
Prov 6:14 . . . perverted hearts **p** evil,
Prov 6:18 . . . a heart that **p-s** evil,

PLOWS (v) to turn, break up, or work with a plow
1 Cor 9:10 . . . the one who **p** and the one

PLOWSHARES (n) a part of a plow that cuts the furrow
Isa 2:4 . . . will hammer their swords into **p**
Joel 3:10 . . . Hammer your **p** into swords
Mic 4:3 . . . hammer their swords into **p**

PLUNDER (v) to take by force (as in war)
Matt 12:29 . . . like Satan and **p** his goods?

PLUNGE (v) to cause to enter a state or course of action usually suddenly, unexpectedly, or violently; to act with reckless haste
1 Tim 6:9 . . . desires that **p** them into ruin
1 Pet 4:4 . . . no longer **p** into the flood of

POINT (n) a particular place; a particular step, stage, or degree in development
Matt 4:5 . . . the highest **p** of the Temple,
Matt 26:38 . . . grief to the **p** of death.

POINT (v) to indicate the fact or probability of something specified
John 5:39 . . . But the Scriptures **p** to me!

POISON (n) a substance that usually kills, injures, or impairs an organism; something destructive or harmful
2 Kgs 4:40 . . . there's **p** in this stew!
Jas 3:8 . . . and evil, full of deadly **p.**

POISONOUS (adj) destructive, harmful; venomous
Mark 16:18 . . . **p,** it won't hurt them.

POLISHED (adj) smooth or glossy; burnished
Dan 10:6 . . . feet shone like **p** bronze,
Rev 1:15 . . . feet were like **p** bronze refined
Rev 2:18 . . . feet are like **p** bronze:

POLLUTE, POLLUTES, POLLUTING (v) to make ceremonially, physically, or morally impure
Num 35:33 . . . for murder **p-s** the land.
Prov 25:26 . . . it's like **p-ing** a fountain
Isa 41:24 . . . who choose you **p** themselves.

POMEGRANATES (n) a several-celled reddish berry that is about the size of an orange with a thick, leathery skin and many tartish seeds
Song 4:3 . . . Your cheeks are like rosy **p**

PONDER, PONDERED (v) to think or consider especially quietly, soberly, and deeply
see also MEDITATE
Ps 111:2 . . . delight in him should **p**
Ps 119:59 . . . I **p-ed** the direction of my life,
Ps 143:5 . . . I **p** all your great works

POOR (adj) characterized by poverty or insufficient resources; humble
Lev 19:10 . . . Leave them for the **p**
Deut 15:4 . . . should be no **p** among you,
Deut 15:11 . . . some in the land who are **p.**
Deut 24:12 . . . If your neighbor is **p**
1 Sam 2:7 . . . The LORD makes some **p**
Job 5:16 . . . at last the **p** have hope,
Ps 35:10 . . . protects the helpless and **p**
Ps 41:1 . . . those who are kind to the **p!**
Ps 82:3 . . . Give justice to the **p** and the
Prov 10:4 . . . Lazy people are soon **p;**
Prov 13:7 . . . Some who are **p** pretend
Prov 14:21 . . . those who help the **p.**
Prov 17:5 . . . mock the **p** insult
Prov 21:13 . . . cries of the **p** will be ignored
Prov 22:2 . . . rich and **p** have this
Prov 22:22 . . . Don't rob the **p** just because
Prov 28:27 . . . Whoever gives to the **p** will
Prov 31:20 . . . helping hand to the **p**
Isa 3:14 . . . things stolen from the **p.**
Isa 14:30 . . . I will feed the **p** in my pasture;
Isa 32:7 . . . They lie to convict the **p,**
Isa 61:1 . . . to bring good news to the **p.**
Jer 22:16 . . . help to the **p** and needy,
Amos 4:1 . . . who oppress the **p** and crush
Amos 5:11 . . . trample the **p,** stealing their
Zech 7:10 . . . foreigners, and the **p.**
Matt 11:5 . . . is being preached to the **p.**
Matt 19:21 . . . and give the money to the **p,**
Mark 12:42 . . . Then a **p** widow came and
Mark 14:7 . . . You will always have the **p**
Luke 4:18 . . . to bring Good News to the **p.**
Luke 14:13 . . . Instead, invite the **p,** the
John 12:8 . . . You will always have the **p**
Rom 15:26 . . . an offering for the **p** among
2 Cor 8:9 . . . for your sakes he became **p,**
Jas 2:2 . . . another comes in who is **p**
Jas 2:6 . . . you dishonor the **p!**

PORTIONS (n) an often limited part set off or abstracted from a whole; share
Num 18:29 . . . give to the LORD the best **p**

POSITION (n) social or official rank or status; job
Ps 109:8 . . . let someone else take his **p.**
Acts 1:20 . . . Let someone else take his **p.**
1 Tim 3:1 . . . elder, he desires an honorable **p.**

POSSESS, POSSESSED (v) to seize, gain, or take (control of); to own
see also INHERIT
Ps 37:11 . . . The lowly will **p** the land
Ps 37:29 . . . The godly will **p** the land
John 7:20 . . . You're demon **p-ed!**
John 8:48 . . . you were **p-ed** by a demon?
John 8:52 . . . you are **p-ed** by a demon.
John 10:20 . . . He's demon **p-ed** and out
John 10:21 . . . like a man **p-ed** by a demon!
Phil 3:12 . . . press on to **p** that perfection

POSSESSION, POSSESSIONS (n) something owned, occupied, or controlled
see also INHERITANCE, RICHES, TREASURE(S), WEALTH
Exod 6:8 . . . as your very own **p.**
Deut 4:20 . . . and his special **p,**
Deut 32:9 . . . is his special **p.**
Zech 2:12 . . . the LORD's special **p**
Matt 19:21 . . . sell all your **p-s** and
Mark 10:22 . . . for he had many **p-s.**
1 Pet 2:9 . . . God's very own **p.**

POSSIBLE (adj) being within the limits of ability, capacity, or realization
Matt 19:26 . . . with God everything is **p.**
Matt 26:39 . . . **p,** let this cup of suffering
Mark 9:23 . . . Anything is **p** if a person
Mark 10:27 . . . Everything is **p** with God.
Mark 14:35 . . . if it were **p,** the awful hour
Heb 10:4 . . . it is not **p** for the blood

POTTER (n) one who makes pottery
Isa 29:16 . . . **p** who made me is stupid"?
Isa 64:8 . . . the clay, and you are the **p.**
Zech 11:13 . . . threw them to the **p**

POUR, POURED, POURING, POURS (v) to move or come continuously; to supply or produce freely
Ps 42:8 . . . LORD **p-s** his unfailing love
Ps 45:7 . . . **p-ing** out the oil of joy on
Isa 32:15 . . . Spirit is **p-ed** out on us
Isa 44:3 . . . I will **p** out my Spirit
Ezek 39:29 . . . I will **p** out my Spirit
Joel 2:28 . . . I will **p** out my Spirit
Zech 12:10 . . . I will **p** out a spirit of
Mal 3:10 . . . I will **p** out a blessing
Luke 22:20 . . . blood, which is **p-ed** out
Acts 2:17 . . . I will **p** out my Spirit
Acts 2:33 . . . the Holy Spirit to **p** out
Acts 10:45 . . . Holy Spirit had been **p-ed**
Eph 1:6 . . . grace he has **p-ed** out on us
Phil 2:17 . . . **p-ing** it out like a liquid
Titus 3:6 . . . generously **p-ed** out the Spirit

POVERTY (n) the state of one who lacks money or material possessions
Prov 6:11 . . . **p** will pounce on you like
Prov 13:18 . . . end in **p** and disgrace;
Prov 21:5 . . . hasty shortcuts lead to **p.**
Prov 24:34 . . . **p** will pounce on you like
Prov 31:7 . . . drink to forget their **p**
2 Cor 8:9 . . . by his **p** he could make you
Rev 2:9 . . . your suffering and your **p**—

POWER, POWERS (n) ability to act or produce an effect; possession of control, authority, or influence over others; physical might; mental or moral efficacy; a controlling group
see also STRENGTH
Exod 15:6 . . . LORD, is glorious in **p.**
Deut 8:18 . . . one who gives you **p** to be
Ps 89:7 . . . angelic **p-s** stand in awe of God.
Isa 40:26 . . . great **p** and incomparable
Jer 9:23 . . . the powerful boast in their **p,**
Mic 3:8 . . . I am filled with **p**—
Matt 16:18 . . . all the **p-s** of hell will not
Matt 22:29 . . . don't know the **p** of God.
Luke 1:35 . . . the **p** of the Most High will
Luke 4:14 . . . the Holy Spirit's **p.**
Luke 9:1 . . . gave them **p** and authority
Luke 10:19 . . . over all the **p** of the enemy,
Luke 11:20 . . . demons by the **p** of God,
Acts 1:8 . . . receive **p** when the Holy Spirit
Rom 1:16 . . . the **p** of God at work,
Rom 1:20 . . . his eternal **p** and divine
Rom 6:9 . . . Death no longer has any **p** over
Rom 7:23 . . . another **p** within me that is
Rom 8:38 . . . not even the **p-s** of hell can
Rom 15:13 . . . the **p** of the Holy Spirit.
1 Cor 1:18 . . . is the very **p** of God.
1 Cor 6:14 . . . from the dead by his **p,**
1 Cor 15:24 . . . ruler and authority and **p.**
2 Cor 4:7 . . . our great **p** is from God,
2 Cor 13:4 . . . now lives by the **p** of God.
Eph 6:10 . . . Lord and in his mighty **p.**
Phil 3:10 . . . and experience the mighty **p**
Col 1:11 . . . with all his glorious **p**
Col 1:29 . . . depending on Christ's mighty **p**
1 Thes 1:5 . . . words but also with **p,**
2 Tim 1:7 . . . but of **p,** love, and
2 Tim 3:5 . . . reject the **p** that could make
Heb 2:14 . . . break the **p** of the devil,
Jas 5:16 . . . righteous person has great **p**
1 Pet 1:5 . . . is protecting you by his **p**
1 Pet 3:22 . . . **p-s** accept his authority.
1 Pet 4:11 . . . All glory and **p** to him
2 Pet 1:3 . . . **p,** God has given us everything
Jude 1:25 . . . majesty, **p,** and authority are his
Rev 4:11 . . . receive glory and honor and **p.**
Rev 5:12 . . . receive **p** and riches and
Rev 19:1 . . . glory and **p** belong to our God.
Rev 20:6 . . . the second death holds no **p,**

POWERFUL (adj) having great power, prestige, or influence
Exod 6:6 . . . will redeem you with a **p** arm
Deut 5:15 . . . strong hand and **p** arm.
Job 25:2 . . . God is **p** and dreadful.
Ps 29:4 . . . the LORD is **p;**
Ps 136:12 . . . strong hand and **p** arm.
Jer 9:23 . . . the **p** boast in their power,
Jer 27:5 . . . my great strength and **p** arm
Luke 24:19 . . . who did **p** miracles,
1 Cor 1:27 . . . to shame those who are **p.**

POWERLESS (adj) devoid of strength or resources; lacking the authority or capacity to act
Num 24:13 . . . would be **p** to do anything
1 Cor 1:27 . . . things that are **p** to shame

PRACTICE, PRACTICING (v) to do or perform often, habitually, or customarily; to carry out, apply
Lev 19:26 . . . Do not **p** fortune-telling
Matt 23:3 . . . they don't **p** what they teach.
Rom 12:13 . . . eager to **p** hospitality.
Phil 4:9 . . . putting into **p** all you learned
1 Jn 1:6 . . . we are not **p-ing** the truth.
1 Jn 5:18 . . . not make a **p** of sinning,

PRAISE, PRAISES (n) worship; commendation; value, merit
Deut 26:19 . . . **p,** honor, and renown.
2 Sam 22:4 . . . LORD, who is worthy of **p,**

2 Chr 29:30 . . . So they offered joyous **p**
Ps 7:17 . . . I will sing **p** to the name
Ps 18:49 . . . I will sing **p-s** to your name.
Ps 34:1 . . . will constantly speak his **p-s.**
Ps 65:1 . . . What mighty **p,** O God,
Ps 81:1 . . . Sing **p-s** to God,
Ps 100:4 . . . into his courts with **p.**
Ps 108:1 . . . your **p-s** with all my heart!
Ps 145:3 . . . He is most worthy of **p!**
Ps 149:6 . . . Let the **p-s** of God be in
John 12:43 . . . loved human **p** more than
Rom 2:29 . . . heart seeks **p** from God,
Rom 15:9 . . . will sing **p-s** to your name.
1 Thes 2:6 . . . As for human **p,**
2 Thes 1:10 . . . his holy people—**p** from all
Jas 5:13 . . . You should sing **p-s.**

PRAISE, PRAISED, PRAISES, PRAISING (v) to worship, commend, or give honor to
Exod 15:2 . . . and I will **p** him—
1 Chr 16:35 . . . name and rejoice and **p** you.
2 Chr 5:13 . . . together in unison to **p** and
2 Chr 20:21 . . . **p-ing** him for his holy
Neh 9:5 . . . Stand up and **p** the LORD
Ps 9:1 . . . I will **p** you, LORD,
Ps 12:8 . . . evil is **p-d** throughout the land.
Ps 34:1 . . . I will **p** the LORD
Ps 42:5 . . . I will **p** him again—
Ps 45:17 . . . nations will **p** you forever
Ps 51:15 . . . my mouth may **p** you.
Ps 63:3 . . . how I **p** you!
Ps 71:8 . . . why I can never stop **p-ing** you;
Ps 71:14 . . . I will **p** you more and
Ps 74:21 . . . and needy **p** your name.
Ps 89:5 . . . angels will **p** you for your
Ps 96:2 . . . LORD; **p** his name.
Ps 102:18 . . . not yet born will **p** the
Ps 104:1 . . . all that I am **p** the
Ps 115:18 . . . But we can **p** the LORD
Ps 135:20 . . . LORD, **p** the LORD!
Ps 144:1 . . . **P** the LORD, who is
Ps 148:13 . . . Let them all **p** the name
Ps 150:2 . . . **p** his unequaled greatness!
Prov 27:2 . . . Let someone else **p** you,
Prov 27:21 . . . person is tested by being **p-d.**
Isa 63:7 . . . I will **p** the LORD
Dan 2:19 . . . Daniel **p-d** the God of heaven.
Dan 2:20 . . . He said, "**P** the name
Dan 4:34 . . . **p-d** and worshiped the Most
Matt 5:16 . . . will **p** your heavenly Father.
Mark 11:9 . . . were shouting, "**P** God!
Luke 1:46 . . . how my soul **p-s** the Lord.
Luke 2:13 . . . armies of heaven—**p-ing** God
Luke 2:20 . . . glorifying and **p-ing** God for
Luke 18:43 . . . all who saw it **p-d** God, too.
Luke 19:37 . . . **p-ing** God for all the wonderful
Acts 2:47 . . . all the while **p-ing** God
Acts 10:46 . . . in other tongues and **p-ing** God
1 Cor 14:16 . . . if you **p** God only in
Gal 1:24 . . . they **p-d** God because of me.
Eph 1:6 . . . we **p** God for the glorious
Jas 3:9 . . . Sometimes it **p-s** our Lord
Rev 19:1 . . . heaven shouting, "**P** the LORD!

PRAY, PRAYED, PRAYING, PRAYS (v) to address God with adoration, confession, supplication, or thanksgiving; to intercede
Gen 24:45 . . . I had finished **p-ing** in my
1 Sam 1:12 . . . she was **p-ing** to the LORD,
2 Chr 7:14 . . . humble themselves and **p** and
2 Chr 30:18 . . . King Hezekiah **p-ed** for
Neh 4:9 . . . we **p-ed** to our God and
Job 42:8 . . . servant Job will **p** for you,
Job 42:10 . . . When Job **p-ed** for his friends,
Ps 5:2 . . . I **p** to no one but you.
Ps 32:6 . . . all the godly **p** to you
Ps 34:6 . . . In my desperation I **p-ed,**
Dan 6:10 . . . He **p-ed** three times a day,
Dan 9:4 . . . I **p-ed** to the LORD
Jon 2:1 . . . Jonah **p-ed** to the LORD
Matt 6:5 . . . When you **p,** don't be like
Matt 6:9 . . . **P** like this: Our Father
Matt 26:39 . . . face to the ground, **p-ing,**
Mark 11:24 . . . you can **p** for anything,
Mark 11:25 . . . when you are **p-ing,** first
Luke 3:21 . . . **p-ing,** the heavens opened,
Luke 9:29 . . . he was **p-ing,** the appearance
Luke 11:1 . . . teach us to **p,**
Luke 22:41 . . . and knelt down and **p-ed,**
John 17:20 . . . I am **p-ing** not only for these
Acts 6:6 . . . apostles, who **p-ed** for them
Acts 9:11 . . . He is **p-ing** to me right now.
Acts 16:25 . . . Paul and Silas were **p-ing**
Rom 8:26 . . . the Holy Spirit **p-s** for us
Rom 12:12 . . . and keep on **p-ing.**
Rom 15:30 . . . join in my struggle by **p-ing**
1 Cor 14:14 . . . For if I **p** in tongues,
2 Cor 13:9 . . . We **p** that you will become
Eph 1:18 . . . I **p** that your hearts will be
Eph 3:16 . . . I **p** that from his glorious,
Phil 4:6 . . . instead, **p** about everything.
1 Thes 1:3 . . . As we **p** to our God and
1 Thes 5:17 . . . Never stop **p-ing.**
2 Thes 1:11 . . . we keep on **p-ing** for you,
1 Tim 2:8 . . . to **p** with holy hands
Jas 5:13 . . . You should **p.**
Jas 5:16 . . . **p** for each other so that
Jude 1:20 . . . **p** in the power of the Holy

PRAYER, PRAYERS (n) conversation with God—in praise, thanksgiving, or intercession
2 Chr 30:27 . . . God heard their **p** from
Ps 4:1 . . . mercy on me and hear my **p.**
Ps 17:1 . . . Pay attention to my **p,**
Ps 20:5 . . . LORD answer all your **p-s.**
Ps 86:6 . . . Listen closely to my **p,**
Prov 15:8 . . . in the **p-s** of the upright.
Isa 1:15 . . . Though you offer many **p-s,**
Isa 56:7 . . . will be called a house of **p**
Matt 11:25 . . . Jesus prayed this **p:**
John 17:9 . . . My **p** is not for the world,
Acts 1:14 . . . were constantly united in **p,**
Acts 4:31 . . . After this **p,** the meeting
Acts 6:4 . . . can spend our time in **p**
Acts 10:31 . . . your **p** has been heard,
Acts 13:3 . . . So after more fasting and **p,**
Eph 6:18 . . . persistent in your **p-s** for all
Col 4:2 . . . Devote yourselves to **p** with an
1 Pet 3:7 . . . your **p-s** will not be hindered.
1 Pet 3:12 . . . ears are open to their **p-s.**
Rev 5:8 . . . are the **p-s** of God's people.

PREACH, PREACHED, PREACHES, PREACHING (v) to deliver a sermon; to exhort an idea or course of action
see also PROCLAIM, TEACH
Luke 9:6 . . . **p-ing** the Good News and
Luke 9:60 . . . go and **p** about the Kingdom
Acts 5:42 . . . teach and **p** this message:
Acts 9:20 . . . he began **p-ing** about Jesus
Acts 16:10 . . . to **p** the Good News
Acts 18:5 . . . all his time **p-ing** the word.
Rom 1:15 . . . to **p** the Good News.
1 Cor 2:4 . . . my message and my **p-ing**
1 Cor 9:27 . . . I fear that after **p-ing** to
1 Cor 15:1 . . . Good News I **p-ed** to you
2 Cor 4:5 . . . We **p** that Jesus Christ is Lord,
2 Cor 11:4 . . . Jesus than the one we **p,**
Gal 1:8 . . . **p-es** a different kind of Good
Gal 1:8 . . . than the one we **p-ed** to you.
Gal 1:9 . . . **p-es** any other Good News
Gal 5:11 . . . no longer **p-ing** salvation
Phil 1:18 . . . Christ is being **p-ed** either way,
Col 1:23 . . . Good News has been **p-ed** all
1 Tim 5:17 . . . work hard at both **p-ing** and
2 Tim 4:17 . . . might **p** the Good News
1 Pet 1:25 . . . Good News that was **p-ed** to
1 Pet 3:19 . . . went and **p-ed** to the spirits

PREACHER (n) one who delivers sermons or proclaims the gospel
1 Tim 2:7 . . . chosen as a **p** and apostle
2 Tim 1:11 . . . God chose me to be a **p,**

PRECEPT(S) (KJV)
Ps 119:15 . . . study your *commandments* and
Ps 119:159 . . . how I love your *commandments,*
Mark 10:5 . . . this *commandment* only as a
Heb 9:19 . . . each of God's *commandments*

PRECIOUS (adj) of great value or high price; highly esteemed or cherished
Prov 31:10 . . . She is more **p** than rubies.
Isa 28:16 . . . It is a **p** cornerstone
1 Pet 1:19 . . . was the **p** blood of Christ,
2 Pet 1:4 . . . great and **p** promises.

PREDICTED (v) to declare or indicate in advance; to foretell
Isa 43:12 . . . First I **p** your rescue,
John 12:38 . . . the prophet had **p:**
Acts 7:52 . . . **p** the coming of

PREDICTIONS (n) something that is predicted; forecast
Isa 44:26 . . . I carry out the **p** of my
Jer 28:9 . . . Only when his **p** come true

PREGNANCY (n) the condition of being pregnant
Gen 3:16 . . . sharpen the pain of your **p,**

PREGNANT (adj) containing a developing unborn offspring within the body
Gen 11:30 . . . was unable to become **p**
Matt 24:19 . . . How terrible it will be for **p**
1 Thes 5:3 . . . as a **p** woman's labor

PREPARE, PREPARED (v) to make ready beforehand for some purpose, use, or activity; to get ready
Exod 23:20 . . . to the place I have **p-d** for
Ps 23:5 . . . You **p** a feast for me
Zeph 1:7 . . . LORD has **p-d** his people
Mal 3:1 . . . he will **p** the way before me.
Matt 25:34 . . . inherit the Kingdom **p-d**
John 14:2 . . . I am going to **p** a place
1 Cor 2:9 . . . has **p-d** for those who love
2 Cor 5:5 . . . God himself has **p-d** us for
2 Tim 4:2 . . . the word of God. Be **p-d,**

PRESBYTERY (KJV)
1 Tim 4:14 . . . *elders of the church* laid their hands

PRESENCE (n) company; nearness; (symbolic of) God-with-us
Exod 25:30 . . . Bread of the **P** on the table
1 Sam 6:20 . . . in the **p** of the LORD,
Ps 15:1 . . . enter your **p** on your holy hill?
Ps 21:6 . . . given him the joy of your **p.**
Ps 23:5 . . . in the **p** of my enemies.
Ps 31:20 . . . in the shelter of your **p,**
Ps 89:15 . . . walk in the light of your **p,**
Ps 114:7 . . . at the **p** of the God of Jacob.
Ps 139:7 . . . never get away from your **p!**
Isa 53:2 . . . grew up in the LORD's **p**
Jer 5:22 . . . tremble in my **p?**
Matt 18:10 . . . always in the **p** of my heavenly
1 Thes 3:9 . . . joy as we enter God's **p.**

PRESENT (adj) being in view or at hand; now existing or in progress
Lev 16:2 . . . I myself am **p** in the cloud
1 Cor 7:26 . . . Because of the **p** crisis,

PRESENT, PRESENTED, PRESENTING (v) to give or bestow formally
Gen 28:22 . . . I will **p** to God a tenth
Matt 5:23 . . . you are **p-ing** a sacrifice
Rom 3:25 . . . **p-ed** Jesus as the sacrifice
Rom 15:19 . . . fully **p-ed** the Good News
Eph 5:27 . . . did this to **p** her to himself
2 Tim 2:15 . . . Work hard so you can **p**

PRESERVE, PRESERVES (v) to keep safe from injury, harm, or destruction
see also SAVE
Gen 45:5 . . . ahead of you to **p** your lives.
Deut 33:12 . . . **p-s** them from every harm.
1 Kgs 19:18 . . . I will **p** 7,000 others
Jer 10:12 . . . he **p-s** it by his wisdom.

PRESS (v) to follow through (a course of action)
Phil 3:12 . . . I **p** on to possess that
Phil 3:14 . . . I **p** on to reach the end

PRESSURE (n) the burden of physical or mental distress
Prov 24:10 . . . **p**, your strength is too small.

PRETEND, PRETENDED (v) to give a false appearance of being, possessing, or performing
1 Sam 21:13 . . . So he **p-ed** to be insane,
Zech 13:4 . . . No one will **p** to be a prophet
Rom 12:9 . . . Don't just **p** to love

PRETENSE (n) professed rather than real intention or purpose
Amos 5:21 . . . I hate all your show and **p**—

PREVAIL, PREVAILS (v) to triumph
Prov 19:21 . . . LORD's purpose will **p.**
Isa 42:4 . . . lose heart until justice **p-s**

PRICE (n) the quantity of one thing that is exchanged or demanded in barter or sale for another
Job 28:18 . . . **p** of wisdom is far above
1 Cor 6:20 . . . bought you with a high **p.**

PRIDE (n) inordinate self-esteem or conceit; disdainful behavior or treatment of others
Ps 101:5 . . . will not endure conceit and **p.**
Prov 6:3 . . . Now swallow your **p;**
Prov 8:13 . . . I hate **p** and arrogance,
Mark 7:22 . . . envy, slander, **p,**
1 Jn 2:16 . . . **p** in our achievements and

PRIEST, PRIESTS (n) one authorized to perform the sacred rites of sacrifice and worship; a mediator between God and humans
Exod 19:6 . . . will be my kingdom of **p-s,**
Ps 110:4 . . . You are a **p** forever
Mal 1:6 . . . Armies says to the **p-s:**
Heb 4:14 . . . since we have a great High **P**
Heb 5:6 . . . You are a **p** forever
Heb 6:20 . . . our eternal High **P**
Heb 8:1 . . . a High **P** who sat down
1 Pet 2:5 . . . you are his holy **p-s.**
1 Pet 2:9 . . . You are royal **p-s,**
Rev 5:10 . . . Kingdom of **p-s** for our God.
Rev 20:6 . . . but they will be **p-s** of God

PRIESTHOOD (n) the office, dignity, or character of a priest
Heb 7:24 . . . his **p** lasts forever.

PRINCE, PRINCES (n) a son of a king; the ruler of a principality or state; a man of high rank or high standing in his class or profession
Ps 118:9 . . . LORD than to trust in **p-s.**
Prov 25:15 . . . Patience can persuade a **p,**
Isa 9:6 . . . Everlasting Father, **P** of Peace.
Ezek 34:24 . . . David will be a **p** among
Dan 8:25 . . . take on the **P** of **p-s**
Matt 10:25 . . . called the **p** of demons,
Luke 11:15 . . . the **p** of demons.
Acts 5:31 . . . at his right hand as **P** and

PRINCESS (n) the daughter of a king; a woman having sovereign power
Ps 45:13 . . . The bride, a **p**, looks glorious

PRINCIPLE, PRINCIPLES (n) a comprehensive and fundamental law, doctrine, or assumption
Gal 4:9 . . . useless spiritual **p-s** of this world?
Gal 6:16 . . . all who live by this **p;**

PRISON, PRISONS (n) a state of confinement or captivity; jail
Ps 142:7 . . . Bring me out of **p**
Isa 42:7 . . . will free the captives from **p,**
Matt 25:36 . . . I was in **p**, and you visited
2 Cor 11:23 . . . been put in **p** more often,
Heb 11:36 . . . were chained in **p-s.**
Heb 13:3 . . . Remember those in **p,**
1 Pet 3:19 . . . preached to the spirits in **p**—
Jude 1:6 . . . chained in **p-s** of darkness,
Rev 20:7 . . . Satan will be let out of his **p.**

PRISONER, PRISONERS (n) a person deprived of liberty and kept under involuntary restraint, confinement, or custody
Ps 79:11 . . . to the moaning of the **p-s.**
Ps 146:7 . . . The LORD frees the **p-s.**
Zech 9:12 . . . you **p-s** who still have hope!
Gal 3:22 . . . we are all **p-s** of sin,
Eph 3:1 . . . I, Paul, a **p** of Christ Jesus

PRIVATE (adj) secret, not to be seen by others
Matt 6:4 . . . Give your gifts in **p**, and
Matt 6:6 . . . and pray to your Father in **p.**
1 Cor 4:5 . . . light and will reveal our **p** motives.

PRIVILEGE (n) a right or immunity granted as a peculiar benefit, advantage, or favor
Prov 25:2 . . . God's **p** to conceal things
Rom 5:2 . . . into this place of undeserved **p**
2 Cor 8:4 . . . for the **p** of sharing in

PRIZE (n) something offered or striven for in competitions or in contests
1 Cor 9:24 . . . one person gets the **p**?
1 Cor 9:25 . . . we do it for an eternal **p.**
Phil 3:14 . . . heavenly **p** for which God,
2 Tim 2:5 . . . cannot win the **p** unless
2 Tim 4:8 . . . **p** awaits me—the crown

PRIZE (v) to value highly, esteem
Prov 4:8 . . . If you **p** wisdom,

PROBLEMS (n) a source of perplexity, distress, or vexation
Matt 13:21 . . . as soon as they have **p**
Rom 5:3 . . . we run into **p** and trials,

PROCESSION (n) a group of individuals moving along in an orderly often ceremonial way
Ps 68:24 . . . O God—the **p** of my God
2 Cor 2:14 . . . in Christ's triumphal **p.**

PROCLAIM, PROCLAIMING, PROCLAIMS (v) to declare publicly
see also PREACH
Lev 25:10 . . . a time to **p** freedom
Deut 32:3 . . . I will **p** the name of
1 Chr 16:8 . . . and **p** his greatness.
Ps 2:7 . . . king **p-s** the LORD's decree:
Ps 50:6 . . . heavens **p** his justice,
Ps 97:6 . . . heavens **p** his righteousness;
Ps 145:4 . . . let them **p** your power.
Isa 61:1 . . . to **p** that captives will be
Acts 28:31 . . . **p-ing** the Kingdom of God
Col 1:25 . . . **p-ing** his entire message to you.
1 Thes 3:2 . . . in **p-ing** the Good News
Titus 1:1 . . . I have been sent to **p** faith
1 Jn 1:1 . . . **p** to you the one who existed

PRODUCE, PRODUCES (v) to yield, make, or manufacture
Prov 3:9 . . . best part of everything you **p.**
Isa 55:11 . . . and it always **p-s** fruit.
Matt 7:18 . . . good tree can't **p** bad fruit,
Luke 3:9 . . . tree that does not **p** good fruit
John 15:8 . . . When you **p** much fruit,
John 15:16 . . . to go and **p** lasting fruit,
Rom 7:4 . . . **p** a harvest of good deeds
Eph 5:9 . . . light within you **p-s** only what
Col 1:10 . . . lives will **p** every kind of good
Jas 2:17 . . . Unless it **p-s** good deeds, it is

PRODUCTIVE (adj) yielding results, benefits, or profits
2 Pet 1:8 . . . the more **p** and useful you will

PROFANING (v) to treat (something sacred) with abuse, irreverence, or contempt
Neh 13:17 . . . Why are you **p** the Sabbath

PROFESSIONAL (adj) of, relating to, or characteristic of a profession
Amos 7:14 . . . I'm not a **p** prophet,

PROFIT (n) gain, benefit, or usefulness
Prov 14:23 . . . Work brings **p**, but
2 Cor 2:17 . . . who preach for personal **p.**

PROFITABLE (adj) yielding advantageous returns or results
Prov 31:18 . . . her dealings are **p;**

PROGRESS (n) a forward or onward movement (as to an objective or goal)
Phil 3:16 . . . hold on to the **p** we have
1 Tim 4:15 . . . everyone will see your **p.**

PROLONG (v) to lengthen in time, extent, scope, or range
Ps 85:5 . . . Will you **p** your wrath to all

PROMISCUITY (n) miscellaneous mingling or selection of persons
see also IMMORALITY
Rom 13:13 . . . **p** and immoral living,

PROMISCUOUS (adj) not restricted to one sexual partner
Prov 23:27 . . . a **p** woman is as dangerous

PROMISE, PROMISES (n) a declaration that one will do or refrain from doing something specified
see also COVENANT, VOW
2 Sam 7:25 . . . a **p** that will last forever.
Neh 5:13 . . . If you fail to keep your **p,**
Ps 91:4 . . . faithful **p-s** are your armor
Ps 116:14 . . . keep my **p-s** to the LORD
Ps 145:13 . . . LORD always keeps his **p-s;**
Ps 146:6 . . . He keeps every **p** forever.
Rom 4:20 . . . in believing God's **p.**
Rom 9:4 . . . receiving his wonderful **p-s.**
Rom 15:4 . . . patiently for God's **p-s** to be
2 Cor 1:20 . . . **p-s** have been fulfilled
2 Cor 7:1 . . . Because we have these **p-s,**
Eph 2:12 . . . covenant **p-s** God had made
Heb 6:13 . . . God's **p** to Abraham.
Heb 8:6 . . . based on better **p-s.**
Heb 10:23 . . . be trusted to keep his **p.**
Heb 11:11 . . . that God would keep his **p.**
2 Pet 3:4 . . . **p** that Jesus is coming again?
2 Pet 3:9 . . . being slow about his **p,**

PROMISED, PROMISES, PROMISING (v) to pledge to do, bring about, or provide
Exod 3:17 . . . I have **p-d** to rescue you
Deut 15:6 . . . bless you as he has **p-d.**
Josh 23:15 . . . the good things he **p-d,**
Luke 24:49 . . . as my Father **p-d.**
Acts 1:4 . . . sends you the gift he **p-d,**
Rom 4:21 . . . able to do whatever he **p-s.**
Gal 3:14 . . . blessing he **p-d** to Abraham,
1 Tim 4:8 . . . **p-ing** benefits in this life
Titus 1:2 . . . God—who does not lie—**p-d**
Heb 10:36 . . . receive all that he has **p-d.**
Jas 1:12 . . . of life that God has **p-d**
Jas 2:5 . . . inherit the Kingdom he **p-d**
2 Pet 3:13 . . . new earth he has **p-d,**
1 Jn 2:25 . . . eternal life he **p-d** us.

PROMOTE (v) to further; to advance
Titus 2:1 . . . **p** the kind of living that

PRONOUNCE (v) to declare officially or ceremoniously
1 Chr 23:13 . . . to **p** blessings in his name

PROOF (n) something that induces certainty or establishes validity
John 10:25 . . . The **p** is the work I do

PROPERTY (n) a piece of real estate owned or possessed
Acts 5:1 . . . wife, Sapphira, sold some **p.**

PROPHECY, PROPHECIES (n) the spoken or written word from God; to forthtell (consoling or corrective material) and foretell (predicative material)
Matt 13:14 . . . fulfills the **p** of Isaiah
Acts 13:29 . . . all that the **p-ies** said about
Acts 17:3 . . . **p-ies** and proved that the Messiah
Acts 21:9 . . . who had the gift of **p.**
Acts 21:10 . . . who also had the gift of **p,**
1 Cor 13:2 . . . If I had the gift of **p,**
1 Cor 13:9 . . . gift of **p** reveals only part
1 Cor 14:6 . . . knowledge or **p** or teaching,
Rev 22:18 . . . words of **p** written in

PROPHESY, PROPHESIED, PROPHESIES, PROPHESYING (v) to issue a prophecy
Num 11:25 . . . upon them, they **p-ied.**
1 Sam 19:24 . . . day and all night, **p-ing** in
Isa 42:9 . . . Everything I **p-ied** has come true,
Joel 2:28 . . . sons and daughters will **p.**
Matt 7:22 . . . We **p-ied** in your name and
Acts 2:17 . . . sons and daughters will **p.**
Acts 19:6 . . . in other tongues and **p-ied.**
Rom 12:6 . . . the ability to **p,**
1 Cor 11:4 . . . head while praying or **p-ing.**
1 Cor 12:10 . . . the ability to **p.**
1 Cor 14:1 . . . the ability to **p.**
1 Cor 14:3 . . . one who **p-ies** strengthens
1 Cor 14:39 . . . be eager to **p,**

PROPHET, PROPHETS (n) an interpreter of the times and of people's hearts; one who issues divinely inspired revelations
Exod 7:1 . . . Aaron, will be your **p.**
Exod 15:20 . . . Miriam the **p,** Aaron's
Deut 13:1 . . . there are **p-s** among you
Deut 18:18 . . . I will raise up a **p** like you
1 Sam 9:9 . . . **p-s** used to be called seers.
1 Kgs 18:36 . . . Elijah the **p** walked up to
2 Kgs 5:8 . . . a true **p** here in Israel.
2 Kgs 6:12 . . . Elisha, the **p** in Israel,
Isa 44:26 . . . the predictions of my **p-s!**
Hos 9:7 . . . you say, "The **p-s** are crazy
Amos 7:14 . . . I'm not a professional **p,**
Hab 1:1 . . . that the **p** Habakkuk received
Zech 7:12 . . . through the earlier **p-s.**
Mal 4:5 . . . the **p** Elijah before the great
Matt 5:17 . . . or the writings of the **p-s.**
Matt 7:12 . . . in the law and the **p-s.**
Matt 10:41 . . . the same reward as a **p.**
Matt 11:9 . . . Yes, and he is more than a **p.**
Matt 12:39 . . . sign of the **p** Jonah.
Matt 23:37 . . . the city that kills the **p-s**
Matt 26:56 . . . fulfill the words of the **p-s**
Luke 4:24 . . . no **p** is accepted in his own
Luke 7:16 . . . A mighty **p** has risen
Luke 11:49 . . . will send **p-s** and apostles
Luke 24:19 . . . **p** who did powerful
Luke 24:25 . . . all that the **p-s** wrote in
Luke 24:44 . . . law of Moses and the **p-s**
John 1:21 . . . you the **P** we are expecting?
Acts 7:37 . . . a **P** like me from among your
Acts 10:43 . . . all the **p-s** testified about,
Acts 13:1 . . . Among the **p-s** and teachers
Rom 1:2 . . . long ago through his **p-s**
Rom 3:21 . . . Moses and the **p-s** long ago.
Rom 11:3 . . . they have killed your **p-s**
1 Cor 12:28 . . . second are **p-s,** third are
1 Cor 14:37 . . . If you claim to be a **p** or
Eph 2:20 . . . of the apostles and the **p-s.**
Eph 3:5 . . . to his holy apostles and **p-s.**
Eph 4:11 . . . the apostles, the **p-s,** the
1 Pet 1:10 . . . the **p-s** wanted to know
2 Pet 1:19 . . . proclaimed by the **p-s.**
2 Pet 1:21 . . . those **p-s** were moved by
2 Pet 3:2 . . . what the holy **p-s** said long
Rev 11:10 . . . death of the two **p-s** who
Rev 18:20 . . . God and apostles and **p-s!**

PROPHETIC (adj) of, relating to, or characteristic of a prophet or prophecy
Ezek 37:4 . . . **p** message to these bones
Dan 9:24 . . . to confirm the **p** vision,
1 Tim 1:18 . . . based on the **p** words

PROPITIATION (KJV)
Rom 3:25 . . . Jesus as the *sacrifice* for sin
1 Jn 2:2 . . . the *sacrifice that atones*
1 Jn 4:10 . . . *sacrifice to take away* our sins

PROSELYTE(S) (KJV)
Matt 23:15 . . . and sea to make one *convert*
Acts 2:11 . . . Jews and *converts to Judaism*
Acts 6:5 . . . *convert to the Jewish faith*
Acts 13:43 . . . devout *converts to Judaism*

PROSPER, PROSPERS (v) to achieve economic success; to become strong and flourishing
Deut 28:63 . . . pleasure in causing you to **p**
Ps 37:3 . . . safely in the land and **p.**
Ps 73:3 . . . **p** despite their wickedness.
Prov 16:20 . . . listen to instruction will **p;**
Prov 17:9 . . . Love **p-s** when a fault is forgiven,
Prov 19:8 . . . cherish understanding will **p.**
Isa 53:10 . . . LORD's good plan will **p**
Isa 55:11 . . . it will **p** everywhere I send it.
Dan 4:27 . . . then you will continue to **p.**

PROSPERITY (n) the condition of being successful or thriving
Gen 41:29 . . . will be a period of great **p**
Deut 28:11 . . . LORD will give you **p**
Deut 30:15 . . . life and death, between **p**
1 Sam 25:6 . . . Peace and **p** to you,
Ps 41:2 . . . He gives them **p** in the land
Prov 21:5 . . . and hard work lead to **p,**
Prov 28:25 . . . trusting the LORD leads to **p.**
Jer 33:6 . . . give it **p** and true peace.
Mic 4:4 . . . will live in peace and **p,**

PROSPEROUS (adj) marked by success or economic well-being; flourishing
Deut 5:33 . . . live long and **p** lives
Ps 30:6 . . . When I was **p,** I said,
Ps 34:12 . . . a life that is long and **p?**
Ps 128:2 . . . How joyful and **p** you will be!
Ps 132:15 . . . bless this city and make it **p;**
Jer 12:1 . . . Why are the wicked so **p?**

PROSTITUTE, PROSTITUTES (n) a person who engages in promiscuous sexual relations, especially for money
Josh 6:17 . . . Rahab the **p** and
Prov 6:26 . . . a **p** will bring you to poverty,
Prov 29:3 . . . hangs around with **p-s,**
Ezek 16:15 . . . as a **p** to every man
Ezek 23:3 . . . They became **p-s** in Egypt.
Matt 21:31 . . . **p-s** will get into the
Luke 15:30 . . . your money on **p-s,**
1 Cor 6:16 . . . if a man joins himself to a **p,**
Rev 17:1 . . . going to come on the great **p,**

PROSTITUTING (v) to devote to corrupt or unworthy purposes; debase
Ezek 20:30 . . . **p** yourselves by worshiping

PROSTITUTION (n) the act or practice of engaging in promiscuous sexual relations especially for money
Lev 20:6 . . . who commit spiritual **p** by
Hos 3:3 . . . days and stop your **p.**

PROTECT, PROTECTED, PROTECTING, PROTECTS (v) to cover or shield from exposure, injury, damage, or destruction; to defend
see also KEEP
Gen 15:1 . . . for I will **p** you,
Num 6:24 . . . bless you and **p** you.
Josh 6:17 . . . for she **p-ed** our spies.
1 Sam 2:9 . . . He will **p** his faithful ones,
Ps 23:4 . . . your staff **p** and comfort me.
Ps 27:1 . . . fortress, **p-ing** me from danger,
Ps 41:2 . . . LORD **p-s** them and keeps
Ps 116:6 . . . LORD **p-s** those of childlike
Ps 127:1 . . . Unless the LORD **p-s** a city,
Ps 145:20 . . . LORD **p-s** all those who love
Ps 146:9 . . . LORD **p-s** the foreigners
Prov 2:8 . . . **p-s** those who are faithful
Isa 31:5 . . . like a bird **p-ing** its nest.
Isa 57:1 . . . God is **p-ing** them from the
John 17:11 . . . now **p** them by the power of
Acts 26:22 . . . But God has **p-ed** me
Gal 3:24 . . . **p-ed** us until we could be
1 Pet 1:5 . . . God is **p-ing** you by his power
Rev 3:10 . . . I will **p** you from the great

PROTECTION (n) the act of protecting; the state of being protected
see also REFUGE
2 Sam 22:3 . . . my rock, in whom I find **p.**
2 Sam 22:31 . . . look to him for **p.**
Ps 5:11 . . . Spread your **p** over them,
Ps 31:2 . . . Be my rock of **p,**
Ps 71:1 . . . I have come to you for **p;**
Ps 91:4 . . . promises are your armor and **p.**
Prov 19:23 . . . security and **p** from harm.

PROTECTIVE (adj) of or relating to protection or defense
Ezra 9:9 . . . He has given us a **p** wall

PROUD (adj) having or displaying excessive self-esteem
Ps 5:5 . . . **p** may not stand in your presence,
Prov 16:5 . . . LORD detests the **p;**
Prov 21:4 . . . Haughty eyes, a **p** heart,
Dan 4:37 . . . he is able to humble the **p.**
Rom 1:30 . . . haters of God, insolent, **p,**
1 Cor 13:4 . . . not jealous or boastful or **p**
1 Tim 3:6 . . . he might become **p,**
1 Tim 6:17 . . . rich in this world not to be **p**
2 Tim 3:2 . . . They will be boastful and **p,**
Jas 4:6 . . . God opposes the **p** but favors
1 Pet 5:5 . . . God opposes the **p** but favors

PROVE, PROVED, PROVING (v) to test or establish the truth, validity, or genuineness of
Ps 51:4 . . . **p-d** right in what you say,

Isa 44:25 . . . thus **p-ing** them to be fools.
John 13:35 . . . love for one another will **p**
Acts 1:3 . . . he **p-d** to them in many ways
Acts 17:3 . . . **p-d** that the Messiah
Acts 17:31 . . . **p-d** to everyone who this is
Acts 26:20 . . . **p** they have changed by
Rom 3:4 . . . **p-d** right in what you say,

PROVIDE, PROVIDED, PROVIDES (v) to furnish or supply, implying foresight in making provision for the future
Gen 22:8 . . . God will **p** a sheep
Gen 22:14 . . . means "the LORD will **p**"
Ps 68:10 . . . O God, you **p-d** for your needy
Isa 4:5 . . . the LORD will **p** shade
Jer 5:28 . . . refuse to **p** justice to orphans
Ezek 18:7 . . . and **p-s** clothes for the needy.
2 Cor 9:8 . . . God will generously **p** all you
2 Cor 9:10 . . . he will **p** and increase your

PROVOKE (v) to incite to anger; to stir up purposely
Eph 6:4 . . . do not **p** your children to anger

PROWLS (v) to roam over in a predatory manner
1 Pet 5:8 . . . **p** around like a roaring lion,

PRUDENT (adj) marked by wisdom or judiciousness; discreet
Prov 14:8 . . . **p** understand where they are
Prov 14:18 . . . the **p** are crowned with
Prov 22:3 . . . A **p** person foresees danger

PRUNES (v) to cut back or off for better shape or more fruitful growth
John 15:2 . . . and he **p** the branches

PRUNING HOOKS (n) a pole bearing a curved blade for pruning plants
Isa 2:4 . . . their spears into **p**.
Joel 3:10 . . . your **p** into spears.

PSALMS (n) a sacred song or poem used in worship
Ps 95:2 . . . Let us sing **p** of praise
Eph 5:19 . . . singing **p** and hymns and spiritual
Col 3:16 . . . Sing **p** and hymns and spiritual

PSYCHICS (n) those who claim to have sensitivity to knowledge and forces that lie outside the normal human experience
Deut 18:11 . . . function as mediums or **p**,
2 Kgs 21:6 . . . with mediums and **p**.
2 Kgs 23:24 . . . rid of the mediums and **p**,

PUBLICAN(S) (KJV)
Matt 5:46 . . . Even *corrupt tax collectors*
Matt 9:10 . . . with many *tax collectors*
Matt 10:3 . . . Matthew (the *tax collector*),
Luke 5:30 . . . and drink with *such scum?*
Luke 18:11 . . . not like that *tax collector*

PUNISH, PUNISHED, PUNISHES, PUNISHING (v) to impose a penalty to fit the crime: from corrective measures (fines or scolding) and corporal punishment (spanking or whipping) to capital punishment and eternal damnation
Gen 15:14 . . . But I will **p** the nation
1 Kgs 8:32 . . . **P** the guilty as they deserve.
Prov 11:21 . . . people will surely be **p-ed**,
Jer 25:14 . . . I will **p** them in proportion
Lam 3:39 . . . when we are **p-ed** for our sins?
Mark 12:40 . . . will be more severely **p-ed**.
Acts 7:7 . . . But I will **p** the nation
Rom 2:2 . . . God, in his justice, will **p**
Rom 13:4 . . . they have the power to **p** you.
Rom 13:4 . . . the very purpose of **p-ing**
2 Thes 1:9 . . . **p-ed** with eternal destruction,
Heb 2:2 . . . act of disobedience was **p-ed**.
Heb 12:6 . . . he **p-es** each one he accepts
1 Pet 2:14 . . . sent them to **p** those who
Rev 19:2 . . . has **p-ed** the great prostitute

PUNISHMENT (n) suffering, pain, or loss that serves as retribution
Isa 53:4 . . . troubles were a **p** from God,
Jer 2:19 . . . will bring its own **p**.
Jer 4:18 . . . This **p** is bitter, piercing
Hos 5:9 . . . On your day of **p**, you will
Matt 25:46 . . . will go away into eternal **p**,
Rom 13:5 . . . not only to avoid **p**, but also
2 Pet 2:9 . . . keeping the wicked under **p**

PURCHASE, PURCHASED (v) to gain or acquire; to buy
see also REDEEM
Acts 20:28 . . . **p-d** with his own blood—
Eph 1:7 . . . **p-d** our freedom with the
Eph 1:14 . . . **p-d** us to be his own people.
Col 1:14 . . . who **p-d** our freedom
1 Tim 2:6 . . . gave his life to **p** freedom
Rev 14:4 . . . have been **p-d** from among

PURE (adj) free of contamination or impurities; ritually clean; guileless; faultless; guiltless; chaste
see also CLEAN, HOLY
Ps 19:9 . . . Reverence for the LORD is **p**,
Prov 20:9 . . . I am **p** and free
Matt 5:8 . . . those whose hearts are **p**,
1 Cor 1:30 . . . he made us **p** and holy,
Phil 4:8 . . . right, and **p**, and lovely,
1 Tim 5:22 . . . Keep yourself **p**.
2 Tim 2:21 . . . If you keep yourself **p**,
Titus 1:15 . . . Everything is **p** to those
Titus 2:5 . . . to live wisely and be **p**,
Jas 1:27 . . . **P** and genuine religion
1 Pet 3:2 . . . your **p** and reverent
2 Pet 3:14 . . . are **p** and blameless
1 Jn 3:3 . . . will keep themselves **p**, just as

PURIFICATION (n) the act or an instance of purifying or of being purified
Lev 16:30 . . . offerings of **p** will be made
Acts 21:24 . . . join them in the **p** ceremony,

PURIFY, PURIFIED (v) to make pure or remove (physical or moral) blemishes; to make ritually clean
see also CLEANSE
Exod 30:10 . . . offering made to **p** the people
Exod 30:15 . . . given to the LORD to **p**
Num 25:13 . . . **p-ied** the people of Israel,
1 Chr 15:12 . . . You must **p** yourselves and
2 Chr 30:17 . . . had not **p-ied** themselves,
Neh 12:30 . . . Levites first **p-ied** themselves;
Isa 52:11 . . . and **p** yourselves,
John 15:3 . . . pruned and **p-ied** by the
Heb 9:14 . . . Christ will **p** our consciences
Heb 9:22 . . . everything was **p-ied** with blood.
Jas 4:8 . . . you sinners; **p** your hearts,

PURIM (n) a Jewish holiday in commemoration of the deliverance of the Jews from the massacre plotted by Haman
Esth 9:26 . . . this celebration is called **P**,

PURITY (n) the quality or state of being pure
Job 14:4 . . . Who can bring **p** out of an
Ps 86:11 . . . Grant me **p** of heart,
2 Cor 6:6 . . . by our **p**, our understanding,
1 Tim 4:12 . . . love, your faith, and your **p**.
1 Tim 5:2 . . . younger women with all **p**

PURPLE (adj) of the color purple; symbolic of royalty and wealth
Prov 31:22 . . . fine linen and **p** gowns.
Mark 15:17 . . . They dressed him in a **p** robe,
Acts 16:14 . . . merchant of expensive **p** cloth,

PURPOSE, PURPOSES (n) something set up as an object or end to be attained; resolution, determination
see also PLAN
Exod 9:16 . . . I have spared you for a **p**—
Prov 19:21 . . . the LORD's **p** will prevail.
Rom 8:28 . . . according to his **p** for them.
Rom 9:11 . . . according to his own **p-s**;
Rom 9:17 . . . for the very **p** of displaying
1 Cor 3:8 . . . with the same **p**.
1 Cor 9:26 . . . I run with **p** in every step.
Phil 2:2 . . . together with one mind and **p**.

PURSUE, PURSUES (v) to follow in order to overtake, capture, kill, or defeat; to seek
Ps 23:6 . . . unfailing love will **p** me
Ps 119:32 . . . I will **p** your commands,
Prov 15:9 . . . those who **p** godliness.
Prov 21:21 . . . Whoever **p-s** righteousness
1 Tim 6:11 . . . **P** righteousness and a godly
2 Tim 2:22 . . . Instead, **p** righteous living,

Q

QUAIL (n) in Palestine, a migrating bird that arrives in droves along the shores of the Mediterranean Sea
Exod 16:13 . . . vast numbers of **q** flew
Num 11:31 . . . there were **q** flying

QUAKE (v) to shake or vibrate
Ps 99:1 . . . the whole earth **q!**

QUALIFICATION (n) a condition or standard that must be complied with (as for the attainment of a privilege)
2 Cor 3:5 . . . Our **q** comes from God.

QUALIFIED (v) to declare competent or adequate
2 Cor 3:5 . . . not that we think we are **q**

QUALITIES (n) a distinguishing attribute; characteristic; nature
Rom 1:20 . . . clearly see his invisible **q**—

QUARREL, QUARRELS (n) a usually verbal conflict between antagonists
Prov 10:12 . . . Hatred stirs up **q-s**,
Prov 17:14 . . . Starting a **q** is like opening
Prov 26:20 . . . **q-s** disappear when gossip
Prov 30:33 . . . anger causes **q-s**.
Titus 3:9 . . . **q-s** and fights about
Jas 4:1 . . . causing the **q-s** and fights

QUARREL, QUARRELING (v) to find fault; to contend or dispute actively
Prov 17:19 . . . Anyone who loves to **q** loves
Prov 20:3 . . . fools insist on **q-ing**.
Rom 13:13 . . . or in **q-ing** and jealousy.
1 Cor 3:3 . . . and **q** with each other.
2 Cor 12:20 . . . will find **q-ing**, jealousy,

QUARRELSOME (adj) apt or disposed to quarrel in an often petty manner; contentious
Prov 19:13 . . . **q** wife is as annoying as
Prov 21:9 . . . than with a **q** wife in a lovely
Prov 26:21 . . . A **q** person starts fights
1 Tim 3:3 . . . He must be gentle, not **q**,

QUEEN (n) the wife or widow of a king; a female monarch
1 Kgs 10:1 . . . **q** of Sheba heard
Ps 45:9 . . . your right side stands the **q**,
Matt 12:42 . . . The **q** of Sheba will

QUENCH (v) to put out or extinguish
Song 8:7 . . . Many waters cannot **q** love,

QUICK (KJV)
Heb 4:12 . . . word of God is *alive* and
1 Pet 4:5 . . . the *living* and the dead.

QUICKEN (KJV)
Ps 80:18 . . . *Revive* us so we can call on
Ps 119:37 . . . *give* me *life* through your
Rom 8:11 . . . he will *give life* to your mortal

QUIET (adj) calm; gentle; peaceful, still; free from noise
Prov 11:12 . . . a sensible person keeps **q.**
Eccl 3:7 . . . A time to be **q** and a time
Eccl 9:17 . . . to hear the **q** words of a wise
Luke 19:40 . . . If they kept **q,** the stones
1 Thes 4:11 . . . to live a **q** life,
1 Tim 2:2 . . . peaceful and **q** lives marked

QUIETNESS (n) the state of being quiet; calmness; stillness
Eccl 4:6 . . . one handful with **q** than two
Isa 30:15 . . . **q** and confidence is
Isa 32:17 . . . it will bring **q** and confidence

QUIT, QUITTING (v) to cease normal, expected, or necessary action; to give up
Prov 23:4 . . . wise enough to know when to **q.**
Eccl 10:4 . . . boss is angry at you, don't **q!**
Rev 2:3 . . . suffered for me without **q-ting.**

QUIVER (n) a case for carrying or holding arrows
Ps 127:5 . . . joyful is the man whose **q** is

R

RABBI (n) a title of honor and respect given by the Jews to a teacher of the Law
Matt 23:8 . . . anyone call you '**R,**'
John 3:2 . . . "**R,**" he said, "we all know

RACE (n) an athletic contest; an ethnic classification
Ps 19:5 . . . athlete eager to run the **r.**
Eccl 9:11 . . . doesn't always win the **r,**
Dan 7:14 . . . people of every **r** and nation
1 Cor 9:24 . . . that in a **r** everyone runs,
Gal 2:2 . . . running the **r** for nothing.
Gal 5:7 . . . were running the **r** so well.
2 Tim 4:7 . . . I have finished the **r,**
Heb 12:1 . . . run with endurance the **r** God

RACE (v) to go, move, or function at top speed or out of control
Prov 6:18 . . . feet that **r** to do wrong,

RADIANCE (n) the quality or state of being radiant
Isa 60:3 . . . will come to see your **r.**
Luke 2:9 . . . and the **r** of the Lord's

RADIANT (adj) vividly bright and shining; marked by or expressive of love, confidence, or happiness
Exod 34:29 . . . face had become **r** because
Ps 34:5 . . . help will be **r** with joy;
Ps 80:1 . . . display your **r** glory

RADIATES (v) to spread abroad or around as if from a center; to shine brightly
Heb 1:3 . . . The Son **r** God's own glory

RAGE (n) violent and uncontrolled anger
Isa 14:6 . . . with endless blows of **r**
Col 3:8 . . . rid of anger, **r,** malicious

RAGING (adj) violent, wild
Ps 42:7 . . . tumult of the **r** seas as your
Ps 65:7 . . . You quieted the **r** oceans

RAGS (n) clothes usually in poor or ragged condition
Isa 64:6 . . . are nothing but filthy **r.**

RAIMENT (KJV)
Exod 12:35 . . . for *clothing* and articles of silver
Deut 8:4 . . . your *clothes* didn't wear out
Luke 9:29 . . . and his *clothes* became dazzling

RAIN, RAINS (n) water falling in drops from the sky
Deut 11:14 . . . will send the **r-s** in their
1 Kgs 17:1 . . . no dew or **r** during the next
1 Kgs 18:1 . . . that I will soon send **r!**
Prov 16:15 . . . refreshes like a spring **r.**
Matt 5:45 . . . and he sends **r** on the just
Jas 5:17 . . . earnestly that no **r** would fall,
Jude 1:12 . . . land without giving any **r.**

RAIN (v) to fall as water in drops from the clouds
Gen 7:4 . . . And it will **r** for forty days

RAINBOW (n) an arch of colors in the sky caused by light passing through moisture in the air
Gen 9:13 . . . I have placed my **r** in the

RAISE, RAISED (v) to recall from death
see also RESURRECTION
Luke 7:22 . . . the dead are **r-d** to life,
John 6:39 . . . that I should **r** them up
Acts 2:32 . . . God **r-d** Jesus from the dead,
Acts 24:15 . . . that he will **r** both the
Rom 1:4 . . . he was **r-d** from the dead
Rom 6:5 . . . we will also be **r-d** to life
Rom 10:9 . . . God **r-d** him from the dead,
1 Cor 15:4 . . . he was **r-d** from the dead
Phil 3:10 . . . mighty power that **r-d** him
1 Thes 4:14 . . . died and was **r-d** to life
1 Pet 1:3 . . . because God **r-d** Jesus Christ

RALLY (v) to join in a common cause
Isa 11:10 . . . The nations will **r** to him,

RAM, RAMS (n) a male sheep
Gen 22:13 . . . he took the **r** and sacrificed
1 Sam 15:22 . . . offering the fat of **r-s.**
Dan 8:3 . . . I saw a **r** with two long
Mic 6:7 . . . him thousands of **r-s** and ten

RANSOM (n) price paid or demanded to release someone or something from captivity
Matt 20:28 . . . his life as a **r** for many.
Mark 10:45 . . . his life as a **r** for many.
1 Pet 1:18 . . . that God paid a **r** to save

RANSOM, RANSOMED (v) to deliver especially from sin or its penalty; to free from captivity or punishment by paying a price
see also REDEEM(ED)
Ps 44:26 . . . Help us! **R** us because of
Ps 71:23 . . . for you have **r-ed** me.
Isa 35:10 . . . have been **r-ed** by the LORD
Hos 13:14 . . . Should I **r** them from
Rev 5:9 . . . your blood has **r-ed** people

RAVEN, RAVENS (n) a large, black, corvine bird
Gen 8:7 . . . and released a **r.** The bird
1 Kgs 17:6 . . . The **r-s** brought him bread and meat
Job 38:41 . . . provides food for the **r-s**
Ps 147:9 . . . feeds the young **r-s** when they
Luke 12:24 . . . Look at the **r-s.** They don't

READ, READING, READS (v) to receive and interpret letters or symbols by sight; to utter aloud the printed or written words of
Deut 17:19 . . . with him and **r** it daily
Josh 8:34 . . . Joshua then **r** to them
2 Kgs 23:2 . . . There the king **r** to them
Acts 8:28 . . . carriage, he was **r-ing** aloud
2 Cor 3:2 . . . everyone can **r** it and
1 Tim 4:13 . . . focus on **r-ing** the Scriptures
Rev 1:3 . . . the one who **r-s** the words of

READY (adj) prepared mentally or physically for some experience or action
1 Tim 6:18 . . . always being **r** to share
1 Pet 3:15 . . . always be **r** to explain

REAL (adj) not artificial, fraudulent, or illusory; genuine
1 Kgs 3:26 . . . who was the **r** mother of
1 Jn 4:2 . . . Christ came in a **r** body,

REALITY (n) a real event, entity, or state of affairs
Col 2:17 . . . shadows of the **r** yet to come.

REALIZATION (n) the state of being fully aware of
Mark 5:33 . . . trembling at the **r** of what

REALIZE, REALIZED, REALIZING (v) to be fully aware of; to conceive vividly as real
2 Chr 33:13 . . . Manasseh finally **r-d** that
Job 38:18 . . . Do you **r** the extent of
Ps 64:9 . . . and **r** all the amazing things
Song 6:12 . . . Before I **r-d** it, my strong
Isa 61:9 . . . Everyone will **r** that they are
Heb 13:2 . . . angels without **r-ing** it!
Jas 4:4 . . . Don't you **r** that friendship

REALMS (n) kingdom; sphere, domain
Eph 1:3 . . . in the heavenly **r** because we
Eph 2:6 . . . in the heavenly **r** because we

REAP (v) to harvest or gather; to obtain
Gal 6:9 . . . will **r** a harvest of blessing
Jas 3:18 . . . **r** a harvest of righteousness.

REAPERS (KJV)
Ruth 2:3 . . . grain behind the *harvesters*
2 Kgs 4:18 . . . working with the *harvesters*
Matt 13:30 . . . the *harvesters* to sort out
Matt 13:39 . . . the *harvesters* are the angels

REBEL, REBELLED, REBELLING, REBELS (v) to oppose or disobey one in authority or control
Num 14:9 . . . Do not **r** against the
Num 27:14 . . . of Israel **r-led,** you failed to
1 Sam 12:14 . . . if you do not **r** against the
Ps 78:56 . . . testing and **r-ling** against God
Isa 63:10 . . . But they **r-led** against him
Matt 10:21 . . . children will **r** against their
Rom 13:2 . . . So anyone who **r-s** against

REBELLION (n) opposition to one in authority or dominance; defiance
Exod 34:7 . . . forgive iniquity, **r,** and sin.
Ps 32:5 . . . I will confess my **r** to the
Ps 39:8 . . . Rescue me from my **r.**
Ps 51:3 . . . I recognize my **r;** it haunts
Isa 53:5 . . . was pierced for our **r,**
Isa 53:8 . . . for the **r** of my people.
Dan 9:24 . . . to finish their **r,** to put an
2 Thes 2:3 . . . is a great **r** against God

REBELLIOUS (adj) given to or engaged in rebellion
Isa 65:2 . . . opened my arms to a **r** people.
Luke 1:17 . . . those who are **r** to accept
Rom 10:21 . . . were disobedient and **r.**
1 Tim 1:9 . . . people who are lawless and **r,**
Titus 1:6 . . . reputation for being wild or **r.**

REBELS (n) those who rebel or participate in a rebellion
Ps 51:13 . . . will teach your ways to **r,**
Isa 53:12 . . . He was counted among the **r.**
Luke 22:37 . . . was counted among the **r.**
Rom 11:30 . . . Gentiles were **r** against God,
Rom 11:31 . . . they are the **r,** and God's

REBUILD, REBUILT (v) to reconstruct; to restore to a previous state
Ezra 5:2 . . . again to **r** the Temple of God
Neh 2:17 . . . Let us **r** the wall of
Ps 102:16 . . . the LORD will **r** Jerusalem.
Amos 9:14 . . . and they will **r** their ruined
Zech 1:16 . . . My Temple will be **r-t**, says the
Acts 15:16 . . . I will **r** its ruins and

REBUKE (n) an expression of strong disapproval; reprimand
see also CORRECT, DISCIPLINE
Prov 17:10 . . . A single **r** does more for
Prov 27:5 . . . An open **r** is better than

REBUKE, REBUKED (v) to criticize sharply; to reprimand
Prov 30:6 . . . or he may **r** you and expose
Mark 16:14 . . . He **r-d** them for their
Luke 17:3 . . . believer sins, **r** that person;
2 Tim 4:2 . . . Patiently correct, **r**, and
Jas 1:5 . . . He will not **r** you for asking.

RECEIVE, RECEIVED, RECEIVES (v) to acquire or take possession of; to welcome
Matt 7:8 . . . For everyone who asks, **r-s**.
Matt 19:17 . . . you want to **r** eternal life,
John 20:22 . . . said, "**R** the Holy Spirit.
Acts 1:8 . . . But you will **r** power when the
Acts 2:38 . . . Then you will **r** the gift of
Acts 8:17 . . . they **r-d** the Holy Spirit.
Acts 10:47 . . . they have **r-d** the Holy
Acts 19:2 . . . Did you **r** the Holy Spirit
Rom 8:15 . . . Instead, you **r-d** God's Spirit
1 Tim 1:16 . . . in him and **r** eternal life.
Rev 4:11 . . . our God, to **r** glory and honor

RECKONING (n) a settling of accounts
Jer 51:18 . . . On the day of **r** they will all

RECOGNIZE, RECOGNIZED (v) to admit as being lord or sovereign; to acknowledge or take notice of in some definite way; to perceive to be something or someone previously known
1 Chr 16:28 . . . of the world, **r** the LORD,
Ps 96:7 . . . of the world, **r** the LORD;
Jer 24:7 . . . give them hearts that **r** me
Hos 4:6 . . . refuse to **r** you as my priests.
John 1:26 . . . is someone you do not **r**.
1 Cor 14:38 . . . But if you do not **r** this,
1 Cor 14:38 . . . yourself will not be **r-d**.
2 Cor 3:2 . . . read it and **r** our good work

RECOMMEND (v) to endorse; to advise
Eccl 8:15 . . . So I **r** having fun, because

RECOMMENDATION (n) something that expresses commendation
2 Cor 3:1 . . . to bring you letters of **r**,

RECONCILED, RECONCILING (v) to restore to friendship or harmony, especially between God and human beings
2 Cor 5:18 . . . task of **r-ing** people to him.
Eph 2:16 . . . Christ **r-d** both groups to God
Col 1:20 . . . God **r-d** everything to himself.
Col 1:22 . . . now he has **r-d** you to himself

RECONCILIATION (n) the action of reconciling; the state of being reconciled
Prov 14:9 . . . acknowledge it and seek **r**.
2 Cor 5:19 . . . this wonderful message of **r**.

RECORD (n) an official body of known or recorded facts about someone
1 Cor 13:5 . . . keeps no **r** of being wronged.
Col 2:14 . . . canceled the **r** of the charges

RECORDED (v) to set down in writing
John 20:30 . . . to the ones **r** in this book.

RED (adj) of the color red
Exod 15:4 . . . are drowned in the **R** Sea.
Ps 106:9 . . . He commanded the **R** Sea to
Prov 23:31 . . . wine, seeing how **r** it is,
Isa 1:18 . . . they are **r** like crimson,
Isa 63:1 . . . with his clothing stained **r?**

REDEDICATE (v) to devote or commit oneself or one's possessions again
Num 6:12 . . . They must **r** themselves to

REDEEM, REDEEMED, REDEEMS (v) to buy back; to save by payment of a ransom; to free from the consequences of sin
see also PURCHASE, RANSOM, RESCUE
Exod 6:6 . . . I will **r** you with a powerful
2 Sam 7:23 . . . have you **r-ed** from slavery
Ps 34:22 . . . the LORD will **r** those
Ps 49:15 . . . God will **r** my life.
Ps 74:2 . . . the tribe you **r-ed** as your own
Ps 103:4 . . . He **r-s** me from death and
Ps 107:2 . . . Has the LORD **r-ed** you?
Ps 130:8 . . . He himself will **r** Israel from
Isa 35:9 . . . Only the **r-ed** will walk
Isa 63:9 . . . love and mercy he **r-ed** them.
Hos 7:13 . . . I wanted to **r** them, but they

REDEEMER (n) one who frees or delivers another from difficulty, danger, or bondage, usually by the payment of a ransom price
Ruth 3:9 . . . for you are my family **r**.
Ruth 4:14 . . . has now provided a **r** for
Job 19:25 . . . I know that my **R** lives,
Ps 19:14 . . . LORD, my rock and my **r**.
Prov 23:11 . . . For their **R** is strong;
Isa 44:6 . . . Israel's King and **R**, the LORD
Isa 48:17 . . . your **R**, the Holy One of Israel:
Isa 59:20 . . . The **R** will come to Jerusalem

REDEMPTION (n) the act, process, or an instance of redeeming
Ps 130:7 . . . love. His **r** overflows.
Eph 4:30 . . . be saved on the day of **r**.
Heb 9:12 . . . and secured our **r** forever.

REEDS (n) any of various tall grasses that grow in wet places
Exod 2:5 . . . basket among the **r**,
Isa 35:7 . . . **r** and rushes will flourish
Isa 58:5 . . . bowing your heads like **r**
Ezek 29:6 . . . a staff made of **r**

REFINE, REFINED (v) to remove impurities from metal; figurative of purifying God's people of sin
Isa 48:10 . . . I have **r-d** you in the furnace
Zech 13:9 . . . I will **r** them like silver

REFINER (n) someone or something that refines
Mal 3:3 . . . will sit like a **r** of silver,

REFLECT, REFLECTS (v) to make manifest or apparent; to think quietly and calmly
Ps 119:5 . . . consistently **r** your decrees!
Ps 119:15 . . . and **r** on your ways.
Prov 27:19 . . . the heart **r-s** the real person.
Isa 44:19 . . . never stops to **r**, "Why, it's
Titus 2:7 . . . Let everything you do **r** the

REFRESH, REFRESHED, REFRESHES, REFRESHING (v) to restore strength and animation to; to replenish, arouse, or stimulate
Prov 9:17 . . . Stolen water is **r-ing;** food
Prov 11:25 . . . will themselves be **r-ed.**
Prov 16:15 . . . favor **r-es** like a spring rain.
Phlm 1:7 . . . has often **r-ed** the hearts

REFUGE (n) shelter or protection from danger or distress
see also FORTRESS, PROTECTION, SHELTER
Deut 33:27 . . . eternal God is your **r**,
2 Sam 22:3 . . . He is my **r**, my savior,
Ps 2:12 . . . for all who take **r** in him!
Ps 5:11 . . . But let all who take **r** in you
Ps 17:7 . . . those who seek **r** from their
Ps 34:8 . . . those who take **r** in him!
Ps 46:1 . . . God is our **r** and strength,
Ps 91:2 . . . He alone is my **r**, my place

REFUSE, REFUSED, REFUSING (v) to show or express unwillingness to do or comply with
Lev 26:15 . . . and **r-ing** to obey
Num 14:22 . . . tested me by **r-ing** to listen to
Josh 24:15 . . . But if you **r** to serve the
Prov 13:19 . . . fools **r** to turn from evil
Eccl 11:10 . . . So **r** to worry, and keep
Luke 15:29 . . . never once **r-d** to do a single
Rom 14:6 . . . And those who **r** to eat
2 Thes 2:10 . . . because they **r** to love
2 Thes 3:14 . . . of those who **r** to obey
Heb 12:25 . . . escape when they **r-d** to listen

REFUTE (v) to prove wrong by argument or evidence
Luke 21:15 . . . be able to reply or **r** you!
Acts 9:22 . . . couldn't **r** his proofs that

REGARDED (v) to consider and appraise
Ps 106:31 . . . has been **r** as a righteous

REGENERATION (KJV)
Matt 19:28 . . . world is *made new* and the
Titus 3:5 . . . giving us a *new birth* and new

REGISTERED (v) to make or secure official entry of in a register
Luke 10:20 . . . your names are **r** in heaven.

REGRET (v) to be very sorry for
Nah 3:7 . . . Does anyone **r** your destruction?

REGULAR (adj) formed, built, arranged, or ordered according to some established rule, law, principle, or type
2 Kgs 25:30 . . . gave him a **r** food allowance

REGULATIONS (n) authoritative rules dealing with details or procedure
see also LAW(S)
Exod 21:1 . . . These are the **r** you must
Deut 33:10 . . . They teach your **r** to Jacob;
Ps 119:30 . . . determined to live by your **r**.
Ps 119:43 . . . for your **r** are my only hope.
Ps 119:120 . . . I stand in awe of your **r**.
Ps 119:164 . . . because all your **r** are just.
Ps 119:175 . . . and may your **r** help me.

REIGN, REIGNED, REIGNING, REIGNS (v) to possess or exercise sovereign power; to rule
Exod 15:18 . . . The LORD will **r** forever
Ps 9:7 . . . But the LORD **r-s** forever,
Ps 29:10 . . . LORD **r-s** as king forever.
Ps 96:10 . . . The LORD **r-s!**
Ps 146:10 . . . The LORD will **r** forever.
Isa 52:7 . . . that the God of Israel **r-s!**
1 Cor 4:8 . . . then we would be **r-ing** with you.
1 Cor 15:25 . . . For Christ must **r** until he
Rev 5:10 . . . And they will **r** on the earth.
Rev 11:15 . . . and he will **r** forever
Rev 19:6 . . . our God, the Almighty, **r-s.**
Rev 20:4 . . . again, and they **r-ed** with Christ
Rev 22:5 . . . And they will **r** forever

REIGNS (n) the time during which one (as a sovereign) rules
Dan 2:44 . . . During the **r** of those kings,

REJECT, REJECTED, REJECTING, REJECTS (v) to refuse to accept, consider, submit to, or take for some purpose or use; to refuse to hear, receive, or admit
1 Sam 8:7 . . . me they are **r-ing,** not you.

Ps 51:17 . . . not **r** a broken and repentant
Ps 118:22 . . . stone that the builders **r-ed**
Prov 3:11 . . . My child, don't **r** the LORD's
Mal 1:3 . . . but I **r-ed** his brother,
Matt 21:42 . . . stone that the builders **r-ed**
Luke 10:16 . . . who **r-s** me is **r-ing** God,
John 6:37 . . . I will never **r** them.
John 12:48 . . . But all who **r** me and my
Rom 9:13 . . . loved Jacob, but I **r-ed** Esau.
1 Thes 4:8 . . . teaching but is **r-ing** God,
1 Tim 4:4 . . . we should not **r** any of it
2 Tim 3:5 . . . but they will **r** the power
Heb 6:6 . . . by **r-ing** the Son of God, they
1 Pet 2:4 . . . He was **r-ed** by people,
1 Pet 2:7 . . . stone that the builders **r-ed**

REJECTION (n) the action of rejecting
Rom 11:15 . . . For since their **r** meant that

REJOICE, REJOICED, REJOICES, REJOICING (v) to feel joy or great delight; to gladden
1 Chr 16:31 . . . glad, and the earth **r!**
1 Chr 29:17 . . . **r** when you find integrity
Esth 8:17 . . . decree arrived, the Jews **r-d**
Ps 5:11 . . . who take refuge in you **r;**
Ps 13:5 . . . I will **r** because you
Ps 35:9 . . . I will **r** in the LORD.
Ps 48:2 . . . the whole earth **r-s** to see it!
Ps 58:10 . . . The godly will **r** when they
Ps 66:6 . . . There we **r-d** in him.
Ps 68:4 . . . LORD—**r** in his presence!
Ps 119:14 . . . I have **r-d** in your laws
Ps 119:162 . . . I **r** in your word like one
Prov 8:31 . . . I **r-d** with the human family!
Prov 17:5 . . . who **r** at the misfortune
Prov 29:2 . . . in authority, the people **r.**
Isa 9:3 . . . and its people will **r.**
Isa 35:1 . . . wasteland will **r** and blossom
Isa 62:5 . . . **r** over you as a bridegroom **r-s**
Jer 51:48 . . . the heavens and earth will **r,**
Lam 4:21 . . . Are you **r-ing** in the land
Hab 1:15 . . . while they **r** and celebrate?
Zeph 3:17 . . . He will **r** over you
Zech 2:10 . . . Shout and **r,** O beautiful
Luke 1:14 . . . and many will **r** at his birth,
Luke 1:47 . . . How my spirit **r-s** in God my
Luke 1:58 . . . everyone **r-d** with her.
Luke 10:20 . . . But don't **r** because evil
Luke 13:17 . . . but all the people **r-d** at the
Acts 5:41 . . . high council **r-ing** that God
Acts 16:34 . . . his entire household **r-d**
1 Cor 13:6 . . . **r** about injustice but **r-s**
Phil 2:18 . . . you should **r,** and I will
Phil 3:1 . . . and sisters, **r** in the Lord.
Phil 4:4 . . . I say it again—**r!**
Col 2:5 . . . I **r** that you are living as
Rev 19:7 . . . Let us be glad and **r,** and

RELATIONSHIP (n) a state of affairs existing between those having relations or dealings
Rom 5:11 . . . our wonderful new **r** with God
2 Jn 1:9 . . . teaching has no **r** with God.

RELATIVES (n) a person connected with another by blood or affinity
Lev 19:17 . . . your heart for any of your **r.**
Mark 6:4 . . . among his **r** and his own
Luke 21:16 . . . parents, brothers, **r,** and
1 Tim 5:8 . . . who won't care for their **r,**

RELEASE (n) relief or deliverance from sorrow, suffering, or trouble
Deut 31:10 . . . the Year of **R,** during the
Job 14:14 . . . eagerly await the **r** of death.

RELEASED (v) to set free from restraint, confinement, or servitude
Isa 61:1 . . . that captives will be **r**
Matt 18:27 . . . and he **r** him and forgave
Matt 27:50 . . . and he **r** his spirit.
Luke 4:18 . . . that captives will be **r,**
John 19:30 . . . his head and **r** his spirit.
Rom 7:6 . . . we have been **r** from the law,
Rom 8:23 . . . bodies to be **r** from sin and

RELENT, RELENTED (v) to become less severe, harsh, or strict; to give in
Ps 106:45 . . . **r-ed** because of his unfailing
Joel 2:13 . . . eager to **r** and not punish.

RELIABLE (adj) dependable
1 Chr 9:22 . . . they were **r** men.
Prov 13:17 . . . but a **r** messenger brings
Prov 20:6 . . . find one who is truly **r?**
2 Tim 2:2 . . . by many **r** witnesses.

RELIEF (n) removal or lightening of something oppressive, painful, or distressing
Gen 5:29 . . . he bring us **r** from our work
Ps 94:13 . . . You give them **r** from troubled

RELIEVED, RELIEVING (v) to free from a burden; to discharge the bladder or bowels of
1 Kgs 18:27 . . . or is **r-ing** himself.
Acts 20:12 . . . and everyone was greatly **r-d.**

RELIGION, RELIGIONS (n) a personal set or institutionalized system of religious attitudes, beliefs, and practices; the service and worship of God or the supernatural
Matt 6:7 . . . as people of other **r-s** do.
Acts 25:19 . . . something about their **r** and
Acts 26:5 . . . the strictest sect of our **r.**
Gal 1:13 . . . I followed the Jewish **r**—
Jas 1:26 . . . and your **r** is worthless.

RELIGIOUS (adj) relating to or manifesting faithful devotion to God or a god
Luke 11:46 . . . with unbearable **r** demands,
Acts 13:50 . . . the influential **r** women and
Jas 1:26 . . . you claim to be **r** but don't

RELY, RELIED, RELIES (v) to be dependent
2 Chr 16:8 . . . time you **r-ied** on the LORD,
Ps 22:8 . . . one who **r-ies** on the LORD?
Ps 33:18 . . . those who **r** on his unfailing
Prov 11:7 . . . for they **r** on their own feeble
Isa 50:10 . . . the LORD and **r** on your God.
2 Cor 1:9 . . . and learned to **r** only on God,

REMAIN, REMAINED, REMAINS (v) to stay in the same place or with the same person or group; to continue unchanged
2 Kgs 18:6 . . . He **r-ed** faithful to the LORD
John 15:7 . . . But if you **r** in me and my
John 15:9 . . . loved me. **R** in my love.
Rom 11:5 . . . of Israel have **r-ed** faithful
2 Tim 2:13 . . . unfaithful, he **r-s** faithful,
2 Tim 3:14 . . . But you must **r** faithful
2 Tim 4:7 . . . and I have **r-ed** faithful.
Heb 7:3 . . . He **r-s** a priest forever,
Heb 10:32 . . . how you **r-ed** faithful even
Heb 13:4 . . . and **r** faithful to one another
1 Pet 1:25 . . . word of the Lord **r-s**
1 Jn 2:27 . . . **r** in fellowship with Christ.

REMARRY, REMARRIES (v) to marry again after divorce or being widowed
Rom 7:3 . . . commit adultery when she **r-ies.**
1 Tim 5:11 . . . to Christ and they will want to **r.**

REMEMBER, REMEMBERED, REMEMBERING, REMEMBERS (v) to bring to mind or think of again; to keep in mind for attention or consideration; to retain in the memory
Gen 9:15 . . . I will **r** my covenant with
Exod 2:24 . . . **r-ed** his covenant promise
1 Chr 16:12 . . . **R** the wonders he has
Ps 49:13 . . . though they are **r-ed** as being
Ps 103:14 . . . he **r-s** we are only dust.
Ps 106:45 . . . **r-ed** his covenant with them
Ps 111:5 . . . he always **r-s** his covenant.
Ps 136:23 . . . He **r-ed** us in our weakness.
Jer 31:34 . . . never again **r** their sins.
Jer 32:20 . . . things still **r-ed** to this day!
Hab 3:2 . . . in your anger, **r** your mercy.
Matt 26:13 . . . will be **r-ed** and discussed.
Luke 1:72 . . . **r-ing** his sacred covenant—
Luke 22:19 . . . Do this to **r** me.
1 Cor 11:24 . . . Do this to **r** me.
2 Tim 2:8 . . . Always **r** that Jesus
Heb 8:12 . . . never again **r** their sins.
2 Pet 1:15 . . . you always **r** these things

REMIND, REMINDING (v) to cause to remember
John 14:26 . . . will **r** you of everything
2 Pet 1:12 . . . I will always **r** you about
2 Pet 1:13 . . . keep on **r-ing** you as long

REMINDER, REMINDERS (n) something that causes to remember
Deut 6:8 . . . them on your forehead as **r-s.**
Prov 7:3 . . . Tie them on your fingers as a **r.**

REMISSION (KJV)
Matt 26:28 . . . as a sacrifice *to forgive*
Acts 10:43 . . . sins *forgiven* through his
Rom 3:25 . . . he *held back and did not punish*
Heb 9:22 . . . blood, there is no *forgiveness*

REMNANT (n) a usually small part, member, or trace remaining; the few people left who gathered together after God scattered them into exile
Ezra 9:8 . . . few of us to survive as a **r.**
Isa 6:13 . . . a tenth—a **r**—survive,
Isa 11:11 . . . to bring back the **r** of his
Jer 23:3 . . . gather together the **r** of my
Zech 8:12 . . . will cause the **r** in Judah

REMOVE, REMOVED (v) to get rid of; to eliminate
Ps 103:12 . . . He has **r-d** our sins as far
Isa 6:7 . . . Now your guilt is **r-d,** and your
1 Cor 5:13 . . . You must **r** the evil person

RENEW, RENEWED, RENEWS (v) to restore to freshness, vigor, or perfection; to make new spiritually
Ps 23:3 . . . He **r-s** my strength.
Ps 51:10 . . . **R** a loyal spirit within me.
Isa 57:10 . . . Desire gave you **r-ed** strength,
Eph 4:23 . . . let the Spirit **r** your thoughts
Col 3:10 . . . be **r-ed** as you learn to know

RENOWN (KJV)
Gen 6:4 . . . the heroes and *famous* warriors
Isa 14:20 . . . will never again *receive honor*
Ezek 16:14 . . . *fame* soon spread
Ezek 39:13 . . . a *glorious victory* for Israel

REPAY, REPAYS (v) to give or inflict in return or requital; to pay back (money)
Ps 62:12 . . . Surely you **r** all people
Prov 17:13 . . . If you **r** good with evil,
Prov 19:17 . . . and he will **r** you!
Jer 51:6 . . . he will **r** her in full.
Jer 51:56 . . . he always **r-s** in full.
Luke 6:34 . . . to those who can **r** you,
Luke 7:42 . . . neither of them could **r** him,
1 Tim 5:4 . . . **r** their parents by taking
1 Pet 3:9 . . . Don't **r** evil for evil.

REPENT, REPENTED, REPENTING, REPENTS (v) to turn from sin and change one's heart and behavior; to feel regret and contrition
Matt 3:2 . . . **R** of your sins and turn
Matt 3:8 . . . that you have **r-ed** of your sins
Matt 4:17 . . . began to preach, "**R** of your
Matt 11:21 . . . people would have **r-ed** of

Luke 3:8 . . . that you have **r-ed** of your sins
Luke 15:7 . . . sinner who **r-s** and returns
Luke 15:10 . . . when even one sinner **r-s.**
Acts 2:38 . . . you must **r** of your sins
Acts 17:30 . . . everywhere to **r** of their sins
Acts 20:21 . . . necessity of **r-ing** from sin
Heb 6:1 . . . importance of **r-ing** from evil
2 Pet 3:9 . . . but wants everyone to **r.**
Rev 2:5 . . . If you don't **r,** I will come

REPENTANCE (n) a turning away from sin, disobedience, or rebellion, and a turning back to God
1 Kgs 8:47 . . . to you in **r** and pray,
Job 42:6 . . . dust and ashes to show my **r.**
Luke 17:3 . . . if there is **r,** forgive.
2 Cor 7:10 . . . sorrow, which lacks **r,**

REPENTANT (adj) penitent; expressive of repentance
see also CONTRITE
Ps 51:17 . . . a broken and **r** heart, O God.

REPORT (n) a usually detailed account or statement
Luke 16:2 . . . Get your **r** in order,

REPRESENTATIVE (n) one that represents another as an agent or delegate usually being invested with the authority of the principal
Col 3:17 . . . do it as a **r** of the Lord

REPRIMAND, REPRIMANDED (v) to reprove sharply or censure formally
see also CORRECT, REBUKE
1 Tim 5:20 . . . sin should be **r-ed** in front
Titus 1:13 . . . So **r** them sternly to make

REPROACH (n) a cause or occasion of blame, discredit, or disgrace
1 Tim 3:2 . . . man whose life is above **r.**

REPUTATION (n) overall quality or character as seen or judged by people in general
see also NAME
Ps 109:21 . . . the sake of your own **r!**
Prov 3:4 . . . you will earn a good **r.**
Prov 22:1 . . . Choose a good **r** over great
Eccl 7:1 . . . A good **r** is more valuable
1 Tim 3:2 . . . wisely, and have a good **r.**
Heb 11:39 . . . good **r** because of their

REQUIRE, REQUIRED, REQUIRES (v) to demand as necessary or essential; to feel or be obliged
Ps 40:6 . . . you don't **r** burnt offerings
Mic 6:8 . . . this is what he **r-s** of you:
Luke 12:48 . . . much will be **r-d** in return;
Luke 23:56 . . . they rested as **r-d** by the law.
Rom 1:32 . . . God's justice **r-s** that those
Heb 8:3 . . . high priest is **r-d** to offer

REQUIREMENTS (n) something required; condition
Rom 13:8 . . . will fulfill the **r** of God's
Rom 13:10 . . . love fulfills the **r** of God's

RESCUE, RESCUED, RESCUES, RESCUING (v) to save or deliver
see also REDEEM, SAVE
2 Kgs 13:5 . . . someone to **r** the Israelites
Ps 9:14 . . . rejoice that you have **r-d** me.
Ps 17:7 . . . mighty power you **r** those who
Ps 22:8 . . . let the LORD **r** him!
Ps 31:2 . . . listen to me; **r** me quickly.
Ps 37:39 . . . The LORD **r-s** the godly;
Ps 37:40 . . . LORD helps them, **r-ing** them
Ps 68:20 . . . The Sovereign LORD **r-s** us
Ps 72:12 . . . He will **r** the poor when
Ps 145:19 . . . cries for help and **r-s** them.
Prov 11:8 . . . godly are **r-d** from trouble,
Isa 56:1 . . . coming soon to **r** you and
Dan 6:27 . . . He **r-s** and saves his people;
Zech 8:7 . . . that I will **r** my people from
Matt 6:13 . . . but **r** us from the evil one.
Rom 11:26 . . . The one who **r-s** will come
2 Cor 1:10 . . . And he did **r** us from mortal
Gal 1:4 . . . in order to **r** us from this
Gal 3:13 . . . But Christ has **r-d** us from the
Col 1:13 . . . For he has **r-d** us from the
1 Thes 1:10 . . . the one who has **r-d** us
2 Pet 2:9 . . . knows how to **r** godly people

RESCUER (n) one who frees from confinement, danger, or evil
Judg 3:9 . . . raised up a **r** to save them.
Judg 3:15 . . . raised up a **r** to save them.
Ps 144:2 . . . my tower of safety, my **r.**

RESIST (v) to withstand the force or effect of; to counteract or defeat
Dan 11:32 . . . will be strong and will **r** him.
Matt 5:39 . . . do not **r** an evil person!
Jas 4:7 . . . **R** the devil, and he will flee

RESPECT (n) a high or special regard; esteem
see also AWE, REVERENCE
Prov 11:16 . . . A gracious woman gains **r,**
Mal 1:6 . . . the honor and **r** I deserve?
Titus 2:2 . . . be worthy of **r,** and to live

RESPECT, RESPECTED (v) to consider worthy of high regard; to esteem
Eph 5:33 . . . the wife must **r** her husband.
1 Tim 3:4 . . . children who **r** and obey him.
1 Tim 3:8 . . . deacons must be well **r-ed**
1 Tim 3:11 . . . their wives must be **r-ed**
1 Tim 5:17 . . . work well should be **r-ed**
1 Pet 2:17 . . . Fear God, and **r** the king.

RESPECTFUL (adj) marked by or showing respect or deference
1 Pet 3:16 . . . a gentle and **r** way.

RESPONSIBILITY (n) moral, legal, or mental accountability
1 Cor 5:12 . . . certainly is your **r** to judge
1 Tim 5:16 . . . not put the **r** on the church.

RESPONSIBLE (adj) marked by or involving responsibility or accountability; liable to be called to account as the primary cause, motive, or agent
Exod 32:34 . . . hold them **r** for their sins.
Num 1:53 . . . The Levites are **r** to stand
Ezek 33:6 . . . he is **r** for their captivity.
Jon 1:14 . . . And don't hold us **r** for his
Gal 6:5 . . . For we are each **r** for our own

REST (n) freedom from activity or labor; peace of mind or spirit; repose, sleep
see also SABBATH
Exod 31:15 . . . day of complete **r,** a holy
Exod 33:14 . . . and I will give you **r**—
Ps 91:1 . . . Most High will find **r** in the
Ps 127:2 . . . for God gives **r** to his loved
Jer 6:16 . . . you will find **r** for your
Matt 11:28 . . . and I will give you **r.**
2 Thes 1:7 . . . God will provide **r** for you
Heb 4:3 . . . even though this **r** has been
Heb 4:9 . . . a special **r** still waiting
Heb 4:10 . . . who have entered into God's **r**

REST, RESTED, RESTING, RESTS (v) to sit or lie on; to cease from action or motion; to take relief or respite
Gen 2:2 . . . of creation, so he **r-ed** from all
Ps 16:9 . . . My body **r-s** in safety.
Ps 23:2 . . . He lets me **r** in green
Isa 11:2 . . . Spirit of the LORD will **r**
Isa 30:15 . . . and **r-ing** in me will you
John 1:32 . . . from heaven and **r-ing** upon
Heb 4:4 . . . seventh day God **r-ed** from all
Rev 14:13 . . . will **r** from their hard work;

RESTITUTION (n) a making good of or giving an equivalent for some injury
Lev 6:5 . . . You must make **r** by paying
Num 5:8 . . . relatives to whom **r** can be

RESTLESS (adj) continuously moving
Isa 57:20 . . . are like the **r** sea, which is

RESTORE, RESTORED, RESTORES, RESTORING (v) to give back, return; to renew
Ps 14:7 . . . When the LORD **r-s** his people,
Ps 30:2 . . . and you **r-d** my health.
Isa 58:11 . . . are dry and **r-ing** your strength.
Jer 30:3 . . . when I will **r** the fortunes of
Jer 30:18 . . . from captivity and **r** their
Jer 31:18 . . . Turn me again to you and **r**
Hos 6:2 . . . a short time he will **r** us,
Nah 2:2 . . . but he will **r** its splendor.
Rom 5:10 . . . friendship with God was **r-d**
1 Pet 5:10 . . . he will **r,** support,

RESURRECTION (n) the state of one risen from the dead; the rising again to life of all the human dead before the final judgment
see also RAISE, RISE
Matt 27:53 . . . cemetery after Jesus' **r,**
Mark 12:23 . . . will she be in the **r?**
Luke 20:36 . . . children of the **r.**
John 11:25 . . . I am the **r** and the life.
Acts 1:22 . . . as a witness of Jesus' **r.**
Acts 2:31 . . . speaking of the Messiah's **r.**
Acts 4:2 . . . there is a **r** of the dead.
Acts 4:33 . . . powerfully to the **r** of
Acts 17:32 . . . Paul speak about the **r** of
1 Cor 15:13 . . . if there is no **r** of the
1 Cor 15:42 . . . way with the **r** of the dead.
Phil 3:11 . . . experience the **r** from the
2 Tim 2:18 . . . claiming that the **r** of the
Heb 6:2 . . . of hands, the **r** of the dead,
Heb 11:35 . . . a better life after the **r.**
1 Pet 3:21 . . . because of the **r** of Jesus
Rev 20:5 . . . This is the first **r.**

RETALIATE (v) to repay (as an injury) in kind; to get revenge
1 Pet 2:23 . . . He did not **r** when he

RETURN, RETURNED, RETURNING, RETURNS (v) to go or come back again; to go back in thought, practice, or condition; to repent
2 Sam 12:23 . . . but he cannot **r** to me.
2 Chr 30:9 . . . if you **r** to the LORD,
Neh 1:9 . . . But if you **r** to me and obey
Ps 35:13 . . . my prayers **r-ed** unanswered.
Ps 51:13 . . . and they will **r** to you.
Ps 126:6 . . . they sing as they **r** with the
Isa 52:8 . . . the LORD **r-ing** to Jerusalem.
Jer 24:7 . . . for they will **r** to me
Hos 6:1 . . . let us **r** to the LORD.
Amos 4:6 . . . you would not **r** to me,
Matt 24:46 . . . If the master **r-s** and finds

REVEAL, REVEALED (v) to make known through divine inspiration; to make (something secret or hidden) publicly or generally known; to display
Exod 6:3 . . . did not **r** my name, Yahweh,
Deut 29:29 . . . all that he has **r-ed** to us,
Isa 40:5 . . . the LORD will be **r-ed,**
Isa 53:1 . . . the LORD **r-ed** his powerful
Matt 10:26 . . . is covered will be **r-ed,**
Matt 11:27 . . . Son chooses to **r** him.
Luke 2:32 . . . He is a light to **r** God
John 12:38 . . . the LORD **r-ed** his powerful
John 14:21 . . . love them and **r** myself
John 17:6 . . . I have **r-ed** you to the
Rom 8:18 . . . glory he will **r** to us
Rom 16:25 . . . Christ has **r-ed** his plan

1 Cor 2:10 . . . that God **r-ed** these things
Gal 1:16 . . . to **r** his Son to me so that
Gal 2:2 . . . because God **r-ed** to me
Eph 3:3 . . . himself **r-ed** his mysterious
Col 1:26 . . . it has been **r-ed** to God's
2 Thes 2:3 . . . man of lawlessness is **r-ed**
Titus 2:13 . . . Christ, will be **r-ed.**
Heb 9:8 . . . the Holy Spirit **r-ed** that
1 Pet 1:7 . . . when Jesus Christ is **r-ed**

REVELATION, REVELATIONS (n) something that is revealed by God to humans; an act of revealing or communicating divine truth
1 Cor 14:6 . . . bring you a **r** or some
1 Cor 14:30 . . . person receives a **r** from
2 Cor 12:1 . . . visions and **r-s** from the
2 Cor 12:7 . . . wonderful **r-s** from God.
Gal 1:12 . . . by direct **r** from Jesus
Rev 1:1 . . . This is a **r** from Jesus

REVELRY (n) noisy partying or merrymaking
Exod 32:6 . . . they indulged in pagan **r.**
1 Cor 10:7 . . . they indulged in pagan **r.**

REVENGE (n) an act or instance of retaliating in order to get even
Lev 19:18 . . . Do not seek **r** or bear
Num 31:3 . . . war of **r** against Midian.
Deut 32:35 . . . I will take **r;** I will
Josh 20:3 . . . relatives seeking **r** for
Judg 20:10 . . . will take **r** on Gibeah
Isa 34:8 . . . day of the LORD's **r,**
Heb 10:30 . . . I will take **r.** I will

REVERENCE (n) profound, adoring, awed respect
see also AWE, FEAR, RESPECT
Lev 19:30 . . . of rest, and show **r** toward
Job 15:4 . . . fear of God, no **r** for him?
Job 37:24 . . . who are wise show him **r.**
Eph 5:21 . . . another out of **r** for Christ.
Heb 5:7 . . . of his deep **r** for God.

REVERENT (adj) expressing or characterized by reverence; worshipful
Col 3:22 . . . because of your **r** fear
1 Pet 1:17 . . . must live in **r** fear
1 Pet 3:2 . . . your pure and **r** lives.

REVIVE, REVIVES, REVIVING (v) to become active or flourishing again; to restore from a depressed, inactive, or unused state
Ps 19:7 . . . are perfect, **r-ing** the soul.
Ps 85:6 . . . Won't you **r** us again,
Ps 119:25 . . . lie in the dust; **r** me
Ps 119:50 . . . Your promise **r-s** me;
Prov 25:13 . . . They **r** the spirit of

REVOLUTIONARIES (n) one engaged in a revolution
Mark 15:27 . . . Two **r** were crucified with

REWARD, REWARDS (n) something that is given in return for good or evil done or received or that is offered or given for some service or attainment
Gen 15:1 . . . and your **r** will be
1 Sam 26:23 . . . gives his own **r** for doing
Prov 12:14 . . . and hard work brings **r-s.**
Isa 49:4 . . . I will trust God for my **r.**
Matt 5:12 . . . For a great **r** awaits you
Matt 6:5 . . . all the **r** they will ever
Luke 6:23 . . . For a great **r** awaits you
Luke 6:35 . . . your **r** from heaven will
Phil 4:17 . . . you to receive a **r** for your
1 Thes 2:19 . . . be our proud **r** and crown
Heb 10:35 . . . the great **r** it brings you!
1 Pet 1:9 . . . The **r** for trusting him

REWARD, REWARDED, REWARDS (v) to give a reward to or for; to recompense
2 Sam 22:21 . . . The LORD **r-ed** me for
Prov 13:21 . . . while blessings **r** the
Prov 25:22 . . . the LORD will **r** you.
Jer 31:16 . . . for I will **r** you," says
Matt 6:18 . . . sees everything, will **r** you.
Luke 12:37 . . . for his return will be **r-ed.**
Luke 14:14 . . . God will **r** you for
1 Cor 3:8 . . . both will be **r-ed** for their
Eph 6:8 . . . the Lord will **r** each one
1 Tim 3:13 . . . will be **r-ed** with respect
Heb 11:6 . . . that he **r-s** those who
Rev 11:18 . . . the dead and **r** your servants

RICH (adj) having abundant possessions and especially material wealth
Job 34:19 . . . no more attention to the **r**
Ps 49:16 . . . the wicked grow **r** and
Prov 10:4 . . . poor; hard workers get **r.**
Prov 11:18 . . . Evil people get **r** for
Prov 13:7 . . . are poor pretend to be **r;**
Prov 21:17 . . . and luxury will never be **r.**
Prov 22:2 . . . The **r** and poor have this
Prov 23:4 . . . yourself out trying to get **r.**
Prov 28:6 . . . than to be dishonest and **r.**
Prov 28:22 . . . Greedy people try to get **r**
Eccl 5:12 . . . But the **r** seldom get a
Isa 53:9 . . . put in a **r** man's grave.
Matt 19:23 . . . hard for a **r** person to enter
Luke 1:53 . . . and sent the **r** away with
Luke 6:24 . . . you who are **r,** for you have
Luke 16:1 . . . was a certain **r** man who had
Luke 21:1 . . . watched the **r** people
2 Cor 8:9 . . . Though he was **r,** yet for your
1 Tim 6:9 . . . who long to be **r** fall into
1 Tim 6:17 . . . who are **r** in this world
Jas 1:10 . . . those who are **r** should boast
Jas 2:3 . . . seat to the **r** person, but you
Jas 5:1 . . . Look here, you **r** people:

RICHES (n) things that make one rich; wealth
see also MONEY, POSSESSION(S), TREASURE(S), WEALTH
2 Chr 1:11 . . . ask for wealth, **r,** fame,
Ps 49:6 . . . wealth and boast of great **r.**
Prov 27:24 . . . for **r** don't last forever,
Eccl 5:13 . . . Hoarding **r** harms the
Jer 9:23 . . . rich boast in their **r.**
Luke 8:14 . . . cares and **r** and pleasures
Rom 11:33 . . . great are God's **r** and
2 Cor 6:10 . . . give spiritual **r** to others.
Col 1:27 . . . know that the **r** and glory

RIDER (n) one who sits and travels on the back of an animal
Rev 6:2 . . . Its **r** carried a bow, and a
Rev 19:11 . . . Its **r** was named Faithful and

RIDICULED, RIDICULING (v) to make fun of
2 Kgs 19:22 . . . you been defying and **r-ing?**
1 Cor 4:10 . . . are honored, but we are **r.**

RIDING (v) to sit and travel on the back of an animal that one directs
Zech 9:9 . . . is humble, **r** on a donkey—
Matt 21:5 . . . is humble, **r** on a donkey—

RIGHT (adj) being in accordance with what is good, just, or proper; being in a correct or proper state; located opposite of left; acting or judging in accordance with truth or fact
see also JUST, JUSTIFY, RIGHTEOUS, UPRIGHT
Gen 4:7 . . . do what is **r,** then watch out!
Gen 18:19 . . . by doing what is **r** and just.
Exod 15:26 . . . do what is **r** in his sight,
Num 25:13 . . . making them **r** with me.
Deut 6:18 . . . Do what is **r** and good
Deut 25:1 . . . that one is **r** and the other
Josh 1:7 . . . either to the **r** or to the
Judg 17:6 . . . whatever seemed **r** in their
1 Sam 12:23 . . . what is good and **r.**
1 Kgs 3:9 . . . difference between **r** and
2 Chr 12:6 . . . The LORD is **r** in doing
Ps 19:8 . . . LORD are **r,** bringing joy
Ps 24:5 . . . have a **r** relationship with
Ps 25:8 . . . does what is **r;** he shows the
Ps 37:30 . . . they teach **r** from wrong.
Ps 64:10 . . . do what is **r** will praise him.
Ps 71:2 . . . do what is **r.** Turn your ear
Ps 84:11 . . . from those who do what is **r.**
Ps 97:11 . . . on those whose hearts are **r.**
Ps 106:3 . . . and always do what is **r.**
Ps 119:144 . . . laws are always **r;** help me
Prov 1:3 . . . do what is **r,** just, and fair.
Prov 2:13 . . . men turn from the **r** way
Prov 14:2 . . . who follow the **r** path
Prov 14:12 . . . person that seems **r,** but
Prov 15:21 . . . stays on the **r** path.
Prov 15:23 . . . to say the **r** thing at the
Prov 18:17 . . . in court sounds **r**—until
Eccl 8:5 . . . and a way to do what is **r,**
Eccl 9:11 . . . being in the **r** place at the
Isa 7:15 . . . choose what is **r** and reject
Isa 16:5 . . . be eager to do what is **r.**
Isa 26:7 . . . who does what is **r,** and you
Jer 23:5 . . . is just and **r** throughout the
Ezek 18:5 . . . and does what is just and **r.**
Ezek 18:21 . . . and do what is just and **r,**
Hos 14:9 . . . are true and **r,** and righteous
Mic 3:1 . . . to know **r** from wrong,
Mic 6:8 . . . do what is **r,** to love mercy,
Zeph 2:3 . . . to do what is **r** and to live
Matt 6:3 . . . hand know what your **r** hand is
Matt 22:44 . . . of honor at my **r** hand until
Acts 2:34 . . . the place of honor at my **r** hand
Acts 7:55 . . . honor at God's **r** hand.
Acts 13:39 . . . is declared **r** with God—
Rom 1:17 . . . God makes us **r** in his sight.
Rom 2:13 . . . doesn't make us **r** with God.
Rom 3:4 . . . will be proved **r** in what you
Rom 3:20 . . . ever be made **r** with God by
Rom 3:22 . . . We are made **r** with God by
Rom 3:28 . . . So we are made **r** with God
Rom 3:30 . . . makes people **r** with himself
Rom 4:13 . . . but on a **r** relationship with
Rom 4:25 . . . life to make us **r** with God.
Rom 5:1 . . . we have been made **r** in God's
Rom 5:16 . . . being made **r** with God,
Rom 6:13 . . . to do what is **r** for the glory
Rom 8:10 . . . have been made **r** with God.
Rom 8:30 . . . given them **r** standing,
Rom 9:30 . . . they were made **r** with God.
Rom 10:3 . . . way of getting **r** with God by
Rom 10:10 . . . you are made **r** with God,
1 Cor 6:11 . . . you were made **r** with God
2 Cor 3:9 . . . which makes us **r** with God!
2 Cor 5:21 . . . be made **r** with God
Gal 2:16 . . . person is made **r** with God by
Gal 2:17 . . . to be made **r** with God through
Gal 2:21 . . . law could make us **r** with God,
Gal 3:11 . . . can be made **r** with God by
Gal 3:21 . . . could be made **r** with God by
Gal 3:24 . . . could be made **r** with God
Gal 5:4 . . . to make yourselves **r** with God
Eph 5:9 . . . what is good and **r** and true.
Phil 4:8 . . . honorable, and **r,** and pure,
2 Tim 3:16 . . . teaches us to do what is **r.**
Heb 2:10 . . . it was only **r** that he should
Heb 12:11 . . . harvest of **r** living for those
Jas 2:24 . . . are shown to be **r** with God by
1 Jn 2:29 . . . who do what is **r** are God's

RIGHT, RIGHTS (n) correct or moral behavior; something to which one has a just claim
Job 27:2 . . . has taken away my **r-s,** by
Ps 25:9 . . . in doing **r,** teaching them his
Ps 34:15 . . . those who do **r;** his ears are
Ps 82:3 . . . the **r-s** of the oppressed
Prov 29:7 . . . about the **r-s** of the poor;

Isa 1:17 . . . Fight for the **r-s** of widows.
Isa 10:2 . . . and deny the **r-s** of the needy
Lam 3:35 . . . others of their **r-s** in
Matt 5:10 . . . for doing **r**, for the Kingdom
John 1:12 . . . he gave the **r** to become
Rom 9:21 . . . he have a **r** to use the same
1 Cor 9:4 . . . have the **r** to live in your
1 Pet 3:12 . . . those who do **r**, and his ears

RIGHTEOUS (adj) acting in accord with divine or moral law; free from guilt or sin; morally right or justifiable
see also JUST, JUSTIFY, RIGHT, UPRIGHT
Gen 6:9 . . . Noah was a **r** man, the only
Gen 15:6 . . . counted him as **r** because of
Gen 18:23 . . . sweep away both the **r** and
Ps 7:8 . . . Declare me **r**, O LORD, for
Ps 17:15 . . . Because I am **r**, I will see
Ps 106:31 . . . regarded as a **r** man ever
Ps 119:7 . . . I learn your **r** regulations,
Ps 119:137 . . . O LORD, you are **r**,
Ps 145:17 . . . The LORD is **r** in everything
Prov 4:18 . . . The way of the **r** is like the
Prov 9:9 . . . Teach the **r**, and they
Prov 29:6 . . . but the **r** escape, shouting
Isa 26:2 . . . to all who are **r**; allow the
Isa 42:21 . . . Because he is **r**, the LORD
Isa 64:6 . . . we display our **r** deeds,
Jer 11:20 . . . you make **r** judgments, and
Jer 23:5 . . . raise up a **r** descendant from
Ezek 3:20 . . . None of their **r** acts will be
Amos 5:24 . . . river of **r** living.
Hab 2:4 . . . But the **r** will live
Mal 3:18 . . . between the **r** and the wicked,
Matt 9:13 . . . think they are **r**, but those
Matt 13:43 . . . Then the **r** will shine
Matt 25:37 . . . Then these **r** ones will
Luke 1:6 . . . and Elizabeth were **r** in God's
Luke 16:15 . . . like to appear **r** in public,
Rom 1:17 . . . faith that a **r** person has
Rom 3:5 . . . people see how **r** God is.
Rom 3:10 . . . No one is **r**—not even one.
Rom 4:3 . . . counted him as **r** because of
Rom 4:6 . . . who are declared **r** without
Rom 4:22 . . . God counted him as **r**.
Rom 6:19 . . . be slaves to **r** living so that
Gal 3:6 . . . counted him as **r** because of
Eph 4:24 . . . like God—truly **r** and holy.
Phil 1:11 . . . salvation—the **r** character
2 Tim 2:22 . . . Instead, pursue **r** living,
Titus 3:7 . . . he declared us **r** and gave us
Jas 2:23 . . . counted him as **r** because of
Jas 5:16 . . . prayer of a **r** person has
1 Jn 2:1 . . . the one who is truly **r**.
1 Jn 3:7 . . . that they are **r**, even as

RIGHTEOUSNESS (n) the state or quality of being righteous
see also GODLINESS, JUSTICE
Ps 36:6 . . . Your **r** is like the mighty
Ps 71:15 . . . tell everyone about your **r**.
Ps 85:10 . . . **R** and peace have kissed!
Ps 98:2 . . . has revealed his **r** to every
Ps 111:3 . . . His **r** never fails.
Prov 21:21 . . . Whoever pursues **r** and
Isa 11:5 . . . He will wear **r** like a belt
Isa 42:6 . . . you to demonstrate my **r**.
Isa 45:8 . . . so salvation and **r** can sprout
Isa 56:1 . . . to display my **r** among you.
Isa 59:17 . . . He put on **r** as his body
Jer 9:24 . . . brings justice and **r** to the
Jer 23:6 . . . LORD Is Our **R**.
Hos 10:12 . . . come and shower **r** upon
Mic 7:9 . . . and I will see his **r**.
Mal 4:2 . . . the Sun of **R** will rise
Matt 5:20 . . . unless your **r** is better
John 16:8 . . . and of God's **r**, and of the
Acts 24:25 . . . about **r** and self-control
Rom 3:26 . . . to demonstrate his **r**, for he
Rom 5:18 . . . one act of **r** brings a right
2 Cor 6:7 . . . the weapons of **r** in the
Eph 6:14 . . . the body armor of God's **r**.
Phil 3:6 . . . And as for **r**, I obeyed the
2 Tim 4:8 . . . the crown of **r**, which
Heb 11:7 . . . he received the **r** that comes
Jas 3:18 . . . and reap a harvest of **r**.
2 Pet 3:13 . . . filled with God's **r**.

RIPE (adj) fully grown and developed
John 4:35 . . . are already **r** for harvest.
Rev 14:15 . . . the crop on earth is **r**.

RISE, RISEN, RISES (v) to ascend or extend above other objects; to return from death; to assume an upright position
see also RESURRECTION
Num 24:17 . . . A star will **r** from Jacob;
Isa 26:19 . . . bodies will **r** again!
Mal 4:2 . . . of Righteousness will **r** with
Matt 22:30 . . . when the dead **r**, they will
Matt 27:63 . . . I will **r** from the dead.
Matt 28:6 . . . He is **r-n** from the dead,
Mark 8:31 . . . later he would **r** from the
Mark 16:6 . . . He is **r-n** from the dead!
Luke 18:33 . . . day he will **r** again.
Luke 24:34 . . . The Lord has really **r-n!**
John 5:29 . . . and they will **r** again.
John 11:24 . . . when everyone else **r-s**, at
John 20:9 . . . said Jesus must **r** from the
Acts 17:3 . . . must suffer and **r** from the
1 Thes 4:16 . . . have died will **r** from

RIVER (n) a natural stream of water; large or overwhelming quantities
Isa 66:12 . . . give Jerusalem a **r** of peace
Amos 5:24 . . . an endless **r** of righteous
Rev 22:1 . . . showed me a **r** with the water

RIVERBANK (n) the ground serving as an edge of a river
Ps 1:3 . . . along the **r**, bearing fruit

ROAD (n) an open way for vehicles, persons, and animals; a route or way to an end, conclusion, or circumstance
Ps 25:4 . . . point out the **r** for me to
Prov 22:5 . . . treacherous **r**; whoever values
Isa 35:8 . . . And a great **r** will go through
Matt 3:3 . . . Clear the **r** for him!

ROARING (adj) making or characterized by a sound resembling a roar
1 Pet 5:8 . . . around like a **r** lion, looking

ROB (v) to steal from by force
Ezek 22:29 . . . oppress the poor, **r** the needy,

ROBBERS (n) one who steals usually by violence or threat
John 10:8 . . . before me were thieves and **r**.

ROBBERY (n) the act or practice of stealing by violence or threat
Isa 61:8 . . . I hate **r** and wrongdoing.

ROBE (n) a long, flowing outer garment
Gen 37:3 . . . for Joseph—a beautiful **r**.
Isa 6:1 . . . the train of his **r** filled the

ROBED (adj) clothed or covered with or as if with a robe
Ps 93:1 . . . LORD is **r** in majesty

ROCK (n) a stone; a cliff; foundation, support; refuge
Exod 17:6 . . . Moses struck the **r** as he was
Num 20:8 . . . speak to the **r** over there,
Deut 32:13 . . . honey from the **r** and olive
2 Sam 22:2 . . . LORD is my **r**, my
Ps 18:2 . . . God is my **r**, in whom I
Ps 19:14 . . . LORD, my **r** and my redeemer.
Ps 61:2 . . . to the towering **r** of safety,
Ps 62:7 . . . my refuge, a **r** where no enemy
Ps 92:15 . . . He is my **r!**
Isa 26:4 . . . GOD is the eternal **R**.
Matt 7:24 . . . builds a house on solid **r**.
Matt 16:18 . . . upon this **r** I will build
Rom 9:33 . . . stumble, a **r** that makes them
1 Cor 10:4 . . . and that **r** was Christ.
1 Pet 2:8 . . . stumble, the **r** that makes

ROD, RODS (n) a straight, slender stick used as a walking stick, a club or weapon, a shepherd's crook, a paddling stick, a royal scepter, or a measuring stick; figurative of divine authority
see also STAFF
2 Sam 7:14 . . . him with the **r**, like any
Ps 2:9 . . . will break them with an iron **r**
Ps 23:4 . . . Your **r** and your staff
Prov 13:24 . . . spare the **r** of discipline
2 Cor 11:25 . . . times I was beaten with **r-s**.
Rev 2:27 . . . the nations with an iron **r**
Rev 12:5 . . . rule all nations with an iron **r**.
Rev 19:15 . . . rule them with an iron **r**.

ROMAN (adj) of or relating to Rome or the people of Rome
Acts 16:37 . . . and we are **R** citizens.
Acts 22:25 . . . you to whip a **R** citizen

ROMAN OFFICER (n) a person of some authority in the Roman military
Matt 8:5 . . . a **R** came and pleaded
Luke 23:47 . . . the **R** overseeing the execution
Acts 10:22 . . . sent by Cornelius, a **R**

ROMAN SOLDIERS (n) those actively involved in the Roman military
Mark 15:15 . . . turned him over to the **R** to be crucified
John 18:3 . . . given Judas a contingent of **R**

ROOSTER (n) an adult male domestic chicken
Matt 26:34 . . . before the **r** crows, you will

ROOT, ROOTS (n) the part of a plant usually found underground; something that is an origin or source (as of a condition or quality)
Isa 11:1 . . . bearing fruit from the old **r**.
Isa 53:2 . . . green shoot, like a **r** in dry
Matt 3:10 . . . to sever the **r-s** of the trees.
Matt 13:21 . . . don't have deep **r-s**, they
Eph 3:17 . . . Your **r-s** will grow down
1 Tim 6:10 . . . money is the **r** of all kinds
Jude 1:12 . . . have been pulled up by the **r-s**.

ROPE, ROPES (n) a large stout cord of strands twisted or braided together
Josh 2:18 . . . this scarlet **r** hanging from
Prov 5:22 . . . they are **r-s** that catch
Hos 11:4 . . . with my **r-s** of kindness

ROT (v) to undergo decomposition
Ps 16:10 . . . holy one to **r** in the grave.
Acts 2:27 . . . Holy One to **r** in the grave.
Acts 13:35 . . . Holy One to **r** in the grave.

ROYAL (adj) of, relating to, or subject to the crown
Ps 93:5 . . . Your **r** laws cannot be
Isa 63:1 . . . this in **r** robes, marching
Jas 2:8 . . . you obey the **r** law as found
1 Pet 2:9 . . . You are **r** priests,

RUDDER (n) an underwater blade that steers a boat or ship
Jas 3:4 . . . a small **r** makes a huge ship

RUDE (adj) offensive in manner or action
1 Cor 13:5 . . . or **r**. It does not demand

RUIN (n) physical, moral, economic, or social collapse
Eccl 4:5 . . . idle hands, leading them to **r**.
1 Tim 6:9 . . . them into **r** and destruction.

RUIN, RUINED, RUINING, RUINS (v) to damage irreparably; to subject to frustration, failure, or disaster
Prov 19:3 . . . People **r** their lives by
Prov 19:18 . . . you will **r** their lives.
Prov 22:23 . . . He will **r** anyone who **r-s**
Isa 3:14 . . . You have **r-ed** Israel,
Matt 9:17 . . . the wine and **r-ing** the skins.
2 Tim 2:14 . . . they can **r** those who hear

RULE, RULES (n) a prescribed guide for conduct or action
Isa 29:13 . . . but man-made **r-s** learned by
2 Tim 2:5 . . . unless they follow the **r-s.**
Heb 13:9 . . . not from **r-s** about food,

RULE, RULED, RULES (v) to exert control, direction, or influence on; to exercise authority or power over
Gen 3:16 . . . but he will **r** over you.
Ps 2:4 . . . But the one who **r-s** in heaven
Ps 11:4 . . . LORD still **r-s** from heaven.
Ps 55:19 . . . God, who has **r-d** forever,
Ps 66:7 . . . great power he **r-s** forever.
Ps 89:9 . . . You **r** the oceans.
Ps 103:19 . . . there he **r-s** over everything.
Prov 17:2 . . . wise servant will **r** over the
Isa 9:7 . . . He will **r** with fairness
Isa 40:10 . . . He will **r** with a powerful
Jer 23:5 . . . a King who **r-s** with wisdom.
Zech 6:13 . . . honor and will **r** as king
Rom 5:21 . . . as sin **r-d** over all people
Rom 15:12 . . . come, and he will **r** over
Col 3:15 . . . comes from Christ **r** in your
Rev 19:15 . . . He will **r** them with

RULER, RULERS (n) person with authority; tribal chief; prince or king; city magistrate; powerful spiritual beings; God himself
Judg 8:22 . . . to Gideon, "Be our **r!**
1 Sam 10:1 . . . to be the **r** over Israel,
Prov 19:6 . . . favors from a **r;** everyone is
Prov 23:1 . . . with a **r,** pay attention to
Jer 30:21 . . . have their own **r** again,
Dan 7:27 . . . all **r-s** will serve and obey him.
Dan 9:25 . . . until a **r**—the Anointed One—
Mic 5:2 . . . a **r** of Israel will come from
Matt 2:6 . . . for a **r** will come from
Matt 20:25 . . . that the **r-s** in this world
John 12:31 . . . when Satan, the **r** of this
1 Cor 2:6 . . . or to the **r-s** of this world,
Eph 1:21 . . . far above any **r** or authority
Eph 3:10 . . . the unseen **r-s** and authorities
Eph 6:12 . . . but against evil **r-s** and
Col 1:16 . . . as thrones, kingdoms, **r-s,** and
Col 2:15 . . . disarmed the spiritual **r-s** and
Rev 1:5 . . . and the **r** of all the kings

RUMORS (n) a statement or report without known authority for its truth
Exod 23:1 . . . must not pass along false **r.**
Prov 18:8 . . . **R** are dainty morsels that
Jer 51:46 . . . For **r** will keep coming year

RUN, RUNNING (v) to go faster than a walk; to flee
Ps 19:5 . . . athlete eager to **r** the race.
Prov 4:12 . . . when you **r,** you won't
Isa 40:31 . . . will **r** and not grow weary.
1 Cor 9:26 . . . So I **r** with purpose in
Gal 2:2 . . . and I was **r-ning** the race for
Gal 5:7 . . . You were **r-ning** the race so
Phil 2:16 . . . that I did not **r** the race in
1 Tim 6:11 . . . so **r** from all these evil
2 Tim 2:22 . . . **R** from anything that
Heb 12:1 . . . let us **r** with endurance

RUNNER (n) a messenger
Hab 2:2 . . . so that a **r** can carry

RUST (n) the reddish brittle coating formed on iron
Matt 6:19 . . . them and **r** destroys them,

RUTH Moabitess (Ruth 1:4); widowed daughter-in-law of Naomi (Ruth 1:18); later married Boaz (Ruth 4:10); ancestor of David and Jesus (Ruth 4:13, 21-22; Matt 1:5).

RUTHLESS (adj) having no pity; cruel
Prov 11:16 . . . gains respect, but **r** men gain

S

SABAOTH (KJV)
Rom 9:29 . . . LORD of *Heaven's Armies* had not
Jas 5:4 . . . the LORD of *Heaven's Armies*

SABBATH, SABBATHS (n) cessation of activity; a holy day set aside to honor God through rest and worship
see also REST
Exod 20:8 . . . to observe the **S** day by
Exod 31:14 . . . must keep the **S** day, for it
Lev 25:2 . . . must observe a **S** rest before
Deut 5:12 . . . Observe the **S** day by
2 Chr 2:4 . . . morning and evening, on the **S-s,**
Isa 56:2 . . . who honor my **S** days of rest
Isa 56:6 . . . do not desecrate the **S** day
Isa 58:13 . . . Honor the **S** in everything
Matt 12:1 . . . some grainfields on the **S.**
Luke 13:10 . . . One **S** day as Jesus was
Col 2:16 . . . or new moon ceremonies or **S-s.**

SACKCLOTH (KJV)
Gen 37:34 . . . dressed himself in *burlap.*
Esth 4:1 . . . put on *burlap* and ashes,
Job 16:15 . . . I wear *burlap* to show my grief
Ps 30:11 . . . my *clothes of mourning* and
Luke 10:13 . . . *burlap* and throwing ashes

SACRED (adj) dedicated or set apart for the service or worship of a deity; entitled to reverence and respect
Lev 10:13 . . . eat it in a **s** place, for
Num 4:15 . . . and all the **s** articles.
2 Tim 3:2 . . . They will consider nothing **s.**

SACRIFICE, SACRIFICES (n) worship or atonement offering; something given up or lost
Exod 12:27 . . . It is the Passover **s** to the
1 Sam 15:22 . . . Obedience is better than **s,**
Ps 40:6 . . . no delight in **s-s** or offerings.
Ps 51:16 . . . do not desire a **s,** or I would
Ps 51:17 . . . The **s** you desire is
Ps 107:22 . . . offer **s-s** of thanksgiving
Prov 15:8 . . . LORD detests the **s** of
Hos 6:6 . . . to show love, not offer **s-s.**
Matt 9:13 . . . to show mercy, not offer **s-s.**
Rom 3:25 . . . Jesus as the **s** for sin.
Rom 8:3 . . . Son as a **s** for our sins.
Rom 12:1 . . . a living and holy **s**—the
Eph 5:2 . . . himself as a **s** for us,
Heb 5:3 . . . he must offer **s-s** for his own
Heb 7:27 . . . need to offer **s-s** every day.
Heb 9:28 . . . time as a **s** to take away
Heb 10:5 . . . did not want animal **s-s** or sin
Heb 10:10 . . . holy by the **s** of the body of
Heb 13:15 . . . Jesus a continual **s** of praise
Heb 13:16 . . . These are the **s-s** that please
1 Pet 2:5 . . . offer spiritual **s-s** that please
1 Jn 2:2 . . . himself is the **s** that atones
1 Jn 4:10 . . . his Son as a **s** to take away

SACRIFICE, SACRIFICED, SACRIFICES (v) to suffer loss of, give up, renounce, injure, kill, or destroy, especially for an ideal, belief, or end
Gen 22:2 . . . Go and **s** him as a
John 10:11 . . . good shepherd **s-s** his life
John 10:15 . . . I **s** my life for the sheep.
1 Cor 5:7 . . . Lamb, has been **s-d** for us.
1 Cor 13:3 . . . poor and even **s-d** my body,

SACRILEGIOUS (adj) of, relating to, or characterized by a violation of or gross irreverence toward something holy or sacred
Dan 11:31 . . . and set up the **s** object that
Dan 12:11 . . . stopped and the **s** object that
Matt 24:15 . . . about—the **s** object that
Mark 13:14 . . . will see the **s** object that

SAD (adj) affected with or expressive of grief or unhappiness
Ps 42:5 . . . Why is my heart so **s?**
Luke 18:23 . . . **s,** for he was very rich.

SADDUCEES (n) members of a Jewish faction that rejected doctrines not in the Law (as resurrection, retribution in a future life, and the existence of angels)
Matt 16:6 . . . yeast of the Pharisees and **S.**
Mark 12:18 . . . **S**—religious leaders
Acts 23:8 . . . for the **S** say there is no

SADNESS (n) affected with or expressive of grief or unhappiness
Ps 31:10 . . . my years are shortened by **s.**
Eccl 7:3 . . . **s** has a refining influence
Jas 4:9 . . . **s** instead of laughter

SAFE (adj) free from harm or risk; secure from threat of danger, harm, or loss
Deut 29:19 . . . I am **s,** even though I am
1 Sam 30:23 . . . has kept us **s** and helped
Ps 4:8 . . . O LORD, will keep me **s.**
Ps 28:8 . . . He is a **s** fortress for his
Prov 2:11 . . . will keep you **s.**
Prov 4:26 . . . stay on the **s** path.
Prov 18:10 . . . run to him and are **s.**
Prov 28:26 . . . who walks in wisdom is **s.**
John 17:15 . . . keep them **s** from the evil

SAFETY (n) the condition of being safe from undergoing or causing hurt, injury, or loss
Deut 33:12 . . . and live in **s** beside him.
2 Sam 23:5 . . . ensure my **s** and success.
Ps 16:9 . . . My body rests in **s.**
Ps 59:16 . . . my refuge, a place of **s**
Prov 11:14 . . . is **s** in having many advisers.
Prov 29:25 . . . trusting the LORD means **s.**
Hos 2:18 . . . live unafraid in peace and **s.**

SAINTS (KJV)
Ps 34:9 . . . you his *godly people,* for
Ps 97:10 . . . the lives of his *godly people*
Dan 7:18 . . . *holy people* of the Most High
Rom 8:27 . . . Spirit pleads for *us believers*
1 Cor 6:2 . . . *we believers* will judge the

SAKE (n) personal or social welfare, safety, or benefit; the good, advantage, or enhancement of some entity
Rom 8:36 . . . say, "For your **s** we are
Heb 11:26 . . . to suffer for the **s** of Christ

SALT (n) the mineral sodium chloride used mainly for seasoning and as a preservative
Gen 19:26 . . . she turned into a pillar of **s.**
Matt 5:13 . . . You are the **s** of the earth.

SALVATION (n) deliverance from the power and effects of sin, danger, or difficulty by God's intervention
see also SAVE
2 Sam 22:47 . . . Rock of my **s,** be exalted!

2 Chr 6:41 . . . be clothed with **s**; may your
Ps 18:46 . . . God of my **s** be exalted!
Ps 27:1 . . . light and my **s**—so why should
Ps 40:16 . . . love your **s** repeatedly shout,
Ps 51:12 . . . joy of your **s**, and make me
Ps 62:2 . . . rock and my **s**, my fortress
Ps 69:13 . . . my prayer with your sure **s.**
Ps 74:12 . . . ages past, bringing **s** to
Ps 85:4 . . . us again, O God of our **s.**
Ps 89:26 . . . and the Rock of my **s.**
Ps 91:16 . . . long life and give them my **s.**
Ps 95:1 . . . joyfully to the Rock of our **s.**
Isa 25:9 . . . rejoice in the **s** he brings!
Isa 26:18 . . . We have not given **s** to the
Isa 33:6 . . . rich store of **s**, wisdom,
Isa 45:8 . . . wide so **s** and righteousness
Isa 45:22 . . . the world look to me for **s!**
Isa 49:6 . . . will bring my **s** to the ends
Isa 51:6 . . . but my **s** lasts forever.
Isa 52:7 . . . of peace and **s**, the news that
Isa 59:17 . . . the helmet of **s** on his head.
Isa 62:1 . . . dawn, and her **s** blazes like
Lam 3:26 . . . wait quietly for **s** from the
Jon 2:9 . . . For my **s** comes from the
Luke 1:77 . . . to find **s** through forgiveness
Luke 2:30 . . . I have seen your **s**,
Luke 3:6 . . . will see the **s** sent from
Luke 21:28 . . . up, for your **s** is near!
John 4:22 . . . him, for **s** comes through the
Acts 13:26 . . . this message of **s** has been
Acts 13:47 . . . Gentiles, to bring **s** to the
Acts 28:28 . . . know that this **s** from God
Rom 11:11 . . . so God made **s** available to
Rom 13:11 . . . for our **s** is nearer now
2 Cor 6:2 . . . the day of **s**, I helped you.
2 Cor 7:10 . . . from sin and results in **s.**
Eph 6:17 . . . Put on **s** as your helmet,
Phil 2:12 . . . show the results of your **s**,
2 Thes 2:13 . . . to experience **s**—a **s**
Titus 2:11 . . . bringing **s** to all people.
Heb 2:3 . . . if we ignore this great **s** that
Heb 5:9 . . . source of eternal **s** for all
Heb 9:28 . . . but to bring **s** to all who
1 Pet 1:9 . . . will be the **s** of your souls.
1 Pet 1:13 . . . to the gracious **s** that will
1 Pet 2:2 . . . into a full experience of **s.**
Rev 7:10 . . . a great roar, "**S** comes from

SAMARIA (n) the capital city of the northern kingdom of Israel; a region in the uplands of central Palestine between Galilee and Judea
1 Kgs 16:24 . . . hill now known as **S** from
2 Kgs 17:6 . . . Hoshea's reign, **S** fell,
John 4:4 . . . to go through **S** on the way.

SAMARITAN (n) a native or inhabitant of Samaria
Luke 10:33 . . . a despised **S** came along,
Luke 17:16 . . . man was a **S.**
John 4:5 . . . he came to the **S** village of
John 4:7 . . . a **S** woman came to draw

SAMSON Judge of Israel from tribe of Dan; defeated oppressing Philistines (Judg 14–15); killed lion with bare hands (Judg 14:6); set 300 fox tails on fire (Judg 15:4); killed 1,000 men (Judg 15:15); carried large gates to top of hill (Judg 16:3); seduced and deceived by Delilah (Judg 16:1-22); died as he destroyed many Philistines (Judg 16:23-31).

SAMUEL Judge and prophet of Israel (Heb 11:32); prophet's birth and dedication (1 Sam 1); raised by Eli in the Temple (1 Sam 2:11, 18-21); called as a prophet (1 Sam 3); served as judge over Israel (1 Sam 7:15); warned Israel of the tyranny of kingship (1 Sam 8:10-18); anointed Saul (1 Sam 10:1); rejected Saul (1 Sam 15:23); anointed David (1 Sam 16:13); protected David from Saul (1 Sam 19:18-24); died (1 Sam 25:1); ghost of Samuel rebuked Saul (1 Sam 28:14-19).

SANCTIFY, SANCTIFIED (KJV)
Gen 2:3 . . . and *declared it holy*
Exod 31:13 . . . LORD, who *makes you holy*
Deut 5:12 . . . Sabbath day by *keeping it holy*
John 17:19 . . . myself as a *holy sacrifice*
Heb 10:10 . . . for us to *be made holy* by

SANCTUARY (n) a holy place set apart for worship of God or refuge from danger
see also TABERNACLE, TEMPLE
Exod 25:8 . . . build me a holy **s** so I can
Lev 19:30 . . . show reverence toward my **s.**
Ps 27:5 . . . he will hide me in his **s.**
Ps 63:2 . . . you in your **s** and gazed upon
Ps 68:35 . . . God is awesome in his **s.**
Ps 150:1 . . . Praise God in his **s**; praise
Heb 6:19 . . . curtain into God's inner **s.**

SAND (n) fine grains of rock that are worn away by wind and rain
Gen 22:17 . . . in the sky and the **s** on
Matt 7:26 . . . who builds a house on **s.**

SANDAL, SANDALS (n) a shoe consisting of a sole strapped to the foot
Exod 3:5 . . . Take off your **s-s**, for you are
Exod 12:11 . . . wear your **s-s**, and carry
Deut 25:9 . . . elders, pull his **s** from his
Josh 5:15 . . . Take off your **s-s**, for the
Ruth 4:7 . . . to remove his **s** and hand it
Matt 3:11 . . . his slave and carry his **s-s.**

SANG (v) *see also* SING
Exod 15:1 . . . people of Israel **s** this
Exod 15:21 . . . And Miriam **s** this song:
Num 21:17 . . . the Israelites **s** this song:
Judg 5:1 . . . son of Abinoam **s** this song:
2 Sam 22:1 . . . David **s** this song to
Ezra 3:11 . . . and thanks, they **s** this song
Job 38:7 . . . morning stars **s** together and
Ps 106:12 . . . Then they **s** his praise.
Matt 26:30 . . . Then they **s** a hymn
Rev 5:9 . . . And they **s** a new song
Rev 5:13 . . . They **s**: "Blessing and
Rev 14:3 . . . great choir **s** a wonderful

SAPS (v) to gradually diminish the supply or intensity of
Prov 17:22 . . . broken spirit **s** a person's

SARAH (SARAI) Wife of Abraham (Abram) (Gen 11:30-31); was infertile (Gen 11:30; Rom 4:19) and very beautiful (Gen 12:11); with Abraham, deceived Pharaoh (Gen 12:10-20); dealings with Hagar and Ishmael (Gen 16); name changed (Gen 17:15); Isaac promised (Gen 18:10-15; Rom 9:9); example of faith (Heb 11:11); with Abraham, deceived Abimelech (Gen 20); Isaac born (Gen 21:1-7); Hagar and Ishmael sent away (Gen 21:8-21); died and was buried (Gen 23); Paul's analogy using Sarah and Hagar (Gal 4:25-26).

SARDIS (n) the capital city of Lydia in the province of Asia, in western Asia Minor (modern Turkey)
Rev 3:1 . . . the angel of the church in **S.**

SAT (v) *see also* SIT
Dan 7:9 . . . and the Ancient One **s** down to
Mark 16:19 . . . into heaven and **s** down in
Heb 8:1 . . . High Priest who **s** down in the
Heb 10:12 . . . Then he **s** down in the

SATAN (n) "adversary" of God and man; the personal name of the devil
see also DEVIL
Job 1:6 . . . and the Accuser, **S**, came with
Zech 3:2 . . . your accusations, **S.** Yes,
Matt 12:26 . . . if **S** is casting out **S**, he
Matt 16:23 . . . Get away from me, **S!**
Mark 4:15 . . . only to have **S** come at once
Luke 10:18 . . . told them, "I saw **S** fall from
Luke 22:3 . . . Then **S** entered into Judas
Rom 16:20 . . . soon crush **S** under your
1 Cor 5:5 . . . him over to **S** so that his
2 Cor 11:14 . . . Even **S** disguises himself as
2 Cor 12:7 . . . from **S** to torment
1 Tim 1:20 . . . them over to **S** so they might
Rev 12:9 . . . the devil, or **S**, the one
Rev 20:2 . . . is the devil, **S**—and bound
Rev 20:7 . . . come to an end, **S** will be let

SATISFY, SATISFIED, SATISFIES, SATISFYING (v) to make happy; to gratify to the full
Josh 22:33 . . . Israelites were **s-ied** and
Ps 17:14 . . . But **s** the hunger of your
Ps 17:15 . . . you face to face and be **s-ied.**
Ps 22:26 . . . poor will eat and be **s-ied.**
Ps 63:5 . . . You **s** me more than the richest
Ps 104:28 . . . and they are richly **s-ied.**
Ps 105:40 . . . quail; he **s-ied** their hunger
Ps 107:9 . . . he **s-ies** the thirsty and fills
Ps 145:16 . . . your hand, you **s** the hunger
Ps 147:14 . . . and **s-ies** your hunger with the
Prov 5:19 . . . Let her breasts **s** you always.
Prov 30:8 . . . just enough to **s** my needs.
Prov 30:15 . . . that are never **s-ied**—no, four
Isa 9:12 . . . LORD's anger will not be **s-ied.**
Mic 7:1 . . . be found to **s** my hunger.
Luke 6:21 . . . now, for you will be **s-ied.**
Heb 13:5 . . . be **s-ied** with what you have.
Jas 5:5 . . . in luxury, **s-ing** your every desire.

SAUL 1. First king of Israel (united kingdom), from tribe of Benjamin (1 Sam 9–11); anointed by Samuel (1 Sam 10:1); made unlawful sacrifices (1 Sam 13:1-14); warrior in battles (1 Sam 13:15–14:52); rejected as king (1 Sam 15:26); troubled by evil spirit (1 Sam 16:14-23); resentful of David and tried to kill him (1 Sam 18:5–19:22); gave Michal as wife to David (1 Sam 18:17-30); hunted David (1 Sam 22–24; 26); had priests at Nob killed (1 Sam 22:6-23); consulted medium at Endor, rebuked by Samuel's ghost (1 Sam 28:3-25); wounded in battle, then killed himself (1 Sam 31:4-6; *see also* 2 Sam 1:4-16); body desecrated, burned, and buried (1 Sam 31:12-13).
2. *See* PAUL, also known as Saul.

SAVE, SAVED, SAVES, SAVING (v) to rescue or deliver from danger or harm; to deliver from sin; to preserve or guard from injury, destruction, or loss; to maintain or preserve
see also PRESERVE, RESCUE, SALVATION
2 Sam 22:3 . . . the power that **s-s** me,
1 Chr 16:23 . . . good news that he **s-s.**
Ps 7:10 . . . is my shield, **s-ing** those whose
Ps 18:48 . . . you **s** me from violent
Ps 22:8 . . . let the LORD **s** him!
Ps 25:5 . . . you are the God who **s-s** me.
Ps 33:16 . . . army cannot **s** a king, nor
Ps 34:6 . . . LORD listened; he **s-d** me
Ps 44:6 . . . not count on my sword to **s**
Ps 68:20 . . . Our God is a God who **s-s!**
Ps 109:31 . . . the needy, ready to **s** them
Ps 116:6 . . . death, and he **s-d** me.
Prov 2:16 . . . Wisdom will **s** you from
Prov 10:2 . . . right living can **s** your
Isa 25:9 . . . trusted in him, and he **s-d** us!
Isa 30:15 . . . resting in me will you be **s-d.**

Isa 35:4 . . . He is coming to **s** you.
Isa 59:1 . . . arm is not too weak to **s**
Isa 63:1 . . . who has the power to **s!**
Jer 4:14 . . . your heart that you may be **s-d.**
Jer 17:14 . . . if you **s** me, I will
Jer 51:9 . . . nothing can **s** her now.
Dan 3:17 . . . we serve is able to **s** us.
Joel 2:32 . . . name of the LORD will be **s-d,**
Mic 7:7 . . . wait confidently for God to **s**
Zeph 1:18 . . . gold will not **s** you
Matt 1:21 . . . he will **s** his people
Matt 16:25 . . . my sake, you will **s** it.
Matt 24:13 . . . to the end will be **s-d.**
Luke 17:33 . . . life go, you will **s** it.
Luke 19:10 . . . seek and **s** those who are
John 10:9 . . . in through me will be **s-d.**
John 12:47 . . . I have come to **s** the world
Acts 2:21 . . . name of the LORD will be **s-d.**
Acts 4:12 . . . by which we must be **s-d.**
Acts 15:11 . . . we are all **s-d** the same way,
Acts 16:30 . . . what must I do to be **s-d?**
Rom 1:16 . . . God at work, **s-ing** everyone
Rom 5:9 . . . he will certainly **s** us from
Rom 10:9 . . . the dead, you will be **s-d.**
Rom 10:13 . . . of the LORD will be **s-d.**
1 Cor 1:18 . . . we who are being **s-d** know
1 Cor 5:5 . . . himself will be **s-d** on the
1 Cor 7:16 . . . wives might be **s-d** because
1 Cor 10:33 . . . so that many may be **s-d.**
1 Cor 15:2 . . . this Good News that **s-s**
Eph 1:13 . . . Good News that God **s-s** you.
1 Thes 5:9 . . . God chose to **s** us through
1 Tim 1:15 . . . the world to **s** sinners
1 Tim 2:4 . . . wants everyone to be **s-d** and
1 Tim 2:15 . . . women will be **s-d** through
2 Tim 1:9 . . . For God **s-d** us and called
Titus 3:5 . . . he **s-d** us, not because of the
Heb 7:25 . . . and forever, to **s** those who
Jas 5:20 . . . sinner back will **s** that person
2 Pet 3:15 . . . gives people time to be **s-d.**

SAVING (adj) of or relating to delivering or rescuing
Ps 40:10 . . . faithfulness and **s** power.
Ps 67:2 . . . the earth, your **s** power
Ps 69:29 . . . God, by your **s** power.
Ps 71:15 . . . proclaim your **s** power,
Ps 98:1 . . . has shown his **s** power!

SAVIOR (n) one who delivers from trouble, sin, or judgment
2 Sam 22:2 . . . my fortress, and my **s;**
Ps 38:22 . . . help me, O LORD my **s.**
Ps 40:17 . . . You are my helper and my **s.**
Ps 106:21 . . . They forgot God, their **s,**
Isa 43:11 . . . and there is no other **S.**
Isa 45:21 . . . a righteous God and **S.**
Isa 49:26 . . . the LORD, am your **S** and
Isa 62:11 . . . Look, your **S** is coming.
Jer 14:8 . . . Hope of Israel, our **S** in
Hos 13:4 . . . for there is no other **s.**
Zeph 3:17 . . . He is a mighty **s.**
Luke 1:47 . . . rejoices in God my **S!**
Luke 1:69 . . . He has sent us a mighty **S**
John 4:42 . . . he is indeed the **S** of the
Acts 5:31 . . . right hand as Prince and **S.**
Acts 13:23 . . . God's promised **S** of Israel!
Eph 5:23 . . . He is the **S** of his body,
1 Tim 2:3 . . . good and pleases God our **S,**
1 Tim 4:10 . . . who is the **S** of all people
Titus 2:10 . . . about God our **S** attractive
Titus 3:4 . . . When God our **S** revealed his
2 Pet 3:2 . . . Lord and **S** commanded
1 Jn 4:14 . . . Son to be the **S** of the world.

SAVOUR (KJV)
2 Cor 2:16 . . . a dreadful *smell* of death
Eph 5:2 . . . for us, a pleasing *aroma* to God

SAW (v) *see also* SEE
Ps 139:16 . . . You **s** me before I was born.

SCALES (n) the outer covering of fish or reptiles; an instrument for weighing *see also* BALANCES
Lev 11:9 . . . fins and **s,** whether taken
Lev 19:36 . . . Your **s** and weights
Deut 25:13 . . . must use accurate **s** when you
Prov 11:1 . . . use of dishonest **s,** but he
Rev 6:5 . . . a pair of **s** in his hand.

SCAPEGOAT (n) a goat upon whose head are symbolically placed the sins of the people, after which he is sent into the wilderness on the Day of Atonement
Lev 16:10 . . . other goat, the **s** chosen by

SCARLET (adj) of the color of any various bright reds
Josh 2:21 . . . leaving the **s** rope hanging
Isa 1:18 . . . sins are like **s,** I will make
Matt 27:28 . . . and put a **s** robe on him.

SCARS (n) a mark left (as in the skin) by the healing of injured tissue
Gal 6:17 . . . on my body the **s** that show

SCATTER, SCATTERED (v) to separate and go in various directions; to disperse
Deut 4:27 . . . the LORD will **s** you
Neh 1:8 . . . to me, I will **s** you among
Isa 11:12 . . . will gather the **s-ed** people
Jer 9:16 . . . I will **s** them around
Jer 30:11 . . . where I have **s-ed** you, but I
Jer 31:10 . . . LORD, who **s-ed** his people,
Ezek 34:21 . . . flock until you **s-ed** them to
Zech 2:6 . . . for I have **s-ed** you to the four
Zech 10:9 . . . Though I have **s-ed** them like
Zech 13:7 . . . sheep will be **s-ed,** and I will
Matt 26:31 . . . of the flock will be **s-ed.**
John 11:52 . . . children of God **s-ed** around
Acts 8:4 . . . were **s-ed** preached the Good
Jas 1:1 . . . Jewish believers **s-ed** abroad.

SCEPTER (n) the official staff of a ruler, symbolizing his authority and power
Gen 49:10 . . . The **s** will not depart from
Num 24:17 . . . a **s** will emerge from Israel.
Heb 1:8 . . . rule with a **s** of justice.

SCHEME (v) to make crafty or secret plans
Zech 8:17 . . . Don't **s** against each

SCHEMERS (n) one who plots or schemes
Job 5:12 . . . He frustrates the plans of **s**
Prov 14:17 . . . things, and **s** are hated.

SCHEMES (n) a crafty or secret plan
Job 5:13 . . . cunning **s-s** are thwarted.
Ps 37:7 . . . or fret about their wicked **s-s.**
Ps 140:8 . . . let their evil **s-s** succeed,
Prov 13:11 . . . from get-rich-quick **s-s**
2 Cor 2:11 . . . familiar with his evil **s-s.**

SCOFF (v) to show contempt by derisive acts or language; to mock
Lam 2:15 . . . They **s** and insult
1 Thes 5:20 . . . Do not **s** at prophecies,
2 Pet 2:12 . . . They **s** at things they do not
Jude 1:8 . . . defy authority, and **s** at

SCOFFERS (n) one who scoffs
2 Pet 3:3 . . . the last days **s** will come,

SCORN (n) open dislike, disrespect, or derision often mixed with indignation
Ps 109:25 . . . they shake their heads in **s.**
Isa 51:7 . . . not be afraid of people's **s,**

SCORN, SCORNED (v) to reject or dismiss as contemptible or unworthy
Ps 22:6 . . . I am **s-ed** and despised by all!
Ps 119:22 . . . Don't let them **s** and insult

Prov 9:12 . . . If you **s** wisdom, you will
Jer 6:10 . . . They **s** the word of the LORD.

SCORNFUL (adj) full of scorn; contemptuous
Ezek 28:24 . . . will Israel's **s** neighbors

SCORPION (n) a small crawling animal with eight legs, two sets of pincers, and a tail with a poisonous stinger
Luke 11:12 . . . give them a **s?** Of course
Rev 9:5 . . . pain of a **s** sting.

SCRIPTURE, SCRIPTURES (n) the Law; the writings of Moses; the entire collection of sacred books
Matt 21:16 . . . you ever read the **S-s?**
Matt 22:29 . . . you don't know the **S-s,**
Luke 24:27 . . . from all the **S-s** the things
Luke 24:45 . . . to understand the **S-s.**
John 2:22 . . . believed both the **S-s** and
John 5:39 . . . You search the **S-s** because
John 7:42 . . . the **S-s** clearly state that
John 10:35 . . . know that the **S-s** cannot
Acts 8:32 . . . The passage of **S** he had
1 Cor 4:6 . . . quoted from the **S-s,** you won't
1 Tim 4:13 . . . focus on reading the **S-s** to
2 Tim 3:16 . . . All **S** is inspired by God
Heb 10:7 . . . written about me in the **S-s.**
2 Pet 1:20 . . . no prophecy in **S** ever came
2 Pet 3:16 . . . do with other parts of **S.**

SCROLL (n) a roll (as of papyrus, leather, or parchment) for writing a document
Isa 34:4 . . . disappear like a rolled-up **s.**
Ezek 3:1 . . . giving you—eat this **s!**
Rev 6:14 . . . sky was rolled up like a **s,**
Rev 10:8 . . . take the open **s** from the hand

SEA, SEAS (n) a great body of salt water that covers much of the earth
Exod 14:16 . . . middle of the **s** on dry
Deut 30:13 . . . not kept beyond the **s,**
Job 11:9 . . . and wider than the **s.**
Ps 93:4 . . . violent raging of the **s-s,**
Ps 95:5 . . . The **s** belongs to him,
Eccl 11:1 . . . your grain across the **s-s,**
Isa 57:20 . . . like the restless **s,** which
Jon 1:4 . . . wind over the **s,** causing a
Hab 2:14 . . . waters fill the **s,** the earth
Matt 18:6 . . . in the depths of the **s.**
Jas 1:6 . . . wave of the **s** that is blown
Jude 1:13 . . . waves of the **s,** churning up
Rev 10:2 . . . right foot on the **s** and
Rev 13:1 . . . rising up out of the **s.**
Rev 20:13 . . . The **s** gave up its dead,
Rev 21:1 . . . And the **s** was also gone.

SEAL, SEALS (n) a piece of wax or clay impressed with a device such as a signet ring or cylinder engraved with the owner's name, a design, or both that certifies or authenticates a document
Rev 5:2 . . . break the **s-s** on this scroll
Rev 6:1 . . . the seven **s-s** on the scroll.
Rev 6:3 . . . broke the second **s,** I heard
Rev 6:5 . . . broke the third **s,** I heard
Rev 6:7 . . . broke the fourth **s,** I heard
Rev 6:9 . . . Lamb broke the fifth **s,** I saw
Rev 6:12 . . . broke the sixth **s,** and there
Rev 8:1 . . . broke the seventh **s** on the
Rev 9:4 . . . did not have the **s** of God

SEAL, SEALED (v) to confirm or make secure by or as if by a seal
Dan 12:4 . . . secret; **s** up the book until
Rev 5:1 . . . and it was **s-ed** with seven
Rev 22:10 . . . Do not **s** up the prophetic

SEARCH, SEARCHES (v) to investigate or examine thoroughly in an effort to find or verify something
Ps 34:14 . . . **S** for peace, and work
Ps 139:23 . . . **S** me, O God, and know
Eccl 3:6 . . . A time to **s** and a time to
Jer 17:10 . . . I, the LORD, **s** all hearts
1 Cor 2:10 . . . Spirit **s-es** out everything
1 Pet 3:11 . . . **S** for peace, and work

SEASHORE (n) land adjacent to the sea
Josh 11:4 . . . like the sand on the **s**.
1 Kgs 4:29 . . . vast as the sands of the **s**.

SEASON, SEASONS (n) the period normally characterized by a particular kind of weather; a period associated with some phase or activity of agriculture (as growth or harvesting)
Gen 1:14 . . . signs to mark the **s-s**, days,
Ps 1:3 . . . bearing fruit each **s**.
Gal 4:10 . . . or months or **s-s** or years. . . .

SEASONAL (adj) of, relating to, or varying in occurrence according to the season
Lev 26:4 . . . send you the **s** rains.

SEAT, SEATS (n) a chair, stool, or bench intended to be sat in or on
Luke 11:43 . . . to sit in the **s-s** of honor
Luke 14:9 . . . to take whatever **s** is left

SEATED (v) to put into a sitting position; to take one's seat or place
Matt 26:64 . . . Son of Man **s** in the place
Luke 22:69 . . . of Man will be **s** in the place
Eph 1:20 . . . the dead and **s** him in the
Eph 2:6 . . . with Christ and **s** us with him
Heb 12:2 . . . Now he is **s** in the place of
Rev 14:14 . . . a white cloud, and **s** on the

SECOND (adj) next to the first in place or time
Job 42:12 . . . Job in the **s** half of his life
Rev 20:14 . . . lake of fire is the **s** death.

SECRET (adj) kept from knowledge or view; hidden
Ps 90:8 . . . before you—our **s** sins—
Jer 23:24 . . . from me in a **s** place?
Matt 10:26 . . . all that is **s** will be
Rom 2:16 . . . judge everyone's **s** life.
Rom 16:25 . . . a plan kept **s** from the
1 Cor 13:2 . . . all of God's **s** plans
1 Cor 14:25 . . . their **s** thoughts will be
Col 1:26 . . . was kept **s** for centuries and

SECRET, SECRETS (n) something kept hidden or unexplained; something kept from the knowledge of others or shared only confidentially with a few
see also MYSTERY
Deut 29:29 . . . God has **s-s** known to no
Judg 16:15 . . . don't share your **s-s** with
Ps 44:21 . . . he knows the **s-s** of every
Prov 11:13 . . . goes around telling **s-s**,
Dan 2:28 . . . heaven who reveals **s-s**, and
Dan 2:29 . . . who reveals **s-s** has shown
Mark 4:11 . . . to understand the **s**
Mark 4:22 . . . and every **s** will be brought
Luke 8:10 . . . to understand the **s-s** of
1 Cor 15:51 . . . reveal to you a wonderful **s**.
Phil 4:12 . . . have learned the **s** of living
Col 1:27 . . . the **s**: Christ lives in you.

SECURE (adj) easy in mind; free from danger or the risk of loss; trustworthy, dependable
Job 31:24 . . . felt **s** because of my gold?
Ps 30:7 . . . made me as **s** as a mountain.
Prov 14:26 . . . fear the LORD are **s**;
1 Thes 5:3 . . . is peaceful and **s**," then
2 Pet 3:17 . . . your own **s** footing.

SECURE, SECURED (v) to make fast
Matt 27:65 . . . Take guards and **s** it the
Heb 9:12 . . . all time and **s-d** our redemption

SECURITY (n) something given, deposited, or pledged to make certain the fulfillment of an obligation; freedom from danger; protection
Deut 24:17 . . . widow's garment as **s** for
Ezra 9:8 . . . has given us **s** in this holy
Prov 3:26 . . . the LORD is your **s**.
Prov 19:23 . . . bringing **s** and protection

SEDUCE, SEDUCED (v) to persuade to disobedience or disloyalty; to entice
Deut 4:19 . . . don't be **s-d** into
Job 31:9 . . . has been **s-d** by a woman,
Job 36:18 . . . you may be **s-d** by wealth.
Prov 6:25 . . . her coy glances **s** you.

SEE, SEEING, SEES (v) to perceive by the eye; to understand or recognize; to come to know
see also SAW
Ps 34:8 . . . Taste and **s** that the
Ps 36:2 . . . they cannot **s** how wicked
Ps 90:8 . . . sins—and you **s** them
Ps 119:82 . . . straining to **s** your promises
Prov 5:21 . . . For the LORD **s-s** clearly
Prov 13:19 . . . pleasant to **s** dreams come
Eccl 3:11 . . . people cannot **s** the whole
Matt 6:18 . . . Father, who **s-s** everything,
John 12:45 . . . you are **s-ing** the one who
Rom 1:20 . . . can clearly **s** his invisible
Rom 7:13 . . . So we can **s** how terrible sin
1 Cor 13:12 . . . we will **s** everything with
2 Cor 4:18 . . . things we cannot **s** will last
2 Cor 5:7 . . . by believing and not by **s-ing**.
2 Cor 8:21 . . . everyone else to **s** that we
Phil 4:5 . . . Let everyone **s** that you are
Col 1:16 . . . things we can't **s**—such as
Rev 1:7 . . . everyone will **s** him—even

SEED, SEEDS (n) the grains of plants used for sowing
Gen 1:11 . . . These **s-s** will then produce
Prov 11:30 . . . The **s-s** of good deeds
Matt 13:3 . . . went out to plant some **s-s**.
Matt 13:31 . . . like a mustard **s** planted in
Matt 17:20 . . . as a mustard **s**, you could say
Mark 4:15 . . . The **s** that fell on
Luke 8:12 . . . The **s-s** that fell on
1 Cor 3:6 . . . I planted the **s** in your
2 Cor 9:6 . . . few **s-s** will get a small
2 Cor 9:10 . . . one who provides **s** for the

SEED-BEARING (adj) a plant that produces seeds
Gen 1:11 . . . every sort of **s** plant,

SEEK, SEEKING, SEEKS (v) to go in search of; to ask for; to try to acquire or gain
see also SOUGHT
2 Chr 7:14 . . . pray and **s** my face and
2 Chr 15:2 . . . Whenever you **s** him,
Prov 3:6 . . . **S** his will in all you do,
Prov 25:27 . . . not good to **s** honors
Prov 29:26 . . . Many **s** the ruler's favor,
Isa 55:6 . . . **S** the LORD while you can
Hos 10:12 . . . time to **s** the LORD,
Zeph 2:3 . . . **S** the LORD, all who are
Matt 6:33 . . . **S** the Kingdom of God above
Matt 7:7 . . . Keep on **s-ing**, and you
Matt 7:8 . . . Everyone who **s-s**, finds.
Luke 12:31 . . . **S** the Kingdom of God
Luke 19:10 . . . Son of Man came to **s** and
Rom 3:11 . . . no one is **s-ing** God.
1 Cor 7:27 . . . have a wife, do not **s** to get
Heb 11:6 . . . those who sincerely **s** him.

SEER (n) one who practices divination and predicts events or developments
1 Sam 9:9 . . . ask the **s**," for prophets

SELF-CONTROL (n) restraint exercised over one's own impulses, emotions, or desires
Prov 5:23 . . . He will die for lack of **s**;
Prov 16:32 . . . better to have **s** than to
Acts 24:25 . . . righteousness and **s** and the
Gal 5:23 . . . gentleness, and **s**. There is no
1 Tim 3:2 . . . must exercise **s**, live wisely,
1 Tim 3:11 . . . They must exercise **s** and be
Titus 2:2 . . . older men to exercise **s**,
1 Pet 1:13 . . . think clearly and exercise **s**.
2 Pet 1:6 . . . and knowledge with **s**, and

SELF-DENIAL (n) a restraint or limitation of one's own desires or interests
Col 2:18 . . . insisting on pious **s** or the
Col 2:23 . . . devotion, pious **s**, and severe

SELF-DISCIPLINE (n) correction or regulation of oneself for the sake of improvement
2 Tim 1:7 . . . but of power, love, and **s**.

SELF-INDULGENCE (n) excessive or unrestrained gratification of one's own appetites, desires, or whims
Matt 23:25 . . . full of greed and **s**!

SELFISH (adj) seeking or concentrating on one's own advantage, pleasure, or well-being without regard for others
Matt 16:24 . . . turn from your **s** ways,
Luke 9:23 . . . turn from your **s** ways,
Gal 5:20 . . . of anger, **s** ambition,
Phil 1:17 . . . They preach with **s** ambition,
Jas 3:14 . . . and there is **s** ambition in
Jas 3:16 . . . is jealousy and **s** ambition,

SELFISHNESS (n) the act of being concerned only with oneself
2 Cor 12:20 . . . jealousy, anger, **s**, slander
Jas 3:15 . . . jealousy and **s** are not God's kind

SELL, SELLING (v) to give up (property) to another for something of value (as money)
see also SOLD
Prov 23:23 . . . truth and never **s** it;
Prov 31:24 . . . and sashes to **s** to the
Mark 10:21 . . . and **s** all your possessions
Luke 17:28 . . . buying and **s-ing**, farming and
Rev 13:17 . . . could buy or **s** anything

SEND, SENDING (v) to direct, order, or request to go
see also SENT
Isa 6:8 . . . Here I am. **S** me.
Isa 55:11 . . . with my word. I **s** it out,
Mal 3:1 . . . I am **s-ing** my messenger,
Matt 9:38 . . . ask him to **s** more workers
Mark 1:2 . . . I am **s-ing** my messenger
1 Cor 1:17 . . . For Christ didn't **s** me to

SENSE (n) sound and prudent judgment based on a simple perception of the situation or facts; intelligence
Prov 3:21 . . . common **s** and discernment.
Prov 8:14 . . . Common **s** and success
Prov 12:11 . . . chases fantasies has no **s**.
Prov 15:21 . . . brings joy to those with no **s**;
Prov 18:1 . . . they lash out at common **s**.
Prov 24:30 . . . of one with no common **s**.

SENSIBLE (adj) having, containing, or indicative of good sense or reason; rational, reasonable
Prov 10:23 . . . brings pleasure to the **s**.
Prov 11:12 . . . a **s** person keeps quiet.
Prov 15:21 . . . **s** person stays on the right
Matt 24:45 . . . A faithful, **s** servant is one

SENSITIVE (adj) highly responsive or susceptible
Rom 15:1 . . . those who are **s** about things

SENT (v) *see also* SEND
Exod 3:14 . . . I AM has **s** me
Matt 10:40 . . . the Father who **s** me.
Luke 10:16 . . . God, who **s** me.
John 3:17 . . . God **s** his Son into the
John 20:21 . . . As the Father has **s** me, so
Rom 8:3 . . . He **s** his own Son in a
Rom 10:15 . . . them without being **s**?
Gal 4:4 . . . time came, God **s** his Son,

SEPARATE, SEPARATED, SEPARATES (v) to set or keep apart; to sort
Prov 17:9 . . . on it **s-s** close friends.
Matt 25:32 . . . a shepherd **s-s** the sheep
Rom 8:35 . . . Can anything ever **s** us
Eph 2:14 . . . of hostility that **s-d** us.
Col 1:21 . . . his enemies, **s-d** from him

SERAPHIM (n) six-winged angels standing in the presence of God
Isa 6:2 . . . were mighty **s**, each having
Isa 6:6 . . . Then one of the **s** flew to me

SERIOUSNESS (n) a sober attitude
Titus 2:7 . . . the integrity and **s** of your

SERPENT (n) a snake or crawling reptile often associated with temptation, sin, and evil; Satan
Gen 3:1 . . . The **s** was the shrewdest of
Isa 27:1 . . . **s**, the coiling, writhing **s**.
2 Cor 11:3 . . . the cunning ways of the **s**.
Rev 12:9 . . . the ancient **s** called the devil,
Rev 20:2 . . . that old **s**, who is the devil,

SERVANT, SERVANTS (n) one who performs tasks under the direction of another *see also* SLAVE(S)
Exod 14:31 . . . LORD and in his **s** Moses.
Lev 25:55 . . . They are my **s-s**, whom I
1 Sam 3:10 . . . Speak, your **s** is listening.
2 Kgs 17:13 . . . my **s-s** the prophets.
Job 1:8 . . . Have you noticed my **s** Job?
Ps 19:13 . . . Keep your **s** from deliberate
Ps 31:16 . . . your favor shine on your **s**.
Ps 89:3 . . . with David, my chosen **s**.
Ps 104:4 . . . flames of fire are your **s-s**.
Prov 14:35 . . . king rejoices in wise **s-s**
Prov 17:2 . . . A wise **s** will rule
Prov 22:7 . . . so the borrower is **s** to the
Prov 31:15 . . . work for her **s** girls.
Eccl 7:21 . . . may hear your **s** curse you.
Eccl 10:7 . . . seen **s-s** riding horseback
Isa 53:11 . . . my righteous **s** will make it
Isa 65:8 . . . I still have true **s-s** there.
Zech 3:8 . . . to bring my **s**, the Branch.
Mal 1:6 . . . father, and a **s** respects his
Matt 20:26 . . . among you must be your **s**,
Matt 24:45 . . . faithful, sensible **s** is one
Luke 1:48 . . . of his lowly **s** girl, and
Luke 17:10 . . . We are unworthy **s-s** who
Luke 22:26 . . . leader should be like a **s**.
John 12:26 . . . because my **s-s** must be
Rom 13:4 . . . authorities are God's **s-s**,
1 Cor 3:5 . . . are only God's **s-s** through
Col 1:23 . . . God's **s** to proclaim it.
1 Tim 4:6 . . . be a worthy **s** of Christ
Heb 1:7 . . . his **s-s** like flames of fire.
Heb 1:14 . . . angels are only **s-s**—spirits

SERVE, SERVED, SERVES, SERVING (v) to meet the needs of and subject one's will to that of another
Deut 10:12 . . . love him and **s** him with
Deut 11:13 . . . your God and **s** him with
Deut 28:47 . . . If you do not **s** the LORD
Deut 30:17 . . . drawn away to **s** and
Josh 24:15 . . . family, we will **s** the LORD.
2 Chr 12:8 . . . between **s-ing** me and
Ps 34:22 . . . redeem those who **s** him.
Ps 101:6 . . . be allowed to **s** me.
Ps 103:21 . . . of angels who **s** him and do
Isa 38:3 . . . have **s-d** you single-mindedly
Dan 3:17 . . . the God whom we **s** is able to
Matt 4:10 . . . your God and **s** only him.
Matt 6:24 . . . No one can **s** two masters.
Matt 20:28 . . . not to be **s-d** but to **s**
Luke 22:27 . . . among you as one who **s-s**.
John 12:2 . . . Martha **s-d**, and Lazarus was
John 12:26 . . . honor anyone who **s-s** me.
Acts 17:25 . . . hands can't **s** his needs—
Rom 1:25 . . . worshiped and **s-d** the things
Rom 12:7 . . . your gift is **s-ing** others, **s**
Rom 12:11 . . . work hard and **s** the Lord
Rom 13:6 . . . They are **s-ing** God in what
Rom 14:18 . . . If you **s** Christ with
Rom 16:18 . . . people are not **s-ing** Christ
1 Cor 16:18 . . . to all who **s** so well.
Gal 5:13 . . . your freedom to **s** one another
Col 3:24 . . . Master you are **s-ing** is Christ.
1 Tim 5:10 . . . kind to strangers and **s-d** other
1 Pet 5:5 . . . all of you, **s** each other in

SERVICE (n) employment as a servant; the work performed by one that serves
Num 8:11 . . . dedicating them to the LORD's **s**.
Luke 12:35 . . . Be dressed for **s** and keep
Rom 15:17 . . . through me in my **s** to God.
1 Cor 12:5 . . . different kinds of **s**, but we

SET APART (v) to reserve for a particular use
Exod 16:23 . . . holy Sabbath day **s** for the Lord
Deut 14:2 . . . **s** as holy to the Lord
Heb 7:26 . . . been **s** from sinners

SEVEN (adj) of or relating to the number 7
Josh 6:4 . . . around the town **s** times, with
Prov 6:16 . . . LORD hates—no, **s** things
Prov 24:16 . . . godly may trip **s** times,
Isa 4:1 . . . so few men will be left that **s**
Luke 11:26 . . . spirit finds **s** other spirits
Rev 1:4 . . . John to the **s** churches in the
Rev 6:1 . . . first of the **s** seals on the
Rev 8:2 . . . were given **s** trumpets.
Rev 10:4 . . . what the **s** thunders said,
Rev 15:7 . . . handed each of the **s** angels

SEVEN (n) the number 7
Dan 9:26 . . . period of sixty-two sets of **s**,

SEVENFOLD (adj) having seven units or members
Rev 4:5 . . . This is the **s** Spirit of God.

SEVENTH (adj) of or relating to the number seven
Gen 2:2 . . . On the **s** day God
Exod 20:10 . . . the **s** day is a Sabbath day
Exod 23:11 . . . uncultivated during the **s**
Exod 23:12 . . . but on the **s** day you must
Heb 4:4 . . . On the **s** day God rested

SEVENTY (adj) of or relating to the number 70
Dan 9:24 . . . A period of **s** sets of seven

SEVERE (adj) strict in judgment, discipline, or government; inflicting physical discomfort or hardship
Rom 11:22 . . . God is both kind and **s**.
1 Thes 1:6 . . . in spite of the **s** suffering

SEWED (v) to unite or fasten by stitches
Gen 3:7 . . . So they **s** fig leaves together

SEXUAL (adj) of, relating to, or associated with sex or the sexes; having or involving sex
Exod 22:19 . . . who has **s** relations with
Lev 18:6 . . . never have **s** relations with
Num 25:1 . . . by having **s** relations with
Matt 1:25 . . . did not have **s** relations with
Matt 15:19 . . . adultery, all **s** immorality,
Acts 15:20 . . . to idols, from **s** immorality,
1 Cor 5:1 . . . about the **s** immorality going
1 Cor 5:11 . . . yet indulges in **s** sin
1 Cor 6:9 . . . who indulge in **s** sin, or who
1 Cor 6:18 . . . Run from **s** sin! No other
1 Cor 7:1 . . . to abstain from **s** relations.
1 Cor 10:8 . . . not engage in **s** immorality
2 Cor 12:21 . . . impurity, **s** immorality,
Eph 5:3 . . . be no **s** immorality, impurity,
Col 3:5 . . . nothing to do with **s** immorality,
1 Thes 4:3 . . . stay away from all **s** sin
2 Pet 2:10 . . . own twisted **s** desire, and
2 Pet 2:18 . . . to twisted **s** desires,
Rev 2:14 . . . and by committing **s** sin.
Rev 2:20 . . . teaches them to commit **s** sin

SEXUALLY (adv) of, relating to, or associated with sex or the sexes; having or involving sex
1 Tim 1:10 . . . The law is for people who are **s** immoral
Rev 22:15 . . . the sorcerers, the **s** immoral,

SHADE (n) a place sheltered from the sun
Ps 121:5 . . . you as your protective **s**.

SHADOW, SHADOWS (n) shelter from danger or observation; an imperfect and faint representation; partial darkness or obscurity within a part of space
Ps 17:8 . . . me in the **s** of your wings.
Ps 36:7 . . . shelter in the **s** of your
Ps 39:6 . . . are merely moving **s-s**, and
Ps 91:1 . . . find rest in the **s** of the
Col 2:17 . . . these rules are only **s-s** of
Heb 8:5 . . . only a copy, a **s** of the real
Heb 10:1 . . . was only a **s**, a dim preview

SHADOWBOXING (v) to box with an imaginary opponent especially as a form of training
1 Cor 9:26 . . . I am not just **s**.

SHAKE, SHAKEN, SHAKING (v) to move to and fro or up and down; to cause to quake, quiver, or tremble; to weaken
Ps 16:8 . . . I will not be **s-n**, for he
Ps 22:7 . . . They sneer and **s** their heads,
Ps 62:2 . . . where I will never be **s-n**.
Ps 64:8 . . . see them will **s** their heads
Isa 28:16 . . . believes need never be **s-n**.
Ezek 38:19 . . . I promise a mighty **s-ing** in the
Hag 2:6 . . . I will again **s** the heavens
Matt 24:29 . . . the heavens will be **s-n**.
Mark 15:29 . . . abuse, **s-ing** their heads
Luke 6:38 . . . pressed down, **s-n** together to
Acts 2:25 . . . I will not be **s-n**, for he is
2 Thes 2:2 . . . be so easily **s-n** or alarmed
Heb 12:26 . . . again I will **s** not only
Heb 12:27 . . . will be **s-n** and removed,

SHAME (n) a condition or feeling of humiliating disgrace or disrepute; something that brings censure and reproach
Lev 19:12 . . . Do not bring **s** on the name
Ps 34:5 . . . no shadow of **s** will darken
Prov 28:7 . . . wild friends bring **s** to
Dan 12:2 . . . some to **s** and everlasting
Titus 2:5 . . . not bring **s** on the word
Heb 6:6 . . . holding him up to public **s**.
1 Jn 2:28 . . . shrink back from him in **s**.

SHAME (v) to disgrace
1 Cor 1:27 . . . in order to **s** those who
1 Cor 11:22 . . . church and **s** the poor?

SHAMEFUL (adj) bringing shame
Prov 18:13 . . . facts is both **s** and foolish.
Hab 2:15 . . . over their **s** nakedness.
Rom 1:24 . . . do whatever **s** things their
Rom 1:27 . . . Men did **s** things with
2 Cor 4:2 . . . We reject all **s** deeds
2 Pet 2:2 . . . teaching and **s** immorality.

SHARE (n) a portion belonging to or due to
Deut 10:9 . . . Levites have no **s** of property
2 Kgs 2:9 . . . inherit a double **s** of your
Matt 21:34 . . . to collect his **s** of the crop.
Rev 22:19 . . . remove that person's **s** in

SHARE, SHARED, SHARING (v) to grant or give a share in; to partake of, use, experience, occupy, or enjoy with others; to have in common
Gen 21:10 . . . to **s** the inheritance
1 Sam 30:24 . . . We **s** and **s** alike—
Ps 41:9 . . . the one who **s-d** my food,
Luke 3:11 . . . If you have food, **s** it with
Acts 2:42 . . . fellowship, and to **s-ing** in
Acts 2:45 . . . possessions and **s-d** the
Rom 8:17 . . . we must also **s** his suffering.
Rom 11:31 . . . they, too, will **s** in God's
1 Cor 10:16 . . . aren't we **s-ing** in the blood
1 Cor 12:13 . . . we all **s** the same Spirit.
2 Cor 1:7 . . . as you **s** in our sufferings,
2 Cor 9:8 . . . left over to **s** with others.
Gal 4:30 . . . will not **s** the inheritance
Gal 6:6 . . . teachers, **s-ing** all good things
Phil 3:10 . . . suffer with him, **s-ing** in his
Col 1:12 . . . has enabled you to **s** in the
1 Thes 2:8 . . . much that we **s-d** with you
2 Thes 2:14 . . . you can **s** in the glory
1 Tim 6:18 . . . ready to **s** with others.
Heb 6:4 . . . and **s-d** in the Holy Spirit,
Heb 12:10 . . . we might **s** in his holiness.
Heb 13:16 . . . to **s** with those in need.
Rev 3:20 . . . and we will **s** a meal together

SHARPENS (v) to make sharp or sharper
Prov 27:17 . . . As iron **s** iron, so a

SHAVED, SHAVING (v) to sever the hair from (the skin) close to the roots
Judg 16:17 . . . my head were **s**, my strength
1 Cor 11:5 . . . the same as **s-ing** her head.
1 Cor 11:6 . . . her hair cut or her head **s**,

SHEARERS (n) one who cuts or clips (as hair or wool) from someone or something
Isa 53:7 . . . silent before the **s**, he did
Acts 8:32 . . . silent before the **s**, he did

SHED, SHEDDING (v) to spill; to cause to flow
1 Chr 22:8 . . . you have **s** so much blood
Ps 106:38 . . . They **s** innocent blood,
Rom 3:25 . . . his life, **s-ding** his blood.
Heb 9:22 . . . without the **s-ding** of blood,
1 Jn 5:6 . . . by **s-ding** his blood on the cross
Rev 16:6 . . . they **s** the blood of your holy people

SHEEP (n) a small domesticated animal, representing wealth and livelihood for many Israelites; figurative of God's people
Gen 22:8 . . . God will provide a **s** for
Num 27:17 . . . not be like **s** without a
Deut 17:1 . . . defective cattle, **s**, or
1 Sam 15:14 . . . bleating of **s** and goats
Ps 44:22 . . . being slaughtered like **s**.
Ps 78:52 . . . people like a flock of **s**,
Ps 100:3 . . . We are his people, the **s**
Ps 119:176 . . . wandered away like a lost **s**;
Isa 53:7 . . . as a **s** is silent before
Jer 50:6 . . . people have been lost **s**.
Matt 7:15 . . . disguised as harmless **s** but
Matt 9:36 . . . like **s** without a shepherd.
Matt 10:16 . . . you out as **s** among wolves.
Matt 12:11 . . . a **s** that fell into a well
Matt 25:32 . . . separates the **s** from the
John 10:3 . . . calls his own **s** by name
John 10:7 . . . I am the gate for the **s**.
John 10:15 . . . sacrifice my life for the **s**.
John 21:17 . . . Then feed my **s**.
1 Pet 2:25 . . . were like **s** who wandered

SHEEPFOLD (n) a pen or shelter for sheep
John 10:1 . . . sneaks over the wall of a **s**,

SHELTER, SHELTERS (n) something that covers or affords protection
see also REFUGE
Lev 23:34 . . . the Festival of **S-s** on the
Deut 16:16 . . . the Festival of **S-s**.
Ps 9:9 . . . LORD is a **s** for the
Ps 31:20 . . . hide them in the **s** of your
Ps 36:7 . . . All humanity finds **s** in the
Ps 61:4 . . . safe beneath the **s** of your
Isa 4:6 . . . will be a **s** from daytime heat
Isa 32:2 . . . be like a **s** from the wind
Isa 58:7 . . . give **s** to the homeless.
Zech 14:16 . . . the Festival of **S-s**.

SHEPHERD, SHEPHERDS (n) a person who tends sheep; figurative of political and religious leaders, especially those who care for God's people
Gen 48:15 . . . has been my **s** all my life,
Gen 49:24 . . . by the **S**, the Rock of Israel.
Num 27:17 . . . be like sheep without a **s**.
2 Sam 7:7 . . . tribal leaders, the **s-s** of my
1 Kgs 22:17 . . . like sheep without a **s**.
Ps 23:1 . . . The LORD is my **s**;
Ps 28:9 . . . Lead them like a **s**, and
Isa 40:11 . . . feed his flock like a **s**.
Jer 23:1 . . . my people—the **s-s** of my
Jer 31:10 . . . as a **s** does his flock.
Ezek 34:5 . . . scattered without a **s**, and
Ezek 34:8 . . . you were my **s-s**, you didn't
Ezek 34:12 . . . like a **s** looking for his
Zech 11:9 . . . won't be your **s** any longer.
Zech 13:7 . . . Strike down the **s**, and
Matt 2:6 . . . will be the **s** for my people
Matt 9:36 . . . like sheep without a **s**.
Matt 26:31 . . . God will strike the **S**,
John 10:11 . . . I am the good **s**.
Heb 13:20 . . . Jesus, the great **S** of the
Jude 1:12 . . . are like shameless **s-s** who care
Rev 7:17 . . . on the throne will be their **S**.

SHEWBREAD (KJV)
Exod 25:30 . . . Place the *Bread of the Presence*
Num 4:7 . . . where the *Bread of the Presence* is
1 Chr 23:29 . . . in charge of the *sacred bread*
Matt 12:4 . . . eating the *sacred loaves of bread*
Heb 9:2 . . . and *sacred loaves of bread* on the

SHIELD (n) a broad piece of defensive armor carried on the arm; one that protects or defends
2 Sam 22:3 . . . He is my **s**, the power that
2 Sam 22:36 . . . me your **s** of victory;
Ps 3:3 . . . LORD, are a **s** around me;
Ps 5:12 . . . them with your **s** of love.
Ps 7:10 . . . God is my **s**, saving those
Ps 18:2 . . . He is my **s**, the power that
Ps 28:7 . . . LORD is my strength and **s**.
Ps 33:20 . . . is our help and our **s**.
Ps 35:2 . . . armor, and take up your **s**.
Ps 84:11 . . . God is our sun and our **s**.
Ps 119:114 . . . are my refuge and my **s**;
Ps 144:2 . . . He is my **s**, and I take refuge
Prov 2:7 . . . He is a **s** to those who walk
Eph 6:16 . . . hold up the **s** of faith

SHINE, SHINES, SHINING (v) to emit rays of light; to be eminent, conspicuous, or distinguished; to have a bright, glowing appearance
see also SHONE
Ps 37:6 . . . of your cause will **s** like
Ps 50:2 . . . God **s-s** in glorious radiance.
Ps 112:4 . . . Light **s-s** in the darkness for
Ps 118:27 . . . LORD is God, **s-ing** upon us.
Isa 60:1 . . . Let your light **s** for all
Ezek 1:27 . . . like a burning flame, **s-ing**
Dan 12:3 . . . righteousness will **s** like
Matt 13:43 . . . the righteous will **s** like
John 1:5 . . . The light **s-s** in the darkness,
2 Cor 4:6 . . . has made this light **s** in
Phil 2:15 . . . of God, **s-ing** like bright lights

SHIP (n) a large seagoing vessel
Prov 31:14 . . . a merchant's **s**, bringing

SHIPWRECK, SHIPWRECKED (v) to destroy (a ship) by grounding or foundering
2 Cor 11:25 . . . Three times I was **s-ed**.
1 Tim 1:19 . . . their faith has been **s-ed**.
Jude 1:12 . . . reefs that can **s** you.

SHONE (v) *see also* SHINE
Matt 17:2 . . . his face **s** like the sun,
Rev 21:11 . . . It **s** with the glory of God

SHOP (n) a handicraft establishment; workshop
Jer 18:2 . . . Go down to the potter's **s**,

SHORT (adj) brief; not coming up to a measure or requirement
Ps 89:47 . . . Remember how **s** my life is,
Rom 3:23 . . . all fall **s** of God's glorious
1 Cor 7:29 . . . time that remains is very **s**.

SHORT-LIVED (adj) not living or lasting long
Job 20:5 . . . of the wicked has been **s**

SHORT-TEMPERED (adj) having a quick temper
Prov 14:17 . . . **S** people do foolish things,

SHOULDERS (n) the place on the human body where the arm is joined to the trunk
Isa 9:6 . . . government will rest on his **s**.
Luke 15:5 . . . carry it home on his **s**.

SHOUT, SHOUTED, SHOUTING (v) to utter a loud cry or in a loud voice
Job 38:7 . . . all the angels **s-ed** for joy?
Ps 95:1 . . . Let us **s** joyfully to
Ps 100:1 . . . **S** with joy to the LORD,
Isa 12:6 . . . people of Jerusalem **s** his
Isa 40:3 . . . someone **s-ing**, "Clear the way
Isa 40:9 . . . news, **s** from the mountaintops!
Isa 42:2 . . . He will not **s** or raise his
Zech 9:9 . . . people of Zion! **S** in triumph,
Matt 3:3 . . . a voice **s-ing** in the wilderness,
Matt 10:27 . . . **s** from the housetops for

SHOW (n) an impressive display
Matt 23:5 . . . Everything they do is for **s**.

SHOW, SHOWED, SHOWN, SHOWS (v) to cause or permit to be seen; to point out; to reveal or demonstrate; to bestow
Exod 33:18 . . . Then **s** me your glorious
2 Sam 22:26 . . . To the faithful you **s**
Neh 9:19 . . . pillar of fire **s-ed** them the
Ps 4:6 . . . Who will **s** us better times?
Ps 16:11 . . . You will **s** me the way
Ps 119:132 . . . Come and **s** me your
Prov 3:6 . . . he will **s** you which path
Prov 24:23 . . . wrong to **s** favoritism
Eccl 9:1 . . . God will **s** them favor.
Isa 30:18 . . . so he can **s** you his love

Hos 6:6 . . . I want you to **s** love, not
Zech 7:9 . . . Judge fairly, and **s** mercy
Luke 24:40 . . . **s-ed** them his hands and his
Acts 2:28 . . . You have **s-n** me the way
Acts 10:34 . . . that God **s-s** no favoritism.
Rom 3:20 . . . The law simply **s-s** us how
Rom 3:21 . . . But now God has **s-n** us a way
Rom 5:8 . . . God **s-ed** his great love for us
Rom 9:22 . . . the right to **s** his anger
Eph 2:7 . . . as **s-n** in all he has done
Jas 2:18 . . . I will **s** you my faith
1 Jn 4:9 . . . God **s-ed** how much he loved

SHOWER, SHOWERED (v) to give in abundance
Hos 10:12 . . . come and **s** righteousness
2 Cor 1:5 . . . more God will **s** us with
Eph 1:8 . . . He has **s-ed** his kindness

SHOWERS (n) something resembling a rain shower
Ezek 34:26 . . . will be **s** of blessing.

SHREWD, SHREWDEST (adj) marked by clever discerning awareness and hardheaded acumen
Gen 3:1 . . . serpent was the **s-est** of all
Matt 10:16 . . . So be as **s** as snakes

SHRINK (v) to become smaller or more compacted
Matt 9:16 . . . new patch would **s** and rip

SHUT (v) to close
Isa 6:10 . . . their ears and **s** their eyes.
Dan 6:22 . . . his angel to **s** the lions'
Amos 5:13 . . . keep their mouths **s**, for it
Heb 11:33 . . . They **s** the mouths of lions,

SICK (adj) affected with disease or ill health; lacking vigor
Ps 41:3 . . . when they are **s** and restores
Prov 13:12 . . . deferred makes the heart **s**,
Matt 9:12 . . . need a doctor—**s** people do.
Matt 10:8 . . . Heal the **s**, raise the dead,
Matt 25:36 . . . I was **s**, and you cared for
Mark 3:10 . . . all the **s** people eagerly
1 Cor 11:30 . . . many of you are weak and **s**
Jas 5:14 . . . Are any of you **s?**

SICKLE (n) a small hand tool with a curved metal blade used for cutting stalks of grain
Joel 3:13 . . . Swing the **s**, for the
Rev 14:14 . . . a sharp **s** in his hand.

SICKNESS, SICKNESSES (n) a disordered, weakened, or unsound condition; illness
Matt 4:24 . . . whatever their **s** or disease,
Matt 8:17 . . . He took our **s-es** and removed

SIDE (n) the right or left part of the trunk of the body
John 20:20 . . . in his hands and his **s.**

SIGHT (n) mental or spiritual perception; the act of beholding
Ps 51:4 . . . done what is evil in your **s.**
Hab 1:13 . . . cannot stand the **s** of evil.
Jas 1:27 . . . religion in the **s** of God

SIGN, SIGNS (n) something indicating the presence or existence of something else; something material or external that stands for or signifies something spiritual
Gen 9:12 . . . you a **s** of my covenant
Gen 17:11 . . . your foreskin as a **s** of
Ps 105:27 . . . performed miraculous **s-s**
Isa 55:13 . . . be an everlasting **s** of
Dan 6:27 . . . he performs miraculous **s-s** and
Matt 12:38 . . . a miraculous **s** to prove
Matt 24:3 . . . What **s** will signal your
Matt 24:30 . . . the **s** that the Son of Man
Mark 16:17 . . . These miraculous **s-s** will
Luke 11:29 . . . them is the **s** of Jonah.
John 3:2 . . . Your miraculous **s-s** are
John 20:30 . . . do many other miraculous **s-s**
1 Cor 14:22 . . . in tongues is a **s**, not for
2 Cor 12:12 . . . did many **s-s** and wonders
2 Thes 2:9 . . . counterfeit power and **s-s**

SIGNAL (n) something (as a sound, gesture, or object) that conveys notice or warning
Num 10:5 . . . you sound the **s** to move on,

SILENCE (n) absence of speech, sound, or noise
Ps 39:2 . . . I stood there in **s**—not even
Rev 8:1 . . . there was **s** throughout heaven

SILENCE, SILENCED, SILENCING (v) to compel or reduce to silence; to cause to cease criticism
Ps 8:2 . . . your strength, **s-ing** your enemies
Titus 1:11 . . . They must be **s-d**, because they
1 Pet 2:15 . . . honorable lives should **s**

SILENT (adj) mute, speechless; still
Ps 30:12 . . . praises to you and not be **s.**
Isa 53:7 . . . as a sheep is **s** before the
Isa 62:1 . . . Jerusalem, I cannot remain **s.**
Hab 2:20 . . . the earth be **s** before him.
Acts 8:32 . . . And as a lamb is **s** before
Acts 18:9 . . . Speak out! Don't be **s!**
1 Cor 14:34 . . . Women should be **s** during

SILVER (adj) made of silver
Prov 25:11 . . . apples in a **s** basket.
Dan 2:32 . . . and arms were **s**, its belly

SILVER (n) a silvery-white metal valued next to gold, capable of a high polish; coin made of silver
Ps 66:10 . . . have purified us like **s.**
Prov 3:14 . . . is more profitable than **s**,
Prov 8:10 . . . instruction rather than **s**,
Prov 22:1 . . . is better than **s** or gold.
Isa 48:10 . . . but not as **s** is refined.
Zech 11:12 . . . wages thirty pieces of **s.**
Zech 13:9 . . . refine them like **s** and
Matt 25:15 . . . two bags of **s** to another,
Matt 26:15 . . . gave him thirty pieces of **s.**
Luke 7:41 . . . 500 pieces of **s** to one
Acts 3:6 . . . don't have any **s** or gold
1 Cor 3:12 . . . materials—gold, **s**, jewels,

SILVERSMITH (n) an artisan who makes articles of silver
Acts 19:24 . . . with Demetrius, a **s** who had

SIMON 1. One of the 12 disciples, Simon Peter (Matt 16:16); *see* PETER.
2. One of the 12 disciples, Simon the Zealot (Matt 10:4; Mark 3:18; Luke 6:15; Acts 1:13).
3. Simon the sorcerer, rebuked by Peter (Acts 8:9-24).
4. Simon who had leprosy (Matt 26:6; Mark 14:3).

SIMPLE (n) a person lacking in knowledge or expertise
Ps 19:7 . . . trustworthy, making wise the **s.**

SIMPLEMINDED (adj) foolish
Prov 19:25 . . . the **s** will learn a lesson;

SIN, SINS (n) moral evil; transgression of or rebellion against God's laws
Gen 4:7 . . . **S** is crouching at the door,
Lev 5:5 . . . ways, you must confess your **s.**
Num 32:23 . . . be sure that your **s** will find
Deut 24:16 . . . to death for the **s-s** of their
Ps 19:13 . . . servant from deliberate **s-s!**
Ps 32:1 . . . whose **s** is put out of sight!
Ps 38:18 . . . I confess my **s-s**; I am deeply
Ps 51:1 . . . blot out the stain of my **s-s.**
Ps 51:2 . . . Purify me from my **s.**
Ps 65:3 . . . we are overwhelmed by our **s-s**,
Ps 79:9 . . . Save us and forgive our **s-s**
Ps 103:12 . . . removed our **s-s** as far from
Prov 5:22 . . . held captive by his own **s-s;**
Prov 10:19 . . . Too much talk leads to **s.**
Prov 14:21 . . . **s** to belittle one's neighbor;
Prov 17:19 . . . who loves to quarrel loves **s;**
Prov 28:13 . . . who conceal their **s-s** will
Prov 29:22 . . . commits all kinds of **s.**
Isa 1:18 . . . your **s-s** are like scarlet,
Isa 53:6 . . . laid on him the **s-s** of us all.
Isa 59:2 . . . Because of your **s-s**, he has
Jer 31:30 . . . die for their own **s-s**—
Jer 31:34 . . . again remember their **s-s.**
Ezek 18:19 . . . pay for the parent's **s-s?**
Matt 1:21 . . . save his people from their **s-s.**
Matt 6:12 . . . forgive us our **s-s**, as we
Matt 26:28 . . . to forgive the **s-s** of many.
Mark 3:29 . . . This is a **s** with eternal
Luke 5:24 . . . on earth to forgive **s-s.**
John 1:29 . . . takes away the **s** of the world!
John 20:23 . . . forgive anyone's **s-s**, they
Acts 2:38 . . . repent of your **s-s** and turn
Rom 4:25 . . . because of our **s-s**, and he
Rom 6:2 . . . we have died to **s**, how can
Rom 6:11 . . . the power of **s** and alive to
Rom 6:23 . . . the wages of **s** is death,
Rom 7:7 . . . law that showed me my **s.**
Rom 7:25 . . . nature I am a slave to **s.**
1 Cor 6:18 . . . is a **s** against your own body.
1 Cor 15:3 . . . died for our **s-s**, just as
1 Cor 15:56 . . . the law gives **s** its power.
Gal 1:4 . . . gave his life for our **s-s**, just
Gal 6:1 . . . believer is overcome by some **s**,
Eph 2:5 . . . were dead because of our **s-s**,
1 Tim 5:22 . . . share in the **s-s** of others.
Heb 2:17 . . . would take away the **s-s** of
Heb 9:28 . . . to take away the **s-s** of many
Heb 10:12 . . . sacrifice for **s-s**, good for
Heb 12:1 . . . the **s** that so easily trips
Jas 1:15 . . . when **s** is allowed to grow,
Jas 4:17 . . . is **s** to know what you ought
Jas 5:16 . . . Confess your **s-s** to each other
1 Pet 2:24 . . . carried our **s-s** in his body
1 Pet 3:18 . . . suffered for our **s-s** once for
1 Jn 1:8 . . . claim we have no **s**, we are
1 Jn 1:9 . . . to forgive us our **s-s** and to
1 Jn 2:1 . . . if anyone does **s**, we have
1 Jn 3:5 . . . take away our **s-s**, and
1 Jn 3:5 . . . there is no **s** in him.
1 Jn 5:16 . . . a **s** that leads to death,
Rev 1:5 . . . from our **s-s** by shedding his

SIN, SINNED, SINNING, SINS (v) to commit an offense or fault against God; to break God's law
Exod 20:20 . . . will keep you from **s-ning!**
2 Sam 12:13 . . . I have **s-ned** against the
2 Chr 6:37 . . . We have **s-ned**, done evil,
Job 1:5 . . . my children have **s-ned**
Ps 51:4 . . . and you alone, have I **s-ned;**
Ps 119:11 . . . I might not **s** against you.
Jer 14:20 . . . all have **s-ned** against you.
Dan 9:5 . . . have **s-ned** and done wrong.
Mark 9:43 . . . causes you to **s**, cut it off.
Luke 15:18 . . . I have **s-ned** against both
Luke 17:3 . . . another believer **s-s**, rebuke
John 8:7 . . . who has never **s-ned** throw
John 8:11 . . . Go and **s** no more.
Rom 1:30 . . . invent new ways of **s-ning**,
Rom 3:23 . . . everyone has **s-ned**; we all
Rom 5:12 . . . When Adam **s-ned**, **s** entered
Rom 14:23 . . . is not right, you are **s-ning.**
1 Cor 15:34 . . . is right, and stop **s-ning.**
Heb 4:15 . . . we do, yet he did not **s.**
Heb 10:26 . . . deliberately continue **s-ning**
1 Pet 2:22 . . . He never **s-ned**, nor ever

1 Jn 1:10 . . . we have not **s-ned,** we are
1 Jn 3:6 . . . who keeps on **s-ning** does not
1 Jn 5:18 . . . not make a practice of **s-ning,**

SINCERE (adj) genuine, having no intention to deceive
Prov 27:6 . . . Wounds from a **s** friend are better
2 Cor 6:6 . . . Spirit within us, and by our **s** love.
Jas 3:17 . . . no favoritism and is always **s.**
1 Pet 1:22 . . . show **s** love to each other

SINFUL (adj) tainted with, marked by, or full of sin; wicked
Lev 5:1 . . . is **s** to refuse to testify,
1 Sam 15:23 . . . is as **s** as witchcraft,
Luke 11:13 . . . So if you **s** people know
Rom 5:20 . . . could see how **s** they were.
Rom 7:5 . . . harvest of **s** deeds, resulting
Rom 7:18 . . . is, in my **s** nature.
Rom 7:25 . . . because of my **s** nature I am
Rom 8:4 . . . follow our **s** nature but
Rom 8:13 . . . deeds of your **s** nature,
Gal 5:13 . . . to satisfy your **s** nature.
Col 2:11 . . . away of your **s** nature.

SINLESS (adj) having no moral blemish; having done nothing to incur the wrath of God
1 Pet 1:19 . . . the **s,** spotless Lamb of God.

SING, SINGING (v) to produce musical tones by means of the voice
Exod 15:1 . . . I will **s** to the LORD,
Ps 5:11 . . . let them **s** joyful praises
Ps 13:6 . . . I will **s** to the LORD
Ps 47:6 . . . to our King, **s** praises!
Ps 51:14 . . . I will joyfully **s** of
Ps 63:7 . . . my helper, I **s** for joy
Ps 69:30 . . . praise God's name with **s-ing,**
Ps 89:1 . . . I will **s** of the
Ps 95:1 . . . let us **s** to the LORD!
Ps 96:1 . . . **S** a new song to the LORD!
Ps 98:4 . . . praise and **s** for joy!
Ps 100:2 . . . Come before him, **s-ing** with
Ps 101:1 . . . I will **s** of your love
Ps 108:1 . . . can **s** your praises with all
Ps 147:1 . . . How good to **s** praises to
Isa 35:10 . . . enter Jerusalem **s-ing**
Jer 16:9 . . . to the happy **s-ing** and laughter
Acts 16:25 . . . praying and **s-ing** hymns
1 Cor 14:15 . . . I will also **s** in words
1 Cor 14:26 . . . one will **s,** another will
Col 3:16 . . . **S** psalms and hymns and
Rev 15:3 . . . And they were **s-ing** the song

SINGERS (n) one who sings
2 Chr 5:13 . . . trumpeters and **s** performed
Rev 18:22 . . . of harps, **s,** flutes,

SINNER, SINNERS (n) those guilty of sin
Ps 51:5 . . . I was born a **s**—yes,
Prov 1:10 . . . if **s-s** entice you, turn
Prov 23:17 . . . Don't envy **s-s,** but
Eccl 9:18 . . . one **s** can destroy much that
Isa 59:12 . . . we know what **s-s** we are.
Isa 64:5 . . . We are constant **s-s;** how
Matt 9:13 . . . who know they are **s-s.**
Luke 5:8 . . . I'm too much of a **s** to be
Luke 15:7 . . . over one lost **s** who repents
Luke 18:13 . . . to me, for I am a **s.**
Rom 4:5 . . . faith in God who forgives **s-s.**
Rom 5:6 . . . time and died for us **s-s.**
1 Tim 1:15 . . . into the world to save **s-s**
Jas 5:20 . . . whoever brings the **s** back
1 Pet 3:18 . . . he died for **s-s** to bring

SISTER, SISTERS (n) a female who has one or both parents in common with another; a fellow female Christian
Lev 18:9 . . . relations with your **s** or half
Matt 19:29 . . . or brothers or **s-s** or father
Mark 3:35 . . . my brother and **s** and
1 Tim 5:2 . . . as you would your own **s-s.**
Jas 2:1 . . . dear brothers and **s-s,** how can

SIT, SITS, SITTING (v) to place (the buttocks) on or in a seat
Ps 110:1 . . . to my Lord, "**S** in the place
Matt 19:28 . . . Son of Man **s-s** upon his
Matt 20:23 . . . to say who will **s** on my right
Col 3:1 . . . heaven, where Christ **s-s** in
Rev 3:21 . . . are victorious will **s** with me
Rev 4:9 . . . to the one **s-ting** on the throne

SKILL (n) a developed aptitude or ability
Heb 5:14 . . . have the **s** to recognize

SKILLED (adj) having acquired mastery of or skill in something
Ps 71:15 . . . I am not **s** with words.

SKILLFUL (adj) possessed of or displaying skill
1 Kgs 7:14 . . . was extremely **s** and talented
Ps 45:1 . . . the pen of a **s** poet.
Ps 78:72 . . . led them with **s** hands.

SKY, SKIES (n) the upper atmosphere appearing as a great vault or arch above the earth
Gen 1:8 . . . God called the space "**s.**"
Deut 33:26 . . . across the **s-ies** in majestic
Ps 19:1 . . . **s-ies** display his craftsmanship.
Prov 30:19 . . . eagle glides through the **s,**
Isa 34:4 . . . fall from the **s** like withered
Jer 33:22 . . . the stars of the **s** cannot
Matt 24:29 . . . will fall from the **s,**
Rev 20:11 . . . The earth and **s** fled from

SLANDER (n) the utterance of false charges or misrepresentations that defame and damage another's reputation
Matt 15:19 . . . theft, lying, and **s.**
Mark 7:22 . . . desires, envy, **s,** pride,
2 Cor 12:20 . . . selfishness, **s,** gossip,
Eph 4:31 . . . harsh words, and **s,** as
Col 3:8 . . . malicious behavior, **s,**

SLANDER, SLANDERED, SLANDERING (v) to utter slander; to malign or defame
Prov 10:18 . . . **s-ing** others makes you a
1 Tim 3:11 . . . must not **s** others.
2 Tim 3:3 . . . they will **s** others
Titus 2:3 . . . They must not **s** others
Titus 3:2 . . . They must not **s** anyone
2 Pet 2:2 . . . way of truth will be **s-ed.**

SLANDEROUS (adj) of, relating to, or marked by slander
Lev 19:16 . . . Do not spread **s** gossip

SLAUGHTER (n) the butchering of livestock for market or sacrifice
Isa 53:7 . . . led like a lamb to the **s.**
Jer 11:19 . . . lamb being led to the **s.**
Acts 8:32 . . . led like a sheep to the **s.**

SLAUGHTER, SLAUGHTERED (v) to discredit, defeat, or demolish completely; to kill in a bloody or violent manner
Hos 6:5 . . . to **s** you with my words,
Rev 5:6 . . . looked as if it had been **s-ed,**
Rev 5:12 . . . Lamb who was **s-ed**—to receive

SLAVE, SLAVES (n) a person bound in servitude; one who has lost his liberty and has no rights
see also SERVANT(S)
Matt 20:27 . . . must become your **s.**
John 8:34 . . . who sins is a **s** of sin.
John 15:15 . . . longer call you **s-s,** because
Rom 1:1 . . . is from Paul, a **s** of Christ
Rom 6:6 . . . are no longer **s-s** to sin.
Rom 6:16 . . . you become the **s** of whatever
Rom 6:22 . . . and have become **s-s** of God.
Rom 7:23 . . . makes me a **s** to the sin
1 Cor 6:12 . . . not become a **s** to anything.
1 Cor 9:19 . . . have become a **s** to all
1 Cor 12:13 . . . some are **s-s,** and some
Gal 3:28 . . . Jew or Gentile, **s** or free,
Gal 4:7 . . . no longer a **s** but God's own
Gal 4:8 . . . you were **s-s** to so-called gods
Gal 4:30 . . . rid of the **s** and her son,
Eph 6:5 . . . **S-s,** obey your earthly masters
Phil 2:7 . . . position of a **s** and was born
Col 3:11 . . . barbaric, uncivilized, **s,** or
Col 4:1 . . . be just and fair to your **s-s.**
1 Tim 1:10 . . . or are **s** traders, liars,
Titus 3:3 . . . became **s-s** to many lusts
Phlm 1:16 . . . no longer like a **s** to you.
2 Pet 2:19 . . . For you are a **s** to whatever

SLAVERY (n) submission to a dominating influence; the practice of slaveholding
Exod 2:23 . . . under their burden of **s.**
Rom 6:19 . . . the illustration of **s** to help

SLEEP (n) natural or induced state of rest; a state of lazy inactivity
Gen 2:21 . . . man to fall into a deep **s.**
Gen 15:12 . . . Abram fell into a deep **s,**
Prov 20:13 . . . If you love **s,** you will
Prov 23:21 . . . too much **s** clothes them
Rom 11:8 . . . has put them into a deep **s.**

SLEEP, SLEEPING, SLEEPS (v) to rest in a state of natural unconsciousness
Gen 28:11 . . . against and lay down to **s.**
Ps 4:8 . . . peace I will lie down and **s,**
Ps 121:4 . . . Israel never slumbers or **s-s.**
Prov 6:9 . . . how long will you **s?**
Eccl 5:12 . . . who work hard **s** well,
Mark 13:36 . . . find you **s-ing** when he

SLEEPER (n) one that sleeps
Eph 5:14 . . . said, "Awake, O **s,** rise up

SLEEPLESS (adj) affording no sleep
2 Cor 6:5 . . . exhaustion, endured **s** nights,

SLING (n) an instrument for throwing stones; slingshot
1 Sam 17:50 . . . with only a **s** and a stone,

SLOTHFUL(NESS) (KJV)
Prov 15:19 . . . *lazy* person's way is blocked
Prov 21:25 . . . the *lazy* will come to ruin,
Eccl 10:18 . . . *Laziness* leads to a sagging roof
Rom 12:11 . . . Never be *lazy,* but work hard
Heb 6:12 . . . *spiritually dull and indifferent*

SLUGGARD (KJV)
Prov 6:6 . . . a lesson from the ants, you *lazybones*
Prov 10:26 . . . *Lazy people* irritate their employers
Prov 13:4 . . . *Lazy people* want much but
Prov 20:4 . . . *Those too lazy* to plow
Prov 26:16 . . . *Lazy people* consider themselves smarter

SLUMBER (n) sleep
Prov 6:10 . . . a little more **s,** a little

SLY (adj) clever in concealing one's aims or ends
Prov 7:10 . . . dressed and **s** of heart.

SMALLEST (adj) of little consequence
Matt 5:18 . . . not even the **s** detail

SMASH, SMASHES (v) to break or crush by violence
Ps 2:9 . . . rod and **s** them like clay
Jer 23:29 . . . mighty hammer that **s-es** a rock

SMILE (v) to bestow approval
Num 6:25 . . . May the LORD **s** on you and
Ps 4:6 . . . Let your face **s** on us, LORD.
Ps 67:1 . . . May his face **s** with favor on

SMOKE (n) the gaseous products of burning materials
Exod 19:18 . . . The **s** billowed into the sky
Isa 6:4 . . . building was filled with **s.**
Joel 2:30 . . . and fire and columns of **s.**
Acts 2:19 . . . and fire and clouds of **s.**
Rev 9:2 . . . air turned dark from the **s.**
Rev 15:8 . . . filled with **s** from God's

SMOKE (v) to emit smoke
Ps 104:32 . . . the mountains **s** at his touch.

SMOOTH (adj) having a continuous, even surface
Jer 31:9 . . . **s** paths where they will not
Luke 3:5 . . . and the rough places made **s.**

SMOOTH (v) to make smooth
Isa 26:7 . . . you **s** out the path ahead
Isa 40:4 . . . and **s** out the rough places.

SNAKE, SNAKES (n) any of numerous limbless scaled reptiles; a worthless or treacherous person
Num 21:8 . . . replica of a poisonous **s** and
Prov 23:32 . . . it bites like a poisonous **s;**
Matt 10:16 . . . shrewd as **s-s** and harmless
Luke 3:7 . . . You brood of **s-s!** Who warned
John 3:14 . . . lifted up the bronze **s** on a
Rom 3:13 . . . **S** venom drips from their

SNARE, SNARES (n) something by which one is entangled, involved in difficulties, or impeded
Josh 23:13 . . . they will be a **s** and a trap
Eccl 7:26 . . . passion is a **s,** and her soft
Lam 4:20 . . . was caught in their **s-s.**
Rom 11:9 . . . table become a **s,** a trap that

SNOUT (n) a long projecting nose (as of swine)
Prov 11:22 . . . gold ring in a pig's **s.**

SNOW (n) precipitation in the form of small white ice crystals
Prov 25:13 . . . refresh like **s** in summer.
Isa 1:18 . . . will make them as white as **s.**
Dan 7:9 . . . clothing was as white as **s,**

SNUFFED (v) to extinguish
Prov 13:9 . . . wicked will be **s** out.

SOAP (n) a cleansing and emulsifying agent
Mal 3:2 . . . like a strong **s** that bleaches

SOAR, SOARING (v) to sail or hover in the air often at a great height
2 Sam 22:11 . . . flew, **s-ing** on the wings
Isa 40:31 . . . will **s** high on wings

SODOM (n) a city at the southern end of the Dead Sea destroyed because of its wickedness
Gen 13:12 . . . to a place near **S** and settled
Gen 19:24 . . . the sky on **S** and Gomorrah.
Isa 1:9 . . . have been wiped out like **S,**
Luke 10:12 . . . you, even wicked **S** will be
Rom 9:29 . . . have been wiped out like **S,**
Rev 11:8 . . . figuratively called "**S**"

SOIL (n) firm land, earth
Matt 13:23 . . . on good **s** represents those

SOJOURN (KJV)
Gen 12:10 . . . where he *lived as a foreigner*
Acts 7:6 . . . descendants would *live in a foreign land*

SOJOURNER (KJV)
Gen 23:4 . . . a stranger and a *foreigner* among
Num 35:15 . . . *foreigners* living among you
Ps 39:12 . . . guest—a *traveler* passing through

SOLD (v) *see also* SELL
1 Kgs 21:25 . . . **s** himself to what was evil
Matt 13:44 . . . and **s** everything he owned

SOLDIER (n) one engaged in military service
1 Cor 9:7 . . . What **s** has to pay his own
2 Tim 2:3 . . . a good **s** of Christ Jesus.

SOLID (adj) firm; not liquid
Ps 40:2 . . . set my feet on **s** ground
Heb 5:12 . . . and cannot eat **s** food.

SOLOMON King of Israel (united kingdom), second son of David and Bathsheba (2 Sam 12:24-25); chosen as successor by David (1 Kgs 1:28-40); given final advice by David (1 Kgs 2:1-9); enemies of his rule removed (1 Kgs 2:13-46); prayed for wisdom (1 Kgs 3:3-15; 4:29-34); demonstrated wisdom (1 Kgs 3:16-28); built and dedicated the Temple (1 Kgs 5–8); the LORD's second appearance (1 Kgs 9:1-9); became famous and powerful (9:10–10:29); visited by the queen of Sheba (1 Kgs 10:1-13); practiced idolatry and warned by God (1 Kgs 11:1-13); troubled by enemies (1 Kgs 11:14-40); died (1 Kgs 11:41-43); wrote many things (1 Kgs 4:32; Ps 72; 127; Prov 1:1; 10:1; 25:1; Eccl 1:1; Song 1:1); often mentioned in NT (Matt 6:29; 12:42; Luke 11:31; 12:27; Acts 7:47).

SON, SONS (n) a parent's male child or descendant further removed; spiritual heir (of Christ); relationship of Jesus to the heavenly Father
see also CHILD(REN), DESCENDANT(S)
Gen 17:19 . . . birth to a **s** for you.
Gen 21:10 . . . slave-woman and her **s.**
Gen 22:2 . . . Take your **s,** your only
Ruth 4:15 . . . better to you than seven **s-s!**
Ps 2:7 . . . You are my **s.** Today I have
Isa 7:14 . . . birth to a **s** and will call
Dan 7:13 . . . someone like a **s** of man
Hos 11:1 . . . I called my **s** out of Egypt.
Joel 2:28 . . . **s-s** and daughters will
Matt 1:21 . . . will have a **s,** and you are
Matt 2:15 . . . I called my **S** out of Egypt.
Matt 3:17 . . . my dearly loved **S,** who brings
Matt 4:3 . . . you are the **S** of God, tell
Matt 11:27 . . . truly knows the **S** except the
Matt 13:55 . . . the carpenter's **s,** and we
Matt 14:33 . . . really are the **S** of God!
Matt 16:16 . . . are the Messiah, the **S** of
Matt 17:5 . . . my dearly loved **S,** who brings
Matt 21:9 . . . God for the **S** of David!
Matt 27:54 . . . truly was the **S** of God!
Matt 28:19 . . . Father and the **S** and the
Mark 14:62 . . . will see the **S** of Man seated
Luke 1:32 . . . be called the **S** of the Most
Luke 2:7 . . . first child, a **s.** She wrapped
Luke 9:35 . . . This is my **S,** my Chosen One.
Luke 12:8 . . . on earth, the **S** of Man will
Luke 15:20 . . . ran to his **s,** embraced him,
John 3:16 . . . his one and only **S,** so that
John 3:36 . . . doesn't obey the **S** will never
John 17:1 . . . Glorify your **S** so he
Acts 13:33 . . . You are my **S.** Today I have
Rom 1:4 . . . shown to be the **S** of God
Rom 5:10 . . . death of his **S** while we
Rom 8:3 . . . He sent his own **S** in a body
Rom 8:29 . . . to become like his **S,** so
Rom 8:32 . . . even his own **S** but gave him
1 Cor 15:28 . . . who gave his **S** authority
2 Cor 6:18 . . . be my **s-s** and daughters,
Gal 4:4 . . . God sent his **S,** born of a
Gal 4:30 . . . slave and her **s,** for the **s**
Heb 1:2 . . . and through the **S** he created
Heb 1:5 . . . You are my **S.** Today I have
Heb 7:28 . . . God appointed his **S** with an
Heb 10:29 . . . trampled on the **S** of God,
1 Jn 2:23 . . . acknowledges the **S** has the
1 Jn 4:9 . . . one and only **S** into the world
1 Jn 5:5 . . . Jesus is the **S** of God.
Rev 1:13 . . . someone like the **S** of Man.

SONG, SONGS (n) a short musical composition of words and music; the act of singing
Exod 15:2 . . . my strength and my **s;**
Job 35:10 . . . who gives **s-s** in the night?
Ps 40:3 . . . given me a new **s** to sing,
Ps 63:5 . . . praise you with **s-s** of joy.
Ps 96:1 . . . Sing a new **s** to the LORD!
Ps 119:54 . . . theme of my **s-s** wherever
Ps 137:3 . . . of those **s-s** of Jerusalem!
Ps 149:1 . . . Sing to the LORD a new **s.**
Isa 49:13 . . . Burst into **s,** O mountains!
Isa 55:12 . . . and hills will burst into **s,**
Rev 5:9 . . . they sang a new **s** with these
Rev 15:3 . . . God, and the **s** of the Lamb:

SOON (adv) before long
John 13:32 . . . Son, he will **s** give glory to
2 Cor 4:18 . . . see now will **s** be gone,

SORCERER, SORCERERS (n) a person who practices sorcery
Exod 7:11 . . . his own wise men and **s-s,**
Acts 8:9 . . . a **s** there for many years,
Acts 13:6 . . . a Jewish **s,** a false prophet
Rev 22:15 . . . the dogs—the **s,** the sexually

SORCERY (n) the use of power gained from the assistance or control of evil spirits, especially for divining
Gal 5:20 . . . idolatry, **s,** hostility, quarreling,

SORROW, SORROWS (n) deep distress, sadness, or regret
Ps 116:3 . . . I saw only trouble and **s.**
Isa 65:14 . . . will cry in **s** and despair.
Jer 31:12 . . . all their **s-s** will be gone.
Ezek 34:2 . . . What **s** awaits you
Amos 5:18 . . . What **s** awaits you
Matt 18:7 . . . What **s** awaits the
Matt 23:13 . . . What **s** awaits you
Luke 11:46 . . . what **s** also awaits
Rom 9:2 . . . with bitter **s** and unending
2 Cor 7:10 . . . the kind of **s** God wants
Eph 4:30 . . . do not bring **s** to God's Holy
1 Tim 6:10 . . . themselves with many **s-s.**
Heb 13:17 . . . with joy and not with **s.**
Jude 1:11 . . . What **s** awaits them!
Rev 21:4 . . . more death or **s** or crying

SORRY (adj) feeling sorrow, regret, or penitence; inspiring pity
Gen 6:6 . . . So the LORD was **s** he had
2 Chr 21:20 . . . No one was **s** when he died.
Ps 38:18 . . . I am deeply **s** for what I have
Mal 3:14 . . . that we are **s** for our sins?
Matt 15:32 . . . I feel **s** for these people.
Matt 20:34 . . . Jesus felt **s** for them and
Mark 8:2 . . . I feel **s** for these people.

SOUGHT (v) *see also* SEEK
2 Chr 26:5 . . . the king **s** guidance from
2 Chr 31:21 . . . Hezekiah **s** his God
2 Chr 33:12 . . . Manasseh **s** the LORD
Eccl 12:10 . . . The Teacher **s** to find just
1 Thes 2:6 . . . we have never **s** it from

SOUL, SOULS (n) the inner life of a human being, the seat of emotions, and the center of human personality
Deut 6:5 . . . heart, all your **s,** and all
Deut 28:65 . . . fail, and your **s** to despair.
Deut 30:6 . . . your heart and **s** and so you

Josh 22:5 . . . all your heart and all your **s.**
2 Kgs 23:25 . . . heart and **s** and strength,
Prov 3:22 . . . for they will refresh your **s.**
Prov 16:24 . . . sweet to the **s** and healthy
Jer 6:16 . . . you will find rest for your **s-s.**
Matt 10:28 . . . can destroy both **s** and body
Matt 11:29 . . . you will find rest for your **s-s.**
Matt 22:37 . . . all your heart, all your **s,**
Mark 8:37 . . . worth more than your **s?**
Mark 12:30 . . . heart, all your **s,** all your
Luke 16:23 . . . his **s** went to the place of
Luke 21:19 . . . firm, you will win your **s-s.**
John 12:27 . . . my **s** is deeply troubled.
Heb 4:12 . . . cutting between **s** and spirit,

SOUND (adj) free from error, fallacy, or misapprehension
see also WHOLESOME
2 Tim 4:3 . . . listen to **s** and wholesome

SOUND (n) a particular auditory impression
Job 39:25 . . . snorts at the **s** of the horn.
Ps 98:6 . . . trumpets and the **s** of the
Dan 3:10 . . . they hear the **s** of the horn,
Acts 2:2 . . . there was a **s** from heaven

SOUND (v) to give a summons by sound
Num 10:6 . . . When you **s** the signal a
1 Cor 14:8 . . . the bugler doesn't **s** a clear

SOUR (adj) having an unpleasant, acidic taste
Ezek 18:2 . . . parents have eaten **s** grapes,

SOVEREIGN (adj) possessed of supreme power; unlimited in extent
Ps 71:16 . . . your mighty deeds, O **S** LORD.
Isa 25:8 . . . **S** LORD will wipe away all
Isa 40:10 . . . the **S** LORD is coming
Isa 50:4 . . . **S** LORD has given me his
Isa 61:1 . . . Spirit of the **S** LORD is upon

SOVEREIGNTY (n) supreme power especially over a body politic
Dan 5:18 . . . God gave **s,** majesty, glory,
Dan 7:27 . . . Then the **s,** power, and greatness

SOW(ED), SOWING (KJV)
Lev 25:3 . . . you may *plant* your fields
Ps 126:5 . . . Those who *plant* in tears
Matt 13:4 . . . As he *scattered* them across
Luke 12:24 . . . the ravens. They don't *plant*
Luke 19:21 . . . crops you didn't *plant*

SOWER (KJV)
Isa 55:10 . . . producing seed for the *farmer* and
Jer 50:16 . . . all *those who plant crops*
Matt 13:18 . . . parable about the *farmer planting seeds*
2 Cor 9:10 . . . provides seed for the *farmer*

SPACE (n) a blank or empty area; expanse
Gen 1:8 . . . God called the **s** "sky."

SPANK (v) to strike especially on the buttocks with the open hand
Prov 23:13 . . . won't die if you **s** them.

SPARE, SPARED, SPARES (v) to hold back from destroying, punishing, or harming; to have left over or as margin; to rescue from the necessity of doing or undergoing something
Esth 7:3 . . . lives of my people will be **s-d.**
Prov 13:24 . . . Those who **s** the rod of
Isa 54:2 . . . your home, and **s** no expense!
Mal 3:17 . . . as a father **s-s** an obedient
Rom 8:32 . . . did not **s** even his own Son
Rom 11:21 . . . if God did not **s** the original
2 Pet 2:4 . . . God did not **s** even the angels
2 Pet 2:5 . . . And God did not **s** the ancient

SPARKLED (v) to glitter or shine
Rev 21:11 . . . **s** like a precious stone—

SPARROW, SPARROWS (n) any of several species of birds that eat grain and insects and gather in noisy flocks
Ps 84:3 . . . Even the **s** finds a home,
Matt 10:31 . . . than a whole flock of **s-s.**
Luke 12:6 . . . What is the price of five **s-s**

SPEAK, SPEAKING, SPEAKS (v) to express thoughts, opinions, or feelings orally; to talk
see also SPOKE
Deut 18:22 . . . If the prophet **s-s** in the
Ps 15:3 . . . or **s** evil of their friends.
Ps 78:2 . . . will **s** to you in a parable.
Isa 3:8 . . . they **s** out against
Isa 32:4 . . . stammer will **s** out plainly.
Matt 12:34 . . . men like you **s** what is good
Matt 15:18 . . . the words you **s** come from
Acts 2:11 . . . hear these people **s-ing** in our
1 Cor 14:2 . . . ability to **s** in tongues,
1 Cor 14:19 . . . I would rather **s** five
1 Pet 3:16 . . . if people **s** against you,

SPEAKERS (n) one who makes a public speech
2 Cor 8:7 . . . in your faith, your gifted **s,**

SPECK (n) a small discoloration or spot
Matt 7:3 . . . why worry about a **s** in your

SPEECH (n) the communication or expression of thoughts in spoken words
Prov 16:23 . . . a wise mind comes wise **s;**
Prov 22:11 . . . gracious **s** will have the king
Prov 25:15 . . . soft **s** can break bones.
Zeph 3:9 . . . I will purify the **s** of all
1 Cor 1:17 . . . not with clever **s,** for

SPELL (n) a state of enchantment
Gal 3:1 . . . cast an evil **s** on you?

SPEND, SPENT (v) to use up or pay out; to exhaust or wear out
Prov 21:20 . . . but fools **s** whatever they
Isa 55:2 . . . Why **s** your money on food that
Mark 5:26 . . . she had **s-t** everything she had
2 Cor 12:15 . . . I will gladly **s** myself

SPINS (v) to draw out and twist into yarns or threads
Prov 31:13 . . . flax and busily **s** it.

SPIRIT, SPIRITS (n) "wind" or "breath"; a supernatural being; the third member of the Trinity, with God the Father and Jesus the Son; an attitude, mood, or disposition; an evil presence that can possess or influence a person; invisible, nonmaterial part of humans (as opposed to body or flesh)
see also ADVOCATE, HOLY SPIRIT
Gen 1:2 . . . the **S** of God was hovering
Gen 6:3 . . . My **S** will not put up with
Exod 31:3 . . . filled him with the **S** of God,
Num 11:25 . . . **S** rested upon them, they
Deut 34:9 . . . full of the **s** of wisdom,
Judg 13:25 . . . And the **S** of the LORD
1 Sam 16:13 . . . And the **S** of the LORD
1 Sam 16:14 . . . a tormenting **s** that filled
2 Kgs 2:9 . . . double share of your **s** and
Job 33:4 . . . the **S** of God has made me,
Ps 31:5 . . . I entrust my **s** into your
Ps 34:18 . . . those whose **s-s** are crushed.
Ps 51:10 . . . Renew a loyal **s** within me.
Ps 51:17 . . . you desire is a broken **s.**
Ps 139:7 . . . can never escape from your **S!**
Isa 11:2 . . . **S** of the LORD will rest
Isa 44:3 . . . I will pour out my **S** on your
Isa 63:10 . . . him and grieved his Holy **S.**
Ezek 11:19 . . . put a new **s** within them.
Joel 2:28 . . . I will pour out my **S** upon all
Zech 4:6 . . . by my **S,** says the LORD
Matt 3:11 . . . baptize you with the Holy **S**
Matt 3:16 . . . and he saw the **S** of God
Matt 4:1 . . . was led by the **S** into the
Matt 28:19 . . . and the Son and the Holy **S.**
Mark 1:8 . . . baptize you with the Holy **S!**
Mark 5:12 . . . pigs," the **s-s** begged.
Luke 1:35 . . . The Holy **S** will come upon
John 3:5 . . . born of water and the **S.**
John 6:63 . . . **S** alone gives eternal life.
John 14:26 . . . the Holy **S**—he will teach
John 16:13 . . . When the **S** of truth comes,
Acts 1:8 . . . when the Holy **S** comes
Acts 2:4 . . . as the Holy **S** gave them this
Acts 2:17 . . . will pour out my **S** upon all
Acts 5:3 . . . You lied to the Holy **S,** and
Acts 6:3 . . . full of the **S** and wisdom.
Acts 8:15 . . . to receive the Holy **S.**
Acts 9:17 . . . and be filled with the Holy **S.**
Acts 11:16 . . . be baptized with the Holy **S.**
Acts 19:2 . . . receive the Holy **S** when you
Rom 8:5 . . . controlled by the Holy **S** think
Rom 8:9 . . . do not have the **S** of Christ
Rom 8:26 . . . the Holy **S** prays for us
1 Cor 2:10 . . . For his **S** searches out
1 Cor 12:1 . . . abilities the **S** gives us.
1 Cor 12:13 . . . one body by one **S,** and we
1 Cor 14:1 . . . abilities the **S** gives—
2 Cor 3:6 . . . covenant, the **S** gives life.
2 Cor 3:17 . . . and wherever the **S** of the
2 Cor 5:3 . . . not be **s-s** without bodies.
Gal 3:2 . . . receive the Holy **S** by obeying
Gal 5:22 . . . But the Holy **S** produces this
Eph 4:4 . . . body and one **S,** just as you
Eph 4:30 . . . to God's Holy **S** by the way
Eph 6:12 . . . and against evil **s-s** in the
Eph 6:17 . . . sword of the **S,** which is the
1 Thes 5:19 . . . Do not stifle the Holy **S.**
1 Tim 3:16 . . . vindicated by the **S.**
2 Tim 1:7 . . . not given us a **s** of fear
1 Pet 3:4 . . . gentle and quiet **s,** which
1 Jn 4:1 . . . who claims to speak by the **S.**

SPIRITUAL (adj) having to do with the spirit, usually God's Spirit
Jon 4:11 . . . living in **s** darkness, not
Rom 7:14 . . . for it is **s** and good.
1 Cor 2:14 . . . who are **s** can understand
1 Cor 14:37 . . . think you are **s,** you should
1 Cor 15:44 . . . there are also **s** bodies.
Eph 5:19 . . . and hymns and **s** songs among
1 Pet 2:5 . . . you offer **s** sacrifices that

SPIT (v) to eject (as saliva) from the mouth
Matt 27:30 . . . And they **s** on him and

SPLENDOR (n) great brightness or luster; magnificence
2 Chr 20:21 . . . him for his holy **s.**
Ps 29:2 . . . the LORD in the **s** of
Ps 145:5 . . . majestic, glorious **s** and
Prov 20:29 . . . experience is the **s** of
Isa 33:17 . . . see the king in all his **s,**
Hab 3:3 . . . brilliant **s** fills the heavens,

SPLINTERS (n) a thin piece split or broken off lengthwise; sliver
Num 33:55 . . . will be like **s** in your eyes

SPLIT (v) to tear or rend apart
Matt 19:6 . . . let no one **s** apart what God

SPOKE, SPOKEN (v) *see also* SPEAK
Isa 40:5 . . . The LORD has **s-n!**
Acts 19:37 . . . and have not **s-n** against our
2 Pet 1:21 . . . Spirit, and they **s** from God.

SPOT, SPOTS (n) a small area visibly different (as in color, finish, or material) from the surrounding area; a taint on character or reputation
Jer 13:23 . . . leopard take away its **s-s?**
Eph 5:27 . . . church without a **s** or wrinkle

SPOTLESS (adj) free from impurity; unblemished
1 Pet 1:19 . . . the sinless, **s** Lamb of God.

SPREAD (v) to stretch out; to become distributed, dispersed, or scattered
Isa 25:6 . . . Armies will **s** a wonderful
Acts 6:7 . . . God's message continued to **s.**
Acts 13:49 . . . Lord's message **s** throughout
Acts 19:20 . . . about the Lord **s** widely and
Phil 1:12 . . . helped to **s** the Good News.
2 Thes 3:1 . . . message will **s** rapidly and

SPRING, SPRINGS (n) a source of water issuing from the ground
Ps 107:33 . . . and **s-s** of water into dry,
Jas 3:12 . . . fresh water from a salty **s.**
2 Pet 2:17 . . . useless as dried-up **s-s** or

SPRINKLE, SPRINKLED (v) to scatter in drops or particles
Lev 8:30 . . . and he **s-d** them on Aaron
Lev 16:14 . . . He must **s** blood seven
Heb 10:22 . . . have been **s-d** with Christ's

STAFF (n) a long stick used for walking or a weapon, often a symbol of authority and protection
see also ROD
Gen 49:10 . . . nor the ruler's **s** from his
Exod 7:12 . . . then Aaron's **s** swallowed up
Num 17:6 . . . Aaron, brought Moses a **s.**
2 Kgs 4:29 . . . travel; take my **s** and go!
Ps 23:4 . . . Your rod and your **s** protect

STAGGER (v) to totter
Isa 63:6 . . . and made them **s** and fall

STAIN (n) a soiled or discolored spot
2 Pet 2:13 . . . disgrace and a **s** among you.

STAINED (v) to discolor, soil
Isa 63:1 . . . with his clothing **s** red?

STAIRWAY (n) one or more flights of stairs
Gen 28:12 . . . dreamed of a **s** that reached

STAND, STANDING, STANDS (v) to remain stationary; to remain erect; to maintain one's position; to endure successfully
see also STOOD
Exod 3:5 . . . you are **s-ing** on holy ground.
Josh 5:15 . . . where you are **s-ing** is holy.
Josh 10:12 . . . Let the sun **s** still
2 Chr 20:17 . . . then **s** still and
Ps 24:3 . . . Who may **s** in his holy
Ps 33:11 . . . LORD's plans **s** firm
Ps 76:7 . . . Who can **s** before you
Ps 119:89 . . . word, O LORD, **s-s** firm
Prov 12:7 . . . family of the godly **s-s** firm.
Isa 40:8 . . . word of our God **s-s** forever.
Mal 3:2 . . . be able to **s** and face him
Luke 6:48 . . . that house, it **s-s** firm because
Rom 14:10 . . . all **s** before the judgment
1 Cor 10:12 . . . think you are **s-ing** strong,
1 Cor 10:13 . . . to be more than you can **s.**
2 Cor 5:10 . . . we must all **s** before Christ
Eph 6:14 . . . **S** your ground, putting on the
Phil 1:27 . . . you are **s-ing** together with
2 Tim 2:19 . . . But God's truth **s-s** firm like
1 Pet 5:9 . . . **S** firm against him, and
Rev 3:20 . . . I **s** at the door and knock.

STANDARD, STANDARDS (n) something established by authority, custom, or general consent as a model or example; criterion
Lev 24:22 . . . This same **s** applies both to
Prov 20:23 . . . LORD detests double **s-s;**

STANDING (n) a position or condition
Rom 8:33 . . . us right **s** with himself.

STAR, STARS (n) a natural luminous body visible in the sky especially at night; sometimes symbolic for angels
Gen 1:16 . . . He also made the **s-s.**
Num 24:17 . . . A **s** will rise from Jacob;
Job 38:7 . . . morning **s-s** sang together
Isa 14:12 . . . O shining **s,** son of the
Dan 12:3 . . . shine like the **s-s** forever.
Matt 2:2 . . . We saw his **s** as it rose,
2 Pet 1:19 . . . the Morning **S** shines in
Rev 2:28 . . . also give them the morning **s!**
Rev 22:16 . . . I am the bright morning **s.**

STARLIGHT (n) light given by the stars
Ps 74:16 . . . you made the **s** and the sun.

STARVE, STARVING (v) to suffer extreme hunger
Job 24:10 . . . while they themselves are **s-ing.**
Prov 6:30 . . . who steals because he is **s-ing.**
Luke 15:14 . . . the land, and he began to **s.**

STATUE (n) a three-dimensional representation usually of a person, animal, or mythical being that is produced by sculpturing, modeling, or casting
Dan 3:1 . . . made a gold **s** ninety feet
Rev 13:14 . . . make a great **s** of the

STATURE (n) quality or status gained by growth, development, or achievement
Luke 2:52 . . . wisdom and in **s** and in favor

STATUTES (KJV)
Exod 15:26 . . . keeping all his *decrees*
Deut 4:40 . . . If you obey all the *decrees* and
1 Kgs 3:14 . . . *decrees* and my commands
Ps 19:8 . . . *commandments* of the LORD
Ps 119:112 . . . to keep your *decrees*

STAY, STAYED (v) to continue in a place or condition
Ps 119:9 . . . can a young person **s** pure?
Luke 2:43 . . . but Jesus **s-ed** behind in
Luke 22:28 . . . You have **s-ed** with me
Gal 5:1 . . . make sure that you **s** free,

STEDFAST (KJV)
Ps 78:37 . . . They did not *keep* his covenant
1 Cor 15:58 . . . be *strong* and immovable.
Heb 3:14 . . . if we are *faithful* to the end,
1 Pet 5:9 . . . and be *strong* in your faith

STEAL, STEALING, STEALS (v) to take the property of another wrongfully
see also STOLE
Exod 20:15 . . . You must not **s.**
Lev 19:11 . . . Do not **s.**
Deut 5:19 . . . You must not **s.**
Prov 28:24 . . . who **s-s** from his father
Matt 19:18 . . . You must not **s.**
Matt 27:64 . . . coming and **s-ing** his body
Rom 13:9 . . . You must not **s.**
Eph 4:28 . . . If you are a thief, quit **s-ing.**
1 Pet 4:15 . . . not be for murder, **s-ing,**

STEPS (n) course, way
Ps 37:23 . . . LORD directs the **s** of
Prov 20:24 . . . LORD directs our **s,**
1 Pet 2:21 . . . you must follow in his **s.**

STIFFNECKED (KJV)
Exod 32:9 . . . how *stubborn and rebellious*
Exod 34:9 . . . *stubborn and rebellious* people
Deut 10:16 . . . stop being *stubborn*
2 Chr 30:8 . . . not be *stubborn,* as they
Acts 7:51 . . . You *stubborn* people! You are

STIFFHEARTED (KJV)
Ezek 2:4 . . . stubborn and *hard-hearted*

STILL (adj) devoid of or abstaining from motion; quiet, calm
Ps 46:10 . . . Be **s,** and know that I am
Isa 57:20 . . . never **s** but continually
Mark 4:39 . . . Silence! Be **s!**

STILL (adv) without motion
Exod 14:13 . . . Just stand **s** and watch
Josh 10:13 . . . sun stood **s** and the moon
2 Chr 20:17 . . . then stand **s** and watch

STILLNESS (n) the quality or state of being still
Ps 107:30 . . . What a blessing was that **s**

STING (n) a wound or pain caused by or as if by stinging
1 Cor 15:55 . . . where is your **s?**

STIRS (v) to provoke
Prov 10:12 . . . Hatred **s** up quarrels,

STOLE (v) *see also* STEAL
Lev 6:4 . . . give back whatever you **s,**

STOMACH (n) the digestive tract of the body
1 Cor 6:13 . . . **s,** and the **s** for food.
Phil 4:12 . . . with a full **s** or empty,

STONE (adj) of, relating to, or made of stone
Deut 4:13 . . . he wrote on two **s** tablets.

STONE, STONES (n) hardened mineral or rock; figurative of Christ or of hardened hearts
Exod 28:10 . . . Six names will be on each **s,**
Josh 4:3 . . . Take twelve **s-s** from the very
1 Sam 17:40 . . . picked up five smooth **s-s**
Ps 91:12 . . . even hurt your foot on a **s.**
Ps 118:22 . . . **s** that the builders rejected
Isa 8:14 . . . a **s** that makes people stumble,
Isa 28:16 . . . a foundation **s** in Jerusalem,
Isa 50:7 . . . face like a **s,** determined to
Jer 51:26 . . . Even your **s-s** will never again
Matt 3:9 . . . Abraham from these very **s-s.**
Matt 7:9 . . . give them a **s** instead?
Matt 21:42 . . . **s** that the builders rejected
Matt 24:2 . . . Not one **s** will be left
Mark 16:3 . . . roll away the **s** for us from
Luke 4:3 . . . tell this **s** to become a loaf
John 8:7 . . . sinned throw the first **s!**
1 Pet 2:5 . . . you are living **s-s** that God

STONED, STONING (v) to kill by pelting with stones
2 Cor 11:25 . . . with rods. Once I was **s-d.**
Heb 11:37 . . . Some died by **s-ing,** some were

STONY (adj) insensitive to pity or human feeling
Ezek 11:19 . . . away their **s,** stubborn heart

STOOD (v) *see also* STAND
Josh 10:13 . . . So the sun **s** still and
2 Tim 4:17 . . . But the Lord **s** with me

STOP, STOPS (v) to cease activity or operation; to pause or hesitate; to restrain or prevent
Job 37:14 . . . **S** and consider the wonderful
Prov 15:18 . . . cool-tempered person **s-s**
Jer 7:5 . . . only if you **s** your evil
Jer 32:40 . . . I will never **s** doing good
Lam 3:49 . . . flow endlessly; they will not **s**
Dan 4:35 . . . No one can **s** him or say to
Matt 19:14 . . . come to me. Don't **s** them!
Eph 6:16 . . . shield of faith to **s** the

STORE (n) a large quantity, supply, or number
Isa 33:6 . . . a rich **s** of salvation,

STORE, STORED (v) to lay away; to accumulate
Matt 6:19 . . . Don't **s** up treasures
Matt 6:26 . . . plant or harvest or **s** food
Luke 2:51 . . . And his mother **s-d** all these

STORIES (n) a fictional narrative
2 Pet 1:16 . . . making up clever **s** when

STORM (n) a heavy fall of rain, snow, or hail sometimes accompanied by thunder and lightning; a disturbed or agitated state
see also WHIRLWIND, WIND
Ps 50:3 . . . and a great **s** rages around
Ps 55:8 . . . from this wild **s** of hatred.
Ps 107:29 . . . He calmed the **s** to a whisper
Luke 8:24 . . . **s** stopped and all was calm.

STRAIN (v) to exert (as oneself) to the utmost; to filter
Ps 119:123 . . . My eyes **s** to see your
Jer 14:6 . . . They **s** their eyes
Matt 23:24 . . . You **s** your water so

STRANGE (adj) foreign; not before known, heard, or seen
see also FOREIGN
Isa 28:11 . . . who speak a **s** language!
1 Cor 14:21 . . . people through **s** languages
1 Pet 4:12 . . . something **s** were happening

STRANGER, STRANGERS (n) a person who is unknown or with whom one is unacquainted
see also FOREIGNER(S)
Job 31:32 . . . turned away a **s** but have
Matt 25:35 . . . I was a **s,** and you invited
John 10:5 . . . They won't follow a **s;**
1 Tim 5:10 . . . been kind to **s-s** and served
Heb 13:2 . . . to show hospitality to **s-s,** for

STRANGLED (adj) characterized by choking to death
Acts 15:29 . . . or the meat of **s** animals,

STRATEGIES (n) a careful and clever plan or method
Eph 6:11 . . . against all **s** of the devil.

STRAW (n) stalks of grain after threshing
1 Cor 3:12 . . . jewels, wood, hay, or **s.**

STRAYED (v) to wander
Isa 53:6 . . . like sheep, have **s** away.
Ezek 34:16 . . . lost ones who **s** away, and

STREAMS (n) a body of running water (as a river or brook)
Ps 23:2 . . . leads me beside peaceful **s.**
Jer 31:9 . . . walk beside quiet **s** and

STRENGTH (n) capacity for exertion or endurance; support; the power of a person or of God, measured variously in terms of wealth, wisdom, military might, or physical prowess
Exod 15:2 . . . LORD is my **s** and my
Deut 6:5 . . . your soul, and all your **s.**
2 Kgs 23:25 . . . his heart and soul and **s,**
1 Chr 16:11 . . . LORD and for his **s;**
Neh 8:10 . . . of the LORD is your **s!**
Ps 23:3 . . . He renews my **s.** He guides me
Ps 28:7 . . . LORD is my **s** and shield.
Ps 33:16 . . . nor is great **s** enough to save
Ps 46:1 . . . God is our refuge and **s,**
Ps 59:17 . . . O my **S,** to you I sing
Ps 65:6 . . . armed yourself with mighty **s.**
Ps 84:5 . . . for those whose **s** comes from
Ps 139:10 . . . your **s** will support me.
Isa 31:1 . . . depending on the **s** of human
Isa 40:26 . . . power and incomparable **s,**
Jer 27:5 . . . With my great **s** and powerful
Mic 5:4 . . . with the LORD's **s,** in
Hab 3:19 . . . LORD is my **s!**
Zech 4:6 . . . nor by **s,** but by my Spirit,
Mark 12:30 . . . your mind, and all your **s.**
1 Cor 1:25 . . . the greatest of human **s.**
Phil 4:13 . . . Christ, who gives me **s.**
Heb 11:34 . . . weakness was turned to **s.**
Heb 13:9 . . . Your **s** comes from God's

STRENGTHEN, STRENGTHENED, STRENGTHENS (v) to make or become stronger
2 Chr 16:9 . . . in order to **s** those whose
Isa 41:10 . . . I will **s** you and help you.
1 Cor 8:1 . . . is love that **s-s** the church.
1 Cor 14:4 . . . in tongues is **s-ed** personally,
1 Cor 14:4 . . . word of prophecy **s-s** the
1 Cor 14:5 . . . whole church will be **s-ed.**
1 Cor 14:12 . . . seek those that will **s** the
1 Cor 14:17 . . . but it won't **s** the people
1 Cor 14:26 . . . is done must **s** all of you.
2 Cor 13:10 . . . has given me to **s** you, not
Heb 12:12 . . . tired hands and **s** your weak
1 Pet 5:10 . . . support, and **s** you, and he

STRIKE (v) to aim and deliver a blow, stroke, or thrust (as with the hand, a weapon, or a tool); to inflict
see also STRUCK
Zech 13:7 . . . **S** down the shepherd, and
Matt 26:31 . . . God will **s** the Shepherd,
Rev 19:15 . . . sword to **s** down the nations.

STRIP (v) to remove extraneous or superficial matter from
Heb 12:1 . . . let us **s** off every weight

STRIPS (n) a long narrow piece of a material
Luke 2:12 . . . wrapped snugly in **s** of cloth,

STRIPES (KJV)
Acts 16:33 . . . washed their *wounds*
2 Cor 11:24 . . . gave me thirty-nine *lashes*
1 Pet 2:24 . . . By his *wounds* you are healed

STRONG, STRONGER, STRONGEST (adj) having or marked by great physical power, moral or intellectual power, or great resources (as of wealth or talent); firm
Exod 6:1 . . . force of my **s** hand, he
Deut 5:15 . . . you out with his **s** hand
Deut 7:8 . . . with such a **s** hand from your
Deut 31:6 . . . So be **s** and courageous!
Josh 1:6 . . . Be **s** and courageous,
Judg 16:5 . . . makes him so **s** and how he
2 Sam 22:33 . . . God is my **s** fortress, and
1 Kgs 8:42 . . . and your **s** hand and your
1 Chr 28:20 . . . Be **s** and courageous, and
Ezra 10:4 . . . so be **s** and take action.
Ps 24:8 . . . The LORD, **s** and mighty;
Ps 96:7 . . . LORD is glorious and **s.**
Prov 18:10 . . . LORD is a **s** fortress;
Prov 24:5 . . . wise are mightier than the **s,**
Prov 30:25 . . . Ants—they aren't **s,** but
Prov 31:17 . . . She is energetic and **s,** a
Eccl 9:11 . . . **s-est** warrior doesn't always
Isa 35:4 . . . Be **s,** and do not fear,
Jer 50:34 . . . one who redeems them is **s.**
Zeph 1:14 . . . when even **s** men will cry
Luke 1:80 . . . and became **s** in spirit.
Luke 2:40 . . . grew up healthy and **s.**
Luke 11:22 . . . someone even **s-er** attacks
1 Cor 1:8 . . . keep you **s** to the end
1 Cor 1:25 . . . God's weakness is **s-er** than
1 Cor 16:13 . . . Be courageous. Be **s.**
Eph 6:10 . . . final word: Be **s** in the Lord
1 Thes 3:13 . . . your hearts **s,** blameless,
2 Tim 2:1 . . . dear son, be **s** through the

STRUCK (v) *see also* STRIKE
Job 2:7 . . . presence, and he **s** Job with
Isa 53:8 . . . But he was **s** down for the

STRUGGLE (n) strife; a violent effort or exertion
Rom 15:30 . . . to join in my **s** by praying
Heb 12:4 . . . lives in your **s** against sin.

STRUGGLE (v) to proceed with difficulty or with great effort; to make strenuous or violent efforts in the face of difficulties or opposition
Gen 3:17 . . . will **s** to scratch a living
Col 1:29 . . . why I work and **s** so hard,
1 Tim 4:10 . . . and continue to **s,** for our

STUBBORN (adj) unreasonably or perversely unyielding
Exod 33:5 . . . You are a **s** and rebellious
Exod 34:9 . . . this is a **s** and rebellious
Lev 26:41 . . . at last their **s** hearts will
Deut 10:16 . . . hearts and stop being **s.**
2 Chr 36:13 . . . a hard and **s** man, refusing
Ps 78:8 . . . ancestors—**s,** rebellious,
Prov 28:14 . . . the **s** are headed for serious
Ezek 36:26 . . . out your stony, **s** heart and
Rom 2:5 . . . because you are **s** and refuse

STUDENTS (n) one who studies
Matt 10:24 . . . **S** are not greater than

STUDY (n) application of the mental faculties to the acquisition of knowledge
Eccl 12:12 . . . and much **s** wears you

STUDY (v) to read in detail, especially with the intention of learning
Josh 1:8 . . . **S** this Book of Instruction
Ezra 7:10 . . . had determined to **s** and obey

STUMBLE, STUMBLES, STUMBLING (v) to trip or walk unsteadily; to fall into sin or waywardness
Lev 19:14 . . . or cause the blind to **s.**
Ps 37:24 . . . Though they **s,** they will
Ps 66:9 . . . he keeps our feet from **s-ing.**
Ps 119:165 . . . great peace and do not **s.**
Ps 121:3 . . . He will not let you **s;**
Prov 3:23 . . . and your feet will not **s.**
Prov 24:17 . . . don't be happy when they **s.**
Isa 8:14 . . . stone that makes people **s,**
Jer 13:16 . . . causing you to **s** and fall
Hos 14:9 . . . paths sinners **s** and fall.
Mal 2:8 . . . caused many to **s** into sin.
Matt 21:44 . . . Anyone who **s-s** over that
John 11:10 . . . is danger of **s-ing** because
Rom 9:33 . . . that makes people **s,**
Rom 14:13 . . . believer to **s** and fall.
Rom 14:20 . . . makes another person **s.**
1 Cor 8:9 . . . weaker conscience to **s.**
2 Cor 6:3 . . . no one will **s** because of us,
1 Jn 2:10 . . . does not cause others to **s.**

STUMP (n) the part of a tree remaining attached to the root after the trunk is cut
Isa 6:13 . . . so Israel's **s** will be a
Isa 11:1 . . . Out of the **s** of David's

STUPID (adj) lacking intelligence or reason
Ps 119:70 . . . hearts are dull and **s,**
Prov 12:1 . . . is **s** to hate correction.

STUPIDITY (n) the quality or state of being stupid
Jer 31:19 . . . kicked myself for my **s!**

SUBMISSION (n) the condition of being submissive, humble, or compliant
1 Sam 15:22 . . . **s** is better than offering

SUBMISSIVE (adj) submitting to others
1 Cor 14:34 . . . They should be **s,** just
Titus 2:5 . . . be **s** to their husbands.

SUBMIT, SUBMITS (v) to yield to authority or be accountable to another—God, society, or fellow believers
Ps 2:12 . . . **S** to God's royal son,
Rom 13:1 . . . Everyone must **s** to governing
Rom 13:5 . . . So you must **s** to them, not
Eph 5:21 . . . **s** to one another out of
Eph 5:24 . . . As the church **s-s** to Christ,

Col 3:18 . . . Wives, **s** to your husbands,
Heb 12:9 . . . shouldn't we **s** even more

SUBTRACT (v) to take away
Deut 4:2 . . . Do not add to or **s** from
Deut 12:32 . . . to them or **s** anything

SUBVERT (KJV)
Lam 3:36 . . . they *twist* justice in the courts
Titus 1:11 . . . *turning* whole families *away from the truth*

SUCCEED (v) to turn out well; to attain a desired end
Gen 39:23 . . . everything he did to **s.**
Josh 1:8 . . . prosper and **s** in all you
1 Sam 2:9 . . . No one will **s** by strength
1 Sam 18:14 . . . continued to **s** in
2 Chr 20:20 . . . prophets, and you will **s.**
Ps 20:4 . . . and make all your plans **s.**
Prov 11:10 . . . celebrates when the godly **s;**
Prov 13:13 . . . respect a command will **s.**
Prov 16:3 . . . and your plans will **s.**
Prov 20:18 . . . Plans **s** through good
Prov 28:12 . . . When the godly **s,** everyone
Eccl 10:10 . . . wisdom; it helps you **s.**

SUCCESS (n) the attainment of wealth, favor, or eminence; favorable or desired outcome
1 Chr 12:18 . . . and **s** to all who help
2 Chr 26:5 . . . LORD, God gave him **s.**
Prov 15:22 . . . many advisers bring **s.**

SUCCESSFUL (adj) resulting or terminating in success; gaining or having gained success
Deut 8:18 . . . gives you power to be **s,**
Deut 30:9 . . . make you **s** in everything
1 Kgs 2:3 . . . that you will be **s** in all
2 Kgs 18:7 . . . Hezekiah was **s** in
1 Chr 22:13 . . . For you will be **s** if you
2 Chr 31:21 . . . result, he was very **s.**
Ps 90:17 . . . and make our efforts **s.**
Prov 1:3 . . . disciplined and **s** lives,
Eccl 9:11 . . . don't always lead **s** lives.

SUES (v) to seek justice or right from (a person) by legal process
1 Cor 6:6 . . . one believer **s** another—

SUFFER, SUFFERED, SUFFERING, SUFFERS (v) to endure death, pain, distress, or loss
Job 36:15 . . . rescues those who **s.**
Mark 8:31 . . . Son of Man must **s** many
Luke 24:26 . . . would have to **s** all these
Luke 24:46 . . . Messiah would **s** and die
Rom 8:18 . . . Yet what we **s** now is nothing
1 Cor 12:26 . . . If one part **s-s,** all the parts
2 Cor 1:5 . . . the more we **s** for Christ,
2 Cor 12:10 . . . troubles that I **s** for Christ.
Phil 3:10 . . . I want to **s** with him, sharing
2 Thes 1:4 . . . and hardships you are **s-ing.**
Heb 11:26 . . . better to **s** for the sake
1 Pet 2:21 . . . just as Christ **s-ed** for you.
1 Pet 4:1 . . . since Christ **s-ed** physical pain,
1 Pet 4:16 . . . is no shame to **s** for being
1 Pet 5:10 . . . So after you have **s-ed** a little
Rev 2:3 . . . You have patiently **s-ed** for me

SUFFERING, SUFFERINGS (n) the state or experience of one that suffers; pain, distress
Deut 16:3 . . . the bread of **s**—so that
Job 36:15 . . . means of their **s,** he rescues
Ps 119:71 . . . My **s** was good for me,
Isa 48:10 . . . you in the furnace of **s.**
Isa 49:13 . . . on them in their **s.**
Lam 1:12 . . . if there is any **s** like mine,
Luke 22:15 . . . you before my **s** begins.
2 Cor 1:7 . . . as you share in our **s-s,** you
Phil 1:29 . . . the privilege of **s** for him.
Col 1:24 . . . participating in the **s-s** of
2 Tim 2:3 . . . Endure **s** along with me,
2 Tim 4:5 . . . afraid of **s** for the Lord.
Heb 2:10 . . . through his **s,** a perfect
Heb 2:18 . . . gone through **s** and testing,
1 Pet 1:11 . . . about Christ's **s** and his
1 Pet 4:13 . . . Christ in his **s,** so that

SUMMED (v) to summarize
Rom 13:9 . . . commandments—are **s** up in
Gal 5:14 . . . whole law can be **s** up in this

SUN (n) a star that sustains life on the earth, being the source of heat and light
Josh 10:13 . . . So the **s** stood still and
Judg 5:31 . . . rise like the **s** in all its
Ps 84:11 . . . God is our **s** and our shield.
Ps 121:6 . . . The **s** will not harm you
Ps 136:8 . . . the **s** to rule the day,
Eccl 1:9 . . . Nothing under the **s** is truly
Isa 60:19 . . . you need the **s** to shine by
Mal 4:2 . . . name, the **S** of Righteousness
Matt 13:43 . . . shine like the **s** in their
Matt 17:2 . . . shone like the **s,** and his
Luke 23:45 . . . light from the **s** was gone.
Eph 4:26 . . . Don't let the **s** go down while
Rev 1:16 . . . was like the **s** in all its
Rev 21:23 . . . has no need of **s** or moon,

SUNDAY (n) the first day of the week
Matt 28:1 . . . Early on **S** morning, as

SUNLIGHT (n) the light of the sun; sunshine
Matt 5:45 . . . he gives his **s** to both the

SUPERIOR (adj) of higher rank, quality, or importance
Heb 8:6 . . . that is far **s** to the old

SUPERNATURAL (adj) of or relating to God, a spirit, or the devil
2 Pet 2:10 . . . scoff at **s** beings without
Jude 1:8 . . . and scoff at **s** beings.

SUPPER (n) meal eaten toward the end of the day; communion (i.e., Lord's Supper)
Luke 22:20 . . . After **s** he took another cup of
Acts 2:42 . . . meals (including the Lord's **S**)
1 Cor 11:33 . . . gather for the Lord's **S,**

SUPPORT, SUPPORTS (v) to pay the costs of; to assist or help
Lev 25:35 . . . and cannot **s** himself, **s**
Ps 18:35 . . . Your right hand **s-s** me;
Ps 139:10 . . . your strength will **s** me.
Ps 147:6 . . . The LORD **s-s** the humble,
1 Pet 5:10 . . . he will restore, **s,** and
3 Jn 1:8 . . . we ourselves should **s** them

SUPPRESS (v) to stop or prohibit the publication or revelation of
Rom 1:18 . . . wicked people who **s** the truth

SUPREME (adj) highest in rank, authority, degree, or quality
Col 1:15 . . . was created and is **s** over all
Col 1:18 . . . is the beginning, **s** over all

SURE (adj) admitting of no doubt; careful to remember, attend to, or find out something
Num 32:23 . . . you may be **s** that your sin
1 Sam 12:24 . . . But be **s** to fear the
2 Cor 1:15 . . . Since I was so **s** of your
2 Cor 9:5 . . . of me to make **s** the gift you
Eph 5:5 . . . You can be **s** that no immoral,
2 Tim 1:12 . . . trust, and I am **s** that he is

SURETY (KJV)
Gen 43:9 . . . I *personally guarantee* his safety
Prov 17:18 . . . *put up security* for a friend
Heb 7:22 . . . Jesus is the one who *guarantees*

SURFACE (n) the external or superficial aspect of something
John 7:24 . . . Look beneath the **s** so you can

SURGING (adj) characterized by tossing and swelling
Ps 42:7 . . . your waves and **s** tides sweep

SURPASS (v) to become better, greater, or stronger than
Prov 31:29 . . . world, but you **s** them all!

SURPLUS (n) the amount that remains when use or need is satisfied
Luke 21:4 . . . part of their **s,** but she,

SURPRISED (v) to take unawares; to strike with wonder or amazement especially because it is unexpected
1 Thes 5:4 . . . you won't be **s** when the day
1 Pet 4:4 . . . former friends are **s** when you
1 Jn 3:13 . . . So don't be **s,** dear brothers

SURRENDERED (v) to yield to the power, control, or possession of another upon compulsion or demand
2 Sam 10:19 . . . by Israel, they **s** to Israel
1 Chr 19:19 . . . by Israel, they **s** to David

SURROUND, SURROUNDED, SURROUNDS (v) to envelop; to encircle
Deut 33:12 . . . He **s-s** them continuously
Ps 5:12 . . . O LORD; you **s** them with
Ps 32:10 . . . unfailing love **s-s** those who
Ps 33:22 . . . unfailing love **s** us, LORD,
Ps 89:7 . . . than all who **s** his throne.
Ps 125:2 . . . the mountains **s** Jerusalem,
Ps 125:2 . . . the LORD **s-s** his people,
Heb 12:1 . . . we are **s-ed** by such a huge

SUSTAINS (v) to keep up or prolong
Heb 1:3 . . . God, and he **s** everything by

SWADDLED, SWADDLING (KJV)
Ezek 16:4 . . . salt, and *wrapped in cloth*
Luke 2:7 . . . wrapped him *snugly in strips of cloth*
Luke 2:12 . . . a baby *wrapped snugly* in strips

SWALLOW, SWALLOWED (v) to take through the mouth and esophagus into the stomach; to envelop or absorb
Isa 25:8 . . . He will **s** up death
Jon 1:17 . . . a great fish to **s** Jonah.
Hab 1:13 . . . while the wicked **s** up people
Matt 23:24 . . . a gnat, but you **s** a camel!
1 Cor 15:54 . . . fulfilled: "Death is **s-ed** up
2 Cor 5:4 . . . bodies will be **s-ed** up by life.

SWEAR (v) to affirm by a solemn oath or binding commitment
see also SWORE, SWORN
Lev 19:12 . . . using it to **s** falsely.
Isa 54:9 . . . earth, so now I **s** that I will
Heb 6:13 . . . one greater to **s** by, God took

SWEET, SWEETER (adj) pleasing to the taste; agreeable, gratifying
Job 20:12 . . . They enjoyed the **s** taste of
Ps 19:10 . . . They are **s-er** than honey,
Ps 119:103 . . . How **s** your words taste
Ps 119:103 . . . they are **s-er** than honey.
Prov 20:17 . . . Stolen bread tastes **s,** but
Prov 24:14 . . . wisdom is **s** to your soul.
Prov 27:9 . . . friend is as **s** as perfume
Song 1:2 . . . your love is **s-er** than wine.
Song 4:11 . . . lips are as **s** as nectar,
Isa 5:20 . . . bitter is **s** and **s** is bitter.
Ezek 3:3 . . . it tasted as **s** as honey in my

SWEET-SMELLING (adj) of or relating to a pleasant scent
Phil 4:18 . . . They are a **s** sacrifice that

SWEETNESS (n) the quality or state of being sweet
Song 5:16 . . . His mouth is **s** itself;

SWEPT (v) to clean with a broom or brush
Matt 12:44 . . . former home empty, **s,** and in

SWORD, SWORDS (n) a handheld weapon with a long blade; figurative of war or persecution by government, also of God's word in spiritual warfare
Gen 3:24 . . . a flaming **s** that flashed
Deut 32:41 . . . my flashing **s** and begin
1 Sam 17:45 . . . come to me with **s,** spear,
1 Sam 31:4 . . . Take your **s** and kill me
2 Sam 12:10 . . . live by the **s** because you
1 Kgs 20:11 . . . putting on his **s** for battle
Ps 44:6 . . . not count on my **s** to save me.
Ps 45:3 . . . Put on your **s,** O mighty
Ps 64:3 . . . their tongues like **s-s** and aim
Joel 3:10 . . . plowshares into **s-s** and your
Amos 9:4 . . . I will command the **s** to kill
Mic 4:3 . . . will hammer their **s-s** into
Matt 10:34 . . . not to bring peace, but a **s.**
Matt 26:52 . . . who use the **s** will die by
Luke 2:35 . . . a **s** will pierce your very
Eph 6:17 . . . take the **s** of the Spirit,
Heb 4:12 . . . sharpest two-edged **s,** cutting
Rev 1:16 . . . sharp two-edged **s** came
Rev 19:15 . . . came a sharp **s** to strike

SWORE, SWORN (v) *see also* SWEAR
Exod 33:1 . . . up to the land I **s** to give
Deut 7:8 . . . the oath he had **s-n** to your
Deut 30:20 . . . land the LORD **s** to give
Isa 45:23 . . . I have **s-n** by my own

SYCAMORE-FIG (n) a fig tree that has edible fruit similar but inferior to the common fig
Amos 7:14 . . . take care of **s** trees.
Luke 19:4 . . . and climbed a **s** tree beside

SYMBOL (n) something that stands for or suggests something else
Rom 5:14 . . . Adam is a **s,** a representation

SYMPATHIZE (v) to share in suffering or grief
1 Pet 3:8 . . . **S** with each other. Love each

SYNAGOGUE (n) the house of worship and communal center of a Jewish congregation
Luke 4:16 . . . to the **s** on the Sabbath
Acts 17:2 . . . he went to the **s** service,

T

TABERNACLE (n) portable shrine or tent designated for the worship of God; metaphor for God dwelling among his people
see also SANCTUARY, TEMPLE
Exod 27:21 . . . stand in the **T,** in front of
Exod 40:2 . . . Set up the **T** on the first
Exod 40:34 . . . cloud covered the **T,** and
Exod 40:34 . . . of the LORD filled the **T.**
Num 3:29 . . . area south of the **T** for their
Heb 8:5 . . . to build the **T,** God gave him
Heb 9:11 . . . more perfect **T** in heaven,
Heb 9:21 . . . blood on the **T** and on
Rev 15:5 . . . heaven, God's **T,** was thrown

TABLE, TABLES (n) a piece of furniture consisting of a smooth flat slab fixed on legs
Exod 25:23 . . . Then make a **t** of acacia
John 2:15 . . . and turned over their **t-s.**

TABLETS (n) a flat slab or plaque suited for or bearing an inscription
Exod 31:18 . . . two stone **t** inscribed with
Deut 10:5 . . . and placed the **t** in the Ark
2 Cor 3:3 . . . carved not on **t** of stone,

TAKE, TAKEN, TAKES (v) to exploit; to seize or capture physically; to remove; to move onto or into; to feel or experience; to lead, carry, or cause to go along to another place; to grasp or grip; to accept; to derive
see also TOOK
Gen 2:23 . . . she was **t-n** from 'man.'
Gen 9:6 . . . life will also be **t-n** by human
Lev 25:14 . . . you must not **t** advantage of
Num 13:30 . . . go at once to **t** the land,
Num 19:3 . . . it will be **t-n** outside the camp
1 Chr 17:13 . . . I will never **t** my favor
Ps 2:12 . . . for all who **t** refuge in him!
Ps 5:4 . . . O God, you **t** no pleasure in
Ps 49:17 . . . they die, they **t** nothing with
Ps 51:11 . . . and don't **t** your Holy Spirit
Prov 3:6 . . . show you which path to **t.**
Jer 25:10 . . . I will **t** away your happy
Zech 3:4 . . . See, I have **t-n** away your sins,
Matt 10:38 . . . refuse to **t** up your cross
Matt 11:29 . . . **T** my yoke upon you. Let me
Matt 16:24 . . . selfish ways, **t** up your cross,
Matt 24:40 . . . one will be **t-n,** the other
Matt 26:26 . . . **T** this and eat it, for this
Matt 26:39 . . . cup of suffering be **t-n** away
Mark 14:36 . . . Please **t** this cup of suffering
Mark 16:19 . . . he was **t-n** up into heaven
John 1:29 . . . Lamb of God who **t-s** away the
John 10:18 . . . No one can **t** my life from me.
Acts 1:9 . . . he was **t-n** up into a cloud
1 Tim 3:16 . . . and **t-n** to heaven in glory.

TALK (n) speech; pointless or fruitless discussion
Ps 5:9 . . . Their **t** is foul, like
Prov 10:19 . . . Too much **t** leads to
2 Tim 2:16 . . . worthless, foolish **t** that

TALK BACK (v) to answer impertinently
Titus 2:9 . . . They must not **t**

TALL, TALLER (adj) of a specified or considerable height
1 Sam 2:26 . . . boy Samuel grew **t-er** and
1 Sam 9:2 . . . and shoulders **t-er** than anyone
1 Sam 17:4 . . . He was over nine feet **t!**
1 Chr 11:23 . . . was 7½ feet **t** and whose

TAME (v) to reduce from a wild to a domestic state; to harness
Jas 3:7 . . . People can **t** all kinds of
Jas 3:8 . . . no one can **t** the tongue.

TANGLED (v) to involve so as to hamper, obstruct, or embarrass; to entrap
Exod 4:10 . . . and my words get **t.**
2 Pet 2:20 . . . Christ and then get **t** up and

TASK (n) duty, function
2 Cor 2:16 . . . for such a **t** as this?
2 Cor 5:18 . . . us this **t** of reconciling

TASTE (n) the act of tasting; a sample experience
Prov 24:13 . . . honeycomb is sweet to the **t.**
1 Pet 2:3 . . . a **t** of the Lord's kindness.

TASTE, TASTED, TASTES (v) to become acquainted with by experience; to ascertain the flavor of by taking a little into the mouth
Ps 34:8 . . . **T** and see that the LORD
Prov 9:17 . . . eaten in secret **t-s** the best!
Song 2:3 . . . and **t** his delicious fruit.
Ezek 3:3 . . . I ate it, it **t-d** as sweet as
Col 2:21 . . . Don't handle! Don't **t!**

TATTOOS (n) an indelible mark or figure fixed upon the body
Lev 19:28 . . . not mark your skin with **t.**

TAX, TAXES (n) a charge usually of money imposed by authority on persons or property for public purposes
Matt 17:24 . . . teacher pay the Temple **t?**
Matt 22:17 . . . right to pay **t-es** to Caesar
Rom 13:7 . . . Pay your **t-es** and

TAX COLLECTOR, TAX COLLECTORS (n) one who collects tax or custom on behalf of the government
Matt 5:46 . . . corrupt **t-s** do that
Matt 9:10 . . . along with many **t-s** and
Matt 11:19 . . . a friend of **t-s** and other sinners
Matt 21:31 . . . **t-s** and prostitutes will get into
Luke 5:27 . . . he saw a **t** named Levi
Luke 18:11 . . . I'm certainly not like that **t!**

TEACH, TEACHES, TEACHING (v) to cause to know something; to instruct by precept, example, or experience
see also INSTRUCT, PREACH, TRAIN
Lev 10:11 . . . you must **t** the Israelites
Deut 6:1 . . . commanded me to **t** you.
2 Chr 17:9 . . . of Judah, **t-ing** the people.
Job 21:22 . . . who can **t** a lesson to God,
Ps 37:30 . . . they **t** right from wrong.
Ps 51:13 . . . Then I will **t** your ways
Prov 15:33 . . . the LORD **t-es** wisdom;
Isa 2:3 . . . he will **t** us his ways,
Matt 5:19 . . . obeys God's laws and **t-es**
Matt 11:29 . . . Let me **t** you, because
Matt 15:9 . . . they **t** man-made ideas
Matt 22:16 . . . You **t** the way of God
Matt 28:20 . . . **T** these new disciples to
Mark 10:1 . . . as usual he was **t-ing** them.
Luke 11:1 . . . Lord, **t** us to pray,
Luke 12:12 . . . Holy Spirit will **t** you
John 14:26 . . . he will **t** you everything
Acts 6:4 . . . in prayer and **t-ing** the word.
Rom 15:4 . . . Scriptures long ago to **t**
Rom 15:14 . . . you can **t** each other all
1 Cor 2:16 . . . knows enough to **t** him?
1 Cor 14:26 . . . another will **t,** another
1 Tim 2:12 . . . do not let women **t** men
1 Tim 3:2 . . . he must be able to **t.**
2 Tim 3:16 . . . is useful to **t** us what
2 Tim 3:16 . . . **t-es** us to do what is right.
Titus 2:15 . . . You must **t** these things
Heb 5:12 . . . you ought to be **t-ing** others.
1 Jn 2:27 . . . need anyone to **t** you what

TEACHER, TEACHERS (n) one who teaches
Job 36:22 . . . Who is a **t** like him?
Prov 5:13 . . . didn't I listen to my **t-s?**
Eccl 1:1 . . . words of the **T,** King David's
Matt 10:24 . . . not greater than their **t,**
Matt 23:10 . . . only one **t,** the Messiah.
Luke 6:40 . . . will become like the **t.**
Luke 20:46 . . . these **t-s** of religious law!
John 13:14 . . . Lord and **T,** have washed
Rom 12:7 . . . If you are a **t,** teach well.
1 Cor 12:28 . . . third are **t-s,** then those
Gal 6:6 . . . should provide for their **t-s,**
Eph 4:11 . . . and the pastors and **t-s.**
2 Tim 4:3 . . . look for **t-s** who will tell
Jas 3:1 . . . of you should become **t-s**
3 Jn 1:10 . . . the traveling **t-s,** he also

TEACHING, TEACHINGS (n) something taught; doctrine
see also INSTRUCTION(S), LAW(S)
Isa 8:20 . . . to God's instructions and **t-s!**
Luke 6:47 . . . listens to my **t,** and then
John 7:17 . . . whether my **t** is from God

John 8:31 . . . remain faithful to my **t-s.**
Acts 2:42 . . . themselves to the apostles' **t,**
Eph 4:14 . . . about by every wind of new **t.**
1 Thes 4:8 . . . not disobeying human **t** but
2 Thes 2:15 . . . grip on the **t** we passed on
1 Tim 1:3 . . . those whose **t** is contrary to
1 Tim 1:10 . . . contradicts the wholesome **t**
1 Tim 4:6 . . . and the good **t** you have
1 Tim 4:16 . . . how you live and on your **t.**
1 Tim 6:3 . . . people may contradict our **t,**
2 Tim 4:2 . . . your people with good **t.**
Titus 1:9 . . . with wholesome **t** and show
Titus 3:8 . . . insist on these **t-s** so that
Heb 6:1 . . . stop going over the basic **t-s**

TEAR, TEARS (n) a drop of clear saline fluid secreted from the eye
Job 16:20 . . . I pour out my **t-s** to God.
Isa 25:8 . . . will wipe away all **t-s.**
Rev 7:17 . . . will wipe every **t** from their
Rev 21:4 . . . will wipe every **t** from their

TELL, TELLING, TELLS (v) to divulge or reveal; to give information to
Ps 26:7 . . . thanksgiving and **t-ing** of all
Ps 71:16 . . . I will **t** everyone that
Ps 118:17 . . . live to **t** what the LORD
Jer 1:7 . . . and say whatever I **t** you.
Jer 1:17 . . . Go out and **t** them everything
John 2:25 . . . No one needed to **t** him what
Acts 20:20 . . . shrank back from **t-ing** you
Rom 10:14 . . . him unless someone **t-s** them?
2 Cor 10:12 . . . these other men who **t** you

TEMPER (n) disposition; characteristic state of mind or of emotion; proneness to anger
Ps 37:8 . . . Do not lose your **t**—it only
Prov 14:29 . . . **t** shows great foolishness.
Prov 19:11 . . . people control their **t;**
Eccl 7:9 . . . Control your **t,** for anger

TEMPLE, TEMPLES (n) first built in Solomon's reign as a permanent worship center, which was destroyed then rebuilt under Herod's reign; figurative of the human body and of Christ
see also HOUSE, SANCTUARY, TABERNACLE
1 Kgs 6:1 . . . to construct the **T** of the
1 Kgs 8:10 . . . cloud filled the **T** of the
1 Chr 29:16 . . . to build a **T** to honor your
2 Chr 36:19 . . . his army burned the **T**
Ps 27:4 . . . meditating in his **T.**
Isa 6:1 . . . train of his robe filled the **T.**
Jer 7:8 . . . suffer because the **T** is here.
Joel 3:18 . . . forth from the LORD's **T,**
Hab 2:20 . . . LORD is in his holy **T.**
Hag 2:18 . . . of the LORD's **T** began.
Matt 12:6 . . . is even greater than the **T!**
Matt 26:61 . . . able to destroy the **T** of God
Matt 27:51 . . . sanctuary of the **T** was torn
Luke 21:5 . . . stonework of the **T** and the
John 2:14 . . . the **T** area he saw merchants
Acts 5:20 . . . Go to the **T** and give the
Acts 17:24 . . . live in man-made **t-s,**
1 Cor 3:16 . . . together are the **t** of God
1 Cor 6:19 . . . body is the **t** of the Holy
Eph 2:21 . . . becoming a holy **t** for the
1 Pet 2:5 . . . building into his spiritual **t.**
Rev 21:22 . . . and the Lamb are its **t.**

TEMPT, TEMPTED, TEMPTING (v) to entice to do wrong by promise of pleasure or gain; to test
Isa 13:17 . . . They cannot be **t-ed** by silver
Matt 4:1 . . . wilderness to be **t-ed** there by
Luke 4:2 . . . where he was **t-ed** by the devil
Luke 4:13 . . . finished **t-ing** Jesus, he left
1 Cor 7:5 . . . be able to **t** you because
1 Cor 10:13 . . . When you are **t-ed,** he will
Jas 1:13 . . . you are being **t-ed,** do not say,
Jas 1:13 . . . God is never **t-ed** to do wrong,

TEMPTATION, TEMPTATIONS (n) a cause or occasion of enticement
Matt 6:13 . . . don't let us yield to **t,**
Matt 18:7 . . . **T-s** are inevitable, but what
Matt 26:41 . . . will not give in to **t.**
Luke 8:13 . . . fall away when they face **t.**
1 Cor 10:13 . . . The **t-s** in your life are
1 Cor 10:13 . . . not allow the **t** to be
Gal 6:1 . . . fall into the same **t** yourself.
1 Tim 6:9 . . . to be rich fall into **t** and
Jas 1:12 . . . endure testing and **t.**

TEN (n) the number 10
Exod 34:28 . . . the **T** Commandments—
Deut 10:4 . . . wrote the **T** Commandments on
Luke 15:8 . . . a woman has **t** silver coins
Rev 12:3 . . . seven heads and **t** horns, with

TENDERHEARTED (adj) easily moved to love, pity, or sorrow; compassionate
Deut 28:54 . . . The most **t** man among you
Eph 4:32 . . . each other, **t,** forgiving one
Col 3:12 . . . yourselves with **t** mercy,

TENDERNESS (n) the quality or state of being gentle, fond, or loving
Jas 5:11 . . . is full of **t** and mercy.

TENTH (n) one-tenth of any property or produce
see also TITHE
Gen 14:20 . . . gave Melchizedek a **t** of all
Heb 7:2 . . . Abraham took a **t** of all he

TENTMAKERS (n) one who makes tents
Acts 18:3 . . . for they were **t** just as he

TENTS (n) portable housing made of cloth or skins
see also TABERNACLE
Gen 13:12 . . . Lot moved his **t** to a place

TERRIBLE (adj) extremely bad; terrifying
Jer 8:6 . . . What a **t** thing I have done
Zeph 1:15 . . . a day of **t** distress and
Heb 10:31 . . . It is a **t** thing to fall into

TERRIFY, TERRIFIED, TERRIFIES (v) to scare, deter, or intimidate; to fill with terror
Deut 2:25 . . . the earth **t-ied** because of you.
Deut 28:67 . . . you will be **t-ied** by the awful
1 Sam 12:18 . . . were **t-ied** of the LORD
Prov 21:15 . . . but it **t-ies** evildoers.
Isa 13:8 . . . and people are **t-ied.** Pangs of
Zeph 2:11 . . . The LORD will **t** them
Matt 14:26 . . . on the water, they were **t-ied.**
Matt 17:6 . . . disciples were **t-ied** and fell
Matt 27:54 . . . the crucifixion were **t-ied**
Mark 4:41 . . . disciples were absolutely **t-ied.**
Luke 21:26 . . . will be **t-ied** at what they

TERRIFYING (adj) causing terror or apprehension
Deut 4:34 . . . powerful arm, and **t** acts?
Deut 34:12 . . . Moses performed **t** acts in the
Judg 13:6 . . . of God's angels, **t** to see.

TERRITORY (n) an indeterminate geographic area
2 Cor 10:16 . . . done in someone else's **t.**

TERROR, TERRORS (n) a state of intense fear; a frightening aspect
Deut 7:19 . . . Remember the great **t-s** the
Job 9:34 . . . no longer live in **t** of his
Ps 53:5 . . . will grip them, **t** like they
Ps 91:5 . . . afraid of the **t-s** of the night,
Prov 22:8 . . . their reign of **t** will come to
Isa 51:17 . . . the cup of **t,** tipping out its
Mic 7:17 . . . trembling in **t** at his
Luke 9:34 . . . them, and **t** gripped them
Acts 7:32 . . . Moses shook with **t** and did

TEST, TESTINGS, TESTS (n) a critical examination, observation, or evaluation
see also TRIAL(S), TROUBLE(S)
Deut 29:3 . . . all the great **t-s** of strength,
1 Cor 10:9 . . . should we put Christ to the **t,**
1 Tim 3:10 . . . If they pass the **t,** then let
Heb 4:15 . . . of the same **t-ings** we do, yet

TEST, TESTED, TESTING, TESTS (v) to put to test or proof
Gen 22:1 . . . God **t-ed** Abraham's faith.
Deut 6:16 . . . You must not **t** the LORD your
Judg 3:1 . . . land to **t** those Israelites
1 Kgs 10:1 . . . she came to **t** him with hard
Job 23:10 . . . when he **t-s** me, I will come
Ps 17:3 . . . You have **t-ed** my thoughts
Ps 66:10 . . . You have **t-ed** us,
Ps 78:18 . . . They stubbornly **t-ed** God in
Ps 106:14 . . . ran wild, **t-ing** God's patience
Ps 139:23 . . . **t** me and know my anxious
Prov 17:3 . . . the LORD **t-s** the heart.
Luke 4:12 . . . You must not **t** the LORD your
Acts 5:9 . . . of conspiring to **t** the Spirit
1 Thes 5:21 . . . but **t** everything that is said.
Heb 2:18 . . . suffering and **t-ing,** he is able
Heb 2:18 . . . us when we are being **t-ed.**
Heb 3:8 . . . they **t-ed** me in the wilderness.
Heb 11:17 . . . when God was **t-ing** him.
Jas 1:3 . . . when your faith is **t-ed,** your
Jas 1:12 . . . who patiently endure **t-ing** and
1 Pet 1:7 . . . It is being **t-ed** as fire tests
1 Jn 4:1 . . . You must **t** them to see if
Rev 2:10 . . . you into prison to **t** you.
Rev 3:10 . . . great time of **t-ing** that will

TESTIFY, TESTIFIED, TESTIFIES, TESTIFYING (v) to make a statement based on personal knowledge or belief; to give evidence or proof
Exod 20:16 . . . must not **t** falsely against
Deut 5:20 . . . must not **t** falsely against
Prov 24:28 . . . Don't **t** against your
Luke 18:20 . . . You must not **t** falsely.
John 1:34 . . . Jesus, so I **t** that he is
John 5:32 . . . else is also **t-ing** about me,
John 15:26 . . . Father and will **t** all about
John 18:37 . . . the world to **t** to the truth.
John 21:24 . . . one who **t-ies** to these events
Acts 4:33 . . . The apostles **t-ied** powerfully
Acts 10:43 . . . the prophets **t-ied** about,
1 Jn 4:14 . . . own eyes and now **t** that the

TESTIMONY (n) the evidence given by a witness
see also TESTIFY
Num 35:30 . . . to death on the **t** of only
John 1:7 . . . might believe because of his **t.**
1 Tim 6:13 . . . gave a good **t** before Pontius
1 Jn 5:9 . . . Since we believe human **t,**
Rev 12:11 . . . of the Lamb and by their **t.**

THANK, THANKING (v) to express gratitude to; to acknowledge God's goodness
Ps 35:18 . . . Then I will **t** you in front
Ps 79:13 . . . pasture, will **t** you forever
Ps 145:10 . . . works will **t** you, LORD,
Isa 12:4 . . . sing: "**T** the LORD!
1 Cor 10:30 . . . If I can **t** God for the food
Phil 4:6 . . . and **t** him for all he has done.
1 Thes 2:13 . . . we never stop **t-ing** God
1 Thes 3:9 . . . How we **t** God for you!

THANKFUL (adj) conscious of benefit received; expressive of thanks
Col 3:15 . . . And always be **t.**
Col 3:16 . . . to God with **t** hearts.
1 Thes 5:18 . . . Be **t** in all circumstances,
Heb 12:28 . . . let us be **t** and please God by

THANKFULNESS (n) the quality or state of being thankful
Col 2:7 . . . you will overflow with **t.**

THANKS (n) kindly or grateful thoughts; gratitude
1 Chr 16:4 . . . to give **t,** and to praise
Ps 30:12 . . . I will give you **t** forever!
Ps 107:1 . . . Give **t** to the LORD,
Rom 1:21 . . . as God or even give him **t.**
1 Cor 11:24 . . . gave **t** to God for it.
Phil 1:3 . . . of you, I give **t** to my God.
1 Tim 2:1 . . . behalf, and give **t** for them.
1 Tim 4:3 . . . be eaten with **t** by faithful
Rev 4:9 . . . and honor and **t** to the one

THANKSGIVING (n) a prayer expressing gratitude; a public acknowledgment or celebration of God's goodness
Ps 26:7 . . . singing a song of **t** and telling
Ps 28:7 . . . I burst out in songs of **t.**
Ps 100:4 . . . Enter his gates with **t;** go
Isa 51:3 . . . Songs of **t** will fill the air.

THIEF, THIEVES (n) one who steals, especially stealthily or secretly
Prov 6:30 . . . might be found for a **t**
Prov 29:24 . . . If you assist a **t,** you only
Jer 7:11 . . . has become a den of **t-ves?**
Matt 6:19 . . . where **t-ves** break in and steal.
Luke 19:46 . . . turned it into a den of **t-ves.**
John 10:1 . . . surely be a **t** and a robber!
John 10:8 . . . me were **t-ves** and robbers.
1 Cor 6:10 . . . or are **t-ves,** or greedy people,
1 Thes 5:2 . . . unexpectedly, like a **t** in the
Rev 16:15 . . . as unexpectedly as a **t!**

THINK, THINKING, THINKS (v) to reflect, ponder, or remember; to subject to the processes of logical thought; to have as an opinion; to conceive or reason
see also MEDITATE, THOUGHT
1 Sam 12:24 . . . **T** of all the wonderful
2 Chr 19:6 . . . Always **t** carefully before
Ps 8:4 . . . you should **t** about them,
Ps 63:6 . . . I lie awake **t-ing** of you,
Ps 77:12 . . . I cannot stop **t-ing** about your
Ps 119:97 . . . I **t** about them all day long.
Ps 119:148 . . . the night, **t-ing** about your
Prov 13:16 . . . Wise people **t** before they
Prov 15:28 . . . godly **t-s** carefully before
Prov 21:29 . . . the virtuous **t** before they
Prov 23:7 . . . are always **t-ing** about how
Prov 29:20 . . . who speaks without **t-ing.**
Isa 44:18 . . . are shut, and they cannot **t.**
Matt 22:42 . . . What do you **t** about the
Rom 11:20 . . . So don't **t** highly of
Phil 1:3 . . . Every time I **t** of you, I give
Phil 2:3 . . . Be humble, **t-ing** of others as
Phil 3:19 . . . they **t** only about this life
Heb 10:24 . . . Let us **t** of ways to motivate
1 Pet 1:13 . . . So **t** clearly and exercise

THINKING (n) opinion, judgment
Rom 1:28 . . . them to their foolish **t**
2 Pet 3:1 . . . wholesome **t** and refresh

THIRST (v) to crave vehemently and urgently
Ps 42:2 . . . I **t** for God, the living God.
Matt 5:6 . . . who hunger and **t** for justice,

THIRSTY (adj) feeling a desire for liquids; having a strong desire
Ps 107:9 . . . he satisfies the **t** and fills
Prov 25:21 . . . If they are **t,** give them
Isa 55:1 . . . Is anyone **t?** Come and drink—
Matt 25:35 . . . I was **t,** and you gave
John 4:14 . . . will never be **t** again.
Rom 12:20 . . . If they are **t,** give them
2 Cor 11:27 . . . been hungry and **t** and
Rev 7:16 . . . never again be hungry or **t;**
Rev 22:17 . . . Let anyone who is **t** come.

THOMAS One of the 12 disciples, also known as "the Twin" (Matt 10:3; Mark 3:18; Luke 6:15; Acts 1:13); willing to die with Jesus (John 11:16); queried Jesus (John 14:5); doubted Jesus' resurrection but was convinced by his appearance (John 20:24-28).

THORN, THORNS (n) a woody plant bearing sharp impeding prickles or spines; something that causes distress or irritation
Gen 3:18 . . . It will grow **t-s** and thistles
Num 33:55 . . . in your eyes and **t-s** in your
Matt 13:7 . . . seeds fell among **t-s** that
Matt 27:29 . . . wove **t** branches into a
2 Cor 12:7 . . . I was given a **t** in my flesh,
Heb 6:8 . . . a field bears **t-s** and thistles,

THORNBUSHES (n) any of various spiny or thorny shrubs or small trees
Luke 6:44 . . . never gathered from **t,** nor grapes

THOUGHT, THOUGHTS (n) the action or process of thinking; a developed intention or plan; recollection, remembrance
Ps 77:12 . . . They are constantly in my **t-s.**
Ps 92:5 . . . And how deep are your **t-s.**
Ps 94:11 . . . LORD knows people's **t-s;**
Ps 104:34 . . . May all my **t-s** be pleasing
Ps 139:23 . . . and know my anxious **t-s.**
Ps 142:4 . . . no one gives me a passing **t!**
Isa 26:3 . . . whose **t-s** are fixed on you!
Isa 55:8 . . . My **t-s** are nothing like your
Matt 9:4 . . . you have such evil **t-s** in your
Matt 15:19 . . . heart come evil **t-s,** murder,
1 Cor 14:25 . . . their secret **t-s** will be
Eph 4:23 . . . renew your **t-s** and attitudes.
Rev 2:23 . . . searches out the **t-s** and

THOUGHT (v) *see also* THINK
Ps 39:3 . . . The more I **t** about it,
Luke 2:19 . . . in her heart and **t** about them
1 Cor 13:11 . . . I spoke and **t** and reasoned

THOUSAND (adj) of the number 1,000
Ps 90:4 . . . For you, a **t** years are as
Rev 20:7 . . . When the **t** years come to an

THOUSANDS (n) a very large number
Joel 3:14 . . . Thousands upon **t** are waiting

THREATS (n) an expression of intention to inflict evil, injury, or damage
Matt 24:6 . . . of wars and **t** of wars,

THREE (adj) the number 3
Deut 19:15 . . . of two or **t** witnesses.
Jon 1:17 . . . **t** days and **t** nights.
Matt 12:40 . . . **t** days and **t** nights,
Matt 18:20 . . . where two or **t** gather
Matt 26:34 . . . you will deny **t** times that
Mark 8:31 . . . but **t** days later he would rise
1 Jn 5:7 . . . have these **t** witnesses—

THRILL (v) to cause to experience a sudden sharp feeling of excitement
Ps 92:4 . . . You **t** me, LORD,
Isa 60:5 . . . your heart will **t** with joy,

THRIVING (adj) characterized by success, prosperity, or growth
Ps 52:8 . . . olive tree, **t** in the house

THROAT (n) the front part of the neck
Prov 23:2 . . . put a knife to your **t;**

THRONE, THRONES (n) seat of power for a king or deity; symbolic of royal authority and the king's role as a judge
Deut 17:18 . . . he sits on the **t** as king,
2 Sam 7:16 . . . and your **t** will be secure
1 Chr 17:12 . . . will secure his **t** forever.
Job 36:7 . . . sets them on **t-s** with kings
Ps 45:6 . . . Your **t,** O God, endures
Ps 47:8 . . . nations, sitting on his holy **t.**
Ps 89:14 . . . are the foundation of your **t.**
Ps 99:1 . . . He sits on his **t** between the
Ps 102:12 . . . sit on your **t** forever.
Ps 103:19 . . . has made the heavens his **t;**
Isa 6:1 . . . He was sitting on a lofty **t,**
Isa 66:1 . . . Heaven is my **t,** and the
Dan 7:9 . . . on a fiery **t** with wheels
Matt 19:28 . . . upon his glorious **t,** you who
Matt 19:28 . . . sit on twelve **t-s,** judging
Acts 7:49 . . . Heaven is my **t,** and the
Rom 15:12 . . . heir to David's **t** will come,
Col 1:16 . . . such as **t-s,** kingdoms, rulers,
Heb 12:2 . . . place of honor beside God's **t.**
Rev 3:21 . . . sat with my Father on his **t.**
Rev 4:2 . . . and I saw a **t** in heaven
Rev 4:4 . . . Twenty-four **t-s** surrounded
Rev 5:5 . . . heir to David's **t,** has won
Rev 20:11 . . . a great white **t** and the
Rev 22:3 . . . the **t** of God and of the Lamb

THROUGH (prep) by way of
Eph 2:18 . . . to the Father **t** the same Holy

THROUGHOUT (prep) in or to every part of; during the whole course or period of
Gen 1:29 . . . seed-bearing plant **t** the
Jer 23:40 . . . be infamous **t** the ages.
Rom 10:18 . . . message has gone **t** the earth,

THROW, THROWING (v) to propel through the air by a forward motion of the hand or arm; to discard
Ps 22:18 . . . themselves and **t** dice for my
Prov 16:33 . . . We may **t** the dice,
Isa 41:9 . . . and will not **t** you away.
Matt 27:35 . . . his clothes by **t-ing** dice.
John 8:7 . . . has never sinned **t** the first
John 19:24 . . . apart, let's **t** dice for it.
Heb 10:35 . . . do not **t** away this confident

THUNDER, THUNDERS (n) the sound that follows a flash of lightning
Job 37:5 . . . voice is glorious in the **t.**
Mark 3:17 . . . nicknamed them "Sons of **T**"
Rev 10:3 . . . the seven **t-s** answered.

THUNDERS (v) to give forth a sound that resembles thunder
Ps 29:3 . . . The God of glory **t.**

TIE, TIED (v) to fasten, attach, or close by means of a tie
Prov 3:3 . . . **T** them around your neck as
Matt 18:6 . . . large millstone **t-d** around your

TIES (n) a bond of kinship or affection
Col 2:2 . . . together by strong **t** of love.

TIME, TIMES (n) occasion; an opportune or suitable moment; an appointed, fixed, or customary moment or hour for something to happen, begin, or end; duration; conditions at present or at some specified period; added or accumulated quantities or instances
Esth 4:14 . . . such a **t** like this?"
Ps 9:9 . . . a refuge in **t-s** of trouble.
Ps 62:8 . . . trust in him at all **t-s.**
Eccl 3:1 . . . a **t** for every activity under
Eccl 7:14 . . . when hard **t-s** strike,
Eccl 8:5 . . . wise will find a **t** and a way

Dan 12:7 . . . times, and half a **t.**
Hos 10:12 . . . for now is the **t** to seek the
Amos 5:13 . . . shut, for it is an evil **t.**
Matt 16:3 . . . interpret the signs of the **t-s!**
Matt 18:21 . . . sins against me? Seven **t-s?**
Luke 12:40 . . . ready all the **t,** for the Son
John 4:53 . . . was the very **t** Jesus had told
John 12:23 . . . the **t** has come for the Son
Acts 1:7 . . . those dates and **t-s,** and they
Acts 18:5 . . . spent all his **t** preaching
1 Cor 7:29 . . . The **t** that remains is very
2 Cor 6:2 . . . the "right **t**" is now.
Gal 6:9 . . . just the right **t** we will reap
2 Tim 1:9 . . . the beginning of **t**—to show
Heb 9:28 . . . once for all **t** as a sacrifice
Heb 10:12 . . . for sins, good for all **t.**
1 Pet 4:17 . . . For the **t** has come for
Rev 12:14 . . . for a time, **t-s,** and half a

TIMID (adj) lacking in courage or self-confidence
1 Thes 5:14 . . . Encourage those who are **t.**

TIMIDITY (n) the quality or state of being timid
2 Tim 1:7 . . . of fear and **t,** but of power,

TIMOTHY Paul's student and traveling companion from Lystra (Acts 16:1-3); raised by devout Jewish mother (2 Tim 1:5; 3:15); joined Paul on second missionary journey (Acts 16–20); sent to serve NT churches (1 Cor 4:17; 16:10; Phil 2:19; 1 Thes 3:5-6; 1 Tim 1:3); wrote letters with Paul (2 Cor 1:1; Phil 1:1; Col 1:1; 1 Thes 1:1; 2 Thes 1:1; Phlm 1:1); letters written to him by Paul (1 Tim 1:2; 2 Tim 1:2).

TIRED (adj) drained of strength and energy
Exod 17:12 . . . became so **t** he could no
Isa 35:3 . . . those who have **t** hands,
Gal 6:9 . . . let's not get **t** of doing what
2 Thes 3:13 . . . never get **t** of doing good.
Heb 12:12 . . . new grip with your **t** hands

TITHE, TITHES (n) one-tenth of any property or produce
see also TENTH
Num 18:21 . . . give them the **t-s** from the
Deut 12:17 . . . neither the **t** of your grain
2 Chr 31:12 . . . brought all the **t-s** and
Amos 4:4 . . . bring your **t-s** every three
Mal 3:8 . . . of the **t-s** and offerings due
Mal 3:10 . . . Bring all the **t-s** into the

TITHE (v) to pay or give a tenth of as an offering to God
Matt 23:23 . . . You should **t,** yes,
Luke 11:42 . . . you are careful to **t** even the

TITTLE (KJV)
Matt 5:18 . . . the *smallest detail* of God's
law
Luke 16:17 . . . the *smallest point* of God's
law

TITUS Young Gentile pastor and helper of Paul (Gal 2:1-3; 2 Tim 4:10); sent to Corinth (2 Cor 2:13; 7:6-14; 8:6-23; 12:18); sent to Crete (Titus 1:4-5).

TODAY (adv) on or for this day; at the present time
Ps 2:7 . . . **T** I have become your Father.
Ps 95:7 . . . listen to his voice **t!**
Matt 6:11 . . . Give us **t** the food we
Luke 2:11 . . . born **t** in Bethlehem,
Luke 23:43 . . . I assure you, **t** you will be
Heb 1:5 . . . **T** I have become your Father.
Heb 3:7 . . . **T** when you hear his voice,
Heb 13:8 . . . is the same yesterday, **t,** and

TOGETHER (adv) with each other; as a unit; in or into one place, mass, collection, or group
Ps 133:1 . . . brothers live **t** in harmony!
Jer 3:18 . . . will return **t** from exile
Zeph 3:9 . . . can worship the LORD **t.**
Acts 1:14 . . . They all met **t** and were
Rom 1:12 . . . When we get **t,** I want to
Eph 1:10 . . . bring everything **t** under the

TOLERANT (adj) marked by forbearance and endurance
Rom 2:4 . . . how wonderfully kind, **t,** and

TOLERATE (v) to put up with
Rev 2:2 . . . know you don't **t** evil people.

TOMORROW (n) the day after the present; the future
Prov 27:1 . . . Don't brag about **t,** since you
Isa 22:13 . . . and drink, for **t** we die!
Rom 8:38 . . . our worries about **t**—not
even
1 Cor 15:32 . . . and drink, for **t** we die!

TONGUE, TONGUES (n) part of the mouth that enables speech; dialect or language of a people; a special gift of speech given by the Holy Spirit
see also LANGUAGE(S)
Ps 5:9 . . . Their **t-s** are filled
Ps 34:13 . . . keep your **t** from speaking
Ps 39:1 . . . I will hold my **t** when
Ps 45:1 . . . king, for my **t** is like
Ps 78:36 . . . lied to him with their **t-s.**
Ps 119:172 . . . Let my **t** sing about
Ps 137:6 . . . May my **t** stick to the
Prov 13:3 . . . who control their **t** will have
Prov 15:4 . . . a deceitful **t** crushes the
Prov 17:20 . . . the lying **t** tumbles into
Prov 21:23 . . . Watch your **t** and keep
Luke 16:24 . . . in water and cool my **t.**
Acts 2:3 . . . like flames or **t-s** of fire
Acts 10:46 . . . speaking in other **t-s** and
praising
Acts 19:6 . . . in other **t-s** and prophesied.
Rom 14:11 . . . me, and every **t** will confess
1 Cor 14:2 . . . to speak in **t-s,** you will
1 Cor 14:4 . . . speaks in **t-s** is strengthened
1 Cor 14:5 . . . speak in **t-s,** but even more
1 Cor 14:13 . . . speaks in **t-s** should pray
1 Cor 14:18 . . . I speak in **t-s** more than
1 Cor 14:27 . . . three should speak in **t-s.**
1 Cor 14:39 . . . forbid speaking in **t-s.**
Phil 2:11 . . . and every **t** confess that
Jas 3:2 . . . if we could control our **t-s,** we
Jas 3:5 . . . same way, the **t** is a small

TOOK (v) *see also* TAKE
Matt 8:17 . . . He **t** our sicknesses and
removed
Matt 26:26 . . . eating, Jesus **t** some bread
and
Matt 26:27 . . . And he **t** a cup of wine and
1 Cor 11:23 . . . the Lord Jesus **t** some bread
1 Cor 11:25 . . . the same way, he **t** the
cup of
Phil 2:7 . . . he **t** the humble position of

TOOTH (n) a bonelike structure in the mouth used for chewing
Exod 21:24 . . . eye for an eye, a **t** for a **t,**
Matt 5:38 . . . eye for an eye, and a **t** for a **t.**

TORMENT (n) extreme pain or anguish of body or mind
Luke 16:28 . . . end up in this place of **t.**

TORMENT, TORMENTED (v) to cause severe usually persistent or recurrent distress of body or mind to
2 Cor 12:7 . . . messenger from Satan to **t**

Rev 20:10 . . . they will be **t-ed** day and
night

TORMENTORS (n) one who torments
Ps 137:3 . . . Our **t** insisted on a joyful

TORTURED (v) to punish or coerce by inflicting excruciating pain
Matt 18:34 . . . prison to be **t** until he
Heb 11:35 . . . others were **t,** refusing to

TOSSED (v) to fling or heave continuously about
Jas 1:6 . . . blown and **t** by the wind.

TOUCH, TOUCHED, TOUCHES (v) to reach out or come in contact with; to lay hands upon; to have an influence upon
Gen 3:3 . . . must not eat it or even **t** it;
Exod 19:12 . . . or even **t** its boundaries.
Exod 19:12 . . . Anyone who **t-es** the
mountain
Isa 6:7 . . . this coal has **t-ed** your lips.
Matt 9:21 . . . If I can just **t** his robe,
Matt 14:36 . . . who **t-ed** him were healed.
Luke 8:45 . . . "Who **t-ed** me?" Jesus asked.
Luke 18:15 . . . so he could **t** and bless
Luke 24:39 . . . **T** me and make sure that
2 Cor 6:17 . . . Don't **t** their filthy things,
Col 2:21 . . . Don't taste! Don't **t!**"?
1 Jn 1:1 . . . **t-ed** him with our own hands.
1 Jn 5:18 . . . evil one cannot **t** them.

TOWER (n) a tall building or structure typically higher than its surroundings
Gen 11:4 . . . with a **t** that reaches into

TRADE, TRADED (v) to give one thing in exchange for another
Gen 25:31 . . . Jacob replied, "but **t** me your
Ps 106:20 . . . They **t-d** their glorious God
Rom 1:25 . . . They **t-d** the truth about God

TRADERS (n) a person whose business is buying and selling
1 Tim 1:10 . . . are slave **t,** liars, promise

TRADITION, TRADITIONS (n) an inherited, customary, or established pattern of thought, action, or behavior
Matt 15:6 . . . for the sake of your own **t.**
Mark 7:5 . . . disciples follow our age-old **t?**
Mark 7:8 . . . law and substitute your own **t.**
Mark 7:13 . . . to hand down your own **t.**
Gal 1:14 . . . in my zeal for the **t-s** of my

TRAGEDY (n) a disastrous event; misfortune
Eccl 9:12 . . . are caught by sudden **t.**

TRAGIC (adj) of, marked by, or expressive of tragedy
Eccl 1:13 . . . has dealt a **t** existence to

TRAIN (n) a part of a gown that trails behind the wearer
Isa 6:1 . . . throne, and the **t** of his robe

TRAIN, TRAINED (v) to form by or undergo instruction, discipline, or drill
see also TEACH
Isa 2:4 . . . against nation, nor **t** for war
Luke 6:40 . . . who is fully **t-ed** will become
John 7:15 . . . when he hasn't been **t-ed?**
Acts 22:3 . . . I was carefully **t-ed** in our
1 Tim 4:7 . . . **t** yourself to be godly.
Titus 2:4 . . . women must **t** the younger
Heb 12:11 . . . those who are **t-ed** in this
way.

TRAINING (n) acquired skill, knowledge, or experience; the act, process, or method of one who trains
Acts 4:13 . . . men with no special **t** in the
1 Tim 4:8 . . . Physical **t** is good, but

TRAITORS (n) one who betrays another's trust, is false to an obligation or duty, or commits treason
Ps 59:5 . . . Show no mercy to wicked **t.**
Ps 119:158 . . . Seeing these **t** makes me

TRAMPLE, TRAMPLED (v) to crush, injure, or destroy by or as if by treading
Ps 60:12 . . . for he will **t** down our foes.
Ps 91:13 . . . You will **t** upon lions
Amos 5:11 . . . You **t** the poor,
Amos 8:4 . . . rob the poor and **t** down the
Mic 4:13 . . . so you can **t** many nations to
Mic 7:19 . . . You will **t** our sins under
Matt 7:6 . . . They will **t** the pearls,
Luke 21:24 . . . Jerusalem will be **t-d** down
Heb 10:29 . . . who have **t-d** on the Son
Rev 14:20 . . . The grapes were **t-d** in the

TRANCE (n) a sleeplike state (as of deep hypnosis)
Acts 10:10 . . . prepared, he fell into a **t.**
Acts 11:5 . . . I went into a **t** and saw a
Acts 22:17 . . . the Temple and fell into a **t.**

TRANSFIGURED (KJV)
Matt 17:2 . . . Jesus' appearance was *transformed*
Mark 9:2 . . . Jesus' appearance was *transformed*

TRANSFORM, TRANSFORMED (v) to change the outward appearance of; to change in character or condition
see also CHANGE(D)
Matt 17:2 . . . appearance was **t-ed** so that
Rom 12:2 . . . let God **t** you into a new
1 Cor 15:51 . . . but we will all be **t-ed!**

TRANSGRESSED, TRANSGRESSION (KJV)
Josh 7:11 . . . and *broken* my covenant
1 Chr 5:25 . . . tribes were *unfaithful*
1 Chr 10:13 . . . because he was *unfaithful*
Rom 4:15 . . . to avoid *breaking* the law
1 Jn 3:4 . . . sin *is contrary to* the law

TRAP, TRAPS (n) something by which one is caught or stopped unawares; a position or situation from which it is difficult or impossible to escape; a device for taking game or other animals
Deut 7:25 . . . will become a **t** to you,
Deut 12:30 . . . fall into the **t** of following
Ps 91:3 . . . you from every **t** and protect
Prov 1:17 . . . a bird sees a **t** being set,
Prov 3:26 . . . foot from being caught in a **t.**
Prov 28:10 . . . into their own **t,** but the
Prov 29:5 . . . is to lay a **t** for their feet.
Prov 29:25 . . . a dangerous **t,** but trusting
Isa 8:14 . . . he will be a **t** and a snare.
Isa 24:17 . . . Terror and **t-s** and snares will
Matt 16:23 . . . are a dangerous **t** to me.
Rom 11:9 . . . a snare, a **t** that makes them
1 Tim 3:7 . . . into the devil's **t.**
2 Tim 2:26 . . . from the devil's **t.**

TRAP, TRAPPED, TRAPS (v) to catch or take in or as if in a trap
Ps 7:15 . . . a deep pit to **t** others, then
Ps 9:16 . . . wicked are **t-ped** by their own
Prov 6:2 . . . if you have **t-ped** yourself by
Prov 12:13 . . . wicked are **t-ped** by their
Prov 18:7 . . . they **t** themselves with
Matt 22:15 . . . to plot how to **t** Jesus into
1 Cor 3:19 . . . He **t-s** the wise in the snare
1 Tim 6:9 . . . temptation and are **t-ped** by

TREACHEROUS (adj) characterized by or manifesting treachery
Prov 11:6 . . . ambition of **t** people traps
Prov 13:2 . . . but **t** people have an appetite
Prov 13:15 . . . a **t** person is headed for
Prov 22:12 . . . ruins the plans of the **t.**
Jer 3:8 . . . But that **t** sister Judah had

TREACHERY (n) violation of allegiance or of faith and confidence
Acts 1:18 . . . he received for his **t.**

TREAD, TREADING, TREADS (v) to beat or press with the feet
Deut 25:4 . . . eating as it **t-s** out the grain.
Isa 63:2 . . . have been **t-ing** out grapes?
Joel 3:13 . . . Come, **t** the grapes,
1 Cor 9:9 . . . from eating as it **t-s** out
1 Tim 5:18 . . . from eating as it **t-s** out

TREASURE, TREASURES (n) wealth or a collection of precious things; something of great value
Exod 19:5 . . . my own special **t** from
Deut 7:6 . . . to be his own special **t.**
1 Chr 29:3 . . . my own private **t-s** of gold
Ps 119:111 . . . Your laws are my **t;** they
Ps 135:4 . . . Israel for his own special **t.**
Prov 2:4 . . . seek them like hidden **t-s.**
Prov 18:22 . . . finds a wife finds a **t,**
Song 4:10 . . . delights me, my **t,** my bride.
Isa 10:3 . . . Where will your **t-s** be safe?
Hag 2:7 . . . the **t-s** of all the nations
Mal 3:17 . . . they will be my own special **t.**
Matt 6:19 . . . Don't store up **t-s** here on
Matt 6:21 . . . Wherever your **t** is, there the
Matt 13:44 . . . Heaven is like a **t** that a man
Luke 12:33 . . . will store up **t** for you in
2 Cor 4:7 . . . jars containing this great **t.**
Eph 3:8 . . . the endless **t-s** available to
Col 2:3 . . . hidden all the **t-s** of wisdom
1 Tim 6:19 . . . storing up their **t** as a good
Heb 11:26 . . . to own the **t-s** of Egypt, for

TREASURE, TREASURED (v) to hold or keep as precious
Job 23:12 . . . but have **t-d** his words more
Prov 2:1 . . . I say, and **t** my commands.
Prov 7:1 . . . always **t** my commands.
Prov 10:14 . . . Wise people **t** knowledge,

TREASURY (n) a place in which stores of wealth are kept
Deut 28:12 . . . time from his rich **t** in the
Luke 6:45 . . . things from the **t** of a good

TREAT, TREATED, TREATING (v) to regard and deal with in a specified manner
Gen 18:25 . . . **t-ing** the righteous
Eccl 8:14 . . . people are often **t-ed** as though
Matt 18:17 . . . **t** that person as a pagan
Eph 6:9 . . . Masters, **t** your slaves in the same
Heb 10:29 . . . God, and have **t-ed** the blood of
1 Pet 3:7 . . . **T** your wife with understanding
Heb 12:7 . . . that God is **t-ing** you as his own

TREATY, TREATIES (n) an agreement or arrangement made by negotiation
Exod 34:12 . . . to make a **t** with the people
Deut 7:2 . . . Make no **t-ies** with them and
Dan 9:27 . . . will make a **t** with the people

TREE, TREES (n) woody perennial plants, many of which produce crops; highly treasured natural resource; often linked with worship of pagan gods; symbolic of a growing believer
Gen 2:9 . . . he placed the **t** of life and
Deut 21:23 . . . from the **t** overnight.
Judg 9:8 . . . the **t-s** decided to choose
2 Sam 18:9 . . . got caught in the **t.**
1 Kgs 14:23 . . . and under every green **t.**
Ps 1:3 . . . They are like **t-s** planted along
Ps 52:8 . . . like an olive **t,** thriving in
Ps 92:12 . . . like palm **t-s** and grow
Ps 96:12 . . . Let the **t-s** of the forest
Prov 3:18 . . . Wisdom is a **t** of life to
Prov 11:30 . . . deeds become a **t** of life;
Isa 55:12 . . . and the **t-s** of the field
Isa 65:22 . . . people will live as long as **t-s,**
Jer 17:8 . . . They are like **t-s** planted along
Dan 4:10 . . . saw a large **t** in the middle
Mic 4:4 . . . and fig **t-s,** for there will be
Matt 3:10 . . . sever the roots of the **t-s.**
Matt 3:10 . . . every **t** that does not produce
Matt 12:33 . . . **t** is identified by its fruit.
Mark 8:24 . . . look like **t-s** walking
Luke 19:4 . . . a sycamore-fig **t** beside the
Rom 11:24 . . . cut from a wild olive **t.**
Gal 3:13 . . . everyone who is hung on a **t.**
Jas 3:12 . . . Does a fig **t** produce olives,
Jude 1:12 . . . They are like **t-s** in autumn
Rev 22:2 . . . the river grew a **t** of life,
Rev 22:14 . . . the fruit from the **t** of life.
Rev 22:19 . . . share in the **t** of life and

TREMBLE, TREMBLED, TREMBLES, TREMBLING (v) to be affected with great fear or anxiety; to shake involuntarily
Exod 15:14 . . . hear and **t;** anguish grips
Exod 19:16 . . . horn, and all the people **t-d.**
Exod 20:18 . . . a distance, **t-ing** with fear.
2 Sam 22:8 . . . the earth quaked and **t-d.**
1 Chr 16:30 . . . all the earth **t** before him.
Ps 2:11 . . . fear, and rejoice with **t-ing.**
Ps 97:4 . . . The earth sees and **t-s.**
Ps 102:15 . . . the earth will **t** before his
Ps 104:32 . . . The earth **t-s** at his glance;
Isa 66:2 . . . contrite hearts, who **t** at my
Jer 10:10 . . . whole earth **t-s** at his anger.
Dan 10:10 . . . and lifted me, still **t-ing,**
Joel 2:1 . . . Let everyone **t** in fear
Nah 1:5 . . . hills melt away; the earth **t-s,**
Hab 3:6 . . . the nations **t.** He shatters
Heb 4:1 . . . we ought to **t** with fear that
Heb 12:21 . . . I am terrified and **t-ing.**

TRESPASS(ES) (KJV)
Lev 19:21 . . . a ram as a *guilt* offering
2 Chr 24:18 . . . Because of this *sin,* divine
Matt 6:15 . . . Father will not forgive your *sins*
Matt 18:15 . . . believer *sins* against you,
Eph 2:1 . . . because of your *disobedience*

TRIAL, TRIALS (n) a legal proceeding based in court; a test of faith, patience, or stamina through subjection to suffering or temptation
see also TEMPTATION(S), TEST(S), TROUBLE(S)
Job 42:11 . . . all the **t-s** the LORD had
Ps 26:2 . . . Put me on **t,** LORD,
Ps 37:33 . . . when they are put on **t.**
Ps 143:2 . . . Don't put your servant on **t,**
Mark 13:11 . . . and stand **t,** don't worry in
Luke 22:28 . . . with me in my time of **t.**
John 16:33 . . . have many **t-s** and sorrows.
Rom 5:3 . . . into problems and **t-s,** for we
1 Pet 1:7 . . . through many **t-s,** it will
1 Pet 4:12 . . . the fiery **t-s** you are going
2 Pet 2:9 . . . from their **t-s,** even while

TRIBE, TRIBES (n) family divisions, usually within Israel, but also of other ethnic peoples
Gen 49:28 . . . are the twelve **t-s** of Israel,
Matt 19:28 . . . the twelve **t-s** of Israel.
Heb 7:13 . . . a different **t,** whose members
Rev 5:5 . . . Lion of the **t** of Judah,
Rev 5:9 . . . God from every **t** and language
Rev 11:9 . . . all peoples, **t-s,** languages,
Rev 14:6 . . . to every nation, **t,** language,

TRIBULATION (n) a period of unparalleled suffering in the last days
Rev 7:14 . . . who died in the great **t.**

TRIBUTE (n) a gift or service showing respect, gratitude, or affection
Ps 76:11 . . . Let everyone bring **t** to the

TRICK, TRICKED (v) to deceive or cheat
Gen 27:35 . . . and he **t-ed** me
Gen 29:25 . . . Why have you **t-ed** me
Jer 29:31 . . . has **t-ed** you into believing
2 Cor 4:2 . . . We don't try to **t** anyone
Eph 4:14 . . . people try to **t** us with lies

TRICKERY (n) deception
Isa 29:21 . . . those who use **t** to pervert
2 Cor 12:16 . . . advantage of you by **t.**

TRIED (v) to make an attempt at; to put to test
Ps 73:16 . . . So I **t** to understand
Ps 95:9 . . . tested and **t** my patience,
Ps 119:10 . . . I have **t** hard to find
Heb 3:9 . . . tested and **t** my patience,

TRIUMPH (n) the joy or exultation of victory or success
Ps 118:7 . . . I will look in **t** at those

TRIUMPH, TRIUMPHED (v) to obtain victory
1 Sam 17:50 . . . So David **t-ed** over the
Ps 54:7 . . . and helped me to **t** over my

TRIUMPHAL (adj) of, relating to, or marked by triumph
2 Cor 2:14 . . . in Christ's **t** procession.

TRIUMPHANT (adj) victorious, conquering
Deut 33:29 . . . shield and your **t** sword!

TROUBLE, TROUBLES (n) a state, condition, or cause of distress, annoyance, difficulty, or inconvenience
see also TEST(S), TRIAL(S)
Gen 41:51 . . . made me forget all my **t-s**
Josh 7:25 . . . have you brought **t** on us?
2 Chr 15:4 . . . they were in **t** and turned
Job 5:7 . . . are born for **t** as readily as
Ps 7:14 . . . they are pregnant with **t**
Ps 9:9 . . . a refuge in times of **t.**
Ps 10:14 . . . you see the **t** and grief
Ps 22:11 . . . from me, for **t** is near,
Ps 27:5 . . . me there when **t-s** come;
Ps 32:7 . . . you protect me from **t.**
Ps 34:17 . . . them from all their **t-s.**
Ps 37:39 . . . their fortress in times of **t.**
Ps 40:12 . . . For **t-s** surround me—
Ps 41:1 . . . them when they are in **t.**
Ps 46:1 . . . ready to help in times of **t.**
Ps 49:5 . . . I fear when **t** comes, when
Ps 50:15 . . . when you are in **t,** and I will
Ps 54:7 . . . have rescued me from my **t-s**
Ps 55:3 . . . They bring **t** on me
Ps 66:14 . . . I was in deep **t.**
Ps 81:7 . . . cried to me in **t,** and
Ps 86:7 . . . whenever I'm in **t,** and
Ps 91:15 . . . I will be with them in **t.**
Ps 107:6 . . . they cried in their **t,**
Ps 107:41 . . . rescues the poor from **t**
Ps 116:3 . . . I saw only **t** and sorrow.
Ps 120:1 . . . took my **t-s** to the LORD;
Ps 138:7 . . . I am surrounded by **t-s,** you
Prov 6:14 . . . they constantly stir up **t.**
Prov 10:10 . . . who wink at wrong cause **t,**
Prov 11:8 . . . godly are rescued from **t,**
Prov 11:29 . . . Those who bring **t** on their
Prov 12:13 . . . the godly escape such **t.**
Prov 12:21 . . . wicked have their fill of **t.**
Prov 13:20 . . . with fools and get in **t.**
Prov 25:19 . . . in times of **t** is like chewing
Eccl 4:10 . . . falls alone is in real **t.**
Isa 38:14 . . . I am in **t,** LORD. Help me!
Isa 53:4 . . . And we thought his **t-s** were
Isa 58:10 . . . and help those in **t.**
Hos 5:15 . . . as soon as **t** comes, they
Nah 1:7 . . . strong refuge when **t** comes.
Matt 6:34 . . . Today's **t** is enough
Rom 8:35 . . . if we have **t** or calamity,
1 Cor 7:28 . . . at this time will have **t-s,**
2 Cor 4:17 . . . our present **t-s** are small
2 Cor 6:4 . . . We patiently endure **t-s** and
2 Cor 7:4 . . . me happy despite all our **t-s.**
2 Cor 8:2 . . . being tested by many **t-s,**
1 Thes 3:3 . . . shaken by the **t-s** you were
1 Tim 6:5 . . . These people always cause **t.**
Jas 1:2 . . . when **t-s** come your way,
Jas 5:1 . . . all the terrible **t-s** ahead

TROUBLE (v) to worry or disturb
Luke 7:6 . . . Lord, don't **t** yourself by

TROUBLED (adj) concerned, worried
Dan 6:14 . . . the king was deeply **t,** and he
Mark 14:33 . . . and he became deeply **t** and
John 14:1 . . . Don't let your hearts be **t.**
John 14:27 . . . So don't be **t** or afraid.

TROUBLEMAKERS (n) a person who consciously or unconsciously causes trouble
Judg 19:22 . . . crowd of **t** from the town

TRUE (adj) fully realized or fulfilled; accurate; properly so called; steadfast, loyal, honest, and just; ideal, essential; being in accordance with the actual state of affairs; legitimate, rightful
Num 11:23 . . . my word comes **t!**
Deut 18:22 . . . does not happen or come **t,**
Josh 23:14 . . . your God has come **t.**
1 Sam 9:6 . . . everything he says comes **t.**
1 Kgs 10:6 . . . and wisdom is **t!**
2 Chr 15:3 . . . without the **t** God,
Ps 7:10 . . . hearts are **t** and right.
Ps 19:9 . . . laws of the LORD are **t;**
Ps 119:142 . . . instructions are perfectly **t.**
Ps 119:151 . . . your commands are **t.**
Isa 45:19 . . . speak only what is **t** and
Jer 10:10 . . . is the only **t** God.
Jer 26:15 . . . it is absolutely **t** that
Jer 28:9 . . . when his predictions come **t**
Luke 16:11 . . . the **t** riches of heaven?
Luke 18:31 . . . Son of Man will come **t.**
John 1:9 . . . one who is the **t** light,
John 3:33 . . . can affirm that God is **t.**
John 4:23 . . . **t** worshipers will worship
John 6:32 . . . offers you the **t** bread
John 6:55 . . . my flesh is **t** food, and
John 7:28 . . . one who sent me is **t,**
John 15:1 . . . I am the **t** grapevine,
John 17:3 . . . know you, the only **t** God,
Rom 3:4 . . . else is a liar, God is **t.**
Rom 15:8 . . . God is **t** to the promises
Eph 5:9 . . . is good and right and **t.**
Phil 4:1 . . . stay **t** to the Lord.
Phil 4:8 . . . thoughts on what is **t,**
Jas 1:18 . . . giving us his **t** word.
1 Jn 2:8 . . . the **t** light is already
1 Jn 2:27 . . . to teach you what is **t.**
1 Jn 5:20 . . . He is the only **t** God,
Rev 19:9 . . . These are **t** words that come
Rev 22:6 . . . seen is trustworthy and **t.**

TRUMPET, TRUMPETS (n) a wind instrument made of metal or an animal horn used to rally troops on the battlefield or by priests during sacrifices
Isa 27:13 . . . the great **t** will sound.
Matt 24:31 . . . blast of a **t,** and they will
1 Cor 15:52 . . . when the last **t** is blown.
1 Thes 4:16 . . . with the **t** call of God.
Rev 8:2 . . . they were given seven **t-s.**
Rev 8:7 . . . angel blew his **t,** and hail
Rev 18:22 . . . flutes, and **t-s** will never

TRUST (n) assured reliance on the character, ability, strength, or truth of someone or something; hope
see also BELIEVE, FAITH
Job 31:24 . . . Have I put my **t** in money
Ps 40:3 . . . put their **t** in the LORD.
Ps 56:3 . . . I will put my **t** in you.
Isa 2:22 . . . Don't put your **t** in mere
Jer 13:25 . . . putting your **t** in false
Jer 17:5 . . . who put their **t** in mere
John 12:46 . . . who put their **t** in me
Heb 2:13 . . . will put my **t** in him,
1 Jn 4:16 . . . have put our **t** in his love.

TRUST, TRUSTED, TRUSTING, TRUSTS (v) to place confidence or depend; to commit or place in one's care or keeping; to rely on the truthfulness or accuracy of
see also BELIEVE, FAITH
Gen 39:8 . . . master **t-s** me with everything
Deut 1:32 . . . refused to **t** the LORD
Deut 28:52 . . . walls you **t-ed** to protect
2 Kgs 18:5 . . . Hezekiah **t-ed** in the
2 Kgs 18:19 . . . What are you **t-ing** in that
1 Chr 5:20 . . . because they **t-ed** in him.
2 Chr 13:18 . . . they **t-ed** in the LORD,
Job 4:18 . . . God does not **t** his own angels
Job 15:31 . . . fool themselves by **t-ing** in
Ps 13:5 . . . I **t** in your unfailing love.
Ps 21:7 . . . the king **t-s** in the LORD.
Ps 25:2 . . . I **t** in you, my God!
Ps 25:3 . . . No one who **t-s** in you will ever
Ps 31:14 . . . I am **t-ing** you, O LORD,
Ps 33:4 . . . we can **t** everything he
Ps 37:3 . . . **T** in the LORD and do
Ps 41:9 . . . the one I **t-ed** completely,
Ps 44:6 . . . I do not **t** in my bow;
Ps 55:23 . . . but I am **t-ing** you to save
Ps 62:8 . . . O my people, **t** in him at
Ps 71:5 . . . I've **t-ed** you, O LORD,
Ps 84:12 . . . for those who **t** in you.
Ps 86:2 . . . serve you and **t** you.
Ps 112:7 . . . confidently **t** the LORD
Ps 115:8 . . . as are all who **t** in them.
Ps 118:8 . . . LORD than to **t** in
Ps 119:42 . . . for I **t** in your word.
Prov 3:5 . . . **T** in the LORD with
Prov 21:22 . . . fortress in which they **t.**
Prov 28:25 . . . **t-ing** the LORD leads to
Prov 28:26 . . . who **t** their own insight
Prov 29:25 . . . **t-ing** the LORD means safety.
Prov 31:11 . . . Her husband can **t** her,
Isa 12:2 . . . I will **t** in him and
Isa 25:9 . . . We **t-ed** in him, and he saved
Isa 26:3 . . . peace all who **t** in you,
Isa 31:1 . . . for help, **t-ing** their horses,
Isa 40:31 . . . who **t** in the LORD
Jer 7:14 . . . this Temple that you **t** in
Jer 12:6 . . . Do not **t** them, no matter
Jer 48:7 . . . Because you have **t-ed** in your
Dan 3:28 . . . his servants who **t-ed** in him.
Dan 6:23 . . . for he had **t-ed** in his God.
Nah 1:7 . . . to those who **t** in him.
Hab 2:4 . . . They **t** in themselves,
Hab 2:18 . . . foolish to **t** in your own
Matt 18:6 . . . little ones who **t-s** in me to
John 2:24 . . . Jesus didn't **t** them,
John 12:44 . . . you are **t-ing** not only me,
John 14:1 . . . in God, and **t** also in me.
Rom 9:32 . . . instead of by **t-ing** in him.
Rom 9:33 . . . But anyone who **t-s** in him will
Rom 10:11 . . . Anyone who **t-s** in him will
Rom 15:13 . . . peace because you **t** in
1 Cor 2:5 . . . so you would **t** not in

1 Cor 7:25 . . . wisdom that can be **t-ed,**
Eph 3:17 . . . hearts as you **t** in him.
Phil 1:29 . . . the privilege of **t-ing** in Christ
Col 2:12 . . . because you **t-ed** the mighty
1 Tim 6:17 . . . not to **t** in their money,
2 Tim 1:12 . . . the one in whom I **t,**
2 Tim 3:15 . . . that comes by **t-ing** in Christ
Heb 10:22 . . . hearts fully **t-ing** him.
Heb 10:23 . . . God can be **t-ed** to keep his
1 Pet 1:9 . . . reward for **t-ing** him will be
1 Pet 2:6 . . . anyone who **t-s** in him will
1 Pet 2:7 . . . you who **t** him recognize

TRUSTWORTHY (adj) worthy of confidence; dependable
see also FAITHFUL, LOYAL
2 Kgs 22:7 . . . honest and **t** men.
Ps 19:7 . . . of the LORD are **t,**
Ps 119:86 . . . All your commands are **t.**
Ps 119:138 . . . perfect and completely **t.**
Prov 11:13 . . . those who are **t** can keep
Dan 6:4 . . . responsible, and completely **t.**
Titus 2:10 . . . to be entirely **t** and good.
Heb 6:19 . . . a strong and **t** anchor

TRUTH, TRUTHS (n) the property (as of a statement) of being in accord with fact or reality (natural and spiritual); sincerity in action, character, and utterance
Ps 15:2 . . . speaking the **t** from sincere
Ps 25:5 . . . Lead me by your **t** and teach
Ps 26:3 . . . lived according to your **t.**
Ps 43:3 . . . light and your **t;** let them
Ps 45:4 . . . defending **t,** humility, and
Ps 86:11 . . . live according to your **t!**
Ps 119:160 . . . essence of your words is **t;**
Prov 8:7 . . . for I speak the **t** and detest
Prov 12:17 . . . honest witness tells the **t;**
Prov 12:22 . . . in those who tell the **t.**
Prov 23:23 . . . Get the **t** and never sell
Isa 45:23 . . . I have spoken the **t,**
Isa 59:15 . . . Yes, **t** is gone,
Jer 4:2 . . . do so with **t,** justice,
Jer 9:3 . . . to stand up for the **t.**
Dan 10:21 . . . written in the Book of **T.**
Dan 11:2 . . . I will reveal the **t** to you.
Amos 5:10 . . . people who tell the **t!**
Zech 8:16 . . . Tell the **t** to each other.
Zech 8:19 . . . So love **t** and peace.
Luke 1:4 . . . can be certain of the **t**
John 4:23 . . . Father in spirit and in **t.**
John 7:18 . . . him speaks **t,** not lies.
John 8:32 . . . the **t** will set you free.
John 8:44 . . . there is no **t** in him.
John 14:6 . . . way, the **t,** and the life.
John 14:17 . . . who leads into all **t.**
John 15:26 . . . Advocate—the Spirit of **t.**
John 16:13 . . . the Spirit of **t** comes,
John 17:17 . . . your word, which is **t.**
John 18:37 . . . to testify to the **t.**
Acts 20:30 . . . distort the **t** in order
Acts 21:34 . . . find out the **t** in all
Acts 24:8 . . . can find out the **t** of our
Rom 1:18 . . . who suppress the **t** by their
Rom 1:25 . . . They traded the **t** about God
Rom 2:8 . . . to obey the **t** and instead
Rom 2:20 . . . complete knowledge and **t.**
1 Cor 2:13 . . . to explain spiritual **t-s.**
2 Cor 6:7 . . . We faithfully preach the **t.**
2 Cor 13:8 . . . always stand for the **t.**
Gal 2:5 . . . wanted to preserve the **t**
Gal 5:7 . . . back from following the **t?**
Eph 1:13 . . . also heard the **t,** the Good
Eph 4:15 . . . will speak the **t** in love,
Eph 6:14 . . . the belt of **t** and the body
2 Thes 2:10 . . . **t** that would save them.
2 Thes 2:12 . . . rather than believing the **t.**
1 Tim 2:4 . . . and to understand the **t.**
1 Tim 3:15 . . . and foundation of the **t.**
1 Tim 4:3 . . . people who know the **t.**
1 Tim 6:5 . . . their backs on the **t.**
2 Tim 2:15 . . . explains the word of **t.**
2 Tim 3:7 . . . able to understand the **t.**
Titus 1:14 . . . turned away from the **t.**
Heb 10:26 . . . received knowledge of the **t,**
Jas 3:14 . . . don't cover up the **t** with
Jas 5:19 . . . wanders away from the **t**
1 Pet 1:22 . . . you obeyed the **t,** so now
2 Pet 1:12 . . . standing firm in the **t**
2 Pet 2:2 . . . the way of **t** will be
1 Jn 1:8 . . . and not living in the **t.**
1 Jn 2:20 . . . all of you know the **t.**
1 Jn 3:19 . . . belong to the **t,** so we
1 Jn 4:6 . . . Spirit of **t** or the spirit
1 Jn 5:6 . . . Spirit, who is **t,** confirms
2 Jn 1:2 . . . because the **t** lives
2 Jn 1:3 . . . who live in **t** and love.
3 Jn 1:3 . . . living according to the **t.**
3 Jn 1:8 . . . partners as they teach the **t.**

TRUTHFUL (adj) telling or disposed to tell the truth
Ps 5:9 . . . cannot speak a **t** word.
Prov 12:19 . . . **T** words stand the test
John 8:26 . . . and he is completely **t.**

TRUTHFULNESS (n) the quality or state of being truthful
Rom 3:7 . . . highlights his **t** and brings
Rom 9:1 . . . I speak with utter **t.**

TURMOIL (n) a state or condition of extreme confusion, agitation, or commotion
Prov 15:16 . . . treasure and inner **t.**

TURN, TURNED, TURNING, TURNS (v) to convert or change allegiance; to return or change direction; to face toward or away; to divert one's attention from; to become or transform; to shape or bend
Deut 28:14 . . . You must not **t** away from
Deut 30:10 . . . if you **t** to the LORD
1 Kgs 11:4 . . . old age, they **t-ed** his heart
2 Chr 7:14 . . . seek my face and **t** from
2 Chr 34:33 . . . they did not **t** away from
Esth 9:22 . . . sorrow was **t-ed** into gladness
Ps 14:3 . . . no, all have **t-ed** away; all
Ps 30:11 . . . You have **t-ed** my mourning
Ps 40:1 . . . and he **t-ed** to me and
Ps 119:59 . . . I **t-ed** to follow your
Ps 119:102 . . . I haven't **t-ed** away from
Prov 3:7 . . . fear the LORD and **t** away
Prov 28:13 . . . confess and **t** from them,
Isa 17:7 . . . Creator and **t** their eyes to
Isa 54:8 . . . anger I **t-ed** my face away
Isa 55:7 . . . Let them **t** to the LORD
Isa 59:2 . . . he has **t-ed** away and will
Jer 14:7 . . . We have **t-ed** away from you
Jer 31:13 . . . I will **t** their mourning into
Jer 31:19 . . . I **t-ed** away from God,
Lam 3:40 . . . Let us **t** back to the LORD.
Mal 4:6 . . . preaching will **t** the hearts
Matt 3:8 . . . your sins and **t-ed** to God.
Matt 18:3 . . . truth, unless you **t** from your
Mark 4:12 . . . Otherwise, they will **t** to me
Mark 8:34 . . . must **t** from your selfish
Luke 1:17 . . . He will **t** the hearts of
Luke 22:32 . . . you have repented and **t-ed**
John 12:40 . . . and they cannot **t** to me
John 16:20 . . . will suddenly **t** to wonderful
Acts 3:19 . . . of your sins and **t** to God,
Acts 7:42 . . . Then God **t-ed** away from
Acts 26:18 . . . so they may **t** from darkness
Rom 1:26 . . . Even the women **t-ed** against
Rom 2:4 . . . to **t** you from your sin?
Rom 3:12 . . . All have **t-ed** away;
Gal 1:6 . . . that you are **t-ing** away so
2 Tim 2:19 . . . LORD must **t** away from
Titus 2:12 . . . instructed to **t** from godless
Heb 10:38 . . . in anyone who **t-s** away.
1 Pet 2:25 . . . But now you have **t-ed** to

TURTLEDOVES (n) any of several small wild pigeons noted for plaintive cooing
Lev 12:8 . . . must bring two **t** or two young
Luke 2:24 . . . a pair of **t** or two young

TWELVE (adj) of or relating to the number 12
Gen 35:22 . . . names of the **t** sons of Jacob:
Gen 49:28 . . . These are the **t** tribes of
Matt 10:1 . . . Jesus called his **t** disciples
Luke 9:17 . . . picked up **t** baskets of
Rev 21:12 . . . names of the **t** tribes of
Rev 21:14 . . . names of the **t** apostles of
Rev 21:21 . . . The **t** gates were made of

TWINS (n) two offspring produced at a birth
Gen 25:24 . . . she did indeed have **t!**

TWIST, TWISTED (v) to distort or pervert
Exod 23:8 . . . righteous person **t** the truth.
Deut 16:19 . . . You must never **t** justice or
Job 34:12 . . . will not **t** justice.
Isa 24:5 . . . have **t-ed** God's instructions,
Lam 3:36 . . . if they **t** justice in the courts—
Gal 1:7 . . . who deliberately **t** the truth
2 Pet 3:16 . . . unstable have **t-ed** his letters

TWO-EDGED (adj) marked by having two cutting edges
Heb 4:12 . . . sharpest **t** sword, cutting
Rev 1:16 . . . a sharp **t** sword came from
Rev 2:12 . . . with the sharp **t** sword:

U

UNAFRAID (adv) in a manner not filled with fear
Hos 2:18 . . . you can live **u** in peace

UNBELIEF (n) incredulity or skepticism in matters of religious truth
see also UNFAITHFUL
Matt 13:58 . . . there because of their **u.**
Mark 6:6 . . . he was amazed at their **u.**
Mark 9:24 . . . help me overcome my **u!**
Mark 16:14 . . . them for their stubborn **u**
Rom 11:23 . . . Israel turn from their **u,**
1 Tim 1:13 . . . it in ignorance and **u.**
Heb 3:19 . . . because of their **u** they

UNBELIEVER, UNBELIEVERS (n) one who does not believe; a non-Christian
Matt 6:32 . . . dominate the thoughts of **u-s,**
Luke 12:30 . . . the thoughts of **u-s** all over
1 Cor 6:6 . . . right in front of **u-s!**
1 Cor 14:22 . . . for believers, but for **u-s.**
2 Cor 6:15 . . . a partner with an **u?**
1 Tim 5:8 . . . people are worse than **u-s.**
Rev 21:8 . . . But cowards, **u-s,** the corrupt,

UNBELIEVING (adj) marked by unbelief
1 Pet 2:12 . . . among your **u** neighbors.

UNBREAKABLE (adj) not capable of being broken
Num 18:19 . . . an eternal and **u** covenant

UNCHANGEABLE (adj) not changing or to be changed; immutable
Heb 6:18 . . . two things are **u** because

UNCIRCUMCISED (adj) not circumcised; spiritually impure
Jer 9:26 . . . of Israel also have **u** hearts.
1 Cor 7:18 . . . man who was **u** when he
Gal 5:6 . . . being circumcised or being **u.**
Col 3:11 . . . circumcised or **u,** barbaric,

UNCLEAN (adj) morally or spiritually impure; prohibited by ritual law for use or contact
Lev 10:10 . . . is ceremonially **u** and what is
Lev 11:4 . . . it is ceremonially **u** for you.
Lev 17:15 . . . remain ceremonially **u** until
Lev 27:11 . . . vow involves an **u** animal—
Isa 52:11 . . . everything you touch is **u.**
Acts 10:14 . . . have declared impure and **u.**
Acts 10:15 . . . not call something **u** if God

UNDERGROUND (adj) beneath the surface of the earth
Gen 8:2 . . . The **u** waters stopped

UNDERMINE (v) to weaken or ruin by degrees
Jer 38:4 . . . will **u** the morale of
Ezek 13:11 . . . A heavy rainstorm will **u** it

UNDERSTAND (v) to grasp the meaning or reasonableness of; to be thoroughly familiar with
see also UNDERSTOOD
Job 5:9 . . . things too marvelous to **u.**
Job 36:26 . . . is greater than we can **u.**
Ps 73:16 . . . tried to **u** why the wicked
Ps 119:27 . . . Help me **u** the meaning of
Ps 119:125 . . . then I will **u** your laws.
Ps 119:130 . . . so even the simple can **u.**
Prov 2:5 . . . will **u** what it means to fear
Prov 2:9 . . . you will **u** what is right,
Prov 28:5 . . . the LORD **u** completely.
Prov 30:18 . . . things that I don't **u:**
Eccl 7:25 . . . and to **u** the reason
Isa 6:9 . . . carefully, but do not **u.**
Isa 40:21 . . . you heard? Don't you **u?**
Jer 9:24 . . . truly know me and **u** that
Hos 14:9 . . . who are wise **u** these things.
Matt 13:11 . . . permitted to **u** the secrets
Matt 13:23 . . . truly hear and **u** God's
Luke 19:42 . . . people would **u** the way
Luke 24:45 . . . minds to **u** the Scriptures.
Acts 8:30 . . . Do you **u** what you are
Rom 7:15 . . . I don't really **u** myself,
Rom 15:21 . . . never heard of him will **u.**
1 Cor 2:14 . . . and they can't **u** it,
1 Cor 14:14 . . . but I don't **u** what I am
2 Cor 3:14 . . . they cannot **u** the truth.
Gal 1:11 . . . you to **u** that the gospel
Eph 1:18 . . . you can **u** the confident
Eph 5:17 . . . thoughtlessly, but **u** what
Phil 1:10 . . . want you to **u** what really
Phil 4:7 . . . exceeds anything we can **u.**
Col 2:2 . . . that they **u** God's mysterious
1 Tim 2:4 . . . saved and to **u** the truth.
2 Tim 2:7 . . . will help you **u** all these
Heb 11:3 . . . By faith we **u** that the entire
2 Pet 3:16 . . . are hard to **u,** and those

UNDERSTANDABLE (adj) marked by being able to understand; comprehendible
1 Cor 14:19 . . . rather speak five **u** words

UNDERSTANDING (n) comprehension; explanation, interpretation; sympathy
Job 28:12 . . . Where can they find **u?**
Job 28:28 . . . to forsake evil is real **u.**
Ps 119:32 . . . for you expand my **u.**
Ps 119:34 . . . Give me **u** and I will
Ps 119:104 . . . commandments give me **u;**
Prov 3:5 . . . not depend on your own **u.**
Prov 10:13 . . . lips of people with **u,**
Prov 14:29 . . . People with **u** control
Prov 15:32 . . . correction, you grow in **u.**
Prov 16:21 . . . wise are known for their **u,**
Prov 18:2 . . . Fools have no interest in **u;**
Prov 19:8 . . . who cherish **u** will prosper.
Prov 20:5 . . . a person with **u** will draw
Prov 28:16 . . . ruler with no **u** will oppress
Isa 40:28 . . . the depths of his **u.**
Isa 50:4 . . . opens my **u** to his will.
Jer 10:12 . . . With his own **u** he stretched
Mark 12:33 . . . heart and all my **u** and all
Luke 2:47 . . . were amazed at his **u** and his
1 Cor 14:20 . . . but be mature in **u** matters
2 Cor 6:6 . . . purity, our **u,** our patience,
Eph 1:8 . . . along with all wisdom and **u.**
Phil 1:9 . . . growing in knowledge and **u.**
Col 1:9 . . . you spiritual wisdom and **u.**
2 Thes 3:5 . . . a full **u** and expression
1 Tim 6:4 . . . is arrogant and lacks **u.**
1 Pet 3:7 . . . your wife with **u** as you live
2 Pet 1:20 . . . from the prophet's own **u,**
1 Jn 5:20 . . . he has given us **u** so that

UNDERSTOOD (v) *see also* UNDERSTAND
Neh 8:12 . . . God's words and **u** them.
Ps 73:17 . . . I finally **u** the destiny
1 Cor 13:2 . . . and if I **u** all of God's

UNDERWORLD (n) place of destruction (Hebrew *Sheol*)
see also HELL
Job 26:6 . . . The **u** is naked in God's

UNDESERVED (adj) of, relating to, or being that which one does not deserve
Rom 5:2 . . . place of **u** privilege where

UNDISCIPLINED (adj) marked by or possessing no discipline
Prov 29:15 . . . disgraced by an **u** child.

UNDIVIDED (adj) not directed or moved toward conflicting interests, states, or objects
2 Chr 19:9 . . . faithfulness and an **u** heart.
2 Cor 11:3 . . . your pure and **u** devotion

UNFADING (adj) not losing freshness, value, or effectiveness
1 Pet 3:4 . . . the **u** beauty of a gentle

UNFAILING (adj) constant, everlasting, inexhaustible, sure
see also FAITHFUL
Exod 15:13 . . . With your **u** love you
Ps 6:4 . . . because of your **u** love.
Ps 13:5 . . . trust in your **u** love.
Ps 17:7 . . . Show me your **u** love in
Ps 18:50 . . . you show **u** love to your
Ps 25:6 . . . compassion and **u** love,
Ps 31:16 . . . In your **u** love, rescue
Ps 32:10 . . . but **u** love surrounds
Ps 33:5 . . . the **u** love of the LORD
Ps 33:22 . . . Let your **u** love surround
Ps 36:7 . . . precious is your **u** love,
Ps 36:10 . . . Pour out your **u** love
Ps 48:9 . . . meditate on your **u** love
Ps 51:1 . . . because of your **u** love.
Ps 52:8 . . . trust in God's **u** love.
Ps 57:10 . . . For your **u** love is
Ps 85:7 . . . Show us your **u** love,
Ps 90:14 . . . morning with your **u** love,
Ps 117:2 . . . he loves us with **u** love;
Ps 119:41 . . . give me your **u** love,
Ps 119:76 . . . let your **u** love comfort
Ps 143:8 . . . me hear of your **u** love
Ps 147:11 . . . hope in his **u** love.
Isa 55:3 . . . the **u** love I promised
Isa 63:7 . . . the LORD's **u** love.
Lam 3:32 . . . greatness of his **u** love.
Mic 7:18 . . . in showing **u** love.

UNFAIR (adj) marked by injustice, partiality, or deception
Job 31:13 . . . If I have been **u** to my male
Rom 3:5 . . . Isn't it **u,** then, for him
Rom 9:14 . . . then, that God was **u?**
1 Pet 2:19 . . . endure **u** treatment.

UNFAITHFUL (adj) marked by stubborn disbelief and disloyalty; adulterous
see also TREACHEROUS, UNBELIEF
Ps 78:8 . . . rebellious, and **u,** refusing
Prov 23:28 . . . eager to make more men **u.**
Jer 3:20 . . . you have been **u** to me,
Matt 5:32 . . . unless she has been **u,**
Rom 3:3 . . . some of them were **u;** but
2 Tim 2:13 . . . If we are **u,** he remains

UNFORGIVING (adj) unwilling or unable to forgive
2 Tim 3:3 . . . will be unloving and **u;**

UNGODLY (adj) sinful, wicked
see also GODLESS, WICKED
Eph 5:12 . . . the things that **u** people do
2 Pet 2:6 . . . will happen to **u** people.
Jude 1:15 . . . of all the **u** things they

UNHOLY (adj) showing disregard for what is holy; wicked
Matt 7:6 . . . people who are **u.** Don't throw
Heb 10:29 . . . were common and **u,** and have

UNION (n) an act or instance of uniting two or more things into one
2 Cor 6:16 . . . And what **u** can there be
Col 2:10 . . . through your **u** with Christ,

UNITED (v) to become one or as if one; in one accord or spirit
Gen 2:24 . . . the two are **u** into one.
Mark 10:8 . . . the two are **u** into one.
Rom 6:5 . . . we have been **u** with him
Rom 7:4 . . . now you are **u** with the one
1 Cor 6:16 . . . The two are **u** into one.
Eph 4:3 . . . to keep yourselves **u** in the

UNITY (n) the quality or state of oneness or harmony
John 17:23 . . . perfect **u** that the world
Eph 4:13 . . . come to such **u** in our faith

UNIVERSE (n) the whole body of things created; cosmos
Eph 4:10 . . . the entire **u** with himself.
Heb 1:2 . . . the Son he created the **u.**
Heb 11:3 . . . the entire **u** was formed at

UNJUST (adj) characterized by injustice
Ps 82:2 . . . you hand down **u** decisions
Matt 5:45 . . . the just and the **u** alike.

UNKIND (adj) harsh, cruel
1 Pet 2:1 . . . and all **u** speech.

UNKNOWN (adj) not known or well-known
1 Cor 12:28 . . . who speak in **u** languages.

UNLEAVENED (adj) characterized by being without yeast
Exod 12:17 . . . this Festival of **U** Bread,
Deut 16:16 . . . the Festival of **U** Bread,

UNLOVING (adj) characterized by lack of affection
2 Tim 3:3 . . . be **u** and unforgiving;

UNMARRIED (adj) not married
1 Cor 7:8 . . . it's better to stay **u,**
1 Cor 7:32 . . . An **u** man can spend his

UNPUNISHED (adj) to not pay the consequences for a fault, offense, or violation
Exod 20:7 . . . let you go **u** if you misuse
Deut 5:11 . . . let you go **u** if you misuse
Prov 6:29 . . . embraces her will not go **u.**
Prov 19:5 . . . false witness will not go **u,**
Jer 49:12 . . . You will not go **u!**
Amos 1:3 . . . will not let them go **u!**

UNRELIABLE (adj) not dependable
Prov 25:19 . . . confidence in an **u** person
1 Tim 6:17 . . . money, which is so **u.**

UNSTABLE (adj) not firm, fixed, or constant; unsteady
2 Pet 2:14 . . . They lure **u** people into sin,
2 Pet 3:16 . . . ignorant and **u** have twisted

UNTHANKFUL (adj) showing no gratitude
Luke 6:35 . . . those who are **u** and wicked.

UNTHINKING (adj) not having the power of thought
2 Pet 2:12 . . . like **u** animals, creatures

UNTIE (v) to free from something that ties, fastens, or restrains
Mark 1:7 . . . a slave and **u** the straps
Luke 13:15 . . . Don't you **u** your ox or

UNTRUSTWORTHY (adj) not worthy of confidence; undependable
Luke 16:11 . . . if you are **u** about worldly

UNWORTHILY (adv) in an undeserving manner
1 Cor 11:27 . . . this cup of the Lord **u**

UPHOLD (v) to give support to
Ps 82:3 . . . **u** the rights of the oppressed

UPRIGHT (adj) marked by strong moral integrity
see also GODLY, RIGHT, RIGHTEOUS
Deut 32:4 . . . how just and **u** he is!
Prov 3:33 . . . blesses the home of the **u.**
Prov 15:8 . . . in the prayers of the **u.**

UPROOT (v) to displace from a country or traditional habitat
Ps 52:5 . . . and **u** you from the land of

UPSET (adj) emotionally disturbed or agitated
Prov 3:11 . . . and don't be **u** when he
Luke 10:41 . . . worried and **u** over all

URGE (n) a continuing impulse
Deut 12:20 . . . have the **u** to eat meat,

URGE, URGED, URGES (v) to solicit or entreat; to impel
Job 32:18 . . . spirit within me **u-s** me on.
1 Thes 2:12 . . . encouraged you, and **u-d** you
2 Tim 4:1 . . . I solemnly **u** you in the

URGENCY (n) a force or impulse that impels
Exod 12:11 . . . meal with **u,** for this is

USE (v) to put into action or service
2 Tim 2:21 . . . for the Master to **u** you

USEFUL (adj) serviceable for an end or purpose
2 Tim 3:16 . . . inspired by God and is **u** to
2 Pet 1:8 . . . productive and **u** you will be

USELESS (adj) having or being of no use; ineffectual, inept
Acts 26:14 . . . It is **u** for you to fight
1 Cor 13:8 . . . knowledge will become **u.**
1 Cor 15:14 . . . **u,** and your faith is **u.**
1 Cor 15:58 . . . do for the Lord is ever **u.**
2 Tim 2:14 . . . Such arguments are **u,** and
Titus 1:10 . . . who engage in **u** talk and
Heb 7:18 . . . because it was weak and **u.**

UTTERMOST (KJV)
Isa 24:16 . . . songs of praise from the *ends of the earth*
Acts 1:8 . . . and to the *ends of the earth*

V

VAIN (adj) marked by futility or ineffectualness
Isa 65:23 . . . will not work in **v,** and

VALID (adj) well-grounded or justifiable
John 8:14 . . . claims are **v** even though

VALLEY, VALLEYS (n) a depression in the earth's surface between ranges of mountains, hills, or other uplands
Ps 23:4 . . . through the darkest **v,** I will
Song 2:1 . . . lily of the **v.**
Isa 40:4 . . . Fill in the **v-s,** and level
Joel 3:14 . . . waiting in the **v** of decision.
Luke 3:5 . . . The **v-s** will be filled, and

VALUABLE (adj) having desirable or esteemed characteristics or qualities; of great use or service
Job 28:17 . . . Wisdom is more **v** than gold
Ps 119:72 . . . instructions are more **v**
Prov 8:11 . . . is far more **v** than rubies.
Prov 20:15 . . . words are more **v** than
Matt 10:31 . . . you are more **v** to God than
Luke 12:24 . . . are far more **v** to him than
Phil 3:7 . . . these things were **v,** but now

VALUE (n) monetary worth of something; relative worth, utility, or importance
Matt 13:46 . . . a pearl of great **v,** he sold
1 Cor 3:13 . . . a person's work has any **v.**
Phil 3:8 . . . the infinite **v** of knowing

VALUED (v) to estimate or assign the monetary worth of
Zech 11:13 . . . sum at which they **v** me!

VANISHING (adj) disappearing
Prov 21:6 . . . lying tongue is a **v** mist

VANITY, VANITIES (KJV)
Deut 32:21 . . . with their *useless idols*
Ps 144:4 . . . For we are like *a breath of air*
Eccl 12:8 . . . Everything is *meaningless*
Acts 14:15 . . . turn from these *worthless things*
Eph 4:17 . . . for they are *hopelessly confused*

VEGETABLES (n) a plant or its edible part
Rom 14:2 . . . conscience will eat only **v.**

VEIL (n) a facial covering
Exod 34:33 . . . covered his face with a **v.**
2 Cor 3:14 . . . same **v** covers their minds
2 Cor 3:18 . . . have had that **v** removed can

VENGEANCE (n) punishment inflicted in retaliation for an injury or offense
1 Sam 25:26 . . . taking **v** into your own
1 Sam 25:33 . . . carrying out **v** with my
Ps 94:1 . . . O LORD, the God of **v,**
Isa 66:6 . . . the LORD taking **v** against
Luke 21:22 . . . be days of God's **v,** and the

VENOM (n) poisonous matter secreted by some animals
Ps 140:3 . . . a snake; the **v** of a viper
Rom 3:13 . . . Snake **v** drips from their

VERILY (KJV)
Ps 58:11 . . . There *truly* is a reward
John 16:20 . . . *I tell you the truth*

VICIOUS (adj) dangerously aggressive
Matt 7:15 . . . but are really **v** wolves.
Acts 20:29 . . . teachers, like **v** wolves,

VICTORIOUS (adj) of, relating to, or characteristic of victory; having won a victory
see also OVERCOME
2 Sam 8:6 . . . made David **v** wherever he
Isa 53:12 . . . of a **v** soldier, because he
Matt 12:20 . . . cause justice to be **v.**
Rev 2:11 . . . Whoever is **v** will not be
Rev 2:17 . . . everyone who is **v** I will give
Rev 2:26 . . . To all who are **v,** who obey
Rev 3:5 . . . All who are **v** will be clothed
Rev 3:21 . . . Those who are **v** will sit with
Rev 21:7 . . . All who are **v** will inherit

VICTORY, VICTORIES (n) the overcoming of an enemy, antagonist, or struggle
see also OVERCOME
Exod 15:2 . . . he has given me **v.**
2 Sam 22:51 . . . You give great **v-ies** to your
Ps 18:50 . . . You give great **v-ies** to your
Ps 20:5 . . . we hear of your **v** and
Ps 21:1 . . . because you give him **v.**
Ps 35:3 . . . I will give you **v!**
Ps 44:4 . . . You command **v-ies** for Israel.
Ps 45:4 . . . majesty, ride out to **v,**
Ps 48:10 . . . right hand is filled with **v.**
Ps 62:1 . . . for my **v** comes from him.
Ps 98:3 . . . have seen the **v** of our God.
Ps 118:14 . . . he has given me **v.**
Ps 149:4 . . . crowns the humble with **v.**
Isa 12:2 . . . he has given me **v.**
Isa 52:10 . . . see the **v** of our God.
Rom 8:37 . . . overwhelming **v** is ours
1 Cor 15:54 . . . Death is swallowed up in **v.**
Col 2:15 . . . publicly by his **v** over them
Rev 5:5 . . . David's throne, has won the **v.**

VILLAGE (n) a settlement usually smaller than a town
Mark 6:6 . . . Jesus went from **v** to **v,**

VINDICATED (v) shown to be without blame; prove right
1 Tim 3:16 . . . human body and **v** by the Spirit.

VINE (KJV)
Gen 49:11 . . . He ties his foal to a *grapevine*
Deut 8:8 . . . and barley; of *grapevines*
Ps 80:8 . . . from Egypt like a *grapevine*
John 15:5 . . . I am the *vine;* you are the branches

VINEGAR (n) a liquid made from wine that had been soured or overfermented
Prov 10:26 . . . employers, like **v** to the

VINEYARD (n) a plantation of grapevines
1 Kgs 21:1 . . . who owned a **v** in Jezreel
Prov 31:16 . . . earnings she plants a **v.**
Song 1:6 . . . for myself—my own **v.**
Isa 5:1 . . . beloved had a **v** on a rich
1 Cor 9:7 . . . farmer plants a **v** and

VIOLATE, VIOLATED, VIOLATES, VIOLATING (v) to do harm to the person or especially the chastity of; to fail to show proper respect for; to break or disregard
Lev 18:7 . . . Do not **v** your father
Lev 18:8 . . . for this would **v** your father.
Lev 18:10 . . . this would **v** yourself.
Lev 18:14 . . . Do not **v** your uncle,
Lev 18:16 . . . this would **v** your brother.
Lev 20:11 . . . If a man **v-s** his father by
Lev 20:20 . . . he has **v-d** his uncle.
Lev 20:21 . . . He has **v-d** his brother, and
Num 15:30 . . . who brazenly **v** the LORD's
Deut 22:30 . . . for this would **v** his father.
Deut 27:20 . . . for he has **v-d** his father.
Isa 24:5 . . . instructions, **v-d** his laws,
Mal 2:10 . . . each other, **v-ing** the covenant

VIOLATION (n) infringement, transgression
Heb 2:2 . . . firm, and every **v** of the law

VIOLENCE (n) exertion of physical force so as to injure or abuse
Gen 6:11 . . . and was filled with **v.**
Ps 12:5 . . . I have seen **v** done to the
Ps 72:14 . . . them from oppression and **v,**
Isa 60:18 . . . **V** will disappear from your
Jon 3:8 . . . and stop all their **v.**
Mic 2:2 . . . take it by fraud and **v.**

VIOLENT (adj) emotionally agitated to the point of loss of self-control
1 Tim 3:3 . . . a heavy drinker or be **v.**
Titus 1:7 . . . not be a heavy drinker, **v,**

VIPER (n) a particular species of venomous snakes
Ps 140:3 . . . venom of a **v** drips from

VIRGIN (n) an unmarried woman who has not had sexual intercourse
Gen 24:16 . . . but she was still a **v.**
Isa 7:14 . . . The **v** will conceive a child!
Matt 1:18 . . . while she was still a **v,** she
Matt 1:23 . . . The **v** will conceive a child!
Luke 1:34 . . . this happen? I am a **v.**

VIRGINITY (n) the quality or state of being virgin
Deut 22:15 . . . proof of her **v** to the elders

VIRTUE (KJV)
Phil 4:8 . . . things that are *excellent*
2 Pet 1:5 . . . provision of *moral excellence*

VIRTUOUS (adj) morally excellent; righteous
Ruth 3:11 . . . you are a **v** woman.
Prov 21:29 . . . but the **v** think before they
Prov 31:10 . . . Who can find a **v** and
Prov 31:29 . . . There are many **v** and

VISION, VISIONS (n) a visual form of divine revelation, including dreams, that consists of symbolic images, often accompanied by their interpretation
Num 12:6 . . . would reveal myself in **v-s.**
2 Sam 7:17 . . . LORD had said in this **v.**
Dan 9:24 . . . the prophetic **v,** and to
Dan 10:1 . . . that the **v** concerned events
Joel 2:28 . . . your young men will see **v-s.**
Hab 2:3 . . . This **v** is for a future time.
Acts 2:17 . . . Your young men will see **v-s,**
Acts 26:19 . . . I obeyed that **v** from heaven.
Col 2:18 . . . they have had **v-s** about these

VOICE (n) verbal communication by human and divine means
Isa 40:3 . . . the **v** of someone shouting,
Mark 1:3 . . . He is a **v** shouting in the
John 10:3 . . . sheep recognize his **v** and
John 12:28 . . . a **v** spoke from heaven,
Rev 3:20 . . . If you hear my **v** and open

VOMIT (n) matter disgorged from the stomach
Prov 26:11 . . . returns to its **v,** so a fool
2 Pet 2:22 . . . A dog returns to its **v.**

VOMIT (v) to eject violently or abundantly
Lev 18:28 . . . it will **v** out the people

VOW, VOWS (n) a binding promise or pledge
see also COVENANT, PROMISE
Num 6:2 . . . the special **v** of a Nazirite,
Judg 11:30 . . . Jephthah made a **v** to the
Ps 110:4 . . . and will not break his **v:**
Matt 5:34 . . . do not make any **v-s!**
Heb 7:21 . . . and will not break his **v:**

VOWED (v) to promise solemnly
Eccl 8:2 . . . since you **v** to God that
Mark 7:11 . . . For I have **v** to give to

VULGAR (adj) lewdly or profanely indecent
Ps 101:3 . . . at anything vile and **v.**

VULNERABLE (adj) capable of being physically or emotionally wounded
2 Tim 3:6 . . . the confidence of **v** women

VULTURES (n) any of various large birds that subsist chiefly or entirely on dead flesh
Matt 24:28 . . . gathering of **v** shows there

W

WAGE, WAGES (n) payment for labor or services; compensation
Hag 1:6 . . . Your **w-s** disappear as though
Zech 11:12 . . . give me my **w-s,** whatever
Mal 3:5 . . . cheat employees of their **w-s,**
Matt 20:2 . . . the normal daily **w** and
Rom 4:4 . . . their **w-s** are not a gift,
Rom 6:23 . . . For the **w-s** of sin is death,

WAGE (v) to engage in or carry on
2 Cor 10:3 . . . but we don't **w** war

WAILING (n) the act of expressing sorrow audibly
Amos 5:17 . . . There will be **w** in every

WAIT, WAITED, WAITING (v) to look forward expectantly; to stay in place in expectation of
Ps 40:1 . . . I **w-ed** patiently for the LORD
Ps 62:5 . . . that I am **w** quietly before
Ps 69:3 . . . **w-ing** for my God to help me.
Isa 30:18 . . . Blessed are those who **w** for
Mic 7:7 . . . I **w** confidently for God to
Hab 3:16 . . . I will **w** quietly for the
Luke 12:37 . . . who are ready and **w-ing**
Rom 8:19 . . . all creation is **w-ing** eagerly
Rom 8:23 . . . We, too, **w** with eager hope
Heb 9:28 . . . are eagerly **w-ing** for him.

WAKE (v) to rouse from or as if from sleep
see also AWAKE
Prov 6:22 . . . When you **w** up, they will
Rev 3:3 . . . If you don't **w** up, I will

WAKENS (v) to wake
Isa 50:4 . . . by morning he **w** me and

WALK, WALKED, WALKING (v) to roam, traverse, or advance by steps; to pursue a course of action or way of life
Gen 3:8 . . . God **w-ing** about in the garden.
Lev 26:12 . . . I will **w** among you;
Deut 11:22 . . . God by **w-ing** in his ways
Deut 26:17 . . . promised to **w** in his ways,
Josh 22:5 . . . God, **w** in all his ways,
Ps 23:4 . . . when I **w** through the
Ps 89:15 . . . they will **w** in the light
Prov 4:12 . . . When you **w,** you won't
Prov 6:22 . . . When you **w,** their counsel
Isa 2:3 . . . we will **w** in his paths.
Isa 40:31 . . . They will **w** and not
Isa 43:2 . . . When you **w** through the
Jer 6:16 . . . godly way, and **w** in it.
Dan 3:25 . . . **w-ing** around in the fire
Amos 3:3 . . . two people **w** together
Mic 6:8 . . . to **w** humbly with your God.
Mal 2:6 . . . they **w-ed** with me, living good
Matt 14:29 . . . boat and **w-ed** on the water
Mark 2:9 . . . pick up your mat, and **w**
John 8:12 . . . have to **w** in darkness,

WALL, WALLS (n) a thick, high, continuous structure of stones or brick that formed a defensive barricade around an ancient city
Josh 6:20 . . . Suddenly, the **w-s** of Jericho
Neh 2:17 . . . rebuild the **w** of Jerusalem
Isa 58:12 . . . as a rebuilder of **w-s** and
Heb 11:30 . . . and the **w-s** came crashing
Rev 21:12 . . . city **w** was broad and high,

WANDER, WANDERED, WANDERS (v) to follow a winding course; to stray
Num 32:13 . . . them **w** in the wilderness
Ps 119:10 . . . don't let me **w** from your
Ps 119:67 . . . I used to **w** off until you
Ps 119:176 . . . I have **w-ed** away like a
Matt 18:12 . . . one of them **w-s** away
Eph 4:18 . . . **w** far from the life God
1 Tim 6:10 . . . have **w-ed** from the true
Jas 5:19 . . . someone among you **w-s**
1 Pet 2:25 . . . like sheep who **w-ed** away.
2 Pet 2:15 . . . They have **w-ed** off the

WANT, WANTED, WANTS (v) to desire or wish
Gen 3:6 . . . she **w-ed** the wisdom it would
Job 23:13 . . . Whatever he **w-s** to do,
Ps 51:16 . . . do not **w** a burnt offering.
Ps 119:58 . . . heart I **w** your blessings.
Prov 13:4 . . . Lazy people **w** much but
Eccl 6:2 . . . they could ever **w,** but then
Mic 7:3 . . . get what they **w,** and together
Matt 5:42 . . . from those who **w** to borrow.
Matt 14:20 . . . as they **w-ed,** and afterward,
Matt 19:21 . . . If you **w** to be perfect,
Matt 23:37 . . . I have **w-ed** to gather your
Luke 19:14 . . . We do not **w** him to be
John 3:8 . . . blows wherever it **w-s.**
John 7:17 . . . Anyone who **w-s** to do the
John 15:7 . . . ask for anything you **w,**
Acts 20:27 . . . all that God **w-s** you to know.
Rom 7:15 . . . I **w** to do what is right,
1 Cor 12:18 . . . part just where he **w-s** it.
2 Cor 8:5 . . . just as God **w-ed** them to do.
2 Cor 8:10 . . . the first who **w-ed** to give,
2 Cor 12:14 . . . you have—I **w** you.
Eph 1:5 . . . This is what he **w-ed** to do,
Eph 5:17 . . . what the Lord **w-s** you to do.
1 Tim 2:4 . . . who **w-s** everyone to be saved
Heb 10:5 . . . did not **w** animal sacrifices
Heb 13:18 . . . is clear and we **w** to live
1 Pet 1:10 . . . the prophets **w-ed** to know
1 Pet 3:17 . . . if that is what God **w-s,**

WAR, WARS (n) armed conflict with an opposing military force; a state of hostility, conflict, or antagonism
Josh 11:23 . . . finally had rest from **w.**
Ps 46:9 . . . He causes **w-s** to end
Ps 68:30 . . . nations that delight in **w.**
Ps 120:7 . . . peace, they want **w!**
Ps 144:1 . . . He trains my hands for **w**
Isa 2:4 . . . nor train for **w** anymore.
2 Cor 10:3 . . . we don't wage **w** as humans
1 Pet 2:11 . . . that wage **w** against your
Rev 12:7 . . . Then there was **w** in heaven.
Rev 19:11 . . . and wages a righteous **w.**

WARN, WARNED, WARNING (v) to give notice to beforehand especially of danger or evil; to counsel
Gen 2:16 . . . God **w-ed** him, "You may freely
Gen 31:24 . . . told him, "I'm **w-ing** you—
Gen 31:29 . . . to me last night and **w-ed** me,
Exod 19:21 . . . down and **w** the people
Num 16:40 . . . This would **w** the Israelites
1 Sam 8:9 . . . but solemnly **w** them about
1 Kgs 2:42 . . . LORD and **w** you not to
2 Kgs 17:13 . . . and seers to **w** both Israel
2 Chr 19:10 . . . must **w** them not to sin
Ezek 3:18 . . . If I **w** the wicked,
Ezek 33:3 . . . the alarm to **w** the people.
Matt 16:6 . . . "Watch out!" Jesus **w-ed** them.
Luke 16:28 . . . I want him to **w** them so
Acts 4:17 . . . must **w** them not to speak

1 Cor 4:14 . . . to **w** you as my beloved
1 Cor 10:11 . . . written down to **w** us who
Col 1:28 . . . **w-ing** everyone and teaching
1 Thes 4:6 . . . solemnly **w-ed** you before.
1 Thes 5:14 . . . urge you to **w** those who
2 Thes 3:15 . . . but **w** them as you would
Heb 3:13 . . . You must **w** each other

WARNING, WARNINGS (n) something that warns or serves to warn; the act of warning
Ps 19:11 . . . They are a **w** to your servant,
Ps 81:8 . . . while I give you stern **w-s.**
Jer 6:8 . . . Listen to this **w,** Jerusalem,
Jer 42:19 . . . Don't forget this **w** I have
Zeph 3:7 . . . they will listen to my **w-s.**
1 Cor 10:6 . . . happened as a **w** to us,
1 Tim 5:20 . . . as a strong **w** to others.
Titus 3:10 . . . give a first and second **w.**

WARRIOR, WARRIORS (n) a man engaged or experienced in warfare
Gen 6:4 . . . and famous **w-s** of ancient
Exod 15:3 . . . LORD is a **w;** Yahweh
Josh 1:14 . . . strong **w-s,** fully armed,
1 Chr 28:3 . . . for you are a **w** and
Ps 45:3 . . . your sword, O mighty **w!**
Jer 20:11 . . . beside me like a great **w.**

WASH, WASHED (v) to cleanse—of physical, ceremonial, or spiritual significance
see also BAPTIZE(D), CLEANSE
Ps 51:7 . . . **w** me, and I will be whiter
John 13:5 . . . he began to **w** the disciples'
John 13:10 . . . does not need to **w,** except
Acts 22:16 . . . Have your sins **w-ed** away.
Eph 5:26 . . . holy and clean, **w-ed** by the
Titus 3:5 . . . He **w-ed** away our sins,
Heb 10:22 . . . bodies have been **w-ed**
Jas 4:8 . . . **W** your hands, you sinners;
2 Pet 2:22 . . . **w-ed** pig returns to the mud.
Rev 7:14 . . . They have **w-ed** their robes in
Rev 22:14 . . . those who **w** their robes.

WASHBASIN (n) a large bowl for water that is used to wash
Exod 30:18 . . . Make a bronze **w** with a

WASTE, WASTED (v) to spend or use carelessly or inefficiently
Ps 127:1 . . . work of the builders is **w-d.**
Prov 29:3 . . . prostitutes, his wealth is **w-d.**
Prov 31:3 . . . do not **w** your strength
Luke 15:13 . . . there he **w-d** all his money
John 6:12 . . . so that nothing is **w-d.**
Gal 2:2 . . . all my efforts had been **w-d**

WATCH (n) the act of keeping awake to guard, protect, or attend
Matt 24:42 . . . you, too, must keep **w!**
Acts 20:31 . . . my constant **w** and care

WATCH, WATCHES, WATCHING (v) to diligently wait or keep guard; to observe closely
Judg 18:6 . . . the LORD is **w-ing** over
Job 14:16 . . . my steps, instead of **w-ing**
Job 34:21 . . . God **w-es** how people live;
Ps 1:6 . . . For the LORD **w-es** over the
Ps 17:11 . . . and surround me, **w-ing** for
Ps 61:7 . . . faithfulness **w** over him.
Ps 121:3 . . . one who **w-es** over you will
Prov 2:11 . . . Wise choices will **w** over
Prov 31:27 . . . carefully **w-es** everything
Eccl 11:4 . . . If they **w** every cloud,
Jer 24:6 . . . I will **w** over and care for
Jer 31:10 . . . gather them and **w** over
Acts 1:9 . . . while they were **w-ing,** and
Eph 6:6 . . . just when they are **w-ing** you.
Heb 13:17 . . . is to **w** over your souls,
1 Pet 1:12 . . . eagerly **w-ing** these things
1 Pet 3:12 . . . eyes of the Lord **w** over

WATCHER (n) one who watches
Job 7:20 . . . you, O **w** of all humanity?

WATCHMAN (n) a person who keeps watch; guard
Ezek 3:17 . . . you as a **w** for Israel.
Ezek 33:6 . . . hold the **w** responsible
Ezek 33:7 . . . you a **w** for the people

WATER, WATERS (n) precious resource for drink and irrigation, usually associated with blessing; a body of water
Exod 7:20 . . . struck the **w** of the Nile.
Exod 17:1 . . . there was no **w** there for
Num 20:2 . . . was no **w** for the people
2 Sam 23:15 . . . good **w** from the well
Ps 42:1 . . . streams of **w,** so I long
Prov 25:21 . . . give them **w** to drink.
Song 8:7 . . . Many **w-s** cannot quench
Isa 11:9 . . . for as the **w-s** fill the sea,
Isa 32:2 . . . like streams of **w** in the
Isa 43:2 . . . through deep **w-s,** I will be
Isa 49:10 . . . lead them beside cool **w-s.**
Jer 17:8 . . . reach deep into the **w.**
Jon 2:3 . . . The mighty **w-s** engulfed me;
Hab 2:14 . . . For as the **w-s** fill the sea,
Zech 14:8 . . . life-giving **w-s** will flow
Matt 14:25 . . . them, walking on the **w.**
John 3:5 . . . born of **w** and the Spirit.
John 4:10 . . . would give you living **w.**
John 7:38 . . . Rivers of living **w** will
1 Jn 5:6 . . . his baptism in **w** and by
Rev 7:17 . . . springs of life-giving **w.**
Rev 21:6 . . . springs of the **w** of life.

WATERED, WATERING (v) to moisten, sprinkle, or soak with water
Joel 3:18 . . . **w-ing** the arid valley of acacias.
1 Cor 3:6 . . . hearts, and Apollos **w-d** it,
1 Cor 3:7 . . . planting, or who does the **w-ing.**

WATERPROOF (v) to cover or treat with a material to prevent permeation by water
Gen 6:14 . . . cypress wood and **w** it with

WAVE, WAVES (n) a moving ridge or swell on the surface of a liquid (as of the sea)
Matt 8:27 . . . the winds and **w-s** obey him!
Jas 1:6 . . . unsettled as a **w** of the

WAVER, WAVERED, WAVERING (v) to fluctuate in opinion, allegiance, or direction
Rom 4:20 . . . Abraham never **w-ed** in believing
Jude 1:22 . . . to those whose faith is **w-ing.**

WAY, WAYS (n) characteristic, regular, or habitual manner or mode of being, behaving, or happening; manner or method of doing or happening; a course of action; route
Exod 33:13 . . . let me know your **w-s**
Deut 26:17 . . . to walk in his **w-s,** and
Deut 30:16 . . . by walking in his **w-s.**
Josh 22:5 . . . walk in all his **w-s,** obey
2 Sam 22:31 . . . God's **w** is perfect.
Ps 77:13 . . . O God, your **w-s** are holy.
Ps 86:11 . . . Teach me your **w-s,** O LORD,
Prov 2:9 . . . find the right **w** to go.
Prov 4:11 . . . teach you wisdom's **w-s**
Eccl 8:6 . . . and a **w** for everything,
Isa 2:3 . . . teach us his **w-s,** and we will
Isa 40:3 . . . Clear the **w** through the
Jer 6:16 . . . old, godly **w,** and walk in
Mic 4:2 . . . teach us his **w-s,** and we will
Mal 3:1 . . . prepare the **w** before me.
Matt 3:3 . . . Prepare the **w** for the
Matt 3:8 . . . Prove by the **w** you live
Luke 7:27 . . . prepare your **w** before you.

John 14:6 . . . I am the **w,** the truth,
Acts 9:2 . . . followers of the **W** he
Acts 24:14 . . . I follow the **W,** which
Rom 1:30 . . . invent new **w-s** of sinning,
1 Cor 10:13 . . . will show you a **w** out
1 Cor 12:31 . . . show you a **w** of life
Col 1:10 . . . Then the **w** you live will
Heb 10:20 . . . and life-giving **w** through

WAYWARD (adj) following one's own capricious, wanton, or depraved inclinations
Jer 3:14 . . . Return home, you **w** children,
Jer 3:22 . . . will heal your **w** hearts.

WEAK, WEAKER, WEAKEST (adj) lacking strength; not able to withstand temptation or persuasion
Ps 72:13 . . . pity for the **w** and the
Ps 103:14 . . . he knows how **w** we are;
Isa 59:1 . . . arm is not too **w** to save
Matt 12:20 . . . will not crush the **w-est** reed
Matt 26:41 . . . but the body is **w!**
Rom 14:1 . . . who are **w** in faith,
1 Cor 8:9 . . . others with a **w-er** conscience
1 Cor 9:22 . . . bring the **w** to Christ.
Cor 11:30 . . . many of you are **w** and
1 Cor 12:22 . . . of the body that seem **w-est**
2 Cor 12:10 . . . For when I am **w,** then
1 Thes 5:14 . . . care of those who are **w.**

WEAKNESS, WEAKNESSES (n) the quality or state of being weak
Ps 136:23 . . . He remembered us in our **w.**
Isa 53:4 . . . it was our **w-es** he carried;
Rom 8:3 . . . the **w** of our sinful nature.
Rom 8:26 . . . Spirit helps us in our **w.**
1 Cor 1:25 . . . God's **w** is stronger than
1 Cor 2:3 . . . I came to you in **w**—timid
2 Cor 12:5 . . . boast only about my **w-es.**
2 Cor 12:10 . . . take pleasure in my **w-es,**
2 Cor 13:4 . . . he was crucified in **w,**
Heb 5:2 . . . is subject to the same **w-es.**

WEALTH (n) abundance of valuable material possessions or resources
see also MONEY, POSSESSION(S), RICHES, TREASURE(S)
2 Chr 1:11 . . . not ask for **w,** riches,
Job 36:18 . . . you may be seduced by **w.**
Ps 39:6 . . . We heap up **w,** not knowing
Ps 62:10 . . . if your **w** increases, don't
Prov 3:9 . . . the LORD with your **w**
Prov 10:2 . . . Tainted **w** has no lasting
Prov 13:11 . . . **w** from hard work grows
Prov 21:20 . . . wise have **w** and luxury,
Prov 29:3 . . . prostitutes, his **w** is wasted.
Eccl 4:8 . . . gain as much **w** as he can.
Luke 19:8 . . . give half my **w** to the poor,
Eph 2:7 . . . of the incredible **w** of his
1 Tim 6:6 . . . contentment is itself great **w.**
Jas 5:3 . . . The very **w** you were counting

WEALTHY (adj) characterized by abundance
Prov 11:24 . . . freely and become more **w;**
Eccl 2:26 . . . sinner becomes **w,** God takes
1 Cor 1:26 . . . or **w** when God called you.

WEAPON, WEAPONS (n) something used to injure, defeat, or destroy
Prov 26:18 . . . shooting a deadly **w**
Eccl 9:18 . . . have wisdom than **w-s** of war,
2 Cor 6:7 . . . use the **w-s** of righteousness

WEARY (adj) exhausted in strength, endurance, or vigor
Isa 40:31 . . . They will run and not grow **w.**
Isa 50:4 . . . know how to comfort the **w.**
Matt 11:28 . . . you who are **w** and carry
2 Cor 5:2 . . . We grow **w** in our present
Heb 12:3 . . . won't become **w** and give up.

WEDDING, WEDDINGS (n) a marriage ceremony usually with its accompanying festivities
Matt 11:17 . . . We played **w** songs, and
Matt 22:11 . . . the proper clothes for a **w.**
Matt 24:38 . . . parties and **w-s** right up
Rev 19:7 . . . for the **w** feast of the Lamb,

WEEDS (n) undesirable growth surrounding a plant
Matt 13:25 . . . and planted **w** among the

WEEK (n) a seven-day cycle
1 Cor 16:2 . . . of each **w,** you should

WEEP, WEEPING (v) to cry aloud, often linked with prayer and repentance
2 Sam 1:26 . . . How I **w** for you,
Ps 126:6 . . . They **w** as they go to
Jer 31:15 . . . deep anguish and bitter **w-ing.**
Jer 31:16 . . . Do not **w** any longer,
Jer 50:4 . . . will come **w-ing** and seeking
Matt 2:18 . . . heard in Ramah—**w-ing** and
Matt 8:12 . . . will be **w-ing** and gnashing
Luke 6:21 . . . blesses you who **w** now,
Luke 22:62 . . . the courtyard, **w-ing** bitterly.
Luke 23:28 . . . don't **w** for me, but **w**
Rom 12:15 . . . and **w** with those who **w.**

WEIGH, WEIGHED, WEIGHS (v) to oppress or depress
Ps 146:8 . . . up those who are **w-ed** down.
Prov 12:25 . . . Worry **w-s** a person down;
Isa 53:4 . . . our sorrows that **w-ed** him
Dan 5:27 . . . *Tekel* means '**w-ed**'—you

WEIGHT, WEIGHTS (n) a piece of material (as metal) of known specified weight for use in weighing articles; burden, hindrance
Lev 19:36 . . . Your scales and **w-s** must be
Prov 11:1 . . . he delights in accurate **w-s.**
Heb 12:1 . . . strip off every **w** that slows

WELCOME (n) the state of being accepted with pleasure
Prov 25:17 . . . you will wear out your **w.**

WELCOME, WELCOMED, WELCOMES, WELCOMING (v) to greet hospitably and with courtesy or cordiality
Matt 18:5 . . . And anyone who **w-s** a little
Mark 9:37 . . . Anyone who **w-s** a little child
John 13:20 . . . who **w-s** my messenger
John 13:20 . . . **w-s** me is **w-ing** the Father
Acts 28:7 . . . He **w-d** us and treated us

WELL (adj) completely cured or healed (physically or spiritually)
Isa 38:9 . . . King Hezekiah was **w** again,
Matt 15:31 . . . the crippled were made **w,**
Matt 17:18 . . . that moment the boy was **w.**
Mark 5:34 . . . your faith has made you **w.**
Jas 5:15 . . . the Lord will make you **w.**

WELL (adv) in a prosperous or affluent manner; in a kindly or friendly manner
Deut 6:18 . . . all will go **w** with you.
Eph 6:3 . . . things will go **w** for you,
1 Tim 3:7 . . . church must speak **w** of him

WEPT (v) *see also* WEEP
Ps 137:1 . . . we sat and **w** as we thought
John 11:35 . . . Then Jesus **w.**

WEST (n) the general direction of the sunset
Ps 103:12 . . . as the east is from the **w.**
Ps 107:3 . . . from east and **w,** from north

WHEAT (n) a cereal grain that yields a fine white flour
Matt 3:12 . . . gathering the **w** into his barn
Matt 13:25 . . . among the **w,** then slipped
Mark 4:28 . . . the heads of **w** are formed,
Luke 22:31 . . . sift each of you like **w.**
John 12:24 . . . a kernel of **w** is planted in

WHEELS (n) a circular frame of hard material capable of turning on an axle
Ezek 1:16 . . . All four **w** looked alike

WHIPPED (v) to strike with a lash or rod
2 Cor 11:23 . . . been **w** times without

WHIRLWIND (n) a small rotating windstorm, sometimes violent and destructive
see also STORM, WIND
2 Kgs 2:1 . . . to heaven in a **w,**
Job 38:1 . . . answered Job from the **w:**
Hos 8:7 . . . and will harvest the **w.**
Nah 1:3 . . . in the **w** and the storm.

WHISPER (n) a minor or softer reflection of the original noise; hint, trace
1 Kgs 19:12 . . . sound of a gentle **w.**
Job 26:14 . . . merely a **w** of his power.
Ps 107:29 . . . calmed the storm to a **w**

WHISPER (v) to speak softly with little or no vibration of the vocal cords
Matt 10:27 . . . What I **w** in your ear,

WHITE, WHITER (adj) free from color; of the color white
Ps 51:7 . . . I will be **w-r** than snow.
Isa 1:18 . . . make them as **w** as snow.
Dan 7:9 . . . clothing was as **w** as snow,
Matt 28:3 . . . clothing was as **w** as snow.
Rev 1:14 . . . like wool, as **w** as snow.
Rev 6:2 . . . saw a **w** horse standing
Rev 19:11 . . . a **w** horse was standing
Rev 20:11 . . . saw a great **w** throne

WHITE (n) the absence of color; free from spot or blemish
Rev 3:4 . . . will walk with me in **w,**
Rev 7:13 . . . who are clothed in **w?**

WHITEWASHED (adj) glossed over with whitewash
Matt 23:27 . . . are like **w** tombs—

WHOLE (adj) entire; complete, unmodified; undivided
1 Sam 1:28 . . . LORD his **w** life.
1 Sam 17:46 . . . the **w** world will know
1 Chr 28:9 . . . him with your **w** heart
Ps 72:19 . . . Let the **w** earth be filled
Ps 103:1 . . . with my **w** heart, I will
Prov 4:22 . . . healing to their **w** body.
Eccl 12:13 . . . That's the **w** story.
Isa 6:3 . . . The **w** earth is filled
Isa 14:26 . . . plan for the **w** earth,
Dan 2:35 . . . covered the **w** earth.
Zeph 1:18 . . . For the **w** land will be
Matt 6:22 . . . eye is good, your **w** body
Matt 16:26 . . . gain the **w** world but lose
Matt 24:14 . . . throughout the **w** world,
John 21:25 . . . I suppose the **w** world
Acts 17:26 . . . throughout the **w** earth.
1 Cor 12:17 . . . Or if your **w** body were
Gal 5:3 . . . regulation in the **w** law of

WHOLEHEARTEDLY (adv) in a completely and sincerely devoted, determined, or enthusiastic manner
Num 32:11 . . . they have not obeyed me **w.**
Deut 11:18 . . . commit yourselves **w** to
Deut 26:16 . . . careful to obey them **w.**
Josh 14:8 . . . For my part, I **w** followed
Josh 24:14 . . . LORD and serve him **w.**
1 Chr 29:9 . . . had given freely and **w**
2 Chr 25:2 . . . sight, but not **w.**
2 Chr 31:21 . . . sought his God **w.**
Jer 29:13 . . . look for me **w,** you will
Jer 32:41 . . . faithfully and **w** replant
Phil 2:2 . . . happy by agreeing **w** with

WHOLESOME (adj) promoting health or well-being of mind or spirit
see also SOUND
1 Tim 1:10 . . . contradicts the **w** teaching
1 Tim 6:3 . . . these are the **w** teachings
Titus 1:9 . . . others with **w** teaching and
Titus 2:1 . . . that reflects **w** teaching.
2 Pet 3:1 . . . stimulate your **w** thinking

WHORE (KJV)
Lev 21:7 . . . a woman *defiled by prostitution*
Deut 23:18 . . . from the earnings of a *prostitute*
Prov 23:27 . . . A *prostitute* is a dangerous trap
Hos 4:14 . . . sinning with *whores*
Rev 17:1 . . . *prostitute,* who rules over

WICKED (adj) morally very bad
Gen 13:13 . . . area were extremely **w** and
2 Sam 22:27 . . . but to the **w** you show
Ps 1:1 . . . the advice of the **w,** or stand
Ps 7:9 . . . those who are **w,** and defend
Ps 10:13 . . . Why do the **w** get away with
Ps 12:8 . . . though the **w** strut about,
Ps 14:6 . . . The **w** frustrate the plans
Ps 18:26 . . . but to the **w** you show
Ps 37:1 . . . worry about the **w** or envy
Ps 82:2 . . . by favoring the **w?**
Ps 101:8 . . . ferret out the **w** and free
Ps 139:19 . . . you would destroy the **w!**
Ps 146:9 . . . the plans of the **w.**
Prov 4:14 . . . Don't do as the **w** do,
Prov 9:7 . . . who corrects the **w** will
Prov 10:7 . . . name of a **w** person rots
Prov 10:28 . . . expectations of the **w** come
Prov 11:10 . . . joy when the **w** die.
Prov 12:5 . . . of the **w** is treacherous.
Prov 26:23 . . . may hide a **w** heart, just
Prov 29:7 . . . the **w** don't care at all.
Isa 5:23 . . . to let the **w** go free,
Isa 11:4 . . . mouth will destroy the **w.**
Isa 26:10 . . . the **w** keep doing wrong
Isa 48:22 . . . no peace for the **w,**
Jer 35:15 . . . Turn from your **w** ways,
Ezek 18:21 . . . But if **w** people turn away
Ezek 21:25 . . . you corrupt and **w** prince
Ezek 33:8 . . . that some **w** people are sure
Hos 10:9 . . . not right that the **w** men of
Jon 1:2 . . . I have seen how **w** its people
Mal 4:1 . . . arrogant and the **w** will be
Luke 6:35 . . . who are unthankful and **w.**
1 Jn 5:17 . . . All **w** actions are sin,

WICKEDNESS (n) the quality or state of being wicked; something wicked
Lev 16:21 . . . it all the **w,** rebellion,
Lev 19:29 . . . with prostitution and **w.**
Deut 9:4 . . . because of the **w** of the other
Ps 73:3 . . . them prosper despite their **w.**
Jer 3:2 . . . your prostitution and your **w.**
Jer 14:16 . . . out their own **w** on them.
Jer 14:20 . . . we confess our **w** and that
Ezek 33:19 . . . turn from their **w** and do
Luke 11:39 . . . of greed and **w!**
Rom 1:18 . . . the truth by their **w.**
Rom 1:29 . . . every kind of **w,** sin, greed,
Rom 2:8 . . . and instead live lives of **w.**
2 Cor 6:14 . . . be a partner with **w?**
Heb 8:12 . . . I will forgive their **w,**

WIDE-OPEN (adj) having virtually no limits or restrictions
1 Cor 16:9 . . . a **w** door for a great

WIDE (adj) fully opened; having great extent
Ps 81:10 . . . Open your mouth **w,** and I
Matt 7:13 . . . its gate is **w** for the
Eph 3:18 . . . should, how **w,** how long,

WIDOW, WIDOWS (n) a woman whose husband has died
Deut 10:18 . . . orphans and **w-s** receive
Ps 68:5 . . . defender of **w-s**—this is God,
Ps 146:9 . . . for the orphans and **w-s**, but
Isa 1:17 . . . Fight for the rights of **w-s**.
Luke 21:2 . . . Then a poor **w** came by and
Acts 6:1 . . . that their **w-s** were being
1 Cor 7:8 . . . aren't married and to **w-s**—
1 Tim 5:3 . . . Take care of any **w** who
1 Tim 5:16 . . . care for the **w-s** who are
Jas 1:27 . . . for orphans and **w-s** in their

WIFE (n) the female partner in a marriage
see also WIVES
Gen 2:24 . . . and is joined to his **w**,
Gen 19:26 . . . But Lot's **w** looked back
Exod 20:17 . . . covet your neighbor's **w**,
Lev 20:10 . . . his neighbor's **w**, both
Deut 5:21 . . . not covet your neighbor's **w**.
Deut 24:5 . . . happiness to the **w** he has
Prov 5:18 . . . Rejoice in the **w** of your
Prov 12:4 . . . A worthy **w** is a crown
Prov 18:22 . . . man who finds a **w**
Prov 19:13 . . . a quarrelsome **w** is as
Prov 21:9 . . . a quarrelsome **w** in a
Prov 31:10 . . . a virtuous and capable **w**?
Mal 2:14 . . . vows you and your **w** made
Matt 1:20 . . . to take Mary as your **w**.
Matt 19:3 . . . to divorce his **w** for just
Luke 17:32 . . . happened to Lot's **w**!
Luke 18:29 . . . up house or **w** or brothers
1 Cor 7:2 . . . should have his own **w**,
1 Cor 7:15 . . . the husband or **w** who isn't
1 Cor 7:33 . . . and how to please his **w**.
Eph 5:23 . . . head of his **w** as Christ
Eph 5:33 . . . love his **w** as he loves
1 Tim 3:12 . . . be faithful to his **w**,
Titus 1:6 . . . be faithful to his **w**,
1 Pet 3:7 . . . Treat your **w** with
Rev 21:9 . . . bride, the **w** of the Lamb.

WILD (adj) not tame or domesticated; growing without human aid; uncontrolled, unruly
Gen 1:25 . . . made all sorts of **w** animals,
Gen 8:1 . . . and all the **w** animals
Luke 15:13 . . . his money in **w** living.
Rom 11:17 . . . branches from a **w** olive

WILDERNESS (n) any desolate, barren, or unpopulated area, usually linked with danger
see also DESERT
Num 16:13 . . . kill us here in this **w**,
Num 26:65 . . . all die in the **w**.
Num 32:13 . . . wander in the **w** for forty
Deut 8:16 . . . manna in the **w**, a food
Deut 29:5 . . . led you through the **w**,
Ps 78:19 . . . give us food in the **w**.
Ps 78:52 . . . safely through the **w**.
Isa 32:15 . . . **w** will become a fertile
Isa 35:6 . . . will gush forth in the **w**,
Matt 3:3 . . . the **w**, 'Prepare the way
Luke 5:16 . . . withdrew to the **w** for
Rev 12:6 . . . fled into the **w**, where God

WILDFLOWERS (n) the flower of a wild or uncultivated plant
Ps 103:15 . . . like grass; like **w**, we bloom
Matt 6:30 . . . so wonderfully for **w** that are

WILL (n) desire, wish
Ps 40:8 . . . in doing your **w**, my God,
Ps 143:10 . . . me to do your **w**, for you
Prov 3:6 . . . Seek his **w** in all you do,
Matt 6:10 . . . May your **w** be done on
Matt 7:21 . . . who actually do the **w**
Matt 12:50 . . . does the **w** of my Father
Matt 18:14 . . . heavenly Father's **w** that
Matt 26:39 . . . want your **w** to be done,
Matt 26:42 . . . I drink it, your **w** be done.
John 5:30 . . . carry out the **w** of the one
John 6:38 . . . heaven to do the **w** of God
1 Thes 5:18 . . . this is God's **w** for you
Heb 10:7 . . . come to do your **w**, O God—
Heb 13:21 . . . need for doing his **w**.
1 Pet 4:2 . . . to do the **w** of God.

WILLING (adj) inclined or favorably disposed in mind; done, borne, or accepted by choice or without reluctance
1 Chr 28:9 . . . heart and a **w** mind.
Ps 51:12 . . . and make me **w** to obey you.
Dan 3:28 . . . command and were **w** to die
Matt 26:41 . . . spirit is **w**, but the body
Rom 9:3 . . . I would be **w** to be forever

WIN (v) to be the victor in
1 Jn 5:5 . . . who can **w** this battle
Rev 6:2 . . . rode out to **w** many battles

WIND, WINDS (n) a natural movement of air of any velocity
see also STORM, WHIRLWIND
Ps 1:4 . . . chaff, scattered by the **w**.
Eccl 2:11 . . . like chasing the **w**.
Hos 8:7 . . . have planted the **w** and
Mark 4:41 . . . Even the **w** and waves
John 3:8 . . . The **w** blows wherever
Eph 4:14 . . . blown about by every **w**
Heb 1:7 . . . his angels like the **w-s**,
Jas 1:6 . . . and tossed by the **w**.

WINDOW, WINDOWS (n) an opening in the wall of a building
Josh 2:21 . . . rope hanging from the **w**.
Mal 3:10 . . . will open the **w-s** of heaven
2 Cor 11:33 . . . a basket through a **w**

WINDOWSILL (n) the horizontal member at the bottom of a window opening
Acts 20:9 . . . sitting on the **w**, became

WINE (n) the fermented juice of grapes, linked positively with blessings and negatively with strong drink
Ps 104:15 . . . **w** to make them glad,
Prov 31:6 . . . and **w** for those in bitter
Song 1:2 . . . love is sweeter than **w**.
Isa 28:7 . . . who reel with **w** and stagger
Mark 15:36 . . . with sour **w**, holding it
John 2:3 . . . The **w** supply ran out
Rom 14:21 . . . to eat meat or drink **w**
Eph 5:18 . . . Don't be drunk with **w**,
1 Tim 5:23 . . . drink a little **w** for
Rev 16:19 . . . was filled with the **w**

WINEBIBBER(S) (KJV)
Prov 23:20 . . . not carouse with *drunkards*
Matt 11:19 . . . glutton and a *drunkard*, and
Luke 7:34 . . . glutton and a *drunkard*, and

WINEPRESS (n) a vat in which the juice from grapes is pressed in the process of making wine
Rev 19:15 . . . juice flowing from a **w**.

WINESKINS (n) a bag used for holding wine, made from the skin of an animal
Matt 9:17 . . . stored in new **w** so that
Luke 5:37 . . . new wine into old **w**.

WINGS (n) feathered appendage of a bird, figurative of freedom, strength, and protection from God
Exod 19:4 . . . carried you on eagles' **w**
Ps 17:8 . . . in the shadow of your **w**.
Ps 91:4 . . . shelter you with his **w**.
Isa 6:2 . . . each having six **w**.
Isa 40:31 . . . high on **w** like eagles.
Mal 4:2 . . . rise with healing in his **w**.
Luke 13:34 . . . chicks beneath her **w**,
Rev 4:8 . . . living beings had six **w**,

WIPE, WIPED (v) to clean or dry by rubbing; to expunge completely
Isa 25:8 . . . will **w** away all tears.
Luke 7:38 . . . she **w-d** them off with her
Acts 3:19 . . . your sins may be **w-d** away.
Rev 7:17 . . . And God will **w** every tear
Rev 21:4 . . . He will **w** every tear

WISDOM (n) knowledge, insight, judgment
Gen 3:6 . . . she wanted the **w** it would
1 Kgs 4:29 . . . gave Solomon very great **w**
1 Kgs 10:24 . . . to hear the **w** God had
2 Chr 1:10 . . . Give me the **w** and
Job 11:6 . . . **w**, for true **w** is not
Job 42:3 . . . that questions my **w** with such
Ps 51:6 . . . teaching me **w** even there.
Prov 2:6 . . . the LORD grants **w**!
Prov 3:13 . . . the person who finds **w**,
Prov 8:11 . . . **w** is far more valuable
Prov 11:2 . . . with humility comes **w**.
Prov 16:16 . . . better to get **w** than gold,
Prov 23:23 . . . also get **w**, discipline,
Prov 29:3 . . . man who loves **w** brings joy
Eccl 10:10 . . . the value of **w**; it helps
Isa 11:2 . . . on him—the Spirit of **w**
Isa 50:4 . . . me his words of **w**, so that
Luke 2:52 . . . Jesus grew in **w** and in
Acts 6:3 . . . full of the Spirit and **w**.
1 Cor 1:21 . . . him through human **w**, he
Eph 1:17 . . . you spiritual **w** and insight
Col 2:3 . . . treasures of **w** and knowledge.
Col 3:16 . . . with all the **w** he gives.
2 Tim 3:15 . . . given you the **w** to receive
Titus 2:12 . . . world with **w**, righteousness,
Jas 1:5 . . . If you need **w**, ask our
Rev 5:12 . . . riches and **w** and strength

WISE, WISER, WISEST (adj) marked by deep understanding, keen discernment, and a capacity for sound judgment
1 Kgs 3:12 . . . you a **w** and understanding
Job 9:4 . . . God is so **w** and so mighty.
Ps 14:2 . . . anyone is truly **w**, if anyone
Ps 19:7 . . . are trustworthy, making **w** the
Ps 119:100 . . . I am even **w-r** than my
Prov 4:7 . . . wisdom is the **w-st** thing
Prov 9:8 . . . correct the **w**, and they
Prov 10:1 . . . A **w** child brings joy to
Prov 11:30 . . . a **w** person wins friends.
Prov 12:16 . . . a **w** person stays calm
Prov 12:18 . . . of the **w** bring healing.
Prov 13:1 . . . A **w** child accepts a parent's
Prov 13:10 . . . who take advice are **w**.
Prov 13:20 . . . Walk with the **w** and
Prov 15:5 . . . learns from correction is **w**.
Prov 16:23 . . . From a **w** mind comes **w**
Prov 18:4 . . . wisdom flows from the **w**
Prov 19:25 . . . they will be all the **w-r**.
Prov 24:5 . . . **w** are mightier than the
Prov 28:7 . . . who obey the law are **w**;
Eccl 8:5 . . . who are **w** will find a time
Eccl 9:17 . . . quiet words of a **w** person
Matt 2:1 . . . some **w** men from eastern
Matt 11:25 . . . who think themselves **w**
Matt 25:2 . . . foolish, and five were **w**.
Rom 3:11 . . . No one is truly **w**; no one
1 Cor 1:19 . . . wisdom of the **w** and
1 Cor 1:25 . . . plan of God is **w-r** than
1 Cor 12:8 . . . ability to give **w** advice;
Jas 3:13 . . . If you are **w** and understand

WITCHCRAFT (n) the use of sorcery or magic
Lev 19:26 . . . practice fortune-telling or **w**.
Deut 18:10 . . . omens, or engage in **w**,
Rev 21:8 . . . those who practice **w**, idol

WITHDRAW, WITHDREW (v) to remove; to retreat
Ps 66:20 . . . or **w** his unfailing love from
Luke 5:16 . . . But Jesus often **w-ew** to the

WITHER, WITHERS (v) to shrivel and lose vitality, force, or freshness
Job 14:2 . . . like a flower and then **w.**
Ps 1:3 . . . leaves never **w**, and they
Isa 40:7 . . . grass **w-s** and the flowers
Isa 64:6 . . . autumn leaves, we **w** and fall,
1 Pet 1:24 . . . grass **w-s** and the flower

WITHHELD (v) to refrain from granting, giving, or allowing
Gen 22:12 . . . You have not **w** from me

WITNESS, WITNESSES (n) a person who gives testimony; one asked to be present at a transaction so as to be able to testify to its having taken place
Deut 19:15 . . . of two or three **w-es.**
Prov 19:5 . . . A false **w** will not go
Prov 21:28 . . . but a credible **w** will be
Matt 18:16 . . . by two or three **w-es.**
John 1:8 . . . simply a **w** to tell about
Acts 1:8 . . . will be my **w-es**, telling people
1 Tim 5:19 . . . by two or three **w-es.**
1 Jn 5:7 . . . we have these three **w-es**—

WITNESSED (v) to have personal or direct cognizance of
Mal 2:14 . . . the LORD **w** the vows

WIVES (n) *see also* WIFE
Eph 5:22 . . . For **w**, this means submit
Eph 5:25 . . . this means love your **w**,
1 Pet 3:1 . . . way, you **w** must accept

WOE (KJV)
Isa 6:5 . . . *It's all over!* I am doomed
Matt 18:7 . . . *What sorrow awaits* the world
Matt 23:13 . . . *What sorrow awaits* you
1 Cor 9:16 . . . *How terrible* for me if I didn't
Rev 8:13 . . . *Terror, terror, terror* to all who

WOLVES (n) any of several wild, predatory animals that resemble large dogs
Matt 7:15 . . . but are really vicious **w.**
Matt 10:16 . . . you out as sheep among **w.**

WOMAN (n) an adult female person
see also WOMEN
Gen 2:22 . . . God made a **w** from the rib,
Gen 3:6 . . . The **w** was convinced.
Gen 3:12 . . . It was the **w** you gave me
Gen 3:16 . . . he said to the **w**, "I will
Exod 3:22 . . . Every Israelite **w** will ask
Lev 12:2 . . . If a **w** becomes pregnant
Lev 15:19 . . . a **w** has her menstrual
Lev 15:25 . . . a **w** has a flow of blood
Num 5:29 . . . If a **w** goes astray and defiles
Judg 4:9 . . . be at the hands of a **w.**
Judg 16:4 . . . love with a **w** named Delilah,
Ruth 3:11 . . . knows you are a virtuous **w.**
2 Sam 11:2 . . . he noticed a **w** of unusual
2 Sam 20:16 . . . But a wise **w** in the town
Prov 11:16 . . . A gracious **w** gains respect,
Prov 11:22 . . . A beautiful **w** who lacks
Prov 14:1 . . . A wise **w** builds her
Prov 30:19 . . . how a man loves a **w.**
Prov 30:23 . . . a bitter **w** who finally gets
Prov 31:30 . . . **w** who fears the LORD
Matt 5:28 . . . looks at a **w** with lust
Matt 9:20 . . . Just then a **w** who had
Matt 26:7 . . . was eating, a **w** came in
Mark 7:25 . . . Right away a **w** who had
Luke 7:39 . . . what kind of **w** is touching
John 4:7 . . . Soon a Samaritan **w** came to
John 8:3 . . . Pharisees brought a **w** who
Rom 7:2 . . . when a **w** marries, the law
1 Cor 7:2 . . . and each **w** should have
1 Cor 7:34 . . . a married **w** has to think
1 Cor 11:3 . . . the head of **w** is man, and
1 Cor 11:6 . . . shameful for a **w** to have
1 Cor 11:13 . . . it right for a **w** to pray
Gal 4:4 . . . born of a **w**, subject to the
Gal 4:31 . . . are children of the free **w.**
Rev 12:1 . . . I saw a **w** clothed with the
Rev 12:13 . . . he pursued the **w** who had
Rev 17:3 . . . There I saw a **w** sitting on a

WOMB (n) uterus
Ps 139:13 . . . together in my mother's **w.**
Prov 31:2 . . . O son of my **w**, O son
Jer 1:5 . . . you in your mother's **w.**
Luke 1:44 . . . baby in my **w** jumped for joy.
John 3:4 . . . into his mother's **w** and be

WOMEN (n) *see also* WOMAN
Gen 6:2 . . . saw the beautiful **w** and took
Song 1:3 . . . all the young **w** love you!
Mark 15:41 . . . Many other **w** who had
Luke 1:42 . . . you above all **w**, and your
Luke 23:27 . . . many grief-stricken **w.**
Rom 1:26 . . . Even the **w** turned against
1 Cor 7:25 . . . the young **w** who are not
1 Tim 2:9 . . . I want **w** to be modest in
2 Tim 3:6 . . . of vulnerable **w** who are
Titus 2:3 . . . teach the older **w** to live in
Titus 2:4 . . . train the younger **w** to love
1 Pet 3:5 . . . how the holy **w** of old made

WON (v) *see also* WIN
1 Kgs 20:11 . . . warrior who has already **w.**
1 Pet 3:1 . . . They will be **w** over
1 Jn 2:13 . . . you have **w** your battle

WONDERFUL (adj) marked by a marvelous, amazing, or extraordinary quality
1 Chr 16:9 . . . about his **w** deeds.
Job 37:14 . . . consider the **w** miracles
Ps 16:6 . . . What a **w** inheritance!
Ps 17:7 . . . unfailing love in **w** ways.
Ps 71:17 . . . about the **w** things you
Ps 72:18 . . . does such **w** things.
Ps 75:1 . . . tell of your **w** deeds.
Ps 105:2 . . . about his **w** deeds.
Ps 118:23 . . . it is **w** to see.
Ps 119:18 . . . to see the **w** truths in
Ps 119:27 . . . meditate on your **w** deeds.
Ps 119:129 . . . Your laws are **w.**
Ps 139:6 . . . knowledge is too **w** for
Ps 145:5 . . . and your **w** miracles.
Eccl 11:9 . . . Young people, it's **w** to be
Isa 9:6 . . . be called: **W** Counselor,
Isa 12:5 . . . he has done **w** things.
Isa 25:1 . . . You do such **w** things!
Matt 21:15 . . . saw these **w** miracles
Matt 21:42 . . . and it is **w** to see.
Luke 13:17 . . . rejoiced at the **w** things
Acts 2:11 . . . about the **w** things God has
Acts 20:24 . . . News about the **w** grace of
2 Cor 10:12 . . . we are as **w** as these
Titus 2:13 . . . hope to that **w** day when

WONDERS (n) mighty works, miracles
1 Chr 16:12 . . . Remember the **w** he has
Ps 26:7 . . . and telling of all your **w.**
Ps 31:21 . . . has shown me the **w** of his
Ps 77:14 . . . are the God of great **w!**
Ps 89:5 . . . your great **w**, LORD;
Mark 13:22 . . . perform signs and **w** so
Acts 2:19 . . . will cause **w** in the heavens
Acts 5:12 . . . signs and **w** among the people.
2 Cor 12:12 . . . signs and **w** and miracles
Heb 2:4 . . . signs and **w** and various

WORD, WORDS (n) something that is said; special revelation from God; commands
Deut 8:3 . . . live by every **w** that comes
Deut 11:18 . . . to these **w-s** of mine. Tie
Job 38:2 . . . with such ignorant **w-s?**
Ps 19:3 . . . speak without a sound or **w;**
Ps 52:4 . . . others with your **w-s**, you liar!
Ps 119:9 . . . pure? By obeying your **w.**
Ps 119:11 . . . hidden your **w** in my heart,
Ps 119:103 . . . How sweet your **w-s** taste
Ps 119:160 . . . essence of your **w-s** is
Ps 119:162 . . . I rejoice in your **w** like
Prov 12:19 . . . Truthful **w-s** stand the test
Prov 12:25 . . . an encouraging **w** cheers
Prov 16:24 . . . Kind **w-s** are like honey—
Prov 17:27 . . . wise person uses few **w-s;**
Prov 26:23 . . . Smooth **w-s** may hide a
Isa 40:21 . . . deaf to the **w-s** of God—
Jer 15:16 . . . your **w-s**, I devoured
Jer 23:29 . . . Does not my **w** burn like
Amos 8:13 . . . for the LORD's **w.**
Matt 4:4 . . . but by every **w** that comes
Matt 15:6 . . . you cancel the **w** of God
Matt 24:35 . . . **w-s** will never disappear.
John 1:1 . . . the beginning the **W** already
John 6:68 . . . the **w-s** that give eternal life.
John 15:7 . . . and my **w-s** remain in you,
John 17:17 . . . teach them your **w**, which
Rom 10:18 . . . the **w-s** to all the world.
1 Cor 2:1 . . . use lofty **w-s** and impressive
1 Cor 2:13 . . . do not use **w-s** that come
1 Cor 14:9 . . . to people in **w-s** they don't
1 Cor 14:19 . . . than ten thousand **w-s** in
2 Cor 2:17 . . . We preach the **w** of God
2 Cor 4:2 . . . or distort the **w** of God.
Eph 6:17 . . . which is the **w** of God.
Phil 2:16 . . . firmly to the **w** of life;
2 Tim 2:15 . . . explains the **w** of truth.
Titus 2:5 . . . shame on the **w** of God.
Heb 4:12 . . . For the **w** of God is
Heb 5:12 . . . things about God's **w.**
Jas 1:22 . . . listen to God's **w.**
1 Pet 1:23 . . . eternal, living **w** of God.
1 Pet 2:8 . . . not obey God's **w**, and so
1 Pet 3:1 . . . to them without any **w-s.**
2 Pet 3:5 . . . the heavens by the **w** of
Rev 19:13 . . . title was the **W** of God.
Rev 22:19 . . . of the **w-s** from this book

WORK, WORKS (n) one's occupation; physical or creative effort
see also DEEDS
Gen 2:2 . . . finished his **w** of creation,
Exod 20:9 . . . week for your ordinary **w**,
Deut 5:13 . . . week for your ordinary **w**,
Ps 77:12 . . . about your mighty **w-s.**
Ps 107:24 . . . impressive **w-s** on the
Ps 127:1 . . . **w** of the builders is wasted.
Ps 150:2 . . . Praise him for his mighty **w-s;**
Prov 21:5 . . . planning and hard **w** lead
Eccl 2:19 . . . my skill and hard **w** under
Eccl 5:19 . . . To enjoy your **w** and accept
John 4:34 . . . and from finishing his **w.**
John 5:36 . . . Father gave me these **w-s** to
John 10:32 . . . have done many good **w-s.**
Acts 13:2 . . . for the special **w** to which
Acts 20:24 . . . finishing the **w** assigned
Rom 4:5 . . . not because of their **w**, but
1 Cor 3:5 . . . the **w** the Lord gave us.
Gal 6:4 . . . attention to your own **w**, for
Eph 4:12 . . . people to do his **w** and build
Eph 4:16 . . . part does its own special **w**,
Eph 4:28 . . . your hands for good hard **w**,
Phil 1:6 . . . began the good **w** within you,
1 Tim 6:18 . . . rich in good **w-s** and
2 Tim 3:17 . . . people to do every good **w.**
Heb 10:24 . . . acts of love and good **w-s.**

Jas 2:26 . . . faith is dead without good **w-s.**
Rev 15:3 . . . marvelous are your **w-s,** O

WORK, WORKED, WORKING (v) to exert oneself physically or mentally
Prov 13:4 . . . but those who **w** hard will
Eccl 5:12 . . . who **w** hard sleep well,
Matt 6:28 . . . They don't **w** or make their
Matt 12:30 . . . anyone who isn't **w-ing** with
Luke 10:7 . . . who **w** deserve their pay.
Luke 13:24 . . . **W** hard to enter the narrow
Rom 4:6 . . . righteous without **w-ing** for
Rom 8:28 . . . to **w** together for the good
Rom 12:11 . . . Never be lazy, but **w** hard
1 Cor 15:10 . . . I have **w-ed** harder than
1 Cor 15:58 . . . Always **w** enthusiastically
2 Cor 11:27 . . . I have **w-ed** hard and
Eph 6:7 . . . you were **w-ing** for the Lord
1 Thes 4:11 . . . and **w-ing** with your hands,
2 Thes 3:10 . . . unwilling to **w** will not
1 Tim 5:18 . . . Those who **w** deserve their
1 Tim 6:2 . . . slaves should **w** all the harder
Heb 6:10 . . . how hard you have **w-ed** for
2 Pet 1:10 . . . **w** hard to prove that you

WORKER, WORKERS (n) one who works; laborer
Prov 10:4 . . . poor; hard **w-s** get rich.
Prov 12:11 . . . A hard **w** has plenty of
Prov 22:29 . . . see any truly competent **w-s?**
Prov 27:18 . . . **w-s** who protect
Prov 31:17 . . . and strong, a hard **w.**
Matt 9:37 . . . great, but the **w-s** are few.
Matt 20:1 . . . one morning to hire **w-s** for
1 Cor 3:9 . . . For we are both God's **w-s.**
2 Tim 2:15 . . . Be a good **w,** one who does

WORLD (n) the earth and its inhabitants; the human race; the current age and its value system
Ps 33:9 . . . he spoke, the **w** began!
Ps 50:12 . . . for all the **w** is mine
Ps 96:13 . . . judge the **w** with justice,
Isa 13:11 . . . will punish the **w** for its
Matt 16:26 . . . you gain the whole **w** but
John 1:29 . . . away the sin of the **w!**
John 3:16 . . . God loved the **w** so much
John 8:12 . . . I am the light of the **w.**
John 13:35 . . . prove to the **w** that you
John 16:33 . . . I have overcome the **w.**
John 17:5 . . . shared before the **w** began.
John 17:14 . . . And the **w** hates them
John 18:36 . . . Kingdom is not of this **w.**
Rom 3:19 . . . the entire **w** is guilty
1 Cor 1:27 . . . things the **w** considers
1 Cor 2:7 . . . glory before the **w** began.
1 Cor 3:1 . . . you belonged to this **w** or
1 Cor 3:19 . . . of this **w** is foolishness
1 Cor 6:2 . . . to judge the **w,** can't you
2 Cor 5:19 . . . reconciling the **w** to himself,
Eph 2:12 . . . lived in this **w** without God
Eph 4:9 . . . also descended to our lowly **w.**
Phil 2:15 . . . lights in a **w** full of crooked
Titus 1:2 . . . them before the **w** began.
Heb 9:26 . . . ever since the **w** began.
Jas 2:5 . . . poor in this **w** to be rich
Jas 4:4 . . . a friend of the **w,** you make
1 Jn 2:2 . . . the sins of all the **w.**
1 Jn 2:15 . . . Do not love this **w** nor
1 Jn 5:4 . . . defeats this evil **w,** and

WORLDLY (adj) belonging to the sphere of human existence only; affected by sin; corrupt
Luke 16:9 . . . Use your **w** resources to benefit
2 Cor 7:10 . . . **w** sorrow, which lacks repentance,
2 Cor 10:4 . . . not **w** weapons, to knock down
1 Pet 2:11 . . . **w** desires that wage war

WORRY, WORRIES (n) mental distress or agitation resulting from concern; anxiety
Prov 12:25 . . . **W** weighs a person down;
Matt 6:27 . . . Can all your **w-ies** add a single
Luke 21:34 . . . and by the **w-ies** of this life.
1 Pet 5:7 . . . Give all your **w-ies** and cares

WORRY, WORRIED, WORRYING (v) to feel or experience concern or anxiety
Deut 20:8 . . . anyone here afraid or **w-ied?**
Ps 37:1 . . . Don't **w** about the wicked
Isa 7:4 . . . Tell him to stop **w-ing.**
Matt 6:25 . . . I tell you not to **w** about
Matt 10:19 . . . don't **w** about how to
Luke 6:41 . . . And why **w** about a speck in
Acts 27:33 . . . You have been so **w-ied** that
Phil 4:6 . . . Don't **w** about anything;

WORSE (adj) of more inferior condition
Matt 12:45 . . . that person is **w** off than
2 Pet 2:20 . . . they are **w** off than

WORSHIP (n) reverent devotion and allegiance pledged to God or a god
1 Cor 10:14 . . . flee from the **w** of idols.

WORSHIP, WORSHIPED, WORSHIPING, WORSHIPS (v) to regard with great respect, honor, or devotion
Gen 12:8 . . . and he **w-ed** the LORD.
Gen 13:4 . . . and there he **w-ed** the LORD
Gen 21:33 . . . and there he **w-ed** the LORD,
Gen 26:25 . . . there and **w-ed** the LORD.
Deut 12:30 . . . and **w-ing** their gods.
2 Kgs 17:36 . . . But **w** only the LORD,
Ps 29:2 . . . **W** the LORD in the splendor
Ps 95:6 . . . Come, let us **w** and bow down.
Ps 105:3 . . . rejoice, you who **w** the LORD.
Isa 44:19 . . . bow down to **w** a piece of
Jer 16:11 . . . **w-ed** other gods and served
Dan 3:28 . . . die rather than serve or **w** any
Hos 9:1 . . . like prostitutes, **w-ing** other
Hos 9:10 . . . as vile as the god they **w-ed.**
Hos 13:1 . . . Ephraim sinned by **w-ing** Baal
Zeph 3:9 . . . everyone can **w** the LORD
Zech 14:17 . . . to Jerusalem to **w** the King,
Matt 2:2 . . . we have come to **w** him.
Matt 4:9 . . . kneel down and **w** me.
Matt 15:25 . . . she came and **w-ed** him,
Matt 28:9 . . . grasped his feet, and **w-ed**
Luke 23:47 . . . he **w-ed** God and said,
John 4:24 . . . **w** in spirit and in truth.
1 Cor 5:11 . . . is greedy, or **w-s** idols,
Heb 9:14 . . . we can **w** the living God.

WORST (adj) most corrupt, bad, or evil
1 Tim 1:15 . . . I am the **w** of them all.

WORTHLESS (adj) valueless, useless, contemptible
1 Sam 12:21 . . . worshiping **w** idols that
Prov 6:12 . . . **w** and wicked people
1 Cor 3:20 . . . he knows they are **w.**
Eph 5:11 . . . part in the **w** deeds of evil
Titus 1:16 . . . **w** for doing anything good.
Jas 5:3 . . . and silver have become **w.**

WORTHY (adj) having sufficient merit or importance; estimable, honorable
Gen 32:10 . . . I am not **w** of all the
Prov 12:4 . . . A **w** wife is a crown
Matt 8:8 . . . Lord, I am not **w** to have
Matt 10:37 . . . are not **w** of being mine;
Matt 22:8 . . . I invited aren't **w** of the
Luke 15:19 . . . I am no longer **w** of being
1 Cor 15:9 . . . I'm not even **w** to be called
Eph 4:1 . . . lead a life **w** of your calling,
Phil 1:27 . . . a manner **w** of the Good News
Rev 5:5 . . . He is **w** to open the scroll

WOUNDS (n) an injury to the body
Isa 30:26 . . . and cure the **w** he gave them.
Zech 13:6 . . . what about those **w** on your
John 20:20 . . . he showed them the **w** in
1 Pet 2:24 . . . By his **w** you are healed.

WRAP (v) to fold cloth, paper, etc. around something, especially in order to cover it
Exod 29:9 . . . **W** the sashes around
Num 4:12 . . . **w** them in a blue cloth

WRAPPINGS (n) something used to wrap an object
John 20:5 . . . saw the linen **w** lying there,

WRATH (n) extreme displeasure, anger, or hostility; God's response to sin
Isa 13:13 . . . Armies displays his **w** in
Rev 6:16 . . . and from the **w** of the Lamb.
Rev 16:19 . . . the wine of his fierce **w.**

WREATH (n) a band of intertwined flowers or leaves worn as a mark of honor or victory
Prov 4:9 . . . will place a lovely **w** on your

WRESTLED (v) to engage in a violent or determined struggle
Gen 32:24 . . . man came and **w** with him

WRITE, WRITING (v) to inscribe or engrave; to record
see also WRITTEN
Deut 10:2 . . . I will **w** on the tablets
Prov 3:3 . . . **W** them deep within your
Prov 7:3 . . . **W** them deep within your
Eccl 12:12 . . . for **w-ing** books is endless,
Jer 31:33 . . . I will **w** them on their hearts.
1 Tim 3:14 . . . I am **w-ing** these things to
Heb 8:10 . . . I will **w** them on their hearts.
Rev 3:12 . . . I will **w** on them the name of

WRITHE (v) to twist (the body or body part) in pain
Jer 4:19 . . . my heart—I **w** in pain!

WRITTEN (v) *see also* WRITE
Deut 28:58 . . . that are **w** in this book,
Josh 1:8 . . . to obey everything **w** in it.
Isa 49:16 . . . See, I have **w** your name
Dan 12:1 . . . whose name is **w** in the book
Mal 3:16 . . . scroll of remembrance was **w**
Luke 24:44 . . . everything **w** about me in
John 20:31 . . . these are **w** so that you
John 21:25 . . . the books that would be **w.**
Rom 2:15 . . . law is **w** in their hearts,
1 Cor 10:11 . . . They were **w** down to warn
Heb 12:23 . . . names are **w** in heaven.
Rev 21:27 . . . whose names are **w** in the

WRONG (adj) incorrect, sinful, immoral, or improper
Prov 14:2 . . . who take the **w** path
Rom 7:19 . . . don't want to do what is **w,**
Rom 12:9 . . . Hate what is **w.** Hold tightly
Rom 14:14 . . . of itself, is **w** to eat.
2 Tim 3:16 . . . make us realize what is **w**

WRONG (adv) in an unsuccessful or unfortunate way
Prov 15:22 . . . Plans go **w** for lack

WRONG (n) an injurious, unfair, or unjust act; something wrong, immoral, or unethical
Exod 23:2 . . . the crowd in doing **w.**
Deut 32:4 . . . faithful God who does no **w;**
Job 34:10 . . . The Almighty can do no **w.**
Ps 141:9 . . . snares of those who do **w.**
Isa 53:9 . . . done no **w** and had never
Rom 13:10 . . . Love does no **w** to others,

Rom 16:19 . . . to stay innocent of any **w.**
1 Cor 6:9 . . . those who do **w** will not
Jas 1:13 . . . God is never tempted to do **w,**
1 Pet 3:17 . . . to suffer for doing **w!**

WRONGDOING (n) evil or improper behavior or action
Prov 26:26 . . . their **w** will be exposed

WRONGED (v) to injure or harm; to malign or discredit
Num 5:7 . . . to the person who was **w.**
Isa 42:3 . . . to all who have been **w.**
1 Cor 13:5 . . . keeps no record of being **w.**

Y

YAHWEH (n) "I AM WHO I AM" or "I WILL BE WHAT I WILL BE"; the personal name of God revealed to Moses in the burning bush
see also LORD
Gen 22:14 . . . named the place **Y**-Yireh
Exod 3:15 . . . **Y,** the God of your ancestors
Exod 6:2 . . . I am **Y**—'the LORD'
Exod 15:3 . . . warrior; **Y** is his name!
Exod 17:15 . . . there and named it **Y**-nissi
Exod 33:19 . . . I will call out my name, **Y,**
Exod 34:5 . . . called out his own name, **Y.**
Judg 6:24 . . . there and named it **Y**-Shalom

YEAR, YEARS (n) the period of about 365 days; a period having special significance; a measure of age or duration
Gen 1:14 . . . the seasons, days, and **y-s.**
Exod 12:40 . . . lived in Egypt for 430 **y-s.**
Exod 16:35 . . . manna for forty **y-s** until
Exod 34:23 . . . Three times each **y** every
Lev 16:34 . . . the LORD once each **y.**
Lev 25:11 . . . During that **y** you must
Job 36:26 . . . His **y-s** cannot be counted.
Ps 90:4 . . . a thousand **y-s** are as a
Luke 3:23 . . . about thirty **y-s** old when
Heb 10:1 . . . again and again, **y** after **y,**
Heb 10:3 . . . of their sins **y** after **y.**
2 Pet 3:8 . . . like a thousand **y-s** to the
Rev 20:2 . . . in chains for a thousand **y-s.**

YEAST (n) a fungus used for making alcohol and bread
Exod 12:8 . . . and bread made without **y.**
Exod 12:15 . . . bread made with **y** during
Matt 16:6 . . . Beware of the **y** of the
1 Cor 5:6 . . . a little **y** that spreads

YESTERDAY (adv) on the day preceding today
Heb 13:8 . . . same **y,** today, and forever.

YIELD, YIELDS (v) to produce; to surrender or submit
Prov 30:33 . . . beating of cream **y-s** butter
Matt 6:13 . . . don't let us **y** to temptation,
Luke 11:4 . . . don't let us **y** to temptation.
Jas 3:17 . . . willing to **y** to others.

YOKE (n) a wooden crossbar linking two load-pulling animals together; figurative of bondage or linkage between people
Hos 11:4 . . . lifted the **y** from his neck,
Matt 11:29 . . . Take my **y** upon you.

YOUNG, YOUNGER (adj) being in the first or an early stage of life, growth, or development
2 Chr 10:14 . . . counsel of his **y-er** advisers.
Ps 119:9 . . . How can a **y** person stay pure?
Prov 20:29 . . . The glory of the **y** is their
Joel 2:28 . . . your **y** men will see visions.
Acts 2:17 . . . Your **y** men will see visions,
Acts 7:58 . . . feet of a **y** man named Saul.
1 Tim 5:1 . . . Talk to **y-er** men as you
Titus 2:4 . . . must train the **y-er** women to
Titus 2:6 . . . encourage the **y** men to live
1 Pet 5:5 . . . same way, you **y-er** men must
1 Jn 2:13 . . . you who are **y** in the faith

YOUTH (n) the period between childhood and maturity
Ps 103:5 . . . My **y** is renewed like the

YOUTHFUL (adj) of, relating to, or characteristic of youth
2 Tim 2:22 . . . that stimulates **y** lusts.

Z

ZEAL (n) eagerness and ardent interest in pursuit of something
Num 25:13 . . . in his **z** for me, his God,
Rom 10:2 . . . but it is misdirected **z.**

NOTES

NOTES

TOPOGRAPHY OF PALESTINE

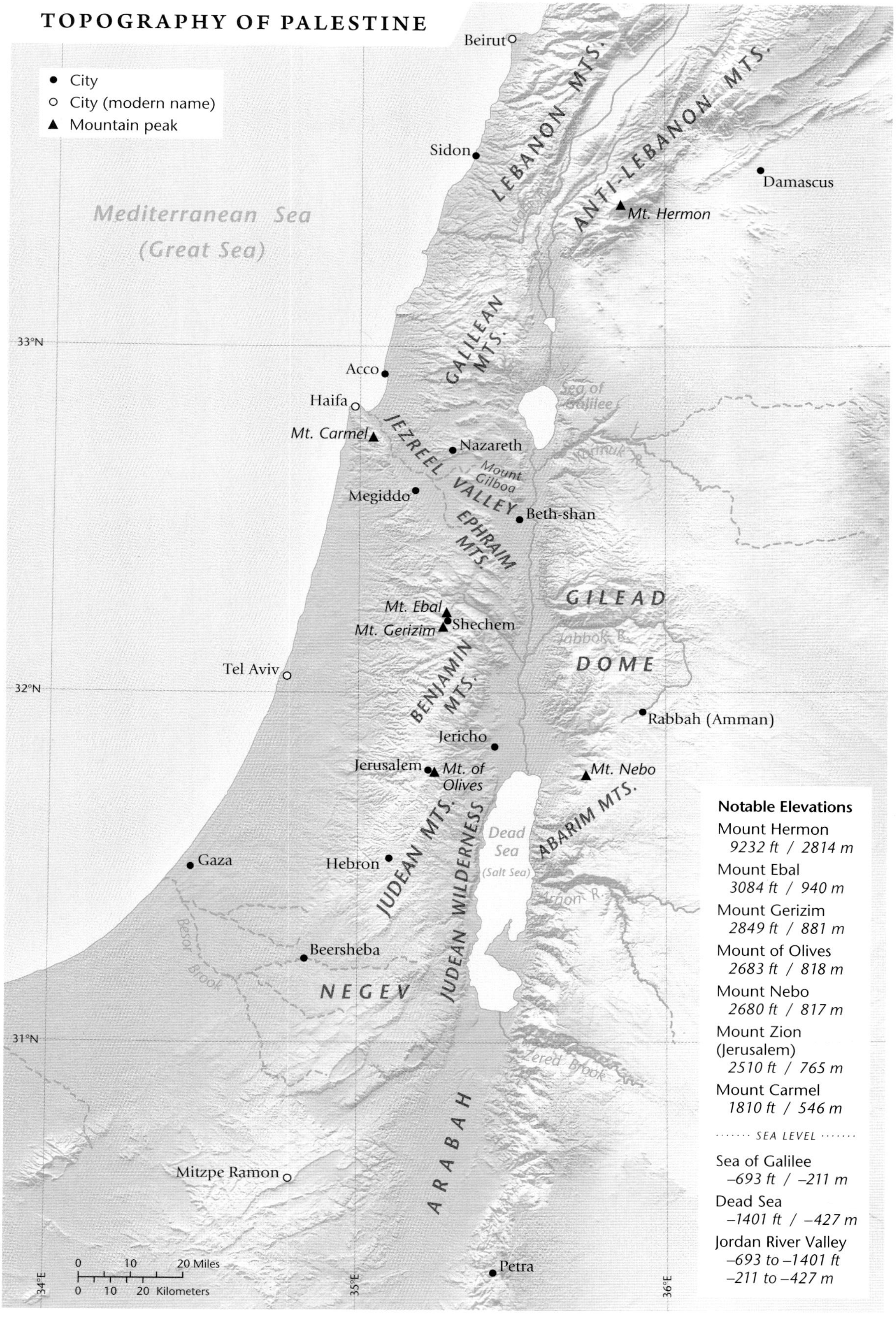
City
City (modern name)
Mountain peak
Beirut
Sidon
Damascus
LEBANON MTS.
ANTI-LEBANON MTS.
Mt. Hermon
Mediterranean Sea
(Great Sea)
GALILEAN MTS.
33°N
Acco
Haifa
Sea of Galilee
Mt. Carmel
JEZREEL VALLEY
Nazareth
Mount Gilboa
Yarmuk R.
Megiddo
Beth-shan
EPHRAIM MTS.
GILEAD
Mt. Ebal
Shechem
Mt. Gerizim
Jabbok R.
DOME
Tel Aviv
32°N
BENJAMIN MTS.
Rabbah (Amman)
Jericho
Jerusalem
Mt. of Olives
Mt. Nebo
ABARIM MTS.
JUDEAN MTS.
JUDEAN WILDERNESS
Dead Sea
(Salt Sea)
Gaza
Hebron
Arnon R.
Besor Brook
Beersheba
NEGEV
31°N
Zered Brook
ARABAH
Mitzpe Ramon
Petra
0 10 20 Miles
0 10 20 Kilometers
34°E
35°E
36°E
Notable Elevations
Mount Hermon
9232 ft / 2814 m
Mount Ebal
3084 ft / 940 m
Mount Gerizim
2849 ft / 881 m
Mount of Olives
2683 ft / 818 m
Mount Nebo
2680 ft / 817 m
Mount Zion (Jerusalem)
2510 ft / 765 m
Mount Carmel
1810 ft / 546 m
SEA LEVEL
Sea of Galilee
–693 ft / –211 m
Dead Sea
–1401 ft / –427 m
Jordan River Valley
–693 to –1401 ft
–211 to –427 m

WORLD OF THE PATRIARCHS

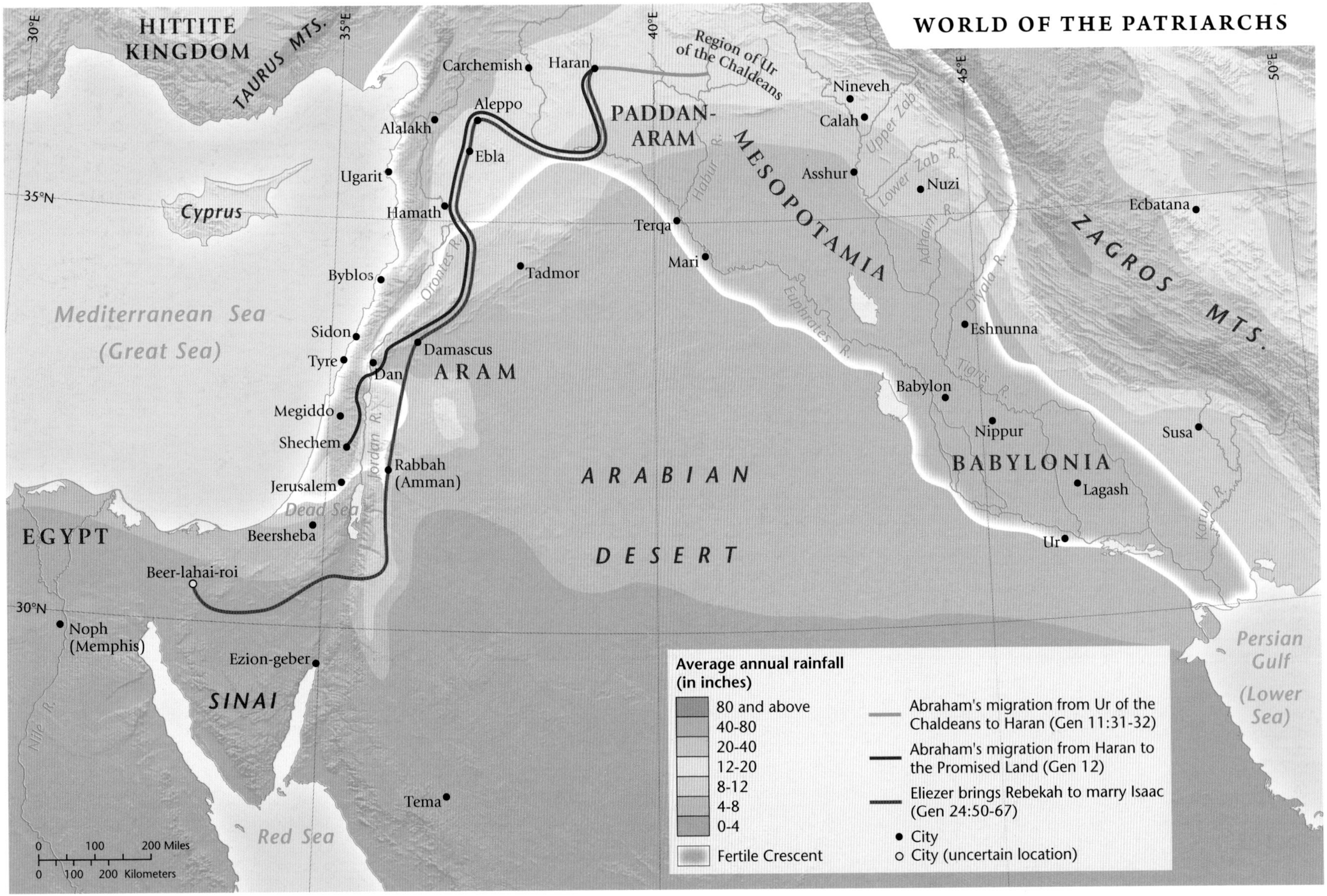
HITTITE KINGDOM
TAURUS MTS.
Cyprus
Mediterranean Sea
(Great Sea)
EGYPT
SINAI
Red Sea
Noph
(Memphis)
Nile R.
Beer-lahai-roi
Ezion-geber
Tema
Carchemish
Haran
Region of Ur of the Chaldeans
Aleppo
Ebla
Alalakh
Ugarit
Hamath
Byblos
Sidon
Tyre
Dan
Megiddo
Shechem
Jerusalem
Dead Sea
Beersheba
Jordan R.
Orontes R.
Damascus
ARAM
Rabbah
(Amman)
Tadmor
PADDAN-ARAM
Habur R.
MESOPOTAMIA
Terqa
Mari
Euphrates R.
ARABIAN
DESERT
Nineveh
Calah
Asshur
Upper Zab R.
Lower Zab R.
Nuzi
Adhaim R.
Diyala R.
Eshnunna
Tigris R.
Babylon
Nippur
BABYLONIA
Lagash
Ur
Susa
Karun R.
Ecbatana
ZAGROS MTS.
Persian Gulf
(Lower Sea)
30°E
35°E
40°E
45°E
50°E
35°N
30°N
0
100
200 Miles
0
100
200 Kilometers
Average annual rainfall
(in inches)
80 and above
40-80
20-40
12-20
8-12
4-8
0-4
Fertile Crescent
Abraham's migration from Ur of the Chaldeans to Haran (Gen 11:31-32)
Abraham's migration from Haran to the Promised Land (Gen 12)
Eliezer brings Rebekah to marry Isaac (Gen 24:50-67)
City
City (uncertain location)

EXODUS FROM EGYPT

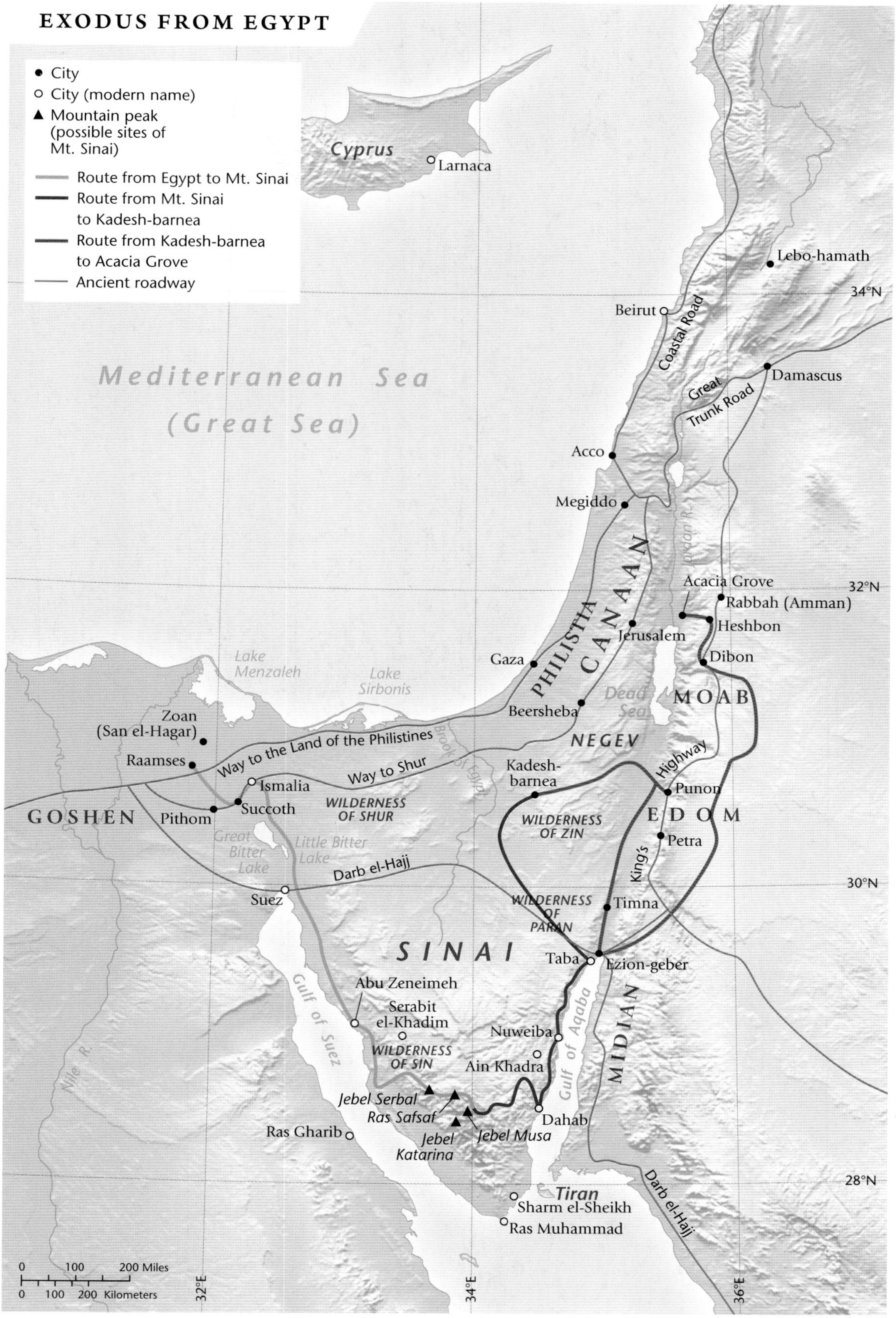
City
City (modern name)
Mountain peak (possible sites of Mt. Sinai)
Route from Egypt to Mt. Sinai
Route from Mt. Sinai to Kadesh-barnea
Route from Kadesh-barnea to Acacia Grove
Ancient roadway
Cyprus
Larnaca
Lebo-hamath
34°N
Beirut
Coastal Road
Damascus
Great Trunk Road
Mediterranean Sea
(Great Sea)
Acco
Megiddo
Jordan R.
CANAAN
PHILISTIA
Acacia Grove
32°N
Rabbah (Amman)
Heshbon
Jerusalem
Dibon
Gaza
Lake Menzaleh
Lake Sirbonis
Dead Sea
MOAB
Beersheba
Zoan
(San el-Hagar)
Way to the Land of the Philistines
Brook of Egypt
NEGEV
Raamses
Way to Shur
Kadesh-barnea
Highway
Punon
Ismalia
Succoth
Pithom
GOSHEN
WILDERNESS OF SHUR
WILDERNESS OF ZIN
EDOM
Petra
King's
Great Bitter Lake
Little Bitter Lake
Darb el-Hajj
Suez
30°N
WILDERNESS OF PARAN
Timna
SINAI
Taba
Ezion-geber
Gulf of Suez
Abu Zeneimeh
Serabit el-Khadim
Nuweiba
Gulf of Aqaba
MIDIAN
WILDERNESS OF SIN
Ain Khadra
Nile R.
Jebel Serbal
Ras Safsaf
Jebel Musa
Jebel Katarina
Dahab
Ras Gharib
28°N
Tiran
Sharm el-Sheikh
Ras Muhammad
Darb el-Hajj
0 100 200 Miles
0 100 200 Kilometers
32°E
34°E
36°E

TWELVE TRIBES OF ISRAEL

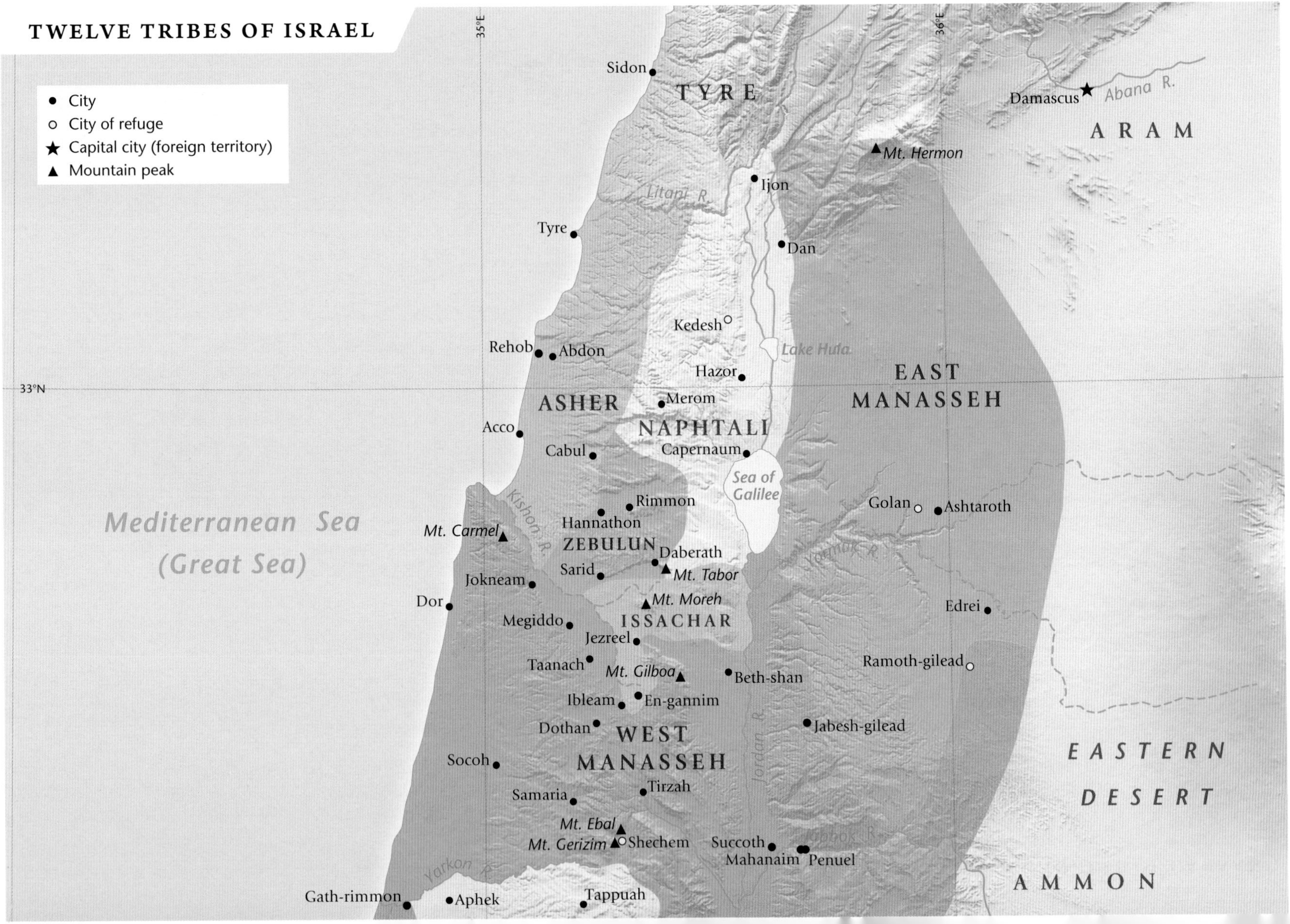

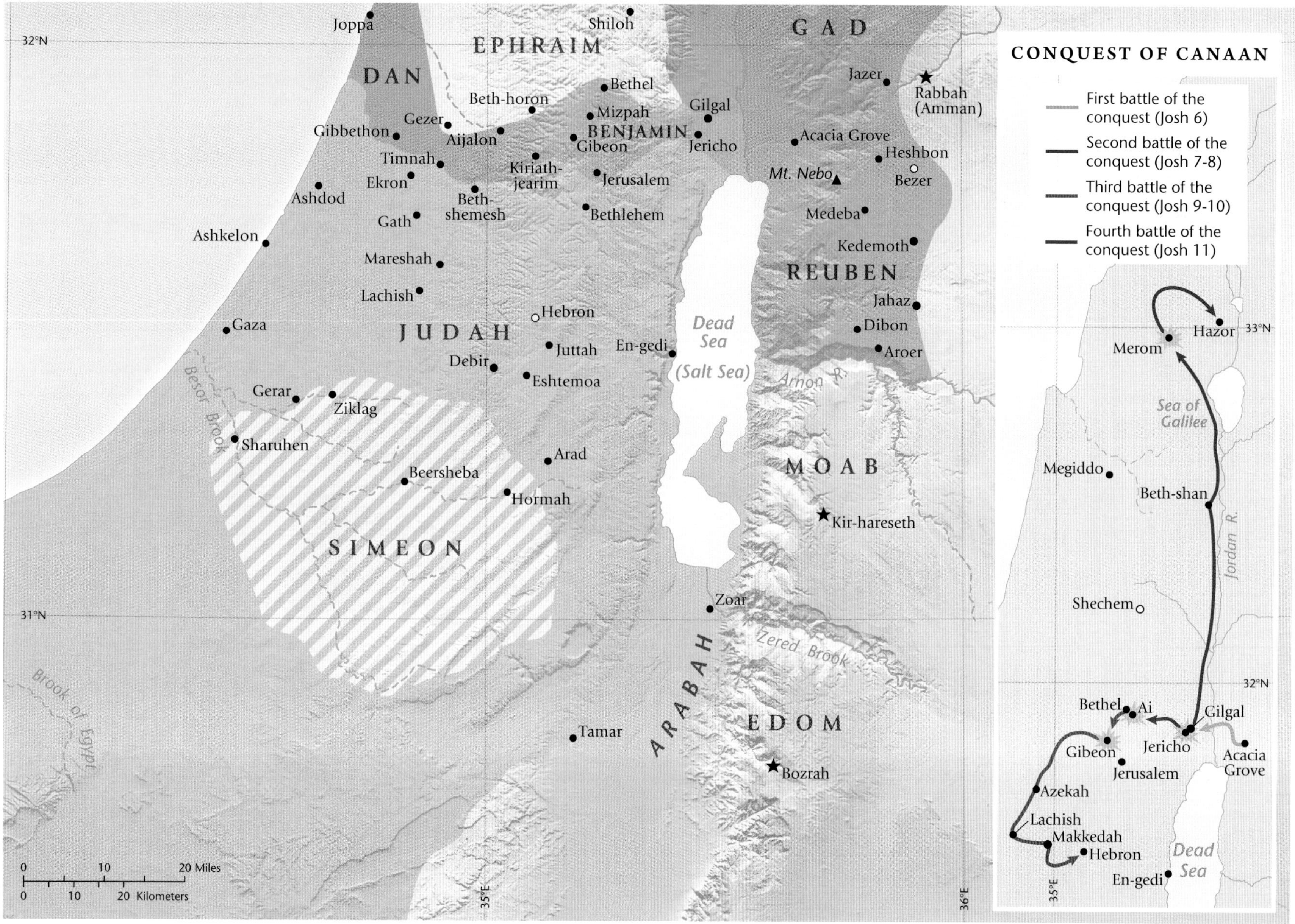
CONQUEST OF CANAAN
First battle of the conquest (Josh 6)
Second battle of the conquest (Josh 7-8)
Third battle of the conquest (Josh 9-10)
Fourth battle of the conquest (Josh 11)
Joppa
Shiloh
GAD
EPHRAIM
DAN
Bethel
Beth-horon
Mizpah
Gilgal
Gezer
Gibbethon
Aijalon
BENJAMIN
Gibeon
Jericho
Timnah
Kiriath-jearim
Jerusalem
Ekron
Ashdod
Beth-shemesh
Bethlehem
Gath
Ashkelon
Mareshah
Lachish
Hebron
Gaza
JUDAH
Juttah
En-gedi
Debir
Eshtemoa
Gerar
Ziklag
Sharuhen
Besor Brook
Arad
Beersheba
Hormah
SIMEON
Dead Sea
(Salt Sea)
Jazer
Rabbah (Amman)
Acacia Grove
Heshbon
Mt. Nebo
Bezer
Medeba
Kedemoth
REUBEN
Jahaz
Dibon
Aroer
Arnon R.
MOAB
Kir-hareseth
Zoar
Zered Brook
ARABAH
EDOM
Bozrah
Tamar
Brook of Egypt
32°N
31°N
35°E
36°E
0 10 20 Miles
0 10 20 Kilometers
Hazor
Merom
33°N
Sea of Galilee
Megiddo
Beth-shan
Jordan R.
Shechem
32°N
Bethel
Ai
Gilgal
Gibeon
Jericho
Acacia Grove
Jerusalem
Azekah
Lachish
Makkedah
Hebron
Dead Sea
En-gedi
35°E

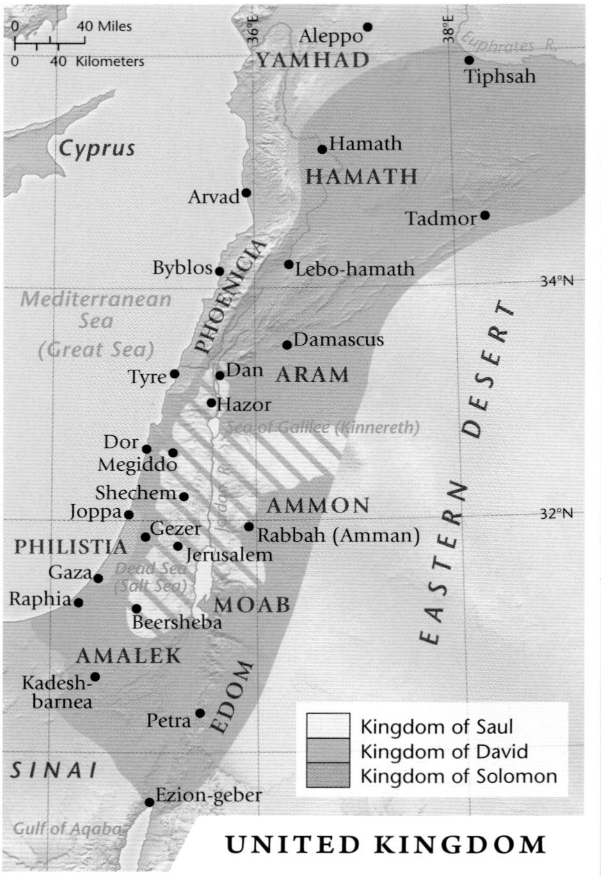

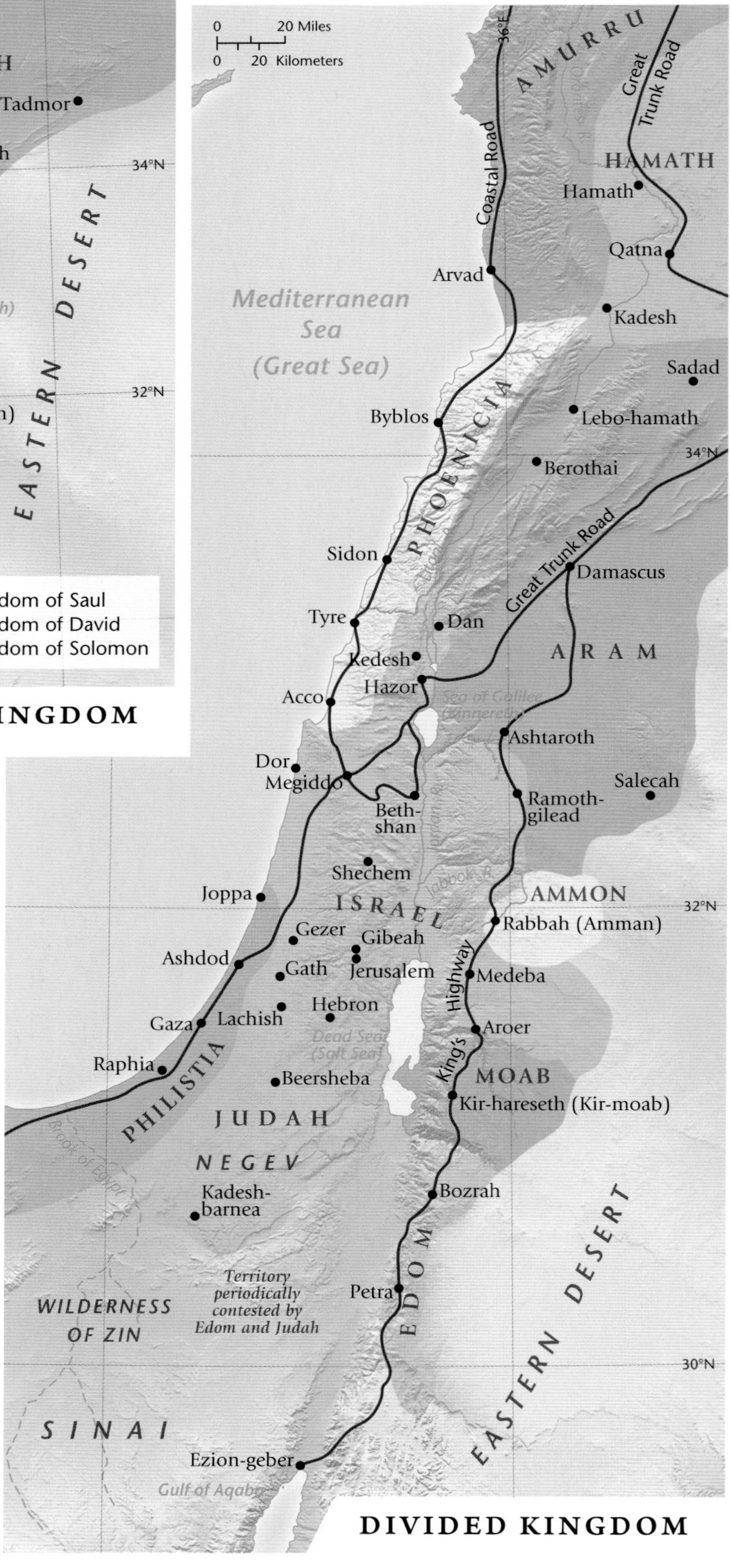

KINGDOMS OF ISRAEL

The United Kingdom of Israel came into being at the coronation of Saul, grew in size and influence under David, and reached its height during Solomon's reign. Solomon inherited a powerful kingdom from his father David, covering the entire area inhabited by the 12 tribes of Israel. Throughout Solomon's reign, his power and influence increased as he also gained control over many of the surrounding nations.

After the death of Solomon, the kingdom of Israel divided. Solomon's son, Rehoboam, remained king of the southern kingdom of Judah, with Jerusalem as its capital. Jeroboam became the king of the northern kingdom of Israel and rebuilt Shechem as his capital. He also built new worship centers in Bethel and Dan, influencing his people to stay away from Jerusalem and its annual religious festivals. The division of the kingdom of Israel began a downward spiral into idolatry and godless leadership for both nations, eventually leading to the exile of the northern kingdom to Assyria and the southern kingdom to Babylon.

ASSYRIAN AND BABYLONIAN EMPIRES

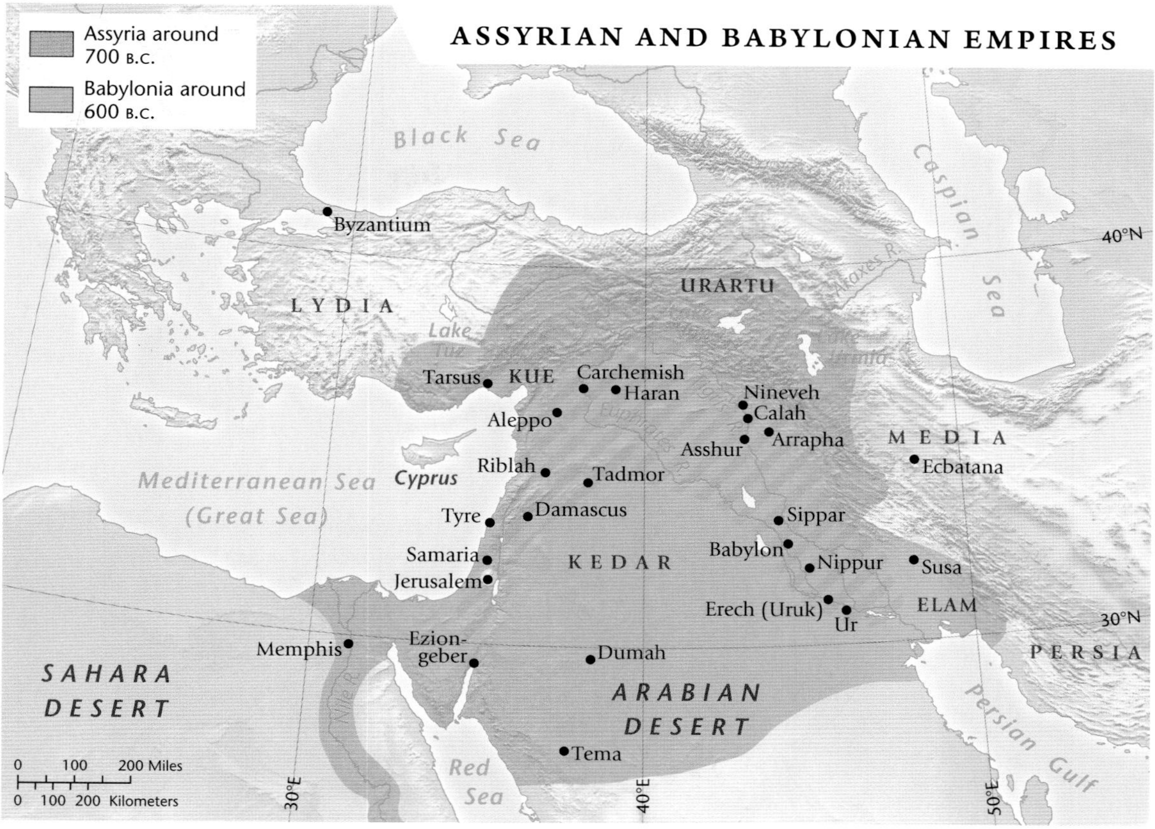

Assyria around 700 B.C.
Babylonia around 600 B.C.
Black Sea
Caspian Sea
Byzantium
40°N
LYDIA
URARTU
Araxes R.
Lake Tuz
Lake Urmia
Tarsus
KUE
Carchemish
Haran
Nineveh
Calah
Aleppo
Euphrates R.
Tigris R.
Asshur
Arrapha
MEDIA
Ecbatana
Riblah
Tadmor
Cyprus
Mediterranean Sea
(Great Sea)
Tyre
Damascus
Sippar
Babylon
Samaria
KEDAR
Nippur
Susa
Jerusalem
Erech (Uruk)
Ur
ELAM
30°N
Memphis
Ezion-geber
Dumah
PERSIA
SAHARA DESERT
ARABIAN DESERT
Nile R.
Persian Gulf
Tema
Red Sea
0 100 200 Miles
0 100 200 Kilometers
30°E
40°E
50°E

GREEK EMPIRE

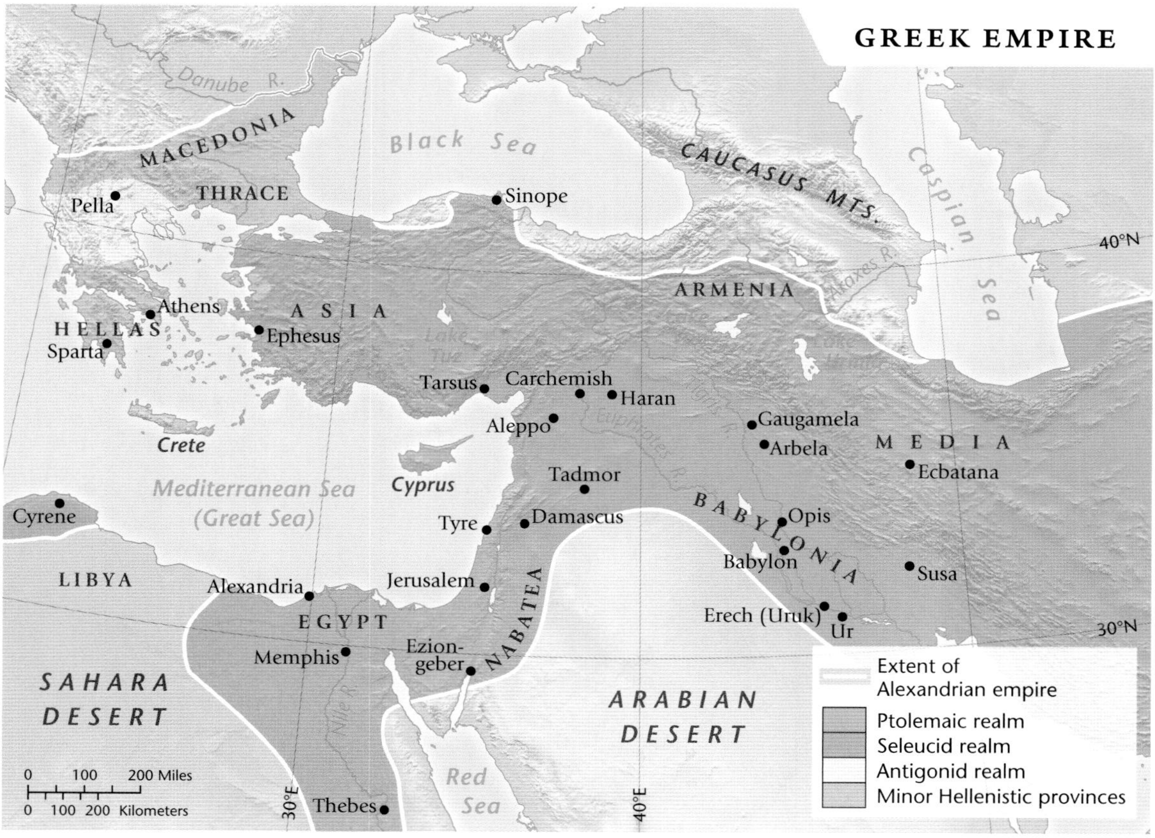

Danube R.
MACEDONIA
Black Sea
CAUCASUS MTS.
Caspian Sea
THRACE
Sinope
Pella
40°N
Araxes R.
ARMENIA
Athens
ASIA
HELLAS
Ephesus
Sparta
Lake Tuz
Lake Urmia
Tarsus
Carchemish
Haran
Euphrates R.
Tigris R.
Gaugamela
Aleppo
Arbela
MEDIA
Crete
Ecbatana
Tadmor
Mediterranean Sea
Cyprus
(Great Sea)
BABYLONIA
Opis
Cyrene
Tyre
Damascus
Babylon
Susa
LIBYA
Alexandria
Jerusalem
NABATEA
EGYPT
Erech (Uruk)
Ur
30°N
Memphis
Ezion-geber
SAHARA DESERT
ARABIAN DESERT
Nile R.
Extent of Alexandrian empire
Ptolemaic realm
Seleucid realm
Antigonid realm
Minor Hellenistic provinces
0 100 200 Miles
0 100 200 Kilometers
Red Sea
Thebes
30°E
40°E

OLD TESTAMENT JERUSALEM

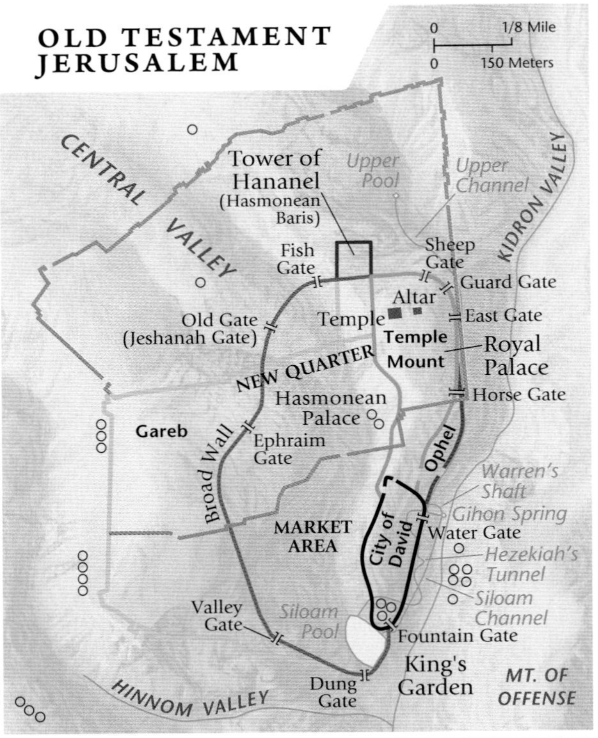

0 1/8 Mile
0 150 Meters
Walls existing today, built in the early 16th century by Suleiman the Magnificent
Jebusite city (captured by David)
Solomon's addition
8th–7th century addition (possibly by Hezekiah)
Manasseh's addition
Postexilic addition (possibly by Nehemiah)
Hasmonean addition
Tombs
CENTRAL VALLEY
KIDRON VALLEY
Tower of Hananel
(Hasmonean Baris)
Upper Pool
Upper Channel
Fish Gate
Sheep Gate
Guard Gate
Altar
Temple
East Gate
Old Gate
(Jeshanah Gate)
Temple Mount
Royal Palace
NEW QUARTER
Horse Gate
Hasmonean Palace
Gareb
Ephraim Gate
Broad Wall
Ophel
Warren's Shaft
Gihon Spring
MARKET AREA
City of David
Water Gate
Hezekiah's Tunnel
Siloam Channel
Valley Gate
Siloam Pool
Fountain Gate
King's Garden
Dung Gate
HINNOM VALLEY
MT. OF OFFENSE

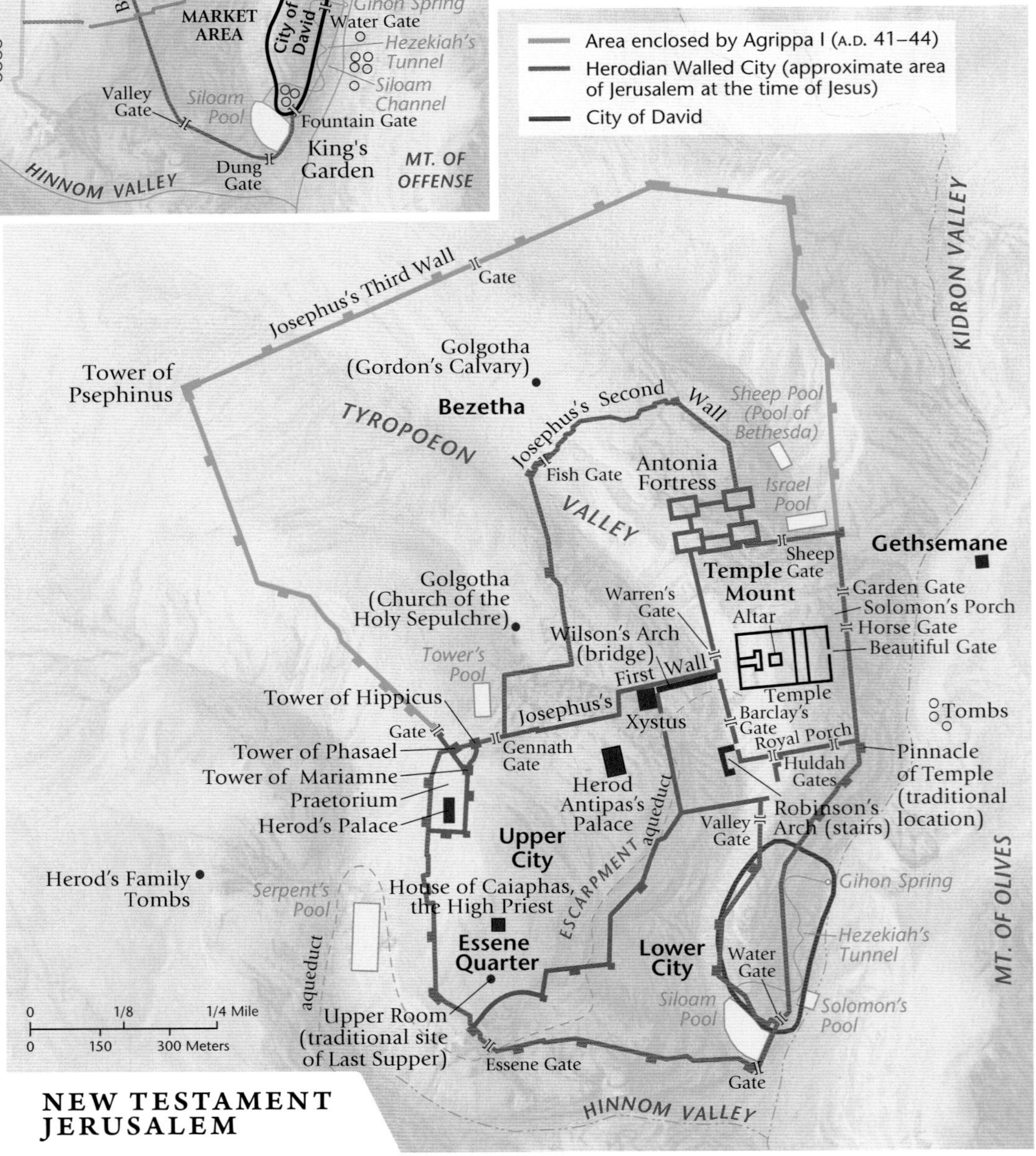

Area enclosed by Agrippa I (A.D. 41–44)
Herodian Walled City (approximate area of Jerusalem at the time of Jesus)
City of David
Josephus's Third Wall
Gate
KIDRON VALLEY
Golgotha
(Gordon's Calvary)
Tower of Psephinus
Bezetha
TYROPOEON
Josephus's Second Wall
Sheep Pool
(Pool of Bethesda)
Fish Gate
Antonia Fortress
Israel Pool
VALLEY
Gethsemane
Sheep Gate
Temple Mount
Garden Gate
Solomon's Porch
Golgotha
(Church of the Holy Sepulchre)
Warren's Gate
Altar
Horse Gate
Beautiful Gate
Wilson's Arch
(bridge)
Tower's Pool
First Wall
Josephus's
Temple
Tombs
Tower of Hippicus
Xystus
Barclay's Gate
Royal Porch
Gate
Tower of Phasael
Gennath Gate
Huldah Gates
Pinnacle of Temple (traditional location)
Tower of Mariamne
Praetorium
Herod Antipas's Palace
Herod's Palace
Upper City
aqueduct
Valley Gate
Robinson's Arch (stairs)
Herod's Family Tombs
Serpent's Pool
House of Caiaphas, the High Priest
ESCARPMENT
Gihon Spring
Essene Quarter
Lower City
Hezekiah's Tunnel
MT. OF OLIVES
Water Gate
aqueduct
Siloam Pool
Solomon's Pool
0 1/8 1/4 Mile
0 150 300 Meters
Upper Room
(traditional site of Last Supper)
Essene Gate
Gate
HINNOM VALLEY

NEW TESTAMENT JERUSALEM

ROMAN DIVISION OF PALESTINE

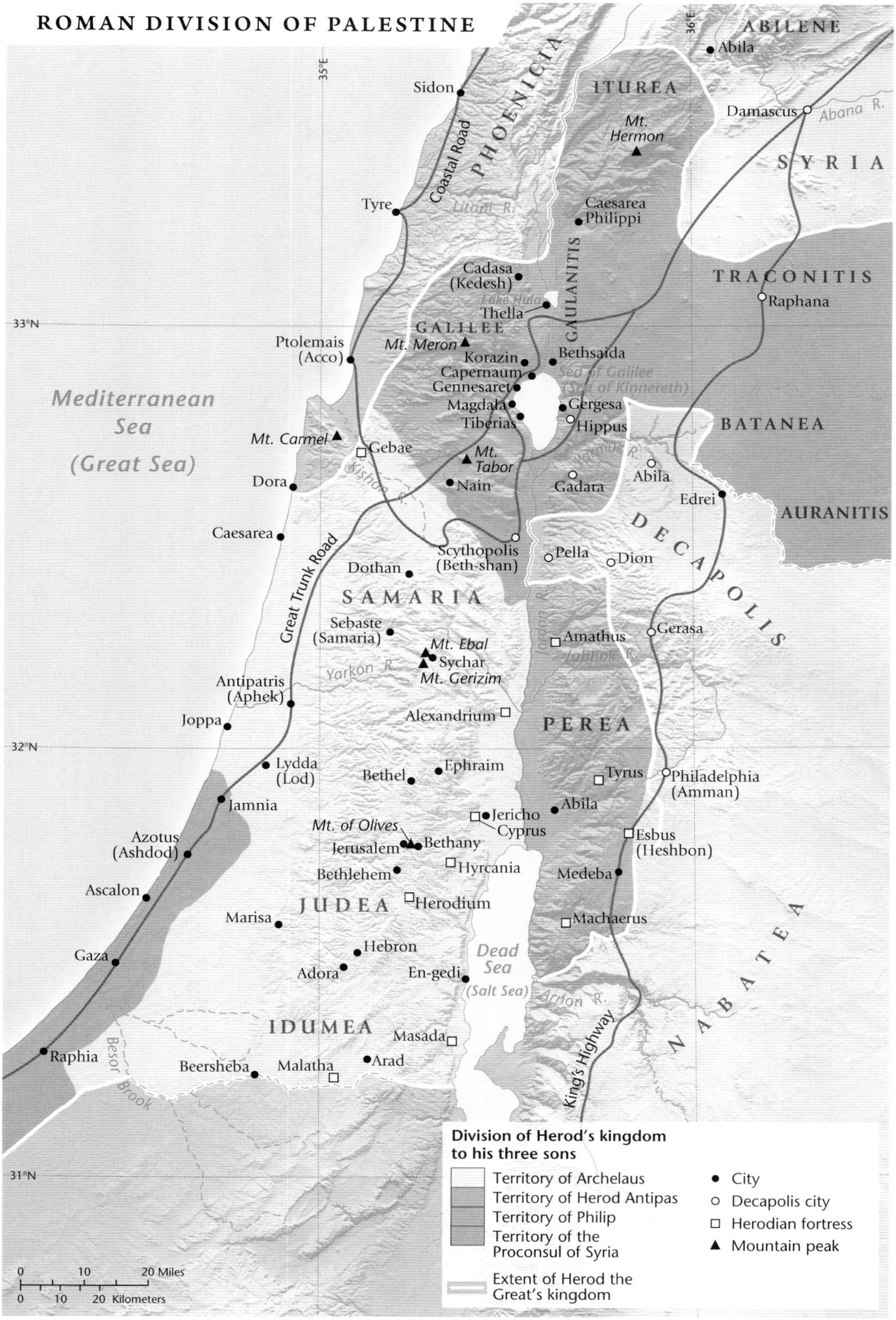

ABILENE
Abila
ITUREA
Sidon
Damascus
Abana R.
Mt. Hermon
PHOENICIA
Coastal Road
SYRIA
Tyre
Litani R.
Caesarea Philippi
GAULANITIS
Cadasa (Kedesh)
TRACONITIS
Lake Hula
Raphana
Thella
GALILEE
Ptolemais (Acco)
Mt. Meron
Bethsaida
Korazin
Capernaum
Sea of Galilee (Sea of Kinnereth)
Gennesaret
Mediterranean Sea (Great Sea)
Magdala
Gergesa
Tiberias
Hippus
BATANEA
Mt. Carmel
Gebae
Mt. Tabor
Yarmuk R.
Kishon R.
Abila
Dora
Gadara
Nain
Edrei
AURANITIS
DECAPOLIS
Caesarea
Great Trunk Road
Scythopolis (Beth-shan)
Pella
Dion
Dothan
SAMARIA
Jordan R.
Gerasa
Sebaste (Samaria)
Amathus
Mt. Ebal
Jabbok R.
Sychar
Yarkon R.
Mt. Gerizim
Antipatris (Aphek)
Alexandrium
Joppa
PEREA
Lydda (Lod)
Ephraim
Bethel
Tyrus
Philadelphia (Amman)
Jamnia
Abila
Jericho
Cyprus
Mt. of Olives
Azotus (Ashdod)
Esbus (Heshbon)
Jerusalem
Bethany
Hyrcania
Bethlehem
Medeba
Ascalon
JUDEA
Herodium
Marisa
Machaerus
Hebron
Gaza
Dead Sea
Adora
En-gedi
(Salt Sea)
Arnon R.
NABATEA
IDUMEA
Masada
King's Highway
Raphia
Besor Brook
Beersheba
Malatha
Arad
35°E
36°E
33°N
32°N
31°N
0 10 20 Miles
0 10 20 Kilometers
Division of Herod's kingdom to his three sons
Territory of Archelaus
Territory of Herod Antipas
Territory of Philip
Territory of the Proconsul of Syria
Extent of Herod the Great's kingdom
City
Decapolis city
Herodian fortress
Mountain peak

MINISTRY OF JESUS

Chronologically speaking, it is not possible to sequentially arrange the events in the life of Christ in any definitive way; none of the New Testament Gospels follows an overtly chronological pattern. Accordingly, the arrangement here follows a geographic order, basically proceeding from north to south on the map. Because the Gospel of Matthew most frequently contains information cited here, and because it is the most geographically particular Gospel, synoptic passages are keyed to the book of Matthew, except where they are unattested there or where more pertinent information about the event cited is available in another Gospel.

Ⓐ *Region of Tyre:* Gentile woman's daughter healed (Mt 15:21-28)

Ⓑ *Caesarea Philippi:* Peter's great declaration (Mt 16:13-20)

Ⓒ *Mt. Meron/Mt. Tabor/Mt. Hermon:* (1) possible location of Transfiguration (Mt 17:1-13); (2) demon-possessed boy healed nearby (Mt 17:14-21)

Ⓓ *Cana of Galilee:* (1) water changed to wine (Jn 2:1-11); (2) Capernaum official's son healed (Jn 4:46-54)

Ⓔ *Gennesaret:* (1) possible location of feeding of multitudes (Mt 14:13-21; 15:32-39); (2) many healings (Mk 6:53-56)

Ⓕ *Area of Korazin:* (1) judgment pronounced on the cities of Korazin, Bethsaida, and Capernaum (Mt 11:20-24); (2) possible area of Sermon on the Mount (Mt 5–7)

Ⓖ *Capernaum:* (1) catch of fish (Lk 5:1-11); (2) evil spirit cast out (Mk 1:21-28); (3) Sermon on the Mount (Mt 5–7); (4) Peter's mother-in-law healed (Mt 8:14-15); (5) Roman officer's servant healed (Mt 8:5-13); (6) paralyzed man healed (Mk 2:1-12); (7) woman with a hemorrhage healed (Mk 5:25-34); (8) Jairus's daughter raised (Lk 8:40-56); (9) two blind men healed (Mt 9:27-31); (10) a mute, demon-possessed man healed (Mt 9:32-34); (11) the twelve apostles sent out (Mt 10:1-15); (12) man with deformed hand healed (Mt 12:9-13); (13) another demon-possessed man healed (Mt 12:22-37); (14) Temple tax provided (Mt 17:24-27); (15) Bread of Life discourse (Jn 6:22-59)

Ⓗ *Bethsaida:* (1) possible location of feeding of multitudes (Mt 14:13-21; 15:32-39); (2) blind man healed (Mk 8:22-26)

Ⓘ *Sea of Galilee near Bethsaida:* walking on water (Mt 14:22-33)

Ⓙ *Sea of Galilee:* storm quieted (Mt 8:23-27)

Ⓚ *Gergesa/Gadara:* possible location of casting out demons, which enter pigs; the pigs then rush down a steep bank and drown (Lk 8:26-39)

Ⓛ *Nazareth:* (1) childhood home (Mt 2:19-23); (2) rejected by townspeople (Lk 4:16-30)

Ⓜ *Nain:* widow's son resurrected (Lk 7:11-17)

Ⓝ *Region of Galilee:* (1) leper cleansed (Mk 1:40-45); (2) post-resurrection appearances to the disciples (Mt 28:16-20)

Ⓞ *Decapolis (Region of Ten Towns):* many healings (Mt 15:29-31; Mk 7:31-37)

Ⓟ *Region between Galilee and Samaria:* (1) refused entry into village (Lk 9:51-56); (2) ten lepers healed (Lk 17:11-19)

Ⓠ *Sychar:* woman at the well of Samaria (Jn 4:1-42)

Ⓡ *Ephraim:* enters into seclusion with the disciples (Jn 11:54)

Ⓢ *Region of Perea:* (1) teaching on marriage (Mt 19:1-12); (2) possible location of healing of woman with infirmity (Lk 13:10-13); (3) possible location of healing of man with swollen limbs (Lk 14:1-6); (4) possible location of the rich young ruler (Lk 18:18-30)

Ⓣ *Jericho:* (1) Bartimaeus healed (Mk 10:46-52); (2) Zacchaeus converted (Lk 19:1-10)

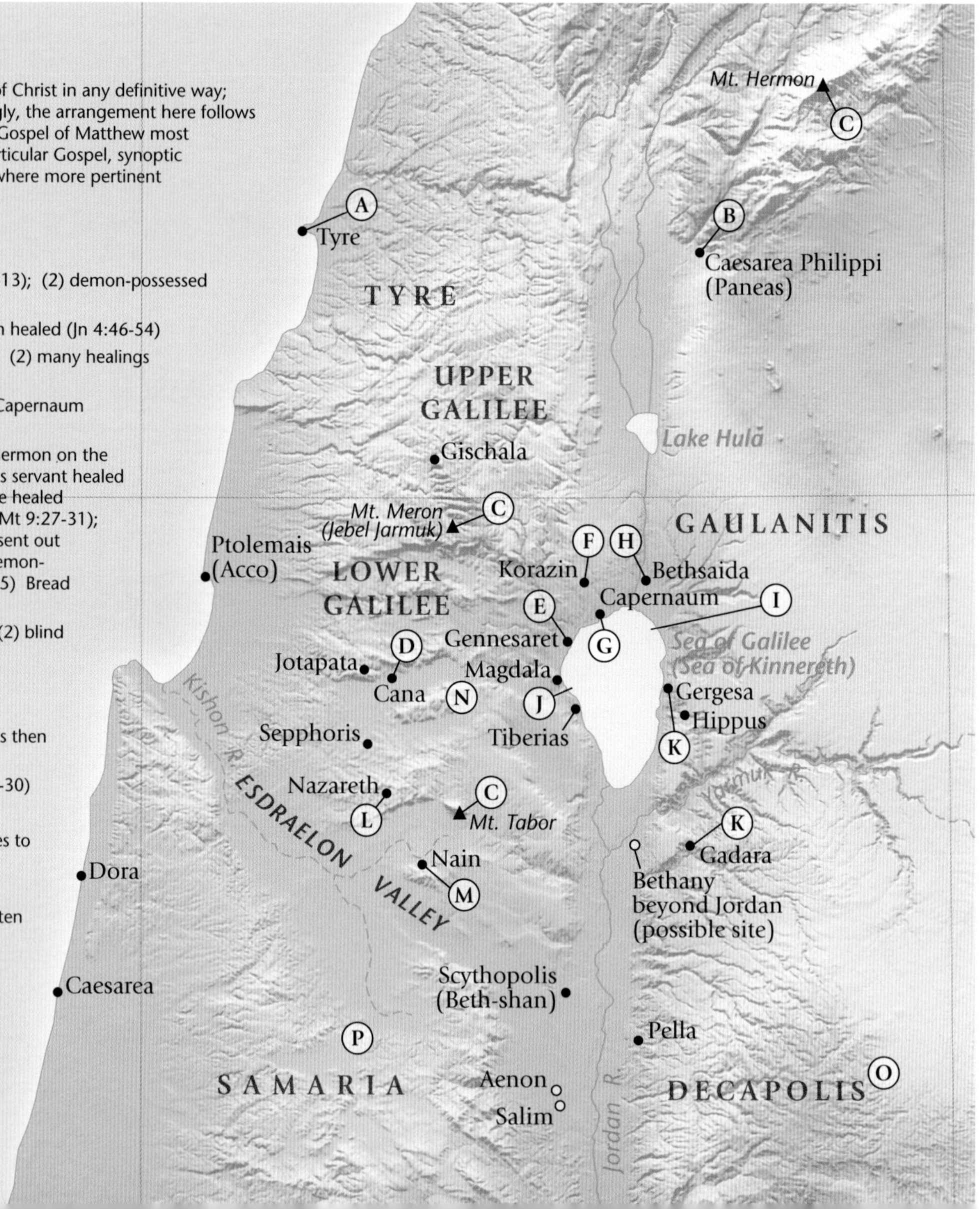

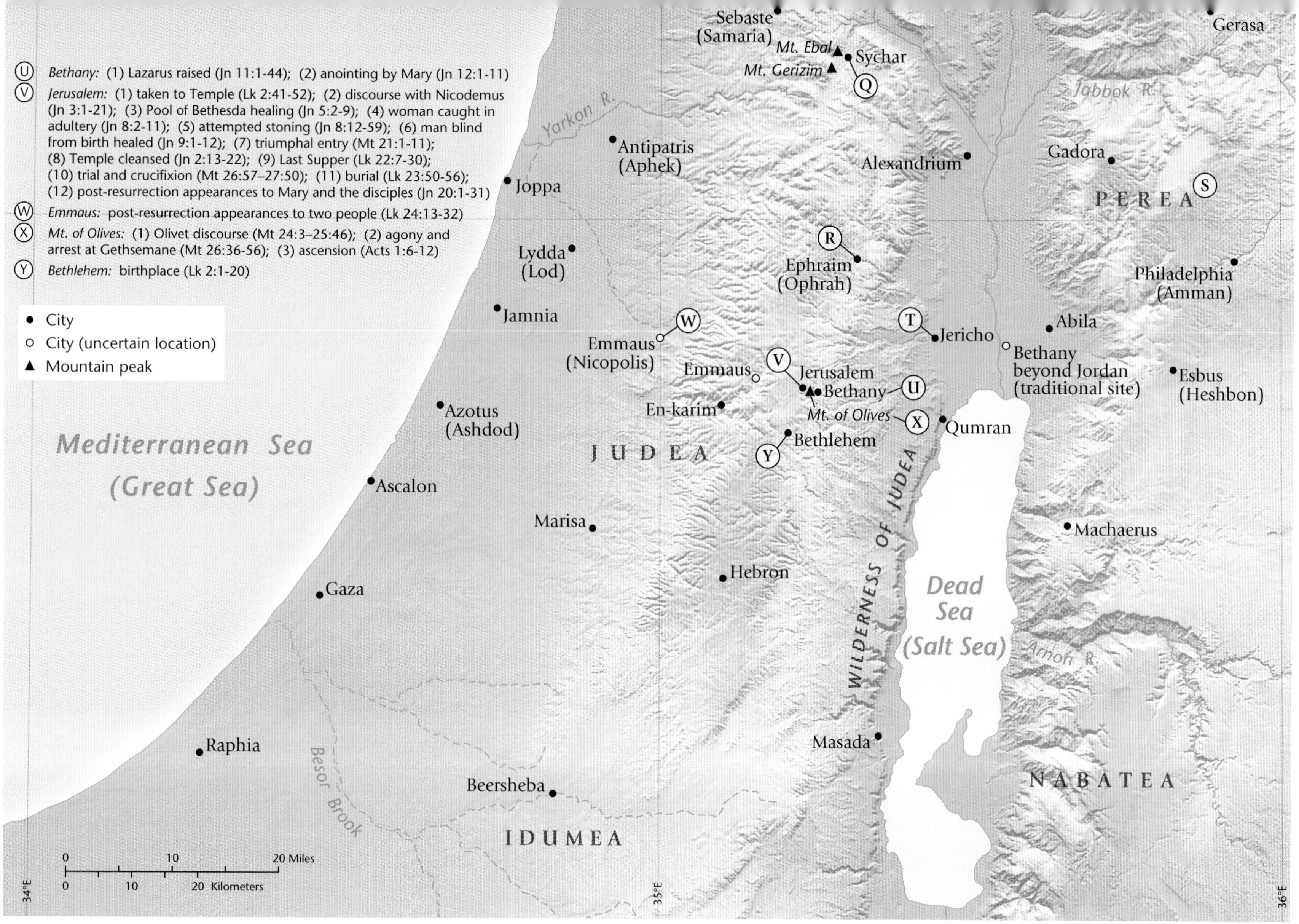
(U) Bethany: (1) Lazarus raised (Jn 11:1-44); (2) anointing by Mary (Jn 12:1-11)
(V) Jerusalem: (1) taken to Temple (Lk 2:41-52); (2) discourse with Nicodemus (Jn 3:1-21); (3) Pool of Bethesda healing (Jn 5:2-9); (4) woman caught in adultery (Jn 8:2-11); (5) attempted stoning (Jn 8:12-59); (6) man blind from birth healed (Jn 9:1-12); (7) triumphal entry (Mt 21:1-11); (8) Temple cleansed (Jn 2:13-22); (9) Last Supper (Lk 22:7-30); (10) trial and crucifixion (Mt 26:57–27:50); (11) burial (Lk 23:50-56); (12) post-resurrection appearances to Mary and the disciples (Jn 20:1-31)
(W) Emmaus: post-resurrection appearances to two people (Lk 24:13-32)
(X) Mt. of Olives: (1) Olivet discourse (Mt 24:3–25:46); (2) agony and arrest at Gethsemane (Mt 26:36-56); (3) ascension (Acts 1:6-12)
(Y) Bethlehem: birthplace (Lk 2:1-20)
City
City (uncertain location)
Mountain peak
Mediterranean Sea
(Great Sea)
Sebaste
(Samaria)
Mt. Ebal
Mt. Gerizim
Sychar
Q
Gerasa
Jabbok R.
Yarkon R.
Antipatris
(Aphek)
Alexandrium
Gadora
Joppa
PEREA
S
R
Ephraim
(Ophrah)
Lydda
(Lod)
Philadelphia
(Amman)
Jamnia
W
Emmaus
(Nicopolis)
T
Jericho
Abila
Bethany
beyond Jordan
(traditional site)
Emmaus
V
Jerusalem
Bethany
U
Esbus
(Heshbon)
En-karim
Mt. of Olives
X
Qumran
Azotus
(Ashdod)
Bethlehem
Y
JUDEA
Ascalon
WILDERNESS OF JUDEA
Marisa
Machaerus
Hebron
Gaza
Dead
Sea
(Salt Sea)
Arnon R.
Raphia
Besor Brook
Masada
Beersheba
NABATEA
IDUMEA
0 10 20 Miles
0 10 20 Kilometers
34°E
35°E
36°E

PAUL'S MISSIONARY JOURNEYS
MACEDONIA
THRACE
BITHYNIA
EPIRUS
MYSIA
ASIA
LYDIA
PHRYGIA
CARIA
LYCIA
PISIDIA
PAMPHYLIA
LYCAONIA
GALATIA
CAPPADOCIA
CILICIA
COMMAGENE
SYRIA
PHOENICIA
ABILENE
ARABIA
JUDEA
EGYPT
ACHAIA
Philippi
Amphipolis
Neapolis
Thessalonica
Berea
Apollonia
Samothrace
Lemnos
Marmara Sea
Aegean Sea
Ionian Sea
Troas
Assos
Mitylene
Pergamum
Thyatira
Sardis
Philadelphia
Smyrna
Ephesus
Laodicea
Colosse
Miletus
Samos
Kios
Patmos
Cos
Cnidus
Rhodes
Delphi
Evvoia
Corinth
Cenchrea
Athens
Sparta
Ancyra (Ankara)
Lake Tuz
Antioch of Pisidia
Iconium
Lystra
Derbe
Attalia
Perga
Patara
Myra
Tarsus
Issus
Antioch
Seleucia
Aleppo
Euphrates R.
Salamis
Cyprus
Paphos
Crete
Phoenix
Fair Havens
Mediterranean Sea
(Great Sea)
Sidon
Tyre
Damascus
Ptolemais
Caesarea
Jordan R.
Jerusalem
Alexandria
40°N
35°N
30°E
35°E
0 50 100 Miles
0 50 100 Kilometers
PAUL'S JOURNEY TO ROME
Rome
Forum of Appius
Puteoli
Three Taverns
ITALY
Ionian Sea
Sicily
Rhegium
Syracuse
Malta
MACEDONIA
Athens
Aegean Sea
Byzantium (Istanbul)
Nicea
PONTUS
GALATIA
ASIA
Ephesus
Tarsus
SYRIA
Cnidus
Myra
Crete
Rhodes
Phoenix
Lasea
Fair Havens
Cyprus
Sidon
Caesarea
Mediterranean Sea
Cyrene
CYRENAICA
EGYPT
Cilician Gates
First journey (outbound)
First journey (inbound)
Second journey (outbound)
Second journey (inbound)
Third journey (outbound)
Third journey (inbound)
Journey to Rome

ROMAN EMPIRE AND THE SPREAD OF CHRISTIANITY

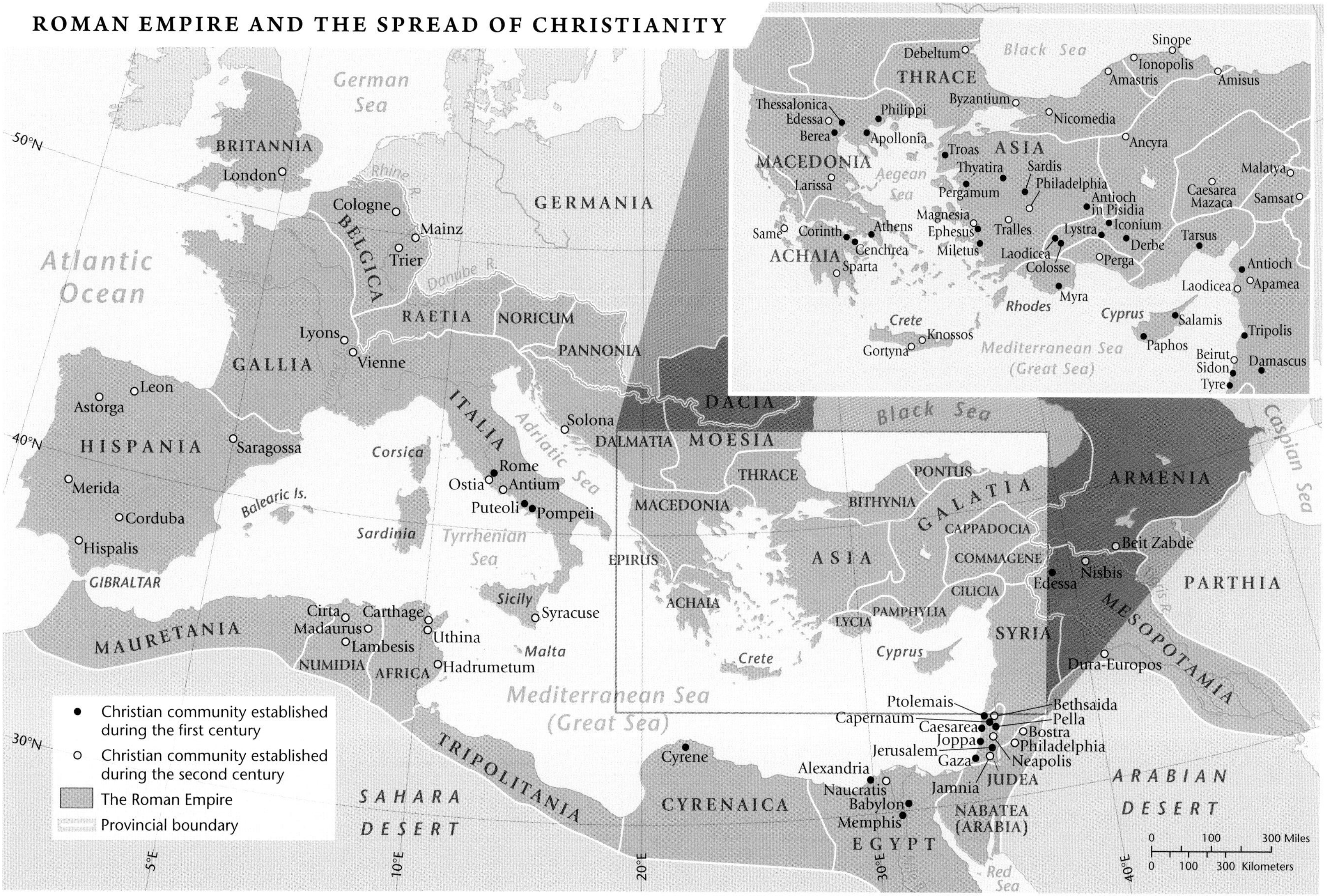

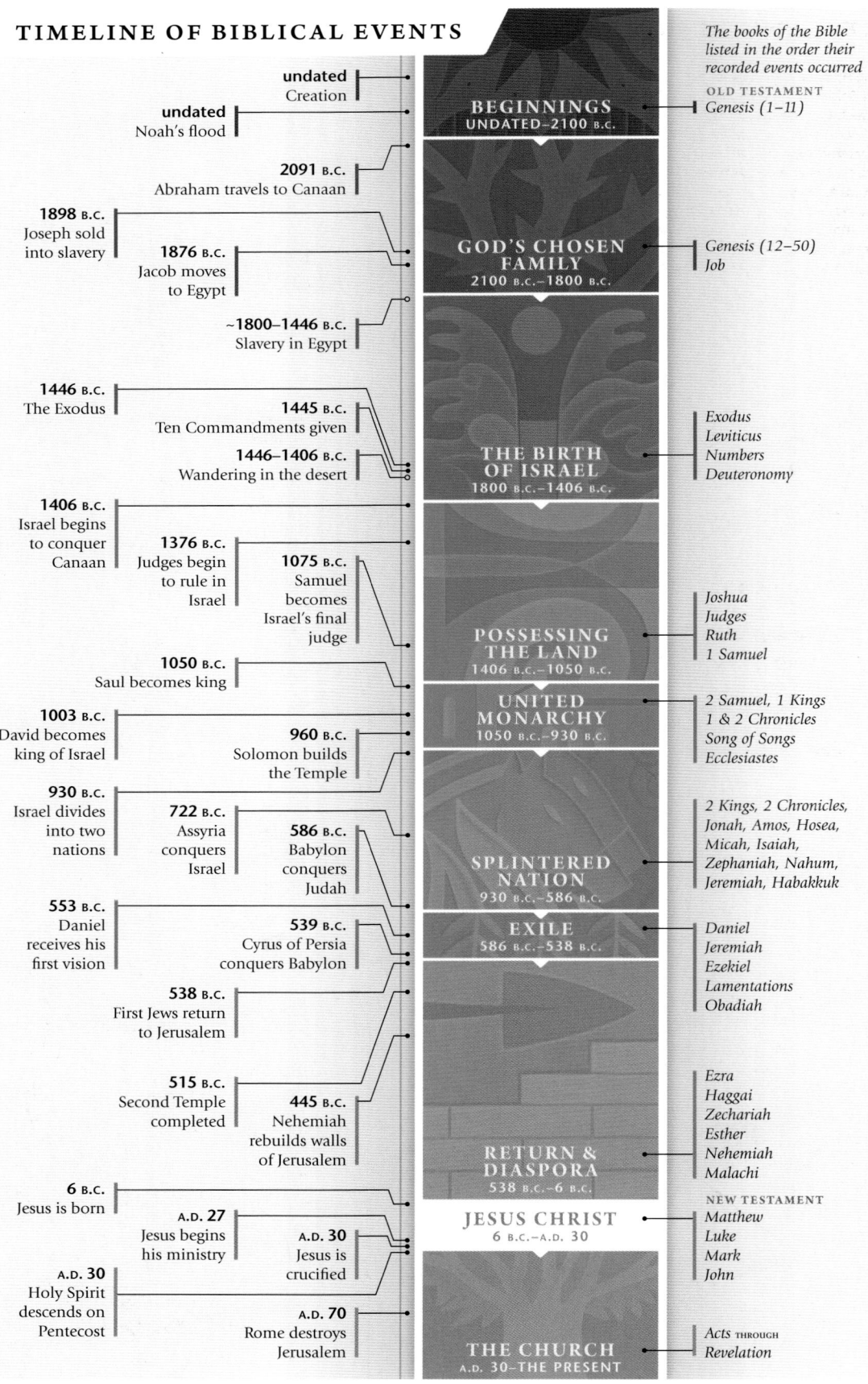

TIMELINE OF BIBLICAL EVENTS

The books of the Bible listed in the order their recorded events occurred

OLD TESTAMENT

BEGINNINGS
UNDATED–2100 B.C.

- **undated** Creation
- **undated** Noah's flood

Genesis (1–11)

GOD'S CHOSEN FAMILY
2100 B.C.–1800 B.C.

- **2091 B.C.** Abraham travels to Canaan
- **1898 B.C.** Joseph sold into slavery
- **1876 B.C.** Jacob moves to Egypt

Genesis (12–50)
Job

THE BIRTH OF ISRAEL
1800 B.C.–1406 B.C.

- **~1800–1446 B.C.** Slavery in Egypt
- **1446 B.C.** The Exodus
- **1445 B.C.** Ten Commandments given
- **1446–1406 B.C.** Wandering in the desert

Exodus
Leviticus
Numbers
Deuteronomy

POSSESSING THE LAND
1406 B.C.–1050 B.C.

- **1406 B.C.** Israel begins to conquer Canaan
- **1376 B.C.** Judges begin to rule in Israel
- **1075 B.C.** Samuel becomes Israel's final judge
- **1050 B.C.** Saul becomes king

Joshua
Judges
Ruth
1 Samuel

UNITED MONARCHY
1050 B.C.–930 B.C.

- **1003 B.C.** David becomes king of Israel
- **960 B.C.** Solomon builds the Temple

2 Samuel, 1 Kings
1 & 2 Chronicles
Song of Songs
Ecclesiastes

SPLINTERED NATION
930 B.C.–586 B.C.

- **930 B.C.** Israel divides into two nations
- **722 B.C.** Assyria conquers Israel
- **586 B.C.** Babylon conquers Judah

2 Kings, 2 Chronicles,
Jonah, Amos, Hosea,
Micah, Isaiah,
Zephaniah, Nahum,
Jeremiah, Habakkuk

EXILE
586 B.C.–538 B.C.

- **553 B.C.** Daniel receives his first vision
- **539 B.C.** Cyrus of Persia conquers Babylon

Daniel
Jeremiah
Ezekiel
Lamentations
Obadiah

RETURN & DIASPORA
538 B.C.–6 B.C.

- **538 B.C.** First Jews return to Jerusalem
- **515 B.C.** Second Temple completed
- **445 B.C.** Nehemiah rebuilds walls of Jerusalem

Ezra
Haggai
Zechariah
Esther
Nehemiah
Malachi

NEW TESTAMENT

JESUS CHRIST
6 B.C.–A.D. 30

- **6 B.C.** Jesus is born
- **A.D. 27** Jesus begins his ministry
- **A.D. 30** Jesus is crucified

Matthew
Luke
Mark
John

THE CHURCH
A.D. 30–THE PRESENT

- **A.D. 30** Holy Spirit descends on Pentecost
- **A.D. 70** Rome destroys Jerusalem

Acts THROUGH *Revelation*

THE TEMPLE IN JESUS' DAY

Herod's Temple followed the basic plan of Solomon's Temple, although its porch was much larger. It was built in the contemporary Greco-Roman architectural style and must therefore be very different from Zerubbabel's reconstruction of the Temple. Work began in 20 B.C.; and while the main sanctuary was quickly erected (it was in full operation in 10 years), the total project was not completed until A.D. 64, only six years before it was destroyed by the Romans.

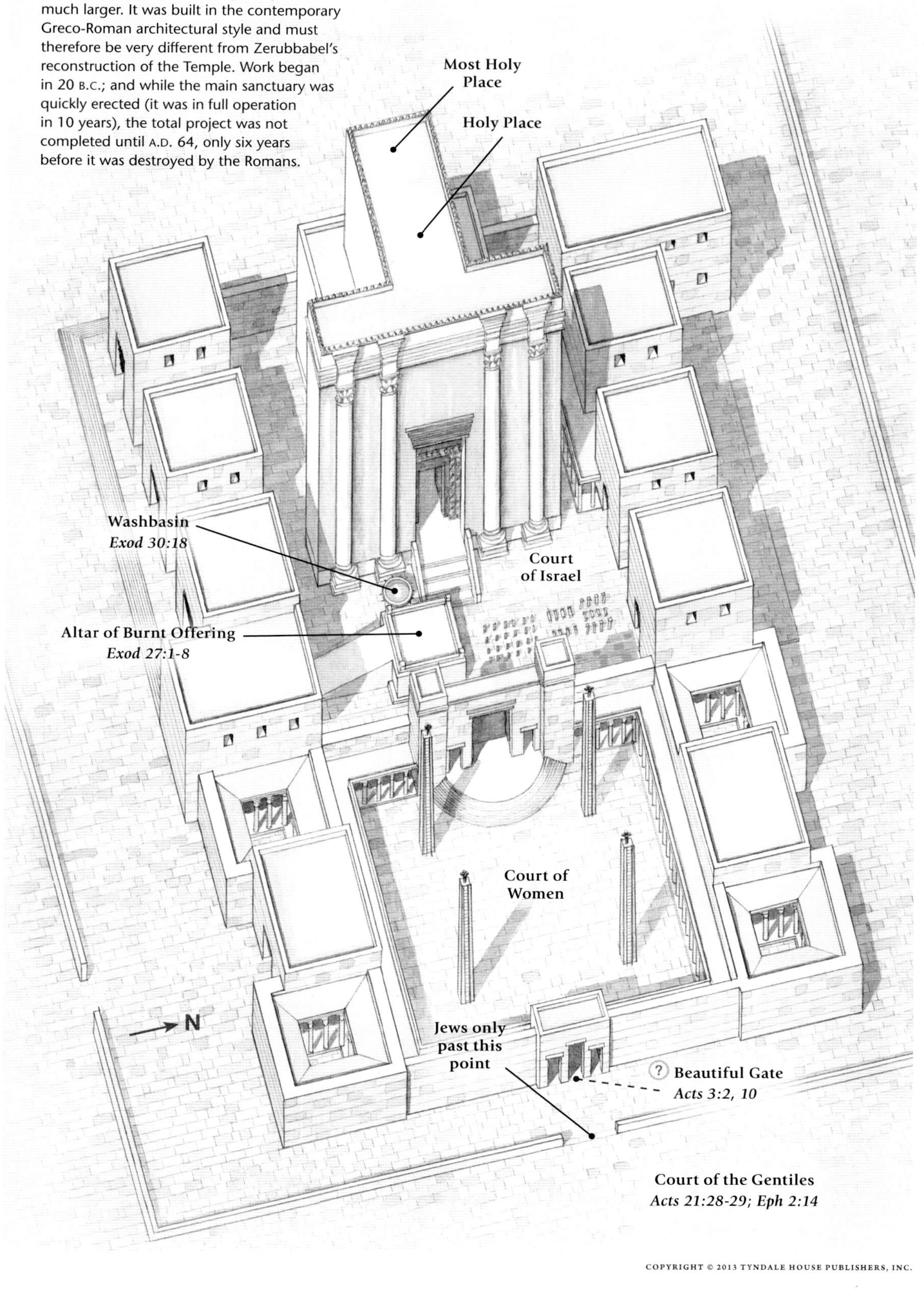

ISRAEL AND THE MIDDLE EAST TODAY

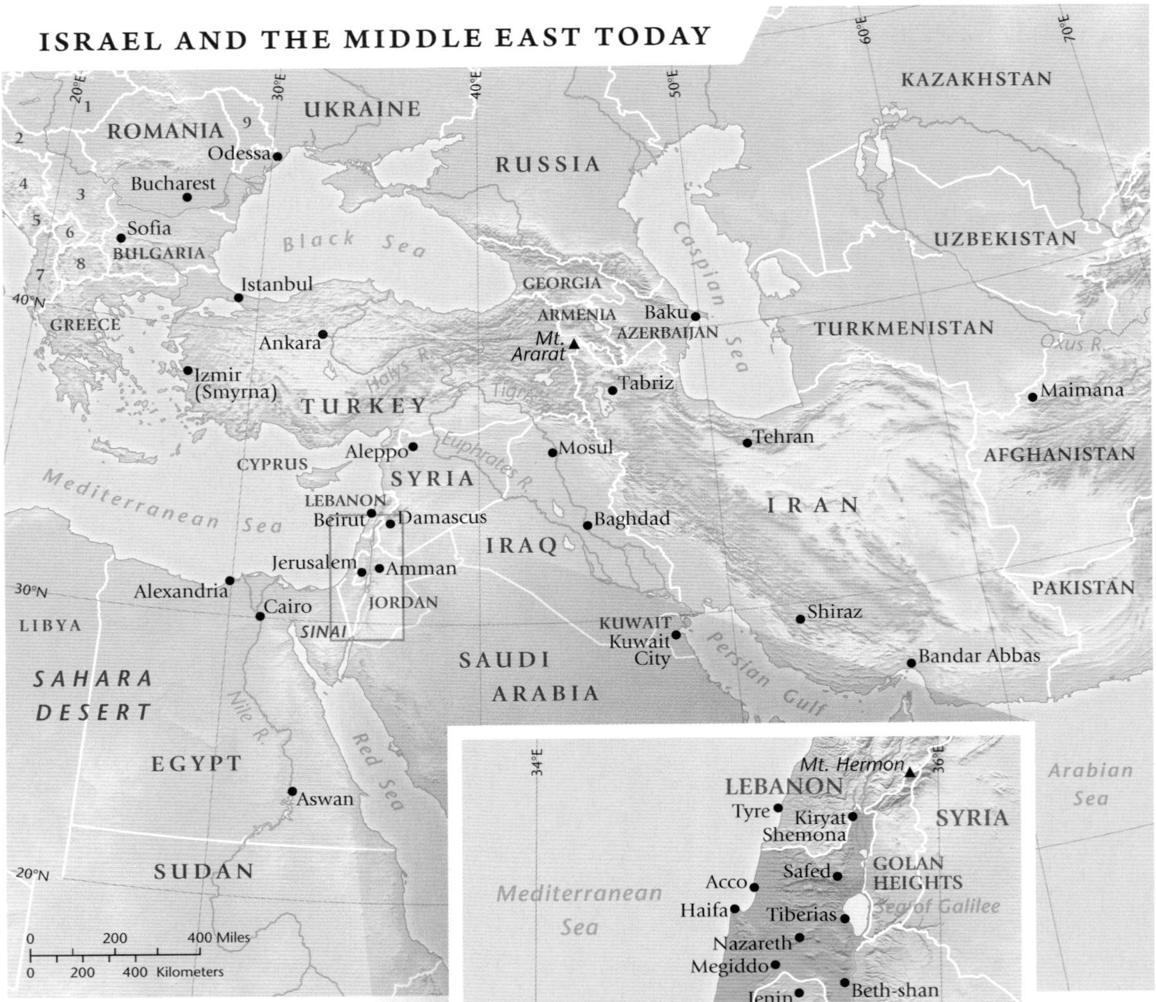

1. HUNGARY 2. CROATIA 3. SERBIA 4. BOSNIA AND HERZEGOVINA
5. MONTENEGRO 6. KOSOVO 7. ALBANIA 8. MACEDONIA 9. MOLDOVA

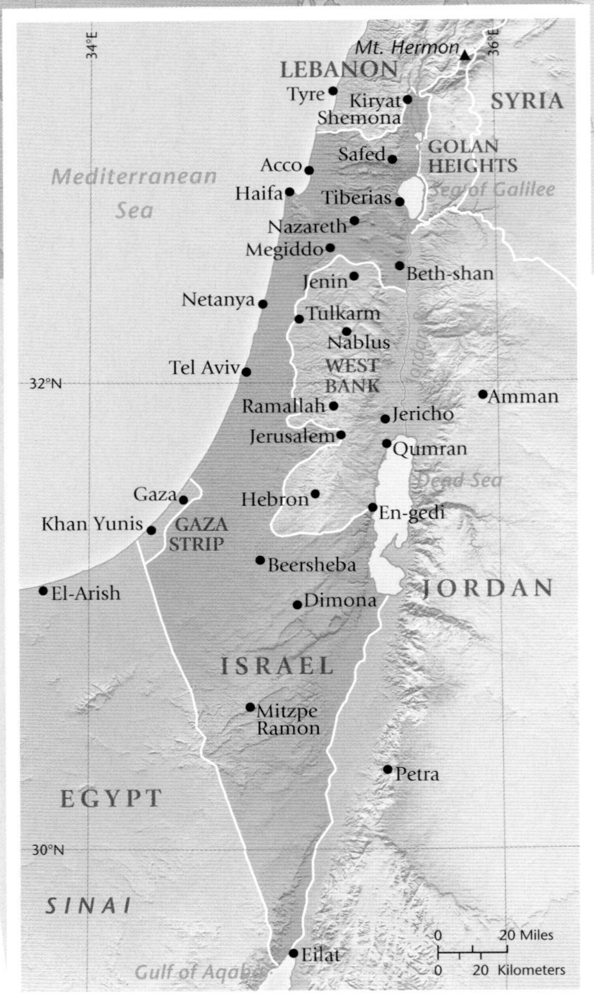

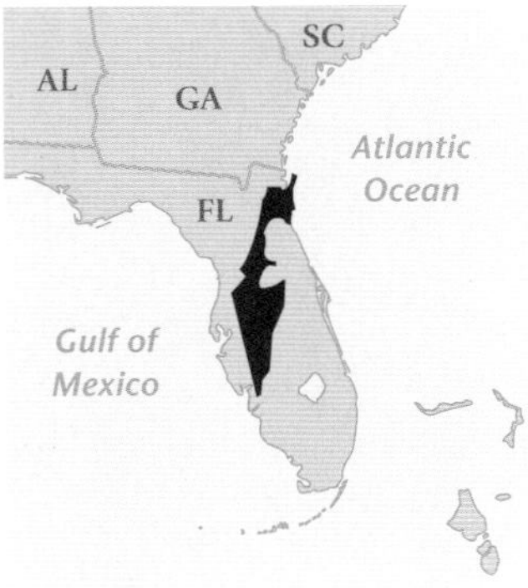

Note the comparative size of Israel to the state of Florida.